NASB® | NEW AMERICAN STANDARD BIBLE

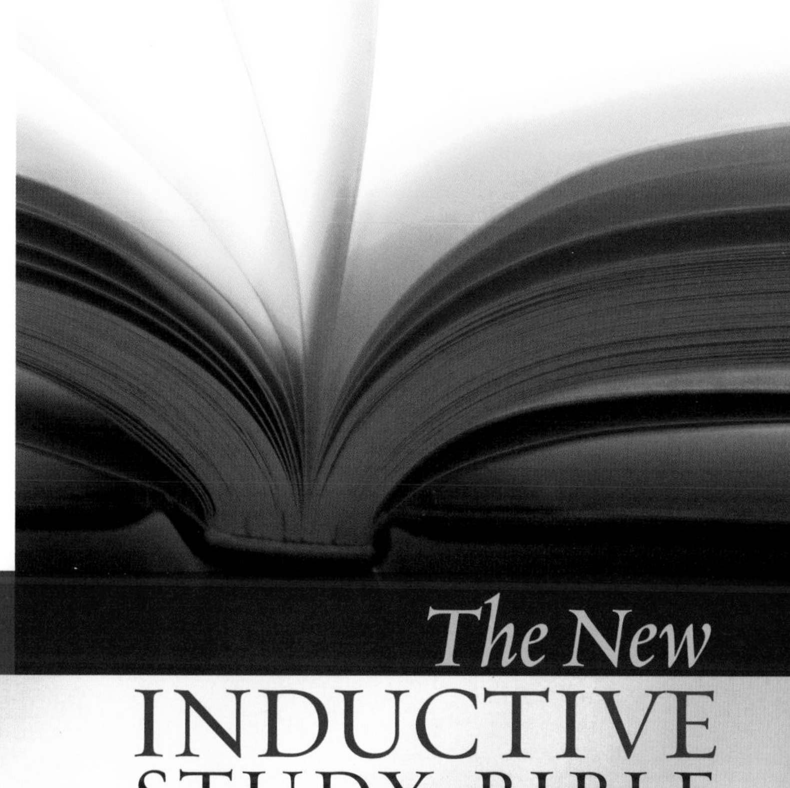

The New INDUCTIVE STUDY BIBLE

HARVEST HOUSE PUBLISHERS
HarvestHousePublishers.com

Precept Ministries International
P.O. Box 182218
Chattanooga, TN 37422

Inductive study material in *The New Inductive Study Bible* compiled by K. Arthur and the staff of Precept Ministries International.

Precept Ministries International exists to serve the body of Jesus Christ by providing inductive Bible studies for individuals, churches, home study groups, and mission organizations.

Cover, interior design, and typesetting by Koechel Peterson and Associates, Inc.

Tabernacle and Temple illustrations by Stanley C. Stein.

THE NEW INDUCTIVE STUDY BIBLE
© 2000 Precept Ministries International
Published by Harvest House Publishers
Eugene, Oregon 97408
www.harvesthousepublishers.com

Library of Congress Cataloging-in-Publication Data
Bible. English. New American Standard. 2013.
The new inductive study Bible (NASB) / Precept Ministries International.
p. cm.
ISBN 978-0-7369-2801-4 (hardcover) -- ISBN 978-0-7369-5710-6 (genuine leather) -- ISBN 978-0-7369-5715-1 (milano softone™ charcoal) -- ISBN 978-0-7369-5717-5 (milano softone™ olive) -- ISBN 978-0-7369-6989-5 (burgundy) -- ISBN 978-0-7369-7730-2 (milano softone™ brown)
I. Precept Ministries International. II. Title.
BS195.N35 2013
220.5'208—dc23 CIP
2013008837

23 / AM / 10 9 8 7

Printed in China

FOREWORD

Scriptural Promise
"The grass withers, the flower fades,
but the word of our God stands forever."
Isaiah 40:8

The New American Standard Bible has been produced with the conviction that the words of Scripture as originally penned in the Hebrew, Aramaic, and Greek were inspired by God. Since they are the eternal Word of God, the Holy Scriptures speak with fresh power to each generation, to give wisdom that leads to salvation, that men may serve Christ to the glory of God.

The purpose of the Editorial Board in making this translation was to adhere as closely as possible to the original languages of the Holy Scriptures, and to make the translation in a fluent and readable style according to current English usage.

The Fourfold Aim of The Lockman Foundation

1. These publications shall be true to the original Hebrew, Aramaic, and Greek.
2. They shall be grammatically correct.
3. They shall be understandable.
4. They shall give the Lord Jesus Christ His proper place, the place which the Word gives Him; therefore, no work will ever be personalized.

PREFACE TO THE NEW AMERICAN STANDARD BIBLE

In the history of English Bible translations, the King James Version is the most prestigious. This time-honored version of 1611, itself a revision of the Bishops' Bible of 1568, became the basis for the English Revised Version appearing in 1881 (New Testament) and 1885 (Old Testament). The American counterpart of this last work was published in 1901 as the American Standard Version. The ASV, a product of both British and American scholarship, has been highly regarded for its scholarship and accuracy. Recognizing the values of the American Standard Version, The Lockman Foundation felt an urgency to preserve these and other lasting values by incorporating recent discoveries of Hebrew and Greek textual sources and by rendering it into more current English. Therefore, in 1959 a new translation project was launched, based on the time-honored principles of translation of the ASV and KJV. The result is the New American Standard Bible.

Translation work for the NASB was begun in 1959. In the preparation of this work numerous other translations have been consulted along with the linguistic tools and literature of biblical scholarship. Decisions about English renderings were made by consensus of a team composed of educators and pastors. Subsequently, review and evaluation by other Hebrew and Greek scholars outside the Editorial Board were sought and carefully considered.

The Editorial Board has continued to function since publication of the complete Bible in 1971. This edition of the NASB represents revisions and refinements recommended over the last several years as well as thorough research based on modern English usage.

Principles of Translation

Modern English Usage: The attempt has been made to render the grammar and terminology in contemporary English. When it was felt that the word-for-word literalness was unacceptable to the modern reader, a change was made in the direction of a more current English idiom. In the instances where this has been done, the more literal rendering has been indicated in the notes.

Alternative Readings: In addition to the more literal renderings, notations have been made to include alternate translations, readings of variant manuscripts and explanatory equivalents of the text. Only such notations have been used as have been felt justified in assisting the reader's comprehension of the terms used by the original author. There are a few exceptions to this procedure. In particular, frequently "And" is not translated at the beginning of sentences because of differences in style between ancient and modern writing. Punctuation is a relatively modern invention, and ancient writers often linked most of their sentences with "and" or other connectives. Also, the Hebrew idiom "answered and said" is sometimes reduced to "answered" or "said" as demanded by the context. For current English the idiom "it came about that" has not been translated in the New Testament except when a major transition is needed.

Hebrew Text: In the present translation the latest edition of Rudolph Kittel's *Biblia Hebraica* has been employed together with the most recent light from lexicography, cognate languages, and the Dead Sea Scrolls.

Hebrew Tenses: Consecution of tenses in Hebrew remains a puzzling factor in translation. The translators have been guided by the requirements of a literal translation, the sequence of tenses, and the immediate and broad contexts.

The Proper Name of God in the Old Testament: In the Scriptures, the name of God is most significant and understandably so. It is inconceivable to think of spiritual matters without a proper designation for the Supreme Deity. Thus the most common name for the Deity is God, a translation of the original *Elohim*. One of the titles for God is Lord, a translation of *Adonai*. There is yet another name which is particularly assigned to God as His special or proper name, that is, the four letters YHWH (Exodus 3:14 and Isaiah 42:8). This name has not been pronounced by the Jews because of reverence for the great sacredness of the divine name. Therefore, it has been consistently translated LORD. The only exception to this translation of YHWH is when it occurs in immediate proximity to the word Lord, that is, *Adonai*. In that case it is regularly translated GOD in order to avoid confusion. It is known that for many years YHWH has been transliterated as Yahweh, however no complete certainty attaches to this pronunciation.

Greek Text: Consideration was given to the latest available manuscripts with a view to determining the best Greek text. In most instances the 26th edition of Eberhard Nestle's *Novum Testamentum Graece* was followed.

Greek Tenses: A careful distinction has been made in the treatment of the Greek aorist tense (usually translated as the English past, "He did") and the Greek imperfect tense (normally rendered either as English past progressive, "He was doing"; or, if inceptive, as "He began to do" or "He started to do"; or else if customary past, as "He used to do"). "Began" is italicized if it renders an imperfect tense, in order to distinguish it from the Greek verb for "begin."

In some contexts the difference between the Greek imperfect and the English past is conveyed better by the choice of vocabulary or by other words in the context, and in such cases the Greek imperfect may be rendered as a simple past tense (e.g. "had an illness for many years" would be preferable to "was having an illness for many years" and would be understood in the same way.

On the other hand, not all aorists have been rendered as English pasts ("He did"), for some of them are clearly to be rendered as English perfects ("He has done"), or even as past perfects ("He had done"), judging from the context in which they occur. Such aorists have been rendered as perfects or past perfects in this translation.

As for the distinction between aorist and present imperatives, the translators have usually rendered these imperatives in the customary manner, rather than attempting any such fine distinction as "Begin to do!" (for the aorist imperative), or, "Continually do!" (for the present imperative).

As for sequence of tenses, the translators took care to follow English rules rather than Greek in translating Greek presents, imperfects and aorists. Thus, where English says, "We knew that he was doing," Greek puts it, "We knew that he does"; similarly, "We knew that he had done" is the Greek, "We knew that he did." Likewise, the English, "When he had come, they met him," is represented in Greek by: "When he came, they met him." In all cases a consistent transfer has been made from the Greek tense in the subordinate clause to the appropriate tense in English.

In the rendering of negative questions introduced by the particle *mē* (which always expects the answer "No") the wording has been altered from a mere, "Will he not do this?" to a more accurate, "He will not do this, will he?"

THE LOCKMAN FOUNDATION

Explanations of General Format

Notes and Cross References are placed in a column adjoining the text on the page and listed under verse numbers to which they refer. Superior numbers refer to literal renderings, alternate translations, or explanations. Superior letters refer to cross references. Cross references in italics are parallel passages.

Paragraphs are designated by bold face numbers or letters.

Quotation marks are used in the text in accordance with modern English usage.

"*Thou*," "*Thee*" and "*Thy*" are not used in this edition and have been rendered as "*You*" and "*Your*."

Personal Pronouns are capitalized when pertaining to Deity.

Italics are used in the text to indicate words which are not found in the original Hebrew, Aramaic, or Greek but implied by it. Italics are used in the marginal notes to signify alternate readings for the text. Roman text in the marginal alternate readings is the same as italics in the Bible text.

Small Caps in the New Testament are used in the text to indicate Old Testament quotations or obvious references to Old Testament texts. Variations of Old Testament wording are found in New Testament citations depending on whether the New Testament writer translated from a Hebrew text, used existing Greek or Aramaic translations, or paraphrased the material. It should be noted that modern rules for the indication of direct quotation were not used in biblical times; thus, the ancient writer would use exact quotations or references to quotation without specific indication of such.

Asterisks are used to mark verbs that are historical presents in the Greek which have been translated with an English past tense in order to conform to modern usage. The translators recognized that in some contexts the present tense seems more unexpected and unjustified to the English reader than a past tense would have been. But Greek authors frequently used the present tense for the sake of heightened vividness, thereby transporting their readers in imagination to the actual scene at the time of occurrence. However, the translators felt that it would be wise to change these historical presents to English past tenses.

Abbreviations and Special Markings

Aram	= Aramaic
DSS	= Dead Sea Scrolls
Gr	= Greek translation of O.T. (Septuagint or LXX) or Greek text of N.T.
Heb	= Hebrew text, usually Masoretic
Lat	= Latin
M.T.	= Masoretic text
Syr	= Syriac
Lit	= A literal translation
Or	= An alternate translation justified by the Hebrew, Aramaic, or Greek
[ ]	= In text, brackets indicate words probably not in the original writings
[ ]	= In margin, brackets indicate references to a name, place or thing similar to, but not identical with that in the text
cf	= compare
f, ff	= following verse or verses
ms, mss	= manuscript, manuscripts
v, vv	= verse, verses

Dedicated to
the church of
the living God...
to those whose
passion is to be
*"the pillar and support
of the truth."*

I TIMOTHY 3:15

THE NEW INDUCTIVE
STUDY BIBLE

Welcome to *The New Inductive Study Bible*

Do you long to know God? Do you yearn for a deep and abiding relationship with Him? Do you want to live the Christian life faithfully—and to know what He requires of you? If so, *The New Inductive Study Bible* is designed for you.

God reveals Himself through His Word. Through it, He shows us how to live. Jesus made it clear: "Man shall not live on bread alone, but on every word that proceeds out of the mouth of God" (Matthew 4:4). And where do we find this divine bread? In the Scriptures.

As you study this Bible with the help of the Holy Spirit, and live out the truths that God reveals to you, you will discover new stability, strength, and confidence. You will be able to say with the prophet Jeremiah: "Your words were found and I ate them, and Your words became for me a joy and the delight of my heart" (Jeremiah 15:16).

Today, many people are convinced they cannot know truth for themselves. A babble of voices surrounds us claiming to know and interpret God's truth for us. Which voices are right? Which are wrong? How can we discern the true from the counterfeit unless we spend time with God and His Word?

Most Christians have been encouraged to study the Word of God, yet many have never been shown how. Others even feel inadequate to do so because they are not ministers or seminary students or scholars. Nothing could be further from the truth.

In fact, if you want to satisfy your hunger and thirst to know God and His Word in a deeper way, you must do more than merely read Scripture and study what someone else has said about it. Just as no one else can eat and digest your food for you, so no one else can feed on God's Word for you. You must interact with the text yourself, absorbing its truths and letting God engrave His truth on your heart and mind and life.

That is the very heart of inductive study: seeing truth for yourself, discerning what it means, and applying that truth to your life. In His inspired Word, God has given us everything we need to know about life and godliness. But He doesn't stop there. He gives every believer a resident teacher—the Holy Spirit—who guides us into His truth.

The Bible is unlike any other book. It is supernatural. It is complete in itself. The Bible needs no other books or truths to supplement it. In inductive study the Bible becomes its own commentary, and it can be understood by any believer.

Anyone who will take the time can see and understand what God has given us in His Word and how it applies to us today.

CONTENTS

The Old Testament

Genesis (B'reshit) 1
Exodus (Shmot) 89
Leviticus (Vayikra) 161
Numbers (Bamidbar) 216
Deuteronomy (Dvarim) 289
Joshua (Yehoshua) 353
Judges (Shofetim) 396
Ruth (Rut) 439
1 Samuel (Shmu'el Aleph) 446
2 Samuel (Shmu'el Bet) 502
1 Kings (M^{e}lakhim Aleph) 547
2 Kings (M^{e}lakhim Bet) 601
1 Chronicles
(Divre Hayyamim Aleph) 656
2 Chronicles (Divre Hayyamim Bet) 707
Ezra (Ezra) 762
Nehemiah (Nechemya) 780
Esther (Ester) 807
Job (Iyyov) 822
Psalms (T^{e}hilim) 876
Proverbs (Mishle) 1018
Ecclesiastes (Qohelet) 1063
Song of Solomon (Shir Hashirim) . . 1078
Isaiah (Yesha' yahu) 1089
Jeremiah (Yirmeyahu) 1195
Lamentations (Ekha) 1303
Ezekiel (Yehezqel) 1316
Daniel (Daniyel) 1403
Hosea (Hoshea) 1434
Joel (Yo'el) 1454
Amos (Amos) 1463
Obadiah (Ovadya) 1479
Jonah (Yona) 1483
Micah (Mikha) 1488
Nahum (Nachum) 1500
Habakkuk (Chavaqquq) 1507
Zephaniah (Tzfanya) 1515
Haggai (Chaggai) 1523
Zechariah (Zekharya) 1528
Malachi (Mal'akhi) 1548

The New Testament

Matthew 1559
Mark 1615
Luke 1651
John 1711
Acts 1761
Romans 1821
1 Corinthians 1848
2 Corinthians 1873
Galatians 1891
Ephesians 1903
Philippians 1914
Colossians 1924
1 Thessalonians 1933
2 Thessalonians 1942
1 Timothy 1948
2 Timothy 1958
Titus 1965
Philemon 1971
Hebrews 1974
James 1996
1 Peter 2006
2 Peter 2015
1 John 2022
2 John 2031
3 John 2033
Jude 2035
Revelation 2040

For a list of the key charts and illustrations in this Bible, see page NISB-12.

Foreword—
Updated New American Standard Bible iii

Welcome to
The New Inductive Study Bible NISB-7

The Books of the Bible NISB-9

How to Use
The New Inductive Study Bible NISB-13
How to Use the Inductive Study Approach NISB-15
Observation—*Discover What It Says!* NISB-17
The Marking Approach—Sample A NISB-19
The Marking Approach—Sample B NISB-21
The AT A GLANCE Charts—Sample C NISB-23
The AT A GLANCE Charts—Sample D NISB-25
A System for Marking Key Words
Throughout Your Bible NISB-26
Interpretation—*Discover What It Means!* NISB-27
Application—*Discover How It Works!* NISB-29
Getting Started NISB-31

The Spiritual Life of Israel
Comparative Timetable of History
The Tabernacle NISB-34
Solomon's Temple NISB-36
Herod's Temple at the Time of Jesus NISB-38
The Temple Mount at the Time of Jesus NISB-40
The History of Israel—*Adam to Modern Times* NISB-42

Bible Study Helps

Understanding the Value of God's Word		2083		
Major Events in Israel's History		2087		
Historical and Grammatical Helps		2099		
The Ark of the Covenant		2099		
Understanding Gnosticism		2100		
Guidelines for Interpreting Predictive Prophecy		2101		
Figures of Speech		2103		
Laws of Composition		2106		
Tense, Voice, and Mood of Greek Verbs		2107		
Read Through the Bible in One Year		2113		
Three-Year Bible Study Plan		2114		
A Harmony of the Gospels		2117		
Indexes to Charts, Maps, and Illustrations				
Historical Charts	(alphabetical)	2123	(Bible book order)	2126
Topical Study Charts	(alphabetical)	2123	(Bible book order)	2126
Maps	(alphabetical)	2124	(Bible book order)	2127
Illustrations	(alphabetical)	2125	(Bible book order)	2128
Index to Color Maps	(alphabetical)	2125	(Bible book order)	2128

Concordance

Concordance 2129

Color Maps

Modern Boundaries of Bible Lands 2241

The Settlements of the Descendants of Shem, Ham, and Japheth 2242

The Ancient and Modern Sites of the Exodus 2243

Ezekiel's Vision of the Promised Land 2244

Israel's Territories: Ancient and Modern 2245

The Relationship of Ancient Empires to Modern Nations 2246

Development of Modern Israel 2248

KEY CHARTS AND ILLUSTRATIONS FOR YOUR USE

Listed below are key charts and illustrations you'll find yourself using again and again as you study your Bible inductively. As soon as you can, you'll find it extremely helpful to look up these charts and illustrations, as they will equip you to make the best use possible of *The New Inductive Study Bible.*

There are many additional charts and illustrations not listed here; you will find the complete lists in the index, on pages 2123-2128.

Key Historical Charts

The History of Israel NISB-42
The Overlapping of the Patriarchs' Lives 10
The Jewish Calendar . . . 201, 560, 809, 1320, 1525, 1531
The Feasts of Israel 214
David's Family Tree Related to 1 Kings. 549
The Historical Chart of the Kings and Prophets
of Israel and Judah. 651
Prophetic Overview of Daniel 1432
The Genealogy of Jesus the Christ 1557
Inside Herod's Temple. 1614
Life of Christ Chart 1710
Sequence of Events in Paul's Life
After His Conversion. 1779, 1893
Overview of the Bible 2085
A Harmony of the Gospels. 2117

Key Illustrations

The Tabernacle NISB-34
Solomon's Temple NISB-36
Herod's Temple at the Time of Jesus NISB-38
The Temple Mount at the Time of Jesus. NISB-40
Inside the Tabernacle 156, 189, 1984
Solomon's Temple and Temple Furnishings 561
Prophetic Overview of Daniel 1432
Inside Herod's Temple. 1614

HOW TO USE

The New INDUCTIVE STUDY BIBLE

How to Use the Inductive Study Approach

If you know there is more to the Word of God than you have discovered so far...

- If you sense there must be concrete answers to the complexities of life...
- If you want a bedrock faith that keeps you from being tossed around by conflicting philosophies in the world and the church...
- If you want to be able to face the uncertainties of the future without fear...

...then *The New Inductive Study Bible* is designed for you.

God's eternal, infallible Word is your guidebook for all of life, and inductive study gives you the key to understanding that guide.

Inductive study, a method that brings you directly to the Word of God apart from another's understanding or interpretation of the text, involves three skills: *observation, interpretation,* and *application*.

OBSERVATION — Discover What It Says!

Observation teaches you to see precisely what the passage says. It is the basis for accurate interpretation and correct application. Observation answers the question: What does the passage say?

INTERPRETATION — Discover What It Means!

Interpretation answers the question: What does the passage mean?

APPLICATION — Discover How It Works!

Application answers the question: What does it mean to me personally? What truths can I put into practice? What changes should I make in my life?

When you know what God says, what He means, and how to put His truths into practice, you will be equipped for every circumstance of life. Ultimately, the goal of personal Bible study is a transformed life and a deep and abiding relationship with Jesus Christ.

The following ten steps provide the basis for inductive study. As you take these steps, observation, interpretation, and application will sometimes happen simultaneously. God can give you insight at any point in your study, so be sensitive to His leading. When words or passages make an impression on you, stop for a moment and meditate on what God has shown you. Record your personal notes and insights in the margin so that you can remember what you've learned.

One of the most valuable aspects of the *NISB* is its wide-margin format, which has been specifically designed to enable you to easily keep a record of what God personally reveals to you from His Word. Although some are hesitant to mark in their Bibles, this interactive Bible has been designed with marking in mind. God wants you to know, understand, and remember His Word, and one of the most profitable ways to do this is to interact with the text through marking and writing.

As you study the Bible chapter by chapter and book by book, you will grow in your ability to comprehend the whole counsel of God. In the future, you will be able to refer to your notes again and again as you study portions of Scripture and grow in your knowledge of Him.

OBSERVATION

Discover What It Says!

STEP ONE

BEGIN WITH PRAYER

Prayer is often the missing element in Bible study. You are about to learn the most effective method of Bible study there is. Yet apart from the work of the Holy Spirit, that's all it will be—a method. It is the indwelling Holy Spirit who guides us into all truth, who takes the things of God and reveals them to us. Always ask God to teach you as you open the Scriptures.

STEP TWO

ASK THE "5 W'S AND AN H"

As you study any passage of Scripture, any book of the Bible, train yourself to constantly ask: *Who? What? When? Where? Why? How?* These questions are the building blocks of precise observation, which is essential for accurate interpretation. Many times Scripture is misinterpreted because the context isn't carefully observed. Asking these questions will help you to stay in the context of the passage.

When we rush into interpretation without laying the vital foundation of observation, our understanding becomes colored by our presuppositions—what we think, what we feel, or what other people have said. We must be careful not to distort the Scriptures to our own destruction (2 Peter 3:16).

Accurate answers to the following questions will help assure correct interpretation.

Who *is speaking? Who is this about? Who are the main characters?* For example, look at the sample passage from 1 Peter 5 (see page NISB-19). In this chapter, "I" is speaking. Verse 1 tells us that "I" is a fellow elder, a witness of the sufferings of Christ, and a partaker of the glory to follow. From reading this and previous chapters (the context), you recognize that the "I" is Peter, the author of this epistle. You'll want to mark the author in a special color (such as blue) to help you with your study.

And, ***to whom*** *is he speaking?* Verse 1 refers to "the elders," verse 5 to "you younger men," and verse 6 to "yourselves" (the recipients of the epistle). You'll find it helpful to mark the recipients in another color.

What *is the subject or event covered in the chapter? What do you learn about the people, the event, or the teaching from the text? What instructions are given?* In 1 Peter 5:2, Peter instructs the elders to shepherd the flock and exercise oversight.

When *do or will the events occur? When did or will something happen to a particular person, people, or nation? When* is a key question in determining the progression of events. In 1 Peter 5:4, we learn that "when the Chief Shepherd appears," the elders will receive their "unfading crown of glory." Mark references to time (such as "when") with a clock 🕒.

Where *did or will this happen? Where was it said?* In 1 Peter 5, the only reference to a place is in verse 13, where there is a greeting from "she who is in Babylon." Mark geographical locations by double-underlining them in green.

Why *is something being said or mentioned? Why would or will this happen? Why* *at this time? Why this person?* First Peter 5:12 explains why and how Peter wrote this epistle, establishing the book's purpose: to exhort and testify that this is the true grace of God, that they may stand firm in it.

How *will it happen? How is it to be done? How is it illustrated?* In 1 Peter 5:2, note *how* the elders are to exercise oversight: voluntarily and eagerly, according to the will of God.

Every time you study a passage of the Bible, you should keep the "5 W's and an H" in mind. Don't be concerned if you can't find the answer to each question every time. Remember, there are many types of literature in the Bible and not all the questions will apply. As you ask *what, when, who, where, why,* and *how,* make notes in the margin of your Bible. Meditate on the truths God reveals to you. Think how they apply to you. This will keep your study from becoming an intellectual pursuit of knowledge for its own sake.

STEP THREE

MARK KEY WORDS AND PHRASES

A key word is one that is essential to the text. It might be a noun, a descriptive word, or an action that plays a part in conveying the author's message. A key word or phrase is one which, when removed, leaves the passage devoid of meaning. Often key words and phrases are repeated in order to convey the author's point or purpose for writing. They may be repeated throughout a chapter, a segment of a book, or the book as a whole. For example, notice that some form of the word *suffering* is used three times in 1 Peter 5.

As you mark key words, ask the same *who, what, when, where, why,* and *how* questions of them as you did of the passage as a whole. For example, *Who* suffers? *What* caused the suffering? etc.

Key words can be marked in several ways:

❧ *Through the use of symbols.*

❧ *Through the use of colors.* Colored pencils and pens with fine tips work best.

SIN COVENANT GRACE

❧ *Through a combination of colors and symbols.*

Always mark each key word the same way every time you observe it. Then, in future study, the visual impact of your marks will help you track key subjects and quickly identify significant truths throughout Scripture. To be sure that you are consistent, list key words, symbols, and color codes on an index card and use it as a bookmark in your Bible.

Be sure to mark pronouns (*I, you, he, she, it, we, our,* and so on) and synonyms (words that have the same meaning in the context) the same way you mark the words to which they refer. For example, a synonym for the devil in 1 Peter 5:8 is *adversary.* The pronoun *him* in verse 9 also refers to the devil. Notice how marking the synonym *adversary* for the devil gives additional insight into his nature.

STEP FOUR

LOOK FOR LISTS

Making lists can be one of the most enlightening things you do as you study a section of Scripture. Lists reveal truths and highlight important concepts. The best way to discover lists in the text is to observe how a key word is described, note what is said about someone or something, or group related thoughts or instructions together. (Develop lists on a separate piece of paper, then if you want, record the significant lists in the margin of your Bible.)

The Inductive Marking Approach

1 PETER 5 ~ SAMPLE A

IN THE EPISTLES, MARK EVERY REFERENCE TO THE AUTHOR IN ONE COLOR, AND EVERY REFERENCE TO THE RECIPIENTS IN ANOTHER

IDENTIFY SIMPLE LISTS

MARK KEY WORDS AND SYNONYMS, SUCH AS GOD, CHRIST, DEVIL, SUFFERING

MARK PRONOUNS

DOUBLE-UNDERLINE IN GREEN ALL GEOGRAPHICAL LOCATIONS

Chapter 5 Theme ______________________

5 [a]Therefore, I exhort the elders among you, as *your* [b]fel-
low elder and [c]witness of the sufferings of Christ, and
a [d]partaker also of the glory that is to be revealed,
2 shepherd [a]the flock of God among you, exercising
oversight [b]not under compulsion, but voluntarily, according
to *the will of* God; and [c]not for sordid gain, but with
eagerness;
3 nor yet as [a]lording it over [1]those allotted to your charge,
but [2]proving to be [b]examples to the flock.
4 And when the Chief [a]Shepherd appears, you will receive
the [b]unfading [1c]crown of glory.
5 [a]You younger men, likewise, [b]be subject to *your* elders;
and all of you, clothe yourselves with [c]humility toward one
another, for [d]GOD IS OPPOSED TO THE PROUD, BUT GIVES GRACE
TO THE HUMBLE.
6 Therefore [a]humble yourselves under the mighty hand
of God, that He may exalt you at the proper time,
7 casting all your [a]anxiety on Him, because He cares for
you.
8 [a]Be of sober *spirit,* [b]be on the alert. Your adversary,
[c]the devil, prowls around like a roaring [d]lion, seeking
someone to devour.
9 [1a]But resist him, [b]firm in *your* faith, knowing that [c]the
same experiences of suffering are being accomplished by
your [2]brethren who are in the world.
10 After you have suffered [a]for a little while, the [b]God of
all grace, who [c]called you to His [d]eternal glory in Christ,
will Himself [e]perfect, [f]confirm, strengthen *and* establish
you.
11 [a]To Him *be* dominion forever and ever. Amen.
12 Through [a]Silvanus, our faithful brother [1](for so I regard
him), [b]I have written to you briefly, exhorting and testifying
that this is [c]the true grace of God. [d]Stand firm in it!
13 She who is in Babylon, chosen together with you,
sends you greetings, and *so does* my son, [a]Mark.
14 [a]Greet one another with a kiss of love.
[b]**P**eace be to you all who are in Christ.

Suffering:
1. Christ Suffered.
2. Brethren are suffering.
3. You will suffer.
4. But God perfects, confirms, strengthens, and establishes those who suffer!

MAKE TOPICAL LISTS FROM KEY WORDS—COMPILE IN THE MARGIN

First Peter 5:2, 3, for example, contains a *simple list* instructing the elders how to shepherd their flock. You can number simple lists within the text for easy reference (Sample A).

Topical lists capture a truth, quality, or characteristic of a specific subject throughout a passage. One way to discover a topical list is to follow a key word through a chapter and note what the text says about the word each time it is used. (You may want to develop your lists on a worksheet before transferring them to the margin of your *NISB*.) See sample A for how a list could be made for the key word *suffering.*

As you write your observations on suffering, you will begin to have a better and broader understanding of God's thoughts on this subject. You will learn that:

- Christ suffered
- the brethren in the world are suffering
- the recipients of the letter may also endure suffering

You will also discover that God:

- perfects
- confirms
- strengthens
- establishes those who suffer

The application value of lists such as these is immeasurable. The next time you endure suffering, you will be able to recall more quickly that:

- Christ suffered
- others are suffering
- ultimately God will use suffering to strengthen your own life

Discovering truths that apply to your daily life is what makes lists such an important part of the inductive method.

STEP FIVE

WATCH FOR CONTRASTS AND COMPARISONS

Contrasts and comparisons use highly descriptive language to drive home significant truths and vital lessons. The word pictures they paint make it easier to remember what you've learned.

A *contrast* is a comparison of things that are different or opposite, such as light/darkness or proud/humble. The word *but* often signifies a contrast is being made. You may want to note contrasts in the text or the margin of your Bible.

A *comparison* points out similarities and is often indicated by the use of words such as *like, as,* and *as it were.* For example, Peter says in 1 Peter 5:8: "Your adversary, the devil, prowls around *like* a roaring lion." You may want to highlight comparisons in a distinctive way so you will recognize them quickly when you return to the passage in the future.

STEP SIX

NOTE EXPRESSIONS OF TIME

The relationship of events in time often sheds light on the true meaning of the text. The timing of something can be observed in exact statements such as "on the tenth day of the eleventh month" or "at the feast of Booths." These phrases can be indicated in the margin by drawing a simple clock in a specific color, such as green, and a squiggly line under the phrase.

Time is also indicated by words such as *until, then, when,* and *after*. These words show the relationship of one statement or event to another. Marking them will help you see the sequence of events and lead to accurate interpretation of Scripture.

STEP SEVEN

IDENTIFY TERMS OF CONCLUSION

Terms of conclusion usually follow an important sequence of thought and include words such as *wherefore, therefore, for this reason,* and *finally.* As the saying goes, when you see a *therefore* (or any term of conclusion),

The Inductive Marking Approach

1 PETER 5 ~ SAMPLE B

IDENTIFY TERMS OF CONCLUSION

DEVELOP CHAPTER THEMES

Chapter 5 Theme Be Humble & Sober; Resist & Stand Firm

5 [a]Therefore, I exhort the elders among you, as *your* [b]fel-
low elder and [c]witness of the sufferings of Christ, and
a [d]partaker also of the glory that is to be revealed,
2 shepherd [a]the flock of God among you, exercising
oversight [b]not under compulsion, but voluntarily, according
to *the will of* God; and [c]not for sordid gain, but with
eagerness;
3 nor yet as [a]lording it over [1]those allotted to your charge,
but [2]proving to be [b]examples to the flock.
4 And when the Chief [a]Shepherd appears, you will
receive the [b]unfading [1c]crown of glory.
5 [a]You younger men, likewise, [b]be subject to *your* elders;
and all of you, clothe yourselves with [c]humility toward one
another, for [d]GOD IS OPPOSED TO THE PROUD, BUT GIVES GRACE
TO THE HUMBLE.
6 Therefore [a]humble yourselves under the mighty hand
of God, that He may exalt you at the proper time,
7 casting all your [a]anxiety on Him, because He cares for
you.
8 [a]Be of sober *spirit,* [b]be on the alert. Your adversary,
[c]the devil, prowls around like a roaring [d]lion, seeking
someone to devour.
9 [1a]But resist him, [b]firm in *your* faith, knowing that [c]the
same experiences of suffering are being accomplished by
your [2]brethren who are in the world.
10 After you have suffered [a]for a little while, the [b]God of
all grace, who [c]called you to His [d]eternal glory in Christ,
will Himself [e]perfect, [f]confirm, strengthen *and* establish
you.
11 [a]To Him *be* dominion forever and ever. Amen.
12 Through [a]Silvanus, our faithful brother [1](for so I regard
him), [b]I have written to you briefly, exhorting and testifying
that this is [c]the true grace of God. [d]Stand firm in it!
13 She who is in Babylon, chosen together with you,
sends you greetings, and *so does* my son, [a]Mark.
14 [a]Greet one another with a kiss of love.
[b]**P**eace be to you all who are in Christ.

MARK CONTRASTS

proud / humble
↓ ↓
is opposed / is given grace

MARK COMPARISONS

MARK SIGNIFICANT EXPRESSIONS OF TIME WITH A CLOCK

LFL

Satan may bring suffering but it has an end. God will use it for my good.

DISCOVER LESSONS FOR LIFE

note what it is there for. You should be able to look through the preceding verses and summarize the message. For example, 1 Peter 5:6 says, *"Therefore* humble yourselves...." If you will look, you will discover that you should humble yourself under the hand of God because God "is opposed to the proud, but gives grace to the humble."

STEP EIGHT

DEVELOP CHAPTER THEMES

The theme of a chapter will center on the main person, event, teaching, or subject of that section of Scripture. Themes are often revealed by reviewing the key words and lists you developed. Try to express the theme as briefly as possible, using words found in the text.

Chapter 5 Theme Be Humble & Sober

5 [a]Therefore, I exhort the elders among you, as
elder and [c]witness of the sufferings of Christ
taker also of the glory that is to be revealed,
2 shepherd [a]the flock of God among you, exercis
[b]not under compulsion, but voluntarily, according

For example, possible themes for 1 Peter 5 might be *Exhortations to Elders, Younger Men, and the Suffering,* or *God Gives Grace to the Humble*. The point of observation is to answer the question: What does the passage say? The theme summarizes the answer. If needed, record the themes in pencil so you can adjust them as your study deepens.

STEP NINE

DISCOVER LESSONS FOR LIFE

In the process of observing the text and seeing how God instructed people and dealt with various individuals, the Holy Spirit will bring to your attention truths that God wants you to be aware of and live by in your own life. These "Lessons for Life" can be noted in the margin under the abbreviation "LFL," or you may wish to create a distinctive symbol to mark your Lessons for Life throughout your *NISB*.

Recording these will add a "devotional" element to your Bible and serve as a good reminder (or legacy) of what God has spoken to your heart when you or others read it.

STEP TEN

COMPLETE THE *AT A GLANCE* CHART

The AT A GLANCE chart, found at the end of every book in the *NISB*, provides a compact visual summary of the book that you can return to again and again for easy reference. See the sample AT A GLANCE charts on the following pages.

Record the author of the book. If the author is not mentioned by name, read the introduction for that book. If the author is not mentioned in either place, leave this space blank.

Record the date the book was written. If the date of writing is known, it will be mentioned in the introduction that precedes each book.

Record the key words. If the key words are not already listed on the AT A GLANCE chart, you will find them listed in the THINGS TO DO section at the beginning of each book. Mark these as you will mark them in the Bible text.

In order to notice subjects which run throughout the entire Bible, there are some key words or phrases you will want to consistently mark in a distinctive manner. Write these on a card, color-code them in the way you intend to mark them throughout your Bible, and use the card as a bookmark.

A sample list of key words to mark (already colored) appears on page NISB-26.

Copy the chapter themes that you recorded at the beginning of each chapter. Because chapter divisions were added much later than the Bible was originally written, they do not always fall naturally in the text. Occasionally you will find a chapter with more than one theme. If this is true, record both themes.

1 PETER AT A GLANCE

Theme of 1 Peter: Suffering and Glory

SEGMENT DIVISIONS

	CHAPTER THEMES
	1 Trials Prove Your Faith - Be Holy
	2 You're Chosen: Follow Christ's Example - Submit
	3
	4
	5

Author:
Peter

Date:
63 or 64 A.D.

Purpose:
To exhort to stand firm in true grace (5:12)

Key Words:
suffering, trials (and all synonyms)
grace
glory
salvation
any reference to Jesus' future revelation
love
Holy Spirit
called
chosen
holy

Complete the AT A GLANCE charts throughout the Bible as you discover book and chapter themes

Look for and record segment divisions. See if any of the chapters can be grouped under a common theme or a common event. This is called a *segment division*. Segment divisions help you see the framework of a book.

The number and types of segment divisions will vary. A book might be divided according to dates, geographical locations, reigns of kings, major characters or events, topics, or doctrines.

When you gain a broad view of a book through its segment divisions, it is easier to understand its content and purpose. The AT A GLANCE chart for the Gospel of John (sample D) shows a number of ways this book could be divided. For example, on the last line under "Segment Divisions," you will notice "Structure of Book." This shows you how John presents his material to achieve his purpose for writing this gospel.

Generally the instructions at the beginning of each book in your *NISB* will help you understand how that book might be divided.

Record the purpose of the book. Discerning the author's purpose for writing and then keeping this purpose in mind while you study the text will help you handle the Word of God accurately. Unless the author specifically states his purpose for writing, as in 1 Peter 5:12 and John 20:31, you will have to discover it by other means:

1. Look for the main subjects covered in the book. These can often be recognized as you study the key repeated words.
2. Watch for any problems that are addressed. It may be that the author's purpose in writing was to deal with these problems.
3. Note exhortations and warnings that are given. These may be the reason for the book.
4. Observe what the author did *not* cover in his writing. When you know what the author covered and what was left unsaid, you are better able to narrow down the real purpose of the book.

Record the main theme of the book. Once you have listed the theme for each chapter, evaluated the author's purpose for writing, and observed the content of the book chapter by chapter and segment by segment, you will be prepared to determine the theme of the book. What one statement best describes the book as a whole?

Once you have completed the ten steps of observation, you are ready to move into interpretation and application.

The At A Glance Charts

Gospel of John ~ Sample D

John at a Glance

Theme of John: Eternal life through Jesus Christ, Son of God

Segment Divisions

structure of Book	written	signs and miracles	Ministry		Chapter Themes
Introduces Jesus as Christ, Son of God	That you may believe Jesus is the Christ, Son of God		To Israel	1	Prologue - The Word John the Baptist / calling disciples
		Water to wine		2	wedding Cana / cleansing temple
Gives signs that prove Jesus is Christ, Son of God				3	born again
		Heals noble-man's son		4	woman at well / royal official
		Heals lame man		5	father / son
		Feeds 5,000 walks on water		6	bread / feeding 5,000
				7	feast of tabernacles / thirst-drink
				8	adulterous woman / truth sets free
		Heals blind man		9	blind man
				10	sheep / shepherd
		Raises Lazarus from dead		11	raising Lazarus
Decision time	Hour has come		To Disciples	12	dinner at Bethany / King on donkey
Life that belongs to those who believe God	That you may have life			13	last supper / washing-disciples
				14	Father's house / hearts be troubled
				15	abide / vine and branches
				16	Holy Spirit / another helper
				17	Lord's prayer / high-priestly prayer
Obtaining of that life—by death and resurrection			To All Mankind	18	arrest and trial
				19	crucifixion
		Resurrection appearances		20	resurrection
Purpose of life: love and follow			To Disciples	21	do you love Me?

Author:
John

Date:
about A.D. 85

Purpose:
that his readers would believe that Jesus is the Christ, God's Son, and thus have eternal life

Key Words:
(including synonyms)
signs / miracles
believe
life
judge
judgment
witness
sin
true, truth
king
kingdom
love
works
commandments
fruit
abide
ask
truth, truly, true
devil (Satan, ruler of this world)

A System for Marking Key Words Including Synonyms and Pronouns Throughout Your Bible

Color-coding key words with various color combinations is very helpful, as using too many symbols can clutter the text.

In an epistle, color *the author* in one color, e.g. blue and *the recipient(s)* another; e.g. orange.

As you mark, choose certain colors to represent various things. For example, blue could be your color for Israel, then anything connected with Israel would always have blue in the color combination; yellow your color for God; anything connected with redemption could be red, and so on.

When you mark a key word such as *circumcised,* mark the negative variation, *uncircumcised,* with a line through it like this:

Mark references to time with a green clock like this: and a squiggly green line under the phrase.

Double-underline in green all geographical locations like this:

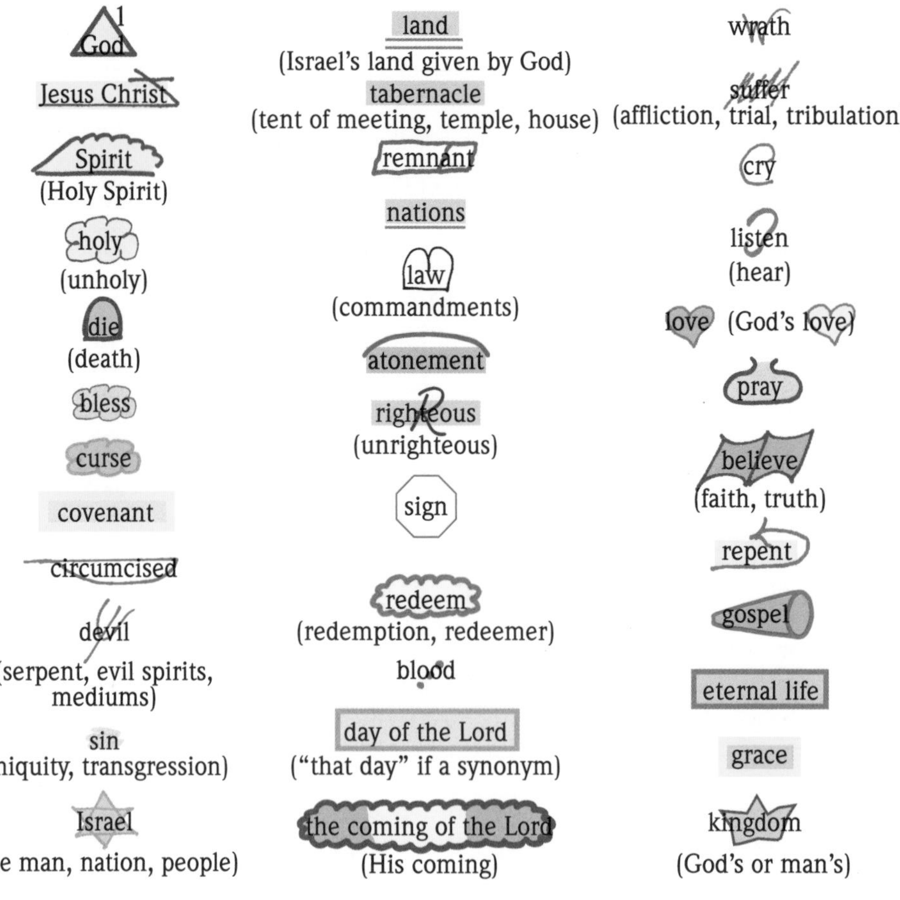

[1]We do not always mark God or Jesus Christ, as sometimes it clutters the text too much.

INTERPRETATION

Discover What It Means!

While observation leads to an accurate understanding of what the Word of God *says*, interpretation goes a step further and helps you understand what it *means*. When you accurately interpret the Word of God, you will be able to confidently put its truths into practice in your daily life.

Like many other people, you may have been taught a system of beliefs before you ever studied God's Word for yourself. Or you may have formed opinions of what the Bible teaches before you carefully examined the Scriptures. As you learn to handle God's Word accurately, you will be able to discern if what you believe is in agreement with Scripture. If this is your desire and you come to the Word of God with a teachable spirit, God will lead you and guide you into all truth.

As you seek to interpret the Bible accurately, the following guidelines will be helpful.

1. **Remember that context rules.**

The word *context* means "that which goes with the text." To understand the context you must be familiar with the Word of God. If you lay the solid foundation of observation, you will be prepared to consider each verse in the light of:

- the surrounding verses
- the book in which it is found
- the entire Word of God

As you study, ask yourself: Is my interpretation of a particular section of Scripture consistent with the theme, purpose, and structure of the book in which it is found? Is it consistent with other Scripture about the same subject, or is there a glaring difference? Am I considering the historic and cultural context of what is being said? Never take a Scripture out of its context to make it say what you want it to say. Discover what the author is saying; don't add to his meaning.

2. **Always seek the full counsel of the Word of God.**

When you know God's Word thoroughly, you will not accept a teaching simply because someone has used one or two isolated verses to support it. Those verses may have been taken out of context, or other important passages might have been overlooked or ignored that would have led to a different understanding. As you read the Bible regularly and extensively, and as you become more familiar with the whole counsel of God's Word, you will be able to discern whether a teaching is biblical or not.

Saturate yourself in the Word of God; it is your safeguard against wrong doctrine.

3. **Remember that Scripture will never contradict Scripture.**

The best interpretation of Scripture is Scripture. Remember, all Scripture is inspired by God; it is God-breathed. Therefore, Scripture will never contradict itself.

The Bible contains all the truth

you will ever need for any situation in life. Sometimes, however, you may find it difficult to reconcile two seemingly contradictory truths taught in Scripture. An example of this would be the sovereignty of God and the responsibility of man. When two or more truths that are clearly taught in the Word seem to be in conflict, remember that we as humans have finite minds. Don't take a teaching to an extreme that God doesn't. Simply humble your heart in faith and believe what God says, even if you can't fully understand or reconcile it at the moment.

4. **Don't base your convictions on an obscure passage of Scripture.**

An obscure passage is one in which the meaning is not easily understood. Because these passages are difficult to understand even when proper principles of interpretation are used, they should not be used as a basis for establishing doctrine.

5. **Interpret Scripture literally.**

The Bible is not a book of mysticism. God spoke to us that we might know truth. Therefore, take the Word of God at face value—in its natural, normal sense. Look first for the clear teaching of Scripture, not a hidden meaning. Understand and recognize figures of speech and interpret them accordingly (see Bible Study Helps, p. 2103).

Consider what is being said in the light of its literary style. For example, you will find more similes and metaphors in poetical and prophetic literature than in historical or biographical books. Interpret portions of Scripture according to their literary style.

Some literary styles in the Bible are:

- Historical—Acts
- Prophetic—Revelation
- Biographical—Luke
- Didactic (teaching)—Romans
- Poetic—Psalms
- Epistle (letter)—2 Timothy
- Proverbial—Proverbs

6. **Look for the single meaning of the passage.**

Always try to understand what the author had in mind when you interpret a portion of the Bible. Don't twist verses to support a meaning that is not clearly taught. Unless the author of a particular book indicates that there is another meaning to what he says, let the passage speak for itself.

APPLICATION

Discover How It Works!

No matter how much you know *about* God's Word, if you don't apply what you learn, Scripture will never benefit your life. To be a hearer of the Word and not a doer is to deceive yourself (James 1:22-25). This is why application is so vital. Observation and interpretation are the "hearing" of God's Word. With *application*, you will be transformed into Christ's image. Application is the embracing of the truth, the "doing" of God's Word. It is this process which allows God to work in your life.

Second Timothy 3:16, 17 says: "All Scripture is inspired by God and profitable for teaching, for reproof, for correction, for training in righteousness, so that the man of God may be adequate, equipped for every good work." Here is the key to application: Apply Scripture in the light of its teaching, reproof, correction, and instructions on life.

Teaching (doctrine) is what the Word of God says on any particular subject. That teaching, whatever the subject, is always true. Therefore, everything that God says in His Bible about any given subject is absolute truth.

The first step in application is to find out what the Word of God says on any particular subject through accurate observation and correct interpretation of the text. Once you understand what the Word of God teaches, you are then obligated before God to accept that truth and to live by it. When you have adjusted any false concepts or teaching you may have believed, and embraced the truth revealed in God's Word, then you have *applied* what you have learned.

Reproof exposes areas in your thinking and behavior that do not align with God's Word. Reproof is finding out where you have thought wrongly or have not been doing what God says is right. The application of reproof is to accept it and agree with God, acknowledging where you are wrong in thought or in behavior. This is how you are set free from unbelief, from sin.

Correction is the next step in application, and often the most difficult. Many times we can see what is wrong, but we are reluctant to take the necessary steps to correct it. God has not left you without help or without answers in this step of correcting what is wrong. Sometimes the answers are difficult to find, but they are always there, and any child of God who wants to please his or her Father, and asks for help, will be shown by the Spirit of God how to do so.

Many times correction comes by simply confessing and forsaking what is wrong. Other times, God gives very definite steps to take. An example of this is in Matthew 18:15-17, in which God tells us how to approach a brother when he sins. When you apply correction to your actions and attitudes, God will work in you to do His good pleasure (Philippians 2:13). Joy will follow obedience.

Training in righteousness: Although God's Word is profitable for reproof and correction, the Bible was also given to us as a handbook for living. As we spend time studying His Word, God equips us through:

- teachings
- commands
- promises

- exhortations
- warnings
- and the lives of biblical characters and insights into God's character and dealings with man

Scripture has everything you need to meet any and all situations of life, so that you "may be adequate, equipped for every good work." The most effective application takes place as you go before the Lord and talk with Him about those things that you have read, studied, seen, and heard.

INSIGHTS ON APPLYING SCRIPTURE

In applying Scripture to your life, the following questions may be helpful:

1. **What does the passage teach?** Is it general or specific? Does it apply only to specific people? To a cultural problem of the day? To a certain time in history? Has it been superseded by a broader teaching? For example, in the Old Testament, Jews were not allowed to eat certain foods or to wear a certain combination of materials. Are those prohibitions applicable to Christians today?

2. **Does this section of Scripture expose any error in my beliefs or in my behavior?** Are there any commandments that I have not obeyed? Are there any wrong attitudes or motives in my life that the Scriptures bring to light?

3. **What is God's instruction to me as His child?** Are there any new truths to be believed? Are there any new commandments to be acted upon? Are there any new insights I am to pursue? Are there any promises I am to embrace?

4. **When applying Scripture, beware of the following:**
   - Applying cultural standards rather than biblical standards
   - Attempting to strengthen a legitimate truth by using a Scripture incorrectly
   - Applying Scripture out of prejudice from past training or teaching

One of the apostle Paul's concerns for Timothy, his son in the faith, was that Timothy learn to handle God's Word in a way that would please the Lord (2 Timothy 2:15). Someday we too will want to give a good account of our stewardship of God's Word. Did we handle it accurately? Were we gentle and reasonable about our faith, giving honor to those whom God has called to lead us, while at the same time searching Scripture ourselves to understand its truths? Did we allow God's living and active Word to change our lives?

Observation, interpretation, and application lead to *transformation*. This is the goal of our study of the Word of God. Through it we are changed from glory to glory into the image of Jesus.

GETTING STARTED

With this basic understanding of the inductive process, you are ready to begin a lifetime of personal Bible study. Prayerfully choose one of the Bible's 66 books, and then begin your study.

As you begin, quickly read through the THINGS TO DO section for an overview, but don't let the instructions overwhelm you. Taken one by one, chapter by chapter, and book by book, they become very manageable.

The THINGS TO THINK ABOUT section encourages you to get alone with God to consider how the truths of the book apply to you.

Old Testament historical and prophetic books have a HISTORICAL CHART usually located just before the first chapter to help you see where the book fits historically and chronologically. And many of the books in the New Testament contain an OBSERVATIONS CHART on which to record information you are instructed to look for in the THINGS TO DO section.

Finally, each book of the Bible ends with an AT A GLANCE chart, as discussed earlier.

For added insights on particular topics relevant to your personal Bible study, you will find a BIBLE STUDY HELPS section at the end of the Bible. This section includes an overview of major events in Israel's history, a concordance, and color maps to provide a geographical frame of reference for your study of God's Word.

Also, in the index on pages 2123-2128, you will find very useful lists of all the maps, charts, and study helps in this Bible, along with their accompanying page numbers. You may find it helpful to remember that this index is right before the concordance in the back of the Bible.

As you study the Bible inductively, you will get to know God in a deep, exciting, and enlightening way—and "the people who know their God will display strength and take action" (Daniel 11:32b).

THE SPIRITUAL LIFE OF ISRAEL

COMPARATIVE TIMETABLE OF HISTORY

The Tabernacle

and the High Priest in his priestly garments

The tabernacle was a sanctuary, built for God according to the pattern of His throne in heaven, where He chose to dwell among His people. It was the focal point of Israel's national life from the time God brought them out of the land of Egypt under Moses until they settled in the land of Canaan. For more than four centuries this elect nation would worship God in the tabernacle—yet from a distance, separated by the veil from the presence of His glory, which hovered over the mercy seat on the ark of the covenant. Only the high priest in his priestly garments could enter, and that only once a year on the Day of Atonement.

*S*OLOMON'S *T*EMPLE

~ King David was grieved because he lived in Jerusalem in a house of cedar while the ark of the Lord was covered by curtains in the tabernacle. However, because David was a man of war, God gave the privilege of building the temple to David's son Solomon, who was a man of peace.
~ Solomon's magnificent work was overshadowed only when God's glory itself filled His temple. God's presence remained there for more than 350 years, until the days of Ezekiel the prophet. Then because of Judah's sin and God's impending judgment, the glory of the Lord departed.
~ In 586 B.C. the temple lay in ruins, destroyed by the Babylonians.

HEROD'S TEMPLE

at the Time of Jesus During the Feast of Tabernacles

When the remnant of Israel returned after the Babylonian captivity, the task of rebuilding the temple was overwhelming. The work began in 536 B.C. but stopped two years later. The people found it easier to rebuild their own houses rather than the house of God. Then the Lord spoke through the prophet Haggai. Convicted, the people completed the temple.

Although this temple, built under Zerubbabel's leadership, could not compare with Solomon's Temple, and although God did not fill this temple with His glory, He honored the people's obedience. ~ When Herod became king of Judea, he aspired to make this second temple more glorious than Solomon's. Magnificent as it was, the temple remained void of God's glory until Joseph and his wife, Mary, took their son, Jesus, there to present Him to the Lord. The glory of God in the person of Jesus Christ (John 1:14) would frequent Herod's Temple until the day He walked out for the last time, leaving the temple desolate. The day they crucified Him, the veil in the temple was torn in two, for a new covenant had begun. ~ In A.D. 70 Herod's Temple was destroyed, as Jesus prophesied it would be, by the Roman general Titus.

THE TEMPLE MOUNT
During the Second Temple Period

1. Second Temple (*Herod's*)
2. Western Wall
3. Wilson's Arch*
4. Barclay's Gate*
5. Small Shops
6. Main N-S Street
7. Robinson's Arch*
8. Upper City
9. Royal Porch
10. Pilasters
11. Double Gate
12. Triple Gate
13. Plaza
14. Ritual Bathhouse
15. Council House
16. Herodian Tower
17. Largest Ashlars
18. Antonia Fortress
19. Warren's Gate*
20. Court of the Gentiles
21. Eastern Gate

**Named after nineteenth-century explorers* *Note: See page 1614 for a floor plan of Herod's Temple*

THE HISTORY OF ISRAEL

ADAM TO SOLOMON

5000 4000 3000 2000 1800 1600 1400 1200 1150 1100 1050 1000

To truly appreciate and fully comprehend the totality of God's revelation to man in the Word of God, one needs a clear understanding of the whole counsel of God. Keeping events, revelations, truths, and peoples in perspective is essential. This easy-to-understand guide to Israel's history from the beginning to modern times is designed to help you place Scripture in its proper historical and chronological context. It is a tool which will make your inductive study even more rewarding and enlightening.

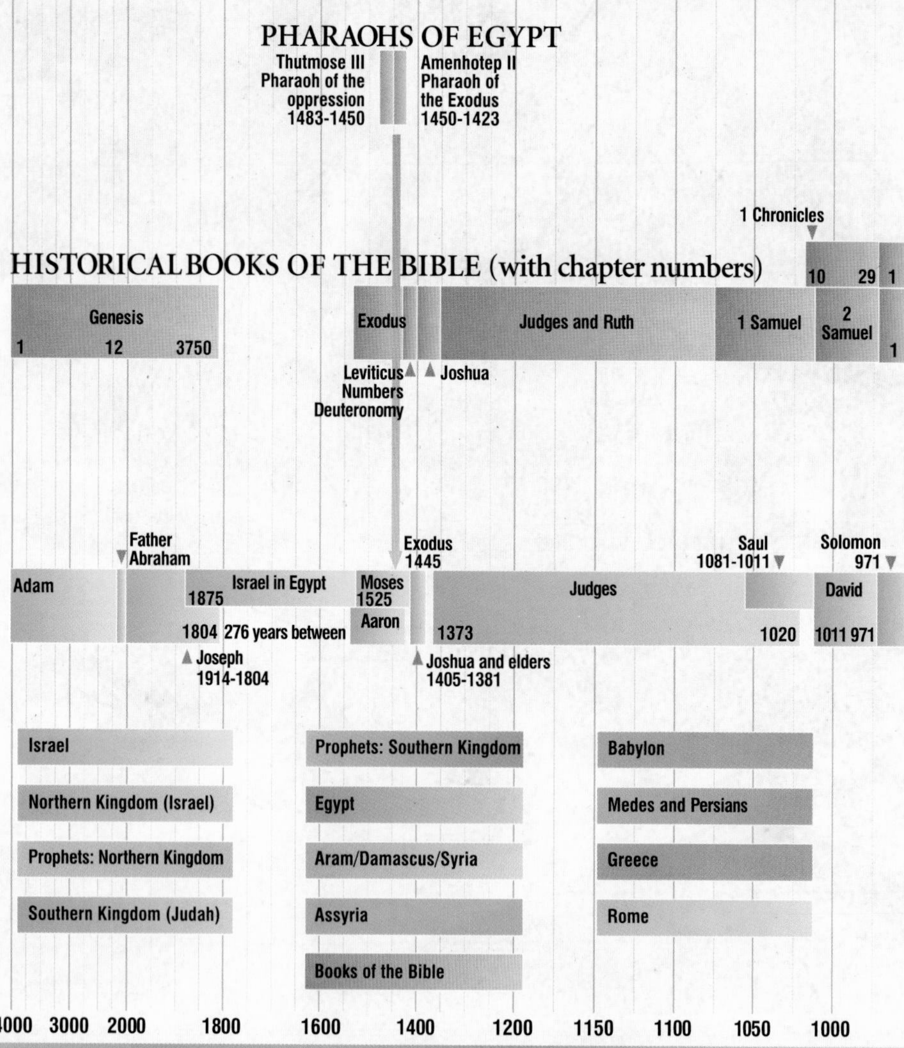

5000 4000 3000 2000 1800 1600 1400 1200 1150 1100 1050 1000

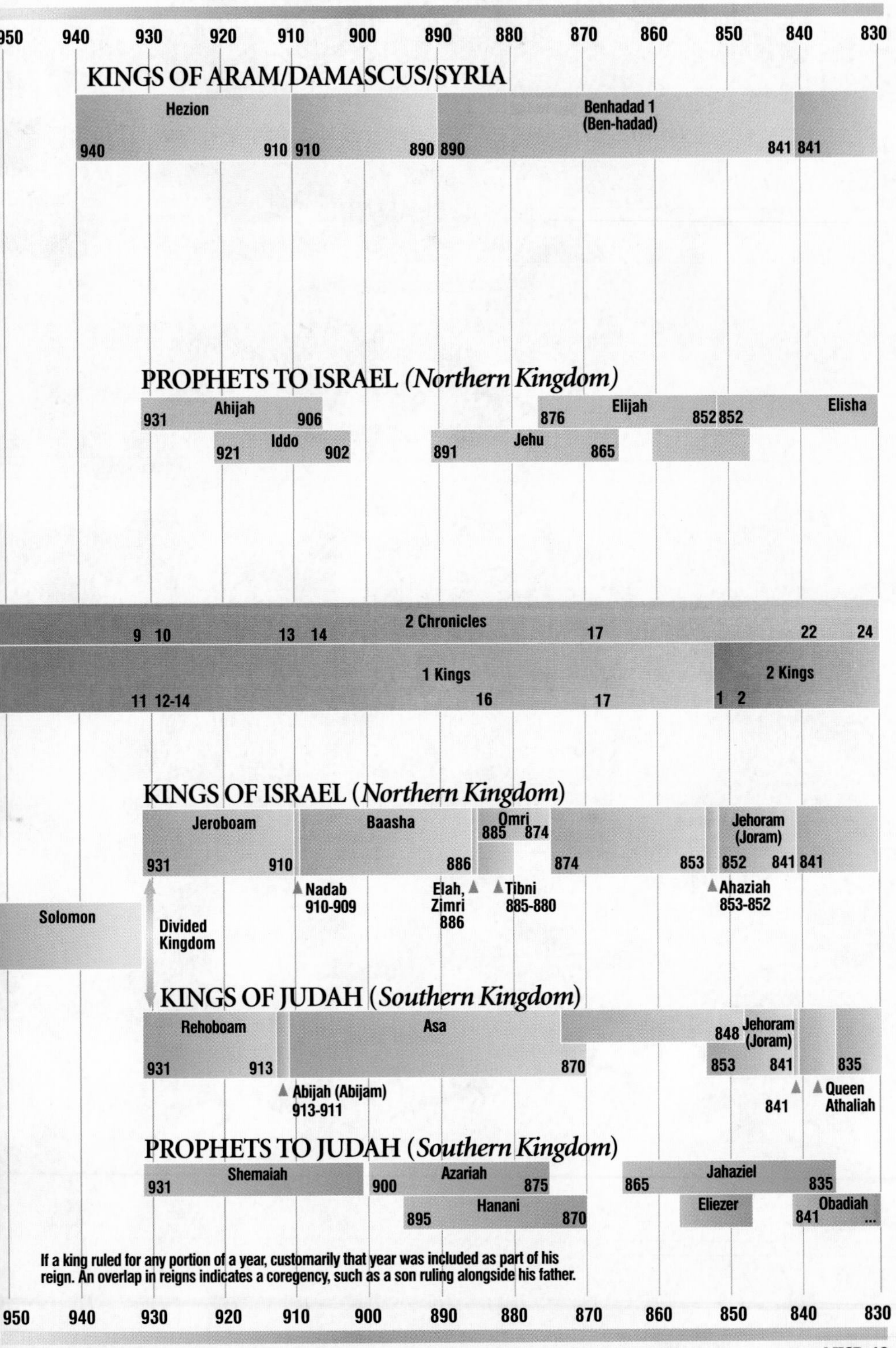

Scholars vary in the dating systems they use. The NISB generally follows John Whitcomb's system throughout for the sake of consistency.

THE ASSYRIAN CAPTIVITY

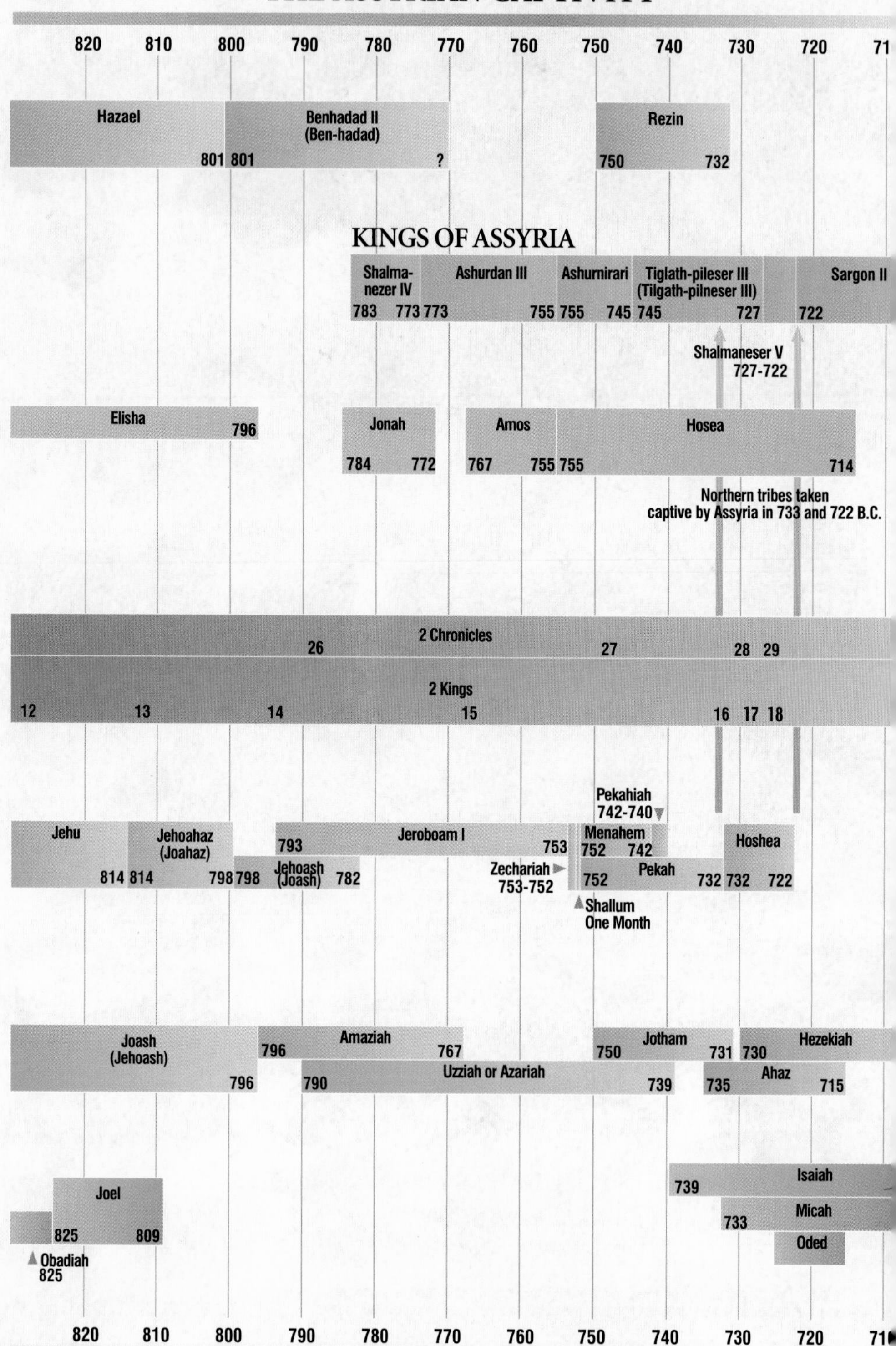

820 810 800 790 780 770 760 750 740 730 720 71
Hazael 801
Benhadad II (Ben-hadad) 801 ?
Rezin 750 732
KINGS OF ASSYRIA
Shalmanezer IV 783 773
Ashurdan III 773 755
Ashurnirari 755 745
Tiglath-pileser III (Tilgath-pilneser III) 745 727
Sargon II 722
Shalmaneser V 727-722
Elisha 796
Jonah 784 772
Amos 767 755
Hosea 755 714
Northern tribes taken captive by Assyria in 733 and 722 B.C.
2 Chronicles
26 27 28 29
2 Kings
12 13 14 15 16 17 18
Pekahiah 742-740
Jehu 814
Jehoahaz (Joahaz) 814 798
Jeroboam I 793 753
Jehoash (Joash) 798 782
Menahem 752 742
Zechariah 753-752
Pekah 752 732
Hoshea 732 722
Shallum One Month
Joash (Jehoash) 796
Amaziah 796 767
Uzziah or Azariah 790 739
Jotham 750 731
Ahaz 735 715
Hezekiah 730
Isaiah 739
Joel 825 809
Micah 733
Oded
Obadiah 825
820 810 800 790 780 770 760 750 740 730 720 71

THE BABYLONIAN CAPTIVITY

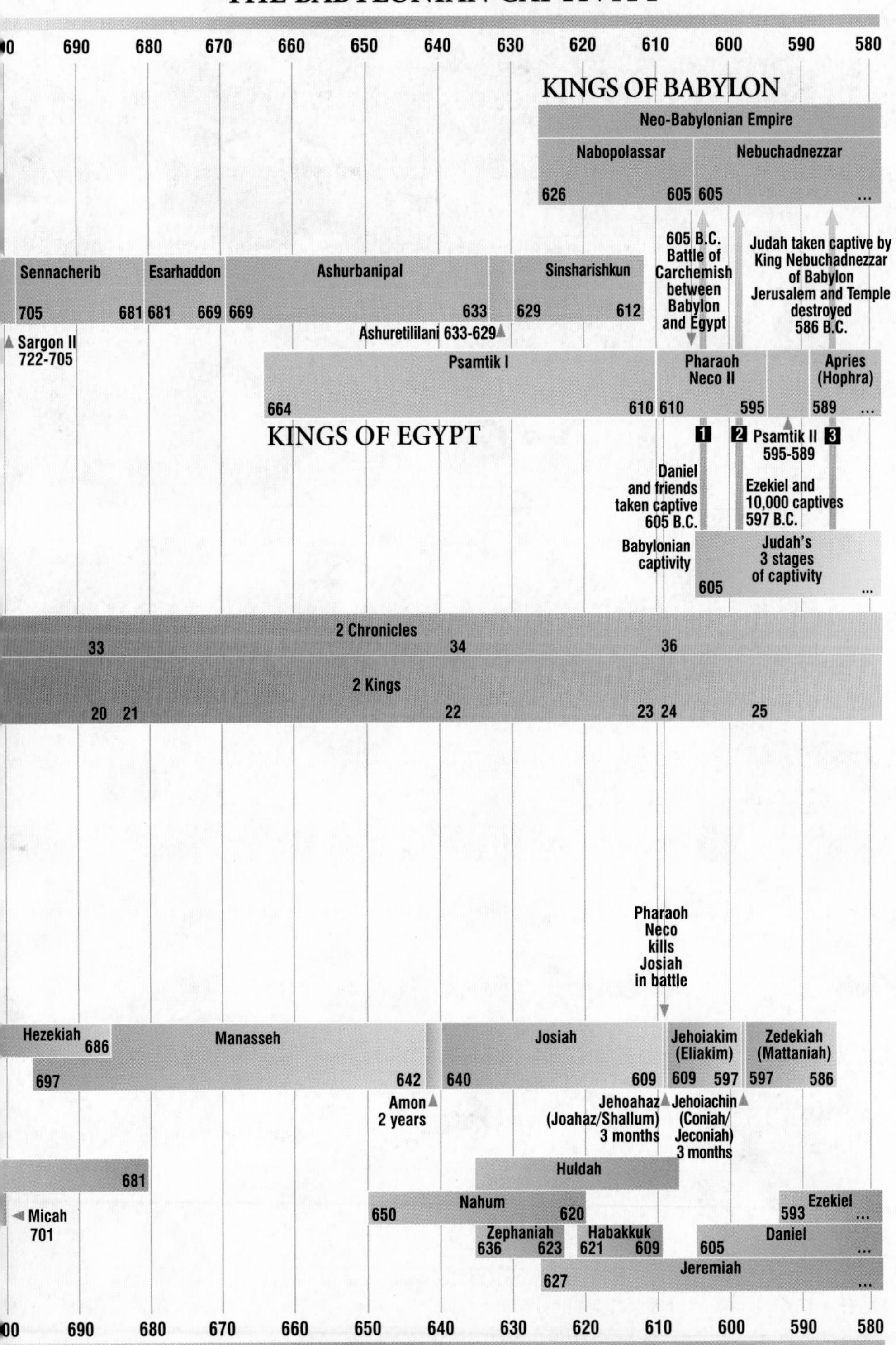

THE REBUILDING OF THE TEMPLE

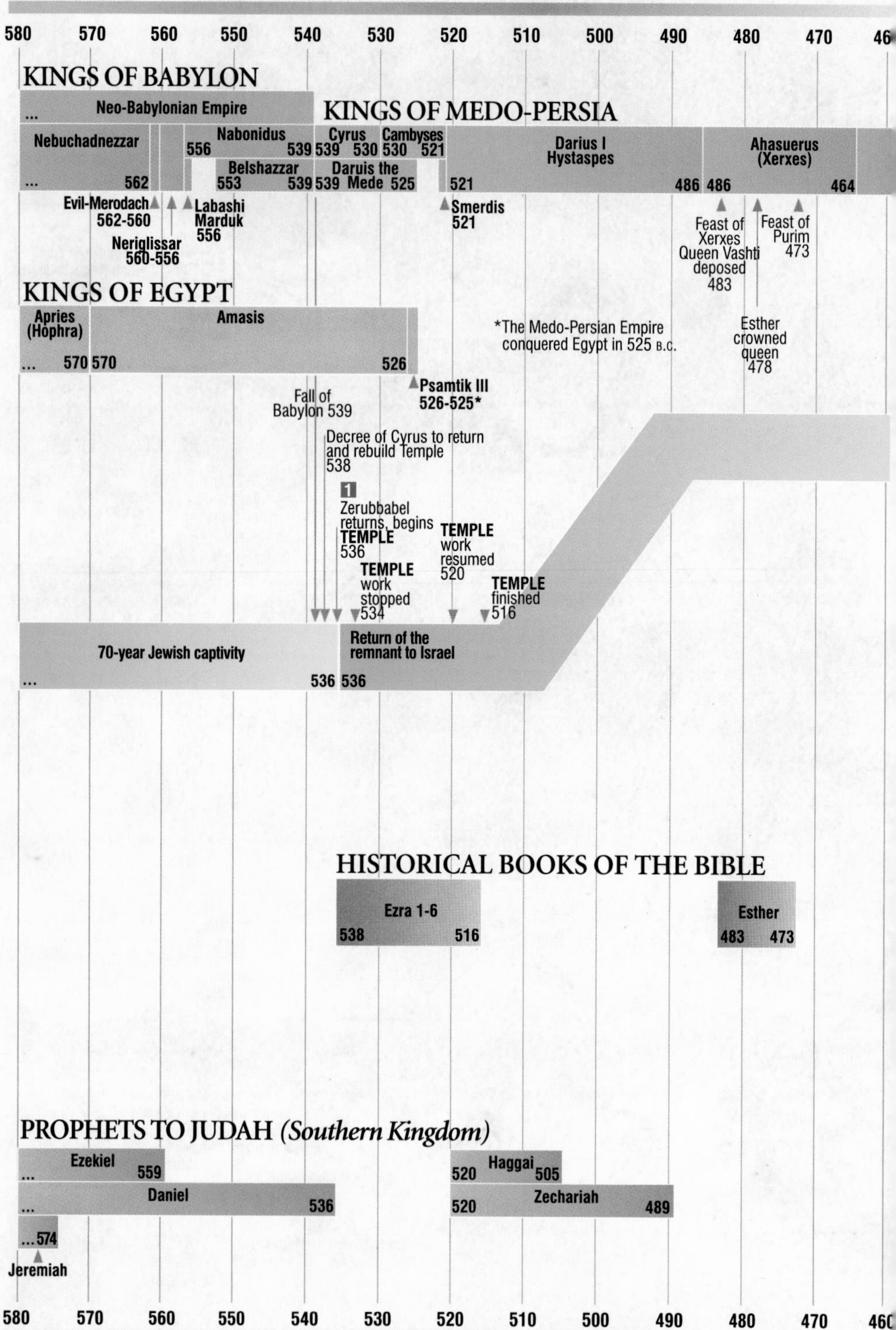

580 570 560 550 540 530 520 510 500 490 480 470 460
KINGS OF BABYLON
Neo-Babylonian Empire
Nebuchadnezzar ... 562
Evil-Merodach 562-560
Neriglissar 560-556
Labashi Marduk 556
Nabonidus 556 539
Belshazzar 553 539
KINGS OF MEDO-PERSIA
Cyrus 539 530
Daruis the Mede 539 525
Cambyses 530 521
Smerdis 521
Darius I Hystaspes 521 486
Ahasuerus (Xerxes) 486 464
Feast of Xerxes Queen Vashti deposed 483
Esther crowned queen 478
Feast of Purim 473
KINGS OF EGYPT
Apries (Hophra) ... 570
Amasis 570 526
Psamtik III 526-525*
*The Medo-Persian Empire conquered Egypt in 525 B.C.
Fall of Babylon 539
Decree of Cyrus to return and rebuild Temple 538
1
Zerubbabel returns, begins TEMPLE 536
TEMPLE work stopped 534
TEMPLE work resumed 520
TEMPLE finished 516
70-year Jewish captivity ... 536
Return of the remnant to Israel 536
HISTORICAL BOOKS OF THE BIBLE
Ezra 1-6 538 516
Esther 483 473
PROPHETS TO JUDAH (Southern Kingdom)
Ezekiel ... 559
Daniel ... 536
... 574
Jeremiah
Haggai 520 505
Zechariah 520 489
580 570 560 550 540 530 520 510 500 490 480 470 460

THE GREEK AND ROMAN PERIODS

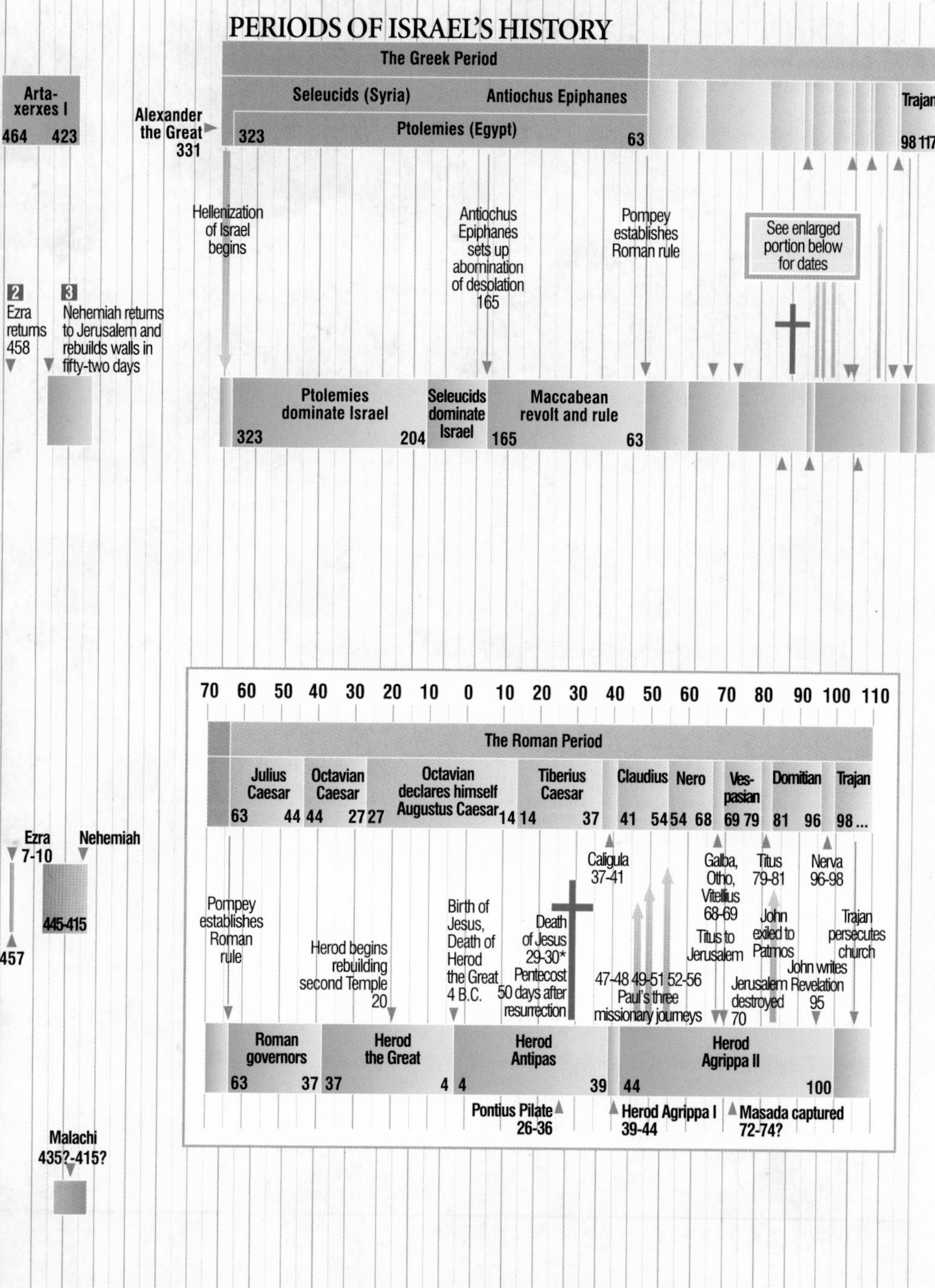

450 430 410 390 370 350 330 310 290 270 250 230 210 190 170 150 130 110 90 70 50 30 10 10 30 50 70 90 110
PERIODS OF ISRAEL'S HISTORY
The Greek Period
Arta-xerxes I
464 423
Seleucids (Syria)
Antiochus Epiphanes
Trajan
Alexander the Great 331
323
Ptolemies (Egypt)
63
98 117
Hellenization of Israel begins
Antiochus Epiphanes sets up abomination of desolation 165
Pompey establishes Roman rule
See enlarged portion below for dates
2 Ezra returns 458
3 Nehemiah returns to Jerusalem and rebuilds walls in fifty-two days
Ptolemies dominate Israel
323 204
Seleucids dominate Israel
Maccabean revolt and rule
165 63
70 60 50 40 30 20 10 0 10 20 30 40 50 60 70 80 90 100 110
The Roman Period
Julius Caesar 63 44
Octavian Caesar 44 27
Octavian declares himself Augustus Caesar 27 14
Tiberius Caesar 14 37
Claudius 41 54
Nero 54 68
Ves-pasian 69 79
Domitian 81 96
Trajan 98...
Caligula 37-41
Galba, Otho, Vitellius 68-69
Titus 79-81
Nerva 96-98
Ezra 7-10
Nehemiah
445-415
457
Pompey establishes Roman rule
Herod begins rebuilding second Temple 20
Birth of Jesus, Death of Herod the Great 4 B.C.
Death of Jesus 29-30*
Pentecost 50 days after resurrection
47-48 49-51 52-56
Paul's three missionary journeys
Titus to Jerusalem
Jerusalem destroyed 70
John exiled to Patmos
John writes Revelation 95
Trajan persecutes church
Roman governors 63 37
Herod the Great 37 4
Herod Antipas 4 39
Herod Agrippa II 44 100
Pontius Pilate 26-36
Herod Agrippa I 39-44
Masada captured 72-74?
Malachi 435?-415?
450 430 410 390 370 350 330 310 290 270 250 230 210 190 170 150 130 110 90 70 50 30 10 10 30 50 70 90 110

*Some scholars say A.D. 33.

A.D. 110 TO MODERN TIMES

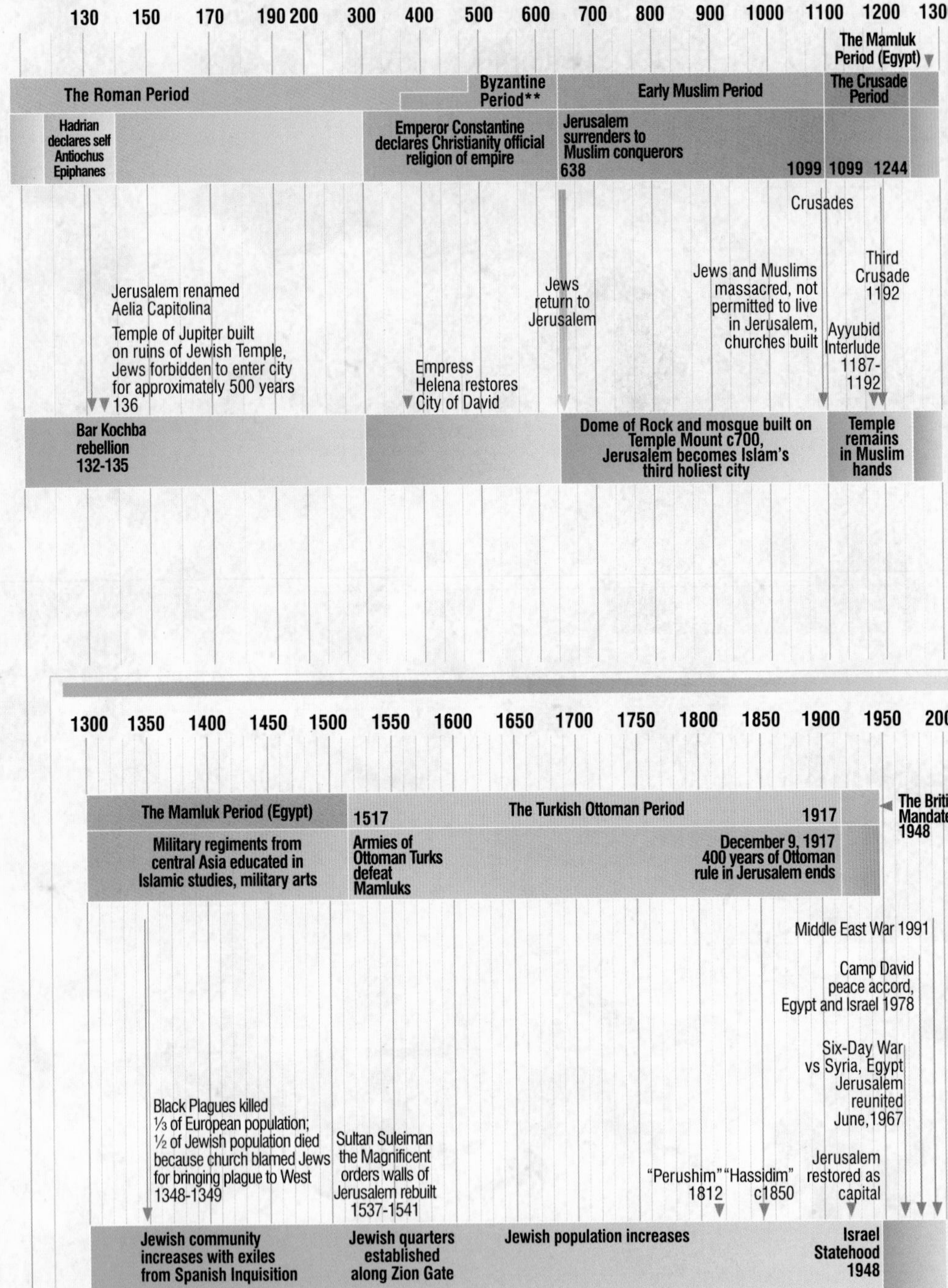

130 150 170 190 200 300 400 500 600 700 800 900 1000 1100 1200 1300
The Mamluk Period (Egypt)
The Roman Period
Byzantine Period**
Early Muslim Period
The Crusade Period
Hadrian declares self Antiochus Epiphanes
Emperor Constantine declares Christianity official religion of empire
Jerusalem surrenders to Muslim conquerors 638
1099 1099 1244
Crusades
Third Crusade 1192
Jews and Muslims massacred, not permitted to live in Jerusalem, churches built
Jews return to Jerusalem
Jerusalem renamed Aelia Capitolina
Temple of Jupiter built on ruins of Jewish Temple, Jews forbidden to enter city for approximately 500 years 136
Ayyubid Interlude 1187-1192
Empress Helena restores City of David
Bar Kochba rebellion 132-135
Dome of Rock and mosque built on Temple Mount c700, Jerusalem becomes Islam's third holiest city
Temple remains in Muslim hands
1300 1350 1400 1450 1500 1550 1600 1650 1700 1750 1800 1850 1900 1950 2000
The Mamluk Period (Egypt)
1517
The Turkish Ottoman Period
1917
The British Mandate 1948
Military regiments from central Asia educated in Islamic studies, military arts
Armies of Ottoman Turks defeat Mamluks
December 9, 1917 400 years of Ottoman rule in Jerusalem ends
Middle East War 1991
Camp David peace accord, Egypt and Israel 1978
Six-Day War vs Syria, Egypt Jerusalem reunited June, 1967
Black Plagues killed 1/3 of European population; 1/2 of Jewish population died because church blamed Jews for bringing plague to West 1348-1349
Sultan Suleiman the Magnificent orders walls of Jerusalem rebuilt 1537-1541
"Perushim" 1812
"Hassidim" c1850
Jerusalem restored as capital
Jewish community increases with exiles from Spanish Inquisition
Jewish quarters established along Zion Gate
Jewish population increases
Israel Statehood 1948
Sinai Campaign 1956
Yom Kippur War 1973

* *The dates from the Byzantine Period are taken from ***The Tower of David,*** *Museum of the History of Jerusalem.*

THE OLD TESTAMENT

GENESIS בְּרֵאשִׁית
B'RESHIT

When there was nothing, there was God. Then God spoke.

THINGS TO DO

General Instructions

Genesis falls into two segments. The first, chapters 1 through 11, covers four major events. The second segment, chapters 12 through 50, covers the lives of four major characters. The instructions on how to study this book will be divided according to these two segments.

1. As you read chapter by chapter, ask the "5 W's and an H" about the text: Who? What? When? Where? Why? and How? Ask questions such as: Who is speaking? What is happening? When is it happening? Where will it happen? Why was this said or done and what were the consequences? How did it happen? How was it to be done? etc.

2. Mark in a distinctive way any repeated words or phrases that are key to understanding the content of the chapter. There are several key words you should look for throughout the book of Genesis. These are listed on the GENESIS AT A GLANCE chart on page 87. Write these on an index card and use it as a bookmark while you study Genesis.

3. The timing and location of events can be very important. Mark time phrases with a clock ⏲, and double-underline every geographical location in green.

4. In the margin of your Bible, summarize the main things that occur in the chapter. List them in the order in which they occur. You may want to number them. For example, in Genesis 1 you could summarize what happens on each of the six days of creation.

5. If you learn something significant about God or His ways, you may want to put a triangle like this △ in the margin and color it yellow. This will act as an indicator of an important truth you've learned about God.

6. Look for the theme (the main subject) of each chapter. Record it on GENESIS AT A GLANCE. Also record the theme at the beginning of each chapter in your Bible.

7. Genesis is often referred to as the book of beginnings; it is the seedbed of truth. This is because the Word of God is a progressive revelation. *Progressive revelation* means that truth is unveiled over a period of time throughout various books of the Bible. God doesn't say everything He has to say about a particular subject at one time or in one place. Rather, He will introduce a truth and then reveal more and more about it.

   Since Genesis is the book of beginnings, when you come to the "first" of anything, record it in the chapter margin in a special way or color so you can spot it easily. For example, next to Genesis 1:26-27 you could write: "First man and woman."

8. Watch for the origins of various people groups.

Chapters 1–11

1. Genesis 1–2
   a. Note what is created on each day. Notice when a day begins and ends.
   b. There are a number of key repeated phrases in Genesis 1. Mark each in a distinctive color.

c. Chapter 2 gives a detailed explanation of the creation of mankind. Note the order of events and the man's relationship and responsibilities to God and to the woman.

2. Genesis 3–5

a. In chapter 3 list all you learn about the serpent and his tactics: how he tempts Eve, what he says. Then note what happens to Satan because he deceives Eve.

b. Note Eve's progression into sin. List what happens before and after she sins.

c. Watch what happens to Adam and Eve's relationship with God. Note the consequence of Adam's disobedience.

d. In chapters 3 through 5 note the consequences of sin's entrance into the world. Genesis 3:15 is the first promise of a Redeemer. Also, in chapter 4, observe the occupations and abilities of the people.

e. When you read chapter 5, you'll find the chart "The Overlapping of the Patriarchs' Lives" on page 10 very helpful.

3. Genesis 6–9

a. As you study these chapters observe the reasons for the flood, how and when it came, who was affected and how.

b. Watch the timing of events. Mark time phrases with a clock or record them in the margin; e.g., "Rains forty days and nights."

c. Mark the word *covenant* and list all you learn from the text about covenant.

4. Genesis 10–11

a. Observe who was separated, why and how they were separated, when and where this occurred, and what happened as a result (see map on page 2242).

b. Babylon plays an intermittently prominent role throughout the Bible, and of course its roots are in Genesis. Therefore whenever you come to any mention of Babel or Babylon, note what you learn on the chart on pages 2074, 2075.

5. When you finish reading Genesis 11, look at GENESIS AT A GLANCE. Next to "Chapter Themes" you will find a place for segment divisions. Fill in the four main events covered in Genesis 1 through 11. The chapter divisions are noted on the chart.

Chapters 12–50

1. Genesis 12 through 50 covers the biographical segment of Genesis, which focuses on the lives of four main characters: Abraham, Isaac, Jacob (also called Israel), and Joseph. When you read:

a. Follow the "General Instructions" for studying each chapter (see page 1).

b. Watch for and mark every reference to time in the life of each of the major characters (including their wives and children) in these chapters. God will often tell how old the person was when certain events occurred in his or her life.

c. The word *covenant* is more prominent in this last segment. Mark each occurrence of this word and then list all you learn about covenant from observing the text. Read the insight about covenant on page 24.

d. Note any insights or lessons you learned from the way these people lived. Note how and why God deals with these men, their families, and their associates, and what happens as a result.

2. Watch when the focus of a chapter moves from Abraham to Isaac, then to Jacob, and then to Joseph. Then on GENESIS AT A GLANCE, on the line where you recorded the

four major events of Genesis 1 through 11, divide the chapters into segments that cover the lives of Abraham, Isaac, Jacob, and Joseph. Look at the chapter themes to see where the focus moves from one of these men to the other.

3. When you finish reading Genesis 50, record on GENESIS AT A GLANCE the theme of Genesis. Under Segment Divisions, record the "firsts" that you marked throughout Genesis. (There is a blank line for any other segment divisions you might want to note.)

THINGS TO THINK ABOUT

1. What have you learned about God—His character, His attributes, and the ways He moves in the lives of men and nations? Since God never changes, can you trust Him? Can you rely on what the Word of God reveals about Him even though you may not fully understand His ways?

2. What can you learn from the lives of those mentioned in Genesis? Romans 15:4 says the things written in the Old Testament were written for our instruction, that through perseverance and the encouragement of Scripture we might have hope. What are the blessings of obedience and the consequences of disobedience?

3. Jesus took the book of Genesis at face value and attributed its authorship to Moses. As you study the Gospels, you will see that Jesus referred to the creation of Adam and Eve, to the flood, and to the destruction of Sodom and Gomorrah. He even referred to Satan as a murderer from the beginning. Jesus never contradicted the teachings of Genesis; He only affirmed them. Are you going to take God's Word at face value and believe as Jesus did, or are you going to listen to the philosophies of men? Are you going to follow men with finite minds who critique God and His Word, or are you going to accept the Bible as the Word of God and then think and live accordingly?

Chapter 1 Theme ______________________________

1 [a]In the beginning [b]God [c]created the heavens and the earth.
2 The earth was [1][a]formless and void, and [b]darkness was
over the [2]surface of the deep, and [c]the Spirit of God [d]was
[3]moving over the [2]surface of the waters.
3 Then [a]God said, "Let there be light"; and there was light.
4 God saw that the light was [a]good; and God [b]separated the
light from the darkness.
5 [a]God called the light day, and the darkness He called night.
And [b]there was evening and there was morning, one day.
6 Then God said, "Let there be [1]an [a]expanse in the midst of
the waters, and let it separate the waters from the waters."
7 God made the [1]expanse, and separated [a]the waters which
were below the [1]expanse from the waters [b]which were above
the [1]expanse; and it was so.
8 God called the [1]expanse heaven. And there was evening
and there was morning, a second day.
9 Then God said, "[a]Let the waters below the heavens be

1:1 [a]Ps 102:25; Is 40:21; John 1:1, 2; Heb 1:10 [b]Ps 89:11; 90:2; Acts 17:24; Rom 1:20; Heb 11:3 [c]Job 38:4; Is 42:5; 45:18; Rev 4:11
2 [1]Or *a waste and emptiness* [2]Lit *face of* [3]Or *hovering* [a]Jer 4:23 [b]Job 38:9 [c]Ps 104:30; Is 40:13, 14 [d]Deut 32:11; Is 31:5
3 [a]Ps 33:6, 9; 2 Cor 4:6
4 [a]Ps 145:9, 10 [b]Is 45:7
5 [a]Ps 74:16 [b]Ps 65:8
6 [1]Or *a firmament* [a]Is 40:22; Jer 10:12; 2 Pet 3:5
7 [1]Or *firmament* [a]Job 38:8-11 [b]Ps 148:4
8 [1]Or *firmament*
9 [a]Ps 104:6-9; Jer 5:22; 2 Pet 3:5

INSIGHT

The first five books of the Bible—Genesis, Exodus, Leviticus, Numbers, and Deuteronomy—are referred to as the ***Torah*** or the ***Pentateuch***. ***Torah***, a term used by the Jews, refers to the law or the teaching. ***Pentateuch***, a word coined about A.D. 200, means "the five scrolls" or the "five-volume book."

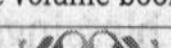

gathered into one place, and let [b]the dry land appear"; and it
was so.
10 God called the dry land earth, and the [a]gathering of the
waters He called seas; and God saw that it was good.
11 Then God said, "Let the earth sprout [1a]vegetation, [2]plants
yielding seed, *and* fruit trees on the earth bearing fruit after
[3]their kind [4]with seed in them"; and it was so.
12 The earth brought forth [1]vegetation, [2]plants yielding seed
after [3]their kind, and trees bearing fruit [4]with seed in them,
after [3]their kind; and God saw that it was good.
13 There was evening and there was morning, a third day.
14 Then God said, "Let there be [1a]lights in the [2b]expanse of
the heavens to separate the day from the night, and let them
be for [c]signs and for [d]seasons and for days and years;
15 and let them be for [1]lights in the [2]expanse of the heavens
to give light on the earth"; and it was so.
16 God made the two [1]great lights, the [a]greater [2]light [3]to
govern the day, and the lesser [2]light [3]to govern the night; *He*
made [b]the stars also.
17 [a]God placed them in the [1]expanse of the heavens to give
light on the earth,
18 and [1]to [a]govern the day and the night, and to separate the
light from the darkness; and God saw that it was good.
19 There was evening and there was morning, a fourth day.
20 Then God said, "Let the waters [1]teem with swarms of
living creatures, and let birds fly above the earth [2]in the open
[3]expanse of the heavens."
21 God created [a]the great sea monsters and every living
creature that moves, with which the waters swarmed after
their kind, and every winged bird after its kind; and God saw
that it was good.
22 God blessed them, saying, "Be fruitful and multiply, and fill
the waters in the seas, and let birds multiply on the earth."
23 There was evening and there was morning, a fifth day.
24 [a]Then God said, "Let the earth bring forth living creatures
after [1]their kind: cattle and creeping things and beasts of the
earth after [1]their kind"; and it was so.
25 God made the [a]beasts of the earth after [1]their kind, and the
cattle after [1]their kind, and everything that creeps on the
ground after its kind; and God saw that it was good.
26 Then God said, "Let [a]Us make [b]man in Our image, according
to Our likeness; and let them [c]rule over the fish of the sea and
over the birds of the [1]sky and over the cattle and over all the
earth, and over every creeping thing that creeps on the earth."
27 God created man [a]in His own image, in the image of God
He created him; [b]male and female He created them.
28 God blessed them; and God said to them, "[a]Be fruitful and
multiply, and fill the earth, and subdue it; and rule over the fish
of the sea and over the birds of the [1]sky and over every living
thing that [2]moves on the earth."
29 Then God said, "Behold, [a]I have given you every plant

9 [b]Ps 24:1, 2; 95:5

10 [a]Ps 33:7; 95:5; 146:6

11 [1]Or *grass* [2]Or *herbs* [3]Lit *its* [4]Lit *in which is its seed* [a]Ps 65:9-13; 104:14; Heb 6:7

12 [1]Or *grass* [2]Or *herbs* [3]Lit *its* [4]Lit *in which is its seed*

14 [1]Or *luminaries, light-bearers* [2]Or *firmament* [a]Ps 74:16; 136:7 [b]Ps 19:1; 150:1 [c]Jer 10:2 [d]Ps 104:19

15 [1]Or *luminaries, light-bearers* [2]Or *firmament*

16 [1]Or *luminaries, light-bearers* [2]Or *luminary, light-bearer* [3]Lit *for the dominion of* [a]Ps 136:8, 9 [b]Job 38:7; Ps 8:3; Is 40:26

17 [1]Or *firmament* [a]Jer 33:20, 25

18 [1]Lit *for the dominion of* [a]Jer 31:35

20 [1]Or *swarm* [2]Lit *on the face of* [3]Or *firmament*

21 [a]Ps 104:25-28

24 [1]Lit *its* [a]Gen 2:19; 6:20; 7:14; 8:19

25 [1]Lit *its* [a]Gen 7:21, 22; Jer 27:5

26 [1]Lit *heavens* [a]Gen 3:22; 11:7 [b]Gen 5:1; 9:6; 1 Cor 11:7; Eph 4:24; James 3:9 [c]Ps 8:6-8

27 [a]Gen 5:1f; 1 Cor 11:7; Eph 4:24; Col 3:10 [b]Matt 19:4; Mark 10:6

28 [1]Lit *heavens* [2]Or *creeps* [a]Gen 9:1, 7; Lev 26:9; Ps 127:3, 5

29 [a]Ps 104:14; 136:25

yielding seed that is on the [1]surface of all the earth, and every
tree [2]which has fruit yielding seed; it shall be food for you;
30 and [a]to every beast of the earth and to every bird of the
[1]sky and to every thing that [2]moves on the earth [3]which has
life, *I have given* every green plant for food"; and it was so.
31 God saw all that He had made, and behold, it was very [a]good.
And there was evening and there was morning, the sixth day.

Chapter 2 Theme ________________________

2 Thus the heavens and the earth were completed, and all
[a]their hosts.
2 By [a]the seventh day God completed His work which He
had done, and [b]He rested on the seventh day from all His work
which He had done.
3 Then God blessed the seventh day and sanctified it,
because in it He rested from all His work which God had
created [1]and made.
4 [1a]This is the account of the heavens and the earth when
they were created, in [b]the day that the LORD God made earth
and heaven.

5 [a]Now no shrub of the field was yet in the earth, and no
plant of the field had yet sprouted, [b]for the LORD God had not
sent rain upon the earth, and there was no man to [1]cultivate
the ground.
6 But a [1]mist used to rise from the earth and water the
whole [2]surface of the ground.
7 Then the LORD God formed man of [a]dust from the ground,
and breathed into his nostrils the breath of life; and [b]man
became a living [1]being.
8 The LORD God planted a [a]garden toward the east, in Eden;
and there He placed the man whom He had formed.
9 Out of the ground the LORD God caused to grow [a]every tree
that is pleasing to the sight and good for food; [b]the tree of life
also in the midst of the garden, and the tree of the knowledge
of good and evil.

29 [1]Lit *face of* [2]Lit *in which is the fruit of a tree yielding seed*

30 [1]Lit *heavens* [2]Or *creeps* [3]Lit *in which is a living soul* [a]Ps 145:15, 16; 147:9

31 [a]Ps 104:24, 28; 119:68; 1 Tim 4:4

2:1 [a]Deut 4:19; 17:3

2 [a]Ex 20:8-11; 31:17 [b]Heb 4:4, 10

3 [1]Lit *to make*

4 [1]Lit *These are the generations* [a]Job 38:4-11 [b]Gen 1:3-31

5 [1]Lit *work, serve* [a]Gen 1:11 [b]Ps 65:9, 10; Jer 10:12, 13

6 [1]Or *flow* [2]Lit *face of*

7 [1]Lit *soul* [a]Gen 3:19 [b]1 Cor 15:45

8 [a]Gen 13:10; Is 51:3; Ezek 28:13

9 [a]Ezek 47:12 [b]Gen 3:22; Rev 2:7; 22:2, 14

INSIGHT

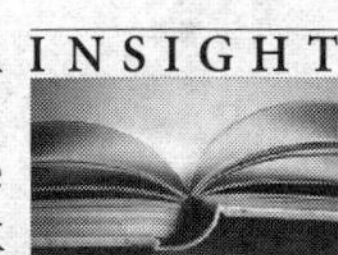

Key Words
Read footnote 1 for verse 4. As you continue reading, mark *generations of.* This is the first occurrence.

The Garden of Eden

10 Now a [a]river [1]flowed out of Eden to water the garden; and
from there it divided and became four [2]rivers.
11 The name of the first is Pishon; it [1]flows around the whole
land of [a]Havilah, where there is gold.
12 The gold of that land is good; the bdellium and the onyx
stone are there.
13 The name of the second river is Gihon; it [1]flows around the
whole land of Cush.
14 The name of the third river is [1a]Tigris; it [2]flows east of
Assyria. And the fourth river is the [3b]Euphrates.
15 Then the LORD God took the man and put him into the
garden of Eden to cultivate it and keep it.
16 The LORD God [a]commanded the man, saying, "From any
tree of the garden you may eat freely;
17 but from the tree of the knowledge of good and evil you shall
not [1]eat, for in the day that you eat from it [a]you will surely die."
18 Then the LORD God said, "It is not good for the man to be
alone; [a]I will make him a helper [1]suitable for him."
19 [a]Out of the ground the LORD God formed every beast of the
field and every bird of the [1]sky, and [b]brought *them* to the man
to see what he would call them; and whatever the man called a
living creature, that was its name.
20 The man gave names to all the cattle, and to the birds of
the [1]sky, and to every beast of the field, but for [2]Adam there
was not found [a]a helper [3]suitable for him.
21 So the LORD God caused a [a]deep sleep to fall upon the man,
and he slept; then He took one of his ribs and closed up the
flesh at that place.
22 The LORD God [1]fashioned into a woman [a]the rib which He
had taken from the man, and brought her to the man.
23 The man said,
"[a]This is now bone of my bones,
And flesh of my flesh;
[1]She shall be called [2]Woman,
Because [1]she was taken out of [3]Man."
24 [a]For this reason a man shall leave his father and his mother,
and be joined to his wife; and they shall become one flesh.
25 [a]And the man and his wife were both naked and were not
ashamed.

Chapter 3 Theme ______________________________

3 Now [a]the serpent was more crafty than any beast of the field
which the LORD God had made. And he said to the woman,
"Indeed, has God said, 'You shall not eat from [1]any tree of the
garden'?"
2 The woman said to the serpent, "[a]From the fruit of the
trees of the garden we may eat;
3 but from the fruit of the tree which is in the middle of the
garden, God has said, 'You shall not eat from it or touch it, or
you will die.'"

10 [1]Lit *was going out* [2]Lit *heads* [a]Ps 46:4

11 [1]Lit *surrounds* [a]Gen 25:18

13 [1]Lit *is the one surrounding*

14 [1]Heb *Hiddekel* [2]Lit *is the one going* [3]Heb *Perath* [a]Dan 10:4 [b]Gen 15:18

16 [a]Gen 3:2, 3

17 [1]Lit *eat from it* [a]Deut 30:15, 19, 20; Rom 6:23; 1 Tim 5:6; James 1:15

18 [1]Lit *corresponding to* [a]1 Cor 11:9

19 [1]Lit *heavens* [a]Gen 1:24 [b]Gen 1:26

20 [1]Lit *heavens* [2]Or *man* [3]Lit *corresponding to* [a]Gen 2:18

21 [a]Gen 15:12

22 [1]Lit *built* [a]1 Cor 11:8, 9

23 [1]Lit *This one* [2]Heb *Ishshah* [3]Heb *Ish* [a]Gen 29:14; Eph 5:28, 29

24 [a]Matt 19:5; Mark 10:7, 8; 1 Cor 6:16; Eph 5:31

25 [a]Gen 3:7, 10, 11

3:1 [1]Or *every* [a]2 Cor 11:3; Rev 12:9; 20:2

2 [a]Gen 2:16, 17

RETURN TO INSTRUCTIONS

4 [a]The serpent said to the woman, "You surely will not die!
5 "For God knows that in the day you eat from it your eyes
will be opened, and [a]you will be like God, knowing good and
evil."
6 [a]When the woman saw that the tree was good for food,
and that it was a delight to the eyes, and that the tree was
desirable to make *one* wise, she took from its fruit and ate; and
she gave also to her husband with her, and he ate.
7 Then the eyes of both of them were opened, and they
[a]knew that they were naked; and they sewed fig leaves
together and made themselves [1]loin coverings.
8 They heard the sound of [a]the LORD God walking in the
garden in the [1]cool of the day, [b]and the man and his wife hid
themselves from the presence of the LORD God among the trees
of the garden.
9 Then the LORD God called to the man, and said to him,
"[a]Where are you?"
10 He said, "[a]I heard the sound of You in the garden, and I
was afraid because I was naked; so I hid myself."
11 And He said, "Who told you that you were naked? Have
you eaten from the tree of which I commanded you not to
eat?"
12 [a]The man said, "The woman whom You gave *to be* with
me, she gave me from the tree, and I ate."
13 Then the LORD God said to the woman, "What is this you
have done?" And the woman said, "[a]The serpent deceived me,
and I ate."
14 The LORD God said to the serpent,
"[a]Because you have done this,
Cursed are you more than all cattle,
And more than every beast of the field;
On your belly you will go,
And [b]dust you will eat
All the days of your life;
15 And I will put [a]enmity
Between you and the woman,
And between your seed and her seed;
[b]He shall [1]bruise you on the head,
And you shall bruise him on the heel."
16 To the woman He said,
"I will greatly multiply
Your pain [1]in childbirth,
In pain you will [a]bring forth children;
Yet your desire will be for your husband,
And [b]he will rule over you."
17 Then to Adam He said, "Because you have listened to the
voice of your wife, and have eaten from the tree about which I
commanded you, saying, 'You shall not eat from it';
[a]Cursed is the ground because of you;
[b]In [1]toil you will eat of it
All the days of your life.

4 [a]John 8:44; 2 Cor 11:3
5 [a]Is 14:14; Ezek 28:2, 12-17
6 [a]Rom 5:12-19; 1 Tim 2:14; James 1:14, 15; 1 John 2:16
7 [1]Or *girdles* [a]Is 47:3; Lam 1:8
8 [1]Lit *wind, breeze* [a]Gen 18:33; Lev 26:12; Deut 23:14 [b]Job 31:33; Ps 139:1-12; Hos 10:8; Amos 9:3; Rev 6:15-17
9 [a]Gen 4:9; 18:9
10 [a]Ex 20:18, 19; Deut 5:25
12 [a]Job 31:33; Prov 28:13
13 [a]2 Cor 11:3; 1 Tim 2:14
14 [a]Deut 28:15-20 [b]Is 65:25; Mic 7:17
15 [1]Or *crush* [a]Rev 12:17 [b]Rom 16:20
16 [1]Lit *and your pregnancy, conception* [a]John 16:21; 1 Tim 2:15 [b]1 Cor 14:34
17 [1]Or *sorrow* [a]Gen 5:29; Rom 8:20-22; Heb 6:8 [b]Job 5:7; 14:1; Eccl 2:23

18 "Both thorns and thistles it shall grow for you;
And you will eat the [1]plants of the field;
19 By the sweat of your face
You will eat bread,
Till you [a]return to the ground,
Because [b]from it you were taken;
For you are dust,
And to dust you shall return."
20 Now the man called his wife's name [1a]Eve, because she
was the mother of all *the* living.
21 The LORD God made garments of skin for Adam and his
wife, and clothed them.
22 Then the LORD God said, "Behold, the man has become
like one of [a]Us, knowing good and evil; and now, he might
stretch out his hand, and take also from [b]the tree of life, and
eat, and live forever"—
23 therefore the LORD God sent him out from the garden of
Eden, to cultivate the ground from which he was taken.
24 So [a]He drove the man out; and at the [b]east of the garden of
Eden He stationed the [c]cherubim and the flaming sword which
turned every direction to guard the way to [d]the tree of life.

Chapter 4 Theme ____________________

4 Now the man [1]had relations with his wife Eve, and she
conceived and gave birth to [2]Cain, and she said, "I have
gotten a [3]manchild with *the help of* the LORD."
2 Again, she gave birth to his brother Abel. And [a]Abel was [b]a
keeper of flocks, but Cain was a tiller of the ground.
3 So it came about [1]in the course of time that Cain brought
an offering to the LORD of the fruit of the ground.
4 [a]Abel, on his part also brought of the firstlings of his flock
and of their fat portions. And [b]the LORD had regard for Abel and
for his offering;
5 but [a]for Cain and for his offering He had no regard. So
[b]Cain became very angry and his countenance fell.
6 Then the LORD said to Cain, "[a]Why are you angry? And
why has your countenance fallen?
7 "[a]If you do well, [1]will not *your countenance* be lifted up?
[b]And if you do not do well, sin is crouching at the door; and its
desire is for you, [c]but you must master it."
8 Cain [1]told Abel his brother. And it came about when they
were in the field, that Cain rose up against Abel his brother
and [a]killed him.
9 Then the LORD said to Cain, "[a]Where is Abel your
brother?" And he said, "I do not know. Am I my brother's
keeper?"
10 He said, "What have you done? [a]The voice of your
brother's blood is crying to Me from the ground.
11 "Now [a]you are cursed from the ground, which has opened
its mouth to receive your brother's blood from your hand.

18 [1]Lit *plant*
19 [a]Ps 90:3; 104:29; Eccl 12:7 [b]Gen 2:7
20 [1]I.e. living; or life [a]2 Cor 11:3; 1 Tim 2:13
22 [a]Gen 1:26 [b]Gen 2:9; Rev 22:14
24 [a]Ezek 31:11 [b]Gen 2:8 [c]Ex 25:18-22; Ps 104:4; Ezek 10:1-20; Heb 1:7 [d]Gen 2:9
4:1 [1]Lit *knew* [2]I.e. gotten one [3]Or *man, the LORD*
2 [a]Luke 11:50, 51 [b]Gen 46:32; 47:3
3 [1]Lit *at the end of days*
4 [a]Heb 11:4 [b]1 Sam 15:22
5 [a]1 Sam 16:7 [b]Is 3:9; Jude 11
6 [a]Jon 4:4
7 [1]Or *surely you will be accepted* [a]Jer 3:12; Mic 7:18 [b]Num 32:23 [c]Job 11:14, 15; Rom 6:12, 16
8 [1]Lit *said to* [a]Matt 23:35; Luke 11:51; 1 John 3:12-15; Jude 11
9 [a]Gen 3:9
10 [a]Num 35:33; Deut 21:1-9; Heb 12:24; Rev 6:9, 10
11 [a]Gen 3:14; Deut 28:15-20; Gal 3:10

12 “[a]When you cultivate the ground, it will no longer yield its
strength to you; [b]you will be a vagrant and a wanderer on the
earth.”
13 Cain said to the LORD, “My punishment is too great to bear!
14 “Behold, You have [a]driven me this day from the face of the
ground; and from Your face I will be hidden, and [b]I will be a
vagrant and a wanderer on the earth, and [c]whoever finds me
will kill me.”
15 So the LORD said to him, “Therefore whoever kills Cain,
vengeance will be taken on him [a]sevenfold.” And the LORD
[1b]appointed a sign for Cain, so that no one finding him would
slay him.
16 Then Cain went out from the presence [a]of the LORD, and
[1]settled in the land of [2]Nod, east of Eden.
17 Cain [1]had relations with his wife and she conceived, and
gave birth to Enoch; and he built a city, and called the name of
the city Enoch, after the name of his son.
18 Now to Enoch was born Irad, and Irad [1]became the father
of Mehujael, and Mehujael [1]became the father of Methushael,
and Methushael [1]became the father of Lamech.
19 Lamech took to himself [a]two wives: the name of the one
was Adah, and the name of the other, Zillah.
20 Adah gave birth to Jabal; he was the father of those who
dwell in tents and *have* livestock.
21 His brother’s name was Jubal; he was the father of all those
who play the lyre and pipe.
22 As for Zillah, she also gave birth to Tubal-cain, the forger of
all implements of bronze and iron; and the sister of Tubal-cain
was Naamah.
23 Lamech said to his wives,
“Adah and Zillah,
Listen to my voice,
You wives of Lamech,
Give heed to my speech,
[a]For I [1]have killed a man for wounding me;
And a boy for striking me;
24 If Cain is avenged [a]sevenfold,
Then Lamech seventy-sevenfold.”
25 [a]Adam [1]had relations with his wife again; and she gave
birth to a son, and named him [2]Seth, for, *she said,* “God [3]has
appointed me another [4]offspring in place of Abel, [b]for Cain
killed him.”
26 To Seth, to him also [a]a son was born; and he called his name
Enosh. Then *men* began [b]to call [1]upon the name of the LORD.

Chapter 5 Theme ______________________________

5 This is the book of the generations of Adam. In the day when
God created man, He made him [a]in the likeness of God.
2 He created them [a]male and female, and He [b]blessed them
and named them [1]Man in the day when they were created.

12 [a]Deut 28:15-24; Joel 1:10-20 [b]Lev 26:17, 36
14 [a]Gen 3:24; Jer 52:3 [b]Deut 28:64-67 [c]Num 35:19
15 [1]Or *set a mark on* [a]Gen 4:24 [b]Ezek 9:4, 6
16 [1]Lit *dwelt* [2]I.e. wandering [a]2 Kin 24:20; Jer 23:39; 52:3
17 [1]Lit *knew*
18 [1]Lit *begot*
19 [a]Gen 2:24
23 [1]Or *kill* [a]Ex 20:13; Lev 19:18; Deut 32:35; Ps 94:1
24 [a]Gen 4:15
25 [1]Lit *knew* [2]Heb *Sheth* [3]Heb *shath* [4]Lit *seed* [a]Gen 5:3 [b]Gen 4:8
26 [1]Or *by* [a]Luke 3:38 [b]Gen 12:8; 26:25; 1 Kin 18:24; Ps 116:17; Joel 2:32; Zeph 3:9; 1 Cor 1:2
5:1 [a]Gen 1:26, 27; Eph 4:24; Col 3:10
2 [1]Lit *Adam* [a]Matt 19:4; Mark 10:6 [b]Gen 1:28

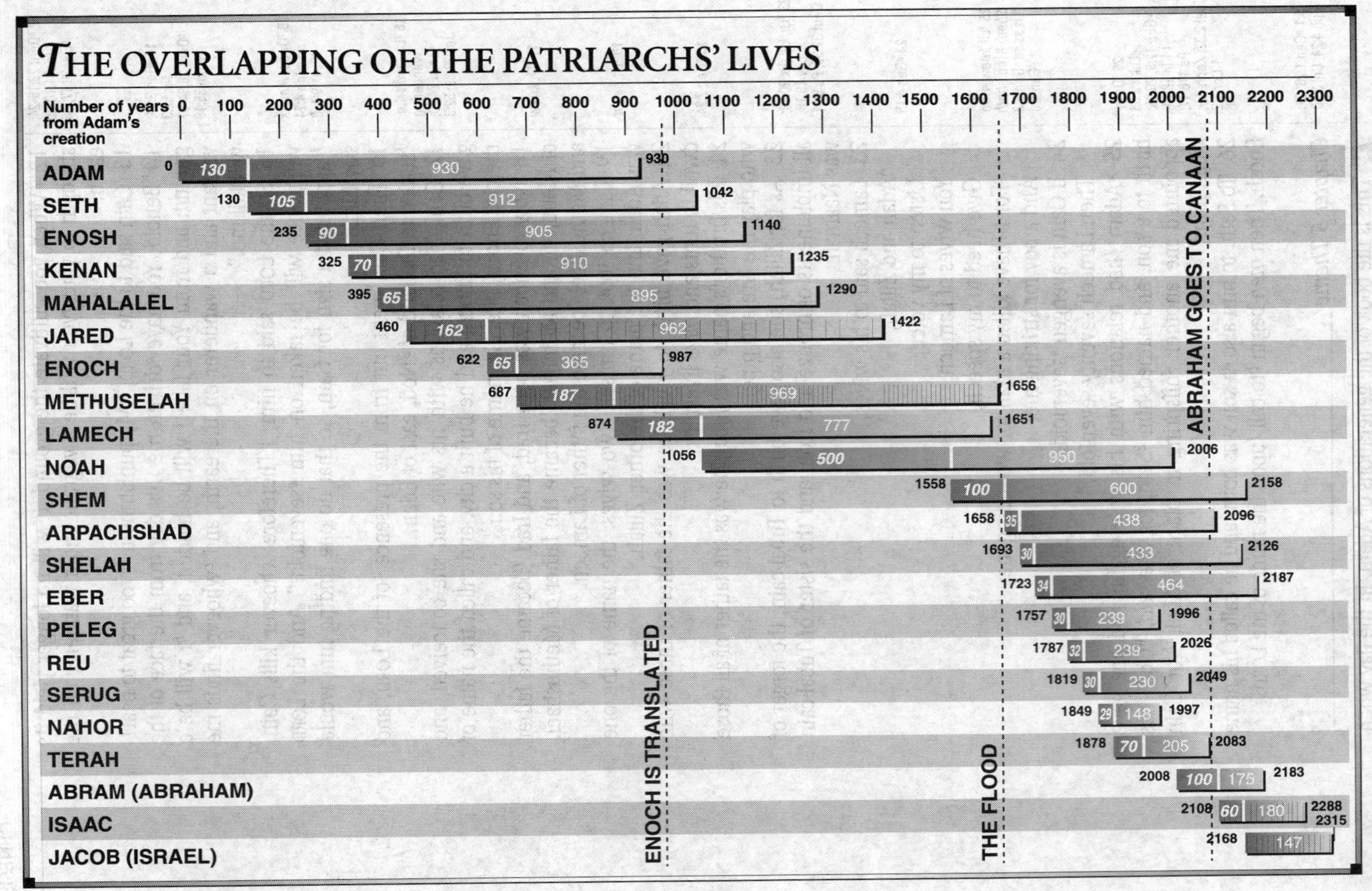

KEY: The first number inside the block is the man's age when his son (whose name is in the next line below) was born. The second number in the block is the number of years the man lived. The numbers preceding and following each block are the number of years from Adam's creation. (Note also: Shem's 1558 birth reflects Genesis 11:10's note that he was 100 two years after the flood, and Abram's 2008 birth is based on his trip to Canaan [Gen. 11:32; 12:1] at 75 [12:4].)

3 [1]Lit *begot,* and so throughout the ch

3 When Adam had lived one hundred and thirty years, he
[1]became the father of *a son* in his own likeness, according to
his image, and named him Seth.
4 Then the days of Adam after he became the father of Seth
were eight hundred years, and he had *other* sons and daughters.
5 So all the days that Adam lived were nine hundred and
thirty years, and he died.
6 Seth lived one hundred and five years, and became the
father of Enosh.
7 Then Seth lived eight hundred and seven years after he
became the father of Enosh, and he had *other* sons and
daughters.
8 So all the days of Seth were nine hundred and twelve
years, and he died.
9 Enosh lived ninety years, and became the father of Kenan.
10 Then Enosh lived eight hundred and fifteen years after he
became the father of Kenan, and he had *other* sons and
daughters.
11 So all the days of Enosh were nine hundred and five years,
and he died.
12 Kenan lived seventy years, and became the father of
Mahalalel.
13 Then Kenan lived eight hundred and forty years after he
became the father of Mahalalel, and he had *other* sons and
daughters.
14 So all the days of Kenan were nine hundred and ten years,
and he died.
15 Mahalalel lived sixty-five years, and became the father of
Jared.
16 Then Mahalalel lived eight hundred and thirty years after
he became the father of Jared, and he had *other* sons and
daughters.
17 So all the days of Mahalalel were eight hundred and ninety-
five years, and he died.
18 Jared lived one hundred and sixty-two years, and became
the father of Enoch.
19 Then Jared lived eight hundred years after he became the
father of Enoch, and he had *other* sons and daughters.
20 So all the days of Jared were nine hundred and sixty-two
years, and he died.
21 Enoch lived sixty-five years, and became the father of
Methuselah.
22 Then Enoch [a]walked with God three hundred years after
he became the father of Methuselah, and he had *other* sons
and daughters.
23 So all the days of Enoch were three hundred and sixty-five
years.
24 [a]Enoch walked with God; and he was not, for God [b]took
him.
25 Methuselah lived one hundred and eighty-seven years, and
became the father of Lamech.

22 [a]Gen 6:9; 17:1; 24:40; 48:15; Mic 6:8; Mal 2:6; 1 Thess 2:12

24 [a]2 Kin 2:11; Jude 14 [b]2 Kin 2:10; Ps 49:15; 73:24; Heb 11:5

26 Then Methuselah lived seven hundred and eighty-two years
after he became the father of Lamech, and he had *other* sons
and daughters.
27 So all the days of Methuselah were nine hundred and sixty-
nine years, and he died.
28 Lamech lived one hundred and eighty-two years, and
became the father of a son.
29 Now he called his name Noah, saying, "This one will [1]give us
rest from our work and from the toil of our hands *arising* from
[a]the ground which the LORD has cursed."
30 Then Lamech lived five hundred and ninety-five years after
he became the father of Noah, and he had *other* sons and
daughters.
31 So all the days of Lamech were seven hundred and seventy-
seven years, and he died.
32 Noah was [a]five hundred years old, and Noah became the
father of Shem, Ham, and Japheth.

Chapter 6 Theme ____________________________

6 Now it came about, when men began to multiply on the
face of the land, and daughters were born to them,
2 that the sons of God saw that the daughters of men were
[1]beautiful; and they took wives for themselves, whomever they
chose.

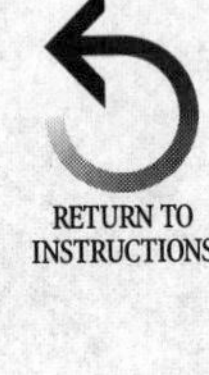

3 Then the LORD said, "[a]My Spirit shall not [1]strive with man
forever, [2b]because he also is flesh; [3]nevertheless his days shall
be one hundred and twenty years."
4 The [a]Nephilim were on the earth in those days, and also
afterward, when the sons of God came in to the daughters of
men, and they bore *children* to them. Those were the mighty
men who *were* of old, men of renown.
5 Then the LORD saw that the wickedness of man was great
on the earth, and that [a]every intent of the thoughts of his heart
was only evil continually.
6 [a]The LORD was sorry that He had made man on the earth,
and He was [b]grieved [1]in His heart.
7 The LORD said, "[a]I will blot out man whom I have created
from the face of the land, from man to animals to creeping things
and to birds of the [1]sky; for [b]I am sorry that I have made them."
8 But [a]Noah [b]found favor in the eyes of the LORD.
9 These are *the records of* the generations of Noah. Noah
was a [a]righteous man, [1b]blameless in his [2]time; Noah [c]walked
with God.
10 Noah [1]became the father of three sons: Shem, Ham, and
Japheth.
11 Now the earth was [a]corrupt in the sight of God, and the
earth was [b]filled with violence.
12 God looked on the earth, and behold, it was corrupt; for
[a]all flesh had corrupted their way upon the earth.
13 Then God said to Noah, "[a]The end of all flesh has come

29 [1]Lit *comfort us in* [a]Gen 3:17-19; 4:11

32 [a]Gen 7:6

6:2 [1]Lit *good*

3 [1]Or *rule in;* some ancient versions read *abide in* [2]Or *in his going astray he is flesh* [3]Or *therefore* [a]Gal 5:16, 17; 1 Pet 3:20 [b]Ps 78:39

4 [a]Num 13:33

5 [a]Gen 8:21; Ps 14:1-3; Prov 6:18; Matt 15:19; Rom 1:28-32

6 [1]Lit *to* [a]Gen 6:7; Jer 18:7-10 [b]Is 63:10; Eph 4:30

7 [1]Lit *heavens* [a]Deut 28:63; 29:20 [b]Gen 6:6; Amos 7:3, 6

8 [a]Matt 24:37; Luke 17:26; 1 Pet 3:20 [b]Gen 19:19; Ex 33:17; Luke 1:30

9 [1]Lit *complete, perfect;* or *having integrity* [2]Lit *generations* [a]Ps 37:39; 2 Pet 2:5 [b]Gen 17:1; Deut 18:13; Job 1:1 [c]Gen 5:24

10 [1]Lit *begot*

11 [a]Deut 31:29; Judg 2:19 [b]Ezek 8:17

12 [a]Ps 14:1-3

13 [a]Is 34:1-4; Ezek 7:2, 3; Amos 8:2; 1 Pet 4:7

before Me; for the earth is filled with violence because of them;
and behold, I am about to destroy them with the earth.
14 "Make for yourself an ark of gopher wood; you shall make
the ark with rooms, and shall [1]cover it inside and out with pitch.
15 "This is how you shall make it: the length of the ark three
hundred [1]cubits, its breadth fifty [1]cubits, and its height thirty
[1]cubits.
16 "You shall make a [1]window for the ark, and finish it to a
cubit from [2]the top; and set the door of the ark in the side of it;
you shall make it with lower, second, and third decks.
17 "Behold, [a]I, even I am bringing the flood of water upon the
earth, to destroy all flesh in which is the breath of life, from
under heaven; everything that is on the earth shall perish.
18 "But I will establish [a]My covenant with you; and [b]you shall
enter the ark—you and your sons and your wife, and your
sons' wives with you.
19 "[a]And of every living thing of all flesh, you shall bring two of
every *kind* into the ark, to keep *them* alive with you; they shall
be male and female.
20 "[a]Of the birds after their kind, and of the animals after their
kind, of every creeping thing of the ground after its kind, two
of every *kind* will come to you to keep *them* alive.
21 "As for you, take for yourself some of all [a]food which is
edible, and gather *it* to yourself; and it shall be for food for you
and for them."
22 [a]Thus Noah did; according to all that God had commanded
him, so he did.

Chapter 7 Theme ______________________

7 Then the LORD said to Noah, "Enter the ark, you and all your
household, for you *alone* I have seen *to be* [a]righteous before
Me in this [1]time.
2 "You shall take [1]with you of every [a]clean animal [2]by sevens,
a male and his female; and of the animals that are not clean
two, a male and his female;
3 also of the birds of the [1]sky, [2]by sevens, male and female,
to keep [3]offspring alive on the face of all the earth.
4 "For after [a]seven more days, I will send rain on the earth
[b]forty days and forty nights; and I will blot out from the face of
the land [c]every living thing that I have made."
5 [a]Noah did according to all that the LORD had commanded
him.
6 Now Noah was [a]six hundred years old when the flood of
water [1]came upon the earth.
7 Then [a]Noah and his sons and his wife and his sons' wives
with him entered the ark because of the water of the flood.
8 [a]Of clean animals and animals that are not clean and birds
and everything that creeps on the ground,
9 there went into the ark to Noah [1]by twos, male and female,
as God had commanded Noah.

14 [1]Or *pitch*
15 [1]I.e. One cubit equals approx 18 in.
16 [1]Or *roof* [2]Lit *above*
17 [a]2 Pet 2:5
18 [a]Gen 9:9-16; 17:7 [b]Gen 7:7
19 [a]Gen 7:2, 14, 15
20 [a]Gen 7:3
21 [a]Gen 1:29, 30
22 [a]Gen 7:5; Heb 11:7
7:1 [1]Lit *generation* [a]Gen 6:9
2 [1]Lit *to* [2]Lit *seven seven* [a]Lev 11:1-31; Deut 14:3-20
3 [1]Lit *heavens* [2]Lit *seven seven* [3]Lit *seed*
4 [a]Gen 7:10 [b]Gen 7:12, 17 [c]Gen 6:7, 13
5 [a]Gen 6:22
6 [1]Lit *was* [a]Gen 5:32
7 [a]Gen 6:18; 7:13; Matt 24:38f; Luke 17:27
8 [a]Gen 6:19, 20; 7:2, 3
9 [1]Lit *two two*

10 It came about after [a]the seven days, that the water of the
flood [1]came upon the earth.
11 In the [a]six hundredth year of Noah's life, in the second
month, on the seventeenth day of the month, on the same day
all [b]the fountains of the great deep burst open, and the
[1]floodgates of the sky were opened.
12 [a]The rain [1]fell upon the earth for forty days and forty nights.
13 On the very same day [a]Noah and Shem and Ham and
Japheth, the sons of Noah, and Noah's wife and the three wives
of his sons with them, entered the ark,
14 they and every beast after its kind, and all the cattle after
[1]their kind, and every creeping thing that creeps on the earth
after its kind, and every bird after its kind, [2]all sorts of birds.
15 So they went into the ark to Noah, [a]by twos of all flesh in
which was the breath of life.
16 Those that entered, male and female of all flesh, entered as
God had commanded him; and the LORD closed *it* behind him.
17 Then the flood [1]came upon the earth for [a]forty days, and
the water increased and lifted up the ark, so that it rose above
the earth.
18 The water prevailed and increased greatly upon the earth,
and the ark [1]floated on the [2]surface of the water.
19 The water prevailed more and more upon the earth, so that
all the high mountains [1]everywhere under the heavens were
covered.
20 The water prevailed fifteen [1]cubits higher, [a]and the
mountains were covered.
21 [a]All flesh that [1]moved on the earth perished, birds and
cattle and beasts and every swarming thing that swarms upon
the earth, and all mankind;
22 of all that was on the dry land, all [a]in whose nostrils was
the breath of the spirit of life, died.
23 Thus He blotted out [1]every living thing that was upon the
face of the land, from man to animals to creeping things and to
birds of the [2]sky, and they were blotted out from the earth; and
only [a]Noah was left, together with those that were with him in
the ark.
24 [a]The water prevailed upon the earth one hundred and fifty
days.

Chapter 8 Theme ______________________

8 But [a]God remembered Noah and all the beasts and all the
cattle that were with him in the ark; and [b]God caused a
wind to pass over the earth, and the water subsided.
2 Also [a]the fountains of the deep and the [1]floodgates of the
sky were closed, and [b]the rain from the sky was restrained;
3 and the water receded steadily from the earth, and at the
end [a]of one hundred and fifty days the water decreased.
4 In the seventh month, on the seventeenth day of the
month, [a]the ark rested upon the mountains of Ararat.

10 [1]Lit *were* [a]Gen 7:4

11 [1]Or *windows of the heavens* [a]Gen 7:6 [b]Gen 8:2

12 [1]Lit *was* [a]Gen 7:4, 17

13 [a]Gen 6:18; 7:7

14 [1]Lit *its* [2]Lit *every bird, every wing*

15 [a]Gen 6:19; 7:9

17 [1]Lit *was* [a]Gen 7:4

18 [1]Lit *went* [2]Lit *face*

19 [1]Lit *which were under all the heavens*

20 [1]I.e. One cubit equals approx 18 in. [a]Gen 8:4

21 [1]Or *crept* [a]Gen 6:7, 13, 17; 7:4

22 [a]Gen 2:7

23 [1]Lit *all existence* [2]Lit *heavens* [a]Matt 24:38, 39; Luke 17:26, 27; Heb 11:7; 1 Pet 3:20; 2 Pet 2:5

24 [a]Gen 8:3

8:1 [a]Gen 19:29; Ex 2:24; 1 Sam 1:19; Ps 105:42 [b]Ex 14:21; 15:10; Job 12:15; Ps 29:10; Is 44:27; Nah 1:4

2 [1]Or *windows of the heavens* [a]Gen 7:11 [b]Gen 7:4, 12

3 [a]Gen 7:24

4 [a]Gen 7:20

5 The water decreased steadily until the tenth month; in the tenth month, on the first day of the month, the tops of the mountains became visible.

6 Then it came about at the end of forty days, that Noah opened the [a]window of the ark which he had made;

7 and he sent out a raven, and it [1]flew here and there until the water was dried up [2]from the earth.

8 Then he sent out a dove from him, to see if the water was abated from the face of the land;

9 but the dove found no resting place for the sole of her foot, so she returned to him into the ark, for the water was on the [1]surface of all the earth. Then he put out his hand and took her, and brought her into the ark to himself.

10 So he waited yet another seven days; and again he sent out the dove from the ark.

11 The dove came to him toward [1]evening, and behold, in her [2]beak was a freshly picked olive leaf. So Noah knew that the water was abated from the earth.

12 Then he waited yet another seven days, and sent out [a]the dove; but she did not return to him again.

13 Now it came about in the [a]six hundred and first year, in the first *month,* on the first of the month, the water was dried up [1]from the earth. Then Noah removed the covering of the ark, and looked, and behold, the [2]surface of the ground was dried up.

14 In the second month, on the twenty-seventh day of the month, the earth was dry.

15 Then God spoke to Noah, saying,

16 "Go out of the ark, you and your wife and your sons and your sons' wives with you.

17 "Bring out with you every living thing of all flesh that is with you, birds and animals and every creeping thing that creeps on the earth, that they may [1a]breed abundantly on the earth, and be fruitful and multiply on the earth."

18 So Noah went out, and his sons and his wife and his sons' wives with him.

19 Every beast, every creeping thing, and every bird, everything that moves on the earth, went out [1]by their families from the ark.

20 Then Noah built [a]an altar to the LORD, and took of every [b]clean animal and of every clean bird and offered [c]burnt offerings on the altar.

21 The LORD [a]smelled the soothing aroma; and the LORD said [1]to Himself, "I will never again [b]curse the ground on account of man, for [c]the [2]intent of man's heart is evil from his youth; [d]and I will never again [3]destroy every living thing, as I have done.

22 "While the earth remains,
Seedtime and harvest,
And cold and heat,
And [a]summer and winter,
And [b]day and night
Shall not cease."

6 [a]Gen 6:16
7 [1]Lit *went out, going and returning* [2]Lit *from upon*
9 [1]Lit *face*
11 [1]Lit *the time of evening* [2]Lit *mouth*
12 [a]Jer 48:28
13 [1]Lit *from upon* [2]Lit *face* [a]Gen 7:6
17 [1]Or *swarm* [a]Gen 1:22, 28
19 [1]Or *according to their kind*
20 [a]Gen 12:7, 8; 13:18; 22:9 [b]Gen 7:2; Lev 11:1-47 [c]Gen 22:2; Ex 10:25
21 [1]Lit *to His heart* [2]Or *inclination* [3]Lit *smite* [a]Ex 29:18, 25 [b]Gen 3:17; 6:7, 13, 17; Is 54:9 [c]Gen 6:5; Ps 51:5; Jer 17:9; Rom 1:21; 3:23; Eph 2:1-3 [d]Gen 9:11, 15
22 [a]Ps 74:17 [b]Jer 33:20, 25

Chapter 9 Theme ______________________________

9 And God blessed Noah and his sons and said to them, "[a]Be
fruitful and multiply, and fill the earth.
2 "The fear of you and the terror of you will be on every beast
of the earth and on every bird of the [1]sky; with everything that
creeps on the ground, and all the fish of the sea, into your hand
they are given.
3 "Every moving thing that is alive shall be food for you; I give
all to you, [a]as *I gave* the green plant.
4 "Only you shall not eat flesh with its life, *that is,* [a]its blood.
5 "Surely I will require [1a]your lifeblood; [2b]from every beast I
will require it. And [2]from *every* man, [2]from every man's
brother I will require the life of man.
6 "[a]Whoever sheds man's blood,
By man his blood shall be shed,
For [b]in the image of God
He made man.
7 "As for you, [a]be fruitful and multiply;
[1]Populate the earth abundantly and multiply in it."
8 Then God spoke to Noah and to his sons with him, saying,
9 "Now behold, [a]I Myself do establish My covenant with you,
and with your [1]descendants after you;
10 and with every living creature that is with you, the birds, the
cattle, and every beast of the earth with you; of all that comes
out of the ark, even every beast of the earth.
11 "I establish My covenant with you; and all flesh shall [a]never
again be cut off by the water of the flood, [b]neither shall there
again be a flood to destroy the earth."
12 God said, "This is [a]the sign of the covenant which I am
making between Me and you and every living creature that is
with you, for [1]all successive generations;
13 I set My [a]bow in the cloud, and it shall be for a sign of a
covenant between Me and the earth.
14 "It shall come about, when I bring a cloud over the earth,
that the bow will be seen in the cloud,
15 and [a]I will remember My covenant, which is between Me
and you and every living creature of all flesh; and [b]never again
shall the water become a flood to destroy all flesh.
16 "When the bow is in the cloud, then I will look upon it, to
remember the [a]everlasting covenant between God and every
living creature of all flesh that is on the earth."
17 And God said to Noah, "This is the sign of the covenant
which I have established between Me and all flesh that is on
the earth."
18 Now the sons of Noah who came out of the ark were Shem
and Ham and Japheth; and [a]Ham was the father of Canaan.
19 These three *were* the sons of Noah, and [a]from these the
whole earth was [1]populated.
20 Then Noah began [1]farming and planted a vineyard.
21 He drank of the wine and [a]became drunk, and uncovered
himself inside his tent.

9:1 [a]Gen 1:28; 9:7
2 [1]Lit *heavens*
3 [a]Gen 1:29
4 [a]Lev 7:26f; 17:10-16; 19:26; Deut 12:16, 23; 15:23; 1 Sam 14:34; Acts 15:20, 29
5 [1]Lit *your blood of your lives* [2]Lit *from the hand of* [a]Ex 20:13; 21:12 [b]Ex 21:28, 29
6 [a]Ex 21:12-14; Lev 24:17; Num 35:33; Matt 26:52 [b]Gen 1:26, 27
7 [1]Lit *Swarm in the earth* [a]Gen 9:1
9 [1]Lit *seed* [a]Gen 6:18
11 [a]Gen 8:21 [b]Is 54:9
12 [1]Or *everlasting generations* [a]Gen 9:13, 17; 17:11
13 [a]Ezek 1:28
15 [a]Lev 26:42, 45; Deut 7:9; Ezek 16:60 [b]Gen 9:11
16 [a]Gen 17:13, 19; 2 Sam 23:5
18 [a]Gen 9:25-27; 10:6
19 [1]Lit *scattered* [a]Gen 9:1, 7; 10:32; 1 Chr 1:4
20 [1]Lit *to be a farmer*
21 [a]Prov 20:1

22 Ham, the father of Canaan, [a]saw the nakedness of his
father, and told his two brothers outside.
23 But Shem and Japheth took a garment and laid it upon both
their shoulders and walked backward and covered the nakedness
of their father; and their faces were [1]turned away, so that they
did not see their father's nakedness.
24 When Noah awoke from his wine, he knew what his
youngest son had done to him.
25 So he said,

"[a]Cursed be Canaan;
[1b]A servant of servants
He shall be to his brothers."

26 He also said,

"[a]Blessed be the LORD,
The God of Shem;
And let Canaan be [1]his servant.

27 "[a]May God enlarge Japheth,
And let him dwell in the tents of Shem;
And let Canaan be [1]his servant."

28 Noah lived three hundred and fifty years after the flood.
29 So all the days of Noah were nine hundred and fifty years,
and he died.

Chapter 10 Theme ____________________

10 Now these are *the records of* the generations of Shem,
Ham, and Japheth, the sons of Noah; and sons were born
to them after the flood.
2 [a]The sons of Japheth *were* [b]Gomer and Magog and [c]Madai
and [d]Javan and Tubal and [e]Meshech and Tiras.
3 The sons of Gomer *were* [a]Ashkenaz and [1]Riphath and
[b]Togarmah.
4 The sons of Javan *were* Elishah and [a]Tarshish, Kittim and
[1]Dodanim.
5 From these the coastlands of the nations [1]were separated
into their lands, every one according to his language, according
to their families, into their nations.
6 [a]The sons of Ham *were* Cush and Mizraim and Put and
Canaan.
7 The sons of Cush *were* [a]Seba and Havilah and Sabtah and
[b]Raamah and Sabteca; and the sons of Raamah *were* [b]Sheba and
[c]Dedan.
8 Now Cush [1]became the father of Nimrod; he [2]became a
mighty one on the earth.
9 He was a mighty hunter before the LORD; therefore it is
said, "Like Nimrod a mighty hunter before the LORD."
10 The beginning of his kingdom was [1a]Babel and Erech and
Accad and Calneh, in the land of [b]Shinar.
11 From that land he went forth [a]into Assyria, and built
Nineveh and Rehoboth-Ir and Calah,
12 and Resen between Nineveh and Calah; that is the great city.

22 [a]Hab 2:15
23 [1]Lit *backward*
25 [1]I.e. The lowest of servants [a]Deut 27:16 [b]Josh 9:23
26 [1]Or *their* [a]Gen 14:20; 24:27
27 [1]Or *their* [a]Gen 10:2-5; Is 66:19
10:2 [a]1 Chr 1:5-7 [b]Ezek 38:2, 6 [c]2 Kin 17:6 [d]Is 66:19 [e]Ezek 38:2
3 [1]I.e. In 1 Chr 1:6, *Diphath* [a]Jer 51:27 [b]Ezek 27:14
4 [1]I.e. In 1 Chr 1:7, *Rodanim* [a]Ezek 27:12, 25
5 [1]Or *separated themselves*
6 [a]1 Chr 1:8-10
7 [a]Is 43:3 [b]Ezek 27:22 [c]Ezek 27:15, 20
8 [1]Lit *begot* [2]Lit *began to be*
10 [1]Or *Babylon* [a]Gen 11:9 [b]Gen 11:2; 14:1
11 [a]Mic 5:6

RETURN TO INSTRUCTIONS

INSIGHT

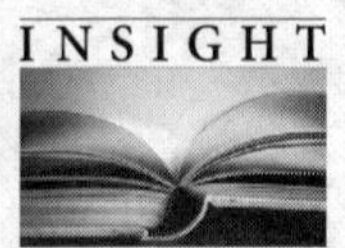

In order to see where the sons of Shem, Ham, and Japheth settled, refer to the map **The Settlement of the Descendants of Shem, Ham, and Japheth** on page 2242.

13 Mizraim [1]became the father of [a]Ludim and Anamim and
Lehabim and Naphtuhim
14 and [a]Pathrusim and Casluhim (from which came the Philistines) and Caphtorim.
15 Canaan [1]became the father of [a]Sidon, his firstborn, and [b]Heth
16 and [a]the Jebusite and the Amorite and the Girgashite
17 and the Hivite and the Arkite and the Sinite
18 and the Arvadite and the Zemarite and the Hamathite; and
afterward the families of the Canaanite were spread abroad.
19 [a]The territory of the Canaanite [1]extended from Sidon as
you go toward Gerar, as far as Gaza; as you go toward [b]Sodom
and Gomorrah and Admah and Zeboiim, as far as Lasha.
20 These are the sons of Ham, according to their families,
according to their languages, by their lands, by their nations.
21 Also to Shem, the father of all the children of Eber, *and* the
[1]older brother of Japheth, children were born.
22 [a]The sons of Shem *were* [b]Elam and Asshur and [c]Arpachshad
and [d]Lud and Aram.
23 The sons of Aram *were* [a]Uz and Hul and Gether and Mash.
24 Arpachshad [1]became the father of [a]Shelah; and Shelah
[1]became the father of Eber.
25 [a]Two sons were born to Eber; the name of the one *was*
[1]Peleg, for in his days the earth was divided; and his brother's
name *was* Joktan.
26 Joktan [1]became the father of Almodad and Sheleph and
Hazarmaveth and Jerah
27 and Hadoram and Uzal and Diklah
28 and [1]Obal and Abimael and Sheba
29 and Ophir and Havilah and Jobab; all these were the sons
of Joktan.
30 Now their [1]settlement [2]extended from Mesha as you go
toward Sephar, the hill country of the east.
31 These are the sons of Shem, according to their families,
according to their languages, by their lands, according to their
nations.
32 These are the families of the sons of Noah, according to
their genealogies, by their nations; and [a]out of these the
nations were separated on the earth after the flood.

Chapter 11 Theme _____________________________

11 Now the whole earth [1]used the same language and [2]the
same words.
2 It came about as they journeyed east, that they found a
plain in the land [a]of Shinar and [1]settled there.
3 They said to one another, "Come, let us make bricks and
burn *them* thoroughly." And they used brick for stone, and they
used [a]tar for mortar.
4 They said, "Come, let us build for ourselves a city, and a
tower whose top [a]*will reach* into heaven, and let us make for
ourselves [b]a name, otherwise we [c]will be scattered abroad over
the face of the whole earth."

13 [1]Lit *begot* [a]Jer 46:9

14 [a]1 Chr 1:12

15 [1]Lit *begot* [a]1 Chr 1:13; Jer 47:4 [b]Gen 23:3

16 [a]Gen 15:19-21

19 [1]Lit *was* [a]Num 34:2-12 [b]Gen 14:2, 3

21 [1]Or *the brother of Japheth the elder*

22 [a]1 Chr 1:17 [b]Gen 14:1, 9 [c]Gen 11:10 [d]Is 66:19

23 [a]Job 1:1; Jer 25:20

24 [1]Lit *begot* [a]Gen 11:12; Luke 3:35

25 [1]I.e. division [a]1 Chr 1:19

26 [1]Lit *begot*

28 [1]I.e. In 1 Chr 1:22, *Ebal*

30 [1]Lit *dwelling* [2]Lit *was*

32 [a]Gen 9:19

11:1 [1]Lit *was one lip* [2]Or *few* or *one set of words*

2 [1]Lit *dwelt* [a]Gen 10:10; 14:1; Dan 1:2

3 [a]Gen 14:10

4 [a]Deut 1:28; 9:1; Ps 107:26 [b]Gen 6:4; 2 Sam 8:13 [c]Deut 4:27

5 [a]The LORD came down to see the city and the tower which
the sons of men had built.
6 The LORD said, "Behold, they are one people, and they all
have [1a]the same language. And this is what they began to do,
and now nothing which they purpose to do will be [2]impossible
for them.
7 "Come, [a]let Us go down and there [b]confuse their [1]language,
so that they will not understand one another's [1]speech."
8 So the LORD [a]scattered them abroad from there over the
face of the whole earth; and they stopped building the city.
9 Therefore its name was called [1a]Babel, because there the
LORD confused the [2]language of the whole earth; and from there
the LORD scattered them abroad over the face of the whole earth.
10 [a]These are *the records of* the generations of Shem. Shem
was one hundred years old, and [1]became the father of
Arpachshad two years after the flood;
11 and Shem lived five hundred years after he became the
father of Arpachshad, and he had *other* sons and daughters.
12 Arpachshad lived thirty-five years, and became the father of
Shelah;
13 and Arpachshad lived four hundred and three years after
he became the father of Shelah, and he had *other* sons and
daughters.
14 Shelah lived thirty years, and became the father of Eber;
15 and Shelah lived four hundred and three years after he
became the father of Eber, and he had *other* sons and daughters.
16 Eber lived thirty-four years, and became the father of Peleg;
17 and Eber lived four hundred and thirty years after he
became the father of Peleg, and he had *other* sons and
daughters.
18 Peleg lived thirty years, and became the father of Reu;
19 and Peleg lived two hundred and nine years after he
became the father of Reu, and he had *other* sons and
daughters.
20 Reu lived thirty-two years, and became the father of Serug;
21 and Reu lived two hundred and seven years after he became
the father of Serug, and he had *other* sons and daughters.
22 Serug lived thirty years, and became the father of Nahor;
23 and Serug lived two hundred years after he became the
father of Nahor, and he had *other* sons and daughters.
24 Nahor lived twenty-nine years, and became the father of
[a]Terah;
25 and Nahor lived one hundred and nineteen years after he
became the father of Terah, and he had *other* sons and daughters.
26 Terah lived seventy years, and became [a]the father of
Abram, Nahor and Haran.
27 Now these are *the records of* the generations of Terah.
Terah became the father of Abram, Nahor and Haran; and
[a]Haran became the father of [b]Lot.
28 Haran died [1]in the presence of his father Terah in the land
of his birth, in [a]Ur of the Chaldeans.

5 [a]Gen 18:21; Ex 3:8; 19:11, 18, 20

6 [1]Lit *one lip* [2]Lit *withheld from* [a]Gen 11:1

7 [1]Lit *lip* [a]Gen 1:26 [b]Gen 42:23; Ex 4:11; Deut 28:49; Is 33:19; Jer 5:15

8 [a]Gen 11:4; Ps 92:9; Luke 1:51

9 [1]Or *Babylon;* cf Heb *balal,* confuse [2]Lit *lip* [a]Gen 10:10

10 [1]Lit *begot,* and so throughout the ch [a]Gen 10:22-25

24 [a]Josh 24:2

26 [a]Josh 24:2

27 [a]Gen 11:31; 12:4 [b]Gen 13:10; 14:12; 19:1, 29

28 [1]Or *during the lifetime of* [a]Gen 11:31

Journeys of Abraham

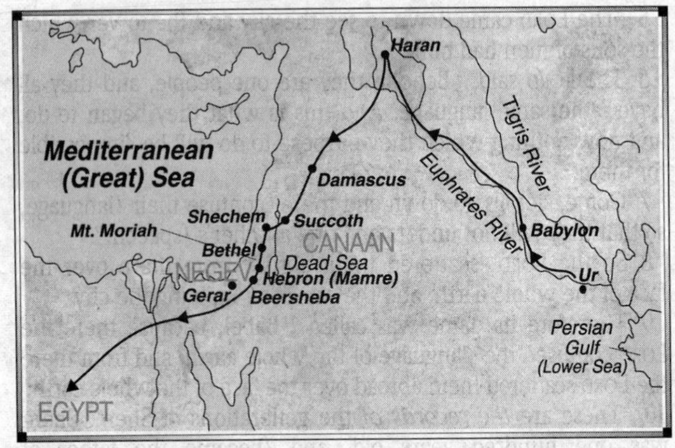

29 Abram and [a]Nahor took wives for themselves. The name of
Abram's wife was [b]Sarai; and the name of Nahor's wife was
[c]Milcah, the daughter of Haran, the father of Milcah [1]and Iscah.
30 [a]Sarai was barren; she had no child.
31 Terah took Abram his son, and Lot the son of Haran, his
grandson, and Sarai his daughter-in-law, his son Abram's wife;
and they went out [1]together from [a]Ur of the Chaldeans in
order to enter the land of Canaan; and they went as far as
Haran, and [2]settled there.
32 The days of Terah were two hundred and five years; and
Terah died in Haran.

Chapter 12 Theme ______________________

12 Now [a]the LORD said to Abram,
"[1]Go forth from your country,
And from your relatives
And from your father's house,
To the land which I will show you;
2 And [a]I will make you a great nation,
And [b]I will bless you,
And make your name great;
And so [1][c]you shall be a blessing;
3 And [a]I will bless those who bless you,
And the one who [1]curses you I will [2]curse.
[b]And in you all the families of the earth will be blessed."
4 So Abram went forth as the LORD had spoken to him; and
[a]Lot went with him. Now Abram was seventy-five years old
when he departed from Haran.
5 Abram took Sarai his wife and Lot his nephew, and all their
[a]possessions which they had accumulated, and [b]the [1]persons
which they had acquired in Haran, and they [2]set out for the
land of Canaan; [c]thus they came to the land of Canaan.
6 Abram passed through the land as far as the site of
[a]Shechem, to the [1]oak of Moreh. Now the Canaanite *was* then
in the land.

RETURN TO INSTRUCTIONS

29 [1]Lit *and the father of* [a]Gen 24:10 [b]Gen 17:15; 20:12 [c]Gen 22:20, 23; 24:15

30 [a]Gen 16:1

31 [1]Lit *with them* [2]Lit *dwelt* [a]Gen 15:7; Neh 9:7; Acts 7:4

12:1 [1]Lit *Go for yourself* [a]Gen 15:7; Acts 7:3; Heb 11:8

2 [1]Lit *be a blessing* [a]Gen 17:4-6; 18:18; 46:3; Deut 26:5 [b]Gen 22:17 [c]Zech 8:13

3 [1]Or *reviles* [2]Or *bind under a curse* [a]Gen 24:35; 27:29; Num 24:9 [b]Gen 22:18; 26:4; 28:14; Acts 3:25; Gal 3:8

4 [a]Gen 11:27, 31

5 [1]Lit *souls* [2]Lit *went forth to go to* [a]Gen 13:6 [b]Gen 14:14; Lev 22:11 [c]Gen 11:31; Heb 11:8

6 [1]Or *terebinth* [a]Gen 35:4; Deut 11:30

7 The LORD [a]appeared to Abram and said, "[b]To your
[1]descendants I will give this land." So he built [c]an altar there to
the LORD who had appeared to him.
8 Then he proceeded from there to the mountain on the east
of Bethel, and pitched his tent, with [a]Bethel on the west and Ai
on the east; and there he built an altar to the LORD and [b]called
upon the name of the LORD.
9 Abram journeyed on, continuing toward [a]the [1]Negev.
10 Now there was [a]a famine in the land; so Abram went down
to Egypt to sojourn there, for the famine was [b]severe in the land.
11 It came about when he [1]came near to Egypt, that he said to
Sarai his wife, "See now, I know that you are a [2a]beautiful
woman;
12 [a]and when the Egyptians see you, they will say, 'This is his
wife'; and they will kill me, but they will let you live.
13 "Please say that you are [a]my sister so that it may go well with
me because of you, and that [1b]I may live on account of you."
14 It came about when Abram came into Egypt, the Egyptians
[1]saw that the woman was very beautiful.
15 Pharaoh's officials saw her and praised her to Pharaoh; and
[a]the woman was taken into Pharaoh's house.
16 Therefore [a]he treated Abram well for her sake; and [1b]gave
him sheep and oxen and donkeys and male and female servants
and female donkeys and camels.
17 But the LORD [a]struck Pharaoh and his house with great
plagues because of Sarai, Abram's wife.
18 Then Pharaoh called Abram and said, "[a]What is this you have
done to me? Why did you not tell me that she was your wife?
19 "Why did you say, 'She is my sister,' so that I took her for
my wife? Now then, [1]here is your wife, take her and go."
20 Pharaoh commanded *his* men concerning him; and they
[1]escorted him away, with his wife and all that belonged to him.

Chapter 13 Theme ____________________

13 So Abram went up from Egypt to [a]the [1]Negev, he and his
wife and all that belonged to him, and Lot with him.
2 Now Abram was [a]very rich in livestock, in silver and in gold.
3 He went [1]on his journeys from the [2]Negev as far as Bethel,
to the place where his tent had been at the beginning,
[a]between Bethel and Ai,
4 to the place of the [a]altar which he had made there
formerly; and there Abram called on the name of the LORD.
5 Now [a]Lot, who went with Abram, also had flocks and
herds and tents.
6 And [a]the land could not [1]sustain them [2]while dwelling
together, [b]for their possessions were so great that they were
not able to remain together.
7 [a]And there was strife between the herdsmen of Abram's
livestock and the herdsmen of Lot's livestock. Now [b]the
Canaanite and the Perizzite were dwelling then in the land.

7 [1]Lit *seed* [a]Gen 17:1; 18:1 [b]Gen 13:15; 15:18; Deut 34:4; Ps 105:9-12; Acts 7:5; Gal 3:16 [c]Gen 13:4, 18; 22:9

8 [a]Josh 8:9, 12 [b]Gen 4:26; 21:33

9 [1]I.e. South country [a]Gen 13:1, 3; 20:1; 24:62

10 [a]Gen 26:1 [b]Gen 43:1

11 [1]Lit *drew near to enter* [2]Lit *woman of beautiful appearance* [a]Gen 26:7; 29:17

12 [a]Gen 20:11

13 [1]Lit *my soul* [a]Gen 20:2, 5, 12; 26:7 [b]Jer 38:17, 20

14 [1]Lit *saw the woman that she was*

15 [a]Gen 20:2

16 [1]Lit *he had* [a]Gen 20:14 [b]Gen 13:2

17 [a]Gen 20:18; 1 Chr 16:21; Ps 105:14

18 [a]Gen 20:9, 10; 26:10

19 [1]Or *behold*

20 [1]Lit *sent*

13:1 [1]I.e. South country [a]Gen 12:9

2 [a]Gen 24:35

3 [1]Lit *by his stages* [2]I.e. South country [a]Gen 12:8

4 [a]Gen 12:7, 8

5 [a]Gen 12:5

6 [1]Lit *bear* [2]Lit *to dwell* [a]Gen 36:7 [b]Gen 12:5, 16; 13:2

7 [a]Gen 26:20 [b]Gen 12:6; 15:20, 21

8 [a]So Abram said to Lot, "Please let there be no strife between
you and me, nor between my herdsmen and your herdsmen,
for we are brothers.
9 "Is not the whole land before you? Please separate from me;
if *to* the left, then I will go to the right; or if *to* the right, then I
will go to the left."
10 Lot lifted up his eyes and saw all the [1a]valley of the Jordan,
that it was well watered everywhere—*this was* before the LORD
[b]destroyed Sodom and Gomorrah—like [c]the garden of the
LORD, [d]like the land of Egypt as you go to [e]Zoar.
11 So Lot chose for himself all the [1]valley of the Jordan, and
Lot journeyed eastward. Thus they separated from each other.
12 Abram [1]settled in the land of Canaan, while Lot [1]settled in
[a]the cities of the [2]valley, and moved his tents as far as Sodom.
13 Now [a]the men of Sodom were wicked [1]exceedingly and
[b]sinners against the LORD.
14 The LORD said to Abram, after Lot had separated from him,
"[a]Now lift up your eyes and look from the place where you are,
[b]northward and southward and eastward and westward;
15 [a]for all the land which you see, [b]I will give it to you and to
your [1]descendants forever.
16 "I will make your [1]descendants [a]as the dust of the earth, so
that if anyone can number the dust of the earth, then your
[1]descendants can also be numbered.
17 "Arise, [a]walk about the land through its length and breadth;
for [b]I will give it to you."
18 Then Abram moved his tent and came and dwelt by the
[1a]oaks of Mamre, which are in Hebron, and there he built [b]an
altar to the LORD.

Chapter 14 Theme ________________

14 And it came about in the days of Amraphel king of [a]Shinar,
Arioch king of Ellasar, Chedorlaomer king of [b]Elam, and
Tidal king of [1]Goiim,
2 *that* they made war with Bera king of Sodom, and with
Birsha king of Gomorrah, Shinab king of [a]Admah, and
Shemeber king of [b]Zeboiim, and the king of Bela (that is, [c]Zoar).
3 All these [1]came as allies to [a]the valley of Siddim (that is,
[b]the Salt Sea).
4 Twelve years they had served Chedorlaomer, but the
thirteenth year they rebelled.
5 In the fourteenth year Chedorlaomer and the kings that
were with him, came and [1]defeated the [a]Rephaim in
[b]Ashteroth-karnaim and the Zuzim in Ham and the Emim in
[2c]Shaveh-kiriathaim,
6 and the [a]Horites in their Mount Seir, as far as [b]El-paran,
which is by the wilderness.
7 Then they turned back and came to En-mishpat (that is,
[a]Kadesh), and [1]conquered all the country of the Amalekites,
and also the Amorites, who lived in [b]Hazazon-tamar.

8 [a]Prov 15:18; 20:3

10 [1]Lit *circle* [a]Gen 19:17-29; Deut 34:3 [b]Gen 19:24 [c]Gen 2:8, 10 [d]Gen 47:6 [e]Gen 14:2, 8; 19:22; Deut 34:3

11 [1]Lit *circle*

12 [1]Lit *dwelt* [2]Lit *circle* [a]Gen 14:2; 19:24, 25, 29

13 [1]Lit *wicked and sinners exceedingly* [a]Gen 18:20; Ezek 16:49 [b]Gen 39:9; Num 32:23; 2 Pet 2:7, 8

14 [a]Deut 3:27; 34:1-4; Is 49:18 [b]Gen 28:14

15 [1]Lit *seed* [a]Gen 12:7 [b]Gen 13:17; 15:7; 17:8; 2 Chr 20:7; Acts 7:5

16 [1]Lit *seed* [a]Gen 16:10; 28:14; Num 23:10

17 [a]Num 13:17-24 [b]Gen 13:15

18 [1]Or *terebinths* [a]Gen 14:13 [b]Gen 8:20; 12:7, 8

14:1 [1]Or *nations* [a]Gen 10:10; 11:2 [b]Gen 10:22; Is 11:11; Dan 8:2

2 [a]Gen 10:19 [b]Deut 29:23 [c]Gen 13:10; 19:22

3 [1]Lit *joined together* [a]Gen 14:8, 10 [b]Num 34:12; Deut 3:17; Josh 3:16

5 [1]Lit *smote* [2]Or *the plain of Kiriathaim* [a]Deut 3:11, 13 [b]Deut 1:4; Josh 9:10 [c]Num 32:37

6 [a]Gen 36:20; Deut 2:12, 22 [b]Gen 21:21; Num 10:12

7 [1]Lit *smote* [a]Num 13:26 [b]2 Chr 20:2

8 And the king of Sodom and the king of Gomorrah and the
king of Admah and the king of Zeboiim and the king of Bela
(that is, Zoar) came out; and they arrayed for battle against
them in [a]the valley of Siddim,
9 against Chedorlaomer king of Elam and Tidal king of
[1]Goiim and Amraphel king of Shinar and Arioch king of
Ellasar—four kings against five.
10 Now the valley of Siddim was full of tar pits; and [a]the kings
of Sodom and Gomorrah fled, and they fell [1]into them. But
those who survived fled to the [b]hill country.
11 Then they took all the goods of Sodom and Gomorrah and
all their food supply, and departed.
12 They also took Lot, [a]Abram's nephew, and his possessions
and departed, [b]for he was living in Sodom.
13 Then [1]a fugitive came and told Abram the [a]Hebrew. Now he
was [2]living by the [3b]oaks of Mamre the Amorite, brother of
Eshcol and brother of Aner, and these were [4c]allies with Abram.
14 When Abram heard that [a]his [1]relative had been taken
captive, he [2]led out his trained men, [b]born in his house, three
hundred and eighteen, and went in pursuit as far as [c]Dan.
15 [a]He divided [1]his forces against them by night, he and his
servants, and [2]defeated them, and pursued them as far as
Hobah, which is [3]north of [b]Damascus.
16 He [a]brought back all the goods, and also brought back [b]his
[1]relative Lot with his possessions, and also the women, and the
people.
17 Then after his return from the [1]defeat of Chedorlaomer and
the kings who were with him, [a]the king of Sodom went out to
meet him at the valley of Shaveh (that is, [b]the King's Valley).
18 And [a]Melchizedek king of Salem brought out [b]bread and
wine; now he was a [c]priest of [1]God Most High.
19 He blessed him and said,
"Blessed be Abram of [1]God Most High,
[2a]Possessor of heaven and earth;
20 And blessed be [1]God Most High,
Who has delivered your enemies into your hand."
[a]He gave him a tenth of all.
21 The king of Sodom said to Abram, "Give the [1]people to me
and take the goods for yourself."
22 Abram said to the king of Sodom, "I have [1]sworn to the
LORD [2a]God Most High, [3b]possessor of heaven and earth,
23 that [a]I will not take a thread or a sandal thong or anything
that is yours, for fear you would say, 'I have made Abram rich.'
24 "[1]I will take nothing except what the young men have eaten,
and the share of the men who went with me, [a]Aner, Eshcol, and
Mamre; let them take their share."

Chapter 15 Theme ______________________

15 After these things [a]the word of the LORD came to Abram
in a vision, saying,
"[b]Do not fear, Abram,

8 [a]Gen 14:3
9 [1]Or *nations*
10 [1]Lit *there* [a]Gen 14:17, 21, 22 [b]Gen 19:17
12 [a]Gen 11:27 [b]Gen 13:12
13 [1]Lit *the* [2]Lit *abiding* [3]Or *terebinths* [4]Lit *possessors of the covenant* [a]Gen 40:15; Ex 3:18 [b]Gen 13:18; 14:24 [c]Gen 21:27, 32
14 [1]Lit *brother* [2]Or *mustered* [a]Gen 14:12 [b]Gen 12:5; 15:3; 17:27; Eccl 2:7 [c]Deut 34:1; Judg 18:29; 1 Kin 15:20
15 [1]Lit *himself* [2]Lit *smote* [3]Lit *on the left* [a]Judg 7:16 [b]Gen 15:2
16 [1]Lit *brother* [a]1 Sam 30:8, 18, 19 [b]Gen 14:12, 14
17 [1]Lit *smiting* [a]Gen 14:10 [b]2 Sam 18:18
18 [1]Heb *El Elyon* [a]Heb 7:1-10 [b]Ps 104:15 [c]Ps 110:4; Heb 5:6, 10
19 [1]Heb *El Elyon* [2]Or *Creator* [a]Gen 14:22
20 [1]Heb *El Elyon* [a]Heb 7:4
21 [1]Lit *soul*
22 [1]Lit *lifted up my hand* [2]Heb *El Elyon* [3]Or *Creator* [a]Gen 14:19 [b]Ps 24:1
23 [a]2 Kin 5:16
24 [1]Lit *Not to me except* [a]Gen 14:13
15:1 [a]Gen 15:4; 46:2; 1 Sam 15:10 [b]Gen 21:17; 26:24; Is 41:10

I am [c]a shield to you;
[1]Your [d]reward shall be very great."

2 Abram said, "O Lord [1]GOD, what will You give me, since I [2]am childless, and the [3]heir of my house is Eliezer of Damascus?"

3 And Abram said, "[1]Since You have given no [2]offspring to me, [3]one [a]born in my house is my heir."

4 Then behold, the word of the LORD came to him, saying, "This man will not be your heir; [a]but one who will come forth from your own [1]body, he shall be your heir."

5 And He took him outside and said, "Now look toward the heavens, and [a]count the stars, if you are able to count them." And He said to him, "[b]So shall your [1]descendants be."

6 [a]Then he believed in the LORD; and He reckoned it to him as righteousness.

7 And He said to him, "I am the LORD who brought you out of [a]Ur of the Chaldeans, to [b]give you this land to [1]possess it."

8 He said, "O Lord [1]GOD, [a]how may I know that I will [2]possess it?"

9 So He said to him, "[1]Bring Me a three year old heifer, and a three year old female goat, and a three year old ram, and a turtledove, and a young pigeon."

10 Then he [1]brought all these to Him and [a]cut them [2]in two, and laid each half opposite the other; but he [b]did not cut the birds.

11 The birds of prey came down upon the carcasses, and Abram drove them away.

12 Now when the sun was going down, [a]a deep sleep fell upon Abram; and behold, [1]terror *and* great darkness fell upon him.

13 *God* said to Abram, "Know for certain that [a]your [1]descendants will be strangers in a land that is not theirs, [2]where [b]they will be enslaved and oppressed [c]four hundred years.

14 "But I will also judge the nation whom they will serve, and afterward they will come out [a]with [1]many possessions.

15 "As for you, [a]you shall go to your fathers in peace; you will be buried at a good old age.

16 "Then in [a]the fourth generation they will return here, for [b]the iniquity of the Amorite is not yet complete."

17 It came about when the sun had set, that it was very dark, and behold, *there appeared* a smoking oven and a flaming torch which [a]passed between these pieces.

18 On that day the LORD made a covenant with Abram, saying,
"[a]To your [1]descendants I have given this land,
From [b]the river of Egypt as far as the great river, the river
Euphrates:

19 [a]the Kenite and the Kenizzite and the Kadmonite
20 and the Hittite and the Perizzite and the Rephaim
21 and the Amorite and the Canaanite and the Girgashite and the Jebusite."

INSIGHT

Beriyth, the Hebrew word for covenant, is a solemn binding agreement made by passing through pieces of flesh. The Greek word for covenant, ***diatheke***, means a testament or an agreement. The Bible is divided into the Old and New Testaments—or covenants. Everything God does is based on covenant. For example, see Exodus 2:23-24, 32:9-14, Jeremiah 34:12-21.

1 [1]Or *Your very great reward* [c]Deut 33:29 [d]Num 18:20; Ps 58:11

2 [1]Heb *YHWH*, usually rendered LORD [2]Lit *go* [3]Lit *son of acquisition*

3 [1]Lit *Behold* [2]Lit *seed* [3]Lit *and behold, a son of* [a]Gen 14:14

4 [1]Lit *inward parts* [a]Gal 4:28

5 [1]Lit *seed* [a]Gen 22:17; 26:4; Deut 1:10 [b]Ex 32:13; Rom 4:18; Heb 11:12

6 [a]Rom 4:3, 20-22; Gal 3:6; James 2:23

7 [1]Or *inherit* [a]Gen 11:31 [b]Gen 13:15, 17

8 [1]Heb *YHWH*, usually rendered LORD [2]Or *inherit* [a]Judg 6:36-40; Luke 1:18

9 [1]Lit *Take*

10 [1]Lit *took* [2]Lit *in the midst* [a]Gen 15:17 [b]Lev 1:17

12 [1]Or *a terror of great darkness* [a]Gen 2:21; 28:11; Job 33:15

13 [1]Lit *seed* [2]Lit *and shall serve them; and they shall afflict them* [a]Acts 7:6, 17 [b]Ex 1:11; Deut 5:15 [c]Ex 12:40; Gal 3:17

14 [1]Lit *great* [a]Ex 12:32-38

15 [a]Gen 25:8; 47:30

16 [a]Gen 15:13 [b]Lev 18:24-28

17 [a]Jer 34:18, 19

18 [1]Lit *seed* [a]Gen 17:8; Josh 21:43; Acts 7:5 [b]Ex 23:31; Num 34:1-15; Deut 1:7, 8

19 [a]Ex 3:17; 23:28; Josh 24:11; Neh 9:8

Chapter 16 Theme ______________________

16 Now [a]Sarai, Abram's wife had borne him no *children,*
and she had [b]an Egyptian maid whose name was Hagar.
2 So Sarai said to Abram, "Now behold, the LORD has prevented
me from bearing *children.* [a]Please go in to my maid; perhaps I
will [1]obtain children through her." And Abram listened to the
voice of Sarai.
3 After Abram had [1]lived [a]ten years in the land of Canaan,
Abram's wife Sarai took Hagar the Egyptian, her maid, and gave
her to her husband Abram as his wife.
4 He went in to Hagar, and she conceived; and when she saw
that she had conceived, her mistress was despised in her sight.
5 And Sarai said to Abram, "[a]May the wrong done me be
upon you. I gave my maid into your [1]arms, but when she saw
that she had conceived, I was despised in her [2]sight. [b]May the
LORD judge between [3]you and me."
6 But Abram said to Sarai, "Behold, your maid is in your
[1]power; do to her what is good in your [2]sight." So Sarai treated
her harshly, and [a]she fled from her presence.
7 Now [a]the angel of the LORD found her by a spring of water
in the wilderness, by the spring on the way to [b]Shur.
8 He said, "Hagar, Sarai's maid, [a]where have you come from
and where are you going?" And she said, "I am fleeing from
the presence of my mistress Sarai."
9 Then the angel of the LORD said to her, "Return to your
mistress, and submit yourself [1]to her authority."
10 Moreover, the [a]angel of the LORD said to her, "[b]I will greatly
multiply your [1]descendants so that [2]they will be too many to count."
11 The angel of the LORD said to her further,
"Behold, you are with child,
And you will bear a son;
And you shall call his name [1]Ishmael,
Because [a]the LORD [2]has given heed to your affliction.
12 "He will be a [a]wild donkey of a man,
His hand *will be* against everyone,
And everyone's hand *will be* against him;
And he will [1]live [2b]to the east of all his brothers."
13 Then she called the name of the LORD who spoke to her,
"[1]You are [2]a God who sees"; for she said, "[a]Have I even
[3]remained alive here after seeing Him?"
14 Therefore the well was called [1]Beer-lahai-roi; behold, it is
between [a]Kadesh and Bered.
15 So Hagar bore Abram a son; and Abram called the name of
his son, whom Hagar bore, Ishmael.
16 Abram was [a]eighty-six years old when Hagar bore Ishmael
to [1]him.

Chapter 17 Theme ______________________

17 Now when Abram was ninety-nine years old, [a]the LORD
appeared to Abram and said to him,

16:1 [a]Gen 11:30 [b]Gen 12:16
2 [1]Lit *be built from her* [a]Gen 30:3, 4, 9, 10
3 [1]Lit *dwelt* [a]Gen 12:4
5 [1]Lit *bosom* [2]Lit *eyes* [3]Lit *me and you* [a]Jer 51:35 [b]Gen 31:53; Ex 5:21
6 [1]Lit *hand* [2]Lit *eyes* [a]Gen 16:9
7 [a]Gen 21:17, 18; 22:11, 15; 31:11 [b]Gen 20:1; 25:18
8 [a]Gen 3:9; 1 Kin 19:9, 13
9 [1]Lit *under her hands*
10 [1]Lit *seed* [2]Or *it shall not be counted for multitude* [a]Gen 22:15-18 [b]Gen 17:20
11 [1]I.e. God hears [2]Lit *has heard* [a]Ex 2:23, 24; 3:7, 9
12 [1]Lit *dwell* [2]Lit *before the face of;* or *in defiance of* [a]Job 24:5; 39:5-8 [b]Gen 25:18
13 [1]Or *You, God, see me* [2]Heb *Elroi* [3]Lit *seen here after the one who saw me* [a]Gen 32:30; Ps 139:1-12
14 [1]I.e. the well of the living one who sees me [a]Gen 14:7
16 [1]Lit *Abram* [a]Gen 12:4; 16:3
17:1 [a]Gen 12:7; 18:1

"I am [1]God [b]Almighty;
Walk before Me, and be [2c]blameless.
2 "I will [1]establish My [a]covenant between Me and you,
And I will [b]multiply you exceedingly."
3 Abram [a]fell on his face, and God talked with him, saying,
4 "As for Me, behold, My covenant is with you,
And you will be the father of a [a]multitude of nations.
5 "No longer shall your name be called [1]Abram,
But [a]your name shall be [2]Abraham;
For [b]I have made you the father of a multitude of nations.
6 "I will make you exceedingly fruitful, and I will make
nations of you, and [a]kings will come forth from you.
7 "I will establish My covenant between Me and you and your
[1]descendants after you throughout their generations for an [a]ever-
lasting covenant, [b]to be God to you and [c]to your [1]descendants
after you.
8 "[a]I will give to you and to your [1]descendants after you, the
land of your sojournings, all the land of Canaan, for an everlasting possession; and [b]I will be their God."
9 God said further to Abraham, "Now as for you, [a]you shall
keep My covenant, you and your [1]descendants after you
throughout their generations.
10 "[a]This is My covenant, which you shall keep, between Me
and you and your [1]descendants after you: every male among
you shall be circumcised.
11 "And [a]you shall be circumcised in the flesh of your foreskin,
and it shall be the sign of the covenant between Me and you.
12 "And every male among you who is [a]eight days old shall be
circumcised throughout your generations, a *servant* who is
born in the house or who is bought with money from any
foreigner, who is not of your [1]descendants.
13 "A *servant* who is born in your house or [a]who is bought
with your money shall surely be circumcised; thus shall My
covenant be in your flesh for an everlasting covenant.
14 "But an uncircumcised male who is not circumcised in the
flesh of his foreskin, that person shall be [a]cut off from his people;
he has broken My covenant."
15 Then God said to Abraham, "As for Sarai your wife, you
shall not call her name Sarai, but [1]Sarah *shall be* her name.
16 "I will bless her, and indeed I will give you [a]a son by her.
Then I will bless her, and she shall be *a mother of* nations;
[b]kings of peoples will [1]come from her."
17 Then Abraham [a]fell on his face and laughed, and said in his
heart, "Will a child be born to a man one hundred years old?
And [b]will Sarah, who is ninety years old, bear *a child?*"
18 And Abraham said to God, "Oh that Ishmael might live
before You!"
19 But God said, "No, but Sarah your wife will bear you [a]a
son, and you shall call his name [1]Isaac; and [b]I will establish My
covenant with him for an everlasting covenant for his
[2]descendants after him.

1 [1]Heb *El Shaddai* [2]Lit *complete, perfect;* or *having integrity* [b]Gen 28:3; 35:11 [c]Gen 6:9; Deut 18:13

2 [1]Lit *give* [a]Gen 15:18 [b]Gen 13:16; 15:5

3 [a]Gen 17:17; 18:2

4 [a]Gen 35:11; 48:19

5 [1]I.e. exalted father [2]I.e. father of a multitude [a]Neh 9:7 [b]Rom 4:17

6 [a]Gen 17:16; 35:11

7 [1]Lit *seed* [a]Gen 17:13, 19; Ps 105:9, 10; Luke 1:55 [b]Gen 26:24; Lev 11:45; 26:12, 45; Heb 11:16 [c]Gen 28:13; Gal 3:16

8 [1]Lit *seed* [a]Gen 12:7; 13:15, 17; Acts 7:5 [b]Ex 6:7; 29:45; Lev 26:12; Deut 29:13; Rev 21:7

9 [1]Lit *seed* [a]Ex 19:5

10 [1]Lit *seed* [a]John 7:22; Acts 7:8; Rom 4:11

11 [a]Ex 12:48; Deut 10:16; Acts 7:8; Rom 4:11

12 [1]Lit *seed* [a]Lev 12:3

13 [a]Ex 12:44

14 [a]Ex 4:24-26

15 [1]I.e. princess

16 [1]Lit *be* [a]Gen 18:10 [b]Gen 17:6; 36:31

17 [a]Gen 17:3; 18:12; 21:6 [b]Gen 21:7

19 [1]I.e. he laughs [2]Lit *seed* [a]Gen 17:16; 18:10; 21:2 [b]Gen 26:2-5

20 "As for Ishmael, I have heard you; behold, I will bless him, and [a]will make him fruitful and will multiply him exceedingly. [b]He shall [1]become the father of twelve princes, and I will make him a [c]great nation.

21 "But My covenant I will establish with [a]Isaac, whom [b]Sarah will bear to you at this season next year."

22 When He finished talking with him, [a]God went up from Abraham.

23 Then Abraham took Ishmael his son, and all *the servants* who were [a]born in his house and all who were bought with his money, every male among the men of Abraham's household, and circumcised the flesh of their foreskin in the very same day, [b]as God had said to him.

24 Now Abraham was ninety-nine years old when [a]he was circumcised in the flesh of his foreskin.

25 And [a]Ishmael his son was thirteen years old when he was circumcised in the flesh of his foreskin.

26 In the very same day Abraham was circumcised, and Ishmael his son.

27 All the men of his household, who were [a]born in the house or bought with money from a foreigner, were circumcised with him.

Chapter 18 Theme ________________

18 Now [a]the LORD appeared to him by the [1b]oaks of Mamre, while he was sitting at the tent door in the heat of the day.

2 When he lifted up his eyes and looked, behold, three [a]men were standing opposite him; and when he saw *them,* he ran from the tent door to meet them and bowed himself to the earth,

3 and said, "[1]My Lord, if now I have found favor in Your sight, please do not [2]pass Your servant by.

4 "Please let a little water be brought and [a]wash your feet, and [1]rest yourselves under the tree;

5 and I will [1a]bring a piece of bread, that you may [2]refresh yourselves; after that you may go on, since you have [3]visited your servant." And they said, "So do, as you have said."

6 So Abraham hurried into the tent to Sarah, and said, "[1]Quickly, prepare three [2]measures of fine flour, knead *it* and make bread cakes."

7 Abraham also ran to the herd, and took a tender and [1]choice calf and gave *it* to the servant, and he hurried to prepare it.

8 He took curds and milk and the calf which he had prepared, and placed *it* before them; and he was standing by them under the tree [1]as they ate.

9 Then they said to him, "Where is Sarah your wife?" And he said, "There, in the tent."

10 He said, "[a]I will surely return to you [1]at this time next year; and behold, Sarah your wife will have a son." And Sarah was listening at the tent door, which was behind him.

20 [1]Lit *beget twelve princes* [a]Gen 16:10 [b]Gen 25:12-16 [c]Gen 21:18

21 [a]Gen 17:19; 18:10, 14 [b]Gen 21:2

22 [a]Gen 18:33; 35:13

23 [a]Gen 14:14 [b]Gen 17:9-11

24 [a]Rom 4:11

25 [a]Gen 16:16

27 [a]Gen 14:14

18:1 [1]Or *terebinths* [a]Gen 12:7; 17:1 [b]Gen 13:18; 14:13

2 [a]Gen 18:16, 22; 32:24; Josh 5:13; Judg 13:6-11; Heb 13:2

3 [1]Or *O Lord* [2]Lit *pass away from Your servant*

4 [1]Lit *support* [a]Gen 19:2; 24:32; 43:24

5 [1]Lit *take* [2]Lit *sustain your heart* [3]Lit *come to* [a]Judg 6:18, 19; 13:15, 16

6 [1]Lit *Hasten three measures* [2]Heb *seah;* i.e. one seah equals approx eleven qts

7 [1]Lit *good*

8 [1]Lit *and*

10 [1]Lit *when the time revives* [a]Gen 21:2; Rom 9:9

11 Now [a]Abraham and Sarah were old, advanced in age; Sarah
was [b]past [1]childbearing.
12 Sarah laughed [1]to herself, saying, "[a]After I have become
old, shall I have pleasure, my [b]lord being old also?"
13 And the LORD said to Abraham, "Why did Sarah laugh,
saying, 'Shall I indeed [1]bear *a child,* when I am *so* old?'
14 "[a]Is anything too [1]difficult for the LORD? At the [b]appointed
time I will return to you, [2]at this time next year, and Sarah will
have a son."
15 Sarah denied *it* however, saying, "I did not laugh"; for she
was afraid. And He said, "No, but you did laugh."
16 Then [a]the men rose up from there, and looked down toward
Sodom; and Abraham was walking with them to send them off.
17 [a]The LORD said, "Shall I hide from Abraham [b]what I am
about to do,
18 since Abraham will surely become a great and [1]mighty
nation, and in him [a]all the nations of the earth will be blessed?
19 "For I have [1a]chosen him, so that he may [b]command his
children and his household after him to [c]keep the way of the
LORD by doing righteousness and justice, so that the LORD may
bring upon Abraham [d]what He has spoken about him."
20 And the LORD said, "[a]The outcry of Sodom and Gomorrah
is indeed great, and their sin is exceedingly grave.
21 "I will [a]go down now, and see if they have done entirely
according to its outcry, which has come to Me; and if not, I will
know."
22 Then [a]the men turned away from there and went toward
Sodom, while Abraham was still standing before [b]the LORD.
23 Abraham came near and said, "[a]Will You indeed sweep
away the righteous with the wicked?
24 "Suppose there are fifty righteous within the city; will You
indeed sweep *it* away and not [1]spare the place for the sake of
the fifty righteous who are in it?
25 "Far be it from You to do [1]such a thing, to slay the righteous
with the wicked, so that the righteous and the wicked are
treated alike. Far be it from You! Shall not [a]the Judge of all the
earth [2]deal justly?"
26 So the LORD said, "[a]If I find in Sodom fifty righteous within
the city, then I will [1]spare the whole place on their account."
27 And Abraham replied, "Now behold, I have [1]ventured to
speak to the Lord, although I am *but* [a]dust and ashes.
28 "Suppose the fifty righteous are lacking five, will You destroy
the whole city because of five?" And He said, "I will not
destroy *it* if I find forty-five there."
29 He spoke to Him yet again and said, "Suppose forty are
found there?" And He said, "I will not do *it* on account of the
forty."
30 Then he said, "Oh may the Lord not be angry, and I shall
speak; suppose thirty are found there?" And He said, "I will
not do *it* if I find thirty there."
31 And he said, "Now behold, I have [1]ventured to speak to

11 [1]Lit *the manner of women* [a]Gen 17:17; Rom 4:19 [b]Heb 11:11

12 [1]Lit *within* [a]Gen 17:17; Luke 1:18 [b]1 Pet 3:6

13 [1]Lit *surely bear*

14 [1]Or *wonderful* [2]Lit *when the time revives* [a]Jer 32:17, 27; Zech 8:6; Matt 19:26; Luke 1:37; Rom 4:21 [b]Gen 17:21; 18:10

16 [a]Gen 18:2, 22; 19:1

17 [a]Gen 18:22, 26, 33; Amos 3:7 [b]Gen 18:21; 19:24

18 [1]Or *populous* [a]Gen 12:3; 22:18; Acts 3:25; Gal 3:8

19 [1]Lit *known* [a]Neh 9:7; Amos 3:2 [b]Deut 6:6, 7 [c]Gen 17:9 [d]Gen 12:2, 3

20 [a]Gen 19:13; Ezek 16:49, 50

21 [a]Gen 11:5; Ex 3:8; Ps 14:2

22 [a]Gen 18:16; 19:1 [b]Gen 18:1, 17

23 [a]Ex 23:7; Num 16:22; 2 Sam 24:17; Ps 11:4-7

24 [1]Or *forgive*

25 [1]Lit *after this manner* [2]Lit *do justice* [a]Deut 1:16, 17; 32:4; Job 8:3, 20; Ps 58:11; 94:2; Is 3:10, 11; Rom 3:5, 6

26 [1]Or *forgive* [a]Jer 5:1

27 [1]Lit *undertaken* [a]Gen 3:19; Job 30:19; 42:6

31 [1]Lit *undertaken*

the Lord; suppose twenty are found there?" And He said, "I will
not destroy *it* on account of the twenty."
32 Then he said, "[a]Oh may the Lord not be angry, and I shall
speak only this once; suppose ten are found there?" And He
said, "I will not destroy *it* on account of the ten."
33 As soon as He had finished speaking to Abraham [a]the LORD
departed, and Abraham returned to his place.

Chapter 19 Theme ____________________

19 Now the [a]two angels came to Sodom in the evening as
Lot was sitting in the gate of Sodom. When [b]Lot saw
them, he rose to meet them and [1]bowed down *with his* face to
the ground.
2 And he said, "Now behold, my lords, please turn aside into
your servant's house, and spend the night, and wash your feet;
then you may rise early and go on your way." They said however,
"No, but we shall spend the night in the square."
3 Yet he urged them strongly, so they turned aside to him and
entered his house; [a]and he prepared a feast for them, and baked
unleavened bread, and they ate.
4 Before they lay down, [a]the men of the city, the men of
Sodom, surrounded the house, both young and old, all the
people [1]from every quarter;
5 and they called to Lot and said to him, "[a]Where are the
men who came to you tonight? Bring them out to us that we
may [1]have relations with them."
6 But Lot went out to them at the doorway, and shut the
door behind him,
7 and said, "Please, my brothers, do not act wickedly.
8 "Now behold, [a]I have two daughters who have not [1]had
relations with man; please let me bring them out to you, and
do to them [2]whatever you like; only do nothing to these men,
inasmuch as they have come under the [3]shelter of my roof."
9 But they said, "Stand aside." Furthermore, they said, "This
one came in [1]as an alien, and already [a]he is acting like a judge;
now we will treat you worse than them." So they pressed hard
against [2]Lot and came near to break the door.
10 But [a]the men reached out their [1]hands and brought Lot into
the house [2]with them, and shut the door.
11 [a]They [1]struck the men who were at the doorway of the
house with blindness, both small and great, so that they
wearied *themselves trying* to find the doorway.
12 Then the *two* men said to Lot, "Whom else have you here?
A son-in-law, and your sons, and your daughters, and whomever you have in the city, bring *them* out of the place;
13 for we are about to destroy this place, because [a]their outcry
has become so great before the LORD that [b]the LORD has sent us
to destroy it."
14 Lot went out and spoke to his sons-in-law, who [1]were to
marry his daughters, and said, "Up, [a]get out of this place, for

32 [a]Judg 6:39

33 [a]Gen 17:22; 35:13

19:1 [1]Lit *bowed himself* [a]Gen 18:2, 22 [b]Gen 18:2-5

3 [a]Gen 18:6-8

4 [1]Or *without exception;* lit *from every end* [a]Gen 13:13; 18:20

5 [1]I.e. have intercourse [a]Lev 18:22; Judg 19:22

8 [1]I.e. had intercourse [2]Lit *as is good in your sight* [3]Lit *shadow* [a]Judg 19:24

9 [1]Lit *to sojourn* [2]Lit *the man, against Lot* [a]Ex 2:14

10 [1]Lit *hand* [2]Lit *to* [a]Gen 19:1

11 [1]Lit *smote* [a]Deut 28:28, 29; 2 Kin 6:18; Acts 13:11

13 [a]Gen 18:20 [b]Lev 26:30-33; Deut 4:26; 28:45; 1 Chr 21:15

14 [1]Or *had married;* lit *were taking* [a]Num 16:21, 45; Rev 18:4

the LORD will destroy the city." [b]But he appeared to his sons-in-
law [2]to be jesting.
15 When morning dawned, the angels urged Lot, saying, "Up,
take your wife and your two daughters who are here, or you
will be swept away in the [1]punishment of the city."
16 But he hesitated. So the men [a]seized his hand and the
hand of his wife and the [1]hands of his two daughters, for [b]the
compassion of the LORD *was* upon him; and they brought him
out, and put him outside the city.
17 When they had brought them outside, [1]one said, "[a]Escape
for your life! [b]Do not look behind you, and do not stay [2]anywhere
in the [c]valley; escape to [d]the [3]mountains, or you will be swept
away."
18 But Lot said to them, "Oh no, my lords!
19 "Now behold, your servant has found favor in your sight,
and you have magnified your lovingkindness, which you have
shown me by saving my life; but I cannot escape to the
[1]mountains, for the disaster will overtake me and I will die;
20 now behold, this town is near *enough* to flee to, and it is
small. Please, let me escape there (is it not small?) [1]that my life
may be saved."
21 He said to him, "Behold, I grant you this [1]request also, not
to overthrow the town of which you have spoken.
22 "Hurry, escape there, for I cannot do anything until you
arrive there." Therefore the name of the town was called [1a]Zoar.
23 The sun had risen over the earth when Lot came to Zoar.
24 Then the LORD [a]rained on Sodom and Gomorrah brimstone
and fire from the LORD out of heaven,
25 and [a]He overthrew those cities, and all the [1]valley, and all
the inhabitants of the cities, and what grew on the ground.
26 But his wife, from behind him, [a]looked *back,* and she
became a pillar of salt.
27 Now Abraham arose early in the morning *and went* to [a]the
place where he had stood before the LORD;
28 and he looked down toward Sodom and Gomorrah, and
toward all the land of the [1]valley, and he saw, and behold, [a]the
smoke of the land ascended like the smoke of a [2]furnace.
29 Thus it came about, when God destroyed the cities of the
[1]valley, that [a]God remembered Abraham, and [b]sent Lot out of
the midst of the overthrow, when He overthrew the cities in
which Lot lived.
30 Lot went up from Zoar, and [1a]stayed in the [2]mountains,
and his two daughters with him; for he was afraid to [3]stay in
Zoar; and he [1]stayed in a cave, he and his two daughters.
31 Then the firstborn said to the younger, "Our father is old,
and there is not a man [1]on earth to [a]come in to us after the
manner of the earth.
32 "Come, [a]let us make our father drink wine, and let us lie
with him that we may preserve [1]our family through our
father."
33 So they made their father drink wine that night, and the

14 [2]Lit *like one who was jesting* [b]Jer 43:1, 2
15 [1]Or *iniquity*
16 [1]Lit *hand* [a]Deut 5:15; 6:21; 7:8; 2 Pet 2:7 [b]Ex 34:7; Ps 32:10; 33:18, 19
17 [1]Lit *he* [2]Lit *in all the circle* [3]Lit *mountain* [a]Jer 48:6 [b]Gen 19:26 [c]Gen 13:10 [d]Gen 14:10
19 [1]Lit *mountain*
20 [1]Lit *and my soul will live*
21 [1]Lit *thing*
22 [1]I.e. small [a]Gen 13:10; 14:2
24 [a]Deut 29:23; Ps 11:6; Is 13:19; Ezek 16:49, 50; Luke 17:29; Jude 7
25 [1]Lit *circle* [a]Deut 29:23; Ps 107:34; Is 13:19; Lam 4:6; 2 Pet 2:6
26 [a]Gen 19:17; Luke 17:32
27 [a]Gen 18:22
28 [1]Lit *circle* [2]Lit *kiln* [a]Rev 9:2; 18:9
29 [1]Lit *circle* [a]Deut 7:8; 9:5, 27 [b]2 Pet 2:7
30 [1]Lit *dwelt* [2]Lit *mountain* [3]Lit *dwell* [a]Gen 19:17, 19
31 [1]Or *in the land* [a]Gen 16:2, 4; 38:8; Deut 25:5
32 [1]Lit *seed from our father* [a]Luke 21:34

firstborn went in and lay with her father; and he did not know when she lay down or when she arose.

34 On the following day, the firstborn said to the younger, "Behold, I lay last night with my father; let us make him drink wine tonight also; then you go in and lie with him, that we may preserve [1]our family through our father."

35 So they made their father drink wine that night also, and the younger arose and lay with him; and he did not know when she lay down or when she arose.

36 Thus both the daughters of Lot were with child by their father.

37 The firstborn bore a son, and called his name [a]Moab; he is the father of the Moabites to this day.

38 As for the younger, she also bore a son, and called his name Ben-ammi; he is the father of the [1]sons of [a]Ammon to this day.

Chapter 20 Theme ______________________________

20 Now Abraham journeyed from [a]there toward the land of [b]the [1]Negev, and [2]settled between Kadesh and Shur; then he sojourned in [c]Gerar.

2 Abraham said of Sarah his wife, "[a]She is my sister." So [b]Abimelech king of Gerar sent and took Sarah.

3 [a]But God came to Abimelech in a dream of the night, and said to him, "Behold, [b]you are a dead man because of the woman whom you have taken, for she is [1]married."

4 Now Abimelech had not come near her; and he said, "Lord, [a]will You slay a nation, even *though* [1]blameless?

5 "Did he not himself say to me, 'She is my sister'? And she [a]herself said, 'He is my brother.' In [b]the integrity of my heart and the innocence of my [1]hands I have done this."

6 Then God said to him in the dream, "Yes, I know that in the integrity of your heart you have done this, and I also [1][a]kept you from sinning against Me; therefore I did not let you touch her.

7 "Now therefore, restore the man's wife, for [a]he is a prophet, and he will pray for you and you will live. But if you do not restore *her*, know that you shall surely die, you and all who are yours."

8 So Abimelech arose early in the morning and called all his servants and told all these things in their hearing; and the men were greatly frightened.

9 [a]Then Abimelech called Abraham and said to him, "What have you done to us? And [1]how have I sinned against you, that you have brought on me and on my kingdom [b]a great sin? You have done to me [2]things that ought not to be done."

10 And Abimelech said to Abraham, "What have you [1]encountered, that you have done this thing?"

11 Abraham said, "Because I thought, surely there is no [a]fear of God in this place, and [b]they will kill me because of my wife.

34 [1]Lit *seed from our father*
37 [a]Deut 2:9
38 [1]Heb *Bene-Ammon* [a]Deut 2:19
20:1 [1]I.e. South country [2]Lit *dwelt* [a]Gen 18:1 [b]Gen 12:9 [c]Gen 26:1, 6
2 [a]Gen 12:11-13; 20:12; 26:7 [b]Gen 12:15
3 [1]Lit *married to a husband* [a]Gen 12:17, 18 [b]Gen 20:7
4 [1]Lit *righteous* [a]Gen 18:23-25
5 [1]Lit *palms* [a]Gen 20:13 [b]1 Kin 9:4; Ps 7:8; 26:6
6 [1]Lit *restrained* [a]1 Sam 25:26, 34
7 [a]1 Sam 7:5; 2 Kin 5:11; Job 42:8
9 [1]Lit *what* [2]Lit *deeds* [a]Gen 12:18 [b]Gen 39:9
10 [1]Lit *seen*
11 [a]Neh 5:15; Prov 16:6 [b]Gen 12:12; 26:7

12 "Besides, she actually is my sister, the daughter of my father,
but not the daughter of my mother, and she became my wife;
13 and it came about, when [a]God caused me to wander from
my father's house, that I said to her, 'This is [1]the kindness
which you will show to me: [2]everywhere we go, [b]say of me,
"He is my brother."'"
14 [a]Abimelech then took sheep and oxen and male and female
servants, and gave them to Abraham, and restored his wife
Sarah to him.
15 Abimelech said, "[a]Behold, my land is before you; [1]settle
wherever [2]you please."
16 To Sarah he said, "Behold, I have given your [a]brother a
thousand pieces of silver; behold, it is [1]your vindication before
all who are with you, and before all men you are cleared."
17 [a]Abraham prayed to God, and God healed Abimelech and
his wife and his maids, so that they bore *children.*
18 [a]For the LORD had closed fast all the wombs of the household
of Abimelech because of Sarah, Abraham's wife.

Chapter 21 Theme ____________

21 [a]Then the LORD took note of Sarah as He had said, and
the LORD did for Sarah as He had [1]promised.
2 [a]So Sarah conceived and bore a son to Abraham in his old
age, at [b]the appointed time of which God had spoken to him.
3 Abraham called the name of his son who was born to him,
whom Sarah bore to him, [a]Isaac.
4 Then Abraham circumcised his son Isaac when he was
[a]eight days old, as God had commanded him.
5 Now Abraham was [a]one hundred years old when his son
Isaac was born to him.
6 Sarah said, "God has made [a]laughter for me; everyone who
hears will laugh [1]with me."
7 And she said, "[a]Who would have said to Abraham that
Sarah would nurse children? Yet I have borne him a son in his
old age."
8 The child grew and was weaned, and Abraham made a
great feast on the day that Isaac was weaned.
9 Now Sarah saw [a]the son of Hagar the Egyptian, whom she
had borne to Abraham, [1b]mocking.
10 Therefore she said to Abraham, "[a]Drive out this maid and
her son, for the son of this maid shall not be an heir with my
son [1]Isaac."
11 [a]The matter [1]distressed Abraham greatly because of his son.
12 But God said to Abraham, "[1]Do not be distressed because
of the lad and your maid; whatever Sarah tells you, listen to
her, for [a]through Isaac [2]your descendants shall be named.
13 "And of [a]the son of the maid I will make a nation also,
because he is your [1]descendant."
14 So Abraham rose early in the morning and took bread and
a [1]skin of water and gave *them* to Hagar, putting *them* on her

13 [1]Lit *your* [2]Lit *at every place where* [a]Gen 12:1-9 [b]Gen 12:13; 20:5

14 [a]Gen 12:16

15 [1]Lit *dwell* [2]Lit *it is good in your sight* [a]Gen 13:9; 34:10; 47:6

16 [1]Lit *for you a covering of the eyes* [a]Gen 20:5

17 [a]Num 12:13; 21:7; James 5:16

18 [a]Gen 12:17

21:1 [1]Lit *spoken* [a]Gen 17:16, 21; 18:10, 14; Gal 4:23

2 [a]Acts 7:8; Gal 4:22; Heb 11:11 [b]Gen 17:21; 18:10, 14

3 [a]Gen 17:19, 21

4 [a]Gen 17:12; Acts 7:8

5 [a]Gen 17:17

6 [1]Lit *for* [a]Gen 18:13; Ps 126:2; Is 54:1

7 [a]Gen 18:11, 13

9 [1]Or *playing* [a]Gen 16:1, 4, 15 [b]Gal 4:29

10 [1]Lit *with Isaac* [a]Gal 4:30

11 [1]Lit *was very grievous in Abraham's sight* [a]Gen 17:18

12 [1]Lit *Do not let it be grievous in your sight* [2]Lit *your seed will be called* [a]Rom 9:7; Heb 11:18

13 [1]Lit *seed* [a]Gen 16:10; 21:18; 25:12-18

14 [1]I.e. a skin used as a bottle

shoulder, and *gave her* the boy, and sent her away. And she departed and wandered about in the wilderness of Beersheba.

15 When the water in the skin was used up, she [1]left the boy under one of the bushes.

16 Then she went and sat down opposite him, about a bowshot away, for she said, "Do not let me [1]see the boy die." And she sat opposite him, and [a]lifted up her voice and wept.

17 God [a]heard the lad crying; and the angel of God called to Hagar from heaven and said to her, "What is the matter with you, Hagar? [b]Do not fear, for God has heard the voice of the lad where he is.

18 "Arise, lift up the lad, and hold him by [1]the hand, [a]for I will make a great nation of him."

19 Then God [a]opened her eyes and she saw [b]a well of water; and she went and filled the [1]skin with water and gave the lad a drink.

20 [a]God was with the lad, and he grew; and he [1]lived in the wilderness and became an archer.

21 [a]He [1]lived in the wilderness of Paran, and his mother took a wife for him from the land of Egypt.

22 Now it came about at that time that [a]Abimelech and Phicol, the commander of his army, spoke to Abraham, saying, "[b]God is with you in all that you do;

23 now therefore, [a]swear to me here by God that you will not deal falsely with me or with my offspring or with my posterity, but according to the kindness that I have shown to you, you shall show to me and to the land in which you have sojourned."

24 Abraham said, "I swear it."

25 But Abraham [1]complained to Abimelech because of the well of water which the servants of Abimelech [a]had seized.

26 And Abimelech said, "I do not know who has done this thing; you did not tell me, nor did I hear of it [1]until today."

27 Abraham took sheep and oxen and gave them to Abimelech, and [a]the two of them made a covenant.

28 Then Abraham set seven ewe lambs of the flock by themselves.

29 Abimelech said to Abraham, "What do these seven ewe lambs mean, which you have set by themselves?"

30 He said, "You shall take these seven ewe lambs from my hand so that it may be a [a]witness to me, that I dug this well."

31 Therefore he called that place [a]Beersheba, because there the two of them took an oath.

32 So they made a covenant at Beersheba; and Abimelech and Phicol, the commander of his army, arose and returned to the land of the Philistines.

33 *Abraham* planted a tamarisk tree at Beersheba, and there [a]he called on the name of the LORD, the [b]Everlasting God.

34 And Abraham sojourned [a]in the land of the Philistines for many days.

15 [1]Lit *cast*
16 [1]Lit *look upon the death of the child* [a]Jer 6:26; Amos 8:10
17 [a]Ex 3:7; Deut 26:7; Ps 6:8 [b]Gen 26:24
18 [1]Lit *your* [a]Gen 16:10; 21:13; 25:12-16
19 [1]V 14, note 1 [a]Num 22:31; 2 Kin 6:17 [b]Gen 16:7, 14
20 [1]Lit *dwelt* [a]Gen 28:15; 39:2, 3, 21
21 [1]Lit *dwelt* [a]Gen 25:18
22 [a]Gen 20:2, 14; 26:26 [b]Gen 26:28; Is 8:10
23 [a]Josh 2:12; 1 Sam 24:21
25 [1]Lit *reproved* [a]Gen 26:15, 18, 20-22
26 [1]Lit *except*
27 [a]Gen 26:31
30 [a]Gen 31:48
31 [a]Gen 21:14; 26:33
33 [a]Gen 12:8 [b]Ex 15:18; Deut 32:40; Ps 90:2; 93:2; Is 40:28; Jer 10:10; Hab 1:12; Heb 13:8
34 [a]Gen 22:19

Chapter 22 Theme ______________________________

22 Now it came about after these things, that [a]God tested
Abraham, and said to him, "[b]Abraham!" And he said,
"Here I am."
2 He said, "Take now [a]your son, your only son, whom you
love, Isaac, and go to the land of [b]Moriah, and offer him there
as a [c]burnt offering on one of the mountains of which I will tell
you."
3 So Abraham rose early in the morning and saddled his
donkey, and took two of his young men with him and Isaac his
son; and he split wood for the burnt offering, and arose and
went to the place of which God had told him.
4 On the third day Abraham raised his eyes and saw the
place from a distance.
5 Abraham said to his young men, "Stay here with the
donkey, and I and the lad will go over there; and we will
worship and return to you."
6 Abraham took the wood of the burnt offering and [a]laid it
on Isaac his son, and he took in his hand the fire and the knife.
So the two of them walked on together.
7 Isaac spoke to Abraham his father and said, "My father!"
And he said, "Here I am, my son." And he said, "Behold, the
fire and the wood, but where is the [a]lamb for the burnt
offering?"
8 Abraham said, "God will [1]provide for Himself the lamb for
the burnt offering, my son." So the two of them walked on
together.
9 Then they came to [a]the place of which God had told him;
and Abraham built [b]the altar there and arranged the wood, and
bound his son Isaac and [c]laid him on the altar, on top of the
wood.
10 Abraham stretched out his hand and took the knife to slay
his son.
11 But [a]the angel of the LORD called to him from heaven and
said, "Abraham, Abraham!" And he said, "Here I am."
12 He said, "Do not stretch out your hand against the lad, and
do nothing to him; for now [a]I know that you [1]fear God, since
you have not withheld [b]your son, your only son, from Me."
13 Then Abraham raised his eyes and looked, and behold,
behind *him* a ram caught in the thicket by his horns; and
Abraham went and took the ram and offered him up for a
burnt offering in the place of his son.
14 Abraham called the name of that place [1]The LORD Will
Provide, as it is said to this day, "In the mount of the LORD [a]it
will [2]be provided."
15 Then the angel of the LORD called to Abraham a second
time from heaven,
16 and said, "[a]By Myself I have sworn, declares the LORD,
because you have done this thing and have not withheld your
son, your only son,
17 indeed I will greatly bless you, and I will greatly [a]multiply

INSIGHT

The words ***love***, ***worship***, and ***obey*** are first used in Genesis 22. Note their context.

22:1 [a]Deut 8:2, 16; Heb 11:17; James 1:12-14 [b]Gen 22:11

2 [a]Gen 22:12, 16; John 3:16; 1 John 4:9 [b]2 Chr 3:1 [c]Gen 8:20

6 [a]John 19:17

7 [a]Ex 29:38-42; John 1:29, 36; Rev 13:8

8 [1]Lit *see*

9 [a]Gen 22:2 [b]Gen 12:7, 8; 13:18 [c]Heb 11:17-19; James 2:21

11 [a]Gen 16:7-11; 21:17, 18

12 [1]Or *reverence;* lit *are a fearer of God* [a]James 2:21, 22 [b]Gen 22:2, 16

14 [1]Heb *YHWH-jireh* [2]Lit *be seen* [a]Gen 22:8

16 [a]Ps 105:9; Luke 1:73; Heb 6:13, 14

17 [a]Gen 15:5; 26:4; Jer 33:22; Heb 11:12

your [1]seed as the stars of the heavens and as [b]the sand which is
on the seashore; and [c]your [1]seed shall possess the gate of [2]their
enemies.
18 "[a]In your [1]seed all the nations of the earth shall [2]be blessed,
because you have [b]obeyed My voice."
19 [a]So Abraham returned to his young men, and they arose and
went together to Beersheba; and Abraham lived at Beersheba.
20 Now it came about after these things, that it was told
Abraham, saying, "Behold, [a]Milcah [1]also has borne children to
your brother Nahor:
21 Uz his firstborn and Buz his brother and Kemuel the father
of Aram
22 and Chesed and Hazo and Pildash and Jidlaph and
Bethuel."
23 Bethuel [1]became the father of [a]Rebekah; these eight Milcah
bore to Nahor, Abraham's brother.
24 His concubine, whose name was Reumah, [1]also bore Tebah
and Gaham and Tahash and Maacah.

Chapter 23 Theme ________________________________

23 Now [1]Sarah lived one hundred and twenty-seven years;
these were the years of the life of Sarah.
2 Sarah died in [a]Kiriath-arba (that is, Hebron) in the land of
Canaan; and Abraham [1]went in to mourn for Sarah and to weep
for her.
3 Then Abraham rose from before his dead, and spoke to the
[a]sons of Heth, saying,
4 "I am [a]a stranger and a sojourner among you; [b]give me [1]a
[c]burial site among you that I may bury my dead out of my sight."
5 The sons of Heth answered Abraham, saying to him,
6 "Hear us, my lord, you are a [1a]mighty prince among us; bury
your dead in the choicest of our graves; none of us will refuse
you his grave for burying your dead."
7 So Abraham rose and bowed to the people of the land, the
sons of Heth.
8 And he spoke with them, saying, "If it is your [1]wish *for me*
to bury my dead out of my sight, hear me, and approach
[a]Ephron the son of Zohar for me,
9 that he may give me the cave of Machpelah which he
owns, which is at the end of his field; for the full price let him
give it to me in [1]your presence for [2]a burial site."
10 Now Ephron was sitting among the sons of Heth; and
Ephron the Hittite answered Abraham in the hearing of the
sons of Heth; *even* [a]of all who went in at the gate of his city,
saying,
11 "No, my lord, hear me; [a]I give you the field, and I give you
the cave that is in it. In the presence of the sons of my people I
give it to you; bury your dead."
12 And Abraham bowed before the people of the land.
13 He spoke to Ephron in the hearing of the people of the

17 [1]Or *descendants* [2]Lit *his* [b]Gen 32:12 [c]Gen 24:60

18 [1]Or *descendants* [2]Or *bless themselves* [a]Gen 12:3; 18:18; Acts 3:25; Gal 3:8, 16 [b]Gen 18:19; 22:3, 10; 26:5

19 [a]Gen 22:5

20 [1]Lit *she also* [a]Gen 11:29

23 [1]Lit *begot* [a]Gen 24:15

24 [1]Lit *she also*

23:1 [1]Lit *the life of Sarah was*

2 [1]Or *proceeded* [a]Josh 14:15; 15:13; 21:11

3 [a]Gen 10:15; 15:20

4 [1]Lit *possession of a grave* [a]Gen 17:8; Lev 25:23; 1 Chr 29:15; Ps 39:12; 105:12; 119:19; Heb 11:9, 13 [b]Acts 7:16 [c]Gen 49:30

6 [1]Lit *prince of God* [a]Gen 14:14; 20:7

8 [1]Lit *soul* [a]Gen 25:9

9 [1]Lit *the midst of you* [2]Lit *possession of a burial place*

10 [a]Gen 23:18; 34:20, 24; Ruth 4:1, 11

11 [a]2 Sam 24:21-24

land, saying, "If you will only please listen to me; I will give the
price of the field, accept *it* from me that I may bury my dead
there."
14 Then Ephron answered Abraham, saying to him,
15 "My lord, listen to me; a piece of land worth four hundred
[a]shekels of silver, what is that between me and you? So bury
your dead."
16 Abraham listened to Ephron; and Abraham [a]weighed out
for Ephron the silver which he had named in the [1]hearing of
the sons of Heth, four hundred shekels of silver, [2]commercial
standard.
17 So [a]Ephron's field, which was in Machpelah, which faced
Mamre, the field and cave which was in it, and all the trees
which were in the field, that were [1]within all the confines of
its border, [2]were deeded over
18 to Abraham for a possession [a]in the presence of the sons of
Heth, before all who went in at the gate of his city.
19 After this, Abraham buried Sarah his wife in the cave of
the field at Machpelah facing Mamre (that is, Hebron) in the
land of Canaan.
20 So the field and the cave that is in it, [1]were [a]deeded over to
Abraham for [2]a burial site by the sons of Heth.

Chapter 24 Theme ______________________

24 Now [a]Abraham was old, advanced in age; and the LORD
had [b]blessed Abraham in every way.
2 Abraham said to his servant, the oldest of his household,
who had [a]charge of all that he owned, "[b]Please place your hand
under my thigh,
3 and I will make you swear by the LORD, [a]the God of heaven
and the God of earth, that you [b]shall not take a wife for my son
from the daughters of [c]the Canaanites, among whom I live,
4 but you will go to [a]my country and to my relatives, and
take a wife for my son Isaac."
5 The servant said to him, "Suppose the woman is not
willing to follow me to this land; should I take your son back to
the land from where you came?"
6 Then Abraham said to him, "[a]Beware that you do not take
my son back there!
7 "[a]The LORD, the God of heaven, who took me from my
father's house and from the land of my birth, and who spoke to
me and who swore to me, saying, '[b]To your [1]descendants I will
give this land,' He will send [c]His angel before you, and you will
take a wife for my son from there.
8 "But if the woman is not willing to follow you, then you will
[a]be free from this my oath; [b]only do not take my son back
there."
9 So the servant [a]placed his hand under the thigh of
Abraham his master, and swore to him concerning this matter.
10 Then the servant took ten camels from the camels of his

15 [a]Ex 30:13; Ezek 45:12

16 [1]Lit *ears* [2]Lit *current according to the merchant* [a]2 Sam 14:26; Jer 32:9, 10; Zech 11:12

17 [1]Lit *in all its border around* [2]Or *were ratified* [a]Gen 25:9; 49:29, 30; 50:13

18 [a]Gen 23:10

20 [1]Or *were ratified* [2]Lit *possession of a burial place* [a]Jer 32:10-14

24:1 [a]Gen 18:11 [b]Gen 12:2; 13:2; 24:35; Gal 3:9

2 [a]Gen 39:4-6 [b]Gen 24:9; 47:29

3 [a]Gen 14:19, 22 [b]Deut 7:3; 2 Cor 6:14-17 [c]Gen 10:15-19; 26:34, 35; 28:1, 8

4 [a]Gen 12:1; Heb 11:15

6 [a]Gen 24:8

7 [1]Lit *seed* [a]Gen 24:3 [b]Gen 12:7; 13:15; 15:18; Ex 32:13 [c]Gen 16:7; 21:17; 22:11; Ex 23:20, 23

8 [a]Josh 2:17-20 [b]Gen 24:6

9 [a]Gen 24:2

master, and set out with a variety of [a]good things of his master's
in his hand; and he arose and went to [1]Mesopotamia, to [b]the
city of Nahor.
11 He made the camels kneel down outside the city by [a]the
well of water at evening time, [b]the time when women go out
to draw water.
12 He said, "[a]O LORD, the God of my master Abraham, please
[1b]grant me success today, and show lovingkindness to my
master Abraham.
13 "Behold, [a]I am standing by the [1]spring, and the daughters of
the men of the city are coming out to draw water;
14 now may it be that the girl to whom I say, 'Please let down
your jar so that I may drink,' and [1]who answers, 'Drink, and I
will water your camels also'—*may* she *be the one* whom You
have appointed for Your servant Isaac; and by this I will know
that You have shown lovingkindness to my master."
15 [a]Before he had finished speaking, behold, [b]Rebekah who
was born to Bethuel the son of [c]Milcah, the wife of Abraham's
brother Nahor, came out with her jar on her shoulder.
16 The girl was [a]very beautiful, a virgin, and no man had [1]had
relations with her; and she went down to the spring and filled
her jar and came up.
17 Then the servant ran to meet her, and said, "[a]Please let me
drink a little water from your jar."
18 [a]She said, "Drink, my lord"; and she quickly lowered her
jar to her hand, and gave him a drink.
19 Now when she had finished giving him a drink, [a]she said, "I
will draw also for your camels until they have finished drinking."
20 So she quickly emptied her jar into the trough, and ran
back to the well to draw, and she drew for all his camels.
21 [a]Meanwhile, the man was gazing at her [1]in silence, to know
whether the LORD had made his journey successful or not.
22 When the camels had finished drinking, the man took a
[a]gold ring weighing a half-shekel and two bracelets for her
[1]wrists weighing ten shekels in gold,
23 and said, "Whose daughter are you? Please tell me, is there
room for us to lodge in your father's house?"
24 She said to him, "[a]I am the daughter of Bethuel, the son of
Milcah, whom she bore to Nahor."
25 Again she said to him, "We have plenty of both straw and
feed, and room to lodge in."
26 Then the man [a]bowed low and worshiped the LORD.
27 He said, "[a]Blessed be the LORD, the God of my master
Abraham, who has not forsaken [b]His lovingkindness and His
truth toward my master; as for me, [c]the LORD has guided me in
the way to the house of my master's brothers."
28 Then [a]the girl ran and told her mother's household about
these things.
29 Now Rebekah had a brother whose name was [a]Laban; and
Laban ran outside to the man at the spring.
30 When he saw the ring and the bracelets on his sister's

10 [1]Heb *Aram-naharaim, Aram of the two rivers* [a]Gen 24:22, 53 [b]Gen 11:31, 32
11 [a]Gen 24:42 [b]Ex 2:16; 1 Sam 9:11
12 [1]Lit *cause to occur for me* [a]Gen 24:27, 42, 48; 26:24; Ex 3:6, 15 [b]Gen 27:20
13 [1]Lit *fountain of water* [a]Gen 24:43
14 [1]Lit *she will say*
15 [a]Gen 24:45 [b]Gen 22:20, 23 [c]Gen 11:29
16 [1]Lit *known* [a]Gen 12:11; 26:7; 29:17
17 [a]John 4:7
18 [a]Gen 24:14, 46
19 [a]Gen 24:14
21 [1]Lit *keeping silent* [a]Gen 24:12-14, 27, 52
22 [1]Lit *hands* [a]Gen 24:47; Ex 32:2, 3
24 [a]Gen 24:15
26 [a]Gen 24:48, 52; Ex 4:31
27 [a]Gen 24:12, 42, 48; Ex 18:10; Ruth 4:14; 1 Sam 25:32; 2 Sam 18:28; Luke 1:68 [b]Gen 32:10; Ps 98:3 [c]Gen 24:21, 48
28 [a]Gen 29:12
29 [a]Gen 29:5, 13

[1]wrists, and when he heard the words of Rebekah his sister,
saying, "[2]This is what the man said to me," he went to the
man; and behold, he was standing by the camels at the spring.
31 And he said, "[a]Come in, [b]blessed of the LORD! Why do you
stand outside since [c]I have prepared the house, and a place for
the camels?"
32 So the man entered the house. Then [1a]Laban unloaded the
camels, and he gave straw and feed to the camels, and water to
wash his feet and the feet of the men who were with him.
33 But when *food* was set before him to eat, he said, "I will
not eat until I have told my business." And he said, "Speak on."
34 So he said, "I am [a]Abraham's servant.
35 "The LORD has greatly [a]blessed my master, so that he has
become [1]rich; and He has given him [b]flocks and herds, and silver
and gold, and servants and maids, and camels and donkeys.
36 "Now [a]Sarah my master's wife bore a son to my master [1]in
her old age, and [b]he has given him all that he has.
37 "[a]My master made me swear, saying, 'You shall not take a
wife for my son from the daughters of the Canaanites, in whose
land I [1]live;
38 but you shall go to my father's house and to my relatives,
and take a wife for my son.'
39 "[a]I said to my master, 'Suppose the woman does not follow
me.'
40 "He said to me, '[a]The LORD, before whom I have [b]walked,
will send [c]His angel with you to make your journey successful,
and you will take a wife for my son from my relatives and from
my father's house;
41 [a]then you will be free from my oath, when you come to my
relatives; and if they do not give her to you, you will be free
from my oath.'
42 "So [a]I came today to the spring, and said, 'O LORD, the God
of my master Abraham, if now You will make my journey on
which I go [b]successful;
43 behold, [a]I am standing by the [1]spring, and may it be that
the maiden who comes out to draw, and to whom I say,
"[b]Please let me drink a little water from your jar";
44 and she will say to me, "You drink, and I will draw for your
camels also"; let her be the woman whom the LORD has
appointed for my master's son.'
45 "Before I had finished [a]speaking in my heart, behold,
[b]Rebekah came out with her jar on her shoulder, and went
down to the spring and drew, and [c]I said to her, 'Please let me
drink.'
46 "She quickly lowered her jar from her *shoulder,* and said,
'[a]Drink, and I will water your camels also'; so I drank, and she
watered the camels also.
47 "[a]Then I asked her, and said, 'Whose daughter are you?'
And she said, 'The daughter of Bethuel, Nahor's son, whom
Milcah bore to him'; and I put the [b]ring on her nose, and the
bracelets on her [1]wrists.

30 [1]Lit *hands* [2]Lit *Thus the man*
31 [a]Gen 29:13 [b]Gen 26:29; Ruth 3:10; Ps 115:15 [c]Gen 18:3-5; 19:2, 3
32 [1]Lit *he* [a]Gen 43:24; Judg 19:21
34 [a]Gen 24:2
35 [1]Lit *great* [a]Gen 24:1 [b]Gen 13:2
36 [1]Lit *after she was old* [a]Gen 21:1-7 [b]Gen 25:5
37 [1]Lit *dwell* [a]Gen 24:2-4
39 [a]Gen 24:5
40 [a]Gen 24:7 [b]Gen 5:22, 24; 17:1 [c]Ex 23:20
41 [a]Gen 24:8
42 [a]Gen 24:11, 12 [b]Neh 1:11
43 [1]Lit *fountain of water* [a]Gen 24:13 [b]Gen 24:14
45 [a]1 Sam 1:13 [b]Gen 24:15 [c]Gen 24:17
46 [a]Gen 24:18, 19
47 [1]Lit *hands* [a]Gen 24:23, 24 [b]Ezek 16:11, 12

48 "And I [a]bowed low and worshiped the LORD, and blessed
the LORD, the God of my master Abraham, [b]who had guided me
in the right way to take the daughter of my master's [1]kinsman
for his son.
49 "So now if you are going to [1a]deal kindly and truly with my
master, tell me; and if not, let me know, that I may turn to the
right hand or the left."
50 Then Laban and Bethuel replied, "[a]The matter comes from
the LORD; [b]*so* we cannot speak to you bad or good.
51 "Here is Rebekah before you, take *her* and go, and let her be
the wife of your master's son, as the LORD has spoken."
52 When Abraham's servant heard their words, he [a]bowed
himself to the ground [1]before the LORD.
53 The servant brought out [a]articles of silver and articles of
gold, and garments, and gave them to Rebekah; he also gave
precious things to her brother and to her mother.
54 Then he and the men who were with him ate and drank
and spent the night. When they arose in the morning, he said,
"[a]Send me away to my master."
55 But her brother and her mother said, "[a]Let the girl stay
with us *a few* days, say ten; afterward she may go."
56 He said to them, "Do not delay me, since [a]the LORD has
prospered my way. Send me away that I may go to my master."
57 And they said, "We will call the girl and [1]consult her
wishes."
58 Then they called Rebekah and said to her, "Will you go
with this man?" And she said, "I will go."
59 Thus they sent away their sister Rebekah and [a]her nurse
with Abraham's servant and his men.
60 They blessed Rebekah and said to her,

"May you, our sister,
[a]Become thousands of ten thousands,
And may [b]your [1]descendants possess
The gate of those who hate them."

61 Then Rebekah arose with her maids, and they mounted the
camels and followed the man. So the servant took Rebekah and
departed.
62 Now Isaac had come from going to [a]Beer-lahai-roi; for he
[1]was living in [b]the [2]Negev.
63 Isaac went out [a]to [1]meditate in the field toward evening;
and [b]he lifted up his eyes and looked, and behold, camels were
coming.
64 Rebekah lifted up her eyes, and when she saw Isaac she
dismounted from the camel.
65 She said to the servant, "Who is that man walking in the field
to meet us?" And the servant said, "He is my master." Then she
took her [1]veil and covered herself.
66 The servant told Isaac all the things that he had done.
67 Then Isaac brought her into his mother Sarah's tent, and
[a]he took Rebekah, and she became his wife, and [b]he loved her;
thus Isaac was comforted after [c]his mother's death.

48 [1]Lit *brother* [a]Gen 24:26, 52 [b]Gen 24:27; Ps 32:8; 48:14; Is 48:17

49 [1]Lit *show lovingkindness and truth* [a]Gen 47:29; Josh 2:14

50 [a]Ps 118:23; Mark 12:11 [b]Gen 31:24, 29

52 [1]Lit *to* [a]Gen 24:26, 48

53 [a]Gen 24:10, 22; Ex 3:22; 11:2; 12:35

54 [a]Gen 24:56, 59; 30:25

55 [a]Judg 19:4

56 [a]Gen 24:40

57 [1]Lit *ask her mouth*

59 [a]Gen 35:8

60 [1]Lit *seed* [a]Gen 17:16 [b]Gen 22:17

62 [1]Lit *was dwelling* [2]I.e. South country [a]Gen 16:14; 25:11 [b]Gen 20:1

63 [1]Or *stroll;* meaning uncertain [a]Josh 1:8; Ps 1:2; 77:12; 119:15, 27, 48; 143:5; 145:5 [b]Gen 18:2

65 [1]Or *shawl*

67 [a]Gen 25:20 [b]Gen 29:18 [c]Gen 23:1, 2

Chapter 25 Theme ______________________

25 Now Abraham took another wife, [1]whose name was
Keturah.
2 [a]She bore to him Zimran and Jokshan and Medan and
Midian and Ishbak and Shuah.
3 Jokshan [1]became the father of Sheba and Dedan. And the
sons of Dedan were Asshurim and Letushim and Leummim.
4 The sons of Midian *were* Ephah and Epher and Hanoch
and Abida and Eldaah. All these *were* the sons of Keturah.
5 [a]Now Abraham gave all that he had to Isaac;
6 but to the sons of [1]his concubines, Abraham gave gifts
while he was still living, and [a]sent them away from his son
Isaac eastward, to the land of the east.
7 These are [1]all the years of Abraham's life that he lived,
[a]one hundred and seventy-five years.
8 Abraham breathed his last and died [a]in a [1]ripe old age, an
old man and satisfied *with life;* and he was [b]gathered to his
people.
9 Then his sons Isaac and Ishmael buried him in [a]the cave of
Machpelah, in the field of Ephron the son of Zohar the Hittite,
facing Mamre,
10 [a]the field which Abraham purchased from the sons of
Heth; there Abraham was buried with Sarah his wife.
11 It came about after the death of Abraham, that [a]God
blessed his son Isaac; and Isaac [1]lived by [b]Beer-lahai-roi.
12 Now these are *the records of* the generations of [a]Ishmael,
Abraham's son, whom Hagar the Egyptian, Sarah's maid, bore
to Abraham;
13 and these are the names of [a]the sons of Ishmael, by their
names, [1]in the order of their birth: Nebaioth, the firstborn of
Ishmael, and Kedar and Adbeel and Mibsam
14 and Mishma and Dumah and Massa,
15 Hadad and Tema, Jetur, Naphish and Kedemah.
16 These are the sons of Ishmael and these are their names,
by their villages, and by their camps; [a]twelve princes according
to their [1]tribes.
17 These are the years of the life of Ishmael, [a]one hundred
and thirty-seven years; and he breathed his last and died, and
was [b]gathered to his people.
18 They [1]settled from [a]Havilah to [b]Shur which is [2]east of
Egypt [3]as one goes toward Assyria; [c]he [4]settled in defiance of
all his [5]relatives.
19 Now these are *the records of* [a]the generations of Isaac,
Abraham's son: Abraham [1]became the father of Isaac;
20 and Isaac was forty years old when he took [a]Rebekah, the
[b]daughter of Bethuel the [1]Aramean of Paddan-aram, the [c]sister
of Laban the [1]Aramean, to be his wife.
21 Isaac prayed to the LORD on behalf of his wife, because she
was barren; and [a]the LORD [1]answered him and Rebekah his
wife [b]conceived.
22 But the children struggled together within her; and she

25:1 [1]Lit *and her name*
2 [a]1 Chr 1:32, 33
3 [1]Lit *begot*
5 [a]Gen 24:35, 36
6 [1]Lit *concubines which belonged to Abraham* [a]Gen 21:14
7 [1]Lit *the days of* [a]Gen 12:4
8 [1]Lit *good* [a]Gen 15:15; 47:8, 9 [b]Gen 25:17; 35:29; 49:29, 33
9 [a]Gen 23:17, 18; 49:29, 30; 50:13
10 [a]Gen 23:3-16
11 [1]Lit *dwelt* [a]Gen 12:2, 3; 22:17; 26:3 [b]Gen 16:14; 24:62
12 [a]Gen 16:15
13 [1]Lit *in regard to their generations* [a]1 Chr 1:29-31
16 [1]Or *peoples* [a]Gen 17:20
17 [a]Gen 16:16 [b]Gen 25:8; 49:33
18 [1]Lit *dwelt* [2]Lit *before* [3]Lit *as you go* [4]Lit *fell over against* [5]Lit *brothers* [a]1 Sam 15:7 [b]Gen 20:1 [c]Gen 16:12
19 [1]Lit *begot* [a]Matt 1:2
20 [1]I.e. Syrian [a]Gen 24:15, 29, 67 [b]Gen 22:23 [c]Gen 24:29
21 [1]Lit *was entreated of him* [a]1 Sam 1:17; 1 Chr 5:20; 2 Chr 33:13; Ezra 8:23; Ps 127:3 [b]Rom 9:10

said, "If it is so, why then am I *this way?*" So she went to
[a]inquire of the LORD.
23 The LORD said to her,
"[a]Two nations are in your womb;
[b]And two peoples will be separated from your body;
And one people shall be stronger than the other;
And [c]the older shall serve the younger."
24 When her days to be delivered were fulfilled, behold, there
were twins in her womb.
25 Now the first came forth red, [a]all over like a hairy garment;
and they named him Esau.
26 Afterward his brother came forth with [a]his hand holding
on to Esau's heel, so [b]his name was called [1]Jacob; and Isaac was
[c]sixty years old when she gave birth to them.
27 When the boys grew up, Esau became a skillful hunter, a
man of the field, but Jacob was a [1]peaceful man, [2a]living in tents.
28 Now Isaac loved Esau, because [1]he had [a]a taste for game,
[b]but Rebekah loved Jacob.
29 When Jacob had cooked [a]stew, Esau came in from the field
and he was [1]famished;
30 and Esau said to Jacob, "Please let me have a swallow of
[1]that red stuff there, for I am [2]famished." Therefore his name
was called [3]Edom.
31 But Jacob said, "[1]First sell me your [a]birthright."
32 Esau said, "Behold, I am about to die; so of what *use* then
is the birthright to me?"
33 And Jacob said, "[1]First swear to me"; so he swore to him,
and [a]sold his birthright to Jacob.
34 Then Jacob gave Esau bread and lentil stew; and he ate and
drank, and rose and went on his way. Thus Esau despised his
birthright.

Chapter 26 Theme

26 Now there was [a]a famine in the land, besides the previous famine that had occurred in the days of Abraham.
So Isaac went to Gerar, to [b]Abimelech king of the Philistines.
2 The LORD [a]appeared to him and said, "Do not go down to
Egypt; [1b]stay in the land of which I shall tell you.
3 "Sojourn in this land and [a]I will be with you and [b]bless you,
for [c]to you and to your [1]descendants I will give all these lands,
and I will establish [d]the oath which I swore to your father
Abraham.
4 "[a]I will multiply your [1]descendants as the stars of heaven,
and will give your [1]descendants all these lands; and [b]by your
[1]descendants all the nations of the earth [2]shall be blessed;
5 because Abraham [1a]obeyed Me and kept My charge, My
commandments, My statutes and My laws."
6 So Isaac [1]lived in Gerar.
7 When the men of the place asked about his wife, he said,
"[a]She is my sister," for he was [b]afraid to say, "my wife,"

22 [a]1 Sam 9:9; 10:22
23 [a]Gen 17:4-6, 16; Num 20:14; Deut 2:4, 8 [b]Gen 27:29 [c]Gen 27:40; Mal 1:2, 3; Rom 9:12
25 [a]Gen 27:11
26 [1]I.e. one who takes by the heel or supplants [a]Hos 12:3 [b]Gen 27:36 [c]Gen 25:20
27 [1]Lit *complete* [2]Lit *dwelling* [a]Heb 11:9
28 [1]Lit *game was in his mouth* [a]Gen 27:19 [b]Gen 27:6-10
29 [1]Lit *weary* [a]2 Kin 4:38
30 [1]Lit *the red, this red* [2]Lit *weary* [3]I.e. red
31 [1]Lit *Today* [a]Deut 21:16, 17; 1 Chr 5:1, 2
33 [1]Lit *Today* [a]Heb 12:16
26:1 [a]Gen 12:10 [b]Gen 20:1, 2
2 [1]Lit *dwell* [a]Gen 12:7; 17:1; 18:1 [b]Gen 12:1
3 [1]Lit *seed* [a]Gen 26:24; 28:15; 31:3 [b]Gen 12:2 [c]Gen 12:7; 13:15; 15:18 [d]Gen 22:16-18; Ps 105:9
4 [1]Lit *seed* [2]Or *bless themselves* [a]Gen 15:5; 22:17; Ex 32:13 [b]Gen 22:18; Gal 3:8
5 [1]Lit *hearkened to My voice* [a]Gen 22:16
6 [1]Lit *dwelt*
7 [a]Gen 12:13; 20:2, 12 [b]Prov 29:25

thinking, "[1]the men of the place might kill me on account of
Rebekah, for she is [c]beautiful."
8 It came about, when he had been there a long time, that
Abimelech king of the Philistines looked out through a
window, and saw, and behold, Isaac was caressing his wife
Rebekah.
9 Then Abimelech called Isaac and said, "Behold, certainly she
is your wife! How then did you say, 'She is my sister'?" And Isaac
said to him, "Because I said, 'I might die on account of her.'"
10 [a]Abimelech said, "What is this you have done to us? One
of the people might easily have lain with your wife, and you
would have brought guilt upon us."
11 So Abimelech charged all the people, saying, "He who
[a]touches this man or his wife shall surely be put to death."
12 Now Isaac sowed in that land and [1]reaped in the same year
a hundredfold. And [a]the LORD blessed him,
13 and the man [a]became rich, and continued to grow [1]richer
until he became very [1]wealthy;
14 for [a]he had possessions of flocks [1]and herds and a great
household, so that the Philistines envied him.
15 Now [a]all the wells which his father's servants had dug in
the days of Abraham his father, the Philistines stopped up [1]by
filling them with earth.
16 Then Abimelech said to Isaac, "Go away from us, for you
are [1a]too powerful for us."
17 And Isaac departed from there and camped in the valley of
Gerar, and [1]settled there.
18 Then Isaac dug again the wells of water which [1]had been
dug in the days of his father Abraham, for the Philistines had
stopped them up after the death of Abraham; and he [2]gave
them the same names which his father had [3]given them.
19 But when Isaac's servants dug in the valley and found there
a well of [1]flowing water,
20 the herdsmen of Gerar [a]quarreled with the herdsmen of
Isaac, saying, "The water is ours!" So he named the well [1]Esek,
because they contended with him.
21 Then they dug another well, and they quarreled over it too,
so he named it [1]Sitnah.
22 He moved away from there and dug another well, and they
did not quarrel over it; so he named it [1]Rehoboth, for he said,
"[2a]At last the LORD has made [3]room for us, and we will be
[b]fruitful in the land."
23 Then he went up from there to [a]Beersheba.
24 The LORD [a]appeared to him the same night and said,

"[b]I am the God of your father Abraham;
[c]Do not fear, for I am with you.
I [d]will bless you, and multiply your [1]descendants,
For the sake of My servant Abraham."

25 So he built an [a]altar there and called upon the name of the
LORD, and pitched his tent there; and there Isaac's servants dug
a well.

7 [1]Lit *lest . . . place* [c]Gen 12:11; 24:16; 29:17

10 [a]Gen 20:9

11 [a]Ps 105:15

12 [1]Lit *found* [a]Gen 24:1; 26:3; Job 42:12; Prov 10:22

13 [1]Lit *great* [a]Prov 10:22

14 [1]Lit *and possessions of herds* [a]Gen 24:35; 25:5

15 [1]Lit *and filled them* [a]Gen 21:25, 30

16 [1]Lit *much mightier than we* [a]Ex 1:9

17 [1]Lit *dwelt*

18 [1]Lit *they had dug* [2]Lit *called their names as the names* [3]Lit *called*

19 [1]Lit *living*

20 [1]I.e. contention [a]Gen 21:25

21 [1]I.e. enmity

22 [1]I.e. broad places [2]Lit *Truly now* [3]Or *broad* [a]Ps 4:1; Is 54:2, 3 [b]Gen 17:6; Ex 1:7

23 [a]Gen 22:19

24 [1]Lit *seed* [a]Gen 26:2 [b]Gen 17:7, 8; 24:12; Ex 3:6; Acts 7:32 [c]Gen 15:1 [d]Gen 22:17; 26:3, 4

25 [a]Gen 12:7, 8; 13:4, 18; Ps 116:17

26 Then [a]Abimelech came to him from Gerar [1]with his
adviser Ahuzzath and Phicol the commander of his army.
27 Isaac said to them, "[a]Why have you come to me, since you
hate me and have sent me away from you?"
28 They said, "We see plainly [a]that the LORD has been with
you; so we said, 'Let there now be an oath between us, *even*
between [1]you and us, and let us make a covenant with you,
29 that you will do us no harm, just as we have not touched
you [1]and have done to you nothing but good and have sent you
away in peace. You are now the [a]blessed of the LORD.'"
30 Then [a]he made them a feast, and they ate and drank.
31 In the morning they arose early and [1a]exchanged oaths; then
Isaac sent them away and they departed from him in peace.
32 Now it came about on the same day, that Isaac's servants
came in and told him about the well which they had dug, and
said to him, "We have found water."
33 So he called it Shibah; therefore the name of the city is
[a]Beersheba to this day.
34 When Esau was forty years old [a]he [1]married Judith the
daughter of Beeri the Hittite, and Basemath the daughter of
Elon the Hittite;
35 and [a]they [1]brought grief to Isaac and Rebekah.

Chapter 27 Theme ______________________

27 Now it came about, when Isaac was old and [a]his eyes
were too dim to see, that he called his [b]older son Esau
and said to him, "My son." And he said to him, "Here I am."
2 [1a]Isaac said, "Behold now, I am old *and* I do not know the
day of my death.
3 "Now then, please take your gear, your quiver and your
bow, and go out to the field and [a]hunt game for me;
4 and prepare a savory dish for me such as I love, and bring
it to me that I may eat, so that [a]my soul may bless you before I
die."
5 Rebekah was listening while Isaac spoke to his son Esau. So
when Esau went to the field to hunt for game to bring *home*,
6 [a]Rebekah said to her son Jacob, "Behold, I heard your
father speak to your brother Esau, saying,
7 'Bring me *some* game and prepare a savory dish for me,
that I may eat, and bless you in the presence of the LORD before
my death.'
8 "Now therefore, my son, [a]listen to [1]me [2]as I command you.
9 "Go now to the flock and [1]bring me two choice [2]young
goats from there, that I may prepare them *as* a savory dish for
your father, such as he loves.
10 "Then you shall bring *it* to your father, that he may eat, so
that he may bless you before his death."
11 Jacob [1]answered his mother Rebekah, "Behold, Esau my
brother is a [a]hairy man and I am a smooth man.
12 "[a]Perhaps my father will feel me, then I will be as a [1]deceiver

26 [1]Lit *and his confidential friend* [a]Gen 21:22
27 [a]Judg 11:7
28 [1]Lit *us and you* [a]Gen 21:22, 23
29 [1]Lit *and just as we* [a]Gen 24:31; Ps 115:15
30 [a]Gen 19:3
31 [1]Lit *swore one to another* [a]Gen 21:31
33 [a]Gen 21:31
34 [1]Lit *took as wife* [a]Gen 28:8; 36:2
35 [1]Lit *were a bitterness of spirit to* [a]Gen 27:46
27:1 [a]Gen 48:10; 1 Sam 3:2 [b]Gen 25:25, 33, 34
2 [1]Lit *He* [a]Gen 47:29
3 [a]Gen 25:28
4 [a]Gen 27:19, 25, 31; 48:9, 15, 16; Deut 33:1; Heb 11:20
6 [a]Gen 25:28
8 [1]Lit *my voice* [2]Lit *according to what* [a]Gen 27:13, 43
9 [1]Lit *take* [2]Lit *kids of goats*
11 [1]Lit *said to* [a]Gen 25:25
12 [1]Lit *mocker* [a]Gen 27:21, 22

in his sight, and I will bring upon myself a curse and not a
blessing."
13 But his mother said to him, "Your curse be on me, my son;
only [a]obey my voice, and go, get *them* for me."
14 So he went and got *them,* and brought *them* to his mother;
and his mother made savory food such as his father loved.
15 Then Rebekah took the [1]best [a]garments of Esau her elder
son, which were with her in the house, and put them on Jacob
her younger son.
16 And she put the skins of the [1]young goats on his hands and
on the smooth part of his neck.
17 She also gave the savory food and the bread, which she had
made, [1]to her son Jacob.
18 Then he came to his father and said, "My father." And he
said, "Here I am. Who are you, my son?"
19 Jacob said to his father, "I am Esau your firstborn; I have
done as you told me. [a]Get up, please, sit and eat of my game,
that [1b]you may bless me."
20 Isaac said to his son, "How is it that you have *it* so quickly,
my son?" And he said, "[a]Because the LORD your God caused *it*
to happen to me."
21 Then Isaac said to Jacob, "Please come close, that [a]I may
feel you, my son, whether you are really my son Esau or not."
22 So Jacob came close to Isaac his father, and he felt him and
said, "The voice is the voice of Jacob, but the hands are the
hands of Esau."
23 He did not recognize him, because his hands were [a]hairy
like his brother Esau's hands; so he blessed him.
24 And he said, "Are you really my son Esau?" And he said, "I
am."
25 So he said, "Bring *it* to me, and I will eat of my son's game,
that [1a]I may bless you." And he brought *it* to him, and he ate;
he also brought him wine and he drank.
26 Then his father Isaac said to him, "Please come close and
kiss me, my son."
27 So he came close and kissed him; and when he smelled the
smell of his garments, he [a]blessed him and said,

"See, [b]the smell of my son
Is like the smell of a field [c]which the LORD has blessed;
28 Now may [a]God give you of the dew of heaven,
And of the [b]fatness of the earth,
And an abundance of grain and new wine;
29 [a]May peoples serve you,
And nations bow down to you;
[b]Be master of your brothers,
[c]And may your mother's sons bow down to you.
[d]Cursed be those who curse you,
And blessed be those who bless you."

30 Now it came about, as soon as Isaac had finished blessing
Jacob, and Jacob had hardly gone out from the presence of Isaac
his father, that Esau his brother came in from his hunting.

13 [a]Gen 27:8

15 [1]Lit *desirable;* or *choice* [a]Gen 27:27

16 [1]Lit *kids of the goats*

17 [1]Lit *into the hand of*

19 [1]Lit *your soul* [a]Gen 27:31 [b]Gen 27:4

20 [a]Gen 24:12

21 [a]Gen 27:12

23 [a]Gen 27:16

25 [1]Lit *my soul* [a]Gen 27:4

27 [a]Heb 11:20 [b]Song 4:11 [c]Ps 65:10

28 [a]Gen 27:39; Deut 33:13, 28; Prov 3:20; Zech 8:12 [b]Num 18:12

29 [a]Gen 25:23; Is 45:14; 49:7, 23; 60:12, 14 [b]Gen 9:26, 27; 27:37 [c]Gen 37:7, 10 [d]Gen 12:3; Num 24:9

31 Then he also made savory food, and brought it to his father;
and he said to his father, "[a]Let my father arise and eat of his son's
game, that [1][b]you may bless me."
32 Isaac his father said to him, "[a]Who are you?" And he said,
"I am your son, [b]your firstborn, Esau."
33 Then Isaac [1]trembled violently, and said, "[a]Who was he
then that hunted game and brought *it* to me, so that I ate of all
of it before you came, and blessed him? [b]Yes, and he shall be
blessed."
34 When Esau heard the words of his father, [a]he cried out with
an exceedingly great and bitter cry, and said to his father,
"Bless me, *even* me also, O my father!"
35 And he said, "[a]Your brother came deceitfully and has taken
away your blessing."
36 Then he said, "[1]Is he not rightly named [a]Jacob, for he has
supplanted me these two times? He took away my birthright,
and behold, now he has taken away my blessing." And he said,
"Have you not reserved a blessing for me?"
37 But Isaac replied to Esau, "Behold, I have made him [a]your
master, and all his [1]relatives I have given to him [2]as servants;
and with grain and new wine I have sustained him. Now as for
you then, what can I do, my son?"
38 Esau said to his father, "Do you have only one blessing, my
father? Bless me, *even* me also, O my father." So Esau lifted his
voice and [a]wept.
39 Then [a]Isaac his father answered and said to him,

"Behold, [1][b]away from the [2]fertility of the earth shall be your dwelling,
And [1]away from the dew of heaven from above.

40 "By your sword you shall live,
And your brother [a]you shall serve;
But it shall come about [b]when you become restless,
That you will [1]break his yoke from your neck."

41 So Esau [a]bore a grudge against Jacob because of the
blessing with which his father had blessed him; and Esau said
[1]to himself, "[b]The days of mourning for my father are near;
then I will kill my brother Jacob."
42 Now when the words of her elder son Esau were reported
to Rebekah, she sent and called her younger son Jacob, and
said to him, "Behold your brother Esau is consoling himself
concerning you *by planning* to kill you.
43 "Now therefore, my son, [a]obey my voice, and arise, [1]flee to
[b]Haran, to my brother [c]Laban!
44 "Stay with him [a]a few days, until your brother's fury [1]subsides,
45 until your brother's anger [1]against you subsides and he
forgets [a]what you did to him. Then I will send and get you from
there. Why should I be bereaved of you both in one day?"
46 Rebekah said to Isaac, "I am tired of [1]living because of [a]the
daughters of Heth; [b]if Jacob takes a wife from the daughters of
Heth, like these, from the daughters of the land, what good will
my life be to me?"

31 [1]Lit *your soul* [a]Gen 27:19 [b]Gen 27:4
32 [a]Gen 27:18 [b]Gen 25:33, 34
33 [1]Lit *trembled with a very great trembling* [a]Gen 27:35 [b]Gen 25:23; 28:3, 4; Num 23:20
34 [a]Heb 12:17
35 [a]Gen 27:19
36 [1]Or *Was he then named Jacob that he has* [a]Gen 25:26, 32-34
37 [1]Lit *brothers* [2]Lit *for* [a]Gen 27:28, 29
38 [a]Heb 12:17
39 [1]Or *of* [2]Lit *fatness* [a]Heb 11:20 [b]Gen 27:28; Deut 33:13, 28
40 [1]Lit *tear off* [a]Gen 25:23; 27:29 [b]2 Kin 8:20-22
41 [1]Lit *in his heart* [a]Gen 32:3-11; 37:4, 8 [b]Gen 50:2-4, 10
43 [1]Lit *flee for yourself* [a]Gen 27:8, 13 [b]Gen 11:31 [c]Gen 24:29
44 [1]Lit *turns away* [a]Gen 31:41
45 [1]Lit *turns away from you* [a]Gen 27:12, 19, 35
46 [1]Lit *my life* [a]Gen 26:34, 35; 28:8 [b]Gen 24:3

Chapter 28 Theme ________________________________

28 So Isaac called Jacob and [a]blessed him and charged him, and said to him, "[b]You shall not take a wife from the daughters of Canaan.

2 "Arise, go to Paddan-aram, to the house of [a]Bethuel your mother's father; and from there take to yourself a wife from the daughters of Laban your mother's brother.

3 "May [1a]God Almighty [b]bless you and [c]make you fruitful and [d]multiply you, that you may become a [e]company of peoples.

4 "May He also give you the [a]blessing of Abraham, to you and to your [1]descendants with you, that you may [b]possess the land of your [c]sojournings, which God gave to Abraham."

5 Then [a]Isaac sent Jacob away, and he went to Paddan-aram to Laban, son of Bethuel the Aramean, the brother of Rebekah, the mother of Jacob and Esau.

6 Now Esau saw that Isaac had blessed Jacob and sent him away to Paddan-aram to take to himself a wife from there, *and that* when he blessed him he charged him, saying, "[a]You shall not take a wife from the daughters of Canaan,"

7 and that Jacob had obeyed his father and his mother and had gone to Paddan-aram.

8 So Esau saw that [a]the daughters of Canaan displeased [1]his father Isaac;

9 and Esau went to Ishmael, and [1]married, [a]besides the wives that he had, Mahalath the daughter of Ishmael, Abraham's son, the sister of Nebaioth.

10 Then Jacob departed from [a]Beersheba and went toward [b]Haran.

11 He [1]came to [2]a [a]certain place and spent the night there, because the sun had set; and he took one of the stones of the place and put it [3]under his head, and lay down in that place.

12 [a]He had a dream, and behold, a ladder was set on the earth with its top reaching to heaven; and behold, [b]the angels of God were ascending and descending on it.

13 And behold, [a]the LORD stood [1]above it and said, "I am the LORD, [b]the God of your father Abraham and the God of Isaac; the land on which you lie, I will give it [c]to you and to [d]your [2]descendants.

14 "Your [1]descendants will also be like [a]the dust of the earth, and you will [2]spread out [b]to the west and to the east and to the north and to the south; and [c]in you and in your [1]descendants shall all the families of the earth be blessed.

15 "Behold, [a]I am with you and [b]will keep you wherever you go, and [c]will bring you back to this land; for [d]I will not leave you until I have done what I have [1]promised you."

16 Then Jacob [a]awoke from his sleep and said, "[b]Surely the LORD is in this place, and I did not know it."

17 He was afraid and said, "[a]How awesome is this place! This is none other than the house of God, and this is the gate of heaven."

18 So Jacob rose early in the morning, and took [a]the stone that

28:1 [a]Gen 27:33 [b]Gen 24:3, 4

2 [a]Gen 25:20

3 [1]Heb *El Shaddai* [a]Gen 17:1; 35:11; 48:3 [b]Gen 22:17 [c]Gen 17:6, 20 [d]Gen 17:2; 26:4, 24 [e]Gen 35:11; 48:4

4 [1]Lit *seed* [a]Gen 12:2; 22:17 [b]Gen 15:7, 8; 17:8 [c]1 Chr 29:15; Ps 39:12

5 [a]Gen 27:43

6 [a]Gen 28:1

8 [1]Lit *in the eyes of his* [a]Gen 24:3; 26:34, 35; 27:46

9 [1]Lit *took for his wife* [a]Gen 26:34; 36:2

10 [a]Gen 26:23 [b]Gen 12:4, 5; 27:43

11 [1]Lit *lighted on* [2]Lit *the place* [3]Lit *at his head-place* [a]Gen 28:19

12 [a]Gen 41:1; Num 12:6 [b]John 1:51

13 [1]Or *beside him* [2]Lit *seed* [a]Gen 35:1; Amos 7:7 [b]Gen 26:3, 24 [c]Gen 13:15, 17; 26:3 [d]Gen 12:7; 15:18

14 [1]Lit *seed* [2]Lit *break through* [a]Gen 13:16; 22:17 [b]Gen 13:14, 15 [c]Gen 12:3; 18:18; 22:18; 26:4

15 [1]Lit *spoken to* [a]Gen 26:3, 24; 31:3 [b]Num 6:24; Ps 121:5, 7, 8 [c]Gen 48:21; Deut 30:3 [d]Num 23:19; Deut 7:9; 31:6, 8

16 [a]1 Kin 3:15; Jer 31:26 [b]Ex 3:4-6; Josh 5:13-15; Ps 139:7-12

17 [a]Ps 68:35

18 [a]Gen 28:11; 35:14

he had put [1]under his head and set it up as a pillar and poured
oil on its top.
19 He called the name of that place [1a]Bethel; however,
[2]previously the name of the city had been [b]Luz.
20 Then Jacob [a]made a vow, saying, "[b]If God will be with me
and will keep me on this journey that I [1]take, and will give me
[2c]food to eat and garments to wear,
21 and [a]I return to my father's house in [1]safety, [b]then the LORD
will be my God.
22 "This stone, which I have set up as a pillar, [a]will be God's
house, and [b]of all that You give me I will surely give a tenth to
You."

Chapter 29 Theme ____

29 Then Jacob [1]went on his journey, and came to the land
of [a]the sons of the east.
2 He looked, and [1]saw [a]a well in the field, and behold, three
flocks of sheep were lying there beside it, for from that well
they watered the flocks. Now the stone on the mouth of the
well was large.
3 When all the flocks were gathered there, they would then
roll the stone from the mouth of the well and water the sheep,
and put the stone back in its place on the mouth of the well.
4 Jacob said to them, "My brothers, where are you from?"
And they said, "We are from [a]Haran."
5 He said to them, "Do you know Laban the [a]son of Nahor?"
And they said, "We know *him.*"
6 And he said to them, "Is it well with him?" And they said,
"It is well, and here is [a]Rachel his daughter coming with the
sheep."
7 He said, "Behold, it is still high day; it is not time for the
livestock to be gathered. Water the sheep, and go, pasture them."
8 But they said, "We cannot, until all the flocks are gathered,
and they roll the stone from the mouth of the well; then we
water the sheep."
9 While he was still speaking with them, Rachel came with
her father's sheep, for she was a shepherdess.
10 When Jacob saw Rachel the daughter of Laban his mother's
brother, and the sheep of Laban his mother's brother, Jacob
went up and rolled the stone from the mouth of the well and
watered the flock of Laban his mother's brother.
11 Then Jacob [a]kissed Rachel, and lifted his voice and wept.
12 Jacob told Rachel that he was a [1a]relative of her father and
that he was Rebekah's son, and [b]she ran and told her father.
13 So when [a]Laban heard the news of Jacob his sister's son, he
ran to meet him, and [b]embraced him and kissed him and
brought him to his house. Then he related to Laban all these
things.
14 Laban said to him, "Surely you are [a]my bone and my flesh."
And he stayed with him a month.

18 [1]Lit *at his head-place*
19 [1]I.e. the house of God [2]Lit *at the first* [a]Judg 1:23 [b]Gen 35:6; 48:3
20 [1]Lit *go* [2]Lit *bread* [a]Gen 31:13; Judg 11:30; 2 Sam 15:8 [b]Gen 28:15 [c]1 Tim 6:8
21 [1]Lit *peace* [a]Judg 11:31 [b]Deut 26:17
22 [a]Gen 35:7 [b]Lev 27:30; Deut 14:22
29:1 [1]Lit *lifted up his feet* [a]Judg 6:3, 33
2 [1]Lit *behold* [a]Gen 24:10, 11; Ex 2:15, 16
4 [a]Gen 28:10
5 [a]Gen 24:24, 29
6 [a]Ex 2:16
11 [a]Gen 33:4
12 [1]Lit *brother* [a]Gen 28:5 [b]Gen 24:28
13 [a]Gen 24:29-31 [b]Gen 33:4
14 [a]Gen 2:23; Judg 9:2; 2 Sam 5:1; 19:12, 13

15 Then Laban said to Jacob, "Because you are my [1]relative,
should you therefore serve me for nothing? Tell me, what shall
[a]your wages be?"
16 Now Laban had two daughters; the name of the older was
Leah, and the name of the younger was Rachel.
17 And Leah's eyes were weak, but Rachel was [a]beautiful of
form and [1]face.
18 Now Jacob [a]loved Rachel, so he said, "[b]I will serve you seven
years for your younger daughter Rachel."
19 Laban said, "It is better that I give her to you than to give
her to another man; stay with me."
20 So Jacob served seven years for Rachel and they seemed to
him but a few days [a]because of his love for her.
21 Then Jacob said to Laban, "Give *me* my wife, for my [1]time
is completed, that I may [a]go in to her."
22 Laban gathered all the men of the place and made a feast.
23 Now in the evening he took his daughter Leah, and
brought her to him; and *Jacob* went in to her.
24 Laban also gave his maid Zilpah to his daughter Leah as a
maid.
25 So it came about in the morning that, behold, it was Leah!
And he said to Laban, "[a]What is this you have done to me?
Was it not for Rachel that I served with you? Why then have
you [b]deceived me?"
26 But Laban said, "It is not [1]the practice in our place to
[2]marry off the younger before the firstborn.
27 "Complete the week of this one, and we will give you the
other also for the service which [a]you shall serve with me for
another seven years."
28 Jacob did so and completed her week, and he gave him his
daughter Rachel as his wife.
29 Laban also gave his maid Bilhah to his daughter Rachel as
her maid.
30 So *Jacob* went in to Rachel also, and indeed [a]he loved Rachel
more than Leah, and he served with [1]Laban for [b]another seven
years.
31 Now the LORD saw that Leah was [1]unloved, and He opened
her womb, but Rachel was barren.
32 Leah conceived and bore a son and named him [1]Reuben,
for she said, "Because the LORD has [2a]seen my affliction; surely
now my husband will love me."
33 Then she conceived again and bore a son and said, "[a]Because
the LORD has [1]heard that I am [2]unloved, He has therefore given
me this *son* also." So she named him Simeon.
34 She conceived again and bore a son and said, "Now this
time my husband will become [1]attached to me, because I have
borne him three sons." Therefore he was named [a]Levi.
35 And she conceived again and bore a son and said, "This time
I will [1]praise the LORD." Therefore she named him [2a]Judah.
Then she stopped bearing.

15 [1]Lit *brother* [a]Gen 31:41
17 [1]Lit *beautiful of appearance* [a]Gen 12:11, 14; 26:7
18 [a]Gen 24:67 [b]Hos 12:12
20 [a]Song 8:7
21 [1]Lit *days are* [a]Judg 15:1
25 [a]Gen 12:18; 20:9; 26:10 [b]1 Sam 28:12
26 [1]Lit *done thus in* [2]Lit *give*
27 [a]Gen 31:41
30 [1]Lit *him* [a]Gen 29:17, 18 [b]Gen 31:41
31 [1]Lit *hated*
32 [1]I.e. see, a son [2]Lit *looked upon* [a]Gen 16:11; 31:42; Ex 3:7; 4:31; Deut 26:7; Ps 25:18
33 [1]Heb *shama,* related to Simeon [2]Lit *hated* [a]Deut 21:15
34 [1]Heb *lavah,* related to Levi [a]Gen 49:5
35 [1]Heb *Jadah,* related to Judah [2]Heb *Jehudah* [a]Gen 49:8; Matt 1:2

Chapter 30 Theme ____

30 Now when Rachel saw that [a]she bore Jacob no children, [1]she became jealous of her sister; and she said to
Jacob, "[b]Give me children, or else I die."
2 Then Jacob's anger burned against Rachel, and he said,
"Am I in the place of God, who has [a]withheld from you the
fruit of the womb?"
3 She said, "[a]Here is my maid Bilhah, go in to her that she
may [b]bear on my knees, that [1a]through her I too may have
children."
4 So [a]she gave him her maid Bilhah as a wife, and Jacob
went in to her.
5 Bilhah conceived and bore Jacob a son.
6 Then Rachel said, "God has [1a]vindicated me, and has
indeed heard my voice and has given me a son." Therefore she
named him [2]Dan.
7 Rachel's maid Bilhah conceived again and bore Jacob a
second son.
8 So Rachel said, "With [1]mighty wrestlings I have [2]wrestled
with my sister, *and* I have indeed prevailed." And she named
him Naphtali.
9 When Leah saw that she had stopped bearing, she took her
maid Zilpah and gave her to Jacob as a wife.
10 Leah's maid Zilpah bore Jacob a son.
11 Then Leah said, "[1]How fortunate!" So she named him [2]Gad.
12 Leah's maid Zilpah bore Jacob a second son.
13 Then Leah said, "[1]Happy am I! For women [a]will call me
happy." So she named him [2]Asher.
14 Now in the days of wheat harvest Reuben went and found
[a]mandrakes in the field, and brought them to his mother Leah.
Then Rachel said to Leah, "Please give me some of your son's
mandrakes."
15 But she said to her, "Is it a small matter for you to take my
husband? And would you take my son's mandrakes also?" So
Rachel said, "Therefore he may lie with you tonight in return
for your son's mandrakes."
16 When Jacob came in from the field in the evening, then
Leah went out to meet him and said, "You must come in to
me, for I have surely hired you with my son's mandrakes." So
he lay with her that night.
17 God gave heed to Leah, and she conceived and bore Jacob
a fifth son.
18 Then Leah said, "God has given me my [1]wages because I
gave my maid to my husband." So she named him Issachar.
19 Leah conceived again and bore a sixth son to Jacob.
20 Then Leah said, "God has endowed me with a good gift;
now my husband [1]will dwell with me, because I have borne
him six sons." So she named him Zebulun.
21 Afterward she bore a daughter and named her Dinah.
22 Then [a]God remembered Rachel, and God gave heed to her
and [b]opened her womb.

30:1 [1]Lit *Rachel* [a]Gen 29:31 [b]1 Sam 1:5, 6
2 [a]Gen 20:18; 29:31
3 [1]Lit *from her I too may be built* [a]Gen 16:2 [b]Gen 50:23; Job 3:12
4 [a]Gen 16:3, 4
6 [1]Lit *judged* [2]I.e. He judged [a]Ps 35:24; 43:1; Lam 3:59
8 [1]Lit *wrestlings of God* [2]Heb *niphtal,* related to Naphtali
11 [1]Lit *With fortune!* Some versions read *Fortune has come* [2]I.e. Fortune
13 [1]Lit *With my happiness!* [2]I.e. happy [a]Luke 1:48
14 [a]Song 7:13
18 [1]Heb *sachar,* related to Issachar
20 [1]Heb *zabal,* related to Zebulun. Some translate *will honor*
22 [a]1 Sam 1:19, 20 [b]Gen 29:31

23 So she conceived and bore a son and said, "God has [a]taken
away my reproach."
24 She named him Joseph, saying, "[a]May the LORD [1]give me
another son."
25 Now it came about when Rachel had borne Joseph, that
Jacob said to Laban, "[a]Send me away, that I may go to my own
place and to my own country.
26 "Give *me* my wives and my children [a]for whom I have
served you, and let me depart; for you yourself know my service
which I have [1]rendered you."
27 But Laban said to him, "If now [1]it pleases you, *stay with
me;* I have divined [a]that the LORD has blessed me on your
account."
28 He [1]continued, "[a]Name me your wages, and I will give it."
29 But he said to him, "[a]You yourself know how I have served
you and how your cattle have [1]fared with me.
30 "For you had little before [1]I came and it has [2]increased to a
multitude, and the LORD has blessed you [3]wherever I turned.
But now, when shall I provide for my own household also?"
31 So he said, "What shall I give you?" And Jacob said, "You
shall not give me anything. If you will do this *one* thing for me,
I will again pasture *and* keep your flock:
32 let me pass through your entire flock today, removing from
there every [a]speckled and spotted sheep and every black [1]one
among the lambs and the spotted and speckled among the
goats; and *such* shall be my wages.
33 "So my [1]honesty will answer for me later, when you come
concerning my [2]wages. Every one that is not speckled and
spotted among the goats and black among the lambs, *if found*
with me, will be considered stolen."
34 Laban said, "[1]Good, let it be according to your word."
35 So he removed on that day the striped and spotted male
goats and all the speckled and spotted female goats, every one
with white in it, and all the black ones among the sheep, and
gave them into the [1]care of his sons.
36 And he put *a distance of* three days' journey between
himself and Jacob, and Jacob fed the rest of Laban's flocks.
37 Then Jacob [1]took fresh rods of poplar and almond and
plane trees, and peeled white stripes in them, exposing the
white which *was* [2]in the rods.
38 He set the rods which he had peeled in front of the flocks
in the gutters, *even* in the watering troughs, where the flocks
came to drink; and they [1]mated when they came to drink.
39 So the flocks [1]mated by the rods, and the flocks brought
forth striped, speckled, and spotted.
40 Jacob separated the lambs, and [1]made the flocks face toward
the striped and all the black in the flock of Laban; and he put his
own herds apart, and did not put them with Laban's flock.
41 Moreover, whenever the [1]stronger of the flock [2]were
mating, Jacob would place the rods in the sight of the flock in
the gutters, so that they might [3]mate by the rods;

23 [a]Is 4:1; Luke 1:25

24 [1]Lit *add to me;* Heb *Joseph* [a]Gen 35:17

25 [a]Gen 24:54, 56

26 [1]Lit *served* [a]Gen 29:18, 20, 27; Hos 12:12

27 [1]Lit *I have found favor in your eyes* [a]Gen 26:24; 39:3, 5; Is 61:9

28 [1]Lit *said* [a]Gen 29:15; 31:7, 41

29 [1]Lit *been* [a]Gen 31:6

30 [1]Lit *me* [2]Lit *broken forth* [3]Lit *at my foot*

32 [1]Lit *sheep* [a]Gen 31:8

33 [1]Lit *righteousness* [2]Lit *wages which are before you*

34 [1]Lit *Behold, would that it might be*

35 [1]Lit *hand*

37 [1]Lit *took to himself* [2]Lit *on*

38 [1]Or *conceived*

39 [1]Or *conceived*

40 [1]Lit *set the faces*

41 [1]Lit *bound ones;* i.e. firm and compact [2]Or *conceived* [3]Or *conceive*

42 but when the flock was feeble, he did not put *them* in; so
the feebler were Laban's and the [1]stronger Jacob's.
43 So [a]the man [1]became exceedingly prosperous, and had large
flocks and female and male servants and camels and donkeys.

Chapter 31 Theme ______________________________

31 Now [1]Jacob heard the words of Laban's sons, saying,
"Jacob has taken away all that was our father's, and from
what belonged to our father he has made all this [2]wealth."
2 Jacob saw the [1]attitude of Laban, and behold, it was not
friendly toward him as formerly.
3 Then the LORD said to Jacob, "[a]Return to the land of your
fathers and to your relatives, and [b]I will be with you."
4 So Jacob sent and called Rachel and Leah to his flock in the
field,
5 and said to them, "[a]I see your father's [1]attitude, that it is not
friendly toward me as formerly, but [b]the God of my father has
been with me.
6 "[a]You know that I have served your father with all my
strength.
7 "Yet your father has [a]cheated me and [b]changed my wages
ten times; however, [c]God did not allow him to hurt me.
8 "If [a]he spoke thus, 'The speckled shall be your wages,' then
all the flock brought forth speckled; and if he spoke thus, 'The
striped shall be your wages,' then all the flock brought forth
striped.
9 "Thus God has [a]taken away your father's livestock and given
them to me.
10 "And it came about at the time when the flock were
[1]mating that I lifted up my eyes and saw in a dream, and
behold, the male goats which were [2]mating *were* striped,
speckled, and mottled.
11 "Then [a]the angel of God said to me in the dream, 'Jacob,'
and I said, 'Here I am.'
12 "He said, 'Lift up now your eyes and see *that* all the male
goats which are [1]mating are striped, speckled, and mottled; for
[a]I have seen all that Laban has been doing to you.
13 'I am [a]the God *of* Bethel, where you [b]anointed a pillar,
where you made a vow to Me; now arise, [1]leave this land, and
[c]return to the land of your birth.'"
14 Rachel and Leah said to him, "Do we still have any portion
or inheritance in our father's house?
15 "Are we not reckoned by him as foreigners? For [a]he has sold
us, and has also [1]entirely consumed [2]our purchase price.
16 "Surely all the wealth which God has taken away from our
father belongs to us and our children; now then, do whatever
God has said to you."
17 Then Jacob arose and put his children and his wives upon
camels;
18 and he drove away all his livestock and all his property

42 [1]Lit *bound ones;* i.e. firm and compact

43 [1]Lit *broke forth* [a]Gen 12:16; 13:2; 24:35; 26:13, 14; 30:30

31:1 [1]Lit *he* [2]Lit *glory*

2 [1]Lit *face*

3 [a]Gen 32:9 [b]Gen 28:15

5 [1]Lit *face* [a]Gen 31:2 [b]Gen 21:22; 28:13, 15; 31:29, 42, 53; Is 41:10; Heb 13:5

6 [a]Gen 30:29

7 [a]Gen 29:25 [b]Gen 31:41 [c]Gen 15:1; 31:29

8 [a]Gen 30:32

9 [a]Gen 31:1, 16

10 [1]Or *conceiving* [2]Lit *leaping upon the flock*

11 [a]Gen 16:7-11; 22:11, 15; 31:13; 48:16

12 [1]Lit *leaping upon the flock* [a]Ex 3:7

13 [1]Lit *go out from* [a]Gen 28:13, 19 [b]Gen 28:18, 20 [c]Gen 28:15; 32:9

15 [1]I.e. enjoyed the benefit of [2]Lit *our money* [a]Gen 29:20, 23, 27

which he had gathered, his acquired livestock which he had
gathered in Paddan-aram, [a]to go to the land of Canaan to his
father Isaac.
19 When Laban had gone to shear his flock, then Rachel stole
the [1a]household idols that were her father's.
20 And Jacob [1]deceived Laban the Aramean by not telling him
that he was fleeing.
21 So he fled with all that he had; and he arose and crossed
the *Euphrates* River, and set his face toward the hill country of
[a]Gilead.
22 When it was told Laban on the third day that Jacob had
fled,
23 then he took his [1]kinsmen with him and pursued him *a
distance of* seven days' journey, and he overtook him in the hill
country of Gilead.
24 [a]God came to Laban the Aramean in a [b]dream of the night
and said to him, "[1c]Be careful that you do not speak to Jacob
either good or bad."
25 Laban caught up with Jacob. Now Jacob had pitched his tent
in the hill country, and Laban with his [1]kinsmen camped in the
hill country of Gilead.
26 Then Laban said to Jacob, "What have you done [1]by
deceiving me and carrying away my daughters like captives of
the sword?
27 "Why did you flee secretly and [1]deceive me, and did not tell
me so that I might have sent you away with joy and with
songs, with [a]timbrel and with [b]lyre;
28 and did not allow me [a]to kiss my sons and my daughters?
Now you have done foolishly.
29 "It is in [1]my power to do you harm, but [a]the God of your
father spoke to me last night, saying, '[2b]Be careful not to speak
either good or bad to Jacob.'
30 "Now you have indeed gone away because you longed
greatly for your father's house; *but* why did you steal [a]my
gods?"
31 Then Jacob replied to Laban, "Because I was afraid, for I
thought that you would take your daughters from me by force.
32 "[a]The one with whom you find your gods shall not live; in
the presence of our [1]kinsmen [2]point out what is yours [3]among
my belongings and take *it* for yourself." For Jacob did not know
that Rachel had stolen them.
33 So Laban went into Jacob's tent and into Leah's tent and
into the tent of the two maids, but he did not find *them*. Then
he went out of Leah's tent and entered Rachel's tent.
34 Now Rachel had taken the [1]household idols and put them
in the camel's saddle, and she sat on them. And Laban felt
through all the tent but did not find *them*.
35 She said to her father, "Let not my lord be angry that I
cannot [a]rise before you, for the manner of women is upon
me." So he searched but did not find the [1b]household idols.
36 Then Jacob became angry and contended with Laban; and

18 [a]Gen 35:27

19 [1]Heb *teraphim* [a]Gen 31:30, 34; 35:2; Judg 17:5; 1 Sam 19:13; Hos 3:4

20 [1]Lit *stole the heart of*

21 [a]Gen 37:25

23 [1]Lit *brothers*

24 [1]Lit *Take heed to yourself* [a]Gen 20:3; 31:29 [b]Gen 20:3, 6; 31:11 [c]Gen 24:50; 31:7, 29

25 [1]Lit *brothers*

26 [1]Lit *and you have stolen my heart*

27 [1]Lit *steal me* [a]Ex 15:20 [b]Gen 4:21

28 [a]Gen 31:55

29 [1]Lit *the power of my hand* [2]Lit *Take heed to yourself* [a]Gen 31:5, 24, 42, 53 [b]Gen 31:24

30 [a]Gen 31:19; Josh 24:2; Judg 18:24

32 [1]Lit *brothers* [2]Lit *recognize* [3]Lit *with me* [a]Gen 44:9

34 [1]Heb *teraphim*

35 [1]Heb *teraphim* [a]Lev 19:32 [b]Gen 31:19

Jacob said to Laban, "What is my transgression? What is my sin
that you have hotly pursued me?
37 "Though you have felt through all my goods, what have you
found of all your household goods? Set *it* here before my [1]kinsmen
and your [1]kinsmen, that they may decide between us two.
38 "These twenty years I *have been* with you; your ewes and
your female goats have not miscarried, nor have I eaten the
rams of your flocks.
39 "That which was torn *of beasts* I did not bring to you; I bore
the loss of it myself. You required it of my hand *whether* stolen
by day or stolen by night.
40 "*Thus* I was: by day the [1]heat consumed me and the frost by
night, and my sleep fled from my eyes.
41 "These twenty years I have been in your house; [a]I served
you fourteen years for your two daughters and six years for
your flock, and you [b]changed my wages ten times.
42 "If [a]the God of my father, the God of Abraham, and the fear
of Isaac, had not been for me, surely now you would have sent
me away empty-handed. [b]God has seen my affliction and the
toil of my hands, so He [c]rendered judgment last night."
43 Then Laban replied to Jacob, "The daughters are my
daughters, and the children are my children, and [a]the flocks
are my flocks, and all that you see is mine. But what can I do
this day to these my daughters or to their children whom they
have borne?
44 "So now come, let us [a]make a covenant, [1]you and I, and [b]let
it be a witness between [2]you and me."
45 Then Jacob took [a]a stone and set it up *as* a pillar.
46 Jacob said to his [1]kinsmen, "Gather stones." So they took
stones and made a heap, and they ate there by the heap.
47 Now Laban [a]called it [1]Jegar-sahadutha, but Jacob called it
[2]Galeed.
48 Laban said, "[a]This heap is a witness between [1]you and me
this day." Therefore it was named Galeed,
49 and [1a]Mizpah, for he said, "May the LORD watch between
[2]you and me when we are [3]absent one from the other.
50 "If you mistreat my daughters, or if you take wives besides
my daughters, *although* no man is with us, see, [a]God is witness
between [1]you and me."
51 Laban said to Jacob, "Behold this heap and behold the
pillar which I have set between [1]you and me.
52 "This heap is a witness, and the pillar is a witness, that I
will not pass by this heap to you for harm, and you will not
pass by this heap and this pillar to me, for harm.
53 "[a]The God of Abraham and the God of Nahor, the God of
their father, [b]judge between us." So Jacob swore by [c]the fear of
his father Isaac.
54 Then Jacob [a]offered a sacrifice on the mountain, and called
his [1]kinsmen to [2]the meal; and they ate [3]the meal and spent
the night on the mountain.
55 [1]Early in the morning Laban arose, and [a]kissed his sons and

37 [1]Lit *brothers*
40 [1]Or *drought*
41 [a]Gen 29:27, 30 [b]Gen 31:7
42 [a]Gen 31:5, 29, 53 [b]Gen 29:32; Ex 3:7 [c]Gen 31:24, 29
43 [a]Gen 31:1
44 [1]Lit *I and you* [2]Lit *me and you* [a]Gen 21:27, 32; 26:28 [b]Josh 24:27
45 [a]Gen 28:18; Josh 24:26, 27
46 [1]Lit *brothers*
47 [1]I.e. the heap of witness, in Aram [2]I.e. the heap of witness, in Heb [a]Josh 22:34
48 [1]Lit *me and you* [a]Josh 24:27
49 [1]Lit *the Mizpah;* i.e. the watch-tower [2]Lit *me and you* [3]Lit *hidden* [a]Judg 11:29; 1 Sam 7:5, 6
50 [1]Lit *me and you* [a]Jer 29:23; 42:5
51 [1]Lit *me and you*
53 [a]Gen 28:13 [b]Gen 16:5 [c]Gen 31:42
54 [1]Lit *brothers* [2]Lit *eat bread* [3]Lit *bread* [a]Ex 18:12
55 [1]Ch 32:1 in Heb [a]Gen 31:28, 43

his daughters and blessed them. Then Laban departed and
returned to his place.

Chapter 32 Theme ______________________________

32 Now as Jacob went on his way, [a]the angels of God met
him.
2 Jacob said when he saw them, "This is God's [1]camp." So
he named that place [2a]Mahanaim.
3 Then Jacob [a]sent messengers before him to his brother
Esau in the land of [b]Seir, the [1]country of [c]Edom.
4 He also commanded them saying, "Thus you shall say to
my lord Esau: 'Thus says your servant Jacob, "I have sojourned
with Laban, and [a]stayed until now;
5 [a]I have oxen and donkeys *and* flocks and male and female
servants; and I have sent to tell my lord, [b]that I may find favor
in your sight."'"
6 The messengers returned to Jacob, saying, "We came to
your brother Esau, and furthermore [a]he is coming to meet you,
and four hundred men are with him."
7 Then Jacob was [a]greatly afraid and distressed; and he
divided the people who were with him, and the flocks and the
herds and the camels, into two companies;
8 for he said, "If Esau comes to the one company and [1]attacks
it, then the company which is left will escape."
9 Jacob said, "O [a]God of my father Abraham and God of my
father Isaac, O LORD, who said to me, '[b]Return to your country
and to your relatives, and I will [1]prosper you,'
10 [1]I am unworthy [a]of all the lovingkindness and of all the
[2]faithfulness which You have shown to Your servant; for with
my staff *only* I crossed this Jordan, and now I have become two
companies.
11 "[a]Deliver me, I pray, [b]from the hand of my brother, from the
hand of Esau; for I fear him, that he will come and [1]attack me
and the [c]mothers with the children.
12 "For You said, '[a]I will surely [1]prosper you and [b]make your
[2]descendants as the sand of the sea, which is too great to be
numbered.'"
13 So he spent the night there. Then he [1]selected from what
[2]he had with him a [a]present for his brother Esau:
14 two hundred female goats and twenty male goats, two
hundred ewes and twenty rams,
15 thirty milking camels and their colts, forty cows and ten
bulls, twenty female donkeys and ten male donkeys.
16 He delivered *them* into the hand of his servants, every drove
by itself, and said to his servants, "Pass on before me, and put a
space between droves."
17 He commanded the [1]one in front, saying, "When my
brother Esau meets you and asks you, saying, 'To whom do you
belong, and where are you going, and to whom do these
animals in front of you belong?'

32:1 [a]2 Kin 6:16, 17; Ps 34:7

2 [1]Or *company* [2]I.e. Two Camps, or Two Companies [a]Josh 21:38; 2 Sam 2:8

3 [1]Lit *field* [a]Gen 27:41, 42; 32:7, 11 [b]Gen 14:6; 33:14 [c]Gen 25:30; 36:8, 9

4 [a]Gen 31:41

5 [a]Gen 30:43 [b]Gen 33:8

6 [a]Gen 33:1

7 [a]Gen 32:11

8 [1]Lit *smites*

9 [1]Lit *do good with you* [a]Gen 28:13; 31:42 [b]Gen 28:15; 31:3, 13

10 [1]Lit *I am less than all* [2]Or *truth* [a]Gen 24:27

11 [1]Lit *smite* [a]Ps 59:1, 2 [b]Gen 27:41, 42; 33:4 [c]Hos 10:14

12 [1]Lit *do good with* [2]Lit *seed* [a]Gen 28:14 [b]Gen 22:17

13 [1]Lit *took* [2]Lit *had come to his hand* [a]Gen 43:11

17 [1]Lit *first*

18 then you shall say, '*These* belong to your servant Jacob; it is
a present sent to my lord Esau. And behold, he also is behind
us.'"
19 Then he commanded also the second and the third, and all
those who followed the droves, saying, "After this manner you
shall speak to Esau when you find him;
20 and you shall say, 'Behold, your servant Jacob also is behind
us.'" For he said, "I will appease him with the present that
goes before me. Then afterward I will see his face; perhaps he
will accept me."
21 So the present passed on before him, while he himself
spent that night in the camp.
22 Now he arose that same night and took his two wives and
his two maids and his eleven children, and crossed the ford of
the [a]Jabbok.
23 He took them and sent them across the stream. And he
sent across whatever he had.
24 Then Jacob was left alone, and a man [a]wrestled with him
until daybreak.
25 When he saw that he had not prevailed against him, he
touched the socket of his thigh; so the socket of Jacob's thigh
was dislocated while he wrestled with him.
26 Then he said, "Let me go, for the dawn is breaking." But
he said, "[a]I will not let you go unless you bless me."
27 So he said to him, "What is your name?" And he said,
"Jacob."
28 [a]He said, "Your name shall no longer be Jacob, but [1]Israel; for
you have striven with God and with men and have prevailed."
29 Then [a]Jacob asked him and said, "Please tell me your
name." But he said, "Why is it that you ask my name?" And he
blessed him there.
30 So Jacob named the place [1]Peniel, for *he said,* "[a]I have
seen God face to face, yet my [2]life has been preserved."
31 Now the sun rose upon him just as he crossed over
[a]Penuel, and he was limping on his thigh.
32 Therefore, to this day the sons of Israel do not eat the
sinew of the hip which is on the socket of the thigh, because
he touched the socket of Jacob's thigh in the sinew of the hip.

Chapter 33 Theme ______________________

33 Then Jacob lifted his eyes and looked, and behold,
[a]Esau was coming, and four hundred men with him. So
he divided the children [1]among Leah and Rachel and the two
maids.
2 He put the maids and their children [1]in front, and Leah
and her children [2]next, and Rachel and Joseph [2]last.
3 But he himself passed on ahead of them and [a]bowed down
to the ground seven times, until he came near to his brother.
4 Then Esau ran to meet him and embraced him, and [a]fell on
his neck and kissed him, and they wept.

22 [a]Deut 3:16; Josh 12:2
24 [a]Hos 12:3, 4
26 [a]Hos 12:4
28 [1]I.e. he who strives with God; or God strives [a]Gen 35:10; 1 Kin 18:31
29 [a]Judg 13:17, 18
30 [1]I.e. the face of God [2]Lit *soul* [a]Gen 16:13; Ex 24:10, 11; 33:20; Num 12:8; Judg 6:22; 13:22
31 [a]Judg 8:8
33:1 [1]Or *to* [a]Gen 32:6
2 [1]Lit *first* [2]Lit *behind*
3 [a]Gen 42:6; 43:26
4 [a]Gen 45:14, 15

5 He lifted his eyes and saw the women and the children,
and said, "[1]Who are these with you?" So he said, "[a]The children
whom God has graciously given your servant."
6 Then the maids came near [1]with their children, and they
bowed down.
7 Leah likewise came near with her children, and they
bowed down; and afterward Joseph came near with Rachel,
and they bowed down.
8 And he said, "What do you mean by [a]all this company
which I have met?" And he said, "[b]To find favor in the sight of
my lord."
9 But Esau said, "[a]I have plenty, my brother; let what you
have be your own."
10 Jacob said, "No, please, if now I have found favor in your
sight, then take my present from my hand, [1]for I see your face as
one sees the face of God, and you have received me favorably.
11 "Please take my [1a]gift which has been brought to you,
[b]because God has dealt graciously with me and because I have
[2]plenty." Thus he urged him and he took *it.*
12 Then [1]Esau said, "Let us take our journey and go, and I will
go before you."
13 But he said to him, "My lord knows that the children are
frail and that the flocks and herds which are nursing are [1]a care
to me. And if they are driven hard one day, all the flocks will die.
14 "Please let my lord pass on before his servant, and I will
proceed at my leisure, according to the pace of the cattle that
are before me and according to the pace of the children, until I
come to my lord at [a]Seir."
15 Esau said, "Please let me leave with you some of the people
who are with me." But he said, "[1]What need is there? [a]Let me
find favor in the sight of my lord."
16 So Esau returned that day on his way to Seir.
17 Jacob journeyed to [1a]Succoth, and built for himself a house
and made booths for his livestock; therefore the place is named
Succoth.
18 Now Jacob came safely to the city of [a]Shechem, which is in
the land of Canaan, when he came from [b]Paddan-aram, and
camped before the city.
19 [a]He bought the piece of land where he had pitched his tent
from the hand of the sons of Hamor, Shechem's father, for one
hundred [1]pieces of money.
20 Then he erected there an altar and called it [1]El-Elohe-Israel.

Chapter 34 Theme ____________________

34 Now [a]Dinah the daughter of Leah, whom she had borne
to Jacob, went out to [1]visit the daughters of the land.
2 When Shechem the son of Hamor [a]the Hivite, the prince of
the land, saw her, he took her and lay with her [1]by force.
3 [1]He was deeply attracted to Dinah the daughter of Jacob,
and he loved the girl and [2]spoke tenderly to her.

5 [1]Or *What relation are these to you?* [a]Gen 48:9; Ps 127:3; Is 8:18

6 [1]Lit *they and*

8 [a]Gen 32:13-16 [b]Gen 32:5

9 [a]Gen 27:39, 40

10 [1]Lit *for therefore I have seen your face like seeing God's face*

11 [1]Lit *blessing* [2]Lit *all* [a]1 Sam 25:27 [b]Gen 30:43

12 [1]Lit *he*

13 [1]Lit *upon me*

14 [a]Gen 32:3

15 [1]Lit *Why this?* [a]Ruth 2:13

17 [1]I.e. booths [a]Josh 13:27; Judg 8:5, 14; Ps 60:6

18 [a]Gen 12:6; Josh 24:1; Judg 9:1 [b]Gen 25:20; 28:2

19 [1]Heb *qesitah* [a]Josh 24:32; John 4:5

20 [1]I.e. God, the God of Israel

34:1 [1]Lit *see* [a]Gen 30:21

2 [1]Lit *and humbled her* [a]Gen 34:30

3 [1]Lit *His soul clung* [2]Lit *spoke to the heart of the girl*

4 So Shechem [a]spoke to his father Hamor, saying, "Get me
this young girl for a wife."
5 Now Jacob heard that he had defiled Dinah his daughter;
but his sons were with his livestock in the field, so Jacob kept
silent until they came in.
6 Then Hamor the father of Shechem went out to Jacob to
speak with him.
7 Now the sons of Jacob came in from the field when they
heard *it;* and the men were grieved, and they were very angry
because he had done a [1a]disgraceful thing in Israel [2]by lying
with Jacob's daughter, for such a thing ought not to be done.
8 But Hamor spoke with them, saying, "The soul of my son
Shechem longs for your daughter; please give her to him [1]in
marriage.
9 "Intermarry with us; give your daughters to us and take our
daughters for yourselves.
10 "Thus you shall [1]live with us, and [a]the land shall be *open*
before you; [1]live and [b]trade in it and [c]acquire property in it."
11 Shechem also said to her father and to her brothers, "If I
find favor in your sight, then I will give whatever you say to me.
12 "Ask me ever so much bridal payment and gift, and I will give
according as you say to me; but give me the girl [1]in marriage."
13 But Jacob's sons answered Shechem and his father Hamor
with deceit, because he had defiled Dinah their sister.
14 They said to them, "We cannot do this thing, to give our sister
to [a]one who is uncircumcised, for that would be a disgrace to us.
15 "Only on this *condition* will we consent to you: if you will
become like us, in that every male of you be circumcised,
16 then we will give our daughters to you, and we will take
your daughters for ourselves, and we will [1]live with you and
become one people.
17 "But if you will not listen to us to be circumcised, then we
will take our daughter and go."
18 Now their words seemed [1]reasonable to Hamor and
Shechem, Hamor's son.
19 The young man did not delay to do the thing, because he
was delighted with Jacob's daughter. Now he was more
respected than all the household of his father.
20 So Hamor and his son Shechem came to the [a]gate of their
city and spoke to the men of their city, saying,
21 "These men are [1]friendly with us; therefore let them [2]live in
the land and trade in it, for behold, the land is [3]large enough
for them. Let us take their daughters [4]in marriage, and give our
daughters to them.
22 "Only on this *condition* will the men consent to us to [1]live
with us, to become one people: that every male among us be
circumcised as they are circumcised.
23 "Will not their livestock and their property and all their
animals be ours? Only let us consent to them, and they will
[1]live with us."
24 [a]All who went out of the gate of his city listened to Hamor

4 [a]Judg 14:2
7 [1]Lit *senseless* [2]Lit *to lie* [a]Deut 22:20-30; Judg 20:6; 2 Sam 13:12
8 [1]Lit *for a wife*
10 [1]Lit *dwell* [a]Gen 13:9; 20:15 [b]Gen 42:34 [c]Gen 47:27
12 [1]Lit *for a wife*
14 [a]Gen 17:14
16 [1]Lit *dwell*
18 [1]Lit *good*
20 [a]Ruth 4:1; 2 Sam 15:2
21 [1]Lit *peaceful* [2]Lit *dwell* [3]Lit *wide of hands before them* [4]Lit *to us for wives*
22 [1]Lit *dwell*
23 [1]Lit *dwell*
24 [a]Gen 23:10

and to his son Shechem, and every male was circumcised, all
who went out of the gate of his city.
25 Now it came about on the third day, when they were in
pain, that two of Jacob's sons, [a]Simeon and Levi, Dinah's
brothers, each took his sword and came upon the city unawares,
and killed every male.
26 They killed Hamor and his son Shechem with the edge of the
sword, and took Dinah from Shechem's house, and went forth.
27 Jacob's sons came upon the slain and looted the city,
because they had defiled their sister.
28 They took their flocks and their herds and their donkeys,
and that which was in the city and that which was in the field;
29 and they captured and looted all their wealth and all their
little ones and their wives, even all that *was* in the houses.
30 Then Jacob said to Simeon and Levi, "You have [a]brought
trouble on me by [b]making me odious among the inhabitants of
the land, among [c]the Canaanites and the Perizzites; and [1d]my
men being few in number, they will gather together against me
and [2]attack me and I will be destroyed, I and my household."
31 But they said, "Should he [1]treat our sister as a harlot?"

Chapter 35 Theme ____________________

35 Then God said to Jacob, "Arise, go up to [a]Bethel and
[1]live there, and make an altar there to [b]God, who
appeared to you [c]when you fled [2]from your brother Esau."
2 So Jacob said to his [a]household and to all who were with
him, "Put away [b]the foreign gods which are among you, and
[c]purify yourselves and change your garments;
3 and let us arise and go up to Bethel, and I will make [a]an
altar there to God, [b]who answered me in the day of my distress
and [c]has been with me [1]wherever I have gone."
4 So they gave to Jacob all the foreign gods which [1]they had
and the rings which were in their ears, and Jacob hid them
under the [2]oak which was near Shechem.
5 As they journeyed, there was [1a]a great terror upon the cities
which were around them, and they did not pursue the sons of
Jacob.
6 So Jacob came to [a]Luz (that is, Bethel), which is in the land
of Canaan, he and all the people who were with him.
7 [a]He built an altar there, and called the place [1]El-bethel,
because there God had revealed Himself to him when he fled
[2]from his brother.
8 Now [a]Deborah, Rebekah's nurse, died, and she was buried
below Bethel under the oak; it was named [1]Allon-bacuth.
9 Then God appeared to Jacob again when he came from
Paddan-aram, and He [a]blessed him.
10 [a]God said to him,

"Your name is Jacob;
[1]You shall no longer be called Jacob,
But Israel shall be your name."

25 [a]Gen 49:5-7

30 [1]Lit *I, few in number* [2]Lit *smite* [a]Josh 7:25 [b]Ex 5:21; 1 Sam 13:4; 2 Sam 10:6 [c]Gen 13:7; 34:2 [d]Gen 46:26, 27; Deut 4:27; 1 Chr 16:19; Ps 105:12

31 [1]Or *make*

35:1 [1]Lit *dwell* [2]Lit *from the face of* [a]Gen 28:19 [b]Gen 28:13 [c]Gen 27:43

2 [a]Gen 18:19; Josh 24:15 [b]Gen 31:19, 30, 34 [c]Ex 19:10, 14

3 [1]Lit *in the way which* [a]Gen 28:20-22 [b]Ps 107:6 [c]Gen 28:15; 31:3, 42

4 [1]Lit *were in their hand* [2]Or *terebinth*

5 [1]Or *a terror of God* [a]Ex 15:16; 23:27; Deut 2:25

6 [a]Gen 28:19; 48:3

7 [1]I.e. the God of Bethel [2]Lit *from the face of* [a]Gen 35:3

8 [1]I.e. oak of weeping [a]Gen 24:59

9 [a]Gen 32:29

10 [1]Lit *Your name* [a]Gen 17:5; 32:28

Thus He called [2]him Israel.
11 God also said to him,
"I am [1a]God Almighty;
[b]Be fruitful and multiply;
A nation and a [c]company of nations shall [2]come from you,
And [d]kings shall [2]come forth from [3]you.
12 "[a]The land which I gave to Abraham and Isaac,
I will give it to you,
And I will give the land to your [1]descendants after you."
13 Then [a]God went up from him in the place where He had
spoken with him.
14 Jacob set up [a]a pillar in the place where He had spoken
with him, a pillar of stone, and he poured out a drink offering
on it; he also poured oil on it.
15 So Jacob named the place where God had spoken with
him, [1a]Bethel.
16 Then they journeyed from Bethel; and when there was still
some distance to go to [a]Ephrath, Rachel began to give birth and
she [1]suffered severe labor.
17 When she was in severe labor the midwife said to her, "Do
not fear, for now [a]you have another son."
18 It came about as her soul was departing (for she died), that
she named him [1]Ben-oni; but his father called him [2]Benjamin.
19 So [a]Rachel died and was buried on the way to [b]Ephrath
(that is, Bethlehem).
20 Jacob set up a pillar over her grave; that is the [a]pillar of
Rachel's grave to this day.
21 Then Israel journeyed on and pitched his tent beyond the
[1a]tower of [2]Eder.
22 It came about while Israel was dwelling in that land, that
[a]Reuben went and lay with Bilhah his father's concubine, and
Israel heard *of it.*

Now there were twelve sons of Jacob—
23 [a]the sons of Leah: Reuben, Jacob's firstborn, then Simeon
and Levi and Judah and Issachar and Zebulun;
24 [a]the sons of Rachel: Joseph and Benjamin;
25 and [a]the sons of Bilhah, Rachel's maid: Dan and Naphtali;
26 and [a]the sons of Zilpah, Leah's maid: Gad and Asher. These
are the sons of Jacob who were born to him in Paddan-aram.
27 Jacob came to his father Isaac at [a]Mamre of [b]Kiriath-arba
(that is, Hebron), where Abraham and Isaac had sojourned.
28 Now the days of Isaac were [a]one hundred and eighty years.
29 Isaac breathed his last and died and was [a]gathered to his
people, an [b]old man [1]of ripe age; and [c]his sons Esau and Jacob
buried him.

Chapter 36 Theme ________________________

36 Now these are *the records of* the generations of [a]Esau
(that is, Edom).
2 Esau [a]took his wives from the daughters of Canaan: Adah

10 [2]Lit *his name*
11 [1]Heb *El Shaddai* [2]Or *come into being* [3]Lit *your loins* [a]Gen 17:1; 28:3; Ex 6:3 [b]Gen 9:1, 7 [c]Gen 48:4 [d]Gen 17:6, 16; 36:31
12 [1]Lit *seed* [a]Gen 12:7; 13:15; 26:3, 4; 28:13; Ex 32:13
13 [a]Gen 17:22; 18:33
14 [a]Gen 28:18, 19; 31:45
15 [1]I.e. the house of God [a]Gen 28:19
16 [1]Lit *had difficulty in her giving birth* [a]Gen 35:19; 48:7; Ruth 4:11; Mic 5:2
17 [a]Gen 30:24
18 [1]I.e. the son of my sorrow [2]I.e. the son of the right hand
19 [a]Gen 48:7 [b]Ruth 1:2; 4:11; Mic 5:2
20 [a]1 Sam 10:2
21 [1]Heb *Migdal-eder* [2]Or *flock* [a]Mic 4:8
22 [a]Gen 49:4; 1 Chr 5:1
23 [a]Gen 29:31-35; 30:18-20; 46:8; Ex 1:1-4
24 [a]Gen 30:22-24; 35:18
25 [a]Gen 30:5-8
26 [a]Gen 30:10-13
27 [a]Gen 13:18; 18:1; 23:19 [b]Josh 14:15
28 [a]Gen 25:26
29 [1]Lit *and satisfied with days* [a]Gen 25:8; 49:33 [b]Gen 15:15 [c]Gen 25:9
36:1 [a]Gen 25:30
2 [a]Gen 28:9

INSIGHT

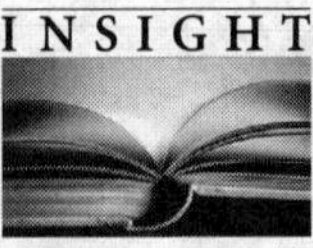

The Birth Order of Jacob's (Israel's) Sons

Mother	Son
Leah	Reuben (born 1921 B.C.) Simeon Levi Judah
Bilhah *(Rachel's maid)*	Dan Naphtali
Zilpah *(Leah's maid)*	Gad Asher
Leah	Issachar Zebulun
Rachel	Joseph (born 1914 B.C.) Benjamin

the daughter of Elon the Hittite, and [b]Oholibamah the daughter
of Anah and the [c]granddaughter of Zibeon the Hivite;
3 also Basemath, Ishmael's daughter, the sister of Nebaioth.
4 Adah bore [a]Eliphaz to Esau, and Basemath bore Reuel,
5 and Oholibamah bore Jeush and Jalam and Korah. These are
the sons of Esau who were born to him in the land of Canaan.
6 [a]Then Esau took his wives and his sons and his daughters
and all [1]his household, and his livestock and all his cattle and
all his goods which he had acquired in the land of Canaan, and
went to *another* land away from his brother Jacob.
7 [a]For their property had become too great for them to [1]live
together, and the [b]land where they [c]sojourned could not sustain
them because of their livestock.
8 So Esau lived in the hill country of [a]Seir; Esau is [b]Edom.
9 These then are *the records of* the generations of Esau the
father of [1]the Edomites in the hill country of Seir.
10 These are the names of Esau's sons: Eliphaz the son of
Esau's wife Adah, Reuel the son of Esau's wife Basemath.
11 The sons of Eliphaz were Teman, Omar, [1]Zepho and Gatam
and Kenaz.
12 Timna was a concubine of Esau's son Eliphaz and she bore
[a]Amalek to Eliphaz. These are the sons of Esau's wife Adah.
13 These are the sons of Reuel: Nahath and Zerah, Shammah
and Mizzah. These were the sons of Esau's wife Basemath.
14 These were the sons of Esau's wife Oholibamah, the daughter
of Anah and the [1]granddaughter of Zibeon: [2]she bore to Esau,
Jeush and Jalam and Korah.
15 These are the chiefs of the sons of Esau. The sons of Eliphaz,
the firstborn of Esau, are chief Teman, chief Omar, chief Zepho,
chief Kenaz,
16 chief Korah, chief Gatam, chief Amalek. These are the
chiefs [1]descended from Eliphaz in the land of Edom; these are
the sons of Adah.
17 These are the sons of Reuel, Esau's son: chief Nahath, chief
Zerah, chief Shammah, chief Mizzah. These are the chiefs
[1]descended from Reuel in the land of Edom; these are the sons
of Esau's wife Basemath.
18 These are the sons of Esau's wife Oholibamah: chief Jeush,
chief Jalam, chief Korah. These are the chiefs [1]descended from
Esau's wife Oholibamah, the daughter of Anah.
19 These are the sons of Esau (that is, Edom), and these are
their chiefs.
20 These are the sons of Seir [a]the Horite, the inhabitants of
the land: Lotan and Shobal and Zibeon and Anah,
21 and Dishon and Ezer and Dishan. These are the chiefs
[1]descended from the Horites, the sons of Seir in the land of
Edom.
22 The sons of Lotan were Hori and [1]Hemam; and Lotan's
sister was Timna.
23 These are the sons of Shobal: [1]Alvan and Manahath and
Ebal, [2]Shepho and Onam.

2 [b]Gen 36:24 [c]Gen 36:25
4 [a]1 Chr 1:35
6 [1]Lit *the souls of his house* [a]Gen 12:5
7 [1]Lit *dwell* [a]Gen 13:6 [b]Gen 17:8; Heb 11:9 [c]1 Chr 29:15; Ps 39:12
8 [a]Gen 32:3 [b]Gen 36:1, 19
9 [1]Lit *Edom*
11 [1]In 1 Chr 1:36, *Zephi*
12 [a]Ex 17:8-16; Num 24:20; Deut 25:17-19; 1 Sam 15:2, 3
14 [1]Gr *son* [2]Lit *and she*
16 [1]Lit *of Eliphaz*
17 [1]Lit *of Reuel*
18 [1]Lit *of Oholibamah, Esau's wife*
20 [a]Gen 14:6; Deut 2:12, 22; 1 Chr 1:38-42
21 [1]Lit *of the Horites*
22 [1]In 1 Chr 1:39, *Homam*
23 [1]In 1 Chr 1:40, *Alian* [2]In 1 Chr 1:40, *Shephi*

24 These are the sons of Zibeon: Aiah and Anah—he is the
Anah who found the hot springs in the wilderness when he
was pasturing the donkeys of his father Zibeon.
25 These are the children of Anah: Dishon, and Oholibamah,
the daughter of Anah.
26 These are the sons of [1a]Dishon: [2]Hemdan and Eshban and
Ithran and Cheran.
27 These are the sons of Ezer: Bilhan and Zaavan and [1]Akan.
28 These are the sons of Dishan: Uz and Aran.
29 These are the chiefs [1]descended from the Horites: chief
Lotan, chief Shobal, chief Zibeon, chief Anah,
30 chief Dishon, chief Ezer, chief Dishan. These are the chiefs
[1]descended from the Horites, according to their *various* chiefs
in the land of Seir.
31 Now these are the kings who reigned in the land of Edom
before any [a]king reigned over the sons of Israel.
32 [1a]Bela the son of Beor reigned in Edom, and the name of
his city was Dinhabah.
33 Then Bela died, and Jobab the son of Zerah of Bozrah
became king in his place.
34 Then Jobab died, and Husham of the land of the Temanites
became king in his place.
35 Then Husham died, and Hadad the son of Bedad, who
[1]defeated Midian in the field of Moab, became king in his
place; and the name of his city was Avith.
36 Then Hadad died, and Samlah of Masrekah became king in
his place.
37 Then Samlah died, and Shaul of Rehoboth on the *Euphrates*
River became king in his place.
38 Then Shaul died, and Baal-hanan the son of Achbor became
king in his place.
39 Then Baal-hanan the son of Achbor died, and [1]Hadar became
king in his place; and the name of his city was [2]Pau; and his
wife's name was Mehetabel, the daughter of Matred, daughter
of Mezahab.
40 Now these are the names of the chiefs [1]descended from
Esau, according to their families *and* their localities, by their
names: chief Timna, chief [2]Alvah, chief Jetheth,
41 chief Oholibamah, chief Elah, chief Pinon,
42 chief Kenaz, chief Teman, chief Mibzar,
43 chief Magdiel, chief Iram. These are the chiefs of Edom
(that is, Esau, the father of [1]the Edomites), according to their
habitations in the land of their possession.

Chapter 37 Theme ____________________

37 Now Jacob lived in [a]the land [1]where his father had
sojourned, in the land of Canaan.
2 These are *the records of* the generations of Jacob.
Joseph, when [a]seventeen years of age, was pasturing the flock
with his brothers while he was *still* a youth, along with [b]the

26 [1]Heb *Dishan* [2]In 1 Chr 1:41, *Hamran* [a]1 Chr 1:41

27 [1]In 1 Chr 1:42, *Jaakan*

29 [1]Lit *of the Horites*

30 [1]Lit *of the Horites*

31 [a]Gen 17:6, 16; 35:11; 1 Chr 1:43

32 [1]Lit *And Bela* [a]1 Chr 1:43

35 [1]Or *smote*

39 [1]In 1 Chr 1:50, *Hadad* [2]In 1 Chr 1:50, *Pai*

40 [1]Lit *of Esau* [2]In 1 Chr 1:51, *Aliah*

43 [1]Heb *Edom*

37:1 [1]Lit *of his father's sojournings* [a]Gen 17:8; 28:4

2 [a]Gen 41:46 [b]Gen 35:25, 26

sons of Bilhah and the sons of Zilpah, his father's wives. And Joseph brought back a [c]bad report about them to their father.

3 Now Israel loved Joseph more than all his sons, because he was [a]the son of his old age; and he made him a [1b]varicolored tunic.

4 His brothers saw that their father loved him more than all his brothers; and *so* they [a]hated him and could not speak to him [1]on friendly terms.

5 Then Joseph [1a]had a dream, and when he told it to his brothers, they hated him even more.

6 He said to them, "Please listen to this dream which I have [1]had;

7 for behold, we were binding sheaves in the field, and lo, my sheaf rose up and also stood erect; and behold, your sheaves gathered around and [a]bowed down to my sheaf."

8 Then his brothers said to him, "[a]Are you actually going to reign over us? Or are you really going to rule over us?" So they hated him even more for his dreams and for his words.

9 Now he [1]had still another dream, and related it to his brothers, and said, "Lo, I have [1]had still another dream; and behold, the sun and the moon and eleven stars were bowing down to me."

10 He related *it* to his father and to his brothers; and his father rebuked him and said to him, "What is this dream that you have [1]had? Shall I and your mother and [a]your brothers actually come to bow ourselves down before you to the ground?"

11 [a]His brothers were jealous of him, but his father [b]kept the saying *in mind.*

12 Then his brothers went to pasture their father's flock in Shechem.

13 Israel said to Joseph, "Are not your brothers pasturing *the flock* in [a]Shechem? Come, and I will send you to them." And he said to him, "[1]I will go."

14 Then he said to him, "Go now and see about the welfare of your brothers and the welfare of the flock, and bring word back to me." So he sent him from the valley of [a]Hebron, and he came to Shechem.

15 A man found him, and behold, he was wandering in the field; and the man asked him, "[1]What are you looking for?"

16 He said, "I am looking for my brothers; please tell me where they are pasturing *the flock.*"

17 Then the man said, "They have moved from here; for I heard *them* say, 'Let us go to [a]Dothan.'" So Joseph went after his brothers and found them at Dothan.

18 [1]When they saw him from a distance and before he came close to them, they [a]plotted against him to put him to death.

19 They said to one another, "[1]Here comes this dreamer!

20 "Now then, come and let us kill him and throw him into one of the pits; and [a]we will say, 'A wild beast devoured him.' Then let us see what will become of his dreams!"

21 But [a]Reuben heard *this* and rescued him out of their hands and said, "Let us not [1]take his life."

2 [c]1 Sam 2:22-24

3 [1]Or *full-length robe* [a]Gen 44:20 [b]Gen 37:23, 32

4 [1]Lit *in peace* [a]Gen 27:41; 1 Sam 17:28

5 [1]Lit *dreamed* [a]Gen 28:12; 31:10, 11, 24

6 [1]Lit *dreamed*

7 [a]Gen 42:6, 9; 43:26; 44:14

8 [a]Gen 49:26; Deut 33:16

9 [1]Lit *dreamed*

10 [1]Lit *dreamed* [a]Gen 27:29

11 [a]Acts 7:9 [b]Dan 7:28; Luke 2:19, 51

13 [1]Lit *Behold me* [a]Gen 33:18-20

14 [a]Gen 13:18; 23:2, 19; 35:27; Josh 14:14, 15; Judg 1:10

15 [1]Lit *saying, "What . . . ?"*

17 [a]2 Kin 6:13

18 [1]Or *And* [a]Ps 31:13; 37:12, 32; Mark 14:1; John 11:53; Acts 23:12

19 [1]Lit *Behold, this master of dreams comes*

20 [a]Gen 37:32, 33

21 [1]Lit *smite his soul* [a]Gen 42:22

22 Reuben further said to them, "Shed no blood. Throw him into this pit that is in the wilderness, but do not lay hands on him"—that he might rescue him out of their hands, to restore him to his father.
23 So it came about, when Joseph [1]reached his brothers, that they stripped Joseph of his [2]tunic, the varicolored tunic that was on him;
24 and they took him and threw him into the pit. Now the pit was empty, without any water in it.
25 Then they sat down to eat [1]a meal. And as they raised their eyes and looked, behold, a caravan of [a]Ishmaelites was coming from Gilead, with their camels bearing [2b]aromatic gum and [3c]balm and [4]myrrh, [5]on their way to bring *them* down to Egypt.
26 Judah said to his brothers, "What profit is it for us to kill our brother and [a]cover up his blood?
27 "[a]Come and let us sell him to the Ishmaelites and not lay our hands on him, for he is our brother, our *own* flesh." And his brothers listened *to him.*
28 Then some [a]Midianite traders passed by, so they pulled *him* up and lifted Joseph out of the pit, and [b]sold [1]him to the Ishmaelites for twenty *shekels* of silver. Thus [c]they brought Joseph into Egypt.
29 Now Reuben returned to the pit, and behold, Joseph was not in the pit; so he [a]tore his garments.
30 He returned to his brothers and said, "[a]The boy is not *there;* as for me, where am I to go?"
31 So [a]they took Joseph's tunic, and slaughtered a male goat and dipped the tunic in the blood;
32 and they sent the varicolored tunic and brought it to their father and said, "We found this; please [1]examine *it* to *see* whether it is your son's tunic or not."
33 Then he [1]examined it and said, "It is my son's tunic. [a]A wild beast has devoured him; [b]Joseph has surely been torn to pieces!"
34 So Jacob [a]tore his clothes, and put sackcloth on his loins and mourned for his son many days.
35 Then all his sons and all his daughters arose to comfort him, but he refused to be comforted. And he said, "Surely I will [a]go down to Sheol in mourning for my son." So his father wept for him.
36 Meanwhile, the [1]Midianites [a]sold him in Egypt to Potiphar, Pharaoh's officer, the captain of the bodyguard.

Chapter 38 Theme ____________________

38 And it came about at that time, that Judah [1]departed from his brothers and [2]visited a certain [a]Adullamite, whose name was Hirah.
2 Judah saw there a daughter of a certain Canaanite whose name was [a]Shua; and he took her and went in to her.
3 So she conceived and bore a son and he named him [a]Er.
4 Then she conceived again and bore a son and named him [a]Onan.

23 [1]Lit *came to* [2]Or *full-length robe*
25 [1]Lit *bread* [2]Or *ladanum spice* [3]Or *mastic* [4]Or *resinous bark* [5]Lit *going* [a]Gen 16:11, 12; 37:28; 39:1 [b]Gen 43:11 [c]Jer 8:22; 46:11
26 [a]Gen 37:20
27 [a]Gen 42:21
28 [1]Lit *Joseph* [a]Gen 37:25; Judg 6:1-3; 8:22, 24 [b]Gen 45:4, 5; Ps 105:17; Acts 7:9 [c]Gen 39:1
29 [a]Gen 37:34; 44:13
30 [a]Gen 42:13, 36
31 [a]Gen 37:3, 23
32 [1]Or *recognize*
33 [1]Or *recognized* [a]Gen 37:20 [b]Gen 44:28
34 [a]Gen 37:29
35 [a]Gen 25:8; 35:29; 42:38; 44:29, 31
36 [1]Lit *Medanites* [a]Gen 39:1
38:1 [1]Lit *went down* [2]Lit *turned aside to* [a]Josh 15:35; 1 Sam 22:1
2 [a]1 Chr 2:3
3 [a]Gen 46:12; Num 26:19
4 [a]Gen 46:12

5 She bore still another son and named him [a]Shelah; and it
was at Chezib [1]that she bore him.
6 Now Judah took a wife for Er his firstborn, and her name
was Tamar.
7 But [a]Er, Judah's firstborn, was evil in the sight of the LORD,
so the LORD took his life.
8 Then Judah said to Onan, "[a]Go in to your brother's wife,
and perform your duty as a brother-in-law to her, and raise up
[1]offspring for your brother."
9 Onan knew that the [1a]offspring would not be his; so when
he went in to his brother's wife, he [2]wasted his seed on the
ground in order not to give [1]offspring to his brother.
10 But what he did was displeasing in the sight of the LORD; so
He [a]took his life also.
11 Then Judah said to his daughter-in-law Tamar, "[a]Remain a
widow in your father's house until my son Shelah grows up";
for he [1]thought, "*I am afraid* that he too may die like his
brothers." So Tamar went and lived in her father's house.
12 Now [1]after a considerable time Shua's daughter, the wife of
Judah, died; and when [2]the time of mourning was ended, Judah
went up to his sheepshearers at [a]Timnah, he and his friend
Hirah the Adullamite.
13 It was told to Tamar, "[1]Behold, your father-in-law is going
up to [a]Timnah to shear his sheep."
14 So she [1]removed her widow's garments and [a]covered *herself*
with a [2]veil, and wrapped herself, and sat in the gateway of
[3]Enaim, which is on the road to Timnah; for she saw that Shelah
had grown up, and [b]she had not been given to him as a wife.
15 When Judah saw her, he thought she *was* a harlot, for she
had covered her face.
16 So he turned aside to her by the road, and said, "[1]Here now,
let me come in to you"; for he did not know that she was his
daughter-in-law. And she said, "What will you give me, that
you may come in to me?"
17 He said, therefore, "I will send you a [1]young goat from the
flock." She said, moreover, "Will you give a pledge until you
send *it?*"
18 He said, "What pledge shall I give you?" And she said, "[a]Your
seal and your cord, and your staff that is in your hand." So he gave
them to her and went in to her, and she conceived by him.
19 Then she arose and departed, and [1]removed her [2]veil and
put on her widow's garments.
20 When Judah sent the [1]young goat by his friend the
Adullamite, to receive the pledge from the woman's hand, he did
not find her.
21 He asked the men of her place, saying, "Where is the
temple prostitute who was by the road at Enaim?" But they
said, "There has been no temple prostitute here."
22 So he returned to Judah, and said, "I did not find her; and
furthermore, the men of the place said, 'There has been no
temple prostitute here.'"

5 [1]Lit *when* [a]Num 26:20

7 [a]Gen 46:12; Num 26:19; 1 Chr 2:3

8 [1]Lit *seed* [a]Deut 25:5, 6; Matt 22:24

9 [1]Lit *seed* [2]Lit *spilled on the ground* [a]Deut 25:6

10 [a]Gen 46:12; Num 26:19

11 [1]Lit *said* [a]Ruth 1:12, 13

12 [1]Lit *the days became many and* [2]Lit *Judah was comforted, he* [a]Josh 15:10, 57

13 [1]Lit *saying, Behold* [a]Josh 15:10, 57; Judg 14:1

14 [1]Lit *removed from herself* [2]Or *shawl* [3]In Josh 15:34, *Enam* [a]Gen 24:65 [b]Gen 38:11, 26

16 [1]Or *Come, now*

17 [1]Lit *kid of goats*

18 [a]Gen 38:25; 41:42

19 [1]Lit *removed from herself* [2]Or *shawl*

20 [1]Lit *kid of goats by the hand of*

23 Then Judah said, "Let her [1]keep them, otherwise we will become a laughingstock. [2]After all, I sent this young goat, but you did not find her."

24 Now it was about three months later that Judah was informed, "[1]Your daughter-in-law Tamar has played the harlot, and behold, she is also with child by harlotry." Then Judah said, "Bring her out and [a]let her be burned!"

25 It was while she was being brought out that she sent to her father-in-law, saying, "I am with child by the man to whom these things belong." And she said, "[a]Please examine and see, whose signet ring and cords and staff are these?"

26 Judah recognized *them,* and said, "[a]She is more righteous than I, inasmuch as [b]I did not give her to my son Shelah." And he did not [1]have relations with her again.

27 It came about at the time she was giving birth, that behold, there were [a]twins in her womb.

28 Moreover, it took place while she was giving birth, one put out a hand, and the midwife took and tied a scarlet *thread* on his hand, saying, "This one came out first."

29 But it came about as he drew back his hand, that behold, his brother came out. Then she said, "What a breach you have made for yourself!" So he was named [1a]Perez.

30 Afterward his brother came out who had the scarlet *thread* on his hand; and he was named [1a]Zerah.

Chapter 39 Theme ________________________

39 Now Joseph had been taken down to Egypt; and Potiphar, an Egyptian officer of Pharaoh, the captain of the bodyguard, bought him [1]from the [a]Ishmaelites, who had taken him down there.

2 [a]The LORD was with Joseph, so he became a [1]successful man. And he was in the house of his master, the Egyptian.

3 Now his master [a]saw that the LORD was with him and *how* the LORD [b]caused all that he did to prosper in his hand.

4 So Joseph [a]found favor in his sight and [1]became his personal servant; and he made him overseer over his house, and [b]all that he owned he put in his [2]charge.

5 It came about that from the time he made him overseer in his house and over all that he owned, the LORD [a]blessed the Egyptian's house on account of Joseph; thus [b]the LORD's blessing was upon all that he owned, in the house and in the field.

6 So he left everything he owned in Joseph's [1]charge; and with him *there* he did not [2]concern himself with anything except the [3]food which he [4]ate.

Now Joseph was [a]handsome in form and appearance.

7 It came about after these events [a]that his master's wife [1]looked with desire at Joseph, and she said, "[b]Lie with me."

8 But [a]he refused and said to his master's wife, "Behold, with me *here,* my master [1]does not concern himself with anything in the house, and he has put all that he owns in my [2]charge.

23 [1]Lit *take for herself* [2]Lit *Behold*

24 [1]Lit *saying, Your* [a]Lev 21:9

25 [a]Gen 37:32

26 [1]Lit *know her yet again* [a]1 Sam 24:17 [b]Gen 38:14

27 [a]Gen 25:24-26

29 [1]I.e. a breach [a]Gen 46:12; Ruth 4:12

30 [1]I.e. a dawning or brightness [a]1 Chr 2:4

39:1 [1]Lit *from the hand of* [a]Gen 37:25, 28, 36; Ps 105:17

2 [1]Or *prosperous* [a]Gen 39:3, 21, 23; Acts 7:9

3 [a]Gen 21:22; 26:28 [b]Ps 1:3

4 [1]Or *ministered to him* [2]Lit *hand* [a]Gen 18:3; 19:19 [b]Gen 24:2; 39:8, 22

5 [a]Gen 30:27 [b]Deut 28:3, 4, 11

6 [1]Lit *hand* [2]Lit *know* [3]Lit *bread* [4]Or *used to eat* [a]Gen 29:17; 1 Sam 16:12

7 [1]Lit *lifted up her eyes at* [a]Prov 7:15-20 [b]2 Sam 13:11

8 [1]Lit *does not know what is in the house* [2]Lit *hand* [a]Prov 6:23, 24

9 "[1a]There is no one greater in this house than I, and he has
withheld nothing from me except you, because you are his
wife. How then could I do this great evil and [b]sin against God?"
10 As she spoke to Joseph day after day, he did not listen to
her to lie beside her *or* be with her.
11 Now it happened [1]one day that he went into the house to
do his work, and none of the men of the household was there
inside.
12 She caught him by his garment, saying, "Lie with me!"
And he left his garment in her hand and fled, and went
outside.
13 [1]When she saw that he had left his garment in her hand
and had fled outside,
14 she called to the men of her household and said to them,
"See, he has brought in a [1]Hebrew to us to make sport of us;
he came in to me to lie with me, and I [2]screamed.
15 "When he heard that I raised my voice and [1]screamed, he
left his garment beside me and fled and went outside."
16 So she [1]left his garment beside her until his master came
home.
17 Then she [a]spoke to him [1]with these words, "[2]The Hebrew
slave, whom you brought to us, came in to me to make sport of
me;
18 and as I raised my voice and [1]screamed, he left his garment
beside me and fled outside."
19 Now when his master heard the words of his wife, which
she spoke to him, saying, "[1]This is what your slave did to me,"
[a]his anger burned.
20 So Joseph's master took him and [a]put him into the jail, the
place where the king's prisoners were confined; and he was
there in the jail.
21 But [a]the LORD was with Joseph and extended kindness to
him, and [b]gave him favor in the sight of the chief jailer.
22 The chief jailer [a]committed to Joseph's [1]charge all the
prisoners who were in the jail; so that whatever was done
there, he was [2]responsible *for it.*
23 [a]The chief jailer did not supervise anything under [1]Joseph's
charge because [b]the LORD was with him; and whatever he did,
[c]the LORD made to prosper.

Chapter 40 Theme ________________________

40 Then it came about after these things, [a]the cupbearer
and the baker for the king of Egypt offended their lord,
the king of Egypt.
2 Pharaoh was [a]furious with his two officials, the chief cupbearer and the chief baker.
3 So he put them in confinement in the house of the [a]captain
of the bodyguard, in the jail, the *same* place where Joseph was
imprisoned.
4 The captain of the bodyguard put Joseph in charge of them,

9 [1]Or *He is not greater* [a]Gen 41:40 [b]Gen 20:6; 42:18; 2 Sam 12:13; Ps 51:4

11 [1]Lit *about this day*

13 [1]Lit *And it came about when*

14 [1]Lit *Hebrew man* [2]Lit *called with a great voice*

15 [1]Lit *called out*

16 [1]Lit *let . . . lie beside*

17 [1]Lit *according to* [2]Lit *saying, "The* [a]Ex 23:1; Prov 26:28

18 [1]Lit *called out*

19 [1]Lit *According to these things your slave* [a]Prov 6:34

20 [a]Gen 40:3; Ps 105:18

21 [a]Gen 39:2; Ps 105:19; Acts 7:9 [b]Ex 3:21; 11:3; 12:36

22 [1]Lit *hand* [2]Lit *the doer* [a]Gen 39:4; 40:3, 4

23 [1]Lit *his hand* [a]Gen 39:3, 8 [b]Gen 39:2, 3 [c]Gen 39:3

40:1 [a]Gen 40:11, 13; Neh 1:11

2 [a]Prov 16:14

3 [a]Gen 39:1, 20

and he [1]took care of them; and they were in confinement for
[2]some time.
5 Then the cupbearer and the baker for the king of Egypt,
who were confined in jail, both had a dream the same night,
each man with his *own* dream *and* each dream with its *own*
interpretation.
6 [1]When Joseph came to them in the morning and observed
them, [2]behold, they were dejected.
7 He asked Pharaoh's officials who were with him in
confinement in his master's house, "[1a]Why are your faces so
sad today?"
8 Then they said to him, "[a]We have [1]had a dream and there
is no one to interpret it." Then Joseph said to them, "[b]Do not
interpretations belong to God? Tell *it* to me, please."
9 So the chief cupbearer told his dream to Joseph, and said to
him, "In my dream, [1]behold, *there was* a vine in front of me;
10 and on the vine *were* three branches. And as it was
budding, its blossoms came out, *and* its clusters produced ripe
grapes.
11 "Now Pharaoh's cup was in my hand; so I took the grapes
and squeezed them into Pharaoh's cup, and I put the cup into
Pharaoh's [1]hand."
12 Then Joseph said to him, "This is the [a]interpretation of it:
the three branches are three days;
13 within three more days Pharaoh will [1]lift up your head and
restore you to your [2]office; and you will put Pharaoh's cup into
his hand according to your former custom when you were his
cupbearer.
14 "Only [1]keep me in mind when it goes well with you, and
please [a]do me a kindness [2]by mentioning me to Pharaoh and
get me out of this house.
15 "For [a]I was in fact kidnapped from the land of the Hebrews,
and even here I have done nothing that they should have put
me into the [1]dungeon."
16 When the chief baker saw that he had interpreted
favorably, he said to Joseph, "I also *saw* in my dream, and
behold, *there were* three baskets of white bread on my head;
17 and in the top basket *there were* some of all [1]sorts of baked
food for Pharaoh, and the birds were eating them out of the
basket on my head."
18 Then Joseph answered and said, "This is its interpretation:
the three baskets are three days;
19 within three more days Pharaoh will lift up your head from
you and will hang you on a tree, and the birds will eat your
flesh off you."
20 Thus it came about on the third day, *which was* [a]Pharaoh's
birthday, that he made a feast for all his servants; [b]and he lifted
up the head of the chief cupbearer and the head of the chief
baker among his servants.
21 He restored the chief cupbearer to his [1]office, and [a]he put
the cup into Pharaoh's [2]hand;

4 [1]Lit *ministered to* [2]Lit *days*
6 [1]Or *And* [2]Lit *and behold*
7 [1]Lit *saying, Why* [a]Neh 2:2
8 [1]Lit *dreamed* [a]Gen 41:15 [b]Gen 41:16; Dan 2:27, 28
9 [1]Lit *and behold*
11 [1]Lit *palm*
12 [a]Dan 2:36; 4:18, 19
13 [1]Or possibly *forgive you* [2]Lit *place*
14 [1]Lit *remember me with yourself* [2]Lit *and mention* [a]Josh 2:12; 1 Sam 20:14; 1 Kin 2:7
15 [1]Or *pit* [a]Gen 37:26-28
17 [1]Lit *food for Pharaoh made by a baker*
20 [a]Matt 14:6 [b]2 Kin 25:27; Jer 52:31
21 [1]Lit *wine-pouring* [2]Lit *palm* [a]Gen 40:13

22 but [a]he hanged the chief baker, just as Joseph had
interpreted to them.
23 Yet the chief cupbearer did not remember Joseph, but
[a]forgot him.

Chapter 41 Theme ______________________

41 Now it happened at the end of two full years that Pharaoh
had a dream, and behold, he was standing by the Nile.
2 And lo, from the Nile there came up seven cows, sleek and
[1]fat; and they grazed in the [a]marsh grass.
3 Then behold, seven other cows came up after them from
the Nile, ugly and [1]gaunt, and they stood by the *other* cows on
the bank of the Nile.
4 The ugly and [1]gaunt cows ate up the seven sleek and fat
cows. Then Pharaoh awoke.
5 He fell asleep and dreamed a second time; and behold, seven
ears of grain came up on a single stalk, plump and good.
6 Then behold, seven ears, thin and scorched by the east
wind, sprouted up after them.
7 The thin ears swallowed up the seven plump and full ears.
Then Pharaoh awoke, and behold, *it was* a dream.
8 Now in the morning [a]his spirit was troubled, so he sent
and called for all the [1b]magicians of Egypt, and all its [c]wise
men. And Pharaoh told them his [2]dreams, but [d]there was no
one who could interpret them to Pharaoh.
9 Then the chief cupbearer spoke to Pharaoh, saying, "I
would make mention today of [a]my *own* [1]offenses.
10 "Pharaoh was [a]furious with his servants, and [b]he put me in
confinement in the house of the captain of the bodyguard, *both*
me and the chief baker.
11 "[a]We had a dream [1]on the same night, [2]he and I; each of us
dreamed according to the interpretation of his *own* dream.
12 "Now a Hebrew youth *was* with us there, a [a]servant of the
captain of the bodyguard, and we related *them* to him, and [b]he
interpreted our dreams for us. To each one he interpreted
according to his *own* dream.
13 "And just [a]as he interpreted for us, so it happened; he
restored me in my [1]office, but he hanged him."
14 Then Pharaoh sent and [a]called for Joseph, and they
[b]hurriedly brought him out of the dungeon; and when he had
shaved himself and changed his clothes, he came to Pharaoh.
15 Pharaoh said to Joseph, "I have had a dream, [a]but no one
can interpret it; and [b]I have heard [1]it said about you, that
[2]when you hear a dream you can interpret it."
16 Joseph then answered Pharaoh, saying, "[1a]It is not in me;
[b]God will [2]give Pharaoh a favorable answer."
17 So Pharaoh spoke to Joseph, "In my dream, behold, I was
standing on the bank of the Nile;
18 and behold, seven cows, [1]fat and sleek came up out of the
Nile, and they grazed in the marsh grass.

22 [a]Gen 40:19; Esth 7:10

23 [a]Job 19:14; Ps 31:12; Eccl 9:15

41:2 [1]Lit *fat of flesh* [a]Job 8:11; Is 19:6, 7

3 [1]Lit *lean of flesh*

4 [1]Lit *lean of flesh*

8 [1]Or *soothsayer priests* [2]Lit *dream* [a]Dan 2:1, 3 [b]Ex 7:11, 22; Dan 1:20; 2:2 [c]Matt 2:1 [d]Dan 2:27; 4:7

9 [1]Or *sins* [a]Gen 40:14, 23

10 [a]Gen 40:2, 3 [b]Gen 39:20

11 [1]Lit *one night* [2]Lit *I and he* [a]Gen 40:5

12 [a]Gen 37:36 [b]Gen 40:12

13 [1]Lit *place* [a]Gen 40:21, 22

14 [a]Ps 105:20 [b]Dan 2:25

15 [1]Lit *about you, saying* [2]Lit *you hear a dream to interpret it* [a]Gen 41:8 [b]Dan 5:16

16 [1]Lit *Apart from me* [2]Lit *answer the peace of Pharaoh* [a]Dan 2:30; Zech 4:6; Acts 3:12; 2 Cor 3:5 [b]Gen 40:8; 41:25, 28, 32; Deut 29:29; Dan 2:22, 28, 47

18 [1]Lit *fat of flesh*

19 "Lo, seven other cows came up after them, poor and very ugly
and [1]gaunt, such as I had never seen for [2]ugliness in all the
land of Egypt;
20 and the lean and [1]ugly cows ate up the first seven fat cows.
21 "Yet when they had [1]devoured them, it could not be
[2]detected that they had [1]devoured them, [3]for they were just as
ugly as [4]before. Then I awoke.
22 "I saw also in my dream, and behold, seven ears, full and
good, came up on a single stalk;
23 and lo, seven ears, withered, thin, *and* scorched by the east
wind, sprouted up after them;
24 and the thin ears swallowed the seven good ears. Then [a]I
told it to the [1]magicians, but there was no one who could
explain it to me."
25 Now Joseph said to Pharaoh, "Pharaoh's [1]dreams are one
and the same; [a]God has told to Pharaoh what He is about to do.
26 "The seven good cows are seven years; and the seven good
ears are seven years; the [1]dreams are one *and the same.*
27 "The seven lean and ugly cows that came up after them are
seven years, and the seven thin ears scorched by the east wind
[a]will be seven years of famine.
28 "[1]It is as I have spoken to Pharaoh: [a]God has shown to
Pharaoh what He is about to do.
29 "Behold, [a]seven years of great abundance are coming in all
the land of Egypt;
30 and after them [a]seven years of famine will [1]come, and all
the abundance will be forgotten in the land of Egypt, and the
famine will [2]ravage the land.
31 "So the abundance will be unknown in the land because of
that subsequent famine; for it *will be* very severe.
32 "Now as for the repeating of the dream to Pharaoh twice, *it
means* that [a]the matter is determined by God, and God will
quickly bring it about.
33 "Now let Pharaoh look for a man [a]discerning and wise, and
set him over the land of Egypt.
34 "Let Pharaoh take action to appoint overseers [1]in charge of
the land, and let him exact a fifth *of the produce* of the land of
Egypt in the seven years of abundance.
35 "Then let them [a]gather all the food of these good years that
are coming, and store up the grain for food in the cities under
Pharaoh's authority, and let them guard *it.*
36 "Let the food become as a reserve for the land for the seven
years of famine which will occur in the land of Egypt, so that
the land will not perish during the famine."
37 Now the [1]proposal seemed good [2]to Pharaoh and [2]to all his
servants.
38 Then Pharaoh said to his servants, "Can we find a man like
this, [a]in whom is a divine spirit?"
39 So Pharaoh said to Joseph, "Since God has informed you of
all this, there is no one so [a]discerning and wise as you are.
40 "[a]You shall be over my house, and according to your

19 [1]Lit *lean of flesh* [2]Lit *badness*
20 [1]Lit *bad*
21 [1]Lit *entered their inward parts* [2]Or *known* [3]Lit *and* [4]Lit *in the beginning*
24 [1]Or *soothsayer priests* [a]Is 8:19; Dan 4:7
25 [1]Lit *dream is* [a]Gen 41:28, 32; Dan 2:28, 29, 45
26 [1]Lit *dream is*
27 [a]2 Kin 8:1
28 [1]Lit *That is the thing which I spoke* [a]Gen 41:25, 32
29 [a]Gen 41:47
30 [1]Lit *arise* [2]Lit *destroy* [a]Gen 41:54, 56; 47:13; Ps 105:16
32 [a]Gen 41:25, 28
33 [a]Gen 41:39
34 [1]Lit *over*
35 [a]Gen 41:48
37 [1]Lit *word* [2]Lit *in the sight of*
38 [a]Job 32:8; Dan 4:8, 9, 18; 5:11, 14
39 [a]Gen 41:33
40 [a]Ps 105:21; Acts 7:10

[1]command all my people shall [2]do homage; only in the throne I
will be greater than you."
41 Pharaoh said to Joseph, "See, I have set you [a]over all the
land of Egypt."
42 Then Pharaoh [a]took off his signet ring from his hand and
put it on Joseph's hand, and clothed him in garments of fine
linen and [b]put the gold necklace around his neck.
43 He had him ride in [1]his second chariot; and they
proclaimed before him, "[2]Bow the knee!" And he set him over
all the land of Egypt.
44 Moreover, Pharaoh said to Joseph, "*Though* I am Pharaoh,
yet [a]without [1]your permission no one shall raise his hand or
foot in all the land of Egypt."
45 Then Pharaoh named Joseph [1]Zaphenath-paneah; and he
gave him Asenath, the daughter of Potiphera priest of [2a]On, as
his wife. And Joseph went forth over the land of Egypt.
46 Now Joseph was [a]thirty years old when he [1]stood before
Pharaoh, king of Egypt. And Joseph went out from the
presence of Pharaoh and went through all the land of Egypt.
47 During the seven years of plenty the land brought forth
[1]abundantly.
48 So he gathered all the food of *these* seven years which
occurred in the land of Egypt and placed the food in the cities;
he placed in every city the food from its own surrounding
fields.
49 Thus Joseph stored up grain [1]in great abundance like the
sand of the sea, until he stopped [2]measuring *it,* for it was
[3]beyond measure.
50 Now before the year of famine came, [a]two sons were born
to Joseph, whom Asenath, the daughter of Potiphera priest of
[1]On, bore to him.
51 Joseph named the firstborn [1]Manasseh, "For," *he said,*
"God has made me forget all my trouble and all my father's
household."
52 He named the second [1]Ephraim, "For," *he said,* "[a]God has
made me fruitful in the land of my affliction."
53 When the seven years of plenty which had been in the
land of Egypt came to an end,
54 and [a]the seven years of famine began to come, just as
Joseph had said, then there was famine in all the lands, but in
all the land of Egypt there was bread.
55 So when all the land of Egypt was famished, the people
cried out to Pharaoh for bread; and Pharaoh said to all the
Egyptians, "Go to Joseph; [a]whatever he says to you, you shall
do."
56 When the famine was *spread* over all the face of the earth,
then Joseph opened all [1]the storehouses, and sold to the
Egyptians; and the famine was severe in the land of Egypt.
57 *The people of* all the earth came to Egypt to buy grain from
Joseph, because [a]the famine was severe in all the earth.

40 [1]Lit *mouth* [2]Lit *kiss*

41 [a]Gen 42:6; Ps 105:21; Dan 6:3; Acts 7:10

42 [a]Esth 3:10; 8:2 [b]Dan 5:7, 16, 29

43 [1]Lit *the second . . . which was his* [2]Heb *Abreck: Attention* or *Make way*

44 [1]Lit *you no one* [a]Ps 105:22

45 [1]Probably Egyptian for "God speaks; he lives" [2]Or *Heliopolis* [a]Jer 43:13; Ezek 30:17

46 [1]Or *entered the service of* [a]Gen 37:2

47 [1]Lit *by handfuls*

49 [1]Lit *very much* [2]Lit *numbering* [3]Or *without number*

50 [1]Or *Heliopolis* [a]Gen 48:5

51 [1]I.e. making to forget

52 [1]I.e. fruitfulness [a]Gen 17:6; 28:3; 49:22

54 [a]Gen 41:30; Ps 105:16; Acts 7:11

55 [a]John 2:5

56 [1]Lit *that which was in them*

57 [a]Gen 12:10

Chapter 42 Theme ________________________________

42 Now [a]Jacob saw that there was grain in Egypt, and
Jacob said to his sons, "Why are you staring at one
another?"
2 He said, "Behold, [a]I have heard that there is grain in Egypt;
go down there and buy *some* for us [1]from that place, [b]so that
we may live and not die."
3 Then ten brothers of Joseph went down to buy grain from
Egypt.
4 But Jacob did not send Joseph's brother [a]Benjamin with his
brothers, for he said, "[b]I am afraid that harm may befall him."
5 So the sons of Israel came to buy grain among those who
were coming, [a]for the famine was in the land of Canaan *also.*
6 Now [a]Joseph was the ruler over the land; he was the one
who sold to all the people of the land. And Joseph's brothers
came and [b]bowed down to him with *their* faces to the ground.
7 When Joseph saw his brothers he recognized them, but he
disguised himself to them and [a]spoke to them harshly. And he
said to them, "Where have you come from?" And they said,
"From the land of Canaan, to buy food."
8 But Joseph had recognized his brothers, although [a]they did
not recognize him.
9 Joseph [a]remembered the dreams which he [1]had about
them, and said to them, "You are spies; you have come to look
at the [2]undefended parts of our land."
10 Then they said to him, "No, [a]my lord, but your servants
have come to buy food.
11 "We are all sons of one man; we are [a]honest men, your
servants are not spies."
12 Yet he said to them, "No, but you have come to look at the
[1]undefended parts of our land!"
13 But they said, "Your servants are twelve brothers *in all,* the
sons of one man in the land of Canaan; and behold, the
youngest is with [a]our father today, and [b]one is no longer alive."
14 Joseph said to them, "It is as I said [1]to you, you are spies;
15 by this you will be tested: [a]by the life of Pharaoh, you shall
not go from this place unless your youngest brother comes here!
16 "Send one of you that he may get your brother, while you
remain confined, that your words may be tested, whether
there is [a]truth in you. But if not, by the life of Pharaoh, surely
you are spies."
17 So he put them all together in [a]prison for three days.
18 Now Joseph said to them on the third day, "Do this and
live, for [a]I fear God:
19 if you are honest men, let one of your brothers be confined
in [1]your prison; but as for *the rest of* you, go, carry grain for the
famine of your households,
20 and [a]bring your youngest brother to me, so your words
may be verified, and you will not die." And they did so.
21 Then they said to one another, "[a]Truly we are guilty
concerning our brother, because we saw the distress of his soul

42:1 [a]Acts 7:12
2 [1]Lit *from there* [a]Acts 7:12 [b]Gen 43:8; Ps 33:18, 19
4 [a]Gen 35:24 [b]Gen 42:38
5 [a]Gen 12:10; 26:1; 41:57; Acts 7:11
6 [a]Gen 41:41, 55 [b]Gen 37:7-10; 41:43; Is 60:14
7 [a]Gen 42:30
8 [a]Gen 37:2; 41:46
9 [1]Lit *had dreamed* [2]Lit *nakedness of the land* [a]Gen 37:6-9
10 [a]Gen 37:8
11 [a]Gen 42:16, 19, 31, 34
12 [1]Lit *nakedness of the land*
13 [a]Gen 43:7 [b]Gen 37:30; 42:32; 44:20
14 [1]Lit *to you, saying*
15 [a]1 Sam 17:55
16 [a]Gen 42:11
17 [a]Gen 40:4, 7
18 [a]Gen 39:9; Lev 25:43; Neh 5:15
19 [1]Lit *the house of your prison*
20 [a]Gen 42:34; 43:5; 44:23
21 [a]Gen 37:26-28; 45:3; Hos 5:15

when he pleaded with us, yet we would not listen; therefore
this distress has come upon us."
22 Reuben answered them, saying, "[a]Did I not tell [1]you, 'Do
not sin against the boy'; and you would not listen? [2b]Now
comes the reckoning for his blood."
23 They did not know, however, that Joseph understood, for
there was an interpreter between them.
24 He turned away from them and [a]wept. But when he
returned to them and spoke to them, he [b]took Simeon from
them and bound him before their eyes.
25 [a]Then Joseph gave orders to fill their bags with grain and to
restore every man's money in his sack, and to give them
provisions for the journey. And thus it was done for them.
26 So they loaded their donkeys with their grain and departed
from there.
27 As one *of them* opened his sack to give his donkey fodder
at the lodging place, he saw his [a]money; and behold, it was in
the mouth of his sack.
28 Then he said to his brothers, "My money has been returned,
and behold, it is even in my sack." And their hearts [1]sank, and
they *turned* [2]trembling to one another, saying, "[a]What is this
that God has done to us?"
29 When they came to their father Jacob in the land of
Canaan, they told him all that had happened to them, saying,
30 "The man, the lord of the land, [a]spoke harshly with us, and
took us for spies of the country.
31 "But we said to him, 'We are [a]honest men; we are not spies.
32 'We are twelve brothers, sons of our father; one is no longer
alive, and the youngest is with our father today in the land of
Canaan.'
33 "The man, the lord of the land, said to us, '[a]By this I will
know that you are honest men: leave one of your brothers with
me and take *grain for* the famine of your households, and go.
34 'But bring your youngest brother to me that I may know
that you are not spies, but [1]honest men. I will give your
brother to you, and you may [a]trade in the land.'"
35 Now it came about as they were emptying their sacks, that
behold, [a]every man's bundle of money *was* in his sack; and
when they and their father saw their bundles of money, they
were dismayed.
36 Their father Jacob said to them, "You have [a]bereaved me of
my children: Joseph is no more, and Simeon is no more, and
you would take Benjamin; all these things are against me."
37 Then Reuben spoke to his father, saying, "You may put my
two sons to death if I do not bring him *back* to you; put him in
my [1]care, and I will return him to you."
38 But [1]Jacob said, "My son shall not go down with you; for
his [a]brother is dead, and he alone is left. [b]If harm should befall
him on the journey [2]you are taking, then you will [c]bring my
gray hair down to Sheol in sorrow."

22 [1]Lit *you saying* [2]Lit *And behold, his blood also is required* [a]Gen 37:21, 22 [b]Gen 9:5, 6; 1 Kin 2:32; 2 Chr 24:22; Ps 9:12

24 [a]Gen 43:30; 45:14, 15 [b]Gen 43:14, 23

25 [a]Gen 44:1; Rom 12:17, 20, 21; 1 Pet 3:9

27 [a]Gen 43:21, 22

28 [1]Lit *went out* [2]Lit *trembled* [a]Gen 43:23

30 [a]Gen 42:7

31 [a]Gen 42:11

33 [a]Gen 42:19, 20

34 [1]Lit *you are honest* [a]Gen 34:10

35 [a]Gen 43:12, 15, 21

36 [a]Gen 43:14

37 [1]Lit *hand*

38 [1]Lit *he* [2]Lit *on which you are going* [a]Gen 37:33, 34; 42:13; 44:27, 28 [b]Gen 42:4 [c]Gen 37:35; 44:29, 31

Chapter 43 Theme __________________________

43 [a]Now the famine was severe in the land.

2 So it came about when they had finished eating the grain which they had brought from Egypt, that their father said to them, "Go back, buy us a little food."

3 Judah spoke to him, however, saying, "[a]The man solemnly warned [1]us, 'You shall not see my face unless your brother is with you.'

4 "If you send our brother with us, we will go down and buy you food.

5 "But if you do not send *him,* we will not go down; for the man said to us, 'You will not see my face unless your brother is with you.'"

6 Then Israel said, "Why did you treat me so badly [1]by telling the man whether you still had *another* brother?"

7 But they said, "The man questioned particularly about us and our relatives, saying, '[a]Is your father still alive? Have you *another* brother?' So we [1]answered his questions. Could we possibly know that he would say, 'Bring your brother down'?"

8 Judah said to his father Israel, "Send the lad with me and we will arise and go, [a]that we may live and not die, we as well as you and our little ones.

9 "[a]I myself will be surety for him; [1]you may hold me responsible for him. If I do not bring him *back* to you and set him before you, then [2]let me bear the blame before you forever.

10 "For if we had not delayed, surely by now we could have returned twice."

11 Then their father Israel said to them, "If *it must be* so, then do this: take some of the best products of the land in your [1]bags, and carry down to the man [a]as a present, a little [2b]balm and a little honey, [3]aromatic gum and [4]myrrh, pistachio nuts and almonds.

12 "Take double *the* money in your hand, and take back in your hand [a]the money that was returned in the mouth of your sacks; perhaps it was a mistake.

13 "Take your brother also, and arise, return to the man;

14 and may [1a]God Almighty [b]grant you compassion in the sight of the man, so that he will release to you [c]your other brother and Benjamin. And as for me, [d]if I am bereaved of my children, I am bereaved."

15 So the men took [a]this present, and they took double *the* money in their hand, and Benjamin; then they arose and went down to Egypt and stood before Joseph.

16 When Joseph saw Benjamin with them, he said to his [a]house steward, "Bring the men into the house, and slay an animal and make ready; for the men are to dine with me at noon."

17 So the man did as Joseph said, and [1]brought the men to Joseph's house.

43:1 [a]Gen 12:10; 26:1; 41:56, 57

3 [1]Lit *us, saying* [a]Gen 43:5; 44:23

6 [1]Lit *to tell*

7 [1]Lit *told him according to these words* [a]Gen 42:13; 43:27

8 [a]Gen 42:2

9 [1]Lit *from my hand you may require him* [2]Lit *I shall have sinned before you all the days* [a]Gen 42:37; 44:32; Philem 18, 19

11 [1]Or *vessels* [2]Or *mastic* [3]Or *ladanum spice* [4]Or *resinous bark* [a]Gen 32:20; 43:25, 26 [b]Gen 37:25; Jer 8:22; Ezek 27:17

12 [a]Gen 42:25, 35; 43:21, 22

14 [1]Heb *El Shaddai* [a]Gen 17:1; 28:3; 35:11 [b]Ps 106:46 [c]Gen 42:24 [d]Gen 42:36

15 [a]Gen 43:11

16 [a]Gen 44:1

17 [1]Lit *the man brought*

18 Now the men were afraid, because they were brought to
Joseph's house; and they said, "*It is* because of the money that
was returned in our sacks the first time that we are being
brought in, that he may [1]seek occasion against us and fall upon
us, and take us for slaves with our donkeys."
19 So they came near to Joseph's house steward, and spoke to
him at the entrance of the house,
20 and said, "Oh, my lord, we indeed came down the first time
to buy food,
21 and it came about when we came to the lodging place, that
we opened our sacks, and behold, [a]each man's money was in
the mouth of his sack, our money in [1]full. So [b]we have brought
it back in our hand.
22 "We have also brought down other money in our hand to
buy food; we do not know who put our money in our sacks."
23 He said, "[1]Be at ease, do not be afraid. [a]Your God and the
God of your father has given you treasure in your sacks; [2]I had
your money." Then [b]he brought Simeon out to them.
24 Then the man brought the men into Joseph's house and
[a]gave them water, and they [b]washed their feet; and he gave
their donkeys fodder.
25 So they prepared [a]the present [1]for Joseph's coming at noon;
for they had heard that they were to eat [2]a meal there.
26 When Joseph came home, they brought into the house to
him the present which was in their hand and [a]bowed to the
ground before him.
27 Then he asked them about their welfare, and said, "[a]Is
your old father well, of whom you spoke? Is he still alive?"
28 They said, "Your servant our father is well; he is still alive."
[a]They bowed down [1]in homage.
29 As he lifted his eyes and saw his brother Benjamin, his
mother's son, he said, "Is this [a]your youngest brother, of whom
you spoke to me?" And he said, "[b]May God be gracious to you,
my son."
30 Joseph hurried *out* for [1a]he was deeply stirred over his
brother, and he sought *a place* to weep; and he entered his
chamber and [b]wept there.
31 Then he washed his face and came out; and he [a]controlled
himself and said, "[1]Serve the meal."
32 So they served him by himself, and them by themselves,
and the Egyptians who ate with him by themselves, because
the Egyptians could not eat bread with the Hebrews, for that is
[1a]loathsome to the Egyptians.
33 Now they [1]were seated before him, [a]the firstborn
according to his birthright and the youngest according to his
youth, and the men looked at one another in astonishment.
34 He took portions to them from [1]his own table, [a]but
Benjamin's portion was five times as much as any of theirs. So
they feasted and drank freely with him.

18 [1]Lit *roll himself upon us*

21 [1]Lit *its weight* [a]Gen 42:27, 35 [b]Gen 43:12, 15

23 [1]Lit *Peace be to you* [2]Lit *your money had come to me* [a]Gen 42:28 [b]Gen 42:24

24 [a]Gen 18:4; 19:2; 24:32 [b]Luke 7:44; John 13:5; 1 Tim 5:10

25 [1]Lit *until* [2]Lit *bread* [a]Gen 43:11, 15

26 [a]Gen 37:7, 10

27 [a]Gen 43:7; 45:3

28 [1]Lit *and prostrated themselves* [a]Gen 37:7, 10

29 [a]Gen 42:13 [b]Num 6:25; Ps 67:1

30 [1]Lit *his compassion grew warm* [a]1 Kin 3:26 [b]Gen 42:24; 45:2, 14, 15; 46:29

31 [1]Lit *Set on bread* [a]Gen 45:1

32 [1]Lit *an abomination* [a]Gen 46:34; Ex 8:26

33 [1]Lit *sat* [a]Gen 42:7

34 [1]Lit *his face* [a]Gen 35:24; 45:22

Chapter 44 Theme ________________________

44 [a]Then he commanded his house steward, saying, "Fill
the men's sacks with food, as much as they can carry,
and put each man's money in the mouth of his sack.
2 "Put my cup, the silver cup, in the mouth of the sack of the
youngest, and his money for the grain." And he did [1]as Joseph
had told *him.*
3 [1]As soon as it was light, the men were sent away, they
with their donkeys.
4 They had *just* gone out of [a]the city, *and* were not far off,
when Joseph said to his house steward, "Up, follow the men;
and when you overtake them, say to them, 'Why have you
repaid evil for good?
5 'Is not this the one from which my lord drinks and which
he indeed uses for [a]divination? You have done wrong in doing
this.'"
6 So he overtook them and spoke these words to them.
7 They said to him, "Why does my lord speak such words as
these? Far be it from your servants to do such a thing.
8 "Behold, [a]the money which we found in the mouth of our
sacks we have brought back to you from the land of Canaan.
How then could we steal silver or gold from your lord's house?
9 "[a]With whomever of your servants it is found, let him die,
and we also will be my lord's [b]slaves."
10 So he said, "Now let it also be according to your words; he
with whom it is found shall be my slave, and *the rest of* you
shall be innocent."
11 Then they hurried, each man lowered his sack to the
ground, and each man opened his sack.
12 He searched, beginning with the oldest and ending with
the youngest, and [a]the cup was found in Benjamin's sack.
13 Then they [a]tore their clothes, and when each man loaded
his donkey, they returned to [b]the city.
14 When Judah and his brothers came to Joseph's house, he
was still there, and [a]they fell to the ground before him.
15 Joseph said to them, "What is this deed that you have
done? Do you not know that such a man as I can indeed
practice [a]divination?"
16 So Judah said, "What can we say to my lord? What can we
speak? And how can we justify ourselves? God has found out
the iniquity of your servants; behold, we are my lord's [a]slaves,
both we and the one in whose [1]possession the cup has been
found."
17 But he said, "Far be it from me to do this. The man in whose
[1]possession the cup has been found, he shall be my slave; but
as for you, go up in peace to your father."
18 Then Judah approached him, and said, "Oh my lord, may
your servant please speak a word in my lord's ears, and [1][a]do
not be angry with your servant; for [b]you are equal to Pharaoh.
19 "[a]My lord asked his servants, saying, 'Have you a father or a
brother?'

44:1 [a]Gen 42:25
2 [1]Or *according to the word*
3 [1]Lit *The morning was light*
4 [a]Gen 44:13
5 [a]Gen 30:27; 44:15; Lev 19:26; Deut 18:10-14
8 [a]Gen 43:21
9 [a]Gen 31:32 [b]Gen 44:16
12 [a]Gen 44:2
13 [a]Gen 37:29, 34; Num 14:6; 2 Sam 1:11 [b]Gen 44:4
14 [a]Gen 37:7, 10
15 [a]Gen 44:5
16 [1]Lit *hand* [a]Gen 44:9
17 [1]Lit *hand*
18 [1]Lit *let not your anger burn against* [a]Gen 18:30, 32; Ex 32:22 [b]Gen 37:7, 8; 41:40-44
19 [a]Gen 43:7

20 "We said to my lord, 'We have an old father and [a]a little
child of *his* old age. Now [b]his brother is dead, so he alone is left
of his mother, and his father loves him.'
21 "Then you said to your servants, '[a]Bring him down to me
that I may set my eyes on him.'
22 "But we said to my lord, 'The lad cannot leave his father, for
if he should leave his father, [1]his father would die.'
23 "You said to your servants, however, '[a]Unless your youngest
brother comes down with you, you will not see my face again.'
24 "Thus it came about when we went up to your servant my
father, we told him the words of my lord.
25 "[a]Our father said, 'Go back, buy us a little food.'
26 "But we said, 'We cannot go down. If our youngest brother
is with us, then we will go down; for we cannot see the man's
face unless our youngest brother is with us.'
27 "Your servant my father said to us, 'You know that [a]my wife
bore me two sons;
28 and the one went out from me, and [a]I said, "Surely he is
torn in pieces," and I have not seen him since.
29 'If you take this one also from [1]me, and harm befalls him,
you will [a]bring my gray hair down to Sheol in [2]sorrow.'
30 "Now, therefore, when I come to your servant my father,
and the lad is not with us, since [1a]his life is bound up in the
lad's life,
31 when he sees that the lad is not *with us,* he will die. Thus
your servants will [a]bring the gray hair of your servant our
father down to Sheol in sorrow.
32 "For your servant [a]became surety for the lad to my father,
saying, 'If I do not bring him *back* to you, then [1]let me bear the
blame before my father forever.'
33 "Now, therefore, please let your servant remain instead of
the lad a slave to my lord, and let the lad go up with his
brothers.
34 "For how shall I go up to my father if the lad is not with
me—for fear that I see the evil that would [1]overtake my
father?"

Chapter 45 Theme ____________________

45 Then Joseph could not control himself before all those
who stood by him, and he cried, "Have everyone go out
from me." So there [1]was no man with him [a]when Joseph made
himself known to his brothers.
2 [a]He [1]wept so loudly that the Egyptians heard *it,* and the
household of Pharaoh heard *of it.*
3 Then Joseph said to his brothers, "[a]I am Joseph! [b]Is my
father still alive?" But his brothers could not answer him, for
[c]they were dismayed at his presence.
4 Then Joseph said to his brothers, "Please come [1]closer to
me." And they came [1]closer. And he said, "I am your brother
Joseph, whom you [a]sold into Egypt.

20 [a]Gen 37:3; 43:8; 44:30 [b]Gen 37:33; 42:13, 38
21 [a]Gen 42:15, 20
22 [1]Lit *he would*
23 [a]Gen 43:3, 5
25 [a]Gen 43:2
27 [a]Gen 46:19
28 [a]Gen 37:31-35
29 [1]Lit *my face* [2]Lit *evil* [a]Gen 42:38; 44:31
30 [1]Lit *his soul is bound with his soul* [a]1 Sam 18:1
31 [a]Gen 44:29
32 [1]Lit *and I shall have sinned for all the days before my father* [a]Gen 43:9
34 [1]Lit *find*
45:1 [1]Lit *stood* [a]Acts 7:13
2 [1]Lit *gave forth his voice in weeping* [a]Gen 45:14, 15; 46:29
3 [a]Acts 7:13 [b]Gen 43:27 [c]Gen 37:20-28; 42:21, 22
4 [1]Lit *near* [a]Gen 37:28

5 "Now do not be grieved or angry [1]with yourselves, because
[a]you sold me here, for [b]God sent me before you to preserve life.
6 "For the famine *has been* in the land [a]these two years, and
there are still five years in which there will be neither plowing
nor harvesting.
7 "[a]God sent me before you to preserve for you a remnant in
the earth, and to keep you alive by a great [1]deliverance.
8 "Now, therefore, it was not you who sent me here, but God;
and He has made me a [a]father to Pharaoh and lord of all his
household and ruler over all the land of Egypt.
9 "Hurry and go up to my father, and [a]say to him, 'Thus says
your son Joseph, "God has made me lord of all Egypt; come
down to me, do not delay.
10 "You shall [1]live in the land of [a]Goshen, and you shall be near
me, you and your children and your children's children and
your flocks and your herds and all that you have.
11 "There I will also [a]provide for you, for there are still five
years of famine *to come,* and you and your household and all
that you have would be impoverished."'
12 "Behold, your eyes see, and the eyes of my brother
Benjamin *see,* that it is my mouth which is speaking to you.
13 "Now you must tell my father of all my splendor in Egypt,
and all that you have seen; and you must hurry and [a]bring my
father down here."
14 Then he fell on his brother Benjamin's neck and [a]wept, and
Benjamin wept on his neck.
15 He kissed all his brothers and wept on them, and afterward
his brothers talked with him.
16 Now when [a]the [1]news was heard in Pharaoh's house [2]that
Joseph's brothers had come, it [3]pleased Pharaoh and his servants.
17 Then Pharaoh said to Joseph, "Say to your brothers, 'Do
this: load your beasts and [1]go to the land of Canaan,
18 and take your father and your households and come to me,
and [a]I will give you the [1]best of the land of Egypt and you will
eat the fat of the land.'
19 "Now you are ordered, 'Do this: [1]take [a]wagons from the
land of Egypt for your little ones and for your wives, and bring
your father and come.
20 'Do not [1]concern yourselves with your goods, for the [2]best
of all the land of Egypt is yours.'"
21 Then the sons of Israel did so; and Joseph gave them
[a]wagons according to the [1]command of Pharaoh, and gave
them provisions for the journey.
22 To [1]each of them he gave [a]changes of garments, but to
Benjamin he gave three hundred *pieces of* silver and [b]five
changes of garments.
23 To his father he sent [1]as follows: ten donkeys loaded with
the [2]best things of Egypt, and ten female donkeys loaded with
grain and bread and sustenance for his father [3]on the journey.
24 So he sent his brothers away, and [1]as they departed, he
said to them, "Do not [2]quarrel on the journey."

5 [1]Lit *in your eyes* [a]Gen 37:28 [b]Gen 45:7, 8; 50:20; Ps 105:17
6 [a]Gen 37:2; 41:46, 53
7 [1]Lit *escaped company* [a]Gen 45:5
8 [a]Judg 17:10
9 [a]Acts 7:14
10 [1]Lit *dwell* [a]Gen 46:28, 34; 47:1
11 [a]Gen 47:12
13 [a]Acts 7:14
14 [a]Gen 45:2
16 [1]Lit *voice* [2]Lit *saying, "Joseph's brothers have come"* [3]Lit *was good in the eyes of* [a]Acts 7:13
17 [1]Lit *come, go*
18 [1]Lit *good* [a]Gen 27:28
19 [1]Lit *take for yourselves* [a]Gen 45:21, 27; 46:5; Num 7:3-8
20 [1]Lit *let your eye look with regret upon your vessels* [2]Lit *good*
21 [1]Lit *mouth* [a]Gen 45:19
22 [1]Lit *all of them he gave each man* [a]2 Kin 5:5 [b]Gen 43:34
23 [1]Lit *like this* [2]Lit *good* [3]Lit *for*
24 [1]Lit *they departed; and he said* [2]Lit *be agitated*

25 Then they went up from Egypt, and came to the land of Canaan to their father Jacob.

26 They told him, saying, "Joseph is still alive, and indeed he is ruler over all the land of Egypt." But [1]he was stunned, for [a]he did not believe them.

27 When they told him all the words of Joseph that he had spoken to them, and when he saw the [a]wagons that Joseph had sent to carry him, the spirit of their father Jacob revived.

28 Then Israel said, "It is enough; my son Joseph is still alive. I will go and see him before I die."

Chapter 46 Theme ______________________

46 So Israel set out with all that he had, and came to [a]Beersheba, and offered sacrifices to the [b]God of his father Isaac.

2 [a]God spoke to Israel [1]in visions of the night and said, "[b]Jacob, Jacob." And he said, "Here I am."

3 He said, "[a]I am God, the God of your father; do not be afraid to go down to Egypt, for I will [b]make you a great nation there.

4 "[a]I will go down with you to Egypt, and [b]I will also surely bring you up again; and [c]Joseph will [1]close your eyes."

5 Then Jacob arose from Beersheba; and the sons of Israel carried their father Jacob and their little ones and their wives in the [a]wagons which Pharaoh had sent to carry him.

6 They took their livestock and their property, which they had acquired in the land of Canaan, and [a]came to Egypt, Jacob and all his [1]descendants with him:

7 his sons and his grandsons with him, his daughters and his granddaughters, and all his [1]descendants he brought with him to Egypt.

8 Now these are the [a]names of the sons of Israel, Jacob and his sons, who went to Egypt: Reuben, Jacob's firstborn.

9 The sons of Reuben: Hanoch and Pallu and Hezron and Carmi.

10 The [a]sons of Simeon: [1]Jemuel and Jamin and Ohad and [2]Jachin and [3]Zohar and Shaul the son of a Canaanite woman.

11 The sons of Levi: [1]Gershon, Kohath, and Merari.

12 The sons of Judah: Er and Onan and Shelah and Perez and Zerah (but Er and Onan died in the land of Canaan). And the [a]sons of Perez were Hezron and Hamul.

13 The sons of Issachar: Tola and [1]Puvvah and [2]Iob and Shimron.

14 The sons of Zebulun: Sered and Elon and Jahleel.

15 These are the sons of Leah, whom she bore to Jacob in Paddan-aram, with his daughter Dinah; [1]all his sons and his daughters *numbered* thirty-three.

16 The [a]sons of Gad: [1]Ziphion and Haggi, Shuni and [2]Ezbon, Eri and [3]Arodi and Areli.

17 The [a]sons of Asher: Imnah and Ishvah and Ishvi and Beriah and their sister Serah. And the [b]sons of Beriah: Heber and Malchiel.

26 [1]Lit *his heart grew numb* [a]Gen 37:31-35

27 [a]Gen 45:19

46:1 [a]Gen 21:31; 28:10 [b]Gen 26:24; 28:13; 31:42

2 [1]Lit *in the visions* [a]Gen 15:1; Num 12:6; Job 33:14, 15 [b]Gen 22:11; 31:11

3 [a]Gen 17:1; 28:13 [b]Gen 12:2; Ex 1:9; Deut 26:5

4 [1]Lit *put his hand on* [a]Gen 28:15; 48:21 [b]Gen 50:24; Ex 3:8 [c]Gen 50:1

5 [a]Gen 45:21

6 [1]Lit *seed* [a]Deut 26:5; Josh 24:4; Ps 105:23; Is 52:4; Acts 7:15

7 [1]Lit *seed*

8 [a]Ex 1:1-4; Num 26:4, 5; 1 Chr 2:1ff

10 [1]In Num 26:12 and 1 Chr 4:24, *Nemuel* [2]In 1 Chr 4:24, *Jarib* [3]In Num 26:13 and 1 Chr 4:24, *Zerah* [a]Ex 6:15

11 [1]In 1 Chr 6:16, *Gershom*

12 [a]1 Chr 2:5

13 [1]In Num 26:23, *Puvah;* in 1 Chr 7:1, *Puah* [2]In Num 26:24 and 1 Chr 7:1, *Jashub*

15 [1]Lit *all the souls of*

16 [1]In Num 26:15, *Zephon* [2]In Num 26:16, *Ozni* [3]In Num 26:17, *Arod* [a]Num 26:15-18

17 [a]1 Chr 7:30 [b]1 Chr 7:31

18 These are the sons of Zilpah, whom Laban gave to his
daughter Leah; and she bore to Jacob these sixteen persons.
19 The sons of Jacob's wife Rachel: Joseph and Benjamin.
20 [a]Now to Joseph in the land of Egypt were born Manasseh
and Ephraim, whom Asenath, the daughter of Potiphera, priest
of On, bore to him.
21 The [a]sons of Benjamin: Bela and Becher and Ashbel, Gera
and Naaman, [1]Ehi and Rosh, [2]Muppim and [3]Huppim and Ard.
22 These are the sons of Rachel, who were born to Jacob;
there were fourteen persons in all.
23 The sons of Dan: [1]Hushim.
24 The sons of Naphtali: [1]Jahzeel and Guni and Jezer and
[2]Shillem.
25 These are the [a]sons of Bilhah, whom [b]Laban gave to his
daughter Rachel, and she bore these to Jacob; *there were* seven
persons in all.
26 [a]All the persons belonging to Jacob, who came to Egypt,
[1]his direct descendants, not including the wives of Jacob's sons,
were sixty-six persons in all,
27 and the sons of Joseph, who were born to him in Egypt
were [1]two; [a]all the persons of the house of Jacob, who came to
Egypt, *were* seventy.
28 Now he sent Judah before him to Joseph, to point out *the way*
before him to [a]Goshen; and they came into the land of Goshen.
29 Joseph [1]prepared his chariot and went up to Goshen to
meet his father Israel; as soon as he appeared [2]before him, he
fell on his neck and [a]wept on his neck a long time.
30 Then Israel said to Joseph, "Now let me die, since I have
seen your face, that you are still alive."
31 Joseph said to his brothers and to his father's household,
"[a]I will go up and tell Pharaoh, and will say to him, 'My
brothers and my father's household, who *were* in the land of
Canaan, have come to me;
32 and the men are shepherds, for they have been [1]keepers of
livestock; and they have brought their flocks and their herds
and all that they have.'
33 "When Pharaoh calls you and says, '[a]What is your occupation?'
34 you shall say, 'Your servants have been [1a]keepers of
livestock from our youth even until now, both we and our
fathers,' that you may [2]live in the land of [b]Goshen; for every
shepherd is [3c]loathsome to the Egyptians."

Chapter 47 Theme ______________________

47 Then [a]Joseph went in and told Pharaoh, and said, "My
father and my brothers and their flocks and their herds
and all that they have, have come out of the land of Canaan;
and behold, they are in the land of [b]Goshen."
2 He took five men from among his brothers and [a]presented
them to Pharaoh.
3 Then Pharaoh said to his brothers, "[a]What is your

20 [a]Gen 41:50-52
21 [1]In Num 26:38, *Ahiram* [2]In Num 26:39, *Shephupham;* in 1 Chr 7:12, *Shuppim* [3]In Num 26:39, *Hupham* [a]1 Chr 7:6
23 [1]In Num 26:42, *Shuham*
24 [1]In 1 Chr 7:13, *Jahziel* [2]In 1 Chr 7:13, *Shallum*
25 [a]Gen 30:5, 7 [b]Gen 29:29
26 [1]Lit *who came out of his loins* [a]Ex 1:5
27 [1]Lit *two souls* [a]Ex 1:5; Deut 10:22; Acts 7:14
28 [a]Gen 45:10
29 [1]Lit *tied, harnessed* [2]Lit *to* [a]Gen 45:14, 15
31 [a]Gen 47:1
32 [1]Lit *men*
33 [a]Gen 47:2, 3
34 [1]Lit *men* [2]Lit *dwell* [3]Lit *an abomination* [a]Gen 13:7, 8; 26:20; 37:2 [b]Gen 45:10, 18; 47:6, 11 [c]Gen 43:32; Ex 8:26
47:1 [a]Gen 46:31 [b]Gen 45:10; 46:28
2 [a]Acts 7:13
3 [a]Gen 46:33

occupation?" So they said to Pharaoh, "Your servants are
[b]shepherds, both we and our fathers."
4 They said to Pharaoh, "[a]We have come to sojourn in the
land, for there is no pasture for your servants' flocks, for [b]the
famine is severe in the land of Canaan. Now, therefore, please
let your servants [1c]live in the land of Goshen."
5 Then Pharaoh said to [1]Joseph, "Your father and your
brothers have come to you.
6 "The land of Egypt is [1]at your disposal; [2]settle your father
and your brothers in [a]the best of the land, let them [3]live in the
land of Goshen; and if you know any [b]capable men among
them, then [4]put them in charge of my livestock."
7 Then Joseph brought his father Jacob and [1]presented him
to Pharaoh; and Jacob [a]blessed Pharaoh.
8 Pharaoh said to Jacob, "How many [1]years have you lived?"
9 So Jacob said to Pharaoh, "The [1a]years of my sojourning are
one hundred and [2]thirty; few and [3]unpleasant have been the
[1]years of my life, nor have they [4]attained [b]the [1]years [5]that my
fathers lived during the days of their sojourning."
10 And Jacob [a]blessed Pharaoh, and went out from [1]his
presence.
11 So Joseph [1]settled his father and his brothers and gave
them a possession in the land of Egypt, in [a]the best of the land,
in the land of [b]Rameses, as Pharaoh had ordered.
12 Joseph [a]provided his father and his brothers and all his
father's household with [1]food, according to their little ones.
13 Now there was no [1]food in all the land, because the famine
was very severe, so that [a]the land of Egypt and the land of
Canaan languished because of the famine.
14 [a]Joseph gathered all the money that was found in the land
of Egypt and in the land of Canaan for the grain which they
bought, and Joseph brought the money into Pharaoh's house.
15 When the money was all spent in the land of Egypt and in
the land of Canaan, all the Egyptians came to Joseph [1]and said,
"Give us [2]food, for [a]why should we die in your presence? For
our money [3]is gone."
16 Then Joseph said, "Give up your livestock, and I will give
you *food* for your livestock, since *your* money [1]is gone."
17 So they brought their livestock to Joseph, and Joseph gave
them [1]food in exchange for the horses and the [2]flocks and the
herds and the donkeys; and he [3]fed them with [1]food in
exchange for all their livestock [4]that year.
18 When that year was ended, they came to him the [1]next
year and said to him, "We will not hide from my lord that our
money is all spent, and the [2]cattle are my lord's. There is nothing
left [3]for my lord except our bodies and our lands.
19 "Why should we die before your eyes, both we and our
land? Buy us and our land for [1]food, and we and our land will
be slaves to Pharaoh. So give us seed, that we may live and not
die, and that the land may not be desolate."
20 So Joseph bought all the land of Egypt for Pharaoh, for

3 [b]Gen 46:34

4 [1]Lit *dwell* [a]Gen 15:13; Deut 26:5; Ps 105:23 [b]Gen 43:1; Acts 7:11 [c]Gen 46:34

5 [1]Lit *Joseph, saying*

6 [1]Lit *before you* [2]Lit *cause them to dwell* [3]Lit *dwell* [4]Lit *appoint them rulers* [a]Gen 45:10, 18; 47:11 [b]Ex 18:21, 25; 1 Kin 11:28; Prov 22:29

7 [1]Lit *set him before* [a]Gen 47:10; 2 Sam 14:22; 1 Kin 8:66

8 [1]Lit *are the days of the years of your life*

9 [1]Lit *days of the years* [2]Lit *thirty years* [3]Lit *evil* [4]Lit *reached* [5]Lit *of the life of my fathers* [a]Heb 11:9, 13 [b]Gen 25:7; 35:28

10 [1]Lit *Pharaoh's* [a]Gen 47:7

11 [1]Lit *caused to dwell* [a]Gen 47:6, 27 [b]Ex 1:11; 12:37

12 [1]Or *bread* [a]Gen 45:11

13 [1]Or *bread* [a]Gen 41:30; Acts 7:11

14 [a]Gen 41:56

15 [1]Lit *saying* [2]Or *bread* [3]Lit *ceases* [a]Gen 47:19

16 [1]Lit *ceases*

17 [1]Or *bread* [2]Lit *livestock of the flocks and livestock of the herds* [3]Lit *led them as a shepherd* [4]Lit *in that year*

18 [1]Lit *second* [2]Lit *livestock of the cattle* [3]Lit *in the presence of*

19 [1]Or *bread*

[1]every Egyptian sold his field, because the famine was severe
upon them. Thus the land became Pharaoh's.
21 As for the people, he removed them to the cities from one
end of Egypt's border to the other.
22 Only the land of the priests he did not buy, for the priests
had an allotment from Pharaoh, and they [1]lived off the allotment
which Pharaoh gave them. Therefore, they did not sell their
land.
23 Then Joseph said to the people, "Behold, I have today
bought you and your land for Pharaoh; now, *here* is seed for
you, and you may sow the land.
24 "[1]At the harvest you shall give a [a]fifth to Pharaoh, and [2]four-
fifths shall be your own for seed of the field and for your food and
for those of your households and as food for your little ones."
25 So they said, "You have saved our lives! Let us find favor in
the sight of my lord, and we will be Pharaoh's slaves."
26 Joseph made it a statute concerning the land of Egypt *valid*
to this day, that Pharaoh should have the fifth; [a]only the land of
the priests [1]did not become Pharaoh's.
27 Now Israel [1]lived in the land of Egypt, in [2]Goshen, and
they [a]acquired property in it and [b]were fruitful and became
very numerous.
28 Jacob lived in the land of Egypt [a]seventeen years; so the
[1]length of Jacob's life was one hundred and forty-seven years.
29 When [1a]the time for Israel to die drew near, he called his son
Joseph and said to him, "Please, if I have found favor in your
sight, [b]place now your hand under my thigh and [c]deal with me
in kindness and [2]faithfulness. Please do not bury me in Egypt,
30 but when I [a]lie down with my fathers, you shall carry me
out of Egypt and bury me in [b]their burial place." And he said,
"I will do as you have said."
31 He said, "[a]Swear to me." So he swore to him. Then [b]Israel
bowed *in worship* at the head of the bed.

Chapter 48 Theme ______________________________

48 Now it came about after these things that [1]Joseph was
told, "Behold, your father is sick." So he took his two
sons [a]Manasseh and Ephraim with him.
2 When [1]it was told to Jacob, "Behold, your son Joseph has
come to you," Israel [2]collected his strength and sat [3]up in the
bed.
3 Then Jacob said to Joseph, "[1a]God Almighty appeared to
me at [b]Luz in the land of Canaan and blessed me,
4 and He said to me, 'Behold, I will make you fruitful and
numerous, and I will make you a company of peoples, and will
give this land to your [1]descendants after you for [a]an everlasting
possession.'
5 "Now your two sons, who were born to you in the land of
Egypt before I came to you in Egypt, are mine; [a]Ephraim and
Manasseh shall be mine, as [b]Reuben and Simeon are.

20 [1]Lit *Egypt, every man*

22 [1]Lit *ate their allotment*

24 [1]Lit *It shall come about . . . that you shall* [2]Lit *four parts* [a]Gen 41:34

26 [1]Lit *alone did* [a]Gen 47:22

27 [1]Lit *dwelt* [2]Lit *in the land of Goshen* [a]Gen 47:11 [b]Gen 17:6; 26:4; 35:11; Ex 1:7; Deut 26:5; Acts 7:17

28 [1]Lit *days of Jacob, the years of his life* [a]Gen 47:9

29 [1]Lit *the days of Israel to die drew near* [2]Lit *truth* [a]Deut 31:14; 1 Kin 2:1 [b]Gen 24:2 [c]Gen 24:49

30 [a]Gen 15:15; Deut 31:16 [b]Gen 23:17-20; 25:9, 10; 35:29; 49:29-32; 50:5, 13; Acts 7:15, 16

31 [a]Gen 21:23, 24; 24:3; 31:53; 50:25 [b]1 Kin 1:47

48:1 [1]Lit *one said to Joseph* [a]Gen 41:51, 52; Josh 14:4

2 [1]Lit *one told Jacob and said* [2]Lit *strengthened himself* [3]Lit *upon the bed*

3 [1]Heb *El Shaddai* [a]Gen 28:13f; 35:9-12 [b]Gen 28:19; 35:6

4 [1]Lit *seed* [a]Gen 17:8

5 [a]Gen 41:50-52; 46:20; 48:1; Josh 14:4 [b]1 Chr 5:1, 2

6 "But your offspring that [1]have been born after them shall be
yours; they shall be called by the [2]names of their brothers in
their inheritance.
7 "Now as for me, when I came from [a]Paddan, [b]Rachel died,
[1]to my sorrow, in the land of Canaan on the journey, when
there was still some distance to go to Ephrath; and I buried her
there on the way to Ephrath (that is, Bethlehem)."
8 When Israel [a]saw Joseph's sons, he said, "Who are these?"
9 Joseph said to his father, "[a]They are my sons, whom God
has given me here." So he said, "Bring them to me, please,
that [b]I may bless them."
10 Now [a]the eyes of Israel were *so* dim from age *that* he could
not see. Then [1]Joseph brought them close to him, and he
[b]kissed them and embraced them.
11 Israel said to Joseph, "I never [1]expected to see your face,
and behold, God has let me see your [2]children as well."
12 Then Joseph [1]took them from his knees, and [a]bowed with
his face to the ground.
13 Joseph took them both, Ephraim with his right hand
toward Israel's left, and Manasseh with his left hand toward
Israel's right, and brought them close to him.
14 But Israel stretched out his right hand and laid it on the
head of Ephraim, who was the younger, and his left hand on
Manasseh's head, [1]crossing his hands, [2]although [a]Manasseh
was the firstborn.
15 He blessed Joseph, and said,
"[a]The God before whom my fathers Abraham and
Isaac walked,
[b]The God who has been my shepherd [1]all my life to this day,
16 [a]The angel who has redeemed me from all evil,
[b]Bless the lads;
And may my name [1]live on in them,
And the [2]names of my fathers Abraham and Isaac;
And [c]may they grow into a multitude in the midst of
the earth."
17 When Joseph saw that his father [a]laid his right hand on
Ephraim's head, it displeased him; and he grasped his father's
hand to remove it from Ephraim's head to Manasseh's head.
18 Joseph said to his father, "Not so, my father, for this one is
the firstborn. Place your right hand on his head."
19 But his father refused and said, "I know, my son, I know; he
also will become a people and he also will be great. However,
his younger brother shall be greater than he, and [a]his
[1]descendants shall become a [2]multitude of nations."
20 [a]He blessed them that day, saying,
"By you Israel will pronounce blessing, saying,
'May God make you like Ephraim and Manasseh!'"
Thus he put Ephraim before Manasseh.
21 Then Israel said to Joseph, "Behold, I am about to die, but
[a]God will be with you, and [b]bring you back to the land of your
fathers.

6 [1]Lit *you have begotten* [2]Lit *name*

7 [1]Lit *upon me* [a]Gen 33:18 [b]Gen 35:19, 20

8 [a]Gen 48:10

9 [a]Gen 33:5 [b]Gen 27:4

10 [1]Lit *he* [a]Gen 27:1 [b]Gen 27:27

11 [1]Lit *meditated, judged* [2]Lit *seed*

12 [1]Lit *made them come out* [a]Gen 42:6

14 [1]Or *consciously directing* [2]Lit *when* [a]Gen 41:51, 52

15 [1]Lit *from the continuance of me* [a]Gen 17:1 [b]Gen 49:24

16 [1]Lit *be called* [2]Lit *name* [a]Gen 22:11, 15-18; 28:13-15; 31:11 [b]Heb 11:21 [c]Gen 28:14; 46:3

17 [a]Gen 48:14

19 [1]Lit *seed* [2]Lit *fullness* [a]Gen 28:14; 46:3

20 [a]Heb 11:21

21 [a]Gen 26:3 [b]Gen 28:15; 46:4; 50:24

22 "I give you one [1]portion more than your brothers, [a]which I took from the hand of the Amorite with my sword and my bow."

22 [1]Or *ridge;* lit *shoulder;* Heb *Shechem* [a]Josh 24:32; John 4:5

Chapter 49 Theme ______________________

49 Then Jacob summoned his sons and said, "Assemble
yourselves that I may tell you what will befall you [a]in
the [1]days to come.
2 "Gather together and hear, O sons of Jacob;
And [a]listen to Israel your father.

3 "Reuben, you are my firstborn;
My might and [a]the beginning of my strength,
[1]Preeminent in dignity and [1]preeminent in power.
4 "[1]Uncontrolled as water, you shall not have preeminence,
[a]Because you went up to your father's bed;
Then you defiled *it*—he went up to my couch.

5 "[a]Simeon and Levi are brothers;
Their swords are implements of violence.
6 "[a]Let my soul not enter into their council;
Let not my glory be united with their assembly;
Because in their anger they slew [1]men,
And in their self-will they lamed [2]oxen.
7 "Cursed be their anger, for it is fierce;
And their wrath, for it is cruel.
[a]I will [1]disperse them in Jacob,
And scatter them in Israel.

8 "Judah, your brothers shall praise you;
Your hand shall be on the neck of your enemies;
[a]Your father's sons shall bow down to you.
9 "Judah is a [a]lion's whelp;
From the prey, my son, you have gone up.
[b]He [1]couches, he lies down as a lion,
And as a [2]lion, who [3]dares rouse him up?
10 "[a]The scepter shall not depart from Judah,
Nor the ruler's staff from between his feet,
[1]Until Shiloh comes,
And [b]to him *shall be* the obedience of the peoples.
11 "[1a]He ties *his* foal to the vine,
And his donkey's colt to the choice vine;
[b]He washes his garments in wine,
And his robes in the blood of grapes.
12 "His eyes are [1]dull from wine,
And his teeth [2]white from milk.

13 "[a]Zebulun will dwell at the seashore;
And he *shall be* [1]a haven for ships,
And his flank *shall be* toward Sidon.

49:1 [1]Lit *end of the days* [a]Num 24:14
2 [a]Ps 34:11
3 [1]Lit *preeminence* [a]Deut 21:17; Ps 78:51; 105:36
4 [1]Or *Boiling over;* lit *Recklessness* [a]Gen 35:22; Deut 27:20; 1 Chr 5:1
5 [a]Gen 34:25-30
6 [1]Lit *a man* [2]Lit *an ox* [a]Ps 64:2
7 [1]Lit *divide* [a]Josh 19:1, 9; 21:1-42
8 [a]Gen 27:29; 1 Chr 5:2
9 [1]Lit *bows down* [2]Or *lioness* [3]Lit *shall* [a]Ezek 19:5-7; Mic 5:8 [b]Num 24:9
10 [1]Or *Until he comes to Shiloh;* or *Until he comes to whom it belongs* [a]Num 24:17; Ps 60:7; 108:8 [b]Ps 2:6-9; 72:8-11; Is 42:1, 4; 49:6
11 [1]Lit *Binding of* [a]Deut 8:7, 8; 2 Kin 18:32 [b]Is 63:2
12 [1]Or *darker than* [2]Or *whiter than*
13 [1]Lit *for a shore of ships* [a]Deut 33:18, 19

14 "Issachar is [1]a strong donkey,
[a]Lying down between the [2]sheepfolds.
15 "When he saw that a resting place was good
And that the land was pleasant,
He bowed his shoulder to bear *burdens,*
And became a slave at forced labor.

16 "[a]Dan shall [b]judge his people,
As one of the tribes of Israel.
17 "Dan shall be a serpent in the way,
A horned snake in the path,
That bites the horse's heels,
So that his rider falls backward.
18 "[a]For Your salvation I wait, O LORD.

19 "[a]As for Gad, [1]raiders shall raid him,
But he will raid *at* their [2]heels.

20 "[1a]As for [b]Asher, his [2]food shall be [3]rich,
And he will yield royal dainties.

21 "[a]Naphtali is a doe let loose,
He gives beautiful words.

22 "[a]Joseph is a fruitful [1]bough,
A fruitful [1]bough by a spring;
Its [2]branches run over a wall.
23 "The archers bitterly attacked him,
And shot *at him* and harassed him;
24 But his [a]bow remained [1]firm,
And [2b]his arms were agile,
From the hands of the [c]Mighty One of Jacob
(From there is [d]the Shepherd, [e]the Stone of Israel),
25 From [a]the God of your father who helps you,
And [1b]by the [2]Almighty who blesses you
With [c]blessings of heaven above,
Blessings of the deep that lies beneath,
Blessings of the breasts and of the womb.
26 "The blessings of your father
Have surpassed the blessings of my ancestors
Up to the [1]utmost bound of [a]the everlasting hills;
May they be on the head of Joseph,
And on the crown of the head of the one distinguished
among his brothers.

27 "Benjamin is a [1]ravenous wolf;
In the morning he devours the prey,
And in the evening he divides the spoil."

28 All these are the twelve tribes of Israel, and this is what
their father said to them [1]when he blessed them. He blessed
them, every one [2]with the blessing appropriate to him.

14 [1]Lit *a donkey of bone* [2]Or *saddlebags* [a]Judg 5:16; Ps 68:13

16 [a]Deut 33:22; Judg 18:26, 27 [b]Gen 30:6

18 [a]Ex 15:2; Ps 25:5; 40:1-3; 119:166, 174; Is 25:9; Mic 7:7

19 [1]Lit *a raiding band* [2]Lit *heel* [a]Deut 33:20

20 [1]Lit *From* [2]Or *bread* [3]Lit *fat* [a]Deut 33:24, 25 [b]Gen 30:13

21 [a]Deut 33:23

22 [1]Lit *son* [2]Lit *daughters* [a]Deut 33:13-17

24 [1]I.e. in an unyielding position [2]Lit *the arms of his hands* [a]Job 29:20 [b]Ps 18:34; 73:23; Is 41:10 [c]Ps 132:2, 5; Is 1:24; 49:26 [d]Ps 23:1; 80:1 [e]Ps 118:22; Is 28:16; 1 Pet 2:6-8

25 [1]Or *with* [2]Heb *Shaddai* [a]Gen 28:13; 32:9 [b]Gen 28:3; 48:3 [c]Gen 27:28

26 [1]Lit *limit;* or *desire* [a]Deut 33:15, 16

27 [1]Lit *a wolf that tears*

28 [1]Lit *and* [2]Lit *according to his blessing*

29 Then he charged them and said to them, "I am about to be
[a]gathered to my people; [b]bury me with my fathers in the cave
that is in [c]the field of Ephron the Hittite,
30 in the [a]cave that is in the field of Machpelah, which is
before Mamre, in the land of Canaan, which Abraham bought
along with the field from Ephron the Hittite for a [1]burial site.
31 "There they buried [a]Abraham and his wife [b]Sarah, there
they buried [c]Isaac and his wife Rebekah, and there I buried
Leah—
32 the field and the cave that is in it, purchased from the sons
of Heth."
33 When Jacob finished charging his sons, he drew his feet
into the bed and [a]breathed his last, and was [b]gathered to his
people.

Chapter 50 Theme ____________________

50 Then Joseph fell on his father's face, and wept over him
and kissed him.
2 Joseph commanded his servants the physicians to embalm
his father. So the physicians [a]embalmed Israel.
3 Now forty days were [1]required for [2]it, for [3]such is the
period required for embalming. And the Egyptians [a]wept for
him seventy days.
4 When the days of [1]mourning for him were past, Joseph spoke
to the household of Pharaoh, saying, "If now I have found favor
in your sight, please speak [2]to Pharaoh, saying,
5 '[a]My father made me swear, saying, "Behold, I am about to
die; in my grave [b]which I dug for myself in the land of Canaan,
there you shall bury me." Now therefore, please let me go up
and bury my father; then I will return.'"
6 Pharaoh said, "Go up and bury your father, as he made you
swear."
7 So Joseph went up to bury his father, and with him went
up all the servants of Pharaoh, the elders of his household and
all the elders of the land of Egypt,
8 and all the household of Joseph and his brothers and his
father's household; they left only their little ones and their
flocks and their herds in the land of Goshen.
9 There also went up with him both chariots and horsemen;
and it was a very great company.
10 When they came to the [1]threshing floor of Atad, which is
beyond the Jordan, they [a]lamented there with a very great and
[2]sorrowful lamentation; and he [3]observed seven days mourning
for his father.
11 Now when the inhabitants of the land, the Canaanites, saw
the mourning at [1]the threshing floor of Atad, they said, "This is
a [2]grievous [3]mourning for the Egyptians." Therefore it was
named [4]Abel-mizraim, which is beyond the Jordan.
12 Thus his sons did for him as he had charged them;
13 for his sons carried him to the land of Canaan and buried

29 [a]Gen 25:8 [b]Gen 47:30 [c]Gen 23:16-20; 50:13

30 [1]Lit *possession of a burial place* [a]Gen 23:3-20

31 [a]Gen 25:9 [b]Gen 23:19 [c]Gen 35:29

33 [a]Gen 25:8; Acts 7:15 [b]Gen 49:29

50:2 [a]Gen 50:26; 2 Chr 16:14; Matt 26:12; Mark 16:1; John 19:39, 40

3 [1]Lit *fulfilled* [2]Or *him* [3]Lit *so are fulfilled the days of embalming* [a]Gen 50:10; Num 20:29; Deut 34:8

4 [1]Lit *weeping* [2]Lit *In the ears of*

5 [a]Gen 47:29-31 [b]2 Chr 16:14; Is 22:16; Matt 27:60

10 [1]Heb *Goren ha-Atad* [2]Lit *heavy* [3]Lit *made a mourning for seven days* [a]Acts 8:2

11 [1]Heb *Goren ha-Atad* [2]Lit *heavy* [3]Heb *ebel* [4]I.e. the meadow (or mourning) of Egypt

him in [a]the cave of the field of Machpelah before Mamre,
which Abraham had bought along with the field for a [1]burial
site from Ephron the Hittite.
14 After he had buried his father, Joseph returned to Egypt, he
and his brothers, and all who had gone up with him to bury his
father.
15 When Joseph's brothers saw that their father was dead,
they said, "[a]What if Joseph bears a grudge against us and pays
us back in full for all the wrong which we did to him!"
16 So they [1]sent *a message* to Joseph, saying, "Your father
charged before he died, saying,
17 'Thus you shall say to Joseph, "Please forgive, I beg you, the
transgression of your brothers and their sin, for they did you
wrong."' And now, please forgive the transgression of the
servants of the God of your father." And Joseph wept when
they spoke to him.
18 Then his brothers also came and [a]fell down before him and
said, "Behold, we are your servants."
19 But Joseph said to them, "Do not be afraid, for am I in
God's place?
20 "As for you, [a]you meant evil against me, *but* God meant it
for good in order to bring about [1]this present result, to preserve
many people alive.
21 "So therefore, do not be afraid; [a]I will provide for you and
your little ones." So he comforted them and spoke [1]kindly to
them.
22 Now Joseph stayed in Egypt, he and his father's household,
and Joseph lived one hundred and ten years.
23 Joseph saw the third generation of Ephraim's sons; also the
sons of Machir, the son of Manasseh, were [a]born on Joseph's
knees.
24 Joseph said to his brothers, "[a]I am about to die, but God
will surely [1]take care of you and bring you up from this land to
the land which He [2]promised on oath to [b]Abraham, to [c]Isaac
and to [d]Jacob."
25 Then Joseph made the sons of Israel swear, saying, "God
will surely [1]take care of you, and [a]you shall carry my bones up
from here."
26 So Joseph died at the age of one hundred and ten years;
and [1]he was [a]embalmed and placed in a coffin in Egypt.

13 [1]Lit *possession of a burial place* [a]Gen 23:16-20; Acts 7:16

15 [a]Gen 37:28; 42:21, 22

16 [1]Lit *commanded*

18 [a]Gen 37:8-10; 41:43

20 [1]Lit *as it is this day* [a]Gen 37:26, 27; 45:5, 7

21 [1]Lit *to their heart* [a]Gen 45:11; 47:12

23 [a]Gen 30:3

24 [1]Or *visit* [2]Lit *swore* [a]Gen 48:21; Ex 3:16, 17; Heb 11:22 [b]Gen 13:15, 17; 15:7, 8, 18 [c]Gen 26:3 [d]Gen 28:13; 35:12

25 [1]Or *visit* [a]Gen 47:29, 30; Ex 13:19; Josh 24:32; Heb 11:22

26 [1]Lit *they embalmed him* [a]Gen 50:2

Genesis at a Glance

Theme of Genesis:

Author:	Segment Divisions					Chapter Themes
Moses (Luke 24:27)		The Firsts		4 Main Events/4 Characters	Time Spans	
Date:		Man	Beginnings of Man		Approximately 2080 Years	1
		Marriage				2
Purpose:						3
						4
						5
Key Words: (include synonyms)						6
God said (or commanded)						7
						8
the generations of						9
covenant (oath)						10
altar						11
land (when it refers to the land promised to Abraham, Isaac, and Jacob)			Beginnings of Israel *(continued next page)*		Approximately 300 Years *(continued next page)*	12
						13
						14
circumcised						15
Abram (or Abraham)						16
						17
bless (blessed, blessing)						18
sin (do evil, act wicked)						19
						20
dream						21
died						22
						23
						24
						25

SEGMENT DIVISIONS

	THE FIRSTS		4 CHARACTERS	TIME SPANS	CHAPTER THEMES
		BEGINNINGS OF ISRAEL		APPROXIMATELY 300 YEARS	26
					27
					28
					29
					30
					31
					32
					33
					34
					35
					36
					37
					38
					39
					40
					41
					42
					43
					44
					45
					46
					47
					48
					49
					50

EXODUS שמות
SHMOT

When Jacob and his family, a relatively small group, went into Egypt, they were welcomed and honored because they were relatives of Joseph. Four hundred and thirty years later the children of Israel were Egypt's slaves, a people so numerous it frightened the Egyptians.

The Israelites were God's covenant people, different from all the nations, a people of His own choosing. And because God is a covenant-keeping God, He could not leave Jacob's people in Egypt—they had to be redeemed by the blood of a lamb, a Passover lamb.

Things to Do

General Instructions

1. As Genesis comes to a close, the children of Israel are living in Egypt rather than in Canaan, the land of promise. The book that began with the creation of man in Eden ends with the children of Israel looking into a coffin in Egypt—but not without a promise that someday they would leave Egypt. Read Genesis 50:22-26 and Exodus 1:1-7 and notice how the book of Exodus relates chronologically to the book of Genesis.

2. Exodus can be divided into three segments according to the location of the children of Israel. In Exodus 1 through 12 they are in Egypt. In Exodus 13 through 18 they journey to Sinai, and then in Exodus 19 through 40 they camp at Sinai. Record this information on the EXODUS AT A GLANCE chart on pages 159, 160 on the first line for segment divisions. This division will be the basis of some of your instructions.

3. Read through Exodus one chapter at a time. As you read do the following:

   a. Remember that you are reading a historical account. As you read, ask the "5 W's and an H": Who? What? When? Where? Why? and How? Ask questions such as: Who are the main characters in this chapter? What is happening? When and where is it happening? What were the consequences of their actions? How and why did this occur?

   b. Mark key repeated words. Although a list of the key words for Exodus is recorded on EXODUS AT A GLANCE, remember that other words will be predominant in specific chapters. Don't miss these. Write the key words on an index card and use it as a bookmark.

   c. List insights you glean from the repeated use of a key word.

   d. Mark references to time with a clock. Geographical locations are very important in the Old Testament. Do not forget to double-underline them in green.

   e. List the main points or events covered in a particular chapter or group of chapters. This will give you a concise analysis of the content of the chapter.

   For example, Exodus 2 gives an account of Moses from his birth to the birth of his first son. In the margin you could list the major events in this chapter: Moses' birth, Moses' adoption by Pharaoh's daughter, Moses kills Egyptian, Moses flees to Midian, etc.

4. When you finish reading a chapter, record the main theme or subject of the chapter on EXODUS AT A GLANCE under "Chapter Themes." Also record it in your Bible at the beginning of the chapter.

Chapters 1–12

1. As you study these chapters, add *Pharaoh, heart, staff,* and *sign (miracle)* to your list of key words. Mark these words and their synonyms in a distinctive way.

2. You can gain insights into God's character, power, and dealings with mankind from these chapters. As you read each chapter, in the margin note what you learn about God. You may want to put a distinguishing mark such as this △ in the margin and then color it yellow so you can easily recognize it.

3. There are lessons to be learned from Moses' life in these chapters. Record these lessons on the chart on pages 351, 352.

4. As you read chapters 7 through 12, in the margin of your Bible list the plagues as they appear in the text, numbering each one in the order in which they appear.

5. When you come to Exodus 12, mark *Passover lamb.* Then list what you learn by asking the "5 W's and an H."

Chapters 13–18

1. As you read:

   a. Watch for the key words, including those you marked in the first segment. Add *first-born, test,* and *grumble*, along with their synonyms. In the margin note what the tests were and why the people grumbled. Also continue your list of insights on Pharaoh and on Moses' staff.

   b. Mark references to time with a symbol and note where events occur. Locate these places on the map on page 94.

2. Note what God is called in 15:26 and 17:15 and the circumstances in which these names are revealed.

3. In chapter 16, mark *bread* and *manna.* Make a list of all you learn from the text about manna and why it was given. When you finish you might compare this with Deuteronomy 8:1-3. Add *sabbath (seventh day)* to your list of key words.

4. In chapter 17 note the conditions under which Moses strikes the rock. Compare this with 1 Corinthians 10:1-4 and John 7:37-39.

Chapters 19–40

1. In chapters 19 through 24 God gives Moses the law. Watch for and mark key words.

   a. Chapter 20 presents the ten commandments. Number these within the text.

   b. In chapters 21–23, list the various ordinances in the margin for easy reference. Note what is to be done if these are violated.

   c. Chapter 24 is very important because it deals with the inauguration of the law, the old covenant. In the margin note the circumstances and procedure connected with its inauguration and how the people respond.

2. In chapters 25 through 31 God gives the pattern for the tabernacle and all that is necessary for the priests.

   a. Note in the margin the main points of these chapters.

   b. Watch for other key words that are predominant in specific chapters. Mark them.

   c. In chapter 31 list everything you learn about the sabbath from the text. Compare Exodus 35:1-3 with Numbers 15:32-36.

3. Chapters 32–34 are very significant. Mark every reference to the *calf (god).*

   a. Note how Moses deals with this situation and record insights on the chart on pages 351, 352.

   b. Read 2 Corinthians 3:12-18 for additional insights regarding the veil over Moses' face.

4. Chapters 35 through 40 are an account of the construction of the tabernacle and the making of the priests' garments. As you read, highlight or mark in a distinguishable way the first reference to each piece of furniture.

5. After you have recorded all the chapter themes on EXODUS AT A GLANCE, see if any of the chapters can be grouped according to main events. Record these segment divisions on the appropriate line next to the chapter themes. Then record the theme of Exodus on the chart.

Things to Think About

1. Daniel 11:32b says, "The people who know their God will display strength and take action." What have you learned about God, His character, and His ways? What have you seen of His power and sovereignty? When we speak of God as being sovereign, we mean He rules over all. How do you see God's sovereignty and power manifested in Exodus? Meditate on what you have learned and then make it a matter of prayer and application.

2. Since the Bible is a progressive revelation of truth, keep in mind what you have observed about redemption and the Passover. These are Old Testament pictures of the salvation to be offered through the Lord Jesus Christ; therefore, they are pictures of truths to be applied to your life (1 Corinthians 5:6-8). Are you a slave to sin? Jesus Christ has provided for your redemption from sin through His blood. Have you been redeemed?

3. What have you learned from Moses' life and his example as a leader? How did he deal with difficult situations and people? What was his overriding passion? What did you learn about Moses' relationship with God that you can apply to your own life today?

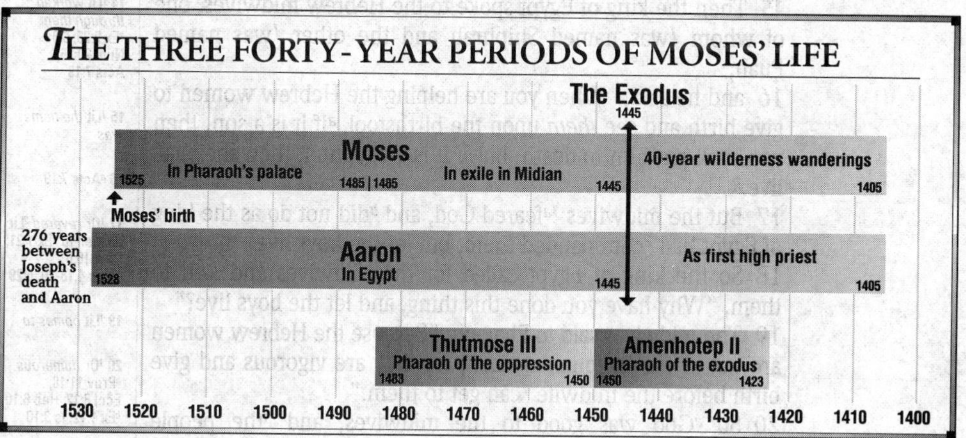

1:1 [1]Lit *and* [a]Gen 46:8-27

Chapter 1 Theme ____________________

1 Now these are the [a]names of the sons of Israel who came to Egypt with Jacob; they came each one [1]with his household:
2 Reuben, Simeon, Levi and Judah;
3 Issachar, Zebulun and Benjamin;
4 Dan and Naphtali, Gad and Asher.
5 All the [1]persons who came from the loins of Jacob were [a]seventy [2]in number, but Joseph was *already* in Egypt.

5 [1]Lit *souls* [2]Lit *as to souls* [a]Gen 46:26, 27; Deut 10:22

6 [a]Joseph died, and all his brothers and all that generation.
7 But the sons of Israel [a]were fruitful and [1]increased greatly,
and multiplied, and became exceedingly [2]mighty, so that the land
was filled with them.
8 Now a new [a]king arose over Egypt, who did not know
Joseph.
9 [a]He said to his people, "Behold, the people of the sons of
Israel are [1]more and mightier than we.
10 "Come, let us [a]deal wisely with them, or else they will
multiply and [1]in the event of war, they will also join
themselves to those who hate us, and fight against us and
[2]depart from the land."
11 So they appointed [a]taskmasters over them to afflict them
with [1b]hard labor. And they built for Pharaoh [c]storage cities,
Pithom and [d]Raamses.
12 But the more they afflicted them, [a]the more they multiplied
and the more they [1]spread out, so that they were in dread of
the sons of Israel.
13 The Egyptians compelled the sons of Israel [a]to labor
rigorously;
14 and they made [a]their lives bitter with hard labor in mortar
and bricks and at all *kinds* of labor in the field, all their labors
which they rigorously [1]imposed on them.
15 Then the king of Egypt spoke to the Hebrew midwives, one
of whom [1]was named Shiphrah and the other [1]was named
Puah;
16 and he said, "When you are helping the Hebrew women to
give birth and see *them* upon the birthstool, [a]if it is a son, then
you shall put him to death; but if it is a daughter, then she shall
live."
17 But the midwives [1a]feared God, and [b]did not do as the king
of Egypt had [2]commanded them, but let the boys live.
18 So the king of Egypt called for the midwives and said to
them, "Why have you done this thing, and let the boys live?"
19 The midwives said to Pharaoh, "Because the Hebrew women
are not as the Egyptian women; for they are vigorous and give
birth before the midwife [1]can get to them."
20 So [a]God was good to the midwives, and [b]the people
multiplied, and became very [1]mighty.
21 Because the midwives [1a]feared God, He [2b]established
[3]households for them.
22 Then Pharaoh commanded all his people, saying, "[a]Every
son who is born [1]you are to cast into [b]the Nile, and every
daughter you are to keep alive."

Chapter 2 Theme ________________________

2 Now a man from [a]the house of Levi went and [1]married a
daughter of Levi.
2 The woman conceived and bore a son; and when she saw
[1]that he was [2a]beautiful, she hid him for three months.

6 [a]Gen 50:26

7 [1]Lit *swarmed* [2]Or *numerous* [a]Gen 12:2; 28:3; 35:11; 46:3; 47:27; 48:4; Deut 26:5; Ps 105:24; Acts 7:17

8 [a]Acts 7:18, 19

9 [1]Or *too many and too mighty for us* [a]Ps 105:24, 25

10 [1]Lit *it came about when war befalls that* [2]Lit *go up from* [a]Acts 7:19

11 [1]Lit *their burdens* [a]Gen 15:13; Ex 3:7; 5:6 [b]Ex 1:14; 2:11; 5:4-9; 6:6f [c]1 Kin 9:19; 2 Chr 8:4 [d]Gen 47:11

12 [1]Lit *broke forth* [a]Ex 1:7

13 [a]Gen 15:13; Deut 4:20

14 [1]Lit *worked through them* [a]Ex 2:23; 6:9; Num 20:15; Acts 7:19

15 [1]Lit *the name was*

16 [a]Acts 7:19

17 [1]Or *revered* [2]Lit *spoken to* [a]Ex 1:21; Prov 16:6 [b]Acts 4:18-20; 5:29

19 [1]Lit *comes to*

20 [1]Or *numerous* [a]Prov 11:18; Eccl 8:12; Heb 6:10 [b]Ex 1:12; Is 3:10

21 [1]Or *revered* [2]Lit *made* [3]Or *families* [a]Ex 1:17 [b]1 Sam 2:35; 2 Sam 7:11, 27; 1 Kin 2:24; 11:38

22 [1]Some versions insert *to the Hebrews* [a]Acts 7:19 [b]Gen 41:1

2:1 [1]Lit *took* [a]Ex 6:16, 18, 20

2 [1]Lit *him that* [2]Lit *good* [a]Acts 7:20; Heb 11:23

3 But when she could hide him no longer, she got him a
[1a]wicker [2]basket and covered it over with tar and pitch. Then
she put the child into it and set *it* among the [b]reeds by the
bank of the Nile.
4 [a]His sister stood at a distance to [1]find out what would
[2]happen to him.
5 The daughter of Pharaoh came down [a]to bathe at the Nile,
with her maidens walking alongside the Nile; and she saw the
[1]basket among the reeds and sent her maid, and she brought it
to her.
6 When she opened *it,* she [1]saw the child, and behold, *the*
[2]boy was crying. And she had pity on him and said, "This is
one of the Hebrews' children."
7 Then his sister said to Pharaoh's daughter, "Shall I go and
call [1]a nurse for you from the Hebrew women that she may
nurse the child for you?"
8 Pharaoh's daughter said to her, "Go *ahead.*" So the girl
went and called the child's mother.
9 Then Pharaoh's daughter said to her, "Take this child away
and nurse him for me and I will give *you* your wages." So the
woman took the child and nursed him.
10 The child grew, and she brought him to Pharaoh's daughter
and [a]he became her son. And she named him [1]Moses, and
said, "Because I [2]drew him out of the water."
11 Now it came about in those days, [a]when Moses had grown
up, that he went out to his brethren and looked on their [1b]hard
labors; and [c]he saw an Egyptian beating a Hebrew, one of his
brethren.
12 So he [1]looked this way and that, and when he saw there
was no one *around,* he [a]struck down the Egyptian and hid him
in the sand.
13 He went out [a]the next day, and behold, two Hebrews were
[1]fighting with each other; and he said to the [2]offender, "Why
are you striking your companion?"
14 But he said, "[a]Who made you a [1]prince or a judge over us?
Are you [2]intending to kill me as you killed the Egyptian?" Then
Moses was afraid and said, "Surely the matter has become
known."
15 When Pharaoh heard of this matter, he tried to kill Moses.
But [a]Moses fled from the presence of Pharaoh and [1]settled in
the land of Midian, and he sat down [b]by a well.
16 Now [a]the priest of Midian had seven daughters; and [b]they
came to draw water and filled the troughs to water their
father's flock.
17 Then the shepherds came and drove them away, but
[a]Moses stood up and helped them and watered their flock.
18 When they came to [a]Reuel their father, he said, "Why have
you come *back* so soon today?"
19 So they said, "An Egyptian delivered us from the hand of
the shepherds, and what is more, he even drew the water for
us and watered the flock."

3 [1]I.e. papyrus reeds [2]Or *chest* [a]Is 18:2 [b]Is 19:6

4 [1]Lit *know* [2]Lit *be done* [a]Ex 15:20; Num 26:59

5 [1]Or *chest* [a]Ex 7:15; 8:20

6 [1]Heb *saw it, the child* [2]Or *lad*

7 [1]Lit *a woman giving suck*

10 [1]Heb *Mosheh,* from *mashah* [2]Heb *mashah* [a]Acts 7:21

11 [1]Lit *burdens* [a]Acts 7:23; Heb 11:24-26 [b]Ex 1:11; 5:4, 5; 6:6, 7 [c]Acts 7:24

12 [1]Lit *turned* [a]Acts 7:24, 25

13 [1]Or *quarreling* [2]Or *the guilty one* [a]Acts 7:26-28

14 [1]Lit *man, a prince* [2]Lit *saying in your heart* [a]Gen 19:9; Acts 7:27, 28

15 [1]Lit *dwelt* [a]Acts 7:29; Heb 11:27 [b]Gen 24:11; 29:2

16 [a]Ex 3:1; 18:12 [b]Gen 24:11, 13, 19; 29:9, 10; 1 Sam 9:11

17 [a]Gen 29:3, 10

18 [a]Ex 3:1; Num 10:29

20 He said to his daughters, "Where is he then? Why is it that
you have left the man behind? Invite him [1]to have something
to eat."
21 [a]Moses was willing to dwell with the man, and he gave his
daughter [b]Zipporah to Moses.
22 Then she gave birth to [a]a son, and he named him [1]Gershom,
for he said, "I have been [b]a [2]sojourner in a foreign land."
23 Now it came about in *the course of* those many days that
the king of Egypt died. And the sons of Israel [a]sighed because
of the bondage, and they cried out; and [b]their cry for help
because of *their* bondage rose up to God.
24 So [a]God heard their groaning; and God remembered [b]His
covenant with Abraham, Isaac, and Jacob.
25 [a]God saw the sons of Israel, and God [1]took notice *of them.*

20 [1]Lit *that he may eat bread*

21 [a]Acts 7:29 [b]Ex 4:25; 18:2

22 [1]Cf Heb *ger sham, a stranger there* [2]Heb *ger* [a]Ex 4:20; 18:3, 4 [b]Gen 23:4; Lev 25:23; Acts 7:29; Heb 11:13, 14

23 [a]Ex 6:5, 9 [b]Ex 3:7, 9; Deut 26:7; James 5:4

24 [a]Ex 6:5; Acts 7:34 [b]Gen 15:13f; 22:16-18; 26:2-5; 28:13-15; Ps 105:8, 42

25 [1]Lit *knew* them [a]Ex 3:7; 4:31; Acts 7:34

The Exodus from Egypt to Canaan

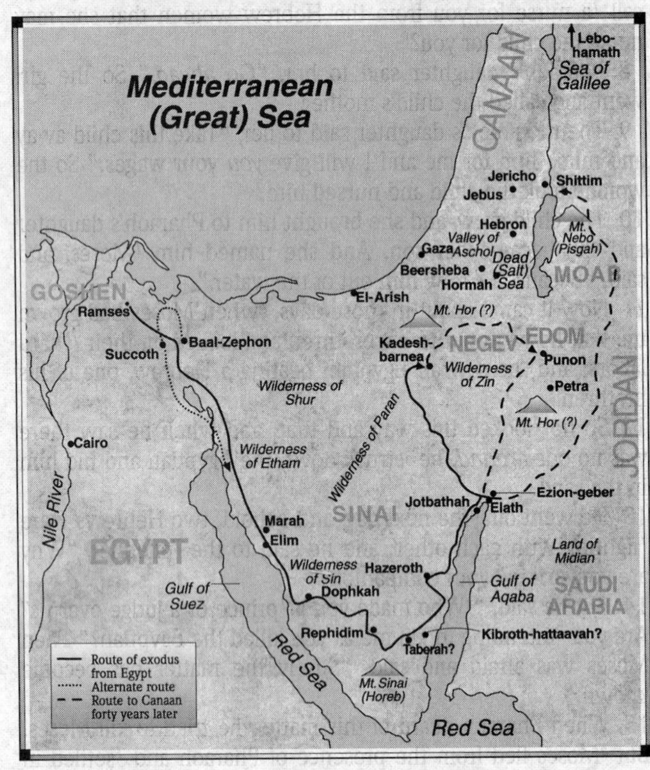

Chapter 3 Theme ____________

3 Now Moses was pasturing the flock of [a]Jethro his father-in-law, the priest of Midian; and he led the flock to the [1]west side of the wilderness and came to [b]Horeb, the [c]mountain of God.

2 [a]The angel of the LORD appeared to him in a blazing fire from the midst of [1]a [b]bush; and he looked, and behold, the bush was burning with fire, yet the bush was not consumed.

3 So Moses said, "[1a]I must turn aside now and see this [2]marvelous sight, why the bush is not burned up."

3:1 [1]Or *rear part* [a]Ex 2:18; 4:18; 18:12; Num 10:29 [b]Ex 3:12; 17:6; 33:6; 1 Kin 19:8 [c]Ex 4:27; 18:5; 24:13

2 [1]Lit *the* [a]Gen 16:7-11; 21:17; 22:11, 15; Ex 3:4-11, 16; Judg 13:13-21; Acts 7:30 [b]Deut 33:16; Mark 12:26; Luke 20:37; Acts 7:30

3 [1]Lit *Let me turn* [2]Lit *great* [a]Acts 7:31

4 When the LORD saw that he turned aside to look, [a]God called to him from the midst of the bush and said, "Moses, Moses!" And he said, "Here I am."

5 Then He said, "Do not come near here; [a]remove your sandals from your feet, for the place on which you are standing is holy ground."

6 He said also, "[a]I am the God of your father, the God of Abraham, the God of Isaac, and the God of Jacob." [b]Then Moses hid his face, for he was [c]afraid to look at God.

7 The LORD said, "I have surely [a]seen the affliction of My people who are in Egypt, and have given heed to their cry because of their taskmasters, for I am aware of their sufferings.

8 "So I have come down [a]to deliver them from the [1]power of the Egyptians, and to bring them up from that land to a [b]good and spacious land, to a land flowing with milk and honey, to the place of [c]the Canaanite and the Hittite and the Amorite and the Perizzite and the Hivite and the Jebusite.

9 "Now, behold, [a]the cry of the sons of Israel has come to Me; furthermore, I have seen the oppression with which the Egyptians are oppressing them.

10 "Therefore, come now, and I will send you to Pharaoh, [a]so that you may bring My people, the sons of Israel, out of Egypt."

11 But Moses said to God, "[a]Who am I, that I should go to Pharaoh, and that I should bring the sons of Israel out of Egypt?"

12 And He said, "Certainly [a]I will be with you, and this shall be the sign to you that it is I who have sent you: [b]when you have brought the people out of Egypt, [c]you shall [1]worship God at this mountain."

13 Then Moses said to God, "Behold, I am going to the sons of Israel, and I will say to them, 'The God of your fathers has sent me to you.' Now they may say to me, 'What is His name?' What shall I say to them?"

14 God said to Moses, "[1a]I AM WHO [1]I AM"; and He said, "Thus you shall say to the sons of Israel, '[1]I AM has sent me to you.'"

15 God, furthermore, said to Moses, "Thus you shall say to the sons of Israel, '[a]The LORD, the God of your fathers, the God of Abraham, the God of Isaac, and the God of Jacob, has sent me to you.' This is My name forever, and this is My [b]memorial-name [1]to all generations.

16 "Go and [a]gather the elders of Israel together and say to them, '[b]The LORD, the God of your fathers, the God of Abraham, Isaac and Jacob, has appeared to me, saying, "[1c]I am indeed concerned about you and what has been done to you in Egypt.

17 "So [a]I said, I will bring you up out of the affliction of Egypt to the land of [b]the Canaanite and the Hittite and the Amorite and the Perizzite and the Hivite and the Jebusite, to a land [c]flowing with milk and honey."'

18 "[a]They will [1]pay heed to what you say; and [b]you with the elders of Israel will come to the king of Egypt and you will say to him, 'The LORD, the God of the Hebrews, has met with us.

4 [a]Ex 4:5
5 [a]Josh 5:15; Acts 7:33
6 [a]Gen 28:13; Ex 3:16; 4:5; Matt 22:32; Mark 12:26; Luke 20:37 [b]Acts 7:32 [c]Judg 13:22; Rev 1:17
7 [a]Ex 2:25; Neh 9:9; Ps 106:44; Is 63:9; Acts 7:34
8 [1]Lit *hand* [a]Gen 15:13-16; 46:4; 50:24, 25; Ex 6:6-8; 12:51 [b]Ex 3:17; 13:5; Num 13:27; Deut 1:25; 8:7-9; Jer 11:5; Ezek 20:6 [c]Gen 15:19-21; Josh 24:11
9 [a]Ex 2:23
10 [a]Gen 15:13, 14; Ex 12:40, 41; Mic 6:4; Acts 7:6, 7
11 [a]Ex 4:10; 6:12; 1 Sam 18:18
12 [1]Or *serve* [a]Gen 31:3; Ex 4:12, 15; 33:14-16; Deut 31:23; Josh 1:5; Is 43:2 [b]Ex 19:1 [c]Ex 19:2, 3; Acts 7:7
14 [1]Related to the name of God, *YHWH,* rendered *LORD,* which is derived from the verb *HAYAH, to be* [a]Ex 6:3; John 8:24, 28, 58; Heb 13:8; Rev 1:8; 4:8
15 [1]Lit *to generation of generation* [a]Ex 3:6, 13 [b]Ps 30:4; 97:12; 102:12; 135:13; Hos 12:5
16 [1]Lit *Visiting I have visited* [a]Ex 4:29 [b]Gen 28:13; 48:15; Ex 3:2, 6; 4:5 [c]Ex 4:31; Ps 33:18f
17 [a]Gen 15:13-21; 46:4; 50:24, 25 [b]Josh 24:11 [c]Ex 3:8
18 [1]Lit *hear your voice* [a]Ex 4:31 [b]Ex 5:1

So now, please, let us go a [c]three days' journey into the
wilderness, that we may sacrifice to the LORD our God.'
19 "But I know that the king of Egypt [a]will not permit you to
go, [b]except [1]under compulsion.
20 "So I will stretch out [a]My hand and strike Egypt with all My
[b]miracles which I shall do in the midst of it; and [c]after that he
will let you go.
21 "I will grant this people [a]favor in the sight of the Egyptians;
and it shall be that when you go, you will not go empty-
handed.
22 "But every woman [a]shall ask of her neighbor and the
woman who lives in her house, articles of silver and articles of
gold, and clothing; and you will put them on your sons and
daughters. Thus you will [b]plunder the Egyptians."

Chapter 4 Theme ______________________________

4 Then Moses said, "What if they will not believe me or [a]lis-
ten [1]to what I say? For they may say, '[b]The LORD has not
appeared to you.'"
2 The LORD said to him, "What is that in your hand?" And he
said, "[a]A staff."
3 Then He said, "Throw it on the ground." So he threw it on
the ground, and [a]it became a serpent; and Moses fled from it.
4 But the LORD said to Moses, "Stretch out your hand and
grasp *it* by its tail"—so he stretched out his hand and caught it,
and it became a staff in his [1]hand—
5 "that [a]they may believe that [b]the LORD, the God of their
fathers, the God of Abraham, the God of Isaac, and the God of
Jacob, has appeared to you."
6 The LORD furthermore said to him, "Now put your hand
into your bosom." So he put his hand into his bosom, and
when he took it out, behold, his hand was [a]leprous like snow.
7 Then He said, "Put your hand into your bosom again." So
he put his hand into his bosom again, and when he took it out
of his bosom, behold, [a]it was restored like *the rest of* his flesh.
8 "If they will not believe you or [1]heed the [2]witness of the
first sign, they may believe the [2]witness of the last sign.
9 "But if they will not believe even these two signs or heed
what you say, then you shall take some water from the Nile and
pour it on the dry ground; and the water which you take from
the Nile [a]will become blood on the dry ground."
10 Then Moses said to the LORD, "Please, Lord, [a]I have never
been [1]eloquent, neither [2]recently nor in time past, nor since
You have spoken to Your servant; for I am [3]slow of speech and
[3]slow of tongue."
11 The LORD said to him, "Who has made man's mouth? Or
[a]who makes *him* mute or deaf, or seeing or blind? Is it not I,
the LORD?
12 "Now then go, and [a]I, even I, will be with your mouth, and
[b]teach you what you are to say."

18 [c]Ex 5:3; 8:27

19 [1]Lit *by a strong hand* [a]Ex 5:2 [b]Ex 6:1

20 [a]Ex 6:1; 7:4, 5; 9:15; 13:3, 9, 14 [b]Ex 7:3; 15:11; Deut 6:22; Neh 9:10; Ps 105:27; 135:9; Jer 32:20; Acts 7:36 [c]Ex 11:1; 12:31-33

21 [a]Ex 11:3; 12:36; 1 Kin 8:50; Ps 105:37f; 106:46; Prov 16:7

22 [a]Gen 15:14; Ex 11:2; 12:35 [b]Ezek 39:10

4:1 [1]Lit *to my voice* [a]Ex 3:18; 6:30 [b]Ex 3:15, 16

2 [a]Ex 4:17, 20

3 [a]Ex 7:10-12

4 [1]Lit *palm*

5 [a]Ex 4:31; 19:9 [b]Gen 28:13; 48:15; Ex 3:6, 15

6 [a]Num 12:10; 2 Kin 5:27

7 [a]Num 12:13-15; Deut 32:39; 2 Kin 5:14; Matt 8:3; Luke 17:12-14

8 [1]Lit *listen to* [2]Lit *voice*

9 [a]Ex 7:19, 20

10 [1]Lit *a man of words* [2]Lit *yesterday* [3]Lit *heavy* [a]Ex 3:11; 4:1; 6:12; Jer 1:6

11 [a]Ps 94:9; 146:8; Matt 11:5; Luke 1:20, 64

12 [a]Ex 4:15, 16; Deut 18:18; Is 50:4; Jer 1:9 [b]Matt 10:19, 20; Mark 13:11; Luke 12:11, 12; 21:14, 15

13 But he said, "Please, Lord, now [1]send *the message* by
whomever You will."
14 Then the anger of the LORD burned against Moses, and He
said, "Is there not your brother Aaron the Levite? I know that
[1]he speaks fluently. And moreover, behold, [a]he is coming out to
meet you; when he sees you, he will be glad in his heart.
15 "You are to speak to him and [a]put the words in his mouth;
and I, even I, will be with your mouth and his mouth, and I
will teach you what you are to do.
16 "Moreover, [a]he shall speak for you to the people; and he will
be as a mouth for you and you will be as God to him.
17 "You shall take in your hand [a]this staff, [b]with which you
shall perform the signs."
18 Then Moses departed and returned to [1]Jethro [a]his father-in-
law and said to him, "Please, let me go, that I may return to my
brethren who are in Egypt, and see if they are still alive." And
Jethro said to Moses, "Go in peace."
19 Now the LORD said to Moses in Midian, "Go [1]back to
Egypt, for [a]all the men who were seeking your life are dead."
20 So Moses took his wife and his [a]sons and mounted them
on a donkey, and returned to the land of Egypt. Moses also took
the [b]staff of God in his hand.
21 The LORD said to Moses, "When you go [1]back to Egypt see
that you perform before Pharaoh all [a]the wonders which I have
put in your [2]power; but [b]I will harden his heart so that he will
not let the people go.
22 "Then you shall say to Pharaoh, 'Thus says the LORD, "[a]Israel
is My son, My firstborn.
23 "So I said to you, '[a]Let My son go that he may serve Me';
but you have refused to let him go. Behold, [b]I will kill your son,
your firstborn."'"
24 Now it came about at the lodging place on the way that the
LORD met him and [a]sought to put him to death.
25 Then Zipporah took [a]a flint and cut off her son's foreskin
and [1]threw it at Moses' feet, and she said, "You are indeed a
bridegroom of blood to me."
26 So He let him alone. At that time she said, "*You are* a
bridegroom of blood"—[1]because of the circumcision.
27 [a]Now the LORD said to Aaron, "Go to meet Moses in the
wilderness." So he went and met him at the [b]mountain of God
and kissed him.
28 [a]Moses told Aaron all the words of the LORD with which He
had sent him, and [b]all the signs that He had commanded him
to do.
29 Then Moses and Aaron went and [a]assembled all the elders
of the sons of Israel;
30 and [a]Aaron spoke all the words which the LORD had spoken
to Moses. He then performed the [b]signs in the sight of the people.
31 So [a]the people believed; and when they heard that the
LORD [1b]was concerned about the sons of Israel and that He had
seen their affliction, then [c]they bowed low and worshiped.

13 [1]Lit *send by the hand which You send*
14 [1]Lit *speaking he speaks* [a]Ex 4:27
15 [a]Ex 4:12, 30; 7:1f; Num 23:5, 12, 16; Deut 18:18; Is 51:16; 59:21; Jer 1:9
16 [a]Ex 7:1, 2
17 [a]Ex 4:2, 20; 17:9 [b]Ex 7:9-20; 14:16
18 [1]Heb *Jether* [a]Ex 2:21; 3:1
19 [1]Lit *return* [a]Ex 2:15, 23
20 [a]Ex 18:3, 4; Acts 7:29 [b]Ex 4:17; 17:9; Num 20:8, 9, 11
21 [1]Lit *to return* [2]Lit *hand* [a]Ex 3:20; 11:9, 10 [b]Ex 7:3, 13; 9:12, 35; 10:1, 20, 27; 14:4, 8; Deut 2:30; Josh 11:20; 1 Sam 6:6; Is 63:17; John 12:40; Rom 9:18
22 [a]Is 63:16; 64:8; Jer 31:9; Hos 11:1; Rom 9:4
23 [a]Ex 5:1; 6:11; 7:16 [b]Ex 11:5; 12:29; Ps 105:36; 135:8; 136:10
24 [a]Num 22:22
25 [1]Lit *made it touch at his feet* [a]Gen 17:14; Josh 5:2, 3
26 [1]Lit *with reference to*
27 [a]Ex 4:14 [b]Ex 3:1; 18:5; 24:13
28 [a]Ex 4:15f [b]Ex 4:8f
29 [a]Ex 3:16
30 [a]Ex 4:15, 16 [b]Ex 4:1-9
31 [1]Lit *had visited* [a]Ex 3:18; 4:8f; 19:9 [b]Gen 50:24; Ex 3:16 [c]Gen 24:26; Ex 12:27; 1 Chr 29:20

Chapter 5 Theme ______

5 And afterward Moses and Aaron came and said to Pharaoh,
"[a]Thus says the LORD, the God of Israel, '[b]Let My people go
that they may celebrate a feast to Me in the wilderness.'"
2 But Pharaoh said, "[a]Who is the LORD that I should obey His
voice to let Israel go? I do not know the LORD, and besides, [b]I
will not let Israel go."
3 Then they said, "[a]The God of the Hebrews has met with
us. Please, let us go a three days' journey into the wilderness
that we may sacrifice to the LORD our God, otherwise He will
fall upon us with pestilence or with the sword."
4 But the king of Egypt said to them, "Moses and Aaron, why
do you [1]draw the people away from their [2]work? Get *back* to
your [3a]labors!"
5 Again Pharaoh said, "Look, [a]the people of the land are now
many, and you would have them cease from their labors!"
6 So the same day Pharaoh commanded [a]the taskmasters
over the people and their [b]foremen, saying,
7 "You are no longer to give the people straw to make brick as
previously; let them go and gather straw for themselves.
8 "But the quota of bricks which they were making previously,
you shall impose on them; you are not to reduce any of it.
Because they are [a]lazy, therefore they cry out, '[1]Let us go and
sacrifice to our God.'
9 "Let the labor be heavier on the men, and let them work at
it so that they will pay no attention to false words."
10 So [a]the taskmasters of the people and their foremen went
out and spoke to the people, saying, "Thus says Pharaoh, 'I am
not going to give you *any* straw.
11 'You go *and* get straw for yourselves wherever you can find
it, but none of your labor will be reduced.'"
12 So the people scattered through all the land of Egypt to
gather stubble for straw.
13 The taskmasters pressed them, saying, "Complete your
[1]work quota, [2]*your* daily amount, just as when [3]you had straw."
14 Moreover, [a]the foremen of the sons of Israel, whom
Pharaoh's taskmasters had set over them, [b]were beaten [1]and were
asked, "Why have you not completed your required amount
either yesterday or today in making brick as previously?"
15 Then the foremen of the sons of Israel came and cried out to
Pharaoh, saying, "Why do you deal this way with your servants?
16 "There is no straw given to your servants, yet they keep
saying to us, 'Make bricks!' And behold, your servants are
being beaten; but it is the fault of your *own* people."
17 But he said, "You are [a]lazy, *very* lazy; therefore you say, 'Let
us go *and* sacrifice to the LORD.'
18 "So go now *and* work; for you will be given no straw, yet
you must deliver the quota of bricks."
19 The foremen of the sons of Israel saw that they were in
trouble [1]because they were told, "You must not reduce [2]*your*
daily amount of bricks."

INSIGHT

Pharaoh is a title that was given to the kings of Egypt. An ancient Pharaoh had absolute power; and during his reign, he was considered a god who owned the lands and the people. He was also the high priest of all religions in Egypt. The Pharaoh mentioned in Exodus chapters 5–12 is believed to have been Amenhotep II.

5:1 [a]Ex 3:18 [b]Ex 4:23; 6:11; 7:16

2 [a]2 Kin 18:35; 2 Chr 32:14; Job 21:15 [b]Ex 3:19

3 [a]Ex 3:18

4 [1]Lit *loose* [2]Lit *works* [3]Lit *burdens* [a]Ex 1:11; 2:11; 6:5-7

5 [a]Ex 1:7, 9

6 [a]Ex 1:11; 3:7; 5:10, 13, 14 [b]Ex 5:10, 14, 15, 19

8 [1]Lit *saying, 'Let* [a]Ex 5:17

10 [a]Ex 1:11; 3:7; 5:6

13 [1]Lit *works* [2]Lit *the matter of a day in its day* [3]Lit *there was*

14 [1]Lit *saying* [a]Ex 5:6 [b]Is 10:24

17 [a]Ex 5:8

19 [1]Lit *saying* [2]Lit *from your bricks the matter of a day in its day*

20 When they left Pharaoh's presence, they met Moses and
Aaron as they were [1]waiting for them.
21 [a]They said to them, "[b]May the LORD look upon you and judge
you, for you have [c]made [1]us odious in Pharaoh's sight and in the
sight of his servants, to put a sword in their hand to kill us."
22 Then Moses returned to the LORD and said, "[a]O Lord, why
have You brought harm to this people? Why did You ever send
me?
23 "Ever since I came to Pharaoh to speak in Your name, he
has done harm to this people, [a]and You have not delivered Your
people at all."

Chapter 6 Theme ______________________________

6 Then the LORD said to Moses, "Now you shall see what I
will do to Pharaoh; for [1a]under compulsion he will let them
go, and [1]under compulsion he will drive them out of his land."
2 God spoke further to Moses and said to him, "I am [a]the LORD;
3 and I appeared to Abraham, Isaac, and Jacob, as [1a]God
Almighty, but *by* [b]My name, [2]LORD, I did not make Myself
known to them.
4 "I also established [a]My covenant with them, to give them
the land of Canaan, the [1]land in which they sojourned.
5 "Furthermore I have [a]heard the groaning of the sons of
Israel, because the Egyptians are holding them in bondage, and
I have remembered My covenant.
6 "Say, therefore, to the sons of Israel, '[a]I am the LORD, and [b]I
will bring you out from under the burdens of the Egyptians,
and I will deliver you from their bondage. I will also [c]redeem
you with [d]an outstretched arm and with great judgments.
7 'Then I will take you [1a]for My people, and [b]I will be [2]your
God; and [c]you shall know that I am the LORD your God, who
brought you out from under the burdens of the Egyptians.
8 'I will bring you to the land which [a]I [1]swore to give to
Abraham, Isaac, and Jacob, and [b]I will give it to you *for* a
possession; [c]I am the LORD.'"
9 So Moses spoke thus to the sons of Israel, but they did not
listen to Moses on [a]account of *their* [1]despondency and cruel
bondage.
10 Now the LORD spoke to Moses, saying,
11 "[a]Go, [1]tell Pharaoh king of Egypt [2]to let the sons of Israel go
out of his land."
12 But Moses spoke before the LORD, saying, "Behold, the
sons of Israel have not listened to me; [a]how then will Pharaoh
listen to me, for I am [1b]unskilled in speech?"
13 Then the LORD spoke to Moses and to Aaron, and gave them
a charge to the sons of Israel and to Pharaoh king of Egypt, to
bring the sons of Israel out of the land of Egypt.
14 These are the heads of their fathers' households. [a]The sons
of Reuben, Israel's firstborn: Hanoch and Pallu, Hezron and
Carmi; these are the families of Reuben.

20 [1]Lit *standing to meet*
21 [1]Lit *our savor to stink* [a]Ex 14:11; 15:24; 16:2 [b]Gen 16:5; 31:53 [c]Gen 34:30; 1 Sam 13:4; 27:12; 2 Sam 10:6; 1 Chr 19:6
22 [a]Num 11:11; Jer 4:10
23 [a]Ex 3:8
6:1 [1]Lit *by a strong hand* [a]Ex 3:19, 20; 7:4, 5; 11:1; 12:31, 33, 39; 13:3
2 [a]Ex 3:14, 15
3 [1]Heb *El Shaddai* [2]Heb *YHWH,* usually rendered LORD [a]Gen 17:1; 35:11; 48:3 [b]Ps 68:4; 83:18; Is 52:6; Jer 16:21; Ezek 37:6, 13
4 [1]Lit *land of their sojournings in which...* [a]Gen 12:7; 15:18; 17:4, 7; 26:3, 4; 28:4, 13
5 [a]Ex 2:24
6 [a]Ex 13:3, 14; 20:2; Deut 6:12 [b]Ex 3:17; 7:4; 12:51; 16:6; 18:1; Deut 26:8; Ps 136:11 [c]Ex 15:13; Deut 7:8; 1 Chr 17:21; Neh 1:10 [d]Deut 4:34; 5:15; 26:8; Ps 136:11f
7 [1]Lit *to Me for a people* [2]Lit *to you for a God* [a]Ex 19:5; Deut 4:20; 7:6; 2 Sam 7:24 [b]Gen 17:7f; Ex 29:45f; Lev 11:45; 26:12, 13, 45; Deut 29:13 [c]Ex 16:12; Is 41:20; 49:23, 26; 60:16
8 [1]Lit *lifted up My hand* [a]Gen 15:18; 26:3; Num 14:30; Neh 9:15; Ezek 20:5, 6 [b]Josh 24:13; Ps 136:21, 22 [c]Ex 6:6
9 [1]Lit *shortness of spirit* [a]Ex 2:23
11 [1]Lit *speak to* [2]Lit *that he let* [a]Ex 4:22, 23
12 [1]Lit *uncircumcised of lips* [a]Ex 4:1, 10; 6:30 [b]Jer 1:6
14 [a]Gen 46:9; Num 26:5-11; 1 Chr 5:3

15 The [a]sons of Simeon: Jemuel and Jamin and Ohad and Jachin
and Zohar and Shaul the son of a Canaanite woman; these are
the families of Simeon.
16 These are the names of [a]the sons of Levi according to their
generations: Gershon and Kohath and Merari; and the [1]length
of Levi's life was one hundred and thirty-seven years.
17 [a]The sons of Gershon: [1]Libni and Shimei, according to
their families.
18 [a]The sons of Kohath: Amram and Izhar and Hebron and
Uzziel; and the [1]length of Kohath's life was one hundred and
thirty-three years.
19 [a]The sons of Merari: Mahli and Mushi. These are the
families of the Levites according to their generations.
20 [a]Amram [1]married his father's sister Jochebed, and she bore
him Aaron and Moses; and the [2]length of Amram's life was one
hundred and thirty-seven years.
21 [a]The sons of Izhar: Korah and Nepheg and Zichri.
22 [a]The sons of Uzziel: Mishael and [1]Elzaphan and Sithri.
23 Aaron [1]married Elisheba, the daughter of [a]Amminadab, the
sister of [b]Nahshon, and she bore him [c]Nadab and Abihu,
Eleazar and Ithamar.
24 The [a]sons of Korah: Assir and Elkanah and [1]Abiasaph;
these are the families of the Korahites.
25 Aaron's son [a]Eleazar [1]married one of the daughters of
Putiel, and she bore him [b]Phinehas. These are the heads of the
fathers' *households* of the Levites according to their families.
26 It was *the same* Aaron and Moses to whom the LORD said,
"[a]Bring out the sons of Israel from the land of Egypt according
to their [b]hosts."
27 They were the ones [a]who spoke to Pharaoh king of Egypt
[1]about bringing out the sons of Israel from Egypt; it was *the
same* Moses and Aaron.
28 Now it came about on the day when the LORD spoke to
Moses in the land of Egypt,
29 that the LORD spoke to Moses, saying, "[a]I am the LORD;
[b]speak to Pharaoh king of Egypt all that I speak to you."
30 But Moses said before the LORD, "Behold, I am [1a]unskilled
in speech; how then will Pharaoh listen to me?"

Chapter 7 Theme ____________________________

7 Then the LORD said to Moses, "[a]See, I make you *as* God to
Pharaoh, and your brother Aaron shall be your prophet.
2 "You shall speak all that I command you, and your brother
[a]Aaron shall speak to Pharaoh that he let the sons of Israel go
out of his land.
3 "But [a]I will harden Pharaoh's heart that I may [b]multiply My
signs and My wonders in the land of Egypt.
4 "When [a]Pharaoh does not listen to you, then I will lay My
hand on Egypt and [b]bring out My hosts, My people the sons of
Israel, from the land of Egypt by [c]great judgments.

15 [a]Gen 46:10; 1 Chr 4:24

16 [1]Lit *years* [a]Gen 46:11; Num 3:17; 26:57f; 1 Chr 6:1, 16-19

17 [1]In 1 Chr 23:7, *Ladan* [a]Num 3:18-20; 1 Chr 6:17-19

18 [1]Lit *years* [a]Num 3:19; 1 Chr 6:2, 18

19 [a]Num 3:20; 1 Chr 6:19; 23:21

20 [1]Lit *took to him to wife* [2]Lit *years* [a]Ex 2:1, 2; Num 26:59

21 [a]Num 16:1; 1 Chr 6:37, 38

22 [1]In Num 3:30, *Elizaphan* [a]Lev 10:4; Num 3:30

23 [1]Lit *took to him to wife* [a]Ruth 4:19, 20; 1 Chr 2:10 [b]Num 1:7; 2:3 [c]Lev 10:1; Num 3:2; 26:60; 1 Chr 6:3; 24:1

24 [1]In 1 Chr 6:23 and 9:19, *Ebiasaph* [a]Num 26:11; 1 Chr 6:22, 23, 37

25 [1]Lit *took to him to wife* [a]Josh 24:33 [b]Num 25:7-13; Josh 24:33; Ps 106:30

26 [a]Ex 3:10; 6:13 [b]Ex 7:4; 12:17, 51

27 [1]Lit *to bring out* [a]Ex 5:1

29 [a]Ex 6:2, 6, 8 [b]Ex 6:11; 7:2

30 [1]Lit *uncircumcised of lips* [a]Ex 4:10; 6:12; Jer 1:6

7:1 [a]Ex 4:16

2 [a]Ex 4:15

3 [a]Ex 4:21 [b]Ex 11:9; Acts 7:36

4 [a]Ex 3:19, 20; 7:13, 16, 22; 8:15, 19; 9:12; 11:9 [b]Ex 12:51; 13:3, 9 [c]Ex 6:6

Some of the Gods of Egypt

The god:	Ruled over:	How symbolized:
Aker	Earth-god • Helper of the dead	*Two lion heads*
Aton	Sun-god	
Bes	Protection at birth • Dispenser of virility	*Group of demons*
Heket	Primordial goddess	*Frog*
Isis	Goddess of life and healing	*Human*
Khepri	Primordial god • Rising sun	*Scarabaeus (beetle)*
Khnum	Giver of the Nile • Creator of mankind	*Human with ram's head*
Mut	"Eye of the sun"	*Vulture or human*
Nut	Sky goddess • Mother of heavenly bodies	
Osiris	Dead Pharaohs • Ruler of dead, life, vegetation	
Ra	God of sun, earth, and sky • National god	*Human with falcon head*
Selket	Guardian of life • Protector of dead	*Scorpion*
Seth	God of chaos, desert and storm, crops	
Sothis	God of Nile floodwaters	
Thermuthis	Goddess of fertility and harvest; fate	*Serpent*

5 “[a]The Egyptians shall know that I am the LORD, when I
[b]stretch out My hand on Egypt and bring out the sons of Israel
from their midst.”
6 So Moses and Aaron did *it;* [a]as the LORD commanded them,
thus they did.
7 Moses was [a]eighty years old and Aaron [1]eighty-three, when
they spoke to Pharaoh.
8 Now the LORD spoke to Moses and Aaron, saying,
9 “When Pharaoh speaks to you, saying, ‘[1a]Work a miracle,’
then you shall say to Aaron, ‘[b]Take your staff and throw *it*
down before Pharaoh, *that* it may become a serpent.’”
10 So Moses and Aaron came to Pharaoh, and thus they did
just as the LORD had commanded; and Aaron threw his staff
down before Pharaoh and [1]his servants, and it [a]became a
serpent.
11 Then Pharaoh also [a]called for *the* wise men and *the*
sorcerers, and they also, the [1b]magicians of Egypt, did [2]the
same with [c]their secret arts.
12 For each one threw down his staff and they turned into
serpents. But Aaron's staff swallowed up their staffs.
13 Yet [a]Pharaoh's heart was [1]hardened, and he did not listen
to them, as the LORD had said.
14 Then the LORD said to Moses, “Pharaoh's heart is
[1]stubborn; he refuses to let the people go.
15 “Go to Pharaoh in the morning [1]as [a]he is going out to the
water, and station yourself to meet him on the bank of the
Nile; and you shall take in your hand [b]the staff that was turned
into a serpent.
16 “[a]You shall say to him, ‘The LORD, the God of the Hebrews,
sent me to you, saying, “[b]Let My people go, that they may
serve Me in the wilderness. But behold, you have not listened
until now.”
17 ‘Thus says the LORD, “[a]By this you shall know that I am the
LORD: behold, I will strike [1]the water that is in the Nile with
the staff that is in my hand, and [b]it will be turned to blood.

5 [a]Ex 7:17; 8:19, 22; 10:7; 14:4, 18, 25 [b]Ex 3:20

6 [a]Gen 6:22; 7:5; Ex 7:2

7 [1]Lit *83 years old* [a]Deut 29:5; 31:2; 34:7; Acts 7:23, 30

9 [1]Lit *Show a wonder for yourselves* [a]Is 7:11; John 2:18; 6:30 [b]Ex 4:2, 17

10 [1]Lit *before his* [a]Ex 4:3; 7:9

11 [1]Or *soothsayer priests* [2]Lit *thus* [a]Dan 2:2; 4:6; 5:7 [b]Gen 41:8; Ex 7:22; Dan 2:2; 2 Tim 3:8 [c]Ex 7:22; 8:7, 18; 2 Tim 3:9; Rev 13:13, 14

13 [1]Lit *strong* [a]Ex 4:21; 7:3, 22; 8:15, 19, 32; 9:7, 12, 34, 35; 10:1, 20, 27

14 [1]Or *hard;* lit *heavy*

15 [1]Lit *behold* [a]Ex 2:5; 8:20 [b]Ex 4:2, 3; 7:10

16 [a]Ex 3:13, 18; 4:22; 5:1 [b]Ex 4:23; 5:1, 3

17 [1]Lit *upon the waters* [a]Ex 5:2; 7:5; 10:2; Ps 9:16; Ezek 25:17 [b]Ex 4:9; 7:20; Rev 11:6; 16:4, 6

18"[a]The fish that are in the Nile will die, and the Nile will
[1]become foul, and the Egyptians will [2b]find difficulty in drinking
water from the Nile."'"
19 Then the LORD said to Moses, "Say to Aaron, 'Take your staff
and [a]stretch out your hand over the waters of Egypt, over their
rivers, over their [1]streams, and over their pools, and over all their
reservoirs of water, that they may become blood; and there will
be blood throughout all the land of Egypt, both in *vessels of*
wood and in *vessels of* stone.'"
20 So Moses and Aaron did even as the LORD had commanded.
And he lifted up [1a]the staff and struck the water that *was* in the
Nile, in the sight of Pharaoh and in the sight of his servants,
and [b]all the water that *was* in the Nile was turned to blood.
21 The fish that *were* in the Nile died, and the Nile [1]became
foul, so that the Egyptians could not drink water from the Nile.
And the blood was through all the land of Egypt.
22 [a]But the [1]magicians of Egypt did [2]the same with their secret
arts; and Pharaoh's heart was [3]hardened, and he did not listen
to them, as the LORD had said.
23 Then Pharaoh turned and went into his house [1]with no
concern even for this.
24 So all the Egyptians dug around the Nile for water to drink,
for they could not drink of the water of the Nile.
25 Seven days [1]passed after the LORD had struck the Nile.

Chapter 8 Theme ______________________

8 [1]Then the LORD said to Moses, "Go to Pharaoh and say to
him, 'Thus says the LORD, "[a]Let My people go, that they may
serve Me.
2"But if you refuse to let *them* go, behold, I will smite your
whole territory with frogs.
3"The Nile will [a]swarm with frogs, which will come up and
go into your house and into your bedroom and on your bed,
and into the houses of your servants and on your people, and
into your ovens and into your kneading bowls.
4"So the frogs will come up on you and your people and all
your servants."'"
5 [1]Then the LORD said to Moses, "Say to Aaron, '[a]Stretch out
your hand with your staff over the rivers, over the [2]streams and
over the pools, and make frogs come up on the land of Egypt.'"
6 So Aaron stretched out his hand over the waters of Egypt,
and the [1a]frogs came up and covered the land of Egypt.
7 [a]The [1]magicians did [2]the same with their secret arts,
[3]making frogs come up on the land of Egypt.
8 Then Pharaoh [a]called for Moses and Aaron and said,
"[b]Entreat the LORD that He remove the frogs from me and from
my people; and [c]I will let the people go, that they may sacrifice
to the LORD."
9 Moses said to Pharaoh, "[1]The honor is yours to tell me:
when shall I entreat for you and your servants and your people,

18 [1]I.e. have a bad smell [2]Or *be weary of* [a]Ex 7:21 [b]Ex 7:24

19 [1]Or *canals* [a]Ex 8:5, 6, 16; 9:22; 10:12, 21; 14:21, 26

20 [1]Lit *with the staff* [a]Ex 17:5 [b]Ps 78:44; 105:29

21 [1]I.e. had a bad smell

22 [1]Or *soothsayer priests* [2]Lit *thus* [3]Lit *strong* [a]Ex 7:11; 8:7

23 [1]Lit *and he did not set his heart even to this*

25 [1]Lit *were fulfilled*

8:1 [1]Ch 7:26 in Heb [a]Ex 3:18; 4:23; 5:1, 3

3 [a]Ps 105:30

5 [1]Ch 8:1 in Heb [2]Or *canals* [a]Ex 7:19

6 [1]Lit *frog* [a]Ps 78:45; 105:30

7 [1]Or *soothsayer priests* [2]Lit *thus* [3]Lit *and made* [a]Ex 7:11, 22

8 [a]Ex 8:25; 9:27; 10:16 [b]Ex 8:28; 9:28; 10:17; Num 21:7; 1 Kin 13:6 [c]Ex 8:15, 29, 32

9 [1]Lit *Glory over me*

that the frogs be [2]destroyed from you and your houses, *that*
they may be left only in the Nile?"
10 Then he said, "Tomorrow." So he said, "*May it be*
according to your word, that you may know that there is [a]no
one like the LORD our God.
11 "The [a]frogs will depart from you and your houses and your
servants and your people; they will be left only in the Nile."
12 Then Moses and Aaron went out from Pharaoh, and
[a]Moses cried to the LORD concerning the frogs which He had
[1]inflicted upon Pharaoh.
13 The LORD did according to the word of Moses, and the
frogs died out of the houses, the courts, and the fields.
14 So they piled them in heaps, and the land [1]became foul.
15 But when Pharaoh saw that there was relief, he [1]hardened
his heart and [a]did not listen to them, as the LORD had said.
16 Then the LORD said to Moses, "Say to Aaron, 'Stretch out
your staff and strike the dust of the earth, that it may become
[1]gnats through all the land of Egypt.'"
17 They did so; and Aaron stretched out his hand with his staff,
and struck the dust of the earth, and there were [1]gnats on man
and beast. All the dust of the earth became [1a]gnats through all
the land of Egypt.
18 The [1]magicians tried with their secret arts to bring forth
[2]gnats, but [a]they could not; so there were [2]gnats on man and
beast.
19 Then the [1]magicians said to Pharaoh, "[a]This is the finger of
God." But Pharaoh's heart was [2]hardened, and he did not listen
to them, as the LORD had said.
20 Now the LORD said to Moses, "[a]Rise early in the morning
and present yourself before Pharaoh, [1]as [b]he comes out to the
water, and say to him, 'Thus says the LORD, "[c]Let My people
go, that they may serve Me.
21 "For if you do not let My people go, behold, I will send
swarms of flies on you and on your servants and on your
people and into your houses; and the houses of the Egyptians
will be full of swarms of flies, and also the ground on which
they *dwell.*
22 "[a]But on that day I will set apart the land of Goshen, where
My people are [1]living, so that no swarms of flies will be there,
in order that you may know that [2b]I, the LORD, am in the midst
of the land.
23 "I will [1]put a division between My people and your people.
Tomorrow this sign will occur."'"
24 Then the LORD did so. And there came [1]great swarms of
flies into the house of Pharaoh and the houses of his servants
and the land was [a]laid waste because of the swarms of flies in
all the land of Egypt.
25 Pharaoh [a]called for Moses and Aaron and said, "[b]Go,
sacrifice to your God within the land."
26 But Moses said, "It is not right to do so, for we will
sacrifice to the LORD our God [1]what is [a]an abomination to the

9 [2]Lit *cut off*
10 [a]Ex 9:14; Deut 4:35, 39; 33:26; 2 Sam 7:22; 1 Chr 17:20; Ps 86:8; Is 46:9; Jer 10:6, 7
11 [a]Ex 8:13
12 [1]Lit *placed* [a]Ex 8:30; 9:33; 10:18
14 [1]I.e. had a bad smell
15 [1]Lit *made heavy* [a]Ex 7:4
16 [1]Or *lice*
17 [1]Or *lice* [a]Ps 105:31
18 [1]Or *soothsayer priests* [2]Or *lice* [a]Ex 7:11, 12; 8:7; 9:11
19 [1]Or *soothsayer priests* [2]Lit *strong* [a]Ex 7:5; 10:7; Ps 8:3; Luke 11:20
20 [1]Lit *behold* [a]Ex 7:15; 9:13 [b]Ex 2:5; 7:15 [c]Ex 3:18; 4:23; 5:1, 3; 8:1
22 [1]Lit *standing* [2]Or *I am the LORD in the midst of the earth* [a]Ex 9:4, 6, 24; 10:23; 11:7 [b]Ex 9:29; 19:5; 20:11
23 [1]Lit *set a ransom*
24 [1]Lit *heavy* [a]Ps 78:45; 105:31
25 [a]Ex 8:8; 9:27; 10:16 [b]Ex 9:28; 10:8, 24; 12:31
26 [1]Lit *the abomination of Egypt* [a]Gen 43:32; 46:34; Deut 7:25f

Egyptians. If we sacrifice [1]what is an abomination to the
Egyptians before their eyes, will they not then stone us?
27 "We must go a [a]three days' journey into the wilderness and
sacrifice to the LORD our God as He [1]commands us."
28 Pharaoh said, "[a]I will let you go, that you may sacrifice to
the LORD your God in the wilderness; only you shall not go very
far away. [b]Make supplication for me."
29 Then Moses said, "Behold, I am going out from you, and I
shall make supplication to the LORD that the swarms of flies
may depart from Pharaoh, from his servants, and from his people
tomorrow; only do not let Pharaoh [a]deal deceitfully again in not
letting the people go to sacrifice to the LORD."
30 So [a]Moses went out from Pharaoh and made supplication
to the LORD.
31 The LORD did [1]as Moses asked, and removed the swarms of
flies from Pharaoh, from his servants and from his people; not
one remained.
32 But Pharaoh [1]hardened his heart this time also, and [a]he did
not let the people go.

Chapter 9 Theme ________________________

9 Then the LORD said to Moses, "Go to Pharaoh and speak to
him, 'Thus says the LORD, the God of the Hebrews, "[a]Let
My people go, that they may serve Me.
2 "For [a]if you refuse to let *them* go and [1]continue to hold them,
3 behold, [a]the hand of the LORD [1]will come *with* a very
severe pestilence on your livestock which are in the field, on
the horses, on the donkeys, on the camels, on the herds, and
on the flocks.
4 "[a]But the LORD will make a distinction between the livestock
of Israel and the livestock of Egypt, so that [b]nothing will die of
all that belongs to the sons of Israel."'"
5 The LORD set a definite time, saying, "Tomorrow the LORD
will do this thing in the land."
6 So the LORD did this thing on the next day, and [a]all the
livestock of Egypt died; [b]but of the livestock of the sons of
Israel, not one died.
7 Pharaoh sent, and behold, there was not even one of the
livestock of Israel dead. But [a]the heart of Pharaoh was
[1]hardened, and he did not let the people go.
8 Then the LORD said to Moses and Aaron, "Take for
yourselves handfuls of soot from a kiln, and let Moses throw it
toward the sky in the sight of Pharaoh.
9 "It will become fine dust over all the land of Egypt, and will
become [a]boils breaking out with sores on man and beast
through all the land of Egypt."
10 So they took soot from a kiln, and stood before Pharaoh;
and Moses threw it toward the sky, and it became boils
breaking out with sores on man and beast.

26 [1]Lit *the abomination of Egypt*

27 [1]Lit *says to us* [a]Ex 3:18; 5:3

28 [a]Ex 8:8, 15, 29, 32 [b]Ex 8:8; 9:28; 1 Kin 13:6

29 [a]Ex 8:8, 15

30 [a]Ex 8:12

31 [1]Lit *according to the word of Moses*

32 [1]Lit *made heavy* [a]Ex 4:21; 8:8, 15

9:1 [a]Ex 4:23; 8:1

2 [1]Lit *still hold* [a]Ex 8:2

3 [1]Lit *will be* [a]Ex 7:4; 1 Sam 5:6; Ps 39:10; Acts 13:11

4 [a]Ex 8:22 [b]Ex 9:6

6 [a]Ex 9:19, 20, 25; Ps 78:48 [b]Ex 9:4

7 [1]Lit *heavy* [a]Ex 7:14; 8:32

9 [a]Deut 28:27; Rev 16:2

11 [a]The [1]magicians could not stand before Moses because of the boils, for the boils were on the magicians [2]as well as on all the Egyptians.

12 And [a]the LORD [1]hardened Pharaoh's heart, and he did not listen to them, just as the LORD had spoken to Moses.

13 Then the LORD said to Moses, "[a]Rise up early in the morning and stand before Pharaoh and say to him, 'Thus says the LORD, the God of the Hebrews, "[b]Let My people go, that they may serve Me.

14 "For this time I will send all My plagues [1]on you and your servants and your people, so that [a]you may know that there is no one like Me in all the earth.

15 "For *if by* now I had put forth My hand and struck you and your people with pestilence, you would then have been cut off from the earth.

16 "But, indeed, [a]for this reason I have allowed you to [1]remain, in order to show you My power and in order to proclaim My name through all the earth.

17 "Still you exalt yourself against My people [1]by not letting them go.

18 "Behold, about this time tomorrow, [a]I will [1]send a very heavy hail, such as has not been *seen* in Egypt from the day it was founded [2]until now.

19 "Now therefore send, bring [a]your livestock and whatever you have in the field to safety. [b]Every man and beast that is found in the field and is not brought home, when the hail comes down on them, will die."'"

20 [a]The one among the servants of Pharaoh who [1]feared the word of the LORD made his servants and his livestock flee into the houses;

21 but he who [1]paid no regard to the word of the LORD [2]left his servants and his livestock in the field.

22 Now the LORD said to Moses, "Stretch out your hand toward the sky, that [1a]hail may fall on all the land of Egypt, on man and on beast and on every plant of the field, throughout the land of Egypt."

23 Moses stretched out his staff toward the sky, and the LORD [1]sent [2]thunder and [a]hail, and fire ran down to the earth. And the LORD rained hail on the land of Egypt.

24 So there was hail, and fire [1]flashing continually in the midst of the hail, very severe, such as had not been in all the land of Egypt since it became a nation.

25 [a]The hail struck all that was in the field through all the land of Egypt, both man and beast; the hail also struck every plant of the field and shattered every tree of the field.

26 [a]Only in the land of Goshen, where the sons of Israel *were,* there was no hail.

27 Then Pharaoh [1a]sent for Moses and Aaron, and said to them, "[b]I have sinned this time; the LORD is the righteous one, and I and my people are the wicked ones.

28 "[a]Make supplication to the LORD, for there has been enough

11 [1]Or *soothsayer priests* [2]Lit *and on all* [a]Ex 8:18

12 [1]Lit *made strong* [a]Ex 4:21; 10:1, 20; 14:8; Josh 11:20; John 12:40

13 [a]Ex 8:20 [b]Ex 4:23

14 [1]Lit *to your heart* [a]Ex 8:10; Deut 3:24; 2 Sam 7:22; 1 Chr 17:20; Ps 86:8; Is 45:5-8; 46:9; Jer 10:6, 7

16 [1]Lit *stand* [a]Prov 16:4; Rom 9:17

17 [1]Lit *so as not to let*

18 [1]Lit *cause to rain* [2]Lit *and until now* [a]Ex 9:23, 24

19 [a]Ex 9:6 [b]Ex 9:25

20 [1]Or *revered* [a]Prov 13:13

21 [1]Lit *did not set his heart to* [2]Lit *then left*

22 [1]Lit *there may be hail* [a]Rev 16:21

23 [1]Lit *gave* [2]Lit *sounds* [a]Gen 19:24; Josh 10:11; Ps 18:13; 78:47; 105:32; Is 30:30; Ezek 38:22; Rev 8:7

24 [1]Lit *taking hold of itself*

25 [a]Ex 9:19; Ps 78:47, 48; 105:32, 33

26 [a]Ex 8:22; 9:4, 6; 11:7

27 [1]Lit *sent and called* [a]Ex 8:8 [b]Ex 10:16, 17; 2 Chr 12:6; Ps 129:4; 145:17; Lam 1:18

28 [a]Ex 8:8, 28; 10:17

of God's [1]thunder and hail; and [b]I will let you go, and you shall
stay no longer."
29 Moses said to him, "As soon as I go out of the city, I will
[a]spread out my [1]hands to the LORD; the [2]thunder will cease and
there will be hail no longer, that you may know that [b]the earth
is the LORD's.
30 "[a]But as for you and your servants, I know that [b]you do not
yet [1]fear [2]the LORD God."
31 (Now the flax and the [a]barley were [1]ruined, for the barley
was in the ear and the flax was in bud.
32 But the wheat and the spelt were not [1]ruined, for they
ripen late.)
33 [a]So Moses went out of the city from Pharaoh, and spread
out his [1]hands to the LORD; and the [2]thunder and the hail ceased,
and rain [3]no longer poured on the earth.
34 But when Pharaoh saw that the rain and the hail and the
[1]thunder had ceased, he sinned again and [2]hardened his heart,
he and his servants.
35 Pharaoh's heart was [1]hardened, and he did not let the sons
of Israel go, just as the [a]LORD had spoken through Moses.

Chapter 10 Theme ______________________

10 Then the LORD said to Moses, "Go to Pharaoh, for [a]I have
[1]hardened his heart and the heart of his servants, that I
may [2]perform these signs of Mine [3]among them,
2 and [a]that you may tell in the [1]hearing of your son, and of
your grandson, how I made a mockery of the Egyptians and
how I [2]performed My signs among them, [b]that you may know
that I am the LORD."
3 Moses and Aaron went to Pharaoh and said to him, "Thus
says the LORD, the God of the Hebrews, 'How long will you
refuse to [a]humble yourself before Me? [b]Let My people go, that
they may serve Me.
4 'For if you refuse to let My people go, behold, tomorrow I
will bring locusts into your territory.
5 'They shall cover the surface of the land, so that no one will
be able to see the land. [a]They will also eat the rest of what has
escaped—what is left to you from the hail—and they will eat
every tree which sprouts for you out of the field.
6 'Then [a]your houses shall be filled and the houses of all your
servants and the houses of all the Egyptians, *something* which
neither your fathers nor your grandfathers have seen, from the
day that they [1]came upon the earth until this day.'" And he
turned and went out from Pharaoh.
7 [a]Pharaoh's servants said to him, "How long will this man
be [b]a snare to us? Let the men go, that they may serve the
LORD their God. Do you not [1]realize that Egypt is destroyed?"
8 So Moses and Aaron [a]were brought back to Pharaoh, and
he said to them, "[b]Go, serve the LORD your God! [1]Who are the
ones that are going?"

28 [1]Lit *sounds* [b]Ex 8:25; 10:8, 24

29 [1]Lit *palms* [2]Lit *sounds* [a]1 Kin 8:22, 38; Ps 143:6; Is 1:15 [b]Ex 8:22; 19:5; 20:11; Ps 24:1; 1 Cor 10:26

30 [1]Or *reverence* [2]Lit *before the LORD* [a]Ex 8:29 [b]Is 26:10

31 [1]Lit *smitten* [a]Ruth 1:22; 2:23

32 [1]Lit *smitten*

33 [1]Lit *palms* [2]Lit *sounds* [3]Lit *was not poured* [a]Ex 8:12; 9:29

34 [1]Lit *sounds* [2]Lit *made heavy*

35 [1]Lit *strong* [a]Ex 4:21

10:1 [1]Lit *made heavy* [2]Lit *put* [3]Lit *in his midst* [a]Ex 4:21; 7:13; Josh 11:20; John 12:40; Rom 9:18

2 [1]Lit *ears* [2]Lit *put* [a]Ex 12:26, 27; 13:8, 14, 15; Deut 4:9; Ps 44:1; 78:5; Joel 1:3 [b]Ex 7:5, 17

3 [a]1 Kin 21:29; 2 Chr 34:27; James 4:10; 1 Pet 5:6 [b]Ex 4:23

5 [a]Joel 1:4; 2:25

6 [1]Lit *were* [a]Ex 8:3, 21

7 [1]Lit *know* [a]Ex 7:5; 8:19; 12:33 [b]Ex 23:33; Josh 23:13; 1 Sam 18:21; Eccl 7:26

8 [1]Lit *Who and who are* [a]Ex 8:8 [b]Ex 8:25

9 Moses said, "[a]We shall go with our young and our old; with
our sons and our daughters, [b]with our flocks and our herds we
shall go, for we [1]must hold a feast to the LORD."
10 Then he said to them, "Thus may the LORD be with you, [1]if
ever I let you and your little ones go! Take heed, for evil is [2]in
your mind.
11 "Not so! Go now, the men *among you,* and serve the LORD,
for [1]that is what you desire." So [a]they were driven out from
Pharaoh's presence.
12 Then the LORD said to Moses, "[a]Stretch out your hand over
the land of Egypt for the locusts, that they may come up on the
land of Egypt and [b]eat every plant of the land, *even* all that the
hail has left."
13 So Moses stretched out his staff over the land of Egypt, and
the LORD directed an east wind on the land all that day and all
that night; and when it was morning, the east wind [1]brought
the [a]locusts.
14 [a]The locusts came up over all the land of Egypt and settled in
all the territory of Egypt; *they were* very [1]numerous. There had
never been so *many* [2]locusts, nor would there be so *many* [3]again.
15 For they covered the surface of the whole land, so that the
land was darkened; and they [a]ate every plant of the land and all
the fruit of the trees that the hail had left. Thus nothing green
was left on tree or plant of the field through all the land of Egypt.
16 Then Pharaoh hurriedly [a]called for Moses and Aaron, and he
said, "[b]I have sinned against the LORD your God and against you.
17 "Now therefore, please forgive my sin only this once, and
[a]make supplication to the LORD your God, that He would only
remove this death from me."
18 [a]He went out from Pharaoh and made supplication to the
LORD.
19 So the LORD shifted *the wind* to a very strong west wind
which took up the locusts and drove them into the [1]Red Sea;
not one locust was left in all the territory of Egypt.
20 But [a]the LORD [1]hardened Pharaoh's heart, and he did not
let the sons of Israel go.
21 Then the LORD said to Moses, "[a]Stretch out your hand
toward the sky, that there may be darkness over the land of
Egypt, even a darkness [b]which may be felt."
22 So Moses stretched out his hand toward the sky, and there
was [a]thick darkness in all the land of Egypt for three days.
23 They did not see one another, nor did anyone rise from his
place for three days, [a]but all the sons of Israel had light in their
dwellings.
24 Then Pharaoh [a]called to Moses, and said, "Go, serve the
LORD; only let your flocks and your herds be detained. Even
[b]your little ones may go with you."
25 But Moses said, "You must also [1]let us have sacrifices and
burnt offerings, that we may [2]sacrifice *them* to the LORD our God.
26 "[a]Therefore, our livestock too shall go with us; not a hoof
shall be left behind, for we shall take some of them to serve the

9 [1]Lit *have a feast* [a]Ex 12:37, 38 [b]Ex 10:26
10 [1]Lit *when I* [2]Lit *before your face*
11 [1]Lit *you desire it* [a]Ex 10:28
12 [a]Ex 7:19 [b]Ex 10:5, 15
13 [1]Lit *carried* [a]Ps 78:46; 105:34
14 [1]Lit *heavy* [2]Lit *locusts like them before them* [3]Lit *after them* [a]Deut 28:38; Ps 78:46; 105:34; Joel 1:4, 7; 2:1-11; Rev 9:3
15 [a]Ex 10:5; Ps 105:34f
16 [a]Ex 8:8 [b]Ex 9:27
17 [a]Ex 8:8, 28; 9:28; 1 Kin 13:6
18 [a]Ex 8:30
19 [1]Lit *Sea of Reeds*
20 [1]Lit *made strong* [a]Ex 4:21; 11:10
21 [a]Ex 9:22 [b]Deut 28:29
22 [a]Ps 105:28; Rev 16:10
23 [a]Ex 8:22
24 [a]Ex 8:8, 25 [b]Ex 10:10
25 [1]Lit *give into our hand* [2]Lit *make*
26 [a]Ex 10:9

LORD our God. And until we arrive there, we ourselves do not
know with what we shall serve the LORD."
27 But [a]the LORD [1]hardened Pharaoh's heart, and he was not
willing to let them go.
28 Then Pharaoh said to him, "[a]Get away from me! [1]Beware,
do not see my face again, for in the day you see my face you
shall die!"
29 Moses said, "You are right; [a]I shall never see your face again!"

27 [1]Lit *made strong* [a]Ex 4:21; 10:20; 14:4, 8

28 [1]Lit *Take heed to yourself* [a]Ex 10:11

29 [a]Ex 11:8; Heb 11:27

Chapter 11 Theme ______________________

11 Now the LORD said to Moses, "One more plague I will
bring on Pharaoh and on Egypt; [a]after that he will let you
go from here. When he lets you go, he will surely drive you out
from here completely.
2 "Speak now in the [1]hearing of the people that [a]each man
ask from his neighbor and each woman from her neighbor for
articles of silver and articles of gold."
3 [a]The LORD gave the people favor in the sight of the Egyptians.
[b]Furthermore, the man Moses *himself* was [1]greatly esteemed
in the land of Egypt, *both* in the sight of Pharaoh's servants and
in the sight of the people.
4 Moses said, "Thus says the LORD, 'About [a]midnight I am
going out into the midst of Egypt,
5 and [a]all the firstborn in the land of Egypt shall die, from
the firstborn of the Pharaoh who sits on his throne, even to the
firstborn of the slave girl who is behind the millstones; all the
firstborn of the cattle as well.
6 'Moreover, there shall be [a]a great cry in all the land of
Egypt, such as there has not been *before* and such as shall
never be again.
7 '[a]But against any of the sons of Israel a dog will not *even*
[1]bark, whether against man or beast, that you may [2]understand
how the LORD makes a distinction between Egypt and Israel.'
8 "[a]All these your servants will come down to me and bow
themselves [1]before me, saying, 'Go out, you and all the people
who [2]follow you,' and after that I will go out." [b]And he went
out from Pharaoh in hot anger.
9 Then the LORD said to Moses, "[a]Pharaoh will not listen to
you, so [b]that My wonders will be multiplied in the land of
Egypt."
10 [a]Moses and Aaron performed all these wonders before
Pharaoh; yet [b]the LORD [1]hardened Pharaoh's heart, and he did
not let the sons of Israel go out of his land.

11:1 [a]Ex 12:31, 33, 39

2 [1]Lit *ears* [a]Ex 3:22; 12:35, 36

3 [1]Lit *very great* [a]Ex 3:21; 12:36; Ps 106:46 [b]Deut 34:10-12

4 [a]Ex 12:29

5 [a]Ex 12:12, 29; Ps 78:51; 105:36; 135:8; 136:10

6 [a]Ex 12:30

7 [1]Lit *sharpen his tongue* [2]Lit *know* [a]Ex 8:22; Josh 10:21

8 [1]Lit *to* [2]Lit *are at your feet* [a]Ex 12:31-33 [b]Heb 11:27

9 [a]Ex 7:4 [b]Ex 7:3

10 [1]Lit *made strong* [a]Ex 4:21 [b]Ex 7:3; 9:12; 10:20, 27; Josh 11:20; Is 63:17; John 12:40

Chapter 12 Theme ______________________

12 Now the LORD said to Moses and Aaron in the land of
[1]Egypt,
2 "[a]This month shall be the beginning of months for you; it is
to be the first month of the year to you.
3 "Speak to all the congregation of Israel, saying, 'On the tenth

12:1 [1]Lit *Egypt, saying*

2 [a]Ex 13:4; 23:15; 34:18; Deut 16:1

of this month they are each one to take a [1]lamb for themselves,
according to their fathers' households, a [1]lamb for [2]each
household.
4 'Now if the household is too small for a [1]lamb, then he and
his neighbor nearest to his house are to take one according to
the [2]number of persons *in them;* according to [3]what each man
should eat, you are to [4]divide the lamb.
5 'Your [1]lamb shall be [a]an unblemished male a year old; you
may take it from the sheep or from the goats.
6 '[1]You shall keep it until the [a]fourteenth day of the same
month, then the whole assembly of the congregation of Israel is
to kill it [2b]at twilight.
7 '[a]Moreover, they shall take some of the blood and put it on
the two doorposts and on the lintel [1]of the houses in which they
eat it.
8 'They shall eat the flesh [a]that *same* night, [b]roasted with fire,
and they shall eat it with [c]unleavened bread [1d]and bitter herbs.
9 'Do not eat any of it raw or boiled at all with water, but
rather [a]roasted with fire, *both* its head and its legs along with
[b]its entrails.
10 '[a]And you shall not leave any of it over until morning, but
whatever is left of it until morning, you shall burn with fire.
11 'Now you shall eat it in this manner: *with* your loins girded,
your sandals on your feet, and your staff in your hand; and you
shall eat it in haste—it is [a]the LORD's Passover.
12 'For [a]I will go through the land of Egypt on that night, and
will strike down all the firstborn in the land of Egypt, both man
and beast; and [b]against all the gods of Egypt I will execute
judgments—[c]I am the LORD.
13 '[a]The blood shall be a sign for you on the houses where you
[1]live; and when I see the blood I will pass over you, and no
plague will befall you [2]to destroy *you* when I strike the land of
Egypt.
14 'Now [a]this day will be [b]a memorial to you, and you shall
celebrate it *as* a feast to the LORD; throughout your generations
you are to celebrate it *as* [1c]a permanent ordinance.
15 '[a]Seven days you shall eat unleavened bread, but on the first
day you shall [1]remove leaven from your houses; for whoever
eats anything leavened from the first day until the seventh day,
[b]that [2]person shall be cut off from Israel.
16 '[a]On the first day you shall have a holy assembly, and
another holy assembly on the seventh day; no work at all shall
be done on them, except what must be eaten [1]by every person,
that alone may be [2]prepared by you.
17 'You shall also observe [a]the *Feast of* Unleavened Bread, for
on this [b]very day I brought your hosts out of the land of Egypt;
therefore you shall observe this day throughout your generations
as [c]a [1]permanent ordinance.
18 '[a]In the first *month,* on the fourteenth day of the month at
evening, you shall eat unleavened bread, until the twenty-first
day of the month at evening.

3 [1]Or *kid* [2]Lit *the*
4 [1]Or *kid* [2]Or *amount* [3]Lit *each man's eating* [4]Lit *compute for*
5 [1]Or *kid* [a]Lev 22:18-21; 23:12; Heb 9:14; 1 Pet 1:19
6 [1]Lit *It shall be to you for a guarding* [2]Lit *between the two evenings* [a]Ex 12:14, 17; Lev 23:5; Num 9:1-3, 11; 28:16 [b]Ex 16:12; Deut 16:4, 6
7 [1]Lit *upon* [a]Ex 12:22
8 [1]Lit *in addition to* [a]Ex 34:25; Num 9:12 [b]Deut 16:7 [c]Deut 16:3, 4; 1 Cor 5:8 [d]Num 9:11
9 [a]Ex 12:8 [b]Ex 29:13, 17, 22
10 [a]Ex 16:19; 23:18; 34:25
11 [a]Ex 12:13, 21, 27, 43
12 [a]Ex 11:4, 5 [b]Num 33:4; Ps 82:1 [c]Ex 6:2
13 [1]Lit *are* [2]Lit *for destruction* [a]Heb 11:28
14 [1]Or *an eternal* [a]Ex 12:6; Lev 23:4, 5; 2 Kin 23:21 [b]Ex 13:9 [c]Ex 12:17, 24; 13:10
15 [1]Lit *cause to cease* [2]Lit *soul* [a]Ex 13:6, 7; 23:15; 34:18; Lev 23:6; Num 28:17; Deut 16:3, 8 [b]Gen 17:14; Ex 12:19; Num 9:13
16 [1]Lit *pertaining to* [2]Lit *done* [a]Lev 23:7, 8; Num 28:18, 25
17 [1]Or *eternal* [a]Deut 16:3-8 [b]Ex 12:41 [c]Ex 12:14; 13:3, 10
18 [a]Ex 12:2; Lev 23:5-8; Num 28:16-25

19 '[a]Seven days there shall be no leaven found in your houses;
for whoever eats what is leavened, that [1b]person shall be cut
off from the congregation of Israel, whether *he is* an alien or a
native of the land.
20 'You shall not eat anything leavened; in all your dwellings
you shall eat unleavened bread.'"
21 Then [a]Moses called for all the elders of Israel and said to
them, "[1]Go and [b]take for yourselves [2]lambs according to your
families, and slay [c]the Passover *lamb.*
22 "[a]You shall take a bunch of hyssop and dip it in the blood
which is in the basin, and [1]apply some of the blood that is in the
basin to the lintel and the two doorposts; and none of you shall
go outside the door of his house until morning.
23 "For [a]the LORD will pass through to smite the Egyptians; and
when He sees the blood on the lintel and on the two doorposts,
the LORD will pass over the door and will [b]not allow the
[c]destroyer to come in to your houses to smite *you.*
24 "And [a]you shall observe this event as an ordinance for you
and your children forever.
25 "When you enter the land which the LORD will give you, as
He has [1]promised, you shall observe this [2]rite.
26 "[a]And when your children say to you, '[1]What does this rite
mean to you?'
27 you shall say, 'It is a Passover sacrifice to [a]the LORD [1]who
passed over the houses of the sons of Israel in Egypt when He
smote the Egyptians, but [2]spared our homes.'" [b]And the people
bowed low and worshiped.
28 Then the sons of Israel went and did *so;* just as the LORD
had commanded Moses and Aaron, so they did.
29 Now it came about at [a]midnight that [b]the LORD struck all
[c]the firstborn in the land of Egypt, from the firstborn of Pharaoh
who sat on his throne to the firstborn of the captive who was
in the dungeon, and all the firstborn of [d]cattle.
30 Pharaoh arose in the night, he and all his servants and all
the Egyptians, and there was [a]a great cry in Egypt, for there
was no home where there was not someone dead.
31 Then [a]he called for Moses and Aaron at night and said,
"Rise up, [b]get out from among my people, both you and the
sons of Israel; and go, [1]worship the LORD, as you have said.
32 "Take [a]both your flocks and your herds, as you have said,
and go, and bless me also."
33 [a]The Egyptians urged the people, to send them out of the
land in haste, for they said, "We will all be dead."
34 So the people took [a]their dough before it was leavened, *with*
their kneading bowls bound up in the clothes on their shoulders.
35 [a]Now the sons of Israel had done according to the word of
Moses, for they had requested from the Egyptians articles of
silver and articles of gold, and clothing;
36 and the LORD had given the people favor in the sight of the
Egyptians, so that they let them have their request. Thus they
[a]plundered the Egyptians.

19 [1]Lit *soul* [a]Ex 12:15; 23:15; 34:18 [b]Num 9:13

21 [1]Lit *Draw out* [2]Lit *sheep* [a]Num 9:4; Heb 11:28 [b]Ex 12:3 [c]Ex 12:11

22 [1]Lit *cause to touch* [a]Ex 12:7

23 [a]Ex 11:4; 12:12, 13 [b]Rev 7:3; 9:4 [c]1 Cor 10:10; Heb 11:28

24 [a]Ex 12:14, 17; 13:5, 10

25 [1]Lit *spoken* [2]Lit *service*

26 [1]Lit *What is this service to you?* [a]Ex 10:2; 13:8, 14, 15; Deut 32:7; Josh 4:6; Ps 78:6

27 [1]Lit *because He* [2]Lit *delivered* [a]Ex 12:11 [b]Ex 4:31

29 [a]Ex 11:4, 5 [b]Num 8:17; 33:4; Ps 135:8; 136:10 [c]Ex 4:23; Ps 78:51; 105:36 [d]Ex 9:6

30 [a]Ex 11:6

31 [1]Or *serve* [a]Ex 8:8 [b]Ex 8:25

32 [a]Ex 10:9, 26

33 [a]Ex 10:7; 11:1; 12:39; Ps 105:38

34 [a]Ex 12:39

35 [a]Ex 3:21, 22; 11:2, 3; Ps 105:37

36 [a]Ex 3:22

37 Now the [a]sons of Israel journeyed from [b]Rameses to Succoth,
about [c]six hundred thousand men on foot, aside from children.
38 A [a]mixed multitude also went up with them, [1]along with
flocks and herds, a [b]very large number of livestock.
39 They baked the dough which they had brought out of Egypt
into cakes of unleavened bread. For it had not become leavened,
since they were [a]driven out of Egypt and could not delay, nor
had they [1]prepared any provisions for themselves.
40 Now the time [1]that the sons of Israel lived in Egypt was
[a]four hundred and thirty years.
41 And at the end of four hundred and thirty years, [1]to [a]the
very day, [b]all the hosts of the LORD went out from the land of
Egypt.
42 [a]It is a night [1]to be observed for the LORD for having
brought them out from the land of Egypt; this night is for the
LORD, [1]to be observed [2]by all the sons of Israel throughout their
generations.
43 The LORD said to Moses and Aaron, "This is the ordinance
of [a]the Passover: no [1b]foreigner is to eat of it;
44 but every man's [a]slave purchased with money, after you
have circumcised him, then he may eat of it.
45 "[a]A sojourner or a hired servant shall not eat of it.
46 "It is to be eaten in a single house; you are not to bring forth
any of the flesh outside of the house, [a]nor are you to break any
bone of it.
47 "[a]All the congregation of Israel are to [1]celebrate this.
48 "But [a]if a [1]stranger sojourns with you, and [2]celebrates the
Passover to the LORD, let all his males be circumcised, and then
let him come near to [3]celebrate it; and he shall be like a native
of the land. But no uncircumcised person may eat of it.
49 "[1a]The same law shall [2]apply to the native as to the [3]stranger
who sojourns among you."
50 Then all the sons of Israel did *so;* they did just as the LORD
had commanded Moses and Aaron.
51 And on that same day [a]the LORD brought the sons of Israel
out of the land of Egypt [1b]by their hosts.

Chapter 13 Theme ________________________

13 Then the LORD spoke to Moses, saying,
2 "[a]Sanctify to Me every firstborn, the first [1]offspring of
every womb among the sons of Israel, both of man and beast; it
belongs to Me."
3 Moses said to the people, "[a]Remember this day in which
you went out from Egypt, from the house of [1]slavery; for [b]by [2]a
powerful hand the LORD brought you out from this place. [c]And
nothing leavened shall be eaten.
4 "On this day in the [a]month of Abib, you are about to go
forth.
5 "It shall be when the LORD [a]brings you to the land of the
Canaanite, the Hittite, the Amorite, the Hivite and the Jebusite,

37 [a]Num 33:3, 5 [b]Gen 47:11 [c]Ex 38:26; Num 1:46; 2:32; 11:21; 26:51

38 [1]Lit *and* [a]Num 11:4 [b]Ex 17:3; Num 20:19; 32:1; Deut 3:19

39 [1]Lit *made* [a]Ex 6:1; 11:1; 12:31-33

40 [1]Or *of the sons of Israel who dwelt* [a]Gen 15:13, 16; Acts 7:6; Gal 3:17

41 [1]Lit *that it happened on this very day* [a]Ex 12:17 [b]Ex 3:8, 10; 6:6

42 [1]Or *of vigil* [2]Lit *to the sons* [a]Ex 13:10; 34:18; Deut 16:1

43 [1]Lit *son of a stranger* [a]Ex 12:11; Num 9:14 [b]Ex 12:48

44 [a]Gen 17:12, 13; Lev 22:11

45 [a]Lev 22:10

46 [a]Num 9:12; Ps 34:20; John 19:33, 36

47 [1]Lit *do* [a]Ex 12:6; Num 9:13, 14

48 [1]Lit *sojourner* [2]Lit *does* [3]Lit *do* [a]Num 9:14

49 [1]Lit *One law* [2]Lit *be* [3]Lit *sojourner* [a]Lev 24:22; Num 15:15, 16, 29

51 [1]Lit *according to* [a]Ex 12:41 [b]Ex 6:26

13:2 [1]Lit *opening* [a]Ex 13:12, 13, 15; 22:29; Lev 27:26; Num 3:13; 8:16f; 18:15; Deut 15:19; Luke 2:23

3 [1]Lit *slaves* [2]Lit *strength of hand* [a]Ex 12:42; Deut 16:3 [b]Ex 3:20; 6:1 [c]Ex 12:19

4 [a]Ex 12:2; 23:15; 34:18; Deut 16:1

5 [a]Ex 3:8, 17;

RETURN TO INSTRUCTIONS

which [b]He swore to your fathers to give you, a land flowing
with milk and honey, [c]that you shall [1]observe this rite in this
month.
6 "For [a]seven days you shall eat unleavened bread, and on the
seventh day there shall be a feast to the LORD.
7 "Unleavened bread shall be eaten throughout the seven
days; and [a]nothing leavened shall be seen [1]among you, nor
shall any leaven be seen [1]among you in all your borders.
8 "[a]You shall tell your son on that day, saying, 'It is because of
what the LORD did for me when I came out of Egypt.'
9 "And [a]it shall [1]serve as a sign to you on your hand, and as a
reminder [2]on your forehead, that the law of the LORD may be
in your mouth; for with [b]a powerful hand the LORD brought you
out of Egypt.
10 "Therefore, you shall [a]keep this ordinance at its appointed
time from [1]year to year.
11 "Now when [a]the LORD brings you to the land of the Canaanite,
as [b]He swore to you and to your fathers, and gives it to you,
12 [a]you shall [1]devote to the LORD the first [2]offspring of every
womb, and [3]the first offspring of every beast that you own; the
males belong to the LORD.
13 "But [a]every first [1]offspring of a donkey you shall redeem with
a lamb, but if you do not redeem *it,* then you shall break its neck;
and [b]every firstborn of man among your sons you shall redeem.
14 "[a]And it shall be when your son asks you in time to come,
saying, 'What is this?' then you shall say to him, '[b]With a
[1]powerful hand the LORD brought us out of Egypt, from the
house of [2]slavery.
15 'It came about, when Pharaoh was stubborn about letting
us go, that the [a]LORD killed every firstborn in the land of Egypt,
both the firstborn of man and the firstborn of beast. Therefore,
I sacrifice to the LORD the males, the first [1]offspring of every
womb, but every firstborn of my sons I redeem.'
16 "So [a]it shall [1]serve as a sign on your hand and as [2]phylacteries
[3]on your forehead, for with a [4]powerful hand the LORD brought
us out of Egypt."
17 Now when Pharaoh had let the people go, God did not lead
them by the way of the land of the Philistines, even though it
was near; for God said, "[a]The people might change their minds
when they see war, and return to Egypt."
18 Hence God led the people around by the way of the
wilderness to the [1]Red Sea; and the sons of Israel went up [a]in
martial array from the land of Egypt.
19 Moses took [a]the bones of Joseph with him, for he had made
the sons of Israel solemnly swear, saying, "God will surely [1]take
care of you, and you shall carry my bones from here with you."
20 Then they set out from [a]Succoth and camped in Etham on
the edge of the wilderness.
21 [a]The LORD was going before them in a pillar of cloud by day
to lead them on the way, and in a pillar of fire by night to give
them light, that they might [1]travel by day and by night.

5 [1]Lit *serve this service* [b]Ex 6:8 [c]Ex 12:25

6 [a]Ex 12:15-20

7 [1]Lit *to* [a]Ex 12:19

8 [a]Ex 10:2; 12:26f; 13:14; Ps 44:1

9 [1]Lit *be for* [2]Lit *between your eyes* [a]Ex 12:14; 13:16; Num 15:39; Deut 6:8; 11:18 [b]Ex 13:3

10 [1]Lit *days to days* [a]Ex 12:24, 25; 13:5

11 [a]Ex 13:5 [b]Gen 15:18; 17:8; 28:15; Ps 105:42-45

12 [1]Lit *cause to pass over* [2]Lit *opening* [3]Lit *every issue the offspring of a beast* [a]Ex 13:1, 2; 22:29; 34:19; Lev 27:26; Num 18:15; Ezek 44:30; Luke 2:23

13 [1]Lit *opening* [a]Ex 34:20; Num 18:15 [b]Num 3:46

14 [1]Lit *strength of hand* [2]Lit *slaves* [a]Ex 10:2; 12:26, 27; 13:8; Deut 6:20; Josh 4:6, 21 [b]Ex 13:3, 9

15 [1]Lit *opening* [a]Ex 12:29

16 [1]Lit *be for* [2]Or *frontlet-bands* [3]Lit *between your eyes* [4]Lit *strength of hand* [a]Ex 13:9; Deut 6:8

17 [a]Ex 14:11, 12; Num 14:1-4; Deut 17:16

18 [1]Lit *Sea of Reeds* [a]Josh 1:14; 4:12, 13

19 [1]Lit *visit* [a]Gen 50:24, 25; Josh 24:32; Acts 7:15, 16

20 [a]Ex 12:37; Num 33:6

21 [1]Lit *go* [a]Ex 14:19, 24; 33:9, 10; Num 9:15; 14:14; Deut 1:33; Neh 9:12; Ps 78:14; 99:7; 105:39; Is 4:5; 1 Cor 10:1

22 [1]He [a]did not take away the pillar of cloud by day, nor the
pillar of fire by night, from before the people.

Chapter 14 Theme ______________________________

14 Now the LORD spoke to Moses, saying,
2 "Tell the sons of Israel to turn back and camp before
[a]Pi-hahiroth, between [b]Migdol and the sea; you shall camp in
front of Baal-zephon, opposite it, by the sea.
3 "For Pharaoh will say of the sons of Israel, 'They are wandering
aimlessly in the land; the wilderness has shut them in.'
4 "Thus [a]I will [1]harden Pharaoh's heart, and [b]he will chase after
them; and I will be honored through Pharaoh and all his army, and
[c]the Egyptians will know that I am the LORD." And they did so.
5 When the king of Egypt was told that the people had fled,
[1]Pharaoh and his servants had a change of heart toward the
people, and they said, "What is this we have done, that we
have let Israel go from serving us?"
6 So he made his chariot ready and took his people with him;
7 and he took six hundred select chariots, and all the *other*
chariots of Egypt with officers over all of them.
8 [a]The LORD [1]hardened the heart of Pharaoh, king of Egypt,
and he chased after the sons of Israel as the sons of Israel were
going out [2b]boldly.
9 Then [a]the Egyptians chased after them *with* all the horses
and chariots of Pharaoh, his horsemen and his army, and they
overtook them camping by the sea, [b]beside Pi-hahiroth, in front
of Baal-zephon.
10 As Pharaoh drew near, the sons of Israel [1]looked, and behold,
the Egyptians were marching after them, and they became very
frightened; [a]so the sons of Israel cried out to the LORD.
11 Then [a]they said to Moses, "Is it because there were no
graves in Egypt that you have taken us away to die in the
wilderness? Why have you dealt with us in this way, [1]bringing
us out of Egypt?
12 "[a]Is this not the word that we spoke to you in Egypt, saying,
'[1]Leave us alone that we may serve the Egyptians'? For it
would have been better for us to serve the Egyptians than to
die in the wilderness."
13 But Moses said to the people, "[a]Do not fear! [1]Stand by and
see [b]the salvation of the LORD which He will accomplish for you
today; for the Egyptians whom you have seen today, you will
never see them again forever.
14 "[a]The LORD will fight for you while [b]you keep silent."
15 Then the LORD said to Moses, "Why are you crying out to
Me? Tell the sons of Israel to go forward.
16 "As for you, lift up [a]your staff and stretch out your hand over
the sea and divide it, and the sons of Israel shall [1]go through
the midst of the sea on dry land.
17 "As for Me, behold, [a]I will [1]harden the hearts of the
Egyptians so that they will go in after them; and I will be

22 [1]Or *The pillar of cloud by day and the pillar of fire by night did not depart* [a]Neh 9:19

14:2 [a]Num 33:7 [b]Jer 44:1

4 [1]Lit *make strong* [a]Ex 4:21; 7:3; 14:17 [b]Ex 14:23 [c]Ex 7:5; 14:25

5 [1]Lit *the heart of Pharaoh . . . was changed*

8 [1]Lit *made strong* [2]Lit *with a high hand* [a]Ex 14:4 [b]Num 33:3; Acts 13:17

9 [a]Ex 15:9; Josh 24:6 [b]Ex 14:2

10 [1]Lit *lifted up their eyes* [a]Josh 24:7; Neh 9:9; Ps 34:17; 107:6

11 [1]Lit *so as to bring* [a]Ex 5:21; 15:24; 16:2; Ps 106:7, 8

12 [1]Lit *Cease from us* [a]Ex 6:9

13 [1]Or *Take your stand* [a]Gen 15:1; 46:3; Ex 20:20; 2 Chr 20:15, 17; Is 41:10, 13, 14 [b]Ex 14:30; 15:2

14 [a]Ex 14:25; 15:3; Deut 1:30; 3:22; Josh 23:3; 2 Chr 20:29; Neh 4:20 [b]Is 30:15

16 [1]Lit *enter the* [a]Ex 4:17, 20; 7:19; 14:21, 26; 17:5, 6, 9; Num 20:8, 9, 11; Is 10:26

17 [1]Lit *make strong* [a]Ex 14:4, 8

honored through Pharaoh and all his army, through his
chariots and his horsemen.
18 "[a]Then the Egyptians will know that I am the LORD, when I
am honored through Pharaoh, through his chariots and his
horsemen."
19 [a]The angel of God, who had been going before the camp of
Israel, moved and went behind them; and the pillar of cloud
moved from before them and stood behind them.
20 So it came between the camp of Egypt and the camp of Israel;
and there was the cloud [1]along with the darkness, yet it gave light
at night. Thus the one did not come near the other all night.
21 [a]Then Moses stretched out his hand over the sea; and the
LORD [1]swept the sea *back* by a strong east wind all night and
turned the sea into [b]dry land, so [c]the waters were divided.
22 [a]The sons of Israel [1]went through the midst of the sea on
the dry land, and [b]the waters *were like* a wall to them on their
right hand and on their left.
23 Then [a]the Egyptians took up the pursuit, and all Pharaoh's
horses, his chariots and his horsemen went in after them into
the midst of the sea.
24 At the morning watch, [a]the LORD looked down on the
[1]army of the Egyptians [2]through the pillar of fire and cloud and
brought the [1]army of the Egyptians into confusion.
25 He [1]caused their chariot wheels to swerve, and He made
them drive with difficulty; so the Egyptians said, "Let [2]us flee
from Israel, [a]for the LORD is fighting for them against the
Egyptians."
26 Then the LORD said to Moses, "[a]Stretch out your hand over
the sea so that the waters may come back over the Egyptians,
over their chariots and their horsemen."
27 So Moses stretched out his hand over the sea, and [a]the sea
returned to its normal state at daybreak, while the Egyptians
were fleeing [1]right into it; then the LORD [2b]overthrew the
Egyptians in the midst of the sea.
28 The waters returned and covered the chariots and the
horsemen, [1]even Pharaoh's entire army that had gone into the
sea after them; [a]not even one of them remained.
29 But the sons of Israel walked on [a]dry land through the
midst of the sea, and the waters *were like* a wall to them on
their right hand and on their left.
30 [a]Thus the LORD saved Israel that day from the hand of the
Egyptians, and Israel [b]saw the Egyptians dead on the seashore.
31 When Israel saw the great [1]power which the LORD had
[2]used against the Egyptians, the people [3]feared the LORD, and
[a]they believed in the LORD and in His servant Moses.

Chapter 15 Theme ________________

15 [a]Then Moses and the sons of Israel sang this song to the
LORD, [1]and said,
"[2b]I will sing to the LORD, for He [3]is highly exalted;
[c]The horse and its rider He has hurled into the sea.

18 [a]Ex 14:25
19 [a]Ex 13:21, 22
20 [1]Lit *and the darkness*
21 [1]Lit *caused to go* [a]Ex 7:19; 14:16 [b]Ps 66:6; 106:9; 136:13, 14 [c]Ex 15:8; Josh 3:16; 4:23; Neh 9:11; Ps 74:13; 78:13; 114:3, 5; Is 63:12, 13
22 [1]Lit *entered the* [a]Ex 15:19; Josh 3:17; 4:22; Neh 9:11; Ps 66:6; 78:13; Heb 11:29 [b]Ex 14:29; 15:8
23 [a]Ex 14:4, 17
24 [1]Lit *camp* [2]Or *in* [a]Ex 13:21
25 [1]Or *removed* [2]Lit *me* [a]Ex 14:4, 14, 18
26 [a]Ex 14:16
27 [1]Lit *to meet it* [2]Lit *shook off* [a]Josh 4:18 [b]Ex 15:1, 7; Deut 11:4; Neh 9:11; Ps 78:53; Heb 11:29
28 [1]Lit *in respect to* [a]Ps 78:53; 106:11
29 [a]Ex 14:22; Ps 66:6; Is 11:15
30 [a]Ex 14:13; Ps 106:8, 10; Is 63:8, 11 [b]Ps 58:10; 59:10
31 [1]Lit *hand* [2]Lit *done* [3]Or *revered* [a]Ex 4:31; 19:9; Ps 106:12; John 2:11; 11:45
15:1 [1]Lit *and said, saying* [2]Or *Let me sing* [3]Or *triumphed gloriously* [a]Ps 106:12; Rev 15:3 [b]Is 12:5; 42:10-12 [c]Jer 51:21

2 "[1][a]The LORD is my strength and song,
And He has become my salvation;
[b]This is my God, and I will praise Him;
[c]My father's God, and I will [d]extol Him.
3 "[a]The LORD is a warrior;
[1][b]The LORD is His name.
4 "[a]Pharaoh's chariots and his army He has cast into the sea;
And the choicest of his officers are [1]drowned in the [2]Red Sea.
5 "The deeps cover them;
[a]They went down into the depths like a stone.
6 "[a]Your right hand, O LORD, is majestic in power,
[b]Your right hand, O LORD, shatters the enemy.
7 "And in the greatness of Your [1]excellence You [a]overthrow
those who rise up against You;
[b]You send forth Your burning anger, *and* it [c]consumes them
as chaff.
8 "[a]At the blast of Your nostrils the waters were piled up,
[b]The flowing waters stood up like a heap;
The deeps were congealed in the heart of the sea.
9 "[a]The enemy said, 'I will pursue, I will overtake, I will
[b]divide the spoil;
My [1]desire shall be [2]gratified against them;
I will draw out my sword, my hand will [3]destroy them.'
10 "[a]You blew with Your wind, the sea covered them;
[b]They sank like lead in the [1]mighty waters.
11 "[a]Who is like You among the gods, O LORD?
Who is like You, [b]majestic in holiness,
[c]Awesome in praises, [d]working wonders?
12 "[a]You stretched out Your right hand,
The earth swallowed them.
13 "In Your lovingkindness You have [a]led the people whom You
have [b]redeemed;
In Your strength You have guided *them* [c]to Your holy
habitation.
14 "[a]The peoples have heard, they tremble;
Anguish has gripped the inhabitants of Philistia.
15 "Then the [a]chiefs of Edom were dismayed;
[b]The leaders of Moab, trembling grips them;
[c]All the inhabitants of Canaan have melted away.
16 "[a]Terror and dread fall upon them;
[b]By the greatness of Your arm they are motionless as stone;
Until Your people pass over, O LORD,
Until the people pass over whom You [c]have purchased.
17 "[a]You will bring them and [b]plant them in [c]the mountain of
Your inheritance,
[d]The place, O LORD, which You have made for Your
dwelling,
[e]The sanctuary, O Lord, which Your hands have
established.
18 "[a]The LORD shall reign forever and ever."
19 [a]For the horses of Pharaoh with his chariots and his

---

2 [1]Heb *YAH* [a]Ps 18:1, 2; Is 12:2; Hab 3:18f [b]Ps 48:14 [c]Ex 3:6, 15, 16 [d]2 Sam 22:47; Ps 99:5; Is 25:1
3 [1]Heb *YHWH,* usually rendered *LORD* [a]Ex 14:14; Rev 19:11 [b]Ex 3:15; 6:2, 3, 7, 8; Ps 24:8; 83:18
4 [1]Lit *sunk* [2]Lit *Sea of Reeds* [a]Ex 14:6, 7, 17, 28
5 [a]Ex 15:10; Neh 9:11
6 [a]Ex 3:20; 6:1 [b]Ps 118:15, 16
7 [1]Or *exaltation* [a]Ex 14:27 [b]Ps 78:49, 50 [c]Deut 4:24; Is 5:24; Heb 12:29
8 [a]Ex 14:22, 29; Job 4:9 [b]Ps 78:13
9 [1]Lit *soul* [2]Lit *be filled with them* [3]Or *dispossess, bring to ruin* [a]Ex 14:5, 8, 9 [b]Judg 5:30; Is 53:12; Luke 11:22
10 [1]Or *majestic* [a]Ex 14:27, 28 [b]Ex 15:5
11 [a]Ex 8:10; 9:14; Deut 3:24; 2 Sam 7:22; 1 Kin 8:23; Ps 71:19; 86:8; Mic 7:18 [b]Is 6:3; Rev 4:8 [c]Ps 22:23 [d]Ps 72:18; 136:4
12 [a]Ex 15:6
13 [a]Neh 9:12; Ps 77:20 [b]Ex 15:16; Ps 77:15 [c]Ex 15:17; Ps 78:54
14 [a]Deut 2:25; Hab 3:7
15 [a]Gen 36:15, 40 [b]Num 22:3, 4 [c]Josh 2:9, 11, 24; 5:1
16 [a]Ex 23:27; Deut 2:25; Josh 2:9 [b]Ex 15:5, 6 [c]Ex 15:13; Ps 74:2; Is 43:1; Jer 31:11; Titus 2:14; 2 Pet 2:1
17 [a]Ex 23:20; 32:34 [b]Ps 44:2; 80:8, 15 [c]Ps 2:6; 78:54, 68 [d]Ps 68:16; 76:2; 132:13, 14 [e]Ps 78:69
18 [a]Ps 10:16; 29:10; Is 57:15
19 [a]Ex 14:23, 28

horsemen went into the sea, and the LORD brought back the
waters of the sea on them, but the sons of Israel walked on [b]dry
land through the midst of the sea.
20 [a]Miriam the prophetess, Aaron's sister, took the [b]timbrel in
her hand, and all the women went out after her with timbrels
and with [1c]dancing.
21 Miriam answered them,
"[a]Sing to the LORD, for He [1]is highly exalted;
The horse and his rider He has hurled into the sea."
22 [a]Then Moses [1]led Israel from the [2]Red Sea, and they went
out into [b]the wilderness of [c]Shur; and they went three days in
the wilderness and found no water.
23 When they came to [a]Marah, they could not drink the
waters [1]of Marah, for they were [2]bitter; therefore it was named
[3]Marah.
24 So the people [a]grumbled at Moses, saying, "What shall we
drink?"
25 Then he [a]cried out to the LORD, and the LORD showed him
[b]a tree; and he threw *it* into the waters, and the waters became
sweet.

There He [c]made for them a statute and regulation, and
there He [d]tested them.
26 And He said, "[a]If you will give earnest heed to the voice of
the LORD your God, and do what is right in His sight, and give
ear [b]to His commandments, and keep all His statutes, [c]I will
put none of the diseases on you which I have put on the
Egyptians; for I, [d]the LORD, am your healer."
27 Then they came to [a]Elim where there *were* twelve springs
of water and seventy date palms, and they camped there beside
the waters.

Chapter 16 Theme ____________________________

16 Then they set out from Elim, and all the congregation of
the sons of Israel came to the wilderness of [a]Sin, which
is between Elim and Sinai, on [b]the fifteenth day of the second
month after their departure from the land of Egypt.
2 The whole congregation of the sons of Israel [a]grumbled
against Moses and Aaron in the wilderness.
3 The sons of Israel said to them, "[a]Would that we had died
by the LORD's hand in the land of Egypt, [b]when we sat by the
pots of [1]meat, when we ate bread to the full; for you have
brought us out into this wilderness to kill this whole assembly
with hunger."
4 Then the LORD said to Moses, "Behold, [a]I will rain bread
from heaven for you; and the people shall go out and gather a
day's portion every day, that I may [b]test them, whether or not
they will walk in My [1]instruction.
5 "[a]On the sixth day, when they prepare what they bring in, it
will be twice as much as they gather daily."
6 So Moses and Aaron said to all the sons of Israel, "At evening

19 [b]Ex 14:22, 29

20 [1]Lit *dances* [a]Ex 2:4; Num 26:59; 1 Chr 6:3; Mic 6:4 [b]Judg 11:34; 1 Sam 18:6; 1 Chr 15:16; Ps 68:25; 81:2; 149:3; Jer 31:4 [c]Judg 11:34; 21:21; 1 Sam 18:6; Ps 30:11; 150:4

21 [1]Or *has triumphed gloriously* [a]Ex 15:1

22 [1]Lit *caused Israel to journey* [2]Lit *Sea of Reeds* [a]Ps 77:20; 78:52, 53 [b]Num 33:8 [c]Gen 16:7; 20:1; 25:18

23 [1]Lit *from* [2]Heb *Marim* [3]I.e. bitterness [a]Num 33:8; Ruth 1:20

24 [a]Ex 14:11; 16:2; Ps 106:13

25 [a]Ex 14:10 [b]Ezek 47:7, 8 [c]Josh 24:25 [d]Ex 16:4; Deut 8:2, 16; Judg 2:22; 3:1, 4; Ps 66:10

26 [a]Ex 19:5, 6; Deut 7:12 [b]Ex 20:2-17 [c]Deut 7:15; 28:58, 60 [d]Ex 23:25; Deut 32:39; Ps 41:3, 4; 103:3; 147:3

27 [a]Num 33:9

16:1 [a]Num 33:10, 11; Ezek 30:15 [b]Ex 12:6, 51; 19:1

2 [a]Ex 14:11; 15:24; Ps 106:25; 1 Cor 10:10

3 [1]Or *flesh* [a]Ex 17:3; Num 14:2, 3; 20:3; Lam 4:9 [b]Num 11:4, 5

4 [1]Or *law* [a]Neh 9:15; Ps 78:23-25; 105:40; John 6:31; 1 Cor 10:3 [b]Ex 15:25; Deut 8:2, 16

5 [a]Ex 16:22

[1a]you will know that the LORD has brought you out of the land
of Egypt;
7 and in the morning [1]you will see [a]the glory of the LORD, for
[b]He hears your grumblings against the LORD; and [c]what are we,
that you grumble against us?"
8 Moses said, "*This will happen* when the LORD gives you
[1]meat to eat in the evening, and bread to the full in the morning;
for the LORD hears your grumblings which you grumble against
Him. And what are we? Your grumblings are [a]not against us
but against the LORD."
9 Then Moses said to Aaron, "Say to all the congregation of
the sons of Israel, '[a]Come near before the LORD, for He has
heard your grumblings.'"
10 It came about as Aaron spoke to the whole congregation of
the sons of Israel, that they [1]looked toward the wilderness, and
behold, [a]the glory of the LORD appeared in the cloud.
11 And the LORD spoke to Moses, saying,
12 "[a]I have heard the grumblings of the sons of Israel; speak to
them, saying, '[1]At twilight you shall eat [2]meat, and in the
morning you shall be filled with bread; and [b]you shall know
that I am the LORD your God.'"
13 So it came about at evening that [a]the quails came up and
covered the camp, and in the morning [b]there was a layer of
dew around the camp.
14 [a]When the layer of dew [1]evaporated, behold, on the
[2]surface of the wilderness [b]there was a fine flake-like thing, fine
as the frost on the ground.
15 When the sons of Israel saw *it,* they said to one another,
"[1]What is it?" For they did not know what it was. And Moses
said to them, "[a]It is the bread which the LORD has given you to
eat.
16 "This is [1]what the LORD has commanded, 'Gather of it every
man [2]as much as he should eat; you shall take [3a]an omer apiece
according to the number of persons each of you has in his
tent.'"
17 The sons of Israel did so, and *some* gathered much and
some little.
18 When they measured it with an omer, [a]he who had
gathered much had no excess, and he who had gathered little
had no lack; every man gathered [1]as much as he should eat.
19 Moses said to them, "[a]Let no man leave any of it until
morning."
20 But they did not listen to Moses, and some left part of it
until morning, and it bred worms and became foul; and Moses
was angry with them.
21 They gathered it morning by morning, every man [1]as much
as he should eat; but when the sun grew hot, it would melt.
22 [a]Now on the sixth day they gathered twice as much bread,
two omers for each one. When all the [b]leaders of the congregation came and told Moses,
23 then he said to them, "This is what the LORD [1]meant:

6 [1]Lit *and you* [a]Ex 6:7
7 [1]Lit *and you* [a]Ex 16:10, 12; Is 35:2; 40:5; John 11:4, 40 [b]Num 14:27; 17:5 [c]Num 16:11
8 [1]Or *flesh* [a]1 Sam 8:7; Luke 10:16; Rom 13:2; 1 Thess 4:8
9 [a]Num 16:16
10 [1]Lit *turned* [a]Ex 13:21; 16:7; Num 16:19; 1 Kin 8:10f
12 [1]Lit *Between the two evenings* [2]Or *flesh* [a]Ex 16:8; Num 14:27 [b]Ex 6:7; 16:7; 1 Kin 20:28; Joel 3:17
13 [a]Num 11:31; Ps 78:27-29; 105:40 [b]Num 11:9
14 [1]Lit *had gone up* [2]Lit *face of* [a]Num 11:7-9 [b]Ex 16:31; Neh 9:15; Ps 78:24; 105:40
15 [1]Heb *Man hu*, cf v 31 [a]Ex 16:4; Neh 9:15; Ps 78:24; John 6:31; 1 Cor 10:3
16 [1]Lit *the thing which* [2]Lit *according to his eating* [3]Lit *an omer for a head* [a]Ex 16:32, 36
18 [1]Lit *according to his eating* [a]2 Cor 8:15
19 [a]Ex 12:10; 16:23; 23:18
21 [1]Lit *according to his eating*
22 [a]Ex 16:5 [b]Ex 34:31
23 [1]Lit *spoke*

[a]Tomorrow is a sabbath observance, a holy sabbath to the LORD.
Bake what you will bake and boil what you will boil, and [b]all
that is left over [2]put aside to be kept until morning."
24 So they [1]put it aside until morning, as Moses had ordered,
and [a]it did not become foul nor was there any worm in it.
25 Moses said, "Eat it today, for today is a sabbath to the LORD;
today you will not find it in the field.
26 "[a]Six days you shall gather it, but on the seventh day, *the*
sabbath, there will be [1]none."
27 It came about on the seventh day that some of the people
went out to gather, but they found none.
28 Then the LORD said to Moses, "[a]How long do you refuse to
keep My commandments and My [1]instructions?
29 "See, [1]the LORD has given you the sabbath; therefore He gives
you bread for two days on the sixth day. Remain every man in
his place; let no man go out of his place on the seventh day."
30 So the people rested on the seventh day.
31 The house of [a]Israel named it [1]manna, and it was like
[b]coriander seed, white, and its taste was like wafers with honey.
32 Then Moses said, "This is [1]what the LORD has commanded,
'Let an omerful of it be kept throughout your generations, that
they may see the bread that I fed you in the wilderness, when I
brought you out of the land of Egypt.'"
33 Moses said to Aaron, "[a]Take a jar and put an omerful of
manna in it, and place it before the LORD to be kept throughout
your generations."
34 As the LORD commanded Moses, so Aaron placed it before
[a]the Testimony, to be kept.
35 [a]The sons of Israel ate the manna forty years, until they
came to an inhabited land; they ate the manna until they came
to the border of the land of Canaan.
36 (Now [a]an omer is a tenth of an [1]ephah.)

Chapter 17 Theme ____________________

17 Then all the congregation of the sons of Israel journeyed
by [1]stages from the wilderness of [a]Sin, according to the
[2]command of the LORD, and camped at [b]Rephidim, and there
was no water for the people to drink.
2 Therefore the people [a]quarreled with Moses and said,
"Give us water that we may drink." And Moses said to them,
"[b]Why do you quarrel with me? [c]Why do you test the LORD?"
3 But the people thirsted there for water; and [1]they
[a]grumbled against Moses and said, "Why, now, have you
brought us up from Egypt, to kill [2]us and [3]our children and
[3b]our livestock with thirst?"
4 So Moses cried out to the LORD, saying, "What shall I do to
this people? A [a]little more and they will stone me."
5 Then the LORD said to Moses, "Pass before the people and
take with you some of [a]the elders of Israel; and take in your
hand your staff with which [b]you struck the Nile, and go.

23 [2]Lit *lay up for you* [a]Gen 2:3; Ex 20:8-11; 23:12; 31:15; 35:2; Lev 23:3; Neh 9:13, 14 [b]Ex 16:19

24 [1]Lit *laid it up* [a]Ex 16:20

26 [1]Lit *none on it* [a]Ex 20:9, 10

28 [1]Or *laws* [a]2 Kin 17:14; Ps 78:10; 106:13

29 [1]Lit *for the LORD*

31 [1]Heb *man,* cf v 15 [a]Num 11:7-9; Deut 8:3, 16 [b]Ex 16:14

32 [1]Lit *the thing which*

33 [a]Heb 9:4; Rev 2:17

34 [a]Ex 25:16, 21; 27:21; 40:20; Num 17:10

35 [a]Deut 8:2f; Josh 5:12; Neh 9:20, 21

36 [1]I.e. Approx one bu [a]Ex 16:16

17:1 [1]Lit *their journeyings* [2]Lit *mouth* [a]Ex 16:1; Num 33:12 [b]Ex 19:2; Num 33:14

2 [a]Ex 14:11; Num 20:2, 3, 13 [b]Ex 16:8 [c]Deut 6:16; Ps 78:18, 41; Matt 4:7; 1 Cor 10:9

3 [1]Lit *the people* [2]Lit *me* [3]Lit *my* [a]Ex 16:2, 3 [b]Ex 12:38

4 [a]Num 14:10; 1 Sam 30:6

5 [a]Ex 3:16, 18 [b]Ex 7:20

6 "Behold, I will stand before you there on the rock at [a]Horeb;
and [b]you shall strike the rock, and water will come out of it, that
the people may drink." And Moses did so in the sight of the
elders of Israel.
7 He named the place [1a]Massah and [2b]Meribah because of the
quarrel of the sons of Israel, and because they [c]tested the LORD,
saying, "Is the LORD among us, or not?"
8 Then [a]Amalek came and fought against Israel at [b]Rephidim.
9 So Moses said to [a]Joshua, "Choose men for us and go out,
fight against Amalek. Tomorrow I will station myself on the top
of the hill with [b]the staff of God in my hand."
10 Joshua did as Moses [1]told him, [2]and fought against Amalek;
and Moses, Aaron, and [a]Hur went up to the top of the hill.
11 So it came about when Moses held his hand up, that Israel
prevailed, and when he let his hand [1]down, Amalek prevailed.
12 But Moses' hands were heavy. Then they took a stone and
put it under him, and he sat on it; and Aaron and Hur [a]sup-
ported his hands, one on one side and one on the other. Thus
his hands were steady until the sun set.
13 So Joshua [1]overwhelmed Amalek and his people with the
edge of the sword.
14 Then the LORD said to Moses, "[a]Write this in [1]a book as a
memorial and [2]recite it to Joshua, [3]that [b]I will utterly blot out
the memory of Amalek from under heaven."
15 Moses built an [a]altar and named it [b]The LORD is My
Banner;
16 and he said, "[1a]The LORD has sworn; the LORD will have
war against Amalek from generation to generation."

Chapter 18 Theme ______

18 Now [a]Jethro, the priest of Midian, Moses' father-in-law,
heard of all that God had done for Moses and for Israel
His people, how the LORD had brought Israel out of Egypt.
2 Jethro, Moses' father-in-law, took Moses' wife [a]Zipporah,
after he had sent her away,
3 and her [a]two sons, of whom [1]one was named Gershom, for
Moses said, "I have been [b]a [2]sojourner in a foreign land."
4 [1]The other was named [2a]Eliezer, for *he said,* "[b]The God of
my father was my help, and delivered me from the sword of
Pharaoh."
5 Then Jethro, Moses' father-in-law, came with his sons and
his wife to Moses [1]in the wilderness where he was camped, at
[a]the mount of God.
6 He [1]sent word to Moses, "I, your father-in-law Jethro, am
coming to you with your wife and her two sons with her."
7 Then Moses went out to meet his father-in-law, and [a]he
bowed down and [b]kissed him; and they [c]asked each other of
their welfare and went into the tent.
8 Moses told his father-in-law all that the LORD had done to
Pharaoh and to the Egyptians [a]for Israel's sake, all the [b]hardship

---

6 [a]Ex 3:1 [b]Num 20:10, 11; Deut 8:15; Neh 9:15; Ps 78:15; 105:41; 114:8; 1 Cor 10:4

7 [1]I.e. test [2]I.e. quarrel [a]Deut 6:16; 9:22; Ps 95:8 [b]Num 20:13, 24; 27:14; Ps 81:7 [c]Num 14:22; Deut 33:8

8 [a]Gen 36:12; Num 24:20; Deut 25:17-19; 1 Sam 15:2 [b]Ex 17:1

9 [a]Ex 24:13 [b]Ex 4:20

10 [1]Lit *said to* [2]Lit *to fight* [a]Ex 24:14; 31:2

11 [1]Lit *rest*

12 [a]Is 35:3

13 [1]Lit *weakened*

14 [1]Lit *the book* [2]Lit *place it in the ears of* [3]Or *for* [a]Ex 24:4; 34:27; Num 33:2 [b]Deut 25:19; 1 Sam 15:3

15 [a]Ex 24:4 [b]Gen 22:14; Judg 6:24

16 [1]Or *Because a hand is against the throne of the LORD;* lit *Because a hand upon the throne of YAH* [a]Gen 22:16

18:1 [a]Ex 2:16, 18; 3:1

2 [a]Ex 2:21; 4:25

3 [1]Lit *the name of the one was* [2]Heb *ger* [a]Ex 2:22; 4:20; Acts 7:29 [b]Ex 2:22

4 [1]Lit *The name of the other was* [2]Heb *El-ezer;* i.e. my God is help [a]1 Chr 23:15, 17 [b]Gen 49:25

5 [1]Lit *unto* [a]Ex 3:1, 12; 4:27; 24:13

6 [1]Lit *said*

7 [a]Gen 43:26, 28 [b]Gen 29:13; Ex 4:27 [c]Gen 43:27; 2 Sam 11:7

8 [a]Ex 4:23; 7:4, 5 [b]Num 20:14; Neh 9:32

that had befallen them on the journey, and *how* [c]the LORD had
delivered them.
9 Jethro rejoiced over all [a]the goodness which the LORD had
done to Israel, [1]in delivering [2]them from the hand of the
Egyptians.
10 So Jethro said, "[a]Blessed be the LORD who delivered you
from the hand of the Egyptians and from the hand of Pharaoh,
and who delivered the people from under the hand of the
Egyptians.
11 "Now I know that [a]the LORD is greater than all the gods;
[1]indeed, [b]it was proven when they dealt proudly against [2]the
people."
12 [a]Then Jethro, Moses' father-in-law, took a burnt offering
and sacrifices for God, and Aaron came with all the elders of
Israel to eat [1]a meal with Moses' father-in-law before God.
13 It came about the next day that Moses sat to judge the
people, and the people stood about Moses from the morning
until the evening.
14 Now when Moses' father-in-law saw all that he was doing
for the people, he said, "What is this thing that you are doing for
the people? Why do you alone sit *as judge* and all the people
stand about you from morning until evening?"
15 Moses said to his father-in-law, "Because the people come
to me [a]to inquire of God.
16 "When they have a [1a]dispute, it comes to me, and I judge
between a man and his neighbor and make known the statutes
of God and His laws."
17 Moses' father-in-law said to him, "The thing that you are
doing is not good.
18 "[a]You will surely wear out, both yourself and [1]these people
who are with you, for the [2]task is too heavy for you; [b]you
cannot do it alone.
19 "Now listen to [1]me: I will give you counsel, and God be with
you. [2]You be the people's representative before God, and you
[a]bring the [3]disputes to God,
20 [a]then teach them the statutes and the laws, and make
known to them [b]the way in which they are to walk and the
work they are to do.
21 "Furthermore, you shall [1]select out of all the people [a]able
men [b]who fear God, men of truth, those who [c]hate dishonest
gain; and you shall place *these* over them *as* leaders of
thousands, [2]of hundreds, [2]of fifties and [2]of tens.
22 "Let them judge the people at all times; and let it be [a]that
every major [1]dispute they will bring to you, but every minor
[1]dispute they themselves will judge. So it will be easier for you,
and [b]they will bear *the burden* with you.
23 "If you do this thing and God *so* commands you, then you
will be able to [1]endure, and all [2]these people also will go to
[3]their place in peace."
24 So Moses listened [1]to his father-in-law and did all that he
had said.

8 [c]Ex 15:6, 16

9 [1]Lit *in that He had delivered* [2]Lit *him* [a]Is 63:7-14

10 [a]Gen 14:20; 2 Sam 18:28; 1 Kin 8:56; Ps 68:19, 20

11 [1]Lit *indeed, in the thing in which they* [2]Lit *them* [a]Ex 12:12; 15:11; 2 Chr 2:5; Ps 95:3; 97:9; 135:5 [b]Luke 1:51

12 [1]Lit *bread* [a]Gen 31:54; Ex 24:5

15 [a]Num 9:6, 8; 27:5; Deut 17:8-13

16 [1]Lit *matter* [a]Ex 24:14

18 [1]Lit *this* [2]Lit *matter* [a]Num 11:14, 17; Deut 1:12 [b]Deut 1:9

19 [1]Lit *my voice* [2]Lit *You be for the people in front of God* [3]Lit *matters* [a]Num 27:5

20 [a]Deut 1:18; 4:1, 5; 5:1 [b]Ps 143:8

21 [1]Lit *see* [2]Lit *leaders of* [a]Ex 18:25; Deut 1:13, 15; 2 Chr 19:5-10; Ps 15:1-5; Acts 6:3 [b]Gen 42:18; 2 Sam 23:3 [c]Deut 16:19

22 [1]Lit *matter* [a]Deut 1:17, 18 [b]Num 11:17

23 [1]Lit *stand* [2]Lit *this* [3]Lit *his*

24 [1]Lit *to the voice of*

25 Moses chose [a]able men out of all Israel and made them
heads over the people, leaders of thousands, [1]of hundreds, [1]of
fifties and [1]of tens.
26 They judged the people at all times; [a]the difficult [1]dispute
they would bring to Moses, but every minor [1]dispute they
themselves would judge.
27 Then Moses [1a]bade his father-in-law farewell, and he went
his way into his own land.

Chapter 19 Theme ______________________

19 [a]In the third month after the sons of Israel had gone out
of the land of Egypt, [1]on that very day they came into the
wilderness of [b]Sinai.
2 When they set out from [a]Rephidim, they came to the
wilderness of Sinai and camped in the wilderness; and there
Israel camped in front of [b]the mountain.
3 Moses went up to God, and [a]the LORD called to him from
the mountain, saying, "Thus you shall say to the house of Jacob
and tell the sons of Israel:
4 '[a]You yourselves have seen what I did to the Egyptians, and
how I bore you on [b]eagles' wings, and brought you to Myself.
5 'Now then, [a]if you will indeed obey My voice and [b]keep My
covenant, then you shall be [c]My [1]own possession among all the
peoples, for [d]all the earth is Mine;
6 and you shall be to Me [a]a kingdom of priests and [b]a holy
nation.' These are the words that you shall speak to the sons of
Israel."
7 [a]So Moses came and called the elders of the people, and set
before them all these words which the LORD had commanded him.
8 [a]All the people answered together and said, "All that the
LORD has spoken we will do!" And Moses brought back the
words of the people to the LORD.
9 The LORD said to Moses, "Behold, I will come to you in [a]a
thick cloud, so that the [b]people may hear when I speak with
you and may also believe in you forever." Then Moses told the
words of the people to the LORD.
10 The LORD also said to Moses, "Go to the people and
[a]consecrate them today and tomorrow, and let them [b]wash
their garments;
11 and let them be ready for the third day, for on [a]the third
day the LORD will come down on Mount Sinai in the sight of all
the people.
12 "You shall set bounds for the people all around, saying,
'[1]Beware that you do not go up on the mountain or touch the
border of it; [a]whoever touches the mountain shall surely be put
to death.
13 'No hand shall touch him, but [a]he shall surely be stoned or
[1]shot through; whether beast or man, he shall not live.' When
the ram's horn sounds a long blast, they shall come up to [b]the
mountain."

25 [1]Lit *leaders of* [a]Ex 18:21; Deut 1:15
26 [1]Lit *matter* [a]Ex 18:22
27 [1]Lit *sent off his father-in-law* [a]Num 10:29, 30
19:1 [1]Lit *on this day* [a]Ex 12:6, 51; 16:1 [b]Deut 1:6; 4:10, 15; 5:2
2 [a]Ex 17:1; Num 33:15 [b]Ex 3:1, 12; 18:5
3 [a]Ex 3:4
4 [a]Deut 29:2 [b]Deut 32:11; Rev 12:14
5 [1]Or *special treasure* [a]Ex 15:26; Deut 5:2f [b]Ps 78:10 [c]Deut 4:20; 7:6; 14:2; 26:18; Ps 135:4; Titus 2:14; 1 Pet 2:9 [d]Ex 9:29; Deut 10:14; Job 41:11; Ps 50:12; 1 Cor 10:26
6 [a]1 Pet 2:5, 9; Rev 1:6; 5:10 [b]Deut 7:6; 14:21; 26:19; Is 62:12
7 [a]Ex 4:29, 30
8 [a]Ex 4:31; 24:3, 7; Deut 5:27; 26:17
9 [a]Ex 19:16; 24:15, 16; Deut 4:11; Ps 99:7 [b]Deut 4:12, 36
10 [a]Lev 11:44, 45 [b]Gen 35:2; Lev 15:5; Num 8:7, 21; 19:19; Rev 22:14
11 [a]Ex 19:16
12 [1]Lit *Take heed to yourselves* [a]Heb 12:20
13 [1]I.e. with arrows [a]Heb 12:20 [b]Ex 19:17

14 So Moses went down from the mountain to the people and consecrated the people, and they washed their garments.

15 He said to the people, "Be ready for the third day; do not go near a woman."

16 [a]So it came about on the third day, when it was morning, that there were [1]thunder and lightning flashes and a thick cloud upon the mountain and a very loud trumpet sound, so that all the people who *were* in the camp trembled.

17 And Moses brought the people out of the camp to meet God, and they stood at the [1]foot of the mountain.

18 [a]Now Mount Sinai *was* all in smoke because the LORD descended upon it [b]in fire; and its smoke ascended like [c]the smoke of a furnace, and [d]the whole mountain [1]quaked violently.

19 When the sound of the trumpet grew louder and louder, Moses spoke and [a]God answered him with [1]thunder.

20 [a]The LORD came down on Mount Sinai, to the top of the mountain; and the LORD called Moses to the top of the mountain, and Moses went up.

21 Then the LORD spoke to Moses, "Go down, [1]warn the people, so that [a]they do not break through to the LORD to gaze, and many of them [2]perish.

22 "Also let the [a]priests who come near to the LORD consecrate themselves, or else the LORD will break out against them."

23 Moses said to the LORD, "The people cannot come up to Mount Sinai, for You [1]warned us, saying, '[a]Set bounds about the mountain and consecrate it.'"

24 Then the LORD said to him, "[1]Go down and come up *again,* [a]you and Aaron with you; but do not let the [b]priests and the people break through to come up to the LORD, or He will break forth upon them."

25 So Moses went down to the people and told them.

Chapter 20 Theme ____________________

20 Then God spoke all these words, saying,

2 "[a]I am the LORD your God, [b]who brought you out of the land of Egypt, out of the house of [1]slavery.

3 "[a]You shall have no other [b]gods [1]before Me.

4 "[a]You shall not make for yourself [1]an idol, or any likeness of what is in heaven above or on the earth beneath or in the water under the earth.

5 "[a]You shall not worship them or serve them; for I, the LORD your God, am a [b]jealous God, [c]visiting the iniquity of the fathers on the children, on the third and the fourth generations of those who hate Me,

6 but showing lovingkindness to [a]thousands, to those who love Me and keep My commandments.

7 "[a]You shall not take the name of the LORD your God in vain, for the LORD will not [1]leave him unpunished who takes His name in vain.

8 "Remember [a]the sabbath day, to keep it holy.

16 [1]Lit *sounds* [a]Heb 12:18, 19, 21

17 [1]Lit *lower part*

18 [1]Or *trembled* [a]Deut 4:11; Ps 104:32; 144:5 [b]Ex 3:2; 24:17; Deut 5:4; 2 Chr 7:1-3; Heb 12:18 [c]Gen 15:17; 19:28 [d]Judg 5:5; Ps 68:7, 8; Jer 4:24

19 [1]Or *a voice;* lit *a sound* [a]Ps 81:7

20 [a]Neh 9:13

21 [1]Lit *testify to* [2]Lit *fall* [a]Ex 3:5; 1 Sam 6:19

22 [a]Ex 19:24; 24:5; Lev 10:3; 21:6-8

23 [1]Lit *testified to* [a]Ex 19:12

24 [1]Lit *Go, descend* [a]Ex 24:1, 9, 12 [b]Ex 19:22

20:2 [1]Lit *slaves* [a]Lev 26:1; Deut 5:6; Ps 81:10 [b]Ex 13:3; 15:13, 16; Deut 7:8

3 [1]Or *besides Me* [a]Deut 6:14; 2 Kin 17:35; Jer 25:6; 35:15 [b]Ex 15:11; 20:23

4 [1]Or *a graven image* [a]Lev 19:4; 26:1; Deut 4:15-19; 27:15

5 [a]Ex 23:24; Josh 23:7; 2 Kin 17:35 [b]Ex 34:14; Deut 4:24; Josh 24:19; Nah 1:2 [c]Ex 34:6, 7; Num 14:18, 33; Deut 5:9, 10; 1 Kin 21:29; Jer 32:18

6 [a]Deut 7:9

7 [1]Or *hold him guiltless* [a]Lev 19:12; Deut 6:13; 10:20

8 [a]Ex 23:12; 31:13-16; Lev 26:2; Deut 5:12

9 “[a]Six days you shall labor and do all your work,
10 but the seventh day is a sabbath of the LORD your God; *in it*
[a]you shall not do any work, you or your son or your daughter,
your male or your female servant or your cattle or your sojourner
who [1]stays with you.
11 “[a]For in six days the LORD made the heavens and the earth,
the sea and all that is in them, and rested on the seventh day;
therefore the LORD blessed the sabbath day and made it holy.
12 “[a]Honor your father and your mother, that your [b]days may
be prolonged in the land which the LORD your God gives you.
13 “[a]You shall not murder.
14 “[a]You shall not commit adultery.
15 “[a]You shall not steal.
16 “[a]You shall not bear false witness against your [b]neighbor.
17 “[a]You shall not covet your neighbor’s house; [b]you shall not
covet your neighbor’s wife or his male servant or his female
servant or his ox or his donkey or anything that belongs to your
neighbor.”
18 [a]All the people perceived the [1]thunder and the lightning
flashes and the sound of the trumpet and the mountain
smoking; and when the people saw *it,* they trembled and stood
at a distance.
19 [a]Then they said to Moses, “Speak [1]to us yourself and we
will listen; but let not God speak [1]to us, or we will die.”
20 Moses said to the people, “[a]Do not be afraid; for God has
come in order [b]to test you, and in order that [c]the fear of Him
may [1]remain with you, so that you may not sin.”
21 So the people stood at a distance, while Moses approached
[a]the thick cloud where God *was.*
22 Then the LORD said to Moses, “Thus you shall say to the
sons of Israel, ‘You yourselves have seen that [a]I have spoken [1]to
you from heaven.
23 ‘[a]You shall not make *other gods* besides Me; [b]gods of silver
or gods of gold, you shall not make for yourselves.
24 ‘You shall make [a]an altar of earth for Me, and you shall
sacrifice on it your [b]burnt offerings and your [c]peace offerings,
[d]your sheep and your oxen; in every place [e]where I cause My
name to be remembered, I will come to you and bless you.
25 ‘If you make an altar of stone for Me, [a]you shall not build it
of cut stones, for if you wield your tool on it, you will profane it.
26 ‘And you shall not go up by steps to My altar, so that [a]your
nakedness will not be exposed on it.’

Chapter 21 Theme ____________________

21 “Now these are the [a]ordinances which you are to set
before them:
2 “If you buy [a]a Hebrew slave, he shall serve for six years; but
on the seventh he shall go out as a free man without payment.
3 “If he comes [1]alone, he shall go out [1]alone; if he is the
husband of a wife, then his wife shall go out with him.

9 [a]Ex 34:21; 35:2, 3; Lev 23:3; Deut 5:13; Luke 13:14
10 [1]Lit *is in your gates* [a]Neh 13:16-19
11 [a]Gen 2:2, 3; Ex 31:17
12 [a]Lev 19:3; Deut 27:16; Matt 15:4; 19:19; Mark 7:10; 10:19; Luke 18:20; Eph 6:2 [b]Deut 5:16, 33; 6:2; 11:8, 9; Jer 35:7
13 [a]Gen 9:6; Ex 21:12; Lev 24:17; Matt 5:21; 19:18; Mark 10:19; Luke 18:20; Rom 13:9; James 2:11
14 [a]Lev 20:10; Deut 5:18; Matt 5:27; 19:18; Rom 13:9
15 [a]Ex 21:16; Lev 19:11, 13; Matt 19:18; Rom 13:9
16 [a]Ex 23:1, 7; Deut 5:20; Matt 19:18 [b]Lev 19:18
17 [a]Deut 5:21; Rom 7:7; 13:9; Eph 5:3, 5 [b]Prov 6:29; Matt 5:28
18 [1]Lit *sounds* [a]Ex 19:16, 18; Heb 12:18, 19
19 [1]Lit *with* [a]Deut 5:5, 23-27; Gal 3:19; Heb 12:19
20 [1]Lit *be before* [a]Ex 14:13; Is 41:10, 13 [b]Ex 15:25; Deut 13:3 [c]Deut 4:10; 6:24; Prov 3:7; 16:6; Is 8:13
21 [a]Ex 19:16; Deut 5:22
22 [1]Lit *with* [a]Deut 4:36; 5:24, 26; Neh 9:13
23 [a]Ex 20:3 [b]Ex 32:1, 2, 4; Deut 29:17
24 [a]Ex 20:25; 27:1-8 [b]Ex 10:25; 18:12 [c]Ex 24:5; Lev 1:2 [d]Deut 12:5; 16:6, 11; 26:2; 2 Chr 6:6 [e]Deut 12:5; 26:2
25 [a]Deut 27:5, 6; Josh 8:31
26 [a]Ex 28:42, 43
21:1 [a]Ex 24:3, 4; Deut 4:14; 6:1
2 [a]Lev 25:39-43; Deut 15:12-18; Jer 34:14
3 [1]Lit *by himself*

RETURN TO INSTRUCTIONS

4 "If his master gives him a wife, and she bears him sons or
daughters, the wife and her children shall belong to her master,
and he shall go out [1]alone.
5 "But [a]if the slave plainly says, 'I love my master, my wife
and my children; I will not go out as a free man,'
6 then his master shall bring him to [1]God, then he shall
bring him to the door or the doorpost. And his master shall
pierce his ear with an awl; and he shall serve him permanently.
7 "[a]If a man sells his daughter as a female slave, she is not to
[1]go free [b]as the male slaves [1]do.
8 "If she is [1]displeasing in the eyes of her master [2]who
designated her for himself, then he shall let her be redeemed.
He does not have authority to sell her to a foreign people
because of his [3]unfairness to her.
9 "If he designates her for his son, he shall deal with her
according to the custom of daughters.
10 "If he takes to himself another woman, he may not reduce
her [1]food, her clothing, or [a]her conjugal rights.
11 "If he will not do these three *things* for her, then she shall
go out for nothing, without *payment of* money.
12 "[a]He who strikes a man so that he dies shall surely be put to
death.
13 "[a]But [1]if he did not lie in wait *for him,* but [b]God let *him* fall
into his hand, then I will appoint you a place to which he may
flee.
14 "[a]If, however, a man acts presumptuously toward his
neighbor, so as to kill him craftily, you are to take him *even*
from My altar, that he may die.
15 "He who strikes his father or his mother shall surely be put
to death.
16 "[a]He who [1]kidnaps a man, whether he sells him or he is
found in his [2]possession, shall surely be put to death.
17 "[a]He who curses his father or his mother shall surely be put
to death.
18 "If men have a quarrel and one strikes the other with a
stone or with *his* fist, and he does not die but [1]remains in bed,
19 if he gets up and walks around outside on his staff, then he
who struck him shall go unpunished; he shall only pay for his
[1]loss of time, and [2]shall take care of him until he is completely
healed.
20 "If a man strikes his male or female slave with a rod and he
dies [1]at his hand, he shall [2]be punished.
21 "If, however, he [1]survives a day or two, no vengeance shall
be taken; [a]for he is his [2]property.
22 "If men struggle with each other and strike a woman with
child so that [1]she gives birth prematurely, yet there is no
injury, he shall surely be fined as the woman's husband [2]may
demand of him, and he shall [a]pay [3]as the judges *decide.*
23 "But if there is *any further* injury, [a]then you shall appoint *as
a penalty* life for life,
24 [a]eye for eye, tooth for tooth, hand for hand, foot for foot,

4 [1]Lit *by himself*
5 [a]Deut 15:16, 17
6 [1]Or *the judges who acted in God's name*
7 [1]Lit *go out* [a]Neh 5:5 [b]Ex 21:2, 3
8 [1]Lit *bad* [2]Another reading is *so that he did not designate her* [3]Lit *dealing treacherously*
10 [1]Lit *flesh* [a]1 Cor 7:3, 5
12 [a]Gen 9:6; Lev 24:17; Num 35:30; Matt 26:52
13 [1]Lit *he who* [a]Num 35:10-34; Deut 19:1-13; Josh 20:1-9 [b]1 Sam 24:4, 10, 18
14 [a]Deut 19:11, 12; 1 Kin 2:28-34
16 [1]Lit *steals* [2]Lit *hand* [a]Deut 24:7
17 [a]Lev 20:9; Prov 20:20; Matt 15:4; Mark 7:10
18 [1]Lit *lies*
19 [1]Lit *his sitting* [2]Lit *healing, he shall cause to be healed*
20 [1]Lit *under* [2]Lit *suffer vengeance*
21 [1]Lit *stands* [2]Lit *money* [a]Lev 25:44-46
22 [1]Or *an untimely birth occurs;* lit *her children come out* [2]Lit *lays on him* [3]Lit *by arbitration* [a]Ex 21:30; Deut 22:18, 19
23 [a]Lev 24:19; Deut 19:21
24 [a]Lev 24:20; Deut 19:21; Matt 5:38

25 burn for burn, wound for wound, [1]bruise for bruise.

26 "If a man strikes the eye of his male or female slave, and destroys it, he shall let him go free on account of his eye.

27 "And if he [1]knocks out a tooth of his male or female slave, he shall let him go free on account of his tooth.

28 "If an ox gores a man or a woman [1]to death, [a]the ox shall surely be stoned and its flesh shall not be eaten; but the owner of the ox shall go unpunished.

29 "If, however, an ox was previously in the habit of goring and its owner has been warned, yet he does not confine it and it kills a man or a woman, the ox shall be stoned and its owner also shall be put to death.

30 "If a ransom is [1]demanded of him, then he shall give for the redemption of his life whatever is [1]demanded of him.

31 "Whether it gores a son or [1]a daughter, it shall be done to him according to [2]the same rule.

32 "If the ox gores a male or female slave, [1]the owner shall give his *or her* master [a]thirty shekels of silver, and the ox shall be stoned.

33 "If a man opens a pit, or [1]digs a pit and does not cover it over, and an ox or a donkey falls into it,

34 the owner of the pit shall make restitution; he shall [1]give money to its owner, and the dead *animal* shall become his.

35 "If one man's ox hurts another's so that it dies, then they shall sell the live ox and divide its price equally; and also they shall divide the dead *ox*.

36 "Or *if* it is known that the ox was previously in the habit of goring, yet its owner has not confined it, he shall surely pay ox for ox, and the dead *animal* shall become his.

Chapter 22 Theme ________________________

22 "[1]If a man steals an ox or a sheep and slaughters it or sells it, he shall pay five oxen for the ox and [a]four sheep for the sheep.

2 "[1]If the [a]thief is [2]caught while breaking in and is struck so that he dies, there will be no bloodguiltiness on his account.

3 "*But* if the sun has risen on him, there will be bloodguiltiness on his account. He shall surely make restitution; if he owns nothing, then he shall be [a]sold for his theft.

4 "If what he stole is actually found alive in his [1]possession, whether an ox or a donkey or a sheep, [a]he shall pay double.

5 "If a man lets a field or vineyard be grazed *bare* and lets his animal loose so that it grazes in another man's field, he shall make restitution from the best of his own field and the best of his own vineyard.

6 "If a fire breaks out and spreads to thorn bushes, so that stacked grain or the standing grain or the field *itself* is consumed, he who started the fire shall surely make restitution.

7 "[a]If a man gives his neighbor money or goods to keep *for him* and it is stolen from the man's house, if the thief is [1]caught, he shall pay double.

25 [1]Lit *welt*

27 [1]Lit *causes to fall*

28 [1]Lit *so that he dies* [a]Gen 9:5; Ex 21:32

30 [1]Lit *laid on him*

31 [1]Lit *gores a daughter* [2]Lit *this judgment*

32 [1]Lit *he* [a]Zech 11:12; Matt 26:15; 27:3, 9

33 [1]Lit *if a man digs*

34 [1]Lit *give back*

22:1 [1]Ch 21:37 in Heb [a]2 Sam 12:6; Luke 19:8

2 [1]Ch 22:1 in Heb [2]Lit *found* [a]Matt 6:19; 24:43; 1 Pet 4:15

3 [a]Matt 18:25

4 [1]Lit *hand* [a]Ex 22:7

7 [1]Lit *found* [a]Lev 6:1-7

8 "If the thief is not [1]caught, then the owner of the house
shall [2]appear before [3a]the judges, *to* determine whether he
[4]laid his hands on his neighbor's property.
9 "For every [1]breach of trust, *whether it is* for ox, for donkey,
for sheep, for clothing, *or* for any lost thing about which one
says, 'This is it,' the [2]case of both parties shall come before
[3a]the judges; he whom [3]the judges condemn shall pay double
to his neighbor.
10 "If a man gives his neighbor a donkey, an ox, a sheep, or any
animal to keep *for him,* and it dies or is hurt or is driven away
while no one is looking,
11 an [a]oath before the LORD shall be made by the two of them
[1]that he has not [2]laid hands on his neighbor's property; and its
owner shall accept *it,* and he shall not make restitution.
12 "But if it is actually stolen from him, he shall make restitution
to its owner.
13 "If it is all torn to pieces, let him bring it as evidence; he
shall not make restitution for what has been torn to pieces.
14 "If a man [1]borrows *anything* from his neighbor, and it is
injured or dies while its owner is not with it, he shall make full
restitution.
15 "If its owner is with it, he shall not make restitution; if it is
hired, it came for its hire.
16 "[a]If a man seduces a virgin who is not engaged, and lies with
her, he must pay a dowry for her *to be* his wife.
17 "If her father absolutely refuses to give her to him, he shall
[1]pay money equal to the [a]dowry for virgins.
18 "You shall not allow a [a]sorceress to live.
19 "[a]Whoever lies with an animal shall surely be put to death.
20 "[a]He who sacrifices to [1]any god, other than to the LORD
alone, shall be [2]utterly destroyed.
21 "[a]You shall not wrong a stranger or oppress him, for you were
strangers in the land of Egypt.
22 "[a]You shall not afflict any widow or orphan.
23 "If you afflict him at all, *and* [a]if he does cry out to Me, [b]I will
surely hear his cry;
24 and My anger will be kindled, and I will kill you with the
sword, [a]and your wives shall become widows and your children
fatherless.
25 "[a]If you lend money to My people, to the poor [1]among you,
you are not to [2]act as a creditor to him; you shall not [3]charge
him [b]interest.
26 "If you ever take your neighbor's cloak [a]as a pledge, you are
to return it to him before the sun sets,
27 for that is his only covering; it is his cloak for his [1]body.
What else shall he sleep in? And it shall come about that [a]when
he cries out to Me, I will hear *him,* for [b]I am gracious.
28 "You shall not [1a]curse God, [b]nor curse a ruler of your people.
29 "[a]You shall not delay *the offering from* [1]your harvest and
your vintage. [b]The firstborn of your sons you shall give to Me.
30 "[a]You shall do the same with your oxen *and* with your sheep.

8 [1]Lit *found* [2]Lit *approach to* [3]Or *God* [4]Lit *stretched his hand* [a]Ex 22:9; Deut 17:8, 9; 19:17

9 [1]Or *matter of transgression* [2]Lit *matter* [3]Or *God* [a]Ex 22:8, 28; Deut 25:1

11 [1]Lit *whether* [2]Lit *stretched his hand* [a]Heb 6:16

14 [1]Lit *asks*

16 [a]Deut 22:28, 29

17 [1]Lit *weigh out silver* [a]Gen 34:12; 1 Sam 18:25

18 [a]Lev 19:31; 20:6, 27; Deut 18:10, 11; 1 Sam 28:3; Jer 27:9, 10

19 [a]Lev 18:23; 20:15, 16; Deut 27:21

20 [1]Lit *the gods* [2]Lit *put under the ban* [a]Ex 32:8; 34:15; Lev 17:7; Num 25:2; Deut 17:2, 3, 5; 1 Kin 18:40; 2 Kin 10:25

21 [a]Ex 23:9; Lev 19:33, 34; 25:35; Deut 1:16; 10:19; 27:19; Zech 7:10

22 [a]Deut 24:17, 18; Prov 23:10, 11; Jer 7:6, 7

23 [a]Deut 15:9; Job 35:9; Luke 18:7 [b]Deut 10:18; Job 34:28; Ps 10:14, 17, 18; 18:6; 68:5; James 5:4

24 [a]Ps 109:2, 9

25 [1]Lit *with* [2]Lit *be* [3]Lit *lay upon* [a]Lev 25:35-37; Deut 15:7-11 [b]Deut 23:19, 20; Neh 5:7; Ps 15:5; Ezek 18:8

26 [a]Deut 24:6, 10-13; Job 24:3; Prov 20:16; Amos 2:8

27 [1]Lit *skin* [a]Ex 22:23 [b]Ex 34:6

28 [1]Or *revile* [a]Lev 24:15, 16 [b]Eccl 10:20; Acts 23:5

29 [1]Lit *your fullness and your tears* [a]Ex 23:16, 19; Deut 26:2-11; Prov 3:9 [b]Ex 13:2, 12

30 [a]Deut 15:19; Lev 22:27

It shall be with its mother seven days; [b]on the eighth day you
shall give it to Me.
31 "[a]You shall be holy men to Me, therefore [b]you shall not eat
any flesh torn to pieces in the field; you shall throw it to the
dogs.

Chapter 23 Theme ______________________

23 "[a]You shall not bear a false report; do not join your hand
with a wicked man to be a [b]malicious witness.
2 "You shall not follow [1]the masses in doing evil, nor shall you
[2]testify in a dispute so as to turn aside after [1]a multitude in
order to [a]pervert *justice;*
3 [a]nor shall you [1]be partial to a poor man in his dispute.
4 "[a]If you meet your enemy's ox or his donkey wandering
away, you shall surely return it to him.
5 "[a]If you see the donkey of one who hates you lying *helpless*
under its load, you shall refrain from leaving it to him, you shall
surely release *it* with him.
6 "[a]You shall not pervert the justice *due* to your needy *brother*
in his dispute.
7 "[a]Keep far from a false charge, and [b]do not kill the innocent
or the righteous, for [c]I will not acquit the guilty.
8 "[a]You shall not take a bribe, for a bribe blinds the clear-
sighted and [1]subverts the cause of the just.
9 "[a]You shall not oppress a [1]stranger, since you yourselves
know the [2]feelings of a [1]stranger, for you *also* were [1]strangers
in the land of Egypt.
10 "[a]You shall sow your land for six years and gather in its yield,
11 but *on* the seventh year you shall let it [1]rest and lie fallow,
so that the needy of your people may eat; and whatever they
leave the beast of the field may eat. You are to do the same
with your vineyard *and* your olive grove.
12 "[a]Six days you are to do your work, but on the seventh day
you shall cease *from labor* so that your ox and your donkey may
rest, and the son of your female slave, as well as [1]your stranger,
may refresh themselves.
13 "Now [a]concerning everything which I have said to you, be
on your guard; and [b]do not mention the name of other gods,
nor let *them* be heard [1]from your mouth.
14 "[a]Three times a year you shall celebrate a feast to Me.
15 "You shall observe [a]the Feast of Unleavened Bread; for seven
days you are to eat unleavened bread, as I commanded you, at
the appointed time in the [b]month Abib, for in it you came out
of Egypt. And [1c]none shall appear before Me empty-handed.
16 "Also *you shall observe* [a]the Feast of the Harvest *of* the first
fruits of your labors *from* what you sow in the field; also the
Feast of the Ingathering at the end of the year [b]when you
gather in *the fruit of* your labors from the field.
17 "[a]Three times a year all your males shall appear before the
Lord [1]GOD.

30 [b]Gen 17:12; Lev 12:3
31 [a]Ex 19:6; Lev 11:44; 19:2 [b]Lev 7:24; 17:15; Ezek 4:14
23:1 [a]Ex 20:16; Lev 19:11f; Deut 5:20; Ps 101:5; Prov 10:18 [b]Deut 19:16-21; Ps 35:11; Prov 19:5; Acts 6:11
2 [1]Lit *many men* [2]Or *answer* [a]Deut 16:19; 24:17
3 [1]Lit *honor* [a]Ex 23:6; Lev 19:15; Deut 1:17; 16:19
4 [a]Deut 22:1-4
5 [a]Deut 22:4
6 [a]Ex 23:2, 3; Lev 19:15
7 [a]Ex 20:16; Ps 119:29; Eph 4:25 [b]Ex 20:13; Deut 27:25 [c]Ex 34:7; Deut 25:1; Rom 1:18
8 [1]Or *distorts the words* [a]Deut 10:17; 16:19; Prov 15:27; 17:8, 23; Is 5:22, 23
9 [1]Or *sojourner(s)* [2]Lit *soul* [a]Ex 22:21; Lev 19:33f; Deut 24:17f; 27:19
10 [a]Lev 25:1-7
11 [1]Lit *drop*
12 [1]Lit *the sojourner* [a]Ex 20:8-11; 31:15; 34:21; 35:2, 3; Lev 23:3; Deut 5:13f
13 [1]Lit *on* [a]Deut 4:9, 23; 1 Tim 4:16 [b]Josh 23:7; Ps 16:4; Hos 2:17
14 [a]Ex 23:17; 34:22-24; Deut 16:16
15 [1]Lit *they . . . not* [a]Ex 12:14-20; Lev 23:6-8; Num 28:16-25 [b]Ex 12:2; 13:4 [c]Ex 22:29; 34:20
16 [a]Ex 34:22; Lev 23:10; Num 28:26 [b]Lev 23:39
17 [1]Heb *YHWH,* usually rendered LORD [a]Ex 23:14; 34:23; Deut 16:16

18 "[a]You shall not offer the blood of My sacrifice with leavened
bread; [b]nor is the fat of My [1]feast to remain overnight until
morning.
19 "You shall bring [a]the choice first fruits of your soil into the
house of the LORD your God.
"[b]**Y**ou are not to boil a young goat in the milk of its mother.
20 "Behold, I am going to send [a]an angel before you to guard
you along the way and [b]to bring you into the place which I
have prepared.
21 "Be on your guard before him and obey his voice; [a]do not be
rebellious toward him, for he will not pardon your transgression, since [b]My name is in him.
22 "But if you truly obey his voice and do all that I say, then [a]I will
be an enemy to your enemies and an adversary to your adversaries.
23 "[a]For My angel will go before you and bring you in to *the land
of* the Amorites, the Hittites, the Perizzites, the Canaanites, the
Hivites and the Jebusites; and I will completely destroy them.
24 "[a]You shall not worship their gods, nor serve them, nor do
according to their deeds; [b]but you shall utterly overthrow them
and break their [c]*sacred* pillars in pieces.
25 "[a]But you shall serve the LORD your God, [1]and He will bless
your bread and your water; and [b]I will remove sickness from
your midst.
26 "There shall be no one miscarrying or [a]barren in your land;
[b]I will fulfill the number of your days.
27 "I will [a]send My terror ahead of you, and [b]throw into
confusion all the people among whom you come, and I will
[c]make all your enemies turn *their* backs to you.
28 "I will send [a]hornets ahead of you so that they will [b]drive
out the Hivites, the Canaanites, and the Hittites before you.
29 "[a]I will not drive them out before you in a single year, that
the land may not become desolate and the beasts of the field
become too numerous for you.
30 "I will drive them out before you [a]little by little, until you
become fruitful and take possession of the land.
31 "[a]I will fix your boundary from the [1]Red Sea to the sea of
the Philistines, and from the wilderness to the River *Euphrates;*
[b]for I will deliver the inhabitants of the land into your hand,
and you will [c]drive them out before you.
32 "[a]You shall [1]make no covenant with them [b]or with their gods.
33 "[a]They shall not live in your land, because they will make
you sin against Me; for *if* you serve their gods, [b]it will surely be
a snare to you."

Chapter 24 Theme ______________________

24 Then He said to Moses, "[a]Come up to the LORD, you
and Aaron, [b]Nadab and Abihu and [c]seventy of the elders of Israel, and you shall worship at a distance.
2 "Moses alone, however, shall come near to the LORD, but they
shall not come near, nor shall the people come up with him."

18 [1]Or *festival* [a]Ex 34:25; Lev 2:11 [b]Ex 12:10; Lev 7:15; Deut 16:4

19 [a]Ex 22:29; 34:26; Deut 26:2, 10; Neh 10:35; Prov 3:9 [b]Deut 14:21

20 [a]Ex 3:2; 14:19; 23:23; 32:34; 33:2 [b]Ex 15:16, 17

21 [a]Deut 9:7; Ps 78:40, 56 [b]Ex 3:14; 6:3; 34:5-7

22 [a]Gen 12:3; Num 24:9; Deut 30:7

23 [a]Ex 23:20; Josh 24:8, 11

24 [a]Ex 20:5; 23:13, 33; Deut 12:30f [b]Num 33:52; Deut 7:5; 12:3; 2 Kin 18:4 [c]Ex 34:13; Lev 26:1; 2 Kin 3:2

25 [1]Or *that He may bless* [a]Lev 26:3-13; Deut 6:13; 10:12; 28:1-14; Josh 22:5; 1 Sam 12:20; Matt 4:10 [b]Ex 15:26; Deut 7:15

26 [a]Deut 7:14 [b]Deut 4:40; Job 5:26

27 [a]Gen 35:5; Ex 15:16; Deut 2:25; Josh 2:9 [b]Deut 7:23 [c]Ps 18:40; 21:12

28 [a]Deut 7:20; Josh 24:12 [b]Ex 33:2; 34:11

29 [a]Deut 7:22

30 [a]Deut 7:22

31 [1]Lit *Sea of Reeds* [a]Gen 15:18; Deut 1:7, 8; 11:24 [b]Deut 2:36; Josh 21:44 [c]Josh 24:12, 18

32 [1]Lit *cut* [a]Ex 34:12; Deut 7:2 [b]Ex 23:13, 24

33 [a]Deut 7:1-5, 16 [b]Ex 34:12; Deut 12:30; Josh 23:13; Judg 2:3; Ps 106:36

24:1 [a]Ex 19:24 [b]Ex 6:23; 28:1; Lev 10:1, 2 [c]Num 11:16

RETURN TO INSTRUCTIONS

3 Then Moses came and recounted to the people all the
words of the LORD and all the [1]ordinances; and all the people
answered with one voice and said, "[a]All the words which the
LORD has spoken we will do!"
4 [a]Moses wrote down all the words of the LORD. Then he
arose early in the morning, and built an [b]altar [1]at the foot of the
mountain with twelve pillars for the twelve tribes of Israel.
5 He sent young men of the sons of Israel, [a]and they offered
burnt offerings and sacrificed young bulls as peace offerings to
the LORD.
6 [a]Moses took half of the blood and put *it* in basins, and the
other half of the blood he sprinkled on the altar.
7 Then he took [a]the book of the covenant and read *it* in the
hearing of the people; and they said, "[b]All that the LORD has
spoken we will do, and we will be obedient!"
8 So [a]Moses took the blood and sprinkled *it* on the people, and
said, "Behold [b]the blood of the covenant, which the LORD has
[1]made with you [2]in accordance with all these words."
9 Then Moses went up [1]with Aaron, [a]Nadab and Abihu, and
seventy of the elders of Israel,
10 and [a]they saw the God of Israel; and under His feet [1b]there
appeared to be a pavement of sapphire, [2]as clear as the sky itself.
11 Yet He did not stretch out His hand against the nobles of
the sons of Israel; and [a]they saw God, and they ate and drank.
12 Now the LORD said to Moses, "Come up to Me on the
mountain and [1]remain there, and [a]I will give you the stone
tablets [2]with the law and the commandment which I have
written for their instruction."
13 So Moses arose [1]with [a]Joshua his [2]servant, and Moses
went up to [b]the mountain of God.
14 But to the elders he said, "[a]Wait here for us until we return
to you. And behold, [b]Aaron and Hur are with you; whoever
[1]has a legal matter, let him approach them."
15 Then Moses went up to the mountain, and [a]the cloud
covered the mountain.
16 [a]The glory of the LORD [1]rested on Mount Sinai, and the
cloud covered it for six days; and on the seventh day He [b]called
to Moses from the midst of the cloud.
17 [a]And to the eyes of the sons of Israel the appearance of the
glory of the LORD was like a [b]consuming fire on the mountain top.
18 Moses entered the midst of the cloud [1]as he went up to the
mountain; and Moses was on the mountain [a]forty days and
forty nights.

Chapter 25 Theme ______________________

25 Then the LORD spoke to Moses, saying,
2 "[a]Tell the sons of Israel to [1]raise a [2]contribution for Me;
[b]from every man whose heart moves him you shall [1]raise My
[2]contribution.

3 [1]Or *judgments* [a]Ex 19:8; 24:7; Deut 5:27
4 [1]Lit *under* [a]Ex 17:14; 34:27; Deut 31:9 [b]Ex 17:15
5 [a]Ex 18:12
6 [a]Heb 9:18
7 [a]Ex 24:4; Heb 9:19 [b]Ex 24:3
8 [1]Lit *cut* [2]Lit *on all* [a]Heb 9:19, 20 [b]Zech 9:11; Matt 26:28; Mark 14:24; Luke 22:20; 1 Cor 11:25; Heb 13:20
9 [1]Lit *and* [a]Ex 24:1
10 [1]Lit *like a pavement* [2]Lit *and as* [a]Ex 24:11; Num 12:8; Is 6:5; John 1:18; 6:46 [b]Ezek 1:26; 10:1; Rev 4:3
11 [a]Gen 16:13; 32:30; Ex 24:10
12 [1]Lit *be* [2]Lit *and* [a]Ex 31:18; 32:15; Deut 5:22
13 [1]Lit *and* [2]Or *minister* [a]Ex 17:9-14; 33:11 [b]Ex 3:1
14 [1]Lit *is a master of matters* [a]Gen 22:5 [b]Ex 17:10, 12
15 [a]Ex 19:9
16 [1]Lit *dwelt* [a]Ex 16:10; Num 14:10 [b]Ps 99:7
17 [a]Ex 3:2; Ezek 1:28 [b]Deut 4:24; 9:3; Heb 12:29
18 [1]Lit *and* [a]Ex 34:28; Deut 9:9; 10:10
25:2 [1]Lit *take* [2]Or *heave offering* [a]Ex 35:4-9 [b]Ex 35:21; 1 Chr 29:3, 5, 9; Ezra 2:68; 2 Cor 8:11, 12; 9:7

RETURN TO INSTRUCTIONS

INSIGHT

Each piece of furniture in the tabernacle was a picture of the work of the Lord Jesus Christ. Think about how each portrays this.

3 "This is the [1]contribution which you are to [2]raise from them:
gold, silver and bronze,
4 [1a]blue, purple and scarlet *material,* fine linen, goat *hair,*
5 rams' skins dyed red, porpoise skins, acacia wood,
6 [a]oil for lighting, [b]spices for the anointing oil and for the
fragrant incense,
7 onyx stones and setting stones for the [a]ephod and for the
[1b]breastpiece.
8 "Let them [a]construct a sanctuary for Me, [b]that I may dwell
among them.
9 "[a]According to all that I am going to show you, *as* the
pattern of the tabernacle and the pattern of all its furniture, just
so you shall construct *it.*
10 "[a]They shall construct an ark of acacia wood two and a half
[1]cubits [2]long, and one and a half cubits [3]wide, and one and a
half cubits [4]high.
11 "You shall [a]overlay it with pure gold, inside and out you
shall overlay it, and you shall make a gold molding [1]around it.
12 "You shall cast four gold rings for it and [1]fasten them on its
four feet, and two rings shall be on one side of it and two rings
on the other side of it.
13 "You shall make poles of acacia wood and overlay them with
gold.
14 "You shall put the poles into the rings on the sides of the
ark, to carry the ark with them.
15 "The [a]poles shall [1]remain in the rings of the ark; they shall
not be removed from it.
16 "You shall [a]put into the ark the testimony which I shall give
you.
17 "You shall [a]make a [1]mercy seat of pure gold, two and a half
[2]cubits [3]long and one and a half cubits [4]wide.
18 "You shall make two cherubim of gold, make them of
hammered work [1]at the two ends of the mercy seat.
19 "Make one cherub [1]at one end and one cherub [1]at the other
end; you shall make the cherubim *of one piece* with the mercy
seat at its two ends.
20 "[a]The cherubim shall have *their* wings spread upward, covering
the mercy seat with their wings and [1]facing one another; the
faces of the cherubim are to be *turned* toward the mercy seat.
21 "[a]You shall put the mercy seat [1]on top of the ark, and [b]in the
ark you shall put the testimony which I will give to you.
22 "[a]There I will meet with you; and from above the mercy
seat, from [b]between the two cherubim which are upon the ark
of the testimony, I will speak to you about all that I will give
you in commandment for the sons of Israel.
23 "[a]You shall make a table of acacia wood, two cubits [1]long
and one cubit [2]wide and one and a half cubits [3]high.
24 "You shall overlay it with pure gold and make a gold [a]border
around it.
25 "You shall make for it a rim of a handbreadth around *it;* and
you shall make a gold border for the rim around it.

Ark of the Covenant (or Testimony)

Table of Showbread

3 [1]Or *heave offering* [2]Lit *take*
4 [1]Or *violet* [a]Ex 28:5, 6, 8
6 [a]Ex 27:20 [b]Ex 30:23f
7 [1]Or *pouch* [a]Ex 28:4, 6-14 [b]Ex 28:4, 15-30
8 [a]Ex 36:1-5 [b]Ex 29:45, 46; Num 5:3; Deut 12:11; 1 Kin 6:13; 2 Cor 6:16; Rev 21:3
9 [a]Ex 25:40; 26:30; Acts 7:44; Heb 8:2, 5
10 [1]I.e. One cubit equals approx 18 in. [2]Lit *its length* [3]Lit *its width* [4]Lit *its height* [a]Ex 37:1-9; Deut 10:3; Heb 9:4
11 [1]Lit *on it round about* [a]Heb 9:4
12 [1]Or *put*
15 [1]Lit *be* [a]1 Kin 8:8
16 [a]Ex 40:20; Deut 10:2; 31:26; 1 Kin 8:9; Heb 9:4
17 [1]Lit *propitiatory,* and so through v 22 [2]I.e. One cubit equals approx 18 in. [3]Lit *its length* [4]Lit *its width* [a]Ex 37:6
18 [1]Lit *from*
19 [1]Lit *from*
20 [1]Lit *their faces to* [a]1 Kin 8:7; 1 Chr 28:18; Heb 9:5
21 [1]Lit *above, upon* [a]Ex 26:34; 40:20 [b]Ex 25:16
22 [a]Ex 29:42, 43; Lev 16:2; Num 17:4 [b]Num 7:89; 1 Sam 4:4; 2 Sam 6:2; 2 Kin 19:15; Ps 80:1; Is 37:16
23 [1]Lit *its length* [2]Lit *its width* [3]Lit *its height* [a]Ex 37:10-16
24 [a]Ex 25:11

26 "You shall make four gold rings for it and put rings on the
four corners which are on its four feet.
27 "The rings shall be close to the rim as holders for the poles
to carry the table.
28 "You shall make the poles of acacia wood and overlay them
with gold, so that with them the table may be carried.
29 "You shall make its [1a]dishes and its pans and its jars and its
[2]bowls with which to pour drink offerings; you shall make them
of pure gold.
30 "You shall set [a]the bread of the [1]Presence on the table before
Me [2]at all times.
31 "[a]Then you shall make a lampstand of pure gold. The lampstand *and* its base and its shaft are to be made of hammered
work; its cups, its [1]bulbs and its flowers shall be *of one piece*
with it.
32 "[a]Six branches shall go out from its sides; three branches of
the lampstand from its one side and three branches of the
lampstand from its [1]other side.
33 "[a]Three cups *shall be* shaped like almond *blossoms* in the
one branch, a [1]bulb and a flower, and three cups shaped like
almond *blossoms* in the [2]other branch, a [1]bulb and a flower—
so for six branches going out from the lampstand;
34 and [a]in the lampstand four cups shaped like almond
blossoms, its [1]bulbs and its flowers.
35 "[a]A [1]bulb shall be under the *first* pair of branches *coming*
out of it, and a [1]bulb under the *second* pair of branches *coming*
out of it, and a [1]bulb under the *third* pair of branches *coming*
out of it, for the six branches coming out of the lampstand.
36 "[a]Their [1]bulbs and their branches *shall be of one piece* with
it; all of it shall be one piece of hammered work of pure gold.
37 "Then you shall make its lamps seven *in number;* and [a]they
shall [1]mount its lamps so as to shed light on the space in front
of it.
38 "Its snuffers and [1]their trays *shall be* of pure gold.
39 "It shall be made from a talent of pure gold, with all these
utensils.
40 "[a]See that you make *them* [b]after the pattern for them, which
was shown to you on the mountain.

Lampstand

Chapter 26 Theme ______________________

26 "[a]Moreover you shall make the tabernacle with ten
curtains of fine twisted linen and [1]blue and purple and
scarlet *material;* you shall make them with cherubim, the work
of a skillful workman.
2 "The length of each curtain shall be twenty-eight [1]cubits,
and the width of each curtain four [1]cubits; all the curtains shall
have [2]the same measurements.
3 "Five curtains shall be [1]joined to one another, and *the other*
five curtains *shall be* [1]joined to one another.
4 "You shall make loops of [1]blue on the edge of the [2]outermost

29 [1]Or *platters* [2]Lit *libation bowls* [a]Ex 37:16; Num 4:7
30 [1]Lit *Face* [2]Or *continually* [a]Ex 39:36; 40:23; Lev 24:5-9
31 [1]Or *calyx* [a]Ex 37:17-24; 1 Kin 7:49; Zech 4:2
32 [1]Lit *second* [a]Ex 37:18
33 [1]Or *calyx* [2]Lit *one branch* [a]Ex 37:19
34 [1]Or *calyxes* [a]Ex 37:20
35 [1]Or *calyx* [a]Ex 37:21
36 [1]Or *calyxes* [a]Ex 37:22
37 [1]Lit *raise up* [a]Num 8:2
38 [1]Lit *its snuff dishes*
40 [a]Heb 8:5 [b]Ex 25:9; 26:30; Num 8:4; Acts 7:44
26:1 [1]Or *violet* [a]Ex 36:8-19
2 [1]I.e. One cubit equals approx 18 in. [2]Lit *one measure*
3 [1]Or *coupled*
4 [1]Or *violet* [2]Lit *one curtain from the end in the coupling*

curtain in the *first* set, and likewise you shall make *them* on
the edge of the curtain that is outermost in the second [3]set.
5 "You shall make fifty loops in the one curtain, and you shall
make fifty loops on the [1]edge of the curtain that is in the second
[2]set; the loops shall be opposite each other.
6 "You shall make fifty clasps of gold, and [1]join the curtains to
one another with the clasps so that the [2]tabernacle will be a
unit.

Curtains

7 "Then [a]you shall make curtains of goats' *hair* for a tent over
the tabernacle; you shall make eleven curtains in all.
8 "The length of each curtain *shall be* thirty [1]cubits, and the
width of each curtain four cubits; the eleven curtains shall have
[2]the same measurements.
9 "You shall [1]join five curtains by themselves and the *other* six
curtains by themselves, and you shall double over the sixth
curtain [2]at the front of the tent.
10 "You shall make fifty loops on the edge of the [1]curtain that is
outermost in the *first* [2]set, and fifty loops on the edge of the
curtain *that is outermost in* the second [2]set.
11 "You shall make fifty clasps of [1]bronze, and you shall put the
clasps into the loops and [2]join the tent together so that it will
be [3]a unit.
12 "The [1]overlapping part that is left over in the curtains of the
tent, the half curtain that is left over, shall lap over the back of
the tabernacle.
13 "The cubit on one side and the cubit on the other, of what is
left over in the length of the curtains of the tent, shall lap over
the sides of the tabernacle on one side and on the other, to
cover it.
14 "[a]You shall make a covering for the tent of rams' skins [1]dyed
red and a covering of porpoise skins above.
15 "Then you shall make [a]the boards for the tabernacle of
acacia wood, standing upright.
16 "Ten cubits *shall be* the length of [1]each board and one and a
half cubits the width of each board.
17 "*There shall be* two tenons for each board, [1]fitted to one
another; thus you shall do for all the boards of the tabernacle.
18 "You shall make the boards for the tabernacle: twenty
boards [1]for the south side.
19 "You shall make forty [1a]sockets of silver under the twenty
boards, two [1]sockets under one board for its two tenons and
two [1]sockets under another board for its two tenons;
20 and for the second side of the tabernacle, on the north
side, twenty boards,
21 and their forty [1]sockets of silver; two [1]sockets under one
board and two [1]sockets under another board.
22 "For the [1]rear of the tabernacle, to the west, you shall make
six boards.
23 "You shall make two boards for the corners of the tabernacle
at the [1]rear.
24 "They shall be double beneath, and together they shall be

4 [3]Lit *coupling*

5 [1]Lit *end* [2]Lit *coupling*

6 [1]Or *couple* [2]Or *dwelling place,* and so throughout the ch

7 [a]Ex 36:14

8 [1]I.e. One cubit equals approx 18 in. [2]Lit *one measure*

9 [1]Or *couple* [2]Lit *toward the front of the face of the tent*

10 [1]Lit *one curtain* [2]Lit *coupling*

11 [1]Or *copper* [2]Or *couple* [3]Lit *one*

12 [1]Lit *excess*

14 [1]Or *tanned* [a]Ex 36:19

15 [a]Ex 36:20-34

16 [1]Lit *the*

17 [1]Lit *bound*

18 [1]Lit *toward the side of the Negev to the south*

19 [1]Or *bases* [a]Ex 38:27

21 [1]Or *bases*

22 [1]Lit *extreme parts*

23 [1]Lit *extreme parts*

complete [1]to its top [2]to the first ring; thus it shall be with both of them: they shall form the two corners.

25 "There shall be eight boards with their [1]sockets of silver, sixteen [1]sockets; two [1]sockets under one board and two [1]sockets under another board.

26 "Then you shall make [a]bars of acacia wood, five for the boards of one side of the tabernacle,

27 and five bars for the boards of the [1]other side of the tabernacle, and five bars for the boards of the side of the tabernacle for the [2]rear *side* to the west.

28 "The middle bar in the [1]center of the boards shall pass through from end to end.

29 "You shall overlay the boards with gold and make their rings of gold *as* holders for the bars; and you shall overlay the bars with gold.

30 "Then you shall erect the tabernacle [a]according to its plan which you have been shown in the mountain.

31 "You shall make [a]a veil of [1]blue and purple and scarlet *material* and fine twisted linen; it shall be made with cherubim, the work of a skillful workman.

The Veil

32 "You shall [1]hang it on four pillars of acacia overlaid with gold, their hooks *also being of* gold, on four [2]sockets of silver.

33 "You shall [1]hang up the veil under the clasps, and shall bring in [a]the ark of the testimony there within the veil; and the veil shall [2]serve for you as a partition [b]between the holy place and the holy of holies.

34 "[a]You shall put the mercy seat on the ark of the testimony in the holy of holies.

35 "[a]You shall set the table outside the veil, and the [b]lampstand opposite the table on the side of the tabernacle toward the south; and you shall put the table on the north side.

36 "[a]You shall make a screen for the doorway of the tent of [1]blue and purple and scarlet *material* and fine twisted linen, the work of a [2]weaver.

37 "[a]You shall make five pillars of acacia for the screen and overlay them with gold, their hooks *also being of* gold; and you shall cast five [1]sockets of [2]bronze for them.

Chapter 27 Theme ____________________

27 "And you shall make [a]the altar of acacia wood, five [1]cubits long and five cubits wide; the altar shall be square, and its height shall be three cubits.

2 "You shall make [a]its horns on its four corners; its horns shall be of one piece with it, and you shall overlay it with [1]bronze.

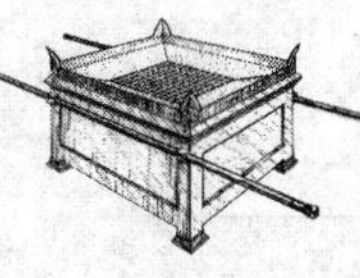

Bronze Altar

3 "You shall make its pails for removing its ashes, and its shovels and its basins and its forks and its firepans; you shall make all its utensils of bronze.

4 "You shall make for it a grating of network of bronze, and on the net you shall make four bronze rings [1]at its four corners.

24 [1]Or *at its head* [2]Or *with reference to*
25 [1]Or *bases*
26 [a]Ex 36:31
27 [1]Lit *second* [2]Lit *extreme parts*
28 [1]Lit *midst*
30 [a]Ex 25:9, 40; Acts 7:44; Heb 8:5
31 [1]Or *violet* [a]Ex 36:35, 36; 2 Chr 3:14; Matt 27:51; Heb 9:3
32 [1]Lit *put* [2]Or *bases*
33 [1]Lit *put* [2]Lit *separate for you between* [a]Ex 25:16; 40:21 [b]Heb 9:2f
34 [a]Ex 25:21; 40:20; Lev 16:2
35 [a]Ex 40:22 [b]Ex 40:24
36 [1]Or *violet* [2]Lit *variegator;* i.e. a weaver in colors [a]Ex 36:37
37 [1]Or *bases* [2]Or *copper* [a]Ex 36:38
27:1 [1]I.e. One cubit equals approx 18 in. [a]Ex 38:1-7
2 [1]Or *copper,* and so for *bronze* throughout the ch [a]Ps 118:27
4 [1]Lit *on*

5 "You shall put it beneath, under the ledge of the altar, so
that the net will reach halfway up the altar.
6 "You shall make poles for the altar, poles of acacia wood, and
overlay them with bronze.
7 "Its poles shall be inserted into the rings, so that the poles
shall be on the two sides of the altar [a]when it is carried.
8 "You shall make it hollow with planks; [a]as it was shown to
you in the mountain, so they shall make *it.*
9 "You shall make [a]the court of the [1]tabernacle. [2]On the south
side *there shall be* hangings for the court of fine twisted linen
one hundred cubits long for one side;
10 and its pillars *shall be* twenty, with their twenty [1]sockets of
bronze; the hooks of the pillars and their [2]bands *shall be* of silver.
11 "Likewise for the north side in length *there shall be* hangings
one hundred *cubits* long, and its twenty pillars with their twenty
[1]sockets of bronze; the hooks of the pillars and their bands *shall
be* of silver.
12 "*For* the width of the court on the west side *shall be* hangings
of fifty cubits *with* their ten pillars and their ten [1]sockets.
13 "The width of the court on the [1]east side *shall be* fifty cubits.
14 "The hangings for the *one* [1]side *of the gate shall be* fifteen
cubits *with* their three pillars and their three [2]sockets.
15 "And for the [1]other [2]side *shall be* hangings of fifteen cubits
with their three pillars and their three [3]sockets.
16 "For the gate of the court *there shall be* a screen of twenty
cubits, of [1]blue and purple and scarlet *material* and fine twisted
linen, the work of a [2]weaver, *with* their four pillars and their
four [3]sockets.
17 "All the pillars around the court shall be furnished with silver
bands *with* their hooks of silver and their [1]sockets of bronze.
18 "The length of the court *shall be* one hundred cubits, and
the width fifty throughout, and the height five cubits of fine
twisted linen, and their [1]sockets of bronze.
19 "All the utensils of the tabernacle *used* in all its service, and
all its pegs, and all the pegs of the court, *shall be* of bronze.
20 "You shall charge the sons of Israel, that they bring you
[a]clear oil of beaten olives for the [1]light, to make a lamp [2]burn
continually.
21 "In the [a]tent of meeting, outside [b]the veil which is before
the testimony, [c]Aaron and his sons shall keep it in order from
evening to morning before the LORD; *it shall be* a perpetual
[d]statute throughout their generations [1]for the sons of Israel.

Chapter 28 Theme ________________________

28 "Then [a]bring near to yourself Aaron your brother, and
his sons with him, from among the sons of Israel, to
minister as priest to Me—Aaron, [b]Nadab and Abihu, Eleazar
and Ithamar, Aaron's sons.
2 "You shall make [a]holy garments for Aaron your brother, for
glory and for beauty.

7 [a]Num 4:15

8 [a]Ex 25:40; 26:30; Acts 7:44; Heb 8:5

9 [1]Or *dwelling place* [2]Lit *For the side of the Negev to the south* [a]Ex 38:9-20

10 [1]Or *bases* [2]Or *fillets, rings*

11 [1]Or *bases*

12 [1]Or *bases*

13 [1]Lit *east side eastward*

14 [1]Lit *shoulder* [2]Or *bases*

15 [1]Lit *second* [2]Lit *shoulder* [3]Or *bases*

16 [1]Or *violet* [2]Lit *variegator;* i.e. a weaver in colors [3]Or *bases*

17 [1]Or *bases*

18 [1]Or *bases*

20 [1]Or *luminary* [2]Lit *ascend* [a]Ex 35:8, 28; Lev 24:1-4

21 [1]Lit *from* [a]Ex 25:22; 29:42; 30:36 [b]Ex 26:31, 33 [c]Ex 30:8; 1 Sam 3:3; 2 Chr 13:11 [d]Ex 28:43; 29:9; Lev 3:17; 16:34; Num 18:23; 19:21; 1 Sam 30:25

28:1 [a]Num 18:7; Ps 99:6; Heb 5:1, 4 [b]Ex 24:1, 9

2 [a]Ex 29:5, 29; 31:10; 39:1-31; Lev 8:7-9, 30

3 "You shall speak to all the [1a]skillful persons [b]whom I have endowed with [2]the spirit of wisdom, that they make Aaron's garments to consecrate him, that he may minister as priest to Me.

4 "These are the garments which they shall make: a [1a]breastpiece and an ephod and a robe and a tunic of checkered work, a turban and a sash, and they shall make holy garments for Aaron your brother and his sons, that he may minister as priest to Me.

5 "They shall take [a]the gold and the [1]blue and the purple and the scarlet *material* and the fine linen.

6 "They shall also make [a]the ephod of gold, of [1]blue and purple *and* scarlet *material* and fine twisted linen, the work of the skillful workman.

7 "It shall have two shoulder pieces joined to its two ends, that it may be joined.

8 "The skillfully woven band, which is on it, shall be like its workmanship, [1]of the same material: of gold, of [2]blue and purple and scarlet *material* and fine twisted linen.

9 "You shall take two onyx stones and engrave on them the names of the sons of Israel,

10 six of their names on the one stone and the names of the remaining six on the [1]other stone, according to their birth.

11 "[1]As a jeweler engraves a signet, you shall engrave the two stones according to the names of the sons of Israel; you shall [2]set them in filigree *settings* of gold.

12 "You shall put the two stones on the shoulder pieces of the ephod, *as* stones of memorial for the sons of Israel, and Aaron shall [a]bear their names before the LORD on his two shoulders [b]for a memorial.

13 "[a]You shall make filigree *settings* of gold,

14 and two chains of pure gold; you shall make them of twisted cordage work, and you shall put the corded chains on the filigree *settings*.

15 "[a]You shall make a [1]breastpiece of judgment, the work of a skillful workman; like the work of the ephod you shall make it: of gold, of [2]blue and purple and scarlet *material* and fine twisted linen you shall make it.

16 "It shall be square *and* folded double, a span [1]in length and a span [1]in width.

17 "You shall [1]mount on it four rows of stones; the first row *shall be* a row of ruby, topaz and emerald;

18 and the second row a turquoise, a sapphire and a diamond;

19 and the third row a jacinth, an agate and an amethyst;

20 and the fourth row a beryl and an onyx and a jasper; they shall be [1]set in gold filigree.

21 "The stones shall be according to the names of the sons of Israel: twelve, according to their names; they shall be *like* the engravings of a seal, each [a]according to his name for the twelve tribes.

22 "You shall make on the [1]breastpiece chains of twisted cordage work in pure gold.

INSIGHT

The ***ephod*** was used to seek guidance from God. Described in Exodus 28, it was a linen garment worn by the priest and also by David when he was king (2 Samuel 6:14). The ephod was fastened on each shoulder by onyx clasps which had the names of six tribes engraved on one clasp and six tribes engraved on the other. The ***breastpiece***, which was fastened to the ephod, had a linen pouch which held the ***Urim*** and ***Thummim***, which may have been used as sacred lots to reveal God's will (1 Samuel 28:6).

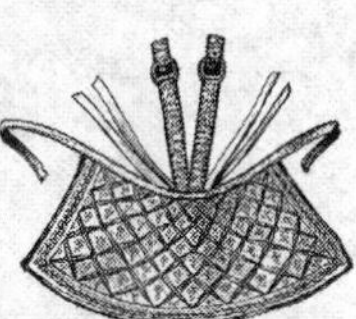

Ephod (viewed from the back)

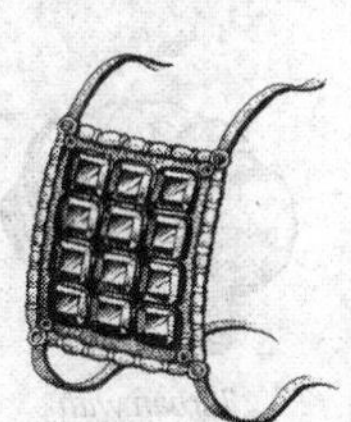

Breastplate

3 [1]Lit *wise of heart* [2]I.e. artistic skill [a]Ex 31:6; 35:25, 31-35; 36:1 [b]Ex 31:3; Is 11:2; 1 Cor 12:7-11; Eph 1:17

4 [1]Or *pouch* [a]Ex 28:15-43

5 [1]Or *violet* [a]Ex 25:3

6 [1]Or *violet* [a]Ex 39:2-7; Lev 8:7

8 [1]Lit *from it* [2]Or *violet*

10 [1]Lit *second*

11 [1]Lit *A work of a lapidary, engravings of a seal* [2]Lit *make them to be surrounded*

12 [a]Ex 28:29; 39:6f [b]Ex 39:7; Lev 24:7; Num 31:54; Josh 4:7; 1 Cor 11:24f

13 [a]Ex 39:16-18

15 [1]Or *pouch* [2]Or *violet* [a]Ex 39:8-21

16 [1]Lit *its*

17 [1]Lit *fill in a setting of stones, four rows of stones*

20 [1]Lit *interwoven with gold in their settings*

21 [a]Rev 7:4-8; 21:12

22 [1]Or *pouch,* and so through v 30

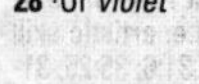

High Priest's Garments

Robe of the Ephod

Turban with Plate of Gold

23 "You shall make on the breastpiece two rings of gold, and shall put the two rings on the two ends of the breastpiece.

24 "You shall put the two cords of gold on the two rings at the ends of the breastpiece.

25 "You shall put the *other* two ends of the two cords on the two filigree *settings,* and put them on the shoulder pieces of the ephod, at the front of it.

26 "You shall make two rings of gold and shall place them on the two ends of the breastpiece, on the edge of it, which is toward the inner side of the ephod.

27 "You shall make two rings of gold and put them on the bottom of the two shoulder pieces of the ephod, on the front of it close to the place where it is joined, above the skillfully woven band of the ephod.

28 "They shall bind the breastpiece by its rings to the rings of the ephod with a [1]blue cord, so that it will be on the skillfully woven band of the ephod, and that the breastpiece will not come loose from the ephod.

29 "Aaron shall carry the names of the sons of Israel in the breastpiece of judgment over his heart when he enters the holy place, for a memorial before the LORD continually.

30 "[a]You shall put in the breastpiece of judgment the [1b]Urim and the Thummim, and they shall be over Aaron's heart when he goes in before the LORD; and Aaron shall carry the judgment of the sons of Israel over his heart before the LORD continually.

31 "[a]You shall make the robe of the ephod all of [1]blue.

32 "There shall be an opening [1]at its top in the middle of it; around its opening there shall be a binding of woven work, like the opening of a coat of mail, so that it will not be torn.

33 "You shall make on its hem pomegranates of blue and purple and scarlet *material,* all around on its hem, and bells of gold between them all around:

34 a golden bell and a pomegranate, a golden bell and a pomegranate, all around on the hem of the robe.

35 "It shall be on Aaron [1]when he ministers; and [2]its tinkling shall be heard when he enters and [3]leaves the holy place before the LORD, so that he will not die.

36 "You shall also make [a]a plate of pure gold and shall engrave on it, like the engravings of a seal, '[b]Holy to the LORD.'

37 "You shall [1]fasten it on a [2]blue cord, and it shall be on the turban; it shall be at the front of the turban.

38 "It shall be on Aaron's forehead, and Aaron shall [1a]take away the iniquity of the holy things which the sons of Israel consecrate, with regard to all their holy gifts; and it shall always be on his forehead, that [b]they may be accepted before the LORD.

39 "You shall weave [a]the tunic of checkered work of fine linen, and shall make a turban of fine linen, and you shall make a sash, the work of a [1]weaver.

40 "For Aaron's sons you shall make [a]tunics; you shall also make sashes for them, and you shall make [1b]caps for them, for glory and for beauty.

28 [1]Or *violet*

30 [1]I.e. lights and perfections [a]Lev 8:8 [b]Num 27:21; Deut 33:8; Ezra 2:63; Neh 7:65

31 [1]Or *violet* [a]Ex 39:22-26

32 [1]Or *for his head*

35 [1]Lit *for ministering* [2]Lit *its sound* [3]Lit *comes out from*

36 [a]Ex 39:30, 31; Lev 8:9 [b]Zech 14:20

37 [1]Lit *place* [2]Or *violet*

38 [1]Or *bear* [a]Lev 10:17; 22:16; Num 18:1 [b]Lev 1:4; 22:27; 23:11; Is 56:7

39 [1]Lit *variegator;* i.e. a weaver in colors [a]Ex 39:27-29

40 [1]Lit *headgear* [a]Ex 28:4; 39:27, 41 [b]Ex 29:9; 39:28; Lev 8:13; Ezek 44:18

41 "You shall put them on Aaron your brother and on his sons with him; and you shall [a]anoint them and [1]ordain them and consecrate them, that they may serve Me as priests.

42 "You shall make for them [a]linen breeches to cover *their* bare flesh; they shall [1]reach from the loins even to the thighs.

43 "They shall be on Aaron and on his sons when they enter the tent of meeting, or [a]when they approach the altar to minister in the holy place, so that they do not incur [1]guilt and die. [b]It *shall be* a statute forever to him and to his [2]descendants after him.

Chapter 29 Theme ______________________________

29 "[a]Now this is [1]what you shall do to them to consecrate them to minister as priests to Me: take one young bull and two rams without blemish,

2 and [a]unleavened bread and unleavened cakes mixed with oil, and unleavened wafers [1]spread with oil; you shall make them of fine wheat flour.

3 "You shall put them in one basket, and present them in the basket along with the bull and the two rams.

4 "Then [a]you shall bring Aaron and his sons to the doorway of the tent of meeting and wash them with water.

5 "You shall take the garments, and put on Aaron the [a]tunic and [b]the robe of the ephod and [c]the ephod and [d]the [1]breastpiece, and gird him with the skillfully [e]woven band of the ephod;

6 and you shall set the [a]turban on his head and put [b]the holy crown on the turban.

7 "Then you shall take [a]the anointing oil and pour it on his head and anoint him.

8 "You shall bring his sons and put [a]tunics on them.

9 "You shall gird them with [a]sashes, Aaron and his sons, and bind [1]caps on them, and they shall have [b]the priesthood by a perpetual statute. So you shall [2c]ordain Aaron and his sons.

10 "Then you shall bring the bull before the tent of meeting, and Aaron and his sons shall [a]lay their hands on the head of the bull.

11 "You shall slaughter the bull before the LORD at the doorway of the tent of meeting.

12 "You shall [a]take some of the blood of the bull and put *it* on [b]the horns of the altar with your finger; and you shall pour out all the blood at the base of the altar.

13 "You shall [a]take all the fat that covers the entrails and the [1]lobe of the liver, and the two kidneys and the fat that is on them, and offer them up in smoke on the altar.

14 "But [a]the flesh of the bull and its hide and its refuse, you shall burn with fire outside the camp; it is a sin offering.

15 "[a]You shall also take the one ram, and Aaron and his sons shall lay their hands on the head of the ram;

16 and you shall slaughter the ram and shall take its blood and sprinkle it around on the altar.

41 [1]Lit *fill their hand* [a]Ex 29:7, 9; 30:30; 40:15; Lev 8:1-36; 10:7
42 [1]Lit *be* [a]Ex 39:28; Lev 6:10; 16:4; Ezek 44:18
43 [1]Or *iniquity* [2]Lit *seed* [a]Ex 20:26 [b]Ex 27:21
29:1 [1]Lit *the thing which* [a]Lev 8:1-34
2 [1]Or *anointed* [a]Lev 2:4; 6:19-23
4 [a]Ex 40:12; Lev 8:6
5 [1]Or *pouch* [a]Ex 28:39; Lev 8:7 [b]Ex 28:31 [c]Ex 28:6 [d]Ex 28:15 [e]Ex 28:8
6 [a]Ex 28:4, 39 [b]Ex 28:36, 37; Lev 8:9
7 [a]Ex 30:25; Lev 8:12; 21:10; Num 35:25; Ps 133:2
8 [a]Ex 28:39, 40; Lev 8:13
9 [1]Lit *headgear* [2]Lit *fill the hand of* [a]Ex 28:40 [b]Ex 40:15; Num 3:10; 18:7; 25:13; Deut 18:5 [c]Ex 28:41; Lev 8:1-36
10 [a]Lev 1:4; 8:14
12 [a]Lev 8:15 [b]Ex 27:2; 30:2
13 [1]Or *appendage on* [a]Lev 3:3, 4
14 [a]Lev 4:11, 12, 21; Heb 13:11
15 [a]Lev 8:18

17 "Then you shall cut the ram into its pieces, and wash its
entrails and its legs, and put *them* [1]with its pieces and [2]its head.
18 "You shall offer up in smoke the whole ram on the altar; it is
a burnt offering to the LORD: [a]it is a soothing aroma, an offering
by fire to the LORD.
19 "Then [a]you shall take the [1]other ram, and Aaron and his
sons shall lay their hands on the head of the ram.
20 "You shall slaughter the ram, and take some of its blood and
put *it* on the lobe of Aaron's right ear and on the lobes of his
sons' right ears and on the thumbs of their right hands and on
the big toes of their right feet, and sprinkle the *rest of the*
blood around on the altar.
21 "Then you shall take some of the blood that is on the altar
and some of the [a]anointing oil, and sprinkle *it* on Aaron and on
his garments and on his sons and on his sons' garments with
him; so he and his garments shall be consecrated, as well as his
sons and his sons' garments with him.
22 "You shall also take the fat from the ram and the fat tail, and
the fat that covers the entrails and the [1]lobe of the liver, and
the two kidneys and the fat that is on them and the right thigh
(for it is a ram of [2]ordination),
23 and one cake of bread and [a]one cake of bread *mixed with*
oil and one wafer from the basket of unleavened bread which
is *set* before the LORD;
24 and you shall put [1]all these [2]in the [3]hands of Aaron and [2]in
the [3]hands of his sons, and shall wave them as a wave offering
before the LORD.
25 "[a]You shall take them from their hands, and offer them up in
smoke on the altar on the burnt offering for a soothing aroma
before the LORD; it is an offering by fire to the LORD.
26 "Then you shall take [a]the breast of Aaron's ram of [1]ordination,
and wave it as a wave offering before the LORD; and it shall be
your portion.
27 "You shall consecrate the breast of the wave offering and the
thigh of the heave offering which was waved and which was
[1]offered from the ram of [2]ordination, from the one which was
for Aaron and from the one which was for his sons.
28 "It shall be for Aaron and his sons as *their* portion forever
from the sons of Israel, for it is a heave offering; and it shall be
a heave offering from the sons of Israel from the sacrifices of
their peace offerings, *even* their heave offering to the LORD.
29 "[a]The holy garments of Aaron shall be for his sons after him,
[1]that in them they may be anointed and ordained.
30 "For seven days the one of his sons who is priest in his stead
shall put them on when he enters the tent of meeting to
minister in the holy place.
31 "You shall take the ram of [1]ordination and [a]boil its flesh in a
holy place.
32 "Aaron and his sons shall eat the flesh of the ram and the
bread that is in the basket, at the doorway of the tent of
meeting.

17 [1]Lit *on* [2]Lit *on its*

18 [a]Gen 8:21; Ex 29:25

19 [1]Lit *second* [a]Lev 8:22f

21 [a]Ex 30:25, 31; Lev 8:30

22 [1]Or *appendage on* [2]Lit *filling*

23 [a]Lev 8:26

24 [1]Lit *the whole* [2]Lit *on* [3]Lit *palms*

25 [a]Lev 8:28

26 [1]Lit *filling* [a]Lev 7:31, 34; 8:29

27 [1]Lit *heaved;* or *lifted up* [2]Lit *filling*

29 [1]Lit *for anointing in them and filling their hand in them* [a]Num 20:26, 28

31 [1]Lit *filling* [a]Lev 8:31

33 “Thus [a]they shall eat [1]those things by which atonement was
made [2]at their ordination *and* consecration; but a [3b]layman shall
not eat *them,* because they are holy.
34 “[a]If any of the flesh of [1]ordination or any of the bread
remains until morning, then you shall burn the remainder with
fire; it shall not be eaten, because it is holy.
35 “Thus you shall do to Aaron and to his sons, according to all
that I have commanded you; you shall [1]ordain them through
[a]seven days.
36 “[a]Each day you shall offer a bull as a sin offering for atonement,
and you shall [1]purify the altar when you make atonement [2]for
it, and [b]you shall anoint it to consecrate it.
37 “For seven days you shall make atonement [1]for the altar and
consecrate it; then [a]the altar shall be most holy, *and* whatever
touches the altar shall be holy.
38 “Now [a]this is what you shall offer on the altar: two one year
old lambs each day, continuously.
39 “The [a]one lamb you shall offer in the morning and the
[1]other lamb you shall offer at [2]twilight;
40 and there *shall be* one-tenth *of an ephah* of fine flour
mixed with one-fourth of a hin of beaten oil, and one-fourth of
a hin of wine for a drink offering with one lamb.
41 “The [1]other lamb you shall offer at [2]twilight, and shall offer
with it [3]the same grain offering and [4]the same drink offering as
in the morning, for a soothing aroma, an offering by fire to the
LORD.
42 “It shall be a continual burnt offering throughout your
generations at the doorway of the tent of meeting before the
LORD, [a]where I will meet with you, to speak to you there.
43 “I will meet there with the sons of Israel, and it shall be
consecrated by My glory.
44 “I will consecrate the tent of meeting and the altar; I will
also consecrate Aaron and his sons to minister as priests to Me.
45 “[a]I will dwell among the sons of Israel and will be their God.
46 “They shall know that [a]I am the LORD their God who
brought them out of the land of Egypt, that I might dwell
among them; I am the LORD their God.

Chapter 30 Theme ________________________

30 “Moreover, you shall make [a]an altar as a place for burning incense; you shall make it of acacia wood.
2 “Its length *shall be* a [1]cubit, and its width a cubit, it shall be
square, and its height *shall be* two cubits; its horns *shall be* [2]of
one piece with it.
3 “You shall overlay it with pure gold, its top and its [1]sides all
around, and its horns; and you shall make a gold molding all
around for it.
4 “You shall make two gold rings for it under its molding; you
shall make *them* on its two side walls—on [1]opposite sides—
and [2]they shall be holders for poles with which to carry it.

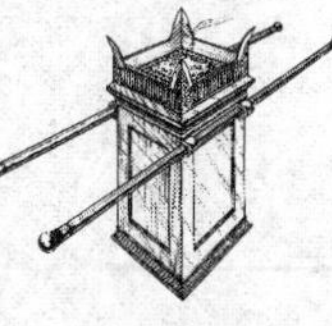

Altar of Incense (Golden Altar)

33 [1]Lit *them* [2]Lit *to fill their hand to sanctify them* [3]Lit *stranger* [a]Lev 10:14 [b]Lev 22:10, 13
34 [1]Lit *filling* [a]Ex 12:10; 23:18; 34:25; Lev 8:32
35 [1]Lit *fill their hand* [a]Lev 8:33
36 [1]Or *offer a sin offering on the altar* [2]Lit *upon* [a]Heb 10:11 [b]Ex 40:10
37 [1]Lit *upon* [a]Ex 30:28f
38 [a]Num 28:3-31; 29:6-38
39 [1]Lit *second* [2]Lit *between the two evenings* [a]Ezek 46:13-15
41 [1]Lit *second* [2]Lit *between the two evenings* [3]Lit *according to the grain offering of the morning* [4]Lit *according to its*
42 [a]Ex 25:22; Num 17:4
45 [a]Ex 25:8; Lev 26:12; Num 5:3; Deut 12:11; Zech 2:10; 2 Cor 6:16; Rev 21:3
46 [a]Ex 20:2
30:1 [a]Ex 37:25-29
2 [1]I.e. One cubit equals approx 18 in. [2]Lit *from itself*
3 [1]Lit *walls*
4 [1]Lit *its two* [2]Lit *it*

5 "You shall make the poles of acacia wood and overlay them
with gold.
6 "You shall put [1]this altar in front of the veil that is [2]near the
ark of the testimony, in front of the [3a]mercy seat that is over
the ark of the testimony, where I will meet with you.
7 "Aaron shall burn fragrant incense on it; he shall burn it
every morning when he trims the lamps.
8 "When Aaron [1]trims the lamps at [2]twilight, he shall burn
incense. *There shall be* perpetual incense before the LORD
throughout your generations.
9 "You shall not offer any strange incense on [1]this altar, or
burnt offering or meal offering; and you shall not pour out a
drink offering on it.
10 "Aaron shall [a]make atonement on its horns once a year; he
shall make atonement on it with the blood of the sin offering of
atonement once a year throughout your generations. It is most
holy to the LORD."
11 The LORD also spoke to Moses, saying,
12 "When you take [a]a [1]census of the sons of Israel [2]to number
them, then each one of them shall give [b]a ransom for [3]himself
to the LORD, when you [4]number them, so that there will be no
plague among them when you [4]number them.
13 "This is what everyone who [1]is numbered shall give: half a
shekel according to the shekel of the sanctuary ([a]the shekel is
twenty gerahs), half a shekel as a [2]contribution to the LORD.
14 "Everyone who [1]is numbered, from twenty years old and
over, shall give the [2]contribution to the LORD.
15 "The rich shall not pay more and the poor shall not pay less
than the half shekel, when you give the [1]contribution to the
LORD to make atonement for [2]yourselves.
16 "You shall take the atonement money from the sons of Israel
and shall give it for the service of the tent of meeting, that it
may be a memorial for the sons of Israel before the LORD, to
make atonement for [1]yourselves."
17 The LORD spoke to Moses, saying,
18 "You shall also make [a]a laver of [1]bronze, with its base of
bronze, for washing; and you shall [b]put it between the tent of
meeting and the altar, and you shall put water in it.
19 "Aaron and his sons shall [a]wash their hands and their feet
from it;
20 when they enter the tent of meeting, they shall wash with
water, so that they will not die; or when they approach the altar
to minister, by offering up in smoke a fire *sacrifice* to the LORD.
21 "So they shall wash their hands and their feet, so that they
will not die; and [a]it shall be a perpetual statute for them, for
[1]Aaron and his [2]descendants throughout their generations."
22 Moreover, the LORD spoke to Moses, saying,
23 "Take also for yourself the finest of spices: of flowing myrrh
five hundred *shekels,* and of fragrant cinnamon half as much,
two hundred and fifty, and of fragrant cane two hundred and
fifty,

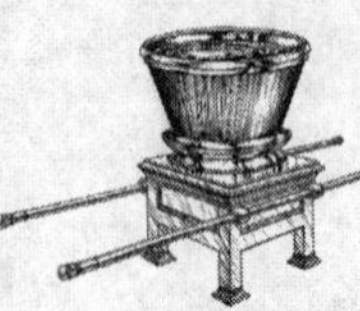
Bronze Laver

6 [1]Lit *it* [2]Lit *upon* or *over* [3]Lit *propitiatory* [a]Ex 25:21f

8 [1]Lit *causes to ascend* [2]Lit *between the two evenings*

9 [1]Lit *it*

10 [a]Lev 16:18

12 [1]Lit *sum* [2]Lit *for their being mustered* [3]Lit *his soul* [4]Lit *muster* [a]Ex 38:25, 26; Num 1:2; 26:2 [b]Num 31:50

13 [1]Lit *passes over to those who are mustered* [2]Lit *heave offering* [a]Lev 27:25; Num 3:47; Ezek 45:12

14 [1]V 13, note 1 [2]Lit *heave offering of the LORD*

15 [1]Lit *heave offering of the LORD* [2]Lit *your souls*

16 [1]Lit *your souls*

18 [1]Or *copper* [a]Ex 38:8 [b]Ex 40:30

19 [a]Ex 40:31f; Is 52:11

21 [1]Lit *him* [2]Lit *seed* [a]Ex 28:43

25 [1]Lit *it* [a]Ex 37:29; 40:9; Lev 8:10

26 [a]Ex 40:9; Lev 8:10; Num 7:1

30 [a]Ex 29:7; Lev 8:12

32 [1]Lit *the flesh of man* [2]Lit *its proportion* [a]Ex 30:25, 37

33 [1]Lit *stranger* [2]Lit *even he shall* [a]Ex 30:38 [b]Gen 17:14; Ex 12:15; Lev 7:20f

36 [a]Ex 29:42

37 [1]Lit *its proportion* [a]Ex 30:32

38 [1]Lit *smell of it* [2]Lit *even he shall* [a]Ex 30:33

31:1 [a]Ex 35:30-36:1

2 [a]1 Chr 2:20

3 [1]Or *workmanship* [a]Ex 35:31; 1 Kin 7:14; 1 Cor 12:4-8

4 [1]Lit *devise devices* [2]Or *copper*

5 [1]Lit *to fill in (for a setting)* [2]Or *workmanship*

6 [1]Lit *given* [2]Lit *wise of heart* [3]Lit *wisdom* [a]Ex 35:34

24 and of cassia five hundred, according to the shekel of the
sanctuary, and of olive oil a hin.
25 "You shall make [1]of these a holy anointing oil, a perfume
mixture, the work of a perfumer; it shall be [a]a holy anointing oil.
26 "With it [a]you shall anoint the tent of meeting and the ark of
the testimony,
27 and the table and all its utensils, and the lampstand and its
utensils, and the altar of incense,
28 and the altar of burnt offering and all its utensils, and the
laver and its stand.
29 "You shall also consecrate them, that they may be most holy;
whatever touches them shall be holy.
30 "[a]You shall anoint Aaron and his sons, and consecrate them,
that they may minister as priests to Me.
31 "You shall speak to the sons of Israel, saying, 'This shall be a
holy anointing oil to Me throughout your generations.
32 'It shall not be poured on [1]anyone's body, nor shall you make
any like it in [2]the same proportions; [a]it is holy, *and* it shall be
holy to you.
33 '[a]Whoever shall mix *any* like it or whoever puts any of it on
a [1]layman [2b]shall be cut off from his people.'"
34 Then the LORD said to Moses, "Take for yourself spices, stacte
and onycha and galbanum, spices with pure frankincense; there
shall be an equal part of each.
35 "With it you shall make incense, a perfume, the work of a
perfumer, salted, pure, *and* holy.
36 "You shall beat some of it very fine, and put part of it before
the testimony in the tent of meeting [a]where I will meet with
you; it shall be most holy to you.
37 "The incense which you shall make, [a]you shall not make in
[1]the same proportions for yourselves; it shall be holy to you for
the LORD.
38 "[a]Whoever shall make *any* like it, to [1]use as perfume, [2]shall
be cut off from his people."

Chapter 31 Theme ____________________

31 [a]Now the LORD spoke to Moses, saying,
2 "See, I have called by name Bezalel, the [a]son of Uri, the
son of Hur, of the tribe of Judah.
3 "I have [a]filled him with the Spirit of God in wisdom, in
understanding, in knowledge, and in all *kinds of* [1]craftsmanship,
4 to [1]make artistic designs for work in gold, in silver, and in
[2]bronze,
5 and in the cutting of stones [1]for settings, and in the carving
of wood, that he may work in all *kinds of* [2]craftsmanship.
6 "And behold, I Myself have [1]appointed with him [a]Oholiab,
the son of Ahisamach, of the tribe of Dan; and in the hearts of
all who are [2]skillful I have put [3]skill, that they may make all
that I have commanded you:

RETURN TO INSTRUCTIONS

7 [a]the tent of meeting, and [b]the ark of testimony, and [c]the [1]mercy seat upon it, and all the furniture of the tent,

8 [a]the table also and its [1]utensils, and the [b]pure *gold* lampstand with all its [1]utensils, and [c]the altar of incense,

9 [a]the altar of burnt offering also with all its [1]utensils, and [b]the laver and its stand,

10 the [1a]woven garments as well, and the holy garments for Aaron the priest, and the garments of his sons, *with which* to [2]carry on their priesthood;

11 [a]the anointing oil also, and the [b]fragrant incense for the holy place, they are to make *them* according to all that I have commanded you."

12 The LORD spoke to Moses, saying,

13 "But as for you, speak to the sons of Israel, saying, '[a]You shall surely observe My sabbaths; for *this* is [b]a sign between Me and you throughout your generations, that you may know that I am the LORD who sanctifies you.

14 'Therefore you are to observe the sabbath, for it is holy to you. [a]Everyone who profanes it shall surely be put to death; for whoever does any work on it, that person shall be cut off from among his people.

15 '[a]For six days work may be done, but on the seventh day there is a [b]sabbath of complete rest, holy to the LORD; [c]whoever does any work on the sabbath day shall surely be put to death.

16 'So the sons of Israel shall observe the sabbath, to [1]celebrate the sabbath throughout their generations as a perpetual covenant.'

17 "[a]It is a sign between Me and the sons of Israel forever; [b]for in six days the LORD made heaven and earth, but on the seventh day He ceased *from labor,* and was refreshed."

18 When He had finished speaking with him upon Mount Sinai, He gave Moses [a]the two tablets of the testimony, tablets of stone, [b]written by the finger of God.

Chapter 32 Theme ____________________

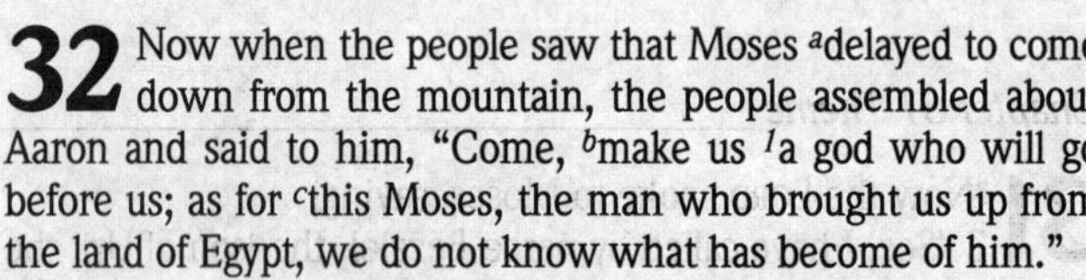

32 Now when the people saw that Moses [a]delayed to come down from the mountain, the people assembled about Aaron and said to him, "Come, [b]make us [1]a god who will go before us; as for [c]this Moses, the man who brought us up from the land of Egypt, we do not know what has become of him."

2 Aaron said to them, "[a]Tear off the gold rings which are in the ears of your wives, your sons, and your daughters, and bring *them* to me."

3 Then all the people tore off the gold rings which were in their ears and brought *them* to Aaron.

4 He took *this* from their hand, and fashioned it with a graving tool and made it into a [a]molten calf; and they said, "[1]This is your god, O Israel, who brought you up from the land of Egypt."

5 Now when Aaron saw *this,* he built an altar before it; and Aaron made a proclamation and said, "Tomorrow *shall be* a feast to the LORD."

7 [1]Lit *propitiatory* [a]Ex 36:8-38 [b]Ex 37:1-5 [c]Ex 37:6-9

8 [1]Or *vessels* [a]Ex 37:10-16 [b]Ex 37:17-24; Lev 24:4 [c]Ex 37:25-29

9 [1]Or *vessels* [a]Ex 38:1-7 [b]Ex 38:8

10 [1]Or *service garments* [2]Lit *minister as priests* [a]Ex 39:1

11 [a]Ex 30:23-32 [b]Ex 30:34-38

13 [a]Ex 20:8 [b]Ex 31:17; Ezek 20:12, 20

14 [a]Ex 31:15; 35:2; Num 15:32, 35; John 7:23

15 [a]Ex 20:9-11; 23:12; 34:21; 35:2; Lev 23:3; Deut 5:12-14 [b]Gen 2:2f; Ex 16:23; 20:8; 35:2, 3 [c]Ex 31:14

16 [1]Lit *do*

17 [a]Ex 31:13; Ezek 20:12 [b]Gen 1:31; 2:2, 3; Ex 20:11

18 [a]Ex 24:12; 34:29; Deut 4:13; 5:22; 9:10f [b]Ex 32:15, 16; 34:1, 28; Deut 9:10

32:1 [1]Or *gods* [a]Ex 24:18; Deut 9:11, 12 [b]Acts 7:40 [c]Ex 14:11

2 [a]Ex 35:22

4 [1]Or *These are your gods* [a]Deut 9:16; Neh 9:18; Ps 106:19; Acts 7:41

6 So the next day they rose early and [a]offered burnt offerings,
and brought peace offerings; and [b]the people sat down to eat
and to drink, and rose up [c]to play.
7 Then the LORD spoke to Moses, "Go [1]down at once, for your
people, whom [a]you brought up from the land of Egypt, have
[b]corrupted *themselves.*
8 "They have quickly turned aside from the way which I
commanded them. [a]They have made for themselves a molten
calf, and have worshiped it and [b]have sacrificed to it and said,
'[1c]This is your god, O Israel, who brought you up from the land
of Egypt!'"
9 [a]The LORD said to Moses, "I have seen this people, and
behold, they are [1b]an obstinate people.
10 "Now then [a]let Me alone, that My anger may burn against
them and that I may destroy them; and [b]I will make of you a
great nation."
11 Then [a]Moses entreated the LORD his God, and said, "O LORD,
why does Your anger burn against Your people whom You have
brought out from the land of Egypt with great power and with
a mighty hand?
12 "Why should [a]the Egyptians speak, saying, 'With evil *intent*
He brought them out to kill them in the mountains and to destroy
them from the face of the earth'? Turn from Your burning
anger and change Your mind about *doing* harm to Your people.
13 "Remember Abraham, Isaac, and Israel, Your servants to
whom You [a]swore by Yourself, and said to them, 'I will [b]multiply
your [1]descendants as the stars of the heavens, and [c]all this land
of which I have spoken I will give to your [1]descendants, and
they shall inherit *it* forever.'"
14 [a]So the LORD changed His mind about the harm which He
said He would do to His people.
15 [a]Then Moses turned and went down from the mountain
with the two tablets of the testimony in his hand, [b]tablets
which were written on both [1]sides; they were written on one
side and the other.
16 The tablets were God's work, and the writing was God's
writing engraved on the tablets.
17 Now when Joshua heard the sound of the people [1]as they
shouted, he said to Moses, "There is a sound of war in the
camp."
18 But he said,

"It is not the sound of the cry of triumph,
Nor is it the sound of the cry of defeat;
But the sound of singing I hear."

19 It came about, as soon as [1]Moses came near the camp, that
[a]he saw the calf and *the* dancing; and Moses' anger burned,
and [b]he threw the tablets from his hands and shattered them
[2]at the foot of the mountain.
20 [a]He took the calf which they had made and burned *it* with
fire, and ground it to powder, and scattered it over the surface
of the water and made the sons of Israel drink *it.*

6 [a]Acts 7:41 [b]1 Cor 10:7 [c]Ex 32:17-19; Num 25:2
7 [1]Lit *go down* [a]Ex 32:4, 11; Deut 9:12 [b]Gen 6:11f
8 [1]Or *These are your gods* [a]Ex 20:3, 4, 23 [b]Ex 22:20; 34:15; Deut 32:17 [c]1 Kin 12:28
9 [1]Or *a stiff-necked* [a]Num 14:11-20 [b]Ex 33:3, 5; 34:9; Is 48:4; Acts 7:51
10 [a]Deut 9:14 [b]Num 14:12
11 [a]Deut 9:18, 26
12 [a]Num 14:13-19; Deut 9:28; Josh 7:9
13 [1]Lit *seed* [a]Gen 22:16-18; Heb 6:13 [b]Gen 15:5; 26:4 [c]Gen 12:7; 13:15; 15:18; 17:8; 35:12; Ex 13:5, 11; 33:1
14 [a]Ps 106:45
15 [1]Lit *their sides* [a]Deut 9:15 [b]Ex 31:18
17 [1]Lit *in its shouting*
19 [1]Lit *he* [2]Lit *beneath* [a]Ex 32:6; Deut 9:16 [b]Deut 9:17
20 [a]Deut 9:21

21 Then Moses said to Aaron, "What did this people do to you, that you have brought *such* great sin upon them?"
22 Aaron said, "Do not let the anger of my lord burn; you know the people yourself, [a]that they are [1]prone to evil.
23 "For [a]they said to me, 'Make [1]a god for us who will go before us; for this Moses, the man who brought us up from the land of Egypt, we do not know what has become of him.'
24 "I said to them, 'Whoever has any gold, let them tear it off.' So they gave *it* to me, and [a]I threw it into the fire, and out came this calf."
25 Now when Moses saw that the people were [1]out of control—for Aaron had [a]let them [2]get out of control to be a derision among [3]their enemies—
26 then Moses stood in the gate of the camp, and said, "Whoever is for the LORD, *come* to me!" And all the sons of Levi gathered together to him.
27 He said to them, "Thus says the LORD, the God of Israel, 'Every man *of you* put his sword upon his thigh, and go back and forth from gate to gate in the camp, and kill every man his brother, and every man his friend, and every man his [1]neighbor.'"
28 So [a]the sons of Levi did [1]as Moses instructed, and about three thousand men of the people fell that day.
29 Then Moses said, "[1]Dedicate yourselves today to the LORD—for every man has been against his son and against his brother—in order that He may bestow a blessing upon you today."
30 On the next day Moses said to the people, "[a]You yourselves have [1]committed a great sin; and now I am going up to the LORD, perhaps I can [b]make atonement for your sin."
31 Then Moses returned to the LORD, and said, "Alas, this people has [1]committed a great sin, and they have made [2]a [a]god of gold for themselves.
32 "But now, if You will, forgive their sin—and if not, please blot me out from Your [a]book which You have written!"
33 The LORD said to Moses, "Whoever has sinned against Me, [a]I will blot him out of My book.
34 "But go now, lead the people [a]where I told you. Behold, [b]My angel shall go before you; nevertheless [c]in the day when I [1]punish, [d]I will [2]punish them for their sin."
35 [a]Then the LORD smote the people, because of [b]what they did with the calf which Aaron had made.

Chapter 33 Theme ______________________

33 Then the LORD spoke to Moses, "Depart, go up from here, you and the people whom you have brought up from the land of Egypt, to the land of which [a]I swore to Abraham, [b]Isaac, and [c]Jacob, saying, '[d]To your [1]descendants I will give it.'
2 "I will send [a]an angel before you and [b]I will drive out the Canaanite, the Amorite, the Hittite, the Perizzite, the Hivite and the Jebusite.

22 [1]Lit *in evil* [a]Deut 9:24
23 [1]Or *gods* [a]Ex 32:1-4
24 [a]Ex 32:4
25 [1]Lit *let loose* [2]Lit *go loose* [3]Lit *those who rise against them* [a]1 Kin 12:28-30; 14:16
27 [1]Or *kin*
28 [1]Lit *according to Moses' word* [a]Num 25:7-13; Deut 33:9
29 [1]Lit *Fill your hand*
30 [1]Lit *sinned* [a]1 Sam 12:20, 23 [b]Num 25:13
31 [1]Lit *sinned* [2]Or *gods* [a]Ex 20:23
32 [a]Ps 69:28; Is 4:3; Dan 12:1; Mal 3:16, 17; Phil 4:3; Rev 3:5; 21:27
33 [a]Ex 17:14; Deut 29:20; Ps 9:5; Rev 3:5
34 [1]Lit *visit* [2]Lit *visit their sin upon them* [a]Ex 3:17 [b]Ex 23:20 [c]Deut 32:35; Rom 2:5, 6 [d]Ps 99:8
35 [a]Ex 32:28 [b]Ex 32:4, 24
33:1 [1]Lit *seed* [a]Ex 32:13 [b]Gen 26:1-3 [c]Gen 28:10 [d]Gen 12:7
2 [a]Ex 32:34 [b]Ex 23:27-31; Josh 24:11

3 "*Go up* to a land [a]flowing with milk and honey; for I will not
go up in your midst, because you are [1b]an obstinate people, and
[c]I might destroy you on the way."
4 When the people heard this [1]sad word, [a]they went into
mourning, and none of them put on his ornaments.
5 For the LORD had said to Moses, "Say to the sons of Israel,
'You are [1a]an obstinate people; should I go up in your midst for
one moment, I would destroy you. Now therefore, put off your
ornaments from you, that I may know what I shall do with you.'"
6 So the sons of Israel stripped themselves of their ornaments,
from Mount Horeb *onward.*
7 Now Moses used to take [a]the tent and pitch it outside the
camp, a good distance from the camp, and he called it the tent
of meeting. And [b]everyone who sought the LORD would go out
to the tent of meeting which was outside the camp.
8 And it came about, whenever Moses went out to the tent,
that all the people would arise and stand, each at the entrance
of his tent, and gaze after Moses until he entered the tent.
9 Whenever Moses entered the tent, [a]the pillar of cloud
would descend and stand at the entrance of the tent; [b]and [1]the
LORD would speak with Moses.
10 When all the people saw the pillar of cloud standing at the
entrance of the tent, all the people would arise and worship,
each at the entrance of his tent.
11 Thus [a]the LORD used to speak to Moses face to face, just as
a man speaks to his friend. When [1]Moses returned to the
camp, [b]his servant Joshua, the son of Nun, a young man, would
not depart from the tent.
12 Then Moses said to the LORD, "See, You say to me, '[a]Bring
up this people!' But You Yourself have not let me know [b]whom
You will send with me. [c]Moreover, You have said, 'I have known
you by name, and you have also found favor in My sight.'
13 "Now therefore, I pray You, if I have found favor in Your
sight, [a]let me know Your ways that I may know You, so that I
may find favor in Your sight. [b]Consider too, that this nation is
Your people."
14 And He said, "[a]My presence shall go *with you,* and [b]I will
give you rest."
15 Then he said to Him, "[a]If Your presence does not go *with
us,* do not lead us up from here.
16 "For how then can it be known that I have found favor in
Your sight, I and Your people? Is it not by Your going with us,
so that [a]we, I and Your people, may be distinguished from all
the *other* people who are upon the face of the [1]earth?"
17 The LORD said to Moses, "I will also do this thing of which
you have spoken; [a]for you have found favor in My sight and I
have known you by name."
18 [a]Then [1]Moses said, "I pray You, show me Your glory!"
19 And He said, "[a]I Myself will make all My goodness pass
before you, and will proclaim the name of the LORD before you;
and [b]I will be gracious to whom I will be gracious, and will
show compassion on whom I will show compassion."

3 [1]Lit *a stiff-necked* [a]Ex 3:8, 17 [b]Ex 32:9; 33:5 [c]Ex 32:10
4 [1]Lit *evil* [a]Num 14:1, 39
5 [1]Lit *a stiff-necked* [a]Ex 33:3
7 [a]Ex 18:7, 12-16 [b]Ex 29:42f
9 [1]Lit *He* [a]Ex 13:21 [b]Ps 99:7
11 [1]Lit *he* [a]Num 12:8; Deut 34:10 [b]Ex 24:13
12 [a]Ex 3:10; 32:34 [b]Ex 33:2 [c]Ex 33:17
13 [a]Ps 25:4; 27:11; 51:13; 86:11; 119:33 [b]Ex 3:7, 10; 5:1; 32:12, 14; Deut 9:26, 29
14 [a]Deut 4:37; Is 63:9 [b]Deut 12:10; 25:19; Josh 21:44; 22:4
15 [a]Ps 80:3, 7, 19
16 [1]Lit *ground* [a]Lev 20:24, 26
17 [a]Ex 33:12
18 [1]Lit *he* [a]Ex 33:20-23
19 [a]Ex 34:6, 7 [b]Rom 9:15

20 But He said, "You cannot see My face, [a]for no man can see
Me and live!"
21 Then the LORD said, "Behold, there is a place [1]by Me, and
[a]you shall stand *there* on the rock;
22 and it will come about, while My glory is passing by, that I
will put you in the cleft of the rock and [a]cover you with My
hand until I have passed by.
23 "Then I will take My hand away and you shall see My back,
but [a]My face shall not be seen."

Chapter 34 Theme ______________________

34 Now the LORD said to Moses, "Cut out for yourself [a]two
stone tablets like the former ones, and [b]I will write on
the tablets the words that were on the former tablets which
you shattered.
2 "So be ready by morning, and come up in the morning to
[a]Mount Sinai, and [1]present yourself there to Me on the top of
the mountain.
3 "[a]No man is to come up with you, nor let any man be seen
[1]anywhere on the mountain; even the flocks and the herds
may not graze in front of that mountain."
4 So he cut out [a]two stone tablets like the former ones, and
Moses rose up early in the morning and went up to Mount
Sinai, as the LORD had commanded him, and he took two stone
tablets in his hand.
5 [a]The LORD descended in the cloud and stood there with
him as [1]he called upon the name of the LORD.
6 Then the LORD passed by in front of him and proclaimed,
"The LORD, the LORD God, [a]compassionate and gracious, slow
to anger, and abounding in lovingkindness and [1]truth;
7 who [a]keeps lovingkindness for thousands, who forgives
iniquity, transgression and sin; yet He [b]will by no means leave *the*
guilty unpunished, [c]visiting the iniquity of fathers on the children
and on the grandchildren to the third and fourth generations."
8 Moses made haste [1a]to bow low toward the earth and
worship.
9 He said, "[a]If now I have found favor in Your sight, O Lord, I
pray, let the Lord go along in our midst, even though [1b]the
people are so obstinate, and [c]pardon our iniquity and our sin,
and [d]take us as Your own [2]possession."
10 Then [1]God said, "Behold, [a]I am going to make a covenant.
Before all your people [b]I will perform miracles which have not
been [2]produced in all the earth nor among any of the nations;
and all the people [3]among whom you live will see the working
of the LORD, for it is a fearful thing that I am going to perform
with you.
11 "[1]Be sure to observe what I am commanding you this day:
behold, [a]I am going to drive out the Amorite before you, and
the Canaanite, the Hittite, the Perizzite, the Hivite and the
Jebusite.

20 [a]Is 6:5; 1 Tim 6:16

21 [1]Lit *with* [a]Ps 18:2, 46; 27:5; 61:2; 62:7

22 [a]Ps 91:1, 4; Is 49:2; 51:16

23 [a]Ex 33:20; John 1:18

34:1 [a]Ex 24:12; 31:18; 32:16, 19 [b]Deut 10:2, 4

2 [1]Or *place yourself before* [a]Ex 19:11, 18, 20

3 [1]Lit *on all* [a]Ex 19:12, 13

4 [a]Ex 34:1

5 [1]Or *he called out with the name of the LORD* [a]Ex 19:9; 33:9

6 [1]Or *faithfulness* [a]Num 14:18; Deut 4:31; Neh 9:17; Ps 86:15; 103:8; 108:4; 145:8; Joel 2:13; Rom 2:4

7 [a]Ex 20:5, 6; Deut 5:10; 7:9; Ps 103:3; 130:3, 4; 1 John 1:9 [b]Ex 23:7; Deut 7:10; Job 10:14; Nah 1:3 [c]Deut 5:9

8 [1]Lit *and bowed . . . worshiped* [a]Ex 4:31

9 [1]Lit *it is a people stiff-necked* [2]Or *inheritance* [a]Ex 33:13 [b]Ex 32:9 [c]Ex 34:7 [d]Deut 4:20; 9:26, 29; 32:9; Ps 33:12

10 [1]Lit *He* [2]Lit *created* [3]Lit *in whose midst you are* [a]Ex 34:27, 28; Deut 5:2 [b]Deut 4:32; Ps 72:18; 136:4

11 [1]Lit *Observe for yourself* [a]Ex 33:2

12 "[a]Watch yourself that you make no covenant with the
inhabitants of the land into which you are going, or it will
become a snare in your midst.
13 "[a]But *rather,* you are to tear down their altars and smash
their *sacred* pillars and cut down their [1b]Asherim
14 —for [a]you shall not worship any other god, for the LORD,
whose name is Jealous, is a jealous God—
15 otherwise you might make a covenant with the inhabitants
of the land and they would play the harlot with their gods and
[a]sacrifice to their gods, and someone [b]might invite you [1]to eat
of his sacrifice,
16 and [a]you might take some of his daughters for your sons,
and his daughters might play the harlot with their gods and
cause your sons *also* to play the harlot with their gods.
17 "[a]You shall make for yourself no molten gods.
18 "You shall observe [a]the Feast of Unleavened Bread. For
[b]seven days you are to eat unleavened bread, [1]as I commanded
you, at the appointed time in the [c]month of Abib, for in the
month of Abib you came out of Egypt.
19 "[a]The first offspring from every womb belongs to Me, and all
your male livestock, the first offspring from [1]cattle and sheep.
20 "[a]You shall redeem with a lamb the [1]first offspring from a
donkey; and if you do not redeem *it,* then you shall break its
neck. You shall redeem [b]all the firstborn of your sons. [2c]None
shall appear before Me empty-handed.
21 "You shall work [a]six days, but on the seventh day you shall
rest; *even* during plowing time and harvest you shall rest.
22 "You shall celebrate [a]the Feast of Weeks, *that is,* the first
fruits of the wheat harvest, and the Feast of Ingathering at the
turn of the year.
23 "[a]Three times a year all your males are to appear before the
Lord [1]GOD, the God of Israel.
24 "For I will [1a]drive out nations before you and enlarge your
borders, and no man shall covet your land when you go up
three times a year to appear before the LORD your God.
25 "[a]You shall not [1]offer the blood of My sacrifice with
leavened bread, [b]nor is the sacrifice of the Feast of the Passover
to [2]be left over until morning.
26 "You shall bring [a]the very first of the first fruits of your soil
into the house of the LORD your God.

"You shall not boil a young goat in its mother's milk."

27 Then the LORD said to Moses, "[a]Write [1]down these words,
for in accordance with these words I have made [b]a covenant
with you and with Israel."
28 So he was there with the LORD [a]forty days and forty nights;
he did not eat bread or drink water. And [1b]he wrote on the
tablets the words of the covenant, [c]the Ten [2]Commandments.
29 It came about when Moses was coming down from Mount
Sinai (and the [a]two tablets of the testimony *were* in Moses'
hand as he was coming down from the mountain), that Moses
did not know that [b]the skin of his face shone because of his
speaking with Him.

12 [a]Ex 23:32, 33

13 [1]I.e. wooden symbols of a female deity [a]Ex 23:24; Deut 12:3 [b]Deut 16:21; Judg 6:25, 26; 2 Kin 18:4; 2 Chr 34:3f

14 [a]Ex 20:3, 5; Deut 4:24

15 [1]Lit *and you eat* [a]Ex 22:20; 32:8 [b]Num 25:1, 2; Deut 32:37, 38

16 [a]Deut 7:3; Josh 23:12, 13; 1 Kin 11:1-4

17 [a]Ex 20:4, 23; Lev 19:4; Deut 5:8

18 [1]Or *which* [a]Ex 12:17; Lev 23:6; Num 28:16f [b]Ex 12:15, 16 [c]Ex 12:2; 13:4

19 [1]Or *oxen* [a]Ex 13:2; 22:29f

20 [1]Lit *first opening of* [2]Lit *They shall not* [a]Ex 13:13 [b]Ex 13:15; Num 3:45 [c]Ex 22:29; 23:15; Deut 16:16

21 [a]Ex 20:9f; 23:12; 31:15; 35:2; Lev 23:3; Deut 5:13f

22 [a]Ex 23:16; Num 28:26

23 [1]Heb *YHWH,* usually rendered *LORD* [a]Ex 23:14-17

24 [1]Or *dispossess* [a]Ex 33:2; Ps 78:55

25 [1]Lit *slaughter* [2]Lit *remain overnight* [a]Ex 23:18 [b]Ex 12:10

26 [a]Ex 23:19; Deut 26:2

27 [1]Lit *for yourself* [a]Ex 17:14; 24:4 [b]Ex 34:10

28 [1]Or *He,* i.e. The LORD [2]Lit *Words* [a]Ex 24:18 [b]Ex 31:18; 34:1 [c]Deut 4:13; 10:4

29 [a]Ex 32:15 [b]Matt 17:2; 2 Cor 3:7

30 So when Aaron and all the sons of Israel saw Moses,
behold, the skin of his face shone, and [a]they were afraid to
come near him.
31 Then Moses called to them, and Aaron and all the rulers in
the congregation returned to him; and Moses spoke to them.
32 Afterward all the sons of Israel came near, and he
commanded them *to do* everything that the LORD had spoken
[1]to him on Mount Sinai.
33 When Moses had finished speaking with them, [a]he put a
veil over his face.
34 But whenever Moses went in before the LORD to speak
with Him, [a]he would take off the veil until he came out; and
whenever he came out and spoke to the sons of Israel what he
had been commanded,
35 [a]the sons of Israel would see the face of Moses, that the
skin of Moses' face shone. So Moses would replace the veil
over his face until he went in to speak with Him.

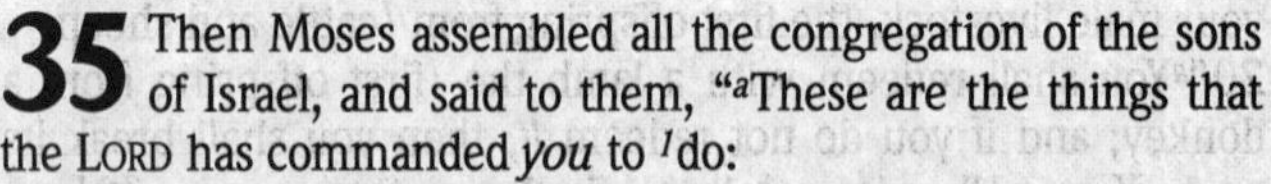
Chapter 35 Theme _____________________________________

35 Then Moses assembled all the congregation of the sons
of Israel, and said to them, "[a]These are the things that
the LORD has commanded *you* to [1]do:
2 "[a]For six days work may be done, but on the seventh day
you shall have a holy *day*, [b]a sabbath of complete rest to the
LORD; [c]whoever does any work on it shall be put to death.
3 "[a]You shall not kindle a fire in any of your dwellings on the
sabbath day."
4 Moses spoke to all the congregation of the sons of Israel,
saying, "This is the thing which the LORD has commanded,
saying,
5 '[a]Take from among you a [1]contribution to the LORD; whoever is of a willing heart, let him bring it as the LORD'S
[1]contribution: gold, silver, and [2]bronze,
6 and [1]blue, purple and scarlet *material*, fine linen, goats' *hair*,
7 and rams' skins [1]dyed red, and porpoise skins, and acacia
wood,
8 and oil for lighting, and spices for the anointing oil, and for
the fragrant incense,
9 and onyx stones and setting stones for the ephod and for
the [1]breastpiece.
10 '[a]Let every skillful man among you come, and make all that
the LORD has commanded:
11 the [1a]tabernacle, its tent and its covering, its hooks and its
boards, its bars, its pillars, and its [2]sockets;
12 the [a]ark and its poles, the [1]mercy seat, and the curtain of
the screen;
13 the [a]table and its poles, and all its [1]utensils, and the bread
of the [2]Presence;
14 the [a]lampstand also for the light and its utensils and its
lamps and the oil for the light;

30 [a]2 Cor 3:7
32 [1]Lit *with*
33 [a]2 Cor 3:13
34 [a]2 Cor 3:16
35 [a]2 Cor 3:13
35:1 [1]Lit *do them* [a]Ex 34:32
2 [a]Ex 20:9, 10; 23:12; 31:15; 34:21; Lev 23:3; Deut 5:13f [b]Ex 16:23 [c]Num 15:32-36
3 [a]Ex 12:16; 16:23
5 [1]Or *heave offering* [2]Or *copper* [a]Ex 25:1-9
6 [1]Or *violet*
7 [1]Or *tanned*
9 [1]Or *pouch*
10 [a]Ex 31:6
11 [1]Lit *dwelling place* [2]Or *bases* [a]Ex 26:1-30
12 [1]Lit *propitiatory* [a]Ex 25:10-22
13 [1]Or *vessels* [2]Lit *Face* [a]Ex 25:23-30
14 [a]Ex 25:31ff

15 and the [a]altar of incense and its poles, and the [b]anointing oil and the [c]fragrant incense, and the screen for the doorway at the [1]entrance of the tabernacle;

16 [a]the altar of burnt offering with its [1]bronze grating, its poles, and all its [2]utensils, the [3]basin and its stand;

17 [a]the hangings of the court, its pillars and its [1]sockets, and the screen for the gate of the court;

18 the pegs of the tabernacle and the pegs of the court and their cords;

19 the [1a]woven garments for ministering in the holy place, the holy garments for Aaron the priest and the garments of his sons, to minister as priests.'"

20 Then all the congregation of the sons of Israel departed from Moses' presence.

21 [a]Everyone whose heart [1]stirred him and everyone whose spirit [2]moved him came *and* brought the LORD's [3]contribution for the work of the tent of meeting and for all its service and for the holy garments.

22 Then all [1]whose hearts moved them, both men and women, came *and* brought brooches and [2]earrings and signet rings and bracelets, all articles of gold; so *did* every man who [3]presented an offering of gold to the LORD.

23 Every man, [1]who had in his possession [2]blue and purple and scarlet *material* and fine linen and goats' *hair* and rams' skins [3]dyed red and porpoise skins, brought them.

24 Everyone who could make a [1]contribution of silver and [2]bronze brought the LORD's [1]contribution; and every man [3]who had in his possession acacia wood for any work of the service brought it.

25 All the [1]skilled women spun with their hands, and brought what they had spun, *in* [2]blue and purple *and* scarlet *material* and *in* fine linen.

26 All the women whose heart [1]stirred with a skill spun the goats' *hair.*

27 The rulers brought the onyx stones and the stones for setting for the ephod and for the [1]breastpiece;

28 and [a]the spice and the oil for the light and for the anointing oil and for the fragrant incense.

29 The [1]Israelites, all the men and women, whose heart [2]moved them to bring *material* for all the work, which the LORD had commanded through Moses to be done, brought a [a]freewill offering to the LORD.

30 [a]Then Moses said to the sons of Israel, "See, the LORD has called by name Bezalel the son of Uri, the son of Hur, of the tribe of Judah.

31 "And He has filled him with the Spirit of God, in wisdom, in understanding and in knowledge and in all [1]craftsmanship;

32 [1]to make designs for working in gold and in silver and in [2]bronze,

33 and in the cutting of stones for settings and in the carving of wood, so as to perform in every inventive work.

34 "He also has put in his heart to teach, both he and [a]Oholiab, the son of Ahisamach, of the tribe of Dan.

15 [1]Or *doorway* [a]Ex 30:1-6 [b]Ex 30:25 [c]Ex 30:34-38

16 [1]Or *copper* [2]Or *vessels* [3]Or *laver* [a]Ex 27:1-8

17 [1]Or *bases* [a]Ex 27:9-18

19 [1]Or *service garments* [a]Ex 31:10; 39:1

21 [1]Lit *lifted up* [2]Or *made him willing* [3]Or *heave offering* [a]Ex 25:2; 35:5, 22, 26, 29; 36:2

22 [1]Or *who were willing-hearted* [2]Or *nose rings* [3]Lit *waved a wave offering*

23 [1]Lit *with whom was found* [2]Or *violet* [3]Or *tanned*

24 [1]Or *heave offering* [2]Or *copper* [3]Lit *with whom was found*

25 [1]Lit *women wise of heart* [2]Or *violet*

26 [1]Lit *lifted them up in wisdom*

27 [1]Or *pouch*

28 [a]Ex 30:23ff

29 [1]Lit *sons of Israel* [2]Lit *made them willing* [a]Ex 35:21; 1 Chr 29:9

30 [a]Ex 31:1-6

31 [1]Or *work*

32 [1]Lit *devise devices* [2]Or *copper*

34 [a]Ex 31:6

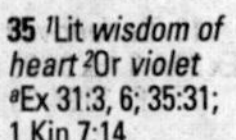

35 “[a]He has filled them with [1]skill to perform every work of an
engraver and of a designer and of an embroiderer, in [2]blue and
in purple *and* in scarlet *material,* and in fine linen, and of a
weaver, as performers of every work and makers of designs.

Chapter 36 Theme ____________________________

36 “Now Bezalel and Oholiab, and every [1]skillful person in
whom the LORD has put [2]skill and understanding to
know how to perform all the work [3]in the construction of the
sanctuary, shall perform in accordance with all that the LORD
has commanded.”
2 Then Moses called Bezalel and Oholiab and every [1]skillful
person in [2]whom the LORD had put [3]skill, [a]everyone whose
heart stirred him, to come to the work to perform it.
3 They received from Moses all the [1]contributions which the
sons of Israel had brought [2]to perform the work [3]in the
construction of the sanctuary. And they still *continued* bringing
to him freewill offerings every morning.
4 And all the [1]skillful men who were performing all the work
of the sanctuary came, each from [2]the work which [3]he was
performing,
5 and they said to [1]Moses, “[a]The people are bringing much
more than enough for the [2]construction work which the LORD
commanded *us* to [3]perform.”
6 So Moses issued a command, and a [1]proclamation was
circulated throughout the camp, saying, “Let no man or woman
any longer perform work for the [2]contributions of the sanctuary.”
Thus the people were restrained from bringing *any more.*
7 [a]For the [1]material they had was sufficient and more than
enough for all the work, to perform it.
8 [a]All the [1]skillful men among those who were performing the
work made the [2]tabernacle with ten curtains; of fine twisted
linen and [3]blue and purple and scarlet *material,* with cherubim,
the work of a skillful workman, [4]Bezalel made them.
9 The length of each curtain was twenty-eight [1]cubits and
the width of each curtain four [1]cubits; all the curtains had [2]the
same measurements.
10 He [1]joined five curtains to one another and *the other* five
curtains he [1]joined to one another.
11 He made loops of [1]blue on the edge of the [2]outermost curtain
in the first [3]set; he did likewise on the edge of the curtain that
was [2]outermost in the second [3]set.
12 He made [a]fifty loops in the one curtain and he made fifty
loops on the [1]edge of the curtain that was in the second [2]set; the
loops were opposite each other.
13 He made [a]fifty clasps of gold and [1]joined the curtains to one
another with the clasps, so the tabernacle was [2]a unit.
14 Then [a]he made curtains of goats' *hair* for a tent over the
tabernacle; he made eleven curtains [1]in all.
15 The length of each curtain *was* thirty cubits and four cubits
the width of each curtain; the eleven curtains had [1]the same
measurements.

Curtains

35 [1]Lit *wisdom of heart* [2]Or *violet* [a]Ex 31:3, 6; 35:31; 1 Kin 7:14

36:1 [1]Lit *man wise of heart* [2]Lit *wisdom* [3]Or *connected with the service of;* lit *of the service of*

2 [1]Lit *man wise of heart* [2]Lit *whose heart* [3]Lit *wisdom* [a]Ex 35:21, 26

3 [1]Lit *lifted offering* [2]Lit *to perform it for the work* [3]Lit *of the service of*

4 [1]Lit *wise* [2]Lit *his* [3]Lit *they were*

5 [1]Lit *Moses, saying,* [2]Lit *service for the work* [3]Lit *perform it* [a]2 Chr 24:14; 31:6-10

6 [1]Lit *voice* [2]Lit *heave offering*

7 [1]Lit *work* [a]1 Kin 8:64

8 [1]Lit *wise of heart* [2]Lit *dwelling place* [3]Or *violet* [4]Lit *he* [a]Ex 26:1-14

9 [1]I.e. One cubit equals approx 18 in. [2]Lit *one measure*

10 [1]Or *coupled*

11 [1]Or *violet* [2]Lit *one curtain from the end in the coupling* [3]Lit *coupling*

12 [1]Lit *end* [2]Lit *coupling* [a]Ex 26:5

13 [1]Or *coupled* [2]Lit *one* [a]Ex 26:6

14 [1]Lit *in number* [a]Ex 26:7-14

15 [1]Lit *one measure*

16 He [1]joined five curtains by themselves and *the other* six curtains by themselves.
17 Moreover, he made fifty loops on the edge of the curtain that was outermost in the *first* [1]set, and he made fifty loops on the edge of the curtain *that was outermost in* the second [1]set.
18 He made fifty clasps of [1]bronze to [2]join the tent together so that it would be [3]a unit.
19 He made a covering for the tent of rams' skins [1]dyed red, and a covering of porpoise skins above.
20 [a]Then he made the boards for the tabernacle of acacia wood, standing upright.
21 Ten cubits *was* the length of [1]each board and one and a half cubits the width of each board.
22 *There were* two tenons for each board, [1]fitted to one another; thus he did for all the boards of the tabernacle.
23 He made the boards for the tabernacle: twenty boards [1]for the south side;
24 and he made forty [1]sockets of silver under the twenty boards; two [1]sockets under one board for its two tenons and two [1]sockets under another board for its two tenons.
25 Then for the second side of the tabernacle, on the north side, he made twenty boards,
26 and their forty [1]sockets of silver; two [1]sockets under one board and two [1]sockets under another board.
27 For the [1]rear of the tabernacle, to the west, he made six boards.
28 He made two boards for the corners of the [1]tabernacle at the [2]rear.
29 They were double beneath, and together they were complete to its [1]top [2]to the first ring; thus he did with both of them for the two corners.
30 There were eight boards with their [1]sockets of silver, sixteen [1]sockets, [2]two under every board.
31 Then he made [a]bars of acacia wood, five for the boards of one side of the tabernacle,
32 and five bars for the boards of the [1]other side of the tabernacle, and five bars for the boards of the tabernacle for the [2]rear *side* to the west.
33 He made the middle bar to pass through in the [1]center of the boards from end to end.
34 He overlaid the boards with gold and made their rings of gold *as* holders for the bars, and overlaid the bars with gold.
35 [a]Moreover, he made the veil of [1]blue and purple and scarlet *material,* and fine twisted linen; he made it with cherubim, the work of a skillful workman.
36 He made four pillars of acacia for it, and overlaid them with gold, with their hooks of gold; and he cast four [1]sockets of silver for them.
37 He made a [a]screen for the doorway of the tent, of [1]blue and purple and scarlet *material,* and fine twisted linen, the work of a [2]weaver;

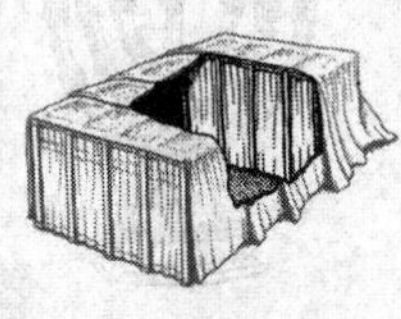
The Veil

16 [1]Or *coupled*
17 [1]Lit *coupling*
18 [1]Or *copper* [2]Or *couple* [3]Lit *one*
19 [1]Or *tanned*
20 [a]Ex 26:15-29
21 [1]Lit *the*
22 [1]Lit *bound*
23 [1]Lit *to the side of the Negev, to the south*
24 [1]Or *bases*
26 [1]Or *bases*
27 [1]Lit *extreme parts*
28 [1]Lit *dwelling place* [2]Lit *extreme parts*
29 [1]Or *head* [2]Or *with reference to*
30 [1]Or *bases* [2]Lit *two sockets*
31 [a]Ex 26:26-29
32 [1]Or *second* [2]Lit *extreme parts*
33 [1]Lit *midst*
35 [1]Or *violet* [a]Ex 26:31-37
36 [1]Or *bases*
37 [1]Or *violet* [2]Lit *variegator;* i.e. a weaver in colors [a]Ex 26:36

38 and *he made* its [a]five pillars with their hooks, and he
overlaid their tops and their [1]bands with gold; but their five
[2]sockets were of [3]bronze.

Chapter 37 Theme ________________________________

37 [a]Now Bezalel made the ark of acacia wood; its length
was two and a half [1]cubits, and its width one and a half
cubits, and its height one and a half cubits;
2 and he overlaid it with pure gold inside and out, and made
a gold molding for it all around.
3 He cast four rings of gold for it on its four feet; even two
rings on one side of it, and two rings on the [1]other side of it.
4 He made poles of acacia wood and overlaid them with gold.
5 He put the poles into the rings on the sides of the ark, to
carry [1]it.

Ark of the Covenant (or Testimony)

6 He made a [1]mercy seat of pure gold, two and a half cubits
[2]long and one and a half cubits [3]wide.
7 He made two cherubim of gold; he made them of hammered
work [1]at the two ends of the mercy seat;
8 one cherub [1]at the one end and one cherub [1]at the other
end; he made the cherubim *of one piece* with the mercy seat
[1]at the two ends.
9 The cherubim had *their* wings spread upward, covering the
[1]mercy seat with their wings, with their faces toward each
other; the faces of the cherubim were toward the mercy seat.
10 [a]Then he made the table of acacia wood, two [1]cubits [2]long
and a cubit [3]wide and one and a half cubits [4]high.

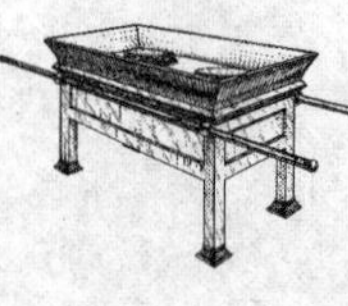

Table of Showbread

11 He overlaid it with pure gold, and made a gold molding for
it all around.
12 He made a rim for it of a handbreadth all around, and made
a gold molding for its rim all around.
13 He cast four gold rings for it and put the rings on the four
corners that were on its four feet.
14 Close by the rim were the rings, the holders for the poles
to carry the table.
15 He made the poles of acacia wood and overlaid them with
gold, to carry the table.
16 He made the utensils which were on the table, its [1]dishes
and its pans and its [2]bowls and its jars, with which to pour out
drink offerings, of pure gold.
17 [a]Then he made the lampstand of pure gold. He made the
lampstand of hammered work, its base and its shaft; its cups,
its [1]bulbs and its flowers were *of one piece* with it.

Lampstand

18 There were six branches going out of its sides; three branches
of the lampstand from the one side of it and three branches of
the lampstand from the [1]other side of it;
19 three cups shaped like almond *blossoms,* a [1]bulb and a
flower in one branch, and three cups shaped like almond
blossoms, a [1]bulb and a flower in the other branch—so for the
six branches going out of the lampstand.

38 [1]Or *fillets, rings* [2]Or *bases* [3]Or *copper* [a]Ex 26:37

37:1 [1]I.e. One cubit equals approx 18 in. [a]Ex 25:10-20

3 [1]Lit *second*

5 [1]Lit *the ark*

6 [1]Lit *propitiatory* [2]Lit *its length* [3]Lit *its width*

7 [1]Lit *from*

8 [1]Lit *from*

9 [1]Lit *propitiatory*

10 [1]I.e. One cubit equals approx 18 in. [2]Lit *its length* [3]Lit *its width* [4]Lit *its height* [a]Ex 25:23-29

16 [1]Or *platters* [2]Lit *libation bowls*

17 [1]Or *calyxes* [a]Ex 25:31-39

18 [1]Lit *second*

19 [1]Or *calyx*

31 and the [1]sockets of the court all around and the [1]sockets of the gate of the court, and all the pegs of the [2]tabernacle and all the pegs of the court all around.

Chapter 39 Theme ______________________________

39 Moreover, from the [1a]blue and purple and scarlet *material,* they made finely [b]woven garments for ministering in the holy place [2]as well as the holy garments which were for Aaron, just as the LORD had commanded Moses.

2 [a]He made the ephod of gold, *and* of [1]blue and purple and scarlet *material,* and fine twisted linen.

3 Then they hammered out gold sheets and cut *them* into threads [1]to be woven in *with* the [2]blue and the purple and the scarlet *material,* and the fine linen, the work of a skillful workman.

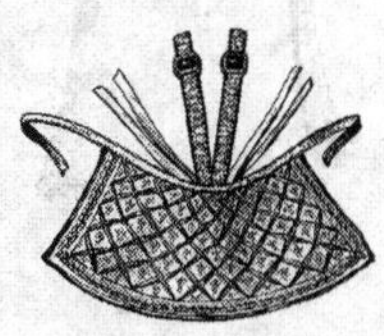
Ephod (viewed from the back)

4 They made attaching shoulder pieces for [1]the ephod; it was attached at its two *upper* ends.

5 The skillfully woven band which was on it was like its workmanship, [1]of the same material: of gold *and* of [2]blue and purple and scarlet *material,* and fine twisted linen, just as the LORD had commanded Moses.

6 [a]They made the onyx stones, set in gold filigree *settings;* they were engraved *like* the engravings of a signet, according to the names of the sons of Israel.

7 And [a]he placed them on the shoulder pieces of the ephod, *as* memorial stones for the sons of Israel, just as the LORD had commanded Moses.

8 [a]He made the breastpiece, the work of a skillful workman, like the workmanship of the ephod: of gold *and* of [1]blue and purple and scarlet *material* and fine twisted linen.

High Priest's Garments

9 It was square; they made the breastpiece folded double, a span [1]long and a span [2]wide when folded double.

10 And they [1]mounted four rows of stones on it. The first row *was* a row of ruby, topaz, and emerald;

11 and the second row, a turquoise, a sapphire and a diamond;

12 and the third row, a jacinth, an agate, and an amethyst;

13 and the fourth row, a beryl, an onyx, and a jasper. They were set in gold filigree *settings* when they were [1]mounted.

14 The stones were corresponding to the names of the sons of Israel; they were twelve, corresponding to their names, *engraved with* the engravings of a signet, each with its name for the twelve tribes.

15 They made on the breastpiece chains like cords, of twisted cordage work in pure gold.

16 They made two gold filigree *settings* and two gold rings, and put the two rings on the two ends of the breastpiece.

17 Then they put the two gold cords in the two rings at the ends of the breastpiece.

18 They put the *other* two ends of the two cords on the two filigree *settings,* and put them on the shoulder pieces of the ephod at the front of it.

31 [1]Or *bases* [2]Lit *dwelling place*

39:1 [1]Or *violet* [2]Lit *and they made* [a]Ex 35:23 [b]Ex 31:10; 35:19

2 [1]Or *violet* [a]Ex 28:6-12

3 [1]Lit *to work* [2]Or *violet*

4 [1]Lit *it*

5 [1]Lit *from it* [2]Or *violet*

6 [a]Ex 28:9-11

7 [a]Ex 28:12

8 [1]Or *violet* [a]Ex 28:15-28

9 [1]Lit *its length* [2]Lit *its width*

10 [1]Lit *filled*

13 [1]Lit *filled*

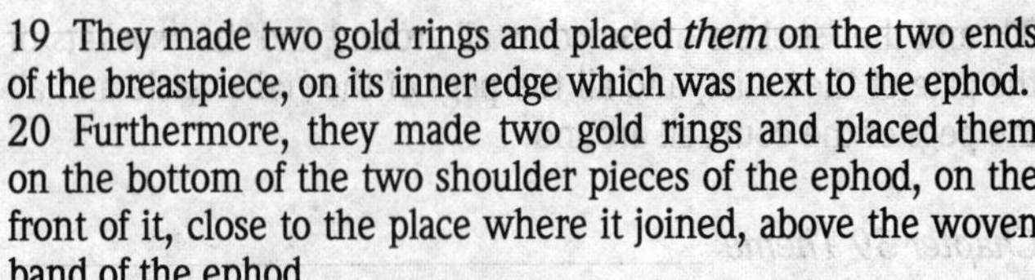
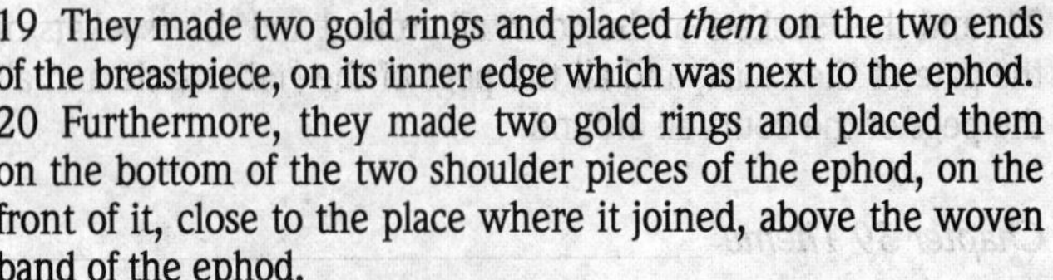

19 They made two gold rings and placed *them* on the two ends
of the breastpiece, on its inner edge which was next to the ephod.
20 Furthermore, they made two gold rings and placed them
on the bottom of the two shoulder pieces of the ephod, on the
front of it, close to the place where it joined, above the woven
band of the ephod.
21 They bound the breastpiece by its rings to the rings of the
ephod with a [1]blue cord, so that it would be on the woven
band of the ephod, and that the breastpiece would not come
loose from the ephod, just as the LORD had commanded Moses.
22 [a]Then he made the robe of the ephod of woven work, all of
[1]blue;
23 [a]and the opening of the robe was *at the top* in the center,
as the opening of a coat of mail, with a binding all around its
opening, so that it would not be torn.
24 They made pomegranates of [1]blue and purple and scarlet
material and twisted *linen* on the hem of the robe.
25 They also made bells of pure gold, and put the bells between
the pomegranates all around on the hem of the [1]robe,
26 [1]alternating a bell and a pomegranate all around on the hem
of the robe for the service, just as the LORD had commanded Moses.
27 [a]They made the tunics of finely woven linen for Aaron and
his sons,
28 and the turban of fine linen, and the decorated [1]caps of
fine linen, and the linen breeches of fine twisted linen,
29 and the sash of fine twisted linen, and [1]blue and purple
and scarlet *material,* the work of the [2]weaver, just as the LORD
had commanded Moses.
30 [a]They made the plate of the holy crown of pure gold, and
[1]inscribed it like the engravings of a signet, "Holy to the LORD."
31 They [1]fastened a [2]blue cord to it, to [1]fasten it on the turban
above, just as the LORD had commanded Moses.
32 Thus all the work of the [1]tabernacle of the tent of meeting
was completed; and the sons of Israel did according to all that
the LORD had commanded Moses; so they did.
33 They brought the tabernacle to Moses, the tent and all its
[1]furnishings: its clasps, its boards, its bars, and its pillars and its
[2]sockets;
34 and the covering of rams' skins [1]dyed red, and the covering
of porpoise skins, and the screening veil;
35 the ark of the testimony and its poles and the [1]mercy seat;
36 the table, all its utensils, and the bread of the [1]Presence;
37 the pure *gold* lampstand, [1]with its arrangement of lamps
and all its utensils, and the oil for the light;
38 and the gold altar, and the anointing oil and the fragrant
incense, and the veil for the doorway of the tent;
39 the [1]bronze altar and its [1]bronze grating, its poles and all
its utensils, the laver and its stand;
40 the hangings for the court, its pillars and its [1]sockets, and
the screen for the gate of the court, its cords and its pegs and
all the [2]equipment for the service of the tabernacle, for the tent
of meeting;

Robe of the Ephod

Turban with Plate of Gold

21 [1]Or *violet*
22 [1]Or *violet* [a]Ex 28:31, 34
23 [a]Ex 28:32
24 [1]Or *violet*
25 [1]Lit *robe, between the pomegranates*
26 [1]Lit *a bell and a pomegranate, a bell . . .*
27 [a]Ex 28:39, 40, 42
28 [1]Lit *headgear*
29 [1]Or *violet* [2]Lit *variegator;* i.e. a weaver in colors
30 [1]Lit *wrote on it a writing* [a]Ex 28:36, 37
31 [1]Lit *put* [2]Or *violet*
32 [1]Lit *dwelling place*
33 [1]Or *utensils* [2]Or *bases*
34 [1]Or *tanned*
35 [1]Lit *propitiatory*
36 [1]Lit *Face*
37 [1]Lit *its lamps, the lamps set in order*
39 [1]Or *copper*
40 [1]Or *bases* [2]Or *utensils*

43 [1]Lit *saw* [a]Lev 9:22, 23; Num 6:23-26

41 the woven garments for ministering in the holy place and
the holy garments for Aaron the priest and the garments of his
sons, to minister as priests.
42 So the sons of Israel did all the work according to all that
the LORD had commanded Moses.
43 And Moses [1]examined all the work and behold, they had
done it; just as the LORD had commanded, this they had done.
So Moses [a]blessed them.

40:2 [1]Lit *dwelling place* [a]Ex 19:1; 40:17; Num 1:1

3 [a]Ex 26:33; 40:21; Num 4:5

Chapter 40 Theme ____________________

40 Then the LORD spoke to Moses, saying,
2 "[a]On the first day of the first month you shall set up
the [1]tabernacle of the tent of meeting.
3 "[a]You shall place the ark of the testimony there, and you
shall screen the ark with the veil.
4 "You shall [a]bring in the table and [1b]arrange what belongs on
it; and you shall [c]bring in the lampstand and [2]mount its lamps.
5 "Moreover, you shall [a]set the gold altar of incense before the
ark of the testimony, and set up the veil for the doorway to the
tabernacle.

4 [1]Lit *arrange its arrangement* [2]Or *light* [a]Ex 26:35; 40:22 [b]Ex 25:30; 40:23 [c]Ex 40:24f

5 [a]Ex 40:26

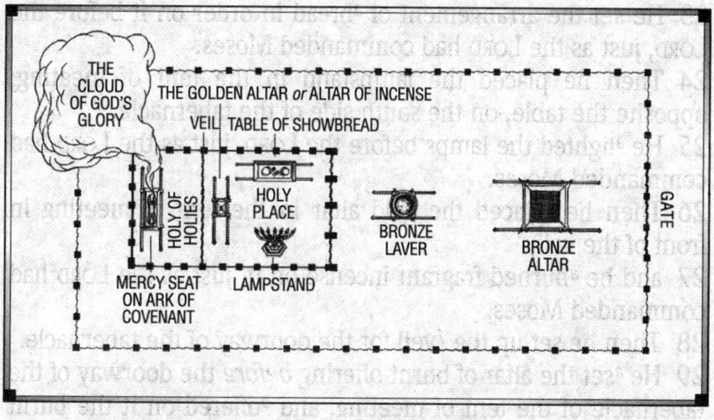

Inside the Tabernacle

7 [1]Lit *there* [a]Ex 30:18; 40:30

8 [1]Lit *put the screen*

6 "You shall set the altar of burnt offering in front of the
doorway of the tabernacle of the tent of meeting.
7 "You shall [a]set the laver between the tent of meeting and
the altar and put water [1]in it.
8 "You shall set up the court all around and [1]hang up the veil
for the gateway of the court.
9 "Then you shall take the anointing oil and [a]anoint the
tabernacle and all that is in it, and shall consecrate it and all its
[1]furnishings; and it shall be holy.
10 "You shall anoint the altar of burnt offering and all its utensils,
and consecrate the altar, and [a]the altar shall be most holy.
11 "You shall anoint the laver and its stand, and consecrate it.
12 "Then you shall [a]bring Aaron and his sons to the doorway of
the tent of meeting and wash them with water.
13 "[a]You shall put the holy garments on Aaron and anoint him
and consecrate him, that he may minister as a priest to Me.
14 "You shall bring his sons and put tunics on them;

9 [1]Or *utensils* [a]Ex 30:26; Lev 8:10

10 [a]Ex 29:37

12 [a]Lev 8:1-6

13 [a]Ex 28:41; Lev 8:13

15 and you shall anoint them even as you have anointed their father, that they may minister as priests to Me; and their anointing will [1]qualify them for a [a]perpetual priesthood throughout their generations."

16 Thus Moses did; according to all that the LORD had commanded him, so he did.

17 Now [a]in the first month [1]of the second year, on the first *day* of the month, the [2]tabernacle was erected.

18 Moses erected the tabernacle and [1]laid its [2]sockets, and set up its boards, and [1]inserted its bars and erected its pillars.

19 He spread the tent over the tabernacle and put the covering of the tent [1]on top of it, just as the LORD had commanded Moses.

20 Then he took [a]the testimony and put *it* into the ark, and [1]attached the poles to the ark, and put the [2]mercy seat [3]on top of the ark.

21 He brought the ark into the tabernacle, and [a]set up a veil for the screen, and screened off the ark of the testimony, just as the LORD had commanded Moses.

22 Then he [a]put the table in the tent of meeting on the north side of the tabernacle, outside the veil.

23 He set the arrangement of [a]bread in order on it before the LORD, just as the LORD had commanded Moses.

24 Then he placed the lampstand in the tent of meeting, opposite the table, on the south side of the tabernacle.

25 He [a]lighted the lamps before the LORD, just as the LORD had commanded Moses.

26 Then he [a]placed the gold altar in the tent of meeting in front of the veil;

27 and he [a]burned fragrant incense on it, just as the LORD had commanded Moses.

28 Then he set up the [1]veil for the doorway of the tabernacle.

29 He [a]set the altar of burnt offering *before* the doorway of the tabernacle of the tent of meeting, and [b]offered on it the burnt offering and the meal offering, just as the LORD had commanded Moses.

30 He placed the laver between the tent of meeting and the altar and put water in it for washing.

31 [a]From it Moses and Aaron and his sons washed their hands and their feet.

32 When they entered the tent of meeting, and when they approached the altar, they washed, just as the LORD had commanded Moses.

33 He [a]erected the court all around the [1]tabernacle and the altar, and [2]hung up the veil for the gateway of the court. Thus Moses finished the work.

34 [a]Then the cloud covered the tent of meeting, and the [b]glory of the LORD filled the tabernacle.

35 Moses [a]was not able to enter the tent of meeting because the cloud had settled on it, and the glory of the LORD filled the tabernacle.

15 [1]Lit *be for them* [a]Ex 29:9; Num 25:13

17 [1]Lit *in* [2]Lit *dwelling place* [a]Ex 40:2

18 [1]Lit *put* [2]Or *bases*

19 [1]Lit *over it above*

20 [1]Lit *set* [2]Lit *propitiatory* [3]Lit *over the ark above* [a]Ex 25:16; Deut 10:5; 1 Kin 8:9; 2 Chr 5:10; Heb 9:4

21 [a]Ex 26:33

22 [a]Ex 26:35

23 [a]Ex 25:30; Lev 24:5, 6

25 [a]Ex 25:37; 40:4

26 [a]Ex 30:6; 40:5

27 [a]Ex 30:7

28 [1]Or *screen*

29 [a]Ex 40:6 [b]Ex 29:38-42

31 [a]Ex 30:19, 20

33 [1]Or *dwelling place* [2]Lit *put the screen* [a]Ex 27:9-18; 40:8

34 [a]Num 9:15-23 [b]1 Kin 8:11; Ezek 43:4f; Rev 15:8

35 [a]1 Kin 8:11; 2 Chr 5:13, 14

36 [a]Num 9:17; Neh 9:19
37 [a]Num 9:19-22
38 [a]Ex 13:21; Num 9:12, 15; Ps 78:14; Is 4:5

36 Throughout all their journeys [a]whenever the cloud was
taken up from over the tabernacle, the sons of Israel would set out;
37 but [a]if the cloud was not taken up, then they did not set
out until the day when it was taken up.
38 For throughout all their journeys, [a]the cloud of the LORD
was on the tabernacle by day, and there was fire in it by night,
in the sight of all the house of Israel.

EXODUS AT A GLANCE

Theme of Exodus:

Author:

Date:

Purpose:

Key Words:
(including synonyms)

slave(s) (bondage)

cry

deliver (delivered)

Mount Sinai (Horeb, Mountain of God)

die (death)

holy

the Lord commanded (I commanded)

covenant

cloud

test(ed)

law

tabernacle (tent, tent of meeting)

SEGMENT DIVISIONS

			CHAPTER THEMES
			1
			2
			3
			4
			5
			6
			7
			8
			9
			10
			11
			12
			13
			14
			15
			16
			17

Exodus at a Glance

Segment Divisions

			Chapter Themes
			18
			19
			20
			21
			22
			23
			24
			25
			26
			27
			28
			29
			30
			31
			32
			33
			34
			35
			36
			37
			38
			39
			40

LEVITICUS ויקרא
VAYIKRA

In Genesis we see the ruin of man as a result of listening to the serpent rather than to God. The human race is condemned to sin's awful wage—death. Yet through the mercy and grace of God comes the promise of redemption through the seed of the woman, through the seed of Abraham, as God calls out a people for Himself. God makes a covenant with Abraham, which He confirms to Isaac and then to Jacob, later to be renamed Israel.

The book of Genesis begins with the creation of man in Eden and ends with the children of Israel looking into a coffin in Egypt, yet not without a promise that someday they would leave Egypt. As Genesis comes to a close, the children of Israel are living in Egypt rather than in Canaan, the land of promise.

Exodus plays out the drama of redemption as Israel is redeemed from slavery through the blood of the Passover lamb. After the descendants of Abraham were enslaved and oppressed for 400 years, just as God promised, they left Egypt with great possessions, and God went before them in His cloud of glory.

And what follows the redemption of ruined man? That is what the book of Leviticus is all about. Study it well, for Leviticus shows us in pictorial form what God expects from those who have been redeemed.

THINGS TO DO

General Instructions

1. As you read Leviticus watch for the verses that attribute the authorship of this book to Moses. When you come across those references, record them under "Author" on the LEVITICUS AT A GLANCE chart on page 213.
2. Read Exodus 40:17,32-38 and Leviticus 1:1-2 and note the uninterrupted transition from one book to the other. Then compare Numbers 1:1 with these verses. As you do this you will see that the book of Leviticus covers a period of one month.
3. As you read through Leviticus one chapter at a time, do the following:
   a. Ask the "5 W's and an H": Who? What? When? Where? Why? and How? For example: Who is to do what? When are they to do it? How are they to do it? Why? What if they didn't know why? Questions that interrogate the text help you see what is being said.
   b. Mark the key repeated words listed on LEVITICUS AT A GLANCE. You will find it helpful to list these key words on an index card that you can use as a bookmark while you study Leviticus. Also watch for any other key words that might be used in that particular chapter. If you gain insights from marking these words, list pertinent insights in your notebook.
   c. Record the main theme or subject of the chapter at the beginning of the chapter in your Bible. Then record it on LEVITICUS AT A GLANCE.
   d. You may want to summarize the main points or the order of events covered in the chapter. Record them in the margin.
   e. Record any new insights about the character and ways of God. You could identify your insights on God with this symbol △ and then color it yellow, which would make it easy to recognize.

Chapters 1–7

1. As you read chapters 1 through 7, which give instructions regarding the various sacrifices or offerings, mark the text as instructed under "General Instructions" and then record what you learn about each of the offerings on the chart THE OFFERINGS AND THEIR PURPOSES on page 212.

2. Watch what God says about unintentional sin, guilt, and restitution. Note what is to be done when a leader sins and when the congregation sins. Mark it in the text.

Chapters 8–10

This segment covers the consecration of Aaron and his sons. Add *ordination, eat, clean,* and *unclean* to your key word list. In chapter 10 note what happened, why it happened, and who was involved. Chapter 10 has the first reference in the Bible to God's holiness.

Chapters 11–15

This segment deals with laws of cleanliness. In the margin record what each law covers. For example: food, women, infections, etc. Mark *leprosy* and *discharge* as key words.

Chapters 16–17

These chapters cover the day of atonement and regulations regarding the blood of the sacrifice.

1. In the margin of chapter 16 or in your notebook carefully outline what is to be done on the day of atonement. Note what you learn about the scapegoat.

2. Note the regulations in chapter 17 regarding sacrifices and blood.

Chapters 18–27

This segment lays out statutes on issues regarding moral laws, the priests, the celebration of annual feasts, the land, etc.

1. As you read each chapter, in the margin list the main topics or situations.

2. If moral laws are given, note the consequences of breaking the laws and the reason for the consequences.

3. In chapter 23 note the feasts, when they are to be celebrated, and how. When you finish studying the chapter, consult the chart THE FEASTS OF ISRAEL on pages 214, 215.

4. Give special attention to any mention of the land—its sabbath rest, principles of redemption, etc. Mark the words *redeem*, *redemption*, and any other related words. Record your insights in the margin.

5. When you finish reading through Leviticus, complete LEVITICUS AT A GLANCE.
   a. See if any of the chapters can be grouped categorically. If so, record this under "Segment Divisions" on the chart. Record any other possible segment divisions. For instance, you could do a segment division titled "Laws Regarding."
   b. Record the theme of Leviticus.

Things to Think About

1. What have you learned about God and His attitude toward sin? What happens when sin goes unpunished?

2. What have you learned about the occult and about the types of sexual sin? How severely were these sins to be dealt with? What does this tell you about how God feels regarding these sins and their consequences? What do you think would happen in your country if these sins were dealt with according to God's law? Read 1 Timothy 1:8-11.

3. Jesus told the Jews that the Scriptures—the Old Testament—testified of Him. Think about how Jesus Christ and His work are foreshadowed in Leviticus.

4. What have you learned about holiness from Leviticus? If you want to be holy, how will you live your life? Are there any changes you need to make? Are you willing? If not, why not?

Chapter 1 Theme ______________________________

1 Then [a]the LORD called to Moses and spoke to him from the
tent of meeting, saying,
2 "Speak to the sons of Israel and say to them, 'When any man
of you brings an [1a]offering to the LORD, you shall bring your
[1]offering of animals from [b]the herd or the flock.
3 'If his offering is a [a]burnt offering from the herd, he shall offer
it, a male [b]without defect; he shall offer it [c]at the doorway of
the tent of meeting, that he may be accepted before the LORD.
4 '[a]He shall lay his hand on the head of the burnt offering, that
it may be accepted for him to make [b]atonement on his behalf.
5 '[a]He shall slay the [1]young bull before the LORD; and Aaron's
sons the priests shall offer up [b]the blood and [c]sprinkle the blood
around on the altar that is at the doorway of the tent of meeting.
6 '[a]He shall then skin the burnt offering and cut it into its
pieces.
7 '[a]The sons of Aaron the priest shall put fire on the altar and
arrange wood on the fire.
8 'Then Aaron's sons the priests shall arrange the pieces, the
head and the [a]suet over the wood which is on the fire that is
on the altar.
9 'Its [a]entrails, however, and its legs he shall wash with
water. And [b]the priest shall offer up in smoke all of it on the
altar for a burnt offering, an offering by fire of [c]a soothing
aroma to the LORD.
10 'But if his offering is from the flock, of the sheep or of the
goats, for a burnt offering, he shall offer it a [a]male without
defect.
11 '[a]He shall slay it on the side of the altar northward before
the LORD, and Aaron's sons the priests shall sprinkle its blood
around on the altar.
12 'He shall then cut it into its pieces with its head and its
[a]suet, and the priest shall arrange them on the wood which is
on the fire that is on the altar.
13 'The entrails, however, and the legs he shall wash with
water. And [a]the priest shall offer all of it, and offer it up in
smoke on the altar; it is a burnt offering, an offering by fire of a
soothing aroma to the LORD.
14 'But if his offering to the LORD is a burnt offering of birds,
then he shall bring his offering from the [a]turtledoves or from
young pigeons.

1:1 [a]Ex 19:3; 25:22; Num 7:89

2 [1]Heb *qorban* [a]Mark 7:11 [b]Lev 22:18f

3 [a]Lev 6:8-13 [b]Ex 12:5; Lev 22:20-24; Deut 15:21; 17:1 [c]Lev 17:8, 9; Deut 12:5, 6, 11

4 [a]Ex 29:10, 15, 19; Lev 3:2, 8 [b]Ex 29:33; Lev 4:20, 26, 31; 2 Chr 29:23, 24

5 [1]Or *one of the herd;* lit *son of the herd* [a]Ex 29:11, 16, 20 [b]Lev 17:11 [c]Lev 1:11; 3:2, 8, 13; Heb 12:24; 1 Pet 1:2

6 [a]Lev 7:8

7 [a]Lev 6:8-13

8 [a]Lev 1:12; 3:3, 4; 8:20

9 [a]Ex 12:9 [b]Num 15:8-10; 28:11-14 [c]Gen 8:21; Ex 29:18, 25; Lev 1:13; Num 15:3; Eph 5:2

10 [a]Ex 12:5; Lev 1:3; Ezek 43:22; 1 Pet 1:19

11 [a]Ex 24:6; Lev 1:5; 8:19; 9:12

12 [a]Lev 3:3, 4

13 [a]Num 15:4-7; 28:11-14

14 [a]Gen 15:9; Lev 5:7, 11; 12:8; Luke 2:24

15 'The priest shall bring it to the altar, and wring off its head
and offer it up in smoke on the altar; and its blood is to be
drained out [a]on the side of the altar.
16 'He shall also take away its crop with its feathers and cast it
beside the altar eastward, to the place of the [1a]ashes.
17 'Then he shall tear it by its wings, *but* [a]shall not sever *it*.
And the priest shall offer it up in smoke on the altar on the
wood which is on the fire; [b]it is a burnt offering, an offering by
fire of a soothing aroma to the LORD.

Chapter 2 Theme ________________________________

2 'Now when anyone presents a [a]grain offering as an offering
to the LORD, his offering shall be of fine flour, and he shall
pour oil on it and put frankincense on it.
2 'He shall then bring it to Aaron's sons the priests; and shall
take from it [a]his handful of its fine flour and of its oil with all of
its frankincense. And the priest shall offer *it* up in smoke *as* its
[b]memorial portion on the altar, an offering by fire of a soothing
aroma to the LORD.
3 '[a]The remainder of the grain offering belongs to [b]Aaron and
his sons: a thing most holy, of the offerings to the LORD by fire.
4 'Now when you bring an offering of a grain offering baked
in an oven, *it shall be* [a]unleavened cakes of fine flour mixed
with oil, or unleavened wafers [1]spread with oil.
5 'If your offering is a grain offering *made* [a]on the griddle, *it*
shall be of fine flour, unleavened, mixed with oil;
6 you shall break it into bits and pour oil on it; it is a grain
offering.
7 'Now if your offering is a grain offering *made* [a]in a [1]pan, it
shall be made of fine flour with oil.
8 'When you bring in the grain offering which is made of
these things to the LORD, it shall be presented to the priest and
he shall bring it to the altar.
9 'The priest then shall take up from the grain offering [a]its
memorial portion, and shall offer *it* up in smoke on the altar *as*
an offering by fire of a soothing aroma to the LORD.
10 '[a]The remainder of the grain offering belongs to Aaron and
his sons: a thing most holy of the offerings to the LORD by fire.
11 '[a]No grain offering, which you bring to the LORD, shall be
made with leaven, for you shall not offer [1]up in smoke any
leaven or any honey as an [b]offering by fire to the LORD.
12 '[a]As an offering of first fruits you shall bring them to the
LORD, but they shall not ascend for a soothing aroma on the altar.
13 'Every grain offering of yours, moreover, you shall season
with salt, so that [a]the salt of the covenant of your God shall not
be lacking from your grain offering; with all your offerings you
shall offer salt.
14 'Also if you bring a grain offering of early ripened things to
the LORD, you shall bring [a]fresh heads of grain roasted in the
fire, grits of new growth, for the grain offering of your early
ripened things.

15 [a]Lev 5:9
16 [1]Or *fat ashes* [a]Lev 6:10
17 [a]Gen 15:10; Lev 5:8 [b]Lev 9:13
2:1 [a]Lev 6:14-18; Num 15:4
2 [a]Lev 5:12; 6:15 [b]Lev 2:9, 16; 5:12; 24:7; Acts 10:4
3 [a]Lev 2:10; 6:16 [b]Lev 10:12, 13
4 [1]Lit *anointed* [a]Ex 29:2
5 [a]Lev 6:21; 7:9
7 [1]Lit *lidded cooking pan* [a]Lev 7:9
9 [a]Lev 2:2, 16; 5:12
10 [a]Lev 2:3; 6:16
11 [1]Lit *up from it* [a]Ex 23:18; 34:25; Lev 6:16, 17 [b]Ex 29:25; Lev 1:13
12 [a]Ex 34:22; Lev 7:13; 23:10, 17, 18
13 [a]Num 18:19; 2 Chr 13:5; Ezek 43:24
14 [a]Lev 23:14

15 'You shall then put oil on it and lay incense on it; it is a
grain offering.
16 'The priest shall offer up in smoke [a]its memorial portion,
part of its grits and its oil with all its incense as an offering by
fire to the LORD.

Chapter 3 Theme ______________________________

3

'Now if his offering is a [a]sacrifice of peace offerings, if he is
going to offer out of the herd, whether male or female, he
shall offer it [b]without defect before the LORD.
2 '[a]He shall lay his hand on the head of his offering and [b]slay
it at the doorway of the tent of meeting, and Aaron's sons the
priests shall sprinkle the blood around on the altar.
3 'From the sacrifice of the peace offerings he shall present an
offering by fire to the LORD, the fat that covers the entrails and
all the fat that is on the entrails,
4 and the two kidneys with the fat that is on them, which is
on the loins, and the [1]lobe of the liver, which he shall remove
with the kidneys.
5 'Then [a]Aaron's sons shall offer *it* up in smoke on the altar
[b]on the burnt offering, which is on the wood that is on the fire;
[c]it is an offering by fire of a soothing aroma to the LORD.
6 'But if his offering for a sacrifice of peace offerings to the
LORD is from the flock, he shall offer it, male or female,
[a]without defect.
7 'If he is going to offer [a]a lamb for his offering, then he shall
offer it [b]before the LORD,
8 and [a]he shall lay his hand on the head of his offering and
[b]slay it before the tent of meeting, and Aaron's sons shall
[c]sprinkle its blood around on the altar.
9 'From the [a]sacrifice of peace offerings he shall bring as an
offering by fire to the LORD, its fat, [1]the entire fat tail which he
shall remove close to the backbone, and the fat that covers the
entrails and all the fat that is on the entrails,
10 and the two kidneys with the fat that is on them, which is
on the loins, and the [1]lobe of the liver, which he shall remove
[a]with the kidneys.
11 'Then the priest shall offer *it* up in smoke [a]on the altar *as*
[b]food, an offering by fire to the LORD.
12 'Moreover, if his offering is [a]a goat, then he shall offer it
before the LORD,
13 and he shall lay his hand on its head and slay it before the
tent of meeting, and the sons of Aaron shall sprinkle its blood
around on the altar.
14 'From it he shall present his offering as an offering by fire to
the LORD, the fat that covers the entrails and all the fat that is
on the entrails,
15 and the two kidneys with the fat that is on them, which is
on the loins, and the [1]lobe of the liver, which he shall remove
[a]with the kidneys.

16 [a]Lev 2:2
3:1 [a]Lev 7:11-34; 17:5 [b]Lev 1:3; 22:20-24
2 [a]Lev 1:4 [b]Ex 29:11, 16, 20
4 [1]Or *appendage on*
5 [a]Lev 7:28-34 [b]Ex 29:38-42; Num 28:3-10 [c]Num 15:8-10; 28:12-14
6 [a]Lev 3:1; 22:20-24
7 [a]Num 15:4, 5; 28:4-8 [b]Lev 17:8, 9; 1 Kin 8:62
8 [a]Lev 1:4 [b]Lev 3:2 [c]Lev 1:5
9 [1]Lit *the fat tail, entire* [a]Lev 17:5; Num 7:88; 1 Sam 10:8; 2 Sam 6:17; 1 Kin 3:15; 8:63, 64; 1 Chr 16:1
10 [1]Or *appendage on* [a]Lev 3:4, 15
11 [a]Lev 3:5 [b]Lev 3:16; 21:6, 8, 17, 22
12 [a]Num 15:6-11
15 [1]Or *appendage on* [a]Lev 3:4; 7:4

16 'The priest shall offer them up in smoke on the altar *as* food,
an offering by fire for a soothing aroma; [a]all fat is the LORD's.
17 'It is a [a]perpetual statute throughout your generations in all
your dwellings: you shall not eat any fat [b]or any blood.'"

Chapter 4 Theme ______________________________

4 Then the LORD spoke to Moses, saying,
2 "Speak to the sons of Israel, saying, 'If a person sins [a]un-
intentionally in any of the [1]things which the LORD has [b]com-
manded not to be done, and commits any of them,
3 [a]if the anointed priest sins so as to bring guilt on the
people, then let him offer to the LORD a [1]bull without defect as
a sin offering for the sin he has [2]committed.
4 'He shall bring the bull to the doorway of the tent of
meeting before the LORD, and [a]he shall lay his hand on the
head of the bull and slay the bull before the LORD.
5 'Then the [a]anointed priest is to take some of the blood of
the bull and bring it to the tent of meeting,
6 and the priest shall dip his finger in the blood and sprinkle
some of the blood seven times before the LORD, in front of [a]the
veil of the sanctuary.
7 'The priest shall also put some of the blood on the horns of
[a]the altar of fragrant incense which is before the LORD in the
tent of meeting; and all the blood of the bull he shall pour out at
the base of the altar of burnt offering which is at the doorway
of the tent of meeting.
8 '[a]He shall remove from it all the fat of the bull of the sin
offering: the fat that covers the entrails, and all the fat which is
on the entrails,
9 and the two kidneys with the fat that is on them, which is
on the loins, and the [1]lobe of the liver, which he shall remove
[a]with the kidneys
10 (just as it is removed from the ox of the sacrifice of peace
offerings), and the priest is to offer them up in smoke on the
altar of burnt offering.
11 'But [a]the hide of the bull and all its flesh with its head and
its legs and its entrails and its refuse,
12 [1]that is, all *the rest of* the bull, he is to bring out to [a]a clean
place outside the camp where the [2]ashes are poured out, and
burn it on wood with fire; where the [2]ashes are poured out it
shall be burned.
13 '[a]Now if the whole congregation of Israel commits error and
the matter [1]escapes the notice of the assembly, and they
commit any of the [2]things which the LORD has commanded not
to be done, and they become guilty;
14 [a]when the sin [1]which they have [2]committed becomes
known, then the assembly shall offer [b]a [3]bull of the herd for a
sin offering and bring it before the tent of meeting.
15 'Then [a]the elders of the congregation shall lay their hands
on the head of the bull before the LORD, and the bull shall be
slain [b]before the LORD.

16 [a]Lev 7:23-25

17 [a]Lev 6:18, 22; 7:34, 36; 10:9, 15; 16:29; 17:7; 23:14, 21; 24:3 [b]Lev 7:26; 17:10-16

4:2 [1]Lit *commands of the LORD which are not to be done* [a]Lev 4:22, 27; 5:15-18; 22:14 [b]Lev 4:13

3 [1]Or *bull of the herd* [2]Lit *sinned* [a]Lev 4:14, 23, 28

4 [a]Lev 1:4; 4:15; Num 8:12

5 [a]Lev 4:3, 17

6 [a]Ex 40:21, 26

7 [a]Lev 4:18, 25, 30, 34; 8:15; 9:9; 16:18

8 [a]Lev 3:3, 4

9 [1]Or *appendage on* [a]Lev 3:4

11 [a]Lev 9:11; Num 19:5

12 [1]Lit *and* [2]Or *fat ashes are* [a]Lev 4:21; 6:10, 11; 16:27

13 [1]Lit *is hidden from the eyes of* [2]Lit *commands of the LORD which are not to be done* [a]Num 15:24-26

14 [1]Lit *concerning which* [2]Lit *sinned* [3]Lit *son of the herd* [a]Lev 4:3 [b]Lev 4:3, 23, 28

15 [a]Lev 8:14, 18, 22; Num 8:10, 12 [b]Lev 1:3

16 'Then the anointed priest is to bring some of the blood of
the bull to the tent of meeting;
17 and [a]the priest shall dip his finger in the blood and sprinkle
it seven times before the LORD, in front of the veil.
18 'He shall put some of the blood on the horns of [a]the altar
which is before the LORD [1]in the tent of meeting; and all the
blood he shall pour out at the base of the altar of burnt offering
which is at the doorway of the tent of meeting.
19 '[a]He shall remove all its fat from it and offer it up in smoke
on the altar.
20 'He shall also do with the bull just as he did with [a]the bull
of the sin offering; thus he shall do with it. So [b]the priest shall
make atonement for them, and they will be forgiven.
21 'Then he is to bring out the bull to *a place* outside the camp
and burn it as he burned the first bull; it is [a]the sin offering for
the assembly.
22 'When [a]a leader [b]sins and unintentionally does any one of
all the [1]things which the LORD his God has commanded not to
be done, and he becomes guilty,
23 [1a]if his sin [2]which he has committed is made known to him,
he shall bring for his offering a [3b]goat, [c]a male without defect.
24 'He shall lay his hand on the head of the male goat and slay
it in the place where [1]they slay the burnt offering before the
LORD; it is a sin offering.
25 'Then the priest is to take some of the blood of the sin
offering with his finger and put it on [a]the horns of the altar of
burnt offering; and *the rest of* its blood he shall pour out at the
base of the altar of burnt offering.
26 '[a]All its fat he shall offer up in smoke on the altar as *in the
case of* the fat of the sacrifice of peace offerings. Thus [b]the priest
shall make atonement for him in regard to his sin, and he will
be forgiven.
27 'Now if [1]anyone of [2]the common people sins [a]unintentionally
in doing any of the [3]things which the LORD has commanded
not to be done, and becomes guilty,
28 [1a]if his sin which he has [2]committed is made known to
him, then he shall bring for his offering a [3b]goat, a [c]female
without defect, for his sin which he has [2]committed.
29 '[a]He shall lay his hand on the head of the sin offering and
[b]slay the sin offering at the place of the burnt offering.
30 'The priest shall take some of its blood with his finger and
put it on the horns of [a]the altar of burnt offering; and [b]all *the
rest of* its blood he shall pour out at the base of the altar.
31 '[a]Then he shall remove all its fat, just as the fat was removed
from the sacrifice of peace offerings; and the priest shall offer it up
in smoke on the altar for [b]a soothing aroma to the LORD. Thus the
priest shall make atonement for him, [1]and he will be forgiven.
32 'But if he brings [a]a lamb as his offering for a sin offering, he
shall bring it, a female without defect.
33 '[a]He shall lay his hand on the head of the sin offering and
slay it for a sin offering [b]in the place where [1]they slay the burnt
offering.

17 [a]Lev 4:6
18 [1]Lit *which is in* [a]Lev 4:7, 25, 30, 34
19 [a]Lev 4:8
20 [a]Lev 4:8, 21 [b]Num 15:25, 28
21 [a]Lev 4:13f; 16:15-17; Num 15:24-26
22 [1]Lit *commands of the LORD which are not to be done* [a]Num 31:13; 32:2 [b]Lev 4:2, 27
23 [1]Lit *or* [2]Lit *in which he has sinned* [3]Lit *buck of the goats* [a]Lev 4:3 [b]Lev 4:3, 14, 28 [c]Lev 4:28
24 [1]Lit *one slays*
25 [a]Lev 4:7, 18, 30, 34
26 [a]Lev 4:19 [b]Lev 4:20, 31; 5:10, 13, 16, 18; 6:7
27 [1]Lit *one soul* [2]Lit *the people of the land* [3]Lit *commands of the LORD which are not to be done* [a]Lev 4:2; Num 15:27
28 [1]Lit *or* [2]Lit *sinned* [3]Or *female goat* [a]Lev 4:3 [b]Lev 4:3, 14, 23, 32 [c]Lev 4:23
29 [a]Lev 1:4; 4:4, 24 [b]Lev 1:5, 11
30 [a]Lev 4:7, 18, 25, 34 [b]Lev 4:7
31 [1]Or *so that he may be* [a]Lev 4:8 [b]Gen 8:21; Ex 29:18; Lev 1:9, 13; 2:2, 9, 12
32 [a]Lev 4:28
33 [1]Lit *one slays* [a]Lev 1:4, 5 [b]Lev 4:29

34 'The priest is to take some of the blood of the sin offering
with his finger and put it on the horns of [a]the altar of burnt
offering, and [b]all *the rest of* its blood he shall pour out at the
base of the altar.
35 'Then he shall remove [a]all its fat, just as the fat of the lamb is
removed from the sacrifice of the peace offerings, and the priest
shall offer them up in smoke on the altar, on the offerings by fire
to the LORD. Thus [b]the priest shall make atonement for him in
regard to his sin which he has [1]committed, and he will be forgiven.

Chapter 5 Theme ______________________

5 'Now if a person sins after he hears a [1]public [a]adjuration *to testify* when he is a witness, whether he has seen or *otherwise* known, if he does not tell *it,* then he will bear his [2]guilt.
2 'Or if a person touches [a]any unclean thing, whether a
carcass of an unclean beast or the carcass of unclean cattle or a
carcass of unclean swarming things, though it is hidden from
him and he is unclean, then he will be guilty.
3 'Or if he touches human uncleanness, of whatever *sort* his
uncleanness *may* be with which he becomes unclean, and it is
hidden from him, and then he comes to know *it,* he will be guilty.
4 'Or if a person [a]swears thoughtlessly with his lips to do evil or
to do good, in whatever matter a man may speak thoughtlessly
with an oath, and it is hidden from him, and then he comes to
know *it,* he will be guilty in one of these.
5 'So it shall be when he becomes guilty in one of these, that
he shall [a]confess that in which he has sinned.
6 'He shall also bring his guilt offering to the LORD for his sin
which he has [1]committed, [a]a female from the flock, a lamb or a
[2]goat as a sin offering. So the priest shall make atonement on
his behalf for his sin.
7 'But if [1]he cannot afford a lamb, then he shall bring to the
LORD his guilt offering for that in which he has sinned, two
turtledoves or two young pigeons, [a]one for a sin offering and
the other for a burnt offering.
8 'He shall bring them to the priest, who shall offer first that
which is for the sin offering and shall nip its head at the front
of its neck, but he [a]shall not sever *it.*
9 'He shall also sprinkle some of the blood of the sin offering
[a]on the side of the altar, while the rest of the blood shall be
drained out [b]at the base of the altar: it is a sin offering.
10 'The second he shall then prepare as a burnt offering
[a]according to the ordinance. [b]So the priest shall make atonement
on his behalf for his sin which he has [1]committed, and it will
be forgiven him.
11 'But [a]if his [1]means are insufficient for two turtledoves or
two young pigeons, then for his offering for that which he has
sinned, he shall bring the tenth of an [2]ephah of fine flour for a
sin offering; [b]he shall not put oil on it or place incense on it, for
it is a sin offering.

34 [a]Lev 4:7, 18, 25, 30 [b]Lev 4:7

35 [1]Lit *sinned* [a]Lev 4:26, 31 [b]Lev 4:20

5:1 [1]Lit *voice of an oath* [2]Or *iniquity* [a]Prov 29:24; Jer 23:10

2 [a]Lev 11:8, 11, 24-40; Num 19:11-16; Deut 14:8

4 [a]Num 30:6, 8; Ps 106:33

5 [a]Lev 16:21; 26:40; Num 5:7; Prov 28:13

6 [1]Lit *sinned* [2]Lit *female goat* [a]Lev 4:28, 32

7 [1]Lit *his hand does not reach enough for* [a]Lev 12:6, 8; 14:22, 30, 31

8 [a]Lev 1:17

9 [a]Lev 1:15 [b]Lev 4:7, 18

10 [1]Lit *sinned* [a]Lev 1:14-17 [b]Lev 4:20, 26; 5:13, 16

11 [1]Lit *hand does not reach* [2]I.e. Approx one bu [a]Lev 14:21-32; 27:8 [b]Lev 2:1, 2

12 [1]Lit *upon*

12 'He shall bring it to the priest, and the priest shall take his
handful of it as its memorial portion and offer *it* up in smoke on
the altar, [1]with the offerings of the LORD by fire: it is a sin offering.

13 [1]Lit *sinned* [a]Lev 5:4, 5 [b]Lev 2:3

13 'So the priest shall make atonement for him concerning his
sin which he has [1]committed from [a]one of these, and it will be
forgiven him; then [b]*the rest* shall become the priest's, like the
grain offering.'"

14 Then the LORD spoke to Moses, saying,

15 [a]Num 5:5-8 [b]Lev 4:2; 22:14 [c]Lev 7:1-10 [d]Lev 6:6 [e]Ex 30:13

15 "[a]If a person acts unfaithfully and sins [b]unintentionally against
the LORD's holy things, then he shall bring his [c]guilt offering to
the LORD: [d]a ram without defect from the flock, according to
your valuation in silver by shekels, in *terms of* the [e]shekel of
the sanctuary, for a guilt offering.

16 [a]Lev 6:5; 22:14; Num 5:7, 8 [b]Lev 7:2-7

16 "[a]He shall make restitution for that which he has sinned
against the holy thing, and shall add to it a fifth part of it and give
it to the priest. [b]The priest shall then make atonement for him
with the ram of the guilt offering, and it will be forgiven him.

17 [1]Lit *the commands of the* LORD *which are* [a]Lev 4:2; 5:19

17 "Now if a person sins and does any of the things [1]which the
LORD has commanded not to be done, [a]though he was unaware,
still he is guilty and shall bear his punishment.

18 [a]Lev 5:15 [b]Lev 5:17

18 "He is then to bring to the priest [a]a ram without defect from
the flock, according to your valuation, for a guilt offering. So
the priest shall make atonement for him concerning his error
in which he sinned [b]unintentionally and did not know *it*, and it
will be forgiven him.
19 "It is a guilt offering; he was certainly guilty before the LORD."

6:1 [1]Ch 5:20 in Heb

Chapter 6 Theme ______________________

2 [a]Ex 22:7-15

6 [1]Then the LORD spoke to Moses, saying,
2 "[a]When a person sins and acts unfaithfully against the
LORD, and deceives his companion in regard to a deposit or a
security entrusted *to him*, or through robbery, or *if* he has
extorted from his companion,

3 [a]Ex 23:4; Deut 22:1-4

3 or [a]has found what was lost and lied about it and sworn
falsely, so that he sins in regard to any one of the things a man
may do;

4 [1]Or *deposited with* [a]Lev 24:18, 21

4 then it shall be, when he sins and becomes guilty, that he
shall [a]restore what he took by robbery or what he got by
extortion, or the deposit which was [1]entrusted to him or the
lost thing which he found,

5 [1]Lit *in its sum* [a]Lev 5:16 [b]Num 5:8

5 or anything about which he swore falsely; [a]he shall make
restitution for it [1]in full and add to it one-fifth more. [b]He shall
give it to the one to whom it belongs on the day *he presents*
his guilt offering.

6 [a]Lev 5:15

6 "Then he shall bring to the priest his guilt offering to the
LORD, [a]a ram without defect from the flock, according to your
valuation, for a guilt offering,

7 [a]Lev 7:2-5

7 and [a]the priest shall make atonement for him before the
LORD, and he will be forgiven for any one of the things which he
may have done to incur guilt."

8 [1]Then the LORD spoke to Moses, saying,
9 "Command Aaron and his sons, saying, 'This is [a]the law for
the burnt offering: the burnt offering itself *shall remain* on the
hearth on the altar all night until the morning, and [b]the fire on
the altar is to be kept burning on it.
10 'The priest is to put on [a]his linen robe, and he shall put on
undergarments next to his flesh; and he shall take up the
[1]ashes *to* which the fire [2]reduces the burnt offering on the altar
and place them beside the altar.
11 'Then he shall take off his garments and put on other
garments, and carry the [1]ashes outside the camp to a clean place.
12 'The fire on the altar shall be kept burning on it. It shall not
go out, but the priest shall burn wood on it every morning; and
he shall lay out the burnt offering on it, and offer up in smoke
the fat portions of the peace offerings [a]on it.
13 'Fire shall be kept burning continually on the altar; it is not
to go out.
14 'Now this is the law of the grain offering: the sons of Aaron
shall present it before the LORD in front of the altar.
15 '[a]Then one *of them* shall lift up from it a handful of the fine
flour of the grain offering, [1]with its oil and all the incense that
is on the grain offering, and he shall offer *it* up in smoke on the
altar, a soothing aroma, as its memorial offering to the LORD.
16 '[a]What is left of it Aaron and his sons are to eat. It shall be
eaten as unleavened cakes in a holy place; they are to eat it in
the court of the tent of meeting.
17 '[a]It shall not be baked with leaven. I have given it as their
share from My offerings by fire; [b]it is most holy, like the sin
offering and [c]the guilt offering.
18 '[a]Every male among the sons of Aaron may eat it; it is a
permanent ordinance throughout your generations, from the
offerings by fire to the LORD. [b]Whoever touches them will
become consecrated.'"
19 Then the LORD spoke to Moses, saying,
20 "This is the offering which Aaron and his sons are to
present to the LORD on the day when he is anointed; the tenth
of an [a]ephah of fine flour as [b]a [1]regular grain offering, half of it
in the morning and half of it in the evening.
21 "It shall be prepared with oil on a [a]griddle. When it is *well*
stirred, you shall bring it. You shall present the grain offering in
baked pieces as a soothing aroma to the LORD.
22 "The anointed priest who will be in his place [1]among his sons
shall [2]offer it. By a permanent ordinance it shall be entirely
offered up in smoke to the LORD.
23 "So every grain offering of the priest shall be burned entirely.
It shall not be eaten."
24 Then the LORD spoke to Moses, saying,
25 "Speak to Aaron and to his sons, saying, 'This is the law of
the sin offering: [a]in the place where the burnt offering is slain
the sin offering shall be slain before the LORD; it is most holy.
26 '[a]The priest who offers it for sin shall eat it. It shall be eaten
in a holy place, in the court of the tent of meeting.

8 [1]Ch 6:1 in Heb

9 [a]Ex 29:38-42; Num 28:3-10 [b]Lev 6:12, 13

10 [1]Or *fat ashes* [2]Lit *consumes* [a]Ex 28:39, 42; 39:27, 28

11 [1]Or *fat ashes*

12 [a]Lev 3:5

15 [1]Lit *and some of* [a]Lev 2:2, 9

16 [a]Lev 2:3; 10:12-14; Ezek 44:29

17 [a]Lev 2:11 [b]Ex 40:10; Lev 6:25, 26, 29, 30; Num 18:9 [c]Lev 7:7; 10:16-18

18 [a]Lev 6:29; 7:6; Num 18:10; 1 Cor 9:13 [b]Lev 6:27

20 [1]Lit *grain offering continually* [a]Lev 5:11 [b]Num 4:16

21 [a]Lev 2:5

22 [1]Lit *from among* [2]Lit *do*

25 [a]Lev 1:11

26 [a]Lev 6:29

27 '[a]Anyone who touches its flesh will become consecrated;
and when any of its blood [1]splashes on a garment, in a holy
place you shall wash what was splashed on.
28 'Also [a]the earthenware vessel in which it was boiled shall
be broken; and if it was boiled in a bronze vessel, then it shall
be scoured and rinsed in water.
29 '[a]Every male among the priests may eat of it; [b]it is most
holy.
30 'But no sin offering [a]of which any of the blood is brought
into the tent of meeting to make atonement [b]in the holy place
shall be eaten; [c]it shall be burned with fire.

Chapter 7 Theme ______________________

7 'Now this is the law of the [a]guilt offering; it is most holy.
2 'In [a]the place where they slay the burnt offering they are
to slay the guilt offering, and he shall sprinkle its blood around
on the altar.
3 'Then he shall offer from it all its fat: the [a]fat tail and the fat
that covers the entrails,
4 and the two kidneys with the fat that is on them, which is
on the loins, and the lobe on the liver he shall remove [a]with
the kidneys.
5 'The priest shall offer them up in smoke on the altar as an
offering by fire to the LORD; it is a guilt offering.
6 '[a]Every male among the priests may eat of it. It shall be eaten
in a holy place; it is most holy.
7 'The guilt offering is like the [a]sin offering, there is one law for
them; the [b]priest who makes atonement with it [1]shall have it.
8 'Also the priest who presents any man's burnt offering, [1]that
priest shall have for himself the skin of the burnt offering
which he has presented.
9 'Likewise, every grain offering that is baked in the oven and
everything prepared in a [1]pan or on a [a]griddle [2]shall belong to
the priest who presents it.
10 'Every grain offering, mixed with oil or dry, shall [1]belong to
all the sons of Aaron, [2]to all alike.
11 'Now this is the law of the [a]sacrifice of peace offerings which
shall be presented to the LORD.
12 'If he offers it by way of [a]thanksgiving, then along with the
sacrifice of thanksgiving he shall offer [b]unleavened cakes mixed
with oil, and unleavened wafers [1]spread with oil, and cakes *of
well* stirred fine flour mixed with oil.
13 'With the sacrifice of his peace offerings for thanksgiving,
he shall present his offering with cakes of [a]leavened bread.
14 'Of [1]this he shall present one of every offering as a [2]con-
tribution to the LORD; [a]it shall [3]belong to the priest who sprinkles
the blood of the peace offerings.
15 '[a]Now *as for* the flesh of the sacrifice of his thanksgiving
peace offerings, it shall be eaten on the day of his offering; he
shall not leave any of it over until morning.

27 [1]Lit *one sprinkles* [a]Lev 7:19
28 [a]Lev 11:33; 15:12
29 [a]Lev 6:18 [b]Lev 6:17, 25
30 [a]Lev 4:1-21 [b]Lev 4:7, 18 [c]Lev 4:11, 12, 21
7:1 [a]Lev 5:14-6:7
2 [a]Lev 1:11
3 [a]Lev 3:9
4 [a]Lev 3:4
6 [a]Lev 6:18, 29; Num 18:9
7 [1]Lit *it shall be for him* [a]Lev 6:25, 26, 30 [b]1 Cor 9:13; 10:18
8 [1]Lit *for the priest, it shall be for him*
9 [1]Lit *lidded cooking pan* [2]Lit *for the priest, it shall be for him* [a]Lev 2:5
10 [1]Lit *be* [2]Lit *a man as his brother*
11 [a]Lev 3:1
12 [1]Or *anointed* [a]Lev 7:15 [b]Lev 2:4; Num 6:15
13 [a]Lev 2:12; 23:17, 18; Amos 4:5
14 [1]Lit *it* [2]Or *heave offering* [3]Lit *be for* [a]Num 18:8, 11, 19
15 [a]Lev 22:29, 30

16 'But if the sacrifice of his offering is a [a]votive or a freewill
offering, it shall be eaten on the day that he offers his sacrifice,
and on the [1]next day what is left of it may be eaten;
17 [a]but what is left over from the flesh of the sacrifice on the
third day shall be burned with fire.
18 'So if any of the flesh of the sacrifice of his peace offerings
should *ever* be eaten on the third day, he who offers it will not
be accepted, *and* it will not be reckoned to his *benefit.* It shall
be an [a]offensive thing, and the person who eats of it will bear
his *own* iniquity.
19 'Also the flesh that touches anything unclean shall not be
eaten; it shall be burned with fire. [1]As for *other* flesh, anyone
who is clean may eat *such* flesh.
20 '[a]But the person who eats the flesh of the sacrifice of peace
offerings which belong to the LORD, [1]in his uncleanness, that
person [b]shall be cut off from his people.
21 '[a]When anyone touches anything unclean, whether human
uncleanness, or an unclean animal, or any unclean [1]detestable
thing, and eats of the flesh of the sacrifice of peace offerings
which belong to the LORD, that person shall be cut off from his
people.'"
22 Then the LORD spoke to Moses, saying,
23 "Speak to the sons of Israel, saying, 'You shall not eat [a]any
fat *from* an ox, a sheep or a goat.
24 'Also the fat of *an animal* which dies and the fat of an animal
[a]torn *by beasts* may be put to any other use, but you must
certainly not eat it.
25 'For whoever eats the fat of the animal from which [1]an
offering by fire is offered to the LORD, even the person who eats
shall be cut off from his people.
26 '[a]You are not to eat any blood, either of bird or animal, in
any of your dwellings.
27 'Any person who eats any blood, even that person shall be
cut off from his people.'"
28 Then the LORD spoke to Moses, saying,
29 "Speak to the sons of Israel, saying, 'He who offers [a]the
sacrifice of his peace offerings to the LORD shall bring his
offering to the LORD from the sacrifice of his peace offerings.
30 'His own hands are to bring offerings by fire to the LORD.
He shall bring the fat with the breast, that the [a]breast may be
[1]presented as a wave offering before the LORD.
31 'The priest shall offer up the fat in smoke on the altar, but
[a]the breast shall belong to Aaron and his sons.
32 'You shall give [a]the right thigh to the priest as a [1]contribution
from the sacrifices of your peace offerings.
33 'The one among the sons of Aaron who offers the blood of
the peace offerings and the fat, the right thigh shall be his as
his portion.
34 'For I have taken [a]the breast of the wave offering and the
thigh of the [1]contribution from the sons of Israel from the
sacrifices of their peace offerings, and have given them to Aaron

16 [1]Lit *morrow and what* [a]Lev 19:5-8
17 [a]Ex 12:10
18 [a]Lev 19:7; Prov 15:8
19 [1]Lit *And the flesh*
20 [1]Lit *and his uncleanness is on him* [a]Lev 22:3-7; Num 19:13 [b]Lev 7:25
21 [1]Some mss read *swarming thing* [a]Lev 5:2, 3
23 [a]Lev 3:17
24 [a]Ex 22:31; Lev 17:15; 22:8
25 [1]Lit *he offers an offering by fire*
26 [a]Gen 9:4; Lev 17:10-16; 19:26; Deut 12:23; 1 Sam 14:33; Acts 15:20
29 [a]Lev 3:1
30 [1]Lit *waved* [a]Ex 29:26, 27; Lev 8:29; Num 6:20
31 [a]Num 18:11; Deut 18:3
32 [1]Or *heave offering* [a]Ex 29:27; Lev 7:34; 9:21; Num 6:20
34 [1]Or *heave offering* [a]Ex 29:27; Lev 10:14, 15; Num 18:18

the priest and to his sons as *their* due forever from the sons of
Israel.
35 'This is [1]that which is consecrated to Aaron and [1]that [a]which
is consecrated to his sons from the offerings by fire to the LORD, in
that day when he presented them to serve as priests to the LORD.
36 '[1]These the LORD had commanded to be given them from
the sons of Israel in the day that He [a]anointed them. It is *their*
due forever throughout their generations.'"
37 This is the law of the burnt offering, the grain offering and
the sin offering and the guilt offering and [a]the ordination
offering and the sacrifice of peace offerings,
38 [a]which the LORD commanded Moses at Mount Sinai in the
day that He commanded the sons of Israel to [1]present their
offerings to the LORD in the wilderness of Sinai.

Chapter 8 Theme ______________________

8 Then the LORD spoke to Moses, saying,
2 "[a]Take Aaron and his sons with him, and the [b]garments
and [c]the anointing oil and the bull of the sin offering, and the
two rams and the basket of unleavened bread,
3 and assemble all the congregation at the doorway of the
tent of meeting."
4 So Moses did just as the LORD commanded him. When the
congregation was assembled at the doorway of the tent of
meeting,
5 Moses said to the congregation, "This is the thing which
the LORD has commanded to do."
6 Then [a]Moses had Aaron and his sons come near and
[b]washed them with water.
7 He [a]put the tunic on him and girded him with the sash,
and clothed him with the robe and put the ephod on him; and
he girded him with the artistic band of the ephod, [1]with which
he tied *it* to him.
8 He then placed the [1]breastpiece on him, and in the [1]breast-
piece he put [2a]the Urim and the Thummim.
9 He also placed the turban on his head, and on the turban,
at its front, he placed [a]the golden plate, the holy crown, just as
the LORD had commanded Moses.
10 Moses then took [a]the anointing oil and anointed the [1]taber-
nacle and all that was in it, and consecrated them.
11 He sprinkled some of it on the altar seven times and
anointed the altar and all its utensils, and the basin and its
stand, to [a]consecrate them.
12 Then he poured some of the [a]anointing oil on Aaron's head
and anointed him, to consecrate him.
13 [a]Next Moses had Aaron's sons come near and clothed them
with tunics, and girded them with sashes and bound [1]caps on
them, just as the LORD had commanded Moses.
14 Then he brought [a]the bull of the sin offering, and Aaron and
his sons laid their hands on the head of the bull of the sin offering.

35 [1]Lit *the anointed portion of* [a]Num 18:8
36 [1]Lit *Which* [a]Ex 40:13-15; Lev 8:12, 30
37 [a]Ex 29:22-34; Lev 8:22, 23
38 [1]Or *offer* [a]Lev 1:1; 26:46; 27:34; Deut 4:5
8:2 [a]Ex 28:1 [b]Lev 6:10 [c]Ex 30:25
6 [a]Ex 29:4-6 [b]Ex 30:19, 20; Ps 26:6; 1 Cor 6:11; Eph 5:26
7 [1]Lit *and with it* [a]Ex 28:4
8 [1]Lit *pouch* [2]I.e. the lights and perfections [a]Ex 28:30; Num 27:21; Deut 33:8; 1 Sam 28:6; Ezra 2:63; Neh 7:65
9 [a]Ex 28:36
10 [1]Or *dwelling place* [a]Ex 30:26-29; Lev 8:2
11 [a]Ex 29:36, 37; 30:29
12 [a]Ex 29:7; 30:30; Lev 21:10, 12; Ps 133:2
13 [1]Lit *headgear* [a]Ex 29:8, 9
14 [a]Ex 29:10; Lev 4:4; Ps 66:15; Ezek 43:19

15 Next [1]Moses slaughtered *it* and took the blood and with his
finger [a]put *some of it* around on the horns of the altar, and
purified the altar. Then he poured out *the rest of* the blood at the
base of the altar and consecrated it, to make atonement for it.
16 He also [a]took all the fat that was on the entrails and the
[1]lobe of the liver, and the two kidneys and their fat; and Moses
offered it up in smoke on the altar.
17 [a]But the bull and its hide and its flesh and its refuse he
burned in the fire outside the camp, just as the LORD had
commanded Moses.
18 Then he presented [a]the ram of the burnt offering, and
Aaron and his sons laid their hands on the head of the ram.
19 [1]Moses slaughtered *it* and sprinkled the blood around on
the altar.
20 When he had cut the ram into its pieces, Moses [a]offered up
the head and the pieces and the suet in smoke.
21 After he had washed the entrails and the legs with water,
Moses [a]offered up the whole ram in smoke on the altar. It was
a burnt offering for a soothing aroma; it was an offering by fire
to the LORD, just as the LORD had commanded Moses.
22 Then he presented the second ram, [a]the ram of [1]ordination,
and Aaron and his sons laid their hands on the head of the ram.
23 [1]Moses slaughtered *it* and took some of its blood and [a]put it
on the lobe of Aaron's right ear, and on the thumb of his right
hand and on the big toe of his right foot.
24 He also had Aaron's sons come near; and Moses put some
of the blood on the lobe of their right ear, and on the thumb of
their right hand and on the big toe of their right foot. Moses
then [a]sprinkled *the rest of* the blood around on the altar.
25 He took the fat, and the fat tail, and all the fat that was on
the entrails, and the [1]lobe of the liver and the two kidneys and
their fat and the right thigh.
26 [a]From the basket of unleavened bread that was before the
LORD, he took one unleavened cake and one cake of bread
mixed with oil and one wafer, and placed *them* on the portions
of fat and on the right thigh.
27 He then [a]put all *these* on the hands of Aaron and on the
hands of his sons and presented them as a wave offering before
the LORD.
28 Then Moses [a]took them from their hands and offered them
up in smoke on the altar with the burnt offering. They were an
ordination offering for [b]a soothing aroma; it was an offering by
fire to the LORD.
29 Moses also took [a]the breast and presented it for a wave
offering before the LORD; it was [b]Moses' portion of the ram of
ordination, just as the LORD had commanded Moses.
30 So Moses [a]took some of the anointing oil and some of the
blood which was on the altar and sprinkled it on Aaron, on his
garments, on his sons, and on the garments of his sons with
him; and he consecrated Aaron, his garments, and his sons,
and the garments of his sons with him.

15 [1]Lit *he slaughtered it and Moses took* [a]Ex 29:12; Lev 4:7; Ezek 43:20
16 [1]Or *appendage on* [a]Ex 29:13
17 [a]Ex 29:14; Lev 4:11, 12
18 [a]Ex 29:15; Lev 8:2
19 [1]Lit *He slaughtered it and Moses sprinkled*
20 [a]Lev 1:8
21 [a]Ex 29:18
22 [1]Lit *filling,* and so throughout the ch [a]Ex 29:31; Lev 8:2
23 [1]Lit *He slaughtered it and Moses took* [a]Ex 29:20, 21
24 [a]Heb 9:18-22
25 [1]Or *appendage on*
26 [a]Ex 29:23
27 [a]Ex 29:24
28 [a]Ex 29:25 [b]Gen 8:21
29 [a]Lev 7:31-34 [b]Ex 29:26; Ps 99:6
30 [a]Ex 29:21

31 Then Moses said to Aaron and to his sons, "[a]Boil the flesh at the doorway of the tent of meeting, and eat it there together with the bread which is in the basket of the ordination offering, just as I commanded, [b]saying, 'Aaron and his sons shall eat it.'

32 "[a]The remainder of the flesh and of the bread you shall burn in the fire.

33 "[a]You shall not go outside the doorway of the tent of meeting for seven days, until the day that the period of your ordination is fulfilled; for he will [1]ordain you through seven days.

34 "The LORD has commanded to do as has been done this day, to make atonement on your behalf.

35 "At the doorway of the tent of meeting, moreover, you shall remain day and night for seven days and [a]keep the charge of the LORD, so that you will not die, for so I have been commanded."

36 Thus Aaron and his sons did all the things which the LORD had commanded through Moses.

Chapter 9 Theme ____________________

9 Now it came about [a]on the eighth day that Moses called Aaron and his sons and the elders of Israel;

2 and he said to Aaron, "[a]Take for yourself a calf, a bull, for a sin offering and a ram for a burnt offering, *both* without defect, and offer *them* before the LORD.

3 "Then to the sons of Israel you shall speak, saying, 'Take a male goat for a sin offering, and a calf and a lamb, both one year old, without defect, for a burnt offering,

4 and an ox and a ram for peace offerings, to sacrifice before the LORD, and a grain offering mixed with oil; for today [a]the LORD will appear to you.'"

5 So they took what Moses had commanded to the front of the tent of meeting, and the whole congregation came near and stood before the LORD.

6 Moses said, "This is the thing which the LORD has commanded you to do, that [a]the glory of the LORD may appear to you."

7 Moses then said to Aaron, "Come near to the altar and [1][a]offer your sin offering and your burnt offering, that you may make atonement for yourself and for the people; then make the offering [2]for the people, that you may make atonement for them, just as the LORD has commanded."

8 [a]So Aaron came near to the altar and slaughtered the calf of the sin offering which was for himself.

9 [a]Aaron's sons presented the blood to him; and he dipped his finger in the blood and [b]put *some* on the horns of the altar, and poured out *the rest of* the blood at the base of the altar.

10 The fat and the kidneys and the [1]lobe of the liver of the sin offering, he then offered up in smoke on the altar just as the LORD had commanded Moses.

11 [a]The flesh and the skin, however, he burned with fire outside the camp.

31 [a]Ex 29:31 [b]Ex 29:32
32 [a]Ex 29:34
33 [1]Lit *fill your hands* [a]Ex 29:35
35 [a]Num 3:7; 9:19; Deut 11:1; 1 Kin 2:3; Ezek 48:11
9:1 [a]Ezek 43:27
2 [a]Ezek 29:1; Lev 4:3
4 [a]Ex 29:43
6 [a]Ex 24:16; Lev 9:23
7 [1]Lit *make* [2]Lit *of* [a]Heb 5:3; 7:27
8 [a]Lev 4:1-12
9 [a]Lev 9:12, 18 [b]Lev 4:7
10 [1]Or *appendage on*
11 [a]Lev 4:11, 12; 8:17

12 Then he slaughtered the burnt offering; and Aaron's sons
handed the blood to him and he sprinkled it around on the altar.
13 They handed the burnt offering to him in [1]pieces, with the
head, and he offered *them* up in smoke on the altar.
14 He also washed the entrails and the legs, and offered *them*
up in smoke with the burnt offering on the altar.
15 Then he presented the people's offering, and took the [a]goat
of the sin offering which was for the people, and slaughtered it
and offered it for sin, like the first.
16 He also presented the burnt offering, and [1]offered it
according to [a]the ordinance.
17 Next he presented [a]the grain offering, and filled his [1]hand
with some of it and offered *it* up in smoke on the altar, [b]besides
the burnt offering of the morning.
18 Then [a]he slaughtered the ox and the ram, the sacrifice of
peace offerings which was for the people; and Aaron's sons
handed the blood to him and he sprinkled it around on the altar.
19 As for the portions of fat from the ox and from the ram, the
fat tail, and the *fat* [a]covering, and the kidneys and the [1]lobe of
the liver,
20 they now placed the portions of fat on the breasts; and he
offered [1]them up in smoke on the altar.
21 But [a]the breasts and the right thigh Aaron [1]presented as a
wave offering before the LORD, just as Moses had commanded.
22 Then Aaron lifted up his hands toward the people and
[a]blessed them, and he stepped down after making the sin
offering and the burnt offering and the peace offerings.
23 Moses and Aaron went into the tent of meeting. When they
came out and blessed the people, [a]the glory of the LORD appeared
to all the people.
24 [a]Then fire came out from before the LORD and consumed
the burnt offering and the portions of fat on the altar; and
when all the people saw *it,* they shouted and fell on their faces.

Chapter 10 Theme ______________________________

10 Now [a]Nadab and Abihu, the sons of Aaron, took their
respective [b]firepans, and after putting fire in them,
placed incense on it and offered strange fire before the LORD,
which He had not commanded them.
2 [a]And fire came out from the presence of the LORD and
consumed them, and they died before the LORD.
3 Then Moses said to Aaron, "It is what the LORD spoke, saying,
'By those who [a]come near Me I [1b]will be treated
as holy,
And before all the people I will [c]be honored.'"
So Aaron, therefore, kept silent.
4 Moses called also to [a]Mishael and Elzaphan, the sons of
Aaron's uncle Uzziel, and said to them, "Come forward, carry
your [1]relatives away from the front of the sanctuary to the
outside of the camp."

13 [1]Lit *its pieces*

15 [a]Lev 4:27-31

16 [1]Lit *made* [a]Lev 1:1-13

17 [1]Lit *palm* [a]Lev 2:1-3 [b]Lev 3:5

18 [a]Lev 3:1-11

19 [1]Or *appendage on* [a]Lev 3:9

20 [1]Lit *the portions of fat*

21 [1]Lit *waved* [a]Ex 29:26, 27; Lev 7:30-34

22 [a]Num 6:22-26; Deut 21:5; Luke 24:50

23 [a]Lev 9:6; Num 16:19

24 [a]1 Kin 18:38, 39; 2 Chr 7:1

10:1 [a]Ex 24:1, 9; Num 3:2; 26:61 [b]Lev 16:12

2 [a]Num 3:4; 16:35; 26:61

3 [1]Or *will show Myself holy* [a]Ex 19:22; Lev 21:6 [b]Ex 30:30; Ezek 38:16 [c]Ex 14:4, 17; Is 49:3; Ezek 28:22

4 [1]Lit *brothers* [a]Ex 6:22

5 So they came forward and carried them still in their [a]tunics
to the outside of the camp, as Moses had said.
6 Then Moses said to Aaron and to his sons Eleazar and
Ithamar, "[a]Do not [1]uncover your heads nor tear your clothes, so
that you will not die and that He will not [b]become wrathful
against all the congregation. But your [2]kinsmen, the whole house
of Israel, shall bewail the burning which the LORD has [3]brought
about.
7 "You shall not even go out from the doorway of the tent of
meeting, or you will die; for [a]the LORD's anointing oil is upon
you." So they did according to the word of Moses.
8 The LORD then spoke to Aaron, saying,
9 "[a]Do not drink wine or strong drink, neither you nor your
sons with you, when you come into the tent of meeting, so that
you will not die—it is a perpetual statute throughout your
generations—
10 and [a]so as to make a distinction between the holy and the
profane, and between the unclean and the clean,
11 and [a]so as to teach the sons of Israel all the statutes which
the LORD has spoken to them through Moses."
12 Then Moses spoke to Aaron, and to his surviving sons,
[a]Eleazar and Ithamar, "[b]Take the grain offering that is left over
from the LORD's offerings by fire and eat it unleavened beside
the altar, for it is most holy.
13 "You shall eat it, moreover, in a holy place, because it is your
due and your sons' due out of the LORD's offerings by fire; for
thus I have been commanded.
14 "[a]The breast of the wave offering, however, and the thigh of
the offering you may eat in a clean place, you and your sons and
your daughters with you; for they have been given as your due
and your sons' due out of the sacrifices of the peace offerings of
the sons of Israel.
15 "[a]The thigh offered by lifting up and the breast offered by
waving they shall bring along with the offerings by fire of the
portions of fat, to present as a wave offering before the LORD; so
it shall be a thing perpetually due you and your sons with you,
just as the LORD has commanded."
16 But Moses searched carefully for the [a]goat of the sin
offering, and behold, it had been burned up! So he was angry
with Aaron's surviving sons Eleazar and Ithamar, saying,
17 "Why [a]did you not eat the sin offering at the holy place? For
it is most holy, and [1]He gave it to you to bear away [b]the guilt of
the congregation, to make atonement for them before the LORD.
18 "Behold, [a]since its blood had not been brought inside, into
the sanctuary, you should certainly have [b]eaten it in the
sanctuary, just as I commanded."
19 But Aaron spoke to Moses, "Behold, this very day they
[a]presented their sin offering and their burnt offering before the
LORD. When things like these happened to me, if I had eaten a sin
offering today, would it have been good in the sight of the LORD?"
20 When Moses heard *that*, it seemed good in his sight.

5 [a]Ex 29:5; Lev 8:13
6 [1]Lit *unbind* [2]Lit *brothers* [3]Lit *burned* [a]Lev 21:1-5, 10-12 [b]Num 1:53; 16:22, 46; 18:5; Josh 7:1; 22:18, 20; 2 Sam 24:1
7 [a]Ex 28:41; Lev 21:12
9 [a]Prov 20:1; 31:5; Is 28:7; Ezek 44:21; Hos 4:11; Luke 1:15; Eph 5:18; 1 Tim 3:3; Titus 1:7
10 [a]Lev 11:47; 20:25; Ezek 22:26
11 [a]Deut 17:10, 11; 33:10
12 [a]Ex 6:23; Num 3:2 [b]Lev 6:14-18
14 [a]Lev 7:30-34; Num 18:11
15 [a]Lev 7:34
16 [a]Lev 9:3, 15
17 [1]Or *was given* [a]Lev 6:24-30 [b]Ex 28:38; Lev 22:16; Num 18:1
18 [a]Lev 6:30 [b]Lev 6:26
19 [a]Lev 9:8, 12

Chapter 11 Theme ________________________________

11 The LORD spoke again to Moses and to Aaron, saying to
them,
2 "Speak to the sons of Israel, saying, '[a]These are the creatures
which you may eat from all the animals that are on the earth.
3 'Whatever divides a hoof, thus making split hoofs, *and* chews
the cud, among the animals, that you may eat.
4 'Nevertheless, [a]you are not to eat of these, among those
which chew the cud, or among those which divide the hoof: the
camel, for though it chews cud, it does not divide the hoof, it is
unclean to you.
5 'Likewise, the [1]shaphan, for though it chews cud, it does not
divide the hoof, it is unclean to you;
6 the [1]rabbit also, for though it chews cud, it does not divide
the hoof, it is unclean to you;
7 and the pig, for though it divides the hoof, thus making a
split hoof, it does not chew cud, it is unclean to you.
8 'You shall not eat of their flesh nor touch their carcasses;
they are unclean to you.
9 '[a]These you may eat, whatever is in the water: all that have
fins and scales, those in the water, in the seas or in the rivers,
you may eat.
10 '[a]But whatever is in the seas and in the rivers that does not
have fins and scales among all the teeming life of the water, and
among all the living creatures that are in the water, they are
detestable things to you,
11 and they shall be [1]abhorrent to you; you may not eat of their
flesh, and their carcasses you shall detest.
12 'Whatever in the water does not have fins and scales is
[1]abhorrent to you.
13 'These, moreover, [a]you shall detest among the birds; they are
[1]abhorrent, not to be eaten: the [2]eagle and the vulture and the
[3]buzzard,
14 and the kite and the falcon in its kind,
15 every raven in its kind,
16 and the ostrich and the owl and the sea gull and the hawk
in its kind,
17 and the little owl and the cormorant and the [1]great owl,
18 and the white owl and the [1]pelican and the carrion vulture,
19 and the stork, the heron in its kinds, and the hoopoe, and
the bat.
20 'All the [1]winged insects that walk on *all* fours are detestable
to you.
21 'Yet these you may eat among all the [1]winged insects which
walk on *all* fours: those which have above their feet jointed
legs with which to jump on the earth.
22 'These of them you may eat: the locust in its kinds, and the
devastating locust in its kinds, and the cricket in its kinds, and
the grasshopper in its kinds.
23 'But all other [1]winged insects which are four-footed are
detestable to you.

11:2 [a]Deut 14:3-21

4 [a]Acts 10:14

5 [1]A small, shy, furry animal *(Hyrax syriacus)* found in the peninsula of the Sinai, northern Israel, and the region round the Dead Sea; KJV *coney,* orig NASB *rock badger*

6 [1]Or *hare*

9 [a]Deut 14:9

10 [a]Deut 14:10

11 [1]Lit *detestable things*

12 [1]Lit *detestable things*

13 [1]Lit *a detestable thing* [2]Or *vulture* [3]Or *black vulture* [a]Deut 14:12-19

17 [1]Specifically, *great horned owl*

18 [1]Or *owl* or *jackdaw*

20 [1]Lit *swarming things with wings*

21 [1]V 20, note 1

23 [1]V 20, note 1

24 'By these, moreover, you will be made unclean: whoever
touches their carcasses becomes unclean until evening,
25 and [a]whoever picks up any of their carcasses shall wash his
clothes and be unclean until evening.
26 'Concerning all the animals which divide the hoof but do
not make a split *hoof,* or which do not chew cud, they are
unclean to you: whoever touches them becomes unclean.
27 'Also whatever walks on its paws, among all the creatures
that walk on *all* fours, are unclean to you; whoever touches
their carcasses becomes unclean until evening,
28 and the one who picks up their carcasses shall wash his
clothes and be unclean until evening; they are unclean to you.
29 'Now these are to you the unclean among the swarming
things which swarm on the earth: the mole, and the mouse,
and the [1]great lizard in its kinds,
30 and the gecko, and the [1]crocodile, and the lizard, and the
[2]sand reptile, and the chameleon.
31 'These are to you the unclean among all the swarming things;
whoever touches them when they are dead becomes unclean
until evening.
32 'Also anything on which one of them may fall when they are
dead becomes unclean, including any wooden article, or clothing,
or a skin, or a sack—any article [1]of which use is made—[a]it shall
be put in the water and be unclean until evening, then it
becomes clean.
33 'As for any [a]earthenware vessel into which one of them
may fall, whatever is in it becomes unclean and you shall break
[1]the vessel.
34 'Any of the [1]food which may be eaten, on which water
comes, shall become unclean, and any [1]liquid which may be
drunk in every vessel shall become unclean.
35 'Everything, moreover, on which part of their carcass may
fall becomes unclean; an oven or a [1]stove shall be smashed;
they are unclean and shall continue as unclean to you.
36 'Nevertheless a spring or a cistern [1]collecting water shall be
clean, though the one who touches their carcass shall be unclean.
37 'If a part of their carcass falls on any seed for sowing which
is to be sown, it is clean.
38 'Though if water is put on the seed and a part of their
carcass falls on it, it is unclean to you.
39 'Also if one of the animals dies which you have for food, the
one who touches its carcass becomes unclean until evening.
40 '[a]He too, who eats some of its carcass shall wash his clothes
and be unclean until evening, and the one who picks up its
carcass shall wash his clothes and be unclean until evening.
41 '[a]Now every swarming thing that swarms on the earth is
detestable, not to be eaten.
42 'Whatever crawls on its belly, and whatever walks on *all*
fours, whatever has many feet, in respect to every swarming
thing that swarms on the earth, you shall not eat them, for they
are detestable.

25 [a]Lev 11:40
29 [1]Or *thorn-tailed lizard*
30 [1]Or *lizard* [2]Species as yet undefined
32 [1]Lit *with which work is done* [a]Lev 15:12
33 [1]Lit *it* [a]Lev 6:28; 15:12
34 [1]I.e. if touched by a carcass; cf vv 29-32
35 [1]Lit *hearth for supporting (two) pots*
36 [1]Lit *of a gathering of*
40 [a]Lev 17:15; 22:8; Deut 14:21; Ezek 44:31
41 [a]Lev 11:29

43 '[a]Do not render [1]yourselves detestable through any of the
swarming things that swarm; and you shall not make yourselves
unclean with them so that you become unclean.
44 'For [a]I am the LORD your God. Consecrate yourselves therefore, and [b]be holy, for I am holy. And you shall not make yourselves unclean with any of the swarming things that swarm on
the earth.
45 '[a]For I am the LORD who brought you up from the land of
Egypt to be your God; thus [b]you shall be holy, for I am holy.'"
46 This is the law regarding the animal and the bird, and
every living thing that moves in the waters and everything that
swarms on the earth,
47 [a]to make a distinction between the unclean and the clean,
and between the edible creature and the creature which is not
to be eaten.

Chapter 12 Theme ____________________

12 Then the LORD spoke to Moses, saying,
2 "Speak to the sons of Israel, saying:
'When a woman [1]gives birth and bears a male *child,* then
she shall be unclean for seven days, [a]as in the days of [2]her
menstruation she shall be unclean.
3 'On [a]the eighth day the flesh of his foreskin shall be circumcised.
4 'Then she shall remain in the blood of *her* purification for
thirty-three days; she shall not touch any consecrated thing,
nor enter the sanctuary until the days of her purification are
completed.
5 'But if she bears a female *child,* then she shall be unclean
for two weeks, as in her [1]menstruation; and she shall remain
in the blood of *her* purification for sixty-six days.
6 '[a]When the days of her purification are completed, for a son
or for a daughter, she shall bring to the priest at the doorway of
the tent of meeting a one year old lamb for a burnt offering and
a young pigeon or a turtledove [b]for a sin offering.
7 'Then he shall offer it before the LORD and make atonement for
her, and she shall be cleansed from the [1]flow of her blood. This is
the law for her who bears *a child, whether* a male or a female.
8 'But if [1]she cannot afford a lamb, then she shall take [a]two
turtledoves or two young pigeons, [b]the one for a burnt offering
and the other for a sin offering; and the [c]priest shall make
atonement for her, and she will be clean.'"

Chapter 13 Theme ____________________

13 Then the LORD spoke to Moses and to Aaron, saying,
2 "When a man has on the skin of his [1]body a swelling or
a scab or a bright spot, and it becomes [2]an infection of leprosy
on the skin of his [1]body, [a]then he shall be brought to Aaron the
priest or to one of his sons the priests.

43 [1]Lit *your souls* [a]Lev 20:25

44 [a]Ex 6:7; 16:12; 23:25; Is 43:3; 51:15 [b]Lev 19:2; 1 Pet 1:16

45 [a]Ex 6:7; 20:2; Lev 22:33; 25:38; 26:45 [b]Lev 19:2; 1 Pet 1:16

47 [a]Lev 10:10; Ezek 22:26; 44:23

12:2 [1]Lit *produces seed* [2]Lit *the impurity of her sickness* [a]Lev 15:19; 18:19

3 [a]Gen 17:12; Luke 1:59; 2:21

5 [1]Lit *impurity*

6 [a]Luke 2:22 [b]Lev 5:7

7 [1]Lit *fountain*

8 [1]Lit *her hand does not find a sufficiency of a lamb* [a]Luke 2:22-24 [b]Lev 5:7 [c]Lev 4:26

13:2 [1]Lit *flesh* [2]Lit *a mark, stroke,* and so throughout the ch [a]Deut 24:8

3 "The priest shall look at the mark on the skin of the [1]body,
and if the hair in the infection has turned white and the infection
appears to be deeper than the skin of his [1]body, it is an infection
of leprosy; when the priest has looked at him, he shall pronounce
him unclean.
4 "But if the bright spot is white on the skin of his [1]body, and
[2]it does not appear to be deeper than the skin, and the hair on
it has not turned white, then the priest shall [3]isolate *him who
has* the infection for seven days.
5 "The priest shall look at him on the seventh day, and if in
his eyes the infection [1]has not changed *and* the infection has
not spread on the skin, then the priest shall [2]isolate him for
seven more days.
6 "The priest shall look at him again on the seventh day, and if
the infection has faded and the mark has not spread on the
skin, then the priest shall pronounce him clean; it is *only* a
scab. And he shall [a]wash his clothes and be clean.
7 "But if the scab spreads farther on the skin after he has shown
himself to the priest for his cleansing, he shall appear again to
the priest.
8 "The priest shall look, and if the scab has spread on the skin,
then the priest shall pronounce him unclean; it is leprosy.
9 "When the infection of leprosy is on a man, then he shall be
brought to the priest.
10 "The priest shall then look, and if there is a [a]white swelling
in the skin, and it has turned the hair white, and there is quick
raw flesh in the swelling,
11 it is [1]a chronic leprosy on the skin of his [2]body, and the
priest shall pronounce him unclean; he shall not [3]isolate him,
for he is unclean.
12 "If the leprosy breaks out farther on the skin, and the
leprosy covers all the skin of *him who has* the infection from
his head even to his feet, [1]as far as the priest can see,
13 then the priest shall look, and behold, *if* the leprosy has
covered all his [1]body, he shall pronounce clean *him who has* the
infection; it has all turned white *and* he is clean.
14 "But whenever raw flesh appears on him, he shall be unclean.
15 "The priest shall look at the raw flesh, and he shall
pronounce him unclean; the raw flesh is unclean, it is leprosy.
16 "Or if the raw flesh turns again and is changed to white,
then he shall [a]come to the priest,
17 and the priest shall look at him, and behold, *if* the infection
has turned to white, then the priest shall pronounce clean *him
who has* the infection; he is clean.
18 "When the [1]body has a boil on its skin and it is healed,
19 and in the place of the boil there is a white swelling or a
reddish-white, bright spot, then it shall be shown to the priest;
20 and the priest shall look, and behold, *if* [1]it appears to be
lower than the skin, and the hair on it has turned white, then
the priest shall pronounce him unclean; it is the infection of
leprosy, it has broken out in the boil.

3 [1]Lit *flesh*
4 [1]Lit *flesh* [2]Lit *the appearance of it is not deeper* [3]Lit *shut up*
5 [1]Lit *has stood* [2]Lit *shut up*
6 [a]Lev 11:25; 14:8
10 [a]Num 12:10; 2 Kin 5:27; 2 Chr 26:19, 20
11 [1]Lit *an old* [2]Lit *flesh* [3]Lit *shut up*
12 [1]Lit *with regard to the whole sight of the priest's eyes*
13 [1]Lit *flesh*
16 [a]Luke 5:12-14
18 [1]Lit *flesh*
20 [1]Lit *the appearance of it is lower*

21 "But if the priest looks at it, and behold, there are no white
hairs in it and it is not lower than the skin and is faded, then
the priest shall [1]isolate him for seven days;
22 and if it spreads farther on the skin, then the priest shall
pronounce him unclean; it is an infection.
23 "But if the bright spot remains in its place and does not
spread, it is *only* the scar of the boil; and the priest shall
pronounce him clean.
24 "Or if the [1]body sustains in its skin a burn by fire, and the raw
flesh of the burn becomes a bright spot, reddish-white, or white,
25 then the priest shall look at it. And if the hair in the bright
spot has [a]turned white and it appears to be deeper than the
skin, it is leprosy; it has broken out in the burn. Therefore, the
priest shall pronounce him unclean; it is an infection of leprosy.
26 "But if the priest looks at it, and indeed, there is no white
hair in the bright spot and it is no [1]deeper than the skin, but is
dim, then the priest shall [2]isolate him for seven days;
27 and the priest shall look at him on the seventh day. If it
spreads farther in the skin, then the priest shall pronounce him
unclean; it is an infection of leprosy.
28 "But if the bright spot remains in its place and has not spread
in the skin, but is dim, it is the swelling from the burn; and the
priest shall pronounce him clean, for it is *only* the scar of the
burn.
29 "Now if a man or woman has an infection on the head or on
the beard,
30 then the priest shall look at the infection, and if it appears
to be deeper than the skin and there is thin yellowish hair in it,
then the priest shall pronounce him unclean; it is a scale, it is
leprosy of the head or of the beard.
31 "But if the priest looks at the infection of the scale, and
indeed, it appears to be no deeper than the skin and there is no
black hair in it, then the priest shall [1]isolate *the person* with
the scaly infection for seven days.
32 "On the seventh day the priest shall look at the infection, and
if the scale has not spread and no yellowish hair has [1]grown in
it, and the appearance of the scale is no deeper than the skin,
33 then he shall shave himself, but he shall not shave the scale;
and the priest shall [1]isolate *the person* with the scale seven more
days.
34 "Then on the seventh day the priest shall look at the scale,
and if the scale has not spread in the skin and it appears to be
no deeper than the skin, the priest shall pronounce him clean;
and he shall wash his clothes and be clean.
35 "But if the scale spreads farther in the skin after his cleansing,
36 then the priest shall look at him, and if the scale has spread
in the skin, the priest need not seek for the yellowish hair; he
is unclean.
37 "If in his sight the scale has remained, however, and black
hair has grown in it, the scale has healed, he is clean; and the
priest shall pronounce him clean.

21 [1]Lit *shut up*

24 [1]Lit *flesh*

25 [a]Ex 4:6; Num 12:10; 2 Kin 5:27

26 [1]Lit *lower* [2]Lit *shut up*

31 [1]Lit *shut up*

32 [1]Lit *been*

33 [1]Lit *shut up*

38 "When a man or a woman has bright spots on the skin of
the [1]body, *even* white bright spots,
39 then the priest shall look, and if the bright spots on the skin
of their [1]bodies are a faint white, it is [2]eczema that has broken
out on the skin; he is clean.
40 "Now if a [1]man loses the hair of his head, he is [a]bald; he is
clean.
41 "If his head becomes bald at the [1]front and sides, he is bald on
the forehead; he is clean.
42 "But if on the bald head or the bald forehead, there occurs a
reddish-white infection, it is leprosy breaking out on his bald
head or on his bald forehead.
43 "Then [a]the priest shall look at him; and if the swelling of the
infection is reddish-white on his bald head or on his bald
forehead, like the appearance of leprosy in the skin of the [1]body,
44 he is a leprous man, he is unclean. The priest shall surely
pronounce him unclean; his infection is on his head.
45 "As for the leper who has the infection, his clothes shall be
torn, and [a]the hair of his head shall be [1]uncovered, and he shall
[b]cover his mustache and cry, '[c]Unclean! Unclean!'
46 "He shall remain unclean all the days during which he has
the infection; he is unclean. He shall live alone; his dwelling
shall be [a]outside the camp.
47 "When a garment has a [1]mark of leprosy in it, whether it is
a wool garment or a linen garment,
48 whether in [1]warp or woof, of linen or of wool, whether in
leather or in any article made of leather,
49 if the mark is greenish or reddish in the garment or in the
leather, or in the [1]warp or in the woof, or in any article of
leather, it is a leprous mark and shall be shown to the priest.
50 "Then [a]the priest shall look at the mark and shall [1]quarantine
the article with the mark for seven days.
51 "He shall then look at the mark on the seventh day; if the
mark has spread in the garment, whether in the warp or in the
woof, or in the leather, whatever the purpose for which the
leather is used, the mark is a [1]leprous malignancy, it is unclean.
52 "So he shall burn the garment, whether the warp or the woof,
in wool or in linen, or any article of leather in which the mark
occurs, for it is a [1]leprous malignancy; it shall be burned in the fire.
53 "But if the priest shall look, and indeed the mark has not
spread in the garment, either in the warp or in the woof, or in
any article of leather,
54 then the priest shall order them to wash the thing in which
the mark occurs and he shall [1]quarantine it for seven more days.
55 "After the article with the mark has been washed, the priest
shall again look, and if the mark has not changed its appearance,
even though the mark has not spread, it is unclean; you shall
burn it in the fire, whether an eating away has produced
bareness on the top or on the front of it.
56 "Then if the priest looks, and if the mark has faded after it
has been washed, then he shall tear it out of the garment or
out of the leather, whether from the warp or from the woof;

38 [1]Lit *flesh*
39 [1]Lit *flesh* [2]Lit *tetter*
40 [1]Lit *man's head becomes bald* [a]2 Kin 2:23; Is 15:2; Amos 8:10
41 [1]Lit *border of his face*
43 [1]Lit *flesh* [a]Lev 10:10; Ezek 22:26
45 [1]Or *disheveled* [a]Lev 10:6 [b]Ezek 24:17, 22; Mic 3:7 [c]Lam 4:15
46 [a]Num 5:1-4; 12:14
47 [1]Lit *infection,* and so throughout the ch
48 [1]Or *weaving or texture*
49 [1]Or *weaving or texture*
50 [1]Lit *shut up* [a]Ezek 44:23
51 [1]Lit *malignant leprosy*
52 [1]Lit *malignant leprosy*
54 [1]Lit *shut up*

57 and if it appears again in the garment, whether in the warp
or in the woof, or in any article of leather, it is an outbreak; the
article with the mark shall be burned in the fire.
58 "The garment, whether the warp or the woof, or any article of
leather from which the mark has departed when you washed
it, it shall then be washed a second time and will be clean."
59 This is the law for the mark of leprosy in a garment of wool
or linen, whether in the warp or in the woof, or in any article
of leather, for pronouncing it clean or unclean.

Chapter 14 Theme ______________________________

14 Then the LORD spoke to Moses, saying,
2 "This shall be the law of the leper in the day of his
cleansing. [a]Now he shall be brought to the priest,
3 and the priest shall go [a]out to the outside of the camp. Thus
the priest shall look, and if the [1]infection of leprosy has been
healed in the leper,
4 then the priest shall give orders to take two live clean birds
and [a]cedar wood and a [1]scarlet string and hyssop for the one
who is to be cleansed.
5 "The priest shall also give orders to slay the one bird in an
earthenware vessel over [1]running water.
6 "*As for* the live bird, he shall take it together with [a]the cedar
wood and the [1]scarlet string and the [b]hyssop, and shall dip them
and the live bird in the blood of the bird that was slain over the
[2]running water.
7 "[a]He shall then sprinkle seven times the one who is to be
cleansed from the leprosy and shall pronounce him clean, and
shall let the live bird go free over the open field.
8 "[a]The one to be cleansed shall then wash his clothes and
shave off all his hair and bathe in water and [b]be clean. Now
afterward, he may enter the camp, but he [c]shall stay outside
his tent for seven days.
9 "It will be on the seventh day that he shall shave off all his
hair: he shall shave his head and his beard and his eyebrows,
even all his hair. He shall then wash his clothes and bathe his
[1]body in water and [a]be clean.
10 "Now on the eighth day he is to take two male lambs without
defect, and a yearling ewe lamb without defect, and three-tenths
of an [1]*ephah* of fine flour mixed with oil for a grain offering, and
one [2a]log of oil;
11 and the priest who pronounces him clean shall present the
man to be cleansed and the [1]aforesaid before the LORD at the
doorway of the tent of meeting.
12 "Then the priest shall take the one male lamb and bring it
for a [a]guilt offering, with the [1b]log of oil, and present them as a
[c]wave offering before the LORD.
13 "Next he shall slaughter the male lamb in [a]the place where
they slaughter the sin offering and the burnt offering, at the
place of the sanctuary—for the guilt offering, [b]like the sin offering,
belongs to the priest; it is most holy.

14:2 [a]Matt 8:4; Mark 1:44; Luke 5:14; 17:14

3 [1]Lit *mark, stroke,* and so throughout the ch [a]Lev 13:46

4 [1]Lit *scarlet color and* [a]Lev 14:6, 49, 51, 52; Num 19:6

5 [1]Lit *living*

6 [1]Lit *scarlet color and* [2]Lit *living* [a]Lev 14:4 [b]Ps 51:7

7 [a]Ezek 36:25

8 [a]Lev 11:25; 13:6; Num 8:7 [b]Lev 14:9, 20 [c]Num 5:2, 3; 12:14, 15; 2 Chr 26:21

9 [1]Lit *flesh* [a]Lev 14:8, 20

10 [1]I.e. Approx one bu [2]I.e. Approx one pt [a]Lev 14:12, 15, 21, 24

11 [1]Lit *them*

12 [1]I.e. Approx one pt [a]Lev 5:6, 18; 6:6; 14:19 [b]Lev 14:10 [c]Ex 29:22-24, 26

13 [a]Ex 29:11; Lev 1:11; 4:24 [b]Lev 6:24-30; 7:7

14 "The priest shall then take some of the blood of the [a]guilt
offering, and the priest shall put *it* on [b]the lobe of the right ear
of the one to be cleansed, and on the thumb of his right hand
and on the big toe of his right foot.
15 "The priest shall also take some of the [1a]log of oil, and pour
it into his left palm;
16 the priest shall then dip his right-hand finger into the oil
that is in his left palm, and with his finger sprinkle some of the
oil seven times before the LORD.
17 "Of the remaining oil which is in his palm, the priest shall
put some on the right ear lobe of the one to be cleansed, and
on the thumb of his right hand, and on the big toe of his right
foot, on the blood of the guilt offering;
18 while the rest of the oil that is in the priest's palm, he shall
put on the head of the one to be cleansed. So the priest shall
make [a]atonement on his behalf before the LORD.
19 "The priest shall next offer the [a]sin offering and make
atonement for the one to be cleansed from his uncleanness.
Then afterward, he shall slaughter the burnt offering.
20 "The priest shall offer up the burnt offering and the grain
offering on the altar. Thus the priest shall make atonement for
him, and [a]he will be clean.
21 "[a]But if he is poor and his [1]means are insufficient, then he is
to take one male lamb for a [b]guilt offering as a wave offering to
make atonement for him, and one-tenth *of an [2]ephah* of fine
flour mixed with oil for a grain offering, and a [3c]log of oil,
22 and two turtledoves or two young pigeons which [1]are
within his means, [a]the one shall be a [b]sin offering and the
other a burnt offering.
23 "[a]Then the eighth day he shall bring them for his cleansing to
the priest, at the doorway of the tent of meeting, before the LORD.
24 "The priest shall take the lamb of the guilt offering and [a]the
[1]log of oil, and the priest shall offer them for a wave offering
before the LORD.
25 "Next he shall slaughter the lamb of the guilt offering; and
the priest is to take some of the blood of the guilt offering and put
it on [a]the lobe of the right ear of the one to be cleansed and on
the thumb of his right hand and on the big toe of his right foot.
26 "The priest shall also pour some of the oil into his left palm;
27 and with his right-hand finger the priest shall sprinkle some
of the oil that is in his left palm seven times before the LORD.
28 "The priest shall then put some of the oil that is in his palm
on the lobe of the right ear of the one to be cleansed, and on
the thumb of his right hand and on the big toe of his right foot,
on the place of the blood of the guilt offering.
29 "Moreover, the rest of the oil that is in the priest's palm he
shall put on the head of the one to be cleansed, to make
atonement on his behalf before the LORD.
30 "He shall then offer one of the turtledoves or young pigeons,
[1]which are within his means.
31 "*He shall offer* what [1]he can afford, [a]the one for a sin offering
and the other for a burnt offering, together with the grain

14 [a]Lev 14:19 [b]Ex 29:20; Lev 8:23, 24
15 [1]I.e. Approx one pt [a]Lev 14:10
18 [a]Lev 4:26; Num 15:28; Heb 2:17
19 [a]Lev 14:12
20 [a]Lev 14:8, 9
21 [1]Lit *hand is not reaching* [2]I.e. Approx one bu [3]I.e. Approx one pt [a]Lev 5:11; 12:8; 27:8 [b]Lev 14:22 [c]Lev 14:10
22 [1]Lit *his hand reaches* [a]Lev 5:7 [b]Lev 14:21, 24, 25
23 [a]Lev 14:10, 11
24 [1]I.e. Approx one pt [a]Lev 14:10
25 [a]Lev 14:14
30 [1]Lit *from those which his hand can reach*
31 [1]Lit *his hand can reach* [a]Lev 5:7

offering. So the priest shall make atonement before the LORD
on behalf of the one to be cleansed.
32 "This is the law *for him* in whom there is an infection of
leprosy, whose [1]means are limited for his cleansing."
33 The LORD further spoke to Moses and to Aaron, saying:
34 "[a]When you enter the land of Canaan, which I give you for
a possession, and I put a mark of leprosy on a house in the land
of your possession,
35 then the one who owns the house shall come and tell the
priest, saying, '*Something* like [a]a mark *of leprosy* has become
visible to me in the house.'
36 "The priest shall then command that they empty the house
before the priest goes in to look at the mark, so that everything
in the house need not become unclean; and afterward the
priest shall go in to look at the house.
37 "So he shall look at the mark, and if the mark on the walls of
the house has greenish or reddish depressions and appears
deeper than the [1]surface,
38 then the priest shall come out of the house, to the [1]doorway,
and [2]quarantine the house for seven days.
39 "The priest shall return on the seventh day and [1]make an
inspection. If the mark has indeed spread in the walls of the house,
40 then the priest shall order them to tear out the stones with
the mark in them and throw them away [1]at an unclean place
outside the city.
41 "He shall have the house scraped all around [1]inside, and
they shall dump the plaster that they scrape off at an unclean
place outside the city.
42 "Then they shall take other stones and replace *those* stones,
and he shall take other plaster and replaster the house.
43 "If, however, the mark breaks out again in the house after
he has torn out the stones and scraped the house, and after it
has been replastered,
44 then the priest shall come in and [1]make an inspection. If
he sees that the mark has indeed spread in the house, it is [a]a
malignant mark in the house; it is unclean.
45 "He shall therefore tear down the house, its stones, and its
timbers, and all the plaster of the house, and he shall take *them*
outside the city to an [a]unclean place.
46 "Moreover, whoever goes into the house during the time
that he has [1]quarantined it, becomes [a]unclean until evening.
47 "Likewise, whoever lies down in the house shall wash his
clothes, and whoever eats in the house shall wash his clothes.
48 "If, on the other hand, the priest comes in and [1]makes an
inspection and the mark has not indeed spread in the house after
the house has been replastered, then the priest shall pronounce
the house clean because the mark has [2]not reappeared.
49 "To cleanse the house then, he shall take [a]two birds and
cedar wood and a [1]scarlet string and hyssop,
50 and he shall slaughter the one bird in an earthenware
vessel over [1]running water.

32 [1]Lit *hand does not reach*
34 [a]Gen 17:8; Num 32:22; Deut 7:1; 32:49
35 [a]Ps 91:10
37 [1]Lit *wall*
38 [1]Lit *doorway of the house* [2]Lit *shut up*
39 [1]Lit *look*
40 [1]Lit *to*
41 [1]Lit *from the house around*
44 [1]Lit *look* [a]Lev 13:51
45 [a]Lev 14:41
46 [1]Lit *shut up* [a]Num 19:7, 10, 21, 22
48 [1]Lit *looks* [2]Lit *healed*
49 [1]Lit *scarlet color* [a]Lev 14:4
50 [1]Lit *living*

51 "Then he shall take the cedar wood and the [a]hyssop and the
[1]scarlet string, with the live bird, and dip them in the blood of
the slain bird as well as in the [2]running water, and sprinkle the
house seven times.
52 "He shall thus cleanse the house with the blood of the bird
and with the [1]running water, along with the live bird and with
the cedar wood and with the hyssop and with the [2]scarlet
string.
53 "However, he shall let the live bird go free outside the city
into the open field. So he shall make atonement for the house,
and it will be clean."
54 This is the law for any mark of leprosy—even for a [a]scale,
55 and for the [a]leprous garment or house,
56 and [a]for a swelling, and for a scab, and for a bright spot—
57 to teach [1]when they are unclean and [2]when they are clean.
This is the law of leprosy.

Chapter 15 Theme ____________________

15 The LORD also spoke to Moses and to Aaron, saying,
2 "Speak to the sons of Israel, and say to them, '[a]When any
man has a discharge from his [1]body, [2]his discharge is unclean.
3 'This, moreover, shall be his uncleanness in his discharge: it
is his uncleanness whether his body allows its discharge to
flow or whether his body obstructs its discharge.
4 'Every bed on which the person with the discharge lies
becomes unclean, and everything on which he sits becomes
unclean.
5 'Anyone, moreover, who touches his bed shall wash his
clothes and bathe in water and be unclean until evening;
6 and whoever sits on the thing on which the man with the
discharge has been sitting, shall wash his clothes and bathe in
water and be unclean until evening.
7 'Also whoever touches the [1]person with the discharge shall
wash his clothes and bathe in water and be unclean until
evening.
8 'Or if the man with the discharge spits on one who is clean,
he too shall wash his clothes and bathe in water and be
unclean until evening.
9 'Every saddle on which the person with the discharge rides
becomes unclean.
10 'Whoever then touches any of the things which were under
him shall be unclean until evening, and he who carries them
shall wash his clothes and bathe in water and be unclean until
evening.
11 'Likewise, whomever the one with the discharge touches
without having rinsed his hands in water shall wash his clothes
and bathe in water and be unclean until evening.
12 'However, an [a]earthenware vessel which the person with
the discharge touches shall be broken, and every wooden vessel
shall be rinsed in water.

51 [1]Lit *scarlet color* [2]Lit *living* [a]1 Kin 4:33; Ps 51:7

52 [1]Lit *living* [2]Lit *scarlet color*

54 [a]Lev 13:30

55 [a]Lev 13:47-52

56 [a]Lev 13:2

57 [1]Lit *in the day of uncleanness* [2]Lit *in the day of cleanness*

15:2 [1]Lit *flesh,* and so throughout the ch [2]Or *by his discharge, he is unclean* [a]Lev 22:4; Num 5:2; 2 Sam 3:29

7 [1]Lit *flesh*

12 [a]Lev 6:28; 11:33

13 'Now when the man with the discharge becomes cleansed
from his discharge, then he [a]shall count off for himself seven
days for his cleansing; he shall then wash his clothes and bathe
his body in [1]running water and will become clean.
14 'Then on the eighth day he shall take for himself [a]two
turtledoves or two young pigeons, and come before the LORD to
the doorway of the tent of meeting and give them to the priest;
15 and the priest shall offer them, [a]one for a sin offering and the
other for a burnt offering. So [b]the priest shall make atonement
on his behalf before the LORD because of his discharge.
16 '[a]Now if a [1]man has a seminal emission, he shall bathe all
his body in water and be unclean until evening.
17 'As for any garment or any leather on which there is seminal
emission, it shall be washed with water and be unclean until
evening.
18 'If a man lies with a woman *so that* there is a seminal
emission, they shall both bathe in water and be [a]unclean until
evening.
19 '[a]When a woman has a discharge, *if* her discharge in her
body is blood, she shall continue in her menstrual impurity for
seven days; and whoever touches her shall be unclean until
evening.
20 'Everything also on which she lies during her menstrual
impurity shall be unclean, and everything on which she sits
shall be unclean.
21 'Anyone who touches her bed shall wash his clothes and
bathe in water and be unclean until evening.
22 'Whoever touches any thing on which she sits shall wash
his clothes and bathe in water and be unclean until evening.
23 'Whether it be on the bed or on the thing on which she is
sitting, when he touches it, he shall be unclean until evening.
24 '[a]If a man actually lies with her so that her menstrual
impurity is on him, he shall be unclean seven days, and every
bed on which he lies shall be unclean.
25 '[a]Now if a woman has a discharge of her blood many days,
not at the period of her menstrual impurity, or if she has a
discharge beyond [1]that period, all the days of her impure
discharge she shall continue as though [2]in her menstrual
impurity; she is unclean.
26 'Any bed on which she lies all the days of her discharge
shall be to her like [1]her bed at menstruation; and every thing on
which she sits shall be unclean, like [2]her uncleanness at that
time.
27 'Likewise, whoever touches them shall be unclean and shall
wash his clothes and bathe in water and be unclean until
evening.
28 'When she becomes clean from her discharge, she shall
count off for herself seven days; and afterward she will be clean.
29 'Then on the eighth day she shall take for herself two
turtledoves or two young pigeons and bring them in to the
priest, to the doorway of the tent of meeting.

13 [1]Lit *living* [a]Lev 8:33; 14:8

14 [a]Lev 14:22, 23

15 [a]Lev 5:7; 14:31 [b]Lev 14:19, 31

16 [1]Lit *man's . . . goes out from him* [a]Lev 22:4; Deut 23:10, 11

18 [a]1 Sam 21:4

19 [a]Lev 12:2

24 [a]Lev 18:19; 20:18

25 [1]Lit *her menstrual impurity* [2]Lit *in the days of* [a]Matt 9:20; Mark 5:25; Luke 8:43

26 [1]Lit *the bed of her menstrual impurity* [2]Lit *the uncleanness of her menstrual impurity*

30 [a]Lev 5:7

31 [1]Or *dwelling place* [a]Lev 20:3; Num 19:13, 20; Ezek 5:11; 36:17

32 [1]Lit *whose seminal emission goes out from him*

16:1 [a]Lev 10:1, 2

2 [1]Lit *propitiatory* [a]Ex 30:10; Heb 6:19; 9:7, 25 [b]Ex 25:21, 22; 40:34; 1 Kin 8:10-12

3 [1]Or *bull of the herd* [a]Lev 4:1-12; 16:6; Heb 9:7

4 [1]Lit *flesh* [a]Ex 28:39, 42 [b]Ex 30:20; Lev 16:24; Heb 10:22

5 [a]Lev 4:13-21; 2 Chr 29:21; Ezek 45:22

6 [a]Heb 5:3

30 'The priest shall offer the [a]one for a sin offering and the
other for a burnt offering. So the priest shall make atonement
on her behalf before the LORD because of her impure
discharge.'
31 "Thus you shall keep the sons of Israel separated from their
uncleanness, so that they will not die in their uncleanness by
their [a]defiling My [1]tabernacle that is among them."
32 This is the law for the one with a discharge, and for the
man [1]who has a seminal emission so that he is unclean by it,
33 and for the woman who is ill because of menstrual impurity,
and for the one who has a discharge, whether a male or a
female, or a man who lies with an unclean woman.

Chapter 16 Theme ____________

16 Now the LORD spoke to Moses after [a]the death of the two
sons of Aaron, when they had approached the presence
of the LORD and died.
2 The LORD said to Moses:
"**T**ell your brother Aaron that he shall not enter [a]at any time
into the holy place inside the veil, before the [1]mercy seat which
is on the ark, or he will die; for [b]I will appear in the cloud over
the [1]mercy seat.
3 "Aaron shall enter the holy place with this: with a [1]bull for a
[a]sin offering and a ram for a burnt offering.
4 "He shall put on the [a]holy linen tunic, and the linen undergarments shall be next to his [1]body, and he shall be girded with
the linen sash and attired with the linen turban (these are holy
garments). Then he shall [b]bathe his [1]body in water and put
them on.
5 "He shall take from the congregation of the sons of Israel
[a]two male goats for a sin offering and one ram for a burnt
offering.
6 "Then [a]Aaron shall offer the bull for the sin offering which
is for himself, that he may make atonement for himself and for
his household.
7 "He shall take the two goats and present them before the
LORD at the doorway of the tent of meeting.

RETURN TO INSTRUCTIONS

INSIGHT

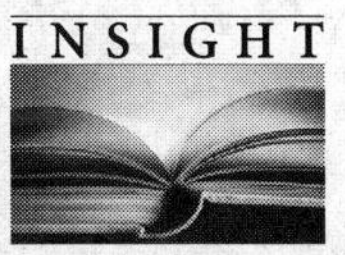

As you study the day of atonement in Leviticus, consult the chart **The Feasts of Israel** on pages 214, 215.

Inside the Tabernacle

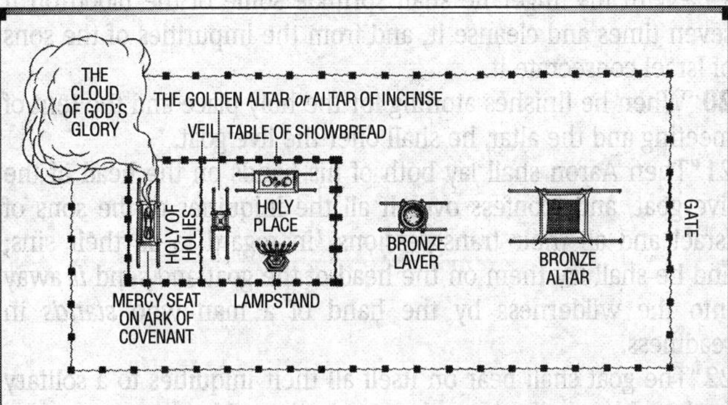

8 "Aaron shall cast lots for the two goats, one lot for the LORD
and the other lot for the [1]scapegoat.
9 "Then Aaron shall offer the goat on which the lot for the
LORD fell, and make it a sin offering.
10 "But the goat on which the lot for the [1]scapegoat fell shall
be presented alive before the LORD, to make [a]atonement upon
it, to send it into the wilderness as the [1]scapegoat.
11 "Then Aaron shall offer the bull of the sin offering [a]which is
for himself and make atonement for himself and [b]for his
household, and he shall slaughter the bull of the sin offering
which is for himself.
12 "He shall take a [a]firepan full of coals of fire from upon the
altar before the LORD and [1]two handfuls of finely ground [b]sweet
incense, and bring *it* inside the veil.
13 "He shall put the incense on the fire before the LORD, that
the cloud of incense may cover the [1a]mercy seat that is on *the*
ark of the testimony, [b]otherwise he will die.
14 "Moreover, [a]he shall take some of the blood of the bull and
sprinkle *it* [b]with his finger on the [1]mercy seat on the east *side;*
also in front of the [1]mercy seat he shall sprinkle some of the
blood with his finger seven times.
15 "Then he shall slaughter the goat of the sin offering [a]which
is for the people, and bring its blood inside the veil and do with
its blood as he did with the blood of the bull, and sprinkle it on
the [1]mercy seat and in front of the [1]mercy seat.
16 "[a]He shall make atonement for the holy place, because of
the impurities of the sons of Israel and because of their
transgressions in regard to all their sins; and thus he shall do
for the tent of meeting which abides with them in the midst of
their impurities.
17 "When he goes in to make atonement in the holy place, no
one shall be in the tent of meeting until he comes out, that he
may make atonement for himself and for his household and for
all the assembly of Israel.
18 "Then he shall go out to the altar that is before the LORD and
make atonement for it, and shall take some of the blood of the
bull and of the blood of the goat and [a]put it on the horns of the
altar on all sides.
19 "[a]With his finger he shall sprinkle some of the blood on it
seven times and cleanse it, and from the impurities of the sons
of Israel consecrate it.
20 "When he finishes atoning for the holy place and the tent of
meeting and the altar, he shall offer the live goat.
21 "Then Aaron shall lay both of his hands on the head of the
live goat, and [a]confess over it all the iniquities of the sons of
Israel and all their transgressions [1]in regard to all their sins;
and he shall lay them on the head of the goat and send *it* away
into the wilderness by the hand of a man who *stands* in
readiness.
22 "The goat shall bear on itself all their iniquities to a solitary
land; and he shall release the goat in the wilderness.

8 [1]Lit *goat of removal,* or else a name: *Azazel*

10 [1]Lit *goat of removal,* or else a name: *Azazel* [a]Is 53:4-10; Rom 3:25; 1 John 2:2

11 [a]Heb 7:27; 9:7 [b]Lev 16:33

12 [1]Lit *the filling of the hollow of his hands* [a]Lev 10:1; Num 16:18 [b]Ex 30:34-38

13 [1]Lit *propitiatory* [a]Ex 25:21 [b]Ex 28:43; Lev 22:9; Num 4:15, 20

14 [1]Lit *propitiatory* [a]Heb 9:25 [b]Lev 4:6, 17

15 [1]Lit *propitiatory* [a]Heb 7:27; 9:7, 12

16 [a]Ex 29:36, 37; 30:10; Heb 2:17

18 [a]Lev 4:25; Ezek 43:20, 22

19 [a]Lev 16:14; Ezek 43:20

21 [1]Lit *in addition to* [a]Lev 5:5

23 "Then Aaron shall come into the tent of meeting and take
off [a]the linen garments which he put on when he went into
the holy place, and shall leave them there.
24 "[a]He shall bathe his [1]body with water in a holy place and
put on [b]his clothes, and come forth and offer his burnt offering
and the burnt offering of the people and make atonement for
himself and for the people.
25 "Then he shall offer up in smoke the fat of the sin offering
on the altar.
26 "The one who released the goat as the [1]scapegoat [a]shall wash
his clothes and bathe his [2]body with water; then afterward he
shall come into the camp.
27 "But the bull of the sin offering and the goat of the sin
offering, [a]whose blood was brought in to make atonement in
the holy place, shall be taken outside the camp, and they shall
burn their hides, their flesh, and their refuse in the fire.
28 "Then the [a]one who burns them shall wash his clothes and
bathe his body with water, then afterward he shall come into
the camp.
29 "*This* shall be a permanent statute for you: [a]in the seventh
month, on the tenth day of the month, you shall humble your
souls and not [b]do any work, whether the native, or the alien
who sojourns among you;
30 for it is on this day that [1]atonement shall be made for you
to [a]cleanse you; you will be clean from all your sins before the
LORD.
31 "It is to be a sabbath of solemn rest for you, that you may
[a]humble your souls; it is a permanent statute.
32 "So the priest who is anointed and [1]ordained to serve as
priest in his father's place shall make atonement: he shall thus
put on [a]the linen garments, the holy garments,
33 and make atonement for the holy sanctuary, and he shall
make atonement for the tent of meeting and for the altar. He
shall also make atonement for [a]the priests and for all the people
of the assembly.
34 "Now you shall have this as a [a]permanent statute, to [b]make
atonement for the sons of Israel for all their sins once every
year." And just as the LORD had commanded Moses, *so* he did.

Chapter 17 Theme ______________________________

17 Then the LORD spoke to Moses, saying,
2 "Speak to Aaron and to his sons and to all the sons of
Israel and say to them, 'This is what the LORD has commanded,
saying,
3 "Any man from the house of Israel who slaughters an ox or a
lamb or a goat in the camp, or who slaughters it outside the camp,
4 and [a]has not brought it to the doorway of the tent of meeting
to present *it* as an offering to the LORD before the [1]tabernacle of
the LORD, bloodguiltiness is to be reckoned to that man. He has
shed blood and that man shall be cut off from among his people.

23 [a]Lev 16:4; Ezek 42:14; 44:19
24 [1]Lit *flesh* [a]Lev 16:4 [b]Ex 28:40, 41
26 [1]Lit *goat of removal,* or else a name: *Azazel* [2]Lit *flesh* [a]Lev 11:25, 40
27 [a]Lev 6:30; Heb 13:11
28 [a]Num 19:8
29 [a]Lev 23:27; Num 29:7 [b]Ex 31:14, 15
30 [1]Lit *he shall make atonement* [a]Ps 51:2; Jer 33:8; Eph 5:26
31 [a]Lev 23:32; Ezra 8:21; Is 58:3, 5; Dan 10:12
32 [1]Lit *whose hand is filled* [a]Lev 16:4
33 [a]Lev 16:11
34 [a]Lev 23:31 [b]Heb 9:7
17:4 [1]Lit *dwelling place* [a]Deut 12:5-21

5 “[1]The reason is so that the sons of Israel may bring their sacrifices which they were sacrificing in the open field, that they may bring them in to the LORD, at the doorway of the tent of meeting to the priest, and sacrifice them as sacrifices of peace offerings to the LORD.

6 “The priest shall sprinkle the blood on the altar of the LORD at the doorway of the tent of meeting, and [a]offer up the fat in smoke as a soothing aroma to the LORD.

7 “[a]They shall no longer sacrifice their sacrifices to the [1]goat demons with which they play the harlot. This shall be a permanent statute to them throughout their generations.”’

8 “Then you shall say to them, ‘Any man from the house of Israel, or from the aliens who sojourn among them, who offers a burnt offering or sacrifice,

9 and [a]does not bring it to the doorway of the tent of meeting to [1]offer it to the LORD, that man also shall be cut off from his people.

10 ‘[a]And any man from the house of Israel, or from the aliens who sojourn among them, who eats any blood, [b]I will set My face against that person who eats blood and will cut him off from among his people.

11 ‘For [a]the [1]life of the flesh is in the blood, and I have given it to you on the altar to make atonement for your souls; for [b]it is the blood by reason of the [1]life that makes atonement.’

12 “Therefore I said to the sons of Israel, ‘No person among you may eat blood, nor may any alien who sojourns among you eat blood.’

13 “So when any man from the sons of Israel, or from the aliens who sojourn among them, [1]in hunting catches a beast or a bird which may be eaten, [a]he shall pour out its blood and cover it with earth.

14 “[a]For *as for the* [1]life of all flesh, its blood is *identified* with its [1]life. Therefore I said to the sons of Israel, ‘You are not to eat the blood of any flesh, for the [1]life of all flesh is its blood; whoever eats it shall be cut off.’

15 “[a]When any person eats *an animal* which dies or is torn *by beasts,* whether he is a native or an alien, he shall wash his clothes and bathe in water, and remain unclean until evening; then he will become clean.

16 “But if he does not wash *them* or bathe his body, then [a]he shall bear his [1]guilt.”

Chapter 18 Theme ________________________________

18 Then the LORD spoke to Moses, saying,
2 “Speak to the sons of Israel and say to them, ‘[a]I am the LORD your God.

3 ‘You shall not do [1]what is [a]done in the land of Egypt where you lived, nor are you to do [1]what is [b]done in the land of Canaan where I am bringing you; you shall not walk in their statutes.

4 ‘You are to perform My judgments and keep My statutes, [1]to live in accord with them; [a]I am the LORD your God.

5 [1]Lit *In order that*

6 [a]Num 18:17

7 [1]Or *goat-idols* [a]Ex 22:20; 32:8; 34:15; Deut 32:17; 2 Chr 11:15; Ps 106:37f; 1 Cor 10:20

9 [1]Lit *do* [a]Ex 20:24; Lev 17:4

10 [a]Gen 9:4; Lev 3:17; 7:26, 27; Deut 12:16, 23-25; 1 Sam 14:33 [b]Lev 20:3, 6; Jer 44:11

11 [1]Lit *soul* [a]Gen 9:4; Lev 17:14 [b]Heb 9:22

13 [1]Lit *who in hunting* [a]Deut 12:16

14 [1]Lit *soul* [a]Gen 9:4; Lev 17:11

15 [a]Ex 22:31; Lev 7:24; 22:8; Deut 14:21

16 [1]Or *iniquity* [a]Num 19:20

18:2 [a]Ex 6:7; Lev 11:44; Ezek 20:5

3 [1]Lit *according to the deed of* [a]Ezek 20:7, 8 [b]Lev 18:24-30; 20:23

4 [1]Lit *to walk in them* [a]Lev 18:2

5 'So you shall keep My statutes and My judgments, [a]by
which a man may live if he does them; I am the LORD.
6 'None of you shall approach any blood relative [1]of his to
uncover nakedness; I am the LORD.
7 '[a]You shall not uncover the nakedness of your father, that is,
the nakedness of your mother. She is your mother; you are not
to uncover her nakedness.
8 '[a]You shall not uncover the nakedness of your father's wife; it
is your father's nakedness.
9 '[a]The nakedness of your sister, *either* your father's daughter or
your mother's daughter, whether born at home or born outside,
their nakedness you shall not uncover.
10 'The nakedness of your son's daughter or your daughter's
daughter, their nakedness you shall not uncover; for [1]their nakedness is yours.
11 'The nakedness of your father's wife's daughter, [1]born to your
father, she is your sister, you shall not uncover her nakedness.
12 '[a]You shall not uncover the nakedness of your father's sister;
she is your father's blood relative.
13 'You shall not uncover the nakedness of your mother's sister,
for she is your mother's blood relative.
14 '[a]You shall not uncover the nakedness of your father's
brother; you shall not approach his wife, she is your aunt.
15 '[a]You shall not uncover the nakedness of your daughter-in-
law; she is your son's wife, you shall not uncover her nakedness.
16 '[a]You shall not uncover the nakedness of your brother's wife;
it is your brother's nakedness.
17 '[a]You shall not uncover the nakedness of a woman and of her
daughter, nor shall you take her son's daughter or her daughter's
daughter, to uncover her nakedness; they are blood relatives. It
is [1]lewdness.
18 'You shall not [1]marry a woman in addition to [2]her sister [3]as
a rival while she is alive, to uncover her nakedness.
19 '[a]Also you shall not approach a woman to uncover her
nakedness during her [b]menstrual impurity.
20 '[a]You shall not have intercourse with your neighbor's wife,
to be defiled with her.
21 'You shall not give any of your offspring [a]to [1]offer them to
Molech, nor shall you [b]profane the name of your God; I am the
LORD.
22 '[a]You shall not lie with a male as [1]one lies with a female; it
is an abomination.
23 '[a]Also you shall not have intercourse with any animal to be
defiled with it, nor shall any woman stand before an animal to
[1]mate with it; it is a perversion.
24 'Do not defile yourselves by any of these things; for by all
these [a]the nations which I am casting out before you have
become defiled.
25 'For the land has become defiled, [a]therefore I have brought
its [1]punishment upon it, so the land [b]has spewed out its
inhabitants.

5 [a]Neh 9:29; Ezek 18:9; 20:11; Luke 10:28; Rom 10:5; Gal 3:12
6 [1]Lit *of his flesh*
7 [a]Lev 20:11; Deut 27:20; Ezek 22:10
8 [a]Lev 20:11; Deut 22:30; 27:20; 1 Cor 5:1
9 [a]Lev 18:11; 20:17; Deut 27:22
10 [1]Lit *they are your nakedness*
11 [1]Lit *begotten of*
12 [a]Lev 20:19
14 [a]Lev 20:20
15 [a]Lev 20:12
16 [a]Lev 20:21
17 [1]Or *wickedness* [a]Lev 20:14
18 [1]Lit *take a wife* [2]Or *another* [3]Lit *to be*
19 [a]Lev 15:24; 20:18 [b]Lev 12:2
20 [a]Lev 20:10; Prov 6:29; Matt 5:27, 28; 1 Cor 6:9; Heb 13:4
21 [1]Lit *cause to pass over* [a]Lev 20:2-5; Deut 12:31 [b]Lev 19:12; 20:3; 21:6; Ezek 36:20; Mal 1:12
22 [1]Lit *those who lie* [a]Lev 20:13; Deut 23:18 mg; Rom 1:27
23 [1]Or *lie* [a]Ex 22:19; Lev 20:15, 16; Deut 27:21
24 [a]Lev 18:3; Deut 18:12
25 [1]Lit *iniquity* [a]Lev 20:23; Deut 9:5; 18:12 [b]Lev 18:28; 20:22

26 'But as for you, you are to keep My statutes and My judgments and shall not do any of these abominations, *neither* the native, nor the alien who sojourns among you
27 (for the men of the land who have been before you have done all these abominations, and the land has become defiled);
28 so that the land will not spew you out, should you defile it, as it has spewed out the nation which has been before you.
29 'For whoever does any of these abominations, [1]those persons who do *so* shall be cut off from among their people.
30 'Thus you are to keep [a]My charge, that you do not practice any of the abominable customs which have been practiced before you, so as not to defile yourselves with them; [b]I am the LORD your God.'"

29 [1]Or *and the*
30 [a]Lev 22:9; Deut 11:1 [b]Lev 18:2

Chapter 19 Theme ______________________

19 Then the LORD spoke to Moses, saying:
2 "Speak to all the congregation of the sons of Israel and
say to them, '[a]You shall be holy, for I the LORD your God am holy.
3 'Every one of you [a]shall reverence his mother and his father,
and you shall keep [b]My sabbaths; [c]I am the LORD your God.
4 'Do not turn to [a]idols or make for yourselves molten [b]gods; I
am the LORD your God.
5 'Now when you offer a sacrifice of peace offerings to the
LORD, you shall offer it so that you may be accepted.
6 'It shall be eaten the same day you offer *it,* and the next
day; but what remains until the third day shall be burned with
fire.
7 'So if it is eaten at all on the third day, it is an offense; it will
not be accepted.
8 'Everyone who eats it will bear his iniquity, for he has
profaned the holy thing of the LORD; and that person shall be
cut off from his people.
9 '[a]Now when you reap the harvest of your land, you shall
not reap to the very corners of your field, nor shall you gather
the gleanings of your harvest.
10 'Nor shall you glean your vineyard, nor shall you gather the
fallen fruit of your vineyard; you shall leave them for the needy
and for the stranger. I am the LORD your God.
11 '[a]You shall not steal, nor deal falsely, [b]nor lie to one another.
12 '[a]You shall not swear falsely by My name, so as to [b]profane
the name of your God; I am the LORD.
13 '[a]You shall not oppress your neighbor, nor rob *him.* [b]The
wages of a hired man are not to remain with you all night until
morning.
14 'You shall not curse a deaf man, nor [a]place a stumbling
block before the blind, but you shall revere your God; I am the
LORD.
15 '[a]You shall do no injustice in judgment; you shall not be
partial to the poor nor defer to the great, but you are to judge
your neighbor fairly.

19:2 [a]Ex 19:6; Lev 11:44; 20:7, 26; Eph 1:4; 1 Pet 1:16
3 [a]Ex 20:12; 31:13; Deut 5:16 [b]Ex 20:8 [c]Lev 11:44
4 [a]Lev 26:1; Ps 96:5; 115:4-7 [b]Ex 20:23; 34:17
9 [a]Lev 23:22; Deut 24:20-22
11 [a]Ex 20:15, 16 [b]Jer 9:3-5; Eph 4:25
12 [a]Ex 20:7; Deut 5:11; Matt 5:33 [b]Lev 18:21
13 [a]Ex 22:7-15, 21-27 [b]Deut 24:15; James 5:4
14 [a]Deut 27:18
15 [a]Ex 23:3, 6; Deut 1:17; 10:17; 16:19

16 'You shall not go about as [a]a slanderer among your people,
and you are not to [1]act against the [2b]life of your neighbor; I am
the LORD.
17 'You [a]shall not hate your [1]fellow countryman in your heart;
you [b]may surely reprove your neighbor, but shall not incur sin
because of him.
18 '[a]You shall not take vengeance, [b]nor bear any grudge against
the sons of your people, but [c]you shall love your neighbor as
yourself; I am the LORD.
19 'You are to keep My statutes. You shall not breed together
two kinds of your cattle; [a]you shall not sow your field with two
kinds of seed, nor wear a garment upon you of two kinds of
material mixed together.
20 '[a]Now if a man lies carnally with a woman who is a slave
acquired for *another* man, but who has in no way been redeemed
nor given her freedom, there shall be punishment; they shall
not, *however,* be put to death, because she was not free.
21 'He shall bring his guilt offering to the LORD to the doorway
of the tent of meeting, [a]a ram for a guilt offering.
22 'The priest shall also make atonement for him with the ram
of the guilt offering before the LORD for his sin which he has
committed, and the sin which he has committed will be
forgiven him.
23 'When you enter the land and plant all kinds of trees for
food, then you shall count their fruit as [1]forbidden. Three years
it shall be [1]forbidden to you; *it* shall not be eaten.
24 'But in the fourth year all its fruit shall be holy, an offering
of praise to the LORD.
25 'In the fifth year you are to eat of its fruit, that its yield may
increase for you; I am the LORD your God.
26 'You shall not eat *anything* [a]with the blood, nor practice
[b]divination or soothsaying.
27 '[a]You shall not round off the side-growth of your heads nor
harm the edges of your beard.
28 'You shall not make any cuts in your [1]body for the [2]dead nor
make any tattoo marks on yourselves: I am the LORD.
29 '[a]Do not [1]profane your daughter by making her a harlot, so
that the land will not fall to harlotry and the land become full of
lewdness.
30 'You shall [a]keep My sabbaths and [b]revere My sanctuary; I am
the LORD.
31 'Do not turn to [1a]mediums or spiritists; do not seek them out
to be defiled by them. I am the LORD your God.
32 '[a]You shall rise up before the grayheaded and honor the
[1]aged, and you shall revere your God; I am the LORD.
33 '[a]When a stranger resides with you in your land, you shall
not do him wrong.
34 'The stranger who resides with you shall be to you as the
native among you, and [a]you shall love him as yourself, for you
were aliens in the land of Egypt; I am the LORD your God.
35 '[a]You shall do no wrong in judgment, in measurement of
weight, or capacity.

16 [1]Lit *stand* [2]Lit *blood* [a]Ps 15:3; Jer 6:28; 9:4; Ezek 22:9 [b]Ex 23:7; Deut 27:25

17 [1]Lit *brother* [a]1 John 2:9, 11; 3:15 [b]Matt 18:15; Luke 17:3

18 [a]Deut 32:35; Rom 12:19; Heb 10:30 [b]Ps 103:9 [c]Matt 19:19; Mark 12:31; Luke 10:27; Rom 13:9; Gal 5:14; James 2:8

19 [a]Deut 22:9, 11

20 [a]Deut 22:23-27

21 [a]Lev 6:1-7

23 [1]Lit *uncircumcised*

26 [a]Gen 9:4; Lev 7:26f; 17:10; Deut 12:16, 23 [b]Deut 18:10; 2 Kin 17:17

27 [a]Lev 21:5; Deut 14:1

28 [1]Lit *flesh* [2]Lit *soul*

29 [1]Or *degrade* [a]Lev 21:9; Deut 22:21; 23:17, 18

30 [a]Lev 19:3 [b]Lev 26:2

31 [1]Or *ghosts or spirits* [a]Lev 20:6, 27; Deut 18:11; 1 Sam 28:3; Is 8:19

32 [1]Lit *face of the aged* [a]Prov 23:22; Lam 5:12; 1 Tim 5:1

33 [a]Ex 22:21; Deut 24:17, 18

34 [a]Lev 19:18

35 [a]Deut 25:13-16; Ezek 45:10

36 'You shall have [a]just balances, just weights, a just [1]ephah,
and a just [2]hin; I am the LORD your God, who brought you out
from the land of Egypt.
37 'You shall thus observe all My statutes and all My ordinances
and do them; I am the LORD.'"

Chapter 20 Theme ______________________

20 Then the LORD spoke to Moses, saying,
2 "You shall also say to the sons of Israel:
'Any man from the sons of Israel or from the aliens
sojourning in Israel [a]who gives any of his [1]offspring to Molech,
shall surely be put to death; [b]the people of the land shall stone
him with stones.
3 'I will also set My face against that man and will cut him off
from among his people, because he has given some of his
[1]offspring to Molech, [a]so as to defile My sanctuary and [b]to
profane My holy name.
4 'If the people of the land, however, [1]should ever disregard
that man when he gives any of his [2]offspring to Molech, so as
not to put him to death,
5 then I Myself will set My face against that man and against
his family, and I will cut off from among their people both him
and all those who play the harlot after him, by playing the
harlot after Molech.
6 'As for the person who turns to [1a]mediums and to spiritists,
to play the harlot after them, I will also set My face against that
person and will cut him off from among his people.
7 'You shall consecrate yourselves therefore and [a]be holy, for I
am the LORD your God.
8 '[a]You shall keep My statutes and practice them; I am the
LORD who sanctifies you.
9 '[a]If *there is* anyone who curses his father or his mother, he
shall surely be put to death; he has cursed his father or his
mother, his bloodguiltiness is upon him.
10 '[a]If *there is* a man who commits adultery with another man's
wife, one who commits adultery with his friend's wife, the
adulterer and the adulteress shall surely be put to death.
11 '[a]If *there is* a man who lies with his father's wife, he has
uncovered his father's nakedness; both of them shall surely be
put to death, their bloodguiltiness is upon them.
12 '[a]If *there is* a man who lies with his daughter-in-law, both of
them shall surely be put to death; they have committed [1]incest,
their bloodguiltiness is upon them.
13 '[a]If *there is* a man who lies with a male as those who lie with
a woman, both of them have committed a detestable act; they
shall surely be put to death. Their bloodguiltiness is upon them.
14 '[a]If *there is* a man who [1]marries a woman and her mother,
it is immorality; both he and they shall be burned with fire, so
that there will be no immorality in your midst.
15 '[a]If *there is* a man who lies with an animal, he shall surely
be put to death; you shall also kill the animal.

36 [1]I.e. Approx one bu [2]I.e. Approx one gal. [a]Deut 25:13-15; Prov 20:10

20:2 [1]Lit *seed* [a]Lev 18:21 [b]Lev 20:27; 24:14-23; Num 15:35, 36; Deut 21:21

3 [1]Lit *seed* [a]Lev 15:31 [b]Lev 18:21

4 [1]Lit *hiding they hide their eyes from* [2]Lit *seed*

6 [1]Or *ghosts and spirits* [a]Lev 19:31

7 [a]Eph 1:4; 1 Pet 1:16

8 [a]Ex 31:13

9 [a]Ex 21:17; Deut 27:16

10 [a]Ex 20:14; Lev 18:20; Deut 5:18

11 [a]Lev 18:7, 8; Deut 27:20

12 [1]Lit *confusion;* i.e. a violation of divine order [a]Lev 18:15

13 [a]Lev 18:22

14 [1]Lit *takes* [a]Lev 18:17; Deut 27:23

15 [a]Lev 18:23; Deut 27:21

16 'If *there is* a woman who approaches any animal to [1]mate
with it, you shall kill the woman and the animal; they shall
surely be put to death. Their bloodguiltiness is upon them.
17 '[a]If *there is* a man who takes his sister, his father's daughter
or his mother's daughter, so that he sees her nakedness and
she sees his nakedness, it is a disgrace; and they shall be cut off
in the sight of the sons of their people. He has uncovered his
sister's nakedness; he bears his guilt.
18 '[a]If *there is* a man who lies with a [1]menstruous woman and
uncovers her nakedness, he has laid bare her flow, and she has
[2]exposed the flow of her blood; thus both of them shall be cut
off from among their people.
19 '[a]You shall also not uncover the nakedness of your mother's
sister or of your father's sister, for such a one has made naked
his [1]blood relative; they will bear their guilt.
20 '[a]If *there is* a man who lies with his uncle's wife he has
uncovered his uncle's nakedness; they will bear their sin. They
will die childless.
21 '[a]If *there is* a man who takes his brother's wife, it is
[1]abhorrent; he has uncovered his brother's nakedness. They
will be childless.
22 'You are therefore to keep all My statutes and all My
ordinances and do them, so that the land to which I am bringing
you to [1]live will not [a]spew you out.
23 'Moreover, you shall not [1]follow [a]the customs of the nation
which I will drive out before you, for they did all these things,
and [b]therefore I have abhorred them.
24 'Hence I have said to you, "[a]You are to possess their land,
and I Myself will give it to you to possess it, a land flowing with
milk and honey." I am the LORD your God, who has [b]separated
you from the peoples.
25 '[a]You are therefore to make a distinction between the clean
animal and the unclean, and between the unclean bird and the
clean; and you shall not make [1]yourselves detestable by animal
or by bird or by anything [2]that creeps on the ground, which I
have separated for you as unclean.
26 'Thus you are to be holy to Me, for I the LORD am holy; and
I [a]have set you apart from the peoples to be Mine.
27 'Now a man or a woman [a]who is a medium or a [1]spiritist
shall surely be put to death. They shall be stoned with stones,
their bloodguiltiness is upon them.'"

Chapter 21 Theme ______________________

21 Then the LORD said to Moses, "Speak to the priests, the
sons of Aaron, and say to them:
'[a]**N**o one shall defile himself for a *dead* person among his
people,
2 [a]except for his relatives who are nearest to him, his mother
and his father and his son and his daughter and his brother,
3 also for his virgin sister, who is near to him [1]because she
has had no husband; for her he may defile himself.

16 [1]Lit *lie*
17 [a]Lev 18:9; Deut 27:22
18 [1]Lit *sick* [2]Or *uncovered* [a]Lev 15:24; 18:19
19 [1]Lit *flesh* [a]Lev 18:12, 13
20 [a]Lev 18:14
21 [1]Or *an impure deed* [a]Lev 18:16
22 [1]Lit *dwell in it* [a]Lev 18:28
23 [1]Lit *walk in the statutes* [a]Lev 18:3 [b]Lev 18:25
24 [a]Ex 13:5; 33:1-3 [b]Ex 33:16; Lev 20:26
25 [1]Lit *your souls* [2]Lit *with which the ground creeps* [a]Lev 10:10; 11:1-47; Deut 14:3-21
26 [a]Lev 20:24
27 [1]Lit *spiritist among them* [a]Lev 19:31
21:1 [a]Lev 19:28; Ezek 44:25
2 [a]Lev 21:11
3 [1]Or *whom no man has had*

4 'He shall not defile himself as a [1]relative by marriage among
his people, and so profane himself.
5 '[a]They shall not make any baldness on their heads, [b]nor shave
off the edges of their beards, [c]nor make any cuts in their flesh.
6 'They shall be holy to their God and [a]not profane the name
of their God, for they present the offerings by fire [1]to the LORD,
[b]the food of their God; so they shall be holy.
7 '[a]They shall not take a woman who is profaned by harlotry,
nor shall they take a woman divorced from her husband; for he
is holy to his God.
8 'You shall consecrate him, therefore, for he offers [a]the food of
your God; he shall be holy to you; for I the LORD, who sanctifies
you, am holy.
9 '[a]Also the daughter of any priest, if she profanes herself by
harlotry, she profanes her father; she shall be burned with fire.
10 'The priest who is the highest among his brothers, on whose
head the anointing oil has been poured and [1]who has been
consecrated to wear the garments, [a]shall not [2]uncover his head
nor tear his clothes;
11 [a]nor shall he approach any dead person, nor defile himself
even for his father or his mother;
12 [a]nor shall he go out of the sanctuary nor profane the
sanctuary of his God, for [b]the consecration of the anointing oil
of his God is on him; I am the LORD.
13 'He shall take a wife in her virginity.
14 '[a]A widow, or a divorced woman, or one who is profaned by
harlotry, these he may not take; but rather he is to [1]marry a
virgin of his own people,
15 so that he will not profane his [1]offspring among his people;
for I am the LORD who sanctifies him.'"
16 Then the LORD spoke to Moses, saying,
17 "Speak to Aaron, saying, 'No man of your [1]offspring
throughout their generations who has a defect shall approach
to offer the [a]food of his God.
18 '[a]For no one who has a defect shall approach: a blind man,
or a lame man, or he who has a [1a]disfigured *face,* or any
deformed *limb,*
19 or a man who has a broken foot or broken hand,
20 or a hunchback or a dwarf, or *one who has* a [1]defect in his
eye or eczema or scabs or [a]crushed testicles.
21 'No man among the [1]descendants of Aaron the priest who
has a defect is to come near to offer the LORD's offerings by fire;
since he has a defect, he shall not come near to offer [a]the food
of his God.
22 'He may eat [a]the food of his God, *both* of the most holy and
of the holy,
23 only he shall not go in to the veil or come near the altar
because he has a defect, so that he will not profane My
sanctuaries. For I am the LORD who sanctifies them.'"
24 So Moses spoke to Aaron and to his sons and to all the sons
of Israel.

4 [1]Lit *husband among*
5 [a]Deut 14:1; Ezek 44:20 [b]Lev 19:27 [c]Deut 14:1
6 [1]Lit *of* [a]Lev 18:21 [b]Lev 3:11
7 [a]Lev 21:13, 14
8 [a]Lev 21:6
9 [a]Gen 38:24; Lev 19:29
10 [1]Lit *whose hand has been filled* [2]Lit *unbind* [a]Lev 10:6
11 [a]Lev 19:28; Num 19:14
12 [a]Lev 10:7 [b]Ex 29:6, 7
14 [1]Lit *take as wife* [a]Lev 21:7; Ezek 44:22
15 [1]Lit *seed*
17 [1]Lit *seed* [a]Lev 21:6
18 [1]Lit *slit* [a]Lev 22:19-25
20 [1]Lit *obscurity* [a]Deut 23:1; Is 56:3-5
21 [1]Lit *seed* [a]Lev 21:6
22 [a]1 Cor 9:13

Chapter 22 Theme ______________________

22 Then the LORD spoke to Moses, saying,
2 "Tell Aaron and his sons to be careful with the holy
gifts of the sons of Israel, which they dedicate to Me, so as not
to profane My holy name; I am the LORD.
3 "Say to them, '[a]If any man among all your [1]descendants
throughout your generations approaches the holy *gifts* which
the sons of Israel dedicate to the LORD, while he has an
uncleanness, that person shall be cut off from before Me; I am
the LORD.
4 '[a]No man of the [1]descendants of Aaron, who is a leper or
who has a discharge, may eat of the holy *gifts* until he is clean.
[b]And if one touches anything made unclean by a corpse or if [c]a
man has a seminal emission,
5 or [a]if a man touches any teeming things by which he is made
unclean, or any man by whom he is made unclean, whatever
his uncleanness;
6 a [1]person who touches any such shall be unclean until
evening, and shall not eat of the holy *gifts* unless he has bathed
his [2]body in water.
7 'But when the sun sets, he will be clean, and afterward he
shall eat of the holy *gifts,* for [a]it is his [1]food.
8 'He shall not eat [a]*an animal* which dies or is torn *by beasts,*
becoming unclean by it; I am the LORD.
9 'They shall therefore keep [a]My charge, so that [b]they will not
bear sin because of it and die thereby because they profane it; I
am the LORD who sanctifies them.
10 '[a]No [1]layman, however, is to eat the holy *gift;* a sojourner
with the priest or a hired man shall not eat of the holy *gift.*
11 '[a]But if a priest buys a [1]slave as *his* property with his
money, [2]that one may eat of it, and those who are born in his
house may eat of his [3]food.
12 'If a priest's daughter is married to a [1]layman, she shall not
eat of the [2]offering of the *gifts.*
13 'But if a priest's daughter becomes a widow or divorced, and
has no child and returns to her father's house as in her youth,
she shall eat of her father's [1]food; [a]but no [2]layman shall eat of it.
14 '[a]But if a man eats a holy *gift* unintentionally, then he shall
add to it a fifth of it and shall give the holy *gift* to the priest.
15 '[a]They shall not profane the holy *gifts* of the sons of Israel
which they offer to the LORD,
16 and *so* cause them [a]to bear [1]punishment for guilt by eating
their holy *gifts;* for I am the LORD who sanctifies them.'"
17 Then the LORD spoke to Moses, saying,
18 "Speak to Aaron and to his sons and to all the sons of Israel
and say to them, '[a]Any man of the house of Israel or of the aliens
in Israel who presents his offering, whether it is any of their
[1]votive or any of their freewill offerings, which they present to
the LORD for a burnt offering—
19 [a]for you to be accepted—*it must be* a male without defect
from the cattle, the sheep, or the goats.

22:3 [1]Lit *seed* [a]Lev 7:20, 21; Num 19:13

4 [1]Lit *seed* [a]Lev 14:1-32 [b]Lev 11:24-28, 39, 40 [c]Lev 15:16, 17

5 [a]Lev 11:23-28

6 [1]Lit *soul* [2]Lit *flesh*

7 [1]Lit *bread* [a]Num 18:11

8 [a]Lev 7:24; 11:39, 40; 17:15

9 [a]Lev 18:30 [b]Ex 28:43; Lev 22:16; Num 18:22

10 [1]Lit *stranger* [a]Ex 29:33; Lev 22:13; Num 3:10

11 [1]Lit *soul* [2]Lit *he may* [3]Lit *bread* [a]Gen 17:13; Ex 12:44

12 [1]Lit *stranger* [2]Lit *heave offering*

13 [1]Lit *bread* [2]Lit *stranger* [a]Lev 22:10

14 [a]Lev 5:15, 16

15 [a]Num 18:32

16 [1]Or *iniquity requiring a guilt offering* [a]Lev 10:17; 22:9

18 [1]Lit *vows* [a]Num 15:14

19 [a]Lev 21:18-21; Deut 15:21

20 '[a]Whatever has a defect, you shall not offer, for it will not be
accepted for you.
21 'When a man offers a sacrifice of peace offerings to the LORD
[a]to [1]fulfill a special vow or for a freewill offering, of the herd or
of the flock, it must be perfect to be accepted; there shall be no
defect in it.
22 'Those *that are* blind or fractured or maimed or having a
running sore or eczema or scabs, you shall not offer to the LORD,
nor make of them an offering by fire on the altar to the LORD.
23 'In respect to an ox or a lamb which has an [1]overgrown or
stunted *member*, you may present it for a freewill offering, but
for a vow it will not be accepted.
24 'Also [a]anything *with its testicles* bruised or crushed or torn
or cut, you shall not offer to the LORD, or [1]sacrifice in your land,
25 nor shall you accept any such from the hand of a foreigner
for offering [a]as the [1]food of your God; for their corruption is in
them, they have a defect, they shall not be accepted for you.'"
26 Then the LORD spoke to Moses, saying,
27 "When an ox or a sheep or a goat is born, it shall [1]remain
[a]seven days [2]with its mother, and from the eighth day on it shall
be accepted as a sacrifice of an offering by fire to the LORD.
28 "[a]But, *whether* it is an ox or a sheep, you shall not kill *both*
it and its young in one day.
29 "When you sacrifice [a]a sacrifice of thanksgiving to the LORD,
you shall sacrifice it so that you may be accepted.
30 "It shall be eaten on the same day, you shall leave none of it
until morning; I am the LORD.
31 "[a]So you shall keep My commandments, and do them; I am
the LORD.
32 "You shall not profane My holy name, but I will be sanctified
among the sons of Israel; I am the LORD who sanctifies you,
33 [a]who brought you out from the land of Egypt, to be your
God; I am the LORD."

Chapter 23 Theme ____________________

23 The LORD spoke again to Moses, saying,
2 "Speak to the sons of Israel and say to them, '[a]The
LORD's appointed times which you shall [b]proclaim as holy
convocations—My appointed times are these:
3 '[a]For six days work may be done, but on the seventh day
there is a sabbath of complete rest, a holy convocation. You
shall not do any work; it is a sabbath to the LORD in all your
dwellings.
4 'These are the [a]appointed times of the LORD, holy convocations which you shall proclaim at the times appointed for them.
5 '[a]In the first month, on the fourteenth day of the month [1]at
twilight is the LORD's Passover.
6 'Then on the fifteenth day of the same month there is the
[a]Feast of Unleavened Bread to the LORD; for seven days you
shall eat unleavened bread.

INSIGHT

See the chart **The Feasts of Israel** on pages 214, 215.

20 [a]Deut 15:21; 17:1; Mal 1:8, 14; Heb 9:14; 1 Pet 1:19
21 [1]Or *make a special votive offering* [a]Num 15:3, 8
23 [1]Or *a deformed*
24 [1]Lit *do* [a]Lev 21:20
25 [1]Lit *bread* [a]Lev 21:22
27 [1]Lit *be* [2]Lit *under* [a]Ex 22:30
28 [a]Deut 22:6, 7
29 [a]Lev 7:12
31 [a]Lev 19:37; Num 15:40; Deut 4:40
33 [a]Lev 11:45
23:2 [a]Lev 23:4, 37, 44; Num 29:39 [b]Lev 23:21
3 [a]Ex 20:9, 10; 23:12; 31:13-17; 35:2, 3; Lev 19:3; Deut 5:13, 14
4 [a]Ex 23:14; Lev 23:2
5 [1]Lit *between the two evenings* [a]Ex 12:18, 19; Num 28:16-25; Deut 16:1; Josh 5:10
6 [a]Ex 12:14-20; 23:15; 34:18; Deut 16:3-8

7 [a]Lev 23:8, 21, 25, 35, 36

The Jewish Calendar

Babylonian names (B) for the months are still used today for the Jewish calendar. Canaanite names (C) were used prior to the Babylonian captivity in 586 B.C. Four are mentioned in the Old Testament. **Adar-Sheni** is an intercalary month used every two to three years or seven times in 19 years.

1st month	2nd month	3rd month	4th month
Nisan (B) Abib (C) March-April	Iyyar (B) Ziv (C) April-May	Sivan (B) May-June	Tammuz (B) June-July
7th month	*8th month*	*9th month*	*10th month*
5th month	**6th month**	**7th month**	**8th month**
Ab (B) July-August	Elul (B) August-September	Tishri (B) Ethanim (C) September-October	Marcheshvan (B) Bul (C) October-November
11th month	*12th month*	*1st month*	*2nd month*
9th month	**10th month**	**11th month**	**12th month**
Chislev (B) November-December	Tebeth (B) December-January	Shebat (B) January-February	Adar (B) February-March
3rd month	*4th month*	*5th month*	*6th month*

Sacred calendar appears in black • Civil calendar appears in gray

10 [a]Ex 23:19; 34:26

13 [1]I.e. Approx one gal. [a]Lev 6:20

14 [a]Ex 34:26; Num 15:20, 21

15 [a]Num 28:26-31; Deut 16:9-12

16 [a]Num 28:26

17 [1]I.e. Approx one bu [a]Lev 2:12; 7:13

7 'On the first day you shall have a holy convocation; you
shall [a]not do any laborious work.
8 'But for seven days you shall present an offering by fire to
the LORD. On the seventh day is a holy convocation; you shall
not do any laborious work.'"
9 Then the LORD spoke to Moses, saying,
10 "Speak to the sons of Israel and say to them, 'When you
enter the land which I am going to give to you and [a]reap its
harvest, then you shall bring in the sheaf of the first fruits of
your harvest to the priest.
11 'He shall wave the sheaf before the LORD for you to be
accepted; on the day after the sabbath the priest shall wave it.
12 'Now on the day when you wave the sheaf, you shall offer a
male lamb one year old without defect for a burnt offering to
the LORD.
13 'Its [a]grain offering shall then be two-tenths *of an ephah* of fine
flour mixed with oil, an offering by fire to the LORD *for* a soothing
aroma, with its drink offering, a fourth of a [1]hin of wine.
14 'Until this same day, until you have brought in the offering
of your God, [a]you shall eat neither bread nor roasted grain nor
new growth. It is to be a perpetual statute throughout your
generations in all your dwelling places.
15 '[a]You shall also count for yourselves from the day after the
sabbath, from the day when you brought in the sheaf of the
wave offering; there shall be seven complete sabbaths.
16 'You shall count fifty days to the day after the seventh
sabbath; then you shall present a [a]new grain offering to the LORD.
17 'You shall bring in from your dwelling places two *loaves* of
bread for a wave offering, made of two-tenths *of an* [1]*ephah;* they
shall be of a fine flour, baked [a]with leaven as first fruits to the LORD.
18 'Along with the bread you shall present seven one year old
male lambs without defect, and a bull of the herd and two
rams; they are to be a burnt offering to the LORD, with their
grain offering and their drink offerings, an offering by fire of a
soothing aroma to the LORD.

19 'You shall also offer [a]one male goat for a sin offering and
two male lambs one year old for a sacrifice of peace offerings.
20 'The priest shall then wave them with the bread of the first
fruits for a wave offering with two lambs before the LORD; they
are to be holy to the LORD for the priest.
21 'On this same day you shall [a]make a proclamation as well;
you are to have a holy convocation. You shall do no laborious
[b]work. It is to be a perpetual statute in all your dwelling places
throughout your generations.
22 '[a]When you reap the harvest of your land, moreover, you
shall not reap to the very corners of your field nor gather the
gleaning of your harvest; you are to leave them for the needy
and the alien. I am the LORD your God.'"
23 Again the LORD spoke to Moses, saying,
24 "Speak to the sons of Israel, saying, '[a]In the seventh month
on the first of the month you shall have a [1]rest, a [b]reminder by
blowing *of trumpets,* a holy convocation.
25 'You shall [a]not do any laborious work, but you shall present
an offering by fire to the LORD.'"
26 The LORD spoke to Moses, saying,
27 "On exactly [a]the tenth day of this seventh month is [b]the day of
atonement; it shall be a holy convocation for you, and you shall
humble your souls and present an offering by fire to the LORD.
28 "You shall not do any work on this same day, for it is a [a]day
of atonement, [b]to make atonement on your behalf before the
LORD your God.
29 "If there is any [1]person who will not humble himself on this
same day, [a]he shall be cut off from his people.
30 "As for any person who does any work on this same day,
that person I will destroy from among his people.
31 "You shall do no work at all. It is to be a perpetual statute
throughout your generations in all your dwelling places.
32 "It is to be a sabbath of complete rest to you, and you shall
humble your souls; on the ninth of the month at evening, from
evening until evening you shall keep your sabbath."
33 Again the LORD spoke to Moses, saying,
34 "Speak to the sons of Israel, saying, 'On [a]the fifteenth of this
seventh month is the [b]Feast of Booths for seven days to the LORD.
35 'On the first day is a holy convocation; you shall do [a]no
laborious work of any kind.
36 '[a]For seven days you shall present an offering by fire to the
LORD. On [b]the eighth day you shall have a holy convocation and
present an offering by fire to the LORD; it is an assembly. You
shall do no laborious work.
37 'These are [a]the appointed times of the LORD which you shall
proclaim as holy convocations, to present offerings by fire to
the LORD—burnt offerings and grain offerings, sacrifices and
drink offerings, [b]*each* day's matter on its own day—
38 besides *those of* the sabbaths of the LORD, and besides your
gifts and besides all your [1]votive and freewill offerings, which
you give to the LORD.

19 [a]Lev 4:23; Num 28:30
21 [a]Lev 23:2, 4 [b]Lev 23:7
22 [a]Lev 19:9, 10; Deut 24:19; Ruth 2:15f
24 [1]Lit *sabbath rest* [a]Num 29:1 [b]Num 10:9, 10
25 [a]Lev 23:21
27 [a]Lev 16:29; 25:9; Num 29:7 [b]Ex 30:10; Lev 16:30; 23:28; Num 29:7-11
28 [a]Lev 23:27 [b]Lev 16:34
29 [1]Lit *soul* [a]Gen 17:14; Lev 13:46; Num 5:2
34 [a]Num 29:12 [b]Lev 23:42, 43; Deut 16:13, 16; Ezra 3:4; Neh 8:14; Zech 14:16; John 7:2
35 [a]Lev 23:25
36 [a]Num 29:12-34 [b]Num 29:35-38
37 [a]Lev 23:2 [b]Num 28:1-29:38
38 [1]Lit *vows, and besides all your*

39 [1]Lit *sabbath rest* [a]Ex 23:16
40 [1]Lit *products, fruit*
42 [1]Lit *dwell* [a]Lev 23:34
43 [a]Deut 31:13; Ps 78:5f
44 [a]Lev 23:37
24:2 [1]Or *luminary* [2]Lit *ascend* [a]Ex 27:20, 21
4 [a]Ex 25:31; 31:8; 37:17
5 [a]Ex 25:30; 39:36; 40:23
6 [a]Ex 25:24; 1 Kin 7:48
7 [a]Lev 2:2, 9, 16
8 [1]Lit *from* [a]Matt 12:5 [b]Ex 25:30; Num 4:7; 2 Chr 2:4
9 [a]Matt 12:4; Mark 2:26; Luke 6:4
11 [a]Ex 3:15; 22:28; Job 2:5, 9; Is 8:21
12 [1]Or *prison* [2]Lit *to declare distinctly to them according to the mouth of the* LORD [a]Ex 18:15; Num 15:34

39 'On exactly the fifteenth day of the seventh month, [a]when you have gathered in the crops of the land, you shall celebrate the feast of the LORD for seven days, with a [1]rest on the first day and a [1]rest on the eighth day.

40 'Now on the first day you shall take for yourselves the [1]foliage of beautiful trees, palm branches and boughs of leafy trees and willows of the brook, and you shall rejoice before the LORD your God for seven days.

41 'You shall thus celebrate it *as* a feast to the LORD for seven days in the year. It *shall be* a perpetual statute throughout your generations; you shall celebrate it in the seventh month.

42 'You shall [1]live [a]in booths for seven days; all the native-born in Israel shall [1]live in booths,

43 so that [a]your generations may know that I had the sons of Israel live in booths when I brought them out from the land of Egypt. I am the LORD your God.'"

44 So Moses declared to the sons of Israel [a]the appointed times of the LORD.

Chapter 24 Theme ____________________

24 Then the LORD spoke to Moses, saying,
2 "Command the sons of Israel that they bring to you [a]clear oil from beaten olives for the [1]light, to make a lamp [2]burn continually.

3 "Outside the veil of testimony in the tent of meeting, Aaron shall keep it in order from evening to morning before the LORD continually; *it shall be* a perpetual statute throughout your generations.

4 "He shall keep the lamps in order on the [a]pure *gold* lampstand before the LORD continually.

5 "[a]Then you shall take fine flour and bake twelve cakes with it; two-tenths *of an ephah* shall be *in* each cake.

6 "You shall set them *in* two rows, six *to* a row, on the [a]pure *gold* table before the LORD.

7 "You shall put pure frankincense on each row that it may be [a]a memorial portion for the bread, *even* an offering by fire to the LORD.

8 "[a]Every sabbath day he shall set it in order before the LORD [b]continually; it is an everlasting covenant [1]for the sons of Israel.

9 "[a]It shall be for Aaron and his sons, and they shall eat it in a holy place; for it is most holy to him from the LORD's offerings by fire, *his* portion forever."

10 Now the son of an Israelite woman, whose father was an Egyptian, went out among the sons of Israel; and the Israelite woman's son and a man of Israel struggled with each other in the camp.

11 The son of the Israelite woman blasphemed the [a]Name and cursed. So they brought him to Moses. (Now his mother's name was Shelomith, the daughter of Dibri, of the tribe of Dan.)

12 They put him in [1]custody [2]so that [a]the command of the LORD might be made clear to them.

Lampstand

13 Then the LORD spoke to Moses, saying,
14 "Bring the one who has cursed outside the camp, and let all
who heard him [a]lay their hands on his head; then [b]let all the
congregation stone him.
15 "You shall speak to the sons of Israel, saying, '[a]If anyone
curses his God, then he will bear his sin.
16 'Moreover, the one who [a]blasphemes the name of the LORD
shall surely be put to death; all the congregation shall certainly
stone him. The alien as well as the native, when he blasphemes
the Name, shall be put to death.
17 '[a]If a man [1]takes the life of any human being, he shall surely
be put to death.
18 '[a]The one who [1]takes the life of an animal shall make it
good, life for life.
19 'If a man [1]injures his neighbor, just as he has done, so it
shall be done to him:
20 [a]fracture for fracture, [b]eye for eye, tooth for tooth; just as
he has [1]injured a man, so it shall be [2]inflicted on him.
21 'Thus the one who [1]kills an animal shall make it good, but
[a]the one who [1]kills a man shall be put to death.
22 'There shall be [a]one [1]standard for you; it shall be for the
stranger as well as the native, for I am the LORD your God.'"
23 Then Moses spoke to the sons of Israel, and they brought
the one who had cursed outside the camp and stoned him with
stones. Thus the sons of Israel did, just as the LORD had
commanded Moses.

Chapter 25 Theme ______________________

25 The LORD then spoke to Moses [1]at Mount Sinai, saying,
2 "Speak to the sons of Israel and say to them, 'When
you come into the land which I shall give you, then the land
shall have a sabbath to the LORD.
3 '[a]Six years you shall sow your field, and six years you shall
prune your vineyard and gather in its crop,
4 but during [a]the seventh year the land shall have a sabbath
rest, a sabbath to the LORD; you shall not sow your field nor
prune your vineyard.
5 'Your harvest's [1]aftergrowth you shall not reap, and your
grapes of untrimmed vines you shall not gather; the land shall
have a sabbatical year.
6 '[a]All of you shall have the sabbath *products* of the land for
food; yourself, and your male and female slaves, and your hired
man and your foreign resident, those who live as aliens with you.
7 'Even your cattle and the animals that are in your land shall
have all its crops to eat.
8 'You are also to count off seven sabbaths of years for yourself, seven times seven years, so that you have the time of the
seven sabbaths of years, *namely,* forty-nine years.
9 'You shall then sound a ram's horn abroad on [a]the tenth day
of the seventh month; on the day of atonement you shall sound
a horn all through your land.

14 [a]Deut 13:9; 17:7 [b]Lev 20:2, 27; Deut 21:21
15 [a]Ex 22:28
16 [a]1 Kin 21:10; Matt 12:31; Mark 3:28f
17 [1]Lit *smites* [a]Gen 9:6; Ex 21:12; Num 35:30, 31; Deut 27:24
18 [1]Lit *smites* [a]Lev 24:21
19 [1]Lit *gives a blemish*
20 [1]Lit *given a blemish* [2]Lit *given* [a]Ex 21:23; Deut 19:21 [b]Matt 5:38
21 [1]Lit *smites* [a]Lev 24:17
22 [1]Lit *judgment* [a]Ex 12:49; Num 9:14; 15:15, 16, 29
25:1 [1]Or *on*
3 [a]Ex 23:10, 11
4 [a]Lev 25:20
5 [1]Lit *growth from spilled kernels*
6 [a]Lev 25:20, 21
9 [a]Lev 23:27

10 'You shall thus consecrate the fiftieth year and [a]proclaim [1]a
release through the land to all its inhabitants. It shall be a
jubilee for you, [2]and [b]each of you shall return to his own
property, [2]and each of you shall return to his family.
11 'You shall have the fiftieth year as a jubilee; you shall not sow,
nor reap its aftergrowth, nor gather in *from* its untrimmed vines.
12 'For it is a jubilee; it shall be holy to you. You shall eat its
crops out of the field.
13 '[a]On this year of jubilee each of you shall return to his own
property.
14 'If you make a sale, moreover, to your friend or buy from your
friend's hand, [a]you shall not wrong one another.
15 'Corresponding to the number of years after the jubilee, you
shall buy from your [1]friend; he is to sell to you according to the
number of years of crops.
16 '[a]In proportion to the [1]extent of the years you shall increase
its price, and in proportion to the fewness of the years you
shall diminish its price, for *it is* a number of crops he is selling
to you.
17 'So [a]you shall not wrong one another, but you shall [1]fear
your God; for I am the LORD your God.
18 'You shall thus observe My statutes and keep My judgments,
so as to carry them out, that [a]you may live securely on the land.
19 'Then the land will yield its produce, so that you can eat
your fill and live securely on it.
20 'But if you say, "[a]What are we going to eat on the seventh
year [1]if we do not sow or gather in our crops?"
21 then [a]I will so order My blessing for you in the sixth year
that it will bring forth the crop for three years.
22 'When you are sowing the eighth year, you can still eat [a]old
things from the crop, eating *the old* until the ninth year when
its crop comes in.
23 'The land, moreover, shall not be sold permanently, for [a]the
land is Mine; for [b]you are *but* aliens and sojourners with Me.
24 'Thus for every [1]piece of your property, you are to provide
for the redemption of the land.
25 '[a]If a [1]fellow countryman of yours becomes so poor he has
to sell part of his property, then his nearest kinsman is to come
and buy back what his [1]relative has sold.
26 'Or in case a man has no kinsman, but so [1]recovers his
means as to find sufficient for its redemption,
27 [a]then he shall calculate the years since its sale and refund
the balance to the man to whom he sold it, and so return to his
property.
28 'But if [1]he has not found sufficient means to get it back for
himself, then what he has sold shall remain in the hands of its
purchaser until the year of jubilee; but at the jubilee it shall
[2]revert, that [a]he may return to his property.
29 'Likewise, if a man sells a dwelling house in a walled city,
then his redemption right remains valid until a full year from
its sale; his right of redemption lasts a full year.

10 [1]Or *liberty* [2]Or *when* [a]Jer 34:8, 15, 17 [b]Lev 25:13, 28, 54
13 [a]Lev 25:10; 27:24
14 [a]Lev 25:17
15 [1]Lit *friend's hands*
16 [1]Lit *multitude* [a]Lev 25:27, 51, 52
17 [1]Or *reverence* [a]Lev 25:14; Prov 14:31; 22:22; Jer 7:5, 6; 1 Thess 4:6
18 [a]Lev 26:5; Deut 12:10; Jer 23:6
20 [1]Or *behold* [a]Lev 25:4
21 [a]Deut 28:8
22 [a]Lev 26:10
23 [a]Ex 19:5 [b]Gen 23:4; 1 Chr 29:15; Ps 39:12; Heb 11:13; 1 Pet 2:11
24 [1]Lit *land*
25 [1]Lit *brother* [a]Ruth 2:20; 4:4, 6
26 [1]Lit *his hand reaches*
27 [a]Lev 25:16
28 [1]Lit *his hand has not found sufficient to* [2]Lit *go out* [a]Lev 25:10, 13

30 'But if it is not bought back for him within the space of a full
year, then the house that is in the walled city passes permanently
to its purchaser throughout his generations; it does not [1]revert
in the jubilee.
31 'The houses of the villages, however, which have no
surrounding wall shall be considered [1]as open fields; they have
redemption rights and [2]revert in the jubilee.
32 'As for [a]cities of the Levites, the Levites have a permanent
right of redemption for the houses of the cities which are their
possession.
33 'What, therefore, [1]belongs to the Levites may be redeemed
and a house sale [2]in the city of this possession [3]reverts in the
jubilee, for the houses of the cities of the Levites are their
possession among the sons of Israel.
34 '[a]But pasture fields of their cities shall not be sold, for that is
their perpetual possession.
35 '[a]Now in case a [1]countryman of yours becomes poor and his
[2]means with regard to you falter, then you are to sustain him,
like a stranger or a sojourner, that he may live with you.
36 '[a]Do not take [1]usurious interest from him, but revere your
God, that your [2]countryman may live with you.
37 'You shall not give him your silver at interest, nor your food
for gain.
38 '[a]I am the LORD your God, who brought you out of the land
of Egypt to give you the land of Canaan *and* [b]to be your God.
39 '[a]If a [1]countryman of yours becomes so poor with regard to
you that he sells himself to you, you shall not subject him to a
slave's service.
40 'He shall be with you as a hired man, as [a]if he were a
sojourner; he shall serve with you until the year of jubilee.
41 'He shall then go out from you, he and his sons with him,
and shall go back to his family, that he may return to the
property of his forefathers.
42 'For they are My servants whom I brought out from the
land of Egypt; they are not to be sold *in* a slave sale.
43 '[a]You shall not rule over him with severity, but are to revere
your God.
44 'As for your male and female slaves whom you may have—
you may acquire male and female slaves from the pagan nations
that are around you.
45 'Then, too, *it is* out of the sons of the sojourners who live as
aliens among you that you may gain acquisition, and out of their
families who are with you, whom they will have [1]produced in
your land; they also may become your possession.
46 'You may even bequeath them to your sons after you, to
receive as a possession; you can use them as permanent slaves.
[a]But in respect to your [1]countrymen, the sons of Israel, you
shall not rule with severity over one another.
47 'Now if the [1]means of a stranger or of a sojourner with you
becomes sufficient, and a [2]countryman of yours becomes so
poor with regard to him as to sell himself to a stranger who is

30 [1]Lit *go out*

31 [1]Lit *according to* [2]Lit *go out*

32 [a]Num 35:1-8; Josh 21:2

33 [1]Lit *is from* [2]Lit *and* [3]Lit *goes out*

34 [a]Num 35:2-5

35 [1]Lit *brother* [2]Lit *hand* [a]Deut 15:7-11; 24:14, 15

36 [1]Lit *interest and usury* [2]Lit *brother* [a]Ex 22:25; Deut 23:19, 20

38 [a]Lev 11:45 [b]Gen 17:7

39 [1]Lit *brother* [a]Ex 21:2-6; Deut 15:12-18; 1 Kin 9:22

40 [a]Ex 21:2

43 [a]Ex 1:13, 14; Lev 25:46, 53; Ezek 34:4; Col 4:1

45 [1]Lit *begotten*

46 [1]Lit *brothers* [a]Lev 25:43

47 [1]Lit *hand . . . reaches* [2]Lit *brother*

sojourning with you, or to the descendants of a stranger's family,
48 then he shall have redemption right after he has been sold.
One of his brothers may redeem him,
49 or his uncle, or his uncle's son, may redeem him, or one of
his blood relatives from his family may redeem him; or [1a]if he
prospers, he may redeem himself.
50 'He then with his purchaser shall calculate from the year
when he sold himself to him up to the year of jubilee; and the
price of his sale shall correspond to the number of years. *It is*
like the days of a hired man *that* he shall be with him.
51 'If there are still many years, [a]he shall refund part of his
purchase price in proportion to them for his own redemption;
52 and if few years remain until the year of jubilee, he shall so
calculate with him. In proportion to his years he is to refund
the amount for his redemption.
53 'Like a man hired year by year he shall be with him; [a]he
shall not rule over him with severity in your sight.
54 'Even if he is not redeemed by [1]these *means,* [a]he shall still
go out in the year of jubilee, he and his sons with him.
55 'For the sons of Israel are My servants; they are My servants
whom I brought out from the land of Egypt. I am the LORD your
God.

Chapter 26 Theme ____________________

26 'You shall not make for yourselves [1a]idols, nor shall you
set up for yourselves [b]an image or [c]a *sacred* pillar, nor
shall you place a [d]figured stone in your land to bow down [2]to
it; for I am the LORD your God.
2 '[a]You shall keep My sabbaths and reverence My sanctuary; I
am the LORD.
3 '[a]If you walk in My statutes and keep My commandments
so as to carry them out,
4 then [a]I shall give you rains in their season, so that the land
will yield its produce and the trees of the field will bear their fruit.
5 '[a]Indeed, your threshing will last for you until grape
gathering, and grape gathering will last until sowing time. You
will thus eat your [1]food to the full and [b]live securely in your land.
6 '[a]I shall also grant peace in the land, so that [b]you may lie
down with no one making *you* tremble. [c]I shall also eliminate
harmful beasts from the land, and [d]no sword will pass through
your land.
7 'But you will chase your enemies and they will fall before
you by the sword;
8 [a]five of you will chase a hundred, and a hundred of you will
chase ten thousand, and your enemies will fall before you by
the sword.
9 'So I will turn toward you and [a]make you fruitful and
multiply you, and I will [b]confirm My covenant with you.
10 '[a]You will eat the old supply and clear out the old because of
the new.

49 [1]Lit *if his hand has reached and* [a]Lev 25:26, 27
51 [a]Lev 25:16
53 [a]Lev 25:43
54 [1]Or *these years* [a]Lev 25:10, 13, 28
26:1 [1]Or *graven images* [2]Lit *over* [a]Lev 19:4; Deut 5:8 [b]Ex 20:4; Deut 16:21f [c]Ex 23:24 [d]Num 33:52
2 [a]Lev 19:30
3 [a]Deut 7:12-26; 11:13; 28:1-14
4 [a]Deut 11:14
5 [1]Lit *bread* [a]Deut 11:15; Joel 2:19, 26; Amos 9:13 [b]Lev 25:18, 19; Ezek 34:25
6 [a]Ps 29:11; 85:8; 147:14 [b]Zeph 3:13 [c]Lev 26:22 [d]Lev 26:25
8 [a]Deut 32:30
9 [a]Gen 17:6; 22:17; 48:4 [b]Gen 17:7
10 [a]Lev 25:22

11 '[a]Moreover, I will make My [1]dwelling among you, and My
soul will not [2]reject you.
12 '[a]I will also walk among you and be your God, and you shall
be My people.
13 '[a]I am the LORD your God, who brought you out of the land
of Egypt so that *you* would not be their slaves, and [b]I broke the
bars of your yoke and made you walk erect.
14 '[a]But if you do not obey Me and do not carry out all these
commandments,
15 if, instead, you [a]reject My statutes, and if your soul abhors
My ordinances so as not to carry out all My commandments,
and so [b]break My covenant,
16 I, in turn, will do this to you: I will appoint over you a
[a]sudden terror, consumption and fever that will waste away the
eyes and cause the [b]soul to pine away; also, [c]you will sow your
seed uselessly, for your enemies will eat it up.
17 'I will set My face against you so that you will be struck
down before your enemies; and [a]those who hate you will rule
over you, and [b]you will flee when no one is pursuing you.
18 'If also after these things you do not obey Me, then I will
punish you [a]seven times more for your sins.
19 'I will also [a]break down your pride of power; I will also
make your sky like iron and your earth like bronze.
20 '[a]Your strength will be spent uselessly, for your land will not
yield its produce and the trees of the land will not yield their
fruit.
21 'If then, you [1a]act with hostility against Me and are unwilling
to obey Me, I will increase the plague on you [b]seven times
according to your sins.
22 '[a]I will let loose among you the beasts of the field, which
will bereave you of your children and destroy your cattle and
reduce your number so that [b]your roads lie deserted.
23 '[a]And if by these things you are not turned to Me, but act
with hostility against Me,
24 then I will [a]act with hostility against you; and I, even I, will
strike you [b]seven times for your sins.
25 'I will also bring upon you a sword which will execute
[a]vengeance for the covenant; and when you gather together
into your cities, I will send [b]pestilence among you, so that you
shall be delivered into enemy hands.
26 '[a]When I break your staff of bread, ten women will bake your
bread in one oven, and they will bring back your bread [1]in
rationed amounts, so that you will [b]eat and not be satisfied.
27 'Yet if in spite of this you do not obey Me, but act with
hostility against Me,
28 then [a]I will act with wrathful hostility against you, and I,
even I, will punish you seven times for your sins.
29 'Further, [a]you will eat the flesh of your sons and the flesh of
your daughters you will eat.
30 'I then [a]will destroy your high places, and cut down your
[b]incense altars, and heap your [1]remains on the [1]remains of your
idols, for My soul shall abhor you.

11 [1]Or *tabernacle* [2]Lit *abhor* [a]Ex 25:8; 29:45, 46; Ezek 37:26
12 [a]Gen 3:8; Deut 23:14; 2 Cor 6:16
13 [a]Ex 20:2 [b]Ezek 34:27
14 [a]Deut 28:15-68; Josh 23:15
15 [a]Lev 26:11; 2 Kin 17:15 [b]Lev 26:9
16 [a]Deut 28:22; Ps 78:33 [b]1 Sam 2:33; Ezek 24:23; 33:10 [c]Judg 6:3-6; Job 31:8
17 [a]Ps 106:41 [b]Lev 26:36, 37; Ps 53:5; Prov 28:1
18 [a]Lev 26:21, 24, 28
19 [a]Is 28:1-3; Ezek 24:21
20 [a]Ps 127:1; Is 17:10, 11; 49:4; Jer 12:13
21 [1]Lit *walk,* and so throughout the ch [a]Lev 26:23, 27, 40 [b]Lev 26:18
22 [a]2 Kin 17:25 [b]Judg 5:6
23 [a]Lev 26:21; Jer 5:3
24 [a]Lev 26:28, 41 [b]Lev 26:21
25 [a]Jer 50:28; 51:11 [b]Num 14:12
26 [1]Lit *by weight* [a]Is 3:1; Ezek 4:16, 17; 5:16 [b]Mic 6:14
28 [a]Lev 26:24, 41; Is 59:18
29 [a]2 Kin 6:29
30 [1]Lit *corpses* [a]2 Kin 23:20; Ezek 6:3, 6; Amos 7:9 [b]2 Chr 34:4, 7; Is 27:9

31 'I will [1]lay [a]waste your cities as well and will make your [b]sanctuaries desolate, and I will not [c]smell your soothing aromas.

32 'I will make [a]the land desolate [b]so that your enemies who settle in it will be appalled over it.

33 'You, however, I [a]will scatter among the nations and will draw out a sword after you, as your land becomes desolate and your cities become waste.

34 '[a]Then the land will [1]enjoy its sabbaths all the days of the desolation, while you are in your enemies' land; then the land will rest and [1]enjoy its sabbaths.

35 'All the days of *its* desolation it will observe the rest which it did not observe on your sabbaths, while you were living on it.

36 'As for those of you who may be left, I will also bring [a]weakness into their hearts in the lands of their enemies. And the sound of a driven leaf will chase them, and even when no one is pursuing they will flee [1]as though from the sword, and they will fall.

37 '[a]They will therefore stumble over each other as if *running* from the sword, although no one is pursuing; and you will have *no strength* [1]to stand up before your enemies.

38 'But [a]you will perish among the nations, and your enemies' land will consume you.

39 '[a]So those of you who may be left will rot away because of their iniquity in the lands of your enemies; and also because of the iniquities of their forefathers they will rot away with them.

40 '[a]If they confess their iniquity and the iniquity of their forefathers, in their unfaithfulness which they committed against Me, and also in their acting with hostility against Me—

41 I also was acting with hostility against them, to bring them into the land of their enemies—[a]or if their uncircumcised heart becomes humbled so that [b]they then make amends for their iniquity,

42 then I will remember [a]My covenant with Jacob, and I will remember also [b]My covenant with Isaac, and [c]My covenant with Abraham as well, and I will remember the land.

43 '[a]For the land will be abandoned by them, and will make up for its sabbaths while it is made desolate without them. They, meanwhile, will be making amends for their iniquity, [1]because they rejected My ordinances and their [b]soul abhorred My statutes.

44 'Yet in spite of this, when they are in the land of their enemies, I will not reject them, nor will I so [a]abhor them as [b]to destroy them, [c]breaking My covenant with them; for I am the LORD their God.

45 'But I will remember for them the [a]covenant with their ancestors, whom I brought out of the land of Egypt in the sight of the nations, that [b]I might be their God. I am the LORD.'"

46 [a]These are the statutes and ordinances and laws which the LORD established between Himself and the sons of Israel [1]through Moses at Mount Sinai.

31 [1]Lit *give desolation to* [a]Neh 2:3; Jer 44:2, 6, 22 [b]Is 63:18; Lam 2:7 [c]Amos 5:21

32 [a]Jer 9:11; 12:11; 25:11; 33:10 [b]Jer 18:16; 19:8

33 [a]Deut 4:27; 28:64; Ps 44:11; 106:27; Jer 31:10; Ezek 12:15; 20:23; Zech 7:14

34 [1]Lit *satisfy* [a]Lev 26:43; 2 Chr 36:21

36 [1]Lit *the flight of the sword* [a]Is 30:17; Lam 1:3, 6; 4:19; Ezek 21:7

37 [1]Lit *you will stand* [a]Jer 6:21; Nah 3:3

38 [a]Deut 4:26

39 [a]Ezek 4:17; 33:10

40 [a]Jer 3:12-15; 14:20; Hos 5:15

41 [a]Jer 4:4; 9:25, 26; Ezek 44:7, 9; Acts 7:51 [b]Ezek 20:43

42 [a]Gen 28:13-15; 35:11, 12 [b]Gen 26:2-5 [c]Gen 22:15-18

43 [1]Lit *because and by the cause* [a]Lev 26:34 [b]Lev 26:11

44 [a]Lev 26:11 [b]Deut 4:31; Jer 30:11 [c]Jer 33:20-26

45 [a]Ex 6:6-8 [b]Gen 17:7

46 [1]Lit *by the hand of* [a]Lev 7:38; 27:34; Deut 4:5; 29:1

Chapter 27 Theme ______________________________

27 Again, the LORD spoke to Moses, saying,
2 "Speak to the sons of Israel and say to them, '[a]When a
man makes a difficult vow, he *shall be valued* according to your
valuation of persons belonging to the LORD.
3 'If your valuation is of the male from twenty years even to
sixty years old, then your valuation shall be fifty shekels of
silver, after [a]the shekel of the sanctuary.
4 'Or if it is a female, then your valuation shall be thirty shekels.
5 'If it be from five years even to twenty years old then your
valuation for the male shall be twenty shekels and for the
female ten shekels.
6 'But if *they are* from a month even up to five years old, then
your valuation shall be [a]five shekels of silver for the male, and
for the female your valuation shall be three shekels of silver.
7 'If *they are* from sixty years old and upward, if it is a male,
then your valuation shall be fifteen shekels, and for the female
ten shekels.
8 'But if he is poorer than your valuation, then he shall be
placed before the priest and the priest shall value him; [a]according
to [1]the means of the one who vowed, the priest shall value him.
9 'Now if it is an animal of the kind which [1]men can present
as an offering to the LORD, any such that one gives to the LORD
shall be holy.
10 '[a]He shall not replace it or exchange it, a good for a bad, or
a bad for a good; or if he does exchange animal for animal, then
both it and its substitute shall become holy.
11 'If, however, it is any unclean animal of the kind which
[1]men do not present as an offering to the LORD, then he shall
place the animal before the priest.
12 'The priest shall value it [1]as either good or bad; as you, the
priest, value it, so it shall be.
13 'But if he should ever *wish to* redeem it, then he shall add
one-fifth of it to your valuation.
14 'Now if a man consecrates his house as holy to the LORD, then
the priest shall value it [1]as either good or bad; as the priest
values it, so it shall stand.
15 'Yet if the one who consecrates it should *wish to* redeem
his house, then he shall add one-fifth of your valuation price to
it, so that it may be his.
16 'Again, if a man consecrates to the LORD part of the fields of his
own property, then your valuation shall be [1]proportionate to the
seed needed for it: a homer of barley seed at fifty shekels of silver.
17 'If he consecrates his field as of the year of jubilee, according
to your valuation it shall stand.
18 'If he consecrates his field after the jubilee, however, then
the priest shall calculate the price for [1]him [2]proportionate to
the years that are left until the year of jubilee; and it shall be
deducted from your valuation.
19 'If the one who consecrates it should ever wish to redeem
the field, then he shall add one-fifth of your valuation price to
it, so that it may pass to him.

27:2 [a]Num 6:2; Deut 23:21-23
3 [a]Ex 30:13; Lev 27:25; Num 3:47; 18:16
6 [a]Num 18:16
8 [1]Lit *what the hand reaches* [a]Lev 5:11; 14:21-24
9 [1]Lit *they*
10 [a]Lev 27:33
11 [1]Lit *they*
12 [1]Lit *between*
14 [1]Lit *between good*
16 [1]Lit *according to its seed*
18 [1]Or *it* [2]Lit *according to the years*

20 'Yet if he will not redeem the field, [1]but has sold the field to
another man, it may no longer be redeemed;
21 and when it [1]reverts in the jubilee, the field shall be holy
to the LORD, like a field [2]set apart; [a]it shall be for the priest as
his [3]property.
22 'Or if he consecrates to the LORD a field which he has
bought, which is not a part of the field of his own [1]property,
23 then the priest shall calculate for [1]him the amount of your
valuation up to the year of jubilee; and he shall on that day give
your valuation as holy to the LORD.
24 'In the year of jubilee the field shall return to the one from
whom he bought it, to whom the possession of the land
belongs.
25 'Every valuation of yours, moreover, shall be after [a]the
shekel of the sanctuary. The shekel shall be twenty gerahs.
26 '[a]However, a firstborn among animals, which as a firstborn
belongs to the LORD, no man may consecrate it; whether ox or
sheep, it is the LORD'S.
27 'But if *it is* among the unclean animals, then he shall
[1]redeem it according to your valuation and add to it one-fifth of
it; and if it is not redeemed, then it shall be sold according to
your valuation.
28 'Nevertheless, [a]anything which a man [1]sets apart to the
LORD out of all that he has, of man or animal or of the fields of
his own property, shall not be sold or redeemed. Anything
[2]devoted to destruction is most holy to the LORD.
29 'No [1]one who may have been [2]set apart among men shall
be ransomed; he shall surely be put to death.
30 'Thus [a]all the tithe of the land, of the seed of the land or of
the fruit of the tree, is the LORD'S; it is holy to the LORD.
31 'If, therefore, a man wishes to redeem part of his tithe, he
shall add to it one-fifth of it.
32 'For every tenth part of herd or flock, whatever [a]passes
under the rod, the tenth one shall be holy to the LORD.
33 '[a]He is not to be concerned whether *it is* good or bad, nor
shall he exchange it; or if he does exchange it, then both it and
its substitute shall become holy. It shall not be redeemed.'"
34 [a]These are the commandments which the LORD commanded
Moses for the sons of Israel at Mount Sinai.

20 [1]Or *if he*
21 [1]Lit *goes out* [2]Or *devoted, banned* [3]Lit *possession* [a]Num 18:14; Ezek 44:29
22 [1]Lit *possession*
23 [1]Or *it*
25 [a]Ex 30:13; Lev 27:3; Num 3:47; 18:16
26 [a]Ex 13:2
27 [1]Or *ransom*
28 [1]Lit *anything devoted;* or *banned* [2]Or *puts under the ban* [a]Num 18:14; Josh 6:17-19
29 [1]Lit *one devoted;* or *banned* [2]Or *put under the ban*
30 [a]Gen 28:22; 2 Chr 31:5; Neh 13:12
32 [a]Jer 33:13; Ezek 20:37
33 [a]Lev 27:10
34 [a]Lev 26:46; Deut 4:5

THE OFFERINGS AND THEIR PURPOSES

THE OFFERING	CHAPTER/ VERSE	VOLUNTARY/ INVOLUNTARY	REASON/PURPOSE

Theme of Leviticus:

Author:

Date:

Purpose:

Key Words:
(including synonyms)

- the Lord spoke to Moses saying
- offering
- tabernacle (tent of meeting)
- fat
- law
- restitution
- sacrifice
- anoint
- sin (iniquity)
- death (die)
- blood
- atonement
- consecrate
- holy
- covenant
- land (when it refers to that given by God)
- sabbath
- jubilee

Segment Divisions				
	Laws Regarding	Main Division		Chapter Themes
		Worshiping a Holy God	1	
			2	
			3	
			4	
			5	
			6	
			7	
			8	
			9	
			10	
			11	
			12	
			13	
			14	
			15	
			16	
			17	
		Living a Holy Life	18	
			19	
			20	
			21	
			22	
			23	
			24	
			25	
			26	
			27	

The Feasts of Israel

	1st Month (Nisan) Festival of Passover *(Pesach)*				3rd Month (Sivan) Fes[tival] of Pentecost *(Shavu[ot])*
Slaves in Egypt 	**Passover** 	**Unleavened Bread** 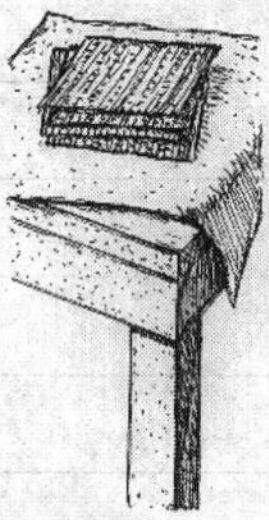	**First fruits** 		**Pentecost or Feast of Weeks** 
	Kill lamb & put blood on doorpost Exodus 12:6, 7	*Purging of all leaven* (symbol of sin)	*Wave offering of sheaf* (promise of harvest to come)		*Wave offering of tw[o] loaves of leavened br[ead]*
Whosoever commits sin is the slave to sin	1st month, 14th day Leviticus 23:5	1st month, 15th day for 7 days Leviticus 23:6-8	Day after Sabbath Leviticus 23:9-14		50 days after first frui[ts] Leviticus 23:15-21
	Christ our Passover has been sacrificed 	**Clean out old leaven... just as you are in fact unleavened**	**Christ has been raised...the first fruits** 	**Going away so Comforter can come**  Mount of Olives	**Promise of the Spi[rit] mystery of church Jews-Gentiles in one** 
John 8:34	1 Corinthians 5:7	1 Corinthians 5:7, 8	1 Corinthians 15:20-23	John 16:7 Acts 1:9-12	Acts 2:1-47 1 Corinthians 12:13 Ephesians 2:11-22

Months: Nisan—*March, April* • **Sivan**—*May, June* • **Tishri**—*September, October*

7th Month (Tishri)
Festival of Tabernacles *(Succoth)*

Feast of Trumpets	Day of Atonement	Feast of Booths or Tabernacles
Trumpet blown — a holy convocation	*Atonement shall be made to cleanse you* Leviticus 16:30	*Harvest celebration memorial of tabernacles in wilderness*
7th month, 1st day Leviticus 23:23-25 *(It is a Sabbath)*	7th month, 10th day Leviticus 23:26-32 *(It is a Sabbath)*	7th month, 15th day, for 7 days; 8th day, Holy Convocation Leviticus 23:33-44 *(The 1st and 8th days are Sabbaths)*
Regathering of Israel in preparation for final day of atonement Jeremiah 32:37-41	**Israel will repent and look to Messiah in one day** Zechariah 3:9,10; 12:10; 13:1; 14:9	**Families of the earth will come to Jerusalem to celebrate the Feast of Booths** Zechariah 14:16-19
Ezekiel 36:24	Ezekiel 36:25-27 Hebrews 9, 10 Romans 11:25-29	Ezekiel 36:28

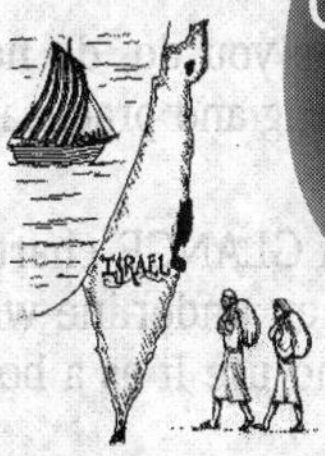

nterlude etween estivals

Coming of Christ

New heaven and new earth

God tabernacles with men

Revelation 21:1-3

Israel had two harvests each year—spring and autumn

NUMBERS במדבר BAMIDBAR

The Israelites cried out to God. The Lord heard their cry and raised up Moses to deliver the children of Israel out of the land of Egypt. They had lived in Egypt for 430 years, 400 of those years as slaves. After camping at Sinai, they were to go to Canaan, the land promised to Abraham, Isaac, and Jacob. At last they would see the land with their own eyes. And God would go with them in a pillar of cloud by day and a pillar of fire by night.

Soon the journey would begin, but first there must be a numbering of all the sons of Israel from 20 years of age on up.

Things to Do

General Instructions

The book of Numbers can be divided into three segments according to the journeys and encampments of the children of Israel. In Numbers 1 through 10:10 they are encamped at Sinai. In Numbers 10:11 the cloud lifts and their journeying begins and does not end for about 39 years. In Numbers 22 Israel camps on the plains of Moab, opposite Jericho, as they prepare to enter the land of promise.

Chapters 1–10:10

1. The first five books of the Bible, Genesis through Deuteronomy, are closely related. They follow each other chronologically. To put Numbers into context:

   a. Read Exodus 40:1-2,17,33-38, which gives an account of the building of the tabernacle at Mount Sinai.

   b. Read Leviticus 1:1 and then 27:34. All of the book of Leviticus takes place at Mount Sinai.

   c. Compare where Leviticus ends and Numbers begins. Read Numbers 1:1-2.

   d. Look at Exodus 40:17 again and Numbers 1:1, and you will see one month elapsed between the close of Exodus and the beginning of Numbers. Leviticus covers a period of only one month.

2. Read through this first segment chapter by chapter. As you do, do not become discouraged and quit; Numbers becomes delightfully interesting and practical after this segment. As you read:

   a. Mark the key words listed on the NUMBERS AT A GLANCE chart on page 288. Also mark *number* or *census* and *of the sons of* (then underline whose sons they were). Write all the key words on an index card and use it as a bookmark as you study Numbers.

   b. Mark every reference to time with a clock ⏲, and double-underline all geographical locations in green.

   c. In the margin of each chapter make lists of key truths you want to be able to find with ease. For instance, next to 9:15 you might write: "Instructions re: Cloud" or simply "The Cloud."

   d. Note the theme of each chapter and record it on the NUMBERS AT A GLANCE chart and at the beginning of the chapter in your Bible.

Chapters 10:11–21:35

1. This segment covers about 39 years. As you study you will discover why it takes so long to cover such a relatively short distance. Do the following as you study chapter by chapter:

   a. Since much of what you will read in this segment is historical, you can learn a lot simply by asking the "5 W's and an H." Ask: Who are the main characters in this chapter? What is happening? Why is it happening? When and where is it happening? Why are they told to do something? What were the consequences of their actions? How and why did this occur?

      1) You might want to note in the margin when and where events occur.

      2) Follow the movements of the Israelites on the map on page 240.

   b. Mark key repeated words. Add *grumbled (complain)* and *anger* to your list. Watch for key words that are not on the list but will be significant in a particular chapter.

   c. Write on a piece of paper what you learn about the land the Israelites are to possess and what you learn about Korah and Balaam. (Balaam appears in Numbers 22.) These two men will be mentioned again, even in the New Testament, so it will be helpful to mark them in a distinctive color and then to summarize all you learn about them on the chart INSIGHTS FROM NUMBERS on page 287.

   d. There are lessons to be learned from Moses' life about leadership and about our relationship to God. You will also find it profitable to summarize what you learn by making a chart in your notebook called LESSONS FROM THE LIFE OF MOSES on pages 351, 352. When you record your insights, make sure you note the book, chapter, and verse from which you took your insight.

2. As you did before, record each chapter theme on NUMBERS AT A GLANCE and in the text.

Chapters 22–36

1. This final segment of Numbers is a mixture of historical events, instructions, and numberings. As you read each chapter, remember to ask the "5 W's and an H" and to record any pertinent insights in the margin.

2. To your list of key words add the following: *Moab* (Moab is first mentioned in Numbers 21, so go back and mark *Moab* in that chapter also), *Midian (Midianites), burnt offering,* and *sin offering*.

3. Balaam plays a major role in this last segment. Note all you learn about him on INSIGHTS FROM NUMBERS on page 287. As you near the end of Numbers you will read more about Balaam, so note in the margin where these final verses on Balaam can be found.

4. Record the main points or events of these chapters in the margin. In Numbers 35 mark every reference to *murderer* and *blood avenger*. See what you learn.

5. Record what you learn about Moses. Give special attention to Numbers 27:12-23 in the light of Numbers 20. Next to Numbers 20:1-13 you might want to write Numbers 27:12-23 as a cross-reference.

6. Record your chapter themes as you did before.

7. Record the predominant theme or event in each of the three segments of Numbers on NUMBERS AT A GLANCE. See if any of the chapters can be grouped according to the types of commands, ordinances, and/or events. In other words, do several chapters cover similar topics or events? For example, chapters 1 and 2 cover the census. Note

these in the first column under "Segment Divisions" and complete the NUMBERS AT A GLANCE chart.

THINGS TO THINK ABOUT

1. Review all you learned from Moses' life and then pray about how it applies to your own life.

2. Remember, God is the same yesterday, today, and forever. His character did not change between the Old Testament and the New Testament. Think about what you have learned about God from the book of Numbers. Are you living according to His standard of righteousness?

3. Are you jealous because the children of Israel had a cloud to guide them? Have you realized that God's presence in the form of the indwelling Spirit is available to guide you? Do you seek and ask for His Spirit to lead and guide you just as surely as He led the children of Israel? What can you learn from the children of Israel so you won't make the same mistakes?

Chapter 1 Theme ____________________

1 Then the LORD spoke to Moses in the wilderness of Sinai, in
the tent of meeting, on [a]the first of the second month, in the
second year after they had come out of the land of Egypt, saying,
2 "[a]Take a [1]census of all the congregation of the sons of Israel,
by their families, by their fathers' households, according to the
number of names, every male, head by head
3 from [a]twenty years old and upward, whoever *is able to* go
out to war in Israel, you and Aaron shall [1]number them by
their armies.
4 "With you, moreover, there shall be a man of each tribe,
[a]each one head of his father's household.
5 "These then are the names of the men who shall stand with
you: [a]of Reuben, Elizur the son of Shedeur;
6 of Simeon, Shelumiel the son of Zurishaddai;
7 of Judah, [a]Nahshon the son of Amminadab;
8 of Issachar, Nethanel the son of Zuar;
9 of Zebulun, Eliab the son of Helon;
10 of the sons of Joseph: of Ephraim, Elishama the son of
Ammihud; of Manasseh, Gamaliel the son of Pedahzur;
11 of Benjamin, Abidan the son of Gideoni;
12 of Dan, Ahiezer the son of Ammishaddai;
13 of Asher, Pagiel the son of Ochran;
14 of Gad, Eliasaph the son of [a]Deuel;
15 of Naphtali, Ahira the son of Enan.
16 "These are they who were [a]called of the congregation, the
leaders of their fathers' tribes; they were the [b]heads of
[1]divisions of Israel."
17 So Moses and Aaron took these men who had been
designated by name,
18 and they assembled all the congregation together on the
[a]first of the second month. Then they registered by [b]ancestry in

1:1 [a]Ex 40:2, 17
2 [1]Lit *sum* [a]Ex 12:37; 38:25, 26; Num 26:2
3 [1]Lit *muster,* and so throughout the ch [a]Ex 30:14; 38:26
4 [a]Ex 18:21, 25; Num 1:16; Deut 1:15
5 [a]Gen 29:32; Ex 1:2; Deut 33:6; Rev 7:5
7 [a]Ruth 4:20; 1 Chr 2:10; Luke 3:32
14 [a]Num 2:14
16 [1]Lit *thousands;* or *clans* [a]Ex 18:21; Num 7:2; 16:2; 26:9 [b]Ex 18:25
18 [a]Num 1:1 [b]Ezra 2:59; Heb 7:3

their families, by their fathers' households, according to the number of names, from twenty years old and upward, head by head,
19 just as [a]the LORD had commanded Moses. So he numbered them in the wilderness of Sinai.
20 [a]Now the sons of Reuben, Israel's firstborn, their genealogical registration by their families, by their fathers' households, according to the number of names, head by head, every male from twenty years old and upward, whoever *was able to* go out to war,
21 their numbered men of the tribe of Reuben *were* 46,500.
22 [a]Of the sons of Simeon, their genealogical registration by their families, by their fathers' households, their numbered men, according to the number of names, head by head, every male from twenty years old and upward, [b]whoever *was able to* go out to war,
23 their numbered men of the tribe of Simeon *were* 59,300.
24 [a]Of the sons of Gad, their genealogical registration by their families, by their fathers' households, according to the number of names, from twenty years old and upward, whoever *was able to* go out to war,
25 their numbered men of the tribe of Gad *were* 45,650.
26 [a]Of the sons of Judah, their genealogical registration by their families, by their fathers' households, according to the number of names, from twenty years old and upward, whoever *was able to* go out to war,
27 their numbered men of the tribe of Judah *were* 74,600.
28 [a]Of the sons of Issachar, their genealogical registration by their families, by their fathers' households, according to the number of names, from twenty years old and upward, whoever *was able to* go out to war,
29 their numbered men of the tribe of Issachar *were* 54,400.
30 [a]Of the sons of Zebulun, their genealogical registration by their families, by their fathers' households, according to the number of names, from twenty years old and upward, whoever *was able to* go out to war,
31 their numbered men of the tribe of Zebulun *were* 57,400.
32 [a]Of the sons of Joseph, *namely,* of the sons of Ephraim, their genealogical registration by their families, by their fathers' households, according to the number of names, from twenty years old and upward, whoever *was able to* go out to war,
33 their numbered men of the tribe of Ephraim *were* 40,500.
34 [a]Of the sons of Manasseh, their genealogical registration by their families, by their fathers' households, according to the number of names, from twenty years old and upward, whoever *was able to* go out to war,
35 their numbered men of the tribe of Manasseh *were* 32,200.
36 [a]Of the sons of Benjamin, their genealogical registration by their families, by their fathers' households, according to the number of names, from twenty years old and upward, whoever *was able to* go out to war,

19 [a]2 Sam 24:1
20 [a]Num 26:5-7
22 [a]Num 26:12-14 [b]Ps 144:1
24 [a]Gen 30:11; Num 26:15-18; Josh 4:12; Jer 49:1
26 [a]Gen 29:35; Num 26:19-22; 2 Sam 24:9; Ps 78:68; Matt 1:2
28 [a]Num 26:23-25
30 [a]Num 26:26, 27
32 [a]Num 26:35-37; Deut 33:13-17; Jer 7:15; Obad 19
34 [a]Num 26:28-34
36 [a]Gen 49:27; Num 26:38-41; 2 Chr 17:17; Rev 7:8

37 their numbered men of the tribe of Benjamin *were* 35,400.
38 [a]Of the sons of Dan, their genealogical registration by their
families, by their fathers' households, according to the number
of names, from twenty years old and upward, whoever *was*
able to go out to war,
39 their numbered men of the tribe of Dan *were* 62,700.
40 [a]Of the sons of Asher, their genealogical registration by
their families, by their fathers' households, according to the
number of names, from twenty years old and upward, whoever
was able to go out to war,
41 their numbered men of the tribe of Asher *were* 41,500.
42 [a]Of the sons of Naphtali, their genealogical registration by
their families, by their fathers' households, according to the
number of names, from twenty years old and upward, whoever
was able to go out to war,
43 their numbered men of the tribe of Naphtali *were* 53,400.
44 These are the ones who were numbered, whom Moses
and Aaron numbered, with the leaders of Israel, twelve men,
each of whom was of his father's household.
45 So all the numbered men of the sons of Israel by their
fathers' households, from twenty years old and upward, whoever
was able to go out to war in Israel,
46 even all the numbered men were [a]603,550.
47 [a]The Levites, however, were not numbered among them
by their fathers' tribe.
48 For the LORD had spoken to Moses, saying,
49 "Only the tribe of Levi [a]you shall not number, nor shall you
take their [1]census among the sons of Israel.
50 "But you shall [a]appoint the Levites over the [1]tabernacle of
the testimony, and over all its furnishings and over all that belongs
to it. They shall carry the tabernacle and all its furnishings, and
they shall take care of it; they shall also camp around the [1]taber-
nacle.
51 "[a]So when the tabernacle is to set out, the Levites shall take
it down; and when the tabernacle encamps, the Levites shall set
it up. But [b]the [1]layman who comes near shall be put to death.
52 "[a]The sons of Israel shall camp, each man by his own camp,
and each man by his own standard, according to their armies.
53 "[a]But the Levites shall camp around the tabernacle of the
testimony, so that there will be [b]no wrath on the congregation
of the sons of Israel. [c]So the Levites shall keep charge of the
tabernacle of the testimony."
54 Thus the sons of Israel did; according to all which the LORD
had commanded Moses, so they did.

Chapter 2 Theme ________________________

2 Now the LORD spoke to Moses and to Aaron, saying,
2 "[a]The sons of Israel shall camp, each by his own standard,
with the [1]banners of their fathers' households; they shall camp
around the tent of meeting [2]at a distance.

38 [a]Gen 30:6; 46:23; Num 2:25; 26:42, 43
40 [a]Num 26:44-47
42 [a]Num 26:48-50
46 [a]Ex 12:37; 38:26; Num 2:32; 26:51
47 [a]Num 2:33; 3:14-39; 4:49; 26:57-64
49 [1]Lit *sum* [a]Num 26:62
50 [1]Lit *dwelling place,* and so throughout the ch [a]Ex 38:21; Num 3:6-8, 25-37; 4:15, 25-27, 31, 32
51 [1]Lit *stranger* [a]Num 4:1-33 [b]Num 3:10, 38; 4:15, 19, 20
52 [a]Num 2:2, 34
53 [a]Num 3:23, 29, 35, 38 [b]Lev 10:6; Num 16:46; 18:5 [c]Num 8:24; 18:2-4; 1 Chr 23:32
2:2 [1]Lit *signs* [2]Or *facing it* [a]Num 1:52; 24:2

3 “Now those who camp on the east side toward the sunrise
shall be of the standard of the camp of Judah, by their armies, and
the leader of the sons of Judah: [a]Nahshon the son of Amminadab,
4 and his army, even their [1]numbered men, 74,600.
5 “Those who camp next to him *shall be* the tribe of Issachar,
and the leader of the sons of Issachar: [a]Nethanel the son of Zuar,
6 and his army, even their numbered men, 54,400.
7 “*Then comes* the tribe of Zebulun, and the leader of the
sons of Zebulun: [a]Eliab the son of Helon,
8 and his army, even his numbered men, 57,400.
9 “The total of the numbered men of the camp of Judah:
186,400, by their armies. [a]They shall set out first.
10 “On the south side *shall be* the standard of the camp of
Reuben by their armies, and the leader of the sons of Reuben:
[a]Elizur the son of Shedeur,
11 and his army, even their numbered men, 46,500.
12 “Those who camp next to him *shall be* the tribe of Simeon,
and the leader of the sons of Simeon: [a]Shelumiel the son of
Zurishaddai,
13 and his army, even their numbered men, 59,300.
14 “Then *comes* the tribe of Gad, and the leader of the sons of
Gad: [a]Eliasaph the son of [1]Deuel,
15 and his army, even their
numbered men, 45,650.
16 “The total of the numbered men
of the camp of Reuben: 151,450
by their armies. And [a]they shall set
out second.
17 “[a]Then the tent of meeting
shall set out *with* the camp of the
Levites in the midst of the camps;
just as they camp, so they shall set
out, every man in his place by their
standards.
18 “On the west side *shall be* the
standard of the camp of [a]Ephraim
by their armies, and the leader of
the sons of Ephraim *shall be*
[b]Elishama the son of Ammihud,
19 and his army, even their numbered men, 40,500.
20 “Next to him *shall be* the tribe of Manasseh, and the leader
of the sons of Manasseh: [a]Gamaliel the son of Pedahzur,
21 and his army, even their numbered men, 32,200.
22 “Then *comes* the tribe of [a]Benjamin, and the leader of the
sons of Benjamin: [b]Abidan the son of Gideoni,
23 and his army, even their numbered men, 35,400.
24 “The total of the numbered men of the camp of Ephraim:
108,100, by their armies. And [a]they shall set out third.
25 “On the north side *shall be* the standard of the camp of Dan
by their armies, and the leader of the sons of Dan: [a]Ahiezer the
son of Ammishaddai,

3 [a]Num 1:7; 10:14; Ruth 4:20; 1 Chr 2:10; Luke 3:32, 33
4 [1]Lit *mustered,* and so throughout the ch
5 [a]Num 1:8; 7:18, 23
7 [a]Num 1:9
9 [a]Num 10:14
10 [a]Num 1:5
12 [a]Num 1:6
14 [1]Many mss read *Reuel* [a]Num 1:14; 7:42
16 [a]Num 10:18
17 [a]Num 1:53
18 [a]Gen 48:14-20; Jer 31:9, 18-20 [b]Num 1:10
20 [a]Num 1:10
22 [a]Ps 68:27 [b]Num 1:11
24 [a]Num 10:22
25 [a]Num 1:12

Camp Arrangement of Israel’s Tribes

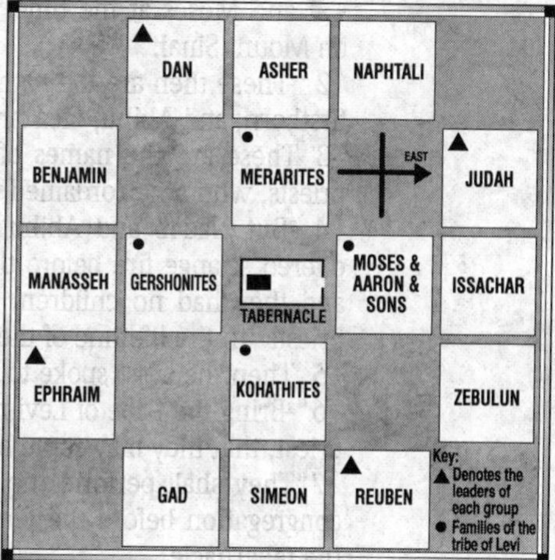

26 and his army, even their numbered men, 62,700.
27 "Those who camp next to him *shall be* the tribe of Asher,
and the leader of the sons of Asher: [a]Pagiel the son of Ochran,
28 and his army, even their numbered men, 41,500.
29 "Then *comes* the tribe of [a]Naphtali, and the leader of the
sons of Naphtali: [b]Ahira the son of Enan,
30 and his army, even their numbered men, 53,400.
31 "The total of the numbered men of the camp of Dan *was*
157,600. [a]They shall set out last by their standards."
32 These are the numbered men of the sons of Israel by their
fathers' households; the total of the numbered men of the
camps by their armies, [a]603,550.
33 [a]The Levites, however, were not numbered among the sons
of Israel, just as the LORD had commanded Moses.
34 Thus the sons of Israel did; according to all that the LORD
commanded Moses, so they camped by their standards, and so
they set out, every one by his family according to his father's
household.

Chapter 3 Theme ________________

3 [a]Now these are *the records of* the generations of Aaron
and Moses at the time when the LORD spoke with Moses
on Mount Sinai.
2 [a]These then are the names of the sons of Aaron: Nadab the
firstborn, and Abihu, Eleazar and Ithamar.
3 These are the names of the sons of Aaron, the [a]anointed
priests, whom he [1]ordained to serve as priests.
4 [a]But Nadab and Abihu died before the LORD when they
offered strange fire before the LORD in the wilderness of Sinai;
and they had no children. So Eleazar and Ithamar served as
priests [1]in the lifetime of their father Aaron.
5 Then the LORD spoke to Moses, saying,
6 "[a]Bring the tribe of Levi near and set them before Aaron the
priest, that they may serve him.
7 "They shall perform the duties for [1]him and for the whole
congregation before the tent of meeting, to do the [a]service of
the tabernacle.
8 "They shall also keep all the furnishings of the tent of
meeting, along with the duties of the sons of Israel, to do the
service of the tabernacle.
9 "You shall thus [a]give the Levites to Aaron and to his sons;
they are wholly given to him from among the sons of Israel.
10 "So you shall appoint Aaron and his sons that [a]they may
keep their priesthood, but [b]the [1]layman who comes near shall
be put to death."
11 Again the LORD spoke to Moses, saying,
12 "Now, behold, I [a]have taken the Levites from among the
sons of Israel instead of every [b]firstborn, the first issue of the
womb among the sons of Israel. So the Levites shall be Mine.
13 "For [a]all the firstborn are Mine; on the day that I struck

27 [a]Num 1:13
29 [a]Gen 30:8 [b]Num 1:15
31 [a]Num 10:25
32 [a]Ex 38:26; Num 1:46
33 [a]Num 1:47; 26:57-62
3:1 [a]Ex 6:20-27
2 [a]Ex 6:23; Num 26:60
3 [1]Lit *filled their hand* [a]Ex 28:41
4 [1]Lit *before the face* [a]Lev 10:1, 2; Num 26:61
6 [a]Num 8:6-22; 18:1-7; Deut 10:8
7 [1]Lit *him and the duties of the whole congregation* [a]Num 1:50
9 [a]Num 18:6
10 [1]Lit *stranger* [a]Ex 29:9 [b]Num 1:51
12 [a]Num 3:45; 8:14 [b]Ex 13:2
13 [a]Ex 13:2; Lev 27:26; Neh 10:36

14 [a]Ex 19:1

down all the firstborn in the land of Egypt, I sanctified to Myself
all the firstborn in Israel, from man to beast. They shall be
Mine; I am the LORD."
14 Then the LORD spoke to Moses [a]in the wilderness of Sinai,
saying,
15 "[1][a]Number the sons of Levi by their fathers' households, by
their families; every male from a month old and upward you
shall number."
16 So Moses numbered them according to the [1]word of the
LORD, just as he had been commanded.
17 [a]These then are the sons of Levi by their names: Gershon
and Kohath and Merari.
18 These are the names of the [a]sons of Gershon by their
families: Libni and Shimei;
19 and the sons of Kohath by their families: Amram and Izhar,
Hebron and Uzziel;
20 and the sons of Merari by their families: Mahli and Mushi.
These are the families of the Levites according to their fathers'
households.
21 Of Gershon *was* the family of the Libnites and the family of
the Shimeites; these *were* the families of the Gershonites.
22 Their numbered men, in the numbering of every male from
a month old and upward, *even* their numbered men *were* 7,500.
23 The families of the Gershonites were to camp behind the
[1]tabernacle westward,
24 and the leader of the fathers' households of the
Gershonites *was* Eliasaph the son of Lael.

Duties of the Gershonites:

25 Now [a]the duties of the sons of Gershon in the tent of
meeting *involved* the tabernacle and [b]the tent, its covering, and
[c]the screen for the doorway of the tent of meeting,
26 and [a]the hangings of the court, and [b]the screen for the
doorway of the court which is around the tabernacle and the
altar, and its cords, according to all the service [1]concerning them.
27 Of Kohath *was* the family of the Amramites and the family
of the Izharites and the family of the Hebronites and the family
of the Uzzielites; these were the families of the Kohathites.
28 In the numbering of every male from a month old and
upward, *there were* 8,600, performing the duties of the sanctuary.
29 The families of the sons of Kohath were to camp on the
southward side of the tabernacle,
30 and the leader of the fathers' households of the Kohathite
families was [1]Elizaphan the son of Uzziel.

Duties of the Kohathites:

31 Now [a]their duties *involved* [b]the ark, [c]the table, [d]the
lampstand, [e]the altars, and the utensils of the sanctuary with
which they minister, and the screen, and all the service
[1]concerning them;
32 and Eleazar the son of Aaron the priest *was* the chief of the
leaders of Levi, *and had* the oversight of those who perform
the duties of the sanctuary.
33 Of Merari *was* the family of the Mahlites and the family of
the Mushites; these *were* the families of Merari.

15 [1]Lit *muster,* and so throughout the ch [a]Num 1:47

16 [1]Lit *mouth*

17 [a]Ex 6:16-22

18 [a]Ex 6:17

23 [1]Lit *dwelling place,* and so throughout the ch

25 [a]Num 4:24-26 [b]Ex 26:1, 7, 14 [c]Ex 26:36

26 [1]Lit *of it* [a]Ex 27:9, 12, 14, 15 [b]Ex 27:16

30 [1]In Ex 6:22, *Elzaphan*

31 [1]Lit *of it* [a]Num 4:15 [b]Ex 25:10-22 [c]Ex 25:23-28 [d]Ex 25:31-40 [e]Ex 27:1, 2; 30:1-5

34 Their numbered men in the numbering of every male from a month old and upward, *were* 6,200.

35 The leader of the fathers' households of the families of Merari *was* Zuriel the son of Abihail. They *were* to [a]camp on the northward side of the tabernacle.

Duties of the Merarites:

36 Now the appointed duties of the sons of Merari *involved* the frames of the tabernacle, its bars, its pillars, its sockets, all its equipment, and the service concerning them,

37 and the pillars around the court with their sockets and their pegs and their cords.

38 Now those who were to [a]camp before the tabernacle eastward, before the tent of meeting toward the sunrise, are Moses and Aaron and his sons, performing the duties of the sanctuary for the obligation of the sons of Israel; but [b]the [1]layman coming near was to be put to death.

39 All the numbered men of the Levites, whom Moses and Aaron numbered at the [1]command of the LORD by their families, every male from a month old and upward, *were* [a]22,000.

40 Then the LORD said to Moses, "[a]Number every firstborn male of the sons of Israel from a month old and upward, and [1]make a list of their names.

41 "You [a]shall take the Levites for Me, I am the LORD, instead of all the firstborn among the sons of Israel, and the cattle of the Levites instead of all the firstborn among the cattle of the sons of Israel."

42 So Moses numbered all the firstborn among the sons of Israel, just as the LORD had commanded him;

43 and all the firstborn males by the number of names from a month old and upward, for their numbered men were [a]22,273.

44 Then the LORD spoke to Moses, saying,

45 "[a]Take the Levites instead of all the firstborn among the sons of Israel and the cattle of the Levites. And the Levites shall be Mine; I am the LORD.

46 "[a]For the ransom of the 273 of the firstborn of the sons of Israel who are in excess beyond the Levites,

47 you shall take [a]five shekels apiece, per head; you shall take *them* in [b]terms of the shekel of the sanctuary ([c]the shekel is twenty [1]gerahs),

48 and give the money, the ransom of those who are in excess among them, to Aaron and to his sons."

49 So Moses took the ransom money from those who were in excess, beyond those ransomed by the Levites;

50 from the firstborn of the sons of Israel he took the money in terms of the shekel of the sanctuary, 1,365.

51 Then Moses gave the ransom money to Aaron and to his sons, at the [1]command of the LORD, just as the LORD had commanded Moses.

Chapter 4 Theme __________________________________

4 Then the LORD spoke to Moses and to Aaron, saying,

2 "Take [1]a census of the [2]descendants of Kohath from among the sons of Levi, by their families, by their fathers' households,

35 [a]Num 1:53; 2:25

38 [1]Lit *stranger* [a]Num 1:53; 2:3 [b]Num 1:51

39 [1]Lit *word* [a]Num 3:43; 4:48; 26:62

40 [1]Lit *take the number* [a]Num 3:15

41 [a]Num 3:12, 45

43 [a]Num 3:39

45 [a]Num 3:12

46 [a]Ex 13:13, 15; Num 18:15, 16

47 [1]I.e. A gerah equals approx one-fortieth oz [a]Lev 27:6; Num 18:16 [b]Ex 30:13 [c]Lev 27:25; Ezek 45:12

51 [1]Lit *mouth*

4:2 [1]Lit *the sum* [2]Lit *sons*

3 from [a]thirty years and upward, even to fifty years old, all who
enter the service to do the work in the tent of meeting.
4 "This is the work of the [1]descendants of Kohath in the tent
of meeting, *concerning* the most holy things.
5 "When the camp sets out, Aaron and his sons shall go in
and they shall take down [a]the veil of the screen and cover the
[b]ark of the testimony with it;
6 and they shall lay a [a]covering of porpoise skin on it, and shall
spread over *it* a cloth of pure [1]blue, and shall insert its poles.
7 "Over the table of the bread of the Presence they shall also
spread a cloth of [1]blue and put on it the dishes and the pans
and the sacrificial bowls and the jars for the drink offering, and
[a]the continual bread shall be on it.
8 "They shall spread over them a cloth of scarlet *material,* and
cover the same with a covering of porpoise skin, and they shall
insert its poles.
9 "Then they shall take a [1]blue cloth and cover the [a]lampstand
for the light, [b]along with its lamps and its snuffers, and its
[2]trays and all its oil vessels, by which they serve it;
10 and they shall put it and all its utensils in a covering of
porpoise skin, and shall put it on the carrying bars.
11 "Over the golden altar they shall spread a [1]blue cloth and
cover it with a covering of porpoise skin, and shall insert its poles;
12 and they shall take all the utensils of service, with which
they serve in the sanctuary, and put them in a [1]blue cloth and
cover them with a covering of porpoise skin, and put them on
the carrying bars.
13 "Then they shall take away the [1]ashes from the [a]altar, and
spread a purple cloth over it.
14 "They shall also put on it all its utensils by which they serve
in connection with it: the firepans, the forks and shovels and
the basins, all the utensils of the altar; and they shall spread a
cover of porpoise skin over it and insert its poles.
15 "When Aaron and his sons have finished covering the holy
objects and all the furnishings of the sanctuary, when the camp
is to set out, after that the sons of Kohath shall come to carry
them, so that they will not touch the holy *objects* [a]and die.
These are the [1]things in the tent of meeting which the sons of
Kohath are to carry.
16 "The responsibility of Eleazar the son of Aaron the priest is
[a]the oil for the light and the [b]fragrant incense and [c]the continual
grain offering and [d]the anointing oil—the responsibility of all
the [1]tabernacle and of all that is in it, with the sanctuary and its
furnishings."
17 Then the LORD spoke to Moses and to Aaron, saying,
18 "Do not let the tribe of the families of the Kohathites be cut
off from among the Levites.
19 "But do this to them that they may live and [a]not die when
they approach the most holy *objects:* Aaron and his sons
shall go in and assign each of them to his work and to his
load;

3 [a]Num 4:23, 30, 35; 8:24; 1 Chr 23:3, 24, 27; Ezra 3:8

4 [1]Lit *sons*

5 [a]Ex 40:5; Lev 16:2; 2 Chr 3:14; Matt 27:51; Heb 9:3 [b]Ex 25:10-16

6 [1]Or *violet* [a]Num 4:25

7 [1]Or *violet* [a]Ex 25:30; Lev 24:5-9

9 [1]Or *violet* [2]Lit *snuff dishes* [a]Ex 25:31 [b]Ex 25:37, 38

11 [1]Or *violet*

12 [1]Or *violet*

13 [1]Or *fat ashes;* i.e. soaked with fat [a]Ex 27:1-8

15 [1]Lit *burden . . . of the sons* [a]Num 1:51; 4:19, 20; 2 Sam 6:6, 7

16 [1]Lit *dwelling place,* and so throughout the ch [a]Lev 24:1-3 [b]Ex 30:34-38 [c]Lev 6:20 [d]Ex 30:22-33

19 [a]Num 4:15

20 but [a]they shall not go in to see the holy *objects* even for a
moment, or they will die."
21 Then the LORD spoke to Moses, saying,
22 "Take [1]a census of the sons of Gershon [2]also, by their
fathers' households, by their families;
23 from [a]thirty years and upward to fifty years old, you shall
[1]number them; all who enter to perform the service to do the
work in the tent of meeting.
24 "This is the service of the families of the Gershonites, in
serving and in carrying:
25 they shall carry [a]the curtains of the tabernacle and the tent
of meeting *with* its covering and [b]the covering of porpoise skin
that is on top of it, and the screen for the doorway of the tent
of meeting,
26 and [a]the hangings of the court, and the screen for the doorway
of the gate of the court which is around the tabernacle and the
altar, and their cords and all the equipment for their service; and
all that is to be done, [1]they shall perform.
27 "All the service of the sons of the Gershonites, in all their
loads and in all their work, shall be *performed* at the
[1]command of Aaron and his sons; and you shall assign to them
as a duty all their loads.
28 "This is the service of the families of the sons of the
Gershonites in the tent of meeting, and their duties *shall be*
[1]under the direction of Ithamar the son of Aaron the priest.
29 "*As for* the sons of Merari, you shall number them by their
families, by their fathers' households;
30 from [a]thirty years and upward even to fifty years old, you
shall number them, everyone who enters the service to do the
work of the tent of meeting.
31 "Now this is the duty of their loads, for all their service in
the tent of meeting: the boards of the tabernacle and its bars
and its pillars and its [1]sockets,
32 and the pillars around the court and their [1]sockets and
their pegs and their cords, with all their equipment and with
all their service; and you shall assign *each man* by name the
items [2]he is to carry.
33 "This is the service of the families of the sons of Merari,
according to all their service in the tent of meeting, [1]under the
direction of Ithamar the son of Aaron the priest."
34 So Moses and Aaron and the leaders of the congregation
numbered the sons of the Kohathites by their families and by
their fathers' households,
35 from [a]thirty years and upward even to fifty years old,
everyone who entered the service for work in the tent of
meeting.
36 Their numbered men by their families were 2,750.
37 These are the numbered men of the Kohathite families,
everyone who was serving in the tent of meeting, whom
Moses and Aaron numbered according to the [1]commandment
of the LORD [2]through Moses.

20 [a]Ex 19:21; 1 Sam 6:19

22 [1]Lit *the sum* [2]Lit *also them*

23 [1]Lit *muster,* and so throughout the ch [a]Num 4:3; 1 Chr 23:3, 24, 27

25 [a]Ex 40:19 [b]Ex 26:14; Num 4:6

26 [1]Lit *so they shall serve* [a]Ex 38:9

27 [1]Lit *mouth*

28 [1]Lit *in the hand*

30 [a]Num 4:3; 8:24-26

31 [1]Or *bases*

32 [1]Or *bases* [2]Lit *of the duty of their loads*

33 [1]Lit *in the hand*

35 [a]1 Chr 23:24

37 [1]Lit *mouth* [2]Lit *by the hand of*

38 The numbered men of the sons of Gershon by their families
and by their fathers' households,
39 from thirty years and upward even to fifty years old, everyone
who entered the service for work in the tent of meeting.
40 Their numbered men by their families, by their fathers'
households, were 2,630.
41 These are the numbered men of the families of the sons of
Gershon, everyone who was serving in the tent of meeting, whom
Moses and Aaron numbered according to the [1]commandment
of the LORD.
42 The numbered men of the families of the sons of Merari by
their families, by their fathers' households,
43 from [a]thirty years and upward even to fifty years old, everyone
who entered the service for work in the tent of meeting.
44 Their numbered men by their families were 3,200.
45 These are the numbered men of the families of the sons of
Merari, whom Moses and Aaron numbered according to the
[1]commandment of the LORD [2]through Moses.
46 All the numbered men of the Levites, whom Moses and
Aaron and the leaders of Israel numbered, by their families and
by their fathers' households,
47 from thirty years and upward even to fifty years old,
everyone who could enter to do the work of service and the
work of carrying in the tent of meeting.
48 Their numbered men were [a]8,580.
49 According to the [1]commandment of the LORD [2]through
Moses, they [a]were numbered, everyone by his serving or
carrying; thus *these were* his numbered men, just as the LORD
had commanded Moses.

Chapter 5 Theme

5 Then the LORD spoke to Moses, saying,
2 "Command the sons of Israel that they [a]send away from
the camp every leper and everyone having a [b]discharge and everyone who is [c]unclean because of a *dead* person.
3 "You shall send away both male and female; you shall send
them outside the camp so that they will not defile their camp
where I dwell [a]in their midst."
4 The sons of Israel did so and sent them outside the camp;
just as the LORD had spoken to Moses, thus the sons of Israel did.
5 Then the LORD spoke to Moses, saying,
6 "Speak to the sons of Israel, '[a]When a man or woman
commits any of the sins of mankind, acting unfaithfully against
the LORD, and that person is guilty,
7 then [1]he shall [a]confess [2]his sins which [3]he has committed,
and he [b]shall make restitution in full for his wrong and add to it
one-fifth of it, and give *it* to him whom he has wronged.
8 'But if the man has no [1]relative to whom restitution may be
made for the wrong, the restitution which is made for the
wrong *must go* to the LORD for the priest, besides the ram of
atonement, by which atonement is made for him.

41 [1]Lit *mouth*
43 [a]Num 8:24-26
45 [1]Lit *mouth* [2]Lit *by the hand of*
48 [a]Num 3:39
49 [1]Lit *mouth* [2]Lit *by the hand of* [a]Num 1:47
5:2 [a]Lev 13:8, 46; Num 12:10, 14, 15 [b]Lev 15:2 [c]Lev 21:1; Num 9:6-10; 19:11
3 [a]Lev 26:12; Num 35:34
6 [a]Lev 5:14-6:7
7 [1]Lit *they* [2]Lit *their* [3]Lit *they have* [a]Lev 5:5; 26:40, 41; Josh 7:19 [b]Lev 6:4, 5
8 [1]Lit *redeemer*

9 'ᵃAlso every [1]contribution pertaining to all the holy *gifts* of
the sons of Israel, which they offer to the priest, shall be his.
10 'So every man's holy *gifts* shall be his; whatever any man
gives to the priest, it [a]becomes his.'"
11 Then the LORD spoke to Moses, saying,
12 "Speak to the sons of Israel and say to them, 'If any man's
wife [a]goes astray and is unfaithful to him,
13 and a man has [a]intercourse with her and it is hidden from
the eyes of her husband and she is [1]undetected, although she
has defiled herself, and there is no witness against her and she
has not been caught in the act,
14 [1]if a spirit of [a]jealousy comes over him and he is jealous of
his wife when she has defiled herself, or if a spirit of jealousy
comes over him and he is jealous of his wife when she has not
defiled herself,
15 the man shall then bring his wife to the priest, and shall
bring *as* [1]an offering for her one-tenth of an [2]ephah of barley
meal; he shall not pour oil on it nor put frankincense on it, for
it is a grain offering of jealousy, a grain offering of memorial, [a]a
reminder of iniquity.
16 'Then the priest shall bring her near and have her stand
before the LORD,
17 and the priest shall take holy water in an earthenware
vessel; and [1]he shall take some of the dust that is on the floor
of the tabernacle and put *it* into the water.
18 'The priest shall then have the woman stand before the
LORD and let *the hair of* the woman's head go loose, and place
the grain offering of memorial [1]in her hands, which is the grain
offering of jealousy, and in the hand of the priest is to be the
water of bitterness that brings a curse.
19 'The priest shall have her take an oath and shall say to the
woman, "If no man has lain with you and if you have not [a]gone
astray into uncleanness, *being* under *the authority of* your
husband, be [1]immune to this water of bitterness that brings a
curse;
20 if you, however, have [a]gone astray, *being* under *the authority
of* your husband, and if you have defiled yourself and a man
other than your husband has had intercourse with you"
21 (then the priest shall have the woman [a]swear with the oath
of the curse, and the priest shall say to the woman), "the LORD
make you a curse and an oath among your people by the LORD'S
making your thigh [1]waste away and your abdomen swell;
22 and this water that brings a curse shall go into your
[1]stomach, and make your abdomen swell and your thigh
[2]waste away." And the woman [a]shall say, "Amen. Amen."
23 'The priest shall then write these curses on a scroll, and he
shall [1]wash them off into the water of bitterness.
24 'Then he shall make the woman drink the water of
bitterness that brings a curse, so that the water which brings a
curse will go into her [1]and *cause* bitterness.
25 'The priest shall take the grain offering of jealousy from the

9 [1]Lit *heave offering* [a]Lev 7:32, 34; 10:14, 15
10 [a]Lev 10:13
12 [a]Num 5:19-21, 29
13 [1]Lit *concealed* [a]Lev 18:20; 20:10
14 [1]Lit *and* [a]Prov 6:34; Song 8:6
15 [1]Lit *her* [2]I.e. Approx one bu [a]1 Kin 17:18; Ezek 29:16
17 [1]Lit *the priest*
18 [1]Lit *on her palms*
19 [1]Lit *free from* [a]Num 5:12
20 [a]Num 5:12
21 [1]Lit *fall* [a]Josh 6:26; 1 Sam 14:24; Neh 10:29
22 [1]Or *inward parts* [2]Lit *fall* [a]Deut 27:15
23 [1]Lit *wipe*
24 [1]Lit *to*

woman's hand, and he shall wave the grain offering before the
LORD and bring it to the altar;
26 and [a]the priest shall take a handful of the grain offering as
its memorial offering and offer *it* up in smoke on the altar, and
afterward he shall make the woman drink the water.
27 'When he has made her drink the water, then it shall come
about, if she has defiled herself and has been unfaithful to her
husband, that the water which brings a curse will go into her [1]and
cause bitterness, and her abdomen will swell and her thigh will
[2]waste away, and the woman will become [a]a curse among her
people.
28 'But if the woman has not defiled herself and is clean, she
will then be free and conceive [1]children.
29 'This is the law of jealousy: when a wife, *being* under *the*
authority of her husband, [a]goes astray and defiles herself,
30 or when a spirit of jealousy comes over a man and he is
jealous of his wife, he shall then make the woman stand before
the LORD, and the priest shall apply all this law to her.
31 'Moreover, the man will be free from [1]guilt, but that woman
shall [a]bear her [1]guilt.'"

Chapter 6 Theme ______________________________

6 Again the LORD spoke to Moses, saying,
2 "Speak to the sons of Israel and say to them, 'When a man
or woman makes a [1]special vow, the vow of [a]a [2]Nazirite, to
[3]dedicate himself to the LORD,
3 he shall [a]abstain from wine and strong drink; he shall drink
no vinegar, whether made from wine or strong drink, nor shall
he drink any grape juice nor eat fresh or dried grapes.
4 'All the days of his [1]separation he shall not eat anything that
is produced by the grape vine, from *the* seeds even to *the* skin.
5 'All the days of his vow of separation [a]no razor shall pass
over his head. He shall be holy until the days are fulfilled for
which he separated himself to the LORD; he shall let the locks
of hair on his head grow long.
6 '[a]All the days of his separation to the LORD he shall not go
near to a dead person.
7 'He [a]shall not make himself unclean for his father or for his
mother, for his brother or for his sister, when they die, because
his separation to God is on his head.
8 'All the days of his separation he is holy to the LORD.
9 'But if a man dies very suddenly beside him and he defiles his
dedicated head *of hair,* then [a]he shall shave his head on the day
when he becomes clean; [b]he shall shave it on the seventh day.
10 'Then on the eighth day he shall bring [a]two turtledoves or
two young pigeons to the priest, to the doorway of the tent of
meeting.
11 'The priest shall offer [a]one for a sin offering and *the* other
for a burnt offering, and make atonement for him [1]concerning
his sin because of the *dead* person. And that same day he shall
consecrate his head,

26 [a]Lev 2:2, 9
27 [1]Lit *to* [2]Lit *fall* [a]Jer 29:18; 42:18; 44:12
28 [1]Lit *seed*
29 [a]Num 5:12
31 [1]Or *iniquity* [a]Lev 20:17
6:2 [1]Or *difficult* [2]I.e. one separated [3]Or *live as a Nazirite* [a]Judg 13:5; 16:17; Amos 2:11, 12
3 [a]Luke 1:15
4 [1]Or *living as a Nazirite,* and so through v 21
5 [a]1 Sam 1:11
6 [a]Lev 21:1-3; Num 19:11-22
7 [a]Num 9:6
9 [a]Lev 14:8, 9 [b]Num 6:18
10 [a]Lev 5:7; 14:22
11 [1]Lit *because of that which he sinned* [a]Lev 5:7

12 and shall dedicate to the LORD his days [1]as a [2]Nazirite, and
shall bring a male lamb a year old for a guilt offering; but the
former days will be void because his separation was defiled.
13 'Now this is the law of the Nazirite [a]when the days of his
separation are fulfilled, he shall bring [1]the offering to the
doorway of the tent of meeting.
14 'He shall present his offering to the LORD: one male lamb a
year old without defect for a burnt offering and one [a]ewe-lamb
a year old without defect for a sin offering and one ram without
defect for a peace offering,
15 and a basket of [a]unleavened cakes of fine flour mixed with
oil and unleavened wafers spread with oil, along with [b]their
grain offering and their drink offering.
16 'Then the priest shall present *them* before the LORD and
shall offer his sin offering and his burnt offering.
17 'He shall also offer the ram for a sacrifice of peace offerings
to the LORD, together with the basket of unleavened cakes; the
priest shall likewise offer its grain offering and its drink offering.
18 '[a]The Nazirite shall then shave his dedicated head *of hair* at
the doorway of the tent of meeting, and take the dedicated hair
of his head and put *it* on the fire which is under the sacrifice of
peace offerings.
19 '[a]The priest shall take the ram's shoulder *when it has been*
boiled, and one unleavened cake out of the basket and one
unleavened wafer, and shall put *them* on the [1]hands of the
Nazirite after he has shaved his [2]dedicated *hair.*
20 'Then the priest shall wave them for a wave offering before
the LORD. It is holy for the priest, together with the breast
offered by waving and the thigh offered by lifting up; and
[a]afterward the Nazirite may drink wine.'
21 "This is the law of the Nazirite who vows his offering to the
LORD according to his separation, in addition to what *else* [1]he
can afford; according to his vow which he takes, so he shall do
according to the law of his separation."
22 Then the LORD spoke to Moses, saying,
23 "Speak to Aaron and to his sons, saying, 'Thus [a]you shall
bless the sons of Israel. You shall say to them:
24 The LORD [a]bless you, and [b]keep you;
25 The LORD [a]make His face shine on you,
And [b]be gracious to you;
26 The LORD [a]lift up His countenance on you,
And [b]give you peace.'
27 "So they shall [1a]invoke My name on the sons of Israel, and I
then will bless them."

Chapter 7 Theme ____________________

7 Now on [a]the day that Moses had finished setting up the
tabernacle, he [b]anointed it and consecrated it with all its
furnishings and the altar and all its utensils; he anointed them
and consecrated them also.

12 [1]Or *of dedication* [2]I.e. one separated
13 [1]Lit *it* [a]Acts 21:26
14 [a]Lev 14:10; Num 15:27
15 [a]Ex 29:2; Lev 2:4 [b]Num 15:1-7
18 [a]Num 6:9; Acts 21:23, 24
19 [1]Lit *palms* [2]Or *separated* [a]Lev 7:28-34
20 [a]Eccl 9:7
21 [1]Lit *his hand can reach*
23 [a]1 Chr 23:13
24 [a]Deut 28:3-6; Ps 28:9 [b]1 Sam 2:9; Ps 17:8
25 [a]Ps 80:3, 7, 19 [b]Ps 86:16
26 [a]Ps 4:6; 44:3 [b]Ps 29:11; 37:37
27 [1]Lit *put* [a]2 Sam 7:23; 2 Chr 7:14
7:1 [a]Ex 40:17 [b]Ex 40:9-11; Num 7:10, 84, 88

2 Then [a]the leaders of Israel, the heads of their fathers'
households, [b]made an offering (they were the leaders of the
tribes; they were the ones who [1]were over the [2]numbered men).
3 When they brought their offering before the LORD, six [a]covered
carts and twelve oxen, a cart for *every* two of the leaders and an
ox for each one, then they presented them before the tabernacle.
4 Then the LORD spoke to Moses, saying,
5 "Accept *these things* from them, that they may be [1]used in
the service of the tent of meeting, and you shall give them to
the Levites, *to* each man according to his service."
6 So Moses took the carts and the oxen and gave them to the
Levites.
7 Two carts and four oxen he gave to the sons of Gershon,
according to [a]their service,
8 and four carts and eight oxen he gave to the sons of
Merari, according to [a]their service, under the [1]direction of
Ithamar the son of Aaron the priest.
9 But he did not give *any* to the sons of Kohath because
theirs *was* [a]the service of the holy *objects, which* they carried
on the shoulder.
10 The leaders offered the dedication *offering* [1]for the altar
[2]when [a]it was anointed, so the leaders offered their offering
before the altar.
11 Then the LORD said to Moses, "Let them present their
offering, one leader each day, for the dedication of the altar."
12 Now the one who presented his offering on the first day
was Nahshon the son of Amminadab, of the tribe of Judah;
13 and his offering *was* one silver [1a]dish whose weight *was* one
hundred and thirty *shekels,* one silver bowl of seventy shekels,
[b]according to [2]the shekel of the sanctuary, both of them full of
fine flour mixed with oil for a grain offering;
14 one gold pan of ten *shekels,* full of incense;
15 one [1]bull, one ram, one male lamb one year old, for a burnt
offering;
16 [a]one male goat for a sin offering;
17 and for the sacrifice of peace offerings, two oxen, five rams,
five male goats, five male lambs one year old. This *was* the
offering of [a]Nahshon the son of Amminadab.
18 On the second day Nethanel the son of Zuar, leader of
Issachar, presented *an offering;*
19 he presented as his offering one silver dish whose weight
was one hundred and thirty *shekels,* one silver bowl of seventy
shekels, according to the shekel of the sanctuary, both of them
full of fine flour mixed with oil for a grain offering;
20 one gold pan of ten *shekels,* full of incense;
21 one bull, one ram, one male lamb one year old, for a burnt
offering;
22 one male goat for a sin offering;
23 and for the sacrifice of [a]peace offerings, two oxen, five rams,
five male goats, five male lambs one year old. This *was* the
offering of Nethanel the son of Zuar.

2 [1]Lit *stood* [2]Lit *mustered* [a]Num 1:5-16 [b]2 Chr 35:8
3 [a]Is 66:20
5 [1]Lit *for serving*
7 [a]Num 4:24-26
8 [1]Lit *hand* [a]Num 4:31, 32
9 [a]Num 4:5-15
10 [1]Lit *of* [2]Lit *in the day that* [a]Num 7:1; 2 Chr 7:9
13 [1]Or *platter,* and so through v 85 [2]I.e. Approx one-half oz, and so through v 86 [a]Ex 25:29; 37:16 [b]Num 3:47
15 [1]Or *bull of the herd,* and so through v 81
16 [a]Lev 4:23
17 [a]Luke 3:32, 33
23 [a]Lev 7:11-13

24 On the third day *it was* Eliab the son of Helon, leader of the sons of Zebulun;
25 his offering *was* one silver dish whose weight *was* one hundred and thirty *shekels,* one silver bowl of seventy shekels, according to the shekel of the sanctuary, both of them full of fine flour mixed with oil for a grain offering;
26 one gold pan of ten *shekels,* full of incense;
27 one young bull, one ram, one [a]male lamb one year old, for a burnt offering;
28 one male goat for a sin offering;
29 and for the sacrifice of peace offerings, two oxen, five rams, five male goats, five male lambs one year old. This *was* the offering of Eliab the son of Helon.
30 On the fourth day *it was* Elizur the son of Shedeur, leader of the sons of Reuben;
31 his offering *was* one silver dish whose weight *was* one hundred and thirty *shekels,* one silver bowl of seventy shekels, according to the shekel of the sanctuary, both of them full of fine flour mixed with oil for a grain offering;
32 one gold pan of ten *shekels,* full of incense;
33 one bull, one ram, one [a]male lamb one year old, for a burnt offering;
34 one male goat for a sin offering;
35 and for the sacrifice of peace offerings, two oxen, five rams, five male goats, five male lambs one year old. This *was* the offering of Elizur the son of Shedeur.
36 On the fifth day *it was* Shelumiel the son of Zurishaddai, leader of the children of Simeon;
37 his offering *was* one silver dish whose weight *was* one hundred and thirty *shekels,* one silver bowl of seventy shekels, according to the shekel of the sanctuary, both of them full of fine flour mixed with oil for a grain offering;
38 one gold pan of ten *shekels,* full of incense;
39 one bull, one ram, one male lamb one year old, for a burnt offering;
40 one male goat for a sin offering;
41 and for the sacrifice of peace offerings, two oxen, five rams, five male goats, five male lambs one year old. This *was* the offering of Shelumiel the son of Zurishaddai.
42 On the sixth day *it was* [a]Eliasaph the son of Deuel, leader of the sons of Gad;
43 his offering *was* one silver dish whose weight *was* one hundred and thirty *shekels,* one silver bowl of seventy shekels, according to the shekel of the sanctuary, both of them full of [a]fine flour mixed with oil for a grain offering;
44 one gold pan of ten *shekels,* full of incense;
45 [a]one bull, one ram, one male lamb one year old, for a burnt offering;
46 one male goat for a sin offering;
47 and for the sacrifice of peace offerings, two oxen, five rams,

27 [a]Is 53:7; John 1:29; 1 Pet 1:19
33 [a]Heb 9:28
42 [a]Num 1:14; 10:20
43 [a]Lev 2:5; 14:10
45 [a]Ps 50:8-14; Is 1:11

five male goats, five male lambs one year old. This *was* the
offering of Eliasaph the son of Deuel.
48 On the seventh day *it was* [a]Elishama the son of Ammihud,
leader of the sons of Ephraim;
49 his offering *was* one silver dish whose weight *was* one
hundred and thirty *shekels,* one silver bowl of seventy shekels,
according to the shekel of the sanctuary, both of them full of
fine flour mixed with oil for a grain offering;
50 one gold pan of ten *shekels,* full of [a]incense;
51 [a]one bull, one ram, one male lamb one year old, for a burnt
offering;
52 one male goat for a sin offering;
53 and for the sacrifice of peace offerings, two oxen, five rams,
five male goats, five male lambs one year old. This *was* the
offering of Elishama the son of Ammihud.
54 On the eighth day *it was* [a]Gamaliel the son of Pedahzur,
leader of the sons of Manasseh;
55 his offering *was* one silver dish whose weight *was* one
hundred and thirty *shekels,* one silver bowl of seventy shekels,
according to the shekel of the sanctuary, both of them full of
fine flour mixed with oil for a grain offering;
56 one gold pan of ten *shekels,* full of [a]incense;
57 one bull, one ram, one [a]male lamb one year old, for a burnt
offering;
58 one male goat for a sin offering;
59 and for the [a]sacrifice of peace offerings, two oxen, five
rams, five male goats, five male lambs one year old. This *was*
the offering of Gamaliel the son of Pedahzur.
60 On the ninth day *it was* [a]Abidan the son of Gideoni, leader
of the sons of Benjamin;
61 his offering *was* one silver dish whose weight *was* one
hundred and thirty *shekels,* one silver bowl of seventy shekels,
according to the shekel of the sanctuary, both of them full of
fine flour mixed with oil for a grain offering;
62 one gold pan of ten *shekels,* full of [a]incense;
63 one bull, one ram, one male lamb one year old, for a burnt
offering;
64 one male goat for a [a]sin offering;
65 and for the sacrifice of [a]peace offerings, two oxen, five
rams, five male goats, five male lambs one year old. This *was*
the offering of Abidan the son of Gideoni.
66 On the tenth day *it was* [a]Ahiezer the son of Ammishaddai,
leader of the sons of Dan;
67 his offering *was* one silver dish whose weight *was* one
hundred and thirty *shekels,* one silver bowl of seventy shekels,
according to the [a]shekel of the sanctuary, both of them full of
fine flour mixed with oil for a grain offering;
68 one gold pan of ten *shekels,* full of [a]incense;
69 one bull, one ram, one male lamb one year old, for a burnt
offering;
70 one male goat for a sin offering;

48 [a]Num 1:10; 2:18; 1 Chr 7:26
50 [a]Deut 33:10; Ezek 8:11; Luke 1:10
51 [a]Mic 6:6-8
54 [a]Num 2:20
56 [a]Ex 30:7
57 [a]Ex 12:5; Acts 8:32; Rev 5:6
59 [a]Lev 3:1-17
60 [a]Num 1:11; 2:22
62 [a]Rev 5:8; 8:3, 4
64 [a]2 Cor 5:21
65 [a]Col 1:20
66 [a]Num 1:12; 2:25
67 [a]Ex 30:13; Lev 27:25
68 [a]Ps 141:2

71 and for the sacrifice of peace offerings, two oxen, five rams,
five male goats, five male lambs one year old. This *was* the
offering of Ahiezer the son of Ammishaddai.
72 On the eleventh day *it was* [a]Pagiel the son of Ochran,
leader of the sons of Asher;
73 his offering *was* one silver dish whose weight *was* one
hundred and thirty *shekels,* one silver bowl of seventy shekels,
according to the shekel of the sanctuary, both of them full of
fine flour mixed with oil for a grain offering;
74 one gold pan of ten *shekels,* full of [a]incense;
75 one bull, one ram, one male lamb one year old, for a burnt
offering;
76 one male goat for a sin offering;
77 and for the sacrifice of peace offerings, two oxen, five rams,
five male goats, five male lambs one year old. This *was* the
offering of Pagiel the son of Ochran.
78 On the twelfth day *it was* [a]Ahira the son of Enan, leader of
the sons of Naphtali;
79 his offering *was* one [a]silver dish whose weight *was* one
hundred and thirty *shekels,* one silver bowl of seventy shekels,
according to the shekel of the sanctuary, both of them full of
fine flour mixed with oil for a grain offering;
80 one gold pan of ten *shekels,* full of incense;
81 one bull, one ram, one male lamb one year old, for a burnt
offering;
82 one male goat for a sin offering;
83 and for the sacrifice of peace offerings, two oxen, five rams,
five male goats, five male lambs one year old. This *was* the
offering of Ahira the son of Enan.
84 This *was* [a]the dedication *offering* [1]for the altar from the
leaders of Israel [2]when [b]it was anointed: twelve silver dishes,
twelve silver bowls, twelve gold pans,
85 each silver dish *weighing* one hundred and thirty *shekels*
and each bowl seventy; all the silver of the utensils *was* 2,400
shekels, according to the shekel of the sanctuary;
86 the twelve gold pans, full of incense, *weighing* ten *shekels*
apiece, according to the [a]shekel of the sanctuary, all the gold of
the pans 120 *shekels;*
87 all the oxen for the burnt offering twelve bulls, *all* the rams
twelve, the male lambs one year old with their grain offering
twelve, and the male goats for a sin offering twelve;
88 and all the oxen for the sacrifice of peace offerings 24
bulls, *all* the rams 60, the male goats 60, the male lambs one
year old 60. [a]This *was* the dedication *offering* for the altar after
it was anointed.
89 Now when [a]Moses went into the tent of meeting to speak
with Him, he heard the voice speaking to him from above [b]the
[1]mercy seat that was on the ark of the testimony, from
[c]between the two cherubim, so He spoke to him.

72 [a]Num 1:13; 2:27

74 [a]Mal 1:11

78 [a]Num 1:15; 2:29

79 [a]Ezra 1:9, 10; Dan 5:2

84 [1]Lit *of* [2]Lit *in the day that* [a]Num 7:10 [b]Num 7:1

86 [a]Ex 30:13

88 [a]Num 7:1, 10

89 [1]Lit *propitiatory* [a]Ex 40:34, 35 [b]Ex 25:21, 22 [c]Ps 80:1; 99:1

8:2 [1]Lit *raise up* [a]Ex 25:37; Lev 24:2, 4
3 [1]Lit *raised up*
4 [a]Ex 25:31-40 [b]Ex 25:9, 31-40; 26:30; 37:17-24
6 [a]Is 52:11
7 [1]Lit *this their cleansing* [2]Lit *water of sin* [3]Lit *cause to pass* [4]Lit *flesh* [a]Num 19:9, 13, 20 [b]Lev 14:8, 9 [c]Num 8:21
8 [1]Or *bull of the herd* [a]Lev 2:1; Num 15:8-10
9 [a]Ex 29:4; 40:12 [b]Lev 8:3
10 [a]Lev 1:4
11 [1]Lit *wave,* and so throughout the ch [2]Lit *be able* [a]Lev 7:30, 34
12 [a]Ex 29:10
14 [a]Num 3:12; 16:9
15 [a]Ex 29:24
16 [a]Num 3:9 [b]Ex 13:2; Num 3:12, 45
17 [a]Ex 13:2, 12, 13, 15; Luke 2:23
19 [1]Lit *given ones* [2]Lit *the sons of Israel's* [a]Num 3:9 [b]Num 1:53; 16:46

Chapter 8 Theme ____

8 Then the LORD spoke to Moses, saying,
2 "Speak to Aaron and say to him, 'When you [1]mount the
lamps, the seven lamps will [a]give light in the front of the lampstand.'"
3 Aaron therefore did so; he [1]mounted its lamps at the front
of the lampstand, just as the LORD had commanded Moses.
4 [a]Now this was the workmanship of the lampstand,
hammered work of gold; from its base to its flowers it was
hammered work; [b]according to the pattern which the LORD had
shown Moses, so he made the lampstand.
5 Again the LORD spoke to Moses, saying,
6 "Take the Levites from among the sons of Israel and [a]cleanse
them.
7 "Thus you shall do to them, for their [1]cleansing: *sprinkle*
[2]purifying [a]water on them, and let them [3b]use a razor over their
whole [4]body and [c]wash their clothes, and they will be clean.
8 "Then let them take a [1]bull with [a]its grain offering, fine flour
mixed with oil; and a second [1]bull you shall take for a sin offering.
9 "So [a]you shall present the Levites before the tent of
meeting. [b]You shall also assemble the whole congregation of
the sons of Israel,
10 and present the Levites before the LORD; and the sons of
Israel [a]shall lay their hands on the Levites.
11 "Aaron then shall [1]present the Levites before the LORD as a
[a]wave offering from the sons of Israel, that they may [2]qualify to
perform the service of the LORD.
12 "Now [a]the Levites shall lay their hands on the heads of the
bulls; then offer the one for a sin offering and the other for a
burnt offering to the LORD, to make atonement for the Levites.
13 "You shall have the Levites stand before Aaron and before
his sons so as to present them as a wave offering to the LORD.
14 "Thus you shall separate the Levites from among the sons of
Israel, and [a]the Levites shall be Mine.
15 "Then after that the Levites may go in to serve the tent of
meeting. But you shall cleanse them and [a]present them as a
wave offering;
16 for they are [a]wholly given to Me from among the sons of
Israel. I have taken them for Myself [b]instead of every first issue
of the womb, the firstborn of all the sons of Israel.
17 "For [a]every firstborn among the sons of Israel is Mine, among
the men and among the animals; on the day that I struck down
all the firstborn in the land of Egypt I sanctified them for Myself.
18 "But I have taken the Levites instead of every firstborn
among the sons of Israel.
19 "[a]I have given the Levites as [1]a gift to Aaron and to his sons
from among the sons of Israel, to perform the service of the sons
of Israel at the tent of meeting and to make atonement on behalf
of the sons of Israel, so that there will be no [b]plague among the
sons of Israel by [2]their coming near to the sanctuary."
20 Thus did Moses and Aaron and all the congregation of the

Lampstand

sons of Israel to the Levites; according to all that the LORD had
commanded Moses concerning the Levites, so the sons of
Israel did to them.
21 [a]The Levites, too, purified themselves from sin and washed
their clothes; and Aaron presented them as a wave offering before
the LORD. Aaron also made atonement for them to cleanse them.
22 Then after that the Levites went in to perform their service
in the tent of meeting before Aaron and before his sons; just as
the LORD had commanded Moses concerning the Levites, so
they did to them.
23 Now the LORD spoke to Moses, saying,
24 "This is what *applies* to the Levites: from [a]twenty-five years
old and upward [1]they shall enter to perform service in the
work of the tent of meeting.
25 "But at the age of fifty years they shall [1]retire from service in
the work and not work any more.
26 "They may, however, [1]assist their brothers in the tent of
meeting, [a]to keep an obligation, but they *themselves* shall do
no work. Thus you shall deal with the Levites concerning their
obligations."

Chapter 9 Theme ______________________________

9 Thus the LORD spoke to Moses in the wilderness of Sinai,
in [a]the first month of the second year after they had come
out of the land of Egypt, saying,
2 "Now, let the sons of Israel observe the Passover at [a]its
appointed time.
3 "On the fourteenth day of this month, [1]at twilight, you shall
observe it at its appointed time; you shall observe it according
to all its statutes and according to all its ordinances."
4 So Moses [1]told the sons of Israel to observe the Passover.
5 [a]They observed the Passover in the first *month,* on the
fourteenth day of the month, at twilight, in the wilderness of
Sinai; [b]according to all that the LORD had commanded Moses,
so the sons of Israel did.
6 But there were *some* men who were [a]unclean because of
the [1]dead person, so that they could not observe Passover on
that day; so [b]they came before Moses and Aaron on that day.
7 Those men said to him, "*Though* we are unclean because of
the [1]dead person, why are we restrained from presenting the
offering of the LORD at its appointed time among the sons of Israel?"
8 Moses therefore said to them, "[1a]Wait, and I will listen to
what the LORD will command concerning you."
9 Then the LORD spoke to Moses, saying,
10 "Speak to the sons of Israel, saying, 'If any one of you or of
your generations becomes unclean because of a *dead* [1]person,
or is on a distant journey, he may, however, observe the
Passover to the LORD.
11 'In the second month on the [a]fourteenth day at twilight,
they shall observe it; they [b]shall eat it with unleavened bread
and bitter herbs.

21 [a]Num 8:7

24 [1]Lit *he* [a]Num 4:3; 1 Chr 23:3, 24, 27

25 [1]Lit *return*

26 [1]Lit *serve* [a]Num 1:53

9:1 [a]Ex 40:2, 17; Num 1:1

2 [a]Ex 12:6; Lev 23:5; Deut 16:1, 2

3 [1]Lit *between the two evenings,* and so throughout the ch

4 [1]Lit *spoke to*

5 [a]Josh 5:10 [b]Ex 12:1-13

6 [1]Lit *soul of man* [a]Num 5:2; 19:11-22 [b]Ex 18:15; Num 27:2

7 [1]Lit *soul of man*

8 [1]Lit *Stand* [a]Ex 18:15; Ps 85:8

10 [1]Lit *soul*

11 [a]2 Chr 30:2, 15 [b]Ex 12:8

12 'They [a]shall leave none of it until morning, [b]nor break a
bone of it; according to all the statute of the Passover they shall
observe it.
13 '[a]But the man who is clean and is not on a journey, and yet
[1]neglects to observe the Passover, that [2]person shall then be
cut off from his people, for he did not present the offering of
the LORD at its appointed time. That man [b]will bear his sin.
14 '[a]If an alien sojourns among you and [1]observes the Passover to
the LORD, according to the statute of the Passover and according
to its ordinance, so he shall do; you shall have [b]one statute, both
for the alien and for the native of the land.'"
15 Now on [a]the day that the tabernacle was erected [b]the cloud
covered the tabernacle, the [c]tent of the testimony, and [d]in the
evening it was like the appearance of fire over the tabernacle,
until morning.
16 So it was continuously; [a]the cloud would cover it *by day,*
and the appearance of fire by night.
17 [a]Whenever the cloud was lifted from over the tent, afterward
the sons of Israel would then set out; and in the place where the
cloud settled down, there the sons of Israel would camp.
18 At the [1]command of the LORD the sons of Israel would set
out, and at the [1]command of the LORD they would camp; [a]as long
as the cloud settled over the tabernacle, they remained camped.
19 Even when the cloud lingered over the tabernacle for many
days, [1]the sons of Israel would keep the LORD's charge and not
set out.
20 If [1]sometimes the cloud remained a few days over the
tabernacle, [a]according to the [2]command of the LORD they
remained camped. Then according to the [2]command of the
LORD they set out.
21 If [1]sometimes the cloud [2]remained from evening until
morning, when the cloud was lifted in the morning, they
would move out; or *if it remained* in the daytime and at night,
whenever the cloud was lifted, they would set out.
22 Whether it was two days or a month or a year that the
cloud lingered over the tabernacle, staying above it, the sons of
Israel remained camped and did not set out; but [a]when it was
lifted, they did set out.
23 [a]At the [1]command of the LORD they camped, and at the
[1]command of the LORD they set out; they kept the LORD's
charge, according to the [1]command of the LORD through Moses.

Chapter 10 Theme ____________________

10 The LORD spoke further to Moses, saying,
2 "Make yourself two trumpets of silver, of hammered
work you shall make them; and you shall use them for [a]sum-
moning the congregation and for having the camps set out.
3 "[a]When both are blown, all the congregation shall gather
themselves to you at the doorway of the tent of meeting.
4 "Yet if *only* one is blown, then the [a]leaders, the heads of the
[1]divisions of Israel, shall assemble before you.

12 [a]Ex 12:10 [b]Ex 12:46; John 19:36
13 [1]Or *ceases* [2]Lit *soul* [a]Gen 17:14; Ex 12:15, 47 [b]Num 5:31
14 [1]Or *would observe* [a]Ex 12:48 [b]Ex 12:49; Lev 24:22; Num 15:15, 16, 29
15 [a]Ex 40:2, 17 [b]Ex 40:34 [c]Num 17:7 [d]Ex 13:21, 22
16 [a]Ex 40:34; Neh 9:12
17 [a]Ex 40:36-38; Num 10:11, 12
18 [1]Lit *mouth* [a]1 Cor 10:1
19 [1]Lit *and the*
20 [1]Lit *it was that* [2]Lit *mouth* [a]Ps 48:14; Prov 3:5, 6
21 [1]Lit *it was that* [2]Lit *was*
22 [a]Ex 40:36, 37
23 [1]Lit *mouth* [a]Ps 73:24; 107:7; Is 63:14
10:2 [a]Is 1:13
3 [a]Jer 4:5; Joel 2:15
4 [1]Lit *thousands;* or *clans* [a]Ex 18:21; Num 1:16; 7:2

5 "But when you blow an alarm, the camps that are pitched [a]on the east side shall set out.

6 "When you blow an alarm the second time, the camps that are pitched on [a]the south side shall set out; an alarm is to be blown for them to set out.

7 "When convening the assembly, however, you shall blow without [a]sounding an alarm.

8 "[a]The priestly sons of Aaron, moreover, shall blow the trumpets; and [1]this shall be for you a perpetual statute throughout your generations.

9 "When you go to war in your land against the adversary who [a]attacks you, then you shall sound an alarm with the trumpets, that you may be [b]remembered before the LORD your God, and be saved from your enemies.

10 "Also in the day of your gladness and in your appointed [1]feasts, and on the first *days* of your months, [a]you shall blow the trumpets over your burnt offerings, and over the sacrifices of your peace offerings; and they shall be as a reminder of you before your God. I am the LORD your God."

RETURN TO INSTRUCTIONS

11 Now in [a]the second year, in the second month, on the twentieth of the month, the cloud was lifted from over the [1]tabernacle of the testimony;

12 and the sons of Israel set out on [a]their journeys from the wilderness of Sinai. Then the cloud settled down in the [b]wilderness of Paran.

13 [a]So they moved out for the first time according to the [1]commandment of the LORD through Moses.

14 The standard of the camp of the sons of Judah, according to their armies, [a]set out first, with Nahshon the son of Amminadab, over its army,

15 and Nethanel the son of Zuar, over the tribal army of the sons of Issachar;

16 and Eliab the son of Helon over the tribal army of the sons of Zebulun.

17 [a]Then the tabernacle was taken down; and the sons of Gershon and the sons of Merari, who were carrying the tabernacle, set out.

18 Next [a]the standard of the camp of Reuben, according to their armies, set out with Elizur the son of Shedeur, over its army,

19 and Shelumiel the son of Zurishaddai over the tribal army of the sons of Simeon,

20 and Eliasaph the son of Deuel was over the tribal army of the sons of Gad.

21 [a]Then the Kohathites set out, carrying the holy *objects;* and [b]the tabernacle was set up before their arrival.

22 [a]Next the standard of the camp of the sons of Ephraim, according to their armies, was set out, with Elishama the son of Ammihud over its army,

23 and Gamaliel the son of Pedahzur over the tribal army of the sons of Manasseh;

5 [a]Num 10:14
6 [a]Num 10:18
7 [a]Joel 2:1
8 [1]Lit *it* [a]Num 31:6; Josh 6:4; 2 Chr 13:12
9 [a]Judg 2:18; 1 Sam 10:18; Ps 106:42 [b]Gen 8:1; Ps 106:4
10 [1]Or *times* [a]Ps 81:3-5
11 [1]Lit *dwelling place,* and so throughout the ch [a]Ex 40:17
12 [a]Ex 40:36 [b]Gen 21:21; Num 12:16
13 [1]Lit *mouth* [a]Deut 1:6
14 [a]Num 2:3-9
17 [a]Num 4:21-32
18 [a]Num 2:10-16
21 [a]Num 4:4-20 [b]Num 10:17
22 [a]Num 2:18-24

24 and Abidan the son of Gideoni over the tribal army of the
sons of Benjamin.
25 [a]Then the standard of the camp of the sons of Dan, according
to their armies, *which formed* the [b]rear guard for all the camps,
set out, with Ahiezer the son of Ammishaddai over its army,
26 and Pagiel the son of Ochran over the tribal army of the
sons of Asher;
27 and Ahira the son of Enan over the tribal army of the sons
of Naphtali.
28 [1]This was the order of march of the sons of Israel by their
armies as they set out.
29 Then Moses said to [a]Hobab the son of [b]Reuel the
Midianite, Moses' father-in-law, "We are setting out to the
place of which the LORD said, '[c]I will give it to you'; [d]come with
us and we will do you good, for the LORD [e]has [1]promised good
concerning Israel."
30 But he said to him, "[a]I will not come, but rather will go to
my *own* land and relatives."
31 Then he said, "Please do not leave us, inasmuch as you
know where we should camp in the wilderness, and you [a]will
be as eyes for us.
32 "So it will be, if you go with us, that [1a]whatever good the
LORD [2]does for us, [b]we will [3]do for you."
33 [a]Thus they set out from the mount of the LORD three days'
journey, with [b]the ark of the covenant of the LORD journeying
in front of them for the [1]three days, to seek out [c]a resting place
for them.
34 [a]The cloud of the LORD was over them by day when they
set out from the camp.
35 Then it came about when the ark set out that Moses said,
"[a]Rise up, O LORD!
And let Your enemies be scattered,
And let those [b]who hate You flee [1]before You."
36 When it came to rest, he said,
"[a]Return, O LORD,
To the myriad [b]thousands of Israel."

Chapter 11 Theme ______

11 Now the people became like [a]those who complain of
adversity [b]in the hearing of the LORD; and when the LORD
heard *it,* His anger was kindled, and the fire of the LORD burned
among them and consumed *some* of the outskirts of the camp.
2 [a]The people therefore cried out to Moses, and Moses
prayed to the LORD and the fire [1]died out.
3 So the name of that place was called [1a]Taberah, because
the fire of the LORD burned among them.
4 The [a]rabble who were among them [1]had greedy desires;
and also the sons of Israel wept again and said, "[b]Who will give
us [2]meat to eat?
5 "[a]We remember the fish which we used to eat free in Egypt,

25 [a]Num 2:25-31 [b]Josh 6:9, 13
28 [1]Lit *These are the settings out of the sons*
29 [1]Lit *spoken* [a]Judg 4:11 [b]Ex 2:18; 3:1; 18:12 [c]Gen 12:7; Ex 6:4-8 [d]Ps 95:1-7; 100:1-5 [e]Deut 4:40; 30:5
30 [a]Judg 1:16; Matt 21:28, 29
31 [a]Job 29:15
32 [1]Lit *that good which* [2]Lit *does good* [3]Lit *do good* [a]Ps 22:27-31; 67:5-7 [b]Lev 19:34; Deut 10:18
33 [1]Lit *three days' journey* [a]Num 10:12 [b]Deut 1:33 [c]Is 11:10
34 [a]Num 9:15-23
35 [1]Or *from Your presence* [a]Ps 68:1, 2; Is 17:12-14 [b]Deut 7:10; 32:41
36 [a]Is 63:17 [b]Deut 1:10
11:1 [a]Num 14:2; 16:11; 17:5 [b]Num 11:18; 14:28
2 [1]Lit *sank down* [a]Num 12:11, 13; 21:7
3 [1]I.e. burning [a]Deut 9:22
4 [1]Lit *desired a desire* [2]Lit *flesh, and so throughout the ch* [a]Ex 12:38; 1 Cor 10:6 [b]Ps 78:20
5 [a]Ex 16:3

The Exodus from Egypt to Canaan

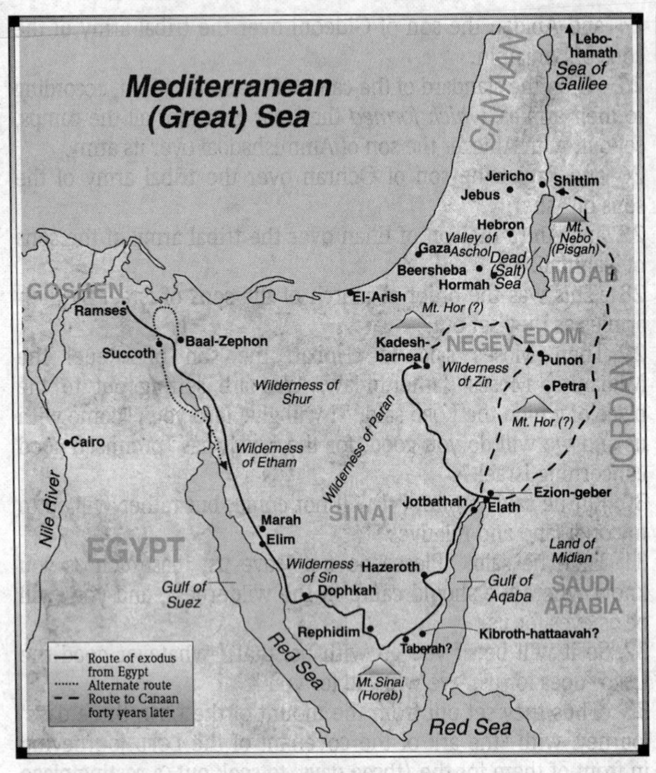

the cucumbers and the melons and the leeks and the onions
and the garlic,
6 but now [a]our [1]appetite is gone. There is nothing at all [2]to
look at except this manna."
7 [a]Now the manna was like coriander seed, and its appearance
like that of [b]bdellium.
8 The people would go about and gather *it* and grind *it*
[1]between two millstones or beat *it* in the mortar, and boil *it* in
the pot and make cakes with it; and its taste was as the taste of
[2]cakes baked with oil.
9 [a]When the dew fell on the camp at night, the manna
would fall [1]with it.
10 Now Moses heard the people weeping throughout their
families, each man at the doorway of his tent; and the anger of
the LORD was kindled greatly, and [1]Moses was displeased.
11 [a]So Moses said to the LORD, "Why have You [1]been so hard
on Your servant? And why have I not found favor in Your sight,
that You have laid the burden of all this people on me?
12 "Was it I who conceived all this people? Was it I who
brought them forth, that You should say to me, 'Carry them in
your bosom as a [1a]nurse carries a nursing infant, to the land
which [b]You swore to their fathers'?
13 "Where am I to get meat to give to [a]all this people? For they
weep before me, saying, 'Give us meat that we may eat!'
14 "[a]I alone am not able to carry all this people, because it is
too [1]burdensome for me.

6 [1]Lit *soul is dried up* [2]Lit *for our eyes* [a]Num 21:5

7 [a]Ex 16:31 [b]Gen 2:12

8 [1]Lit *with* [2]Lit *juice of oil*

9 [1]Lit *on* [a]Ex 16:13, 14

10 [1]Lit *it was evil in Moses' sight*

11 [1]Lit *dealt ill with* [a]Ex 5:22; Deut 1:12

12 [1]Or *foster-father* [a]2 Kin 10:1, 5; Is 49:23 [b]Gen 24:7; Ex 13:5, 11; 33:1

13 [a]Num 11:21, 22; John 6:5-9

14 [1]Lit *heavy* [a]Ex 18:18; Deut 1:12

15 “[a]So if You are going to deal thus with me, please kill me at
once, if I have found favor in Your sight, and do not let me see
my wretchedness.”
16 The LORD therefore said to Moses, “Gather for Me [a]seventy
men from the elders of Israel, [b]whom you know to be the
elders of the people and their officers and bring them to the
tent of meeting, and let them take their stand there with you.
17 “[a]Then I will come down and speak with you there, and I
will take of [b]the Spirit who is upon you, and will put *Him* upon
them; and they shall bear the burden of the people with you,
so that you will not bear *it* all alone.
18 “Say to the people, ‘[a]Consecrate yourselves for tomorrow,
and you shall eat meat; for you have wept [b]in the ears of the
LORD, saying, “Oh that someone would give us meat to eat! For
we were well-off in Egypt.” Therefore the LORD will give you
meat and you shall eat.
19 ‘You shall eat, not one day, nor two days, nor five days, nor
ten days, nor twenty days,
20 [1]but a whole month, until it comes out of your nostrils and
becomes loathsome to you; because [a]you have rejected the
LORD who is among you and have wept before Him, saying,
“Why did we ever leave Egypt?”’”
21 But Moses said, “The people, among whom I am, are
600,000 on foot; yet You have said, ‘I will give them meat, so
that they may eat for a whole month.’
22 “Should flocks and herds be slaughtered for them, to be
sufficient for them? Or should all the fish of the sea be
gathered together for them, to be sufficient for them?”
23 The LORD said to Moses, “Is [a]the LORD’s [1]power limited? Now
you shall see whether [b]My word will [2]come true for you or not.”
24 So Moses went out and [a]told the people the words of the
LORD. Also, he gathered seventy men of the elders of the
people, and stationed them around the tent.
25 [a]Then the LORD came down in the cloud and spoke to him;
and He took of the Spirit who was upon him and placed *Him*
upon the seventy elders. And when the Spirit rested upon
them, they prophesied. But they did not do *it* again.
26 But two men had remained in the camp; the name of one
was Eldad and the name of the [1]other Medad. And [a]the Spirit
rested upon them (now they were among those who had been
registered, but had not gone out to the tent), and they
prophesied in the camp.
27 So a young man ran and told Moses and said, “Eldad and
Medad are prophesying in the camp.”
28 Then [a]Joshua the son of Nun, the attendant of Moses from
his youth, said, “[b]Moses, my lord, restrain them.”
29 But Moses said to him, “Are you jealous for my sake?
[a]Would that all the LORD’s people were prophets, that the LORD
would put His Spirit upon them!”
30 Then Moses [1]returned to the camp, *both* he and the elders
of Israel.

15 [a]Ex 32:32
16 [a]Ex 24:1, 9 [b]Ex 18:25
17 [a]Num 11:25 [b]1 Sam 10:6; Joel 2:28
18 [a]Ex 19:10, 22 [b]Num 11:1
20 [1]Lit *until* [a]Josh 24:27; 1 Sam 10:19
23 [1]Lit *hand short* [2]Lit *befall you* [a]Is 50:2; 59:1 [b]Ezek 12:25; 24:14
24 [a]Num 11:16
25 [a]Num 11:17; 12:5
26 [1]Lit *second* [a]Num 24:2; 1 Sam 10:6; 2 Chr 15:1; Neh 9:30
28 [a]Ex 33:11; Josh 1:1 [b]Mark 9:38-40
29 [a]1 Cor 14:5
30 [1]Lit *removed himself*

31 [a]Now there went forth a wind from the LORD and it
brought quail from the sea, and let *them* fall beside the camp,
about a day's journey on this side and a day's journey on the
other side, all around the camp and [1]about two [2]cubits *deep* on
the surface of the ground.
32 The people [1]spent all day and all night and all the next day, and
gathered the quail (he who gathered least gathered ten [2a]homers)
and they spread *them* out for themselves all around the camp.
33 [a]While the meat was still between their teeth, before it was
chewed, the anger of the LORD was kindled against the people,
and the LORD struck the people with a very severe plague.
34 So the name of that place was called [1a]Kibroth-hattaavah,
because there they buried the people who had been greedy.
35 From Kibroth-hattaavah [a]the people set out for Hazeroth,
and they [1]remained at Hazeroth.

Chapter 12 Theme ____

12 Then Miriam and Aaron spoke against Moses because of
the Cushite woman whom he had married (for he had
married a [a]Cushite woman);
2 [a]and they said, "Has the LORD indeed spoken only through
Moses? Has He not spoken through us as well?" And the LORD
heard it.
3 (Now the man Moses was [a]very humble, more than any
man who was on the face of the earth.)
4 Suddenly the LORD said to Moses and Aaron and to Miriam,
"You three come out to the tent of meeting." So the three of
them came out.
5 [a]Then the LORD came down in a pillar of cloud and stood at
the doorway of the tent, and He called [1]Aaron and Miriam.
When they had both come forward,
6 He said,

"Hear now My words:
If there is a prophet among you,
I, the LORD, shall make Myself known to him in a [a]vision.
I shall speak with him in a [b]dream.
7 "Not so, with [a]My servant Moses,
[b]He is faithful in all My household;
8 [a]With him I speak mouth to mouth,
Even openly, and not in dark sayings,
And he beholds [b]the form of the LORD.
Why then were you not afraid
To speak against My servant, against Moses?"

9 So the anger of the LORD burned against them and [a]He
departed.
10 But when the cloud had withdrawn from over the tent,
behold, [a]Miriam *was* leprous, as [b]*white as* snow. As Aaron
turned toward Miriam, behold, she *was* leprous.
11 Then Aaron said to Moses, "Oh, my lord, I beg you, [a]do
not account *this* sin to us, in which we have acted foolishly and
in which we have sinned.

31 [1]Or from *about two cubits above* [2]I.e. One cubit equals approx 18 in. [a]Ex 16:13; Ps 78:26-28; 105:40

32 [1]Lit *rose* [2]I.e. One homer equals approx 11 bu [a]Ezek 45:11

33 [a]Ps 78:29-31; 106:15

34 [1]I.e. the graves of greediness [a]Deut 9:22

35 [1]Lit *were* [a]Num 33:17

12:1 [a]Ex 2:21

2 [a]Num 16:3

3 [a]Matt 11:29

5 [1]Or *"Aaron and Miriam!"* [a]Ex 19:9; 34:5

6 [a]Gen 46:2; 1 Sam 3:15 [b]Gen 31:11; 1 Kin 3:5, 15

7 [a]Josh 1:1 [b]Heb 3:2, 5

8 [a]Deut 34:10; Hos 12:13 [b]Ex 20:4; 24:10, 11; Deut 5:8; Ps 17:15

9 [a]Gen 17:22; 18:33

10 [a]Deut 24:9 [b]Ex 4:6; 2 Kin 5:27

11 [a]2 Sam 19:19; 24:10

12 "Oh, do not let her be like one dead, whose flesh is half
eaten away when he comes from his mother's womb!"
13 Moses cried out to the LORD, saying, "O God, [a]heal her, I pray!"
14 But the LORD said to Moses, "If her father had but [a]spit in
her face, would she not bear her shame for seven days? Let her
be shut up for seven days [b]outside the camp, and afterward she
may be received again."
15 So [a]Miriam was shut up outside the camp for seven days, and
the people did not move on until Miriam was received again.
16 Afterward, however, the people moved out from Hazeroth
and camped in the wilderness of Paran.

Chapter 13 Theme ______________________

13 Then [a]the LORD spoke to Moses saying,
2 "[a]Send out for yourself men so that they may spy out the
land of Canaan, which I am going to give to the sons of Israel; you
shall send a man from each of their fathers' tribes, every one a
leader among them."
3 So Moses sent them from the wilderness of Paran at the
[1]command of the LORD, all of them men who were heads of the
sons of Israel.
4 These then *were* their names: from the tribe of Reuben,
Shammua the son of Zaccur;
5 from the tribe of Simeon, Shaphat the son of Hori;
6 from the tribe of Judah, [a]Caleb the son of Jephunneh;
7 from the tribe of Issachar, Igal the son of Joseph;
8 from the tribe of Ephraim, [a]Hoshea the son of Nun;
9 from the tribe of Benjamin, Palti the son of Raphu;
10 from the tribe of Zebulun, Gaddiel the son of Sodi;
11 from the tribe of Joseph, from the tribe of Manasseh, Gaddi
the son of Susi;
12 from the tribe of Dan, Ammiel the son of Gemalli;
13 from the tribe of Asher, Sethur the son of Michael;
14 from the tribe of Naphtali, Nahbi the son of Vophsi;
15 from the tribe of Gad, Geuel the son of Machi.
16 These are the names of the men whom Moses sent to spy
out the land; but Moses called [a]Hoshea the son of Nun, Joshua.
17 When Moses sent them to spy out the land of Canaan, he
said to them, "Go up [1]there into [a]the [2]Negev; then go up into
the hill country.
18 "See what the land is like, and whether the people who live
in it are strong *or* weak, whether they are few or many.
19 "How is the land in which they live, is it good or bad? And
how are the cities in which they live, are *they* [1]like *open*
camps or with fortifications?
20 "[a]How is the land, is it fat or lean? Are there trees in it or
not? [1]Make an [b]effort then to get some of the fruit of the land."
Now the time was the time of the first ripe grapes.
21 So they went up and spied out the land from [a]the wilderness
of Zin as far as Rehob, [1b]at Lebo-hamath.

13 [a]Ps 30:2; 41:4; Is 30:26; Jer 17:14
14 [a]Deut 25:9; Job 17:6; 30:10; Is 50:6 [b]Num 5:1-4
15 [a]Deut 24:9
13:1 [a]Deut 1:22, 23
2 [a]Deut 1:22; 9:23
3 [1]Lit *mouth*
6 [a]Num 14:6, 30; Josh 14:6
8 [a]Num 13:16; Deut 32:44
16 [a]Num 13:8; Deut 32:44
17 [1]Lit *here* [2]I.e. South country, and so throughout the ch [a]Gen 12:9; 13:1, 3
19 [1]Lit *in*
20 [1]Lit *Use your strength* [a]Deut 1:24, 25 [b]Deut 31:6, 23
21 [1]Or *to the entrance of Hamath* [a]Num 20:1; 27:14; 33:36 [b]Josh 13:5

22 When they had gone up into [a]the Negev, [1]they came to Hebron where [b]Ahiman, Sheshai and Talmai, the [2]descendants of [c]Anak were. (Now Hebron was built seven years before [d]Zoan in Egypt.)

23 Then they came to the [1]valley of [2a]Eshcol and from there cut down a branch with a single cluster of grapes; and they carried it on a pole between two *men,* with some of the pomegranates and the figs.

24 That place was called the valley of [1]Eshcol, because of the cluster which the sons of Israel cut down from there.

25 When they returned from spying out the land, at the end of forty days,

26 they proceeded to come to Moses and Aaron and to all the congregation of the sons of Israel [1]in the wilderness of Paran, at [a]Kadesh; and they brought back word to them and to all the congregation and showed them the fruit of the land.

27 Thus they told him, and said, "We went in to the land where you sent us; and [a]it certainly does flow with milk and honey, and [b]this is its fruit.

28 "Nevertheless, [a]the people who live in the land are strong, and the cities are fortified *and* very large; and moreover, we saw [b]the [1]descendants of Anak there.

29 "Amalek is living in the land of [a]the Negev and the Hittites and the Jebusites and [b]the Amorites are living in the hill country, and [c]the Canaanites are living by the sea and by the side of the Jordan."

30 Then Caleb quieted the people [1]before Moses and said, "We should by all means go up and take possession of it, for we will surely overcome it."

31 But the men who had gone up with him said, "[a]We are not able to go up against the people, for they are too strong for us."

32 So they gave out to the sons of Israel [a]a bad report of the land which they had spied out, saying, "The land through which we have gone, in spying it out, is [b]a land that devours its [1]inhabitants; and [c]all the people whom we saw in it are men of *great* size.

33 "There also we saw the [a]Nephilim (the sons of Anak are part of the Nephilim); and [b]we became like grasshoppers in our own sight, and so we were in their sight."

Chapter 14 Theme ______________________________

14 Then all the congregation [1]lifted up their voices and cried, and the people wept [2]that night.

2 All the sons of Israel [a]grumbled against Moses and Aaron; and the whole congregation said to them, "[b]Would that we had died in the land of Egypt! Or would that we had died in this wilderness!

3 "Why is the LORD bringing us into this land, [a]to fall by the sword? [b]Our wives and our little ones will become plunder; would it not be better for us to return to Egypt?"

4 So they said to one another, "[a]Let us appoint a leader and return to Egypt."

22 [1]Lit Most mss read *one came* [2]Lit *children* [a]Num 13:17 [b]Josh 15:14 [c]Num 13:28, 33 [d]Ps 78:12, 43

23 [1]Or *wadi* [2]I.e. cluster [a]Gen 14:13; Num 13:24; 32:9; Deut 1:24

24 [1]I.e. cluster

26 [1]Lit *to* [a]Num 20:1, 14; 32:8

27 [a]Ex 3:8, 17; 13:5 [b]Deut 1:25

28 [1]Lit *born ones* [a]Deut 1:28; 9:1, 2 [b]Num 13:33

29 [a]Num 13:17; 14:25, 45 [b]Josh 10:6 [c]Num 14:43, 45

30 [1]Lit *toward*

31 [a]Deut 1:28; 9:1-3

32 [1]Or *settlers* [a]Num 14:36, 37; Ps 106:24 [b]Ezek 36:13, 14 [c]Amos 2:9

33 [a]Gen 6:4 [b]Deut 1:28; 9:2; Josh 11:21

14:1 [1]Lit *lifted and gave their voice* [2]Lit *in that*

2 [a]Num 11:1 [b]Num 11:5; 16:13; 20:3, 4; 21:5

3 [a]Ex 5:21; 16:3 [b]Num 14:31; Deut 1:39

4 [a]Neh 9:17

5 [a]Then Moses and Aaron fell on their faces in the presence
of all the assembly of the congregation of the sons of Israel.
6 Joshua the son of Nun and Caleb the son of Jephunneh, of
those who had spied out the land, tore their clothes;
7 and they spoke to all the congregation of the sons of Israel,
saying, "[a]The land which we passed through to spy out is an
exceedingly good land.
8 "[a]If the LORD is pleased with us, then He will bring us into this
land and give it to us—[b]a land which flows with milk and honey.
9 "Only [a]do not rebel against the LORD; and do not [b]fear the
people of the land, for they will be our [1]prey. Their [2]protection
has been removed from them, and the LORD is with us; do not
fear them."
10 [a]But all the congregation said to stone them with stones.
Then [b]the glory of the LORD appeared in the tent of meeting to
all the sons of Israel.
11 [a]The LORD said to Moses, "How long will this people spurn
Me? And how long will [b]they not believe in Me, despite all the
signs which I have performed in their midst?
12 "I will smite them with [1a]pestilence and dispossess them, and
I [b]will make you into a nation greater and mightier than they."
13 [a]But Moses said to the LORD, "Then the Egyptians will hear of
it, for by Your strength You brought up this people from their midst,
14 and they will tell *it* to the inhabitants of this land. They
have heard that You, O LORD, are in the midst of this people,
for [a]You, O LORD, are seen eye to eye, while Your cloud stands
over them; and You go before them in a pillar of cloud by day
and in a pillar of fire by night.
15 "Now if You slay this people as one man, [a]then the nations
who have heard of Your fame will [1]say,
16 'Because the LORD [a]could not bring this people into the land
which He promised them by oath, therefore He slaughtered
them in the wilderness.'
17 "But now, I pray, let the power of the Lord be great, just as
You have [1]declared,
18 '[a]The LORD is slow to anger and abundant in lovingkindness,
forgiving iniquity and transgression; but [b]He will by no means
clear *the guilty,* [c]visiting the iniquity of the fathers on the
children [1]to the third and the fourth *generations.*'
19 "[a]Pardon, I pray, the iniquity of this people according to the
greatness of Your lovingkindness, just as You also have forgiven
this people, from Egypt even until now."
20 So the LORD said, "[a]I have pardoned *them* according to
your word;
21 but indeed, [a]as I live, [1b]all the earth will be filled with the
glory of the LORD.
22 "Surely [a]all the men who have seen My glory and My signs
which I performed in Egypt and in the wilderness, yet [b]have put
Me to the test these ten times and have not listened to My voice,
23 [a]shall by no means see the land which I swore to their
fathers, nor shall any of those who spurned Me see it.

5 [a]Num 16:4
7 [a]Num 13:27; Deut 1:25
8 [a]Deut 10:15 [b]Ex 3:8; Num 13:27
9 [1]Lit *food* [2]Lit *shadow* [a]Deut 1:26; 9:23, 24 [b]Deut 1:21, 29
10 [a]Ex 17:4 [b]Ex 16:10; Lev 9:23
11 [a]Ex 32:9-13 [b]Ps 106:24
12 [1]Lit *the pestilence* [a]Lev 26:25; Deut 28:21 [b]Ex 32:10
13 [a]Ex 32:11-14; Ps 106:23
14 [a]Ex 13:21; Deut 5:4
15 [1]Lit *speak, saying* [a]Ex 32:12
16 [a]Josh 7:7
17 [1]Lit *spoken, saying*
18 [1]Lit *on* [a]Ex 20:6; 34:6, 7; Deut 5:10; 7:9; Ps 103:8; 145:8; Jon 4:2 [b]Ex 20:5; Deut 5:9; 7:10 [c]Ex 34:7
19 [a]Ex 32:32; 34:9
20 [a]Mic 7:18-20
21 [1]Lit *and all* [a]Num 14:28; Deut 32:40; Is 49:18 [b]Is 6:3; Hab 2:14
22 [a]1 Cor 10:5 [b]Ex 5:21; 14:11; 15:24; 16:2; 17:2, 3; 32:1; Num 11:1, 4; 12:1; 14:2
23 [a]Num 26:65; 32:11; Heb 3:18

24 "But My servant Caleb, [a]because he has had a different spirit
and has followed Me fully, [1b]I will bring into the land [2]which he
entered, and his [3]descendants shall take possession of it.
25 "[a]Now the Amalekites and the Canaanites live in the valleys;
turn tomorrow and set out to the wilderness by the way of the
[1]Red Sea."
26 The LORD spoke to Moses and Aaron, saying,
27 "How long *shall I bear* with this evil congregation who are
[a]grumbling against Me? I have heard the complaints of the sons
of Israel, which they are [1]making against Me.
28 "Say to them, '[a]As I live,' says the LORD, 'just as [b]you have
spoken in My hearing, so I will surely do to you;
29 [a]your corpses will fall in this wilderness, even all [b]your
[1]numbered men, according to your complete number from
twenty years old and upward, who have grumbled against Me.
30 'Surely you shall not come into the land in which I [1]swore
to settle you, [a]except Caleb the son of Jephunneh and Joshua
the son of Nun.
31 '[a]Your children, however, whom you said would become a
prey—I will bring them in, and they will know the land which
you have rejected.
32 '[a]But as for you, your corpses will fall in this wilderness.
33 'Your sons shall be shepherds for [a]forty years in the
wilderness, and they will [1]suffer *for* your [2]unfaithfulness, until
your corpses [3]lie in the wilderness.
34 'According to the [a]number of days which you spied out the
land, forty days, for every day you shall bear your [1]guilt a year,
even forty years, and you will know My opposition.
35 '[a]I, the LORD, have spoken, surely this I will do to all this
evil congregation who are gathered together against Me. In this
wilderness they shall be destroyed, and there they will die.'"
36 [a]As for the men whom Moses sent to spy out the land and
who returned and made all the congregation grumble against
him by bringing out a bad report concerning the land,
37 even [a]those men who brought out the very bad report of
the land died by a [b]plague before the LORD.
38 But Joshua the son of Nun and Caleb the son of Jephunneh
remained alive out of those men who went to spy out the land.
39 When Moses spoke [a]these words to all the sons of Israel,
[b]the people mourned greatly.
40 In the morning, however, they rose up early and went up
to the [1]ridge of the hill country, saying, "[a]Here we are; [2]we
have indeed sinned, but we will go up to the place which the
LORD has promised."
41 But Moses said, "[a]Why then are you transgressing the
[1]commandment of the LORD, when it will not succeed?
42 "[a]Do not go up, or you will be struck down before your
enemies, for the LORD is not among you.
43 "For the Amalekites and the Canaanites will be there in front
of you, and you will fall by the sword, inasmuch as you have

24 [1]Lit *him* [2]Lit *where* [3]Lit *seed* [a]Num 14:6-9 [b]Num 26:65; 32:12; Deut 1:36; Josh 14:6-15

25 [1]Lit *Sea of Reeds* [a]Num 13:29

27 [1]Lit *complaining* [a]Num 11:1

28 [a]Num 14:21 [b]Num 14:2; Deut 2:14, 15; Heb 3:17

29 [1]Lit *mustered* [a]Heb 3:17 [b]Num 1:45, 46

30 [1]Lit *raised My hand* [a]Num 14:24

31 [a]Num 14:3

32 [a]Num 26:64, 65; 32:13; 1 Cor 10:5

33 [1]Lit *bear* [2]Lit *fornications* [3]Lit *are finished* [a]Deut 2:7; 8:2, 4; 29:5

34 [1]Or *iniquities* [a]Num 13:25

35 [a]Num 23:19

36 [a]Num 13:4-16, 32

37 [a]1 Cor 10:10; Heb 3:17, 18 [b]Num 16:49

39 [a]Num 14:28-35 [b]Ex 33:4

40 [1]Or *top of the mountain* [2]Or *and we will go up . . . for we have sinned* [a]Deut 1:41-44

41 [1]Lit *mouth* [a]2 Chr 24:20

42 [a]Deut 1:42

turned back from following the LORD. And the LORD will not be
with you."
44 But they went up heedlessly to the [1]ridge of the hill country;
neither [a]the ark of the covenant of the LORD nor Moses left the
camp.
45 Then the Amalekites and the Canaanites who lived in that
hill country came down, and struck them and beat them down
as far as [a]Hormah.

Chapter 15 Theme ______________________

15 Now the LORD spoke to Moses, saying,
2 "[a]Speak to the sons of Israel and say to them, 'When you
enter the land [1]where you are to live, which I am giving you,
3 then make [a]an offering by fire to the LORD, a burnt offering
or a sacrifice to [1b]fulfill a special vow, or as a freewill offering or
in your [c]appointed times, to make a [d]soothing aroma to the
LORD, from the herd or from the flock.
4 '[a]The one who presents his offering shall present to the
LORD a grain offering of one-tenth *of an ephah* of fine flour
mixed with one-fourth of a [1]hin of oil,
5 and you shall prepare wine for the drink offering, one-
fourth of a hin, with the burnt offering or for the sacrifice, for
[a]each lamb.
6 'Or for a ram you shall prepare as a grain offering two-tenths
of an ephah of fine flour mixed with one-third of a hin of oil;
7 and for the drink offering you shall offer one-third of a hin
of wine as a soothing aroma to the LORD.
8 'When you prepare [a]a bull as a burnt offering or a sacrifice,
to [1]fulfill a special vow, or for peace offerings to the LORD,
9 then you shall offer with the bull a grain offering of three-
tenths *of an ephah* of fine flour mixed with one-half a hin of oil;
10 and you shall offer as the drink offering one-half a hin of
wine as an offering by fire, as a soothing aroma to the LORD.
11 'Thus it shall be done for each ox, or for each ram, or for
each of the male lambs, or of the goats.
12 'According to the number that you prepare, so you shall do
for everyone according to their number.
13 'All who are native shall do these things in this manner, in
presenting an offering by fire, as a soothing aroma to the LORD.
14 'If an alien sojourns with you, or one who may be among
you throughout your generations, and he *wishes to* make an
offering by fire, as a soothing aroma to the LORD, just as you do
so he shall do.
15 '*As for* the assembly, there shall be [a]one statute for you and
for the alien who sojourns *with you,* a perpetual statute
throughout your generations; as you are, so shall the alien be
before the LORD.
16 'There is to be [a]one law and one ordinance for you and for
the alien who sojourns with you.'"
17 Then the LORD spoke to Moses, saying,

44 [1]Or *top of the mountain* [a]Num 31:6
45 [a]Num 21:3
15:2 [1]Lit *of your dwellings* [a]Lev 23:10
3 [1]Or *make a special votive offering* [a]Lev 1:2, 3 [b]Lev 22:21 [c]Lev 23:1-44 [d]Gen 8:21; 2 Cor 2:15, 16; Phil 4:18
4 [1]I.e. Approx one gal., and so through v 10 [a]Num 28:1-29:40
5 [a]Lev 1:10; 3:6; Num 15:11
8 [1]Or *make a special votive offering* [a]Lev 1:3; 3:1
15 [a]Num 9:14; 15:29
16 [a]Lev 24:22

18 "Speak to the sons of Israel and say to them, 'When you
enter the land where I bring you,
19 then it shall be, that when you eat of the [1][a]food of the land,
you shall lift up [2]an offering to the LORD.
20 '[a]Of the first of your [1]dough you shall lift up a cake as an
[2]offering; as [b]the [2]offering of the threshing floor, so you shall lift
it up.
21 'From the first of your [1]dough you shall give to the LORD an
[2]offering throughout your generations.
22 'But when you [a]unwittingly fail and do not observe all these
commandments, which the LORD has spoken to Moses,
23 *even* all that the LORD has commanded you [1]through Moses,
from the day when the LORD gave commandment and onward
throughout your generations,
24 then it shall be, if it is done [a]unintentionally, [1]without the
knowledge of the congregation, that all the congregation shall
offer one bull for a burnt offering, as a soothing aroma to the
LORD, [b]with its grain offering and its drink offering, according
to the ordinance, and one male goat for a sin offering.
25 'Then [a]the priest shall make atonement for all the congregation
of the sons of Israel, and they will be forgiven; for it was an error,
and they have brought their offering, an offering by fire to the
LORD, and their sin offering before the LORD, for their error.
26 'So all the congregation of the sons of Israel will be forgiven,
with the alien who sojourns among them, for *it happened* to all
the people through [a]error.
27 'Also if one person sins [a]unintentionally, then he shall offer
a one year old female goat for a sin offering.
28 '[a]The priest shall make atonement before the LORD for the
person who goes astray when he sins unintentionally, making
atonement for him [1]that he may be forgiven.
29 'You shall have one law for him who does *anything* unintentionally, for him who is native among the sons of Israel and for
the alien who sojourns among them.
30 'But the person who does *anything* [a]defiantly, whether he is
native or an alien, that one is blaspheming the LORD; and that
person shall be cut off from among his people.
31 'Because he has [a]despised the word of the LORD and has
broken His commandment, that person shall be completely cut
off; [b]his [1]guilt *will be* on him.'"
32 Now while the sons of Israel were in the wilderness, they
found a man [a]gathering wood on the sabbath day.
33 Those who found him gathering wood brought him to
Moses and Aaron and to all the congregation;
34 and they put him in [1]custody [a]because it had not been
[2]declared what should be done to him.
35 Then the LORD said to Moses, "The man shall surely be put
to death; [a]all the congregation shall stone him with stones
outside the camp."
36 So all the congregation brought him outside the camp and
stoned him [1]to death with stones, just as the LORD had
commanded Moses.

19 [1]Lit *bread* [2]Or *a heave offering* [a]Josh 5:11, 12

20 [1]Or *coarse meal* [2]Or *heave offering* [a]Ex 34:26; Lev 23:14 [b]Deut 14:22, 23; 16:13

21 [1]Or *coarse meal* [2]Or *offering lifted up*

22 [a]Lev 4:2

23 [1]Lit *by the hand of*

24 [1]Lit *from the eyes of the congregation* [a]Lev 4:2, 22, 27; 5:15, 18 [b]Num 15:8-10

25 [a]Lev 4:20; Heb 2:17

26 [a]Num 15:24

27 [a]Lev 4:27-31; Luke 12:48

28 [1]Or *and he shall* [a]Lev 4:35

30 [a]Num 14:40-44; Deut 1:43; 17:12, 13

31 [1]Or *iniquity* [a]2 Sam 12:9; Prov 13:13 [b]Ezek 18:20

32 [a]Ex 31:14, 15; 35:2, 3

34 [1]Or *prison* [2]Lit *declared distinctly* [a]Num 9:8

35 [a]Lev 20:2, 27; 24:14-23; Deut 21:21

36 [1]Lit *with stones and he died*

37 The LORD also spoke to Moses, saying,
38 "Speak to the sons of Israel, and tell them that they shall
make for themselves [a]tassels on the corners of their garments
throughout their generations, and that they shall put on the
tassel of each corner a cord of blue.
39 "It shall be a tassel for you [1]to look at and [a]remember all the
commandments of the LORD, so as to do them and not [2]follow
after your own heart and your own eyes, after which you played
the harlot,
40 so that you may remember to do all My commandments
and [a]be holy to your God.
41 "I am the LORD your God who brought you out from the
land of Egypt to be your God; I am the LORD your God."

Chapter 16 Theme ______________________

16 Now [a]Korah the son of Izhar, the son of Kohath, the son
of Levi, with [b]Dathan and Abiram, the sons of Eliab, and
On the son of Peleth, sons of Reuben, took *action,*
2 and they rose up before Moses, [1]together with some of the
sons of Israel, two hundred and fifty leaders of the congregation,
[2a]chosen in the assembly, men of renown.
3 They assembled together [a]against Moses and Aaron, and said
to them, "[1b]You have gone far enough, for all the congregation
are holy, every one of them, and [c]the LORD is in their midst; so
why do you exalt yourselves above the assembly of the LORD?"
4 When Moses heard *this,* [a]he fell on his face;
5 and he spoke to Korah and all his company, saying,
"Tomorrow morning the LORD will show who is His, and [a]who
is holy, and will bring *him* near to Himself; even [b]the one
whom He will choose, He will bring near to Himself.
6 "Do this: take censers for yourselves, Korah and all [1]your
company,
7 and put fire in them, and lay incense upon them in the
presence of the LORD tomorrow; and the man whom the LORD
chooses *shall be* the one who is holy. [1a]You have gone far
enough, you sons of Levi!"
8 Then Moses said to Korah, "Hear now, you sons of Levi,
9 [a]is it [1]not enough for you that the God of Israel has separated
you from the *rest of* the congregation of Israel, [b]to bring you
near to Himself, to do the service of the tabernacle of the LORD,
and to stand before the congregation to minister to them;
10 and that He has brought you near, *Korah,* and all your
brothers, sons of Levi, with you? And are you [a]seeking for the
priesthood also?
11 "Therefore you and all your company are gathered together
[a]against the LORD; but as for Aaron, [1]who is he that [b]you
grumble against him?"
12 Then Moses sent [1]a summons to Dathan and Abiram, the
sons of Eliab; but they said, "We will not come up.
13 "Is it [1]not enough that you have brought us up out of a [a]land

38 [a]Deut 22:12; Matt 23:5
39 [1]Lit *and you shall look at it* [2]Lit *seek* [a]Deut 4:23; 6:12; 8:11, 14, 19
40 [a]Lev 11:44, 45
16:1 [a]Ex 6:21; Jude 11 [b]Num 26:9; Deut 11:6
2 [1]Lit *and men from* [2]Lit *called ones of* [a]Num 1:16; 26:9
3 [1]Lit *It is much for you* [a]Num 12:2; Ps 106:16 [b]Num 16:7 [c]Num 5:3
4 [a]Num 14:5
5 [a]Lev 10:3; Ps 65:4 [b]Num 17:5, 8
6 [1]Lit *his*
7 [1]Lit *It is much for you* [a]Num 16:3
9 [1]Or *too little for you* [a]Is 7:13 [b]Num 3:6, 9; Deut 10:8
10 [a]Num 3:10; 18:1-7
11 [1]Lit *what* [a]Ex 16:7 [b]1 Cor 10:10
12 [1]Lit *to call*
13 [1]Lit *a little thing* [a]Ex 16:3; Num 11:4-6

flowing with milk and honey [b]to have us die in the wilderness,
but you would also lord it over us?
14 "Indeed, you have not brought us [a]into a land flowing with
milk and honey, nor have you given us an inheritance of [b]fields
and vineyards. Would you [1][c]put out the eyes of [2]these men?
We will not come up!"
15 Then Moses became very angry and said to the LORD, "[a]Do
not regard their offering! [b]I have not taken a single donkey
from them, nor have I done harm to any of them."
16 Moses said to Korah, "You and all your company be present
before the LORD tomorrow, both you and they along with Aaron.
17 "Each of you take his firepan and put incense on [1]it, and
each of you bring his censer before the LORD, two hundred and
fifty firepans; also you and Aaron *shall* each *bring* his firepan."
18 So they each took his *own* censer and put fire on [1]it, and
laid incense on [1]it; and they stood at the doorway of the tent of
meeting, with Moses and Aaron.
19 Thus Korah assembled all the congregation against them at
the doorway of the tent of meeting. And [a]the glory of the LORD
appeared to all the congregation.
20 Then the LORD spoke to Moses and Aaron, saying,
21 "[a]Separate yourselves from among this congregation, [b]that I
may consume them instantly."
22 But they fell on their faces and said, "O God, [a]God of the
spirits of all flesh, [b]when one man sins, will You be angry with
the entire congregation?"
23 Then the LORD spoke to Moses, saying,
24 "Speak to the congregation, saying, '[a]Get back from around
the dwellings of Korah, Dathan and Abiram.'"
25 Then Moses arose and went to Dathan and Abiram, with the
elders of Israel following him,
26 and he spoke to the congregation, saying, "[a]Depart now
from the tents of these wicked men, and touch nothing that
belongs to them, [b]or you will be swept away in all their sin."
27 So they got back from around the dwellings of Korah,
Dathan and Abiram; and Dathan and Abiram came out *and*
stood at the doorway of their tents, along with their wives and
[a]their sons and their little ones.
28 Moses said, "By this you shall know that [a]the LORD has sent
me to do all these deeds; for this is not [1]my doing.
29 "If these men die [1]the death of all men or [2]if they suffer the
[a]fate of all men, *then* the LORD has not sent me.
30 "But [a]if the LORD [1]brings about an entirely new thing and
the ground opens its mouth and swallows them up with all that
is theirs, and they [b]descend alive into [2]Sheol, then you will
understand that these men have spurned the LORD."
31 As he finished speaking all these words, the ground that
was under them split open;
32 and [a]the earth opened its mouth and swallowed them up,
and their households, and [b]all the men who belonged to Korah
with *their* possessions.

13 [b]Num 14:2, 3

14 [1]Lit *bore out* [2]Lit *those* [a]Num 13:27; 14:8 [b]Ex 22:5; 23:10, 11; Num 20:5 [c]Judg 16:21; 1 Sam 11:2

15 [a]Gen 4:4, 5 [b]1 Sam 12:3

17 [1]Lit *them*

18 [1]Lit *them*

19 [a]Num 14:10; 16:42; 20:6

21 [a]Num 16:45 [b]Ex 32:10, 12

22 [a]Num 27:16 [b]Gen 18:23-32; Lev 4:3

24 [a]Num 16:45

26 [a]Is 52:11 [b]Gen 19:15, 17

27 [a]Num 26:11

28 [1]Lit *from my heart* [a]Ex 3:12-15; 4:12, 15

29 [1]Lit *like the death* [2]Lit *the visitation of all men be visited upon them* [a]Eccl 3:19

30 [1]Lit *creates a new creation* [2]I.e. the nether world [a]Job 31:2, 3 [b]Ps 55:15

32 [a]Num 26:10; Deut 11:6; Ps 106:17 [b]Num 26:11

33 So they and all that belonged to them went down alive to
[1]Sheol; and the earth closed over them, and they perished from
the midst of the assembly.
34 All Israel who *were* around them fled at their [1]outcry, for
they said, "The earth may swallow us up!"
35 [a]Fire also came forth from the LORD and consumed the
[b]two hundred and fifty men who were offering the incense.
36 [1]Then the LORD spoke to Moses, saying,
37 "Say to Eleazar, the son of Aaron the priest, that he shall
take up the censers out of the midst of the [1]blaze, for they are
holy; and you scatter the [2]burning coals abroad.
38 "As for the censers of these [1]men who have sinned at the
cost of their lives, let them be made into hammered sheets for
a plating of the altar, since they did present them before the
LORD and they are holy; and [a]they shall be for a sign to the sons
of Israel."
39 So Eleazar the priest took the bronze censers which the men
who were burned had offered, and they hammered them out
as a plating for the altar,
40 as a [1]reminder to the sons of Israel that [a]no [2]layman who is
not of the [3]descendants of Aaron should come near [b]to burn
incense before the LORD; so that he will not become like Korah
and his company—just as the LORD had spoken to him
[4]through Moses.
41 But on the next day all the congregation of the sons of
Israel [a]grumbled against Moses and Aaron, saying, "You are the
ones who have caused the death of the LORD'S people."
42 It came about, however, when the congregation had
assembled against Moses and Aaron, that they turned toward
the tent of meeting, and behold, the cloud covered it and [a]the
glory of the LORD appeared.
43 Then Moses and Aaron came to the front of the tent of
meeting,
44 and the LORD spoke to Moses, saying,
45 "[1a]Get away from among this congregation, that I may
consume them instantly." Then they fell on their faces.
46 Moses said to Aaron, "Take your censer and put in it fire
from the altar, and lay incense *on it;* then bring it quickly to the
congregation and [a]make atonement for them, for [b]wrath has
gone forth from the LORD, the plague has begun!"
47 Then Aaron took *it* as Moses had spoken, and ran into the
midst of the assembly, for behold, the plague had begun among
the people. [a]So he put *on* the incense and made atonement for
the people.
48 He took his stand between the dead and the living, so that
the plague was checked.
49 [a]But those who died by the plague were 14,700, besides
those who [b]died on account of Korah.
50 Then Aaron returned to Moses at the doorway of the tent
of meeting, for the plague had been checked.

33 [1]I.e. the nether world
34 [1]Or *voice*
35 [a]Num 11:1-3; 26:10 [b]Num 16:2
36 [1]Ch 17:1 in Heb
37 [1]Or *place of burning* [2]Lit *the fire*
38 [1]Lit *sinners against their lives* [a]Ezek 14:8; 2 Pet 2:6
40 [1]Or *memorial* [2]Lit *stranger* [3]Lit *seed* [4]Lit *by the hand of* [a]Num 1:51 [b]Ex 30:7-10
41 [a]Num 16:3
42 [a]Num 16:19
45 [1]Or *Arise* [a]Num 16:21, 24
46 [a]Num 25:13; Is 6:6, 7 [b]Num 18:5; Deut 9:22
47 [a]Num 25:6-8, 13
49 [a]Num 25:9 [b]Num 16:32, 35

Chapter 17 Theme ____________________

17 [1]Then the LORD spoke to Moses, saying,

2 "Speak to the sons of Israel, and get from them a rod for each father's household: twelve rods, from all their leaders according to their fathers' households. You shall write each name on his rod,

3 and write Aaron's name on the rod of Levi; for there is one rod for the head *of each* of their fathers' households.

4 "You shall then deposit them in the tent of meeting in front of [a]the testimony, where I meet with you.

5 "It will come about that the rod of [a]the man whom I choose will sprout. Thus I will lessen from upon Myself the grumblings of the sons of Israel, who are grumbling against you."

6 Moses therefore spoke to the sons of Israel, and all their leaders gave him a rod apiece, for each leader according to their fathers' households, twelve rods, with the rod of Aaron among their rods.

7 So Moses deposited the rods before the LORD in [a]the tent of the testimony.

8 Now on the next day Moses went into the tent of the testimony; and behold, [a]the rod of Aaron for the house of Levi had sprouted and put forth buds and produced blossoms, and it bore ripe almonds.

9 Moses then brought out all the rods from the presence of the LORD to all the sons of Israel; and they looked, and each man took his rod.

10 But the LORD said to Moses, "Put back the rod of Aaron [a]before the testimony [1]to be kept as a sign against the [2b]rebels, that you may put an end to their grumblings against Me, so that they will not die."

11 Thus Moses did; just as the LORD had commanded him, so he did.

12 Then the sons of Israel spoke to Moses, saying, "[a]Behold, we perish, we are dying, we are all dying!

13 "[a]Everyone who comes near, who comes near to the tabernacle of the LORD, must die. Are we to perish completely?"

Chapter 18 Theme ____________________

18 So the LORD said to Aaron, "You and your sons and your father's household with you shall [a]bear the guilt [1]in connection with the sanctuary, and you and your sons with you shall bear the guilt [2]in connection with your priesthood.

2 "But bring with you also your brothers, the tribe of Levi, the tribe of your father, that they may be [a]joined with you and serve you, while you and your sons with you are before the tent of the testimony.

3 "And they shall thus attend to your obligation and the obligation of all the tent, but [a]they shall not come near to the furnishings of the sanctuary and [b]the altar, or both they and you will die.

17:1 [1]Ch 17:16 in Heb
4 [a]Ex 25:16, 21, 22; Num 17:7
5 [a]Num 16:5
7 [a]Num 1:50, 53; 9:15
8 [a]Ezek 17:24; Heb 9:4
10 [1]Lit *for preserving* [2]Lit *sons of rebellion* [a]Num 17:4 [b]Deut 9:7, 24
12 [a]Is 6:5
13 [a]Num 1:51
18:1 [1]Lit *of the sanctuary* [2]Lit *of your priesthood* [a]Ex 28:38; Lev 10:17; 22:16
2 [a]Num 3:5-10
3 [a]Num 4:15-20 [b]Num 1:51; 18:7

4 "They shall be joined with you and attend to the obligations
of the tent of meeting, for all the service of the tent; but an
[1]outsider may not come near you.
5 "So you shall attend to the [a]obligations of the sanctuary and
the obligations of the altar, [b]so that there will no longer be
wrath on the sons of Israel.
6 "Behold, I Myself [a]have taken your [1]fellow Levites from
among the sons of Israel; they are [b]a gift to you, [2]dedicated to
the LORD, to perform the service for the tent of meeting.
7 "But you and your sons with you shall [a]attend to your
priesthood for everything concerning the altar and inside the veil,
and you are to perform service. I am giving you the priesthood
as [b]a [1]bestowed service, but [c]the [2]outsider who comes near
shall be put to death."
8 Then the LORD spoke to Aaron, "Now behold, I Myself
have given you charge of My [1a]offerings, even all the holy gifts
of the sons of Israel I have given them to you as a portion and
to your sons as a perpetual allotment.
9 "This shall be yours from the most holy *gifts reserved* from
the fire; every offering of theirs, even [a]every grain offering and
every [b]sin offering and every guilt offering, which they shall
render to Me, shall be most holy for you and for your sons.
10 "As the most holy *gifts* you shall eat it; every male shall eat
it. It shall be holy to you.
11 "This also is yours, [a]the offering of their gift, even all the
wave offerings of the sons of Israel; I have [b]given them to you
and to your sons and daughters with you as a perpetual
allotment. Everyone of your household who is clean may eat it.
12 "[a]All the [1]best of the fresh oil and all the [1]best of the fresh
wine and of the grain, the first fruits of those which they give
to the LORD, I give them to you.
13 "[a]The first ripe fruits of all that is in their land, which they
bring to the LORD, shall be yours; everyone of your household
who is clean may eat it.
14 "[a]Every devoted thing in Israel shall be yours.
15 "[1a]Every first issue of the womb of all flesh, whether man or
animal, which they offer to the LORD, shall be yours; nevertheless the firstborn of man you shall surely redeem, and the
firstborn of unclean animals you shall redeem.
16 "As to their redemption price, from a month old you shall
redeem them, by your valuation, five [1]shekels in silver, according
to the [1]shekel of the sanctuary, which is twenty gerahs.
17 "But [a]the firstborn of an ox or the firstborn of a sheep or the
firstborn of a goat, you shall not redeem; they are holy. [b]You shall
sprinkle their blood on the altar and shall offer up their fat in
smoke *as* an offering by fire, for a soothing aroma to the LORD.
18 "Their [1]meat shall be yours; it shall be yours like the [a]breast
of a wave offering and like the right thigh.
19 "[a]All the offerings of the holy *gifts,* which the sons of Israel
offer to the LORD, I have given to you and your sons and your
daughters with you, as a perpetual allotment. It is [b]an everlasting

4 [1]Lit *a stranger*
5 [a]Ex 27:21; Lev 24:3 [b]Num 16:46
6 [1]Lit *brethren the* [2]Lit *given* [a]Num 3:12, 45 [b]Num 3:9
7 [1]Lit *service of gift* [2]Lit *stranger* [a]Ex 29:9 [b]Num 18:20; Deut 18:2; Matt 10:8; 1 Pet 5:2, 3 [c]Num 1:51
8 [1]Lit *heave offerings,* and so throughout the ch [a]Lev 6:16, 18; 7:28-34
9 [a]Lev 2:1-16 [b]Lev 6:30
11 [a]Num 18:1; Deut 18:3 [b]Lev 22:1-16
12 [1]Lit *fat* [a]Deut 18:4; 32:14; Ps 81:16; 147:14
13 [a]Ex 22:29; 23:19; 34:26
14 [a]Lev 27:1-33
15 [1]Lit *Everything that opens* [a]Ex 13:13, 15; Num 3:46
16 [1]I.e. A shekel equals approx one-half oz
17 [a]Deut 15:19 [b]Lev 3:2
18 [1]Lit *flesh* [a]Lev 7:31
19 [a]Num 18:11 [b]2 Chr 13:5

covenant of salt before the LORD to you and your [1]descendants
with you."
20 Then the LORD said to Aaron, "[a]You shall have no inheritance
in their land nor own any portion among them; [b]I am your
portion and your inheritance among the sons of Israel.
21 "To the sons of Levi, behold, I have given all the [a]tithe in
Israel for an inheritance, in return for their service which they
perform, the service of the tent of meeting.
22 "[a]The sons of Israel shall not come near the tent of meeting
again, or they will bear sin and die.
23 "Only the Levites shall perform the service of the tent of
meeting, and they shall [a]bear their iniquity; it shall be a
perpetual statute throughout your generations, and among the
sons of Israel [b]they shall have no inheritance.
24 "For the tithe of the sons of Israel, which they offer as an
offering to the LORD, I have given to the Levites for an
inheritance; therefore I have said concerning them, '[a]They
shall have no inheritance among the sons of Israel.'"
25 Then the LORD spoke to Moses, saying,
26 "Moreover, you shall speak to the Levites and say to them,
'When you take from the sons of Israel [a]the tithe which I have
given you from them for your inheritance, then you shall
present an offering from it to the LORD, a [b]tithe of the tithe.
27 'Your offering shall be reckoned to you as the grain from the
threshing floor or the full produce from the wine vat.
28 'So you shall also present an offering to the LORD from your
tithes, which you receive from the sons of Israel; and from it
you shall give the LORD's offering to Aaron the priest.
29 'Out of all your gifts you shall present every offering due to
the LORD, from all the [1]best of them, [2]the sacred part from them.'
30 "You shall say to them, 'When you have [1]offered from it the
best of it, then *the rest* shall be reckoned to the Levites as the
product of the threshing floor, and as the product of the wine vat.
31 'You may eat it anywhere, you and your households, for it is
your compensation in return for your service in the tent of
meeting.
32 'You will bear no sin by reason of it when you have [1]offered
the [2]best of it. But you shall not [a]profane the sacred gifts of the
sons of Israel, or you will die.'"

Chapter 19 Theme ____________________

19 Then the LORD spoke to Moses and Aaron, saying,
2 "This is the statute of the law which the LORD has commanded, saying, 'Speak to the sons of Israel that they bring you
an [a]unblemished red heifer in which is no defect *and* [b]on which
a yoke has never [1]been placed.
3 'You shall give it to [a]Eleazar the priest, and it shall [b]be
brought outside the camp and be slaughtered in his presence.
4 'Next Eleazar the priest shall take some of its blood with his
finger and [a]sprinkle some of its blood toward the front of the
tent of meeting seven times.

19 [1]Lit *seed*
20 [a]Deut 10:9; 12:12; 14:27, 29 [b]Deut 18:2; Josh 13:33; Ezek 44:28
21 [a]Lev 27:30-33; Deut 14:22-29
22 [a]Num 1:51
23 [a]Num 18:1 [b]Num 18:20
24 [a]Deut 10:9
26 [a]Num 18:21 [b]Neh 10:38
29 [1]Lit *fat* [2]Lit *its*
30 [1]Lit *lifted*
32 [1]Lit *lifted* [2]Lit *fat* [a]Lev 22:15, 16
19:2 [1]Lit *come up* [a]Lev 22:20-25 [b]Deut 21:3
3 [a]Num 3:4 [b]Lev 4:11, 12, 21; Num 19:9
4 [a]Lev 4:6, 17; 16:14

5 'Then the heifer shall be burned in his sight; [a]its hide and its flesh and its blood, with its refuse, shall be burned.

6 'The priest shall take [a]cedar wood and hyssop and scarlet *material* and cast it into the midst of the [1]burning heifer.

7 'The priest [a]shall then wash his clothes and bathe his [1]body in water, and afterward come into the camp, but the priest shall be unclean until evening.

8 'The one who burns it shall also wash his clothes in water and bathe his [1]body in water, and shall be unclean until evening.

9 'Now a man who is clean shall gather up the ashes of the heifer and deposit them outside the camp in a clean place, and [1]the congregation of the sons of Israel shall keep it as [a]water to remove impurity; it is [2]purification from sin.

10 'The one who gathers the ashes of the heifer [a]shall wash his clothes and be unclean until evening; and it shall be a perpetual statute to the sons of Israel and to the alien who sojourns among them.

11 '[a]The one who touches the corpse of any [1]person shall be unclean for seven days.

12 'That one shall [a]purify himself from uncleanness with [1]the water on the third day and on the seventh day, *and then* he will be clean; but if he does not purify himself on the third day and on the seventh day, he will not be clean.

13 '[a]Anyone who touches a corpse, the [1]body of a man who has died, and does not purify himself, [b]defiles the [2]tabernacle of the LORD; and that person shall be cut off from Israel. Because the water for impurity was not [3c]sprinkled on him, he shall be unclean; his uncleanness is still on him.

14 'This is the law when a man dies in a tent: everyone who comes into the tent and everyone who is in the tent shall be unclean for seven days.

15 'Every open vessel, which has no covering [1]tied down on it, shall be unclean.

16 '[a]Also, anyone who in the open field touches one who has been slain with a sword or who has died *naturally,* or a human bone or a grave, shall be unclean for seven days.

17 'Then for the unclean *person* they shall take some of the [1]ashes of the [2]burnt [3a]purification from sin and [4]flowing water shall be [5]added to them in a vessel.

18 'A clean person shall take hyssop and dip *it* in the water, and sprinkle *it* on the tent and on all the furnishings and on the persons who were there, and on the one who touched the bone or the one slain or the one dying *naturally* or the grave.

19 'Then the clean *person* [a]shall sprinkle on the unclean on the third day and on the seventh day; and on the seventh day he shall purify him from uncleanness, and he shall wash his clothes and bathe *himself* in water and shall be clean by evening.

20 'But the man who is unclean and does not purify himself from uncleanness, that person shall be cut off from the midst of the assembly, because he has [a]defiled the sanctuary of the LORD; the water for impurity has not been sprinkled on him, he is unclean.

5 [a]Ex 29:14; Lev 4:11, 12

6 [1]Lit *burning of the heifer* [a]Lev 14:4

7 [1]Lit *flesh* [a]Lev 16:26, 28; 22:6

8 [1]Lit *flesh*

9 [1]Lit *it shall be to the congregation . . . Israel, for a guarding as water of impurity* [2]Or *a sin offering* [a]Num 8:7; 31:23

10 [a]Num 19:7

11 [1]Lit *soul of man* [a]Lev 21:1, 11; Num 5:2; 6:6; Acts 21:26, 27

12 [1]Lit *it* [a]Num 19:19; 31:19

13 [1]Lit *soul* [2]Lit *dwelling place* [3]Or *thrown* [a]Lev 7:21; 22:3-7 [b]Lev 15:31; 20:3; Num 19:20 [c]Num 19:19

15 [1]Lit *cord*

16 [a]Num 31:19

17 [1]Lit *dust* [2]Lit *burning of the* [3]Or *sin offering* [4]Lit *living* [5]Lit *put* [a]Num 19:9

19 [a]Ezek 36:25; Heb 10:22

20 [a]Num 19:13

21 'So it shall be a perpetual statute for them. And he [a]who sprinkles the water for impurity shall wash his clothes, and he who touches the water for impurity shall be unclean until evening.

22 '[a]Furthermore, anything that the unclean *person* touches shall be unclean; and the person who touches *it* shall be unclean until evening.'"

Chapter 20 Theme ____

20 Then the sons of Israel, the whole congregation, came to the [a]wilderness of Zin in the first month; and the people stayed at Kadesh. Now Miriam died there and was buried there.

2 [a]There was no water for the congregation, [b]and they assembled themselves against Moses and Aaron.

3 [a]The people thus contended with Moses and spoke, saying, "[b]If only we had perished [c]when our brothers perished before the LORD!

4 "[a]Why then have you brought the LORD's assembly into this wilderness, for us and our beasts to die [1]here?

5 "Why have you made us come up from Egypt, to bring us in to this wretched place? [a]It is not a place of [1]grain or figs or vines or pomegranates, nor is there water to drink."

6 Then Moses and Aaron came in from the presence of the assembly to the doorway of the tent of meeting and [a]fell on their faces. Then the glory of the LORD appeared to them;

7 and the LORD spoke to Moses, saying,

8 "Take [a]the rod; and you and your brother Aaron assemble the congregation and speak to the rock before their eyes, that it may yield its water. You shall thus bring forth water for them out of the rock and let the congregation and their beasts drink."

9 So Moses took the rod [a]from before the LORD, just as He had commanded him;

10 and Moses and Aaron gathered the assembly before the rock. And he said to them, "[a]Listen now, you rebels; shall we bring forth water for you out of this rock?"

11 Then Moses lifted up his hand and struck the rock twice with his rod; and [a]water came forth abundantly, and the congregation and their beasts drank.

12 But the LORD said to Moses and Aaron, "[a]Because you have not believed Me, to treat Me as holy in the sight of the sons of Israel, therefore you shall not bring this assembly into the land which I have given them."

13 Those *were* the waters of [1a]Meribah, [2]because the sons of Israel contended with the LORD, and He proved Himself holy among them.

14 From Kadesh Moses then sent messengers to [a]the king of Edom: "Thus your brother Israel has said, 'You [b]know all the hardship that has befallen us;

15 that our fathers went down to Egypt, and we stayed in Egypt a long time, and the Egyptians treated us and our fathers badly.

16 'But [a]when we cried out to the LORD, He heard our voice

21 [a]Num 19:7
22 [a]Lev 5:2, 3; 7:21; 22:5, 6
20:1 [a]Num 13:21; 27:14; 33:36
2 [a]Ex 17:1 [b]Num 16:19, 42
3 [a]Ex 17:2 [b]Num 14:2, 3 [c]Num 16:31-35
4 [1]Lit *there* [a]Ex 17:3
5 [1]Lit *seed* [a]Num 16:14
6 [a]Num 14:5
8 [a]Ex 4:17, 20; 17:5, 6
9 [a]Num 17:10
10 [a]Ps 106:33
11 [a]Ps 78:16; Is 48:21; 1 Cor 10:4
12 [a]Num 20:24; 27:14; Deut 1:37; 3:26, 27
13 [1]I.e. contention [2]Or *where* [a]Ex 17:7; Ps 95:8
14 [a]Gen 36:31-39; Deut 2:4 [b]Josh 2:9, 10; 9:9, 10, 24
16 [a]Ex 2:23; 3:7

and sent [b]an angel and brought us out from Egypt; now behold,
we are at Kadesh, a town on the edge of your territory.
17 'Please [a]let us pass through your land. We will not pass
through field or through vineyard; we will not even drink water
from a well. We will go along the king's highway, not turning to
the right or left, until we pass through your territory.'"
18 [a]Edom, however, said to him, "You shall not pass through
[1]us, or I will come out with the sword against you."
19 Again, the sons of Israel said to him, "We will go up by the
highway, and if I and [a]my livestock do drink any of your water,
[b]then I will [1]pay its price. Let me only pass through on my feet,
[2]nothing *else.*"
20 But he said, "[a]You shall not pass through." And Edom came
out against him with a heavy [1]force and with a strong hand.
21 [a]Thus Edom refused to allow Israel to pass through his
territory; [b]so Israel turned away from him.
22 Now when they set out from [a]Kadesh, the sons of Israel,
the whole congregation, came to Mount Hor.
23 Then the LORD spoke to Moses and Aaron at [a]Mount Hor
by the border of the land of Edom, saying,
24 "Aaron will be [a]gathered to his people; for he shall not enter
the land which I have given to the sons of Israel, because [b]you
rebelled against My [1]command at the waters of Meribah.
25 "Take Aaron and his son [a]Eleazar and bring them up to
Mount Hor;
26 and strip Aaron of his garments and put them on his son
Eleazar. So Aaron will be [a]gathered *to his people,* and will die
there."
27 So Moses did just as the LORD had commanded, and they
went up to Mount Hor in the sight of all the congregation.
28 After Moses had stripped Aaron of his garments and [a]put
them on his son Eleazar, [b]Aaron died there on the mountain
top. Then Moses and Eleazar came down from the mountain.
29 When all the congregation saw that Aaron had died, all the
house of Israel wept for Aaron thirty [a]days.

Chapter 21 Theme ______________________________

21 When the Canaanite, the king of [a]Arad, who lived in the
[1]Negev, heard that Israel was coming by the way of
[2]Atharim, then he fought against Israel and took some of them
captive.
2 So [a]Israel made a vow to the LORD and said, "If You will
indeed deliver this people into my hand, then I will [1]utterly
destroy their cities."
3 The LORD heard the voice of Israel and delivered up the
Canaanites; then they [1]utterly destroyed them and their cities.
Thus the name of the place was called [2a]Hormah.
4 Then they set out from Mount Hor by the way of the [1]Red
Sea, to [a]go around the land of Edom; and the [2]people became
impatient because of the journey.
5 The people spoke against God and Moses, "[a]Why have you

16 [b]Ex 14:19
17 [a]Num 21:22
18 [1]Lit *me* [a]Num 24:18
19 [1]Lit *give* [2]Or *no great thing* [a]Ex 12:38 [b]Deut 2:6, 28
20 [1]Lit *people* [a]Judg 11:17
21 [a]Judg 11:17 [b]Deut 2:8
22 [a]Num 20:1, 14
23 [a]Num 33:37
24 [1]Lit *mouth* [a]Gen 25:8 [b]Num 20:5, 10
25 [a]Num 3:4
26 [a]Num 20:24
28 [a]Ex 29:29 [b]Num 33:38; Deut 10:6; 32:50
29 [a]Gen 1:5; 50:3, 10; Deut 34:8
21:1 [1]I.e. South country [2]Or *the spies* [a]Num 33:40; Josh 12:14; Judg 1:16
2 [1]Lit *devote to destruction* [a]Gen 28:20; Judg 11:30
3 [1]Lit *devoted to destruction* [2]I.e. a devoted thing; or Destruction [a]Num 14:45
4 [1]Lit *Sea of Reeds* [2]Lit *soul of the people was short* [a]Deut 2:8
5 [a]Num 14:2, 3

brought us up out of Egypt to die in the wilderness? For there
is no [1]food and no water, and [2b]we loathe this miserable food."
6 [a]The LORD sent fiery serpents among the people and [b]they
bit the people, so that [c]many people of Israel died.
7 [a]So the people came to Moses and said, "We have sinned,
because we have spoken against the LORD and you; [b]intercede
with the LORD, that He may remove the serpents from us." And
Moses interceded for the people.
8 Then the LORD said to Moses, "[1]Make a [a]fiery *serpent,* and
set it on a standard; and it shall come about, that everyone who
is bitten, when he looks at it, he will live."
9 And Moses made a [a]bronze serpent and set it on the
standard; and it came about, that if a serpent bit any man,
when he looked to the bronze serpent, he lived.
10 [a]Now the sons of Israel moved out and camped in Oboth.
11 They journeyed from Oboth and camped at Iyeabarim, in
the wilderness which is opposite Moab, to the [1]east.
12 [a]From there they set out and camped in [1]Wadi Zered.
13 From there they journeyed and camped on the other side
of the Arnon, which is in the wilderness that comes out of the
border of the Amorites, [a]for the Arnon is the border of Moab,
between Moab and the Amorites.
14 Therefore it is said in the Book of the Wars of the LORD,
"Waheb in Suphah,
And the wadis of the Arnon,
15 And the slope of the wadis
That extends to the site of [a]Ar,
And leans to the border of Moab."
16 [a]From there *they continued* to [1]Beer, that is the well where
the LORD said to Moses, "Assemble the people, that I may give
them water."
17 [a]Then Israel sang this song:
"Spring up, O well! Sing to it!
18 "The well, which the leaders sank,
Which the nobles of the people dug,
With the scepter *and* with their staffs."
And from the wilderness *they continued* to Mattanah,
19 and from Mattanah to Nahaliel, and from Nahaliel to Bamoth,
20 and from Bamoth to the valley that is in the land of Moab,
at the top of Pisgah which overlooks the [1]wasteland.
21 [a]Then Israel sent messengers to Sihon, king of the Amorites,
saying,
22 "[a]Let me pass through your land. We will not turn off into field
or vineyard; we will not drink water from wells. We will go by the
king's highway until we have passed through your border."
23 [a]But Sihon would not permit Israel to pass through his
border. So Sihon gathered all his people and went out against
Israel in the wilderness, and came to [b]Jahaz and fought against
Israel.
24 Then [a]Israel [1]struck him with the edge of the sword, and took
possession of his land from the Arnon to the Jabbok, as far as

5 [1]Lit *bread* [2]Lit *our soul loathes* [b]Num 11:6
6 [a]Deut 8:15 [b]Jer 8:17 [c]1 Cor 10:9
7 [a]Num 11:2; Ps 78:34; Is 26:16; Hos 5:15 [b]Ex 8:8; 1 Sam 12:19; Acts 8:24
8 [1]Lit *Make for yourself* [a]Is 14:29; 30:6; John 3:14
9 [a]2 Kin 18:4; John 3:14, 15
10 [a]Num 33:43, 44
11 [1]Lit *sunrise*
12 [1]I.e. a dry ravine except during rainy season [a]Num 33:45
13 [a]Num 22:36; Judg 11:18
15 [a]Num 21:28; Deut 2:9, 18, 29
16 [1]I.e. a well [a]Num 33:46-49
17 [a]Ex 15:1; Ps 105:2
20 [1]Or *Jeshimon*
21 [a]Deut 2:26-37; Judg 11:19
22 [a]Num 20:16, 17
23 [a]Num 20:21 [b]Deut 2:32
24 [1]Lit *smote,* so with Gr and Lat [a]Amos 2:9

the sons of Ammon; for the [b]border of the sons of Ammon *was*
[2]Jazer.
25 Israel took all these cities and [a]Israel lived in all the cities of
the Amorites, in Heshbon, and in all her [1]villages.
26 For Heshbon was the city of Sihon, king of the Amorites,
who had fought against the former king of Moab and had taken
all his land out of his hand, as far as the Arnon.
27 Therefore those who use proverbs say,
"Come to Heshbon! Let it be built!
So let the city of Sihon be established.
28 "[a]For a fire went forth from Heshbon,
A flame from the town of Sihon;
It devoured [b]Ar of Moab,
The [1c]dominant [2]heights of the Arnon.
29 "[a]Woe to you, O Moab!
You are ruined, O people of [b]Chemosh!
[c]He has given his sons as fugitives,
[d]And his daughters into captivity,
To an Amorite king, Sihon.
30 "But we have cast them down,
Heshbon is ruined as far as [a]Dibon,
Then we have laid waste even to Nophah,
Which *reaches* to Medeba."
31 Thus Israel lived in the land of the Amorites.
32 Moses sent to spy out [a]Jazer, and they captured its villages
and dispossessed the Amorites who *were* there.
33 [a]Then they turned and went up by the way of Bashan, and
Og the king of Bashan went out [1]with all his people, for battle
at [b]Edrei.
34 But the LORD said to Moses, "[a]Do not fear him, for I have
given him into your hand, and all his people and his land; and
you shall do to him as you did to Sihon, king of the Amorites,
who lived at Heshbon."
35 So [a]they [1]killed him and his sons and all his people, until
there was no remnant left him; and they possessed his land.

Chapter 22 Theme ________________________

22 [a]Then the sons of Israel journeyed, and camped in the
plains of Moab beyond the Jordan *opposite* Jericho.
2 Now [a]Balak the son of Zippor saw all that Israel had done
to the Amorites.
3 [a]So Moab was in great fear because of the people, for they
were numerous; and Moab was in dread of the sons of Israel.
4 Moab said to the elders of [a]Midian, "Now this [1]horde will lick
up all that is around us, as the ox licks up the grass of the field."
And Balak the son of Zippor was king of Moab at that time.
5 So he sent messengers to [a]Balaam the son of Beor, at [b]Pethor,
which is near the [1]River, *in* the land of the sons of his people,
to call him, saying, "Behold, a people came out of Egypt; behold,
they cover the surface of the land, and they are living opposite me.
6 "[a]Now, therefore, please come, [b]curse this people for me since

24 [2]M.T. reads *strong* [b]Deut. 2:37
25 [1]Lit *daughters* [a]Amos 2:10
28 [1]Lit *lords of the* [2]Or *Bamoth* [a]Jer 48:45 [b]Num 21:15 [c]Num 22:41; Is 15:2; 16:12
29 [a]Jer 48:46 [b]Judg 11:24; 1 Kin 11:33; 2 Kin 23:13 [c]Is 15:5 [d]Is 16:2
30 [a]Num 32:3, 34; Jer 48:18, 22
32 [a]Num 32:1, 3, 35; Jer 48:32
33 [1]Lit *he and* [a]Deut 3:1-7 [b]Josh 13:12
34 [a]Deut 3:2
35 [1]Lit *smote* [a]Deut 3:3, 4
22:1 [a]Num 33:48, 49
2 [a]Judg 11:25
3 [a]Ex 15:15
4 [1]Lit *assembly* [a]Num 25:15-18; 31:1-3
5 [1]I.e. Euphrates [a]Josh 24:9; 2 Pet 2:15f; Jude 11 [b]Deut 23:4
6 [a]Num 22:17; 23:7, 8 [b]Num 22:12; 24:9

RETURN TO INSTRUCTIONS

The Lands of Israel's Journey from Mt. Hor to Moab (for details see map on page 356)

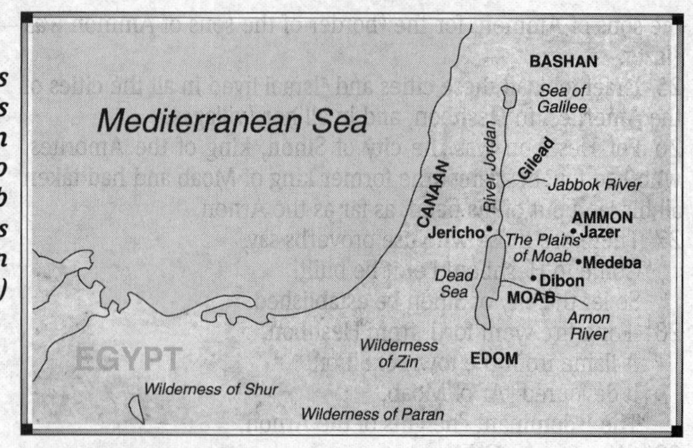

they are too [1]mighty for me; perhaps I may be able to [2]defeat
them and drive them out of the land. For I know that he whom
you bless is blessed, and he whom you curse is cursed."
7 So the elders of Moab and the elders of Midian departed with
the *fees for* [a]divination in their hand; and they came to Balaam
and [1]repeated Balak's words to him.
8 He said to them, "Spend the night here, and I will bring word
back to you as the LORD may speak to me." And the leaders of
Moab stayed with Balaam.
9 Then [a]God came to Balaam and said, "Who are these men
with you?"
10 Balaam said to God, "Balak the son of Zippor, king of Moab,
has sent *word* to me,
11 'Behold, there is a people who came out of Egypt and they
cover the surface of the land; now come, curse them for me;
perhaps I may be able to fight against them and drive them out.'"
12 God said to Balaam, "Do not go with them; [a]you shall not
curse the people, for they [b]are blessed."
13 So Balaam arose in the morning and said to Balak's leaders,
"Go back to your land, for the LORD has refused to let me go
with you."
14 The leaders of Moab arose and went to Balak and said,
"Balaam refused to come with us."
15 Then Balak again sent leaders, more numerous and more
distinguished than [1]the former.
16 They came to Balaam and said to him, "Thus says Balak the
son of Zippor, 'Let nothing, I beg you, hinder you from coming
to me;
17 for I will indeed honor you richly, and I will do whatever you
say to me. [a]Please come then, curse this people for me.'"
18 Balaam replied to the servants of Balak, "[a]Though Balak
were to give me his house full of silver and gold, I could not do
anything, either small or great, contrary to the [1]command of
the LORD my God.
19 "Now please, you also stay here tonight, and I will find out
what else the LORD will speak to me."
20 God came to Balaam at night and said to him, "If the men

INSIGHT

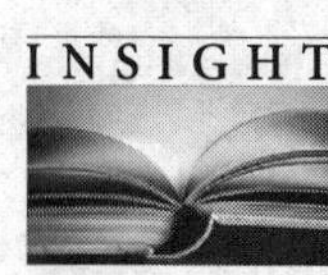

Midian was the son of Abraham by his wife Keturah (Genesis 25:2). Midian's descendants, the Midianites, took Joseph to Egypt (Genesis 37:28, 36). After killing the Egyptian, Moses fled to Midian and there married the daughter of a priest.

6 [1]Or *numerous* [2]Lit *smite*

7 [1]Lit *spoke* [a]Num 23:23; 24:1; Josh 13:22

9 [a]Gen 20:3

12 [a]Num 23:8; 24:9 [b]Gen 12:2; 22:17

15 [1]Lit *these*

17 [a]Num 22:6

18 [1]Lit *mouth* [a]Num 22:38; 24:13; 1 Kin 22:14; 2 Chr 18:13

have come to call you, rise up *and* go with them; but [a]only the
word which I speak to you shall you do."
21 [a]So Balaam arose in the morning, and saddled his donkey
and went with the leaders of Moab.
22 But God was angry because he was going, [a]and the angel of the
LORD took his stand in the way as an adversary against him. Now
he was riding on his donkey and his two servants were with him.
23 When the donkey saw the angel of the LORD standing in
the way with his drawn sword in his hand, the donkey turned
off from the way and went into the field; but Balaam struck the
donkey to turn her back into the way.
24 Then the angel of the LORD stood in a narrow path of the
vineyards, *with* a wall on this side and a wall on that side.
25 When the donkey saw the angel of the LORD, she pressed
herself to the wall and pressed Balaam's foot against the wall,
so he struck her again.
26 The angel of the LORD went further, and stood in a narrow
place where there was no way to turn to the right hand or the left.
27 When the donkey saw the angel of the LORD, she lay down
under Balaam; so [a]Balaam was angry and struck the donkey
with his stick.
28 And [a]the LORD opened the mouth of the donkey, and she
said to Balaam, "What have I done to you, that you have struck
me these three times?"
29 Then Balaam said to the donkey, "Because you have made
a mockery of me! If there had been a sword in my hand, [a]I
would have killed you by now."
30 The donkey said to Balaam, "Am I not your donkey on
which you have ridden all your life to this day? Have I ever
been accustomed to do so to you?" And he said, "No."
31 Then the LORD opened the eyes of Balaam, and he saw [a]the
angel of the LORD standing in the way with his drawn sword in
his hand; and he bowed [1]all the way to the ground.
32 The angel of the LORD said to him, "Why have you struck
your donkey these three times? Behold, I have come out as an
adversary, because your way was [1a]contrary to me.
33 "But the donkey saw me and turned aside from me these
three times. If she had not turned aside from me, I would
surely have killed you just now, and let her live."
34 Balaam said to the angel of the LORD, "[a]I have sinned, for I
did not know that you were standing in the way against me.
Now then, if it is displeasing to you, I will turn back."
35 But the angel of the LORD said to Balaam, "Go with the
men, but [a]you shall speak only the word which I [1]tell you." So
Balaam went along with the leaders of Balak.
36 When Balak heard that Balaam was coming, he went out to
meet him at the city of Moab, which is on the Arnon border,
[1]at the extreme end of the border.
37 Then Balak said to Balaam, "Did I not urgently send to you
to call you? Why did you not come to me? Am I really unable to
honor you?"

20 [a]Num 22:35; 23:5, 12, 16, 26; 24:13
21 [a]2 Pet 2:15
22 [a]Ex 23:20
27 [a]James 1:19
28 [a]2 Pet 2:16
29 [a]Prov 12:10; Matt 15:19
31 [1]Lit *and prostrated himself to his face* [a]Josh 5:13-15
32 [1]Lit *reckless* [a]2 Pet 2:15
34 [a]Num 14:40
35 [1]Or *speak to* [a]Num 22:20
36 [1]Lit *which is at*

38 So Balaam said to Balak, "Behold, I have come now to you!
[a]Am I able to speak anything at all? The word that God puts in
my mouth, that I shall speak."
39 And Balaam went with Balak, and they came to Kiriath-
huzoth.
40 Balak sacrificed oxen and sheep, and sent *some* to Balaam
and the leaders who were with him.
41 Then it came about in the morning that Balak took Balaam
and brought him up to [1a]the high places of Baal, and he saw
from there [2]a [b]portion of the people.

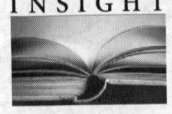

INSIGHT

This is the first mention of ***Baal,*** the principal male god of the Canaanites.

Chapter 23 Theme ________________________________

23 Then Balaam said to Balak, "Build seven altars for me here,
and prepare seven bulls and seven rams for me here."
2 Balak did just as Balaam had spoken, and Balak and Balaam
offered up a bull and a ram on each altar.
3 Then Balaam said to Balak, "Stand beside your burnt offering,
and I will go; perhaps the LORD will come to meet me, and
whatever He shows me I will tell you." So he went to a bare hill.
4 Now God met Balaam, and he said to Him, "I have set up
the seven altars, and I have offered up a bull and a ram on each
altar."
5 Then the LORD [a]put a word in Balaam's mouth and said,
"Return to Balak, and you shall speak thus."
6 So he returned to him, and behold, he was standing beside
his burnt offering, he and all the leaders of Moab.
7 He took up his [1]discourse and said,
"From [a]Aram Balak has brought me,
Moab's king from the mountains of the East,
'[b]Come curse Jacob for me,
And come, denounce Israel!'
8 "[a]How shall I curse whom God has not cursed?
And how can I denounce whom the LORD has not denounced?
9 "As I see him from the top of the rocks,
And I look at him from the hills;
[a]Behold, a people *who* dwells apart,
And will not be reckoned among the nations.
10 "[a]Who can count the dust of Jacob,
Or number the fourth part of Israel?
[b]Let [1]me die the death of the upright,
[c]And let my end be like his!"
11 Then Balak said to Balaam, "What have you done to me? [a]I
took you to curse my enemies, but behold, you have actually
blessed them!"
12 He replied, "Must I not be careful to speak [a]what the LORD
puts in my mouth?"
13 Then Balak said to him, "Please come with me to another
place from where you may see them, although you will only
see the extreme end of them and will not see all of them; and
curse them for me from there."
14 So he took him to the field of Zophim, to the top of Pisgah,

38 [a]Num 22:18

41 [1]*Or Bamoth-baal* [2]*Lit the end of the camp* [a]Num 21:28 [b]Num 23:13

23:5 [a]Num 22:20; Deut 18:18; Jer 1:9

7 [1]*Lit parable* [a]Num 22:5; Deut 23:4 [b]Num 22:6

8 [a]Num 22:12

9 [a]Deut 32:8; 33:28

10 [1]*Lit my soul* [a]Gen 13:16; 28:14 [b]Is 57:1 [c]Ps 37:37

11 [a]Neh 13:2

12 [a]Num 22:20

and built seven altars and offered a bull and a ram on *each*
altar.
15 And he said to Balak, "Stand here beside your burnt offering
while I myself meet *the LORD* over there."
16 Then the LORD met Balaam and [a]put a word in his mouth
and said, "Return to Balak, and thus you shall speak."
17 He came to him, and behold, he was standing beside his
burnt offering, and the leaders of Moab with him. And Balak
said to him, "What has the LORD spoken?"
18 Then he took up his [1]discourse and said,
"Arise, O Balak, and hear;
Give ear to me, O son of Zippor!
19 "[a]God is not a man, that He should lie,
Nor a son of man, that He should repent;
[b]Has He said, and will He not do it?
Or has He spoken, and will He not make it good?
20 "Behold, I have received *a command* to bless;
[a]When He has blessed, then [b]I cannot revoke it.
21 "[a]He has not observed [1]misfortune in Jacob;
[b]Nor has He seen trouble in Israel;
[c]The LORD his God is with him,
[d]And the shout of a king is among them.
22 "[a]God brings them out of Egypt,
He is for them like the [b]horns of the wild ox.
23 "[a]For there is no omen against Jacob,
Nor is there any divination against Israel;
At the proper time it shall be said to Jacob
And to Israel, what God has done!
24 "[a]Behold, a people rises like a lioness,
And as a lion it lifts itself;
It will not lie down until it devours the prey,
And drinks the blood of the slain."
25 Then Balak said to Balaam, "Do not curse them at all nor
bless them at all!"
26 But Balaam replied to Balak, "Did I not tell you,
'[1a]Whatever the LORD speaks, that I must do'?"
27 Then Balak said to Balaam, "Please come, I will take you to
another place; perhaps it will be [1]agreeable with God that you
curse them for me from there."
28 So Balak took Balaam to the top of Peor which overlooks
the [1]wasteland.
29 Balaam said to Balak, "Build seven altars for me here and
prepare seven bulls and seven rams for me here."
30 Balak did just as Balaam had said, and offered up a bull and
a ram on *each* altar.

Chapter 24 Theme ____________________

24 When Balaam saw that it [1]pleased the LORD to bless
Israel, he did not go as at other times to [2]seek [a]omens
but he set his face toward the [b]wilderness.

16 [a]Num 22:20
18 [1]Lit *parable*
19 [a]1 Sam 15:29 [b]Is 40:8; 55:11
20 [a]Gen 12:2; 22:17; Num 22:12 [b]Is 43:13
21 [1]Or *iniquity* [a]Num 14:18, 19, 34; Ps 32:2, 5 [b]Deut 9:24; 32:5; Jer 50:20 [c]Ex 3:12; Deut 31:23 [d]Deut 33:5; Ps 89:15-18
22 [a]Num 24:8 [b]Deut 33:17
23 [a]Num 22:7; 24:1; Josh 13:22
24 [a]Gen 49:9; Nah 2:11, 12
26 [1]Lit *saying, Whatever* [a]Num 22:18
27 [1]Lit *right in the sight of God*
28 [1]Or *Jeshimon*
24:1 [1]Lit *was good in the eyes of* [2]Lit *encounter* [a]Num 22:7; 23:23 [b]Num 23:28

2 And Balaam lifted up his eyes and saw Israel [1]camping
tribe by tribe; and [a]the Spirit of God came upon him.
3 He took up his [1]discourse and said,
"[a]The oracle of Balaam the son of Beor,
And the oracle of the man whose eye is opened;
4 The oracle of him who [a]hears the [1]words of God,
Who sees the [b]vision of [2]the Almighty,
Falling down, yet having his eyes uncovered,
5 How fair are your tents, O Jacob,
Your dwellings, O Israel!
6 "Like [1]valleys that stretch out,
Like gardens beside the river,
Like [a]aloes planted by the LORD,
Like [b]cedars beside the waters.
7 "Water will flow from his buckets,
And his seed *will be* by many waters,
And his king shall be higher than [a]Agag,
[b]And his kingdom shall be exalted.
8 "[a]God brings him out of Egypt,
He is for him like the horns of the wild ox.
[b]He will devour the nations *who are* his adversaries,
And will crush their bones in pieces,
And shatter *them* with his [c]arrows.
9 "[a]He [1]couches, he lies down as a lion,
And as a [2]lion, who [3]dares rouse him?
[b]Blessed is everyone who blesses you,
And cursed is everyone who curses you."
10 Then Balak's anger burned against Balaam, and he struck
his [1]hands together; and Balak said to Balaam, "I called you to
curse my enemies, but behold, you have persisted in blessing
them these three times!
11 "Therefore, [1]flee to your place now. I said I would honor you
greatly, but behold, the LORD has held you back from honor."
12 Balaam said to Balak, "[a]Did I not tell your messengers
whom you had sent to me, saying,
13 'Though Balak were to give me his house full of silver and
gold, I could not do anything contrary to the [1]command of the
LORD, either good or bad, [a]of my own [2]accord. [b]What the LORD
speaks, that I will speak'?
14 "And now, behold, [a]I am going to my people; come, *and* I
will advise you what this people will do to your people in the
[1]days to come."
15 He took up his discourse and said,
"[a]The oracle of Balaam the son of Beor,
And the oracle of the man whose eye is opened,
16 The oracle of him who hears the [1]words of God,
And knows the knowledge of the [2]Most High,
Who sees the vision of [3]the Almighty,
Falling down, yet having his eyes uncovered.
17 "I see him, but not now;
I behold him, but not near;

2 [1]Lit *dwelling* [a]Num 11:26; 1 Sam 19:20; Rev 1:10

3 [1]Lit *parable,* and so throughout the ch [a]Num 24:15, 16

4 [1]Lit *sayings* [2]Heb *Shaddai* [a]Num 22:20 [b]Gen 15:1; Num 12:6

6 [1]Or possibly *palm trees* [a]Ps 45:8 [b]Ps 1:3

7 [a]Num 24:20; 1 Sam 15:8 [b]Ps 145:11-13

8 [a]Num 23:22 [b]Num 23:24; Ps 2:9 [c]Ps 45:5

9 [1]Lit *bows down* [2]Or *lioness* [3]Lit *shall* [a]Gen 49:9; Num 23:24 [b]Gen 12:3; 27:29

10 [1]Lit *palms*

11 [1]Lit *flee for yourself*

12 [a]Num 22:18

13 [1]Lit *mouth* [2]Lit *heart* [a]Num 16:28 [b]Num 22:20

14 [1]Lit *end of the days* [a]Num 31:8, 16; Josh 13:22

15 [a]Num 24:3, 4

16 [1]Lit *sayings* [2]Heb *Elyon* [3]Heb *Shaddai*

A star shall come forth from Jacob,
[a]A scepter shall rise from Israel,
[b]And shall crush through the [1]forehead of Moab,
And [2]tear down all the sons of [3]Sheth.
18 “[a]Edom shall be a possession,
[b]Seir, its enemies, also will be a possession,
While Israel performs valiantly.
19 “One from Jacob shall have dominion,
And will destroy the remnant from the city.”

20 And he looked at Amalek and took up his discourse and said,
“Amalek was the first of the nations,
[a]But his end *shall be* [1]destruction.”

21 And he looked at the [a]Kenite, and took up his discourse and said,
“Your dwelling place is enduring,
And your nest is set in the cliff.
22 “Nevertheless Kain will be consumed;
How long will [a]Asshur [1]keep you captive?”

23 Then he took up his discourse and said,
“Alas, who can live except God has ordained it?
24 “But ships *shall come* from the coast of [a]Kittim,
And they shall afflict Asshur and will afflict [b]Eber;
[c]So they also *will come* to destruction.”

25 Then Balaam arose and departed and returned to [a]his place, and Balak also went his way.

Chapter 25 Theme ______________________

25 While Israel remained at [a]Shittim, the people began [b]to play the harlot with the daughters of Moab.

2 For [a]they invited the people to the sacrifices of their gods, and the people ate and bowed down to their gods.

3 So [a]Israel joined themselves to [1]Baal of Peor, and the LORD was angry against Israel.

4 The LORD said to Moses, “Take all the leaders of the people and execute them [1]in broad daylight before the LORD, [a]so that the fierce anger of the LORD may turn away from Israel.”

5 So Moses said to the judges of Israel, “Each of you [a]slay his men who have joined themselves to [1]Baal of Peor.”

6 Then behold, one of the sons of Israel came and brought to his [1]relatives a [a]Midianite woman, in the sight of Moses and in the sight of all the congregation of the sons of Israel, [b]while they were weeping at the doorway of the tent of meeting.

7 [a]When Phinehas the son of Eleazar, the son of Aaron the priest, saw it, he arose from the midst of the congregation and took a spear in his hand,

8 and he went after the man of Israel into the [1]tent and pierced both of them through, the man of Israel and the woman, through the [2]body. [a]So the plague on the sons of Israel was checked.

9 [a]Those who died by the plague were 24,000.

10 Then the LORD spoke to Moses, saying,

17 [1]Lit *corners* [2]Another reading is *the crown of the head of* [3]I.e. tumult [a]Gen 49:10 [b]Num 21:29; Is 15:1-16:14
18 [a]Gen 27:29; Amos 9:11, 12 [b]Gen 32:3
20 [1]Lit *to destroying* [a]Num 24:24
21 [a]Gen 15:19
22 [1]Lit *take* [a]Gen 10:21, 22
24 [a]Gen 10:4; Ezek 27:6 [b]Gen 10:21 [c]Num 24:20
25 [a]Num 24:14
25:1 [a]Num 33:49; Josh 2:1 [b]Num 31:16; 1 Cor 10:8; Rev 2:14
2 [a]Ex 34:15; Deut 32:38
3 [1]Or *Baal-peor* [a]Ps 106:28, 29; Hos 9:10
4 [1]Lit *in front of the sun* [a]Deut 13:17
5 [1]Or *Baal-peor* [a]Ex 32:27
6 [1]Lit *brothers* [a]Num 22:4 [b]Joel 2:17
7 [a]Ps 106:30
8 [1]Or *inner rooms* [2]Or *belly* [a]Num 16:46-48
9 [a]Num 14:37; 16:48-50; 31:16

11 “[a]Phinehas the son of Eleazar, the son of Aaron the priest,
has turned away My wrath from the sons of Israel in that he was
jealous with My jealousy among them, so that I did not destroy
the sons of Israel [b]in My jealousy.
12 “Therefore say, ‘[a]Behold, I give him My [b]covenant of peace;
13 and it shall be for him and his [1]descendants after him, a
covenant of a [a]perpetual priesthood, because he was jealous for
his God and [b]made atonement for the sons of Israel.’”
14 Now the name of the [1]slain man of Israel who was [1]slain
with the Midianite woman, was Zimri the son of Salu, a leader
of a father’s household among the Simeonites.
15 The name of the Midianite woman who was [1]slain was
[a]Cozbi the daughter of [b]Zur, [2]who was head of the people of a
father’s household in Midian.
16 Then the LORD spoke to Moses, saying,
17 “[a]Be hostile to the Midianites and strike them;
18 for they have been hostile to you with their tricks, with
which they have deceived you in the affair of Peor and in the
affair of Cozbi, the daughter of the leader of Midian, their sister
who was slain on the day of the plague because of Peor.”

Chapter 26 Theme ______________________

26 [1]Then it came about after the [a]plague, [2]that the LORD
spoke to Moses and to Eleazar the son of Aaron the
priest, saying,
2 “[a]Take a [1]census of all the congregation of the sons of Israel
from twenty years old and upward, by their fathers’ households,
whoever is able to go out to war in Israel.”
3 So Moses and Eleazar the priest spoke with them [a]in the
plains of Moab by the Jordan at Jericho, saying,
4 “*Take a census of the people* from twenty years old and
upward, as the LORD has commanded Moses.”
Now the sons of Israel who came out of the land of Egypt
were:
5 Reuben, Israel’s firstborn, the sons of Reuben: *of* Hanoch,
the family of the Hanochites; of Pallu, the family of the Palluites;
6 of Hezron, the family of the Hezronites; of Carmi, the family
of the Carmites.
7 These are the families of the Reubenites, and those who
were numbered of them were [a]43,730.
8 The son of Pallu: Eliab.
9 The sons of Eliab: Nemuel and Dathan and Abiram. These are
the Dathan and Abiram who were [a]called by the congregation,
who contended against Moses and against Aaron in the
company of Korah, when they contended against the LORD,
10 and [a]the earth opened its mouth and swallowed them up
along with Korah, when that company died, [b]when the fire
devoured 250 men, so that they became a [1]warning.
11 [a]The sons of Korah, however, did not die.
12 The sons of Simeon according to their families: of [1]Nemuel,

11 [a]Ps 106:30 [b]Ex 20:5

12 [a]Ps 106:30, 31 [b]Is 54:10; Ezek 34:25; 37:26

13 [1]Lit *seed* [a]Ex 29:9 [b]Num 16:46

14 [1]Lit *smitten*

15 [1]Lit *smitten* [2]Lit *he* [a]Num 25:18 [b]Num 31:8

17 [a]Num 25:1; 22:4; 31:1-3

26:1 [1]Ch 25:19 in Heb [2]Ch 26:1 in Heb [a]Num 25:9

2 [1]Lit *sum* [a]Ex 30:11-16; 38:25, 26; Num 1:2

3 [a]Num 22:1; 33:48; 35:1

7 [a]Num 1:21

9 [a]Num 1:16; 16:2

10 [1]Lit *sign* [a]Num 16:32 [b]Num 16:35, 38

11 [a]Num 16:27, 33; Deut 24:16

12 [1]In Gen 46:10 and Ex 6:15, *Jemuel*

the family of the Nemuelites; of Jamin, the family of the Jaminites;
of [2]Jachin, the family of the Jachinites;
13 of [1]Zerah, the family of the Zerahites; of Shaul, the family
of the Shaulites.
14 These are the families of the Simeonites, [a]22,200.
15 The sons of Gad according to their families: of [1]Zephon, the
family of the Zephonites; of Haggi, the family of the Haggites; of
Shuni, the family of the Shunites;
16 of [1]Ozni, the family of the Oznites; of Eri, the family of the
Erites;
17 of [1]Arod, the family of the Arodites; of Areli, the family of
the Arelites.
18 These are the families of the sons of Gad according to those
who were numbered of them, [a]40,500.
19 The [a]sons of Judah *were* Er and Onan, but Er and Onan
died in the land of Canaan.
20 The [a]sons of Judah according to their families were: of Shelah,
the family of the Shelanites; of Perez, the family of the Perezites;
of Zerah, the family of the Zerahites.
21 The sons of Perez were: of Hezron, the family of the
Hezronites; of Hamul, the family of the Hamulites.
22 These are the families of Judah according to those who
were numbered of them, [a]76,500.
23 The [a]sons of Issachar according to their families: *of* Tola,
the family of the Tolaites; of [1]Puvah, the family of the Punites;
24 of [1]Jashub, the family of the Jashubites; of Shimron, the
family of the Shimronites.
25 These are the families of Issachar according to those who
were numbered of them, [a]64,300.
26 The [a]sons of Zebulun according to their families: of Sered,
the family of the Seredites; of Elon, the family of the Elonites;
of Jahleel, the family of the Jahleelites.
27 These are the families of the Zebulunites according to
those who were numbered of them, [a]60,500.
28 The [a]sons of Joseph according to their families: Manasseh
and Ephraim.
29 The sons of Manasseh: of Machir, the family of the
Machirites; and [a]Machir [1]became the father of Gilead: of
Gilead, the family of the Gileadites.
30 These are the sons of Gilead: *of* [1]Iezer, the family of the
[a]Iezerites; of Helek, the family of the Helekites;
31 and *of* Asriel, the family of the Asrielites; and *of* Shechem,
the family of the Shechemites;
32 and *of* Shemida, the family of the Shemidaites; and *of*
Hepher, the family of the Hepherites.
33 Now Zelophehad the son of Hepher had no sons, but only
daughters; and [a]the names of the daughters of Zelophehad
were Mahlah, Noah, Hoglah, Milcah and Tirzah.
34 These are the families of Manasseh; and those who were
numbered of them were [a]52,700.
35 These are the sons of Ephraim according to their families:

12 [2]In 1 Chr 4:24, *Jarib*
13 [1]In Gen 46:10, *Zohar*
14 [a]Num 1:23
15 [1]In Gen 46:16, *Ziphion*
16 [1]In Gen 46:16, *Ezbon*
17 [1]In Gen 46:16, *Arodi*
18 [a]Num 1:25
19 [a]Gen 38:2; 46:12
20 [a]Gen 49:8; 1 Chr 2:3; Rev 7:5
22 [a]Num 1:27
23 [1]In Gen 46:13, *Puvvah;* in 1 Chr 7:1, *Puah* [a]Gen 46:13; 1 Chr 7:1
24 [1]In Gen 46:13, *Iob*
25 [a]Num 1:29
26 [a]Gen 46:14
27 [a]Num 1:31
28 [a]Gen 46:20; Deut 33:16f
29 [1]Lit *begot* [a]Josh 17:1; 1 Chr 7:14f
30 [1]In Josh 17:2, *Abiezer* [a]Judg 6:11, 24, 34
33 [a]Num 27:1
34 [a]Num 1:35

of Shuthelah, the family of the Shuthelahites; of [1]Becher, the
family of the Becherites; of Tahan, the family of the Tahanites.
36 These are the sons of Shuthelah: of Eran, the family of the
Eranites.
37 These are the families of the sons of Ephraim according to
those who were numbered of them, [a]32,500. These are the
sons of Joseph according to their families.
38 The sons of Benjamin according to their families: of Bela,
the family of the Belaites; of Ashbel, the family of the Ashbelites;
of [1]Ahiram, the family of the Ahiramites;
39 of [1]Shephupham, the family of the Shuphamites; of
[2]Hupham, the family of the Huphamites.
40 The sons of Bela were [1]Ard and Naaman: *of Ard,* the family
of the Ardites; of Naaman, the family of the Naamites.
41 These are the sons of Benjamin according to their families;
and those who were numbered of them were [a]45,600.
42 These are the sons of Dan according to their families: of
[1]Shuham, the family of the Shuhamites. These are the families
of Dan according to their families.
43 All the families of the Shuhamites, according to those who
were numbered of them, were [a]64,400.
44 The [a]sons of Asher according to their families: of Imnah,
the family of the Imnites; of Ishvi, the family of the Ishvites; of
Beriah, the family of the Beriites.
45 Of the sons of Beriah: of Heber, the family of the Heberites;
of Malchiel, the family of the Malchielites.
46 The name of the daughter of Asher *was* Serah.
47 These are the families of the sons of Asher according to
those who were numbered of them, [a]53,400.
48 The [a]sons of Naphtali according to their families: of Jahzeel,
the family of the Jahzeelites; of Guni, the family of the Gunites;
49 of Jezer, the family of the Jezerites; of [a]Shillem, the family
of the Shillemites.
50 These are the families of Naphtali according to their families;
and those who were numbered of them were [a]45,400.
51 These are those who were numbered of the sons of Israel,
[a]601,730.
52 Then the LORD spoke to Moses, saying,
53 "[1]Among these the land shall be divided for an inheritance
according to the number of names.
54 "[a]To the larger *group* you shall increase their inheritance,
and to the smaller *group* you shall diminish their inheritance;
each shall be given their inheritance according to those who
were numbered of them.
55 "But the land shall be [a]divided by lot. They shall [1]receive
their inheritance according to the names of the tribes of their
fathers.
56 "According to the selection by lot, their inheritance shall be
divided between the larger and the smaller *groups.*"
57 [a]These are those who were numbered of the Levites
according to their families: of Gershon, the family of the

35 [1]In 1 Chr 7:20, *Bered*
37 [a]Num 1:33
38 [1]In Gen 46:21, *Ehi;* in 1 Chr 8:1, *Aharah*
39 [1]In Gen 46:21, *Muppim;* in 1 Chr 7:12, *Shuppim* [2]In Gen 46:21, *Muppim* and *Huppim*
40 [1]In 1 Chr 8:3, *Addar*
41 [a]Num 1:37
42 [1]In Gen 46:23, *Hushim*
43 [a]Num 1:39
44 [a]Gen 46:17; 1 Chr 7:30
47 [a]Num 1:41
48 [a]Gen 46:24; 1 Chr 7:13
49 [a]1 Chr 7:13
50 [a]Num 1:43
51 [a]Ex 12:37; 38:26; Num 1:46; 11:21
53 [1]Lit *To*
54 [a]Num 33:54
55 [1]Lit *inherit according to* [a]Num 33:54; 34:13
57 [a]Gen 46:11; Ex 6:16; 1 Chr 6:1, 16

Gershonites; of Kohath, the family of the Kohathites; of Merari,
the family of the Merarites.
58 These are the families of Levi: the family of the Libnites, the
family of the Hebronites, the family of the Mahlites, the family
of the Mushites, the family of the Korahites. [a]Kohath [1]became
the father of Amram.
59 The name of Amram's wife [a]was Jochebed, the daughter of
Levi, who was born to Levi in Egypt; and she bore to Amram:
Aaron and Moses and their sister Miriam.
60 [a]To Aaron were born Nadab and Abihu, Eleazar and Ithamar.
61 [a]But Nadab and Abihu died when they offered strange fire
before the LORD.
62 Those who were numbered of them were [a]23,000, every
male from a month old and upward, for [b]they were not
numbered among the sons of Israel [c]since no inheritance was
given to them among the sons of Israel.
63 These are those who were numbered by Moses and Eleazar
the priest, who numbered the sons of Israel in the plains of
Moab by the Jordan at Jericho.
64 [a]But among these there was not a man of those who were
numbered by Moses and Aaron the priest, who numbered the
sons of Israel in the wilderness of Sinai.
65 For the LORD had said [1]of them, "[a]They shall surely die in
the wilderness." And not a man was left of them, [b]except
Caleb the son of Jephunneh and Joshua the son of Nun.

Chapter 27 Theme ____________________

27 Then [a]the daughters of Zelophehad, the son of Hepher,
the son of Gilead, the son of Machir, the son of Manasseh, of the families of Manasseh the son of Joseph, came near;
and these are [b]the names of his daughters: Mahlah, Noah and
Hoglah and Milcah and Tirzah.
2 They stood before Moses and before Eleazar the priest and
before the leaders and all the congregation, at the doorway of
the tent of meeting, saying,
3 "Our father [a]died in the wilderness, yet he was not among
the company of those who gathered themselves together
against the LORD in the company of Korah; but he died in his
own sin, and [b]he had no sons.
4 "Why should the name of our father be withdrawn from
among his family because he had no son? Give us a possession
among our father's brothers."
5 [a]So Moses brought their case before the LORD.
6 Then the LORD spoke to Moses, saying,
7 "[a]The daughters of Zelophehad are right in *their* statements.
You shall surely give them a hereditary possession among their
father's brothers, and you shall transfer the inheritance of their
father to them.
8 "Further, you shall speak to the sons of Israel, saying, 'If a man
dies and has no son, then you shall transfer his inheritance to
his daughter.

58 [1]Lit *begot* [a]Ex 6:20
59 [a]Ex 2:1, 2; 6:20
60 [a]Num 3:2
61 [a]Lev 10:1, 2; Num 3:4
62 [a]Num 3:39 [b]Num 1:47 [c]Num 18:23, 24
64 [a]Num 14:29-35; Deut 2:14-16; Heb 3:17
65 [1]Or *to* [a]Num 14:26-35; Ps 90:3-10; 1 Cor 10:5 [b]Deut 1:36; Josh 14:6-10
27:1 [a]Num 26:33; 36:1 [b]Num 26:33
3 [a]Num 26:64, 65 [b]Num 26:33
5 [a]Num 9:8; 27:21
7 [a]Num 36:2; Josh 17:4

9 'If he has no daughter, then you shall give his inheritance to
his brothers.
10 'If he has no brothers, then you shall give his inheritance to
his father's brothers.
11 'If his father has no brothers, then you shall give his
inheritance to his nearest relative in his own family, and he
shall possess it; and it shall be a [a]statutory ordinance to the
sons of Israel, just as the LORD commanded Moses.'"
12 [a]Then the LORD said to Moses, "Go up to this [b]mountain of
Abarim, and see the land which I have given to the sons of Israel.
13 "When you have seen it, you too [a]will be gathered to your
people, [b]as Aaron your brother [1]was;
14 for in the wilderness of Zin, during the strife of the
congregation, [a]you rebelled against My [1]command [2]to treat Me
as holy before their eyes at the water." (These are the waters of
Meribah of Kadesh in the wilderness of Zin.)
15 Then Moses spoke to the LORD, saying,
16 "[a]May the LORD, the God of the spirits of all flesh, appoint a
man over the congregation,
17 who [a]will go out [1]and come in before them, and who will
lead them out and [2]bring them in, so that the congregation of
the LORD will not be [b]like sheep which have no shepherd."
18 So the LORD said to Moses, "[1]Take Joshua the son of Nun, a
man [a]in whom is the Spirit, and [b]lay your hand on him;
19 and have him stand before Eleazar the priest and before all
the congregation, and [a]commission him in their sight.
20 "You shall put some of your [1]authority on him, in order that
all the congregation of the sons of Israel may obey *him.*
21 "Moreover, he shall stand before Eleazar the priest, who
shall inquire for him [a]by the judgment of the Urim before the
LORD. At his [1]command they shall go out and at his [1]command
they shall come in, *both* he and the sons of Israel with him,
even all the congregation."
22 Moses did just as the LORD commanded him; and he took
Joshua and set him before Eleazar the priest and before all the
congregation.
23 Then he laid his hands on him and [a]commissioned him,
just as the LORD had spoken [1]through Moses.

Chapter 28 Theme ______________________

28 Then the LORD spoke to Moses, saying,
2 "Command the sons of Israel and say to them, 'You shall
[1]be careful to present My offering, My [a]food for My offerings by
fire, of a soothing aroma to Me, at their appointed time.'
3 "[a]You shall say to them, 'This is the offering by fire which you
shall offer to the LORD: two male lambs one year old without
defect *as* a continual burnt offering every day.
4 'You shall offer the one lamb in the morning and the other
lamb you shall offer [1]at twilight;
5 also [a]a tenth of an ephah of fine flour for a [b]grain offering,
mixed with a fourth of a hin of beaten oil.

11 [a]Num 35:29

12 [a]Deut 3:23-27; 32:48-52 [b]Num 33:47, 48

13 [1]Lit *was gathered* [a]Num 31:2 [b]Num 20:24, 28; Deut 10:6

14 [1]Lit *mouth* [2]Lit *for My sanctity* [a]Num 20:12; Deut 32:51; Ps 106:32

16 [a]Num 16:22

17 [1]Lit *before them and who will* [2]Lit *who will bring* [a]Deut 31:2; 2 Chr 1:10 [b]1 Kin 22:17; Ezek 34:5; Matt 9:36; Mark 6:34

18 [1]Lit *Take for yourself* [a]Num 11:25-29; Deut 34:9 [b]Num 27:23

19 [a]Deut 3:28; 31:3, 7, 8, 23

20 [1]Lit *majesty*

21 [1]Lit *mouth* [a]Ex 28:30; 1 Sam 28:6

23 [1]Lit *by the hand of* [a]Deut 31:23

28:2 [1]Lit *watch* [a]Lev 3:11

3 [a]Ex 29:38-42

4 [1]Lit *between the two evenings*

5 [a]Ex 16:36; Num 15:4 [b]Lev 2:1

7 [a]Ex 29:42
8 [1]Lit *between the two evenings*
9 [1]I.e. Approx one bu
10 [a]Num 28:3
11 [1]Lit *bulls of the herd* [a]Num 10:10; Ezek 46:6, 7
12 [1]I.e. Approx one bu [a]Num 15:4-12
13 [1]I.e. Approx one bu
15 [a]Num 28:3
16 [a]Ex 12:1-20; Lev 23:5-8; Deut 16:1-8
17 [a]Lev 23:6 [b]Ex 23:15; 34:18; Deut 16:3-8
18 [a]Lev 23:7
19 [1]Or *bulls of the herd* [a]Deut 15:21
20 [1]I.e. Approx one bu
21 [1]I.e. Approx one bu [2]Lit *each lamb*
22 [a]Lev 16:18; Rom 8:3; Gal 4:4f
23 [a]Num 28:3
24 [a]Lev 3:11 [b]Num 28:3

6 'It is a continual burnt offering which was ordained in
Mount Sinai as a soothing aroma, an offering by fire to the LORD.
7 'Then the drink offering with it *shall be* a fourth of a hin for
each lamb, [a]in the holy place you shall pour out a drink offering
of strong drink to the LORD.
8 'The other lamb you shall offer [1]at twilight; as the grain
offering of the morning and as its drink offering, you shall offer
it, an offering by fire, a soothing aroma to the LORD.
9 'Then on the sabbath day two male lambs one year old
without defect, and two-tenths *of an* [1]*ephah* of fine flour mixed
with oil as a grain offering, and its drink offering:
10 '*This is* the burnt offering of every sabbath in addition to
the [a]continual burnt offering and its drink offering.
11 'Then [a]at the beginning of each of your months you shall
present a burnt offering to the LORD: two [1]bulls and one ram,
seven male lambs one year old without defect;
12 [a]and three-tenths *of an* [1]*ephah* of fine flour mixed with oil
for a grain offering, for each bull; and two-tenths of fine flour
mixed with oil for a grain offering, for the one ram;
13 and a tenth *of an* [1]*ephah* of fine flour mixed with oil for a
grain offering for each lamb, for a burnt offering of a soothing
aroma, an offering by fire to the LORD.
14 'Their drink offerings shall be half a hin of wine for a bull
and a third of a hin for the ram and a fourth of a hin for a lamb;
this is the burnt offering of each month throughout the months
of the year.
15 'And one male goat for a sin offering to the LORD; it shall be
offered with its drink offering in addition to the [a]continual
burnt offering.
16 '[a]Then on the fourteenth day of the first month shall be the
LORD'S Passover.
17 '[a]On the fifteenth day of this month *shall be* a [b]feast,
unleavened bread *shall be* eaten for seven days.
18 'On the [a]first day *shall be* a holy convocation; you shall do
no laborious work.
19 'You shall present an offering by fire, a burnt offering to the
LORD: two [1]bulls and one ram and seven male lambs one year
old, [a]having them without defect.
20 'For their grain offering, you shall offer fine flour mixed
with oil: three-tenths *of an* [1]*ephah* for a bull and two-tenths for
the ram.
21 'A tenth *of an* [1]*ephah* you shall offer for [2]each of the seven
lambs;
22 and one male goat for a [a]sin offering to make atonement for
you.
23 'You shall present these besides [a]the burnt offering of the
morning, which is for a continual burnt offering.
24 'After this manner you shall present daily, for seven days,
[a]the food of the offering by fire, of a soothing aroma to the
LORD; it shall be presented with its drink offering in addition to
the [b]continual burnt offering.

25 'On the seventh day you shall have a holy convocation; [a]you shall do no laborious work.

26 'Also on [a]the day of the first fruits, when you present a new grain offering to the LORD in your *Feast of* Weeks, you shall have a holy convocation; [b]you shall do no laborious work.

27 'You shall offer a burnt offering for a soothing aroma to the LORD: two young bulls, one ram, seven male lambs one year old;

28 and their grain offering, fine flour mixed with oil: three-tenths *of an* [1]*ephah* for each bull, two-tenths for the one ram,

29 a tenth for [1]each of the seven lambs;

30 *also* one male goat to make atonement for you.

31 '[a]Besides the continual burnt offering and its grain offering, you shall present *them* with their drink offerings. They shall be [1]without defect.

Chapter 29 Theme ________________

29 '[a]Now in the seventh month, on the first day of the month, you shall also have a holy convocation; [b]you shall do no laborious work. It will be to you a day for blowing trumpets.

2 'You shall offer a burnt offering as a soothing aroma to the LORD: one [1]bull, one ram, *and* seven male lambs one year old without defect;

3 also their grain offering, fine flour mixed with oil: three-tenths *of an* [1]*ephah* for the bull, two-tenths for the ram,

4 and one-tenth for [1]each of the seven lambs.

5 '*Offer* one male goat for a sin offering, to make atonement for you,

6 [a]besides the burnt offering of the new moon and its grain offering, and the [b]continual burnt offering and its grain offering, and their drink offerings, according to their ordinance, for a soothing aroma, an offering by fire to the LORD.

7 'Then on [a]the tenth day of this seventh month you shall have a holy convocation, and you shall humble yourselves; you shall not do any work.

8 'You shall present a burnt offering to the LORD *as* a soothing aroma: one bull, one ram, seven male lambs one year old, [a]having them without defect;

9 and their grain offering, fine flour mixed with oil: three-tenths *of an* [1]*ephah* for the bull, two-tenths for the one ram,

10 a tenth for each of the seven lambs;

11 one male goat for a sin offering, besides [a]the sin offering of atonement and [b]the continual burnt offering and its grain offering, and their drink offerings.

12 'Then on [a]the fifteenth day of the seventh month you shall have a holy convocation; you [b]shall do no laborious work, and you shall observe a feast to the LORD for seven days.

13 'You shall present a burnt offering, an offering by fire as a soothing aroma to the LORD: thirteen bulls, two rams, fourteen male lambs one year old, which are without defect;

14 and their grain offering, fine flour mixed with oil: three-

25 [a]Num 28:18

26 [a]Ex 23:16; 34:22; Lev 23:15-21; Deut 16:9-12 [b]Num 28:18

28 [1]I.e. Approx one bu

29 [1]Lit *each lamb*

31 [1]Lit *without defect to you* [a]Num 28:3

29:1 [a]Ex 23:16; 34:22; Lev 23:23-25 [b]Num 28:26

2 [1]Or *bull of a herd,* and so throughout the ch

3 [1]I.e. Approx one bu

4 [1]Lit *each lamb,* and so throughout the ch

6 [a]Num 28:27 [b]Num 28:3

7 [a]Lev 16:29-34; 23:26-32

8 [a]Lev 22:20; Deut 15:21; 17:1

9 [1]I.e. Approx one bu

11 [a]Lev 16:3, 5 [b]Num 28:3

12 [a]Lev 23:33-35; Deut 16:13-15 [b]Num 29:1

tenths *of an* [1]*ephah* for [2]each of the thirteen bulls, two-tenths
for [3]each of the two rams,
15 and a tenth for each of the fourteen lambs;
16 and one male goat for a sin offering, [a]besides the continual
burnt offering, its grain offering and its drink offering.
17 'Then on [a]the second day: twelve bulls, two rams, fourteen
male lambs one year old without defect;
18 and their grain offering and their drink offerings for the bulls,
for the rams and for the lambs, by their number [a]according to
the ordinance;
19 and one male goat for a sin offering, [a]besides the continual
burnt offering and its grain offering, and their drink offerings.
20 'Then on the third day: eleven bulls, two rams, fourteen
male lambs one year old without defect;
21 and their grain offering and their drink offerings for the
bulls, for the rams and for the lambs, by their number according to the ordinance;
22 and one male goat for a sin offering, besides the continual
burnt offering and its grain offering and its drink offering.
23 'Then on the fourth day: ten bulls, two rams, fourteen male
lambs one year old without defect;
24 their grain offering and their drink offerings for the bulls,
for the rams and for the lambs, by their number according to
the ordinance;
25 and one male goat for a sin offering, besides the continual
burnt offering, its grain offering and its drink offering.
26 'Then on the fifth day: nine bulls, two rams, fourteen male
lambs one year old [a]without defect;
27 and their grain offering and their drink offerings for the
bulls, for the rams and for the lambs, by their number according to the ordinance;
28 and one male goat for a sin offering, besides the continual
burnt offering and its grain offering and its drink offering.
29 'Then on the sixth day: eight bulls, two rams, fourteen male
lambs one year old without defect;
30 and their grain offering and their drink offerings for the bulls,
for the rams and for the lambs, by their number according to
the ordinance;
31 and one male goat for a sin offering, besides the continual
burnt offering, its grain offering and its drink offerings.
32 'Then on the seventh day: seven bulls, two rams, fourteen
male lambs one year old without defect;
33 and their grain offering and their drink offerings for the
bulls, for the rams and for the lambs, by their number according to the ordinance;
34 and one male goat for a sin offering, besides the continual
burnt offering, its grain offering and its drink offering.
35 '[a]On the eighth day you shall have a solemn assembly; you
shall do no laborious work.
36 'But you shall present a burnt offering, an offering by fire, as
a soothing aroma to the LORD: one bull, one ram, seven male
lambs one year old without defect;

14 [1]I.e. Approx one bu [2]Lit *each bull* [3]Lit *each ram*
16 [a]Num 28:3
17 [a]Lev 23:36
18 [a]Lev 2:1-16
19 [a]Num 28:8
26 [a]Heb 7:26
35 [a]Lev 23:36

37 their grain offering and their drink offerings for the bull, for
the ram and for the lambs, by their number according to the
ordinance;
38 and one male goat for a sin offering, besides the continual
burnt offering and its grain offering and its drink offering.
39 'You shall present these to the LORD at your [a]appointed
times, besides your [1]votive offerings and your freewill
offerings, for your burnt offerings and for your grain offerings
and for your drink offerings and for your peace offerings.'"
40 [1]Moses spoke to the sons of Israel in accordance with all
that the LORD had commanded Moses.

Chapter 30 Theme ____________________

30 Then Moses spoke to [a]the heads of the tribes of the
sons of Israel, saying, "This is the word which the LORD
has commanded.
2 "[a]If a man makes a vow to the LORD, or takes an oath to bind
himself with a binding obligation, he shall not violate his word;
he shall do according to all that proceeds out of his mouth.
3 "Also if a woman makes a vow to the LORD, and binds
herself by an obligation in her father's house in her youth,
4 and her father hears her vow and her obligation by which
she has bound herself, and her father [1]says nothing to her, then
all her vows shall stand and every obligation by which she has
bound herself shall stand.
5 "But if her father should forbid her on the day he hears *of it,*
none of her vows or her obligations by which she has bound
herself shall stand; and the LORD will forgive her because her
father had forbidden her.
6 "However, if she should [1]marry while [2]under her vows or
the rash statement of her lips by which she has bound herself,
7 and her husband hears of it and says nothing to her on the
day he hears *it,* then her vows shall stand and her obligations
by which she has bound herself shall stand.
8 "But if on the day her husband hears *of it,* he forbids her,
then he shall annul her vow which [1]she is under and the rash
statement of her lips by which she has bound herself; and the
LORD will forgive her.
9 "But the vow of a widow or of a divorced woman, everything
by which she has bound herself, shall stand against her.
10 "However, if she vowed in her husband's house, or bound
herself by an obligation with an oath,
11 and her husband heard *it,* but said nothing to her *and* did
not forbid her, then all her vows shall stand and every
obligation by which she bound herself shall stand.
12 "But if her husband indeed annuls them on the day he hears
them, then whatever proceeds out of her lips concerning her
vows or concerning the obligation of herself shall not stand;
her husband has annulled them, and the LORD will forgive her.
13 "Every vow and every binding oath to humble herself, her
husband may confirm it or her husband may annul it.

39 [1]Lit *vows* [a]Lev 23:2

40 [1]Ch 30:1 in Heb

30:1 [a]Num 1:4, 16; 7:2

2 [a]Deut 23:21-23; Matt 5:33

4 [1]Lit *is silent to her,* and so throughout the ch

6 [1]Lit *be to a husband* [2]Lit *her vows are on her*

8 [1]Lit *is on her*

31:2 [a]Num 25:1, 16, 17 [b]Num 20:24, 26; 27:13

14 "But if her husband indeed says nothing to her from day to
day, then he confirms all her vows or all her obligations which
are on her; he has confirmed them, because he said nothing to
her on the day he heard them.
15 "But if he indeed annuls them after he has heard them, then
he shall bear her guilt."

3 [1]Lit *be* [a]Lev 26:25

16 These are the statutes which the LORD commanded Moses,
as between a man and his wife, *and as* between a father and
his daughter, *while she is* in her youth in her father's house.

Chapter 31 Theme ____________________

5 [1]Lit *delivered*

31 Then the LORD spoke to Moses, saying,
2 "[a]Take full vengeance for the sons of Israel on the
Midianites; afterward you will be [b]gathered to your people."
3 Moses spoke to the people, saying, "Arm men from among
you for the war, that they may [1]go against Midian to execute
[a]the LORD's vengeance on Midian.

6 [a]Num 14:44 [b]Num 10:8, 9

4 "A thousand from each tribe of all the tribes of Israel you
shall send to the war."
5 So there were [1]furnished from the thousands of Israel, a
thousand from each tribe, twelve thousand armed for war.
6 Moses sent them, a thousand from each tribe, to the war, and

7 [a]Deut 20:13; Judg 21:11; 1 Kin 11:15, 16

Phinehas the son of Eleazar the priest, to the war with them, [a]and
the holy vessels and [b]the trumpets for the alarm in his hand.
7 So they made war against Midian, just as the LORD had
commanded Moses, and [a]they killed every male.
8 They killed the kings of Midian along with the *rest of* their
slain: [a]Evi and Rekem and [b]Zur and Hur and Reba, the five
kings of Midian; they also killed [c]Balaam the son of Beor with
the sword.

8 [a]Josh 13:21 [b]Num 25:15 [c]Num 31:16; Josh 13:22

9 The sons of Israel captured the women of Midian and their
little ones; and all their cattle and all their flocks and all their
goods they plundered.
10 Then they burned all their cities where they lived and all
their camps with fire.

11 [a]Deut 20:14

11 [a]They took all the spoil and all the prey, both of man and of
beast.
12 They brought the captives and the prey and the spoil to
Moses, and to Eleazar the priest and to the congregation of the
sons of Israel, to the camp at the plains of Moab, which are by
the Jordan *opposite* Jericho.

15 [1]Lit *let . . . live* [a]Deut 20:14

13 Moses and Eleazar the priest and all the leaders of the
congregation went out to meet them outside the camp.
14 Moses was angry with the officers of the army, the captains
of thousands and the captains of hundreds, who had come from
service in the war.
15 And Moses said to them, "Have you [1]spared [a]all the women?

16 [1]Lit *were to* [2]Lit *word* [3]Possibly *defect from the Lord* [a]Num 25:1-9 [b]Num 31:8

16 "[a]Behold, these [1]caused the sons of Israel, through the
[2]counsel of [b]Balaam, to [3]trespass against the LORD in the matter
of Peor, so the plague was among the congregation of the LORD.

17 "[a]Now therefore, kill every male among the little ones, and
kill every woman who has known man [1]intimately.
18 "But all the [1]girls who have not known man [2]intimately,
[3]spare for yourselves.
19 "[a]And you, camp outside the camp seven days; whoever has
killed any person and whoever has touched any slain, purify
yourselves, you and your captives, on the third day and on the
seventh day.
20 "You shall purify for yourselves every garment and every article
of [1]leather and all the work of goats' *hair,* and all articles of wood."
21 Then Eleazar the priest said to the men of war who had
gone to battle, "This is the statute of the law which the LORD
has commanded Moses:
22 only the gold and the silver, the bronze, the iron, the tin
and the lead,
23 everything that can stand the fire, you shall pass through
the fire, and it shall be clean, but it shall be purified with
[a]water for impurity. But whatever cannot stand the fire you
shall pass through the water.
24 "And you shall wash your clothes on the seventh day and be
clean, and afterward you may enter the camp."
25 Then the LORD spoke to Moses, saying,
26 "You and Eleazar the priest and the heads of the fathers'
households of the congregation take a count of the booty [1]that
was captured, both of man and of animal;
27 and [a]divide the booty between the warriors who went out
to battle and all the congregation.
28 "[a]Levy a tax for the LORD from the men of war who went
out to battle, one [1]in five hundred of the persons and of the
cattle and of the donkeys and of the sheep;
29 take it from their half and give it to Eleazar the priest, as an
[1]offering to the LORD.
30 "From the sons of Israel's half, you shall take one drawn out
of every fifty of the persons, of the cattle, of the donkeys and of
the sheep, from all the animals, and give them to the Levites
who [a]keep charge of the tabernacle of the LORD."
31 Moses and Eleazar the priest did just as the LORD had
commanded Moses.
32 Now the booty that remained from the spoil which the
[1]men of war had plundered was 675,000 sheep,
33 and 72,000 cattle,
34 and 61,000 donkeys,
35 and of human beings, of the women who had not known
man [1]intimately, all the persons were 32,000.
36 The half, the portion of those who went out to war, was *as
follows:* the number of sheep was 337,500,
37 and the LORD's levy of the sheep was 675;
38 and the cattle were 36,000, from which the LORD's levy
was 72;
39 and the donkeys were 30,500, from which the LORD's levy
was 61;

17 [1]Lit *by lying with a man* [a]Deut 7:2; 20:16-18

18 [1]Lit *female children* [2]Lit *by lying with a man* [3]Lit *keep alive*

19 [a]Num 19:11-22

20 [1]Or *skin*

23 [a]Num 19:9, 17

26 [1]Lit *of captives*

27 [a]Josh 22:8

28 [1]Lit *soul from* [a]Num 18:21-30

29 [1]Lit *heave offering,* and so throughout the ch

30 [a]Num 3:7, 8, 25, 26, 31, 36, 37; 18:3, 4

32 [1]Lit *people*

35 [1]Lit *by lying with a man*

41 [a]Num 5:9, 10; 18:19

40 and the human beings were 16,000, from whom the
LORD's levy was 32 persons.
41 Moses gave the levy *which was* the LORD's offering to
Eleazar the priest, just [a]as the LORD had commanded Moses.
42 As for the sons of Israel's half, which Moses [1]separated
from the men who had gone to war—
43 now the congregation's half was 337,500 sheep,

42 [1]Or *divided*

44 and 36,000 cattle,
45 and 30,500 donkeys,
46 and the human beings were 16,000—
47 and from the sons of Israel's half, Moses took one drawn
out of every fifty, both of man and of animals, and gave them to
the Levites, who kept charge of the tabernacle of the LORD, just
as the LORD had commanded Moses.

50 [a]Ex 30:12-16

48 Then the officers who were over the thousands of the
army, the captains of thousands and the captains of hundreds,
approached Moses,
49 and they said to Moses, "Your servants have taken a census of
men of war who are in our charge, and no man of us is missing.
50 "So we have brought as an offering to the LORD what each
man found, articles of gold, armlets and bracelets, signet rings,

53 [a]Num 31:32; Deut 20:14

earrings and necklaces, [a]to make atonement for ourselves
before the LORD."
51 Moses and Eleazar the priest took the gold from them, all
kinds of wrought articles.
52 All the gold of the offering which they offered up to the
LORD, from the captains of thousands and the captains of
hundreds, was 16,750 shekels.

54 [a]Ex 30:16

53 [a]The men of war had taken booty, every man for himself.
54 So Moses and Eleazar the priest took the gold from the
captains of thousands and of hundreds, and brought it to the tent
of meeting as [a]a memorial for the sons of Israel before the LORD.

Chapter 32 Theme __________________________

32:1 [1]Lit *behold, the place, a place for* [a]Ex 12:38 [b]Num 21:32

32 Now the sons of Reuben and the sons of Gad had an
[a]exceedingly large number of livestock. So when they
saw the land of [b]Jazer and the land of Gilead, that [1]it was
indeed a place suitable for livestock,
2 the sons of Gad and the sons of Reuben came and spoke to
Moses and to Eleazar the priest and to the leaders of the
congregation, saying,
3 "[a]Ataroth, Dibon, Jazer, Nimrah, Heshbon, Elealeh, Sebam,
Nebo and Beon,

3 [a]Num 32:34-38

4 the land [a]which the LORD [1]conquered before the
congregation of Israel, is a land for livestock, and your servants
have livestock."
5 They said, "If we have found favor in your sight, let this
land be given to your servants as a possession; do not take us
across the Jordan."

4 [1]Lit *smote* [a]Num 21:34

6 But Moses said to the sons of Gad and to the sons of Reuben,
"Shall your brothers go to war while you yourselves sit here?

7 "[a]Now why are you [1]discouraging the sons of Israel from
crossing over into the land which the LORD has given them?
8 "[1]This is what your fathers did when I sent them from
[a]Kadesh-barnea to see the land.
9 "For when they went up to [a]the [1]valley of Eshcol and saw
the land, they [2]discouraged the sons of Israel so that they did
not go into the land which the LORD had given them.
10 "So [a]the LORD'S anger burned in that day, and He swore, saying,
11 '[a]None of the men who came up from Egypt, from twenty
years old and upward, shall see the land which I swore to
Abraham, to Isaac and to Jacob; for they did not follow Me fully,
12 except Caleb the son of Jephunneh the Kenizzite and
Joshua the son of Nun, [a]for they have followed the LORD fully.'
13 "[a]So the LORD'S anger burned against Israel, and He made
them wander in the wilderness forty years, until the entire
generation of those who had done evil in the sight of the LORD
was destroyed.
14 "Now behold, you have risen up in your fathers' place, a
brood of sinful men, to add still more to the burning [a]anger of
the LORD against Israel.
15 "For if you [a]turn away from following Him, He will once
more abandon them in the wilderness, and you will destroy all
these people."
16 Then they came near to him and said, "We will build here
sheepfolds for our livestock and cities for our little ones;
17 [a]but we ourselves will be armed ready *to go* before the sons
of Israel, until we have brought them to their place, while our
little ones live in the fortified cities because of the inhabitants
of the land.
18 "[a]We will not return to our homes until every one of the
sons of Israel has possessed his inheritance.
19 "For we will not have an inheritance with them on the
other side of the Jordan and beyond, because our inheritance
has fallen to us [a]on this side of the Jordan toward the east."
20 [a]So Moses said to them, "If you will do [1]this, if you will
arm yourselves before the LORD for the war,
21 and all of you armed men cross over the Jordan before the
LORD until He has driven His enemies out from before Him,
22 [a]and the land is subdued before the LORD, then afterward
you shall return and be free of obligation toward the LORD and
toward Israel, and this land shall be yours for a possession
before the LORD.
23 "But if you will not do so, behold, you have sinned against
the LORD, and be sure [a]your sin will find you out.
24 "Build yourselves cities for your little ones, and sheepfolds
for your sheep, and [a]do [1]what you have promised."
25 The sons of Gad and the sons of Reuben spoke to Moses,
saying, "Your servants will do just as my lord commands.
26 "[a]Our little ones, our wives, our livestock and all our cattle
shall [1]remain there in the cities of Gilead;
27 while your servants, everyone who is armed for war, will

7 [1]Lit *restraining the hearts of* [a]Num 13:27-14:4

8 [1]Lit *Thus your fathers* [a]Num 13:3, 26; Deut 1:19-25

9 [1]Or *wadi* [2]Lit *restrained the hearts of* [a]Num 13:24; Deut 1:24

10 [a]Num 14:11f; Deut 1:34

11 [a]Num 14:28-30

12 [a]Deut 1:36; Josh 14:8f

13 [a]Num 14:33-35

14 [a]Deut 1:34f

15 [a]Deut 30:17, 18; 2 Chr 7:19, 20

17 [a]Josh 4:12, 13

18 [a]Josh 22:1-4

19 [a]Josh 12:1; 13:8

20 [1]Lit *this thing* [a]Deut 3:18

22 [a]Deut 3:20

23 [a]Gen 4:7; 44:16; Is 59:12

24 [1]Lit *that which has come out of your mouth* [a]Num 30:2

26 [1]Lit *be* [a]Josh 1:14

[a]cross over in the presence of the LORD to battle, just as my lord says."

28 So Moses gave command concerning them to Eleazar the priest, and to Joshua the son of Nun, and to the heads of the fathers' *households* of the tribes of the sons of Israel.

29 Moses said to them, "If the sons of Gad and the sons of Reuben, everyone who is armed for battle, will cross with you over the Jordan in the presence of the LORD, and the land is subdued before you, then you shall give them the land of Gilead for a possession;

30 but if they will not cross over with you armed, they shall have possessions among you in the land of Canaan."

31 The sons of Gad and the sons of Reuben answered, saying, "As the LORD has said to your servants, so we will do.

32 "We ourselves will cross over armed in the presence of the LORD into the land of Canaan, and the possession of our inheritance *shall remain* with us across the Jordan."

33 [a]So Moses gave to them, to the sons of Gad and to the sons of Reuben and to the half-tribe of Joseph's son Manasseh, the kingdom of Sihon, king of the Amorites and the kingdom of Og, the king of Bashan, the land with its cities with *their* [1]territories, the cities of the surrounding land.

34 The sons of Gad built Dibon and Ataroth and [a]Aroer,

35 and Atroth-shophan and Jazer and Jogbehah,

36 and [a]Beth-nimrah and Beth-haran as fortified cities, and sheepfolds for sheep.

37 The sons of Reuben built Heshbon and Elealeh and Kiriathaim,

38 and [a]Nebo and Baal-meon—*their* names being changed—and Sibmah, and they gave *other* names to the cities which they built.

39 The sons of [a]Machir the son of Manasseh went to Gilead and took it, and dispossessed the Amorites who were in it.

40 So Moses gave [a]Gilead to Machir the son of Manasseh, and he lived in it.

41 Jair the son of Manasseh went and took its [1]towns, and called them [2a]Havvoth-jair.

42 Nobah went and took Kenath and its villages, and called it Nobah after [a]his own name.

Chapter 33 Theme ____

33 These are the journeys of the sons of Israel, by which they came out from the land of Egypt by their armies, under [a]the [1]leadership of Moses and Aaron.

2 Moses recorded their starting places according to their journeys by the [1]command of the LORD, and these are their journeys according to their starting places.

3 [a]They journeyed from Rameses in the first month, on the fifteenth day of the first month; on the [1]next day after the Passover the sons of Israel [b]started out [2]boldly in the sight of all the Egyptians,

4 while the Egyptians were burying all their firstborn whom

27 [a]Josh 4:12
33 [1]Lit *borders* [a]Deut 3:8-17; Josh 12:1-6
34 [a]Deut 2:36
36 [a]Num 32:3
38 [a]Is 46:1
39 [a]Gen 50:23
40 [a]Deut 3:12, 13, 15; Josh 17:1
41 [1]Lit *tent villages* [2]I.e. the towns of Jair [a]Deut 3:14; Judg 10:4
42 [a]2 Sam 18:18; Ps 49:11
33:1 [1]Lit *hand* [a]Ps 77:20; 105:26; Mic 6:4
2 [1]Lit *mouth*
3 [1]Lit *morrow* [2]Lit *with a high hand* [a]Ex 12:37 [b]Ex 14:8

the LORD had struck down among them. The LORD had also
executed judgments [a]on their gods.
5 Then [a]the sons of Israel journeyed from Rameses and camped
in Succoth.
6 [a]They journeyed from Succoth and camped in Etham, which
is on the edge of the wilderness.
7 [a]They journeyed from Etham and turned back to Pi-hahiroth,
which faces Baal-zephon, and they camped before Migdol.
8 [a]They journeyed [1]from before Hahiroth and passed through
the midst of the sea into the wilderness; and [b]they went three
days' journey in the wilderness of Etham and camped at Marah.
9 [a]They journeyed from Marah and came to Elim; and in
Elim there were twelve springs of water and seventy palm
trees, and they camped there.
10 They journeyed from Elim and camped by the [1]Red Sea.
11 They journeyed from the [1]Red Sea and camped in [a]the
wilderness of Sin.
12 They journeyed from the wilderness of Sin and camped at
Dophkah.
13 They journeyed from Dophkah and camped at Alush.
14 They journeyed from Alush and camped [a]at Rephidim; now
it was there that the people had no water to drink.
15 They journeyed from Rephidim and camped in [a]the wilderness of Sinai.
16 They journeyed from the wilderness of Sinai and camped at
[a]Kibroth-hattaavah.
17 They journeyed from Kibroth-hattaavah and camped at
[a]Hazeroth.
18 They journeyed from Hazeroth and camped at Rithmah.
19 They journeyed from Rithmah and camped at Rimmon-perez.
20 They journeyed from Rimmon-perez and camped at [a]Libnah.
21 They journeyed from Libnah and camped at Rissah.
22 They journeyed from Rissah and camped in Kehelathah.
23 They journeyed from Kehelathah and camped at Mount
Shepher.
24 They journeyed from Mount Shepher and camped at Haradah.
25 They journeyed from Haradah and camped at Makheloth.
26 They journeyed from Makheloth and camped at Tahath.
27 They journeyed from Tahath and camped at Terah.
28 They journeyed from Terah and camped at Mithkah.
29 They journeyed from Mithkah and camped at Hashmonah.
30 They journeyed from Hashmonah and camped at [a]Moseroth.
31 They journeyed from Moseroth and camped at Bene-jaakan.
32 They journeyed from [a]Bene-jaakan and camped at Hor-
haggidgad.
33 They journeyed from Hor-haggidgad and camped at [a]Jotbathah.
34 They journeyed from Jotbathah and camped at Abronah.
35 They journeyed from Abronah and camped at [a]Ezion-geber.
36 They journeyed from Ezion-geber and camped in the
wilderness of [a]Zin, that is, Kadesh.
37 They journeyed from Kadesh and camped at [a]Mount Hor,
[b]at the edge of the land of Edom.

4 [a]Ex 12:12
5 [a]Ex 12:37
6 [a]Ex 13:20
7 [a]Ex 14:1, 2
8 [1]Many mss read *from Pi-hahiroth* [a]Ex 14:22 [b]Ex 15:22, 23
9 [a]Ex 15:27
10 [1]Lit *Sea of Reeds*
11 [1]Lit *Sea of Reeds* [a]Ex 16:1
14 [a]Ex 17:1
15 [a]Ex 19:1
16 [a]Num 11:34
17 [a]Num 11:35
20 [a]Deut 1:1
30 [a]Deut 10:6
32 [a]Gen 36:27; Deut 10:6; 1 Chr 1:42
33 [a]Deut 10:7
35 [a]Deut 2:8
36 [a]Num 20:1
37 [a]Num 20:22 [b]Num 20:16

38 [a]Then Aaron the priest went up to Mount Hor at the
[1]command of the LORD, and died there in the fortieth year after
the sons of Israel had come from the land of Egypt, on the first
day in the fifth month.
39 Aaron was one hundred twenty-three years old when he
died on Mount Hor.
40 Now the Canaanite, the king of [a]Arad [1]who lived in the
[2]Negev in the land of Canaan, heard of the coming of the sons
of Israel.
41 Then they journeyed from Mount Hor and camped at
Zalmonah.
42 They journeyed from Zalmonah and camped at Punon.
43 They journeyed from Punon and camped at [a]Oboth.
44 They journeyed from Oboth and camped at Iye-abarim, at
the border of Moab.
45 They journeyed from Iyim and camped at Dibon-gad.
46 They journeyed from Dibon-gad and camped at Almon-
diblathaim.
47 They journeyed from Almon-diblathaim and camped in the
mountains of [a]Abarim, before Nebo.
48 They journeyed from the mountains of Abarim and [a]camped
in the plains of Moab by the Jordan *opposite* Jericho.
49 They camped by the Jordan, from Beth-jeshimoth as far as
[a]Abel-shittim in the plains of Moab.
50 Then the LORD spoke to Moses in the plains of Moab by the
Jordan *opposite* Jericho, saying,
51 "Speak to the sons of Israel and say to them, '[a]When you
cross over the Jordan into the land of Canaan,
52 then you shall drive out all the inhabitants of the land from
before you, and [a]destroy all their figured stones, and destroy all
their molten images and demolish all their high places;
53 [a]and you shall take possession of the land and live in it, for
I have given the land to you to possess it.
54 '[a]You shall inherit the land by lot according to your families;
to the larger you shall give more inheritance, and to the smaller
you shall give less inheritance. Wherever the lot falls to anyone,
that shall be his. You shall inherit according to the tribes of
your fathers.
55 'But if you do not drive out the inhabitants of the land from
before you, then it shall come about that those whom you let
remain of them *will become* [a]as pricks in your eyes and as
thorns in your sides, and they will trouble you in the land in
which you live.
56 'And as I plan to do to them, so I will do to you.'"

Chapter 34 Theme ______

34
Then the LORD spoke to Moses, saying,
2 "Command the sons of Israel and say to them, 'When
you enter [a]the land of Canaan, this is the land that shall fall to you
as an inheritance, *even the* land of Canaan according to its borders.
3 '[a]Your southern [1]sector shall [2]extend from the wilderness of

38 [1]Lit *mouth* [a]Num 20:28; Deut 10:6
40 [1]Lit *and he* [2]I.e. South country [a]Num 21:1
43 [a]Num 21:10, 11
47 [a]Num 27:12
48 [a]Num 22:1
49 [a]Num 25:1
51 [a]Josh 3:17
52 [a]Ex 23:24; Lev 26:1; Deut 7:5; 12:3, 30; Ps 106:34-36
53 [a]Deut 11:31; 17:14; Josh 21:43
54 [a]Num 26:53-56
55 [a]Josh 23:13
34:2 [a]Gen 17:8; Ps 78:54, 55; 105:11
3 [1]Lit *side* [2]Lit *be* [a]Josh 15:1-3

Border of Canaan (to be distributed to the nine and a half tribes—Numbers 34:13)

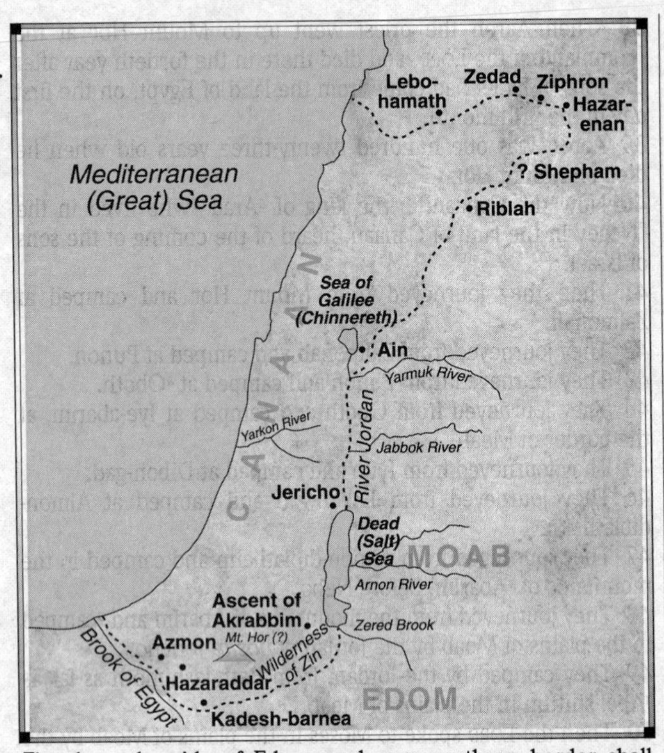

Zin along the side of Edom, and your southern border shall
[2]extend from the end of the Salt Sea [b]eastward.
4 'Then your border shall turn *direction* from the south to the
ascent of Akrabbim and [1]continue to Zin, and its [2]termination
shall be to the south of [a]Kadesh-barnea; and it shall [3]reach
Hazaraddar and [1]continue to Azmon.
5 'The border shall turn *direction* from Azmon to the brook of
Egypt, and its termination shall be at [a]the sea.
6 'As for the western border, you shall have the Great Sea,
that is, *its* [1]coastline; this shall be your west border.
7 '[a]And this shall be your north border: you shall draw your
border line from the Great Sea to Mount Hor.
8 'You shall draw a line from Mount Hor to [a]the [1]Lebo-
hamath, and the termination of the border shall be at Zedad;
9 and the border shall proceed to Ziphron, and its termination
shall be at Hazar-enan. This shall be your north border.
10 'For your eastern border you shall also draw a line from
Hazar-enan to Shepham,
11 and the border shall go down from Shepham to [a]Riblah on
the east side of Ain; and the border shall go down and reach to
the [1]slope on the east side of the Sea of [b]Chinnereth.
12 'And the border shall go down to the Jordan and its
termination shall be at the Salt Sea. This shall be your land
according to its borders all around.'"
13 So Moses commanded the sons of Israel, saying, "[a]This is
the land that you are to apportion by lot among you as a

3 [2]Lit *be* [b]Josh 15:5

4 [1]Lit *pass along* [2]Lit *goings out,* and so throughout the ch [3]Lit *go forth to* [a]Num 32:8

5 [a]Josh 15:4

6 [1]Lit *border*

7 [a]Ezek 47:15-17

8 [1]Or *entrance of Hamath* [a]Josh 13:5

11 [1]Lit *shoulder* [a]2 Kin 23:33 [b]Deut 3:17; Josh 13:27

13 [a]Gen 15:18; Num 26:52-56; Deut 11:24; Josh 14:1-5

14 aNum 32:33

possession, which the LORD has commanded to give to the nine
and a half tribes.
14 "[a]For the tribe of the sons of Reuben have received *theirs*
according to their fathers' households, and the tribe of the sons
of Gad according to their fathers' households, and the half-tribe
of Manasseh have received their possession.
15 "The two and a half tribes have received their possession
across the Jordan opposite Jericho, eastward toward the sunrising."

17 aJosh 14:1, 2

16 Then the LORD spoke to Moses, saying,
17 "[a]These are the names of the men who shall apportion the
land to you for inheritance: Eleazar the priest and Joshua the son
of Nun.
18 "You shall take one leader of every tribe to apportion the
land for inheritance.
19 "These are the names of the men: of the tribe of [a]Judah, [b]Caleb
the son of Jephunneh.

19 aGen 29:35; Deut 33:7; Ps 60:7 bNum 13:6, 30; 26:65; Deut 1:36

20 "Of the tribe of the sons of [a]Simeon, Samuel the son of
Ammihud.
21 "Of the tribe of [a]Benjamin, Elidad the son of Chislon.
22 "Of the tribe of the sons of Dan a leader, Bukki the son of Jogli.
23 "Of the sons of Joseph: of the tribe of the sons of Manasseh
a leader, Hanniel the son of Ephod.
24 "Of the tribe of the sons of Ephraim a leader, Kemuel the
son of Shiphtan.
25 "Of the tribe of the sons of Zebulun a leader, Elizaphan the
son of Parnach.

20 aGen 29:33; 49:5; Ezek 48:24

26 "Of the tribe of the sons of Issachar a leader, Paltiel the son
of Azzan.
27 "Of the tribe of the sons of Asher a leader, Ahihud the son
of Shelomi.
28 "Of the tribe of the sons of Naphtali a leader, Pedahel the
son of Ammihud."
29 These are those whom the LORD commanded to apportion
the inheritance to the sons of Israel in the land of Canaan.

21 aGen 49:27; Deut 33:12; Ps 68:27

Chapter 35 Theme ____________________

35 [a]Now the LORD spoke to Moses in the plains of Moab by
the Jordan *opposite* Jericho, saying,
2 "Command the sons of Israel that they give to the Levites
from the inheritance of their possession cities to live in; and
you shall give to the Levites pasture lands around the cities.
3 "The cities shall be theirs to live in; and their pasture lands
shall be for their cattle and for their herds and for all their beasts.

35:1 aLev 25:32-34

4 "The pasture lands of the cities which you shall give to the
Levites *shall extend* from the wall of the city [1]outward a
thousand cubits around.
5 "You shall also measure outside the city on the east side two
thousand cubits, and on the south side two thousand cubits,
and on the west side two thousand cubits, and on the north
side two thousand cubits, with the city in the center. This shall
become theirs as pasture lands for the cities.

4 [1]Lit *and outward*

6 "The cities which you shall give to the Levites *shall be* the
[a]six cities of refuge, which you shall give for the manslayer to
flee to; and in addition to them you shall give forty-two cities.

Cities of Refuge

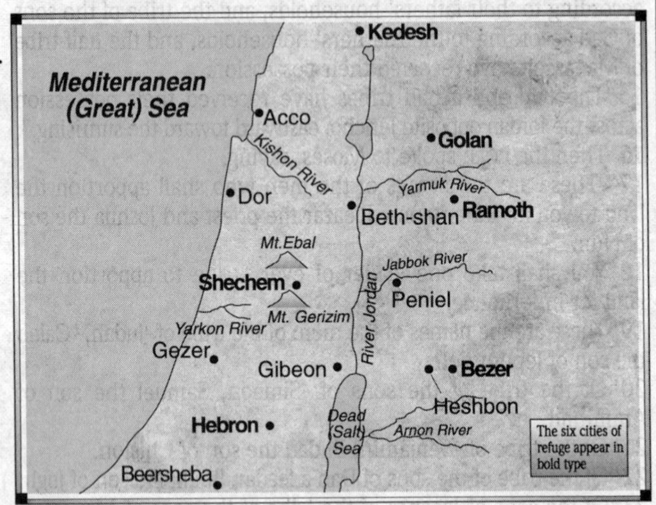

7 "All the cities which you shall give to the Levites *shall be*
[a]forty-eight cities, [1]together with their pasture lands.
8 "[a]As for the cities which you shall give from the possession
of the sons of Israel, you shall take more from the larger and
you shall take less from the smaller; each shall give some of his
cities to the Levites in proportion to his possession which he
inherits."
9 Then the LORD spoke to Moses, saying,
10 "[a]Speak to the sons of Israel and say to them, 'When you
cross the Jordan into the land of Canaan,
11 [a]then you shall select for yourselves cities to be your [b]cities
of refuge, that the manslayer who has [1]killed any person
[c]unintentionally may flee there.
12 '[a]The cities shall be to you as a refuge from the avenger, so
that the manslayer will not die until he stands before the
congregation for [1]trial.
13 'The cities which you are to give shall be your six cities of
refuge.
14 'You [a]shall give three cities across the Jordan and three
cities [1]in the land of Canaan; they are to be cities of refuge.
15 'These six cities shall be for refuge for the sons of Israel,
and for the alien and for the sojourner among them; that
anyone who [1]kills a person [a]unintentionally may flee there.
16 '[a]But if he struck him down with an iron object, so that he
died, he is a murderer; the murderer shall surely be put to death.
17 'If he struck him down with a stone in the hand, by which
he will die, and *as a result* he died, he is a murderer; the
murderer [a]shall surely be put to death.
18 'Or if he struck him with a wooden object in the hand, by
which he might die, and *as a result* he died, he is a murderer;
the murderer shall surely be put to death.

6 [a]Josh 20:7-9
7 [1]Lit *them* [a]Josh 21:41
8 [a]Lev 25:32-34; Num 26:54; 33:54; Josh 21:1-42
10 [a]Josh 20:1-9
11 [1]Lit *smote* [a]Deut 19:1-13 [b]Josh 20:2f [c]Ex 21:13; Lev 4:2f, 22f; Num 35:22-25
12 [1]Lit *judgment* [a]Deut 19:4-6; Josh 20:2, 3
14 [1]Lit *you shall give in* [a]Deut 4:41
15 [1]Lit *smites* [a]Num 35:11
16 [a]Ex 21:12, 14; Lev 24:17
17 [a]Num 35:31

19 'The blood avenger himself shall put the murderer to death;
he shall put him to death when he meets him.
20 '[a]If he pushed him of hatred, or threw something at him
[b]lying in wait and *as a result* he died,
21 or if he struck him down with his hand in enmity, and *as a*
result he died, the one who struck him shall surely be put to
death, he is a murderer; the blood avenger shall put the murderer to death when he meets him.
22 '[a]But if he pushed him suddenly without enmity, or threw
something at him without lying in wait,
23 or with any [1]deadly object of stone, and without seeing it
dropped on him so that he died, while he was not his enemy nor
seeking his injury,
24 then [a]the congregation shall judge between the slayer and
the blood avenger according to these ordinances.
25 'The congregation shall deliver the manslayer from the
hand of the blood avenger, and the congregation shall restore
him to his city of refuge to which he fled; and he shall live in it
until the death of the high priest who was anointed with the
holy oil.
26 'But if the manslayer at any time goes beyond the border of
his city of refuge to which he may flee,
27 and the blood avenger finds him outside the border of his
city of refuge, and the blood avenger kills the manslayer, he
will not be guilty of blood
28 because he should have remained in his city of refuge until
the death of the high priest. But after the death of the high
priest the manslayer shall return to the land of his possession.
29 'These things shall be for a [a]statutory ordinance to you
throughout your generations in all your dwellings.
30 '[a]If anyone kills a person, the murderer shall be put to
death at the [1]evidence of witnesses, but [b]no person shall be put
to death on the testimony of one witness.
31 'Moreover, you shall not take ransom for the life of a murderer
who is guilty of death, but he shall surely be put to death.
32 'You shall not take ransom for him who has fled to his city
of refuge, that he may return to live in the land [1]before the
death of the priest.
33 '[a]So you shall not pollute the land in which you are; for
blood pollutes the land and no expiation can be made for the
land for the blood that is shed on it, except [b]by the blood of
him who shed it.
34 'You shall not [a]defile the land in which you live, in the
midst of which [b]I dwell; for I the LORD am dwelling in the
midst of the sons of Israel.'"

Chapter 36 Theme ______________________________

36 [a]And the heads of the fathers' *households* of the family
of the sons of Gilead, the son of Machir, the son of
Manasseh, of the families of the sons of Joseph, came near and

20 [a]Gen 4:8; 2 Sam 3:27; 20:10 [b]Ex 21:14; Deut 19:11
22 [a]Num 35:11
23 [1]Lit *by which he may die*
24 [a]Josh 20:6
29 [a]Num 27:11
30 [1]Lit *mouth* [a]Num 35:16 [b]Deut 17:6; 19:15; Matt 18:16; John 7:51; 8:17, 18
32 [1]Or *until*
33 [a]Deut 21:7, 8; Ps 106:38 [b]Gen 9:6
34 [a]Lev 18:24, 25 [b]Num 5:3
36:1 [a]Num 27:1

spoke before Moses and before the leaders, the heads of the
fathers' *households* of the sons of Israel,
2 and they said, "The LORD commanded my lord to give the
land by lot to the sons of Israel as an inheritance, and my lord
[a]was commanded by the LORD to give the inheritance of
Zelophehad our brother to his daughters.
3 "But if they [1]marry one of the sons of the *other* tribes of the
sons of Israel, their inheritance will be withdrawn from the
inheritance of our fathers and will be added to the inheritance
of the tribe to which they belong; thus it will be withdrawn
from our allotted inheritance.
4 "When the [a]jubilee of the sons of Israel [1]comes, then their
inheritance will be added to the inheritance of the tribe to
which they belong; so their inheritance will be withdrawn
from the inheritance of the tribe of our fathers."
5 Then Moses commanded the sons of Israel according to the
[1]word of the LORD, saying, "The tribe of the sons of Joseph are
right in *their* statements.
6 "[a]This is [1]what the LORD has commanded concerning the
daughters of Zelophehad, saying, 'Let them marry [2]whom they
wish; only they must marry within the family of the tribe of
their father.'
7 "Thus [a]no inheritance of the sons of Israel shall [1]be
transferred from tribe to tribe, for the sons of Israel shall each
[2]hold to the inheritance of the tribe of his fathers.
8 "[a]Every daughter who comes into possession of an
inheritance of any tribe of the sons of Israel shall be wife to one
of the family of the tribe of her father, so that the sons of Israel
each may possess the inheritance of his fathers.
9 "Thus no inheritance shall [1]be transferred from one tribe to
another tribe, for the tribes of the sons of Israel shall each
[2]hold to his own inheritance."
10 Just as the LORD had commanded Moses, so the daughters
of Zelophehad did:
11 [a]Mahlah, Tirzah, Hoglah, Milcah and Noah, the daughters
of Zelophehad married their uncles' sons.
12 They married *those* from the families of the sons of
Manasseh the son of Joseph, and their inheritance [1]remained
with the tribe of the family of their father.
13 [a]These are the commandments and the ordinances which
the LORD commanded to the sons of Israel through Moses in
the plains of Moab by the Jordan *opposite* Jericho.

2 [a]Num 27:5-7

3 [1]Lit *become wives to,* in this ch

4 [1]Lit *shall be* [a]Lev 25:10

5 [1]Lit *mouth*

6 [1]Lit *the thing which* [2]Lit *to the good one in their eyes* [a]Num 27:7

7 [1]Lit *turn about* [2]Lit *cleave* [a]1 Kin 21:3

8 [a]1 Chr 23:22

9 [1]Lit *turn about* [2]Lit *cleave*

11 [a]Num 26:33

12 [1]Lit *was*

13 [a]Lev 26:46; 27:34; Num 22:1

Insights from Numbers

Land of Canaan	Balaam	Korah

Theme of Numbers:

SEGMENT DIVISIONS

	JOURNEYS/ ENCAMP- MENTS	CHAPTER THEMES
		1
		2
		3
		4
		5
		6
		7
		8
		9
		10
		11
		12
		13
		14
		15
		16
		17
		18
		19
		20
		21
		22
		23
		24
		25
		26
		27
		28
		29
		30
		31
		32
		33
		34
		35
		36

Author:

Date:

Purpose:

Key Words:

the Lord spok

service

cloud

wilderness

tent (tabernac

offering

atonement

Passover

sin (iniquity)

curse

covenant

DEUTERONOMY 

DVARIM

Deuteronomy is the crown jewel of the Pentateuch. It lays before us clearly what God expects from those whom He redeems: a life of uncompromising obedience.

God raised up Moses to deliver His people from the land of Egypt, the land of bondage. That had been accomplished. Now he stood at Pisgah, near the land of promise. He was 120 years old.

When Moses struck the rock a second time, he failed to respect God's holiness. Therefore, he could not enter the land of promise. But the people who survived and whom he had led so faithfully for the last 40 years would go in and possess it.

Moses had to do one more thing before God took him home: tell God's children how to live in the land that the God of their fathers was giving them.

Things to Do

General Instructions

1. For the book's historical context, read Numbers 21:21–22:1; 36:13; Deuteronomy 1:1-5.
   a. Record the author, date, and geographical setting of the book on the DEUTERONOMY AT A GLANCE chart on page 350.
   b. When you study Deuteronomy, watch for any verses that confirm Moses' authorship. Although the last chapter tells of Moses' death, this doesn't negate the fact that Moses wrote the rest of the book. The last chapter would be an appropriate postscript after his death.
2. Read Romans 15:4 and 1 Corinthians 10:1-14 and keep these verses in mind as you study.
   a. As you study each chapter, note in the margin of your Bible (under the symbol △) insights you glean about the character of God and the ways He deals with His children and with unbelievers.
   b. Also note in the margin any specific instructions or admonitions that are to be followed in respect to God—for example, "Fear Him."
   c. Record in the margin any "Lessons for Life" you learn from the text under the heading "LFL."
3. There are insightful lessons to be learned from Moses' life about leadership and about our relationship to God. As you study Deuteronomy, note these on the chart on pages 351, 352. When you record your insights, make sure you note the book, chapter, and verse from which they came.
4. Double-underline all geographical locations in green, and look them up on the map on page 292 to see where the events took place.

Chapters 1–3

Moses rehearses what happened from the time they left Horeb (Mount Sinai) until they camped in the valley opposite Beth-peor at the foot of Mount Nebo (Pisgah).

1. As you read these three chapters:
   a. Ask the "5 W's and an H." Watch what happens in each chapter, where it happens and to whom, why it happens, and what the consequences or results are. Also note how things are accomplished.
   b. Mark every reference to time and every use of *then* so you can see the sequence of events.

2. In a distinctive way mark these key words and their synonyms: *covenant*, *fear*, *heart*, *command (commanded)*, and *listen*. Write these on an index card to use as a bookmark while studying Deuteronomy.

3. Choose the theme of each chapter and record it at the beginning of the chapter and on DEUTERONOMY AT A GLANCE.

Chapters 4–11

Moses instructs the children of Israel regarding what they are to do when they enter the land.

1. Read this segment chapter by chapter, keeping in mind the "5 W's and an H." Words such as *when*, *then*, *watch*, *hear*, *listen*, *beware*, and *you shall therefore* will come to your attention. When you see the word "when," look and see if "then" eventually follows it. If so, circle each word and connect them with a line.

2. Mark the following key words when you come to them in the text: *observe (keep, do)*, *love*, *remember*, *commandment (statutes)*, *nations*, *blessing*, and *curse*.

3. Record the main points of each chapter in the margin or number them in the text.

4. Record the chapter themes as you did previously.

Chapters 12–26

Moses gives the people the statutes and the judgments they are to observe.

1. Make sure you mark every occurrence of the phrase *you shall purge (remove) the evil*. Also mark the words *life* and *death*. Mark every reference to the *feasts.*

2. As you read these chapters, note in the margin of the text what the people are to do and why.

3. Record the theme of the chapters on DEUTERONOMY AT A GLANCE and in your Bible.

Chapters 27–30

Moses tells the people about the necessity of obedience and that if they obey they will be blessed, but if they disobey they will be cursed.

1. Carefully mark the words on your key words list. Underline every reference to *the* LORD *will*. Think about what you observe from marking the text.

2. As you read these chapters, keep asking the "5 W's and an H." Note who Moses speaks to, who he's making a covenant with, and who or what will be affected by their obedience or disobedience. Also note everything that will happen if they obey or disobey.

3. Don't forget to note what you learn about God from these chapters and to record the theme of each chapter.

Chapters 31–34

This segment contains Moses' parting words, song, and blessing, as well as the account of his death.

1. Mark the key repeated words listed on your index card.

2. As Moses sings his song in chapter 32, he recounts Israel's relationship to God and God's dealings with them. *Jeshurun* in 32:15 is a reference to Israel.

   a. Pay attention to what you learn about Israel. Observe what leads to Israel's downfall and what the consequences are.

   b. Remember that although Moses begged God to change His mind and allow him to enter the promised land, God said no. Keep this in mind as you read these chapters and see Moses' heart and hear his words in respect to God. Take note of all you learn about God from these significant chapters. List what you learn about "the Rock" in your notebook.

3. Observe what Moses says will happen after his death and note this in the margin.

4. When you study chapter 33, mark the name of each of the tribes of Israel and carefully observe how they are described and what is said about each one of them. Underline every occurrence of *they shall* (NIV *he*) in 33:10.

5. Complete DEUTERONOMY AT A GLANCE and record what you learn about Moses from chapter 34 on the chart on pages 351, 352.

Things to Think About

1. Since we are under the new covenant of grace, what is our relationship to the blessings and curses set forth in Deuteronomy? Read Hebrews 8–10.

2. What kind of allegiance does God call for from Israel? Do you think He expects anything less from the Church, the body of the Lord Jesus Christ? Do you think grace allows us to continue in sin and disobedience without any consequences or chastening from the Father?

3. What have you learned regarding the long-suffering of God and His gracious ways with His covenant people?

4. How does a follower of God demonstrate his love for the Lord?

Chapter 1 Theme ______________________

1 These are the words which Moses spoke to all Israel [a]across
the Jordan in the wilderness, in the [b]Arabah opposite [1]Suph,
between Paran and Tophel and Laban and Hazeroth and Dizahab.
2 It is eleven days' *journey* from [a]Horeb by the way of Mount
[b]Seir to [c]Kadesh-barnea.
3 In the [a]fortieth year, on the first *day* of the eleventh month,
Moses spoke to the children of Israel, [b]according to all that the
LORD had commanded him *to give* to them,
4 after he had [1a]defeated Sihon the king of the Amorites, who
lived in Heshbon, and [b]Og the king of Bashan, who lived in
[c]Ashtaroth [2]and Edrei.
5 Across the Jordan in the land of Moab, Moses undertook to
expound this law, saying,
6 "The LORD our God [a]spoke to us at Horeb, saying, 'You have
[1]stayed long enough at this mountain.
7 'Turn and set your journey, and go to [a]the hill country of the
Amorites, and to all their neighbors in the Arabah, in the hill
country and in the lowland and in [b]the [1]Negev and by the
seacoast, the land of the Canaanites, and Lebanon, as far as the
great river, the river Euphrates.
8 'See, I have placed the land before you; go in and possess the
land which the LORD [a]swore to give to your fathers, to Abraham,
to Isaac, and to Jacob, to them and their [1]descendants after them.'

1:1 [1]Perhaps Red Sea [a]Deut 4:46 [b]Deut 2:8

2 [a]Ex 3:1; 17:6 [b]Gen 32:3 [c]Num 13:26; 32:8; Deut 9:23

3 [a]Num 33:38 [b]Deut 4:1, 2

4 [1]Lit *smitten* [2]So with ancient versions; M.T. omits *and* [a]Num 21:21-26; Deut 2:26-35; Josh 13:10; Neh 9:22 [b]Num 21:33-35; Josh 13:12 [c]Josh 12:4

6 [1]Lit *dwelt* [a]Num 10:11-13

7 [1]I.e. South country [a]Gen 15:18; Deut 11:24; Josh 10:40 [b]Gen 12:9

8 [1]Lit *seed* [a]Gen 12:7; 26:3; 28:13; Ex 33:1; Num 14:23; 32:11; Heb 6:13, 14

The Lands of Israel's Journeys after the Exodus

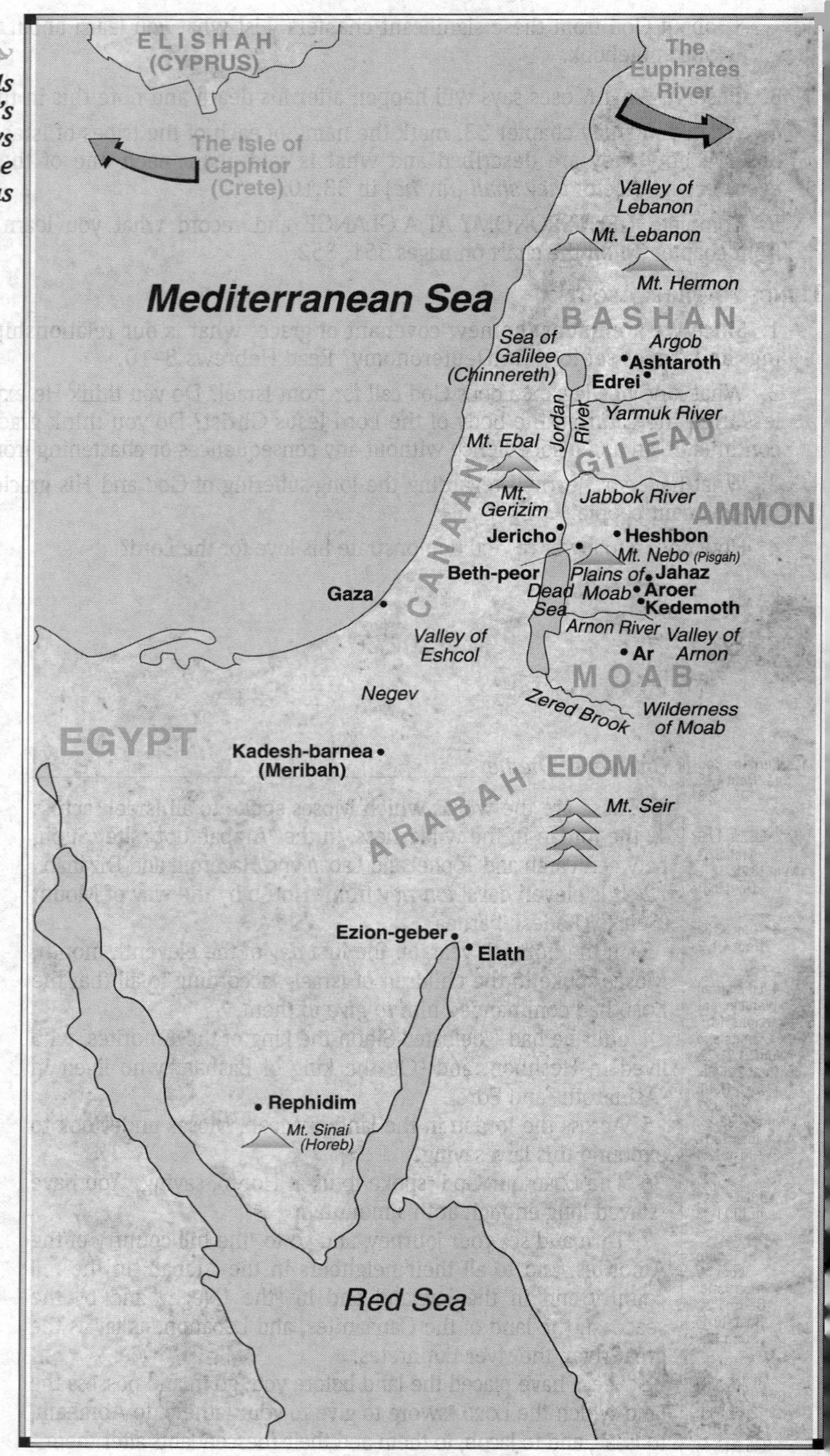

ELISHAH
(CYPRUS)
The Euphrates River
The Isle of Caphtor
(Crete)
Valley of Lebanon
Mt. Lebanon
Mt. Hermon
Mediterranean Sea
BASHAN
Sea of Galilee
(Chinnereth)
Argob
Ashtaroth
Edrei
Jordan River
Yarmuk River
Mt. Ebal
GILEAD
Mt. Gerizim
Jabbok River
AMMON
CANAAN
Jericho
Heshbon
Mt. Nebo (Pisgah)
Beth-peor
Plains of Moab
Jahaz
Aroer
Kedemoth
Dead Sea
Gaza
Arnon River
Valley of Arnon
Valley of Eshcol
Ar
MOAB
Negev
Zered Brook
Wilderness of Moab
EGYPT
Kadesh-barnea
(Meribah)
EDOM
Mt. Seir
ARABAH
Ezion-geber
Elath
Rephidim
Mt. Sinai
(Horeb)
Red Sea

9 "I spoke to you at that time, saying, '[a]I am not able to bear
the burden of you alone.
10 'The LORD your God has [a]multiplied you, and behold, you
are this day like the stars of heaven in number.
11 'May the LORD, the God of your fathers, increase you a
thousand-fold more than you are and bless you, [a]just as He has
[1]promised you!
12 'How can I alone bear the load and burden of you and your
strife?
13 '[1a]Choose wise and discerning and experienced men from
your tribes, and I will appoint them as your heads.'
14 "You answered me and said, 'The thing which you have said
to do is good.'
15 "So I took the heads of your tribes, wise and experienced men,
and [1]appointed them heads over you, leaders of thousands and [2]of
hundreds, [2]of fifties and [2]of tens, and officers for your tribes.
16 "Then I charged your judges at that time, saying, 'Hear *the cases*
between your [1]fellow countrymen, and [a]judge righteously between
a man and his [2]fellow countryman, or the alien who is with him.
17 '[a]You shall not show partiality in judgment; you shall hear the
small and the great alike. You shall [b]not fear [1]man, for the judgment is God's. [c]The case that is too hard for you, you shall
bring to me, and I will hear it.'
18 "[a]I commanded you at that time all the things that you
should do.
19 "Then we set out from [a]Horeb, and went through all that
[b]great and terrible wilderness which you saw on the way to the
[c]hill country of the Amorites, just as the LORD our God had
commanded us; and we came to [a]Kadesh-barnea.
20 "I said to you, 'You have come to the hill country of the
Amorites which the LORD our God is about to give us.
21 'See, the LORD your God has placed the land before you; go
up, take possession, as the LORD, the God of your fathers, has
spoken to you. [a]Do not fear or be dismayed.'
22 "[a]Then all of you approached me and said, 'Let us send men
before us, that they may search out the land for us, and bring
back to us word of the way by which we should go up and the
cities which we shall enter.'
23 "The thing pleased me and I took twelve of your men, one
man for each tribe.
24 "[a]They turned and went up into the hill country, and came
to the valley of Eshcol and spied it out.
25 "Then they took *some* of the fruit of the land in their hands
and brought it down to us; and they brought us back a report and
said, 'It is a good land which the LORD our God is about to give us.'
26 "[a]Yet you were not willing to go up, but [b]rebelled against
the [1]command of the LORD your God;
27 and [a]you grumbled in your tents and said, 'Because the LORD
hates us, He has brought us out of the land of Egypt to deliver
us into the hand of the Amorites to destroy us.
28 'Where can we go up? Our brethren have made our hearts
melt, saying, "The people are bigger and taller than we; the cities

9 [a]Ex 18:18, 24; Num 11:14
10 [a]Gen 15:5; 22:17; Ex 32:13; Deut 7:7; 10:22; 26:5; 28:62
11 [1]Lit *spoken to* [a]Deut 1:8, 10
13 [1]Lit *Give for yourselves* [a]Ex 18:21
15 [1]Lit *gave* [2]Lit *leaders of*
16 [1]Lit *brothers* [2]Lit *brother* [a]Deut 16:18; John 7:24
17 [1]Lit *because of man* [a]Deut 10:17; 16:19; 24:17; 2 Chr 19:5, 6; Prov 24:23-26; Acts 10:34; James 2:1, 9 [b]Prov 29:25 [c]Ex 18:22, 26
18 [a]Ex 18:20
19 [a]Deut 1:2 [b]Deut 2:7; 8:15; 32:10; Jer 2:6 [c]Deut 1:7
21 [a]Josh 1:6, 9
22 [a]Num 13:1-3
24 [a]Num 13:21-25
26 [1]Lit *mouth* [a]Num 14:1-4 [b]Deut 9:23
27 [a]Deut 9:28; Ps 106:25

are large and fortified to heaven. And besides, we saw [a]the sons
of the Anakim there."'
29 "Then I said to you, 'Do not be shocked, nor fear them.
30 'The LORD your God who goes before you will [a]Himself fight
on your behalf, [1]just as He did for you in Egypt before your eyes,
31 and in the wilderness where you saw how [a]the LORD your
God carried you, just as a man carries his son, in all the way
which you have walked until you came to this place.'
32 "But [1a]for all this, you did not trust the LORD your God,
33 [a]who goes before you on *your* way, [b]to seek out a place for
you to encamp, in fire by night and cloud by day, to show you
the way in which you should go.
34 "Then the LORD heard the sound of your words, and He was
angry and [a]took an oath, saying,
35 '[a]Not one of these men, this evil generation, shall see the good
land which I swore to give your fathers,
36 except Caleb the son of Jephunneh; he shall see it, and [a]to
him and to his sons I will give the land on which he has set
foot, because he has followed the LORD fully.'
37 "[a]The LORD was angry with me also on your account, saying,
'[b]Not even you shall enter there.
38 'Joshua the son of Nun, who stands before you, [a]he shall enter
there; encourage him, for [b]he will cause Israel to inherit it.
39 'Moreover, [a]your little ones who you said would become a
prey, and your sons, who this day have [b]no knowledge of good
or evil, shall enter there, and I will give it to them and they
shall possess it.
40 'But as for you, [a]turn around and set out for the wilderness
by the way to the [1]Red Sea.'
41 "[a]Then you said to me, 'We have sinned against the LORD; we
will indeed go up and fight, just as the LORD our God commanded
us.' And every man of you girded on his weapons of war, and
regarded it as easy to go up into the hill country.
42 "[a]And the LORD said to me, 'Say to them, "Do not go up nor
fight, for I am not among you; otherwise you will be [1]defeated
before your enemies."'
43 "So I spoke to you, but you would not listen. Instead [a]you
rebelled against the [1]command of the LORD, and acted presumptuously and went up into the hill country.
44 "[a]The Amorites who [1]lived in that hill country came out
against you and chased you [b]as bees do, and crushed you from
Seir to Hormah.
45 "Then you returned and wept before the LORD; but the [a]LORD
did not listen to your voice nor give ear to you.
46 "So you remained in [a]Kadesh many days, [1]the days that you
spent *there.*

Chapter 2 Theme ______________________________

2 "[a]Then we turned and set out for the wilderness by the way
to the [1]Red Sea, as the LORD spoke to me, and circled
[b]Mount Seir for many days.

28 [a]Num 13:28, 33; Deut 9:2

30 [1]Lit *according to all that* [a]Ex 14:14; Deut 3:22; 20:4; Neh 4:20

31 [a]Deut 32:10-12; Is 46:3, 4; 63:9; Hos 11:3; Acts 13:18

32 [1]Lit *in this matter* [a]Num 14:11; Ps 106:24; Heb 3:19; 4:2; Jude 5

33 [a]Ex 13:21; Num 9:15-23; Neh 9:12; Ps 78:14 [b]Num 10:33

34 [a]Num 14:28-30; Heb 3:18

35 [a]Ps 95:11; 106:26; Ezek 20:15; 1 Cor 10:5; Heb 3:14-19

36 [a]Num 14:24; Josh 14:9

37 [a]Num 20:12; Deut 3:26; 4:21 [b]Num 27:13, 18

38 [a]Num 14:30 [b]Num 34:17; Deut 3:28; 31:7; Josh 11:23

39 [a]Num 14:3, 31 [b]Is 7:15, 16

40 [1]Lit *Sea of Reeds* [a]Num 14:25

41 [a]Num 14:40

42 [1]Lit *smitten* [a]Num 14:41-43

43 [1]Lit *mouth* [a]Num 14:40

44 [1]Lit *dwelt* [a]Num 14:45 [b]Ps 118:12

45 [a]Job 27:8, 9; Ps 66:18; John 9:31

46 [1]Lit *as the days* [a]Num 20:1, 22; Deut 2:7, 14; Judg 11:17

2:1 [1]Lit *Sea of Reeds* [a]Num 21:4 [b]Deut 1:2

2 "And the LORD spoke to me, saying,
3 'You have circled this mountain long enough. *Now* turn north,
4 [a]and command the people, saying, "You will pass through
the [b]territory of your brothers the sons of Esau who live in Seir;
and [c]they will be afraid of you. So be very careful;
5 do not [1]provoke them, for I will not give you any of their
land, even *as little as* a [2]footstep [a]because I have given Mount
Seir to Esau as a possession.
6 "You shall buy food from them with money so that you may
eat, and you shall also purchase water from them with money
so that you may drink.
7 "For the LORD your God has blessed you in all [1]that you have
done; He has known your [2]wanderings through this [a]great
wilderness. These [b]forty years the LORD your God has been
with you; you have not lacked a thing."'
8 "So we passed beyond our brothers the sons of Esau, who
live in Seir, away from the [a]Arabah road, away from Elath and
[b]from Ezion-geber. And we turned and passed through by the
way of the wilderness of Moab.
9 "Then the LORD said to me, 'Do not harass Moab, nor provoke
them to war, for I will not give you any of [1]their land as a
possession, because I have given [a]Ar to [b]the sons of Lot as a
possession.'
10 (The [a]Emim lived there formerly, a people as great, numerous,
and tall as the Anakim.
11 Like the Anakim, they are also regarded as [a]Rephaim, but
the Moabites call them Emim.
12 [a]The Horites formerly lived in Seir, but the sons of Esau
dispossessed them and destroyed them from before them and
settled in their place, [b]just as Israel did to the land of [1]their
possession which the LORD gave to them.)
13 'Now arise and cross over the [1]brook Zered yourselves.' So
we crossed over the [1]brook Zered.
14 "Now the [1]time that it took for us to come from Kadesh-
barnea until we crossed over the [2]brook Zered was [a]thirty-eight
years, until [b]all the generation of the men of war perished from
within the camp, as [c]the LORD had sworn to them.
15 "[a]Moreover the hand of the LORD was against them, to
destroy them from within the camp until they all perished.
16 "So it came about when [a]all the men of war had finally
perished from among the people,
17 that the LORD spoke to me, saying,
18 'Today you shall cross over [a]Ar, the border of Moab.
19 'When you come opposite the [a]sons of Ammon, do not
harass them nor provoke them, for I will not give you any of
the land of the sons of Ammon as a possession, because I have
given it to [b]the sons of Lot as a possession.'
20 (It is also regarded as the land of the [a]Rephaim, *for* Rephaim
formerly lived in it, but the Ammonites call them Zamzummin,
21 a people as great, numerous, and tall as the Anakim, but
the LORD destroyed them before them. And they dispossessed
them and settled in their place,

4 [a]Num 20:14-21 [b]Gen 36:8 [c]Ex 15:15, 16
5 [1]Or *engage in strife with* [2]Lit *treading of a sole of a foot* [a]Gen 36:8; Josh 24:4
7 [1]Lit *the work of your hand* [2]Lit *goings* [a]Deut 1:19 [b]Num 14:33, 34; 32:13; Deut 2:14
8 [a]Deut 1:1 [b]Num 33:35; 1 Kin 9:26
9 [1]Lit *his* [a]Num 21:15, 28; Deut 2:18, 29 [b]Gen 19:36, 37
10 [a]Gen 14:5
11 [a]Gen 14:5; Deut 2:20
12 [1]Lit *his* [a]Gen 36:20; Deut 2:22 [b]Num 21:25, 35
13 [1]Or *wadi*
14 [1]Lit *days in which we went* [2]Or *wadi* [a]Deut 2:7 [b]Num 14:29-35; 26:64, 65; Ps 106:26; 1 Cor 10:5 [c]Deut 1:34, 35
15 [a]Jude 5
16 [a]Deut 2:14
18 [a]Deut 2:9
19 [a]Gen 19:38 [b]Deut 2:9
20 [a]Deut 2:11

22 just as He did for the sons of Esau, who [a]live in Seir, when
He destroyed [b]the Horites from before them; they dispossessed
them and settled in their place even to this day.
23 And the [a]Avvim, who lived in villages as far as Gaza, the
[1b]Caphtorim who came from [2c]Caphtor, destroyed them and
lived in their place.)
24 'Arise, set out, and pass through the [1a]valley of Arnon. Look!
I have given Sihon the Amorite, king of Heshbon, and his land
into your hand; begin to take possession and contend with him
in battle.
25 'This day I will begin to put [a]the dread and fear of you [1]upon
the peoples [2]everywhere under the heavens, who, when they hear
the report of you, [b]will tremble and be in anguish because of you.'
26 "[a]So I sent messengers from the wilderness of Kedemoth to
Sihon king of Heshbon with words of peace, saying,
27 'Let me pass through your land, I will [1]travel only on the
highway; I will not turn aside to the right or to the left.
28 'You will sell me food for money so that I may eat, and give
me water for money so that I may drink, [a]only let me pass
through on [1]foot,
29 just as the sons of Esau who live in Seir and the Moabites
who live in [a]Ar did for me, until I cross over the Jordan into
the land which the LORD our God is giving to us.'
30 "But [a]Sihon king of Heshbon was not willing for us to pass
[1]through his land; for the [b]LORD your God hardened his spirit
and made his heart obstinate, in order to deliver him into your
hand, as *he is* today.
31 "The LORD said to me, 'See, I have begun to deliver Sihon and his
land [1]over to you. Begin to [2]occupy, that you may possess his land.'
32 "Then Sihon [1]with all his people came out to meet us in
battle at Jahaz.
33 "[a]The LORD our God delivered him [1]over to us, and we
[2b]defeated him with his sons and all his people.
34 "So we captured all his cities at that time and [1a]utterly
destroyed [2]the men, women and children of every city. We left
no survivor.
35 "We took [a]only the animals as our booty and the spoil of the
cities which we had captured.
36 "From [a]Aroer which is on the edge of the [1]valley of Arnon
and *from* the city which is in the [1]valley, even to Gilead, there
was no city that was too high for us; the LORD our God delivered all [2]over to us.
37 "[a]Only you did not go near to the land of the sons of
Ammon, all along the [1]river [b]Jabbok and the cities of the hill
country, and wherever the LORD our God had commanded us.

Chapter 3 Theme ____________________

3 "[a]Then we turned and went up the road to Bashan, and Og,
king of Bashan, [1]with all his people came out to meet us in
battle at Edrei.

22 [a]Gen 36:8; Deut 2:5 [b]Deut 2:12

23 [1]I.e. Philistines [2]I.e. Crete [a]Josh 13:3 [b]Gen 10:14; 1 Chr 1:12 [c]Jer 47:4; Amos 9:7

24 [1]Or *wadi* [a]Num 21:13, 14; Judg 11:18

25 [1]Lit *in front of* [2]Lit *under all the heavens* [a]Ex 23:27; Deut 11:25; Josh 2:9 [b]Ex 15:14-16

26 [a]Num 21:21-32; Deut 1:4; Judg 11:19-21

27 [1]Lit *go by the way*

28 [1]Lit *my feet* [a]Num 20:19

29 [a]Deut 2:9

30 [1]Lit *by him* [a]Num 21:23 [b]Ex 4:21; Josh 11:20

31 [1]Lit *before you* [2]Lit *possess*

32 [1]Lit *he and*

33 [1]Lit *before us* [2]Lit *smote* [a]Ex 23:31; Deut 7:2 [b]Deut 29:7

34 [1]Or *put under the ban* [2]Lit *every city of man . . .* [a]Deut 3:6; 7:2

35 [a]Deut 3:7

36 [1]Or *wadi* [2]Lit *before us* [a]Deut 3:12; 4:48; Josh 12:2; 13:9

37 [1]Or *wadi* [a]Deut 2:19 [b]Gen 32:22; Num 21:24; Deut 3:16

3:1 [1]Lit *he and* [a]Num 21:33-35

3 [1]Lit *him* [2]Lit *left to him*

4 [a]Deut 3:13, 14; 1 Kin 4:13

5 [1]Or *rural*

6 [1]Or *put them under the ban* [2]Or *putting under the ban* [3]Lit *every city of men . . .* [a]Deut 1:4 [b]Deut 2:34

7 [a]Deut 2:35

8 [1]Or *wadi* [a]Num 32:33; Josh 12:1-7; 13:8-12

9 [a]Deut 4:48; Josh 11:17; Ps 42:6; 133:3 [b]Ps 29:6 [c]1 Chr 5:23

10 [a]Josh 13:11

11 [1]Or *couch* [2]Lit *by a man's forearm* [a]Gen 14:5; Deut 2:11, 20 [b]2 Sam 11:1; 12:26; Jer 49:2

12 [1]Or *wadi* [a]Deut 2:36 [b]Num 32:32-38; Josh 13:8-13

14 [1]Lit *them* [2]I.e. the towns of Jair [a]Num 32:41; 1 Chr 2:22

15 [a]Num 32:39, 40

16 [1]Or *wadi* [2]Lit *and* [a]Num 21:24; Deut 2:37

17 [1]Lit *and* [2]I.e. the Sea of Galilee [3]Lit *under* [a]Num 34:11; Josh 13:27 [b]Josh 12:3 [c]Gen 14:3; Josh 3:16

18 [a]Josh 1:13 [b]Num 32:20; Josh 4:12, 13

19 [a]Josh 1:14 [b]Ex 12:38

2 "But the LORD said to me, 'Do not fear him, for I have
delivered him and all his people and his land into your hand;
and you shall do to him just as you did to Sihon king of the
Amorites, who lived at Heshbon.'
3 "So the LORD our God delivered Og also, king of Bashan,
with all his people into our hand, and we smote [1]them until no
survivor was [2]left.
4 "We captured all his cities at that time; there was not a city
which we did not take from them: sixty cities, all the region of
[a]Argob, the kingdom of Og in Bashan.
5 "All these were cities fortified with high walls, gates and
bars, besides a great many [1]unwalled towns.
6 "We [1]utterly destroyed them, as we did to [a]Sihon king of
Heshbon, [2b]utterly destroying [3]the men, women and children
of every city.
7 "[a]But all the animals and the spoil of the cities we took as
our booty.
8 "[a]Thus we took the land at that time from the hand of the
two kings of the Amorites who were beyond the Jordan, from
the [1]valley of Arnon to Mount Hermon
9 (Sidonians [a]call Hermon [b]Sirion, and the Amorites call it
[c]Senir):
10 all the cities of the plateau and all Gilead and [a]all Bashan,
as far as Salecah and Edrei, cities of the kingdom of Og in Bashan.
11 (For only Og king of Bashan was left of the remnant of the
[a]Rephaim. Behold, his [1]bedstead was an iron [1]bedstead; it is in
[b]Rabbah of the sons of Ammon. Its length was nine cubits and
its width four cubits [2]by ordinary cubit.)
12 "So we took possession of this land at that time. From [a]Aroer,
which is by the [1]valley of Arnon, and half the hill country of
[b]Gilead and its cities I gave to the Reubenites and to the Gadites.
13 "The rest of Gilead and all Bashan, the kingdom of Og, I gave
to the half-tribe of Manasseh, all the region of Argob (concerning
all Bashan, it is called the land of Rephaim.
14 [a]Jair the son of Manasseh took all the region of Argob as far as
the border of the Geshurites and the Maacathites, and called
[1]it, *that is,* Bashan, after his own name, [2]Havvoth-jair, *as it is* to
this day.)
15 "[a]To Machir I gave Gilead.
16 "To the Reubenites and to the Gadites I gave from Gilead even
as far as the [1]valley of Arnon, the middle of the [1]valley [2]as a border
and as far as the [1]river [a]Jabbok, the border of the sons of Ammon;
17 the Arabah also, with the Jordan [1]as *a* border, from
[2a]Chinnereth [b]even as far as the sea of the Arabah, [c]the Salt
Sea, [3]at the foot of the slopes of Pisgah on the east.
18 "Then I commanded you at that time, saying, '[a]The LORD your
God has given you this land to possess it; [b]all you valiant men
shall cross over armed before your brothers, the sons of Israel.
19 '[a]But your wives and your little ones and your livestock (I
know that you have [b]much livestock) shall remain in your cities
which I have given you,

20 [a]until the LORD gives rest to your fellow countrymen as to
you, and they also possess the land which the LORD your God
will give them beyond the Jordan. [b]Then you may return every
man to his possession which I have given you.'
21 "I commanded Joshua at that time, saying, 'Your eyes have seen
all that the LORD your God has done to these two kings; so the LORD
shall do to all the kingdoms into which you are about to cross.
22 'Do not fear them, for the LORD your God [a]is the one fighting for you.'
23 "I also pleaded with the LORD at that time, saying,
24 'O Lord [1]GOD, You have begun to show Your servant [a]Your
greatness and Your strong hand; for what [b]god is there in heaven
or on earth who can do such works and mighty acts as Yours?
25 'Let me, I pray, cross over and see the [a]fair land that is
beyond the Jordan, [1]that good hill country and Lebanon.'
26 "But [a]the LORD was angry with me on your account, and would
not listen to me; and the LORD said to me, '[1]Enough! Speak to Me
no more of this matter.
27 'Go up to the top of [a]Pisgah and lift up your eyes to the west
and north and south and east, and see *it* with your eyes, [b]for
you shall not cross over this Jordan.
28 '[a]But charge Joshua and encourage him and strengthen him,
[b]for he shall go across [1]at the head of this people, and he will
give them as an inheritance the land which you will see.'
29 "So we remained in the valley opposite [a]Beth-peor.

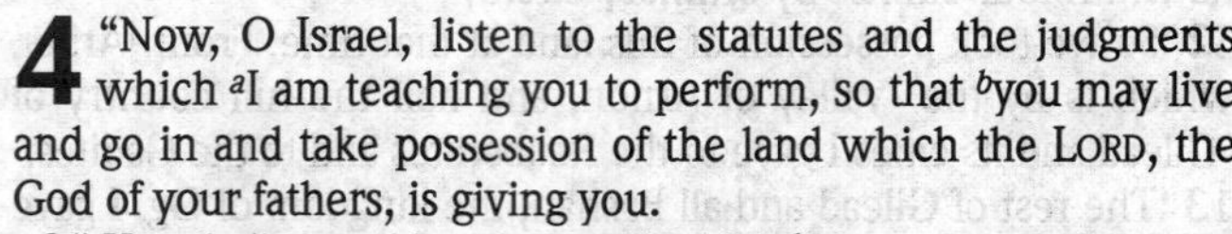

Chapter 4 Theme ______________________________

4 "Now, O Israel, listen to the statutes and the judgments
which [a]I am teaching you to perform, so that [b]you may live
and go in and take possession of the land which the LORD, the
God of your fathers, is giving you.

2 "[a]You shall not add to the word which [b]I am commanding you,
nor take away from it, that you may keep the commandments
of the LORD your God which I command you.
3 "[a]Your eyes have seen what the LORD has done in the case of
Baal-peor, for all the men who followed Baal-peor, the LORD
your God has destroyed [1]them from among you.
4 "But you who held fast to the LORD your God are alive today,
every one of you.
5 "See, I have taught you statutes and judgments [a]just as the
LORD my God commanded me, that you should do thus in the
land where you are entering to possess it.
6 "So keep and do *them,* [a]for that is your wisdom and your
understanding in the sight of the peoples who will hear all
these statutes and say, 'Surely this great nation is a wise and
understanding people.'
7 "For [a]what great nation is there that has a god [b]so near to it
as is the LORD our God [c]whenever we call on Him?
8 "Or what great nation is there that has [a]statutes and judgments
as righteous as this whole law which I am setting before you today?

20 [a]Josh 1:15 [b]Josh 22:4

22 [a]Ex 14:14; Deut 1:30; 20:4; Neh 4:20

24 [1]Heb *YHWH,* usually rendered *LORD* [a]Deut 11:2 [b]Ex 8:10; 15:11; 2 Sam 7:22; Ps 71:19; 86:8

25 [1]Lit *this* [a]Deut 4:22

26 [1]Lit *Enough for you* [a]Deut 1:37

27 [a]Num 23:14; 27:12 [b]Deut 1:37

28 [1]Lit *before this people* [a]Num 27:18; Deut 31:3, 7, 8, 23 [b]Deut 1:38

29 [a]Num 25:1-3; Deut 4:46; 34:6

4:1 [a]Deut 1:3 [b]Lev 18:5; Deut 5:33; 8:1; 16:20; 30:16, 19; Ezek 20:11; Rom 10:5

2 [a]Deut 12:32; Prov 30:6; Rev 22:18 [b]Deut 4:5, 14, 40

3 [1]Lit *him* [a]Num 25:1-9

5 [a]Lev 26:46; 27:34

6 [a]Deut 30:19, 20; 32:46, 47; Job 28:28; Ps 19:7; 111:10; Prov 1:7; 2 Tim 3:15

7 [a]Deut 4:32-34; 2 Sam 7:23 [b]Ps 34:17, 18; 145:18; 148:14; Is 55:6 [c]Ps 34:18; 85:9

8 [a]Ps 89:14; 97:2; 119:144, 160, 172

9 "Only [a]give heed to yourself and keep your soul diligently,
so that you do not forget the things which your eyes have seen
and they do not depart from your heart [b]all the days of your
life; but [c]make them known to your sons and your grandsons.
10 "*Remember* the day you stood before the LORD your God at
Horeb, when the LORD said to me, 'Assemble the people to Me,
that I may let them hear My words [a]so they may learn to [1]fear
Me all the days they live on the earth, and that they may [b]teach
their children.'
11 "You came near and stood at the foot of the mountain, [a]and
the mountain burned with fire to the *very* heart of the heavens:
darkness, cloud and thick gloom.
12 "Then the LORD spoke to you from the midst of the fire; you
heard the sound of words, but you saw no form—only a voice.
13 "So He declared to you His covenant which He commanded
you to perform, *that is,* [a]the Ten [1]Commandments; and [b]He
wrote them on two tablets of stone.
14 "The LORD commanded me at that time to teach you statutes
and judgments, that you might perform them in the land where
you are going over to possess it.
15 "So [a]watch yourselves carefully, since you did not see any
[b]form on the day the LORD spoke to you at Horeb from the midst
of the fire,
16 so that you do not [a]act corruptly and [b]make a graven image for
yourselves in the form of any figure, the likeness of male or female,
17 the likeness of any animal that is on the earth, the likeness
of [a]any winged bird that flies in the sky,
18 the likeness of anything that creeps on the ground, the
likeness of any fish that is in the water below the earth.
19 "And *beware* not to lift up your eyes to heaven and see the
sun and the moon and the stars, [a]all the host of heaven, [b]and
be drawn away and worship them and serve them, those
which the LORD your God has allotted to all the peoples under
the whole heaven.
20 "But the LORD has taken you and brought you out of [a]the iron
furnace, from Egypt, to [b]be a people for His own possession, as
today.
21 "[a]Now the LORD was angry with me on your account, and
swore that I would not cross the Jordan, and that I would not
enter the good land which the LORD your God is giving you as
an inheritance.
22 "For [a]I will die in this land, I shall not cross the Jordan, but
you shall cross and take possession of this [b]good land.
23 "So watch yourselves, [a]that you do not forget the covenant
of the LORD your God which He made with you, and [b]make for
yourselves a graven image in the form of anything *against*
which the LORD your God has commanded you.
24 "For the LORD your God is a [a]consuming fire, a [b]jealous God.
25 "When you [1]become the father of children and children's
children and have remained long in the land, and [a]act corruptly, and
[b]make an [2]idol in the form of anything, and [c]do that which is evil
in the sight of the LORD your God *so as* to provoke Him to anger,

9 [a]Deut 4:23; 6:12; 8:11, 14, 19; Prov 4:23; 23:19 [b]Deut 6:2; 12:1; 16:3 [c]Gen 18:19; Deut 4:10; 6:7, 20-25; 11:19; 32:46; Ps 78:5, 6; Prov 22:6; Eph 6:4

10 [1]Or *reverence* [a]Deut 14:23; 17:19; 31:12, 13 [b]Deut 4:9

11 [a]Ex 19:18; Heb 12:18, 19

13 [1]Lit *Words* [a]Ex 34:28; Deut 10:4 [b]Ex 31:18; 34:1, 28

15 [a]Josh 23:11 [b]Is 40:18

16 [a]Deut 4:25; 9:12; 31:29 [b]Ex 20:4; Lev 26:1; Deut 5:8, 9; 27:15; Rom 1:23

17 [a]Rom 1:23

19 [a]Gen 2:1; Deut 17:3; 2 Kin 17:16; 21:3 [b]Deut 13:5, 10; Job 31:26-28

20 [a]1 Kin 8:51; Jer 11:4 [b]Ex 19:5; Deut 7:6; 14:2; 26:18; Titus 2:14; 1 Pet 2:9

21 [a]Num 20:12; Deut 1:37

22 [a]Num 27:13, 14 [b]Deut 3:25

23 [a]Deut 4:9 [b]Deut 4:16

24 [a]Ex 24:17; Deut 9:3; Is 30:27; 33:14; Heb 12:29 [b]Deut 5:9; 6:15

25 [1]Lit *beget* [2]Or *a graven image* [a]Deut 4:16 [b]Deut 4:23 [c]2 Kin 17:17

26 I [a]call heaven and earth to witness against you today, that you will [b]surely perish quickly from the land where you are going over the Jordan to possess it. You shall not [1]live long on it, but will be utterly destroyed.

27 "The LORD will [a]scatter you among the peoples, and you will be left few in number among the nations where the LORD drives you.

28 "[a]There you will serve gods, the work of man's hands, [b]wood and stone, [c]which neither see nor hear nor eat nor smell.

29 "[a]But from there you will seek the LORD your God, and you will find *Him* if you search for Him [b]with all your heart and all your soul.

30 "When you [a]are in distress and all these things have come upon you, [b]in the latter days [c]you will return to the LORD your God and listen to His voice.

31 "For the LORD your God is a [a]compassionate God; [b]He will not fail you nor [c]destroy you nor [d]forget the covenant with your fathers which He swore to them.

32 "Indeed, [a]ask now concerning the former days which were before you, since the [b]day that God created [1]man on the earth, and *inquire* [c]from one end of the heavens to the other. [d]Has *anything* been done like this great thing, or has *anything* been heard like it?

33 "[a]Has *any* people heard the voice of God speaking from the midst of the fire, as you have heard *it*, and survived?

34 "[a]Or has a god tried to go to take for himself a nation from within *another* nation [b]by trials, by signs and wonders and by war and [c]by a mighty hand and by an outstretched arm and by great terrors, [1]as the LORD your God did for you in Egypt before your eyes?

35 "To you it was shown that you might know that the LORD, He is God; [a]there is no other besides Him.

36 "[a]Out of the heavens He let you hear His voice [b]to discipline you; and on earth He let you see His great fire, and you heard His words from the midst of the fire.

37 "[1a]Because He loved your fathers, therefore He chose [2]their descendants after them. And He [3b]personally brought you from Egypt by His great power,

38 driving out from before you nations greater and mightier than you, to bring you in *and* [a]to give you their land for an inheritance, as it is today.

39 "Know therefore today, and take it to your heart, that [a]the LORD, He is God in heaven above and on the earth below; there is no other.

40 "[a]So you shall keep His statutes and His commandments which I am [1]giving you today, that [b]it may go well with you and with your children after you, and [c]that you may [2]live long on the land which the LORD your God is giving you for all time."

41 [a]Then Moses set apart three cities across the Jordan to the [1]east,

42 that a manslayer might flee there, who unintentionally slew his neighbor without having enmity toward him in time past; and by fleeing to one of these cities he might live:

26 [1]Lit *prolong your days* [a]Deut 30:19; 31:28; 32:1; Is 1:2; Mic 6:2 [b]Deut 7:4; 8:19, 20

27 [a]Lev 26:33; Deut 28:64; 29:28; Neh 1:8

28 [a]Deut 28:36, 64; Jer 16:13 [b]Deut 29:17 [c]Ps 115:4-8; 135:15-18; Is 44:12-20

29 [a]Deut 30:1-3, 10; 2 Chr 15:4; Is 55:6; Jer 29:13 [b]Deut 6:5; 10:12

30 [a]Ps 18:6; 59:16; 107:6, 13 [b]Deut 31:29; Jer 23:20; Hos 3:5; Heb 1:2 [c]Jer 4:1, 2

31 [a]Ex 34:6; 2 Chr 30:9; Neh 9:31; Ps 103:8; 111:4; 116:5; Jon 4:2 [b]Deut 31:6, 8; Josh 1:5; 1 Chr 28:20; Heb 13:5 [c]Jer 30:11 [d]Lev 26:45

32 [1]Or *Adam* [a]Deut 32:7; Job 8:8 [b]Gen 1:27; Is 45:12 [c]Deut 28:64; Matt 24:31 [d]Deut 4:7; 2 Sam 7:23

33 [a]Ex 20:22; Deut 5:24, 26

34 [1]Lit *according to all that* [a]Ex 14:30; Deut 33:29 [b]Deut 7:19 [c]Deut 5:15; 6:21; Ps 136:12

35 [a]Ex 8:10; 9:14; Deut 4:39; 32:12, 39; 1 Sam 2:2; Is 43:10-12; 44:6-8; 45:5-7; Mark 12:32

36 [a]Ex 19:9, 19; 20:18, 22; Deut 4:33; Neh 9:13; Heb 12:25 [b]Deut 8:5

37 [1]Lit *And instead, because* [2]Lit *his seed* [3]Lit *with His presence* [a]Deut 7:7, 8; 10:15; 33:3 [b]Ex 33:14; Is 63:9

38 [a]Num 32:4; 34:14, 15

39 [a]Deut 4:35; Josh 2:11

40 [1]Lit *commanding* [2]Lit *prolong your days* [a]Lev 22:31; Deut 4:2; Ps 105:45 [b]Deut 4:1; 5:16, 29, 33; 6:3, 18; 12:25, 28; 22:7 [c]Ex 23:26; Deut 32:47

41 [1]Lit *sunrise* [a]Num 35:6; Deut 19:2-13; Josh 20:7-9

43 [a]Bezer in the wilderness on the plateau for the Reubenites,
and Ramoth in Gilead for the Gadites, and Golan in Bashan for
the Manassites.
44 Now this is the law which Moses set before the sons of Israel;
45 these are the testimonies and the statutes and the ordinances
which Moses spoke to the sons of Israel, when they came out
from Egypt,
46 across the Jordan, in the valley [a]opposite Beth-peor, in the
land of [b]Sihon king of the Amorites who lived at Heshbon, whom
Moses and the sons of Israel [1]defeated when they came out
from Egypt.
47 They took possession of his land and the land of [a]Og king of
Bashan, the two kings of the Amorites, *who were* across the
Jordan to the [1]east,
48 from [a]Aroer, which is on the edge of the [1]valley of Arnon,
even as far as [b]Mount Sion (that is, Hermon),
49 with all the Arabah across the Jordan to the east, even as
far as the sea of the Arabah, [1]at the foot of the slopes of Pisgah.

Chapter 5 Theme ______________________

5 Then Moses summoned all Israel and said to them:
"Hear, O Israel, the statutes and the ordinances which I
am speaking today in your [1]hearing, that you may learn them
and observe [2]them carefully.
2 "The LORD our God made [a]a covenant with us at Horeb.
3 "[a]The LORD did not make this covenant with our fathers, but
with us, *with* all those of [1]us alive here today.
4 "The LORD spoke to you [a]face to face at the mountain [b]from
the midst of the fire,
5 *while* [a]I was standing between the LORD and you at that time,
to declare to you the word of the LORD; [b]for you were afraid
because of the fire and did not go up the mountain. [1]He said,
6 '[a]I am the LORD your God who brought you out of the land
of Egypt, out of the house of [1]slavery.
7 '[a]You shall have no other gods [1]before Me.
8 '[a]You shall not make for yourself [1]an idol, *or* any likeness *of*
what is in heaven above [2]or on the earth beneath [2]or in the
water under the earth.
9 'You shall not worship them or serve them; for I, the LORD
your God, am a jealous God, [a]visiting the iniquity of the fathers
on the children, and on the third and the fourth *generations* of
those who hate Me,
10 but [a]showing lovingkindness to thousands, to those who
love Me and keep My commandments.
11 '[a]You shall not take the name of the LORD your God in vain,
for the LORD will not [1]leave him unpunished who takes His
name in vain.
12 '[a]Observe the sabbath day to keep it holy, as the LORD your
God commanded you.
13 'Six days you shall labor and do all your work,

43 [a]Josh 20:8
46 [1]Lit *smote* [a]Deut 3:29 [b]Num 21:21-25
47 [1]Lit *sunrise* [a]Deut 1:4; 3:3, 4
48 [1]Or *wadi* [a]Deut 2:36; 3:12 [b]Deut 3:9; Ps 133:3
49 [1]Lit *under*
5:1 [1]Lit *ears* [2]Lit *to do them*
2 [a]Ex 19:5; Mal 4:4
3 [1]Lit *us ourselves* [a]Jer 31:32; Heb 8:9
4 [a]Num 14:14; Deut 34:10 [b]Deut 4:33
5 [1]Lit *saying* [a]Gal 3:19 [b]Ex 19:16, 21-24; 20:18; Heb 12:18-21
6 [1]Lit *slaves* [a]Ex 20:2-17; Lev 26:1; Deut 6:4; Ps 81:10
7 [1]Or *besides* [a]Ex 20:3
8 [1]Or *a graven image* [2]Lit *or what is* [a]Ex 20:4-6; Lev 26:1; Deut 4:15-18; 27:15; Ps 97:7
9 [a]Ex 34:7; Num 14:18; Deut 7:10
10 [a]Num 14:18; Deut 7:9; Jer 32:18
11 [1]Or *hold him guiltless* [a]Ex 20:7; Lev 19:12; Deut 6:13; 10:20; Matt 5:33
12 [a]Ex 16:23-30; 20:8-11; 31:13f; Mark 2:27f

14 but [a]the seventh day is a sabbath of the LORD your God; *in it*
you shall not do any work, you or your son or your daughter or your
male servant or your female servant or your ox or your donkey or
any of your cattle or your sojourner who [1]stays with you, so that
your male servant and your female servant may rest as well as you.
15 '[a]You shall remember that you were a slave in the land of
Egypt, and the LORD your God brought you out of there by a
mighty hand and by an outstretched arm; therefore the LORD
your God commanded you to observe the sabbath day.
16 '[a]Honor your father and your mother, as the LORD your God has
commanded you, [b]that your days may be prolonged and that it may
go well with you on the land which the LORD your God gives you.
17 '[a]You shall not murder.
18 '[a]You shall not commit adultery.
19 '[a]You shall not steal.
20 '[a]You shall not bear false witness against your neighbor.
21 '[a]You shall not covet your neighbor's wife, and you shall not
desire your neighbor's house, his field or his male servant or his
female servant, his ox or his donkey or anything that belongs to
your neighbor.'
22 "These words the LORD spoke to all your assembly at the
mountain from the midst of the fire, *of* the cloud and *of* the
thick gloom, with a great voice, and He added no more. [a]He
wrote them on two tablets of stone and gave them to me.
23 "And when you heard the voice from the midst of the darkness,
while the mountain was burning with fire, you came near to me,
all the heads of your tribes and your elders.
24 "You said, 'Behold, the LORD our God has shown us His
glory and His greatness, and we have heard His voice from the
midst of the fire; we have seen today that God speaks with
man, yet he lives.
25 '[a]Now then why should we die? For this great fire will
consume us; if we hear the voice of the LORD our God any longer,
then we will die.
26 'For [a]who is there of all flesh who has heard the voice of
the living God speaking from the midst of the fire, as we *have,*
and lived?
27 '[1]Go near and hear all that the LORD our God says; then speak
to us all that the LORD our God speaks to you, and we will hear
and do *it*.'
28 "The LORD heard the voice of your words when you spoke
to me, [a]and the LORD said to me, 'I have heard the voice of the
words of this people which they have spoken to you. They
have done well in all that they have spoken.
29 '[a]Oh that they had such a heart in them, that they would
fear Me and [b]keep all My commandments always, that [c]it may
be well with them and with their sons forever!
30 'Go, say to them, "Return to your tents."
31 '[a]But as for you, stand here by Me, that I may speak to you
all the commandments and the statutes and the judgments
which you shall teach them, that they may observe *them* in the
land which I give them to possess.'

14 [1]Lit *is in your gates* [a]Gen 2:2; Heb 4:4
15 [a]Ex 20:11
16 [a]Ex 20:12; Lev 19:3; Deut 27:16; Matt 15:4; 19:19; Mark 7:10; 10:19; Luke 18:20; Eph 6:2, 3; Col 3:20 [b]Deut 4:40
17 [a]Gen 9:6; Ex 20:13; Lev 24:17; Matt 5:21f; 19:18; Mark 10:19; Rom 13:9; James 2:11
18 [a]Ex 20:14; Lev 20:10; Matt 5:27f; 19:18; Mark 10:19; Luke 18:20; Rom 13:9; James 2:11
19 [a]Ex 20:15; Lev 19:11
20 [a]Ex 20:16; 23:1; Matt 19:18
21 [a]Ex 20:17; Rom 7:7; 13:9
22 [a]Ex 24:12; 31:18; Deut 4:13
25 [a]Ex 20:18, 19; Deut 18:16
26 [a]Deut 4:33
27 [1]Lit *Go yourself*
28 [a]Deut 18:17
29 [a]Ps 81:13; Is 48:18 [b]Deut 11:1 [c]Deut 5:16, 33
31 [a]Ex 24:12

32 "So you shall observe to do just as the LORD your God has
commanded you; [a]you shall not turn aside to the right or to the left.
33 "[a]You shall walk in all the way which the LORD your God has
commanded you, [b]that you may live and that it may be well
with you, and that you may prolong *your* days in the land
which you will possess.

Chapter 6 Theme ____________________

6 "Now this is the commandment, the statutes and the judgments which the LORD your God has commanded *me* to
teach you, that you might do *them* in the land where you are
going over to possess it,
2 so that you and your son and your grandson might [a]fear the
LORD your God, to keep all His statutes and His commandments
which I command you, [b]all the days of your life, and that your
days may be prolonged.
3 "O Israel, you should listen and [1]be careful to do *it,* that [a]it
may be well with you and that you may multiply greatly, just as
the LORD, the God of your fathers, has promised you, *in* [b]a land
flowing with milk and honey.
4 "[a]Hear, O Israel! The LORD is our God, the [b]LORD is one!
5 "[a]You shall love the LORD your God [b]with all your heart and
with all your soul and with all your might.
6 "[a]These words, which I am commanding you today, shall be
on your heart.
7 "[a]You shall teach them diligently to your sons and shall talk
of them when you sit in your house and when you walk by the
way and when you lie down and when you rise up.
8 "[a]You shall bind them as a sign on your hand and they shall
be as [1]frontals [2]on your forehead.
9 "[a]You shall write them on the doorposts of your house and
on your gates.
10 "Then it shall come about when the LORD your God brings
you into the land which He swore to your fathers, Abraham,
Isaac and Jacob, to give you, [a]great and splendid cities which
you did not build,
11 and houses full of all good things which you did not fill,
and hewn cisterns which you did not dig, vineyards and olive
trees which you did not plant, and [a]you eat and are satisfied,
12 then watch yourself, that [a]you do not forget the LORD who
brought you from the land of Egypt, out of the house of [1]slavery.
13 "[a]You shall [1]fear *only* the LORD your God; and you shall
[2]worship Him and [b]swear by His name.
14 "[a]You shall not follow other gods, any of the gods of the
peoples who surround you,
15 for the LORD your God in the midst of you is a [a]jealous God;
otherwise the anger of the LORD your God will be kindled
against you, and He will [1]wipe you off the face of the earth.
16 "[a]You shall not put the LORD your God to the test, [b]as you
tested *Him* at Massah.

32 [a]Deut 17:20; 28:14; Josh 1:7; 23:6; Prov 4:27
33 [a]Deut 10:12; Jer 7:23; Luke 1:6 [b]Deut 4:1, 40; 12:25, 28; 22:7; Eph 6:3
6:2 [a]Ex 20:20; Deut 10:12; Ps 111:10; 128:1; Eccl 12:13 [b]Deut 4:9
3 [1]Lit *keep* [a]Deut 5:33 [b]Ex 3:8, 17
4 [a]Matt 22:37; Mark 12:29, 30; Luke 10:27 [b]Deut 4:35, 39; John 10:30; 1 Cor 8:4; Eph 4:6
5 [a]Matt 22:37; Mark 12:30; Luke 10:27 [b]Deut 4:29; 10:12
6 [a]Deut 11:18
7 [a]Deut 4:9; 11:19; Eph 6:4
8 [1]Or *frontlet bands* [2]Lit *between your eyes* [a]Ex 12:14; 13:9, 16; Deut 11:18; Prov 3:3; 6:21; 7:3
9 [a]Deut 11:20
10 [a]Deut 9:1; 19:1; Josh 24:13; Ps 105:44
11 [a]Deut 8:10; 11:15; 14:29
12 [1]Lit *slaves* [a]Deut 4:9
13 [1]Or *reverence* [2]Or *serve* [a]Deut 13:4; Matt 4:10; Luke 4:8 [b]Deut 5:11; 10:20; Ps 63:11; Matt 5:33
14 [a]Jer 25:6
15 [1]Lit *destroy* [a]Deut 4:24; 5:9
16 [a]Matt 4:7; Luke 4:12 [b]Ex 17:7

17 "[a]You should diligently keep the commandments of the LORD
your God, and His testimonies and His statutes which He has
commanded you.
18 "You shall do what is right and good in the sight of the LORD,
that [a]it may be well with you and that you may go in and possess
the good land which the LORD swore to *give* your fathers,
19 by driving out all your enemies from before you, as the
LORD has spoken.
20 "[a]When your son asks you in time to come, saying, 'What
do the testimonies and the statutes and the judgments *mean*
which the LORD our God commanded you?'
21 then you shall say to your son, 'We were slaves to Pharaoh in
Egypt, and the LORD brought us from Egypt with a mighty hand.
22 'Moreover, the LORD showed great and distressing signs and
wonders before our eyes against Egypt, Pharaoh and all his
household;
23 He brought us out from there in order to bring us in, to
give us the land which He had sworn to our fathers.'
24 "So the LORD commanded us to observe all these statutes, [a]to
fear the LORD our God for our good always and [b]for our survival,
as *it is* today.
25 "[a]It will be righteousness for us if we [1]are careful to observe
all this commandment before the LORD our God, just as He
commanded us.

Chapter 7 Theme ____________________

7 "[a]When the LORD your God brings you into the land where
you are entering to possess it, and clears away many nations
before you, the Hittites and the Girgashites and the Amorites
and the Canaanites and the Perizzites and the Hivites and the
Jebusites, [b]seven nations greater and stronger than you,
2 and when the LORD your God delivers them before you and
you [1]defeat them, [a]then you shall [2]utterly destroy them. [b]You
shall make no covenant with them [c]and show no favor to them.
3 "Furthermore, [a]you shall not intermarry with them; you
shall not give your [1]daughters to [2]their sons, nor shall you take
[3]their daughters for your [4]sons.
4 "For [1]they will turn your [2]sons away from [3]following Me to
serve other gods; then the anger of the LORD will be kindled
against you and [a]He will quickly destroy you.
5 "But thus you shall do to them: [a]you shall tear down their
altars, and smash their *sacred* pillars, and hew down their
[1]Asherim, and burn their graven images with fire.
6 "For you are [a]a holy people to the LORD your God; the LORD
your God has chosen you to be [b]a people for His [1]own possession
out of all the peoples who are on the face of the [2]earth.
7 "[a]The LORD did not set His love on you nor choose you
because you were more in number than any of the peoples, for
you were the fewest of all peoples,
8 but because the LORD loved you and kept the [a]oath which
He swore to your forefathers, [b]the LORD brought you out by a

17 [a]Deut 11:22; Ps 119:4

18 [a]Deut 4:40

20 [a]Ex 13:8, 14

24 [a]Deut 10:12; Jer 32:39 [b]Ps 41:2; Luke 10:28

25 [1]Lit *keep* [a]Deut 24:13; Rom 10:3

7:1 [a]Deut 20:16-18 [b]Acts 13:19

2 [1]Lit *smite* [2]Lit *surely devote to the ban* [a]Num 31:17; Josh 11:11 [b]Ex 23:32 [c]Deut 7:16; 13:8

3 [1]Lit *daughter* [2]Lit *his son* [3]Lit *his daughter* [4]Lit *son* [a]Ex 34:15, 16; Josh 23:12; Ezra 9:2

4 [1]Lit *he* [2]Lit *son* [3]Lit *after* [a]Deut 4:26

5 [1]I.e. wooden symbols of a female deity [a]Ex 23:24; 34:13; Deut 12:3

6 [1]Or *special treasure* [2]Lit *ground* [a]Ex 19:6; Deut 14:2, 21; Ps 50:5; Jer 2:3 [b]Ex 19:5; Deut 4:20; 14:2; 26:18; Ps 135:4; Titus 2:14; 1 Pet 2:9

7 [a]Deut 4:37

8 [a]Ex 32:13 [b]Ex 13:3

mighty hand and redeemed you from the house of [1]slavery,
from the hand of Pharaoh king of Egypt.
9 "Know therefore that the LORD your God, [a]He is God, [b]the
faithful God, [c]who keeps [1]His covenant and [1]His lovingkindness
to a thousandth generation with those who [d]love Him and keep
His commandments;
10 but [a]repays those who hate Him to [1]their faces, to destroy
[2]them; He will not delay [3]with him who hates Him, He will
repay him to his face.
11 "Therefore, you shall keep the commandment and the statutes
and the judgments which I am commanding you today, to do them.
12 "[a]Then it shall come about, because you listen to these
judgments and keep and do them, that the LORD your God will
keep with you [1]His covenant and [1]His lovingkindness which
He swore to your forefathers.
13 "He will [a]love you and bless you and [b]multiply you; He will
also bless the fruit of your womb and the fruit of your ground,
your grain and your new wine and your oil, the increase of
your herd and the young of your flock, [1]in the land which He
swore to your forefathers to give you.
14 "You shall be blessed above all peoples; there will be no
male or female [a]barren among you or among your cattle.
15 "[a]The LORD will remove from you all sickness; and He will
not put on you any of the harmful diseases of Egypt which you
have known, but He will lay them on all who hate you.
16 "You shall consume all the peoples whom the LORD your
God will deliver to you; [a]your eye shall not pity them, nor shall
you serve their gods, for that *would be* [b]a snare to you.
17 "If you should say in your heart, 'These nations are greater
than I; how can I [a]dispossess them?'
18 you shall not be afraid of them; you shall well [a]remember
what the LORD your God did to Pharaoh and to all Egypt:
19 [a]the great trials which your eyes saw and the signs and the
wonders and the mighty hand and the outstretched arm by
which the LORD your God brought you out. So shall the LORD
your God do to all the peoples of whom you are afraid.
20 "Moreover, the LORD your God will send [a]the hornet against
them, until those who are left and hide themselves from you perish.
21 "You shall not dread [1]them, for [a]the LORD your God is in
your midst, [b]a great and awesome God.
22 "[a]The LORD your God will clear away these nations before
you little by little; you will not be able to put an end to them
quickly, for the [1]wild beasts would grow too numerous for you.
23 "[a]But the LORD your God will deliver them before you, and
will [1]throw them into great confusion until they are destroyed.
24 "[a]He will deliver their kings into your hand so that you will
make their name perish from under heaven; [b]no man will be
able to stand before you until you have destroyed them.
25 "The graven images of their gods you are to [a]burn with fire;
you shall [b]not covet the silver or the gold that is on them, nor
take it for yourselves, or you will be [c]snared by it, for it is an
[d]abomination to the LORD your God.

8 [1]Lit *slaves*

9 [1]Lit *the* [a]Deut 4:35, 39 [b]Is 49:7; 1 Cor 1:9; 1 Thess 5:24; 2 Tim 2:13 [c]Ex 20:6; Dan 9:4 [d]Deut 5:10

10 [1]Lit *his face* [2]Lit *him* [3]Lit *to* [a]Is 59:18; Nah 1:2

12 [1]Lit *the* [a]Lev 26:3-13; Deut 28:1-14

13 [1]Lit *on the ground* [a]Ps 146:8; Prov 15:9; John 14:21 [b]Lev 26:9; Deut 13:17; 30:5

14 [a]Ex 23:26

15 [a]Ex 15:26

16 [a]Deut 7:2 [b]Ex 23:33; Judg 8:27; Ps 106:36

17 [a]Num 33:53

18 [a]Ps 105:5

19 [a]Deut 4:34

20 [a]Ex 23:28; Josh 24:12

21 [1]Lit *from before them* [a]Ex 29:45; Josh 3:10 [b]Deut 10:17; Neh 1:5; 9:32

22 [1]Lit *beasts of the field* [a]Ex 23:29, 30

23 [1]Lit *confuse them with* [a]Ex 23:27; Josh 10:10

24 [a]Josh 6:2; 10:23-25 [b]Deut 11:25; Josh 1:5; 10:8; 23:9

25 [a]Ex 32:20; Deut 12:3; 1 Chr 14:12 [b]Ex 20:17 [c]Deut 7:16; Judg 8:27 [d]Deut 17:1

26 "You shall not bring an abomination into your house, and like
it come under the [a]ban; you shall utterly detest it and you shall
utterly abhor it, for it is something banned.

Chapter 8 Theme ______________________

8 "All the commandments that I am commanding you today
you shall be careful to do, that you [a]may live and multiply,
and go in and possess the land which the LORD swore *to give* to
your forefathers.
2 "[a]You shall remember all the way which the LORD your God
has [b]led you in the wilderness these forty years, that He might
humble you, [c]testing you, to know what was in your heart,
whether you would keep His commandments or not.
3 "He humbled you and let you be hungry, and fed you with
manna which you did not know, nor did your fathers know, that
He might make you [1]understand that [a]man does not live by bread
alone, but man lives by everything that proceeds out of the
mouth of the LORD.
4 "[a]Your clothing did not wear out on you, nor did your foot
swell these forty years.
5 "[a]Thus you are to know in your heart that the LORD your God
was disciplining you just as a man disciplines his son.
6 "Therefore, you shall keep the commandments of the LORD
your God, to walk in His ways and to [1]fear Him.
7 "For [a]the LORD your God is bringing you into a good land, a
land of brooks of water, of fountains and springs, flowing forth
in valleys and hills;
8 a land of wheat and barley, of vines and fig trees and
pomegranates, a land of olive oil and honey;
9 a land where you will eat food without scarcity, in which
you will not lack anything; a land whose stones are iron, and
out of whose hills you can dig copper.
10 "When [a]you have eaten and are satisfied, you shall bless the
LORD your God for the good land which He has given you.
11 "[1]Beware that you do not [a]forget the LORD your God by not
keeping His commandments and His ordinances and His
statutes which I am commanding you today;
12 otherwise, [a]when you have eaten and are satisfied, and have
built good houses and lived *in them,*
13 and when your herds and your flocks multiply, and your silver
and gold multiply, and all that you have multiplies,
14 then your heart will become [1]proud and you will [a]forget the
LORD your God who brought you out from the land of Egypt,
out of the house of [2]slavery.
15 "He led you through [a]the great and terrible wilderness, *with
its* [b]fiery serpents and scorpions and thirsty ground where there
was no water; He [c]brought water for you out of the rock of flint.
16 "In the wilderness He fed you manna [a]which your fathers
did not know, that He might humble you and that He might
[b]test you, to do good for you [1]in the end.

26 [a]Lev 27:28f

8:1 [a]Deut 4:1

2 [a]Deut 8:16 [b]Ps 136:16; Amos 2:10 [c]Ex 15:25; 20:20; 2 Chr 32:31

3 [1]Lit *know* [a]Matt 4:4; Luke 4:4

4 [a]Deut 29:5; Neh 9:21

5 [a]Deut 4:36; 2 Sam 7:14; Prov 3:12; Heb 12:6; Rev 3:19

6 [1]Or *reverence*

7 [a]Deut 11:9-12; Jer 2:7

10 [a]Deut 6:11

11 [1]Lit *Take heed to yourself* [a]Deut 4:9

12 [a]Prov 30:9; Hos 13:6

14 [1]Lit *lifted up* [2]Lit *slaves* [a]Deut 8:11; Ps 106:21

15 [a]Deut 1:19; Jer 2:6 [b]Num 21:6 [c]Ex 17:6; Num 20:11; Deut 32:13; Ps 78:15; 114:8

16 [1]Lit *at your end* [a]Ex 16:15 [b]Deut 8:2

17“Otherwise, [a]you may say in your heart, ‘My power and the
strength of my hand made me this wealth.’
18“But you shall remember the LORD your God, for [a]it is He
who is giving you power to make wealth, that He may confirm
His covenant which He swore to your fathers, as *it is* this day.
19“It shall come about if you ever forget the LORD your God
and go after other gods and serve them and worship them, [a]I
testify against you today that you will surely perish.
20“Like the nations that the LORD makes to perish before you,
so [a]you shall perish; because you would not listen to the voice
of the LORD your God.

Chapter 9 Theme ______________________

9 “Hear, O Israel! You are crossing over the Jordan today to
go in to dispossess [a]nations greater and mightier than you,
great cities [1b]fortified to heaven,
2 a people great and tall, the sons of the Anakim, whom you
know and of whom you have heard *it said,* ‘[a]Who can stand
before the sons of Anak?’
3“Know therefore today that [a]it is the LORD your God who is
crossing over before you as [b]a consuming fire. He will destroy them
and He will subdue them before you, so that [c]you may drive them
out and destroy them quickly, just as the LORD has spoken to you.
4“[a]Do not say in your heart when the LORD your God has driven
them out before [1]you, ‘Because of my righteousness the LORD has
brought me in to possess this land,’ but *it is* [b]because of the
wickedness of these nations *that* the LORD is dispossessing them
before you.
5“It is [a]not for your righteousness or for the uprightness of your
heart that you are going to possess their land, but *it is* because of
the wickedness of these nations *that* the LORD your God is driving
them out before you, in order to confirm [b]the [1]oath which the
LORD swore to your fathers, to Abraham, Isaac and Jacob.
6“Know, then, *it is* not because of your righteousness *that* the
LORD your God is giving you this good land to possess, for you
are [a]a [1]stubborn people.
7“Remember, do not forget how you provoked the LORD your
God to wrath in the wilderness; [a]from the day that you left the
land of Egypt until you arrived at this place, you have been
rebellious against the LORD.
8“Even [a]at Horeb you provoked the LORD to wrath, and the
LORD was so angry with you that He would have destroyed you.
9“When I went up to the mountain to receive the tablets of
stone, the tablets of the covenant which the LORD had made
with you, then I remained on the mountain forty days and
nights; [a]I neither ate bread nor drank water.
10“The LORD gave me the two tablets of stone [a]written by the
finger of God; and on them *were* all the words which the LORD
had spoken with you at the mountain from the midst of the fire
on the day of the assembly.

17 [a]Deut 9:4
18 [a]Prov 10:22; Hos 2:8
19 [a]Deut 4:26; 30:18
20 [a]Ezek 5:5-17
9:1 [1]Lit *and fortified* [a]Deut 4:38; 7:1; 11:23 [b]Deut 1:28
2 [a]Num 13:22, 28, 33; Josh 11:21, 22
3 [a]Deut 31:3; Josh 3:11 [b]Deut 4:24; Heb 12:29 [c]Ex 23:31; Deut 7:24
4 [1]Lit *you saying* [a]Deut 8:17; 9:7, 24; 31:27 [b]Lev 18:3, 24-30; Deut 12:31; 18:9-14
5 [1]Lit *word* [a]Titus 3:5 [b]Gen 12:7; 13:15; 15:7; 17:8; 26:4; 28:13
6 [1]Or *stiff-necked* [a]Deut 9:13; 10:16; 31:27
7 [a]Ex 14:10f; Num 14:22
8 [a]Ex 32:7-10; Ps 106:19
9 [a]Ex 24:18; 34:28; Deut 8:3; 9:18
10 [a]Deut 4:13

11 "It came about [a]at the end of forty days and nights that the
LORD gave me the two tablets of stone, the tablets of the covenant.
12 "[a]Then the LORD said to me, 'Arise, go down from here quickly,
for your people whom you brought out of Egypt have acted corruptly. They have [b]quickly turned aside from the way which I
commanded them; they have made a molten image for themselves.'
13 "The [a]LORD spoke further to me, saying, 'I have seen this
people, and indeed, it is a [1b]stubborn people.
14 '[a]Let Me alone, that I may destroy them and [b]blot out their
name from under heaven; and I will make of you a nation
mightier and greater than they.'
15 "[a]So I turned and came down from the mountain while the
mountain was burning with fire, and the two tablets of the
covenant were in my two hands.
16 "And I saw that you had indeed sinned against the LORD your
God. You had made for yourselves a molten calf; you had turned
aside quickly from the way which the LORD had commanded you.
17 "I took hold of the two tablets and threw them from my
hands and smashed them before your eyes.
18 "[a]I fell down before the LORD, [b]as at the first, forty days and
nights; [c]I neither ate bread nor drank water, [d]because of all
your sin which you had committed in doing what was evil in
the sight of the LORD to provoke Him to anger.
19 "For [a]I was afraid of the anger and hot displeasure with which
the LORD was wrathful against you in order to destroy you, [b]but
the LORD listened to me that time also.
20 "The LORD was angry enough with Aaron to destroy him; so
I also prayed for Aaron at the same time.
21 "[a]I took your [1]sinful *thing,* the calf which you had made,
and burned it with fire and crushed it, grinding it very small
until it was as fine as dust; and I threw its dust into the brook
that came down from the mountain.
22 "Again at [a]Taberah and at [b]Massah and at [c]Kibroth-hattaavah
you provoked the LORD to wrath.
23 "When the LORD sent you from [a]Kadesh-barnea, saying, '[b]Go
up and possess the land which I have given you,' then you
rebelled against the [1]command of the LORD your God; [c]you
neither believed Him nor listened to His voice.
24 "[a]You have been rebellious against the LORD from the day I
knew you.
25 "[a]So I fell down before the LORD the forty days and nights,
which I [1]did because the LORD had said He would destroy you.
26 "[a]I prayed to the LORD and said, 'O Lord GOD, do not destroy
Your people, even Your inheritance, whom You have redeemed
through Your greatness, whom You have brought out of Egypt
with a mighty hand.
27 'Remember Your servants, Abraham, Isaac, and Jacob; do
not look at the stubbornness of this people or at their wickedness
or their sin.
28 'Otherwise the land from which You brought us may say,
"[a]Because the LORD was not able to bring them into the land

11 [a]Deut 9:9
12 [a]Ex 32:7, 8 [b]Judg 2:17
13 [1]Or *stiff-necked* [a]Ex 32:9 [b]Deut 10:16; 31:27; 2 Kin 17:14
14 [a]Ex 32:10 [b]Ps 9:5; 109:13
15 [a]Ex 32:15-19
18 [a]Ex 34:28 [b]Deut 10:10 [c]Deut 9:9 [d]Ex 34:9
19 [a]Ex 32:10f; Heb 12:21 [b]Ex 34:10; Deut 10:10
21 [1]Lit *sin* [a]Ex 32:20
22 [a]Num 11:3 [b]Ex 17:7 [c]Num 11:34
23 [1]Lit *mouth* [a]Deut 1:2 [b]Deut 1:21 [c]Deut 1:26; Ps 106:24
24 [a]Deut 9:7; 31:27
25 [1]Lit *fell down* [a]Deut 9:18
26 [a]Ex 32:11-13; 1 Sam 7:9; Jer 15:1
28 [a]Ex 32:12; Num 14:16

which He had [1]promised them and because He hated them He
has brought them out to slay them in the wilderness."
29 'Yet they are Your people, even [a]Your inheritance, whom You
have brought out by Your [b]great power and Your outstretched arm.'

Chapter 10 Theme ______________________________

10 "At that time the LORD said to me, '[a]Cut out for yourself
two tablets of stone like the former ones, and come up to
Me on the mountain, and [b]make an ark of wood for yourself.
2 '[a]I will write on the tablets the words that were on the former
tablets which you shattered, and [b]you shall put them in the ark.'
3 "So [a]I made an ark of acacia wood and [b]cut out two tablets
of stone like the former ones, and went up on the mountain
with the two tablets in my hand.
4 "He wrote on the tablets, like the former writing, [a]the Ten
[1]Commandments [b]which the LORD had spoken to you on the
mountain from the midst of the fire [c]on the day of the assembly;
and the LORD gave them to me.
5 "Then I turned and [a]came down from the mountain and
[b]put the tablets in the ark which I had made; [c]and there they
are, as the LORD commanded me."
6 (Now the sons of Israel set out from [1]Beeroth [a]Bene-jaakan
to Moserah. [b]There Aaron died and there he was buried and
Eleazar his son ministered as priest in his place.
7 [a]From there they set out to Gudgodah, and from Gudgodah
to Jotbathah, a land of brooks of water.
8 [a]At that time the LORD set apart the tribe of Levi to carry
the ark of the covenant of the LORD, to stand before the LORD
[b]to serve Him and to bless in His name until this day.
9 [a]Therefore, Levi does not have a portion or inheritance
with his brothers; the LORD is his inheritance, just as the LORD
your God spoke to him.)
10 "[a]I, moreover, stayed on the mountain forty days and forty
nights like the first time, and the LORD listened to me that time
also; the LORD was not willing to destroy you.
11 "Then the LORD said to me, 'Arise, proceed on your journey
ahead of the people, that they may go in and possess the land
which I swore to their fathers to give them.'
12 "[a]Now, Israel, what does the LORD your God require from
you, but to [1]fear the LORD your God, to walk in all His ways and
[b]love Him, and to serve the LORD your God with [c]all your heart
and with all your soul,
13 *and* to keep the LORD'S commandments and His statutes
which I am commanding you today for your good?
14 "Behold, [a]to the LORD your God belong heaven and the
[1]highest heavens, [b]the earth and all that is in it.
15 "[a]Yet on your fathers did the LORD set His affection to love
them, and He chose their [1]descendants after them, *even* you
above all peoples, as *it is* this day.
16 "[a]So circumcise [1]your heart, and [b]stiffen your neck no longer.

28 [1]Lit *spoken to*
29 [a]Deut 4:20; 1 Kin 8:51; Neh 1:10; Ps 106:40 [b]Deut 4:34
10:1 [a]Ex 34:1 [b]Ex 25:10
2 [a]Deut 4:13 [b]Ex 25:16
3 [a]Ex 25:5; 37:1-9 [b]Ex 34:4
4 [1]Lit *Words* [a]Ex 34:28; Deut 4:13 [b]Ex 20:1 [c]Deut 9:10; 18:16
5 [a]Ex 34:29 [b]Ex 40:20 [c]1 Kin 8:9
6 [1]Or *the wells of the sons of Jaakan* [a]Num 33:30, 31 [b]Num 20:25-28; 33:38
7 [a]Num 33:33, 34
8 [a]Num 3:6; 18:1-7; Deut 31:9 [b]Deut 17:12; 18:5; 21:5
9 [a]Num 18:20, 24; Deut 18:1, 2; Ezek 44:28
10 [a]Ex 34:28; Deut 9:18
12 [1]Or *reverence* [a]Mic 6:8 [b]Deut 6:5; Matt 22:37; 1 Tim 1:5 [c]Deut 4:29
14 [1]Lit *heaven of heavens* [a]1 Kin 8:27; Neh 9:6; Ps 68:33; 115:16 [b]Ps 24:1
15 [1]Lit *seed* [a]Deut 4:37
16 [1]Lit *the foreskin of your heart* [a]Lev 26:41; Jer 4:4 [b]Deut 9:6

17 "[a]For the LORD your God is the God of gods and the [b]Lord of
lords, the great, the mighty, and the awesome God [c]who does
not show partiality nor [d]take a bribe.
18 "He executes justice for [a]the orphan and the widow, and
shows His love for the alien by giving him food and clothing.
19 "[a]So show your love for the alien, for you were aliens in the
land of Egypt.
20 "You shall fear the LORD your God; you shall serve Him and
[a]cling to Him, and [b]you shall swear by His name.
21 "He is [a]your praise and He is your God, who has done these
great and awesome things for you which your eyes have seen.
22 "[a]Your fathers went down to Egypt seventy persons *in all,*
[b]and now the LORD your God has made you as numerous as the
stars of heaven.

Chapter 11 Theme ____________________

11 "You shall therefore [a]love the LORD your God, and always
[b]keep His charge, His statutes, His ordinances, and His
commandments.
2 "Know this day [a]that I *am* not *speaking* with your sons who
have not known and who have not seen the [1]discipline of the
LORD your God—His greatness, His mighty hand and His outstretched arm,
3 and [a]His signs and His works which He did in the midst of
Egypt to Pharaoh the king of Egypt and to all his land;
4 and what He did to Egypt's army, to its horses and its
chariots, [a]when He made the water of the [1]Red Sea to [2]engulf
them while they were pursuing you, and the LORD [3]completely
destroyed them;
5 and what He did to you in the wilderness until you came to
this place;
6 and [a]what He did to Dathan and Abiram, the sons of Eliab,
the son of Reuben, when the earth opened its mouth and
swallowed them, their households, their tents, and [b]every
living thing that [1]followed them, among all Israel—
7 but your own eyes have seen all the great work of the LORD
which He did.
8 "You shall therefore keep every commandment which I am
commanding you today, [a]so that you may be strong and go in
and possess the land into which you are about to cross to
possess it;
9 [a]so that you may prolong *your* days on the land which the
LORD swore to your fathers to give to them and to their
[1]descendants, [b]a land flowing with milk and honey.
10 "For the land, into which you are entering to possess it, is
not like the land of Egypt from which you came, where you
used to sow your seed and water it with your [1]foot like a
vegetable garden.
11 "But [a]the land into which you are about to cross to possess it,
a land of hills and valleys, drinks water from the rain of heaven,

17 [a]Josh 22:22; Ps 136:2; Dan 2:47; 1 Tim 6:15; Rev 19:16 [b]Rev 17:14 [c]Deut 1:17; Acts 10:34; Rom 2:11; Gal 2:6; Eph 6:9 [d]Deut 16:19

18 [a]Ex 22:22-24; Ps 68:5; 146:9

19 [a]Lev 19:34; Ezek 47:22, 23

20 [a]Deut 11:22; 13:4 [b]Deut 5:11; 6:13; Ps 63:11

21 [a]Ps 109:1; 148:14; Jer 17:14

22 [a]Gen 46:27 [b]Gen 15:5; 22:17; Deut 1:10

11:1 [a]Deut 6:5; 10:12 [b]Lev 18:30; 22:9

2 [1]Or *instruction* [a]Deut 4:34

3 [a]Ex 7:8-21

4 [1]Lit *Sea of Reeds* [2]Lit *flow over their faces* [3]Lit *to this day* [a]Ex 14:28; Deut 1:40; 2:1

6 [1]Lit *was at their feet* [a]Num 16:1-35; Ps 106:16-18 [b]Num 26:10, 11

8 [a]Deut 31:6, 7, 23; Josh 1:6, 7

9 [1]Lit *seed* [a]Deut 4:40; 5:16, 33; 6:2; Prov 10:27 [b]Ex 3:8

10 [1]I.e. probably a treadmill

11 [a]Deut 8:7

12 a land for which the LORD your God cares; [a]the eyes of the
LORD your God are always on it, from the [1]beginning even to
the end of the year.
13 "It shall come about, [a]if you listen obediently to my commandments which I am commanding you today, [b]to love the LORD
your God and to serve Him [c]with all your heart and all your soul,
14 that [1a]He will give the rain for your land in its season, the
[2b]early and [3]late rain, that you may gather in your grain and your
new wine and your oil.
15 "[1a]He will give grass in your fields for your cattle, and [b]you
will eat and be satisfied.
16 "[1a]Beware that your hearts are not deceived, and that you
do not turn away and serve other gods and worship them.
17 "Or [a]the anger of the LORD will be kindled against you, and
He will [b]shut up the heavens [c]so that there will be no rain and
the ground will not yield its fruit; and [d]you will perish quickly
from the good land which the LORD is giving you.
18 "[a]You shall therefore [1]impress these words of mine on your
heart and on your soul; and you shall bind them as a sign on
your hand, and they shall be as [2]frontals [3]on your forehead.
19 "[a]You shall teach them to your sons, talking of them when
you sit in your house and when you walk along the road and
when you lie down and when you rise up.
20 "[a]You shall write them on the doorposts of your house and
on your gates,
21 so that [a]your days and the days of your sons may be
multiplied on the land which the LORD swore to your fathers to
give them, as [1b]long as the heavens *remain* above the earth.
22 "For if you are [a]careful to keep all this commandment which
I am commanding you to do, [b]to love the LORD your God, to
walk in all His ways and [c]hold fast to Him,
23 then the LORD will [a]drive out all these nations from before you,
and you will [b]dispossess nations greater and mightier than you.
24 "[a]Every place on which the sole of your foot treads shall be
yours; [b]your border will be from the wilderness to Lebanon, *and*
from the river, the river Euphrates, as far as [1]the western sea.
25 "[a]No man will be able to stand before you; the LORD your
God will lay the dread of you and the fear of you on all the land
on which you set foot, as He has spoken to you.
26 "[a]See, I am setting before you today a blessing and a curse:
27 the [a]blessing, if you listen to the commandments of the
LORD your God, which I am commanding you today;
28 and the [a]curse, if you do not listen to the commandments
of the LORD your God, but turn aside from the way which I am
commanding you today, [1]by following other gods which you
have not known.
29 "It shall come about, when the LORD your God brings you into
the land where you are entering to possess it, [a]that you shall place
the blessing on Mount Gerizim and the curse on Mount Ebal.
30 "Are they not across the Jordan, west of the way toward the
sunset, in the land of the Canaanites who live in the Arabah,
opposite [a]Gilgal, beside [b]the [1]oaks of Moreh?

12 [1]Lit *beginning of the year* [a]1 Kin 9:3
13 [a]Lev 26:3; Deut 7:12 [b]Deut 11:1 [c]Deut 4:29
14 [1]So some ancient versions; M.T. reads *I* [2]I.e. autumn [3]I.e. spring [a]Lev 26:4; Deut 28:12 [b]Joel 2:23; James 5:7
15 [1]So some ancient versions; M.T. reads *I* [a]Ps 104:14 [b]Deut 6:11
16 [1]Lit *Watch yourselves* [a]Job 31:27
17 [a]Deut 6:15; 9:19 [b]1 Kin 8:35; 2 Chr 6:26; 7:13 [c]Deut 28:24 [d]Deut 4:26
18 [1]Lit *put* [2]Lit *frontlet bands* [3]Lit *between your eyes* [a]Ex 13:9, 16; Deut 6:8
19 [a]Deut 4:9, 10; 6:7; Prov 22:6
20 [a]Deut 6:9
21 [1]Lit *the days of the heavens* [a]Prov 3:2; 4:10; 9:11 [b]Ps 72:5
22 [a]Deut 6:17 [b]Deut 11:1 [c]Deut 10:20
23 [a]Deut 4:38 [b]Deut 9:1
24 [1]I.e. the Mediterranean [a]Josh 1:3; 14:9 [b]Gen 15:18; Ex 23:31; Deut 1:7, 8
25 [a]Ex 23:27; Deut 7:24
26 [a]Deut 30:1, 19
27 [a]Deut 28:1-14
28 [1]Lit *to follow* [a]Deut 28:15-68
29 [a]Deut 27:12; Josh 8:33
30 [1]Lit *terebinths* [a]Josh 4:19 [b]Gen 12:6

31 "For you are about to cross the Jordan to go in to possess the
land which the LORD your God is giving you, and [a]you shall
possess it and live in it,
32 and you shall be careful to do all the statutes and the
judgments which I am setting before you today.

Chapter 12 Theme ______________________

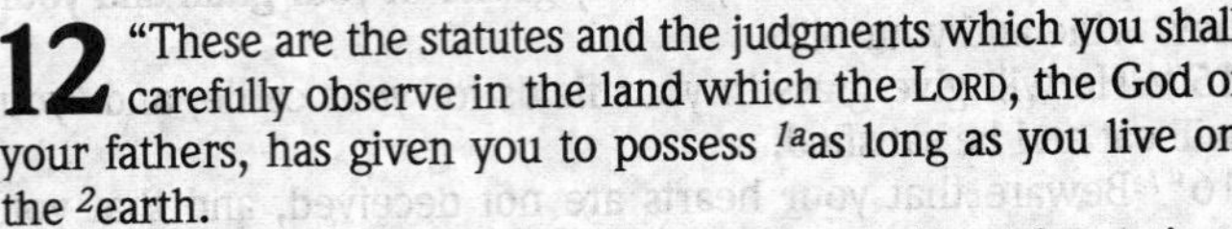

12 "These are the statutes and the judgments which you shall
carefully observe in the land which the LORD, the God of
your fathers, has given you to possess [1a]as long as you live on
the [2]earth.

RETURN TO INSTRUCTIONS

2 "You shall utterly destroy all the places where the nations
whom you shall dispossess serve their gods, on the [a]high
mountains and on the hills and under every green tree.
3 "[a]You shall tear down their altars and smash their *sacred* pillars
and burn their [1]Asherim with fire, and you shall cut down the
engraved images of their gods and [b]obliterate their name from
that place.
4 "You shall not act like this toward the LORD your God.
5 "[a]But you shall seek *the LORD* at the place which the LORD
your God will choose from all your tribes, to establish His
name there for His dwelling, and there you shall come.
6 "There you shall bring your burnt offerings, your sacrifices,
[a]your tithes, the [1]contribution of your hand, your votive offerings,
your freewill offerings, and the firstborn of your herd and of
your flock.
7 "There also you and your households shall eat before the
LORD your God, and [a]rejoice in all [1]your undertakings in which
the LORD your God has blessed you.
8 "You shall not do at all what we are doing here today, every
man *doing* whatever is right in his own eyes;
9 for you have not as yet come to [a]the resting place and the
[b]inheritance which the LORD your God is giving you.
10 "When you cross the Jordan and live in the land which the
LORD your God is giving you to inherit, and [a]He gives you rest
from all your enemies around *you* so that you live in security,
11 [a]then it shall come about that the place in which the LORD
your God will choose for His name to dwell, there you shall
bring all that I command you: your burnt offerings and your
sacrifices, your tithes and the [1]contribution of your hand, and
all your choice votive offerings which you will vow to the LORD.
12 "And you shall [a]rejoice before the LORD your God, you and
your sons and daughters, your male and female servants, and
the [b]Levite who is within your gates, since [c]he has no portion
or inheritance with you.
13 "[a]Be careful that you do not offer your burnt offerings in
every *cultic* place you see,
14 but in the place which the LORD chooses in one of your
tribes, there you shall offer your burnt offerings, and there you
shall do all that I command you.

31 [a]Deut 17:14; Josh 21:43

12:1 [1]Lit *all the days* [2]Lit *ground* [a]Deut 4:9, 10; 1 Kin 8:40

2 [a]2 Kin 16:4; 17:10, 11

3 [1]I.e. wooden symbols of a female deity [a]Num 33:52; Deut 7:5; Judg 2:2 [b]Ex 23:13; Ps 16:4; Zech 13:2

5 [a]Ex 20:24; Deut 12:11, 13; 2 Chr 7:12; Ps 78:68

6 [1]Or *heave offering* [a]Deut 14:22

7 [1]Lit *the putting forth of your hand* [a]Lev 23:40; Deut 12:12, 18; 14:26; 28:47; Eccl 3:12, 13; 5:18-20

9 [a]Deut 3:20; 25:19; Ps 95:11 [b]Deut 4:21

10 [a]Josh 11:23

11 [1]Or *heave offering* [a]Deut 12:5; 15:20; 16:2; 17:8; 18:6

12 [a]Deut 12:7 [b]Deut 12:18, 19; 26:11-13 [c]Deut 10:9; 14:29

13 [a]Deut 12:5, 11

15 "[a]However, you may slaughter and eat meat within any of
your gates, [1]whatever you desire, according to the blessing of
the LORD your God which He has given you; the unclean and
the clean may eat of it, as of [b]the gazelle and the deer.
16 "[a]Only you shall not eat the blood; [b]you are to pour it out on
the ground like water.
17 "[a]You are not allowed to eat within your gates the tithe of
your grain or new wine or oil, or the firstborn of your herd or
flock, or any of your votive offerings which you vow, or your
freewill offerings, or the [1]contribution of your hand.
18 "But [a]you shall eat them before the LORD your God in [b]the
place which the LORD your God will choose, you and your son
and daughter, and your male and female servants, and the
[c]Levite who is within your gates; and you shall [d]rejoice before
the LORD your God in all [1]your undertakings.
19 "[a]Be careful that you do not forsake the Levite [1]as long as
you live in your land.
20 "When the LORD your God extends your border [a]as He has
promised you, and you say, 'I will eat meat,' because [1]you desire
to eat meat, *then* you may eat meat, [2]whatever you desire.
21 "If the place which the LORD your God chooses to put His
name is too far from you, then you may slaughter of your herd
and flock which the LORD has given you, as I have commanded
you; and you may eat within your gates [1]whatever you desire.
22 "Just as a gazelle or a deer is eaten, so you will eat it; the
unclean and the clean alike may eat of it.
23 "Only be sure [a]not to eat the blood, for the blood is the [1]life,
and you shall not eat the [1]life with the flesh.
24 "You shall not eat it; you shall pour it out on the ground like
water.
25 "You shall not eat it, so that [a]it may be well with you and
your sons after you, for [b]you will be doing what is right in the
sight of the LORD.
26 "[a]Only your holy things which you may have and your
votive offerings, you shall take and go to the place which the
LORD chooses.
27 "And [a]you shall offer your burnt offerings, the flesh and the
blood, on the altar of the LORD your God; and the blood of your
sacrifices shall be poured out on the altar of the LORD your God,
and [b]you shall eat the flesh.
28 "Be careful to listen to all these words which I command
you, so that [a]it may be well with you and your sons after you
forever, for you will be doing what is good and right in the
sight of the LORD your God.
29 "When [a]the LORD your God cuts off before you the nations
which you are going in to dispossess, and you dispossess them
and dwell in their land,
30 beware that you are not ensnared [1]to follow them, after
they are destroyed before you, and that you do not inquire after
their gods, saying, 'How do these nations serve their gods, that
I also may do likewise?'

15 [1]Lit *in every desire of your soul* [a]Deut 12:20-23 [b]Deut 12:22; 14:5; 15:22

16 [a]Gen 9:4; Lev 7:26; 17:10-12; 1 Sam 14:33f; Acts 15:20, 29 [b]Deut 15:23

17 [1]Lit *heave offering* [a]Deut 12:26

18 [1]Lit *the putting forth of your hand* [a]Deut 14:23 [b]Deut 12:5 [c]Deut 12:12 [d]Deut 12:7; Eccl 3:12f; 5:18-20

19 [1]Lit *all your days upon your land* [a]Deut 14:27

20 [1]Lit *your soul desires* [2]Lit *in every desire of your soul* [a]Gen 15:18; Deut 11:24; 19:8

21 [1]Lit *in every desire of your soul*

23 [1]Lit *soul* [a]Gen 9:4; Lev 17:10-14; Deut 12:16

25 [a]Deut 4:40; Is 3:10 [b]Ex 15:26; 1 Kin 11:38

26 [a]Num 5:9f; 18:19; Deut 12:17

27 [a]Lev 1:9, 13 [b]Lev 3:1-17

28 [a]Deut 4:40; Eccl 8:12

29 [a]Josh 23:4

30 [1]Lit *after them*

31 "[a]You shall not behave thus toward the LORD your God, for every abominable act which the LORD hates they have done for their gods; for [b]they even burn their sons and daughters in the fire to their gods.

32 "[1a]Whatever I command you, you shall be careful to do; [b]you shall not add to nor take away from it.

Chapter 13 Theme ____________________

13

"[1a]If a prophet or a dreamer of dreams arises among you and gives you a sign or a wonder,

2 and the sign or the wonder comes true, concerning which he spoke to you, saying, '[a]Let us go after other gods (whom you have not known) and let us serve them,'

3 you shall not listen to the words of that prophet or that dreamer of dreams; for the LORD your God is [a]testing you to find out if [b]you love the LORD your God with all your heart and with all your soul.

4 "[a]You shall follow the LORD your God and fear Him; and you shall keep His commandments, listen to His voice, serve Him, and [b]cling to Him.

5 "But that prophet or that dreamer of dreams shall be [a]put to death, because he has [1]counseled [2]rebellion against the LORD your God who brought you from the land of Egypt and redeemed you from the house of [3]slavery, [b]to seduce you from the way in which the LORD your God commanded you to walk. [c]So you shall purge the evil from among you.

6 "[a]If your brother, your mother's son, or your son or daughter, or the wife [1]you cherish, or your friend who is as your own soul, entice you secretly, saying, '[b]Let us go and serve other gods' (whom neither you nor your fathers have known,

7 of the gods of the peoples who are around you, near you or far from you, from one end of the earth to the other end),

8 [a]you shall not yield to him or listen to him; [b]and your eye shall not pity him, nor shall you spare or conceal him.

9 "[a]But you shall surely kill him; [b]your hand shall be first against him to put him to death, and afterwards the hand of all the people.

10 "So you shall stone him [1]to death because he has sought [a]to seduce you from the LORD your God who brought you out from the land of Egypt, out of the house of [2]slavery.

11 "Then [a]all Israel will hear and be afraid, and will never again do such a wicked thing among you.

12 "If you hear in one of your cities, which the LORD your God is giving you to live in, *anyone* saying *that*

13 some worthless men have gone out from among you and have seduced the inhabitants of their city, saying, '[a]Let us go and serve other gods' (whom you have not known),

14 then you shall investigate and search out and inquire thoroughly. If it is true *and* the matter established that this abomination has been done among you,

---

31 [a]Deut 9:5 [b]Lev 18:21; Deut 18:10; Ps 106:37; Jer 32:35

32 [1]Lit *Everything that* [a]Deut 4:2; Josh 1:7 [b]Prov 30:6; Rev 22:18

13:1 [1]Ch 13:2 in Heb [a]Matt 24:24; Mark 13:22; 2 Thess 2:9

2 [a]Deut 13:6, 13

3 [a]Ex 20:20; Deut 8:2, 16; 1 Cor 11:19 [b]Deut 6:5

4 [a]2 Kin 23:3; 2 Chr 34:31; 2 John 6 [b]Deut 10:20

5 [1]Lit *spoken* [2]Lit *turning aside* [3]Lit *slaves* [a]Deut 13:9, 15; 17:5; 1 Kin 18:40 [b]Deut 4:19; 13:10 [c]1 Cor 5:13

6 [1]Lit *of your bosom* [a]Deut 17:2-7; 29:18 [b]Deut 13:2

8 [a]Prov 1:10 [b]Deut 7:2

9 [a]Deut 13:5 [b]Lev 24:14; Deut 17:7

10 [1]Lit *with stones so that he dies* [2]Lit *slaves* [a]Deut 13:5

11 [a]Deut 19:20

13 [a]Deut 13:2

15 [1]Or *putting it under the ban* [a]Deut 13:5

15 [a]you shall surely strike the inhabitants of that city with the
edge of the sword, [1]utterly destroying it and all that is in it and
its cattle with the edge of the sword.

16 [1]Lit *mound* [a]Deut 7:25, 26 [b]Josh 8:28; Is 17:1; 25:2; Jer 49:2

16 "[a]Then you shall gather all its booty into the middle of its
open square and burn the city and all its booty with fire as a
whole burnt offering to the LORD your God; and it shall be a
[1b]ruin forever. It shall never be rebuilt.

17 [a]Ex 32:12; Num 25:4 [b]Deut 30:3 [c]Deut 7:13 [d]Gen 22:17; 26:4, 24; 28:14

17 "Nothing from that which is put under the ban shall cling to
your hand, in order that the LORD may turn from [a]His burning
anger and [b]show mercy to you, and have compassion on you
and [c]make you increase, just [d]as He has sworn to your fathers,

18 [1]Or *for* [2]Lit *to keep* [3]Lit *to do*

18 [1]if you will listen to the voice of the LORD your God,
[2]keeping all His commandments which I am commanding you
today, [3]and doing what is right in the sight of the LORD your God.

14:1 [1]Lit *make a baldness between your eyes* [a]Rom 8:16; 9:8, 26; Gal 3:26; 1 John 3:1 [b]Lev 19:28; 21:5; Jer 16:6; 41:5

Chapter 14 Theme ____________________

14 "You are [a]the sons of the LORD your God; [b]you shall not cut
yourselves nor [1]shave your forehead for the sake of the dead.

2 [1]Or *special treasure* [a]Lev 20:26; Deut 7:6; Rom 12:1 [b]Ex 19:5; Deut 4:20; 26:18; Titus 2:14; 1 Pet 2:9

2 "For you are [a]a holy people to the LORD your God, and the
LORD has chosen you to be a [b]people for His [1]own possession
out of all the peoples who are on the face of the earth.

3 [a]Ezek 4:14

3 "[a]You shall not eat any detestable thing.

4 [a]Lev 11:2-45; Acts 10:14

4 "[a]These are the animals which you may eat: the ox, the sheep,
the goat,

5 [1]Exact identification of these animals is uncertain

5 [1]the deer, the gazelle, the roebuck, the wild goat, the ibex,
the antelope and the mountain sheep.

6 [1]Lit *two hoofs* [2]Lit *brings up*

6 "Any animal that divides the hoof and has the hoof split in
[1]two *and* [2]chews the cud, among the animals, that you may eat.

7 [1]Lit *brings up* [2]Lit *a cleaving* [3]Or *hare* [4]A small, shy, furry animal *(Hyrax syriacus)* found in the peninsula of the Sinai, northern Israel, and the region round the Dead Sea; KJV *coney*, orig NASB *rock-badger*

7 "Nevertheless, you are not to eat of these among those which
[1]chew the cud, or among those that divide the hoof in [2]two: the
camel and the [3]rabbit and the [4]shaphan, for though they [1]chew
the cud, they do not divide the hoof; they are unclean for you.

8 "The pig, because it divides the hoof but *does* not *chew* the
cud, it is unclean for you. You shall not eat any of their flesh
nor touch their carcasses.

9 "These you may eat of all that are in water: anything that
has fins and scales you may eat,

10 but anything that does not have fins and scales you shall
not eat; it is unclean for you.

11 "You may eat any clean bird.

12 [1]Or *vulture* [2]Or *black vulture* [a]Lev 11:13

12 "But [a]these are the ones which you shall not eat: the [1]eagle
and the vulture and the [2]buzzard,

13 and the red kite, the falcon, and the kite in their kinds,

14 and every raven in its kind,

15 and the ostrich, the owl, the sea gull, and the hawk in their
kinds,

16 [1]Or *great horned owl*

16 the little owl, the [1]great owl, the white owl,

17 the pelican, the carrion vulture, the cormorant,

18 the stork, and the heron in their kinds, and the hoopoe and
the bat.

19 "And all the [1]teeming life with wings are unclean to you;
they shall not be eaten.
20 "You may eat any clean bird.
21 "[a]You shall not eat anything which dies *of itself.* You may give
it to the alien who is in your [1]town, so that he may eat it, or you
may sell it to a foreigner, for you are [b]a holy people to the LORD
your God. [c]You shall not boil a young goat in its mother's milk.
22 "You [a]shall surely tithe all the produce from [1]what you sow,
which comes out of the field every year.
23 "You shall eat in the presence of the LORD your God, [a]at the
place where He chooses to establish His name, the tithe of your
grain, your new wine, your oil, and the firstborn of your herd
and your flock, so that you may [b]learn to fear the LORD your
God always.
24 "If the [1]distance is so great for you that you are not able to
[2]bring *the tithe,* since the place where the LORD your God
chooses [a]to set His name is too far away from you when the
LORD your God blesses you,
25 then you shall [1]exchange *it* for money, and bind the money in
your hand and go to the place which the LORD your God chooses.
26 "You may spend the money for whatever your [1]heart desires:
for oxen, or sheep, or wine, or strong drink, or whatever your
[1]heart [2]desires; and [a]there you shall eat in the presence of the
LORD your God and rejoice, you and your household.
27 "Also you shall not neglect [a]the Levite who is in your [1]town,
[b]for he has no portion or inheritance among you.
28 "[a]At the end of every third year you shall bring out all the tithe
of your produce in that year, and shall deposit *it* in your [1]town.
29 "The Levite, [a]because he has no portion or inheritance among
you, and [b]the alien, the [1]orphan and the widow who are in your
[2]town, shall come and [c]eat and be satisfied, in order that [d]the
LORD your God may bless you in all the work of your hand
which you do.

Chapter 15 Theme ______________________________

15
"[a]At the end of *every* seven years you shall [1]grant a remission *of debts.*
2 "This is the manner of remission: every creditor shall
release what he has loaned to his neighbor; he shall not exact
it of his neighbor and his brother, because the LORD's remission
has been proclaimed.
3 "[a]From a foreigner you may exact *it,* but your hand shall
release whatever of yours is with your brother.
4 "However, there will be no poor among you, since [a]the LORD
will surely bless you in the land which the LORD your God is
giving you as an inheritance to possess,
5 if only you listen obediently to the voice of the LORD your
God, to observe carefully all this commandment which I am
commanding you today.
6 "[a]For the LORD your God will bless you as He has promised
you, and you will lend to many nations, but you will not

19 [1]I.e. flying insects

21 [1]Lit *gates* [a]Lev 17:15; 22:8; Ezek 4:14; 44:31 [b]Deut 14:2 [c]Ex 23:19; 34:26

22 [1]Lit *your seed* [a]Lev 27:30; Deut 12:6, 17; Neh 10:37

23 [a]Deut 12:5 [b]Deut 4:10; Ps 2:11; 111:10; 147:11; Is 8:13; Jer 32:38-40

24 [1]Lit *way* [2]Lit *carry* it [a]Deut 12:5, 21

25 [1]Lit *give in money*

26 [1]Lit *soul* [2]Lit *asks of you* [a]Deut 12:7

27 [1]Lit *gates* [a]Deut 12:12 [b]Num 18:20; Deut 10:9; 18:12

28 [1]Lit *gates* [a]Deut 26:12

29 [1]Or *fatherless* [2]Lit *gates* [a]Deut 10:9 [b]Deut 16:11, 14; 24:19-21; 26:12; Ps 94:6; Is 1:17 [c]Deut 6:11 [d]Deut 15:10; Mal 3:10

15:1 [1]Lit *make a release* [a]Deut 31:10

3 [a]Deut 23:20

4 [a]Deut 28:8

6 [a]Deut 28:12, 13

borrow; and you will rule over many nations, but they will not
rule over you.
7 "If there is [a]a poor man with you, one of your brothers, in
any of your [1]towns in your land which the LORD your God is
giving you, [b]you shall not harden your heart, nor close your
hand from your poor brother;
8 but [a]you shall freely open your hand to him, and shall
generously lend him sufficient for his need *in* whatever he lacks.
9 "Beware that there is no base [1]thought in your heart, saying,
'[a]The seventh year, the year of remission, is near,' and [b]your eye is
hostile toward your poor brother, and you give him nothing; then
he [c]may cry to the LORD against you, and it will be a sin in you.
10 "You shall generously give to him, and your heart shall not
be grieved when you give to him, because [a]for this thing the
LORD your God will bless you in all your work and in all [1]your
undertakings.
11 "[a]For the poor will never cease *to be* [1]in the land; therefore
I command you, saying, 'You shall freely open your hand to
your brother, to your needy and poor in your land.'
12 "[a]If your [1]kinsman, a Hebrew man or woman, is sold to you,
then he shall serve you six years, but in the seventh year you
shall set him [2]free.
13 "When you set him [1]free, you shall not send him away
empty-handed.
14 "You shall furnish him liberally from your flock and from
your threshing floor and from your wine vat; you shall give to
him as the LORD your God has blessed you.
15 "You shall remember that you were a slave in the land of
Egypt, and the LORD your God redeemed you; therefore I
command you [1]this today.
16 "It shall come about [a]if he says to you, 'I will not go out from
you,' because he loves you and your household, since he fares
well with you;
17 then you shall take an awl and pierce it through his ear
into the door, and he shall be your servant forever. Also you
shall do likewise to your maidservant.
18 "It shall not seem hard to you when you set him [1]free, for
he has given you six years *with* [2]double the service of a hired
man; so the LORD your God will bless you in whatever you do.
19 "[a]You shall consecrate to the LORD your God all the firstborn
males that are born of your herd and of your flock; you shall
not work with the firstborn of your herd, nor shear the firstborn of your flock.
20 "[a]You and your household shall eat it every year before the
LORD your God in the place which the LORD chooses.
21 "[a]But if it has any [1]defect, *such as* lameness or blindness, *or*
any serious [1]defect, you shall not sacrifice it to the LORD your God.
22 "You shall eat it within your gates; [a]the unclean and the
clean alike *may eat it,* as [a]a gazelle or a deer.
23 "Only [a]you shall not eat its blood; you are to pour it out on
the ground like water.

7 [1]Lit *gates* [a]Lev 25:35; Deut 15:11 [b]1 John 3:17
8 [a]Matt 5:42; Luke 6:34; Gal 2:10
9 [1]Lit *word* [a]Deut 15:1 [b]Matt 20:15 [c]Ex 22:23; Deut 24:15; Job 34:28; Ps 12:5; James 5:4
10 [1]Lit *the putting forth of your hand* [a]Deut 14:29; Ps 41:1; Prov 22:9
11 [1]Lit *in the midst of* [a]Matt 26:11; Mark 14:7; John 12:8
12 [1]Lit *brother* [2]Lit *free from you* [a]Ex 21:2-6; Lev 25:39-43; Jer 34:14
13 [1]Lit *free from you*
15 [1]Lit *this thing*
16 [a]Ex 21:5, 6
18 [1]Lit *free from you* [2]Lit *double the amount*
19 [a]Ex 13:2, 12
20 [a]Lev 7:15-18; Deut 12:5; 14:23
21 [1]Lit *blemish* [a]Lev 22:19-25; Deut 17:1
22 [a]Deut 12:15, 16, 22
23 [a]Gen 9:4; Lev 7:26; 17:10; 19:26; Deut 12:16, 23

Chapter 16 Theme ______________________________

16 "Observe [a]the month of Abib and [1b]celebrate the Passover
to the LORD your God, for in the month of Abib the LORD
your God brought you out of Egypt by night.
2 "You shall sacrifice the Passover to the LORD your God from
the flock and the herd, in the place where the LORD chooses to
establish His name.
3 "[a]You shall not eat leavened bread with it; seven days you
shall eat with it unleavened bread, the bread of affliction (for
you came out of the land of Egypt in haste), so that you may
remember [b]all the days of your life the day when you came out
of the land of Egypt.
4 "For seven days no leaven shall be seen with you in all your
territory, and [a]none of the flesh which you sacrifice on the
evening of the first day shall remain overnight until morning.
5 "You are not allowed to sacrifice the Passover in any of your
[1]towns which the LORD your God is giving you;
6 but [a]at the place where the LORD your God chooses to
establish His name, you shall sacrifice the Passover in the evening
at sunset, at the time that you came out of Egypt.
7 "You shall [a]cook and eat *it* in the place which the LORD your
God chooses. In the morning you are to return to your tents.
8 "Six days you shall eat unleavened bread, and [a]on the
seventh day there shall be [b]a solemn assembly to the LORD your
God; you shall do no work *on it*.
9 "[a]You shall count seven weeks for yourself; you shall begin
to count seven weeks from the time you begin to put the sickle
to the standing grain.
10 "Then you shall [1]celebrate the Feast of Weeks to the LORD
your God with a tribute of a freewill offering of your hand,
which you shall give just as the LORD your God blesses you;
11 and you shall [a]rejoice before the LORD your God, you and
your son and your daughter and your male and female servants
and [b]the Levite who is in your [1]town, and [c]the stranger and the
[2]orphan and the widow who are in your midst, in the place
where the LORD your God chooses to establish His name.
12 "[a]You shall remember that you were a slave in Egypt, and
you shall be careful to observe these statutes.
13 "[a]You shall [1]celebrate the Feast of Booths seven days after
you have gathered in from your threshing floor and your wine vat;
14 and you shall [a]rejoice in your feast, you and your son and your
daughter and your male and female servants and the Levite and the
stranger and the [1]orphan and the widow who are in your [2]towns.
15 "Seven days you shall celebrate a feast to the LORD your God
in the place which the LORD chooses, because the LORD your
God will bless you in all your produce and in all the work of
your hands, so that you will be altogether joyful.
16 "[a]Three times in a year all your males shall appear before the
LORD your God in the place which He chooses, at the Feast of
Unleavened Bread and at the Feast of Weeks and at the Feast of
Booths, and [b]they shall not appear before the LORD empty-handed.

16:1 [1]Lit *perform* [a]Ex 12:2 [b]Num 28:16
3 [a]Ex 12:8, 15, 19, 39; 13:3; 34:18 [b]Deut 4:9
4 [a]Ex 12:8, 10; 34:25
5 [1]Lit *gates*
6 [a]Deut 12:5
7 [a]Ex 12:8; 2 Chr 35:13
8 [a]Num 28:25 [b]Ex 12:16; 13:6; Lev 23:8, 36
9 [a]Ex 23:16; 34:22; Lev 23:15; Num 28:26
10 [1]Lit *perform*
11 [1]Lit *gates* [2]Or *fatherless* [a]Deut 12:7 [b]Deut 12:12 [c]Deut 14:29
12 [a]Deut 15:15
13 [1]Lit *perform* [a]Lev 23:34-43
14 [1]Or *fatherless* [2]Lit *gates* [a]Deut 16:11
16 [a]Ex 23:14-17; 34:23, 24 [b]Ex 34:20

17 “Every man [1]shall give as he is able, according to the
blessing of the LORD your God which He has given you.
18 “You shall appoint for yourself judges and officers in all your
[1]towns which the LORD your God is giving you, according to your
tribes, and they shall judge the people with righteous judgment.
19 “[a]You shall not distort justice; [b]you shall not [1]be partial, and
[c]you shall not take a bribe, for a bribe blinds the eyes of the
wise and perverts the words of the righteous.
20 “Justice, *and only* justice, you shall pursue, that [a]you may
live and possess the land which the LORD your God is giving you.
21 “[a]You shall not plant for yourself an [1]Asherah of any kind of
tree beside the altar of the LORD your God, which you shall
make for yourself.
22 “[a]You shall not set up for yourself a *sacred* pillar which the
LORD your God hates.

Chapter 17 Theme ______________________________

17 “[a]You shall not sacrifice to the LORD your God an ox or a
sheep which has a blemish *or* any [1]defect, for that is a
detestable thing to the LORD your God.
2 “[a]If there is found in your midst, in any of your [1]towns,
which the LORD your God is giving you, a man or a woman
who does what is evil in the sight of the LORD your God, by
transgressing His covenant,
3 and has gone and [a]served other gods and worshiped them,
[b]or the sun or the moon or any of the heavenly host, [c]which I
have not commanded,
4 and if it is told you and you have heard of it, then you shall
inquire thoroughly. Behold, if it is true and the thing certain
that this detestable thing has been done in Israel,
5 then you shall bring out that man or that woman who has
done this evil deed to your gates, *that is,* the man or the woman,
and [a]you shall stone them to [1]death.
6 “[a]On the [1]evidence of two witnesses or three witnesses, he
who is to die shall be put to death; he shall not be put to death
on the [1]evidence of one witness.
7 “[a]The hand of the witnesses shall be first against him to put
him to death, and afterward the hand of all the people. [b]So you
shall purge the evil from your midst.
8 “[a]If any case is too difficult for you to decide, between [1]one
kind of homicide or another, between [2]one kind of lawsuit or
another, and between [3]one kind of assault or another, being
cases of dispute in your [4]courts, then you shall arise and go up
to [b]the place which the LORD your God chooses.
9 “So you shall come to [a]the Levitical priest or the judge who
is *in office* in those days, and you shall inquire *of them* and
they will declare to you the verdict in the case.
10 “You shall do according to the [1]terms of the verdict which they
declare to you from that place which the LORD chooses; and you
shall be careful to observe according to all that they teach you.

17 [1]Lit *according to the gift of his hand*

18 [1]Lit *gates*

19 [1]Lit *regard persons* [a]Ex 23:2; Lev 19:15; Deut 1:17; 10:17 [b]Prov 24:23 [c]Ex 23:8; Prov 17:23; Eccl 7:7

20 [a]Deut 4:1

21 [1]I.e. wooden symbol of a female deity [a]Deut 7:5; 2 Kin 17:16; 21:3; 2 Chr 33:3

22 [a]Lev 26:1

17:1 [1]Lit *evil thing* [a]Deut 15:21

2 [1]Lit *gates* [a]Deut 13:6-11

3 [a]Ex 22:20 [b]Job 31:26-28 [c]Jer 7:22

5 [1]Lit *death with stones* [a]Lev 24:14; Josh 7:25

6 [1]Lit *mouth* [a]Num 35:30; Deut 19:15; Matt 18:16; John 8:17; 2 Cor 13:1; 1 Tim 5:19; Heb 10:28

7 [a]Lev 24:14; Deut 13:9 [b]1 Cor 5:13

8 [1]Lit *blood to blood* [2]Lit *judgment to judgment* [3]Lit *stroke to stroke* [4]Lit *gates* [a]2 Chr 19:10; Hag 2:11 [b]Deut 12:5; Ps 122:5

9 [a]Deut 19:17

10 [1]Lit *mouth*

11 "[a]According to the [1]terms of the law which they teach you,
and according to the verdict which they tell you, you shall do;
you shall not turn aside from the word which they declare to
you, to the right or the left.
12 "The man who acts [a]presumptuously by not listening to the
priest who stands there to serve the LORD your God, nor to the
judge, that man shall die; thus you shall purge the evil from Israel.
13 "Then all the people will hear and be afraid, and will not act
[a]presumptuously again.
14 "When you enter the land which the LORD your God gives
you, and you [a]possess it and live in it, and you say, '[b]I will set a
king over me like all the nations who are around me,'
15 you shall surely set a king over you whom the LORD your
God chooses, *one* [a]from among your [1]countrymen you shall set
as king over yourselves; you may not put a foreigner over
yourselves who is not your [1]countryman.
16 "[a]Moreover, he shall not multiply horses for himself, nor shall
he [b]cause the people to return to Egypt to multiply horses, since
[c]the LORD has said to you, 'You shall never again return that way.'
17 "[a]He shall not multiply wives for himself, [1]or else his heart
will turn away; nor shall he greatly increase silver and gold for
himself.
18 "Now it shall come about when he sits on the throne of his
kingdom, he shall write for himself a copy of this law on a
scroll [1][a]in the presence of the Levitical priests.
19 "It shall be with him and he shall read it [a]all the days of his
life, that he may learn to fear the LORD his God, [1]by carefully
observing all the words of this law and these statutes,
20 that his heart may not be lifted up above his [1]countrymen
[a]and that he may not turn aside from the commandment, to
the right or the left, so that he and his sons may continue long
in his kingdom in the midst of Israel.

Chapter 18 Theme ____________________

18 "[a]The Levitical priests, the whole tribe of Levi, shall
have no portion or inheritance with Israel; they shall eat
the LORD's offerings by fire and His [1]portion.
2 "[a]They shall have no inheritance among their [1]countrymen;
the LORD is their inheritance, as He [2]promised them.
3 "[a]Now this shall be the priests' due from the people, from
those who offer a sacrifice, either an ox or a sheep, of which
they shall give to the priest the shoulder and the two cheeks
and the stomach.
4 "You shall give him the [a]first fruits of your grain, your new
wine, and your oil, and the first shearing of your sheep.
5 "[a]For the LORD your God has chosen him and his sons from all
your tribes, to [b]stand [1]and serve in the name of the LORD forever.
6 "Now if a Levite comes from any of your [1]towns throughout
Israel where he [a]resides, and comes [2]whenever he desires to
the place which the LORD chooses,

11 [1]Lit *mouth* [a]Deut 25:1

12 [a]Num 15:30; Deut 1:43; 17:13; 18:20; Hos 4:4

13 [a]Deut 17:12

14 [a]Deut 11:31; Josh 21:43 [b]1 Sam 8:5, 19, 20; 10:19

15 [1]Lit *brother(s)* [a]Jer 30:21

16 [a]1 Kin 4:26; 10:26-29; Ps 20:7 [b]Is 31:1; Ezek 17:15 [c]Ex 13:17, 18; Hos 11:5

17 [1]Lit *nor* [a]2 Sam 5:13; 12:11; 1 Kin 11:3, 4

18 [1]Lit *from before* [a]Deut 31:24-26

19 [1]Lit *to keep to do them* [a]Deut 4:9, 10; Josh 1:8

20 [1]Lit *brothers* [a]Deut 5:32; 1 Kin 15:5

18:1 [1]Or *inheritance* [a]Deut 10:9; 1 Cor 9:13

2 [1]Lit *brothers* [2]Lit *spoke to* [a]Num 18:20

3 [a]Lev 7:32-34; Num 18:11, 12

4 [a]Num 18:12

5 [1]Lit *to* [a]Ex 29:9 [b]Deut 10:8

6 [1]Lit *gates* [2]Lit *with all the desire of his soul* [a]Num 35:2, 3

7 then he shall serve in the name of the LORD his God, like
all his fellow Levites who stand there before the LORD.
8 “[a]They shall eat [1]equal portions, except *what they receive*
from the sale of their fathers’ *estates.*
9 “When you enter the land which the LORD your God gives
you, you shall not learn to [1a]imitate the detestable things of
those nations.
10 “There shall not be found among you anyone [a]who makes
his son or his daughter pass through the fire, one who uses
divination, one [b]who practices witchcraft, or one who interprets
omens, or a sorcerer,
11 or one who casts a spell, [a]or a medium, or a spiritist, or one
who calls up the dead.
12 “For whoever does these things is detestable to the LORD;
and [a]because of these detestable things the LORD your God will
drive them out before you.
13 “[a]You shall be [1]blameless before the LORD your God.
14 “For those nations, which you shall dispossess, listen to
those who [a]practice witchcraft and to diviners, but as for you,
the LORD your God has not allowed you *to do* so.
15 “[a]The LORD your God will raise up for you a prophet like me
from among you, from your [1]countrymen, you shall listen to him.
16 “This is [a]according to all that you asked of the LORD your
God in Horeb on the day of the assembly, saying, ‘Let me not
hear again the voice of the LORD my God, let me not see this
great fire anymore, or I will die.’
17 “[a]The LORD said to me, ‘They have [1]spoken well.
18 ‘I will raise up a prophet from among their [1]countrymen
like you, and [a]I will put My words in his mouth, and [b]he shall
speak to them all that I command him.
19 ‘[a]It shall come about that whoever will not listen to My words
which he shall speak in My name, I Myself will require *it* of him.
20 ‘But the prophet who speaks a word [a]presumptuously in My
name which I have not commanded him to speak, or [b]which
he speaks in the name of other gods, [1]that prophet shall die.’
21 “[1]You may say in your heart, ‘How will we know the word
which the LORD has not spoken?’
22 “[a]When a prophet speaks in the name of the LORD, if the
thing does not come about or come true, that is the thing
which the LORD has not spoken. The prophet has spoken it
[b]presumptuously; you shall not be afraid of him.

Chapter 19 Theme ____________________

19 “[a]When the LORD your God cuts off the nations, whose
land the LORD your God gives you, and you dispossess
them and settle in their cities and in their houses,
2 [a]you shall set aside three cities for yourself in the midst of
your land, which the LORD your God gives you to [1]possess.
3 “You shall prepare the [1]roads for yourself, and divide into three
parts the territory of your land which the LORD your God will
give you as a possession, [2]so that any manslayer may flee there.

8 [1]Lit *portion like portion* [a]Lev 27:30-33; Num 18:21-24; 2 Chr 31:4; Neh 12:44

9 [1]Lit *do according to* [a]Deut 9:5

10 [a]Deut 12:31 [b]Ex 22:18; Lev 19:26, 31; 20:6; Jer 27:9, 10; Mal 3:5

11 [a]Lev 19:31

12 [a]Lev 18:24

13 [1]Lit *complete, perfect;* or *having integrity* [a]Gen 6:9; 17:1; Matt 5:48

14 [a]2 Kin 21:6

15 [1]Lit *brothers* [a]Matt 21:11; Luke 2:25-34; 7:16; 24:19; John 1:21, 25; 4:19; Acts 3:22; 7:37

16 [a]Ex 20:18, 19; Deut 5:23-27

17 [1]Lit *done well what they have spoken* [a]Deut 5:28

18 [1]Lit *brothers* [a]Is 51:16; John 17:8 [b]John 4:25; 8:28; 12:49, 50

19 [a]Acts 3:23; Heb 12:25

20 [1]Lit *and that* [a]Deut 13:5; 17:12 [b]Deut 13:1, 2; Jer 14:14; Zech 13:3

21 [1]Lit *if you say*

22 [a]Jer 28:9 [b]Deut 18:20

19:1 [a]Deut 6:10, 11

2 [1]Lit *possess it* [a]Deut 4:41; Josh 20:2

3 [1]Lit *road* [2]Lit *and it shall be for every manslayer to flee there*

4 "[a]Now this is the case of the manslayer who may flee there
and live: when he [1]kills his friend [2]unintentionally, [3]not hating
him previously—
5 as when *a man* goes into the forest with his friend to cut
wood, and his hand [1]swings the axe to cut down the tree, and
the iron *head* slips off the [2]handle and [3]strikes his friend so
that he dies—he may flee to one of these cities and live;
6 otherwise the avenger of blood might pursue the manslayer
[1]in the heat of his anger, and overtake him, because the way is
long, and [2]take his life, though he was not deserving of death,
since he had not hated him previously.
7 "Therefore, I command you, saying, 'You shall set aside three
cities for yourself.'
8 "If the LORD your God [a]enlarges your territory, just as He has
sworn to your fathers, and gives you all the land which He
[1]promised to give your fathers—
9 if you [1]carefully observe all this commandment which I
command you today, [a]to love the LORD your God, and to walk
in His ways always—[b]then you shall add three more cities for
yourself, besides these three.
10 "So innocent blood will not be shed in the midst of your
land which the LORD your God gives you as an inheritance, and
[a]bloodguiltiness be on you.
11 "But [a]if there is a man who hates his neighbor and lies in
wait for him and rises up against him and strikes [1]him so that
he dies, and he flees to one of these cities,
12 then the elders of his city shall send and take him from
there and deliver him into the hand of the avenger of blood,
that he may die.
13 "[1a]You shall not pity him, but [b]you shall purge the blood of
the innocent from Israel, that it may go well with you.
14 "[a]You shall not move your neighbor's boundary mark, which
the ancestors have set, in your inheritance which you will
inherit in the land that the LORD your God gives you to [1]possess.
15 "[a]A single witness shall not rise up against a man on account
of any iniquity or any sin [1]which he has committed; on the
[2]evidence of two or three witnesses a matter shall be confirmed.
16 "[a]If a malicious witness rises up against a man to [1]accuse
him of [2]wrongdoing,
17 then both the men who have the dispute shall stand
[a]before the LORD, before the priests and the judges who will be
in office in those days.
18 "The judges [a]shall investigate thoroughly, and if the witness
is a false witness *and* he has [1]accused his brother falsely,
19 then [a]you shall do to him just as he had intended to do to
his brother. Thus you shall purge the evil from among you.
20 "[a]The rest will hear and be afraid, and will never again do
such an evil thing among you.
21 "Thus [1a]you shall not show pity: [b]life for life, [c]eye for eye,
tooth for tooth, hand for hand, foot for foot.

4 [1]Lit *smites* [2]Lit *without knowledge* [3]Lit *and he was not hating him previously* [a]Num 35:9-34

5 [1]Lit *is thrust with* [2]Lit *wood* [3]Lit *finds*

6 [1]Lit *while his heart is hot* [2]Lit *smite him in the soul*

8 [1]Lit *spoke* [a]Gen 15:18

9 [1]Lit *keep . . . to do it* [a]Deut 6:5 [b]Josh 20:7

10 [a]Num 35:33; Deut 21:1-9

11 [1]Lit *him in the soul* [a]Ex 21:12; Num 35:16; 1 John 3:15

13 [1]Lit *Your eye* [a]Deut 7:2 [b]1 Kin 2:31

14 [1]Lit *possess it* [a]Deut 27:17; Job 24:2; Prov 22:28; Hos 5:10

15 [1]Lit *in any sin, which he sins* [2]Lit *mouth of two witnesses, or by the mouth of three* [a]Num 35:30; Deut 17:6; Matt 18:16; John 8:17; 2 Cor 13:1; 1 Tim 5:19; Heb 10:28

16 [1]Lit *testify against* [2]Lit *turning aside* [a]Ex 23:1; Ps 27:12

17 [a]Deut 17:9

18 [1]Lit *testified against* [a]Deut 25:1

19 [a]Prov 19:5

20 [a]Deut 17:13; 21:21

21 [1]Lit *your eye* [a]Deut 19:13 [b]Ex 21:23; Lev 24:20 [c]Matt 5:38

Chapter 20 Theme

20 "When you go out to battle against your enemies and
see [a]horses and chariots *and* people more numerous
than you, [b]do not be afraid of them; for the LORD your God,
who brought you up from the land of Egypt, is with you.
2 "When you are approaching the battle, the priest shall come
near and speak to the people.
3 "He shall say to them, 'Hear, O Israel, you are approaching
the battle against your enemies today. Do not be fainthearted.
[a]Do not be afraid, or panic, or tremble before them,
4 for the LORD your God [a]is the one who goes with you, to
fight for you against your enemies, to save you.'
5 "The officers also shall speak to the people, saying, 'Who is
the man that has built a new house and has not [a]dedicated it?
Let him depart and return to his house, otherwise he might die
in the battle and another man would dedicate it.
6 'Who is the man that has planted a vineyard and has not
[1]begun to use its fruit? Let him depart and return to his house,
otherwise he might die in the battle and another man [1]would
begin to use its fruit.
7 '[a]And who is the man that is engaged to a woman and has
not [1]married her? Let him depart and return to his house,
otherwise he might die in the battle and another man [2]would
marry her.'
8 "Then the officers shall speak further to the people and say,
'[a]Who is the man that is afraid and fainthearted? Let him
depart and return to his house, so that [1]he might not make his
brothers' hearts melt like his heart.'
9 "When the officers have finished speaking to the people, they
shall appoint commanders of armies at the head of the people.
10 "When you approach a city to fight against it, you shall [1]offer
it terms of peace.
11 "If it [1]agrees to make peace with you and opens to you, then
all the people who are found in it shall become your [a]forced
labor and shall serve you.
12 "However, if it does not make peace with you, but makes
war against you, then you shall besiege it.
13 "When the LORD your God gives it into your hand, [a]you shall
strike all the [1]men in it with the edge of the sword.
14 "Only the women and the children and [a]the animals and all
that is in the city, all its spoil, you shall take as booty for
yourself; and you shall [1]use the spoil of your enemies which
the LORD your God has given you.
15 "Thus you shall do to all the cities that are very far from you,
which are not of the cities of these nations [1]nearby.
16 "[a]Only in the cities of these peoples that the LORD your God
is giving you as an inheritance, you shall not leave alive anything that breathes.
17 "But you shall [1]utterly destroy them, the Hittite and the
Amorite, the Canaanite and the Perizzite, the Hivite and the
Jebusite, as the LORD your God has commanded you,

20:1 [a]Deut 3:22; 7:18; 31:6, 8; Ps 20:7; Is 31:1 [b]2 Chr 32:7, 8; Ps 23:4; Is 41:10
3 [a]Deut 20:1; Josh 23:10
4 [a]Deut 1:30; 3:22; Josh 23:10
5 [a]Neh 12:27
6 [1]Lit *treat(ed) it as common*
7 [1]Lit *taken* [2]Lit *take* [a]Deut 24:5
8 [1]So with Gr and other ancient versions [a]Judg 7:3
10 [1]Lit *call to it for peace*
11 [1]Lit *answers peace* [a]1 Kin 9:21
13 [1]Lit *males* [a]Num 31:7
14 [1]Lit *eat* [a]Josh 8:2
15 [1]Lit *here*
16 [a]Ex 23:31-33; Num 21:2, 3; Deut 7:1-5; Josh 11:14
17 [1]Or *put them under the ban*

18 so that they may not teach you to do [a]according to all their
detestable things which they have done for their gods, so that
you would [b]sin against the LORD your God.
19 "When you besiege a city a long time, to make war against it
in order to capture it, you shall not destroy its trees by
swinging an axe against them; for you may eat from them, and
you shall not cut them down. [1]For is the tree of the field a
man, that it should [2]be besieged by you?
20 "Only the trees which you know [1]are not fruit trees you
shall destroy and cut down, that you may construct siegeworks
against the city that is making war with you until it falls.

Chapter 21 Theme ____________________

21 "If a slain person is found lying in the open country in
the land which the LORD your God gives you to [1]possess,
and it is not known who has struck him,
2 then your elders and your judges shall go out and measure
the distance to the cities which are around the slain one.
3 "It shall be that the city which is nearest to the slain man,
that is, the elders of that city, shall take a heifer of the herd,
which has not been worked and which has not pulled in a
yoke;
4 and the elders of that city shall bring the heifer down to a
valley with running water, which has not been plowed or
sown, and shall break the heifer's neck there in the valley.
5 "Then [a]the priests, the sons of Levi, shall come near, for the
LORD your God has chosen them to serve Him and to bless in
the name of the LORD; and every dispute and every [1]assault
[2]shall be settled by them.
6 "All the elders of that city [1]which is nearest to the slain man
shall [a]wash their hands over the heifer whose neck was broken
in the valley;
7 and they shall answer and say, 'Our hands did not shed this
blood, nor did our eyes see *it*.
8 '[1]Forgive Your people Israel whom You have redeemed, O
LORD, and do not place the guilt of [a]innocent blood in the midst
of Your people Israel.' And the bloodguiltiness shall be [2]forgiven
them.
9 "[a]So you shall remove the guilt of innocent blood from your
midst, when you do what is right in the eyes of the LORD.
10 "When you go out to battle against your enemies, and [a]the
LORD your God delivers them into your hands and you take
them away captive,
11 and see among the captives a beautiful woman, and have a
desire for her and would take her as a wife for yourself,
12 then you shall bring her home to your house, and she shall
[a]shave her head and [1]trim her nails.
13 "She shall also [1]remove the clothes of her captivity and shall
remain in your house, and [a]mourn her father and mother a full

18 [a]Ex 34:12-16; Deut 7:4; 9:5; 12:30, 31 [b]Ex 23:33; 2 Kin 21:3-15; Ps 106:34-41

19 [1]Read as interrogative with ancient versions [2]Lit *come before you in the siege*

20 [1]Lit *they are not trees for food*

21:1 [1]Lit *possess it*

5 [1]Lit *stroke* [2]Lit *shall be according to their mouth* [a]Deut 17:9-11; 19:17; 1 Chr 23:13

6 [1]Lit *who are* [a]Matt 27:24

8 [1]Lit *Cover over, atone for* [2]Lit *covered over, atoned for* [a]Num 35:33, 34; Jon 1:14

9 [a]Deut 19:13

10 [a]Josh 21:44

12 [1]Lit *do* [a]Lev 14:8, 9; Num 6:9

13 [1]Lit *remove from her* [a]Ps 45:10

month; and after that you may go in to her and be her husband
and she shall be your wife.
14 "It shall be, if you are not pleased with her, then you shall
let her go [1]wherever she wishes; but you shall certainly not sell
her for money, you shall not [2]mistreat her, because you have
[a]humbled her.
15 "If a man has two wives, the one loved and [a]the other
[1]unloved, and *both* the loved and the [1]unloved have borne him
sons, if the firstborn son belongs to the [1]unloved,
16 then it shall be in the day he [1]wills what he has to his sons,
he cannot make the son of the loved the firstborn before the
son of the [2]unloved, who is the firstborn.
17 "But he shall acknowledge the firstborn, the son of the
[1]unloved, by giving him a double portion of all that [2]he has, for
he is the [a]beginning of his strength; [b]to him belongs the right
of the firstborn.
18 "If any man has a stubborn and rebellious son who will [a]not
obey his father or his mother, and when they chastise him, he
will not even listen to them,
19 then his father and mother shall seize him, and bring him
out to the elders of his city [1]at the gateway of his hometown.
20 "They shall say to the elders of his city, 'This son of ours is
stubborn and rebellious, he will not obey us, he is a glutton
and a drunkard.'
21 "[a]Then all the men of his city shall stone him to death; so
[b]you shall remove the evil from your midst, and [c]all Israel will
hear *of it* and fear.
22 "If a man has committed a sin [a]worthy of death and he is
put to death, and you hang him on a tree,
23 [a]his corpse shall not hang all night on the tree, but you
shall surely bury him on the same day (for [b]he who is hanged is
[1]accursed of God), so that you [c]do not defile your land which
the LORD your God gives you as an inheritance.

Chapter 22 Theme ____________________

22 "[a]You shall not see your [1]countryman's ox or his sheep
straying away, and [2]pay no attention to them; you shall
certainly bring them back to your countryman.
2 "If your countryman is not near you, or if you do not know
him, then you shall bring it home to your house, and it shall
remain with you until your countryman looks for it; then you
shall restore it to him.
3 "Thus you shall do with his donkey, and you shall do the
same with his garment, and you shall do likewise with anything lost by your countryman, which he has lost and you have
found. You are not allowed to [1]neglect *them.*
4 "You shall not see your countryman's donkey or his ox fallen
down on the way, and [1]pay no attention to them; you shall
certainly help him to raise *them* up.

14 [1]Lit *according to her soul* [2]Or *enslave* [a]Gen 34:2
15 [1]Lit *hated* [a]Gen 29:33
16 [1]Lit *makes to inherit* [2]Lit *hated*
17 [1]Lit *hated* [2]Lit *is found with him* [a]Gen 49:3 [b]Gen 25:31
18 [a]Ex 20:12; Lev 19:3; Prov 1:8; Eph 6:1-3
19 [1]Lit *and to the gate of his place*
21 [a]Lev 20:2, 27; 24:14-23; Num 15:25, 36 [b]Deut 19:19 [c]Deut 13:11
22 [a]Deut 22:26; Matt 26:66; Mark 14:64; Acts 23:29
23 [1]Lit *the curse of God* [a]Josh 8:29; 10:26, 27; John 19:31 [b]Gal 3:13 [c]Lev 18:25; Num 35:34
22:1 [1]Lit *brother*, and so through v 4 [2]Lit *hide yourself from them* [a]Ex 23:4, 5; Prov 27:10; Zech 7:9
3 [1]Lit *hide yourself*
4 [1]Lit *hide yourself from them*

5 "A woman shall not wear man's clothing, nor shall a man
put on a woman's clothing; for whoever does these things is an
abomination to the LORD your God.
6 "If you happen to come upon a bird's nest along the way, in
any tree or on the ground, with young ones or eggs, and the
mother sitting on the young or on the eggs, [a]you shall not take
the mother with the young;
7 you shall certainly let the mother go, but the young you
may take for yourself, [a]in order that it may be well with you
and that you may prolong your days.
8 "When you build a new house, you shall make a parapet for
your roof, so that you will not bring bloodguilt on your house if
anyone falls from it.
9 "[a]You shall not sow your vineyard with two kinds of seed, or
[1]all the produce of the seed which you have sown and the
increase of the vineyard will become defiled.
10 "[a]You shall not plow with an ox and a donkey together.
11 "[a]You shall not wear a material mixed of wool and linen
together.
12 "[a]You shall make yourself tassels on the four corners of your
garment with which you cover yourself.
13 "[a]If any man takes a wife and goes in to her and *then* [1]turns
against her,
14 and charges her with shameful deeds and [1]publicly defames
her, and says, 'I took this woman, *but* when I came near her, I
did not find her a virgin,'
15 then the girl's father and her mother shall take and bring
out the *evidence* of the girl's virginity to the elders of the city at
the gate.
16 "The girl's father shall say to the elders, 'I gave my daughter
to this man for a wife, but he [1]turned against her;
17 and behold, he has charged her with shameful deeds,
saying, "I did not find your daughter a virgin." But [1]this is the
evidence of my daughter's virginity.' And they shall spread the
garment before the elders of the city.
18 "So [a]the elders of that city shall take the man and chastise him,
19 and they shall fine him a hundred *shekels* of silver and give
it to the girl's father, because he [1]publicly defamed a virgin of
Israel. And she shall remain his wife; he cannot [2]divorce her all
his days.
20 "But if this [1a]charge is true, that the girl was not found a virgin,
21 then they shall bring out the girl to the doorway of her
father's house, and the men of her city shall stone her [1]to death
because she has [a]committed an act of folly in Israel by playing
the harlot in her father's house; thus [b]you shall purge the evil
from among you.
22 "[a]If a man is found lying with a married woman, then both
of them shall die, the man who lay with the woman, and the
woman; thus you shall purge the evil from Israel.
23 "[a]If there is a girl who is a virgin engaged to a man, and
another man finds her in the city and lies with her,

6 [a]Lev 22:28
7 [a]Deut 4:40
9 [1]Lit *the fullness* [a]Lev 19:19
10 [a]2 Cor 6:14-16
11 [a]Lev 19:19
12 [a]Num 15:37-41; Matt 23:5
13 [1]Lit *hates her* [a]Gen 29:21; Deut 24:1; Judg 15:1
14 [1]Lit *causes an evil name to go out against her*
16 [1]Lit *hated her*
17 [1]Lit *these are*
18 [a]Ex 18:21; Deut 1:9-18
19 [1]Lit *caused an evil name to go out against a virgin* [2]Lit *send her away*
20 [1]Lit *matter* [a]Deut 17:4
21 [1]Lit *with stones so that she dies* [a]Gen 34:7; Lev 19:29; 21:9; Deut 23:17, 18; Judg 20:5-10; 2 Sam 13:12, 13 [b]Deut 13:5; 17:7; 19:19
22 [a]Lev 20:10; Ezek 16:38; Matt 5:27, 28; John 8:5; 1 Cor 6:9; Heb 13:4
23 [a]Lev 19:20-22; Matt 1:18, 19

24 then you shall bring them both out to the gate of that city
and you shall stone them [1]to death; the girl, because she did not
cry out in the city, and the man, because he has violated his
neighbor's wife. Thus you shall purge the evil from among you.
25 "But if in the field the man finds the girl who is engaged,
and the man forces her and lies with her, then only the man
who lies with her shall die.
26 "But you shall do nothing to the girl; there is no sin in the
girl worthy of death, for just as a man rises against his neighbor
and murders him, so is this case.
27 "When he found her in the field, the engaged girl cried out,
but there was no one to save her.
28 "[a]If a man finds a girl who is a virgin, who is not engaged,
and seizes her and lies with her and they are discovered,
29 then the man who lay with her shall give to the girl's father
fifty *shekels* of silver, and she shall become his wife because he
has violated her; he cannot divorce her all his days.
30 "[1a]A man shall not take his father's wife so that he will not
uncover his father's skirt.

Chapter 23 Theme ______________________

23 "[a]No one who is [1]emasculated or has his male organ
cut off shall enter the assembly of the LORD.
2 "No one of illegitimate birth shall enter the assembly of the
LORD; none of his *descendants,* even to the tenth generation,
shall enter the assembly of the LORD.
3 "[a]No Ammonite or Moabite shall enter the assembly of the
LORD; none of their *descendants,* even to the tenth generation,
shall ever enter the assembly of the LORD,
4 [a]because they did not meet you with [1]food and water on
the way when you came out of Egypt, and because they hired
against you [b]Balaam the son of Beor from Pethor of [2]Meso-
potamia, to curse you.
5 "Nevertheless, the LORD your God was not willing to listen
to Balaam, but the LORD your God [a]turned the curse into a
blessing for you because the LORD your God [b]loves you.
6 "[a]You shall never seek their peace or their prosperity all
your days.
7 "You shall not detest an Edomite, for [a]he is your brother;
you shall not detest an Egyptian, [b]because you were an alien in
his land.
8 "The sons of the third generation who are born to them may
enter the assembly of the LORD.
9 "When you go out as [1]an army against your enemies, you
shall keep yourself from every evil thing.
10 "[a]If there is among you any man who is unclean because of a
nocturnal emission, then he must go outside the camp; he may
not [1]reenter the camp.
11 "But it shall be when evening approaches, he shall bathe
himself with water, and at sundown he may [1]reenter the camp.

24 [1]Lit *with stones so that they die*
28 [a]Ex 22:16
30 [1]Ch 23:1 in Heb [a]Lev 18:8; 20:11; Deut 27:20; 1 Cor 5:1
23:1 [1]Lit *wounded by crushing* of testicles [a]Lev 21:20; 22:24
3 [a]Neh 13:1, 2
4 [1]Lit *bread* [2]Heb *Aram-naharaim* [a]Neh 13:2 [b]Num 22:5; 23:7; Josh 24:9; 2 Pet 2:15; Jude 11
5 [a]Prov 26:2 [b]Deut 4:37
6 [a]Ezra 9:12
7 [a]Gen 25:24-26; Obad 10, 12 [b]Ex 22:21; 23:9; Lev 19:34; Deut 10:19
9 [1]Or *a camp*
10 [1]Lit *come to the midst of* [a]Lev 15:16
11 [1]Lit *come to the midst of*

12 "You shall also have a place outside the camp and go out
there,
13 and you shall have a [1]spade among your tools, and it shall
be when you sit down outside, you shall dig with it and shall
turn [2]to cover up your excrement.
14 "Since [a]the LORD your God walks in the midst of your camp
to deliver you and to [1]defeat your enemies before you, therefore
your camp must be [b]holy; and He must not see [2]anything
indecent among you [3]or He will turn away from you.
15 "[a]You shall not hand over to his master a slave who has
[1]escaped from his master to you.
16 "He shall live with you in your midst, in the place which he
shall choose in one of your [1]towns where it pleases him; [a]you
shall not mistreat him.
17 "[a]None of the daughters of Israel shall be a cult prostitute,
[b]nor shall any of the sons of Israel be a cult prostitute.
18 "You shall not bring the hire of a harlot or the wages of a
[1a]dog into the house of the LORD your God for any votive
offering, for both of these are an abomination to the LORD your
God.
19 "[a]You shall not charge interest to your [1]countrymen: interest
on money, food, *or* anything that may be loaned at interest.
20 "[a]You may charge interest to a foreigner, but to your
[1]countrymen you shall not charge interest, so that [b]the LORD
your God may bless you in all [2]that you undertake in the land
which you are about to enter to [3]possess.
21 "[a]When you make a vow to the LORD your God, you shall
not delay to pay it, for it would be sin in you, [1]and the LORD
your God will surely require it of you.
22 "However, if you refrain from vowing, it would not be sin in
you.
23 "You shall be careful to perform what goes out from your
lips, just as you have voluntarily vowed to the LORD your God,
what you have [1]promised.
24 "When you enter your neighbor's vineyard, then you may
eat grapes [1]until you are fully satisfied, but you shall not put
any in your [2]basket.
25 "[a]When you enter your neighbor's standing grain, then you
may pluck the heads with your hand, but you shall not wield a
sickle in your neighbor's standing grain.

Chapter 24 Theme ______________________

24 "When a man takes a wife and marries her, and it happens [1]that she finds no favor in his eyes because he has
found some [a]indecency in her, and [b]he writes her a certificate
of divorce and puts *it* in her hand and sends her out from his
house,
2 and she leaves his house and goes and becomes another
man's *wife*,

13 [1]Lit *peg* [2]Lit *and*

14 [1]Lit *give* [2]Lit *nakedness of anything* [3]Lit *and* [a]Lev 26:12 [b]Ex 3:5

15 [1]Lit *delivered himself* [a]1 Sam 30:15

16 [1]Lit *gates* [a]Ex 22:21; Prov 22:22

17 [a]Lev 19:29; Deut 22:21 [b]Gen 19:5; 2 Kin 23:7

18 [1]I.e. male prostitute, sodomite [a]Lev 18:22; 20:13

19 [1]Lit *brother* [a]Ex 22:25; Lev 25:35-37; Neh 5:2-7; Ps 15:5

20 [1]Lit *brother* [2]Lit *the putting forth of your hand* [3]Lit *possess it* [a]Deut 28:12 [b]Deut 15:10

21 [1]Lit *for* [a]Num 30:1, 2; Job 22:27; Ps 61:8; Eccl 5:4, 5; Matt 5:33

23 [1]Lit *spoken with your mouth*

24 [1]Lit *according to your satisfaction of your soul* [2]Or *vessel*

25 [a]Matt 12:1; Mark 2:23; Luke 6:1

24:1 [1]Lit *if* [a]Num 5:12, 28; Deut 22:13-21 [b]Matt 5:31; 19:7-9; Mark 10:4, 5

3 and if the latter husband [1]turns against her and writes her
a certificate of divorce and puts *it* in her hand and sends her
out of his house, or if the latter husband dies who took her to
be his wife,
4 *then* her [a]former husband who sent her away is not allowed
to take her again to be his wife, since she has been defiled; for
that is an abomination before the LORD, and you shall not bring
sin on the land which the LORD your God gives you as an
inheritance.
5 "[a]When a man takes a new wife, he shall not go out with
the army nor be charged with any duty; he shall be free at
home one year and shall [b]give happiness to his wife whom he
has taken.
6 "No one shall take a handmill or an upper millstone in
pledge, for he would be taking a life in pledge.
7 "[a]If a man is [1]caught kidnapping any of his [2]countrymen of
the sons of Israel, and he deals with him violently or sells him,
then that thief shall die; so you shall purge the evil from among
you.
8 "[a]Be careful against [1]an infection of leprosy, that you diligently
observe and do according to all that the Levitical priests teach
you; as I have commanded them, so you shall be careful to do.
9 "Remember what the LORD your God did [a]to Miriam on the
way as you came out of Egypt.
10 "[a]When you make your neighbor a loan of any sort, you shall
not enter his house to take his pledge.
11 "You shall remain outside, and the man to whom you make
the loan shall bring the pledge out to you.
12 "If he is a poor man, you shall not sleep with his pledge.
13 "[a]When the sun goes down you shall surely return the
pledge to him, that he may sleep in his cloak and bless you;
and [b]it will be righteousness for you before the LORD your God.
14 "[a]You shall not oppress a hired servant *who is* poor and
needy, whether *he is* one of your [1]countrymen or one of your
aliens who is in your land in your [2]towns.
15 "[a]You shall give him his wages on his day [1]before the sun
sets, for he is poor and sets his [2]heart on it; so that [b]he will not
cry against you to the LORD and it become sin in you.
16 "[a]Fathers shall not be put to death [1]for *their* sons, nor shall
sons be put to death [1]for *their* fathers; everyone shall be put to
death for his own sin.
17 "[a]You shall not pervert the justice [1]due an alien *or* [2]an
orphan, nor [b]take a widow's garment in pledge.
18 "But you shall remember that you were a slave in Egypt, and
that the LORD your God redeemed you from there; therefore I
am commanding you to do this thing.
19 "[a]When you reap your harvest in your field and have
forgotten a sheaf in the field, you shall not go back to get it; it
shall be [b]for the alien, for the [1]orphan, and for the widow, in
order that the LORD your God [c]may bless you in all the work of
your hands.

3 [1]Lit *hates her*
4 [a]Jer 3:1
5 [a]Deut 20:7 [b]Prov 5:18
7 [1]Lit *found stealing* [2]Lit *brothers* [a]Ex 21:16
8 [1]Lit *a mark* or *stroke* [a]Lev 13:1-14, 57
9 [a]Num 12:10
10 [a]Ex 22:26, 27
13 [a]Ex 22:26 [b]Deut 6:25; Ps 106:31; Dan 4:27
14 [1]Lit *brothers* [2]Lit *gates* [a]Lev 19:13; 25:35-43; Deut 15:7-18; Prov 14:31; Amos 4:1; 1 Tim 5:18
15 [1]Lit *that the sun shall not go down on it* [2]Lit *soul* [a]Lev 19:13; Jer 22:13; James 5:4 [b]Ex 22:23; Deut 15:9; Job 35:9; James 5:4
16 [1]Or *with* [a]2 Kin 14:6; 2 Chr 25:4; Jer 31:29, 30; Ezek 18:20
17 [1]Lit *of* [2]Or *the fatherless* [a]Ex 23:9; Lev 19:33; Deut 1:17; 10:17; 16:19; 27:19 [b]Ex 22:22
19 [1]Or *fatherless* [a]Lev 19:9, 10; 23:22 [b]Deut 14:29 [c]Prov 19:17

20 "[a]When you beat your olive tree, you shall not go over the
boughs [1]again; it shall be [b]for the alien, for the [2]orphan, and for
the widow.
21 "When you gather the grapes of your vineyard, you shall not
[1]go over it again; it shall be for the alien, for the [2]orphan, and
for the widow.
22 "You shall remember that you were a slave in the land of
Egypt; therefore I am commanding you to do this thing.

Chapter 25 Theme ______________________

25 "[a]If there is a dispute between men and they go to
[1]court, and [2]the judges decide their case, [b]and they justify the righteous and condemn the wicked,
2 then it shall be if the wicked man [1a]deserves to be beaten,
the judge shall then make him lie down and be beaten in his
presence with the number of stripes according to his [2]guilt.
3 "[a]He may beat him forty times *but* no more, so that he does
not beat him with many more stripes than these and your
brother is not [b]degraded in your eyes.
4 "[a]You shall not muzzle the ox while he is threshing.
5 "When brothers live together and one of them dies and has
no son, the wife of the deceased shall not be *married* outside
the family to a strange man. [a]Her husband's brother shall go in
to her and take her to himself as wife and perform the duty of a
husband's brother to her.
6 "It shall be that the firstborn whom she bears shall [1]assume
the name of his dead brother, so that [a]his name will not be
blotted out from Israel.
7 "[a]But if the man does not desire to take his brother's wife,
then his brother's wife shall go up to the gate to the elders and
say, 'My husband's brother refuses to establish a name for his
brother in Israel; he is not willing to perform the duty of a
husband's brother to me.'
8 "Then the elders of his city shall summon him and speak to
him. And *if* he persists and says, 'I do not desire to take her,'
9 [a]then his brother's wife shall come to him in the sight of
the elders, and pull his sandal off his foot and [b]spit in his face;
and she shall [1]declare, 'Thus it is done to the man who does
not build up his brother's house.'
10 "In Israel his name shall be called, 'The house of him whose
sandal is removed.'
11 "If *two* men, a man and his [1]countryman, are struggling
together, and the wife of one comes near to deliver her husband
from the hand of the one who is striking him, and puts out her
hand and seizes his genitals,
12 then you shall cut off her [1]hand; [2a]you shall not show pity.
13 "[a]You shall not have in your bag [1]differing weights, a large
and a small.
14 "You shall not have in your house [1]differing measures, a
large and a small.

20 [1]Lit *after yourself* [2]Or *fatherless* [a]Lev 19:10 [b]Deut 24:19

21 [1]Lit *glean it after yourself* [2]Or *fatherless*

25:1 [1]Lit *the judgment* [2]Lit *they judge them* [a]Deut 17:8-13; 19:17 [b]Deut 1:16, 17

2 [1]Lit *is a son of beating* [2]Or *wickedness* [a]Prov 19:29; Luke 12:48

3 [a]2 Cor 11:24 [b]Job 18:3

4 [a]Prov 12:10; 1 Cor 9:9; 1 Tim 5:18

5 [a]Matt 22:24; Mark 12:19; Luke 20:28

6 [1]Lit *stand on* [a]Ruth 4:5, 10

7 [a]Ruth 4:5, 6

9 [1]Lit *answer and say* [a]Ruth 4:7, 8 [b]Num 12:14

11 [1]Lit *brother*

12 [1]Lit *palm* [2]Lit *your eye* [a]Deut 7:2; 19:13

13 [1]Lit *a stone and a stone* [a]Lev 19:35-37; Prov 11:1; 20:23; Ezek 45:10; Mic 6:11

14 [1]Lit *an ephah and an ephah*

15 "You shall have a full and just weight; you shall have a full
and just [1]measure, [a]that your days may be prolonged in the
[2]land which the LORD your God gives you.
16 "For [a]everyone who does these things, everyone who acts
unjustly is an abomination to the LORD your God.
17 "[a]Remember what Amalek did to you along the way when
you came out from Egypt,
18 how he met you along the way and attacked among you all
the stragglers at your rear when you were faint and weary; and
he [a]did not [1]fear God.
19 "Therefore it shall come about when the LORD your God has
given you [a]rest from all your surrounding enemies, in the land
which the LORD your God gives you as an inheritance to
[1]possess, you shall blot out the memory of Amalek from under
heaven; you must not forget.

Chapter 26 Theme ____________________

26 "Then it shall be, when you enter the land which the
LORD your God gives you as an inheritance, and you
possess it and live in it,
2 that you shall take some of [a]the first of all the produce of
the ground which you bring in from your land that the LORD your
God gives you, and you shall put *it* in a basket and [b]go to the
place where the LORD your God chooses to establish His name.
3 "You shall go to the priest who is in office at that time and say
to him, 'I declare this day to the LORD [1]my God that I have
entered the land which the LORD swore to our fathers to give us.'
4 "Then the priest shall take the basket from your hand and
set it down before the altar of the LORD your God.
5 "You shall answer and say before the LORD your God, '[a]My
father was a [1]wandering Aramean, and he went down to Egypt
and [2]sojourned there, [b]few in number; but there he became a
[c]great, mighty and populous nation.
6 'And the [a]Egyptians treated us harshly and afflicted us, and
imposed hard labor on us.
7 'Then [a]we cried to the LORD, the God of our fathers, and the
LORD heard our voice and saw our affliction and our toil and
our oppression;
8 [a]and the LORD brought us out of Egypt with a mighty hand
and an outstretched arm and with great terror and with signs
and wonders;
9 and He has brought us to this place and has given us this
land, [a]a land flowing with milk and honey.
10 'Now behold, I have brought the first of the produce of the
ground [a]which You, O LORD have given me.' And you shall set
it down before the LORD your God, and worship before the
LORD your God;
11 and you and [a]the Levite and the alien who is among you
shall [b]rejoice in all the good which the LORD your God has
given you and your household.

15 [1]Lit *ephah* [2]Lit *ground* [a]Ex 20:12
16 [a]Prov 11:1
17 [a]Ex 17:8-16
18 [1]Or *reverence* [a]Ps 36:1; Rom 3:18
19 [1]Lit *possess it* [a]Deut 12:9
26:2 [a]Ex 22:29; 23:16, 19; Num 18:13; Prov 3:9 [b]Deut 12:5
3 [1]So with Gr; Heb *your*
5 [1]Or *perishing* [2]Or *lived as an alien* [a]Gen 43:1-14 [b]Gen 46:27 [c]Deut 1:10; 10:22
6 [a]Ex 1:8-11
7 [a]Ex 2:23-25; 3:9
8 [a]Deut 4:34; 34:11, 12
9 [a]Ex 3:8, 17
10 [a]Deut 8:18; Prov 10:22
11 [a]Deut 12:12 [b]Deut 12:7; 16:11; Eccl 3:12, 13; 5:18-20

12“[a]When you have finished [1]paying all the tithe of your
increase in the third year, the year of tithing, then you shall
give it to the Levite, to the stranger, to the [2]orphan and to the
widow, that they may eat in your [3]towns and be satisfied.
13“You shall say before the LORD your God, ‘I have removed
the sacred *portion* from *my* house, and also have given it to the
Levite and the alien, the [1]orphan and the widow, according to
all Your commandments which You have commanded me; [a]I
have not transgressed or forgotten any of Your commandments.
14 ‘I have not eaten of it [1]while mourning, nor have I removed
any of it while I was unclean, nor offered any of it to the dead.
I have listened to the voice of the LORD my God; I have done
according to all that You have commanded me.
15 ‘[a]Look down from Your holy habitation, from heaven, and
bless Your people Israel, and the ground which You have given
us, [b]a land flowing with milk and honey, as You swore to our
fathers.’
16“This day the LORD your God commands you to do these
statutes and ordinances. You shall therefore be careful to do
them [a]with all your heart and with all your soul.
17“[a]You have today declared the LORD to be your God, and
[1]that you would walk in His ways and keep His statutes, His
commandments and His ordinances, and listen to His voice.
18“The LORD has today declared you to be [a]His people, a
treasured possession, as He promised you, and [1]that you should
keep all His commandments;
19 and [1]that He will [a]set you high above all nations which He
has made, for praise, fame, and honor; and that you shall be [b]a
consecrated people to the LORD your God, as He has spoken.”

Chapter 27 Theme ______________________

27 Then Moses and the elders of Israel charged the people,
saying, “Keep all the commandments which I command you today.

2“[a]So it shall be on the day when you cross the Jordan to the
land which the LORD your God gives you, that you shall set up
for yourself large stones and coat them with lime
3 and write on them all the words of this law, when you
cross over, so that you may enter the land which the LORD your
God gives you, [a]a land flowing with milk and honey, as the
LORD, the God of your fathers, [1]promised you.
4“So it shall be when you cross the Jordan, you shall set up
[a]on Mount Ebal, these stones, [1]as I am commanding you today,
and you shall coat them with lime.
5“Moreover, you shall build there an altar to the LORD your
God, an altar of stones; you [a]shall not [1]wield an iron *tool* on
them.
6“You shall build the altar of the LORD your God of [1]uncut
stones, and you shall offer on it burnt offerings to the LORD your
God;

12 [1]Lit *tithing* [2]Or *fatherless* [3]Lit *gates* [a]Lev 27:30; Num 18:24; Deut 14:28, 29; Heb 7:5, 9, 10

13 [1]Or *fatherless* [a]Ps 119:141, 153, 176

14 [1]Lit *while in my*

15 [a]Ps 80:14; Is 63:15; Zech 2:13 [b]Deut 26:9

16 [a]Deut 4:29

17 [1]Lit *to walk in* [a]Ps 48:14

18 [1]Lit *to keep all* [a]Ex 6:7; 19:5; Deut 4:20; 7:6; 14:2; 28:9; 29:13; Titus 2:14; 1 Pet 2:9

19 [1]Lit *to set you* [a]Deut 4:7, 8; 28:1, 13 [b]Ex 19:6; Deut 7:6; Is 62:12; Jer 2:3; 1 Pet 2:9

27:2 [a]Josh 8:30-32

3 [1]Lit *spoke to* [a]Deut 26:9

4 [1]Lit *which* [a]Deut 11:29; Josh 8:30

5 [1]Lit *lift up* [a]Ex 20:25; Josh 8:31

6 [1]Lit *whole*

7 and you shall sacrifice peace offerings and eat there, and
[a]rejoice before the LORD your God.
8 "You shall write on the [1]stones all the words of this law very
distinctly."
9 Then Moses and the Levitical priests spoke to all Israel,
saying, "Be silent and listen, O Israel! This day you have become
a people for the LORD your God.
10 "You shall therefore [1]obey the LORD your God, and do His
commandments and His statutes which I command you today."
11 Moses also charged the people on that day, saying,
12 "When you cross the Jordan, these shall stand on [a]Mount
Gerizim to bless the people: [b]Simeon, Levi, Judah, Issachar,
Joseph, and Benjamin.
13 "For the curse, these shall stand on Mount Ebal: Reuben,
Gad, Asher, Zebulun, Dan, and Naphtali.
14 "The Levites shall then answer and say to all the men of
Israel with a loud voice,
15 'Cursed is the man who makes [1a]an idol or a molten image,
an abomination to the LORD, the work of the hands of the
craftsman, and sets *it* up in secret.' And [b]all the people shall
answer and say, 'Amen.'
16 '[a]Cursed is he who dishonors his father or mother.' And all
the people shall say, 'Amen.'
17 '[a]Cursed is he who moves his neighbor's boundary mark.'
And all the people shall say, 'Amen.'
18 '[a]Cursed is he who misleads a blind *person* on the road.'
And all the people shall say, 'Amen.'
19 '[a]Cursed is he who distorts the justice due an alien,
[1]orphan, and widow.' And all the people shall say, 'Amen.'
20 '[a]Cursed is he who lies with his father's wife, because he
has uncovered his father's skirt.' And all the people shall say,
'Amen.'
21 '[a]Cursed is he who lies with any animal.' And all the people
shall say, 'Amen.'
22 '[a]Cursed is he who lies with his sister, the daughter of his
father or of his mother.' And all the people shall say, 'Amen.'
23 '[a]Cursed is he who lies with his mother-in-law.' And all the
people shall say, 'Amen.'
24 '[a]Cursed is he who strikes his neighbor in secret.' And all
the people shall say, 'Amen.'
25 '[a]Cursed is he who accepts a bribe to strike down an
innocent person.' And all the people shall say, 'Amen.'
26 '[a]Cursed is he who does not confirm the words of this law
by doing them.' And all the people shall say, 'Amen.'

Chapter 28 Theme ______________________________

28 "[a]Now it shall be, if you diligently [1]obey the LORD your
God, being careful to do all His commandments which
I command you today, the LORD your God [b]will set you high
above all the nations of the earth.

7 [a]Deut 26:11
8 [1]I.e. stones coated with lime, cf v 4
10 [1]Lit *listen to the voice of*
12 [a]Deut 11:29 [b]Josh 8:33-35
15 [1]Or *a graven image* [a]Ex 20:4, 23; 34:17; Lev 19:4; 26:1; Deut 4:16, 23; 5:8; Is 44:9 [b]1 Cor 14:16
16 [a]Ex 20:12; 21:17; Lev 19:3; 20:9; Deut 5:16; Ezek 22:7
17 [a]Deut 19:14; Prov 22:28
18 [a]Lev 19:14
19 [1]Or *fatherless* [a]Ex 22:21; 23:9; Lev 19:33; Deut 10:18; 24:17
20 [a]Lev 18:8; 20:11; Deut 22:30; 1 Cor 5:1
21 [a]Ex 22:19; Lev 18:23; 20:15
22 [a]Lev 18:9; 20:17
23 [a]Lev 20:14
24 [a]Ex 21:12; Lev 24:17; Num 35:30, 31
25 [a]Ex 23:7; Deut 10:17; Ps 15:5; Ezek 22:12
26 [a]Ps 119:21; Jer 11:3; Gal 3:10
28:1 [1]Lit *listen to the voice of* [a]Ex 15:26; 23:22-27; Lev 26:3-13; Deut 7:12-26; 11:13 [b]Deut 28:13; 26:19; 1 Chr 14:2

2 "All these blessings will come upon you and [a]overtake you if
you [1]obey the LORD your God:
3 "Blessed *shall* you *be* in the city, and blessed *shall* you *be* [a]in
the [1]country.
4 "Blessed *shall be* the [1]offspring of your [2]body and the
[1]produce of your ground and the [1]offspring of your beasts, the
increase of your herd and the young of your flock.
5 "Blessed *shall be* your basket and your kneading bowl.
6 "Blessed *shall* you *be* [a]when you come in, and blessed *shall*
you *be* when you go out.
7 "The LORD shall cause your enemies who rise up against you
to be [1]defeated before you; they will come out against you one
way and will flee before you seven ways.
8 "The LORD will command the blessing upon you in your
barns and in [a]all that you put your hand to, and He will bless
you in the land which the LORD your God gives you.
9 "[a]The LORD will establish you as a holy people to Himself, as
He swore to you, if you keep the commandments of the LORD
your God and walk in His ways.
10 "So all the peoples of the earth will see that [1a]you are called
by the name of the LORD, and they will be afraid of you.
11 "[a]The LORD will make you abound in prosperity, in the
[1]offspring of your [2]body and in the [1]offspring of your beast and
in the [1]produce of your ground, in the land which the LORD
swore to our fathers to give you.
12 "The LORD will open for you His good storehouse, the
heavens, to give rain to your land in its season and to bless all
the work of your hand; and [a]you shall lend to many nations,
but you shall not borrow.
13 "[a]The LORD will make you the head and not the tail, and you
only will be above, and you will not be underneath, if you
listen to the commandments of the LORD your God, which I
charge you today, to [1]observe *them* carefully,
14 and [a]do not turn aside from any of the words which I
command you today, to the right or to the left, to go after other
gods to serve them.
15 "[a]But it shall come about, if you do not [1]obey the LORD your
God, to observe to do all His commandments and His statutes
with which I charge you today, that all these curses will come
upon you and overtake you:
16 "[a]Cursed *shall* you *be* in the city, and cursed *shall* you *be* in
the [1]country.
17 "[a]Cursed *shall be* your basket and your kneading bowl.
18 "[a]Cursed *shall be* the [1]offspring of your [2]body and the
[1]produce of your ground, the increase of your herd and the
young of your flock.
19 "[a]Cursed *shall* you *be* when you come in, and cursed *shall*
you *be* when you go out.
20 "[a]The LORD will send upon you curses, confusion, and
[b]rebuke, in all [1]you undertake to do, until you are destroyed
and until [c]you perish quickly, on account of the evil of your
deeds, because you have forsaken Me.

2 [1]Lit *listen to the voice of* [a]Zech 1:6
3 [1]Or *field* [a]Gen 39:5
4 [1]Lit *fruit* [2]Lit *womb*
6 [a]Ps 121:8
7 [1]Lit *smitten*
8 [a]Deut 15:10
9 [a]Ex 19:5
10 [1]Lit *the name of the LORD is called upon you* [a]2 Chr 7:14
11 [1]Lit *fruit* [2]Or *womb* [a]Deut 28:4; Prov 10:22
12 [a]Deut 23:20
13 [1]Lit *keep and do* [a]Deut 28:1, 44
14 [a]Deut 5:32; Josh 1:7
15 [1]Lit *listen to the voice of* [a]Lev 26:14-43; Josh 23:15; Dan 9:11
16 [1]Or *field* [a]Deut 28:3
17 [a]Deut 28:5
18 [1]Lit *fruit* [2]Or *womb* [a]Deut 28:4
19 [a]Deut 28:6
20 [1]Lit *the putting forth of your hand which you do* [a]Deut 28:8; Mal 2:2 [b]Ps 80:16; Is 51:20; 66:15 [c]Deut 4:26

21 "[a]The LORD will make the pestilence cling to you until He has consumed you from the land where you are entering to possess it.

22 "[a]The LORD will smite you with consumption and with fever and with inflammation and with fiery heat and with [1]the sword and [b]with blight and with mildew, and they will pursue you until [c]you perish.

23 "[1]The heaven which is over your head shall be bronze, and the earth which is under you, iron.

24 "[a]The LORD will make the rain of your land powder and dust; from heaven it shall come down on you until you are destroyed.

25 "[a]The LORD shall cause you to be [1]defeated before your enemies; you will go out one way against them, but you will flee seven ways before them, and you will [b]be *an example of* terror to all the kingdoms of the earth.

26 "[a]Your carcasses will be food to all birds of the sky and to the beasts of the earth, and there will be no one to frighten *them* away.

27 "[a]The LORD will smite you with the boils of Egypt and with [b]tumors and with the scab and with the itch, from which you cannot be healed.

28 "The LORD will smite you with madness and with blindness and with bewilderment of heart;

29 and you will [1a]grope at noon, as the blind man gropes in darkness, and you will not prosper in your ways; but you shall only be oppressed and robbed continually, with none to save you.

30 "[a]You shall betroth a wife, but another man will violate her; [b]you shall build a house, but you will not live in it; you shall plant a vineyard, but you will not [1]use its fruit.

31 "Your ox shall be slaughtered before your eyes, but you will not eat of it; your donkey shall be torn away from you, and will not be restored to you; your sheep shall be given to your enemies, and you will have none to save you.

32 "[a]Your sons and your daughters shall be given to another people, while your eyes look on and yearn for them continually; but there will be nothing [1]you can do.

33 "[a]A people whom you do not know shall eat up the produce of your ground and all your labors, and you will never be anything but oppressed and crushed continually.

34 "You shall be driven mad by the sight of [1]what you see.

35 "[a]The LORD will strike you on the knees and legs with sore boils, from which you cannot be healed, from the sole of your foot to the crown of your head.

36 "[a]The LORD will bring you and your king, whom you set over you, to a nation which neither you nor your fathers have known, and there you shall serve other gods, [b]wood and stone.

37 "[a]You shall become a horror, a proverb, and a taunt among all the people where the LORD drives you.

21 [a]Lev 26:25; Num 14:12; Jer 24:10; Amos 4:10

22 [1]Another reading is *drought* [a]Lev 26:16 [b]Amos 4:9 [c]Deut 4:26

23 [1]Lit *Your*

24 [a]Deut 11:17; 28:12

25 [1]Lit *smitten* [a]Deut 28:7; Is 30:17 [b]2 Chr 29:8; Jer 15:4; 24:9; Ezek 23:46

26 [a]Jer 7:33; 16:4; 19:7; 34:20

27 [a]Ex 9:9; Deut 7:15; 28:60, 61 [b]1 Sam 5:6

29 [1]Lit *be groping* [a]Ex 10:21

30 [1]Lit *begin it* [a]Job 31:10; Jer 8:10 [b]Amos 5:11

32 [1]Lit *in the power of your hand* [a]Deut 28:41

33 [a]Jer 5:15, 17

34 [1]Lit *your eyes which you*

35 [a]Deut 28:27

36 [a]2 Kin 17:4, 6; 24:12, 14; 25:7, 11; 2 Chr 36:1-21; Jer 39:1-9 [b]Deut 4:28; Jer 16:13

37 [a]1 Kin 9:7, 8; Jer 19:8; 24:9; 25:9; 29:18

38 "[a]You shall bring out much seed to the field but you will
gather in little, for [b]the locust will consume it.
39 "[a]You shall plant and cultivate vineyards, but you will
neither drink of the wine nor gather *the grapes,* for the worm
will devour them.
40 "[a]You shall have olive trees throughout your territory but you
will not anoint yourself with the oil, for your olives will drop off.
41 "[a]You shall [1]have sons and daughters but they will not be
yours, for they will go into captivity.
42 "[a]The cricket shall possess all your trees and the produce of
your ground.
43 "[a]The alien who is among you shall rise above you higher
and higher, but you will go down lower and lower.
44 "[a]He shall lend to you, but you will not lend to him; [b]he
shall be the head, and you will be the tail.
45 "So all these curses shall come on you and pursue you and
overtake you [a]until you are destroyed, because you would not
[1]obey the LORD your God by keeping His commandments and
His statutes which He commanded you.
46 "They shall become [a]a sign and a wonder on you and your
[1]descendants forever.
47 "[a]Because you did not serve the LORD your God with joy and
a glad heart, for the abundance of all things;
48 therefore you shall serve your enemies whom the LORD will
send against you, [a]in hunger, in thirst, in nakedness, and in the
lack of all things; and He [b]will put an iron yoke on your neck
until He has destroyed you.
49 "[a]The LORD will bring a nation against you from afar, from
the end of the earth, [b]as the eagle swoops down, a nation
whose language you shall not understand,
50 a nation of fierce countenance who will [a]have no respect
for the old, nor show favor to the young.
51 "Moreover, it shall eat the [1]offspring of your herd and the
produce of your ground until you are destroyed, who also leaves
you no grain, new wine, or oil, nor the increase of your herd or
the young of your flock until they have caused you to perish.
52 "[a]It shall besiege you in all your [1]towns until your high and
fortified walls in which you trusted come down throughout your
land, and it shall besiege you in all your [1]towns throughout your
land which the LORD your God has given you.
53 "[a]Then you shall eat the [1]offspring of your own body, the
flesh of your sons and of your daughters whom the LORD your
God has given you, during the siege and the distress by which
your enemy will [2]oppress you.
54 "The man who is [1]refined and very delicate among you
[2]shall be hostile toward his brother and toward the wife [3]he
cherishes and toward the rest of his children who remain,
55 so that he will not give *even* one of them any of the flesh of
his children which he will eat, since he has nothing *else* left,
during the siege and the distress by which your enemy will
[1]oppress you in all your [2]towns.

38 [a]Is 5:10; Mic 6:15; Hag 1:6 [b]Ex 10:4; Joel 1:4

39 [a]Is 5:10; 17:10, 11

40 [a]Jer 11:16; Mic 6:15

41 [1]Lit *beget* [a]Deut 28:32

42 [a]Deut 28:38

43 [a]Deut 28:13

44 [a]Deut 28:12 [b]Deut 28:13

45 [1]Lit *listen to the voice of* [a]Deut 4:25, 26

46 [1]Lit *seed* [a]Num 26:10; Is 8:18; Ezek 5:15; 14:8

47 [a]Deut 12:7; Neh 9:35-37

48 [a]Lam 4:4-6 [b]Jer 28:13, 14

49 [a]Is 5:26-30; 7:18-20; Jer 5:15; 6:22, 23 [b]Jer 48:40; 49:22; Lam 4:19; Hos 8:1

50 [a]Is 47:6

51 [1]Lit *fruit*

52 [1]Lit *gates* [a]Jer 10:17, 18; Zeph 1:15, 16

53 [1]Lit *fruit* [2]Or *distress* [a]Lev 26:29; 2 Kin 6:28, 29; Jer 19:9; Lam 2:20; 4:10

54 [1]Lit *tender* [2]Lit *his eye shall be evil toward* [3]Lit *of his bosom*

55 [1]Or *distress* [2]Lit *gates*

56 "[a]The [1]refined and delicate woman among you, who would
not venture to set the sole of her foot on the ground for
delicateness and [2]refinement, [3]shall be hostile toward the
husband [4]she cherishes and toward her son and daughter,
57 and toward her afterbirth which issues from between her
[1]legs and toward her children whom she bears; for [a]she will eat
them secretly for lack of anything *else,* during the siege and the
distress by which your enemy will [2]oppress you in your [3]towns.
58 "If you are not careful to observe all the words of this law
which are written in this book, to [1a]fear this honored and
awesome [b]name, [2]the LORD your God,
59 then the LORD will bring extraordinary plagues on you and
[1]your descendants, even [2]severe and lasting plagues, and
miserable and chronic sicknesses.
60 "[a]He will bring back on you all the diseases of Egypt of
which you were afraid, and they will cling to you.
61 "Also every sickness and every plague which, not written in
the book of this law, the LORD will bring on you [a]until you are
destroyed.
62 "Then you shall be left few in number, [a]whereas you were
as numerous as the stars of heaven, because you did not [1]obey
the LORD your God.
63 "It shall come about that as the LORD [a]delighted over you to
prosper you, and multiply you, so the LORD will [b]delight over
you to make you perish and destroy you; and you will be [c]torn
from the land where you are entering to possess it.
64 "Moreover, the LORD will [a]scatter you among all peoples,
from one end of the earth to the other end of the earth; and
there you shall [b]serve other gods, wood and stone, which you
or your fathers have not known.
65 "[a]Among those nations you shall find no rest, and there will
be no resting place for the sole of your foot; but there [b]the LORD
will give you a trembling heart, failing of eyes, and despair of
soul.
66 "So your life shall [1]hang in doubt before you; and you will be
in dread night and day, and shall have no assurance of your life.
67 "[a]In the morning you shall say, 'Would that it were evening!'
And at evening you shall say, 'Would that it were morning!'
because of the dread of your heart which you dread, and for
the sight of your eyes which you will see.
68 "The LORD will bring you back to Egypt in ships, by the way
about which I spoke to you, 'You will never see it again!' And
there you will offer yourselves for sale to your enemies as male
and female slaves, but there will be no buyer."

Chapter 29 Theme ______________________________

29 [1a]These are the words of the covenant which the LORD
commanded Moses to make with the sons of Israel in
the land of Moab, besides the [b]covenant which He had made
with them at Horeb.

56 [1]Lit *tender* [2]Lit *tenderness* [3]Lit *her eye shall be evil toward* [4]Lit *of her bosom* [a]Lam 4:10

57 [1]Lit *feet* [2]Or *distress* [3]Lit *gates* [a]2 Kin 6:28, 29; Lam 4:10

58 [1]Or *reverence* [2]Heb *YHWH* [a]Ps 99:3; Mal 1:14 [b]Is 42:8

59 [1]Lit *plague on your seed* [2]Lit *great*

60 [a]Deut 28:27

61 [a]Deut 4:25, 26

62 [1]Lit *listen to the voice of* [a]Deut 1:10; Neh 9:23

63 [a]Jer 32:41 [b]Prov 1:26 [c]Jer 12:14; 45:4

64 [a]Lev 26:33; Deut 4:27; Neh 1:8 [b]Deut 4:28; 29:26; 32:17

65 [a]Lam 1:3 [b]Lev 26:36

66 [1]Lit *be hung for you in front*

67 [a]Job 7:4

29:1 [1]Ch 28:69 in Heb [a]Lev 26:46; 27:34 [b]Deut 5:2, 3

2 [1]And Moses summoned all Israel and said to them, "You
have seen all that the LORD did before your eyes in the land of
Egypt to Pharaoh and all his servants and all his land;
3 [a]the great trials which your eyes have seen, those great
signs and wonders.
4 "Yet to this day [a]the LORD has not given you a heart to know,
nor eyes to see, nor ears to hear.
5 "I have led you forty years in the wilderness; [a]your clothes
have not worn out on you, and your sandal has not worn out
on your foot.
6 "[a]You have not eaten bread, nor have you drunk wine or
strong drink, in order that you might know that I am the LORD
your God.
7 "[a]When you [1]reached this place, Sihon the king of Heshbon
and Og the king of Bashan came out to meet us for battle, but
we [2]defeated them;
8 and we took their land and [a]gave it as an inheritance to the
Reubenites, the Gadites, and the half-tribe of the Manassites.
9 "[a]So keep the words of this covenant to do them, [b]that you
may prosper in all that you do.
10 "You stand today, all of you, before the LORD your God: your
chiefs, your tribes, your elders and your officers, *even* all the
men of Israel,
11 your little ones, your wives, and the alien who is within
your camps, from [a]the one who chops your wood to the one
who draws your water,
12 that you may enter into the covenant with the LORD your
God, and into His oath which the LORD your God is making
with you today,
13 in order that He may establish you today as His people and
that [a]He may be your God, just as He spoke to you and as He
swore to your fathers, to Abraham, Isaac, and Jacob.
14 "Now not with you alone am I [a]making this covenant and
this oath,
15 [a]but both with those who stand here with us today in the
presence of the LORD our God and with those who are not with
us here today
16 (for you know how we lived in the land of Egypt, and how
we came through the midst of the nations through which you
passed;
17 moreover, you have seen their abominations and their idols
of [a]wood, stone, silver, and gold, which *they had* with them);
18 [a]so that there will not be among you a man or woman, or
family or tribe, whose heart turns away today from the LORD
our God, to go and serve the gods of those nations; that there
will not be among you [b]a root bearing poisonous fruit and
wormwood.
19 "It shall be when he hears the words of this curse, that he
will [1]boast, saying, 'I have peace though I walk in the stubbornness of my heart in order [2]to destroy the watered *land* with the
dry.'

2 [1]Ch 29:1 in Heb
3 [a]Deut 4:34; 7:19
4 [a]Is 6:9, 10; Ezek 12:2; Matt 13:14; Acts 28:26, 27; Rom 11:8
5 [a]Deut 8:4
6 [a]Deut 8:3
7 [1]Lit *came to* [2]Lit *smote* [a]Num 21:21-24, 33, 35; Deut 2:26-3:17
8 [a]Num 32:32, 33; Deut 3:12, 13
9 [a]Deut 4:6; 1 Kin 2:3 [b]Josh 1:7
11 [a]Josh 9:21, 23, 27
13 [a]Gen 17:7; Ex 6:7
14 [a]Jer 31:31; Heb 8:7, 8
15 [a]Acts 2:39
17 [a]Ex 20:23; Deut 4:28; 28:36
18 [a]Deut 13:6 [b]Deut 32:32; Heb 12:15
19 [1]Lit *bless himself in his heart* [2]I.e. to destroy everything

20 [1]Lit *smoke* [2]Lit *lie down* [a]Ps 79:5; Ezek 23:25 [b]Ps 74:1; 80:4 [c]Ex 32:33; Deut 9:14; 2 Kin 14:27

20 "The LORD shall never be willing to forgive him, but rather
the anger of the LORD and [a]His jealousy will [1b]burn against that
man, and every curse which is written in this book will [2]rest
on him, and the LORD will [c]blot out his name from under
heaven.

21 [1]Lit *evil* [a]Deut 30:10

21 "Then the LORD will single him out for [1]adversity from all
the tribes of Israel, according to all the curses of the covenant
[a]which are written in this book of the law.

22 [1]Lit *made it sick* [a]Jer 19:8; 49:17; 50:13

22 "Now the generation to come, your sons who rise up after
you and [a]the foreigner who comes from a distant land, when
they see the plagues of the land and the diseases with which
the LORD has [1]afflicted it, will say,

23 [1]Lit *it is not sown and does not cause to sprout* [a]Gen 19:24; Is 34:9; Jer 17:6; Zeph 2:9 [b]Is 1:7; 64:11 [c]Jude 7

23 'All its land is [a]brimstone and salt, [b]a burning waste, [1]unsown
and unproductive, and no grass grows in it, like the overthrow
of [c]Sodom and Gomorrah, Admah and Zeboiim, which the LORD
overthrew in His anger and in His wrath.'

24 [1]Lit *heat* [a]1 Kin 9:8; Jer 22:8

24 "All the nations will say, '[a]Why has the LORD done thus to
this land? Why this great [1]outburst of anger?'

25 [a]2 Kin 17:9-23; 2 Chr 36:13-21

25 "Then *men* will say, '[a]Because they forsook the covenant of
the LORD, the God of their fathers, which He made with them
when He brought them out of the land of Egypt.

26 [1]Lit *portioned*

26 'They went and served other gods and worshiped them,
gods whom they have not known and whom He had not
[1]allotted to them.

27 [a]Dan 9:11

27 'Therefore, the anger of the LORD burned against that land,
[a]to bring upon it every curse which is written in this book;

28 [a]2 Chr 7:20; Ps 52:5; Prov 2:22; Ezek 19:12, 13

28 and [a]the LORD uprooted them from their land in anger and
in fury and in great wrath, and cast them into another land, as
it is this day.'

29 [a]Acts 1:7 [b]John 5:39; Acts 17:11; 2 Tim 3:16

29 "[a]The secret things belong to the LORD our God, but [b]the
things revealed belong to us and to our sons forever, that we
may observe all the words of this law.

Chapter 30 Theme ____________________

30:1 [1]Lit *cause them to return to your heart* [a]Deut 11:26; 30:15, 19 [b]Lev 26:40-45; Deut 28:64; 29:28; 1 Kin 8:47

30 "So it shall be when all of these things have come upon
you, [a]the blessing and the curse which I have set
before you, and you [1]call *them* to mind [b]in all nations where
the LORD your God has banished you,

2 [1]Lit *listen to His voice* [a]Deut 4:29, 30; Neh 1:9 [b]Deut 4:29

2 and you [a]return to the LORD your God and [1]obey Him [b]with
all your heart and soul according to all that I command you
today, you and your sons,

3 [1]Lit *your captivity* [a]Gen 28:15; 48:21; Ps 126:1, 4; Jer 29:14 [b]Ps 147:2; Jer 32:37; Ezek 34:13 [c]Deut 4:27

3 then the LORD your God will [a]restore [1]you from captivity,
and have compassion on you, and [b]will gather you again from
all the peoples where the LORD your God has [c]scattered you.

4 [1]Lit *sky* [2]Lit *take you* [a]Neh 1:9; Is 43:6; 48:20; 62:11

4 "If your outcasts are at the ends of the [1]earth, [a]from there
the LORD your God will gather you, and from there He will
[2]bring you back.

5 [a]Jer 29:14; 30:3 [b]Deut 7:13; 13:17

5 "[a]The LORD your God will bring you into the land which
your fathers possessed, and you shall possess it; and He will
prosper you and [b]multiply you more than your fathers.

6 "Moreover [a]the LORD your God will circumcise your heart and the heart of your [1]descendants, [b]to love the LORD your God with all your heart and with all your soul, so that you may live.

7 "[a]The LORD your God will [1]inflict all these curses on your enemies and on those who hate you, who persecuted you.

8 "And you shall again [1]obey the LORD, and observe all His commandments which I command you today.

9 "[a]Then the LORD your God will [1]prosper you abundantly in all the work of your hand, in the [2]offspring of your [3]body and in the [2]offspring of your cattle and in the [2]produce of your ground, for [b]the LORD will again rejoice over you for good, just as He rejoiced over your fathers;

10 [1]if you [2]obey the LORD your God to keep His commandments and His statutes which [a]are written in this book of the law, [1]if you turn to the LORD your God [b]with all your heart and soul.

11 "For this commandment which I command you today is not too difficult for you, nor is it [1]out of reach.

12 "It is not in heaven, [1]that you should say, '[a]Who will go up to heaven for us to get it for us and make us hear it, that we may observe it?'

13 "Nor is it beyond the sea, [1]that you should say, 'Who will cross the sea for us to get it for us and make us hear it, that we may observe it?'

14 "But the word is very near you, in your mouth and in your heart, that you may observe it.

15 "See, [a]I have set before you today life and [1]prosperity, and death and [2]adversity;

16 in that I command you today [a]to love the LORD your God, to walk in His ways and to keep His commandments and His statutes and His judgments, that you [b]may live and multiply, and that the LORD your God may bless you in the land where you are entering to possess it.

17 "But if your heart turns away and you will not obey, but are drawn away and worship other gods and serve them,

18 I declare to you today that [a]you shall surely perish. You will not prolong *your* days in the land where you are crossing the Jordan to enter [1]and possess it.

19 "[a]I call heaven and earth to witness against you today, that I have set before you life and death, [b]the blessing and the curse. So choose life in order that you may live, you and your [1]descendants,

20 [a]by loving the LORD your God, by obeying His voice, and [b]by holding fast to Him; [c]for [1]this is your life and the length of your days, [2]that you may live in [d]the land which the LORD swore to your fathers, to Abraham, Isaac, and Jacob, to give them."

Chapter 31 Theme

31 So Moses went and spoke these words to all Israel.

2 And he said to them, "I am [a]a hundred and twenty years old today; [b]I am no longer able to come and go, and the LORD has said to me, '[c]You shall not cross this Jordan.'

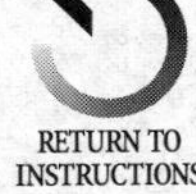

6 [1]Lit *seed* [a]Deut 10:16 [b]Deut 6:5

7 [1]Lit *put* [a]Deut 7:15

8 [1]Lit *listen to the voice of*

9 [1]Lit *make you have excess for good* [2]Lit *fruit* [3]Lit *womb* [a]Jer 31:27, 28 [b]Jer 32:41

10 [1]Or *for you will* [2]Lit *listen to the voice of* [a]Deut 29:21 [b]Deut 4:29

11 [1]Lit *far off*

12 [1]Lit *to say* [a]Rom 10:6-8

13 [1]Lit *to say*

15 [1]Lit *good* [2]Lit *evil* [a]Deut 11:26

16 [a]Deut 6:5 [b]Deut 4:1; 30:19

18 [1]Lit *to* [a]Deut 4:26; 8:19

19 [1]Lit *seed* [a]Deut 4:26 [b]Deut 30:1

20 [1]Lit *that* [2]Lit *to dwell* [a]Deut 6:5 [b]Deut 10:20 [c]Deut 4:1; 32:47; Acts 17:25, 28 [d]Gen 12:7; 17:1-8

31:2 [a]Deut 34:7 [b]Num 27:17; 1 Kin 3:7 [c]Deut 1:37; 3:27

3 "[a]It is the LORD your God who will cross ahead of you; He
will destroy these nations before you, and you shall dispossess
them. [b]Joshua is the one who will cross ahead of you, just as
the LORD has spoken.
4 "The LORD will do to them just as He did to Sihon and Og,
the kings of the Amorites, and to their land, when He destroyed
them.
5 "[a]The LORD will deliver them up before you, and you shall
do to them according to all the commandments which I have
commanded you.
6 "[a]Be strong and courageous, [b]do not be afraid or tremble at
them, for [c]the LORD your God is the one who goes with you.
[d]He will not fail you or forsake you."
7 Then Moses called to Joshua and said to him in the sight of
all Israel, "[a]Be strong and courageous, for you shall go with this
people into the land which the LORD has sworn to their fathers
to give them, and you shall give it to them as an inheritance.
8 "[a]The LORD is the one who goes ahead of you; He will be
with you. [b]He will not fail you or forsake you. Do not fear or be
dismayed."
9 So Moses wrote this law and gave it to the priests, the sons
of Levi [a]who carried the ark of the covenant of the LORD, and to
all the elders of Israel.
10 Then Moses commanded them, saying, "At the end of
every seven years, at the time of [a]the year of remission of debts,
at the [b]Feast of Booths,
11 when all Israel comes [a]to appear before the LORD your God
at [b]the place which He will choose, [c]you shall read this law in
front of all Israel in their hearing.
12 "Assemble the people, the men and the women and children
and [1]the alien who is in your [2]town, so that they may hear and
[a]learn and fear the LORD your God, and be careful to observe all
the words of this law.
13 "Their children, who have not known, will hear and learn
to fear the LORD your God, as long as you live on the land
[1]which you are about to cross the Jordan to [2]possess."
14 Then the LORD said to Moses, "Behold, [1a]the time for you
to die is near; call Joshua, and present yourselves at the tent of
meeting, that I may commission him." [b]So Moses and Joshua
went and presented themselves at the tent of meeting.
15 [a]The LORD appeared in the tent in a pillar of cloud, and the
pillar of cloud stood at the doorway of the tent.
16 The LORD said to Moses, "Behold, [a]you are about to lie
down with your fathers; and [b]this people will arise and play the
harlot with the strange gods of the land, into the midst of
which they are going, and [c]will forsake Me and break My
covenant which I have made with them.
17 "[a]Then My anger will be kindled against them in that day,
and [b]I will forsake them and [c]hide My face from them, and
they will be consumed, and many evils and troubles will come
upon them; so that they will say in that day, '[d]Is it not because
our God is not among us that these evils have come upon us?'

3 [a]Deut 9:3 [b]Num 27:18
5 [a]Deut 7:2
6 [a]Josh 10:25; 1 Chr 22:13 [b]Deut 1:29; 7:18; 20:1 [c]Deut 20:4 [d]Josh 1:5; Heb 13:5
7 [a]Deut 1:38; 3:28
8 [a]Ex 13:21; 33:14 [b]Deut 31:6; Josh 1:5; Heb 13:5
9 [a]Num 4:5, 6, 15; Deut 10:8; 31:25, 26; Josh 3:3
10 [a]Deut 15:1, 2 [b]Lev 23:34; Deut 16:13
11 [a]Deut 16:16 [b]Deut 12:5 [c]Josh 8:34; 2 Kin 23:2
12 [1]Lit *your alien* [2]Lit *gates* [a]Deut 4:10
13 [1]Lit *where* [2]Lit *possess it*
14 [1]Lit *your days to die are* [a]Num 27:12, 13; Deut 4:22; 32:50 [b]Ex 33:9-11
15 [a]Ex 33:9
16 [a]Gen 15:15 [b]Ex 34:15; Deut 4:25-28; Judg 2:11, 12, 17 [c]Judg 10:6; 1 Kin 18:18; 19:10; Jer 2:13
17 [a]Judg 2:14; 6:13 [b]2 Chr 15:2; 24:20 [c]Ps 104:29; Is 8:17 [d]Num 14:42

18 "But I will surely hide My face in that day because of all the
evil which they will do, for they will turn to other gods.
19 "Now therefore, [a]write this song for yourselves, and teach it
to the sons of Israel; put it [1]on their lips, so that this song may
be a witness for Me against the sons of Israel.
20 "[a]For when I bring them into the land flowing with milk and
honey, which I swore to their fathers, and they have eaten and are
satisfied and [b]become [1]prosperous, then they will turn to other
gods and serve them, and spurn Me and break My covenant.
21 "Then it shall come about, [a]when many evils and troubles
have come upon them, that this song will testify before them as a
witness (for it shall not be forgotten from the [1]lips of their
descendants); for [b]I know their intent which they are [2]developing
today, before I have brought them into the land which I swore."
22 [a]So Moses wrote this song the same day, and taught it to
the sons of Israel.
23 [a]Then He commissioned Joshua the son of Nun, and said,
"[b]Be strong and courageous, for you shall bring the sons of
Israel into the land which I swore to them, and [c]I will be with
you."
24 It came about, when Moses finished writing the words of
this law in a book until they were complete,
25 that Moses commanded the Levites [a]who carried the ark of
the covenant of the LORD, saying,
26 "Take this book of the law and place it beside the ark of the
covenant of the LORD your God, that it may [1]remain there as a
witness against you.
27 "For I know [a]your rebellion and [b]your [1]stubbornness; behold,
while I am still alive with you today, you have been rebellious
against the LORD; how much more, then, after my death?
28 "Assemble to me all the elders of your tribes and your
officers, that I may speak these words in their hearing and [a]call
the heavens and the earth to witness against them.
29 "For I know that after my death you will [a]act corruptly and
turn from the way which I have commanded you; and evil will
befall you in the latter days, for you will do that which is evil in
the sight of the LORD, provoking Him to anger with the work of
your hands."
30 Then Moses spoke in the hearing of all the assembly of
Israel the words of this song, until they were complete:

Chapter 32 Theme ______________________

32 "[a]Give ear, O heavens, and let me speak;
And let the earth hear the words of my mouth.
2 "[a]Let my teaching drop as the rain,
My speech distill as the dew,
[b]As the droplets on the fresh grass
And as the showers on the herb.
3 "[a]For I proclaim the name of the LORD;
[b]Ascribe greatness to our God!

19 [1]Lit *in their mouths* [a]Deut 31:22

20 [1]Lit *fat* [a]Deut 6:10-12; 8:10, 19; 11:16, 17 [b]Deut 32:15-17

21 [1]Lit *mouth of its seed* [2]Lit *making* [a]Lev 26:41; Deut 4:30 [b]1 Chr 28:9; John 2:24, 25

22 [a]Deut 31:19

23 [a]Num 27:23; Deut 31:7 [b]Josh 1:6 [c]Ex 3:12

25 [a]Deut 31:9

26 [1]Lit *be*

27 [1]Lit *stiff neck* [a]Deut 9:7, 24 [b]Ex 32:9; Deut 9:6, 13

28 [a]Deut 4:26; 30:19; 32:1

29 [a]Judg 2:19

32:1 [a]Deut 4:26; Ps 50:4; Is 1:2; Jer 6:19

2 [a]Is 55:10, 11 [b]Ps 72:6

3 [a]Ex 33:19; 34:5, 6 [b]Deut 3:24; 5:24

4 [1]Or *judgment* [a]Deut 32:15, 18, 30; 2 Sam 22:31 [b]Gen 18:25; Dan 4:37 [c]Deut 7:9

5 [1]Lit *It has* [a]Deut 4:25; 31:29 [b]Matt 17:17

6 [a]Ps 116:12 [b]Deut 32:28 [c]Deut 1:31; Ps 74:2; Is 63:16 [d]Deut 32:15

7 [a]Ex 12:26; Ps 78:5-8

8 [1]Or *Adam* [a]Acts 17:26 [b]Num 23:9; Deut 33:28

9 [a]1 Sam 10:1; 1 Kin 8:51, 53; Jer 10:16

10 [a]Deut 1:19 [b]Ps 17:8; Prov 7:2; Zech 2:8

11 [a]Ex 19:4; Deut 33:12 [b]Ps 18:10-18

12 [a]Deut 4:35, 39 [b]Deut 32:39; Is 43:12

13 [a]Is 58:14 [b]Deut 8:8; Ps 81:16 [c]Job 29:6

14 [a]Ps 81:16; 147:14 [b]Gen 49:11

15 [1]I.e. Israel [a]Deut 31:20 [b]Judg 10:6 [c]Deut 32:6 [d]Deut 32:4; Ps 89:26

16 [a]Ps 78:58 [b]Ps 106:29

17 [a]Lev 17:7; 1 Cor 10:20 [b]Deut 28:64 [c]Judg 5:8

4 "[a]The Rock! His work is perfect,
[b]For all His ways are [1]just;
[c]A God of faithfulness and without injustice,
Righteous and upright is He.
5 "[1a]They have acted corruptly toward Him,
They are not His children, because of their defect;
[b]*But are* a perverse and crooked generation.
6 "Do you thus [a]repay the LORD,
[b]O foolish and unwise people?
[c]Is not He your Father who has bought you?
[d]He has made you and established you.
7 "Remember the days of old,
Consider the years of all generations.
[a]Ask your father, and he will inform you,
Your elders, and they will tell you.
8 "[a]When the Most High gave the nations their inheritance,
When He separated the sons of [1]man,
He set the boundaries of the peoples
[b]According to the number of the sons of Israel.
9 "[a]For the LORD's portion is His people;
Jacob is the allotment of His inheritance.
10 "[a]He found him in a desert land,
And in the howling waste of a wilderness;
He encircled him, He cared for him,
He guarded him as [b]the pupil of His eye.
11 "[a]Like an eagle that stirs up its nest,
That hovers over its young,
[b]He spread His wings and caught them,
He carried them on His pinions.
12 "[a]The LORD alone guided him,
[b]And there was no foreign god with him.
13 "[a]He made him ride on the high places of the earth,
And he ate the produce of the field;
[b]And He made him suck honey from the rock,
And [c]oil from the flinty rock,
14 Curds of cows, and milk of the flock,
With fat of lambs,
And rams, the breed of Bashan, and goats,
[a]With the finest of the wheat—
And of the [b]blood of grapes you drank wine.

15 "[a]But [1]Jeshurun grew fat and kicked—
You are grown fat, thick, and sleek—
[b]Then he forsook God [c]who made him,
And scorned [d]the Rock of his salvation.
16 "[a]They made Him jealous with strange *gods;*
[b]With abominations they provoked Him to anger.
17 "[a]They sacrificed to demons who were not God,
[b]To gods whom they have not known,
[c]New *gods* who came lately,
Whom your fathers did not dread.

18 "You neglected [a]the Rock who begot you,
[b]And forgot the God who gave you birth.

19 "[a]The LORD saw *this,* and spurned *them*
[b]Because of the provocation of His sons and daughters.
20 "Then He said, 'I will hide My face from them,
[a]I will see what their end *shall be;*
[b]For they are a perverse generation,
[c]Sons in whom is no faithfulness.
21 '[a]They have made Me jealous with *what* is not God;
They have provoked Me to anger with their [1][b]idols.
[c]So I will make them jealous with *those who* are not a people;
I will provoke them to anger with a foolish nation,
22 [a]For a fire is kindled in My anger,
And burns to the lowest part of [1]Sheol,
[b]And consumes the earth with its yield,
And sets on fire the foundations of the mountains.

23 '[a]I will heap misfortunes on them;
[b]I will use My arrows on them.
24 '[a]*They will be* wasted by famine, and consumed by [1]plague
[b]And bitter destruction;
[c]And the teeth of beasts I will send upon them,
[d]With the venom of crawling things of the dust.
25 '[a]Outside the sword will bereave,
And inside terror—
[b]Both young man and virgin,
The nursling with the man of gray hair.
26 'I would have said, "[a]I will cut them to pieces,
[b]I will remove the memory of them from men,"
27 Had I not feared the provocation by the enemy,
That their adversaries would misjudge,
That they would say, "[a]Our hand is [1]triumphant,
And the LORD has not done all this."'

28 "[a]For they are a nation [1]lacking in counsel,
And there is no understanding in them.
29 "[a]Would that they were wise, that they understood this,
[b]That they would discern their [1]future!
30 "[a]How could one chase a thousand,
And two put ten thousand to flight,
Unless their [b]Rock had sold them,
And the LORD had given them up?
31 "Indeed their rock is not like our Rock,
[a]Even our enemies [1]themselves judge this.
32 "For their vine is from the vine of Sodom,
And from the fields of Gomorrah;
Their grapes are grapes of [a]poison,
Their clusters, bitter.
33 "Their wine is the venom of [1]serpents,
And the [2]deadly poison of cobras.

18 [a]Deut 32:4 [b]Ps 106:21

19 [a]Lev 26:30; Ps 106:40 [b]Jer 44:21-23

20 [a]Deut 31:29 [b]Deut 32:5 [c]Deut 9:23

21 [1]Lit *vanities* [a]Deut 32:16; 1 Cor 10:22 [b]Deut 32:17; 1 Kin 16:13, 26 [c]Rom 10:19

22 [1]I.e. the nether world [a]Num 16:33-35; Ps 18:7, 8; Lam 4:11 [b]Lev 26:20

23 [a]Deut 29:21 [b]Ps 18:14; 45:5

24 [1]Lit *burning heat* [a]Deut 28:22, 48 [b]Ps 91:6 [c]Lev 26:22 [d]Amos 5:18, 19

25 [a]Lam 1:20; Ezek 7:15 [b]2 Chr 36:17; Lam 2:21

26 [a]Deut 4:27; 28:64 [b]Deut 9:14

27 [1]Lit *high* [a]Num 15:30

28 [1]Lit *perishing* [a]Deut 32:6

29 [1]Or *latter end* [a]Deut 5:29 [b]Deut 31:29

30 [a]Lev 26:7, 8 [b]Deut 32:4; Ps 44:12

31 [1]Lit *are judges* [a]Ex 14:25

32 [a]Deut 29:18

33 [1]Lit *dragons* [2]Lit *cruel*

34 '[a]Is it not laid up in store with Me,
Sealed up in My treasuries?
35 '[a]Vengeance is Mine, and retribution,
[b]In due time their foot will slip;
[c]For the day of their calamity is near,
And the impending things are hastening upon them.'
36 "[a]For the LORD will vindicate His people,
[b]And will have compassion on His servants,
When He sees that *their* [1]strength is gone,
And there is none *remaining,* bond or free.
37 "And He will say, '[a]Where are their gods,
The rock in which they sought refuge?
38 '[a]Who ate the fat of their sacrifices,
And drank the wine of their drink offering?
[b]Let them rise up and help you,
Let them be your hiding place!
39 '[a]See now that I, I am He,
[b]And there is no god besides Me;
[c]It is I who put to death and give life.
[d]I have wounded and it is I who heal,
[e]And there is no one who can deliver from My hand.
40 'Indeed, [a]I lift up My hand to heaven,
And say, as I live forever,
41 [a]If I sharpen My [1]flashing sword,
And My hand takes hold on justice,
[b]I will render vengeance on My adversaries,
And I will repay those who hate Me.
42 '[a]I will make My arrows drunk with blood,
[b]And My sword will devour flesh,
With the blood of the slain and the captives,
From the long-haired [1]leaders of the enemy.'
43 "[a]Rejoice, O nations, *with* His people;
[b]For He will avenge the blood of His servants,
[c]And will render vengeance on His adversaries,
[d]And will atone for His land *and* His people."
44 Then Moses came and spoke all the words of this song in
the hearing of the people, he, with [1a]Joshua the son of Nun.
45 When Moses had finished speaking all these words to all Israel,
46 he said to them, "[a]Take to your heart all the words with
which I am warning you today, which you shall command [b]your
sons to observe [1]carefully, *even* all the words of this law.
47 "For it is not an idle word for you; indeed [a]it is your life.
And [b]by this word you will prolong your days in the land,
[1]which you are about to cross the Jordan to [2]possess."
48 [a]The LORD spoke to Moses that very same day, saying,
49 "[a]Go up to this mountain of the Abarim, Mount Nebo, which
is in the land of Moab [1]opposite Jericho, and look at the land of
Canaan, which I am giving to the sons of Israel for a possession.
50 "Then die on the mountain where you ascend, and be
[a]gathered to your people, as Aaron your brother died on Mount
Hor and was gathered to his people,

34 [a]Job 14:17; Jer 44:21
35 [a]Ps 94:1; Rom 12:19; Heb 10:30 [b]Jer 23:12 [c]Ezek 7:5-10
36 [1]Lit *hand* [a]Ps 135:14; Heb 10:30 [b]Lev 26:43-45; Deut 30:1-3
37 [a]Judg 10:14; Jer 2:28
38 [a]Num 25:1, 2 [b]Jer 11:12
39 [a]Is 41:4; 43:10 [b]Deut 32:12; Is 45:5 [c]1 Sam 2:6; Ps 68:20 [d]Ps 51:8 [e]Ps 50:22
40 [a]Ezek 20:5, 6; 21:4, 5
41 [1]Or *lightning* [a]Is 34:6-8 [b]Jer 50:28-32
42 [1]Lit *head* [a]Deut 32:23 [b]Jer 12:12; 46:10, 14
43 [a]Rom 15:10 [b]2 Kin 9:7; Rev 6:10; 19:2 [c]Is 1:24, 25 [d]Ps 65:3; 79:9; 85:1
44 [1]Lit *Hoshea* [a]Num 13:8, 16
46 [1]Lit *to do* [a]Ezek 40:4; 44:5 [b]Deut 4:9
47 [1]Lit *where* [2]Lit *possess it* [a]Deut 8:3; 30:20 [b]Deut 4:40; 33:25
48 [a]Num 27:12
49 [1]Lit *which is opposite* [a]Num 27:12-14; Deut 3:27
50 [a]Gen 25:8

51 [a]because you broke faith with Me in the midst of the sons
of Israel at the waters of Meribah-kadesh, in the [b]wilderness of
Zin, because you did not treat Me as holy in the midst of the
sons of Israel.
52 "[a]For you shall see the land at a distance, but [b]you shall not
go there, into the land which I am giving the sons of Israel."

Chapter 33 Theme ____________________

33 Now this is the blessing with which Moses [a]the man of God blessed the sons of Israel before his death.

2 He said,
"[a]The LORD came from Sinai,
[b]And [1]dawned on them from Seir;
[c]He shone forth from Mount Paran,
And He came from [d]the [2]midst of ten thousand holy ones;
[e]At His right hand there was [3]flashing lightning for them.
3 "[a]Indeed, He loves [1]the people;
[b]All [2]Your holy ones are in Your hand,
[c]And they [3]followed in Your steps;
Everyone receives of Your words.
4 "[a]Moses charged us with a law,
[b]A possession for the assembly of Jacob.
5 "[a]And He was king in Jeshurun,
When the heads of the people were gathered,
The tribes of Israel together.

6 "[a]May Reuben live and not die,
Nor his men be few."

7 [a]And this regarding Judah; so he said,
"Hear, O LORD, the voice of Judah,
And bring him to his people.
With his hands he contended for [1]them,
And may You be a help against his adversaries."

8 Of Levi he said,
"*Let* Your [a]Thummim and Your Urim *belong* to [1]Your [b]godly man,
[c]Whom You proved at Massah,
With whom You contended at the waters of Meribah;
9 [a]Who said of his father and his mother,
'I did not consider them';
And he did not acknowledge his brothers,
Nor did he regard his own sons,
For [b]they observed Your word,
And kept Your covenant.
10 "[a]They shall teach Your ordinances to Jacob,
And Your law to Israel.
[b]They shall put incense [1]before You,
And [c]whole burnt offerings on Your altar.

51 [a]Num 20:12 [b]Num 27:14

52 [a]Deut 34:1-3 [b]Deut 1:37; 3:27

33:1 [a]Josh 14:6

2 [1]Lit *rose to* [2]Lit *myriads of holiness* [3]Or *a fiery law* [a]Ex 19:18, 20; Ps 68:8, 17 [b]Judg 5:4 [c]Num 10:12; Hab 3:3 [d]Dan 7:10; Acts 7:53 [e]Ex 23:20-22

3 [1]Lit *peoples* [2]Lit *His* [3]Or *lie down at Your feet* [a]Deut 4:37; Mal 1:2 [b]Deut 7:6; 14:2 [c]Deut 6:1-9; Luke 10:39

4 [a]Deut 4:2; John 7:19 [b]Ps 119:111

5 [a]Num 23:21

6 [a]Gen 49:3, 4

7 [1]Lit *him* [a]Gen 49:8-12

8 [1]Lit *him* [a]Ex 28:30; Lev 8:8 [b]Ps 106:16 [c]Ex 17:7; Num 20:13, 24; Deut 6:16

9 [a]Ex 32:27-29 [b]Mal 2:5

10 [1]Lit *in Your nostrils* [a]Lev 10:11; Deut 31:9-13 [b]Lev 16:12, 13 [c]Ps 51:19

12 [a]Deut 4:37f; 12:10 [b]Deut 32:11 [c]Ex 28:12

11 "O LORD, bless his substance,
And accept the work of his hands;
Shatter the loins of those who rise up against him,
And those who hate him, so that they will not rise *again*."

13 [a]Gen 27:27, 28; 49:22-26

12 Of Benjamin he said,
"[a]May the beloved of the LORD dwell in security by Him,
[b]Who shields him all the day,
[c]And he dwells between His shoulders."

15 [1]Or *chief* [a]Hab 3:6

13 Of Joseph he said,
"[a]Blessed of the LORD *be* his land,
With the choice things of heaven, with the dew,
And from the deep lying beneath,
14 And with the choice yield of the sun,
And with the choice produce of the months.

16 [a]Ex 2:2-6; 3:2, 4

15 "And with the [1]best things of [a]the ancient mountains,
And with the choice things of the everlasting hills,
16 And with the choice things of the earth and its fullness,
And the favor [a]of Him who dwelt in the bush.

17 [1]Or *together* [a]Num 23:22 [b]1 Kin 22:11; Ps 44:5

Let it come to the head of Joseph,
And to the crown of the head of the one distinguished
among his brothers.
17 "As the firstborn of his ox, majesty is his,
And his horns are the horns of [a]the wild ox;
With them he will [b]push the peoples,

18 [a]Gen 49:13-15

All [1]at once, *to* the ends of the earth.
And those are the ten thousands of Ephraim,
And those are the thousands of Manasseh."

19 [1]Lit *suck* [a]Ex 15:17; Ps 2:6; Is 2:3 [b]Ps 4:5; 51:19 [c]Is 60:5

18 [a]Of Zebulun he said,
"Rejoice, Zebulun, in your going forth,
And, Issachar, in your tents.
19 "[a]They will call peoples *to* the mountain;
There they will offer [b]righteous sacrifices;
For they will [1]draw out [c]the abundance of the seas,
And the hidden treasures of the sand."

20 [1]Or *lioness* [a]Gen 49:19 [b]Gen 49:9

20 [a]Of Gad he said,
"Blessed is the one who enlarges Gad;
He lies down [b]as a [1]lion,
And tears the arm, also the crown of the head.

21 [1]Lit *saw* [2]Or *covered up* [a]Num 32:1-5 [b]Num 34:14 [c]Josh 4:12 [d]Josh 22:1-3

21 "[a]Then he [1]provided the first *part* for himself,
[b]For there the ruler's portion was [2]reserved;
[c]And he came *with* the leaders of the people;
[d]He executed the justice of the LORD,
And His ordinances with Israel."

22 [a]Of Dan he said,
"Dan is [b]a lion's whelp,
That leaps forth from Bashan."

22 [a]Gen 49:16 [b]Ezek 19:2, 3

23 Of Naphtali he said,
"[a]O Naphtali, satisfied with favor,
And full of the blessing of the LORD,
Take possession of the sea and the south."

24 [a]Of Asher he said,
"More blessed than sons is Asher;
May he be favored by his brothers,
[b]And may he dip his foot in oil.
25 "[a]Your locks will be iron and bronze,
[b]And according to your days, so will your leisurely
walk be.

26 "[a]There is none like the God of [1]Jeshurun,
[b]Who rides the heavens [2]to your help,
And through the skies in His majesty.
27 "[a]The eternal God is a [1]dwelling place,
[b]And underneath are the everlasting arms;
[c]And He drove out the enemy from before you,
[d]And said, 'Destroy!'
28 "[a]So Israel dwells in security,
[b]The fountain of Jacob secluded,
[c]In a land of grain and new wine;
[d]His heavens also drop down dew.
29 "[a]Blessed are you, O Israel;
[b]Who is like you, a people saved by the LORD,
[c]Who is the shield of your help
[d]And the sword of your majesty!
[e]So your enemies will cringe before you,
[f]And you will tread upon their high places."

Chapter 34 Theme ____________________

34 [a]Now Moses went up from the plains of Moab to
Mount Nebo, to the top of Pisgah, which is opposite
Jericho. And the LORD [b]showed him all the land, Gilead as far
as Dan,
2 and all Naphtali and the land of Ephraim and Manasseh,
and all the land of Judah as far as the [1a]western sea,
3 and the [1]Negev and the plain in the valley of Jericho, [a]the
city of palm trees, as far as Zoar.
4 Then the LORD said to him, "This is the land which [a]I
swore to Abraham, Isaac, and Jacob, saying, 'I will give it to
your [1]descendants'; I have let you see *it* with your eyes, but
you shall not go over there."
5 So Moses [a]the servant of the LORD [b]died there in the land
of Moab, according to the [1]word of the LORD.
6 And He buried him in the valley in the land of Moab,
[a]opposite Beth-peor; but [b]no man knows his burial place to this
day.
7 Although Moses was [a]one hundred and twenty years old

23 [a]Gen 49:21

24 [a]Gen 49:20 [b]Job 29:6

25 [a]Ps 147:13 [b]Deut 4:40; 32:47

26 [1]I.e. Israel [2]Lit *in* [a]Ex 15:11; Deut 4:35; Ps 86:8; Jer 10:6 [b]Deut 10:14; Ps 68:33, 34; 104:3; Hab 3:8

27 [1]Or *refuge* [a]Ps 90:1, 2 [b]Gen 49:24 [c]Ex 34:11; Josh 24:18 [d]Deut 7:2

28 [a]Deut 33:12; Jer 23:6 [b]Num 23:9; Deut 32:8 [c]Gen 27:28, 37 [d]Deut 33:13

29 [a]Ps 1:1; 32:1, 2 [b]Deut 4:32; 2 Sam 7:23 [c]Gen 15:1; Ps 33:20; 115:9-11 [d]Ps 68:34 [e]Ps 66:3 [f]Num 33:52

34:1 [a]Deut 32:49 [b]Deut 32:52

2 [1]I.e. Mediterranean Sea [a]Deut 11:24

3 [1]I.e. South country [a]Judg 1:16; 3:13; 2 Chr 28:15

4 [1]Lit *seed* [a]Gen 12:7; 26:3; 28:13

5 [1]Lit *mouth* [a]Num 12:7; Josh 1:1, 2 [b]Deut 32:50

6 [a]Deut 3:29; 4:46 [b]Jude 9

7 [a]Deut 31:2

7 [b]Gen 27:1; 48:10

when he died, [b]his eye was not dim, nor his vigor abated.
8 So the sons of Israel wept for Moses in the plains of Moab
thirty days; then the days of weeping *and* mourning for Moses
came to an end.

9 [a]Num 27:18, 23; Is 11:2

9 Now Joshua the son of Nun was [a]filled with the spirit of
wisdom, for Moses had laid his hands on him; and the sons of
Israel listened to him and did as the LORD had commanded
Moses.

10 [a]Deut 18:15, 18 [b]Ex 33:11; Num 12:8; Deut 5:4

10 Since that time [a]no prophet has risen in Israel like Moses,
whom [b]the LORD knew face to face,
11 for all the signs and wonders which the LORD sent him to
perform in the land of Egypt against Pharaoh, all his servants,
and all his land,
12 and for all the mighty [1]power and for all the great terror
which Moses performed in the sight of all Israel.

12 [1]Lit *hand*

Deuteronomy at a Glance

Theme of Deuteronomy:

Segment Divisions

		Chapter Themes
		1
		2
		3
		4
		5
		6
		7
		8
		9
		10
		11
		12
		13
		14
		15
		16
		17
		18
		19
		20
		21
		22
		23
		24
		25
		26
		27
		28
		29
		30
		31
		32
		33
		34

Author:

Date:

Geographical Location:

Purpose:

Key Words:

covenant

fear

heart

command (commanded)

listen

observe (keep, do)

love

remember

commandment (statutes)

nations

blessing

curse

you shall purge (remove) the evil

life

death

the Lord will

Book/ Chapter/ Verse	Lessons

(continued)

BOOK/ CHAPTER/ VERSE	LESSONS

JOSHUA יהושע
YEHOSHUA

For years Joshua had faithfully served Moses—and God. How well Joshua had come to understand the meaning of his name, "The Lord is salvation." All his contemporaries except Caleb had died in the wilderness because they had not believed God. But God had spared Joshua and Caleb because they had followed Him fully.

After Moses died, God appointed Joshua to lead the children of Israel into the land of promise. Their salvation from their enemies would not come from the east nor from the west but from the One who made the heaven and the earth!

God's encouragement rang in Joshua's heart: "Be strong and courageous."

Things to Do

General Instructions

1. If you are not familiar with who Joshua is, before you begin studying the book, read Numbers 13; 14; 27:18-23; Deuteronomy 34:9.

2. As you study Joshua one chapter at a time, it will help you keep everything in context if you keep in mind that the book of Joshua falls into four segments. In chapters 1 through 5 the children of Israel prepare to enter the land. Chapters 6 through 12 describe the conquest of the land. Chapters 13 through 21 tell of the allocation of the land. In chapters 22 through 24 Joshua calls Israel to serve the Lord, who gave them the land.

3. As you read each chapter, ask the "5 W's and an H": Who? What? When? Where? Why? and How? For example, in a historical book such as Joshua, ask: What is this chapter about? Who are the main characters? What is taking place? Where is it happening and when? Who is involved? Why is this occurring, being said, or to be done? What are the consequences? How is it going to happen? How should it be done? Record the main points or events of the chapter in the margin of your Bible. Double-underline every geographical location in green.

4. Look at the map on page 356 to find the various cities and places mentioned throughout this book. This will help you keep the book in its geographical context.

5. Mark every reference to time with a clock 🕒. This will help you see when events occurred and the chronological relationship of one event to another.

6. After you finish studying each chapter, write the theme or event covered in that chapter at the beginning of the chapter in your Bible. Then record it on the JOSHUA AT A GLANCE chart on page 395.

Chapters 1–5

1. As you read these chapters, mark the following key words and their synonyms: *Joshua*, *land*, *strong*, *courageous*, *firm*, *command (commanded, as the Lord commanded, in accordance with the command of the Lord)*, *possess*, *covenant*, *ark of the Lord (ark of the covenant)*, and *Israel*. Write these on an index card that you can use as a bookmark while studying this segment.

2. Watch how the events or the instructions prepare the Israelites to enter the land. Also note the procedure for entering the land and the requirements placed on them as they arrive in the land. You might list these in the margin under the heading "Possessing the Land."

3. If while reading chapter 5 you need a review of circumcision, read Genesis 17 and Exodus 4:24-26.

4. Don't forget to record the theme of each chapter in your Bible and on JOSHUA AT A GLANCE.

Chapters 6–12

1. As you study this section keep in mind the general instructions above.

2. Although you will mark many of the same key words, make a new bookmark with the following key words: *God, Lord, Joshua, covenant, strong, courageous, land, fear, command (commanded), fight (fought), captured, ark of the Lord (of the covenant),* and *Israel.*

3. Carefully observe what God tells the people to do when they conquer a city. Read Genesis 15:7-21 and note that God told Abraham He would bring his descendants into Canaan when the iniquity of the Amorites was complete. Also recall the covenant God made with Abraham on that day. You might write "Genesis 15:7-21" in the margin of this section as a cross-reference.

4. As you read, watch what happens when the people fail to consult God or to obey His commands regarding the inhabitants of the land. Note this in the margin.

5. When you come to chapter 8, note where Mount Ebal and Mount Gerizim are located and what takes place there. Refer back to Deuteronomy 11:29 and Deuteronomy 27:11-14. Use the map on page 356 to locate these places. Also mark all clues to time with a clock.

6. Record the theme of each chapter.

Chapters 13–21

1. Once again make a new bookmark and write the following key words on it, although some words will remain the same: *Israel, land, Joshua, Caleb, strong, fear, command (commanded, commandments), fought, captured, inheritance, possession, possessed* (also mark *possession* in chapter 12), and *promised.*

2. Double-underline the geographical locations in green, then locate them on the map on page 356. Also mark in the text the name of each tribe as it is allotted its portion of the land.

3. As you read, watch for any mention of Caleb. Remember what you read about Joshua and Caleb in Numbers 13 and 14. There are important lessons to be learned from their example.

4. Pay careful attention to chapter 20 and what you learn about the cities of refuge.

5. Also note the inheritance given to the Levites in Joshua 21.

6. Don't forget to record the chapter themes.

Chapters 22–24

1. Make one final bookmark for the key words you want to mark in the text: *land, possess (possession), covenant, strong, firm, fear, command (commandment, commanded), serve (served), Israel, Joshua, promised, fought,* and *inheritance.*

2. List God's instructions and what the people are to do in order to keep them. Also note the consequences of disobedience.

3. As you read Joshua 23, mark the word *cling.* Then read Jeremiah 13:1-11.

4. Complete JOSHUA AT A GLANCE. Fill in the four main segment divisions and any others you see.

5. Compare what Joshua tells the children of Israel in chapter 23 with God's word to Joshua in chapter 1. You might write "Joshua 1:7-9" in the margin of Joshua 23.

Things to Think About

1. Do you consult the Lord and His Word and then walk in obedience to what He says?

2. Joshua was admonished to be strong and courageous. What do you think this means? Read Revelation 21:8 and note what is said about the cowardly.

3. Have you decided whom you are going to follow? Have you counted the cost? What would cause you to compromise? Could you get away with compromise? What would it cost you? Would it be worth it?

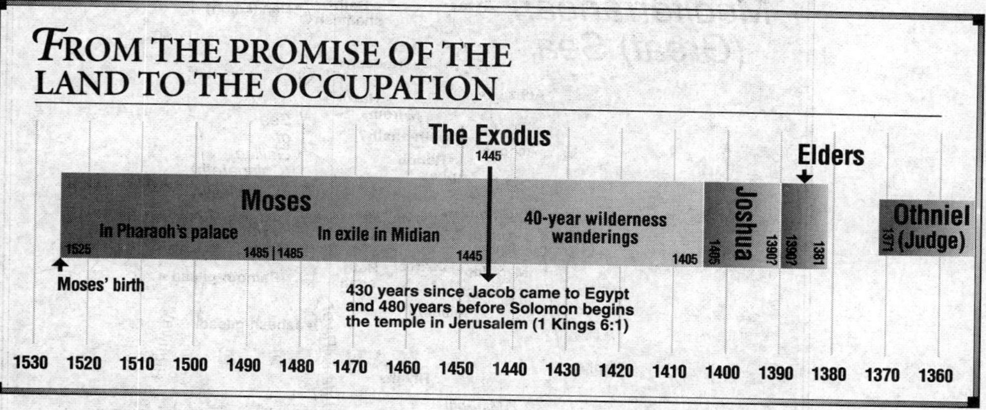

1:1 [1]Or *minister* — *Chapter 1 Theme* ______________________

1 Now it came about after the death of Moses the servant of
2 [a]Num 12:7; Deut 34:5 [b]Josh 1:11 — the LORD, that the LORD spoke to Joshua the son of Nun,
Moses' [1]servant, saying,
2 "Moses [a]My servant is dead; now therefore arise, [b]cross this
Jordan, you and all this people, to the land which I am giving to
3 [a]Deut 11:24 — them, to the sons of Israel.
3 "[a]Every place on which the sole of your foot treads, I have
given it to you, just as I spoke to Moses.
4 [a]Gen 15:18; Num 34:3 — 4 "[a]From the wilderness and this Lebanon, even as far as the
great river, the river Euphrates, all the land of the Hittites, and
as far as the Great Sea toward the setting of the sun will be
your territory.
5 [a]Deut 7:24 [b]Deut 31:6, 7; Heb 13:5 — 5 "[a]No man will *be able to* stand before you all the days of
your life. Just as I have been with Moses, I will be with you; [b]I
will not fail you or forsake you.
6 "[a]Be strong and courageous, for you shall give this people
6 [a]Deut 31:6, 7, 23 — possession of the land which I swore to their fathers to give them.
7 "Only be strong and very courageous; [1a]be careful to do
according to all the law which Moses My servant commanded
7 [1]Lit *observe* [2]Or *act wisely* [a]Deut 5:32 — you; do not turn from it to the right or to the left, so that you
may [2]have success wherever you go.

Joshua: Occupying the Promised Land

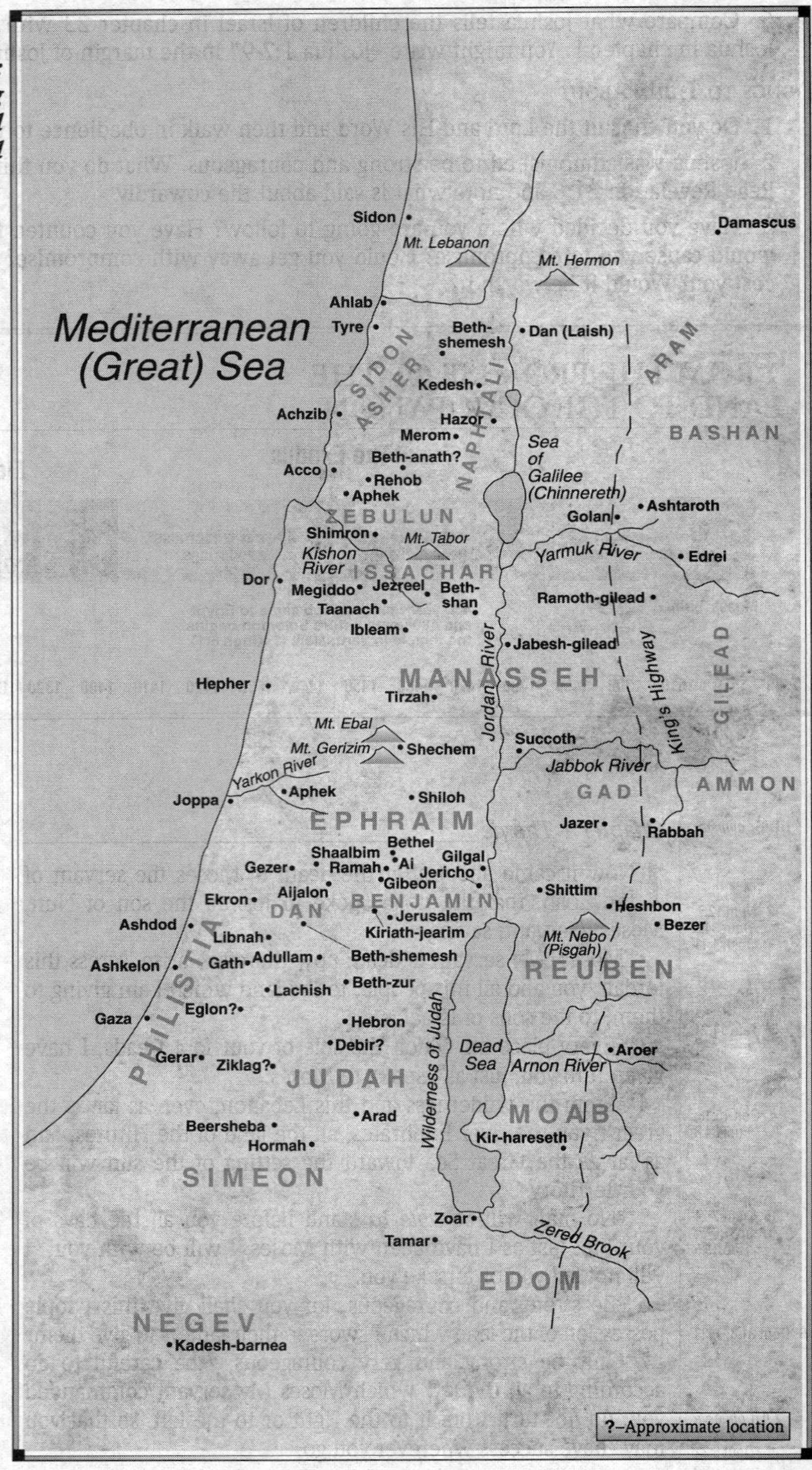
Sidon
Damascus
Mt. Lebanon
Mt. Hermon
Ahlab
Mediterranean
(Great) Sea
Tyre
Beth-shemesh
Dan (Laish)
ARAM
SIDON
ASHER
NAPHTALI
Kedesh
Achzib
Hazor
Merom
BASHAN
Sea of Galilee (Chinnereth)
Beth-anath?
Acco
Rehob
Aphek
ZEBULUN
Golan
Ashtaroth
Shimron
Mt. Tabor
Kishon River
ISSACHAR
Yarmuk River
Edrei
Dor
Megiddo
Jezreel
Beth-shan
Taanach
Ramoth-gilead
Ibleam
Jabesh-gilead
Jordan River
King's Highway
GILEAD
Hepher
MANASSEH
Tirzah
Mt. Ebal
Mt. Gerizim
Shechem
Succoth
Jabbok River
Yarkon River
Aphek
GAD
AMMON
Joppa
Shiloh
EPHRAIM
Jazer
Rabbah
Bethel
Shaalbim
Gilgal
Gezer
Ramah
Ai
Jericho
Gibeon
Aijalon
Ekron
BENJAMIN
Shittim
DAN
Heshbon
Jerusalem
Ashdod
Kiriath-jearim
Mt. Nebo (Pisgah)
Bezer
Libnah
Beth-shemesh
Ashkelon
Gath
Adullam
REUBEN
Beth-zur
PHILISTIA
Lachish
Eglon?
Gaza
Hebron
Wilderness of Judah
Debir?
Dead Sea
Aroer
Gerar
Ziklag?
Arnon River
JUDAH
MOAB
Arad
Beersheba
Kir-hareseth
Hormah
SIMEON
Zoar
Tamar
Zered Brook
EDOM
NEGEV
Kadesh-barnea
?–Approximate location

8 "[a]This book of the law shall not depart from your mouth,
but you shall meditate on it day and night, so that you may [1]be
careful to do according to all that is written in it; [b]for then you
will make your way prosperous, and then you will [2]have success.
9 "Have I not commanded you? [a]Be strong and courageous!
[b]Do not tremble or be dismayed, for the LORD your God is with
you wherever you go."
10 Then Joshua commanded the officers of the people, saying,
11 "Pass through the midst of the camp and command the
people, saying, 'Prepare provisions for yourselves, for within
[a]three days you are to cross this Jordan, to go in to possess the
land which the LORD your God is giving you, to possess it.'"
12 [a]To the Reubenites and to the Gadites and to the half-tribe
of Manasseh, Joshua [1]said,
13 "Remember the word which Moses the servant of the LORD
commanded you, saying, '[a]The LORD your God gives you rest
and will give you this land.'
14 "Your wives, your little ones, and your cattle shall remain in
the land which Moses gave you beyond the Jordan, but you
shall cross before your brothers in battle array, all your valiant
warriors, and shall help them,
15 until the LORD gives your brothers rest, as *He gives* you, and
they also possess the land which the LORD your God is giving
them. [a]Then you shall return to [1]your own land, and possess
[2]that which Moses [b]the servant of the LORD gave you beyond
the Jordan toward the sunrise."
16 They answered Joshua, saying, "All that you have commanded us we will do, and wherever you send us we will go.
17 "Just as we obeyed Moses in all things, so we will obey you;
only [a]may the LORD your God be with you as He was with Moses.
18 "Anyone who rebels against your [1]command and does not
obey your words in all that you command him, shall be put to
death; only be strong and courageous."

Chapter 2 Theme ____________________

2 Then Joshua the son of Nun sent two men as spies secretly
from [a]Shittim, saying, "Go, view the land, especially Jericho."
So they went and came into the house of [b]a harlot whose name
was Rahab, and [1]lodged there.
2 It was told the king of Jericho, saying, "Behold, men from
the sons of Israel have come here tonight to search out the land."
3 And the king of Jericho sent *word* to Rahab, saying, "Bring
out the men who have come to you, who have entered your
house, for they have come to search out all the land."
4 But the [a]woman had taken the two men and hidden them,
and she said, "Yes, the men came to me, but I did not know
where they were from.
5 "It came about when *it was time* to shut the gate at dark,
that the men went out; I do not know where the men went.
Pursue them quickly, for you will overtake them."

8 [1]Lit *observe* [2]Or *act wisely* [a]Deut 31:24; Josh 8:34 [b]Deut 29:9; Ps 1:1-3

9 [a]Josh 1:7 [b]Deut 31:8

11 [a]Josh 3:2

12 [1]Lit *said, saying* [a]Num 32:20-22

13 [a]Deut 3:18-20

15 [1]Lit *the land of your possession* [2]Lit *it* [a]Josh 22:4 [b]Josh 1:1

17 [a]Josh 1:5, 9

18 [1]Lit *mouth*

2:1 [1]Lit *lay down* [a]Num 25:1; Josh 3:1 [b]Heb 11:31; James 2:25

4 [a]2 Sam 17:19

6 But [a]she had brought them up to the roof and hidden them
in the stalks of flax which she had laid in order on the roof.
7 So the men pursued them on the road to the Jordan to the
fords; and as soon as those who were pursuing them had gone
out, they shut the gate.
8 Now before they lay down, [1]she came up to them on the
roof,
9 and said to the men, "[a]I know that the LORD has given you
the land, and that the [b]terror of you has fallen on us, and that
all the inhabitants of the land have [1]melted away before you.
10 "[a]For we have heard how the LORD dried up the water of the
[1]Red Sea before you when you came out of Egypt, and [b]what
you did to the two kings of the Amorites who were beyond the
Jordan, to Sihon and Og, whom you [2]utterly destroyed.
11 "When we heard *it,* [a]our hearts melted and no [1]courage
remained in any man any longer because of you; for the [b]LORD
your God, He is God in heaven above and on earth beneath.
12 "Now therefore, please swear to me by the LORD, since I
have dealt kindly with you, that you also will deal kindly with
my father's household, and give me a [a]pledge of [1]truth,
13 and [1]spare my father and my mother and my brothers and
my sisters, with all who belong to them, and deliver our [2]lives
from death."
14 So the men said to her, "Our [1]life [2]for yours if you do not
tell this business of ours; and it shall come about when the
LORD gives us the land that we will [a]deal kindly and [3]faithfully
with you."
15 Then she let them down by a rope through the window, for
her house was on the city wall, so that she was living on the wall.
16 She said to them, "[a]Go to the hill country, so that the
pursuers will not happen upon you, and hide yourselves there
for three days until the pursuers return. Then afterward you
may go on your way."
17 The men said to her, "[a]We *shall be* free from this oath [1]to
you which you have made us swear,
18 [1]unless, when we come into the land, you tie this cord of
scarlet thread in the window through which you let us down,
and [a]gather to yourself into the house your father and your
mother and your brothers and all your father's household.
19 "It shall come about that anyone who goes out of the doors
of your house into the street, his blood *shall be* on his own
head, and we *shall be* free; but anyone who is with you in the
house, [a]his blood *shall be* on our head if a hand is *laid* on him.
20 "But if you tell this business of ours, then we shall be free
from the oath which you have made us swear."
21 She said, "According to your words, so be it." So she sent
them away, and they departed; and she tied the scarlet cord in
the window.
22 They departed and came to the hill country, and remained
there for three days until the pursuers returned. Now the pursuers
had sought *them* [1]all along the road, but had not found *them.*

6 [a]James 2:25
8 [1]Lit *then she*
9 [1]Or *become demoralized* [a]Num 20:24; Josh 9:24 [b]Ex 23:27; Deut 2:25; Josh 9:9, 10
10 [1]Lit *Sea of Reeds* [2]Or *put under the ban* [a]Ex 14:21; Num 23:22; 24:8 [b]Num 21:21-35
11 [1]Lit *spirit arose* [a]Josh 5:1; 7:5; Ps 22:14; Is 13:7; 19:1 [b]Deut 4:39
12 [1]Or *faithfulness* [a]Josh 2:18, 19
13 [1]Lit *let live* [2]Lit *souls*
14 [1]Lit *soul* [2]Lit *instead of you to die* [3]Or *truly* [a]Gen 24:49
16 [a]James 2:25
17 [1]Lit *of yours* [a]Gen 24:8
18 [1]Lit *behold* [a]Josh 2:12
19 [a]Matt 27:25
22 [1]Lit *through all the road*

23 Then the two men returned and came down from the hill
country and crossed over and came to Joshua the son of Nun,
and they related to him all that had happened to them.
24 They said to Joshua, "Surely the LORD has given all the land
into our hands; moreover, [a]all the inhabitants of the land have
[1]melted away before us."

Chapter 3 Theme ________________________________

3 Then Joshua rose early in the morning; and he and all the
sons of Israel set out from [a]Shittim and came to the Jordan,
and they lodged there before they crossed.
2 [a]At the end of three days the officers went through the
midst of the camp;
3 and they commanded the people, saying, "When you see
the [a]ark of the covenant of the LORD your God with the
Levitical priests carrying it, then you shall set out from your
place and go after it.
4 "However, there shall be between you and it a distance of
about 2,000 [1]cubits by measure. Do not come near it, that you
may know the way by which you shall go, for you have not
passed this way before."
5 Then Joshua said to the people, "[a]Consecrate yourselves,
for tomorrow the LORD will do wonders among you."
6 And Joshua spoke to the priests, saying, "Take up the ark of
the covenant and cross over ahead of the people." So they took
up the ark of the covenant and went ahead of the people.
7 Now the LORD said to Joshua, "This day I will begin to
[a]exalt you in the sight of all Israel, that they may know that just
as I have been with Moses, I will be with you.
8 "You shall, moreover, command the priests who are carrying
the ark of the covenant, saying, 'When you come to the edge of
the waters of the Jordan, you shall stand *still* in the Jordan.'"
9 Then Joshua said to the sons of Israel, "Come here, and
hear the words of the LORD your God."
10 Joshua said, "By this you shall know that [a]the living God is
among you, and that He will assuredly [b]dispossess from before
you the Canaanite, the Hittite, the Hivite, the Perizzite, the
Girgashite, the Amorite, and the Jebusite.
11 "Behold, the ark of the covenant of [a]the Lord of all the earth
is crossing over ahead of you into the Jordan.
12 "Now then, [a]take for yourselves twelve men from the tribes
of Israel, one man for each tribe.
13 "It shall come about when the soles of the feet of the priests
who carry the ark of the LORD, the Lord of all the earth, rest in
the waters of the Jordan, the waters of the Jordan will be cut
off, *and* the waters which are [1]flowing down from above [2]will
[a]stand in one heap."
14 So when the people set out from their tents to cross the
Jordan with the priests carrying [a]the ark of the covenant before
the people,

24 [1]Or *become demoralized* [a]Josh 2:9
3:1 [a]Josh 2:1
2 [a]Josh 1:11
3 [a]Deut 31:9
4 [1]I.e. One cubit equals approx 18 in.
5 [a]Ex 19:10, 11; Josh 7:13
7 [a]Josh 4:14
10 [a]Deut 5:26; 1 Thess 1:9 [b]Ex 33:2; Deut 7:1
11 [a]Job 41:11; Ps 24:1; Zech 6:5
12 [a]Josh 4:2
13 [1]Lit *going* [2]Lit *and they will* [a]Ex 15:8
14 [a]Ps 132:8; Acts 7:44f

15 and when those who carried the ark came into the Jordan,
and the feet of the priests carrying the ark were dipped in the
edge of the water (for the [a]Jordan overflows all its banks all the
days of harvest),
16 [a]the waters which were [1]flowing down from above stood
and rose up in [b]one heap, a great distance away at Adam, the city
that is beside Zarethan; and those which were [1]flowing down
toward the sea of the [c]Arabah, the Salt Sea, were completely
cut off. So the people crossed opposite Jericho.
17 And the priests who carried the ark of the covenant of the
LORD stood firm [a]on dry ground in the middle of the Jordan
while all Israel crossed on dry ground, until all the nation had
finished crossing the Jordan.

Chapter 4 Theme ____________________

4 Now when all the nation had finished crossing the [a]Jordan,
the LORD spoke to Joshua, saying,
2 "[a]Take for yourselves twelve men from the people, one man
from each tribe,
3 and command them, saying, 'Take up for yourselves twelve
stones from here out of the middle of the Jordan, from the
place where the priests' feet are standing firm, and carry them
over with you and lay them down in [a]the lodging place where
you will lodge tonight.'"
4 So Joshua called the twelve men whom he had appointed
from the sons of Israel, one man from each tribe;
5 and Joshua said to them, "[1]Cross again to the ark of the
LORD your God into the middle of the Jordan, and each of you
take up a stone on his shoulder, according to the number of the
tribes of the sons of Israel.
6 "[1]Let this be a sign among you, so that [a]when your children
ask [2]later, saying, 'What do these stones mean to you?'
7 then you shall say to them, 'Because the [a]waters of the
Jordan were cut off before the ark of the covenant of the LORD;
when it crossed the Jordan, the waters of the Jordan were cut
off.' So these stones shall become a [b]memorial to the sons of
Israel forever."
8 Thus the sons of Israel did as Joshua commanded, and took
up twelve stones from the middle of the Jordan, just as the
LORD spoke to Joshua, according to the number of the tribes of
the sons of Israel; and they carried them over with them to
[a]the lodging place and put them down there.
9 Then Joshua set up twelve [a]stones in the middle of the Jordan
at the place where the feet of the priests who carried the ark of
the covenant were standing, and they are there to this day.
10 For the priests who carried the ark were standing in the
middle of the Jordan until everything was completed that the
LORD had commanded Joshua to speak to the people, according
to all that Moses had commanded Joshua. And the people
hurried and crossed;

15 [a]1 Chr 12:15; Jer 12:5; 49:19

16 [1]Lit *going* [a]Ps 66:6; 74:15; 114:3, 5 [b]Josh 3:13 [c]Deut 1:1

17 [a]Ex 14:21, 22, 29

4:1 [a]Deut 27:2; Josh 3:17

2 [a]Josh 3:12

3 [a]Josh 4:20

5 [1]Lit *Cross before the ark*

6 [1]Lit *That this may be* [2]Lit *tomorrow* [a]Ex 12:26; 13:14; Josh 4:21

7 [a]Josh 3:13 [b]Ex 12:14; Num 16:40

8 [a]Josh 4:20

9 [a]Gen 28:18; Josh 24:26f; 1 Sam 7:12

11 and when all the people had finished crossing, the ark of
the LORD and the priests crossed before the people.
12 [a]The sons of Reuben and the sons of Gad and the half-tribe
of Manasseh crossed over in battle array before the sons of
Israel, just as Moses had spoken to them;
13 about 40,000 equipped for war, crossed for battle before
the LORD to the desert plains of Jericho.
14 [a]On that day the LORD exalted Joshua in the sight of all
Israel; so that they [1]revered him, just as they had [1]revered
Moses all the days of his life.
15 Now the LORD said to [1]Joshua,
16 "Command the priests who carry [a]the ark of the testimony
that they come up from the Jordan."
17 So Joshua commanded the priests, saying, "Come up from
the Jordan."
18 It came about when the priests who carried the ark of the
covenant of the LORD had come up from the middle of the
Jordan, and the soles of the priests' feet were [1]lifted up to the
dry ground, that the waters of the Jordan returned to their
place, and went over all its banks as before.
19 Now the people came up from the Jordan on the [a]tenth of the
first month and camped at Gilgal on the eastern edge of Jericho.
20 [1a]Those twelve stones which they had taken from the
Jordan, Joshua set up [b]at Gilgal.
21 He said to the sons of [1]Israel, "When your children ask
their fathers in time to come, saying, 'What are these stones?'
22 then you shall inform your children, saying, 'Israel crossed
this Jordan on [a]dry ground.'
23 "For the LORD your God dried up the waters of the Jordan
before you until you had crossed, just as the LORD your God
had done to the [1]Red Sea, [a]which He dried up before us until
we had crossed;
24 that [a]all the peoples of the earth may know that the [b]hand
of the LORD is mighty, so that you may [1c]fear the LORD your God
[2]forever."

Chapter 5 Theme ______________________

5 Now it came about when all the kings of the Amorites who
were beyond the Jordan to the west, and all the kings of
the [a]Canaanites who *were* by the sea, [b]heard how the LORD had
dried up the waters of the Jordan before the sons of Israel until
[1]they had crossed, that their hearts melted, and there was no
spirit in them any longer because of the sons of Israel.
2 At that time the LORD said to Joshua, "Make for yourself [a]flint
knives and circumcise again the sons of Israel the second time."
3 So Joshua made himself flint knives and circumcised the
sons of Israel at [1]Gibeath-haaraloth.
4 This is the reason why Joshua circumcised them: [a]all the
people who came out of Egypt who were males, all the men of
war, died in the wilderness along the way after they came out
of Egypt.

12 [a]Num 32:17
14 [1]Or *feared* [a]Josh 3:7
15 [1]Lit *Joshua, saying*
16 [a]Ex 25:16
18 [1]Lit *drawn out*
19 [a]Deut 1:3
20 [1]Lit *these* [a]Josh 4:8 [b]Josh 4:3, 8
21 [1]Lit *Israel, saying,*
22 [a]Josh 3:17
23 [1]Lit *Sea of Reeds* [a]Ex 14:21
24 [1]Or *reverence* [2]Lit *all the days* [a]1 Kin 8:42; 2 Kin 19:19; Ps 106:8 [b]Ex 15:16; 1 Chr 29:12; Ps 89:13 [c]Ex 14:31; Ps 76:7f; Jer 10:7
5:1 [1]Other mss read *we* [a]Num 13:29 [b]Josh 2:10, 11
2 [a]Ex 4:25
3 [1]I.e. the hill of the foreskins
4 [a]Deut 2:14

5 For all the people who came out were circumcised, but all
the people who were born in the wilderness along the way as
they came out of Egypt had not been circumcised.
6 For the sons of Israel walked [a]forty years in the wilderness,
until all the nation, *that is,* the men of war who came out of
Egypt, [1]perished because they did not listen to the voice of the
LORD, [b]to whom the LORD had sworn that He would not let
them see the land which the LORD had sworn to their fathers to
give us, a land flowing with milk and honey.
7 Their children whom He raised up in their place, Joshua
[1]circumcised; for they were uncircumcised, because they had
not circumcised them along the way.
8 Now when they had finished circumcising all the nation,
they remained in their places in the camp until they were
[1]healed.
9 Then the LORD said to Joshua, "Today I have rolled away
[a]the reproach of Egypt from you." So the name of that place is
called [1]Gilgal to this day.
10 While the sons of Israel camped at Gilgal [a]they observed
the Passover on the evening of the [b]fourteenth day of the
month on the desert plains of Jericho.
11 On the [1]day after the Passover, on [2]that very day, they ate
some of the produce of the land, unleavened cakes and parched
grain.
12 [a]The manna ceased on the [1]day after they had eaten some
of the produce of the land, so that the sons of Israel no longer
had manna, but they ate some of the yield of the land of
Canaan during that year.
13 Now it came about when Joshua was by Jericho, that he lifted
up his eyes and looked, and behold, [a]a man was standing opposite
him with his sword drawn in his hand, and Joshua went to him
and said to him, "Are you for us or for our adversaries?"
14 He said, "No; rather I indeed come now *as* captain of the host
of the LORD." And Joshua [a]fell on his face to the earth, and bowed
down, and said to him, "What has my lord to say to his servant?"
15 The captain of the LORD'S host said to Joshua, "[a]Remove your
sandals from your feet, for the place where you are standing is
holy." And Joshua did so.

Chapter 6 Theme ________________________

6 Now Jericho was tightly shut because of the sons of Israel;
no one went out and no one came in.
2 The LORD said to Joshua, "See, I have given Jericho into
your hand, with [a]its king *and* the valiant warriors.
3 "You shall march around the city, all the men of war circling
the city once. You shall do so for six days.
4 "Also seven priests shall carry seven [a]trumpets of rams'
horns before the ark; then on the seventh day you shall march
around the city seven times, and the priests shall blow the
trumpets.

RETURN TO INSTRUCTIONS

6 [1]Lit *were finished* [a]Deut 2:7, 14 [b]Num 14:29-35; 26:63-65

7 [1]Lit *circumcised them*

8 [1]Lit *revived*

9 [1]I.e. rolling [a]Zeph 2:8

10 [a]Ex 12:18 [b]Josh 4:19

11 [1]Lit *morrow* [2]Lit *this*

12 [1]Lit *morrow* [a]Ex 16:35

13 [a]Gen 18:1, 2; 32:24, 30; Num 22:31

14 [a]Gen 17:3

15 [a]Ex 3:5

6:2 [a]Deut 7:24

4 [a]Lev 25:9

5 "It shall be that when they make a long blast with the ram's
horn, and when you hear the sound of the trumpet, all the
people shall shout with a great shout; and the wall of the city
will fall down [1]flat, and the people will go up every man
[2]straight ahead."
6 So Joshua the son of Nun called the priests and said to
them, "Take up the ark of the covenant, and let seven priests
carry seven trumpets of rams' horns before the ark of the LORD."
7 Then [1]he said to the people, "Go forward, and march around
the city, and let the armed men go on before the ark of the LORD."
8 And it was *so,* that when Joshua had spoken to the people,
the seven priests carrying the seven trumpets of rams' horns
before the LORD went forward and blew the trumpets; and the
ark of the covenant of the LORD followed them.
9 The armed men went before the priests who blew the
trumpets, and [a]the rear guard came after the ark, while they
continued to blow the trumpets.
10 But Joshua commanded the people, saying, "You shall not
shout nor let your voice be heard nor let a word proceed out of
your mouth, until the day I tell you, 'Shout!' Then you shall
shout!"
11 So he had the ark of the LORD [1]taken around the city,
circling *it* once; then they came into the camp and spent the
night in the camp.
12 Now Joshua rose early in the morning, and the priests took
up the ark of the LORD.
13 [a]The seven priests carrying the seven trumpets of rams'
horns before the ark of the LORD went on continually, and blew
the trumpets; and the armed men went before them and [b]the
rear guard came after the ark of the LORD, while they continued
to blow the trumpets.
14 Thus the second day they marched around the city once
and returned to the camp; they did so for six days.
15 Then on the seventh day they rose early at the dawning of
the day and marched around the city in the same manner seven
times; only on that day they marched around the city seven
times.
16 At the seventh time, when the priests blew the trumpets,
Joshua said to the people, "[a]Shout! For the LORD has given you
the city.
17 "The city shall be [a]under the ban, it and all that is in it
belongs to the LORD; only Rahab the harlot [1]and all who are
with her in the house shall live, because she hid the messengers
whom we sent.
18 "But as for you, only keep yourselves from the things under
the ban, so that you do not [1]covet *them* and [a]take some of the
things under the ban, and make the camp of Israel accursed
and bring trouble on it.
19 "[a]But all the silver and gold and articles of bronze and iron
are holy to the LORD; they shall go into the treasury of the
LORD."

5 [1]Lit *in its place* [2]Lit *before himself*
7 [1]Or *they*
9 [a]Josh 6:13; Is 52:12
11 [1]Lit *to go around*
13 [a]Josh 6:4 [b]Josh 6:9
16 [a]2 Chr 13:14f
17 [1]Lit *she and all* [a]Lev 27:28; Deut 20:17
18 [1]Lit *devote* [a]Josh 7:1
19 [a]Num 31:11, 12, 21-23

20 So the people shouted, and [1]*priests* blew the trumpets; and
when the people heard the sound of the trumpet, the people
shouted with a great shout and the [a]wall fell down [2]flat, so that
the people went up into the city, every man straight [3]ahead,
and they took the city.

20 [1]Or *they* [2]Lit *in its place* [3]Lit *before himself* [a]Heb 11:30

21 [a]They [1]utterly destroyed everything in the city, both man
and woman, young and old, and ox and sheep and donkey,
with the edge of the sword.

21 [1]Or *put under the ban* [a]Deut 20:16

22 Joshua said to the two men who had spied out the land,
"[a]Go into the harlot's house and bring the woman and all she
has out of there, as you have sworn to her."

22 [a]Josh 2:12-19

23 So the young men who were spies went in and [a]brought
out Rahab and her father and her mother and her brothers and
all she had; they also brought out all her relatives and placed
them outside the camp of Israel.

23 [a]Heb 11:31

24 [a]They burned the city with fire, and all that was in it. Only
the silver and gold, and articles of bronze and iron, they put
into the treasury of the [1]house of the LORD.

24 [1]I.e. tabernacle [a]Deut 20:16-18

25 However, [a]Rahab the harlot and her father's household and
all she had, Joshua [1]spared; and she has lived in the midst of
Israel to this day, for [b]she hid the messengers whom Joshua
sent to spy out Jericho.

25 [1]Lit *let live* [a]Heb 11:31 [b]Josh 2:6

26 Then Joshua made them take an oath at that time, saying,
"[a]Cursed before the LORD is the man who rises up and builds
this city Jericho; with *the loss of* his firstborn he shall lay its
foundation, and with *the loss of* his youngest son he shall set
up its gates."

26 [a]1 Kin 16:34

27 So [a]the LORD was with Joshua, and his [b]fame was in all the
land.

27 [a]Gen 39:2; Judg 1:19 [b]Josh 9:1, 3

Chapter 7 Theme ______________________________

7 [a]But the sons of Israel acted unfaithfully in regard to the
things under the ban, for Achan, the son of Carmi, the son
of Zabdi, the son of Zerah, from the tribe of Judah, took some
of the things under the ban, therefore the anger of the LORD
burned against the sons of Israel.

7:1 [a]Josh 6:17-19

2 Now Joshua sent men from Jericho to Ai, which is near
[a]Beth-aven, east of Bethel, and said to them, "[1]Go up and spy
out the land." So the men went up and spied out Ai.

2 [1]Lit *saying, Go* [a]Josh 18:12; 1 Sam 13:5; 14:23

3 They returned to Joshua and said to him, "Do not let all the
people go up; *only* about two or three thousand men need go up
[1]to Ai; do not make all the people toil up there, for they are few."

3 [1]Lit *and smite*

4 So about three thousand men from the people went up
there, but [a]they fled [1]from the men of Ai.

4 [1]Lit *before* [a]Lev 26:17; Deut 28:25

5 The men of Ai struck down about thirty-six of their men,
and pursued them [1]from the gate as far as Shebarim and struck
them down on the descent, so the [a]hearts of the people melted
and became as water.

5 [1]Or *before* [a]Lev 26:36; Josh 2:11; Ezek 21:7; Nah 2:10

6 Then Joshua [a]tore his clothes and fell to the earth on his
face before the ark of the LORD until the evening, *both* he and
the elders of Israel; and [b]they put dust on their heads.

6 [a]Job 2:12 [b]Job 42:6; Lam 2:10; Rev 18:19

7 Joshua said, "Alas, O Lord [1]GOD, why did You ever bring this people over the Jordan, *only* to deliver us into the hand of the Amorites, to destroy us? If only we had been willing [2]to dwell beyond the Jordan!

8 "O Lord, what can I say since Israel has turned *their* [1]back before their enemies?

9 "[a]For the Canaanites and all the inhabitants of the land will hear of it, and they will surround us and cut off our name from the earth. And what will You do for Your great name?"

10 So the LORD said to Joshua, "Rise up! Why is it that you have fallen on your face?

11 "Israel has sinned, and [a]they have also transgressed My covenant which I commanded them. And they have even taken some of the things under the ban and have both stolen and deceived. Moreover, they have also put *them* among their own things.

12 "Therefore the [a]sons of Israel cannot stand before their enemies; they turn *their* [1]backs before their enemies, for they have become accursed. I will not be with you anymore unless you destroy the things under the ban from your midst.

13 "Rise up! [a]Consecrate the people and say, 'Consecrate yourselves for tomorrow, for thus the LORD, the God of Israel, has said, "[b]There are things under the ban in your midst, O Israel. You cannot stand before your enemies until you have removed the things under the ban from your midst."

14 'In the morning then you shall come near by your tribes. And it shall be that the tribe which [a]the LORD takes *by lot* shall come near by families, and the family which the LORD takes shall come near by households, and the household which the LORD takes shall come near man by man.

15 '[a]It shall be that the one who is taken with the things under the ban shall be burned with fire, he and all that belongs to him, because he has transgressed the covenant of the LORD, and because he [b]has committed a disgraceful thing in Israel.'"

16 So Joshua arose early in the morning and brought Israel near by [1]tribes, and the tribe of Judah was taken.

17 He brought the family of Judah near, and he took the family of the Zerahites; and he brought the family of the Zerahites near man by man, and Zabdi was taken.

18 He brought his household near man by man; and [a]Achan, son of Carmi, son of Zabdi, son of Zerah, from the tribe of Judah, was taken.

19 Then Joshua said to Achan, "My son, I implore you, [a]give glory to the LORD, the God of Israel, and give praise to Him; and tell me now what you have done. Do not hide it from me."

20 So Achan answered Joshua and said, "Truly, I have sinned against the LORD, the God of Israel, and [1]this is what I did:

21 when I saw among the spoil a beautiful mantle from Shinar and two hundred shekels of silver and a bar of gold fifty shekels in weight, then I [a]coveted them and took them; and behold, they are concealed in the earth inside my tent with the silver underneath it."

7 [1]Heb *YHWH*, usually rendered LORD [2]Lit *and had dwelt*
8 [1]Lit *neck*
9 [a]Ex 32:12; Deut 9:28
11 [a]Josh 6:18, 19
12 [1]Lit *necks* [a]Num 14:39, 45; Judg 2:14
13 [a]Josh 3:5 [b]Josh 6:18
14 [a]Prov 16:33
15 [a]1 Sam 14:38f [b]Gen 34:7; Judg 20:6
16 [1]Lit *its tribes*
18 [a]Num 32:23; Acts 5:1-10
19 [a]1 Sam 6:5; 2 Chr 30:22; Jer 13:16; John 9:24
20 [1]Lit *thus and thus I did*
21 [a]Eph 5:5; 1 Tim 6:10

22 So Joshua sent messengers, and they ran to the tent; and
behold, it was concealed in his tent with the silver underneath
it.
23 They took them from inside the tent and brought them to
Joshua and to all the sons of Israel, and they poured them out
before the LORD.
24 Then Joshua and all Israel with him, took Achan the son of
Zerah, the silver, the mantle, the bar of gold, his sons, his
daughters, his [1]oxen, his donkeys, his sheep, his tent and all
that belonged to him; and they brought them up to [a]the valley
of [2]Achor.
25 Joshua said, "Why have you [a]troubled us? The LORD will
trouble you this day." And all Israel stoned [1]them with stones;
and they burned them with fire [2]after they had stoned them
with stones.
26 They raised over him a great heap of stones that stands to
this day, and the LORD turned from the fierceness of His anger.
Therefore the name of that place has been called [a]the valley of
[1]Achor to this day.

Chapter 8 Theme ______________________________

8 Now the LORD said to Joshua, "[a]Do not fear or be dismayed. Take all the people of war with you and arise, go
up to Ai; see, [b]I have given into your hand the king of Ai, his
people, his city, and his land.
2 "You shall do to Ai and its king just as you did to Jericho and
its king; you shall [a]take only its spoil and its cattle as plunder
for yourselves. [1]Set an ambush for the city behind it."

Joshua's 3-Pronged Invasion

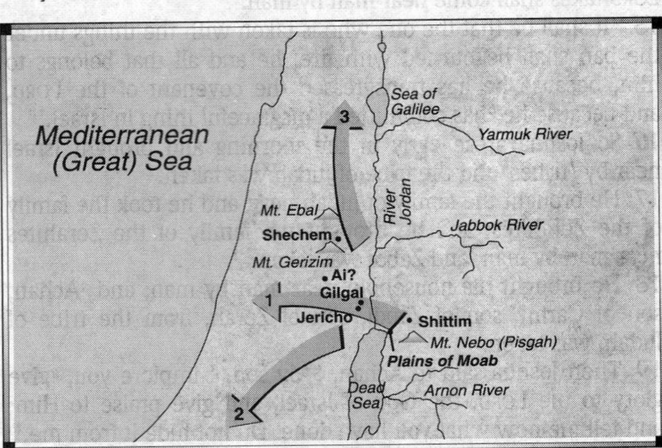

3 So Joshua rose with all the people of war to go up to Ai;
and Joshua chose 30,000 men, valiant warriors, and sent them
out at night.
4 He commanded them, saying, "See, you are [a]going to
ambush the city from behind [1]it. Do not go very far from the
city, but all of you be ready.

24 [1]Or *cattle* [2]I.e. trouble [a]Josh 15:7

25 [1]Lit *him* [2]Lit *and they stoned* [a]Josh 6:18

26 [1]I.e. trouble [a]Is 65:10; Hos 2:15

8:1 [a]Josh 1:9; 10:8 [b]Josh 6:2

2 [1]Lit *Set for yourself* [a]Deut 20:14; Josh 8:27

4 [1]Lit *the city* [a]Judg 20:29

5 "Then I and all the people who are with me will approach
the city. And when they come out to meet us as at the first,
[a]we will flee before them.
6 "They will come out after us until we have drawn them
away from the city, for they will say, '*They* are fleeing before us
as at the first.' So we will flee before them.
7 "And you shall rise from *your* ambush and take possession
of the city, for the LORD your God will deliver it into your hand.
8 "Then it will be when you have seized the city, that you
shall set the city on fire. You shall do *it* [a]according to the word
of the LORD. See, I have commanded you."
9 So Joshua sent them away, and they went to the place of
ambush and remained between Bethel and Ai, on the west side
of Ai; but Joshua spent that night among the people.
10 Now Joshua [a]rose early in the morning and mustered the
people, and he went up with the elders of Israel before the
people to Ai.
11 Then all the people of war who *were* with him went up and
drew near and arrived in front of the city, and camped on the
north side of Ai. Now *there was* a valley between him and Ai.
12 And he took about 5,000 men and set them in ambush
between [a]Bethel and Ai, on the west side of the [1]city.
13 So they stationed the people, all the army that was on the
north side of the city, and its rear guard on the west side of the
city, and Joshua spent that night in the midst of the valley.
14 It came about when the king of Ai saw *it,* that the men of
the city hurried and rose up early and went out to meet Israel
in battle, he and all his people at the appointed place before
the desert plain. But he did not know that *there was* an
ambush against him behind the city.
15 Joshua and all Israel pretended to be beaten before them,
and fled [a]by the way of the wilderness.
16 And all the people who were in the city were called
together to pursue them, and they pursued Joshua and [a]were
drawn away from the city.
17 So not a man was left in Ai or Bethel who had not gone out
after Israel, and they left the city [1]unguarded and pursued Israel.
18 Then the LORD said to Joshua, "[a]Stretch out the javelin that is
in your hand toward Ai, for I will give it into your hand." So Joshua
stretched out the javelin that was in his hand toward the city.
19 The *men in* ambush rose quickly from their place, and
when he had stretched out his hand, they ran and entered the
city and captured it, and they quickly set the city on fire.
20 When the men of Ai turned [1]back and looked, behold, the
smoke of the city ascended to the sky, and they had no place to
flee this way or that, for the people who had been fleeing to
the wilderness turned against the pursuers.
21 When Joshua and all Israel saw that the *men in* ambush
had captured the city and that the smoke of the city ascended,
they turned back and [1]slew the men of Ai.
22 [1]The others came out from the city to encounter them, so
that they were *trapped* in the midst of Israel, [2]some on this

5 [a]Judg 20:32
8 [a]Deut 20:16-18; Josh 8:2
10 [a]Gen 22:3
12 [1]I.e. Ai [a]Gen 12:8; 28:19; Judg 1:22
15 [a]Josh 15:61; 16:1; 18:12
16 [a]Judg 20:31
17 [1]Lit *open*
18 [a]Ex 14:16; 17:9-13; Josh 8:26
20 [1]Lit *behind them*
21 [1]Lit *smote*
22 [1]Lit *These came* [2]Lit *these . . . those*

side and some on that side; and they [3]slew them until [a]no one
was left [4]of those who survived or escaped.
23 But they took alive the king of Ai and brought him to Joshua.
24 Now when Israel had finished killing all the inhabitants of
Ai in the field in the wilderness where they pursued them, and
all of them were fallen by the edge of the sword until they
were destroyed, then all Israel returned to Ai and struck it with
the edge of the sword.
25 [a]All who fell that day, both men and women, were 12,000—
all the [1]people of Ai.
26 For Joshua [a]did not withdraw his hand with which he
stretched out the javelin until he had [1]utterly destroyed all the
inhabitants of Ai.
27 [a]Israel took only the cattle and the spoil of that city as plunder
for themselves, according to the word of the LORD which He
had commanded Joshua.
28 So Joshua burned Ai and made it [a]a heap forever, a desolation
until this day.
29 [a]He hanged the king of Ai on a tree until evening; and at
sunset Joshua gave command and they took his body down
from the tree and threw it at the entrance of the city gate, and
raised over it a great heap of stones *that stands* to this day.
30 Then Joshua built an altar to the LORD, the God of Israel, in
[a]Mount Ebal,
31 just as Moses the servant of the LORD had commanded the
sons of Israel, as it is written in the book of the law of Moses,
[a]an altar of uncut stones on which no man had wielded an iron
tool; and they offered burnt offerings on it to the LORD, and
sacrificed peace offerings.
32 He [a]wrote there on the stones a copy of the law of Moses,
which [1]he had written, in the presence of the sons of Israel.
33 [a]All Israel with their elders and officers and their judges were
standing on both sides of the ark before the Levitical priests who
carried the ark of the covenant of the LORD, the stranger as well as
the native. Half of them *stood* in front of [b]Mount Gerizim and half
of them in front of Mount Ebal, just as Moses the servant of the
LORD had given command at first to bless the people of Israel.
34 Then afterward he read all the words of the law, the
blessing and the curse, according to all that is written in [a]the
book of the law.
35 There was not a word of all that Moses had commanded
which Joshua did not read before all the assembly of Israel
[a]with the women and the little ones and the strangers who
were [1]living among them.

Chapter 9 Theme ______________________________

9 Now it came about when [a]all the kings who were beyond
the Jordan, in the hill country and in the lowland and on
all the [b]coast of the Great Sea toward Lebanon, [c]the Hittite and
the Amorite, the Canaanite, the Perizzite, the Hivite and the
Jebusite, heard of it,

22 [3]Lit *smote* [4]Lit *for it* [a]Josh 8:8
25 [1]Lit *men* [a]Deut 20:16-18
26 [1]Or *put under the ban* [a]Ex 17:11, 12
27 [a]Josh 8:2
28 [a]Deut 13:16
29 [a]Deut 21:22, 23
30 [a]Deut 27:2-8
31 [a]Ex 20:25
32 [1]I.e. Moses [a]Deut 27:2, 3, 8
33 [a]Deut 27:11-14 [b]Deut 11:29
34 [a]Josh 1:8
35 [1]Lit *walking* [a]Ex 12:38; Deut 31:12; Zech 8:23
9:1 [a]Num 13:29; Josh 3:10 [b]Num 34:6 [c]Ex 3:17; 23:23

2 that they gathered themselves together with [1a]one accord
to fight with Joshua and with Israel.
3 When the inhabitants of [a]Gibeon heard what Joshua had
done to Jericho and to Ai,
4 they also acted craftily and [1]set out as envoys, and took
worn-out sacks on their donkeys, and wineskins worn-out and
torn and [2]mended,
5 and worn-out and patched sandals on their feet, and worn-
out clothes on themselves; and all the bread of their provision
was dry *and* had become crumbled.
6 They went to Joshua to the [a]camp at Gilgal and said to him
and to the men of Israel, "We have come from a far country;
now therefore, make a covenant with us."
7 The men of Israel said to the [a]Hivites, "Perhaps you are
living [1]within our land; [b]how then shall we make a covenant
with you?"
8 But they said to Joshua, "[a]We are your servants." Then Joshua
said to them, "Who are you and where do you come from?"
9 They said to him, "Your servants have come from [a]a very
far country because of the [1]fame of the LORD your God; for [b]we
have heard the report of Him and all that He did in Egypt,
10 and all that He did to the two kings of the Amorites who
were beyond the Jordan, to Sihon king of Heshbon and to Og
king of Bashan who was at Ashtaroth.
11 "So our elders and all the inhabitants of our country spoke
to us, saying, 'Take provisions in your hand for the journey, and
go to meet them and say to them, "[a]We are your servants; now
then, make a covenant with us."'
12 "This our bread *was* warm *when* we took it for our
provisions out of our houses on the day that we left to come to
you; but now behold, it is dry and has become crumbled.
13 "These wineskins which we filled were new, and behold,
they are torn; and these our clothes and our sandals are worn
out because of the very long journey."
14 So the men *of Israel* took some of their provisions, and [a]did
not ask for the [1]counsel of the LORD.
15 [a]Joshua made peace with them and made a covenant with
them, to let them live; and the leaders of the congregation
swore *an oath* to them.
16 It came about at the end of three days after they had made
a covenant with them, that they heard that they were
neighbors and that they were living [1]within their land.
17 Then the sons of Israel set out and came to their cities on
the third day. Now their cities *were* [a]Gibeon and Chephirah
and Beeroth and Kiriath-jearim.
18 The sons of Israel did not strike them because the leaders
of the congregation had sworn to them by the LORD the God of
Israel. And the whole congregation grumbled against the leaders.
19 But all the leaders said to the whole congregation, "We
have sworn to them by the LORD, the God of Israel, and now
we cannot touch them.

2 [1]Lit *one mouth* [a]Ps 83:3, 5
3 [a]Josh 9:17, 22; 10:2; 21:17
4 [1]Lit *went and traveled as envoys* [2]Lit *tied up*
6 [a]Josh 5:10
7 [1]Lit *among us* [a]Josh 9:1; 11:19 [b]Ex 23:32; Deut 7:2
8 [a]Deut 20:11; 2 Kin 10:5
9 [1]Or *name* [a]Josh 9:16, 17 [b]Josh 2:9; 9:24
11 [a]Josh 9:8
14 [1]Lit *mouth* [a]Num 27:21
15 [a]Ex 23:32
16 [1]Lit *among them*
17 [a]Josh 18:25

20 "This we will do to them, even let them live, so that wrath
will not be upon us for the oath which we swore to them."
21 The leaders said to them, "Let them live." So they became
[a]hewers of wood and drawers of water for the whole congregation, just as the leaders had spoken to them.
22 Then Joshua called for them and spoke to them, saying,
"Why have you deceived us, saying, 'We are very far from you,'
[a]when you are living [1]within our land?
23 "Now therefore, you are [a]cursed, and [1]you shall never cease
being slaves, both hewers of wood and drawers of water for the
house of my God."
24 So they answered Joshua and said, "[a]Because it was certainly
told your servants that the LORD your God had commanded His
servant Moses to give you all the land, and to destroy all the
inhabitants of the land before you; therefore we feared greatly
for our lives because of you, and have done this thing.
25 "Now behold, [a]we are in your hands; do as it seems good
and right in your sight to do to us."
26 Thus he did to them, and delivered them from the hands of
the sons of Israel, and they did not kill them.
27 But Joshua made them that day hewers of wood and
drawers of water for the congregation and for the altar of the
LORD, to this day, [a]in the place which He would choose.

Chapter 10 Theme ____________________

10 Now it came about when Adoni-zedek king of Jerusalem
heard that Joshua had captured Ai, and had [1]utterly
destroyed it (just [a]as he had done to Jericho and its king, so he
had done to Ai and its king), and that the inhabitants of Gibeon
had [b]made peace with Israel and were [2]within their land,
2 that [1]he [a]feared greatly, because Gibeon *was* a great city,
like one of the royal cities, and because it was greater than Ai,
and all its men *were* mighty.
3 Therefore Adoni-zedek king of Jerusalem sent *word* [a]to
Hoham king of Hebron and to Piram king of Jarmuth and to
Japhia king of Lachish and to Debir king of Eglon, saying,
4 "Come up to me and help me, and let us [1]attack Gibeon, for
it has [a]made peace with Joshua and with the sons of Israel."
5 So the five kings of [a]the Amorites, the king of Jerusalem,
the king of Hebron, the king of Jarmuth, the king of Lachish, *and*
the king of Eglon, gathered together and went up, they with all
their armies, and camped by Gibeon and fought against it.
6 Then the men of Gibeon sent *word* to Joshua to the camp
at Gilgal, saying, "Do not [1]abandon your servants; come up to us
quickly and save us and help us, for all the kings of the Amorites
that live in the hill country have assembled against us."
7 So Joshua went up from Gilgal, he and [a]all the people of
war with him and all the valiant warriors.
8 The LORD said to Joshua, "[a]Do not fear them, for I have given
them into your hands; not [1]one of them shall stand before you."

21 [a]Deut 29:11
22 [1]Lit *among us* [a]Josh 9:16
23 [1]Lit *a servant shall not be cut off from you* [a]Gen 9:25
24 [a]Josh 9:9
25 [a]Gen 16:6
27 [a]Deut 12:5
10:1 [1]Or *put under the ban* [2]Lit *among them* [a]Josh 8:21f [b]Josh 9:15
2 [1]Lit *they* [a]Ex 15:14-16
3 [a]Josh 10:23
4 [1]Lit *smite* [a]Josh 9:15
5 [a]Num 13:29
6 [1]Lit *slacken your hands from*
7 [a]Josh 8:1
8 [1]Lit *a man* [a]Josh 1:5, 9

9 [1]Lit *he went up*

9 So Joshua came upon them suddenly [1]by marching all night from Gilgal.

10 [1]Lit *struck* [a]Deut 7:23

10 [a]And the LORD confounded them before Israel, and He [1]slew them with a great slaughter at Gibeon, and pursued them by the way of the ascent of Beth-horon and struck them as far as Azekah and Makkedah.

11 [1]Lit *with* [a]Ps 18:12f; Is 28:2

11 As they fled from before Israel, *while* they were at the descent of Beth-horon, [a]the LORD threw large stones from heaven on them as far as Azekah, and they died; *there were* more who died [1]from the hailstones than those whom the sons of Israel killed with the sword.

12 [a]Hab 3:11

12 Then Joshua spoke to the LORD in the day when the LORD delivered up the Amorites before the sons of Israel, and he said in the sight of Israel,

"O [a]sun, stand still at Gibeon,
And O moon in the valley of Aijalon."

13 [a]Hab 3:11 [b]2 Sam 1:18 [c]Is 38:8

13 [a]So the sun stood still, and the moon stopped,
Until the nation avenged themselves of their enemies.
Is it not written in [b]the book of Jashar? And [c]the sun stopped in the middle of the sky and did not hasten to go *down* for about a whole day.

14 [a]Ex 14:14; Deut 1:30; Josh 10:42

14 There was no day like that before it or after it, when the LORD listened to the voice of a man; for [a]the LORD fought for Israel.

15 Then Joshua and all Israel with him returned to the camp to Gilgal.

16 [a]Josh 10:5

16 Now these [a]five kings had fled and hidden themselves in the cave at Makkedah.

17 It was told Joshua, saying, "The five kings have been found hidden in the cave at Makkedah."

18 Joshua said, "Roll large stones against the mouth of the cave, and assign men by it to guard them,

19 [1]Lit *smite their tail*

19 but do not stay *there* yourselves; pursue your enemies and [1]attack them in the rear. Do not allow them to enter their cities, for the LORD your God has delivered them into your hand."

20 [1]Lit *striking* [2]Lit *and had* [a]Deut 20:16

20 It came about when Joshua and the sons of Israel had finished [1]slaying them with a very great slaughter, [a]until they were destroyed, and the survivors *who* remained of them [2]had entered the fortified cities,

21 [1]Lit *sharpened his tongue*

21 that all the people returned to the camp to Joshua at Makkedah in peace. No one [1]uttered a word against any of the sons of Israel.

22 Then Joshua said, "Open the mouth of the cave and bring these five kings out to me from the cave."

23 [a]Deut 7:24

23 They did so, and [a]brought these five kings out to him from the cave: the king of Jerusalem, the king of Hebron, the king of Jarmuth, the king of Lachish, *and* the king of Eglon.

24 [a]Mal 4:3

24 When they brought these kings out to Joshua, Joshua called for all the men of Israel, and said to the chiefs of the men of war who had gone with him, "Come near, [a]put your feet on the necks of these kings." So they came near and put their feet on their necks.

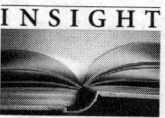

INSIGHT

The ***book of Jashar*** was a collection of poetical writings of important events in Israel's history which was gathered in the time of David or Solomon. It is often compared to "The Book of Wars of the Lord." Bible authors are believed to have quoted from this book.

25 Joshua then said to them, "[a]Do not fear or be dismayed! Be strong and courageous, for thus the LORD will do to all your enemies with whom you fight."
26 So afterward Joshua struck them and put them to death, and he [a]hanged them on five trees; and they hung on the trees until evening.
27 It came about at [1]sunset that Joshua gave a command, and [a]they took them down from the trees and threw them into the cave where they had hidden themselves, and put large stones over the mouth of the cave, to this very day.
28 Now Joshua captured Makkedah on that day, and struck it and its king with the edge of the sword; [a]he [1]utterly destroyed [2]it and every [3]person who was in it. He left no survivor. Thus he did to the king of Makkedah [b]just as he had done to the king of Jericho.
29 Then Joshua and all Israel with him passed on from Makkedah to [a]Libnah, and fought against Libnah.
30 The LORD gave it also with its king into the hands of Israel, and he struck it and every person who *was* in it with the edge of the sword. He left no survivor in it. Thus he did to its king just as he had done to the king of Jericho.
31 And Joshua and all Israel with him passed on from Libnah to Lachish, and they camped by it and fought against it.
32 The LORD gave Lachish into the hands of Israel; and he captured it on the second day, and struck it and every person who *was* in it with the edge of the sword, according to all that he had done to Libnah.
33 Then Horam king of [a]Gezer came up to help Lachish, and Joshua [1]defeated him and his people until he had left him no survivor.
34 And Joshua and all Israel with him passed on from Lachish to Eglon, and they camped by it and fought against it.
35 They captured it on that day and struck it with the edge of the sword; and he [1]utterly destroyed that day every person who *was* in it, according to all that he had done to Lachish.
36 Then Joshua and all Israel with him went up from Eglon to [a]Hebron, and they fought against it.
37 They captured it and struck it and its king and all its cities and all the persons who *were* in it with the edge of the sword. He left no survivor, according to all that he had done to Eglon. And he [1]utterly destroyed it and every person who *was* in it.
38 Then Joshua and all Israel with him returned to [a]Debir, and they fought against it.
39 He captured it and its king and all its cities, and they struck them with the edge of the sword, and [1]utterly destroyed every person *who was* in it. He left no survivor. Just as he had done to Hebron, so he did to Debir and its king, as he had also done to Libnah and its king.
40 Thus Joshua struck all the land, [a]the hill country and the [1]Negev and the lowland and the slopes and [b]all their kings. He left no survivor, but [c]he [2]utterly destroyed all who breathed, just as the LORD, the God of Israel, had commanded.

25 [a]Josh 10:8

26 [a]Josh 8:29

27 [1]Lit *the time of the going of the sun* [a]Deut 21:22, 23

28 [1]Or *put under the ban* [2]Some mss read *them* [3]Lit *soul,* and so throughout the ch [a]Deut 20:16 [b]Josh 6:21

29 [a]Josh 15:42; 21:13

33 [1]Lit *smote* [a]Josh 16:3, 10; Judg 1:29; 1 Kin 9:16f

35 [1]Or *put under the ban*

36 [a]Num 13:22; Judg 1:10, 20; 2 Sam 5:1, 3, 5, 13; 2 Chr 11:10

37 [1]Or *put it under the ban*

38 [a]Josh 15:15; Judg 1:11; 1 Chr 6:58

39 [1]Or *put it under the ban*

40 [1]I.e. South country [2]Or *put it under the ban* [a]Deut 1:7 [b]Deut 7:24 [c]Deut 20:16

41 Joshua struck them from Kadesh-barnea even as far as Gaza,
and all the country of [a]Goshen even as far as Gibeon.
42 Joshua captured all these kings and their lands at one time,
because [a]the LORD, the God of Israel, fought for Israel.
43 So Joshua and all Israel with him returned to the camp at
Gilgal.

Chapter 11 Theme ______________________________

11 Then it came about, when Jabin king of [a]Hazor heard *of
it,* that he sent to Jobab king of Madon and to the king of
Shimron and to the king of Achshaph,
2 and to the kings who were of the north in the hill country,
and in the [a]Arabah—south of [1]Chinneroth and in the lowland
and on the [2]heights of Dor on the west—
3 to the Canaanite on the east and on the west, and the Amorite
and the Hittite and the Perizzite and the Jebusite in the hill
country, and [a]the Hivite [1]at the foot of [b]Hermon in the land of
[c]Mizpeh.
4 They came out, they and all their armies with them, [a]*as*
many people as the sand that is on the seashore, with very
many horses and chariots.
5 So all of these kings having agreed to meet, came and
encamped together at the waters of Merom, to fight against Israel.
6 Then the LORD said to Joshua, "[a]Do not be afraid because of
them, for tomorrow at this time I will deliver all of them slain
before Israel; you shall [b]hamstring their horses and burn their
chariots with fire."
7 So Joshua and all the people of war with him came upon
them suddenly by the waters of Merom, and attacked them.
8 The LORD delivered them into the hand of Israel, so that
they [1]defeated them, and pursued them as far as Great Sidon
and [a]Misrephoth-maim and the valley of [b]Mizpeh to the east;
and they struck them until no survivor was left to them.
9 Joshua did to them as the LORD had told him; he [a]hamstrung
their horses and burned their chariots with fire.
10 Then Joshua turned back at that time, and captured [a]Hazor
and struck its king with the sword; for Hazor formerly was the
head of all these kingdoms.
11 [a]They struck every person who was in it with the edge of
the sword, [1]utterly destroying *them;* there was no one left who
breathed. And he burned Hazor with fire.
12 Joshua captured all the cities of these kings, and all their
kings, and he struck them with the edge of the sword, *and*
utterly destroyed them; just [a]as Moses the servant of the LORD
had commanded.
13 However, Israel did not burn any cities that stood on their
mounds, except Hazor alone, *which* Joshua burned.
14 [a]All the spoil of these cities and the cattle, the sons of Israel
took as their plunder; but they struck every man with the edge
of the sword, until they had destroyed them. They left no one
who breathed.

41 [a]Josh 11:16; 15:51
42 [a]Josh 10:14
11:1 [a]Josh 11:10
2 [1]I.e. Sea of Galilee [2]Or *Naphoth-dor* [a]Josh 12:3; 13:27
3 [1]Lit *under* [a]Deut 7:1; Judg 3:3, 5; 1 Kin 9:20 [b]Josh 11:17; 13:5, 11 [c]Josh 15:38; 18:26
4 [a]Judg 7:12
6 [a]Josh 10:8 [b]2 Sam 8:4
8 [1]Lit *smote* [a]Josh 13:6 [b]Josh 11:3
9 [a]Josh 11:6
10 [a]Josh 11:1
11 [1]Or *putting them under the ban,* and so throughout the ch [a]Deut 20:16
12 [a]Num 33:50-52; Deut 7:2; 20:16f
14 [a]Num 31:11, 12

15 Just as the LORD had commanded Moses his servant, so
Moses commanded Joshua, and so Joshua did; he left nothing
undone of all that the LORD had commanded Moses.
16 Thus Joshua took all that land: [a]the hill country and all the
[1]Negev, all that land of Goshen, the lowland, [b]the Arabah, the
hill country of Israel and its lowland
17 from [a]Mount Halak, that rises toward Seir, even as far as
Baal-gad in the valley of Lebanon [1]at the foot of Mount Hermon.
And he captured [b]all their kings and struck them down and put
them to death.
18 Joshua waged war a long time with all these kings.
19 There was not a city which made peace with the sons of
Israel except [a]the Hivites living in Gibeon; they took them all
in battle.
20 [a]For it was of the LORD to [1]harden their hearts, to meet
Israel in battle in order that he might [b]utterly destroy them,
that they might [2]receive no mercy, but that he might destroy
them, just as the LORD had commanded Moses.
21 Then Joshua came at that time and cut off [a]the Anakim
from the hill country, from Hebron, from Debir, from Anab and
from all the hill country of Judah and from all the hill country
of Israel. Joshua utterly destroyed them with their cities.
22 There were no Anakim left in the land of the sons of Israel;
only in Gaza, in [a]Gath, and in [b]Ashdod some remained.
23 So Joshua took the whole land, according to all that the LORD
had spoken to Moses, and [a]Joshua gave it for an inheritance to
Israel according to their divisions by their tribes. [b]Thus the
land had rest from war.

Chapter 12 Theme ____________________

12 Now these are the [a]kings of the land whom the sons of
Israel [1]defeated, and whose land they possessed beyond
the Jordan toward the sunrise, from the valley of the Arnon as
far as Mount Hermon, and all the Arabah to the east:
2 Sihon king of the Amorites, who lived in Heshbon, *and*
ruled [a]from Aroer, which is on the edge of the valley of the
Arnon, both the middle of the valley and half of Gilead, even as
far as the brook Jabbok, the border of the sons of Ammon;
3 and the [a]Arabah as far as the Sea of [1]Chinneroth toward
the east, and as far as the sea of the Arabah, *even* the Salt Sea,
eastward [2]toward [b]Beth-jeshimoth, and on the south, [3]at the
foot of the slopes of Pisgah;
4 and the territory of Og king of Bashan, one of [a]the remnant
of Rephaim, who lived at [b]Ashtaroth and at Edrei,
5 and ruled over Mount Hermon and [a]Salecah and all Bashan,
as far as [b]the border of the Geshurites and the Maacathites, and
half of Gilead, *as far as* the border of Sihon king of Heshbon.
6 Moses the servant of the LORD and the sons of Israel
[1]defeated them; and [a]Moses the servant of the LORD gave it to
the Reubenites and the Gadites and the half-tribe of Manasseh
as a possession.

16 [1]I.e. South country [a]Josh 10:40, 41 [b]Josh 11:2

17 [1]Lit *under* [a]Josh 12:7 [b]Deut 7:24

19 [a]Josh 9:3, 7

20 [1]Lit *make strong* [2]Lit *have* [a]Ex 14:17 [b]Deut 7:16

21 [a]Num 13:33; Deut 9:2

22 [a]1 Sam 17:4; 1 Kin 2:39; 1 Chr 8:13 [b]Josh 15:46f; 1 Sam 5:1; Is 20:1

23 [a]Deut 1:38 [b]Deut 12:9, 10; 25:19; Heb 4:8

12:1 [1]Lit *smote* [a]Num 32:33; Deut 3:8-17

2 [a]Deut 2:36

3 [1]I.e. Galilee [2]Lit *the way of* [3]Lit *under* [a]Josh 11:2 [b]Josh 13:20

4 [a]Deut 3:11 [b]Deut 1:4

5 [a]Deut 3:10; Josh 13:11; 1 Chr 5:11 [b]Deut 3:14; 1 Sam 27:8

6 [1]Lit *smote* [a]Num 32:33; Deut 3:12

7 Now these are the kings of the land whom Joshua and the
sons of Israel [1]defeated beyond the Jordan toward the west,
from Baal-gad in the valley of Lebanon even as far as [a]Mount
Halak, which rises toward Seir; and Joshua gave it to the tribes
of Israel as a possession according to their divisions,
8 in [a]the hill country, in the lowland, in the Arabah, on the
slopes, and in the wilderness, and in the [1]Negev; the Hittite, the
Amorite and the Canaanite, the Perizzite, the Hivite and the
Jebusite:
9 the [a]king of Jericho, one; the [b]king of Ai, which is beside
Bethel, one;
10 the [a]king of Jerusalem, one; the king of Hebron, one;
11 the king of Jarmuth, one; the king of Lachish, one;
12 the king of Eglon, one; the king of Gezer, one;
13 the king of Debir, one; the king of Geder, one;
14 the king of Hormah, one; the king of [a]Arad, one;
15 the king of Libnah, one; the king of Adullam, one;
16 the king of Makkedah, one; the king of Bethel, one;
17 the king of Tappuah, one; the [a]king of Hepher, one;
18 the king of [a]Aphek, one; the king of Lasharon, one;
19 the king of Madon, one; the king of Hazor, one;
20 the king of Shimron-meron, one; the king of Achshaph, one;
21 the king of Taanach, one; the king of Megiddo, one;
22 the king of [a]Kedesh, one; the king of Jokneam in Carmel, one;
23 the king of Dor in the [1]heights of Dor, one; the king of
[a]Goiim in Gilgal, one;
24 the king of Tirzah, one: [a]in all, thirty-one kings.

7 [1]Lit *smote* [a]Josh 11:17
8 [1]I.e. South country [a]Josh 11:16
9 [a]Josh 6:2 [b]Josh 8:29
10 [a]Josh 10:23
14 [a]Num 21:1
17 [a]1 Kin 4:10
18 [a]Josh 13:4; 2 Kin 13:17
22 [a]Josh 19:37; 20:7; 21:32
23 [1]Or *Naphath-dor* [a]Gen 14:1
24 [a]Deut 7:24

Chapter 13 Theme ____________________

13 Now [a]Joshua was old *and* advanced in years when the
LORD said to him, "You are old *and* advanced in years,
and very much of the land remains to be possessed.
2 "This is the land that remains: all the regions *of* the Philistines
and all *those of* the [a]Geshurites;
3 from the Shihor which is [1]east of Egypt, even as far as the
border of Ekron to the north (it is counted as Canaanite); the
[a]five lords of the Philistines: the Gazite, the Ashdodite, the
Ashkelonite, the Gittite, the Ekronite; and the Avvite
4 [1]to the south, all the land of the Canaanite, and Mearah
that belongs to the Sidonians, as far as [a]Aphek, to the border of
the [b]Amorite;
5 and the land of the [a]Gebalite, and all of Lebanon, toward
the [1]east, [b]from Baal-gad below Mount Hermon as far as [2]Lebo-hamath.
6 "All the inhabitants of the hill country from Lebanon as far
as [a]Misrephoth-maim, all the Sidonians, I will [1]drive them out
from before the sons of Israel; [b]only allot it to Israel for an
inheritance as I have commanded you.
7 "Now therefore, apportion this land for an inheritance to
the nine tribes and the half-tribe of Manasseh."

13:1 [a]Josh 14:10
2 [a]Josh 13:11; 1 Sam 27:8
3 [1]Lit *on the face of* [a]1 Sam 6:4, 16
4 [1]Or *from the Teman* [a]Josh 12:18; 19:30; 1 Sam 4:1; 1 Kin 20:26, 30 [b]Ezek 16:3; Amos 2:10
5 [1]Lit *sunrise* [2]Or *the entrance of Hamath* [a]1 Kin 5:18 [b]Josh 12:7
6 [1]Or *dispossess* [a]Josh 11:8 [b]Num 33:54

8 With [1]the other half-tribe, the Reubenites and the Gadites
received their inheritance which Moses gave them [a]beyond the
Jordan to the east, just as Moses the servant of the LORD gave to
them;
9 from Aroer, which is on the edge of the valley of the
Arnon, with the city which is in the middle of the valley, and
all the plain of Medeba, as far as Dibon;
10 and all the cities of Sihon king of the Amorites, who
reigned in Heshbon, as far as the border of the sons of Ammon;
11 and [a]Gilead, and the [1]territory of the Geshurites and
Maacathites, and all Mount Hermon, and all Bashan as far as
Salecah;
12 all the kingdom of [a]Og in Bashan, who reigned in Ashtaroth
and in Edrei (he alone was left of the remnant of the Rephaim);
for Moses [b]struck them and dispossessed them.
13 But the sons of Israel did not dispossess the Geshurites or
the Maacathites; for Geshur and Maacath live among Israel
until this day.
14 [a]Only to the tribe of Levi he did not give an inheritance;
the offerings by fire to the LORD, the God of Israel, are [1]their
inheritance, as He spoke to him.
15 So Moses gave *an inheritance* to the tribe of the sons of
Reuben according to their families.
16 Their [1]territory was [a]from Aroer, which is on the edge of
the valley of the Arnon, with the city which is in the middle of
the valley and all the plain by Medeba;
17 Heshbon, and all its cities which are on the plain: Dibon
and Bamoth-baal and Beth-baal-meon,
18 and [a]Jahaz and Kedemoth and Mephaath,
19 and [a]Kiriathaim and Sibmah and Zereth-shahar on the hill
of the valley,
20 and Beth-peor and the slopes of Pisgah and Beth-jeshimoth,
21 even all the cities of the plain and all the kingdom of Sihon
king of the Amorites who reigned in Heshbon, whom Moses
struck with the chiefs of Midian, [a]Evi and Rekem and Zur and
Hur and Reba, the princes of Sihon, who lived in the land.
22 The sons of Israel also killed [a]Balaam the son of Beor, the
diviner, with the sword among *the rest of* their slain.
23 The border of the sons of Reuben was the [1]Jordan. This
was the inheritance of the sons of Reuben according to their
families, the cities and their villages.
24 Moses also gave *an inheritance* to the tribe of Gad, to the
sons of Gad, according to their families.
25 Their territory was [a]Jazer, and all the cities of Gilead, and
half the land of the sons of Ammon, as far as Aroer which is
before Rabbah;
26 and from Heshbon as far as Ramath-mizpeh and Betonim,
and from Mahanaim as far as the border of [1]Debir;
27 and in the valley, Beth-haram and Beth-nimrah and Succoth
and Zaphon, the rest of the kingdom of Sihon king of Heshbon,
with the Jordan [1]as a border, as far as the *lower* end of the Sea
of [2a]Chinnereth beyond the Jordan to the east.

8 [1]Lit *it, the* [a]Josh 12:1-6
11 [1]Or *border* [a]Gen 37:25; Num 32:29; Josh 13:25; 17:5f
12 [a]Deut 3:11 [b]Num 21:24
14 [1]Lit *his* [a]Deut 18:1, 2
16 [1]Or *border* [a]Josh 13:9
18 [a]Num 21:23; Judg 11:20; Is 15:4; Jer 48:34
19 [a]Num 32:37; Jer 48:1, 23; Ezek 25:9
21 [a]Num 31:8
22 [a]Num 31:8
23 [1]Lit *Jordan and border*
25 [a]Num 21:32; Josh 21:39; 2 Sam 24:5; 1 Chr 6:81; 26:31; Is 16:8f; Jer 48:32
26 [1]Or *Lidebir*
27 [1]Lit *and border* [2]I.e. Galilee [a]Num 34:11; Deut 3:17

30 [1]Lit *tent villages* [a]Num 32:41

31 [a]Josh 9:10; 12:4; 13:12; Judg 10:6; 1 Sam 7:3f; 12:10; 1 Chr 6:71

33 [1]Lit *spoken to* [a]Deut 18:1f; Josh 13:14

14:1 [1]Lit *fathers'* [a]Num 34:16-29

2 [1]Lit *by the hand of* [a]Num 26:55; 33:54; 34:13

3 [a]Num 32:33 [b]Josh 13:14

4 [a]Gen 41:51f; 46:20; 48:1, 5; Num 26:28; 2 Chr 30:1

5 [a]Num 35:1f; Josh 21:2

6 [1]Lit *me and concerning you* [a]Num 13:6, 30; 14:6, 24, 30

7 [a]Num 13:1-31

8 [1]Lit *become demoralized* [a]Num 14:24; Deut 1:36

9 [a]Deut 1:36

28 This is the inheritance of the sons of Gad according to their
families, the cities and their villages.
29 Moses also gave *an inheritance* to the half-tribe of Manasseh;
and it was for the half-tribe of the sons of Manasseh according to
their families.
30 Their territory was from Mahanaim, all Bashan, all the
kingdom of Og king of Bashan, and all [a]the [1]towns of Jair,
which are in Bashan, sixty cities;
31 also half of Gilead, with [a]Ashtaroth and Edrei, the cities of
the kingdom of Og in Bashan, *were* for the sons of Machir the
son of Manasseh, for half of the sons of Machir according to
their families.
32 These are *the territories* which Moses apportioned for an
inheritance in the plains of Moab, beyond the Jordan at Jericho
to the east.
33 But [a]to the tribe of Levi, Moses did not give an inheritance;
the LORD, the God of Israel, is their inheritance, as He had
[1]promised to them.

Chapter 14 Theme ______________________________

14 Now these are *the territories* which the sons of Israel
inherited in the land of Canaan, which [a]Eleazar the
priest, and Joshua the son of Nun, and the heads of the [1]house-
holds of the tribes of the sons of Israel apportioned to them for
an inheritance,
2 by the [a]lot of their inheritance, as the LORD commanded
[1]through Moses, for the nine tribes and the half-tribe.
3 For [a]Moses had given the inheritance of the two tribes and
the half-tribe beyond the Jordan; but [b]he did not give an
inheritance to the Levites among them.
4 For the sons of Joseph were two tribes, [a]Manasseh and
Ephraim, and they did not give a portion to the Levites in the
land, except cities to live in, with their pasture lands for their
livestock and for their property.
5 Thus the sons of Israel did just [a]as the LORD had commanded
Moses, and they divided the land.
6 Then the sons of Judah drew near to Joshua in Gilgal, and
[a]Caleb the son of Jephunneh the Kenizzite said to him, "You
know the word which the LORD spoke to Moses the man of
God concerning [1]you and me in Kadesh-barnea.
7 "I was forty years old when [a]Moses the servant of the LORD
sent me from Kadesh-barnea to spy out the land, and I brought
word back to him as *it was* in my heart.
8 "Nevertheless my brethren who went up with me made the
heart of the people [1]melt with fear; but [a]I followed the LORD
my God fully.
9 "So Moses swore on that day, saying, 'Surely [a]the land on
which your foot has trodden will be an inheritance to you and to
your children forever, because you have followed the LORD my
God fully.'

10 "Now behold, the LORD has let me live, just as He spoke,
these forty-five years, from the time that the LORD spoke this
word to Moses, when Israel walked in the wilderness; and now
behold, I am eighty-five years old today.
11 "[a]I am still as strong today as I was in the day Moses sent
me; as my strength was then, so my strength is now, for war
and for [b]going out and coming in.
12 "Now then, give me this hill country about which the LORD
spoke on that day, for you heard on that day that [a]Anakim *were*
there, with great fortified cities; perhaps the LORD will be with
me, and I will [1]drive them out as the LORD has spoken."
13 So Joshua [a]blessed him and [b]gave Hebron to Caleb the son
of Jephunneh for an inheritance.
14 Therefore, Hebron became the inheritance of Caleb the
son of Jephunneh the Kenizzite until this day, because he
followed the LORD God of Israel fully.
15 Now the name of Hebron was formerly [1]Kiriath-arba; *for
Arba* was the greatest man among the Anakim. [a]Then the land
had rest from war.

Chapter 15 Theme ______________________

15 Now [a]the lot for the tribe of the sons of Judah according
to their families [1]reached the [b]border of Edom, southward to the [c]wilderness of Zin at the extreme south.
2 Their south border was from the lower end of the Salt Sea,
from the bay that turns to the south.
3 Then it proceeded southward to the ascent of Akrabbim and
continued to Zin, then went up by the south of Kadesh-barnea
and continued to Hezron, and went up to Addar and turned
about to Karka.
4 It [a]continued to Azmon and proceeded to the [1b]brook of Egypt,
and the [2]border ended at the sea. This shall be your south border.
5 The [a]east border *was* the Salt Sea, as far as the [1]mouth of
the Jordan. And the [b]border of the north side was from the bay
of the sea at the [1]mouth of the Jordan.
6 Then the border went up to Beth-hoglah, and continued on
the north of Beth-arabah, and the border went up to the stone
of Bohan the son of Reuben.
7 The border went up to Debir from [a]the valley of Achor, and
turned northward toward Gilgal which is opposite the ascent of
Adummim, which is on the south of the valley; and the border
continued to the waters of En-shemesh and [1]it ended at En-rogel.
8 Then the border went up the valley of Ben-hinnom to the
slope of the [a]Jebusite on the south (that is, Jerusalem); and the
border went up to the top of the mountain which is before the
valley of Hinnom to the west, which is at the end of the valley
of Rephaim toward the north.
9 From the top of the mountain the border curved to the
spring of the waters of Nephtoah and proceeded to the cities of
Mount Ephron, then the border curved to [a]Baalah (that is,
[b]Kiriath-jearim).

11 [a]Deut 34:7 [b]Deut 31:2
12 [1]Or *dispossess* [a]Num 13:33
13 [a]Josh 22:6 [b]Judg 1:20; 1 Chr 6:55f
15 [1]I.e. the city of Arba [a]Josh 11:23
15:1 [1]Lit *was to* [a]Num 34:3, 4 [b]Num 20:16 [c]Deut 32:51
4 [1]Or *wadi* [2]Lit *goings out of the border were* [a]Num 34:5 [b]Gen 15:18; 1 Kin 8:65
5 [1]Lit *end* [a]Num 34:3, 10-12 [b]Josh 18:15-19
7 [1]Lit *the goings out of it were* [a]Josh 7:24
8 [a]Josh 15:63
9 [a]1 Chr 13:6 [b]Judg 18:12

10 [a]Gen 38:13; Judg 14:1
11 [1]Lit *goings out... were*
12 [1]Lit *border* [a]Num 34:6
13 [1]Lit *mouth* [2]I.e. the city of Arba [a]Josh 14:13-15 [b]Num 13:6
14 [1]Or *dispossessed* [a]Josh 11:21, 22 [b]Num 13:33; Deut 9:2
15 [a]Josh 10:38
16 [1]Lit *smites* [2]Lit *and I*
17 [a]Judg 1:13; 3:9
18 [a]Judg 1:14
19 [1]I.e. South country
21 [a]Gen 35:21
28 [a]Gen 21:31
31 [a]1 Sam 27:6; 30:1
33 [a]Judg 13:25; 16:31
35 [a]1 Sam 22:1

10 The border turned about from Baalah westward to Mount
Seir, and continued to the slope of Mount Jearim on the north
(that is, Chesalon), and went down to Beth-shemesh and
continued through [a]Timnah.
11 The border proceeded to the side of Ekron northward. Then
the border curved to Shikkeron and continued to Mount Baalah
and proceeded to Jabneel, and the [1]border ended at the sea.
12 The west border *was* [a]at the Great Sea, even *its* [1]coastline.
This is the border around the sons of Judah according to their
families.
13 Now [a]he gave to Caleb the son of Jephunneh a portion
[b]among the sons of Judah, according to the [1]command of the
LORD to Joshua, *namely,* [2]Kiriath-arba, *Arba being* the father of
Anak (that is, Hebron).
14 [a]Caleb [1]drove out from there the three [b]sons of Anak: Sheshai
and Ahiman and Talmai, the children of Anak.
15 Then [a]he went up from there against the inhabitants of
Debir; now the name of Debir formerly was Kiriath-sepher.
16 And Caleb said, "The one who [1]attacks Kiriath-sepher and
captures it, [2]I will give him Achsah my daughter as a wife."
17 [a]Othniel the son of Kenaz, the brother of Caleb, captured
it; so he gave him Achsah his daughter as a wife.
18 [a]It came about that when she came *to him,* she persuaded
him to ask her father for a field. So she alighted from the
donkey, and Caleb said to her, "What do you want?"
19 Then she said, "Give me a blessing; since you have given
me the land of the [1]Negev, give me also springs of water." So
he gave her the upper springs and the lower springs.
20 This is the inheritance of the tribe of the sons of Judah
according to their families.
21 Now the cities at the extremity of the tribe of the sons of
Judah toward the border of Edom in the south were Kabzeel
and [a]Eder and Jagur,
22 and Kinah and Dimonah and Adadah,
23 and Kedesh and Hazor and Ithnan,
24 Ziph and Telem and Bealoth,
25 and Hazor-hadattah and Kerioth-hezron (that is, Hazor),
26 Amam and Shema and Moladah,
27 and Hazar-gaddah and Heshmon and Beth-pelet,
28 and Hazar-shual and [a]Beersheba and Biziothiah,
29 Baalah and Iim and Ezem,
30 and Eltolad and Chesil and Hormah,
31 and [a]Ziklag and Madmannah and Sansannah,
32 and Lebaoth and Shilhim and Ain and Rimmon; in all,
twenty-nine cities with their villages.
33 In the lowland: [a]Eshtaol and Zorah and Ashnah,
34 and Zanoah and En-gannim, Tappuah and Enam,
35 Jarmuth and [a]Adullam, Socoh and Azekah,
36 and Shaaraim and Adithaim and Gederah and Gederothaim;
fourteen cities with their villages.
37 Zenan and Hadashah and Migdal-gad,

38 and Dilean and Mizpeh and Joktheel,
39 [a]Lachish and Bozkath and Eglon,
40 and Cabbon and Lahmas and Chitlish,
41 and Gederoth, Beth-dagon and Naamah and Makkedah;
sixteen cities with their villages.
42 Libnah and Ether and Ashan,
43 and Iphtah and Ashnah and Nezib,
44 and Keilah and Achzib and Mareshah; nine cities with their
villages.
45 Ekron, with its towns and its villages;
46 from Ekron even to the sea, all that were by the [1]side of
Ashdod, with their villages.
47 Ashdod, its towns and its villages; Gaza, its towns and its
villages; as far as [a]the [1]brook of Egypt and the Great Sea, even
its [2]coastline.
48 In the hill country: Shamir and Jattir and Socoh,
49 and Dannah and Kiriath-sannah (that is, Debir),
50 and Anab and Eshtemoh and Anim,
51 and Goshen and Holon and Giloh; eleven cities with their
villages.
52 Arab and Dumah and Eshan,
53 and Janum and Beth-tappuah and Aphekah,
54 and Humtah and Kiriath-arba (that is, Hebron), and Zior;
nine cities with their villages.
55 Maon, Carmel and Ziph and Juttah,
56 and Jezreel and Jokdeam and Zanoah,
57 Kain, Gibeah and Timnah; ten cities with their villages.
58 Halhul, Beth-zur and Gedor,
59 and Maarath and Beth-anoth and Eltekon; six cities with
their villages.
60 Kiriath-baal (that is, Kiriath-jearim), and Rabbah; two cities
with their villages.
61 In the wilderness: Beth-arabah, Middin and Secacah,
62 and Nibshan and the City of Salt and Engedi; six cities with
their villages.
63 Now as for the [a]Jebusites, the inhabitants of Jerusalem, the
sons of Judah could not [1]drive them out; so the Jebusites live
with the sons of Judah at Jerusalem until this day.

Chapter 16 Theme ____________________

16 Then the lot for the sons of Joseph went from the Jordan at
Jericho to the waters of Jericho on the east into [a]the wilderness, going up from Jericho through the hill country to Bethel.
2 It went from Bethel to Luz, and [a]continued to the border of
the Archites at Ataroth.
3 It went down westward to the territory of the Japhletites,
as far as the territory of lower [a]Beth-horon even to [b]Gezer, and
[1]it ended at the sea.
4 The [a]sons of Joseph, Manasseh and Ephraim, received their
inheritance.

39 [a]Josh 10:3; 2 Kin 14:19
46 [1]Lit *hand*
47 [1]Or *wadi* [2]Lit *border* [a]Josh 15:4
63 [1]Or *dispossess them* [a]Judg 1:21; 2 Sam 5:6; 1 Chr 11:4
16:1 [a]Josh 8:15; 18:12
2 [a]Josh 18:13
3 [1]Lit *the goings out of it were* [a]Josh 18:13; 1 Kin 9:17 [b]Josh 10:33
4 [a]Josh 17:14

5 Now *this* was the territory of the sons of Ephraim according
to their families: the border of their inheritance eastward was
[a]Ataroth-addar, as far as upper Beth-horon.
6 Then the border went westward at [a]Michmethath on the
north, and the border turned about eastward to Taanath-shiloh
and continued *beyond* it to the east of Janoah.
7 It went down from Janoah to Ataroth and to [a]Naarah, then
reached Jericho and came out at the Jordan.
8 From [a]Tappuah the border continued westward to the [1]brook
of Kanah, and [2]it ended at the sea. This is the inheritance of
the tribe of the sons of Ephraim according to their families,
9 *together* with the cities which were set apart for the sons
of Ephraim in the midst of the inheritance of the sons of
Manasseh, all the cities with their villages.
10 [a]But they did not [1]drive out the Canaanites who lived in
Gezer, so [b]the Canaanites live in the midst of Ephraim to this
day, and they became forced laborers.

Chapter 17 Theme ____________

17 Now *this* was the lot for the tribe of [a]Manasseh, for he
was the firstborn of Joseph. To Machir the firstborn of
Manasseh, the father of Gilead, [1]were allotted Gilead and
Bashan, because he was a man of war.
2 So *the lot* was *made* for the rest of the sons of Manasseh
according to their families: for the sons of Abiezer and for the
sons of Helek and for the sons of Asriel and for the sons of
Shechem and for the sons of Hepher and for the sons of
Shemida; these *were* the male [1]descendants of Manasseh the
son of Joseph according to their families.
3 However, [a]Zelophehad, the son of Hepher, the son of
Gilead, the son of Machir, the son of Manasseh, had no sons,
only daughters; and these are the names of his daughters:
Mahlah and Noah, Hoglah, Milcah and Tirzah.
4 They came near before Eleazar the priest and before Joshua
the son of Nun and before the leaders, saying, "The LORD
commanded Moses to give us an inheritance among our
brothers." So [a]according to the [1]command of the LORD he gave
them an inheritance among their father's brothers.
5 Thus there fell ten portions to Manasseh, besides the land
of Gilead and Bashan, which is beyond the Jordan,
6 because the daughters of Manasseh received an inheritance
among his sons. And the [a]land of Gilead belonged to the rest of
the sons of Manasseh.
7 The border of Manasseh [1]ran from Asher to Michmethath
which was east of Shechem; then the border went [2]southward
to the inhabitants of En-tappuah.
8 The land of Tappuah belonged to Manasseh, but [a]Tappuah
on the border of Manasseh *belonged* to the sons of Ephraim.
9 The [a]border went down to the [1]brook of Kanah, southward
of the [1]brook (these cities *belonged* to Ephraim among the

5 [a]Josh 18:13
6 [a]Josh 17:7
7 [a]1 Chr 7:28
8 [1]Or *wadi* [2]Lit *the goings out of it were* [a]Josh 17:8
10 [1]Or *dispossess* [a]Judg 1:29; 1 Kin 9:16 [b]Josh 17:12, 13
17:1 [1]Lit *and there was to him* [a]Gen 41:51; 46:20; 48:17f
2 [1]Lit *sons*
3 [a]Num 26:33; 27:1-7
4 [1]Lit *mouth* [a]Num 27:5-7
6 [a]Josh 13:30, 31
7 [1]Lit *was* [2]Lit *to the right hand*
8 [a]Josh 16:8
9 [1]Or *wadi* [a]Josh 16:8f

cities of Manasseh), and the border of Manasseh *was* on the
north side of the [1]brook and [2]it ended at the sea.
10 The south side *belonged* to Ephraim and the north side to
Manasseh, and the sea was [1]their border; and they reached to
Asher on the north and to Issachar on the east.
11 In Issachar and in Asher, [a]Manasseh had Beth-shean and its
towns and Ibleam and its towns, and the inhabitants of Dor
and its towns, and the inhabitants of En-dor and its towns, and
the inhabitants of Taanach and its towns, and the inhabitants of
Megiddo and its towns, the third is [b]Napheth.
12 [a]But the sons of Manasseh could not take possession of these
cities, because the Canaanites persisted in living in that land.
13 It came about when the sons of Israel became strong, [a]they
put the Canaanites to forced labor, but they did not [1]drive them
out completely.
14 Then the [a]sons of Joseph spoke to Joshua, saying, "Why have
you given me only one lot and one portion for an inheritance,
since I am a numerous people whom the LORD has thus far
blessed?"
15 Joshua said to them, "If you are a numerous people, go [1]up
to the forest and [2]clear a place for yourself there in the land of
the Perizzites and of the Rephaim, since the hill country of
Ephraim is too narrow for you."
16 The sons of Joseph said, "The hill country is not enough for
us, and all the Canaanites who live in the valley land have
[a]chariots of iron, both those who are in Beth-shean and its towns
and those who are in the valley of Jezreel."
17 Joshua spoke to the house of Joseph, to Ephraim and
Manasseh, saying, "You are a numerous people and have great
power; you shall not have one lot *only,*
18 but the hill country shall be yours. For though it is a forest,
you shall [1]clear it, and to its [2]farthest borders it shall be yours;
for you shall [3]drive out the Canaanites, even though they have
[a]chariots of iron *and* though they are strong."

Chapter 18 Theme ______________________

18 Then the whole congregation of the sons of Israel assembled themselves at [a]Shiloh, and set up the tent of meeting there; and the land was subdued before them.
2 There remained among the sons of Israel seven tribes who
had not divided their inheritance.
3 So Joshua said to the sons of Israel, "[a]How long will you
put off entering to take possession of the land which the LORD,
the God of your fathers, has given you?
4 "Provide for yourselves three men from [1]each tribe that I
may send them, and that they may arise and walk through the
land and write a description of it according to their inheritance;
then they shall [2]return to me.
5 "They shall divide it into seven portions; [a]Judah shall stay in
its territory on the south, and the house of Joseph shall stay in
their territory on the north.

9 [1]Or *wadi* [2]Lit *goings out of it were*
10 [1]Lit *its*
11 [a]1 Chr 7:29 [b]Josh 11:2; 12:23
12 [a]Judg 1:27
13 [1]Or *dispossess* [a]Josh 16:10
14 [a]Num 13:7
15 [1]Lit *up for yourself* [2]Lit *cut down*
16 [a]Josh 17:18; Judg 1:19; 4:3, 13
18 [1]Lit *cut it down* [2]Lit *goings out* [3]Or *dispossess* [a]Josh 17:16
18:1 [a]Judg 21:19; Jer 7:12; 26:6, 9
3 [a]Judg 18:9
4 [1]Lit *the* [2]Lit *come*
5 [a]Josh 15:1

6 "You shall describe the land in seven divisions, and bring
the description here to me. [a]I will cast lots for you here before
the LORD our God.
7 "For [a]the Levites have no portion among you, because the
priesthood of the LORD is [1]their inheritance. Gad and Reuben
and the half-tribe of Manasseh also have received their
inheritance eastward beyond the Jordan, which Moses the
servant of the LORD gave them."
8 Then the men arose and went, and Joshua commanded
those who went to describe the land, saying, "Go and walk
through the land and describe it, and return to me; then I will
cast lots for you here before the LORD in [a]Shiloh."
9 So the men went and passed through the land, and
described it by cities in seven divisions in a book; and they
came to Joshua to the camp at Shiloh.
10 And [a]Joshua cast lots for them in Shiloh before the LORD, and
there Joshua divided the land to the sons of Israel according to
their divisions.
11 Now the lot of the tribe of the sons of Benjamin came up
according to their families, and the territory of their lot [1]lay
between the sons of Judah and the sons of Joseph.
12 [a]Their border on the north side was from the Jordan, then
the border went up to the side of Jericho on the north, and
went up through the hill country westward, and [1]it ended at
the wilderness of Beth-aven.
13 From there the border continued to [a]Luz, to the side of Luz
(that is, Bethel) southward; and the border went down to Ataroth-
addar, near the hill which *lies* on the south of [b]lower Beth-
horon.
14 The border extended *from there* and turned round on the
west side southward, from the hill which *lies* before Beth-
horon southward; and [1]it ended at Kiriath-baal (that is, Kiriath-
jearim), a city of the sons of Judah. This *was* the west side.
15 Then the [a]south side *was* from the edge of Kiriath-jearim,
and the border went westward and went to the fountain of the
waters of Nephtoah.
16 The border went down to the edge of the hill which is in
the [a]valley of Ben-hinnom, which is in the valley of Rephaim
northward; and it went down to the valley of Hinnom, to the
slope of the Jebusite southward, and went down to En-rogel.
17 It extended northward and went to En-shemesh and went
to Geliloth, which is opposite the ascent of Adummim, and it
went down to the [a]stone of Bohan the son of Reuben.
18 It continued to the side in front of the Arabah northward
and went down to the Arabah.
19 The border continued to the side of Beth-hoglah northward;
and the [1]border ended at the north bay of the Salt Sea, at the
south end of the Jordan. This *was* the south border.
20 Moreover, the Jordan was its border on the east side. This
was the inheritance of the sons of Benjamin, according to their
families *and* according to its borders all around.

6 [a]Josh 14:2
7 [1]Lit *his* [a]Num 18:7, 20; Josh 13:33
8 [a]Josh 18:1
10 [a]Num 34:16-29; Josh 19:51
11 [1]Lit *went out*
12 [1]Lit *the goings out of it were* [a]Josh 16:1
13 [a]Gen 28:19; Judg 1:23 [b]Josh 16:3
14 [1]Lit *the goings out of it were*
15 [a]Josh 15:5-9
16 [a]2 Kin 23:10
17 [a]Josh 15:6
19 [1]Lit *goings out of the border were*

21 Now the cities of the tribe of the sons of Benjamin
according to their families were Jericho and Beth-hoglah and
Emek-keziz,
22 and Beth-arabah and Zemaraim and Bethel,
23 and Avvim and Parah and Ophrah,
24 and Chephar-ammoni and Ophni and [a]Geba; twelve cities
with their villages.
25 Gibeon and Ramah and Beeroth,
26 and Mizpeh and Chephirah and Mozah,
27 and Rekem and Irpeel and Taralah,
28 and [a]Zelah, Haeleph and the Jebusite (that is, Jerusalem),
Gibeah, Kiriath; fourteen cities with their villages. This is the
inheritance of the [b]sons of Benjamin according to their families.

Chapter 19 Theme ______________________

19 Then the second lot [1]fell to Simeon, to the tribe of the sons
of Simeon according to their families, and their inheritance was in the midst of the inheritance of the sons of Judah.
2 So they had as their inheritance Beersheba or [1]Sheba and
Moladah,
3 and Hazar-shual and Balah and Ezem,
4 and Eltolad and Bethul and Hormah,
5 and Ziklag and Beth-marcaboth and Hazar-susah,
6 and Beth-lebaoth and Sharuhen; thirteen cities with their
villages;
7 Ain, Rimmon and Ether and Ashan; four cities with their
villages;
8 and all the villages which *were* around these cities as far as
Baalath-beer, Ramah of the [1]Negev. This *was* the inheritance of
the tribe of the sons of Simeon according to their families.
9 The inheritance of the sons of Simeon *was taken* from the
portion of the sons of Judah, for the share of the sons of Judah
was too large for them; so the sons of Simeon received *an*
inheritance in the midst of [1]Judah's inheritance.
10 Now the third lot came up for the sons of Zebulun according
to their families. And the territory of their inheritance was as
far as Sarid.
11 Then their border went up to the west and to Maralah, it
then [1]touched Dabbesheth and reached to the [2]brook that is
before Jokneam.
12 Then it turned from Sarid to the east toward the sunrise as
far as the border of Chisloth-tabor, and it proceeded to Daberath
and [1]up to Japhia.
13 From there it continued eastward toward the sunrise to
Gath-hepher, to Eth-kazin, and it proceeded to Rimmon [1]which
stretches to Neah.
14 The border circled around it on the north to Hannathon,
and [1]it ended at the valley of Iphtahel.
15 *Included* also *were* Kattah and Nahalal and Shimron and
Idalah and Bethlehem; twelve cities with their villages.

24 [a]Ezra 2:26; Is 10:29

28 [a]2 Sam 21:14 [b]Num 26:38

19:1 [1]Lit *came out*

2 [1]In Josh 15:26, *Shema*

8 [1]I.e. South country

9 [1]Lit *their*

11 [1]Or *reached to* [2]Or *wadi*

12 [1]Lit *went up*

13 [1]Or *and is marked off*

14 [1]Lit *the goings out of it were*

17 [1]Lit *came out*
16 This *was* the inheritance of the sons of Zebulun according
to their families, these cities with their villages.
17 The fourth lot [1]fell to Issachar, to the sons of Issachar
according to their families.
18 [a]1 Sam 28:4; 2 Kin 4:8
18 Their territory was to Jezreel and *included* Chesulloth and
[a]Shunem,
19 and Hapharaim and Shion and Anaharath,
20 and Rabbith and Kishion and Ebez,
22 [1]Lit *the goings out of their border were* [a]Judg 4:6; Ps 89:12
21 and Remeth and En-gannim and En-haddah and Beth-pazzez.
22 The border reached to [a]Tabor and Shahazumah and Beth-
shemesh, and [1]their border ended at the Jordan; sixteen cities
with their villages.
23 This *was* the inheritance of the tribe of the sons of Issachar
according to their families, the cities with their villages.
24 [1]Lit *came out*
24 Now the fifth lot [1]fell to the tribe of the sons of Asher
according to their families.
25 Their territory was Helkath and Hali and Beten and
Achshaph,
27 [1]Lit *sunrise* [2]Lit *from the left hand* [a]1 Kin 9:13
26 and Allammelech and Amad and Mishal; and it reached to
Carmel on the west and to Shihor-libnath.
27 It turned toward the [1]east to Beth-dagon and reached to
Zebulun, and to the valley of Iphtahel northward to Beth-emek
and Neiel; then it proceeded on [2]north to [a]Cabul,
28 [a]Gen 10:19; Judg 1:31; Acts 27:3
28 and Ebron and Rehob and Hammon and Kanah, as far as
Great [a]Sidon.
29 The border turned to Ramah and to the fortified city of
Tyre; then the border turned to Hosah, and [1]it ended at the sea
by the region of [a]Achzib.
29 [1]Lit *the goings out of it were* [a]Judg 1:31
30 *Included* also *were* Ummah, and Aphek and Rehob; twenty-
two cities with their villages.
31 This *was* the inheritance of the tribe of the sons of Asher
according to their families, these cities with their villages.
32 [1]Lit *came out*
32 The sixth lot [1]fell to the sons of Naphtali; to the sons of
Naphtali according to their families.
33 Their border was from Heleph, from the oak in Zaanannim
and Adami-nekeb and Jabneel, as far as Lakkum, and [1]it ended
at the Jordan.
33 [1]Lit *the goings out of it were*
34 Then the border turned westward to Aznoth-tabor and
proceeded from there to Hukkok; and it reached to Zebulun on
the south and [1]touched Asher on the west, and to Judah at the
Jordan toward the [2]east.
34 [1]Or *reached to* [2]Lit *sunrise*
35 The fortified cities *were* Ziddim, Zer and [a]Hammath, Rakkath
and [b]Chinnereth,
36 and Adamah and Ramah and Hazor,
37 and Kedesh and Edrei and En-hazor,
35 [a]Gen 10:18; 1 Kin 8:65 [b]Deut 3:17
38 and Yiron and Migdal-el, Horem and Beth-anath and Beth-
shemesh; nineteen cities with their villages.
39 This *was* the inheritance of the tribe of the sons of Naphtali
according to their families, the cities with their villages.
40 The seventh lot [1]fell to the tribe of the sons of Dan
40 [1]Lit *came out*
according to their families.

41 The territory of their inheritance was Zorah and Eshtaol
and Ir-shemesh,
42 and Shaalabbin and Aijalon and Ithlah,
43 and Elon and Timnah and Ekron,
44 and Eltekeh and Gibbethon and Baalath,
45 and Jehud and Bene-berak and Gath-rimmon,
46 and Me-jarkon and Rakkon, with the territory over against
[1]Joppa.
47 The territory of the [a]sons of Dan proceeded [1]beyond them;
for the sons of Dan went up and fought with Leshem and
captured it. Then they struck it with the edge of the sword and
possessed it and [2]settled in it; and they called [3b]Leshem Dan
after the name of Dan their father.
48 This *was* the inheritance of the tribe of the sons of Dan
according to their families, these cities with their villages.
49 When they finished apportioning the land for inheritance
by its borders, the sons of Israel gave an inheritance in their
midst to Joshua the son of Nun.
50 In accordance with the [1]command of the LORD they gave
him the city for which he asked, [a]Timnath-serah in the hill
country of Ephraim. So he built the city and [2]settled in it.
51 [a]These are the inheritances which Eleazar the priest, and
Joshua the son of Nun, and the heads of the [1]households of the
tribes of the sons of Israel distributed by lot in Shiloh before the
LORD at the doorway of the tent of meeting. So they finished
dividing the land.

Chapter 20 Theme ____________________

20 Then the LORD spoke to Joshua, saying,
2 "Speak to the sons of Israel, saying, '[1]Designate [a]the
cities of refuge, of which I spoke to you [2]through Moses,
3 that the manslayer who [1]kills any person unintentionally,
without premeditation, may flee there, and they shall become
your refuge from the avenger of blood.
4 'He shall flee to one of these cities, and shall stand at the
entrance of the [a]gate of the city and state his case in the
hearing of the elders of that city; and they shall [1]take him into
the city to them and give him a place, so that he may dwell
among them.
5 'Now [a]if the avenger of blood pursues him, then they shall
not deliver the manslayer into his hand, because he struck his
neighbor without premeditation and did not hate him
beforehand.
6 'He shall dwell in that city [a]until he stands before the
congregation for judgment, until the death of the one who is
high priest in those days. Then the manslayer shall [1]return to his
own city and to his own house, to the city from which he fled.'"
7 So they [1]set apart [a]Kedesh in [2]Galilee in the hill country of
Naphtali and Shechem in the hill country of Ephraim, and
Kiriath-arba (that is, Hebron) in [b]the hill country of Judah.

46 [1]Heb *Japho*

47 [1]Lit *from* [2]Lit *dwelt* [3]I.e. Laish [a]Judg 18:1 [b]Judg 18:29

50 [1]Lit *mouth* [2]Lit *dwelt* [a]Num 13:8; Josh 24:30

51 [1]Lit *fathers* [a]Josh 18:10

20:2 [1]Lit *Set for yourselves* [2]Lit *by the hand of* [a]Num 35:6-34; Deut 4:41-43; 19:2ff

3 [1]Lit *smites*

4 [1]Lit *gather* [a]Ruth 4:1; Job 5:4; Jer 38:7

5 [a]Num 35:12

6 [1]Lit *return and come* [a]Num 35:12

7 [1]Lit *sanctified* [2]Heb *Galil* [a]Josh 21:32; 1 Chr 6:76 [b]Josh 21:11; Luke 1:39

8 [1]Lit *set*

8 Beyond the Jordan east of Jericho, they [1]designated Bezer in the wilderness on the plain from the tribe of Reuben, and Ramoth in Gilead from the tribe of Gad, and Golan in Bashan from the tribe of Manasseh.

9 [1]Lit *smites* [a]Num 35:13ff

9 [a]These were the appointed cities for all the sons of Israel and for the stranger who sojourns among them, that whoever [1]kills any person unintentionally may flee there, and not die by the hand of the avenger of blood until he stands before the congregation.

21:1 [1]Lit *fathers* [a]Num 35:1-8

Chapter 21 Theme ____________________

21 Then the heads of [1]households of [a]the Levites approached Eleazar the priest, and Joshua the son of Nun, and the heads of [1]households of the tribes of the sons of Israel.

2 [1]Lit *by the hand of* [a]Num 35:2

2 They spoke to them at Shiloh in the land of Canaan, saying, "[a]The LORD commanded [1]through Moses to give us cities to live in, with their pasture lands for our cattle."

3 [1]Lit *mouth*

3 So the sons of Israel gave the Levites from their inheritance these cities with their pasture lands, according to the [1]command of the LORD.

4 [1]Lit *had*

4 Then the lot came out for the families of the Kohathites. And the sons of Aaron the priest, who were of the Levites, [1]received thirteen cities by lot from the tribe of Judah and from the tribe of the Simeonites and from the tribe of Benjamin.

5 [1]Lit *had*

5 The rest of the sons of Kohath [1]received ten cities by lot from the families of the tribe of Ephraim and from the tribe of Dan and from the half-tribe of Manasseh.

6 [1]Lit *had*

6 The sons of Gershon [1]received thirteen cities by lot from the families of the tribe of Issachar and from the tribe of Asher and from the tribe of Naphtali and from the half-tribe of Manasseh in Bashan.

7 [1]Lit *had*

7 The sons of Merari according to their families [1]received twelve cities from the tribe of Reuben and from the tribe of Gad and from the tribe of Zebulun.

8 [1]Lit *by the hand of* [a]Gen 49:5ff

8 Now the [a]sons of Israel gave by lot to the Levites these cities with their pasture lands, as the LORD had commanded [1]through Moses.

9 They gave these cities which are *here* mentioned by name from the tribe of the sons of Judah and from the tribe of the sons of Simeon;

10 and they were for the sons of Aaron, one of the families of the Kohathites, of the sons of Levi, for the lot was theirs first.

11 [a]1 Chr 6:55 [b]Josh 14:15; 15:13

11 Thus [a]they gave them Kiriath-arba, *Arba being* the [b]father of Anak (that is, Hebron), in the hill country of Judah, with its surrounding pasture lands.

12 But the fields of the city and its villages they gave to Caleb the son of Jephunneh as his possession.

13 [a]1 Chr 6:57 [b]Josh 15:54 [c]Josh 15:42

13 So [a]to the sons of Aaron the priest they gave [b]Hebron, the city of refuge for the manslayer, with its pasture lands, and [c]Libnah with its pasture lands,

14 and [a]Jattir with its pasture lands and [b]Eshtemoa with its pasture lands,
15 and [1]Holon with its pasture lands and [a]Debir with its pasture lands,
16 and [1]Ain with its pasture lands and [a]Juttah with its pasture lands *and* [b]Beth-shemesh with its pasture lands; nine cities from these two tribes.
17 From the tribe of Benjamin, [a]Gibeon with its pasture lands, [b]Geba with its pasture lands,
18 Anathoth with its pasture lands and [1]Almon with its pasture lands; four cities.
19 All the cities of the sons of Aaron, the priests, were thirteen cities with their pasture lands.
20 Then the cities from the tribe of Ephraim were allotted to the [a]families of the sons of Kohath, the Levites, *even to* the rest of the sons of Kohath.
21 They gave them [a]Shechem, the city of refuge for the manslayer, with its pasture lands, in the hill country of Ephraim, and Gezer with its pasture lands,
22 and Kibzaim with its pasture lands and Beth-horon with its pasture lands; four cities.
23 From the tribe of Dan, Elteke with its pasture lands, Gibbethon with its pasture lands,
24 Aijalon with its pasture lands, Gath-rimmon with its pasture lands; four cities.
25 From the half-tribe of Manasseh, *they allotted* Taanach with its pasture lands and Gath-rimmon with its pasture lands; two cities.
26 All the cities with their pasture lands for the families of the rest of the sons of Kohath were ten.
27 [a]To the sons of Gershon, one of the families of the Levites, from the half-tribe of Manasseh, *they gave* Golan in Bashan, the city of refuge for the manslayer, with its pasture lands, and Be-eshterah with its pasture lands; two cities.
28 From the tribe of Issachar, *they gave* Kishion with its pasture lands, Daberath with its pasture lands,
29 Jarmuth with its pasture lands, En-gannim with its pasture lands; four cities.
30 From the tribe of Asher, *they gave* Mishal with its pasture lands, Abdon with its pasture lands,
31 Helkath with its pasture lands and Rehob with its pasture lands; four cities.
32 From the tribe of Naphtali, *they gave* [a]Kedesh in Galilee, the city of refuge for the manslayer, with its pasture lands and Hammoth-dor with its pasture lands and Kartan with its pasture lands; three cities.
33 All the cities of the Gershonites according to their families were thirteen cities with their pasture lands.
34 To the families of [a]the sons of Merari, the rest of the Levites, *they gave* from the tribe of Zebulun, Jokneam with its pasture lands and Kartah with its pasture lands.

14 [a]Josh 15:48 [b]Josh 15:50
15 [1]In 1 Chr 6:58, *Hilen* [a]Josh 15:49
16 [1]In 1 Chr 6:59, *Ashan* [a]Josh 15:55 [b]Josh 15:10
17 [a]Josh 18:25 [b]Josh 18:24
18 [1]In 1 Chr 6:60, *Allemeth*
20 [a]1 Chr 6:66
21 [a]Josh 20:7
27 [a]1 Chr 6:71
32 [a]Josh 20:7
34 [a]1 Chr 6:77

36 [a]Deut 4:43; Josh 20:8

35 Dimnah with its pasture lands, Nahalal with its pasture
lands; four cities.
36 From the tribe of Reuben, *they gave* [a]Bezer with its pasture
lands and Jahaz with its pasture lands,

38 [a]Deut 4:43; 1 Kin 4:13 [b]Gen 32:2; 2 Sam 2:8

37 Kedemoth with its pasture lands and Mephaath with its
pasture lands; four cities.
38 From the tribe of Gad, *they gave* [a]Ramoth in Gilead, the
city of refuge for the manslayer, with its pasture lands and
[b]Mahanaim with its pasture lands,

41 [a]Num 35:7

39 Heshbon with its pasture lands, Jazer with its pasture lands;
four cities in all.
40 All *these were* the cities of the sons of Merari according to
their families, the rest of the families of the Levites; and their
lot was twelve cities.

43 [a]Deut 34:4 [b]Num 33:53; Deut 11:31; 17:14

41 [a]All the cities of the Levites in the midst of the possession of
the sons of Israel were forty-eight cities with their pasture lands.
42 These cities each had its surrounding pasture lands; thus *it
was* with all these cities.

44 [a]Josh 1:13; 23:1 [b]Deut 7:24 [c]Ex 23:31

43 [a]So the LORD gave Israel all the land which He had sworn
to give to their fathers, and [b]they possessed it and lived in it.
44 And the LORD [a]gave them rest on every side, according to
all that He had sworn to their fathers, and [b]no one of all their
enemies stood before them; [c]the LORD gave all their enemies
into their hand.

45 [1]Lit *a word from every good word* [2]Lit *spoken* [a]Josh 23:14; 1 Kin 8:56

45 [a]Not [1]one of the good promises which the LORD had [2]made
to the house of Israel failed; all came to pass.

Chapter 22 Theme ______________________________

22:1 [a]Num 32:20-22

22 [a]Then Joshua summoned the Reubenites and the Gadites
and the half-tribe of Manasseh,
2 and said to them, "You have kept all that Moses the servant
of the LORD commanded you, [a]and have listened to my voice in
all that I commanded you.

2 [a]Josh 1:12-18

RETURN TO INSTRUCTIONS

3 "You have not forsaken your brothers these many days to
this day, but have kept the charge of the commandment of the
LORD your God.

4 [a]Num 32:18; Deut 3:20

4 "And now [a]the LORD your God has given rest to your brothers,
as He spoke to them; therefore turn now and go to your tents,
to the land of your possession, which Moses the servant of the
LORD gave you beyond the Jordan.

5 [a]Deut 5:10 [b]Deut 4:29

5 "Only be very careful to observe the commandment and the
law which Moses the servant of the LORD commanded you, to
[a]love the LORD your God and walk in all His ways and keep His
commandments and hold fast to Him and serve Him [b]with all
your heart and with all your soul."

6 [a]Gen 47:7; Josh 14:13; 2 Sam 6:18; Luke 24:50

6 So Joshua [a]blessed them and sent them away, and they
went to their tents.
7 Now [a]to the one half-tribe of Manasseh Moses had given *a
possession* in Bashan, but [b]to the other half Joshua gave *a
possession* among their brothers westward beyond the Jordan.
So when Joshua sent them away to their tents, he blessed them,

7 [a]Num 32:33 [b]Josh 17:1-13

8 and said to [1]them, "Return to your tents with great riches
and with very much livestock, with silver, gold, bronze, iron,
and with very many clothes; [a]divide the spoil of your enemies
with your brothers."
9 The sons of Reuben and the sons of Gad and the half-tribe of
Manasseh returned *home* and departed from the sons of Israel
at Shiloh which is in the land of Canaan, to go to the [a]land of
Gilead, to the land of their possession which they had possessed,
according to the [1]command of the LORD [2]through Moses.
10 When they came to the region of the Jordan which is in the
land of Canaan, the sons of Reuben and the sons of Gad and
the half-tribe of Manasseh built an altar there by the Jordan, a
large altar in appearance.
11 And the sons of Israel heard *it* [1]said, "Behold, the sons of
Reuben and the sons of Gad and the half-tribe of Manasseh
have [a]built an altar at the [2]frontier of the land of Canaan, in the
region of the Jordan, on the side *belonging to* the sons of Israel."
12 When the sons of Israel heard *of it,* the whole congregation
of the sons of Israel gathered themselves at [a]Shiloh to go up
against them in war.
13 Then the sons of Israel sent to the sons of Reuben and to
the sons of Gad and to the half-tribe of Manasseh, into the land
of Gilead, [a]Phinehas the son of Eleazar the priest,
14 and with him ten chiefs, one chief for each father's
household from each of the tribes of Israel; and [a]each one of
them *was* the head of his father's household among the
[1]thousands of Israel.
15 They came to the sons of Reuben and to the sons of Gad
and to the half-tribe of Manasseh, to the land of Gilead, and
they spoke with them saying,
16 "Thus says the whole congregation of the LORD, 'What is
this unfaithful act which you have committed against the God
of Israel, turning away from following the LORD this day, by
[a]building yourselves an altar, to rebel against the LORD this day?
17 'Is not [a]the iniquity of Peor [1]enough for us, from which we
have not cleansed ourselves to this day, although a plague came
on the congregation of the LORD,
18 that you must turn away this day from following the LORD?
If you rebel against the LORD today, [a]He will be angry with the
whole congregation of Israel tomorrow.
19 'If, however, the land of your possession is unclean, then
[1]cross into the land of the possession of the LORD, where the
LORD's tabernacle [2]stands, and take possession among us. Only
do not rebel against the LORD, or rebel against us by [a]building
an altar for yourselves, besides the altar of the LORD our God.
20 'Did not [a]Achan the son of Zerah act unfaithfully in the
things under the ban, and wrath fall on all the congregation of
Israel? And that man did not perish alone in his iniquity.'"
21 Then the sons of Reuben and the sons of Gad and the half-
tribe of Manasseh answered and spoke to the heads of the
[1]families of Israel.

8 [1]Lit *them, saying, "Return* [a]Num 31:27; 1 Sam 30:16

9 [1]Lit *mouth* [2]Lit *by the hand of* [a]Num 32:1, 26, 29

11 [1]Lit *saying* [2]Lit *front* [a]Deut 12:5; Josh 22:19

12 [a]Josh 18:1

13 [a]Num 25:7, 11; 31:6

14 [1]Or *families* [a]Num 1:4

16 [a]Josh 22:11

17 [1]Lit *little for us* [a]Num 25:1-9

18 [a]Num 16:22

19 [1]Lit *cross for yourselves* [2]Lit *abides* [a]Josh 22:11

20 [a]Josh 7:1-26

21 [1]Lit *thousands*

22 [a]Deut 10:17 [b]1 Kin 8:39; Job 10:7; Ps 44:21

23 [a]Deut 12:11

24 [1]Lit *from* [2]Lit *sons, saying*

26 [1]Lit *prepare to build for ourselves*

27 [a]Gen 31:48; Josh 24:27 [b]Deut 12:6, 11, 26f

29 [1]Lit *dwelling place* [a]Deut 12:13f

30 [1]Lit *thousands*

31 [a]Ex 25:8; Lev 26:11f; 2 Chr 15:2

33 [a]1 Chr 29:20; Dan 2:19; Luke 2:28

34 [a]Gen 31:47-49

22 "The [a]Mighty One, God, the LORD, the Mighty One, God, the
LORD! [b]He knows, and may Israel itself know. If *it was* in rebellion,
or if in an unfaithful act against the LORD do not save us this day!
23 "If we have built us an altar to turn away from following the
LORD, or if to [a]offer a burnt offering or grain offering on it, or if
to offer sacrifices of peace offerings on it, may the LORD Himself
require it.
24 "But truly we have done this out of concern, [1]for a reason,
saying, 'In time to come your sons may say to our [2]sons, "What
have you to do with the LORD, the God of Israel?
25 "For the LORD has made the Jordan a border between us and
you, *you* sons of Reuben and sons of Gad; you have no portion
in the LORD." So your sons may make our sons stop fearing the
LORD.'
26 "Therefore we said, 'Let us [1]build an altar, not for burnt
offering or for sacrifice;
27 rather it shall be [a]a witness between us and you and
between our generations after us, that we are to [b]perform the
service of the LORD before Him with our burnt offerings, and
with our sacrifices and with our peace offerings, so that your
sons will not say to our sons in time to come, "You have no
portion in the LORD."'
28 "Therefore we said, 'It shall also come about if they say *this*
to us or to our generations in time to come, then we shall say,
"See the copy of the altar of the LORD which our fathers made,
not for burnt offering or for sacrifice; rather it is a witness
between us and you."'
29 "Far be it from us that we should rebel against the LORD and
turn away from following the LORD this day, by [a]building an altar
for burnt offering, for grain offering or for sacrifice, besides the
altar of the LORD our God which is before His [1]tabernacle."
30 So when Phinehas the priest and the leaders of the
congregation, even the heads of the [1]families of Israel who *were*
with him, heard the words which the sons of Reuben and the
sons of Gad and the sons of Manasseh spoke, it pleased them.
31 And Phinehas the son of Eleazar the priest said to the sons
of Reuben and to the sons of Gad and to the sons of Manasseh,
"Today we know that the [a]LORD is in our midst, because you
have not committed this unfaithful act against the LORD; now you
have delivered the sons of Israel from the hand of the LORD."
32 Then Phinehas the son of Eleazar the priest and the leaders
returned from the sons of Reuben and from the sons of Gad,
from the land of Gilead to the land of Canaan, to the sons of
Israel, and brought back word to them.
33 The word pleased the sons of Israel, and the sons of Israel
[a]blessed God; and they did not speak of going up against them
in war to destroy the land in which the sons of Reuben and the
sons of Gad were living.
34 The sons of Reuben and the sons of Gad [a]called the altar
Witness; "For," *they said,* "it is a witness between us that the
LORD is God."

Chapter 23 Theme ________________________________

23 Now it came about after many days, when the LORD had given [a]rest to Israel from all their enemies [1]on every side, and Joshua was old, advanced in years,
2 that [a]Joshua called for all Israel, for their elders and their heads and their judges and their officers, and said to them, "I am old, advanced in years.
3 "And you have seen all that the LORD your God has done to all these nations because of you, for [a]the LORD your God is He who has been fighting for you.
4 "See, [a]I have apportioned to you these nations which remain as an inheritance for your tribes, with all the nations which I have cut off, from the Jordan even to the Great Sea toward the setting of the sun.
5 "The LORD your God, He will thrust them out from before you and [1a]drive them from before you; and [b]you will possess their land, just as the LORD your God [2]promised you.
6 "[a]Be very firm, then, to keep and do all that is written in the book of the law of Moses, so that you may not turn aside from it to the right hand or to the left,
7 so that you will not [1]associate with these nations, these which remain among you, or [a]mention the name of their gods, or [b]make *anyone* swear *by them,* or [c]serve them, or bow down to them.
8 "But you are to cling to the LORD your God, as you have done to this day.
9 "[a]For the LORD has [1]driven out great and strong nations from before you; and as for you, [b]no man has stood before you to this day.
10 "[a]One of your men puts to flight a thousand, for the LORD your God is [b]He who fights for you, just as He [1]promised you.
11 "So take diligent heed to yourselves to love the LORD your God.
12 "For if you ever go back and [a]cling to the rest of these nations, these which remain among you, and [b]intermarry with them, so that you [1]associate with them and they with you,
13 know with certainty that the LORD your God will not continue to [1]drive these nations out from before you; but they will be a [a]snare and a trap to you, and a whip on your sides and thorns in your eyes, until you perish from off this good land which the LORD your God has given you.
14 "Now behold, today [a]I am going the way of all the earth, and you know in all your hearts and in all your souls that [b]not one word of all the good words which the LORD your God spoke concerning you has failed; all have [1]been fulfilled for you, not [2]one of them has failed.
15 "It shall come about that just as all the good words which the LORD your God spoke to you have come upon you, so [a]the LORD will bring upon you all the threats, until He has destroyed you from off this good land which the LORD your God has given you.
16 "[a]When you transgress the covenant of the LORD your God, which He commanded you, and go and serve other gods and bow down to them, then the anger of the LORD will burn

23:1 [1]Lit *from round about* [a]Josh 21:44

2 [a]Josh 24:1

3 [a]Deut 1:30

4 [a]Ex 23:30

5 [1]Or *dispossess* [2]Lit *spoke to* [a]Ex 23:20 [b]Num 33:53

6 [a]Deut 5:32; Josh 1:7

7 [1]Lit *go among* [a]Ex 23:13; Ps 16:4 [b]Deut 6:13; 10:20 [c]Ex 20:5

9 [1]Or *dispossessed* [a]Ex 23:23, 30 [b]Deut 7:24

10 [1]Lit *spoke to* [a]Lev 26:8; Deut 28:7; 32:20 [b]Deut 3:22; Josh 23:3

12 [1]Lit *go among* [a]Ex 34:15, 16; Ps 106:34, 35 [b]Deut 7:3, 4; Ezra 9:2; Neh 13:25

13 [1]Or *dispossess* [a]Ex 23:33; 34:12; Deut 7:16

14 [1]Lit *come* [2]Lit *one word* [a]1 Kin 2:2 [b]Josh 21:45

15 [a]Lev 26:14-33; Deut 28:15

16 [a]Deut 4:25, 26

against you, and you will perish quickly from off the good land
which He has given you."

Chapter 24 Theme ______________________________

24 Then [a]Joshua gathered all the tribes of Israel to Shechem,
and called for the elders of Israel and for their heads
and their judges and their officers; and they presented themselves before God.
2 Joshua said to all the people, "Thus says the LORD, the God
of Israel, 'From ancient times your fathers lived beyond the
[1]River, *namely,* [a]Terah, the father of Abraham and the father of
Nahor, and they served other gods.
3 'Then [a]I took your father Abraham from beyond the [1]River,
and led him through all the land of Canaan, and [b]multiplied his
[2]descendants and gave him [c]Isaac.
4 'To Isaac I gave [a]Jacob and Esau, and [b]to Esau I gave Mount
Seir to possess it; but [c]Jacob and his sons went down to Egypt.
5 'Then [a]I sent Moses and Aaron, and I plagued Egypt [1]by
what I did in its midst; and afterward I brought you out.
6 'I brought your fathers out of Egypt, and [a]you came to the sea;
and Egypt pursued your fathers with chariots and horsemen to
the [1]Red Sea.
7 'But when they cried out to the LORD, He put darkness
between you and the Egyptians, and brought the sea upon
them and covered them; and your own eyes saw what I did in
Egypt. And [a]you lived in the wilderness for a long time.
8 'Then [a]I brought you into the land of the Amorites who
lived beyond the Jordan, and they fought with you; and I gave
them into your hand, and you took possession of their land
when I destroyed them before you.
9 'Then [a]Balak the son of Zippor, king of Moab, arose and
fought against Israel, and he sent and summoned Balaam the
son of Beor to curse you.
10 'But I [a]was not willing to listen to Balaam. So he had to
bless you, and I delivered you from his hand.
11 '[a]You crossed the Jordan and came to Jericho; and the
citizens of Jericho fought against you, *and* [b]the Amorite and the
Perizzite and the Canaanite and the Hittite and the Girgashite,
the Hivite and the Jebusite. Thus [c]I gave them into your hand.
12 'Then I [a]sent the hornet before you and it [1]drove out the
two kings of the Amorites from before you, *but* [b]not by your
sword or your bow.
13 '[a]I gave you a land on which you had not labored, and cities
which you had not built, and you have lived in them; you are
eating of vineyards and olive groves which you did not plant.'
14 "Now, therefore, [1a]fear the LORD and serve Him in sincerity
and [2]truth; and put away the gods which your fathers served
beyond the [3]River and in Egypt, and serve the LORD.
15 "If it is disagreeable in your sight to serve the LORD, choose
for yourselves today whom you will serve: whether the gods
which your fathers served which were beyond the River, or

24:1 [a]Josh 23:2
2 [1]I.e. Euphrates [a]Gen 11:27-32
3 [1]I.e. Euphrates [2]Lit *seed* [a]Gen 12:1; 24:7 [b]Gen 15:5 [c]Gen 21:3
4 [a]Gen 25:25, 26 [b]Gen 36:8; Deut 2:5 [c]Gen 46:6, 7
5 [1]Lit *according to* [a]Ex 4:14-17
6 [1]Lit *Sea of Reeds* [a]Ex 14:2-31
7 [a]Deut 1:46; 2:14
8 [a]Num 21:21-32
9 [a]Num 22:2-6
10 [a]Deut 23:5
11 [a]Josh 3:14-17 [b]Ex 23:23, 28; Deut 7:1 [c]Ex 23:31
12 [1]Lit *drove them out* [a]Ex 23:28; Deut 7:20 [b]Ps 44:3
13 [a]Deut 6:10, 11
14 [1]Or *reverence* [2]Or *faithfulness* [3]I.e. Euphrates [a]Deut 10:12; 18:13; 1 Sam 12:24

[a]the gods of the Amorites in whose land you are living; but as
for me and my house, we will serve the LORD."
16 The people answered and said, "Far be it from us that we
should forsake the LORD to serve other gods;
17 for the LORD our God is He who brought us and our fathers
up out of the land of Egypt, from the house of [1]bondage, and
who did these great signs in our sight and preserved us
through all the way in which we went and among all the
peoples through whose midst we passed.
18 "The LORD drove out from before us all the peoples, even
the Amorites who lived in the land. We also will serve the
LORD, for He is our God."
19 Then Joshua said to the people, "You will not be able to
serve the LORD, [a]for He is a holy God. He is [b]a jealous God; [c]He
will not forgive your transgression or your sins.
20 "[a]If you forsake the LORD and serve foreign gods, then He
will turn and do you harm and consume you after He has done
good to you."
21 The people said to Joshua, "No, but we will serve the LORD."
22 Joshua said to the people, "You are witnesses against
yourselves that [a]you have chosen for yourselves the LORD, to
serve Him." And they said, "We are witnesses."
23 "Now therefore, put away the foreign gods which are in your
midst, and [a]incline your hearts to the LORD, the God of Israel."
24 [a]The people said to Joshua, "We will serve the LORD our
God and we will [1]obey His voice."
25 [a]So Joshua made a covenant with the people that day, and
made for them a statute and an ordinance in Shechem.
26 And Joshua [a]wrote these words in the book of the law of
God; and he took a large stone and set it up there under the
oak that was by the sanctuary of the LORD.
27 Joshua said to all the people, "Behold, [a]this stone shall be
for a witness against us, for it has heard all the words of the
LORD which He spoke [1]to us; thus it shall be for a witness
against you, so that you do not deny your God."
28 Then Joshua dismissed the people, each to his inheritance.
29 It came about after these things that Joshua the son of Nun, the
servant of the LORD, died, being one hundred and ten years old.
30 And they buried him in the territory of his inheritance in
[a]Timnath-serah, which is in the hill country of Ephraim, on the
north of Mount Gaash.
31 [a]Israel served the LORD all the days of Joshua and all the
days of the elders who [1]survived Joshua, and had known all the
deeds of the LORD which He had done for Israel.
32 Now [a]they buried the bones of Joseph, which the sons of
Israel brought up from Egypt, at Shechem, in the piece of
ground [b]which Jacob had bought from the sons of Hamor the
father of Shechem for one hundred [1]pieces of money; and they
became the inheritance of Joseph's sons.
33 And Eleazar the son of Aaron died; and they buried him [1]at
Gibeah of [a]Phinehas his son, which was given him in the hill
country of Ephraim.

15 [a]Judg 6:10
17 [1]Lit *bondmen*
19 [a]Lev 19:2; 20:7, 26 [b]Ex 20:5; 34:14 [c]Ex 23:21
20 [a]Deut 4:25, 26
22 [a]Ps 119:173
23 [a]1 Kin 8:57, 58; Ps 119:36; 141:4
24 [1]Lit *listen to* [a]Ex 19:8; 24:3, 7; Deut 5:27
25 [a]Ex 24:8
26 [a]Deut 31:24
27 [1]Lit *with* [a]Josh 22:27, 34
30 [a]Josh 19:50
31 [1]Lit *prolonged days after* [a]Judg 2:6f
32 [1]Heb *qesitah* [a]Gen 50:24, 25; Ex 13:19 [b]Gen 33:19; John 4:5; Acts 7:15f
33 [1]Or *on the hill* [a]Josh 22:13

JOSHUA AT A GLANCE

heme of Joshua:

uthor:

ate:

urpose:

ey Words:

SEGMENT DIVISIONS			CHAPTER THEMES
			1
			2
			3
			4
			5
			6
			7
			8
			9
			10
			11
			12
			13
			14
			15
			16
			17
			18
			19
			20
			21
			22
			23
			24

JUDGES שופטים SHOFTIM

During Joshua's leadership, Israel finally entered the land that had been promised to Abraham. There were giants in the land, but none who were greater than God. The Captain of the Host was able to subdue all Israel's enemies. In one battle, the sun stood still until the people of Israel had avenged themselves on their enemies.

Then there arose a generation that did not know war, nor did they know the Lord or the work He had done for His children. Israel went from victory to defeat, plunging into more than 300 years of darkness. These were the days of the judges, days from which we can learn valuable lessons.

Things to Do

Chapters 1–2

1. Because the book of Judges is not strictly chronological, it is helpful to understand the setting of the book. Read chapters 1 and 2. Then go to the end of Judges and read Judges 17:6; 18:1; 19:1; 21:25 and look for the key repeated phrase. Mark this phrase in a distinctive way and record it on the JUDGES AT A GLANCE chart on page 438 under "Key Words."

2. Now read chapters 1 and 2 again and do the following:

   a. Mark in the text the key words and phrases listed on JUDGES AT A GLANCE. Put these on an index card that you can use as a bookmark while you study Judges.

   b. Judges 1:21-33 contains an important key phrase that is not on this list because it is not used afterward. Look for that phrase and mark its repeated use in a distinctive way. Then look up Exodus 23:20-33, Deuteronomy 7:1-11,16, and Joshua 23:5-13. Record these references in the margin of chapter 1 for cross-references.

   c. As you read each chapter, question the text with the "5 W's and an H": Who? What? When? Where? Why? and How? You will not always find the answer to every question. As you read, make sure you note who does what and why. Watch for where events take place and when. Always ask how something was accomplished, happened, or is to be done.

   d. On a separate piece of paper, list everything you learn from chapter 2 about the sons of Israel, Joshua, the elders, and the judges.

3. When you finish your observations of chapter 2, review all you have learned, especially from verses 11 through 23. Notice the cycle of events. Make sure you record this in the margin; it sets the pattern for chapters 3 through 16.

4. Discern the themes of these chapters and record them on JUDGES AT A GLANCE and in your Bible next to the chapter number.

Chapters 3–16

1. Study chapters 3 through 16 the same way you did chapters 1 and 2: Mark key words, ask the "5 W's and an H," list your insights in the margin, and record the theme of each chapter in the appropriate places.

2. As you read Judges 3 through 16, note the names of the judges and record them in the chapter margin where they appear. Then record what you learn about them on the chart on page 437. To understand when these judges ruled and what their relationship was to one another, carefully study the historical chart on page 397.

3. As you study each judge, note where the judge is from and write his or her name on the map on page 398 next to the proper location.

Chapters 17–21

1. There is no indication that chapters 17 through 21 chronologically follow chapters 3 through 16. Rather, they give an overview of the moral setting of the time. Examine each chapter carefully as you have done the other chapters of Judges and note your insights. Watch the progression of events.

2. As you read these chapters, keep in mind the key phrase you marked when you began your study. Note how this phrase describes how the people are living.

3. Record the chapter themes as you have done previously on JUDGES AT A GLANCE. Also record the main theme of each segment division and any other segment division you may see. Finally, record the main theme of Judges.

Things to Think About

1. What have you learned from Judges about carefully listening to and obeying the commands of the Lord? What have you seen about the consequences of doing what is right in your own eyes? What parallels do you see between the sins committed in Judges 17 through 21 and today? What does this tell you?

2. Think about why the cycle of sin wasn't broken in the days of the judges. Are you caught in a cycle of sin in your own life? What will it take to break it?

3. What have you learned by studying the lives of the judges? Carefully review your charts on pages 437, 438 and meditate on the lessons you can apply to your own life.

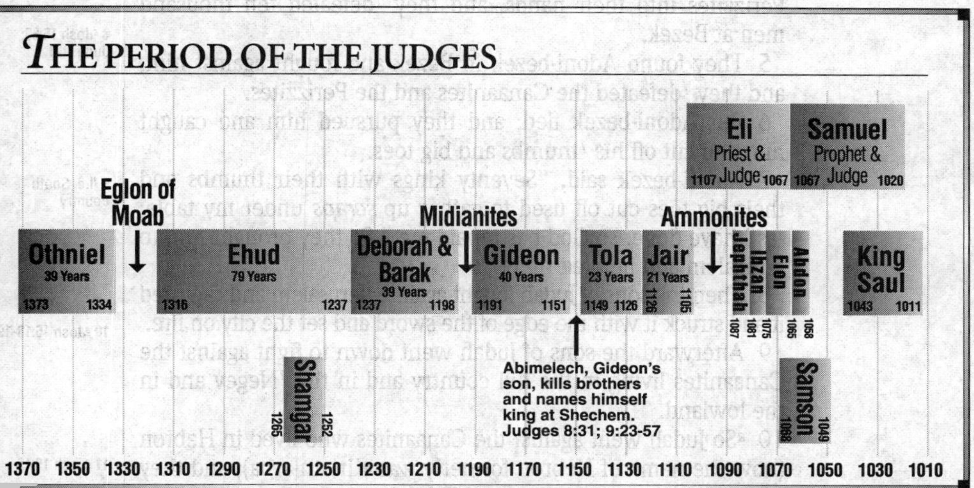

Chapter 1 Theme

1:1 [a]Num 27:21 [b]Judg 1:27; 2:21-23; 3:1-6

2 [a]Gen 49:8

1 Now it came about after the death of Joshua that the sons of
Israel [a]inquired of the LORD, saying, "Who shall go up first
for us [b]against the Canaanites, to fight against them?"
2 The LORD said, "[a]Judah shall go up; behold, I have given
the land into his hand."

Israelite Cities and Settlements in the Time of the Judges

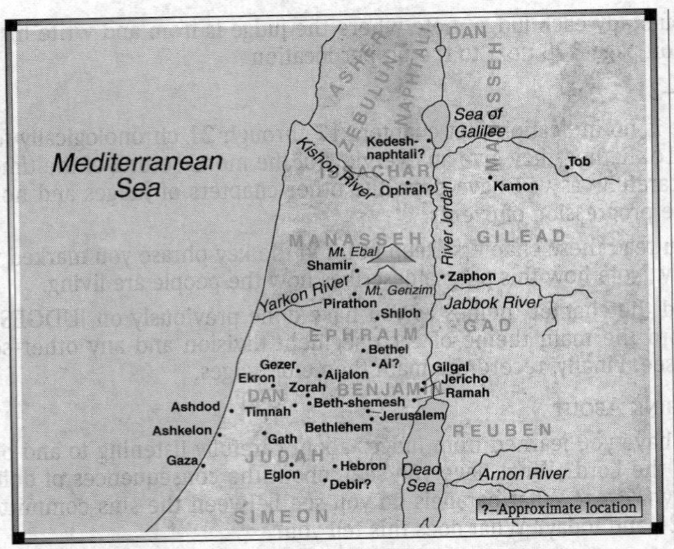

3 Then Judah said to Simeon his brother, "Come up with me
into [1]the territory allotted me, that we may fight against the
Canaanites; and [2]I in turn will go with you into [3]the territory
allotted you." So Simeon went with him.
4 Judah went up, and [a]the LORD gave the Canaanites and the
Perizzites into their hands, and they [1]defeated ten thousand
men at Bezek.
5 They found Adoni-bezek in Bezek and fought against him,
and they [1]defeated the Canaanites and the Perizzites.
6 But Adoni-bezek fled; and they pursued him and caught
him and cut off his [1]thumbs and big toes.
7 Adoni-bezek said, "Seventy kings with their thumbs and
their big toes cut off used to gather up *scraps* under my table;
[a]as I have done, so God has repaid me." So they brought him to
Jerusalem and he died there.
8 Then the sons of Judah fought against [a]Jerusalem and captured
it and struck it with the edge of the sword and set the city on fire.
9 Afterward the sons of Judah went down to fight against the
Canaanites living in the hill country and in the [1]Negev and in
the lowland.
10 [a]So Judah went against the Canaanites who lived in Hebron
(now the name of Hebron formerly *was* Kiriath-arba); and they
struck Sheshai and Ahiman and Talmai.
11 Then [a]from there he went against the inhabitants of Debir
(now the name of Debir formerly *was* Kiriath-sepher).
12 And Caleb said, "The one who attacks Kiriath-sepher and
captures it, I will even give him my daughter Achsah for a wife."
13 [a]Othniel the son of Kenaz, Caleb's younger brother, captured
it; so he gave him his daughter Achsah for a wife.
14 Then [a]it came about when she came *to him,* that she
persuaded him to ask her father for a field. Then she alighted
from [1]her donkey, and Caleb said to her, "What [2]do you want?"

3 [1]Lit *my lot* [2]Lit *I, even I* [3]Lit *your lot*
4 [1]Lit *smote them* [a]Ps 44:2; 78:55
5 [1]Lit *smote*
6 [1]Lit *thumbs of his hands and his feet*
7 [a]Lev 24:19
8 [a]Josh 15:63; Judg 1:21
9 [1]I.e. South country
10 [a]Josh 15:13-19
11 [a]Josh 15:15
13 [a]Judg 3:9
14 [1]Lit *the* [2]Lit *for yourself* [a]Josh 15:18

15 She said to him, "Give me a blessing, since you have given
me the land of the [1]Negev, give me also springs of water." So
Caleb gave her the upper springs and the lower springs.
16 The [1]descendants of [a]the Kenite, Moses' father-in-law, went
up from the [b]city of palms with the sons of Judah, to the
wilderness of Judah which is in the south of [c]Arad; and they
went and lived with the people.
17 Then Judah went with Simeon his brother, and they struck
the Canaanites living in Zephath, and utterly destroyed it. So
the name of the city was called [a]Hormah.
18 And Judah took [a]Gaza with its territory and Ashkelon with
its territory and Ekron with its territory.
19 Now the LORD was with Judah, and they took possession of
the hill country; but they could not [1]drive out the inhabitants
of the valley because they had [a]iron chariots.
20 Then they gave Hebron to Caleb, [a]as Moses had [1]promised;
and he drove out from there [b]the three sons of Anak.
21 [a]But the sons of Benjamin did not drive out the [b]Jebusites
who lived in Jerusalem; so the Jebusites have lived with the
sons of Benjamin in Jerusalem to this day.
22 Likewise the house of Joseph went up against Bethel, and
the LORD was with them.
23 The house of Joseph spied out Bethel ([a]now the name of
the city was formerly Luz).
24 The spies saw a man coming out of the city and they said to
him, "Please show us the entrance to the city and [a]we will treat
you kindly."
25 So he showed them the entrance to the city, and they struck
the city with the edge of the sword, [a]but they let the man and
all his family go free.
26 The man went into the land of the Hittites and built a city
and named it Luz [1]which is its name to this day.
27 [a]But Manasseh did not take possession of Beth-shean and
its villages, or Taanach and its villages, or the inhabitants of
Dor and its villages, or the inhabitants of Ibleam and its
villages, or the inhabitants of Megiddo and its villages; so [b]the
Canaanites persisted in living in that land.
28 It came about when Israel became strong, that they put the
Canaanites to forced labor, but they did not drive them out
completely.
29 [a]Ephraim did not drive out the Canaanites who were living
in Gezer; so the Canaanites lived in Gezer among them.
30 Zebulun did not drive out the inhabitants of Kitron, or the
inhabitants of [1]Nahalol; so the Canaanites lived among them
and became subject to forced labor.
31 Asher did not drive out the inhabitants of Acco, or the
inhabitants of Sidon, or of Ahlab, or of Achzib, or of Helbah, or
of Aphik, or of Rehob.
32 So the Asherites lived among the Canaanites, the inhabitants
of the land; for they did not drive them out.
33 Naphtali did not drive out the inhabitants of Beth-shemesh,
or the inhabitants of Beth-anath, but lived among the Canaanites,

15 [1]I.e. South country
16 [1]Lit *sons* [a]Num 10:29-32; Judg 4:11 [b]Deut 34:3; Judg 3:13 [c]Num 21:1
17 [a]Num 21:3
18 [a]Josh 11:22
19 [1]Or *dispossess* [a]Josh 17:16; Judg 4:3, 13
20 [1]Lit *spoken* [a]Josh 14:9 [b]Josh 15:14; Judg 1:10
21 [a]Josh 15:63; Judg 1:8 [b]1 Chr 11:4
23 [a]Gen 28:19
24 [a]Josh 2:12
25 [a]Josh 6:25
26 [1]Lit *it*
27 [a]Josh 17:12 [b]Judg 1:1
29 [a]Josh 16:10
30 [1]Perhaps same as *Nahalal*

the inhabitants of the land; and the inhabitants of Beth-shemesh
and Beth-anath became forced labor for them.
34 Then the Amorites [1]forced the sons of Dan into the hill
country, for they did not allow them to come down to the valley;
35 yet the Amorites persisted in [1]living in Mount Heres, in
Aijalon and in Shaalbim; but when the [2]power of the house of
Joseph [3]grew strong, they became forced labor.
36 The border of the Amorites ran from the [a]ascent of
Akrabbim, from Sela and upward.

Chapter 2 Theme ______________________

2 Now [a]the angel of the LORD came up from Gilgal to [b]Bochim.
And he said, "[c]I brought you up out of Egypt and led you
into the land which I have sworn to your fathers; and I said, '[d]I
will never break My covenant with you,
2 and as for you, [a]you shall make no covenant with the
inhabitants of this land; [b]you shall tear down their altars.' But
you have not [1]obeyed Me; what is this you have done?
3 "Therefore I also said, '[a]I will not drive them out before you;
but they will [1]become [b]*as thorns* in your sides and their gods
will be a snare to you.'"
4 When the angel of the LORD spoke these words to all the
sons of Israel, the people lifted up their voices and wept.
5 So they named that place [1]Bochim; and there they sacrificed
to the LORD.
6 [a]When Joshua had dismissed the people, the sons of Israel
went each to his inheritance to possess the land.
7 The people served the LORD all the days of Joshua, and all
the days of the elders who [1]survived Joshua, who had seen all
the great work of the LORD which He had done for Israel.
8 Then Joshua the son of Nun, the servant of the LORD, died
at the age of one hundred and ten.
9 And they buried him in the territory of [a]his inheritance in
Timnath-heres, in the hill country of Ephraim, north of Mount
Gaash.
10 All that generation also were gathered to their fathers; and
there arose another generation after them who [a]did not know
the LORD, nor yet the work which He had done for Israel.
11 Then the sons of Israel did [a]evil in the sight of the LORD and
[1]served the [b]Baals,
12 and [a]they forsook the LORD, the God of their fathers, who
had brought them out of the land of Egypt, and followed other
gods from *among* the gods of the peoples who were around
them, and bowed themselves down to them; thus they provoked
the LORD to anger.
13 So they forsook the LORD and [a]served Baal and the Ashtaroth.
14 [a]The anger of the LORD burned against Israel, and He gave
them into the hands of plunderers who plundered them; and
[b]He sold them into the hands of their enemies around *them,* so
that they could no longer stand before their enemies.

INSIGHT

Baal, which meant "lord, owner, possessor, or husband," was the Canaanite god of fertility. ***Baal*** was part of several compound names for locations where Canaanite deities were worshiped, such as Baal-peor.

Baal is first mentioned in Numbers 22:31.

Ashtoreth–the plural form is Ashtaroth–is the Canaanite goddess of fertility, love, and war. According to Greek mythology she was the wife of Baal.

34 [1]Lit *pressed*

35 [1]Lit *dwelling* [2]Lit *hand* [3]Lit *was heavy*

36 [a]Josh 15:3

2:1 [a]Judg 6:11; 13:2-21 [b]Judg 2:5 [c]Ex 20:2 [d]Gen 17:7, 8; Lev 26:42, 44; Deut 7:9

2 [1]Lit *listened to My voice* [a]Ex 23:32; Deut 7:2-5 [b]Ex 34:12, 13

3 [1]Some ancient mss read *be adversaries, and* [a]Josh 23:13 [b]Num 33:55

5 [1]I.e. weepers

6 [a]Josh 24:28-31

7 [1]Lit *prolonged days after*

9 [a]Josh 19:49f

10 [a]Ex 5:2; 1 Sam 2:12

11 [1]Or *worshiped* [a]Judg 3:7, 12; 4:1; 6:1 [b]Judg 6:25; 8:33; 10:6

12 [a]Deut 31:16

13 [a]Judg 10:6

14 [a]Deut 31:17; Ps 106:40-42 [b]Deut 28:25; 32:30

15 Wherever they went, the hand of the LORD was against them
for evil, as the LORD had spoken and [a]as the LORD had sworn to
them, so that they were severely distressed.
16 [a]Then the LORD raised up judges [1]who delivered them from
the hands of those who plundered them.
17 Yet they did not listen to their judges, for they played the
harlot after other gods and bowed themselves down to them.
They turned aside quickly from the way [a]in which their fathers
had walked in obeying the commandments of the LORD; they
did not do as *their fathers.*
18 When the LORD raised up judges for them, [a]the LORD was
with the judge and delivered them from the hand of their
enemies all the days of the judge; for the LORD was [b]moved to
pity by their groaning because of those who oppressed and
afflicted them.
19 But it came about when the judge died, that they would turn
back and act more corruptly than their fathers, in following
other gods to serve them and bow down to them; they did not
abandon their practices or their stubborn ways.
20 [a]So the anger of the LORD burned against Israel, and He said,
"Because this nation has transgressed My covenant which I
commanded their fathers and has not listened to My voice,
21 [a]I also will no longer drive out before them any of the
nations which Joshua left when he died,
22 in order to [a]test Israel by them, whether they will keep the
way of the LORD to walk in it as their fathers [1]did, or not."
23 So the LORD allowed those nations to remain, not driving
them out quickly; and He did not give them into the hand of
Joshua.

Chapter 3 Theme ____________________

3 [a]Now these are the nations which the LORD left, to test
Israel by them (*that is,* all who had not [1]experienced any
of the wars of Canaan;
2 only in order that the generations of the sons of Israel might
[1]be taught war, [2]those who had not [3]experienced it formerly).
3 *These nations are:* the five lords of the Philistines and all
the Canaanites and the Sidonians and [a]the Hivites who lived
in Mount Lebanon, from Mount Baal-hermon as far as [1]Lebo-
hamath.
4 They were for [1a]testing Israel, to find out if they would [2]obey
the commandments of the LORD, which He had commanded
their fathers [3]through Moses.
5 [a]The sons of Israel lived among the Canaanites, the Hittites,
the Amorites, the Perizzites, the Hivites, and the Jebusites;
6 and [a]they took their daughters for themselves as wives, and
gave their own daughters to their sons, and served their gods.
7 The sons of Israel did [a]what was evil in the sight of the
LORD, and [b]forgot the LORD their God and [c]served the Baals and
the [1]Asheroth.

15 [a]Lev 26:14-39; Deut 28:15-68
16 [1]Lit *and they* [a]Ps 106:43-45
17 [a]Judg 2:7
18 [a]Josh 1:5 [b]Deut 32:36; Ps 106:44
20 [a]Judg 2:14
21 [a]Josh 23:4, 5, 13
22 [1]Lit *kept* [a]Deut 8:2; 13:3
3:1 [1]Lit *known* [a]Judg 1:1; 2:21, 22
2 [1]Lit *know, to teach them* [2]Lit *only* [3]Lit *known*
3 [1]Or *the entrance of Hamath* [a]Josh 9:7; 11:19
4 [1]Lit *testing by them* [2]Lit *hear* [3]Lit *by the hand of* [a]Deut 8:2
5 [a]Ps 106:35
6 [a]Ex 34:15, 16; Deut 7:3, 4; Josh 23:12
7 [1]I.e. wooden symbol of a female deity [a]Judg 2:11 [b]Deut 4:9 [c]Judg 2:13

RETURN TO INSTRUCTIONS

8 Then the anger of the LORD was kindled against Israel, so
that He sold them into the hands of Cushan-rishathaim king of
[1]Mesopotamia; and the sons of Israel served Cushan-rishathaim
eight years.
9 When the sons of Israel cried to the LORD, the LORD raised
up a deliverer for the sons of Israel to deliver them, [a]Othniel
the son of Kenaz, Caleb's younger brother.
10 [a]The Spirit of the LORD came upon him, and he judged Israel.
When he went out to war, the LORD gave Cushan-rishathaim
king of [1]Mesopotamia into his hand, so that [2]he prevailed over
Cushan-rishathaim.
11 Then the land had rest forty years. And Othniel the son of
Kenaz died.
12 Now the sons of Israel again [a]did evil in the sight of the
LORD. So [b]the LORD strengthened Eglon the king of Moab against
Israel, because they had done evil in the sight of the LORD.
13 And he gathered to himself the sons of Ammon and Amalek;
and he went and [1]defeated Israel, and they possessed [a]the city
of the palm trees.
14 The sons of Israel served Eglon the king of Moab eighteen
years.
15 But when the sons of Israel [a]cried to the LORD, the LORD
raised up a deliverer for them, Ehud the son of Gera, the
Benjamite, a left-handed man. And the sons of Israel sent
tribute by [1]him to Eglon the king of Moab.
16 Ehud made himself a sword which had two edges, a cubit
in length, and he bound it on his right thigh under his cloak.
17 He presented the tribute to Eglon king of Moab. Now Eglon
was a very fat man.
18 It came about when he had finished presenting the tribute,
that he sent away the people who had carried the tribute.
19 But he himself turned back from the idols which were at
Gilgal, and said, "I have a secret message for you, O king." And
he said, "Keep silence." And all who attended him left him.
20 Ehud came to him while he was sitting alone in his cool roof
chamber. And Ehud said, "I have a message from God for you."
And he arose from his seat.
21 Ehud stretched out his left hand, took the sword from his
right thigh and thrust it into his belly.
22 The handle also went in after the blade, and the fat closed
over the blade, for he did not draw the sword out of his belly;
and the refuse came out.
23 Then Ehud went out into the vestibule and shut the doors
of the roof chamber behind him, and locked *them.*
24 When he had gone out, his servants came and looked, and
behold, the doors of the roof chamber were locked; and they
said, "[a]He is only [1]relieving himself in the cool room."
25 They waited until they [1]became anxious; but behold, he did
not open the doors of the roof chamber. Therefore they took the
key and opened them, and behold, their master had fallen to
the [2]floor dead.

8 [1]Heb *Aram-naharaim*

9 [a]Judg 1:13

10 [1]Heb *Aram* [2]Lit *his hand was strong* [a]Num 11:25-29; 24:2

12 [a]Judg 2:11 [b]Judg 2:14

13 [1]Lit *smote* [a]Deut 34:3; Judg 1:16

15 [1]Lit *his hand* [a]Ps 78:34

24 [1]Lit *covering his feet* [a]1 Sam 24:3

25 [1]Lit *were ashamed* [2]Lit *earth*

26 Now Ehud escaped while they were delaying, and he passed
by the idols and escaped to Seirah.
27 It came about when he had arrived, that [a]he blew the trumpet
in the hill country of Ephraim; and the sons of Israel went down
with him from the hill country, and he *was* in front of them.
28 He said to them, "Pursue *them,* for the LORD has given your
enemies the Moabites into your hands." So they went down
after him and seized [a]the fords of the Jordan opposite Moab,
and did not allow anyone to cross.
29 They struck down at that time about ten thousand Moabites,
all robust and valiant men; and no one escaped.
30 So Moab was subdued that day under the hand of Israel.
And the land was undisturbed for eighty years.
31 After him came [a]Shamgar the son of Anath, who struck down
six hundred Philistines with an oxgoad; and he also saved Israel.

Chapter 4 Theme ______________________________________

4 Then [a]the sons of Israel again did evil in the sight of the
LORD, after Ehud died.
2 And the LORD sold them into the hand of [a]Jabin king of
Canaan, who reigned in Hazor; and the commander of his
army was Sisera, who lived in [b]Harosheth-hagoyim.
3 The sons of Israel cried to the LORD; for he had nine
hundred [a]iron chariots, and he oppressed the sons of Israel
severely for twenty years.
4 Now Deborah, a [1]prophetess, the wife of Lappidoth, was
judging Israel at that time.
5 She used to [1]sit under the [a]palm tree of Deborah between
Ramah and Bethel in the hill country of Ephraim; and the sons
of Israel came up to her for judgment.
6 Now she sent and summoned [a]Barak the son of Abinoam
from Kedesh-naphtali, and said to him, "[1]Behold, the LORD, the
God of Israel, has commanded, 'Go and march to Mount Tabor,
and take with you ten thousand men from the sons of Naphtali
and from the sons of Zebulun.
7 'I will draw out to you Sisera, the commander of Jabin's army,
with his chariots and his [1]many *troops* to the river Kishon, and
[a]I will give him into your hand.'"
8 Then Barak said to her, "If you will go with me, then I will
go; but if you will not go with me, I will not go."
9 She said, "I will surely go with you; nevertheless, the
honor shall not be yours on the journey that you are about to
take, [a]for the LORD will sell Sisera into the hands of a woman."
Then Deborah arose and went with Barak to Kedesh.
10 Barak called [a]Zebulun and Naphtali together to Kedesh,
and ten thousand men went up [1b]with him; Deborah also went
up with him.
11 Now Heber [a]the Kenite had separated himself from the
Kenites, from the sons of Hobab the father-in-law of Moses,
and had pitched his tent as far away as the [1]oak in [b]Zaanannim,
which is near Kedesh.

27 [a]Judg 6:34; 1 Sam 13:3
28 [a]Judg 7:24; 12:5
31 [a]Judg 5:6
4:1 [a]Judg 2:19
2 [a]Josh 11:1, 10 [b]Judg 4:13, 16
3 [a]Judg 1:19
4 [1]Lit *woman prophetess*
5 [1]Or *live* [a]Gen 35:8
6 [1]Or *Has not... commanded...?* [a]Heb 11:32
7 [1]Lit *multitude* [a]Ps 83:9
9 [a]Judg 4:21
10 [1]Lit *at his feet* [a]Judg 5:18 [b]Judg 4:14; 5:15
11 [1]Or *terebinth* [a]Judg 1:16 [b]Josh 19:33

12 Then they told Sisera that Barak the son of Abinoam had
gone up to Mount Tabor.
13 Sisera called together all his chariots, [a]nine hundred iron
chariots, and all the people who *were* with him, from [b]Harosheth-
hagoyim to the river Kishon.
14 Deborah said to Barak, "Arise! For this is the day in which
the LORD has given Sisera into your hands; [1]behold, [a]the LORD
has gone out before you." So Barak went down from Mount
Tabor with ten thousand men following him.
15 [a]The LORD [1]routed Sisera and all *his* chariots and all *his*
army with the edge of the sword before Barak; and Sisera
alighted from *his* chariot and fled away on foot.
16 But Barak pursued the chariots and the army as far as
Harosheth-hagoyim, and all the army of Sisera fell by the edge
of the sword; [a]not even one was left.
17 Now Sisera fled away on foot to the tent of Jael the wife of
Heber the Kenite, for *there was* peace between Jabin the king
of Hazor and the house of Heber the Kenite.
18 Jael went out to meet Sisera, and said to him, "Turn aside,
my master, turn aside to me! Do not be afraid." And he turned
aside to her into the tent, and she covered him with a [1]rug.
19 [a]He said to her, "Please give me a little water to drink, for I
am thirsty." So she opened a [1]bottle of milk and gave him a
drink; then she covered him.
20 He said to her, "Stand in the doorway of the tent, and it
shall be if anyone comes and inquires of you, and says, 'Is there
anyone here?' that you shall say, 'No.'"
21 But Jael, Heber's wife, [a]took a tent peg and [1]seized a
hammer in her hand, and went secretly to him and drove the
peg into his temple, and it went through into the ground; for
he was sound asleep and exhausted. So he died.
22 And behold, as Barak pursued Sisera, Jael came out to meet
him and said to him, "Come, and I will show you the man
whom you are seeking." And he entered [1]with her, and behold
Sisera was lying dead with the tent peg in his temple.
23 So [a]God subdued on that day Jabin the king of Canaan
before the sons of Israel.
24 The hand of the sons of Israel pressed heavier and heavier
upon Jabin the king of Canaan, until they had [1]destroyed Jabin
the king of Canaan.

Chapter 5 Theme ________________________

5 [a]Then Deborah and Barak the son of Abinoam sang on that
day, saying,

2 "[a]That [1]the leaders led in Israel,
That [b]the people volunteered,
Bless the LORD!
3 "Hear, O kings; give ear, O rulers!
[a]I—to the LORD, I will sing,
I will sing praise to the LORD, the God of Israel.

13 [a]Judg 4:3 [b]Judg 4:2

14 [1]Or *has not the LORD gone . . . ?* [a]Deut 9:3; 2 Sam 5:24; Ps 68:7

15 [1]Lit *confused* [a]Deut 7:23; Josh 10:10

16 [a]Ex 14:28; Ps 83:9

18 [1]Or *blanket*

19 [1]I.e. skin container [a]Judg 5:24-27

21 [1]Lit *placed* [a]Judg 5:26

22 [1]Lit *to*

23 [a]Neh 9:24; Ps 18:47

24 [1]Lit *cut off*

5:1 [a]Ex 15:1

2 [1]Or *locks hung loose in* [a]Judg 5:9 [b]Ps 110:3

3 [a]Ps 27:6

4 "[a]LORD, when You went out from Seir,
When You marched from the field of Edom,
[b]The earth quaked, the heavens also dripped,
Even the clouds dripped water.
5 "[a]The mountains [1]quaked at the presence of the LORD,
[b]This Sinai, at the presence of the LORD, the God of
Israel.

6 "In the days of [a]Shamgar the son of Anath,
In the days of [b]Jael, the highways [1]were deserted,
And travelers [2]went by [3]roundabout ways.
7 "The peasantry ceased, they ceased in Israel,
Until I, Deborah, arose,
Until I arose, a mother in Israel.
8 "[a]New gods were chosen;
Then war *was* in the gates.
Not a shield or a spear was seen
Among forty thousand in Israel.
9 "My heart *goes out* to [a]the commanders of Israel,
The volunteers among the people;
Bless the LORD!
10 "[a]You who ride on [1]white donkeys,
You who sit on *rich* carpets,
And you who travel on the road—[2]sing!
11 "At the sound of those who divide *flocks* among [a]the
watering places,
There they shall recount [b]the righteous deeds of
the LORD,
The righteous deeds for His [1]peasantry in Israel.
Then the people of the LORD went down [c]to the gates.

12 "[a]Awake, awake, Deborah;
Awake, awake, [1]sing a song!
Arise, Barak, and [b]take away your captives, O son of
Abinoam.
13 "Then survivors came down to the nobles;
The people of the LORD came down to me as warriors.
14 "From Ephraim those whose root is [a]in Amalek *came
down,*
Following you, Benjamin, with your peoples;
From Machir commanders came down,
And from Zebulun those who wield the staff of [1]office.
15 "And the [1]princes of Issachar *were* with Deborah;
As *was* Issachar, so *was* Barak;
Into the valley they rushed [a]at his [2]heels;
Among the divisions of Reuben
There were great resolves of heart.
16 "Why did you sit among [a]the [1]sheepfolds,
To hear the piping for the flocks?
Among the divisions of Reuben
There were great searchings of heart.

---

4 [a]Deut 33:2; Ps 68:7 [b]Ps 68:8, 9
5 [1]Lit *flowed* [a]Ex 19:18 [b]Ps 68:8
6 [1]Lit *had ceased* [2]Lit *walked* [3]Lit *twisted* [a]Judg 3:31 [b]Judg 4:17
8 [a]Deut 32:17
9 [a]Judg 5:2
10 [1]Or *tawny* [2]Or *declare it* [a]Judg 10:4; 12:14
11 [1]Or *rural dwellers* [a]Gen 24:11; 29:2, 3 [b]1 Sam 12:7; Mic 6:5 [c]Judg 5:8
12 [1]Or *utter* [a]Ps 57:8 [b]Ps 68:18; Eph 4:8
14 [1]Lit *the scribe* [a]Judg 12:15
15 [1]So with ancient versions; Heb *My princes* [2]Lit *feet* [a]Judg 4:10
16 [1]Or *saddlebags* [a]Num 32:1, 2, 24, 36

17 "[a]Gilead [1]remained across the Jordan;
And why did Dan stay in ships?
Asher sat at the seashore,
And [1]remained by its landings.
18 "[a]Zebulun *was* a people who despised their lives *even* to death,
And Naphtali also, on the high places of the field.

19 "[a]The kings came *and* fought;
Then fought the kings of Canaan
[b]At Taanach near the waters of Megiddo;
[c]They took no plunder in silver.
20 "[a]The stars fought from heaven,
From their courses they fought against Sisera.
21 "The torrent of Kishon swept them away,
The ancient torrent, the torrent Kishon.
[a]O my soul, march on with strength.
22 "[a]Then the horses' hoofs beat
From the dashing, the dashing of his [1]valiant steeds.
23 'Curse Meroz,' said the angel of the LORD,
'Utterly curse its inhabitants;
[a]Because they did not come to the help of the LORD,
To the help of the LORD against the warriors.'

24 "[a]Most blessed of women is Jael,
The wife of Heber the Kenite;
Most blessed is she of women in the tent.
25 "He asked for water *and* she gave him milk;
In a magnificent bowl she brought him curds.
26 "She reached out her hand for the tent peg,
And her right hand for the workmen's hammer.
Then she struck Sisera, she smashed his head;
And she shattered and pierced his temple.
27 "Between her feet he bowed, he fell, he lay;
Between her feet he bowed, he fell;
Where he bowed, there he fell [1]dead.

28 "Out of the window she looked and lamented,
The mother of Sisera through the [1]lattice,
'Why does his chariot delay in coming?
Why do the [2]hoofbeats of his chariots tarry?'
29 "Her wise princesses would answer her,
Indeed she repeats her words to herself,
30 '[a]Are they not finding, are they not dividing the spoil?
A maiden, two maidens for every warrior;
To Sisera a spoil of dyed work,
A spoil of dyed work embroidered,
Dyed work of double embroidery on the [1]neck of the spoiler?'
31 "[a]Thus let all Your enemies perish, O LORD;
[b]But let those who love Him be like the rising of the sun in its might."
And the land was undisturbed for forty years.

17 [1]Or *dwelt* [a]Josh 22:9

18 [a]Judg 4:6, 10

19 [a]Josh 11:1-5; Judg 4:13 [b]Judg 1:27 [c]Judg 5:30

20 [a]Josh 10:12-14

21 [a]Ex 15:2; Ps 44:5

22 [1]Lit *mighty ones* [a]Job 39:19-25

23 [a]Judg 5:13

24 [a]Judg 4:19-21

27 [1]Lit *devastated*

28 [1]Or *window* [2]Lit *steps*

30 [1]Lit *necks of the spoil* [a]Ex 15:9

31 [a]Ps 68:2; 92:9 [b]Ps 19:4-6; 89:36, 37

Chapter 6 Theme ______________________

6 Then the sons of Israel [a]did what was evil in the sight of
the LORD; and the LORD gave them into the hands of [b]Midian
seven years.
2 The [1]power of Midian prevailed against Israel. Because of
Midian the sons of Israel made for themselves [a]the dens which
were in the mountains and the caves and the strongholds.
3 For it was when Israel had sown, that the Midianites would
come up with the Amalekites and the sons of the east and [1]go
against them.
4 So they would camp against them and [a]destroy the produce
of the earth [1]as far as Gaza, and [b]leave no sustenance in Israel
as well as no sheep, ox, or donkey.
5 For they would come up with their livestock and their
tents, they would come in [a]like locusts for number, both they
and their camels were innumerable; and they came into the
land to devastate it.
6 So Israel was brought [a]very low because of Midian, and the
sons of Israel cried to the LORD.
7 Now it came about when the sons of Israel cried to the
LORD on account of Midian,
8 that the LORD sent a prophet to the sons of Israel, and [a]he
said to them, "Thus says the LORD, the God of Israel, 'It was I
who brought you up from Egypt and brought you out from the
house of [1]slavery.
9 'I delivered you from the hands of the Egyptians and from
the hands of all your oppressors, and dispossessed them before
you and gave you their land,
10 and I said to you, "I am the LORD your God; you [a]shall not
fear the gods of the Amorites in whose land you live. But you
have not [1]obeyed Me."'"
11 Then [a]the angel of the LORD came and sat under the [1]oak
that was in Ophrah, which belonged to Joash the [b]Abiezrite as
his son [c]Gideon was beating out wheat in the wine press in
order to save *it* from the Midianites.
12 The angel of the LORD appeared to him and said to him,
"The LORD is with you, O valiant warrior."
13 Then Gideon said to him, "O my lord, if the LORD is with
us, why then has all this happened to us? And where are all
His miracles which our fathers told us about, saying, 'Did not
the LORD bring us up from Egypt?' But [a]now the LORD has
abandoned us and given us into the hand of Midian."
14 The LORD [1]looked at him and said, "[a]Go in this your strength
and deliver Israel from the hand of Midian. Have I not sent
you?"
15 [a]He said to Him, "O Lord, [1]how shall I deliver Israel? Behold,
my family is the least in [b]Manasseh, and I am the youngest in
my father's house."
16 [a]But the LORD said to him, "Surely I will be with you, and
you shall [1]defeat Midian as one man."

6:1 [a]Judg 2:11 [b]Num 22:4; 25:15-18; 31:1-3
2 [1]Lit *hand* [a]1 Sam 13:6; Heb 11:38
3 [1]Lit *go up*
4 [1]Lit *until your coming to* [a]Lev 26:16 [b]Deut 28:31
5 [a]Judg 7:12; 8:10
6 [a]Deut 28:43
8 [1]Lit *slaves* [a]Judg 2:1, 2
10 [1]Lit *listened to My voice* [a]2 Kin 17:35; Jer 10:2
11 [1]Or *terebinth* [a]Judg 2:1; 6:14; 13:3 [b]Josh 17:2; Judg 6:15 [c]Heb 11:32
13 [a]Judg 6:1; Ps 44:9
14 [1]Or *turned toward* [a]Heb 11:32-34
15 [1]Lit *with what* [a]Ex 3:11 [b]Judg 6:11
16 [1]Lit *smite* [a]Ex 3:12; Josh 1:5

17 So [1]Gideon said to Him, "If now I have found favor in Your
sight, then show me [a]a sign that it is You who speak with me.
18 "Please do not depart from here, until I come *back* to You,
and bring out my offering and lay it before You." And He said,
"I will remain until you return."
19 Then Gideon went in and [a]prepared a young goat and
unleavened bread from an [1]ephah of flour; he put the meat in a
basket [2]and the broth in a pot, and brought *them* out to him
under the [3]oak and presented *them*.
20 The angel of God said to him, "Take the meat and the
unleavened bread and lay them on this rock, and pour out the
broth." And he did so.
21 Then the angel of the LORD put out the end of the staff that
was in his hand and touched the meat and the unleavened
bread; and [a]fire sprang up from the rock and consumed the
meat and the unleavened bread. Then the angel of the LORD
[1]vanished from his sight.
22 [a]When Gideon saw that he was the angel of the LORD, [1]he
said, "Alas, O Lord [2]GOD! For now I have seen the angel of the
LORD face to face."
23 The LORD said to him, "Peace to you, do not fear; you shall
not die."
24 Then Gideon built an altar there to the LORD and named it
[1]The LORD is Peace. To this day it is still [a]in Ophrah of the
Abiezrites.
25 Now on the same night the LORD said to him, "Take your
father's bull [1]and a second bull seven years old, and pull down
the altar of Baal which belongs to your father, and cut down the
[2a]Asherah that is beside it;
26 and build an altar to the LORD your God on the top of this
stronghold in an orderly manner, and take a second bull and
offer a burnt offering with the wood of the Asherah which you
shall cut down."
27 Then Gideon took ten men of his servants and did as the
LORD had spoken to him; and because he was too afraid of his
father's household and the men of the city to do it by day, he
did it by night.
28 When the men of the city arose early in the morning,
behold, the altar of Baal was torn down, and the Asherah which
was beside it was cut down, and the second bull was offered on
the altar which had been built.
29 They said to one another, "Who did this thing?" And when
they searched about and inquired, they said, "Gideon the son
of Joash did this thing."
30 Then the men of the city said to Joash, "Bring out your son,
that he may die, for he has torn down the altar of Baal, and
indeed, he has cut down the Asherah which was beside it."
31 But Joash said to all who stood against him, "Will you
contend for Baal, or will you deliver him? Whoever will [1]plead
for him shall be put to death by morning. If he is a god, let him
contend for himself, because someone has torn down his altar."

17 [1]Lit *he* [a]Judg 6:37; Is 38:7, 8

19 [1]I.e. Approx one bu [2]Lit *and he put* [3]Or *terebinth* [a]Gen 18:6-8

21 [1]Or *departed* [a]Lev 9:24

22 [1]Lit *Gideon* [2]Heb *YHWH,* usually rendered *LORD* [a]Gen 32:30; Ex 33:20; Judg 13:21, 22

24 [1]Heb *Yahweh-shalom* [a]Judg 8:32

25 [1]Or *even* [2]I.e. wooden symbol of a female deity, also vv 26, 28, 30 [a]Ex 34:13

31 [1]Or *contend*

32 Therefore on that day he named him [a]Jerubbaal, that is to
say, "Let Baal contend against him," because he had torn down
his altar.
33 Then all the Midianites and the Amalekites and the sons of
the east assembled themselves; and they crossed over and
camped in [a]the valley of Jezreel.
34 So [a]the Spirit of the LORD [1]came upon Gideon; and he [b]blew
a trumpet, and the Abiezrites were called together to follow him.
35 He sent messengers throughout Manasseh, and they also
were called together to follow him; and he sent messengers to
Asher, [a]Zebulun, and Naphtali, and [b]they came up to meet them.
36 Then Gideon said to God, "[a]If You will deliver Israel [1]through
me, as You have spoken,
37 behold, I will put a fleece of wool on the threshing floor. If
there is dew on the fleece only, and it is dry on all the ground,
then I will know that You will deliver Israel [1]through me, as
You have spoken."
38 And it was so. When he arose early the next morning and
squeezed the fleece, he drained the dew from the fleece, a
bowl full of water.
39 Then Gideon said to God, "[a]Do not let Your anger burn
against me that I may speak once more; please let me make a
test once more with the fleece, let it now be dry only on the
fleece, and let there be dew on all the ground."
40 God did so that night; for it was dry only on the fleece, and
dew was on all the ground.

Chapter 7 Theme ________________________

7 Then [a]Jerubbaal (that is, Gideon) and all the people who
were with him, rose early and camped beside [1]the spring
of Harod; and the camp of Midian was on the north side of
[2]them by the hill of [b]Moreh in the valley.
2 The LORD said to Gideon, "The people who are with you
are too many for Me to give Midian into their hands, [a]for Israel
[1]would become boastful, saying, 'My own [2]power has delivered
me.'
3 "Now therefore [1]come, proclaim in the hearing of the people,
saying, '[a]Whoever is afraid and trembling, let him return and
depart from Mount Gilead.'" So 22,000 people returned, but
10,000 remained.
4 [a]Then the LORD said to Gideon, "The people are still too
many; bring them down to the water and I will test them for
you there. Therefore it shall be that he of whom I say to you,
'This one shall go with you,' he shall go with you; but everyone
of whom I say to you, 'This one shall not go with you,' he shall
not go."
5 So he brought the people down to the water. And the LORD
said to Gideon, "You shall separate everyone who laps the water
with his tongue as a dog laps, as well as everyone who kneels
to drink."

32 [a]Judg 7:1
33 [a]Josh 17:16
34 [1]Lit *clothed* [a]Judg 3:10 [b]Judg 3:27
35 [a]Judg 4:6, 10; 5:18 [b]Judg 7:3
36 [1]Lit *by my hand* [a]Judg 6:14, 16, 17
37 [1]Lit *by my hand*
39 [a]Gen 18:32
7:1 [1]Or *En-Harod* [2]Lit *him* [a]Judg 6:32 [b]Gen 12:6; Deut 11:30
2 [1]Lit *glorify itself against me* [2]Lit *hand* [a]Deut 8:17, 18
3 [1]Or *please* [a]Deut 20:8
4 [a]1 Sam 14:6

6 Now the number of those who lapped, putting their hand
to their mouth, was 300 men; but all the rest of the people
kneeled to drink water.
7 The LORD said to Gideon, "I will deliver you [a]with the 300
men who lapped and will give the Midianites into your hands;
so let all the *other* people go, each man to his [1]home."
8 So [1]the 300 men took the people's provisions and their
trumpets into their hands. And [2]Gideon sent all the *other* men
of Israel, each to his tent, but retained the 300 men; and the
camp of Midian was below him in the valley.
9 Now the same night it came about that the LORD said to
him, "Arise, go down against the camp, [a]for I have given it into
your hands.
10 "But if you are afraid to go down, go with Purah your
servant down to the camp,
11 and you will hear what they say; and [a]afterward your hands
will be strengthened that you may go down against the camp."
So he went with Purah his servant down to the [1]outposts of the
army that was in the camp.
12 Now the Midianites and the Amalekites and all the sons of
the east were lying in the valley [a]as numerous as locusts; and
their camels were without number, [b]as numerous as the sand
on the seashore.
13 When Gideon came, behold, a man was relating a dream to
his friend. And he said, "Behold, I [1]had a dream; [2]a loaf of barley
bread was tumbling into the camp of Midian, and it came to the
tent and struck it so that it fell, and turned it [3]upside down so
that the tent lay flat."
14 His friend replied, "This is nothing less than the sword of
Gideon the son of Joash, a man of Israel; God has given Midian
and all the camp [a]into his hand."
15 When Gideon heard the account of the dream and its
interpretation, he bowed in worship. He returned to the camp
of Israel and said, "Arise, for the LORD has given the camp of
Midian into your hands."
16 He divided the 300 men into three [1]companies, and he put
trumpets and empty pitchers into the hands of all of them, with
torches inside the pitchers.
17 He said to them, "Look at me and do likewise. And behold,
when I come to the outskirts of the camp, [1]do as I do.
18 "When I and all who are with me blow the trumpet, then
you also blow the trumpets all around the camp and say, 'For
the LORD and for Gideon.'"
19 So Gideon and the hundred men who were with him came
to the outskirts of the camp at the beginning of the middle
watch, when they had just posted the watch; and they blew the
trumpets and smashed the pitchers that were in their hands.
20 When the three [1]companies blew the trumpets and broke
the pitchers, they held the torches in their left hands and the
trumpets in their right hands for blowing, and cried, "A sword
for the LORD and for Gideon!"

7 [1]Lit *place* [a]1 Sam 14:6
8 [1]Lit *they* [2]Lit *he*
9 [a]Josh 2:24; 10:8; 11:6
11 [1]Lit *extremity of the battle array* [a]Judg 7:15; 1 Sam 14:9, 10
12 [a]Judg 6:5; 8:10 [b]Josh 11:4
13 [1]Lit *dreamed* [2]Lit *and behold, a loaf* [3]Lit *upwards*
14 [a]Josh 2:9
16 [1]Lit *heads*
17 [1]Lit *it shall come about that just as I do, so you shall do*
20 [1]Lit *heads*

21 Each stood in his place around the camp; and [a]all the [1]army ran, crying out as they fled.

22 When they blew 300 trumpets, the [a]LORD set the sword of one against another even throughout the whole [1]army; and the [1]army fled as far as Beth-shittah toward Zererah, as far as the edge of [b]Abel-meholah, by Tabbath.

23 The men of Israel were summoned from [a]Naphtali and Asher and all Manasseh, and they pursued Midian.

24 Gideon sent messengers throughout all the hill country of Ephraim, saying, "Come down [1]against Midian and [a]take the waters before them, as far as Beth-barah and the Jordan." So all the men of Ephraim were summoned and they took the waters as far as Beth-barah and the Jordan.

25 They captured the two leaders of Midian, [a]Oreb and Zeeb, and they killed Oreb at the rock of Oreb, and they killed Zeeb at the wine press of Zeeb, while they pursued Midian; and they brought the heads of Oreb and Zeeb to Gideon [b]from across the Jordan.

Chapter 8 Theme ____________________

8 Then the men of Ephraim said to him, "[a]What is this thing you have done to us, not calling us when you went to fight against Midian?" And they contended with him vigorously.

2 But he said to them, "What have I done now in comparison with you? Is not the gleaning *of the grapes* of Ephraim better than the vintage of Abiezer?

3 "God has given the leaders of Midian, Oreb and Zeeb into your hands; and what was I able to do in comparison with you?" Then their [1]anger toward him subsided when he said [2]that.

4 Then Gideon and the 300 men who were with him came [a]to the Jordan *and* crossed over, weary yet pursuing.

5 He said to the men of [a]Succoth, "Please give loaves of bread to the people who are following me, for they are weary, and I am pursuing Zebah and Zalmunna, the kings of Midian."

6 The leaders of Succoth said, "[1a]Are the hands of Zebah and Zalmunna already in your hands, that we should give bread to your army?"

7 Gideon said, "[1]All right, [a]when the LORD has given Zebah and Zalmunna into my hand, then I will [2]thrash your [3]bodies with the thorns of the wilderness and with briers."

8 He went up from there to [1a]Penuel and spoke similarly to them; and the men of Penuel answered him just as the men of Succoth had answered.

9 So he spoke also to the men of Penuel, saying, "When I return safely, [a]I will tear down this tower."

10 Now Zebah and Zalmunna were in Karkor, and their [1]armies with them, about 15,000 men, all who were left of the entire [2]army of the sons of the east; [a]for the fallen were 120,000 [3]swordsmen.

21 [1]Or *camp* [a]2 Kin 7:7
22 [1]Or *camp* [a]1 Sam 14:20 [b]1 Kin 4:12; 19:16
23 [a]Judg 6:35
24 [1]Lit *to meet* [a]Judg 3:28
25 [a]Ps 83:11; Is 10:26 [b]Judg 8:4
8:1 [a]Judg 12:1
3 [1]Lit *spirit* [2]Lit *this thing*
4 [a]Judg 7:25
5 [a]Gen 33:17
6 [1]Lit *Is the palm* [a]Judg 8:15
7 [1]Lit *For thus* [2]Or *trample* [3]Lit *flesh* [a]Judg 7:15
8 [1]In Gen 32:30, *Peniel* [a]Gen 32:31
9 [a]Judg 8:17
10 [1]Or *camps* [2]Or *camp* [3]Lit *men who drew sword* [a]Judg 6:5; 7:12; Is 9:4

11 Gideon went up by the way of those who lived in tents on
the east of Nobah and Jogbehah, and [1]attacked the camp when
the camp was [2]unsuspecting.
12 When Zebah and Zalmunna fled, he pursued them and
captured the two kings of Midian, Zebah and Zalmunna, and
routed the whole [1]army.
13 Then Gideon the son of Joash returned from the battle [1]by
the ascent of Heres.
14 And he captured a youth [1]from Succoth and questioned him.
Then *the youth* wrote down for him the princes of Succoth and
its elders, seventy-seven men.
15 He came to the men of Succoth and said, "Behold Zebah
and Zalmunna, concerning whom you taunted me, saying,
'[1a]Are the hands of Zebah and Zalmunna already in your hand,
that we should give bread to your men who are weary?'"
16 He took the elders of the city, and thorns of the wilderness
and briers, and he [1]disciplined the men of Succoth with them.
17 [a]He tore down the tower of Penuel and killed the men of
the city.
18 Then he said to Zebah and Zalmunna, "What kind of men
were they whom you killed at Tabor?" And they said, "They
were like you, each one [1]resembling the son of a king."
19 He said, "They *were* my brothers, the sons of my mother.
As the LORD lives, if only you had let them live, I would not kill
you."
20 So he said to Jether his firstborn, "Rise, kill them." But the
youth did not draw his sword, for he was afraid, because he
was still a youth.
21 Then Zebah and Zalmunna said, "Rise up yourself, and fall
on us; for as the man, so is his strength." [a]So Gideon arose and
killed Zebah and Zalmunna, and [b]took the crescent ornaments
which were on their camels' necks.
22 Then the men of Israel said to Gideon, "Rule over us, both
you and your son, also your son's son, for you have delivered us
from the hand of Midian."
23 But Gideon said to them, "I will not rule over you, nor shall
my son rule over you; [a]the LORD shall rule over you."
24 Yet Gideon said to them, "I would [1]request of you, that
each of you give me [2]an earring from his spoil." (For they had
gold earrings, because they were [a]Ishmaelites.)
25 They said, "We will surely give *them.*" So they spread out a
garment, and every one of them threw an earring there from
his spoil.
26 The weight of the gold earrings that he requested was
1,700 *shekels* of gold, besides the crescent ornaments and the
pendants and the purple robes which *were* on the kings of
Midian, and besides the neck bands that *were* on their camels'
necks.
27 Gideon made it into [a]an ephod, and placed it in his city,
Ophrah, and all Israel played the harlot with it there, so that it
became a snare to Gideon and his household.

11 [1]Lit *smote* [2]Or *secure*
12 [1]Or *camp*
13 [1]Or *from*
14 [1]Lit *of the men of*
15 [1]Lit *Is the palm* [a]Judg 8:6
16 [1]Lit *made the men . . . to know*
17 [a]Judg 8:9
18 [1]Lit *like the form of the sons*
21 [a]Ps 83:11 [b]Judg 8:26
23 [a]1 Sam 8:7; 10:19; 12:12; Ps 10:16
24 [1]Lit *request a request* [2]Or *a nose ring* [a]Gen 25:13-16
27 [a]Ex 28:6-35; Judg 17:5; 18:14-20

28 So Midian was subdued before the sons of Israel, and they did not lift up their heads anymore. And the land was undisturbed for forty years in the days of Gideon.
29 Then [a]Jerubbaal the son of Joash went and lived in his own house.
30 Now Gideon had [a]seventy sons who [1]were his direct descendants, for he had many wives.
31 His concubine who was in Shechem also bore him a son, and he [1]named him Abimelech.
32 And Gideon the son of Joash died at a ripe old age and was buried in the tomb of his father Joash, in Ophrah of the Abiezrites.
33 Then it came about, as soon as Gideon was dead, [a]that the sons of Israel again played the harlot with the Baals, and made [b]Baal-berith their god.
34 Thus the sons of Israel [a]did not remember the LORD their God, who had delivered them from the hands of all their enemies on every side;
35 [a]nor did they show kindness to the household of Jerubbaal (*that is,* Gideon) in accord with all the good that he had done to Israel.

Chapter 9 Theme ________________________

9 And [a]Abimelech the son of Jerubbaal went to Shechem to his mother's [1]relatives, and spoke to them and to the whole clan of the household of his mother's father, saying,
2 "Speak, now, in the hearing of all the leaders of Shechem, 'Which is better for you, that [a]seventy men, all the sons of Jerubbaal, rule over you, or that one man rule over you?' Also, remember that I am [b]your bone and your flesh."
3 And his mother's [1]relatives spoke all these words on his behalf in the hearing of all the leaders of Shechem; and [2]they were inclined to follow Abimelech, for they said, "He is [a]our [3]relative."
4 They gave him seventy *pieces* of silver from the house of [a]Baal-berith with which Abimelech hired worthless and reckless fellows, and they followed him.
5 Then he went to his father's house at Ophrah and [a]killed his brothers the sons of Jerubbaal, [b]seventy men, on one stone. But Jotham the youngest son of Jerubbaal was left, for he hid himself.
6 All the men of Shechem and all [1]Beth-millo assembled together, and they went and made Abimelech king, by the [2]oak of the pillar which was in Shechem.
7 Now when they told Jotham, he went and stood on the top of [a]Mount Gerizim, and lifted his voice and called out. Thus he said to them, "Listen to me, O men of Shechem, that God may listen to you.
8 "Once the trees went forth to anoint a king over them, and they said to the olive tree, 'Reign over us!'

29 [a]Judg 7:1
30 [1]Lit *came from his loins* [a]Judg 9:2, 5
31 [1]Lit *appointed his name*
33 [a]Judg 2:11, 12 [b]Judg 9:4, 27, 46
34 [a]Deut 4:9; Judg 3:7
35 [a]Judg 9:16-18
9:1 [1]Lit *brothers* [a]Judg 8:31, 35
2 [a]Judg 8:30; 9:5, 18 [b]Gen 29:14
3 [1]Lit *brothers* [2]Lit *their hearts inclined after* [3]Lit *brother* [a]Gen 29:15
4 [a]Judg 8:33
5 [a]2 Kin 11:1, 2 [b]Judg 8:30; 9:2, 18
6 [1]Or *the house of Millo* [2]Or *terebinth*
7 [a]Deut 11:29, 30

9“But the olive tree said to them, ‘Shall I leave my fatness
with [1]which God and men are honored, and go to wave over
the trees?’
10“Then the trees said to the fig tree, ‘You come, reign over us!’
11“But the fig tree said to them, ‘Shall I leave my sweetness
and my good [1]fruit, and go to wave over the trees?’
12“Then the trees said to the vine, ‘You come, reign over us!’
13“But the vine said to them, ‘Shall I leave my new wine,
which cheers God and men, and go to wave over the trees?’
14“Finally all the trees said to the bramble, ‘You come, reign
over us!’
15“The bramble said to the trees, ‘If in [1]truth you are anointing
me as king over you, come and take refuge in my shade; but if
not, may fire come out from the bramble and consume the
cedars of Lebanon.’
16“Now therefore, if you have dealt in [1]truth and integrity in
making Abimelech king, and if you have dealt well with [a]Jerubbaal
and his house, and [2]have dealt with him [3]as he deserved—
17 for my father fought for you and [1]risked his life and delivered
you from the hand of Midian;
18 but you have risen against my father’s house today and
have killed [a]his sons, seventy men, on one stone, and have
made Abimelech, [b]the son of his maidservant, king over the
men of Shechem, because he is your [1]relative—
19 if then you have dealt in [1]truth and integrity with Jerubbaal
and his house this day, rejoice in Abimelech, and let him also
rejoice in you.
20“But if not, let fire come out from Abimelech and consume
the men of Shechem and [1]Beth-millo; and let fire come out
from the men of Shechem and from [1]Beth-millo, and consume
Abimelech.”
21 Then Jotham escaped and fled, and went to Beer and
remained there because of Abimelech his brother.
22 Now Abimelech ruled over Israel three years.
23 [a]Then God sent an evil spirit between Abimelech and the
men of Shechem; and the men of Shechem [b]dealt treacherously
with Abimelech,
24 [a]so that the violence [1]done to the seventy sons of Jerubbaal
might come, and [b]their blood might be laid on Abimelech their
brother, who killed them, and on the men of Shechem, who
strengthened his hands to kill his brothers.
25 The men of Shechem set [1]men in ambush against him on
the tops of the mountains, and they robbed all who might pass
by them along the road; and it was told to Abimelech.
26 Now Gaal the son of Ebed came with his [1]relatives, and
crossed over into Shechem; and the men of Shechem put their
trust in him.
27 They went out into the field and gathered *the grapes of*
their vineyards and trod *them,* and held a [1]festival; and they
went into the house of [a]their god, and ate and drank and cursed
Abimelech.

9 [1]Lit *which by me*
11 [1]Or *produce*
15 [1]Or *sincerity*
16 [1]Or *sincerity* [2]Lit *if you have* [3]Lit *according to the dealing of his hands* [a]Judg 8:35
17 [1]Lit *cast his soul in front*
18 [1]Lit *brother* [a]Judg 8:30; 9:2, 5 [b]Judg 8:31
19 [1]Or *sincerity*
20 [1]Or *the house of Millo*
23 [a]1 Sam 16:14; Is 19:2, 14 [b]Is 33:1
24 [1]Lit *of the seventy* [a]Deut 27:25; Judg 9:56, 57 [b]Num 35:33
25 [1]Lit *liers-in-wait for*
26 [1]Lit *brothers*
27 [1]Lit *rejoicing* [a]Judg 8:33; 9:46

28 Then Gaal the son of Ebed said, "Who is Abimelech, and
who is Shechem, that we should serve him? Is he not the son
of Jerubbaal, and *is* Zebul *not* his [1]lieutenant? Serve the men of
[a]Hamor the father of Shechem; but why should we serve him?
29 "[1a]Would, therefore, that this people were under my authority!
Then I would remove Abimelech." And he said to Abimelech,
"Increase your army and come out."
30 When Zebul the ruler of the city heard the words of Gaal
the son of Ebed, his anger burned.
31 He sent messengers to Abimelech [1]deceitfully, saying,
"Behold, Gaal the son of Ebed and his [2]relatives have come to
Shechem; and behold, they are [3]stirring up the city against you.
32 "Now therefore, arise by night, you and the people who are
with you, and lie in wait in the field.
33 "In the morning, as soon as the sun is up, you shall rise
early and rush upon the city; and behold, when he and the
people who are with him come out against you, you shall [a]do
to them [1]whatever you can."
34 So Abimelech and all the people who *were* with him arose
by night and lay in wait against Shechem in four [1]companies.
35 Now Gaal the son of Ebed went out and stood in the
entrance of the city gate; and Abimelech and the people who
were with him arose from the ambush.
36 When Gaal saw the people, he said to Zebul, "[1]Look, people
are coming down from the tops of the mountains." But Zebul
said to him, "You are seeing the shadow of the mountains as *if
they were* men."
37 Gaal spoke again and said, "Behold, people are coming
down from [a]the [1]highest part of the land, and one [2]company
comes by the way of [3]the diviners' [4]oak."
38 Then Zebul said to him, "Where is your [1]boasting now with
which you said, 'Who is Abimelech that we should serve him?'
Is this not the people whom you despised? Go out now and
fight with them!"
39 So Gaal went out before the leaders of Shechem and fought
with Abimelech.
40 Abimelech chased him, and he fled before him; and many
fell wounded up to the entrance of the gate.
41 Then Abimelech remained at Arumah, but Zebul drove out
Gaal and his [1]relatives so that they could not remain in
Shechem.
42 Now it came about the next day, that the people went out
to the field, and it was told to Abimelech.
43 So he took [1]his people and divided them into three
[2]companies, and lay in wait in the field; when he looked and
[3]saw the people coming out from the city, he arose against them
and [4]slew them.
44 Then Abimelech and the [1]company who was with him
dashed forward and stood in the entrance of the city gate; the
other two [2]companies then dashed against all who *were* in the
field and [3]slew them.

28 [1]Lit *overseer* [a]Gen 34:2

29 [1]Lit *And who will give this people into my hand* [a]2 Sam 15:4

31 [1]Or *in Tormah* [2]Lit *brothers* [3]Lit *besieging*

33 [1]Lit *as your hand can find* [a]1 Sam 10:7

34 [1]Lit *heads*

36 [1]Lit *Behold*

37 [1]Or *center* [2]Lit *head* [3]Heb *Elommeonenim* [4]Or *terebinth* [a]Ezek 38:12

38 [1]Lit *mouth*

41 [1]Lit *brothers*

43 [1]Lit *the* [2]Lit *heads* [3]Lit *behold* [4]Lit *smote*

44 [1]Singular with Gr; Heb plural, *heads* [2]Lit *heads* [3]Lit *smote*

45 Abimelech fought against the city all that day, and he
captured the city and killed the people who *were* in it; then he
[a]razed the city and sowed it with salt.
46 When all the leaders of the tower of Shechem heard of *it,*
they entered the inner chamber of the [1]temple of [a]El-berith.
47 It was told Abimelech that all the leaders of the tower of
Shechem were gathered together.
48 So Abimelech went up to Mount [a]Zalmon, he and all the
people who *were* with him; and Abimelech took [1]an axe in his
hand and cut down a branch from the trees, and lifted it and laid
it on his shoulder. Then he said to the people who *were* with
him, "What you have seen me do, hurry *and* do [2]likewise."
49 All the people also cut down each one his branch and
followed Abimelech, and put *them* on the inner chamber and
set the inner chamber on fire over those *inside,* so that all the
men of the tower of Shechem also died, about a thousand men
and women.
50 Then Abimelech went to Thebez, and he camped against
Thebez and captured it.
51 But there was a strong tower in the center of the city, and
all the men and women with all the leaders of the city fled
there and shut themselves in; and they went up on the roof of
the tower.
52 So Abimelech came to the tower and fought against it, and
approached the entrance of the tower to burn it with fire.
53 But [a]a certain woman threw an upper millstone on
Abimelech's head, crushing his skull.
54 Then [a]he called quickly to the young man, his armor bearer,
and said to him, "Draw your sword and kill me, so that it will
not be said of me, 'A woman slew him.'" So [1]the young man
pierced him through, and he died.
55 When the men of Israel saw that Abimelech was dead,
each departed to his [1]home.
56 Thus [a]God repaid the wickedness of Abimelech, which he
had done to his father in killing his seventy brothers.
57 Also God returned all the wickedness of the men of Shechem
on their heads, and the curse of Jotham the son of Jerubbaal
came [1]upon them.

Chapter 10 Theme ____________________________

10 Now after Abimelech died, Tola the son of Puah, the son
of Dodo, a man of Issachar, [a]arose to save Israel; and he
lived in Shamir in the hill country of Ephraim.
2 He judged Israel twenty-three years. Then he died and was
buried in Shamir.
3 After him, Jair the Gileadite arose and judged Israel twenty-
two years.
4 He had thirty sons who rode on thirty donkeys, and they had
thirty cities [1]in the land of Gilead [a]that are called [2]Havvoth-jair
to this day.

45 [a]2 Kin 3:25
46 [1]Lit *house* [a]Judg 8:33
48 [1]Lit *the axes* [2]Lit *like me* [a]Ps 68:14
53 [a]2 Sam 11:21
54 [1]Lit *his* [a]1 Sam 31:4
55 [1]Lit *place*
56 [a]Gen 9:5, 6; Ps 94:23
57 [1]Lit *to*
10:1 [a]Judg 2:16
4 [1]Lit *which are in* [2]I.e. the towns of Jair [a]Num 32:41

5 And Jair died and was buried in Kamon.

6 Then the sons of Israel again did evil in the sight of the LORD, [a]served the Baals and the Ashtaroth, the gods of Aram, the gods of Sidon, the gods of Moab, [b]the gods of the sons of Ammon, and the gods of the Philistines; thus [c]they forsook the LORD and did not serve Him.

7 The anger of the LORD burned against Israel, and He [a]sold them into the hands of the Philistines and into the hands of the sons of Ammon.

8 They [1]afflicted and crushed the sons of Israel [2]that year; for eighteen years they *afflicted* all the sons of Israel who were beyond the Jordan [3]in Gilead in the land of the Amorites.

9 The sons of Ammon crossed the Jordan to fight also against Judah, Benjamin, and the house of Ephraim, so that Israel was greatly distressed.

10 Then the [a]sons of Israel cried out to the LORD, saying, "We have sinned against You, for indeed, we have forsaken our God and served the Baals."

11 The LORD said to the sons of Israel, "*Did I* not *deliver you* [a]from the Egyptians, [b]the Amorites, [c]the sons of Ammon, and the Philistines?

12 "Also when the Sidonians, the Amalekites and the Maonites [a]oppressed you, you cried out to Me, and I delivered you from their hands.

13 "Yet [a]you have forsaken Me and served other gods; therefore I will no longer deliver you.

14 "[a]Go and cry out to the gods which you have chosen; let them deliver you in the time of your distress."

15 The sons of Israel said to the LORD, "We have sinned, [a]do to us whatever seems good to You; only please deliver us this day."

16 [a]So they put away the foreign gods from among them and served the LORD; and [1b]He could bear the misery of Israel no longer.

17 Then the sons of Ammon were summoned and they camped in Gilead. And the sons of Israel gathered together and camped in [a]Mizpah.

18 The people, the leaders of Gilead, said to one another, "Who is the man who will begin to fight against the sons of Ammon? He shall become head over all the inhabitants of Gilead."

Chapter 11 Theme ______________________

11 Now [a]Jephthah the Gileadite was a [1]valiant warrior, but he was the son of a harlot. And Gilead [2]was the father of Jephthah.

2 Gilead's wife bore him sons; and when his wife's sons grew up, they drove Jephthah out and said to him, "You shall not have an inheritance in our father's house, for you are the son of another woman."

6 [a]Judg 2:13 [b]Judg 11:24 [c]Deut 31:16, 17; 32:15

7 [a]1 Sam 12:9

8 [1]Lit *shattered* [2]Lit *in that* [3]Lit *which is in*

10 [a]1 Sam 12:10

11 [a]Judg 2:12 [b]Num 21:21-25 [c]Judg 3:13

12 [a]Ps 106:42

14 [a]Deut 32:37

13 [a]Jer 2:13

15 [a]1 Sam 3:18

16 [1]Lit *His soul was short with the misery* [a]Josh 24:23 [b]Deut 32:36

17 [a]Judg 11:29

11:1 [1]Or *mighty man of valor* [2]Lit *begat* [a]Heb 11:32

3 So Jephthah fled from his brothers and lived in the land of
[a]Tob; and worthless fellows gathered themselves [1]about Jephthah,
and they went out with him.
4 It came about after a while that [a]the sons of Ammon fought
against Israel.
5 When the sons of Ammon fought against Israel, the elders
of Gilead went to get Jephthah from the land of Tob;
6 and they said to Jephthah, "Come and be our chief that we
may fight against the sons of Ammon."
7 Then Jephthah said to the elders of Gilead, "[a]Did you not
hate me and drive me from my father's house? So why have
you come to me now when you are in trouble?"
8 The elders of Gilead said to Jephthah, "For this reason we
have now returned to you, that you may go with us and fight
with the sons of Ammon and [a]become head over all the
inhabitants of Gilead."
9 So Jephthah said to the elders of Gilead, "If you take me
back to fight against the sons of Ammon and the LORD gives
them up [1]to me, will I become your head?"
10 The elders of Gilead said to Jephthah, "[a]The LORD is
[1]witness between us; surely we will do [2]as you have said."
11 Then Jephthah went with the elders of Gilead, and the
people made him head and chief over them; and Jephthah
spoke all his words before the LORD at [a]Mizpah.
12 Now Jephthah sent messengers to the king of the sons of
Ammon, saying, "What is between you and me, that you have
come to me to fight against my land?"
13 The king of the sons of Ammon said to the messengers of
Jephthah, "Because Israel [a]took away my land when they came
up from Egypt, from the Arnon as far as the [b]Jabbok and the
Jordan; therefore, return them peaceably now."
14 But Jephthah sent messengers again to the king of the sons
of Ammon,
15 and they said to him, "Thus says Jephthah, 'Israel did not
take away the land of Moab nor the land of the sons of Ammon.
16 'For when they came up from Egypt, and Israel [a]went
through the wilderness to the [1]Red Sea and [b]came to Kadesh,
17 then Israel [a]sent messengers to the king of Edom, saying,
"Please let us pass through your land," but the king of Edom
would not listen. [b]And they also sent to the king of Moab, but
he would not consent. So Israel remained at Kadesh.
18 'Then they went through the wilderness and [a]around the
land of Edom and the land of Moab, and came to the east side
of the land of Moab, and they camped beyond the Arnon; but
they [b]did not enter the territory of Moab, for the Arnon *was*
the border of Moab.
19 'And Israel sent [a]messengers to Sihon king of the Amorites,
the king of Heshbon, and Israel said to him, "Please let us pass
through your land to our place."
20 'But Sihon did not trust Israel to pass through his territory;
so Sihon gathered all his people and camped in Jahaz and
fought with Israel.

3 [1]Lit *to* [a]2 Sam 10:6, 8
4 [a]Judg 10:9, 17
7 [a]Gen 26:27
8 [a]Judg 10:18
9 [1]Lit *before*
10 [1]Lit *hearer* [2]Lit *according to your word* [a]Gen 31:50; Jer 29:23; 42:5; Mic 1:2
11 [a]Judg 10:17; 11:29; 20:1; 1 Sam 10:17
13 [a]Num 21:24 [b]Gen 32:22
16 [1]Lit *Sea of Reeds* [a]Num 14:25; Deut 1:40 [b]Num 20:1, 4-21
17 [a]Num 20:14-21 [b]Josh 24:9
18 [a]Num 21:4; Deut 2:8 [b]Deut 2:9, 18, 19
19 [a]Num 21:21-32; Deut 2:26-36

21 'The LORD, the God of Israel, gave Sihon and all his people into
the hand of Israel, and they [1a]defeated them; so Israel possessed
all the land of the Amorites, the inhabitants of that country.
22 '[a]So they possessed all the territory of the Amorites, from
the Arnon as far as the Jabbok, and from the wilderness as far
as the Jordan.
23 'Since now the LORD, the God of Israel, drove out the
Amorites from before His people Israel, are you then to possess it?
24 'Do you not possess what [a]Chemosh your god gives you to
possess? So whatever the LORD our God has driven out before
us, we will possess it.
25 'Now are you any better than [a]Balak the son of Zippor, king
of Moab? Did he ever strive with Israel, or did he ever fight
against them?
26 '[a]While Israel lived in Heshbon and its villages, and in Aroer
and its villages, and in all the cities that are on the banks of the
Arnon, three hundred years, why did you not recover them
within that time?
27 'I therefore have not sinned against you, but you are doing
me wrong by making war against me; [a]may the LORD, the
Judge, judge today between the sons of Israel and the sons of
Ammon.'"
28 But the king of the sons of Ammon [1]disregarded the
message which Jephthah sent him.
29 Now [a]the Spirit of the LORD came upon Jephthah, so that
he passed through Gilead and Manasseh; then he passed
through Mizpah of Gilead, and from Mizpah of Gilead he went
on to the sons of Ammon.
30 Jephthah made a vow to the LORD and said, "If You will
indeed give the sons of Ammon into my hand,
31 then it shall be that whatever comes out of the doors of my
house to meet me when I return in peace from the sons of
Ammon, it shall be the LORD'S, and I will offer it up as a burnt
offering."
32 So Jephthah crossed over to the sons of Ammon to fight
against them; and the LORD gave them into his hand.
33 He struck them with a very great slaughter from Aroer [1]to
the entrance of [a]Minnith, twenty cities, and as far as Abel-
keramim. So the sons of Ammon were subdued before the sons
of Israel.
34 When Jephthah came to his house at [a]Mizpah, behold, his
daughter was coming out to meet him [b]with tambourines and
with dancing. Now she was his one *and* only child; besides her
he had no son or daughter.
35 When he saw her, he tore his clothes and said, "Alas, my
daughter! You have brought me very low, and you are among
those who trouble me; for I have [1]given my word to the LORD,
and [a]I cannot take *it* back."
36 So she said to him, "My father, you have [1]given your word
to the LORD; [a]do to me [2]as you have said, since the LORD has
avenged you of your enemies, the sons of Ammon."

21 [1]Lit *smote* [a]Num 21:24; Deut 2:32-34
22 [a]Deut 2:36, 37
24 [a]Num 21:29; 1 Kin 11:7
25 [a]Num 22:2; Josh 24:9; Mic 6:5
26 [a]Num 21:25, 26; Deut 2:36
27 [a]Gen 16:5; 18:25; 31:53; 1 Sam 24:12, 15
28 [1]Lit *did not listen to the words*
29 [a]Judg 3:10
33 [1]Lit *even until you are coming to* [a]Ezek 27:17
34 [a]Judg 10:17; 11:11 [b]Ex 15:20; 1 Sam 18:6; Jer 31:4
35 [1]Lit *opened my mouth* [a]Num 30:2; Eccl 5:4, 5
36 [1]Lit *opened your mouth* [2]Lit *according to what has proceeded from your mouth* [a]Num 30:2

37 She said to her father, "Let this thing be done for me; let me alone two months, that I may [1]go to the mountains and weep because of [a]my virginity, I and my companions."

38 Then he said, "Go." So he sent her away for two months; and she left with her companions, and wept on the mountains because of her virginity.

39 At the end of two months she returned to her father, who did to her according to the vow which he had made; and she [1]had no relations with a man. Thus it became a custom in Israel,

40 that the daughters of Israel went yearly to [1]commemorate the daughter of Jephthah the Gileadite four days in the year.

Chapter 12 Theme ________________________________

12 Then the men of Ephraim were summoned, and they crossed [1]to Zaphon and [a]said to Jephthah, "Why did you cross over to fight against the sons of Ammon without calling us to go with you? We will burn your house down on you."

2 Jephthah said to them, "I and my people were at great strife with the sons of Ammon; when I called you, you did not deliver me from their hand.

3 "When I saw that you would not deliver *me,* I [1a]took my life in my hands and crossed over against the sons of Ammon, and the LORD gave them into my hand. Why then have you come up to me this day to fight against me?"

4 Then Jephthah gathered all the men of Gilead and fought Ephraim; and the men of Gilead [1]defeated Ephraim, because they said, "You are fugitives of Ephraim, O Gileadites, in the midst of Ephraim *and* in the midst of Manasseh."

5 The Gileadites [a]captured the fords of the Jordan opposite Ephraim. And it happened when *any of* the fugitives of Ephraim said, "Let me cross over," the men of Gilead would say to him, "Are you an Ephraimite?" If he said, "No,"

6 then they would say to him, "Say now, 'Shibboleth.'" But he said, "Sibboleth," for he could not [1]pronounce it correctly. Then they seized him and slew him at the fords of the Jordan. Thus there fell at that time 42,000 of Ephraim.

7 Jephthah judged Israel six years. Then Jephthah the Gileadite died and was buried in *one of* the cities of Gilead.

8 Now Ibzan of Bethlehem judged Israel after him.

9 He had thirty sons, and thirty daughters *whom* he [1]gave in marriage outside *the family,* and he brought in thirty daughters from outside for his sons. And he judged Israel seven years.

10 Then Ibzan died and was buried in Bethlehem.

11 Now Elon the Zebulunite judged Israel after him; and he judged Israel ten years.

12 Then Elon the Zebulunite died and was buried at Aijalon in the land of Zebulun.

13 Now Abdon the son of Hillel the Pirathonite judged Israel after him.

14 He had forty sons and thirty grandsons who rode on seventy donkeys; and he judged Israel eight years.

37 [1]Lit *go and go down on* [a]Gen 30:23; Luke 1:25

39 [1]Lit *knew no man*

40 [1]Lit *recount;* ancient versions, *lament*

12:1 [1]Or *northward* [a]Judg 8:1

3 [1]Lit *put my soul in my palm* [a]1 Sam 19:5; 28:21; Job 13:14

4 [1]Lit *smote*

5 [a]Judg 3:28

6 [1]Lit *speak so*

9 [1]Lit *sent outside*

15 Then Abdon the son of Hillel the Pirathonite died and was
buried at Pirathon in the land of Ephraim, in the hill country of
the Amalekites.

Chapter 13 Theme ______________________

13 Now the sons of Israel [a]again did evil in the sight of the
LORD, so that the LORD gave them into the hands of the
Philistines forty years.
2 There was a certain man of [a]Zorah, of the family of the
Danites, whose name was Manoah; and his wife was barren
and had borne no *children.*
3 [a]Then the angel of the LORD appeared to the woman and
said to her, "Behold now, you are barren and have borne no
children, but you shall conceive and give birth to a son.
4 "Now therefore, be careful [a]not to drink wine or strong
drink, nor eat any unclean thing.
5 "[a]For behold, you shall conceive and give birth to a son, and
no razor shall come upon his head, for the boy shall be a
[b]Nazirite to God from the womb; and he shall begin to deliver
Israel from the hands of the Philistines."
6 Then the woman came and told her husband, saying, "[a]A
man of God came to me and his appearance was like the
appearance of the angel of God, very awesome. And I did not
ask him where he *came* from, nor did he tell me his name.
7 "But he said to me, 'Behold, you shall conceive and give
birth to a son, and now you shall not drink wine or strong drink
nor eat any unclean thing, for the boy shall be a Nazirite to
God from the womb to the day of his death.'"
8 Then Manoah entreated the LORD and said, "O Lord, please
let [a]the man of God whom You have sent come to us again that
he may teach us what to do for the boy who is to be born."
9 God listened to the voice of Manoah; and [a]the angel of God
came again to the woman as she was sitting in the field, but
Manoah her husband was not with her.
10 So the woman ran quickly and told her [1]husband, "Behold,
[a]the man who [2]came the *other* day has appeared to me."
11 Then Manoah arose and followed his wife, and when he
came to the man he said to him, "Are you [a]the man who spoke
to the woman?" And he said, "I am."
12 Manoah said, "Now when your words come *to pass,* what
shall be the boy's mode of life and his vocation?"
13 So [a]the angel of the LORD said to Manoah, "[b]Let the woman
pay attention [1]to all that I said.
14 "She should not eat anything that comes from the [a]vine nor
drink wine or strong drink, nor eat any unclean thing; let her
observe all that I commanded."
15 Then Manoah said to [a]the angel of the LORD, "Please let us
detain you so that we may prepare a young goat for you."
16 The angel of the LORD said to Manoah, "Though you detain
me, [a]I will not eat your [1]food, but if you prepare a burnt offering,

13:1 [a]Judg 2:11
2 [a]Josh 19:41
3 [a]Judg 6:11, 14; 13:6, 8, 10, 11; Luke 1:11-13
4 [a]Num 6:2, 3; Luke 1:15
5 [a]Luke 1:15 [b]Num 6:2-5
6 [a]Judg 6:11; 13:8, 10, 11
8 [a]Judg 13:3, 7
9 [a]Judg 13:8
10 [1]Lit *husband, and said to him* [2]Lit *came to me* [a]Judg 13:9
11 [a]Judg 13:8
13 [1]Lit *from* [a]Judg 13:11 [b]Judg 13:4
14 [a]Num 6:4
15 [a]Judg 13:3
16 [1]Lit *bread* [a]Judg 6:20

then offer it to the LORD." For Manoah did not know that he
was the angel of the LORD.
17 Manoah said to the angel of the LORD, "[a]What is your
name, so that when your words come *to pass,* we may honor
you?"
18 But the angel of the LORD said to him, "Why do you ask my
name, seeing it is [1a]wonderful?"
19 So [a]Manoah took the young goat with the grain offering
and offered it on the rock to the LORD, and He performed
wonders while Manoah and his wife looked on.
20 For it came about when the flame went up from the altar
toward heaven, that the angel of the LORD ascended in the
flame of the altar. When Manoah and his wife saw *this,* they
[a]fell on their faces to the ground.
21 Now the angel of the LORD did not appear to Manoah or his
wife again. [a]Then Manoah knew that he was the angel of the
LORD.
22 So Manoah said to his wife, "[a]We will surely die, for we
have seen God."
23 But his wife said to him, "If the LORD had desired to kill us,
He would not have accepted a burnt offering and a grain offering
from our hands, nor would He have [a]shown us all these things,
nor would He have let us hear *things* like this at this time."
24 Then the woman gave birth to a son and named him
Samson; and the [a]child grew up and the LORD blessed him.
25 And [a]the Spirit of the LORD began to stir him in [1b]Mahaneh-
dan, between Zorah and Eshtaol.

Chapter 14 Theme ____________________

14 Then Samson went down to Timnah and saw a woman
in Timnah, *one* of the daughters of the Philistines.
2 So he came [1]back and told his father and [2]mother, "I saw a
woman in Timnah, *one* of the daughters of the Philistines; now
therefore, get her for me as a wife."
3 Then his father and his mother said to him, "Is there no
woman among the daughters of your [1a]relatives, or among all
[2]our people, that you go to [b]take a wife from the uncircumcised
Philistines?" But Samson said to his father, "Get her for me, for
she [3]looks good to me."
4 However, his father and mother did not know that [a]it was
of the LORD, for He was seeking an occasion against the
Philistines. Now at that time the Philistines were ruling over
Israel.
5 Then Samson went down to Timnah with his father and
mother, and came as far as the vineyards of Timnah; and behold,
a young lion *came* roaring toward him.
6 [a]The Spirit of the LORD [1]came upon him mightily, so that
[b]he tore him as one tears a young goat though he had nothing in
his hand; but he did not tell his father or mother what he had
done.

17 [a]Gen 32:29
18 [1]I.e. incomprehensible [a]Is 9:6
19 [a]Judg 6:20, 21
20 [a]Lev 9:24; 1 Chr 21:16; Ezek 1:28; Matt 17:6
21 [a]Judg 13:16
22 [a]Gen 32:30; Deut 5:26; Judg 6:22
23 [a]Ps 25:14
24 [a]1 Sam 3:19; Luke 1:80
25 [1]I.e. the camp of Dan [a]Judg 3:10 [b]Judg 18:11, 12
14:2 [1]Lit *up* [2]Lit *mother, saying,*
3 [1]Lit *brothers* [2]Lit *my* [3]Lit *is right in my eyes* [a]Gen 24:3, 4 [b]Ex 34:16; Deut 7:3
4 [a]Josh 11:20
6 [1]Lit *rushed upon* [a]Judg 3:10 [b]1 Sam 17:34-36

7 So he went down and talked to the woman; and she [1]looked
good to Samson.
8 When he returned later to take her, he turned aside to look
at the carcass of the lion; and behold, a swarm of bees and
honey were in the body of the lion.
9 So he scraped [1]the honey into his [2]hands and went on,
eating as he went. When he came to his father and mother, he
gave *some* to them and they ate *it;* but he did not tell them that
he had scraped the honey out of the body of the lion.
10 Then his father went down to the woman; and Samson
made a feast there, for the young men customarily did this.
11 When they saw him, they brought thirty companions to be
with him.
12 Then Samson said to them, "Let me now [a]propound a
riddle to you; if you will indeed tell it to me within the seven
days of the feast, and find it out, then I will give you thirty
linen wraps and thirty [b]changes of clothes.
13 "But if you are unable to tell me, then you shall give me
thirty linen wraps and thirty changes of clothes." And they said
to him, "Propound your riddle, that we may hear it."
14 So he said to them,

"Out of the eater came something to eat,
And out of the strong came something sweet."

But they could not tell the riddle in three days.
15 Then it came about on the [1]fourth day that they said to
Samson's wife, "[a]Entice your husband, so that he will tell us the
riddle, [b]or we will burn you and your father's house with fire.
Have you invited us to impoverish us? Is this not *so?*"
16 Samson's wife wept before him and said, "[a]You only hate
me, and you do not love me; you have propounded a riddle to
the sons of my people, and have not told *it* to me." And he said
to her, "Behold, I have not told *it* to my father or mother; so
should I tell you?"
17 However she wept before him seven days while their feast
lasted. And on the seventh day he told her because she pressed
him so hard. She then told the riddle to the sons of her people.
18 So the men of the city said to him on the seventh day
before the sun went down,

"What is sweeter than honey?
And what is stronger than a lion?"

And he said to them,

"If you had not plowed with my heifer,
You would not have found out my riddle."

19 Then [a]the Spirit of the LORD [1]came upon him mightily, and
he went down to Ashkelon and killed thirty of them and took
their spoil and gave the changes *of clothes* to those who told
the riddle. And his anger burned, and he went up to his
father's house.
20 But Samson's wife was [a]*given* to his companion who had
been his [1]friend.

7 [1]Lit *was right in Samson's eyes*

9 [1]Lit *it* [2]Lit *palms*

12 [a]Ezek 17:2 [b]Gen 45:22; 2 Kin 5:22

15 [1]So with some ancient versions; Heb *seventh* [a]Judg 16:5 [b]Judg 15:6

16 [a]Judg 16:15

19 [1]Lit *rushed upon* [a]Judg 3:10; 13:25

20 [1]Or *best man* [a]Judg 15:2

Chapter 15 Theme ________________________

15 But after a while, in the time of wheat harvest, Samson
visited his wife [a]with a young goat, and said, "I will go in
to my wife in *her* room." But her father did not let him enter.
2 Her father said, "I really thought that you hated her
intensely; so I [a]gave her to your companion. Is not her younger
sister [1]more beautiful than she? Please let her be yours [2]instead."
3 Samson then said to them, "This time I shall be blameless
in regard to the Philistines when I do them harm."
4 Samson went and caught three hundred foxes, and took
torches, and turned *the foxes* tail to tail and put one torch in
the middle between two tails.
5 When he had set fire to the torches, he released [1]the foxes
into the standing grain of the Philistines, thus burning up both
the shocks and the standing grain, along with the vineyards
and groves.
6 Then the Philistines said, "Who did this?" And they said,
"Samson, the son-in-law of the Timnite, because [1]he took his
wife and gave her to his companion." So the Philistines came
up and [a]burned her and her father with fire.
7 Samson said to them, "Since you act like this, I will surely
take revenge on you, but after that I will quit."
8 He struck them [1]ruthlessly with a great slaughter; and he
went down and lived in the cleft of the rock of Etam.
9 Then the Philistines went up and camped in Judah, and
spread out in Lehi.
10 The men of Judah said, "Why have you come up against
us?" And they said, "We have come up to bind Samson in
order to do to him as he did to us."
11 Then 3,000 men of Judah went down to the cleft of the
rock of Etam and said to Samson, "Do you not know [a]that the
Philistines are rulers over us? What then is this that you have
done to us?" And he said to them, "As they did to me, so I
have done to them."
12 They said to him, "We have come down to bind you so that
we may give you into the hands of the Philistines." And Samson
said to them, "Swear to me that you will not [1]kill me."
13 So they said to [1]him, "No, but we will bind you fast and give
you into their hands; yet surely we will not kill you." Then
they bound him with two new ropes and brought him up from
the rock.
14 When he came to Lehi, the Philistines shouted as they met
him. And [a]the Spirit of the LORD [1]came upon him mightily so
that the ropes that were on his arms were as flax that is burned
with fire, and his bonds [2]dropped from his hands.
15 He found a fresh jawbone of a donkey, so he [1]reached out
and took it and [2]killed [a]a thousand men with it.
16 Then Samson said,

"With the jawbone of a donkey,
[1]Heaps upon heaps,
With the jawbone of a donkey
I have [2]killed a thousand men."

15:1 [a]Gen 38:17

2 [1]Lit *better* [2]Lit *instead of her* [a]Judg 14:20

5 [1]Lit *them*

6 [1]I.e. the Timnite [a]Judg 14:15

8 [1]Lit *leg on thigh*

11 [a]Lev 26:25; Deut 28:43f; Judg 13:1; 14:4; Ps 106:40-42

12 [1]Lit *fall upon me yourselves*

13 [1]Lit *him, saying*

14 [1]Lit *rushed upon* [2]Lit *were melted* [a]Judg 14:19; 1 Sam 11:6

15 [1]Lit *stretched out his hand* [2]Lit *smote* [a]Lev 26:8; Josh 23:10

16 [1]Lit *Heap, two heaps;* Heb is same root as donkey [2]Lit *smitten*

17 When he had finished speaking, he threw the jawbone from his hand; and he named that place [1]Ramath-lehi.
18 Then he became very thirsty, and he [a]called to the LORD and said, "You have given this great deliverance by the hand of Your servant, and now [1]shall I die of thirst [2]and fall into the hands of the uncircumcised?"
19 But God split the hollow place that is in Lehi so that water came out of it. When he drank, [a]his [1]strength returned and he revived. Therefore he named it [2]En-hakkore, which is in Lehi to this day.
20 So [a]he judged Israel twenty years in [b]the days of the Philistines.

Chapter 16 Theme ____________________

16 Now Samson went to [a]Gaza and saw a harlot there, and went in to her.
2 *When it was told* to the Gazites, saying, "Samson has come here," they [a]surrounded *the place* and lay in wait for him all night at the gate of the city. And they kept silent all night, saying, "*Let us wait* until the morning light, then we will kill him."
3 Now Samson lay until midnight, and at midnight he arose and took hold of the doors of the city gate and the two posts and pulled them up along with the bars; then he put them on his shoulders and carried them up to the top of the mountain which is opposite Hebron.
4 After this it came about that he loved a woman in the valley of Sorek, whose name was Delilah.
5 The [a]lords of the Philistines came up to her and said to her, "[b]Entice him, and see where his great strength *lies* and [1]how we may overpower him that we may bind him to afflict him. Then we will each give you eleven hundred *pieces* of silver."
6 So Delilah said to Samson, "Please tell me where your great strength is and [1]how you may be bound to afflict you."
7 Samson said to her, "If they bind me with seven fresh cords that have not been dried, then I will become weak and be like any *other* man."
8 Then the lords of the Philistines brought up to her seven fresh cords that had not been dried, and she bound him with them.
9 Now she had *men* lying in wait in an inner room. And she said to him, "The Philistines are upon you, Samson!" But he snapped the cords as a string of tow snaps when it [1]touches fire. So his strength was not discovered.
10 Then Delilah said to Samson, "Behold, you have deceived me and told me lies; now please tell me [1]how you may be bound."
11 He said to her, "If they bind me tightly with new ropes [1]which have not been used, then I will become weak and be like any *other* man."
12 So Delilah took new ropes and bound him with them and said to him, "The Philistines are upon you, Samson!" For the

17 [1]I.e. the high place of the jawbone

18 [1]Or *I shall . . . uncircumcised* [2]Or *or* [a]Judg 16:28

19 [1]Lit *spirit* [2]I.e. the spring of him who called [a]Is 40:29

20 [a]Judg 16:31; Heb 11:32 [b]Judg 13:1

16:1 [a]Josh 15:47

2 [a]1 Sam 23:26; Ps 118:10-12

5 [1]Lit *by what* [a]Josh 13:3 [b]Judg 14:15

6 [1]Lit *by what*

9 [1]Lit *smells*

10 [1]Lit *by what*

11 [1]Lit *with which work has not been done*

men were lying in wait in the inner room. But he snapped [1]the
ropes from his arms like a thread.
13 Then Delilah said to Samson, "Up to now you have deceived
me and told me lies; tell me [1]how you may be bound." And he
said to her, "If you weave the seven locks of my [2]hair with the
web [3][and fasten it with a pin, then I will become weak and be
like any other man."
14 So while he slept, Delilah took the seven locks of his [1]hair
and wove them into the web]. And she fastened *it* with the pin
and said to him, "The Philistines are upon you, Samson!" But
he awoke from his sleep and pulled out the pin of the loom and
the web.
15 Then she said to him, "[a]How can you say, 'I love you,'
when your heart is not with me? You have deceived me these
three times and have not told me where your great strength is."
16 It came about when she pressed him daily with her words
and urged him, that his soul was [1]annoyed to death.
17 So he told her all *that was* in his heart and said to her, "A
razor has never come on my head, for I have been a [a]Nazirite
to God from my mother's womb. If I am shaved, then my
strength will leave me and I will become weak and be like any
other man."
18 When Delilah saw that he had told her all *that was* in his
heart, she sent and called the lords of the Philistines, saying,
"Come up once more, for he has told me all *that is* in his heart."
Then the lords of the Philistines came up to her and brought
the money in their hands.
19 She made him sleep on her knees, and called for a man
and had him shave off the seven locks of his [1]hair. Then she
began to afflict him, and his strength left him.
20 She said, "The Philistines are upon you, Samson!" And he
awoke from his sleep and said, "I will go out as at other times
and shake myself free." But he did not know that [a]the LORD
had departed from him.
21 Then the Philistines seized him and gouged out his eyes;
and they brought him down to Gaza and bound him with
bronze chains, and he was a grinder in the prison.
22 However, the hair of his head began to grow again after it
was shaved off.
23 Now the lords of the Philistines assembled to offer a great
sacrifice to [a]Dagon their god, and to rejoice, for they said,
"Our god has given Samson our enemy into our hands."
24 When the people saw him, [a]they praised their god, for they
said,
"Our god has given our enemy into our hands,
Even the destroyer of our country,
Who has slain many of us."
25 It so happened when [1]they were in high spirits, that they
said, "Call for Samson, that he may amuse us." So they called
for Samson from the prison, and he [2]entertained them. And
they made him stand between the pillars.

12 [1]Lit *them*

13 [1]Lit *by what* [2]Lit *head* [3]The passage in brackets is found in Gr but not in any Heb mss

14 [1]Lit *head*

15 [a]Judg 14:16

16 [1]Lit *impatient to the point of*

17 [a]Num 6:2, 5; Judg 13:5

19 [1]Lit *head*

20 [a]Num 14:42, 43; Josh 7:12; 1 Sam 16:14

23 [a]1 Sam 5:2

24 [a]1 Sam 31:9; 1 Chr 10:9; Ps 97:7

25 [1]Lit *their heart was pleasant* [2]Lit *made sport before them*

28 [1]Heb *YHWH*, usually rendered *LORD* [a]Judg 15:18 [b]Jer 15:15

30 [1]Lit *strength*

31 [a]Judg 15:20

17:2 [1]Lit *and also spoke it in my ears*

3 [1]Lit *it* [a]Ex 20:4, 23; 34:17

4 [1]Lit *it* [2]Lit *it was*

5 [1]Lit *house of gods* [2]Heb *teraphim* [3]Lit *filled the hand of* [a]Judg 18:24 [b]Judg 8:27; 18:14 [c]Gen 31:19 [d]Num 3:10

6 [a]Judg 18:1; 19:1 [b]Deut 12:8; Judg 21:25

7 [1]Or *sojourning* [a]Judg 19:1; Ruth 1:1, 2; Mic 5:2; Matt 2:1

8 [1]Or *sojourn* [a]Josh 24:33

26 Then Samson said to the boy who was holding his hand,
"Let me feel the pillars on which the house rests, that I may
lean against them."
27 Now the house was full of men and women, and all the lords
of the Philistines were there. And about 3,000 men and women
were on the roof looking on while Samson was amusing *them.*
28 [a]Then Samson called to the LORD and said, "O Lord [1]GOD,
please remember me and please strengthen me just this time,
O God, that I may at once [b]be avenged of the Philistines for my
two eyes."
29 Samson grasped the two middle pillars on which the house
rested, and braced himself against them, the one with his right
hand and the other with his left.
30 And Samson said, "Let me die with the Philistines!" And
he bent with [1]all his might so that the house fell on the lords
and all the people who were in it. So the dead whom he killed
at his death were more than those whom he killed in his life.
31 Then his brothers and all his father's household came down,
took him, brought him up and buried him between Zorah and
Eshtaol in the tomb of Manoah his father. [a]Thus he had judged
Israel twenty years.

Chapter 17 Theme ______________________

17 Now there was a man of the hill country of Ephraim
whose name was Micah.
2 He said to his mother, "The eleven hundred *pieces* of silver
which were taken from you, about which you uttered a curse
[1]in my hearing, behold, the silver is with me; I took it." And
his mother said, "Blessed be my son by the LORD."
3 He then returned the eleven hundred *pieces* of silver to his
mother, and his mother said, "I wholly dedicate the silver from
my hand to the LORD for my son [a]to make a graven image and a
molten image; now therefore, I will return [1]them to you."
4 So when he returned the silver to his mother, his mother
took two hundred *pieces* of silver and gave them to the
silversmith who made [1]them into a graven image and a molten
image, and [2]they were in the house of Micah.
5 And the man Micah had a [1a]shrine and he made an [b]ephod
and [2c]household idols and [3]consecrated one of his sons, [d]that
he might become his priest.
6 In those days [a]there was no king in Israel; [b]every man did
what was right in his own eyes.
7 Now there was a young man from [a]Bethlehem in Judah, of
the family of Judah, who was a Levite; and he was [1]staying
there.
8 Then the man departed from the city, from Bethlehem in
Judah, to [1]stay wherever he might find *a place;* and as he made
his journey, he came to the [a]hill country of Ephraim to the
house of Micah.

9 Micah said to him, "Where do you come from?" And he
said to him, "I am a Levite from Bethlehem in Judah, and I am
going to [1]stay wherever I may find *a place.*"
10 Micah then said to him, "Dwell with me and be [a]a father
and a priest to me, and I will give you ten *pieces* of silver a year,
a suit of clothes, and your maintenance." So the Levite went *in.*
11 The Levite agreed to live with the man, and the young man
became to him like one of his sons.
12 So Micah [1]consecrated the Levite, and the young man
[a]became his priest and [2]lived in the house of Micah.
13 Then Micah said, "Now I know that the LORD will prosper
me, seeing I have a Levite as priest."

Chapter 18 Theme ____________________________

18 [a]In those days there was no king of Israel; and [b]in those
days the tribe of the Danites was seeking an inheritance
for themselves to live in, for until that day [1]an inheritance had
not [2]been allotted to them as a possession among the tribes of
Israel.
2 So the sons of Dan sent from their family five men out of
their whole number, [1]valiant men from [a]Zorah and Eshtaol, to
spy out the land and to search it; and they said to them, "Go,
search the land." And they came to [b]the hill country of Ephraim,
to the house of Micah, and lodged there.
3 When they were near the house of Micah, they recognized
the voice of the young man, the Levite; and they turned aside
there and said to him, "Who brought you here? And what are
you doing in this *place?* And what do you have here?"
4 He said to them, "Thus and so has Micah done to me, and
he has hired me and [a]I have become his priest."
5 They said to him, "Inquire of God, please, that we may know
whether our way on which we are going will be prosperous."
6 The priest said to them, "Go in peace; your way in which
you are going [1]has the LORD's approval."
7 Then the five men departed and came to [a]Laish and saw
the people who were in it living in security, after the manner
of the Sidonians, quiet and secure; for there was no [1]ruler
humiliating *them* for anything in the land, and they were far
from the Sidonians and had no dealings with anyone.
8 When they came back to their brothers at Zorah and
Eshtaol, their brothers said to them, "What *do* you *report?*"
9 They said, "Arise, and let us go up against them; for we
have seen the land, and behold, it is very good. And will you
[1]sit still? Do not delay to go, to enter, to possess the land.
10 "When you enter, you will come to a secure people with a
spacious land; for God has given it into your hand, [a]a place
where there is no lack of anything that is on the earth."
11 Then from the family of the Danites, from Zorah and from
Eshtaol, six hundred men armed with weapons of war set out.

9 [1]Or *sojourn*

10 [a]Judg 18:19

12 [1]Lit *filled the hand of* [2]Lit *was* [a]Num 16:10; 18:1-7

18:1 [1]Lit *it* [2]Lit *fallen* [a]Judg 17:6; 19:1 [b]Josh 19:40-48

2 [1]Lit *men, sons of valor* [a]Judg 13:25 [b]Judg 17:1

4 [a]Judg 17:12

6 [1]Lit *is before the LORD*

7 [1]Lit *possessor of restraint* [a]Josh 19:47; Judg 18:29

9 [1]Lit *be*

10 [a]Deut 8:9

12 They went up and camped at Kiriath-jearim in Judah.
Therefore they called that place [1a]Mahaneh-dan to this day;
behold, it is [2]west of Kiriath-jearim.
13 They passed from there to the hill country of Ephraim and
came to the house of Micah.
14 Then the five men who went to spy out the country of
Laish said to their kinsmen, "Do you know that there are in
these houses [a]an ephod and [1]household idols and a graven
image and a molten image? Now therefore, consider what you
should do."
15 They turned aside there and came to the house of the
young man, the Levite, to the house of Micah, and asked him
of his welfare.
16 The six hundred men armed with their weapons of war,
who were of the sons of Dan, stood by the entrance of the gate.
17 Now the five men who went to spy out the land went up
and entered there, *and* took [a]the graven image and the ephod
and [1]household idols and the molten image, while the priest
stood by the entrance of the gate with the six hundred men
armed with weapons of war.
18 When these went into Micah's house and took the graven
image, the ephod and [1]household idols and the molten image,
the priest said to them, "What are you doing?"
19 They said to him, "Be silent, [a]put your hand over your
mouth and come with us, and be to us [b]a father and a priest. Is
it better for you to be a priest to the house of one man, or to be
priest to a tribe and a family in Israel?"
20 The priest's heart was glad, and he took the ephod and
[1]household idols and the graven image and went among the
people.
21 Then they turned and departed, and put the little ones and
the livestock and the valuables in front of them.
22 When they had gone some distance from the house of
Micah, the men who *were* in the houses near Micah's house
assembled and overtook the sons of Dan.
23 They cried to the sons of Dan, who turned [1]around and said
to Micah, "What is *the matter* with you, that you have assembled
together?"
24 He said, "You have taken away my gods which I made, and
the priest, and have gone away, and what do I have besides? So
how can you say to me, 'What is *the matter* with you?'"
25 The sons of Dan said to him, "Do not let your voice be
heard among us, or else [1]fierce men will fall upon you and you
will [2]lose your life, with the lives of your household."
26 So the sons of Dan went on their way; and when Micah
saw that they were too strong for him, he turned and went
back to his house.
27 Then they took what Micah had made and the priest who
had belonged to him, and came to [a]Laish, to a people quiet and
secure, and struck them with the edge of the sword; and they
burned the city with fire.

12 [1]I.e. the camp of Dan [2]Lit *behind* [a]Judg 13:25
14 [1]Heb *teraphim* [a]Judg 17:5
17 [1]Heb *teraphim* [a]Gen 31:19, 30; Is 41:29; Mic 5:13
18 [1]Heb *teraphim*
19 [a]Job 21:5; 29:9; 40:4 [b]Judg 17:10
20 [1]Heb *teraphim*
23 [1]Lit *their faces*
25 [1]Lit *bitter of soul* [2]Lit *gather*
27 [a]Josh 19:47; Judg 18:7

28 And there was no one to deliver *them,* because it was far from Sidon and they had no dealings with anyone, and it was in the valley which is near [a]Beth-rehob. And they rebuilt the city and lived in it.

29 [a]They called the name of the city Dan, after the name of Dan their father who was born in Israel; however, the name of the city formerly was Laish.

30 The sons of Dan set up for themselves [a]the graven image; and Jonathan, the son of [b]Gershom, the son of [1]Manasseh, [a]he and his sons were priests to the tribe of the Danites until the day of the captivity of the land.

31 So they set up for themselves Micah's graven image which he had made, all the time that the [a]house of God was at Shiloh.

Chapter 19 Theme ______________________

19 Now it came about in those days, when [a]there was no king in Israel, that there was a certain Levite [1]staying in the remote part of the hill country of Ephraim, who took a concubine for himself from Bethlehem in Judah.

2 But his concubine played the harlot against him, and she went away from him to her father's house in Bethlehem in Judah, and was there for a period of four months.

3 Then her husband arose and went after her to [a]speak [1]tenderly to her in order to bring her back, [2]taking with him his servant and a pair of donkeys. So she brought him into her father's house, and when the girl's father saw him, he was glad to meet him.

4 His father-in-law, the girl's father, detained him; and he remained with him three days. So they ate and drank and lodged there.

5 Now on the fourth day they got up early in the morning, and he [1]prepared to go; and the girl's father said to his son-in-law, "[a]Sustain [2]yourself with a piece of bread, and afterward you may go."

6 So both of them sat down and ate and drank together; and the girl's father said to the man, "Please be willing to spend the night, and [a]let your heart be merry."

7 Then the man arose to go, but his father-in-law urged him so that he spent the night there again.

8 On the fifth day he arose to go early in the morning, and the girl's father said, "Please sustain [1]yourself, and wait until [2]afternoon"; so both of them ate.

9 When the man arose to go along with his concubine and servant, his father-in-law, the girl's father, said to him, "Behold now, the day has drawn [1]to a close; please spend the night. Lo, the day is [2]coming to an end; spend the night here that your heart may be merry. Then tomorrow you may arise early for your journey so that you may go [3]home."

10 But the man was not willing to spend the night, so he arose and departed and came to *a place* opposite [a]Jebus (that is,

28 [a]2 Sam 10:6

29 [a]Josh 19:47

30 [1]Some ancient versions read *Moses* [a]Judg 17:3, 5 [b]Ex 2:22; 18:3

31 [a]Josh 18:1

19:1 [1]Or *sojourning* [a]Judg 18:1

3 [1]Lit *to her heart* [2]Lit *and* [a]Gen 34:3; 50:21

5 [1]Lit *arose* [2]Lit *your heart* [a]Gen 18:5; Judg 19:8

6 [a]Judg 16:25; 19:9, 22; Ruth 3:7; 1 Kin 21:7; Esth 1:10

8 [1]Lit *your heart* [2]Lit *the day declines*

9 [1]Lit *toward evening* [2]Lit *declining* [3]Lit *to your tent*

10 [a]1 Chr 11:4, 5

Jerusalem). And there were with him a pair of saddled donkeys;
his concubine also was with him.
11 When they *were* near Jebus, the day was almost gone; and
[a]the servant said to his master, "Please come, and let us turn
aside into this city of the Jebusites and spend the night in it."
12 However, his master said to him, "We will not turn aside
into the city of foreigners who are not of the sons of Israel; but
we will go on as far as Gibeah."
13 He said to his servant, "Come and let us approach one of
these places; and we will spend the night in Gibeah or Ramah."
14 So they passed along and went their way, and the sun set
on them near Gibeah which belongs to Benjamin.
15 They turned aside there in order to enter *and* lodge in
Gibeah. When [1]they entered, [1]they sat down in the open square
of the city, for no one took them into *his* house to spend the
night.
16 Then behold, an old man was coming out of the field from
his work at evening. Now the man was from [a]the hill country
of Ephraim, and he was [1]staying in Gibeah, but the men of the
place [b]were Benjamites.
17 And he lifted up his eyes and saw the traveler in the open
square of the city; and the old man said, "Where are you going,
and where do you come from?"
18 He said to him, "We are passing from Bethlehem in Judah
to the remote part of the hill country of Ephraim, *for* I am from
there, and I went to Bethlehem in Judah. But I am *now* going
to [1]my house, and no man will take me into his house.
19 "Yet there is both straw and fodder for our donkeys, and also
bread and wine for me, [1]your maidservant, and [a]the young man
who is with your servants; there is no lack of anything."
20 The old man said, "[a]Peace to you. Only let me *take care of* all
your needs; however, do not spend the night in the open square."
21 [a]So he took him into his house and gave the donkeys fodder,
and they washed their feet and ate and drank.
22 While they were [1]celebrating, behold, [a]the men of the city,
certain [2b]worthless fellows, surrounded the house, pounding
the door; and they spoke to the owner of the house, the old
man, saying, "Bring out the man who came into your house
that we may have [3]relations with him."
23 Then the man, the owner of the house, went out to them
and said to them, "No, my fellows, please do not act so wickedly;
since this man has come into my house, [a]do not commit this
act of folly.
24 "[a]Here is my virgin daughter and his concubine. Please let
me bring them out that you may ravish them and do to them
[1]whatever you wish. But do not commit such an act of folly
against this man."
25 But the men would not listen to him. So the man seized his
concubine and brought *her* out to them; and they raped her
and abused her all night until morning, then let her go at the
approach of dawn.

11 [a]Judg 19:19
15 [1]So with Gr; M.T. *he*
16 [1]Or *sojourning* [a]Judg 19:1 [b]Judg 19:14
18 [1]Heb *the house of the LORD*, cf v 29
19 [1]I.e. my concubine [a]Judg 19:11
20 [a]Gen 43:23; Judg 6:23
21 [a]Gen 24:32, 33
22 [1]Lit *making their hearts merry* [2]Lit *sons of Belial* [3]Lit *intercourse* [a]Gen 19:4, 5; Ezek 16:46-48 [b]Deut 13:13; 1 Sam 2:12; 1 Kin 21:10; 2 Cor 6:15
23 [a]Gen 34:7; Deut 22:21; Judg 20:6; 2 Sam 13:12
24 [1]Lit *the good in your eyes* [a]Gen 19:8

26 [1]As the day began to dawn, the woman came and fell down at the doorway of the man's house where her master was, until *full* daylight.

27 When her master arose in the morning and opened the doors of the house and went out to go on his way, then behold, his concubine was lying at the doorway of the house with her hands on the threshold.

28 He said to her, "Get up and let us go," [a]but there was no answer. Then he placed her on the donkey; and the man arose and went to his [1]home.

29 When he entered his house, he took a knife and laid hold of his concubine and [a]cut her in twelve pieces, limb by limb, and sent her throughout the territory of Israel.

30 All who saw *it* said, "Nothing like this has *ever* happened or been seen from the day when the sons of Israel came up from the land of Egypt to this day. Consider it, [a]take counsel and speak up!"

Chapter 20 Theme ________________________

20 Then all the sons of Israel from Dan to Beersheba, including the land of Gilead, came out, and the congregation assembled as one man to the LORD at [a]Mizpah.

2 The [1]chiefs of all the people, *even* of all the tribes of Israel, took their stand in the assembly of the people of God, 400,000 foot [2]soldiers [a]who drew the sword.

3 (Now the sons of Benjamin heard that the sons of Israel had gone up to Mizpah.) And the sons of Israel said, "Tell *us,* how did this wickedness take place?"

4 So the Levite, the husband of the woman who was murdered, answered and said, "I came with my concubine to spend the night at Gibeah which belongs to Benjamin.

5 "But the [a]men of Gibeah rose up against me and surrounded the house at night because of me. They intended to kill me; instead, they [b]ravished my concubine so that she died.

6 "And I [a]took hold of my concubine and cut her in pieces and sent her throughout the land of Israel's inheritance; for [b]they have committed a lewd and disgraceful act in Israel.

7 "Behold, all you sons of Israel, [a]give your advice and counsel here."

8 Then all the people arose as one man, saying, "Not one of us will go to his tent, nor will any of us return to his house.

9 "But now this is the thing which we will do to Gibeah; *we will go up* against it by lot.

10 "And we will take 10 men out of 100 throughout the tribes of Israel, and 100 out of 1,000, and 1,000 out of 10,000 to [1]supply food for the people, that when they come to [2]Gibeah of Benjamin, they may [3]punish *them* for all the disgraceful acts that they have committed in Israel."

11 Thus all the men of Israel were gathered against the city, united as one man.

26 [1]Lit *At the turning of the morning*

28 [1]Lit *place* [a]Judg 20:5

29 [a]1 Sam 11:7

30 [a]Judg 20:7; Prov 13:10

20:1 [a]1 Sam 7:5

2 [1]Lit *cornerstones* [2]Lit *men* [a]Judg 8:10

5 [a]Judg 19:22 [b]Judg 19:25f

6 [a]Judg 19:29 [b]Gen 34:7; Josh 7:15

7 [a]Judg 19:30

10 [1]Lit *take* [2]Heb *Geba* [3]Lit *do*

12 Then the tribes of Israel sent men through the entire [1]tribe
of Benjamin, saying, "What is this wickedness that has taken
place among you?
13 "Now then, deliver up the men, the [1a]worthless fellows in
Gibeah, that we may put them to death and [b]remove *this*
wickedness from Israel." But the sons of Benjamin would not
listen to the voice of their brothers, the sons of Israel.
14 The sons of Benjamin gathered from the cities to Gibeah,
to go out to battle against the sons of Israel.
15 From the cities on that day the [a]sons of Benjamin were
[1]numbered, 26,000 men who draw the sword, besides the
inhabitants of Gibeah who were [1]numbered, 700 choice men.
16 Out of all these people 700 [a]choice men were left-handed;
each one could sling a stone at a hair and not miss.
17 Then the men of Israel besides Benjamin were [1]numbered,
400,000 men who draw the sword; all these were men of war.
18 Now the sons of Israel arose, went up to Bethel, and
[a]inquired of God and said, "Who shall go up first for us to battle
against the sons of Benjamin?" Then the LORD said, "Judah
shall go up first."
19 So the sons of Israel arose in the morning and camped
against Gibeah.
20 The men of Israel went out to battle against Benjamin, and
the men of Israel arrayed for battle against them at Gibeah.
21 Then the sons of Benjamin came out of Gibeah and [1a]felled
to the ground on that day 22,000 men of Israel.
22 But the people, the men of Israel, encouraged themselves
and arrayed for battle again in the place where they had
arrayed themselves the first day.
23 [a]The sons of Israel went up and wept before the LORD until
evening, and [b]inquired of the LORD, saying, "Shall we again
draw near for battle against the sons of my brother Benjamin?"
And the LORD said, "Go up against him."
24 Then the sons of Israel [1]came against the sons of Benjamin
the second day.
25 Benjamin went out [1]against them from Gibeah the second
day and [2]felled to the ground again 18,000 men of the sons of
Israel; all these drew the sword.
26 Then [a]all the sons of Israel and all the people went up and
came to Bethel and wept; thus they remained there before the
LORD and fasted that day until evening. And they offered burnt
offerings and peace offerings before the LORD.
27 The sons of Israel [a]inquired of the LORD (for the ark of the
covenant of God *was* there in those days,
28 and Phinehas the son of Eleazar, Aaron's son, stood before
it to *minister* in those days), saying, "Shall I yet again go out to
battle against the sons of my brother Benjamin, or shall I cease?"
And the LORD said, "Go up, [a]for tomorrow I will deliver them
into your hand."
29 [a]So Israel set men in ambush around Gibeah.

12 [1]Lit *tribes*
13 [1]Lit *sons of Belial* [a]2 Cor 6:15 [b]Deut 13:5; 17:12; 1 Cor 5:13
15 [1]Or *mustered* [a]Num 1:36, 37; 2:23; 26:41
16 [a]Judg 3:15; 1 Chr 12:2
17 [1]Or *mustered*
18 [a]Num 27:21; Judg 20:23, 27
21 [1]Lit *destroyed* [a]Judg 20:25
23 [a]Josh 7:6, 7 [b]Judg 20:18
24 [1]Lit *approached*
25 [1]Lit *to meet* [2]Lit *destroyed*
26 [a]Judg 20:23; 21:2
27 [a]Judg 20:18
28 [a]Judg 7:9
29 [a]Josh 8:4

30 The sons of Israel went up against the sons of Benjamin on
the third day and arrayed themselves against Gibeah as at other
times.
31 [a]The sons of Benjamin went out [1]against the people and
were drawn away from the city, and they began to strike [2]and
kill some of the people as at other times, on the highways, one
of which goes up to Bethel and the other to Gibeah, *and* in the
field, about thirty men of Israel.
32 The sons of Benjamin said, "They are struck down before
us, as at the first." But the sons of Israel said, "Let us flee that
we may draw them away from the city to the highways."
33 Then all the men of Israel arose from their place and
arrayed themselves at Baal-tamar; [a]and the men of Israel in
ambush broke out of their place, even out of Maareh-geba.
34 When ten thousand choice men from all Israel came
against Gibeah, the battle became [1]fierce; [a]but [2]Benjamin did
not know that [3]disaster was [4]close to them.
35 And the LORD struck Benjamin before Israel, so that the
sons of Israel destroyed 25,100 men of Benjamin that day, all
[1]who draw the sword.
36 So the sons of Benjamin saw that they were [1]defeated.
[a]When the men of Israel gave [2]ground to Benjamin because
they relied on the men in ambush whom they had set against
Gibeah,
37 [a]the men in ambush hurried and rushed against Gibeah;
the men in ambush also deployed and struck all the city with
the edge of the sword.
38 Now the appointed sign between the men of Israel and the
men in ambush was [a]that they would make a great cloud of
smoke rise from the city.
39 Then the men of Israel turned in the battle, and Benjamin
began to strike [1]and kill about thirty men of Israel, [a]for they
said, "Surely they are [2]defeated before us, as in the first battle."
40 But when the cloud began to rise from the city in a column
of smoke, Benjamin looked [a]behind them; and behold, the
whole city was going up *in smoke* to heaven.
41 Then the men of Israel turned, and the men of Benjamin
were terrified; for they saw that [1a]disaster was [2]close to them.
42 Therefore, they turned their backs before the men of Israel
[a]toward the direction of the wilderness, but the battle overtook
them while those who came out of the cities destroyed them in
the midst of them.
43 [a]They surrounded Benjamin, pursued them without rest
and trod them down opposite Gibeah toward the [1]east.
44 Thus 18,000 men of Benjamin fell; all these were valiant
warriors.
45 [1]The rest turned and fled toward the wilderness to the rock
of [a]Rimmon, but they [2]caught 5,000 of them on the highways
and overtook them [3]at Gidom and [4]killed 2,000 of them.
46 So all of Benjamin who fell that day were 25,000 men who
draw the sword; all these were valiant warriors.

31 [1]Lit *to meet* [2]Lit *slain ones* [a]Josh 8:16

33 [a]Josh 8:19

34 [1]Lit *heavy* [2]Lit *they* [3]Lit *evil* [4]Lit *touching* [a]Josh 8:14; Job 21:13

35 [1]Lit *these*

36 [1]Lit *smitten* [2]Lit *place* [a]Josh 8:15

37 [a]Josh 8:19

38 [a]Josh 8:20

39 [1]Lit *slain ones* [2]Lit *smitten* [a]Judg 20:32

40 [a]Josh 8:20

41 [1]Lit *evil* [2]Lit *touching* [a]Prov 5:22; 11:5, 6; 29:6

42 [a]Josh 8:15, 24

43 [1]Lit *sunrise* [a]Hos 9:9; 10:9

45 [1]So with Gr; Heb *And they* [2]Lit *gleaned* [3]Lit *as far as* [4]Lit *smote* [a]Judg 21:13

47 But 600 men turned and fled toward the wilderness to the
rock of Rimmon, and they remained at the rock of Rimmon
four months.
48 The men of Israel then turned back against the sons of
Benjamin and struck them with the edge of the sword, both
the entire city with the cattle and all that they found; they also
set on fire all the cities which they found.

Chapter 21 Theme ______________________

21 Now the men of Israel [a]had sworn in Mizpah, saying,
"None of us shall give his daughter to Benjamin [1]in
marriage."
2 [a]So the people came to Bethel and sat there before God until
evening, and lifted up their voices and wept [1]bitterly.
3 They said, "Why, O LORD, God of Israel, has this come about
in Israel, so that one tribe should be *missing* today in Israel?"
4 It came about the next day that the people arose early and
built [a]an altar there and offered burnt offerings and peace
offerings.
5 Then the sons of Israel said, "Who is there among all the
tribes of Israel who did not come up in the assembly to the
LORD?" For [1]they had taken a great oath concerning him [a]who
did not come up to the LORD at Mizpah, saying, "He shall
surely be put to death."
6 And the sons of Israel were sorry for their brother Benjamin
and said, "One tribe is cut off from Israel today.
7 "What shall we do for wives for those who are left, since we
have [a]sworn by the LORD not to give them any of our daughters
in marriage?"
8 And they said, "What one is there of the tribes of Israel
who did not come up to the LORD at Mizpah?" And behold, no
one had come to the camp from Jabesh-gilead to the assembly.
9 For when the people were [1]numbered, behold, not one of
the inhabitants of Jabesh-gilead was there.
10 And the congregation sent 12,000 of the valiant warriors
there, and commanded them, saying, "Go and [a]strike the
inhabitants of Jabesh-gilead with the edge of the sword, with
the women and the little ones.
11 "This is the thing that you shall do: you [a]shall utterly destroy
every man and every woman who has [1]lain with a man."
12 And they found among the inhabitants of Jabesh-gilead 400
young virgins who had not known a man by lying with [1]him;
and they brought them to the camp at Shiloh, which is in the
land of Canaan.
13 Then the whole congregation sent *word* and spoke to the
sons of Benjamin who were [a]at the rock of Rimmon, and
[b]proclaimed peace to them.
14 Benjamin returned at that time, and they gave them the
women whom they had kept alive from the women of Jabesh-
gilead; yet they [1]were not enough for them.

21:1 [1]Lit *for a wife* [a]Judg 21:7, 18
2 [1]Lit *with great weeping* [a]Judg 20:26
4 [a]Deut 12:5; 2 Sam 24:25
5 [1]Lit *there was a great oath* [a]Judg 5:23
7 [a]Judg 21:1
9 [1]Or *mustered*
10 [a]Num 31:17; Judg 5:23; 1 Sam 11:7
11 [1]Lit *known lying with* [a]Num 31:17
12 [1]Lit *a male*
13 [a]Judg 20:47 [b]Deut 20:10
14 [1]Lit *did not find it so*

15 And the people were sorry for Benjamin because the LORD
had made a breach in the tribes of Israel.
16 Then the elders of the congregation said, "What shall we
do for wives for those who are left, since the women are
destroyed out of Benjamin?"
17 They said, "*There must be* an inheritance for the survivors
of Benjamin, so that a tribe will not be blotted out from Israel.
18 "But we cannot give them wives of our daughters." For the
sons of Israel [a]had sworn, saying, "Cursed is he who gives a
wife to Benjamin."
19 So they said, "Behold, there is a feast of the LORD from year
to year in [a]Shiloh, which is on the north side of Bethel, on the
east side of the highway that goes up from Bethel to Shechem,
and on the south side of Lebonah."
20 And they commanded the sons of Benjamin, saying, "Go
and lie in wait in the vineyards,
21 and watch; and behold, if the daughters of Shiloh come out
to [1a]take part in the dances, then you shall come out of the
vineyards and each of you shall catch his wife from the
daughters of Shiloh, and go to the land of Benjamin.
22 "It shall come about, when their fathers or their brothers
come to complain to us, that we shall say to them, 'Give them
to us voluntarily, because we did not take for each man *of
Benjamin* [1]a wife in battle, [2a]nor did you give *them* to them,
else you would now be guilty.'"
23 The sons of Benjamin did so, and took wives according to
their number from those who danced, whom they carried
away. And they went and returned to their inheritance and
[a]rebuilt the cities and lived in them.
24 The sons of Israel departed from there at that time, every
man to his tribe and family, and each one of them went out
from there to his inheritance.
25 [a]In those days there was no king in Israel; everyone did
what was right in his own eyes.

18 [a]Judg 21:1

19 [a]Josh 18:1; Judg 18:31; 1 Sam 1:3

21 [1]Lit *dance* [a]Ex 15:20; Judg 11:34

22 [1]Lit *his* [2]Lit *because* [a]Judg 21:1, 18

23 [a]Judg 20:48

25 [a]Judg 17:6; 18:1; 19:1

The Judges of Israel

Judge	Chapter/ Verse	Years Judged	Major Facts/Accomplishments	Lessons for My Life

Theme of Judges:

SEGMENT DIVISIONS

OPPRESSOR	JUDGE AND YEARS RULED	CHAPTER THEMES
		1
		2
		3
		4
		5
		6
		7
		8
		9
		10
		11
		12
		13
		14
		15
		16
		17
		18
		19
		20
		21

Author:

Date:

Purpose:

Key Words:

covenant

sons of Israel di[d] evil

sold (served)

sons of Israel c[ried]

the Lord raised a deliverer (or judge)

judge(s)

RUTH רות
RUT

The events recorded in the book of Ruth take place during the dark years of the judges. This book offers encouragement and hope to those who decide to follow God. This story of love and dedication revolves around three people who determine in their hearts to walk in integrity, clinging to their God and His precepts—three people who know who their King is and who do what is right in His eyes.

Things to Do

1. As you read Ruth one chapter at a time:
   a. First read each chapter simply to catch the flavor of the lives of these people.
   b. Then read each chapter again, focusing on the "who" and the "what." Look at the main characters mentioned in each chapter. Note the sequence of events and how each character confronts and deals with his or her situations. Note how chapter 1 gives you the historical context of Ruth.
   c. Watch for and mark the key repeated words listed on the RUTH AT A GLANCE chart on page 445. After you finish marking key words in a chapter, observe what you learn about each. If there is something significant you want to remember, write it in the margin.

2. Determine the theme of each chapter and record it on RUTH AT A GLANCE and at the beginning of each chapter in your Bible.

3. When you finish reading Ruth and marking every reference to *redeem*, *kinsman*, and *closest relative:*
   a. List everything you learn about the process of redeeming a close relative. Pay attention to the process in chapter 4.
   b. Look up the laws regarding redemption in Leviticus 25:23-28 and Deuteronomy 25:5-10. You may want to record these cross-references next to your insights on *redemption.*

4. Complete RUTH AT A GLANCE.

Things to Think About

1. What have you learned about loyalty from the story of Ruth? What does it mean to be loyal to God, to His people, to His precepts, and to trust God to do what He says He will do?

2. As you think of Boaz redeeming Ruth, remember that you have a Kinsman Redeemer, the Lord Jesus Christ. Think of how the Lord has acted on your behalf as your Kinsman Redeemer by becoming a man so He could break death's hold by paying for your sin (Hebrews 2:14-15). Remember that you were not redeemed from your empty way of life with silver or gold, but with the precious blood of the Lamb of God, a Lamb without spot or blemish (1 Peter 1:18-19).

3. The final verses of Ruth show us that Ruth was included in the genealogy of David and therefore in the human lineage of our Lord Jesus Christ. Not only did a sovereign God include Rahab the harlot in the genealogy of His Son, but He also chose a Gentile, Ruth. Both of these women chose to believe God when those around them didn't! Consider how their example might apply to your life.

4. In the book of Judges, Israel forsook the true God and turned to idols, while in Ruth we see the opposite. One Gentile woman turns from idols to serve the only true God. In which category do you find yourself?

Chapter 1 Theme ______________________________

1:1 [1]Or *judged* [2]Lit *he, and* [a]Judg 2:16-18 [b]Gen 12:10; 26:1; 2 Kin 8:1 [c]Judg 17:8; Mic 5:2

1 Now it came about in the days [a]when the judges [1]governed,
that there was [b]a famine in the land. And a certain man [c]of
Bethlehem in Judah went to sojourn in the land of Moab [2]with
his wife and his two sons.
2 The name of the man *was* Elimelech, and the name of his
wife, Naomi; and the names of his two sons *were* Mahlon and
Chilion, Ephrathites of Bethlehem in Judah. Now they [a]entered
the land of Moab and remained there.
3 Then Elimelech, Naomi's husband, died; and she was left
with her two sons. 2 [a]Judg 3:30
4 They took for themselves Moabite women *as* wives; the
name of the one was Orpah and the name of the other Ruth.
And they lived there about ten years.
5 Then [1]both Mahlon and Chilion also died, and the woman
was bereft of her two children and her husband.
6 Then she arose with her daughters-in-law that she might
return from the land of Moab, for she had heard in the land of
Moab that the LORD had [a]visited His people in [b]giving them food. 5 [1]Lit *both of them*
7 So she departed from the
place where she was, and her two
daughters-in-law with her; and
they went on the way to return to
the land of Judah.
8 And Naomi said to her two
daughters-in-law, "Go, return each
of you to her mother's house. [a]May 6 [a]Ex 4:31; Jer 29:10; Zeph 2:7 [b]Ps 132:15; Matt 6:11
the LORD deal kindly with you as
you have dealt with the dead and
with me.
9 "May the LORD grant that you
may find rest, each in the house
of her husband." Then she kissed
them, and they lifted up their
voices and wept.

Ruth's Journey from Moab to Bethlehem

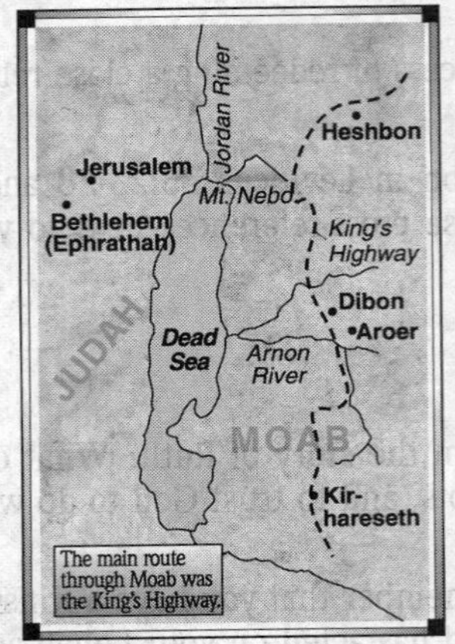

10 And they said to her, "*No,* but we will surely return with 8 [a]2 Tim 1:16
you to your people."
11 But Naomi said, "Return, my daughters. Why should you go
with me? Have I yet sons in my womb, that [a]they may be your
husbands?
12 "Return, my daughters! Go, for I am too old to have a
husband. If I said I have hope, if I should even have a husband
tonight and also bear sons,
13 would you therefore wait until they were grown? Would 11 [a]Gen 38:11; Deut 25:5

you therefore refrain from marrying? No, my daughters; for it is
[1]harder for me than for you, for [a]the hand of the LORD has gone
forth against me."
14 And they lifted up their voices and wept again; and Orpah
kissed her mother-in-law, but Ruth clung to her.
15 Then she said, "Behold, your sister-in-law has gone back to
her people and her [a]gods; return after your sister-in-law."
16 But Ruth said, "Do not urge me to leave you *or* turn back from
following you; for where you go, I will go, and where you lodge, I
will lodge. Your people *shall be* my people, and your God, my God.
17 "Where you die, I will die, and there I will be buried. Thus
may [a]the LORD do to me, and worse, if *anything but* death parts
you and me."
18 When [a]she saw that she was determined to go with her,
she [1]said no more to her.
19 So they both went until they came to Bethlehem. And when
they had come to Bethlehem, [a]all the city was stirred because
of them, and [1]the women said, "Is this Naomi?"
20 She said to them, "Do not call me [1]Naomi; call me [2]Mara,
for [3a]the Almighty has dealt very bitterly with me.
21 "I went out full, but [a]the LORD has brought me back empty.
Why do you call me Naomi, since the LORD has witnessed
against me and [1]the Almighty has afflicted me?"
22 So Naomi returned, and with her Ruth the Moabitess, her
daughter-in-law, who returned from the land of Moab. And
they came to Bethlehem at [a]the beginning of barley harvest.

Chapter 2 Theme ______________________

2 Now Naomi had [1]a kinsman of her husband, a [2]man of great
wealth, of the family of [a]Elimelech, whose name was Boaz.
2 And Ruth the Moabitess said to Naomi, "Please let me go
to the field and [a]glean among the ears of grain after one in whose
sight I may find favor." And she said to her, "Go, my daughter."
3 So she departed and went and gleaned in the field after the
reapers; and [1]she happened to come to the portion of the field
belonging to Boaz, who was of the family of Elimelech.
4 Now behold, Boaz came from Bethlehem and said to the
reapers, "[a]May the LORD be with you." And they said to him,
"May the LORD bless you."
5 Then Boaz said to his servant who was [1]in charge of the
reapers, "Whose young woman is this?"
6 The servant [1]in charge of the reapers replied, "She is the
young Moabite woman who returned with Naomi from the
land of Moab.
7 "And she said, 'Please let me glean and gather after the
reapers among the sheaves.' Thus she came and has remained
from the morning until now; she has been sitting in the house
for a little while."
8 Then Boaz said to Ruth, "[1]Listen carefully, my daughter. Do
not go to glean in another field; furthermore, do not go on from
this one, but stay here with my maids.

13 [1]Lit *more bitter* [a]Judg 2:15; Job 19:21; Ps 32:4
15 [a]Josh 24:15; Judg 11:24
17 [a]1 Sam 3:17; 2 Kin 6:31
18 [1]Lit *ceased to speak* [a]Acts 21:14
19 [1]Lit *they* [a]Matt 21:10
20 [1]I.e. pleasant [2]I.e. bitter [3]Heb *Shaddai* [a]Ex 6:3; Job 6:4
21 [1]Heb *Shaddai* [a]Job 1:21
22 [a]Ex 9:31; Lev 23:10, 11
2:1 [1]Or *an acquaintance* [2]Or *mighty, valiant man* [a]Ruth 1:2
2 [a]Lev 19:9, 10; 23:22; Deut 24:19; Ruth 2:7
3 [1]Lit *her chance chanced upon*
4 [a]Judg 6:12; Ps 129:8; Luke 1:28; 2 Thess 3:16
5 [1]Lit *appointed over*
6 [1]Lit *who was appointed over*
8 [1]Lit *Have you not heard*

9 "Let your eyes be on the field which they reap, and go after
them. Indeed, I have commanded the servants not to touch
you. When you are thirsty, go to the [1]water jars and drink from
what the servants draw."
10 Then she [a]fell on her face, bowing to the ground and said
to him, "Why have I found favor in your sight that you should
take notice of me, since I am a foreigner?"
11 Boaz replied to her, "All that you have done for your
mother-in-law after the death of your husband has been fully
reported to me, and how you left your father and your mother
and the land of your birth, and came to a people that you did
not previously know.
12 "[a]May the LORD reward your work, and your wages be full
from the LORD, the God of Israel, [b]under whose wings you have
come to seek refuge."
13 Then she said, "I have found favor in your sight, my lord, for
you have comforted me and indeed have spoken [1]kindly to your
maidservant, though I am not like one of your maidservants."
14 At mealtime Boaz said to her, "[1]Come here, that you may
eat of the bread and dip your piece of bread in the vinegar." So
she sat beside the reapers; and he [2]served her roasted grain,
and she ate and was satisfied [a]and had some left.
15 When she rose to glean, Boaz commanded his servants,
saying, "Let her glean even among the sheaves, and do not
insult her.
16 "Also you shall purposely pull out for her *some grain* from the
bundles and leave *it* that she may glean, and do not rebuke her."
17 So she gleaned in the field until evening. Then she beat out
what she had gleaned, and it was about an ephah of barley.
18 She took *it* up and went into the city, and her mother-in-
law saw what she had gleaned. She also took *it* out and [a]gave
[1]Naomi what she had left after [2]she was satisfied.
19 Her mother-in-law then said to her, "Where did you glean
today and where did you work? May he who [a]took notice of
you be blessed." So she told her mother-in-law with whom she
had worked and said, "The name of the man with whom I
worked today is Boaz."
20 Naomi said to her daughter-in-law, "[a]May he be blessed of
the LORD who has not withdrawn his kindness to the living and
to the dead." Again Naomi said to her, "The man is [1]our relative,
he is one of our [2]closest relatives."
21 Then Ruth the Moabitess said, "[1]Furthermore, he said to me,
'You should stay close to my servants until they have finished
all my harvest.'"
22 Naomi said to Ruth her daughter-in-law, "It is good, my
daughter, that you go out with his maids, so that *others* do not
fall upon you in another field."
23 So she stayed close by the maids of Boaz in order to glean
until [a]the end of the barley harvest and the wheat harvest. And
she lived with her mother-in-law.

9 [1]Lit *vessels*
10 [a]1 Sam 25:23
12 [a]1 Sam 24:19 [b]Ruth 1:16; Ps 17:8; 36:7; 57:1; 61:4; 63:7; 91:4
13 [1]Lit *to the heart of your*
14 [1]Lit *Draw near* [2]Lit *held out to* [a]Ruth 2:18
18 [1]Lit *her* [2]Lit *her satiety* [a]Ruth 2:14
19 [a]Ps 41:1
20 [1]Lit *near to us* [2]Lit *redeemers* [a]2 Sam 2:5
21 [1]Lit *Also that*
23 [a]Deut 16:9

Chapter 3 Theme ______________________________

3 Then Naomi her mother-in-law said to her, "My daughter, shall I not seek [1]security for you, that it may be well with you?

2 "Now is not Boaz [a]our [1]kinsman, with whose maids you were? Behold, he winnows barley at the threshing floor tonight.

3 "Wash yourself therefore, and anoint yourself and put on your *best* clothes, and go down to the threshing floor; *but* do not make yourself known to the man until he has finished eating and drinking.

4 "It shall be when he lies down, that you shall [1]notice the place where he lies, and you shall go and uncover his feet and lie down; then he will tell you what you shall do."

5 She said to her, "[a]All that you say I will do."

6 So she went down to the threshing floor and did according to all that her mother-in-law had commanded her.

7 When Boaz had eaten and drunk and [a]his heart was merry, he went to lie down at the end of the heap of grain; and she came secretly, and uncovered his feet and lay down.

8 It happened in the middle of the night that the man was startled and [1]bent forward; and behold, a woman was lying at his feet.

9 He said, "Who are you?" And she answered, "I am Ruth your maid. So spread your covering over your maid, for you are a [1]close relative."

10 Then he said, "[a]May you be blessed of the LORD, my daughter. You have shown your last kindness to be better than the first by not going after young men, whether poor or rich.

11 "Now, my daughter, do not fear. I will do for you whatever you [1]ask, for all my people in the [2]city know that you are [a]a woman of excellence.

12 "Now it is true I am a [1]close relative; however, there is a [1]relative closer than I.

13 "Remain this night, and when morning comes, [a]if he will [1]redeem you, good; let him redeem you. But if he does not wish to [1]redeem you, then I will redeem you, [b]as the LORD lives. Lie down until morning."

14 So she lay at his feet until morning and rose before one could recognize another; and he said, "[a]Let it not be known that the woman came to the threshing floor."

15 Again he said, "Give me the cloak that is on you and hold it." So she held it, and he measured six *measures* of barley and laid *it* on her. Then [1]she went into the city.

16 When she came to her mother-in-law, she said, "[1]How did it go, my daughter?" And she told her all that the man had done for her.

17 She said, "These six *measures* of barley he gave to me, for he said, 'Do not go to your mother-in-law empty-handed.'"

18 Then she said, "Wait, my daughter, until you know how the matter [1]turns out; for the man will not rest until he has [2]settled it today."

3:1 [1]Lit *rest*
[1]Or *acquaintance* [a]Deut 25:5-10
4 [1]Lit *know*
5 [a]Eph 6:1; Col 3:20
7 [a]Judg 19:6, 9; 2 Sam 13:28; 1 Kin 21:7; Esth 1:10
8 [1]Lit *twisted himself*
9 [1]Or *redeemer*
10 [a]Ruth 2:20
11 [1]Lit *say* [2]Lit *gate* [a]Prov 12:4; 31:10
12 [1]Or *redeemer*
13 [1]Or *act as close relative to* [a]Deut 25:5; Matt 22:24 [b]Judg 8:19; Jer 4:2; 12:16
14 [a]Rom 14:16; 2 Cor 8:21
15 [1]So with many mss; M.T. *he*
16 [1]Lit *Who are you?*
18 [1]Lit *falls* [2]Lit *finished the matter*

Chapter 4 Theme ________________________________

4 Now Boaz went up to the gate and sat down there, and
behold, [a]the [1]close relative of whom Boaz spoke was passing by, so he said, "Turn aside, [2]friend, sit down here." And he
turned aside and sat down.
2 He took ten men of the [a]elders of the city and said, "Sit
down here." So they sat down.
3 Then he said to the [1]closest relative, "Naomi, who has come
back from the land of Moab, has to sell the piece of land
[a]which belonged to our brother Elimelech.
4 "So I thought to [1]inform you, saying, '[a]Buy *it* before those
who are sitting *here,* and before the elders of my people. If you
will redeem *it,* redeem *it;* but if [2]not, tell me that I may know;
for [b]there is no one but you to redeem *it,* and I am after you.'"
And he said, "I will redeem *it.*"
5 Then Boaz said, "On the day you buy the field from the
hand of Naomi, you must also acquire Ruth the Moabitess, the
widow of the deceased, in order [a]to raise up the name of the
deceased on his inheritance."
6 [a]The [1]closest relative said, "I cannot redeem *it* for myself,
because I would [2]jeopardize my own inheritance. Redeem *it* for
yourself; you *may have* my right of redemption, for I cannot
redeem *it.*"
7 Now this was [a]*the custom* in former times in Israel
concerning the redemption and the exchange *of land* to confirm
any matter: a man removed his sandal and gave it to another;
and this was the *manner of* attestation in Israel.
8 So the [1]closest relative said to Boaz, "Buy *it* for yourself."
And he removed his sandal.
9 Then Boaz said to the elders and all the people, "You are
witnesses today that I have bought from the hand of Naomi all
that belonged to Elimelech and all that belonged to Chilion and
Mahlon.
10 "Moreover, I have acquired Ruth the Moabitess, the widow
of Mahlon, to be my wife in order to raise up the name of the
deceased on his inheritance, so [a]that the name of the deceased
will not be cut off from his brothers or from the [1]court of his
birth place; you are witnesses today."
11 All the people who were in the [1]court, and the elders, said,
"*We are* witnesses. May the LORD make the woman who is
coming into your home [a]like Rachel and Leah, both of whom
built the house of Israel; and may you achieve [2]wealth in
Ephrathah and [3]become famous in Bethlehem.
12 "Moreover, may your house be like the house of [a]Perez
whom Tamar bore to Judah, through the [1]offspring which the
LORD will give you by this young woman."
13 So Boaz took Ruth, and she became his wife, and he went
in to her. And [a]the LORD [1]enabled her to conceive, and she
gave birth to a son.
14 Then the [a]women said to Naomi, "Blessed is the LORD who
has not left you without a [1]redeemer today, and may his name
[2]become famous in Israel.

INSIGHT

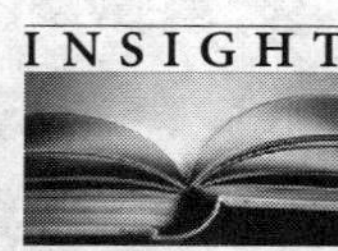

The Genealogy of Boaz

Abram + Sarai (Abraham + Sarah)
↓
Isaac + Rebekah
↓
Jacob + Leah
↓
Judah + Tamar
↓
Perez
↓
Hezron
↓
Ram
↓
Admin
↓
Amminadab
↓
Nahshon
↓
Salmon + ***Rahab*** (the harlot)
↓
Boaz + ***Ruth*** (the Gentile)
↓
Obed
↓
Jesse
↓
David "from whom came Mary the mother of Jesus"

See **The Genealogy of Jesus the Christ** on page 1557.

4:1 [1]Or *redeemer* [2]Lit *a certain one* [a]Ruth 3:12

2 [a]1 Kin 21:8; Prov 31:23

3 [1]Lit *redeemer* [a]Lev 25:25

4 [1]Lit *uncover your ear* [2]Lit *no one w... redeem* [a]Jer 32:7 [b]Lev 25:25

5 [a]Gen 38:8; Deut 25:5f; Matt 22:24

6 [1]Lit *redeemer* [2]Lit *ruin* [a]Lev 25:25

7 [a]Deut 25:8-10

8 [1]Lit *redeemer*

10 [1]Lit *gate* [a]Deut 25:6

11 [1]Lit *gate* [2]Or *power* [3]Lit *call the name in* [a]Gen 29:25-30

12 [1]Lit *seed* [a]Gen 38:29; 46:12; Ruth 4:18

13 [1]Lit *gave her conception* [a]Gen 29:31; 33:5

14 [1]Or *closest relative* [2]Lit *be called in* [a]Luke 1:58

15 "May he also be to you a restorer of life and a sustainer of
your old age; for your daughter-in-law, who loves you [1a]and is
better to you than seven sons, has given birth to him."
16 Then Naomi took the child [1]and laid him in her lap, and
became his nurse.
17 The neighbor women gave him a name, saying, "A son has
been born to Naomi!" So they named him Obed. He is the
father of Jesse, the father of David.
18 Now these are the generations of Perez: [a]to Perez [1]was
born Hezron,
19 and to Hezron was born Ram, and to Ram, Amminadab,
20 and to Amminadab was born Nahshon, and to Nahshon,
Salmon,
21 and to Salmon was born Boaz, and to Boaz, Obed,
22 and to Obed was born Jesse, and to Jesse, David.

15 [1]Lit *who* [a]Ruth 1:16, 17; 2:11, 12

16 [1]I.e. as her own

18 [1]Lit *begot,* and so through v 22 [a]Matt 1:3-6

Ruth at a Glance

Theme of Ruth:

Author:

Date:

Purpose:

Key Words:

redeem (redemption)

relative (closest relative, kinsman)

Naomi

Ruth

Boaz

Segment Divisions	Chapter Themes
	1
	2
	3
	4

1 SAMUEL שמואל א
SHMU'EL ALEPH

The days of the judges were dark until God raised up Samuel as a prophet, priest, and judge. Samuel was committed to doing what was right in God's eyes. But the people weren't satisfied. They cried, "Now appoint a king for us to judge us like all the nations!" With that plea they rejected the Lord as their King. What would it be like to live under a monarchy rather than a theocracy? The children of Israel were soon to find out. The kingdom, at first united, eventually was divided because of the disobedience of the kings.

The books of 1 and 2 Samuel, 1 and 2 Kings, and 1 and 2 Chronicles record the days of the kings of Israel. God's children can learn many valuable lessons from these books. The lessons begin when God rejects Saul and chooses as king a man after His own heart. And what will such a man be like? Will he live a perfect life? Is this what will make him a man after God's own heart?

Things to Do

General Instructions

As you study this book, never forget that these are actual people, frail but with access to God and His precepts and statutes of life. Observe the text prayerfully and carefully, and as you study, note in the margin God's lessons for life.

Chapters 1–7: Samuel, the Last Judge

1. As you observe these first seven chapters, mark the following words in a distinctive way and then record in the margin key insights that you want to remember.

   a. *Ark (of the Lord, of God, of the covenant), ephod, judge (judged), king, Ichabod,* and *Ebenezer*. The last three words are used only one time in these chapters but are significant. *Ephod* is used only twice in this segment but will have greater significance in the last segment of 1 Samuel. List these key words on 1 SAMUEL AT A GLANCE and on an index card you can use as a bookmark for this segment.

   b. Double-underline in green every geographical location. Then locate these places on the map on page 501.

2. Since 1 Samuel is a historical account, note the focus of each chapter. Who and/or what event does the chapter center on?

   a. You might want to list your insights about the main characters and what they do in the margin of each chapter.

   b. Read the insights on Nazirites and the ephod on pages 449 and 451.

   c. Using an easily recognizable symbol such as △, note in the margin your insights about God and His ways. For instance, in chapter 1 God closes the womb and opens the womb.

3. Record the theme of each chapter next to each chapter number in your Bible and on the 1 SAMUEL AT A GLANCE chart on page 500.

Chapters 8–15: From Samuel to Saul, from Judge to King

1. As you observe this segment of 1 Samuel:

   a. Mark the following key words: *judge (judges)*, *king* (don't include foreign kings), *sin (sins, sinned), evil, Spirit of God (of the Lord), ark of God*, and *ephod*. Put them on 1 SAMUEL AT A GLANCE and on an index card to use as a bookmark.

b. List what you learn about Samuel, Saul, King Agag, and the Amalekites. See the chart "Saul's Family Tree" on page 470.

c. Note all you learn about God and His ways.

d. Mark the references to time (when Saul begins his reign, etc.) and geographical locations.

e. There are no references to the ark in 1 Samuel after this segment. Review what you learned about the ark in this book and note in the margin where it is last mentioned and its location. Read "The Ark of the Covenant" on page 2099.

2. Carefully observe all you learn from marking the word *king*. Watch for the following and record your insights.

a. Why the people wanted a king, how they perceived the kingship, and what kind of king they wanted.

b. How God responded to the people's request, what God desired in a kingship, and how the success or failure of a king was determined. Compare this with Deuteronomy 17:14-20.

3. Examine each chapter as you did in the previous segment, watching for and recording the main event of each chapter and any pertinent subpoints. Don't forget to record the chapter theme on 1 SAMUEL AT A GLANCE and in the text.

Chapters 16–31: The Preparation of Another King

1. In this segment:

a. Make a new bookmark and mark the following key words: *king* (not foreign kings), *evil, evil spirit, sin (sinned), judge, covenant, inquire (inquired)*, and *ephod*. Don't forget to record what you are learning from marking *king* and *ephod*.

b. Mark all references to time and to geographical locations as before.

2. Observe and record in the margin of each chapter the major points you learn about Samuel, Saul, and David. Observe all that happens to David and how he responds to God and to man. Watch for and note in the margin the "LFL" (Lessons for Life).

3. In the margin write "Covenant" and list what you have observed from the text. Ask the "5 W's and an H": Who makes the covenant? How is it made? What is done? What is promised? What are the conditions? When is it made? Where is it made? Why? Remember that you are in covenant with God if you are a child of God (Matthew 26:26-29); watch for any principles which might apply to you. Read the "Insight" on covenant at Genesis 15:10.

4. As you read each chapter, watch for insights about God, note the events of each chapter and the subpoints of the chapter, and record the chapter themes.

5. Complete 1 SAMUEL AT A GLANCE. Watch for any additional segment divisions in 1 Samuel. Look at the chapter themes and see if there is any other way 1 Samuel might be segmented: Can any chapters be grouped in respect to David's relationship to Saul, to Jonathan, to the Philistines, or to others? Or is there any geographical segmentation, such as where Samuel, Saul, and David spend their time?

6. Record the theme of 1 Samuel on 1 SAMUEL AT A GLANCE.

Things to Think About

1. What lessons did you learn from Eli's dealings with his sons? Do you see your accountability before God to discipline your children?

2. What do you learn from Samuel's, Saul's, and David's lives regarding seeking God, listening to Him, and obeying Him? Are there consequences when you don't?

3. Did you notice how much time has elapsed since David was anointed to be king? Still, as 1 Samuel comes to a close, David is not king over Israel. Think about all that transpired since Samuel anointed David. What can you learn from this about God's promises, His purpose, and His timing? Are you waiting patiently on God for the fulfillment of His promises to you?

4. Review the "Lessons for Life" you observed and the insights you recorded about God in the margins of 1 Samuel. Make these a matter of prayer.

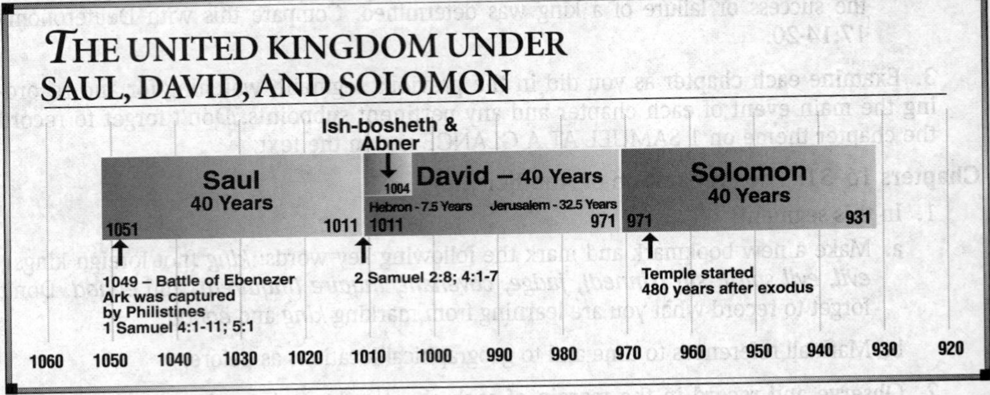

Chapter 1 Theme ______________________

1100 B.C.

1 Now there was a certain man from [a]Ramathaim-zophim
from the [b]hill country of Ephraim, and his name was
[c]Elkanah the son of Jeroham, the son of Elihu, the son of Tohu,
the son of Zuph, an Ephraimite.
2 He had [a]two wives: the name of one was [b]Hannah and the
name of the other Peninnah; and Peninnah had children, but
Hannah had no children.
3 Now this man would go up from his city [a]yearly [b]to worship
and to sacrifice to the LORD of hosts in [c]Shiloh. And the two sons
of Eli, Hophni and Phinehas, were priests to the LORD there.

1:1 [a]1 Sam 1:19 [b]Josh 17:17, 18; 24:33 [c]1 Chr 6:22-28, 33-38

2 [a]Deut 21:15-17 [b]Luke 2:36

3 [a]Ex 34:23; 1 Sam 1:21; Luke 2:41 [b]Ex 23:14; Deut 12:5-7; 16:16 [c]Josh 18:1

4 When the day came that Elkanah sacrificed, he [a]would give
portions to Peninnah his wife and to all her sons and her
daughters;
5 but to Hannah he would give a double portion, for he loved
Hannah, [a]but the LORD had closed her womb.
6 Her rival, however, [a]would provoke her bitterly to irritate
her, because the LORD had closed her womb.
7 It happened year after year, as often as she went up to the
house of the LORD, she would provoke her; so she wept and
would not eat.
8 Then Elkanah her husband said to her, "Hannah, why do
you weep and why do you not eat and why is your heart sad?
[a]Am I not better to you than ten sons?"
9 Then Hannah rose after eating and drinking in Shiloh. Now
Eli the priest was sitting on the seat by the doorpost of [a]the
temple of the LORD.
10 She, [1]greatly distressed, prayed to the LORD and wept bitterly.
11 She [a]made a vow and said, "O LORD of hosts, if You will
indeed [b]look on the affliction of Your maidservant and remember
me, and not forget Your maidservant, but will give Your maidservant a [1]son, then I will give him to the LORD all the days of
his life, and [c]a razor shall never come on his head."
12 Now it came about, as she [1]continued praying before the
LORD, that Eli was watching her mouth.
13 As for Hannah, [a]she was speaking in her heart, only her lips
were moving, but her voice was not heard. So Eli thought she
was drunk.
14 Then Eli said to her, "[a]How long will you make yourself
drunk? Put away your wine from you."
15 But Hannah replied, "No, my lord, I am a woman [1]oppressed
in spirit; I have drunk neither wine nor strong drink, but I [a]have
poured out my soul before the LORD.
16 "Do not [1]consider your maidservant as a worthless woman,
for I have spoken until now out of my great concern and
[2]provocation."
17 Then Eli answered and said, "[a]Go in peace; and may the
God of Israel [b]grant your petition that you have asked of Him."
18 She said, "[a]Let your maidservant find favor in your sight."
So the woman went her way and ate, and [b]her face was no
longer *sad*.
19 Then they arose early in the morning and worshiped before
the LORD, and returned again to their house in [a]Ramah. And
Elkanah [1]had relations with Hannah his wife, and [b]the LORD
remembered her.
20 It came about [1]in due time, after Hannah had conceived,
that she gave birth to a son; and she named him Samuel,
saying, "[a]Because I have asked him of the LORD."
21 Then the man Elkanah [a]went up with all his household to
offer to the LORD the yearly sacrifice and *pay* his vow.
22 But Hannah did not go up, for she said to her husband, "*I
will not go up* until the child is weaned; then I will [a]bring him,
that he may appear before the LORD and [b]stay there forever."

4 [a]Deut 12:17, 18
5 [a]Gen 16:1; 30:1
6 [a]Job 24:21
8 [a]Ruth 4:15
9 [a]1 Sam 3:3
10 [1]Lit *bitter of soul*
11 [1]Lit *seed of men* [a]Num 30:6-11 [b]Gen 29:32 [c]Num 6:5; Judg 13:5
12 [1]Lit *multiplied*
13 [a]Gen 24:42-45
14 [a]Acts 2:4, 13
15 [1]Lit *severe* [a]Job 30:16; Ps 42:4; 62:8; Lam 2:19
16 [1]Lit *give* [2]Lit *my provocation*
17 [a]Judg 18:6; 1 Sam 25:35; 2 Kin 5:19; Mark 5:34; Luke 7:50 [b]Ps 20:3-5
18 [a]Gen 33:15; Ruth 2:13 [b]Rom 15:13
19 [1]Lit *knew* [a]1 Sam 1:1; 2:11 [b]Gen 21:1; 30:22
20 [1]Lit *at the circuit of the days* [a]Gen 41:51, 52; Ex 2:10, 22; Matt 1:21
21 [a]Deut 12:11; 1 Sam 1:3
22 [a]Luke 2:22 [b]1 Sam 1:11, 28

INSIGHT

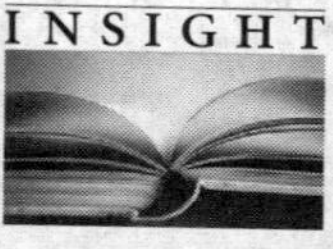

A ***Nazirite*** (which means "consecration, devotion, and separation") was someone who was bound by a vow of consecration to God's service for either a specific period of time or for life. A Nazirite's devotion to God was evidenced outwardly by not cutting the hair, abstaining from wine and alcoholic drinks, and avoiding contact with the dead. Violation of these brought defilement and need of purification.

In 1 Samuel 1:11, when Hannah made her vow, she was making a Nazirite vow.

23 [a]Elkanah her husband said to her, "Do what seems best [1]to
you. Remain until you have weaned him; only [b]may the LORD
confirm His word." So the woman remained and nursed her
son until she weaned him.
24 Now when she had weaned him, [a]she took him up with
her, with a three-year-old bull and one ephah of flour and a jug
of wine, and brought him to [b]the house of the LORD in Shiloh,
although the child was young.
25 Then [a]they slaughtered the bull, and [b]brought the boy to Eli.
26 She said, "Oh, my lord! [a]As your soul lives, my lord, I am
the woman who stood here beside you, praying to the LORD.
27 "[a]For this boy I prayed, and the LORD has given me my petition
which I asked of Him.
28 "[a]So I have also [1]dedicated him to the LORD; as long as he lives
he is [1]dedicated to the LORD." And [b]he worshiped the LORD there.

Chapter 2 Theme ______________________

2 Then Hannah [a]prayed and said,
"My heart exults in the LORD;
[b]My [1]horn is exalted in the LORD,
My mouth [2]speaks boldly against my enemies,
Because [c]I rejoice in Your salvation.
2 "[a]There is no one holy like the LORD,
Indeed, [b]there is no one besides You,
[c]Nor is there any rock like our God.
3 "[1]Boast no more so very proudly,
[a]Do not let arrogance come out of your mouth;
[b]For the LORD is a God of knowledge,
[c]And with Him actions are weighed.
4 "[a]The bows of the mighty are shattered,
[b]But the feeble gird on strength.
5 "Those who were full hire themselves out for bread,
But those who were hungry cease *to hunger.*
[a]Even the barren gives birth to seven,
But [b]she who has many children languishes.
6 "[a]The LORD kills and makes alive;
[b]He brings down to [1]Sheol and raises up.
7 "[a]The LORD makes poor and rich;
[b]He brings low, He also exalts.
8 "[a]He raises the poor from the dust,
[b]He lifts the needy from the ash heap
[c]To make them sit with nobles,
And inherit a seat of honor;
[d]For the pillars of the earth are the LORD's,
And He set the world on them.
9 "[a]He keeps the feet of His godly ones,
[b]But the wicked ones are silenced in darkness;
[c]For not by might shall a man prevail.
10 "[a]Those who contend with the LORD will be shattered;
[b]Against them He will thunder in the heavens,

23 [1]Lit *in your eyes* [a]Num 30:7, 10, 11 [b]1 Sam 1:17
24 [a]Num 15:9, 10; Deut 12:5, 6 [b]Josh 18:1; 1 Sam 4:3, 4
25 [a]Lev 1:5 [b]Luke 2:22
26 [a]2 Kin 2:2, 4, 6; 4:30
27 [a]1 Sam 1:11-13; Ps 6:9; 66:19, 20
28 [1]Lit *lent* [a]1 Sam 1:11, 22 [b]Gen 24:26, 52
2:1 [1]I.e. strength [2]Lit *is enlarged* [a]1 Sam 2:1-10; Luke 1:46-55 [b]Deut 33:17; Job 16:15; Ps 75:10; 89:17, 24; 92:10; 112:9 [c]Ps 9:14; 13:5; 35:9; Is 12:2, 3
2 [a]Ex 15:11; Lev 19:2; Ps 86:8 [b]2 Sam 22:32 [c]Deut 32:30, 31
3 [1]Lit *Talk much* [a]Prov 8:13 [b]1 Sam 16:7; 1 Kin 8:39 [c]Prov 16:2; 24:12
4 [a]Ps 37:15; 46:9 [b]Ps 18:39; Heb 11:32-34
5 [a]Ruth 4:15; Ps 113:9 [b]Jer 15:9
6 [1]I.e. the nether world [a]Deut 32:39; 2 Kin 5:7; Rev 1:18 [b]Is 26:19
7 [a]Deut 8:17, 18 [b]Job 5:11; Ps 75:7; James 4:10
8 [a]Job 42:10-12; Ps 75:7; 113:7 [b]2 Sam 7:8; Dan 2:48; James 2:5 [c]Job 36:7; Ps 113:8 [d]Job 38:4-6; Ps 75:3; 104:5
9 [a]Ps 91:11, 12; 121:3; Prov 3:26; 1 Pet 1:5 [b]Matt 8:12 [c]Ps 33:16, 17
10 [a]Ex 15:6; Ps 2:9 [b]1 Sam 7:10; 2 Sam 22:14; Ps 18:13, 14

[c]The LORD will judge the ends of the earth;
[d]And He will give strength to His king,
[e]And will exalt the [1]horn of His anointed."
11 Then Elkanah went to his home at [a]Ramah. [b]But the boy
ministered to the LORD before Eli the priest.
12 Now the sons of Eli were [1a]worthless men; they did not
know the LORD
13 [a]and the custom of the priests with the people. When any
man was offering a sacrifice, the priest's servant would come
while the meat was boiling, with a three-pronged fork in his
hand.
14 Then he would thrust it into the pan, or kettle, or caldron, or
pot; all that the fork brought up the priest would take for himself.
Thus they did in Shiloh to all the Israelites who came there.
15 Also, before [a]they burned the fat, the priest's servant would
come and say to the man who was sacrificing, "Give the priest
meat for roasting, as he will not take boiled meat from you,
only raw."
16 If the man said to him, "They must surely [1]burn the fat [2]first,
and then take as much as [3]you desire," then he would say,
"No, but you shall give *it to me* now; and if not, I will take it by
force."
17 Thus the sin of the young men was very great before the
LORD, for the men [a]despised the offering of the LORD.
18 Now [a]Samuel was ministering before the LORD, *as* a boy
[1b]wearing a linen ephod.
19 And his mother would make him a little [a]robe and bring it
to him from year to year when she would come up with her
husband to offer [b]the yearly sacrifice.
20 Then Eli would [a]bless Elkanah and his wife and say, "May
the LORD give you [1]children from this woman in place of [2]the one
she [b]dedicated to the LORD." And they went to their own [3]home.
21 [a]The LORD visited Hannah; and she conceived and gave
birth to three sons and two daughters. And [b]the boy Samuel
grew before the LORD.
22 Now Eli was very old; and he heard [a]all that his sons were
doing to all Israel, and how they lay with [b]the women who
served at the doorway of the tent of meeting.
23 He said to them, "Why do you do such things, the evil
things that I hear from all these people?
24 "No, my sons; for the report is not good [a]which I hear [1]the
LORD'S people circulating.
25 "If one man sins against another, [a]God will mediate for him;
but [b]if a man sins against the LORD, who can intercede for
him?" But they would not listen to the voice of their father, for
the [c]LORD desired to put them to death.
26 Now the boy [a]Samuel [1]was growing in stature and in favor
both with the LORD and with men.
27 Then [a]a man of God came to Eli and said to him, "Thus says
the LORD, '[b]Did I *not* indeed reveal Myself to the house of your
father when they were in Egypt *in bondage* to Pharaoh's house?

10 [1]I.e. strength [c]Ps 96:13; 98:9; Matt 25:31, 32 [d]Ps 21:1, 7 [e]Ps 89:24
11 [a]1 Sam 1:1, 19 [b]1 Sam 1:28; 2:18; 3:1
12 [1]Lit *sons of Belial* [a]Jer 2:8; 9:3, 6; 2 Cor 6:15
13 [a]Lev 7:29-34
15 [a]Lev 3:3-5, 16
16 [1]Lit *offer up in smoke* [2]Lit *like the day* [3]Lit *your soul*
17 [a]Mal 2:7-9
18 [1]Lit *girded with* [a]1 Sam 2:11; 3:1 [b]1 Sam 2:28; 22:18; 2 Sam 6:14; 1 Chr 15:27
19 [a]Ex 28:31 [b]1 Sam 1:3, 21
20 [1]Lit *seed* [2]Lit *the one asked for which was lent* [3]Lit *place* [a]Luke 2:34 [b]1 Sam 1:11, 27, 28
21 [a]Gen 21:1 [b]Judg 13:24; 1 Sam 2:26; 3:19-21; Luke 1:80; 2:40
22 [a]1 Sam 2:13-17 [b]Ex 38:8
24 [1]Or *making the LORD's people transgress* [a]1 Kin 15:26
25 [a]Deut 1:17 [b]Num 15:30; 1 Sam 3:14; Heb 10:26, 27 [c]Josh 11:20
26 [1]Lit *was going on both great and good* [a]1 Sam 2:21; Luke 2:52
27 [a]Deut 33:1; Judg 13:6 [b]Ex 4:14-16; 12:1, 43

INSIGHT

The ***ephod*** was used to seek guidance from God. Described in Exodus 28, it was a linen garment worn by the priest and also by David when he was king (2 Samuel 6:14). The ephod was fastened on each shoulder by onyx clasps which had the names of six tribes engraved on one clasp and six tribes engraved on the other. The ***breastpiece***, which was fastened to the ephod, had a linen pouch which held the ***Urim*** and ***Thummim***, which may have been used as sacred lots to reveal God's will (1 Samuel 28:6).

28 ‘[a]Did I *not* choose them from all the tribes of Israel to be My priests, to go up to My altar, to burn incense, to carry an ephod before Me; and did I *not* [b]give to the house of your father all the fire *offerings* of the sons of Israel?

29 ‘Why do you [a]kick at My sacrifice and at My offering [b]which I have commanded *in My* [c]dwelling, and [d]honor your sons above Me, by making yourselves fat with the [1]choicest of every offering of My people Israel?’

30 “Therefore the LORD God of Israel declares, ‘[a]I did indeed say that your house and the house of your father should walk before Me forever’; but now the LORD declares, ‘Far be it from Me—for [b]those who honor Me I will honor, and those [c]who despise Me will be lightly esteemed.

31 ‘Behold, [a]the days are coming when I will break your [1]strength and the [1]strength of your father’s house so that there will not be an old man in your house.

32 ‘You will see [a]the distress of *My* dwelling, in *spite of* all the good that [1]I do for Israel; and an [b]old man will not be in your house forever.

33 ‘Yet I will not cut off every man of yours from My altar [1]so that your eyes will fail *from weeping* and your soul grieve, and all the increase of your house will die [2]in the prime of life.

34 ‘This will be [a]the sign to you which will come concerning your two sons, Hophni and Phinehas: [b]on the same day both of them will die.

35 ‘But [a]I will raise up for Myself a faithful priest who will do according to what is in My heart and in My soul; and [b]I will build him an enduring house, and he will walk before [c]My anointed always.

36 ‘Everyone who is left in your house will come and bow down to him for a [1]piece of silver or a loaf of bread and say, “Please [2]assign me to one of the priest’s offices so that I may eat a piece of bread.”’”

Chapter 3 Theme ________________________________

3 Now [a]the boy Samuel was ministering to the LORD before Eli. And [b]word from the LORD was rare in those days, [1]visions were infrequent.

2 It happened at that time as Eli was lying down in his place (now [a]his eyesight had begun to grow dim *and* he could not see *well*),

3 and [a]the lamp of God had not yet gone out, and Samuel was lying down in the temple of the LORD where the ark of God *was,*

4 that the LORD called Samuel; and he said, “[a]Here I am.”

5 Then he ran to Eli and said, “Here I am, for you called me.” But he said, “I did not call, lie down again.” So he went and lay down.

6 The LORD called yet again, “Samuel!” So Samuel arose and went to Eli and said, “Here I am, for you called me.” But he [1]answered, “I did not call, my son, lie down again.”

28 [a]Ex 28:1-4; 30:7, 8; Lev 8:7, 8 [b]Lev 7:35, 36

29 [1]Or *first* [a]1 Sam 2:13-17 [b]Deut 12:5-9 [c]Ps 26:8 [d]Matt 10:37

30 [a]Ex 29:9; Num 25:13 [b]Ps 50:23 [c]Mal 2:9

31 [1]Or *arm* [a]1 Sam 4:11-18; 22:17-20

32 [1]Lit *He does* [a]1 Kin 2:26, 27 [b]Zech 8:4

33 [1]Lit *to waste away your eyes and to grieve your soul* [2]Lit *as men*

34 [a]1 Sam 10:7-9; 1 Kin 13:3 [b]1 Sam 4:11, 17

35 [a]1 Sam 3:1; 7:9; 9:12, 13 [b]1 Sam 8:3-5; 25:28; 2 Sam 7:11, 27; 1 Kin 11:38 [c]1 Sam 10:9, 10; 12:3; 16:13

36 [1]Or *payment* [2]Lit *attach*

3:1 [1]Lit *no vision spread abroad* [a]1 Sam 2:11, 18 [b]Ps 74:9; Ezek 7:26; Amos 8:11, 12

2 [a]Gen 27:1; 48:10; 1 Sam 4:15

3 [a]Ex 25:31-37; Lev 24:2, 3

4 [a]Is 6:8

6 [1]Lit *said*

7 [a]Now Samuel did not yet know the LORD, nor had the word
of the LORD yet been revealed to him.
8 So the LORD called Samuel again for the third time. And he
arose and went to Eli and said, "Here I am, for you called me."
Then Eli discerned that the LORD was calling the boy.
9 And Eli said to Samuel, "Go lie down, and it shall be if He
calls you, that you shall say, 'Speak, LORD, for Your servant is
listening.'" So Samuel went and lay down in his place.
10 Then the LORD came and stood and called as at other times,
"Samuel! Samuel!" And Samuel said, "Speak, for Your servant
is listening."
11 The LORD said to Samuel, "Behold, [a]I am about to do a thing
in Israel at which both ears of everyone who hears it will tingle.
12 "In that day [a]I will carry out against Eli all that I have spoken
concerning his house, from beginning to end.
13 "For [a]I have told him that I am about to judge his house
forever for [b]the iniquity which he knew, because [c]his sons
brought a curse on themselves and [d]he did not rebuke them.
14 "Therefore I have sworn to the house of Eli that [a]the iniquity
of Eli's house shall not be atoned for by sacrifice or offering
forever."
15 So Samuel lay down until morning. Then he [a]opened the
doors of the house of the LORD. But Samuel was afraid to tell
[b]the vision to Eli.
16 Then Eli called Samuel and said, "Samuel, my son." And
he said, "Here I am."
17 He said, "What is the word that He spoke to you? Please do
not hide it from me. [a]May God do so to you, and more also, if you
hide anything from me of all the words that He spoke to you."
18 So Samuel told him everything and hid nothing from him.
And he said, "[a]It is the LORD; let Him do what seems good to
Him."
19 Thus [a]Samuel grew and [b]the LORD was with him and [c]let
none of his words [1]fail.
20 All Israel [a]from Dan even to Beersheba knew that Samuel
was confirmed as a prophet of the LORD.
21 And [a]the LORD appeared again at Shiloh, [b]because the LORD
revealed Himself to Samuel at Shiloh by the word of the LORD.

Chapter 4 Theme ____________________

4 Thus the word of Samuel came to all Israel. Now Israel went 1075 B.C.
out to meet the Philistines in battle and camped beside
[a]Ebenezer while the Philistines camped in [b]Aphek.
2 The Philistines drew up in battle array to meet Israel. When
the battle spread, Israel was [1]defeated before the Philistines
who killed about four thousand men on the battlefield.
3 When the people came into the camp, the elders of Israel
said, "[a]Why has the LORD defeated us today before the Philistines? [b]Let us take to ourselves from Shiloh the ark of the
covenant of the LORD, that [1]it may come among us and deliver
us from the power of our enemies."

7 [a]Acts 19:2; 1 Cor 13:11
11 [a]2 Kin 21:12; Jer 19:3
12 [a]1 Sam 2:27-36
13 [a]1 Sam 2:29-31 [b]1 Sam 2:22 [c]1 Sam 2:12, 17, 22 [d]Deut 17:12; 21:18
14 [a]Lev 15:31; Is 22:14
15 [a]1 Chr 15:23 [b]1 Sam 3:10
17 [a]2 Sam 3:35
18 [a]Ex 34:5-7; Lev 10:3; Job 2:10; Is 39:8
19 [1]Lit *fall to the ground* [a]1 Sam 2:21 [b]Gen 21:22; 28:15; 39:2 [c]1 Sam 9:6
20 [a]Judg 20:1
21 [a]Gen 12:7 [b]1 Sam 3:10
4:1 [a]1 Sam 7:12 [b]Josh 12:18; 1 Sam 29:1
2 [1]Lit *smitten*
3 [1]Or *he* [a]Josh 7:7, 8 [b]Num 10:35; Josh 6:6

4 So the people sent to Shiloh, and from there they carried
the ark of the covenant of the LORD of hosts [a]who sits *above* the
cherubim; and the two sons of Eli, Hophni and Phinehas, *were*
there with the ark of the covenant of God.
5 As the ark of the covenant of the LORD came into the camp,
[a]all Israel shouted with a great shout, so that the earth resounded.
6 When the Philistines heard the noise of the shout, they said,
"What *does* the noise of this great shout in the camp of the
Hebrews *mean?*" Then they understood that the ark of the LORD
had come into the camp.
7 The Philistines were afraid, for they said, "God has come
into the camp." And they said, "[a]Woe to us! For nothing like
this has happened before.
8 "Woe to us! Who shall deliver us from the hand of these
mighty gods? These are the gods who smote the Egyptians with
all *kinds of* plagues in the wilderness.
9 "[a]Take courage and be men, O Philistines, or you will become
slaves to the Hebrews, [b]as they have been slaves to you; therefore, be men and fight."
10 So the Philistines fought and [a]Israel was [1]defeated, and [b]every
man fled to his tent; and the slaughter was very great, for there
fell of Israel thirty thousand foot soldiers.
11 And the ark of God was taken; and [a]the two sons of Eli,
Hophni and Phinehas, died.
12 Now a man of Benjamin ran from the battle line and came to
Shiloh the same day with [a]his clothes torn and [1]dust on his head.
13 When he came, behold, [a]Eli was sitting on *his* seat [1]by the
road eagerly watching, because his heart was trembling for the
ark of God. So the man came to tell *it* in the city, and all the
city cried out.
14 When Eli heard the noise of the outcry, he said, "What
does the noise of this commotion *mean?*" Then the man came
hurriedly and told Eli.
15 Now Eli was ninety-eight years old, and [a]his eyes were set
so that he could not see.
16 The man said to Eli, "I am the one who came from the
battle line. Indeed, I escaped from the battle line today." And
he said, "[a]How did things go, my son?"
17 Then the one who brought the news replied, "Israel has
fled before the Philistines and there has also been a great
slaughter among the people, and your two sons also, Hophni
and Phinehas, are dead, and the ark of God has been taken."
18 When he mentioned the ark of God, [1a]Eli fell off the seat
backward beside the gate, and his neck was broken and he died,
for [2]he was old and heavy. Thus he judged Israel forty years.
19 Now his daughter-in-law, Phinehas's wife, was pregnant and
about to give birth; and when she heard the news that the ark of
God was taken and that her father-in-law and her husband had
died, she kneeled down and gave birth, for her pains came
upon her.
20 And about the time of her death the women who stood by

4 [a]Ex 25:22; 2 Sam 6:2; Ps 80:1

5 [a]Josh 6:5, 20

7 [a]Ex 15:14

9 [a]1 Cor 16:13 [b]Judg 13:1; 1 Sam 14:21

10 [1]Lit *smitten* [a]Deut 28:15, 25; 1 Sam 4:2 [b]2 Sam 18:17; 19:8; 2 Kin 14:12; 2 Chr 25:22

11 [a]1 Sam 2:34; Ps 78:56-64

12 [1]Lit *ground* [a]Josh 7:6; 2 Sam 1:2; 15:32; Neh 9:1; Job 2:12

13 [1]Gr version reads *beside the gate watching the road* [a]1 Sam 1:9; 4:18

15 [a]1 Sam 3:2; 1 Kin 14:4

16 [a]2 Sam 1:4

18 [1]Lit *he* [2]Lit *the man* [a]1 Sam 4:13

20 [a]Gen 35:16-19

her said to her, "[a]Do not be afraid, for you have given birth to a
son." But she did not answer or pay attention.
21 And she called the boy [1]Ichabod, saying, "[a]The glory has
departed from Israel," because [b]the ark of God was taken and
because of her father-in-law and her husband.
22 She said, "The glory has departed from Israel, for the ark of
God was taken."

21 [1]I.e. No glory [a]Ps 26:8; Jer 2:11 [b]1 Sam 4:11

Chapter 5 Theme ________________________

5:1 [a]1 Sam 4:1; 7:12 [b]Josh 13:3

5 Now the Philistines took the ark of God and [a]brought it from
Ebenezer to [b]Ashdod.
2 Then the Philistines took the ark of God and brought it to
[a]the house of Dagon and set it by Dagon.
3 When the Ashdodites arose early the next morning, behold,
[a]Dagon had fallen on his face to the ground before the ark of
the LORD. So they took Dagon and [b]set him in his place again.
4 But when they arose early the next morning, behold, [a]Dagon
had fallen on his face to the ground before the ark of the LORD.
And the head of Dagon and both the palms of his hands *were* cut
off on the threshold; [1]only the trunk of Dagon was left to him.
5 Therefore neither the
priests of Dagon nor all who
enter Dagon's house [a]tread
on the threshold of Dagon
in Ashdod to this day.
6 Now [a]the hand of the
LORD was heavy on the Ashdodites, and [b]He ravaged
them and smote them with
[c]tumors, both Ashdod and
its territories.
7 When the men of Ashdod
saw that it was so, they said,
"The ark of the God of
Israel must not remain with
us, for His hand is severe
on us and on Dagon our
god."
8 So they sent and
[a]gathered all the lords of the Philistines to them and said,
"What shall we do with the ark of the God of Israel?" And they
said, "Let the ark of the God of Israel be brought around to
Gath." And they brought the ark of the God of Israel *around.*
9 After they had brought it around, [a]the hand of the LORD
was against the city with very great confusion; and He smote
the men of the city, both young and old, so that [b]tumors broke
out on them.
10 So they sent the ark of God to Ekron. And as the ark of God
came to Ekron the Ekronites cried out, saying, "They have
brought the ark of the God of Israel around to [1]us, to kill [1]us
and [2]our people."

2 [a]Judg 16:23-30; 1 Chr 10:8-10

3 [a]Is 19:1; 46:1, 2 [b]Is 46:7

4 [1]So with ancient versions; Heb *only Dagon* [a]Ezek 6:4, 6; Mic 1:7

5 [a]Zeph 1:9

6 [a]Ex 9:3; 1 Sam 5:7, 11; Ps 32:4; 145:20; 147:6; Acts 13:11 [b]1 Sam 6:5 [c]Deut 28:27; Ps 78:66

8 [a]1 Sam 5:11; 29:6-11

9 [a]Deut 2:15; 1 Sam 5:11; 7:13; 12:15 [b]1 Sam 5:6

10 [1]Lit *me* [2]Lit *my*

INSIGHT

Dagon, the chief deity of the Philistines, dates back to Mesopotamia and the third millennium B.C. According to ancient literature Dagon was the father of Baal. (See Judges 16:23; 1 Chronicles 10:10.)

The Wanderings of the Ark
(see page 2099)

11 They [a]sent therefore and gathered all the lords of the
Philistines and said, "Send away the ark of the God of Israel,
and let it return to its own place, so that it will not kill [1]us and
[2]our people." For there was a deadly confusion throughout the
city; [b]the hand of God was very heavy there.
12 And the men who did not die were smitten with tumors
and [a]the cry of the city went up to heaven.

Chapter 6 Theme ______________________________

6 Now the ark of the LORD had been in the [1]country of the
Philistines seven months.
2 And [a]the Philistines called for the priests and the diviners,
saying, "What shall we do with the ark of the LORD? Tell us
[1]how we shall send it to its place."
3 They said, "If you send away the ark of the God of Israel,
[a]do not send it empty; but you shall surely [b]return to Him a
guilt offering. Then you will be healed and it will be known to
you why His hand is not removed from you."
4 Then they said, "What shall be the guilt offering which we
shall return to Him?" And they said, "Five golden [a]tumors and
five golden mice [b]*according to* the number of the lords of the
Philistines, for one plague was on all of [1]you and on your lords.
5 "So you shall make likenesses of your tumors and likenesses
of your mice that ravage the land, and [a]you shall give glory to
the God of Israel; perhaps [b]He will ease His hand from you,
[c]your gods, and your land.
6 "Why then do you harden your hearts [a]as the Egyptians and
Pharaoh hardened their hearts? When He had severely dealt
with them, [b]did they not allow [1]the people to go, and they
departed?
7 "Now therefore, take and [a]prepare a new cart and two milch
cows on which there [b]has never been a yoke; and hitch the
cows to the cart and take their calves home, away from them.
8 "Take the ark of the LORD and place it on the cart; and put
[a]the articles of gold which you return to Him as [b]a guilt offering
in a box by its side. Then send it away that it may go.
9 "Watch, if it goes up by the way of its own territory to [a]Beth-
shemesh, then He has done us this great evil. But if not, then
[b]we will know that it was not His hand that struck us; it
happened to us by chance."
10 Then the men did so, and took two milch cows and hitched
them to the cart, and shut up their calves at home.
11 They put the ark of the LORD on the cart, and the box with
the golden mice and the likenesses of their tumors.
12 And the cows took the straight way in the [1]direction of [a]Beth-
shemesh; they went along [b]the highway, lowing as they went,
and did not turn aside to the right or to the left. And the lords
of the Philistines followed them to the border of Beth-shemesh.
13 Now *the people of* Beth-shemesh were reaping their wheat
harvest in the valley, and they raised their eyes and saw the ark
and were glad to see *it*.

11 [1]Lit *me* [2]Lit *my* [a]1 Sam 5:8 [b]1 Sam 5:6, 9

12 [a]Ex 12:30; Is 15:3

6:1 [1]Lit *field*

2 [1]Or *with what* [a]Gen 41:8; Ex 7:11; Is 2:6

3 [a]Ex 23:15; Deut 16:16 [b]Lev 5:15, 16

4 [1]Lit *them* [a]1 Sam 5:6, 9, 12; 6:17 [b]Josh 13:3; Judg 3:3; 1 Sam 6:17, 18

5 [a]Josh 7:19; 1 Chr 16:28, 29; Is 42:12; Jer 13:16; John 9:24; Rev 14:7 [b]1 Sam 5:6, 11 [c]1 Sam 5:3, 4, 7

6 [1]Lit *them* [a]Ex 7:13; 8:15, 32; 9:34; 14:17 [b]Ex 12:31

7 [a]2 Sam 6:3 [b]Num 19:2; Deut 21:3, 4

8 [a]1 Sam 6:4, 5 [b]1 Sam 6:3

9 [a]Josh 15:10; 21:16 [b]1 Sam 6:3

12 [1]Lit *way* [a]1 Sam 6:9 [b]Num 20:19

14 [a]2 Sam 24:22; 1 Kin 19:21
14 The cart came into the field of Joshua the Beth-shemite and
stood there where there *was* a large stone; and they split the wood
of the cart and [a]offered the cows as a burnt offering to the LORD.

15 [a]Josh 3:3
15 [a]The Levites took down the ark of the LORD and the box
that was with it, in which were the articles of gold, and put
them on the large stone; and the men of Beth-shemesh offered
burnt offerings and sacrificed sacrifices that day to the LORD.

16 [a]Josh 13:3; Judg 3:3
16 When the [a]five lords of the Philistines saw it, they returned
to Ekron that day.

17 [a]1 Sam 6:4
17 [a]These are the golden tumors which the Philistines returned
for a guilt offering to the LORD: one for Ashdod, one for Gaza,
one for Ashkelon, one for Gath, one for Ekron;

18 [1]So some mss and versions; Heb *Abel* [a]Deut 3:5 [b]1 Sam 6:14, 15
18 and the golden mice, *according* to the number of all the cities
of the Philistines belonging to the five lords, [a]both of fortified
cities and of country villages. [b]The large [1]stone on which they
set the ark of the LORD *is a witness* to this day in the field of
Joshua the Beth-shemite.

19 [a]Ex 19:21; Num 4:5, 15, 20; 2 Sam 6:7
19 [a]He struck down some of the men of Beth-shemesh because
they had looked into the ark of the LORD. He struck down of all
the people, 50,070 men, and the people mourned because the
LORD had struck the people with a great slaughter.

20 [a]Lev 11:44, 45; 2 Sam 6:9; Mal 3:2; Rev 6:17
20 The men of Beth-shemesh said, "[a]Who is able to stand before
the LORD, this holy God? And to whom shall He go up from us?"

21 [a]Josh 9:17; 15:9, 60; 1 Chr 13:5, 6
21 So they sent messengers to the inhabitants of [a]Kiriath-jearim,
saying, "The Philistines have brought back the ark of the LORD;
come down and take it up to you."

Chapter 7 Theme ____________________

7:1 [a]2 Sam 6:3, 4
7 And the men of Kiriath-jearim came and took the ark of the
LORD and [a]brought it into the house of Abinadab on the hill,
and consecrated Eleazar his son to keep the ark of the LORD.

2 From the day that the ark remained at Kiriath-jearim, the
time was long, for it was twenty years; and all the house of
Israel lamented after the LORD.

3 [a]1 Kin 8:48; Is 55:7; Hos 6:1; Joel 2:12-14 [b]Gen 35:2; Josh 24:14, 23; Judg 10:16 [c]Judg 2:13; 1 Sam 31:10 [d]Deut 13:4; 2 Chr 19:3 [e]Deut 6:13; 10:20; 13:4; Josh 24:14; Matt 4:10; Luke 4:8
3 Then Samuel spoke to all the house of Israel, saying, "[a]If you
return to the LORD with all your heart, [b]remove the foreign gods
and the [c]Ashtaroth from among you and [d]direct your hearts to
the LORD and [e]serve Him alone; and He will deliver you from
the hand of the Philistines."

4 So the sons of Israel removed the Baals and the Ashtaroth
and served the LORD alone.

5 [a]Judg 10:17; 20:1 [b]1 Sam 8:6; 12:17-19
5 Then Samuel said, "Gather all Israel to [a]Mizpah and [b]I will
pray to the LORD for you."

6 [a]1 Sam 1:15; Ps 62:8; Lam 2:19 [b]Lev 16:29; Neh 9:1 [c]Judg 10:10; 1 Kin 8:47; Ps 106:6
6 They gathered to Mizpah, and drew water and [a]poured it
out before the LORD, and [b]fasted on that day and said there,
"[c]We have sinned against the LORD." And Samuel judged the
sons of Israel at Mizpah.

7 [a]1 Sam 13:6; 17:11
7 Now when the Philistines heard that the sons of Israel had
gathered to Mizpah, the lords of the Philistines went up against
Israel. And when the sons of Israel heard it, [a]they were afraid
of the Philistines.

8 Then the sons of Israel said to Samuel, "[a]Do not cease to
cry to the LORD our God for us, that He may save us from the
hand of the Philistines."
9 Samuel took [a]a suckling lamb and offered it for a whole
burnt offering to the LORD; and Samuel cried to the LORD for
Israel and [b]the LORD answered him.
10 Now Samuel was offering up the burnt offering, and the
Philistines drew near to battle against Israel. But [a]the LORD
thundered with a great [1]thunder on that day against the
Philistines and [b]confused them, so that they were [2]routed
before Israel.
11 The men of Israel went out of Mizpah and pursued the
Philistines, and struck them down as far as below Beth-car.
12 Then Samuel [a]took a stone and set it between Mizpah and
Shen, and named it [1]Ebenezer, saying, "Thus far the LORD has
helped us."
13 [a]So the Philistines were subdued and [b]they did not come
anymore within the border of Israel. And the hand of the LORD
was against the Philistines all the days of Samuel.
14 The cities which the Philistines had taken from Israel were
restored to Israel, from Ekron even to Gath; and Israel delivered
their territory from the hand of the Philistines. So there was
peace between Israel and [a]the Amorites.
15 Now Samuel [a]judged Israel all the days of his life.
16 He used to go annually on circuit to [a]Bethel and [b]Gilgal and
[c]Mizpah, and he judged Israel in all these places.
17 Then his return *was* to [a]Ramah, for his house *was* there, and
there he judged Israel; and he [b]built there an altar to the LORD.

Chapter 8 Theme ______________________________

8 And it came about when Samuel was old that [a]he appointed
his sons judges over Israel.
2 Now the name of his firstborn was Joel, and the name of
his second, Abijah; *they* were judging in [a]Beersheba.
3 His sons, however, did not walk in his ways, but turned
aside after dishonest gain and [a]took bribes and perverted justice.
4 Then all the elders of Israel gathered together and came to
Samuel at [a]Ramah;
5 and they said to him, "Behold, you have grown old, and
your sons do not walk in your ways. Now [a]appoint a king for us
to judge us like all the nations."
6 But the thing was [1a]displeasing in the sight of Samuel when
they said, "Give us a king to judge us." And [b]Samuel prayed to
the LORD.
7 The LORD said to Samuel, "Listen to the voice of the people
in regard to all that they say to you, for [a]they have not rejected
you, but they have rejected Me from being king over them.
8 "Like all the deeds which they have done since the day that I
brought them up from Egypt even to this day—in that they have
forsaken Me and served other gods—so they are doing to you also.

8 [a]1 Sam 12:19-24; Is 37:4
9 [a]Lev 22:27 [b]Ps 99:6; Jer 15:1
10 [1]Lit *voice* [2]Lit *smitten* [a]1 Sam 2:10; 2 Sam 22:14, 15; Ps 29:3, 4 [b]Josh 10:10; Ps 18:14
12 [1]I.e. The stone of help [a]Gen 35:14; Josh 4:9; 24:26
13 [a]Judg 13:1-15 [b]1 Sam 13:5
14 [a]Num 13:29; Josh 10:5-10
15 [a]1 Sam 7:6
16 [a]Gen 28:19; 35:6 [b]Josh 5:9, 10 [c]1 Sam 7:5
17 [a]1 Sam 1:1, 19; 2:11 [b]Judg 21:4
8:1 [a]Deut 16:18, 19
2 [a]Gen 22:19; 1 Kin 19:3; Amos 5:5
3 [a]Ex 23:6, 8; Deut 16:19
4 [a]1 Sam 7:17
5 [a]Deut 17:14, 15
6 [1]Or *evil* [a]1 Sam 12:17 [b]1 Sam 15:11
7 [a]Ex 16:8; 1 Sam 10:19

9 “Now then, listen to their voice; [a]however, you shall solemnly
[1]warn them and tell them of [b]the [2]procedure of the king who
will reign over them.”
10 So Samuel spoke all the words of the LORD to [a]the people
who had asked of him a king.
11 He said, “[a]This will be the [1]procedure of the king who will
reign over you: [b]he will take your sons and place *them* for
himself in his chariots and among his horsemen and [c]they will
run before his chariots.
12 “[a]He will appoint for himself commanders of thousands and
of fifties, and *some* to [1]do his plowing and to reap his harvest
and to make his weapons of war and equipment for his chariots.
13 “He will also take your daughters for perfumers and cooks
and bakers.
14 “[a]He will take the best of your fields and your vineyards and
your olive groves and give *them* to his servants.
15 “He will take a tenth of your seed and of your vineyards and
give to his officers and to his servants.
16 “He will also take your male servants and your female servants
and your best young men and your donkeys and [1]use *them* for
his work.
17 “He will take a tenth of your flocks, and you yourselves will
become his servants.
18 “Then [a]you will cry out in that day because of your king
whom you have chosen for yourselves, but [b]the LORD will not
answer you in that day.”
19 Nevertheless, the people [a]refused to listen to the voice of
Samuel, and they said, “No, but there shall be a king over us,
20 [a]that we also may be like all the nations, that our king may
judge us and go out before us and fight our battles.”
21 Now after Samuel had heard all the words of the people,
[a]he repeated them in the LORD’s hearing.
22 The LORD said to Samuel, “[a]Listen to their voice and [1]appoint
them a king.” So Samuel said to the men of Israel, “Go every
man to his city.”

Chapter 9 Theme ____________________

9 Now there was a man of Benjamin whose name was [a]Kish
the son of Abiel, the son of Zeror, the son of Becorath, the
son of Aphiah, the son of a Benjamite, a mighty man of [1]valor.
2 He had a son whose name was Saul, a [a]choice and handsome
man, and there was not a more handsome person than he
among the sons of Israel; [b]from his shoulders and up he was
taller than any of the people.
3 Now the donkeys of Kish, Saul’s father, were lost. So Kish
said to his son Saul, “Take now with you one of the servants,
and arise, go search for the donkeys.”
4 He passed through [a]the hill country of Ephraim and passed
through the land of [b]Shalishah, but they did not find *them.*
Then they passed through the land of [c]Shaalim, but *they were*

9 [1]Lit *testify to* [2]Lit *custom* [a]Ezek 3:18 [b]1 Sam 8:11-18; 10:25
10 [a]1 Sam 8:4
11 [1]Lit *custom* [a]Deut 17:14-20; 1 Sam 10:25 [b]1 Sam 14:52 [c]2 Sam 15:1
12 [1]Lit *plow his plowing* [a]Num 31:14; 1 Sam 22:7
14 [a]1 Kin 21:7; Ezek 46:18
16 [1]Lit *make*
18 [a]Is 8:21 [b]Prov 1:25-28; Is 1:15; Mic 3:4
19 [a]Is 66:4; Jer 44:16
20 [a]1 Sam 8:5
21 [a]Judg 11:11
22 [1]Lit *cause a king to reign for them* [a]1 Sam 8:7
9:1 [1]Or *wealth* or *influence* [a]1 Sam 14:51; 1 Chr 8:33; 9:36-39
2 [a]1 Sam 10:24 [b]1 Sam 10:23
4 [a]Josh 24:33 [b]2 Kin 4:42 [c]Josh 19:42

not *there.* Then he passed through the land of the Benjamites,
but they did not find *them.*
5 When they came to the land of [a]Zuph, Saul said to his
servant who was with him, "Come, and let us return, [b]or else
my father will cease *to be concerned* about the donkeys and
will become anxious for us."
6 He said to him, "Behold now, there is [a]a man of God in this
city, and the man is held in honor; [b]all that he says surely
comes true. Now let us go there, [c]perhaps he can tell us about
our journey on which we have set out."
7 Then Saul said to his servant, "But behold, if we go, what
shall we bring the man? For the bread is gone from our sack and
there is [a]no present to bring to the man of God. What do we
have?"
8 The servant answered Saul again and said, "Behold, I have
in my hand a fourth of a shekel of silver; I will give *it* to the
man of God and he will [a]tell us our way."
9 (Formerly in Israel, when a man went to inquire of God, he
used to say, "Come, and let us go to the seer"; for *he who is*
called a prophet now was formerly called [a]a seer.)
10 Then Saul said to his servant, "Well said; come, let us go."
So they went to the city where the man of God was.
11 As they went up the slope to the city, [a]they found young
women going out to draw water and said to them, "Is the seer
here?"
12 They answered them and said, "He is; [1]see, *he is* ahead of
you. Hurry now, for he has come into the city today, for [a]the
people have a sacrifice on [b]the high place today.
13 "As soon as you enter the city you will find him before he
goes up to the high place to eat, for the people will not eat until
he comes, because [a]he must bless the sacrifice; afterward those
who are invited will eat. Now therefore, go up for you will find
him at once."
14 So they went up to the city. As they came into the city,
behold, Samuel was coming out toward them to go up to the
high place.
15 Now a day before Saul's coming, [a]the LORD had [1]revealed
this to Samuel saying,
16 "About this time tomorrow I will send you a man from the
land of Benjamin, and [a]you shall anoint him to be prince over
My people Israel; and he will deliver My people from the hand
of the Philistines. For [b]I have regarded My people, because
their cry has come to Me."
17 When Samuel saw Saul, the LORD [1]said to him, "[a]Behold,
the man of whom I spoke to you! This one shall rule over My
people."
18 Then Saul approached Samuel in the gate and said, "Please
tell me where the seer's house is."
19 Samuel answered Saul and said, "I am the seer. Go up
before me to the high place, for you shall eat with me today;
and in the morning I will let you go, and will tell you all that is
on your mind.

5 [a]1 Sam 1:1 [b]1 Sam 10:2
6 [a]Deut 33:1; 1 Kin 13:1; 2 Kin 5:8 [b]1 Sam 3:19 [c]Gen 24:42
7 [a]1 Kin 14:3; 2 Kin 5:15; 8:8, 9; Ezek 13:19
8 [a]1 Sam 9:6
9 [a]2 Sam 24:11; 2 Kin 17:13; 1 Chr 9:22; 26:28; 29:29; Is 30:10; Amos 7:12
11 [a]Gen 24:11, 15; 29:8, 9; Ex 2:16
12 [1]Or *behold* [a]Gen 31:54; Num 28:11-15; 1 Kin 3:2 [b]1 Sam 7:17; 10:5
13 [a]Luke 9:16; John 6:11
15 [1]Lit *uncovered the ear* [a]1 Sam 15:1; Acts 13:21
16 [a]1 Sam 10:1 [b]Ex 3:7, 9
17 [1]Lit *answered* [a]1 Sam 16:12

20 [a]1 Sam 9:3 [b]1 Sam 8:5; 12:13

20 "[a]As for your donkeys which were lost three days ago, do
not set your mind on them, for they have been found. And [b]for
whom is all that is desirable in Israel? Is it not for you and for
all your father's household?"

21 [1]So some ancient versions; Heb *tribes* [a]1 Sam 15:17 [b]Judg 20:46-48

21 Saul replied, "[a]Am I not a Benjamite, of [b]the smallest of the
tribes of Israel, and my family the least of all the families of the
[1]tribe of Benjamin? Why then do you speak to me in this way?"
22 Then Samuel took Saul and his servant and brought them
into the hall and gave them a place at the head of those who
were invited, who were about thirty men.

23 [1]Lit *Give* [2]Lit *with you*

23 Samuel said to the cook, "[1]Bring the portion that I gave
you, concerning which I said to you, 'Set it [2]aside.'"

24 [1]Lit *saying* [a]Ex 29:22, 27; Lev 7:32, 33; Num 18:18

24 Then the cook [a]took up the leg with what was on it and set
it before Saul. And *Samuel* said, "Here is what has been
reserved! Set *it* before you *and* eat, because it has been kept for
you until the appointed time, [1]since I said I have invited the
people." So Saul ate with Samuel that day.

25 [1]Gr adds *and they spread a bed for Saul on the roof and he slept* [a]Deut 22:8; Luke 5:19; Acts 10:9

25 When they came down from the high place into the city,
Samuel spoke with Saul [a]on the [1]roof.
26 And they arose early; and at daybreak Samuel called to Saul
on the roof, saying, "Get up, that I may send you away." So Saul
arose, and both he and Samuel went out into the street.
27 As they were going down to the edge of the city, Samuel
said to Saul, "Say to the servant that he might go ahead of us
and pass on, but you remain standing now, that I may proclaim
the word of God to you."

10:1 [a]Ex 30:23-33; 1 Sam 16:13; 2 Kin 9:3, 6 [b]Ps 2:12 [c]1 Sam 16:13; 26:9; 2 Sam 1:14 [d]Deut 32:9; Ps 78:71

Chapter 10 Theme ______________________________

10 Then [a]Samuel took the flask of oil, poured it on his head,
[b]kissed him and said, "Has not [c]the LORD anointed you a
ruler over [d]His inheritance?

2 [1]Lit *abandoned the matter of* [a]Gen 35:16-20; 48:7 [b]1 Sam 9:3-5

2 "When you go from me today, then you will find two men
close to [a]Rachel's tomb in the territory of Benjamin at Zelzah;
and they will say to you, '[b]The donkeys which you went to look
for have been found. Now behold, your father has [1]ceased to
be concerned about the donkeys and is anxious for you, saying,
"What shall I do about my son?"'

3 [1]Or *terebinth* [a]Gen 35:8 [b]Gen 28:19; 35:1, 3, 7

3 "Then you will go on further from there, and you will come as
far as the [1a]oak of Tabor, and there three men going up [b]to God at
Bethel will meet you, one carrying three young goats, another
carrying three loaves of bread, and another carrying a jug of wine;
4 and they will greet you and give you two *loaves* of bread,
which you will accept from their hand.

5 [1]Or *Gibeath-haelohim* [a]1 Sam 13:2, 3 [b]1 Sam 19:20; 2 Kin 2:3, 5, 15 [c]2 Kin 3:15; 1 Chr 25:1-6; 1 Cor 14:1

5 "Afterward you will come to [1a]the hill of God where the
Philistine garrison is; and it shall be as soon as you have come
there to the city, that you will meet [b]a group of prophets
coming down from the high place with harp, tambourine, flute,
and a lyre before them, and [c]they will be prophesying.

6 [a]Num 11:25, 29; Judg 14:6 [b]1 Sam 10:10; 19:23, 24

6 "Then [a]the Spirit of the LORD will come upon you mightily, and
[b]you shall prophesy with them and be changed into another man.

7 "It shall be when these signs come to you, [a]do for yourself
what [1]the occasion requires, for [b]God is with you.
8 "And [a]you shall go down before me to Gilgal; and behold, I
will come down to you to offer burnt offerings and [b]sacrifice
peace offerings. [c]You shall wait seven days until I come to you
and show you what you should do."
9 Then it happened when he turned his back to leave Samuel,
God [a]changed [1]his heart; and all those signs came about on
that day.
10 [a]When they came to [1]the hill there, behold, a group of
prophets met him; and the Spirit of God came upon him
mightily, so that he prophesied among them.
11 It came about, when all who knew him previously saw that
he prophesied now with the prophets, that the people said to
one another, "What has happened to the son of Kish? [a]Is Saul
also among the prophets?"
12 A man there said, "Now, who is their father?" Therefore it
became a proverb: "[a]Is Saul also among the prophets?"
13 When he had finished prophesying, he came to the high
place.
14 Now [a]Saul's uncle said to him and his servant, "Where did
you go?" And he said, "[b]To look for the donkeys. When we saw
that they could not be found, we went to Samuel."
15 Saul's uncle said, "Please tell me what Samuel said to you."
16 So Saul said to his uncle, "[a]He told us plainly that the
donkeys had been found." But he did not tell him about the
matter of the kingdom which Samuel had mentioned.
17 Thereafter Samuel called the [a]people together to the LORD
at Mizpah;
18 and he said to the sons of Israel, "[a]Thus says the LORD, the
God of Israel, 'I brought Israel up from Egypt, and I delivered
you from the hand of the Egyptians and from the [1]power of all
the kingdoms that were oppressing you.'
19 "But you [a]have today rejected your God, who delivers you
from all your calamities and your distresses; yet you have [1]said,
'No, but set a king over us!' Now therefore, [b]present yourselves
before the LORD by your tribes and by your clans."
20 Thus Samuel brought all the tribes of Israel near, and the
tribe of Benjamin was taken by lot.
21 Then he brought the tribe of Benjamin near by its families,
and the Matrite family was taken. And Saul the son of Kish was
taken; but when they looked for him, he could not be found.
22 Therefore [a]they inquired further of the LORD, "Has the man
come here yet?" So the LORD said, "Behold, he is hiding himself
by the baggage."
23 So they ran and took him from there, and when he stood
among the people, [a]he was taller than any of the people from
his shoulders upward.
1051 B.C. 24 Samuel said to all the people, "Do you see him [a]whom the
LORD has chosen? Surely there is no one like him among all the
people." So all the people shouted and said, "[1][b]*Long* live the king!"

7 [1]Lit *your hand finds* [a]Eccl 9:10 [b]Josh 1:5; Judg 6:12; Heb 13:5

8 [a]1 Sam 11:14; 13:8 [b]1 Sam 11:15 [c]1 Sam 13:8

9 [1]Lit *for him another heart* [a]1 Sam 10:6

10 [1]Or *Gibeath* [a]1 Sam 10:5, 6; 19:20

11 [a]1 Sam 19:24; Amos 7:14, 15; Matt 13:54-57; John 7:15

12 [a]1 Sam 19:23, 24

14 [a]1 Sam 14:50 [b]1 Sam 9:3-6

16 [a]1 Sam 9:20

17 [a]Judg 20:1; 1 Sam 7:5

18 [1]Lit *hand* [a]Judg 6:8, 9

19 [1]So with several mss and versions; M.T. *said to Him* [a]1 Sam 8:6, 7; 12:12 [b]Josh 7:14-18; 24:1; Prov 16:33

22 [a]1 Sam 23:2, 4

23 [a]1 Sam 9:2

24 [1]Lit *May the king live* [a]Deut 17:15; 2 Sam 21:6 [b]1 Kin 1:25, 34, 39

25 Then Samuel told the people [a]the ordinances of the kingdom,
and wrote *them* in the book and [b]placed *it* before the LORD.
And Samuel sent all the people away, each one to his house.
26 Saul also went [a]to his house at Gibeah; and the valiant *men*
whose hearts God had touched went with him.
27 But certain [1][a]worthless men said, "How can this one deliver
us?" And they despised him and [b]did not bring him any present.
But he kept silent.

Chapter 11 Theme ________________________

11 Now [a]Nahash the Ammonite came up and [1]besieged
[b]Jabesh-gilead; and all the men of Jabesh said to Nahash,
"Make [c]a covenant with us and we will serve you."
2 But Nahash the Ammonite said to them, "I will make *it*
with you on this condition, [a]that I will gouge out the right eye of
every one of you, thus I will make it [b]a reproach on all Israel."
3 [a]The elders of Jabesh said to him, "Let us alone for seven days,
that we may send messengers throughout the territory of Israel.
Then, if there is no one to deliver us, we will come out to you."
4 Then the messengers
came [a]to Gibeah of Saul and
spoke these words in the
hearing of the people, and
all the people [b]lifted up
their voices and wept.
5 Now behold, Saul was
coming from the field
[a]behind the oxen, and [1]he
said, "What is *the matter*
with the people that they
weep?" So they related to
him the words of the men
of Jabesh.
6 Then [a]the Spirit of God
came upon Saul mightily
when he heard these words,
and [1]he became very angry.
7 He took a yoke of oxen
and [a]cut them in pieces, and sent *them* throughout the territory
of Israel by the hand of messengers, saying, "[b]Whoever does not
come out after Saul and after Samuel, so shall it be done to his
oxen." Then the dread of the LORD fell on the people, and they
came out [c]as one man.
8 He [1]numbered them in [a]Bezek; and the [b]sons of Israel
were 300,000, and the men of Judah 30,000.
9 They said to the messengers who had come, "Thus you
shall say to the men of Jabesh-gilead, 'Tomorrow, by the time
the sun is hot, you will have deliverance.'" So the messengers
went and told the men of Jabesh; and they were glad.
10 Then the men of Jabesh said, "[a]Tomorrow we will come out
to you, and you may do to us whatever seems good [1]to you."

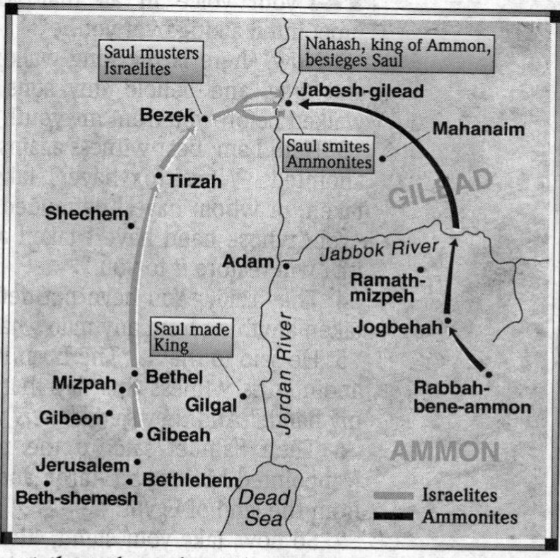

Saul's Ascent to Kingship

25 [a]Deut 17:14-20; 1 Sam 8:11-18 [b]Deut 31:26
26 [a]1 Sam 11:4; 15:34
27 [1]Lit *sons of Belial,* cf 2 Cor 6:15 [a]Deut 13:13; 1 Sam 25:17 [b]1 Kin 10:25; 2 Chr 17:5
11:1 [1]Lit *camped against* [a]1 Sam 12:12 [b]Judg 21:8; 1 Sam 31:11 [c]Gen 26:28; 1 Kin 20:34; Job 41:4; Ezek 17:13
2 [a]Num 16:14 [b]1 Sam 17:26; Ps 44:13
3 [a]1 Sam 8:4
4 [a]1 Sam 10:26; 15:34 [b]Gen 27:38; Judg 2:4; 20:23, 26; 21:2; 1 Sam 30:4
5 [1]Lit *Saul* [a]1 Kin 19:19
6 [1]Lit *his anger burned exceedingly* [a]Judg 3:10; 6:34; 11:29; 13:25; 14:6; 1 Sam 10:10; 16:13
7 [a]Judg 19:29 [b]Judg 21:5, 8 [c]Judg 20:1
8 [1]Lit *mustered* [a]Judg 1:5 [b]Judg 20:2
10 [1]Lit *in your sight* [a]1 Sam 11:3

11 The next morning Saul put the people [a]in three companies;
and they came into the midst of the camp at the morning
watch and struck down the Ammonites until the heat of the
day. Those who survived were scattered, so that no two of
them were left together.
12 Then the people said to Samuel, "[a]Who is he that said, 'Shall
Saul reign over us?' [1b]Bring the men, that we may put them to
death."
13 But Saul said, "[a]Not a man shall be put to death this day,
for today [b]the LORD has accomplished deliverance in Israel."
14 Then Samuel said to the people, "Come and let us go to
[a]Gilgal and [b]renew the kingdom there."
15 So all the people went to Gilgal, and there they made Saul
king [a]before the LORD in Gilgal. There they also [b]offered sacrifices
of peace offerings before the LORD; and there Saul and all the
men of Israel rejoiced greatly.

Chapter 12 Theme ________________________

12 Then Samuel said to all Israel, "Behold, [a]I have listened to
your voice in all that you said to me and I [b]have
[1]appointed a king over you.
2 "Now, [a]here is the king walking before you, but [b]I am old
and gray, and behold [c]my sons are with you. And [d]I have
walked before you from my youth even to this day.
3 "Here I am; bear witness against me before the LORD and [a]His
anointed. [b]Whose ox have I taken, or whose donkey have I
taken, or whom have I defrauded? Whom have I oppressed, or
[c]from whose hand have I taken a bribe to blind my eyes with
it? I will restore *it* to you."
4 They said, "You have not defrauded us or oppressed us or
taken anything from any man's hand."
5 He said to them, "The LORD is witness against you, and His
anointed is witness this day that [a]you have found nothing [b]in
my hand." And they said, "*He is* witness."
6 Then Samuel said to the people, "It is the LORD who
[1a]appointed Moses and Aaron and who brought your fathers up
from the land of Egypt.
7 "So now, take your stand, [a]that I may plead with you before
the LORD concerning all the righteous acts of the LORD which
He did for you and your fathers.
8 "[a]When Jacob went into Egypt and [b]your fathers cried out to
the LORD, then [c]the LORD sent Moses and Aaron [1d]who brought
your fathers out of Egypt and settled them in this place.
9 "But [a]they forgot the LORD their God, so [b]He sold them into
the hand of Sisera, captain of the army of Hazor, and [c]into the
hand of the Philistines and [d]into the hand of the king of Moab,
and they fought against them.
10 "[a]They cried out to the LORD and said, 'We have sinned
because we have forsaken the LORD and have served [b]the Baals
and the Ashtaroth; but [c]now deliver us from the hands of our
enemies, and we will serve You.'

11 [a]Judg 7:16, 20
12 [1]Lit *Give* [a]1 Sam 10:27 [b]Luke 19:27
13 [a]1 Sam 10:27; 2 Sam 19:22 [b]Ex 14:13, 30; 1 Sam 19:5
14 [a]1 Sam 7:16; 10:8 [b]1 Sam 10:25
15 [a]1 Sam 10:17 [b]1 Sam 10:8
12:1 [1]Lit *made* [a]1 Sam 8:7, 9, 22 [b]1 Sam 10:24; 11:14, 15
2 [a]1 Sam 8:20 [b]1 Sam 8:1, 5 [c]1 Sam 8:3, 5 [d]1 Sam 3:10, 19, 20
3 [a]1 Sam 10:1; 24:6; 2 Sam 1:14 [b]Ex 20:17; Num 16:15; Acts 20:33 [c]Ex 23:8; Deut 16:19
5 [a]Acts 23:9; 24:20 [b]Ex 22:4
6 [1]Lit *made* [a]Ex 6:26; Mic 6:4
7 [a]Ezek 20:35; Mic 6:1-5
8 [1]Lit *and they brought* [a]Gen 46:5, 6 [b]Ex 2:23-25 [c]Ex 3:10; 4:14-16 [d]1 Sam 10:18
9 [a]Deut 32:18; Judg 3:7 [b]Judg 4:2 [c]Judg 3:31; 10:7; 13:1 [d]Judg 3:12-30
10 [a]Judg 10:10 [b]Judg 2:13; 3:7 [c]Judg 10:15, 16

11 "Then the LORD sent [a]Jerubbaal and [1b]Bedan and [c]Jephthah
and [d]Samuel, and delivered you from the hands of your enemies
all around, so that you lived in security.
12 "When you saw [a]that Nahash the king of the sons of Ammon
came against you, you said to me, '[b]No, but a king shall reign
over us,' [c]although the LORD your God *was* your king.
13 "Now therefore, [a]here is the king whom you have chosen,
[b]whom you have asked for, and behold, the LORD has set a king
over you.
14 "[a]If you will fear the LORD and serve Him, and listen to His
voice and not rebel against the [1]command of the LORD, then
both you and also the king who reigns over you will follow the
LORD your God.
15 "[a]If you will not listen to the voice of the LORD, but rebel
against the [1]command of the LORD, then [b]the hand of the LORD
will be against you, [c]*as it was* against your fathers.
16 "Even now, [a]take your stand and see this great thing which
the LORD will do before your eyes.
17 "[a]Is it not the wheat harvest today? [b]I will call to the LORD,
that He may send [1]thunder and rain. Then you will know and
see that [c]your wickedness is great which you have done in the
sight of the LORD by asking for yourselves a king."
18 So Samuel called to the LORD, and the LORD sent [1]thunder
and rain that day; and [a]all the people greatly feared the LORD
and Samuel.
19 Then all the people said to Samuel, "[a]Pray for your servants
to the LORD your God, so that we may not die, for we have
added to all our sins [b]*this* evil by asking for ourselves a king."
20 Samuel said to the people, "Do not fear. You have committed
all this evil, yet [a]do not turn aside from following the LORD, but
serve the LORD with all your heart.
21 "You must not turn aside, for *then you would go* after [a]futile
things which can not profit or deliver, because they are futile.
22 "For [a]the LORD will not abandon His people [b]on account of
His great name, because the LORD [c]has been pleased to make
you a people for Himself.
23 "Moreover, as for me, [a]far be it from me that I should sin
against the LORD by ceasing to pray for you; but [b]I will instruct
you in the good and right way.
24 "[a]Only [1]fear the LORD and serve Him in truth with all your
heart; for consider [b]what great things He has done for you.
25 "[a]But if you still do wickedly, [b]both you and your king [c]will
be swept away."

Chapter 13 Theme

13 Saul was [1]*thirty* years old when he began to reign, and
he reigned [2]*forty* two years over Israel. 1051 B.C.
2 Now Saul chose for himself 3,000 men of Israel, of which
2,000 were with Saul in [a]Michmash and in the hill country of
Bethel, while 1,000 were with Jonathan at [b]Gibeah of Benjamin.
But he sent away the rest of the people, each to his tent.

11 [1]Gr and Syr read *Barak* [a]Judg 6:31, 32; 7:1 [b]Judg 4:6; 11:1 [c]Judg 11:29 [d]1 Sam 3:20
12 [a]1 Sam 11:1, 2 [b]1 Sam 8:6, 19 [c]Judg 8:23; 1 Sam 8:7
13 [a]1 Sam 10:24 [b]1 Sam 8:5; 12:17, 19; Hos 13:11
14 [1]Lit *mouth* [a]Josh 24:14
15 [1]Lit *mouth* [a]Lev 26:14, 15; Josh 24:20; Is 1:20 [b]1 Sam 5:9 [c]1 Sam 12:9
16 [a]Ex 14:13, 31
17 [1]Lit *sounds* [a]Prov 26:1 [b]1 Sam 7:9, 10; James 5:16ff [c]1 Sam 8:7
18 [1]Lit *sounds* [a]Ex 14:31
19 [a]Ex 9:28; 1 Sam 12:23; Jer 15:1; 1 John 5:16 [b]1 Sam 12:17, 20
20 [a]Deut 11:16
21 [a]Deut 11:16; Is 41:29; Hab 2:18
22 [a]Deut 31:6; 1 Kin 6:13 [b]Ex 32:12; Num 14:13; Josh 7:9; Ps 106:8; Jer 14:21 [c]Deut 7:6-11; 1 Pet 2:9
23 [a]Rom 1:9; 1 Cor 9:16; Col 1:9; 1 Thess 3:10; 2 Tim 1:3 [b]1 Kin 8:36; Ps 34:11; Prov 4:11
24 [1]Or *reverence* [a]Eccl 12:13 [b]Deut 10:21; Is 5:12
25 [a]Is 1:20; 3:11 [b]Josh 24:20 [c]1 Sam 31:1-5; Hos 10:3
13:1 [1]As in some mss of the LXX; Heb omits *thirty* [2]See Acts 13:21; Heb omits *forty*
2 [a]1 Sam 13:5; 14:31 [b]1 Sam 10:26

3 Jonathan smote [a]the garrison of the Philistines that was in
[b]Geba, and the Philistines heard of *it.* Then Saul [c]blew the
trumpet throughout the land, saying, "Let the Hebrews hear."
4 All Israel heard [1]the news that Saul had smitten the
garrison of the Philistines, and also that Israel [a]had become
odious to the Philistines. The people were then summoned [2]to
Saul at Gilgal.

The Philistines' Attack on the Israelites

5 Now the Philistines assembled to fight with Israel, 30,000
chariots and 6,000 horsemen, and [a]people like the sand which
is on the seashore in abun-
dance; and they came up and
camped in Michmash, east of
[b]Beth-aven.

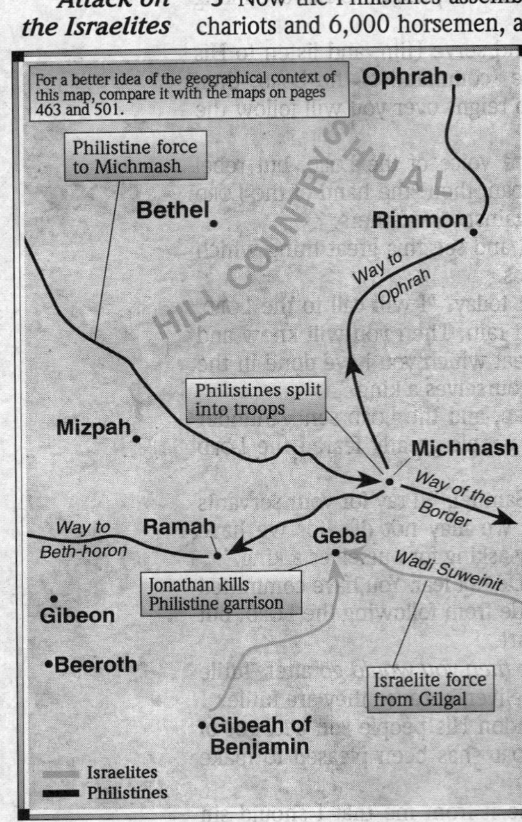

6 When the men of Israel
saw that they were in a
strait (for the people were
hard-pressed), then [a]the people hid themselves in caves,
in thickets, in cliffs, in cellars,
and in pits.
7 Also *some of* the He-
brews crossed the Jordan into
the land of [a]Gad and Gilead.
But as for Saul, he *was* still
in Gilgal, and all the people
followed him trembling.
8 Now [a]he waited seven
days, according to the appointed time set by Samuel, but
Samuel did not come to Gilgal;
and the people were scat-
tering from him.
9 So Saul said, "Bring to
me the burnt offering and
the peace offerings." And [a]he
offered the burnt offering.
10 As soon as he finished
offering the burnt offering, behold, Samuel came; and [a]Saul went
out to meet him *and* to [1]greet him.
11 But Samuel said, "What have you done?" And Saul said,
"Because I saw that the people were scattering from me, and
that you did not come within the appointed days, and that [a]the
Philistines were assembling at Michmash,
12 therefore I said, 'Now the Philistines will come down
against me at Gilgal, and I have not asked the favor of the
LORD.' So I forced myself and offered the burnt offering."
13 Samuel said to Saul, "[a]You have acted foolishly; [b]you have
not kept the commandment of the LORD your God, which He
commanded you, for now the LORD would have established
your kingdom [1]over Israel [c]forever.
14 "But [a]now your kingdom shall not endure. [b]The LORD has
sought out for Himself a man after His own heart, and the LORD

3 [a]1 Sam 10:5 [b]1 Sam 13:16; 14:5 [c]Judg 3:27; 6:34
4 [1]Lit *saying* [2]Lit *after* [a]Gen 34:30; Ex 5:21; 2 Sam 10:6
5 [a]Josh 11:4 [b]Josh 18:12; 1 Sam 14:23
6 [a]Judg 6:2
7 [a]Num 32:33
8 [a]1 Sam 10:8
9 [a]Deut 12:5-14; 2 Sam 24:25; 1 Kin 3:4
10 [1]Lit *bless* [a]1 Sam 15:13
11 [a]1 Sam 13:2, 5, 16, 23
13 [1]Lit *to* [a]2 Chr 16:9 [b]1 Sam 15:11, 22, 28 [c]1 Sam 1:22
14 [a]1 Sam 15:28 [b]Acts 7:46; 13:22

has appointed him as ruler over His people, because you have
not kept what the LORD commanded you."
15 Then Samuel arose and went up from Gilgal to [a]Gibeah of
Benjamin. And Saul [1]numbered the people who were present
with him, [b]about six hundred men.
16 Now Saul and his son Jonathan and the people who were
present with them were staying in [a]Geba of Benjamin while
the Philistines camped at Michmash.
17 And [a]the [1]raiders came from the camp of the Philistines in
three [2]companies: one [3]company turned [4]toward [b]Ophrah, to
the land of Shual,
18 and another [1]company turned [2]toward [a]Beth-horon, and
another [1]company turned [2]toward the border which overlooks
the valley of [b]Zeboim toward the wilderness.
19 Now [a]no blacksmith could be found in all the land of Israel,
for the Philistines said, "Otherwise the Hebrews will make
[1b]swords or spears."
20 So all Israel went down to the Philistines, each to sharpen
his plowshare, his mattock, his axe, and his hoe.
21 The charge was [1]two-thirds of a shekel for the plowshares,
the mattocks, the forks, and the axes, and to fix the hoes.
22 So it came about on the day of battle that [a]neither sword
nor spear was found in the hands of any of the people who
were with Saul and Jonathan, but they were found with Saul
and his son Jonathan.
23 And [a]the garrison of the Philistines went out to [b]the pass of
Michmash.

Chapter 14 Theme ______________________________

14 Now the day came that Jonathan, the son of Saul, said to
the young man who was carrying his armor, "Come and
let us cross over to the Philistines' garrison that is on the other
side." But he did not tell his father.
2 Saul was staying in the outskirts of [a]Gibeah under the
pomegranate tree which is in [b]Migron. And the people who
were with him *were* [c]about six hundred men,
3 and Ahijah, the [a]son of Ahitub, [b]Ichabod's brother, the son of
Phinehas, the son of Eli, the priest of the LORD at [c]Shiloh, [d]was
[1]wearing an ephod. And the people did not know that Jonathan
had gone.
4 [a]Between the passes by which Jonathan sought to cross
over to the Philistines' garrison, there was a sharp crag on the
one side and a sharp crag on the other side, and the name of
the one was Bozez, and the name of the other Seneh.
5 The one crag rose on the north opposite Michmash, and
the other on the south opposite Geba.
6 Then Jonathan said to the young man who was carrying his
armor, "Come and let us cross over to the garrison of [a]these
uncircumcised; perhaps the LORD will work for us, for [b]the
LORD is not restrained to save by many or by few."

15 [1]Lit *mustered* [a]1 Sam 13:2 [b]1 Sam 13:2, 6, 7; 14:2
16 [a]1 Sam 13:2, 3
17 [1]Lit *destroyers* [2]Lit *heads* [3]Lit *head* [4]Lit *toward the direction of* [a]1 Sam 14:15 [b]Josh 18:23
18 [1]Lit *head* [2]Lit *the direction of* [a]Josh 16:3; 18:13, 14 [b]Neh 11:34
19 [1]Lit *sword or spear* [a]Judg 5:8; 2 Kin 24:14; Jer 24:1; 29:2 [b]Judg 5:8
21 [1]Heb *pim*
22 [a]Judg 5:8
23 [a]1 Sam 14:1; 2 Sam 23:14 [b]1 Sam 14:4, 5; Is 10:28
14:2 [a]1 Sam 13:15, 16 [b]Is 10:28 [c]1 Sam 13:15
3 [1]Lit *carrying* [a]1 Sam 22:9-12, 20 [b]1 Sam 4:21 [c]1 Sam 1:3 [d]1 Sam 2:28
4 [a]1 Sam 13:23
6 [a]1 Sam 17:26, 36; Jer 9:25, 26 [b]Judg 7:4, 7; 1 Sam 17:46, 47; Ps 115:3; 135:6; Zech 4:6; Matt 19:26

7 His armor bearer said to him, "Do all that is in your heart;
turn yourself, *and* here I am with you according to your
[1]desire."
8 Then Jonathan said, "[a]Behold, we will cross over to the
men and reveal ourselves to them.

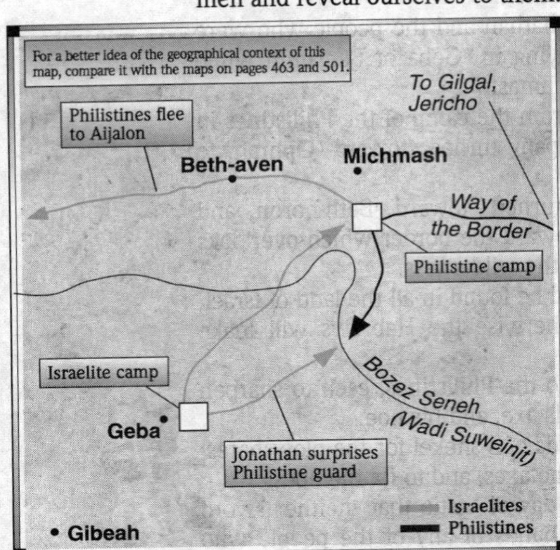

The Battle at Michmash

9 "If they [1]say to us, 'Wait
until we come to you'; then
we will stand in our place
and not go up to them.
10 "But if they [1]say, 'Come
up to us,' then we will go
up, for the LORD has given
them into our hands; and
[a]this shall be the sign to us."
11 When both of them
revealed themselves to the
garrison of the Philistines,
the Philistines said, "Behold, [a]Hebrews are coming
out of the holes where they
have hidden themselves."
12 So the men of the gar-
rison [1]hailed Jonathan and
his armor bearer and said,
"Come up to us and [a]we will tell you something." And
Jonathan said to his armor bearer, "Come up after me, for [b]the
LORD has given them into the hands of Israel."
13 Then Jonathan climbed up on his hands and feet, with his
armor bearer behind him; and they fell before Jonathan, and
his armor bearer put some to death after him.
14 That first slaughter which Jonathan and his armor bearer
made was about twenty men within about half a furrow in an
acre of land.
15 And there was a trembling in the camp, in the field, and
among all the people. Even the garrison and [a]the raiders
trembled, and [b]the earth quaked so [c]that it became a [1]great
trembling.
16 Now Saul's watchmen in Gibeah of Benjamin looked, and
behold, the multitude melted away; and they went here and
there.
17 Saul said to the people who *were* with him, "[1]Number
now and see who has gone from us." And when they had
[1]numbered, behold, Jonathan and his armor bearer were not
there.
18 Then Saul said to Ahijah, "[a]Bring the ark of God here." For
the ark of God was at that time with the sons of Israel.
19 [a]While Saul talked to the priest, the commotion in the
camp of the Philistines continued and increased; so Saul said to
the priest, "Withdraw your hand."
20 Then Saul and all the people who *were* with him rallied
and came to the battle; and behold, [a]every man's sword was
against his fellow, *and there was* very great confusion.

7 [1]Lit *heart*
8 [a]Judg 7:9-14
9 [1]Lit *say thus*
10 [1]Lit *say thus* [a]Gen 24:14; Judg 6:36
11 [a]1 Sam 13:6; 14:22
12 [1]Lit *answered* [a]1 Sam 17:43, 44 [b]2 Sam 5:24
15 [1]Lit *trembling of God* [a]1 Sam 13:17, 18 [b]1 Sam 7:10 [c]Gen 35:5; 2 Kin 7:6
17 [1]Lit *muster(ed)*
18 [a]1 Sam 23:9; 30:7
19 [a]Num 27:21
20 [a]Judg 7:22; 2 Chr 20:23

21 Now the Hebrews *who* were with the Philistines previously,
who went up with them all around in the camp, even [a]they also
turned to be with the Israelites who *were* with Saul and Jonathan.
22 When all the [a]men of Israel who had hidden themselves in
the hill country of Ephraim heard that the Philistines had fled,
even they also pursued them closely in the battle.
23 So [a]the LORD delivered Israel that day, and the battle [1]spread
beyond [b]Beth-aven.
24 Now the men of Israel were hard-pressed on that day, for
Saul had [a]put the people under oath, saying, "Cursed be the
man who eats food [1]before evening, and until I have avenged
myself on my enemies." So none of the people tasted food.
25 All *the people of* the land entered the forest, and there was
honey on the ground.
26 When the people entered the forest, behold, [a]*there was* a
flow of honey; but no man put his hand to his mouth, for the
people feared the oath.
27 But Jonathan had not heard when his father put the people
under oath; therefore, [a]he put out the end of the staff that *was*
in his hand and dipped it in the honeycomb, and put his hand
to his mouth, and [b]his eyes brightened.
28 Then one of the people said, "Your father strictly put the
people under oath, saying, 'Cursed be the man who eats food
today.'" And the people were weary.
29 Then Jonathan said, "[a]My father has troubled the land. See
now, how my eyes have brightened because I tasted a little of
this honey.
30 "How much more, if only the people had eaten freely today
of the spoil of their enemies which they found! For now the
slaughter among the Philistines has not been great."
31 They struck among the Philistines that day from [a]Michmash
to [b]Aijalon. And the people were very weary.
32 [a]The people [1]rushed greedily upon the spoil, and took
sheep and oxen and calves, and slew *them* on the ground; and
the people ate *them* [b]with the blood.
33 Then they told Saul, saying, "Behold, the people are
[a]sinning against the LORD by eating with the blood." And he
said, "You have acted treacherously; roll a great stone to me
today."
34 Saul said, "Disperse yourselves among the people and say
to them, 'Each one of you bring me his ox or his sheep, and
slaughter *it* here and eat; and do not sin against the LORD by
eating with the blood.'" So all the people that night brought
each one his ox [1]with him and slaughtered *it* there.
35 And [a]Saul built an altar to the LORD; it was the first altar
that he built to the LORD.
36 Then Saul said, "Let us go down after the Philistines by
night and take spoil among them until the morning light, and
let us not leave a man of them." And they said, "Do whatever
seems good [1]to you." So [a]the priest said, "Let us draw near to
God here."

21 [a]1 Sam 29:4
22 [a]1 Sam 13:6
23 [1]Lit *passed over* [a]Ex 14:30; 1 Sam 10:19; 14:23; 1 Chr 11:14; 2 Chr 32:22; Ps 44:7 [b]1 Sam 13:5
24 [1]Lit *until* [a]Josh 6:26
26 [a]Matt 3:4
27 [a]1 Sam 14:43 [b]1 Sam 30:12
29 [a]Josh 7:25; 1 Kin 18:18
31 [a]1 Sam 14:5 [b]Josh 10:12
32 [1]Lit *did with regard to the spoil* [a]1 Sam 15:19 [b]Gen 9:4; Lev 3:17; 17:10-14; 19:26; Deut 12:16, 23; Acts 15:20
33 [a]Lev 7:26, 27; 19:26; Deut 12:16, 23-25; 15:23
34 [1]Lit *in his hand*
35 [a]1 Sam 7:12, 17; 2 Sam 24:25; James 4:8
36 [1]Lit *in your eyes* [a]1 Sam 14:3, 18, 19

37 Saul [a]inquired of God, "Shall I go down after the Philistines?
Will You give them into the hand of Israel?" But [b]He did not
answer him on that day.
38 Saul said, "[a]Draw near here, all you [1]chiefs of the people,
and investigate and see how this sin has happened today.
39 "For [a]as the LORD lives, who delivers Israel, though it is in
Jonathan my son, he shall surely die." But not one of all the
people answered him.
40 Then he said to all Israel, "You shall be on one side and I
and Jonathan my son will be on the other side." And the
people said to Saul, "Do what seems good [1]to you."
41 Therefore, Saul said to the LORD, the God of Israel, "[a]Give a
perfect *lot.*" And Jonathan and Saul were taken, but the people
escaped.
42 Saul said, "Cast *lots* between me and Jonathan my son."
And Jonathan was taken.
43 Then Saul said to Jonathan, "[a]Tell me what you have done."
So Jonathan told him and said, "[b]I indeed tasted a little honey
with the end of the staff that was in my hand. Here I am, I
must die!"
44 Saul said, "[a]May God do [1]this *to me* and more also, for [b]you
shall surely die, Jonathan."
45 But the people said to Saul, "Must Jonathan die, who has
[1]brought about this great deliverance in Israel? Far from it! As
the LORD lives, [a]not one hair of his head shall fall to the ground,
for [b]he has worked with God this day." So the people [2]rescued
Jonathan and he did not die.
46 Then Saul went up from [1]pursuing the Philistines, and the
Philistines went to their own place.
47 Now when Saul had taken the kingdom over Israel, he
fought against all his enemies on every side, against Moab, [a]the
sons of Ammon, Edom, [b]the kings of Zobah, and [c]the Philistines;
and wherever he turned, he [1]inflicted punishment.
48 He acted valiantly and [1a]defeated the Amalekites, and
delivered Israel from the hands of [2]those who plundered them.
49 Now [a]the sons of Saul were Jonathan and Ishvi and Malchi-
shua; and the names of his two daughters *were these:* the name
of the firstborn [b]Merab and the name of the younger [c]Michal.
50 The name of Saul's wife was Ahinoam the daughter of
Ahimaaz. And [a]the name of the captain of his army was Abner
the son of Ner, Saul's uncle.

37 [a]1 Sam 10:22 [b]1 Sam 28:6

38 [1]Lit *corners* [a]Josh 7:11, 12; 1 Sam 10:19, 20

39 [a]1 Sam 14:24, 44; 2 Sam 12:5

40 [1]Lit *in your eyes*

41 [a]Acts 1:24

43 [a]Josh 7:19 [b]1 Sam 14:27

44 [1]Lit *thus* [a]Ruth 1:17; 1 Sam 25:22 [b]1 Sam 14:39

45 [1]Lit *worked* [2]Lit *ransomed* [a]2 Sam 14:11; 1 Kin 1:52; Luke 21:18; Acts 27:34 [b]2 Cor 6:1

46 [1]Lit *after*

47 [1]Or *condemned* [a]1 Sam 11:1-13 [b]2 Sam 8:3-10 [c]1 Sam 14:52

48 [1]Lit *smote* [2]Lit *its plunderers* [a]1 Sam 15:3, 7

49 [a]1 Sam 31:2; 1 Chr 8:33; 10:2 [b]1 Sam 18:17-19 [c]1 Sam 18:20, 27; 19:12; 2 Sam 6:20-23

50 [a]2 Sam 2:8

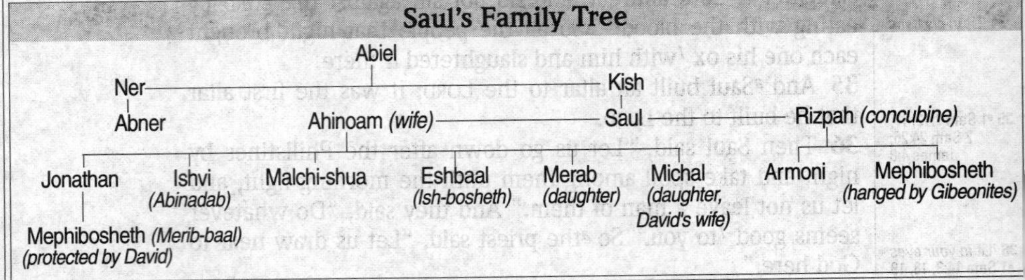

51 [a]Kish *was* the father of Saul, and Ner the father of Abner
was the son of Abiel.
52 Now the war against the Philistines was severe all the days
of Saul; and when Saul saw any mighty man or any valiant
man, he [1a]attached him to [2]his staff.

Chapter 15 Theme ______________________________

15 Then Samuel said to Saul, "[a]The LORD sent me to anoint
you as king over His people, over Israel; now therefore,
listen to the [1]words of the LORD.
2 "Thus says the LORD of hosts, 'I will [1]punish Amalek [a]*for*
what he did to Israel, how he set himself against him on the
way while he was coming up from Egypt.
3 'Now go and strike Amalek and [a]utterly destroy all that he
has, and do not spare him; but [b]put to death both man and
woman, child and infant, ox and sheep, camel and donkey.'"
4 Then Saul summoned the people and [1]numbered them in
[a]Telaim, 200,000 foot soldiers and 10,000 men of Judah.
5 Saul came to the city of Amalek and set an ambush in the
valley.
6 Saul said to [a]the Kenites, "Go, depart, go down from
among the Amalekites, so that I do not destroy you with them;
for [b]you showed kindness to all the sons of Israel when they
came up from Egypt." So the Kenites departed from among the
Amalekites.
7 So [a]Saul [1]defeated the Amalekites, from [b]Havilah as you go
to [c]Shur, which is [2]east of Egypt.
8 He captured [a]Agag the king of the Amalekites alive, and
[b]utterly destroyed all the people with the edge of the sword.
9 But Saul and the people [a]spared Agag and the best of the
sheep, the oxen, the fatlings, the lambs, and all that was good,
and were not willing to destroy them utterly; but everything
despised and worthless, that they utterly destroyed.
10 Then the word of the LORD came to Samuel, saying,
11 "[a]I regret that I have made Saul king, for [b]he has turned back
from [1]following Me and has not carried out My commands."
And Samuel was distressed and [c]cried out to the LORD all night.
12 Samuel rose early in the morning to meet Saul; and it was
told Samuel, saying, "Saul came to [a]Carmel, and behold, he set
up a monument for himself, then turned and proceeded on
[1]down to [b]Gilgal."
13 Samuel came to Saul, and Saul said to him, "[a]Blessed are
you of the LORD! I have carried out the command of the LORD."
14 But Samuel said, "[a]What then is this [1]bleating of the sheep
in my ears, and the [1]lowing of the oxen which I hear?"
15 Saul said, "They have brought them from the Amalekites, for
[a]the people spared the best of the sheep and oxen, to sacrifice to
the LORD your God; but the rest we have utterly destroyed."
16 Then Samuel said to Saul, "Wait, and let me tell you what
the LORD said to me last night." And he said to him, "Speak!"

51 [a]1 Sam 9:1, 21

52 [1]Lit *gathered* [2]Lit *himself* [a]1 Sam 8:11

15:1 [1]Lit *sound of the words* [a]1 Sam 9:16; 10:1

2 [1]Or *visit* [a]Ex 17:8-16; Num 24:20; Deut 25:17-19

3 [a]Num 24:20; Deut 20:16-18; Josh 6:17-21 [b]1 Sam 22:19

4 [1]Lit *mustered* [a]Josh 15:24

6 [a]Num 24:21; Judg 1:16; 4:11 [b]Ex 18:9, 10; Num 10:29-32

7 [1]Lit *smote* [2]Lit *before* [a]1 Sam 14:48 [b]Gen 25:18 [c]Gen 16:7; Ex 15:22; 1 Sam 27:8

8 [a]Num 24:7; 1 Sam 15:20; Esth 3:1 [b]1 Sam 27:8, 9; 30:1; 2 Sam 8:12

9 [a]1 Sam 15:3, 15, 19

11 [1]Lit *after* [a]Gen 6:6, 7; Ex 32:14; 1 Sam 15:35; 2 Sam 24:16 [b]Josh 22:16; 1 Sam 13:13; 1 Kin 9:6, 7 [c]Ex 32:11-13; Luke 6:12

12 [1]Lit *and went down* [a]Josh 15:55; 1 Sam 25:2 [b]1 Sam 13:12, 15

13 [a]Gen 14:19; Judg 17:2; Ruth 3:10; 2 Sam 2:5

14 [1]Lit *sound* [a]Ex 32:21-24

15 [a]Gen 3:12, 13; Ex 32:22, 23; 1 Sam 15:9, 21

17 Samuel said, "Is it not true, [a]though you were little in your
own eyes, you were *made* the head of the tribes of Israel? And
the LORD anointed you king over Israel,
18 and the LORD sent you on a [1]mission, and said, '[a]Go and
utterly destroy the sinners, the Amalekites, and fight against
them until they are exterminated.'
19 "Why then did you not obey the voice of the LORD, [a]but rushed
upon the spoil and did what was evil in the sight of the LORD?"
20 Then Saul said to Samuel, "[a]I did obey the voice of the
LORD, and went on the [1]mission on which the LORD sent me,
and have brought back Agag the king of Amalek, and have
utterly destroyed the Amalekites.
21 "But [a]the people took *some* of the spoil, sheep and oxen,
the choicest of the things devoted to destruction, to sacrifice to
the LORD your God at Gilgal."
22 Samuel said,

"[a]Has the LORD as much delight in burnt offerings and
sacrifices
As in obeying the voice of the LORD?
Behold, [b]to obey is better than sacrifice,
And to heed than the fat of rams.

23 "For rebellion is as the sin of [a]divination,
And insubordination is as [b]iniquity and idolatry.
Because you have rejected the word of the LORD,
[c]He has also rejected you from *being* king."

24 Then Saul said to Samuel, "[a]I have sinned; [b]I have indeed
transgressed the [1]command of the LORD and your words,
because I feared the people and listened to their voice.
25 "Now therefore, [a]please pardon my sin and return with me,
that I may worship the LORD."
26 But Samuel said to Saul, "I will not return with you; for [a]you
have rejected the word of the LORD, and the LORD has rejected
you from being king over Israel."
27 As Samuel turned to go, [a]*Saul* seized the edge of his robe,
and it tore.
28 So Samuel said to him, "[a]The LORD has torn the kingdom of
Israel from you today and has given it to your neighbor, who is
better than you.
29 "Also the [1a]Glory of Israel [b]will not lie or change His mind;
for He is not a man that He should change His mind."
30 Then he said, "I have sinned; [a]*but* please honor me now
before the elders of my people and before Israel, and go back
with me, [b]that I may worship the LORD your God."
31 So Samuel went back following Saul, and Saul worshiped
the LORD.
32 Then Samuel said, "Bring me Agag, the king of the
Amalekites." And Agag came to him [1]cheerfully. And Agag said,
"Surely the bitterness of death is past."
33 But Samuel said, "[a]As your sword has made women childless,
so shall your mother be childless among women." And Samuel
hewed Agag to pieces before the LORD at Gilgal.

17 [a]1 Sam 9:21; 10:22
18 [1]Lit *way* [a]1 Sam 15:3
19 [a]1 Sam 14:32
20 [1]Lit *way* [a]1 Sam 15:13
21 [a]Ex 32:22, 23; 1 Sam 15:15
22 [a]Ps 40:6-8; 51:16, 17; Is 1:11-15; Mic 6:6-8; Heb 10:6-9 [b]Jer 7:22, 23; Hos 6:6; Matt 12:7; Mark 12:33
23 [a]Deut 18:10 [b]Gen 31:19, 34 [c]1 Sam 13:14
24 [1]Lit *mouth* [a]Num 22:34; 2 Sam 12:13; Ps 51:4 [b]Prov 29:25; Is 51:12, 13
25 [a]Ex 10:17
26 [a]1 Sam 13:14; 16:1
27 [a]1 Kin 11:30, 31
28 [a]1 Sam 28:17, 18; 1 Kin 11:31
29 [1]Or *Eminence* [a]1 Chr 29:11 [b]Num 23:19; Ezek 24:14; Titus 1:2
30 [a]John 5:44; 12:43 [b]Is 29:13
32 [1]Or *in bonds*
33 [a]Gen 9:6; Judg 1:7; Matt 7:2

34 Then Samuel went to [a]Ramah, but Saul went up to his house
at [b]Gibeah of Saul.
35 [a]Samuel did not see Saul again until the day of his death;
for Samuel [b]grieved over Saul. And the LORD regretted that He
had made Saul king over Israel.

Chapter 16 Theme ______________________

16 Now the LORD said to Samuel, "[a]How long will you
grieve over Saul, since [b]I have rejected him from being
king over Israel? [c]Fill your horn with oil and go; I will send you
to [d]Jesse the Bethlehemite, for I have [e]selected a king for
Myself among his sons."
2 But Samuel said, "How can I go? When Saul hears *of it,* he
will kill me." And the LORD said, "[a]Take a heifer with you and
say, 'I have come to sacrifice to the LORD.'
3 "You shall invite Jesse to the sacrifice, and [a]I will show you
what you shall do; and [b]you shall anoint for Me the one whom
I [1]designate to you."
4 So Samuel did what the LORD said, and came to [a]Bethlehem.
And the elders of the city came trembling to meet him and
said, "[b]Do you come in peace?"
5 He said, "In peace; I have come to sacrifice to the LORD.
[a]Consecrate yourselves and come with me to the sacrifice." He
also consecrated Jesse and his sons and invited them to the
sacrifice.
6 When they entered, he looked at [a]Eliab and thought,
"Surely the LORD's anointed is before Him."
7 But the LORD said to Samuel, "Do not look at his appearance
or at the height of his stature, because I have rejected him; for
[1]God *sees* not as man sees, for man looks at the outward
appearance, [a]but the LORD looks at the heart."
8 Then Jesse called [a]Abinadab and made him pass before
Samuel. And he said, "The LORD has not chosen this one either."
9 Next Jesse made [1a]Shammah pass by. And he said, "The
LORD has not chosen this one either."
10 Thus Jesse made seven of his sons pass before Samuel. But
Samuel said to Jesse, "The LORD has not chosen these."
11 And Samuel said to Jesse, "Are these all the children?" And
he said, "[a]There remains yet the youngest, and behold, he is
tending the sheep." Then Samuel said to Jesse, "Send and
[1]bring him; for we will not sit down until he comes here."
12 So he sent and brought him in. Now he was ruddy, with
[a]beautiful eyes and a handsome appearance. And the LORD said,
"[b]Arise, anoint him; for this is he."
13 Then Samuel took the horn of oil and [a]anointed him in the
midst of his brothers; and [b]the Spirit of the LORD came mightily
upon David from that day forward. And Samuel arose and went
to Ramah.
14 [a]Now the Spirit of the LORD departed from Saul, and [b]an
evil spirit from the LORD terrorized him.

34 [a]1 Sam 7:17 [b]1 Sam 11:4
35 [a]1 Sam 19:24 [b]1 Sam 16:1
16:1 [a]1 Sam 15:35 [b]1 Sam 13:13, 14; 15:23 [c]1 Sam 9:16; 10:1; 2 Kin 9:1 [d]Ruth 4:17-22 [e]Ps 78:70, 71; Acts 13:22
2 [a]1 Sam 20:29
3 [1]Lit *say to you* [a]Ex 4:15; Acts 9:6 [b]Deut 17:14, 15; 1 Sam 9:16
4 [a]Gen 48:7; Luke 2:4 [b]1 Kin 2:13; 2 Kin 9:22; 1 Chr 12:17, 18
5 [a]Gen 35:2; Ex 19:10
6 [a]1 Sam 17:13
7 [1]So with Gr; Heb He does *not* see *what man sees* [a]1 Sam 2:3; 1 Kin 8:39; 1 Chr 28:9; Luke 16:15
8 [a]1 Sam 17:13
9 [1]In 2 Sam 13:3, *Shimeah;* in 1 Chr 2:13, *Shimea* [a]1 Sam 17:13
11 [1]Lit *take* [a]1 Sam 17:12; 2 Sam 13:3
12 [a]Gen 39:6; Ex 2:2; Acts 7:20 [b]1 Sam 9:17
13 [a]1 Sam 10:1 [b]Num 27:18; 1 Sam 10:6, 9, 10
14 [a]Judg 16:20; 1 Sam 11:6; 18:12; 28:15 [b]Judg 9:23; 1 Sam 16:15, 16; 18:10; 19:9; 1 Kin 22:19-22

15 Saul's servants then said to him, "Behold now, an evil spirit
from God is terrorizing you.
16 "Let our lord now command your servants who are before
you. Let them seek a man who is a skillful player on the harp; and
it shall come about when the evil spirit from God is on you, that
[a]he shall play *the harp* with his hand, and you will be well."
17 So Saul said to his servants, "Provide for me now a man
who can play well and bring *him* to me."
18 Then one of the young men said, "Behold, I have seen a son
of Jesse the Bethlehemite who is a skillful musician, [a]a mighty
man of valor, a warrior, one prudent in speech, and a handsome
man; and [b]the LORD is with him."
19 So Saul sent messengers to Jesse and said, "Send me your
son David who is with the flock."
20 Jesse [a]took a donkey *loaded with* bread and a jug of wine
and a young goat, and sent *them* to Saul by David his son.
21 Then David came to Saul and [1a]attended him; and [2]Saul
loved him greatly, and he became his armor bearer.
22 Saul sent to Jesse, saying, "Let David now stand before me,
for he has found favor in my sight."
23 So it came about whenever [a]the *evil* spirit from God came
to Saul, David would take the harp and play *it* with his hand;
and Saul would be refreshed and be well, and the evil spirit
would depart from him.

Chapter 17 Theme ____________________________

17 Now [a]the Philistines gathered their armies for battle; and
they were gathered at Socoh which belongs to Judah, and
they camped between [b]Socoh and [c]Azekah, in [d]Ephes-dammim.
2 Saul and the men of Israel were gathered and camped in
[a]the valley of Elah, and drew up in battle array to encounter
the Philistines.
3 The Philistines stood on the mountain on one side while
Israel stood on the mountain on the other side, with the valley
between them.
4 Then a champion came out from the armies of the
Philistines named [a]Goliath, from [b]Gath, whose height was six
[1]cubits and a span.
5 *He had* a bronze helmet on his head, and he was clothed
with scale-armor [1]which weighed five thousand shekels of
bronze.
6 *He* also *had* bronze [1]greaves on his legs and a [a]bronze
javelin *slung* between his shoulders.
7 [a]The shaft of his spear was like a weaver's beam, and the
head of his spear *weighed* six hundred shekels of iron; [b]his
shield-carrier also walked before him.
8 He stood and shouted to the ranks of Israel and said to
them, "Why do you come out to draw up in battle array? Am I
not the Philistine and you [a]servants of Saul? Choose a man for
yourselves and let him come down to me.

16 [a]1 Sam 18:10; 19:9; 2 Kin 3:15

18 [a]1 Sam 17:32-36 [b]1 Sam 3:19

20 [a]1 Sam 10:4, 27; Prov 18:16

21 [1]Lit *stood before him* [2]Lit *he* [a]Gen 41:46; Prov 22:29

23 [a]1 Sam 16:14-16

17:1 [a]1 Sam 13:5 [b]Josh 15:35; 2 Chr 28:18 [c]Josh 10:10 [d]1 Chr 11:13

2 [a]1 Sam 21:9

4 [1]I.e. One cubit equals approx 18 in. [a]2 Sam 21:19 [b]Josh 11:22

5 [1]Lit *and the weight of the armor* was

6 [1]Or *shin guards* [a]1 Sam 17:45

7 [a]2 Sam 21:19; 1 Chr 11:23 [b]1 Sam 17:41

8 [a]1 Sam 8:17

9 “[a]If he is able to fight with me and [1]kill me, then we will
become your servants; but if I prevail against him and [1]kill him,
then you shall become our servants and serve us.”
10 Again the Philistine said, “[a]I defy the ranks of Israel this
day; give me a man that we may fight together.”
11 When Saul and all Israel heard these words of the
Philistine, they were dismayed and greatly afraid.
12 Now David was [a]the son of [1]the [b]Ephrathite of Bethlehem in
Judah, whose name was Jesse, and [c]he had eight sons. And
[2]Jesse was old in the days of Saul, advanced *in years* among men.
13 The three older sons of Jesse had [1]gone after Saul to the
battle. And [a]the names of his three sons who went to the battle
were Eliab the firstborn, and the second to him Abinadab, and
the third Shammah.
14 [a]David was the youngest. Now the three oldest followed Saul,
15 [a]but David went back and forth from Saul [b]to tend his
father’s flock at Bethlehem.
16 The Philistine came [1]forward morning and evening for forty
days and took his stand.
17 Then Jesse said to David his son, “[a]Take now for your
brothers an ephah of this roasted grain and these ten loaves
and run to the camp to your brothers.
18 “[a]Bring also these ten cuts of cheese to the commander of
their thousand, [b]and look into the welfare of your brothers, and
bring back [1]news of them.
19 “For Saul and they and all the men of Israel are in the valley
of Elah, fighting with the Philistines.”
20 So David arose early in the morning and left the flock with
a keeper and took *the supplies* and went as Jesse had
commanded him. And he came to the [a]circle of the camp while
the army was going out in battle array shouting the war cry.
21 Israel and the Philistines drew up in battle array, army
against army.
22 Then David left his [a]baggage in the [1]care of the baggage
keeper, and ran to the battle line and entered in order to greet
his brothers.
23 As he was talking with them, behold, the champion, the
Philistine from Gath named Goliath, was coming up from the
army of the Philistines, and he spoke [a]these same words; and
David heard *them.*
24 When all the men of Israel saw the man, they fled from
him and were greatly afraid.
25 The men of Israel said, “Have you seen this man who is
coming up? Surely he is coming up to defy Israel. And it will be
that the king will enrich the man who kills him with great
riches and [a]will give him his daughter and make his father’s
house [1]free in Israel.”
26 Then David spoke to the men who were standing by him,
saying, “What will be done for the man who kills this Philistine
and takes away [a]the reproach from Israel? For who is this
[b]uncircumcised Philistine, that he should [c]taunt the armies of
[d]the living God?”

9 [1]Lit *smite* [a]2 Sam 2:12-16

10 [a]1 Sam 17:26, 36, 45; 2 Sam 21:21

12 [1]Lit *this* [2]Lit *the man* [a]Ruth 4:22; 1 Sam 16:18 [b]Gen 35:19 [c]1 Sam 16:10, 11; 1 Chr 2:13-15

13 [1]Lit *gone; they went* [a]1 Sam 16:6, 8, 9

14 [a]1 Sam 16:11

15 [a]1 Sam 16:21-23 [b]1 Sam 16:11, 19

16 [1]Lit *near*

17 [a]1 Sam 25:18

18 [1]Lit *their pledge* [a]1 Sam 16:20 [b]Gen 37:13, 14

20 [a]1 Sam 26:5, 7

22 [1]Lit *hand* [a]Judg 18:21; Is 10:28

23 [a]1 Sam 17:8-10

25 [1]I.e. free from taxes and public service [a]Josh 15:16

26 [a]1 Sam 11:2 [b]1 Sam 14:6; 17:36; Jer 9:25, 26 [c]1 Sam 17:10 [d]Deut 5:26; 2 Kin 19:4; Jer 10:10

27 The people [1]answered him in accord with this word,
saying, "[a]Thus it will be done for the man who kills him."
28 Now Eliab his oldest brother heard when he spoke to the
men; and [a]Eliab's anger burned against David and he said,
"Why have you come down? And with whom have you left
those few sheep in the wilderness? I know your insolence and
the wickedness of your heart; for you have come down in
order to see the battle."
29 But David said, "What have I done now? Was it not just a
[1]question?"
30 Then he turned [1]away from him to another and [a]said the
same thing; and the people answered the same thing as [2]before.
31 When the words which David spoke were heard, they told
them [1]to Saul, and he sent for him.
32 David said to Saul, "[a]Let no man's heart fail on account of
him; [b]your servant will go and fight with this Philistine."
33 Then Saul said to David, "[a]You are not able to go against
this Philistine to fight with him; for you are *but* a youth while
he has been a warrior from his youth."
34 But David said to Saul, "Your servant was tending his
father's sheep. When a lion or a bear came and took a lamb
from the flock,
35 I went out after him and [1]attacked him, and [a]rescued *it* from
his mouth; and when he rose up against me, I seized *him* by
his beard and [1]struck him and killed him.
36 "Your servant has [1]killed both the lion and the bear; and this
uncircumcised Philistine will be like one of them, since he has
taunted the armies of the living God."
37 And David said, "[a]The LORD who delivered me from the
paw of the lion and from the paw of the bear, He will deliver
me from the hand of this Philistine." And Saul said to David,
"[b]Go, and may the LORD be with you."
38 Then Saul clothed David with his garments and put a
bronze helmet on his head, and he clothed him with armor.
39 David girded his sword over his armor and tried to walk, for
he had not tested *them*. So David said to Saul, "I cannot go with
these, for I have not tested *them*." And David took them [1]off.
40 He took his stick in his hand and chose for himself five
smooth stones from the brook, and put them in the shepherd's
bag which he had, even in *his* pouch, and [a]his sling was in his
hand; and he approached the Philistine.
41 Then the Philistine came on and approached David, with
the shield-bearer in front of him.
42 When the Philistine looked and saw David, [a]he disdained
him; for he was *but* a youth, and [b]ruddy, with a handsome
appearance.
43 The Philistine said to David, "[a]Am I a dog, that you come
to me with sticks?" And [b]the Philistine cursed David by his gods.
44 The Philistine also said to David, "Come to me, and I will
give your flesh [a]to the birds of the sky and the beasts of the
field."

27 [1]Lit *said to* [a]1 Sam 17:25

28 [a]Gen 37:4, 8-36; Prov 18:19; Matt 10:36

29 [1]Lit *word*

30 [1]Lit *from beside him* [2]Lit *the former word* [a]1 Sam 17:26, 27

31 [1]Lit *before*

32 [a]Deut 20:1-4 [b]1 Sam 16:18

33 [a]Num 13:31

35 [1]Lit *smote* [a]Amos 3:12

36 [1]Lit *smitten*

37 [a]2 Cor 1:10; 2 Tim 4:17, 18 [b]1 Sam 20:13; 1 Chr 22:11, 16

39 [1]Lit *off from himself*

40 [a]Judg 20:16

42 [a]Ps 123:4; Prov 16:18 [b]1 Sam 16:12

43 [a]1 Sam 24:14; 2 Sam 3:8; 2 Kin 8:13 [b]1 Kin 20:10

44 [a]1 Sam 17:46

45 Then David said to the Philistine, "You come to me with a
sword, a spear, and a javelin, [a]but I come to you in the name of
the LORD of hosts, the God of the armies of Israel, whom you
have taunted.
46 "This day the LORD will deliver you up into my hands, and I
will strike you down and remove your head from you. And I
will give the [a]dead bodies of the army of the Philistines this day
to the birds of the sky and the wild beasts of the earth, [b]that all
the earth may know that there is a God in Israel,
47 and that all this assembly may know that [a]the LORD does
not deliver by sword or by spear; [b]for the battle is the LORD'S
and He will give you into our hands."
48 Then it happened when the Philistine rose and came and
drew near to meet David, that [a]David ran quickly toward the
battle line to meet the Philistine.
49 And David put his hand into his bag and took from it a stone
and slung *it,* and struck the Philistine on his forehead. And the
stone sank into his forehead, so that he fell on his face to the
ground.
50 Thus David prevailed over the Philistine with a sling and a
stone, and he struck the Philistine and killed him; but there
was no sword in David's hand.
51 Then David ran and stood over the Philistine and [a]took his
sword and drew it out of its sheath and killed him, and cut off his
head with it. [b]When the Philistines saw that their champion was
dead, they fled.
52 The men of Israel and Judah arose and shouted and pursued
the Philistines [1]as far as the valley, and to the gates of [a]Ekron.
And the slain Philistines [2]lay along the way to [b]Shaaraim, even to
Gath and Ekron.
53 The sons of Israel returned from chasing the Philistines and
plundered their camps.
54 Then David took the Philistine's head and brought it to
Jerusalem, but he put his weapons in his tent.
55 Now when Saul saw David going out against the Philistine,
he said to Abner the commander of the army, "Abner, whose
son is [a]this young man?" And Abner said, "By your life, O king,
I do not know."
56 The king said, "You inquire whose son the youth is."
57 So when David returned from killing the Philistine, Abner
took him and [a]brought him before Saul with the Philistine's
head in his hand.
58 Saul said to him, "Whose son are you, young man?" And
David answered, "[a]*I am* the son of your servant Jesse the
Bethlehemite."

Chapter 18 Theme ______________________

18 Now it came about when he had finished speaking to
Saul, that [a]the soul of Jonathan was knit to the soul of
David, and [b]Jonathan loved him as himself.

45 [a]2 Sam 22:35; 2 Chr 32:8; Ps 124:8; Heb 11:32-34
46 [a]Deut 28:26 [b]Josh 4:24; 1 Kin 8:43; 18:36; 2 Kin 19:19; Is 37:20
47 [a]1 Sam 14:6; 2 Chr 14:11; 20:15; Ps 44:6; Hos 1:7; Zech 4:6 [b]2 Chr 20:15
48 [a]Ps 27:3
51 [a]1 Sam 21:9; 2 Sam 23:21 [b]Heb 11:34
52 [1]Lit *until your coming to* [2]Lit *fell* [a]Josh 15:11 [b]Josh 15:36
55 [a]1 Sam 16:12, 21, 22
57 [a]1 Sam 17:54
58 [a]1 Sam 17:12
18:1 [a]Gen 44:30 [b]Deut 13:6; 1 Sam 20:17; 2 Sam 1:26

2 Saul took him that day and [a]did not let him return to his
father's house.
3 Then [a]Jonathan made a covenant with David because he
loved him as himself.
4 [a]Jonathan stripped himself of the robe that was on him and
gave it to David, with his armor, including his sword and his
bow and his belt.
5 So David went out wherever Saul sent him, *and* [1]prospered;
and Saul set him over the men of war. And it was pleasing in
the sight of all the people and also in the sight of Saul's servants.
6 It happened as they were coming, when David returned
from killing the Philistine, that [a]the women came out of all the
cities of Israel, singing and dancing, to meet King Saul, with
tambourines, with joy and with [1]musical instruments.
7 The women [a]sang as they [1]played, and said,
"[b]Saul has slain his thousands,
[c]And David his ten thousands."
8 Then Saul became very angry, for this saying [1]displeased
him; and he said, "They have ascribed to David ten thousands,
but to me they have ascribed thousands. Now [a]what more can
he have but the kingdom?"
9 Saul looked at David with suspicion from that day on.
10 Now it came about on the next day that [a]an evil spirit from
God came mightily upon Saul, and [b]he raved in the midst of
the house, while David was playing *the harp* with his hand,
[1c]as usual; and [2d]a spear *was* in Saul's hand.
11 [a]Saul hurled the spear for he thought, "I will [1]pin David to
the wall." But David [2]escaped from his presence twice.
12 Now [a]Saul was afraid of David, [b]for the LORD was with him
but [c]had departed from Saul.
13 Therefore Saul removed him from [1]his presence and
appointed him as his commander of a thousand; and [a]he went
out and came in before the people.
14 David was [1]prospering in all his ways for [a]the LORD *was*
with him.
15 When Saul saw that he was [1]prospering greatly, he dreaded
him.
16 But [a]all Israel and Judah loved David, and he went out and
came in before them.
17 Then Saul said to David, "[a]Here is my older daughter
Merab; I will give her to you as a wife, only be a valiant man for
me and fight [b]the LORD's battles." For Saul thought, "My hand
shall not be against him, but [c]let the hand of the Philistines be
against him."
18 But David said to Saul, "[a]Who am I, and what is my life *or*
my father's family in Israel, that I should be the king's son-in-law?"
19 So it came about at the time when Merab, Saul's daughter,
should have been given to David, that she was given to [a]Adriel
[b]the Meholathite for a wife.
20 Now [a]Michal, Saul's daughter, loved David. When they told
Saul, the thing was agreeable [1]to him.

2 [a]1 Sam 17:15
3 [a]1 Sam 20:8-17
4 [a]Gen 41:42; 1 Sam 17:38; Esth 6:8
5 [1]Or *acted wisely*
6 [1]I.e. triangles; or three-stringed instruments [a]Ex 15:20, 21; Judg 11:34; Ps 68:25; 149:3
7 [1]Or *danced* [a]Ex 15:21; 1 Sam 21:11; 29:5 [b]1 Sam 21:11 [c]2 Sam 18:3
8 [1]Lit *was evil in his eyes* [a]1 Sam 15:28
10 [1]Lit *day by day* [2]Lit *the* [a]1 Sam 16:14 [b]1 Sam 19:23, 24 [c]1 Sam 16:23 [d]1 Sam 19:9
11 [1]Lit *strike David and the wall* [2]Lit *turned about* [a]1 Sam 19:10; 20:33
12 [a]1 Sam 18:15, 29 [b]1 Sam 16:13, 18 [c]1 Sam 16:14; 28:15
13 [1]Lit *with him* [a]Num 27:17; 1 Sam 18:16; 2 Sam 5:2
14 [1]Or *acting wisely* [a]Gen 39:2, 3, 23; Josh 6:27; 1 Sam 16:18
15 [1]Or *acting very wisely*
16 [a]1 Sam 18:5
17 [a]1 Sam 17:25 [b]Num 21:14; 1 Sam 17:36, 47; 25:28 [c]1 Sam 18:21, 25
18 [a]1 Sam 9:21; 18:23; 2 Sam 7:18
19 [a]2 Sam 21:8 [b]Judg 7:22; 1 Kin 19:16
20 [1]Lit *in his sight* [a]1 Sam 18:28

21 [a]1 Sam 18:17 [b]1 Sam 18:26

21 Saul thought, "I will give her to him that she may become
a snare to him, and [a]that the hand of the Philistines may be
against him." Therefore Saul said to David, "[b]For a second time
you may be my son-in-law today."

23 [1]Lit *in the ears of* [a]Gen 29:20; 34:12

22 Then Saul commanded his servants, "Speak to David secretly,
saying, 'Behold, the king delights in you, and all his servants
love you; now therefore, become the king's son-in-law.'"
23 So Saul's servants spoke these words [1]to David. But David

24 [1]Lit *by saying according*

said, "Is it trivial in your sight to become the king's son-in-law,
[a]since I am a poor man and lightly esteemed?"
24 The servants of Saul reported to him [1]according to these
words *which* David spoke.

25 [a]Gen 34:12; Ex 22:17 [b]1 Sam 14:24 [c]1 Sam 18:17

25 Saul then said, "Thus you shall say to David, 'The king
does not desire any [a]dowry except a hundred foreskins of the
Philistines, [b]to take vengeance on the king's enemies.'" Now
[c]Saul planned to make David fall by the hand of the Philistines.
26 When his servants told David these words, [1]it pleased David

26 [1]Lit *it was agreeable in the sight of* [2]Lit *And the days had not expired* [a]1 Sam 18:21

to become the king's son-in-law. [2a]Before the days had expired
27 David rose up and went, [a]he and his men, and struck down
two hundred men among the Philistines. Then [b]David brought
their foreskins, and they gave them in full number to the king,
that he might become the king's son-in-law. So Saul gave him
Michal his daughter for a wife.

27 [a]1 Sam 18:17 [b]2 Sam 3:14

28 When Saul saw and knew that the LORD was with David,
and *that* Michal, Saul's daughter, loved him,
29 then Saul was even more afraid of David. Thus Saul was
David's enemy continually.

30 [a]2 Sam 11:1 [b]1 Sam 18:5

30 Then the commanders of the Philistines [a]went out *to*
battle, and it happened as often as they went out, that David
[b]behaved himself more wisely than all the servants of Saul. So
his name was highly esteemed.

19:1 [a]1 Sam 18:8, 9 [b]1 Sam 18:1-3

Chapter 19 Theme ______________

19 Now Saul told Jonathan his son and all his servants [a]to
put David to death. But [b]Jonathan, Saul's son, greatly
delighted in David.

3 [1]Lit *see* [a]1 Sam 20:9, 13

2 So Jonathan told David saying, "Saul my father is seeking to
put you to death. Now therefore, please be on guard in the
morning, and stay in a secret place and hide yourself.

4 [1]Lit *good* [a]1 Sam 20:32; Prov 31:8, 9 [b]Gen 42:22; Prov 17:13; Jer 18:20

3 "I will go out and stand beside my father in the field where
you are, and I will speak with my father about you; [a]if I [1]find
out anything, then I will tell you."
4 Then Jonathan [a]spoke well of David to Saul his father and
said to him, "[b]Do not let the king sin against his servant David,
since he has not sinned against you, and since his deeds *have*
been very [1]beneficial to you.

5 [a]Judg 9:17; 1 Sam 17:49, 50; 28:21; Ps 119:109 [b]1 Sam 11:13; 1 Chr 11:14 [c]Deut 19:10-13; 1 Sam 20:32; Ps 94:21; Matt 27:4

5 "For [a]he took his life in his hand and struck the Philistine,
and [b]the LORD brought about a great deliverance for all Israel;
you saw *it* and rejoiced. [c]Why then will you sin against
innocent blood by putting David to death without a cause?"

6 Saul listened to the voice of Jonathan, and Saul vowed, "As
the LORD lives, he shall not be put to death."
7 Then Jonathan called David, and Jonathan told him all
these words. And Jonathan brought David to Saul, and he was
in his presence as [a]formerly.
8 When there was war again, David went out and fought
with the Philistines and [1]defeated them with great slaughter, so
that they fled before him.
9 Now there was [a]an evil spirit from the LORD on Saul as he
was sitting in his house [b]with his spear in his hand, [c]and David
was playing *the harp* with *his* hand.
10 [a]Saul tried to [1]pin David to the wall with the spear, but he
slipped away out of Saul's presence, so that he [2]stuck the spear
into the wall. And David fled and escaped that night.
11 Then [a]Saul sent messengers to David's house to watch him,
in order to put him to death in the morning. But Michal,
David's wife, told him, saying, "If you do not save your life
tonight, tomorrow you will be put to death."
12 [a]So Michal let David down through a window, and he went
out and fled and escaped.
13 Michal took [a]the [1]household idol and laid *it* on the bed, and
put a quilt of goats' *hair* at its head, and covered *it* with clothes.
14 When Saul sent messengers to take David, she said, "[a]He is
sick."
15 Then Saul sent messengers to see David, saying, "Bring
him up to me on [1]his bed, that I may put him to death."
16 When the messengers entered, behold, the [1]household idol
was on the bed with the quilt of goats' *hair* at its head.
17 So Saul said to Michal, "Why have you deceived me like this
and let my enemy go, so that he has escaped?" And Michal said to
Saul, "He said to me, 'Let me go! [a]Why should I put you to
death?'"
18 Now David fled and escaped and came [a]to Samuel at Ramah,
and told him all that Saul had done to him. And he and Samuel
went and stayed in [b]Naioth.
19 It was told Saul, saying, "Behold, David is at Naioth in
Ramah."
20 Then [a]Saul sent messengers to take David, but when they
saw [b]the company of the prophets prophesying, with Samuel
standing *and* presiding over them, the Spirit of God came upon
the messengers of Saul; and [c]they also prophesied.
21 When it was told Saul, he sent other messengers, and they
also prophesied. So Saul sent messengers again the third time,
and they also prophesied.
22 Then he himself went to Ramah and came as far as the
large well that is in Secu; and he asked and said, "Where are
Samuel and David?" And *someone* said, "Behold, they are at
Naioth in Ramah."
23 He [1]proceeded there to Naioth in Ramah; and [a]the Spirit of
God came upon him also, so that he went along prophesying
continually until he came to Naioth in Ramah.

7 [a]1 Sam 16:21; 18:2, 10, 13
8 [1]Lit *smote*
9 [a]1 Sam 16:14; 18:10, 11 [b]1 Sam 18:10 [c]1 Sam 16:16
10 [1]Lit *strike David and the wall* [2]Lit *struck* [a]1 Sam 18:11; 20:33; Prov 1:16
11 [a]Judg 16:2; Ps 59: title
12 [a]Josh 2:15; Acts 9:25; 2 Cor 11:33
13 [1]Heb *teraphim* [a]Gen 31:19; Judg 18:14, 17
14 [a]Josh 2:5
15 [1]Lit *the*
16 [1]Heb *teraphim*
17 [a]2 Sam 2:22
18 [a]1 Sam 7:17 [b]1 Sam 19:22, 23
20 [a]1 Sam 19:11, 14; John 7:32 [b]1 Sam 10:5, 6, 10 [c]Num 11:25; Joel 2:28
23 [1]Lit *went* [a]1 Sam 10:10

24 He also stripped off his clothes, and he too prophesied
before Samuel and [1]lay down [2a]naked all that day and all that
night. Therefore they say, "[b]Is Saul also among the prophets?"

Chapter 20 Theme ______________________

20 Then David fled from Naioth in Ramah, and came and [a]said
[1]to Jonathan, "What have I done? What is my iniquity?
And what is my sin before your father, that he is seeking my life?"
2 He said to him, "Far from it, you shall not die. Behold, my
father does nothing either great or small [1]without disclosing it
to me. So why should my father hide this thing from me? It is
not so!"
3 Yet David [a]vowed again, [1]saying, "Your father knows well
that I have found favor in your sight, and he has said, 'Do not
let Jonathan know this, or he will be grieved.' But truly [b]as the
LORD lives and as your soul lives, there is [2]hardly a step
between me and death."
4 Then Jonathan said to David, "Whatever [1]you say, I will do
for you."
5 So David said to Jonathan, "Behold, tomorrow is [a]the new
moon, and I ought [b]to sit down to eat with the king. But let me
go, [c]that I may hide myself in the field until the third evening.
6 "If your father misses me at all, then say, 'David earnestly
asked *leave* of me to run to [a]Bethlehem his city, because it is
[b]the yearly sacrifice there for the whole family.'
7 "If he [1]says, 'It is good,' your servant *will be* safe; but if he is
very angry, [a]know that he has decided on evil.
8 "Therefore deal kindly with your servant, for [a]you have
brought your servant into a covenant of the LORD with you. But
[b]if there is iniquity in me, put me to death yourself; for why
then should you bring me to your father?"
9 Jonathan said, "Far be it from you! For if I should indeed
learn that evil has been decided by my father to come upon
you, then would I not tell you about it?"
10 Then David said to Jonathan, "Who will tell me [1]if your
father answers you harshly?"
11 Jonathan said to David, "Come, and let us go out into the
field." So both of them went out to the field.
12 Then Jonathan said to David, "The LORD, the God of Israel, *be
witness!* When I have sounded out my father about this time
tomorrow, *or* the third day, behold, if there is good *feeling* toward
David, shall I not then send to you and [1]make it known to you?
13 "If it please my father *to do* you harm, [a]may the LORD do so
to Jonathan and more also, if I do not [1]make it known to you
and send you away, that you may go in safety. And [b]may the
LORD be with you as He has been with my father.
14 "If I am still alive, will you not show me the lovingkindness
of the LORD, that I may not die?
15 "[a]You shall not cut off your lovingkindness from my house
forever, not even when the LORD cuts off every one of the
enemies of David from the face of the earth."

24 [1]Lit *fell* [2]I.e. without outward garments [a]2 Sam 6:20; Is 20:2; Mic 1:8 [b]1 Sam 10:10-12

20:1 [1]Lit *before* [a]1 Sam 24:9

2 [1]Lit *and he does not uncover my ear*

3 [1]Lit *and said* [2]Lit *about* [a]Deut 6:13 [b]1 Sam 25:26; 2 Kin 2:6

4 [1]Lit *your soul says*

5 [a]Num 10:10; 28:11-15; Amos 8:5 [b]1 Sam 20:24, 27 [c]1 Sam 19:2

6 [a]1 Sam 17:58 [b]Deut 12:5; 1 Sam 9:12

7 [1]Lit *says thus* [a]1 Sam 25:17

8 [a]1 Sam 18:3; 23:18 [b]2 Sam 14:32

10 [1]Lit *or what*

12 [1]Lit *uncover your ear*

13 [1]Lit *uncover your ear* [a]Ruth 1:17; 1 Sam 3:17 [b]Josh 1:5; 1 Sam 17:37; 18:12; 1 Chr 22:11, 16

15 [a]2 Sam 9:1, 3

16 So Jonathan made a *covenant* with the house of David, *saying,*
"[a]May the LORD require *it* at the hands of David's enemies."
17 Jonathan made David vow again because of his love for
him, because [a]he loved him as he loved his own life.
18 Then Jonathan said to him, "[a]Tomorrow is the new moon,
and you will be missed because your seat will be empty.
19 "When you have stayed for three days, you shall go down
quickly and come to the place where you hid yourself on that
eventful day, and you shall remain by the stone Ezel.
20 "I will shoot three arrows to the side, as though I shot at a
target.
21 "And behold, I will send the lad, *saying,* 'Go, find the
arrows.' If I specifically say to the lad, 'Behold, the arrows are
on this side of you, get them,' then come; for there is safety for
you and [1]no harm, as the LORD lives.
22 "But if I [1]say to the youth, '[a]Behold, the arrows are beyond
you,' go, for the LORD has sent you away.
23 "[a]As for the [1]agreement of which you and I have spoken,
behold, [b]the LORD is between you and me forever."
24 So David hid in the field; and when the new moon came,
the king sat down to eat food.
25 The king sat on his seat as usual, the seat by the wall; then
Jonathan rose up and Abner sat down by Saul's side, but
[a]David's place was empty.
26 Nevertheless Saul did not speak anything that day, for he
thought, "It is an accident, [a]he is not clean, surely *he is* not clean."
27 It came about the next day, the second *day* of the new moon,
that David's place was empty; so Saul said to Jonathan his son,
"Why has the son of Jesse not come to the meal, either
yesterday or today?"
28 Jonathan then answered Saul, "[a]David earnestly asked
leave of me *to go* to Bethlehem,
29 for he said, 'Please [1]let me go, since our family has a
sacrifice in the city, and my brother has commanded me to
attend. And now, if I have found favor in your sight, please let
me get away that I may see my brothers.' For this reason he
has not come to the king's table."
30 Then Saul's anger burned against Jonathan and he said to
him, "You son of a perverse, rebellious woman! Do I not know
that you are choosing the son of Jesse to your own shame and
to the shame of your mother's nakedness?
31 "For [1]as long as the son of Jesse lives on the earth, neither
you nor your kingdom will be established. Therefore now, send
and bring him to me, for [a]he [2]must surely die."
32 But Jonathan answered Saul his father and said to him,
"[a]Why should he be put to death? What has he done?"
33 Then [a]Saul hurled his spear at him to strike him down; [b]so
Jonathan knew that his father had decided to put David to death.
34 Then Jonathan arose from the table in fierce anger, and did
not eat food on the second day of the new moon, for he was
grieved over David because his father had dishonored him.

16 [a]Deut 23:21; 1 Sam 25:22
17 [a]1 Sam 18:1
18 [a]1 Sam 20:5, 25
21 [1]Lit *there is nothing*
22 [1]Lit *say thus* [a]1 Sam 20:37
23 [1]Lit *word* [a]1 Sam 20:14, 15 [b]Gen 31:49, 53; 1 Sam 20:42
25 [a]1 Sam 20:18
26 [a]Lev 7:20, 21; 15:5; 1 Sam 16:5
28 [a]1 Sam 20:6
29 [1]Lit *send me away*
31 [1]Lit *all the days which* [2]Lit *is a son of death* [a]2 Sam 12:5
32 [a]Gen 31:36; 1 Sam 19:5; Prov 31:9; Matt 27:23
33 [a]1 Sam 18:11; 19:10 [b]1 Sam 20:7

35 Now it came about in the morning that Jonathan went out
into the field for the appointment with David, and a little lad
was with him.
36 He said to his lad, "[a]Run, find now the arrows which I am
about to shoot." As the lad was running, he shot [1]an arrow past
him.
37 When the lad reached the place of the arrow which Jonathan
had shot, Jonathan called after the lad and said, "[a]Is not the
arrow beyond you?"
38 And Jonathan called after the lad, "Hurry, be quick, do not
stay!" And Jonathan's lad picked up the arrow and came to his
master.
39 But the lad was not aware of anything; only Jonathan and
David knew about the matter.
40 Then Jonathan gave his weapons to his lad and said to him,
"Go, bring *them* to the city."
41 When the lad was gone, David rose from the south side and
fell on his face to the ground, and [a]bowed three times. And they
kissed each other and wept together, but [b]David *wept* the more.
42 Jonathan said to David, "[a]Go in safety, inasmuch as we
have sworn to each other in the name of the LORD, saying,
'[b]The LORD will be between me and you, and between my
[1]descendants and your [1]descendants forever.'" [2]Then he rose
and departed, while Jonathan went into the city.

Chapter 21 Theme ______________________________

21 Then David came to [a]Nob to Ahimelech the priest; and
Ahimelech [b]came trembling to meet David and said to
him, "Why are you alone and no one with you?"
2 David said to Ahimelech the priest, "The king has
commissioned me with a matter and has said to me, '[a]Let no
one know anything about the matter on which I am sending
you and with which I have commissioned you; and I have
directed the young men to a certain place.'
3 "Now therefore, what [1]do you have on hand? Give [2]me five
loaves of bread, or whatever can be found."
4 The priest answered David and said, "There is no ordinary
bread [1]on hand, but there is [a]consecrated bread; if only the
young men have [b]kept themselves from women."
5 David answered the priest and said to him, "[a]Surely women
have been kept from us as previously when I set out and the
[b]vessels of the young men were holy, though it was an ordinary
journey; how much more then today will [1]their vessels *be holy?*"
6 So [a]the priest gave him consecrated *bread;* for there was no
bread there but the [b]bread of the Presence which was removed
from before the LORD, in order to put hot bread *in its place*
when it was taken away.
7 Now one of the servants of Saul was there that day, detained
before the LORD; and his name was [a]Doeg the Edomite, the
[b]chief of Saul's shepherds.

36 [1]Lit *the* [a]1 Sam 20:20, 21
37 [a]1 Sam 20:22
41 [a]Gen 42:6 [b]1 Sam 18:3
42 [1]Lit *seed* [2]Ch 21:1 in Heb [a]1 Sam 20:22 [b]1 Sam 20:15, 16, 23
21:1 [a]1 Sam 22:19; Neh 11:32; Is 10:32 [b]1 Sam 16:4
2 [a]Ps 141:3
3 [1]Lit *is under your hand?* [2]Lit *in my hand*
4 [1]Lit *under my hand* [a]Ex 25:30; Lev 24:5-9; Matt 12:4 [b]Ex 19:15
5 [1]Lit *it* be holy *in the vessel* [a]Ex 19:14, 15 [b]1 Thess 4:4
6 [a]Matt 12:3, 4; Luke 6:3, 4 [b]Lev 24:5-9
7 [a]1 Sam 14:47; 22:9; Ps 52: title [b]1 Chr 27:29, 31

8 David said to Ahimelech, "Now is there not a spear or a
sword [1]on hand? For I brought neither my sword nor my
weapons [2]with me, because the king's matter was urgent."
9 Then the priest said, "[a]The sword of Goliath the Philistine,
whom you [1]killed [b]in the valley of Elah, behold, it is wrapped
in a cloth behind the ephod; if you would take it for yourself,
take *it.* For there is no other except it here." And David said,
"There is none like it; give it to me."
10 Then David arose and fled that day from Saul, and went to
[a]Achish king of Gath.
11 But the [a]servants of Achish said to him, "Is this not David
the king of the land? [b]Did they not sing of this one as they
danced, saying,
'Saul has slain his thousands,
And David his ten thousands'?"
12 David [a]took these words [1]to heart and greatly feared Achish
king of Gath.
13 So he [a]disguised his sanity before them, and acted insanely
in their hands, and scribbled on the doors of the gate, and let
his saliva run down into his beard.
14 Then Achish said to his servants, "Behold, you see the man
behaving as a madman. Why do you bring him to me?
15 "Do I lack madmen, that you have brought this one to act the
madman in my presence? Shall this one come into my house?"

8 [1]Lit *under your hand* [2]Lit *in my hand*
9 [1]Lit *smote* [a]1 Sam 17:51, 54 [b]1 Sam 17:2
10 [a]Ps 34: title
11 [a]Ps 56: title [b]1 Sam 18:7; 29:5
12 [1]Lit *in his* [a]Luke 2:19
13 [a]Ps 34: title

Chapter 22 Theme ______________________________

22 So David departed from there and [a]escaped to [b]the cave
of Adullam; and when his brothers and all his father's
household heard *of it,* they went down there to him.
2 Everyone who was in distress, and everyone who [1]was in
debt, and everyone who was [2]discontented gathered to him;
and he became captain over them. Now there were [a]about four
hundred men with him.
3 And David went from there to Mizpah of Moab; and he
said to the king of Moab, "Please let my father and my mother
come *and stay* with you until I know what God will do for me."
4 Then he left them with the king of Moab; and they stayed
with him all the time that David was in the stronghold.
5 [a]The prophet Gad said to David, "Do not stay in the
stronghold; depart, and go into the land of Judah." So David
departed and went into the forest of Hereth.
6 Then Saul heard that David and the men who were with
him had been discovered. Now [a]Saul was sitting in Gibeah,
under the tamarisk tree on the height with his spear in his
hand, and all his servants were standing around him.
7 Saul said to his servants who stood around him, "Hear
now, O Benjamites! Will the son of Jesse also give to all of you
fields and vineyards? [a]Will he make you all commanders of
thousands and commanders of hundreds?
8 "For all of you have conspired against me so that there is no
one who [1]discloses to me [a]when my son makes *a covenant* with

INSIGHT
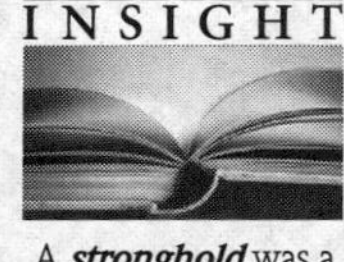
A ***stronghold*** was a fortified or secure location.

22:1 [a]Ps 57: title [b]Josh 12:15; 15:35; 2 Sam 23:13; Ps 142: title
2 [1]Lit *had a creditor* [2]Lit *bitter of soul* [a]1 Sam 23:13; 25:13
5 [a]2 Sam 24:11; 1 Chr 21:9; 29:29; 2 Chr 29:25
6 [a]Judg 4:5; 1 Sam 14:2
7 [a]1 Sam 8:12; 1 Chr 12:16-18
8 [1]Lit *uncovers my ear* [a]1 Sam 18:3; 20:16

the son of Jesse, and there
is none of you [b]who is sorry
for me or [1]discloses to me
that my son has stirred up
my servant against me to lie
in ambush, as *it is* this day."
9 Then [a]Doeg the Edom-
ite, who was [1]standing by
the servants of Saul, said, "[b]I
saw the son of Jesse coming
to Nob, to [c]Ahimelech the
son of Ahitub.
10 "[a]He inquired of the
LORD for him, [b]gave him
provisions, and [c]gave him
the sword of Goliath the
Philistine."
11 Then the king sent someone to summon Ahimelech
the priest, the son of Ahitub, and all his father's household, the
priests who were in Nob; and all of them came to the king.
12 Saul said, "Listen now, son of Ahitub." And he [1]answered,
"Here I am, my lord."
13 Saul then said to him, "Why have you and the son of Jesse
conspired against me, in that you have given him bread and a
sword and have inquired of God for him, so that he would rise
up against me [a]by lying in ambush as *it is* this day?"
14 [a]Then Ahimelech answered the king and said, "And who
among all your servants is as faithful as David, even the king's
son-in-law, who [1]is captain over your guard, and is honored in
your house?
15 "Did I *just* begin [a]to inquire of God for him today? Far be it
from me! [b]Do not let the king impute anything to his servant *or*
to any of the household of my father, for your servant knows
nothing [1]at all of this whole affair."
16 But the king said, "You shall surely die, Ahimelech, you
and all your father's household!"
17 And [a]the king said to the [1]guards who were attending him,
"Turn around and put the priests of the LORD to death, because
their hand also is with David and because they knew that he
was fleeing and did not [2]reveal it to me." But the [b]servants of
the king were not willing to put forth their hands to [3]attack the
priests of the LORD.
18 Then the king said to Doeg, "You turn around and [1]attack the
priests." And Doeg the Edomite turned around and [2]attacked
the priests, and [a]he killed that day eighty-five men [b]who wore
the linen ephod.
19 And [a]he struck Nob the city of the priests with the edge of
the sword, both men and women, children and infants; also oxen,
donkeys, and sheep *he struck* with the edge of the sword.
20 But [a]one son of Ahimelech the son of Ahitub, named
Abiathar, [b]escaped and fled after David.

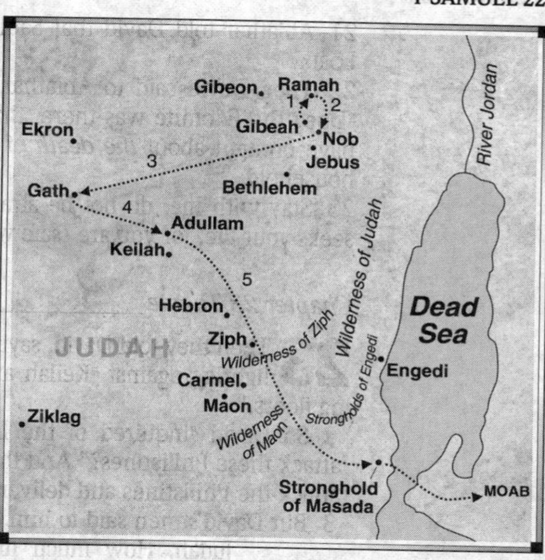

David's Journeys: 1 Samuel 21, 22
(Numbers on the following maps indicate the progression of David's journey.)

8 [1]Lit *uncovers my ear* [b]1 Sam 23:21
9 [1]Or *set over* [a]Ps 52: title [b]1 Sam 21:1 [c]1 Sam 14:3; 21:1
10 [a]Num 27:21; 1 Sam 10:22 [b]1 Sam 21:6 [c]1 Sam 21:9
12 [1]Lit *said*
13 [a]1 Sam 22:8
14 [1]So with Gr; Heb *turns aside to* [a]1 Sam 19:4, 5; 20:32
15 [1]Lit *small or great* [a]2 Sam 5:19, 23 [b]2 Sam 19:18, 19
17 [1]Lit *runners* [2]Lit *uncover my ear* [3]Lit *fall upon* [a]2 Kin 10:25 [b]Ex 1:17
18 [1]Lit *smite* [2]Lit *smote* [a]1 Sam 2:31 [b]1 Sam 2:18
19 [a]1 Sam 15:3
20 [a]1 Sam 23:6, 9; 30:7; 1 Kin 2:26, 27 [b]1 Sam 23:6

21 Abiathar told David that Saul had killed the priests of the
LORD.
22 Then David said to Abiathar, "I knew on that day, when
[a]Doeg the Edomite was there, that he would surely tell Saul. I
have brought about *the death* of every person in your father's
household.
23 "Stay with me; do not be afraid, for [a]he who seeks my life
seeks your life, for you are [1]safe with me."

Chapter 23 Theme ______________________________

23 Then they told David, saying, "Behold, the Philistines are
fighting against [a]Keilah and are plundering the threshing floors."
2 So David [a]inquired of the LORD, saying, "Shall I go and
[1]attack these Philistines?" And the LORD said to David, "Go and
[1]attack the Philistines and deliver Keilah."
3 But David's men said to him, "Behold, we are afraid here in
Judah. How much more then if we go to Keilah
against the ranks of the Philistines?"

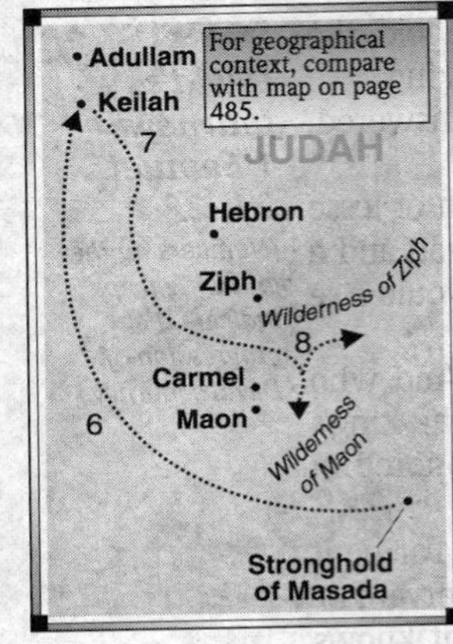

4 Then David inquired of the LORD once more.
And the LORD answered him and said, "Arise, go
down to Keilah, for [a]I will give the Philistines into
your hand."
5 So David and his men went to Keilah and
fought with the Philistines; and he led away their
livestock and struck them with a great slaughter.
Thus David delivered the inhabitants of Keilah.
6 Now it came about, when Abiathar the son of
Ahimelech [a]fled to David at Keilah, *that* he came
down *with* an ephod in his hand.
7 When it was told Saul that David had come to
Keilah, Saul said, "God has [1]delivered him into my
hand, for he shut himself in by entering a city with
double gates and bars."
8 So Saul summoned all the people for war, to go down to
Keilah to besiege David and his men.
9 Now David knew that Saul was plotting evil against him; so
he said to [a]Abiathar the priest, "[b]Bring the ephod here."
10 Then David said, "O LORD God of Israel, Your servant has
heard for certain that Saul is seeking to come to Keilah to
destroy the city on my account.
11 "Will the men of Keilah surrender me into his hand? Will Saul
come down just as Your servant has heard? O LORD God of Israel,
I pray, tell Your servant." And the LORD said, "He will come down."
12 Then David said, "Will the men of Keilah surrender me
and my men into the hand of Saul?" And the LORD said, "[a]They
will surrender you."
13 Then David and his men, [a]about six hundred, arose and
departed from Keilah, and they went [b]wherever they could go.
When it was told Saul that David had escaped from Keilah, he
[1]gave up the pursuit.

David's Journeys: 1 Samuel 23

22 [a]1 Sam 21:7

23 [1]Lit *a charge* [a]1 Kin 2:26

23:1 [a]Josh 15:44; Neh 3:17, 18

2 [1]Lit *smite* [a]1 Sam 23:4, 6, 9-12; 2 Sam 5:19, 23

4 [a]Josh 8:7; Judg 7:7

6 [a]1 Sam 22:20

7 [1]Lit *alienated*

9 [a]1 Sam 22:20 [b]1 Sam 23:6; 30:7

12 [a]Judg 15:10-13; 1 Sam 23:20

13 [1]Lit *ceased going out* [a]1 Sam 22:2; 25:13 [b]2 Sam 15:20

14 David stayed in the wilderness in the strongholds, and
remained in the hill country in the wilderness of [a]Ziph. And
Saul sought him every day, but [b]God did not deliver him into
his hand.
15 Now David [1]became aware that Saul had come out to seek
his life while David was in the wilderness of Ziph at Horesh.
16 And Jonathan, Saul's son, arose and went to David at
Horesh, and [1a]encouraged him in God.
17 Thus he said to him, "[a]Do not be afraid, because the hand of
Saul my father will not find you, and you will be king over Israel
and I will be next to you; and [b]Saul my father knows that also."
18 So [a]the two of them made a covenant before the LORD; and
David stayed at Horesh while Jonathan went to his house.
19 Then [a]Ziphites came up to Saul at Gibeah, saying, "Is David
not hiding with us in the strongholds at Horesh, on [b]the hill of
Hachilah, which is on the [1]south of [2]Jeshimon?
20 "Now then, O king, come down according to all the desire
of your soul to [1]do so; and [a]our part *shall be* to surrender him
into the king's hand."
21 Saul said, "May you be blessed of the LORD, [a]for you have
had compassion on me.
22 "Go now, make more sure, and investigate and see his place
where his [1]haunt is, *and* who has seen him there; for I am told
that he is very cunning.
23 "So look, and learn about all the hiding places where he
hides himself and return to me with certainty, and I will go
with you; and if he is in the land, I will search him out among
all the thousands of Judah."
24 Then they arose and went to Ziph before Saul. Now David
and his men were in the wilderness of [a]Maon, in the Arabah to
the [1]south of [2]Jeshimon.
25 When Saul and his men went to seek *him,* they told David,
and he came down to the rock and stayed in the wilderness of
Maon. And when Saul heard *it,* he pursued David in the
wilderness of Maon.
26 Saul went on one side of the mountain, and David and his
men on the other side of the mountain; and David was hurrying
to get away from Saul, for Saul and his men [a]were surrounding
David and his men to seize them.
27 But a messenger came to Saul, saying, "Hurry and come,
for the Philistines have made a raid on the land."
28 So Saul returned from pursuing David and went to meet the
Philistines; therefore they called that place [1]the Rock of Escape.
29 [1]David went up from there and stayed in the strongholds of
[a]Engedi.

Chapter 24 Theme ______________________

24 Now [a]when Saul returned from pursuing the Philistines,
[b]he was told, saying, "Behold, David is in the wilderness
of Engedi."

14 [a]Josh 15:55; 2 Chr 11:8 [b]Ps 32:7
15 [1]Lit *saw*
16 [1]Lit *strengthened his hand* [a]1 Sam 30:6; Neh 2:18
17 [a]Ps 27:1, 3; 118:6; Is 54:17; Heb 13:6 [b]1 Sam 20:31; 24:20
18 [a]1 Sam 18:3; 20:12-17, 42; 2 Sam 9:1; 21:7
19 [1]Lit *right side* [2]Or *the desert* [a]1 Sam 26:1; Ps 54: title [b]1 Sam 26:3
20 [1]Lit *come down* [a]1 Sam 23:12
21 [a]1 Sam 22:8
22 [1]Lit *foot*
24 [1]Lit *right side* [2]Or *the desert* [a]Josh 15:55; 1 Sam 25:2
26 [a]Ps 17:9
28 [1]Heb *Selahammahlekoth*
29 [1]Ch 24:1 in Heb [a]Josh 15:62; 2 Chr 20:2
24:1 [a]1 Sam 23:28, 29 [b]1 Sam 23:19

2 Then [a]Saul took three thousand chosen men from all Israel
and went to seek David and his men in front of the Rocks of
the Wild Goats.
3 He came to the sheepfolds on the way, where there *was* a
cave; and Saul [a]went in to [1]relieve himself. Now [b]David and his
men were sitting in the inner recesses of the cave.
4 The men of David said to him, "Behold, [a]*this is* the day of
which the LORD said to you, 'Behold; [b]I am about to give your
enemy into your hand, and you shall do to him as it seems
good [1]to you.'" Then David arose and cut off the edge of Saul's
robe secretly.
5 It came about afterward that [a]David's [1]conscience
bothered him because he had cut off the edge of
Saul's *robe.*
6 So he said to his men, "[a]Far be it from me
because of the LORD that I should do this thing to my
lord, the LORD's anointed, to stretch out my hand
against him, since he is the LORD's anointed."
7 David [1]persuaded his men with *these* words
and did not allow them to rise up against Saul. And
Saul arose, [2]left the cave, and went on *his* way.
8 Now afterward David arose and went out of the
cave and called after Saul, saying, "My lord the king!"
And when Saul looked behind him, [a]David bowed
with his face to the ground and prostrated himself.
9 David said to Saul, "Why do you listen to the
words of men, saying, 'Behold, David seeks [1]to harm you'?
10 "[a]Behold, this day your eyes have seen that the LORD had
given you today into my hand in the cave, and [b]some said to kill
you, but *my eye* had pity on you; and I said, 'I will not stretch
out my hand against my lord, for he is the LORD's anointed.'
11 "Now, [a]my father, see! Indeed, see the edge of your robe in
my hand! For in that I cut off the edge of your robe and did not
kill you, know and perceive that there is no evil or [1]rebellion in
my hands, and I have not sinned against you, though you [b]are
lying in wait for my life to take it.
12 "[a]May the LORD judge between [1]you and me, and may the
LORD avenge me on you; but my hand shall not be against you.
13 "As the proverb of the ancients says, '[a]Out of the wicked
comes forth wickedness'; but my hand shall not be against you.
14 "After whom has the king of Israel come out? Whom are
you pursuing? [a]A dead dog, [b]a single flea?
15 "[a]The LORD therefore be judge and decide between [1]you and
me; and may He see and [b]plead my cause and [2]deliver me from
your hand."
16 When David had finished speaking these words to Saul,
Saul said, "[a]Is this your voice, my son David?" Then Saul lifted
up his voice and wept.
17 [a]He said to David, "You are more righteous than I; for [b]you
have dealt well with me, while I have dealt wickedly with you.
18 "You have declared today that you have done good to me, that
[a]the LORD delivered me into your hand and *yet* you did not kill me.

Strongholds of Engedi
Engedi
Dead Sea
9
Stronghold of Masada

David's Journeys: 1 Samuel 24

2 [a]1 Sam 26:2

3 [1]Lit *cover his feet* [a]Judg 3:24 [b]Ps 57: title; 142: title

4 [1]Lit *in your sight* [a]1 Sam 23:17; 25:28-30 [b]1 Sam 26:8, 11

5 [1]Lit *heart struck* [a]2 Sam 24:10

6 [a]1 Sam 26:11

7 [1]Lit *tore apart* [2]Lit *from*

8 [a]1 Sam 25:23, 24; 1 Kin 1:31

9 [1]Lit *your hurt*

10 [a]Ps 7:3, 4 [b]1 Sam 24:4

11 [1]Lit *transgression* [a]2 Kin 5:13 [b]1 Sam 23:14, 23; 26:20

12 [1]Lit *me and you* [a]Gen 16:5; 31:53; Judg 11:27; 1 Sam 26:10, 23

13 [a]Matt 7:16-20

14 [a]2 Sam 9:8 [b]1 Sam 26:20

15 [1]Lit *me and you* [2]Lit *vindicate* [a]1 Sam 24:12 [b]Ps 35:1; 43:1; 119:154; Mic 7:9

16 [a]1 Sam 26:17

17 [a]1 Sam 26:21 [b]Matt 5:44

18 [a]1 Sam 26:23

19 "For if a man [a]finds his enemy, will he let him go away [1]safely?
May the LORD therefore reward you with good in return for
what you have done to me this day.
20 "Now, behold, [a]I know that you will surely be king, and that
[b]the kingdom of Israel will be established in your hand.
21 "So now [a]swear to me by the LORD that you will not cut off
my [1]descendants after me and that you will not destroy my
name from my father's household."
22 David swore to Saul. And Saul went to his home, but David
and his men went up to [a]the stronghold.

Chapter 25 Theme ______________________

25 [a]Then Samuel died; and all Israel gathered together and
[b]mourned for him, and [c]buried him at his house in Ramah.
And David arose and went down to the [d]wilderness of Paran.
2 Now *there was* a man in [a]Maon whose business was in
[b]Carmel; and the man was very [1]rich, and he had three thousand
sheep and a thousand goats. And it came about while [c]he was
shearing his sheep in Carmel
3 (now the man's name was Nabal, and his [a]wife's name was
Abigail. And the woman was [1]intelligent and beautiful in
appearance, but the man was harsh and evil in *his* dealings,
and he was [b]a Calebite),
4 that David heard in the wilderness that Nabal was shearing
his sheep.
5 So David sent ten young men; and David said to the young
men, "Go up to Carmel, [1]visit Nabal and greet him in my name;
6 and thus you shall say, '[1]Have a long life, [a]peace be to you,
and peace be to your house, and peace be to all that you have.
7 'Now I have heard [a]that you have shearers; now
your shepherds have been with us and we have not
insulted them, [b]nor have they missed anything all
the days they were in Carmel.
8 'Ask your young men and they will tell you.
Therefore let *my* young men find favor in your
eyes, for we have come on [a]a [1]festive day. Please
give whatever you find at hand to your servants
and to your son David.'"
9 When David's young men came, they spoke to
Nabal according to all these words in David's name;
then they waited.
10 But Nabal answered David's servants and said,
"[a]Who is David? And who is the son of Jesse? There
are many servants today who are each breaking
away from his master.
11 "Shall I then [a]take my bread and my water and my meat that
I have slaughtered for my shearers, and give it to men [1]whose
origin I do not know?"
12 So David's young men retraced their way and went back;
and they came and told him according to all these words.
13 David said to his men, "Each *of you* gird on his sword." So

For geographical context, see map on page 485.

David's Journeys: 1 Samuel 25:1–27:2

19 [1]Lit *on a good road* [a]1 Sam 23:17
20 [a]1 Sam 23:17 [b]1 Sam 13:14
21 [1]Lit *seed* [a]Gen 21:23; 1 Sam 20:14-17; 2 Sam 21:6-8
22 [a]1 Sam 23:29
25:1 [a]1 Sam 28:3 [b]Num 20:29; Deut 34:8 [c]2 Kin 21:18; 2 Chr 33:20 [d]Gen 21:21; Num 10:12; 13:3
2 [1]Lit *great* [a]1 Sam 23:24 [b]Josh 15:55 [c]Gen 38:13; 2 Sam 13:23
3 [1]Lit *of good understanding* [a]Prov 31:10 [b]Josh 15:13; 1 Sam 30:14
5 [1]Lit *go into*
6 [1]Lit *To life* [a]1 Chr 12:18; Ps 122:7; Luke 10:5
7 [a]2 Sam 13:23, 24 [b]1 Sam 25:15, 21
8 [1]Lit *good* [a]Neh 8:10-12; Esth 9:19, 22
10 [a]Judg 9:28
11 [1]Lit *from where they are* [a]Judg 8:6, 15

each man girded on his sword. And David also girded on his
sword, and about [a]four hundred men went up behind David
while two hundred [b]stayed with the baggage.
14 But one of the young men told Abigail, Nabal's wife, saying,
"Behold, David sent messengers from the wilderness to [1][a]greet
our master, and he scorned them.
15 "Yet the men were very good to us, and we were not
[a]insulted, nor did we miss anything [1]as long as we went about
with them, while we were in the fields.
16 "[a]They were a wall to us both by night and by day, all the
time we were with them tending the sheep.
17 "Now therefore, know and [1]consider what you should do, for
evil is plotted against our master and against all his household;
and he is such a [2]worthless man that no one can speak to him."
18 Then Abigail hurried and [a]took two hundred *loaves* of
bread and two jugs of wine and five sheep already prepared and
five measures of roasted grain and a hundred clusters of raisins
and two hundred cakes of figs, and loaded *them* on donkeys.
19 She said to her young men, "[a]Go on before me; behold, I
am coming after you." But she did not tell her husband Nabal.
20 It came about as she was riding on her donkey and coming
down by the hidden part of the mountain, that behold, David
and his men were coming down toward her; so she met them.
21 Now David had said, "Surely in vain I have guarded all that
this *man* has in the wilderness, so that nothing was missed of
all that belonged to him; and he has [a]returned me evil for good.
22 "[a]May God do so to the enemies of David, and more also, [b]if by
morning I leave *as much as* one [1]male of any who belong to him."
23 When Abigail saw David, she hurried and dismounted from
her donkey, and fell on her face before David [a]and bowed
herself to the ground.
24 She fell at his feet and said, "On me [1]alone, my lord, be the
blame. And please let your maidservant speak [2]to you, and
listen to the words of your maidservant.
25 "Please do not let my lord [1]pay attention to this [2]worthless
man, Nabal, for as his name is, so is he. [3]Nabal is his name and
folly is with him; but I your maidservant did not see the young
men of my lord whom you sent.
26 "Now therefore, my lord, as the LORD lives, and as your soul
lives, since the LORD has restrained you from [1]shedding blood, and
[a]from [2]avenging yourself by your own hand, now then [b]let your
enemies and those who seek evil against my lord, be as Nabal.
27 "Now let [a]this [1]gift which your maidservant has brought to
my lord be given to the young men who [2]accompany my lord.
28 "Please forgive [a]the transgression of your maidservant; for
[b]the LORD will certainly make for my lord an enduring house,
because my lord is [c]fighting the battles of the LORD, and [d]evil
will not be found in you all your days.
29 "Should anyone rise up to pursue you and to seek your [1]life,
then the [1]life of my lord shall be bound in the bundle of the
living with the LORD your God; but the [1]lives of your enemies
[a]He will sling out [2]as from the hollow of a sling.

13 [a]1 Sam 23:13 [b]1 Sam 30:24
14 [1]Lit *bless* [a]1 Sam 13:10; 15:13
15 [1]Lit *all the days* [a]1 Sam 25:7, 21
16 [a]Ex 14:22; Job 1:10
17 [1]Lit *see* [2]Lit *son of Belial*
18 [a]2 Sam 16:1; 1 Chr 12:40
19 [a]Gen 32:16, 20
21 [a]Ps 109:5; Prov 17:13
22 [1]Lit *who urinates against the wall* [a]1 Sam 3:17; 20:13 [b]1 Kin 14:10
23 [a]1 Sam 20:41
24 [1]Lit *even me* [2]Lit *in your ears*
25 [1]Lit *set his heart to* [2]Lit *man of Belial* [3]I.e. Fool
26 [1]Lit *coming in with blood* [2]Lit *saving* [a]Heb 10:30 [b]2 Sam 18:32
27 [1]Lit *blessing* [2]Lit *walk at the feet of* [a]Gen 33:11; 1 Sam 30:26
28 [a]1 Sam 25:24 [b]1 Sam 22:14; 2 Sam 7:11, 16 [c]1 Sam 18:17 [d]1 Sam 24:11; Ps 7:3
29 [1]Lit *soul* [2]Lit *in the midst* [a]Jer 10:18

30 "And when the LORD does for my lord according to all the
good that He has spoken concerning you, and [a]appoints you
ruler over Israel,
31 this will not [1]cause grief or a troubled heart to my lord,
both by having shed blood without cause and by my lord
having [2]avenged himself. [a]When the LORD deals well with my
lord, then remember your maidservant."
32 Then David said to Abigail, "[a]Blessed be the LORD God of
Israel, who sent you this day to meet me,
33 and blessed be your discernment, and blessed be you, [a]who
have kept me this day from [1]bloodshed and from [2]avenging
myself by my own hand.
34 "Nevertheless, as the LORD God of Israel lives, [a]who has
restrained me from harming you, unless you had come quickly
to meet me, surely there would not have been left to Nabal
until the morning light *as much as* one [1]male."
35 So David received from her hand what she had brought
him and said to her, "[a]Go up to your house in peace. See, I
have listened to [1]you and [2b]granted your request."
36 Then Abigail came to Nabal, and behold, he was holding [a]a
feast in his house, like the feast of a king. And Nabal's heart
was merry within him, [b]for he was very drunk; so [c]she did not
tell him anything [1]at all until the morning light.
37 But in the morning, when the wine had gone out of Nabal,
his wife told him these things, and his heart died within him
so that he became *as* a stone.
38 About ten days later, [a]the LORD struck Nabal and he died.
39 When David heard that Nabal was dead, he said, "Blessed be
the LORD, who has [a]pleaded the cause of my reproach from the
hand of Nabal and [b]has kept back His servant from evil. The LORD
has also returned the evildoing of Nabal on his own head."
Then David sent [1c]a proposal to Abigail, to take her as his wife.
40 When the servants of David came to Abigail at Carmel,
they spoke to her, saying, "David has sent us to you to take you
as his wife."
41 She arose [a]and bowed with her face to the ground and said,
"Behold, your maidservant is a maid [b]to wash the feet of my
lord's servants."
42 Then [a]Abigail quickly arose, and rode on a donkey, with
her five maidens who [1]attended her; and she followed the
messengers of David and became his wife.
43 David had also taken Ahinoam of [a]Jezreel, and [b]they both
became his wives.
44 Now Saul had given [a]Michal his daughter, David's wife, to
Palti the son of Laish, who was from [b]Gallim.

Chapter 26 Theme ______________________

26 Then the Ziphites came to Saul at Gibeah, saying, "[a]Is
not David hiding on the hill of Hachilah, *which is* before
[1]Jeshimon?"

30 [a]1 Sam 13:14

31 [1]Lit *become staggering to you or a stumbling of the heart* [2]Lit *saved* [a]Gen 40:14; 1 Sam 25:30

32 [a]Ex 18:10; 1 Kin 1:48; Ps 41:13; 72:18; 106:48; Luke 1:68

33 [1]Lit *coming in with blood* [2]Lit *saving* [a]1 Sam 25:26

34 [1]Lit *who urinates against the wall* [a]1 Sam 25:26

35 [1]Lit *your voice* [2]Lit *lifted up your face* [a]1 Sam 20:42; 2 Kin 5:19 [b]Gen 19:21

36 [1]Lit *small or large* [a]2 Sam 13:28 [b]Prov 20:1; Is 5:11; Hos 4:11 [c]1 Sam 25:19

38 [a]1 Sam 26:10; 2 Sam 6:7; Ps 104:29

39 [1]Lit *and spoke* [a]1 Sam 24:15; Prov 22:23 [b]1 Sam 25:26, 34 [c]Song 8:8

41 [a]1 Sam 25:23 [b]Mark 1:7

42 [1]Lit *walked at her feet* [a]Gen 24:61-67

43 [a]Josh 15:56 [b]1 Sam 27:3; 30:5

44 [a]1 Sam 18:27; 2 Sam 3:14 [b]Is 10:30

26:1 [1]Or *the desert* [a]1 Sam 23:19; Ps 54: title

2 So Saul arose and went down to the wilderness of Ziph,
having with him [a]three thousand chosen men of Israel, to
search for David in the wilderness of Ziph.
3 Saul camped in the hill of Hachilah, which is before
[1]Jeshimon, [a]beside the road, and David was staying in the
wilderness. When [b]he saw that Saul came after him into the
wilderness,
4 David sent out spies, and he knew that Saul was definitely
coming.
5 David then arose and came to the place where Saul had
camped. And David saw the place where Saul lay, and [a]Abner
the son of Ner, the commander of his army; and Saul was lying in
the circle of the camp, and the people were camped around him.
6 Then David said to Ahimelech [a]the Hittite and to [b]Abishai
the son of Zeruiah, Joab's brother, saying, "Who [c]will go down
with me to Saul in the camp?" And Abishai said, "I will go
down with you."
7 So David and Abishai came to the people by night, and
behold, Saul lay sleeping inside the circle of the camp with his
spear stuck in the ground at his head; and Abner and the
people were lying around him.
8 Then Abishai said to David, "Today God has delivered your
enemy into your hand; now therefore, please let me strike him
with the spear [1]to the ground with one stroke, and I will not
[2]strike him the second time."
9 But David said to Abishai, "Do not destroy him, for [a]who
can stretch out his hand against the LORD's anointed and be
without guilt?"
10 David also said, "As the LORD lives, [a]surely the LORD will
strike him, or [b]his day will come that he dies, or [c]he will go
down into battle and perish.
11 "[a]The LORD forbid that I should stretch out my hand against
the LORD's anointed; but now please take the spear that is at his
head and the jug of water, and let us go."
12 So David took the spear and the jug of water from *beside*
Saul's head, and they went away, but no one saw or knew *it,*
nor did any awake, for they were all asleep, because [a]a sound
sleep from the LORD had fallen on them.
13 Then David crossed over to the other side and stood on top
of the mountain at a distance *with* a large area between them.
14 David called to the people and to Abner the son of Ner,
saying, "Will you not answer, Abner?" Then Abner replied,
"Who are you who calls to the king?"
15 So David said to Abner, "Are you not a man? And who is
like you in Israel? Why then have you not guarded your lord
the king? For one of the people came to destroy the king your
lord.
16 "This thing that you have done is not good. As the LORD
lives, *all* of you [1a]must surely die, because you did not guard
your lord, the LORD's anointed. And now, see where the king's
spear is and the jug of water that was at his head."

2 [a]1 Sam 13:2; 24:2

3 [1]Or *the desert* [a]1 Sam 24:3 [b]1 Sam 23:15

5 [a]1 Sam 14:50, 51; 17:55

6 [a]Gen 23:3; 26:34; Josh 3:10; 1 Kin 10:29; 2 Kin 7:6 [b]1 Chr 2:16 [c]Judg 7:10, 11

8 [1]Lit *even into* [2]Lit *repeat with respect to him*

9 [a]1 Sam 24:6, 7; 2 Sam 1:14, 16

10 [a]Deut 32:35; 1 Sam 25:26, 38; Rom 12:19; Heb 10:30 [b]Gen 47:29; Deut 31:14; Ps 37:13 [c]1 Sam 31:6

11 [a]1 Sam 24:6, 12; Rom 12:17, 19; 1 Pet 3:9

12 [a]Gen 2:21; 15:12; Is 29:10

16 [1]Lit *are surely sons of death* [a]1 Sam 20:31

17 Then Saul recognized David's voice and said, "[a]Is this your
voice, my son David?" And David said, "It is my voice, my lord
the king."
18 He also said, "[a]Why then is my lord pursuing his servant?
For what have I done? Or what evil is in my hand?
19 "Now therefore, please let my lord the king listen to the
words of his servant. If [a]the LORD has stirred you up against
me, [b]let Him [1]accept an offering; but [c]if it is [2]men, cursed are
they before the LORD, for [d]they have driven me out today so
that I would have no attachment with the inheritance of the
LORD, saying, 'Go, serve other gods.'
20 "Now then, do not let my blood fall to the ground away
from the presence of the LORD; for the king of Israel has come
out to search for [a]a single flea, just as one hunts a partridge in
the mountains."
21 Then Saul said, "[a]I have sinned. Return, my son David, for
I will not harm you again because my life was precious in your
sight this day. Behold, I have played the fool and have committed
a serious error."
22 David replied, "Behold the spear of the king! Now let one
of the young men come over and take it.
23 "[a]The LORD will repay each man *for* his righteousness and
his faithfulness; for the LORD delivered you into *my* hand today,
but [b]I refused to stretch out my hand against the LORD's anointed.
24 "Now behold, as your life was [a]highly valued in my sight
this day, so may my life be highly valued in the sight of the
LORD, and may He [b]deliver me from all distress."
25 Then Saul said to David, "[a]Blessed are you, my son David;
you will both accomplish much and surely prevail." So [b]David
went on his way, and Saul returned to his place.

Chapter 27 Theme ________________________

27 Then David said [1]to himself, "Now I will perish one day
by the hand of Saul. [a]There is nothing better for me
than [2]to escape into the land of the Philistines. Saul then will
despair of searching for me anymore in all the territory of
Israel, and I will escape from his hand."
2 So David arose and crossed over, he and [a]the six hundred men
who were with him, to [b]Achish the son of Maoch, king of Gath.
3 And David lived with Achish at Gath, he and his men, [a]each
with his household, *even* David with [b]his two wives, Ahinoam
the Jezreelitess, and Abigail the Carmelitess, Nabal's [1]widow.
4 Now it was told Saul that David had fled to Gath, so he no
longer searched for him.
5 Then David said to Achish, "If now I have found favor in
your sight, let them give me a place in one of the cities in the
country, that I may live there; for why should your servant live
in the royal city with you?"
6 So Achish gave him Ziklag that day; therefore [a]Ziklag has
belonged to the kings of Judah to this day.

17 [a]1 Sam 24:16
18 [a]1 Sam 24:9, 11-14
19 [1]Lit *smell* [2]Lit *sons of men* [a]2 Sam 16:11 [b]Gen 8:21 [c]1 Sam 24:9 [d]Josh 22:25-27
20 [a]1 Sam 24:14
21 [a]Ex 9:27; 1 Sam 15:24, 30; 24:17
23 [a]1 Sam 24:19; Ps 7:8; 18:20; 62:12 [b]1 Sam 24:12
24 [a]1 Sam 18:30 [b]Ps 54:7
25 [a]1 Sam 24:19 [b]1 Sam 24:22
27:1 [1]Lit *in his heart* [2]Lit *that I should surely escape* [a]1 Sam 26:19
2 [a]1 Sam 25:13 [b]1 Sam 21:10; 1 Kin 2:39
3 [1]Lit *wife* [a]1 Sam 30:3; 2 Sam 2:3 [b]1 Sam 25:42, 43
6 [a]Josh 15:31; 19:5; Neh 11:28

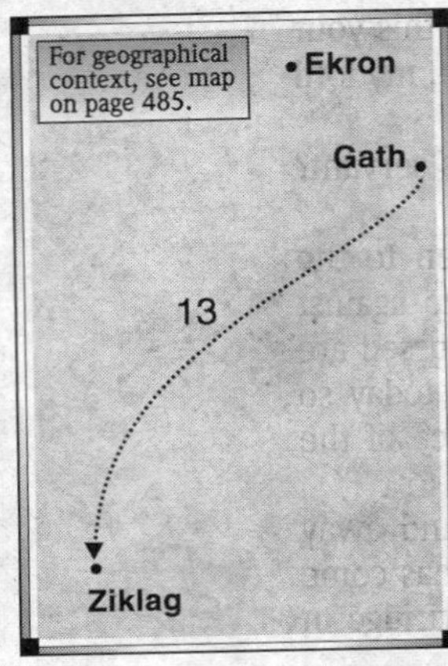

David's Journeys: 1 Samuel 27

7 The number of days that David lived in the
country of the Philistines was [a]a year and four months.
8 Now David and his men went up and raided
[a]the Geshurites and the Girzites and [b]the
Amalekites; for they were the inhabitants of the
land from ancient times, as you come to [c]Shur even
as far as the land of Egypt.
9 David [1]attacked the land and did not leave a man
or a woman alive, and he [a]took away the sheep, the
cattle, the donkeys, the camels, and the clothing.
Then he returned and came to Achish.
10 Now Achish said, "Where have you [a]made a raid
today?" And David said, "Against the [1]Negev of
Judah and against the [1]Negev of [b]the Jerahmeelites
and against the [1]Negev of [c]the Kenites."
11 David did not leave a man or a woman alive to bring to
Gath, saying, "Otherwise they will tell about us, saying, 'So has
David done and so *has been* his practice all the time he has
lived in the country of the Philistines.'"
12 So Achish believed David, saying, "He has surely made
himself odious among his people Israel; therefore he will become
my servant forever."

Chapter 28 Theme ______________________

28 Now it came about in those days that [a]the Philistines
gathered their armed camps for war, to fight against
Israel. And Achish said to David, "Know assuredly that you will
go out with me in the camp, you and your men."
2 David said to Achish, "Very well, you shall know what your
servant can do." So Achish said to David, "Very well, I will
make you [1]my bodyguard [a]for life."
3 Now [a]Samuel was dead, and all Israel had lamented him
and buried him [b]in Ramah, his own city. And Saul had removed
from the land those who [c]were mediums and spiritists.
4 So the Philistines gathered together and came and camped
[a]in Shunem; and Saul gathered all Israel together and they
camped in [b]Gilboa.
5 When Saul saw the camp of the Philistines, he was afraid
and his heart trembled greatly.
6 [a]When Saul inquired of the LORD, [b]the LORD did not answer
him, either by [c]dreams or by [d]Urim or by prophets.
7 Then Saul said to his servants, "Seek for me a woman who
is a medium, that I may go to her and inquire of her." And his
servants said to him, "Behold, [a]there is a woman who is a
medium at [b]En-dor."
8 Then Saul [a]disguised himself by putting on other clothes,
and went, he and two men with him, and they came to the
woman by night; and he said, "[b]Conjure up for me, please, and
[c]bring up for me whom I shall [1]name to you."
9 But the woman said to him, "Behold, you know [a]what Saul
has done, how he has cut off those who are mediums and

7 [a]1 Sam 29:3
8 [a]Josh 13:2, 13 [b]Ex 17:8; 1 Sam 15:7, 8 [c]Ex 15:22
9 [1]Lit *smote* [a]1 Sam 15:3; Job 1:3
10 [1]I.e. South country [a]1 Sam 23:27 [b]1 Sam 30:29; 1 Chr 2:9, 25 [c]Judg 1:16; 4:11
28:1 [a]1 Sam 29:1
2 [1]Lit *keeper of my head* [a]1 Sam 1:22, 28
3 [a]1 Sam 25:1 [b]1 Sam 7:17 [c]Lev 19:31; 20:27; Deut 18:10; 1 Sam 15:23
4 [a]Josh 19:18; 1 Sam 28:4; 1 Kin 1:3; 2 Kin 4:8 [b]1 Sam 31:1
6 [a]1 Chr 10:13, 14 [b]1 Sam 14:37; Prov 1:24-31 [c]Num 12:6; Joel 2:28 [d]Ex 28:30; Num 27:21
7 [a]Acts 16:16 [b]Josh 17:11; Ps 83:10
8 [1]Lit *say* [a]2 Chr 18:29; 35:22 [b]1 Chr 10:13; Is 8:19 [c]Deut 18:10, 11
9 [a]1 Sam 28:3

spiritists from the land. Why are you then laying a snare for my
life to bring about my death?"
10 Saul vowed to her by the LORD, saying, "As the LORD lives,
no punishment shall come upon you for this thing."
11 Then the woman said, "Whom shall I bring up for you?"
And he said, "Bring up Samuel for me."
12 When the woman saw Samuel, she cried out with a loud
voice; and the woman spoke to Saul, saying, "Why have you
deceived me? For you are Saul."
13 The king said to her, "Do not be afraid; but what do you
see?" And the woman said to Saul, "I see a [1]divine being
coming up out of the earth."
14 He said to her, "What is his form?" And she said, "An old
man is coming up, and [a]he is wrapped with a robe." And Saul
knew that it was Samuel, and [b]he bowed with his face to the
ground and did homage.
15 Then Samuel said to Saul, "Why have you disturbed me by
bringing me up?" And Saul answered, "I am greatly distressed;
for the Philistines are waging war against me, and [a]God has
departed from me and [b]no longer answers me, either through
prophets or by dreams; therefore I have called you, that you
may make known to me what I should do."
16 Samuel said, "Why then do you ask me, since the LORD has
departed from you and has become your adversary?
17 "The LORD has done [1]accordingly [a]as He spoke through me;
for the LORD has torn the kingdom out of your hand and given
it to your neighbor, to David.
18 "As [a]you did not [1]obey the LORD and did not execute His fierce
wrath on Amalek, so the LORD has done this thing to you this day.
19 "Moreover the LORD will also give over Israel along with you
into the hands of the Philistines, therefore tomorrow [a]you and
your sons will be with me. Indeed the LORD will give over the
army of Israel into the hands of the Philistines!"
20 Then Saul immediately fell full length upon the ground and
was very afraid because of the words of Samuel; also there was no
strength in him, for he had eaten no [1]food all day and all night.
21 The woman came to Saul and saw that he was terrified,
and said to him, "Behold, your maidservant has [1]obeyed you,
and [a]I have [2]taken my life in my hand and have listened to
your words which you spoke to me.
22 "So now also, please listen to the voice of your maidservant,
and let me set a piece of bread before you that *you may* eat and
have strength when you go on *your* way."
23 But he refused and said, "[a]I will not eat." [b]However, his
servants together with the woman urged him, and he listened
to [1]them. So he arose from the ground and sat on [c]the bed.
24 The woman had a [a]fattened calf in the house, and she
quickly slaughtered it; and she [b]took flour, kneaded it and
baked unleavened bread from it.
25 She brought *it* before Saul and his servants, and they ate.
Then they arose and went away that night.

13 [1]Or *god*
14 [a]1 Sam 15:27 [b]1 Sam 24:8
15 [a]1 Sam 16:14; 18:12 [b]1 Sam 28:6
17 [1]Lit *for himself* [a]1 Sam 15:28
18 [1]Lit *listen to the voice of* [a]1 Sam 15:20, 26; 1 Kin 20:42
19 [a]1 Sam 31:2; Job 3:17-19
20 [1]Lit *bread*
21 [1]Lit *listened to your voice* [2]Lit *put* [a]Judg 12:3; 1 Sam 19:5; Job 13:14
23 [1]Lit *their voices* [a]1 Kin 21:4 [b]2 Kin 5:13 [c]Esth 1:6; Ezek 23:41
24 [a]Gen 18:7; Luke 15:23, 27, 30 [b]Gen 18:6

Chapter 29 Theme ______________________________

29 Now [a]the Philistines gathered together all their armies
to [b]Aphek, while the Israelites were camping by the
spring which is in [c]Jezreel.

29:1 [a]1 Sam 28:1 [b]Josh 12:18; 19:30; 1 Sam 4:1; 1 Kin 20:30 [c]1 Kin 21:1; 2 Kin 9:30

2 And the lords of the Philistines were proceeding on by
hundreds and by thousands, and [a]David and his men were
proceeding on in the rear with Achish.

2 [a]1 Sam 28:1, 2

3 Then the commanders of the Philistines said, "What *are*
these Hebrews *doing here?*" And Achish said to the commanders
of the Philistines, "Is this not David, the servant of Saul the
king of Israel, [a]who has been with me these days, or *rather*
these years, and [b]I have found no fault in him from the day he
[1]deserted *to me* to this day?"

3 [1]Lit *fell* [a]1 Sam 27:7 [b]1 Sam 27:1-6; 1 Chr 12:19, 20; Dan 6:5

4 But the commanders of the Philistines were angry with
him, and the commanders of the Philistines said to him, "Make
the man go back, that he may return [a]to his place where you
have assigned him, and do not let him go down to battle with
us, [b]or in the battle he may become an adversary to us. For
with what could this *man* make himself acceptable to his lord?
Would it not *be* with the heads of [1]these men?

4 [1]Lit *those* [a]1 Sam 27:6 [b]1 Sam 14:21

5 "Is this not David, [a]of whom they sing in the dances, saying,
'Saul has slain his thousands,
And David his ten thousands'?"

5 [a]1 Sam 18:7; 21:11

6 Then Achish called David and said to him, "*As* the LORD lives,
you *have been* upright, and [a]your going out and your coming in
with me in the army are pleasing in my sight; [b]for I have not
found evil in you from the day of your coming to me to this
day. Nevertheless, you are not pleasing in the sight of the lords.
7 "Now therefore return and go in peace, that you may not
displease the lords of the Philistines."

6 [a]2 Sam 3:25; 2 Kin 19:27; Is 37:28 [b]1 Sam 27:8-12; 29:3

8 David said to Achish, "[a]But what have I done? And what
have you found in your servant from the day when I came
before you to this day, that I may not go and fight against the
enemies of my lord the king?"

8 [a]1 Sam 27:10-12

9 But Achish replied to David, "I know that you are pleasing in
my sight, [a]like an angel of God; nevertheless [b]the commanders of
the Philistines have said, 'He must not go up with us to the
battle.'

9 [a]2 Sam 14:17, 20; 19:27 [b]1 Sam 29:4

10 "Now then arise early in the morning [a]with the servants of
your lord who have come with you, and as soon as you have
arisen early in the morning and have light, depart."
11 So David arose early, he and his men, to depart in the
morning to return to the land of the Philistines. And the
Philistines went up to Jezreel.

10 [a]1 Chr 12:19, 22

Chapter 30 Theme ______________________________

30 Then it happened when David and his men came to
[a]Ziklag on the third day, that [b]the Amalekites had made
a raid on the [1]Negev and on [c]Ziklag, and had [2]overthrown Ziklag
and burned it with fire;

30:1 [1]I.e. South country [2]Lit *smote* [a]1 Sam 29:4, 11 [b]1 Sam 15:7; 27:8-10 [c]1 Sam 27:6, 8

2 [1]Lit *they did not kill* [a]1 Sam 27:11

4 [a]Num 14:1

5 [1]Lit *wife* [a]1 Sam 25:42, 43; 2 Sam 2:2

6 [1]Lit *bitter in soul* [a]Ex 17:4; John 8:59 [b]1 Sam 23:16; Ps 18:2; 27:14; 31:24; 71:4, 5; Rom 4:20

7 [a]1 Sam 23:6, 9 [b]1 Sam 22:20-23

8 [a]1 Sam 23:2, 4; Ps 50:15; 91:15 [b]Ex 15:9 [c]1 Sam 30:18

9 [a]1 Sam 27:2

10 [a]1 Sam 30:9, 21

12 [1]Lit *returned to him* [a]Judg 15:19

14 [1]I.e. South country [a]1 Sam 30:1, 16; 2 Sam 8:18; 1 Kin 1:38, 44; Ezek 25:16; Zeph 2:5 [b]Josh 14:13; 15:13; 21:12 [c]1 Sam 30:1

2 and they took captive the women *and all* who were in it,
both small and great, [1a]without killing anyone, and carried
them off and went their way.
3 When David and his men came to the city, behold, it was
burned with fire, and their wives and their sons and their
daughters had been taken captive.
4 Then David and the people who were with him [a]lifted their
voices and wept until there was no strength in them to weep.
5 Now [a]David's two wives had been taken captive, Ahinoam
the Jezreelitess and Abigail the [1]widow of Nabal the Carmelite.
6 Moreover David was greatly distressed because [a]the people
spoke of stoning him, for all the people were [1]embittered, each
one because of his sons and his daughters. But [b]David
strengthened himself in the LORD his God.
7 Then [a]David said to [b]Abiathar the priest, the son of
Ahimelech, "Please bring me the ephod." So Abiathar brought
the ephod to David.
8 [a]David inquired of the LORD, saying, "[b]Shall I pursue this
band? Shall I overtake them?" And He said to him, "Pursue, for
you will surely overtake them, [c]and you will surely rescue *all.*"
9 So David went, [a]he
and the six hundred men
who were with him, and
came to the brook Besor,
where those left behind
remained.
10 But David pursued, he
and four hundred men, for
[a]two hundred who were
too exhausted to cross the
brook Besor remained *behind.*
11 Now they found an
Egyptian in the field and
brought him to David, and
gave him bread and he ate,
and they provided him
water to drink.
12 They gave him a piece
of fig cake and two clusters of raisins, and he ate; [a]then his
spirit [1]revived. For he had not eaten bread or drunk water for
three days and three nights.
13 David said to him, "To whom do you belong? And where
are you from?" And he said, "I am a young man of Egypt, a
servant of an Amalekite; and my master left me behind when I
fell sick three days ago.
14 "We made a raid on [a]the [1]Negev of the Cherethites, and on
that which belongs to Judah, and on [b]the [1]Negev of Caleb, and
[c]we burned Ziklag with fire."
15 Then David said to him, "Will you bring me down to this
band?" And he said, "Swear to me by God that you will not kill

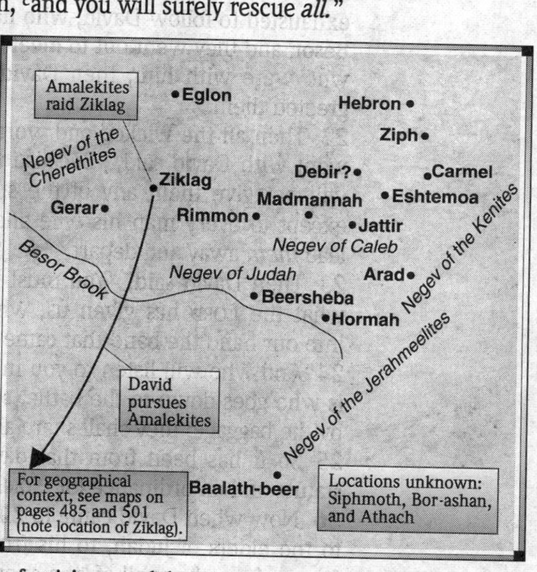

Ziklag and the Spoils

me or deliver me into the hands of my master, and I will bring
you down to this band."
16 When he had brought him down, behold, they were [1]spread
over all the land, [a]eating and drinking and [2]dancing because of
[b]all the great spoil that they had taken from the land of the
Philistines and from the land of Judah.
17 David [1]slaughtered them [a]from the twilight [2]until the
evening of [3]the next day; and not a man of them escaped,
except four hundred young men who rode on [b]camels and
fled.
18 So David [a]recovered all that the Amalekites had taken, and
[1]rescued his two wives.
19 But nothing of theirs was missing, whether small or great,
sons or daughters, spoil or anything that they had taken for
themselves; [a]David brought *it* all back.
20 So David had [1]captured all the sheep and the cattle *which
the people* drove ahead of [2]the *other* livestock, and they said,
"[a]This is David's spoil."
21 When [a]David came to the two hundred men who were too
exhausted to follow David, who had also been left at the brook
Besor, and they went out to meet David and to meet the people
who were with him, then David approached the people and
greeted them.
22 Then all the wicked and worthless men among those who
went with David said, "Because they did not go with [1]us, we
will not give them any of the spoil that we have recovered,
except to every man his wife and his children, that they may
lead *them* away and depart."
23 Then David said, "You must not do so, my brothers, with
what the LORD has given us, who has kept us and delivered
into our hand the band that came against us.
24 "And who will listen to you in this matter? For [a]as his share
is who goes down to the battle, so shall his share be who stays
by the baggage; they shall share alike."
25 So it has been from that day forward, that he made it a
statute and an ordinance for Israel to this day.
26 Now when David came to Ziklag, he sent *some* of the spoil
to the elders of Judah, to his friends, saying, "Behold, [a]a [1]gift
for you from the spoil of [b]the enemies of the LORD:
27 to those who were in [a]Bethel, and to those who were in
[b]Ramoth of the [1]Negev, and to those who were in [c]Jattir,
28 and to those who were in [a]Aroer, and to those who were in
Siphmoth, and to those who were in [b]Eshtemoa,
29 and to those who were in Racal, and to those who were in
the cities of [a]the Jerahmeelites, and to those who were in the
cities of [b]the Kenites,
30 and to those who were in [a]Hormah, and to those who were
in [b]Bor-ashan, and to those who were in Athach,
31 and to those who were in [a]Hebron, and to all the places
where David himself and his men were accustomed to [b]go."

16 [1]Lit *left* [2]Lit *keeping a pilgrim-feast* [a]Luke 12:19; 17:27f [b]1 Sam 30:14

17 [1]Lit *smote* [2]Lit *even until* [3]Lit *their* [a]1 Sam 11:11 [b]Judg 7:12; 1 Sam 15:3

18 [1]Lit *David rescued* [a]Gen 14:16

19 [a]1 Sam 30:8

20 [1]Lit *taken* [2]Lit *those livestock* [a]1 Sam 30:26-31

21 [a]1 Sam 30:10

22 [1]Lit *me*

24 [a]Num 31:27; Josh 22:8

26 [1]Lit *blessing* [a]1 Sam 25:27 [b]1 Sam 18:17; 25:28

27 [1]I.e. South country [a]Gen 12:8; Josh 7:2; 8:9; 16:1 [b]Josh 19:8 [c]Josh 15:48; 21:14

28 [a]Josh 13:16; 1 Chr 11:44 [b]Josh 15:50

29 [a]1 Sam 27:10 [b]Judg 1:16; 1 Sam 15:6

30 [a]Num 14:45; 21:3; Josh 12:14; 15:30; 19:4; Judg 1:17 [b]Josh 15:42; 19:7

31 [a]Num 13:22; Josh 14:13-15; 21:11-13; 2 Sam 2:1 [b]1 Sam 23:22

31:1 [a]1 Chr 10:1-12 [b]1 Sam 28:4
2 [1]Lit *smote* [a]1 Chr 8:33f
3 [1]Lit *found* [a]2 Sam 1:6
4 [a]Judg 9:54; 1 Chr 10:4 [b]Judg 14:3; 1 Sam 14:6; 17:26, 36 [c]2 Sam 1:6, 10
8 [1]Lit *morrow*
9 [1]Lit *into . . . around* [a]2 Sam 1:20 [b]Judg 16:23, 24
10 [1]Lit *house* [a]Judg 2:13; 1 Sam 7:3 [b]1 Sam 31:12; 2 Sam 21:12 [c]Josh 17:11
11 [1]Lit *about him what* [a]1 Sam 11:1-13
12 [a]2 Sam 2:4-7 [b]2 Chr 16:14
13 [a]2 Sam 21:12-14 [b]1 Sam 22:6 [c]2 Sam 1:12

Chapter 31 Theme ______________________

1 Chronicles 10

31 [a]Now the Philistines were fighting against Israel, and the
men of Israel fled from before the Philistines and fell
slain [b]on Mount Gilboa.
2 The Philistines overtook Saul and his sons; and the Philistines
[1]killed [a]Jonathan and Abinadab and Malchi-shua the sons of Saul.
3 [a]The battle went heavily against Saul, and the archers [1]hit
him; and he was badly wounded by the archers.
4 [a]Then Saul said to his armor bearer, "Draw your sword and
pierce me through with it, otherwise [b]these uncircumcised will
come and pierce me through and make sport of me." But his
armor bearer would not, for he was greatly afraid. [c]So Saul took
his sword and fell on it.
5 When his armor bearer saw that Saul was dead,
he also fell on his sword and died with him.
6 Thus Saul died with his three sons, his armor
bearer, and all his men on that day together.
7 When the men of Israel who were on the other
side of the valley, with those who were beyond the
Jordan, saw that the men of Israel had fled and that
Saul and his sons were dead, they abandoned the
cities and fled; then the Philistines came and lived
in them.
8 It came about on the [1]next day when the
Philistines came to strip the slain, that they found
Saul and his three sons fallen on Mount Gilboa.
9 They cut off his head and stripped off his
weapons, and sent *them* [1]throughout the land of the Philistines,
[a]to carry the good news [b]to the house of their idols and to the
people.
10 They put his weapons in the [1]temple of [a]Ashtaroth, and
[b]they fastened his body to the wall of [c]Beth-shan.
11 Now when [a]the inhabitants of Jabesh-gilead heard [1]what
the Philistines had done to Saul,
12 [a]all the valiant men rose and walked all night, and took the
body of Saul and the bodies of his sons from the wall of Beth-
shan, and they came to Jabesh and [b]burned them there.
13 They took their bones and [a]buried them under [b]the tamarisk
tree at Jabesh, and [c]fasted seven days.

The Death of Saul and His Sons

1011 B.C.

1 Samuel at a Glance

Theme of 1 Samuel:

Segment Divisions

		Main Divisions	Chapter Themes
		Samuel, the Last Judge	1
			2
			3
			4
			5
			6
			7
		From Samuel to Saul From Judges to Kings	8
			9
			10
			11
			12
			13
			14
			15
		The Preparation of Another King	16
			17
			18
			19
			20
			21
			22
			23
			24
			25
			26
			27
			28
			29
			30
			31

Author:

Date:

Purpose:

Key Words:

Israel in the Days of Samuel, Saul, and David

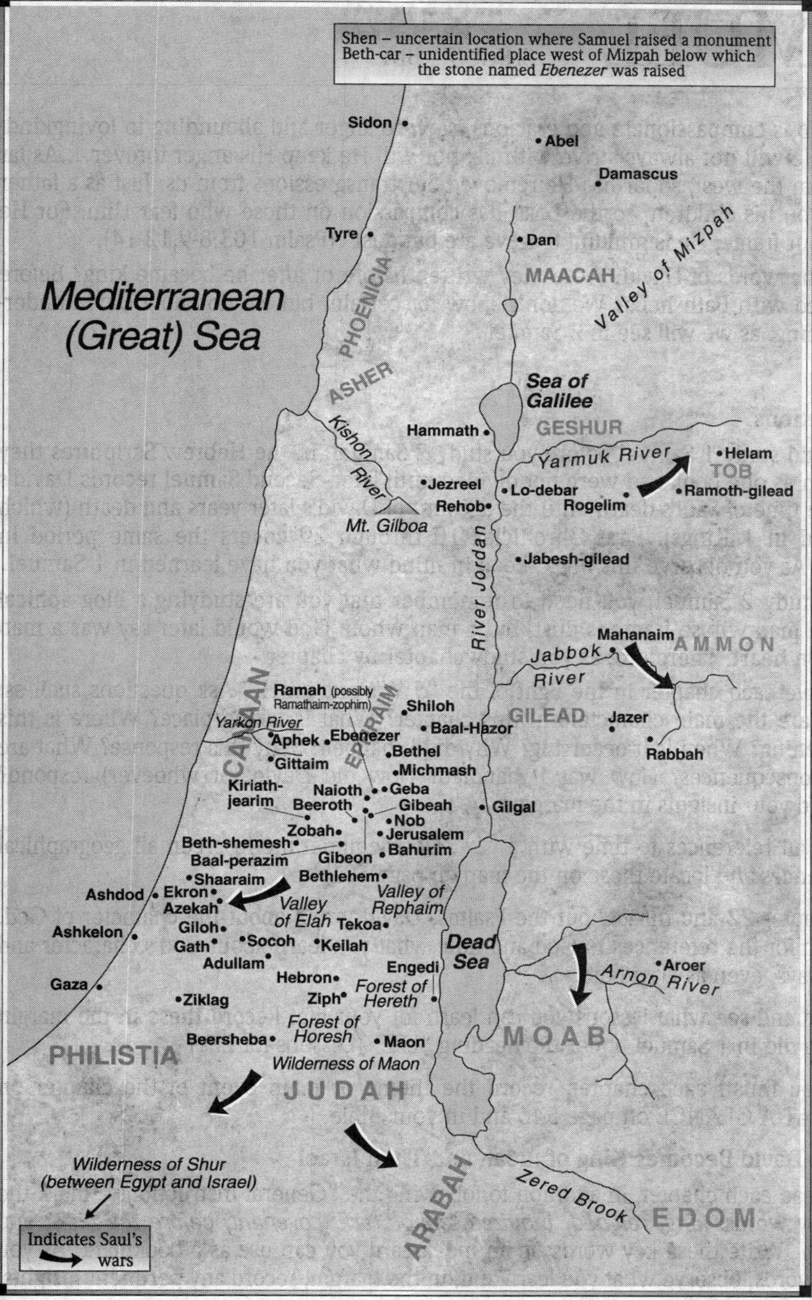
Shen – uncertain location where Samuel raised a monument
Beth-car – unidentified place west of Mizpah below which the stone named *Ebenezer* was raised
Mediterranean (Great) Sea
Sidon
Abel
Damascus
Tyre
Dan
PHOENICIA
MAACAH
Valley of Mizpah
ASHER
Sea of Galilee
Kishon River
Hammath
GESHUR
Yarmuk River
Helam
TOB
Jezreel
Lo-debar
Rogelim
Ramoth-gilead
Rehob
Mt. Gilboa
Jabesh-gilead
River Jordan
Mahanaim
AMMON
Jabbok River
Ramah (possibly Ramathaim-zophim)
Shiloh
GILEAD
Jazer
Yarkon River
Aphek
Ebenezer
Baal-Hazor
CANAAN
EPHRAIM
Gittaim
Bethel
Rabbah
Michmash
Kiriath-jearim
Naioth
Geba
Beeroth
Gibeah
Nob
Gilgal
Zobah
Jerusalem
Beth-shemesh
Baal-perazim
Gibeon
Bahurim
Shaaraim
Bethlehem
Ashdod
Ekron
Azekah
Valley of Elah
Valley of Rephaim
Ashkelon
Giloh
Tekoa
Gath
Socoh
Keilah
Dead Sea
Adullam
Engedi
Aroer
Arnon River
Hebron
Gaza
Ziklag
Ziph
Forest of Hereth
Forest of Horesh
MOAB
Beersheba
Maon
PHILISTIA
Wilderness of Maon
JUDAH
Wilderness of Shur (between Egypt and Israel)
ARABAH
Zered Brook
EDOM
Indicates Saul's wars

2 SAMUEL שמואל ב
SHMU'EL BET

"The LORD is compassionate and gracious, slow to anger and abounding in lovingkindness. He will not always strive with us, nor will He keep His anger forever....As far as the east is from the west, so far has He removed our transgressions from us. Just as a father has compassion on his children, so the LORD has compassion on those who fear Him. For He Himself knows our frame; He is mindful that we are but dust" (Psalm 103:8-9,12-14).

These are the words of David. Were they written before or after he became king? Before or after he sinned with Bathsheba? We don't know for certain, but we do know David understood their meaning, as we will see in 2 Samuel.

THINGS TO DO

General Instructions

1. You should study 1 Samuel before you study 2 Samuel. In the Hebrew Scriptures they were written as one book and were not divided until later. Second Samuel records David's life from the time of Saul's death until the account of David's later years and death (which are recorded in 1 Kings). First Chronicles 10 through 29 covers the same period in David's life. As you observe this book, keep in mind what you have learned in 1 Samuel.

2. As you study 2 Samuel, you need to remember that you are studying a biographical account of a man whose frame is dust, but a man whom God would later say was a man after His own heart. Therefore, as you study chapter by chapter:

   a. Observe each chapter in the light of the "5 W's and an H." Ask questions such as: Who are the main characters in this chapter? What is taking place? Where is this happening? When is it occurring? Why did it happen? Why this response? What are the consequences? How was it handled? How did David (or whoever) respond? Record your insights in the margin.

   b. Mark all references to time with a ⏲. Double-underline in green all geographical references and locate these on the map on page 501.

   c. In chapter 22 and throughout the Psalms, David wrote about the character of God. Watch for the references to God and note what you learn about God's character and His ways, even as David did.

   d. Watch and see what lessons you can learn for your life. Record these in the margin as you did in 1 Samuel under the heading "LFL" (Lessons for Life).

3. When you finish each chapter, record the theme or main event of the chapter on 2 SAMUEL AT A GLANCE on page 546 and in your Bible.

Chapters 1–10: David Becomes King of Judah and Then Israel

1. As you read each chapter, in addition to following the "General Instructions," mark the following key words: *king, reigned, inquired, ephod, ark, covenant, before the Lord,* and *evil (iniquity)*. Write these key words on an index card you can use as a bookmark. As you mark these words, observe what you learn and, in the margin, record any pertinent insights.

2. In chapter 5, refer to the chart "David's Family Tree" on page 511.

3. When you study chapter 7, give special attention to the Lord's promises to David. This is referred to as a covenant in 2 Chronicles 13:5; 21:7. Then observe what David does and how he responds to the Lord.

4. In 1 Samuel you marked every reference to *covenant*. In 1 Samuel 20 Jonathan and

David make a covenant between their "houses" (families). When you study chapters 4 and 9 of 2 Samuel, keep in mind the covenant David and Jonathan made in regard to their houses and notice how David fulfills this covenant. Also when you study Mephibosheth, remember 2 Samuel 5:6-8. Mark *Mephibosheth* in a distinctive way.

Chapters 11–12: David's Sins

1. Make a new bookmark for this segment. Mark the following key words: *inquired, ark, evil (sinned, sin),* and every reference to fasting.
2. Carefully watch the progression of events in these two chapters. Note the progression of sin and the things which could have served as admonitions against sin had David heeded them. Also list the consequences of David's sin and how the consequences parallel his sin.
3. Remember to follow the "General Instructions." Don't forget the "Lessons for Life" (LFL).
4. Study Psalm 51. Note when the psalm was written.

Chapters 13–24: Consequences of David's Sins

1. Mark the following key words: *Absalom, Mephibosheth, inquired, ark, covenant (oath), before the Lord, evil (iniquity, sinned),* and *Spirit*. Make a new bookmark for this segment.
2. Follow the "General Instructions." Pay attention to who's who in these chapters—there are many key characters. Record their names in the margin. Note how they are described and observe the consequences of their actions.
3. Note who David's children are and how he deals with them. Watch Absalom carefully and keep a running record in the margin of what you learn about him. Record your "LFL" in the margin.
4. As you study these final chapters, give special attention to David's relationship to the Lord and to what David has to say about God even after God told him He would chasten him. Spend time meditating on chapter 22 and 23:1-7. When you come to *covenant*, review what you learned in chapter 7 and add any new insights.
5. Then complete 2 SAMUEL AT A GLANCE.

THINGS TO THINK ABOUT

1. What have you learned about sin and its consequences? Did you think that if God forgave you, you would never reap sin's harvest? What do you think now?
2. In light of all you have learned, why do you think God referred to David as a man after His own heart (1 Samuel 13:14; Acts 13:22)? Give this some serious thought. Then think about what such a statement about David, made after his death, would mean to you. If you wanted to be a man, a woman, a teen, a child after God's own heart, what do you think it would require on your part?
3. Review the "Lessons for Life" you marked in the margin. What did you see that you can make a matter of prayer? Did you learn anything about inquiring or sitting before the Lord? Did you learn anything from marking "before the Lord"?

Chapter 1 Theme ____________________

1011 B.C.

1 Now it came about after [a]the death of Saul, when David had
returned from [b]the slaughter of the Amalekites, that David
remained two days in Ziklag.
2 On the third day, behold, [a]a man came out of the camp from
Saul, [b]with his clothes torn and [1]dust on his head. And it came

1:1 [a]1 Sam 31:6 [b]1 Sam 30:1, 17, 26

2 [1]Lit *ground* [a]2 Sam 4:10 [b]1 Sam 4:12

about when he came to David that [c]he fell to the ground and
prostrated himself.
3 Then David said to him, "From where do you come?" And
he said to him, "I have escaped from the camp of Israel."
4 David said to him, "[a]How did things go? Please tell me."
And he said, "The people have fled from the battle, and also
many of the people have fallen and are dead; and Saul and
Jonathan his son are dead also."
5 So David said to the young man who told him, "How do
you know that Saul and his son Jonathan are dead?"
6 The young man who told him said, "By chance I happened to
be on [a]Mount Gilboa, and behold, [b]Saul was leaning on his spear.
And behold, the chariots and the horsemen pursued him closely.
7 "When he looked behind him, he saw me and called to me.
And I said, 'Here I am.'
8 "He said to me, 'Who are you?' And I [1]answered him, '[a]I am
an Amalekite.'
9 "Then he said to me, 'Please stand beside me and kill me,
for agony has seized me because my [1]life still lingers in me.'
10 "So I stood beside him [a]and killed him, because I knew that
he could not live after he had fallen. And [b]I took the crown
which *was* on his head and the bracelet which *was* on his arm,
and I have brought them here to my lord."
11 Then [a]David took hold of his clothes and tore them, and *so*
also *did* all the men who *were* with him.
12 They mourned and wept and [a]fasted until evening for Saul
and his son Jonathan and for the people of the LORD and the
house of Israel, because they had fallen by the sword.
13 David said to the young man who told him, "Where are
you from?" And he [1]answered, "[a]I am the son of an alien, an
Amalekite."
14 Then David said to him, "How is it you were not afraid [a]to
stretch out your hand to destroy the LORD's anointed?"
15 And David called one of the young men and said, "Go, [1]cut
him down." [a]So he struck him and he died.
16 David said to him, "[a]Your blood is on your head, for [b]your
mouth has testified against you, saying, 'I have killed the LORD's
anointed.'"
17 Then David [a]chanted with this lament over Saul and Jonathan
his son,
18 and he told *them* to teach the sons of Judah *the song of* the
bow; behold, it is written in [a]the book of Jashar.
19 "[1]Your beauty, O Israel, is slain on your high places!
[a]How have the mighty fallen!
20 "[a]Tell *it* not in Gath,
Proclaim it not in the streets of Ashkelon,
Or [b]the daughters of the Philistines will rejoice,
The daughters of [c]the uncircumcised will exult.
21 "[a]O mountains of Gilboa,
[b]Let not dew or rain be on you, nor fields of offerings;
For there the shield of the mighty was defiled,
The shield of Saul, not [c]anointed with oil.

INSIGHT

The ***book of Jashar*** was a collection of poetical writings of important events in Israel's history which was gathered in the time of David or Solomon. It is often compared to "The Book of the Wars of the Lord." Bible authors are believed to have quoted occasionally from this book.

2 [c]1 Sam 25:23
4 [a]1 Sam 4:16
6 [a]1 Sam 28:4; 31:1-6; 1 Chr 10:4-10 [b]1 Sam 31:2-4
8 [1]Lit *said to* [a]1 Sam 15:3; 30:1, 13, 17
9 [1]Lit *whole life is still in me*
10 [a]Judg 9:54 [b]2 Kin 11:12
11 [a]Gen 37:29, 34; Josh 7:6; 2 Chr 34:27; Ezra 9:3
12 [a]2 Sam 3:35
13 [1]Lit *said* [a]2 Sam 1:8
14 [a]1 Sam 24:6; 26:9, 11, 16
15 [1]Lit *fall upon him* [a]2 Sam 4:10, 12
16 [a]1 Sam 26:9; 2 Sam 3:28, 29; 1 Kin 2:32 [b]2 Sam 1:10; Luke 19:22
17 [a]2 Chr 35:25
18 [a]Josh 10:13
19 [1]Lit *The* [a]2 Sam 1:25, 27
20 [a]1 Sam 31:8-13; Mic 1:10 [b]Ex 15:20, 21; 1 Sam 18:6 [c]1 Sam 14:6
21 [a]1 Sam 31:1 [b]Ezek 31:15 [c]Is 21:5

22 “[a]From the blood of the slain, from the fat of the mighty,
[b]The bow of Jonathan did not turn back,
And the sword of Saul did not return empty.
23 “Saul and Jonathan, beloved and pleasant in their life,
And in their death they were not parted;
[a]They were swifter than eagles,
[b]They were stronger than lions.
24 “O daughters of Israel, weep over Saul,
Who clothed you luxuriously in scarlet,
Who put ornaments of gold on your apparel.
25 “[a]How have the mighty fallen in the midst of the battle!
Jonathan is slain on your high places.
26 “I am distressed for you, my brother Jonathan;
You have been very pleasant to me.
[a]Your love to me was more wonderful
Than the love of women.
27 “[a]How have the mighty fallen,
And [b]the weapons of war perished!”

Chapter 2 Theme ______________________

2 Then it came about afterwards that [a]David inquired of the
LORD, saying, “Shall I go up to one of the cities of Judah?”
And the LORD said to him, “Go up.” So David said, “Where shall
I go up?” And He said, “[b]To Hebron.”
2 So David went up there, and [a]his two wives also, Ahinoam
the Jezreelitess and Abigail the [1]widow of Nabal the Carmelite.
3 And [a]David brought up his men who *were* with him, each
with his household; and they lived in the cities of Hebron.
4 Then the men of Judah came and there [a]anointed David
king over the house of Judah.
And they told David, saying, “It was [b]the men of Jabesh-gilead
who buried Saul.”
5 David sent messengers to the men of Jabesh-gilead, and
said to them, “[a]May you be blessed of the LORD because you
have [1]shown this kindness to Saul your lord, and have buried
him.
6 “Now [a]may the LORD [1]show lovingkindness and truth to you;
and I also will [1]show this goodness to you, because you have
done this thing.
7 “Now therefore, let your hands be strong and be [1]valiant; for
Saul your lord is dead, and also the house of Judah has anointed
me king over them.”
8 But [a]Abner the son of Ner, commander of Saul’s army, had
taken [1]Ish-bosheth the son of Saul and brought him over to
[b]Mahanaim.
9 He made him king over [a]Gilead, over the [b]Ashurites, over
[c]Jezreel, over Ephraim, and over Benjamin, even over all Israel.
10 Ish-bosheth, Saul’s son, was forty years old when he became
king over Israel, and he was king for two years. The house of
Judah, however, followed David.

22 [a]Deut 32:42; Is 34:6 [b]1 Sam 18:4
23 [a]Jer 4:13 [b]Judg 14:18
25 [a]2 Sam 1:19, 27
26 [a]1 Sam 18:1-4
27 [a]2 Sam 1:19, 25 [b]Is 13:5
2:1 [a]1 Sam 23:2, 4, 9-12 [b]Josh 14:13; 1 Sam 30:31
2 [1]Lit *wife* [a]1 Sam 25:42, 43
3 [a]1 Sam 30:9; 1 Chr 12:1
4 [a]1 Sam 16:13; 2 Sam 5:3, 5 [b]1 Sam 31:11-13
5 [1]Lit *done* [a]1 Sam 23:21; Ps 115:15
6 [1]Lit *do* [a]Ex 34:6; 2 Tim 1:16
7 [1]Lit *sons of valor*
8 [1]I.e. man of shame; cf 1 Chr 8:33, *Eshbaal* [a]1 Sam 14:50 [b]Gen 32:2; 2 Sam 17:24
9 [a]Josh 22:9 [b]Judg 1:32 [c]1 Sam 29:1

11 [a]The [1]time that David was king in Hebron over the house
of Judah was seven years and six months.
12 Now Abner the son of Ner, went out from Mahanaim to
[a]Gibeon with the servants of Ish-bosheth the son of Saul.
13 And [a]Joab the son of Zeruiah and the servants of David
went out and met [1]them by the pool of Gibeon; and they sat
down, [2]one on the one side of the pool and [2]the other on the
other side of the pool.
14 Then Abner said to Joab, "Now let the young men arise
and [1a]hold a contest before us." And Joab said, "Let them arise."
15 So they arose and went over by count, twelve for Benjamin
and Ish-bosheth the son of Saul, and twelve of the servants of
David.
16 Each one of them seized his [1]opponent by the head and
thrust his sword in his [2]opponent's side; so they fell down
together. Therefore that place was called [3]Helkath-hazzurim,
which is in Gibeon.
17 That day the battle was very severe, and [a]Abner and the
men of Israel were beaten before the servants of David.
18 Now [a]the three sons of Zeruiah were there, Joab and Abishai
and Asahel; and Asahel *was* [b]*as* [1]swift-footed as one of the
gazelles which is in the field.
19 Asahel pursued Abner and did not [1]turn to the right or to
the left from following Abner.
20 Then Abner looked behind him and said, "Is that you,
Asahel?" And he answered, "It is I."
21 So Abner said to him, "[1]Turn to your right or to your left,
and take hold of one of the young men for yourself, and take for
yourself his spoil." But Asahel was not willing to turn aside
from following him.
22 Abner repeated again to Asahel, "Turn [1]aside from following
me. Why should I strike you to the ground? [a]How then could I
lift up my face to your brother Joab?"
23 However, he refused to turn aside; therefore Abner struck
him in the belly with the butt end of the spear, so that the
spear came out at his back. And he fell there and died on the
spot. And it came about that all who came to the place where
[a]Asahel had fallen and died, stood still.
24 But Joab and Abishai pursued Abner, and when the sun
was going down, they came to the hill of Ammah, which is in
front of Giah by the way of the wilderness of Gibeon.
25 The sons of Benjamin gathered together behind Abner and
became one band, and they stood on the top of a certain hill.
26 Then Abner called to Joab and said, "Shall the sword devour
forever? Do you not know that it will be bitter in the end? How
long will you [1]refrain from telling the people to turn back from
following their brothers?"
27 Joab said, "As God lives, if you had not spoken, surely then
the people would have gone away in the morning, each from
following his brother."
28 So Joab blew the trumpet; and all the people halted and

11 [1]Lit *number of days* [a]2 Sam 5:5

12 [a]Josh 10:12; 18:25

13 [1]Lit *them together* [2]Lit *these* [a]2 Sam 8:16; 1 Chr 2:16; 11:6

14 [1]Lit *make sport* [a]2 Sam 2:16, 17

16 [1]Lit *fellow* [2]Lit *fellow's* [3]I.e. the field of sword-edges

17 [a]2 Sam 3:1

18 [1]Lit *light in his feet* [a]1 Chr 2:16 [b]1 Chr 12:8; Hab 3:19

19 [1]Lit *turn to go to*

21 [1]Lit *Turn for yourself*

22 [1]Lit *aside for yourself* [a]2 Sam 3:27

23 [a]2 Sam 20:12

26 [1]Lit *not tell the people*

pursued Israel no longer, [a]nor did they continue to fight anymore.
29 Abner and his men then went through the Arabah all that
night; so they crossed the Jordan, walked all morning, and came
to [a]Mahanaim.
30 Then Joab returned from following Abner; when he had
gathered all the people together, [1]nineteen of David's servants
besides Asahel were missing.
31 But the servants of David had struck down many of Benjamin
and Abner's men, *so that* three hundred and sixty men died.
32 And they took up Asahel and buried him [a]in his father's
tomb which was in Bethlehem. Then Joab and his men went
all night until the day [1]dawned at Hebron.

Chapter 3 Theme ______________________

3 Now [a]there was a long war between the house of Saul and
the house of David; and David grew steadily stronger, but
the house of Saul grew weaker continually.
2 [a]Sons were born to David at Hebron: his firstborn was
Amnon, by [b]Ahinoam the Jezreelitess;
3 and his second, Chileab, by Abigail the [1]widow of Nabal the
Carmelite; and the third, Absalom the son of [a]Maacah, the
daughter of Talmai, king of [b]Geshur;
4 and the fourth, [a]Adonijah the son of Haggith; and the fifth,
Shephatiah the son of Abital;
5 and the sixth, Ithream, by David's wife Eglah. These were
born to David at Hebron.
6 It came about while there was war between the house of
Saul and the house of David that [a]Abner was making himself
strong in the house of Saul.
7 Now Saul had a concubine whose name was [a]Rizpah, the
daughter of Aiah; and [1]Ish-bosheth said to Abner, "Why have
you gone in to my father's concubine?"
8 Then Abner was very angry over the words of Ish-bosheth
and said, "[a]Am I a dog's head that belongs to Judah? Today I show
kindness to the house of Saul your father, to his brothers and to
his friends, and have not delivered you into the hands of David;
and yet today you charge me with a guilt concerning the woman.
9 "[a]May God do so to Abner, and more also, if [b]as the LORD
has sworn to David, I do not accomplish this for him,
10 [a]to transfer the kingdom from the house of Saul and to
establish the throne of David over Israel and over Judah, [b]from
Dan even to Beersheba."
11 And he could no longer answer Abner a word, because he
was afraid of him.
12 Then Abner sent messengers to David in his place, saying,
"Whose is the land? Make your covenant with me, and behold,
my hand shall be with you to bring all Israel over to you."
13 He said, "Good! I will make a covenant with you, but I demand
one thing of you, [1]namely, [a]you shall not see my face unless you
[b]first bring Michal, Saul's daughter, when you come to see [2]me."

1 Chronicles 3

28 [a]2 Sam 3:1
29 [a]2 Sam 2:8
30 [1]Lit *nineteen men*
32 [1]Lit *lighted on them* [a]Gen 47:29, 30; Judg 8:32
3:1 [a]1 Kin 14:30; Ps 46:9
2 [a]1 Chr 3:1-3 [b]1 Sam 25:42, 43
3 [1]Lit *wife* [a]1 Sam 27:8; 1 Chr 3:2 [b]2 Sam 14:32; 15:8
4 [a]1 Kin 1:5
6 [a]2 Sam 2:8, 9
7 [1]So some ancient mss and versions; M.T. *he* [a]2 Sam 21:8-11
8 [a]1 Sam 24:14; 2 Sam 9:8
9 [a]1 Kin 19:2 [b]1 Sam 15:28
10 [a]1 Sam 15:28 [b]1 Sam 3:20
13 [1]Lit *saying* [2]Lit *my face* [a]Gen 43:3 [b]1 Sam 18:20; 19:11

14 So David sent messengers to Ish-bosheth, Saul's son, saying,
"Give me my wife Michal, to whom I was betrothed [a]for a
hundred foreskins of the Philistines."
15 Ish-bosheth sent and took her from *her* husband, from [1]Paltiel
the son of Laish.
16 But her husband went with her, weeping as he went, and
followed her as far as [a]Bahurim. Then Abner said to him, "Go,
return." So he returned.
17 Now Abner had [1]consultation with [a]the elders of Israel, saying,
"In times past you were seeking for David to be king over you.
18 "Now then, do *it!* For the LORD has spoken of David, saying,
'[a]By the hand of My servant David [1]I will save My people Israel
from the hand of the Philistines and from the hand of all their
enemies.'"
19 Abner also spoke in the hearing of Benjamin; and in addition
Abner went to speak in the hearing of David in Hebron all that
seemed good to Israel and to [a]the whole house of Benjamin.
20 Then Abner and twenty men with him came to David at
Hebron. And David made a feast for Abner and the men who
were with him.
21 Abner said to David, "Let me arise and go and [a]gather all
Israel to my lord the king, that they may make a covenant with
you, and that [b]you may be king over all that your soul desires."
So David sent Abner away, and he went in peace.
22 And behold, [a]the servants of David and Joab came from a raid
and brought much spoil with them; but Abner was not with
David in Hebron, for he had sent him away, and he had gone
in peace.
23 When Joab and all the army that was with him arrived,
they told Joab, saying, "Abner the son of Ner came to the king,
and he has sent him away, and he has gone in peace."
24 Then Joab came to the king and said, "What have you
done? Behold, Abner came to you; why then have you sent
him away and he is already gone?
25 "You know Abner the son of Ner, that he came to deceive
you and to learn of [a]your going out and coming in and to find
out all that you are doing."
26 When Joab came out from David, he sent messengers after
Abner, and they brought him back from the well of Sirah; but
David did not know *it.*
27 So when Abner returned to Hebron, Joab took him aside
into the middle of the gate to speak with him privately, and
there [a]he struck him in the belly so that he died on account of
the blood of Asahel his brother.
28 Afterward when David heard it, he said, "I and my
kingdom are innocent before the LORD forever of the blood of
Abner the son of Ner.
29 "[a]May it [1]fall on the head of Joab and on all his father's house;
and may there not fail from the house of Joab [b]one who has a
discharge, or who is a leper, or who takes hold of a distaff, or
who falls by the sword, or who lacks bread."

14 [a]1 Sam 18:25, 27
15 [1]In 1 Sam 25:44, *Palti*
16 [a]2 Sam 16:5; 19:16
17 [1]Lit *a word* [a]1 Sam 8:4
18 [1]So many ancient mss and versions; M.T. *he* [a]1 Sam 9:16; 15:28
19 [a]1 Sam 10:20, 21; 1 Chr 12:29
21 [a]2 Sam 3:10, 12 [b]1 Kin 11:37
22 [a]1 Sam 27:8
25 [a]Deut 28:6; 1 Sam 29:6; Is 37:28
27 [a]2 Sam 2:23; 20:9, 10; 1 Kin 2:5
29 [1]Lit *whirl* [a]Deut 21:6-9; 1 Kin 2:31-33 [b]Lev 13:46

30 So Joab and Abishai his brother killed Abner [a]because he
had put their brother Asahel to death in the battle at Gibeon.
31 Then David said to Joab and to all the people who were
with him, "[a]Tear your clothes and gird on sackcloth and lament
before Abner." And King David walked behind the bier.
32 Thus they buried Abner in Hebron; and the king lifted up his
voice and wept at [a]the grave of Abner, and all the people wept.
33 [a]The king chanted a *lament* for Abner and said,
"Should Abner die as a fool dies?
34 "Your hands were not bound, nor your feet put in fetters;
As one falls before the [1]wicked, you have fallen."
And all the people wept again over him.
35 Then all the people came [a]to [1]persuade David to eat bread
while it was still day; but David vowed, saying, "[b]May God do
so to me, and more also, if I taste bread or anything else [c]before
the sun goes down."
36 Now all the people took note *of it,* and it [1]pleased them,
just as everything the king did [2]pleased all the people.
37 So all the people and all Israel understood that day that it had
not been *the will* of the king to put Abner the son of Ner to death.
38 Then the king said to his servants, "Do you not know that
a prince and a great man has fallen this day in Israel?
39 "I am [a]weak today, though anointed king; and these men [b]the
sons of Zeruiah are too difficult for me. [c]May the LORD repay the
evildoer according to his evil."

Chapter 4 Theme ______________________

4 Now when [1]Ish-bosheth, Saul's son, heard that [a]Abner had
died in Hebron, [2b]he lost courage, and all Israel was disturbed.
2 Saul's son *had* two men who were commanders of bands:
the name of the one was Baanah and the name of the other
Rechab, sons of Rimmon the Beerothite, of the sons of Benjamin
(for [a]Beeroth is also considered [b]*part* of Benjamin,
3 and the Beerothites fled to [a]Gittaim and have been aliens
there until this day).
4 Now [a]Jonathan, Saul's son, had a son crippled in his feet. He
was five years old when the [b]report of Saul and Jonathan came
from Jezreel, and his nurse took him up and fled. And it
happened that in her hurry to flee, he fell and became lame.
And his name was [1c]Mephibosheth.
5 So the sons of Rimmon the Beerothite, Rechab and Baanah,
departed and came to the house of [a]Ish-bosheth in the heat of
the day while he was taking his midday rest.
6 [1]They came to the middle of the house as [2]if to get wheat,
and [a]they struck him in the belly; and Rechab and Baanah his
brother escaped.
7 Now when they came into the house, as he was lying on
his bed in his bedroom, they struck him and killed him and
beheaded him. And they took his head and [1a]traveled by way
of the Arabah all night.

30 [a]2 Sam 2:23
31 [a]Gen 37:34; Judg 11:35
32 [a]Job 31:28, 29; Prov 24:17
33 [a]2 Sam 1:17; 2 Chr 35:25
34 [1]Lit *sons of wickedness*
35 [1]Lit *cause* [a]2 Sam 12:17 [b]1 Sam 3:17 [c]2 Sam 1:12
36 [1]Lit *was good in their eyes* [2]Lit *was good in the eyes of all*
39 [a]1 Chr 29:1; 2 Chr 13:7 [b]2 Sam 19:5-7 [c]1 Kin 2:32-34
4:1 [1]So some ancient mss; M.T. *he* [2]Lit *his hands dropped* [a]2 Sam 3:27 [b]Ezra 4:4
2 [a]Josh 9:17 [b]Josh 18:25
3 [a]Neh 11:33
4 [1]I.e. Merib-baal [a]2 Sam 9:3, 6 [b]1 Sam 31:1-4 [c]1 Chr 8:34; 9:40
5 [a]2 Sam 2:8
6 [1]Lit *And here* [2]Lit *takers of wheat* [a]2 Sam 2:23
7 [1]Lit *went* [a]2 Sam 2:29

8 Then they brought the head of Ish-bosheth to David at
Hebron and said to the king, "Behold, the head of Ish-bosheth
[a]the son of Saul, your enemy, who sought your life; thus the
LORD has given my lord the king vengeance this day on Saul
and his [1]descendants."
9 David answered Rechab and Baanah his brother, sons of
Rimmon the Beerothite, and said to them, "As the LORD lives,
[a]who has redeemed my life from all distress,
10 [a]when one told me, saying, 'Behold, Saul is dead,' and
[1]thought he was bringing good news, I seized him and killed
him in Ziklag, which was the reward I gave him for *his* news.
11 "How much more, when wicked men have killed a righteous
man in his own house on his bed, shall I not now [a]require his
blood from your hand and [1]destroy you from the earth?"
12 Then [a]David commanded the young men, and they killed
them and cut off their hands and feet and hung them up beside
the pool in Hebron. But they took the head of Ish-bosheth [b]and
buried it in the grave of Abner in Hebron.

Chapter 5 Theme ______

1 Chronicles 11

5 [a]Then all the tribes of Israel came to David at Hebron and
[1]said, "Behold, we are [b]your bone and your flesh.
2 "Previously, when Saul was king over us, [a]you were the one
who led Israel out and in. And the LORD said to you, '[b]You will
shepherd My people Israel, and you will be [c]a ruler over Israel.'"
3 So all the elders of Israel came to the king at Hebron, and
King David [a]made a covenant with them before the LORD at
Hebron; then [b]they anointed David king over Israel.
4 David was [a]thirty years old when he became king, *and* [b]he
reigned forty years.
5 At Hebron [a]he reigned over Judah seven years and six
months, and in Jerusalem he reigned thirty-three years over all
Israel and Judah.
6 [a]Now the king and his men went to [b]Jerusalem against the
Jebusites, the inhabitants of the land, and they said to [1]David,
"You shall not come in here, but the blind and lame will turn
you away"; [2]thinking, "David cannot enter here."
7 Nevertheless, David captured the stronghold of Zion, that
is [a]the city of David.
8 David said on that day, "Whoever would strike the Jebusites,
let him reach the lame and the blind, who are hated by David's
soul, through the water tunnel." Therefore they say, "The blind
or the lame shall not come into the house."
9 So David lived in the stronghold and called it [a]the city of
David. And David built all around from the [1b]Millo and inward.
10 [a]David became greater and greater, for the LORD God of hosts
was with him.

1 Chronicles 14

11 [a]Then Hiram king of Tyre sent messengers to David with
cedar trees and carpenters and stonemasons; and [b]they built a
house for David.

8 [1]Lit *seed* [a]1 Sam 24:4; 25:29
9 [a]Gen 48:16; 1 Kin 1:29; Ps 31:7
10 [1]Lit *he was as a bearer of good news in his own eyes* [a]2 Sam 1:2, 4, 15
11 [1]Lit *burn* [a]Gen 9:5; Ps 9:12
12 [a]2 Sam 1:15 [b]2 Sam 3:32
5:1 [1]Lit *said, saying* [a]1 Chr 11:1-3 [b]2 Sam 19:13
2 [a]1 Sam 18:5, 13, 16 [b]Gen 49:24; 2 Sam 7:7 [c]1 Sam 25:30
3 [a]2 Sam 3:21 [b]1 Sam 16:13; 2 Sam 2:4
4 [a]Gen 41:46; Num 4:3; Luke 3:23 [b]1 Kin 2:11; 1 Chr 26:31
5 [a]2 Sam 2:11; 1 Chr 3:4; 29:27
6 [1]Lit *David, saying* [2]Lit *saying* [a]1 Chr 11:4-9 [b]Josh 15:63; 18:28; Judg 1:21
7 [a]2 Sam 6:12, 16; 1 Kin 2:10; 9:24
9 [1]I.e. citadel [a]2 Sam 5:7 [b]1 Kin 9:15, 24
10 [a]2 Sam 3:1
11 [a]1 Kin 5:1, 10, 18; 1 Chr 14:1 [b]Ps 30: title

13 aDeut 17:17; 1 Chr 3:9
14 a1 Chr 3:5-8

12 And David realized that the LORD had established him as king
over Israel, and that He had exalted his kingdom for the sake of
His people Israel.
13 Meanwhile aDavid took more concubines and wives from
Jerusalem, after he came from Hebron; and more sons and
daughters were born to David.
14 Now athese are the names of those who were born to him
in Jerusalem: Shammua, Shobab, Nathan, Solomon,
15 Ibhar, Elishua, Nepheg, Japhia,
16 Elishama, Eliada and Eliphelet.

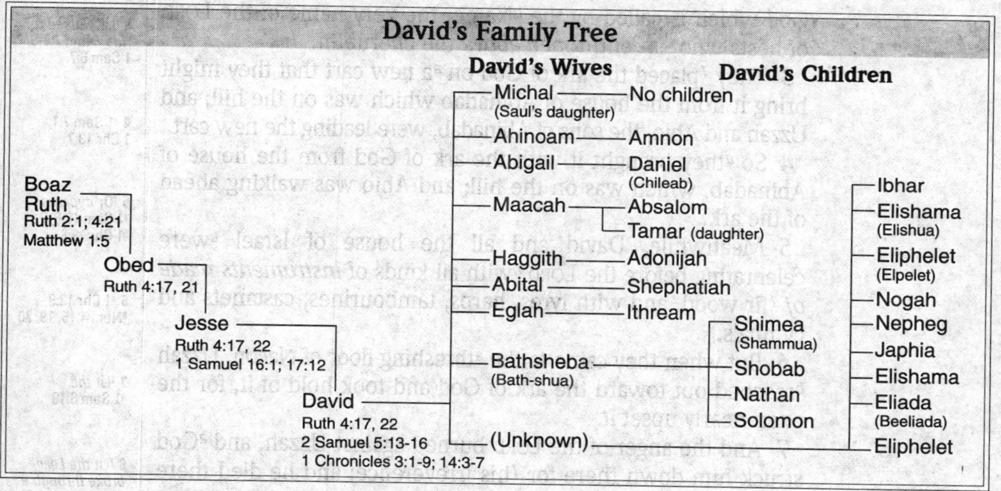

17 a1 Sam 29:1 b2 Sam 23:14; 1 Chr 11:16
18 aGen 14:5; Josh 15:8; 17:15; 18:16
19 a1 Sam 23:2 b2 Sam 2:1
20 [1]Lit *David smote* [2]I.e. the master of breakthrough a1 Chr 14:11; Is 28:21
21 a1 Chr 14:12
22 a2 Sam 5:18
23 [1]Or *baka-shrubs* a2 Sam 5:19
24 [1]Or *baka-shrubs* a2 Kin 7:6 bJudg 4:14

17 When the Philistines heard that they had anointed David
king over Israel, aall the Philistines went up to seek out David;
and when David heard *of it,* he went down to the bstronghold.
18 Now the Philistines came and spread themselves out in
athe valley of Rephaim.
19 Then aDavid inquired of the LORD, saying, "Shall I go up
against the Philistines? Will You give them into my hand?" And
bthe LORD said to David, "Go up, for I will certainly give the
Philistines into your hand."
20 So David came to aBaal-perazim and [1]defeated them there;
and he said, "The LORD has broken through my enemies before
me like the breakthrough of waters." Therefore he named that
place [2]Baal-perazim.
21 They abandoned their idols there, so aDavid and his men
carried them away.
22 Now athe Philistines came up once again and spread themselves out in the valley of Rephaim.
23 When aDavid inquired of the LORD, He said, "You shall not
go *directly* up; circle around behind them and come at them in
front of the [1]balsam trees.
24 "It shall be, when ayou hear the sound of marching in the
tops of the [1]balsam trees, then you shall act promptly, for then

[b]the LORD will have gone out before you to strike the army of
the Philistines."
25 Then David did so, just as the LORD had commanded him,
and struck down the Philistines from [1a]Geba [2]as far as [b]Gezer.

Chapter 6 Theme ______________________________

1 Chronicles 13

6 [a]Now David again gathered all the chosen men of Israel,
thirty thousand.
2 And David arose and went with all the people who were
with him to [1a]Baale-judah, to bring up from there the ark of
God which is called by the [b]Name, the very name of the LORD
of hosts who [c]is [2]enthroned *above* the cherubim.
3 They [1]placed the ark of God on [a]a new cart that they might
bring it from the house of Abinadab which was on the hill; and
Uzzah and Ahio, the sons of Abinadab, were leading the new cart.
4 So [a]they brought it with the ark of God from the house of
Abinadab, which was on the hill; and Ahio was walking ahead
of the ark.
5 Meanwhile, David and all the house of Israel [a]were
celebrating before the LORD [b]with all kinds of *instruments made
of* [1]fir wood, and with lyres, harps, tambourines, castanets and
cymbals.
6 But when they came to the [a]threshing floor of Nacon, Uzzah
[b]reached out toward the ark of God and took hold of it, for the
oxen nearly upset *it.*
7 And the anger of the LORD burned against Uzzah, and [a]God
struck him down there for [1]his irreverence; and he died there
by the ark of God.
8 David became angry because [1]of the LORD's outburst
against Uzzah, and that place is called [2]Perez-uzzah to this day.
9 So [a]David was afraid of the LORD that day; and he said, "How
can the ark of the LORD come to me?"
10 And David was unwilling to move the ark of the LORD into
the city of David with him; but David took it aside to the house
of [a]Obed-edom the Gittite.
11 Thus the ark of the LORD remained in the house of Obed-
edom the Gittite three months, and the LORD [a]blessed Obed-
edom and all his household.

1 Chronicles 15

12 Now it was told King David, saying, "The LORD has blessed
the house of Obed-edom and all that belongs to him, on account of
the ark of God." [a]David went and brought up the ark of God from
the house of Obed-edom into [b]the city of David with gladness.
13 And so it was, that when the [a]bearers of the ark of the LORD
had gone six paces, he sacrificed an [b]ox and a fatling.
14 And [a]David was dancing before the LORD with all *his* might,
and David was [1b]wearing a linen ephod.
15 So David and all the house of Israel were bringing up the
ark of the LORD with shouting and the sound of the trumpet.
16 Then it happened *as* the ark of the LORD came into the city
of David that [a]Michal the daughter of Saul looked out of the

25 [1]In 1 Chr 14:16, *Gibeon* [2]Lit *until you are coming to* [a]Is 28:21 [b]Josh 12:12; 21:21

6:1 [a]1 Chr 13:5-14

2 [1]I.e. Kiriath-jearim [2]Lit *sitting* [a]Josh 15:9, 10; 1 Sam 7:1 [b]Lev 24:16 [c]Ex 25:22

3 [1]Lit *caused to ride* [a]Num 7:4-9; 1 Sam 6:7

4 [a]1 Sam 7:1; 1 Chr 13:7

5 [1]Or *cypress* [a]1 Sam 18:6, 7 [b]1 Chr 13:8

6 [a]1 Chr 13:9 [b]Num 4:15, 19, 20

7 [1]Lit *the* [a]1 Sam 6:19

8 [1]Lit *the LORD broke through a breakthrough* [2]I.e. the breakthrough of Uzzah

9 [a]Ps 119:120; Luke 5:8

10 [a]1 Chr 26:4-8

11 [a]Gen 30:27; 39:5

12 [a]1 Chr 15:25-16:3 [b]1 Kin 8:1

13 [a]Num 4:15; Josh 3:3; 1 Chr 15:2, 15 [b]1 Kin 8:5

14 [1]Lit *girded with* [a]Ex 15:20, 21; Judg 11:34 [b]Ex 19:6; 1 Sam 2:18, 28

16 [a]2 Sam 3:14

17 [a]1 Chr 15:1; 2 Chr 1:4 [b]1 Kin 8:62-65
window and saw King David leaping and dancing before the
LORD; and she despised him in her heart.
17 So they brought in the ark of the LORD and set it [a]in its place
1 Chronicles 16
inside the tent which David had pitched for it; and [b]David
offered burnt offerings and peace offerings before the LORD.
18 [a]1 Kin 8:14, 15
18 When David had finished offering the burnt offering and the
peace offering, [a]he blessed the people in the name of the LORD
of hosts.
19 Further, he distributed to all the people, to all the multitude
20 [a]2 Sam 6:14, 16; Eccl 7:17 [b]Judg 9:4
of Israel, both to men and women, a cake of bread and one of
dates and one of raisins to each one. Then all the people departed
each to his house.
20 But when David returned to bless his household, Michal
1 Chronicles 15:29
the daughter of Saul came out to meet David and said, "How
21 [a]1 Sam 13:14; 15:28
the king of Israel distinguished himself today! [a]He uncovered
himself today in the eyes of his servants' maids as one of the
[b]foolish ones shamelessly uncovers himself!"
21 So David said to Michal, "[a]*It was* before the LORD, who
7:1 [a]1 Chr 17:1-27
chose me above your father and above all his house, to appoint
me ruler over the people of the LORD, over Israel; therefore I
will celebrate before the LORD.
22"I will be more lightly esteemed than this and will be
2 [a]2 Sam 7:17; 12:1; 1 Kin 1:22; 1 Chr 29:29; 2 Chr 9:29 [b]2 Sam 5:11 [c]Ex 26:1
humble in my own eyes, but with the maids of whom you have
spoken, with them I will be distinguished."
23 Michal the daughter of Saul had no child to the day of her
death.

Chapter 7 Theme ____________________

7 [a]Now it came about when the king lived in his house, and
1 Chronicles 17
3 [a]1 Kin 8:17, 18; 1 Chr 22:7
the LORD had given him rest on every side from all his
enemies,
2 that the king said to [a]Nathan the prophet, "See now, I
dwell in [b]a house of cedar, but the ark of God [c]dwells within
tent curtains."
5 [a]1 Kin 5:3, 4; 8:19
3 Nathan said to the king, "[a]Go, do all that is in your mind,
for the LORD is with you."
4 But in the same night the word of the LORD came to Nathan,
saying,
6 [1]Lit *dwelling place* [a]Josh 18:1; 1 Kin 8:16 [b]Ex 40:18, 34
5"Go and say to My servant David, 'Thus says the LORD, "[a]Are
you the one who should build Me a house to dwell in?
6"For [a]I have not dwelt in a house since the day I brought up
the sons of Israel from Egypt, even to this day; but I have been
moving about [b]in a tent, even in a [1]tabernacle.
7 [a]Lev 26:11, 12 [b]2 Sam 5:2
7"[a]Wherever I have gone with all the sons of Israel, did I speak
a word with one of the tribes of Israel, [b]which I commanded to
shepherd My people Israel, saying, 'Why have you not built Me
a house of cedar?'"'
8"Now therefore, thus you shall say to My servant David,
8 [a]1 Sam 16:11, 12; Ps 78:70, 71 [b]2 Sam 6:21
'Thus says the LORD of hosts, "[a]I took you from the pasture,
from following the sheep, [b]to be ruler over My people Israel.

9 “[a]I have been with you wherever you have gone and [b]have
cut off all your enemies from before you; and I will make you a
great name, like the names of the great men who are on the
earth.
10 “I will also appoint a place for My people Israel and [a]will plant
them, that they may live in their own place and not be disturbed
again, [b]nor will the [1]wicked afflict them any more as formerly,
11 even [a]from the day that I commanded judges to be over My
people Israel; and [b]I will give you rest from all your enemies.
The LORD also declares to you that [c]the LORD will make a house
for you.
12 “[a]When your days are complete and you [b]lie down with
your fathers, [c]I will raise up your [1]descendant after you, who
will come forth from [2]you, and I will establish his kingdom.
13 “[a]He shall build a house for My name, and [b]I will establish
the throne of his kingdom forever.
14 “[a]I will be a father to him and he will be a son to Me; [b]when
he commits iniquity, I will correct him with the rod of men and
the strokes of the sons of men,
15 but My lovingkindness shall not depart from him, [a]as I took
it away from Saul, whom I removed from before you.
16 “[a]Your house and your kingdom shall endure before [1]Me
forever; your throne shall be established forever.”’”
17 In accordance with all these words and all this vision, so
Nathan spoke to David.
18 Then David the king went in and sat before the LORD, and
he said, “[a]Who am I, O Lord [1]GOD, and what is my house, that
You have brought me this far?
19 “And yet this was insignificant in Your eyes, O Lord GOD, [a]for
You have spoken also of the house of Your servant concerning
the distant future. And [b]this is the [1]custom of man, O Lord GOD.
20 “Again what more can David say to You? For [a]You know
Your servant, O Lord GOD!
21 “[a]For the sake of Your word, and according to Your own heart,
You have done all this greatness to let Your servant know.
22 “For this reason [a]You are great, O Lord GOD; for [b]there is
none like You, and there is no God besides You, [c]according to
all that we have heard with our ears.
23 “And [a]what one nation on the earth is like Your people Israel,
whom God went to redeem for Himself as a people and to make
a name for Himself, and [b]to do a great thing for You and awesome
things for Your land, before [c]Your people whom [d]You have
redeemed for Yourself from Egypt, *from* nations and their gods?
24 “For [a]You have established for Yourself Your people Israel as
Your own people forever, and [b]You, O LORD, have become their
God.
25 “Now therefore, O LORD God, the word that You have spoken
concerning Your servant and his house, confirm *it* forever, and
do as You have spoken,
26 [a]that Your name may be magnified forever, by saying, ‘The
LORD of hosts is God over Israel’; and may the house of Your

9 [a]1 Sam 5:10 [b]Ps 18:37-42

10 [1]Lit *sons of wickedness* [a]Ex 15:17; Is 5:2, 7 [b]Ps 89:22, 23; Is 60:18

11 [a]Judg 2:14-16; 1 Sam 12:9-11 [b]2 Sam 7:1 [c]1 Sam 25:28; 2 Sam 7:27

12 [1]Lit *seed* [2]Lit *your bowels* [a]1 Kin 2:1 [b]Deut 31:16; Acts 13:36 [c]1 Kin 8:20; Ps 132:11

13 [a]1 Kin 6:12; 8:19 [b]Is 9:7; 49:8

14 [a]Ps 89:26, 27; 2 Cor 6:18; Heb 1:5 [b]1 Kin 11:34; Ps 89:30-33

15 [a]1 Sam 15:23; 16:14

16 [1]So with Gr and some ancient mss; M.T. *you* [a]2 Sam 7:13; Ps 89:36, 37

18 [1]Heb *YHWH,* usually rendered *LORD,* and so throughout the ch [a]Ex 3:11; 1 Sam 18:18

19 [1]Or *law* [a]2 Sam 7:11-16; 1 Chr 17:17 [b]Is 55:8, 9

20 [a]1 Sam 16:7; John 21:17

21 [a]1 Chr 17:19; Eph 4:32

22 [a]Deut 3:24; Ps 48:1; 86:10 [b]Ex 15:11; 1 Sam 2:2 [c]Ex 10:2; Ps 44:1

23 [a]Deut 4:32-38 [b]Deut 10:21 [c]Deut 15:15 [d]Deut 9:26

24 [a]Deut 32:6 [b]Gen 17:7, 8; Ex 6:7

26 [a]Ps 72:18, 19; Matt 6:9

servant David be established before You.
27 "For You, O LORD of hosts, the God of Israel, have [1]made a
revelation to Your servant, saying, '[a]I will build you a house';
therefore Your servant has found [2]courage to pray this prayer to
You.
28 "Now, O Lord GOD, You are God, and [a]Your words are truth,
and You have [1]promised this good thing to Your servant.
29 "Now therefore, may it please You to bless the house of Your
servant, that it may continue forever before You. For You, O
Lord GOD, have spoken; and [a]with Your blessing may the house
of Your servant be blessed forever."

Chapter 8 Theme ____

8 [a]Now after this it came about that David [1]defeated the
Philistines and subdued them; and David took [2]control of
the chief city from the hand of the Philistines.

1 Chronicles 18

2 [a]He [1]defeated [b]Moab, and measured them with the line,
making them lie down on the ground; and he measured two
lines to put to death and one full line to keep alive. And [c]the
Moabites became servants to David, [d]bringing tribute.
3 Then David [1]defeated [a]Hadadezer, the son of Rehob king of
Zobah, as [b]he went to restore his [2]rule at the [3]River.
4 David captured from him 1,700 horsemen and 20,000 foot
soldiers; and David [a]hamstrung the chariot horses, but reserved
enough of them for 100 chariots.
5 When [a]the Arameans of Damascus came to help Hadadezer,
king of Zobah, David [1]killed 22,000 Arameans.
6 Then David put garrisons among the Arameans of Damascus,
and [a]the Arameans became servants to David, bringing tribute.
And [b]the LORD helped David wherever he went.
7 David took the shields of gold which were [1]carried by the
servants of Hadadezer and brought them to Jerusalem.
8 From [1]Betah and from [a]Berothai, cities of Hadadezer, King
David took a very large amount of bronze.
9 Now when Toi king of [a]Hamath heard that David had
[1]defeated all the army of Hadadezer,
10 Toi sent [1]Joram his son to King David to [2]greet him and bless
him, because he had fought against Hadadezer and [3]defeated
him; for Hadadezer [4]had been at war with Toi. And [5]*Joram*
brought with him articles of silver, of gold and of bronze.
11 King David also [a]dedicated these to the LORD, with the silver
and gold that he had dedicated from all the nations which he
had subdued:
12 from [1]Aram and [a]Moab and [b]the sons of Ammon and [c]the
Philistines and [d]Amalek, and from the spoil of Hadadezer, son
of Rehob, king of Zobah.
13 So [a]David made a name *for himself* when he returned from
[1]killing 18,000 [2]Arameans in [b]the Valley of Salt.
14 He put garrisons in Edom. In all Edom he put garrisons,
and [a]all the Edomites became servants to David. And [b]the LORD

27 [1]Lit *uncovered the ear of* [2]Lit *his heart* [a]2 Sam 7:13
28 [1]Or *spoken* [a]Ex 34:6; John 17:17
29 [a]Num 6:24-26
8:1 [1]Lit *smote* [2]Lit *the bridle of the mother city* [a]1 Chr 18
2 [1]Lit *smote* [a]Num 24:17 [b]1 Sam 22:3, 4
2 [c]2 Sam 8:6; 1 Kin 4:21 [d]2 Kin 3:4; 17:3
3 [1]Lit *smote* [2]Lit *hand* [3]I.e. Euphrates [a]1 Sam 14:47; 2 Sam 10:16, 19 [b]2 Sam 10:15-19
4 [a]Josh 11:6, 9
5 [1]Lit *smote* [a]1 Kin 11:23-25
6 [a]2 Sam 8:2 [b]2 Sam 3:18
7 [1]Lit *on*
8 [1]In 1 Chr 18:8, *Tibhath* [a]Ezek 47:16
9 [1]Lit *smitten* [a]1 Kin 8:65; 2 Chr 8:4
10 [1]In 1 Chr 18:10, *Hadoram* [2]Lit *ask him of his welfare* [3]Lit *smitten* [4]Lit *was a man of wars* [5]Lit *there were in his hand*
11 [a]1 Kin 7:51
12 [1]Some mss read *Edom* [a]2 Sam 8:2 [b]2 Sam 10:14 [c]2 Sam 5:17-25 [d]1 Sam 27:8; 30:17-20
13 [1]Lit *smiting* [2]Some mss read *Edom* [a]2 Sam 7:9 [b]2 Kin 14:7
14 [a]Gen 27:37-40; Num 24:17, 18 [b]2 Sam 8:6

helped David wherever he went.
15 So David reigned over all Israel; and David [1]administered
justice and righteousness for all his people.
16 [a]Joab the son of Zeruiah *was* over the army, and [b]Jehoshaphat
the son of Ahilud *was* [c]recorder.
17 [a]Zadok the son of Ahitub and Ahimelech the son of Abiathar
were [b]priests, and Seraiah *was* [c]secretary.
18 [a]Benaiah the son of Jehoiada [1]was over the [b]Cherethites
and the Pelethites; and David's sons were [2c]chief ministers.

Chapter 9 Theme ______________________________

9 Then David said, "Is there yet [1]anyone left of the house of
Saul, [a]that I may show him kindness for Jonathan's sake?"
2 Now there was a servant of the house of Saul whose name
was Ziba, and they called him to David; and the king said to
him, "Are you [a]Ziba?" And he said, "*I am* your servant."
3 The king said, "Is there not yet anyone of the house of Saul
to whom I may show the [a]kindness of God?" And Ziba said to
the king, "[b]There is still a son of Jonathan who is crippled in
both feet."
4 So the king said to him, "Where is he?" And Ziba said to
the king, "Behold, he is [a]in the house of Machir the son of
Ammiel in Lo-debar."
5 Then King David sent and brought him from the house of
Machir the son of Ammiel, from Lo-debar.
6 [a]Mephibosheth, the son of Jonathan the son of Saul, came
to David and [b]fell on his face and prostrated himself. And David
said, "Mephibosheth." And he said, "Here is your servant!"
7 David said to him, "Do not fear, for [a]I will surely show
kindness to you for the sake of your father Jonathan, and [b]will
restore to you all the [1]land of your [2]grandfather Saul; and [c]you
shall [3]eat at my table regularly."
8 Again he prostrated himself and said, "What is your servant,
that you should regard [a]a dead dog like me?"
9 Then the king called Saul's servant Ziba and said to him,
"[a]All that belonged to Saul and to all his house I have given to
your master's [1]grandson.
10 "You and your sons and your servants shall cultivate the land
for him, and you shall bring in *the produce* so that your
master's grandson may have food; nevertheless [a]Mephibosheth
your master's grandson [b]shall [1]eat at my table regularly." Now
Ziba had fifteen sons and twenty servants.
11 Then Ziba said to the king, "According [a]to all that my lord
the king commands his servant so your servant will do." So
Mephibosheth ate at [1]David's table as one of the king's sons.
12 Mephibosheth had a young son whose name was Mica.
And all who lived in the house of Ziba were servants to
Mephibosheth.
13 So Mephibosheth lived in Jerusalem, for [a]he ate at the king's
table regularly. Now [b]he was lame in both feet.

15 [1]Lit *was doing*

16 [a]1 Chr 11:6 [b]1 Kin 4:3 [c]2 Kin 18:18, 37

17 [a]1 Chr 6:4-8 [b]1 Chr 16:39, 40 [c]2 Kin 18:18

18 [1]Lit *and the Cherethites* [2]Lit *priests* [a]1 Kin 4:4 [b]1 Sam 30:14; 2 Sam 15:18; 20:7, 23; 1 Kin 1:38, 44 [c]1 Chr 18:17

9:1 [1]Lit *he who is* [a]1 Sam 20:14-17, 42

2 [a]2 Sam 16:1-4; 19:17, 29

3 [a]1 Sam 20:14

3 [b]2 Sam 4:4

4 [a]2 Sam 17:27-29

6 [a]2 Sam 16:4; 19:24-30 [b]1 Sam 25:23

7 [1]Lit *field* [2]Lit *father* [3]Lit *eat bread* [a]2 Sam 9:1, 3 [b]2 Sam 12:8 [c]2 Sam 19:28; 1 Kin 2:7; 2 Kin 25:29

8 [a]2 Sam 16:9; 24:14

9 [1]Lit *son* [a]2 Sam 16:4; 19:29

10 [1]Lit *eat bread* [a]2 Sam 9:7, 11, 13 [b]2 Sam 19:28; 1 Kin 2:7

11 [1]Lit *my* [a]2 Sam 16:1-4; 19:24-30

13 [a]2 Sam 9:7, 11 [b]2 Sam 9:3

Chapter 10 Theme ____________________

1 Chronicles 19

10 [a]Now it happened afterwards that [b]the king of the Ammonites died, and Hanun his son became king in his place.
2 Then David said, "I will show kindness to Hanun the son of
[a]Nahash, just as his father showed kindness to me." So David
sent [1]some of his servants to console him concerning his father.
But when David's servants came to the land of the Ammonites,
3 the princes of the Ammonites said to Hanun their lord,
"[1]Do you think that David is honoring your father because he
has sent consolers to you? [a]Has David not sent his servants to
you in order to search the city, to spy it out and overthrow it?"
4 So Hanun took David's servants and [a]shaved off half of their
beards, and [b]cut off their garments in the middle as far as their
hips, and sent them away.
5 When they told *it* to David, he sent to meet them, for the
men were greatly humiliated. And the king said, "[1]Stay at
Jericho until your beards grow, and *then* return."
6 Now when the sons of Ammon saw that [a]they had become
odious to David, the sons of Ammon sent and [b]hired the
Arameans of [c]Beth-rehob and the [d]Arameans of Zobah, 20,000
foot soldiers, and the king of [e]Maacah with 1,000 men, and the
men of Tob with 12,000 men.
7 When David heard *of it,* he sent Joab and all the army, the
mighty men.
8 The sons of Ammon came out and drew up in battle array
[a]at the entrance of the [1]city, while the Arameans of Zobah and
of Rehob and the men of [b]Tob and Maacah *were* by themselves
in the field.
9 Now when Joab saw that [1]the battle was set against him in
front and in the rear, he selected from all the choice men of Israel,
and arrayed *them* against the Arameans.
10 But the remainder of the people he placed in the hand of
Abishai his brother, and he arrayed *them* against the sons of
Ammon.
11 He said, "If the Arameans are too strong for me, then you
shall help me, but if the sons of Ammon are too strong for you,
then I will come to help you.
12 "[a]Be strong, and let us show ourselves courageous for the
sake of our people and for the cities of our God; and [b]may the
LORD do what is good in His sight."
13 So Joab and the people who were with him drew near to
the battle against the Arameans, and [a]they fled before him.
14 When the sons of Ammon saw that the Arameans fled, they
also fled before Abishai and entered the city. [a]Then Joab returned
from *fighting* against the sons of Ammon and came to Jerusalem.
15 When the Arameans saw that they had been [1]defeated by
Israel, they gathered themselves together.
16 [a]And Hadadezer sent and brought out the Arameans who
were beyond the [1]River, and they came to Helam; and
[b]Shobach the commander of the army of Hadadezer [2]led them.
17 Now when it was told David, he gathered all Israel together

10:1 [a]1 Chr 19:1-19 [b]1 Sam 11:1
2 [1]Lit *by the hand of* [a]1 Sam 11:1
3 [1]Lit *In your eyes is David honoring* [a]Gen 42:9, 16
4 [a]Is 15:2; Jer 41:5 [b]Is 20:4
5 [1]Lit *Return to*
6 [a]Gen 34:30; 1 Sam 27:12 [b]2 Sam 8:3, 5; 2 Kin 7:6 [c]Judg 18:28 [d]2 Sam 8:3 [e]Deut 3:14
8 [1]Lit *gate* [a]1 Chr 19:9 [b]Judg 11:3, 5
9 [1]Lit *the faces of the battle were against*
12 [a]Deut 31:6; Josh 1:6; 1 Cor 16:13 [b]1 Sam 3:18
13 [a]1 Kin 20:13-21
14 [a]2 Sam 11:1
15 [1]Lit *smitten before*
16 [1]I.e. Euphrates [2]Lit *before* [a]2 Sam 8:3-8 [b]1 Chr 19:16

and crossed the Jordan, and came to Helam. And the Arameans
arrayed themselves to meet David and fought against him.
18 But the Arameans fled before Israel, and David killed [a]700
charioteers of the Arameans and 40,000 horsemen and struck
down Shobach the commander of their army, and he died there.
19 When all the kings, servants of Hadadezer, saw that they
were [1]defeated by Israel, [a]they made peace with Israel and served
them. So the Arameans feared to help the sons of Ammon
anymore.

Chapter 11 Theme ______________________________

1 Chronicles 20

RETURN TO INSTRUCTIONS

11 [a]Then it happened [1b]in the spring, at the time when kings
go out *to battle,* that David sent Joab and his servants with
him and all Israel, and they destroyed the sons of Ammon and
[c]besieged Rabbah. But David stayed at Jerusalem.
2 Now when evening came David arose from his bed and
walked around on [a]the roof of the king's house, and from the roof
he saw a woman bathing; and the woman was very beautiful in
appearance.
3 So David sent and inquired about the woman. And one said,
"Is this not [a]Bathsheba, the daughter of Eliam, the wife of [b]Uriah
the Hittite?"
4 David sent messengers and took her, and when she came to
him, [a]he lay with her; [b]and when she had purified herself from
her uncleanness, she returned to her house.
5 The woman conceived; and she sent and told David, and
said, "[a]I am pregnant."
6 Then David sent to Joab, *saying,* "Send me Uriah the Hittite."
So Joab sent Uriah to David.
7 When Uriah came to him, [a]David asked concerning the
welfare of Joab and [1]the people and the state of the war.
8 Then David said to Uriah, "Go down to your house, and
[a]wash your feet." And Uriah went out of the king's house, and
a present from the king [1]was sent out after him.
9 But Uriah slept [a]at the door of the king's house with all the
servants of his lord, and did not go down to his house.
10 Now when they told David, saying, "Uriah did not go down
to his house," David said to Uriah, "Have you not come from a
journey? Why did you not go down to your house?"
11 Uriah said to David, "[a]The ark and Israel and Judah are
staying in [1]temporary shelters, and my lord Joab and [b]the
servants of my lord are camping in the open field. Shall I then
go to my house to eat and to drink and to lie with my wife? By
your life and the life of your soul, I will not do this thing."
12 Then David said to Uriah, "[a]Stay here today also, and
tomorrow I will let you go." So Uriah remained in Jerusalem
that day and the [1]next.
13 Now David called him, and he ate and drank before him, and
he [a]made him drunk; and in the evening he went out to lie on his
bed [b]with his lord's servants, but he did not go down to his house.

18 [a]1 Chr 19:18

19 [1]Lit *smitten before* [a]2 Sam 8:6

11:1 [1]Lit *at the return of the year* [a]1 Chr 20:1 [b]2 Sam 10:14; 1 Kin 20:22, 26 [c]2 Sam 12:26-29; Jer 49:2, 3; Amos 1:14

2 [a]Deut 22:8; 1 Sam 9:25; Matt 24:17; Acts 10:9

3 [a]1 Chr 3:5 [b]2 Sam 23:39

4 [a]Ps 51: title; James 1:14, 15 [b]Lev 12:2-5; 15:18-28; 18:19

5 [a]Lev 20:10; Deut 22:22

7 [1]Lit *welfare of* [a]Gen 37:14; 1 Sam 17:22

8 [1]Lit *went out* [a]Gen 43:24; Luke 7:44

9 [a]1 Kin 14:27, 28

11 [1]Or *booths* [a]2 Sam 7:2, 6 [b]2 Sam 20:6

12 [1]Lit *morrow* [a]Job 20:12-14

13 [a]Prov 20:1; 23:29-35 [b]2 Sam 11:9

14 Now in the morning David [a]wrote a letter to Joab and sent
it by the hand of Uriah.
15 [a]He had written in the letter, saying, "[1]Place Uriah in the
front line of the [2]fiercest battle and withdraw from him, [b]so
that he may be struck down and die."
16 So it was as Joab kept watch on the city, that he put Uriah
at the place where he knew there *were* valiant men.
17 The men of the city went out and fought against Joab, and
some of the people among David's servants fell; and [a]Uriah the
Hittite also died.
18 Then Joab sent and reported to David all the events of the war.
19 He charged the messenger, saying, "When you have finished
telling all the events of the war to the king,
20 and if it happens that the king's wrath rises and he says to
you, 'Why did you go so near to the city to fight? Did you not
know that they would shoot from the wall?
21 'Who [a]struck down Abimelech the son of Jerubbesheth? Did
not a woman throw an upper millstone on him from the wall so
that he died at Thebez? Why did you go so near the wall?'—then
you shall say, 'Your servant Uriah the Hittite is dead also.'"
22 So the messenger departed and came and reported to
David all that Joab had sent him *to tell.*
23 The messenger said to David, "The men prevailed against
us and came out against us in the field, but we [1]pressed them
as far as the entrance of the gate.
24 "Moreover, the archers shot at your servants from the wall;
so some of the king's servants are dead, and your servant Uriah
the Hittite is also dead."
25 Then David said to the messenger, "Thus you shall say to
Joab, 'Do not let this thing [1]displease you, for the sword devours
one as well as another; make your battle against the city stronger
and overthrow it'; and *so* encourage him."
26 Now when the wife of Uriah heard that Uriah her husband
was dead, [a]she mourned for her husband.
27 When the *time of* mourning was over, David sent and
[1]brought her to his house and [a]she became his wife; then she
bore him a son. But [b]the thing that David had done was evil in
the sight of the LORD.

Chapter 12 Theme ______________________

12 Then the LORD sent [a]Nathan to David. And [b]he came to
him and [1]said,
"There were two men in one city, the one rich and the
other poor.
2 "The rich man had a great many flocks and herds.
3 "But the poor man had nothing except [a]one little ewe lamb
Which he bought and nourished;
And it grew up together with him and his children.
It would eat of his [1]bread and drink of his cup and lie in his
bosom,

14 [a]1 Kin 21:8-10
15 [1]Lit *Give* [2]Lit *strong* [a]Eccl 8:11; Jer 17:9 [b]2 Sam 12:9
17 [a]2 Sam 11:21
21 [a]Judg 9:50-54
23 [1]Lit *were upon*
25 [1]Lit *be evil in your sight*
26 [a]Gen 50:10; Deut 34:8; 1 Sam 31:13
27 [1]Lit *gathered* [a]2 Sam 12:9 [b]Ps 51:4, 5
12:1 [1]Lit *said to him* [a]2 Sam 7:2, 4, 17 [b]Ps 51: title
3 [1]Lit *morsel* [a]2 Sam 11:3

And was like a daughter to him.
4 "Now a traveler came to the rich man,
And he [1]was unwilling to take from his own flock or his
own herd,
To prepare for the wayfarer who had come to him;
Rather he took the poor man's ewe lamb and prepared it
for the man who had come to him."
5 Then David's anger burned greatly against the man, and he
said to Nathan, "As the LORD lives, surely the man who has done
this [1a]deserves to die.
6 "He must make restitution for the lamb [a]fourfold, because
he did this thing and had no compassion."
7 Nathan then said to David, "[a]You are the man! Thus says
the LORD God of Israel, '[b]It is I who anointed you king over
Israel and it is I who delivered you from the hand of Saul.
8 'I also gave you [a]your master's house and your master's wives
into your [1]care, and I gave you the house of Israel and Judah;
and if *that had been* too little, I would have added to you many
more things like these!
9 'Why [a]have you despised the word of the LORD by doing evil
in His sight? [b]You have struck down Uriah the Hittite with the
sword, [c]have taken his wife to be your wife, and have killed
him with the sword of the sons of Ammon.
10 'Now therefore, [a]the sword shall never depart from your
house, because you have despised Me and have taken the wife
of Uriah the Hittite to be your wife.'
11 "Thus says the LORD, 'Behold, I will raise up evil against you
from your own household; [a]I will even take your wives before
your eyes and give *them* to your companion, and he will lie
with your wives in [1]broad daylight.
12 'Indeed [a]you did it secretly, but [b]I will do this thing before
all Israel, and [1]under the sun.'"
13 Then David said to Nathan, "[a]I have sinned against the
LORD." And Nathan said to David, "The LORD also has [1b]taken
away your sin; you shall not die.
14 "However, because by this deed you have [a]given occasion to
the enemies of the LORD to blaspheme, the child also that is
born to you shall surely die."
15 So Nathan went to his house.
Then the LORD struck the child that Uriah's [1]widow bore to
David, so that he was *very* sick.
16 David therefore inquired of God for the child; and David
[a]fasted and went and [b]lay all night on the ground.
17 [a]The elders of his household stood beside him in order to
raise him up from the ground, but he was unwilling and would
not eat food with them.
18 Then it happened on the seventh day that the child died. And
the servants of David were afraid to tell him that the child was
dead, for they said, "Behold, while the child was *still* alive, we
spoke to him and he did not listen to our voice. How then can we
tell him that the child is dead, since he might do *himself* harm!"

4 [1]Lit *spared*

5 [1]Lit *is a son of death* [a]1 Sam 26:16

6 [a]Ex 22:1; Luke 19:8

7 [a]1 Kin 20:42 [b]1 Sam 16:13

8 [1]Lit *bosom* [a]2 Sam 9:7

9 [a]1 Sam 15:23, 26 [b]2 Sam 11:14-17 [c]2 Sam 11:27

10 [a]2 Sam 13:28; 18:14; 1 Kin 2:25

11 [1]Lit *the sight of this sun* [a]Deut 28:30; 2 Sam 16:21, 22

12 [1]Lit *before* [a]2 Sam 11:4-15 [b]2 Sam 16:22

13 [1]Lit *caused your sin to pass away* [a]1 Sam 15:24, 30; 2 Sam 24:10; Luke 18:13 [b]Lev 20:10; 24:17; Prov 28:13; Mic 7:18

14 [a]Is 52:5; Rom 2:24

15 [1]Lit *wife*

16 [a]Neh 1:4 [b]2 Sam 13:31

17 [a]Gen 24:2

20 [a]Ruth 3:3; Matt 6:17 [b]Ps 95:6-8; 103:1, 8-17; Prov 3:7

19 But when David saw that his servants were whispering
together, David perceived that the child was dead; so David said
to his servants, "Is the child dead?" And they said, "He is dead."
20 So David arose from the ground, [a]washed, anointed *himself,*
and changed his clothes; and he came into the house of the LORD
and [b]worshiped. Then he came to his own house, and when he
requested, they set food before him and he ate.
21 Then his servants said to him, "What is this thing that you
have done? [1]While the child was alive, you fasted and wept; but
when the child died, you arose and ate food."
22 He said, "While the child was *still* alive, [a]I fasted and wept;
for I said, '[b]Who knows, the LORD may be gracious to me, that
the child may live.'
23 "But now he has died; why should I fast? Can I bring him
back again? [a]I will go to him, but [b]he will not return to me."
24 Then David comforted his wife Bathsheba, and went in to
her and lay with her; and she gave birth to a son, and [1a]he
named him Solomon. Now the LORD loved him
25 and sent *word* through Nathan the prophet, and he named
him [1]Jedidiah for the LORD's sake.
26 [a]Now Joab fought against [b]Rabbah of the sons of Ammon and
captured the royal city.
27 Joab sent messengers to David and said, "I have fought
against Rabbah, I have even captured the city of waters.
28 "Now therefore, gather the rest of the people together and
camp against the city and capture it, or I will capture the city
myself and it will be named after me."
29 So David gathered all the people and went to Rabbah, fought
against it and captured it.
30 Then [a]he took the crown of [1]their king from his head; and
its weight *was* a talent of gold, and *in it* [2]*was* a precious stone;
and it was *placed* on David's head. And he brought out the
spoil of the city in great amounts.
31 He also brought out the people who were in it, and [a]set *them*
under saws, sharp iron instruments, and iron axes, and made
them pass through the brickkiln. And thus he did to all the
cities of the sons of Ammon. Then David and all the people
returned *to* Jerusalem.

21 [1]Lit *On account of*

22 [a]Is 38:1-3 [b]Jon 3:9

23 [a]Gen 37:35 [b]Job 7:8-10

24 [1]Some mss read *she* [a]1 Chr 22:9; Matt 1:6

25 [1]I.e. beloved of the LORD

26 [a]1 Chr 20:1-3 [b]Deut 3:11

30 [1]Or *Malcam;* cf Zeph 1:5 [2]Or were *precious stones* [a]1 Chr 20:2

31 [a]1 Chr 20:3; Heb 11:37

1 Chronicles 20

INSIGHT

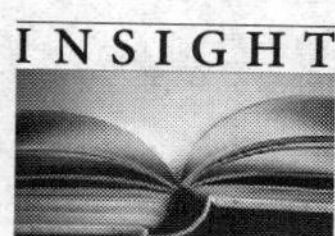

A **brickkiln** was an oven, furnace, or heated enclosure which was used for drying or firing bricks.

Chapter 13 Theme ____________________

13 Now it was after this that [a]Absalom the son of David had
a beautiful sister whose name was [b]Tamar, and [c]Amnon
the son of David loved her.
2 Amnon was so frustrated because of his sister Tamar that
he made himself ill, for she was a virgin, and it seemed [1]hard
to Amnon to do anything to her.
3 But Amnon had a friend whose name was Jonadab, the son of
[1a]Shimeah, David's brother; and Jonadab was a very shrewd man.
4 He said to him, "O son of the king, why are you so depressed
morning after morning? Will you not tell me?" Then Amnon

13:1 [a]2 Sam 3:2, 3; 1 Chr 3:2 [b]1 Chr 3:9 [c]2 Sam 3:2

2 [1]Lit *hard in Amnon's eyes*

3 [1]In 1 Sam 16:9, *Shammah;* in 1 Chr 2:13, *Shimea* [a]1 Sam 16:9

RETURN TO INSTRUCTIONS

said to him, "I am in love with Tamar, the sister of my brother
Absalom."
5 Jonadab then said to him, "Lie down on your bed and
pretend to be ill; when your father comes to see you, say to
him, 'Please let my sister Tamar come and give me *some* food
to eat, and let her prepare the food in my sight, that I may see
it and eat from her hand.'"
6 So Amnon lay down and pretended to be ill; when the king
came to see him, Amnon said to the king, "Please let my sister
Tamar come and [a]make me a couple of cakes in my sight, that I
may eat from her hand."
7 Then David sent to the house for Tamar, saying, "Go now
to your brother Amnon's house, and prepare food for him."
8 So Tamar went to her brother Amnon's house, and he was
lying down. And she took dough, kneaded *it,* made cakes in his
sight, and baked the cakes.
9 She took the pan and [1]dished *them* out before him, but he
refused to eat. And Amnon said, "[a]Have everyone go out from
me." So everyone went out from him.
10 Then Amnon said to Tamar, "Bring the food into the
[1]bedroom, that I may eat from your hand." So Tamar took the
cakes which she had made and brought them into the bedroom
to her brother Amnon.
11 When she brought *them* to him to eat, he [a]took hold of her
and said to her, "Come, lie with me, my sister."
12 But she answered him, "No, my brother, do not violate me,
for [a]such a thing is not done in Israel; do not do this
[b]disgraceful thing!
13 "As for me, where could I [1]get rid of my reproach? And as for
you, you will be like one of the [2]fools in Israel. Now therefore,
please speak to the king, for [a]he will not withhold me from you."
14 However, he would not listen to [1]her; since he was
stronger than she, he [a]violated her and lay with her.
15 Then Amnon hated her with a very great hatred; for the
hatred with which he hated her was greater than the love with
which he had loved her. And Amnon said to her, "Get up, go
away!"
16 But she said to him, "No, because this wrong in sending
me away is greater than the other that you have done to me!"
Yet he would not listen to her.
17 Then he called his young man who attended him and said,
"Now throw this woman out of my *presence,* and lock the
door behind her."
18 Now she had on [a]a [1]long-sleeved garment; for in this manner
the virgin daughters of the king dressed themselves in robes.
Then his attendant took her out and locked the door behind her.
19 [a]Tamar put [1]ashes on her head and [b]tore her [2]long-sleeved
garment which *was* on her; and [c]she put her hand on her head
and went away, crying aloud as she went.
20 Then Absalom her brother said to her, "Has Amnon your
brother been with you? But now keep silent, my sister, he is

6 [a]Gen 18:6

9 [1]Lit *poured* [a]Gen 45:1

10 [1]Or *inner room*

11 [a]Gen 39:12

12 [a]Lev 20:17 [b]Judg 19:23; 20:6

13 [1]Lit *cause to go* [2]Or *disgraceful ones* [a]Gen 20:12

14 [1]Lit *her voice* [a]Lev 18:9; Deut 22:25; 27:22; 2 Sam 12:11

18 [1]Lit *a varicolored tunic* [a]Gen 37:3, 23

19 [1]Or *dust* [2]Lit *varicolored tunic* [a]1 Sam 4:12; Esth 4:1 [b]Gen 37:29; 2 Sam 1:11 [c]Jer 2:37

your brother; do not take this matter to heart." So Tamar
remained and was desolate in her brother Absalom's house.
21 Now when King David heard of all these matters, he was
very angry.
22 But Absalom did not speak to Amnon [a]either good or bad; for
[b]Absalom hated Amnon because he had violated his sister Tamar.
23 Now it came about after two full years that Absalom [a]had
sheepshearers in Baal-hazor, which is near Ephraim, and Absalom
invited all the king's sons.
24 Absalom came to the king and said, "Behold now, your
servant has sheepshearers; please let the king and his servants
go with your servant."
25 But the king said to Absalom, "No, my son, we should not
all go, for we will be burdensome to you." Although he [1]urged
him, he would not go, but blessed him.
26 Then [a]Absalom said, "If not, please let my brother Amnon go
with us." And the king said to him, "Why should he go with you?"
27 But when Absalom [1]urged him, he let Amnon and all the
king's sons go with him.
28 Absalom commanded his servants, saying, "See now,
[a]when Amnon's heart is merry with wine, and when I say to
you, 'Strike Amnon,' then put him to death. Do not fear; have
not I myself commanded you? Be courageous and be [1]valiant."
29 The servants of Absalom did to Amnon just as Absalom had
commanded. Then all the king's sons arose and each mounted
[a]his mule and fled.
30 Now it was while they were on the way that the report
came to David, saying, "Absalom has struck down all the king's
sons, and not one of them is left."
31 Then the king arose, [a]tore his clothes and [b]lay on the ground;
and all his servants were standing by with clothes torn.
32 [a]Jonadab, the son of Shimeah, David's brother, [1]responded,
"Do not let my lord [2]suppose they have put to death all the
young men, the king's sons, for Amnon alone is dead; because
by the [3]intent of Absalom this has been determined since the
day that he violated his sister Tamar.
33 "Now therefore, do not let my lord the king [a]take the report
to [1]heart, namely, 'all the king's sons are dead,' for only Amnon
is dead."
34 Now [a]Absalom had fled. And [b]the young man who was the
watchman raised his eyes and looked, and behold, many people
were coming from the road behind him by the side of the
mountain.
35 Jonadab said to the king, "Behold, the king's sons have
come; according to your servant's word, so it happened."
36 As soon as he had finished speaking, behold, the king's sons
came and lifted their voices and wept; and also the king and all
his servants wept [1]very bitterly.
37 Now [a]Absalom fled and went to [b]Talmai the son of
Ammihud, the king of [c]Geshur. And *David* mourned for his son
every day.

22 [a]Gen 31:24 [b]Lev 19:17; 1 John 2:9, 11; 3:10, 12, 15
23 [a]1 Sam 25:7
25 [1]Lit *broke through*
26 [a]2 Sam 3:27; 11:13-15
27 [1]Lit *broke through*
28 [1]Lit *sons of valor* [a]Judg 19:6, 9, 22; 1 Sam 25:36-38
29 [a]2 Sam 18:9; 1 Kin 1:33, 38
31 [a]2 Sam 1:11 [b]2 Sam 12:16
32 [1]Lit *answered and said* [2]Lit *say* [3]Lit *mouth* [a]2 Sam 13:3-5
33 [1]Lit *his heart* [a]2 Sam 19:19
34 [a]2 Sam 13:37, 38 [b]2 Sam 18:24
36 [1]Lit *with a very great weeping*
37 [a]2 Sam 13:34 [b]2 Sam 3:3 [c]2 Sam 14:23, 32

38 [a]So Absalom had fled and gone to Geshur, and was there three years.

39 *The heart of* King David longed to go out to Absalom; for [a]he was comforted concerning Amnon, since he was dead.

Chapter 14 Theme ______________________________

14 Now Joab the son of Zeruiah perceived that [a]the king's heart *was inclined* toward Absalom.

2 So Joab sent to [a]Tekoa and [1]brought a wise woman from there and said to her, "Please pretend to be a mourner, and put on mourning garments now, and do not [b]anoint yourself with oil, but be like a woman who has been mourning for the dead many days;

3 then go to the king and speak to him in this manner." So Joab put [a]the words in her mouth.

4 Now when the woman of Tekoa [1]spoke to the king, she fell on her face to the ground and [a]prostrated herself and said, "[b]Help, O king."

5 The king said to her, "What is your trouble?" And she [1]answered, "Truly I am a widow, for my husband is dead.

6 "Your maidservant had two sons, but the two of them struggled together in the field, and there was no [1]one to separate them, so one struck the other and killed him.

7 "Now behold, [a]the whole family has risen against your maidservant, and they say, 'Hand over the one who struck his brother, that we may put him to death for the life of his brother whom he killed, [b]and destroy the heir also.' Thus they will extinguish my coal which is left, so as to [1]leave my husband neither name nor remnant on the face of the earth."

8 Then the king said to the woman, "Go to your house, and I will give orders concerning you."

9 The woman of Tekoa said to the king, "O my lord, the king, [a]the iniquity is on me and my father's house, but [b]the king and his throne are guiltless."

10 So the king said, "Whoever speaks to you, bring him to me, and he will not touch you anymore."

11 Then she said, "Please let the king remember the LORD your God, [a]*so that* the avenger of blood will not continue to destroy, otherwise they will destroy my son." And he said, "[b]As the LORD lives, not one hair of your son shall fall to the ground."

12 Then the woman said, "Please let your maidservant speak a word to my lord the king." And he said, "Speak."

13 The woman said, "[a]Why then have you planned such a thing against the people of God? For in speaking this word the king is as one who is guilty, *in that* the king does not bring back [b]his banished one.

14 "For [a]we will surely die and are [b]like water spilled on the ground which cannot be gathered up again. Yet God does not take away life, but plans [1]ways so that [c]the banished one will not be cast out from him.

38 [a]2 Sam 13:34

39 [a]2 Sam 12:19-23

14:1 [a]2 Sam 13:39

2 [1]Lit *took* [a]2 Sam 23:26; 2 Chr 11:6; Amos 1:1 [b]2 Sam 12:20

3 [a]2 Sam 14:19

4 [1]Many mss and ancient versions read *came* [a]1 Sam 25:23 [b]2 Kin 6:26-28

5 [1]Lit *said*

6 [1]Lit *deliverer between*

7 [1]Lit *set* [a]Num 35:19; Deut 19:12, 13 [b]Matt 21:38

9 [a]Gen 43:9; 1 Sam 25:24 [b]1 Kin 2:33

11 [a]Num 35:19, 21; Deut 19:4-10 [b]1 Sam 14:45; 1 Kin 1:52; Matt 10:30

13 [a]2 Sam 12:7; 1 Kin 20:40-42 [b]2 Sam 13:37, 38

14 [1]Lit *devices* [a]Job 30:23; 34:15; Heb 9:27 [b]Ps 58:7 [c]Num 35:15, 25, 28

15 [1]Lit *that* [2]Lit *word*

15 "Now [1]the reason I have come to speak this word to my lord
the king is that the people have made me afraid; so your maidservant said, 'Let me now speak to the king, perhaps the king
will perform the [2]request of his maidservant.

16 [1]Lit *to* [2]Lit *palm* [3]Lit *together* [a]Deut 32:9; 1 Sam 26:19

16 'For the king will hear [1]and deliver his maidservant from the
[2]hand of the man who would destroy [3]both me and my son from
[a]the inheritance of God.'
17 "Then your maidservant said, 'Please let the word of my lord
the king be [1]comforting, for as [a]the angel of God, so is my lord the

17 [1]Lit *for rest* [a]1 Sam 29:9; 2 Sam 14:20; 19:27

king to discern good and evil. And may the LORD your God be
with you.'"
18 Then the king answered and said to the woman, "Please do
not hide anything from me that I am about to ask you." And
the woman said, "Let my lord the king please speak."

19 [a]2 Sam 14:3

19 So the king said, "Is the hand of Joab with you in all this?"
And the woman replied, "As your soul lives, my lord the king,
no one can turn to the right or to the left from anything that my

20 [a]2 Sam 14:17; 19:27

lord the king has spoken. Indeed, it was [a]your servant Joab who
commanded me, and it was he who put all these words in the
mouth of your maidservant;
20 in order to change the appearance of things your servant Joab

21 [a]2 Sam 14:11

has done this thing. But my lord is wise, [a]like the wisdom of
the angel of God, to know all that is in the earth."
21 Then the king said to Joab, "Behold now, [a]I will surely do

22 [1]Lit *word*

this thing; go therefore, bring back the young man Absalom."
22 Joab fell on his face to the ground, prostrated himself and
blessed the king; then Joab said, "Today your servant knows
that I have found favor in your sight, O my lord, the king, in

23 [a]Deut 3:14; 2 Sam 13:37, 38

that the king has performed the [1]request of his servant."
23 So Joab arose and went to [a]Geshur and brought Absalom to
Jerusalem.
24 However the king said, "Let him turn to [a]his own house,

24 [a]2 Sam 13:20

and let him not see my face." So Absalom turned to his own
house and did not see the king's face.
25 Now in all Israel was no one as handsome as Absalom, so

25 [a]Deut 28:35; Job 2:7; Is 1:6

highly praised; [a]from the sole of his foot to the crown of his
head there was no defect in him.
26 When he [a]cut the hair of his head (and it was at the end of
every year that he cut *it*, for it was heavy on him so he cut it), he

26 [a]Ezek 44:20

weighed the hair of his head at 200 shekels by the king's weight.
27 [a]To Absalom there were born three sons, and one daughter
whose name was [b]Tamar; she was a woman of beautiful

27 [a]2 Sam 18:18 [b]2 Sam 13:1

appearance.
28 Now Absalom lived two full years in Jerusalem, [a]and did
not see the king's face.
29 Then Absalom sent for Joab, to send him to the king, but

28 [a]2 Sam 14:24

he would not come to him. So he sent again a second time, but
he would not come.
30 Therefore he said to his servants, "See, [a]Joab's [1]field is next
to mine, and he has barley there; go and set it on fire." So

30 [1]Lit *portion* [a]Judg 15:3-5

Absalom's servants set the [1]field on fire.

31 Then Joab arose, came to Absalom at his house and said to
him, "Why have your servants set my [1]field on fire?"
32 Absalom [1]answered Joab, "Behold, I sent for you, saying,
'Come here, that I may send you to the king, to say, "Why have I
come from Geshur? It would be better for me still to be there."'
Now therefore, let me see the king's face, [a]and if there is
iniquity in me, let him put me to death."
33 So when Joab came to the king and told him, he called for
Absalom. Thus he came to the king and prostrated himself on his
face to the ground before the king, and [a]the king kissed Absalom.

Chapter 15 Theme ____

15 Now it came about after this that [a]Absalom provided for
himself a chariot and horses and fifty men as runners
before him.
2 Absalom used to rise early and [a]stand beside the way to the
gate; and when any man had a suit to come to the king for
judgment, Absalom would call to him and say, "From what city
are you?" And he would say, "Your servant is from one of the
tribes of Israel."
3 Then Absalom would say to him, "See, [a]your [1]claims are good
and right, but no man listens to you on the part of the king."
4 Moreover, Absalom would say, "[a]Oh that one would appoint
me judge in the land, then every man who has any suit or cause
could come to me and I would give him justice."
5 And when a man came near to prostrate himself before him,
he would put out his hand and take hold of him and [a]kiss him.
6 In this manner Absalom dealt with all Israel who came to
the king for judgment; [a]so Absalom stole away the hearts of the
men of Israel.
7 Now it came about at the end of [1]forty years that Absalom
said to the king, "Please let me go and pay my vow which I
have vowed to the LORD, in [a]Hebron.
8 "For your servant [a]vowed a vow while I was living at Geshur
in Aram, saying, '[b]If the LORD shall indeed bring me back to
Jerusalem, then I will serve the LORD.'"
9 The king said to him, "Go in peace." So he arose and went
to Hebron.
10 But Absalom sent spies throughout all the tribes of Israel,
saying, "As soon as you hear the sound of the trumpet, then you
shall say, '[a]Absalom is king in Hebron.'"
11 Then two hundred men went with Absalom from Jerusalem,
[a]who were invited and [b]went [1]innocently, and they did not
know anything.
12 And Absalom sent for [a]Ahithophel the Gilonite, David's
counselor, from his city [b]Giloh, while he was offering the
sacrifices. And the conspiracy was strong, for [c]the people
increased continually with Absalom.
13 Then a messenger came to David, saying, "[a]The hearts of
the men of Israel are [1]with Absalom."

31 [1]Lit *portion*
32 [1]Lit *said to* [a]1 Sam 20:8; Prov 28:13
33 [a]Gen 33:4; Luke 15:20
15:1 [a]1 Kin 1:5
2 [a]Ruth 4:1; 2 Sam 19:8
3 [1]Lit *words* [a]Prov 12:2
4 [a]Judg 9:29
5 [a]2 Sam 14:33; 20:9
6 [a]Rom 16:18
7 [1]Some ancient versions render *four* [a]2 Sam 3:2, 3
8 [a]2 Sam 13:37, 38 [b]Gen 28:20, 21
10 [a]1 Kin 1:34; 2 Kin 9:13
11 [1]Lit *in their integrity* [a]1 Sam 9:13 [b]1 Sam 22:15
12 [a]2 Sam 15:31 [b]Josh 15:51 [c]Ps 3:1
13 [1]Lit *after* [a]Judg 9:3; 2 Sam 15:6

14 David said to all his servants who were with him at Jerusalem, "[a]Arise and let us flee, for *otherwise* none of us will escape
from Absalom. Go in haste, or he will overtake us quickly and
bring down calamity on us and strike the city with the edge of
the sword."
15 Then the king's servants said to the king, "Behold, your
servants *are ready to do* whatever my lord the king chooses."
16 So the king went out and all his household [1]with him. But
[a]the king left ten concubines to keep the house.
17 The king went out and all the people [1]with him, and they
stopped at the last house.
18 Now all his servants passed on beside him, [a]all the
Cherethites, all the Pelethites and all the Gittites, [b]six hundred men
who had come [1]with him from Gath, passed on before the king.
19 Then the king said to [a]Ittai the Gittite, "Why will you also go
with us? Return and remain with the king, for you are a foreigner
and also an exile; *return* to your own place.
20 "You came *only* yesterday, and shall I today make you wander
with us, while [a]I go where I will? Return and take back your
brothers; [b]mercy and [1]truth be with you."
21 But Ittai answered the king and said, "As the LORD lives, and
as my lord the king lives, surely [a]wherever my lord the king may
be, whether for death or for life, there also your servant will be."
22 Therefore David said to Ittai, "Go and pass over." So Ittai
the Gittite passed over with all his men and all the little ones
who *were* with him.
23 While all the country was weeping with a loud voice, all the
people passed over. The king also passed over [a]the brook Kidron,
and all the people passed over toward [b]the way of the wilderness.
24 Now behold, [a]Zadok also *came,* and all the Levites with him
[b]carrying the ark of the covenant of God. And they set down
the ark of God, and [c]Abiathar came up until all the people had
finished passing from the city.
25 The king said to Zadok, "Return the ark of God to the city.
If I find favor in the sight of the LORD, then [a]He will bring me
back again and show me both it and [b]His habitation.
26 "But if He should say thus, '[a]I have no delight in you,' behold,
here I am, [b]let Him do to me as seems good [1]to Him."
27 The king said also to Zadok the priest, "Are you *not* [a]a
seer? Return to the city in peace and your [b]two sons with you,
your son Ahimaaz and Jonathan the son of Abiathar.
28 "See, I am going to wait [a]at the fords of the wilderness until
word comes from you to inform me."
29 Therefore Zadok and Abiathar returned the ark of God to
Jerusalem and remained there.
30 And David went up the ascent of the *Mount of* Olives, and
wept as he went, and [a]his head was covered and he walked
[b]barefoot. Then all the people who were with him each
covered his head and went up weeping as they went.
31 Now someone told David, saying, "[a]Ahithophel is among the
conspirators with Absalom." And David said, "O LORD, I pray,
[b]make the counsel of Ahithophel foolishness."

14 [a]2 Sam 12:11; Ps 3: title
16 [1]Lit *at his feet* [a]2 Sam 16:21, 22
17 [1]Lit *at his feet*
18 [1]Lit *at his feet* [a]2 Sam 8:18 [b]1 Sam 23:13; 25:13; 30:1, 9
19 [a]2 Sam 18:2
20 [1]Or *faithfulness* [a]1 Sam 23:13 [b]2 Sam 2:6
21 [a]Ruth 1:16, 17; Prov 17:17
23 [a]1 Kin 15:13; 2 Chr 29:16 [b]2 Sam 15:28; 16:2
24 [a]2 Sam 8:17; 20:25 [b]Num 4:15; 1 Sam 4:4, 5 [c]1 Sam 22:20
25 [a]Ps 43:3 [b]Ex 15:13; Jer 25:30
26 [1]Lit *in His sight* [a]2 Sam 11:27; 1 Chr 21:7 [b]1 Sam 3:18
27 [a]1 Sam 9:6-9 [b]2 Sam 17:17
28 [a]Josh 5:10; 2 Sam 17:16
30 [a]Esth 6:12; Ezek 24:17, 23 [b]Is 20:2-4
31 [a]2 Sam 15:12 [b]2 Sam 16:23; 17:14, 23

32 It happened as David was coming to the summit, where
God was worshiped, that behold, Hushai the [a]Archite met him
with his [1]coat torn and [2]dust on his head.
33 David said to him, "If you pass over with me, then you will
be [a]a burden to me.
34 "But if you return to the city, and [a]say to Absalom, 'I will be
your servant, O king; as I have been your father's servant in
time past, so I will now be your servant,' then you can thwart
the counsel of Ahithophel for me.
35 "Are not Zadok and Abiathar the priests with you there? So
it shall be that [a]whatever you hear from the king's house, you
shall report to Zadok and Abiathar the priests.
36 "Behold [a]their two sons are with them there, Ahimaaz,
Zadok's son and Jonathan, Abiathar's son; and [b]by them you shall
send me everything that you hear."
37 So Hushai, [a]David's friend, came into the city, and [b]Absalom
came into Jerusalem.

Chapter 16 Theme ______________________________

16 Now when David had passed [a]a little beyond the summit, behold, [b]Ziba the servant of Mephibosheth met him
[c]with a couple of saddled donkeys, and on them *were* two hundred loaves of bread, a hundred clusters of raisins, a hundred
summer fruits, and a jug of wine.
2 The king said to Ziba, "Why do you have these?" And Ziba
said, "[a]The donkeys are for the king's household to ride, and
the bread and summer fruit for the young men to eat, and the
wine, [b]for whoever is faint in the wilderness to drink."
3 Then the king said, "And where is [a]your master's son?"
And [b]Ziba said to the king, "Behold, he is staying in Jerusalem,
for he said, 'Today the house of Israel will restore the kingdom
of my father to me.'"
4 So the king said to Ziba, "Behold, all that belongs to
Mephibosheth is yours." And Ziba said, "I prostrate myself; let
me find favor in your sight, O my lord, the king!"
5 When King David came to [a]Bahurim, behold, there came
out from there a man of the family of the house of Saul [b]whose
name was Shimei, the son of Gera; he came out [c]cursing
continually as he came.
6 He threw stones at David and at all the servants of King
David; and all the people and all the mighty men were at his
right hand and at his left.
7 Thus Shimei said when he cursed, "Get out, get out, [a]you
man of bloodshed, and worthless fellow!
8 "[a]The LORD has returned upon you all [b]the bloodshed of the
house of Saul, in whose place you have reigned; and the LORD
has given the kingdom into the hand of your son Absalom. And
behold, you are *taken* in your own evil, for you are a man of
bloodshed!"
9 Then [a]Abishai the son of Zeruiah said to the king, "Why

32 [1]Or *tunic* [2]Lit *ground* [a]Josh 16:2
33 [a]2 Sam 19:35
34 [a]2 Sam 16:19
35 [a]2 Sam 17:15, 16
36 [a]2 Sam 15:27 [b]2 Sam 17:17
37 [a]2 Sam 16:16; 1 Chr 27:33 [b]2 Sam 16:15
16:1 [a]2 Sam 15:32 [b]2 Sam 9:2-13 [c]1 Sam 25:18
2 [a]Judg 10:4 [b]2 Sam 17:29
3 [a]2 Sam 9:9, 10 [b]2 Sam 19:26, 27
5 [a]2 Sam 3:16; 17:18 [b]2 Sam 19:16-23; 1 Kin 2:8, 9, 44 [c]Ex 22:28; 1 Sam 17:43
7 [a]2 Sam 12:9
8 [a]2 Sam 21:1-9 [b]2 Sam 1:16; 3:28, 29; 4:11, 12
9 [a]1 Sam 26:8; 2 Sam 19:21; Luke 9:54

should [b]this dead dog [c]curse my lord the king? Let me go over
now and [1]cut off his head."
10 But the king said, "[a]What have I to do with you, O sons of
Zeruiah? [b]If he curses, and if the LORD has told him, 'Curse
David,' [c]then who shall say, 'Why have you done so?'"
11 Then David said to Abishai and to all his servants, "Behold,
[a]my son who came out from [1]me seeks my life; how much
more now this Benjamite? Let him alone and let him curse,
[b]for the LORD has told him.
12 "Perhaps the LORD will look on my affliction and [1a]return
good to me instead of his cursing this day."
13 So David and his men went on the way; and Shimei went
along on the hillside parallel with him and as he went he cursed
and cast stones and threw dust at him.
14 The king and all the people who were with him arrived
weary and he refreshed himself there.
15 [a]Then Absalom and all the people, the men of Israel,
entered Jerusalem, and Ahithophel with him.
16 Now it came about when [a]Hushai the Archite, David's
friend, came to Absalom, that [b]Hushai said to Absalom, "[c]*Long*
live the king! *Long* live the king!"
17 Absalom said to Hushai, "Is this your [1]loyalty to your
friend? [a]Why did you not go with your friend?"
18 Then Hushai said to Absalom, "No! For whom the LORD,
this people, and all the men of Israel have chosen, his I will be,
and with him I will remain.
19 "Besides, [a]whom should I serve? *Should I* not *serve* in the
presence of his son? As I have served in your father's presence,
so I will be in your presence."
20 Then Absalom said to Ahithophel, "Give your advice.
What shall we do?"
21 Ahithophel said to Absalom, "[a]Go in to your father's
concubines, whom he has left to keep the house; then all Israel
will hear that you have made yourself odious to your father.
The hands of all who are with you will also be strengthened."
22 So they pitched a tent for Absalom on the roof, [a]and Absalom
went in to his father's concubines [b]in the sight of all Israel.
23 [a]The advice of Ahithophel, which he [1]gave in those days,
was as if one inquired of the word of God; [b]so was all the
advice of Ahithophel *regarded* by both David and Absalom.

Chapter 17 Theme ________________________________

17 Furthermore, Ahithophel said to Absalom, "Please let me
choose 12,000 men that I may arise and pursue David
tonight.
2 "[a]I will come upon him while he is weary and [1]exhausted
and terrify him, so that all the people who are with him will
flee. Then [b]I will strike down the king alone,
3 and I will bring back all the people to you. [1]The return of
everyone depends on the man you seek; *then* all the people will
be at [a]peace."

9 [1]Lit *take off* [b]2 Sam 9:8 [c]Ex 22:28
10 [a]2 Sam 3:39; 19:22 [b]John 18:11 [c]Rom 9:20
11 [1]Lit *my body* [a]2 Sam 12:11 [b]Gen 45:5; 1 Sam 26:19
12 [1]Lit *the LORD will return* [a]Deut 23:5; Rom 8:28
15 [a]2 Sam 15:12, 37
16 [a]2 Sam 15:37 [b]2 Sam 15:34 [c]1 Sam 10:24; 2 Kin 11:12
17 [1]Or *kindness* [a]2 Sam 19:25
19 [a]2 Sam 15:34
21 [a]2 Sam 15:16; 20:3
22 [a]2 Sam 15:16; 20:3 [b]2 Sam 12:11, 12
23 [1]Lit *advised* [a]2 Sam 17:14, 23 [b]2 Sam 15:12
17:2 [1]Lit *slack of hands* [a]2 Sam 16:14 [b]1 Kin 22:31
3 [1]Lit *Like the return of the whole is the man whom you seek* [a]Jer 6:14

4 So the [1]plan pleased Absalom and all the elders of Israel.
5 Then Absalom said, "Now call [a]Hushai the Archite also,
and let us hear what [1]he has to say."
6 When Hushai had come to Absalom, Absalom said to [1]him,
"Ahithophel has spoken [2]thus. Shall we [3]carry out his plan? If
not, you speak."
7 So Hushai said to Absalom, "[a]This time the advice that
Ahithophel has [1]given is not good."
8 Moreover, Hushai said, "You know your father and his
men, that they are mighty men and they are [1]fierce, [a]like a bear
robbed of her cubs in the field. And your father is an [2]expert in
warfare, and will not spend the night with the people.
9 "Behold, he has now hidden himself in one of the [1]caves or
in another place; and it will be [2]when he falls on them at the
first attack, that whoever hears *it* will say, 'There has been a
slaughter among the people who follow Absalom.'
10 "And even the one who is valiant, whose heart is like the
heart of a lion, [a]will completely [1]lose heart; for all Israel knows
that your father is a mighty man and those who are with him
are valiant men.
11 "But I counsel that all Israel be surely gathered to you, [a]from
Dan even to Beersheba, [b]as the sand that is by the sea in
abundance, and that [1]you personally go into battle.
12 "So we shall come to him in one of the places where he can
be found, and we will [1]fall on him [a]as the dew falls on the
ground; and of him and of all the men who are with him, not
even one will be left.
13 "If he withdraws into a city, then all Israel shall bring ropes
to that city, and we will [a]drag it into the [1]valley until not even a
small stone is found there."
14 Then Absalom and all the men of Israel said, "The counsel of
Hushai the Archite is better than the counsel of Ahithophel."
For [a]the LORD had ordained to thwart the good counsel of
Ahithophel, so that the LORD might bring calamity on Absalom.
15 Then [a]Hushai said to Zadok and to Abiathar the priests,
"[1]This is what Ahithophel counseled Absalom and the elders of
Israel, and [1]this is what I have counseled.
16 "Now therefore, send quickly and tell David, saying, '[a]Do
not spend the night at the fords of the wilderness, but by all
means cross over, or else the king and all the people who are
with him will be [1]destroyed.'"
17 [a]Now Jonathan and Ahimaaz were staying at [b]En-rogel, and
a maidservant would go and tell them, and they would go and
tell King David, for they could not be seen entering the city.
18 But a lad did see them and told Absalom; so the two of them
departed quickly and came to the house of a man [a]in Bahurim,
who had a well in his courtyard, and they went down [1]into it.
19 And [a]the woman [1]took a covering and spread it over the well's
mouth and scattered grain on it, so that nothing was known.
20 Then Absalom's servants came to the woman at the house
and said, "Where are Ahimaaz and Jonathan?" And [a]the woman

4 [1]Lit *word was pleasing in the sight of*
5 [1]Lit *is in his mouth—even he* [a]2 Sam 15:32-34
6 [1]Lit *him, saying* [2]Lit *according to this word* [3]Lit *do his word*
7 [1]Lit *advised* [a]2 Sam 16:21
8 [1]Lit *bitter of soul* [2]Lit *man of war* [a]Hos 13:8
9 [1]Lit *pits* [2]Lit *according to a falling among them*
10 [1]Lit *melt* [a]Josh 2:9-11
11 [1]Lit *your face go* [a]1 Sam 3:20 [b]Gen 22:17; 1 Sam 13:5
12 [1]Lit *settle down* [a]Ps 110:3; Mic 5:7
13 [1]Or *wadi* [a]Mic 1:6
14 [a]2 Sam 15:31, 34; Ps 9:15, 16
15 [1]Lit *Thus and thus* [a]2 Sam 15:35, 36
16 [1]Lit *swallowed up* [a]2 Sam 15:28
17 [a]2 Sam 15:27, 36 [b]Josh 15:7; 18:16
18 [1]Lit *there* [a]2 Sam 3:16; 16:5
19 [1]Lit *took and spread the covering* [a]Josh 2:4-6
20 [a]Lev 19:11; Josh 2:3-5; 1 Sam 19:12-17

said to them, "They have crossed the brook of water." And
when they searched and could not find *them,* they returned to
Jerusalem.
21 It came about after they had departed that they came up out
of the well and went and told King David; and they said to David,
"[a]Arise and cross over the water quickly for thus Ahithophel
has counseled against you."
22 Then David and all the people who *were* with him arose
and crossed the Jordan; and by [1]dawn not even one remained
who had not crossed the Jordan.
23 Now when Ahithophel saw that his counsel was not
[1]followed, he [2]saddled *his* donkey and arose and went to his
home, to [a]his city, and [3b]set his house in order, and [c]strangled
himself; thus he died and was buried in the grave of his father.
24 Then David came to [a]Mahanaim. And Absalom crossed the
Jordan, he and all the men of Israel with him.
25 Absalom set [a]Amasa over the army in place of Joab. Now
Amasa was the son of a man whose name was [1]Ithra the
Israelite, who went in to Abigail the daughter of [b]Nahash, sister
of Zeruiah, Joab's mother.
26 And Israel and Absalom camped in the land of Gilead.
27 Now when David had come to Mahanaim, Shobi [a]the son of
Nahash from [b]Rabbah of the sons of Ammon, [c]Machir the son of
Ammiel from Lo-debar, and [d]Barzillai the Gileadite from Rogelim,
28 brought [a]beds, basins, pottery, wheat, barley, flour, parched
grain, beans, lentils, parched *seeds,*
29 honey, curds, sheep, and cheese of the herd, for David and
for the people who *were* with him, [a]to eat; for they said, "The
people are hungry and weary and thirsty in the wilderness."

Chapter 18 Theme ______________________________

18 Then David [1]numbered the people who were with him
and [a]set over them commanders of thousands and commanders of hundreds.
2 David sent the people out, [a]one third under the [1]command
of Joab, one third under the [1]command of Abishai the son of
Zeruiah, Joab's brother, and one third under the [1]command of
[b]Ittai the Gittite. And the king said to the people, "I myself will
surely go out with you also."
3 But the people said, "[a]You should not go out; for if we indeed
flee, they will not care about us; even if half of us die, they will
not care about us. But [1]you are worth ten thousand of us; therefore now it is better that you *be ready* to help us from the city."
4 Then the king said to them, "Whatever seems best to you I
will do." So [a]the king stood beside the gate, and all the people
went out by hundreds and thousands.
5 The king charged Joab and Abishai and Ittai, saying, "*Deal*
gently for my sake with the young man Absalom." And [a]all the
people heard when the king charged all the commanders
concerning Absalom.

21 [a]2 Sam 17:15, 16
22 [1]Lit *the light of the morning*
23 [1]Lit *done* [2]Lit *bound* [3]Lit *gave charge to* [a]2 Sam 15:12 [b]2 Kin 20:1 [c]Matt 27:5
24 [a]Gen 32:2, 10; 2 Sam 2:8
25 [1]In 1 Chr 2:17, *Jether the Ishmaelite* [a]2 Sam 19:13; 20:9-12; 1 Kin 2:5, 32 [b]1 Chr 2:16
27 [a]1 Sam 11:1; 2 Sam 10:1, 2 [b]2 Sam 12:26, 29 [c]2 Sam 9:4 [d]2 Sam 19:31-39; 1 Kin 2:7
28 [a]Prov 11:25; Matt 5:7
29 [a]2 Sam 16:2, 14; Prov 21:26; Eccl 11:1; Rom 12:13
18:1 [1]Lit *mustered* [a]Ex 18:25; Num 31:14; 1 Sam 22:7
2 [1]Lit *hand* [a]Judg 7:16; 1 Sam 11:11 [b]2 Sam 15:19-22
3 [1]So with some ancient versions; M.T. *for now there are ten thousand like us* [a]2 Sam 21:17
4 [a]2 Sam 18:24
5 [a]2 Sam 18:12

6 Then the people went out into the field against Israel, and
the battle took place in [a]the forest of Ephraim.
7 The people of Israel were [1]defeated there before the servants
of David, and the slaughter there that day was great, 20,000 men.
8 For the battle there was spread over the whole countryside, and the forest devoured more people that day than the
sword devoured.
9 Now Absalom happened to meet the servants of David. For
Absalom was riding on *his* mule, and the mule went under the
thick branches of a great oak. And [a]his head caught fast in the
oak, so he was [1]left hanging between heaven and earth, while
the mule that was under him kept going.
10 When a certain man saw *it,* he told Joab and said, "Behold,
I saw Absalom hanging in an oak."
11 Then Joab said to the man who had told him, "Now behold,
you saw *him!* Why then did you not strike him there to the
ground? And I would have given you ten *pieces* of silver and a
belt."
12 The man said to Joab, "Even if I should receive a thousand
pieces of silver in my hand, I would not put out my hand
against the king's son; for [a]in our hearing the king charged you
and Abishai and Ittai, saying, '[1]Protect for me the young man
Absalom!'
13 "Otherwise, if I had dealt treacherously against his life (and
[a]there is nothing hidden from the king), then you yourself
would have stood aloof."
14 Then Joab said, "I will not [1]waste time here with you." [a]So
he took three spears in his hand and thrust them through the
heart of Absalom while he was yet alive in the [2]midst of the oak.
15 And ten young men who carried Joab's armor gathered
around and struck Absalom and killed him.
16 Then [a]Joab blew the trumpet, and the people returned
from pursuing Israel, for Joab restrained the people.
17 They took Absalom and cast him into [1]a deep pit in the
forest and [a]erected over him a very great heap of stones. And
[b]all Israel fled, each to his tent.
18 Now Absalom in his lifetime had taken and [a]set up for
himself a pillar which is in [b]the King's Valley, for he said, "[c]I have
no son [1]to preserve my name." So he named the pillar after his
own name, and it is called Absalom's Monument to this day.
19 Then [a]Ahimaaz the son of Zadok said, "Please let me run
and bring the king news [b]that the LORD has [1]freed him from
the hand of his enemies."
20 But Joab said to him, "You are not the man to carry news
this day, but you shall carry news another day; however, you
shall carry no news today because the king's son is dead."
21 Then Joab said to the Cushite, "Go, tell the king what you
have seen." So the Cushite bowed to Joab and ran.
22 Now Ahimaaz the son of Zadok said once more to Joab, "But
whatever happens, please let me also run after the Cushite."
And Joab said, "Why would you run, my son, since [a]you will
have no reward for going?"

6 [a]Josh 17:15, 18; 2 Sam 17:26
7 [1]Lit *smitten*
9 [1]Lit *placed* [a]2 Sam 14:26
12 [1]So with some mss and the ancient versions; M.T. *Take care whoever* you are *of* [a]2 Sam 18:5
13 [a]2 Sam 14:19, 20
14 [1]Lit *tarry thus* [2]Lit *heart* [a]2 Sam 14:30
16 [a]2 Sam 2:28; 20:22
17 [1]Lit *the great* [a]Deut 21:20, 21; Josh 7:26; 8:29 [b]2 Sam 19:8; 20:1, 22
18 [1]Lit *for the sake of remembering* [a]1 Sam 15:12 [b]Gen 14:17 [c]2 Sam 14:27
19 [1]Lit *vindicated* [a]2 Sam 15:36 [b]2 Sam 18:31
22 [a]2 Sam 18:29

23 "But whatever happens," *he said,* "I will run." So he said to
him, "Run." Then Ahimaaz ran by way of the plain and passed
up the Cushite.
24 Now [a]David was sitting between the two gates; and [b]the
watchman went up to the roof of the gate by the wall, and raised
his eyes and looked, and behold, a man running by himself.
25 The watchman called and told the king. And the king said,
"If he is by himself there is good news in his mouth." And he
came nearer and nearer.
26 Then the watchman saw another man running; and the
watchman called to the gatekeeper and said, "Behold, *another*
man running by himself." And the king said, "This one also is
bringing good news."
27 The watchman said, "I [1]think the running of the first one
[a]is like the running of Ahimaaz the son of Zadok." And the
king said, "[b]This is a good man and comes with good news."
28 Ahimaaz called and said to the king, "[1]All is well." And [a]he
prostrated himself before the king with his face to the ground.
And he said, "[b]Blessed is the LORD your God, who has delivered
up the men who lifted their hands against my lord the king."
29 The king said, "[a]Is it well with the young man Absalom?" And
Ahimaaz answered, "When Joab sent the king's servant, and your
servant, I saw a great tumult, but [b]I did not know what *it was.*"
30 Then the king said, "Turn aside and stand here." So he
turned aside and stood still.
31 Behold, the Cushite arrived, and the Cushite said, "Let my
lord the king receive good news, for [a]the LORD has [1]freed you
this day from the hand of all those who rose up against you."
32 Then the king said to the Cushite, "[a]Is it well with the
young man Absalom?" And the Cushite answered, "[b]Let the
enemies of my lord the king, and all who rise up against you
for evil, be as that young man!"
33 [1]The king was deeply moved and went up to the chamber
over the gate and wept. And thus he said as he walked, "[a]O my
son Absalom, my son, my son Absalom! [b]Would I had died
instead of you, O Absalom, my son, my son!"

Chapter 19 Theme ______________________

19 Then it was told Joab, "Behold, [a]the king is weeping and
mourns for Absalom."
2 The [1]victory that day was turned to mourning for all the
people, for the people heard *it* said that day, "The king is
grieved for his son."
3 So the people went by stealth into the city that day, as people
who are humiliated steal away when they flee in battle.
4 The king [a]covered his face and [1]cried out with a loud voice,
"[b]O my son Absalom, O Absalom, my son, my son!"
5 Then Joab came into the house to the king and said,
"Today you have covered with shame the faces of all your
servants, who today have saved your life and the lives of your

24 [a]2 Sam 19:8 [b]2 Sam 13:34; 2 Kin 9:17
27 [1]Lit *see* [a]2 Kin 9:20 [b]1 Kin 1:42
28 [1]Lit *Peace* [a]1 Sam 25:23; 2 Sam 14:4 [b]1 Sam 17:46
29 [a]2 Sam 20:9; 2 Kin 4:26 [b]2 Sam 18:22
31 [1]Lit *vindicated* [a]Judg 5:31; 2 Sam 18:19
32 [a]2 Sam 18:29 [b]1 Sam 25:26
33 [1]Ch 19:1 in Heb [a]2 Sam 19:4 [b]Ex 32:32; Rom 9:3
19:1 [a]2 Sam 18:5, 14
2 [1]Lit *salvation*
4 [1]Lit *the king cried* [a]2 Sam 15:30 [b]2 Sam 18:33

sons and daughters, the lives of your wives, and the lives of
your concubines,
6 by loving those who hate you, and by hating those who
love you. For you have shown today that [1]princes and servants
are nothing to you; for I know this day that if Absalom were alive
and all of us were dead today, then [2]you would be pleased.
7 "Now therefore arise, go out and speak [1]kindly to your servants,
for I swear by the LORD, if you do not go out, surely [a]not a man
will pass the night with you, and this will be worse for you than
all the evil that has come upon you from your youth until now."
8 So the king arose and sat in the gate. When they told all
the people, saying, "Behold, the king is [a]sitting in the gate,"
then all the people came before the king.
Now [b]Israel had fled, each to his tent.
9 All the people were quarreling throughout all the tribes of
Israel, saying, "[a]The king delivered us from the [1]hand of our
enemies and [b]saved us from the [1]hand of the Philistines, but
now [c]he has fled out of the land from Absalom.
10 "However, Absalom, whom we anointed over us, has died
in battle. Now then, why are you silent about bringing the king
back?"
11 Then King David sent to [a]Zadok and Abiathar the priests,
saying, "Speak to the elders of Judah, saying, 'Why are you the
last to bring the king back to his house, since the word of all
Israel has come to the king, *even* to his house?
12 'You are my brothers; [a]you are my bone and my flesh. Why
then should you be the last to bring back the king?'
13 "Say to [a]Amasa, 'Are you not my bone and my flesh? [b]May
God do so to me, and more also, if you will not be [c]commander
of the army before me continually [d]in place of Joab.'"
14 Thus he turned the hearts of all the men of Judah [a]as one
man, so that they sent *word* to the king, *saying,* "Return, you
and all your servants."
15 The king then returned and came as far as the Jordan. And
Judah came to [a]Gilgal in order to go to meet the king, to bring
the king across the Jordan.
16 Then [a]Shimei the son of Gera, the Benjamite who was from
Bahurim, hurried and came down with the men of Judah to
meet King David.
17 There were a thousand men of Benjamin with him, with
[a]Ziba the servant of the house of Saul, and his fifteen sons and
his twenty servants with him; and they rushed to the Jordan
before the king.
18 Then they kept crossing the ford to bring over the king's
household, and to do what was good in his sight. And Shimei
the son of Gera fell down before the king as he was about to
cross the Jordan.
19 So he said to the king, "[a]Let not my lord consider me
guilty, nor remember what your servant did wrong on the day
when my lord the king came out from Jerusalem, so that the
king would [1]take *it* to heart.

6 [1]Or *commanders* [2]Lit *it would be right in your eyes*

7 [1]Lit *to the heart* [a]Prov 14:28

8 [a]2 Sam 15:2; 18:24 [b]2 Sam 18:17

9 [1]Lit *palm* [a]2 Sam 8:1-14 [b]2 Sam 5:20; 8:1 [c]2 Sam 15:14

11 [a]2 Sam 15:29

12 [a]2 Sam 5:1

13 [a]2 Sam 17:25 [b]1 Kin 19:2 [c]2 Sam 8:16 [d]2 Sam 3:27-39; 19:5-7

14 [a]Judg 20:1

15 [a]Josh 5:9; 1 Sam 11:14, 15

16 [a]2 Sam 16:5-13; 1 Kin 2:8

17 [a]2 Sam 16:1-4; 19:26, 27

19 [1]Lit *set* [a]1 Sam 22:15; 2 Sam 16:6-8

20 "For your servant knows that I have sinned; therefore
behold, I have come today, [a]the first of all the house of Joseph
to go down to meet my lord the king."
21 But Abishai the son of Zeruiah said, "[a]Should not Shimei be
put to death for this, [b]because he cursed the LORD'S anointed?"
22 David then said, "[a]What have I to do with you, O sons of
Zeruiah, that you should this day be an adversary to me?
[b]Should any man be put to death in Israel today? For do I not
know that I am king over Israel today?"
23 The king said to Shimei, "[a]You shall not die." Thus the king
swore to him.
24 Then [a]Mephibosheth the [1]son of Saul came down to meet
the king; and [b]he had neither [2]cared for his feet, nor [2]trimmed
his mustache, nor [c]washed his clothes, from the day the king
departed until the day he came *home* in peace.
25 It was when he came from Jerusalem to meet the king, that
the king said to him, "[a]Why did you not go with me,
Mephibosheth?"
26 So he answered, "O my lord, the king, my servant deceived
me; for your servant said, 'I will saddle a donkey for myself that
I may ride on it and go with the king,' [a]because your servant is
lame.
27 "Moreover, [a]he has slandered your servant to my lord the king;
but my lord the king is [b]like the angel of God, therefore do
what is good in your sight.
28 "For [a]all my father's household was nothing but dead men
before my lord the king; [b]yet you set your servant among those
who ate at your own table. What right do I have yet that I should
[1]complain anymore to the king?"
29 So the king said to him, "Why do you still speak of your
affairs? I have [1]decided, 'You and Ziba shall divide the land.'"
30 Mephibosheth said to the king, "Let him even take it all,
since my lord the king has come safely to his own house."
31 Now [a]Barzillai the Gileadite had come down from Rogelim;
and he went on to the Jordan with the king to [1]escort him over
the Jordan.
32 Now Barzillai was very old, being eighty years old; and he
had [1a]sustained the king while he stayed at Mahanaim, for he
was a very great man.
33 The king said to Barzillai, "You cross over with me and I
will [1]sustain you in Jerusalem with me."
34 But Barzillai said to the king, "[a]How long [1]have I yet to
live, that I should go up with the king to Jerusalem?
35 "I am [1]now [a]eighty years old. Can I distinguish between good
and bad? Or can your servant taste what I eat or what I drink?
Or can I hear anymore [b]the voice of singing men and women?
[c]Why then should your servant be an added burden to my lord
the king?
36 "Your servant would merely cross over the Jordan with the
king. Why should the king compensate me *with* this reward?
37 "Please let your servant return, that I may die in my own
city near the grave of my father and my mother. However, here

20 [a]2 Sam 16:5
21 [a]2 Sam 16:7, 8 [b]Ex 22:28
22 [a]2 Sam 3:39; 16:9, 10 [b]1 Sam 11:13
23 [a]1 Kin 2:8
24 [1]I.e. grandson [2]Lit *done* [a]2 Sam 9:6-10 [b]2 Sam 12:20 [c]Ex 19:10
25 [a]2 Sam 16:17
26 [a]2 Sam 9:3
27 [a]2 Sam 16:3, 4 [b]2 Sam 14:17, 20
28 [1]Lit *cry out* [a]2 Sam 21:6-9 [b]2 Sam 9:7, 10, 13
29 [1]Lit *said*
31 [1]Lit *send* [a]2 Sam 17:27-29; 1 Kin 2:7
32 [1]Or *provided food for* [a]2 Sam 17:27-29
33 [1]Or *provide food for*
34 [1]Lit *are the days of the years of my life* [a]Gen 47:8
35 [1]Lit *today* [a]Ps 90:10 [b]Eccl 2:8; Is 5:11, 12 [c]2 Sam 15:33

is your servant [a]Chimham, let him cross over with my lord the
king, and do for him what is good in your sight."
38 The king answered, "Chimham shall cross over with me,
and I will do for him what is good in your sight; and whatever
you [1]require of me, I will do for you."
39 All the people crossed over the Jordan and the king crossed
too. The king then [a]kissed Barzillai and blessed him, and he
returned to his place.
40 Now the king went on to Gilgal, and Chimham went on
with him; and all the people of Judah and also [a]half the people
of Israel [1]accompanied the king.
41 And behold, all the men of Israel came to the king and said to
the king, "[a]Why had our brothers [b]the men of Judah stolen you
away, and brought the king and his household and all David's
men with him over the Jordan?"
42 Then all the men of Judah answered the men of Israel,
"Because [a]the king is a close relative to [1]us. Why then [2]are you
angry about this matter? Have we eaten at all at the king's
expense, or has [3]anything been taken for us?"
43 But the men of Israel answered the men of Judah and said,
"[1a]We have ten parts in the king, therefore [1]we also have more
claim on David than you. Why then did you treat us with
contempt? Was it not [1]our advice first to bring back [1]our king?"
Yet the words of the men of Judah were harsher than the
words of the men of Israel.

Chapter 20 Theme ________________

20 Now [a]a worthless fellow happened to be there whose
name was Sheba, the son of [b]Bichri, a Benjamite; and
he blew the trumpet and said,

"[c]We have no portion in David,
Nor do we have inheritance in [d]the son of Jesse;
[e]Every man to his tents, O Israel!"

2 So all the men of Israel [1]withdrew from following David *and*
followed Sheba the son of Bichri; but the men of Judah [2]remained
steadfast to their king, from the Jordan even to Jerusalem.
3 Then David came to his house at Jerusalem, and [a]the king
took the ten women, the concubines whom he had left to keep
the house, and placed them under guard and provided them
with sustenance, but did not go in to them. So they were shut
up until the day of their death, living as widows.
4 Then the king said to [a]Amasa, "Call out the men of Judah
for me within three days, and be present here yourself."
5 So Amasa went to call out *the men of* Judah, but he
[a]delayed longer than the set time which he had appointed him.
6 And David said to [a]Abishai, "Now Sheba the son of Bichri
will do us more harm than Absalom; [b]take your lord's servants
and pursue him, so that he does not find for himself fortified
cities and escape from our sight."
7 So Joab's men went out after him, [a]along with the Cherethites

37 [a]2 Sam 19:40; 1 Kin 2:7; Jer 41:17
38 [1]Lit *choose*
39 [a]Gen 31:55; Ruth 1:14; 2 Sam 14:33
40 [1]Lit *crossed over with* [a]2 Sam 19:9, 10
41 [a]Judg 8:1; 12:1 [b]2 Sam 19:11, 12
42 [1]Lit *me* [2]Lit *is it hot to you* [3]Or *a gift* [a]2 Sam 19:12
43 [1]Singular in Heb [a]2 Sam 5:1; 1 Kin 11:30, 31
20:1 [a]2 Sam 16:7 [b]Gen 46:21 [c]2 Sam 19:43; 1 Kin 12:16 [d]1 Sam 22:7-9 [e]1 Sam 13:2; 2 Sam 18:17; 2 Chr 10:16
2 [1]Lit *went up* [2]Lit *clung to*
3 [a]2 Sam 15:16; 16:21, 22
4 [a]2 Sam 17:25; 19:13
5 [a]1 Sam 13:8
6 [a]2 Sam 21:17 [b]2 Sam 11:11; 1 Kin 1:33
7 [a]2 Sam 8:18; 1 Kin 1:38

and the Pelethites and all the mighty men; and they went out
from Jerusalem to pursue Sheba the son of Bichri.
8 When they were at the large stone which is in [a]Gibeon,
Amasa came [1]to meet them. Now Joab was [2]dressed in his
military attire, and over it was a belt with a sword in its sheath
fastened at his waist; and as he went forward, it fell out.
9 Joab said to Amasa, "Is it well with you, my brother?" And
[a]Joab took Amasa by the beard with his right hand to kiss him.
10 But Amasa was not on guard against the sword which was
in Joab's hand so [a]he struck him in the belly with it and poured
out his inward parts on the ground, and did not *strike* him
again, and he died. Then Joab and Abishai his brother pursued
Sheba the son of Bichri.
11 Now there stood by him one of Joab's young men, and said,
"Whoever favors Joab and whoever is for David, [a]*let him* follow
Joab."
12 But Amasa lay wallowing in *his* blood in the middle of the
highway. And when the man saw that all the people stood still,
he [1]removed Amasa from the highway into the field and threw
a garment over him when he saw that everyone who came by
him stood still.
13 As soon as he was removed from the highway, all the men
passed on after Joab to pursue Sheba the son of Bichri.
14 Now he went through all the tribes of Israel to Abel, even
Beth-maacah, and all the Berites; and they were gathered
together and also went after him.
15 They came and besieged him in [a]Abel Beth-maacah, and
[b]they [1]cast up a siege ramp against the city, and it stood by the
rampart; and all the people who were with Joab were wreaking
destruction in order to topple the wall.
16 Then [a]a wise woman called from the city, "Hear, hear!
Please tell Joab, 'Come here that I may speak with you.'"
17 So he approached her, and the woman said, "Are you Joab?"
And he answered, "I am." Then she said to him, "Listen to the
words of your maidservant." And he answered, "I am listening."
18 Then she spoke, saying, "Formerly they used to say, 'They
will surely ask *advice* at Abel,' and thus they ended *the dispute.*
19 "I am of those who are peaceable *and* faithful in Israel. [a]You
are seeking to destroy a city, even a mother in Israel. Why
would you swallow up [b]the inheritance of the LORD?"
20 Joab replied, "Far be it, far be it from me that I should swallow
up or destroy!
21 "Such is not the case. But a man from [a]the hill country of
Ephraim, [b]Sheba the son of Bichri by name, has lifted up his
hand against King David. Only hand him over, and I will depart
from the city." And the woman said to Joab, "Behold, his head
will be thrown to you over the wall."
22 Then the woman [a]wisely came to all the people. And they
cut off the head of Sheba the son of Bichri and threw it to Joab.
So [b]he blew the trumpet, and they were dispersed from the
city, each to his tent. Joab also returned to the king at Jerusalem.

8 [1]Lit *before* [2]Lit *girded with military garment as clothing* [a]2 Sam 2:13; 3:30
9 [a]Matt 26:49
10 [a]2 Sam 2:23; 3:27; 1 Kin 2:5
11 [a]2 Sam 20:13
12 [1]Lit *caused to turn*
15 [1]Lit *poured out* [a]1 Kin 15:20; 2 Kin 15:29 [b]2 Kin 19:32; Ezek 4:2
16 [a]2 Sam 14:2
19 [a]Deut 20:10 [b]1 Sam 26:19; 2 Sam 14:16; 21:3
21 [a]Josh 24:33 [b]2 Sam 20:2
22 [a]2 Sam 20:16; Eccl 9:13-16 [b]2 Sam 20:1

23 [a]Now Joab was over the whole army of Israel, and Benaiah the son of Jehoiada was over the Cherethites and the Pelethites;
24 and Adoram was over the forced labor, and [a]Jehoshaphat the son of Ahilud was the recorder;
25 and Sheva was scribe, and Zadok and [a]Abiathar were priests;
26 and Ira the Jairite was also a priest to David.

Chapter 21 Theme ______________________

21 Now there was [a]a famine in the days of David for three years, year after year; and [b]David sought the presence of the LORD. And the LORD said, "It is for Saul and his bloody house, because he put the Gibeonites to death."
2 So the king called the Gibeonites and spoke to them (now the Gibeonites were not of the sons of Israel but of the remnant of the Amorites, and [a]the sons of Israel [1]made a covenant with them, but Saul had sought to [2]kill them in his zeal for the sons of Israel and Judah).
3 Thus David said to the Gibeonites, "What should I do for you? And how can I make atonement that you may bless [a]the inheritance of the LORD?"
4 Then the Gibeonites said to him, "[a]We have no *concern* of silver or gold with Saul or his house, nor is it for us to put any man to death in Israel." And he said, "I will do for you whatever you say."
5 So they said to the king, "[a]The man who consumed us and who planned [1]to exterminate us from remaining within any border of Israel,
6 let seven men from his sons be given to us, and we will [1]hang them [a]before the LORD in Gibeah of Saul, [b]the chosen of the LORD." And the king said, "I will give *them*."
7 But the king spared [a]Mephibosheth, the son of Jonathan the son of Saul, [b]because of the oath of the LORD which was between them, between David and Saul's son Jonathan.
8 So the king took the two sons of [a]Rizpah the daughter of Aiah, Armoni and Mephibosheth whom she had borne to Saul, and the five sons of [1b]Merab the daughter of Saul, whom she had borne to Adriel the son of Barzillai the [c]Meholathite.
9 Then he gave them into the hands of the Gibeonites, and they [1]hanged them in the mountain before the LORD, so that the seven of them fell together; and they were put to death in the first days of harvest at [a]the beginning of barley harvest.
10 [a]And Rizpah the daughter of Aiah took sackcloth and spread it for herself on the rock, from the beginning of harvest until [1]it rained on them from the sky; and [b]she [2]allowed neither the birds of the sky to rest on them by day nor the beasts of the field by night.
11 When it was told David what Rizpah the daughter of Aiah, the concubine of Saul, had done,
12 then David went and took [a]the bones of Saul and the bones of Jonathan his son from the men of Jabesh-gilead, who had

23 [a]2 Sam 8:16-18; 1 Kin 4:3-6

24 [a]1 Kin 4:3

25 [a]1 Kin 4:4

21:1 [a]Gen 12:10; 26:1; 42:5 [b]Num 27:21

2 [1]Lit *had sworn to* [2]Lit *smite* [a]Josh 9:3, 15-20

3 [a]1 Sam 26:19; 2 Sam 20:19

4 [a]Num 35:31, 32

5 [1]Lit *against us that we should be exterminated* [a]2 Sam 21:1

6 [1]Lit *expose them* [a]Num 25:4 [b]1 Sam 10:24

7 [a]2 Sam 4:4; 9:10 [b]1 Sam 18:3; 20:12-17; 23:18; 2 Sam 9:1-7

8 [1]So Gr and Heb mss [a]2 Sam 3:7 [b]1 Sam 18:19 [c]1 Kin 19:16

9 [1]Lit *exposed them* [a]Ex 9:31, 32

10 [1]Lit *water was poured* [2]Lit *gave* [a]Deut 21:23 [b]1 Sam 17:44, 46

12 [a]1 Sam 31:11-13

12 [b]Josh 17:11 [c]1 Sam 31:10 [d]1 Sam 31:3, 4

stolen them from the open square of [b]Beth-shan, [c]where the
Philistines had hanged them on the day [d]the Philistines struck
down Saul in Gilboa.

13 [1]Lit *exposed*

13 He brought up the bones of Saul and the bones of Jonathan
his son from there, and they gathered the bones of those who
had been [1]hanged.

14 [a]Josh 18:28 [b]Josh 7:26; 2 Sam 24:25

14 They buried the bones of Saul and Jonathan his son in the
country of Benjamin in [a]Zela, in the grave of Kish his father;
thus they did all that the king commanded, and after that [b]God
was moved by prayer for the land.

15 [a]2 Sam 5:17-25

15 Now when [a]the Philistines were at war again with Israel, 1 Chronicles 20:4
David went down and his servants with him; and as they fought
against the Philistines, David became weary.

16 [1]Heb *Raphah* [2]Lit *and he was* [3]Lit *said* [a]Num 13:22, 28; Josh 15:14; 2 Sam 21:18-22

16 Then Ishbi-benob, who was [a]among the descendants of the
[1]giant, the weight of whose spear was three hundred *shekels* of
bronze in weight, [2]was girded with a new *sword*, and he
[3]intended to kill David.

17 [a]2 Sam 20:6-10 [b]2 Sam 18:3 [c]2 Sam 22:29 1 Kin 11:36

17 But [a]Abishai the son of Zeruiah helped him, and struck the
Philistine and killed him. Then the men of David swore to him,
saying, "[b]You shall not go out again with us to battle, so that
you do not extinguish [c]the lamp of Israel."

18 [1]Heb *Raphah* [a]1 Chr 20:4-8 [b]1 Chr 11:29; 27:11

18 [a]Now it came about after this that there was war again with
the Philistines at Gob; then [b]Sibbecai the Hushathite struck
down Saph, who was among the descendants of the [1]giant.

19 [1]Lit *smote* [2]In 1 Chr 20:5, *Lahmi, the brother of Goliath* [a]1 Sam 17:7

19 There was war with the Philistines again at Gob, and Elhanan
the son of Jaare-oregim the Bethlehemite [1]killed [2]Goliath the
Gittite, [a]the shaft of whose spear was like a weaver's beam.

20 [1]Heb *Raphah* [a]2 Sam 21:16, 18

20 There was war at Gath again, where there was a man of
great stature who had six fingers on each hand and six toes on
each foot, twenty-four in number; and he also had been born
[a]to the [1]giant.

22 [1]Heb *Raphah* [a]1 Chr 20:8

21 When he defied Israel, Jonathan the son of Shimei, David's
brother, struck him down.
22 [a]These four were born to the [1]giant in Gath, and they fell
by the hand of David and by the hand of his servants.

22:1 [1]Lit *palm* [a]Ps 18:2-50 [b]Ex 15:1; Deut 31:30

Chapter 22 Theme ________________________

2 [1]Lit *crag* [a]1 Sam 23:25; 24:2; Ps 31:3; 71:3

22 [a]And David spoke [b]the words of this song to the LORD
in the day that the LORD delivered him from the [1]hand
of all his enemies and from the [1]hand of Saul.

3 [1]Lit *God of my rock* [a]Deut 32:4, 37; 1 Sam 2:2 [b]Gen 15:1; Deut 33:29 [c]Luke 1:69 [d]Ps 9:9

2 He said, Psalm 18
"[a]The LORD is my [1]rock and my fortress and my deliverer;
3 [1a]My God, my rock, in whom I take refuge,
My [b]shield and [c]the horn of my salvation, my stronghold
and [d]my refuge;
My savior, You save me from violence.

4 [a]Ps 48:1; 96:4

4 "I call upon the LORD, [a]who is worthy to be praised,
And I am saved from my enemies.

5 [1]Heb *Belial* [2]Or *terrified* [a]Ps 93:4; Jon 2:3 [b]Ps 69:14, 15

5 "For [a]the waves of death encompassed me;
[b]The torrents of [1]destruction [2]overwhelmed me;

6 [a]The cords of [1]Sheol surrounded me;
The snares of death confronted me.
7 "[a]In my distress I called upon the LORD,
Yes, I [1]cried to my God;
And from His temple He heard my voice,
And my cry for help *came* into His ears.
8 "Then [a]the earth shook and quaked,
[b]The foundations of heaven were trembling
And were shaken, because He was angry.
9 "Smoke went up [1]out of His nostrils,
[a]Fire from His mouth devoured;
[b]Coals were kindled by it.
10 "He bowed the heavens also, and came down
With [a]thick darkness under His feet.
11 "[a]And He rode on a cherub and flew;
And He [1]appeared on [b]the wings of the wind.
12 "[a]And He made darkness [1]canopies around Him,
A mass of waters, thick clouds of the sky.
13 "From the brightness before Him
[a]Coals of fire were kindled.
14 "[a]The LORD thundered from heaven,
And the Most High uttered His voice.
15 "[a]And He sent out arrows, and scattered them,
Lightning, and [1]routed them.
16 "Then the channels of the sea appeared,
The foundations of the world were [1]laid bare
By the rebuke of the LORD,
[a]At the blast of the breath of His nostrils.
17 "[a]He sent from on high, He took me;
[b]He drew me out of many waters.
18 "He delivered me from my strong enemy,
From those who hated me, for they were too strong for me.
19 "They confronted me in the day of my calamity,
[a]But the LORD was my support.
20 "[a]He also brought me forth into a broad place;
He rescued me, [b]because He delighted in me.
21 "[a]The LORD has rewarded me according to my
righteousness;
[b]According to the cleanness of my hands He has
recompensed me.
22 "[a]For I have kept the ways of the LORD,
And have not acted wickedly against my God.
23 "[a]For all His ordinances *were* before me,
And *as for* His statutes, I did not depart from [1]them.
24 "[a]I was also [1]blameless toward Him,
And I kept myself from my iniquity.
25 "[a]Therefore the LORD has recompensed me according to my
righteousness,
According to my cleanness before His eyes.
26 "[a]With the [1]kind You show Yourself [1]kind,
With the [2]blameless You show Yourself [2]blameless;

6 [1]I.e. the nether world [a]Ps 116:3
7 [1]Or *called* [a]Ps 116:4; 120:1
8 [a]Judg 5:4; Ps 97:4 [b]Job 26:11
9 [1]Or *in His wrath* [a]Ps 97:3; Heb 12:29 [b]2 Sam 22:13
10 [a]Ex 19:16; 1 Kin 8:12; Ps 97:2; Nah 1:3
11 [1]Many mss read *sped* [a]2 Sam 6:2 [b]Ps 104:3
12 [1]Or *pavilions* [a]Job 36:29
13 [a]2 Sam 22:9
14 [a]Job 37:2-5; Ps 29:3
15 [1]Lit *confused* [a]Deut 32:23; Josh 10:10; 1 Sam 7:10
16 [1]Or *uncovered* [a]Ex 15:8; Nah 1:4
17 [a]Ps 144:7 [b]Ex 2:10
19 [a]Ps 23:4
20 [a]Ps 31:8; 118:5 [b]2 Sam 15:26
21 [a]1 Sam 26:23; 1 Kin 8:32 [b]Ps 24:4
22 [a]Gen 18:19; Ps 128:1; Prov 8:32
23 [1]Lit *it* [a]Deut 6:6-9; Ps 119:30, 102
24 [1]Lit *complete;* or *having integrity* [a]Gen 6:9; 7:1; Eph 1:4; Col 1:21, 22
25 [a]2 Sam 22:21
26 [1]Or *loyal* [2]Lit *complete;* or *having integrity* [a]Matt 5:7

27 [a]With the pure You show Yourself pure,
[b]And with the perverted You show Yourself [1]astute.
28 "[a]And You save an afflicted people;
[b]But Your eyes are on the haughty *whom* You abase.
29 "[a]For You are my lamp, O LORD;
And the LORD illumines my darkness.
30 "[a]For by You I can [1]run upon a troop;
By my God I can leap over a wall.
31 "[a]As for God, His way is [1]blameless;
[b]The word of the LORD is tested;
[c]He is a shield to all who take refuge in Him.
32 "[a]For who is God, besides the LORD?
[b]And who is a rock, besides our God?
33 "[a]God is my strong fortress;
And He [1]sets the [2]blameless in [3]His way.
34 "[a]He makes [1]my feet like hinds' *feet,*
[b]And sets me on my high places.
35 "[a]He trains my hands for battle,
[b]So that my arms can bend a bow of bronze.
36 "You have also given me [a]the shield of Your salvation,
And Your [1]help makes me great.
37 "[a]You enlarge my steps under me,
And my [1]feet have not slipped.
38 "I pursued my enemies and [a]destroyed them,
And I did not turn back until they were consumed.
39 "And I have devoured them and shattered them, so that
they did not rise;
And [a]they fell under my feet.
40 "For You have girded me with strength for battle;
You have [1]subdued under me [a]those who rose up against me.
41 "You have also [a]made my enemies turn *their* backs to me,
And I [1]destroyed those who hated me.
42 "[a]They looked, but there was none to save;
[b]*Even* to the LORD, but He did not answer them.
43 "[a]Then I pulverized them as the dust of the earth;
[b]I crushed *and* stamped them as the mire of the streets.
44 "[a]You have also delivered me from the contentions of my
people;
[b]You have kept me as head of the nations;
[c]A people whom I have not known serve me.
45 "[a]Foreigners pretend obedience to me;
As soon as they hear, they obey me.
46 "Foreigners [1]lose heart,
[a]And [2]come trembling out of their [3]fortresses.
47 "The LORD lives, and blessed be my rock;
And exalted be [1][a]God, the rock of my salvation,
48 [a]The God who executes vengeance for me,
[b]And brings down peoples under me,
49 Who also brings me out from my enemies;
You even lift me above [a]those who rise up against me;
[b]You rescue me from the violent man.

27 [1]Lit *twisted* [a]Matt 5:8; 1 John 3:3 [b]Lev 26:23, 24; Rom 1:28
28 [a]Ex 3:7, 8; Ps 72:12, 13 [b]Is 2:11, 12, 17; 5:15
29 [a]2 Sam 21:17; 1 Kin 11:36; Ps 27:1
30 [1]Or *crush a troop* [a]2 Sam 5:6-8
31 [1]Lit *complete;* or *having integrity* [a]Deut 32:4; Matt 5:48 [b]Ps 12:6; 119:140; Prov 30:5 [c]2 Sam 22:3; Ps 84:9
32 [a]1 Sam 2:2 [b]2 Sam 22:2
33 [1]Or *sets free* [2]Lit *complete;* or *having integrity* [3]Another reading is *my* [a]2 Sam 22:2; Ps 31:3, 4
34 [1]Another reading is *His* [a]2 Sam 2:18; Hab 3:19 [b]Deut 32:13
35 [a]Ps 144:1 [b]Job 20:24
36 [1]Lit *answering* [a]Eph 6:16, 17
37 [1]Lit *ankles* [a]2 Sam 22:20; Prov 4:12
38 [a]Ex 15:9
39 [a]Mal 4:3
40 [1]Lit *caused to bow down* [a]Ps 44:5
41 [1]Or *silenced* [a]Ex 23:27; Josh 10:24
42 [a]Is 17:7, 8 [b]1 Sam 28:6; Is 1:15
43 [a]2 Kin 13:7 [b]Is 10:6; Mic 7:10
44 [a]2 Sam 3:1; 19:9, 14 [b]2 Sam 8:1-14 [c]Is 55:5
45 [a]Ps 66:3; 81:15
46 [1]Lit *languish* [2]Lit *gird themselves* [3]Lit *fastnesses* [a]1 Sam 14:11; Mic 7:17
47 [1]Lit *the God of the rock* [a]2 Sam 22:3; Ps 89:26
48 [a]1 Sam 24:12; 25:39; 2 Sam 4:8; Ps 94:1 [b]Ps 144:2
49 [a]Ps 44:5 [b]Ps 140:1, 4, 11

50 "[a]Therefore I will give thanks to You, O LORD, among the
nations,
And I will sing praises to Your name.
51 "[a]*He* is a tower of [1]deliverance to His king,
And [b]shows lovingkindness to His anointed,
[c]To David and his [2]descendants forever."

Chapter 23 Theme ___________________________________

23 Now these are the last words of David.
David the son of Jesse declares,
[a]The man who was raised on high declares,
[b]The anointed of the God of Jacob,
And the sweet psalmist of Israel,
2 "[a]The Spirit of the LORD spoke by me,
And His word was on my tongue.
3 "The God of Israel said,
[a]The Rock of Israel spoke to me,
'[b]He who rules over men righteously,
[c]Who rules in the fear of God,
4 [a]Is as the light of the morning *when* the sun rises,
A morning without clouds,
When the tender grass *springs* out of the earth,
Through sunshine after rain.'
5 "Truly is not my house so with God?
For [a]He has made an everlasting covenant with me,
Ordered in all things, and secured;
For all my salvation and all *my* desire,
Will He not indeed make *it* grow?
6 "[a]But the worthless, every one of them will be thrust away
like thorns,
Because they cannot be taken in hand;
7 But the man who touches them
Must be [1]armed with iron and the shaft of a spear,
And [a]they will be completely burned with fire in *their*
[2]place."

1 Chronicles 11

8 [a]These are the names of the mighty men whom David had:
Josheb-basshebeth a Tahchemonite, chief of the [1]captains, he
was *called* Adino the Eznite, because of eight hundred slain *by*
him at one time;
9 and after him was Eleazar the son of [a]Dodo the [b]Ahohite,
one of the three mighty men with David when they [1]defied the
Philistines who were gathered there to battle and the men of
Israel had [2]withdrawn.
10 [a]He arose and struck the Philistines until his hand was
weary and [1]clung to the sword, and [b]the LORD brought about a
great [2]victory that day; and the people returned after him only
to strip *the slain.*
11 Now after him was Shammah the son of Agee a [a]Hararite. And
the Philistines were gathered [1]into a troop where there was a plot
of ground full of lentils, and the people fled from the Philistines.

50 [a]Rom 15:9

51 [1]I.e. victories; lit *salvation* [2]Lit *seed* [a]Ps 144:10 [b]Ps 89:24 [c]2 Sam 7:12-16

23:1 [a]2 Sam 7:8, 9; Ps 78:70, 71 [b]1 Sam 16:12, 13; Ps 89:20

2 [a]Matt 22:43; 2 Pet 1:21

3 [a]2 Sam 22:2, 3, 32 [b]Ps 72:1-3; Is 11:1-5 [c]2 Chr 19:7, 9

4 [a]Judg 5:31; Ps 72:6

5 [a]2 Sam 7:12-16; Ps 89:29; Is 55:3

6 [a]Matt 13:41

7 [1]Lit *filled* [2]Lit *sitting* [a]Matt 3:10; 13:30; Heb 6:8

8 [1]Or *three* [a]1 Chr 11:11-47

9 [1]Lit *reproached* [2]Lit *gone up* [a]1 Chr 27:4 [b]1 Chr 8:4

10 [1]Lit *his hand clung* [2]Lit *salvation* [a]1 Chr 11:13 [b]1 Sam 11:13; 19:5

11 [1]Possibly, *at Lehi* [a]2 Sam 23:33

12 But he took his stand in the midst of the plot, defended it
and struck the Philistines; and [a]the LORD brought about a great
[1]victory.
13 Then three of the thirty chief men went down and came to
David in the harvest time to the [a]cave of Adullam, while the
troop of the Philistines was camping in [b]the valley of Rephaim.
14 David was then [a]in the stronghold, while the garrison of
the Philistines was then in Bethlehem.
15 [a]David had a craving and said, "Oh that someone would give
me water to drink from the well of Bethlehem which is by the
gate!"
16 [a]So the three mighty men broke through the camp of the
Philistines, and drew water from the well of Bethlehem which
was by the gate, and took *it* and brought *it* to David. Nevertheless he would not drink it, but [b]poured it out to the LORD;
17 and he said, "Be it far from me, O LORD, that I should do
this. [a]*Shall I drink* the blood of the men who went in *jeopardy*
of their lives?" Therefore he would not drink it. These things
the three mighty men did.
18 [a]Abishai, the brother of Joab, the son of Zeruiah, was [b]chief
of the [1]thirty. And he swung his spear against three hundred
[2]and killed *them,* and had a name as well as the three.
19 He was most honored of the thirty, therefore he became
their commander; however, he did not attain to the three.
20 Then [a]Benaiah the son of Jehoiada, the son of a valiant
man of [b]Kabzeel, who had done mighty deeds, [1]killed the [2]two
sons of Ariel of Moab. He also went down and killed a lion in
the middle of a pit on a snowy day.
21 He [1]killed an Egyptian, [2]an impressive man. Now the
Egyptian *had* a spear in his hand, but he went down to him
with a club and snatched the spear from the Egyptian's hand
and killed him with his own spear.
22 These *things* [a]Benaiah the son of Jehoiada did, and had a
name as well as the three mighty men.
23 He was honored among the thirty, but he did not attain to
the three. And David appointed him over his guard.
24 [a]Asahel the brother of Joab was among the thirty; Elhanan
the son of Dodo of Bethlehem,
25 [a]Shammah the [b]Harodite, Elika the Harodite,
26 Helez the Paltite, Ira the son of Ikkesh the [a]Tekoite,
27 Abiezer the [a]Anathothite, Mebunnai the Hushathite,
28 Zalmon the Ahohite, Maharai the [a]Netophathite,
29 [a]Heleb the son of Baanah the Netophathite, Ittai the son of
Ribai of [b]Gibeah of the sons of Benjamin,
30 Benaiah a [a]Pirathonite, Hiddai of the brooks of [b]Gaash,
31 Abi-albon the Arbathite, Azmaveth the [a]Barhumite,
32 Eliahba the [a]Shaalbonite, the sons of Jashen, Jonathan,
33 [a]Shammah the Hararite, Ahiam the son of Sharar the Ararite,
34 Eliphelet the son of Ahasbai, the son of [a]the Maacathite,
[b]Eliam the son of [c]Ahithophel the Gilonite,
35 [a]Hezro the [b]Carmelite, Paarai the Arbite,

12 [1]Lit *salvation* [a]2 Sam 23:10
13 [a]1 Sam 22:1 [b]2 Sam 5:18
14 [a]1 Sam 22:4, 5
15 [a]1 Chr 11:17
16 [a]1 Chr 11:18 [b]Gen 35:14
17 [a]Lev 17:10
18 [1]So two Heb mss and Syriac; M.T. *three* [2]Lit *slain ones* [a]2 Sam 10:10, 14; 18:2 [b]1 Chr 11:20, 21
20 [1]Lit *smote* [2]Or *two lion-like heroes* [a]2 Sam 8:18; 20:23 [b]Josh 15:21
21 [1]Lit *smote* [2]Lit *a man of appearance*
22 [a]2 Sam 23:20
24 [a]2 Sam 2:18; 1 Chr 27:7
25 [a]1 Chr 11:27 [b]Judg 7:1
26 [a]2 Sam 14:2
27 [a]Josh 21:18
28 [a]2 Kin 25:23
29 [a]1 Chr 11:30 [b]Josh 18:28
30 [a]Judg 12:13, 15 [b]Josh 24:30
31 [a]2 Sam 3:16
32 [a]Josh 19:42
33 [a]2 Sam 23:11
34 [a]2 Sam 10:6, 8; 20:14 [b]2 Sam 11:3 [c]2 Sam 15:12
35 [a]1 Chr 11:37 [b]Josh 15:55

36 Igal the son of Nathan of [a]Zobah, Bani the Gadite,
37 Zelek the Ammonite, Naharai the [a]Beerothite, armor bearers
of Joab the son of Zeruiah,
38 Ira the [a]Ithrite, Gareb the Ithrite,
39 [a]Uriah the Hittite; thirty-seven in all.

Chapter 24 Theme ______________________________

1 Chronicles 21

24 [a]Now [b]again the anger of the LORD burned against Israel,
and it incited David against them to say, "[c]Go, number
Israel and Judah."
2 The king said to Joab the commander of the army who was
with him, "Go about now through all the tribes of Israel, [a]from
Dan to Beersheba, and [1]register the people, that I may know the
number of the people."
3 But Joab said to the king, "[a]Now may the LORD your God
add to the people a hundred times as many as they are, while
the eyes of my lord the king *still* see; but why does my lord the
king delight in this thing?"
4 Nevertheless, the king's word prevailed against Joab and
against the commanders of the army. So Joab and the
commanders of the army went out from the presence of the
king to [1]register the people of Israel.
5 They crossed the Jordan and camped in [a]Aroer, on the right
side of the city that is in the middle of the valley of Gad and
toward [b]Jazer.
6 Then they came to Gilead and to [1]the land of Tahtim-hodshi,
and they came to Dan-jaan and around to [a]Sidon,
7 and came to the [a]fortress of Tyre and to all the cities of the
[b]Hivites and of the Canaanites, and they went out to the south
of Judah, *to* [c]Beersheba.
8 So when they had gone about through the whole land, they
came to Jerusalem at the end of nine months and twenty days.
9 And Joab gave [a]the number of the [1]registration of the
people to the king; and there were in Israel [b]eight hundred
thousand valiant men who drew the sword, and the men of
Judah were five hundred thousand men.
10 Now [a]David's heart [1]troubled him after he had numbered
the people. So David said to the LORD, "[b]I have sinned greatly
in what I have done. But now, O LORD, please [2]take away the
iniquity of Your servant, for [c]I have acted very foolishly."
11 When David arose in the morning, the word of the LORD
came to [a]the prophet Gad, David's [b]seer, saying,
12 "Go and speak to David, 'Thus the LORD says, "I am offering
you three things; choose for yourself one of them, which I will
do to you."'"
13 So Gad came to David and told him, and said to him, "Shall
[a]seven years of famine come to you in your land? Or will you flee
three months before your foes while they pursue you? Or shall
there be three days' pestilence in your land? Now consider and
see what answer I shall return to Him who sent me."

36 [a]2 Sam 8:3
37 [a]2 Sam 4:2
38 [a]1 Chr 2:53
39 [a]2 Sam 11:3, 6
24:1 [a]1 Chr 21:1 [b]2 Sam 21:1, 2 [c]1 Chr 27:23, 24
2 [1]Lit *muster* [a]Judg 20:1; 2 Sam 3:10
3 [a]Deut 1:11
4 [1]Lit *muster*
5 [a]Deut 2:36; Josh 13:9, 16 [b]Num 21:32; 32:35
6 [1]Or *Kadesh in the land of the Hittite* [a]Josh 19:28; Judg 1:31
7 [a]Josh 19:29 [b]Josh 11:3; Judg 3:3 [c]Gen 21:22-33
9 [1]Lit *muster* [a]Num 1:44-46 [b]1 Chr 21:5
10 [1]Lit *smote* [2]Lit *cause to pass away* [a]1 Sam 24:5 [b]2 Sam 12:13 [c]1 Sam 13:13; 2 Chr 16:9
11 [a]1 Sam 22:5; 1 Chr 29:29 [b]1 Sam 9:9
13 [a]1 Chr 21:12; Ezek 14:21

14 [a]Ps 51:1; 130:4, 7

14 Then David said to Gad, “I am in great distress. Let us now
fall into the hand of the LORD [a]for His mercies are great, but do
not let me fall into the hand of man.”
15 So [a]the LORD [1]sent a pestilence upon Israel from the
morning until the appointed time, and seventy thousand men
of the people [b]from Dan to Beersheba died.
16 [a]When the angel stretched out his hand toward Jerusalem
to destroy it, [b]the LORD relented from the calamity and said to
the angel who destroyed the people, “It is enough! Now relax
your hand!” And the angel of the LORD was by the threshing
floor of Araunah the Jebusite.
17 Then David spoke to the LORD when he saw the angel who
was striking down the people, and said, “Behold, [a]it is I who
have sinned, and it is I who have done wrong; but [b]these
sheep, what have they done? Please let Your hand be against
me and against my father’s house.”
18 So Gad came to David that day and said to him, “[a]Go up,
erect an altar to the LORD on the threshing floor of [1]Araunah the
Jebusite.”
19 David went up according to the word of Gad, just as the
LORD had commanded.
20 Araunah looked down and saw the king and his servants
crossing over toward him; and Araunah went out and bowed
his face to the ground before the king.
21 Then Araunah said, “Why has my lord the king come to his
servant?” And David said, “To buy the threshing floor from
you, in order to build an altar to the LORD, [a]that the plague may
be held back from the people.”
22 Araunah said to David, “Let my lord the king take and offer
up what is good in his sight. Look, [a]the oxen for the burnt
offering, the threshing sledges and the yokes of the oxen for
the wood.
23 “Everything, O king, Araunah gives to the king.” And Araunah
said to the king, “May the LORD your God [a]accept you.”
24 However, the king said to Araunah, “No, but I will surely
buy *it* from you for a price, for [a]I will not offer burnt offerings
to the LORD my God [1]which cost me nothing.” So [b]David bought
the threshing floor and the oxen for fifty shekels of silver.
25 David built there an altar to the LORD and offered burnt
offerings and peace offerings. [a]Thus the LORD was moved by
prayer for the land, and the plague was held back from Israel.

15 [1]Lit *gave* [a]1 Chr 21:14; 27:24 [b]2 Sam 24:2

16 [a]Ex 12:23; 2 Kin 19:35; Acts 12:23 [b]Ex 32:14; 1 Sam 15:11

17 [a]2 Sam 24:10 [b]2 Sam 7:8; Ps 74:1

18 [1]In 2 Chr 3:1, *Ornan* [a]1 Chr 21:18

21 [a]Num 16:44-50

22 [a]1 Sam 6:14; 1 Kin 19:21

23 [a]Ezek 20:40, 41

24 [1]Lit *gratuitously* [a]Mal 1:13, 14 [b]1 Chr 21:24, 25

25 [a]2 Sam 21:14

INSIGHT

This purchase by David is significant. Compare this with 1 Chronicles 21:18-30 and 2 Chronicles 3:1. To whom does the Temple Mount in Jerusalem belong?

972 B.C.

Theme of 2 Samuel:

Segment Divisions		Chapter Themes
		1
		2
		3
		4
		5
		6
		7
		8
		9
		10
		11
		12
		13
		14
		15
		16
		17
		18
		19
		20
		21
		22
		23
		24

Author:

Date:

Purpose:

Key Words:

1 KINGS מלכים א

M^e^LAKHIM ALEPH

David—the warrior, the great king, the man whom God both loved and chastised—was getting old. By the end of his life many people were vying for his throne. First Kings, which records the final events of David's life, marks the beginning of a new era for Israel, one that opens in resplendent glory and ends with apostasy.

The account of the kings who followed David is full of sobering lessons. It is an important chapter in the history of Israel and their God, who made them a people of His own possession.

We don't know who wrote 1 Kings. We only know that this is God's Word preserved "for our instruction, so that through perseverance and the encouragement of the Scriptures we might have hope" (Romans 15:4).

THINGS TO DO

General Instructions

Chapter 12 of 1 Kings records a dramatic, pivotal point in the history of Israel. Therefore, as we study 1 Kings, we will divide it into two segments with two sets of instructions.

Chapters 1–11

Read through this first segment of 1 Kings one chapter at a time.

1. Remember, you are studying the lives of real people. Observe the opportunities God gives them, His instructions to them, and how they respond. Watch when they succeed and when they fail; note why—and learn! Ask God to speak to your heart. In the margin of each chapter, if applicable, make a list of these two things: "Lessons for Life" (LFL) and "Insights about God" (△). Your insights on God will be most enlightening.

2. Mark in a distinctive way the following words and phrases: *word* (or any reference to *the word of the Lord), heart, pray (cry, cried), covenant, wisdom (wise), command (commandments), prophet, promise (promised), high places, house* (when it refers to God's house), and *sin (sinned)*. The first occurrence of the word *sin* is in chapter 8.

   a. List the key words on an index card and use it as a bookmark while you study. You might want to mark the beginning of a king's reign with a crown.

   b. When you read *"the Lord said,"* highlight or underline what the Lord said. Then underline anything you want to remember.

3. The main characters of these first chapters are David and Solomon.

   a. When you come to Solomon's reign, read Deuteronomy 7:2-6 and 17:14-20 to understand Solomon's actions as he took over the kingdom. Remember that sin was to be judged and murderers were to be put to death; otherwise the land would be polluted.

   b. Second Chronicles 1 through 9 is an excellent cross-reference on 1 Kings 1 through 11.

4. Mark every reference to time with a 🕒 and double-underline in green every geographical reference.

5. After you finish reading a chapter, record the theme or subject of that chapter in your Bible and on the appropriate place on 1 KINGS AT A GLANCE on page 600.

6. When you finish chapter 11, see if any of the first 11 chapters can be grouped under a common theme or as part of an event: e.g. the building of the temple. These are called segment divisions and can be recorded in the designated place on 1 KINGS AT A GLANCE.

Chapters 12–22

1. As you read chapter 12, study the chart ISRAEL'S DIVISION AND CAPTIVITY on page 576. Note the division of the kingdom, which occurred in 931 B.C. From this point on, whenever "Israel" is used, you will need to distinguish whether it is a reference to the ten tribes of the northern kingdom (which it usually will be) or to the nation of Israel as a whole.

2. Add *according to* to your key word list. When you come to this phrase, note what was "according to" what. You will gain some important insights. Also add *did evil, Elijah,* and *Elisha.* Mark your key words in this section.

3. Watch for insights the Lord gives you about Himself, His ways, and about life in general through the example of the kings and God's people. Record these in the margin under "Insights about God" or "Lessons for Life" just as you did in the first segment of 1 Kings.

4. When you read of a king or another key figure, consult THE HISTORICAL CHART OF THE KINGS AND PROPHETS OF ISRAEL AND JUDAH on pages 651 through 653. You might want to mark the beginning of each king's reign with a crown.

5. Each time you finish reading about a king, record your insights on the chart THE KINGS OF ISRAEL AND JUDAH on pages 654 and 655. Also fill in the information on Solomon.

   a. Make sure you note on the chart whether each king ruled over the northern kingdom (Israel) or southern kingdom (Judah) and whether they did good or evil.

   b. Mark every reference to time.

6. Compare 17:1 with Deuteronomy 28:1-2,12,15,23-24 and James 5:17-18. What could be the scriptural basis for Elijah's prayer and word to Ahab? Think about it.

7. Record the chapter themes and any segment divisions you see on 1 KINGS AT A GLANCE. Also fill in any other pertinent information. Choose a theme for 1 Kings that best describes what happens during this period in Israel's history.

8. Second Kings is a continuation of 1 Kings. You will want to study it next.

Things to Think About

1. Have you seen God's graciousness and long-suffering? God doesn't retaliate; rather, He seeks to bring us to repentance and obedience. What does this provoke in your heart? And how should you live if God is in control of your life?

2. Have you seen how a person can start well in his walk with the Lord and then turn away? What do you think causes this? What can you do to prevent this in your own life? Go back and review what you have listed in the margin regarding the kings and their relationship with the Lord. What lessons have you learned that you can apply to your life?

3. Did you notice the sovereignty of God—how He turns hearts, directs spirits, raises up and puts down kings and others in order to accomplish His purpose and will? Are you living in the light of this truth about God?

4. Have you been thinking that you had to be absolutely perfect before God could use you? Did you see how Elijah was a man "of like passions" just like you and yet God used him? What have you learned about this in 1 Kings? When David's life was over, didn't God call David a man after His own heart? Frailties and all, David was a man of God because he believed and obeyed God.

David's Family Tree Related to 1 Kings

David					According to 2 Samuel 5:13-16; 1 Chronicles 3:1-9; 14:3-7, there were fourteen other sons:
Amnon (killed by Absalom)	**Chileab** (Daniel) (died in youth)	**Absalom** (killed by Joab)	**Adonijah** (deposed by Solomon and killed by Benaiah, son of Jehoiada, by order of Solomon)	**Solomon**	**Shephatiah, Ithream, Eliphelet, Shimea, Shobab, Nathan, Ibhar, Elishama, Eliphelet, Nogah, Nepheg, Japhia, Eliada, Elishama.**

Also see chart on page 511.

Chapter 1 Theme ____________________

972 B.C.

1 Now King David was old, advanced in age; and they covered
him with clothes, but he could not keep warm.
2 So his servants said to him, "Let them seek a young virgin for
my lord the king, and let her [1]attend the king and become his
nurse; and let her lie in your bosom, that my lord the king may
keep warm."
3 So they searched for a beautiful girl throughout all the
territory of Israel, and found Abishag the [a]Shunammite, and
brought her to the king.
4 The girl was very beautiful; and she became the king's nurse
and served him, but the king did not [1]cohabit with her.
5 Now [a]Adonijah the son of Haggith exalted himself, saying,
"I will be king." So [b]he prepared for himself chariots and horsemen with fifty men to run before him.
6 His father had never [1]crossed him at any time by asking,
"Why have you done so?" And he was also a very handsome
man, and [2a]he was born after Absalom.
7 [1]He had conferred with [a]Joab the son of Zeruiah and with
[b]Abiathar the priest; and following [c]Adonijah they helped him.
8 But [a]Zadok the priest, [b]Benaiah the son of Jehoiada, [c]Nathan
the prophet, [d]Shimei, Rei, and [e]the mighty men who belonged to
David, were not with Adonijah.
9 Adonijah sacrificed sheep and oxen and fatlings by the [1]stone
of Zoheleth, which is beside [a]En-rogel; and he invited all his
brothers, the king's sons, and all the men of Judah, the king's
servants.
10 But he did not invite Nathan the prophet, Benaiah, the
mighty men, and [a]Solomon his brother.
11 Then Nathan spoke to [a]Bathsheba the mother of Solomon,
saying, "Have you not heard that Adonijah the son of Haggith
has become king, and David our lord does not know *it?*
12 "So now come, please let me [a]give you counsel and save your
life and the life of your son Solomon.
13 "Go [1]at once to King David and say to him, 'Have you not,
my lord, O king, sworn to your maidservant, saying, "[a]Surely
Solomon your son shall be king after me, and he shall sit on my
throne"? Why then has Adonijah become king?'
14 "Behold, while you are still there speaking with the king, I
will come in after you and confirm your words."

1:2 [1]Lit *stand before*
3 [a]Josh 19:18; 1 Sam 28:4
4 [1]Lit *know her*
5 [a]2 Sam 3:4 [b]2 Sam 15:1
6 [1]Lit *pained him* [2]Lit *she gave him birth* [a]2 Sam 3:3, 4
7 [1]Lit *his words were* [a]1 Chr 11:6 [b]1 Sam 22:20, 23; 2 Sam 20:25 [c]1 Kin 2:22
8 [a]2 Sam 20:25; 1 Chr 16:39 [b]2 Sam 8:18 [c]2 Sam 12:1 [d]1 Kin 4:18 [e]2 Sam 23:8-39
9 [1]Or *Gliding* or *Serpent Stone* [a]Josh 15:7; 18:16; 2 Sam 17:17
10 [a]2 Sam 12:24
11 [a]2 Sam 12:24
12 [a]Prov 15:22
13 [1]Lit *and enter* [a]1 Kin 1:30; 1 Chr 22:9-13

15 So Bathsheba went in to the king in the bedroom. Now [a]the
king was very old, and Abishag the Shunammite was ministering
to the king.
16 Then Bathsheba bowed and prostrated herself [1]before the
king. And the king said, "What [2]do you wish?"
17 She said to him, "My lord, you swore to your maidservant by
the LORD your God, *saying,* '[a]Surely your son Solomon shall be
king after me and he shall sit on my throne.'
18 "Now, behold, Adonijah is king; and now, my lord the king,
you do not know *it.*
19 "[a]He has sacrificed oxen and fatlings and sheep in abundance,
and has invited all the sons of the king and Abiathar the priest
and Joab the commander of the army, but he has not invited
Solomon your servant.
20 "As for you now, my lord the king, the eyes of all Israel are
on you, to tell them who shall sit on the throne of my lord the
king after him.
21 "Otherwise it will come about, [a]as soon as my lord the king
sleeps with his fathers, that I and my son Solomon will be
considered [1]offenders."
22 Behold, while she was still speaking with the king, Nathan
the prophet came in.
23 They told the king, saying, "Here is Nathan the prophet."
And when he came in before the king, he prostrated himself
[1]before the king with his face to the ground.
24 Then Nathan said, "My lord the king, have you said,
'Adonijah shall be king after me, and he shall sit on my throne'?
25 "[a]For he has gone down today and has sacrificed oxen and
fatlings and sheep in abundance, and has invited all the king's
sons and the commanders of the army and Abiathar the priest,
and behold, they are eating and drinking before him; and they
say, '[b]*Long* live King Adonijah!'
26 "[a]But me, *even* me your servant, and Zadok the priest and
Benaiah the son of Jehoiada and your servant Solomon, he has
not invited.
27 "Has this thing been done by my lord the king, and you have
not shown to your [1]servants who should sit on the throne of
my lord the king after him?"
28 Then King David said, "Call Bathsheba to me." And she
came into the king's presence and stood before the king.
29 The king vowed and said, "[a]As the LORD lives, who has
redeemed my life from all distress,
30 surely as [a]I vowed to you by the LORD the God of Israel,
saying, 'Your son Solomon shall be king after me, and he shall
sit on my throne in my place'; I will indeed do so this day."
31 Then Bathsheba bowed with her face to the ground, and
prostrated herself [1]before the king and said, "[a]May my lord King
David live forever."
32 Then King David said, "Call to me [a]Zadok the priest, Nathan
the prophet, and Benaiah the son of Jehoiada." And they came
into the king's presence.

15 [a]1 Kin 1:1
16 [1]Lit *to* [2]Lit *to you*
17 [a]1 Kin 1:13
19 [a]1 Kin 1:9
21 [1]Lit *sinners* [a]Deut 31:16; 2 Sam 7:12; 1 Kin 2:10
23 [1]Lit *to*
25 [a]1 Kin 1:9 [b]1 Sam 10:24
26 [a]1 Kin 1:8, 10
27 [1]Some mss read *servant*
29 [a]2 Sam 4:9
30 [a]1 Kin 1:13, 17
31 [1]Lit *to* [a]Dan 2:4; 3:9
32 [a]1 Kin 1:8

33 The king said to them, "Take with you [a]the servants of your
lord, and have my son Solomon ride on my own mule, and
bring him down to [b]Gihon.
34 "Let Zadok the priest and Nathan the prophet [a]anoint him
there as king over Israel, and [b]blow the trumpet and say, '[c]*Long*
live King Solomon!'
35 "Then you shall come up after him, and he shall come and
sit on my throne and be king in my place; for I have appointed
him to be ruler over Israel and Judah."
36 Benaiah the son of Jehoiada answered the king and said,
"Amen! Thus may the LORD, the God of my lord the king, say.
37 "[a]As the LORD has been with my lord the king, so may He be
with Solomon, and [b]make his throne greater than the throne of
my lord King David!"
38 So [a]Zadok the priest, Nathan the prophet, Benaiah the son of
Jehoiada, [b]the Cherethites, and the Pelethites went down and had
Solomon ride on King David's mule, and brought him to [c]Gihon.
39 Zadok the priest then [a]took the horn of oil from the tent
and [b]anointed Solomon. Then they [c]blew the trumpet, and all
the people said, "[d]*Long* live King Solomon!"
40 All the people went up after him, and the people [1]were
playing on flutes and rejoicing with great joy, so that the earth
[2]shook at their noise.
41 Now Adonijah and all the guests who *were* with him heard
it as they finished eating. When Joab heard the sound of the
trumpet, he said, "Why [1]is the city making such an uproar?"
42 While he was still speaking, behold, [a]Jonathan the son of
Abiathar the priest came. Then Adonijah said, "Come in, for [b]you
are a valiant man and bring good news."
43 But Jonathan replied to Adonijah, "No! Our lord King David
has made Solomon king.
44 "The king has also sent with him Zadok the priest, Nathan the
prophet, Benaiah the son of Jehoiada, the Cherethites, and the
Pelethites; and they have made him ride on the king's mule.
45 "Zadok the priest and Nathan the prophet have anointed him
king in Gihon, and they have come up from there rejoicing, [a]so
that the city is in an uproar. This is the noise which you have
heard.
46 "Besides, [a]Solomon has even taken his seat on the throne of
the kingdom.
47 "Moreover, the king's servants came to bless our lord King
David, saying, 'May [a]your God make the name of Solomon better
than your name and his throne greater than your throne!' And
[b]the king bowed himself on the bed.
48 "The king has also said thus, 'Blessed be the LORD, the God of
Israel, who [a]has granted one to sit on my throne today while my
own eyes see *it*.'"
49 Then all the guests of Adonijah were terrified; and they arose
and each went on his way.
50 And Adonijah was afraid of Solomon, and he arose, went
and [a]took hold of the horns of the altar.

33 [a]2 Sam 20:6, 7 [b]2 Chr 32:30; 33:14
34 [a]1 Sam 10:1; 16:3, 12; 2 Sam 5:3; 1 Kin 19:16; 2 Kin 9:3 [b]2 Sam 15:10 [c]1 Kin 1:25
37 [a]Josh 1:5, 17; 1 Sam 20:13 [b]1 Kin 1:47
38 [a]1 Kin 1:8 [b]2 Sam 8:18 [c]1 Kin 1:33
39 [a]Ex 30:23-32; Ps 89:20 [b]1 Chr 29:22 [c]1 Kin 1:34 [d]1 Sam 10:24
40 [1]Lit *fluting* [2]Lit *was split*
41 [1]Lit *is the sound of the city an uproar*
42 [a]2 Sam 15:27, 36; 17:17 [b]2 Sam 18:27
45 [a]1 Kin 1:40
46 [a]1 Chr 29:23
47 [a]1 Kin 1:37 [b]Gen 47:31
48 [a]2 Sam 7:12; 1 Kin 3:6
50 [a]Ex 27:2; 30:10; 1 Kin 2:28

51 Now it was told Solomon, saying, “Behold, Adonijah is
afraid of King Solomon, for behold, he has taken hold of the
horns of the altar, saying, ‘Let King Solomon swear to me today
that he will not put his servant to death with the sword.’”
52 Solomon said, “If he is a worthy man, [a]not one of his hairs
will fall to the ground; but if wickedness is found in him, he
will die.”
53 So King Solomon sent, and they brought him down from the
altar. And he came and prostrated himself [1]before King Solomon,
and Solomon said to him, “Go to your house.”

Chapter 2 Theme ____________________

1 Chronicles 28:20

2 As David’s [1a]time to die drew near, he charged Solomon his
son, saying,
2 “[a]I am going the way of all the earth. [b]Be strong, therefore,
and [1]show yourself a man.
3 “Keep the charge of the LORD your God, to walk in His ways,
to keep His statutes, His commandments, His ordinances, and His
testimonies, [a]according to what is written in the Law of Moses,
that [b]you may succeed in all that you do and wherever you turn,
4 so that [a]the LORD may carry out His promise which He spoke
concerning me, saying, ‘[b]If your sons are careful of their way,
[c]to walk before Me in [1]truth with all their heart and with all
their soul, [2d]you shall not lack a man on the throne of Israel.’
5 “Now you also know what Joab the [a]son of Zeruiah did to me,
what he did to the two commanders of the armies of Israel, to
[b]Abner the son of Ner, and to [c]Amasa the son of Jether, whom
he killed; he also [1]shed the blood of war in peace. And he put the
blood of war on his belt [2]about his waist, and on his sandals
[3]on his feet.
6 “[a]So act according to your wisdom, and do not let his gray
hair go down to [1]Sheol in peace.
7 “But [a]show kindness to the sons of Barzillai the Gileadite,
and [b]let them be among those who eat at your table; [c]for they
[1]assisted me when I fled from Absalom your brother.
8 “Behold, [a]there is with you Shimei the son of Gera the
Benjamite, of Bahurim; now it was he who cursed me with a
[1]violent curse on the day I went to Mahanaim. But when [b]he
came down to me at the Jordan, I swore to him by the LORD,
saying, ‘I will not put you to death with the sword.’
9 “Now therefore, do not let him go unpunished, [a]for you are
a wise man; and you will know what you ought to do to him,
and you will bring his gray hair down to [1]Sheol with blood.”
10 Then [a]David slept with his fathers and was buried in [b]the city
of David.
11 [a]The days that David reigned over Israel *were* forty years:
[b]seven years he reigned in Hebron and thirty-three years he
reigned in Jerusalem.
12 And [a]Solomon sat on the throne of David his father, and his
kingdom was firmly established.

52 [a]1 Sam 14:45; 2 Sam 14:11; Acts 27:34

53 [1]Lit *to*

2:1 [1]Lit *days* [a]Gen 47:29; Deut 31:14

2 [1]Lit *become a man* [a]Josh 23:14 [b]Deut 31:7, 23; Josh 1:6, 7

3 [a]Deut 17:18-20 [b]1 Chr 22:12, 13

4 [1]Or *faithfulness* [2]Lit *there shall not be cast off to you a man from before Me* [a]2 Sam 7:25 [b]Ps 132:12 [c]2 Kin 20:3 [d]2 Sam 7:12, 13; 1 Kin 8:25; 9:5

5 [1]Lit *made* [2]Lit *that was about* [3]Lit *that were on* [a]2 Sam 2:13, 18 [b]2 Sam 3:27; 1 Kin 2:32 [c]2 Sam 20:10

6 [1]I.e. the nether world [a]1 Kin 2:9

7 [1]Lit *came near to* [a]2 Sam 19:31-38 [b]2 Sam 9:7, 10 [c]2 Sam 17:27-29

8 [1]Or *grievous* [a]2 Sam 16:5-8 [b]2 Sam 19:18-23

9 [1]I.e. the nether world [a]1 Kin 2:6

10 [a]Acts 2:29; 13:36 [b]2 Sam 5:7; 1 Kin 3:1

11 [a]2 Sam 5:4, 5; 1 Chr 3:4; 29:26, 27 [b]2 Sam 5:5

12 [a]1 Chr 29:23; 2 Chr 1:1

13 Now Adonijah the son of Haggith came to Bathsheba the
mother of Solomon. And she said, "[a]Do you come peacefully?"
And he said, "Peacefully."
14 Then he said, "I have something *to say* to you." And she
said, "Speak."
15 So he said, "You know that [a]the kingdom was mine and
[b]that all Israel [1]expected me to be king; [c]however, the kingdom
has turned about and become my brother's, [d]for it was his from
the LORD.
16 "Now I am making one request of you; do not [1]refuse me."
And she said to him, "Speak."
17 Then he said, "Please speak to Solomon the king, for he will
not [1]refuse you, that he may give me [a]Abishag the Shunammite
as a wife."
18 Bathsheba said, "Very well; I will speak to the king for you."
19 So Bathsheba went to King Solomon to speak to him for
Adonijah. And the king arose to meet her, bowed before her, and
sat on his throne; then he [a]had a throne set for the king's mother,
and [b]she sat on his right.
20 Then she said, "I am making one small request of you; [a]do
not [1]refuse me." And the king said to her, "Ask, my mother, for I
will not [2]refuse you."
21 So she said, "[a]Let Abishag the Shunammite be given to
Adonijah your brother as a wife."
22 King Solomon answered and said to his mother, "And why
are you asking Abishag the Shunammite for Adonijah? [a]Ask for
him also the kingdom—[b]for he is my older brother—even for
him, for [c]Abiathar the priest, and for Joab the son of Zeruiah!"
23 Then King Solomon swore by the LORD, saying, "May God
do so to me and more also, if Adonijah has [a]not spoken this word
against his own [1]life.
24 "Now therefore, as the LORD lives, who has established me and
set me on the throne of David my father and [a]who has made me
a house as He promised, surely Adonijah shall be put to death
today."
25 So King Solomon [a]sent Benaiah the son of Jehoiada; and he
fell upon him so that he died.
26 Then to Abiathar the priest the king said, "[a]Go to Anathoth
to your own field, [b]for you [1]deserve to die; but I will not put
you to death at this time, because [c]you carried the ark of the
Lord [2]GOD before my father David, and because [d]you were
afflicted in everything with which my father was afflicted."
27 So Solomon dismissed Abiathar from being priest to the
LORD, in order to fulfill [a]the word of the LORD, which He had
spoken concerning the house of Eli in Shiloh.
28 Now the news came to Joab, [a]for Joab had followed
Adonijah, [b]although he had not followed Absalom. And Joab fled
to the tent of the LORD and [c]took hold of the horns of the altar.
29 It was told King Solomon that Joab had fled to the tent of the
LORD, and behold, he is beside the altar. Then Solomon [a]sent
Benaiah the son of Jehoiada, saying, "[b]Go, fall upon him."

13 [a]1 Sam 16:4
15 [1]Lit *set their faces on me* [a]2 Sam 3:3, 4; 1 Kin 2:22 [b]1 Kin 1:5-25 [c]1 Kin 1:38-50 [d]1 Chr 22:9, 10; 28:5-7
16 [1]Lit *turn away my face*
17 [1]Lit *turn away your face* [a]1 Kin 1:3, 4
19 [a]1 Kin 15:13 [b]Ps 45:9
20 [1]Lit *turn away my face* [2]Lit *turn away your face* [a]1 Kin 2:16
21 [a]1 Kin 1:3, 4
22 [a]2 Sam 12:8 [b]1 Kin 1:6; 2:15; 1 Chr 3:2, 5 [c]1 Kin 1:7
23 [1]Lit *soul* [a]Ruth 1:17
24 [a]2 Sam 7:11, 13; 1 Chr 22:10
25 [a]2 Sam 8:18
26 [1]Lit *are a man of death* [2]Heb *YHWH,* usually rendered *LORD* [a]Josh 21:18; Jer 1:1 [b]1 Sam 26:16 [c]1 Sam 23:6; 2 Sam 15:24-29 [d]1 Sam 22:20-23; 23:8, 9
27 [a]1 Sam 2:27-36
28 [a]1 Kin 1:7 [b]2 Sam 17:25; 18:2 [c]1 Kin 1:50
29 [a]1 Kin 2:25 [b]Ex 21:14

30 So Benaiah came to the tent of the LORD and said to him,
"Thus the king has said, 'Come out.'" But he said, "No, for I will
die here." And Benaiah brought the king word again, saying,
"Thus spoke Joab, and thus he answered me."
31 The king said to him, "[a]Do as he has spoken and fall upon
him and bury him, [b]that you may remove from me and from
my father's house the blood which Joab shed without cause.
32 "[a]The LORD will return his blood on his own head, [b]because
he fell upon two men more righteous and better than he and
killed them with the sword, while my father David did not know
it: [c]Abner the son of Ner, commander of the army of Israel, and
[d]Amasa the son of Jether, commander of the army of Judah.
33 "[a]So shall their blood return on the head of Joab and on the
head of his [1]descendants forever; but to David and his [1]de-
scendants and his house and his throne, may there be peace
from the LORD forever."
34 Then [a]Benaiah the son of Jehoiada went up and fell upon him
and put him to death, and he was buried at his own house [b]in
the wilderness.
35 [a]The king appointed Benaiah the son of Jehoiada over the
army in his place, and the king appointed [b]Zadok the priest [c]in
the place of Abiathar.
36 Now the king sent and called for [a]Shimei and said to him,
"Build for yourself a house in Jerusalem and live there, and do
not go out from there to any place.
37 "For on the day you go out and [a]cross over the [1]brook Kidron,
you will know for certain that you shall surely die; [b]your blood
shall be on your own head."
38 Shimei then said to the king, "The word is good. As my
lord the king has said, so your servant will do." So Shimei lived
in Jerusalem many days.
39 But it came about at the end of three years, that two of the
servants of Shimei ran away [a]to Achish son of Maacah, king of
Gath. And they told Shimei, saying, "Behold, your servants are
in Gath."
40 Then Shimei arose and saddled his donkey, and went to
Gath to Achish to look for his servants. And Shimei went and
brought his servants from Gath.
41 It was told Solomon that Shimei had gone from Jerusalem
to Gath, and had returned.
42 So the king sent and called for Shimei and said to him,
"Did I not make you swear by the LORD and solemnly warn you,
saying, 'You will know for certain that on the day you depart and
go anywhere, you shall surely die'? And you said to me, 'The
word which I have heard is good.'
43 "Why then have you not kept the oath of the LORD, and the
command which I [1]have laid on you?"
44 The king also said to Shimei, "[a]You know all the evil which
[1]you acknowledge in your heart, which you did to my father
David; therefore [b]the LORD shall return your evil on your own
head.

31 [a]Ex 21:14 [b]Num 35:33; Deut 19:13; 21:8, 9

32 [a]Gen 9:6; Judg 9:24, 57; Ps 7:16 [b]2 Chr 21:13, 14 [c]2 Sam 3:27 [d]2 Sam 20:9, 10

33 [1]Lit *seed* [a]2 Sam 3:29

34 [a]1 Kin 2:25 [b]Josh 15:61; Matt 3:1

35 [a]1 Kin 4:4 [b]1 Chr 6:53; 24:3; 29:22 [c]1 Kin 2:27

36 [a]2 Sam 16:5; 1 Kin 2:8

37 [1]Or *wadi* [a]2 Sam 15:23; 2 Kin 23:6; John 18:1 [b]Josh 2:19; 2 Sam 1:16; Ezek 18:13

39 [a]1 Sam 27:2

43 [1]Lit *commanded*

44 [1]Lit *your heart acknowledges* [a]2 Sam 16:5-13 [b]1 Sam 25:39; 2 Kin 11:1, 12-16; Ps 7:16

45 "But King Solomon shall be blessed, and [a]the throne of
David shall be established before the LORD forever."
46 [a]So the king commanded Benaiah the son of Jehoiada, and
he went out and fell upon him so that he died.
[b]Thus the kingdom was established in the hands of Solomon.

Chapter 3 Theme ______________________

2 Chronicles 1

3 Then [a]Solomon [1]formed a marriage alliance with Pharaoh
king of Egypt, and took Pharaoh's daughter [b]and brought her
to the city of David [c]until he had finished building his own house
and the house of the LORD and [d]the wall around Jerusalem.
2 [a]The people were still sacrificing on the high places, because
there was no house built for the name of the LORD until those days.
3 Now [a]Solomon loved the LORD, [b]walking in the statutes of
his father David, except he sacrificed and burned incense on
the high places.
4 [a]The king went to [b]Gibeon to sacrifice there, [c]for that was
the great high place; Solomon offered a thousand burnt offerings
on that altar.
5 [a]In Gibeon the LORD appeared to Solomon [b]in a dream at
night; and God said, "[c]Ask what *you wish* me to give you."
6 Then Solomon said, "[a]You have shown great lovingkindness
to Your servant David my father, [b]according as he walked before
You in [1]truth and righteousness and uprightness of heart toward
You; and [c]You have [2]reserved for him this great lovingkindness,
that You have given him a son to sit on his throne, as *it is* this day.
7 "Now, O LORD my God, [a]You have made Your servant king
in place of my father David, yet [b]I am but a little child; [c]I do not
know how to go out or come in.
8 "[a]Your servant is in the midst of Your people which You have
chosen, [b]a great people who are too many to be numbered or
counted.
9 "So [a]give Your servant [1]an understanding heart to judge Your
people [b]to discern between good and evil. For who is able to
judge this [2]great people of Yours?"
10 [1]It was pleasing in the sight of the Lord that Solomon had
asked this thing.
11 God said to him, "Because you have asked this thing and
have [a]not asked for yourself [1]long life, nor have asked riches for
yourself, nor have you asked for the life of your enemies, but
have asked for yourself [2]discernment to understand justice,
12 behold, [a]I have done according to your words. Behold, [b]I have
given you a wise and discerning heart, so that there has been no
one like you before you, nor shall one like you arise after you.
13 "[a]I have also given you what you have not asked, both [b]riches
and honor, so that there will not be any among the kings like you
all your days.
14 "[a]If you walk in My ways, keeping My statutes and commandments, as your father David walked, then I will [b]prolong your
days."

45 [a]2 Sam 7:13; Prov 25:5

46 [a]1 Kin 2:25, 34 [b]1 Kin 2:12; 2 Chr 1:1

3:1 [1]Lit *made himself a son-in-law of Pharaoh* [a]1 Kin 7:8; 9:16, 24; 2 Chr 8:11 [b]1 Kin 9:24 [c]1 Kin 7:1; 9:10 [d]1 Kin 9:15

2 [a]Lev 17:3-5; Deut 12:2, 13, 14; 1 Kin 22:43

3 [a]Deut 6:5; 10:12, 13; 11:13; 30:16; Ps 31:23; 145:20; 1 Cor 8:3 [b]1 Kin 2:3; 9:4; 11:4, 6, 38

4 [a]2 Chr 1:3 [b]Josh 18:21-25 [c]1 Chr 16:39; 21:29

5 [a]1 Kin 9:2; 11:9 [b]Num 12:6; Matt 1:20; 2:13 [c]John 15:7

6 [1]Or *faithfulness* [2]Lit *kept* [a]2 Sam 7:8-17; 2 Chr 1:8 [b]1 Kin 9:4 [c]1 Kin 1:48

7 [a]1 Chr 22:9-13 [b]1 Chr 29:1; Jer 1:6, 7 [c]Num 27:17

8 [a]Ex 19:6; Deut 7:6 [b]Gen 15:5; 22:17

9 [1]Lit *a hearing* [2]Lit *heavy* [a]2 Chr 1:10; Ps 72:1, 2; Prov 2:3-9; James 1:5 [b]2 Sam 14:17; Heb 5:14

10 [1]Lit *the thing*

11 [1]Lit *many days* [2]Lit *hearing* [a]James 4:3

12 [a]1 John 5:14, 15 [b]1 Kin 4:29-31; 5:12; 10:23, 24; Eccl 1:16

13 [a]1 Kin 4:21-24; 10:23, 27; Matt 6:33; Eph 3:20 [b]Prov 3:16

14 [a]1 Kin 3:6 [b]Ps 91:16; Prov 3:2

15 Then [a]Solomon awoke, and behold, it was a dream. And he
came to Jerusalem and stood before the ark of the covenant of
the Lord, and offered burnt offerings and made peace offerings,
and [b]made a feast for all his servants.
16 Then two women who were harlots came to the king and
stood before him.
17 The one woman said, "Oh, my lord, [1]this woman and I live
in the same house; and I gave birth to a child while she *was* in
the house.
18 "It happened on the third day after I gave birth, that this
woman also gave birth to a child, and we were together. There
was no stranger with us in the house, only the two of us in the
house.
19 "This woman's son died in the night, because she lay on it.
20 "So she arose in the middle of the night and took my son
from beside me while your maidservant slept, and laid him in
her bosom, and laid her dead son in my bosom.
21 "When I rose in the morning to nurse my son, behold, he
was dead; but when I looked at him carefully in the morning,
behold, he was not my son, whom I had borne."
22 Then the other woman said, "No! For the living one is my
son, and the dead one is your son." But [1]the first woman said,
"No! For the dead one is your son, and the living one is my
son." Thus they spoke before the king.
23 Then the king said, "[1]The one says, 'This is my son who is
living, and your son is the dead one'; and [1]the other says, 'No!
For your son is the dead one, and my son is the living one.'"
24 The king said, "Get me a sword." So they brought a sword
before the king.
25 The king said, "Divide the living child in two, and give half
to the one and half to the other."
26 Then the woman whose child *was* the living one spoke to
the king, for [1a]she was deeply stirred over her son and said,
"Oh, my lord, give her the living child, and by no means kill
him." But the other said, "He shall be neither mine nor yours;
divide *him!*"
27 Then the king said, "Give [1]the first woman the living child,
and by no means kill him. She is his mother."
28 When all Israel heard of the judgment which the king had
[1]handed down, they feared the king, for [a]they saw that the
wisdom of God was in him to [2]administer justice.

Chapter 4 Theme ______________________

4 Now King Solomon was king over all Israel.
2 These were his officials: Azariah the son of Zadok *was*
[a]the priest;
3 Elihoreph and Ahijah, the sons of Shisha *were* secretaries;
[a]Jehoshaphat the son of Ahilud *was* the recorder;
4 and [a]Benaiah the son of Jehoiada *was* over the army; and
Zadok and [b]Abiathar *were* priests;

15 [a]Gen 41:7 [b]1 Kin 8:65

17 [1]Lit *I and this woman*

22 [1]Lit *this one was saying*

23 [1]Lit *this one*

26 [1]Lit *her compassion grew warm* [a]Gen 43:30; Is 49:15; Jer 31:20; Hos 11:8

27 [1]Lit *her the living child*

28 [1]Lit *judged* [2]Lit *do* [a]1 Kin 3:9, 11, 12; Dan 1:17; Col 2:2, 3

4:2 [a]1 Chr 6:10

3 [a]2 Sam 8:16

4 [a]1 Kin 2:35 [b]1 Kin 2:27

5 and Azariah the son of
Nathan *was* over [a]the deputies;
and Zabud the son of Nathan,
a priest, *was* the king's friend;
6 and Ahishar was over the
household; and Adoniram the
son of Abda *was* over the men
subject to forced labor.
7 Solomon had twelve
deputies over all Israel, who
[1]provided for the king and his
household; each man had to
[2]provide for a month in the
year.
8 These are their names:
Ben-hur, in the [a]hill country of
Ephraim;
9 Ben-deker in Makaz and
[a]Shaalbim and [b]Beth-shemesh
and Elonbeth-hanan;
10 Ben-hesed, in Arubboth
([a]Socoh *was* his and all the land
of [b]Hepher);
11 Ben-abinadab, *in* all [1]the
[a]height of Dor (Taphath the
daughter of Solomon was his
wife);
12 Baana the son of Ahilud,
in [a]Taanach and Megiddo, and
all [b]Beth-shean which is beside [c]Zarethan below Jezreel, from
Beth-shean to [d]Abel-meholah as far as the other side of
[e]Jokmeam;
13 Ben-geber, in [a]Ramoth-gilead ([b]the towns of Jair, the son of
Manasseh, which are in Gilead were his: [c]the region of Argob,
which is in Bashan, sixty great cities with walls and bronze
bars *were* his);
14 Ahinadab the son of Iddo, *in* [a]Mahanaim;
15 [a]Ahimaaz, in Naphtali (he also married Basemath the
daughter of Solomon);
16 Baana the son of [a]Hushai, in Asher and [1]Bealoth;
17 Jehoshaphat the son of Paruah, in Issachar;
18 [a]Shimei the son of Ela, in Benjamin;
19 Geber the son of Uri, in the land of Gilead, [a]the country of
Sihon king of the Amorites and of Og king of Bashan; and *he*
was the only deputy who *was* in the land.
20 [a]Judah and Israel *were* as numerous as the sand that is on
the [1]seashore in abundance; *they* were eating and drinking and
rejoicing.
21 [1a]Now Solomon ruled over all the kingdoms [b]from the [2]River
to the land of the Philistines and to the border of Egypt; [c]*they*
brought tribute and served Solomon all the days of his life.

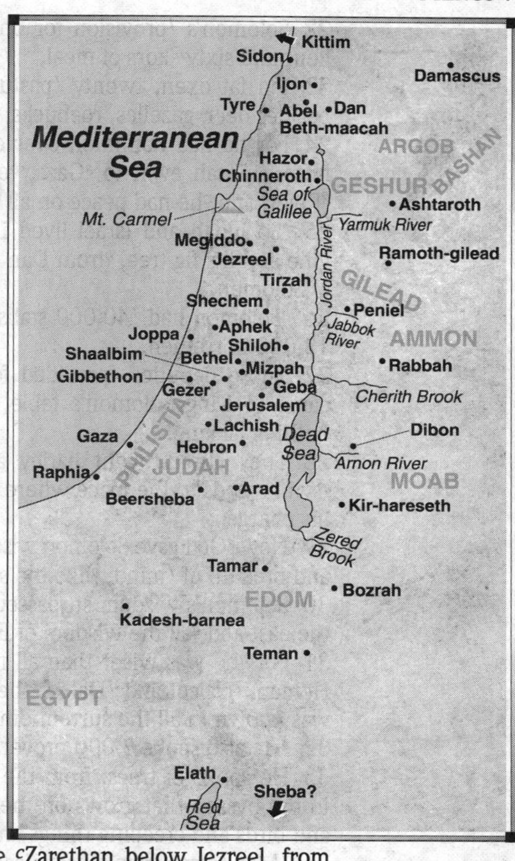

Solomon's Kingdom

5 [a]1 Kin 4:7
7 [1]Lit *nourished* [2]Lit *nourish*
8 [a]Josh 24:33
9 [a]Judg 1:35 [b]Josh 21:16
10 [a]Josh 15:35 [b]Josh 12:17
11 [1]Or *Naphoth-dor* [a]Josh 11:1, 2
12 [a]Judg 5:19 [b]Josh 17:11 [c]Josh 3:16 [d]1 Kin 19:16 [e]1 Chr 6:68
13 [a]1 Kin 22:3-15 [b]Num 32:41 [c]Deut 3:4
14 [a]Josh 13:26
15 [a]2 Sam 15:27
16 [1]Or *in Aloth* [a]2 Sam 15:32
18 [a]1 Kin 1:8
19 [a]Deut 3:8-10
20 [1]Lit *sea* [a]Gen 22:17; 32:12; 1 Kin 3:8
21 [1]Ch 5:1 in Heb [2]I.e. Euphrates [a]2 Chr 9:26 [b]Gen 15:18; Josh 1:4 [c]2 Sam 8:2, 6

22 Solomon's [1]provision for one day was thirty [2]kors of fine
flour and sixty [2]kors of meal,
23 ten fat oxen, twenty [1]pasture-fed oxen, a hundred sheep
besides deer, gazelles, roebucks, and fattened fowl.
24 For he had dominion over everything [1]west of the [2]River,
from Tiphsah even to [a]Gaza, [b]over all the kings [1]west of the
[2]River; and [c]he had peace on all sides around about him.
25 [a]So Judah and Israel lived in safety, every man under his
vine and his fig tree, [b]from Dan even to Beersheba, all the days
of Solomon.
26 [a]Solomon had [1]40,000 stalls of horses for his chariots, and
12,000 horsemen.
27 Those deputies [1]provided for King Solomon and all who
came to King Solomon's table, each in his month; they left
nothing lacking.
28 They also brought barley and straw for the horses and
[a]swift steeds to the place where it should be, each according to
his charge.
29 Now [a]God gave Solomon wisdom and very great discernment
and breadth of [1]mind, [b]like the sand that is on the seashore.
30 Solomon's wisdom surpassed the wisdom of all [a]the sons of
the east and [b]all the wisdom of Egypt.
31 For [a]he was wiser than all men, than [b]Ethan the Ezrahite,
Heman, [c]Calcol and [1]Darda, the sons of Mahol; and his [2]fame
was *known* in all the surrounding nations.
32 [a]He also spoke 3,000 proverbs, and his songs were 1,005.
33 He spoke of trees, from the cedar that is in Lebanon even
to the hyssop that grows on the wall; he spoke also of animals
and birds and creeping things and fish.
34 [1]Men [a]came from all peoples to hear the wisdom of Solomon,
from all the kings of the earth who had heard of his wisdom.

Chapter 5 Theme ______________________

2 Chronicles 2

5 [1][a]Now Hiram king of Tyre sent his servants to Solomon,
when he heard that they had anointed him king in place of
his father, for [b]Hiram had [2]always been a friend of David.
2 Then [a]Solomon sent *word* to Hiram, saying,
3 "You know that [a]David my father was unable to build a
house for the name of the LORD his God because of the wars
which surrounded him, until the LORD put them under the
soles of his feet.
4 "But now [a]the LORD my God has given me rest on every
side; there is neither adversary nor [1]misfortune.
5 "Behold, [a]I [1]intend to build a house for the name of the
LORD my God, as the LORD spoke to David my father, saying,
'Your son, whom I will set on your throne in your place, he will
build the house for My name.'
6 "Now therefore, command that they cut for me [a]cedars from
Lebanon, and my servants will be with your servants; and I will
give you wages for your servants according to all that you say,

22 [1]Lit *bread* [2]I.e. One kor equals approx 10 bu

23 [1]Lit *oxen of the pasture*

24 [1]Lit *beyond* [2]I.e. Euphrates [a]Judg 1:18 [b]Ps 72:11 [c]1 Chr 22:9

25 [a]Jer 23:6; Mic 4:4; Zech 3:10 [b]1 Sam 3:20

26 [1]One ms reads *4000,* cf 2 Chr 9:25 [a]1 Kin 10:26; 2 Chr 1:14

27 [1]Or *nourished*

28 [a]Esth 8:10, 14; Mic 1:13

29 [1]Lit *heart* [a]1 Kin 3:12 [b]1 Kin 4:20

30 [a]Gen 29:1; Judg 6:33 [b]Is 19:11; Acts 7:22

31 [1]In 1 Chr 2:6, *Dara* [2]Lit *name* [a]1 Kin 3:12 [b]1 Chr 15:19; Ps 89: title [c]1 Chr 2:6

32 [a]Prov 1:1; 10:1; 25:1; Eccl 12:9; Song 1:1

34 [1]Lit *they* [a]1 Kin 10:1; 2 Chr 9:23

5:1 [1]Ch 5:15 in Heb [2]Lit *all the day* [a]2 Chr 2:3 [b]2 Sam 5:11; 1 Chr 14:1

2 [a]2 Chr 2:3

3 [a]2 Sam 7:5; 1 Chr 28:2, 3

4 [1]Lit *evil occurrence* [a]1 Kin 4:24; 1 Chr 22:9

5 [1]Lit *say* [a]2 Sam 7:12, 13; 1 Chr 17:12; 22:10; 28:6; 2 Chr 2:4

6 [a]2 Chr 2:8

for you know that there is no one among us who knows how to
cut timber like the Sidonians."
7 When Hiram heard the words of Solomon, he rejoiced
greatly and said, "Blessed be the LORD today, who has given to
David a wise son over this great people."
8 So Hiram sent *word* to Solomon, saying, "I have heard *the
message* which you have sent me; I will do [1]what you desire
concerning the cedar and cypress timber.
9 "My servants will bring *them* down from Lebanon to the
sea; and I will make them into rafts *to go* by sea [a]to the place
where you [1]direct me, and I will have them broken up there,
and you shall carry *them* away. Then [b]you shall accomplish my
desire by giving food to my household."
10 So [1]Hiram [2]gave Solomon [3]as much as he desired of the
cedar and cypress timber.
11 [a]Solomon then gave Hiram 20,000 [1]kors of wheat as food
for his household, and twenty [1]kors of beaten oil; thus Solomon
would give Hiram year by year.
12 [a]The LORD gave wisdom to Solomon, just as He [1]promised
him; and there was peace between Hiram and Solomon, and
the two of them made a covenant.
13 Now [a]King Solomon [1]levied forced laborers from all Israel;
and the forced laborers [2]numbered 30,000 men.
14 He sent them to Lebanon, 10,000 a month in relays; they
were in Lebanon a month *and* two months at home. And
[a]Adoniram *was* over the forced laborers.
15 Now [a]Solomon had 70,000 [1]transporters, and 80,000 hewers
of stone in the mountains,
16 [a]besides Solomon's 3,300 chief deputies who *were* over the
[1]project *and* who ruled over the people who were doing the work.
17 Then [a]the king commanded, and they quarried great
stones, costly stones, to lay the foundation of the house with
cut stones.
18 So Solomon's builders and [1]Hiram's builders and [a]the
Gebalites [2]cut them, and prepared the timbers and the stones
to build the house.

Chapter 6 Theme ________________________

6 [a]Now it came about in the four hundred and eightieth year
after the sons of Israel came out of the land of Egypt, in the
fourth year of Solomon's reign over Israel, in the month of Ziv
which is the second month, that he [1]began to build the house
of the LORD.
2 As for the house which King Solomon built for the LORD, its
length *was* sixty [1]cubits and its width twenty *cubits* and its height
thirty cubits.
3 The porch in front of the nave of the house *was* twenty
cubits [1]in length, [2]corresponding to the width of the house,
and its [3]depth along the front of the house *was* ten cubits.
4 Also for the house [a]he made windows with *artistic* frames.

968 B.C.

2 Chronicles 3

8 [1]Lit *all your pleasure*
9 [1]Lit *send* [a]2 Chr 2:16 [b]Ezra 3:7; Ezek 27:17
10 [1]Heb *Hirom* [2]Lit *was giving* [3]Lit *all his desire*
11 [1]I.e. One kor equals approx 10 bu [a]2 Chr 2:10
12 [1]Lit *spoke to* [a]1 Kin 3:12
13 [1]Lit *raised up* [2]Lit *was* [a]1 Kin 4:6; 9:15
14 [a]1 Kin 4:6; 12:18
15 [1]Or *burden bearers* [a]1 Kin 9:20-22; 2 Chr 2:17, 18
16 [1]Lit *work* [a]1 Kin 9:23
17 [a]1 Kin 6:7; 1 Chr 22:2
18 [1]Heb *Hirom's* [2]Or *chiseled* [a]Josh 13:5; Ezek 27:9
6:1 [1]Lit *built* [a]2 Chr 3:1, 2
2 [1]I.e. One cubit equals approx 18 in.
3 [1]Lit *in its length* [2]Lit *on the face of* [3]Lit *width*
4 [a]Ezek 40:16; 41:16

The Jewish Calendar

Babylonian names (B) for the months are still used today for the Jewish calendar. Canaanite names (C) were used prior to the Babylonian captivity in 586 B.C. Four are mentioned in the Old Testament. **Adar-Sheni** is an intercalary month used every two to three years or seven times in 19 years.

1st month	2nd month	3rd month	4th month
Nisan (B) Abib (C) March-April	Iyyar (B) Ziv (C) April-May	Sivan (B) May-June	Tammuz (B) June-July
7th month	*8th month*	*9th month*	*10th month*
5th month	**6th month**	**7th month**	**8th month**
Ab (B) July-August	Elul (B) August-September	Tishri (B) Ethanim (C) September-October	Marcheshvan (B) Bul (C) October-November
11th month	*12th month*	*1st month*	*2nd month*
9th month	**10th month**	**11th month**	**12th month**
Chislev (B) November-December	Tebeth (B) December-January	Shebat (B) January-February	Adar (B) February-March
3rd month	*4th month*	*5th month*	*6th month*

Sacred calendar appears in black • Civil calendar appears in gray

5 [a]Against the wall of the house he built stories encompassing the walls of the house around both the nave and the [b]inner sanctuary; thus he made [c]side chambers all around.

6 The lowest story *was* five cubits wide, and the middle *was* six cubits wide, and the third *was* seven cubits wide; for on the outside he [1]made offsets *in the wall* of the house all around in order that *the beams* would not [2]be inserted in the walls of the house.

7 [a]The house, while it was being built, was built of stone [1]prepared at the quarry, and there was neither hammer nor axe nor any iron tool heard in the house while it was being built.

8 The doorway for the [1]lowest side chamber *was* on the right side of the house; and they would go up by winding stairs to the middle *story,* and from the middle to the third.

9 So [a]he built the house and finished it; and he covered the house with beams and [1]planks of cedar.

10 He also built the stories against the whole house, each five [1]cubits high; and they [2]were fastened to the house with timbers of cedar.

11 Now the word of the LORD came to Solomon saying,

12 "*Concerning* this house which you are building, [a]if you will walk in My statutes and execute My ordinances and keep all My commandments by walking in them, then I will carry out My word with you which I spoke to David your father.

13 "[a]I will dwell among the sons of Israel, and [b]will not forsake My people Israel."

14 [a]So Solomon built the house and finished it.

15 Then he [a]built the walls of the house on the inside with boards of cedar; from the floor of the house to the [1]ceiling he overlaid *the walls* on the inside with wood, and he overlaid the floor of the house with boards of cypress.

16 [a]He built twenty cubits on the rear part of the house with boards of cedar from the floor to the [1]ceiling; he built *them* for it on the inside as an inner sanctuary, *even* as [b]the most holy place.

5 [a]Ezek 41:6 [b]1 Kin 6:16, 19, 20 [c]Ezek 41:5

6 [1]Lit *gave* [2]Lit *take hold*

7 [1]Lit *finished* [a]Ex 20:25; Deut 27:5, 6

8 [1]So with Gr and versions; M.T. *middle*

9 [1]Lit *rows* [a]1 Kin 6:14, 38

10 [1]I.e. One cubit equals approx 18 in. [2]Lit *took hold*

12 [a]2 Sam 7:5-16; 1 Kin 9:4

13 [a]Ex 25:8; 29:45; Lev 26:11 [b]Deut 31:6; Josh 1:5; Heb 13:5

14 [a]1 Kin 6:9, 38

15 [1]Lit *walls of ceiling* [a]1 Kin 7:7

16 [1]Lit *walls* [a]2 Chr 3:8 [b]Ex 26:33, 34; Lev 16:2; 1 Kin 8:6; Heb 9:3

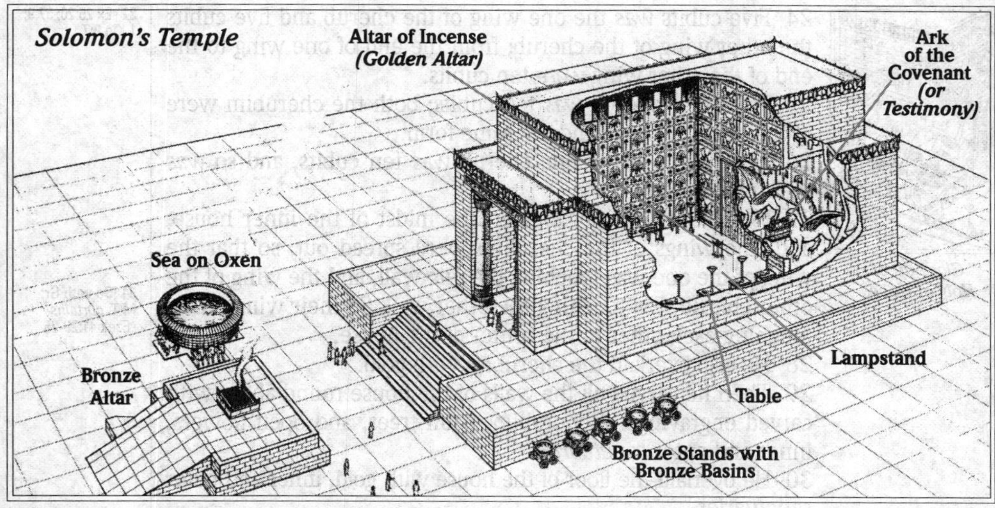

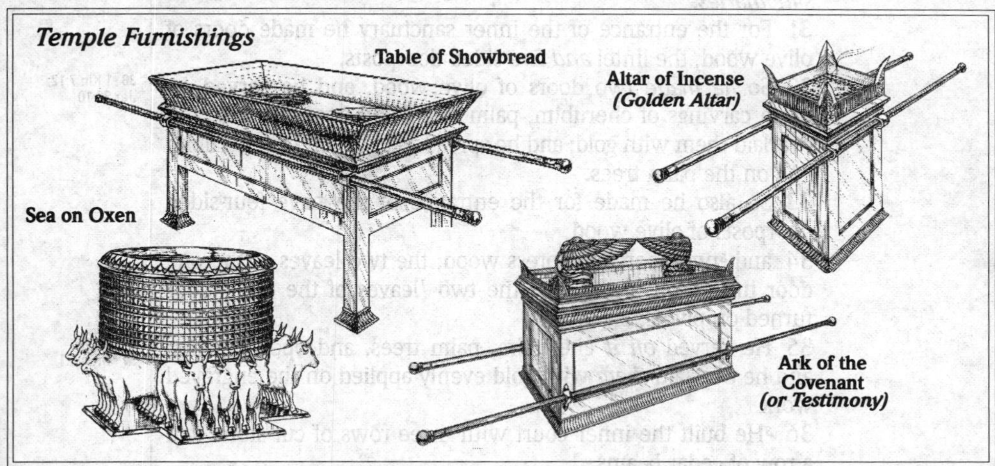

17 The house, that is, the nave in front of *the inner sanctuary,*
was forty [1]cubits *long.*
18 There was cedar on the house within, carved *in the shape* of
[a]gourds and open flowers; all was cedar, there was no stone seen.
19 Then he prepared an inner sanctuary within the house in
order to place there the ark of the covenant of the LORD.
20 [1]The inner sanctuary *was* twenty cubits in length, twenty
cubits in width, and twenty cubits in height, and he overlaid it
with pure gold. He also overlaid the altar with cedar.
21 So Solomon overlaid the inside of the house with pure
gold. And he drew chains of gold across the front of the inner
sanctuary, and he overlaid it with gold.
22 He overlaid the whole house with gold, until all the house
was finished. Also [a]the whole altar which was by the inner
sanctuary he overlaid with gold.
23 [a]Also in the inner sanctuary he made two cherubim of
olive wood, each ten cubits high.

17 [1]I.e. One cubit equals approx 18 in.

18 [a]1 Kin 7:24

20 [1]Lit *before*

22 [a]Ex 30:1, 3, 6

23 [a]Ex 37:7-9; 2 Chr 3:10-12

Close-up of Holy of Holies

24 Five cubits *was* the one wing of the cherub and five cubits
the other wing of the cherub; from the end of one wing to the
end of the other wing *were* ten cubits.
25 The other cherub *was* ten cubits; both the cherubim were
of the same measure and the same form.
26 The height of the one cherub *was* ten cubits, and so *was*
the other cherub.
27 He placed the cherubim in the midst of the inner house,
and [a]the wings of the cherubim were spread out, so that the
wing of the one was touching the *one* wall, and the wing of the
other cherub was touching the other wall. So their wings were
touching each other in the center of the house.
28 He also overlaid the cherubim with gold.
29 Then he carved all the walls of the house round about with
carved engravings of cherubim, palm trees, and open flowers,
inner and outer *sanctuaries.*
30 He overlaid the floor of the house with gold, inner and outer
sanctuaries.
31 For the entrance of the inner sanctuary he made doors of
olive wood, the lintel *and* five-sided doorposts.
32 So *he made* two doors of olive wood, and he carved on
them carvings of cherubim, palm trees, and open flowers, and
overlaid them with gold; and he spread the gold on the cherubim
and on the palm trees.
33 So also he made for the entrance of the nave four-sided
doorposts of olive wood
34 and [a]two doors of cypress wood; the two leaves of the one
door turned on pivots, and the two [1]leaves of the other door
turned on pivots.
35 He carved *on it* cherubim, palm trees, and open flowers;
and he overlaid *them* with gold evenly applied on the engraved
work.
36 [a]He built the inner court with three rows of cut stone and
a row of cedar beams.
37 [a]In the fourth year the foundation of the house of the LORD
was laid, in the month of Ziv.
38 In the eleventh year, in the month of Bul, which is the eighth
month, the house was finished throughout all its parts and
961 B.C. according to all its plans. So he was seven years in building it.

Chapter 7 Theme

948 B.C. **7** Now [a]Solomon was building his own house thirteen years,
and he finished all his house.
2 [a]He built the house of the forest of Lebanon; its length was
100 [1]cubits and its width 50 cubits and its height 30 cubits, on
four rows of cedar pillars with cedar beams on the pillars.
3 It was paneled with cedar above the side chambers which
were on the 45 pillars, 15 in each row.
4 *There were artistic window* frames in three rows, and
window was opposite window in three ranks.

27 [a]Ex 25:20; 37:9; 1 Kin 8:7

34 [1]So with Gr; M.T. *curtains* [a]Ezek 41:23-25

36 [a]1 Kin 7:12; Jer 36:10

37 [a]1 Kin 6:1

7:1 [a]1 Kin 3:1; 9:10; 2 Chr 8:1

2 [1]I.e. One cubit equals approx 18 in. [a]1 Kin 10:17, 21; 2 Chr 9:16

5 All the doorways and doorposts *had* squared *artistic* frames,
and window was opposite window in three ranks.
6 Then he made [a]the hall of pillars; its length was 50 cubits
and its width 30 cubits, and a porch *was* in front of them and
pillars and a [b]threshold in front of them.
7 He made the hall of the [a]throne where he was to judge, the
hall of judgment, and [b]it was paneled with cedar from floor to
floor.
8 His house where he was to live, the other court inward
from the hall, was of the same workmanship. [a]He also made a
house like this hall for Pharaoh's daughter, [b]whom Solomon
had married.
9 All these were of costly stones, of stone cut according to
measure, sawed with saws, inside and outside; even from the
foundation to the coping, and so on the outside to the great
court.
10 The foundation was of costly stones, *even* large stones,
stones of ten cubits and stones of eight cubits.
11 And above were costly stones, stone cut according to
measure, and cedar.
12 So [a]the great court all around *had* three rows of cut stone and
a row of cedar beams even as the inner court of the house of
the LORD, and [b]the porch of the house.
13 Now [a]King Solomon sent and brought Hiram from Tyre.
14 [a]He was a widow's son from the tribe of Naphtali, and his
father was a man of Tyre, a worker in bronze; and [b]he was filled
with wisdom and understanding and skill for doing any work in
bronze. So he came to King Solomon and [c]performed all his work.
15 He fashioned [a]the two pillars of bronze; [b]eighteen cubits was
the height of one pillar, and a line of twelve cubits [1]measured
the circumference of both.
16 He also made two capitals of molten bronze to set on the
tops of the pillars; the height of the one capital was five [1]cubits
and the height of the other capital was five cubits.
17 *There were* nets of network and twisted threads of chain-
work for the capitals which were on the top of the pillars;
seven for the one capital and seven for the other capital.
18 So he made the pillars, and two rows around on the one
network to cover the capitals which were on the top of the
pomegranates; and so he did for the other capital.
19 The capitals which *were* on the top of the pillars in the
porch were of lily design, four cubits.
20 *There were* capitals on the two pillars, even above *and*
close to the [1]rounded projection which was beside the network;
and [a]the pomegranates *numbered* two hundred in rows around
[2]both capitals.
21 [a]Thus he set up the pillars at the [b]porch of the nave; and he
set up the right pillar and named it [1]Jachin, and he set up the
left pillar and named it [2]Boaz.
22 On the top of the pillars was lily design. So the work of the
pillars was finished.

6 [a]1 Kin 7:12 [b]Ezek 41:25, 26

7 [a]Ps 122:5; Prov 20:8 [b]1 Kin 6:15, 16

8 [a]1 Kin 9:24; 2 Chr 8:11 [b]1 Kin 3:1

12 [a]1 Kin 6:36 [b]1 Kin 7:6

13 [a]2 Chr 2:13, 14; 4:11

14 [a]2 Chr 2:14 [b]Ex 28:3; 31:3-5; 35:31; 36:1 [c]2 Chr 4:11-16

15 [1]Lit *went around the other pillar* [a]2 Kin 25:17; 2 Chr 3:15; 4:12; Jer 52:21 [b]1 Kin 7:41

16 [1]I.e. One cubit equals approx 18 in.

20 [1]Lit *belly* [2]Lit *on the other capital* [a]1 Kin 7:42; 2 Chr 3:16; 4:13; Jer 52:23

21 [1]I.e. he shall establish [2]I.e. in it is strength [a]2 Chr 3:17 [b]1 Kin 6:3

2 Chronicles 4

23 [a]Now he made the sea of [b]cast *metal* ten cubits from brim to brim, circular in form, and its height was five cubits, and [1]thirty cubits in circumference.

24 Under its brim [a]gourds went around encircling it ten to a cubit, [b]completely surrounding the sea; the gourds were in two rows, cast [1]with the rest.

25 [a]It stood on twelve oxen, three facing north, three facing west, three facing south, and three facing east; and the sea *was set* on top of them, and all their rear parts *turned* inward.

Sea on Oxen

26 It was a handbreadth thick, and its brim was made like the brim of a cup, *as* a lily blossom; it could hold two thousand baths.

27 Then [a]he made the ten stands of bronze; the length of each stand was four cubits and its width four cubits and its height three cubits.

28 This was the design of the stands: they had borders, even borders between the [1]frames,

29 and on the borders which were between the [1]frames *were* lions, oxen and cherubim; and on the [1]frames there *was* a pedestal above, and beneath the lions and oxen *were* wreaths of hanging work.

30 Now each stand had four bronze wheels with bronze axles, and its four feet had supports; beneath the basin *were* cast supports with wreaths at each side.

31 Its opening inside the crown at the top *was* a cubit, and its opening *was* round like the design of a pedestal, a cubit and a half; and also on its opening *there were* engravings, and their borders were square, not round.

32 The four wheels *were* underneath the borders, and the axles of the wheels *were* on the stand. And the height of a wheel *was* a cubit and a half.

33 The workmanship of the wheels *was* like the workmanship of a chariot wheel. Their axles, their rims, their spokes, and their hubs *were* all cast.

34 Now *there were* four supports at the four corners of each stand; its supports *were* part of the stand itself.

35 On the top of the stand *there was* a circular form half a [1]cubit high, and on the top of the stand its [2]stays and its borders *were* part of it.

36 He engraved on the plates of its stays and on its borders, cherubim, lions and palm trees, according to the clear space on each, with wreaths *all* around.

37 [a]He made the ten stands like this: all of them had one casting, one measure and one form.

Bronze Stand with Bronze Basin

38 [a]He made ten basins of bronze, one basin held forty baths; each basin *was* four cubits, *and* on each of the ten stands *was* one basin.

39 Then he set the stands, five on the right side of the house and five on the left side of the house; and he set the sea *of cast metal* on the right side of the house eastward toward the south.

40 Now Hiram made the basins and the shovels and the bowls. So Hiram finished doing all the work which he performed for King Solomon *in* the house of the LORD:

23 [1]Lit *a line of 30 cubits went around it* [a]2 Chr 4:2 [b]2 Kin 16:17; 25:13

24 [1]Lit *in its casting* [a]1 Kin 6:18 [b]2 Chr 4:3

25 [a]2 Chr 4:4, 5; Jer 52:20

27 [a]1 Kin 7:38; 2 Kin 25:13; 2 Chr 4:14

28 [1]Or *crossbars*

29 [1]Or *crossbars*

35 [1]I.e. One cubit equals approx 18 in. [2]Lit *hands*

37 [a]2 Chr 4:14

38 [a]Ex 30:18; 2 Chr 4:6

41 the two pillars and the *two* bowls of the capitals which
were on the top of the [a]two pillars, and the two networks to
cover the two bowls of the capitals which *were* on the top of
the pillars;
42 and the [a]four hundred pomegranates for the two networks,
two rows of pomegranates for each network to cover the two
bowls of the capitals which *were* on the tops of the pillars;
43 and the ten stands with the ten basins on the stands;
44 and [a]the one sea and the twelve oxen under the sea;
45 and [a]the pails and the shovels and the bowls; even all these
utensils which Hiram made for King Solomon *in* the house of
the LORD *were* of polished bronze.
46 [a]In the plain of the Jordan the king cast them, in the clay
ground between [b]Succoth and [c]Zarethan.
47 Solomon left all the utensils *unweighed,* because *they were*
too many; [a]the weight of the bronze could not be ascertained.
48 Solomon made all the furniture which *was in* the house of
the LORD: [a]the golden altar and the golden table on which *was*
the [b]bread of the Presence;
49 and the lampstands, five on the right side and five on the
left, in front of the inner sanctuary, of pure gold; and [a]the
flowers and the lamps and the tongs, of gold;
50 and the cups and the snuffers and the bowls and the
spoons and the [a]firepans, of pure gold; and the hinges both for
the doors of the inner house, the most holy place, *and* for the
doors of the house, *that is,* of the nave, of gold.
51 [a]Thus all the work that King Solomon performed *in* the
house of the LORD was finished. And [b]Solomon brought in the
things dedicated by his father David, the silver and the gold
and the utensils, *and* he put them in the treasuries of the
house of the LORD.

41 [a]1 Kin 7:17, 18
42 [a]1 Kin 7:20
44 [a]1 Kin 7:23, 25
45 [a]Ex 27:3; 2 Chr 4:16
46 [a]2 Chr 4:17 [b]Gen 33:17; Josh 13:27 [c]Josh 3:16
47 [a]1 Chr 22:3, 14
48 [a]Ex 30:1-3; 37:10-29; 2 Chr 4:8 [b]Ex 25:30
49 [a]Ex 25:31-38
50 [a]Ex 27:3; 2 Kin 25:15
51 [a]2 Chr 5:1 [b]2 Sam 8:11; 1 Chr 18:11; 2 Chr 5:1

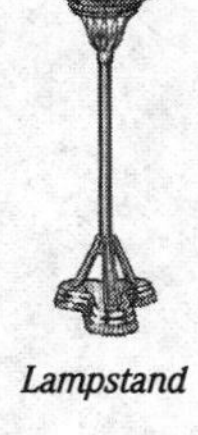
Lampstand

Chapter 8 Theme ____________________

2 Chronicles 5

8 [a]Then Solomon assembled the elders of Israel and all [b]the
heads of the tribes, the leaders of the fathers' *households*
of the sons of Israel, to King Solomon in Jerusalem, [c]to bring up
the ark of the covenant of the LORD from [d]the city of David,
which is Zion.
2 All the men of Israel assembled themselves to King Solomon
at [a]the feast, in the month Ethanim, which is the seventh
month.
3 Then all the elders of Israel came, and [a]the priests took up
the ark.
4 They brought up the ark of the LORD and [a]the tent of
meeting and all the holy utensils, which were in the tent, and
the priests and the Levites brought them up.
5 And King Solomon and all the congregation of Israel, who
were assembled to him, [a]were with him before the ark,
sacrificing [1]so many sheep and oxen they could not be counted
or numbered.

8:1 [a]2 Chr 5:2-10 [b]Num 1:4; 7:2 [c]2 Sam 6:12-17; 1 Chr 15:25-29 [d]2 Sam 5:7
2 [a]Lev 23:34; 1 Kin 8:65; 2 Chr 7:8-10
3 [a]Num 7:9; Deut 31:9; Josh 3:3, 6
4 [a]1 Kin 3:4; 2 Chr 1:3
5 [1]Lit *sheep and oxen...numbered for multitude* [a]2 Sam 6:13; 2 Chr 1:6

INSIGHT

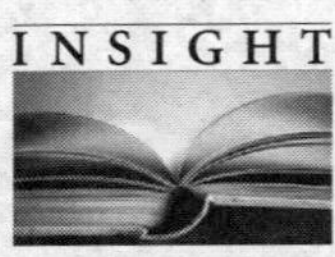

See the illustration of Solomon's Temple on page NISB-36.

6 Then [a]the priests brought the ark of the covenant of the
LORD [b]to its place, into the inner sanctuary of the house, to the
most holy place, [c]under the wings of the cherubim.
7 For the cherubim spread *their* wings over the place of the
ark, and the cherubim made a covering over the ark and its
poles from above.
8 But [a]the poles were so long that the ends of the poles could
be seen from the holy place before the inner sanctuary, but
they could not be seen outside; they are there to this day.
9 [a]There was nothing in the ark except the two tablets of
stone which Moses put there at Horeb, where [b]the LORD made
a covenant with the sons of Israel, when they came out of the
land of Egypt.
10 It happened that when the priests came from the holy
place, [a]the cloud filled the house of the LORD,
11 so that the priests could not stand to minister because of
the cloud, for the glory of the LORD filled the house of the LORD.
12 [a]Then Solomon said,
"The LORD has said that [b]He would dwell in the thick cloud.
13 "[a]I have surely built You a lofty house,
[b]A place for Your dwelling forever."
14 Then the king [1]faced about and [a]blessed all the assembly of
Israel, while all the assembly of Israel was standing.
15 He said, "[a]Blessed be the LORD, the God of Israel, [b]who
spoke with His mouth to my father David and has fulfilled *it*
with His hand, saying,
16 '[a]Since the day that I brought My people Israel from Egypt, I
did not choose a city out of all the tribes of Israel *in which* to
build a house that [b]My name might be there, but [c]I chose
David to be over My people Israel.'
17 "[a]Now it was [1]in the heart of my father David to build a
house for the name of the LORD, the God of Israel.
18 "But the LORD said to my father David, 'Because it was [1]in
your heart to build a house for My name, you did well that it
was [1]in your heart.
19 '[a]Nevertheless you shall not build the house, but your son
who [1]will be born to you, he will build the house for My name.'
20 "Now the LORD has fulfilled His word which He spoke; for [a]I
have risen in place of my father David and sit on the throne of
Israel, as the LORD [1]promised, and have built the house for the
name of the LORD, the God of Israel.
21 "There I have set a place for the ark, [a]in which is the
covenant of the LORD, which He made with our fathers when
He brought them from the land of Egypt."
22 Then [a]Solomon stood before the altar of the LORD in the
presence of all the assembly of Israel and [b]spread out his hands
toward heaven.

2 Chronicles 6

23 He said, "O LORD, the God of Israel, [a]there is no God like
You in heaven above or on earth beneath, [b]keeping covenant
and *showing* lovingkindness to Your servants who walk before
You with all their heart,

6 [a]1 Kin 8:3 [b]1 Kin 6:19 [c]1 Kin 6:27
8 [a]Ex 25:13-15; 37:4, 5
9 [a]Ex 25:16, 21; Deut 10:2-5; Heb 9:4 [b]Ex 24:7, 8; 40:20; Deut 4:13
10 [a]Ex 40:34, 35; 2 Chr 7:1, 2
12 [a]2 Chr 6:1 [b]Lev 16:2; Ps 18:11; 97:2
13 [a]2 Sam 7:13 [b]Ex 15:17; Ps 132:14
14 [1]Lit *turned his face about* [a]2 Sam 6:18; 1 Kin 8:55
15 [a]1 Chr 29:10, 20; Neh 9:5; Luke 1:68 [b]2 Sam 7:12, 13; 1 Chr 22:10
16 [a]2 Sam 7:4, 5; 1 Chr 17:3-10; 2 Chr 6:5 [b]Deut 12:5, 11 [c]1 Sam 16:1; 2 Sam 7:8
17 [1]Lit *with* [a]2 Sam 7:2, 3; 1 Chr 17:1, 2
18 [1]Lit *with*
19 [1]Lit *will come forth from your loins* [a]2 Sam 7:5, 12, 13; 1 Kin 5:3, 5; 1 Chr 17:11, 12; 22:8-10
20 [1]Lit *spoke* [a]1 Chr 28:5, 6
21 [a]Deut 31:26; 1 Kin 8:9
22 [a]1 Kin 8:54; 2 Chr 6:12 [b]Ex 9:33; Ezra 9:5
23 [a]1 Sam 2:2; 2 Sam 7:22 [b]Deut 7:9; Neh 1:5; 9:32; Dan 9:4

24 who have kept with Your servant, my father David, that
which You have [1]promised him; indeed, You have spoken
with Your mouth and have fulfilled it with Your hand as it is
this day.
25 "Now therefore, O LORD, the God of Israel, keep with Your
servant David my father that which You have [1]promised him,
saying, '[2a]You shall not lack a man to sit on the throne of Israel,
if only your sons take heed to their way to walk before Me as
you have walked.'
26 "Now therefore, O God of Israel, let Your word, I pray, be
confirmed [a]which You have spoken to Your servant, my father
David.
27 "But will God indeed dwell on the earth? Behold, [a]heaven
and the [1]highest heaven cannot contain You, how much less
this house which I have built!
28 "Yet have regard to the [a]prayer of Your servant and to his
supplication, O LORD my God, to listen to the cry and to the
prayer which Your servant prays before You today;
29 [a]that Your eyes may be open toward this house night and
day, toward [b]the place of which You have said, 'My name shall
be there,' to listen to the prayer which Your servant shall pray
toward this place.
30 "[a]Listen to the supplication of Your servant and of Your
people Israel, [b]when they pray toward this place; hear in
heaven Your dwelling place; hear and [c]forgive.
31 "[a]If a man sins against his neighbor and is made to take an
oath, and he comes *and* takes an oath before Your altar in this
house,
32 then hear in heaven and act and judge Your servants,
[a]condemning the wicked by bringing his way on his own head
and justifying the righteous by giving him according to his
righteousness.
33 "[a]When Your people Israel are [1]defeated before an enemy,
because they have sinned against You, [b]if they turn to You
again and confess Your name and pray and make supplication
to You in this house,
34 then hear in heaven, and forgive the sin of Your people
Israel, and bring them back to the land which You gave to their
fathers.
35 "[a]When the heavens are shut up and there is no rain,
because they have sinned against You, and they pray toward
this place and confess Your name and turn from their sin when
You afflict them,
36 then hear in heaven and forgive the sin of Your servants
and of Your people Israel, [a]indeed, teach them the good way in
which they should walk. And [b]send rain on Your land, which
You have given Your people for an inheritance.
37 "[a]If there is famine in the land, if there is pestilence, if there
is blight *or* mildew, locust *or* grasshopper, if their enemy besieges
them in the land of their [1]cities, whatever plague, whatever
sickness *there is,*

24 [1]Lit *spoken to*
25 [1]Lit *spoken to* [2]Lit *There shall not be cut off to you a man from before Me* [a]1 Kin 2:4
26 [a]2 Sam 7:25
27 [1]Lit *heaven of heavens* [a]2 Chr 2:6; Ps 139:7-16; Is 66:1; Jer 23:24; Acts 7:49
28 [a]Phil 4:6
29 [a]2 Chr 7:15; Neh 1:6 [b]Deut 12:11
30 [a]Neh 1:6 [b]Dan 6:10 [c]Ex 34:6, 7; Ps 85:2; Dan 9:9; 1 John 1:9
31 [a]Ex 22:8-11
32 [a]Deut 25:1
33 [1]Lit *smitten* [a]Lev 26:17, 25; Deut 28:25, 48 [b]Lev 26:40-42
35 [a]Lev 26:19; Deut 11:16, 17; 2 Sam 24:10-13
36 [a]1 Sam 12:23; Ps 5:8; 25:4, 5; 27:11; 86:11; 119:133; Jer 6:16 [b]1 Kin 18:1, 41-45; Jer 14:22
37 [1]Lit *gates* [a]Lev 26:16, 25, 26; Deut 28:21-23, 38-42

38 whatever prayer or supplication is made by any man *or* by
all Your people Israel, [1]each knowing the [2]affliction of his own
heart, and spreading his [3]hands toward this house;
39 then hear in heaven Your dwelling place, and forgive and
act and render to each according to all his ways, [a]whose heart
You know, for [b]You alone know the hearts of all the sons of
men,
40 that they may [1]fear You all the days that they live [2]in the
land which You have given to our fathers.
41 "Also concerning the foreigner who is not of Your people
Israel, when he comes from a far country for Your name's sake
42 (for they will hear of Your great name [a]and Your mighty
hand, and of Your outstretched arm); when he comes and prays
toward this house,
43 hear in heaven Your dwelling place, and do according to all
for which the foreigner calls to You, in order [a]that all the
peoples of the earth may know Your name, to [1]fear You, as *do*
Your people Israel, and that they may know that [2]this house
which I have built is called by Your name.
44 "When Your people go out to battle against [1]their enemy, by
whatever way You shall send them, and [a]they pray to the LORD
[2]toward the city which You have chosen and the house which I
have built for Your name,
45 then hear in heaven their prayer and their supplication,
and maintain their [1]cause.
46 "When they sin against You (for [a]there is no man who does
not sin) and You are angry with them and deliver them to an
enemy, so that [1]they take them away captive [b]to the land of the
enemy, far off or near;
47 [a]if they [1]take thought in the land where they have been
taken captive, and repent and make supplication to You in the
land of those who have taken them captive, saying, '[b]We have
sinned and have committed iniquity, we have acted wickedly';
48 [a]if they return to You with all their heart and with all their
soul in the land of their enemies who have taken them captive,
and [b]pray to You toward their land which You have given to
their fathers, the city which You have chosen, and the house
which I have built for Your name;
49 then hear their prayer and their supplication in heaven
Your dwelling place, and maintain their [1]cause,
50 and forgive Your people who have sinned against You and
all their transgressions which they have transgressed against
You, and [a]make them *objects of* compassion before those who
have taken them captive, that they may have compassion on
them
51 ([a]for they are Your people and Your inheritance which You
have brought forth from Egypt, [b]from the midst of the iron
furnace),
52 [a]that Your eyes may be open to the supplication of Your
servant and to the supplication of Your people Israel, to listen
to them whenever they call to You.

38 [1]Lit *who shall know each* [2]Lit *plague* [3]Lit *palms*

39 [a]1 Sam 2:3; 16:7 [b]1 Chr 28:9; Ps 11:4; Jer 17:10; John 2:24, 25; Acts 1:24

40 [1]Or *revere* [2]Lit *on the face of the land*

42 [a]Ex 13:3; Deut 3:24

43 [1]Or *reverence* [2]Lit *Your name is called upon this house which I have built* [a]Josh 4:23, 24; 1 Sam 17:46; Ps 67:2

44 [1]Lit *his* [2]Lit in *the way of* [a]2 Chr 14:11

45 [1]Lit *right* or *justice*

46 [1]Lit *their captors take them captive* [a]Ps 130:3, 4; 143:2; Prov 20:9; Eccl 7:20; Rom 3:23; 1 John 1:8-10 [b]Lev 26:34-39; 2 Kin 17:6, 18; 25:21

47 [1]Lit *return to their heart* [a]Lev 26:40-42; Neh 9:2 [b]Ezra 9:6, 7; Neh 1:6; Ps 106:6; Dan 9:5

48 [a]Deut 4:29; 1 Sam 7:3, 4; Neh 1:9 [b]Dan 6:10; Jon 2:4

49 [1]Lit *judgment*

50 [a]2 Chr 30:9; Ps 106:46; Acts 7:10

51 [a]Ex 32:11, 12; Deut 9:26-29 [b]Deut 4:20; Jer 11:4

52 [a]1 Kin 8:29

53 “For You have separated them from all the peoples of the earth
as Your inheritance, [a]as You spoke through Moses Your servant,
when You brought our fathers forth from Egypt, O Lord [1]GOD.”
54 [a]When Solomon had finished praying this entire prayer
and supplication to the LORD, [b]he arose from before the altar of
the LORD, from kneeling on his knees with his [1]hands spread
toward heaven.
55 And he stood and [a]blessed all the assembly of Israel with a
loud voice, saying:
56 “Blessed be the LORD, who has given rest to His people
Israel, [a]according to all that He [1]promised; [b]not one word has
[2]failed of all His good [3]promise, which He [1]promised through
Moses His servant.
57 “May the LORD our God be with us, as He was with our
fathers; [a]may He not leave us or forsake us,
58 that [a]He may incline our hearts to Himself, to walk in all
His ways and to keep His commandments and His statutes and
His ordinances, which He commanded our fathers.
59 “And may these words of mine, with which I have made
supplication before the LORD, be near to the LORD our God day
and night, that He may maintain the [1]cause of His servant and
the [1]cause of His people Israel, [2]as each day requires,
60 so [a]that all the peoples of the earth may know that [b]the
LORD is God; there is no one else.
61 “[a]Let your heart therefore be [1]wholly devoted to the LORD
our God, to walk in His statutes and to keep His commandments,
as at this day.”
62 [a]Now the king and all Israel with him [b]offered sacrifice
before the LORD.
63 Solomon offered for the sacrifice of peace offerings, which
he offered to the LORD, 22,000 oxen and 120,000 sheep. [a]So the
king and all the sons of Israel dedicated the house of the LORD.
64 On the same day the king consecrated the middle of the
court that *was* before the house of the LORD, because there he
[1]offered the burnt offering and the grain offering and the fat of
the peace offerings; for [a]the bronze altar that *was* before the
LORD *was* too small to hold the burnt offering and the grain
offering and the fat of the peace offerings.
65 So [a]Solomon observed the feast at that time, and all Israel
with him, a great assembly [b]from the entrance of Hamath [c]to
the brook of Egypt, before the LORD our God, for seven days
and seven *more* days, *even* fourteen days.
66 On the eighth day he sent the people away and they
blessed the king. Then they went to their tents joyful and glad
of heart for all the goodness that the LORD had [1]shown to David
His servant and to Israel His people.

Chapter 9 Theme ____________________

9 [a]Now it came about when Solomon had finished building
the house of the LORD, and [b]the king's house, and [c]all [1]that
Solomon desired to do,

2 Chronicles 7:11

53 [1]Heb *YHWH,* usually rendered LORD [a]Ex 19:5, 6; Deut 9:26-29
54 [1]Lit *palms* [a]2 Chr 7:1 [b]2 Chr 6:13
55 [a]Num 6:23-26; 2 Sam 6:18; 1 Kin 8:14
56 [1]Lit *spoke* [2]Lit *fallen* [3]Lit *word* [a]Deut 12:10 [b]Josh 21:45; 23:14, 15
57 [a]Deut 31:6, 17; Josh 1:5; 1 Sam 12:22; Rom 8:31; Heb 13:5
58 [a]Ps 119:36; Jer 31:33
59 [1]Lit *judgment* [2]Lit *the thing of a day in its day*
60 [a]Josh 4:24; 1 Sam 17:46; 1 Kin 8:43; 2 Kin 19:19 [b]Deut 4:35; 1 Kin 18:39; Jer 10:10-12
61 [1]Lit *complete with* [a]Deut 18:13; 1 Kin 11:4; 2 Kin 20:3
62 [a]2 Chr 7:4-10 [b]2 Sam 6:17-19; Ezra 6:16, 17
63 [a]Ezra 6:15-18; Neh 12:27
64 [1]Lit *made* [a]2 Chr 4:1
65 [a]Lev 23:34-42; 1 Kin 8:2 [b]Num 34:8; Josh 13:5; Judg 3:3; 2 Kin 14:25 [c]Gen 15:18; Ex 23:31; Num 34:5; Josh 13:3
66 [1]Lit *done*
9:1 [1]Lit *Solomon's desire which he was pleased to do* [a]2 Chr 7:11 [b]1 Kin 7:1, 2 [c]2 Chr 8:6

2 that [a]the LORD appeared to Solomon a second time, as He
had appeared to him at Gibeon.
3 The LORD said to him, "[a]I have heard your prayer and your
supplication, which you have made before Me; I have consecrated
this house which you have built [b]by putting My name there
forever, and [c]My eyes and My heart will be there perpetually.
4 "As for you, [a]if you will walk before Me as your father David
walked, in integrity of heart and uprightness, doing according
to all that I have commanded you *and* will keep My statutes
and My ordinances,
5 then [a]I will establish the throne of your kingdom over
Israel forever, just as I [1]promised to your father David, saying,
'[2]You shall not lack a man on the throne of Israel.'
6 "[a]But if you or your sons indeed turn away from following
Me, and do not keep My commandments and My statutes
which I have set before you, and go and serve other gods and
worship them,
7 [a]then I will cut off Israel from the land which I have given
them, and [b]the house which I have consecrated for My name, I
will [1]cast out of My sight. So [c]Israel will become a proverb and
a byword among all peoples.
8 "And this house will become [1a]a heap of ruins; everyone
who passes by will be astonished and hiss and say, '[b]Why has
the LORD done thus to this land and to this house?'
9 "And they will say, '[a]Because they forsook the LORD their
God, who brought their fathers out of the land of Egypt, and
adopted other gods and worshiped them and served them,
therefore the LORD has brought all this adversity on them.'"
948 B.C. **10** [a]It came about [b]at the end of twenty years in which
Solomon had built the two houses, the house of the LORD and
2 Chronicles 8 the king's house
11 (Hiram king of Tyre had supplied Solomon with cedar and
cypress timber and gold according to all his desire), then King
Solomon gave Hiram twenty cities in the land of Galilee.
12 So Hiram came out from Tyre to see the cities which
Solomon had given him, and they [1]did not please him.
13 He said, "What are these cities which you have given me,
my brother?" So [1]they were called the land of [2a]Cabul to this
day.
14 [a]And Hiram sent to the king 120 talents of gold.
15 Now this is the account of the forced labor which King
Solomon [a]levied to build the house of the LORD, his own house,
the [1b]Millo, the wall of Jerusalem, [c]Hazor, [d]Megiddo, and
[e]Gezer.
16 *For* Pharaoh king of Egypt had gone up and captured Gezer
and burned it with fire, and killed the [a]Canaanites who lived in
the city, and had [b]given it *as* a dowry to his daughter,
Solomon's wife.
17 So Solomon rebuilt Gezer and the lower [a]Beth-horon
18 and [a]Baalath and Tamar in the wilderness, in the land *of
Judah,*

2 [a]1 Kin 3:5; 11:9; 2 Chr 1:7
3 [a]2 Kin 20:5; Ps 10:17; 34:17 [b]1 Kin 8:29 [c]Deut 11:12; 2 Chr 6:40
4 [a]1 Kin 3:6, 14; 11:4, 6, 8; 2 Kin 20:3; Ps 128:1
5 [1]Lit *spoke* [2]Lit *There shall not be cut off to you a man* [a]2 Sam 7:12, 16; 1 Kin 2:4; 6:12; 1 Chr 22:10
6 [a]2 Sam 7:14-16; 1 Chr 28:9; Ps 89:30ff
7 [1]Lit *send* [a]Lev 18:24-29; Deut 4:26; 2 Kin 17:23 [b]Jer 7:4-14 [c]Deut 28:37; Ps 44:14; Jer 24:9
8 [1]Heb *high* [a]2 Kin 25:9; 2 Chr 36:19 [b]Deut 29:24-26; 2 Chr 7:21; Jer 22:8, 9, 28
9 [a]Deut 29:25-28; Jer 2:10-13
10 [a]2 Chr 8:1 [b]1 Kin 6:37, 38; 7:1; 9:1
12 [1]Lit *were not right in his sight*
13 [1]Lit *he called them* [2]I.e. as good as nothing [a]Josh 19:27
14 [a]1 Kin 9:11
15 [1]I.e. citadel [a]1 Kin 5:13 [b]2 Sam 5:9; 1 Kin 9:24 [c]Josh 11:1; 19:36 [d]Josh 17:11 [e]Judg 1:29
16 [a]Josh 16:10 [b]1 Kin 3:1; 7:8
17 [a]Josh 10:10; 16:3; 21:22; 2 Chr 8:5
18 [a]Josh 19:44

19 and all the storage cities which Solomon had, even [a]the
cities for [1]his chariots and the cities for [1b]his horsemen, and
[2c]all that it pleased Solomon to build in Jerusalem, in Lebanon,
and in all the land [3]under his rule.
20 *As for* all the people who were left of the Amorites, the
Hittites, the Perizzites, the Hivites and the Jebusites, who were
not of the sons of Israel,
21 [a]their descendants who were left after them in the land
[b]whom the sons of Israel were unable to destroy utterly, [c]from
them Solomon levied [d]forced laborers, even to this day.
22 But Solomon [a]did not make slaves of the sons of Israel; for
they were men of war, his servants, his princes, his captains,
his chariot commanders, and his horsemen.
23 These *were* the [1a]chief officers who *were* over Solomon's
work, five hundred and fifty, [b]who ruled over the people doing
the work.
24 As soon as [a]Pharaoh's daughter came up from the city of
David to her house which *Solomon* had built for her, [b]then he
built the Millo.
25 Now [a]three times in a year Solomon offered burnt offerings
and peace offerings on the altar which he built to the LORD,
burning incense with them *on the altar* which *was* before the
LORD. So he finished the house.
26 King Solomon also built a [a]fleet of ships in [b]Ezion-geber,
which is near Eloth on the shore of the [1]Red Sea, in the land of
Edom.
27 [a]And Hiram sent his servants with the fleet, sailors who
knew the sea, along with the servants of Solomon.
28 They went to [a]Ophir and took four hundred and twenty
talents of gold from there, and brought *it* to King Solomon.

Chapter 10 Theme ____________________

10 [a]Now when the [a]queen of [b]Sheba heard about the fame
of Solomon concerning the name of the LORD, she came
[c]to test him with difficult questions.
2 Chronicles 9

2 So she came to Jerusalem with a very large retinue, with
camels [a]carrying spices and very much gold and precious
stones. When she came to Solomon, she spoke with him about
all that was in her heart.
3 Solomon [1]answered all her questions; nothing was hidden
from the king which he did not [2]explain to her.
4 When the queen of Sheba perceived all the wisdom of
Solomon, the house that he had built,
5 the food of his table, the seating of his servants, the
attendance of his waiters and their attire, his cupbearers, and
[1]his stairway by which he went up to the house of the LORD,
there was no more spirit in her.
6 Then she said to the king, "It was a true report which I
heard in my own land about your words and your wisdom.

19 [1]Lit *the* [2]Lit *the desire of Solomon which he desired to build in Jerusalem* [3]Lit *of* [a]1 Kin 10:26; 2 Chr 1:14 [b]1 Kin 4:26 [c]1 Kin 9:1

21 [a]Judg 1:21-29; 3:1 [b]Josh 15:63; 17:12, 13 [c]Judg 1:28, 35 [d]Gen 9:25, 26; Ezra 2:55, 58

22 [a]Lev 25:39

23 [1]Or *officers of the deputies* [a]2 Chr 8:10 [b]1 Kin 5:16

24 [a]1 Kin 3:1; 7:8 [b]2 Sam 5:9; 1 Kin 9:15; 11:27; 2 Chr 32:5

25 [a]Ex 23:14-17; Deut 16:16

26 [1]Lit *Sea of Reeds* [a]1 Kin 22:48 [b]Num 33:35; Deut 2:8; 1 Kin 22:48

27 [a]1 Kin 5:6, 9; 10:11

28 [a]1 Chr 29:4; 2 Chr 8:18

10:1 [a]2 Chr 9:1; Matt 12:42; Luke 11:31 [b]Gen 10:7, 28; Ps 72:10, 15 [c]Judg 14:12-14; Ps 49:4

2 [a]1 Kin 10:10

3 [1]Lit *told her all her words* [2]Lit *tell her*

5 [1]Or *his burnt offering which he offered*

7 "Nevertheless I did not believe the [1]reports, until I came and my eyes had seen it. And behold, the half was not told me. You exceed *in* wisdom and prosperity the report which I heard.

8 "How [a]blessed are your men, how blessed are these your servants who stand before you continually *and* hear your wisdom.

9 "[a]Blessed be the LORD your God who delighted in you to set you on the throne of Israel; [b]because the LORD loved Israel forever, therefore He made you king, [c]to do justice and righteousness."

10 [a]She gave the king a hundred and twenty talents of gold, and a very great *amount* of spices and precious stones. Never again did such abundance of spices come in as that which the queen of Sheba gave King Solomon.

11 [a]Also the ships of Hiram, which brought gold from Ophir, brought in from Ophir a very great *number of* almug trees and precious stones.

12 [a]The king made of the almug trees supports for the house of the LORD and for the king's house, also lyres and harps for the singers; such almug trees have not come in *again* nor have they been seen to this day.

13 King Solomon gave to the queen of Sheba all her desire which she requested, besides what he gave her according to [1]his royal bounty. Then she turned and went to her own land [2]together with her servants.

14 [a]Now the weight of gold which came in to Solomon in one year was 666 talents of gold,

15 besides *that* from the traders and the [1]wares of the merchants and all the kings of the [a]Arabs and the governors of the country.

16 [a]King Solomon made 200 large shields of beaten gold, [1]using 600 *shekels of* gold on each large shield.

17 *He made* [a]300 shields of beaten gold, [1]using three minas of gold on each shield, and [b]the king put them in the house of the forest of Lebanon.

18 Moreover, the king made a great throne of [a]ivory and overlaid it with refined gold.

19 *There were* six steps to the throne and a round top to the throne at its rear, and [1]arms [2]on each side of the seat, and two lions standing beside the [1]arms.

20 Twelve lions were standing there on the six steps on the one side and on the other; nothing like *it* was made for any other kingdom.

21 All King Solomon's drinking vessels *were* of gold, and all the vessels of the house of the forest of Lebanon *were* of pure gold. None was of silver; it was not considered [1]valuable in the days of Solomon.

22 For [a]the king had at sea the ships of Tarshish with the ships of Hiram; once every three years the ships of Tarshish came bringing gold and silver, ivory and apes and peacocks.

23 [a]So King Solomon became greater than all the kings of the earth in riches and in wisdom.

7 [1]Lit *words*

8 [a]Prov 8:34

9 [a]1 Kin 5:7 [b]1 Chr 17:22; 2 Chr 2:11 [c]2 Sam 8:15; 23:3; Ps 72:2

10 [a]1 Kin 10:2

11 [a]1 Kin 9:27, 28; Job 22:24

12 [a]2 Chr 9:11

13 [1]Lit *the hand of King Solomon* [2]Lit *she and*

14 [a]2 Chr 9:13-28

15 [1]Or *traffic* [a]2 Chr 9:14

16 [1]Lit *he brought up* [a]1 Kin 14:26-28; 2 Chr 12:9, 10

17 [1]Lit *he brought up* [a]1 Kin 14:26 [b]1 Kin 7:2

18 [a]1 Kin 10:22; 2 Chr 9:17; Ps 45:8

19 [1]Lit *hands* [2]Lit *on this side and on this at the place of the seat*

21 [1]Lit *anything*

22 [a]1 Kin 9:26-28; 22:48; 2 Chr 20:36

23 [a]1 Kin 3:12, 13; 4:30

24 [a]1 Kin 3:9, 12, 28

24 All the earth was seeking the presence of Solomon, [a]to hear his wisdom which God had put in his heart.

25 [a]Ps 68:29

25 [a]They brought every man his gift, articles of silver and gold, garments, weapons, spices, horses, and mules, so much year by year.

26 [1]So with ancient versions; Heb *led* [a]1 Kin 4:26; 2 Chr 1:14-17; 9:25 [b]1 Kin 9:19

26 [a]Now Solomon gathered chariots and horsemen; and he had 1,400 chariots and 12,000 horsemen, and he [1]stationed them in the [b]chariot cities and with the king in Jerusalem.

27 [1]Heb *Shephelah* [a]Deut 17:17; 2 Chr 1:15

27 [a]The king made silver *as common* as stones in Jerusalem, and he made cedars as plentiful as sycamore trees that are in the [1]lowland.

28 [a]Deut 17:16; 2 Chr 1:16; 9:28

28 [a]Also Solomon's import of horses was from Egypt and Kue, *and* the king's merchants procured *them* from Kue for a price.

29 [1]Lit *came up and went out from* [2]Lit *in like manner by their hand* [a]2 Kin 7:6, 7

29 A chariot [1]was imported from Egypt for 600 *shekels* of silver, and a horse for 150; and [2]by the same means they exported them [a]to all the kings of the Hittites and to the kings of the Arameans.

Chapter 11 Theme ______________________

11:1 [a]Deut 17:17; Neh 13:23-27

11 Now [a]King Solomon loved many foreign women along with the daughter of Pharaoh: Moabite, Ammonite, Edomite, Sidonian, and Hittite women,

2 [1]Lit *go among* [a]Ex 23:31-33; 34:12-16; Deut 7:3

2 from the nations concerning which the LORD had said to the sons of Israel, "[a]You shall not [1]associate with them, nor shall they [1]associate with you, *for* they will surely turn your heart away after their gods." Solomon held fast to these in love.

3 [a]2 Sam 5:13-16

3 [a]He had seven hundred wives, princesses, and three hundred concubines, and his wives turned his heart away.

4 [1]Lit *complete with* [a]1 Kin 9:4

4 For when Solomon was old, his wives turned his heart away after other gods; and [a]his heart was not [1]wholly devoted to the LORD his God, as the heart of David his father *had been.*

5 [1]In Jer 49:1, 3, *Malcam* [a]Judg 2:13; 10:6; 1 Sam 7:3, 4 [b]1 Kin 11:7

5 For Solomon went after [a]Ashtoreth the goddess of the Sidonians and after [1b]Milcom the detestable idol of the Ammonites.

6 Solomon did what was evil in the sight of the LORD, and did not follow the LORD fully, as David his father *had done.*

7 [1]Lit *before* [a]Num 21:29; Judg 11:24; 2 Kin 23:13 [b]Lev 20:2-5; 2 Kin 23:10; Acts 7:43

7 Then Solomon built a high place for [a]Chemosh the detestable idol of Moab, on the mountain which is [1]east of Jerusalem, and for [b]Molech the detestable idol of the sons of Ammon.

8 Thus also he did for all his foreign wives, who burned incense and sacrificed to their gods.

9 [a]Ps 90:7 [b]1 Kin 11:2, 4 [c]1 Kin 3:5; 9:2

9 Now [a]the LORD was angry with Solomon [b]because his heart was turned away from the LORD, the God of Israel, [c]who had appeared to him twice,

10 [a]1 Kin 6:12; 9:6, 7

10 and [a]had commanded him concerning this thing, that he should not go after other gods; but he did not observe what the LORD had commanded.

11 [1]Lit *this is with you* [a]1 Sam 2:30; 1 Kin 11:29-31; 12:15, 16, 20; 2 Kin 17:15, 21

11 So the LORD said to Solomon, "Because [1]you have done this, and you have not kept My covenant and My statutes, which I have commanded you, [a]I will surely tear the kingdom from you, and will give it to your servant.

INSIGHT

Religious Influences of Solomon's Wives

1. The Gods of Egypt (see page 101).
2. Ashtoreth—*Sidonian* (Canaanite) goddess of fertility, love, and war. Later she became the spouse of Baal (2 Kings 23:13).
3. Milcom—*Ammonite* god whose name means "king." At the request of his pagan wives, Solomon built sanctuaries to Milcom on the Mount of Olives (2 Kings 23:13).
4. Chemosh—*god of Moab*—meaning "to subdue." Solomon erected a sanctuary for Chemosh on a mountain east of Jerusalem (2 Kings 23:13; Jeremiah 48:7, 13, 46).
5. Molech—a pagan god from Ammon to whom human sacrifices, usually children, were made. This practice was condemned by God (Leviticus 18:21; 20:3-5; 2 Kings 23:10; Jeremiah 32:35). Compare with 2 Kings 17:31 and Jeremiah 7:31; 19:5.

For more information, look up these names in a Bible dictionary.

12 "Nevertheless I will not do it in your days for the sake of
your father David, *but* I will tear it out of the hand of your son.
13 "However, [a]I will not tear away all the kingdom, *but* [b]I will
give one tribe to your son for the sake of My servant David and
[c]for the sake of Jerusalem which I have chosen."
14 Then the LORD raised up an adversary to Solomon, Hadad
the Edomite; he was of the [1]royal line in Edom.
15 For it came about, [a]when David was in Edom, and Joab the
commander of the army had gone up to bury the slain, and had
[b]struck down every male in Edom
16 (for Joab and all Israel stayed there six months, until he had
cut off every male in Edom),
17 that Hadad fled [1]to Egypt, he and certain Edomites of his
father's servants with him, while Hadad *was* a young boy.
18 They arose from Midian and came to [a]Paran; and they took
men with them from Paran and came to Egypt, to Pharaoh king
of Egypt, who gave him a house and assigned him food and
gave him land.
19 Now Hadad found great favor [1]before Pharaoh, so that he
gave him in marriage the sister of his own wife, the sister of
Tahpenes the queen.
20 The sister of Tahpenes bore him his son Genubath, whom
Tahpenes weaned in Pharaoh's house; and Genubath was in
Pharaoh's house among the sons of Pharaoh.
21 But [a]when Hadad heard in Egypt that David slept with his
fathers and that Joab the commander of the army was dead,
Hadad said to Pharaoh, "Send me away, that I may go to my
own country."
22 Then Pharaoh said to him, "But what have you lacked with
me, that behold, you are seeking to go to your own country?" And
he answered, "Nothing; nevertheless you must surely [1]let me go."
23 [a]God also raised up *another* adversary to him, Rezon the son
of Eliada, who had fled from his lord [b]Hadadezer king of Zobah.
24 He gathered men to himself and became leader of a
marauding band, [a]after David slew them of *Zobah;* and they
went to Damascus and stayed [1]there, and reigned in Damascus.
25 So he was an adversary to Israel all the days of Solomon,
along with the evil that Hadad *did;* and he abhorred Israel and
reigned over Aram.
26 Then [a]Jeroboam the son of Nebat, an Ephraimite of Zeredah,
Solomon's servant, whose mother's name was Zeruah, a widow,
[b]also [1]rebelled against the king.
27 Now this was the reason why he [1]rebelled against the king:
[a]Solomon built the [2]Millo, *and* closed up the breach of the city
of his father David.
28 Now the man Jeroboam was a valiant warrior, and when
[a]Solomon saw that the young man was [1]industrious, he
appointed him over all the [2]forced labor of the house of Joseph.
29 It came about at that time, when Jeroboam went out of
Jerusalem, that [a]the prophet Ahijah the Shilonite found him on
the road. Now [1]Ahijah had clothed himself with a new cloak;
and both of them were alone in the field.

13 [a]2 Sam 7:15; 1 Chr 17:13; Ps 89:33 [b]1 Kin 11:32, 36; 12:20 [c]1 Kin 8:29
14 [1]Lit *king's seed*
15 [a]2 Sam 8:14; 1 Chr 18:12, 13 [b]Deut 20:13
17 [1]Lit *to go into*
18 [a]Num 10:12; Deut 1:1
19 [1]Lit *in the sight of*
21 [a]1 Kin 2:10
22 [1]Lit *send me away*
23 [a]1 Kin 11:14 [b]2 Sam 8:3; 10:16
24 [1]Lit *in it* [a]2 Sam 10:8, 18
26 [1]Lit *lifted up a hand* [a]1 Kin 11:11, 28; 12:2, 20; 2 Chr 13:6 [b]2 Sam 20:21
27 [1]Lit *lifted up a hand* [2]I.e. citadel [a]1 Kin 9:15, 24
28 [1]Lit *a doer of work* [2]Lit *burden* [a]Prov 22:29
29 [1]Lit *he* [a]1 Kin 12:15; 14:2; 2 Chr 9:29

30 Then [a]Ahijah took hold of the new cloak which was on
him and tore it into twelve pieces.
31 He said to Jeroboam, "Take for yourself ten pieces; for thus
says the LORD, the God of Israel, 'Behold, [a]I will tear the
kingdom out of the hand of Solomon and give you ten tribes
32 ([a]but he will have one tribe, for the sake of My servant
David and for the sake of Jerusalem, [b]the city which I have
chosen from all the tribes of Israel),
33 because they have forsaken Me, and [a]have worshiped
Ashtoreth the goddess of the Sidonians, [b]Chemosh the god of
Moab, and Milcom the god of the sons of Ammon; and they have
not walked in My ways, doing what is right in My sight and
observing My statutes and My ordinances, as his father David *did.*
34 'Nevertheless I will not take the whole kingdom out of his
hand, but I will make him [1]ruler all the days of his life, for the
sake of My servant David whom I chose, who observed My
commandments and My statutes;
35 but [a]I will take the kingdom from his son's hand and give it
to you, *even* ten tribes.
36 'But [a]to his son I will give one tribe, [b]that My servant David
may have a lamp always before Me in Jerusalem, [a]the city
where I have chosen for Myself to put My name.
37 'I will take you, and you shall reign over whatever [1]you
desire, and you shall be king over Israel.
38 'Then it will be, that if you listen to all that I command you
and walk in My ways, and do what is right in My sight by
observing My statutes and My commandments, as My servant
David did, then [a]I will be with you and [b]build you an enduring
house as I built for David, and I will give Israel to you.
39 'Thus I will afflict the [1]descendants of David for this, but
not always.'"
40 Solomon sought therefore to put Jeroboam to death; but
Jeroboam arose and fled to Egypt to [a]Shishak king of Egypt, and
he was in Egypt until the death of Solomon.
41 [a]Now the rest of the acts of Solomon and whatever he did,
and his wisdom, are they not written in the book of the acts of
Solomon?
42 Thus [a]the time that Solomon reigned in Jerusalem over all
Israel was forty years.
43 And Solomon [a]slept with his fathers and was buried in the city
of his father David, and his son [b]Rehoboam reigned in his place.

931 B.C.

Chapter 12 Theme ______________________

2 Chronicles 10

12 [a]Then Rehoboam went to Shechem, for all Israel had
come to [b]Shechem to make him king.

931 B.C.

2 Now [a]when Jeroboam the son of Nebat heard *of it,* [1]he was
living in Egypt (for he was yet in Egypt, where he had fled from
the presence of King Solomon).
3 Then they sent and called him, and Jeroboam and all the
assembly of Israel came and spoke to Rehoboam, saying,

30 [a]1 Sam 15:27, 28
31 [a]1 Kin 11:11, 12
32 [a]1 Kin 11:13; 12:21 [b]1 Kin 11:13; 14:21
33 [a]1 Sam 7:3; 1 Kin 11:5-8 [b]Num 21:29; Jer 48:7, 13
34 [1]Or *prince*
35 [a]1 Kin 11:12; 12:16, 17
36 [a]1 Kin 11:13 [b]1 Kin 15:4; 2 Kin 8:19; Ps 132:17
37 [1]Lit *your soul desires*
38 [a]Deut 31:8; Josh 1:5 [b]2 Sam 7:11, 27
39 [1]Lit *seed*
40 [a]1 Kin 14:25; 2 Chr 12:2-9
41 [a]2 Chr 9:29
42 [a]2 Chr 9:30
43 [a]1 Kin 2:10; 2 Chr 9:31 [b]1 Kin 14:21; Matt 1:7
12:1 [a]2 Chr 10:1 [b]Judg 9:6
2 [1]Lit *Jeroboam* [a]1 Kin 11:26, 40

RETURN TO INSTRUCTIONS

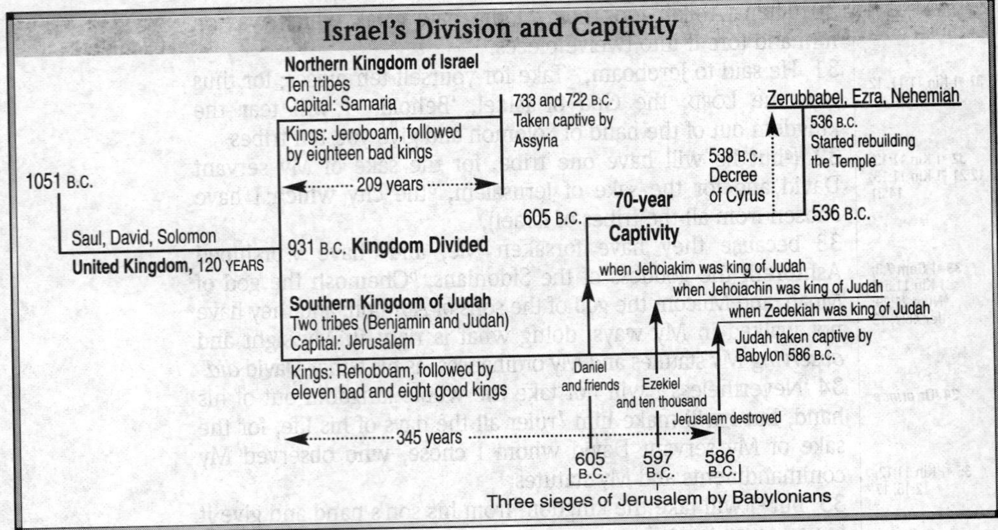

4 "[a]Your father made our yoke hard; now therefore lighten the
hard service of your father and his heavy yoke which he put on
us, and we will serve you."
5 Then he said to them, "[a]Depart [1]for three days, then return
to me." So the people departed.
6 King Rehoboam [a]consulted with the elders who had [1]served
his father Solomon while he was still alive, saying, "How do
you counsel *me* to answer this people?"
7 Then they spoke to him, saying, "[a]If you will be a servant
to this people today, and will serve them and [1]grant them their
petition, and speak good words to them, then they will be your
servants forever."
8 But he forsook the counsel of the elders which they had
given him, and consulted with the young men who grew up
with him [1]and served him.
9 So he said to them, "What counsel do you give that we
may answer this people who have spoken to me, saying,
'Lighten the yoke which your father put on us'?"
10 The young men who grew up with him spoke to him,
saying, "Thus you shall say to this people who spoke to you,
saying, 'Your father made our yoke heavy, now you make it
lighter for us!' But you shall speak to them, 'My little finger is
thicker than my father's loins!
11 'Whereas my father loaded you with a heavy yoke, I will
add to your yoke; my father disciplined you with whips, but I
will discipline you with scorpions.'"
12 Then Jeroboam and all the people came to Rehoboam on
the third day as the king had [1]directed, saying, "[a]Return to me
on the third day."
13 The king answered the people harshly, for he forsook the
advice of the elders which they had [1]given him,
14 and he spoke to them according to the advice of the young

4 [a]1 Sam 8:11-18; 1 Kin 4:7, 21-25; 9:15

5 [1]Lit *yet three* [a]1 Kin 12:12

6 [1]Lit *stood before* [a]1 Kin 4:1-6; Job 12:12; 32:7

7 [1]Lit *answer them* [a]2 Chr 10:7; Prov 15:1

8 [1]Lit *who stood before*

12 [1]Lit *spoken* [a]1 Kin 12:5

13 [1]Lit *advised*

men, saying, "[a]My father made your yoke heavy, but I will add
to your yoke; my father disciplined you with whips, but I will
discipline you with scorpions."
15 So the king did not listen to the people; [a]for it was a turn *of*
events from the LORD, [b]that He might establish His word, which
the LORD spoke through Ahijah the Shilonite to Jeroboam the
son of Nebat.
16 When all Israel *saw* that the king did not listen to them,
the people answered the king, saying,
"What portion do we have in David?
We have no inheritance in the son of Jesse;
[a]To your tents, O Israel!
Now look after your own house, David!"
So Israel departed to their tents.
17 But [a]as for the sons of Israel who lived in the cities of
Judah, Rehoboam reigned over them.
18 Then King Rehoboam sent [a]Adoram, who was over the
forced labor, and all Israel stoned him [1]to death. And King
Rehoboam made haste to mount his chariot to flee to Jerusalem.
19 [a]So Israel has been in rebellion against the house of David
to this day.
20 It came about when all Israel heard that Jeroboam had
returned, that they sent and called him to the assembly and
made him king over all Israel. [a]None but the tribe of Judah
followed the house of David.
21 [a]Now when Rehoboam had come to Jerusalem, he assembled
all the house of Judah and the tribe of Benjamin, 180,000
chosen men who were warriors, to fight against the house of
Israel to restore the kingdom to Rehoboam the son of Solomon.
22 But the word of God came to [a]Shemaiah the
man of God, saying,
23 "Speak to Rehoboam the son of Solomon, king of
Judah, and to all the house of Judah and Benjamin
and to the [a]rest of the people, saying,
24 'Thus says the LORD, "You must not go up and
fight against your [1]relatives the sons of Israel;
return every man to his house, [a]for this thing has
come from Me."'" So they listened to the word of
the LORD, and returned and went *their way* according
to the word of the LORD.
25 Then [a]Jeroboam built Shechem in the hill
country of Ephraim, and lived [1]there. And he went
out from there and built [b]Penuel.
26 Jeroboam said in his heart, "Now the kingdom
will return to the house of David.
27 "[a]If this people go up to offer sacrifices in the house of the
LORD at Jerusalem, then the heart of this people will return to
their lord, *even* to Rehoboam king of Judah; and they will kill
me and return to Rehoboam king of Judah."
28 So the king [1]consulted, and [a]made two golden [b]calves, and
he said to them, "It is too much for you to go up to Jerusalem;

14 [a]Ex 1:13, 14; 5:5-9, 16-18
15 [a]Deut 2:30; Judg 14:4; 1 Kin 12:24; 2 Chr 10:15 [b]1 Kin 11:11, 31
16 [a]2 Sam 20:1
17 [a]1 Kin 11:13, 36
18 [1]Lit *with stones that he died* [a]2 Sam 20:24; 1 Kin 4:6; 5:14
19 [a]2 Kin 17:21
20 [a]1 Kin 11:13, 32, 36
21 [a]2 Chr 11:1
22 [a]2 Chr 11:2; 12:5-7
23 [a]1 Kin 12:17
24 [1]Lit *brothers* [a]1 Kin 12:15
25 [1]Lit *in it* [a]Gen 12:6; Judg 9:45-49 [b]Gen 32:30, 31; Judg 8:8, 17
27 [a]Deut 12:5-7, 14
28 [1]Lit *took counsel* [a]2 Kin 10:29; 17:16; Hos 8:4-7 [b]Hos 10:5

The Divided Kingdom 931–586 B.C.

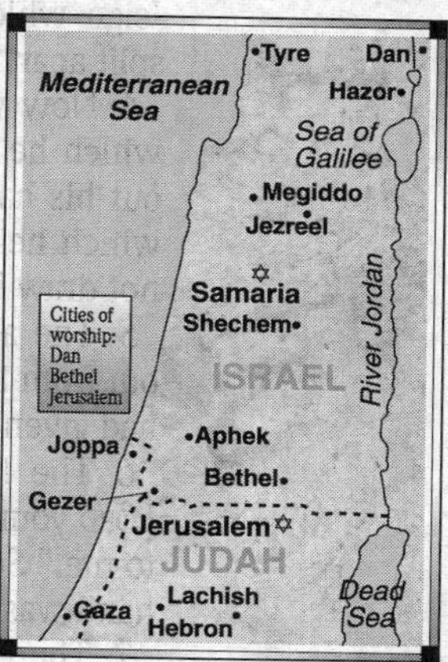

[c]behold your gods, O Israel, that brought you up from the land
of Egypt."
29 He set [a]one in [b]Bethel, and the other he put in [c]Dan.
30 Now [a]this thing became a sin, for the people went *to*
worship before the one as far as Dan.
31 And [a]he made houses on high places, and [b]made priests
from among [1]all the people who were not of the sons of Levi.
32 Jeroboam [1]instituted a feast in the eighth month on the
fifteenth day of the month, [a]like the feast which is in Judah,
and he [2]went up to the altar; thus he did in Bethel, sacrificing
to the calves which he had made. And he stationed in Bethel
[b]the priests of the high places which he had made.
33 Then he [1]went up to the altar which he had made in
Bethel on the fifteenth day in the eighth month, even in the
month which he had [2a]devised [3]in his own heart; and he
[2]instituted a feast for the sons of Israel and [1]went up to the
altar [b]to burn [4]incense.

Chapter 13 Theme ______________________

13 Now behold, there came [a]a man of God from Judah to
Bethel by the word of the LORD, while Jeroboam was
standing by the altar [b]to burn incense.
2 [a]He cried against the altar by the word of the LORD, and
said, "O altar, altar, thus says the LORD, 'Behold, a son shall be
born to the house of David, [b]Josiah by name; and on you he
shall sacrifice the priests of the high places who burn incense
on you, and human bones shall be burned on you.'"
3 Then he gave a [1]sign the same day, saying, "[a]This is the
[1]sign which the LORD has spoken, 'Behold, the altar shall be
split apart and the [2]ashes which are on it shall be poured out.'"
4 Now when the king heard the saying of the man of God,
which he cried against the altar in Bethel, Jeroboam stretched
out his hand from the altar, saying, "Seize him." But his hand
which he stretched out against him dried up, so that he could
not draw it back to himself.
5 The altar also was split apart and the [1]ashes were poured
out from the altar, according to the [2]sign which the man of God
had given by the word of the LORD.
6 The king said to the man of God, "Please [1a]entreat the
LORD your God, and pray for me, that my hand may be restored
to me." So [b]the man of God [2]entreated the LORD, and the king's
hand was restored to him, and it became as it was before.
7 Then the king said to the man of God, "Come home with
me and refresh yourself, and [a]I will give you a reward."
8 But the man of God said to the king, "[a]If you were to give
me half your house I would not go with you, nor would I eat
bread or drink water in this place.
9 "For so [1]it was commanded me by the word of the LORD,
saying, 'You shall eat no bread, nor drink water, nor return by
the way which you came.'"

28 [c]Ex 32:4, 8

29 [a]Hos 10:5 [b]Gen 28:19 [c]Judg 18:26-31

30 [a]1 Kin 13:34; 2 Kin 17:21

31 [1]Or *extremities of* [a]1 Kin 13:32 [b]1 Kin 13:33; 2 Kin 17:32; 2 Chr 11:15; 13:9

32 [1]Lit *made* [2]Or *offered upon* [a]Lev 23:33, 34; Num 29:12; 1 Kin 8:2, 5 [b]Amos 7:10-13

33 [1]Or *offered upon* [2]Lit *made* [3]Lit *from* [4]Or *sacrifices* [a]Num 15:39 [b]1 Kin 13:1

13:1 [a]1 Kin 12:22; 2 Kin 23:17 [b]1 Kin 12:33

2 [a]1 Kin 13:32 [b]2 Kin 23:15, 16

3 [1]Lit *wonder* [2]Lit *ashes of fat* [a]Ex 4:1-5; Judg 6:17; Is 38:7; John 2:18; 1 Cor 1:22

5 [1]Lit *ashes of fat* [2]Lit *wonder*

6 [1]Lit *soften the face of* [2]Lit *softened the face of* [a]Ex 8:8, 28; 9:28; 10:17; Acts 8:24; James 5:16 [b]Luke 6:27, 28

7 [a]1 Sam 9:7, 8; 2 Kin 5:15

8 [a]Num 22:18; 24:13; 1 Kin 13:16, 17

9 [1]Lit *he commanded me*

10 So he went another way and did not return by the way
which he came to Bethel.
11 Now [a]an old prophet was living in Bethel; and his [1]sons
came and told him all the deeds which the man of God had
done that day in Bethel; the words which he had spoken to the
king, these also they related to their father.
12 Their father said to them, "[1]Which way did he go?" Now
his sons [2]had seen the way which the man of God who came
from Judah had gone.
13 Then he said to his sons, "Saddle the donkey for me." So
they saddled the donkey for him and he rode away on it.
14 So he went after the man of God and found him sitting
under [1]an oak; and he said to him, "Are you the man of God
who came from Judah?" And he said, "I am."
15 Then he said to him, "Come home with me and eat bread."
16 He said, "[a]I cannot return with you, nor go with you, nor
will I eat bread or drink water with you in this place.
17 "For a command *came* to me [a]by the word of the LORD, 'You
shall eat no bread, nor drink water there; do not return by
going the way which you came.'"
18 He said to him, "[a]I also am a prophet like you, and [b]an
angel spoke to me by the word of the LORD, saying, 'Bring him
back with you to your house, that he may eat bread and drink
water.'" *But* [c]he lied to him.
19 So he went back with him, and ate bread in his house and
drank water.
20 Now it came about, as they were sitting down at the table,
that the word of the LORD came to the prophet who had
brought him back;
21 and he cried to the man of God who came from Judah,
saying, "Thus says the LORD, 'Because you have [1]disobeyed the
[2]command of the LORD, and have not observed the commandment which the LORD your God commanded you,
22 but have returned and eaten bread and drunk water in the
place of which He said to you, "Eat no bread and drink no
water"; your body shall not come to the grave of your fathers.'"
23 It came about after he had eaten bread and after he had
drunk, that he saddled the donkey for him, for the prophet
whom he had brought back.
24 Now when he had gone, [a]a lion met him on the way and
killed him, and his body was thrown on the road, with the
donkey standing beside it; the lion also was standing beside the
body.
25 And behold, men passed by and saw the body thrown on
the road, and the lion standing beside the body; so they came
and told *it* in the city where [a]the old prophet lived.
26 Now when the prophet who brought him back from the
way heard *it*, he said, "It is the man of God, who [1]disobeyed
the [2]command of the LORD; therefore the LORD has given him
to the lion, which has torn him and killed him, according to
the word of the LORD which He spoke to him."

11 [1]Lit *son* [a]1 Kin 13:25; 2 Kin 23:18
12 [1]Lit *Where is the way he went* [2]Some ancient versions read *showed him*
14 [1]Or a *terebinth*
16 [a]1 Kin 13:8, 9
17 [a]1 Kin 20:35
18 [a]Matt 7:15; 1 John 4:1 [b]Gal 1:8 [c]Prov 12:19, 22; 19:5; Jer 29:31, 32; Ezek 13:8, 9; 1 Tim 4:1, 2
21 [1]Lit *rebelled against* [2]Lit *mouth*
24 [a]1 Kin 20:36
25 [a]1 Kin 13:11
26 [1]Lit *rebelled against* [2]Lit *mouth*

27 Then he spoke to his sons, saying, "Saddle the donkey for
me." And they saddled *it.*
28 He went and found his body thrown on the road with the
donkey and the lion standing beside the body; the lion had not
eaten the body nor torn the donkey.
29 So the prophet took up the body of the man of God and laid
it on the donkey and brought it back, and he came to the city
of the old prophet to mourn and to bury him.
30 He laid his body in his own grave, and they mourned over
him, *saying,* "[a]Alas, my brother!"
31 After he had buried him, he spoke to his sons, saying,
"When I die, bury me in the grave in which the man of God is
buried; [a]lay my bones beside his bones.
32 "[a]For the thing shall surely come to pass which he cried by
the word of the LORD against the altar in Bethel and [b]against all
the houses of the high places which are in the cities of [c]Samaria."
33 After this event Jeroboam did not return from his evil way,
but [a]again he made priests of the high places from among [1]all
the people; [b]any who would, he ordained, to be priests of the
high places.
34 [1a]This event became sin to the house of Jeroboam, [b]even to
blot *it* out and destroy *it* from off the face of the earth.

Chapter 14 Theme ______________________

14 At that time Abijah the son of Jeroboam became sick.
2 Jeroboam said to his wife, "Arise now, and [a]disguise
yourself so that they will not know that you are the wife of
Jeroboam, and go to [b]Shiloh; behold, Ahijah the prophet is
there, who [c]spoke concerning me *that I would be* king over
this people.
3 "[a]Take ten loaves with you, *some* cakes and a jar of honey,
and go to him. He will tell you what will happen to the boy."
4 Jeroboam's wife did so, and arose and went to [a]Shiloh, and
came to the house of [b]Ahijah. Now Ahijah could not see, [c]for
his eyes were [1]dim because of his age.
5 Now the LORD had said to Ahijah, "Behold, the wife of
Jeroboam is coming to [1]inquire of you concerning her son, for
he is sick. You shall say thus and thus to her, for it will be when
she arrives that [a]she will pretend to be another woman."
6 When Ahijah heard the sound of her feet coming in the
doorway, he said, "Come in, wife of Jeroboam, why do you
pretend to be another woman? For I am sent to you *with* a
harsh *message.*
7 "Go, say to Jeroboam, 'Thus says the LORD God of Israel,
"[a]Because I exalted you from among the people and made you
leader over My people Israel,
8 and [a]tore the kingdom away from the house of David and
gave it to you—[b]yet you have not been like My servant David,
who kept My commandments and who followed Me with all
his heart, [c]to do only that which was right in My sight;

30 [a]Jer 22:18
31 [a]Ruth 1:17; 2 Kin 23:17, 18
32 [a]1 Kin 13:2 [b]Lev 26:30; 1 Kin 12:31 [c]1 Kin 16:24; John 4:5; Acts 8:14
33 [1]Or *extremities of* [a]1 Kin 12:31, 32 [b]Judg 17:5
34 [1]Lit *by this thing he became* [a]1 Kin 12:30; 2 Kin 17:21 [b]1 Kin 14:10; 15:29, 30
14:2 [a]1 Sam 28:8; 2 Sam 14:2; 2 Chr 18:29 [b]Josh 18:1 [c]1 Kin 11:29-31
3 [a]1 Sam 9:7, 8; 1 Kin 13:7; 2 Kin 4:42
4 [1]Lit *set* [a]1 Kin 14:2 [b]1 Kin 11:29 [c]1 Sam 3:2; 4:15
5 [1]Lit *seek a word from* [a]2 Sam 14:2
7 [a]2 Sam 12:7; 1 Kin 11:28-31; 16:2
8 [a]1 Kin 11:31 [b]1 Kin 11:33, 38 [c]1 Kin 15:5

9 [a]1 Kin 12:28; 2 Chr 11:15 [b]Ex 34:17 [c]Neh 9:26; Ps 50:17; Ezek 23:35

9 you also have done more evil than all who were before you, and [a]have gone and made for yourself other gods and [b]molten images to provoke Me to anger, and have [c]cast Me behind your back—

10 [1]Lit *him who urinates against the wall* [a]1 Kin 21:21; 2 Kin 9:8 [b]Deut 32:36; 2 Kin 14:26 [c]1 Kin 15:29

10 therefore behold, I am bringing calamity on the house of Jeroboam, and [a]will cut off from Jeroboam [1]every male person, [b]both bond and free in Israel, and I [c]will make a clean sweep of the house of Jeroboam, as one sweeps away dung until it is all gone.

11 [a]1 Kin 16:4; 21:24

11 "[a]Anyone belonging to Jeroboam who dies in the city the dogs will eat. And he who dies in the field the birds of the heavens will eat; for the LORD has spoken *it*."'

12 [a]1 Kin 14:17

12 "Now you, arise, go to your house. [a]When your feet enter the city the child will die.

13 [1]Lit *the one* [a]2 Chr 19:3

13 "All Israel shall mourn for him and bury him, for [1]he alone of Jeroboam's *family* will come to the grave, because in him [a]something good was found toward the LORD God of Israel in the house of Jeroboam.

14 [1]Lit *and what even now?* [a]1 Kin 15:27-29

14 "Moreover, [a]the LORD will raise up for Himself a king over Israel who will cut off the house of Jeroboam this day [1]and from now on.

15 [1]I.e. wooden symbols of a female deity [a]Deut 29:28; 2 Kin 17:6; Ps 52:5 [b]Josh 23:15, 16 [c]2 Kin 15:29 [d]Ex 34:13, 14; Deut 12:3, 4

15 "For the LORD will strike Israel, as a reed is shaken in the water; and [a]He will uproot Israel from [b]this good land which He gave to their fathers, and [c]will scatter them beyond the *Euphrates* River, [d]because they have made their [1]Asherim, provoking the LORD to anger.

16 [1]Lit *sinned* [a]1 Kin 12:30; 13:34; 15:30, 34; 16:2

16 "He will give up Israel [a]on account of the sins of Jeroboam, which he [1]committed and with which he made Israel to sin."

17 [a]1 Kin 15:21, 33; 16:6-9, 15, 23; Song 6:4 [b]1 Kin 14:12

17 Then Jeroboam's wife arose and departed and came to [a]Tirzah. [b]As she was entering the threshold of the house, the child died.

18 [a]1 Kin 14:13

18 [a]All Israel buried him and mourned for him, according to the word of the LORD which He spoke through His servant Ahijah the prophet.

19 [a]1 Kin 14:30; 2 Chr 13:2-20

19 Now the rest of the acts of Jeroboam, [a]how he made war and how he reigned, behold, they are written in the Book of the Chronicles of the Kings of Israel.

20 The time that Jeroboam reigned *was* twenty-two years; and 910 B.C.
he slept with his fathers, and Nadab his son reigned in his place.

21 [a]2 Chr 12:13 [b]1 Kin 11:32, 36

21 [a]Now Rehoboam the son of Solomon reigned in Judah. 931 B.C.
Rehoboam was forty-one years old when he became king, and he reigned seventeen years in Jerusalem, [b]the city which the LORD had chosen from all the tribes of Israel to put His name there. And his mother's name was Naamah the Ammonitess.

22 [1]Lit *their* [2]Lit *sinned* [a]2 Chr 12:1, 14 [b]Deut 32:21; Ps 78:58; 1 Cor 10:22

22 [a]Judah did evil in the sight of the LORD, and they [b]provoked Him to jealousy more than all that their fathers had done, with [1]the sins which they [2]committed.

23 [1]I.e. wooden symbols of a female deity [a]Deut 12:2; Ezek 16:24 [b]Deut 16:22 [c]1 Kin 14:15 [d]2 Kin 17:10; Is 57:5; Jer 2:20

23 For they also built for themselves [a]high places and *sacred* [b]pillars and [1c]Asherim on every high hill and [d]beneath every luxuriant tree.

24 There were also [a]male cult prostitutes in the land. They did according to all the abominations of the nations which the LORD dispossessed before the sons of Israel.

927 B.C.

2 Chronicles 12

25 [a]Now it happened in the fifth year of King Rehoboam, that Shishak the king of Egypt came up against Jerusalem.

26 He took away the treasures of the house of the LORD and the treasures of the king's house, and [a]he took everything, [1b]even taking all the shields of gold which Solomon had made.

27 So King Rehoboam made shields of bronze in their place, and [a]committed them to the [1]care of the commanders of the [2]guard who guarded the doorway of the king's house.

28 Then it happened as often as the king entered the house of the LORD, that the [1]guards would carry them and would bring them back into the [1]guards' room.

29 [a]Now the rest of the acts of Rehoboam and all that he did, are they not written in the Book of the Chronicles of the Kings of Judah?

30 [a]There was war between Rehoboam and Jeroboam continually.

913 B.C.

31 And Rehoboam slept with his fathers and was buried with his fathers in the city of David; and [a]his mother's name was Naamah the Ammonitess. And Abijam his son became king in his place.

Chapter 15 Theme ______________________

913 B.C.

2 Chronicles 13

15 [a]Now in the eighteenth year of King Jeroboam, the son of Nebat, Abijam became king over Judah.

2 He reigned three years in Jerusalem; and his mother's name was [1a]Maacah the daughter of [2b]Abishalom.

3 He walked in all the sins of his father which he had committed before him; and [a]his heart was not [1]wholly devoted to the LORD his God, like the heart of his father David.

4 But for David's sake the LORD his God gave him a [a]lamp in Jerusalem, to raise up his son after him and to establish Jerusalem;

5 [a]because David did what was right in the sight of the LORD, and had not turned aside from anything that He commanded him all the days of his life, [b]except in the case of Uriah the Hittite.

6 [a]There was war between Rehoboam and Jeroboam all the days of his life.

7 Now [a]the rest of the acts of Abijam and all that he did, are they not written in the Book of the Chronicles of the Kings of Judah? [b]And there was war between Abijam and Jeroboam.

911 B.C.

8 [a]And Abijam slept with his fathers and they buried him in the city of David; and Asa his son became king in his place.

9 So in the twentieth year of Jeroboam the king of Israel, Asa began to reign as king of Judah.

10 He reigned forty-one years in Jerusalem; and [a]his mother's name was Maacah the daughter of Abishalom.

24 [a]Gen 19:5; Deut 23:17; 1 Kin 15:12; 22:46; 2 Kin 23:7

25 [a]1 Kin 11:40; 2 Chr 12:2, 9

26 [1]Lit *and he took away* [a]1 Kin 15:18; 2 Chr 12:9 [b]1 Kin 10:17; 2 Chr 9:15, 16

27 [1]Lit *hand* [2]Lit *runner* [a]1 Sam 8:11; 22:17

28 [1]Lit *runners*

29 [a]2 Chr 12:15, 16

30 [a]1 Kin 12:21; 15:6

31 [a]1 Kin 14:21

15:1 [a]2 Chr 13:1

2 [1]In 2 Chr 13:2, *Micaiah, the daughter of Uriel* [2]In 2 Chr 11:20, *Absalom* [a]2 Chr 13:2 [b]2 Chr 11:21

3 [1]Lit *complete with* [a]1 Kin 11:4; Ps 119:80

4 [a]2 Sam 21:17; 1 Kin 11:36; 2 Chr 21:7

5 [a]1 Kin 9:4; 14:8; Luke 1:6 [b]2 Sam 11:3f, 15-17; 12:9, 10

6 [a]1 Kin 14:30; 2 Chr 12:15-13:20

7 [a]2 Chr 13:2, 21, 22 [b]2 Chr 13:3-20

8 [a]2 Chr 14:1

10 [a]1 Kin 15:2

11 [a]Asa did what was right in the sight of the LORD, like David
his father.
12 [a]He also put away the male cult prostitutes from the land
and [b]removed all the idols which his fathers had made.
13 [1a]He also removed Maacah his mother from *being* queen
mother, because she had made a horrid image [2]as an Asherah; and
Asa cut down her horrid image and [b]burned *it* at the brook Kidron.
14 [a]But the high places were not taken away; nevertheless
[b]the heart of Asa was [1]wholly devoted to the LORD all his days.
15 [a]He brought into the house of the LORD the dedicated things
of his father and his own dedicated things: silver and gold and
utensils.
16 [a]Now there was war between Asa and Baasha king of Israel
all their days.
17 [a]Baasha king of Israel went up against Judah and [1b]fortified
Ramah [c]in order to prevent *anyone* from going out or coming
in to Asa king of Judah.
18 Then [a]Asa took all the silver and the gold which were left
in the treasuries of the house of the LORD and the treasuries of the
king's house, and delivered them into the hand of his servants.
And [b]King Asa sent them to Ben-hadad the son of Tabrimmon,
the son of Hezion, king of Aram, who lived in [c]Damascus, saying,
19 "*Let there be* a [a]treaty between [1]you and me, *as* between
my father and your father. Behold, I have sent you a present of
silver and gold; go, break your treaty with Baasha king of Israel
so that he will withdraw from me."
20 So Ben-hadad listened to King Asa and sent the commanders
of his armies against the cities of Israel, and [1]conquered [a]Ijon,
[b]Dan, [c]Abel-beth-maacah and all [d]Chinneroth, besides all the
land of Naphtali.
21 When Baasha heard *of it,* [a]he ceased [1]fortifying Ramah and
remained in [b]Tirzah.
22 Then King Asa made a proclamation to all Judah—none
was exempt—and they carried away the stones of Ramah and
its timber with which Baasha had built. And King Asa built
with them [a]Geba of Benjamin and Mizpah.
23 [a]Now the rest of all the acts of Asa and all his might and all
that he did and the cities which he built, are they not written
in the Book of the Chronicles of the Kings of Judah? But in the
time of his old age he was diseased in his feet.
24 And Asa slept with his fathers and was buried with his 870 B.C.
fathers in the city of David his father; and [a]Jehoshaphat his son
reigned in his place.
25 Now [a]Nadab the son of Jeroboam became king over Israel 910 B.C.
in the second year of Asa king of Judah, and he reigned over
Israel two years.
26 He did evil in the sight of the LORD, and [a]walked in the way
of his father and [b]in his sin which he made Israel sin.
27 Then [a]Baasha the son of Ahijah of the house of Issachar
conspired against him, and Baasha struck him down at
[b]Gibbethon, which belonged to the Philistines, while Nadab and
all Israel were laying siege to Gibbethon.

11 [a]2 Chr 14:2
12 [a]Deut 23:17; 1 Kin 14:24; 22:46 [b]1 Kin 11:7, 8; 14:23; 2 Chr 14:2-5
13 [1]Lit *also Maacah his mother and he removed her* [2]Or *for Asherah* [a]2 Chr 15:16-18 [b]Ex 32:20
14 [1]Lit *complete with* [a]1 Kin 22:43; 2 Kin 12:3 [b]1 Kin 8:61; 15:3
15 [a]1 Kin 7:51
16 [a]1 Kin 15:32
17 [1]Lit *built* [a]2 Chr 16:1-6 [b]Josh 18:25; 1 Kin 15:21, 22 [c]1 Kin 12:26-29
18 [a]1 Kin 14:26; 15:15 [b]2 Kin 12:17, 18; 2 Chr 16:2 [c]Gen 14:15; 1 Kin 11:23, 24
19 [1]Lit *me and you* [a]2 Chr 16:7
20 [1]Lit *smote* [a]2 Kin 15:29 [b]Judg 18:29; 1 Kin 12:29 [c]2 Sam 20:15; 2 Kin 15:29 [d]Josh 11:2; 12:3
21 [1]Lit *building* [a]1 Kin 15:17 [b]1 Kin 14:17; 16:15-18
22 [a]Josh 18:24; 21:17
23 [a]2 Chr 16:11-14
24 [a]1 Kin 22:41-44; 2 Chr 17:1; Matt 1:8
25 [a]1 Kin 14:20
26 [a]1 Kin 12:28-33; 13:33, 34 [b]1 Kin 14:16; 15:30, 34
27 [a]1 Kin 14:14 [b]Josh 19:44; 21:23; 1 Kin 16:15

28 So Baasha killed him in the third year of Asa king of Judah
and reigned in his place.
29 It came about as soon as he was king, he struck down all
the household of Jeroboam. He did not leave to Jeroboam [1]any
persons alive, until he had destroyed them, [a]according to the
word of the LORD, which He spoke by His servant Ahijah the
Shilonite,
30 *and* because of the sins of Jeroboam which he sinned, and
[a]which he made Israel sin, because of his provocation with
which he provoked the LORD God of Israel to anger.
31 [a]Now the rest of the acts of Nadab and all that he did, are they
not written in the Book of the Chronicles of the Kings of Israel?
32 [a]There was war between Asa and Baasha king of Israel all
their days.
909 B.C. **33** In the third year of Asa king of Judah, Baasha the son of
Ahijah became king over all Israel at Tirzah, *and reigned* twenty-
four years.
34 He did evil in the sight of the LORD, and [a]walked in the way
of Jeroboam and in his sin which he made Israel sin.

Chapter 16 Theme ______________________________

16 Now the word of the LORD came to [a]Jehu the son of
[b]Hanani against Baasha, saying,
2 "Inasmuch as I [a]exalted you from the dust and made you
leader over My people Israel, and [b]you have walked in the way
of Jeroboam and have made My people Israel sin, provoking
Me to anger with their sins,
3 behold, [a]I will consume [b]Baasha and his house, and [c]I will
make your house like the house of Jeroboam the son of Nebat.
4 "[a]Anyone of Baasha who dies in the city the dogs will eat,
and anyone of his who dies in the field the birds of the heavens
will eat."
5 [a]Now the rest of the acts of Baasha and what he did and his
might, are they not written in the Book of the Chronicles of
the Kings of Israel?
6 And Baasha slept with his fathers and was buried in [a]Tirzah,
and Elah his son became king in his place.
7 Moreover, the word of the LORD through [a]the prophet Jehu
the son of Hanani also came against Baasha and his household,
both because of all the evil which he did in the sight of the
LORD, provoking Him to anger with [b]the work of his hands, in
being like the house of Jeroboam, and because [c]he struck [1]it.
886 B.C. **8** In the twenty-sixth year of Asa king of Judah, Elah the son of
Baasha became king over Israel at Tirzah, *and reigned* two years.
9 His servant [a]Zimri, commander of half his chariots, conspired
against him. Now he *was* at Tirzah drinking himself drunk in
the house of Arza, [b]who *was* over the household at Tirzah.
885 B.C. 10 Then Zimri went in and struck him and put him to death
in the twenty-seventh year of Asa king of Judah, and became
king in his place.

29 [1]Lit *any breath*
[a]1 Kin 14:9-16
30 [a]1 Kin 15:26
31 [a]1 Kin 14:19
32 [a]1 Kin 15:16
34 [a]1 Kin 15:26
16:1 [a]1 Kin 16:7; 2 Chr 19:2; 20:34
[b]2 Chr 16:7-10
2 [a]1 Sam 2:8; 1 Kin 14:7
[b]1 Kin 15:34
3 [a]1 Kin 14:10; 21:21
[b]1 Kin 16:11
[c]1 Kin 15:29
4 [a]1 Kin 14:11; 21:24
5 [a]1 Kin 14:19; 15:31
6 [a]1 Kin 14:17; 15:21
7 [1]Or *him*
[a]1 Kin 16:1
[b]Ps 115:4; Is 2:8
[c]1 Kin 14:14; 15:27, 29
9 [a]2 Kin 9:30-33
[b]Gen 24:2; 39:4; 1 Kin 18:3

11 It came about when he became king, as soon as he sat on his
throne, that [a]he [1]killed all the household of Baasha; he did not
leave [2]a single male, neither of his [3]relatives nor of his friends.
12 Thus Zimri destroyed all the household of Baasha, [a]according
to the word of the LORD, which He spoke against Baasha through
[b]Jehu the prophet,
13 for all the sins of Baasha and the sins of Elah his son, which
they sinned and which they made Israel sin, [a]provoking the
LORD God of Israel to anger with their [1]idols.
14 [a]Now the rest of the acts of Elah and all that he did, are they
not written in the Book of the Chronicles of the Kings of Israel?
15 In the twenty-seventh year of Asa king of Judah, Zimri
reigned seven days at Tirzah. Now the people were camped
against [a]Gibbethon, which belonged to the Philistines.
16 The people who were camped heard [1]it said, "Zimri has
conspired and has also struck down the king." Therefore all
Israel made Omri, the commander of the army, king over Israel
that day in the camp.
17 Then Omri and all Israel with him went up from Gibbethon
and besieged Tirzah.
18 When Zimri saw that the city was taken, he went into the
citadel of the king's house and burned the king's house over
him with fire, and [a]died,
19 because of his sins which he sinned, doing evil in the sight
of the LORD, [a]walking in the way of Jeroboam, and in his sin
which he did, making Israel sin.
20 [a]Now the rest of the acts of Zimri and his conspiracy which
he [1]carried out, are they not written in the Book of the Chronicles
of the Kings of Israel?
21 Then the people of Israel were divided into two parts: half
of the people followed Tibni the son of Ginath, to make him
king; the *other* half followed Omri.
22 But the people who followed Omri prevailed over the people
who followed Tibni the son of Ginath. And Tibni died and
Omri became king.
23 In the thirty-first year of Asa king of Judah, Omri became 881 B.C.
king over Israel *and reigned* twelve years; he reigned six years
at [a]Tirzah.
24 He bought the hill [1]Samaria from Shemer for two talents of
silver; and he built on the hill, and named the city which he
built [1a]Samaria, after the name of Shemer, the owner of the hill.
25 [a]Omri did evil in the sight of the LORD, and [b]acted more
wickedly than all who *were* before him.
26 For he [a]walked in all the way of Jeroboam the son of Nebat
and in his sins which he made Israel sin, provoking the LORD
God of Israel with their [1]idols.
27 Now the rest of the acts of Omri which he did and his
might which he [1]showed, are they not written in the Book of
the Chronicles of the Kings of Israel?
28 So Omri slept with his fathers and was buried in Samaria;
and Ahab his son became king in his place.

11 [1]Lit *smote* [2]Lit *him who urinates against the wall* [3]Lit *redeemers* [a]1 Kin 15:29; 16:3
12 [a]1 Kin 16:3 [b]2 Chr 19:2; 20:34
13 [1]Lit *vanities* [a]Deut 32:21; 1 Kin 15:30
14 [a]1 Kin 16:5
15 [a]1 Kin 15:27
16 [1]Lit *saying*
18 [a]1 Sam 31:4, 5; 2 Sam 17:23
19 [a]1 Kin 12:28; 14:16; 15:26
20 [1]Lit *conspired* [a]1 Kin 16:5, 14, 27
23 [a]1 Kin 15:21
24 [1]Heb *Shomeron* [a]1 Kin 16:28, 29, 32
25 [a]Mic 6:16 [b]1 Kin 14:9; 16:30-33
26 [1]Lit *vanities* [a]1 Kin 16:19
27 [1]Lit *did*

874 B.C.
29 Now Ahab the son of Omri became king over Israel in the
thirty-eighth year of Asa king of Judah, and Ahab the son of
Omri reigned over Israel in Samaria twenty-two years.
30 Ahab the son of Omri did evil in the sight of the LORD [a]more
than all who were before him.
31 It came about, as though it had been a trivial thing for him
to walk in the sins of Jeroboam the son of Nebat, that [a]he
married Jezebel the daughter of Ethbaal king of the [b]Sidonians,
and went to serve Baal and worshiped him.
32 So he erected an altar for Baal in [a]the house of Baal which
he built in Samaria.
33 Ahab also made [a]the [1]Asherah. Thus [b]Ahab did more to
provoke the LORD God of Israel than all the kings of Israel who
were before him.
34 [a]In his days Hiel the Bethelite built Jericho; he laid its
foundations with the *loss of* Abiram his firstborn, and set up its
gates with the *loss of* his youngest son Segub, according to the
word of the LORD, which He spoke by Joshua the son of Nun.

Chapter 17 Theme ______________________________

17 Now Elijah the Tishbite, who was of [1a]the settlers of
Gilead, said to Ahab, "[b]As the LORD, the God of Israel lives,
before whom I stand, surely [c]there shall be neither dew nor
rain these years, except by my word."
2 The word of the LORD came to him, saying,
3 "Go away from here and turn eastward, and hide yourself by
the brook Cherith, which is [1]east of the Jordan.
4 "It shall be that you will drink of the brook, and [a]I have
commanded the ravens to provide for you there."
5 So he went and did according to the word of the LORD, for
he went and lived by the brook Cherith, which is [1]east of the
Jordan.
6 The ravens brought him bread and meat in the morning and
bread and meat in the evening, and he would drink from the
brook.
7 It happened after a while that the brook dried up, because
there was no rain in the land.
8 Then the word of the LORD came to him, saying,
9 "Arise, go to [a]Zarephath, which belongs to Sidon, and stay
there; behold, [b]I have commanded a widow there to provide
for you."
10 So he arose and went to Zarephath, and when he came to
the gate of the city, behold, a widow was there gathering sticks;
and [a]he called to her and said, "Please get me a little water in a
[1]jar, that I may drink."
11 As she was going to get *it,* he called to her and said,
"Please bring me a piece of bread in your hand."
12 But she said, "[a]As the LORD your God lives, [b]I have no
[1]bread, only a handful of flour in the [2]bowl and a little oil in the
jar; and behold, I am gathering [3]a few sticks that I may go in
and prepare for me and my son, that we may eat it and [c]die."

30 [a]1 Kin 14:9; 16:25

31 [a]Deut 7:1-5 [b]Judg 18:7; 1 Kin 11:1-5; 2 Kin 10:18; 17:16

32 [a]2 Kin 10:21, 26, 27

33 [1]I.e. wooden symbol of a female deity [a]2 Kin 13:6 [b]1 Kin 14:9; 16:29, 30; 21:25

34 [a]Josh 6:26

17:1 [1]Or *Tishbe in Gilead* [a]Judg 12:4 [b]1 Kin 18:10; 22:14; 2 Kin 3:14; 5:20 [c]1 Kin 18:1; Luke 4:25; James 5:17

3 [1]Lit *before*

4 [a]1 Kin 17:9

5 [1]Lit *before*

9 [a]Obad 20; Luke 4:26 [b]1 Kin 17:4

10 [1]Or *vessel* [a]Gen 24:17; John 4:7

12 [1]Lit *cake* [2]Lit *pitcher* [3]Lit *two* [a]1 Kin 17:1 [b]2 Kin 4:2-7 [c]Gen 21:15, 16

13 [1]Lit *there*

14 [1]Lit *pitcher* [2]Lit *lack*

16 [1]Lit *pitcher* [2]Lit *lack*

18 [1]Or *Have you come...death?* [a]2 Sam 16:10; 2 Kin 3:13; Luke 4:34; John 2:4 [b]1 Kin 12:22

20 [1]Lit *sojourning*

21 [1]Lit *upon his inward part* [a]2 Kin 4:34, 35; Acts 20:10

22 [1]Lit *upon his inward part* [a]Luke 7:14; Heb 11:35

24 [a]John 2:11; 3:2; 16:30

18:1 [a]1 Kin 17:1; Luke 4:25; James 5:17 [b]Deut 28:12

3 [1]Or *revered* [a]1 Kin 16:9 [b]Neh 7:2; Job 28:28

4 [1]Lit *cut off* [a]1 Kin 18:13 [b]Matt 10:40-42

5 [1]Lit *cut off*

13 Then Elijah said to her, "Do not fear; go, do as you have
said, but make me a little bread cake from [1]it first and bring *it*
out to me, and afterward you may make *one* for yourself and
for your son.
14 "For thus says the LORD God of Israel, 'The [1]bowl of flour
shall not be exhausted, nor shall the jar of oil [2]be empty, until
the day that the LORD sends rain on the face of the earth.'"
15 So she went and did according to the word of Elijah, and
she and he and her household ate for *many* days.
16 The [1]bowl of flour was not exhausted nor did the jar of oil
[2]become empty, according to the word of the LORD which He
spoke through Elijah.
17 Now it came about after these things that the son of the
woman, the mistress of the house, became sick; and his sickness
was so severe that there was no breath left in him.
18 So she said to Elijah, "[a]What do I have to do with you, O
[b]man of God? [1]You have come to me to bring my iniquity to
remembrance and to put my son to death!"
19 He said to her, "Give me your son." Then he took him
from her bosom and carried him up to the upper room where
he was living, and laid him on his own bed.
20 He called to the LORD and said, "O LORD my God, have You
also brought calamity to the widow with whom I am [1]staying,
by causing her son to die?"
21 [a]Then he stretched himself upon the child three times, and
called to the LORD and said, "O LORD my God, I pray You, let
this child's life return [1]to him."
22 The LORD heard the voice of Elijah, [a]and the life of the child
returned [1]to him and he revived.
23 Elijah took the child and brought him down from the upper
room into the house and gave him to his mother; and Elijah
said, "See, your son is alive."
24 Then the woman said to Elijah, "[a]Now I know that you are a
man of God and that the word of the LORD in your mouth is truth."

Chapter 18 Theme

18 Now it happened [a]*after* many days that the word of the
LORD came to Elijah in the third year, saying, "Go, show
yourself to Ahab, and [b]I will send rain on the face of the earth."
2 So Elijah went to show himself to Ahab. Now the famine
was severe in Samaria.
3 Ahab called Obadiah [a]who *was* over the household. (Now
Obadiah [1b]feared the LORD greatly;
4 for [a]when Jezebel [1]destroyed the prophets of the LORD,
Obadiah took a hundred prophets and hid them by fifties in a
cave, and [b]provided them with bread and water.)
5 Then Ahab said to Obadiah, "Go through the land to all the
springs of water and to all the valleys; perhaps we will find
grass and keep the horses and mules alive, and not [1]have to kill
some of the cattle."

871 B.C.

6 So they divided the land between them to [1]survey it; Ahab
went one way by himself and Obadiah went another way by
himself.
7 Now as Obadiah was on the way, behold, Elijah [1]met him,
[a]and he recognized him and fell on his face and said, "Is this
you, Elijah my master?"
8 He said to him, "It is I. Go, say to your master, 'Behold, Elijah
is here.'"
9 He said, "What [1]sin have I committed, that you are giving
your servant into the hand of Ahab to put me to death?
10 "[a]As the LORD your God lives, there is no nation or kingdom
where my master has not sent to search for you; and when
they said, 'He is not *here,*' he made the kingdom or nation
swear that they could not find you.
11 "And now you are saying, 'Go, say to your master, "Behold,
Elijah *is here.*"'
12 "It will come about when I leave you [a]that the Spirit of the
LORD will carry you where I do not know; so when I come and
tell Ahab and he cannot find you, he will kill me, although *I*
your servant have [1]feared the LORD from my youth.
13 "[a]Has it not been told to my master what I did when Jezebel
killed the prophets of the LORD, that I hid [1]a hundred prophets
of the LORD by fifties in a cave, and provided them with bread
and water?
14 "And now you are saying, 'Go, say to your master, "Behold,
Elijah *is here*"'; he will then kill me."
15 Elijah said, "[a]As the LORD of hosts lives, before whom I
stand, I will surely show myself to him today."
16 So Obadiah went to meet Ahab and told him; and Ahab
went to meet Elijah.
17 When Ahab saw Elijah, [a]Ahab said to him, "Is this you, you
troubler of Israel?"
18 He said, "I have not troubled Israel, but you and your father's
house *have,* because [a]you have forsaken the commandments of
the LORD and [b]you have followed the Baals.
19 "Now then send *and* gather to me all Israel at [a]Mount Carmel,
[b]*together* with 450 prophets of Baal and 400 prophets of [c]the
Asherah, who eat at Jezebel's table."
20 So Ahab sent *a message* among all the sons of Israel and
brought the prophets together at Mount Carmel.
21 Elijah came near to all the people and said, "[a]How long *will*
you [1]hesitate between two opinions? [b]If the LORD is God,
follow Him; but if Baal, follow him." But the people did not
answer him a word.
22 Then Elijah said to the people, "I [a]alone am left a prophet
of the LORD, but Baal's prophets are [b]450 men.
23 "Now let them give us two oxen; and let them choose one
ox for themselves and cut it up, and place it on the wood, but
put no fire *under it;* and I will prepare the other ox and lay it
on the wood, and I will not put a fire *under it.*

6 [1]Lit *pass through*

7 [1]Lit *to meet* [a]2 Kin 1:6-8

9 [1]Lit *have I sinned*

10 [a]1 Kin 17:1

12 [1]Or *revered* [a]2 Kin 2:16; Ezek 3:12, 14; Acts 8:39

13 [1]Lit *a hundred men of the prophets* [a]1 Kin 18:4

15 [a]1 Kin 17:1

17 [a]Josh 7:25; 1 Kin 21:20

18 [a]1 Kin 9:9; 2 Chr 15:2 [b]1 Kin 16:31; 21:25, 26

19 [a]Josh 19:26; 2 Kin 2:25 [b]1 Kin 18:22 [c]1 Kin 16:33

21 [1]Lit *limp on the two divided opinions* [a]2 Kin 17:41; Matt 6:24 [b]Josh 24:15

22 [a]1 Kin 19:10, 14 [b]1 Kin 18:19

24 "Then you call on the name of your god, and I will call on
the name of the LORD, and [a]the God who answers by fire, He is
God." And all the people said, "[1]That is a good idea."
25 So Elijah said to the prophets of Baal, "Choose one ox for
yourselves and prepare it first for you are many, and call on the
name of your god, but put no fire *under it.*"
26 Then they took the ox which [1]was given them and they
prepared it and called on the name of Baal from morning until
noon saying, "O Baal, answer us." But there was [a]no voice and
no one answered. And they [2]leaped about the altar which
[3]they made.
27 It came about at noon, that Elijah mocked them and said,
"Call out with a loud voice, for he is a god; either he is occupied
or gone aside, or is on a journey, or perhaps he is asleep and
needs to be awakened."
28 So they cried with a loud voice and [a]cut themselves according
to their custom with swords and lances until the blood gushed
out on them.
29 When midday was past, they [1]raved [a]until the time of the
offering of the *evening* sacrifice; but there was no voice, no one
answered, and no [2]one paid attention.
30 Then Elijah said to all the people, "Come near to me." So
all the people came near to him. And [a]he repaired the altar of
the LORD which had been torn down.
31 Elijah took twelve stones according to the number of the
tribes of the sons of Jacob, to whom the word of the LORD had
come, saying, "[a]Israel shall be your name."
32 So with the stones he built an altar in [a]the name of the
LORD, and he made a trench around the altar, large enough to
hold two [1]measures of seed.
33 [a]Then he arranged the wood and cut the ox in pieces and
laid *it* on the wood.
34 And he said, "Fill four pitchers with water and pour *it* on
the burnt offering and on the wood." And he said, "Do it a
second time," and they did it a second time. And he said, "Do
it a third time," and they did it a third time.
35 The water flowed around the altar and he also filled the
trench with water.
36 [a]At the time of the offering of the *evening* sacrifice, Elijah the
prophet came near and said, "[b]O LORD, the God of Abraham,
Isaac and Israel, today let it be known that [c]You are God in
Israel and that I am Your servant and [d]I have done all these
things at Your word.
37 "Answer me, O LORD, answer me, that this people may
know that You, O LORD, are God, and *that* You have turned
their heart back again."
38 Then the [a]fire of the LORD fell and consumed the burnt
offering and the wood and the stones and the dust, and licked
up the water that was in the trench.
39 When all the people saw it, they fell on their faces; and
they said, "[a]The LORD, He is God; the LORD, He is God."

24 [1]Lit *The matter is good* [a]1 Kin 18:38
26 [1]Lit *he gave* [2]Lit *limped;* i.e. a type of ceremonial dance [3]So some mss and the ancient versions; M.T. *he* [a]Ps 115:4, 5; Jer 10:5
28 [a]Lev 19:28; Deut 14:1
29 [1]Lit *prophesied* [2]Lit *attentiveness* [a]Ex 29:39, 41
30 [a]1 Kin 19:10, 14; 2 Chr 33:16
31 [a]Gen 32:28; 35:10; 2 Kin 17:34
32 [1]Heb *seahs;* i.e. one seah equals approx 11 qts [a]Col 3:17
33 [a]Gen 22:9; Lev 1:7, 8
36 [a]1 Kin 18:29 [b]Gen 28:13; Ex 3:6; 4:5; Matt 22:32 [c]1 Kin 8:43 [d]Num 16:28-32
38 [a]Gen 15:17; Lev 9:24; 10:1, 2; Judg 6:21; 2 Kin 1:12; 1 Chr 21:26; 2 Chr 7:1; Job 1:16
39 [a]1 Kin 18:21, 24

40 Then Elijah said to them, "Seize the prophets of Baal; do not
let one of them escape." So they seized them; and Elijah brought
them down to [a]the brook Kishon, [b]and slew them there.
41 Now Elijah said to Ahab, "Go up, eat and drink; for there is
the sound of the roar of a *heavy* shower."
42 So Ahab went up to eat and drink. But Elijah went up to
the top of [a]Carmel; and he [b]crouched down on the earth and
put his face between his knees.
43 He said to his servant, "Go up now, look toward the sea." So
he went up and looked and said, "There is nothing." And he
said, "Go back" seven times.
44 It came about at the seventh *time,* that he said, "Behold, [a]a
cloud as small as a man's hand is coming up from the sea." And
he said, "Go up, say to Ahab, '[1]Prepare *your chariot* and go
down, so that the *heavy* shower does not stop you.'"
45 In a little while the sky grew black with clouds and wind, and
there was a heavy shower. And Ahab rode and went to [a]Jezreel.
46 Then [a]the hand of the LORD was on Elijah, and [b]he girded
up his loins and [1]outran Ahab [2]to Jezreel.

Chapter 19 Theme ____________________

19 Now Ahab told Jezebel all that Elijah had done, and
[1a]how he had killed all the prophets with the sword.
2 Then Jezebel sent a messenger to Elijah, saying, "[a]So may
the gods do to me and even more, if I do not make your [1]life as
the [1]life of one of them by tomorrow about this time."
3 And he [1]was afraid and arose and ran for his [2]life and came
to [a]Beersheba, which belongs to Judah, and left his servant there.
4 But he himself went a day's journey into the wilderness, and
came and sat down under a [1]juniper tree; and [a]he requested for
himself that he might die, and said, "It is enough; now, O
LORD, take my [2]life, for I am not better than my fathers."
5 He lay down and slept under a [1]juniper tree; and behold, there
was [a]an angel touching him, and he said to him, "Arise, eat."
6 Then he looked and behold, there was at his head a bread
cake *baked on* hot stones, and a jar of water. So he ate and
drank and lay down again.
7 The angel of the LORD came again a second time and
touched him and said, "Arise, eat, because the journey is too
great for you."
8 So he arose and ate and drank, and went in the strength of
that food [a]forty days and forty nights to [b]Horeb, the mountain
of God.
9 Then he came there to a cave and lodged there; and
behold, [a]the word of the LORD *came* to him, and He said to
him, "What are you doing here, Elijah?"
10 He said, "[a]I have been very zealous for the LORD, the God
of hosts; for the sons of Israel have forsaken Your covenant,
[b]torn down Your altars and killed Your prophets with the sword.
And [c]I alone am left; and they seek my life, to take it away."

40 [a]Judg 4:7; 5:21 [b]Deut 13:5; 18:20; 2 Kin 10:24, 25

42 [a]1 Kin 18:19, 20 [b]James 5:18

44 [1]Lit *Tie, harness* [a]Luke 12:54

45 [a]Josh 17:16; Judg 6:33

46 [1]Lit *ran before* [2]Lit *until you are coming to* [a]2 Kin 3:15; Is 8:11; Ezek 3:14 [b]2 Kin 4:29; Jer 1:17; 1 Pet 1:13

19:1 [1]Lit *all* about *how* [a]1 Kin 18:40

2 [1]Lit *soul* [a]Ruth 1:17; 1 Kin 20:10; 2 Kin 6:31

3 [1]Reading of many mss; Heb text may read *saw* [2]Lit *soul* [a]Gen 21:31

4 [1]Or *broom-tree* [2]Lit *soul* [a]Num 11:15; Jer 20:14-18; Jon 4:3, 8

5 [1]Or *broom-tree* [a]Gen 28:12

8 [a]Ex 24:18; 34:28; Deut 9:9-11, 18; Matt 4:2 [b]Ex 3:1; 4:27

9 [a]Ex 33:21, 22

10 [a]Ex 20:5; 34:14 [b]Rom 11:3, 4 [c]1 Kin 18:22

11 [a]Ex 19:20; 24:12, 18 [b]Ezek 1:4
12 [a]Job 4:16; Zech 4:6
13 [a]Ex 3:6 [b]1 Kin 19:9
14 [a]1 Kin 19:10
15 [a]2 Kin 8:8-15
16 [a]2 Kin 9:1-10 [b]1 Kin 19:19-21; 2 Kin 2:9, 15
17 [a]2 Kin 8:12; 13:3, 22 [b]2 Kin 9:14-10:25
18 [a]Rom 11:4 [b]Hos 13:2
19 [a]1 Sam 28:14; 2 Kin 2:8, 13, 14
20 [a]Matt 8:21, 22; Luke 9:61, 62; Acts 20:37

11 So He said, "[a]Go forth
and stand on the mountain
before the LORD." And
behold, the LORD was
passing by! And [b]a great and
strong wind was rending
the mountains and breaking
in pieces the rocks before
the LORD; *but* the LORD *was*
not in the wind. And after
the wind an earthquake,
but the LORD *was* not in the
earthquake.
12 After the earthquake a
fire, *but* the LORD *was* not in
the fire; and after the fire [a]a
sound of a gentle blowing.
13 When Elijah heard *it,*
[a]he wrapped his face in his
mantle and went out and
stood in the entrance of the
cave. And behold, [b]a voice
came to him and said,
"What are you doing here,
Elijah?"
14 Then he said, "[a]I have
been very zealous for the
LORD, the God of hosts; for
the sons of Israel have forsaken Your covenant, torn
down Your altars and killed Your prophets with the sword. And
I alone am left; and they seek my life, to take it away."
15 The LORD said to him, "Go, return on your way to the
wilderness of Damascus, and when you have arrived, [a]you shall
anoint Hazael king over Aram;
16 and [a]Jehu the son of Nimshi you shall anoint king over
Israel; and [b]Elisha the son of Shaphat of Abel-meholah you shall
anoint as prophet in your place.
17 "It shall come about, the [a]one who escapes from the sword
of Hazael, Jehu [b]shall put to death, and the one who escapes
from the sword of Jehu, Elisha shall put to death.
18 "[a]Yet I will leave 7,000 in Israel, all the knees that have not
bowed to Baal and every mouth that has not [b]kissed him."
19 So he departed from there and found Elisha the son of
Shaphat, while he was plowing with twelve pairs *of oxen*
before him, and he with the twelfth. And Elijah passed over to
him and threw [a]his mantle on him.
20 He left the oxen and ran after Elijah and said, "Please [a]let
me kiss my father and my mother, then I will follow you." And
he said to him, "Go back again, for what have I done to you?"
21 So he returned from following him, and took the pair of oxen

Elijah's Ministry

and sacrificed them and [a]boiled their flesh with the implements
of the oxen, and gave *it* to the people and they ate. Then he
arose and followed Elijah and ministered to him.

Chapter 20 Theme ________________________

20 Now [a]Ben-hadad king of Aram gathered all his army,
[b]and there *were* thirty-two kings with him, and horses
and chariots. And he went up and [c]besieged Samaria and
fought against it.
2 Then he sent messengers to the city to Ahab king of Israel
and said to him, "Thus says Ben-hadad,
3 'Your silver and your gold are mine; your most beautiful
wives and children are also mine.'"
4 The king of Israel replied, "It is according to your word, my
lord, O king; I am yours, and all that I have."
5 Then the messengers returned and said, "Thus says [1]Ben-
hadad, 'Surely, I sent to you saying, "You shall give me your
silver and your gold and your wives and your children,"
6 but about this time tomorrow I will send my servants to
you, and they will search your house and the houses of your
servants; and [1]whatever is desirable in your eyes, they will
[2]take in their hand and carry away.'"
7 Then the king of Israel called all the elders of the land and
said, "Please observe and [a]see how this man is looking for
trouble; for he sent to me for my wives and my children and
my silver and my gold, and I did not refuse him."
8 All the elders and all the people said to him, "Do not listen
or consent."
9 So he said to the messengers of Ben-hadad, "Tell my lord
the king, 'All that you sent for to your servant at the first I will
do, but this thing I cannot do.'" And the messengers departed
and brought him word again.
10 Ben-hadad sent to him and said, "May [a]the gods do so to
me and more also, if the dust of Samaria will suffice for
handfuls for all the people who [1]follow me."
11 Then the king of Israel replied, "Tell *him,* '[a]Let not him
who girds on *his armor* boast like him who takes *it* off.'"
12 When *Ben-hadad* heard this message, as [a]he was drinking
[1]with the kings in the [2]temporary shelters, he said to his servants,
"Station *yourselves.*" So they stationed *themselves* against the city.
13 Now behold, a prophet approached Ahab king of Israel and
said, "Thus says the LORD, 'Have you seen all this great multitude?
Behold, [a]I will deliver them into your hand today, and [b]you
shall know that I am the LORD.'"
14 Ahab said, "By whom?" So he said, "Thus says the LORD,
'By the young men of the rulers of the provinces.'" Then he
said, "Who shall [1]begin the battle?" And he [2]answered, "You."
15 Then he mustered the young men of the rulers of the
provinces, and there were 232; and after them he mustered all
the people, *even* all the sons of Israel, 7,000.

21 [a]2 Sam 24:22

20:1 [a]1 Kin 15:18, 20; 2 Kin 6:24 [b]1 Kin 22:31 [c]1 Kin 16:24; 2 Kin 6:24

5 [1]Lit *Ben-hadad, saying*

6 [1]Lit *all the desire of your eyes* [2]Lit *put*

7 [a]2 Kin 5:7

10 [1]Lit *are at my feet* [a]1 Kin 19:2; 2 Kin 6:31

11 [a]Prov 27:1

12 [1]Lit *he and* [2]Or *booths* [a]1 Kin 16:9; Prov 31:4, 5

13 [a]1 Kin 20:28 [b]1 Kin 18:36

14 [1]Lit *bind* [2]Lit *said*

16 [1]Or *booths* [2]Lit *he and the 32 kings* [a]1 Kin 16:9; 20:12; Prov 20:1

18 [a]2 Kin 14:8-12

20 [1]Lit *smote*

21 [1]Lit *smote*

22 [a]1 Kin 20:13 [b]2 Sam 11:1; 1 Kin 20:26

23 [a]1 Kin 14:23; Jer 16:19-21; Rom 1:21-23

25 [1]Lit *number*

26 [a]1 Kin 20:22 [b]2 Kin 13:17

27 [a]Judg 6:3-5; 1 Sam 13:5-8

28 [a]1 Kin 17:18 [b]1 Kin 20:23 [c]1 Kin 20:13

29 [1]Lit *smote*

30 [a]1 Kin 20:26 [b]1 Kin 22:25; 2 Chr 18:24

31 [1]Lit *soul* [a]1 Kin 20:23-26 [b]Gen 37:34; 2 Sam 3:31

16 They went out at noon, while [a]Ben-hadad was drinking
himself drunk in the [1]temporary shelters [2]with the thirty-two
kings who helped him.
17 The young men of the rulers of the provinces went out
first; and Ben-hadad sent out and they told him, saying, "Men
have come out from Samaria."
18 [a]Then he said, "If they have come out for peace, take them
alive; or if they have come out for war, take them alive."
19 So these went out from the city, the young men of the
rulers of the provinces, and the army which followed them.
20 They [1]killed each his man; and the Arameans fled and
Israel pursued them, and Ben-hadad king of Aram escaped on a
horse with horsemen.
21 The king of Israel went out and [1]struck the horses and
chariots, and [1]killed the Arameans with a great slaughter.
22 Then [a]the prophet came near to the king of Israel and said
to him, "Go, strengthen yourself and observe and see what you
have to do; for [b]at the turn of the year the king of Aram will
come up against you."
23 Now the servants of the king of Aram said to him, "[a]Their
gods are gods of the mountains, therefore they were stronger
than we; but rather let us fight against them in the plain, *and*
surely we will be stronger than they.
24 "Do this thing: remove the kings, each from his place, and
put captains in their place,
25 and [1]muster an army like the army that you have lost,
horse for horse, and chariot for chariot. Then we will fight
against them in the plain, and surely we will be stronger than
they." And he listened to their voice and did so.
26 [a]At the turn of the year, Ben-hadad mustered the Arameans
and went up to [b]Aphek to fight against Israel.
27 The sons of Israel were mustered and were provisioned
and went to meet them; and the sons of Israel camped before
them like two little flocks of goats, [a]but the Arameans filled the
country.
28 Then [a]a man of God came near and spoke to the king of
Israel and said, "Thus says the LORD, 'Because the Arameans
have said, "[b]The LORD is a god of *the* mountains, but He is
not a god of *the* valleys," therefore [c]I will give all this great
multitude into your hand, and you shall know that I am the
LORD.'"
29 So they camped one over against the other seven days. And
on the seventh day the battle was joined, and the sons of Israel
[1]killed *of* the Arameans 100,000 foot soldiers in one day.
30 But the rest fled to [a]Aphek into the city, and the wall fell on
27,000 men who were left. And Ben-hadad fled and came into
the city [b]into an inner chamber.
31 [a]His servants said to him, "Behold now, we have heard that
the kings of the house of Israel are merciful kings, please let us
[b]put sackcloth on our loins and ropes on our heads, and go out
to the king of Israel; perhaps he will save your [1]life."

32 So [a]they girded sackcloth on their loins and *put* ropes on
their heads, and came to the king of Israel and said, "[b]Your
servant Ben-hadad says, 'Please let me live.'" And he said, "Is
he still alive? He is my brother."
33 Now the men [1]took this as an omen, and quickly [2]catching
his word said, "Your brother Ben-hadad." Then he said, "Go,
bring him." Then Ben-hadad came out to him, and he [3]took
him up into the chariot.
34 *Ben-hadad* said to him, "[a]The cities which my father took
from your father I will restore, and you shall make streets for
yourself in Damascus, as my father made in Samaria." *Ahab
said,* "And I will let you go with this covenant." So he made a
covenant with him and let him go.
35 Now a certain man of [a]the sons of the prophets said to
[1]another [b]by the word of the LORD, "Please strike me." But the
man refused to strike him.
36 Then he said to him, "Because you have not listened to the
voice of the LORD, behold, as soon as you have departed from
me, [a]a lion will [1]kill you." And as soon as he had departed from
him a lion found him and [2]killed him.
37 Then he found another man and said, "Please [1]strike me."
And the man [2]struck him, [3]wounding him.
38 So the prophet departed and waited for the king by the
way, and [a]disguised himself with a bandage over his eyes.
39 As the king passed by, he cried to the king and said, "Your
servant went out into the midst of the battle; and behold, a
man turned aside and brought a man to me and said, 'Guard
this man; if for any reason he is missing, [a]then your life shall be
for his life, or else you shall pay a talent of silver.'
40 "While your servant was busy here and there, he was gone."
And the king of Israel said to him, "So shall your judgment be;
you yourself have decided *it.*"
41 Then he hastily took the bandage away from his eyes, and
the king of Israel recognized him that he was of the prophets.
42 He said to him, "Thus says the LORD, 'Because you have let
go out of *your* hand the man whom I had devoted to destruction,
therefore [a]your [1]life shall go for his [1]life, and your people for
his people.'"
43 So [a]the king of Israel went to his house sullen and vexed,
and came to Samaria.

Chapter 21 Theme ____________________

21 Now it came about after these things that Naboth the
Jezreelite had a vineyard which *was* in [a]Jezreel beside
the palace of Ahab king of Samaria.
2 Ahab spoke to Naboth, saying, "[a]Give me your vineyard,
that I may have it for a vegetable garden because it is close
beside my house, and I will give you a better vineyard than it in
its place; if [1]you like, I will give you the price of [2]it in money."
3 But Naboth said to Ahab, "The LORD forbid me [a]that I
should give you the inheritance of my fathers."

32 [a]1 Kin 20:31 [b]1 Kin 20:3-6
33 [1]Lit *divined* [2]Lit *caught from him* [3]Lit *caused him to come up*
34 [a]1 Kin 15:20
35 [1]Lit *his neighbor* [a]2 Kin 2:3-7 [b]1 Kin 13:17, 18
36 [1]Lit *smite* [2]Lit *smote* [a]1 Kin 13:24
37 [1]Lit *smite* [2]Lit *smote* [3]Lit *striking and wounding*
38 [a]1 Kin 14:2
39 [a]2 Kin 10:24
42 [1]Lit *soul* [a]1 Kin 20:39
43 [a]1 Kin 21:4
21:1 [a]Judg 6:33; 1 Kin 18:45, 46
2 [1]Lit *it is good in your eyes* [2]Lit *this* [a]1 Sam 8:14
3 [a]Lev 25:23; Num 36:7; Ezek 46:18

4 [a]So Ahab came into his house sullen and vexed because of the word which Naboth the Jezreelite had spoken to him; for he said, "I will not give you the inheritance of my fathers." And he lay down on his bed and turned away his face and ate no [1]food.

5 But Jezebel his wife came to him and said to him, "How is it that your spirit is so sullen that you are not eating [1]food?"

6 So he said to her, "Because I spoke to Naboth the Jezreelite and said to him, 'Give me your vineyard for money; or else, if it pleases you, I will give you a vineyard in its place.' But he said, 'I will not give you my vineyard.'"

7 Jezebel his wife said to him, "[a]Do you now [1]reign over Israel? Arise, eat bread, and let your heart be joyful; I will give you the vineyard of Naboth the Jezreelite."

8 [a]So she wrote letters in Ahab's name and sealed them with his seal, and sent letters to [b]the elders and to the nobles who were living with Naboth in his city.

9 Now she wrote in the letters, saying, "Proclaim a fast and seat Naboth at the head of the people;

10 and seat two [a]worthless men before him, and let them testify against him, saying, '[b]You cursed God and the king.' Then take him out and [c]stone him [1]to death."

11 So the men of his city, the elders and the nobles who lived in his city, did as Jezebel had sent *word* to them, just as it was written in the letters which she had sent them.

12 They [a]proclaimed a fast and seated Naboth at the head of the people.

13 Then the two worthless men came in and sat before him; and the worthless men testified against him, even against Naboth, before the people, saying, "Naboth cursed God and the king." [a]So they took him outside the city and stoned him [1]to death with stones.

14 Then they sent *word* to Jezebel, saying, "Naboth has been stoned and is dead."

15 When Jezebel heard that Naboth had been stoned and was dead, Jezebel said to Ahab, "Arise, take possession of the vineyard of Naboth, the Jezreelite, which he refused to give you for money; for Naboth is not alive, but dead."

16 When Ahab heard that Naboth was dead, Ahab arose to go down to the vineyard of Naboth the Jezreelite, to take possession of it.

17 Then the word of the LORD came to Elijah the Tishbite, saying,

18 "Arise, go down to meet Ahab king of Israel, [a]who is in Samaria; behold, he is in the vineyard of Naboth where he has gone down to take possession of it.

19 "You shall speak to him, saying, 'Thus says the LORD, "[a]Have you murdered and also taken possession?"' And you shall speak to him, saying, 'Thus says the LORD, "[b]In the place where the dogs licked up the blood of Naboth the dogs will lick up your blood, even yours."'"

4 [1]Lit *bread* [a]1 Kin 20:43
5 [1]Lit *bread*
7 [1]Lit *exercise kingship* [a]1 Sam 8:14
8 [a]Esth 3:12; 8:8, 10 [b]1 Kin 20:7
10 [1]Lit *so that he dies* [a]1 Sam 2:12; 2 Sam 20:1 [b]Ex 22:28; Lev 24:15, 16; Acts 6:11 [c]Lev 24:14
12 [a]Is 58:4
13 [1]Lit *with stones so that he died* [a]2 Kin 9:26; 2 Chr 24:21; Acts 7:58, 59; Heb 11:37
18 [a]1 Kin 16:29
19 [a]2 Sam 12:9 [b]1 Kin 22:38; 2 Kin 9:26

20 Ahab said to Elijah, "[a]Have you found me, O my enemy?"
And he [1]answered, "I have found *you,* [b]because you have sold
yourself to do evil in the sight of the LORD.
21 "Behold, I will bring evil upon you, and [a]will utterly sweep
you away, and will cut off from Ahab every male, both bond
and free in Israel;
22 and [a]I will make your house [b]like the house of Jeroboam
the son of Nebat, and like the house of Baasha the son of Ahijah,
because of the provocation with which you have provoked *Me*
to anger, and *because* you [c]have made Israel sin.
23 "Of Jezebel also has the LORD spoken, saying, '[a]The dogs will
eat Jezebel in the [1]district of Jezreel.'
24 "[a]The one belonging to Ahab, who dies in the city, the dogs
will eat, and the one who dies in the field the birds of heaven
will eat."
25 [a]Surely there was no one like Ahab who sold himself to do
evil in the sight of the LORD, [1]because Jezebel his wife incited
him.
26 [a]He acted very abominably in following idols, [b]according to
all that the Amorites had done, whom the LORD cast out before
the sons of Israel.
27 It came about when Ahab heard these words, that [a]he tore
his clothes and put [1]on sackcloth and fasted, and he lay in sackcloth and went about [2]despondently.
28 Then the word of the LORD came to Elijah the Tishbite, saying,
29 "Do you see how Ahab has humbled himself before Me?
Because he has humbled himself before Me, I will not bring
the evil in his days, *but* I will bring the evil upon his house [a]in
his son's days."

Chapter 22 Theme ______________________

2 Chronicles 18

22
Three [1]years passed without war between Aram and
Israel.
2 [a]In the third year [b]Jehoshaphat the king of Judah came
down to the king of Israel.
3 Now the king of Israel said to his servants, "Do you know
that [a]Ramoth-gilead belongs to us, and we [1]are still doing
nothing to take it out of the hand of the king of Aram?"
4 And he said to Jehoshaphat, "Will you go with me to battle
at Ramoth-gilead?" And Jehoshaphat said to the king of Israel,
"[a]I am as you are, my people as your people, my horses as your
horses."
5 Moreover, Jehoshaphat said to the king of Israel, "Please
inquire [1]first for the word of the LORD."
6 Then [a]the king of Israel gathered the prophets together,
about four hundred men, and said to them, "Shall I go against
Ramoth-gilead to battle or shall I refrain?" And they said, "Go
up, for the Lord will give *it* into the hand of the king."
7 But [a]Jehoshaphat said, "Is there not yet a prophet of the
LORD here that we may inquire of him?"

20 [1]Lit *said* [a]1 Kin 18:17 [b]1 Kin 21:25; 2 Kin 17:17; Rom 7:14

21 [a]1 Kin 14:10; 2 Kin 9:8

22 [a]1 Kin 15:29 [b]1 Kin 16:3, 11 [c]1 Kin 12:30; 13:34; 14:16

23 [1]Lit *portion;* some mss read *rampart* [a]2 Kin 9:10, 30-37

24 [a]1 Kin 14:11; 16:4

25 [1]Or *whom Jezebel his wife incited* [a]1 Kin 16:30-33; 21:20

26 [a]1 Kin 15:12; 2 Kin 17:12 [b]Gen 15:16; Lev 18:25-30; 2 Kin 21:11

27 [1]Lit *sackcloth on his flesh* [2]Or *softly* [a]Gen 37:34; 2 Sam 3:31; 2 Kin 6:30

29 [a]2 Kin 9:25-37

22:1 [1]Lit *they sat for three years*

2 [a]2 Chr 18:2 [b]1 Kin 15:24

3 [1]Lit *are silent so as not* [a]Deut 4:43; Josh 21:38; 1 Kin 4:13

4 [a]2 Kin 3:7

5 [1]Lit *as the day*

6 [a]1 Kin 18:19

7 [a]2 Kin 3:11

9 [1]Lit *Hasten Micaiah*
10 [a]1 Kin 22:6
11 [a]Zech 1:18-21 [b]Deut 33:17
14 [a]1 Kin 18:10, 15 [b]Num 22:18; 24:13
15 [1]Lit *said to* [a]1 Kin 22:12
17 [a]Num 27:17; 1 Kin 22:34-36; 2 Chr 18:16; Matt 9:36; Mark 6:34
18 [a]1 Kin 22:8
19 [1]Lit *he* [a]Is 6:1; Ezek 1:26-28; Dan 7:9, 10 [b]Job 1:6; 2:1; Ps 103:20, 21; Dan 7:10; Matt 18:10; Heb 1:7, 14
22 [a]Judg 9:23; 1 Sam 16:14; 18:10; 19:9; Ezek 14:9; 2 Thess 2:11
23 [a]Ezek 14:9

8 The king of Israel said to Jehoshaphat, "There is yet one
man by whom we may inquire of the LORD, but I hate him,
because he does not prophesy good concerning me, but evil.
He is Micaiah son of Imlah." But Jehoshaphat said, "Let not the
king say so."
9 Then the king of Israel called an officer and said, "[1]Bring
quickly Micaiah son of Imlah."
10 Now the king of Israel and Jehoshaphat king of Judah were
sitting each on his throne, arrayed in *their* robes, at the
threshing floor at the entrance of the gate of Samaria; and [a]all
the prophets were prophesying before them.
11 Then Zedekiah the son of Chenaanah made [a]horns of iron
for himself and said, "Thus says the LORD, '[b]With these you will
gore the Arameans until they are consumed.'"
12 All the prophets were prophesying thus, saying, "Go up to
Ramoth-gilead and prosper, for the LORD will give *it* into the
hand of the king."
13 Then the messenger who went to summon Micaiah spoke
to him saying, "Behold now, the words of the prophets are
uniformly favorable to the king. Please let your word be like
the word of one of them, and speak favorably."
14 But Micaiah said, "[a]As the LORD lives, what [b]the LORD says
to me, that I shall speak."
15 When he came to the king, the king said to him, "Micaiah,
shall we go to Ramoth-gilead to battle, or shall we refrain?"
And he [1]answered him, "[a]Go up and succeed, and the LORD
will give *it* into the hand of the king."
16 Then the king said to him, "How many times must I adjure
you to speak to me nothing but the truth in the name of the
LORD?"
17 So he said,
"I saw all Israel
Scattered on the mountains,
[a]Like sheep which have no shepherd.
And the LORD said, 'These have no master.
Let each of them return to his house in peace.'"
18 Then the king of Israel said to Jehoshaphat, "[a]Did I not tell
you that he would not prophesy good concerning me, but evil?"
19 [1]Micaiah said, "Therefore, hear the word of the LORD. [a]I
saw the LORD sitting on His throne, and [b]all the host of heaven
standing by Him on His right and on His left.
20 "The LORD said, 'Who will entice Ahab to go up and fall at
Ramoth-gilead?' And one said this while another said that.
21 "Then a spirit came forward and stood before the LORD and
said, 'I will entice him.'
22 "The LORD said to him, 'How?' And he said, 'I will go out
and [a]be a deceiving spirit in the mouth of all his prophets.' Then
He said, 'You are to entice *him* and also prevail. Go and do so.'
23 "Now therefore, behold, [a]the LORD has put a deceiving spirit
in the mouth of all these your prophets; and the LORD has
proclaimed disaster against you."

24 Then [a]Zedekiah the son of Chenaanah came near and
struck Micaiah on the cheek and said, "[b]How did the Spirit of
the LORD pass from me to speak to you?"
25 Micaiah said, "Behold, you shall see on that day when you
[a]enter an inner room to hide yourself."
26 Then the king of Israel said, "Take Micaiah and return him
to Amon the governor of the city and to Joash the king's son;
27 and say, 'Thus says the king, "[a]Put this man in prison and
feed him [1]sparingly with bread and water until I return safely."'"
28 Micaiah said, "[a]If you indeed return safely the LORD has not
spoken by me." And he said, "[b]Listen, all you people."
29 So [a]the king of Israel and Jehoshaphat king of Judah went
up against Ramoth-gilead.
30 The king of Israel said to Jehoshaphat, "[a]I will disguise
myself and go into the battle, but you put on your robes." So
the king of Israel disguised himself and went into the battle.
31 Now [a]the king of Aram had commanded the thirty-two
captains of his chariots, saying, "Do not fight with small or
great, but with the king of Israel alone."
32 So when the captains of the chariots saw Jehoshaphat, they
said, "Surely it is the king of Israel," and they turned aside to
fight against him, and Jehoshaphat cried out.
33 When the captains of the chariots saw that it was not the
king of Israel, they turned back from pursuing him.
34 Now a certain man drew his bow at random and struck the
king of Israel [1]in a joint of the armor. So he said to the driver of
his chariot, "Turn [2]around and take me out of the [3]fight; [a]for I
am severely wounded."
35 The battle [1]raged that day, and the king was propped up in
his chariot in front of the Arameans, and died at evening, and
the blood from the wound ran into the bottom of the chariot.
36 [a]Then a cry passed throughout the army close to sunset,
saying, "Every man to his city and every man to his [1]country."
37 So the king died and was brought to Samaria, and they
buried the king in Samaria.
38 They washed the chariot by the pool of Samaria, and the
dogs licked up his blood (now the harlots bathed themselves
there), [a]according to the word of the LORD which He spoke.
39 Now the rest of the acts of Ahab and all that he did and
[a]the ivory house which he built and all the cities which he
built, are they not written in the Book of the Chronicles of the
Kings of Israel?
40 So Ahab slept with his fathers, and Ahaziah his son became
king in his place.
870 B.C. **41** [a]Now Jehoshaphat the son of Asa became king over Judah
in the fourth year of Ahab king of Israel.
42 Jehoshaphat was thirty-five years old when he became
king, and he reigned twenty-five years in Jerusalem. And his
mother's name was Azubah the daughter of Shilhi.
43 [a]He walked in all the way of Asa his father; he did not turn
aside from it, doing right in the sight of the LORD. [b]However,

24 [a]1 Kin 22:11; Matt 5:39; Acts 23:2, 3 [b]2 Chr 18:23

25 [a]1 Kin 20:30

27 [1]Lit *with bread of affliction and water of affliction* [a]2 Chr 16:10; 18:25-27

28 [a]Deut 18:22 [b]Mic 1:2

29 [a]1 Kin 22:3, 4

30 [a]2 Chr 35:22

31 [a]1 Kin 20:1, 16, 24; 2 Chr 18:30

34 [1]Lit *between the scale-armor and the breastplate* [2]Lit *your hand* [3]Lit *camp* [a]2 Chr 35:23

35 [1]Lit *went up*

36 [1]Lit *land* [a]2 Kin 14:12

38 [a]1 Kin 21:19

39 [a]Amos 3:15

41 [a]2 Chr 20:31

43 [a]2 Chr 17:3 [b]1 Kin 15:14; 2 Kin 12:3

the high places were not taken away; the people still sacrificed
and burnt incense on the high places.
44 [a]Jehoshaphat also made peace with the king of Israel.
45 Now the rest of the acts of Jehoshaphat, and his might
which he showed and how he warred, are they not written [a]in
the Book of the Chronicles of the Kings of Judah?
46 The remnant of [a]the sodomites who remained in the days
of his father Asa, he [1]expelled from the land.
47 Now [a]there was no king in Edom; a deputy was king.
48 Jehoshaphat made [a]ships of Tarshish to go to [b]Ophir for
gold, but [c]they did not go for the ships were broken at [d]Ezion-
geber.
49 Then Ahaziah the son of Ahab said to Jehoshaphat, "Let my
servants go with your servants in the ships." But Jehoshaphat
was not willing.
50 [a]And Jehoshaphat slept with his fathers and was buried
with his fathers in the city of his father David, and Jehoram his
son became king in his place.
51 Ahaziah the son of Ahab [a]became king over Israel in 853 B.C.
Samaria in the seventeenth year of Jehoshaphat king of Judah,
and he reigned two years over Israel.
52 He did evil in the sight of the LORD and [a]walked in the way
of his father and in the way of his mother and in the way of
Jeroboam the son of Nebat, who caused Israel to sin.
53 [a]So he served Baal and worshiped him and provoked the
LORD God of Israel to anger, according to all that his father had
done.

44 [a]1 Kin 22:2; 2 Kin 8:16, 18; 2 Chr 19:2
45 [a]2 Chr 20:34
46 [1]Lit *consumed* [a]Gen 19:5; Deut 23:17; 1 Kin 14:24; 15:12; Jude 7
47 [a]2 Sam 8:14; 2 Kin 3:9
48 [a]1 Kin 10:22; 2 Chr 20:36 [b]1 Kin 9:28 [c]2 Chr 20:37 [d]1 Kin 9:26
50 [a]2 Chr 21:1
51 [a]1 Kin 22:40
52 [a]1 Kin 15:26; 21:25
53 [a]Judg 2:11; 1 Kin 16:30-32

1 Kings at a Glance

Theme of 1 Kings:

Segment Divisions

		Chapter Themes
		1
		2
		3
		4
		5
		6
		7
		8
		9
		10
		11
		12
		13
		14
		15
		16
		17
		18
		19
		20
		21
		22

Author:

Date:

Purpose:

Key Words

2 KINGS מלכים ב

MeLAKHIM BET

"Where is the LORD, the God of Elijah?" As you study 2 Kings, the continuation of 1 Kings, you will see God at work setting up and removing kings and kingdoms. And in the process you will be introduced to His spokesmen, the prophets, who faithfully speak forth His Word until Israel, and then Judah, are taken into captivity...because they did not listen.

THINGS TO DO

1. As you read through 2 Kings one chapter at a time:
   a. Mark the following key repeated words: *according to the Word of the Lord, Aram, Assyria, prophet, did evil, did right, heart, sin,* references to *mediums, spiritists,* and related terms, *high places, idols (gods),* and *covenant.* Always watch for and mark words which are distinctive to a particular chapter, such as *customs* in chapter 17. Write these key words on an index card you can use as a bookmark while studying 2 Kings.
   b. Mark references to time with a clock 🕒 and double-underline in green all geographical locations.
   c. Observe what you learn about God: His requirements, His ways, His judgments, and His character. Record your insights in the margin of the text under a △. Also, be sure to note "Lessons for Life" (LFL).
   d. Watch for any reforms instituted by a king such as "he removed the high places". In the margin, note these reforms and the results. Mark the beginning of a king's reign with a crown. Record what you learn about each king on the chart THE KINGS OF ISRAEL AND JUDAH on pages 654 and 655.
   e. Record the theme or main event of each chapter on 2 KINGS AT A GLANCE on page 650 and in your Bible.
2. Second Kings has some key or pivotal events:
   a. In 1:1 through 8:15 the prophetic ministries of Elijah and then Elisha are prominent. Mark *Elijah* and *Elisha* and then list in the margin the miracles accomplished through these men. Several miraculous things occur after 8:15; watch for them.
   b. Second Kings gives the account of the Assyrian invasion and subsequent captivity of the northern kingdom of Israel. Give special attention to the details of this invasion and why it came about, and mark in the margin when it happens.
   c. After the Assyrian captivity all that remains of the Hebrew nation is the southern kingdom—Judah. Watch how Judah conducts herself after seeing God's judgment on the northern kingdom. All this came to pass just as God's prophets said it would!
   d. Watch for the account of the Babylonian sieges of the southern kingdom (Judah) and the ensuing events. Record these in the margin as you did the Assyrian captivity.
3. Two charts identify the major characters and events of 2 Kings.
   a. The first chart, ISRAEL'S DIVISION AND CAPTIVITY, on page 649, gives a broad overview of the division of the kingdom through the three sieges of Jerusalem by the Babylonians.
   b. The second is a three-part chart: THE HISTORICAL CHART OF THE KINGS AND

PROPHETS OF ISRAEL AND JUDAH, on pages 651 through 653. This chart shows the relationship of the kings and prophets to one another and to other foreign kings and their kingdoms. You might color these charts so that the kings of the northern and southern kingdoms and the prophets can be readily distinguished from one another.

c. When you read of key figures or events in 2 Kings, consult these charts.

4. Complete the chart 2 KINGS AT A GLANCE. Considering the key events or personages featured in 2 Kings, see which chapters of 2 Kings can be grouped together under a common theme or topic. Record the theme of each segment under "Segment Divisions." Also, you might want to note on the chart the chapters that tell when the Assyrian and Babylonian invasions occur. Remember to record the theme of 2 Kings.

Things to Think About

1. As you consider the lives of Elijah and Elisha, what do you learn about trusting God?

2. As you think about the captivity of Israel and Judah, and the reasons for their captivity, what do you learn about the necessity of living a righteous life? What practical applications can you make to your own life? Remember, walking your own way may be pleasurable for a while, but a just God must hold you accountable.

3. As you studied 1 and 2 Kings you saw that what God says will happen eventually comes to pass. Since His Word stands and none can alter it, can you see how critical it is that you believe God and hold to His Word no matter what others say or do?

Chapter 1 Theme ______________________

853 B.C.

1 Now [a]Moab rebelled against Israel after the death of Ahab.
2 And Ahaziah fell through the lattice in his upper chamber
which *was* in Samaria, and became ill. So he sent messengers
and said to them, "Go, [a]inquire of Baal-zebub, the god of Ekron,
[b]whether I will recover from this sickness."
3 But the angel of the LORD said to [a]Elijah the Tishbite,
"Arise, go up to meet the messengers of the king of Samaria
and say to them, 'Is it because there is no God in Israel *that*
you are going to inquire of [b]Baal-zebub, the god of Ekron?'
4 "Now therefore thus says the LORD, '[1a]You shall not come
down from the bed where you have gone up, but you shall surely
die.'" Then Elijah departed.
5 When the messengers returned to him he said to them,
"[1]Why have you returned?"
6 They said to him, "A man came up to meet us and said to
us, 'Go, return to the king who sent you and say to him, "Thus
says the LORD, 'Is it because there is no God in Israel *that* you
are sending [a]to inquire of Baal-zebub, the god of Ekron? Therefore [1]you shall not come down from the bed where you have
gone up, but shall surely die.'"'"
7 He said to them, "What kind of man was he who came up
to meet you and spoke these words to you?"
8 They [1]answered him, "[a]*He was* a hairy man with a leather
girdle [2]bound about his loins." And he said, "It is Elijah the
Tishbite."

1:1 [a]2 Sam 8:2; 2 Kin 3:5

2 [a]2 Kin 1:3, 6, 16; Matt 10:25; Mark 3:22 [b]2 Kin 8:7-10

3 [a]1 Kin 17:1; 21:17 [b]2 Kin 1:2

4 [1]Lit *The bed where you went up, you shall not come down from it* [a]2 Kin 1:6, 16

5 [1]Lit *What is this that you have returned?*

6 [1]V 4, note 1 [a]2 Kin 1:2

8 [1]Lit *said* [2]Or *girt* [a]Zech 13:4; Matt 3:4; Mark 1:6

9 Then *the king* [a]sent to him a captain of fifty with his fifty.
And he went up to him, and behold, he was sitting on the top
of the hill. And he said to him, "O man of God, the king says,
'Come down.'"
10 Elijah replied to the captain of fifty, "If I am a man of God, [a]let
fire come down from heaven and consume you and your fifty."
[b]Then fire came down from heaven and consumed him and his
fifty.
11 So he again sent to him another captain of fifty with his
fifty. And he said to him, "O man of God, thus says the king,
'Come down quickly.'"
12 Elijah replied to them, "If I am a man of God, let fire come
down from heaven and consume you and your fifty." Then the
fire of God came down from heaven and consumed him and
his fifty.
13 So he [a]again sent the captain of a third fifty with his fifty.
When the third captain of fifty went up, he came and bowed
down on his knees before Elijah, and begged him and said to
him, "O man of God, please let my life and the lives of these
fifty servants of yours be precious in your sight.
14 "Behold fire came down from heaven and consumed the
first two captains of fifty with their fifties; but now let my [1]life
be precious in your sight."
15 [a]The angel of the LORD said to Elijah, "Go down with him;
[b]do not be afraid of him." So he arose and went down with
him to the king.
16 Then he said to him, "Thus says the LORD, 'Because you have
sent messengers [a]to inquire of Baal-zebub, the god of Ekron—is
it because there is no God in Israel to inquire of His word?—
therefore [1]you shall not come down from the bed where you
have gone up, but shall surely die.'"
17 So Ahaziah died according to the word of the LORD which 852 B.C.
Elijah had spoken. And because he had no son, Jehoram became
king in his place [a]in the second year of Jehoram the son of
Jehoshaphat, king of Judah.
18 Now the rest of the acts of Ahaziah which he did, are they
not written in the Book of the Chronicles of the Kings of Israel?

Chapter 2 Theme ______________________

2 And it came about when the LORD was about to [a]take up
Elijah by a [1]whirlwind to heaven, that Elijah went with
[b]Elisha from [c]Gilgal.
2 Elijah said to Elisha, "[a]Stay here please, for the LORD has
sent me as far as [b]Bethel." But Elisha said, "[c]As the LORD lives and
as you yourself live, I will not leave you." So they went down
to Bethel.
3 Then [a]the sons of the prophets who *were at* Bethel came out
to Elisha and said to him, "Do you know that the LORD will take
away your master from over [1]you today?" And he said, "Yes, I
know; be still."

9 [a]2 Kin 6:13, 14
10 [a]1 Kin 18:36-38; Luke 9:54 [b]Job 1:16
13 [a]Is 1:5; Jer 5:3
14 [1]Lit *soul*
15 [a]2 Kin 1:3 [b]Is 51:12; Jer 1:17; Ezek 2:6
16 [1]V 4, note 1 [a]2 Kin 1:3
17 [a]2 Kin 3:1; 8:16
2:1 [1]Or *windstorm* [a]Gen 5:24; Heb 11:5 [b]1 Kin 19:16-21 [c]Josh 4:19
2 [a]Ruth 1:15 [b]1 Kin 12:28, 29 [c]1 Sam 1:26; 2 Kin 2:4, 6
3 [1]Lit *your head* [a]2 Kin 4:1, 38; 5:22

4 Elijah said to him, "Elisha, please [a]stay here, for the LORD has
sent me to [b]Jericho." But he said, "[a]As the LORD lives, and as
you yourself live, I will not leave you." So they came to Jericho.
5 [a]The sons of the prophets who *were* at Jericho approached
Elisha and said to him, "[b]Do you know that the LORD will take
away your master from over [1]you today?" And he [2]answered,
"Yes, I know; be still."
6 Then Elijah said to him, "Please [a]stay here, for the LORD has
sent me to [b]the Jordan." And he said, "As the LORD lives, and
as you yourself live, I will not leave you." So the two of them
went on.
7 Now [a]fifty men of the sons of the prophets went and stood
opposite *them* at a distance, while the two of them stood by
the Jordan.
8 Elijah [a]took his mantle and folded it together and [b]struck
the waters, and they were divided here and there, so that the
two of them crossed over on dry ground.
9 When they had crossed over, Elijah said to Elisha, "Ask
what I shall do for you before I am taken from you." And Elisha
said, "Please, let a [a]double portion of your spirit be upon me."
10 He said, "You have asked a hard thing. *Nevertheless,* if you
[a]see me when I am taken
from you, it shall be so for
you; but if not, it shall not
be *so.*"
11 As they were going
along and talking, behold,
there appeared [a]a chariot of
fire and horses of fire
which separated the two of
them. And Elijah went up
by a [1]whirlwind to heaven.
12 Elisha saw *it* and cried
out, "[a]My father, my father,
the [1]chariots of Israel and
its horsemen!" And he saw
[2]Elijah no more. Then [b]he
took hold of his own clothes
and tore them in two
pieces.
13 He also took up the
mantle of Elijah that fell
from him and returned and
stood by the bank of the
Jordan.
14 He took the mantle of
Elijah that fell from him
and struck the waters and
said, "Where is the LORD,
the God of Elijah?" And
when he also had [a]struck

Elisha's Ministry

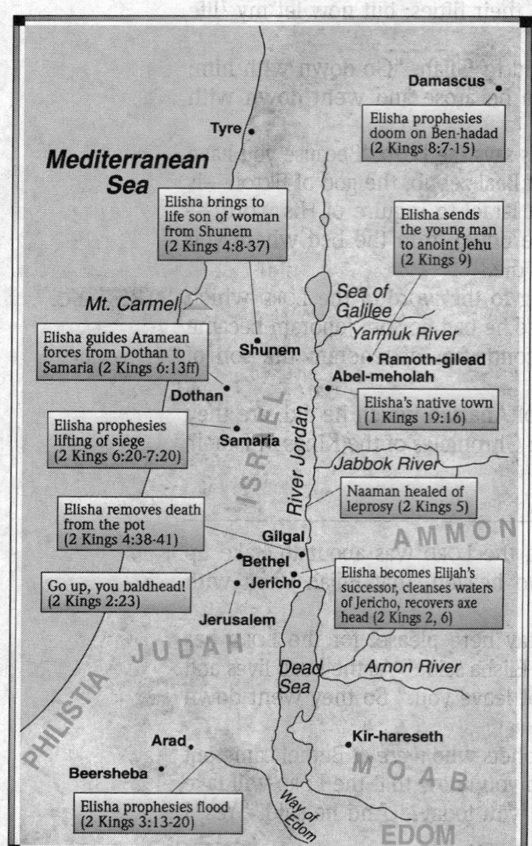

4 [a]2 Kin 2:2 [b]Josh 6:26
5 [1]Lit *your head* [2]Lit *said* [a]2 Kin 2:3 [b]2 Kin 2:3
6 [a]2 Kin 2:2 [b]Josh 3:8, 15-17
7 [a]2 Kin 2:15, 16
8 [a]1 Kin 19:13, 19 [b]Ex 14:21, 22; 2 Kin 2:14
9 [a]Num 11:17-25; Deut 21:17
10 [a]Acts 1:10
11 [1]Or *windstorm* [a]2 Kin 6:17
12 [1]Lit *chariot* [2]Lit *him* [a]2 Kin 13:14 [b]Gen 37:34; Job 1:20
14 [a]2 Kin 2:8

the waters, they were divided here and there; and Elisha
crossed over.
15 Now when [a]the sons of the prophets who *were* at Jericho
opposite *him* saw him, they said, "The spirit of Elijah rests on
Elisha." And they came to meet him and bowed themselves to
the ground before him.
16 They said to him, "Behold now, there are with your servants
fifty strong men, please let them go and search for your master;
perhaps [a]the Spirit of the LORD has taken him up and cast him
on some mountain or into some valley." And he said, "You shall
not send."
17 But when [a]they urged him until he was ashamed, he said,
"Send." They sent therefore fifty men; and they searched three
days but did not find him.
18 They returned to him while he was staying at Jericho; and
he said to them, "Did I not say to you, 'Do not go'?"
19 Then the men of the city said to Elisha, "Behold now, the
situation of this city is pleasant, as my lord sees; but the water
is bad and the land [1]is unfruitful."
20 He said, "Bring me a new jar, and put salt [1]in it." So they
brought *it* to him.
21 He went out to the spring of water and [a]threw salt [1]in it and
said, "Thus says the
LORD, 'I have [2]purified
these waters; there shall
not be from there death
or [3]unfruitfulness any
longer.'"
22 So the waters have
been [1]purified to this day,
according to the word of
Elisha which he spoke.
23 Then he went up
from there to Bethel; and
as he was going up by the
way, young lads came out
from the city and [a]mocked
him and said to him, "Go
up, you baldhead; go up,
you baldhead!"
24 When he looked be-
hind him and saw them,
he [a]cursed them in the
name of the LORD. Then
two female bears came
out of the woods and tore
up forty-two lads of [1]their
number.
25 He went from there
to [a]Mount Carmel, and
from there he returned
to Samaria.

15 [a]2 Kin 2:7
16 [a]1 Kin 18:12; Acts 8:39
17 [a]2 Kin 8:11
19 [1]Lit *causes barrenness*
20 [1]Lit *there*
21 [1]Lit *there* [2]Lit *healed* [3]Lit *barrenness* [a]Ex 15:25, 26; 2 Kin 4:41; 6:6
22 [1]Lit *healed*
23 [a]2 Chr 36:16; Ps 31:17, 18
24 [1]Lit *them* [a]Neh 13:25-27
25 [a]1 Kin 18:19, 20; 2 Kin 4:25

The Cities and Geography of 2 Kings

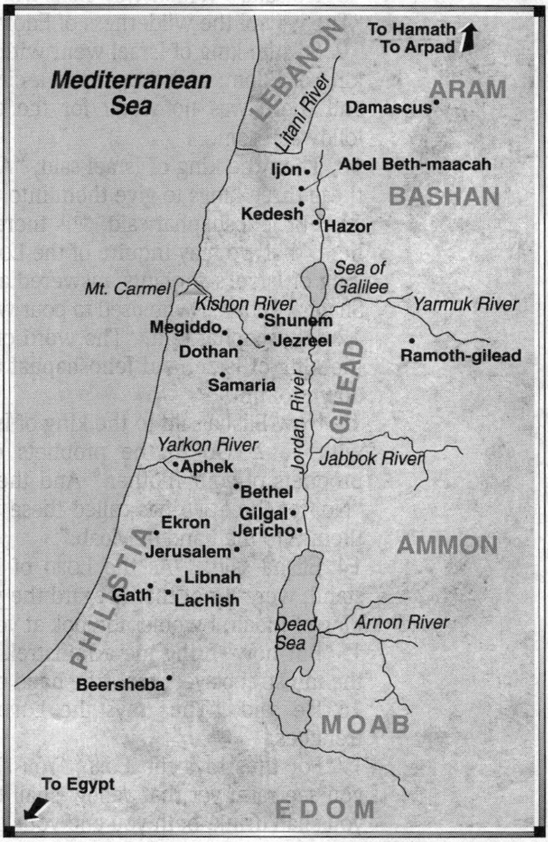

Chapter 3 Theme ______________________

852 B.C.

3 Now Jehoram the son of Ahab became king over Israel at
Samaria [a]in the eighteenth year of Jehoshaphat king of
Judah, and reigned twelve years.
2 He did evil in the sight of the LORD, though not like his
father and his mother; for [a]he put away the *sacred* pillar of Baal
[b]which his father had made.
3 Nevertheless, [a]he clung to the sins of Jeroboam the son of
Nebat, [b]which he made Israel sin; he did not depart from them.
4 Now Mesha king of Moab was a sheep breeder, and [a]used to
pay the king of Israel 100,000 lambs and the wool of 100,000
rams.
5 But [a]when Ahab died, the king of Moab rebelled against the
king of Israel.
6 And King Jehoram went out of Samaria [1]at that time and
mustered all Israel.
7 Then he went and sent *word* to Jehoshaphat the king of
Judah, saying, "The king of Moab has rebelled against me. Will
you go with me to fight against Moab?" And he said, "I will go
up; [a]I am as you are, my people as your people, my horses as
your horses."
8 He said, "Which way shall we go up?" And he [1]answered,
"The way of the wilderness of Edom."
9 So [a]the king of Israel went with [b]the king of Judah and [c]the
king of Edom; and they made a circuit of seven days' journey,
and there was no water for the army or for the cattle that
followed them.
10 Then the king of Israel said, "Alas! For the LORD has called
these three kings to give them into the hand of Moab."
11 But Jehoshaphat said, "[a]Is there not a prophet of the LORD
here, that we may inquire of the LORD by him?" And one of the
king of Israel's servants answered and said, "[b]Elisha the son of
Shaphat is here, [c]who used to pour water on the hands of Elijah."
12 Jehoshaphat said, "The word of the LORD is with him." So
the king of Israel and Jehoshaphat and the king of Edom went
down to him.
13 Now Elisha said to the king of Israel, "What do I have to do
with you? [a]Go to the prophets of your father and to the
prophets of your mother." And the king of Israel said to him,
"No, for the LORD has called these three kings *together* to give
them into the hand of Moab."
14 Elisha said, "[a]As the LORD of hosts lives, before whom I
stand, were it not that I regard the presence of Jehoshaphat the
king of Judah, I would not look at you nor see you.
15 "But now [a]bring me a minstrel." And it came about, when
the minstrel played, that [b]the hand of the LORD came upon him.
16 He said, "Thus says the LORD, 'Make this valley full of
trenches.'
17 "For thus says the LORD, 'You shall not see wind nor shall
you see rain; yet that valley [a]shall be filled with water, so that
you shall drink, both you and your cattle and your beasts.

3:1 [a]2 Kin 1:17

2 [a]Ex 23:24; 2 Kin 10:18, 26-28 [b]1 Kin 16:31, 32

3 [a]1 Kin 12:28-32 [b]1 Kin 14:9, 16

4 [a]2 Sam 8:2; Is 16:1, 2

5 [a]2 Kin 1:1

6 [1]Lit *in that day*

7 [a]1 Kin 22:4

8 [1]Lit *said*

9 [a]2 Kin 3:1 [b]2 Kin 3:7 [c]1 Kin 22:47

11 [a]1 Kin 22:7 [b]2 Kin 2:25 [c]1 Kin 19:21; John 13:4, 5, 13, 14

13 [a]1 Kin 18:19; 22:6-11, 22-25

14 [a]1 Kin 17:1; 2 Kin 5:16

15 [a]1 Sam 16:23; 1 Chr 25:1 [b]1 Kin 18:46; Ezek 1:3

17 [a]Ps 107:35

18 'This is but a [a]slight thing in the sight of the LORD; He will
also give the Moabites into your hand.
19 '[a]Then you shall strike every fortified city and every choice
city, and fell every good tree and stop all springs of water, and
mar every good piece of land with stones.'"
20 It happened in the morning [a]about the time of offering the
sacrifice, that behold, water came by the way of Edom, and the
country was filled with water.
21 Now all the Moabites heard that the kings had come up to
fight against them. And all who were able to [1]put on armor and
older were summoned and stood on the border.
22 They rose early in the morning, and the sun shone on the
water, and the Moabites saw the water opposite *them* as red as
blood.
23 Then they said, "This is blood; the kings have surely fought
together, and they have slain one another. Now therefore, Moab,
to the spoil!"
24 But when they came to the camp of Israel, the Israelites
arose and struck the Moabites, so that they fled before them; and
they went forward [1]into the land, [2]slaughtering the Moabites.
25 [a]Thus they destroyed the cities; and each one threw a
stone on every piece of good land and filled it. So they stopped
all the springs of water and felled all the good trees, until in
[b]Kir-hareseth *only* they left its stones; however, the slingers
went about *it* and struck it.
26 When the king of Moab saw that the battle was too fierce
for him, he took with him 700 men who drew swords, to
break through to the king of Edom; but they could not.
27 Then he took his oldest son who was to reign in his place,
and [a]offered him as a burnt offering on the wall. And there
came great wrath against Israel, and they departed from him
and returned to their own land.

Chapter 4 Theme ____________________

4 Now a certain woman of the wives of [a]the sons of the
prophets cried out to [1]Elisha, "Your servant my husband is
dead, and you know that your servant feared the LORD; and [b]the
creditor has come to take my two children to be his slaves."
2 Elisha said to her, "What shall I do for you? Tell me, what
do you have in the house?" And she said, "Your maidservant
has nothing in the house except [a]a jar of oil."
3 Then he said, "Go, borrow vessels at large for yourself from
all your neighbors, *even* empty vessels; do not get a few.
4 "And you shall go in and shut the door behind you and your
sons, and pour out into all these vessels, and you shall set aside
what is full."
5 So she went from him and shut the door behind her and
her sons; they were bringing *the vessels* to her and she poured.
6 When [a]the vessels were full, she said to her son, "Bring me
another vessel." And he said to her, "There is not one vessel
more." And the oil stopped.

18 [a]Jer 32:17, 27; Mark 10:27; Luke 1:37
19 [a]2 Kin 3:25
20 [a]Ex 29:39, 40
21 [1]Lit *gird themselves with a belt*
24 [1]Lit *into it* [2]Lit *smiting*
25 [a]2 Kin 3:19 [b]Is 16:7; Jer 48:31, 36
27 [a]Amos 2:1; Mic 6:7
4:1 [1]Lit *Elisha, saying* [a]2 Kin 2:3 [b]Lev 25:39-41, 48; 1 Sam 22:2; Neh 5:2-5
2 [a]1 Kin 17:12
6 [a]Matt 14:20

7 Then she came and told [a]the man of God. And he said,
"Go, sell the oil and pay your debt, and you *and* your sons can
live on the rest."
8 Now there came a day when Elisha passed over to [a]Shunem,
where there was a [1]prominent woman, and she persuaded him
to eat [2]food. And so it was, as often as he passed by, he turned
in there to eat [2]food.
9 She said to her husband, "Behold now, I perceive that this
is a holy [a]man of God passing by us continually.
10 "Please, let us [a]make a little walled upper chamber and let
us set a bed for him there, and a table and a chair and a
lampstand; and it shall be, when he comes to us, *that* he can
turn in there."
11 [1]One day he came there and turned in to the upper chamber
and [2]rested.
12 Then he said to [a]Gehazi his servant, "Call this Shunammite."
And when he had called her, she stood before him.
13 He said to him, "Say now to her, 'Behold, you have been
[1]careful for us with all this [2]care; what can I do for you? Would
you be spoken for to the king or to the captain of the army?'"
And she [3]answered, "I live among my own people."
14 So he said, "What then is to be done for her?" And Gehazi
[1]answered, "Truly she has no son and her husband is old."
15 He said, "Call her." When he had called her, she stood in
the doorway.
16 Then he said, "[a]At this season [1]next year you will embrace
a son." And she said, "No, my lord, O man of God, [b]do not lie
to your maidservant."
17 The woman conceived and bore a son at that season [1]the
next year, as Elisha had said to her.
18 When the child was grown, the day came that he went out
to his father to the reapers.
19 He said to his father, "My head, my head." And he said to
his servant, "Carry him to his mother."
20 When he had taken him and brought him to his mother, he
sat on her [1]lap until noon, and *then* died.
21 She went up and [a]laid him on the bed of [b]the man of God,
and shut *the door* behind him and went out.
22 Then she called to her husband and said, "Please send me
one of the servants and one of the donkeys, that I may run to
the man of God and return."
23 He said, "Why will you go to him today? It is neither [a]new
moon nor sabbath." And she said, "*It will be* well."
24 Then she saddled a donkey and said to her servant, "Drive and
go forward; do not slow down [1]the pace for me unless I tell you."
25 So she went and came to the man of God to [a]Mount Carmel.
When the man of God saw her at a distance, he said to
Gehazi his servant, "Behold, [1]there is the Shunammite.
26 "Please run now to meet her and say to her, 'Is it well with
you? Is it well with your husband? Is it well with the child?'"
And she [1]answered, "It is well."

7 [a]1 Kin 12:22
8 [1]Lit *great* [2]Lit *bread* [a]Josh 19:18
9 [a]2 Kin 4:7
10 [a]Matt 10:41, 42; 25:40; Rom 12:13
11 [1]Lit *Now a day came that* [2]Lit *lay there*
12 [a]2 Kin 4:29-31; 5:20-27; 8:4, 5
13 [1]Lit *fearful* [2]Lit *fear* [3]Lit *said*
14 [1]Lit *said*
16 [1]Lit *when the time revives* [a]Gen 18:14 [b]2 Kin 4:28
17 [1]Lit *when the time revived*
20 [1]Lit *knees*
21 [a]2 Kin 4:32 [b]2 Kin 4:7
23 [a]Num 10:10; 28:11; 1 Chr 23:31
24 [1]Lit *riding*
25 [1]Lit *this Shunammite* [a]2 Kin 2:25
26 [1]Lit *said*

27 When she came to the man of God [a]to the hill, she caught
hold of his feet. And Gehazi came near to push her away; but the
man of God said, "Let her alone, for her soul is [1]troubled within
her; and the LORD has hidden it from me and has not told me."
28 Then she said, "Did I ask for a son from my lord? Did I not
say, '[a]Do not deceive me'?"
29 Then he said to Gehazi, "[a]Gird up your loins and [b]take my
staff in your hand, and go your way; if you meet any man, do
not [c]salute him, and if anyone salutes you, do not answer him;
and [d]lay my staff on the lad's face."
30 The mother of the lad said, "[a]As the LORD lives and as you
yourself live, I will not leave you." And he arose and followed her.
31 Then Gehazi passed on before them and laid the staff on the
lad's face, but there was no sound or [1]response. So he returned
to meet him and told [2]him, "The lad [a]has not awakened."
32 When Elisha came into the house, behold the lad was dead
and laid on his bed.
33 So he entered and [a]shut the door behind them both and
prayed to the LORD.
34 And [a]he went up and lay on the child, and put his mouth
on his mouth and his eyes on his eyes and his hands on his
hands, and he stretched himself on him; and the flesh of the
child became warm.
35 Then he returned and walked in the house once back and
forth, and went up and [a]stretched himself on him; and the lad
sneezed seven times and the lad opened his eyes.
36 He called Gehazi and said, "Call this Shunammite." So he
called her. And when she came in to him, he said, "Take up
your son."
37 Then she went in and fell at his feet and bowed herself to
the ground, and [a]she took up her son and went out.
38 When Elisha returned to [a]Gilgal, *there was* [b]a famine in the
land. [1]As [c]the sons of the prophets [d]were sitting before him, he
said to his servant, "[e]Put on the large pot and boil stew for the
sons of the prophets."
39 Then one went out into the field to gather herbs, and found
a wild vine and gathered from it his lap full of wild gourds, and
came and sliced them into the pot of stew, for they did not
know *what they were.*
40 So they poured *it* out for the men to eat. And as they were
eating of the stew, they cried out and said, "O man of God,
there is [a]death in the pot." And they were unable to eat.
41 But he said, "Now bring meal." [a]He threw it into the pot
and said, "Pour *it* out for the people that they may eat." Then
there was no harm in the pot.
42 Now a man came from Baal-shalishah, and brought the
man of God bread of the first fruits, twenty loaves of barley and
fresh ears of grain in his sack. And he said, "[a]Give *them* to the
people that they may eat."
43 His attendant said, "What, [a]will I set this before a hundred
men?" But he said, "Give *them* to the people that they may eat,
for thus says the LORD, 'They shall eat and have *some* left over.'"

27 [1]Lit *bitter* [a]2 Kin 4:25
28 [a]2 Kin 4:16
29 [a]1 Kin 18:46; 2 Kin 9:1 [b]Ex 4:17; 2 Kin 2:14 [c]Luke 10:4 [d]Ex 7:19, 20; 14:16
30 [a]2 Kin 2:2, 4
31 [1]Lit *attentiveness* [2]Lit *him, saying* [a]John 11:11
33 [a]2 Kin 4:4; Matt 6:6; Luke 8:51
34 [a]1 Kin 17:21-23
35 [a]1 Kin 17:21
37 [a]Heb 11:35
38 [1]Lit *And* [a]2 Kin 2:1 [b]2 Kin 8:1 [c]2 Kin 2:3 [d]Luke 10:39; Acts 22:3 [e]Ezek 11:3, 7, 11; 24:3
40 [a]Ex 10:17
41 [a]Ex 15:25; 2 Kin 2:21
42 [a]Matt 14:16-21; 15:32-38
43 [a]Luke 9:13; John 6:9

INSIGHT

The land of ***Baal-shalishah***, meaning "the third," was evidently the tribal territory of Ephraim (1 Samuel 9:4). Modern-day Kefr Thilth may be on the site of the ancient city. However, the exact location of Baal-shalishah has recently been questioned.

44 So he set *it* before them, and they ate and [a]had *some* left
over, according to the word of the LORD.

Chapter 5 Theme ____________________

5 Now [a]Naaman, captain of the army of the king of Aram,
was a great man [1]with his master, and highly respected,
because by him the LORD had given victory to Aram. The man
was also a valiant warrior, *but he was* a leper.
2 Now the Arameans had gone out [a]in bands and had taken
captive a little girl from the land of Israel; and she [1]waited on
Naaman's wife.
3 She said to her mistress, "I wish that my master were [1]with
the prophet who is in Samaria! Then he would cure him of his
leprosy."
4 [1]Naaman went in and told his master, saying, "Thus and
thus spoke the girl who is from the land of Israel."
5 Then the king of Aram said, "Go [1]now, and I will send a
letter to the king of Israel." He departed and [a]took with him
ten talents of silver and six thousand *shekels* of gold and ten
[b]changes of clothes.
6 He brought the letter to the king of Israel, saying, "And now
as this letter comes to you, behold, I have sent Naaman my
servant to you, that you may cure him of his leprosy."
7 When the king of Israel read the letter, [a]he tore his clothes
and said, "[b]Am I God, to kill and to make alive, that this man is
sending *word* to me to cure a man of his leprosy? But [c]consider
now, and see how he is seeking [1]a quarrel against me."
8 It happened when Elisha [a]the man of God heard that the king
of Israel had torn his clothes, that he sent *word* to the king,
saying, "Why have you torn your clothes? Now let him come to
me, and he shall know that there is a prophet in Israel."
9 So Naaman came with his horses and his chariots and stood
at the doorway of the house of Elisha.
10 Elisha sent a messenger to him, saying, "[a]Go and wash in
the Jordan seven times, and your flesh will be restored to you
and *you will* be clean."
11 But Naaman was furious and went away and said, "Behold,
I [1]thought, 'He will surely come out to me and stand and call
on the name of the LORD his God, and wave his hand over the
place and cure the leper.'
12 "Are not [1]Abanah and Pharpar, the rivers of Damascus, better
than all the waters of Israel? Could I not wash in them and be
clean?" So he turned and [a]went away in a rage.
13 [a]Then his servants came near and spoke to him and said,
"[b]My father, had the prophet told you *to do some* great thing,
would you not have done *it?* How much more *then,* when he
says to you, 'Wash, and be clean'?"
14 So he went down and dipped *himself* seven times in the
Jordan, according to the word of the man of God; and [a]his flesh
was restored like the flesh of a little child and [b]he was clean.

44 [a]Matt 14:20; 15:37; John 6:13

5:1 [1]Lit *before* [a]Luke 4:27

2 [1]Lit *was before* [a]2 Kin 6:23; 13:20

3 [1]Lit *before*

4 [1]Lit *He*

5 [1]Lit *enter* [a]1 Sam 9:7; 2 Kin 4:42 [b]Judg 14:12; 2 Kin 5:22, 23

7 [1]Lit *an occasion* [a]Gen 37:29 [b]Gen 30:2; 1 Sam 2:6 [c]1 Kin 20:7; Luke 11:54

8 [a]1 Kin 12:22

10 [a]John 9:7

11 [1]Lit *said*

12 [1]Another reading is *Amanah* [a]Prov 14:17; 16:32; 19:11

13 [a]1 Sam 28:23 [b]2 Kin 2:12; 6:21; 8:9

14 [a]2 Kin 5:10; Job 33:25 [b]Luke 4:27; 5:13

15 When he returned to the man of God [1]with all his company,
and came and stood before him, he said, "Behold now, [a]I know
that there is no God in all the earth, but in Israel; so please
[b]take a [2]present from your servant now."
16 But he said, "[a]As the LORD lives, before whom I stand, [b]I
will take nothing." And he urged him to take *it,* but he refused.
17 Naaman said, "If not, please let your servant at least be given
two mules' load of [a]earth; for your servant will no longer offer
burnt offering nor will he sacrifice to other gods, but to the LORD.
18 "In this matter may the LORD pardon your servant: when my
master goes into the house of Rimmon to worship there, and
[a]he leans on my hand and I bow myself in the house of Rimmon,
when I bow myself in the house of Rimmon, the LORD pardon
your servant in this matter."
19 He said to him, "[a]Go in peace." So he departed from him
some distance.
20 But [a]Gehazi, the servant of Elisha the man of God, [1]thought,
"Behold, my master has spared this Naaman the Aramean, [2]by
not receiving from his hands what he brought. [b]As the LORD lives,
I will run after him and take something from him."
21 So Gehazi pursued Naaman. When Naaman saw one running
after him, he came down from the chariot to meet him and
said, "Is all well?"
22 He said, "[a]All is well. My master has sent me, saying,
'Behold, just now two young men of the sons of the prophets
have come to me from [b]the hill country of Ephraim. Please give
them a talent of silver and [c]two changes of clothes.'"
23 Naaman said, "[a]Be pleased to take two talents." And he urged
him, and bound two talents of silver in two bags with two
changes of clothes and gave them to two of his servants; and
they carried *them* before him.
24 When he came to the [1]hill, he took them from their hand
and [a]deposited them in the house, and he sent the men away,
and they departed.
25 But he went in and stood before his master. And Elisha said
to him, "Where have you been, Gehazi?" And he said, "[a]Your
servant went nowhere."
26 Then he said to him, "Did not my heart go *with you,* when
the man turned from his chariot to meet you? [a]Is it a time to
receive money and to receive clothes and olive groves and
vineyards and sheep and oxen and male and female servants?
27 "Therefore, the leprosy of Naaman shall cling to you and to
your [1]descendants forever." So he went out from his presence
[a]a leper *as white* as snow.

Chapter 6 Theme

6 Now [a]the sons of the prophets said to Elisha, "Behold now,
the place before you where we are living is too limited for us.
2 "Please let us go to the Jordan and each of us take from there
a beam, and let us make a place there for ourselves where we
may live." So he said, "Go."

15 [1]Lit *he and* [2]Lit *blessing* [a]Josh 2:11; 1 Sam 17:46, 47; 2 Kin 5:8 [b]1 Sam 25:27
16 [a]2 Kin 3:14 [b]Gen 14:22, 23; 2 Kin 5:20, 26
17 [a]Ex 20:24
18 [a]2 Kin 7:2, 17
19 [a]Ex 4:18; 1 Sam 1:17; Mark 5:34
20 [1]Lit *said* [2]Lit *from* [a]2 Kin 4:12, 31, 36 [b]Ex 20:7; 2 Kin 6:31
22 [a]2 Kin 4:26 [b]Josh 24:33 [c]2 Kin 5:5
23 [a]2 Kin 6:3
24 [1]Lit *Ophel* [a]Josh 7:1, 11, 12, 21; 1 Kin 21:16
25 [a]2 Kin 5:22
26 [a]2 Kin 5:16
27 [1]Lit *seed* [a]Ex 4:6; Num 12:10
6:1 [a]2 Kin 2:3

INSIGHT

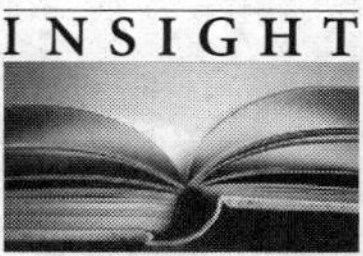

The ***Arameans***, the descendants of Noah through Shem, lived in a confederation of towns and settlements in what is now Syria. Some settled as far as Babylon. Jacob's grandfather, Abraham, was Aramean (Deuteronomy 26:5).

3 Then one said, "Please be willing to go with your servants."
And he [1]answered, "I shall go."
4 So he went with them; and when they came to the Jordan,
they cut down trees.
5 But as one was felling a beam, [1]the axe head fell into the
water; and he cried out and said, "Alas, my master! For it was
borrowed."
6 Then the man of God said, "Where did it fall?" And when
he showed him the place, [a]he cut off a stick and threw *it* in
there, and made the iron float.
7 He said, "Take it up for yourself." So he put out his hand
and took it.
8 Now the king of Aram was warring against Israel; and he
[1]counseled with his servants saying, "In such and such a place
shall be my camp."
9 [a]The man of God sent *word* to the king of Israel saying,
"Beware that you do not pass this place, for the Arameans are
coming down there."
10 The king of Israel sent to the place about which the man of
God had told him; thus he warned him, so that he guarded
himself there, [1]more than once or twice.
11 Now the heart of the king of Aram was enraged over this
thing; and he called his servants and said to them, "Will you
tell me which of us is for the king of Israel?"
12 One of his servants said, "No, my lord, O king; but Elisha,
the prophet who is in Israel, tells the king of Israel the words
that you speak in your bedroom."
13 So he said, "Go and see where he is, that I may send and take
him." And it was told him, saying, "Behold, he is in [a]Dothan."
14 He sent horses and chariots and a great army there, and
they came by night and surrounded the city.
15 Now when the attendant of the man of God had risen early
and gone out, behold, an army with horses and chariots was
circling the city. And his servant said to him, "Alas, my master!
[1]What shall we do?"
16 So he [1]answered, "[a]Do not fear, for [b]those who are with us
are more than those who are with them."
17 Then Elisha prayed and said, "[a]O LORD, I pray, open his
eyes that he may see." And the LORD opened the servant's eyes
and he saw; and behold, the mountain was full of [b]horses and
chariots of fire all around Elisha.
18 When they came down to him, Elisha prayed to the LORD
and said, "Strike this [1]people with blindness, I pray." So He
[a]struck them with blindness according to the word of Elisha.
19 Then Elisha said to them, "This is not the way, nor is this
the city; follow me and I will bring you to the man whom you
seek." And he brought them to Samaria.
20 When they had come into Samaria, Elisha said, "O [a]LORD,
open the eyes of these *men,* that they may see." So the LORD
opened their eyes and they saw; and behold, they were in the
midst of Samaria.

3 [1]Lit *said*
5 [1]Lit *as for the iron, it fell*
6 [a]Ex 15:25; 2 Kin 2:21; 4:41
8 [1]Lit *took counsel*
9 [a]2 Kin 4:1, 7; 6:12
10 [1]Lit *not once or twice*
13 [a]Gen 37:17
15 [1]Lit *How*
16 [1]Lit *said* [a]Ex 14:13 [b]2 Chr 32:7, 8; Rom 8:31
17 [a]2 Kin 6:20 [b]2 Kin 2:11; Ps 68:17; Zech 6:1-7
18 [1]Lit *nation* [a]Gen 19:11
20 [a]2 Kin 6:17

21 Then the king of Israel when he saw them, said to Elisha, “[a]My father, shall I [1]kill them? Shall I [1]kill them?”

22 He [1]answered, “You shall not [2]kill *them.* Would you [2a]kill those you have taken captive with your sword and with your bow? [b]Set bread and water before them, that they may eat and drink and go to their master.”

23 So he prepared a great feast for them; and when they had eaten and drunk he sent them away, and they went to their master. And [a]the marauding bands of Arameans did not come again into the land of Israel.

24 Now it came about after this, that [a]Ben-hadad king of Aram gathered all his army and went up and besieged Samaria.

25 There was a great [a]famine in Samaria; and behold, they besieged it, until a donkey's head was sold for eighty *shekels* of silver, and a fourth of a [1]kab of dove's dung for five *shekels* of silver.

26 As the king of Israel was passing by on the wall a woman cried out to him, saying, “Help, my lord, O king!”

27 He said, “[1]If the LORD does not help you, from where shall I help you? From the threshing floor, or from the wine press?”

28 And the king said to her, “[a]What [1]is the matter with you?” And she [2]answered, “This woman said to me, ‘Give your son that we may eat him today, and we will eat my son tomorrow.’

29 “[a]So we boiled my son and ate him; and I said to her on the next day, ‘Give your son, that we may eat him’; but she has hidden her son.”

30 When the king heard the words of the woman, [a]he tore his clothes—now he was passing by on the wall—and the people looked, and behold, he had sackcloth [1]beneath on his [2]body.

31 Then he said, “May [a]God do so to me and more also, if the head of Elisha the son of Shaphat [1]remains on him today.”

32 Now Elisha was sitting in his house, and [a]the elders were sitting with him. And *the king* sent a man from his presence; but before the messenger came to him, he said to the elders, “Do you [b]see how this son of a murderer has sent to take away my head? Look, when the messenger comes, shut the door and [1]hold the door shut against him. Is not the sound of his master's feet behind him?”

33 While he was still talking with them, behold, the messenger came down to him and he said, “[a]Behold, this evil is from the LORD; why should I wait for the LORD any longer?”

Chapter 7 Theme ______________________________

7 Then Elisha said, “Listen to the word of the LORD; thus says the LORD, ‘[a]Tomorrow about this time a [1]measure of fine flour will be *sold* for a shekel, and two measures of barley for a shekel, in the gate of Samaria.’”

2 [a]The royal officer on whose hand the king was leaning answered the man of God and said, “Behold, [b]if the LORD should make windows in heaven, could this thing be?” Then he said, “Behold, you will see it with your own eyes, but you will not eat [1]of it.”

21 [1]Lit *smite* [a]2 Kin 2:12; 5:13; 8:9

22 [1]Lit *said* [2]Lit *smite* [a]Deut 20:11-16; 2 Chr 28:8-15 [b]Rom 12:20

23 [a]2 Kin 5:2; 24:2

24 [a]1 Kin 20:1

25 [1]I.e. One kab equals approx 2 qts [a]Lev 26:26

27 [1]Lit *No, let the LORD help you*

28 [1]Lit *to you* [2]Lit *said* [a]Judg 18:23

29 [a]Lev 26:27-29; Deut 28:52, 53, 57; Lam 4:10

30 [1]Lit *within* [2]Lit *flesh* [a]1 Kin 21:27

31 [1]Lit *stands* [a]Ruth 1:17; 1 Kin 19:2

32 [1]Lit *press him with the door* [a]Ezek 8:1; 14:1; 20:1 [b]1 Kin 18:4, 13, 14; 21:10, 13

33 [a]Is 8:21

7:1 [1]Heb *seah* [a]2 Kin 7:18

2 [1]Lit *from there* [a]2 Kin 5:18; 7:17, 19 [b]Gen 7:11; Mal 3:10

3 Now there were four [a]leprous men at the entrance of the gate; and they said to one another, "Why do we sit here until we die?

4 "If we say, 'We will enter the city,' then the famine is in the city and we will die there; and if we sit here, we die also. Now therefore come, and let us [1]go over to [a]the camp of the Arameans. If they spare us, we will live; and if they kill us, we will but die."

5 They arose at twilight to go to the camp of the Arameans; when they came to the outskirts of the camp of the Arameans, behold, there was no one there.

6 For [a]the Lord had caused the army of the Arameans to hear a sound of chariots and a sound of horses, *even* the sound of a great army, so that they said to one another, "Behold, the king of Israel has hired against us [b]the kings of the Hittites and [c]the kings of the Egyptians, to come upon us."

7 Therefore they [a]arose and fled in the twilight, and left their tents and their horses and their donkeys, *even* the camp just as it was, and fled for their life.

8 When these lepers came to the outskirts of the camp, they entered one tent and ate and drank, and [a]carried from there silver and gold and clothes, and went and hid *them;* and they returned and entered another tent and carried from there *also,* and went and hid *them.*

9 Then they said to one another, "We are not doing right. This day is a day of good news, but we are keeping silent; if we wait until morning light, punishment will [1]overtake us. Now therefore come, let us go and tell the king's household."

10 So they came and called to the gatekeepers of the city, and they told them, saying, "We came to the camp of the Arameans, and behold, there was no one there, nor the voice of man, only the horses tied and the donkeys tied, and the tents just as they were."

11 The gatekeepers called and told *it* within the king's household.

12 Then the king arose in the night and said to his servants, "I will now tell you what the Arameans have done to us. They know that [a]we are hungry; therefore they have gone from the camp [b]to hide themselves in the field, saying, 'When they come out of the city, we will capture them alive and get into the city.'"

13 One of his servants said, "Please, let some *men* take five of the horses which remain, which are left [1]in the city. Behold, they *will be in any case* like all the multitude of Israel who are left in it; behold, they *will be in any case* like all the multitude of Israel who have already perished, so let us send and see."

14 They took therefore two chariots with horses, and the king sent after the army of the Arameans, saying, "Go and see."

15 They went after them to the Jordan, and behold, all the way was full of clothes and equipment which the Arameans had thrown away in their haste. Then the messengers returned and told the king.

3 [a]Lev 13:45, 46; Num 5:2-4; 12:10-14

4 [1]Lit *fall* [a]2 Kin 6:24

6 [a]2 Sam 5:24 [b]1 Kin 10:29 [c]2 Chr 12:2, 3; Is 31:1; 36:9

7 [a]Ps 48:4-6; Prov 28:1

8 [a]Josh 7:21

9 [1]Lit *find*

12 [a]2 Kin 6:25-29 [b]Josh 8:4-12

13 [1]Lit *in it*

16 So the people went out and plundered the camp of the
Arameans. Then a [1]measure of fine flour *was sold* for a shekel
and two [1]measures of barley for a shekel, [a]according to the
word of the LORD.
17 Now the king appointed [a]the royal officer on whose hand
he leaned [1]to have charge of the gate; but the people trampled
on him at the gate, and he died just as the man of God had
said, [b]who spoke when the king came down to him.
18 It happened just as the man of God had spoken to the king,
saying, "[a]Two [1]measures of barley for a shekel and a [1]measure
of fine flour for a shekel, will be *sold* tomorrow about this time
at the gate of Samaria."
19 Then the royal officer answered the man of God and said,
"Now behold, [a]if the LORD should make windows in heaven,
could such a thing be?" And he said, "Behold, you will see it
with your own eyes, but you will not eat [1]of it."
20 And so it happened to him, for the people trampled on him
at the gate and he died.

Chapter 8 Theme ______________________

8 Now [a]Elisha spoke to the woman whose son he had restored
to life, saying, "Arise and go [1]with your household, and
sojourn wherever you can sojourn; for the [b]LORD has called for
a famine, and [c]it will even come on the land for seven years."
2 So the woman arose and did according to the word of the
man of God, and she went with her household and sojourned
in the land of the Philistines seven years.
3 At the end of seven years, the woman returned from the
land of the Philistines; and she went out to [1]appeal to the king
for her house and for her field.
4 Now the king was talking with [a]Gehazi, the servant of the
man of God, saying, "Please relate to me all the great things
that Elisha has done."
5 As he was relating to the king [a]how he had restored to life
the one who was dead, behold, the woman whose son he had
restored to life [1]appealed to the king for her house and for her
field. And Gehazi said, "My lord, O king, this is the woman
and this is her son, whom Elisha restored to life."
6 When the king asked the woman, she related *it* to him. So
the king appointed for her a certain officer, saying, "Restore all
that was hers and all the produce of the field from the day that
she left the land even until now."
7 Then Elisha came to [a]Damascus. Now [b]Ben-hadad king of
Aram was sick, and it was told him, saying, "[c]The man of God
has come here."
8 The king said to [a]Hazael, "[b]Take a gift in your hand and go
to meet the man of God, and [c]inquire of the LORD by him,
saying, 'Will I recover from this sickness?'"
9 So Hazael went to meet him and took a gift in his hand,
even every kind of good thing of Damascus, forty camels' loads;

16 [1]Heb *seah;* i.e. one seah equals approx 11 qts [a]2 Kin 7:1
17 [1]Lit *over the gate* [a]2 Kin 7:2 [b]2 Kin 6:32
18 [1]Heb *seah;* i.e. one seah equals approx 11 qts [a]2 Kin 7:1
19 [1]Lit *from there* [a]2 Kin 7:2
8:1 [1]Lit *you and your* [a]2 Kin 4:18, 31-35 [b]Ps 105:16; Hag 1:11 [c]Gen 41:27, 54
3 [1]Lit *cry out*
4 [a]2 Kin 4:12; 5:20-27
5 [1]Lit *cried out* [a]2 Kin 4:35
7 [a]1 Kin 11:24 [b]2 Kin 6:24 [c]2 Kin 5:20
8 [a]1 Kin 19:15, 17 [b]1 Kin 14:3 [c]2 Kin 1:2

and he came and stood before him and said, "[a]Your son Ben-
hadad king of Aram has sent me to you, saying, 'Will I recover
from this sickness?'"
10 Then Elisha said to him, "[a]Go, say to him, 'You will surely
recover,' but the [b]LORD has shown me that he will certainly die."
11 He [1]fixed his gaze steadily *on him* [a]until he was ashamed,
and [b]the man of God wept.
12 Hazael said, "Why does my lord weep?" Then he [1]answered,
"Because [a]I know the evil that you will do to the sons of Israel:
their strongholds you will set on fire, and their young men you
will kill with the sword, and their little ones you [b]will dash in
pieces, and their women with child you will rip up."
13 Then Hazael said, "But what is your servant, [a]*who is but* a
dog, that he should do this great thing?" And Elisha [1]answered,
"[b]The LORD has shown me that you will be king over Aram."
14 So he departed from Elisha and returned to his master, who
said to him, "What did Elisha say to you?" And he [1]answered,
"He told me that [a]you would surely recover."
15 On the following day, he took the cover and dipped it in
water and spread it on his face, [a]so that he died. And Hazael
became king in his place.

853 B.C.

2 Chronicles 21

16 Now in the fifth year of [a]Joram the son of Ahab king of
Israel, Jehoshaphat being then the king of Judah, Jehoram the
son of Jehoshaphat king of Judah became king.
17 He was [a]thirty-two years old when he became king, and he
reigned eight years in Jerusalem.
18 He walked in the way of the kings of Israel, just as the house
of Ahab had done, for [a]the daughter of Ahab became his wife;
and he did evil in the sight of the LORD.
19 However, the LORD was not willing to destroy Judah, for
the sake of David His servant, [a]since He had [1]promised him to
give a [2]lamp to him through his sons always.
20 In his days [a]Edom revolted from under the hand of Judah,
and made a king over themselves.
21 Then Joram crossed over to Zair, and all his chariots with
him. And he arose by night and struck the Edomites who had
surrounded him and the captains of the chariots; [a]but *his* [1]army
fled to their tents.
22 [a]So Edom revolted [1]against Judah to this day. Then [b]Libnah
revolted at the same time.
23 The rest of the acts of Joram and all that he did, are they
not written in the Book of the Chronicles of the Kings of
Judah?

841 B.C.

2 Chronicles 22

24 So Joram slept with his fathers and [a]was buried with his
fathers in the city of David; and [b]Ahaziah his son became king
in his place.
25 [a]In the twelfth year of Joram the son of Ahab king of Israel,
Ahaziah the son of Jehoram king of Judah began to reign.
26 [a]Ahaziah *was* twenty-two years old when he became king,
and he reigned one year in Jerusalem. And his mother's name
was Athaliah the granddaughter of Omri king of Israel.

INSIGHT

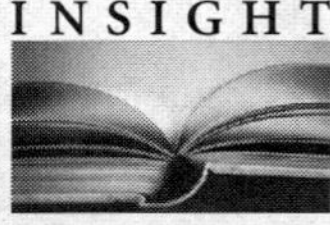

Zair's exact location (see verse 21) is in question. The name means "small." Some believe it was south of the Dead (Salt) Sea near Edom, while others equate it with Zoar (Genesis 13:10) or Zior (Joshua 15:54).

9 [a]2 Kin 5:13

10 [a]2 Kin 8:14 [b]2 Kin 8:15

11 [1]Lit *made his face stand fast and he set* [a]2 Kin 2:17 [b]Luke 19:41

12 [1]Lit *said* [a]2 Kin 10:32, 33; 12:17; 13:3, 7 [b]2 Kin 15:16; Nah 3:10

13 [1]Lit *said* [a]1 Sam 17:43; 2 Sam 9:8 [b]1 Kin 19:15

14 [1]Lit *said* [a]2 Kin 8:10

15 [a]2 Kin 8:10

16 [a]2 Kin 1:17; 3:1

17 [a]2 Chr 21:5-10

18 [a]2 Kin 8:27

19 [1]Lit *said* [2]I.e. descendant on the throne [a]2 Sam 7:12-15; 1 Kin 11:36

20 [a]1 Kin 22:47; 2 Kin 3:9, 26, 27; 8:22

21 [1]Lit *the people* [a]2 Sam 18:17; 19:8

22 [1]Lit *from under the hand of* [a]Gen 27:40 [b]Josh 21:13; 2 Kin 19:8

24 [a]2 Chr 21:20 [b]2 Chr 21:1, 7

25 [a]2 Chr 22:1-6

26 [a]2 Chr 22:2

27 [a]He walked in the way of the house of Ahab and did evil in
the sight of the LORD, like the house of Ahab *had done,* because
he was a son-in-law of the house of Ahab.
28 Then he went with Joram the son of Ahab to war against
[a]Hazael king of Aram at [b]Ramoth-gilead, and the Arameans
[1]wounded Joram.
29 So [a]King Joram returned to be healed in Jezreel of the
wounds which the Arameans had [1]inflicted on him at [b]Ramah
when he fought against Hazael king of Aram. Then [c]Ahaziah
the son of Jehoram king of Judah went down to see Joram the
son of Ahab in Jezreel because he was sick.

Chapter 9 Theme ____________________

9 Now Elisha the prophet called one of [a]the sons of the
prophets and said to him, "[b]Gird up your loins, and [c]take this
flask of oil in your hand and go to [d]Ramoth-gilead.
2 "When you arrive there, [1]search out [a]Jehu the son of
Jehoshaphat the son of Nimshi, and go in and [2b]bid him arise
from among his brothers, and bring him to an inner room.
3 "Then take the flask of oil and pour it on his head and say,
'Thus says the LORD, "[a]I have anointed you king over Israel."'
Then open the door and flee and do not wait."
4 So [a]the young man, the servant of the prophet, went to
Ramoth-gilead.
5 When he came, behold, the captains of the army were sitting,
and he said, "I have a word for you, O captain." And Jehu said,
"[1]For which *one* of us?" And he said, "For you, O captain."
6 He arose and went into the house, and he poured the oil
on his head and said to him, "Thus says the LORD, the God of
Israel, '[a]I have anointed you king over the people of the LORD,
even over Israel.
7 'You shall strike the house of Ahab your master, [a]that I may
avenge [b]the blood of My servants the prophets, and the blood
of all the servants of the LORD, [c]at the hand of Jezebel.
8 'For the whole house of Ahab shall perish, and [a]I will cut off
from Ahab [b]every male person [c]both bond and free in Israel.
9 '[a]I will make the house of Ahab like the house of Jeroboam
the son of Nebat, and [b]like the house of Baasha the son of Ahijah.
10 '[a]The dogs shall eat Jezebel in the territory of Jezreel, and
none shall bury *her.*'" Then he opened the door and fled.
11 Now Jehu came out to the servants of his master, and one
said to him, "[a]Is all well? Why did this [b]mad fellow come to
you?" And he said to them, "You know *very well* the man and
his talk."
12 They said, "It is a lie, tell us now." And he said, "Thus and
thus he said to me, 'Thus says the LORD, "I have anointed you
king over Israel."'"
13 Then [a]they hurried and each man took his garment and
placed it under him on the bare steps, and [b]blew the trumpet,
saying, "Jehu is king!"

27 [a]2 Chr 22:3
28 [1]Lit *smote* [a]2 Kin 8:15 [b]1 Kin 22:3, 29
29 [1]Lit *struck* [a]2 Kin 9:15 [b]2 Kin 8:28; 2 Chr 22:5, 6 [c]2 Kin 9:16
9:1 [a]2 Kin 2:3 [b]2 Kin 4:29 [c]1 Sam 10:1; 16:1; 1 Kin 1:39 [d]2 Kin 8:28, 29
2 [1]Lit *and look there for* [2]Lit *cause him to* [a]1 Kin 19:16, 17; 2 Kin 9:14, 20 [b]2 Kin 9:5, 11
3 [a]2 Chr 22:7
4 [a]2 Kin 9:1
5 [1]Lit *To whom of us all?*
6 [a]1 Sam 2:7, 8; 1 Kin 19:16; 2 Kin 9:3; 2 Chr 22:7
7 [a]Deut 32:35, 43 [b]1 Kin 18:4; 21:15, 21, 25 [c]2 Kin 9:32-37
8 [a]1 Kin 21:21; 2 Kin 10:17 [b]1 Sam 25:22 [c]Deut 32:36; 2 Kin 14:26
9 [a]1 Kin 14:10, 11; 15:29 [b]1 Kin 16:3-5, 11, 12
10 [a]1 Kin 21:23; 2 Kin 9:35, 36
11 [a]2 Kin 9:17, 19, 22 [b]Jer 29:26; Hos 9:7; Mark 3:21
13 [a]Matt 21:7, 8; Mark 11:7, 8 [b]2 Sam 15:10; 1 Kin 1:34, 39

14 So Jehu the son of Jehoshaphat the son of Nimshi conspired
against Joram. [a]Now Joram [1]with all Israel was [2]defending
Ramoth-gilead against Hazael king of Aram,
15 but [a]King [1]Joram had returned to Jezreel to be healed of the
wounds which the Arameans had [2]inflicted on him when he
fought with Hazael king of Aram. So Jehu said, "If this is your
mind, *then* let no one escape *or* [3]leave the city to go tell *it* in
Jezreel."
16 Then Jehu rode in a chariot and went to Jezreel, for Joram
was lying there. [a]Ahaziah king of Judah had come down to see
Joram.
17 Now the watchman was standing on the tower in Jezreel
and he saw the [1]company of Jehu as he came, and said, "I see a
[1]company." And Joram said, "Take a horseman and send him to
meet them and let him say, 'Is it peace?'"
18 So a horseman went to meet him and said, "Thus says the
king, 'Is it peace?'" And Jehu said, "[a]What have you to do with
peace? Turn behind me." And the watchman [1]reported, "The
messenger came to them, but he did not return."
19 Then he sent out a second horseman, who came to them
and said, "Thus says the king, 'Is it peace?'" And Jehu [1]answered,
"What have you to do with peace? Turn behind me."
20 The watchman [1]reported, "He came even to them, and he
did not return; and [a]the driving is like the driving of [b]Jehu the
son of Nimshi, for he drives furiously."
21 Then [1]Joram said, "[2]Get ready." And they made his chariot
ready. [1a]Joram king of Israel and Ahaziah king of Judah went
out, each in his chariot, and they went out to meet Jehu and
found him in the [3b]property of Naboth the Jezreelite.
22 When [1]Joram saw Jehu, he said, "Is it peace, Jehu?" And
he [2]answered, "What peace, [a]so long as the harlotries of your
mother Jezebel and her witchcrafts are so many?"
23 So [1]Joram [2]reined about and fled and said to Ahaziah,
"[a]*There is* treachery, O Ahaziah!"
24 And [a]Jehu [1]drew his bow with his full strength and [2]shot
[3]Joram between his arms; and the arrow went [4]through his
heart and he sank in his chariot.
25 Then *Jehu* said to Bidkar his officer, "Take *him* up and [a]cast
him into the [1]property of the field of Naboth the Jezreelite, for
I remember when [2]you and I were riding together after Ahab
his father, that the [b]LORD laid this [c]oracle against him:
26 'Surely [a]I have seen yesterday the blood of Naboth and the
blood of his sons,' says the LORD, 'and [b]I will repay you in this
[1]property,' says the LORD. Now then, take and cast him into the
[1]property, according to the word of the LORD."
27 [a]When Ahaziah the king of Judah saw *this,* he fled by the
way of the garden house. And Jehu pursued him and said,
"[1]Shoot him too, in the chariot." *So they shot him* at the ascent of
Gur, which is at [b]Ibleam. But he fled to Megiddo and died there.
28 [a]Then his servants carried him in a chariot to Jerusalem
and buried him in his grave with his fathers in the city of David.

14 [1]Lit *he and* [2]Lit *keeping* [a]1 Kin 22:3; 2 Kin 8:28

15 [1]Heb *Jehoram* [2]Lit *struck* [3]Lit *go out from* [a]2 Kin 8:29

16 [a]2 Kin 8:29

17 [1]Lit *multitude*

18 [1]Lit *told, saying* [a]2 Kin 9:19, 22

19 [1]Lit *said*

20 [1]Lit *told, saying* [a]2 Sam 18:27 [b]1 Kin 19:17

21 [1]Heb *Jehoram* [2]Lit *Yoke the chariot* [3]Lit *portion* [a]2 Chr 22:7 [b]1 Kin 21:1-7, 15-19; 2 Kin 9:26

22 [1]Heb *Jehoram* [2]Lit *said* [a]1 Kin 16:30-33; 18:19; 2 Chr 21:13

23 [1]Heb *Jehoram* [2]Lit *turned his hands* [a]2 Kin 11:14

24 [1]Lit *filled his hand with the bow* [2]Lit *smote* [3]Heb *Jehoram* [4]Lit *out at* [a]1 Kin 22:34

25 [1]Lit *portion* [2]Lit *I and you* [a]1 Kin 21:1 [b]1 Kin 21:19, 24-29 [c]Is 13:1

26 [1]Lit *portion* [a]1 Kin 21:13, 19 [b]2 Kin 9:21, 25

27 [1]Lit *smite* [a]2 Chr 22:7, 9 [b]Josh 17:11; Judg 1:27

28 [a]2 Kin 23:30

841 B.C.

29 Now in [a]the eleventh year of Joram, the son of Ahab,
Ahaziah became king over Judah.
30 When Jehu came to Jezreel, Jezebel heard *of it,* and [a]she
painted her eyes and adorned her head and looked out the
window.
31 As Jehu entered the gate, she said, "[a]Is it [1]well, Zimri,
[2]your master's murderer?"
32 Then he lifted up his face to the window and said, "Who is on
my side? Who?" And two or three officials looked down at him.
33 He said, "Throw her down." So they threw her down, and
some of her blood was sprinkled on the wall and on the horses,
and he trampled her under foot.
34 When he came in, he ate and drank; and he said, "See now
to [a]this cursed woman and bury her, for [b]she is a king's daughter."
35 They went to bury her, but they found nothing more of her
than the skull and the feet and the palms of her hands.
36 Therefore they returned and told him. And he said, "This
is the word of the LORD, which He spoke by His servant Elijah
the Tishbite, saying, '[a]In the [1]property of Jezreel the dogs shall
eat the flesh of Jezebel;
37 and [a]the corpse of Jezebel will be as dung on the face of the
field in the [1]property of Jezreel, so they cannot say, "This is
Jezebel."'"

Chapter 10 Theme ____________________

10 Now Ahab had seventy sons in [a]Samaria. And Jehu wrote
letters and sent *them* to Samaria, to the rulers of Jezreel,
the elders, and to the guardians of *the children of* Ahab, saying,
2 "Now, [a]when this letter comes to you, since your master's
sons are with you, [1]as well as the chariots and horses and a
fortified city and the weapons,
3 select the best and [1]fittest of your master's sons, and set
him on his father's throne, and fight for your master's house."
4 But they feared greatly and said, "Behold, [a]the two kings
did not stand before him; how then can we stand?"
5 And the one who *was* over the household, and he who *was*
over the city, the elders, and the guardians of *the children,* sent
word to Jehu, saying, "[a]We are your servants, all that you say to
us we will do, we will not make any man king; do what is good
in your sight."
6 Then he wrote a letter to them a second time saying, "If you
are on my side, and you will listen to my voice, take the heads
of the men, your master's sons, and come to me at Jezreel
tomorrow about this time." Now the king's sons, seventy persons,
were with the great men of the city, *who* were rearing them.
7 When the letter came to them, they took the king's sons
and [a]slaughtered *them,* seventy persons, and put their heads in
baskets, and sent *them* to him at Jezreel.
8 When the messenger came and told him, saying, "They
have brought the heads of the king's sons," he said, "Put them
in two heaps at the entrance of the gate until morning."

29 [a]2 Kin 8:25
30 [a]Jer 4:30; Ezek 23:40
31 [1]Lit *peace* [2]Lit *his* [a]1 Kin 16:9-20; 2 Kin 9:18-22
34 [a]1 Kin 21:25 [b]1 Kin 16:31
36 [1]Lit *portion* [a]1 Kin 21:23
37 [1]Lit *portion* [a]Jer 8:1-3
10:1 [a]1 Kin 16:24-29
2 [1]Lit *and with you the* [a]2 Kin 5:6
3 [1]Lit *most upright*
4 [a]2 Kin 9:24, 27
5 [a]Josh 9:8, 11; 1 Kin 20:4, 32; 2 Kin 18:14
7 [a]Judg 9:5; 2 Kin 11:1

9 Now in the morning he went out and stood and said to all
the people, "You are [1]innocent; behold, [a]I conspired against my
master and killed him, but [b]who [2]killed all these?
10 "Know then that [a]there shall fall to the earth nothing of the
word of the LORD, which the LORD spoke concerning the house
of Ahab, for the LORD has done [b]what He spoke [1]through His
servant Elijah."
11 So Jehu [1]killed all who remained of the house of Ahab in
[a]Jezreel, and all his great men and his acquaintances and his
priests, until he left him without a survivor.
12 Then he arose and departed and went to Samaria. On the
way while he was at [1]Beth-eked of the shepherds,
13 [a]Jehu [1]met the [2]relatives of Ahaziah king of Judah and said,
"Who are you?" And they [3]answered, "We are the [2]relatives of
Ahaziah; and we have come down [4]to greet the sons of the king
and the sons of the queen mother."
14 He said, "Take them alive." So they took them alive and killed
them at the pit of Beth-eked, forty-two men; and he left none of
them.
15 Now when he had departed from there, he [1]met [a]Jehonadab
the son of [b]Rechab *coming* to meet him; and he [2]greeted him
and said to him, "Is your heart right, as my heart is with your
heart?" And Jehonadab [3]answered, "It is." *Jehu said,* "If it is,
[c]give *me* your hand." And he gave him his hand, and he took
him up to him into the chariot.
16 He said, "Come with me and [a]see my zeal for the LORD."
So [1]he made him ride in his chariot.
17 When he came to Samaria, [a]he [1]killed all who remained to
Ahab in Samaria, until he had destroyed him, [b]according to the
word of the LORD which He spoke to Elijah.
18 Then Jehu gathered all the people and said to them, "[a]Ahab
served Baal a little; Jehu will serve him much.
19 "Now, [a]summon all the prophets of Baal, all his worshipers
and all his priests; let no one be missing, for I have a great
sacrifice for Baal; whoever is missing shall not live." But Jehu
did it in [1]cunning, so that he might destroy the worshipers of
Baal.
20 And Jehu said, "[a]Sanctify a solemn assembly for Baal." And
[b]they proclaimed *it.*
21 Then Jehu sent [1]throughout Israel and all the worshipers of
Baal came, so that there was not a man left who did not come.
And when they went into [a]the house of Baal, the house of Baal
was filled from one end to the other.
22 He said to the one who *was* [1]in charge of the wardrobe,
"Bring out garments for all the worshipers of Baal." So he
brought out garments for them.
23 Jehu went into the house of Baal with Jehonadab the son of
Rechab; and he said to the worshipers of Baal, "Search and see
that there is here with you none of the servants of the LORD,
but only the worshipers of Baal."
24 Then they went in to offer sacrifices and burnt offerings.

9 [1]Lit *just* [2]Lit *smote* [a]2 Kin 9:14-24 [b]2 Kin 10:6

10 [1]Lit *by the hand of* [a]2 Kin 9:7-10 [b]1 Kin 21:19-29

11 [1]Lit *smote* [a]Hos 1:4

12 [1]I.e. house of binding

13 [1]Lit *found* [2]Lit *brothers* [3]Lit *said* [4]Lit *about the welfare of* [a]2 Kin 8:24, 29; 2 Chr 21:17; 22:8

15 [1]Lit *found* [2]Lit *blessed* [3]Lit *said* [a]Jer 35:6-19 [b]1 Chr 2:55 [c]Ezra 10:19; Ezek 17:18

16 [1]Lit *they* [a]1 Kin 19:10

17 [1]Lit *smote* [a]2 Kin 9:8 [b]2 Kin 10:10

18 [a]1 Kin 16:31, 32

19 [1]Lit *insidiousness* [a]1 Kin 18:19; 22:6

20 [a]Joel 1:14 [b]Ex 32:4-6

21 [1]Lit *in all* [a]1 Kin 16:32; 2 Kin 11:18

22 [1]Lit *over the*

Now Jehu had stationed for himself eighty men outside, and
he had said, "[a]The one who permits any of the men whom I bring
into your hands to escape [1]shall give up his life in exchange."
25 Then it came about, as soon as he had finished offering the
burnt offering, that Jehu said to the [1a]guard and to the royal
officers, "[b]Go in, [2]kill them; let none come out." And they [3]killed
them with the edge of the sword; and the [1]guard and the royal
officers threw *them* out, and went to the [4]inner room of the
house of Baal.
26 They brought out the *sacred* [a]pillars of the house of Baal
and burned them.
27 They also broke down the *sacred* pillar of Baal and broke
down the house of Baal, and [a]made it a latrine to this day.
28 Thus Jehu eradicated Baal out of Israel.
29 However, [a]*as for* the sins of Jeroboam the son of Nebat,
which he made Israel sin, from these Jehu did not depart, *even*
the [b]golden calves that *were* at Bethel and that *were* at Dan.
30 The LORD said to Jehu, "Because you have done well in
executing what is right in My eyes, *and* have done to the house
of Ahab according to all that *was* in My heart, [a]your sons of the
fourth generation shall sit on the throne of Israel."
31 But Jehu [1a]was not careful to walk in the law of the LORD,
the God of Israel, with all his heart; [b]he did not depart from the
sins of Jeroboam, which he made Israel sin.
32 In those days the [a]LORD began to cut off *portions* [1]from Israel;
and [b]Hazael [2]defeated them throughout the territory of Israel:
33 from the Jordan eastward, all the land of Gilead, the Gadites
and the Reubenites and the Manassites, from [a]Aroer, which is
by the valley of the Arnon, even [b]Gilead and Bashan.
34 Now the rest of the acts of Jehu and all that he did and all his
might, are they not written in the Book of the Chronicles of
the Kings of Israel?
35 And Jehu slept with his fathers, and they buried him in 814 B.C.
Samaria. And Jehoahaz his son became king in his place.
36 Now the [1]time which Jehu reigned over Israel in Samaria
was twenty-eight years.

Chapter 11 Theme ____________________

11 [a]When Athaliah the mother of Ahaziah saw that her son 841 B.C.
was dead, she rose and destroyed all the royal [1]offspring.
2 But Jehosheba, the daughter of King Joram, sister of Ahaziah, 2 Chronicles 22
[a]took Joash the son of Ahaziah and stole him from among the
king's sons who were being put to death, and placed him and
his nurse in the bedroom. So they hid him from Athaliah, and
he was not put to death.
3 So he was hidden with her in the house of the LORD six
years, while Athaliah was reigning over the land.
4 [a]Now in the seventh year Jehoiada sent and brought the
captains of hundreds of [b]the Carites and of the [1]guard, and
brought them to him in the house of the LORD. Then he made a

24 [1]Lit *his soul for his soul* [a]1 Kin 20:30-42

25 [1]Lit *runners* [2]Lit *smite* [3]Lit *smote* [4]Lit *city* [a]1 Sam 22:17 [b]1 Kin 18:40

26 [a]1 Kin 14:23; 2 Kin 3:2

27 [a]Ezra 6:11; Dan 2:5; 3:29

29 [a]1 Kin 12:28-30; 13:33, 34 [b]1 Kin 12:29

30 [a]2 Kin 15:12

31 [1]Lit *did not watch* [a]Prov 4:23 [b]2 Kin 10:29

32 [1]Lit *in* [2]Lit *smote* [a]2 Kin 13:25; 14:25 [b]1 Kin 19:17; 2 Kin 8:12; 13:22

33 [a]Deut 2:36 [b]Amos 1:3-5

36 [1]Lit *days*

11:1 [1]Lit *seed* [a]2 Chr 22:10-12

2 [a]2 Kin 11:21; 12:1

4 [1]Lit *runners* [a]2 Chr 23:1-21 [b]2 Sam 20:23; 2 Kin 11:19

covenant with them and put them under oath in the house of the LORD, and showed them the king's son.

5 He commanded them, saying, "This is the thing that you shall do: [a]one third of you, who come in on the sabbath and keep watch over the king's house

6 (one third also *shall be* at the gate Sur, and one third at the gate behind the [1]guards), [2]shall keep watch over the house for defense.

7 "Two parts of you, *even* all who go out on the sabbath, shall also keep watch over the house of the LORD for the king.

8 "Then you shall surround the king, each with his weapons in his hand; and whoever comes within the ranks shall be put to death. And [a]be with the king when he goes out and when he comes in."

9 So the captains of hundreds [a]did according to all that Jehoiada the priest commanded. And each one of them took his men who were to come in on the sabbath, with those who were to go out on the sabbath, and came to Jehoiada the priest.

10 [a]The priest gave to the captains of hundreds the spears and shields that *had been* King David's, which *were* in the house of the LORD.

11 The [1]guards stood each with his weapons in his hand, from the right [2]side of the house to the left [2]side of the house, by the altar and by the house, around the king.

12 Then he brought the king's son out and [a]put the crown on him and *gave him* [b]the testimony; and they made him king and anointed him, and they clapped their hands and said, "[c]*Long* live the king!"

13 [a]When Athaliah heard the noise of the guard *and of* the people, she came to the people in the house of the LORD.

14 She looked and behold, the king was standing [a]by the pillar, according to the custom, with the captains and the [1]trumpeters beside the king; and [b]all the people of the land rejoiced and blew trumpets. Then Athaliah [c]tore her clothes and cried, "[d]Treason! Treason!"

15 And Jehoiada the priest commanded the captains of hundreds who were appointed over the army and said to them, "Bring her out [1]between the ranks, and whoever follows her put to death with the sword." For the priest said, "Let her not be put to death in the house of the LORD."

16 So they [1]seized her, and when she arrived at the horses' entrance of the king's house, she was [a]put to death there.

17 Then [a]Jehoiada made a covenant between the LORD and the king and the people, that they would be the LORD's people, also [b]between the king and the people.

18 All the people of the land went to [a]the house of Baal, and tore it down; [b]his altars and his images they broke in pieces thoroughly, and [c]killed Mattan the priest of Baal before the altars. And the priest appointed [1]officers over the house of the LORD.

19 He took the captains of hundreds and the [a]Carites and the [1]guards and all the people of the land; and they brought the

5 [a]1 Chr 9:25

6 [1]Lit *runners* [2]Lit *and shall*

8 [a]Num 27:16, 17

9 [a]2 Chr 23:8

10 [a]2 Sam 8:7; 1 Chr 18:7

11 [1]Lit *runners* [2]Lit *shoulder*

12 [a]2 Sam 1:10 [b]Ex 25:16; 31:18 [c]1 Sam 10:24

13 [a]2 Chr 23:12

14 [1]Lit *trumpets* [a]2 Kin 23:3; 2 Chr 34:31 [b]1 Kin 1:39, 40 [c]Gen 37:29; 44:13 [d]2 Kin 9:23

15 [1]Lit *from within*

16 [1]Lit *placed hands to her* [a]Gen 9:6; Lev 24:17

17 [a]Josh 24:25; 2 Chr 15:12-14; 34:31 [b]1 Sam 10:25; 2 Sam 5:3

18 [1]Lit *offices* [a]2 Kin 10:26, 27 [b]Deut 12:2, 3 [c]1 Kin 18:40

19 [1]Lit *runners* [a]2 Kin 11:4

king down from the house of the LORD, and came by the way of
[b]the gate of the [1]guards to the king's house. And he sat on the
throne of the kings.
20 So [a]all the people of the land rejoiced and the city was quiet. 835 B.C.
For they had put Athaliah to death with the sword at the king's
house.
21 [1a]Jehoash was seven years old when he became king.

Chapter 12 Theme ____________

12 In the seventh year of Jehu, [a]Jehoash became king, and 2 Chronicles 24
he reigned forty years in Jerusalem; and his mother's name
was Zibiah of Beersheba.
2 Jehoash did right in the sight of the LORD all his days in
which Jehoiada the priest instructed him.
3 Only [a]the high places were not taken away; the people still
sacrificed and burned incense on the high places.
4 Then Jehoash said to the priests, "All the money of the
sacred things [a]which is brought into the house of the LORD, in
current money, *both* [b]the money of each man's assessment *and*
all the money [1]which any man's heart prompts him to bring
into the house of the LORD,
5 let the priests take it for themselves, each from his
acquaintance; and they shall repair the [1]damages of the house
wherever any damage may be found."
6 But it came about that in the twenty-third year of King 812 B.C.
Jehoash [a]the priests had not repaired the damages of the house.
7 Then King Jehoash called for Jehoiada the priest, and for the
other priests and said to them, "Why do you not repair the
damages of the house? Now therefore take no *more* money from
your acquaintances, but pay it for the damages of the house."
8 So the priests agreed that they would take no *more* money
from the people, nor repair the damages of the house.
9 But [a]Jehoiada the priest took a chest and bored a hole in its
lid and put it beside the altar, on the right side as one comes
into the house of the LORD; and the priests who guarded the
threshold put in it all the money which was brought into the
house of the LORD.
10 When they saw that there was much money in the chest, [a]the
king's scribe and the high priest came up and tied *it* in bags and
counted the money which was found in the house of the LORD.
11 They gave the money which was weighed out into the
hands of those who did the work, who had the oversight of the
house of the LORD; and they [1]paid it out to the carpenters and
the builders who worked on the house of the LORD;
12 and [a]to the masons and the stonecutters, and for buying
timber and hewn stone to repair the damages to the house of
the LORD, and for all that was [1]laid out for the house to repair it.
13 But [a]there were not made for the house of the LORD [b]silver
cups, snuffers, bowls, trumpets, any vessels of gold, or vessels
of silver from the money which was brought into the house of
the LORD;

19 [1]Lit *runners* [b]2 Kin 11:6
20 [a]Prov 11:10
21 [1]Ch 12:1 in Heb [a]2 Chr 24:1-14
12:1 [a]2 Chr 24:1
3 [a]2 Kin 14:4; 15:35
4 [1]Lit *which it comes into . . . to bring* [a]2 Kin 22:4 [b]Ex 30:13-16; 35:5, 22, 29; 1 Chr 29:3-9
5 [1]Lit *breaches,* and so through v 12
6 [a]2 Chr 24:5
9 [a]Mark 12:41; Luke 21:1
10 [a]2 Sam 8:17; 2 Kin 19:2; 22:3, 4, 12
11 [1]Lit *brought*
12 [1]Lit *went out* [a]2 Kin 22:5, 6
13 [a]2 Chr 24:14 [b]1 Kin 7:48, 50

14 for they gave that to those who did the work, and with it
they repaired the house of the LORD.
15 Moreover, [a]they did not require an accounting from the
men into whose hand they gave the money to pay to those
who did the work, for they dealt faithfully.
16 The [a]money from the guilt offerings and [b]the money from
the sin offerings was not brought into the house of the LORD; [c]it
was for the priests.
17 Then [a]Hazael king of Aram went up and fought against Gath
and captured it, and [b]Hazael set his face to go up to Jerusalem.
18 [a]Jehoash king of Judah took all the sacred things that
Jehoshaphat and Jehoram and Ahaziah, his fathers, kings of
Judah, had dedicated, and [b]his own sacred things and all the gold
that was found among the treasuries of the house of the LORD
and of the king's house, and sent *them* to Hazael king of Aram.
Then he went away from Jerusalem.
19 Now the rest of the acts of Joash and all that he did, are they
not written in the Book of the Chronicles of the Kings of Judah?
20 [a]His servants arose and made a conspiracy and [b]struck
down Joash at [c]the house of Millo *as he was* going down to Silla.
21 For Jozacar the son of Shimeath and Jehozabad the son of
[a]Shomer, his servants, struck *him* and he died; and they buried
him with his fathers in the city of David, and [b]Amaziah his son
became king in his place.

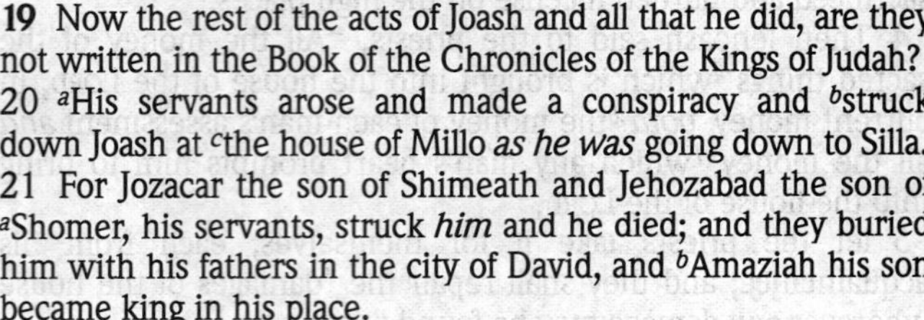

INSIGHT

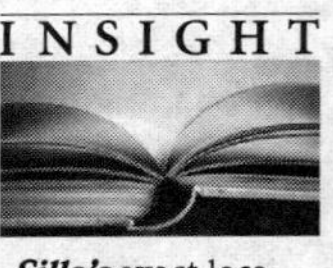

Silla's exact location is indefinite, but is believed to be near Jerusalem.

Chapter 13 Theme ____

814 B.C.

13 In the twenty-third year of Joash the son of Ahaziah, king
of Judah, Jehoahaz the son of Jehu became king over
Israel at Samaria, *and he reigned* seventeen years.
2 He did evil in the sight of the LORD, and followed the sins
of Jeroboam the son of Nebat, [a]with which he made Israel sin;
he did not turn from them.
3 [a]So the anger of the LORD was kindled against Israel, and
He gave them continually into the hand of [b]Hazael king of
Aram, and into the hand of [c]Ben-hadad the son of Hazael.
4 Then [a]Jehoahaz entreated the favor of the LORD, and the
LORD listened to him; for [b]He saw the oppression of Israel, how
the king of Aram oppressed them.
5 The LORD gave Israel a [1a]deliverer, so that they [2]escaped
from under the hand of the Arameans; and the sons of Israel
lived in their tents as formerly.
6 Nevertheless they did not turn away from the sins of the
house of Jeroboam, [a]with which he made Israel sin, but walked
in [1]them; and [b]the Asherah also remained standing in Samaria.
7 For he left to Jehoahaz of the [1]army not more than fifty horsemen and ten chariots and 10,000 footmen, for the king of Aram
had destroyed them and [a]made them like the dust at threshing.
8 Now the rest of the acts of Jehoahaz, and all that he did and
his might, are they not written in the Book of the Chronicles of
the Kings of Israel?

15 [a]2 Kin 22:7; 1 Cor 4:2; 2 Cor 8:20
16 [a]Lev 5:15-18 [b]Lev 4:24, 29 [c]Lev 7:7; Num 18:19
17 [a]1 Kin 19:17; 2 Kin 8:12; 10:32, 33 [b]2 Chr 24:23, 24
18 [a]1 Kin 14:26; 15:18; 2 Kin 16:8; 18:15, 16 [b]2 Kin 12:4
20 [a]2 Chr 24:25-27 [b]2 Kin 14:5 [c]Judg 9:6; 2 Sam 5:9; 1 Kin 11:27
21 [a]2 Chr 24:26 [b]2 Kin 14:1
13:2 [a]1 Kin 12:26-33
3 [a]Judg 2:14 [b]2 Kin 12:17 [c]2 Kin 13:24, 25
4 [a]Num 21:7-9 [b]Ex 3:7, 9; 2 Kin 14:26
5 [1]Or *savior* [2]Lit *went out* [a]2 Kin 13:25; 14:25, 27; Neh 9:27
6 [1]Lit *it* [a]2 Kin 13:2 [b]1 Kin 16:33
7 [1]Lit *people* [a]Amos 1:3

9 And Jehoahaz slept with his fathers, and they buried him
in Samaria; and Joash his son became king in his place.
10 In the thirty-seventh year of Joash king of Judah, Jehoash 798 B.C.
the son of Jehoahaz became king over Israel in Samaria, *and*
reigned sixteen years.
11 He did evil in the sight of the LORD; he did not turn away
from all the sins of Jeroboam the son of Nebat, with which he
made Israel sin, but he walked in [1]them.
12 [a]Now the rest of the acts of Joash and all that he did and his
might with which he fought against Amaziah king of Judah, are
they not written in the Book of the Chronicles of the Kings of
Israel?
13 So Joash slept with his fathers, and Jeroboam sat on his 782 B.C.
throne; and Joash was buried in Samaria with the kings of Israel.
14 When Elisha [1]became sick with the illness of which he was
to die, Joash the king of Israel came down to him and wept over
[2]him and said, "[a]My father, my father, the chariots of Israel and
its horsemen!"
15 Elisha said to him, "Take a bow and arrows." So he [1]took a
bow and arrows.
16 Then he said to the king of Israel, "Put your hand on the
bow." And he put his hand *on it,* then Elisha laid his hands on
the king's hands.
17 He said, "Open the window toward the east," and he
opened *it.* Then Elisha said, "Shoot!" And he shot. And he said,
"The LORD'S arrow of victory, even the arrow of victory over
Aram; for you will [1]defeat the Arameans at [a]Aphek until you
have [2]destroyed *them.*"
18 Then he said, "Take the arrows," and he took them. And
he said to the king of Israel, "Strike the ground," and he struck
it three times and [1]stopped.
19 So [a]the man of God was angry with him and said, "You
should have struck five or six times, then you would have
struck Aram until you would have [1]destroyed *it.* But now you
shall strike Aram [b]*only* three times."
20 Elisha died, and they buried him. Now [a]the bands of the
Moabites would invade the land in the spring of the year.
21 As they were burying a man, behold, they saw a marauding
band; and they cast the man into the grave of Elisha. And
when the man [1]touched the bones of Elisha he [a]revived and
stood up on his feet.
22 Now [a]Hazael king of Aram had oppressed Israel all the days
of Jehoahaz.
23 But the [a]LORD was gracious to them and [b]had compassion on
them and turned to them because of [c]His covenant with Abraham,
Isaac, and Jacob, and would not destroy them or cast them
from His presence until now.
24 When Hazael king of Aram died, Ben-hadad his son became 801 B.C.
king in his place.
25 Then [a]Jehoash the son of Jehoahaz took again from the hand
of Ben-hadad the son of Hazael the cities which he had taken

11 [1]Lit *it*
12 [a]2 Kin 13:14-19; 14:8-15
14 [1]Lit *was sick with his sickness* [2]Lit *his face* [a]2 Kin 2:12
15 [1]Lit *took to himself*
17 [1]Lit *smite* [2]Lit *made an end of* [a]1 Kin 20:26
18 [1]Lit *stood*
19 [1]Lit *made an end of* [a]2 Kin 5:20 [b]2 Kin 13:25
20 [a]2 Kin 3:7; 24:2
21 [1]Lit *went and touched* [a]Matt 27:52
22 [a]2 Kin 8:12, 13
23 [a]2 Kin 14:27 [b]1 Kin 8:28 [c]Gen 13:16, 17; 17:2-5
25 [a]2 Kin 10:32, 33; 14:25

in war from the hand of Jehoahaz his father. [b]Three times Joash
[1]defeated him and recovered the cities of Israel.

Chapter 14 Theme ______________________

796 B.C.

2 Chronicles 25

14 [a]In the second year of Joash son of Joahaz king of Israel,
[b]Amaziah the son of Joash king of Judah became king.
2 He was twenty-five years old when he became king, and he
reigned twenty-nine years in Jerusalem. And his mother's name
was Jehoaddin of Jerusalem.
3 He did right in the sight of the LORD, yet not like David his
father; he did according to all that Joash his father had done.
4 Only [a]the high places were not taken away; [b]the people still
sacrificed and burned incense on the high places.
5 Now it came about, as soon as the kingdom was firmly in his
hand, that he [1a]killed his servants who had slain the king his
father.
6 But the sons of the [1]slayers he did not put to death, according
to what is written in the book of the Law of Moses, as the LORD
commanded, saying, "[a]The fathers shall not be put to death for
the sons, nor the sons be put to death for the fathers; but [b]each
shall be put to death for his own sin."
7 He [1]killed *of* Edom in [a]the Valley of Salt 10,000 and took
[b]Sela by war, and named it [c]Joktheel to this day.
8 [a]Then Amaziah sent messengers to Jehoash, the son of
Jehoahaz son of Jehu, king of Israel, saying, "[b]Come, let us face
each other."
9 Jehoash king of Israel sent to Amaziah king of Judah, saying,
"[a]The thorn bush which was in Lebanon sent to the cedar which
was in Lebanon, saying, 'Give your daughter to my son in
marriage.' But there passed by a wild beast that was in Lebanon,
and trampled the thorn bush.
10 "[a]You have indeed [1]defeated Edom, and [b]your heart has
[2]become proud. Enjoy your glory and stay at home; for why
should you provoke trouble so that you, even you, would fall,
and Judah with you?"
11 But Amaziah would not listen. So Jehoash king of Israel
went up; and he and Amaziah king of Judah faced
each other at [a]Beth-shemesh, which belongs to Judah.
12 Judah was defeated [1]by Israel, and [a]they fled
each to his tent.
13 Then Jehoash king of Israel captured Amaziah
king of Judah, the son of Jehoash the son of
Ahaziah, at Beth-shemesh, and came to Jerusalem
and tore down the wall of Jerusalem from [a]the Gate
of Ephraim to [b]the Corner Gate, 400 [1]cubits.
14 [a]He took all the gold and silver and all the
utensils which were found in the house of the
LORD, and in the treasuries of the king's house, the
hostages also, and returned to Samaria.
15 [a]Now the rest of the acts of Jehoash which he
did, and his might and how he fought with Amaziah

Jerusalem in the Time of the Judean Monarchy

Sheep Gate
Northwestern Hill
Muster Gate
Fish Gate
Temple
East Gate
Altar
Temple Hill
Horse Gate
Ephraim Gate
Corner Gate
MAKTESH
CENTRAL VALLEY
Ophel
Kidron Valley
Gihon Spring
Southeastern Hill (Zion)
Valley Gate
Siloam Channel
Hezekiah's Tunnel
Siloam Pool
Lower Pool
Water Gate (Fountain Gate)
Valley Gate
Dung Gate

25 [1]Lit *smote* [b]2 Kin 13:18, 19
14:1 [a]2 Chr 25:1 [b]2 Kin 13:10
4 [a]2 Kin 12:3 [b]2 Kin 16:4
5 [1]Lit *smote* [a]2 Kin 12:20
6 [1]Lit *smiters* [a]Deut 24:16 [b]Jer 31:30; Ezek 18:4, 20
7 [1]Lit *smote* [a]2 Sam 8:13; 1 Chr 18:12; 2 Chr 25:11 [b]Is 16:1 [c]Josh 15:38
8 [a]2 Chr 25:17-24 [b]2 Sam 2:14-17
9 [a]Judg 9:8-15
10 [1]Lit *smitten* [2]Lit *lifted you up* [a]2 Kin 14:7 [b]Deut 8:14; 2 Chr 26:16
11 [a]Josh 19:38
12 [1]Lit *before* [a]2 Sam 18:17
13 [1]I.e. One cubit equals approx 18 in. [a]Neh 8:16; 12:39 [b]2 Chr 25:23
14 [a]1 Kin 14:26; 2 Kin 12:18
15 [a]2 Kin 13:12, 13

17 [a]2 Chr 25:25-28

king of Judah, are they not written in the Book of the Chronicles
of the Kings of Israel?
16 So Jehoash slept with his fathers and was buried in Samaria
with the kings of Israel; and Jeroboam his son became king in
his place.

19 [a]Josh 10:31; 2 Kin 18:14, 17

17 [a]Amaziah the son of Joash king of Judah lived fifteen years
after the death of Jehoash son of Jehoahaz king of Israel.
18 Now the rest of the acts of Amaziah, are they not written
in the Book of the Chronicles of the Kings of Judah?

21 [1]In 2 Chr 26:1, *Uzziah*

19 They conspired against him in Jerusalem, and he fled to
[a]Lachish; but they sent after him to Lachish and killed him there.
20 Then they brought him on horses and he was buried at
Jerusalem with his fathers in the city of David.
21 All the people of Judah took [1]Azariah, who *was* sixteen years

22 [a]1 Kin 9:26; 2 Kin 16:6; 2 Chr 8:17

old, and made him king in the place of his father Amaziah.
22 [a]He built Elath and restored it to Judah after the king slept
with his fathers.
23 In the fifteenth year of Amaziah the son of Joash king of
Judah, Jeroboam the son of Joash king of Israel became king in

25 [1]Lit *by* [a]2 Kin 10:32; 13:25 [b]1 Kin 8:65 [c]Deut 3:17 [d]Jon 1:1; Matt 12:39, 40 [e]Josh 19:13

Samaria, *and reigned* forty-one years.
24 He did evil in the sight of the LORD; he did not depart from all
the sins of Jeroboam the son of Nebat, which he made Israel sin.
25 [a]He restored the border of Israel from [b]the entrance of
Hamath as far as [c]the Sea of the Arabah, according to the word of
the LORD, the God of Israel, which He spoke [1]through His servant
[d]Jonah the son of Amittai, the prophet, who was of [e]Gath-hepher.

26 [a]2 Kin 13:4 [b]Deut 32:36

26 For the [a]LORD saw the affliction of Israel, *which was* very
bitter; for [b]there was neither bond nor free, nor was there any
helper for Israel.
27 The [a]LORD did not say that He would blot out the name of
Israel from under heaven, but He saved them by the hand of

27 [a]2 Kin 13:23

Jeroboam the son of Joash.
28 Now the rest of the acts of Jeroboam and all that he did
and his might, how he fought and how he recovered for Israel,
[a]Damascus and [b]Hamath, *which had belonged* to Judah, are

28 [a]1 Kin 11:24 [b]2 Chr 8:3

they not written in the Book of the Chronicles of the Kings of
Israel?
29 And Jeroboam slept with his fathers, even with the kings of 753 B.C.
Israel, and Zechariah his son became king in his place.

15:1 [a]2 Kin 14:17

Chapter 15 Theme ____________________

15 [a]In the twenty-seventh year of Jeroboam king of Israel, 767 B.C.
Azariah son of Amaziah king of Judah became king.
2 He was [a]sixteen years old when he became king, and he

2 [1]In 2 Chr 26:3, *Jechiliah* [a]2 Chr 26:3, 4

reigned fifty-two years in Jerusalem; and his mother's name
was [1]Jecoliah of Jerusalem.
3 He did right in the sight of the LORD, according to all that
his father Amaziah had done.
4 Only [a]the high places were not taken away; the people still

4 [a]2 Kin 12:3

sacrificed and burned incense on the high places.

5 [a]The LORD struck the king, so that he was a leper to the day of
his death. And he [b]lived in a separate house, [1]while Jotham the
king's son was over the household, judging the people of the land.
6 Now the rest of the acts of Azariah and all that he did, are they
not written in the Book of the Chronicles of the Kings of Judah?
7 And Azariah slept with his fathers, and they buried him with
his fathers in the city of David, and Jotham his son became
king in his place.
753 B.C. **8** [a]In the thirty-eighth year of Azariah king of Judah, Zechariah
the son of Jeroboam became king over Israel in Samaria *for* six
months.
9 He did evil in the sight of the LORD, as his fathers had
done; he did not depart from the sins of Jeroboam the son of
Nebat, which he made Israel sin.
10 Then Shallum the son of Jabesh conspired against him and
[a]struck him before the people and [1]killed him, and reigned in
his place.
11 Now the rest of the acts of Zechariah, behold they are
written in the Book of the Chronicles of the Kings of Israel.
12 This is [a]the word of the LORD which He spoke to Jehu,
saying, "Your sons to the fourth generation shall sit on the
throne of Israel." And so it was.
752 B.C. **13** Shallum son of Jabesh became king in the [a]thirty-ninth year
of Uzziah king of Judah, and he reigned one month in [b]Samaria.
14 Then Menahem son of Gadi went up from [a]Tirzah and
came to Samaria, and struck Shallum son of Jabesh in Samaria,
and killed him and became king in his place.
15 Now the rest of the acts of Shallum and his conspiracy
which he made, behold they are written in the Book of the
Chronicles of the Kings of Israel.
16 Then Menahem struck Tiphsah and all who were in it and
its borders from Tirzah, because they did not open *to him;*
therefore he struck *it* and ripped up [a]all its women who were
with child.
752 B.C. **17** In the [a]thirty-ninth year of Azariah king of Judah, Menahem
son of Gadi became king over Israel *and reigned* ten years in
Samaria.

5 [1]Lit *and* [a]2 Chr 26:21-23 [b]Lev 13:46; Num 12:14
8 [a]2 Kin 15:1
10 [1]Lit *smote* [a]Amos 7:9
12 [a]2 Kin 10:30
13 [a]2 Kin 15:1, 8 [b]1 Kin 16:24
14 [a]1 Kin 14:17
16 [a]2 Kin 8:12; Hos 13:16
17 [a]2 Kin 15:1, 8, 13

Some of the Pagan Gods Worshiped by the Israelites

The god:	Ruled over / description:	Reference:
Adrammelech	War, love	2 Kings 17:31
Anammelech	Demanded child sacrifice	2 Kings 17:31
Asherah	Wife of Baal	2 Kings 13:6
Ashima	God of Hittites	2 Kings 17:30
Ashtoreth (Astarte, Ishtar)	Sex, fertility, queen of heaven	2 Kings 23:13
Baal	Rain, wind, clouds, fertility of land	2 Kings 3:2
Baal-zebub	God of Ekron	2 Kings 1:2
Chemosh	Provider of land	2 Kings 23:13
Molech (Milcom)	National god of Moabites, worship involved human sacrifice	2 Kings 23:10
Nebo	Wisdom, literature, arts	1 Chronicles 5:8
Nergal	Underworld, death	2 Kings 17:30
Nibhaz	Worshiped by the Avvites *(a people transplanted to Samaria from Assyria)*	2 Kings 17:31
Nisroch	God worshiped in Nineveh	2 Kings 19:37
Rimmon	Thunder, lightning, rain	2 Kings 5:18
Succoth-Benoth	Mistress of Marduk, goddess of war	2 Kings 17:30
Tartak	Fertility (worshiped by Avvites)	2 Kings 17:31

18 He did evil in the sight of the LORD; he did not depart all
his days from the sins of Jeroboam the son of Nebat, which he
made Israel sin.
19 [a]Pul, king of Assyria, came against the land, and Menahem
gave Pul a thousand talents of silver so that his hand might be
with him to [b]strengthen the kingdom [1]under his rule.
20 Then Menahem exacted the money from Israel, even from
all the mighty men of wealth, from each man fifty shekels of
silver to pay the king of Assyria. So the king of Assyria returned
and did not remain there in the land.
21 Now the rest of the acts of Menahem and all that he did,
are they not written in the Book of the Chronicles of the Kings
of Israel?
22 And Menahem slept with his fathers, and Pekahiah his son
became king in his place.
23 In [a]the fiftieth year of Azariah king of Judah, Pekahiah son 742 B.C.
of Menahem became king over Israel in Samaria, *and reigned*
two years.
24 He did evil in the sight of the LORD; he did not depart from
the sins of Jeroboam son of Nebat, which he made Israel sin.
25 Then Pekah son of Remaliah, his officer, conspired against
him and struck him in Samaria, in [a]the castle of the king's
house with Argob and Arieh; and with him were fifty men of
the Gileadites, and he killed him and became king in his place.
26 Now the rest of the acts of Pekahiah and all that he did,
behold they are written in the Book of the Chronicles of the
Kings of Israel.
27 In [a]the fifty-second year of Azariah king of Judah, [b]Pekah son 740 B.C.
of Remaliah became king over Israel in Samaria, *and reigned*
twenty years.
28 He did evil in the sight of the LORD; he did not depart from
the sins of Jeroboam son of Nebat, which he made Israel sin.
29 In the days of Pekah king of Israel, [1a]Tiglath-pileser king of
Assyria came and [2]captured Ijon and Abel-beth-maacah and
Janoah and Kedesh and Hazor and Gilead and Galilee, all the
land of Naphtali; and [b]he carried them captive to Assyria.
30 And Hoshea the son of Elah made a conspiracy against 732 B.C.
Pekah the son of Remaliah, and struck him and put him to death
and became king in his place, in the twentieth year of Jotham
the son of Uzziah.
31 Now the rest of the acts of Pekah and all that he did,
behold, they are written in the Book of the Chronicles of the
Kings of Israel.
32 In the second year of Pekah the son of Remaliah king of
Israel, Jotham the son of [1]Uzziah king of Judah became king.
33 [a]He was twenty-five years old when he became king, and
he reigned sixteen years in Jerusalem; and his mother's name
was Jerusha the daughter of Zadok.
34 [a]He did what was right in the sight of the LORD; he did
according to all that his father Uzziah had done.

19 [1]Lit *in his hand* [a]1 Chr 5:25, 26 [b]2 Kin 14:5
23 [a]2 Kin 15:1, 8, 13, 17
25 [a]1 Kin 16:18
27 [a]2 Kin 15:23 [b]2 Chr 28:6; Is 7:1
29 [1]In 1 Chr 5:6, 26, *Tilgath-pilneser* [2]Lit *took* [a]2 Kin 15:19 [b]2 Kin 17:6
32 [1]I.e. Azariah
33 [a]2 Chr 27:1
34 [a]2 Kin 15:3, 4; 2 Chr 26:4, 5

35 Only [a]the high places were not taken away; the people still
sacrificed and burned incense on the high places. [b]He built the
upper gate of the house of the LORD.
36 Now the rest of the acts of Jotham and all that he did, are
they not written in the Book of the Chronicles of the Kings of
Judah?
37 In those days [a]the LORD began to send Rezin king of Aram
and Pekah the son of Remaliah against Judah.
38 And Jotham slept with his fathers, and he was buried with
his fathers in the city of David his father; and Ahaz his son
became king in his place.

Chapter 16 Theme ______________________

735 B.C.

2 Chronicles 28

16 In the seventeenth year of Pekah the son of Remaliah,
[a]Ahaz the son of Jotham, king of Judah, became king.
2 [a]Ahaz *was* twenty years old when he became king, and he
reigned sixteen years in Jerusalem; and he did not do what was
right in the sight of the LORD his God, as his father David *had
done.*
3 But he walked in the way of the kings of Israel, [a]and even
made his son pass through the fire, [b]according to the
abominations of the nations whom the LORD had [1]driven out
from before the sons of Israel.
4 He [a]sacrificed and burned incense on the high places and
on the hills and under every green tree.
5 Then [a]Rezin king of Aram and Pekah son of Remaliah, king
of Israel, came up to Jerusalem to *wage* war; and they besieged
Ahaz, [b]but could not [1]overcome him.
6 At that time Rezin king of Aram recovered [a]Elath for Aram,
and cleared the Judeans out of [1]Elath entirely; and the [2]Arameans
came to Elath and have lived there to this day.
7 [a]So Ahaz sent messengers to [b]Tiglath-pileser king of
Assyria, saying, "I am your servant and your son; come up and
deliver me from the [1]hand of the king of Aram and from the
[1]hand of the king of Israel, who are rising up against me."
8 [a]Ahaz took the silver and gold that was found in the house
of the LORD and in the treasuries of the king's house, and sent a
present to the king of Assyria.
9 [a]So the king of Assyria listened to him; and the king of
Assyria went up against Damascus and [b]captured it, and carried
the people of it away into exile to [c]Kir, and put Rezin to death.
10 Now King Ahaz went to Damascus to meet [a]Tiglath-pileser
king of Assyria, and saw the altar which *was* at Damascus; and
King Ahaz sent to [b]Urijah the priest the [1]pattern of the altar
and its model, according to all its workmanship.
11 So Urijah the priest built an altar; according to all that King
Ahaz had sent from Damascus, thus Urijah the priest made *it,*
[1]before the coming of King Ahaz from Damascus.
12 When the king came from Damascus, the king saw the
altar; then [a]the king approached the altar and [1]went up to it,

35 [a]2 Kin 12:3 [b]2 Chr 23:20; 27:3
37 [a]2 Kin 16:5; Is 7:1
16:1 [a]2 Chr 28:1
2 [a]2 Chr 28:1-4
3 [1]Or *dispossessed* [a]Lev 18:21; 2 Kin 17:17; 21:6 [b]Deut 12:31; 2 Kin 21:2, 11
4 [a]Deut 12:2; 2 Kin 14:4
5 [1]Lit *fight* [a]2 Kin 15:37; Is 7:1 [b]2 Chr 28:5, 6
6 [1]Heb *Eloth* [2]So with some ancient versions; Heb *Edomites* [a]2 Kin 14:22; 2 Chr 26:2
7 [1]Lit *palm* [a]2 Chr 28:16 [b]2 Kin 15:29
8 [a]2 Kin 12:17, 18; 18:15
9 [a]2 Chr 28:21 [b]Amos 1:3-5 [c]Is 22:6; Amos 9:7
10 [1]Lit *likeness* [a]2 Kin 15:29 [b]Is 8:2
11 [1]Lit *until*
12 [1]Or *offered on it* [a]2 Chr 26:16, 19

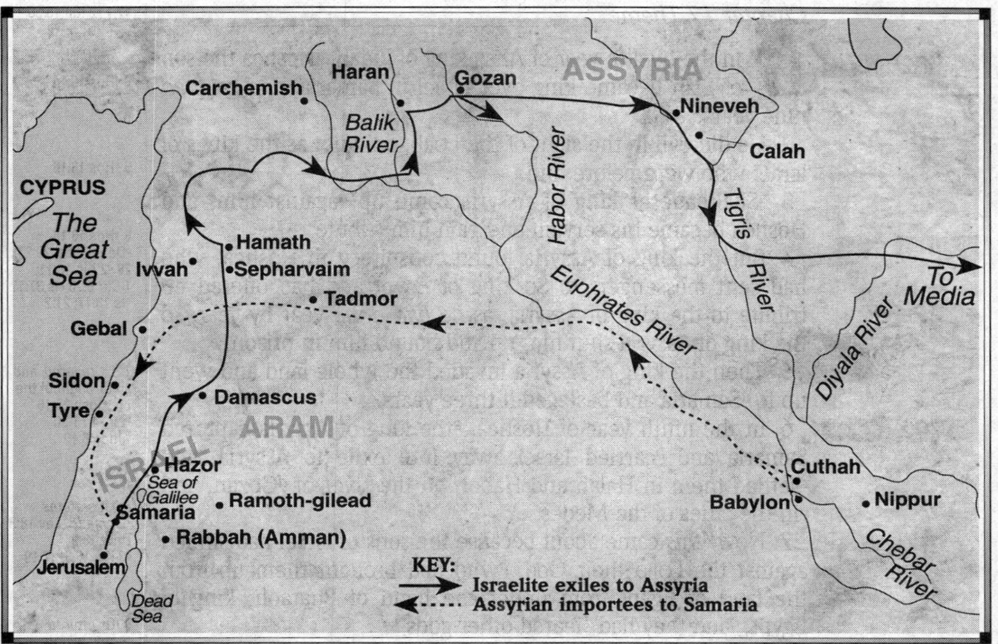

13 [1]Lit *offered in smoke*

14 [1]Lit *he also* [a]Ex 27:1, 2; 40:6, 29; 2 Chr 4:1 [b]2 Kin 16:11

15 [1]Lit *commanded him, Urijah* [2]Lit *offer in smoke* [a]Ex 29:39-41 [b]2 Kin 16:14

17 [a]1 Kin 7:27, 28, 38 [b]1 Kin 7:23, 25

19 [a]2 Chr 28:26

20 [a]Is 14:28 [b]2 Chr 28:27

The Assyrian Captivity of Israel

13 and [1]burned his burnt offering and his meal offering, and
poured his drink offering and sprinkled the blood of his peace
offerings on the altar.
14 [a]The bronze altar, which *was* before the LORD, [1]he brought
from the front of the house, from between [b]*his* altar and the
house of the LORD, and he put it on the north side of *his* altar.
15 Then King Ahaz [1]commanded Urijah the priest, saying,
"Upon the great altar [2]burn [a]the morning burnt offering and the
evening meal offering and the king's burnt offering and his
meal offering, with the burnt offering of all the people of the land
and their meal offering and their drink offerings; and sprinkle on
it all the blood of the burnt offering and all the blood of the
sacrifice. But [b]the bronze altar shall be for me to inquire *by.*"
16 So Urijah the priest did according to all that King Ahaz
commanded.
17 Then King Ahaz [a]cut off the borders of the stands, and
removed the laver from them; he also [b]took down the sea from
the bronze oxen which were under it and put it on a pavement
of stone.
18 The covered way for the sabbath which they had built in
the house, and the outer entry of the king, he removed from
the house of the LORD because of the king of Assyria.
19 Now the rest of the acts of Ahaz which he did, are they not
written [a]in the Book of the Chronicles of the Kings of Judah?
20 So [a]Ahaz slept with his fathers, and [b]was buried with his
fathers in the city of David; and his son Hezekiah reigned in his
place.

715 B.C.

Chapter 17 Theme ______________________

732 B.C.

17 In the twelfth year of Ahaz king of Judah, [a]Hoshea the son of Elah became king over Israel in Samaria, *and reigned* nine years.

2 He did evil in the sight of the LORD, only not as the kings of Israel who were before him.

3 [a]Shalmaneser king of Assyria came up [b]against him, and Hoshea became his servant and paid him tribute.

4 But the king of Assyria found conspiracy in Hoshea, who had sent messengers to So king of Egypt and had offered no tribute to the king of Assyria, as *he had done* year by year; so the king of Assyria shut him up and bound him in prison.

5 Then the king of Assyria invaded the whole land and went up to [a]Samaria and besieged it three years.

722 B.C.

6 In the ninth year of Hoshea, [a]the king of Assyria captured Samaria and [b]carried Israel away into exile to Assyria, and [c]settled them in Halah and Habor, *on* the river of [d]Gozan, and [e]in the cities of the Medes.

7 Now [a]*this* came about because the sons of Israel had sinned against the LORD their God, [b]who had brought them up from the land of Egypt from under the hand of Pharaoh, king of Egypt, [c]and they had [1]feared other gods

8 and [a]walked in the [1]customs of the nations whom the LORD had driven out before the sons of Israel, and *in the customs* [b]of the kings of Israel which they had [2]introduced.

9 The sons of Israel [1]did things secretly which were not right against the LORD their God. Moreover, they built for themselves high places in all their towns, from [a]watchtower to fortified city.

10 [a]They set for themselves *sacred* pillars and [1b]Asherim on every high hill and under every green tree,

11 and there they burned incense on all the high places as the nations *did* which the LORD had carried away to exile before them; and they did evil things provoking the LORD.

12 They served idols, [a]concerning which the LORD had said to them, "You shall not do this thing."

13 Yet the [a]LORD warned Israel and Judah [b]through all His prophets *and* [c]every seer, saying, "[d]Turn from your evil ways and keep My commandments, My statutes according to all the law which I commanded your fathers, and which I sent to you through My servants the prophets."

14 However, they did not listen, but [a]stiffened their neck [1]like their fathers, who did not believe in the LORD their God.

15 [a]They rejected His statutes and [b]His covenant which He made with their fathers and His warnings with which He warned them. And [c]they followed vanity and [d]became vain, and *went* after the nations which surrounded them, concerning which the [e]LORD had commanded them not to do like them.

16 They forsook all the commandments of the LORD their God and made for themselves molten images, *even* [a]two calves, and [b]made an [1]Asherah and [c]worshiped all the host of heaven and [d]served Baal.

17:1 [a]2 Kin 15:30

3 [a]Hos 10:14 [b]2 Kin 18:9-12

5 [a]Hos 13:16

6 [a]Hos 13:16 [b]Deut 28:64; 29:27, 28 [c]2 Kin 18:11; 1 Chr 5:26 [d]Is 37:12 [e]Is 13:17; 21:2

7 [1]Lit *revered,* and so throughout the ch [a]Josh 23:16 [b]Ex 14:15-30 [c]Judg 6:10

8 [1]Lit *statutes* [2]Lit *made* [a]Lev 18:3; Deut 18:9 [b]2 Kin 16:3; 17:19

9 [1]Or *uttered words which* [a]2 Kin 18:8

10 [1]I.e. wooden symbols of a female deity [a]Ex 34:12-14 [b]1 Kin 14:23; Mic 5:14

12 [a]Ex 20:4

13 [a]Neh 9:29, 30 [b]2 Kin 17:23 [c]1 Sam 9:9 [d]Jer 7:3-7; 18:11; Ezek 18:31

14 [1]Lit *like the neck of* [a]Ex 32:9; 33:3; Acts 7:51

15 [a]Jer 8:9 [b]Ex 24:6-8; Deut 29:25 [c]Deut 32:21 [d]Jer 2:5; Rom 1:21-23 [e]Deut 12:30, 31

16 [1]I.e. a wooden symbol of a female deity [a]1 Kin 12:28 [b]1 Kin 14:15, 23 [c]Deut 4:19; 2 Kin 21:3 [d]1 Kin 16:31

17 [a]2 Kin 16:3 [b]Lev 19:26; Deut 18:10-12 [c]1 Kin 21:20

17 Then [a]they made their sons and their daughters pass
through the fire, and [b]practiced divination and enchantments, and
[c]sold themselves to do evil in the sight of the LORD, provoking
Him.

18 [1]Lit *face* [a]2 Kin 17:6 [b]1 Kin 11:13, 32, 36

18 So the LORD was very angry with Israel and [a]removed them
from His [1]sight; [b]none was left except the tribe of Judah.

19 [1]Lit *statutes* [2]Lit *of Israel which they* [3]Lit *made* [a]1 Kin 14:22, 23 [b]2 Kin 16:3

19 Also [a]Judah did not keep the commandments of the LORD
their God, but [b]walked in the [1]customs [2]which Israel had
[3]introduced.

20 [1]Lit *seed* [2]Lit *from His face* [a]2 Kin 15:29

20 The LORD rejected all the [1]descendants of Israel and
afflicted them and [a]gave them into the hand of plunderers,
until He had cast them [2]out of His sight.

21 [1]Lit *sin* [a]1 Kin 11:11, 31 [b]1 Kin 12:20 [c]1 Kin 12:28-33

21 When [a]He had torn Israel from the house of David, [b]they
made Jeroboam the son of Nebat king. Then [c]Jeroboam drove
Israel away from following the LORD and made them [1]commit a
great sin.
22 The sons of Israel walked in all the sins of Jeroboam which
he did; they did not depart from them

23 [a]2 Kin 17:6 [b]2 Kin 17:13

23 [a]until the LORD removed Israel from His sight, [b]as He spoke
through all His servants the prophets. [a]So Israel was carried
away into exile from their own land to Assyria until this day.

24 [1]In 2 Kin 18:34, *Ivvah* [a]Ezra 4:2, 10 [b]2 Kin 18:34 [c]1 Kin 8:65

24 [a]The king of Assyria brought *men* from Babylon and from
Cuthah and from [1b]Avva and from [c]Hamath and Sepharvaim,
and settled *them* in the cities of Samaria in place of the sons of
Israel. So they possessed Samaria and lived in its cities.

25 [a]2 Kin 17:32-41

25 At the beginning of their living there, they [a]did not fear the
LORD; therefore the LORD sent lions among them which killed
some of them.
26 So they spoke to the king of Assyria, saying, "The nations
whom you have carried away into exile in the cities of Samaria
do not know the custom of the god of the land; so he has sent
lions among them, and behold, they kill them because they do
not know the custom of the god of the land."

27 [1]Lit *exile from there* [2]Lit *them*

27 Then the king of Assyria commanded, saying, "Take there
one of the priests whom you carried away into [1]exile and let
[2]him go and live there; and let him teach them the custom of
the god of the land."
28 So one of the priests whom they had carried away into
exile from Samaria came and lived at Bethel, and taught them
how they should fear the LORD.

29 [a]1 Kin 12:31; 13:32

29 But every nation still made gods of its own and put them
[a]in the houses of the high places which the people of Samaria
had made, every nation in their cities in which they lived.

30 [a]2 Kin 17:24

30 [a]The men of Babylon made Succoth-benoth, the men of
Cuth made Nergal, the men of Hamath made Ashima,

31 [a]2 Kin 17:17 [b]2 Kin 19:37 [c]2 Kin 17:24

31 and the Avvites made Nibhaz and Tartak; and [a]the
Sepharvites burned their children in the fire to [b]Adrammelech
and Anammelech the gods of [c]Sepharvaim.

32 [1]Lit *made for themselves from among* [a]Zeph 1:5 [b]1 Kin 12:31

32 [a]They also feared the LORD and [1b]appointed from among
themselves priests of the high places, who acted for them in
the houses of the high places.

INSIGHT

Cuthah (or Cuth), located in Mesopotamia about eighteen miles northeast of Babylon, was the center of worship for Nergal, the god of death or the underworld. The Assyrians took the people of Cuthah captive and exiled them to Israel (2 Kings 17:24). There they made an idol to Nergal (2 Kings 17:30), and became yet another influence upon the people's tendency to worship other gods alongside Yahweh of Israel.

33 They feared the LORD and served their own gods according
to the custom of the nations from among whom they had been
carried away into exile.
34 To this day they do according to the earlier customs: they
do not fear the LORD, nor do they [1]follow their statutes or their
ordinances or the law, or the commandments which the LORD
commanded the sons of Jacob, [a]whom He named Israel;
35 with whom the LORD made a covenant and commanded
them, saying, "[a]You shall not fear other gods, nor [b]bow down
yourselves to them nor [c]serve them nor sacrifice to them.
36 "But the LORD, [a]who brought you up from the land of Egypt
with great power and with [b]an outstretched arm, [c]Him you
shall fear, and to Him you shall bow yourselves down, and to
Him you shall sacrifice.
37 "The statutes and the ordinances and the law and the
commandment which He wrote for you, [a]you shall observe to
do forever; and you shall not fear other gods.
38 "The covenant that I have made with you, [a]you shall not
forget, nor shall you fear other gods.
39 "But the LORD your God you shall fear; and He will deliver
you from the hand of all your enemies."
40 However, they did not listen, but they did according to
their earlier custom.
41 [a]So while these nations feared the LORD, they also served
their [1]idols; their children likewise and their grandchildren, as
their fathers did, so they do to this day.

Chapter 18 Theme ______________________

2 Chronicles 29

18 Now it came about [a]in the third year of Hoshea, the son
of Elah king of Israel, that [b]Hezekiah the son of Ahaz
king of Judah became king.
2 He was [a]twenty-five years old when he became king, and
he reigned twenty-nine years in Jerusalem; and his mother's
name was Abi the daughter of Zechariah.
3 [a]He did right in the sight of the LORD, according to all that
his father David had done.
4 [a]He removed the high places and broke down the *sacred*
pillars and cut down the [1]Asherah. He also broke in pieces [b]the
bronze serpent that Moses had made, for until those days the
sons of Israel burned incense to it; and it was called [2]Nehushtan.
5 [a]He trusted in the LORD, the God of Israel; [b]so that after
him there was none like him among all the kings of Judah, nor
among those who were before him.
6 For he [a]clung to the LORD; he did not depart from following
Him, but kept His commandments, which the LORD had
commanded Moses.
7 [a]And the LORD was with him; wherever he went he prospered.
And [b]he rebelled against the king of Assyria and did not serve him.
8 [a]He [1]defeated the Philistines as far as Gaza and its territory,
from [b]watchtower to fortified city.

34 [1]Lit *do according to* [a]Gen 32:28; 35:10
35 [a]Judg 6:10 [b]Ex 20:5 [c]Deut 5:9
36 [a]Ex 14:15-30 [b]Ex 6:6; 9:15 [c]Lev 19:32; Deut 6:13
37 [a]Deut 5:32
38 [a]Deut 4:23; 6:12
41 [1]Or *graven images* [a]Zeph 1:5; Matt 6:24
18:1 [a]2 Kin 16:2; 17:1 [b]2 Chr 28:27
2 [a]2 Chr 29:1, 2
3 [a]2 Kin 20:3; 2 Chr 31:20
4 [1]I.e. a wooden symbol of a female deity [2]I.e. a piece of bronze [a]2 Kin 18:22; 2 Chr 31:1 [b]Num 21:8, 9
5 [a]2 Kin 19:10 [b]2 Kin 23:25
6 [a]Deut 10:20; Josh 23:8
7 [a]Gen 39:2, 3; 1 Sam 18:14 [b]2 Kin 16:7
8 [1]Lit *smote* [a]2 Chr 28:18; Is 14:29 [b]2 Kin 17:9

9 Now in the fourth year of King Hezekiah, which was the
seventh year of Hoshea son of Elah king of Israel, [a]Shalmaneser
king of Assyria came up against Samaria and besieged it.
10 At the end of three years they captured it; in the sixth year
of Hezekiah, which was [a]the ninth year of Hoshea king of
Israel, Samaria was captured.
11 Then the king of Assyria carried Israel away into exile to
Assyria, and put them in [a]Halah and on the Habor, the river of
Gozan, and in the cities of the Medes,
12 because they [a]did not obey the voice of the LORD their God,
but transgressed His covenant, *even* all that Moses the servant
of the LORD commanded; they would neither listen nor do *it*.
13 [a]Now in the fourteenth year of King Hezekiah, Sennacherib
king of Assyria came up against all the fortified cities of Judah
and seized them.
14 Then Hezekiah king of Judah sent to the king of Assyria at
Lachish, saying, "[a]I have done wrong. [1]Withdraw from me;
whatever you [2]impose on me I will bear." So the king of
Assyria [3]required of Hezekiah king of Judah three hundred
talents of silver and thirty talents of gold.
15 [a]Hezekiah gave *him* all the silver which was found in the
house of the LORD, and in the treasuries of the king's house.
16 At that time Hezekiah cut off *the gold from* the doors of the
temple of the LORD, and *from* the doorposts which Hezekiah
king of Judah had overlaid, and gave it to the king of Assyria.
17 Then the king of Assyria sent [a]Tartan and Rab-saris and
Rabshakeh from Lachish to King Hezekiah with a large army to
Jerusalem. So they went up and came to Jerusalem. And when
they went up, they came and stood by the [b]conduit of the
upper pool, which is on the highway of the [1]fuller's field.
18 When they called to the king, [a]Eliakim the son of Hilkiah,
who was over the household, and [b]Shebnah the scribe and Joah
the son of Asaph the recorder, came out to them.
19 Then Rabshakeh said to them, "Say now to Hezekiah, 'Thus
says the great king, the king of Assyria, "[a]What is this
confidence that you [1]have?
20 "You say (but *they are* [1]only empty words), '*I have* counsel
and strength for the war.' Now on whom do you rely, [a]that you
have rebelled against me?
21 "Now behold, you [1a]rely on the staff of this crushed reed, *even*
on Egypt; on which if a man leans, it will go into his [2]hand and
pierce it. So is Pharaoh king of Egypt to all who rely on him.
22 "But if you say to me, 'We trust in the LORD our God,' is it
not He whose high places and [a]whose altars Hezekiah has
taken away, and has said to Judah and to Jerusalem, 'You shall
worship before this altar in Jerusalem'?
23 "Now therefore, [1]come, make a bargain with my master the
king of Assyria, and I will give you two thousand horses, if you
are able on your part to set riders on them.
24 "How then can you [1]repulse one [2]official of the least of my
master's servants, and [3]rely on Egypt for chariots and for horsemen?

722 B.C.

701 B.C.

2 Chronicles 32

9 [a]2 Kin 17:3-7
10 [a]2 Kin 17:6
11 [a]1 Chr 5:26
12 [a]1 Kin 9:6; Dan 9:6, 10
13 [a]2 Chr 32:1; Is 36:1-39:8
14 [1]Lit *Return* [2]Lit *give* [3]Lit *put on* [a]2 Kin 18:7
15 [a]1 Kin 15:18, 19; 2 Kin 12:18; 16:8
17 [1]I.e. launderer's [a]Is 20:1 [b]2 Kin 20:20; Is 7:3
18 [a]2 Kin 19:2; Is 22:20 [b]Is 22:15
19 [1]Lit *trust* [a]2 Chr 32:10
20 [1]Lit *a word of the lips* [a]2 Kin 18:7
21 [1]Lit *rely for yourself* [2]Lit *palm* [a]Is 30:2, 3, 7; Ezek 29:6, 7
22 [a]2 Kin 18:4; 2 Chr 31:1
23 [1]Lit *please exchange pledges*
24 [1]Lit *turn away the face of* [2]Or *governor* [3]Lit *rely for yourself*

25 "Have I now come up [1]without the LORD's approval against
this place to destroy it? The LORD said to me, 'Go up against
this land and destroy it.'""
26 Then Eliakim the son of Hilkiah, and Shebnah and Joah,
said to Rabshakeh, "Speak now to your servants in Aramaic, for
we [1]understand *it;* and do not speak with us in [2a]Judean in the
hearing of the people who are on the wall."
27 But Rabshakeh said to them, "Has my master sent me only
to your master and to you to speak these words, *and* not to the
men who sit on the wall, *doomed* to eat their own dung and
drink their own urine with you?"
28 Then Rabshakeh stood and cried with a loud voice in Judean,
[1]saying, "Hear the word of the great king, the king of Assyria.
29 "Thus says the king, '[a]Do not let Hezekiah deceive you, for
he will not be able to deliver you from [1]my hand;
30 nor let Hezekiah make you trust in the LORD, saying, "The
LORD will surely deliver us, and this city will not be given into
the hand of the king of Assyria."
31 'Do not listen to Hezekiah, for thus says the king of Assyria,
"[1]Make your peace with me and come out to me, and eat [a]each
of his vine and each of his fig tree and drink each of the waters
of his own cistern,
32 until I come and take you away [a]to a land like your own land,
a land of grain and new wine, a land of bread and vineyards, a
land of olive trees and honey, that you may live and not die."
But do not listen to Hezekiah when he misleads you, saying,
"The LORD will deliver us."
33 '[a]Has any one of the gods of the nations delivered his land
from the hand of the king of Assyria?
34 '[a]Where are the gods of Hamath and [b]Arpad? Where are the
gods of Sepharvaim, Hena and [1c]Ivvah? Have they delivered
Samaria from my hand?
35 'Who among all the gods of the lands [1]have delivered their
land from my hand, [a]that the LORD should deliver Jerusalem from
my hand?'"
36 But the people were silent and answered him not a word,
for the king's commandment was, "Do not answer him."
37 Then [a]Eliakim the son of Hilkiah, who was over the
household, and Shebna the scribe and Joah the son of Asaph,
the recorder, came to Hezekiah [b]with their clothes torn and
told him the words of Rabshakeh.

INSIGHT

Ivvah (also spelled Ava or Avva) refers to the people the Assyrians conquered and took to Israel to replace the people taken into exile (2 Kings 17:24). Since the gods of the Ivvahian people did not come to their rescue against the Assyrians, they were used by Sennacherib as an example to call Jerusalem to surrender in 701 B.C. (2 Kings 18:34). Ivvah is believed to have been in Syria. Sennacherib used the same ploy against the city of Hena, which could possibly have been Ana or Anat on the Euphrates River.

Chapter 19 Theme ____________________

19 [a]And when King Hezekiah heard *it,* he [b]tore his clothes,
[c]covered himself with sackcloth and entered the house
of the LORD.
2 Then he sent Eliakim who was over the household with
Shebna the scribe and the elders of the priests, [a]covered with
sackcloth, to [b]Isaiah the prophet the son of Amoz.

25 [1]Lit *without the LORD*

26 [1]Lit *hear* [2]I.e. Hebrew [a]Ezra 4:7; Dan 2:4

28 [1]Lit *and spoke, saying,*

29 [1]Heb *his* [a]2 Chr 32:15

31 [1]Lit *Make with me a blessing* [a]1 Kin 4:20, 25

32 [a]Deut 8:7-9; 11:12

33 [a]2 Kin 19:12; Is 10:10, 11

34 [1]In 2 Kin 17:24, *Avva* [a]2 Kin 19:13 [b]Is 10:9 [c]2 Kin 17:24

35 [1]Lit *who have* [a]Ps 2:1-3; 59:7

37 [a]2 Kin 18:26 [b]2 Kin 6:30

19:1 [a]2 Chr 32:20-22; Is 37:1 [b]2 Kin 18:37 [c]1 Kin 21:27

2 [a]2 Sam 3:31 [b]Is 1:1; 2:1

3 They said to him, "Thus says Hezekiah, 'This day is a day of distress, rebuke, and rejection; for children have come to birth and there is no strength to *deliver.*

4 '[a]Perhaps the LORD your God will hear all the words of Rabshakeh, whom his master the king of Assyria has sent [b]to reproach the living God, and will rebuke the words which the LORD your God has heard. Therefore, offer a prayer for [c]the remnant that is left.'"

5 So the servants of King Hezekiah came to Isaiah.

6 Isaiah said to them, "Thus you shall say to your master, 'Thus says the LORD, "Do not be afraid because of the words that you have heard, with which the [a]servants of the king of Assyria [b]have blasphemed Me.

7 "Behold, I will put a spirit in him so that [a]he will hear a rumor and return to his own land. And [b]I will make him fall by the sword in his own land."'"

8 Then Rabshakeh returned and found the king of Assyria fighting against [a]Libnah, for he had heard that [1]the king had left [b]Lachish.

9 When he heard *them* say concerning Tirhakah king of [1]Cush, "Behold, he has come out to fight against you," he sent messengers again to Hezekiah saying,

10 "Thus you shall say to Hezekiah king of [1]Judah, 'Do not [a]let your God in whom you trust deceive you saying, "[b]Jerusalem will not be given into the hand of the king of Assyria."

11 'Behold, you have heard what the kings of Assyria have done to all the lands, destroying them completely. So will you be [1]spared?

12 '[a]Did the gods of [1]those nations which my fathers destroyed deliver them, *even* [b]Gozan and [c]Haran and Rezeph and [d]the sons of Eden who *were* in Telassar?

13 '[a]Where is the king of Hamath, the king of Arpad, the king of the city of Sepharvaim, and *of* Hena and Ivvah?'"

14 Then [a]Hezekiah took the [1]letter from the hand of the messengers and read it, and he went up to the house of the LORD and [2]spread it out before the LORD.

15 Hezekiah prayed before the LORD and said, "O LORD, the God of Israel, [a]who are [1]enthroned *above* the cherubim, [b]You are the God, You alone, of all the kingdoms of the earth. You have made heaven and earth.

16 "[a]Incline Your ear, O LORD, and hear; [b]open Your eyes, O LORD, and see; and listen to the words of Sennacherib, which he has sent [c]to reproach the living God.

17 "Truly, O LORD, the kings of Assyria have devastated the nations and their lands

18 and have cast their gods into the fire, [a]for they were not gods but the work of men's hands, wood and stone. So they have destroyed them.

19 "Now, O LORD our God, I pray, deliver us from his hand [a]that all the kingdoms of the earth may know that You alone, O [b]LORD, are God."

4 [a]Josh 14:12; 2 Sam 16:12 [b]2 Kin 18:35 [c]Is 1:9

6 [a]2 Kin 18:17 [b]2 Kin 18:22-25, 30, 35

7 [a]2 Kin 7:6 [b]2 Kin 19:37

8 [1]Lit *he* [a]Josh 10:29 [b]2 Kin 18:14

9 [1]Or *Ethiopia*

10 [1]Lit *Judah, saying,* [a]2 Kin 18:5 [b]2 Kin 18:30

11 [1]Lit *delivered*

12 [1]Lit *the* [a]2 Kin 18:33 [b]2 Kin 17:6 [c]Gen 11:31 [d]Is 37:12

13 [a]2 Kin 18:34

14 [1]Lit *letters...read them* [2]Lit *Hezekiah spread* [a]Is 37:14

15 [1]Lit *seated* [a]Ex 25:22; Is 37:14 [b]2 Kin 5:15

16 [a]Ps 31:2; Is 37:17 [b]1 Kin 8:29; 2 Chr 6:40 [c]2 Kin 19:4

18 [a]Is 44:9-20; Acts 17:29

19 [a]1 Kin 8:42, 43 [b]2 Kin 19:15

20 Then Isaiah the son of Amoz sent to Hezekiah saying,
"Thus says the LORD, the God of Israel, 'Because you have prayed
to Me about Sennacherib king of Assyria, [a]I have heard *you.*'
21 "This is the word that the LORD has spoken against him:
'She has despised you and mocked you,
[a]The virgin daughter of Zion;
She [b]has shaken *her* head behind you,
The daughter of Jerusalem!
22 'Whom have you [a]reproached and [b]blasphemed?
And against whom have you raised *your* voice,
And [1]haughtily lifted up your eyes?
Against the [c]Holy One of Israel!
23 '[a]Through your messengers you have reproached the Lord,
And you have said, "With my many chariots
I came up to the heights of the mountains,
To the remotest parts of Lebanon;
And I [1]cut down its tall cedars *and* its choice cypresses.
And I [1]entered its farthest lodging place, its [b]thickest forest.
24 "I dug *wells* and drank foreign waters,
And with the sole of my feet I [1a]dried up
All the rivers of [2]Egypt."

25 '[a]Have you not heard?
Long ago I did it;
From ancient times I planned it.
[b]Now I have brought it to pass,
That you should turn fortified cities into ruinous heaps.
26 'Therefore their inhabitants were short of strength,
They were dismayed and put to shame;
They were [a]as the vegetation of the field and as the green
herb,
As grass on the housetops is scorched before it is grown up.
27 'But [a]I know your sitting down,
And your going out and your coming in,
And your raging against Me.
28 'Because of your raging against Me,
And because your [1]arrogance has come up to My ears,
Therefore I [a]will put My hook in your nose,
And My bridle in your lips,
And [b]I will turn you back by the way which you came.
29 'Then this shall be [a]the sign for you: [1]you will eat this year
what grows of itself, in the second year what springs from the
same, and in the third year sow, reap, plant vineyards, and eat
their fruit.
30 '[a]The surviving remnant of the house of Judah will again
take root downward and bear fruit upward.
31 'For out of Jerusalem will go forth a remnant, and [a]out of
Mount Zion [1]survivors. [b]The zeal of [2]the LORD will perform this.
32 'Therefore thus says the LORD concerning the king of Assyria,
"[a]He will not come to this city or shoot an arrow there; and he
will not come before it with a shield or throw up a siege ramp
against it.

20 [a]2 Kin 20:5

21 [a]Jer 14:17; Lam 2:13 [b]Ps 109:25; Matt 27:39

22 [1]Lit *on high* [a]2 Kin 19:4 [b]2 Kin 19:6 [c]Is 5:24; 30:11-15

23 [1]So with some ancient versions; M.T. *will cut . . . will enter* [a]2 Kin 18:17 [b]2 Chr 26:10; Is 10:18

24 [1]So with some ancient versions; M.T. *will dry up* [2]Lit *the besieged place* [a]Is 19:6

25 [a]Is 45:7 [b]Is 10:5

26 [a]Ps 129:6

27 [a]Ps 139:1

28 [1]Lit *complacency* [a]Ezek 19:9; 29:4 [b]2 Kin 19:33, 36

29 [1]Lit *eating* [a]Ex 3:12; 2 Kin 20:8, 9

30 [a]2 Kin 19:4; 2 Chr 32:22, 23

31 [1]Lit *those who escape* [2]Some ancient mss read *the LORD of hosts* [a]Is 10:20 [b]Is 9:7

32 [a]Is 8:7-10

33 “[a]By the way that he came, by the same he will return, and
he shall not come to this city,”’ declares the LORD.
34 ‘[a]For I will defend this city to save it for My own sake and
[b]for My servant David’s sake.’”
35 [a]Then it happened that night that the angel of the LORD
went out and struck 185,000 in the camp of the Assyrians; and
when [1]men rose early in the morning, behold, all of them were
[2]dead.
36 So [a]Sennacherib king of Assyria departed and returned 701 B.C.
home, and lived at [b]Nineveh.
37 It came about as he was worshiping in the house of Nisroch
his god, that [1a]Adrammelech and Sharezer killed him with the
sword; and they escaped into [b]the land of Ararat. And 681 B.C.
[c]Esarhaddon his son became king in his place.

Chapter 20 Theme ____________________

20 [a]In those days Hezekiah became [1]mortally ill. And 701 B.C.
Isaiah the prophet the son of Amoz came to him and
said to him, “Thus says the LORD, ‘[b]Set your house in order, for
you shall die and not live.’”
2 Then he turned his face to the wall and prayed to the LORD,
saying,
3 “[a]Remember now, O LORD, I beseech You, [b]how I have walked
before You in truth and with a whole heart and have done
what is good in Your sight.” And [c]Hezekiah wept [1]bitterly.
4 Before Isaiah had gone out of the middle court, the word of
the LORD came to him, saying,
5 “Return and say to [a]Hezekiah the leader of My people, ‘Thus
says the LORD, the God of your father David, “[b]I have heard
your prayer, [c]I have seen your tears; behold, I will heal you. On
the third day you shall go up to the house of the LORD.
6 “I will add fifteen years to your [1]life, and I will deliver you and
this city from the hand of the king of Assyria; and [a]I will defend
this city for My own sake and for My servant David’s sake.”’”
7 Then Isaiah said, “Take a cake of figs.” And they took and
laid *it* on the boil, and he recovered.
8 Now Hezekiah said to Isaiah, “What will be the sign that
the LORD will heal me, and that I shall go up to the house of the
LORD the third day?”
9 Isaiah said, “[a]This shall be the sign to you from the LORD,
that the LORD will do the thing that He has spoken: shall the
shadow go forward ten steps or go back ten steps?”
10 So Hezekiah [1]answered, “It is easy for the shadow to decline
ten steps; no, but let the shadow turn backward ten steps.”
11 Isaiah the prophet cried to the LORD, and [a]He brought the
shadow on the [1]stairway back ten steps by which it had gone
down on the [1]stairway of Ahaz.
12 [a]At that time [1]Berodach-baladan a son of Baladan, king of
Babylon, sent letters and a present to Hezekiah, for he heard
that Hezekiah had been sick.

33 [a]2 Kin 19:28
34 [a]2 Kin 20:6; Is 31:5 [b]1 Kin 11:12, 13
35 [1]Lit *they* [2]Lit *dead bodies* [a]2 Sam 24:16; 2 Chr 32:21
36 [a]2 Kin 19:7, 28, 33 [b]Jon 1:2
37 [1]Some ancient mss read *Adrammelech and Sharezer his sons smote him* [a]2 Kin 19:17, 31 [b]Gen 8:4; Jer 51:27 [c]Ezra 4:2
20:1 [1]Lit *sick to the point of death* [a]2 Chr 32:24; Is 38:1-22 [b]2 Sam 17:23
3 [1]Lit *great weeping* [a]Neh 5:19; 13:14, 22, 31 [b]2 Kin 18:3-6 [c]2 Sam 12:21, 22
5 [a]1 Sam 9:16; 10:1 [b]2 Kin 19:20 [c]Ps 39:12
6 [1]Lit *days* [a]2 Kin 19:34
9 [a]Is 38:7
10 [1]Lit *said*
11 [1]Lit *steps* [a]Josh 10:12-14; Is 38:8
12 [1]Many mss and ancient versions read *Merodach-baladan;* cf Is 39:1 [a]2 Chr 32:31; Is 39:1-8

13 Hezekiah listened to them, and showed them [a]all his
treasure house, the silver and the gold and the spices and the
precious oil and the house of his armor and all that was found
in his treasuries. There was nothing in his house nor in all his
dominion that Hezekiah did not show them.
14 Then Isaiah the prophet came to King Hezekiah and said to
him, "What did these men say, and from where have they
come to you?" And Hezekiah said, "They have come from a far
country, from Babylon."
15 He said, "What have they seen in your house?" So Hezekiah
[1]answered, "They have seen all that is in my house; there is
nothing among my treasuries that I have not shown them."
16 Then Isaiah said to Hezekiah, "Hear the word of the LORD.
17 'Behold, the days are coming when [a]all that is in your
house, and all that your fathers have laid up in store to this day
will be carried to Babylon; nothing shall be left,' says the LORD.
18 'Some [a]of your sons who shall issue from you, whom you
will beget, will be taken away; and they will become [b]officials
in the palace of the king of Babylon.'"
19 Then Hezekiah said to Isaiah, "The word of the LORD which
you have spoken is [a]good." For he [1]thought, "Is it not so, if
there will be peace and truth in my days?"
20 [a]Now the rest of the acts of Hezekiah and all his might, and
how he [b]made the pool and the conduit and brought water into
the city, are they not written in the Book of the Chronicles of
the Kings of Judah?
686 B.C. 21 [a]So Hezekiah slept with his fathers, and Manasseh his son
became king in his place.

Chapter 21 Theme ______________________

697 B.C. **21** [a]Manasseh was twelve years old when he became king,
and he reigned fifty-five years in Jerusalem; and his
2 Chronicles 33 mother's name was Hephzibah.
2 [a]He did evil in the sight of the LORD, [b]according to the
abominations of the nations whom the LORD dispossessed
before the sons of Israel.
3 For [a]he rebuilt the high places which Hezekiah his father
had destroyed; and [b]he erected altars for Baal and made an
[1]Asherah, as Ahab king of Israel had done, and [c]worshiped all
the host of heaven and served them.
4 [a]He built altars in the house of the LORD, of which the LORD
had said, "[b]In Jerusalem I will put My name."
5 For he built altars for [a]all the host of heaven in [b]the two
courts of the house of the LORD.
6 [a]He made his son pass through the fire, [b]practiced witchcraft
and used divination, and dealt with mediums and spiritists. He
did much evil in the sight of the LORD provoking *Him to anger.*
7 Then [a]he set the carved image of Asherah that he had
made, in the house of which the LORD said to David and to his
son Solomon, "[b]In this house and in Jerusalem, which I have
chosen from all the tribes of Israel, I will put My name forever.

13 [a]2 Chr 32:27
15 [1]Lit *said*
17 [a]2 Kin 24:13; 25:13-15; 2 Chr 36:10; Jer 52:17-19
18 [a]2 Kin 24:12; 2 Chr 33:11 [b]Dan 1:3-7
19 [1]Lit *said* [a]1 Sam 3:18
20 [a]2 Chr 32:32 [b]Neh 3:16
21 [a]2 Chr 32:33
21:1 [a]2 Chr 33:1-9
2 [a]Jer 15:4 [b]2 Kin 16:3
3 [1]I.e. a wooden symbol of a female deity [a]2 Kin 18:4 [b]1 Kin 16:31-33 [c]Deut 17:2-5; 2 Kin 17:16; 23:5
4 [a]2 Kin 16:10-16 [b]2 Sam 7:13; 1 Kin 8:29
5 [a]2 Kin 23:4, 5 [b]1 Kin 7:12; 2 Kin 23:12
6 [a]Lev 18:21; 2 Kin 16:3; 17:17 [b]Lev 19:26, 31; Deut 18:10-14
7 [a]Deut 16:21; 2 Kin 23:6 [b]1 Kin 8:29; 9:3; 2 Chr 7:12, 16

8 "And I [a]will not make the feet of Israel wander anymore from the land which I gave their fathers, if only they will observe to do according to all that I have commanded them, and according to all the law that My servant Moses commanded them."

9 But they did not listen, and Manasseh [a]seduced them to do evil more than the nations whom the LORD destroyed before the sons of Israel.

10 Now the LORD spoke through His servants the prophets, saying,

11 "[a]Because Manasseh king of Judah has done these abominations, [b]having done wickedly more than all the Amorites did who *were* before him, and [c]has also made Judah sin [d]with his idols;

12 therefore thus says the LORD, the God of Israel, 'Behold, I am bringing *such* calamity on Jerusalem and Judah, that whoever hears of it, [a]both his ears will tingle.

13 '[a]I will stretch over Jerusalem the line of Samaria and the plummet of the house of Ahab, and I will wipe Jerusalem as one wipes a dish, wiping it and turning it upside down.

14 'I will abandon the remnant of My inheritance and deliver them into the hand of their enemies, and they will become as plunder and spoil to all their enemies;

15 because they have done evil in My sight, and have been provoking Me to anger since the day their fathers came from Egypt, even to this day.'"

16 [a]Moreover, Manasseh shed very much innocent blood until he had filled Jerusalem from one end to another; besides his sin [b]with which he made Judah sin, in doing evil in the sight of the LORD.

17 [a]Now the rest of the acts of Manasseh and all that he did and his sin which he [1]committed, are they not written in the Book of the Chronicles of the Kings of Judah?

18 [a]And Manasseh slept with his fathers and was buried in the garden of his own house, [b]in the garden of Uzza, and Amon his son became king in his place.

19 [a]Amon was twenty-two years old when he became king, and he reigned two years in Jerusalem; and his mother's name *was* Meshullemeth the daughter of Haruz of Jotbah. 642 B.C.

20 He did evil in the sight of the LORD, [a]as Manasseh his father had done.

21 For he walked in all the way that his father had walked, and served the idols that his father had served and worshiped them.

22 So [a]he forsook the LORD, the God of his fathers, and did not walk in the way of the LORD.

23 [a]The servants of Amon conspired against him and killed the king in his own house.

24 Then [a]the people of the land [1]killed all those who had conspired against King Amon, and the people of the land made Josiah his son king in his place.

25 Now the rest of the acts of Amon which he did, are they not written in the Book of the Chronicles of the Kings of Judah?

8 [a]2 Sam 7:10; 2 Kin 18:11, 12
9 [a]Prov 29:12
11 [a]2 Kin 21:2; 24:3, 4 [b]Gen 15:16; 1 Kin 21:26 [c]2 Kin 21:16 [d]2 Kin 21:21
12 [a]1 Sam 3:11; Jer 19:3
13 [a]Is 34:11; Amos 7:7, 8
16 [a]2 Kin 24:4 [b]2 Kin 21:11
17 [1]Lit *sinned* [a]2 Chr 33:11-19
18 [a]2 Chr 33:20 [b]2 Kin 21:26
19 [a]2 Chr 33:21-23
20 [a]2 Kin 21:2-6, 11, 16
22 [a]2 Kin 22:17; 1 Chr 28:9
23 [a]2 Kin 12:20; 14:19
24 [1]Lit *smote* [a]2 Kin 14:5

26 He was buried in his grave [a]in the garden of Uzza, and Josiah his son became king in his place.

26 [a]2 Kin 21:18

Chapter 22 Theme ________________________

640 B.C.

2 Chronicles 34

22 [a]Josiah was eight years old when he became king, and he reigned thirty-one years in Jerusalem; and his mother's name *was* Jedidah the daughter of Adaiah of [b]Bozkath.

2 He did right in the sight of the LORD and walked in all the way of his father David, nor did he [a]turn aside to the right or to the left.

3 Now [a]in the eighteenth year of King Josiah, the king sent Shaphan, the son of Azaliah the son of Meshullam the scribe, to the house of the LORD saying,

4 "[a]Go up to Hilkiah the high priest that he may [1]count the money brought in to the house of the LORD which the doorkeepers have gathered from the people.

5 "[a]Let them deliver it into the hand of the workmen who have the oversight of the house of the LORD, and let them give it to the workmen who are in the house of the LORD to repair the [1]damages of the house,

6 to the carpenters and the builders and the masons and for buying timber and hewn stone to repair the house.

7 "Only [a]no accounting shall be made with them for the money delivered into their hands, for they deal faithfully."

8 Then Hilkiah the high priest said to Shaphan the scribe, "[a]I have found the book of the law in the house of the LORD." And Hilkiah gave the book to Shaphan who read it.

9 Shaphan the scribe came to the king and brought back word to the king and said, "Your servants have emptied out the money that was found in the house, and have delivered it into the hand of the workmen who have the oversight of the house of the LORD."

10 Moreover, Shaphan the scribe told the king saying, "Hilkiah the priest has given me a book." And Shaphan read it in the presence of the king.

11 When the king heard the words of the book of the law, [a]he tore his clothes.

12 Then the king commanded Hilkiah the priest, [a]Ahikam the son of Shaphan, [1b]Achbor the son of Micaiah, Shaphan the scribe, and Asaiah the king's servant saying,

13 "Go, inquire of the LORD for me and the people and all Judah concerning the words of this book that has been found, for [a]great is the wrath of the LORD that burns against us, because our fathers have not listened to the words of this book, to do according to all that is written concerning us."

14 So Hilkiah the priest, Ahikam, Achbor, Shaphan, and Asaiah went to Huldah the prophetess, the wife of Shallum the son of [1a]Tikvah, the son of Harhas, keeper of the wardrobe (now she lived in Jerusalem in the [b]Second Quarter); and they spoke to her.

22:1 [a]2 Chr 34:1 [b]Josh 15:39

2 [a]Deut 5:32; Josh 1:7

3 [a]2 Chr 34:8

4 [1]Or *total* [a]2 Kin 12:4, 9, 10

5 [1]Lit *breach* [a]2 Kin 12:11-14

7 [a]2 Kin 12:15; 1 Cor 4:2

8 [a]Deut 31:24-26; 2 Chr 34:14, 15

11 [a]Gen 37:34; Josh 7:6

12 [1]In 2 Chr 34:20, *Abdon, son of Micah* [a]2 Kin 25:22; Jer 26:24 [b]2 Chr 34:20

13 [a]Deut 29:23-28; 31:17, 18

14 [1]In 2 Chr 34:22, *Tokhath, son of Hasrah* [a]2 Chr 34:22 [b]Zeph 1:10

16 [a]Deut 29:27; Dan 9:11-14

17 [a]Deut 29:25, 26; 2 Kin 21:22

18 [a]2 Chr 34:26

19 [a]1 Sam 24:5; Ps 51:17 [b]Ex 10:3; 1 Kin 21:29 [c]Lev 26:31 [d]Jer 26:6 [e]2 Kin 22:11

20 [a]2 Kin 23:30

15 She said to them, "Thus says the LORD God of Israel, 'Tell the man who sent you to me,

16 thus says the LORD, "Behold, I [a]bring evil on this place and on its inhabitants, *even* all the words of the book which the king of Judah has read.

17 "[a]Because they have forsaken Me and have burned incense to other gods that they might provoke Me to anger with all the work of their hands, therefore My wrath burns against this place, and it shall not be quenched."'

18 "But to [a]the king of Judah who sent you to inquire of the LORD thus shall you say to him, 'Thus says the LORD God of Israel, "*Regarding* the words which you have heard,

19 [a]because your heart was tender and [b]you humbled yourself before the LORD when you heard what I spoke against this place and against its inhabitants that they should become [c]a desolation and a [d]curse, and you have [e]torn your clothes and wept before Me, I truly have heard you," declares the LORD.

20 "Therefore, behold, I will gather you to your fathers, and [a]you will be gathered to your grave in peace, and your eyes will not see all the evil which I will bring on this place."'" So they brought back word to the king.

Chapter 23 Theme ____

23:1 [a]2 Chr 34:29-32

2 [a]Deut 31:10-13 [b]2 Kin 22:8

3 [1]Lit *took a stand in* [a]2 Kin 11:14, 17 [b]Deut 13:4

4 [1]Lit *keepers of the threshold* [2]I.e. a wooden symbol of a female deity, and so throughout the ch [a]2 Kin 25:18; Jer 52:24 [b]2 Kin 21:3, 7; 2 Chr 33:3 [c]2 Kin 23:15

5 [a]2 Kin 21:3

6 [1]Lit *sons of the people* [a]2 Kin 23:15 [b]2 Chr 34:4

23 [a]Then the king sent, and they gathered to him all the elders of Judah and of Jerusalem.

2 The king went up to the house of the LORD and all the men of Judah and all the inhabitants of Jerusalem with him, and the priests and the prophets and all the people, both small and great; and [a]he read in their hearing all the words of the book of the covenant [b]which was found in the house of the LORD.

3 [a]The king stood by the pillar and made a covenant before the LORD, [b]to walk after the LORD, and to keep His commandments and His testimonies and His statutes with all *his* heart and all *his* soul, to carry out the words of this covenant that were written in this book. And all the people [1]entered into the covenant.

4 Then the king commanded Hilkiah the high priest and [a]the priests of the second order and the [1]doorkeepers, [b]to bring out of the temple of the LORD all the vessels that were made for Baal, for [2]Asherah, and for all the host of heaven; and [c]he burned them outside Jerusalem in the fields of the Kidron, and carried their ashes to Bethel.

5 He did away with the idolatrous priests whom the kings of Judah had appointed to burn incense in the high places in the cities of Judah and in the surrounding area of Jerusalem, also those who burned incense to Baal, to the sun and to the moon and to the constellations and to all the [a]host of heaven.

6 He brought out the Asherah from the house of the LORD outside Jerusalem to the brook Kidron, and burned it at the brook Kidron, and [a]ground *it* to dust, and [b]threw its dust on the graves of the [1]common people.

7 He also broke down the houses of the [a]*male* cult prostitutes
which *were* in the house of the LORD, where [b]the women were
weaving [1]hangings for the Asherah.
8 Then he brought all the priests from the cities of Judah, and
defiled the high places where the priests had burned incense,
from [a]Geba to Beersheba; and he broke down the high places of
the gates which *were* at the entrance of the gate of Joshua the
governor of the city, which *were* on one's left at the city gate.
9 Nevertheless [a]the priests of the high places did not go up to
the altar of the LORD in Jerusalem, but they ate unleavened
bread among their brothers.
10 [a]He also defiled [1]Topheth, which is in the valley of the son
of Hinnom, [b]that no man might make his son or his daughter
pass through the fire for [c]Molech.
11 He did away with the horses which the kings of Judah had
given to the [a]sun, at the entrance of the house of the LORD, by
the chamber of Nathan-melech the official, which *was* in the
precincts; and he burned the chariots of the sun with fire.
12 [a]The altars which *were* on the roof, the upper chamber of
Ahaz, which the kings of Judah had made, and [b]the altars
which Manasseh had made in the two courts of the house of
the LORD, the king broke down; and he [1]smashed them there
and [c]threw their dust into the brook Kidron.
13 The high places which *were* before Jerusalem, which *were*
on the right of [a]the mount of destruction which Solomon the
king of Israel had built for [b]Ashtoreth the abomination of the
Sidonians, and for [c]Chemosh the abomination of Moab, and for
Milcom the abomination of the sons of Ammon, the king defiled.
14 [a]He broke in pieces the *sacred* pillars and cut down the
Asherim and [b]filled their places with human bones.
15 Furthermore, [a]the altar that *was* at Bethel *and* the [b]high
place which Jeroboam the son of Nebat, who made Israel sin,
had made, even that altar and the high place he broke down.
Then he [1c]demolished its stones, ground them to dust, and
burned the Asherah.
16 Now when Josiah turned, he saw the graves that *were*
there on the mountain, and he sent and took the bones from the
graves and burned *them* on the altar and defiled it [a]according to
the word of the LORD which the man of God proclaimed, who
proclaimed these things.
17 Then he said, "What is this monument that I see?" And
the men of the city told him, "[a]It is the grave of the man of
God who came from Judah and proclaimed these things which
you have done against the altar of Bethel."
18 He said, "Let him alone; let no one disturb his bones." So
they [1]left his bones undisturbed [a]with the bones of the prophet
who came from Samaria.
19 Josiah also removed all the houses of the high places which
were [a]in the cities of Samaria, which the kings of Israel had
made provoking [1]the LORD; and he did to them [2]just as he had
done in Bethel.

7 [1]Or *tents;* lit *houses* [a]1 Kin 14:24; 15:12 [b]Ex 35:25, 26; Ezek 16:16

8 [a]Josh 21:17; 1 Kin 15:22

9 [a]Ezek 44:10-14

10 [1]I.e. place of burning [a]Is 30:33; Jer 7:31, 32; 19:4-6 [b]Lev 18:21 [c]1 Kin 11:7

11 [a]Deut 4:19; Job 31:26; Ezek 8:16

12 [1]Or *ran from there* [a]Jer 19:13; Zeph 1:5 [b]2 Kin 21:5; 2 Chr 33:5 [c]2 Kin 23:4, 6

13 [a]1 Kin 11:7 [b]1 Kin 11:5 [c]Num 21:29

14 [a]Deut 7:5, 25 [b]2 Kin 23:16

15 [1]So the Gr; Heb *burned the high place* [a]1 Kin 13:1 [b]1 Kin 12:28-33 [c]2 Kin 23:6

16 [a]1 Kin 13:2

17 [a]1 Kin 13:1, 30, 31

18 [1]Lit *let his bones escape with* [a]1 Kin 13:11, 31

19 [1]So with ancient versions [2]Lit *according to all the acts* [a]2 Chr 34:6, 7

20 [a]2 Kin 10:25; 11:18

20 All the priests of the high places who *were* there [a]he
slaughtered on the altars and burned human bones on them;
then he returned to Jerusalem.

21 [a]2 Chr 35:1-17 [b]Num 9:2-4; Deut 16:2-8

21 Then the king commanded all the people saying, "[a]Celebrate
the Passover to the LORD your God [b]as it is written in this book
of the covenant."

22 [a]2 Chr 35:18, 19

22 [a]Surely such a Passover had not been celebrated from the
days of the judges who judged Israel, nor in all the days of the
kings of Israel and of the kings of Judah.
23 But in the eighteenth year of King Josiah, this Passover was 622 B.C.
observed to the LORD in Jerusalem.

24 [1]Lit *consumed* [2]Or *perform* [a]Lev 19:31; 2 Kin 21:6 [b]Gen 31:19 mg [c]2 Kin 21:11, 21 [d]Deut 18:10-22 [e]2 Kin 22:8

24 Moreover, Josiah [1]removed [a]the mediums and the spiritists
and the [b]teraphim and [c]the idols and all the abominations that
were seen in the land of Judah and in Jerusalem, [d]that he
might [2]confirm the words of the law which were written [e]in
the book that Hilkiah the priest found in the house of the LORD.

25 [a]2 Kin 18:5

25 Before him there was no king [a]like him who turned to the
LORD with all his heart and with all his soul and with all his
might, according to all the law of Moses; nor did any like him
arise after him.

26 [a]2 Kin 21:11-13; Jer 15:4

26 However, the LORD did not turn from the fierceness of His
great wrath with which His anger burned against Judah, [a]because
of all the provocations with which Manasseh had provoked Him.

27 [1]Lit *house* [a]2 Kin 18:11 [b]2 Kin 21:13, 14

27 The LORD said, "I will remove Judah also from My sight, [a]as
I have removed Israel. And [b]I will cast off Jerusalem, this city
which I have chosen, and the [1]temple of which I said, 'My
name shall be there.'"
28 Now the rest of the acts of Josiah and all that he did, are
they not written in the Book of the Chronicles of the Kings of
Judah?

29 [a]2 Chr 35:20-24 [b]Jer 46:2 [c]Judg 5:19

29 [a]In his days [b]Pharaoh Neco king of Egypt went up to the
king of Assyria to the river Euphrates. And King Josiah went to
meet him, and when *Pharaoh Neco* saw him he killed him at
[c]Megiddo.

30 [1]Lit *him, dead* [a]2 Kin 9:28 [b]2 Chr 36:1-4

30 [a]His servants drove [1]his body in a chariot from Megiddo,
and brought him to Jerusalem and buried him in his own tomb.
[b]Then the people of the land took Jehoahaz the son of Josiah
and anointed him and made him king in place of his father.

31 [a]1 Chr 3:15; Jer 22:11 [b]2 Kin 24:18

31 [a]Jehoahaz was twenty-three years old when he became king, 609 B.C.
and he reigned three months in Jerusalem; and his mother's
name was [b]Hamutal the daughter of Jeremiah of Libnah.

32 [a]2 Kin 21:2-7

32 He did evil in the sight of the LORD, [a]according to all that
his fathers had done.

33 [a]2 Kin 23:29 [b]2 Kin 25:6 [c]1 Kin 8:65

33 [a]Pharaoh Neco imprisoned him at [b]Riblah in the land of
[c]Hamath, that he might not reign in Jerusalem; and he imposed
on the land a fine of one hundred talents of silver and a talent
of gold.

34 [1]So with Gr; Heb *he came* [a]1 Chr 3:15 [b]2 Kin 24:17; 2 Chr 36:4 [c]Jer 22:11, 12; Ezek 19:3, 4

34 Pharaoh Neco made [a]Eliakim the son of Josiah king in the
place of Josiah his father, and [b]changed his name to Jehoiakim.
But he took Jehoahaz away and [1c]brought *him* to Egypt, and he
died there.

35 So Jehoiakim [a]gave the silver and gold to Pharaoh, but he
taxed the land in order to give the money at the [1]command of
Pharaoh. He exacted the silver and gold from the people of the
land, each according to his valuation, to give it to Pharaoh Neco.
36 [a]Jehoiakim was twenty-five years old when he became
king, and he reigned eleven years in Jerusalem; and his mother's
name *was* Zebidah the daughter of Pedaiah of Rumah.
37 He did evil in the sight of the LORD, [a]according to all that
his fathers had done.

Chapter 24 Theme ____________________

24 [a]In his days Nebuchadnezzar king of Babylon came up,
and Jehoiakim became his servant *for* three years; then
he turned and rebelled against him.
2 The LORD sent against him [a]bands of Chaldeans, [b]bands of
Arameans, [c]bands of Moabites, and bands of Ammonites. So He
sent them against Judah to destroy it, [d]according to the word of
the LORD which He had spoken through His servants the
prophets.
605 B.C. 3 [a]Surely at the [1]command of the LORD it came upon Judah, to
remove *them* from His sight [b]because of the sins of Manasseh,
according to all that he had done,
4 and [a]also for the innocent blood which he shed, for he
filled Jerusalem with innocent blood; and the LORD would not
forgive.
5 Now the rest of the acts of Jehoiakim and all that he did,
are they not written in the Book of the Chronicles of the Kings
of Judah?
6 So [a]Jehoiakim slept with his fathers, and Jehoiachin his son
became king in his place.
7 [a]The king of Egypt did not come out of his land again, [b]for
the king of Babylon had taken all that belonged to the king of
Egypt from [c]the brook of Egypt to the river Euphrates.
597 B.C. **8** [a]Jehoiachin was [b]eighteen years old when he became king,
and he reigned three months in Jerusalem; and his mother's
name *was* Nehushta the daughter of Elnathan of Jerusalem.
9 He did evil in the sight of the LORD, [a]according to all that
his father had done.
10 At that time the servants of Nebuchadnezzar king of
Babylon went up to Jerusalem, and the city came under siege.
11 And Nebuchadnezzar the king of Babylon came to the city,
while his servants were besieging it.
12 [a]Jehoiachin the king of Judah went out to the king of
Babylon, he and his mother and his servants and his captains
and his officials. So [b]the king of Babylon took him captive in
the eighth year of his reign.
13 [a]He carried out from there all the treasures of the house of
the LORD, and the treasures of the king's house, and [b]cut in pieces
all the vessels of gold [c]which Solomon king of Israel had made
in the temple of the LORD, just as the LORD had said.

35 [1]Lit *mouth* [a]2 Kin 23:33
36 [a]2 Chr 36:5; Jer 22:18, 19; 26:1
37 [a]2 Kin 23:32
24:1 [a]2 Chr 36:6; Jer 25:1; Dan 1:1, 2
2 [a]Jer 35:11f [b]2 Kin 6:23 [c]2 Kin 13:20 [d]2 Kin 23:27
3 [1]Lit *mouth* [a]2 Kin 18:25 [b]2 Kin 23:26
4 [a]2 Kin 21:16
6 [a]Jer 22:18, 19
7 [a]Jer 37:5-7 [b]Jer 46:2 [c]Gen 15:18
8 [a]1 Chr 3:16 [b]2 Chr 36:9
9 [a]2 Kin 21:2-7
12 [a]Jer 22:24-30; 24:1; 29:1, 2 [b]2 Chr 36:10
13 [a]2 Kin 20:17; Is 39:6 [b]2 Kin 25:13-15 [c]1 Kin 7:48-50

14 [a]Jer 24:1 [b]2 Kin 24:16; Jer 52:28 [c]Jer 24:1; 29:2 [d]2 Kin 25:12

14 Then [a]he led away into exile all Jerusalem and all the captains and all the mighty men of valor, [b]ten thousand captives, and [c]all the craftsmen and the smiths. None remained [d]except the poorest people of the land.

15 [a]2 Chr 36:10; Jer 22:24-28; Ezek 17:12

15 So [a]he led Jehoiachin away into exile to Babylon; also the king's mother and the king's wives and his officials and the leading men of the land, he led away into exile from Jerusalem to Babylon.

16 [a]2 Kin 24:14

16 All the men of valor, [a]seven thousand, and the craftsmen and the smiths, one thousand, all strong and fit for war, and these the king of Babylon brought into exile to Babylon.

17 [1]I.e. Jehoiachin's uncle [a]2 Chr 36:10-13; Jer 37:1

17 [a]Then the king of Babylon made [1]his uncle Mattaniah king in his place, and changed his name to Zedekiah.

Exiles of Judah to Babylon

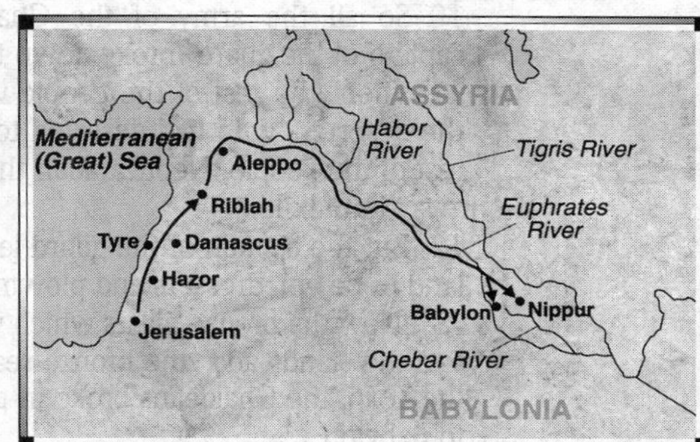

18 [a]Jer 27:1; 28:1; 52:1 [b]2 Kin 23:31

18 [a]Zedekiah was twenty-one years old when he became king, and he reigned eleven years in Jerusalem; and his mother's name was [b]Hamutal the daughter of Jeremiah of Libnah.

19 [a]2 Kin 23:37

19 He did evil in the sight of the LORD, [a]according to all that Jehoiakim had done.

20 [a]Deut 4:24; 29:27; 2 Kin 23:26 [b]2 Chr 36:13; Ezek 17:15

20 For [a]through the anger of the LORD *this* came about in Jerusalem and Judah until He cast them out from His presence. And [b]Zedekiah rebelled against the king of Babylon.

Chapter 25 Theme

25:1 [1]Lit *against it* [a]2 Chr 36:17-20; Jer 39:1-7 [b]Jer 21:2; 34:1, 2; Ezek 24:2 [c]Ezek 21:22

25 [a]Now in the ninth year of his reign, on the tenth day of the tenth month, [b]Nebuchadnezzar king of Babylon came, he and all his army, against Jerusalem, camped against it and [c]built a siege wall all around [1]it.

2 So the city was under siege until the eleventh year of King Zedekiah.

586 B.C.

3 [a]2 Kin 6:24, 25; Lam 4:9, 10

3 On the ninth day of the *fourth* month [a]the famine was so severe in the city that there was no food for the people of the land.

4 [1]So some ancient mss and versions; M.T. *he* [a]Ezek 33:21 [b]Neh 3:15

4 [a]Then the city was broken into, and all the men of war *fled* by night by way of the gate between the two walls beside [b]the king's garden, though the Chaldeans were all around the city. And [1]they went by way of the Arabah.

5 But the army of the Chaldeans pursued the king and overtook him in the plains of Jericho and all his army was scattered from him.

6 [1]Lit *they spoke judgment with him* [a]Jer 34:21, 22 [b]Jer 32:4 [c]2 Kin 23:33

6 Then [a]they captured the king and [b]brought him to the king of Babylon at [c]Riblah, and [1]he passed sentence on him.

7 [a]Jer 39:6, 7 [b]Ezek 12:13

7 [a]They slaughtered the sons of Zedekiah before his eyes, then [b]put out the eyes of Zedekiah and bound him with bronze fetters and brought him to Babylon.

8 [a]Now on the seventh day of the [b]fifth month, which was
the nineteenth year of King Nebuchadnezzar, king of Babylon,
Nebuzaradan the captain of the guard, a servant of the king of
Babylon, came to Jerusalem.
9 [a]He burned the house of the LORD, [b]the king's house, and
all the houses of Jerusalem; even every great house he burned
with fire.
10 So all the army of the Chaldeans who *were with* the
captain of the guard [a]broke down the walls around Jerusalem.
11 Then [a]the rest of the people who were left in the city and
the deserters who had deserted to the king of Babylon and the
rest of the people, Nebuzaradan the captain of the guard carried
away into exile.
12 But the captain of the guard left some of [a]the poorest of the
land to be vinedressers and plowmen.
13 [a]Now the bronze pillars which were in the house of the LORD,
and the stands and [b]the bronze sea which were in the house of
the LORD, the Chaldeans broke in pieces and carried the [1]bronze
to Babylon.
14 [a]They took away the pots, the shovels, the snuffers, the
spoons, and all the bronze vessels which were used in *temple*
service.
15 The captain of the guard also took away the firepans and
the basins, what was fine gold and what was fine silver.
16 The two pillars, the one sea, and the stands which Solomon
had made for the house of the LORD—[a]the bronze of all these
vessels was beyond weight.
17 [a]The height of the one pillar was eighteen [1]cubits, and a
bronze capital was on it; the height of the capital was three
[1]cubits, with a network and pomegranates on the capital all
around, all of bronze. And the second pillar was like these with
network.
18 Then the captain of the guard took [a]Seraiah the chief priest
and [b]Zephaniah the second priest, with the three [1]officers of
the temple.
19 From the city he took one official who was overseer of the
men of war, and [a]five [1]of the king's advisers who were found in
the city; and the [2]scribe of the captain of the army who
mustered the people of the land; and sixty men of the people of
the land who were found in the city.
20 Nebuzaradan the captain of the guard took them and
brought them to the king of Babylon at [a]Riblah.
21 Then the king of Babylon struck them down and put them
to death at Riblah in the land of Hamath. [a]So Judah was led
away into exile from its land.
22 Now *as for* the people who were left in the land of Judah,
whom Nebuchadnezzar king of Babylon had left, he appointed
[a]Gedaliah the son of Ahikam, the son of Shaphan over them.
23 [a]When all the captains of the forces, they and *their* men,
heard that the king of Babylon had appointed Gedaliah
governor, they came to Gedaliah to [b]Mizpah, namely, Ishmael

8 [a]Jer 52:12 [b]Jer 39:8-12

9 [a]1 Kin 9:8; 2 Chr 36:19; Ps 74:3-7 [b]Amos 2:5

10 [a]2 Kin 14:13; Neh 1:3

11 [a]2 Chr 36:20

12 [a]2 Kin 24:14; Jer 40:7

13 [1]Lit *bronze of them* [a]1 Kin 7:15-22; 2 Kin 20:17; 2 Chr 3:15-17; 36:18 [b]1 Kin 7:23-26; 2 Chr 4:2-4

14 [a]Ex 27:3; 1 Kin 7:47-50; 2 Chr 4:16

16 [a]1 Kin 7:47

17 [1]I.e. One cubit equals approx 18 in. [a]1 Kin 7:15-22

18 [1]Lit *keepers of the door* [a]1 Chr 6:14; Ezra 7:1 [b]Jer 21:1; 29:25, 29

19 [1]Lit *men of those seeing the king's face* [2]Or *scribe, a captain* [a]Esth 1:14

20 [a]2 Kin 23:33

21 [a]Deut 28:64; 2 Kin 23:27

22 [a]Jer 39:14; 40:7-9

23 [a]Jer 40:7-9 [b]Josh 18:26

25 [1]Lit *seed* [2]Lit *and ten men with him* [a]Jer 41:1, 2

26 [a]Jer 43:4-7

27 [1]Lit *lifted up the head of* [a]Jer 52:31-34 [b]2 Kin 24:12, 15 [c]Gen 40:13, 20

28 [a]Dan 2:37; 5:18, 19

29 [1]Lit *he* [2]Lit *ate bread* [3]Lit *his presence* [a]2 Sam 9:7

30 [a]Neh 11:23; 12:47

the son of Nethaniah, and Johanan the son of Kareah, and
Seraiah the son of Tanhumeth the Netophathite, and Jaazaniah
the son of the Maacathite, they and their men.
24 Gedaliah swore to them and their men and said to them,
"Do not be afraid of the servants of the Chaldeans; live in the
land and serve the king of Babylon, and it will be well with
you."
25 [a]But it came about in the seventh month, that Ishmael the
son of Nethaniah, the son of Elishama, of the royal [1]family,
came [2]with ten men and struck Gedaliah down so that he died
along with the Jews and the Chaldeans who were with him at
Mizpah.
26 [a]Then all the people, both small and great, and the captains
of the forces arose and went to Egypt; for they were afraid of
the Chaldeans.
27 [a]Now it came about in the thirty-seventh year of [b]the exile
of Jehoiachin king of Judah, in the twelfth month, on the
twenty-seventh *day* of the month, that Evil-merodach king of
Babylon, in the year that he became king, [1c]released Jehoiachin
king of Judah from prison;
28 and he [a]spoke kindly to him and set his throne above the
throne of the kings who *were* with him in Babylon.
29 [1]Jehoiachin changed his prison clothes and [2a]had his meals
in [3]the king's presence regularly all the days of his life;
30 and for his [a]allowance, a regular allowance was given him
by the king, a portion for each day, all the days of his life.

560 B.C.

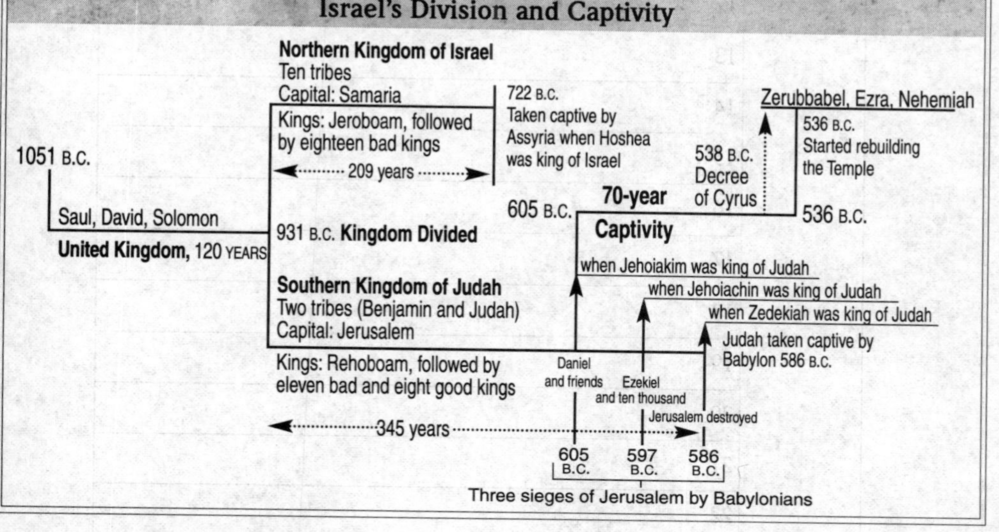

2 Kings at a Glance

Theme of 2 Kings:

Author:

Date:

Purpose:

Key Word

Segment Divisions

		Chapter Themes
		1
		2
		3
		4
		5
		6
		7
		8
		9
		10
		11
		12
		13
		14
		15
		16
		17
		18
		19
		20
		21
		22
		23
		24
		25

THE HISTORICAL CHART OF THE KINGS AND PROPHETS OF ISRAEL AND JUDAH

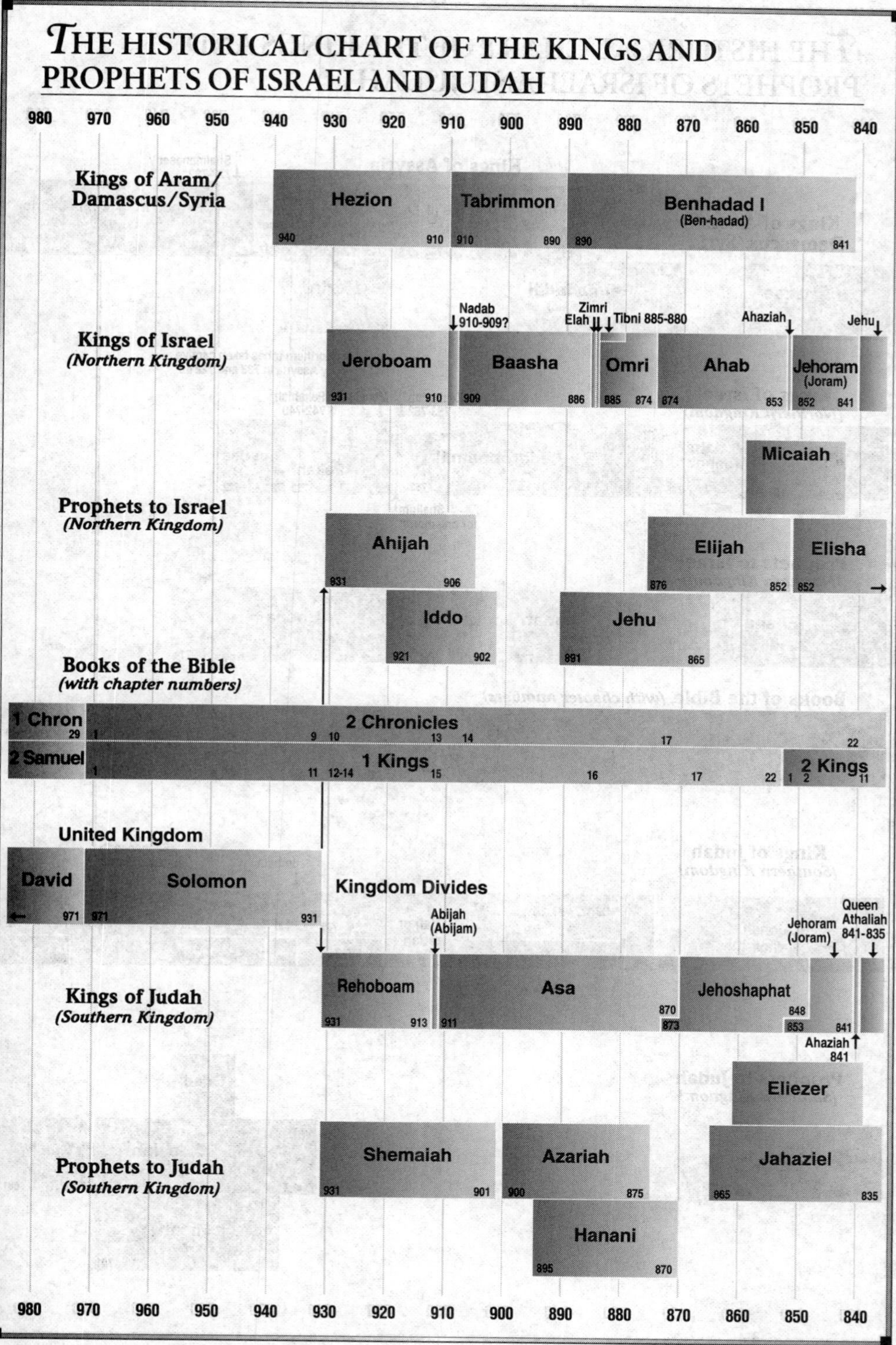

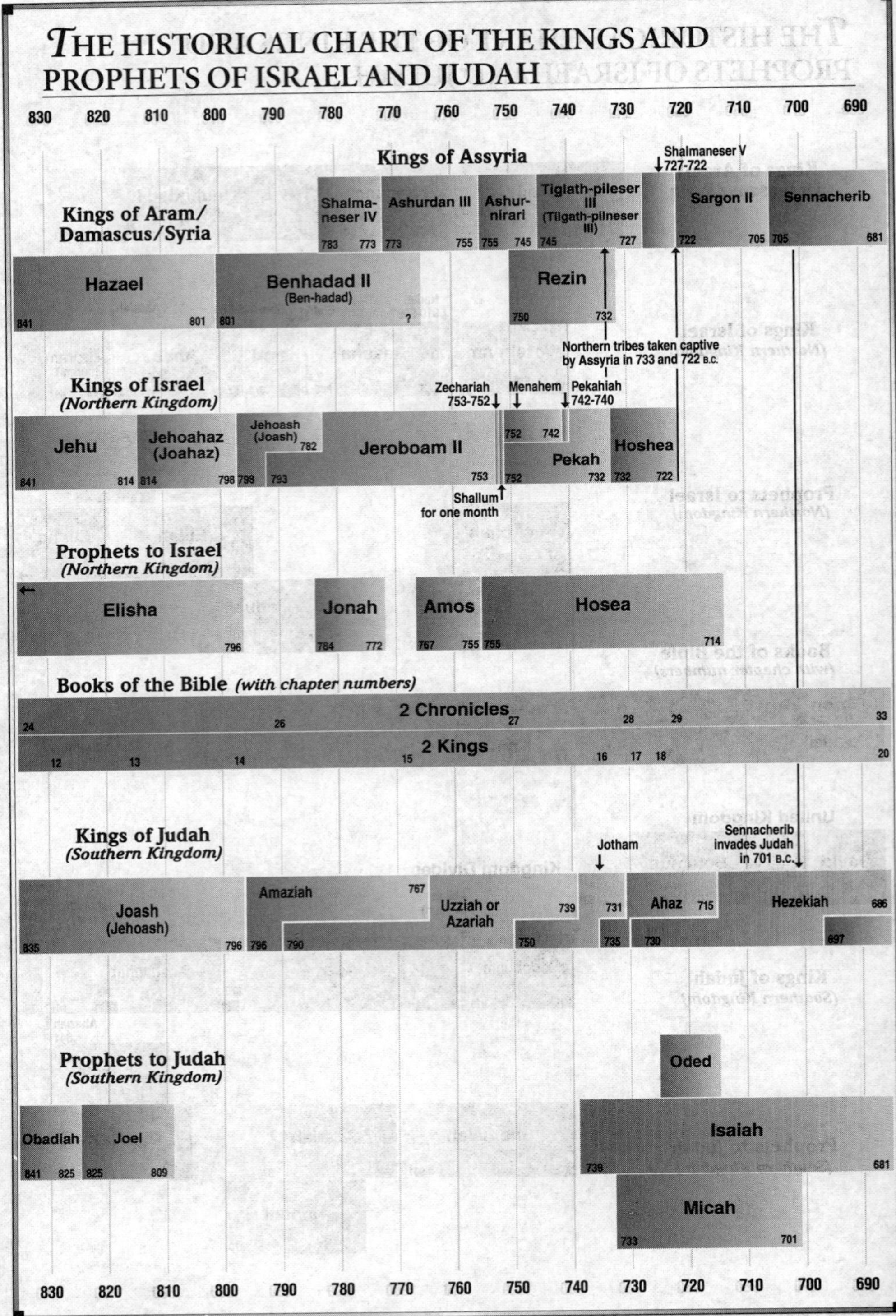
THE HISTORICAL CHART OF THE KINGS AND PROPHETS OF ISRAEL AND JUDAH
830 820 810 800 790 780 770 760 750 740 730 720 710 700 690
Kings of Assyria
Shalmaneser V 727-722
Shalmaneser IV 783 773
Ashurdan III 773 755
Ashur-nirari 755 745
Tiglath-pileser III (Tilgath-pilneser III) 745 727
Sargon II 722 705
Sennacherib 705 681
Kings of Aram/ Damascus/Syria
Hazael 841 801
Benhadad II (Ben-hadad) 801 ?
Rezin 750 732
Northern tribes taken captive by Assyria in 733 and 722 B.C.
Kings of Israel (Northern Kingdom)
Zechariah 753-752
Menahem
Pekahiah 742-740
Jehu 841 814
Jehoahaz (Joahaz) 814 798
Jehoash (Joash) 798 782
Jeroboam II 793 753
752 742
Pekah 752 732
Hoshea 732 722
Shallum for one month
Prophets to Israel (Northern Kingdom)
Elisha 796
Jonah 784 772
Amos 767 755
Hosea 755 714
Books of the Bible (with chapter numbers)
2 Chronicles 24 26 27 28 29 33
2 Kings 12 13 14 15 16 17 18 20
Kings of Judah (Southern Kingdom)
Jotham
Sennacherib invades Judah in 701 B.C.
Joash (Jehoash) 835 796
Amaziah 796 767
Uzziah or Azariah 790 739
750 731
735
Ahaz 730 715
Hezekiah 686
697
Prophets to Judah (Southern Kingdom)
Oded
Obadiah 841 825
Joel 825 809
Isaiah 739 681
Micah 733 701
830 820 810 800 790 780 770 760 750 740 730 720 710 700 690

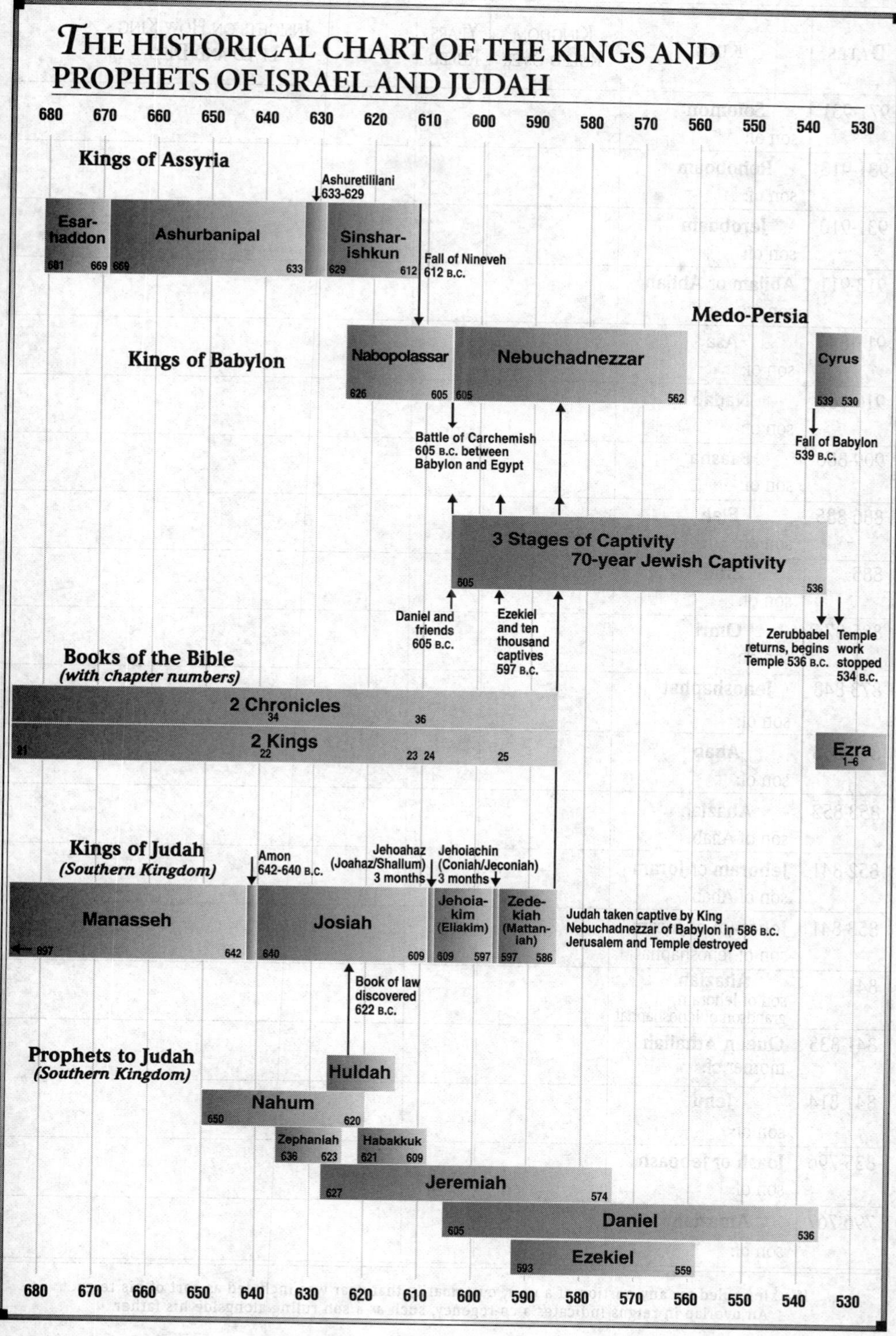
THE HISTORICAL CHART OF THE KINGS AND PROPHETS OF ISRAEL AND JUDAH
680 670 660 650 640 630 620 610 600 590 580 570 560 550 540 530
Kings of Assyria
Ashuretililani 633-629
Esar-haddon 681 669
Ashurbanipal 669 633
Sinshar-ishkun 629 612
Fall of Nineveh 612 B.C.
Medo-Persia
Kings of Babylon
Nabopolassar 626 605
Nebuchadnezzar 605 562
Cyrus 539 530
Battle of Carchemish 605 B.C. between Babylon and Egypt
Fall of Babylon 539 B.C.
3 Stages of Captivity
70-year Jewish Captivity
605 536
Daniel and friends 605 B.C.
Ezekiel and ten thousand captives 597 B.C.
Zerubbabel returns, begins Temple 536 B.C.
Temple work stopped 534 B.C.
Books of the Bible
(with chapter numbers)
2 Chronicles 34 36
2 Kings 21 22 23 24 25
Ezra 1–6
Kings of Judah
(Southern Kingdom)
Amon 642-640 B.C.
Jehoahaz (Joahaz/Shallum) 3 months
Jehoiachin (Coniah/Jeconiah) 3 months
Manasseh 697 642
Josiah 640 609
Jehoia-kim (Eliakim) 609 597
Zede-kiah (Mattan-iah) 597 586
Judah taken captive by King Nebuchadnezzar of Babylon in 586 B.C. Jerusalem and Temple destroyed
Book of law discovered 622 B.C.
Prophets to Judah
(Southern Kingdom)
Huldah
Nahum 650 620
Zephaniah 636 623
Habakkuk 621 609
Jeremiah 627 574
Daniel 605 536
Ezekiel 593 559
680 670 660 650 640 630 620 610 600 590 580 570 560 550 540 530

The Kings of Israel and Judah

Dates	King	Kingdom Ruled over	Years Ruled	Insights on How King Lived and Died
971-931	**Solomon** son of:			
931-913	**Rehoboam** son of:			
931-910	**Jeroboam** son of:			
913-911	**Abijam** or **Abijah** son of:			
911-870	**Asa** son of:			
910-909	**Nadab** son of:			
909-886	**Baasha** son of:			
886-885	**Elah** son of:			
885	**Zimri** son of:			
885-874	**Omri** son of:			
873-848	**Jehoshaphat** son of:			
874-853	**Ahab** son of:			
853-852	**Ahaziah** son of Ahab			
852-841	**Jehoram** or **Joram** son of Ahab			
853-841	**Jehoram** or **Joram** son of Jehoshaphat			
841	**Ahaziah** son of Jehoram, grandson of Jehoshaphat			
841-835	**Queen Athaliah** mother of:			
841-814	**Jehu** son of:			
835-796	**Joash** or **Jehoash** son of:			
796-767	**Amaziah** son of:			

If a king ruled for any portion of a year, customarily that year was included as part of his reign. An overlap in reigns indicates a co-regency, such as a son ruling alongside his father.

THE KINGS OF ISRAEL AND JUDAH

DATES	KING	KINGDOM RULED OVER	YEARS RULED	INSIGHTS ON HOW KING LIVED AND DIED
814-798	**Jehoahaz** or **Joahaz** son of:			
798-782	**Jehoash** or **Joash** son of:			
790-739	**Azariah** or **Uzziah** son of:			
793-753	**Jeroboam II** son of:			
753-752	**Zechariah** son of:			
752	**Shallum** son of:			
752-742	**Menahem** son of:			
742-740	**Pekahiah** son of:			
752-732	**Pekah** son of:			
750-731	**Jotham** son of:			
735-715	**Ahaz** son of:			
732-722	**Hoshea** son of:			
728-686	**Hezekiah** son of:			
697-642	**Manasseh** son of:			
642-640	**Amon** son of:			
640-609	**Josiah** son of:			
609	**Jehoahaz** or **Joahaz** or **Shallum** son of:			
609-597	**Jehoiakim** or **Eliakim** son of:			
597	**Jehoiachin** or **Coniah** or **Jeconiah** son of:			
597-586	**Zedekiah** or **Mattaniah** son of:			

If a king ruled for any portion of a year, customarily that year was included as part of his reign. An overlap in reigns indicates a co-regency, such as a son ruling alongside his father.

1 CHRONICLES דברי הימים א
DIVRE HAYAMIM ALEPH

Judah had watched as Assyria captured the last of Israel in 722 B.C. In 586 B.C., when the Babylonians besieged Jerusalem for the third and final time, Judah lost her temple and the city of David, bringing the reign of the sons of David to a halt. All seemed lost. Judah was held captive for 70 years. Then a Persian king, Cyrus, sent out a decree telling the exiles they could return and rebuild Jerusalem and their temple.

But if they did, could they be assured that the God of Abraham, Isaac, and Jacob would be with them? Had He abandoned His people and His promise to Abraham because of their sin? Would the northern and southern kingdoms ever be united again? Would God still send Messiah? Would David have a descendant who would sit on the throne of David forever?

And the temple? Between the time of Solomon and the Babylonian captivity, king after king had neglected it or desecrated it with idols. If they were to restore it, would it do any good?

What of the prophets? What was God's Word, the prophets' message, regarding Israel, Judah, and their future? Would the Word of God change? Would the words of the prophets be valid after Israel and Judah had so grievously sinned?

On returning from captivity, God's people had to be reminded "of the events or annals of the days, the years," and so Chronicles was written. We don't know for certain who wrote Chronicles; perhaps it was Ezra. However, we do know that it was part of God's plan, for God included it in the canon of Scripture.

THINGS TO DO

General Instructions

1. If possible, study 1 and 2 Samuel and then 1 and 2 Kings before you study 1 and 2 Chronicles. Chronicles is to these other historical books what John is to the synoptic Gospels (Matthew, Mark, and Luke). Both John and Chronicles are supplemental and yet bring unique insight and understanding. Study the HISTORICAL PARALLEL OF SAMUEL, KINGS, AND CHRONICLES on page 659.
2. First and 2 Chronicles have time gaps in them. Keep this in mind as you study. When you wonder about the timing of something, look at the HISTORICAL PARALLEL again.
3. Watch for and mark references to time with a clock 🕒. Double-underline in green all geographical references.
4. When you finish observing each chapter, record its theme on 1 CHRONICLES AT A GLANCE on page 706 and in your Bible.

Chapters 1–9: The Genealogies of the Nation of Israel

1. This section may seem boring because it is primarily genealogies with a few historical sidelights. However, remember that this information has a purpose, and that is why God included it in His Word. Some genealogies, such as 4:1-23, are not included anywhere else.
   a. Don't skip this section; you will gain valuable insights which will help you in the study of the rest of the book.
   b. To discover the scope of the genealogies, read verses 1:1 and 9:1-2. Then write in the margin of 1:1 when the genealogies begin and end according to the historical events they represent. Keeping in mind what was said in the introduction to 1 Chronicles, notice in 9:2 the words "the first who lived in their possessions in their cities."

2. In this segment the key words to mark or underline are the names of people who play vital roles in Israel's history.

   a. Mark the following key words in a distinctive way: *Adam*, *Noah*, and Noah's three sons: *Shem*, *Ham*, and *Japheth*. Then mark the phrases *the sons of Japheth*, *the sons of Ham*, and *the sons of Shem*.

   b. Mark *the sons of Abraham were Isaac and Ishmael*, and *Abraham became the father of Isaac*, and *the sons of Isaac were Esau and Israel* (remember that Israel was called Jacob until God changed his name to Israel).

   c. In chapter 2 mark *these are the sons of Israel*. Then count the sons. How many were there? They became the heads of the tribes of Israel. Record their names on an index card and look for any place where they are repeated in this segment. Use this card as a bookmark. Read Genesis 49:1-28, where Jacob (Israel) gives a prophetic blessing to each of these men (cf. "Insight" on page 661).

   d. In 2:3-15 mark *the sons of Judah* and then look for *David*. In the margin, list David's genealogy from Judah through David's immediate father, Jesse. Remember that the author of Chronicles gives the genealogy of Judah before the other sons of Israel. Why? What would be important to the exiles who now repossessed their cities? Wouldn't it be God's promises to David? Keep this in mind as you study the second-to-last segment of 1 Chronicles.

   e. In 3:1, mark the names of the sons of David and list their names in the margin. Refer to "David's Family Tree" on page 511.

   f. First Chronicles 3:10-16 gives the line of kings that come from David through Solomon. List these names in the margin.

   g. First Chronicles 3:17-24 lists the genealogy through Jeconiah (Jehoiachin). He was the king who reigned three months and ten days before he was taken into exile in Babylon, put in prison, and then released. See 2 Kings 24:8-16 and 2 Chronicles 36:9-10.

3. When you read chapters 4 through 9, watch for any mention of the 12 sons of Israel and their genealogy. As you do:

   a. Notice that not all 12 are mentioned in chapters 4 through 9.

   b. Joseph's sons Manasseh and Ephraim are mentioned in Scripture as part of the 12 tribes of Israel. The reason for this is given in 1 Chronicles 5:1-2. Take special note of this.

      1) Write "Joseph's son" next to any mention of Manasseh and/or Ephraim.

      2) Manasseh is named twice. The tribe split when Canaan was divided. Half the tribe of Manasseh took land east of the Jordan and the other half went west of the Jordan; thus the reference to the "half-tribe of Manasseh."

4. Read the section on the sons of Levi carefully and either underline what they were to do or note it in the margin. Also observe and note what Aaron and his sons were to do. This will help when you come to the final chapters of 1 Chronicles.

5. Don't forget to record the chapter themes in the text and on 1 CHRONICLES AT A GLANCE.

Chapters 10–19: God Turns the Kingdom to David

1. As you read this segment, see how it fits with 1 and 2 Samuel. To do this consult the chart HISTORICAL PARALLEL OF SAMUEL, KINGS, AND CHRONICLES on page 659.

   a. Read 1 Chronicles 10, mark any reference to *kingdom*, and list the events of that chapter.

b. Also note where it says whose son David was. Keep in mind what you just studied in the first segment.

c. Note in the margin why Saul died, who died with him, and what happened to Saul's body.

2. Read this segment chapter by chapter and do the following:

a. Mark the following key words: *city of David, ark, covenant,* and *inquired of God.* Observe what you learn from these words and record your insights in your notebook.

b. Ask the "5 W's and an H" as you read each chapter. Who are the key characters? What happens? When? (Mark references to time with a ◷.) Where do events occur? Why do they occur? How do things happen? Record your insights in your notebook.

c. Don't forget to record the chapter themes on 1 CHRONICLES AT A GLANCE and in the text next to the chapter number.

3. Watch for any prophecies (promises), speeches, songs, or psalms of praise. Who gives them? Why? What is said in each? Record your insights in your notebook. Also ask: How can I apply these truths in my life?

Chapters 20–29: David Builds an Altar and Prepares for God's House

1. Note where this portion of 1 Chronicles comes in respect to 2 Samuel.

a. When you read chapter 20, compare the wording of verse 1 with 2 Samuel 11:1. Then as you look at the content of 2 Samuel 11–12, note what the author of Chronicles leaves out.

b. Now compare 1 Chronicles 21 with 2 Samuel 24. Why was this event included in 1 Chronicles when David's other sin was omitted? Remember, the temple is very important to the returning exiles. (See the "Insight" on page 694.)

2. As you read each chapter, mark the following key words and note in the margin what you learn from each: *house (home, temple, sanctuary)*, *ark*, *heart*, *Levi (Levites),* and *Aaron*.

a. The word *house* has been used numerous times in 1 Chronicles; however, with one or two exceptions "house" referred to someone's family, such as the house of David. In this segment it is used primarily for the house of the Lord. As you mark it, note what you learn. Keep in mind that this is the book for the exiles who had returned to rebuild the temple and thus the emphasis is on the house of God and its importance. When difficulties arose, this historical account would affirm God's enduring purpose and promises.

b. As you mark the references to the *Levites* and to *Aaron and his sons,* observe carefully the types of duties they were to perform and which Levite family was to perform each type of duty.

3. Read each chapter as you did in the last segment, asking the "5 W's and an H." Note in the margin what you observe. Also as you did in the last segment, watch for any speeches, prophecies, etc., and note the same things you looked for previously.

4. Complete 1 CHRONICLES AT A GLANCE. There are two lines for any additional segment divisions you might see and want to mark.

THINGS TO THINK ABOUT

1. Second Timothy 2:13 says, "If we are faithless, He remains faithful; for He cannot deny Himself." What have you seen of the faithfulness of God in the book of 1 Chronicles? What assurance does this give you for your life?

2. You marked the word *heart* in this last segment. Go back over these references in

chapter 29 and review what you observed about the heart. Also review what you observed as David blessed the Lord. Think about your own heart. What is your heart like in respect to the Lord? How can you turn what David did into a prayer to the Lord?

3. As you think about all you learned about the priests and their duties and you think of yourself and other Christians as a kingdom of priests unto God (Revelation 1 and 5), do you see any application you can make to your responsibilities as a priest unto God?

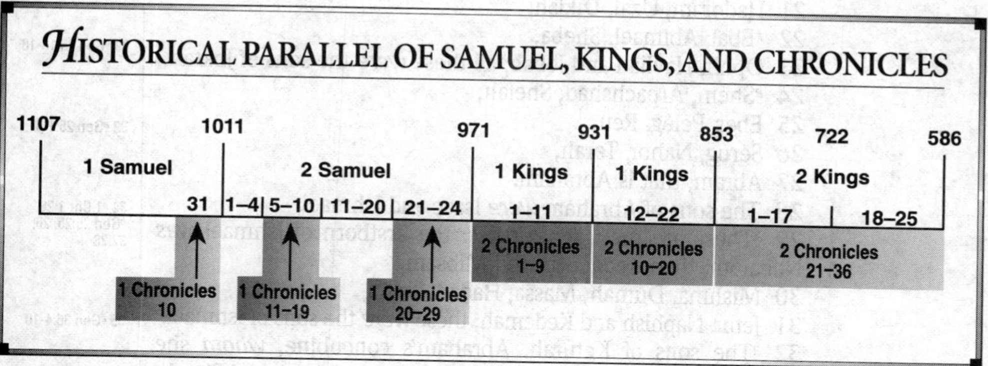

1:1 aGen 4:25-5:32

Chapter 1 Theme ________________________

1 [a]Adam, Seth, Enosh,
2 Kenan, Mahalalel, Jared,
3 Enoch, Methuselah, Lamech,
4 Noah, Shem, Ham and Japheth.
5 [a]The sons of Japheth *were* Gomer, Magog, Madai, Javan,
Tubal, Meshech and Tiras.
6 The sons of Gomer *were* Ashkenaz, [1]Diphath, and Togarmah.
7 The sons of Javan *were* Elishah, Tarshish, Kittim and [1]Rodanim.
8 The sons of Ham *were* Cush, Mizraim, Put, and Canaan.
9 The sons of Cush *were* Seba, Havilah, Sabta, Raama and
Sabteca; and the sons of Raamah *were* Sheba and Dedan.
10 Cush [1]became the father of Nimrod; he began to be a mighty
one in the earth.
11 [a]Mizraim became the father of the people of Lud, Anam,
Lehab, Naphtuh,
12 Pathrus, Casluh, from which the [1]Philistines came, and
Caphtor.
13 Canaan became the father of Sidon, his firstborn, Heth,
14 and the Jebusites, the Amorites, the Girgashites,
15 the Hivites, the Arkites, the Sinites,
16 the Arvadites, the Zemarites and the Hamathites.

5 aGen 10:2-4
6 1In Gen 10:3, *Riphath*
7 1In Gen 10:4, *Dodanim*
10 1Lit *begot*, and so throughout the ch
11 aGen 10:13-18
12 1Or *people of Pelisht*

17 [a]The sons of Shem *were* Elam, Asshur, Arpachshad, Lud,
Aram, Uz, Hul, Gether and [1]Meshech.
18 Arpachshad became the father of Shelah and Shelah
became the father of Eber.
19 Two sons were born to Eber, the name of the one was Peleg,
for in his days the earth was divided, and his brother's name
was Joktan.
20 Joktan became the father of Almodad, Sheleph, Hazarmaveth,
Jerah,
21 Hadoram, Uzal, Diklah,
22 [1]Ebal, Abimael, Sheba,
23 Ophir, Havilah and Jobab; all these *were* the sons of Joktan.
24 [a]Shem, Arpachshad, Shelah,
25 Eber, Peleg, Reu,
26 Serug, Nahor, Terah,
27 Abram, that is Abraham.
28 The sons of Abraham *were* Isaac and Ishmael.
29 [a]These are their genealogies: the firstborn of Ishmael *was*
Nebaioth, then Kedar, Adbeel, Mibsam,
30 Mishma, Dumah, Massa, Hadad, Tema,
31 Jetur, Naphish and Kedemah; these *were* the sons of Ishmael.
32 [a]The sons of Keturah, Abraham's concubine, *whom* she
bore, *were* Zimran, Jokshan, Medan, Midian, Ishbak and Shuah.
And the sons of Jokshan *were* Sheba and Dedan.
33 The sons of Midian were Ephah, Epher, Hanoch, Abida and
Eldaah. All these were the sons of Keturah.
34 [a]Abraham became the father of Isaac. The sons of Isaac
were [b]Esau and Israel.
35 [a]The sons of Esau *were* Eliphaz, Reuel, Jeush, Jalam and
Korah.
36 The sons of Eliphaz *were* Teman, Omar, [1]Zephi, Gatam,
Kenaz, Timna and Amalek.
37 The sons of Reuel *were* Nahath, Zerah, Shammah and
Mizzah.
38 [a]The sons of Seir *were* Lotan, Shobal, Zibeon, Anah, Dishon,
Ezer and Dishan.
39 The sons of Lotan *were* Hori and [1]Homam; and Lotan's
sister *was* Timna.
40 The sons of Shobal *were* [1]Alian, Manahath, Ebal, [2]Shephi
and Onam. And the sons of Zibeon *were* Aiah and Anah.
41 The [1]son of Anah *was* Dishon. And the sons of Dishon
were [2]Hamran, Eshban, Ithran and Cheran.
42 The sons of Ezer *were* Bilhan, Zaavan and [1]Jaakan. The
sons of Dishan *were* Uz and Aran.
43 [a]Now these are the kings who reigned in the land of Edom
before any king of the sons of Israel reigned. Bela was the son
of Beor, and the name of his city was Dinhabah.
44 When Bela died, Jobab the son of Zerah of [a]Bozrah became
king in his place.
45 When Jobab died, Husham of the land of [a]the Temanites
became king in his place.

17 [1]In Gen 10:23, *Mash* [a]Gen 10:22-29
22 [1]In Gen 10:28, *Obal*
24 [a]Gen 11:10-26; Luke 3:34-36
29 [a]Gen 25:13-16
32 [a]Gen 25:1-4
34 [a]1 Chr 1:28 [b]Gen 25:25, 26; 32:28
35 [a]Gen 36:4-10
36 [1]In Gen 36:11, *Zepho*
38 [a]Gen 36:20-28
39 [1]In Gen 36:22, *Hemam*
40 [1]In Gen 36:23, *Alvan* [2]In Gen 36:23, *Shepho*
41 [1]Lit *sons* [2]In Gen 36:26, *Hemdan*
42 [1]Or *Akan*, as in Gen 36:27
43 [a]Gen 36:31-43
44 [a]Is 34:6
45 [a]Job 2:11

46 When Husham died, Hadad the son of Bedad, who
[1]defeated Midian in the field of Moab, became king in his
place; and the name of his city *was* Avith.
47 When Hadad died, Samlah of Masrekah became king in his
place.
48 When Samlah died, Shaul of Rehoboth by the River became
king in his place.
49 When Shaul died, Baal-hanan the son of Achbor became
king in his place.
50 When Baal-hanan died, [1]Hadad became king in his place;
and the name of his city was [2]Pai, and his wife's name was
Mehetabel, the daughter of Matred, the daughter of Mezahab.
51 Then Hadad died.
Now the chiefs of Edom were: chief Timna, chief [1]Aliah,
chief Jetheth,
52 chief Oholibamah, chief Elah, chief Pinon,
53 chief Kenaz, chief Teman, chief Mibzar,
54 chief Magdiel, chief Iram. These *were* the chiefs of Edom.

Chapter 2 Theme _________________________

2 [a]These are the sons of Israel: Reuben, Simeon, Levi, Judah,
Issachar, Zebulun,
2 Dan, Joseph, Benjamin, Naphtali, Gad and Asher.
3 [a]The sons of Judah *were* Er, Onan and Shelah; *these* three
were born to him by Bath-shua the Canaanitess. And Er, Judah's
firstborn, was wicked in the sight of the LORD, so He put him to
death.
4 [a]Tamar his daughter-in-law bore him Perez and Zerah.
Judah had five sons in all.
5 The sons of Perez *were* Hezron and Hamul.
6 The sons of Zerah *were* [1]Zimri, Ethan, Heman, Calcol and
[2]Dara; five of them in all.
7 The [1]son of Carmi *was* [2a]Achar, the troubler of Israel, who
violated the ban.
8 The [1]son of Ethan *was* Azariah.
9 Now the sons of Hezron, who were born to him *were*
Jerahmeel, Ram and Chelubai.
10 Ram [1]became the father of Amminadab, and Amminadab
became the father of Nahshon, leader of the sons of Judah;
11 Nahshon became the father of Salma, Salma became the
father of Boaz,
12 Boaz became the father of Obed, and Obed became the
father of Jesse;
13 and Jesse became the father of Eliab his firstborn, then
Abinadab the second, [1]Shimea the third,
14 Nethanel the fourth, Raddai the fifth,
15 Ozem the sixth, David the seventh;
16 and their sisters *were* Zeruiah and Abigail. And the three
sons of Zeruiah *were* [1]Abshai, Joab and Asahel.
17 Abigail bore Amasa, and the father of Amasa was [1]Jether
the Ishmaelite.

46 [1]Lit *smote*
50 [1]In Gen 36:39, *Hadar* [2]In Gen 36:39, *Pau*
51 [1]In Gen 36:40, *Alvah*
2:1 [a]Gen 35:22-26; 46:8-25
3 [a]Gen 38:2-10
4 [a]Gen 38:13-30
6 [1]In Josh 7:1, *Zabdi* [2]In 1 Kin 4:31, *Darda*
7 [1]Lit *sons* [2]In Josh 7:18, *Achan* [a]Josh 7:1
8 [1]Lit *sons*
10 [1]Lit *begot*, and so throughout the ch
13 [1]In 1 Sam 16:9, *Shammah;* in 2 Sam 13:3, *Shimeah*
16 [1]In 2 Sam 2:18, *Abishai*
17 [1]In 2 Sam 17:25, *Ithra the Israelite*

INSIGHT

The Birth Order of Jacob's (Israel's) Sons

Mother	Son
Leah	Reuben (born 1921 B.C.) Simeon Levi Judah
Bilhah *(Rachel's maid)*	Dan Naphtali
Zilpah *(Leah's maid)*	Gad Asher
Leah	Issachar Zebulun
Rachel	Joseph (born 1914 B.C.) Benjamin

18 Now Caleb the son of Hezron had sons by Azubah *his* wife,
and by Jerioth; and these were her sons: Jesher, Shobab, and
Ardon.
19 When Azubah died, Caleb married Ephrath, who bore him
Hur.
20 Hur became the father of Uri, and Uri became the father of
Bezalel.
21 Afterward Hezron went in to the daughter of Machir the
father of Gilead, whom he married when he was sixty years
old; and she bore him Segub.
22 Segub became the father of Jair, who had twenty-three
cities in the land of Gilead.
23 But Geshur and Aram took [1]the towns of Jair from them,
with Kenath and its villages, *even* sixty cities. All these were
the sons of Machir, the father of Gilead.
24 After the death of Hezron in Caleb-ephrathah, Abijah,
Hezron's wife, bore him Ashhur the father of Tekoa.
25 Now the sons of Jerahmeel the firstborn of Hezron *were*
Ram the firstborn, then Bunah, Oren, Ozem *and* Ahijah.
26 Jerahmeel had another wife, whose name was Atarah; she
was the mother of Onam.
27 The sons of Ram, the firstborn of Jerahmeel, were Maaz,
Jamin and Eker.
28 The sons of Onam were Shammai and Jada. And the sons
of Shammai *were* Nadab and Abishur.
29 The name of Abishur's wife *was* Abihail, and she bore him
Ahban and Molid.
30 The sons of Nadab *were* Seled and Appaim, and Seled died
without sons.
31 The [1]son of Appaim *was* Ishi. And the [1]son of Ishi *was*
Sheshan. And the [1]son of Sheshan *was* Ahlai.
32 The sons of Jada the brother of Shammai *were* Jether and
Jonathan, and Jether died without sons.
33 The sons of Jonathan *were* Peleth and Zaza. These were
the sons of Jerahmeel.
34 Now Sheshan had no sons, only daughters. And Sheshan
had an Egyptian servant whose name was Jarha.
35 Sheshan gave his daughter to Jarha his servant in marriage,
and she bore him Attai.
36 Attai became the father of Nathan, and Nathan became the
father of Zabad,
37 and Zabad became the father of Ephlal, and Ephlal became
the father of Obed,
38 and Obed became the father of Jehu, and Jehu became the
father of Azariah,
39 and Azariah became the father of Helez, and Helez became
the father of Eleasah,
40 and Eleasah became the father of Sismai, and Sismai
became the father of Shallum,
41 and Shallum became the father of Jekamiah, and Jekamiah
became the father of Elishama.

23 [1]Or *Havvoth-jai*

31 [1]Lit *sons*

42 [1]Lit *the sons of*

42 Now the sons of Caleb, the brother of Jerahmeel, *were*
Mesha his firstborn, who was the father of Ziph; and [1]his son
was Mareshah, the father of Hebron.
43 The sons of Hebron *were* Korah and Tappuah and Rekem
and Shema.
44 Shema became the father of Raham, the father of Jorkeam;
and Rekem became the father of Shammai.
45 The son of Shammai was Maon, and Maon *was* the father
of Bethzur.
46 Ephah, Caleb's concubine, bore Haran, Moza and Gazez;
and Haran became the father of Gazez.
47 The sons of Jahdai *were* Regem, Jotham, Geshan, Pelet,

50 [1]Lit *son*

Ephah and Shaaph.
48 Maacah, Caleb's concubine, bore Sheber and Tirhanah.
49 She also bore Shaaph the father of Madmannah, Sheva the
father of Machbena and the father of Gibea; and the daughter
of Caleb *was* Achsah.
50 These were the sons of Caleb.
The [1]sons of Hur, the firstborn of Ephrathah, *were* Shobal
the father of Kiriath-jearim,
51 Salma the father of Bethlehem *and* Hareph the father of
Beth-gader.
52 Shobal the father of Kiriath-jearim had sons: Haroeh, half of

3:1 [a]2 Sam 3:2-5

the Manahathites,
53 and the families of Kiriath-jearim: the Ithrites, the Puthites,
the Shumathites and the Mishraites; from these came the
Zorathites and the Eshtaolites.
54 The sons of Salma *were* Bethlehem and the Netophathites,
Atroth-beth-joab and half of the Manahathites, the Zorites.
55 The families of scribes who lived at Jabez *were* the Tirathites,
the Shimeathites *and* the Sucathites. Those are the Kenites
who came from Hammath, the father of the house of Rechab.

Chapter 3 Theme ____________________

4 [a]2 Sam 2:11; 5:4, 5; 1 Kin 2:11; 1 Chr 29:27

3 [a]Now these were the sons of David who were born to him
in Hebron: the firstborn *was* Amnon, by Ahinoam the
Jezreelitess; the second *was* Daniel, by Abigail the Carmelitess;
2 the third *was* Absalom the son of Maacah, the daughter of
Talmai king of Geshur; the fourth *was* Adonijah the son of
Haggith;
3 the fifth *was* Shephatiah, by Abital; the sixth *was* Ithream,
by his wife Eglah.
4 Six were born to him in Hebron, and [a]there he reigned
seven years and six months. And in Jerusalem he reigned thirty-
three years.
5 [a]These were born to him in Jerusalem: Shimea, Shobab,
Nathan and [b]Solomon, four, by [c]Bath-shua the daughter of

5 [a]2 Sam 5:14-16; 1 Chr 14:4-7 [b]2 Sam 12:24, 25 [c]2 Sam 11:3

Ammiel;
6 and Ibhar, Elishama, Eliphelet,
7 Nogah, Nepheg and Japhia,

2 Samuel 3

8 Elishama, Eliada and Eliphelet, nine.
9 All *these were* the sons of David, besides the sons of the
concubines; and [a]Tamar *was* their sister.
10 Now Solomon's son *was* Rehoboam, Abijah *was* his son,
Asa his son, Jehoshaphat his son,
11 Joram his son, Ahaziah his son, Joash his son,
12 Amaziah his son, Azariah his son, Jotham his son,
13 Ahaz his son, Hezekiah his son, Manasseh his son,
14 Amon his son, Josiah his son.
15 The sons of Josiah *were* Johanan the firstborn, and the
second *was* Jehoiakim, the third Zedekiah, the fourth Shallum.
16 The sons of Jehoiakim *were* Jeconiah his son, Zedekiah his son.
17 The sons of Jeconiah, the prisoner, *were* Shealtiel his son,
18 and Malchiram, Pedaiah, Shenazzar, Jekamiah, Hoshama and
Nedabiah.
19 The sons of Pedaiah *were* Zerubbabel and Shimei. And the
[1]sons of Zerubbabel *were* Meshullam and Hananiah, and
Shelomith *was* their sister;
20 and Hashubah, Ohel, Berechiah, Hasadiah and Jushab-hesed,
five.
21 The [1]sons of Hananiah *were* Pelatiah and Jeshaiah, the sons
of Rephaiah, the sons of Arnan, the sons of Obadiah, the sons
of Shecaniah.
22 The [1]descendants of Shecaniah *were* Shemaiah, and the
sons of Shemaiah: Hattush, Igal, Bariah, Neariah and Shaphat, six.
23 The [1]sons of Neariah *were* Elioenai, Hizkiah and Azrikam,
three.
24 The sons of Elioenai *were* Hodaviah, Eliashib, Pelaiah,
Akkub, Johanan, Delaiah and Anani, seven.

Chapter 4 Theme ______________________

4 [a]The sons of Judah *were* Perez, Hezron, Carmi, Hur and
Shobal.
2 Reaiah the son of Shobal [1]became the father of Jahath, and
Jahath became the father of Ahumai and Lahad. These *were*
the families of the Zorathites.
3 These *were* the [1]sons of Etam: Jezreel, Ishma and Idbash;
and the name of their sister *was* Hazzelelponi.
4 Penuel *was* the father of Gedor, and Ezer the father of
Hushah. These *were* the sons of Hur, the firstborn of Ephrathah,
the father of Bethlehem.
5 Ashhur, the father of Tekoa, had two wives, Helah and
Naarah.
6 Naarah bore him Ahuzzam, Hepher, Temeni and
Haahashtari. These were the sons of Naarah.
7 The sons of Helah *were* Zereth, [1]Izhar and Ethnan.
8 Koz became the father of Anub and Zobebah, and the
families of Aharhel the son of Harum.
9 Jabez was more honorable than his brothers, and his mother
named him Jabez saying, "Because I bore *him* with pain."

9 [a]2 Sam 13:1
19 [1]Lit *son*
21 [1]Lit *son*
22 [1]Lit *sons*
23 [1]Lit *son*
4:1 [a]1 Chr 2:3
2 [1]Lit *begot,* and so throughout the ch
3 [1]So with some ancient versions; Heb *father*
7 [1]Another reading is *Zohar*

10 Now Jabez called on the God of Israel, saying, "Oh that You would bless me indeed and enlarge my border, and that Your hand might be with me, and that You would keep *me* from harm that *it* may not pain me!" And God granted him what he requested.

11 Chelub the brother of Shuhah became the father of Mehir, who was the father of Eshton.

12 Eshton became the father of Beth-rapha and Paseah, and Tehinnah the father of [1]Ir-nahash. These are the men of Recah.

13 Now the sons of Kenaz *were* Othniel and Seraiah. And the sons of Othniel *were* Hathath and Meonothai.

14 Meonothai became the father of Ophrah, and Seraiah became the father of Joab the father of [1]Ge-harashim, for they were craftsmen.

15 The sons of Caleb the son of Jephunneh *were* Iru, Elah and Naam; and the [1]son of Elah *was* [2]Kenaz.

16 The sons of Jehallelel *were* Ziph and Ziphah, Tiria and Asarel.

17 The [1]sons of Ezrah *were* Jether, Mered, Epher and Jalon. ([2]And these are the sons of Bithia the daughter of Pharaoh, whom Mered took) and she conceived *and bore* Miriam, Shammai and Ishbah the father of Eshtemoa.

18 His Jewish wife bore Jered the father of Gedor, and Heber the father of Soco, and Jekuthiel the father of Zanoah.

19 The sons of the wife of Hodiah, the sister of Naham, *were* the [1]fathers of Keilah the Garmite and Eshtemoa the Maacathite.

20 The sons of Shimon *were* Amnon and Rinnah, Benhanan and Tilon. And the sons of Ishi *were* Zoheth and Ben-zoheth.

21 The sons of Shelah the son of Judah *were* Er the father of Lecah and Laadah the father of Mareshah, and the families of the house of the linen workers at Beth-ashbea;

22 and Jokim, the men of Cozeba, Joash, Saraph, who ruled in Moab, and Jashubi-lehem. And the [1]records are ancient.

23 These were the potters and the inhabitants of Netaim and Gederah; they lived there with the king for his work.

24 The sons of Simeon *were* [1]Nemuel and Jamin, [2]Jarib, [3]Zerah, Shaul;

25 Shallum his son, Mibsam his son, Mishma his son.

26 The sons of Mishma *were* Hammuel his son, Zaccur his son, Shimei his son.

27 Now Shimei had sixteen sons and six daughters; but his brothers did not have many sons, nor did all their family multiply like the sons of Judah.

28 They lived at Beersheba, Moladah and Hazar-shual,

29 at Bilhah, Ezem, Tolad,

30 Bethuel, Hormah, Ziklag,

31 Beth-marcaboth, Hazar-susim, Beth-biri and Shaaraim. These *were* their cities until the reign of David.

32 Their villages *were* Etam, Ain, Rimmon, Tochen and Ashan, five cities;

33 and all their villages that *were* around the same cities as far as [1]Baal. These *were* their settlements, and they have their genealogy.

12 [1]Or *the city of Nahash*

14 [1]Or *valley of craftsmen*

15 [1]Lit *sons* [2]Lit *and Kenaz*

17 [1]Lit *son* [2]In the Heb the words in ( ) are at the end of v 18

19 [1]Lit *father*

22 [1]Lit *words*

24 [1]In Gen 46:10 and Ex 6:15, *Jemuel* [2]In Num 26:12, *Jachin* [3]In Gen 46:10 and Ex 6:15, *Zohar*

33 [1]In Josh 19:8, *Baalath*

The Land Settled by the Twelve Tribes

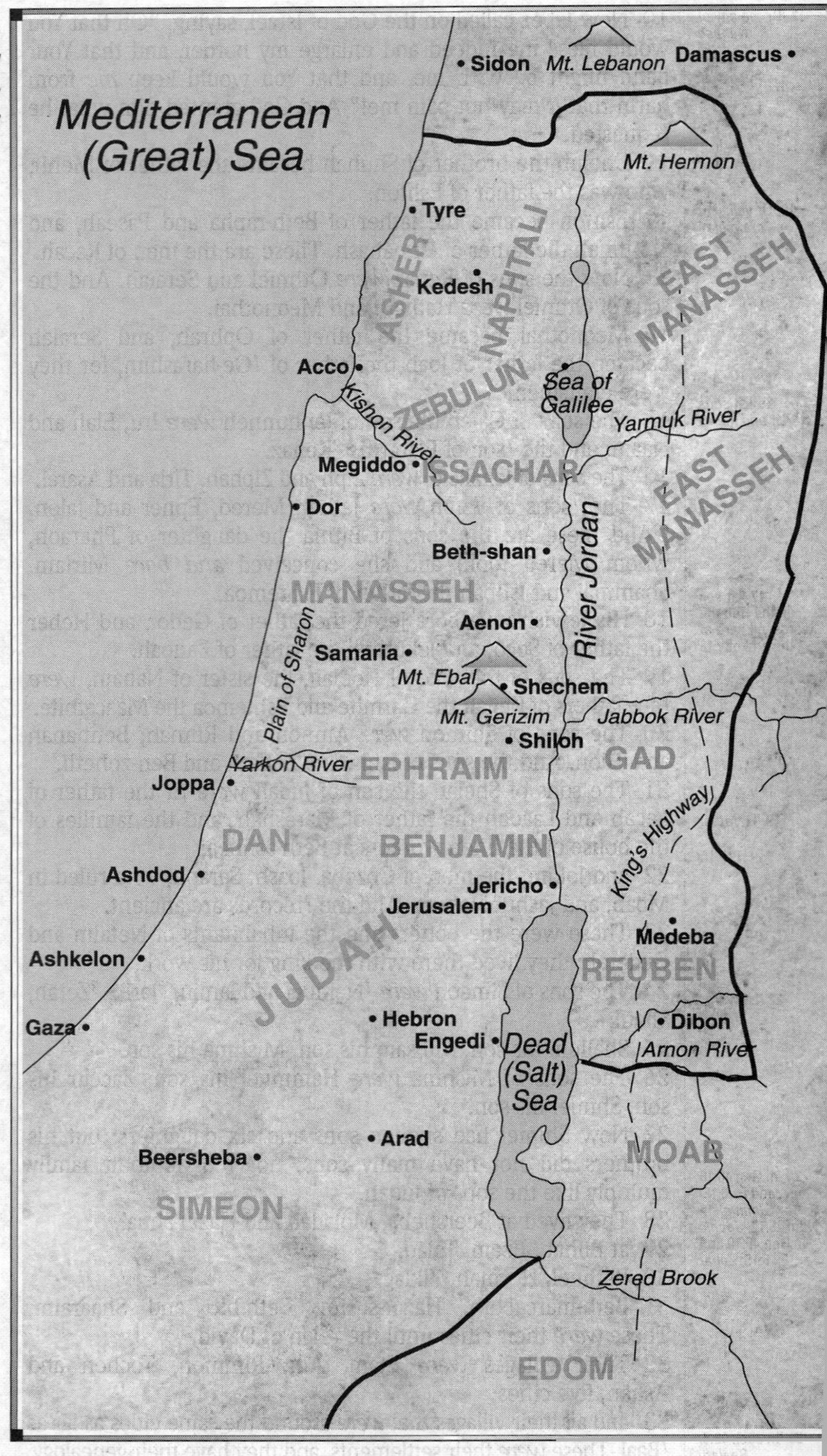

Mediterranean (Great) Sea
Sidon
Mt. Lebanon
Damascus
Mt. Hermon
Tyre
ASHER
NAPHTALI
EAST MANASSEH
Kedesh
Acco
ZEBULUN
Sea of Galilee
Kishon River
Yarmuk River
Megiddo
ISSACHAR
EAST MANASSEH
Dor
River Jordan
Beth-shan
MANASSEH
Plain of Sharon
Aenon
Samaria
Mt. Ebal
Shechem
Mt. Gerizim
Jabbok River
Shiloh
GAD
Yarkon River
EPHRAIM
Joppa
King's Highway
DAN
BENJAMIN
Ashdod
Jericho
Jerusalem
Medeba
JUDAH
Ashkelon
REUBEN
Gaza
Hebron
Dibon
Engedi
Dead (Salt) Sea
Arnon River
Arad
Beersheba
MOAB
SIMEON
Zered Brook
EDOM

34 Meshobab and Jamlech and Joshah the son of Amaziah,
35 and Joel and Jehu the son of Joshibiah, the son of Seraiah,
the son of Asiel,
36 and Elioenai, Jaakobah, Jeshohaiah, Asaiah, Adiel, Jesimiel,
Benaiah,
37 Ziza the son of Shiphi, the son of Allon, the son of Jedaiah,
the son of Shimri, the son of Shemaiah;
38 these mentioned by name *were* leaders in their families;
and their fathers' houses increased greatly.
39 They went to the entrance of Gedor, even to the east side
of the valley, to seek pasture for their flocks.
40 They found rich and good pasture, and [a]the land was broad
and quiet and peaceful; for those who lived there formerly
were Hamites.
41 [a]These, recorded by name, came in the days of Hezekiah king
of Judah, and [1]attacked their tents and the Meunites who were
found there, and destroyed them utterly to this day, and lived
in their place, because there was pasture there for their flocks.
42 From them, from the sons of Simeon, five hundred men
went to [a]Mount Seir, with Pelatiah, Neariah, Rephaiah and
Uzziel, the sons of Ishi, as their leaders.
43 [a]They [1]destroyed the remnant of the Amalekites who
escaped, and have lived there to this day.

Chapter 5 Theme ____

5 Now the sons of Reuben the firstborn of Israel (for [a]he was
the firstborn, but because [b]he defiled his father's bed, [c]his
birthright was given to the sons of Joseph the son of Israel; so that
he is not enrolled in the genealogy according to the birthright.
2 [a]Though Judah prevailed over his brothers, and [b]from him
came the leader, yet the birthright belonged to Joseph),
3 [a]the sons of Reuben the firstborn of Israel *were* Hanoch
and Pallu, Hezron and Carmi.
4 The sons of Joel *were* Shemaiah his son, Gog his son,
[a]Shimei his son,
5 Micah his son, Reaiah his son, Baal his son,
6 Beerah his son, whom [1]Tilgath-pilneser king of Assyria
carried away into exile; he was leader of the Reubenites.
7 His [1]kinsmen by their families, [a]in the genealogy of their
generations, *were* Jeiel the chief, then Zechariah
8 and Bela the son of Azaz, the son of Shema, the son of Joel,
who lived in [a]Aroer, even to Nebo and Baal-meon.
9 To the east he settled as far as the entrance of the wilderness
from the river Euphrates, [a]because their cattle had
increased in the land of Gilead.
10 In the days of Saul [a]they made war with the Hagrites, who
fell by their hand, so that they [1]occupied their tents throughout
[2]all the land east of Gilead.
11 Now the sons of Gad lived opposite them in the land of
[a]Bashan as far as [b]Salecah.

40 [a]Judg 18:7-10
41 [1]Lit *smote* [a]1 Chr 4:33-38
42 [a]Gen 36:8, 9
43 [1]Lit *smote* [a]1 Sam 15:7, 8; 30:17
5:1 [a]Gen 29:32; 1 Chr 2:1 [b]Gen 35:22; 49:4 [c]Gen 48:15-22
2 [a]Gen 49:8-10; Ps 60:7; 108:8 [b]Mic 5:2; Matt 2:6
3 [a]Gen 46:9; Ex 6:14; Num 26:5-9
4 [a]1 Chr 5:8
6 [1]In 2 Kin 15:29, *Tiglath-pileser*
7 [1]Lit *brothers* [a]1 Chr 5:17
8 [a]Num 32:34; Josh 12:2
9 [a]Josh 22:8, 9
10 [1]Lit *dwelt in* [2]Lit *all the face of the east* [a]1 Chr 5:18-21
11 [a]Josh 13:11 [b]Deut 3:10

12 Joel *was* the chief and Shapham the second, then Janai and
Shaphat in Bashan.
13 Their [1]kinsmen of their fathers' households *were* Michael,
Meshullam, Sheba, Jorai, Jacan, Zia and Eber, seven.
14 These *were* the sons of Abihail, the son of Huri, the son of
Jaroah, the son of Gilead, the son of Michael, the son of Jeshishai,
the son of Jahdo, the son of Buz;
15 Ahi the son of Abdiel, the son of Guni, *was* head of their
fathers' households.
16 They lived in Gilead, in Bashan and in its towns, and in all
the pasture lands of [a]Sharon, as far as their [1]borders.
17 All of these were enrolled in the genealogies in the days of
[a]Jotham king of Judah and in the days of [b]Jeroboam king of Israel.
18 The sons of Reuben and the Gadites and the half-tribe of
Manasseh, *consisting* of valiant men, men who bore shield and
sword and shot with bow and *were* skillful in battle, *were*
44,760, who [a]went to war.
19 They made war against [a]the Hagrites, [b]Jetur, Naphish and
Nodab.
20 They were helped against them, and the Hagrites and all
who *were* with them were given into their hand; for [a]they
cried out to God in the battle, and He answered their prayers
because [b]they trusted in Him.
21 They took away their cattle: their 50,000 camels, 250,000
sheep, 2,000 donkeys; and 100,000 [1]men.
22 For many fell slain, because [a]the war *was* of God. And
[b]they settled in their place until the [c]exile.
23 Now the sons of the half-tribe of Manasseh lived in the
land; from Bashan to Baal-hermon and [a]Senir and Mount
Hermon they were numerous.
24 These were the heads of their fathers' households, even
Epher, Ishi, Eliel, Azriel, Jeremiah, Hodaviah and Jahdiel, mighty
men of valor, famous men, heads of their fathers' households.
25 But they [a]acted treacherously against the God of their fathers
and [b]played the harlot [c]after the gods of the peoples of the land,
whom God had destroyed before them.
26 So the God of Israel stirred up the spirit of [a]Pul, king of
Assyria, even the spirit of [1]Tilgath-pilneser king of Assyria, and
he [b]carried them away into exile, namely the Reubenites, the
Gadites and the half-tribe of Manasseh, and brought them to
Halah, Habor, Hara and to the river of Gozan, to this day.

Chapter 6 Theme ____________

6 [1a]The sons of Levi *were* [2]Gershon, Kohath and Merari.
2 The sons of Kohath *were* Amram, Izhar, Hebron and
Uzziel.
3 The children of Amram *were* Aaron, Moses and Miriam.
And the sons of Aaron *were* Nadab, Abihu, Eleazar and Ithamar.
4 Eleazar [1]became the father of Phinehas, *and* Phinehas
became the father of Abishua,

13 [1]Lit *brother*

16 [1]Lit *goings out* [a]1 Chr 27:29; Song 2:1; Is 35:2; 65:10

17 [a]2 Kin 15:5, 32 [b]2 Kin 14:16, 28

18 [a]Num 1:3

19 [a]1 Chr 5:10 [b]Gen 25:15; 1 Chr 1:31

20 [a]2 Chr 14:11-13 [b]Ps 9:10; 20:7, 8; 22:4, 5

21 [1]Lit *souls of men*

22 [a]Josh 23:10; 2 Chr 32:8; Rom 8:31 [b]1 Chr 4:41 [c]2 Kin 15:29; 17:6

23 [a]Deut 3:9

25 [a]Deut 32:15-18 [b]Ex 34:15 [c]2 Kin 17:7

26 [1]In 2 Kin 15:29, *Tiglath-pileser* [a]2 Kin 15:19, 29; 2 Chr 28:20 [b]2 Kin 17:6

6:1 [1]Ch 5:27 in Heb [2]In v 16, *Gershom* [a]Gen 46:11; Ex 6:16-25

4 [1]Lit *begot,* and so throughout the ch

8 [a]2 Sam 8:17 [b]2 Sam 15:27
10 [a]2 Chr 26:17 [b]1 Kin 6:1; 2 Chr 3:1
11 [a]Ezra 7:3
12 [1]In ch 9:11, *Meshullam*
14 [a]Neh 11:11
15 [1]Lit *by the hand of*
16 [1]Ch 6:1 in Heb [2]In v 1, *Gershon* [a]Gen 46:11; Ex 6:16
19 [a]Num 3:33; 1 Chr 23:21
28 [a]1 Sam 8:2; 1 Chr 6:33
31 [a]1 Chr 15:16-22, 27; 16:4-6 [b]2 Sam 6:17; 1 Kin 8:4; 1 Chr 15:25-16:1
32 [1]Lit *stood over*

5 and Abishua became the father of Bukki, and Bukki became
the father of Uzzi,
6 and Uzzi became the father of Zerahiah, and Zerahiah
became the father of Meraioth,
7 Meraioth became the father of Amariah, and Amariah
became the father of Ahitub,
8 and [a]Ahitub became the father of Zadok, and Zadok [b]became
the father of Ahimaaz,
9 and Ahimaaz became the father of Azariah, and Azariah
became the father of Johanan,
10 and Johanan became the father of Azariah ([a]it was he who
served as the priest in the house [b]which Solomon built in
Jerusalem),
11 and [a]Azariah became the father of Amariah, and Amariah
became the father of Ahitub,
12 and Ahitub became the father of Zadok, and Zadok became
the father of [1]Shallum,
13 and Shallum became the father of Hilkiah, and Hilkiah
became the father of Azariah,
14 and Azariah became the father of [a]Seraiah, and Seraiah
became the father of Jehozadak;
15 and Jehozadak went *along* when the LORD carried Judah
and Jerusalem away into exile [1]by Nebuchadnezzar.
16 [1a]The sons of Levi *were* [2]Gershom, Kohath and Merari.
17 These are the names of the sons of Gershom: Libni and
Shimei.
18 The sons of Kohath *were* Amram, Izhar, Hebron and Uzziel.
19 The sons of [a]Merari *were* Mahli and Mushi. And these are
the families of the Levites according to their fathers' *households.*
20 Of Gershom: Libni his son, Jahath his son, Zimmah his son,
21 Joah his son, Iddo his son, Zerah his son, Jeatherai his son.
22 The sons of Kohath *were* Amminadab his son, Korah his
son, Assir his son,
23 Elkanah his son, Ebiasaph his son and Assir his son,
24 Tahath his son, Uriel his son, Uzziah his son and Shaul his
son.
25 The sons of Elkanah *were* Amasai and Ahimoth.
26 *As for* Elkanah, the sons of Elkanah *were* Zophai his son
and Nahath his son,
27 Eliab his son, Jeroham his son, Elkanah his son.
28 The sons of Samuel *were* [a]Joel the firstborn, and Abijah the
second.
29 The sons of Merari *were* Mahli, Libni his son, Shimei his
son, Uzzah his son,
30 Shimea his son, Haggiah his son, Asaiah his son.
31 [a]Now these are those whom David appointed over the service
of song in the house of the LORD, [b]after the ark rested *there.*
32 They ministered with song before the tabernacle of the
tent of meeting, until Solomon had built the house of the LORD
in Jerusalem; and they [1]served in their office according to their
order.

33 These are those who [1]served with their sons: From the sons
of the Kohathites *were* Heman the singer, the son of Joel, the
son of Samuel,
34 the son of Elkanah, the son of Jeroham, the son of Eliel, the
son of Toah,
35 the son of Zuph, the son of Elkanah, the son of Mahath,
the son of Amasai,
36 the son of Elkanah, the son of Joel, the son of Azariah, the
son of Zephaniah,
37 the son of Tahath, the son of Assir, the son of Ebiasaph, the
son of Korah,
38 the son of Izhar, the son of Kohath, the son of Levi, the son
of Israel.
39 *Heman's* brother Asaph stood at his right hand, even
Asaph the son of Berechiah, the son of Shimea,
40 the son of Michael, the son of Baaseiah, the son of Malchijah,
41 the son of Ethni, the son of Zerah, the son of Adaiah,
42 the son of Ethan, the son of Zimmah, the son of Shimei,
43 the son of Jahath, the son of Gershom, the son of Levi.
44 On the left hand *were* their [1]kinsmen the sons of Merari:
Ethan the son of Kishi, the son of Abdi, the son of Malluch,
45 the son of Hashabiah, the son of Amaziah, the son of Hilkiah,
46 the son of Amzi, the son of Bani, the son of Shemer,
47 the son of Mahli, the son of Mushi, the son of Merari, the
son of Levi.
48 Their [1]kinsmen the Levites were [2]appointed for all the
service of the tabernacle of the house of God.
49 But Aaron and his sons [1a]offered on the altar of burnt
offering and [b]on the altar of incense, for all the work of the most
holy place, and [c]to make atonement for Israel, according to all
that Moses the servant of God had commanded.
50 [a]These are the sons of Aaron: Eleazar his son, Phinehas his
son, Abishua his son,
51 Bukki his son, Uzzi his son, Zerahiah his son,
52 Meraioth his son, Amariah his son, Ahitub his son,
53 Zadok his son, Ahimaaz his son.
54 Now these are their settlements according to their camps
within their borders. To the sons of Aaron of the families of the
Kohathites (for theirs was the [a]*first* lot),
55 to them they gave [a]Hebron in the land of Judah and its
pasture lands around it;
56 [a]but the fields of the city and its villages, they gave to Caleb
the son of Jephunneh.
57 [a]To the sons of Aaron they gave the *following* cities of refuge:
Hebron, Libnah also with its pasture lands, Jattir, Eshtemoa
with its pasture lands,
58 [1]Hilen with its pasture lands, Debir with its pasture lands,
59 [1]Ashan with its pasture lands and Beth-shemesh with its
pasture lands;
60 and from the tribe of Benjamin: Geba with its pasture lands,
[1]Allemeth with its pasture lands, and Anathoth with its pasture

33 [1]Lit *stood*

44 [1]Lit *brothers*

48 [1]Lit *brothers* [2]Lit *given*

49 [1]Lit *offered up in smoke* [a]Ex 27:1-8 [b]Ex 30:1-7 [c]Ex 30:10-16

50 [a]1 Chr 6:4-8; Ezra 7:5

54 [a]Josh 21:4, 10

55 [a]Josh 14:13; 21:11f

56 [a]Josh 15:13

57 [a]Josh 21:13, 19

58 [1]In Josh 21:15, *Holon*

59 [1]In Josh 21:16, *Ain*

60 [1]In Josh 21:18, *Almon*

lands. All their cities throughout their families were thirteen
cities.
61 [a]Then to the rest of the sons of Kohath *were given* by lot,
from the family of the tribe, from the half-tribe, the half of
Manasseh, ten cities.
62 To the sons of Gershom, according to their families, *were*
given from the tribe of Issachar and from the tribe of Asher, the
tribe of Naphtali, and the tribe of Manasseh, thirteen cities in
Bashan.
63 [a]To the sons of Merari *were given* by lot, according to their
families, from the tribe of Reuben, the tribe of Gad and the
tribe of Zebulun, twelve cities.
64 [a]So the sons of Israel gave to the Levites the cities with
their pasture lands.
65 They gave by lot from the tribe of the sons of Judah, the
tribe of the sons of Simeon and the tribe of the sons of
Benjamin, [a]these cities which are mentioned by name.
66 [a]Now some of the families of the sons of Kohath had cities
of their territory from the tribe of Ephraim.
67 They gave to them the *following* cities of refuge: Shechem
in the hill country of Ephraim with its pasture lands, Gezer also
with its pasture lands,
68 Jokmeam with its pasture lands, Beth-horon with its pasture
lands,
69 Aijalon with its pasture lands and Gath-rimmon with its
pasture lands;
70 and from the half-tribe of Manasseh: Aner with its pasture
lands and Bileam with its pasture lands, for the rest of the family
of the sons of Kohath.
71 To the sons of Gershom *were given,* from the family of the
half-tribe of Manasseh: Golan in Bashan with its pasture lands
and Ashtaroth with its pasture lands;
72 and from the tribe of Issachar: Kedesh with its pasture lands,
Daberath with its pasture lands
73 and Ramoth with its pasture lands, Anem with its pasture
lands;
74 and from the tribe of Asher: Mashal with its pasture lands,
Abdon with its pasture lands,
75 Hukok with its pasture lands and Rehob with its pasture
lands;
76 and from the tribe of Naphtali: Kedesh in Galilee with its
pasture lands, Hammon with its pasture lands and Kiriathaim
with its pasture lands.
77 To the rest of *the Levites,* the sons of Merari, *were given,*
from the tribe of Zebulun: Rimmono with its pasture lands, Tabor
with its pasture lands;
78 and beyond the Jordan at Jericho, on the east side of the
Jordan, *were given them,* from the tribe of Reuben: Bezer in the
wilderness with its pasture lands, Jahzah with its pasture lands,
79 Kedemoth with its pasture lands and Mephaath with its
pasture lands;

61 [a]Josh 21:5; 1 Chr 6:66-70
63 [a]Josh 21:7, 34-40
64 [a]Num 35:1-8; Josh 21:3, 41, 42
65 [a]1 Chr 6:57-60
66 [a]Josh 21:20-26

80 and from the tribe of Gad: Ramoth in Gilead with its
pasture lands, Mahanaim with its pasture lands,
81 Heshbon with its pasture lands and Jazer with its pasture
lands.

Chapter 7 Theme

7 Now the sons of Issachar *were* four: Tola, [1]Puah, [2]Jashub
and Shimron.
2 The sons of Tola *were* Uzzi, Rephaiah, Jeriel, Jahmai, Ibsam
and Samuel, heads of their fathers' households. *The sons* of
Tola *were* mighty men of valor in their generations; [a]their
number in the days of David was 22,600.
3 The [1]son of Uzzi *was* Izrahiah. And the sons of Izrahiah
were Michael, Obadiah, Joel, Isshiah; all five of them *were*
[a]chief men.
4 With them by their generations according to their fathers'
households were 36,000 [1]troops of the army for war, for they
had many wives and sons.
5 Their [1]relatives among all the families of Issachar *were*
mighty men of valor, enrolled by genealogy, in all 87,000.
6 [a]*The sons of* Benjamin *were* three: Bela and Becher and
Jediael.
7 The sons of Bela were five: Ezbon, Uzzi, Uzziel, Jerimoth
and Iri. They *were* heads of fathers' households, mighty men of
valor, and were 22,034 enrolled by genealogy.
8 The sons of Becher *were* Zemirah, Joash, Eliezer, Elioenai,
Omri, Jeremoth, Abijah, Anathoth and Alemeth. All these *were*
the sons of Becher.
9 They were enrolled by genealogy, according to their
generations, heads of their fathers' households, 20,200 mighty
men of valor.
10 The [1]son of Jediael *was* Bilhan. And the sons of Bilhan
were Jeush, Benjamin, Ehud, Chenaanah, Zethan, Tarshish and
Ahishahar.
11 All these *were* sons of Jediael, according to the heads of
their fathers' households, 17,200 mighty men of valor, who
were [1]ready to go out with the army to war.
12 [1]Shuppim and [2]Huppim *were* the sons of [3]Ir; Hushim *was*
the [4]son of [5]Aher.
13 The sons of Naphtali *were* [1]Jahziel, Guni, Jezer, and [2]Shallum,
the sons of Bilhah.
14 The sons of Manasseh *were* Asriel, whom his Aramean
concubine bore; she bore Machir the father of Gilead.
15 Machir took a wife for Huppim and Shuppim, [1]whose
sister's name was Maacah. And the name of the second was
Zelophehad, and Zelophehad had daughters.
16 Maacah the wife of Machir bore a son, and she named him
Peresh; and the name of his brother *was* Sheresh, and his sons
were Ulam and Rakem.

7:1 [1]In Gen 46:13, *Puvvah;* in Num 26:23, *Puvah* [2]In Gen 46:13, *Iob*

2 [a]2 Sam 24:1-9

3 [1]Lit *sons* [a]1 Chr 5:24

4 [1]Or *bands*

5 [1]Lit *brothers,* and so throughout the ch

6 [a]1 Chr 8:1-40

10 [1]Lit *sons*

11 [1]Lit *going out*

12 [1]In Num 26:39, *Shephupham* [2]In Num 26:39, *Hupham* [3]In v 7, *Iri* [4]Lit *sons* [5]In Num 26:38, *Ahiram*

13 [1]In Gen 46:24, *Jahzeel* [2]In Gen 46:24 and Num 26:49, *Shillem*

15 [1]Lit *and his*

17 The [1]son of Ulam *was* Bedan. These *were* the sons of Gilead
the son of Machir, the son of Manasseh.
18 His sister Hammolecheth bore Ishhod and [1]Abiezer and
Mahlah.
19 The sons of Shemida were Ahian and Shechem and Likhi
and Aniam.
20 [a]The sons of Ephraim *were* Shuthelah and [1]Bered his son,
Tahath his son, Eleadah his son, Tahath his son,
21 Zabad his son, Shuthelah his son, and Ezer and Elead whom
the men of Gath who were born in the land killed, because they
came down to take their livestock.
22 Their father Ephraim [a]mourned many days, and his relatives
[b]came to comfort him.
23 Then he went in to his wife, and she conceived and bore a
son, and he named him [1]Beriah, because misfortune had come
upon his house.
24 His daughter was Sheerah, [a]who built lower and upper
Beth-horon, also Uzzen-sheerah.
25 Rephah was his son *along* with Resheph, Telah his son,
Tahan his son,
26 Ladan his son, Ammihud his son, Elishama his son,
27 [1]Non his son and [a]Joshua his son.
28 [a]Their possessions and settlements *were* Bethel with its
towns, and to the east [1]Naaran, and to the west Gezer with
its towns, and Shechem with its towns as far as [2]Ayyah with its
towns,
29 and along the borders of the sons of Manasseh, Beth-shean
with its towns, Taanach with its towns, Megiddo with its towns,
Dor with its towns. In these lived the [a]sons of Joseph the son of
Israel.
30 [a]The sons of Asher *were* Imnah, Ishvah, Ishvi and Beriah,
and Serah their sister.
31 The sons of Beriah *were* Heber and Malchiel, who was the
father of Birzaith.
32 Heber [1]became the father of Japhlet, [2]Shomer and Hotham,
and Shua their sister.
33 The sons of Japhlet *were* Pasach, Bimhal and Ashvath. These
were the sons of Japhlet.
34 The sons of [1]Shemer *were* Ahi and Rohgah, Jehubbah and
Aram.
35 The [1]sons of his brother Helem *were* Zophah, Imna, Shelesh
and Amal.
36 The sons of Zophah *were* Suah, Harnepher, Shual, Beri and
Imrah,
37 Bezer, Hod, Shamma, Shilshah, Ithran and Beera.
38 The sons of Jether *were* Jephunneh, Pispa and Ara.
39 The sons of Ulla *were* Arah, Hanniel and Rizia.
40 All these *were* the sons of Asher, heads of the fathers'
houses, choice and mighty men of valor, heads of the princes.
And the number of them enrolled by genealogy for service in
war was 26,000 men.

17 [1]Lit *sons*
18 [1]In Num 26:30, *Iezer*
20 [1]In Num 26:35, *Becher* [a]Num 26:35, 36
22 [a]Gen 37:34 [b]Job 2:11; John 11:19
23 [1]I.e. on misfortune
24 [a]Josh 16:3, 5; 2 Chr 8:5
27 [1]In Ex 33:11, *Nun* [a]Ex 17:9-14; 24:13
28 [1]In Josh 16:7, *Naarah* [2]Many mss read *Azzah* [a]Josh 16:2
29 [a]Judg 1:22-29
30 [a]Gen 46:17; Num 26:44-46
32 [1]Lit *begot* [2]In v 34, *Shemer*
34 [1]In v 32, *Shomer*
35 [1]Lit *son*

Chapter 8 Theme ______________________________

8 And [a]Benjamin [1]became the father of Bela his firstborn,
Ashbel the second, [b]Aharah the third,
2 Nohah the fourth and Rapha the fifth.
3 Bela had sons: [1]Addar, Gera, Abihud,
4 Abishua, Naaman, Ahoah,
5 Gera, Shephuphan and Huram.
6 These are the sons of Ehud: these are the heads of fathers'
households of the inhabitants of Geba, and they carried them
into exile to Manahath,
7 namely, Naaman, Ahijah and Gera—he carried them into
exile; and he became the father of Uzza and Ahihud.
8 Shaharaim became the father of children in the [1]country of
Moab after he had [2]sent away Hushim and Baara his wives.
9 By Hodesh his wife he became the father of Jobab, Zibia,
Mesha, Malcam,
10 Jeuz, Sachia, Mirmah. These were his sons, heads of fathers'
households.
11 By Hushim he became the father of Abitub and Elpaal.
12 The sons of Elpaal *were* Eber, Misham, and Shemed, who
built Ono and Lod, with its towns;
13 and Beriah and Shema, who were heads of fathers' *house-*
holds of the inhabitants of Aijalon, who put to flight the
inhabitants of Gath;
14 and [1]Ahio, Shashak and Jeremoth.
15 Zebadiah, Arad, Eder,
16 Michael, Ishpah and Joha *were* the sons of Beriah.
17 Zebadiah, Meshullam, Hizki, Heber,
18 Ishmerai, Izliah and Jobab *were* the sons of Elpaal.
19 Jakim, Zichri, Zabdi,
20 Elienai, Zillethai, Eliel,
21 Adaiah, Beraiah and Shimrath *were* the sons of [1]Shimei.
22 Ishpan, Eber, Eliel,
23 Abdon, Zichri, Hanan,
24 Hananiah, Elam, Anthothijah,
25 Iphdeiah and Penuel *were* the sons of Shashak.
26 Shamsherai, Shehariah, Athaliah,
27 Jaareshiah, Elijah and Zichri *were* the sons of Jeroham.
28 These were heads of the fathers' *households* according to
their generations, chief men [1]who lived in Jerusalem.
29 [a]Now in Gibeon, *Jeiel,* the father of Gibeon lived, and his
wife's name was Maacah;
30 and his firstborn son *was* Abdon, then Zur, Kish, Baal, Nadab,
31 Gedor, Ahio and [1]Zecher.
32 Mikloth became the father of [1]Shimeah. And they also lived
with their [2]relatives in Jerusalem opposite their *other* [2]relatives.
33 [a]Ner became the father of Kish, and Kish became the
father of Saul, and Saul became the father of Jonathan, Malchi-
shua, [1]Abinadab and [2]Eshbaal.
34 The son of Jonathan *was* [1]Merib-baal, and Merib-baal became
the father of Micah.

8:1 [1]Lit *begot,* and so throughout the ch [a]Gen 46:21; 1 Chr 7:6-12 [b]1 Chr 7:12

3 [1]In Gen 46:21 and Num 26:40, *Ard*

8 [1]Lit *field* [2]Lit *sent them away*

14 [1]Or *his brothers*

21 [1]In v 13, *Shema*

28 [1]Lit *these*

29 [a]1 Chr 9:35-38

31 [1]In ch 9:37, *Zechariah*

32 [1]In ch 9:38, *Shimeam* [2]Lit *brothers*

33 [1]1 Sam 14:49, *Ishvi* [2]In 2 Sam 2:8, *Ish-bosheth* [a]1 Chr 9:39-44

34 [1]In 2 Sam 4:4, *Mephibosheth*

35 The sons of Micah *were* Pithon, Melech, [1]Tarea and Ahaz.
36 Ahaz became the father of [1]Jehoaddah, and Jehoaddah
became the father of Alemeth, Azmaveth and Zimri; and Zimri
became the father of Moza.
37 Moza became the father of Binea; [1]Raphah *was* his son,
Eleasah his son, Azel his son.
38 Azel had six sons, and these *were* their names: Azrikam,
Bocheru, Ishmael, Sheariah, Obadiah and Hanan. All these *were*
the sons of Azel.
39 The sons of Eshek his brother *were* Ulam his firstborn, Jeush
the second and Eliphelet the third.
40 The sons of Ulam were mighty men of valor, archers, and
had many sons and grandsons, 150 *of them.* All these *were* of
the sons of Benjamin.

Chapter 9 Theme ____________________

9 So all Israel was enrolled by genealogies; and behold, they
are written in the Book of the Kings of Israel. And [a]Judah
was carried away into exile to Babylon for their unfaithfulness.
2 [a]Now the first who lived in their possessions in their cities
were Israel, the priests, the Levites and [b]the [1]temple servants.

536 B.C.

3 Some of the sons of Judah, of the sons of Benjamin and of
the sons of Ephraim and Manasseh lived in [a]Jerusalem:
4 Uthai the son of Ammihud, the son of Omri, the son of
Imri, the son of Bani, from the sons of Perez the [a]son of Judah.
5 From the Shilonites *were* Asaiah the firstborn and his sons.
6 From the sons of Zerah *were* Jeuel and their [1]relatives, 690
of them.
7 From the sons of Benjamin *were* Sallu the son of Meshullam,
the son of Hodaviah, the son of Hassenuah,
8 and Ibneiah the son of Jeroham, and Elah the son of Uzzi,
the son of Michri, and Meshullam the son of Shephatiah, the
son of Reuel, the son of Ibnijah;
9 and their relatives according to their generations, [a]956. All
these *were* heads of fathers' *households* according to their
fathers' houses.
10 [a]From the priests *were* Jedaiah, Jehoiarib, Jachin,
11 and [1]Azariah the son of Hilkiah, the son of Meshullam, the
son of Zadok, the son of Meraioth, the son of Ahitub, [a]the chief
officer of the house of God;
12 and Adaiah the son of Jeroham, the son of Pashhur, the son
of Malchijah, and Maasai the son of Adiel, the son of Jahzerah,
the son of Meshullam, the son of Meshillemith, the son of
Immer;
13 and their relatives, heads of their fathers' households, 1,760
very able men for the work of the service of the house of God.
14 [a]Of the Levites *were* Shemaiah the son of Hasshub, the son
of Azrikam, the son of Hashabiah, of the sons of Merari;
15 and Bakbakkar, Heresh and Galal and Mattaniah the son of
Mica, the son of [1]Zichri, the son of Asaph,

35 [1]In 9:41, *Tahrea*
36 [1]In 9:42, *Jarah*
37 [1]In 9:43, *Rephaiah*
9:1 [a]1 Chr 5:25, 26
2 [1]Heb *Nethinim* [a]Ezra 2:70; Neh 7:73; 11:3-22 [b]Ezra 2:43, 58; 8:20
3 [a]Neh 11:1
4 [a]Gen 46:12; Num 26:20
6 [1]Lit *brothers,* and so throughout the ch
9 [a]Neh 11:8
10 [a]Neh 11:10-14
11 [1]In Neh 11:11, *Seraiah* [a]Jer 20:1
14 [a]Neh 11:15-19
15 [1]In Neh 11:17, *Zabdi*

16 and [1]Obadiah the son of [2]Shemaiah, the son of Galal, the
son of Jeduthun, and Berechiah the son of Asa, the son of
Elkanah, who lived in the villages of the Netophathites.
17 Now the gatekeepers *were* [1]Shallum and Akkub and Talmon
and Ahiman and their relatives (Shallum the chief
18 *being stationed* until now at [a]the king's gate to the east).
These *were* the gatekeepers for the camp of the sons of Levi.
19 Shallum the son of Kore, the son of [1]Ebiasaph, the son of
Korah, and his relatives of his father's house, the Korahites,
were over the work of the service, keepers of the thresholds of
the tent; and their fathers had been over the camp of the LORD,
keepers of the entrance.
20 [a]Phinehas the son of Eleazar was ruler over them previously,
and the LORD was with him.
21 [a]Zechariah the son of Meshelemiah was gatekeeper of the
entrance of the tent of meeting.
22 All these who were chosen to be gatekeepers at the
thresholds were 212. These were enrolled by genealogy in
their villages, [a]whom David and Samuel the seer appointed [b]in
their office of trust.
23 So they and their sons [1]had charge of the gates of the
house of the LORD, *even* the house of the tent, as guards.
24 The gatekeepers were [1]on the four sides, to the east, west,
north and south.
25 Their relatives in their villages [a]*were* to come in every
seven days from time to time *to be* with [1]them;
26 for the four chief gatekeepers who *were* Levites, were in
an office of trust, and were over the chambers and over the
treasuries in the house of God.
27 They spent the night around the house of God, [a]because
the watch was [1]committed to them; and they *were* [2]in charge
of opening *it* morning by morning.
28 Now some of them [1]had charge of the utensils of service,
for [2]they counted them when they brought them in and when
they took them out.
29 Some of them also were appointed over the furniture and
over all the utensils of the sanctuary and [a]over the fine flour
and the wine and the oil and the frankincense and the spices.
30 Some of [a]the sons of the priests prepared the mixing of the
spices.
31 Mattithiah, one of the Levites, who was the firstborn of
Shallum the Korahite, had [a]the [1]responsibility over the things
which were baked in pans.
32 Some of their relatives of the sons of the Kohathites [a]*were*
over the showbread to prepare it every sabbath.
33 Now these are [a]the singers, heads of fathers' *households* of the
Levites, *who lived* in the chambers *of the temple* free *from other*
service; for they were [1]engaged [b]in their work day and night.
34 These were heads of fathers' *households* of the Levites
according to their generations, chief men, [1]who lived in
Jerusalem.

16 [1]In Neh 11:17, *Abda* [2]In Neh 11:17, *Shammua*
17 [1]In v 21, *Meshelemiah;* in 26:14, *Shelemiah;* in Neh 12:25, *Meshullam*
18 [a]Ezek 44:1; 46:1, 2
19 [1]In Ex 6:24, *Abiasaph*
20 [a]Num 25:7-13
21 [a]1 Chr 26:2, 14
22 [a]1 Chr 26:1 [b]2 Chr 31:15, 18
23 [1]Lit were *over the gates*
24 [1]Lit *to the four winds*
25 [1]Lit *these* [a]2 Kin 11:5, 7; 2 Chr 23:8
27 [1]Lit *on them* [2]Lit *over the opening* [a]1 Chr 23:30-32
28 [1]Lit *were over the* [2]Lit *by count they brought them in and by count they took them out*
29 [a]1 Chr 23:29
30 [a]Ex 30:23-25
31 [1]Lit *office of trust* [a]1 Chr 9:22
32 [a]Lev 24:5-8
33 [1]Lit *over them in the work* [a]1 Chr 6:31-47; 25:1 [b]Ps 134:1
34 [1]Lit *these*

35 [a]In Gibeon Jeiel the father of Gibeon lived, and his wife's name was Maacah,

36 and his firstborn son *was* Abdon, then Zur, Kish, Baal, Ner, Nadab,

37 Gedor, Ahio, Zechariah and Mikloth.

38 Mikloth became the father of Shimeam. And they also lived with their relatives in Jerusalem opposite their *other* relatives.

39 [a]Ner became the father of Kish, and Kish became the father of Saul, and Saul became the father of Jonathan, Malchi-shua, Abinadab and Eshbaal.

40 The son of Jonathan *was* Merib-baal; and Merib-baal became the father of Micah.

41 The sons of Micah *were* Pithon, Melech, Tahrea [a]*and Ahaz.*

42 Ahaz became the father of Jarah, and Jarah became the father of Alemeth, Azmaveth and Zimri; and Zimri became the father of Moza,

43 and Moza became the father of Binea and Rephaiah his son, Eleasah his son, Azel his son.

44 Azel had six sons whose names are these: Azrikam, Bocheru and Ishmael and Sheariah and Obadiah and Hanan. These were the sons of Azel.

Chapter 10 Theme ______________________________

1011 B.C.

1 Samuel 31

10 [a]Now the Philistines fought against Israel; and the men of Israel fled before the Philistines and fell slain on Mount Gilboa.

2 The Philistines closely pursued Saul and his sons, and the Philistines struck down Jonathan, [1a]Abinadab and Malchi-shua, the sons of Saul.

3 The battle became heavy against Saul, and the archers [1]overtook him; and he was wounded by the archers.

4 Then Saul said to his armor bearer, "Draw your sword and thrust me through with it, otherwise these uncircumcised will come and abuse me." But his armor bearer would not, for he was greatly afraid. [a]Therefore Saul took his sword and fell on it.

5 When his armor bearer saw that Saul was dead, he likewise fell on his sword and died.

6 [a]Thus Saul died with his three sons, and all *those* of his house died together.

7 When all the men of Israel who were in the valley saw that they had fled, and that Saul and his sons were dead, they forsook their cities and fled; and the Philistines came and lived in them.

8 It came about the next day, when the Philistines came to strip the slain, that they found Saul and his sons fallen on Mount Gilboa.

9 [a]So they stripped him and took his head and his armor and sent *messengers* around the land of the Philistines to carry the good news to their idols and to the people.

10 They put his armor in the house of their gods and fastened his head in the house of Dagon.

RETURN TO INSTRUCTIONS

35 [a]1 Chr 8:29-32
39 [a]1 Chr 8:33-38
41 [a]1 Chr 8:35-37
10:1 [a]1 Sam 31:1-13
2 [1]In 1 Sam 14:49, *Ishvi* [a]1 Sam 31:2
3 [1]Lit *found him*
4 [a]1 Sam 31:4
6 [a]1 Sam 31:6
9 [a]1 Sam 31:9

11 When all Jabesh-gilead heard all that the Philistines had
done to Saul,
12 [a]all the valiant men arose and took away the body of Saul and
the bodies of his sons and brought them to Jabesh, and they
buried their bones under the oak in Jabesh, and fasted seven days.
13 [a]So Saul died for his trespass which he committed against
the LORD, because of the word of the LORD which he did not
keep; and also [b]because he asked counsel of a medium, making
inquiry *of it,*
14 and did not inquire of the LORD. Therefore He killed him
and [a]turned the kingdom to David the son of Jesse.

Chapter 11 Theme ______________________

2 Samuel 5

11 [a]Then all Israel gathered to David at Hebron [1]and said,
"Behold, we are your bone and your flesh.
2 "In times past, even when Saul was king, you *were* the one
who led out and brought in Israel; and the LORD your God said
to you, '[a]You shall shepherd My people Israel, and you shall be
prince over My people Israel.'"
3 So all the elders of Israel came to the king at Hebron, and
David made a covenant with them in Hebron before the LORD;
and [a]they anointed David king over Israel, [b]according to the
word of the LORD through Samuel.
4 Then David and all Israel went to Jerusalem ([a]that is, Jebus);
and the Jebusites, the inhabitants of the land, *were* there.
5 The inhabitants of Jebus said to David, "You shall not enter
here." Nevertheless David captured the stronghold of Zion
(that is, the city of David).
6 Now David had said, "Whoever strikes down a Jebusite
first shall be chief and commander." [a]Joab the son of Zeruiah
went up first, so he became chief.
7 Then David dwelt in the stronghold; therefore it was called
the city of David.
8 He [1]built the city all around, from the [2]Millo even to the
surrounding area; and Joab [3]repaired the rest of the city.
9 [a]David became greater and greater, for the LORD of hosts
was with him.

2 Samuel 23

10 [a]Now these are the heads of the mighty men whom David
had, who gave him strong support in his kingdom, together
with all Israel, to make him king, [b]according to the word of the
LORD concerning Israel.
11 These *constitute* the list of the mighty men whom David
had: [a]Jashobeam, the son of a Hachmonite, [b]the chief of the
thirty; he lifted up his spear against three hundred [1]whom he
killed at one time.
12 After him was Eleazar the son of [a]Dodo, the Ahohite, who
was [1]one of the three mighty men.
13 He was with David at [1]Pasdammim [a]when the Philistines
were gathered together there to battle, and there was a plot of
ground full of barley; and the people fled before the Philistines.

12 [a]1 Sam 31:12f

13 [a]1 Sam 13:13, 14; 15:23 [b]Lev 19:31; 20:6; 1 Sam 28:7

14 [a]1 Sam 15:28; 1 Chr 12:23

11:1 [1]Lit *saying* [a]2 Sam 5:1, 3, 6-10

2 [a]2 Sam 5:2; 7:7

3 [a]2 Sam 2:4; 5:3, 5 [b]1 Sam 16:1, 3, 12, 13

4 [a]Josh 15:8, 63; Judg 1:21

6 [a]2 Sam 8:16

8 [1]Or *fortified* [2]I.e. citadel [3]Lit *revived*

9 [a]2 Sam 3:1

10 [a]2 Sam 23:8-39 [b]1 Chr 11:3

11 [1]Lit *slain ones* [a]2 Sam 23:8 [b]1 Chr 12:18

12 [1]Lit *among* [a]1 Chr 27:4

13 [1]In 1 Sam 17:1, *Ephesdammim* [a]2 Sam 23:11, 12

14 They took their stand in the midst of the plot and defended it, and struck down the Philistines; and the LORD saved them by a great [1]victory.

15 Now three of the thirty chief men went down to the rock to David, into the cave of Adullam, while [a]the army of the Philistines was camping in the valley of Rephaim.

16 David was then in the stronghold, while [a]the garrison of the Philistines *was* then in Bethlehem.

17 David had a craving and said, "Oh that someone would give me water to drink from the well of Bethlehem, which is by the gate!"

18 So the three broke through the camp of the Philistines and drew water from the well of Bethlehem which *was* by the gate, and took *it* and brought *it* to David; nevertheless David would not drink it, but poured it out to the LORD;

19 and he said, "Be it far from me before my God that I should do this. Shall I drink the blood of these men *who went* [1]at the risk of their lives? For at the risk of their lives they brought it." Therefore he would not drink it. These things the three mighty men did.

20 As for [1]Abshai the brother of Joab, he was chief of the [2]thirty, and he swung his spear against three hundred [3]and killed them; and he had a name as well as the [2]thirty.

21 Of the three in the second *rank* he was the most honored and became their commander; however, he did not attain to the *first* three.

22 [a]Benaiah the son of Jehoiada, the son of a valiant man of Kabzeel, mighty in deeds, struck down the [1]two *sons of* Ariel of Moab. He also went down and [2]killed a lion inside a pit on a snowy day.

23 He [1]killed an Egyptian, a man of *great* stature five [2]cubits tall. Now in the Egyptian's hand *was* [a]a spear like a weaver's beam, but he went down to him with a club and snatched the spear from the Egyptian's hand and [1]killed him with his own spear.

24 These *things* Benaiah the son of Jehoiada did, and had a name as well as the three mighty men.

25 Behold, he was honored among the thirty, but he did not attain to the three; and David appointed him over his guard.

26 Now the mighty men of the armies *were* Asahel the brother of Joab, Elhanan the son of Dodo of Bethlehem,

27 [1]Shammoth the Harorite, Helez the [2]Pelonite,

28 Ira the son of Ikkesh the Tekoite, Abiezer the Anathothite,

29 [1]Sibbecai the Hushathite, [2]Ilai the Ahohite,

30 Maharai the Netophathite, [1]Heled the son of Baanah the Netophathite,

31 Ithai the son of Ribai of Gibeah of the sons of Benjamin, Benaiah the Pirathonite,

32 [1]Hurai of the brooks of Gaash, [2]Abiel the Arbathite,

33 Azmaveth the Baharumite, Eliahba the Shaalbonite,

34 the sons of [1]Hashem the Gizonite, Jonathan the son of Shagee the Hararite,

14 [1]Or *salvation*

15 [a]1 Chr 14:9

16 [a]1 Sam 10:5

19 [1]Lit *with their souls*

20 [1]In 2 Sam 23:18, *Abishai* [2]So Syriac; M.T. *three* [3]Lit *slain ones*

22 [1]Or *two lion-like heroes* of [2]Lit *smote* [a]2 Sam 8:18

23 [1]Lit *smote* [2]I.e. One cubit equals approx 18 in. [a]1 Sam 17:7

27 [1]In 2 Sam 23:25, *Shammah the Harodite* [2]In 2 Sam 23:26, *Paltite*

29 [1]In 2 Sam 23:27, *Mebunnai* [2]In 2 Sam 23:28, *Zalmon*

30 [1]In 2 Sam 23:29, *Heleb*

32 [1]In 2 Sam 23:30, *Hiddai* [2]In 2 Sam 23:31, *Abi-albon*

34 [1]In 2 Sam 23:32, *Jashen*

35 Ahiam the son of [1]Sacar the Hararite, [2]Eliphal the son of Ur,
36 Hepher the Mecherathite, Ahijah the Pelonite,
37 Hezro the Carmelite, [1]Naarai the son of Ezbai,
38 Joel the brother of Nathan, Mibhar the son of Hagri,
39 Zelek the Ammonite, Naharai the Berothite, the armor
bearer of Joab the son of Zeruiah,
40 Ira the Ithrite, Gareb the Ithrite,
41 Uriah the Hittite, Zabad the son of Ahlai,
42 Adina the son of Shiza the Reubenite, a chief of the
Reubenites, and thirty with him,
43 Hanan the son of Maacah and Joshaphat the Mithnite,
44 Uzzia the Ashterathite, Shama and Jeiel the sons of Hotham
the Aroerite,
45 Jediael the son of Shimri and Joha his brother, the Tizite,
46 Eliel the Mahavite and Jeribai and Joshaviah, the sons of
Elnaam, and Ithmah the Moabite,
47 Eliel and Obed and Jaasiel the Mezobaite.

Chapter 12 Theme ____________________________________

12 [a]Now these are the ones who came to David at Ziklag,
while he was still restricted because of Saul the son of
Kish; and they were among the mighty men who helped *him*
in war.
2 They were equipped with bows, [a]using both the right hand
and the left *to sling* stones and *to shoot* arrows from the bow;
[b]*they were* Saul's kinsmen from Benjamin.
3 The chief was Ahiezer, then Joash, the sons of Shemaah
the Gibeathite; and Jeziel and Pelet, the sons of Azmaveth, and
Beracah and Jehu the Anathothite,
4 and Ishmaiah the Gibeonite, a mighty man among the thirty,
and over the thirty. [1]Then Jeremiah, Jahaziel, Johanan, Jozabad
the Gederathite,
5 [1]Eluzai, Jerimoth, Bealiah, Shemariah, Shephatiah the Har-
uphite,
6 Elkanah, Isshiah, Azarel, Joezer, Jashobeam, the Korahites,
7 and Joelah and Zebadiah, the sons of Jeroham of Gedor.
8 From the Gadites there [1]came over to David in the
stronghold in the wilderness, mighty men of valor, men trained
for war, who could handle shield and spear, and whose faces
were like the faces of lions, and [a]*they were* as swift as the
gazelles on the mountains.
9 Ezer *was* the first, Obadiah the second, Eliab the third,
10 Mishmannah the fourth, Jeremiah the fifth,
11 Attai the sixth, Eliel the seventh,
12 Johanan the eighth, Elzabad the ninth,
13 Jeremiah the tenth, Machbannai the eleventh.
14 These of the sons of Gad were [1]captains of the army; [a]he who
was least was equal to a hundred and the greatest to a thousand.
15 [a]These are the ones who crossed the Jordan in the first
month when it was overflowing all its banks and they put to
flight all those in the valleys, both to the east and to the west.

35 [1]In 2 Sam 23:33, *Sharar* [2]In 2 Sam 23:34, *Eliphelet the son of Ahasbai*
37 [1]In 2 Sam 23:35, *Paarai the Arbite*
12:1 [a]1 Sam 27:2-6
2 [a]Judg 3:15; 20:16 [b]1 Chr 12:29
4 [1]In Heb the beginning of v 5, making 41 vv in ch
5 [1]V 6 in Heb
8 [1]Lit *separated themselves* [a]2 Sam 2:18
14 [1]Or *chiefs* [a]Deut 32:30
15 [a]Josh 3:15; 4:18

16 Then some of the sons of Benjamin and Judah came to the
stronghold to David.
17 David went out to meet them, and said to them, "If you
come peacefully to me to help me, my heart shall be united
with you; but if to betray me to my adversaries, since there is
no [1]wrong in my hands, may the God of our fathers look on *it*
and decide."
18 Then [a]the Spirit [1]came upon [b]Amasai, who was the chief of
the thirty, *and he said,*
"*We* are yours, O David,
And with you, O son of Jesse!
[c]Peace, peace to you,
And peace to him who helps you;
Indeed, your God helps you!"
Then David received them and made them [2]captains of the band.
19 [a]From Manasseh also some defected to David when he was
about to go to battle with the Philistines against Saul. But they did
not help them, for the lords of the Philistines after consultation
sent him away, saying, "At *the cost of* our heads he may defect
to his master Saul."
20 As he went to Ziklag there defected to him from Manasseh:
Adnah, Jozabad, Jediael, Michael, Jozabad, Elihu and Zillethai,
[1]captains of thousands who belonged to Manasseh.
21 They helped David against [a]the band of raiders, for they
were all mighty men of valor, and were captains in the army.
22 For day by day *men* came to David to help him, until there
was a great army [a]like the army of God.
23 Now these are the numbers of the [1]divisions equipped for
war, [a]who came to David at Hebron, [b]to turn the kingdom of
Saul to him, [c]according to the [2]word of the LORD.
24 The sons of Judah who bore shield and spear *were* 6,800,
equipped for war.
25 Of the sons of Simeon, mighty men of valor for war, 7,100.
26 Of the sons of Levi 4,600.
27 Now Jehoiada was the leader of *the house of* Aaron, and
with him were 3,700,
28 also [a]Zadok, a young man mighty of valor, and of his
father's house twenty-two captains.
29 Of the sons of Benjamin, [a]Saul's kinsmen, 3,000; for until
now [b]the greatest part of them had kept their allegiance to the
house of Saul.
30 Of the sons of Ephraim 20,800, mighty men of valor, famous
men in their fathers' households.
31 Of the half-tribe of Manasseh 18,000, who were designated
by name to come and make David king.
32 Of the sons of Issachar, [a]men who understood the times,
with knowledge of what Israel should do, their chiefs *were* two
hundred; and all their kinsmen *were* at their command.
33 Of Zebulun, there were 50,000 who went out in the army,
who could draw up in battle formation with all kinds of weapons
of war and helped *David* [1]with [a]an undivided heart.

17 [1]Lit *violence*
18 [1]Lit *clothed* [2]Or *chiefs* [a]Judg 3:10; 6:34 [b]1 Chr 2:17 [c]1 Sam 25:5, 6
19 [a]1 Sam 29:2-9
20 [1]Or *chiefs*
21 [a]1 Sam 30:1
22 [a]Gen 32:2; Josh 5:13-15
23 [1]Lit *heads* [2]Lit *mouth* [a]2 Sam 2:3, 4 [b]1 Chr 10:14 [c]1 Chr 11:10
28 [a]2 Sam 8:17; 1 Chr 6:8, 53
29 [a]1 Chr 12:2 [b]2 Sam 2:8, 9
32 [a]Esth 1:13
33 [1]Lit *not of double heart* [a]Ps 12:2

34 Of Naphtali *there were* 1,000 captains, and with them
37,000 with shield and spear.
35 Of the Danites who could draw up in battle formation, *there*
were 28,600.
36 Of Asher *there were* 40,000 who went out in the army to
draw up in battle formation.
37 From the other side of the Jordan, of the Reubenites and
the Gadites and of the half-tribe of Manasseh, *there were*
120,000 with all *kinds* of weapons of war for the battle.
38 All these, being men of war who could draw up in battle
formation, came to Hebron with [a]a perfect heart to make David
king over all Israel; and all the rest also of Israel were of one
mind to make David king.
39 They were there with David three days, eating and drinking,
for their kinsmen had prepared for them.
40 Moreover those who were near to them, *even* as far as
Issachar and Zebulun and Naphtali, [a]brought food on donkeys,
camels, mules and on oxen, great quantities of flour cakes, fig
cakes and bunches of raisins, wine, oil, oxen and sheep. There
was joy indeed in Israel.

Chapter 13 Theme ____________________

2 Samuel 6

13 Then David consulted with the captains of the thousands
and the hundreds, even with every leader.
2 David said to all the assembly of Israel, "If it seems good to
you, and if it is from the LORD our God, let us send everywhere
to our kinsmen who remain in all the land of Israel, also to the
priests and Levites who are with them in their cities with
pasture lands, that they may meet with us;
3 and let us bring back the ark of our God to us, [a]for we did
not seek it in the days of Saul."
4 Then all the assembly said that they would do so, for the
thing was right in the eyes of all the people.
5 [a]So David assembled all Israel together, from the Shihor of
Egypt even to the entrance of Hamath, [b]to bring the ark of God
from Kiriath-jearim.
6 [a]David and all Israel went up to [b]Baalah, *that is,* to Kiriath-
jearim, which belongs to Judah, to bring up from there the ark
of God, the LORD [c]who is enthroned *above* the cherubim,
where His name is called.
7 They [1]carried the ark of God on a new cart from [a]the house
of Abinadab, and Uzza and Ahio drove the cart.
8 David and all Israel were celebrating before God with all *their*
might, [a]even with songs and with lyres, harps, tambourines,
cymbals and with trumpets.
9 When they came to [a]the threshing floor of Chidon, Uzza put
out his hand to hold the ark, because the oxen nearly upset *it.*
10 The anger of the LORD burned against Uzza, so He struck
him down [a]because he put out his hand to the ark; [b]and he
died there before God.

38 [a]2 Sam 5:1-3; 1 Chr 12:33
40 [a]1 Sam 25:18
13:3 [a]1 Sam 7:1, 2
5 [a]2 Sam 6:1; 1 Kin 8:65; 1 Chr 15:3 [b]1 Sam 6:21; 7:1
6 [a]2 Sam 6:2-11 [b]Josh 15:9 [c]Ex 25:22; 2 Kin 19:15
7 [1]Lit *caused to ride* [a]1 Sam 7:1
8 [a]1 Chr 15:16
9 [a]2 Sam 6:6
10 [a]1 Chr 15:13, 15 [b]Lev 10:2

11 [1]Lit *the LORD had broken through a breakthrough* [2]I.e. the breakthrough of Uzza

11 Then David became
angry because [1]of the LORD's
outburst against Uzza; and
he called that place [2]Perez-
uzza to this day.
12 David was afraid of God
that day, saying, "How can I
bring the ark of God *home*
to me?"
13 So David did not take the
ark with him to the city of
David, but took it aside [a]to
the house of Obed-edom the
Gittite.
14 Thus the ark of God
remained with the family of
Obed-edom in his house
three months; and [a]the LORD
blessed the family of Obed-edom with all that he had.

13 [a]1 Chr 15:25

14 [a]1 Chr 26:4, 5

14:1 [a]2 Sam 5:11

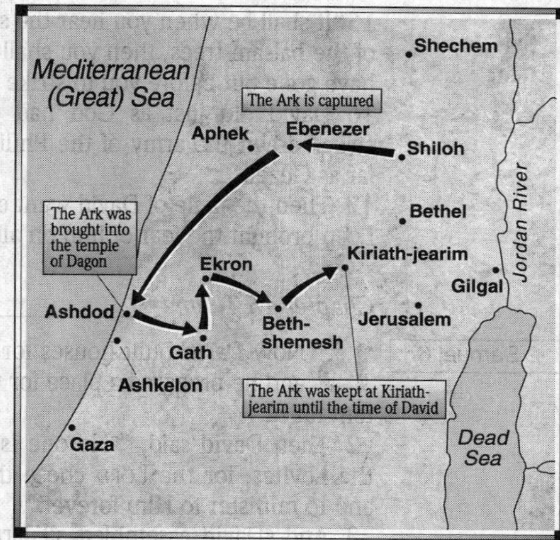

The Wanderings of the Ark
(see page 2099)

2 Samuel 5:11

Chapter 14 Theme ______________________

14 [a]Now Hiram king of Tyre sent messengers to David with
cedar trees, masons and carpenters, to build a house for him.
2 And David realized that the LORD had established him as
king over Israel, *and* that his kingdom was highly exalted, for
the sake of His people Israel.
3 Then David took more wives at Jerusalem, and David
[1]became the father of more sons and daughters.
4 [a]These are the names of the children [1]born *to him* in
Jerusalem: Shammua, Shobab, Nathan, Solomon,
5 Ibhar, Elishua, Elpelet,
6 Nogah, Nepheg, Japhia,
7 Elishama, Beeliada and Eliphelet.
8 When the Philistines heard that David had been anointed
king over all Israel, all the Philistines went up in search of
David; and David heard of it and went out against them.
9 Now the Philistines had come and [a]made a raid in the valley
of Rephaim.
10 David inquired of God, saying, "Shall I go up against the
Philistines? And will You give them into my hand?" Then the
LORD said to him, "Go up, for I will give them into your hand."
11 So they came up to Baal-perazim, and David [1]defeated them
there; and David said, "God has broken through my enemies
by my hand, like the breakthrough of waters." Therefore they
named that place [2]Baal-perazim.
12 They abandoned their gods there; so David gave the order
and they were burned with fire.
13 The Philistines made [a]yet another raid in the valley.
14 David inquired again of God, and God said to him, "You
shall not go up after them; circle around [1]behind them and come
at them in front of the [2]balsam trees.

3 [1]Lit *begot*

4 [1]Lit *were to* [a]1 Chr 3:5-8

9 [a]1 Chr 11:15; 14:13

11 [1]Lit *smote* [2]I.e. the master of breakthrough

13 [a]1 Chr 14:9

14 [1]Lit *from upon* [2]Or *baka shrubs*

15 "It shall be when you hear the sound of marching in the tops of the balsam trees, then you shall go out to battle, for God will have gone out before you to strike the army of the Philistines."
16 David did just as God had commanded him, and they struck down the army of the Philistines from [1]Gibeon even as far as Gezer.
17 Then the fame of David went out into all the lands; and [a]the LORD brought the fear of him on all the nations.

Chapter 15 Theme ____________________________________

2 Samuel 6

15 Now *David* built houses for himself in the city of David; and he prepared a place for the ark of God and [a]pitched a tent for it.
2 Then David said, "[a]No one is to carry the ark of God but the Levites; for the LORD chose them to carry the ark of God and to minister to Him forever."
3 And [a]David assembled all Israel at Jerusalem to bring up the ark of the LORD [b]to its place which he had prepared for it.
4 David gathered together the sons of Aaron and [a]the Levites:
5 of the sons of Kohath, Uriel the chief, and 120 of his [1]relatives;
6 of the sons of Merari, Asaiah the chief, and 220 of his relatives;
7 of the sons of Gershom, Joel the chief, and 130 of his relatives;
8 of the sons of Elizaphan, Shemaiah the chief, and 200 of his relatives;
9 of the sons of Hebron, Eliel the chief, and 80 of his relatives;
10 of the sons of Uzziel, Amminadab the chief, and 112 of his relatives.
11 Then David called for [a]Zadok and [b]Abiathar the priests, and for the Levites, for Uriel, Asaiah, Joel, Shemaiah, Eliel and Amminadab,
12 and said to them, "You are the heads of the fathers' *households* of the Levites; [a]consecrate yourselves both you and your relatives, that you may bring up the ark of the LORD God of Israel [b]to *the place* that I have prepared for it.
13 "[a]Because you did not *carry it* at the first, the LORD our God made an outburst on us, for we did not seek Him according to the ordinance."
14 [a]So the priests and the Levites consecrated themselves to bring up the ark of the LORD God of Israel.
15 The sons of [a]the Levites carried the ark of God on their shoulders with the poles thereon, as Moses had commanded according to the word of the LORD.
16 Then David spoke to the chiefs of the Levites [a]to appoint their relatives the singers, with instruments of music, harps, lyres, loud-sounding cymbals, to raise sounds of joy.

16 [1]In 2 Sam 5:25, *Geba*
17 [a]Ex 15:14-16; Deut 2:25
15:1 [a]1 Chr 15:3; 16:1; 17:1-5
2 [a]Num 4:15; Deut 10:8
3 [a]1 Kin 8:1; 1 Chr 13:5 [b]Ex 40:20f; 2 Sam 6:12, 17; 1 Chr 15:1, 12
4 [a]1 Chr 6:16-30; 12:26
5 [1]Lit *brothers;* i.e. fellow tribesmen, and so throughout the ch
11 [a]1 Chr 12:28 [b]1 Sam 22:20-23; 1 Kin 2:26, 35
12 [a]Ex 19:14, 15; 2 Chr 35:6 [b]1 Chr 15:1, 3
13 [a]2 Sam 6:3; 1 Chr 13:7
14 [a]1 Chr 15:12
15 [a]Ex 25:14; Num 4:5f
16 [a]1 Chr 13:8; 25:1

17 So [a]the Levites appointed Heman the son of Joel, and from his relatives, Asaph the son of Berechiah; and from the sons of Merari their relatives, Ethan the son of Kushaiah,

18 and with them their relatives of the second rank, Zechariah, [1]Ben, Jaaziel, Shemiramoth, Jehiel, Unni, Eliab, Benaiah, Maaseiah, Mattithiah, Eliphelehu, Mikneiah, Obed-edom and Jeiel, the gatekeepers.

19 So the singers, Heman, Asaph and Ethan *were appointed* to sound aloud cymbals of bronze;

20 and Zechariah, Aziel, Shemiramoth, Jehiel, Unni, Eliab, Maaseiah and Benaiah, with [1]harps *tuned* to [a]alamoth;

21 and Mattithiah, Eliphelehu, Mikneiah, Obed-edom, Jeiel and Azaziah, to lead with [1]lyres tuned to [a]the sheminith.

22 Chenaniah, chief of the Levites, was *in charge of* the singing; he gave instruction in singing because he was skillful.

23 Berechiah and Elkanah were gatekeepers for the ark.

24 Shebaniah, Joshaphat, Nethanel, Amasai, Zechariah, Benaiah and Eliezer, the priests, [a]blew the trumpets before the ark of God. Obed-edom and Jehiah also *were* gatekeepers for the ark.

25 [a]So *it was* David, with the elders of Israel and the captains over thousands, who went to bring up the ark of the covenant of the LORD from [b]the house of Obed-edom with joy.

26 Because God was helping the Levites who were carrying the ark of the covenant of the LORD, they sacrificed [a]seven bulls and seven rams.

27 Now David was clothed with a robe of fine linen with all the Levites who were carrying the ark, and the singers and Chenaniah the leader of the singing *with* the singers. [a]David also wore an ephod of linen.

28 Thus all Israel brought up the ark of the covenant of the LORD with shouting, and with sound of the horn, with trumpets, with loud-sounding cymbals, with harps and lyres.

29 It happened when the ark of the covenant of the LORD came to the city of David, that [a]Michal the daughter of Saul looked out of the window and saw King David leaping and celebrating; and she despised him in her heart.

Robe of the Ephod

Chapter 16 Theme ________________________

16 And they brought in the ark of God and [a]placed it inside the tent which David had pitched for it, and they offered burnt offerings and peace offerings before God.

2 When David had finished offering the burnt offering and the peace offerings, he blessed the people in the name of the LORD.

3 He distributed to everyone of Israel, both man and woman, to everyone a loaf of bread and a portion *of meat* and a raisin cake.

4 He appointed some of the Levites *as* ministers before the ark of the LORD, even to celebrate and to thank and praise the LORD God of Israel:

17 [a]1 Chr 25:1
18 [1]Omitted in Gr and many mss
20 [1]Or *harps of maiden-like tone* [a]Ps 46: title
21 [1]Or *octave harps* [a]Ps 6: title
24 [a]1 Chr 15:28; 16:6
25 [a]2 Sam 6:12, 15 [b]1 Chr 13:13
26 [a]Num 23:1-4, 29
27 [a]2 Sam 6:14
29 [a]2 Sam 3:13f; 6:16
16:1 [a]1 Chr 15:1

5 Asaph the chief, and second to him Zechariah, *then* [1]Jeiel,
Shemiramoth, Jehiel, Mattithiah, Eliab, Benaiah, Obed-edom
and Jeiel, with musical instruments, harps, lyres; also Asaph
played loud-sounding cymbals,
6 and Benaiah and Jahaziel the priests *blew* trumpets
continually before the ark of the covenant of God.
7 Then on that day David [a]first assigned [1]Asaph and his
[2]relatives to give thanks to the LORD.

8 [a]Oh give thanks to the LORD, call upon His name;
[b]Make known His deeds among the peoples.
9 Sing to Him, sing praises to Him;
[1]Speak of all His [2]wonders.
10 [1]Glory in His holy name;
Let the heart of those who seek the LORD be glad.
11 [a]Seek the LORD and His strength;
Seek His face continually.
12 [a]Remember His wonderful deeds which He has done,
[b]His marvels and the judgments from His mouth,
13 O seed of Israel His servant,
Sons of Jacob, His chosen ones!
14 He is the LORD our God;
[a]His judgments are in all the earth.
15 Remember His covenant forever,
The word which He commanded to a thousand
generations,
16 [a]*The covenant* which He made with Abraham,
And His oath to Isaac.
17 [a]He also confirmed it to Jacob for a statute,
To Israel as an everlasting covenant,
18 Saying, "[a]To you I will give the land of Canaan,
As the portion of your inheritance."
19 [a]When they were only a few in number,
Very few, and strangers in it,
20 And they wandered about from nation to nation,
And from *one* kingdom to another people,
21 He permitted no man to oppress them,
And [a]He reproved kings for their sakes, *saying,*
22 "Do not touch My anointed ones,
And [a]do My prophets no harm."
23 [a]Sing to the LORD, all the earth;
Proclaim good tidings of His salvation from day to day.
24 Tell of His glory among the nations,
His wonderful deeds among all the peoples.
25 For [a]great is the LORD, and greatly to be praised;
He also is [b]to be feared above all gods.
26 For all the gods of the peoples are [1a]idols,
[b]But the LORD made the heavens.
27 Splendor and majesty are before Him,
Strength and joy are in His place.
28 Ascribe to the LORD, O families of the peoples,
Ascribe to the LORD glory and strength.

5 [1]In 1 Chr 15:18, *Jaaziel*

7 [1]Lit *by the hand of Asaph* [2]Lit *brothers* [a]2 Sam 22:1; 23:1

8 [a]1 Chr 16:8-36; Ps 105:1-15 [b]1 Kin 8:43; 2 Kin 19:19

9 [1]Or *Meditate on* [2]I.e. wonderful acts

10 [1]Or *Boast*

11 [a]Ps 24:6

12 [a]Ps 103:2 [b]Ps 78:43-68

14 [a]Ps 48:10

16 [a]Gen 12:7; 17:2; 22:16-18; 26:3

17 [a]Gen 35:11, 12

18 [a]Gen 13:15

19 [a]Gen 34:30; Deut 7:7

21 [a]Gen 12:17; 20:3; Ex 7:15-18

22 [a]Gen 20:7

23 [a]Ps 96:1-13

25 [a]Ps 144:3-6 [b]Ps 89:7

26 [1]Or *non-existent things* [a]Lev 19:4 [b]Ps 102:25

29 Ascribe to the LORD the glory due His name;
Bring an [1]offering, and come before Him;
[a]Worship the LORD in [2]holy array.
30 Tremble before Him, all the earth;
Indeed, the world is firmly established, it will not be
moved.
31 [a]Let the heavens be glad, and let the earth rejoice;
And let them say among the nations, "[b]The LORD reigns."
32 [a]Let the sea [1]roar, and [2]all it contains;
Let the field exult, and all that is in it.
33 Then the trees of the forest will sing for joy before the LORD;
For He is coming to judge the earth.
34 [a]O give thanks to the LORD, for *He is* good;
For His lovingkindness is everlasting.
35 [a]Then say, "Save us, O God of our salvation,
And gather us and deliver us from the nations,
To give thanks to Your holy name,
And [1]glory in Your praise."
36 [a]Blessed be the LORD, the God of Israel,
From everlasting even to everlasting.
Then all the people [b]said, "Amen," and praised the LORD.
37 So he left Asaph and his [1]relatives there [a]before the ark of
the covenant of the LORD to minister before the ark continually,
[b]as every day's work required;
38 and [a]Obed-edom with [1]his 68 relatives; Obed-edom, also
the son of Jeduthun, and [b]Hosah as gatekeepers.
39 *He left* [a]Zadok the priest and his [1]relatives the priests [b]before
the [2]tabernacle of the LORD in the high place which *was* at
Gibeon,
40 to offer burnt offerings to the LORD on the altar of burnt
offering continually morning and evening, [a]even according to
all that is written in the law of the LORD, which He commanded
Israel.
41 With them *were* [a]Heman and Jeduthun, and [b]the rest who
were chosen, who were designated by name, to [c]give thanks to
the LORD, because His lovingkindness is everlasting.
42 And with them *were* Heman and Jeduthun *with* trumpets
and cymbals for those who should sound aloud, and *with*
instruments *for* [a]the songs of God, and the sons of Jeduthun for
the gate.
43 [a]Then all the people departed each to his house, and David
returned to bless his household.

Chapter 17 Theme ____________

17 [a]And it came about, when David dwelt in his house, that
David said to Nathan the prophet, "Behold, I am
dwelling in a house of cedar, but the ark of the covenant of the
LORD is under curtains."
2 Then Nathan said to David, "Do all that is in your heart, for
God is with you."

2 Samuel 7

29 [1]Or *a grain offering* [2]Or *the splendor of holiness* [a]Ps 29:2
31 [a]Is 44:23; 49:13 [b]Ps 93:1; 96:10
32 [1]Or *thunder* [2]Lit *its fullness* [a]Ps 98:7
34 [a]2 Chr 5:13; 7:3; Ezra 3:11; Ps 106:1; 136:1; Jer 33:11
35 [1]Lit *boast* [a]Ps 106:47, 48
36 [a]1 Kin 8:15, 56; Ps 72:18 [b]Deut 27:15; Neh 8:6
37 [1]Lit *brothers* [a]1 Chr 16:4, 5 [b]2 Chr 8:14; Ezra 3:4
38 [1]Lit *their brothers, 68* [a]1 Chr 13:14 [b]1 Chr 26:10
39 [1]Lit *brothers* [2]Lit *dwelling place* [a]1 Chr 15:11 [b]1 Kin 3:4
40 [a]Ex 29:38-42; Num 28:3, 4
41 [a]1 Chr 6:33 [b]1 Chr 25:1-6 [c]2 Chr 5:13
42 [a]1 Chr 25:7; 2 Chr 7:6; 29:27
43 [a]2 Sam 6:19
17:1 [a]2 Sam 7:1-29

3 It came about the same night that the word of God came to
Nathan, saying,
4 "Go and tell David My servant, 'Thus says the LORD, "[a]You
shall not build a house for Me to dwell in;
5 for I have not dwelt in a house since the day that I brought
up Israel to this day, [a]but I have [1]gone from tent to tent and
from *one* dwelling place *to another.*
6 "In all places where I have walked with all Israel, have I
spoken a word [a]with any of the judges of Israel, whom I
commanded to shepherd My people, saying, 'Why have you
not built for Me a house of cedar?'"'
7 "Now, therefore, thus shall you say to My servant David,
'Thus says the LORD of hosts, "I took you from the pasture,
from following the sheep, to be leader over My people Israel.
8 "I have been with you wherever you have gone, and have
cut off all your enemies from before you; and I will make you a
name like the name of the great ones who are in the earth.
9 "I will appoint a place for My people Israel, and will plant
them, so that they may dwell in their own place and not be
moved again; and the [1]wicked will not waste them anymore as
formerly,
10 even from the day that I commanded judges *to be* over My
people Israel. And I will subdue all your enemies.
Moreover, I tell you that the LORD will build a house for you.
11 "When your days are fulfilled that you must go *to be* with
your fathers, that I will set up *one of* your [1]descendants after
you, who will be of your sons; and I will establish his
kingdom.
12 "He shall build for Me a house, and I will establish his
throne forever.
13 "[a]I will be his father and he shall be My son; and I will not
take My lovingkindness away from him, [b]as I took it from him
who was before you.
14 "But I will settle him in My house and in My kingdom
forever, and his throne shall be established forever."'"
15 According to all these words and according to all this
vision, so Nathan spoke to David.
16 Then David the king went in and sat before the LORD and
said, "[a]Who am I, O LORD God, and what is my house that You
have brought me this far?
17 "This was a small thing in Your eyes, O God; but You have
spoken of Your servant's house for a great while to come, and
have regarded me according to the standard of a man of high
degree, O LORD God.
18 "What more can David still *say* to You concerning the honor
bestowed on Your servant? For You know Your servant.
19 "O LORD, [a]for Your servant's sake, and according to Your
own heart, You have wrought all this greatness, to make
known all these great things.
20 "O LORD, there is none like You, nor is there any God
besides You, according to all that we have heard with our ears.

4 [a]1 Chr 28:2, 3

5 [1]Lit *been* [a]Ex 40:2, 3; 2 Sam 7:6

6 [a]2 Sam 7:7

9 [1]Lit *sons of wickedness*

11 [1]Lit *seed*

13 [a]2 Cor 6:18; Heb 1:5 [b]1 Chr 10:14

16 [a]2 Sam 7:18

19 [a]2 Sam 7:21; Is 37:35

21 "And what one nation in the earth is like Your people Israel,
whom God went to redeem for Himself *as* a people, to make
You a name by great and terrible things, in driving out nations
from before Your people, whom You redeemed out of Egypt?
22 "[a]For Your people Israel You made Your own people forever,
and You, O LORD, became their God.
23 "Now, O LORD, let the word that You have spoken concerning
Your servant and concerning his house be established forever,
and do as You have spoken.
24 "Let Your name be established and magnified forever, saying,
'The LORD of hosts is the God of Israel, *even* a God to Israel;
and the house of David Your servant is established before You.'
25 "For You, O my God, have revealed to Your servant that You
will build for him a house; therefore Your servant has found
courage to pray before You.
26 "Now, O LORD, You are God, and have [1]promised this good
thing to Your servant.
27 "And now it has pleased You to bless the house of Your
servant, that it may [1]continue forever before You; for You, O
LORD, have blessed, and it is blessed forever."

Chapter 18 Theme ____________________

18 Now after this [a]it came about that David [1]defeated the
Philistines and subdued them and took Gath and its
towns from the hand of the Philistines.

2 Samuel 8

2 He defeated Moab, and the Moabites became servants to
David, bringing tribute.
3 David also defeated Hadadezer king of Zobah *as far as*
Hamath, as he went to establish his [1]rule to the Euphrates River.
4 David took from him 1,000 chariots and 7,000 horsemen
and 20,000 foot soldiers, and David hamstrung all the chariot
horses, but reserved *enough* of them for 100 chariots.
5 When the Arameans of [1]Damascus came to help Hadadezer
king [a]of Zobah, David [2]killed 22,000 men of the Arameans.
6 Then David put *garrisons* among the Arameans of
[1]Damascus; and the Arameans became servants to David,
bringing tribute. And the LORD helped David wherever he went.
7 David took the shields of gold which were [1]carried by the
servants of Hadadezer and brought them to Jerusalem.
8 Also from [1]Tibhath and from Cun, cities of Hadadezer,
David took a very large amount of bronze, with which [a]Solomon
made the bronze sea and the pillars and the bronze utensils.
9 Now when [1]Tou king of Hamath heard that David had
[2]defeated all the army of Hadadezer king of Zobah,
10 he sent [1]Hadoram his son to King David to [2]greet him and to
bless him, because he had fought against Hadadezer and had
[3]defeated him; for Hadadezer had been at war with Tou. And
Hadoram brought all kinds of articles of gold and silver and bronze.
11 King David also dedicated these to the LORD with the silver
and the gold which he had carried away from all the nations:

22 [a]Ex 19:5, 6
26 [1]Lit *said*
27 [1]Lit *be*
18:1 [1]Lit *smote,* and so in vv 1-3 [a]2 Sam 8:1-18
3 [1]Lit *hand*
5 [1]Heb *Darmeseq* [2]Lit *smote* [a]1 Chr 19:6
6 [1]Heb *Darmeseq*
7 [1]Lit *on*
8 [1]In 2 Sam 8:8, *Betah* [a]1 Kin 7:40-47; 2 Chr 4:11-18
9 [1]In 2 Sam 8:9, *Toi* [2]Lit *smitten*
10 [1]In 2 Sam 8:10, *Joram* [2]Lit *ask him of his welfare* [3]Lit *smitten*

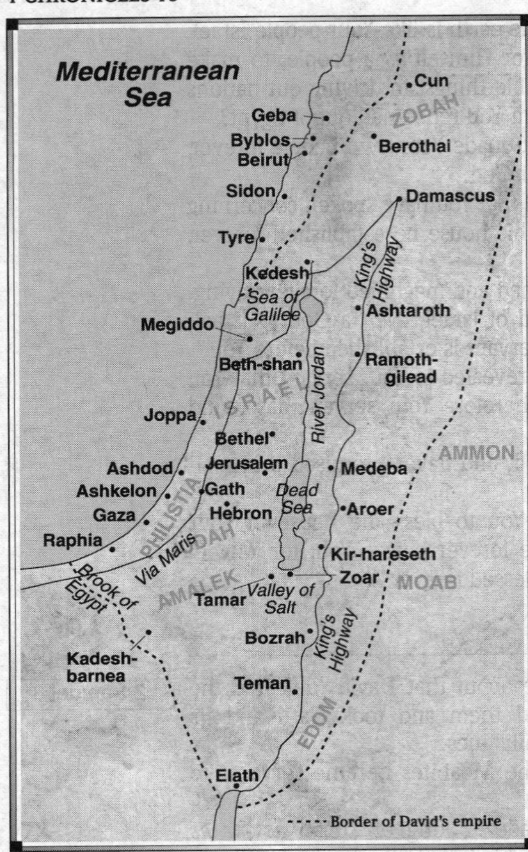

from Edom, Moab, the sons
of Ammon, the Philistines,
and from Amalek.
12 Moreover Abishai the
son of Zeruiah [1]defeated
18,000 Edomites in the
Valley of Salt.
13 Then he put garrisons in
Edom, and all the Edomites
became servants to David.
And the LORD helped David
wherever he went.
14 So David reigned over
all Israel; and he [1]admin-
istered justice and righteousness for all his people.
15 [a]Joab the son of Zeruiah
was over the army, and
Jehoshaphat the son of Ahilud *was* recorder;
16 and Zadok the son of
Ahitub and Abimelech the
son of Abiathar *were* priests,
and Shavsha *was* secretary;
17 and Benaiah the son of
Jehoiada *was* over the Cherethites and the Pelethites,
and the sons of David *were*
chiefs at the king's side.

12 [1]Lit *smote*

14 [1]Lit *was doing*

15 [a]1 Chr 11:6

19:1 [a]2 Sam 10:1-19

The Borders of David's Empire

2 Samuel 10

Chapter 19 Theme ______________

19 [a]Now it came about after this, that Nahash the king of
the sons of Ammon died, and his son became king in his
place.
2 Then David said, "I will show kindness to Hanun the son
of Nahash, because his father showed kindness to me." So
David sent messengers to console him concerning his father.
And David's servants came into the land of the sons of Ammon
to Hanun to console him.
3 But the princes of the sons of Ammon said to Hanun, "[1]Do
you think that David is honoring your father, in that he has
sent comforters to you? Have not his servants come to you to
search and to overthrow and to spy out the land?"
4 So Hanun took David's servants and shaved them and cut
off their garments in the middle as far as their hips, and sent
them away.
5 Then *certain persons* went and told David about the men.
And he sent to meet them, for the men were greatly
humiliated. And the king said, "[1]Stay at Jericho until your
beards grow, and *then* return."

3 [1]Lit *In your eyes is David honoring your father because*

5 [1]Lit *Return to*

6 [a]1 Chr 18:5, 9

6 When the sons of Ammon saw that they had made themselves odious to David, Hanun and the sons of Ammon sent 1,000
talents of silver to hire for themselves chariots and horsemen
from Mesopotamia, from Aram-maacah and [a]from Zobah.
7 So they hired for themselves 32,000 chariots, and the king of
Maacah and his people, who came and camped before [a]Medeba.
And the sons of Ammon gathered together from their cities
and came to battle.
8 When David heard *of it,* he sent Joab and all the army, the
mighty men.
9 The sons of Ammon came out and drew up in battle array
at the entrance of the city, and the kings who had come were
by themselves in the field.
10 Now when Joab saw that the [1]battle was set against him in
front and in the rear, he selected from all the choice men of
Israel and they arrayed themselves against the Arameans.
11 But the remainder of the people he placed in the hand of
[1]Abshai his brother; and they arrayed themselves against the
sons of Ammon.
12 He said, "If the Arameans are too strong for me, then you
shall help me; but if the sons of Ammon are too strong for you,
then I will help you.
13 "Be strong, and let us show ourselves courageous for the
sake of our people and for the cities of our God; and may the
LORD do what is good in His sight."
14 So Joab and the people who were with him drew near to
the battle against the Arameans, and they fled before him.
15 When the sons of Ammon saw that the Arameans fled,
they also fled before Abshai his brother and entered the city.
Then Joab came to Jerusalem.
16 When the Arameans saw that they had been [1]defeated by
Israel, they sent messengers and brought out the Arameans
who were beyond the [2]River, with Shophach the commander
of the army of Hadadezer [3]leading them.
17 When it was told David, he gathered all Israel together and
crossed the Jordan, and came upon them and drew up in
formation against them. And when David drew up in battle
array against the Arameans, they fought against him.
18 The Arameans fled before Israel, and David killed of the
Arameans 7,000 charioteers and 40,000 foot soldiers, and put
to death Shophach the commander of the army.
19 So when the servants of Hadadezer saw that they were
[1]defeated by Israel, they made peace with David and served
him. Thus the Arameans were not willing to help the sons of
Ammon anymore.

7 [a]Num 21:30; Josh 13:9, 16

10 [1]Lit *the face of the battle*

11 [1]In 2 Sam 10:10, *Abishai*

16 [1]Lit *smitten before* [2]I.e. Euphrates [3]Lit *before*

19 [1]Lit *smitten before*

Chapter 20 Theme ______________________

20 [a]Then it happened [1]in the spring, at the time when kings
go out *to battle,* that Joab led out the army and ravaged the
land of the sons of Ammon, and came and besieged Rabbah.
But David stayed at Jerusalem. And [b]Joab struck Rabbah and
overthrew it.

20:1 [1]Lit *at the return of the year* [a]2 Sam 11:1 [b]2 Sam 12:26

2 Samuel 11

2 [a]David took the crown of [1]their king from his head, and he
found it to weigh a talent of gold, and there was a precious
stone in it; and it was placed on David's head. And he brought
out the spoil of the city, a very great amount.
3 He brought out the people who *were* in it, [a]and cut *them*
with saws and with sharp instruments and with axes. And thus
David did to all the cities of the sons of Ammon. Then David
and all the people returned *to* Jerusalem.

2 Samuel 21:18

4 [a]Now it came about after this, that war [1]broke out at [2]Gezer
with the Philistines; then Sibbecai the Hushathite [3]killed Sippai,
one of the descendants of the [4]giants, and they were subdued.
5 And there was war with the Philistines again, and Elhanan
the son of [a]Jair [1]killed Lahmi the brother of Goliath the Gittite,
the [b]shaft of whose spear *was* like a weaver's beam.
6 Again there was war at Gath, where there was a man of
great stature who had twenty-four fingers and toes, six *fingers
on each hand* and six *toes on each foot;* and he also was
descended from the giants.
7 When he taunted Israel, Jonathan the son of Shimea, David's
brother, [1]killed him.
8 These were descended from the giants in Gath, and they
fell by the hand of David and by the hand of his servants.

Chapter 21 Theme ______________________________

2 Samuel 24

21 [a]Then Satan stood up against Israel and moved David to
number Israel.
2 So David said to Joab and to the princes of the people,
"[a]Go, number Israel from Beersheba even to Dan, and bring
me *word* that I may know their number."
3 Joab said, "[a]May the LORD add to His people a hundred
times as many as they are! But, my lord the king, are they not
all my lord's servants? Why does my lord seek this thing? Why
should he be a cause of guilt to Israel?"
4 Nevertheless, the king's word prevailed against Joab.
Therefore, Joab departed and went throughout all Israel, and
came to Jerusalem.
5 Joab gave the number of the [1]census of *all* the people to
David. And [a]all Israel were 1,100,000 men who drew the
sword; and Judah *was* 470,000 men who drew the sword.
6 [a]But he did not [1]number Levi and Benjamin among them,
for the king's [2]command was abhorrent to Joab.
7 [1]God was displeased with this thing, so He struck Israel.
8 David said to God, "I have sinned greatly, in that I have
done this thing. [a]But now, please take away the iniquity of Your
servant, for I have done very foolishly."
9 The LORD spoke to [a]Gad, David's [b]seer, saying,
10 "Go and speak to David, saying, 'Thus says the LORD, "I [1]offer
you three things; choose for yourself one of them, which I will
do to you."'"
11 So Gad came to David and said to him, "Thus says the
LORD, 'Take for yourself

2 [1]In Zeph 1:5, *Malcam* [a]2 Sam 12:30, 31

3 [a]2 Sam 12:31

4 [1]Lit *stood up* [2]In 2 Sam 21:18, *Gob* [3]Lit *smote* [4]Heb *Raphah,* and so in vv 6, 8 [a]2 Sam 21:18-22

5 [1]Lit *smote* [a]2 Sam 21:19 [b]1 Sam 17:7; 1 Chr 11:23

7 [1]Lit *smote*

21:1 [a]2 Sam 24:1-25

2 [a]1 Chr 27:23, 24

3 [a]Deut 1:11

5 [1]Lit *muster* [a]2 Sam 24:9

6 [1]Lit *muster* [2]Lit *word* [a]1 Chr 27:24

7 [1]Lit *it was evil in the sight of God*

8 [a]2 Sam 12:13

9 [a]2 Sam 24:11; 1 Chr 29:29 [b]1 Sam 9:9

10 [1]Lit *stretch out to*

12 [a]2 Sam 24:13
12 [a]either three years of famine, or three months to be swept
away before your foes, while the sword of your enemies
overtakes *you,* or else three days of the sword of the LORD, even
pestilence in the land, and the angel of the LORD destroying
13 [a]Ps 51:1; 130:4, 7
throughout all the territory of Israel.' Now, therefore, consider
what answer I shall return to Him who sent me."
13 David said to Gad, "I am in great distress; please let me fall
into the hand of the LORD, [a]for His mercies are very great. But
do not let me fall into the hand of man."
14 [1]Lit *gave* [a]1 Chr 27:24
14 [a]So the LORD [1]sent a pestilence on Israel; 70,000 men of
Israel fell.
15 And God sent an angel to Jerusalem to destroy it; but as he
was about to destroy *it,* the LORD saw and [a]was sorry over the
calamity, and said to the destroying angel, "It is enough; now
15 [1]In 2 Sam 24:16, *Araunah* [a]Ex 32:14; 1 Sam 15:11; Jon 3:10
relax your hand." And the angel of the LORD was standing by
the threshing floor of [1]Ornan the Jebusite.
16 Then David lifted up his eyes and saw the angel of the
LORD standing between earth and heaven, with his drawn
sword in his hand stretched out over Jerusalem. Then David
and the elders, [a]covered with sackcloth, fell on their faces.
16 [a]1 Kin 21:27
17 David said to God, "Is it not I who [1]commanded to count the
people? Indeed, I am the one who has sinned and done very
wickedly, [a]but these sheep, what have they done? O LORD my
God, please let Your hand be against me and my father's household, but not against Your people that they should be plagued."
17 [1]Lit *said* [a]2 Sam 7:8; Ps 74:1
18 [a]Then the angel of the LORD [1]commanded Gad to say to
David, that David should go up and build an altar to the LORD
on the threshing floor of Ornan the Jebusite.
19 So David went up at the word of Gad, which he spoke in
the name of the LORD.
18 [1]Lit *said to* [a]2 Chr 3:1
20 Now Ornan turned back and saw the angel, and his four
sons *who were* with him hid themselves. And Ornan was
threshing wheat.
21 As David came to Ornan, Ornan looked and saw David,
and went out from the threshing floor and prostrated himself
[1]before David with his face to the ground.
21 [1]Lit *to*
22 Then David said to Ornan, "Give me the [1]site of *this*
threshing floor, that I may build on it an altar to the LORD; for
the full price you shall give it to me, that the plague may be
restrained from the people."
22 [1]Lit *place*
23 Ornan said to David, "Take *it* for yourself; and let my lord
the king do what is good in his sight. See, I will give the oxen
for burnt offerings and the threshing sledges for wood and the
wheat for the grain offering; I will give *it* all."
24 But King David said to Ornan, "No, but I will surely buy *it*
24 [1]Lit *gratuitously*
for the full price; for I will not take what is yours for the LORD,
or offer a burnt offering [1]which costs me nothing."
25 So [a]David gave Ornan 600 shekels of gold by weight for
the [1]site.
26 Then David built an altar to the LORD there and offered burnt
25 [1]Lit *place* [a]2 Sam 24:24
offerings and peace offerings. And he called to the LORD and

INSIGHT

See 2 Chronicles 3:1 for what happened at this threshing floor.

[a]He answered him with fire from heaven on the altar of burnt
offering.
27 The LORD commanded the angel, and he put his sword
back in its sheath.
28 At that time, when David saw that the LORD had answered
him on the threshing floor of Ornan the Jebusite, he offered
sacrifice there.
29 [a]For the tabernacle of the LORD, which Moses had made in
the wilderness, and the altar of burnt offering *were* in the high
place at Gibeon at that time.
30 But David could not go before it to inquire of God, for he
was terrified by the sword of the angel of the LORD.

Chapter 22 Theme ________________________

22 Then David said, "[a]This is the house of the LORD God,
and this is the altar of burnt offering for Israel."
2 So David [1]gave orders to gather [a]the foreigners who were
in the land of Israel, and [b]he set stonecutters to hew out stones
to build the house of God.
3 David [a]prepared large quantities of iron [1]to make the nails
for the doors of the gates and for the clamps, and more [b]bronze
than could be weighed;
4 and timbers of cedar logs beyond number, for [a]the Sidonians
and Tyrians brought large quantities of cedar timber to David.
5 David said, "My son [a]Solomon is young and inexperienced,
and the house that is to be built for the LORD shall be exceedingly
magnificent, famous and glorious throughout all lands. *Therefore*
now I will make preparation for it." So David made ample
preparations before his death.
6 Then [a]he called for his son Solomon, and charged him to
build a house for the LORD God of Israel.
7 David said to Solomon, "[a]My son, [1]I had intended to build
a house to the name of the LORD my God.
8 "But the word of the LORD came to me, saying, '[a]You have
shed much blood and have [1]waged great wars; you shall not
build a house to My name, because you have shed *so* much
blood on the earth before Me.
9 'Behold, a son will be born to you, who shall be a man of
rest; and [a]I will give him rest from all his enemies on every
side; for [b]his name shall be [1]Solomon, and I will give peace and
quiet to Israel in his days.
10 '[a]He shall build a house for My name, and he shall be My
son and I will be his father; and I will establish the throne of
his kingdom over Israel forever.'
11 "Now, my son, [a]the LORD be with you that you may be
successful, and build the house of the LORD your God just as He
has spoken concerning you.
12 "[a]Only the LORD give you discretion and understanding, and
give you charge over Israel, so that you may [b]keep the law of
the LORD your God.

INSIGHT

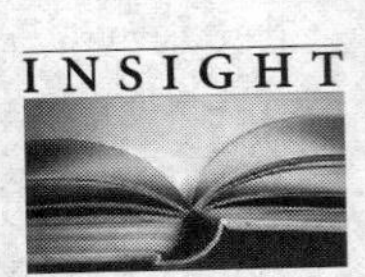

There were basically three historical temples: ***Solomon's*** (pre-exilic), ***Zerubbabel's***, called the second temple (post-exilic), and ***Herod's*** (New Testament). Since Herod's Temple was an expansion/rebuilding of the second temple, it is often referred to as the second temple rather than "the third." All were located on a hill north of David's capital city which he took from the Jebusites (2 Samuel 5:6, 7). David acquired the temple hill to build an altar and offer sacrifices (2 Samuel 24:18-25). Second Chronicles identifies this hill with Mount Moriah, where Abraham was willing to offer Isaac (2 Chronicles 3:1; Genesis 22:1-14).

26 [a]Lev 9:24; Judg 6:21

29 [a]1 Kin 3:4; 1 Chr 16:39

22:1 [a]1 Chr 21:18-28; 2 Chr 3:1

2 [1]Lit *said to* [a]1 Kin 9:20, 21; 2 Chr 2:17 [b]1 Kin 5:17, 18

3 [1]Lit *for* [a]1 Chr 29:2, 7 [b]1 Chr 22:14

4 [a]1 Kin 5:6-10

5 [a]1 Kin 3:7; 1 Chr 29:1

6 [a]1 Kin 2:1

7 [1]Lit *as for me, it was in my heart* [a]2 Sam 7:2, 3; 1 Chr 17:1

8 [1]Lit *made* [a]1 Chr 28:3

9 [1]I.e. peaceful [a]1 Kin 4:20, 25 [b]2 Sam 12:24, 25

10 [a]2 Sam 7:13, 14; 1 Chr 17:12

11 [a]1 Chr 22:16

12 [a]1 Kin 3:9-12; 2 Chr 1:10 [b]1 Kin 2:3

13 "[a]Then you will prosper, if you are careful to observe the
statutes and the ordinances which the LORD commanded Moses
concerning Israel. [b]Be strong and courageous, do not fear nor
be dismayed.
14 "Now behold, [1]with great pains I have prepared for the house of
the LORD [a]100,000 talents of gold and 1,000,000 talents of silver,
and [b]bronze and iron beyond weight, for [2]they are in great
quantity; also timber and stone I have prepared, and you may
add to them.
15 "Moreover, there are many workmen with you, stonecutters
and masons of stone and carpenters, and all men who are skillful
in every kind of work.
16 "Of the gold, the silver and the bronze and the iron there is
no limit. Arise and work, and may [a]the LORD be with you."
17 [a]David also commanded all the leaders of Israel to help his
son Solomon, *saying,*
18 "Is not the LORD your God with you? And [a]has He not given
you rest on every side? For He has given the inhabitants of the
land into my hand, and the land is subdued before the LORD
and before His people.
19 "Now [a]set your heart and your soul to seek the LORD your
God; arise, therefore, and build the sanctuary of the LORD God,
[b]so that you may bring the ark of the covenant of the LORD and
the holy vessels of God into the house that is to be built [c]for
the name of the LORD."

Chapter 23 Theme ______________________________

23 [a]Now when David [1]reached old age, [b]he made his son
Solomon king over Israel.
2 And he gathered together all the leaders of Israel with the
priests and the Levites.
3 [a]The Levites were numbered from thirty years old and
upward, and [b]their number by [1]census of men was 38,000.
4 Of these, 24,000 were [a]to oversee the work of the house
of the LORD; and 6,000 *were* [b]officers and judges,
5 and 4,000 *were* gatekeepers, and [a]4,000 *were* praising the
LORD with the instruments which [1]David made for giving praise.
6 David divided them into divisions [a]according to the sons of
Levi: Gershon, Kohath, and Merari.
7 Of the Gershonites *were* [1]Ladan and Shimei.
8 The sons of Ladan *were* Jehiel the first and Zetham and
Joel, three.
9 The sons of Shimei *were* Shelomoth and Haziel and Haran,
three. These were the heads of the fathers' *households* of Ladan.
10 The sons of Shimei *were* Jahath, [1]Zina, Jeush and Beriah.
These four *were* the sons of Shimei.
11 Jahath was the first and Zizah the second; but Jeush and
Beriah did not have many sons, so they became a father's
household, one [1]class.
12 The sons of Kohath were four: Amram, Izhar, Hebron and
Uzziel.

13 [a]1 Chr 28:7 [b]Josh 1:6-9

14 [1]Lit *in my affliction* [2]Lit *it is* [a]1 Chr 29:4 [b]1 Chr 22:3

16 [a]1 Chr 22:11

17 [a]1 Chr 28:1-6

18 [a]1 Chr 22:9; 23:25

19 [a]1 Chr 28:9 [b]1 Kin 8:6, 21; 2 Chr 5:7 [c]1 Chr 22:7

23:1 [1]Lit *became old and sated with days* [a]1 Chr 29:28 [b]1 Kin 1:1-40; 2:12; 1 Chr 28:5; 29:22

3 [1]Lit *their heads* [a]Num 4:3-49 [b]Num 4:48; 1 Chr 23:24

4 [a]Ezra 3:8, 9 [b]1 Chr 26:29

5 [1]Lit *I made* [a]1 Chr 15:16

6 [a]1 Chr 6:1

7 [1]In Ex 6:17, *Libni*

10 [1]In v 11, *Zizah*

11 [1]Lit *mustering*

13 [a]The sons of Amram were Aaron and Moses. And [b]Aaron
was set apart to sanctify him as most holy, he and his sons
forever, [c]to burn incense before the LORD, to minister to Him
and to bless in His name forever.
14 But *as for* [a]Moses the man of God, his sons were named
among the tribe of Levi.
15 The sons of Moses *were* Gershom and Eliezer.
16 The [1]son of Gershom *was* [2]Shebuel the chief.
17 The [1]son of Eliezer was Rehabiah the chief; and Eliezer had
no other sons, but the sons of Rehabiah were very many.
18 The [1]son of Izhar was [2]Shelomith the chief.
19 The sons of Hebron *were* Jeriah the first, Amariah the second,
Jahaziel the third and Jekameam the fourth.
20 The sons of Uzziel *were* Micah the first and Isshiah the second.
21 The sons of Merari were Mahli and Mushi. The sons of
Mahli *were* Eleazar and Kish.
22 Eleazar died and had no sons, but daughters only, so their
brothers, the sons of Kish, took them *as wives.*
23 The sons of Mushi *were* three: Mahli, Eder and Jeremoth.
24 [a]These were the sons of Levi according to their fathers'
households, *even* the heads of the fathers' *households* of those
of them who were [1]counted, in the number of names by their
[2]census, doing the work for the service of the house of the
LORD, [b]from twenty years old and upward.
25 For David said, "The LORD God of Israel [a]has given rest to
His people, and He dwells in Jerusalem forever.
26 "Also, [a]the Levites will no longer need to carry the tabernacle
and all its utensils for its service."
27 For by the last words of David the sons of Levi *were*
numbered from twenty years old and upward.
28 For their office is [1]to assist the sons of Aaron with the service
of the house of the LORD, in the courts and in the chambers and
in the purifying of all holy things, even the work of the service
of the house of God,
29 [a]and with the showbread, and [b]the fine flour for a grain
offering, and unleavened wafers, or [c]*what is baked in* the pan
or [d]what is well-mixed, and [e]all measures of volume and size.
30 They are to stand every morning to thank and to praise the
LORD, and likewise at evening,
31 and to offer all burnt offerings to the LORD, [a]on the
sabbaths, the new moons and [b]the fixed festivals in the number
set by the ordinance concerning them, continually before the
LORD.
32 Thus [a]they are to keep charge of the tent of meeting, and
charge of the holy place, and [b]charge of the sons of Aaron their
[1]relatives, for the service of the house of the LORD.

13 [a]Ex 6:20 [b]Ex 28:1 [c]Ex 30:6-10

14 [a]Deut 33:1; Ps 90: title

16 [1]Lit *sons* [2]In ch 24:20, *Shubael*

17 [1]Lit *sons...were*

18 [1]Lit *sons* [2]In ch 24:22, *Shelomoth*

24 [1]Lit *mustered* [2]Lit *heads* [a]Num 10:17, 21 [b]1 Chr 23:3

25 [a]1 Chr 22:18

26 [a]Num 4:5, 15; 7:9; Deut 10:8

28 [1]Lit *at the hand of*

29 [a]Lev 24:5-9 [b]Lev 6:20 [c]1 Chr 9:31 [d]Lev 6:21 [e]Lev 19:35, 36

31 [a]Is 1:13, 14 [b]Lev 23:2-4

32 [1]Lit *brothers* [a]Num 1:53; 1 Chr 9:27 [b]Num 3:6-9, 38

Chapter 24 Theme ____________________

24 Now the divisions of the [1]descendants of Aaron *were*
these: [a]the sons of Aaron *were* Nadab, Abihu, Eleazar
and Ithamar.

24:1 [1]Lit *sons* [a]Ex 6:23

2 [a]But Nadab and Abihu died before their father and had no
[1]sons. So Eleazar and Ithamar served as priests.
3 David, with [a]Zadok of the sons of Eleazar and Ahimelech of
the sons of Ithamar, divided them according to their offices [1]for
their ministry.
4 Since more chief men were found from the [1]descendants of
Eleazar than the [1]descendants of Ithamar, they divided them
thus: *there were* sixteen heads of fathers' households of the
[1]descendants of Eleazar and eight of the [1]descendants of
Ithamar, according to their fathers' households.
5 [a]Thus they were divided by lot, the one as the other; for
they were officers of the sanctuary and officers of God, both from
the [1]descendants of Eleazar and the [1]descendants of Ithamar.
6 Shemaiah, the son of Nethanel the scribe, from the Levites,
recorded them in the presence of the king, the princes, Zadok
the priest, [a]Ahimelech the son of Abiathar, and the heads of the
fathers' *households* of the priests and of the Levites; one
father's household taken for Eleazar and one taken for Ithamar.
7 Now the first lot came out for Jehoiarib, the second for
Jedaiah,
8 the third for Harim, the fourth for Seorim,
9 the fifth for Malchijah, the sixth for Mijamin,
10 the seventh for Hakkoz, the eighth for [a]Abijah,
11 the ninth for Jeshua, the tenth for Shecaniah,
12 the eleventh for Eliashib, the twelfth for Jakim,
13 the thirteenth for Huppah, the fourteenth for Jeshebeab,
14 the fifteenth for Bilgah, the sixteenth for Immer,
15 the seventeenth for Hezir, the eighteenth for Happizzez,
16 the nineteenth for Pethahiah, the twentieth for Jehezkel,
17 the twenty-first for Jachin, the twenty-second for Gamul,
18 the twenty-third for Delaiah, the twenty-fourth for Maaziah.
19 [a]These were their offices for their ministry when *they*
came in to the house of the LORD according to the ordinance
given to them through Aaron their father, just as the LORD God
of Israel had commanded him.
20 Now for the rest of the sons of Levi: of the sons of Amram,
[1]Shubael; of the sons of Shubael, Jehdeiah.
21 Of Rehabiah: of the sons of Rehabiah, Isshiah the first.
22 Of the Izharites, [1]Shelomoth; of the sons of Shelomoth,
Jahath.
23 The sons [a]*of Hebron:* Jeriah *the first,* Amariah the second,
Jahaziel the third, Jekameam the fourth.
24 *Of* the sons of Uzziel, Micah; of the sons of Micah, Shamir.
25 The brother of Micah, Isshiah; of the sons of Isshiah,
Zechariah.
26 The sons of Merari, Mahli and Mushi; the sons of Jaaziah,
Beno.
27 The sons of Merari: by Jaaziah *were* Beno, Shoham, Zaccur
and Ibri.
28 By Mahli: Eleazar, who had no sons.
29 By Kish: the sons of Kish, Jerahmeel.

2 [1]Or *children* [a]Lev 10:2
3 [1]Lit *in their service* [a]1 Chr 6:8
4 [1]Lit *sons*
5 [1]Lit *sons* [a]1 Chr 24:31
6 [a]1 Chr 18:16
10 [a]Neh 12:4; Luke 1:5
19 [a]1 Chr 9:25
20 [1]In 23:16, *Shebuel*
22 [1]In 23:18, *Shelomith*
23 [a]1 Chr 23:19

30 The sons of Mushi: Mahli, Eder and Jerimoth. These *were*
the sons of the Levites according to their fathers' households.
31 [a]These also cast lots just as their [1]relatives the sons of
Aaron in the presence of David the king, [b]Zadok, Ahimelech,
and the heads of the fathers' *households* of the priests and of
the Levites—the head of fathers' *households* as well as those of
his younger brother.

Chapter 25 Theme ______________________

25 Moreover, David and the commanders of the army set
apart for the service *some* of the sons of [a]Asaph and of
Heman and of Jeduthun, who *were* to [b]prophesy with lyres,
[c]harps and cymbals; and the number of [1]those who performed
their service was:
2 Of the sons of Asaph: Zaccur, Joseph, Nethaniah and
[1]Asharelah; the sons of Asaph *were* under the [2]direction of
Asaph, who prophesied under the [2]direction of the king.
3 [a]Of Jeduthun, the sons of Jeduthun: Gedaliah, [1]Zeri, Jeshaiah,
[2]Shimei, Hashabiah and Mattithiah, six, under the [3]direction of
their father Jeduthun with the harp, who prophesied in giving
thanks and praising the LORD.
4 Of Heman, the sons of Heman: Bukkiah, Mattaniah, [1]Uzziel,
[2]Shebuel and Jerimoth, Hananiah, Hanani, Eliathah, Giddalti
and Romamti-ezer, Joshbekashah, Mallothi, Hothir, Mahazioth.
5 All these *were* the sons of Heman [a]the king's seer to [1]exalt
him according to the words of God, for God gave fourteen sons
and three daughters to Heman.
6 All these were under the [1]direction of their father to sing
in the house of the LORD, [a]with cymbals, harps and lyres, for
the service of the house of God. [b]Asaph, Jeduthun and Heman
were under the [1]direction of the king.
7 Their number who were trained in singing to the LORD,
with their [1]relatives, all who were skillful, *was* [a]288.
8 [a]They cast lots for their duties, all alike, the small as well as
the great, the teacher *as well* as the pupil.
9 Now the first lot came out for Asaph to Joseph, the second
for Gedaliah, he with his relatives and sons *were* twelve;
10 the third to Zaccur, his sons and his relatives, twelve;
11 the fourth to [1]Izri, his sons and his relatives, twelve;
12 the fifth to Nethaniah, his sons and his relatives, twelve;
13 the sixth to Bukkiah, his sons and his relatives, twelve;
14 the seventh to [1]Jesharelah, his sons and his relatives, twelve;
15 the eighth to Jeshaiah, his sons and his relatives, twelve;
16 the ninth to Mattaniah, his sons and his relatives, twelve;
17 the tenth to Shimei, his sons and his relatives, twelve;
18 the eleventh to Azarel, his sons and his relatives, twelve;
19 the twelfth to Hashabiah, his sons and his relatives, twelve;
20 for the thirteenth, Shubael, his sons and his relatives, twelve;
21 for the fourteenth, Mattithiah, his sons and his relatives,
twelve;

31 [1]Lit *brothers* [a]1 Chr 24:5, 6 [b]1 Chr 24:6

25:1 [1]Lit *workmen according to their service* [a]1 Chr 6:33, 39 [b]2 Kin 3:15 [c]1 Chr 15:16

2 [1]In v 14, *Jesharelah* [2]Lit *hand(s)*

3 [1]In v 11, *Izri* [2]So with mss and ancient versions, cf v 17 [3]Lit *hands* [a]1 Chr 16:41, 42

4 [1]In v 18, *Azarel* [2]In v 20, *Shubael*

5 [1]Lit *lift up the horn* [a]2 Sam 24:11; 1 Chr 21:9

6 [1]Lit *hands* [a]1 Chr 15:16 [b]1 Chr 15:19

7 [1]Lit *brothers,* and so throughout the ch [a]1 Chr 23:5

8 [a]1 Chr 26:13

11 [1]In v 3, *Zeri*

14 [1]In v 2, *Asherelah*

26:1 [1]In v 14, *Shelemiah* [2]In 9:19, *Ebiasaph*

22 for the fifteenth to Jeremoth, his sons and his relatives, twelve;
23 for the sixteenth to Hananiah, his sons and his relatives,
twelve;
24 for the seventeenth to Joshbekashah, his sons and his
relatives, twelve;
25 for the eighteenth to Hanani, his sons and his relatives, twelve;
26 for the nineteenth to Mallothi, his sons and his relatives,
twelve;
27 for the twentieth to Eliathah, his sons and his relatives,
twelve;

4 [a]2 Sam 6:11; 1 Chr 13:14

28 for the twenty-first to Hothir, his sons and his relatives,
twelve;
29 for the twenty-second to Giddalti, his sons and his relatives,
twelve;
30 for the twenty-third to Mahazioth, his sons and his relatives,
twelve;
31 for the twenty-fourth to Romamti-ezer, his sons and his
relatives, twelve.

Chapter 26 Theme

8 [1]Lit *brothers,* and so throughout the ch

26 For the divisions of the gatekeepers *there were* of the
Korahites, [1]Meshelemiah the son of Kore, of the sons
of [2]Asaph.
2 Meshelemiah had sons: Zechariah the firstborn, Jediael the
second, Zebadiah the third, Jathniel the fourth,
3 Elam the fifth, Johanan the sixth, Eliehoenai the seventh.
4 [a]Obed-edom had sons: Shemaiah the firstborn, Jehozabad
the second, Joah the third, Sacar the fourth, Nethanel the fifth,
5 Ammiel the sixth, Issachar the seventh *and* Peullethai the
eighth; God had indeed blessed him.

10 [a]1 Chr 16:38

6 Also to his son Shemaiah sons were born who ruled over
the house of their father, for they were mighty men of valor.
7 The sons of Shemaiah *were* Othni, Rephael, Obed and
Elzabad, whose brothers, Elihu and Semachiah, were valiant men.
8 All these *were* of the sons of Obed-edom; they and their
sons and their [1]relatives *were* able men with strength for the
service, 62 from Obed-edom.
9 Meshelemiah had sons and relatives, 18 valiant men.
10 Also [a]Hosah, *one* of the sons of Merari had sons: Shimri the
first (although he was not the firstborn, his father made him first),

13 [a]1 Chr 24:5, 31; 25:8

11 Hilkiah the second, Tebaliah the third, Zechariah the
fourth; all the sons and relatives of Hosah *were* 13.
12 To these divisions of the gatekeepers, the chief men, *were*
given duties like their relatives to minister in the house of the
LORD.
13 [a]They cast lots, the small and the great alike, according to
their fathers' households, for every gate.
14 The lot to the east fell to [1]Shelemiah. Then they cast lots
for his son Zechariah, a counselor with insight, and his lot
came out to the north.

14 [1]In 9:17, *Shallum*

15 For Obed-edom *it fell* to the south, and to his sons went
the storehouse.
16 For Shuppim and Hosah *it was* to the west, by the gate of
Shallecheth, on the ascending highway. Guard corresponded to
guard.
17 On the east there were six Levites, on the north four daily,
on the south four daily, and at the storehouse two by two.
18 At the [1a]Parbar on the west *there were* four at the highway
and two at the Parbar.
19 These were the divisions of the gatekeepers of the sons of
Korah and of the sons of Merari.
20 [1]The Levites, their relatives, [2]had [a]charge of the treasures
of the house of God and of the treasures of the dedicated gifts.
21 The sons of Ladan, the sons of the Gershonites belonging
to Ladan, *namely,* the Jehielites, *were* the heads of the fathers'
households, belonging to Ladan the Gershonite.
22 The sons of Jehieli, Zetham and Joel his brother, [1]had charge
of the treasures of the house of the LORD.
23 As for the Amramites, the Izharites, the Hebronites and the
Uzzielites,
24 Shebuel the son of Gershom, the son of Moses, was officer
over the treasures.
25 His relatives by Eliezer *were* Rehabiah his son, Jeshaiah his
son, Joram his son, Zichri his son and Shelomoth his son.
26 This Shelomoth and his relatives [1]had charge of all the
treasures of the dedicated gifts [a]which King David and the
heads of the fathers' *households,* the commanders of thousands
and hundreds, and the commanders of the army, had dedicated.
27 They dedicated [1]part of the spoil won in battles to repair
the house of the LORD.
28 And all that Samuel the seer had dedicated and Saul the
son of Kish, Abner the son of Ner and Joab the son of Zeruiah,
everyone who had dedicated *anything, all of this* was [1]in the
care of [2]Shelomoth and his relatives.
29 As for the Izharites, Chenaniah and his sons [a]were
assigned to outside duties for Israel, as [b]officers and judges.
30 As for the Hebronites, [a]Hashabiah and his relatives, 1,700
capable men, had charge of the affairs of Israel [1]west of the
Jordan, for all the work of the LORD and the service of the king.
31 As for the Hebronites, [a]Jerijah the chief [1](these Hebronites
were investigated according to their genealogies and fathers'
households, in the fortieth year of David's reign, and men of
outstanding capability were found among them at [b]Jazer of Gilead)
32 and his relatives, capable men, *were* 2,700 in number, heads
of fathers' *households.* And King David made them overseers of
the Reubenites, the Gadites and the half-tribe of the Manassites
[a]concerning [1]all the affairs of God and of the king.

Chapter 27 Theme ______________________

27 Now *this is* the enumeration of the sons of Israel, the
heads of fathers' *households,* the commanders of

18 [1]Possibly *court or colonnade* [a]2 Kin 23:11

20 [1]So Gr; Heb *As for the Levites, Ahijah had* [2]Lit *were over* [a]1 Chr 26:22, 24, 26; 28:12; Ezra 2:69

22 [1]Lit *were over*

26 [1]Lit *were over* [a]2 Sam 8:11

27 [1]Heb *from the battles and from the spoil*

28 [1]Lit *under the hand* [2]Heb *Shelomith*

29 [a]Neh 11:16 [b]1 Chr 23:4

30 [1]Lit *beyond the Jordan westward* [a]1 Chr 27:17

31 [1]Heb *according to the Hebronites . . . father's households* [a]1 Chr 23:19 [b]1 Chr 6:81

32 [1]Lit *every matter of God and matter of the king* [a]2 Chr 19:11

27:2 [1]*Lit was over,* and so throughout the ch
[a]2 Sam 23:8-30; 1 Chr 11:11-31

thousands and of hundreds, and their officers who served the
king in all the affairs of the divisions which came in and went
out month by month throughout all the months of the year,
each division *numbering* 24,000:
2 Jashobeam the son of Zabdiel [1a]had charge of the first
division for the first month; and in his division *were* 24,000.
3 *He was* from the sons of Perez, *and was* chief of all the
commanders of the army for the first month.
4 Dodai the Ahohite and his division had charge of the division
for the second month, Mikloth *being* the chief officer; and in
his division *were* 24,000.
5 The third commander of the army for the third month *was*
Benaiah, the son of Jehoiada the priest, *as* chief; and in his
division *were* 24,000.
6 This Benaiah *was* the mighty man of the thirty, and had
charge of thirty; and over his division was Ammizabad his son.
7 The fourth for the fourth month *was* Asahel the brother of
Joab, and Zebadiah his son after him; and in his division *were*
24,000.
8 The fifth for the fifth month *was* the commander Shamhuth
the Izrahite; and in his division *were* 24,000.
9 The sixth for the sixth month *was* Ira the son of Ikkesh the
Tekoite; and in his division *were* 24,000.
10 The seventh for the seventh month *was* Helez the Pelonite
of the sons of Ephraim; and in his division *were* 24,000.
11 The eighth for the eighth month *was* Sibbecai the Hushathite
of the Zerahites; and in his division *were* 24,000.
12 The ninth for the ninth month *was* Abiezer the Anathothite
of the Benjamites; and in his division *were* 24,000.
13 The tenth for the tenth month *was* Maharai the
Netophathite of the Zerahites; and in his division *were* 24,000.
14 The eleventh for the eleventh month *was* Benaiah the Pirathonite of the sons of Ephraim; and in his division *were* 24,000.
15 The twelfth for the twelfth month *was* Heldai the Netophathite of Othniel; and in his division *were* 24,000.
16 Now in charge of the tribes of Israel: chief officer for the
Reubenites was Eliezer the son of Zichri; for the Simeonites,
Shephatiah the son of Maacah;
17 for Levi, Hashabiah the son of Kemuel; for Aaron, Zadok;
18 for Judah, Elihu, *one* of David's brothers; for Issachar, Omri
the son of Michael;
19 for Zebulun, Ishmaiah the son of Obadiah; for Naphtali,
Jeremoth the son of Azriel;
20 for the sons of Ephraim, Hoshea the son of Azaziah; for the
half-tribe of Manasseh, Joel the son of Pedaiah;
21 for the half-tribe of Manasseh in Gilead, Iddo the son of
Zechariah; for Benjamin, Jaasiel the son of Abner;
22 for Dan, Azarel the son of Jeroham. [a]These *were* the
princes of the tribes of Israel.
23 But David did not [1]count those twenty years of age and
under, [a]because the LORD had said He would multiply Israel [b]as
the stars of heaven.

22 [a]1 Chr 28:1

23 [1]*Lit take their number from*
[a]1 Chr 21:2-5
[b]Gen 15:5; 22:17; 26:4

24 Joab the son of Zeruiah had begun to count *them,* but did not finish; and because of [a]this, wrath came upon Israel, and the number was not included in the account of the chronicles of King David.

25 Now Azmaveth the son of Adiel had charge of the king's storehouses. And Jonathan the son of Uzziah had charge of the storehouses in the country, in the cities, in the villages and in the towers.

26 Ezri the son of Chelub had charge of the [1]agricultural workers who tilled the soil.

27 Shimei the Ramathite had charge of the vineyards; and Zabdi the Shiphmite had charge of the [1]produce of the vineyards *stored* in the wine cellars.

28 Baal-hanan the Gederite had charge of the olive and [a]sycamore trees in the [1]Shephelah; and Joash had charge of the stores of oil.

29 Shitrai the Sharonite had charge of the cattle which were grazing in [a]Sharon; and Shaphat the son of Adlai had charge of the cattle in the valleys.

30 Obil the Ishmaelite had charge of the camels; and Jehdeiah the Meronothite had charge of the donkeys.

31 Jaziz the [a]Hagrite had charge of the flocks. All these were [1]overseers of the property which belonged to King David.

32 Also Jonathan, David's uncle, *was* a counselor, a man of understanding, and a scribe; and Jehiel the son of Hachmoni [1]tutored the king's sons.

33 [a]Ahithophel *was* counselor to the king; and [b]Hushai the Archite *was* the king's friend.

34 Jehoiada the son of [a]Benaiah, and [b]Abiathar [1]succeeded Ahithophel; and Joab was the [c]commander of the king's army.

Chapter 28 Theme ________________________

28 Now [a]David assembled at Jerusalem all the officials of Israel, the princes of the tribes, and the commanders of the divisions that served the king, and the commanders of thousands, and the commanders of hundreds, and the overseers of all the property and livestock belonging to the king and his sons, with the officials and [b]the mighty men, even all the valiant men.

2 Then King David rose to his feet and said, "Listen to me, my brethren and my people; I [a]*had* [1]intended to build a [2]permanent home for the ark of the covenant of the LORD and for [b]the footstool of our God. So I had made preparations to build *it.*

3 "But God said to me, '[a]You shall not build a house for My name because you are a man of war and have shed blood.'

4 "Yet, the LORD, the God of Israel, [a]chose me from all the house of my father to be king over Israel [b]forever. For [c]He has chosen Judah to be a leader; and [d]in the house of Judah, my father's house, and among the sons of my father He took pleasure in me to make *me* king over all Israel.

24 [a]2 Sam 24:12-15; 1 Chr 21:1-7

26 [1]Lit *doers of the work of the field for the tilling of...*

27 [1]Lit *what was in the vineyards of the storehouses of wine*

28 [1]Or *lowlands* [a]1 Kin 10:27; 2 Chr 1:15

29 [a]1 Chr 5:16

31 [1]Or *rulers* [a]1 Chr 5:10

32 [1]Lit *was with*

33 [a]2 Sam 15:12 [b]2 Sam 15:32, 37

34 [1]Lit *after* [a]1 Chr 27:5 [b]1 Kin 1:7 [c]1 Chr 11:6

28:1 [a]1 Chr 23:2; 27:1-31 [b]1 Chr 11:10-47

2 [1]Lit *in my heart* [2]Lit *house of rest* [a]1 Chr 17:1, 2 [b]Ps 132:7; Is 66:1

3 [a]1 Chr 22:8

4 [a]1 Sam 16:6-13 [b]1 Chr 17:23, 27 [c]Gen 49:8-10; 1 Chr 5:2 [d]1 Sam 16:1

5 [a]1 Chr 3:1-9; 14:3-7 [b]1 Chr 22:9, 10

5 “[a]Of all my sons (for the LORD has given me many sons), [b]He
has chosen my son Solomon to sit on the throne of the kingdom
of the LORD over Israel.
6 “He said to me, ‘Your son [a]Solomon is the one who shall
build My house and My courts; for I have chosen him to be a
son to Me, and I will be a father to him.
7 ‘I will establish his kingdom forever [a]if he resolutely performs
My commandments and My ordinances, as [1]is done now.’
8 “So now, in the sight of all Israel, the assembly of the LORD,
and in the hearing of our God, observe and seek after all the
commandments of the LORD your God so that you may possess
the good land and bequeath *it* to your sons after you forever.
9 “As for you, my son Solomon, know the God of your father,
and [a]serve Him with [1]a whole heart and a willing [2]mind; [b]for
the LORD searches all hearts, and understands every intent of
the thoughts. [c]If you seek Him, He will let you find Him; but if
you forsake Him, He will reject you forever.
10 “Consider now, for the LORD has chosen you to build a house
for the sanctuary; [a]be courageous and act.”
11 Then David gave to his son Solomon [a]the plan of [b]the porch
of the temple, its buildings, its storehouses, its upper rooms, its
inner rooms and [c]the room for the mercy seat;
12 and the plan of all that he had in [1]mind, for the courts of
the house of the LORD, and for all the surrounding rooms, for
[a]the storehouses of the house of God and for the storehouses of
the dedicated things;
13 also for [a]the divisions of the priests and [b]the Levites and for
all the work of the service of the house of the LORD and for all
the utensils of service in the house of the LORD;
14 for the golden *utensils,* the weight of gold for all utensils
for every kind of service; for the silver utensils, the weight *of*
silver for all utensils for every kind of service;
15 and the weight *of gold* for the [a]golden lampstands and their
golden lamps, with the weight of each lampstand and its lamps;
and *the weight of silver* for the silver lampstands, with the
weight of each lampstand and its lamps according to the use of
each lampstand;
16 and the gold by weight for the tables of showbread, for each
table; and silver for the silver tables;
17 and the forks, the basins, and the pitchers of pure gold; and
for the golden bowls with the weight for each bowl; and for the
silver bowls with the weight for each bowl;
18 and for [a]the altar of incense refined gold by weight; and gold
for the model of the chariot, *even* [b]the cherubim that spread out
their wings and covered the ark of the covenant of the LORD.
19 “All *this,*” *said David,* “the LORD made me understand in
writing by His hand upon me, [a]all the [1]details of this pattern.”
20 Then David said to his son Solomon, “[a]Be strong and
courageous, and act; do not fear nor be dismayed, for the LORD
God, my God, is with you. [b]He will not fail you nor forsake you
until all the work for the service of the house of the LORD is
finished.

6 [a]2 Sam 7:13, 14

7 [1]Lit *at this day* [a]1 Chr 22:13

9 [1]Or *the same* [2]Lit *soul* [a]1 Kin 8:61; 1 Chr 29:17-19 [b]1 Sam 16:7 [c]2 Chr 15:2; Jer 29:13

10 [a]1 Chr 22:13

11 [a]Ex 25:40; 1 Chr 28:12, 19 [b]1 Kin 6:3 [c]Ex 25:17-22

12 [1]Lit *the spirit with him* [a]1 Chr 26:20, 28

13 [a]1 Chr 24:1 [b]1 Chr 23:6

15 [a]Ex 25:31-39

18 [a]Ex 30:1-10 [b]Ex 25:18-22

19 [1]Lit *works* [a]1 Chr 28:11, 12

20 [a]1 Chr 22:13 [b]Josh 1:5; Heb 13:5

1 Kings 2

21 "Now behold, [a]*there are* the divisions of the priests and the
Levites for all the service of the house of God, and [b]every
willing man of any skill will be with you in all the work for all
kinds of service. The officials also and all the people will be
entirely at your command."

Chapter 29 Theme ____________________

29 Then King David said to the entire assembly, "My son
Solomon, whom alone God has chosen, [a]is still young
and inexperienced and the work is great; for [b]the [1]temple is
not for man, but for the LORD God.
2 "Now [a]with all my ability I have provided for the house of my
God the gold for the *things of* gold, and the silver for the *things
of* silver, and the bronze for the *things of* bronze, the iron for the
things of iron, and wood for the *things of* wood, onyx stones and
inlaid *stones,* stones of antimony and stones of various colors,
and all kinds of precious stones and alabaster in abundance.
3 "Moreover, in my delight in the house of my God, the treasure
I have of gold and silver, I give to the house of my God, over
and above all that I have already provided for the holy [1]temple,
4 *namely,* [a]3,000 talents of gold, of [b]the gold of Ophir, and 7,000
talents of refined silver, to overlay the walls of the [1]buildings;
5 of gold for the *things of* gold and of silver for the *things of*
silver, that is, for all the work [1]done by the craftsmen. Who
then is willing [2]to consecrate himself this day to the LORD?"
6 Then [a]the rulers of the fathers' *households,* and the princes
of the tribes of Israel, and the commanders of thousands and of
hundreds, with [b]the overseers over the king's work, offered
willingly;
7 and for the service for the house of God they gave 5,000
talents and 10,000 [a]darics of gold, and 10,000 talents of silver,
and 18,000 talents of brass, and 100,000 talents of iron.
8 [1]Whoever possessed *precious* stones gave them to the
treasury of the house of the LORD, [2]in care of [a]Jehiel the
Gershonite.
9 Then the people rejoiced because they had offered so
willingly, for they made their offering to the LORD [a]with a
whole heart, and King David also rejoiced greatly.
10 So David blessed the LORD in the sight of all the assembly;
and David said, "Blessed are You, O LORD God of Israel our
father, forever and ever.
11 "[a]Yours, O LORD, is the greatness and the power and the
glory and the victory and the majesty, indeed everything that is
in the heavens and the earth; Yours is the dominion, O LORD,
and You exalt Yourself as head over all.
12 "[a]Both riches and honor *come* from You, and You rule over
all, and [b]in Your hand is power and might; and it lies in Your
hand to make great and to strengthen everyone.
13 "Now therefore, our God, we thank You, and praise Your
glorious name.

21 [a]1 Chr 28:13 [b]Ex 35:25-35; 36:1, 2

29:1 [1]Lit *palace* [a]1 Chr 22:5 [b]1 Chr 29:19

2 [a]1 Chr 22:3-5

3 [1]Lit *house*

4 [1]Lit *houses* [a]1 Chr 22:14 [b]1 Kin 9:28

5 [1]Lit *by the hand of the craftsmen* [2]Lit *to fill his hand*

6 [a]1 Chr 27:1; 28:1 [b]1 Chr 27:25-31

7 [a]Ezra 2:69; Neh 7:70

8 [1]Lit *those with whom were found* [2]Lit *under the hand of* [a]1 Chr 23:8

9 [a]1 Kin 8:61; 2 Cor 9:7

11 [a]Matt 6:13; Rev 5:13

12 [a]2 Chr 1:12 [b]2 Chr 20:6

14 "But who am I and who are my people that we should [1]be
able to offer as generously as this? For all things come from
You, and from Your hand we have given You.
15 "For [a]we are sojourners before You, and tenants, as all our
fathers were; [b]our days on the earth are like a shadow, and
there is no hope.
16 "O LORD our God, all this abundance that we have provided
to build You a house for Your holy name, it is from Your hand,
and all is Yours.
17 "Since I know, O my God, that [a]You try the heart and [b]delight
in uprightness, I, in the integrity of my heart, have willingly
offered all these *things;* so now with joy I have seen Your people,
who are present here, make *their* offerings willingly to You.
18 "O LORD, the God of Abraham, Isaac and Israel, our fathers,
preserve this forever in the [1]intentions of the heart of Your
people, and direct their heart to You;
19 and [a]give to my son Solomon a perfect heart to keep Your
commandments, Your testimonies and Your statutes, and to do
them all, and [b]to build the [1]temple, for which I have made
provision."
20 Then David said to all the assembly, "Now bless the LORD
your God." And [a]all the assembly blessed the LORD, the God of
their fathers, and [b]bowed low and did homage to the LORD and
to the king.
21 On the next day [a]they [1]made sacrifices to the LORD and
offered burnt offerings to the LORD, 1,000 bulls, 1,000 rams
and 1,000 lambs, with their drink offerings and sacrifices in
abundance for all Israel.
22 So they ate and drank that day before the LORD with great
gladness.
And they made Solomon the son of David king [a]a second time,
and they [b]anointed *him* as ruler for the LORD and Zadok as priest.
23 Then [a]Solomon sat on the throne of the LORD as king
instead of David his father; and he prospered, and all Israel
obeyed him.
24 All the officials, the mighty men, and also all the sons of
King David [1]pledged allegiance to King Solomon.
25 [a]The LORD highly exalted Solomon in the sight of all Israel,
and [b]bestowed on him royal majesty which had not been on
any king before him in Israel.
26 Now [a]David the son of Jesse reigned over all Israel.
27 [a]The period which he reigned over Israel *was* forty years;
he reigned in Hebron seven years and [1]in Jerusalem thirty-
three *years.*
28 Then he died in [a]a [1]ripe old age, [b]full of days, riches and
honor; and his son Solomon reigned in his place.
29 Now the acts of King David, from first to last, are written
in the chronicles of [a]Samuel the seer, in the chronicles of
[b]Nathan the prophet and in the chronicles of [c]Gad the seer,
30 with all his reign, his power, and the circumstances which
came on him, on Israel, and on all the kingdoms of the lands.

971 B.C.

14 [1]Lit *retain strength*
15 [a]Lev 25:23 [b]Job 14:2, 10-12
17 [a]1 Chr 28:9 [b]Ps 15:2
18 [1]Lit *intent of the thoughts of the heart*
19 [1]Lit *palace* [a]1 Chr 28:9; Ps 72:1 [b]1 Chr 29:1, 2
20 [a]Josh 22:33 [b]Ex 4:31
21 [1]Lit *sacrificed* [a]1 Kin 8:62, 63
22 [a]1 Chr 23:1 [b]1 Kin 1:33-39
23 [a]1 Kin 2:12
24 [1]Lit *put a hand under Solomon*
25 [a]2 Chr 1:1 [b]1 Kin 3:13; 2 Chr 1:12
26 [a]1 Chr 18:14
27 [1]Lit *he reigned in* [a]2 Sam 5:4, 5; 1 Kin 2:11; 1 Chr 3:4
28 [1]Lit *good* [a]Gen 15:15; Acts 13:36 [b]1 Chr 23:1
29 [a]1 Sam 9:9 [b]2 Sam 7:2-4; 12:1-7 [c]1 Sam 22:5

1 Chronicles at a Glance

Theme of 1 Chronicles:

Segment Divisions

		Main Divisions	Chapter Themes
		The Genealogies of Israel	1
			2
			3
			4
			5
			6
			7
			8
			9
		God Turns Kingdom to David	10
			11
			12
			13
			14
			15
			16
			17
			18
			19
		David Builds Altar, Prepares for God's House	20
			21
			22
			23
			24
			25
			26
			27
			28
			29

Author:

Date:

Purpose:

Key Words:

2 CHRONICLES דברי הימים ב

DIVRE HAYAMIM BET

King David wanted to build a house for the Lord, but instead the Lord promised David that He would establish David's house forever and that David's son would build the temple. Second Chronicles records for us how this came to pass.

THINGS TO DO

If you haven't studied 1 Chronicles yet, you'll want to do so before you begin your study of 2 Chronicles.

Second Chronicles is filled with truths and lessons for life, which, if heeded, will help you in your pursuit of holiness. Second Chronicles focuses on the reigns of the kings of Judah and their relationship to God and His house from the time of Solomon until the Babylonian exile. Read all the instructions before you begin.

1. Examine every chapter in the light of the "5 W's and an H." Record your insights in the margin.
   a. Look for three *who's*: the king, the prophet, and the Lord. Of the three, the Lord and the king are most prominent. Ask: Who are the associates of the king? Who influences, opposes, or assists him?
   b. Look for *what* each king does, *what* God does in respect to that king, and *what* role the prophet plays, if any. In 2 Chronicles the "house" of God takes center stage; therefore, in each reign observe what the king's relationship is to the Lord and to His house.
   c. Also keep track of *when* events occur. Don't forget to note references to time with a clock 🕒.
   d. This is a historical book; watch *where* things occur and double-underline these references in green.
   e. Observing *why* events occur will bring insight into the character and sovereignty of God in the affairs of men and nations. Keep asking why. If the king does evil, ask why.
   f. Ask *how*. How did the king seek the Lord? How did the king do evil? How did God respond?
2. Record your insights on the kings mentioned in 2 Chronicles. Transfer these insights to the chart THE KINGS OF ISRAEL AND JUDAH located on pages 654 through 655.
3. On an index card make a list of the key repeated words printed on the 2 CHRONICLES AT A GLANCE chart on page 761. Use this list as a bookmark while you study 2 Chronicles.
   a. In your notebook, record all you learn from marking each of these key words. Note that after chapter 8, *ark*, one of the key words, is used once more—in chapter 35.
   b. You will also observe key words and phrases that will play a major role in only one or two chapters. Don't miss these. They will come to the surface as you prayerfully read and meditate on a chapter.
4. As you study each chapter, take notes in the margin of all you learn about God. You will gain rich and perhaps surprising insights. Also mark and record any lessons for life ("LFL").
5. Remember that 1 and 2 Chronicles were written as one book. Second Chronicles is a continuation of 1 Chronicles. Chronicles has a number of speeches, prophecies, and

prayers, some of which are not mentioned in Samuel or Kings. Watch for these and pay attention to what is said, by whom, and why. Highlight or note your insights in the margin.

6. When you finish reading each chapter, record its theme on 2 CHRONICLES AT A GLANCE and in your Bible. Also watch for the major historical events that occur in 2 Chronicles. Highlight these on the chart.

7. Complete 2 CHRONICLES AT A GLANCE. As you review the chapter themes you have recorded, see how this book could be segmented and record this under "Segment Divisions." Also, record the book's theme.

Things to Think About

1. Many lessons about prayer and seeking God can be learned from this book. Review what you have seen from marking the key words. Think about what you learned regarding sin, prayer, confession, and repentance in 2 Chronicles 6.

2. Second Chronicles is filled with illustrations of how people dealt with difficulties and testings. How did you relate to these people? What did you learn from their lives—men such as Asa, Jehoshaphat, Hezekiah, Uzziah? As you studied them, did God prick your heart? With what warnings or cautions?

3. What did you learn about the heart from this book? Do you serve the Lord wholeheartedly or halfheartedly? What did you learn about crying to the Lord? What happened to those who cried out to Him? Did they always deserve to be heard?

4. What did you learn about the sovereignty of God? How active or involved is God in the affairs of men? What were the different ways God afflicted those who disobeyed? Do you have a healthy fear of God?

INSIGHT

Read **The Ark of the Covenant** on page 2099.

1 Kings 3

Chapter 1 Theme ____________________ 1:1 [a]1 Kin 2:12, 46 [b]1 Chr 29:25

1 Now [a]Solomon the son of David established himself securely
over his kingdom, and the LORD his God *was* with him and
[b]exalted him greatly. 2 [a]1 Chr 28:1
2 Solomon spoke to all Israel, [a]to the commanders of thousands
and of hundreds and to the judges and to every leader in all Israel,
the heads of the fathers' *households.* 3 [a]1 Kin 3:4 [b]Ex 36:8
3 Then Solomon and all the assembly with him went to [a]the
high place which was at Gibeon, [b]for God's tent of meeting was
there, which Moses the servant of the LORD had made in the
wilderness. 4 [1]Lit *where David had prepared for it* [a]1 Chr 15:25-28 [b]2 Chr 6:2
4 However, David had brought up [a]the ark of God from
Kiriath-jearim [1]to [b]the place he had prepared for it, for he had
pitched a tent for it in Jerusalem.
5 Now [a]the bronze altar, which Bezalel the son of Uri, the
son of Hur, had made, [1]was there before the tabernacle of the 5 [1]Lit *he put* [a]Ex 31:9; 38:1-7
LORD, and Solomon and the assembly sought it out.
6 Solomon went up there before the LORD to the bronze altar
which *was* at the tent of meeting, and [a]offered a thousand
burnt offerings on it. 6 [a]1 Kin 3:4

7 [a]1 Kin 3:5-14

7 [a]In that night God appeared to Solomon and said to him, "Ask what I shall give you."

8 [a]1 Chr 28:5

8 Solomon said to God, "You have dealt with my father David with great lovingkindness, and [a]have made me king in his place.

9 [1]Lit *word* [a]2 Sam 7:12-16 [b]Gen 13:16; 22:17; 28:14

9 "Now, O LORD God, [a]Your [1]promise to my father David is fulfilled, for You have made me king over [b]a people as numerous as the dust of the earth.

10 [a]1 Kin 3:9 [b]Num 27:17; 2 Sam 5:2

10 "[a]Give me now wisdom and knowledge, [b]that I may go out and come in before this people, for who can rule this great people of Yours?"

11 [1]Lit *this was in your heart* [a]1 Kin 3:11

11 [a]God said to Solomon, "Because [1]you had this in mind, and did not ask for riches, wealth or honor, or the life of those who hate you, nor have you even asked for long life, but you have asked for yourself wisdom and knowledge that you may rule My people over whom I have made you king,

12 [1]Lit *which was not so to the kings who were before you* [2]Lit *be* [a]1 Chr 29:25; 2 Chr 9:22

12 wisdom and knowledge have been granted to you. And [a]I will give you riches and wealth and honor, [1]such as none of the kings who were before you has possessed nor those who will [2]come after you."

13 [1]Lit *to* [a]2 Chr 1:3

13 [a]So Solomon went [1]from the high place which was at Gibeon, from the tent of meeting, to Jerusalem, and he reigned over Israel.

14 [a]1 Kin 10:26-29 [b]1 Kin 4:26 [c]1 Kin 9:19

14 [a]Solomon amassed chariots and horsemen. [b]He had 1,400 chariots and 12,000 horsemen, and he stationed them in [c]the chariot cities and with the king at Jerusalem.

15 [1]Heb *shephelah* [a]1 Kin 10:27 [b]Deut 17:17

15 [a]The king made [b]silver and gold as plentiful in Jerusalem as stones, and he made cedars as plentiful as sycamores in the [1]lowland.

16 [a]Deut 17:16

16 Solomon's [a]horses were imported from Egypt and from Kue; the king's traders procured them from Kue for a price.

17 [1]Lit *brought up and brought out* [2]Lit *and in like manner by their hand* [3]Lit *brought out*

17 They [1]imported chariots from Egypt for 600 *shekels* of silver apiece and horses for 150 apiece, and [2]by the same means they [3]exported them to all the kings of the Hittites and the kings of Aram.

Chapter 2 Theme ______________________

2:1 [1]Ch 1:18 in Heb [2]Lit *said* [3]Lit *house for his royalty* [a]1 Kin 5:5

1 Kings 5

2 [1a]Now Solomon [2]decided to build a house for the name of the LORD and a [3]royal palace for himself.

2 [1]Ch 2:1 in Heb [2]Lit *numbered* [a]1 Kin 5:15, 16; 2 Chr 2:18

2 [1]So [a]Solomon [2]assigned 70,000 men to carry loads and 80,000 men to quarry *stone* in the mountains and 3,600 to supervise them.

3 [1]In 1 Kin 5:18, *Hiram* [a]1 Kin 5:2-11 [b]1 Chr 14:1

3 [a]Then Solomon sent *word* to [1]Huram the king of Tyre, saying, "[b]As you dealt with David my father and sent him cedars to build him a house to dwell in, so do for me.

4 [a]Ex 30:7 [b]Ex 25:30 [c]Ex 29:38-42 [d]Num 28:9, 10

4 "Behold, I am about to build a house for the name of the LORD my God, dedicating it to Him, [a]to burn fragrant incense before Him and *to set out* [b]the showbread continually, and to offer [c]burnt offerings morning and evening, [d]on sabbaths and on new moons and on the appointed feasts of the LORD our God, this *being required* forever in Israel.

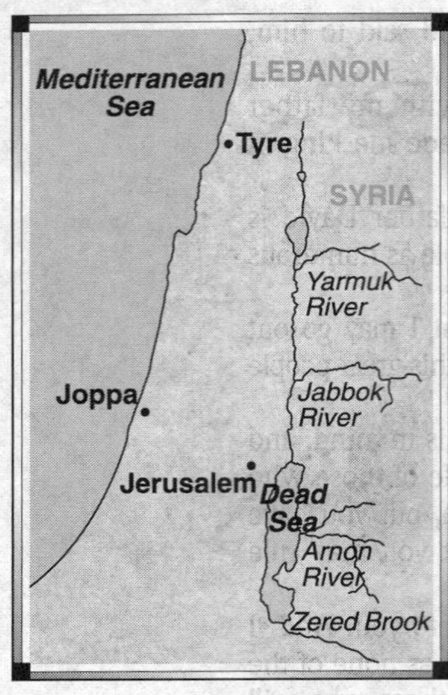

5 "The house which I am about to build *will*
be great, for [a]greater is our God than all the
gods.
6 "But [a]who is able to build a house for Him,
for the heavens and the highest heavens cannot
contain Him? So who am I, that I should build a
house for Him, except to [1]burn *incense* before
Him?
7 "Now [a]send me a skilled man to work in
gold, silver, brass and iron, and in purple,
crimson and violet *fabrics,* and who knows
how to make engravings, to *work* with the
skilled men [1b]whom I have in Judah and
Jerusalem, whom David my father provided.
8 "[a]Send me also cedar, cypress and algum
timber from Lebanon, for I know that your
servants know how to cut timber of Lebanon;
and indeed [b]my servants *will work* with your
servants,

Cedar from Lebanon

9 to prepare timber in abundance for me, for the house which
I am about to build *will be* great and wonderful.
10 "Now behold, [a]I will give to your servants, the woodsmen
who cut the timber, 20,000 [1]kors of crushed wheat and
20,000 [1]kors of barley, and 20,000 baths of wine and 20,000
baths of oil."
11 Then Huram, king of Tyre, [1]answered in a letter sent to
Solomon: "[a]Because the LORD loves His people, He has made
you king over them."
12 Then Huram [1]continued, "Blessed be [a]the LORD, the God of
Israel, who has made heaven and earth, who has given King
David a wise son, [2]endowed with discretion and understanding,
[b]who will build a house for the LORD and a [3]royal palace for
himself.
13 "Now I am sending Huram-abi, a skilled man, [1]endowed
with understanding,
14 [a]the son of a [1]Danite woman and [2]a Tyrian father, who
knows how to work in gold, silver, bronze, iron, stone and
wood, *and* in purple, violet, linen and crimson fabrics, and *who*
knows how to make all kinds of engravings and to [3]execute any
design which may be assigned to him, *to work* with your
skilled men and with [4]those of my lord David your father.
15 "Now then, let my lord send to his servants wheat and
barley, oil and wine, of [a]which he has spoken.
16 "[a]We will cut whatever timber you need from Lebanon and
bring it to you on rafts by sea to Joppa, so that you may carry it
up to Jerusalem."
17 Solomon numbered all the aliens who *were* in the land of
Israel, [a]following the [1]census which his father David had
[2]taken; and 153,600 were found.
18 [a]He appointed 70,000 of them to carry loads and 80,000 to
quarry *stones* in the mountains and 3,600 supervisors to make
the people work.

5 [a]Ex 15:11; 1 Chr 16:25

6 [1]Lit *offer up in smoke* [a]1 Kin 8:27; 2 Chr 6:18

7 [1]Lit *who are with me* [a]Ex 31:3-5; 2 Chr 2:13, 14 [b]1 Chr 22:15

8 [a]1 Kin 5:6 [b]2 Chr 9:10, 11

10 [1]I.e. One kor equals approx 10 bu [a]1 Kin 5:11

11 [1]Lit *said . . . and he sent* [a]1 Kin 10:9; 2 Chr 9:8

12 [1]Lit *said* [2]Lit *knowing discretion* [3]Lit *house for his royalty* [a]Ps 33:6; 102:25 [b]2 Chr 2:1

13 [1]Lit *knowing understanding*

14 [1]Lit *a woman of the daughters of Dan* [2]Lit *whose father is a Tyrian man* [3]Lit *devise any device* [4]Lit *skilled men* [a]1 Kin 7:14

15 [a]2 Chr 2:10

16 [a]1 Kin 5:8, 9

17 [1]Lit *numbering* [2]Lit *numbered of them* [a]1 Chr 22:2

18 [a]2 Chr 2:2

Chapter 3 Theme ______________________________

1 Kings 6

3 [a]Then Solomon began to build the house of the LORD in
Jerusalem on Mount Moriah, where *the LORD* had appeared
to his father David, at the place that David had prepared [b]on
the threshing floor of [1]Ornan the Jebusite.
2 He began to build on the second *day* in the second month
[1]of the fourth year of his reign.
3 Now these are the [1]foundations which [a]Solomon laid for
building the house of God. The length in [2]cubits, according to
the old standard *was* sixty cubits, and the width twenty cubits.
4 The porch which was in front of the house [a]was as long as
the width of the house, twenty cubits, and the height 120; and
inside he overlaid it with pure gold.
5 He overlaid [a]the [1]main room with cypress wood and overlaid
it with fine gold, and [2]ornamented it with palm trees and chains.
6 Further, he [1]adorned the house with precious stones; and
the gold was gold from [2]Parvaim.
7 [a]He also overlaid the house with gold—the beams, the
thresholds and its walls and its doors; and he [b]carved cherubim
on the walls.
8 Now he made [a]the [1]room of the holy of holies: its length
across the width of the house *was* twenty cubits, and its width
was twenty cubits; and he overlaid it with fine gold, *amounting*
to 600 talents.
9 The weight of the nails was fifty shekels of gold. He also
overlaid [a]the upper rooms with gold.
10 [a]Then he made two [1]sculptured cherubim in the room of
the holy of holies and overlaid them with gold.
11 The wingspan of the cherubim *was* twenty cubits; the wing
of one, of five cubits, touched the wall of the house, and *its*
other wing, of five cubits, touched the wing of the other cherub.
12 The wing of the other cherub, of five cubits, touched the
wall of the house; and *its* other wing of five cubits was attached
to the wing of the [1]first cherub.
13 The wings of these cherubim extended twenty cubits, and
they stood on their feet [1]facing the *main* room.
14 [a]He made the veil of violet, purple, crimson and fine linen,
and he worked cherubim on it.
15 [a]He also made two pillars for the front of the house, thirty-five
cubits [1]high, and the capital on the top of each *was* five cubits.
16 He made chains in the inner sanctuary and placed *them* on
the tops of the pillars; and he made one hundred pomegranates
and placed *them* on the chains.
17 [a]He erected the pillars in front of the temple, one on the
right and the other on the left, and named the one on the right
Jachin and the one on the left Boaz.

968 B.C.

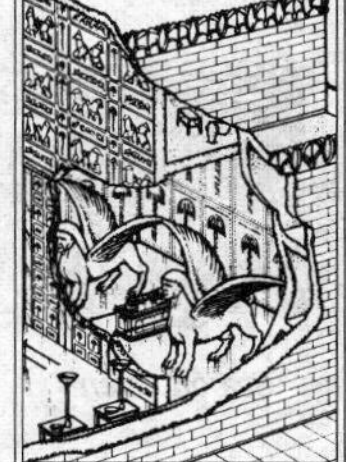

Close-up of Holy of Holies

Chapter 4 Theme ______________________________

1 Kings 7

4 Then [a]he made a bronze altar, twenty cubits in length and
twenty cubits in width and ten cubits in height.
2 [a]Also he made the cast *metal* sea, ten cubits from brim to

3:1 [1]In 2 Sam 24:18, *Araunah* [a]1 Kin 6:1 [b]1 Chr 21:18
2 [1]Lit *in*
3 [1]Lit *founding of Solomon to build* [2]I.e. One cubit equals approx 18 in. [a]1 Kin 6:2
4 [a]1 Kin 6:3
5 [1]Lit *great house* [2]Lit *put on it palm trees* [a]1 Kin 6:17
6 [1]Lit *overlaid . . . for beauty* [2]Or *country of gold*
7 [a]1 Kin 6:20-22 [b]1 Kin 6:29-35
8 [1]Lit *house* [a]Ex 26:33; 1 Kin 6:16
9 [a]1 Chr 28:11
10 [1]Lit *cherubim of sculptured work* [a]Ex 25:18-20; 1 Kin 6:23-28
12 [1]Lit *other*
13 [1]Lit *and their faces to*
14 [a]Ex 26:31
15 [1]Lit *long* [a]1 Kin 7:15-20
17 [a]1 Kin 7:21
4:1 [a]Ex 27:1, 2; 2 Kin 16:14
2 [a]1 Kin 7:23-26

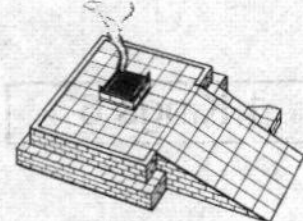
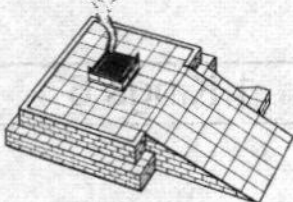

Bronze Altar

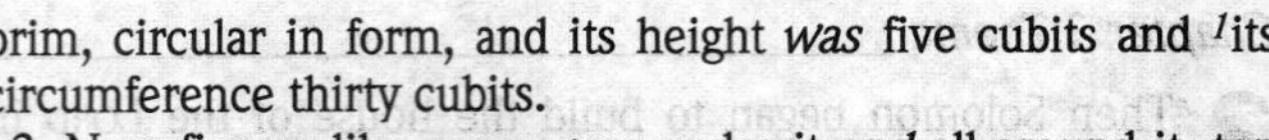
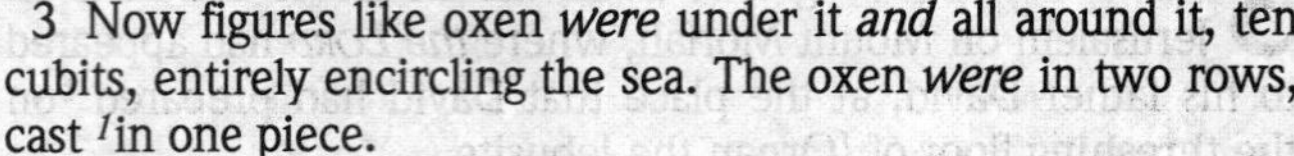

brim, circular in form, and its height *was* five cubits and [1]its
circumference thirty cubits.
3 Now figures like oxen *were* under it *and* all around it, ten
cubits, entirely encircling the sea. The oxen *were* in two rows,
cast [1]in one piece.
4 It stood on twelve oxen, three facing the north, three
facing west, three facing south and three facing east; and the
sea *was set* on top of them and all their hindquarters turned
inwards.
5 It was a handbreadth thick, and its brim was made like the
brim of a cup, *like* a lily blossom; it [a]could hold 3,000 baths.
6 [a]He also made ten basins in which to wash, and he set five
on the right side and five on the left [1]to rinse things for the
burnt offering; but the sea *was* for the priests to wash in.
7 Then [a]he made the ten golden lampstands in the way
prescribed for them and he set them in the temple, five on the
right side and five on the left.
8 He also made [a]ten tables and placed them in the temple,
five on the right side and five on the left. And he made one
hundred golden bowls.
9 Then he made [a]the court of the priests and [b]the great court
and doors for the court, and overlaid their doors with bronze.
10 [a]He set the sea on the right [1]side *of the house* toward the
southeast.
11 [a]Huram also made the pails, the shovels and the bowls. So
Huram finished doing the work which he performed for King
Solomon in the house of God:
12 the two pillars, the bowls and the two capitals on top of the
pillars, and the two networks to cover the two bowls of the
capitals which were on top of the pillars,
13 and [a]the four hundred pomegranates for the two networks,
two rows of pomegranates for each network to cover the two
bowls of the capitals which were on the pillars.
14 [a]He also made the stands and he made the basins on the
stands,
15 *and* the one sea with the twelve oxen under it.
16 The pails, the shovels, the forks and all its utensils,
[a]Huram-abi made of polished bronze for King Solomon for the
house of the LORD.
17 On the plain of the Jordan the king cast them in the clay
ground between Succoth and Zeredah.
18 [a]Thus Solomon made all these utensils in great quantities,
for the weight of the bronze could not be found out.
19 Solomon also made all the things that *were* in the house of
God: even the golden altar, [a]the tables with the bread of the
Presence on them,
20 the lampstands with their lamps of pure gold, [a]to burn in
front of the inner sanctuary in the way prescribed;
21 the flowers, the lamps, and the tongs of gold, of purest
gold;
22 and the snuffers, the bowls, the spoons and the firepans of

Sea on Oxen

Bronze Stand with Bronze Basin

Lampstand

Table

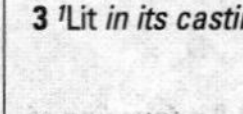

2 [1]Lit *a line of 30 cubits encircling it round about*
3 [1]Lit *in its casting*
5 [a]1 Kin 7:26
6 [1]Lit *in which to* [a]Ex 30:17-21; 1 Kin 7:38, 40
7 [a]Ex 25:31-40; 1 Kin 7:49
8 [a]1 Kin 7:48
9 [a]1 Kin 6:36 [b]2 Kin 21:5
10 [1]Lit *shoulder* [a]1 Kin 7:39
11 [a]1 Kin 7:40-51
13 [a]1 Kin 7:20
14 [a]1 Kin 7:27-43
16 [a]1 Kin 7:14; 2 Chr 2:13
18 [a]1 Kin 7:47
19 [a]2 Chr 4:8
20 [a]Ex 25:31-37; 2 Chr 5:7

5:1 [1]Lit *dedicated things of David,* [a]1 Kin 7:51 [b]2 Sam 8:11; 1 Chr 18:11

pure gold; and the entrance of the house, its inner doors for
the holy of holies and the doors of the house, *that is,* of the
nave, of gold.

Chapter 5 Theme ______________________

1 Kings 8

2 [a]1 Kin 8:1-9 [b]2 Sam 6:12-15; 1 Chr 15:25-28; 2 Chr 1:4

5 [a]Thus all the work that Solomon performed for the house of
the LORD was finished. And Solomon brought in the [1b]things
that David his father had dedicated, even the silver and the gold
and all the utensils, *and* put *them* in the treasuries of the house
of God.
2 [a]Then Solomon assembled to Jerusalem the elders of Israel
and all the heads of the tribes, the leaders of the fathers'
households of the sons of Israel, [b]to bring up the ark of the
covenant of the LORD out of the city of David, which is Zion.

3 [a]1 Kin 8:2 [b]2 Chr 7:8-10

3 [a]All the men of Israel assembled themselves to the king at
[b]the feast, that is *in* the seventh month.

4 [a]Josh 3:6; 2 Chr 5:7

4 Then all the elders of Israel came, and [a]the Levites took up
the ark.
5 They brought up the ark and the tent of meeting and all
the holy utensils which *were* in the tent; the Levitical priests
brought them up.

6 [1]Lit *sheep . . . numbered for multitude*

6 And King Solomon and all the congregation of Israel who
were assembled with him before the ark, were sacrificing [1]so
many sheep and oxen that they could not be counted or
numbered.

8 [1]Lit *poles above*

7 Then the priests brought the ark of the covenant of the
LORD to its place, into the inner sanctuary of the house, to the
holy of holies, under the wings of the cherubim.
8 For the cherubim spread their wings over the place of the ark,
so that the cherubim made a covering over the ark and its [1]poles.

9 [1]Lit *it is* [a]1 Kin 8:8, 9

9 The poles were so long that [a]the ends of the poles of the
ark could be seen in front of the inner sanctuary, but they
could not be seen outside; and [1]they are there to this day.

Ark of the Covenant (or Testimony)

10 [a]Deut 10:2-5; Heb 9:4

10 [a]There was nothing in the ark except the two tablets which
Moses put *there* at Horeb, where the LORD made a covenant
with the sons of Israel, when they came out of Egypt.

11 [a]1 Chr 24:1-5

11 When the priests came forth from the holy place (for all the
priests who were present had sanctified themselves, without
regard [a]to divisions),
12 and all the Levitical singers, [a]Asaph, Heman, Jeduthun, and
their sons and kinsmen, clothed in fine linen, [b]with cymbals,
harps and lyres, standing east of the altar, and with them one
hundred and twenty priests [c]blowing trumpets

12 [a]1 Chr 25:1-4 [b]1 Chr 13:8; 15:16, 24 [c]2 Chr 7:6

13 in unison when the trumpeters and the singers were to
make themselves heard with one voice to praise and to glorify
the LORD, and when they lifted up their voice [a]accompanied by
trumpets and cymbals and instruments of music, and when
they praised the LORD *saying,* "[b]*He* indeed is good for His
lovingkindness is everlasting," then the house, the house of the
LORD, was filled with a cloud,

13 [a]1 Chr 16:42 [b]1 Chr 16:34; 2 Chr 7:3; Ezra 3:11; Ps 100:5; Jer 33:11

14 so that the priests could not stand to minister because of the cloud, for [a]the glory of the LORD filled the house of God.

INSIGHT

See the illustration of Solomon's Temple on page NISB-36.

Chapter 6 Theme ______________________

6 [a]Then Solomon said,
"The LORD has said that He would dwell in the thick cloud.
2 "I have built You a lofty house,
And a place for Your dwelling forever."

3 Then the king [1]faced about and blessed all the assembly of Israel, while all the assembly of Israel was standing.

4 He said, "Blessed be the LORD, the God of Israel, who spoke with His mouth to my father David and has fulfilled *it* with His hands, saying,

5 'Since the day that I brought My people from the land of Egypt, I did not choose a city out of all the tribes of Israel *in which* to build a house that My name might be there, nor did I choose any man for a leader over My people Israel;

6 but [a]I have chosen Jerusalem that My name might be there, and I [b]have chosen David to be over My people Israel.'

7 "[a]Now it was [1]in the heart of my father David to build a house for the name of the LORD, the God of Israel.

8 "But the LORD said to my father David, 'Because it was [1]in your heart to build a house for My name, you did well that it was [1]in your heart.

9 'Nevertheless you shall not build the house, but your son who [1]will be born to you, he shall build the house for My name.'

10 "Now the LORD has fulfilled His word which He spoke; for I have risen in the place of my father David and sit on the throne of Israel, as the LORD [1]promised, and have built the house for the name of the LORD, the God of Israel.

11 "There I have set the ark [a]in which is the covenant of the LORD, which He made with the sons of Israel."

12 Then he stood before the altar of the LORD in the presence of all the assembly of Israel and spread out his hands.

13 [a]Now Solomon had made a bronze platform, five cubits long, five cubits wide and three cubits high, and had set it in the midst of the court; and he stood on it, [b]knelt on his knees in the presence of all the assembly of Israel and spread out his hands toward heaven.

14 He said, "O LORD, the God of Israel, [a]there is no god like You in heaven or on earth, [b]keeping covenant and *showing* lovingkindness to Your servants who walk before You with all their heart;

15 [a]who has kept with Your servant David, my father, that which You have [1]promised him; indeed You have spoken with Your mouth and have fulfilled it with Your hand, as it is this day.

16 "Now therefore, O LORD, the God of Israel, keep with Your servant David, my father, that which You have [1]promised him, saying, '[2][a]You shall not lack a man to sit on the throne of Israel, if only your sons take heed to their way, to walk in My law as you have walked before Me.'

14 [a]Ex 40:35; 1 Kin 8:11

6:1 [a]1 Kin 8:12-50

3 [1]Lit *turned his face about*

6 [a]2 Chr 12:13 [b]1 Chr 28:4

7 [1]Lit *with* [a]1 Kin 5:3; 1 Chr 28:2

8 [1]Lit *with*

9 [1]Lit *will come forth from your loins*

10 [1]Lit *spoke*

11 [a]2 Chr 5:7, 10

13 [a]Neh 8:4 [b]1 Kin 8:54

14 [a]Ex 15:11; Deut 3:24 [b]Deut 7:9

15 [1]Lit *spoken to* [a]1 Chr 22:9, 10

16 [1]Lit *spoken to* [2]Lit *There shall not be cut off to you a man from before Me* [a]1 Kin 2:4; 2 Chr 7:18

17 "Now therefore, O LORD, the God of Israel, let Your word be
confirmed which You have spoken to Your servant David.
18 "But [a]will God indeed dwell with mankind on the earth?
Behold, [b]heaven and the [1]highest heaven cannot contain You;
how much less this house which I have built.
19 "Yet have regard to the prayer of Your servant and to his
supplication, O LORD my God, to listen to the cry and to the
prayer which Your servant prays before You;
20 that Your [a]eye may be open toward this house day and night,
toward [b]the place of which You have said that *You would* put
Your name there, to listen to the prayer which Your servant
shall pray toward this place.
21 "Listen to the supplications of Your servant and of Your
people Israel when they pray toward this place; hear from Your
dwelling place, from heaven; [a]hear and forgive.
22 "If a man sins against his neighbor and is made to take an
oath, and he comes *and* takes an oath before Your altar in this
house,
23 then hear from heaven and act and judge Your servants,
[1a]punishing the wicked by bringing his way on his own head
and justifying the righteous by giving him according to his
righteousness.
24 "If Your people Israel [1]are defeated before an enemy
because [a]they have sinned against You, and they return *to You*
and confess Your name, and pray and make supplication before
You in this house,
25 then hear from heaven and forgive the sin of Your people
Israel, and bring them back to the land which You have given
to them and to their fathers.
26 "When the [a]heavens are shut up and there is no rain because
they have sinned against You, and they pray toward this place
and confess Your name, and turn from their sin when You afflict
them;
27 then hear in heaven and forgive the sin of Your servants
and Your people Israel, indeed, [a]teach them the good way in
which they should walk. And send rain on Your land which
You have given to Your people for an inheritance.
28 "If there is [a]famine in the land, if there is pestilence, if there
is blight or mildew, if there is locust or grasshopper, if their
enemies besiege them in the land of their [1]cities, whatever
plague or whatever sickness *there is,*
29 whatever prayer or supplication is made by any man or by
all Your people Israel, [1]each knowing his own affliction and his
own pain, and spreading his hands toward this house,
30 then hear from heaven Your dwelling place, and forgive,
and render to each according to all his ways, whose heart You
know [a]for You alone know the hearts of the sons of men,
31 that they may [1]fear You, to walk in Your ways [2]as long as
they live in the land which You have given to our fathers.
32 "Also concerning [a]the foreigner who is not from Your people
Israel, when he comes from a far country for Your great name's

18 [1]Lit *heaven of heavens* [a]Ps 113:5, 6 [b]2 Chr 2:6; Is 66:1; Acts 7:49
20 [a]Ps 33:18; 34:15 [b]Deut 12:11
21 [a]Is 43:25; 44:22; Mic 7:18
23 [1]Lit *returning* [a]Is 3:11; Rom 2:8, 9
24 [1]Lit *smitten* [a]Ps 51:4
26 [a]1 Kin 17:1
27 [a]Ps 94:12
28 [1]Lit *gates* [a]2 Chr 20:9
29 [1]Lit *whoever shall know*
30 [a]1 Sam 16:7; 1 Chr 28:9
31 [1]Or *reverence* [2]Lit *all the days that they live on the face of the land*
32 [a]Is 56:3-8

sake and Your mighty hand and Your outstretched arm, when
they come and pray toward this house,
33 then hear from heaven, from Your dwelling place, and do
according to all for which the foreigner calls to You, in order that
all the peoples of the earth may know Your name, and [1]fear
You as *do* Your people Israel, and that they may know that [2]this
house which I have built is [a]called by Your name.
34 "When Your people go out to battle against their enemies,
by whatever way You shall send them, and they pray to You
toward this city which You have chosen and the house which I
have built for Your name,
35 then hear from heaven their prayer and their supplication,
and maintain their cause.
36 "When they sin against You ([a]for there is no man who does
not sin) and You are angry with them and deliver them to an
enemy, so that [1]they take them away captive to a land far off or
near,
37 if they [1]take thought in the land where they are taken captive,
and repent and make supplication to You in the land of their
captivity, saying, 'We have sinned, we have committed iniquity
and have acted wickedly';
38 [a]if they return to You with all their heart and with all their
soul in the land of their captivity, where they have been taken
captive, and pray toward their land which You have given to
their fathers and the city which You have chosen, and toward
the house which I have built for Your name,
39 then hear from heaven, from Your dwelling place, their
prayer and supplications, and maintain their cause and forgive
Your people who have sinned against You.
40 "Now, O my God, I pray, [a]let Your eyes be open and [b]Your
ears attentive to the prayer *offered* in this place.
41 "[a]Now therefore arise, O LORD God, to Your resting place, You
and the ark of Your might; let Your priests, O LORD God, be clothed
with salvation and let Your godly ones rejoice in what is good.
42 "O LORD God, do not turn away the face of Your anointed;
[a]remember *Your* lovingkindness to Your servant David."

Chapter 7 Theme ______________________

7 [a]Now when Solomon had finished praying, [b]fire came
down from heaven and consumed the burnt offering and
the sacrifices, and the glory of the LORD filled the house.
2 [a]The priests could not enter into the house of the LORD
because the glory of the LORD filled the LORD's house.
3 All the sons of Israel, seeing the fire come down and the
glory of the LORD upon the house, bowed down on the
pavement with their faces to the ground, and they worshiped
and gave praise to the LORD, *saying,* "[a]Truly He is good, truly
His lovingkindness is everlasting."
4 [a]Then the king and all the people offered sacrifice before
the LORD.

33 [1]Or *reverence* [2]Lit *Your name is called upon this house* [a]2 Chr 7:14
36 [1]Lit *their captors take them captive* [a]Job 15:14-16; James 3:2; 1 John 1:8-10
37 [1]Lit *return to their heart*
38 [a]Jer 29:12, 13
40 [a]2 Chr 7:15; Neh 1:6, 11 [b]Ps 17:1
41 [a]Ps 132:8, 9
42 [a]Ps 89:24, 28; 132:10-12; Is 55:3
7:1 [a]1 Kin 8:54 [b]Lev 9:23f; 1 Kin 18:24, 38
2 [a]2 Chr 5:14
3 [a]2 Chr 5:13; 20:21
4 [a]1 Kin 8:62, 63

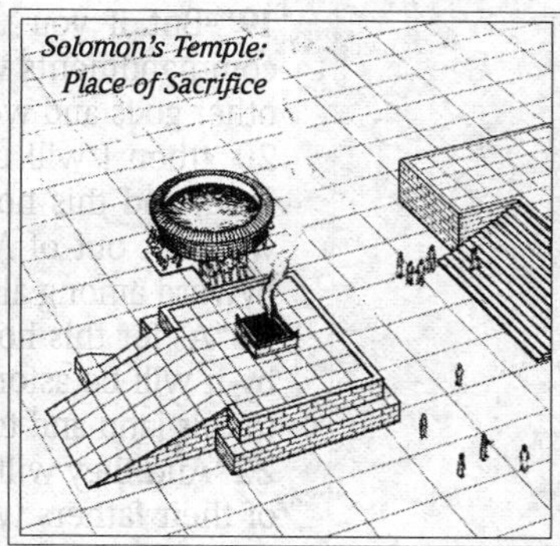
Solomon's Temple: Place of Sacrifice

5 King Solomon offered a sacrifice of 22,000
oxen and 120,000 sheep. Thus the king and
all the people dedicated the house of God.
6 The priests stood at their posts, and [a]the
Levites also, with the instruments of music
to the LORD, which King David had made for
giving praise to the LORD—"for His lovingkindness is everlasting"—whenever [1]he gave
praise by their [2]means, while [b]the priests on
the other side blew trumpets; and all Israel
was standing.
7 [a]Then Solomon consecrated the middle of
the court that *was* before the house of the
LORD, for there he offered the burnt offerings and the fat of the
peace offerings because the bronze altar which Solomon had
made was not able to contain the burnt offering, the grain
offering and the fat.
8 So [a]Solomon observed the feast at that time for seven days,
and all Israel with him, a very great assembly *who came* from
the entrance of Hamath to the [b]brook of Egypt.
9 On the eighth day they held [a]a solemn assembly, for the
dedication of the altar they observed seven days and the feast
seven days.
10 Then on the twenty-third day of the seventh month he sent
the people to their tents, rejoicing and happy of heart because
of the goodness that the LORD had shown to David and to
Solomon and to His people Israel.
11 [a]Thus Solomon finished the house of the LORD and the
king's palace, and successfully completed all that [1]he had
planned on doing in the house of the LORD and in his palace.
12 Then the LORD appeared to Solomon at night and said to
him, "I have heard your prayer and [a]have chosen this place for
Myself as a house of sacrifice.
13 "[a]If I shut up the heavens so that there is no rain, or if I
command the locust to devour the land, or if I send pestilence
among My people,
14 [a]and My people [1]who are called by My name humble
themselves and pray and seek My face and turn from their wicked
ways, then I will hear from heaven, will forgive their sin and
will heal their land.
15 "[a]Now My eyes will be open and My ears attentive to the
[1]prayer *offered* in this place.
16 "For [a]now I have chosen and consecrated this house that
My name may be there forever, and My eyes and My heart will
be there perpetually.
17 "As for you, if you walk before Me as your father David
walked, even to do according to all that I have commanded
you, and will keep My statutes and My ordinances,
18 then I will establish your royal throne as I covenanted with
your father David, saying, '[1a]You shall not lack a man *to be*
ruler in Israel.'

1 Kings 9

6 [1]Lit *David* [2]Lit *hand* [a]1 Chr 15:16-21 [b]2 Chr 5:12
7 [a]1 Kin 8:64-66
8 [a]1 Kin 8:65 [b]Gen 15:18
9 [a]Lev 23:36
11 [1]Lit *came upon the heart of Solomon to do* [a]1 Kin 9:1-9
12 [a]Deut 12:5, 11
13 [a]2 Chr 6:26-28
14 [1]Lit *over whom My name is called* [a]2 Chr 6:37-39; James 4:10
15 [1]Lit *prayer of this place* [a]2 Chr 6:20, 40
16 [a]2 Chr 7:12
18 [1]Lit *There shall not be cut off to you a man* [a]1 Kin 2:4; 2 Chr 6:16

19 "[a]But if you turn away and forsake My statutes and My
commandments which I have set before you, and go and serve
other gods and worship them,
20 [a]then I will uproot you from My land which I have given
[1]you, and this house which I have consecrated for My name I
will cast out of My sight and I will make it [b]a proverb and a
byword among all peoples.
21 "As for this house, which was exalted, everyone who passes
by it will be astonished and say, '[a]Why has the LORD done thus
to this land and to this house?'
22 "And they will say, 'Because [a]they forsook the LORD, the God
of their fathers who brought them from the land of Egypt, and
they adopted other gods and worshiped them and served them;
therefore He has brought all this adversity on them.'"

Chapter 8 Theme ______________________

948 B.C.

8 [a]Now it came about at the end of the twenty years in which
Solomon had built the house of the LORD and his own house
2 that he built the cities which Huram had given to [1]him,
and settled the sons of Israel there.
3 Then Solomon went to Hamath-zobah and captured it.
4 He built Tadmor in the wilderness and all the storage cities
which he had built in Hamath.
5 He also built upper [a]Beth-horon and lower Beth-horon,
[b]fortified cities *with* walls, gates and bars;
6 and Baalath and all the storage cities that Solomon had, and
all the cities for [1]his chariots and cities for [1]his horsemen, and
all that it pleased Solomon to build in Jerusalem, in Lebanon,
and in all the land [2]under his rule.
7 [a]All of the people who were left of the Hittites, the Amorites,
the Perizzites, the Hivites and the Jebusites, who were not of
Israel,
8 *namely,* from their descendants who were left after them in
the land whom the sons of Israel had not destroyed, [a]them
Solomon raised as forced laborers to this day.
9 But Solomon did not make slaves for his work from the
sons of Israel; they were men of war, his chief captains and
commanders of his chariots and his horsemen.
10 These were the chief [1]officers of King Solomon, two
hundred and fifty who ruled over the people.
11 [a]Then Solomon brought Pharaoh's daughter up from the
city of David to the house which he had built for her, for he
said, "My wife shall not dwell in the house of David king of
Israel, because [1]the places are holy where the ark of the LORD
has entered."
12 Then Solomon offered burnt offerings to the LORD on [a]the
altar of the LORD which he had built before the porch;
13 and [a]*did so* according to the daily rule, offering *them* up
[b]according to the commandment of Moses, for [c]the sabbaths,
[d]the new moons and the [e]three annual feasts—the Feast of
Unleavened Bread, the Feast of Weeks and the Feast of Booths.

19 [a]Lev 26:14, 33; Deut 28:15
20 [1]Ancient versions and Heb read *them* [a]Deut 29:28; 1 Kin 14:15 [b]Deut 28:37
21 [a]Deut 29:24-27
22 [a]Judg 2:13
8:1 [a]1 Kin 9:10-28
2 [1]Lit *Solomon*
5 [a]1 Chr 7:24 [b]2 Chr 14:7
6 [1]Lit *the* [2]Lit *of*
7 [a]Gen 15:18-21; 1 Kin 9:20
8 [a]1 Kin 4:6; 9:21
10 [1]Or *deputies*
11 [1]Lit *they are* [a]1 Kin 3:1; 7:8
12 [a]2 Chr 4:1
13 [a]Ex 29:38-42 [b]Num 28:3 [c]Num 28:9, 10 [d]Num 28:11 [e]Ex 23:14-17; 34:22, 23; Deut 16:16

14 [a]1 Chr 24:1 [b]1 Chr 25:1 [c]1 Chr 26:1 [d]Neh 12:24, 36

14 Now according to the ordinance of his father David, he appointed [a]the divisions of the priests for their service, and [b]the Levites for their duties of praise and ministering before the priests according to the daily rule, and [c]the gatekeepers by their divisions at every gate; for [d]David the man of God had so commanded.

15 And they did not depart from the commandment of the king to the priests and Levites in any manner or concerning the storehouses.

16 [1]So ancient versions; M.T. *as far as*

16 Thus all the work of Solomon was carried out [1]from the day of the foundation of the house of the LORD, and until it was finished. So the house of the LORD was completed.

17 Then Solomon went to [a]Ezion-geber and to [b]Eloth on the seashore in the land of Edom.

17 [a]1 Kin 9:26 [b]2 Kin 14:22

18 And Huram by his servants sent him ships and servants who knew the sea; and they went with Solomon's servants to Ophir, and [a]took from there four hundred and fifty talents of gold and brought them to King Solomon.

18 [a]2 Chr 9:10, 13

Chapter 9 Theme ______________________

1 Kings 10

9 [a]Now when the queen of Sheba heard of the fame of Solomon, she came to Jerusalem to test Solomon with difficult questions. She had a very large retinue, with camels carrying spices and a large amount of gold and precious stones; and when she came to Solomon, she spoke with him about all that was on her heart.

9:1 [a]1 Kin 10:1-13; Matt 12:42; Luke 11:31

2 Solomon [1]answered all her questions; nothing was hidden from Solomon which he did not [2]explain to her.

3 When the queen of Sheba had seen the wisdom of Solomon, the house which he had built,

2 [1]Lit *told her all her words* [2]Lit *tell*

4 the food at his table, the seating of his servants, the attendance of his ministers and their attire, his cupbearers and their attire, and [1]his stairway by which he went up to the house of the LORD, she was breathless.

4 [1]Or *his burnt offering which he offered*

5 Then she said to the king, "It was a true report which I heard in my own land about your words and your wisdom.

6 "Nevertheless I did not believe their reports until I came and my eyes had seen it. And behold, the half of the greatness of your wisdom was not told me. You surpass the report that I heard.

7 "How [1]blessed are your men, how [1]blessed are these your servants who stand before you continually and hear your wisdom.

7 [1]Or *happy*

8 "Blessed be the LORD your God who delighted in you, [a]setting you on His throne as king for the LORD your God; [b]because your God loved Israel establishing them forever, therefore He made you king over them, to do justice and righteousness."

8 [a]1 Chr 28:5; 29:23 [b]Deut 7:8; 2 Chr 2:11

9 Then she gave the king one hundred and twenty talents of gold and a very great *amount of* spices and precious stones; there had never been spice like that which the queen of Sheba gave to King Solomon.

10 The servants of Huram and the servants of Solomon [a]who brought gold from Ophir, also brought algum trees and precious stones.

10 [a]1 Kin 10:11; 2 Chr 8:18

11 From the algum trees the king made steps for the house of
the LORD and for the king's palace, and lyres and harps for the
singers; and none like that was seen before in the land of Judah.
12 King Solomon gave to the queen of Sheba all her desire
which she requested besides *a return for* what she had brought
to the king. Then she turned and went to her own land with her
servants.
13 [a]Now the weight of gold which came to Solomon in one
year was 666 talents of gold,
14 besides that which the traders and merchants brought; and
all [a]the kings of Arabia and the governors of the country
brought gold and silver to Solomon.
15 King Solomon made 200 large shields of beaten gold,
[1]using 600 *shekels of* beaten gold on each large shield.
16 *He made* 300 shields of beaten gold, [1]using three hundred
shekels of gold on each shield, and the king put them in the
house of the forest of Lebanon.
17 Moreover, the king made a great throne of ivory and
overlaid it with pure gold.
18 *There were* six steps to the throne and a footstool in gold
attached to the throne, and [1]arms [2]on each side of the seat, and
two lions standing beside the [1]arms.
19 Twelve lions were standing there on the six steps on the
one side and on the other; nothing like *it* was made for any
other kingdom.
20 All King Solomon's drinking vessels *were* of gold, and all
the vessels of the house of the forest of Lebanon *were* of pure
gold; silver was not considered [1]valuable in the days of Solomon.
21 [a]For the king had ships which went to Tarshish with the
servants of Huram; once every three years the ships of Tarshish
came bringing gold and silver, ivory and apes and peacocks.
22 [a]So King Solomon became greater than all the kings of the
earth in riches and wisdom.
23 And all the kings of the earth were seeking the presence of
Solomon, to hear his wisdom which God had put in his heart.
24 [a]They brought every man his gift, articles of silver and gold,
garments, weapons, spices, horses and mules, so much year by
year.
25 Now Solomon had [a]4,000 stalls for horses and chariots and
12,000 horsemen, and he stationed them in the chariot cities
and with the king in Jerusalem.
26 [a]He was the ruler over all the kings from the Euphrates
River even to the land of the Philistines, and as far as the
border of Egypt.
27 [a]The king made silver *as common* as stones in Jerusalem,
and he made cedars as plentiful as sycamore trees that are in
the [1]lowland.
28 [a]And they were bringing horses for Solomon from Egypt
and from all countries.
29 [a]Now the rest of the acts of Solomon, from first to last, [b]are
they not written in the [1]records of Nathan the prophet, and in

13 [a]1 Kin 10:14-28
14 [a]Ps 68:29; 72:10
15 [1]Lit *he brought up*
16 [1]Lit *he brought up*
18 [1]Lit *hands* [2]Lit *on this side and on this at the place of the seat*
20 [1]Lit *anything*
21 [a]2 Chr 20:36, 37
22 [a]1 Kin 3:13; 2 Chr 1:12
24 [a]Ps 72:10
25 [a]Deut 17:16; 1 Kin 4:26; 10:26; 2 Chr 1:14
26 [a]Gen 15:18; 1 Kin 4:21, 24
27 [1]Heb *shephelah* [a]2 Chr 1:15-17
28 [a]2 Chr 1:16
29 [1]Lit *words* [a]1 Kin 11:41-43 [b]1 Chr 29:29

the prophecy of Ahijah the Shilonite, and in the visions of [2]Iddo
the seer concerning Jeroboam the son of Nebat?
30 [a]Solomon reigned forty years in Jerusalem over all Israel.
31 And Solomon slept with his fathers and was buried in [a]the
city of his father David; and his son Rehoboam reigned in his
place.

~931 B.C.

Chapter 10 Theme ________________

1 Kings 12

10 [a]Then Rehoboam went to Shechem, for all Israel had
come to Shechem to make him king.
2 When Jeroboam the son of Nebat heard *of it* (for [a]he was in
Egypt where he had fled from the presence of King Solomon),
Jeroboam returned from Egypt.
3 So they sent and summoned him. When Jeroboam and all
Israel came, they spoke to Rehoboam, saying,
4 "Your father made our [a]yoke hard; now therefore lighten the
hard service of your father and his heavy yoke which he put on
us, and we will serve you."
5 He said to them, "Return to me again in three days." So the
people departed.
6 Then King Rehoboam [a]consulted with the elders who had
[1]served his father Solomon while he was still alive, saying, "How
do you counsel *me* to answer this people?"
7 They spoke to him, saying, "If you will be kind to this people
and please them and [a]speak good words to them, then they will
be your servants forever."
8 But he [a]forsook the counsel of the elders which they had
given him, and consulted with the young men who grew up with
him [1]and served him.
9 So he said to them, "What counsel do you give that we may
answer this people, who have spoken to me, saying, 'Lighten the
yoke which your father put on us'?"
10 The young men who grew up with him spoke to him, saying,
"Thus you shall say to the people who spoke to you, saying,
'Your father made our yoke heavy, but you make it lighter for
us.' Thus you shall say to them, 'My little finger is thicker than
my father's loins!
11 'Whereas my father loaded you with a heavy yoke, I will
add to your yoke; my father disciplined you with whips, but I
will discipline you with scorpions.'"
12 So Jeroboam and all the people came to Rehoboam on the
third day as the king had [1]directed, saying, "Return to me on
the third day."
13 The king answered them harshly, and King Rehoboam
forsook the counsel of the elders.
14 He spoke to them according to the advice of the young
men, saying, "[1]My father made your yoke heavy, but I will add
to it; my father disciplined you with whips, but I *will discipline
you* with scorpions."
15 So the king did not listen to the people, [a]for it was a turn *of*

29 [2]Heb *Jedo*
30 [a]1 Kin 11:42, 43
31 [a]1 Kin 2:10
10:1 [a]1 Kin 12:1-20
2 [a]1 Kin 11:40
4 [a]1 Kin 5:13-16
6 [1]Lit *stood before* [a]Job 8:8, 9; 32:7
7 [a]Prov 15:1
8 [1]Lit *who stood before* [a]2 Sam 17:14; Prov 13:20
12 [1]Lit *spoken*
14 [1]Many mss read *I have made*
15 [a]2 Chr 25:16-20

events from God [b]that the LORD might establish His word, which He spoke through Ahijah the Shilonite to Jeroboam the son of Nebat.

16 When all Israel *saw* that the king did not listen to them the people answered the king, saying,

"[a]What portion do we have in David?
We have no inheritance in the son of Jesse.
Every man to your tents, O Israel;
Now look after your own house, David."

[b]So all Israel departed to their tents.

17 But as for the sons of Israel who lived in the cities of Judah, Rehoboam reigned over them.

18 Then King Rehoboam sent Hadoram, who was [a]over the forced labor, and the sons of Israel stoned him [1]to death. And King Rehoboam made haste to mount his chariot to flee to Jerusalem.

19 So [a]Israel has been in rebellion against the house of David to this day.

Chapter 11 Theme ________________

11 [a]Now when Rehoboam had come to Jerusalem, he assembled the house of Judah and Benjamin, 180,000 chosen men who were warriors, to fight against Israel to restore the kingdom to Rehoboam.

2 But the word of the LORD came to [a]Shemaiah the man of God, saying,

3 "Speak to Rehoboam the son of Solomon, king of Judah, and to all Israel in Judah and Benjamin, saying,

4 'Thus says the LORD, "You shall not go up or fight against [a]your [1]relatives; return every man to his house, [b]for this thing is from Me."'" So they listened to the words of the LORD and returned from going against Jeroboam.

The Divided Kingdom 931–586 B.C.

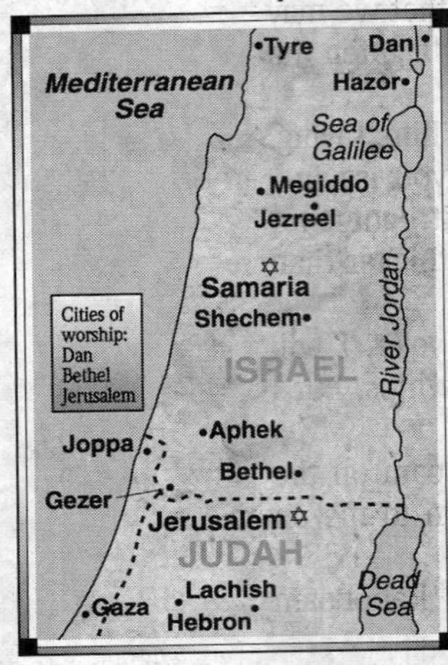

5 Rehoboam lived in Jerusalem and [a]built cities for defense in Judah.

6 Thus he built Bethlehem, Etam, Tekoa,

7 Beth-zur, Soco, Adullam,

8 Gath, Mareshah, Ziph,

9 Adoraim, Lachish, Azekah,

10 Zorah, Aijalon and Hebron, which are fortified cities in Judah and in Benjamin.

11 He also strengthened the fortresses and put officers in them and stores of food, oil and wine.

12 *He put* shields and spears in every city and strengthened them greatly. So he held Judah and Benjamin.

13 Moreover, the priests and the Levites who were in all Israel stood with him from all their districts.

14 For [a]the Levites left their pasture lands and their property and came to Judah and Jerusalem, for [b]Jeroboam and his sons had excluded them from serving as priests to the LORD.

15 [b]1 Kin 11:29-39

16 [a]2 Sam 20:1 [b]2 Chr 10:19

18 [1]Lit *with stones that he died* [a]1 Kin 4:6; 5:14

19 [a]1 Kin 12:19

11:1 [a]1 Kin 12:21-24

2 [a]2 Chr 12:5-7, 15

4 [1]Lit *brothers* [a]2 Chr 28:8-11 [b]2 Chr 10:15

5 [a]2 Chr 8:2-6; 11:23

14 [a]Num 35:2-5 [b]1 Kin 12:28-33; 2 Chr 13:9

15 [a]He set up priests of his own for the high places, for the
satyrs and for the calves which he had made.
16 [a]Those from all the tribes of Israel who set their hearts on
seeking the LORD God of Israel [1]followed them to Jerusalem, to
sacrifice to the LORD God of their fathers.
17 [a]They strengthened the kingdom of Judah and supported
Rehoboam the son of Solomon for three years, for they walked
in the way of David and Solomon for three years.
18 Then Rehoboam took as a wife Mahalath the daughter of
Jerimoth the son of David *and of* Abihail the daughter of [a]Eliab
the son of Jesse,
19 and she bore him sons: Jeush, Shemariah and Zaham.
20 After her he took [a]Maacah the daughter of [1]Absalom, and
she bore him Abijah, Attai, Ziza and Shelomith.
21 Rehoboam loved Maacah the daughter of Absalom more
than all his *other* wives and concubines. For [a]he had taken
eighteen wives and sixty concubines and fathered twenty-eight
sons and sixty daughters.
22 [a]Rehoboam appointed Abijah the son of Maacah as head and
leader among his brothers, for he *intended* to make him king.
23 He acted wisely and distributed [1]some of his sons through
all the territories of Judah and Benjamin to all the fortified cities,
and he gave them food in abundance. And he sought many
wives *for them.*

15 [a]1 Kin 12:31; 13:33
16 [1]Lit *came after* [a]2 Chr 15:9
17 [a]2 Chr 12:1
18 [a]1 Sam 16:6
20 [1]In 1 Kin 15:2, *Abishalom* [a]1 Kin 15:2; 2 Chr 13:2
21 [a]Deut 17:17
22 [a]Deut 21:15-17
23 [1]Lit *from all*

Chapter 12 Theme ______________________

926 B.C.

12 [a]When the kingdom of Rehoboam was established and
strong, [b]he and all Israel with him forsook the law of the
LORD.
2 [a]And it came about in King Rehoboam's fifth year, because
they had been unfaithful to the LORD, that [b]Shishak king of
Egypt came up against Jerusalem
3 with 1,200 chariots and 60,000 horsemen. And the people
who came with him from Egypt were without number: [a]the
Lubim, the Sukkiim and the Ethiopians.
4 He captured [a]the fortified cities of Judah and came as far as
Jerusalem.
5 Then [a]Shemaiah the prophet came to Rehoboam and the
princes of Judah who had gathered at Jerusalem because of
Shishak, and he said to them, "Thus says the LORD, "[b]You have
forsaken Me, so I also have forsaken you [1]to Shishak.'"
6 So the princes of Israel and the king humbled themselves
and said, "The [a]LORD is righteous."
7 When the LORD saw that they humbled themselves, the
word of the LORD came to Shemaiah, saying, "[a]They have
humbled themselves *so* I will not destroy them, but I will grant
them some *measure* of deliverance, and [b]My wrath shall not be
poured out on Jerusalem by means of Shishak.
8 "But they will become his slaves so [a]that they may learn *the
difference between* My service and the service of the kingdoms
of the countries."

1 Kings 14

12:1 [a]2 Chr 11:17; 12:13 [b]2 Chr 26:13-16
2 [a]1 Kin 14:25 [b]1 Kin 11:40
3 [a]2 Chr 16:8; Nah 3:9
4 [a]2 Chr 11:5-12
5 [1]Lit *in the hand of* [a]2 Chr 11:2 [b]Deut 28:15; 2 Chr 15:2
6 [a]Ex 9:27; Dan 9:14
7 [a]1 Kin 21:29 [b]2 Chr 34:25-27; Ps 78:38
8 [a]Deut 28:47, 48

9 [a]So Shishak king of Egypt came up against Jerusalem, and took the treasures of the house of the LORD and the treasures of the king's palace. He took everything; [b]he even took the golden shields which Solomon had made.

10 Then King Rehoboam made shields of bronze in their place and committed them to the [1]care of the commanders of the [2]guard who guarded the door of the king's house.

11 As often as the king entered the house of the LORD, the [1]guards came and carried them and *then* brought them back into the [1]guards' room.

12 And [a]when he humbled himself, the anger of the LORD turned away from him, so as not to destroy *him* completely; and also conditions [b]were good in Judah.

13 [a]So King Rehoboam strengthened himself in Jerusalem and reigned. Now Rehoboam was forty-one years old when he began to reign, and he reigned seventeen years in Jerusalem, the city which the LORD had chosen from all the tribes of Israel, to put His name there. And his mother's name was Naamah the Ammonitess.

14 He did evil [a]because he did not set his heart to seek the LORD.

15 [a]Now the acts of Rehoboam, from first to last, are they not written in the [1]records of [b]Shemaiah the prophet and of [c]Iddo the seer, according to genealogical enrollment? And *there were* wars between Rehoboam and Jeroboam continually.

16 And Rehoboam slept with his fathers and was buried in the city of David; and his son [a]Abijah became king in his place.

Chapter 13 Theme ______________________

912 B.C.

1 Kings 15

13

[a]In the eighteenth year of King Jeroboam, Abijah became king over Judah.

2 He reigned three years in Jerusalem; and his mother's name was Micaiah the daughter of Uriel of Gibeah.

[a]**N**ow there was war between Abijah and Jeroboam.

3 Abijah began the battle with an army of valiant warriors, 400,000 chosen men, while Jeroboam drew up in battle formation against him with 800,000 chosen men *who were* valiant warriors.

4 Then Abijah stood on Mount [a]Zemaraim, which is in the hill country of Ephraim, and said, "Listen to me, Jeroboam and all Israel:

5 "Do you not know that [a]the LORD God of Israel gave the rule over Israel forever to David [1]and his sons by [b]a covenant of salt?

6 "Yet [a]Jeroboam the son of Nebat, the servant of Solomon the son of David, rose up and rebelled against his [1]master,

7 and worthless men gathered about him, scoundrels, who proved too strong for Rehoboam, the son of Solomon, when [1a]he was young and timid and could not hold his own against them.

8 "So now you intend to resist the kingdom of the LORD [1]through the sons of David, [2]being a great multitude and *having* with you [a]the golden calves which Jeroboam made for gods for you.

9 [a]1 Kin 14:26-28 [b]1 Kin 10:16, 17; 2 Chr 9:15, 16

10 [1]Lit *hands* [2]Lit *runners*

11 [1]Lit *runners*

12 [a]2 Chr 12:6, 7 [b]2 Chr 19:3

13 [a]1 Kin 14:21

14 [a]2 Chr 19:3

15 [1]Lit *words* [a]1 Kin 14:29 [b]2 Chr 12:5 [c]2 Chr 9:29

16 [a]2 Chr 11:20

13:1 [a]1 Kin 15:1, 2

2 [a]1 Kin 15:7

4 [a]Josh 18:22

5 [1]Lit *to him and to his sons* [a]2 Sam 7:12-16 [b]Lev 2:13; Num 18:19

6 [1]Or *lord* [a]1 Kin 11:26

7 [1]Lit *Rehoboam* [a]2 Chr 12:13

8 [1]Lit *in the hands of* [2]Lit *and you are a* [a]1 Kin 12:28; 2 Chr 11:15

9 [a]2 Chr 11:14, 15 [b]Ex 29:29-33 [c]Jer 2:11; 5:7
10 [1]Lit *in the work*
11 [1]Lit *offer up in smoke* [a]Ex 29:38; 2 Chr 2:4 [b]Ex 25:30-39; Lev 24:5-9
12 [a]Num 10:8, 9
13 [a]Josh 8:4-9
14 [1]Lit *the battle was before and behind them* [a]2 Chr 14:11
15 [1]Lit *smote* [a]2 Chr 14:12
16 [a]2 Chr 16:8
18 [1]Lit *were strong* [a]2 Chr 14:11
19 [1]Another reading is *Ephrain*
20 [a]1 Sam 25:38 [b]1 Kin 14:20
22 [1]Heb *midrash* [a]2 Chr 24:27 [b]2 Chr 9:29
14:1 [1]Ch 13:23 in Heb [a]1 Kin 15:8
2 [1]Ch 14:1 in Heb
3 [1]I.e. wooden symbols of a female deity [a]Deut 7:5 [b]1 Kin 15:12-14 [c]Ex 34:13

9 "[a]Have you not driven out the priests of the LORD, the sons of Aaron and the Levites, and made for yourselves priests like the peoples of *other* lands? Whoever comes [b]to consecrate himself with a young bull and seven rams, even he may become a priest of *what are* [c]no gods.

10 "But as for us, the LORD is our God, and we have not forsaken Him; and the sons of Aaron are ministering to the LORD as priests, and the Levites [1]attend to their work.

11 "Every morning and evening [a]they [1]burn to the LORD burnt offerings and fragrant incense, and [b]the showbread is *set* on the clean table, and the golden lampstand with its lamps is *ready* to light every evening; for we keep the charge of the LORD our God, but you have forsaken Him.

12 "Now behold, God is with us at *our* head and [a]His priests with the signal trumpets to sound the alarm against you. O sons of Israel, do not fight against the LORD God of your fathers, for you will not succeed."

13 But Jeroboam [a]had set an ambush to come from the rear, so that *Israel* was in front of Judah and the ambush was behind them.

14 When Judah turned around, behold, [1]they were attacked both front and rear; so [a]they cried to the LORD, and the priests blew the trumpets.

15 Then the men of Judah raised a war cry, and when the men of Judah raised the war cry, then it was that God [1a]routed Jeroboam and all Israel before Abijah and Judah.

16 When the sons of Israel fled before Judah, [a]God gave them into their hand.

17 Abijah and his people defeated them with a great slaughter, so that 500,000 chosen men of Israel fell slain.

18 Thus the sons of Israel were subdued at that time, and the sons of Judah [1]conquered [a]because they trusted in the LORD, the God of their fathers.

19 Abijah pursued Jeroboam and captured from him *several* cities, Bethel with its villages, Jeshanah with its villages and [1]Ephron with its villages.

20 Jeroboam did not again recover strength in the days of Abijah; and the [a]LORD struck him and [b]he died.

21 But Abijah became powerful; and took fourteen wives to himself, and became the father of twenty-two sons and sixteen daughters.

22 Now the rest of the acts of Abijah, and his ways and his words are written in [a]the [1]treatise of [b]the prophet Iddo.

Chapter 14 Theme

14 [1a]So Abijah slept with his fathers, and they buried him in the city of David, and his son Asa became king in his place. The land was undisturbed for ten years during his days. 911 B.C.

2 [1]Asa did good and right in the sight of the LORD his God,

3 for he removed [a]the foreign altars and [b]high places, tore down the *sacred* pillars, cut down the [1c]Asherim,

4 and commanded Judah to seek the LORD God of their fathers
and to observe the law and the commandment.
5 He also removed the high places and the [a]incense altars from
all the cities of Judah. And the kingdom was undisturbed under
him.
6 [a]He built fortified cities in Judah, since the land was
undisturbed, and [1]there was no one at war with him during
those years, [b]because the LORD had given him rest.
7 For he said to Judah, "[a]Let us build these cities and
surround *them* with walls and towers, gates and bars. The land
is still [1]ours because we have sought the LORD our God; we
have sought Him, and He has given us rest on every side." So
they built and prospered.
8 Now Asa had an army of [a]300,000 from Judah, bearing
large shields and spears, and 280,000 from Benjamin, bearing
shields and wielding bows; all of them were valiant warriors.
9 Now Zerah the Ethiopian [a]came out against them with an
army of a million men and 300 chariots, and he came to
[b]Mareshah.
10 So Asa went out [1]to meet him, and they drew up in battle
formation in the valley of Zephathah at Mareshah.
11 Then Asa [a]called to the LORD his God and said, "LORD,
there is no one besides You to help *in the battle* between the
powerful and those who have no strength; so help us, O LORD
our God, [b]for we trust in You, and in Your name have come
against this multitude. O LORD, You are our God; let not man
prevail against You."
12 So [a]the LORD [1]routed the Ethiopians before Asa and before
Judah, and the Ethiopians fled.
13 Asa and the people who *were* with him pursued them as
far as [a]Gerar; and so many Ethiopians fell that [1]they could not
recover, for they were shattered before the LORD and before His
army. And they carried away very much plunder.
14 They [1]destroyed all the cities around Gerar, [a]for the dread
of the LORD had fallen on them; and they despoiled all the cities,
for there was much plunder in them.
15 They also struck down [1]those who owned livestock, and
they carried away large numbers of sheep and camels. Then
they returned to Jerusalem.

Chapter 15 Theme ____________________

15 Now [a]the Spirit of God came on Azariah the son of Oded,
2 and he went out [1]to meet Asa and said to him, "Listen
to me, Asa, and all Judah and Benjamin: [a]the LORD is with you
when you are with Him. And [b]if you seek Him, He will let you
find Him; but if you forsake Him, He will forsake you.
3 "[a]For many days Israel was without the true God and
without [b]a teaching priest and without law.
4 "But [a]in their distress they turned to the LORD God of Israel,
and they sought Him, and He let them find Him.

5 [a]2 Chr 34:4, 7

6 [1]Lit *there was not with him war* [a]2 Chr 11:5 [b]2 Chr 15:15

7 [1]Lit *before us* [a]2 Chr 8:5

8 [a]2 Chr 13:3

9 [a]2 Chr 12:2, 3; 16:8 [b]2 Chr 11:8

10 [1]Lit *before him*

11 [a]2 Chr 13:14 [b]2 Chr 13:18

12 [1]Lit *struck* [a]2 Chr 13:15

13 [1]Or *there was none left alive* [a]Gen 10:19

14 [1]Lit *smote* [a]2 Chr 17:10

15 [1]Lit *tents of livestock*

15:1 [a]2 Chr 20:14; 24:20

2 [1]Lit *before Asa* [a]2 Chr 20:17 [b]2 Chr 15:4, 15

3 [a]1 Kin 12:28-33 [b]Lev 10:8-11; 2 Chr 17:9

4 [a]Deut 4:29

5 “[a]In those times there was no peace to him who went out or
to him who came in, for many disturbances [1]afflicted all the
inhabitants of the lands.
6 “[a]Nation was crushed by nation, and city by city, for God
troubled them with every kind of distress.
7 “But you, [a]be strong and do not [1]lose courage, for there is
[b]reward for your work.”
8 Now when Asa heard these words and the [1]prophecy which
Azariah the son of Oded the prophet spoke, he took courage
and removed the abominable idols from all the land of Judah
and Benjamin and from [a]the cities which he had captured in
the hill country of Ephraim. [b]He then restored the altar of the
LORD which was in front of the porch of the LORD.
9 He gathered all Judah and Benjamin and those from
Ephraim, Manasseh and Simeon [a]who resided with them, for
many defected to him from Israel when they saw that the LORD
his God was with him.
10 So they assembled at Jerusalem in the third month of the
fifteenth year of Asa’s reign.
11 [a]They sacrificed to the LORD that day 700 oxen and 7,000
sheep from the spoil they had brought.
12 [a]They entered into the covenant to seek the LORD God of
their fathers with all their heart and soul;
13 and whoever would not seek the LORD God of Israel [a]should
be put to death, whether small or great, man or woman.
14 Moreover, they made an oath to the LORD with a loud
voice, with shouting, with trumpets and with horns.
15 All Judah rejoiced concerning the oath, for they had sworn
with their whole heart and had sought Him [1]earnestly, and He
let them find Him. So [a]the LORD gave them rest on every side.
16 [a]He also removed Maacah, the mother of King Asa, from
the *position of* queen mother, because she had made a horrid
image [1]as [b]an Asherah, and [c]Asa cut down her horrid image,
crushed *it* and burned *it* at the brook Kidron.
17 But the high places were not removed from Israel;
nevertheless Asa’s heart was blameless all his days.
18 He brought into the house of God the dedicated things of
his father and his own dedicated things: silver and gold and
utensils.
19 And there was no more war until the thirty-fifth year of
Asa’s reign.

Chapter 16 Theme ____________________

16 In the thirty-sixth year of Asa’s reign [a]Baasha king of
Israel came up against Judah and [1]fortified Ramah in
order to prevent *anyone* from going out or coming in to Asa
king of Judah.
2 Then Asa brought out silver and gold from the treasuries of
the house of the LORD and the king’s house, and sent them to
Ben-hadad king of Aram, who lived in Damascus, saying,

896 B.C.

5 [1]Lit *were on* [a]Judg 5:6
6 [a]Matt 24:7
7 [1]Lit *let your hands drop* [a]Josh 1:7, 9 [b]Ps 58:11
8 [1]With several ancient versions; Heb *the prophecy, Oded the prophet* [a]2 Chr 13:19 [b]2 Chr 4:1; 8:12
9 [a]2 Chr 11:16
11 [a]2 Chr 14:13-15
12 [a]2 Chr 23:16
13 [a]Ex 22:20; Deut 13:6-9
15 [1]Lit *with their whole desire* [a]2 Chr 14:7
16 [1]Or for *Asherah* [a]1 Kin 15:13-15 [b]Ex 34:13 [c]2 Chr 14:2-5
16:1 [1]Lit *built* [a]1 Kin 15:17-22

3 "*Let there be* a treaty between [1]you and me, *as* between my
father and your father. Behold, I have sent you silver and gold;
go, break your treaty with Baasha king of Israel so that he will
withdraw from me."
4 So Ben-hadad listened to King Asa and sent the commanders
of his armies against the cities of Israel, and they [1]conquered
Ijon, Dan, Abel-maim and all [a]the [2]store cities of Naphtali.
5 When Baasha heard *of it,* he ceased [1]fortifying Ramah and
stopped his work.
6 Then King Asa brought all Judah, and they carried away
the stones of Ramah and its timber with which Baasha had
been building, and with them he [1]fortified Geba and Mizpah.
7 At that time [a]Hanani the seer came to Asa king of Judah
and said to him, "[b]Because you have relied on the king of Aram
and have not relied on the LORD your God, therefore the army
of the king of Aram has escaped out of your hand.
8 "Were not [a]the Ethiopians and the Lubim [b]an immense
army with very many chariots and horsemen? Yet [c]because you
relied on the LORD, He delivered them into your hand.
9 "For [a]the eyes of the LORD move to and fro throughout the
earth that He may strongly support those [b]whose heart is
completely His. You have acted foolishly in this. Indeed, from
now on you will surely have wars."
10 Then Asa was angry with the seer and put him in [1]prison,
for he was enraged at him for this. And Asa oppressed some of
the people at the same time.
11 [a]Now, the acts of Asa from first to last, behold, they are
written in the Book of the Kings of Judah and Israel.
12 In the thirty-ninth year of his reign Asa became diseased in
his feet. His disease was severe, yet even in his disease he [a]did
not seek the LORD, but the physicians.
13 So Asa slept with his fathers, [1]having died in the forty-first
year of his reign.
14 They buried him in his own tomb which he had cut out for
himself in the city of David, and they laid him in the resting
place which he had filled [a]with spices of various kinds blended
by the perfumers' art; and [b]they made a very great fire for him.

Chapter 17 Theme ____________________

873 B.C.

17 [a]Jehoshaphat his son then became king in his place, and
made his position over Israel firm.
2 He placed troops in all [a]the fortified cities of Judah, and set
garrisons in the land of Judah and in the cities of Ephraim
[b]which Asa his father had captured.
3 The LORD was with Jehoshaphat because he [1]followed the
example of his father David's earlier days and did not seek the
Baals,
4 but sought the God of his father, [1]followed His commandments,
[a]and did not act as Israel did.
5 So the LORD established the kingdom in his [1]control, and all

3 [1]Lit *me and you*

4 [1]Lit *smote* [2]Lit *storage places of the cities* [a]Ex 1:11

5 [1]Lit *building*

6 [1]Lit *built*

7 [a]1 Kin 16:1; 2 Chr 19:2 [b]2 Chr 14:11; 32:7, 8

8 [a]2 Chr 14:9 [b]2 Chr 12:3 [c]2 Chr 13:16, 18

9 [a]Prov 15:3; Jer 16:17; Zech 4:10 [b]2 Chr 15:17

10 [1]Lit *the house of the stocks*

11 [a]1 Kin 15:23, 24

12 [a]Jer 17:5

13 [1]Lit *and*

14 [a]Gen 50:2; John 19:39, 40 [b]2 Chr 21:19

17:1 [a]1 Kin 15:24

2 [a]2 Chr 11:5 [b]2 Chr 15:8

3 [1]Lit *walked in the earlier ways of his father*

4 [1]Lit *walked in* [a]1 Kin 12:28

5 [1]Lit *hand*

5 [a]2 Chr 18:1
Judah brought tribute to Jehoshaphat, and [a]he had great riches
and honor.
6 [1]He took great pride in the ways of the LORD and again
[a]removed the high places and the Asherim from Judah.
6 [1]Lit *his heart was high* [a]2 Chr 15:17
7 Then in the third year of his reign he sent his officials, Ben-
hail, Obadiah, Zechariah, Nethanel and Micaiah, [a]to teach in
the cities of Judah;
8 and with them [a]the Levites, Shemaiah, Nethaniah, Zebadiah,
Asahel, Shemiramoth, Jehonathan, Adonijah, Tobijah and
7 [a]2 Chr 15:3; 35:3
Tobadonijah, the Levites; and with them Elishama and
Jehoram, the priests.
9 They taught in Judah, *having* [a]the book of the law of the
LORD with them; and they went throughout all the cities of
Judah and taught among the people.
8 [a]2 Chr 19:8
10 Now [a]the dread of the LORD was on all the kingdoms of the
lands which *were* around Judah, so that they did not make war
against Jehoshaphat.
11 Some of the Philistines [a]brought gifts and silver as tribute to
9 [a]Deut 6:4-9
Jehoshaphat; the Arabians also brought him flocks, 7,700 rams
and 7,700 male goats.
12 So Jehoshaphat grew greater and greater, and he built
fortresses and store cities in Judah.
13 He had large supplies in the cities of Judah, and warriors,
10 [a]2 Chr 14:14
valiant men, in Jerusalem.
14 This was their muster according to their fathers' households:
of Judah, commanders of thousands, Adnah *was* the commander,
and with him 300,000 valiant warriors;
15 and next to him *was* Johanan the commander, and with
11 [a]2 Chr 9:14; 26:8
him 280,000;
16 and next to him Amasiah the son of Zichri, [a]who volunteered
for the LORD, and with him 200,000 valiant warriors;
17 and of Benjamin, Eliada a valiant warrior, and with him
16 [a]Judg 5:2, 9; 1 Chr 29:9
200,000 armed with bow and shield;
18 and next to him Jehozabad, and with him 180,000
equipped for war.
19 These are they who served the king, apart from [a]those
whom the king put in the fortified cities through all Judah.
19 [a]2 Chr 17:2

Chapter 18 Theme ______________________

18 Now [a]Jehoshaphat had great riches and honor; and he
allied himself by marriage with Ahab.
1 Kings 22
18:1 [a]2 Chr 17:5
2 [a]Some years later he went down to *visit* Ahab at Samaria.
And Ahab slaughtered many sheep and oxen for him and the
people who were with him, and induced him to go up against
Ramoth-gilead.
3 Ahab king of Israel said to Jehoshaphat king of Judah, "Will
2 [a]1 Kin 22:2-35
you go with me *against* Ramoth-gilead?" And he said to him, "I
am as you are, and my people as your people, and *we will be*
with you in the battle."
4 Moreover, Jehoshaphat said to the king of Israel, "Please
4 [1]Lit *as the day*
inquire [1]first for the word of the LORD."

5 Then the king of Israel assembled the prophets, four
hundred men, and said to them, "Shall we go against Ramoth-
gilead to battle, or shall I refrain?" And they said, "Go up, for
God will give *it* into the hand of the king."
6 But Jehoshaphat said, "Is there not yet a prophet of the
LORD here that we may inquire of him?"
7 The king of Israel said to Jehoshaphat, "There is yet one
man by whom we may inquire of the LORD, but I hate him, for
he never prophesies good concerning me but always evil. He is
Micaiah, son of Imla." But Jehoshaphat said, "Let not the king
say so."
8 Then the king of Israel called an officer and said, "[1]Bring
quickly Micaiah, Imla's son."
9 Now the king of Israel and Jehoshaphat the king of Judah
were sitting each on his throne, arrayed in *their* robes, and *they*
were sitting [a]at the threshing floor at the entrance of the gate
of Samaria; and all the prophets were prophesying before them.
10 Zedekiah the son of Chenaanah made horns of iron for
himself and said, "Thus says the LORD, 'With these you shall
gore the Arameans until they are consumed.'"
11 All the prophets were prophesying thus, saying, "Go up to
Ramoth-gilead and succeed, for the LORD will give *it* into the
hand of the king."
12 Then the messenger who went to summon Micaiah spoke to
him saying, "Behold, the words of the prophets are uniformly
favorable to the king. So please let your word be like one of
them and speak favorably."
13 But Micaiah said, "As the LORD lives, [a]what my God says,
that I will speak."
14 When he came to the king, the king said to him, "Micaiah,
shall we go to Ramoth-gilead to battle, or shall I refrain?" He
said, "Go up and succeed, for they will be given into your
hand."
15 Then the king said to him, "How many times must I adjure
you to speak to me nothing but the truth in the name of the
LORD?"
16 So he said,
"I saw all Israel
Scattered on the mountains,
[a]Like sheep which have no shepherd;
And the LORD said,
'These have no master.
Let each of them return to his house in peace.'"
17 Then the king of Israel said to Jehoshaphat, "Did I not tell
you that he would not prophesy good concerning me, but evil?"
18 Micaiah said, "Therefore, hear the word of the LORD. [a]I saw
the LORD sitting on His throne, and all the host of heaven
standing on His right and on His left.
19 "The LORD said, 'Who will entice Ahab king of Israel to go
up and fall at Ramoth-gilead?' And one said this while another
said that.

8 [1]Lit *Hasten*
9 [a]Ruth 4:1
13 [a]Num 22:18-20, 35
16 [a]Num 27:17; 1 Kin 22:17; Ezek 34:5; 35:4-8; Matt 9:36; Mark 6:34
18 [a]Is 6:1-5; Dan 7:9, 10

20 "Then a [a]spirit came forward and stood before the LORD and said, 'I will entice him.' And the LORD said to him, 'How?'

21 "He said, 'I will go and be [a]a deceiving spirit in the mouth of all his prophets.' Then He said, 'You are to entice *him* and prevail also. Go and do so.'

22 "Now therefore, behold, [a]the LORD has put a deceiving spirit in the mouth of these your prophets, for the LORD has proclaimed disaster against you."

23 Then Zedekiah the son of Chenaanah came near and [a]struck Micaiah on the cheek and said, "[1]How did the Spirit of the LORD pass from me to speak to you?"

24 Micaiah said, "Behold, you will see on that day when you enter an inner room to hide yourself."

25 Then the king of Israel said, "[a]Take Micaiah and return him to Amon [b]the governor of the city and to Joash the king's son;

26 and say, 'Thus says the king, "[a]Put this *man* in prison and feed him [1]sparingly with bread and water until I return safely."'"

27 Micaiah said, "If you indeed return safely, the LORD has not spoken by me." And he said, "[a]Listen, all you people."

28 So the king of Israel and Jehoshaphat king of Judah went up against Ramoth-gilead.

29 The king of Israel said to Jehoshaphat, "I will disguise myself and go into battle, but you put on your robes." So the king of Israel disguised himself, and they went into battle.

30 Now the king of Aram had commanded the captains of his chariots, saying, "Do not fight with small or great, but with the king of Israel alone."

31 So when the captains of the chariots saw Jehoshaphat, they said, "It is the king of Israel," and they turned aside to fight against him. But Jehoshaphat [a]cried out, and the LORD helped him, and God diverted them from him.

32 When the captains of the chariots saw that it was not the king of Israel, they turned back from pursuing him.

33 A certain man drew his bow at random and struck the king of Israel [1]in a joint of the armor. So he said to the driver of the chariot, "Turn [2]around and take me out of the [3]fight, for I am severely wounded."

34 The battle raged that day, and the king of Israel propped himself up in his chariot in front of the Arameans until the evening; and at sunset he died.

Chapter 19 Theme ____________________

19 Then Jehoshaphat the king of Judah returned in safety to his house in Jerusalem.

2 [a]Jehu the son of Hanani the seer went out to meet him and said to King Jehoshaphat, "[b]Should you help the wicked and love those who hate the LORD and [1c]so *bring* wrath on yourself from the LORD?

3 "But [1a]there is *some* good in you, for [b]you have removed the [2]Asheroth from the land and you [c]have set your heart to seek God."

20 [a]Job 1:6; 2 Thess 2:9
21 [a]John 8:44
22 [a]Is 19:14; Ezek 14:9
23 [1]Lit *Which way* [a]Jer 20:2; Mark 14:65; Acts 23:2
25 [a]2 Chr 18:8 [b]2 Chr 34:8
26 [1]Lit *with bread of affliction and water of affliction* [a]2 Chr 16:10
27 [a]Mic 1:2
31 [a]2 Chr 13:14, 15
33 [1]Lit *between the scale-armor and the breastplate* [2]Lit *your hand* [3]Lit *camp*
19:2 [1]Lit *by this* [a]1 Kin 16:1; 2 Chr 20:34 [b]2 Chr 18:1, 3 [c]2 Chr 24:18
3 [1]Lit *good things are found* [2]I.e. wooden pillars [a]2 Chr 12:12 [b]2 Chr 17:6 [c]2 Chr 12:14

4 So Jehoshaphat lived in Jerusalem and went out again among the people from Beersheba to the hill country of Ephraim and [a]brought them back to the LORD, the God of their fathers.

5 He appointed [a]judges in the land in all the fortified cities of Judah, city by city.

6 He said to the judges, "Consider what you are doing, for [a]you do not judge for man but for the LORD who is with you [1]when you render judgment.

7 "Now then let the fear of the LORD be upon you; [1]be very careful what you do, for [2]the LORD our God will [a]have no part in unrighteousness [b]or partiality or the taking of a bribe."

8 In Jerusalem also Jehoshaphat appointed some [a]of the Levites and priests, and some of the heads of the fathers' *households* of Israel, for the judgment of the LORD and to judge [1]disputes among the inhabitants of Jerusalem.

9 Then he charged them saying, "Thus you shall do in the fear of the LORD, faithfully and wholeheartedly.

10 "[a]Whenever any dispute comes to you from your brethren who live in their cities, between blood and blood, between law and commandment, statutes and ordinances, you shall warn them so that they may not be guilty before the LORD, and [b]wrath may *not* come on you and your brethren. Thus you shall do and you will not be guilty.

11 "Behold, Amariah the chief priest will be over you in [1a]all that pertains to the LORD, and Zebadiah the son of Ishmael, the ruler of the house of Judah, in [1]all that pertains to the king. Also the Levites shall be officers before you. [2b]Act resolutely, and the LORD be with the upright."

Chapter 20 Theme ____________________________

20 Now it came about after this that the sons of Moab and the sons of Ammon, together with some of the [1a]Meunites, came to make war against Jehoshaphat.

2 Then some came and reported to Jehoshaphat, saying, "A great multitude is coming against you from beyond the sea, out of [1]Aram and behold, they are in [a]Hazazon-tamar (that is Engedi)."

3 Jehoshaphat was afraid and [1a]turned his attention to seek the LORD, and [b]proclaimed a fast throughout all Judah.

4 So Judah gathered together to [a]seek help from the LORD; they even came from all the cities of Judah to seek the LORD.

5 Then Jehoshaphat stood in the assembly of Judah and Jerusalem, in the house of the LORD before the new court,

6 and he said, "O LORD, the God of our fathers, [a]are You not God in the heavens? And [b]are You not ruler over all the kingdoms of the nations? Power and might are in Your hand so that no one can stand against You.

7 "Did You not, O our God, drive out the inhabitants of this land before Your people Israel and [a]give it to the descendants of [b]Abraham Your friend forever?

4 [a]2 Chr 15:8-13

5 [a]Deut 16:18-20

6 [1]Lit *in the word of judgment* [a]Lev 19:15; Deut 1:17

7 [1]Lit *be careful and do* [2]Lit *there is not with the LORD our God* [a]Gen 18:25; Deut 32:4 [b]Deut 10:17, 18

8 [1]So the versions; Heb reads *disputes. And they returned to Jerusalem,* or *And they lived in Jerusalem* [a]2 Chr 17:8, 9

10 [a]Deut 17:8 [b]2 Chr 19:2

11 [1]Lit *every matter of* [2]Lit *Be strong and do* [a]2 Chr 19:8 [b]1 Chr 28:20

20:1 [1]So with Gr; Heb *Ammonites* [a]1 Chr 4:41; 2 Chr 26:7

2 [1]Another reading is *Edom* [a]Gen 14:7

3 [1]Lit *set his face* [a]2 Chr 19:3 [b]1 Sam 7:6; Ezra 8:21

4 [a]Joel 1:14

6 [a]Deut 4:39 [b]1 Chr 29:11

7 [a]Is 41:8 [b]James 2:23

9 [a]2 Chr 6:28-30 [b]2 Chr 6:20

8 "They have lived in it, and have built You a sanctuary there
for Your name, saying,
9 '[a]Should evil come upon us, the sword, *or* judgment, or
pestilence, or famine, we will stand before this house and before
You (for [b]Your name is in this house) and cry to You in our
distress, and You will hear and deliver *us.*'

10 [1]I.e. Edom [a]2 Chr 20:1, 22 [b]Num 20:17-21

10 "Now behold, [a]the sons of Ammon and Moab and [1]Mount
Seir, [b]whom You did not let Israel invade when they came out
of the land of Egypt (they turned aside from them and did not
destroy them),

11 [a]Ps 83:12

11 see *how* they are rewarding us by [a]coming to drive us out
from Your possession which You have given us as an inheritance.
12 "O our God, [a]will You not judge them? For we are powerless
before this great multitude who are coming against us; nor do
we know what to do, but [b]our eyes are on You."

12 [a]Judg 11:27 [b]Ps 25:15; 121:1, 2

13 All Judah was standing before the LORD, with their infants,
their wives and their children.
14 Then in the midst of the assembly [a]the Spirit of the LORD
came upon Jahaziel the son of Zechariah, the son of Benaiah, the
son of Jeiel, the son of Mattaniah, the Levite of the sons of Asaph;

14 [a]2 Chr 15:1; 24:20

15 and he said, "Listen, all Judah and the inhabitants of
Jerusalem and King Jehoshaphat: thus says the LORD to you,
'[a]Do not fear or be dismayed because of this great multitude,
for [b]the battle is not yours but God's.

15 [a]Ex 14:13; Deut 20:1-4; 2 Chr 32:7, 8 [b]1 Sam 17:47

16 'Tomorrow go down against them. Behold, they will come
up by the ascent of Ziz, and you will find them at the end of
the valley in front of the wilderness of Jeruel.
17 'You *need* not fight in this *battle;* station yourselves, [a]stand
and see the salvation of the LORD on your behalf, O Judah and
Jerusalem.' Do not fear or be dismayed; tomorrow go out to
face them, [b]for the LORD is with you."

17 [a]Ex 14:13 [b]2 Chr 15:2

18 Jehoshaphat [a]bowed his head with *his* face to the ground,
and all Judah and the inhabitants of Jerusalem fell down before
the LORD, worshiping the LORD.
19 The Levites, from the sons of the Kohathites and of the
sons of the Korahites, stood up to praise the LORD God of Israel,
with a very loud voice.

18 [a]Ex 4:31

20 They rose early in the morning and went out to the
wilderness of Tekoa; and when they went out, Jehoshaphat
stood and said, "Listen to me, O Judah and inhabitants of
Jerusalem, [a]put your trust in the LORD your God and you will be
established. Put your trust in His prophets and succeed."

20 [a]Is 7:9

21 When he had consulted with the people, he appointed
those who sang to the LORD and those who [a]praised *Him* in
holy attire, as they went out before the army and said, "[b]Give
thanks to the LORD, for His lovingkindness is everlasting."

21 [a]1 Chr 16:29; Ps 29:2 [b]1 Chr 16:34

22 When they began singing and praising, the LORD [a]set
ambushes against the sons of [b]Ammon, Moab and Mount Seir,
who had come against Judah; so they were [1]routed.

22 [1]Lit *struck down* [a]2 Chr 13:13 [b]2 Chr 20:10

23 For the sons of Ammon and Moab rose up against the
inhabitants of Mount Seir destroying *them* completely; and when

they had finished with the inhabitants of Seir, [a]they helped to
destroy one another.
24 When Judah came to the lookout of the wilderness, they
looked toward the multitude, and behold, they *were* corpses
lying on the ground, and no one had escaped.
25 When Jehoshaphat and his people came to take their spoil,
they found much among them, *including* goods, [1]garments and
valuable things which they took for themselves, more than they
could carry. And they were three days taking the spoil because
there was so much.
26 Then on the fourth day they assembled in the valley of
Beracah, for there they blessed the LORD. Therefore they have
named that place "The Valley of [1]Beracah" until today.
27 Every man of Judah and Jerusalem returned with Jehoshaphat at their head, returning to Jerusalem with joy, [a]for the
LORD had made them to rejoice over their enemies.
28 They came to Jerusalem with harps, lyres and trumpets to
the house of the LORD.
29 And [a]the dread of God was on all the kingdoms of the lands
when they heard that the LORD had fought against the enemies
of Israel.
30 So the kingdom of Jehoshaphat was at peace, [a]for his God
gave him rest on all sides.
31 [a]Now Jehoshaphat reigned over Judah. He *was* thirty-five
years old when he became king, and he reigned in Jerusalem
twenty-five years. And his mother's name *was* Azubah the
daughter of Shilhi.
32 He walked in the way of his father Asa and did not depart
from it, doing right in the sight of the LORD.
33 [a]The high places, however, were not removed; [b]the people
had not yet directed their hearts to the God of their fathers.
34 Now the rest of the acts of Jehoshaphat, first [1]to last,
behold, they are written in the annals of [a]Jehu the son of
Hanani, which is [2]recorded in the Book of the Kings of Israel.
35 [a]After this Jehoshaphat king of Judah allied himself with
Ahaziah king of Israel. He acted wickedly [1]in so doing.
36 So he allied himself with him to make ships to go [a]to
Tarshish, and they made the ships in Ezion-geber.
37 Then Eliezer the son of Dodavahu of Mareshah prophesied
against Jehoshaphat saying, "Because you have allied yourself
with Ahaziah, the LORD has destroyed your works." So the
ships were broken and could not go to Tarshish.

Chapter 21 Theme ____________________

848 B.C.

2 Kings 8

21 [a]Then Jehoshaphat slept with his fathers and was buried
with his fathers in the city of David, and Jehoram his son
became king in his place.
2 He had brothers, the sons of Jehoshaphat: Azariah, Jehiel,
Zechariah, [1]Azaryahu, Michael and Shephatiah. All these *were*
the sons of Jehoshaphat king [a]of Israel.

23 [a]Judg 7:22; 1 Sam 14:20
25 [1]So several ancient mss; others read *corpses*
26 [1]I.e. blessing
27 [a]Neh 12:43
29 [a]2 Chr 14:14; 17:10
30 [a]2 Chr 14:6, 7; 15:15
31 [a]1 Kin 22:41-43
33 [a]2 Chr 17:6 [b]2 Chr 19:3
34 [1]Lit *and* [2]Lit *taken up* [a]2 Chr 19:2
35 [1]Lit *to do* [a]1 Kin 22:48, 49
36 [a]2 Chr 9:21
21:1 [a]1 Kin 22:50
2 [1]Or *Azariah* [a]2 Chr 12:6; 23:2

3 Their father gave them many gifts of silver, gold and precious
things, [a]with fortified cities in Judah, but he gave the kingdom
to Jehoram because he was the firstborn.
4 Now when Jehoram had [1]taken over the kingdom of his
father and made himself [2]secure, he [a]killed all his brothers with
the sword, and some of the rulers of Israel also.
5 [a]Jehoram *was* thirty-two years old when he became king,
and he reigned eight years in Jerusalem.
6 [a]He walked in the way of the kings of Israel, just as the house
of Ahab did ([b]for Ahab's daughter was his wife), and he did evil
in the sight of the LORD.
7 Yet the LORD was not willing to destroy the house of David
because of the covenant which He had made with David, [a]and
since He had promised to give a lamp to him and his sons forever.
8 In his days [a]Edom revolted [1]against the rule of Judah and
set up a king over themselves.
9 Then Jehoram crossed over with his commanders and all
his chariots with him. And he arose by night and struck down
the Edomites who were surrounding him and the commanders
of the chariots.
10 So Edom revolted [1]against Judah to this day. Then Libnah
revolted at the same time [2]against his rule, because he had
forsaken the LORD God of his fathers.
11 Moreover, [a]he made high places in the mountains of Judah,
and caused the inhabitants of Jerusalem [b]to play the harlot and
led Judah astray.
12 Then a letter came to him from Elijah the prophet saying,
"Thus says the LORD God of your father David, 'Because [a]you
have not walked in the ways of Jehoshaphat your father [b]and
the ways of Asa king of Judah,
13 but [a]have walked in the way of the kings of Israel, and have
caused Judah and the inhabitants of Jerusalem to play the harlot
[b]as the house of Ahab played the harlot, and you [c]have also killed
your brothers, [1]your own family, who were better than you,
14 behold, the LORD is going to strike your people, your sons,
your wives and all your possessions with a great [1]calamity;
15 and [a]you will suffer [1]severe sickness, a disease of your
bowels, until your bowels come out because of the sickness,
day by day.'"
16 Then [a]the LORD stirred up against Jehoram the spirit of the
Philistines and [b]the Arabs who [1]bordered the Ethiopians;
17 and they came against Judah and invaded it, and carried
away all the possessions found in the king's house together
with his sons and his wives, so that no son was left to him
except [1a]Jehoahaz, the youngest of his sons.
18 So after all this the LORD smote him [a]in his bowels with an
incurable sickness.
19 Now it came about in the course of time, at the end of two
years, that his bowels came out because of his sickness and he
died in great pain. And his people made no fire for him like
[a]the fire for his fathers.

3 [a]2 Chr 11:5
4 [1]Lit *risen up* [2]Lit *strong* [a]Gen 4:8; Judg 9:5
5 [a]2 Kin 8:17-22
6 [a]1 Kin 12:28-30 [b]2 Chr 18:1
7 [a]2 Sam 7:12-17; 1 Kin 11:13, 36
8 [1]Lit *from under the hand of* [a]2 Chr 20:22, 23; 21:10
10 [1]Lit *from under the hand of* [2]Lit *from under his hand*
11 [a]1 Kin 11:7 [b]Lev 20:5
12 [a]2 Chr 17:3, 4 [b]2 Chr 14:2-5
13 [1]Lit *your father's house* [a]2 Chr 21:6 [b]1 Kin 16:31-33 [c]2 Chr 21:4
14 [1]Lit *blow*
15 [1]Lit *in many sicknesses* [a]2 Chr 21:18, 19
16 [1]Lit *were at the hand of* [a]2 Chr 33:11 [b]2 Chr 17:11; 22:1
17 [1]In 2 Chr 22:1, *Ahaziah* [a]2 Chr 25:23
18 [a]2 Chr 21:15
19 [a]2 Chr 16:14

20 He was thirty-two years old when he became king, and he reigned in Jerusalem eight years; and he departed [1a]with no one's regret, and they buried him in the city of David, [b]but not in the tombs of the kings.

Chapter 22 Theme ______________________

841 B.C.

2 Kings 8

22 [a]Then the inhabitants of Jerusalem made [1]Ahaziah, his youngest son, king in his place, for the band of men who came with [b]the Arabs to the camp had slain all the older *sons.* So Ahaziah the son of Jehoram king of Judah began to reign.

2 Ahaziah *was* [1]twenty-two years old when he became king, and he reigned one year in Jerusalem. And his mother's name was Athaliah, the [2]granddaughter of Omri.

3 He also walked in the ways of the house of Ahab, for his mother was his counselor to do wickedly.

4 He did evil in the sight of the LORD like the house of Ahab, for they were his counselors after the death of his father, to [a]his destruction.

5 He also walked according to their counsel, and went with Jehoram the son of Ahab king of Israel to wage war against Hazael king of Aram at Ramoth-gilead. But the [1a]Arameans [2]wounded [3]Joram.

6 So he returned to be healed in Jezreel of the wounds [1]which they had inflicted on him at Ramah, when he fought against Hazael king of Aram. And [2]Ahaziah, the son of Jehoram king of Judah, went down to see Jehoram the son of Ahab in Jezreel, because he was sick.

7 Now [a]the destruction of Ahaziah was from God, in that [1]he went to Joram. For when he came, [b]he went out with Jehoram against Jehu the son of Nimshi, [c]whom the LORD had anointed to cut off the house of Ahab.

8 [a]It came about when Jehu was executing judgment on the house of Ahab, he found the princes of Judah and the sons of Ahaziah's brothers ministering to Ahaziah, and slew them.

9 [a]He also sought Ahaziah, and they caught him while he was hiding in Samaria; they brought him to Jehu, put him to death [b]and buried him. For they said, "He is the son of Jehoshaphat, [c]who sought the LORD with all his heart." So there was no one of the house of Ahaziah to retain the power of the kingdom.

2 Kings 11

10 [a]Now when Athaliah the mother of Ahaziah saw that her son was dead, she rose and destroyed all the royal [1]offspring of the house of Judah.

11 But Jehoshabeath the king's daughter took Joash the son of Ahaziah, and stole him from among the king's sons who were being put to death, and placed him and his nurse in the bedroom. So Jehoshabeath, the daughter of King Jehoram, the wife of Jehoiada the priest (for she was the sister of Ahaziah), hid him from Athaliah so that she would not put him to death.

12 He was hidden with them in the house of God six years while Athaliah reigned over the land.

20 [1]Lit *without desire* [a]Jer 22:18, 28 [b]2 Chr 24:25; 28:27

22:1 [1]In 2 Chr 21:17, *Jehoahaz* [a]2 Kin 8:24-29 [b]2 Chr 21:16

2 [1]So some versions and 2 Kin 8:26; Heb *42 years* [2]Lit *daughter*

4 [a]Prov 13:20

5 [1]Heb *archers* [2]Lit *smote* [3]I.e. Jehoram [a]2 Kin 8:28

6 [1]Lit *with which . . . smitten* [2]So with 2 Kin 8:29; Heb *Azariah*

7 [1]Lit *to go* [a]2 Chr 10:15 [b]2 Kin 9:21 [c]2 Kin 9:6, 7

8 [a]2 Kin 10:11-14

9 [a]2 Kin 9:27 [b]2 Kin 9:28 [c]2 Chr 17:4

10 [1]Lit *seed* [a]2 Kin 11:1-3

Chapter 23 Theme ________________________

23 [a]Now in the seventh year Jehoiada strengthened himself, and took captains of hundreds: Azariah the son of
Jeroham, Ishmael the son of Johanan, Azariah the son of Obed,
Maaseiah the son of Adaiah, and Elishaphat the son of Zichri,
and they entered into a covenant with him.
2 They went throughout Judah and gathered the Levites from
all the cities of Judah, and the heads of the fathers' *households*
of [a]Israel, and they came to Jerusalem.
3 Then all the assembly made a covenant with the king in the
house of God. And [1]Jehoiada said to them, "Behold, the king's
son shall reign, [a]as the LORD has spoken concerning the sons of
David.
4 "This is the thing which you shall do: one third of you, of
the priests and Levites [a]who come in on the sabbath, *shall be*
gatekeepers,
5 and one third *shall be* at the king's house, and a third at
the Gate of the Foundation; and all the people *shall be* in the
courts of the house of the LORD.
6 "But let no one enter the house of the LORD except the
priests and [a]the ministering Levites; they may enter, for they
are holy. And let all the people keep the charge of the LORD.
7 "The Levites will surround the king, each man with his
weapons in his hand; and whoever enters the house, let him
be killed. Thus be with the king when he comes in and when
he goes out."
8 So the Levites and all Judah did according to all that
Jehoiada the priest commanded. And each one of them took his
men who were to come in on the sabbath, with those who
were to go out on the sabbath, for Jehoiada the priest did not
dismiss *any of* [a]the divisions.
9 Then Jehoiada the priest gave to the captains of hundreds
the spears and the large and small shields which had been King
David's, which were in the house of God.
10 He stationed all the people, each man with his weapon in
his hand, from the right [1]side of the house to the left [1]side of
the house, by the altar and by the house, around the king.
11 Then they brought out the king's son and put the crown on
him, and *gave him* [a]the testimony and made him king. And
Jehoiada and his sons anointed him and said, "[b]*Long* live the
king!"
12 When Athaliah heard the noise of the people running and
praising the king, she came into the house of the LORD to the
people.
13 She looked, and behold, the king was standing by his pillar
at the entrance, and the captains and the [1]trumpeters *were*
beside the king. And all the people of the land rejoiced and
blew trumpets, the singers with *their* musical instruments
[2]leading the praise. Then Athaliah tore her clothes and said,
"Treason! Treason!"
14 Jehoiada the priest brought out the captains of hundreds

23:1 [a]2 Kin 11:4-20
2 [a]2 Chr 11:13-17; 21:2
3 [1]Lit *he* [a]2 Sam 7:12; 2 Chr 21:7
4 [a]1 Chr 9:25
6 [a]1 Chr 23:28-32
8 [a]1 Chr 24:1
10 [1]Lit *shoulder*
11 [a]Ex 25:16, 21 [b]1 Sam 10:24
13 [1]Lit *trumpets* [2]Lit *and leading for praising*

who were appointed over the army and said to them, "Bring
her out [1]between the ranks; and whoever follows her, put to
death with the sword." For the priest said, "Let her not be put
to death in the house of the LORD."
15 So they [1]seized her, and when she arrived at the entrance
of [a]the Horse Gate of the king's house, they [b]put her to death
there.
16 Then [a]Jehoiada made a covenant between himself and all
the people and the king, that they would be the LORD's people.
17 And all the people went to the house of Baal and tore it
down, and they broke in pieces his altars and his images, and
[a]killed Mattan the priest of Baal before the altars.
18 Moreover, Jehoiada placed the offices of the house of the
LORD under the [1]authority of [a]the Levitical priests, [b]whom
David had assigned over the house of the LORD, to offer the
burnt offerings of the LORD, as it is written in the law of
Moses—[c]with rejoicing and singing according to the [2]order of
David.
19 He stationed [a]the gatekeepers of the house of the LORD, so
that no one would enter *who was* in any way unclean.
20 [a]He took the captains of hundreds, the nobles, the rulers of
the people and all the people of the land, and brought the king
down from the house of the LORD, and came through the upper
gate to the king's house. And they placed the king upon the
royal throne.
21 So [a]all of the people of the land rejoiced and the city was
quiet. For they had put Athaliah to death with the sword.

Chapter 24 Theme ______________________

835 B.C.

2 Kings 12

24 [a]Joash *was* seven years old when he became king, and
he reigned forty years in Jerusalem; and his mother's
name *was* Zibiah from Beersheba.
2 [a]Joash did what was right in the sight of the LORD all the
days of Jehoiada the priest.
3 Jehoiada took two wives for him, and he became the father
of sons and daughters.
4 Now it came about after this that Joash [1]decided [a]to restore
the house of the LORD.
5 He gathered the priests and Levites and said to them, "Go
out to the cities of Judah and collect money from all [a]Israel to
[1]repair the house of your God [2]annually, and you shall do the
matter quickly." But the Levites did not act quickly.
6 So the king summoned Jehoiada the chief *priest* and said to
him, "Why have you not required the Levites to bring in from
Judah and from Jerusalem [a]the levy *fixed by* Moses the servant
of the LORD on the congregation of Israel [b]for the tent of the
testimony?"
7 For [a]the sons of the wicked Athaliah had broken into the
house of God and even [1]used the holy things of the house of the
LORD for the Baals.

14 [1]Lit *from within*
15 [1]Lit *placed hands to her* [a]Neh 3:28; Jer 31:40 [b]2 Chr 22:10
16 [a]2 Kin 11:17
17 [a]Deut 13:6-9; 1 Kin 18:40
18 [1]Lit *hand* [2]Lit *hands of* [a]2 Chr 5:5 [b]1 Chr 23:6, 25-31 [c]1 Chr 25:1
19 [a]1 Chr 9:22
20 [a]2 Kin 11:19
21 [a]2 Kin 11:20
24:1 [a]2 Kin 11:21; 12:1-15
2 [a]2 Chr 26:4, 5
4 [1]Lit *was with a heart* [a]2 Chr 24:7
5 [1]Lit *to strengthen* [2]Lit *from year to year* [a]2 Chr 21:2
6 [a]Ex 30:12-16 [b]Num 1:50
7 [1]Lit *made* [a]2 Chr 21:17

8 [a]2 Kin 12:9
9 [a]2 Chr 36:22 [b]2 Chr 24:6
10 [1]Lit *threw*
11 [a]2 Kin 12:10
12 [1]Lit *to strengthen*
13 [1]Lit *set up* [2]Lit *upon its proportion*
15 [1]Lit *became old and satisfied with days*
16 [1]Lit *with* [a]2 Chr 21:20 [b]2 Chr 21:2
18 [1]I.e. wooden symbols of a female deity [a]2 Chr 24:4 [b]Ex 34:12-14 [c]Josh 22:20
19 [a]Jer 7:25
20 [1]Lit *clothed* [a]2 Chr 20:14 [b]Num 14:41 [c]2 Chr 15:2
21 [1]Lit *with stones* [a]Neh 9:26; Matt 23:34, 35
22 [1]Lit *seek,* or *require* [a]Gen 9:5
23 [a]2 Kin 12:17

8 So the king commanded, and [a]they made a chest and set it
outside by the gate of the house of the LORD.
9 [a]They made a proclamation in Judah and Jerusalem to bring
to the LORD [b]the levy *fixed by* Moses the servant of God on
Israel in the wilderness.
10 All the officers and all the people rejoiced and brought in
their levies and [1]dropped *them* into the chest until they had
finished.
11 It came about whenever the chest was brought in to the
king's officer by the Levites, and when [a]they saw that there
was much money, then the king's scribe and the chief priest's
officer would come, empty the chest, take it, and return it to its
place. Thus they did daily and collected much money.
12 The king and Jehoiada gave it to those who did the work of
the service of the house of the LORD; and they hired masons
and carpenters to restore the house of the LORD, and also workers
in iron and bronze to [1]repair the house of the LORD.
13 So the workmen labored, and the repair work progressed
in their hands, and they [1]restored the house of God [2]according
to its specifications and strengthened it.
14 When they had finished, they brought the rest of the money
before the king and Jehoiada; and it was made into utensils for
the house of the LORD, utensils for the service and the burnt
offering, and pans and utensils of gold and silver. And they
offered burnt offerings in the house of the LORD continually all
the days of Jehoiada.
15 Now when Jehoiada [1]reached a ripe old age he died; he
was one hundred and thirty years old at his death.
16 They buried him [a]in the city of David among the kings,
because he had done well in [b]Israel and [1]to God and His house.
17 But after the death of Jehoiada the officials of Judah came
and bowed down to the king, and the king listened to them.
18 They abandoned [a]the house of the LORD, the God of their
fathers, and [b]served the [1]Asherim and the idols; so [c]wrath
came upon Judah and Jerusalem for this their guilt.
19 Yet [a]He sent prophets to them to bring them back to the
LORD; though they testified against them, they would not listen.
20 [a]Then the Spirit of God [1]came on Zechariah the son of
Jehoiada the priest; and he stood above the people and said to
them, "Thus God has said, '[b]Why do you transgress the
commandments of the LORD and do not prosper? [c]Because you
have forsaken the LORD, He has also forsaken you.'"
21 So [a]they conspired against him and at the command of the
king they stoned him [1]to death in the court of the house of the
LORD.
22 Thus Joash the king did not remember the kindness which
his father Jehoiada had shown him, but he murdered his son.
And as he died he said, "May [a]the LORD see and [1]avenge!"
23 Now it happened at the turn of the year that [a]the army of
the Arameans came up against him; and they came to Judah
and Jerusalem, destroyed all the officials of the people from

among the people, and sent all their spoil to the king of
Damascus.
24 Indeed the army of the Arameans came with a small
number of men; yet [a]the LORD delivered a very great army into
their hands, [b]because they had forsaken the LORD, the God of
their fathers. Thus they executed judgment on Joash.
25 [a]When they had departed from him (for they left him very
sick), his own servants conspired against him because of the
blood of the [1]son of Jehoiada the priest, and murdered him on
his bed. So he died, and they buried him in the city of David,
but they did not bury him in the tombs of the kings.
26 Now these are those who conspired against him: Zabad the
son of Shimeath the Ammonitess, and Jehozabad the son of
Shimrith the Moabitess.
27 As to his sons and the many [1]oracles against him and [a]the
[2]rebuilding of the house of God, behold, they are written in the
[3b]treatise of the Book of the Kings. Then Amaziah his son
became king in his place.

Chapter 25 Theme ______________________

796 B.C.

2 Kings 14

25 [a]Amaziah was twenty-five years old when he became
king, and he reigned twenty-nine years in Jerusalem.
And his mother's name was Jehoaddan of Jerusalem.
2 He did right in the sight of the LORD, [a]yet not with a whole
heart.
3 Now [a]it came about as soon as the kingdom was [1]firmly in
his grasp, that he killed his servants who had slain his father
the king.
4 However, he did not put their children to death, but *did* as
it is written in the law in the book of Moses, which the LORD
commanded, saying, "[a]Fathers shall not be put to death for sons,
nor sons be put to death for fathers, but each shall be put to
death for his own sin."
5 Moreover, Amaziah assembled Judah and appointed them
according to *their* fathers' households under commanders of
thousands and commanders of hundreds throughout Judah and
Benjamin; and he [1]took a census of those [a]from twenty years
old and upward and found them to be [b]300,000 choice men,
able to go to war *and* handle spear and shield.
6 He hired also 100,000 valiant warriors out of Israel for one
hundred talents of silver.
7 But [a]a man of God came to him saying, "O king, do not let
the army of Israel go with you, for the LORD is not with Israel
nor with any of the sons of Ephraim.
8 "But if you do go, do *it,* be strong for the battle; *yet* God will
[1]bring you down before the enemy, [a]for God has power to help
and to [1]bring down."
9 Amaziah said to the man of God, "But what *shall we* do for
the hundred talents which I have given to the troops of Israel?"
And the man of God answered, "[a]The LORD has much more to
give you than this."

24 [a]2 Chr 16:7, 8 [b]2 Chr 24:20

25 [1]So some ancient versions; Heb *sons* [a]2 Kin 12:20, 21

27 [1]Or *burdens upon* [2]Lit *founding* [3]Heb *midrash* [a]2 Chr 24:12 [b]2 Chr 13:22

25:1 [a]2 Kin 14:1-6

2 [a]2 Chr 25:14

3 [1]Lit *firm upon him* [a]2 Kin 14:5

4 [a]Deut 24:16

5 [1]Lit *mustered* [a]Num 1:3 [b]2 Chr 26:13

7 [a]2 Kin 4:9

8 [1]Lit *cause to stumble* [a]2 Chr 14:11; 20:6

9 [a]Deut 8:18; Prov 10:22

10 [1]Lit *separated* [2]Lit *to their own place*

10 Then Amaziah [1]dismissed them, the troops which came to
him from Ephraim, to go home; so their anger burned against
Judah and they returned [2]home in fierce anger.
11 Now Amaziah strengthened himself and led his people forth,
and went to [a]the Valley of Salt and struck down 10,000 of the
sons of Seir.

11 [a]2 Kin 14:7

12 The sons of Judah also captured 10,000 alive and brought
them to the top of the cliff and threw them down from the top of
the cliff, so that they were all dashed to pieces.

13 [1]Lit *sons of the troops*

13 But the [1]troops whom Amaziah sent back from going with
him to battle, raided the cities of Judah, from Samaria to Beth-horon, and struck down 3,000 of them and plundered much
spoil.
14 Now after Amaziah came from slaughtering the Edomites,
[a]he brought the gods of the sons of Seir, set them up as his
gods, bowed down before them and burned incense to them.

14 [a]2 Chr 28:23

15 Then the anger of the LORD burned against Amaziah, and
He sent him a prophet who said to him, "Why have you sought
the gods of the people [a]who have not delivered their own
people from your hand?"

15 [a]2 Chr 25:11, 12

16 As he was talking with him, [1]the king said to him, "Have
we appointed you a royal counselor? Stop! Why should you be
struck down?" Then the prophet stopped and said, "I know
that God has planned to destroy you, because you have done
this and have not listened to my counsel."

16 [1]Lit *he*

17 [a]Then Amaziah king of Judah took counsel and sent to
Joash the son of Jehoahaz the son of Jehu, the king of Israel,
saying, "Come, let us face each other."

17 [a]2 Kin 14:8-14

18 Joash the king of Israel sent to Amaziah king of Judah,
saying, "[a]The thorn bush which was in Lebanon sent to the
cedar which was in Lebanon, saying, 'Give your daughter to
my son in marriage.' But there passed by a wild beast that was
in Lebanon and trampled the thorn bush.

18 [a]Judg 9:8-15

19 "You said, 'Behold, you have [1]defeated Edom.' And [a]your
heart has [2]become proud in boasting. Now stay at home; for
why should you provoke trouble so that you, even you, would
fall and Judah with you?"

19 [1]Lit *smitten* [2]Lit *lifted you up to boast* [a]2 Chr 26:16; 32:25

20 But Amaziah would not listen, for it was from God, that He
might deliver them into the hand *of Joash* because they had
sought the gods of Edom.
21 So Joash king of Israel went up, and he and Amaziah king of
Judah faced each other at Beth-shemesh, which belonged to Judah.
22 Judah was defeated [1]by Israel, and they fled each to his tent.

22 [1]Lit *before*

23 Then Joash king of Israel captured Amaziah king of Judah,
the son of Joash the son of [a]Jehoahaz, at Beth-shemesh, and
brought him to Jerusalem and tore down the wall of Jerusalem
from the Gate of Ephraim to the Corner Gate, 400 [1]cubits.

23 [1]I.e. One cubit equals approx 18 in. [a]2 Chr 21:17; 22:1

24 *He took* all the gold and silver and all the utensils which
were found in the house of God with [a]Obed-edom, and the
treasures of the king's house, the hostages also, and returned to
Samaria.

24 [a]1 Chr 26:15

25 [a]And Amaziah, the son of Joash king of Judah, lived fifteen
years after the death of Joash, son of Jehoahaz, king of Israel.
26 Now the rest of the acts of Amaziah, from first to last,
behold, are they not written in the Book of the Kings of Judah
and Israel?
27 From the time that Amaziah turned away from following
the LORD they conspired against him in Jerusalem, and he fled to
Lachish; but they sent after him to Lachish and killed him there.
28 Then they brought him on horses and buried him with his
fathers in the city of Judah.

Chapter 26 Theme ________________________

790 B.C.

2 Kings 15

26 And all the people of Judah took [1]Uzziah, who *was* sixteen years old, and made him king in the place of his
father Amaziah.
2 He built Eloth and restored it to Judah after the king slept
with his fathers.
3 Uzziah was [a]sixteen years old when he became king, and
he reigned fifty-two years in Jerusalem; and his mother's name
was [1]Jechiliah of Jerusalem.
4 He did right in the sight of the LORD according to all that
his father Amaziah had done.
5 [a]He continued to seek God in the days of Zechariah, [b]who
had understanding [1]through the vision of God; and [2c]as long as
he sought the LORD, God prospered him.
6 Now he went out and [a]warred against the Philistines, and
broke down the wall of Gath and the wall of Jabneh and the
wall of Ashdod; and he built cities in *the area of* Ashdod and
among the Philistines.
7 [a]God helped him against the Philistines, and against the
Arabians who lived in Gur-baal, and the Meunites.
8 The Ammonites also gave [a]tribute to Uzziah, and his [1]fame
extended to the border of Egypt, for he became very strong.
9 Moreover, Uzziah built towers in Jerusalem at [a]the Corner
Gate and at the [b]Valley Gate and at the corner buttress and
fortified them.
10 He built towers in the wilderness and [a]hewed many
cisterns, for he had much livestock, both in the [1]lowland and in
the plain. *He also had* plowmen and vinedressers in the hill
country and the fertile fields, for he loved the soil.
11 Moreover, Uzziah had an army ready for battle, which
[1]entered combat by divisions according to the number of their
muster, [2]prepared by Jeiel the scribe and Maaseiah the official,
under the direction of Hananiah, one of the king's officers.
12 The total number of the heads of the [1]households, of
valiant warriors, was 2,600.
13 Under their direction was an [1]elite army of [a]307,500, who
could wage war with great power, to help the king against the
enemy.
14 Moreover, Uzziah prepared [1]for all the army shields,
spears, helmets, body armor, bows and sling stones.

25 [a]2 Kin 14:17-22

26:1 [1]In 2 Kin 14:21, *Azariah*

3 [1]In 2 Kin 15:2, *Jecoliah* [a]2 Kin 15:2, 3

5 [1]Many mss read *in the fear of God* [2]Lit *in the days of his seeking* [a]2 Chr 24:2 [b]Dan 1:17 [c]2 Chr 15:2

6 [a]Is 14:29

7 [a]2 Chr 21:16

8 [1]Lit *name went to the entering of Egypt* [a]2 Chr 17:11

9 [a]2 Chr 25:23 [b]Neh 2:13, 15; 3:13

10 [1]Heb *shephelah* [a]Gen 26:18-21

11 [1]Lit *goes out to* [2]Lit *by the hand of*

12 [1]Lit *fathers*

13 [1]Lit *powerful* [a]2 Chr 25:5

14 [1]Lit *for them, for all*

15 In Jerusalem he made engines *of war* invented by skillful
men to be on the towers and on the corners for the purpose of
shooting arrows and great stones. Hence his [1]fame spread afar,
for he was marvelously helped until he *was* strong.
16 But [a]when he became strong, his heart was so [1]proud that
he acted corruptly, and he was unfaithful to the LORD his God,
for [b]he entered the temple of the LORD to burn incense on the
altar of incense.
17 Then [a]Azariah the priest entered after him and with him
eighty priests of the LORD, valiant men.
18 [a]They opposed Uzziah the king and said to him, "[b]It is not
for you, Uzziah, to burn incense to the LORD, [c]but for the
priests, the sons of Aaron who are consecrated to burn incense.
Get out of the sanctuary, for you have been unfaithful and will
have no honor from the LORD God."
19 But Uzziah, with a censer in his hand for burning incense,
was enraged; and while he was enraged with the priests, [a]the
leprosy broke out on his forehead before the priests in the
house of the LORD, beside the altar of incense.
20 Azariah the chief priest and all the priests looked at him,
and behold, he *was* leprous on his forehead; and they hurried
him out of there, and he himself also hastened to get out
because the LORD had smitten him.
21 [a]King Uzziah was a leper to the day of his death; and he
lived in [b]a separate house, being a leper, for he was cut off from
the house of the LORD. And Jotham his son *was* over the king's
house judging the people of the land.
22 Now the rest of the acts of Uzziah, first to last, the prophet
[a]Isaiah, the son of Amoz, has written.
23 So Uzziah slept with his fathers, and they buried him with
his fathers [a]in the field of the grave which belonged to the
kings, for they said, "He is a leper." And Jotham his son became
king in his place.

Chapter 27 Theme ____________________

27 [a]Jotham was twenty-five years old when he became
king, and he reigned sixteen years in Jerusalem. And
his mother's name was Jerushah the daughter of Zadok.

750 B.C.

2 He did right in the sight of the LORD, according to all that
his father Uzziah had done; [a]however he did not enter the
temple of the LORD. But the people continued acting corruptly.
3 He built the upper gate of the house of the LORD, and he
built extensively the wall of [a]Ophel.
4 Moreover, he built [a]cities in the hill country of Judah, and
he built fortresses and towers on the wooded *hills*.
5 He fought also with the king of the Ammonites and
prevailed over them so that the Ammonites gave him during
that year one hundred talents of silver, ten thousand [1]kors of
wheat and ten thousand of barley. The Ammonites also paid
him this *amount* in the second and in the third year.

15 [1]Lit *name*
16 [1]Lit *lifted up* [a]Deut 32:15; 2 Chr 25:19 [b]1 Kin 13:1-4
17 [a]1 Chr 6:10
18 [a]2 Chr 19:2 [b]Num 3:10; 16:39, 40 [c]Ex 30:7, 8
19 [a]2 Kin 5:25-27
21 [a]2 Kin 15:5-7 [b]Lev 13:46
22 [a]Is 1:1
23 [a]2 Chr 21:20; 28:27; Is 6:1
27:1 [a]2 Kin 15:33-35
2 [a]2 Chr 26:16
3 [a]2 Chr 33:14; Neh 3:26
4 [a]2 Chr 11:5
5 [1]I.e. One kor equals approx 10 bu

6 [a]So Jotham became mighty because he ordered his ways
before the LORD his God.
7 [a]Now the rest of the acts of Jotham, even all his wars and
his acts, behold, they are written in the Book of the Kings of
Israel and Judah.
8 He was [a]twenty-five years old when he became king, and
he reigned sixteen years in Jerusalem.
9 And Jotham slept with his fathers, and they buried him in
the city of David; and Ahaz his son became king in his place.

Chapter 28 Theme ____________________

735 B.C.

2 Kings 16

28 [a]Ahaz *was* twenty years old when he became king, and
he reigned sixteen years in Jerusalem; and [b]he did not
do right in the sight of the LORD as David his father *had done.*
2 [a]But he walked in the ways of the kings of Israel; he also
[b]made molten images for the Baals.
3 Moreover, [a]he burned incense in the valley of Ben-hinnom
and [b]burned his sons in fire, [c]according to the abominations of the
nations whom the LORD had driven out before the sons of Israel.
4 He sacrificed and [a]burned incense on the high places, on
the hills and under every green tree.
5 Wherefore, [a]the LORD his God delivered him into the hand
of the king of Aram; and they [1]defeated him and carried away
from him a great number of captives and brought *them* to
Damascus. And he was also delivered into the hand of the king
of Israel, who [2]inflicted him with heavy casualties.
6 For [a]Pekah the son of Remaliah slew in Judah 120,000 in
one day, all valiant men, because they had forsaken the LORD
God of their fathers.
7 And Zichri, a mighty man of Ephraim, slew Maaseiah the
king's son and Azrikam the ruler of the house and Elkanah the
second to the king.
8 [a]The sons of Israel carried away captive of [b]their brethren
200,000 women, sons and daughters; and they [1]took also a
great deal of spoil from them, and brought the spoil to Samaria.
9 But a prophet of the LORD was there, whose name *was* Oded;
and [a]he went out to meet the army which came to Samaria and
said to them, "Behold, because the LORD, the God of your fathers,
[b]was angry with Judah, He has delivered them into your hand, and
you have slain them in a rage [c]*which* has even reached heaven.
10 "Now you are proposing to [a]subjugate for yourselves the
people of Judah and Jerusalem for male and female slaves.
Surely, *do* you not *have* transgressions of your own against the
LORD your God?
11 "Now therefore, listen to me and return the captives [a]whom
you captured from your brothers, [b]for the burning anger of the
LORD is against you."
12 Then some of the heads of the sons of Ephraim—Azariah the
son of Johanan, Berechiah the son of Meshillemoth, Jehizkiah
the son of Shallum, and Amasa the son of Hadlai—arose against
those who were coming from the battle,

6 [a]2 Chr 26:5
7 [a]2 Kin 15:36
8 [a]2 Chr 27:1
28:1 [a]2 Kin 16:2-4 [b]2 Chr 27:2
2 [a]2 Chr 22:3 [b]Ex 34:17
3 [a]Josh 15:8 [b]Lev 18:21; 2 Chr 33:6 [c]2 Chr 33:2
4 [a]2 Chr 28:25
5 [1]Lit *smote* [2]Lit *smote him with a great smiting* [a]2 Kin 16:5; 2 Chr 24:24; Is 7:1
6 [a]2 Kin 16:5
8 [1]Lit *plundered* [a]Deut 28:25, 41 [b]2 Chr 11:4
9 [a]2 Chr 25:15 [b]Is 47:6 [c]Ezra 9:6; Rev 18:5
10 [a]Lev 25:39
11 [a]2 Chr 28:8 [b]James 2:13

13 and said to them, "You must not bring the captives in here,
for you are proposing *to bring* upon us guilt against the LORD
adding to our sins and our guilt; for our guilt is great so that *His*
burning anger is against Israel."
14 So the armed men left the captives and the spoil before the
officers and all the assembly.
15 Then [a]the men who were designated by name arose, took the
captives, and they clothed all their naked ones from the spoil;
and they gave them clothes and sandals, fed them and [b]gave
them drink, anointed them *with oil,* led all their feeble ones on
donkeys, and brought them to Jericho, [c]the city of palm trees,
to their brothers; then they returned to Samaria.
16 [a]At that time King Ahaz sent to the [1]kings of Assyria for help.
17 [a]For again the Edomites had come and attacked Judah and
carried away captives.
18 [a]The Philistines also had invaded the cities of the [1]lowland
and of the Negev of Judah, and had taken Beth-shemesh,
Aijalon, Gederoth, and Soco with its villages, Timnah with its
villages, and Gimzo with its villages, and they settled there.
19 For the LORD humbled Judah because of Ahaz king of
[a]Israel, for he had brought about a lack of restraint in Judah and
was very unfaithful to the LORD.
20 So [a]Tilgath-pilneser king of Assyria came against him and
afflicted him instead of strengthening him.
21 [a]Although Ahaz took a portion out of the house of the LORD
and out of the palace of the king and of the princes, and gave *it*
to the king of Assyria, it did not help him.
22 Now in the time of his distress this same King Ahaz
[a]became yet more unfaithful to the LORD.
23 [a]For he sacrificed to the gods of Damascus which had
[1]defeated him, and said, "[b]Because the gods of the kings of
Aram helped them, I will sacrifice to them that they may help
me." But they became the [2]downfall of him and all Israel.
24 Moreover, when Ahaz gathered together the utensils of the
house of God, he [a]cut the utensils of the house of God in
pieces; and he [b]closed the doors of the house of the LORD and
[c]made altars for himself in every corner of Jerusalem.
25 In every city of Judah he made high places to burn
incense to other gods, and provoked the LORD, the God of his
fathers, to anger.
26 [a]Now the rest of his acts and all his ways, from first to last,
behold, they are written in the Book of the Kings of Judah and
Israel.
27 [a]So Ahaz slept with his fathers, and they buried him in the
city, in Jerusalem, for they did not bring him into the tombs of
the kings of [b]Israel; and Hezekiah his son reigned in his place.

Chapter 29 Theme ____________________

29 [a]Hezekiah became king *when he was* twenty-five years
old; and he reigned twenty-nine years in Jerusalem.
And his mother's name *was* Abijah, the daughter of Zechariah.

715 B.C.

2 Kings 18

15 [a]2 Chr 28:12 [b]2 Kin 6:22; Prov 25:21, 22 [c]Deut 34:3
16 [1]Ancient versions read *king* [a]2 Kin 16:7
17 [a]Obad 10, 14
18 [1]Heb *shephelah* [a]Ezek 16:57
19 [a]2 Chr 21:2
20 [a]1 Chr 5:26
21 [a]2 Kin 16:8, 9
22 [a]Is 1:5; Jer 5:3; Rev 16:11
23 [1]Lit *smitten* [2]Lit *stumbling* [a]2 Chr 25:14 [b]Jer 44:17, 18
24 [a]2 Kin 16:17 [b]2 Chr 29:7 [c]2 Chr 30:14; 33:3-5
26 [a]2 Kin 16:19, 20
27 [a]2 Kin 16:20; 2 Chr 24:25; Is 14:28 [b]2 Chr 21:2
29:1 [a]2 Kin 18:1-3

2 [a]He did right in the sight of the LORD, according to all that
his father David had done.
3 In the first year of his reign, in the first month, he [a]opened
the doors of the house of the LORD and repaired them.
4 He brought in the priests and the Levites and gathered them
into the square on the east.
5 Then he said to them, "Listen to me, O Levites. [a]Consecrate
yourselves now, and consecrate the house of the LORD, the God of
your fathers, and carry the uncleanness out from the holy place.
6 "For our fathers have been unfaithful and have done evil in
the sight of the LORD our God, and have forsaken Him and
[a]turned their faces away from the dwelling place of the LORD,
and have [1]turned *their* backs.
7 "They have also [a]shut the doors of the porch and put out the
lamps, and have not burned incense or offered burnt offerings
in the holy place to the God of Israel.
8 "Therefore [a]the wrath of the LORD was against Judah and
Jerusalem, and He has made them an object of terror, of horror,
and of [b]hissing, as you see with your own eyes.
9 "For behold, [a]our fathers have fallen by the sword, and our
sons and our daughters and our wives are in captivity for this.
10 "Now it is in my heart [a]to make a covenant with the LORD
God of Israel, that His burning anger may turn away from us.
11 "My sons, do not be negligent now, for [a]the LORD has chosen
you to stand before Him, to minister to Him, and to be His
ministers and burn incense."
12 Then the Levites arose: [a]Mahath, the son of Amasai and
Joel the son of Azariah, from the sons of [b]the Kohathites; and
from the sons of Merari, Kish the son of Abdi and Azariah the
son of Jehallelel; and from the Gershonites, Joah the son of
Zimmah and Eden the son of Joah;
13 and from the sons of Elizaphan, Shimri and [1]Jeiel; and from
the sons of Asaph, Zechariah and Mattaniah;
14 and from the sons of Heman, [1]Jehiel and Shimei; and from
the sons of Jeduthun, Shemaiah and Uzziel.
15 They assembled their brothers, [a]consecrated themselves, and
went in [b]to cleanse the house of the LORD, according to the
commandment of the king [c]by the words of the LORD.
16 So the priests went in to the inner part of the house of the
LORD to cleanse *it,* and every unclean thing which they found
in the temple of the LORD they brought out to the court of the
house of the LORD. Then the Levites received *it* to carry out to
[a]the Kidron [1]valley.
17 Now they began [1]the consecration [a]on the first *day* of the
first month, and on the eighth day of the month they entered
the porch of the LORD. Then they consecrated the house of the
LORD in eight days, and finished on the sixteenth day of the
first month.
18 Then they went in to King Hezekiah and said, "We have
cleansed the whole house of the LORD, the altar of burnt
offering with all of its utensils, and the table of showbread with
all of its utensils.

2 [a]2 Chr 28:1; 34:2
3 [a]2 Chr 28:24; 29:7
5 [a]2 Chr 29:15, 34; 35:6
6 [1]Lit *given* [a]Ezek 8:16
7 [a]2 Chr 28:24
8 [a]2 Chr 24:20 [b]Jer 25:9, 18
9 [a]2 Chr 28:5-8, 17
10 [a]2 Chr 23:16
11 [a]Num 3:6; 8:6
12 [a]2 Chr 31:13 [b]Num 3:19, 20
13 [1]Or *Jeuel*
14 [1]Or *Jehuel,* 1 Chr 15:18, 20
15 [a]2 Chr 29:5 [b]1 Chr 23:28 [c]2 Chr 30:12
16 [1]Or *wadi* [a]2 Chr 15:16
17 [1]Lit *to consecrate* [a]2 Chr 29:3

19 "Moreover, [a]all the utensils which King Ahaz had discarded
during his reign in his unfaithfulness, we have prepared and
consecrated; and behold, they are before the altar of the LORD."
20 Then King Hezekiah arose early and assembled the princes
of the city and went up to the house of the LORD.
21 They brought seven bulls, seven rams, seven lambs and
seven male goats [a]for a sin offering for the kingdom, the
sanctuary, and Judah. And he ordered the priests, the sons of
Aaron, to offer *them* on the altar of the LORD.
22 So they slaughtered the bulls, and the priests took the blood
and sprinkled it on the altar. They also slaughtered the rams
and sprinkled the blood on the altar; they slaughtered the
lambs also and [a]sprinkled the blood on the altar.
23 Then they brought the male goats of the sin offering before
the king and the assembly, and [a]they laid their hands on them.
24 The priests slaughtered them and purged the altar with
their blood [a]to atone for all Israel, for the king ordered the
burnt offering and the sin offering for all Israel.
25 [a]He then stationed the Levites in the house of the LORD
with cymbals, with harps and with lyres, [b]according to the
command of David and of [c]Gad the king's seer, and of [d]Nathan
the prophet; for the command was from the LORD through His
prophets.
26 The Levites stood with [a]the *musical* instruments of David,
and [b]the priests with the trumpets.
27 Then Hezekiah gave the order to offer the burnt offering
on the altar. When the burnt offering began, [a]the song to the
LORD also began with the trumpets, [1]*accompanied* by the
instruments of David, king of Israel.
28 While the whole assembly worshiped, the singers also sang
and the trumpets sounded; all this *continued* until the burnt
offering was finished.
29 Now at the completion of the burnt offerings, [a]the king and
all who were present with him bowed down and worshiped.
30 Moreover, King Hezekiah and the officials ordered the
Levites to sing praises to the LORD with the words of David and
Asaph the seer. [a]So they sang praises with joy, and bowed
down and worshiped.
31 Then Hezekiah said, "[a]Now *that* you have [1]consecrated
yourselves to the LORD, come near and bring sacrifices and
thank offerings to the house of the LORD." And the assembly
brought sacrifices and thank offerings, and [b]all those who were
[2]willing *brought* burnt offerings.
32 The number of the burnt offerings which the assembly
brought was 70 bulls, 100 rams, and 200 lambs; all these were
for a burnt offering to the LORD.
33 The consecrated things were 600 bulls and 3,000 sheep.
34 But the priests were too few, so that they were unable to
skin all the burnt offerings; [a]therefore their brothers the
Levites helped them until the work was completed and until
the *other* priests had consecrated themselves. For [b]the Levites

19 [a]2 Chr 28:24
21 [a]Lev 4:3-14
22 [a]Lev 4:18
23 [a]Lev 4:15
24 [a]Lev 4:26
25 [a]1 Chr 25:6 [b]2 Chr 8:14 [c]2 Sam 24:11 [d]2 Sam 7:2
26 [a]1 Chr 23:5 [b]2 Chr 5:12
27 [1]Lit *and according to the authority of the instruments* [a]2 Chr 23:18
29 [a]2 Chr 20:18
30 [a]Ps 100:1; 106:12
31 [1]Lit *filled your hands* [2]Lit *willing of heart* [a]2 Chr 13:9 [b]Ex 35:5, 22
34 [a]2 Chr 35:11 [b]2 Chr 30:3

were more [1]conscientious to consecrate themselves than the
priests.
35 There *were* also [1][a]many burnt offerings with [b]the fat of the
peace offerings and with [c]the libations for the burnt offerings.
Thus the service of the house of the LORD was established *again.*
36 Then Hezekiah and all the people rejoiced over what God
had prepared for the people, because the thing came about
suddenly.

Chapter 30 Theme ______________________

30 Now Hezekiah sent to all Israel and Judah and wrote
letters also to Ephraim and Manasseh, that they should
come to the house of the LORD at Jerusalem to [1]celebrate the
Passover to the LORD God of Israel.
2 For the king and his princes and all the assembly in Jerusalem
had decided [a]to celebrate the Passover in the second month,
3 since they could not celebrate it [a]at that time, because the
priests had not consecrated themselves in sufficient numbers,
nor had the people been gathered to Jerusalem.
4 Thus the thing was right in the sight of the king and [1]all
the assembly.
5 So they established a decree to circulate a [1]proclamation
throughout all Israel [a]from Beersheba even to Dan, that they
should come to celebrate the Passover to the LORD God of Israel
at Jerusalem. For they had not celebrated *it* in great numbers as
it was [2]prescribed.
6 [a]The [1]couriers went throughout all Israel and Judah with
the letters from the hand of the king and his princes, even
according to the command of the king, saying, "O sons of
Israel, return to the LORD God of Abraham, Isaac and Israel,
that He may return to those of you who escaped *and* are left
from [b]the [2]hand of the kings of Assyria.
7 "[a]Do not be like your fathers and your brothers, who were
unfaithful to the LORD God of their fathers, so that [b]He made
them a horror, as you see.
8 "Now do not [a]stiffen your neck like your fathers, but [1]yield
to the LORD and enter His sanctuary which He has consecrated
forever, and serve the LORD your God, [b]that His burning anger
may turn away from you.
9 "For [a]if you return to the LORD, your brothers and your sons
will find compassion before those who led them captive and
will return to this land. [b]For the LORD your God is gracious and
compassionate, and will not turn *His* face away from you if you
return to Him."
10 So the [1]couriers passed from city to city through the
country of Ephraim and Manasseh, and as far as Zebulun, but
[a]they laughed them to scorn and mocked them.
11 Nevertheless [a]some men of Asher, Manasseh and Zebulun
humbled themselves and came to Jerusalem.
12 The [a]hand of God was also on Judah to give them one heart

34 [1]Lit *upright of heart*
35 [1]Lit *the burnt offerings to an abundance* [a]2 Chr 29:32 [b]Lev 3:16 [c]Num 15:5-10
30:1 [1]Lit *do*, so in vv 2, 3, 5, 13, 21, 23
2 [a]Num 9:10, 11; 2 Chr 30:13, 15
3 [a]2 Chr 29:17, 34
4 [1]Lit *in the sight of all*
5 [1]Lit *voice* [2]Lit *written* [a]Judg 20:1
6 [1]Lit *runners* [2]Lit *palm* [a]Esth 8:14; Job 9:25; Jer 51:31 [b]2 Chr 28:20
7 [a]Ezek 20:13 [b]2 Chr 29:8
8 [1]Lit *give a hand* [a]Ex 32:9 [b]2 Chr 29:10
9 [a]Deut 30:2 [b]Ex 34:6, 7; Mic 7:18
10 [1]Lit *runners* [a]2 Chr 36:16
11 [a]2 Chr 30:18, 21, 25
12 [a]2 Cor 3:5; Phil 2:13; Heb 13:20, 21

to do what the king and the princes commanded by the word
of the LORD.
13 Now many people were gathered at Jerusalem to celebrate
the Feast of Unleavened Bread [a]in the second month, a very
large assembly.
14 They arose and removed the altars which *were* in Jerusalem;
they also [a]removed all the incense altars and [b]cast *them* into
the brook Kidron.
15 Then [a]they slaughtered the Passover *lambs* on the fourteenth
of the second month. And [b]the priests and Levites were ashamed
of themselves, and consecrated themselves and brought burnt
offerings to the house of the LORD.
16 [a]They stood at their stations after their custom, according
to the law of Moses the man of God; the priests sprinkled the
blood *which they received* from the hand of the Levites.
17 For *there were* many in the assembly who had not
consecrated themselves; therefore, [a]the Levites *were* over the
slaughter of the Passover *lambs* for everyone who *was* unclean,
in order to consecrate *them* to the LORD.
18 For a multitude of the people, [a]*even* many from Ephraim and
Manasseh, Issachar and Zebulun, had not purified themselves, [b]yet
they ate the Passover [c]otherwise than [1]prescribed. For Hezekiah
prayed for them, saying, "May the good LORD pardon
19 [a]everyone who prepares his heart to seek God, the LORD
God of his fathers, though not according to the purification
rules of the sanctuary."
20 So the LORD heard Hezekiah and [a]healed the people.
21 The sons of Israel present in Jerusalem [a]celebrated the
Feast of Unleavened Bread *for* seven days with great joy, and
the Levites and the priests praised the LORD day after day with
loud instruments to the LORD.
22 Then Hezekiah [a]spoke [1]encouragingly to all the Levites
who showed good insight *in the things* of the LORD. So they ate
for the appointed seven days, sacrificing peace offerings and
[b]giving thanks to the LORD God of their fathers.
23 Then the whole assembly [a]decided to celebrate *the feast*
another seven days, so they celebrated the seven days with joy.
24 For [a]Hezekiah king of Judah had contributed to the
assembly 1,000 bulls and 7,000 sheep, and the princes had
contributed to the assembly 1,000 bulls and 10,000 sheep; and
[b]a large number of priests consecrated themselves.
25 All the assembly of Judah rejoiced, with the priests and the
Levites and [a]all the assembly that came from Israel, both the
sojourners who came from the land of Israel and those living in
Judah.
26 So there was great joy in Jerusalem, because there was
nothing like this in Jerusalem [a]since the days of Solomon the
son of David, king of Israel.
27 Then [a]the Levitical priests arose and [b]blessed the people;
and their voice was heard and their prayer came to [c]His holy
dwelling place, to heaven.

13 [a]2 Chr 30:2
14 [a]2 Chr 28:24 [b]2 Chr 29:16
15 [a]2 Chr 30:2, 3 [b]2 Chr 29:34
16 [a]2 Chr 35:10, 15
17 [a]2 Chr 29:34
18 [1]Lit *written* [a]2 Chr 30:11, 25 [b]Num 9:10 [c]Ex 12:43-49
19 [a]2 Chr 19:3
20 [a]James 5:16
21 [a]Ex 12:15; 13:6
22 [1]Lit *to the heart of* [a]2 Chr 32:6 [b]Ezra 10:11
23 [a]1 Kin 8:65
24 [a]2 Chr 35:7, 8 [b]2 Chr 29:34; 30:3
25 [a]2 Chr 30:11, 18
26 [a]2 Chr 7:8-10
27 [a]2 Chr 23:18 [b]Num 6:23 [c]Deut 26:15; Ps 68:5

Chapter 31 Theme ____________________

31 Now when all this was finished, all Israel who were
present went out to the cities of Judah, [a]broke the pillars
in pieces, cut down the [1]Asherim and pulled down the high
places and the altars throughout all Judah and Benjamin, as
well as in Ephraim and Manasseh, [2]until they had destroyed
them all. Then all the sons of Israel returned to their cities,
each to his possession.
2 And Hezekiah appointed [a]the divisions of the priests and
the Levites by their divisions, each according to his service,
both the priests and the Levites, [b]for burnt offerings and for
peace offerings, to minister and to give thanks and to praise in
the gates of the camp of the LORD.
3 *He* also *appointed* [a]the king's portion of his goods for the
burnt offerings, *namely,* for the morning and evening burnt
offerings, and the burnt offerings for the sabbaths and for the
new moons and for the fixed festivals, [b]as it is written in the
law of the LORD.
4 Also he [1]commanded the people who lived in Jerusalem to
give [a]the portion due to the priests and the Levites, that they
might devote themselves to [b]the law of the LORD.
5 As soon as the [1]order spread, the sons of Israel provided in
abundance the first fruits of grain, new wine, oil, honey and of
all the produce of the field; and they brought in abundantly
[a]the tithe of all.
6 The sons of Israel and Judah who lived in the cities of
Judah also brought in the tithe of oxen and sheep, and [a]the
tithe of [1]sacred gifts which were consecrated to the LORD their
God, and placed *them* in heaps.
7 In the third month they began to [1]make the heaps, and
finished *them* by the seventh month.
8 When Hezekiah and the rulers came and saw the heaps,
they blessed the LORD and [a]His people Israel.
9 Then Hezekiah questioned the priests and the Levites
concerning the heaps.
10 Azariah the chief priest [a]of the house of Zadok said to
[1]him, "[b]Since the contributions began to be brought into the
house of the LORD, we have had enough to eat with plenty left
over, for the LORD has blessed His people, and this great
quantity is left over."
11 Then Hezekiah commanded *them* to prepare [a]rooms in the
house of the LORD, and they prepared *them.*
12 They faithfully brought in the contributions and the tithes
and the consecrated things; and Conaniah the Levite *was* the
officer in charge [a]of them and his brother Shimei *was* second.
13 Jehiel, Azaziah, Nahath, Asahel, Jerimoth, Jozabad, Eliel,
Ismachiah, Mahath and Benaiah *were* overseers [1]under the
authority of Conaniah and Shimei his brother by the
appointment of King Hezekiah, and [a]Azariah *was* the *chief*
officer of the house of God.
14 Kore the son of Imnah the Levite, the keeper of the eastern

31:1 [1]I.e. wooden symbols of a female deity [2]Lit *even to completion* [a]2 Kin 18:4

2 [a]1 Chr 24:1 [b]1 Chr 23:28-31

3 [a]2 Chr 35:7 [b]Num 28:1-29:40

4 [1]Lit *said to* [a]Num 18:8 [b]Mal 2:7

5 [1]Lit *word* [a]Neh 13:12

6 [1]Lit *consecrated things* [a]Lev 27:30; Deut 14:28

7 [1]Lit *found*

8 [a]Deut 33:29; Ps 33:12; 144:15

10 [1]Lit *him, and he said* [a]1 Chr 6:8, 9 [b]Mal 3:10

11 [a]1 Kin 6:5, 8

12 [a]2 Chr 35:9

13 [1]Lit *from the hand of* [a]2 Chr 31:10

gate, was over the freewill offerings of God, to apportion the
contributions for the LORD and the most holy things.
15 [1]Under his authority *were* [a]Eden, Miniamin, Jeshua,
Shemaiah, Amariah and Shecaniah in [b]the cities of the priests,
to distribute faithfully *their portions* to their brothers by
divisions, whether great or small,
16 without regard to their genealogical enrollment, to the
males from [1a]thirty years old and upward—everyone who
entered the house of the LORD [b]for his daily obligations—for
their work in their duties according to their divisions;
17 as well as the priests who were enrolled genealogically
according to their fathers' households, and the Levites [a]from
twenty years old and upwards, by their duties *and* their divisions.
18 The genealogical enrollment *included* [1]all their little children,
their wives, their sons and their daughters, for the whole
assembly, for they consecrated themselves [2]faithfully in holiness.
19 Also for the sons of Aaron the priests *who were* in [a]the
pasture lands of their cities, or in each and every city, [b]*there
were* men who were designated by name to distribute portions
to every male among the priests and to everyone genealogically
enrolled among the Levites.
20 Thus Hezekiah did throughout all Judah; and [a]he did what
was good, right and true before the LORD his God.
21 Every work which he began in the service of the house of
God in law and in commandment, seeking his God, he did
with all his heart and [a]prospered.

Chapter 32 Theme ____________________

32 After these [1]acts of faithfulness [a]Sennacherib king of
Assyria came and invaded Judah and besieged the fortified cities, and [2]thought to break into them for himself.
2 Now when Hezekiah saw that Sennacherib had come and
that [1]he intended to make war on Jerusalem,
3 he decided with his officers and his warriors to cut off the
supply of water from the springs which *were* outside the city,
and they helped him.
4 So many people assembled [a]and stopped up all the springs
and [b]the stream which flowed [1]through the region, saying, "Why
should the kings of Assyria come and find abundant water?"
5 And he took courage and [a]rebuilt all the wall that had been
broken down and [1]erected towers on it, and *built* [b]another
outside wall and strengthened the [c]Millo *in* the city of David,
and made weapons and shields in great number.
6 He appointed military officers over the people and gathered
them to him in the square at the city gate, and [a]spoke [1]encour-
agingly to them, saying,
7 "[a]Be strong and courageous, do not fear or be dismayed
because of the king of Assyria nor because of all the horde that is
with him; [b]for the one with us is greater than the one with him.
8 "With him is *only* [a]an arm of flesh, but [b]with us is the LORD

701 B.C.

15 [1]Lit *under his hand* [a]2 Chr 29:12 [b]Josh 21:9-19
16 [1]Heb *three* [a]1 Chr 23:3 [b]Ezra 3:4
17 [a]1 Chr 23:24
18 [1]Lit *with all* [2]Lit *in their faithfulness*
19 [a]Lev 25:34; Num 35:2-5 [b]2 Chr 31:12-15
20 [a]2 Kin 20:3; 22:2
21 [a]Deut 29:9; Prov 3:9, 10
32:1 [1]Lit *things and this faithfulness* [2]Lit *said* [a]2 Kin 18:13-19, 37; Is 36:1-37:38
2 [1]Lit *his face for war against*
4 [1]Lit *in the midst of the land* [a]2 Kin 20:20 [b]2 Chr 32:30
5 [1]Lit *raised on the towers* [a]2 Chr 25:23 [b]2 Kin 25:4 [c]1 Kin 9:24
6 [1]Lit *upon their hearts* [a]2 Chr 30:22
7 [a]1 Chr 22:13 [b]2 Kin 6:16
8 [a]Jer 17:5 [b]2 Chr 20:17

our God to help us and to fight our battles." And the people
relied on the words of Hezekiah king of Judah.
9 After this [a]Sennacherib king of Assyria sent his servants to
Jerusalem while he *was* [1]besieging Lachish with all his forces
with him, against Hezekiah king of Judah and against all Judah
who *were* at Jerusalem, saying,
10 "Thus says Sennacherib king of Assyria, 'On what are you
trusting that you are remaining in Jerusalem under siege?
11 'Is not Hezekiah misleading you to give yourselves over to
die by hunger and by thirst, saying, "The LORD our God will
deliver us from the [1]hand of the king of Assyria"?
12 '[a]Has not the same Hezekiah taken away His high places and
His altars, and said to Judah and [1]Jerusalem, "You shall worship
before one altar, and on it you shall [2]burn incense"?
13 'Do you not know what I and my fathers have done to all
the peoples of the lands? [a]Were the gods of the nations of the
lands able at all to deliver their land from my hand?
14 '[a]Who *was there* among all the gods of those nations which
my fathers utterly destroyed who could deliver his people out
of my hand, that your God should be able to deliver you from
my hand?
15 'Now therefore, do not let Hezekiah deceive you or mislead
you like this, and do not believe him, for [a]no god of any nation or
kingdom was able to deliver his people from my hand or from
the hand of my fathers. How much less will your God deliver
you from my hand?'"
16 His servants spoke further against the LORD God and
against His servant Hezekiah.
17 He also wrote letters to insult the LORD God of Israel, and to
speak against Him, saying, "[a]As the gods of the nations of the
lands [1]have not delivered their people from my hand, so the
God of Hezekiah will not deliver His people from my hand."
18 [a]They called this out with a loud voice in the language of
Judah to the people of Jerusalem who were on the wall, to
frighten and terrify them, so that they might take the city.
19 They spoke [1]of the God of Jerusalem as of [a]the gods of the
peoples of the earth, the work of men's hands.
20 But King Hezekiah and Isaiah the prophet, the son of
Amoz, prayed about this and cried out to heaven.
21 And the LORD sent an angel who destroyed every mighty
warrior, commander and officer in the camp of the king of
Assyria. So he returned [1]in shame to his own land. And when
he had entered the temple of his god, some of his own children
killed him there with the sword.
22 So the LORD [a]saved Hezekiah and the inhabitants of
Jerusalem from the hand of Sennacherib the king of Assyria and
from the hand of all *others,* and [1]guided them on every side.
23 And [a]many were bringing gifts to the LORD at Jerusalem
and choice presents to Hezekiah king of Judah, so that [b]he was
exalted in the sight of all nations thereafter.
24 [a]In those days Hezekiah became [1]mortally ill; and he prayed
to the LORD, and [2]the LORD spoke to him and gave him a sign.

9 [1]Lit *against* [a]2 Kin 18:17
11 [1]Lit *palm*
12 [1]Lit *Jerusalem, saying,* [2]Lit *offer up in smoke* [a]2 Chr 31:1
13 [a]2 Kin 18:33-35
14 [a]Is 10:9-11
15 [a]Ex 5:2; Is 36:18-20; Dan 3:15
17 [1]Lit *who have* [a]2 Chr 32:14
18 [a]2 Kin 18:28
19 [1]Lit *to* [a]Ps 115:4-8
21 [1]Lit *in shame of face*
22 [1]Another reading is *gave them rest* [a]Is 31:5
23 [a]2 Sam 8:10 [b]2 Chr 1:1
24 [1]Lit *sick to the point of death* [2]Lit *He* [a]2 Kin 20:1-11; Is 38:1-8

25 But Hezekiah gave no return for the benefit [1]he received,
[a]because his heart was [2]proud; [b]therefore wrath came on him
and on Judah and Jerusalem.
26 However, [a]Hezekiah [1]humbled the pride of his heart, both
he and the inhabitants of Jerusalem, so that the wrath of the
LORD did not come on them in the days of Hezekiah.
27 Now Hezekiah had immense riches and honor; and he
made for himself treasuries for silver, gold, precious stones,
spices, shields and all kinds of valuable articles,
28 storehouses also for the produce of grain, wine and oil,
pens for all kinds of cattle and [1]sheepfolds for the flocks.
29 He made cities for himself and acquired flocks and herds in
abundance, for [a]God had given him very great [1]wealth.
30 It was Hezekiah who [a]stopped the upper outlet of the
waters of [b]Gihon and directed them to the west side of the city
of David. And Hezekiah prospered in all that he did.
31 Even *in the matter of* [a]the envoys of the rulers of Babylon,
who sent to him to inquire of [b]the wonder that had happened
in the land, God left him *alone only* [c]to test him, that He might
know all that was in his heart.
32 Now the rest of the acts of Hezekiah and his deeds of
devotion, behold, they are written in the vision of Isaiah the
prophet, the son of Amoz, in the Book of the Kings of Judah
and Israel.
33 So Hezekiah slept with his fathers, and they buried him in
the [1]upper section of the tombs of the sons of David; and all
Judah and the inhabitants of Jerusalem [a]honored him at his
death. And his son Manasseh became king in his place.

Chapter 33 Theme

33 [a]Manasseh was twelve years old when he became king,
and he reigned fifty-five years in Jerusalem.

697 B.C.

2 Kings 21

2 [a]He did evil in the sight of the LORD according to the
abominations of the nations whom the LORD dispossessed before
the sons of Israel.
3 For [a]he rebuilt the high places which Hezekiah his father had
broken down; [b]he also erected altars for the Baals and made
[1]Asherim, and worshiped all the host of heaven and served them.
4 [a]He built altars in the house of the LORD of which the LORD
had said, "My name shall be [b]in Jerusalem forever."
5 For he built altars for all the host of heaven in [a]the two
courts of the house of the LORD.
6 [a]He made his sons pass through the fire in the valley of
Ben-hinnom; and he practiced witchcraft, used divination,
practiced sorcery and [b]dealt with mediums and spiritists. He
did much evil in the sight of the LORD, provoking Him *to anger.*
7 Then he put [a]the carved image of the idol which he had
made in the house of God, of which God had said to David and
to Solomon his son, "[b]In this house and in Jerusalem, which I
have chosen from all the tribes of Israel, I will put My name
forever;

25 [1]Lit *to him* [2]Lit *high* [a]2 Chr 26:16; 32:31 [b]2 Chr 24:18
26 [1]Lit *humbled himself in* [a]Jer 26:18, 19
28 [1]So ancient versions; Heb *flocks for the sheepfolds*
29 [1]Lit *possessions, property* [a]1 Chr 29:12
30 [a]2 Kin 20:20 [b]1 Kin 1:33
31 [a]2 Kin 20:12; Is 39:1 [b]2 Chr 32:24; Is 38:7, 8 [c]Deut 8:16
33 [1]Or *ascent to* [a]Ps 112:6; Prov 10:7
33:1 [a]2 Kin 21:1-9
2 [a]2 Chr 28:3; Jer 15:4
3 [1]I.e. wooden symbols of a female deity [a]2 Chr 31:1 [b]Deut 16:21; 2 Kin 23:5, 6
4 [a]2 Chr 28:24 [b]2 Sam 7:13; 2 Chr 7:16
5 [a]2 Chr 4:9
6 [a]2 Chr 28:3 [b]Lev 19:31; 20:27
7 [a]2 Chr 33:15 [b]1 Kin 9:3-5; 2 Chr 7:16; 33:4

8 and I will not again remove the foot of Israel from the land
[a]which I have appointed for your fathers, if only they will
observe to do all that I have commanded them according to all
the law, the statutes and the ordinances *given* through Moses."
9 Thus Manasseh misled Judah and the inhabitants of
Jerusalem to do more evil than the nations whom the LORD
destroyed before the sons of Israel.
10 The LORD spoke to Manasseh and his people, but [a]they paid
no attention.
11 [a]Therefore the LORD brought the commanders of the army of
the king of Assyria against them, and they captured Manasseh with
[l]hooks, [b]bound him with bronze *chains* and took him to Babylon.
12 When [a]he was in distress, he entreated the LORD his God
and [b]humbled himself greatly before the God of his fathers.
13 When he prayed to Him, [a]He was moved by his entreaty
and heard his supplication, and brought him again to Jerusalem
to his kingdom. Then Manasseh [b]knew that the LORD *was* God.
14 Now after this he built the outer wall of the city of David
on the west side of [a]Gihon, in the valley, even to the entrance
of the [b]Fish Gate; and he encircled the [c]Ophel *with it* and
made it very high. Then he put army commanders in all the
fortified cities of Judah.
15 He also [a]removed the foreign gods and the idol from the
house of the LORD, as well as all the altars which he had built
on the mountain of the house of the LORD and in Jerusalem,
and he threw *them* outside the city.
16 He set up the altar of the LORD and sacrificed [a]peace offerings
and thank offerings on it; and he ordered Judah to serve the LORD
God of Israel.
17 Nevertheless [a]the people still sacrificed in the high places,
although only to the LORD their God.
18 Now the rest of the acts of Manasseh even [a]his prayer to his
God, and the words of [b]the seers who spoke to him in the name
of the LORD God of Israel, behold, they are among the records
of the kings of [c]Israel.
19 His prayer also and [a]*how God* was entreated by him, and
all his sin, his unfaithfulness, and [b]the sites on which he built
high places and erected the Asherim and the carved images,
before he humbled himself, behold, they are written in the
records of the [l]Hozai.
20 So Manasseh slept with his fathers, and they buried him in
his own house. And Amon his son became king in his place.
21 [a]Amon *was* twenty-two years old when he became king,
and he reigned two years in Jerusalem.
22 He did evil in the sight of the LORD as Manasseh his father
[a]had done, and Amon sacrificed to all [b]the carved images
which his father Manasseh had made, and he served them.
23 Moreover, he did not humble himself before the LORD [a]as
his father Manasseh had [l]done, but Amon multiplied guilt.
24 Finally [a]his servants conspired against him and put him to
death in his own house.

8 [a]2 Sam 7:10
10 [a]Neh 9:29; Jer 25:4
11 [l]I.e. thongs put through the nose [a]Deut 28:36 [b]2 Chr 36:6
12 [a]Ps 118:5; 120:1; 130:1, 2 [b]2 Chr 32:26
13 [a]1 Chr 5:20; Ezra 8:23 [b]Dan 4:32
14 [a]1 Kin 1:33 [b]Neh 3:3 [c]2 Chr 27:3
15 [a]2 Chr 33:3-7
16 [a]Lev 7:11-18
17 [a]2 Chr 32:12
18 [a]2 Chr 33:12, 13 [b]2 Chr 33:10 [c]2 Chr 21:2
19 [l]Gr reads *seers* [a]2 Chr 33:13 [b]2 Chr 33:3
21 [a]2 Kin 21:19-24
22 [a]2 Chr 33:2-7 [b]2 Chr 34:3, 4
23 [l]Lit *humbled himself* [a]2 Chr 33:12, 19
24 [a]2 Chr 25:27

25 [1]Lit *smote*

25 But the people of the land [1]killed all the conspirators against
King Amon, and the people of the land made Josiah his son king
in his place.

34:1 [a]2 Kin 22:1, 2; Jer 1:2; 3:6

Chapter 34 Theme ____________________

34 [a]Josiah *was* eight years old when he became king, and
he reigned thirty-one years in Jerusalem.

640 B.C.

2 Kings 22

2 [a]2 Chr 29:2

2 [a]He did right in the sight of the LORD, and walked in the
ways of his father David and did not turn aside to the right or
to the left.

3 [a]2 Chr 15:2; Prov 8:17 [b]1 Kin 13:2; 2 Chr 33:22

3 For in the eighth year of his reign while he was still a youth,
he began to [a]seek the God of his father David; and in the twelfth
year he began [b]to purge Judah and Jerusalem of the high places,
the Asherim, the carved images and the molten images.

4 [a]2 Kin 23:4, 5, 11 [b]Ex 32:20

4 They tore down the altars of the Baals in his presence, and
[a]the incense altars that were high above them he chopped down;
also the Asherim, the carved images and the molten images he
broke in pieces and [b]ground to powder and scattered *it* on the
graves of those who had sacrificed to them.

5 [a]1 Kin 13:2; 2 Kin 23:20

5 Then [a]he burned the bones of the priests on their altars and
purged Judah and Jerusalem.

6 [a]2 Kin 23:15, 19

6 [a]In the cities of Manasseh, Ephraim, Simeon, even as far as
Naphtali, in their surrounding ruins,

7 [a]2 Chr 31:1

7 he also tore down the altars and [a]beat the Asherim and the
carved images into powder, and chopped down all the incense
altars throughout the land of Israel. Then he returned to Jerusalem.

8 [a]2 Kin 22:3-20 [b]2 Chr 18:25

8 [a]Now in the eighteenth year of his reign, when he had
purged the land and the house, he sent Shaphan the son of
Azaliah, and Maaseiah [b]an official of the city, and Joah the son
of Joahaz the recorder, to repair the house of the LORD his God.

9 [1]Lit *guardians of the threshold* [2]Lit *from the hand of* [a]2 Chr 35:8 [b]2 Chr 30:10, 18

9 They came to [a]Hilkiah the high priest and delivered the
money that was brought into the house of God, which the
Levites, the [1]doorkeepers, had collected [2]from [b]Manasseh and
Ephraim, and from all the remnant of Israel, and from all Judah
and Benjamin and the inhabitants of Jerusalem.

10 [1]Lit *gave*

10 Then they gave *it* into the hands of the workmen who had
the oversight of the house of the LORD, and the workmen who
were working in the house of the LORD [1]used it to restore and
repair the house.

11 [a]2 Chr 33:4-7

11 They in turn gave *it* to the carpenters and to the builders to
buy quarried stone and timber for couplings and to make beams
for the houses [a]which the kings of Judah had let go to ruin.

12 [a]2 Kin 12:15 [b]1 Chr 25:1

12 [a]The men did the work faithfully with foremen over them
to supervise: Jahath and Obadiah, the Levites of the sons of
Merari, Zechariah and Meshullam of the sons of the Kohathites, and [b]the Levites, all who were skillful with musical
instruments.

13 [a]Neh 4:10

13 *They were* also over [a]the burden bearers, and supervised all
the workmen from job to job; and *some* of the Levites *were*
scribes and officials and gatekeepers.

14 When they were bringing out the money which had been
brought into the house of the LORD, [a]Hilkiah the priest found
the book of the law of the LORD *given* by Moses.
15 Hilkiah responded and said to Shaphan the scribe, "I have
found the book of the law in the house of the LORD." And
Hilkiah gave the book to Shaphan.
16 Then Shaphan brought the book to the king and [1]reported
further word to the king, saying, "Everything that was [2]entrusted
to your servants they are doing.
17 "They have also emptied out the money which was found in
the house of the LORD, and have delivered it into the hands of the
supervisors and the workmen."
18 Moreover, Shaphan the scribe told the king saying,
"Hilkiah the priest gave me a book." And Shaphan read from it
in the presence of the king.
19 When the king heard [a]the words of the law, [b]he tore his
clothes.
20 Then the king commanded Hilkiah, Ahikam the son of
Shaphan, [1]Abdon the son of Micah, Shaphan the scribe, and
Asaiah the king's servant, saying,
21 "Go, inquire of the LORD for me and for those who are left in
Israel and in Judah, concerning the words of the book which has
been found; for [a]great is the wrath of the LORD which is poured
out on us because our fathers have not observed the word of the
LORD, to do according to all that is written in this book."
22 So Hilkiah and *those* whom the king [1]had told went to
Huldah the prophetess, the wife of Shallum the son of [2]Tokhath,
the son of Hasrah, the keeper of the wardrobe (now she lived in
Jerusalem in the Second Quarter); and they spoke to her
regarding this.
23 She said to them, "Thus says the LORD, the God of Israel,
'Tell the man who sent you to Me,
24 thus says the LORD, "Behold, [a]I am bringing evil on this
place and on its inhabitants, *even* all [b]the curses written in the
book which they have read in the presence of the king of Judah.
25 "[a]Because they have forsaken Me and have burned incense
to other gods, that they might provoke Me to anger with all the
works of their hands; therefore My wrath will be poured out
on this place and it shall not be quenched."'
26 "But to the king of Judah who sent you to inquire of the
LORD, thus you will say to him, 'Thus says the LORD God of
Israel *regarding* the words which you have heard,
27 "[a]Because your heart was tender and you humbled yourself
before God when you heard His words against this place and
against its inhabitants, and *because* you humbled yourself
before Me, tore your clothes and wept before Me, I truly have
heard you," declares the LORD.
28 "Behold, I will gather you to your fathers and you shall be
gathered to your grave in peace, so your eyes will not see all the
evil which I will bring on this place and on its inhabitants."'"
And they brought back word to the king.

14 [a]2 Chr 34:9

16 [1]Lit *returned* [2]Lit *given into the hand of*

19 [a]Deut 28:3-68 [b]Josh 7:6

20 [1]In 2 Kin 22:12, *Achbor, son of Micaiah*

21 [a]2 Chr 29:8

22 [1]So with Gr [2]In 2 Kin 22:14 *Tikvah, son of Harhas*

24 [a]2 Chr 36:14-20 [b]Deut 28:15-68

25 [a]2 Chr 33:3

27 [a]2 Kin 22:19; 2 Chr 12:7; 32:26

29 [a]2 Kin 23:1-3

29 [a]Then the king sent and gathered all the elders of Judah
and Jerusalem.
30 The king went up to the house of the LORD and [a]all the men
of Judah, the inhabitants of Jerusalem, the priests, the Levites

30 [a]Neh 8:1-3

and all the people, from the greatest to the least; and he read in
their hearing all the words of the book of the covenant which
was found in the house of the LORD.
31 Then the king [a]stood in his place and [b]made a covenant

31 [a]2 Kin 11:14; 23:3; 2 Chr 30:16 [b]2 Chr 23:16; 29:10

before the LORD to walk after the LORD, and to keep His
commandments and His testimonies and His statutes with all
his heart and with all his soul, to perform the words of the
covenant written in this book.
32 Moreover, he made all who were present in Jerusalem and

33 [1]Lit *days* [a]2 Chr 34:3-7

Benjamin to stand *with him.* So the inhabitants of Jerusalem
did according to the covenant of God, the God of their fathers.
33 Josiah [a]removed all the abominations from all the lands
belonging to the sons of Israel, and made all who were present

35:1 [a]2 Kin 23:21 [b]Ex 12:6; Num 9:3

in Israel to serve the LORD their God. Throughout his [1]lifetime
they did not turn from following the LORD God of their fathers.

Chapter 35 Theme

2 [a]2 Chr 29:11

35 Then Josiah [a]celebrated the Passover to the LORD in
Jerusalem, and [b]they slaughtered the Passover *animals*
on the fourteenth *day* of the first month.

2 Kings 23

2 He set the priests in their offices and [a]encouraged them in

3 [a]2 Chr 17:8, 9; Neh 8:7 [b]1 Chr 23:26

the service of the house of the LORD.
3 He also said to [a]the Levites who taught all Israel *and* who
were holy to the LORD, "Put the holy ark in the house which
Solomon the son of David king of Israel built; [b]it will be a
burden on *your* shoulders no longer. Now serve the LORD your

4 [a]1 Chr 9:10-13 [b]2 Chr 8:14

God and His people Israel.
4 "[a]Prepare *yourselves* by your fathers' households in your
divisions, according to the writing of David king of Israel and
[b]according to the writing of his son Solomon.
5 "Moreover, [a]stand in the holy place according to the sections

5 [1]Lit *sons of the people,* and so throughout the ch [a]Ezra 6:18

of the fathers' households of your brethren the [1]lay people, and
according to the Levites, by division of a father's household.
6 "Now [a]slaughter the Passover *animals,* [b]sanctify yourselves
and prepare for your brethren to do according to the word of
the LORD by Moses."
7 Josiah contributed to the lay people, to all who were

6 [a]2 Chr 35:1 [b]2 Chr 29:5

present, flocks of lambs and young goats, all for the Passover
offerings, numbering 30,000 plus 3,000 bulls; these were from
the king's possessions.
8 His officers also contributed a freewill offering to the

8 [a]2 Chr 31:13

people, the priests and the Levites. Hilkiah and Zechariah and
Jehiel, [a]the officials of the house of God, gave to the priests for
the Passover offerings 2,600 *from the flocks* and 300 bulls.
9 [a]Conaniah also, and Shemaiah and Nethanel, his brothers,

9 [a]2 Chr 31:12

and Hashabiah and Jeiel and Jozabad, the officers of the Levites, contributed to the Levites for the Passover offerings 5,000 *from the flocks* and 500 bulls.

10 [a]2 Chr 35:5

10 So the service was prepared, and [a]the priests stood at their stations and the Levites by their divisions according to the king's command.

11 [1]I.e. the Levites [2]So with Gr [a]2 Chr 35:1, 6 [b]2 Chr 29:22 [c]2 Chr 29:34

11 [1a]They slaughtered the Passover *animals,* and while [b]the priests sprinkled [2]the blood *received* from their hand, [c]the Levites skinned *them.*

12 Then they removed the burnt offerings that *they* might give them to the sections of the fathers' households of the lay people to present to the LORD, as it is written in the book of Moses. *They did* this also with the bulls.

13 [a]Ex 12:8, 9 [b]Lev 6:28

13 So [a]they roasted the Passover *animals* on the fire according to the ordinance, and they boiled [b]the holy things in pots, in kettles, in pans, and carried *them* speedily to all the lay people.

14 Afterwards they prepared for themselves and for the priests, because the priests, the sons of Aaron, *were* offering the burnt offerings and the fat until night; therefore the Levites prepared for themselves and for the priests, the sons of Aaron.

15 [a]1 Chr 25:1 [b]1 Chr 26:12-19

15 The singers, the sons of Asaph, *were* also at their stations [a]according to the command of David, Asaph, Heman, and Jeduthun the king's seer; and [b]the gatekeepers at each gate did not have to depart from their service, because the Levites their brethren prepared for them.

16 So all the service of the LORD was prepared on that day to celebrate the Passover, and to offer burnt offerings on the altar of the LORD according to the command of King Josiah.

17 [a]Ex 12:1-20; 2 Chr 30:21

17 Thus [a]the sons of Israel who were present celebrated the Passover at that time, and the Feast of Unleavened Bread seven days.

18 [a]2 Kin 23:21; 2 Chr 30:5

18 [a]There had not been celebrated a Passover like it in Israel since the days of Samuel the prophet; nor had any of the kings of Israel celebrated such a Passover as Josiah did with the priests, the Levites, all Judah and Israel who were present, and the inhabitants of Jerusalem.

19 In the eighteenth year of Josiah's reign this Passover was celebrated.

20 [1]Lit *house* [a]2 Kin 23:29, 30 [b]Is 10:9; Jer 46:2

20 [a]After all this, when Josiah had set the [1]temple in order, Neco king of Egypt came up to make war at [b]Carchemish on the Euphrates, and Josiah went out to engage him.

21 [1]Lit *he* [a]2 Chr 25:19

21 But [1]Neco sent messengers to him, saying, "[a]What have we to do with each other, O King of Judah? *I am* not *coming* against you today but against the house with which I am at war, and God has ordered me to hurry. Stop for your own sake from *interfering with* God who is with me, so that He will not destroy you."

22 [1]Lit *his face* [a]2 Chr 18:29 [b]2 Chr 35:21 [c]Judg 5:19

22 However, Josiah would not turn [1]away from him, but [a]disguised himself in order to make war with him; nor did he listen to the words of Neco [b]from the mouth of God, but came to make war on the plain of [c]Megiddo.

23 The archers shot King Josiah, and the king said to his servants, "Take me away, for I am badly wounded."

24 So his servants took him out of the chariot and carried him
in the second chariot which he had, and brought him to
Jerusalem [1]where he died and was buried in the tombs of his
fathers. [a]All Judah and Jerusalem mourned for Josiah.
25 Then [a]Jeremiah chanted a lament for Josiah. And all the male
and female singers speak about Josiah in their lamentations to
this day. And they made them an ordinance in Israel; behold,
they are also written in the Lamentations.
26 Now the rest of the acts of Josiah and his deeds of devotion
as written in the law of the LORD,
27 and his acts, first to last, behold, they are written in the
Book of the Kings of Israel and Judah.

Chapter 36 Theme ____________________

36 [a]Then the people of the land took [1b]Joahaz the son of
Josiah, and made him king in place of his father in
Jerusalem.
2 Joahaz was twenty-three years old when he became king, and
he reigned three months in Jerusalem.
3 Then the king of Egypt deposed him at Jerusalem, and
imposed on the land a fine of one hundred talents of silver and
one talent of gold.
4 The king of Egypt made Eliakim his brother king over Judah
and Jerusalem, and changed his name to Jehoiakim. But [a]Neco
took Joahaz his brother and brought him to Egypt.
5 [a]Jehoiakim was twenty-five years old when he became
king, and he reigned eleven years in Jerusalem; and he did evil
in the sight of the LORD his God.
6 Nebuchadnezzar king of Babylon came up [a]against him and
[b]bound him with bronze *chains* to take him to Babylon.
7 [a]Nebuchadnezzar also brought *some* of the articles of the
house of the LORD to Babylon and put them in his temple at
Babylon.
8 [a]Now the rest of the acts of Jehoiakim and [1]the abominations
which he did, and what was found against him, behold, they
are written in the Book of the Kings of Israel and Judah. And
Jehoiachin his son became king in his place.
9 [a]Jehoiachin was eight years old when he became king, and
he reigned three months and ten days in Jerusalem, and he did
evil in the sight of the LORD.
10 [a]At the turn of the year King Nebuchadnezzar sent and
brought him to Babylon with the valuable articles of the house
of the LORD, and he made his kinsman [b]Zedekiah king over
Judah and Jerusalem.
11 [a]Zedekiah was twenty-one years old when he became king,
and he reigned eleven years in Jerusalem.
12 He did evil in the sight of the LORD his God; [a]he did not
humble himself [b]before Jeremiah the prophet [1]who spoke for
the LORD.
13 [a]He also rebelled against King Nebuchadnezzar who had

609 B.C.

597 B.C.

2 Kings 24

597 B.C.

2 Kings 24

24 [1]Lit *and* [a]Zech 12:11
25 [a]Jer 22:10; Lam 4:20
36:1 [1]I.e. short form of Jehoahaz [a]2 Kin 23:30-34 [b]Jer 22:11
4 [a]Jer 22:10-12
5 [a]2 Kin 23:36, 37; Jer 22:13-19; 26:1; 35:1
6 [a]2 Kin 24:1; Jer 25:1-9 [b]2 Chr 33:11
7 [a]2 Kin 24:13
8 [1]Lit *his* [a]2 Kin 24:5
9 [a]2 Kin 24:8-17
10 [a]2 Sam 11:1; Jer 22:25; 24:1; 29:1; Ezek 17:12 [b]Jer 37:1
11 [a]2 Kin 24:18-20; Jer 27:1; 28:1; 52:1
12 [1]Lit *from the mouth of the LORD* [a]2 Chr 33:23 [b]Jer 21:3-7
13 [a]Jer 52:3; Ezek 17:15

made him swear *allegiance* by God. But [b]he stiffened his neck
and hardened his heart against turning to the LORD God of
Israel.
14 Furthermore, all the officials of the priests and the people
were very unfaithful *following* all the abominations of the
nations; and they defiled the house of the LORD which He had
sanctified in Jerusalem.
15 The LORD, the God of their fathers, [a]sent *word* to them
again and again by His messengers, because He had compassion on His people and on His dwelling place;
16 but they *continually* [a]mocked the messengers of God,
[b]despised His words and scoffed at His prophets, [c]until the
wrath of the LORD arose against His people, until there was no
remedy.
17 [a]Therefore He brought up against them the king of the
Chaldeans who slew their young men with the sword in the
house of their sanctuary, and had no compassion on young man
or virgin, old man or infirm; He gave *them* all into his hand.
586 B.C. 18 [a]All the articles of the house of God, great and small, and
2 Kings 25 the treasures of the house of the LORD, and the treasures of the
king and of his officers, he brought *them* all to Babylon.
19 Then [a]they burned the house of God and broke down the
wall of Jerusalem, and burned all its fortified buildings with fire
and destroyed all its valuable articles.
20 Those who had escaped from the sword he [a]carried away
to Babylon; and [b]they were servants to him and to his sons
until the rule of the kingdom of Persia,
21 [a]to fulfill the word of the LORD by the mouth of Jeremiah,
until [b]the land had enjoyed its sabbaths. [c]All the days of its
desolation it kept sabbath [1d]until seventy years were complete.
538 B.C. **22** [a]Now in the first year of Cyrus king of Persia—in order to
fulfill the word of the LORD [b]by the mouth of Jeremiah—the
LORD [c]stirred up the spirit of Cyrus king of Persia, so that he
sent a proclamation throughout his kingdom, and also *put it* in
writing, saying,
23 "Thus says Cyrus king of Persia, 'The LORD, the God of
heaven, has given me all the kingdoms of the earth, and He has
appointed me to build Him a house in Jerusalem, which is in
Judah. Whoever there is among you of all His people, may the
LORD his God be with him, and let him go up!' "

13 [b]2 Chr 30:8
15 [a]Jer 7:13; 25:3
16 [a]2 Chr 30:10; Jer 5:12, 13 [b]Prov 1:24-32 [c]Ezra 5:12
17 [a]2 Kin 25:1-7; Jer 21:1-10
18 [a]2 Chr 36:7, 10
19 [a]1 Kin 9:8; 2 Kin 25:9; Jer 52:13
20 [a]2 Kin 25:11 [b]Jer 27:7
21 [1]Lit *to fulfill seventy years* [a]Jer 29:10 [b]Lev 26:34 [c]Lev 25:4 [d]Jer 25:11
22 [a]Ezra 1:1-3 [b]Jer 25:12; 29:10 [c]Is 44:28

2 Chronicles at a Glance

Theme of 2 Chronicles:

Author:

Date:

Purpose:

Key Words:

house

ark

covenant

cry (cried)

seek (sought)

heart

pray
(prayer, prayed)

prophet(s)

sin

rebellion

glory of the
Lord (cloud)

the Spirit

humble

pride

Segment Divisions			Chapter Themes
			1
			2
			3
			4
			5
			6
			7
			8
			9
			10
			11
			12
			13
			14
			15
			16
			17
			18
			19
			20
			21
			22
			23
			24
			25
			26
			27
			28
			29
			30
			31
			32
			33
			34
			35
			36

EZRA עזרא

EZRA

Every seventh year the land was to lie fallow. This was God's ordinance to His people, part of His law by which they were to govern their lives.

However, for 490 years God's people had not paid attention to this statute, nor to others. The land had missed 70 Sabbaths. As prophesied by Jeremiah, God would exact 70 years for the land. Then the Spirit of God would move on behalf of His people. He would stir up the spirit of Cyrus, king of Persia, so that Cyrus would send out a written decree proclaiming, "The LORD, the God of heaven, has given me all the kingdoms of the earth, and He has appointed me to build Him a house in Jerusalem, which is in Judah. Whoever there is among you of all His people, may the LORD his God be with him, and let him go up!" (2 Chronicles 36:23).

And so a remnant returned from the land of exile to the land promised to Abraham, Isaac, and Jacob as an everlasting possession. Ezra tells us what happened.

THINGS TO DO

To better understand Ezra, look at Isaiah's prophecy in 44:28–45:7. This was written about 100 years before Cyrus was born.

Ezra falls into two main segments: chapters 1 through 6 and chapters 7 through 10. There is a lapse of approximately 58 to 60 years between these two segments.

Chapters 1–6

1. Read this segment chapter by chapter and do the following:
   a. In a distinctive way mark in the text the key words listed on the EZRA AT A GLANCE chart on page 779.
   b. Pay attention to any references to time. Mark these with a clock.
   c. When you come to a reference of a particular king, mark it and consult the historical chart THE TIMES OF EZRA, NEHEMIAH, AND ESTHER on page 764. This will help you appreciate the historical setting of the book of Ezra and see the relationship of Ezra to Esther and Nehemiah, who were contemporaries of Ezra.
   d. If specific people play a significant role, record their names in the margin and briefly describe what they did.

2. There are seven official documents or letters in the book of Ezra, all of which (except the first) were written in Aramaic, the international language of the times. The first document, written by Cyrus, the Persian king, is in Hebrew. These documents or letters are found in Ezra 1:2-4; 4:11-16; 4:17-22; 5:7-17; 6:2-5; and 6:6-12. The last one is in the second segment of the book, 7:12-26.

As you come to each document or letter in the text, underline who presented it. Then in the margin list the major points of the document or letter. This information will help you keep track of the opposition the Jews faced and how God moved on their behalf.

3. After you finish reading each chapter, identify the main subject, theme, or event and record it in your Bible next to the chapter number and on EZRA AT A GLANCE.

4. The book of Ezra records when the temple construction began and when it was completed. Write this information in the margin in bold print so you can easily find it.

5. For a better understanding of the Jewish feasts, consult the chart THE FEASTS OF ISRAEL on pages 214 and 215.

Chapters 7–10

1. This is the first time Ezra's name appears in this book. Note how he is described. Observe this man and the lessons you can learn from his life. List your insights in the margin under LFL, "Lessons for Life."

2. Mark key words as before, but add these to your list: every reference to *sin (iniquity, abomination, unfaithfulness*, etc.), *fast*, *covenant*, *guilt*, and *remnant*. Also, note your insights on the last official document in 7:12-26.

3. Watch for and mark references to time and to kings. Note these as you did before.

4. Record the theme of each chapter as you did in the first segment of Ezra.

5. How does the second segment of Ezra, chapters 7 through 10, differ from the first?

   a. Record the theme or subject of the first six chapters on EZRA AT A GLANCE under "Segment Divisions." Do the same for the last segment, chapters 7 through 10.

   b. On the second line for segment divisions write in the name(s) of the central character(s) of each segment.

   c. Consult the historical chart THE TIMES OF EZRA, NEHEMIAH, AND ESTHER on page 764 and then record on the chart the number of years covered in each segment.

6. What is the theme or teaching of Ezra? Record this and any other requested information in the appropriate place on EZRA AT A GLANCE.

Things to Think About

1. How did the people in Ezra's time deal with their sin? What showed you whether their sorrow led to repentance or simply regret? How do you deal with sin in your own life? How is it dealt with within your church congregation?

2. What did you learn about prayer and fasting? Are either of these integral parts of your walk with the Lord? Why?

3. As you review what you have learned in Ezra, what have you learned about God, His promises, and His ways? What difference can this knowledge make in your life?

Chapter 1 Theme ________________

1:1 [a]2 Chr 36:22; Jer 25:12; 29:10 [b]Ezra 5:13

1 [a]Now in the first year of Cyrus king of Persia, in order to fulfill the word of the LORD by the mouth of Jeremiah, the LORD
stirred up the spirit of Cyrus king of Persia, so that he [b]sent a
proclamation throughout all his kingdom, and also *put it* in
writing, saying:

2 [a]Is 44:28; 45:1, 12, 13

2 "Thus says Cyrus king of Persia, 'The LORD, the God of heaven,
has given me all the kingdoms of the earth and [a]He has appointed
me to build Him a house in Jerusalem, which is in Judah.

3 [a]1 Kin 8:23; 18:39; Is 37:16; Dan 6:26

3 'Whoever there is among you of all His people, may his God
be with him! Let him go up to Jerusalem which is in Judah and
rebuild the house of the LORD, the God of Israel; [a]He is the God
who is in Jerusalem.

4 'Every survivor, at whatever place he may [1]live, let the men
of [2]that place support him with silver and gold, with goods and
cattle, together with a freewill offering for the house of God
which is in Jerusalem.'"

4 [1]Or *reside as an alien* [2]Lit *his*

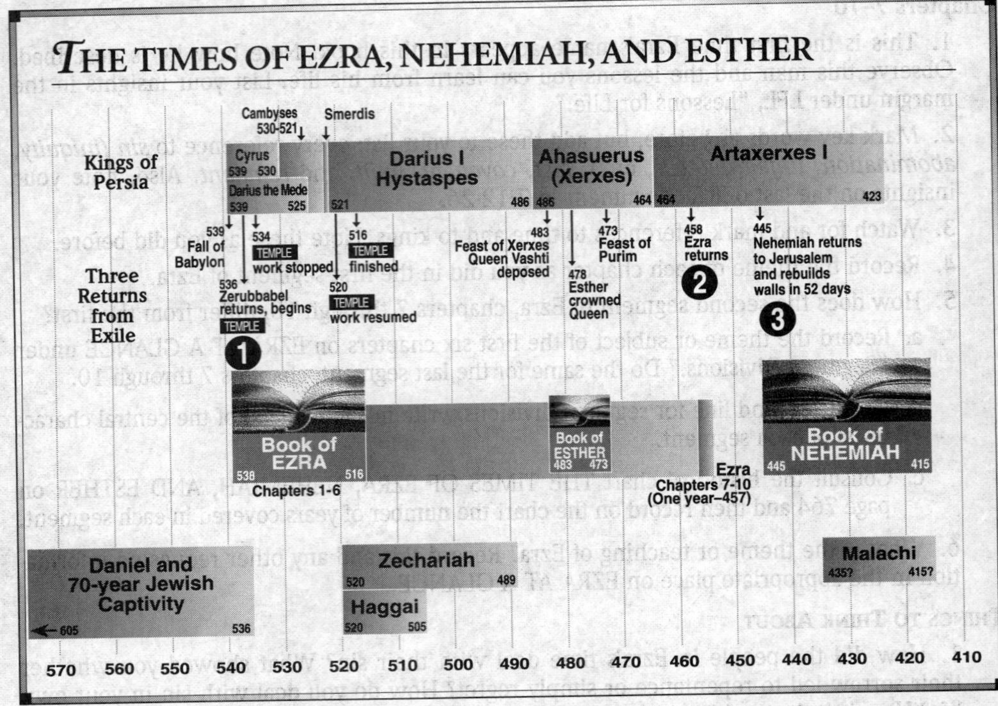

5 Then the heads of fathers' *households* of Judah and Benjamin
and the priests and the Levites arose, [a]even everyone whose
spirit God had stirred to go up and rebuild the house of the
LORD which is in Jerusalem.
6 All those about them [1a]encouraged them with articles of
silver, with gold, with goods, with cattle and with valuables,
aside from all that was given as a freewill offering.
7 [a]Also King Cyrus brought out the articles of the house of
the LORD, [b]which Nebuchadnezzar had carried away from
Jerusalem and put in the house of his gods;
8 and Cyrus, king of Persia, had them brought out by the
hand of Mithredath the treasurer, and he counted them out to
[a]Sheshbazzar, the prince of Judah.
9 Now this *was* their number: 30 [a]gold dishes, 1,000 silver
dishes, 29 [1]duplicates;
10 30 gold bowls, 410 silver bowls of a second *kind and* 1,000
other articles.
11 All the articles of gold and silver *numbered* 5,400. Sheshbazzar brought them all up with the exiles who went up from
Babylon to Jerusalem.

5 [a]Ezra 1:1, 2

6 [1]Lit *strengthened their hands* [a]Neh 6:9; Is 35:3

7 [a]Ezra 5:14; 6:5 [b]2 Kin 24:13; 2 Chr 36:7

8 [a]Ezra 5:14

9 [1]Heb obscure; other possible meanings are *knives, censers* [a]Ezra 8:27

Chapter 2 Theme ______________________

2 [a]Now these are the [1]people of the province who came up
out of the captivity of the exiles whom Nebuchadnezzar

2:1 [1]Lit *sons* [a]2 Kin 24:14-16; 25:11; 2 Chr 36:20; Neh 7:6-73

the king of Babylon had carried away to Babylon, and returned
to Jerusalem and Judah, each to his city.
2 [1]These came with Zerubbabel, Jeshua, Nehemiah, [2]Seraiah,
[3]Reelaiah, Mordecai, Bilshan, [4]Mispar, Bigvai, [5]Rehum *and*
Baanah.

The number of the men of the people of Israel:
3 the sons of Parosh, 2,172;
4 the sons of Shephatiah, 372;
5 the sons of [a]Arah, 775;
6 the sons of [a]Pahath-moab of the sons of Jeshua *and* Joab,
2,812;
7 the sons of Elam, 1,254;
8 the sons of Zattu, 945;
9 the sons of Zaccai, 760;
10 the sons of [1]Bani, 642;
11 the sons of Bebai, 623;
12 the sons of Azgad, 1,222;
13 the sons of [a]Adonikam, 666;
14 the sons of Bigvai, 2,056;
15 the sons of Adin, 454;
16 the sons of Ater of Hezekiah, 98;
17 the sons of Bezai, 323;
18 the sons of [1]Jorah, 112;
19 the sons of Hashum, 223;
20 the sons of [1]Gibbar, 95;
21 the [1]men of [a]Bethlehem, 123;
22 the men of Netophah, 56;
23 the men of Anathoth, 128;
24 the sons of [1]Azmaveth, 42;
25 the sons of [1]Kiriath-arim, Chephirah and Beeroth, 743;
26 the sons of [a]Ramah and Geba, 621;
27 the men of Michmas, 122;
28 the men of Bethel and Ai, 223;
29 the sons of Nebo, 52;
30 the sons of Magbish, 156;
31 the sons of the other Elam, 1,254;
32 the sons of Harim, 320;
33 the sons of Lod, Hadid and Ono, 725;
34 the [1]men of [a]Jericho, 345;
35 the sons of Senaah, 3,630.
36 [a]The priests: the sons of Jedaiah of the house of Jeshua, 973;
37 the sons of [a]Immer, 1,052;
38 [a]the sons of Pashhur, 1,247;
39 the sons of [a]Harim, 1,017.
40 The Levites: the sons of Jeshua and Kadmiel, of the sons of
[1]Hodaviah, 74.
41 The singers: the sons of Asaph, 128.
42 The sons of the gatekeepers: the sons of Shallum, the sons of
Ater, the sons of Talmon, the sons of Akkub, the sons of Hatita,
the sons of Shobai, in all 139.
43 The [a]temple servants: the sons of Ziha, the sons of
Hasupha, the sons of Tabbaoth,

2 [1]Lit *who* [2]In Neh 7:7, *Azariah* [3]In Neh 7:7, *Raamiah* [4]In Neh 7:7, *Mispereth* [5]In Neh 7:7, *Nehum*

5 [a]Neh 7:10

6 [a]Neh 7:11

10 [1]In Neh 7:15, *Binnui*

13 [a]Ezra 8:13

18 [1]In Neh 7:24, *Hariph*

20 [1]In Neh 7:25, *Gibeon*

21 [1]Lit *sons* [a]Gen 35:19; Matt 2:6

24 [1]In Neh 7:28, *Beth-azmaveth*

25 [1]In Neh 7:29, *Kiriath-jearim*

26 [a]Josh 18:25

34 [1]Lit *sons* [a]1 Kin 16:34; 2 Chr 28:15

36 [a]1 Chr 24:7-18

37 [a]1 Chr 24:14

38 [a]1 Chr 9:12

39 [a]1 Chr 24:8

40 [1]In Ezra 3:9, *Judah;* in Neh 7:43, *Hodevah*

43 [a]1 Chr 9:2

44 the sons of Keros, the sons of [1]Siaha, the sons of Padon,
45 the sons of Lebanah, the sons of Hagabah, the sons of Akkub,
46 the sons of Hagab, the sons of Shalmai, the sons of Hanan,
47 the sons of Giddel, the sons of Gahar, the sons of Reaiah,
48 the sons of Rezin, the sons of Nekoda, the sons of Gazzam,
49 the sons of Uzza, the sons of Paseah, the sons of Besai,
50 the sons of Asnah, the sons of Meunim, the sons of [1]Nephisim,
51 the sons of Bakbuk, the sons of Hakupha, the sons of Harhur,
52 the sons of [1]Bazluth, the sons of Mehida, the sons of Harsha,
53 the sons of Barkos, the sons of Sisera, the sons of Temah,
54 the sons of Neziah, the sons of Hatipha.
55 The sons of [a]Solomon's servants: the sons of Sotai, the sons
of [1]Hassophereth, the sons of [2]Peruda,
56 the sons of Jaalah, the sons of Darkon, the sons of Giddel,
57 the sons of Shephatiah, the sons of Hattil, the sons of
Pochereth-hazzebaim, the sons of [1]Ami.
58 All the [a]temple servants and the sons of [b]Solomon's
servants were 392.
59 Now these are those who came up from Tel-melah, Tel-
harsha, Cherub, [1]Addan *and* Immer, but they were not able to
[2]give evidence of their fathers' households and their [3]descendants,
whether they were of Israel:
60 the sons of Delaiah, the sons of Tobiah, the sons of Nekoda,
652.
61 Of the sons of the priests: the sons of [1]Habaiah, the sons of
Hakkoz, the sons of [a]Barzillai, who took a wife from the daughters
of Barzillai the Gileadite, and he was called by their name.
62 These searched *among* their ancestral registration, but they
could not be located; [a]therefore they were considered unclean
and excluded from the priesthood.
63 The [1]governor said to them [a]that they should not eat from the
most holy things until a priest stood up with [b]Urim and Thummim.
64 The whole assembly [1]numbered 42,360,
65 besides their male and female servants [1]who numbered
7,337; and they had 200 [a]singing men and women.
66 Their horses were 736; their mules, 245;
67 their camels, 435; *their* donkeys, 6,720.
68 Some of the heads of fathers' *households,* when they
arrived at the house of the LORD which is in Jerusalem, offered
willingly for the house of God to [1]restore it on its foundation.
69 According to their ability they gave [a]to the treasury for the
work 61,000 gold drachmas and 5,000 silver minas and 100
priestly [1]garments.
70 [a]Now the priests and the Levites, some of the people, the
singers, the gatekeepers and the temple servants lived in their
cities, and all Israel in their cities.

Chapter 3 Theme ______________________________

3 Now when the seventh month came, and [a]the sons of
Israel *were* in the cities, the people gathered together as
one man to Jerusalem.

44 [1]In Neh 7:47, *Sia*

50 [1]In Neh 7:52, *Nephushesim*

52 [1]In Neh 7:54, *Bazlith*

55 [1]In Neh 7:57, *Sophereth* [2]In Neh 7:57, *Perida* [a]1 Kin 9:21

57 [1]In Neh 7:59, *Amon*

58 [a]1 Chr 9:2 [b]1 Kin 9:21

59 [1]In Neh 7:61, *Addon* [2]Lit *tell* [3]Lit *seed*

61 [1]In Neh 7:63, *Hobaiah* [a]2 Sam 17:27; 1 Kin 2:7

62 [a]Num 16:39, 40

63 [1]Heb *Tirshatha,* a Persian title [a]Lev 2:3, 10 [b]Ex 28:30; Num 27:21

64 [1]Lit *together was*

65 [1]Lit *they were* [a]2 Chr 35:25

68 [1]Lit *establish*

69 [1]Or *tunics* [a]Ezra 8:25-34

70 [a]1 Chr 9:2; Neh 11:3

3:1 [a]Neh 7:73; 8:1

2 Then [a]Jeshua the son of Jozadak and his brothers the priests, and [b]Zerubbabel the son [c]of Shealtiel and his brothers arose and [d]built the altar of the God of Israel to offer burnt offerings on it, [e]as it is written in the law of Moses, the man of God.

3 So they set up the altar on its foundation, for [1a]they were terrified because of the peoples of the lands; and they [b]offered burnt offerings on it to the LORD, burnt offerings morning and evening.

4 They celebrated the [a]Feast of [1]Booths, [b]as it is written, and *offered* [2]the fixed number of burnt offerings daily, [c]according to the ordinance, as each day required;

5 and afterward *there was* a [a]continual burnt offering, also [b]for the new moons and [c]for all the fixed festivals of the LORD that were consecrated, and from everyone who offered a freewill offering to the LORD.

6 From the first day of the seventh month they began to offer burnt offerings to the LORD, but the foundation of the temple of the LORD had not been laid.

7 Then they gave money to the masons and carpenters, and [a]food, drink and oil to the Sidonians and to the Tyrians, [b]to bring cedar wood from Lebanon to the sea at [c]Joppa, according to the permission they had [1]from [d]Cyrus king of Persia.

8 Now in the second year of their coming to the house of God at Jerusalem in the second month, [a]Zerubbabel the son of Shealtiel and Jeshua the son of Jozadak and the rest of their brothers the priests and the Levites, and all who came from the captivity to Jerusalem, began *the work* and [b]appointed the Levites from twenty years and older to oversee the work of the house of the LORD.

9 Then [a]Jeshua *with* his sons and brothers stood united *with* Kadmiel and his sons, the sons of [1]Judah *and* the sons of Henadad *with* their sons and brothers the Levites, to oversee the workmen in the temple of God.

10 Now when the builders had [a]laid the foundation of the temple of the LORD, [1]the priests stood in their apparel with trumpets, and the Levites, the sons of Asaph, with cymbals, to praise the LORD [b]according to the [2]directions of King David of Israel.

11 [a]They sang, praising and giving thanks to the LORD, *saying,* "[b]For He is good, for His lovingkindness is upon Israel forever." And all the people shouted with a great shout when they praised the LORD because the foundation of the house of the LORD was laid.

12 Yet many of the priests and Levites and heads of fathers' *households,* [a]the old men who had seen the first [1]temple, wept with a loud voice when the foundation of this house was laid before their eyes, while many shouted aloud for joy,

13 so that the people could not distinguish the sound of the shout of joy from the sound of the weeping of the people, for the people shouted with a loud shout, and the sound was heard far away.

2 [a]Neh 12:1, 8 [b]Ezra 2:2; Hag 1:1; 2:2 [c]1 Chr 3:17 [d]Ex 27:1 [e]Deut 12:5, 6

3 [1]Lit *terror* was *upon them* [a]Ezra 4:4 [b]Num 28:2

4 [1]Or *Tabernacles* [2]Lit *by number* [a]Neh 8:14; Zech 14:16 [b]Ex 23:16 [c]Num 29:12

5 [a]Ex 29:38; Num 28:3 [b]Num 28:11 [c]Num 29:39

7 [1]Lit *of* [a]2 Chr 2:10; Acts 12:20 [b]2 Chr 2:16 [c]Acts 9:36 [d]Ezra 1:2; 6:3

8 [a]Ezra 3:2; 4:3 [b]1 Chr 23:4, 24

9 [1]In Ezra 2:40, *Hodaviah* [a]Ezra 2:40

10 [1]So with the Gr and some mss; M.T. *they set the priests* [2]Lit *hands* [a]Zech 4:6-10 [b]1 Chr 6:31; 25:1

11 [a]2 Chr 7:3; Neh 12:24, 40 [b]1 Chr 16:34; 2 Chr 5:13; Ps 100:5; 106:1; 107:1; 118:1; 131:1; Jer 33:11

12 [1]Lit *house* [a]Hag 2:3

Chapter 4 Theme ______________________________

4 Now when [a]the enemies of Judah and Benjamin heard that
[b]the people of the exile were building a temple to the LORD
God of Israel,
2 they approached Zerubbabel and the heads of fathers' *house-*
holds, and said to them, "Let us build with you, for we, like you,
seek your God; [a]and we have been sacrificing to Him since the
days of [b]Esarhaddon king of Assyria, who brought us up here."
3 But Zerubbabel and Jeshua and the rest of the heads of
fathers' *households* of Israel said to them, "[a]You have nothing
in common with us in building a house to our God; but we
ourselves will together build to the LORD God of Israel, [b]as King
Cyrus, the king of Persia has commanded us."
4 Then [a]the people of the land [1]discouraged the people of
Judah, and frightened them from building,
5 and hired counselors against them to frustrate their counsel
all the days of Cyrus king of Persia, even until the reign of
Darius king of Persia.
6 Now in the reign of [1a]Ahasuerus, in the beginning of his
reign, they wrote an accusation against the inhabitants of Judah
and Jerusalem.
7 And in the days of [1]Artaxerxes, Bishlam, Mithredath, Tabeel
and the rest of his colleagues wrote to Artaxerxes king of
Persia; and the [2]text of the letter was written in Aramaic and
translated [a]*from* Aramaic.
8 [1]Rehum the commander and Shimshai the scribe wrote a
letter against Jerusalem to King Artaxerxes, as follows—
9 then *wrote* Rehum the commander and Shimshai the scribe
and [a]the rest of their colleagues, the judges and [b]the lesser
governors, the officials, the secretaries, the men of Erech, the
Babylonians, the men of Susa, that is, the Elamites,
10 and the rest of the nations which the great and honorable
[1]Osnappar deported and settled in the city of Samaria, and in
the rest of the region beyond the [2]River. [a]Now
11 this is the copy of the letter which they sent to him:
"To King Artaxerxes: Your servants, the men in the region
beyond the River, and now
12 let it be known to the king that the Jews who came up
from you have come to us at Jerusalem; they are rebuilding
[a]the rebellious and evil city and [b]are finishing the walls and
repairing the foundations.
13 "Now let it be known to the king, that if that city is rebuilt
and the walls are finished, [a]they will not pay tribute, custom or
toll, and it will damage the revenue of the kings.
14 "Now because we [1]are in the service of the palace, and it is
not fitting for us to see the king's dishonor, therefore we have
sent and informed the king,
15 so that a search may be made in the record books of your
fathers. And you will discover in the record books and learn
that that city is a rebellious city and damaging to kings and
provinces, and that they have incited revolt within it in past
days; therefore that city was laid waste.

4:1 [a]Ezra 4:7-10 [b]Ezra 1:11

2 [a]2 Kin 17:32 [b]2 Kin 19:37

3 [a]Neh 2:20 [b]Ezra 1:1, 2

4 [1]Lit *weakened the hands of* [a]Ezra 3:3

6 [1]Or *Xerxes;* Heb *Ahash-verosh* [a]Esth 1:1; Dan 9:1

7 [1]Heb *Artah-shashta* [2]Lit *writing* [a]2 Kin 18:26; Dan 2:4

8 [1]Ch 4:8-6:18 is in Aram

9 [a]2 Kin 17:24 [b]Ezra 5:6; 6:6

10 [1]I.e. probably Ashurbanipal [2]I.e. Euphrates River, and so throughout the ch [a]Ezra 4:11, 17; 7:12

12 [a]2 Chr 36:13 [b]Ezra 5:3, 9

13 [a]Ezra 4:20; 7:24

14 [1]Lit *eat the salt*

18 [1]Lit *plainly read before* [a]Neh 8:8
19 [1]Lit *put* forth
20 [1]Lit *been* [a]1 Kin 4:21; 1 Chr 18:3 [b]Gen 15:18; Josh 1:4 [c]Ezra 4:13; 7:24
5:1 [a]Hag 1:1 [b]Zech 1:1
2 [a]Ezra 3:2; Hag 1:12; Zech 4:6-9 [b]Ezra 6:14; Hag 2:4; Zech 3:1
3 [1]I.e. Euphrates River, and so throughout the ch [2]Lit *house,* and so in vv 9, 11, 12 [a]Ezra 6:6, 13 [b]Ezra 1:3; 5:9
4 [a]Ezra 5:10
5 [a]Ezra 7:6, 28
6 [a]Ezra 5:3 [b]Ezra 4:9

16 "We inform the king that if that city is rebuilt and the walls
finished, as a result you will have no possession in *the province*
beyond the River."
17 *Then* the king sent an answer to Rehum the commander, to
Shimshai the scribe, and to the rest of their colleagues who live
in Samaria and in the rest of *the provinces* beyond the River:
"Peace. And now
18 the document which you sent to us has been [1a]translated
and read before me.
19 "A decree has been [1]issued by me, and a search has been
made and it has been discovered that that city has risen up
against the kings in past days, that rebellion and revolt have
been perpetrated in it,
20 [a]that mighty kings have [1]ruled over Jerusalem, governing
all *the provinces* [b]beyond the River, and that [c]tribute, custom
and toll were paid to them.
21 "So, now issue a decree to make these men stop *work,* that
this city may not be rebuilt until a decree is issued by me.
22 "Beware of being negligent in carrying out this *matter;* why
should damage increase to the detriment of the kings?"
23 Then as soon as the copy of King Artaxerxes' document
was read before Rehum and Shimshai the scribe and their
colleagues, they went in haste to Jerusalem to the Jews and
stopped them by force of arms.
24 Then work on the house of God in Jerusalem ceased, and it
was stopped until the second year of the reign of Darius king of
Persia.

Chapter 5 Theme ____________

5 When the prophets, [a]Haggai the prophet and [b]Zechariah the
son of Iddo, prophesied to the Jews who were in Judah and
Jerusalem in the name of the God of Israel, who was over them,
2 then [a]Zerubbabel the son of Shealtiel and Jeshua the son of
Jozadak arose and began to rebuild the house of God which is
in Jerusalem; and [b]the prophets of God were with them
supporting them.
3 At that time [a]Tattenai, the governor of *the province* beyond
the [1]River, and Shethar-bozenai and their colleagues came to
them and spoke to them thus, "[b]Who issued you a decree to
rebuild this [2]temple and to finish this structure?"
4 [a]Then we told them accordingly what the names of the
men were who were reconstructing this building.
5 But [a]the eye of their God was on the elders of the Jews,
and they did not stop them until a report could come to Darius,
and then a written reply be returned concerning it.
6 *This is* the copy of the letter which [a]Tattenai, the governor
of *the province* beyond the River, and Shethar-bozenai and his
colleagues [b]the officials, who were beyond the River, sent to
Darius the king.
7 They sent a report to him in which it was written thus: "To
Darius the king, all peace.

8 "Let it be known to the king that we have gone to the province
of Judah, to the house of the great God, which is being built with
huge stones, and [1]beams are being laid in the walls; and this work
is going on with great care and is succeeding in their hands.
9 "Then we asked those elders and said to them thus, 'Who
issued you a decree to rebuild this temple and to finish this
structure?'
10 "We also asked them their names so as to inform you, and
that we might write down the names of the men who were at
their head.
11 "Thus they [1]answered us, saying, 'We are the servants of
the God of heaven and earth and are rebuilding the temple that
was built many years ago, [a]which a great king of Israel built
and finished.
12 'But [a]because our fathers had provoked the God of heaven
to wrath, [b]He gave them into the hand of Nebuchadnezzar king
of Babylon, the Chaldean, *who* destroyed this temple and
deported the people to Babylon.
13 'However, [a]in the first year of Cyrus king of Babylon, King
Cyrus [b]issued a decree to rebuild this house of God.
14 'Also [a]the gold and silver utensils of the house of God which
Nebuchadnezzar had taken from the temple [1]in Jerusalem, and
brought them to the temple of Babylon, these King Cyrus took
from the temple of Babylon and they were given to one [b]whose
name was Sheshbazzar, whom he had appointed governor.
15 'He said to him, "Take these utensils, go *and* deposit them
in the temple [1]in Jerusalem and let the house of God be rebuilt
in its place."
16 'Then that Sheshbazzar came *and* [a]laid the foundations of
the house of God [1]in Jerusalem; and from then until now it has
been under construction and it is [b]not *yet* completed.'
17 "Now if it pleases the king, [a]let a search be conducted in the
king's treasure house, which is there in Babylon, if it be that a
decree was issued by King Cyrus to rebuild this house of God at
Jerusalem; and let the king send to us his decision concerning
this *matter*."

Chapter 6 Theme ____________________

6 Then King Darius issued a decree, and [a]search was made in
the [1]archives, where the treasures were stored in Babylon.
2 In [1]Ecbatana in the fortress, which is [a]in the province of
Media, a scroll was found and there was written in it as follows:
"Memorandum—
3 "[a]In the first year of King Cyrus, Cyrus the king issued a
decree: '*Concerning* the house of God at Jerusalem, let the
[1]temple, the place where sacrifices are offered, be rebuilt and
let its foundations be [2]retained, its height being 60 cubits and
its width 60 cubits;
4 [a]with three layers of huge stones and [1]one layer of timbers.
And let the cost be paid from the [2]royal treasury.

8 [1]Lit *timber is*

11 [1]Lit *returned us the word* [a]1 Kin 6:1, 38

12 [a]2 Chr 36:16, 17 [b]2 Kin 25:8-11; Jer 52:12-15

13 [a]Ezra 1:1 [b]Ezra 1:1-4

14 [1]Lit *that was in* [a]Ezra 1:7; 6:5; Dan 5:2 [b]Ezra 1:8; 5:16

15 [1]Lit *that is in*

16 [1]Lit *that is in* [a]Ezra 3:8, 10 [b]Ezra 6:15

17 [a]Ezra 6:1, 2

6:1 [1]Lit *house of the books* [a]Ezra 5:17

2 [1]Aram *Achmetha* [a]2 Kin 17:6

3 [1]Lit *house* [2]Or *fixed, laid* [a]Ezra 1:1; 5:13

4 [1]So Gr; Aram *a layer of new timber* [2]Lit *king's house* [a]1 Kin 6:36

5 'Also let [a]the gold and silver utensils of the house of God,
which Nebuchadnezzar took from the temple in Jerusalem and
brought to Babylon, be returned and [1]brought to their places in
the temple in Jerusalem; and you shall put *them* in the house of
God.'
6 "Now *therefore,* [a]Tattenai, governor of *the province* beyond
the [1]River, Shethar-bozenai and [2]your colleagues, the officials of
the provinces beyond the [1]River, [3]keep away from there.
7 "Leave this work on the house of God alone; let the governor
of the Jews and the elders of the Jews rebuild this house of God
on its site.
8 "Moreover, [a]I issue a decree concerning what you are to do
for these elders of Judah in the rebuilding of this house of God:
the full cost is to be paid to these people from the royal treasury
out of the taxes of *the provinces* beyond the River, and that
without delay.
9 "Whatever is needed, both young bulls, rams, and lambs for
a burnt offering to the God of heaven, and wheat, salt, wine
and anointing oil, as the priests in Jerusalem request, *it* is to be
given to them daily without fail,
10 that they may offer [1]acceptable sacrifices to the God of
heaven and [a]pray for the life of the king and his sons.
11 "And I issued a decree that [a]any man who violates this edict,
a timber shall be drawn from his house and he shall be impaled on
it and [b]his house shall be made a refuse heap on account of this.
12 "May the God who [a]has caused His name to dwell there
overthrow any king or people who [1]attempts to change *it,* so as
to destroy this house of God in Jerusalem. I, Darius, have
issued *this* decree, let *it* be carried out with all diligence!"
13 Then [a]Tattenai, the governor of *the province* beyond the
River, Shethar-bozenai and their colleagues carried out *the
decree* with all diligence, just as King Darius had sent.
14 And [a]the elders of the Jews [1]were successful in building
through the prophesying of Haggai the prophet and Zechariah
the son of Iddo. And [2]they finished building according to the
command of the God of Israel and the decree [b]of Cyrus, [c]Darius,
and [d]Artaxerxes king of Persia.
15 This [1]temple was completed [2]on the third day of the
[a]month Adar; it was the sixth year of the reign of King Darius.
16 And the sons of Israel, the priests, the Levites and the rest of
the [1]exiles, [a]celebrated the dedication of this house of God with joy.
17 They offered for the dedication of this temple of God 100
bulls, 200 rams, 400 lambs, and as a sin offering for all Israel [a]12
male goats, corresponding to the number of the tribes of Israel.
18 Then they appointed the priests to [a]their divisions and the
Levites in [b]their orders for the service of God [1]in Jerusalem, [c]as
it is written in the book of Moses.
19 [a]The exiles observed the Passover on [b]the fourteenth of the
first month.
20 [a]For the priests and the Levites had purified themselves
together; all of them were pure. Then [b]they slaughtered the

5 [1]Lit *go* [a]Ezra 1:7; 5:14
6 [1]I.e. Euphrates River, and so throughout the ch [2]Aram *their* [3]Lit *be distant* [a]Ezra 5:3; 6:13
8 [a]Ezra 6:4; 7:14-22
10 [1]Lit *pleasing;* or *sweet-smelling sacrifices* [a]Ezra 7:23; Jer 29:7; 1 Tim 2:1, 2
11 [a]Ezra 7:26 [b]Dan 2:5; 3:29
12 [1]Lit *sends his hand* [a]Deut 12:5, 11; 1 Kin 9:3
13 [a]Ezra 6:6
14 [1]Lit *were building and succeeding* [2]Lit *built and finished* [a]Ezra 5:1, 2 [b]Ezra 1:1; 5:13 [c]Ezra 4:24; 6:12 [d]Ezra 7:1
15 [1]Lit *house* [2]Lit *until* [a]Esth 3:7
16 [1]Lit *sons of the captivity* [a]1 Kin 8:63; 2 Chr 7:5
17 [a]Ezra 8:35
18 [1]Lit *which is in* [a]1 Chr 24:1; 2 Chr 35:5 [b]1 Chr 23:6 [c]Num 3:6; 8:9
19 [a]Ezra 1:11 [b]Ex 12:6
20 [a]2 Chr 29:34; 30:15 [b]2 Chr 35:11

Passover *lamb* for all the exiles, both for their brothers the
priests and for themselves.
21 The sons of Israel who returned from exile and [a]all those
who had separated themselves from [b]the impurity of the
nations of the land to *join* them, to seek the LORD God of Israel,
ate *the Passover.*
22 And [a]they observed the Feast of Unleavened Bread seven
days with joy, for the LORD had caused them to rejoice, and
[b]had turned the heart of [c]the king of Assyria toward them to
[1]encourage them in the work of the house of God, the God of
Israel.

Chapter 7 Theme ________________

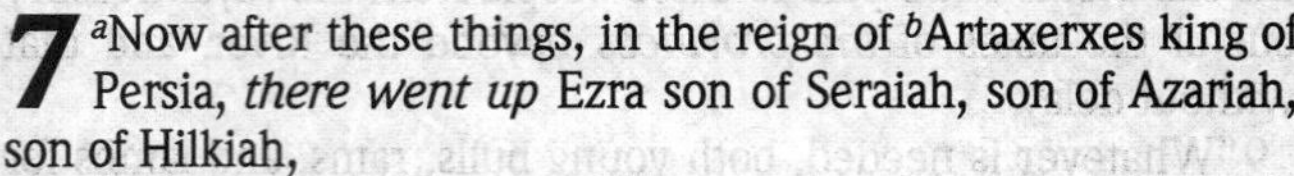

7 [a]Now after these things, in the reign of [b]Artaxerxes king of
Persia, *there went up* Ezra son of Seraiah, son of Azariah,
son of Hilkiah,
2 son of Shallum, son of Zadok, son of Ahitub,
3 son of Amariah, son of Azariah, son of Meraioth,
4 son of Zerahiah, son of Uzzi, son of Bukki,
5 son of Abishua, son of Phinehas, son of Eleazar, son of
Aaron the chief priest.
6 This Ezra went up from Babylon, and he was a [a]scribe
skilled in the law of Moses, which the LORD God of Israel had
given; and the king granted him all [1]he requested [b]because the
hand of the LORD his God *was* upon him.
7 [a]Some of the sons of Israel and some of the priests, the
Levites, the singers, the gatekeepers and the temple servants
went up to Jerusalem in the seventh year of King Artaxerxes.
8 He came to Jerusalem in the fifth month, which was in the
seventh year of the king.
9 For on the first of the first month [1]he began to go up from
Babylon; and on the first of the fifth month he came to
Jerusalem, [a]because the good hand of his God *was* upon him.
10 For Ezra had set his heart to [1]study the law of the LORD
and to practice *it,* and [a]to teach *His* statutes and ordinances in
Israel.
11 Now this is the copy of the decree which King Artaxerxes
gave to Ezra the priest, the scribe, [1]learned in the words of the
commandments of the LORD and His statutes to Israel:
12 "[1]Artaxerxes, [a]king of kings, to Ezra the priest, the scribe of
the law of the God of heaven, perfect *peace.* And now
13 [a]I have issued a decree that any of the people of Israel and
their priests and the Levites in my kingdom who are willing to
go to Jerusalem, may go with you.
14 "Forasmuch as you are sent [1]by the king and his [a]seven
counselors to inquire concerning Judah and Jerusalem according
to the law of your God which is in your hand,
15 and to bring the silver and gold, which the king and his
counselors have freely offered to the God of Israel, [a]whose
dwelling is in Jerusalem,

RETURN TO INSTRUCTIONS

21 [a]Neh 9:2; 10:28 [b]Ezra 9:11

22 [1]Lit *strengthen their hands* [a]Ex 12:15 [b]Ezra 7:27; Prov 21:1 [c]Ezra 1:1; 6:1

7:1 [a]1 Chr 6:4-14 [b]Ezra 7:12, 21; Neh 2:1

6 [1]Lit *his request* [a]Ezra 7:11, 12, 21 [b]Ezra 7:9, 28; 8:22

7 [a]Ezra 8:1-20

9 [1]Lit *was the foundation* [a]Ezra 7:6; Neh 2:8

10 [1]Lit *seek* [a]Deut 33:10; Ezra 7:25; Neh 8:1

11 [1]Lit *the scribe of*

12 [1]Ch 7:12-26 is in Aram [a]Ezek 26:7; Dan 2:37

13 [a]Ezra 6:1

14 [1]Lit *from before* [a]Ezra 7:15, 28; 8:25

15 [a]2 Chr 6:2; Ezra 6:12; Ps 135:21

16 with [a]all the silver and gold which you find in the whole
province of Babylon, along [b]with the freewill offering of the
people and of the priests, who [c]offered willingly for the house
of their God which is in Jerusalem;
17 with this money, therefore, you shall diligently buy bulls,
rams and lambs, [a]with their grain offerings and their drink
offerings and [b]offer them on the altar of the house of your God
which is in Jerusalem.
18 "Whatever seems good to you and to your brothers to do
with the rest of the silver and gold, you may do according to
the will of your God.
19 "Also the utensils which are given to you for the service of the
house of your God, deliver in full before the God of Jerusalem.
20 "The rest of the needs for the house of your God, for which
you may have occasion to provide, [a]provide *for it* from the
royal treasury.
21 "I, even I, King Artaxerxes, issue a decree to all the treasurers
who are *in the provinces* beyond the [1]River, that whatever Ezra
the priest, [a]the scribe of the law of the God of heaven, may
require of you, it shall be done diligently,
22 *even* up to 100 talents of silver, 100 [1]kors of wheat, 100
baths of wine, 100 baths of oil, and salt [2]as needed.
23 "Whatever is [1]commanded by the God of heaven, let it be
done with zeal for the house of the God of heaven, [a]so that there
will not be wrath against the kingdom of the king and his sons.
24 "We also inform you that [a]it is not allowed to [1]impose tax,
tribute or toll [b]*on* any of the priests, Levites, singers, doorkeepers,
Nethinim or servants of this house of God.
25 "You, Ezra, according to the wisdom of your God which is in
your hand, [a]appoint magistrates and judges that they may judge
all the people who are in *the province* beyond the River, *even*
all those who know the laws of your God; and you may [b]teach
anyone who is ignorant *of them.*
26 "[a]Whoever will not observe the law of your God and the law
of the king, let judgment be executed upon him strictly,
whether for death or for [1]banishment or for confiscation of
goods or for imprisonment."
27 Blessed be the LORD, the God of our fathers, [a]who has put
such a thing as this in the king's heart, to adorn the house of
the LORD which is in Jerusalem,
28 and [a]has extended lovingkindness to me before the king
and his counselors and before all the king's mighty princes.
Thus I was strengthened according to [b]the hand of the LORD my
God upon me, and I gathered [1]leading men from Israel to go up
with me.

Chapter 8 Theme ______________________

8 Now these are the heads of their fathers' *households* and
the genealogical enrollment of those who went up with me
from Babylon in the reign of King Artaxerxes:

16 [a]Ezra 8:25 [b]Ezra 1:4, 6 [c]1 Chr 29:6
17 [a]Num 15:4-13 [b]Deut 12:5-11
20 [a]Ezra 6:4
21 [1]I.e. Euphrates River, and so throughout the ch [a]Ezra 7:6
22 [1]I.e. One kor equals approx ten bu [2]Lit *without prescription*
23 [1]Lit *from the decree of* [a]Ezra 6:10
24 [1]Lit *throw on them* [a]Ezra 4:13, 20 [b]Ezra 7:7
25 [a]Ex 18:21; Deut 16:18 [b]Ezra 7:10; Mal 2:7; Col 1:28
26 [1]Lit *rooting out* [a]Ezra 6:11, 12
27 [a]Ezra 6:22
28 [1]Lit *heads* [a]Ezra 9:9 [b]Ezra 5:5

2 of the sons of Phinehas, Gershom; of the sons of Ithamar,
Daniel; of the sons of David, [a]Hattush;
3 of the sons of Shecaniah *who was* of the sons of [a]Parosh,
Zechariah and with him 150 males *who were in* the genealogical
list;
4 of the sons of Pahath-moab, Eliehoenai the son of Zerahiah
and 200 males with him;
5 of the sons of Zattu, Shecaniah, the son of Jahaziel and 300
males with him;
6 and of the sons of [a]Adin, Ebed the son of Jonathan and 50
males with him;
7 and of the sons of Elam, Jeshaiah the son of Athaliah and
70 males with him;
8 and of the sons of Shephatiah, Zebadiah the son of Michael
and 80 males with him;
9 of the sons of Joab, Obadiah the son of Jehiel and 218
males with him;
10 and of the sons of Bani, Shelomith, the son of Josiphiah and
160 males with him;
11 and of the sons of Bebai, Zechariah the son of Bebai and 28
males with him;
12 and of the sons of Azgad, Johanan the son of Hakkatan and
110 males with him;
13 and of the sons of Adonikam, the last ones, these being their
names, Eliphelet, Jeuel and Shemaiah, and 60 males with them;
14 and of the sons of Bigvai, Uthai and [1]Zabbud, and 70 males
with [2]them.
15 Now I assembled them at [a]the river that runs to Ahava,
where we camped for three days; and when I observed the
people and the priests, I [b]did not find any Levites there.
16 So I sent for Eliezer, Ariel, Shemaiah, Elnathan, Jarib,
Elnathan, Nathan, Zechariah and Meshullam, [1]leading men,
and for Joiarib and Elnathan, teachers.
17 I sent them to Iddo the [1]leading man at the place Casiphia;
and I [2]told them what to say to [3]Iddo *and* his brothers, [a]the
temple servants at the place Casiphia, *that is,* to bring ministers
to us for the house of our God.
18 [a]According to the good hand of our God upon us they brought
us a [b]man of insight of the sons of Mahli, the son of Levi, the son
of Israel, namely Sherebiah, and his sons and brothers, 18 men;
19 and Hashabiah and [1]Jeshaiah of the sons of Merari, with
his brothers and their sons, 20 men;
20 and 220 of [a]the temple servants, whom David and the
princes had given for the service of the Levites, all of them
designated by name.
21 Then I proclaimed [a]a fast there at [b]the river of Ahava, that
we might [c]humble ourselves before our God to seek from Him
a [1]safe journey for us, our little ones, and all our possessions.
22 For I was ashamed to request from the king troops and
horsemen to [1]protect us from the enemy on the way, because
we had said to the king, "[a]The hand of our God is [2]favorably

8:2 [a]1 Chr 3:22

3 [a]Ezra 2:3

6 [a]Ezra 2:15; Neh 7:20; 10:16

14 [1]Or *Zakkur* [2]Or *him*

15 [a]Ezra 8:21, 31 [b]Ezra 7:7; 8:2

16 [1]Lit *heads*

17 [1]Lit *head* [2]Lit *put words in their mouth to say* [3]So Gr; Heb *Iddo his brother* [a]Ezra 2:43

18 [a]Ezra 7:6, 28 [b]2 Chr 30:22

19 [1]So Gr; Heb *with him Jeshaiah*

20 [a]Ezra 2:43; 7:7

21 [1]Lit *straight way* [a]1 Sam 7:6; 2 Chr 20:3 [b]Ezra 8:15, 31 [c]Lev 16:29; 23:29; Is 58:3, 5

22 [1]Lit *help* [2]Lit *upon all . . . for good* [a]Ezra 7:6, 9, 28

disposed to all those who seek Him, but [b]His power and His
anger are against all those who [c]forsake Him."
23 So we fasted and sought our God concerning this *matter,*
and He [1a]listened to our entreaty.
24 Then I set apart twelve of the leading priests, [a]Sherebiah,
Hashabiah, and with them ten of their brothers;
25 and I [a]weighed out to them [b]the silver, the gold and the
utensils, the offering for the house of our God which the king
and [c]his counselors and his princes and all Israel present *there*
had offered.
26 [a]Thus I weighed into their hands 650 talents of silver, and
silver utensils *worth* 100 talents, *and* 100 gold talents,
27 and 20 gold bowls *worth* 1,000 darics, and two utensils of
fine shiny bronze, precious as gold.
28 Then I said to them, "[a]You are holy to the LORD, and the
[b]utensils are holy; and the silver and the gold are a freewill
offering to the LORD God of your fathers.
29 "Watch and keep *them* [a]until you weigh *them* before the
leading priests, the Levites and the heads of the fathers'
households of Israel at Jerusalem, *in* the chambers of the house
of the LORD."
30 So the priests and the Levites [a]accepted the weighed out
silver and gold and the utensils, to bring *them* to Jerusalem to
the house of our God.
31 Then we journeyed from [a]the river Ahava on [b]the twelfth
of the first month to go to Jerusalem; and [c]the hand of our God
was over us, and He delivered us from the hand of the enemy
and the ambushes by the way.
32 [a]Thus we came to Jerusalem and remained there three days.
33 On the fourth day the silver and the gold and the utensils
[a]were weighed out in the house of our God into the hand of
[b]Meremoth the son of Uriah the priest, and with him *was*
Eleazar the son of Phinehas; and with them *were* the Levites,
Jozabad the son of Jeshua and Noadiah the son of Binnui.
34 Everything *was* numbered and weighed, and all the weight
was recorded at that time.
35 [a]The exiles who had come from the captivity offered burnt
offerings to the God of Israel: [b]12 bulls for all Israel, 96 rams,
77 lambs, 12 male goats for a sin offering, all as a burnt
offering to the LORD.
36 Then [a]they delivered the king's edicts to [b]the king's satraps
and to the governors *in the provinces* beyond the [1]River, and
they supported the people and the house of God.

Chapter 9 Theme

9 Now when these things had been completed, the princes
approached me, saying, "The people of Israel and the priests
and the Levites have not [a]separated themselves from the peoples
of the lands, [b]according to their abominations, *those* of the
Canaanites, the Hittites, the Perizzites, the Jebusites, the
Ammonites, the Moabites, the Egyptians and the Amorites.

22 [b]Josh 22:16 [c]2 Chr 15:2
23 [1]Lit *was entreated by us* [a]1 Chr 5:20; 2 Chr 33:13
24 [a]Ezra 8:18, 19
25 [a]Ezra 8:33 [b]Ezra 7:15, 16 [c]Ezra 7:14
26 [a]Ezra 1:9-11
28 [a]Lev 21:6-8 [b]Lev 22:2, 3
29 [a]Ezra 8:33, 34
30 [a]Ezra 1:9
31 [a]Ezra 8:15, 21 [b]Ezra 7:9 [c]Ezra 8:22
32 [a]Neh 2:11
33 [a]Ezra 8:30 [b]Neh 3:4, 21
35 [a]Ezra 2:1 [b]Ezra 6:17
36 [1]I.e. Euphrates River [a]Ezra 7:21-24 [b]Ezra 4:7; 5:6
9:1 [a]Ezra 6:21; Neh 9:2 [b]Lev 18:24-30

2 "For [a]they have taken some of their daughters *as wives* for
themselves and for their sons, so that [b]the holy [1]race has
[c]intermingled with the peoples of the lands; indeed, the hands
of the princes and the rulers have been foremost in this
unfaithfulness."
3 When I heard about this matter, I [a]tore my garment and my
robe, and pulled some of the hair from my head and my beard,
and [b]sat down appalled.
4 Then [a]everyone who trembled at the words of the God of
Israel on account of the unfaithfulness of the exiles gathered to
me, and I sat appalled until [b]the evening offering.
5 But at the evening offering I arose from my [1]humiliation,
even with my garment and my robe torn, and I fell on my
knees and [a]stretched out my [2]hands to the LORD my God;
6 and I said, "O my God, I am ashamed and embarrassed to
lift up my face to You, my God, for our iniquities have [1]risen
above our heads and our [a]guilt has grown even to the heavens.
7 "[a]Since the days of our fathers to this day we *have been* in
great guilt, and on account of our iniquities we, our kings *and*
our priests have been given into the hand of the kings of the
lands, to the sword, to captivity and to plunder and to [1b]open
shame, as *it is* this day.
8 "But now for a brief moment grace has been *shown* from
the LORD our God, [a]to leave us an escaped remnant and to give
us a [b]peg in His holy place, that our God may [c]enlighten our
eyes and grant us a little reviving in our bondage.
9 "[a]For we are slaves; yet in our bondage our God has not
forsaken us, but [b]has extended lovingkindness to us in the
sight of the kings of Persia, to give us reviving to raise up the
house of our God, to restore its ruins and to give us a wall in
Judah and Jerusalem.
10 "Now, our God, what shall we say after this? For we have
forsaken Your commandments,
11 which You have commanded by Your servants the prophets,
saying, 'The land which you are entering to possess is an
unclean land with the uncleanness of the peoples of the lands,
with their abominations which have filled it from end to end
and [a]with their impurity.
12 'So now do not [a]give your daughters to their sons nor take
their daughters to your sons, and [b]never seek their peace or
their prosperity, that you may be strong and eat the good *things*
of the land and [c]leave *it* as an inheritance to your sons forever.'
13 "After all that has come upon us for our evil deeds and [a]our
great guilt, since You our God have requited *us* less than our
iniquities *deserve,* and have given us [b]an escaped remnant as this,
14 [a]shall we again break Your commandments and intermarry
with the peoples [1]who commit these abominations? [b]Would You
not be angry with us [2]to the point of destruction, until there is
no remnant nor any who escape?
15 "O LORD God of Israel, [a]You are righteous, for we have been left
an escaped remnant, as *it is* this day; behold, we are before You
in [b]our guilt, for [c]no one can stand before You because of this."

2 [1]Lit *seed* [a]Deut 7:3; Ezra 10:2, 18 [b]Ex 22:31; Deut 14:2; 2 Cor 6:14 [c]Neh 13:3
3 [a]2 Kin 18:37 [b]Neh 1:4
4 [a]Ezra 10:3; Is 66:2 [b]Ex 29:39
5 [1]Or *fasting* [2]Lit *palms* [a]Ex 9:29
6 [1]Lit *multiplied over the head* [a]2 Chr 28:9; Ezra 9:13, 15; Rev 18:5
7 [1]Lit *shame of faces* [a]2 Chr 29:6; Ps 106:6 [b]Dan 9:7
8 [a]Ezra 9:13-15 [b]Is 22:23 [c]Ps 13:3
9 [a]Neh 9:36 [b]Ezra 7:28
11 [a]Ezra 6:21
12 [a]Ex 34:15, 16; Deut 7:3; Ezra 9:2 [b]Deut 23:6 [c]Prov 13:22
13 [a]Ezra 9:6, 7 [b]Ezra 9:8
14 [1]Lit *of these abominations* [2]Lit *to destroy* [a]Ezra 9:2 [b]Deut 9:8, 14
15 [a]Neh 9:33; Dan 9:7 [b]Ezra 9:6 [c]Job 9:2; Ps 130:3

Chapter 10 Theme ______________________

10 Now [a]while Ezra was praying and making confession, weeping and prostrating himself [b]before the house of God, a very large assembly, men, women and children, gathered to him from Israel; for the people wept bitterly.

2 Shecaniah the son of Jehiel, one of the sons of Elam, said to Ezra, "[a]We have been unfaithful to our God and have [1]married foreign women from the peoples of the land; yet now there is hope for Israel in spite of this.

3 "So now [a]let us make a covenant with our God to put away all the wives and [1b]their children, according to the counsel of [2]my lord and of [c]those who tremble at the commandment of our God; and let it be done [d]according to the law.

4 "Arise! For *this* matter is [1]your responsibility, but we will be with you; [a]be courageous and act."

5 Then Ezra rose and [a]made the leading priests, the Levites and all Israel, take oath that they would do according to this [1]proposal; so they took the oath.

6 Then Ezra [a]rose from before the house of God and went into the chamber of Jehohanan the son of Eliashib. Although he went there, [b]he did not eat bread nor drink water, for he was mourning over the unfaithfulness of the exiles.

7 They made a proclamation throughout Judah and Jerusalem to all the exiles, that they should assemble at Jerusalem,

8 and that whoever would not come within three days, according to the counsel of the leaders and the elders, all his possessions should be forfeited and he himself excluded from the assembly of the exiles.

9 So all the men of Judah and Benjamin assembled at Jerusalem within the three days. It was the ninth month on the twentieth of the month, and all the people sat in the open square *before* the house of God, [a]trembling because of this matter and the heavy rain.

10 Then Ezra the priest stood up and said to them, "You have been unfaithful and have married foreign wives adding to the guilt of Israel.

11 "Now therefore, [a]make confession to the LORD God of your fathers and [b]do His will; and [c]separate yourselves from the peoples of the land and from the foreign wives."

12 Then all the assembly replied with a loud voice, "That's right! As you have said, so it is [1]our duty to do.

13 "But there are many people; it is the rainy season and we are not able to stand in the open. Nor *can* the task *be done* in one or two days, for we have transgressed greatly in this matter.

14 "Let our leaders [1]represent the whole assembly and let all those in our cities who have married foreign wives come at appointed times, together with the elders and judges of each city, until the [a]fierce anger of our God on account of this matter is turned away from us."

15 Only Jonathan the son of Asahel and Jahzeiah the son of Tikvah [1]opposed this, with Meshullam and Shabbethai the Levite supporting them.

10:1 [a]Dan 9:4, 20 [b]2 Chr 20:9

2 [1]Lit *given dwelling to* [a]Ezra 9:2; Neh 13:27

3 [1]Lit *that which is born of them* [2]Or *the Lord* [a]2 Chr 34:31 [b]Ezra 10:44 [c]Ezra 9:4 [d]Deut 7:2, 3

4 [1]Lit *upon you* [a]1 Chr 28:10

5 [1]Lit *word, thing* [a]Neh 5:12; 13:25

6 [a]Ezra 10:1 [b]Deut 9:18

9 [a]1 Sam 12:18; Ezra 9:4; 10:3

11 [a]Lev 26:40; Prov 28:13 [b]Rom 12:2 [c]Ezra 10:3

12 [1]Lit *upon us*

14 [1]Lit *stand for* [a]2 Kin 23:26; 2 Chr 28:11-13; 29:10; 30:8

15 [1]Lit *stood against*

16 But the exiles did so. And [1]Ezra the priest selected men
who were heads of fathers' *households* for *each of* their father's
households, all of them by name. So they [2]convened on the
first day of the tenth month to investigate the matter.
17 They finished *investigating* all the men who had married
foreign wives by the first day of the first month.
18 Among the sons of the priests who had married foreign
wives were found of the sons of [a]Jeshua the son of Jozadak, and
his brothers: Maaseiah, Eliezer, Jarib and Gedaliah.
19 They [1]pledged to put away their wives, and being guilty,
[a]*they offered* a ram of the flock for their offense.
20 Of the sons of Immer *there were* Hanani and Zebadiah;
21 and of the sons of Harim: Maaseiah, Elijah, Shemaiah,
Jehiel and Uzziah;
22 and of the sons of Pashhur: Elioenai, Maaseiah, Ishmael,
Nethanel, Jozabad and Elasah.
23 Of Levites *there were* Jozabad, Shimei, Kelaiah (that is,
Kelita), Pethahiah, Judah and Eliezer.
24 Of the singers *there was* Eliashib; and of the gatekeepers:
Shallum, Telem and Uri.
25 Of Israel, of the sons of [a]Parosh *there were* Ramiah, Izziah,
Malchijah, Mijamin, Eleazar, Malchijah and Benaiah;
26 and of the sons of Elam: Mattaniah, Zechariah, Jehiel, Abdi,
Jeremoth and Elijah;
27 and of the sons of [a]Zattu: Elioenai, Eliashib, Mattaniah,
Jeremoth, Zabad and Aziza;
28 and of the sons of Bebai: Jehohanan, Hananiah, Zabbai *and*
Athlai;
29 and of the sons of Bani: Meshullam, Malluch and Adaiah,
Jashub, Sheal *and* Jeremoth;
30 and of the sons of Pahath-moab: Adna, Chelal, Benaiah,
Maaseiah, Mattaniah, Bezalel, Binnui and Manasseh;
31 and *of* the sons of Harim: Eliezer, Isshijah, [a]Malchijah,
Shemaiah, Shimeon,
32 Benjamin, Malluch *and* Shemariah;
33 of the sons of Hashum: Mattenai, Mattattah, Zabad,
Eliphelet, Jeremai, Manasseh *and* Shimei;
34 of the sons of Bani: Maadai, Amram, Uel,
35 Benaiah, Bedeiah, Cheluhi,
36 Vaniah, Meremoth, Eliashib,
37 Mattaniah, Mattenai, Jaasu,
38 Bani, Binnui, Shimei,
39 Shelemiah, Nathan, Adaiah,
40 Machnadebai, Shashai, Sharai,
41 Azarel, Shelemiah, Shemariah,
42 Shallum, Amariah *and* Joseph.
43 Of the sons of [a]Nebo *there were* Jeiel, Mattithiah, Zabad,
Zebina, Jaddai, Joel *and* Benaiah.
44 All these had married [a]foreign wives, and some of them
had wives *by whom* they had children.

16 [1]Heb reads *there were set apart Ezra the priest, men . . .* [2]Lit *sat*

18 [a]Ezra 5:2; Hag 1:1, 12; 2:4; Zech 3:1; 6:11

19 [1]Lit *gave their hand* [a]Lev 5:15; 6:6

25 [a]Ezra 2:3; 8:3; Neh 7:8

27 [a]Ezra 2:8; Neh 7:13

31 [a]Neh 3:11

43 [a]Num 32:38; Ezra 2:29

44 [a]1 Kin 11:1-3; Ezra 10:3

Theme of Ezra:

Author:

Date:

Purpose:

Key Words:

house (or any reference to God's house)

decree

the law (of Moses, of the Lord, of your God)

commandments

SEGMENT DIVISIONS				
	YEARS COVERED	CENTRAL CHARACTERS		CHAPTER THEMES
				1
				2
				3
				4
				5
				6
				7
				8
				9
				10

NEHEMIAH נחמיה NECHEMYA

Since the third millennium B.C., the cities of the Middle East had been surrounded by walls made of stones while guarded gates acted as sentinels. From the tops of these walls, watchmen could survey the landscape for great distances, seeing everyone who approached the city either as visitors or invaders.

The city fathers would gather at the city gates to carry out their business transactions and pass their judgments on civic affairs. The condition of the walls of the city was a matter of either pride or reproach.

Jerusalem's walls had been destroyed during the Babylonian invasion. The walls and their many gates stood in ruins, a rebuke to the newly returned exiles and a cause of mourning to Nehemiah, although he was over 600 miles away serving as cupbearer to Artaxerxes. Nehemiah had not forgotten his beloved city or her people.

While Ezra gives the account of the rebuilding of the temple under Zerubbabel, Nehemiah (Ezra's contemporary) gives the account of the rebuilding of Jerusalem's walls. His account begins in 445 B.C. in Susa, the Persian capital.

THINGS TO DO

1. Nehemiah is a continuation of Ezra. In fact, Ezra and Nehemiah were treated as one book in the earliest Hebrew manuscripts. Therefore, to put this book into context, study the historical chart THE TIMES OF EZRA, NEHEMIAH, AND ESTHER on page 781.
2. As you read Nehemiah chapter by chapter:
   a. Look for the theme of each chapter. Record this next to the chapter number on the NEHEMIAH AT A GLANCE chart on page 806 and record it in your Bible next to the chapter number.

   b. Read each chapter again. This time make a list of the points you want to remember about the main topic or event within each chapter.

      1) For example, in chapter 1 the theme is Nehemiah's concern for Jerusalem. In the margin opposite the first three verses you could write "Remnant's Distress." Then underneath it write "walls broken down, gates burned."

      2) Then next to verses 4 through 11 you could write "Nehemiah's Prayer" and list the main parts or points of his prayer; for example, a) weeps, mourns, fasts, b) reminds God of who He is and His covenant, and c) confesses his and Israel's sins.

      3) As you summarize each chapter, list what you learn about God.

   c. While there are many key repeated words you could mark—such as *wall*, *gate*, *build*, *repairs*, etc.—you may want to observe them without marking them because of the nature of Nehemiah's writing. Some key words are used so many times within specific chapters that you may become overwhelmed by all the markings.

      1) Mark the key words listed on the NEHEMIAH AT A GLANCE chart.

      2) When you mark *command (commandments, ordinances, law)*, note in the margin what you learn.

   d. Note any references to time by drawing a clock 🕒 next to the verse.

   e. As you read through Nehemiah, note in the margin when the wall is started, when it is completed, and when it is dedicated.

3. There are valuable lessons to be learned from observing how Nehemiah handled situations. As you see how Nehemiah related to God in each situation, how he dealt with the people (including those who opposed him), and the example he set, you will see principles you can apply to your life. As you study, record your insights on the chart LESSONS FROM THE LIFE OF NEHEMIAH on page 805.

4. When you finish recording the theme of every chapter on NEHEMIAH AT A GLANCE, look for the main division of the book, where one emphasis ends and another begins. On the line under "Segment Divisions," record this division and the theme or subject of the two segments of the book. Also fill in the rest of the chart and record the theme of Nehemiah.

THINGS TO THINK ABOUT

1. Read Nehemiah chapter 9 again and think about the character of God and how He dealt with Israel. What can you learn about God and also about Israel's behavior that you can apply to your own life?

2. Have you thought about what could happen if the congregation of a church gathered together and publicly confessed their sins and then the sins of their nation?

3. What have you learned from Nehemiah's life? How are you going to apply it to your life in a practical way?

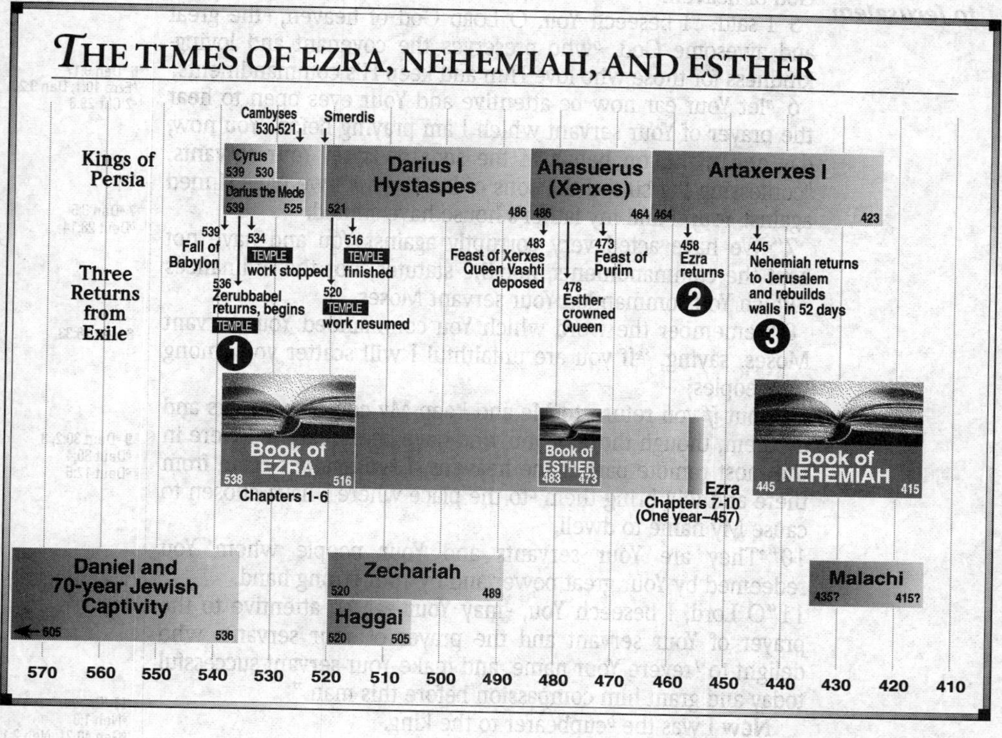

Chapter 1 Theme ____________________

1 The words of [a]Nehemiah the son of Hacaliah.
Now it happened in [b]the month Chislev, [c]*in* the twentieth
year, while I was in [d]Susa the [1]capitol,
2 that [a]Hanani, one of my brothers, and [1]some men from
Judah came; and I asked
them concerning the Jews
who had escaped *and* had
survived the captivity, and
about Jerusalem.
3 They said to me, "The
remnant there in the [a]prov-
ince who survived the captivity are in great distress
and [b]reproach, and [b]the wall
of Jerusalem is broken down
and [c]its gates are burned
with fire."
4 When I heard these words, [a]I sat down and wept and
mourned for days; and I was fasting and praying before [b]the
God of heaven.
5 I said, "I beseech You, O LORD God of heaven, [a]the great
and awesome God, [b]who preserves the covenant and lovingkindness for those who love Him and keep His commandments,
6 [a]let Your ear now be attentive and Your eyes open to hear
the prayer of Your servant which I am praying before You now,
day and night, on behalf of the sons of Israel Your servants,
[b]confessing the sins of the sons of Israel which we have sinned
against You; [c]I and my father's house have sinned.
7 "[a]We have acted very corruptly against You and have not
kept the commandments, nor the statutes, nor the ordinances
[b]which You commanded Your servant Moses.
8 "Remember the word which You commanded Your servant
Moses, saying, '[a]If you are unfaithful I will scatter you among
the peoples;
9 [a]but *if* you return to Me and keep My commandments and
do them, though those of you who have been scattered were in
the most remote part of the heavens, I [b]will gather them from
there and will bring them [c]to the place where I have chosen to
cause My name to dwell.'
10 "[a]They are Your servants and Your people whom You
redeemed by Your great power and by Your strong hand.
11 "O Lord, I beseech You, [a]may Your ear be attentive to the
prayer of Your servant and the prayer of Your servants who
delight to [1]revere Your name, and make Your servant successful
today and grant him compassion before this man."
Now I was the [b]cupbearer to the king.

From Susa to Jerusalem

Chapter 2 Theme ____________________

2 And it came about in the month Nisan, [a]in the twentieth
year of King [b]Artaxerxes, that wine *was* before him, and [c]I

1:1 [1]Or *palace* or *citadel* [a]Neh 10:1 [b]Zech 7:1 [c]Neh 2:1 [d]Esth 1:2; Dan 8:2
2 [1]Lit *he and some* [a]Neh 7:2
3 [a]Neh 7:6 [b]Neh 2:17 [c]Neh 2:3
4 [a]Ezra 9:3; 10:1 [b]Neh 2:4
5 [a]Neh 4:14; 9:32; Dan 9:4 [b]Ex 20:6; Ps 89:2, 3
6 [a]Dan 9:17 [b]Ezra 10:1; Dan 9:20 [c]2 Chr 29:6
7 [a]Dan 9:5 [b]Deut 28:14
8 [a]Lev 26:33
9 [a]Deut 30:2, 3 [b]Deut 30:4 [c]Deut 12:5
10 [a]Ex 32:11; Deut 9:29
11 [1]Or *fear* [a]Neh 1:6 [b]Gen 40:21; Neh 2:1
2:1 [a]Neh 1:1 [b]Ezra 7:1 [c]Neh 1:11

took up the wine and gave it to the king. Now I had not been
sad in his presence.
2 So the king said to me, "Why is your face sad though you
are not sick? [a]This is nothing but sadness of heart." Then I was
very much afraid.
3 I said to the king, "[a]Let the king live forever. Why should
my face not be sad [b]when the city, the place of my fathers'
tombs, lies desolate and its gates have been consumed by fire?"
4 Then the king said to me, "What would you request?" [a]So I
prayed to the God of heaven.
5 I said to the king, "If it please the king, and if your servant
has found favor before you, send me to Judah, to the city of my
fathers' tombs, that I may rebuild it."
6 Then the king said to me, the queen sitting beside him,
"How long will your journey be, and when will you return?" So
it pleased the king to send me, and [a]I gave him a definite time.
7 And I said to the king, "If it please the king, let letters be
given me [a]for the governors *of the provinces* beyond the River,
that they may allow me to pass through until I come to Judah,
8 and a letter to Asaph the keeper of the king's [a]forest, that
he may give me timber to make beams for the gates of [b]the
fortress which is by the [1]temple, for the wall of the city and for
the house to which I will go." And the king granted *them* to
me because [c]the good hand of my God *was* on me.
9 Then I came to [a]the governors *of the provinces* beyond the
River and gave them the king's letters. Now [b]the king had sent
with me officers of the army and horsemen.
10 When [a]Sanballat the Horonite and Tobiah the Ammonite
[1]official heard *about it,* it was very displeasing to them that
someone had come to seek the welfare of the sons of Israel.
11 So I [a]came to Jerusalem and was there three days.
12 And I arose in the night, I and a few men with me. I did
not tell anyone what my God was putting into my [1]mind to do
for Jerusalem and there was no animal with me except the
animal on which I was riding.
13 So I went out at night by [a]the Valley Gate in the direction
of the Dragon's Well and *on* to the [1]Refuse Gate, inspecting the
walls of Jerusalem [b]which were broken down and its [c]gates
which were consumed by fire.
14 Then I passed on to [a]the Fountain Gate and [b]the King's
Pool, but there was no place for [1]my mount to pass.
15 So I went up at night by the [a]ravine and inspected the wall.
Then I entered the Valley Gate again and returned.
16 The officials did not know where I had gone or what I had
done; nor had I as yet told the Jews, the priests, the nobles, the
officials or the rest who did the work.
17 Then I said to them, "You see the bad situation we are in,
that [a]Jerusalem is desolate and its gates burned by fire. Come,
let us rebuild the wall of Jerusalem so that we will no longer be
a reproach."

2 [a]Prov 15:13
3 [a]Dan 2:4 [b]2 Kin 25:8-10; 2 Chr 36:19; Neh 1:3; Jer 52:12-14
4 [a]Neh 1:4
6 [a]Neh 13:6
7 [a]Ezra 7:21; 8:36
8 [1]Lit *house* [a]Eccl 2:5, 6 [b]Neh 7:2 [c]Ezra 7:6; Neh 2:18
9 [a]Neh 2:7 [b]Ezra 8:22
10 [1]Lit *servant* [a]Neh 2:19; 4:1
11 [a]Ezra 8:32
12 [1]Lit *heart*
13 [1]Lit *Gate of Ash-heaps* [a]Neh 3:13 [b]Neh 1:3 [c]Neh 2:3, 17
14 [1]Lit *the animal under me* [a]Neh 3:15 [b]2 Kin 20:20
15 [a]John 18:1
17 [a]Neh 1:3

18 I told them how the hand of my God had been favorable to
me and also about the king's words which he had spoken to
me. Then they said, "Let us arise and build." [a]So they put their
hands to the good *work.*
19 But when Sanballat the Horonite and Tobiah the Ammonite
[1]official, and [a]Geshem the Arab heard *it,* [b]they mocked us and
despised us and said, "What is this thing you are doing? [a]Are
you rebelling against the king?"
20 So I answered them and said to them, "[a]The God of heaven
will give us success; therefore we His servants will arise and
build, [b]but you have no portion, right or memorial in Jerusalem."

Chapter 3 Theme ______________________________

3 Then [a]Eliashib the high priest arose with his brothers the
priests and built [b]the Sheep Gate; they consecrated it and
[c]hung its doors. They consecrated [1]the wall to [d]the Tower of
the Hundred *and* [e]the Tower of Hananel.
2 Next to him [a]the men of Jericho built, and next
to [1]them Zaccur the son of Imri built.
3 Now the sons of Hassenaah built [a]the Fish
Gate; they laid its beams and hung its doors with
its bolts and bars.
4 Next to them Meremoth the son of Uriah the son
of Hakkoz made repairs. And next to him Meshullam
the son of Berechiah the son of Meshezabel made
repairs. And next to [1]him Zadok the son of Baana
also made repairs.
5 Moreover, next to [1]him the Tekoites made
repairs, but their nobles did not [2]support the work
of their masters.
6 Joiada the son of Paseah and Meshullam the
son of Besodeiah repaired [a]the Old Gate; they laid
its beams and hung its doors with its bolts and its bars.
7 Next to them Melatiah the Gibeonite and Jadon the
Meronothite, the men of Gibeon and of Mizpah, [1]also made
repairs for the official seat of the [a]governor *of the province*
beyond the River.
8 Next to him Uzziel the son of Harhaiah of the [a]goldsmiths
made repairs. And next to him Hananiah, one of the perfumers,
made repairs, and they restored Jerusalem as far as [b]the Broad
Wall.
9 Next to them Rephaiah the son of Hur, [a]the official of half
the district of Jerusalem, made repairs.
10 Next to them Jedaiah the son of Harumaph made repairs
opposite his house. And next to him Hattush the son of
Hashabneiah made repairs.
11 Malchijah the son of Harim and Hasshub the son of Pahath-
moab repaired another section and [a]the Tower of Furnaces.
12 Next to him Shallum the son of Hallohesh, [a]the official of
half the district of Jerusalem, made repairs, he and his
daughters.

Jerusalem's Gates in Nehemiah's Time

18 [a]2 Sam 2:7
19 [1]Lit *servant* [a]Neh 6:6 [b]Neh 4:1
20 [a]Ezra 4:3 [b]Neh 2:4; Acts 8:21
3:1 [1]Lit *it* [a]Neh 3:20; 13:28 [b]Neh 3:32; 12:39 [c]Neh 6:1; 7:1 [d]Neh 12:39 [e]Jer 31:38
2 [1]Lit *him* [a]Neh 7:36
3 [a]Neh 12:39
4 [1]Lit *them*
5 [1]Lit *them* [2]Lit *bring their neck to*
6 [a]Neh 12:39
7 [1]Or *which was under the jurisdiction of the governor of the province beyond the River, also made repairs* [a]Neh 2:7
8 [a]Neh 3:31, 32 [b]Neh 12:38
9 [a]Neh 3:12, 17
11 [a]Neh 12:38
12 [a]Neh 3:9

13 Hanun and the inhabitants of Zanoah repaired [a]the Valley
Gate. They built it and hung its doors with its bolts and its
bars, and a thousand cubits of the wall to the [1]Refuse Gate.
14 Malchijah the son of Rechab, the official of the district of
[a]Beth-haccherem repaired the [1b]Refuse Gate. He built it and
hung its doors with its bolts and its bars.
15 Shallum the son of Col-hozeh, the official of the district of
Mizpah, [a]repaired the Fountain Gate. He built it, covered it and
hung its doors with its bolts and its bars, and the wall of the
Pool of Shelah at [b]the king's garden as far as [c]the steps that
descend from the city of David.
16 After him Nehemiah the son of Azbuk, [a]official of half the
district of Beth-zur, made repairs as far as *a point* opposite the
tombs of David, and as far as [b]the artificial pool and the house
of the mighty men.
17 After him the Levites carried out repairs *under* Rehum the
son of Bani. Next to him Hashabiah, the official of half the
district of Keilah, carried out repairs for his district.
18 After him their brothers carried out repairs *under* Bavvai the
son of Henadad, official of *the other* half of the district of Keilah.
19 Next to him Ezer the son of Jeshua, [a]the official of Mizpah,
repaired [1]another section in front of the ascent of the armory
[b]at the Angle.
20 After him Baruch the son of Zabbai zealously repaired
another section, from the Angle to the doorway of the house of
[a]Eliashib the high priest.
21 After him Meremoth the son of Uriah the son of Hakkoz
repaired another section, from the doorway of Eliashib's house
even as far as the end of [1]his house.
22 After him the priests, [a]the men of the [1]valley, carried out
repairs.
23 After [1]them Benjamin and Hasshub carried out repairs in
front of their house. After [1]them Azariah the son of Maaseiah,
son of Ananiah, carried out repairs beside his house.
24 After him Binnui the son of Henadad repaired another
section, from the house of Azariah as far as [a]the Angle and as
far as the corner.
25 Palal the son of Uzai *made repairs* in front of the Angle and
the tower projecting from the upper house of the king, which
is by [a]the court of the guard. After him Pedaiah the son of
Parosh *made repairs.*
26 [a]The temple servants living in [b]Ophel *made repairs* as far as
the front of [c]the Water Gate toward the east and the projecting
tower.
27 After [1]them [a]the Tekoites repaired another section in front
of the great projecting tower and as far as the wall of Ophel.
28 Above [a]the Horse Gate the priests carried out repairs, each
in front of his house.
29 After [1]them Zadok the son of Immer carried out repairs in
front of his house. And after him Shemaiah the son of Shecaniah,
the keeper of the East Gate, carried out repairs.

13 [1]Lit *Gate of Ash-heaps* [a]Neh 2:13
14 [1]Lit *Gate of Ash-heaps* [a]Jer 6:1 [b]Neh 2:13
15 [a]Neh 2:17 [b]2 Kin 25:4 [c]Neh 12:37
16 [a]Neh 3:9, 12, 17 [b]2 Kin 20:20; Is 7:3
19 [1]Lit *a second measure,* and so in vv 20, 21, 24, 30 [a]Neh 3:15 [b]2 Chr 26:9
20 [a]Neh 3:1
21 [1]Lit *Eliashib's*
22 [1]Lit *circle;* i.e. lower Jordan valley [a]Neh 12:28
23 [1]Lit *him*
24 [a]Neh 3:19
25 [a]Jer 32:2
26 [a]Neh 7:46 [b]Neh 11:21 [c]Neh 8:1
27 [1]Lit *him* [a]Neh 3:5
28 [a]2 Kin 11:16; 2 Chr 23:15; Jer 31:40
29 [1]Lit *him*

30 After him Hananiah the son of Shelemiah, and Hanun the
sixth son of Zalaph, repaired another section. After him
Meshullam the son of Berechiah carried out repairs in front of
his own [1]quarters.
31 After him Malchijah, [1]one of [a]the goldsmiths, carried out
repairs as far as the house of the temple servants and of the
merchants, in front of the [2]Inspection Gate and as far as the
upper room of the corner.
32 Between the upper room of the corner and [a]the Sheep
Gate the goldsmiths and the merchants carried out repairs.

Chapter 4 Theme ____________________

4 [1]Now it came about that when [a]Sanballat heard that we
were rebuilding the wall, he became furious and very
angry and mocked the Jews.
2 He spoke in the presence of his brothers and [a]the [1]wealthy
men of Samaria and said, "What are these feeble Jews doing?
Are they going to restore *it* for themselves? Can they offer
sacrifices? Can they finish in a day? Can they revive the stones
from the [2b]dusty rubble even the burned ones?"
3 Now Tobiah the Ammonite *was* near him and he said,
"Even what they are building—[a]if a fox should [1]jump on *it*, he
would break their stone wall down!"
4 [a]Hear, O our God, how we are despised! [b]Return their
reproach on their own heads and give them up for plunder in a
land of captivity.
5 Do not [1a]forgive their iniquity and let not their sin be
blotted out before You, for they have [2]demoralized the builders.
6 So we built the wall and the whole wall was joined together
to half its *height,* for the people had a [1]mind to work.
7 [1]Now when Sanballat, Tobiah, the Arabs, the Ammonites
and the Ashdodites heard that the [2]repair of the walls of
Jerusalem went on, *and* that the breaches began to be closed,
they were very angry.
8 All of them [a]conspired together to come *and* fight against
Jerusalem and to cause a disturbance in it.
9 But we prayed to our God, and because of them we [a]set up
a guard against them day and night.
10 Thus [1]in Judah it was said,

"The strength of the burden bearers is failing,
Yet there is much [2]rubbish;
And we ourselves are unable
To rebuild the wall."

11 Our enemies said, "They will not know or see until we
come among them, kill them and put a stop to the work."
12 When the Jews who lived near them came and told us ten
times, "[1]They will come up against us from every place where
you may turn,"
13 then I stationed *men* in the lowest parts of the space behind
the wall, the [1]exposed places, and I [a]stationed the people in
families with their swords, spears and bows.

30 [1]Or *cell*
31 [1]Lit *son of* [2]Or *Mustering* [a]Neh 3:8, 32
32 [a]Neh 3:1; 12:39
4:1 [1]Ch 3:33 in Heb [a]Neh 2:10
2 [1]Or *army* [2]Lit *heaps of dust* [a]Ezra 4:9, 10 [b]Neh 4:10
3 [1]Lit *go up* [a]Lam 5:18
4 [a]Ps 123:3, 4 [b]Ps 79:12
5 [1]Lit *cover* [2]Lit *offended against* [a]Ps 69:27, 28; Jer 18:23
6 [1]Lit *heart*
7 [1]Ch 4:1 in Heb [2]Lit *healing*
8 [a]Ps 83:3
9 [a]Neh 4:11
10 [1]Lit *Judah said* [2]Lit *dust*
12 [1]So Gr; Heb omits *they . . . up*
13 [1]Lit *bare* [a]Neh 4:17, 18

14 [a]Num 14:9; Deut 1:29, 30 [b]2 Sam 10:12

14 When I saw *their fear,* I rose and spoke to the nobles, the
officials and the rest of the people: "[a]Do not be afraid of them;
remember the Lord who is great and awesome, and [b]fight for your
brothers, your sons, your daughters, your wives and your houses."
15 When our enemies heard that it was known to us, and that
[a]God had frustrated their plan, then all of us returned to the
wall, each one to his work.

15 [a]2 Sam 17:14

16 From that day on, half of my servants carried on the work
while half of them held the spears, the shields, the bows and
the breastplates; and the captains *were* behind the whole
house of Judah.

18 [1]Lit *he who sounded the trumpet*

17 Those who were rebuilding the wall and those who carried
burdens took *their* load with one hand doing the work and the
other holding a weapon.
18 As for the builders, each *wore* his sword girded at his side
as he built, while [1]the trumpeter *stood* near me.

20 [1]Lit *assemble yourselves* [a]Ex 14:14; Deut 1:30

19 I said to the nobles, the officials and the rest of the people,
"The work is great and extensive, and we are separated on the
wall far from one another.
20 "At whatever place you hear the sound of the trumpet,
[1]rally to us there. [a]Our God will fight for us."

21 [1]Lit *rising of the dawn* [2]Lit *came out*

21 So we carried on the work with half of them holding spears
from [1]dawn until the stars [2]appeared.
22 At that time I also said to the people, "Let each man with
his servant spend the night within Jerusalem so that they may
be a guard for us by night and a laborer by day."

5:1 [a]Lev 25:35 [b]Deut 15:7

23 So neither I, my brothers, my servants, nor the men of the
guard who followed me, none of us removed our clothes, each
took his weapon *even to* the water.

2 [a]Hag 1:6

Chapter 5 Theme

5 Now [a]there was a great outcry of the people and of their
wives against their [b]Jewish brothers.
2 For there were those who said, "We, our sons and our
daughters are many; therefore let us [a]get grain that we may eat
and live."

4 [a]Ezra 4:13; 7:24

3 There were others who said, "We are mortgaging our fields,
our vineyards and our houses that we might get grain because
of the famine."

5 [1]Lit *there is not the power in our hands* [a]Gen 37:27 [b]Lev 25:39

4 Also there were those who said, "We have borrowed money
[a]for the king's tax *on* our fields and our vineyards.
5 "Now [a]our flesh is like the flesh of our brothers, our
children like their children. Yet behold, [b]we are forcing our
sons and our daughters to be slaves, and some of our daughters
are forced into bondage *already,* and [1]we are helpless because
our fields and vineyards belong to others."

6 [a]Ex 11:8

6 Then I was very [a]angry when I had heard their outcry and
these words.

7 [a]Ex 22:25; Lev 25:36; Deut 23:19, 20

7 I consulted with myself and contended with the nobles and
the rulers and said to them, "[a]You are exacting usury, each from
his brother!" Therefore, I held a great assembly against them.

8 I said to them, "We according to our ability [a]have [1]redeemed
our Jewish brothers who were sold to the nations; now would
you even sell your brothers that they may be sold to us?" Then
they were silent and could not find a word *to say.*
9 Again I said, "The thing which you are doing is not good;
should you not walk in the fear of our God because of [a]the
reproach of the nations, our enemies?
10 "And likewise I, my brothers and my servants are lending
them money and grain. Please, let us leave off this usury.
11 "Please, give back to them this very day their fields, their
vineyards, their olive groves and their houses, also the
hundredth *part* of the money and of the grain, the new wine
and the oil that you are exacting from them."
12 Then they said, "We [a]will give *it* back and [b]will require
nothing from them; we will do exactly as you say." So I called
the priests and [c]took an oath from them that they would do
according to this [1]promise.
13 I [a]also shook out the [1]front of my garment and said, "Thus
may God shake out every man from his house and from his
possessions who does not fulfill this [2]promise; even thus may
he be shaken out and emptied." And [b]all the assembly said,
"Amen!" And they praised the LORD. Then the people did
according to this [2]promise.
14 Moreover, from the day that I was appointed to be their
governor in the land of Judah, from [a]the twentieth year to the
[b]thirty-second year of King Artaxerxes, *for* twelve years, neither
I nor my [1]kinsmen have eaten the governor's food *allowance.*
15 But the former governors who were before me [1]laid
burdens on the people and took from them bread and wine
besides forty shekels of silver; even their servants domineered
the people. But I did not do so [a]because of the fear of God.
16 I also [1]applied myself to the work on this wall; we did not
buy any land, and all my servants were gathered there for the
work.
17 Moreover, [a]*there were* at my table one hundred and fifty
Jews and officials, besides those who came to us from the
nations that were around us.
18 Now [a]that which was prepared for each day was one ox
and six choice sheep, also birds were prepared for me; and
once in ten days all sorts of wine *were furnished* in abundance.
Yet for all this [b]I did not demand the governor's food *allowance,*
because the servitude was heavy on this people.
19 [a]Remember me, O my God, for good, *according to* all that I
have done for this people.

Chapter 6 Theme ________________________

6 Now when it was reported to Sanballat, Tobiah, to Geshem
the Arab and to the rest of our enemies that I had rebuilt
the wall, and *that* no breach remained in it, [a]although at that
time I had not set up the doors in the gates,

8 [1]Lit *bought* [a]Lev 25:48
9 [a]Neh 4:4
12 [1]Lit *word* [a]2 Chr 28:15 [b]Neh 10:31 [c]Ezra 10:5
13 [1]Lit *bosom* [2]Lit *word* [a]Acts 18:6 [b]Neh 8:6
14 [1]Lit *brothers* [a]Neh 1:1 [b]Neh 13:6
15 [1]Lit *made heavy* [a]Neh 5:9; Job 31:23
16 [1]Or *held fast*
17 [a]1 Kin 18:19
18 [a]1 Kin 4:22, 23 [b]2 Thess 3:8
19 [a]Neh 13:14, 22, 31
6:1 [a]Neh 3:1, 3

2 then Sanballat and Geshem sent *a message* to me, saying,
"Come, let us meet together at [1]Chephirim in the plain of
[a]Ono." But they were planning to [2]harm me.
3 So I sent messengers to them, saying, "I am doing a great
work and I cannot come down. Why should the work stop
while I leave it and come down to you?"
4 They sent *messages* to me four times in this manner, and I
answered them in the same way.
5 Then Sanballat sent his servant to me in the same manner
a fifth time with an open letter in his hand.
6 In it was written, "It is reported among the nations, and
[1]Gashmu says, that [a]you and the Jews are planning to rebel;
therefore you are rebuilding the wall. And you are to be their
king, according to these reports.
7 "You have also appointed prophets to proclaim in Jerusalem
concerning [1]you, 'A king is in Judah!' And now it will be
reported to the king according to these reports. So come now,
let us take counsel together."
8 Then I sent *a message* to him saying, "Such things as you
are saying have not been done, but you are [a]inventing them [1]in
your own mind."
9 For all of them were *trying* to frighten us, [1]thinking, "[2]They
will become discouraged with the work and it will not be
done." But now, [a]*O God,* strengthen my hands.
10 When I entered the house of Shemaiah the son of Delaiah,
son of Mehetabel, [a]who was [1]confined at home, he said, "Let
us meet together in the house of God, within the temple, and
let us close the doors of the temple, for they are coming to kill
you, and they are coming to kill you at night."
11 But I said, "[a]Should a man like me flee? And could one such
as I go into the temple [1]to save his life? I will not go in."
12 Then I perceived [1]that surely God had not sent him, but he
uttered *his* prophecy against me because Tobiah and Sanballat
had hired him.
13 He was hired for this reason, [a]that I might become frightened
and act accordingly and sin, so that they might have an evil
report in order that they could reproach me.
14 [a]Remember, O my God, Tobiah and Sanballat according to
these works of theirs, and also Noadiah [b]the prophetess and
the rest of the prophets who were *trying* to frighten me.
15 So [a]the wall was completed on the twenty-fifth of *the
month* Elul, in fifty-two days.
16 [a]When all our enemies heard *of it,* and all the nations
surrounding us saw *it,* they [1]lost their confidence; for [b]they
recognized that this work had been accomplished [2]with the
help of our God.
17 Also in those days many letters went from the nobles of
Judah to Tobiah, and Tobiah's *letters* came to them.
18 For many in Judah were bound by oath to him because he
was the son-in-law of Shecaniah the son of Arah, and his son
Jehohanan had married the daughter of Meshullam the son of
Berechiah.

2 [1]Another reading is, one of *the villages* [2]Lit *do evil to me* [a]1 Chr 8:12
6 [1]In v 1 and elsewhere, *Geshem* [a]Neh 2:19
7 [1]Lit *you, saying*
8 [1]Lit *from your heart* [a]Job 13:4; Ps 52:2
9 [1]Lit *saying,* [2]Lit *Their hands will drop from* [a]Ps 138:3
10 [1]Lit *shut up* [a]Jer 36:5
11 [1]Lit *and live* [a]Prov 28:1
12 [1]Lit *and behold God*
13 [a]Neh 6:6
14 [a]Neh 13:29 [b]Ezek 13:17
15 [a]Neh 4:1, 2
16 [1]Lit *fell exceedingly in their own eyes* [2]Lit *from our God* [a]Neh 2:10; 4:1, 7 [b]Ex 14:25

19 Moreover, they were speaking about his good deeds in my
presence and reported my words to him. Then Tobiah sent
letters to frighten me.

Chapter 7 Theme __________________________________

7 Now when [a]the wall was rebuilt and I had set up the
doors, and the gatekeepers and the singers and the Levites
were appointed,
2 then I put [a]Hanani my brother, and [b]Hananiah the
commander of [c]the fortress, in charge of Jerusalem, for he was
[d]a faithful man and feared God more than many.
3 Then I said to them, "Do not let the gates of Jerusalem be
opened until the sun is hot, and while they are standing *guard,*
let them shut and bolt the doors. Also appoint guards from the
inhabitants of Jerusalem, each at his post, and each in front of
his own house."
4 Now the city was large and spacious, but the people in it
were few and the houses were not built.
5 [a]Then my God put it into my heart to assemble the nobles,
the officials and the people to be enrolled by genealogies. Then
I found the book of the genealogy of those who came up first
[1]in which I found the following record:
6 [a]These are the [1]people of the province who came up from
the captivity of the exiles whom Nebuchadnezzar the king of
Babylon had carried away, and who returned to Jerusalem and
Judah, each to his city,
7 who came with Zerubbabel, Jeshua, Nehemiah, [1]Azariah,
[2]Raamiah, Nahamani, Mordecai, Bilshan, [3]Mispereth, Bigvai,
[4]Nehum, Baanah.

The number of men of the people of Israel:

8 the sons of Parosh, 2,172;
9 the sons of Shephatiah, 372;
10 the sons of Arah, 652;
11 the sons of Pahath-moab of the sons of Jeshua and Joab,
2,818;
12 the sons of Elam, 1,254;
13 the sons of Zattu, 845;
14 the sons of Zaccai, 760;
15 the sons of [1]Binnui, 648;
16 the sons of Bebai, 628;
17 the sons of Azgad, 2,322;
18 the sons of Adonikam, 667;
19 the sons of Bigvai, 2,067;
20 the sons of Adin, 655;
21 the sons of Ater, of Hezekiah, 98;
22 the sons of Hashum, 328;
23 the sons of Bezai, 324;
24 the sons of [1]Hariph, 112;
25 the sons of [1]Gibeon, 95;
26 the men of Bethlehem and Netophah, 188;

7:1 [a]Neh 6:1, 15

2 [a]Neh 1:2 [b]Neh 10:23 [c]Neh 2:8 [d]Neh 13:13

5 [1]Lit *and I found written in it* [a]Prov 2:6; 3:6

6 [1]Lit *sons* [a]Ezra 2:1-70

7 [1]In Ezra 2:2, *Seraiah* [2]In Ezra 2:2, *Reelaiah* [3]In Ezra 2:2, *Mispar* [4]In Ezra 2:2, *Rehum*

15 [1]In Ezra 2:10, *Bani*

24 [1]In Ezra 2:18, *Jorah*

25 [1]In Ezra 2:20, *Gibbar*

27 the men of Anathoth, 128;
28 the men of [1]Beth-azmaveth, 42;
29 the men of [1]Kiriath-jearim, Chephirah and Beeroth, 743;
30 the men of Ramah and Geba, 621;
31 the men of Michmas, 122;
32 the men of Bethel and Ai, 123;
33 the men of the other Nebo, 52;
34 the sons of the other Elam, 1,254;
35 the sons of Harim, 320;
36 the [1]men of Jericho, 345;
37 the sons of Lod, Hadid and Ono, 721;
38 the sons of Senaah, 3,930.
39 The priests: the sons of Jedaiah of the house of Jeshua, 973;
40 the sons of Immer, 1,052;
41 the sons of Pashhur, 1,247;
42 the sons of Harim, 1,017.
43 The Levites: the sons of Jeshua, of Kadmiel, of the sons of
[1]Hodevah, 74.
44 The singers: the sons of Asaph, 148.
45 The gatekeepers: the sons of Shallum, the sons of Ater, the
sons of Talmon, the sons of Akkub, the sons of Hatita, the sons
of Shobai, 138.
46 The temple servants: the sons of Ziha, the sons of Hasupha,
the sons of Tabbaoth,
47 the sons of Keros, the sons of [1]Sia, the sons of Padon,
48 the sons of Lebana, the sons of Hagaba, the sons of Shalmai,
49 the sons of Hanan, the sons of Giddel, the sons of Gahar,
50 the sons of Reaiah, the sons of Rezin, the sons of Nekoda,
51 the sons of Gazzam, the sons of Uzza, the sons of Paseah,
52 the sons of Besai, the sons of Meunim, the sons of
[1]Nephushesim,
53 the sons of Bakbuk, the sons of Hakupha, the sons of Harhur,
54 the sons of [1]Bazlith, the sons of Mehida, the sons of Harsha,
55 the sons of Barkos, the sons of Sisera, the sons of Temah,
56 the sons of Neziah, the sons of Hatipha.
57 The sons of Solomon's servants: the sons of Sotai, the sons
of [1]Sophereth, the sons of [2]Perida,
58 the sons of Jaala, the sons of Darkon, the sons of Giddel,
59 the sons of Shephatiah, the sons of Hattil, the sons of
Pochereth-hazzebaim, the sons of [1]Amon.
60 All the temple servants and the sons of Solomon's servants
were 392.
61 These *were* they who came up from Tel-melah, Tel-harsha,
Cherub, [1]Addon and Immer; but they could not show their
fathers' houses or their [2]descendants, whether they were of
Israel:
62 the sons of Delaiah, the sons of Tobiah, the sons of Nekoda,
642.
63 Of the priests: the sons of [1]Hobaiah, the sons of Hakkoz, the
sons of Barzillai, who took a wife of the daughters of Barzillai,
the Gileadite, and was named after them.

28 [1]In Ezra 2:24, *Azmaveth*
29 [1]In Ezra 2:25, *Kiriath-arim*
36 [1]Lit *sons*
43 [1]In Ezra 2:40, *Hodaviah*
47 [1]In Ezra 2:44, *Siaha*
52 [1]In Ezra 2:50, *Nephisim*
54 [1]In Ezra 2:52, *Bazluth*
57 [1]In Ezra 2:55, *Hassophereth* [2]In Ezra 2:55, *Peruda*
59 [1]In Ezra 2:57, *Ami*
61 [1]In Ezra 2:59, *Addan* [2]Lit *seed*
63 [1]In Ezra 2:61, *Habaiah*

64 These searched *among* their ancestral registration, but it
could not be located; therefore they were considered unclean
and excluded from the priesthood.
65 [a]The [1]governor said to them that they should not eat from the
most holy things until a priest arose with [b]Urim and Thummim.
66 The whole assembly together *was* 42,360,
67 besides their male and their female servants, [1]of whom
there were 7,337; and they had 245 male and female singers.
68 [1a]Their horses were 736; their mules, 245;
69 *their* camels, 435; *their* donkeys, 6,720.
70 Some from among the heads of fathers' *households* gave to
the work. The [1a]governor gave to the treasury 1,000 gold
drachmas, 50 basins, 530 priests' garments.
71 Some of the heads of fathers' *households* gave into the
treasury of the work 20,000 gold drachmas and 2,200 silver
minas.
72 That which the rest of the people gave was 20,000 gold
drachmas and 2,000 silver minas and 67 priests' garments.
73 Now [a]the priests, the Levites, the gatekeepers, the singers,
some of the people, the temple servants and all Israel, lived in
their cities.
[b]And when the seventh month came, the sons of Israel *were*
in their cities.

Chapter 8 Theme ____________________

8 And all the people gathered as one man at the square
which was in front of [a]the Water Gate, and they [1]asked
[b]Ezra the scribe to bring [c]the book of the law of Moses which
the LORD had [2]given to Israel.
2 Then [a]Ezra the priest brought the law before the assembly
of men, women and all who *could* listen with understanding,
on [b]the first day of the seventh month.
3 He read from it before the square which was in front of
[a]the Water Gate from [1]early morning until midday, in the
presence of men and women, those who could understand;
and all the people were attentive to the book of the law.
4 Ezra the scribe stood at a wooden podium which they had
made for the purpose. And beside him stood Mattithiah, Shema,
Anaiah, Uriah, Hilkiah, and Maaseiah on his right hand; and
Pedaiah, Mishael, Malchijah, Hashum, Hashbaddanah, Zechariah
and Meshullam on his left hand.
5 Ezra opened [a]the book in the sight of all the people for he
was standing above all the people; and when he opened it, all
the people [b]stood up.
6 Then Ezra blessed the LORD the great God. And all the
people answered, "[a]Amen, Amen!" while lifting up their hands;
then [b]they bowed low and worshiped the LORD with *their* faces
to the ground.
7 Also Jeshua, Bani, Sherebiah, Jamin, Akkub, Shabbethai,
Hodiah, Maaseiah, Kelita, Azariah, Jozabad, Hanan, Pelaiah,

65 [1]Heb *Tirshatha,* a Persian title [a]Neh 8:9; 10:1 [b]Ex 28:30; Deut 33:8

67 [1]Lit *these*

68 [1]So with some ancient mss and Gr [a]Ezra 2:66

70 [1]Heb *Tirshatha,* a Persian title [a]Neh 7:65; 8:9

73 [a]1 Chr 9:2 [b]Ezra 3:1

8:1 [1]Lit *said to* [2]Lit *commanded* [a]Neh 3:26 [b]Ezra 7:6 [c]2 Chr 34:15

2 [a]Deut 31:9-11; Neh 8:9 [b]Lev 23:24

3 [1]Lit *the light* [a]Neh 8:1

5 [a]Neh 8:3 [b]Judg 3:20; 1 Kin 8:12-14

6 [a]Neh 5:13 [b]Ex 4:31

8 [1]Or *explaining*

the Levites, explained the law to the people while the people
remained in their place.
8 They read from the book, from the law of God, [1]translating
to give the sense so that they understood the reading.

9 [1]Heb *Tirshatha,* a Persian title [a]Neh 7:65, 70 [b]Neh 12:26 [c]Neh 8:2 [d]Deut 12:7, 12

9 Then Nehemiah, who was the [1a]governor, and Ezra [b]the
priest *and* scribe, and the Levites who taught the people said to
all the people, "[c]This day is holy to the LORD your God; [d]do not
mourn or weep." For all the people were weeping when they
heard the words of the law.

10 [a]Deut 26:11-13

10 Then he said to them, "Go, eat of the fat, drink of the
sweet, and [a]send portions to him who has nothing prepared;
for this day is holy to our Lord. Do not be grieved, for the joy of
the LORD is your strength."

12 [1]Lit *make a great rejoicing* [a]Neh 8:10 [b]Neh 8:7, 8

11 So the Levites calmed all the people, saying, "Be still, for
the day is holy; do not be grieved."
12 All the people went away to eat, to drink, [a]to send portions
and to [1]celebrate a great festival, [b]because they understood the
words which had been made known to them.

14 [a]Lev 23:34, 40, 42

13 Then on the second day the heads of fathers' *households*
of all the people, the priests and the Levites were gathered to
Ezra the scribe that they might gain insight into the words of
the law.

15 [1]Lit *And that they will cause to be heard* [2]Lit *oil tree,* species unknown [a]Lev 23:4 [b]Deut 16:16 [c]Lev 23:40

14 They found written in the law how the LORD had commanded
through Moses that the sons of Israel [a]should live in booths
during the feast of the seventh month.
15 [1a]So they proclaimed and circulated a proclamation in all
their cities and [b]in Jerusalem, saying, "[c]Go out to the hills, and
bring olive branches and [2]wild olive branches, myrtle branches,
palm branches and branches of *other* leafy trees, to make
booths, as it is written."

16 [a]Jer 32:29 [b]Neh 8:1 [c]2 Kin 14:13; Neh 12:39

16 So the people went out and brought *them* and made booths
for themselves, each [a]on his roof, and in their courts and in the
courts of the house of God, and in the square at [b]the Water
Gate and in the square at [c]the Gate of Ephraim.

17 [1]Lit *the booths* [a]2 Chr 7:8; 8:13 [b]2 Chr 30:21

17 The entire assembly of those who had returned from the
captivity made booths and lived in [1]them. The sons of Israel
[a]had indeed not done so from the days of Joshua the son of
Nun to that day. And [b]there was great rejoicing.

18 [a]Deut 31:11 [b]Lev 23:36 [c]Num 29:35

18 [a]He read from the book of the law of God daily, from the
first day to the last day. And they [b]celebrated the feast seven
days, and on [c]the eighth day *there was* a solemn assembly
according to the ordinance.

9:1 [a]Neh 8:2 [b]Ezra 8:23 [c]1 Sam 4:12

Chapter 9 Theme ______________________

9 Now on the twenty-fourth day of [a]this month the sons of
Israel assembled [b]with fasting, in sackcloth and with [c]dirt
upon them.

2 [1]Lit *seed* [a]Ezra 10:11; Neh 13:3 [b]Prov 28:13; Jer 3:13

2 The [1a]descendants of Israel separated themselves from all
foreigners, and stood and [b]confessed their sins and the
iniquities of their fathers.

3 While [a]they stood in their place, they read from the book of
the law of the LORD their God for a fourth of the day; and for
another fourth they confessed and worshiped the LORD their God.
4 [a]Now on the Levites' platform stood Jeshua, Bani, Kadmiel,
Shebaniah, Bunni, Sherebiah, Bani *and* Chenani, and they cried
with a loud voice to the LORD their God.
5 Then the Levites, Jeshua, Kadmiel, Bani, Hashabneiah,
Sherebiah, Hodiah, Shebaniah *and* Pethahiah, said, "Arise, bless
the LORD your God forever and ever!

O may Your glorious name be blessed
And exalted above all blessing and praise!
6 "[a]You alone are the LORD.
[b]You have made the heavens,
The heaven of heavens with all their host,
The earth and all that is on it,
The seas and all that is in them.
[c]You give life to all of them
And the heavenly host bows down before You.
7 "You are the LORD God,
[a]Who chose Abram
And brought him out from [b]Ur of the Chaldees,
And [c]gave him the name Abraham.
8 "You found [a]his heart faithful before You,
And made a covenant with him
To give *him* the land of the Canaanite,
Of the Hittite and the Amorite,
Of the Perizzite, the Jebusite and the Girgashite—
To give *it* to his [1]descendants.
And You [b]have fulfilled Your promise,
For You are righteous.

9 "[a]You saw the affliction of our fathers in Egypt,
And [b]heard their cry by the [1]Red Sea.
10 "Then You performed [a]signs and wonders against Pharaoh,
Against all his servants and all the people of his land;
For You knew that [b]they acted arrogantly toward them,
And [c]made a name for Yourself as *it is* this day.
11 "[a]You divided the sea before them,
So they passed through the midst of the sea on dry ground;
And [b]their pursuers You hurled into the depths,
Like a stone into [1]raging waters.
12 "And with a pillar of cloud [a]You led them by day,
And with a pillar of fire by night
To light for them the way
In which they were to go.
13 "Then [a]You came down on Mount Sinai,
And [b]spoke with them from heaven;
You gave them [c]just ordinances and true laws,
Good statutes and commandments.
14 "So You made known to them [a]Your holy sabbath,
And laid down for them commandments, statutes and law,
Through Your servant Moses.

3 [a]Neh 8:4
4 [a]Neh 8:7
6 [a]Deut 6:4; 2 Kin 19:15 [b]Gen 1:1 [c]Col 1:16f
7 [a]Gen 12:1 [b]Gen 11:31 [c]Gen 17:5
8 [1]Lit *seed* [a]Gen 15:6, 18-21 [b]Josh 21:43-45
9 [1]Lit *Sea of Reeds* [a]Ex 3:7 [b]Ex 14:10-14, 31
10 [a]Ex 7:8-12:32 [b]Ex 5:2 [c]Ex 9:16
11 [1]Lit *strong, mighty* [a]Ex 14:21 [b]Ex 15:1, 5, 10
12 [a]Ex 13:21, 22
13 [a]Ex 19:11, 18-20 [b]Ex 20:1 [c]Ps 19:7-9
14 [a]Ex 16:23; 20:8

15 "You [a]provided bread from heaven for them for their hunger,
You [b]brought forth water from a rock for them for their thirst,
And You [c]told them to enter in order to possess
The land which You [1]swore to give them.

15 [1]Lit *lifted up Your hand* [a]Ex 16:4, 14, 15 [b]Ex 17:6; Num 20:7-13 [c]Deut 1:8, 21

16 "But they, our fathers, [a]acted arrogantly;
They [1b]became stubborn and would not listen to Your commandments.

16 [1]Lit *stiffened their neck;* so also v 17 [a]Neh 9:10 [b]Deut 1:26-33; 31:27; Neh 9:29

17 "They refused to listen,
And [a]did not remember Your wondrous deeds which You had performed among them;
So they became stubborn and [b]appointed a leader to return to their slavery [1]in Egypt.
But You are a God [c]of forgiveness,
Gracious and compassionate,
Slow to anger and abounding in lovingkindness;
And You did not forsake them.

17 [1]So Gr and some Heb mss; Heb reads *in their rebellion* [a]Ps 78:11, 42-55 [b]Num 14:4 [c]Ex 34:6, 7; Num 14:18

18 "Even when they [a]made for themselves
A calf of molten metal
And said, 'This is your God
Who brought you up from Egypt,'
And committed great [1]blasphemies,

18 [1]Lit *acts of contempt* [a]Ex 32:4-8, 31

19 [a]You, in Your great compassion,
Did not forsake them in the wilderness;
[b]The pillar of cloud did not leave them by day,
To guide them on their way,
Nor the pillar of fire by night, to light for them the way in which they were to go.

19 [a]Deut 8:2-4; Neh 9:27, 31 [b]Neh 9:12

20 "[a]You gave Your good Spirit to instruct them,
Your manna You did not withhold from their mouth,
And You gave them water for their thirst.

20 [a]Num 11:17; Neh 9:30; Is 63:11-14

21 "Indeed, [a]forty years You provided for them in the wilderness *and* they were not in want;
Their clothes did not wear out, nor did their feet swell.

21 [a]Deut 2:7

22 "You also gave them kingdoms and peoples,
And allotted *them* to them as a [1]boundary.
[a]They took possession of the land of Sihon [2]the king of Heshbon
And the land of Og the king of Bashan.

22 [1]Lit *side, corner* [2]So the Gr and the Latin; Heb reads *and the land of the king of Heshbon* [a]Num 21:21-35

23 "You made their sons numerous as [a]the stars of heaven,
And You brought them into the land
Which You had told their fathers to enter and possess.

23 [a]Gen 15:5; 22:17

24 "[a]So their sons entered and possessed the land.
And [b]You subdued before them the inhabitants of the land, the Canaanites,
And You gave them into their hand, with their kings and the peoples of the land,
To do with them [1]as they desired.

24 [1]Lit *according to their desire* [a]Josh 11:23; 21:43 [b]Josh 18:1

25 "[a]They captured fortified cities and a [1b]fertile land.
They took possession of [c]houses full of every good thing,
Hewn cisterns, vineyards, olive groves,

25 [1]Lit *fat* [a]Deut 3:5 [b]Num 13:27 [c]Deut 6:11

Fruit trees in abundance.
So they ate, were filled and [d]grew fat,
And [e]reveled in Your great goodness.

26 "[a]But they became disobedient and rebelled against You,
And [b]cast Your law behind their backs
And [c]killed Your prophets who had [d]admonished them
So that they might return to You,
And [e]they committed great [1]blasphemies.
27 "Therefore You [a]delivered them into the hand of their
oppressors who oppressed them,
But when they cried to You [b]in the time of their distress,
You heard from heaven, and according to Your great
compassion
You [c]gave them deliverers who delivered them from the
hand of their oppressors.
28 "But [a]as soon as they had rest, they did evil again before You;
Therefore You abandoned them to the hand of their
enemies, so that they ruled over them.
When they cried again to You, You heard from heaven,
And [b]many times You rescued them according to Your
compassion,
29 And [a]admonished them in order to turn them back to Your
law.
Yet [b]they acted arrogantly and did not listen to Your
commandments but sinned against Your ordinances,
By [c]which if a man observes them he shall live.
And they [1d]turned a stubborn shoulder and stiffened their
neck, and would not listen.
30 "[a]However, You bore with them for many years,
And [b]admonished them by [c]Your Spirit through Your
prophets,
Yet they would not give ear.
Therefore You gave them into the hand of the peoples of
the lands.
31 "Nevertheless, in Your great compassion You [a]did not make
an end of them or forsake them,
For You are [b]a gracious and compassionate God.

32 "Now therefore, our God, [a]the great, the mighty, and the
awesome God, who keeps covenant and
lovingkindness,
Do not let all the hardship seem insignificant before You,
Which has come upon us, our kings, our princes, our
priests, our prophets, our fathers and on all Your
people,
[b]From the days of the kings of Assyria to this day.
33 "However, [a]You are just in all that has come upon us;
For You have dealt faithfully, but we have acted wickedly.
34 "For our kings, our leaders, our priests and our fathers have
not kept Your law

25 [d]Deut 32:15 [e]1 Kin 8:66

26 [1]Lit *acts of contempt* [a]Judg 2:11 [b]1 Kin 14:9 [c]2 Chr 36:16 [d]Neh 9:30 [e]Neh 9:18

27 [a]Judg 2:14 [b]Deut 4:29 [c]Judg 2:16

28 [a]Judg 3:11 [b]Ps 106:43

29 [1]Lit *gave* [a]Neh 9:26, 30 [b]Neh 9:10, 16 [c]Lev 18:5 [d]Zech 7:11

30 [a]Ps 95:10; Acts 13:18 [b]2 Kin 17:13-18; 2 Chr 36:15, 16; Neh 9:26, 29 [c]Neh 9:20

31 [a]Jer 4:27 [b]Neh 9:17

32 [a]Neh 1:5 [b]2 Kin 15:19, 29; 2 Kin 17:3-6; Ezra 4:2, 10

33 [a]Gen 18:25; Jer 12:1

Or paid attention to Your commandments and Your
[1]admonitions with which You have [2]admonished
them.
35 "But [a]they, in their own kingdom,
[b]With Your great goodness which You gave them,
With the broad and rich land which You set before them,
Did not serve You or turn from their evil deeds.
36 "Behold, [a]we are slaves today,
And as to the land which You gave to our fathers to eat of
its fruit and its bounty,
Behold, we are slaves in it.
37 "[a]Its abundant produce is for the kings
Whom You have set over us because of our sins;
They also rule over our bodies
And over our cattle as they please,
So we are in great distress.

38 "[1]Now because of all this
[a]We are making an agreement in writing;
And on the [b]sealed document *are the names of* our leaders,
our Levites *and* our priests."

Chapter 10 Theme ______________________

10 [1]Now on the [a]sealed document *were the names of:* Nehemiah the [2]governor, the son of Hacaliah, and Zedekiah,
2 Seraiah, Azariah, Jeremiah,
3 Pashhur, Amariah, Malchijah,
4 Hattush, Shebaniah, Malluch,
5 Harim, Meremoth, Obadiah,
6 Daniel, Ginnethon, Baruch,
7 Meshullam, Abijah, Mijamin,
8 Maaziah, Bilgai, Shemaiah. These *were* the priests.
9 And the Levites: Jeshua the son of Azaniah, Binnui of the
sons of Henadad, Kadmiel;
10 also their brothers Shebaniah, Hodiah, Kelita, Pelaiah, Hanan,
11 Mica, Rehob, Hashabiah,
12 Zaccur, Sherebiah, Shebaniah,
13 Hodiah, Bani, Beninu.
14 The leaders of the people: Parosh, Pahath-moab, Elam,
Zattu, Bani,
15 Bunni, Azgad, Bebai,
16 Adonijah, Bigvai, Adin,
17 Ater, Hezekiah, Azzur,
18 Hodiah, Hashum, Bezai,
19 Hariph, Anathoth, Nebai,
20 Magpiash, Meshullam, Hezir,
21 Meshezabel, Zadok, Jaddua,
22 Pelatiah, Hanan, Anaiah,
23 Hoshea, Hananiah, Hasshub,
24 Hallohesh, Pilha, Shobek,

34 [1]Lit *testimonies* [2]Or *witnessed*
35 [a]Deut 28:47 [b]Neh 9:25
36 [a]Deut 28:48
37 [a]Deut 28:33
38 [1]Ch 10:1 in Heb [a]Neh 10:29 [b]Neh 10:1
10:1 [1]Ch 10:2 in Heb [2]Heb *Tirshatha,* a Persian title [a]Neh 9:38

25 Rehum, Hashabnah, Maaseiah,
26 Ahiah, Hanan, Anan,
27 Malluch, Harim, Baanah.
28 Now [a]the rest of the people, the priests, the Levites, the
gatekeepers, the singers, the temple servants and [b]all those
who had separated themselves from the peoples of the lands to
the law of God, their wives, their sons and their daughters, all
those who had knowledge and understanding,
29 are joining with their [1]kinsmen, their nobles, and are
[2a]taking on themselves a curse and an oath to walk in God's
law, which was given through Moses, God's servant, and to
keep and to observe all the commandments of [3]GOD our Lord,
and His ordinances and His statutes;
30 and [a]that we will not give our daughters to the peoples of
the land or take their daughters for our sons.
31 As [a]for the peoples of the land who bring wares or any
grain on the sabbath day to sell, we will not buy from them on
the sabbath or a holy day; and we will forego *the crops* the
[b]seventh year and the [c]exaction of every debt.
32 We also [1]placed ourselves under obligation to contribute yearly
[a]one third of a shekel for the service of the house of our God:
33 for the [a]showbread, for the continual grain offering, for the
continual burnt offering, the sabbaths, the new moon, for the
appointed times, for the holy things and for the sin offerings to
make atonement for Israel, and all the work of the house of our
God.
34 Likewise [a]we cast lots [b]for the supply of wood *among* the
priests, the Levites and the people so that they might bring it to
the house of our God, according to our fathers' households, at
fixed times annually, to burn on the altar of the LORD our God,
as it is written in the law;
35 and that they might bring the first fruits of our ground and
[a]the first fruits of all the fruit of every tree to the house of the
LORD annually,
36 and [a]bring to the house of our God the firstborn of our sons
and of our cattle, and the firstborn of our herds and our flocks
as it is written in the law, for the priests who are ministering in
the house of our God.
37 [a]We will also bring the first of our [1]dough, our contributions,
the fruit of every tree, the new wine and the oil [b]to the priests
at the chambers of the house of our God, and the [c]tithe of our
ground to the Levites, for the Levites are they who receive the
tithes in all the rural towns.
38 [a]The priest, the son of Aaron, shall be with the Levites
when the Levites receive tithes, and the Levites shall bring up
the tenth of the tithes to the house of our God, to the
chambers of [b]the storehouse.
39 For the sons of Israel and the sons of Levi shall bring the
[a]contribution of the grain, the new wine and the oil to the
chambers; there are the utensils of the sanctuary, the priests
who are ministering, the gatekeepers and the singers. Thus
[b]we will not [1]neglect the house of our God.

28 [a]Ezra 2:36-58 [b]Neh 9:2

29 [1]Lit *brothers* [2]Lit *entering into a* [3]Heb *YHWH,* usually rendered LORD [a]Neh 5:12

30 [a]Ex 34:16; Deut 7:3

31 [a]Neh 13:15-22 [b]Ex 23:10, 11; Lev 25:1-7 [c]Deut 15:1, 2

32 [1]Lit *imposed commandments on us* [a]Ex 30:11-16; Matt 17:24

33 [a]Lev 24:5, 6; 2 Chr 2:4

34 [a]Neh 11:1 [b]Neh 13:31

35 [a]Ex 23:19; 34:26; Deut 26:2

36 [a]Ex 13:2

37 [1]Or *coarse meal* [a]Lev 23:17 [b]Neh 13:5, 9 [c]Lev 27:30; Num 18:21

38 [a]Num 18:26 [b]Neh 13:12, 13

39 [1]Lit *forsake* [a]Deut 12:6 [b]Neh 13:10, 11

11:1 [a]Neh 7:4 [b]Neh 10:34 [c]Neh 11:18; Is 48:2

2 [a]Judg 5:9

3 [1]Lit *Israel* [2]Heb *Nethinim* [3]Lit *sons* [a]1 Chr 9:2-34 [b]Neh 7:73; 11:20 [c]Ezra 2:43 [d]Neh 7:57

9 [1]Lit *over*

12 [1]Lit *brothers,* and so throughout the ch [2]Lit *house*

14 [1]Or *the great ones*

16 [1]Lit *heads* [2]Lit *over* [a]1 Chr 26:29

17 [1]In 1 Chr 9:15, *Zichri* [2]Lit *head* [3]In 1 Chr 9:16, *Obadiah* [4]In 1 Chr 9:16, *Shemaiah*

Chapter 11 Theme ____________________

11 Now [a]the leaders of the people lived in Jerusalem, but the
rest of the people [b]cast lots to bring one out of ten to live
in Jerusalem, [c]the holy city, while nine-tenths *remained* in the
other cities.
2 And the people blessed all the men who [a]volunteered to
live in Jerusalem.
3 [a]Now these are the heads of the provinces who lived in
Jerusalem, but in the cities of Judah [b]each lived on his own
property in their cities—the [1]Israelites, the priests, the Levites,
the [2c]temple servants and the [3d]descendants of Solomon's
servants.
4 Some of the sons of Judah and some of the sons of Benjamin
lived in Jerusalem. From the sons of Judah: Athaiah the son of
Uzziah, the son of Zechariah, the son of Amariah, the son of
Shephatiah, the son of Mahalalel, of the sons of Perez;
5 and Maaseiah the son of Baruch, the son of Col-hozeh, the
son of Hazaiah, the son of Adaiah, the son of Joiarib, the son of
Zechariah, the son of the Shilonite.
6 All the sons of Perez who lived in Jerusalem were 468 able
men.
7 Now these are the sons of Benjamin: Sallu the son of Meshullam, the son of Joed, the son of Pedaiah, the son of Kolaiah,
the son of Maaseiah, the son of Ithiel, the son of Jeshaiah;
8 and after him Gabbai *and* Sallai, 928.
9 Joel the son of Zichri was their overseer, and Judah the son
of Hassenuah was second [1]in command of the city.
10 From the priests: Jedaiah the son of Joiarib, Jachin,
11 Seraiah the son of Hilkiah, the son of Meshullam, the son
of Zadok, the son of Meraioth, the son of Ahitub, the leader of
the house of God,
12 and their [1]kinsmen who performed the work of the [2]temple,
822; and Adaiah the son of Jeroham, the son of Pelaliah, the son
of Amzi, the son of Zechariah, the son of Pashhur, the son of
Malchijah,
13 and his kinsmen, heads of fathers' *households,* 242; and
Amashsai the son of Azarel, the son of Ahzai, the son of
Meshillemoth, the son of Immer,
14 and their brothers, valiant warriors, 128. And their
overseer was Zabdiel, the son of [1]Haggedolim.
15 Now from the Levites: Shemaiah the son of Hasshub, the
son of Azrikam, the son of Hashabiah, the son of Bunni;
16 and Shabbethai and Jozabad, from the [1]leaders of the
Levites, who were [2]in charge of [a]the outside work of the house
of God;
17 and Mattaniah the son of Mica, the son of [1]Zabdi, the son of
Asaph, who was the [2]leader in beginning the thanksgiving at
prayer, and Bakbukiah, the second among his brethren; and
[3]Abda the son of [4]Shammua, the son of Galal, the son of
Jeduthun.

18 All the Levites in [a]the holy city *were* 284.
19 Also the gatekeepers, Akkub, Talmon and their brethren who kept watch at the gates, *were* 172.
20 The rest of Israel, of the priests *and* of the Levites, *were* in all the cities of Judah, each [a]on his own inheritance.
21 But [a]the temple servants were living in Ophel, and Ziha and Gishpa were [1]in charge of the temple servants.
22 Now [a]the overseer of the Levites in Jerusalem was Uzzi the son of Bani, the son of Hashabiah, the son of Mattaniah, the son of Mica, from the sons of Asaph, who were the singers for the [1]service of the house of God.
23 [a]For *there was* a commandment from the king concerning them and a firm regulation for the song leaders [b]day by day.
24 Pethahiah the son of Meshezabel, of the sons [a]of Zerah the son of Judah, was the [b]king's [1]representative in all matters concerning the people.
25 Now as for the villages with their fields, some of the sons of Judah lived in [a]Kiriath-arba and its [1]towns, in [b]Dibon and its [1]towns, and in Jekabzeel and its villages,
26 and in Jeshua, in Moladah and Beth-pelet,
27 and in Hazar-shual, in Beersheba and its towns,
28 and in Ziklag, in Meconah and in its towns,
29 and in En-rimmon, in Zorah and in Jarmuth,
30 Zanoah, Adullam, and their villages, Lachish and its fields, Azekah and its towns. So they encamped from Beersheba as far as the valley of Hinnom.
31 The sons of Benjamin also *lived* from Geba *onward,* at Michmash and Aija, at Bethel and its towns,
32 at Anathoth, Nob, Ananiah,
33 Hazor, Ramah, Gittaim,
34 Hadid, Zeboim, Neballat,
35 Lod and Ono, the valley of craftsmen.
36 From the Levites, *some* divisions in Judah belonged to Benjamin.

Chapter 12 Theme ______________________________

12 Now these are [a]the priests and the Levites who came up with Zerubbabel the son of Shealtiel, and Jeshua: Seraiah, Jeremiah, Ezra,
2 Amariah, Malluch, Hattush,
3 Shecaniah, Rehum, Meremoth,
4 Iddo, Ginnethoi, Abijah,
5 Mijamin, Maadiah, Bilgah,
6 Shemaiah and Joiarib, Jedaiah,
7 Sallu, Amok, Hilkiah and Jedaiah. These were the heads of the priests and their [1]kinsmen in the days of Jeshua.
8 The Levites *were* Jeshua, Binnui, Kadmiel, Sherebiah, Judah, *and* Mattaniah *who was* [1]in charge of the songs of thanksgiving, he and his brothers.
9 Also Bakbukiah and Unni, their brothers, stood opposite them [a]in *their* service divisions.

18 [a]Neh 11:1
20 [a]Neh 11:3
21 [1]Lit *over* [a]Neh 3:26
22 [1]Or *work* [a]Neh 11:9, 14
23 [a]Ezra 6:8; 7:20 [b]Neh 12:47
24 [1]Lit *hand* [a]Gen 38:30 [b]1 Chr 18:17
25 [1]Lit *daughters,* and so throughout the ch [a]Josh 14:15 [b]Josh 13:9, 17
12:1 [a]Ezra 2:1; 7:7
7 [1]Lit *brothers*
8 [1]Lit *over*
9 [a]Neh 12:24

10 Jeshua [1]became the father of Joiakim, and Joiakim [1]became
the father of Eliashib, and Eliashib [1]became the father of Joiada,
11 and Joiada became the father of Jonathan, and Jonathan
became the father of Jaddua.
12 Now in the days of Joiakim, the priests, the heads of fathers'
households were: of Seraiah, Meraiah; of Jeremiah, Hananiah;
13 of Ezra, Meshullam; of Amariah, Jehohanan;
14 of [1]Malluchi, Jonathan; of Shebaniah, Joseph;
15 of Harim, Adna; of Meraioth, Helkai;
16 of Iddo, Zechariah; of Ginnethon, Meshullam;
17 of Abijah, Zichri; of Miniamin, of Moadiah, Piltai;
18 of Bilgah, Shammua; of Shemaiah, Jehonathan;
19 of Joiarib, Mattenai; of Jedaiah, Uzzi;
20 of Sallai, Kallai; of Amok, Eber;
21 of Hilkiah, Hashabiah; of Jedaiah, Nethanel.
22 As for the Levites, the heads of fathers' *households* were
registered in the days of Eliashib, Joiada, and Johanan and
Jaddua; so *were* the priests in the reign of Darius the Persian.
23 The sons of Levi, the heads of fathers' *households,* were
registered in the Book of the Chronicles up to the days of
Johanan the son of Eliashib.
24 The heads of the Levites *were* Hashabiah, Sherebiah and
Jeshua the son of Kadmiel, with their brothers opposite them,
[a]to praise *and* give thanks, [1]as prescribed by David the man of
God, [b]division corresponding to division.
25 Mattaniah, Bakbukiah, Obadiah, Meshullam, Talmon *and*
Akkub *were* gatekeepers keeping watch at [a]the storehouses of
the gates.
26 These *served* in the days of Joiakim the son of Jeshua, the
son of Jozadak, and in the days of [a]Nehemiah the governor and
of Ezra the priest *and* scribe.
27 Now at the dedication of the wall of Jerusalem they sought
out the Levites from all their places, to bring them to Jerusalem
so that they might celebrate the dedication with gladness, with
hymns of thanksgiving and with songs [a]*to the accompaniment*
of cymbals, harps and lyres.
28 So the sons of the singers were assembled from the district
around Jerusalem, and from [a]the villages of the Netophathites,
29 from Beth-gilgal and from *their* fields in Geba and Azmaveth,
for the singers had built themselves villages around Jerusalem.
30 The priests and the Levites [a]purified themselves; they also
purified the people, the gates and the wall.
31 Then I had the leaders of Judah come up on top of the wall,
and I appointed two great [1]choirs, [2a]the first proceeding to the
right on top of the wall toward [b]the Refuse Gate.
32 Hoshaiah and half of the leaders of Judah followed them,
33 with Azariah, Ezra, Meshullam,
34 Judah, Benjamin, Shemaiah, Jeremiah,
35 and some of the sons of the priests with trumpets; *and*
Zechariah the son of Jonathan, the son of Shemaiah, the son of
Mattaniah, the son of Micaiah, the son of Zaccur, the son of Asaph,

10 [1]Lit *begot,* and so in vv 11, 12
14 [1]In Neh 12:2, *Malluch*
24 [1]Lit *in the commandment of* [a]Neh 11:17 [b]Neh 12:9
25 [a]1 Chr 26:15
26 [a]Neh 8:9
27 [a]1 Chr 15:16, 28
28 [a]1 Chr 9:16
30 [a]Neh 13:22, 30
31 [1]Lit *thanksgiving choirs* [2]Heb *and processions to the right* [a]Neh 12:38 [b]Neh 2:13

36 and his [1]kinsmen, Shemaiah, Azarel, Milalai, Gilalai, Maai,
Nethanel, Judah *and* Hanani, [a]with the musical instruments of
David the man of God. And Ezra the scribe went before them.
37 At [a]the Fountain Gate they went directly up [b]the steps of
the city of David by the stairway of the wall above the house of
David to [c]the Water Gate on the east.
38 [a]The second [1]choir proceeded to the [2]left, while I followed
them with half of the people on the wall, [b]above the Tower of
Furnaces, to [c]the Broad Wall,
39 and above [a]the Gate of Ephraim, by [b]the Old Gate, by the
[c]Fish Gate, [d]the Tower of Hananel and the Tower of the
Hundred, as far as the Sheep Gate; and they stopped at [e]the
Gate of the Guard.
40 Then the two choirs took their stand in the house of God.
So did I and half of the officials with me;
41 and the priests, Eliakim, Maaseiah, Miniamin, Micaiah,
Elioenai, Zechariah and Hananiah, with the trumpets;
42 and Maaseiah, Shemaiah, Eleazar, Uzzi, Jehohanan,
Malchijah, Elam and Ezer. And the singers [1]sang, with Jezrahiah
their leader,
43 and on that day they offered great sacrifices and rejoiced
because [a]God had given them great joy, even the women and
children rejoiced, so that the joy of Jerusalem was heard from
afar.
44 On that day [a]men were also appointed over the chambers
for the stores, the contributions, the first fruits and the tithes,
to gather into them from the fields of the cities the portions
required by the law for the priests and Levites; for Judah
rejoiced over the priests and Levites who [1]served.
45 For they performed the [1]worship of their God and the
service of purification, together with the singers and the
gatekeepers [a]in accordance with the command of David *and* of
his son Solomon.
46 For in the days of David and [a]Asaph, in ancient times,
there were [1b]leaders of the singers, songs of praise and hymns
of thanksgiving to God.
47 So all Israel in the days of Zerubbabel and Nehemiah gave
the portions due the singers and the gatekeepers [a]as each day
required, and [b]set apart the consecrated *portion* for the Levites,
and the Levites set apart the consecrated *portion* for the sons
of Aaron.

Chapter 13 Theme ____________________

13 On that day [a]they read aloud from the book of Moses in
the hearing of the people; and there was found written
in it that [b]no Ammonite or Moabite should ever enter the
assembly of God,
2 because they did not meet the sons of Israel with bread
and water, but [a]hired Balaam against them to curse them.
However, [b]our God turned the curse into a blessing.

36 [1]Lit *brothers* [a]Neh 12:24

37 [a]Neh 2:14 [b]Neh 3:15 [c]Neh 3:26

38 [1]Lit *thanksgiving choir* [2]Lit *front* [a]Neh 12:31 [b]Neh 3:11 [c]Neh 3:8

39 [a]Neh 8:16 [b]Neh 3:6 [c]Neh 3:3 [d]Neh 3:1 [e]Neh 3:25

42 [1]Lit *caused their voices to be heard*

43 [a]Ps 9:2; 92:4

44 [1]Lit *stood* [a]Neh 13:4, 5, 12, 13

45 [1]Lit *service* [a]1 Chr 25:1

46 [1]Lit *heads* [a]2 Chr 29:30 [b]1 Chr 9:33

47 [a]Neh 11:23 [b]Num 18:21

13:1 [a]Neh 9:3 [b]Deut 23:3-5; Neh 13:23

2 [a]Num 22:3-11 [b]Deut 23:5

3 So when they heard the law, [a]they excluded [b]all foreigners
from Israel.
4 Now prior to this, Eliashib the priest, [a]who was appointed
over the chambers of the house of our God, being [1]related to
[b]Tobiah,
5 had prepared a large [1]room for him, where formerly they
put the grain offerings, the frankincense, the utensils and the
tithes of grain, wine and oil [a]prescribed for the Levites, the
singers and the gatekeepers, and the [2]contributions for the
priests.
6 But during all this *time* I was not in Jerusalem, for in [a]the
thirty-second year of [b]Artaxerxes king of Babylon I had gone to
the king. After some time, however, I asked leave from the king,
7 and I came to Jerusalem and [1]learned about the evil that
Eliashib had done for Tobiah, [a]by preparing a [2]room for him in
the courts of the house of God.
8 It was very displeasing to me, so I [a]threw all of Tobiah's
household goods out of the room.
9 Then I gave an order and [a]they cleansed the rooms; and I
returned there the utensils of the house of God with the grain
offerings and the frankincense.
10 I also [1]discovered that [a]the portions of the Levites had not
been given *them,* so that the Levites and the singers who
performed the service had [2]gone away, [b]each to his own field.
11 So I [1a]reprimanded the officials and said, "[b]Why is the
house of God forsaken?" Then I gathered them together and
restored them to their posts.
12 All Judah then brought [a]the tithe of the grain, wine and oil
into the storehouses.
13 In charge of the storehouses I appointed Shelemiah the
priest, Zadok the scribe, and Pedaiah of the Levites, and in
addition to them was Hanan the son of Zaccur, the son of
Mattaniah; for [a]they were considered reliable, and it was [1]their
task to distribute to their [2]kinsmen.
14 [a]Remember me for this, O my God, and do not blot out my
loyal deeds which I have performed for the house of my God
and its services.
15 In those days I saw in Judah some who were treading wine
presses [a]on the sabbath, and bringing in sacks of grain and
loading *them* on donkeys, as well as wine, grapes, figs and all
kinds of loads, [b]and they brought *them* into Jerusalem on the
sabbath day. So [c]I admonished *them* on the day they sold food.
16 Also men of Tyre were living [1]there *who* imported fish and
all kinds of merchandise, and sold *them* to the sons of Judah on
the sabbath, even in Jerusalem.
17 Then [a]I [1]reprimanded the nobles of Judah and said to
them, "What is this evil thing you are doing, [2]by profaning the
sabbath day?
18 "[a]Did not your fathers do the same, so that our God brought
on us and on this city all this trouble? Yet you are adding to the
wrath on Israel by profaning the sabbath."

3 [a]Neh 9:2; 10:28 [b]Ex 12:38
4 [1]Lit *close to* [a]Neh 12:44 [b]Neh 2:10; 6:1, 17, 18
5 [1]Or *chamber* [2]Lit *heave offerings* [a]Num 18:21
6 [a]Neh 5:14 [b]Ezra 6:22
7 [1]Or *understood* [2]Or *chamber,* and so in vv 8, 9 [a]Neh 13:5
8 [a]John 2:13-16
9 [a]2 Chr 29:5, 15, 16
10 [1]Or *knew* [2]Lit *fled* [a]Deut 12:19; Neh 10:37 [b]Neh 12:28, 29
11 [1]Or *contended with* [a]Neh 13:17, 25 [b]Neh 10:39
12 [a]Neh 10:37; 12:44; Mal 3:10
13 [1]Lit *on them to* [2]Lit *brothers* [a]Neh 7:2
14 [a]Neh 5:19; 13:22, 31
15 [a]Ex 20:8; 34:21; Deut 5:12-14; Jer 17:22 [b]Neh 10:31; Jer 17:21 [c]Neh 9:29; 13:21
16 [1]Lit *in it*
17 [1]Or *contended with* [2]Lit *and* [a]Neh 13:11, 25
18 [a]Ezra 9:13; Jer 17:21

19 [a]It came about that just as it grew dark at the gates of
Jerusalem before the sabbath, I commanded that the doors
should be shut [1]and that they should not open them until after
the sabbath. Then I stationed some of my servants at the gates
so that no load would enter on the sabbath day.
20 Once or twice the traders and merchants of every kind of
merchandise spent the night outside Jerusalem.
21 Then [a]I [1]warned them and said to them, "Why do you
spend the night in front of the wall? If you do so again, I will
[2]use force against you." From that time on they did not come
on the sabbath.
22 And I commanded the Levites that [a]they should purify
themselves and come as gatekeepers to sanctify the sabbath day.
For this also [b]remember me, O my God, and have compassion
on me according to the greatness of Your lovingkindness.
23 In those days I also saw that the Jews had [1a]married women
from [b]Ashdod, [c]Ammon *and* Moab.
24 As for their children, half spoke in the language of Ashdod,
and none of them was able to speak the language of Judah, but
[1]the language of his own people.
25 So [a]I contended with them and cursed them and [b]struck
some of them and pulled out their hair, and [c]made them swear
by God, "You shall not give your daughters to their sons, nor
take of their daughters for your sons or for yourselves.
26 "[a]Did not Solomon king of Israel sin regarding these things?
[b]Yet among the many nations there was no king like him, and
[c]he was loved by his God, and God made him king over all
Israel; nevertheless the foreign women caused even him to sin.
27 "[1]Do we then hear about you that you have committed all
this great evil [a]by acting unfaithfully against our God by
[2]marrying foreign women?"
28 Even one of the sons of Joiada, the son of Eliashib the high
priest, was a son-in-law of [a]Sanballat the Horonite, so I drove
him away from me.
29 [a]Remember them, O my God, [1]because they have defiled
the priesthood and the [b]covenant of the priesthood and the
Levites.
30 [a]Thus I purified them from everything foreign and appointed
duties for the priests and the Levites, each in his task,
31 and *I arranged* [a]for the supply of wood at appointed times
and for the first fruits. [b]Remember me, O my God, for good.

19 [1]Lit *and commanded* [a]Lev 23:32

21 [1]Lit *witnessed against* [2]Lit *send a hand against* [a]Neh 13:15

22 [a]1 Chr 15:12; Neh 12:30 [b]Neh 13:14, 31

23 [1]Lit *given dwelling to* [a]Ex 34:11-16; Deut 7:1-5; Ezra 9:2; Neh 10:30 [b]Neh 4:7 [c]Ezra 9:1; Neh 13:1

24 [1]Lit *according to the tongue of people and people*

25 [a]Neh 13:11, 17 [b]Deut 25:2 [c]Neh 10:29, 30

26 [a]1 Kin 11:1 [b]1 Kin 3:13; 2 Chr 1:12 [c]2 Sam 12:24, 25

27 [1]Or *Is it reported* [2]Lit *giving dwelling to* [a]Ezra 10:2; Neh 13:23

28 [a]Neh 2:10, 19; 4:1

29 [1]Lit *for the defilings of* [a]Neh 6:14 [b]Num 25:13

30 [a]Neh 10:30

31 [a]Neh 10:34 [b]Neh 13:14, 22

Lessons from the Life of Nehemiah

The Situation	How Nehemiah Related to God	How Nehemiah Related to People	Nehemiah's Example

Theme of Nehemiah:

SEGMENT DIVISIONS		CHAPTER THEMES
		1
		2
		3
		4
		5
		6
		7
		8
		9
		10
		11
		12
		13

Author:

Date:

Purpose:

Key Words:

remember

command (commandments, ordinances, law)

sin (iniquities)

covenant

fast

prayer

the book (book of the law, law of Moses)

ESTHER אסתר
ESTER

Throughout time people have attempted to destroy the nation of Israel, the "apple of God's eye." Why? Because from the Jews came the covenants, the promises, the law, and the Messiah—salvation for the world. The people of God are the enemy of Satan, the prince of this world, and the conflict is as old as Genesis 3:15.

While a remnant from Judah returned to the land promised to Abraham, Isaac, and Jacob, other Jews remained in the cities of their captivity. Some were welcomed as valued members of their communities, but others were despised and hated. Some were even targeted for extermination.

Esther tells the story. The book of Esther records a ten-year span during the 58- to 60-year interlude in the book of Ezra. Esther tells us of the inauguration of a feast that has endured over 2000 years because of one woman who, for the sake of her people, was willing to say, "If I perish, I perish."

Things to Do

Esther is a story of intrigue—a divinely inspired one. It reveals the sovereignty of God, although God is never mentioned in this book. As you read:

1. Consult the historical chart THE TIMES OF EZRA, NEHEMIAH, AND ESTHER on page 808 in order to see the setting of Esther.

2. Observe the main events that occur in each chapter. Examine each chapter under the scrutiny of the "5 W's and an H": Who? What? When? Where? Why? and How? Ask: Who was involved? What happened? When did it occur? Where did it take place and why? How did it come about? etc.

   a. List in the margin the major points you want to remember about each event under the heading you give that event. For example, Esther 1:3-4 could be titled "King Ahasuerus's Banquet." Under the heading you could list these points: 1) attended by his princes, attendants, etc., 2) given to display riches, 3) lasted 180 days.

   b. While the main event of each chapter will not always be a banquet, banquets play an important role in Esther. So mark in a distinctive way each use of the words *banquet* or *feast*. Ask the "5 W's and an H" about each banquet and list your insights in the margin.

   c. Make sure you underline or mark in a distinctive way the main characters in each chapter. Study each person's character, as there is much to be learned.

3. Mark the key words on the AT A GLANCE chart. When you mark *Jew* or *Jews*, mark the pronouns and synonyms, such as *her people*, *my kindred*, or *people*. *Jews* was a term used to describe the people who came from Judah.

4. Mark every reference to time with a clock 🕒. This will help you quickly identify the timing of the events. Also consult the calendar on page 809 so you can keep track of the references to the various months.

5. When you finish studying each chapter, record the theme of that chapter in the appropriate place on the ESTHER AT A GLANCE chart on page 821. Also record this in your Bible.

6. In your notebook, list all you learn about Esther and then list all you learn about Mordecai.

7. When you finish reading Esther, complete ESTHER AT A GLANCE. See if any of the chapters can be grouped according to events. If so, record these segment divisions on the AT A GLANCE chart.

THINGS TO THINK ABOUT

1. What can you learn from the lives of each of the main characters of this historical event? Review what you have listed about Esther and Mordecai. Have you ever realized that you too have come to the kingdom for such a time as this? What are the good works that God would have you do? Read John 15:16 and Ephesians 2:8-10.

2. Have you thought about why Mordecai was unwilling to bow before Haman? Have you "bowed" to someone or something and in so doing compromised your calling and position as a child of God? Read Galatians 1:10.

3. Esther and Mordecai relied heavily on fasting to turn the tide of events. What about you?

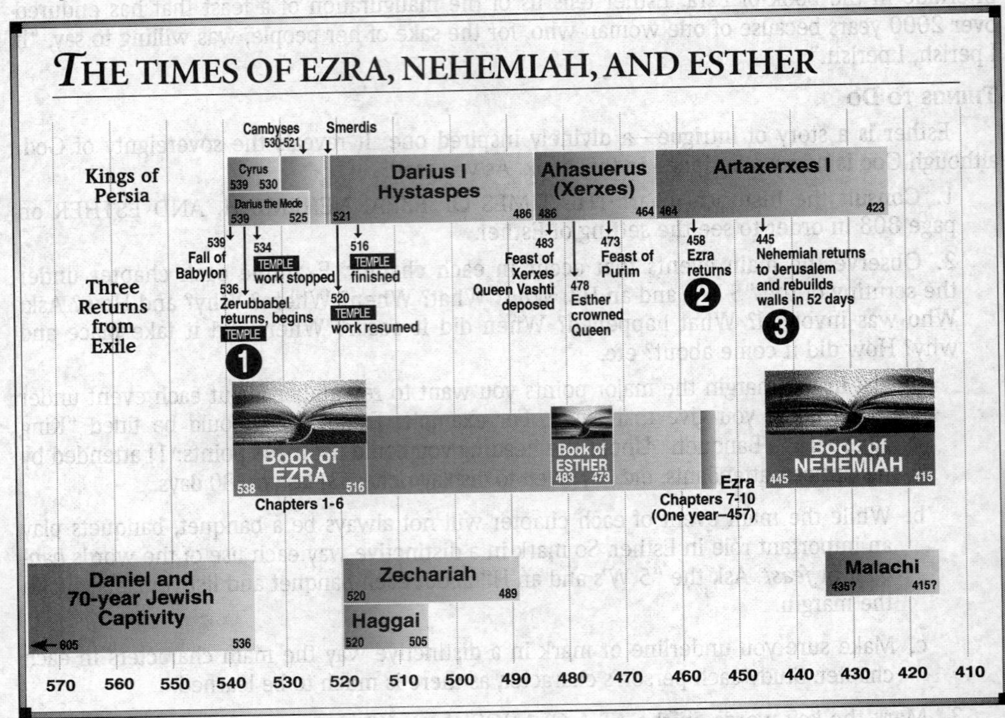

The Jewish Calendar

Babylonian names (B) for the months are still used today for the Jewish calendar. Canaanite names (C) were used prior to the Babylonian captivity in 586 B.C. Four are mentioned in the Old Testament. **Adar-Sheni** is an intercalary month used every two to three years or seven times in 19 years.

1st month	2nd month	3rd month	4th month
Nisan (B) Abib (C) March-April	Iyyar (B) Ziv (C) April-May	Sivan (B) May-June	Tammuz (B) June-July
7th month	*8th month*	*9th month*	*10th month*
5th month	**6th month**	**7th month**	**8th month**
Ab (B) July-August	Elul (B) August-September	Tishri (B) Ethanim (C) September-October	Marcheshvan (B) Bul (C) October-November
11th month	*12th month*	*1st month*	*2nd month*
9th month	**10th month**	**11th month**	**12th month**
Chislev (B) November-December	Tebeth (B) December-January	Shebat (B) January-February	Adar (B) February-March
3rd month	*4th month*	*5th month*	*6th month*

Sacred calendar appears in black • Civil calendar appears in gray

Chapter 1 Theme ______

483 B.C.

1 Now it took place in the days of [a]Ahasuerus, the Ahasuerus
who reigned [b]from India to [1]Ethiopia over [c]127 provinces,
2 in those days as King Ahasuerus [a]sat on his royal throne
which *was* at the citadel in [b]Susa,
3 in the third year of his reign [a]he gave a banquet for all his
princes and attendants, the army *officers* of Persia and Media,
the nobles and the princes of his provinces being in his
presence.
4 [1]And he displayed the riches of his royal glory and the
splendor of his great majesty for many days, 180 days.
5 When these days were completed, the king gave a banquet
lasting seven days for all the people who were present at the
citadel in Susa, from the greatest to the least, in the court of
[a]the garden of the king's palace.
6 *There were hangings of* fine white and violet linen held by
cords of fine purple linen on silver rings and marble columns, *and*
[a]couches of gold and silver on a mosaic pavement of porphyry,
marble, mother-of-pearl and precious stones.
7 Drinks were served in golden vessels of various kinds, and
the royal wine was plentiful [a]according to the king's [1]bounty.
8 The drinking was *done* according to the law, there was no
compulsion, for so the king had given orders to each official of
his household that he should do according to the desires of
each person.
9 Queen Vashti also gave a banquet for the women in the
[1]palace which belonged to King Ahasuerus.
10 On the seventh day, when the heart of the king was [a]merry
with wine, he commanded Mehuman, Biztha, Harbona, Bigtha,
Abagtha, Zethar and Carkas, the seven eunuchs who served in
the presence of King Ahasuerus,

1:1 [1]Lit *Cush* [a]Ezra 4:6; Dan 9:1 [b]Esth 8:9 [c]Esth 9:30
2 [a]1 Kin 1:46 [b]Neh 1:1; Dan 8:2
3 [a]Esth 2:18
4 [1]Lit *When*
5 [a]Esth 7:7, 8
6 [a]Ezek 23:41; Amos 6:4
7 [1]Lit *hand* [a]Esth 2:18
9 [1]Lit *royal house*
10 [a]Judg 16:25

11 to bring Queen Vashti before the king with *her* royal [a]crown
in order to display her beauty to the people and the princes, for
she was beautiful.
12 But Queen Vashti refused to come at the king's command
delivered by the eunuchs. Then the king became very angry
and his wrath burned within him.
13 Then the king said to [a]the wise men [b]who understood the
times—for it was the custom of the king so *to speak* before all
who knew law and justice
14 and were close to him: Carshena, Shethar, Admatha,
Tarshish, Meres, Marsena and Memucan, the seven princes of
Persia and Media [a]who [1]had access to the king's presence and
sat in the first place in the kingdom—
15 "According to law, what is to be done with Queen Vashti,
because she did not [1]obey the command of King Ahasuerus
delivered by the eunuchs?"
16 In the presence of the king and the princes, Memucan said,
"Queen Vashti has wronged not only the king but *also* all the
princes and all the peoples who are in all the provinces of King
Ahasuerus.
17 "For the queen's conduct will [1]become known to all the
women causing them [2]to look with contempt on their husbands
by saying, 'King Ahasuerus commanded Queen Vashti to be
brought in to his presence, but she did not come.'
18 "This day the ladies of Persia and Media who have heard of
the queen's conduct will speak in *the same way* to all the king's
princes, and there will be plenty of contempt and anger.
19 "If it pleases the king, let a royal [1]edict be issued by him and
let it be written in the laws of Persia and Media so [a]that it
cannot [2]be repealed, that Vashti may no longer come into the
presence of King Ahasuerus, and let the king give her royal
position to [3]another who is more worthy than she.
20 "When the king's edict which he will make is heard
throughout all his kingdom, [1]great as it is, then [a]all women will
give honor to their husbands, great and small."
21 *This* word pleased the king and the princes, and the king
did [1]as Memucan proposed.
22 So he sent letters to all the king's provinces, [a]to each province
according to its script and to every people according to their
language, that every man should [b]be the master in his own house
and the one who speaks in the language of his own people.

Chapter 2 Theme ________________________

2 After these things [a]when the anger of King Ahasuerus had
subsided, he remembered Vashti and what she had done
and [b]what had been decreed against her.
2 Then the king's attendants, who served him, said, "[a]Let
beautiful young virgins be sought for the king.
3 "Let the king appoint overseers in [a]all the provinces of his
kingdom that they may gather every beautiful young virgin to

11 [a]Esth 2:17; 6:8
13 [a]Jer 10:7; Dan 2:2 [b]1 Chr 12:32
14 [1]Lit *saw the face of the king* [a]2 Kin 25:19; Matt 18:10
15 [1]Lit *do*
17 [1]Lit *go forth* [2]Lit *to despise . . . in their eyes*
19 [1]Lit *word go forth from* [2]Lit *pass away* [3]Lit *her neighbor* [a]Esth 8:8; Dan 6:8
20 [1]Lit *for great is it* [a]Eph 5:22; Col 3:18
21 [1]Lit *according to the word of*
22 [a]Esth 3:12; 8:9 [b]Eph 5:22-24
2:1 [a]Esth 7:10 [b]Esth 1:19, 20
2 [a]1 Kin 1:2
3 [a]Esth 1:1, 2

the citadel of Susa, to the harem, into the custody of [b]Hegai, the
king's eunuch, who is in charge of the women; and [c]let their
cosmetics be given *them.*
4 "Then let the young lady who pleases the king be queen in
place of Vashti." And the matter pleased the king, and he did
accordingly.
5 *Now* there was at the citadel in Susa a Jew whose name
was [a]Mordecai, the son of Jair, the son of Shimei, the son of
Kish, a Benjamite,
6 [a]who had been taken into exile from Jerusalem with the
captives who had been exiled with Jeconiah king of Judah,
whom Nebuchadnezzar the king of Babylon had exiled.
7 He was bringing up Hadassah, that is [a]Esther, his uncle's
daughter, for she had no father or mother. Now the young lady
was beautiful of form and [1]face, and when her father and her
mother died, Mordecai took her as his own daughter.
8 So it came about when the command and decree of the
king were heard and [a]many young ladies were gathered to the
citadel of Susa into the custody of [b]Hegai, that Esther was taken
to the king's [1]palace into the custody of Hegai, who was in
charge of the women.
9 Now the young lady pleased him and found favor with him.
So he quickly provided her with her [a]cosmetics and [1]food, gave
her seven choice maids from the king's palace and transferred
her and her maids to the best place in the harem.
10 [a]Esther did not make known her people or her kindred, for
Mordecai had instructed her that she should not make *them*
known.
11 Every day Mordecai walked back and forth in front of the
court of the harem to learn how Esther was and how she fared.
12 Now when the turn of each young lady came to go in to
King Ahasuerus, after the end of her twelve months under the
regulations for the women—for the days of their beautification
were completed as follows: six months with oil of myrrh and
six months with spices and the cosmetics for women—
13 the young lady would go in to the king in this way: anything
that she [1]desired was given her to take with her from the harem
to the king's palace.
14 In the evening she would go in and in the morning she
would return to the second harem, to the [1]custody of Shaashgaz,
the king's eunuch who was in charge of the concubines. She
would not again go in to the king unless the king delighted in
her and she was summoned by name.
15 Now when the turn of Esther, [a]the daughter of Abihail the
uncle of Mordecai who had taken her as his daughter, came to go
in to the king, she did not request anything except what [b]Hegai,
the king's eunuch who was in charge of the women, [1]advised.
And Esther found favor in the eyes of all who saw her.
16 So Esther was taken to King Ahasuerus to his royal palace
in the tenth month which is the month Tebeth, in the seventh
year of his reign.

478 B.C.

3 [b]Esth 2:8, 15 [c]Esth 2:9, 12
5 [a]Esth 3:2
6 [a]2 Kin 24:14, 15; 2 Chr 36:10
7 [1]Lit *good of appearance* [a]Esth 2:15
8 [1]Lit *house* [a]Esth 2:3 [b]Esth 2:3, 15
9 [1]Lit *portions* [a]Esth 2:3, 12
10 [a]Esth 2:20
13 [1]Lit *said*
14 [1]Lit *hand*
15 [1]Lit *said* [a]Esth 2:7; 9:29 [b]Esth 2:3, 8

17 The king loved Esther more than all the women, and she
found favor and kindness with him more than all the virgins, so
that [a]he set the royal crown on her head and made her queen
instead of Vashti.
18 Then [a]the king gave a great banquet, Esther's banquet, for
all his princes and his servants; he also made a holiday for the
provinces and gave gifts [b]according to the king's bounty.
19 [a]When the virgins were gathered together the second time,
then Mordecai [b]was sitting at the king's gate.
20 [a]Esther had not yet made known her kindred or her people,
even as Mordecai had commanded her; for Esther did [1]what
Mordecai told her as she had done [b]when under his care.
21 In those days, while Mordecai was sitting at the king's gate,
[a]Bigthan and Teresh, two of the king's officials from those who
guarded the door, became angry and sought to [1]lay hands on
King Ahasuerus.
22 But the [1]plot became known to Mordecai and [a]he told Queen
Esther, and Esther [2]informed the king in Mordecai's name.
23 Now when the plot was investigated and found *to be so,*
they were both hanged on a [1]gallows; and it was written in
[a]the Book of the Chronicles in the king's presence.

17 [a]Esth 1:11

18 [a]Esth 1:3 [b]Esth 1:7

19 [a]Esth 2:3, 4 [b]Esth 2:21; 3:2

20 [1]Lit *the word of Mordecai* [a]Esth 2:10 [b]Esth 2:7

21 [1]Lit *send a hand against* [a]Esth 6:2

22 [1]Lit *matter,* so also v 23 [2]Lit *told* [a]Esth 6:1, 2

23 [1]Lit *tree* [a]Esth 10:2

Chapter 3 Theme ____________________

3 After these events King Ahasuerus [a]promoted Haman, the
son of Hammedatha [b]the Agagite, and [a]advanced him and
[1]established his authority over all the princes who *were* with him.
2 All the king's servants who were at the king's gate bowed
down [1]and paid homage to Haman; for so the king had
commanded concerning him. But [a]Mordecai neither bowed
down nor paid homage.
3 Then the king's servants who were at [a]the king's gate said
to Mordecai, "[b]Why are you transgressing the king's command?"
4 Now it was when they had spoken daily to him and he would
not listen to them, that they told Haman to see whether Mordecai's
reason would stand; for he had told them that he was a Jew.
5 When Haman saw that [a]Mordecai neither bowed down nor
paid homage to him, Haman was filled with rage.
6 But he [1]disdained to [2]lay hands on Mordecai alone, for
they had told him *who* the people of Mordecai *were;* therefore
Haman [a]sought to destroy all the Jews, the people of Mordecai,
who *were* throughout the whole kingdom of Ahasuerus.
7 In the first month, which is the month Nisan, in the
twelfth year of King Ahasuerus, [1]Pur, that is the lot, was [a]cast
before Haman from day to day and from month *to month,*
[2]until the twelfth month, that is [b]the month Adar.
8 Then Haman said to King Ahasuerus, "There is a certain
people scattered and dispersed among the peoples in all the
provinces of your kingdom; [a]their laws are different from *those*
of all *other* people and they do not observe the king's laws, so it
is not in the king's interest to let them remain.

INSIGHT

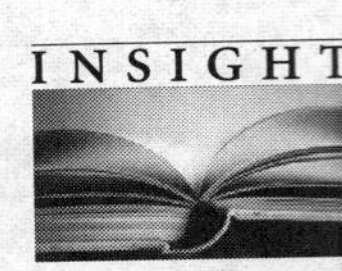

Agagite, possibly a synonym for Amalekite, is a reference to a descendant of Agag. Agag was king of the Amalekites, a tribal people whom the Lord ordered King Saul to destroy completely. Saul disobeyed by sparing King Agag, so Samuel put Agag to death. Haman, the arch villain in Esther, was an Agagite.

3:1 [1]Lit *set his seat* [a]Esth 5:11 [b]Esth 3:10; 8:3

2 [1]Lit *and prostrated themselves before* [a]Esth 2:19; 5:9

3 [a]Esth 2:19 [b]Esth 3:2

5 [a]Esth 5:9

6 [1]Lit *despised in his eyes* [2]Lit *send a hand against* [a]Ps 83:4

7 [1]Lit *he cast Pur . . . before* [2]Gr *and the lot fell on the thirteenth day of* [a]Esth 9:24-26 [b]Ezra 6:15

8 [a]Ezra 4:12-15; Acts 16:20, 21

9 [1]Lit *written*

9 "If it is pleasing to the king, let it be [1]decreed that they be destroyed, and I will pay ten thousand talents of silver into the hands of those who carry on the *king's* business, to put into the king's treasuries."

10 [a]Gen 41:42; Esth 8:2 [b]Esth 3:1 [c]Esth 7:6

10 Then [a]the king took his signet ring from his hand and gave it to Haman, the son of Hammedatha [b]the Agagite, [c]the enemy of the Jews.

11 The king said to Haman, "The silver is [1]yours, and the people *also,* to do with them as you please."

11 [1]Lit *given to you*

12 [a]Then the king's scribes were summoned on the thirteenth day of the first month, and it was written just as Haman commanded to [b]the king's satraps, to the governors who were over each province and to the princes of each people, each province according to its script, each people according to its language, being written [c]in the name of King Ahasuerus and sealed with the king's signet ring.

12 [a]Esth 8:9 [b]Ezra 8:36 [c]1 Kin 21:8; Esth 8:8, 10

13 Letters were sent by [a]couriers to all the king's provinces [b]to destroy, to kill and to annihilate all the Jews, both young and old, women and children, [c]in one day, the thirteenth *day* of the twelfth month, which is the month Adar, and to [d]seize their possessions as plunder.

13 [a]2 Chr 30:6; Esth 8:10, 14 [b]Esth 7:4 [c]Esth 8:12 [d]Esth 8:11; 9:10

14 [a]A copy of the edict to be [1]issued as law in every province was published to all the peoples so that they should be ready for this day.

15 The couriers went out impelled by the king's command while the decree was [1]issued at the citadel in Susa; and while the king and Haman sat down to drink, [a]the city of Susa was in confusion.

14 [1]Lit *given* [a]Esth 8:13, 14

Chapter 4 Theme __________________________

15 [1]Lit *given* [a]Esth 8:15

4 When Mordecai learned [a]all that had been done, [1]he tore his clothes, put on sackcloth and ashes, and went out into the midst of the city and wailed loudly and bitterly.

2 He went as far as the king's gate, for no one was to enter the king's gate clothed in sackcloth.

4:1 [1]Lit *Mordecai* [a]2 Sam 1:11; Esth 3:8-10; Jon 3:5,6

3 In each and every province where the command and decree of the king came, there was great mourning among the Jews, with [a]fasting, weeping and wailing; and many lay on sackcloth and ashes.

4 Then Esther's maidens and her eunuchs came and told her, and the queen writhed in great anguish. And she sent garments to clothe Mordecai that he might remove his sackcloth from him, but he did not accept *them.*

3 [a]Esth 4:16

5 Then Esther summoned Hathach from the king's eunuchs, whom [1]the king had appointed to attend her, and ordered him *to go* to Mordecai to learn what this *was* and why it *was.*

5 [1]Lit *he*

6 So Hathach went out to Mordecai to the city square in front of the king's gate.

7 Mordecai told him all that had happened to him, and [a]the exact amount of money that Haman had promised to pay to the king's treasuries for the destruction of the Jews.

7 [a]Esth 3:9

8 He also gave him [a]a copy of the text of the edict which had
been issued in Susa for their destruction, that he might show
Esther and inform her, and to order her to go in to the king to
implore his favor and to plead with him for her people.
9 Hathach came back and related Mordecai's words to Esther.
10 Then Esther spoke to Hathach and ordered him *to reply* to
Mordecai:
11 "All the king's servants and the people of the king's
provinces know that for any man or woman who [a]comes to the
king to the inner court who is not summoned, [b]he has but one
law, that he be put to death, unless the king holds out [c]to him
the golden scepter so that he may live. And I have not been
summoned to come to the king for these thirty days."
12 They related Esther's words to Mordecai.
13 Then Mordecai told *them* to reply to Esther, "Do not imagine
that you in the king's palace can escape any more than all the Jews.
14 "For if you remain silent at this time, relief and [a]deliverance
will arise for the Jews from another place and you and your
father's house will perish. And who knows whether you have
not attained royalty for such a time as this?"
15 Then Esther told *them* to reply to Mordecai,
16 "Go, assemble all the Jews who are found in Susa, and fast for
me; [a]do not eat or drink for [b]three days, night or day. I and my
maidens also will fast in the same way. And thus I will go in to the
king, which is not according to the law; and if I perish, I perish."
17 So Mordecai went away and did just as Esther had
commanded him.

Chapter 5 Theme ____________________

5 Now it came about [a]on the third day that Esther put on her
royal robes and stood [b]in the inner court of the king's
palace in front of the king's [1]rooms, and the king was sitting on
his royal throne in the [2]throne room, opposite the entrance to
the palace.
2 When the king saw Esther the queen standing in the court,
[a]she obtained favor in his sight; and [b]the king extended to
Esther the golden scepter which *was* in his hand. So Esther
came near and touched the top of the scepter.
3 Then the king said to her, "What is *troubling* you, Queen
Esther? And what is your request? [a]Even to half of the kingdom
it shall be given to you."
4 Esther said, "If it pleases the king, may the king and Haman
come this day to the banquet that I have prepared for him."
5 Then the king said, "[a]Bring Haman quickly that we may do
[1]as Esther desires." So the king and Haman came to the banquet
which Esther had prepared.
6 [1]As they drank their wine at the banquet, [a]the king said to
Esther, "[b]What is your petition, for it shall be granted to you.
And what is your request? Even to half of the kingdom it shall
be done."

8 [a]Esth 3:14
11 [a]Esth 5:1; 6:4 [b]Dan 2:9 [c]Esth 5:2; 8:4
14 [a]Lev 26:42; 2 Kin 13:5
16 [a]Joel 1:14; 2:12 [b]Esth 5:1
5:1 [1]Lit *house* [2]Lit *royal house* [a]Esth 4:16 [b]Esth 4:11; 6:4
2 [a]Esth 2:9 [b]Esth 4:11; 8:4
3 [a]Esth 7:2; Mark 6:23
5 [1]Lit *the word of Esther* [a]Esth 6:14
6 [1]Lit *at the banquet of wine* [a]Esth 7:2 [b]Esth 5:3

7 So Esther replied, "My petition and my request is:
8 [a]if I have found favor in the sight of the king, and if it
pleases the king to grant my petition and do [1]what I request,
may the king and Haman come to [b]the banquet which I will
prepare for them, and tomorrow I will do [2]as the king says."
9 Then Haman went out that day glad and pleased of heart;
but when Haman saw Mordecai [a]in the king's gate and [b]that he
did not stand up or [1]tremble before him, Haman was filled
with anger against Mordecai.
10 Haman controlled himself, however, went to his house and
[1]sent for his friends and his wife [a]Zeresh.
11 Then Haman recounted to them the glory of his riches, and
the [1a]number of his sons, and every *instance* where the king
had magnified him and how he had [2b]promoted him above the
princes and servants of the king.
12 Haman also said, "Even Esther the queen let no one but me
come with the king to the banquet which she had prepared;
and [a]tomorrow also I am [1]invited by her with the king.
13 "Yet all of this [1]does not satisfy me every time I see Mordecai
the Jew sitting at [a]the king's gate."
14 Then Zeresh his wife and all his friends said to him, "[a]Have
a [1]gallows fifty cubits high made and in the morning ask the
king to have Mordecai hanged on it; then go joyfully with the
king to the banquet." And the [2]advice pleased Haman, so he
had the gallows made.

Chapter 6 Theme ______________________________

6 During that night [1]the king [a]could not sleep so he gave an
order to bring [b]the book of records, the chronicles, and
they were read before the king.
2 It was found written what [a]Mordecai had reported concerning
Bigthana and Teresh, two of the king's eunuchs who were doorkeepers, that they had sought to lay hands on King Ahasuerus.
3 The king said, "What honor or dignity has been bestowed
on Mordecai for this?" Then the king's servants who attended
him said, "Nothing has been done for him."
4 So the king said, "Who is in the court?" Now Haman had
just [a]entered the outer court of the king's palace in order to
speak to the king about [b]hanging Mordecai on the gallows
which he had prepared for him.
5 The king's servants said to him, "Behold, Haman is
standing in the court." And the king said, "Let him come in."
6 So Haman came in and the king said to him, "What is to be
done for the man [a]whom the king desires to honor?" And Haman
said [1]to himself, "Whom would the king desire to honor more
than me?"
7 Then Haman said to the king, "For the man whom the
king desires to honor,
8 let them bring a royal robe which the king has worn, and
[a]the horse on which the king has ridden, and on whose head [b]a
royal crown has been placed;

8 [1]Lit *my request* [2]Lit *according to the word of the king* [a]Esth 7:3; 8:5 [b]Esth 6:14

9 [1]Or *move for* [a]Esth 2:19 [b]Esth 3:5

10 [1]Lit *sent and brought* [a]Esth 6:13

11 [1]Lit *multitude* [2]Lit *lifted* [a]Esth 9:7-10 [b]Esth 3:1

12 [1]Lit *summoned to her* [a]Esth 5:8

13 [1]Lit *is not suitable to me* [a]Esth 5:9

14 [1]Lit *tree* [2]Lit *thing* [a]Esth 6:4; 7:9, 10

6:1 [1]Lit *the king's sleep fled* [a]Dan 6:18 [b]Esth 2:23; 10:2

2 [a]Esth 2:21, 22

4 [a]Esth 4:11 [b]Esth 5:14

6 [1]Lit *in his heart* [a]Esth 6:7, 9, 11

8 [a]1 Kin 1:33 [b]Esth 1:11; 2:17

9 and let the robe and the horse be handed over to one of
the king's most noble princes and let them array the man
whom the king desires to honor and lead him on horseback
through the city square, [a]and proclaim before him, 'Thus it
shall be done to the man whom the king desires to honor.'"
10 Then the king said to Haman, "Take quickly the robes and
the horse as you have said, and do so for Mordecai the Jew,
who is sitting at the king's gate; do not fall short in anything of
all that you have said."
11 So Haman took the robe and the horse, and arrayed
Mordecai, and led him *on horseback* through the city square,
and proclaimed before him, "Thus it shall be done to the man
whom the king desires to honor."
12 Then Mordecai returned to the king's gate. But Haman
hurried home, mourning, [a]with *his* head covered.
13 Haman recounted [a]to Zeresh his wife and all his friends
everything that had happened to him. Then his wise men and
Zeresh his wife said to him, "If Mordecai, before whom you
have begun to fall, is [1]of Jewish origin, you will not overcome
him, but will surely fall before him."
14 While they were still talking with him, the king's eunuchs
arrived and hastily [a]brought Haman to the banquet which
Esther had prepared.

Chapter 7 Theme ________________________

7 Now the king and Haman came to drink *wine* with Esther
the queen.
2 And the king said to Esther on the second day also [1]as they
drank their wine at the banquet, "[a]What is your petition, Queen
Esther? It shall be granted you. And what is your request?
[b]Even to half of the kingdom it shall be done."
3 Then Queen Esther replied, "[a]If I have found favor in your
sight, O king, and if it pleases the king, let my life be given me
as my petition, and my people as my request;
4 for [a]we have been sold, I and my people, to be destroyed,
[b]to be killed and to be annihilated. Now if we had only been sold
as slaves, men and women, I would have remained silent, for the
[1]trouble would not be commensurate with the [2]annoyance to
the king."
5 Then King Ahasuerus [1]asked Queen Esther, "Who is he,
and where is he, [2]who would presume to do thus?"
6 Esther said, "[a]A foe and an enemy is this wicked Haman!"
Then Haman became terrified before the king and queen.
7 The king arose [a]in his anger from [1]drinking wine *and went*
into [b]the palace garden; but Haman stayed to beg for his life
from Queen Esther, for he saw that harm had been determined
against him by the king.
8 Now when the king returned from the palace garden into
the [1]place where they were drinking wine, Haman was falling
on [a]the couch where Esther was. Then the king said, "Will he

9 [a]Gen 41:43

12 [a]2 Sam 15:30

13 [1]Lit *from the seed of the Jews* [a]Esth 5:10

14 [a]Esth 5:8

7:2 [1]Lit *at the banquet of wine* [a]Esth 5:6; 9:12 [b]Esth 5:3

3 [a]Esth 5:8; 8:5

4 [1]Or *enemy could not compensate for the loss* [2]Or *damage* [a]Esth 3:9 [b]Esth 3:13

5 [1]Lit *said and said to* [2]Lit *whose heart has been filled*

6 [a]Esth 3:10

7 [1]Lit *the banquet of wine* [a]Esth 1:12 [b]Esth 1:5

8 [1]Lit *house of the banquet of wine* [a]Esth 1:6

9 [a]Esth 5:14 [b]Esth 2:22

even assault the queen with me in the house?" As the word
went out of the king's mouth, they covered Haman's face.
9 Then Harbonah, one of the eunuchs who *were* before the
king said, "Behold indeed, [a]the gallows standing at Haman's
house fifty cubits high, which Haman made for Mordecai [b]who

10 [1]Lit *tree* [a]Ps 7:16; 94:23 [b]Esth 7:7, 8

spoke good on behalf of the king!" And the king said, "Hang
him on it."
10 [a]So they hanged Haman on the [1]gallows which he had
prepared for Mordecai, [b]and the king's anger subsided.

8:1 [a]Esth 7:6 [b]Esth 2:7, 15

Chapter 8 Theme ____________________

8 On that day King Ahasuerus gave the house of Haman,
[a]the enemy of the Jews, to Queen Esther; and Mordecai
came before the king, for Esther had disclosed [b]what he was
to her.

2 [a]Esth 3:10

2 [a]The king took off his signet ring which he had taken away
from Haman, and gave it to Mordecai. And Esther set Mordecai
over the house of Haman.
3 Then Esther spoke again to the king, fell at his feet, wept

4 [a]Esth 4:11; 5:2

and implored him to avert the evil *scheme* of Haman the
Agagite and his plot which he had devised against the Jews.
4 [a]The king extended the golden scepter to Esther. So Esther
arose and stood before the king.
5 Then she said, "[a]If it pleases the king and if I have found

5 [a]Esth 5:8; 7:3 [b]Esth 3:13

favor before him and the matter *seems* proper to the king and I
am pleasing in his sight, let it be written to revoke the [b]letters
devised by Haman, the son of Hammedatha the Agagite, which
he wrote to destroy the Jews who are in all the king's provinces.
6 "For [a]how can I endure to see the calamity which will befall

6 [a]Esth 7:4; 9:1

my people, and how can I endure to see the destruction of my
kindred?"
7 So King Ahasuerus said to Queen Esther and to Mordecai
the Jew, "Behold, [a]I have given the house of Haman to Esther,

7 [a]Esth 8:1

and him they have hanged on the gallows because he had
stretched out his hands against the Jews.
8 "Now you write to the Jews [1]as you see fit, in the king's
name, and [a]seal *it* with the king's signet ring; for a decree
which is written in the name of the king and sealed with the

8 [1]Lit *according to the good in your eyes* [a]Esth 3:12; 8:10 [b]Esth 1:19

king's signet ring [b]may not be revoked."
9 [a]So the king's scribes were called at that time in the third
month (that is, the month Sivan), on the twenty-third [1]day; and
it was written according to all that Mordecai commanded to the
Jews, the satraps, the governors and the princes of the provinces
which *extended* [b]from India to [2]Ethiopia, 127 provinces, to

9 [1]Lit *in it* [2]Lit *Cush* [a]Esth 3:12 [b]Esth 1:1 [c]Esth 1:22; 3:12

[c]every province according to its script, and to every people
according to their language as well as to the Jews according to
their script and their language.
10 He wrote in the name of King Ahasuerus, and sealed it
with the king's signet ring, and sent letters by couriers on

10 [a]1 Kin 4:28

[a]horses, riding on steeds sired by the royal stud.

11 [1]In them the king granted the Jews who were in each and
every city *the right* [a]to assemble and to defend their lives, [b]to
destroy, to kill and to annihilate the entire army of any people
or province which might attack them, including children and
women, and [c]to plunder their spoil,
12 on [a]one day in all the provinces of King Ahasuerus, the
thirteenth *day* of the twelfth month (that is, the month Adar).
13 [a]A copy of the edict to be [1]issued as law in each and every
province was published to all the peoples, so that the Jews would
be ready for this day to avenge themselves on their enemies.
14 The couriers, hastened and impelled by the king's command,
went out, riding on the royal steeds; and the decree was given
out at the citadel in Susa.
15 Then Mordecai went out from the presence of the king [a]in
royal robes of [1]blue and white, with a large crown of gold and
[b]a garment of fine linen and purple; and [c]the city of Susa
shouted and rejoiced.
16 For the Jews there was [a]light and gladness and joy and honor.
17 In each and every province and in each and every city,
wherever the king's commandment and his decree arrived,
there was gladness and joy for the Jews, a feast and a [1a]holiday.
And [b]many among the peoples of the land became Jews, for the
dread of the Jews had fallen on them.

Chapter 9 Theme ______________________________

9 Now [a]in the twelfth month (that is, the month Adar), on
[b]the thirteenth [1]day [c]when the king's command and edict
[2]were about to be executed, on the day when the enemies of
the Jews hoped to gain the mastery over them, it was turned to
the contrary so that the Jews themselves gained the mastery
over those who hated them.
2 [a]The Jews assembled in their cities throughout all the
provinces of King Ahasuerus to lay hands on those who sought
their harm; and no one could stand before them, [b]for the dread
of them had fallen on all the peoples.
3 Even all the princes of the provinces, [a]the satraps, the
governors and those who were doing the king's business [1]assisted
the Jews, because the dread of Mordecai had fallen on them.
4 Indeed, Mordecai was great in the king's house, and his
fame spread throughout all the provinces; for the man
Mordecai [a]became greater and greater.
5 Thus [a]the Jews struck all their enemies with [1]the sword,
killing and destroying; and they did what they pleased to those
who hated them.
6 At the citadel in Susa the Jews killed and destroyed five
hundred men,
7 and Parshandatha, Dalphon, Aspatha,
8 Poratha, Adalia, Aridatha,
9 Parmashta, Arisai, Aridai and Vaizatha,
10 [a]the ten sons of Haman the son of Hammedatha, the Jews'
enemy; but [b]they did not lay their hands on the plunder.

11 [1]Lit *Which* [a]Esth 9:2 [b]Esth 3:13 [c]Esth 9:10

12 [a]Esth 3:13; 9:1

13 [1]Lit *given* [a]Esth 3:14

15 [1]Or *violet* [a]Esth 5:11 [b]Gen 41:42 [c]Esth 3:15

16 [a]Ps 97:11; 112:4

17 [1]Lit *good day* [a]Esth 9:19 [b]Esth 9:27

9:1 [1]Lit *day in it* [2]Lit *drew near* [a]Esth 8:12 [b]Esth 9:17 [c]Esth 3:13

2 [a]Esth 8:11; 9:15-18 [b]Esth 8:17

3 [1]Lit *lifted up* [a]Ezra 8:36

4 [a]2 Sam 3:1; 1 Chr 11:9

5 [1]Lit *the stroke of* [a]Esth 3:13

10 [a]Esth 5:11 [b]Esth 8:11

11 [1]Lit *came*

11 On that day the number of those who were killed at the
citadel in Susa [1]was reported to the king.

12 [a]Esth 5:6; 7:2

12 The king said to Queen Esther, "The Jews have killed and
destroyed five hundred men and the ten sons of Haman at the
citadel in Susa. What then have they done in the rest of the king's
provinces! [a]Now what is your petition? It shall even be granted
you. And what is your further request? It shall also be done."

13 [a]Esth 8:11; 9:15

13 Then said Esther, "If it pleases the king, [a]let tomorrow also be
granted to the Jews who are in Susa to do according to the edict
of today; and let Haman's ten sons be hanged on the gallows."

15 [a]Esth 9:12 [b]Esth 9:10

14 So the king commanded that it should be done so; and an
edict was issued in Susa, and Haman's ten sons were hanged.
15 The Jews who were in Susa assembled also on the fourteenth
day of the month Adar and killed [a]three hundred men in Susa,
but [b]they did not lay their hands on the plunder.

16 [1]Lit *have rest from* [a]Esth 9:2 [b]Lev 26:7, 8; Esth 8:11

16 Now [a]the rest of the Jews who *were* in the king's provinces
[b]assembled, to defend their lives and [1]rid themselves of their
enemies, and kill 75,000 of those who hated them; but they
did not lay their hands on the plunder.

17 [1]Lit *in it* [a]Esth 9:1 [b]Esth 9:21

17 *This was done* on [a]the thirteenth day of the month Adar,
and [b]on the fourteenth [1]day they rested and made it a day of
feasting and rejoicing.

18 [1]Lit *in it* [a]Esth 8:11; 9:2 [b]Esth 9:21

18 But the Jews who were in Susa [a]assembled on the thirteenth
and [b]the fourteenth [1]of the same month, and they rested on
the fifteenth [1]day and made it a day of feasting and rejoicing.

19 [1]Lit *rejoicing and feasting and a good day and sending* [a]Deut 3:5; Zech 2:4 [b]Esth 9:22 [c]Neh 8:10

19 Therefore the Jews of the rural areas, who live in [a]the rural
towns, make the fourteenth day of the month Adar *a* [1b]holiday for
rejoicing and feasting and [c]sending portions *of food* to one another.
20 Then Mordecai recorded these events, and he sent letters
to all the Jews who were in all the provinces of King Ahasuerus,
both near and far,

21 [1]Lit *in it*

21 obliging them to celebrate the fourteenth day of the month
Adar, and the fifteenth day [1]of the same month, annually,

22 [1]Lit *had rest from* [2]Lit *good day* [a]Ps 30:11 [b]Neh 8:12

22 because on those days the Jews [1]rid themselves of their
enemies, and *it was a* month which was [a]turned for them from
sorrow into gladness and from mourning into a [2]holiday; that
they should make them days of feasting and rejoicing and
[b]sending portions *of food* to one another and gifts to the poor.
23 Thus the Jews undertook what they had started to do, and
what Mordecai had written to them.

24 [a]Esth 3:7

24 For Haman the son of Hammedatha, the Agagite, the
adversary of all the Jews, had schemed against the Jews to
destroy them and [a]had cast Pur, that is the lot, to disturb them
and destroy them.

25 [1]Lit *before the king, he* [2]Lit *schemed* [3]Lit *tree* [a]Esth 7:4-10 [b]Esth 3:6-15 [c]Ps 7:16

25 But [a]when it came [1]to the king's attention, he commanded
by letter [b]that his wicked scheme which he had [2]devised
against the Jews, [c]should return on his own head and that he
and his sons should be hanged on the [3]gallows.

26 [1]Lit *Therefore because of all the words* [a]Esth 9:20

26 Therefore they called these days Purim after the name of
Pur. [1]And [a]because of the instructions in this letter, both what
they had seen in this regard and what had happened to them,

27 the Jews established and [1]made a custom for themselves and
for their [2]descendants and for [a]all those who allied themselves
with them, so that [3]they would not fail [b]to celebrate these two
days according to their [4]regulation and according to their
appointed time annually.
28 So these days were to be remembered and celebrated
throughout every generation, every family, every province and
every city; and these days of Purim were not to [1]fail from among
the Jews, or their memory [2]fade from their [3]descendants.
29 Then Queen Esther, [a]daughter of Abihail, with Mordecai
the Jew, wrote with full authority to confirm [b]this second letter
about Purim.
30 He sent letters to all the Jews, [a]to the 127 provinces of the
kingdom of Ahasuerus, *namely,* words of peace and truth,
31 to establish these days of Purim at their appointed times,
just as Mordecai the Jew and Queen Esther had established for
them, and just as they had established for themselves and for
their [1]descendants with [2]instructions [a]for their times of fasting
and their lamentations.
32 The command of Esther established these [1]customs for
[a]Purim, and it was written in the book.

Chapter 10 Theme ____________________

10 Now King Ahasuerus laid a tribute on the land and on
the [a]coastlands of the sea.
2 And all the [1]accomplishments of his authority and strength,
and the full account of the greatness of Mordecai [a]to which the
king [2]advanced him, are they not written in [b]the Book of the
Chronicles of the Kings of Media and Persia?
3 For Mordecai the Jew was [a]second *only* to King Ahasuerus,
and great among the Jews and in favor with his many kinsmen,
[b]one who sought the good of his people and one who spoke for
the welfare of his whole nation.

27 [1]Lit *received* [2]Lit *seed* [3]Lit *it should not pass away* [4]Lit *writing* [a]Esth 8:17 [b]Esth 9:20, 21

28 [1]Lit *pass away* [2]Lit *end* [3]Lit *seed*

29 [a]Esth 2:15 [b]Esth 9:20, 21

30 [a]Esth 1:1

31 [1]Lit *seed* [2]Lit *words* [a]Esth 4:3

32 [1]Lit *words* [a]Esth 9:26

10:1 [a]Is 11:11; 24:15

2 [1]Lit *doings* [2]Lit *made him great* [a]Esth 8:15; 9:4 [b]Esth 2:23

3 [a]Gen 41:43, 44 [b]Neh 2:10

Esther at a Glance

Theme of Esther:

Author:

Date:

Purpose:

Key Words:

- anger (angry)
- banquet, feast
- Jew, Jews
- edict (decree)
- fast
- destroy (destroyed, destruction)

Segment Divisions		Chapter Themes
		1
		2
		3
		4
		5
		6
		7
		8
		9
		10

JOB איוב IYYOV

Job is a book born out of pain. Job's pain was so crushing he wanted to die, so unrelenting he wished he had never been born. His pain was compounded as his friends wrestled with the reason for his suffering. Job's affliction brought God's character and ways into question. Yet ultimately it brought deeper intimacy with God.

Job, the first and probably oldest of the poetical books of the Bible, is for those who need answers from God, for those who want to say with Job, "It is still my consolation, and I rejoice in unsparing pain, that I have not denied the words of the Holy One" (6:10).

Things to Do

1. Chapters 1 and 2 provide the setting of Job's pain. Read through these two chapters. Mark every reference to Satan and to God. On the OBSERVATIONS CHART on page 873:

   a. List what you learn about Satan—his person and his relationship to God and to Job.

   b. List what you learn about God.

   c. List what you learn about Job: what God says about him; what Satan says; how he responds to God, to his pain, and to the counsel of his wife.

2. In order to understand Job and the ensuing discourses of his friends, read Job 1:8 and 2:3,11-13 and then Job 42:7-9. Do this before you proceed any further. Pay attention to what God says about Job and to what God says about what Job's three friends said.

3. In chapter 3 Job pours out his anguish, and then in chapters 4 through 42:6 there is a series of discourses given either by Job, his friends, or God Himself. Read through this section chapter by chapter and do the following:

   a. In your Bible, next to each chapter number, note who is speaking and to whom. Then record this under chapter themes on the JOB AT A GLANCE chart on pages 874, 875. You might want to color-code Job's and his friends' names so you can quickly distinguish who is speaking.

   b. Job 42:7 says that Job's friends did not speak what was right concerning God. Therefore, if one of these three men speaks, in the margin note how his reasoning is wrong in respect to God and to Job's suffering. Watch carefully to see where or how (if it tells) Job's friend came up with his conclusion. Then watch how Job answers each of his friends. Record pertinent notes in the margin.

4. As you read Job 4 through 42 observe what the text says about:

   a. Man and God

   b. What God expects from man and what He does not expect

   c. Nature

   d. Sin and righteousness

   e. Physical life and death

   f. How to deal with those in pain

Record your insights on the OBSERVATIONS CHART on page 873 as you read each chapter.

5. Mark key words or phrases that play a significant role in a particular chapter or which recur throughout the book. These are listed on the AT A GLANCE chart on pages 874, 875. Note in the margin the insights you glean about God by marking *wisdom* and other key words. Also highlight or underline verses which speak to your heart.

6. Don't fail to compare Job's end with his beginning and to notice what came from Satan's challenge.

7. When you finish reading Job and you have filled in JOB AT A GLANCE, note how the book divides itself into a pattern of discourses. Record this under "Segment Divisions."

Things to Think About

1. Think about Job's end compared to his beginning and then ask yourself if Job's suffering was worth it. What about your suffering? What can it produce if you will respond in the proper way? What is the proper way? What did you learn from Job?

2. What have you learned about Satan and Satan's relationship to God from this book? How can those insights comfort you?

3. Read Job 31 again, and if you did not mark it the first time, mark in a distinctive way every *if* and every *if I have*. Think about how Job appealed to his own integrity in various matters of life. Examine those areas carefully. How does your own integrity measure up in those areas? What do you need to remember, do, hold onto, let go of, begin, or stop?

Chapter 1 Theme ______________________

1:1 [a]Jer 25:20; Lam 4:21 [b]Ezek 14:14, 20; James 5:11 [c]Gen 6:9; 17:1; Deut 18:13 [d]Gen 22:12; 42:18; Ex 18:21; Prov 8:13 [e]Job 28:28

1 There was a man in the [a]land of Uz whose name was [b]Job;
and that man was [c]blameless, upright, [d]fearing God and
[e]turning away from evil.
2 [a]Seven sons and three daughters were born to him.

2 [a]Job 42:13

3 [a]His possessions also were 7,000 sheep, 3,000 camels, 500
yoke of oxen, 500 female donkeys, and very many servants;
and that man was [b]the greatest of all the [1]men of the east.

3 [1]Lit *sons* [a]Job 42:12 [b]Job 29:25

4 His sons used to go and hold a feast in the house of each
one on his day, and they would send and invite their three
sisters to eat and drink with them.

5 [a]Gen 8:20; Job 42:8 [b]Job 8:4 [c]1 Kin 21:10, 13

5 When the days of feasting had completed their cycle, Job
would send and consecrate them, rising up early in the
morning and offering [a]burnt offerings *according to* the number
of them all; for Job said, "[b]Perhaps my sons have sinned and
[c]cursed God in their hearts." Thus Job did continually.

6 [1]I.e. the adversary, and so throughout chs 1 and 2 [a]Job 2:1 [b]Job 38:7

6 [a]Now there was a day when the [b]sons of God came to
present themselves before the LORD, and [1]Satan also came
among them.

7 [a]1 Pet 5:8

7 The LORD said to Satan, "From where do you come?" Then
Satan answered the LORD and said, "[a]From roaming about on
the earth and walking around on it."

8 [1]Lit *set your heart to* [2]Or *revering* [a]Num 12:7; Josh 1:2, 7; Job 42:7, 8 [b]Job 1:1

8 The LORD said to Satan, "Have you [1]considered [a]My servant
Job? For there is no one like him on the earth, [b]a blameless and
upright man, [2]fearing God and turning away from evil."

9 [1]Lit *LORD and said* [a]Rev 12:9f

9 Then [a]Satan answered the [1]LORD, "Does Job fear God for
nothing?

10 "[a]Have You not made a hedge about him and his house and
all that he has, on every side? [b]You have blessed the work of his
hands, and his [c]possessions have increased in the land.
11 "[a]But put forth Your hand now and [b]touch all that he has; he
will surely curse You to Your face."
12 Then the LORD said to Satan, "Behold, all that he has is in
your [1]power, only do not put forth your hand on him." So Satan
departed from the presence of the LORD.
13 Now on the day when his sons and his daughters were
eating and drinking wine in their oldest brother's house,
14 a messenger came to Job and said, "The oxen were
plowing and the [1]donkeys feeding beside them,
15 and [1]the [a]Sabeans [2]attacked and took them. They also [3]slew
the servants with the edge of the sword, and [4]I alone have escaped
to tell you."
16 While he was still speaking, another also came and said,
"[a]The fire of God fell from heaven and burned up the sheep and
the servants and consumed them, and I alone have escaped to
tell you."
17 While he was still speaking, another also came and said, "The
[a]Chaldeans formed three bands and made a raid on the camels
and took them and [1]slew the servants with the edge of the
sword, and I alone have escaped to tell you."
18 While he was still speaking, another also came and said,
"Your sons and your daughters were eating and drinking wine
in their oldest brother's house,
19 and behold, a great wind came from across the wilderness
and struck the four corners of the house, and it fell on the young
people and they died, and I alone have escaped to tell you."
20 Then Job arose and [a]tore his robe and shaved his head, and
he fell to the ground and worshiped.
21 He said,
"[a]Naked I came from my mother's womb,
And naked I shall return there.
The [b]LORD gave and the LORD has taken away.
Blessed be the name of the LORD."
22 [a]Through all this Job did not sin nor did he [1]blame God.

Chapter 2 Theme ______________________

2 [a]Again there was a day when the sons of God came to
present themselves before the LORD, and Satan also came
among them to present himself before the LORD.
2 The LORD said to Satan, "Where have you come from?" Then
Satan answered the LORD and said, "From roaming about on
the earth and walking around on it."
3 The LORD said to Satan, "Have you [1]considered My servant
Job? For there is no one like him on the earth, a blameless and
upright man [2]fearing God and turning away from evil. And he
still [a]holds fast his integrity, although you incited Me against
him to [3]ruin him without cause."

10 [a]Job 29:2-6; Ps 34:7 [b]Job 31:25 [c]Job 1:3; 31:25

11 [a]Job 2:5 [b]Job 19:21

12 [1]Lit *hand*

14 [1]Lit *female donkeys*

15 [1]Lit *Sheba* [2]Lit *fell upon* [3]Lit *smote* [4]Lit *only I alone*, and so also vv 16, 17, 19 [a]Gen 10:7; Job 6:19

16 [a]Gen 19:24; Lev 10:2; Num 11:1-3

17 [1]Lit *smote* [a]Gen 11:28, 31

20 [a]Gen 37:29, 34; Josh 7:6

21 [a]Eccl 5:15 [b]1 Sam 2:7, 8; Job 2:10

22 [1]Lit *ascribe unseemliness to* [a]Job 2:10

2:1 [a]Job 1:6-8

3 [1]Lit *set your heart to* [2]Or *revering* [3]Lit *swallow him up* [a]Job 27:5, 6

5 [a]Job 1:11 [b]Job 19:20
6 [1]Lit *hand*
7 [a]Deut 28:35; Job 7:5; 13:28; 30:17, 18, 30
8 [a]Job 42:6; Jer 6:26; Ezek 27:30; Jon 3:6
10 [a]Job 1:21 [b]Job 1:22; Ps 39:1; James 1:12
11 [a]Gen 36:11; Job 6:19; Jer 49:7 [b]Gen 25:2 [c]Job 42:11; Rom 12:15
12 [a]Job 1:20 [b]Josh 7:6; Neh 9:1; Lam 2:10; Ezek 27:30
13 [a]Gen 50:10; Ezek 3:15
3:1 [1]Lit *his day*
2 [1]Lit *answered and said*
3 [1]Lit *man-child* [a]Jer 20:14-18
5 [a]Jer 13:16
8 [1]Or *skillful* [a]Job 41:1, 25
9 [1]Lit *eyelids*

4 Satan answered the LORD and said, "Skin for skin! Yes, all
that a man has he will give for his life.
5 "[a]However, put forth Your hand now, and [b]touch his bone
and his flesh; he will curse You to Your face."
6 So the LORD said to Satan, "Behold, he is in your [1]power,
only spare his life."
7 Then Satan went out from the presence of the LORD and
smote Job with [a]sore boils from the sole of his foot to the
crown of his head.
8 And he took a potsherd to scrape himself while [a]he was
sitting among the ashes.
9 Then his wife said to him, "Do you still hold fast your
integrity? Curse God and die!"
10 But he said to her, "You speak as one of the foolish women
speaks. [a]Shall we indeed accept good from God and not accept
adversity?" [b]In all this Job did not sin with his lips.
11 Now when Job's three friends heard of all this adversity
that had come upon him, they came each one from his own
place, Eliphaz the [a]Temanite, Bildad the [b]Shuhite and Zophar
the Naamathite; and they made an appointment together to
come to [c]sympathize with him and comfort him.
12 When they lifted up their eyes at a distance and did not
recognize him, they raised their voices and wept. And each of
them [a]tore his robe and they [b]threw dust over their heads
toward the sky.
13 [a]Then they sat down on the ground with him for seven
days and seven nights with no one speaking a word to him, for
they saw that *his* pain was very great.

Chapter 3 Theme ______________________________

3

Afterward Job opened his mouth and cursed [1]the day of his
birth.
2 And Job [1]said,
3 "[a]Let the day perish on which I was to be born,
And the night *which* said, 'A [1]boy is conceived.'
4 "May that day be darkness;
Let not God above care for it,
Nor light shine on it.
5 "Let [a]darkness and black gloom claim it;
Let a cloud settle on it;
Let the blackness of the day terrify it.
6 "*As for* that night, let darkness seize it;
Let it not rejoice among the days of the year;
Let it not come into the number of the months.
7 "Behold, let that night be barren;
Let no joyful shout enter it.
8 "Let those curse it who curse the day,
Who are [1]prepared to [a]rouse Leviathan.
9 "Let the stars of its twilight be darkened;
Let it wait for light but have none,
And let it not see the [1]breaking dawn;

10 Because it did not shut the opening of my *mother's* womb,
Or hide trouble from my eyes.

11 "[a]Why did I not die [1]at birth,
Come forth from the womb and expire?
12 "Why did the knees receive me,
And why the breasts, that I should suck?
13 "For now I [a]would have lain down and been quiet;
I would have slept then, I would have been at rest,
14 With [a]kings and *with* [b]counselors of the earth,
Who rebuilt [c]ruins for themselves;
15 Or with [a]princes [b]who had gold,
Who were filling their houses *with* silver.
16 "Or like a miscarriage which is [1]discarded, I would not be,
As infants that never saw light.
17 "There the wicked cease from raging,
And there the [1]weary are at [a]rest.
18 "The prisoners are at ease together;
They do not hear the voice of the taskmaster.
19 "The small and the great are there,
And the slave is free from his master.

20 "Why is [a]light given to him who suffers,
And life to the bitter of soul,
21 Who [1a]long for death, but there is none,
And dig for it more than for [b]hidden treasures,
22 Who rejoice greatly,
And exult when they find the grave?
23 "*Why is light given* to a man [a]whose way is hidden,
And whom [b]God has hedged in?
24 "For [a]my groaning comes at the sight of my food,
And [b]my cries pour out like water.
25 "For [1a]what I fear comes upon me,
And what I dread befalls me.
26 "I [a]am not at ease, nor am I quiet,
And I am not at rest, but turmoil comes."

Chapter 4 Theme ____________________________

4 Then Eliphaz the Temanite [1]answered,
2 "If one ventures a word with you, will you become impatient?
But [a]who can refrain [1]from speaking?
3 "Behold [a]you have admonished many,
And you have strengthened weak hands.
4 "Your words have [1]helped the tottering to stand,
And you have strengthened [2]feeble knees.
5 "But now it has come to you, and you [a]are impatient;
It [b]touches you, and you are dismayed.
6 "Is not your [1a]fear *of God* [b]your confidence,
And the integrity of your ways your hope?

11 [1]Lit *from the womb* [a]Job 10:18, 19
13 [a]Job 3:13-19; 7:8-10, 21; 10:21, 22; 14:10-15, 20-22; 16:22; 17:13-16; 19:25-27; 21:13, 23-26; 24:19, 20; 26:5, 6; 34:22
14 [a]Job 12:18 [b]Job 12:17 [c]Job 15:28; Is 58:12
15 [a]Job 12:21 [b]Job 27:16, 17
16 [1]Lit *hidden*
17 [1]Lit *weary of strength* [a]Job 17:16
20 [a]Jer 20:18
21 [1]Lit *wait* [a]Rev 9:6 [b]Prov 2:4
23 [a]Job 19:6, 8, 12 [b]Job 19:8; Ps 88:8; Lam 3:7
24 [a]Job 6:7; 33:20 [b]Job 30:16; Ps 42:4
25 [1]Lit *the fear I fear and* [a]Job 9:28; 30:15
26 [a]Job 7:13, 14
4:1 [1]Lit *answered and said*
2 [1]Lit *in words* [a]Job 32:18-20
3 [a]Job 4:3, 4; 29:15, 16, 21, 25
4 [1]Lit *caused* [2]Lit *bowing*
5 [a]Job 6:14 [b]Job 19:21
6 [1]Or *reverence* [a]Job 1:1 [b]Prov 3:26

7 "Remember now, [a]who *ever* perished being innocent?
Or where were the upright destroyed?
8 "According to what I have seen, [a]those who plow iniquity
And those who sow trouble harvest it.
9 "By [a]the breath of God they perish,
And [b]by the [1]blast of His anger they come to an end.
10 "The [a]roaring of the lion and the voice of the *fierce* lion,
And the teeth of the young lions are broken.
11 "The [a]lion perishes for lack of prey,
And the [b]whelps of the lioness are scattered.

12 "Now a word [a]was brought to me stealthily,
And my ear received a [b]whisper of it.
13 "Amid disquieting [a]thoughts from the visions of the night,
When deep sleep falls on men,
14 Dread came upon me, and trembling,
And made [1]all my bones shake.
15 "Then a [1]spirit passed by my face;
The hair of my flesh bristled up.
16 "It stood still, but I could not discern its appearance;
A form *was* before my eyes;
There was silence, then I heard a voice:
17 'Can [a]mankind be just [1]before God?
Can a man be pure [1]before his [b]Maker?
18 '[a]He puts no trust even in His servants;
And against His angels He charges error.
19 'How much more those who dwell in [a]houses of clay,
Whose [b]foundation is in the dust,
Who are crushed before the moth!
20 '[a]Between morning and evening they are broken in pieces;
Unobserved, they [b]perish forever.
21 'Is not their [a]tent-cord plucked up within them?
They die, yet [b]without wisdom.'

Chapter 5 Theme ______________________________

5 "Call now, is there anyone who will answer you?
And to which of the [a]holy ones will you turn?
2 "For [a]anger slays the foolish man,
And jealousy kills the simple.
3 "I have seen the [a]foolish taking root,
And I [b]cursed his abode immediately.
4 "His [a]sons are far from safety,
They are even [1]oppressed in the gate,
And there is no deliverer.
5 "[1]His harvest the hungry devour
And take it to a *place of* thorns,
And the [2a]schemer is eager for their wealth.
6 "For [a]affliction does not come from the dust,
Nor does trouble sprout from the ground,
7 For [a]man is born for trouble,
As sparks fly upward.

7 [a]Job 8:20; 36:6, 7; Ps 37:25
8 [a]Job 15:31, 35; Prov 22:8; Hos 10:13; Gal 6:7
9 [1]Lit *wind* [a]Job 15:30; Is 11:4; 30:33; 2 Thess 2:8 [b]Job 40:11-13
10 [a]Job 5:15; Ps 58:6
11 [a]Job 29:17; Ps 34:10 [b]Job 5:4; 20:10; 27:14
12 [a]Job 4:12-17; 33:15-18 [b]Job 26:14
13 [a]Job 33:15
14 [1]Lit *the multitude of*
15 [1]Or *breath passed over*
17 [1]Lit *from* [a]Job 9:2; 25:4 [b]Job 31:15; 32:22; 35:10; 36:3
18 [a]Job 15:15
19 [a]Job 10:9; 33:6 [b]Gen 2:7; 3:19; Job 22:16
20 [a]Job 14:2 [b]Job 14:20; 20:7
21 [a]Job 8:22 [b]Job 18:21; 36:12
5:1 [a]Job 15:15
2 [a]Prov 12:16; 27:3
3 [a]Jer 12:2 [b]Job 24:18; 31:30
4 [1]Lit *crushed* [a]Job 4:11
5 [1]Lit *Whose* [2]Ancient versions read *thirsty* [a]Job 18:8-10; 22:10
6 [a]Job 15:35
7 [a]Job 14:1

8 "But as for me, I would [a]seek God,
And I would place my cause before God;
9 Who [a]does great and unsearchable things,
[1]Wonders without number.
10 "He [a]gives rain on the earth
And sends water on the fields,
11 So that [a]He sets on high those who are lowly,
And those who mourn are lifted to safety.
12 "He [a]frustrates the plotting of the shrewd,
So that their hands cannot attain success.
13 "He [a]captures the wise by their own shrewdness,
And the advice of the cunning is quickly thwarted.
14 "By day they [a]meet with darkness,
And grope at noon as in the night.
15 "But He saves from [a]the sword of their mouth,
And [b]the poor from the hand of the mighty.
16 "So the helpless has hope,
And [a]unrighteousness must shut its mouth.

17 "Behold, how [a]happy is the man whom God reproves,
So do not despise the [b]discipline of [1]the Almighty.
18 "For [a]He inflicts pain, and [1]gives relief;
He wounds, and His hands *also* heal.
19 "[1]From six troubles [a]He will deliver you,
Even in seven [b]evil will not touch you.
20 "In [a]famine He will redeem you from death,
And [b]in war from the power of the sword.
21 "You will be [a]hidden from the scourge of the tongue,
[b]And you will not be afraid of violence when it comes.
22 "You will [a]laugh at violence and famine,
[b]And you will not be afraid of [1]wild beasts.
23 "For you will be in league with the stones of the field,
And [a]the beasts of the field will be at peace with you.
24 "You will know that your [a]tent is secure,
For you will visit your abode and fear no loss.
25 "You will know also that your [1a]descendants will be many,
And [b]your offspring as the grass of the earth.
26 "You will [a]come to the grave in full vigor,
Like the stacking of grain in its season.
27 "Behold this; we have investigated it, *and* so it is.
Hear it, and know for yourself."

Chapter 6 Theme ____________________

6 Then Job [1]answered,
2 "[a]Oh that my grief were actually weighed
And laid in the balances together with my calamity!
3 "For then it would be [a]heavier than the sand of the seas;
Therefore my words have been rash.
4 "For the [a]arrows of the Almighty are within me,
[1]Their [b]poison my spirit drinks;
The [c]terrors of God are arrayed against me.

8 [a]Job 13:2, 3; Ps 50:15
9 [1]Or *Miracles* [a]Job 9:10; 37:14, 16; 42:3
10 [a]Job 36:27-29; 37:6-11; 38:26
11 [a]Job 22:29; 36:7
12 [a]Ps 33:10
13 [a]Job 37:24; 1 Cor 3:19
14 [a]Job 12:25; 15:30; 18:18; 20:26; 24:13
15 [a]Job 4:10, 11; Ps 35:10 [b]Job 29:17; 34:28; 36:6, 15; 38:15
16 [a]Ps 107:42
17 [1]Heb *Shaddai*, and so throughout ch 6 [a]Ps 94:12 [b]Job 36:15, 16; Prov 3:11; Heb 12:5-11; James 1:12
18 [1]Lit *binds* [a]Deut 32:39; 1 Sam 2:6; Is 30:26; Hos 6:1
19 [1]Lit *In* [a]Ps 34:19 [b]Ps 91:10
20 [a]Ps 33:19; 37:19 [b]Ps 144:10
21 [a]Job 5:15; Ps 31:20 [b]Ps 91:5, 6
22 [1]Lit *beasts of the earth* [a]Job 8:21 [b]Ps 91:13; Ezek 34:25; Hos 2:18
23 [a]Is 11:6-9; 65:25
24 [a]Job 8:6
25 [1]Lit *seed* [a]Ps 112:2 [b]Is 44:3, 4; 48:19
26 [a]Job 42:17
6:1 [1]Lit *answered and said*
2 [a]Job 31:6
3 [a]Job 23:2
4 [1]Lit *Whose* [a]Job 16:13; Ps 38:2 [b]Job 20:16; 21:20 [c]Job 30:15

5 "Does the [a]wild donkey bray over *his* grass,
Or does the ox low over his fodder?
6 "Can something tasteless be eaten without salt,
Or is there any taste in the [1]white of an egg?
7 "My soul [a]refuses to touch *them;*
They are like loathsome food to me.

8 "Oh that my request might come to pass,
And that God would grant my longing!
9 "Would that God were [a]willing to crush me,
That He would loose His hand and cut me off!
10 "But it is still my consolation,
And I rejoice in unsparing pain,
That I [a]have not [1]denied the words of the Holy One.
11 "What is my strength, that I should wait?
And what is my end, that I should [1a]endure?
12 "Is my strength the strength of stones,
Or is my flesh bronze?
13 "Is it that my [a]help is not within me,
And that [1b]deliverance is driven from me?

14 "For the [a]despairing man *there should be* kindness from his friend;
So that he does not [b]forsake the [1]fear of the Almighty.
15 "My brothers have acted [a]deceitfully like a [1]wadi,
Like the torrents of [1]wadis which vanish,
16 Which are turbid because of ice
And into which the snow [1]melts.
17 "When [a]they become waterless, they [1]are silent,
When it is hot, they vanish from their place.
18 "The [1]paths of their course wind along,
They go up into nothing and perish.
19 "The caravans of [a]Tema looked,
The travelers of [b]Sheba hoped for them.
20 "They [a]were [1]disappointed for they had trusted,
They came there and were confounded.
21 "Indeed, you have now become such,
[a]You see a terror and are afraid.
22 "Have I said, 'Give me *something,*'
Or, 'Offer a bribe for me from your wealth,'
23 Or, 'Deliver me from the hand of the adversary,'
Or, 'Redeem me from the hand of the tyrants'?

24 "Teach me, and [a]I will be silent;
And show me how I have erred.
25 "How painful are honest words!
But what does your argument prove?
26 "Do you intend to reprove *my* words,
When the [a]words of one in despair belong to the wind?
27 "You would even [a]cast *lots* for [b]the orphans
And [c]barter over your friend.

5 [a]Job 39:5-8
6 [1]Heb *hallamuth,* meaning uncertain. Perhaps the juice of a plant
7 [a]Job 3:24; 33:20
9 [a]Num 11:15; 1 Kin 19:4; Job 7:16; 9:21; 10:1
10 [1]Lit *hidden* [a]Job 22:22; 23:11, 12
11 [1]Lit *prolong my soul* [a]Job 21:4
13 [1]So ancient versions [a]Job 26:2 [b]Job 26:3
14 [1]Or *reverence* [a]Job 4:5 [b]Job 1:5; 15:4
15 [1]Or *brooks* [a]Jer 15:18
16 [1]Lit *hides itself*
17 [1]Or *cease* [a]Job 24:19
18 [1]Or *caravans turn from their course, they go up into the waste and perish*
19 [a]Gen 25:15; Is 21:14; Jer 25:23 [b]Job 1:15
20 [1]Lit *ashamed* [a]Jer 14:3
21 [a]Ps 38:11
24 [a]Ps 39:1
26 [a]Job 8:2; 15:2; 16:3
27 [a]Joel 3:3; Nah 3:10 [b]Job 22:9; 24:3, 9 [c]2 Pet 2:3

28 "Now please look at me,
And *see* if I [a]lie to your face.
29 "Desist now, let there be no injustice;
Even desist, [a]my righteousness is yet in it.
30 "Is there injustice on my tongue?
Cannot [a]my palate discern [1]calamities?

Chapter 7 Theme ______________________

7 "[1]Is not man [a]forced to labor on earth,
And *are not* his days like the days of [b]a hired man?
2 "As a slave who pants for the shade,
And as a hired man who eagerly waits for his wages,
3 So am I allotted months of vanity,
And [a]nights of trouble are appointed me.
4 "When I [a]lie down I say,
'When shall I arise?'
But the night continues,
And I am [1]continually tossing until dawn.
5 "My [a]flesh is clothed with worms and a crust of dirt,
My skin hardens and runs.
6 "My days are [a]swifter than a weaver's shuttle,
And come to an end [b]without hope.

7 "Remember that my life [a]is *but* breath;
My eye will [b]not again see good.
8 "The [a]eye of him who sees me will behold me no longer;
Your eyes *will be* on me, but [b]I will not be.
9 "When a [a]cloud vanishes, it is gone,
So [b]he who goes down to [c]Sheol does not come up.
10 "He will not return again to his house,
Nor will [a]his place know him anymore.

11 "Therefore [a]I will not restrain my mouth;
I will speak in the anguish of my spirit,
I will complain in the bitterness of my soul.
12 "Am I the sea, or [a]the sea monster,
That You set a guard over me?
13 "If I say, '[a]My bed will comfort me,
My couch will [1]ease my complaint,'
14 Then You frighten me with dreams
And terrify me by visions;
15 So that my soul would choose suffocation,
Death rather than my [1]pains.
16 "I [1a]waste away; I will not live forever.
Leave me alone, [b]for my days are *but* a breath.
17 "[a]What is man that You magnify him,
And that You [1]are concerned about him,
18 That [a]You examine him every morning
And try him every moment?
19 "[1a]Will You never turn Your gaze away from me,
Nor let me alone until I swallow my spittle?

28 [a]Job 27:4; 33:3; 36:4
29 [a]Job 13:18; 19:6; 23:10; 27:5, 6; 34:5; 42:1-6
30 [1]Or *words* [a]Job 12:11
7:1 [1]Lit *Has not man compulsory labor* [a]Job 5:7; 10:17; 14:1, 14 [b]Job 14:6
3 [a]Job 16:7
4 [1]Lit *sated with* [a]Deut 28:67; Job 7:13, 14
5 [a]Job 2:7; 17:14
6 [a]Job 9:25 [b]Job 13:15; 14:19; 17:15, 16; 19:10
7 [a]Job 7:16; Ps 78:39; James 4:14 [b]Job 9:25
8 [a]Job 8:18; 20:9 [b]Job 7:21
9 [a]Job 30:15 [b]Job 3:13-19 [c]2 Sam 12:23; Job 11:8; 14:13; 17:13, 16
10 [a]Job 8:18; 20:9; 27:21, 23
11 [a]Job 10:1; 21:4; 23:2; Ps 40:9
12 [a]Ezek 32:2, 3
13 [1]Lit *bear* [a]Job 7:4; Ps 6:6
15 [1]Lit *bones*
16 [1]Or *loathe* [a]Job 6:9; 9:21; 10:1 [b]Job 7:7
17 [1]Lit *set Your heart on* [a]Job 22:2; Ps 8:4; 144:3; Heb 2:6
18 [a]Job 14:3
19 [1]Lit *How long will You not* [a]Job 9:18; 10:20; 14:6

20 [a]Job 35:3, 6 [b]Ps 36:6

21 [a]Job 9:28; 10:14 [b]Job 10:9 [c]Job 7:8

8:1 [1]Lit *answered and said*

2 [a]Job 6:26

3 [1]Heb *Shaddai* [a]Gen 18:25; Deut 32:4; 2 Chr 19:7; Job 34:10, 12; 36:23; 37:23; Rom 3:5

4 [1]Lit *hand* [a]Job 1:5, 18, 19

5 [1]Heb *Shaddai* [a]Job 5:17-27

6 [1]Lit *place* [a]Job 22:27; 34:28; Ps 7:6 [b]Job 5:24

7 [a]Job 42:12

8 [a]Deut 4:32; 32:7; Job 15:18; 20:4

9 [a]Job 14:2

12 [1]Lit *reed*

13 [a]Ps 9:17 [b]Job 11:20; 13:16; 15:34; 20:5; 27:8

14 [1]Lit *house* [a]Is 59:5, 6

15 [1]Lit *leans on* [a]Job 8:22; 27:18; Ps 49:11

16 [1]Lit *is lush* [a]Ps 37:35; Jer 11:16 [b]Ps 80:11

17 [1]Heb *sees*

18 [1]Lit *swallowed up* [a]Job 7:10 [b]Job 7:8

19 [a]Job 20:5

20 "[a]Have I sinned? What have I done to You,
O [b]watcher of men?
Why have You set me as Your target,
So that I am a burden to myself?
21 "Why then [a]do You not pardon my transgression
And take away my iniquity?
For now I will [b]lie down in the dust;
And You will seek me, [c]but I will not be."

Chapter 8 Theme ______________________________

8 Then Bildad the Shuhite [1]answered,
2 "How long will you say these things,
And the [a]words of your mouth be a mighty wind?
3 "Does [a]God pervert justice?
Or does [1]the Almighty pervert what is right?
4 "[a]If your sons sinned against Him,
Then He delivered them into the [1]power of their
transgression.
5 "If you would [a]seek God
And implore the compassion of [1]the Almighty,
6 If you are pure and upright,
Surely now [a]He would rouse Himself for you
And restore your righteous [1b]estate.
7 "Though your beginning was insignificant,
Yet your [a]end will increase greatly.

8 "Please [a]inquire of past generations,
And consider the things searched out by their fathers.
9 "For we are *only* of yesterday and know nothing,
Because [a]our days on earth are as a shadow.
10 "Will they not teach you *and* tell you,
And bring forth words from their minds?

11 "Can the papyrus grow up without a marsh?
Can the rushes grow without water?
12 "While it is still green *and* not cut down,
Yet it withers before any *other* [1]plant.
13 "So are the paths of [a]all who forget God;
And the [b]hope of the godless will perish,
14 Whose confidence is fragile,
And whose trust a [a]spider's [1]web.
15 "He [1]trusts in his [a]house, but it does not stand;
He holds fast to it, but it does not endure.
16 "He [1a]thrives before the sun,
And his [b]shoots spread out over his garden.
17 "His roots wrap around a rock pile,
He [1]grasps a house of stones.
18 "If he is [1]removed from [a]his place,
Then it will deny him, *saying,* '[b]I never saw you.'
19 "Behold, [a]this is the joy of His way;
And out of the dust others will spring.

20 "Lo, [a]God will not reject *a man of* integrity,
Nor [b]will He [1]support the evildoers.
21 "He will yet fill [a]your mouth with laughter
And your lips with shouting.
22 "Those who hate you will be [a]clothed with shame,
And the [b]tent of the wicked will be no longer."

Chapter 9 Theme ______________________

9

Then Job [1]answered,
2 "In truth I know that this is so;
But how can a [a]man be in the right [1]before God?
3 "If one wished to [a]dispute with Him,
He could not answer Him once in a thousand *times.*
4 "[a]Wise in heart and [b]mighty in strength,
Who has [1c]defied Him [2]without harm?
5 "[a]*It is God* who removes the mountains, they know not *how,*
When He overturns them in His anger;
6 Who [a]shakes the earth out of its place,
And its [b]pillars tremble;
7 Who commands the [a]sun [1]not to shine,
And sets a seal upon the stars;
8 Who alone [a]stretches out the heavens
And [1b]tramples down the waves of the sea;
9 Who makes the [a]Bear, Orion and the Pleiades,
And the [b]chambers of the south;
10 Who [a]does great things, [1]unfathomable,
And wondrous works without number.
11 "Were He to pass by me, [a]I would not see Him;
Were He to move past *me,* I would not perceive Him.
12 "Were He to snatch away, who could [a]restrain Him?
Who could say to Him, '[b]What are You doing?'

13 "God will not turn back His anger;
Beneath Him crouch the helpers of [a]Rahab.
14 "How then can [a]I [1]answer Him,
And choose my words [2]before Him?
15 "For [a]though I were right, I could not [1]answer;
I would have to [b]implore the mercy of my judge.
16 "If I called and He answered me,
I could not believe that He was listening to my voice.
17 "For He [a]bruises me with a tempest
And multiplies my wounds without cause.
18 "He will [a]not allow me to get my breath,
But saturates me with [b]bitterness.
19 "If *it is a matter* of power, [a]behold, *He is* the strong one!
And if *it is a matter* of justice, who can summon [1]Him?
20 "[a]Though I am righteous, my mouth will [b]condemn me;
Though I am guiltless, He will declare me guilty.
21 "I am [a]guiltless;
I do not take notice of myself;
I [b]despise my life.

20 [1]Lit *strengthen the hand of* [a]Job 4:7 [b]Job 21:30

21 [a]Job 5:22; Ps 126:1, 2

22 [a]Ps 132:18 [b]Job 8:15; 15:34; 18:14; 21:28

9:1 [1]Lit *answered and said*

2 [1]Lit *with* [a]Job 4:17; 25:4

3 [a]Job 10:2; 13:19; 23:6; 40:2

4 [1]Lit *stiffened his neck against* [2]Lit *and remained safe* [a]Job 11:6; 12:13; 28:23; 38:36, 37 [b]Job 9:19; 23:6 [c]2 Chr 13:12; Prov 29:1

5 [a]Job 9:5-10; 26:6-14; 41:11

6 [a]Is 2:19, 21; 13:13; Hag 2:6 [b]Ps 75:3

7 [1]Lit *and it does not shine* [a]Is 13:10; Ezek 32:7, 8

8 [1]Lit *treads upon the heights of* [a]Gen 1:1; Job 37:18; Ps 104:2; Is 40:22 [b]Job 38:16; Ps 77:19

9 [a]Job 38:31, 32; Amos 5:8 [b]Job 37:9

10 [1]Lit *until there is no searching out* [a]Job 5:9

11 [a]Job 23:8, 9; 35:14

12 [a]Job 10:7; 11:10 [b]Is 45:9

13 [a]Job 26:12; Ps 89:10; Is 30:7; 51:9

14 [1]Or *plead my case* [2]Lit *with* [a]Job 9:3, 32

15 [1]Or *plead my case* [a]Job 9:20, 21; 10:15 [b]Job 8:5

17 [a]Job 16:12, 14; 30:22

18 [a]Job 7:19; 10:20 [b]Job 13:26; 27:2

19 [1]So with Gr; Heb *me* [a]Job 9:4

20 [a]Job 9:15 [b]Job 9:29; 15:6

21 [a]Job 1:1; 12:4; 13:18 [b]Job 7:16

22 "It is *all* one; therefore I say,
'He [a]destroys the guiltless and the wicked.'
23 "If the scourge kills suddenly,
He [a]mocks the despair of the innocent.
24 "The earth [a]is given into the hand of the wicked;
He [b]covers the faces of its judges.
If *it is* not *He,* then who is it?

25 "Now [a]my days are swifter than a runner;
They flee away, [b]they see no good.
26 "They slip by like [a]reed boats,
Like an [b]eagle that swoops on [1]its prey.
27 "Though I say, 'I will forget [a]my complaint,
I will leave off my *sad* countenance and be cheerful,'
28 I am [a]afraid of all my pains,
I know that [b]You will not acquit me.
29 "I am accounted [a]wicked,
Why then should I toil in vain?
30 "If I should [a]wash myself with snow
And cleanse [b]my hands with lye,
31 Yet You would plunge me into the pit,
And my own clothes would abhor me.
32 "For [a]*He is* not a man as I am that [b]I may answer Him,
That we may go to [1]court together.
33 "There is no [a]umpire between us,
Who may lay his hand upon us both.
34 "Let Him [a]remove His rod from me,
And let not dread of Him terrify me.
35 "*Then* I [a]would speak and not fear Him;
But I am not like that in myself.

Chapter 10 Theme ______________________

10 "[1][a]I loathe my own life;
I will give full vent to [b]my complaint;
I will speak in the bitterness of my soul.
2 "I will say to God, '[a]Do not condemn me;
Let me know why You contend with me.
3 'Is it [1]right for You indeed to [a]oppress,
To reject [b]the labor of Your hands,
And [2]to look favorably on [c]the schemes of the wicked?
4 'Have You eyes of flesh?
Or do You [a]see as a man sees?
5 'Are Your days as the days of a mortal,
Or [a]Your years as man's years,
6 That [a]You should seek for my guilt
And search after my sin?
7 'According to Your knowledge [a]I am indeed not guilty,
Yet there is [b]no deliverance from Your hand.

8 '[a]Your hands fashioned and made me [1]altogether,
[b]And would You destroy me?

22 [a]Job 10:7, 8
23 [a]Job 24:12
24 [a]Job 10:3; 12:6; 16:11 [b]Job 12:17
25 [a]Job 7:6 [b]Job 7:7
26 [1]Lit *food* [a]Is 18:2 [b]Job 39:29; Hab 1:8
27 [a]Job 7:11
28 [a]Job 3:25 [b]Job 7:21; 10:14
29 [a]Job 10:2; Ps 37:33
30 [a]Jer 2:22 [b]Job 31:7
32 [1]Lit *judgment* [a]Eccl 6:10 [b]Job 9:3; Rom 9:20
33 [a]1 Sam 2:25; Job 9:19; Is 1:18
34 [a]Job 13:21
35 [a]Job 13:22
10:1 [1]Lit *My soul loathes* [a]Job 7:16 [b]Job 7:11
2 [a]Job 9:29
3 [1]Lit *good* [2]Lit *You shine forth* [a]Job 9:22-24; 16:11; 19:6; 27:2 [b]Job 10:8; 14:15; Ps 138:8; Is 64:8 [c]Job 21:16; 22:18
4 [a]1 Sam 16:7; Job 28:24; 34:21
5 [a]Job 36:26
6 [a]Job 14:16
7 [a]Job 9:21; 13:18 [b]Job 9:12; 23:13; 27:22
8 [1]Lit *together round about* [a]Job 10:3; Ps 119:73 [b]Job 9:22

9 'Remember now, that You have made me as [a]clay;
And would You [b]turn me into dust again?
10 'Did You not pour me out like milk
And curdle me like cheese;
11 Clothe me with skin and flesh,
And knit me together with bones and sinews?
12 'You have [a]granted me life and lovingkindness;
And Your care has preserved my spirit.
13 'Yet [a]these things You have concealed in Your heart;
I know that this is within You:
14 If I sin, then You would [a]take note of me,
And [b]would not acquit me of my guilt.
15 'If [a]I am wicked, woe to me!
And [b]if I am righteous, I dare not lift up my head.
I am sated with disgrace and [1]conscious of my misery.
16 'Should *my head* be lifted up, [a]You would hunt me like a lion;
And again You would show Your [b]power against me.
17 'You renew [a]Your witnesses against me
And increase Your anger toward me;
[1b]Hardship after hardship is with me.

18 '[a]Why then have You brought me out of the womb?
Would that I had died and no eye had seen me!
19 'I should have been as though I had not been,
Carried from womb to tomb.'
20 "Would He not let [a]my few days alone?
[1b]Withdraw from me that I may have a little cheer
21 Before I go—[a]and I shall not return—
[b]To the land of darkness and [c]deep shadow,
22 The land of utter gloom as darkness *itself,*
Of deep shadow without order,
And which shines as the darkness."

Chapter 11 Theme ____________________

11 Then Zophar the Naamathite [1]answered,
2 "Shall a multitude of words go unanswered,
And a [a]talkative man be acquitted?
3 "Shall your boasts silence men?
And shall you [a]scoff and none rebuke?
4 "For [a]you have said, 'My teaching is pure,
And [b]I am innocent in your eyes.'
5 "But would that God might speak,
And open His lips against you,
6 And show you the secrets of wisdom!
For sound wisdom [1a]has two sides.
Know then that God [2]forgets a part of [b]your iniquity.

7 "[a]Can you discover the depths of God?
Can you discover the limits of the Almighty?

9 [a]Job 4:19; 33:6 [b]Job 7:21

12 [a]Job 33:4

13 [a]Job 23:13

14 [a]Job 7:20 [b]Job 7:21; 9:28

15 [1]Lit *see* [a]Job 10:7; Is 3:11 [b]Job 6:29

16 [a]Is 38:13; Lam 3:10; Hos 13:7 [b]Job 5:9

17 [1]Lit *Changes and warfare are with me* [a]Ruth 1:21; Job 16:8 [b]Job 7:1

18 [a]Job 3:11-13

20 [1]Lit *Put* [a]Job 14:1 [b]Job 7:16, 19

21 [a]2 Sam 12:23; Job 3:13-19; 16:22 [b]Ps 88:12 [c]Job 10:22; 34:22; 38:17; Ps 23:4

11:1 [1]Lit *answered and said*

2 [a]Job 8:2; 15:2; 18:2

3 [a]Job 17:2; 21:3

4 [a]Job 6:10 [b]Job 10:7

6 [1]Lit *is double* [2]Lit *causes to be forgotten for you* [a]Job 9:4 [b]Job 15:5; 22:5

7 [a]Job 33:12, 13; 36:26; 37:5, 23; Rom 11:33

8 "*They are* [a]high as [1]the heavens, what can you do?
Deeper than [2b]Sheol, what can you know?
9 "Its measure is longer than the earth
And broader than the sea.
10 "If He passes by or shuts up,
Or calls an assembly, [a]who can restrain Him?
11 "For [a]He knows false men,
And He [b]sees iniquity [1]without investigating.
12 "[1a]An idiot will become intelligent
When the [2]foal of a [b]wild donkey is born a man.

13 "[a]If you would [b]direct your heart right
And [c]spread out your hand to Him,
14 If iniquity is in your hand, [a]put it far away,
And do not let wickedness dwell in your tents;
15 "Then, indeed, you could [a]lift up your face without
moral defect,
And you would be steadfast and [b]not fear.
16 "For you would [a]forget *your* trouble,
As [b]waters that have passed by, you would remember *it.*
17 "Your [1]life would be [2a]brighter than noonday;
Darkness would be like the morning.
18 "Then you would trust, because there is hope;
And you would look around and rest securely.
19 "You would [a]lie down and none would disturb *you,*
And many would [b]entreat your [1]favor.
20 "But the [a]eyes of the wicked will fail,
And [1]there will [b]be no escape for them;
And their [c]hope is [2d]to breathe their last."

Chapter 12 Theme ________________________________

12 Then Job [1]responded,
2 "Truly then [a]you are the people,
And with you wisdom will die!
3 "But [a]I have intelligence as well as you;
I am not inferior to you.
And [1]who does not know such things as these?
4 "I am a [a]joke to [1]my friends,
The one who called on God and He answered him;
The just *and* [b]blameless *man* is a joke.
5 "[1]He who is at ease holds calamity in contempt,
As prepared for those whose feet slip.
6 "The [a]tents of the destroyers prosper,
And those who provoke God [b]are secure,
[1]Whom God brings [c]into their power.

7 "But now ask the beasts, and let them teach you;
And the birds of the heavens, and let them tell you.
8 "Or speak to the earth, and let it teach you;
And let the fish of the sea declare to you.

8 [1]Lit *the heights of heaven* [2]I.e. the nether world [a]Job 22:12; 35:5 [b]Job 26:6; 38:17

10 [a]Job 9:12

11 [1]Or *even He does not consider* [a]Job 34:21-23 [b]Job 24:23; 28:24; 31:4

12 [1]Lit *A hollow man* [2]Lit *donkey* [a]Ps 39:5, 11; 62:9; 144:4; Eccl 1:2; 11:10 [b]Job 39:5

13 [a]Job 5:17-27; 11:13-20 [b]1 Sam 7:3; Ps 78:8 [c]Job 22:27; Ps 88:9; 143:6

14 [a]Job 22:23

15 [a]Job 22:26 [b]Ps 27:3; 46:2

16 [a]Is 65:16 [b]Job 22:11

17 [1]Lit *duration of life* [2]Lit *above noonday* [a]Job 22:26

19 [1]Lit *face* [a]Lev 26:6; Is 17:2; Mic 4:4; Zeph 3:13 [b]Is 45:14

20 [1]Lit *escape has perished from them* [2]Lit *the expiring of the soul* [a]Deut 28:65; Job 17:5 [b]Job 27:22; 34:22 [c]Job 8:13 [d]Job 6:9

12:1 [1]Lit *answered and said*

2 [a]Job 17:10

3 [1]Lit *with whom is there not like these?* [a]Job 13:2

4 [1]Lit *his* [a]Job 17:6; 30:1, 9, 10; 34:7 [b]Job 6:29

5 [1]Lit *Contempt for calamity is the thought of him who is at ease*

6 [1]Or *He who brings God into his hand* [a]Job 9:24; 21:7-9 [b]Job 24:23 [c]Job 22:18

9 "Who among all these does not know
That [a]the hand of the LORD has done this,
10 [a]In whose hand is the life of every living thing,
And [b]the breath of all mankind?
11 "Does not [a]the ear test words,
As the palate [1]tastes its food?
12 "Wisdom is with [a]aged men,
With [1]long life is understanding.

13 "With Him are [a]wisdom and [a]might;
To Him belong counsel and [b]understanding.
14 "Behold, He [a]tears down, and it cannot be rebuilt;
He [1b]imprisons a man, and [2]there can be no release.
15 "Behold, He [a]restrains the waters, and they dry up;
And He [b]sends them out, and they [1]inundate the earth.
16 "With Him are strength and sound wisdom,
The [a]misled and the misleader belong to Him.
17 "He makes [a]counselors walk [1]barefoot
And makes fools of [b]judges.
18 "He [a]loosens the [1]bond of kings
And binds their loins with a girdle.
19 "He makes priests walk [1]barefoot
And overthrows [a]the secure ones.
20 "He deprives the trusted ones of speech
And [a]takes away the discernment of the elders.
21 "He [a]pours contempt on nobles
And [b]loosens the belt of the strong.
22 "He [a]reveals mysteries from the darkness
And brings the deep darkness into light.
23 "He [a]makes the nations great, then destroys them;
He [1]enlarges the nations, then leads them away.
24 "He [a]deprives of intelligence the chiefs of the earth's people
And makes them wander in a pathless waste.
25 "They [a]grope in darkness with no light,
And He makes them [b]stagger like a drunken man.

Chapter 13 Theme ________________

13 "[a]Behold, my eye has seen all *this,*
My ear has heard and understood it.
2 "[a]What you know I also know;
I am not inferior to you.

3 "But [a]I would speak to [1]the Almighty,
And I desire to [b]argue with God.
4 "But you [a]smear with lies;
You are all [b]worthless physicians.
5 "O that you would [a]be completely silent,
And that it would become your wisdom!
6 "Please hear my argument
And listen to the contentions of my lips.

9 [a]Is 41:20

10 [a]Acts 17:28 [b]Job 27:3; 33:4

11 [1]Lit *tastes food for itself* [a]Job 34:3

12 [1]Lit *length of days* [a]Job 15:10; 32:7

13 [a]Job 9:4 [b]Job 11:6; 26:12; 32:8; 36:5; 38:36

14 [1]Lit *shuts against* [2]Lit *it is not opened* [a]Job 19:10; Is 25:2 [b]Job 37:7

15 [1]Lit *overturn* [a]Deut 11:17; 1 Kin 8:35; 17:1 [b]Gen 7:11-24

16 [a]Job 13:7, 9

17 [1]Or *stripped* [a]Job 3:14 [b]Job 9:24

18 [1]Or *discipline* [a]Ps 116:16

19 [1]Or *stripped* [a]Job 24:22; 34:24-28; 35:9

20 [a]Job 17:4; 32:9

21 [a]Job 34:19; Ps 107:40 [b]Job 12:18

22 [a]Dan 2:22; 1 Cor 4:5

23 [1]Or *spreads out* [a]Is 9:3; 26:15

24 [a]Job 12:20

25 [a]Job 5:14 [b]Is 24:20

13:1 [a]Job 12:9

2 [a]Job 12:3

3 [1]Heb *Shaddai* [a]Job 13:22; 23:4 [b]Job 13:15

4 [a]Ps 119:69 [b]Jer 23:32

5 [a]Job 13:13; 21:5; Prov 17:28

7 [a]Job 27:4
8 [a]Lev 19:15; Prov 24:23
9 [a]Job 12:16
10 [a]Job 13:8; 32:21; 34:19
11 [1]Lit *exaltation* [a]Job 31:23
13 [a]Job 13:5
14 [1]Lit *palm* [a]Ps 119:109
15 [1]Lit *to His face* [a]Job 7:6 [b]Job 27:5
16 [a]Job 23:7; Is 12:1, 2 [b]Job 34:21-23
18 [a]Job 23:4 [b]Job 9:21; 10:7; 12:4
19 [a]Is 50:8 [b]Job 7:21; 10:8
21 [1]Lit *palm* [a]Job 9:34; Ps 39:10
22 [a]Job 9:16; 14:15
23 [1]Or *transgression* [a]Job 7:21
24 [a]Ps 13:1; 44:24; 88:14; Is 8:17 [b]Job 19:11; 33:10; Lam 2:5
25 [a]Lev 26:36 [b]Job 21:18
26 [a]Job 9:18 [b]Ps 25:7
27 [1]Lit *carve for* [a]Job 33:11
28 [1]Lit *he is* [a]Job 2:7

7 "Will you [a]speak what is unjust for God,
And speak what is deceitful for Him?
8 "Will you [a]show partiality for Him?
Will you contend for God?
9 "Will it be well when He examines you?
Or [a]will you deceive Him as one deceives
a man?
10 "He will surely reprove you
If you secretly [a]show partiality.
11 "Will not [a]His [1]majesty terrify you,
And the dread of Him fall on you?
12 "Your memorable sayings are proverbs of ashes,
Your defenses are defenses of clay.

13 "[a]Be silent before me so that I may speak;
Then let come on me what may.
14 "Why should I take my flesh in my teeth
And [a]put my life in my [1]hands?
15 "[a]Though He slay me,
I will hope in Him.
Nevertheless I [b]will argue my ways [1]before Him.
16 "This also will be my [a]salvation,
For [b]a godless man may not come before
His presence.
17 "Listen carefully to my speech,
And let my declaration *fill* your ears.
18 "Behold now, I have [a]prepared my case;
I know that [b]I will be vindicated.
19 "[a]Who will contend with me?
For then I would be silent and [b]die.

20 "Only two things do not do to me,
Then I will not hide from Your face:
21 [a]Remove Your [1]hand from me,
And let not the dread of You terrify me.
22 "Then call, and [a]I will answer;
Or let me speak, then reply to me.
23 "[a]How many are my iniquities and sins?
Make known to me my [1]rebellion and my sin.
24 "Why do You [a]hide Your face
And consider me [b]Your enemy?
25 "Will You cause a [a]driven leaf to tremble?
Or will You pursue the dry [b]chaff?
26 "For You write [a]bitter things against me
And [b]make me to inherit the iniquities of my youth.
27 "You [a]put my feet in the stocks
And watch all my paths;
You [1]set a limit for the soles of my feet,
28 While [1]I am decaying like a [a]rotten thing,
Like a garment that is moth-eaten.

Chapter 14 Theme ______________________

14 "[a]Man, who is born of woman,
Is [1]short-lived and [b]full of turmoil.
2 "[a]Like a flower he comes forth and withers.
He also flees like [b]a shadow and does not remain.
3 "You also [a]open Your eyes on him
And [b]bring [1]him into judgment with Yourself.
4 "[a]Who can make the clean out of the unclean?
No one!
5 "Since his days are determined,
The [a]number of his months is with You;
And his limits You have [1]set so that he cannot pass.
6 "[a]Turn Your gaze from him that he may [1]rest,
Until he [2]fulfills his day like a hired man.

7 "For there is hope for a tree,
When it is cut down, that it will sprout again,
And its shoots will not [1]fail.
8 "Though its roots grow old in the ground
And its stump dies in the dry soil,
9 At the scent of water it will flourish
And put forth sprigs like a plant.
10 "But [a]man dies and lies prostrate.
Man [b]expires, and where is he?
11 "*As* [a]water [1]evaporates from the sea,
And a river becomes parched and dried up,
12 So [a]man lies down and does not rise.
Until the heavens are no longer,
[1]He will not awake nor be aroused out of [2]his sleep.

13 "Oh that You would hide me in [1]Sheol,
That You would conceal me [a]until Your wrath returns
to You,
That You would set a limit for me and remember me!
14 "If a man dies, will he live *again?*
All the days of my struggle I will wait
Until my change comes.
15 "You will call, and I will answer You;
You will long for [a]the work of Your hands.
16 "For now You [a]number my steps,
You do not [b]observe my sin.
17 "My transgression is [a]sealed up in a bag,
And You [1]wrap up my iniquity.

18 "But the falling mountain [1]crumbles away,
And the rock moves from its place;
19 Water wears away stones,
Its torrents wash away the dust of the earth;
So You [a]destroy man's hope.
20 "You forever overpower him and he [a]departs;
You change his appearance and send him away.

14:1 [1]Lit *short of days* [a]Job 5:7 [b]Eccl 2:23

2 [a]Ps 90:5, 6; 103:15; Is 40:6, 7; James 1:10; 1 Pet 1:24 [b]Job 8:9

3 [1]So with some ancient versions; M.T. *me* [a]Ps 8:4; 144:3 [b]Ps 143:2

4 [a]Job 15:14; 25:4; Ps 51:5

5 [1]Lit *made* [a]Job 21:21

6 [1]Lit *cease* [2]Lit *makes acceptable* [a]Job 7:19; Ps 39:13

7 [1]Or *cease*

10 [a]Job 3:13; 14:10-15 [b]Job 13:9

11 [1]Lit *disappears* [a]Is 19:5

12 [1]Lit *They* [2]Lit *their* [a]Job 3:13

13 [1]I.e. the nether world [a]Is 26:20

15 [a]Job 10:3

16 [a]Job 31:4; 34:21; Ps 139:1-3; Prov 5:21 [b]Job 10:6

17 [1]Lit *plaster;* or *glue together* [a]Deut 32:32-34

18 [1]Lit *withers*

19 [a]Job 7:6

20 [a]Job 4:20; 20:7

21 [a]Eccl 9:5
22 [1]Lit *flesh*
15:1 [1]Lit *answered and said*
2 [1]Lit *his belly* [a]Job 6:26
4 [1]Lit *fear*
5 [a]Job 22:5 [b]Job 5:12, 13
6 [a]Job 18:7
7 [a]Job 38:4, 21; Prov 8:25
8 [a]Job 29:4; Rom 11:34; 1 Cor 2:11
9 [1]Lit *is not within us?* [a]Job 12:3; 13:2
10 [a]Job 12:12; 32:6, 7
11 [a]Job 5:17-19; 36:15, 16 [b]Job 6:10; 23:12
12 [a]Job 11:13; 36:13
14 [a]Job 14:4; Prov 20:9; Eccl 7:20 [b]Job 25:4
15 [a]Job 5:1 [b]Job 25:5
16 [a]Ps 14:1 [b]Job 34:7; Prov 19:28
18 [a]Job 8:8; 20:4
20 [1]Lit *the number of years are* [a]Job 15:24 [b]Job 24:1; 27:13
21 [1]Lit *A sound of terrors is* [a]Job 15:24; 18:11; 20:25; 24:17; 27:20 [b]Job 20:21; 1 Thess 5:3

21 "His sons achieve honor, but [a]he does not know *it;*
Or they become insignificant, but he does not perceive it.
22 "But his [1]body pains him,
And he mourns only for himself."

Chapter 15 Theme ________________________

15 Then Eliphaz the Temanite [1]responded,
2 "Should a wise man answer with windy knowledge
[a]And fill [1]himself with the east wind?
3 "Should he argue with useless talk,
Or with words which are not profitable?
4 "Indeed, you do away with [1]reverence
And hinder meditation before God.
5 "For [a]your guilt teaches your mouth,
And you choose the language of [b]the crafty.
6 "Your [a]own mouth condemns you, and not I;
And your own lips testify against you.

7 "Were you the first man to be born,
Or [a]were you brought forth before the hills?
8 "Do you hear the [a]secret counsel of God,
And limit wisdom to yourself?
9 "[a]What do you know that we do not know?
What do you understand that [1]we do not?
10 "Both the [a]gray-haired and the aged are among us,
Older than your father.
11 "Are [a]the consolations of God too small for you,
Even the [b]word *spoken* gently with you?
12 "Why does your [a]heart carry you away?
And why do your eyes flash,
13 That you should turn your spirit against God
And allow *such* words to go out of your mouth?
14 "What is man, that [a]he should be pure,
Or [b]he who is born of a woman, that he should
be righteous?
15 "Behold, He puts no trust in His [a]holy ones,
And the [b]heavens are not pure in His sight;
16 How much less one who is [a]detestable and corrupt,
Man, who [b]drinks iniquity like water!

17 "I will tell you, listen to me;
And what I have seen I will also declare;
18 What wise men have told,
And have not concealed from [a]their fathers,
19 To whom alone the land was given,
And no alien passed among them.
20 "The wicked man writhes [a]in pain all *his* days,
And [1]numbered are the years [b]stored up for the ruthless.
21 "[1]Sounds of [a]terror are in his ears;
[b]While at peace the destroyer comes upon him.

22 "He does not believe that he will [a]return from darkness,
And he is destined for [b]the sword.
23 "He wanders about for food, saying, 'Where is it?'
He knows that a day of [a]darkness is [1]at hand.
24 "Distress and anguish terrify him,
They overpower him like a king ready for the attack,
25 Because he has stretched out his hand against God
And conducts himself [a]arrogantly against [1]the Almighty.
26 "He rushes [1]headlong at Him
With [2]his massive shield.
27 "For he has [a]covered his face with his fat
And made his thighs heavy with flesh.
28 "He has [a]lived in desolate cities,
In houses no one would inhabit,
Which are destined to become [1]ruins.
29 "He [a]will not become rich, nor will his wealth endure;
And his grain will not bend down to the ground.
30 "He will [a]not [1]escape from darkness;
The [b]flame will wither his shoots,
And by [c]the breath of His mouth he will go away.
31 "Let him not [a]trust in emptiness, deceiving himself;
For emptiness will be his [1]reward.
32 "It will be accomplished [a]before his time,
And his palm [b]branch will not be green.
33 "He will drop off his unripe grape like the vine,
And will [a]cast off his flower like the olive tree.
34 "For the company of [a]the godless is barren,
And fire consumes [b]the tents of [1]the corrupt.
35 "They [a]conceive [1]mischief and bring forth iniquity,
And their [2]mind prepares deception."

Chapter 16 Theme ________________________

16

Then Job [1]answered,
2 "I have heard many such things;
[1a]Sorry comforters are you all.
3 "Is there *no* limit to [a]windy words?
Or what plagues you that you answer?
4 "I too could speak like you,
If [1]I were in your place.
I could compose words against you
And [a]shake my head at you.
5 "I could strengthen you with my mouth,
And the solace of my lips could lessen *your pain.*

6 "If I speak, [a]my pain is not lessened,
And if I hold back, what has left me?
7 "But now He has [a]exhausted me;
You have laid [b]waste all my company.
8 "You have shriveled me up,
[a]It has become a witness;

22 [a]Job 15:30 [b]Job 19:29; 27:14; 33:18; 36:12
23 [1]Lit *ready at his hand* [a]Job 15:22, 30
25 [1]Heb *Shaddai* [a]Job 36:9
26 [1]Lit *with a stiff neck* [2]Lit *the thick-bossed shields*
27 [a]Ps 73:7; 119:70
28 [1]Or *heaps* [a]Job 3:14; Is 5:8, 9
29 [a]Job 27:16, 17
30 [1]Lit *turn aside* [a]Job 5:14; 15:22 [b]Job 15:34; 20:26; 22:20; 31:12 [c]Job 4:9
31 [1]Lit *exchange* [a]Job 35:13; Is 59:4
32 [a]Job 22:16; Eccl 7:17 [b]Job 18:16
33 [a]Job 14:2
34 [1]Lit *a bribe* [a]Job 8:13 [b]Job 8:22
35 [1]Or *pain* [2]Lit *belly* [a]Ps 7:14; Is 59:4
16:1 [1]Lit *answered and said*
2 [1]Lit *Comforters of trouble* [a]Job 13:4; 21:34
3 [a]Job 6:26
4 [1]Lit *your soul were in place of my soul* [a]Ps 22:7; 109:25; Zeph 2:15; Matt 27:39
6 [a]Job 9:27, 28
7 [a]Job 7:3 [b]Job 16:20; 19:13-15
8 [a]Job 10:17

8 [b]Job 19:20; Ps 109:24

And my [b]leanness rises up against me,
It testifies to my face.

9 [1]Lit *borne a grudge against me* [2]Lit *sharpens his eyes* [a]Job 19:11; Hos 6:1 [b]Ps 35:16; Lam 2:16; Acts 7:54 [c]Job 13:24; 33:10

9 "His anger has [a]torn me and [1]hunted me down,
He has [b]gnashed at me with His teeth;
My [c]adversary [2]glares at me.
10 "They have [a]gaped at me with their mouth,
They have [1b]slapped me on the cheek with contempt;
They have [c]massed themselves against me.

10 [1]Lit *struck* [a]Ps 22:13 [b]Is 50:6; Lam 3:30; Acts 23:2 [c]Job 30:12; Ps 35:15

11 "God hands me over to ruffians
And tosses me into the hands of the wicked.
12 "I was at ease, but [a]He shattered me,
And He has grasped me by the neck and shaken me
to pieces;
He has also set me up as His [b]target.

12 [a]Job 9:17 [b]Job 7:20; Lam 3:12

13 "His [a]arrows surround me.
Without mercy He splits my kidneys open;
He pours out [b]my gall on the ground.

13 [a]Job 6:4; 19:12; 25:3 [b]Job 20:25

14 "He [a]breaks through me with breach after breach;
He [b]runs at me like a warrior.

14 [a]Job 9:17 [b]Joel 2:7

15 "I have sewed [a]sackcloth over my skin
And [b]thrust my horn in the dust.

15 [a]Gen 37:34; Ps 69:11 [b]Ps 7:5

16 "My face is flushed from [a]weeping,
[b]And deep darkness is on my eyelids,

16 [a]Job 16:20 [b]Job 24:17

17 Although there is no [a]violence in my hands,
And [b]my prayer is pure.

17 [a]Is 59:6; Jon 3:8 [b]Job 27:4

18 "O earth, do not cover my blood,
And let there be no *resting* place for my cry.
19 "Even now, behold, [a]my witness is in heaven,
And my [1]advocate is [b]on high.

19 [1]Or *witness* [a]Gen 31:50; Job 19:25-27; Rom 1:9; Phil 1:8; 1 Thess 2:5 [b]Job 31:2

20 "My friends are my scoffers;
[a]My eye [1]weeps to God.

20 [1]Or *drips* [a]Job 17:7

21 "O that a man might plead with God
As a man with his neighbor!
22 "For when a few years are past,
I shall go the way [a]of no return.

22 [a]Job 3:13

Chapter 17 Theme ______________________________

17:1 [1]Lit *graves* [a]Ps 88:3, 4

17

"My spirit is broken, my days are extinguished,
The [1a]grave is *ready* for me.
2 "[a]Surely mockers are with me,
And my eye [1]gazes on their provocation.

2 [1]Lit *lodges* [a]Job 12:4; 17:6

3 "Lay down, now, a pledge [a]for me with Yourself;
Who is there that will [1]be my guarantor?

3 [1]Lit *strike hands with me* [a]Ps 119:122; Is 38:14

4 "For You have [1a]kept their heart from understanding,
Therefore You will not exalt *them.*

4 [1]Lit *hidden* [a]Job 12:20

5 "He who [a]informs against friends for a share *of the spoil,*
The [b]eyes of his children also will languish.

5 [a]Lev 19:13, 16 [b]Job 11:20

6 "But He has made me a [a]byword of the people,
And I am [1]one at whom men [b]spit.
7 "My eye has also grown [a]dim because of grief,
And all my [b]members are as a shadow.
8 "The upright will be appalled at this,
And the [a]innocent will stir up himself against the godless.
9 "Nevertheless [a]the righteous will hold to his way,
And [b]he who has clean hands will grow stronger
and stronger.
10 "But come again all of [1]you now,
For I [a]do not find a wise man among you.
11 "My [a]days are past, my plans are torn apart,
Even the wishes of my heart.
12 "They make night into day, *saying,*
'The light is near,' in the presence of darkness.
13 "If I look for [a]Sheol as my home,
I [1]make my bed in the darkness;
14 If I call to the [a]pit, 'You are my father';
To the [b]worm, 'my mother and my sister';
15 Where now is [a]my hope?
And who regards my hope?
16 "[1]Will it go down with me to Sheol?
Shall we together [a]go down into the dust?"

Chapter 18 Theme ____________________

18 Then Bildad the Shuhite [1]responded,
2 "How long will you hunt for words?
Show understanding and then we can talk.
3 "Why are we [a]regarded as beasts,
As stupid in your eyes?
4 "O [1]you who tear yourself in your anger—
For your sake is the earth to be abandoned,
Or the rock to be moved from its place?

5 "Indeed, the [a]light of the wicked goes out,
And the [1]flame of his fire gives no light.
6 "The light in his tent is [a]darkened,
And his lamp goes out above him.
7 "His [1]vigorous stride is shortened,
And his [a]own scheme brings him down.
8 "For he is [a]thrown into the net by his own feet,
And he steps on the webbing.
9 "A snare seizes *him* by the heel,
And a trap snaps shut on him.
10 "A noose for him is hidden in the ground,
And a trap for him on the path.
11 "All around [a]terrors frighten him,
And [b]harry him at every step.
12 "His strength is [a]famished,
And calamity is ready at his side.

6 [1]Lit *a spitting to the faces* [a]Job 17:2 [b]Job 30:10

7 [a]Job 16:16 [b]Job 16:8

8 [a]Job 22:19

9 [a]Prov 4:18 [b]Job 22:30; 31:7

10 [1]With some ancient mss and versions; M.T. *them* [a]Job 12:2

11 [a]Job 7:6

13 [1]Lit *spread out* [a]Job 3:13

14 [a]Job 7:5; 13:28; 30:30 [b]Job 21:26; 25:6

15 [a]Job 7:6

16 [1]So the Gr; Heb possibly *Let my limbs sink down to Sheol, since there is rest in the dust for all* [a]Job 3:17; 21:33

18:1 [1]Lit *answered and said*

3 [a]Ps 73:22

4 [1]Lit *he . . . tears himself . . . his*

5 [1]Lit *spark* [a]Job 21:17; Prov 13:9; 20:20; 24:20

6 [a]Job 12:25

7 [1]Lit *steps of his strength* [a]Job 15:6

8 [a]Job 22:10; Ps 9:15; 35:8; Is 24:17, 18

11 [a]Job 15:21 [b]Job 18:18; 20:8

12 [a]Is 8:21

13 [1]Heb *It eats parts of his skin* [2]Or *parts* [a]Zech 14:12
14 [1]Lit *his tent his trust* [2]Or *you or she shall march* [a]Job 8:22; 18:6 [b]Job 15:21
15 [1]A suggested reading is *Fire dwells in his tent* [a]Ps 11:6
16 [a]Is 5:24; Hos 9:16; Amos 2:9; Mal 4:1 [b]Job 15:30, 32
17 [a]Job 24:20; Ps 34:16; Prov 10:7
18 [1]Lit *They drive him . . . And chase him* [a]Job 5:14; Is 8:22 [b]Job 20:8; 27:21-23
19 [a]Job 27:14, 15; Is 14:22
20 [1]Lit *who come after* [2]Lit *day* [3]Lit *who have gone before* [a]Ps 37:13; Jer 50:27; Obad 12
21 [a]Job 21:28
19:1 [1]Lit *answered and said*
2 [1]Lit *my soul*
5 [a]Ps 35:26; 38:16; 55:12, 13
6 [a]Job 16:11; 27:2 [b]Job 18:8-10; Ps 66:11; Lam 1:13
7 [a]Job 9:24; 30:20, 24; Hab 1:2
8 [a]Job 3:23; Lam 3:7, 9 [b]Job 30:26
9 [a]Job 12:17, 19; Ps 89:44 [b]Job 16:15; Ps 89:39; Lam 5:16
10 [a]Job 12:14 [b]Job 7:6 [c]Job 24:20
11 [a]Job 16:9 [b]Job 13:24; 33:10
12 [1]I.e. siegework [a]Job 16:13 [b]Job 30:12
13 [a]Job 16:7; Ps 69:8 [b]Job 16:20; Ps 88:8, 18
14 [a]Job 19:19

13 "[1]His skin is devoured by disease,
The firstborn of death [a]devours his [2]limbs.
14 "He is [a]torn from [1]the security of his tent,
And [2]they march him before the king of [b]terrors.
15 "[1]There dwells in his tent nothing of his;
[a]Brimstone is scattered on his habitation.
16 "His [a]roots are dried below,
And his [b]branch is cut off above.
17 "[a]Memory of him perishes from the earth,
And he has no name abroad.
18 "[1]He is driven from light [a]into darkness,
And [b]chased from the inhabited world.
19 "He has no [a]offspring or posterity among his people,
Nor any survivor where he sojourned.
20 "Those [1]in the west are appalled at [a]his [2]fate,
And those [3]in the east are seized with horror.
21 "Surely such are the [a]dwellings of the wicked,
And this is the place of him who does not know God."

Chapter 19 Theme ____________________

19 Then Job [1]responded,
2 "How long will you torment [1]me
And crush me with words?
3 "These ten times you have insulted me;
You are not ashamed to wrong me.
4 "Even if I have truly erred,
My error lodges with me.
5 "If indeed you [a]vaunt yourselves against me
And prove my disgrace to me,
6 Know then that [a]God has wronged me
And has closed [b]His net around me.

7 "Behold, [a]I cry, 'Violence!' but I get no answer;
I shout for help, but there is no justice.
8 "He has [a]walled up my way so that I cannot pass,
And He has put [b]darkness on my paths.
9 "He has [a]stripped my honor from me
And removed the [b]crown from my head.
10 "He [a]breaks me down on every side, and I am gone;
And He has uprooted my [b]hope [c]like a tree.
11 "He has also [a]kindled His anger against me
And [b]considered me as His enemy.
12 "His [a]troops come together,
And [b]build up their [1]way against me
And camp around my tent.

13 "He has [a]removed my brothers far from me,
And my [b]acquaintances are completely estranged from me.
14 "My relatives have failed,
And my [a]intimate friends have forgotten me.

15 "Those who live in my house and my maids consider me
a stranger.
I am a foreigner in their sight.
16 "I call to my servant, but he does not answer;
I have to implore him with my mouth.
17 "My breath is [1]offensive to my wife,
And I am loathsome to my own brothers.
18 "Even young children despise me;
I rise up and they speak against me.
19 "All [1]my [a]associates abhor me,
And those I love have turned against me.
20 "My [a]bone clings to my skin and my flesh,
And I have escaped *only* by the skin of my teeth.
21 "Pity me, pity me, O you my friends,
For the [a]hand of God has struck me.
22 "Why do you [a]persecute me as God *does,*
And are not satisfied with my flesh?

23 "Oh that my words were written!
Oh that they were [a]inscribed in a book!
24 "That with an iron stylus and lead
They were engraved in the rock forever!
25 "As for me, I know that [a]my [1]Redeemer lives,
And [2]at the last He will take His stand on the [3]earth.
26 "Even after my skin [1]is destroyed,
Yet from my flesh I shall [a]see God;
27 Whom I [1]myself shall behold,
And whom my eyes will see and not another.
My [2]heart [a]faints [3]within me!
28 "If you say, 'How shall we [a]persecute him?'
And '[1]What pretext for a case against him can we find?'
29 "*Then* be afraid of [a]the sword for yourselves,
For wrath *brings* the punishment of the sword,
So that you may know [b]there is judgment."

Chapter 20 Theme ______

20 Then Zophar the Naamathite [1]answered,
2 "Therefore my disquieting thoughts make me [1]respond,
Even because of my [2]inward agitation.
3 "I listened to [a]the reproof which insults me,
And the spirit of my understanding makes me answer.
4 "Do you know this from [a]of old,
From the establishment of man on earth,
5 That the [a]triumphing of the wicked is short,
And [b]the joy of the godless momentary?
6 "Though his loftiness [1a]reaches the heavens,
And his head touches the clouds,
7 He [a]perishes forever like his refuse;
Those who have seen him [b]will say, 'Where is he?'
8 "He flies away like a [a]dream, and they cannot find him;
Even like a vision of the night he is [b]chased away.

17 [1]Lit *strange*

19 [1]Lit *the men of my council* [a]Ps 38:11; 55:12, 13

20 [a]Job 16:8; 33:21; Ps 102:5; Lam 4:8

21 [a]Job 1:11; Ps 38:2

22 [a]Job 13:24, 25; 16:11; 19:6; Ps 69:26

23 [a]Is 30:8; Jer 36:2

25 [1]Or *Vindicator, defender;* lit *kinsman* [2]Or *as the Last* [3]Lit *dust* [a]Job 16:19; Ps 78:35; Prov 23:11; Is 43:14; Jer 50:34

26 [1]Lit *which they have cut off* [a]Ps 17:15; Matt 5:8; 1 Cor 13:12; 1 John 3:2

27 [1]Or *on my side* [2]Lit *kidneys* [3]Lit *in my loins* [a]Ps 73:26

28 [1]Or *the root of the matter is found in him* [a]Job 19:22

29 [a]Job 15:22 [b]Job 22:4; Ps 1:5; 9:7; Eccl 12:14

20:1 [1]Lit *answered and said*

2 [1]Lit *return* [2]Lit *haste within me*

3 [a]Job 19:3

4 [a]Job 8:8

5 [a]Job 8:12, 13; Ps 37:35, 36 [b]Job 8:13

6 [1]Lit *goes up to* [a]Is 14:13, 14; Obad 3, 4

7 [a]Job 4:20; 14:20 [b]Job 7:10; 8:18

8 [a]Ps 73:20; 90:5 [b]Job 18:18; 27:21-23

9 "The [a]eye which saw him sees him no longer,
And [b]his place no longer beholds him.
10 "His [a]sons [1]favor the poor,
And his hands [b]give back his wealth.
11 "His [a]bones are full of his youthful vigor,
But it lies down with him [1]in the dust.

12 "Though [a]evil is sweet in his mouth
And he hides it under his tongue,
13 *Though* he [1]desires it and will not let it go,
But holds it [a]in his [2]mouth,
14 *Yet* his food in his stomach is changed
To the [1]venom of cobras within him.
15 "He swallows riches,
But will [a]vomit them up;
God will expel them from his belly.
16 "He sucks [a]the poison of cobras;
The viper's tongue slays him.
17 "He does not look at [a]the streams,
The rivers flowing with honey and curds.
18 "He [a]returns what he has attained
And cannot swallow *it;*
As to the riches of his trading,
He cannot even enjoy *them.*
19 "For he has [a]oppressed *and* forsaken the poor;
He has seized a house which he has not built.

20 "Because he knew no quiet [1]within him,
He does [a]not retain anything he desires.
21 "Nothing remains [1]for him to devour,
Therefore [a]his prosperity does not endure.
22 "In the fullness of his plenty he will be cramped;
The [a]hand of everyone who suffers will come *against* him.
23 "When he [a]fills his belly,
God will send His fierce anger on him
And will [b]rain *it* on him [1]while he is eating.
24 "He may [a]flee from the iron weapon,
But the bronze bow will pierce him.
25 "It is drawn forth and comes out of his back,
Even the glittering point from [a]his gall.
[b]Terrors come upon him,
26 Complete [a]darkness is held in reserve for his treasures,
And unfanned [b]fire will devour him;
It will consume the survivor in his tent.
27 "The [a]heavens will reveal his iniquity,
And the earth will rise up against him.
28 "The [a]increase of his house will depart;
His possessions will flow away [b]in the day of His anger.
29 "This is the wicked man's [a]portion from God,
Even the heritage decreed to him by God."

9 [a]Job 7:8; 8:18 [b]Job 7:10
10 [1]Or *seek the favor of* [a]Job 5:4; 27:14 [b]Job 20:18; 27:16, 17
11 [1]Lit *on* [a]Job 21:23, 24
12 [a]Job 15:16
13 [1]Lit *has compassion on* [2]Lit *palate* [a]Num 11:18-20, 33; Job 20:23
14 [1]Lit *gall*
15 [a]Job 20:10, 20, 21
16 [a]Deut 32:24, 33
17 [a]Deut 32:13, 14; Job 29:6
18 [a]Job 20:10, 15
19 [a]Job 24:2-4; 35:9
20 [1]Lit *in his belly* [a]Eccl 5:13-15
21 [1]Or *of what he devours* [a]Job 15:29
22 [a]Job 5:5
23 [1]Or *as his food* [a]Job 20:13, 14 [b]Num 11:18-20, 33; Ps 78:30, 31
24 [a]Is 24:18; Amos 5:19
25 [a]Job 16:13 [b]Job 18:11, 14
26 [a]Job 18:18 [b]Job 15:30; Ps 21:9
27 [a]Deut 31:28; Is 26:21
28 [a]Deut 28:31 [b]Job 20:15; 21:30
29 [a]Job 27:13; 31:2, 3

Chapter 21 Theme ______________________________

21 Then Job [1]answered,
2 "Listen carefully to my speech,
And let this be your *way of* consolation.
3 "Bear with me that I may speak;
Then after I have spoken, you may [a]mock.
4 "As for me, is [a]my complaint [1]to man?
And [b]why should [2]I not be impatient?
5 "Look at me, and be astonished,
And [a]put *your* hand over *your* mouth.
6 "Even when I remember, I am disturbed,
And [a]horror takes hold of my flesh.
7 "Why [a]do the wicked *still* live,
Continue on, also become very [b]powerful?
8 "Their [1a]descendants are established with them in their sight,
And their offspring before their eyes,
9 Their houses [a]are safe from fear,
And the rod of God is not on them.
10 "His ox mates [1]without fail;
His cow calves and does not abort.
11 "They send forth their little ones like the flock,
And their children skip about.
12 "They [1]sing to the timbrel and harp
And rejoice at the sound of the flute.
13 "They [a]spend their days in prosperity,
And [1]suddenly they go down to [2]Sheol.
14 "They say to God, '[a]Depart from us!
We do not even desire the knowledge of Your ways.
15 '[1]Who is [2]the Almighty, that we should serve Him,
And [a]what would we gain if we entreat Him?'
16 "Behold, their prosperity is not in their hand;
The [a]counsel of the wicked is far from me.

17 "How often is [a]the lamp of the wicked put out,
Or does their [b]calamity fall on them?
Does [1]God apportion destruction in His anger?
18 "Are they as [a]straw before the wind,
And like [b]chaff which the storm carries away?
19 "*You say,* '[a]God stores away [1]a man's iniquity for his sons.'
Let [2]God repay him so that he may know *it.*
20 "Let his [a]own eyes see his decay,
And let him [b]drink of the wrath of [1]the Almighty.
21 "For what does he care for his household [1]after him,
When the number of his months is cut off?
22 "Can anyone [a]teach God knowledge,
In that He [b]judges those on high?
23 "One [a]dies in his full strength,
Being wholly at ease and [1]satisfied;
24 His [1]sides are filled out with fat,
And the [a]marrow of his bones is moist,

21:1 [1]Lit *answered and said*

3 [a]Job 11:3; 17:2

4 [1]Or *against* [2]Lit *my spirit* [a]Job 7:11 [b]Job 6:11

5 [a]Judg 18:19; Job 13:5; 29:9; 40:4

6 [a]Ps 55:5

7 [a]Job 9:24; Ps 73:3; Jer 12:1; Hab 1:13 [b]Job 12:19

8 [1]Lit *seed* [a]Ps 17:14

9 [a]Job 12:6

10 [1]Lit *and does not fail*

12 [1]Lit *lifted up the voice*

13 [1]So with most versions; M.T. *are shattered by Sheol* [2]I.e. the nether world [a]Job 21:23; 36:11

14 [a]Job 22:17

15 [1]Lit *What* [2]Heb *Shaddai* [a]Job 22:17; 34:9

16 [a]Job 22:18

17 [1]Lit *He* [a]Job 18:5, 6 [b]Job 31:2, 3

18 [a]Job 13:25; Ps 83:13 [b]Ps 1:4; 35:5; Is 17:13; Hos 13:3

19 [1]Lit *his* [2]Lit *Him* [a]Ex 20:5; Jer 31:29; Ezek 18:2

20 [1]Heb *Shaddai* [a]Num 14:28-32; Jer 31:30; Ezek 18:4 [b]Ps 60:3; Is 51:17; Jer 25:15; Rev 14:10

21 [1]I.e. after he dies

22 [a]Job 35:11; 36:22; Is 40:14; Rom 11:34 [b]Job 4:18; 15:15; Ps 82:1

23 [1]Or *quiet* [a]Job 20:11; 21:13

24 [1]So with Syr; Heb uncertain. Some render as, *his pails are full of milk* [a]Prov 3:8

25 [1]Lit *eating*

26 [a]Job 3:13; 20:11; Eccl 9:2 [b]Job 24:20; Is 14:11

28 [a]Job 1:3; 31:37 [b]Job 8:22; 18:21

29 [1]Lit *signs*

30 [a]Job 20:29; Prov 16:4; 2 Pet 2:9 [b]Job 21:17, 20; 40:11

31 [1]Lit *declare his way to his face*

33 [1]Lit *be sweet to him* [2]Lit *draw* [a]Job 3:22; 17:16 [b]Job 3:19; 24:24

34 [1]Or *faithlessness* [a]Job 16:2

22:1 [1]Lit *answered and said*

2 [a]Job 35:7; Luke 17:10

3 [1]Heb *Shaddai*

4 [1]Or *fear* [a]Job 14:3; 19:29

5 [a]Job 11:6; 15:5

6 [1]Lit *clothing of the naked* [a]Ex 22:26; Deut 24:6, 17; Job 24:3, 9; Ezek 18:16 [b]Job 31:19, 20

7 [a]Job 31:16, 17 [b]Job 31:31

8 [a]Job 9:24 [b]Job 12:19 [c]Is 3:3; 9:15

9 [1]Lit *arms* [a]Job 24:3, 21; 29:13; 31:16, 18 [b]Job 6:27

10 [a]Job 18:8 [b]Job 15:21

11 [a]Job 5:14 [b]Job 38:34; Ps 69:2; 124:5; Lam 3:54

12 [1]Lit *head, topmost* [a]Job 11:7-9

13 [a]Ps 10:11; 59:7; 64:5; 94:7; Is 29:15; Ezek 8:12

25 While another dies with a bitter soul,
Never even [1]tasting *anything* good.
26 "Together they [a]lie down in the dust,
And [b]worms cover them.

27 "Behold, I know your thoughts,
And the plans by which you would wrong me.
28 "For you say, 'Where is the house of [a]the nobleman,
And where is the [b]tent, the dwelling places of the wicked?'
29 "Have you not asked wayfaring men,
And do you not recognize their [1]witness?
30 "For the [a]wicked is reserved for the day of calamity;
They will be led forth at [b]the day of fury.
31 "Who will [1]confront him with his actions,
And who will repay him for what he has done?
32 "While he is carried to the grave,
Men will keep watch over *his* tomb.
33 "The [a]clods of the valley will [1]gently cover him;
Moreover, [b]all men will [2]follow after him,
While countless ones *go* before him.
34 "How then will you vainly [a]comfort me,
For your answers remain *full of* [1]falsehood?"

Chapter 22 Theme ____________________

22 Then Eliphaz the Temanite [1]responded,
2 "Can a vigorous [a]man be of use to God,
Or a wise man be useful to himself?
3 "Is there any pleasure to [1]the Almighty if you are righteous,
Or profit if you make your ways perfect?
4 "Is it because of your [1]reverence that He reproves you,
That He [a]enters into judgment against you?
5 "Is not [a]your wickedness great,
And your iniquities without end?
6 "For you have [a]taken pledges of your brothers
without cause,
And [b]stripped [1]men naked.
7 "To the weary you have [a]given no water to drink,
And from the hungry you have [b]withheld bread.
8 "But the earth [a]belongs to the [b]mighty man,
And [c]the honorable man dwells in it.
9 "You have sent [a]widows away empty,
And the [1]strength of the [b]orphans has been crushed.
10 "Therefore [a]snares surround you,
And sudden [b]dread terrifies you,
11 Or [a]darkness, so that you cannot see,
And an [b]abundance of water covers you.

12 "Is not God [a]*in* the height of heaven?
Look also at the [1]distant stars, how high they are!
13 "You say, '[a]What does God know?
Can He judge through the thick darkness?

14 '[a]Clouds are a hiding place for Him, so that He cannot see;
And He walks on the [1]vault of heaven.'
15 "Will you keep to the ancient path
Which [a]wicked men have trod,
16 Who were snatched away [a]before their time,
Whose [b]foundations were [1]washed away by a river?
17 "They [a]said to God, 'Depart from us!'
And 'What can [1]the Almighty do to them?'
18 "Yet He [a]filled their houses with good *things;*
But [b]the counsel of the wicked is far from me.
19 "The [a]righteous see and are glad,
And the innocent mock them,
20 *Saying,* 'Truly our adversaries are cut off,
And their [1]abundance [a]the fire has consumed.'

21 "[1a]Yield now and be at peace with Him;
Thereby good will come to you.
22 "Please receive [1a]instruction from His mouth
And establish His words in your heart.
23 "If you [a]return to [1]the Almighty, you will be [2]restored;
If you [b]remove unrighteousness far from your tent,
24 And [a]place *your* [1]gold in the dust,
And *the gold of* Ophir among the stones of the brooks,
25 Then [1]the Almighty will be your [2]gold
And choice silver to you.
26 "For then you will [a]delight in [1]the Almighty
And lift up your face to God.
27 "You will [a]pray to Him, and [b]He will hear you;
And you will pay your vows.
28 "You will also decree a thing, and it will be established
for you;
And [a]light will shine on your ways.
29 "When [1]you are cast down, you will speak
with [2]confidence,
And the [3a]humble person He will save.
30 "He will deliver one who is not innocent,
And he will be [a]delivered through the cleanness of
your hands."

Chapter 23 Theme ____________________

23 Then Job [1]replied,
2 "Even today my [a]complaint is rebellion;
[1]His hand is [b]heavy despite my groaning.
3 "Oh that I knew where I might find Him,
That I might come to His seat!
4 "I would [a]present *my* case before Him
And fill my mouth with arguments.
5 "I would learn the words *which* He would [1]answer,
And perceive what He would say to me.
6 "Would He contend with me by [a]the greatness of *His* power?
No, surely He would pay attention to me.

14 [1]Lit *circle* [a]Job 26:9
15 [a]Job 34:36
16 [1]Lit *poured out* [a]Job 15:32; 21:13, 18 [b]Job 14:19; Ps 90:5; Is 28:2; Matt 7:26, 27
17 [1]Heb *Shaddai* [a]Job 21:14, 15
18 [a]Job 12:6 [b]Job 21:16
19 [a]Ps 52:6; 58:10; 107:42
20 [1]Or *excess* [a]Job 15:30
21 [1]Or *Know intimately* [a]Ps 34:10
22 [1]Or *law* [a]Job 6:10; 23:12; Prov 2:6
23 [1]Heb *Shaddai* [2]Lit *built up* [a]Job 8:5; 11:13; Is 19:22; 31:6; Zech 1:3 [b]Job 11:14
24 [1]Lit *ore* [a]Job 31:24, 25
25 [1]Heb *Shaddai* [2]Lit *ore*
26 [1]Heb *Shaddai* [a]Job 27:10; Ps 37:4; Is 58:14
27 [a]Job 11:13; 33:26; Is 58:9 [b]Job 34:28
28 [a]Job 11:17; Ps 112:4
29 [1]Lit *they cast you down* [2]Lit *pride* [3]Lit *lowly of eyes* [a]Job 5:11; 36:7; Matt 23:12; James 4:6; 1 Pet 5:5
30 [a]Job 42:7, 8; Ps 18:20; 24:3, 4
23:1 [1]Lit *answered and said*
2 [1]So with Gr and Syr; M.T. *My* [a]Job 7:11 [b]Job 6:2, 3; Ps 32:4
4 [a]Job 13:18
5 [1]Lit *answer me*
6 [a]Job 9:4

7 "There the upright would [a]reason with Him;
And I [1]would be [b]delivered forever from my Judge.

8 "Behold, I go forward but He is not *there,*
And backward, but I [a]cannot perceive Him;
9 When He acts on the left, I cannot behold *Him;*
He turns on the right, I cannot see Him.
10 "But He knows the [1]way I take;
When He has [a]tried me, I shall come forth as gold.
11 "My foot has [a]held fast to His path;
I have kept His way and not turned aside.
12 "I have not departed from the command of His lips;
I have treasured the [a]words of His mouth [1]more than my
[2]necessary food.
13 "But He is unique and who can turn Him?
And *what* His soul desires, that He does.
14 "For He performs what is appointed for me,
And many such *decrees* are with Him.
15 "Therefore, I would be dismayed at His presence;
When I consider, I am terrified of Him.
16 "*It is* God *who* has made my [a]heart faint,
And the Almighty *who* has dismayed me,
17 But I [a]am not silenced by the darkness,
Nor [b]deep gloom *which* covers me.

Chapter 24 Theme ______________________________

24 "[a]Why are [1]times not stored up by the Almighty,
And why do those who know Him not see [b]His days?
2 "[1]Some [a]remove the landmarks;
They seize and [2]devour flocks.
3 "They drive away the donkeys of the [a]orphans;
They take the [b]widow's ox for a pledge.
4 "They push [a]the needy aside from the road;
The [b]poor of the land are made to hide
themselves altogether.
5 "Behold, as [a]wild donkeys in the wilderness
They [b]go forth seeking food in their activity,
As [1]bread for *their* children in the desert.
6 "They harvest their fodder in the field
And glean the vineyard of the wicked.
7 "[a]They spend the night naked, without clothing,
And have no covering against the cold.
8 "They are wet with the mountain rains
And hug the rock for want of a shelter.
9 "[1]Others snatch the [a]orphan from the breast,
And against the poor they take a pledge.
10 "They cause *the poor* to go about naked without clothing,
And they take away the sheaves from the hungry.
11 "Within the walls they produce oil;
They tread wine presses but thirst.

7 [1]Or *bring forth my justice forever* [a]Job 13:3 [b]Job 13:16; 23:10

8 [a]Job 9:11; 35:14

10 [1]Lit *way with me* [a]Job 7:18; Ps 7:9; 11:5; 66:10; Zech 13:9; 1 Pet 1:7

11 [a]Job 31:7; Ps 17:5; 44:18

12 [1]Or with some versions, *in my breast* [2]Lit *prescribed portion* [a]Job 6:10; 22:22

16 [a]Deut 20:3; Job 27:2; Jer 51:46

17 [a]Job 10:18, 19 [b]Job 19:8

24:1 [1]I.e. times of judgment [a]Acts 1:7 [b]Is 2:12; Jer 46:10; Obad 15; Zeph 1:7

2 [1]Lit *They* [2]Or *pasture* [a]Deut 19:14; 27:17; Prov 23:10

3 [a]Job 6:27 [b]Deut 24:17; Job 22:9

4 [a]Job 24:14; 29:16; 30:25; 31:19 [b]Job 29:12; Ps 41:1; Prov 14:31; 28:28; Amos 8:4

5 [1]Lit *his bread* [a]Job 39:5-8 [b]Ps 104:23

7 [a]Ex 22:26; Job 22:6

9 [1]Lit *They* [a]Job 6:27

12 "From the city men groan,
And the souls of the wounded cry out;
Yet God [a]does not pay attention to folly.

13 "[1]Others have been with those who rebel against the light;
They do not want to know its ways
Nor abide in its paths.
14 "The murderer [a]arises at dawn;
He [b]kills the poor and the needy,
And at night he is as a thief.
15 "The eye of the [a]adulterer waits for the twilight,
Saying, 'No eye will see me.'
And he [1]disguises his face.
16 "In the dark they [a]dig into houses,
They [b]shut themselves up by day;
They do not know the light.
17 "For the morning is the same to him as thick darkness,
For he is familiar with the [a]terrors of thick darkness.

18 "They are [1a]insignificant on the surface of the water;
Their portion is [b]cursed on the earth.
They do not turn [2]toward the [c]vineyards.
19 "Drought and heat [1a]consume the snow waters,
So does [2b]Sheol *those who* have sinned.
20 "A [1a]mother will forget him;
The [b]worm feeds sweetly till he is [c]no longer remembered.
And wickedness will be broken [d]like a tree.
21 "He wrongs the [1]barren woman
And does no good for [a]the widow.
22 "But He drags off the valiant by [a]His power;
He rises, but [b]no one has assurance of life.
23 "He provides them [a]with security, and they are supported;
And His [b]eyes are on their ways.
24 "They are exalted a [a]little while, then they are gone;
Moreover, they are [b]brought low and like everything
gathered up;
Even like the heads of grain they are cut off.
25 "Now if it is not so, [a]who can prove me a liar,
And make my speech worthless?"

Chapter 25 Theme ______________________

25 Then Bildad the Shuhite [1]answered,
2 "[a]Dominion and awe [1]belong to Him
Who establishes peace in [b]His heights.
3 "Is there any number to [a]His troops?
And upon whom does His light not rise?
4 "How then can a man be [a]just with God?
Or how can he be [b]clean who is born of woman?
5 "If even [a]the moon has no brightness
And the [b]stars are not pure in His sight,
6 How much less [a]man, *that* [b]maggot,
And the son of man, *that* worm!"

12 [a]Job 9:23, 24
13 [1]Lit *They*
14 [a]Mic 2:1 [b]Ps 10:8
15 [1]Or *puts a covering on his face* [a]Prov 7:9
16 [a]Ex 22:2; Matt 6:19 [b]John 3:20
17 [a]Job 15:21
18 [1]Or *light* or *swift* [2]Lit *to the path of* [a]Job 22:11, 16; 27:20 [b]Job 5:3 [c]Job 24:6, 11
19 [1]Lit *seize* [2]I.e. nether world [a]Job 6:16, 17 [b]Job 21:13
20 [1]Lit *womb* [a]Is 49:15 [b]Job 21:26 [c]Job 18:17; Ps 34:16; Prov 10:7 [d]Job 19:10; Dan 4:14
21 [1]Lit *barren who does not bear* [a]Job 22:9
22 [a]Job 9:4 [b]Job 18:20
23 [a]Job 12:6 [b]Job 10:4; 11:11
24 [a]Ps 37:10 [b]Job 14:21
25 [a]Job 6:28; 27:4
25:1 [1]Lit *answered and said*
2 [1]Lit *are with Him* [a]Job 9:4; 36:5, 22; 37:23; 42:2 [b]Job 16:19; 31:2
3 [a]Job 16:13
4 [a]Job 4:17; 9:2 [b]Job 14:4
5 [a]Job 31:26 [b]Job 15:15
6 [a]Job 7:17 [b]Job 17:14

Chapter 26 Theme ______________________________

26

Then Job [1]responded,
2 "What a help you are to [1a]the weak!
How you have saved the arm [b]without strength!
3 "What counsel you have given to *one* without wisdom!
What helpful insight you have abundantly [1]provided!
4 "To whom have you uttered words?
And whose [1]spirit was expressed through you?

5 "The [1a]departed spirits tremble
Under the waters and their inhabitants.
6 "Naked is [1a]Sheol before Him,
And [2b]Abaddon has no covering.
7 "He [a]stretches out the north over empty space
And hangs the earth on nothing.
8 "He [a]wraps up the waters in His clouds,
And the cloud does not burst under them.
9 "He [1a]obscures the face of the [2]full moon
And spreads His cloud over it.
10 "He has inscribed a [a]circle on the surface of the waters
At the [b]boundary of light and darkness.
11 "The pillars of heaven tremble
And are amazed at His rebuke.
12 "He [a]quieted the sea with His power,
And by His [b]understanding He shattered [c]Rahab.
13 "By His breath the [a]heavens are [1]cleared;
His hand has pierced [b]the fleeing serpent.
14 "Behold, these are the fringes of His ways;
And how faint [a]a word we hear of Him!
But His mighty [b]thunder, who can understand?"

Chapter 27 Theme ______________________________

27

Then Job [1]continued his [a]discourse and said,
2 "As God lives, [a]who has taken away my right,
And the Almighty, [b]who has embittered my soul,
3 For as long as [1]life is in me,
And the [2a]breath of God is in my nostrils,
4 My lips certainly will not speak unjustly,
Nor will [a]my tongue mutter deceit.
5 "Far be it from me that I should declare you right;
Till I die [a]I will not put away my integrity from me.
6 "I [a]hold fast my righteousness and will not let it go.
My heart does not reproach any of my days.

7 "May my enemy be as the wicked
And [1]my opponent as the unjust.
8 "For what is [a]the hope of the godless [1]when he is cut off,
When God requires [b]his [2]life?
9 "Will God [a]hear his cry
When [b]distress comes upon him?

26:1 [1]Lit *responded and said*
2 [1]Lit *no power* [a]Job 6:11, 12 [b]Ps 71:9
3 [1]Lit *made known*
4 [1]Lit *breath has gone forth*
5 [1]Or *shades;* Heb *Rephaim* [a]Job 3:13; Ps 88:10
6 [1]I.e. the nether world [2]I.e. place of destruction [a]Job 9:5-10; 26:6-14; 38:17; 41:11 [b]Job 28:22; 31:12
7 [a]Job 9:8
8 [a]Job 37:11; Prov 30:4
9 [1]Lit *covers* [2]Or *throne* [a]Job 22:14; Ps 97:2; 105:39
10 [a]Job 38:1-11; Prov 8:29 [b]Job 38:19, 20, 24
12 [a]Is 51:15; Jer 31:35 [b]Job 12:13 [c]Job 9:13
13 [1]Lit *made beautiful* [a]Job 9:8 [b]Is 27:1
14 [a]Job 4:12 [b]Job 36:29; 37:4, 5
27:1 [1]Or *again took up* [a]Job 13:12; 29:1
2 [a]Job 16:11; 34:5 [b]Job 9:18
3 [1]Lit *breath* [2]Or *spirit* [a]Job 32:8; 33:4
4 [a]Job 6:28; 33:3
5 [a]Job 6:29
6 [a]Job 2:3; 13:18
7 [1]Lit *he who rises up against me*
8 [1]Or *though he gains* [2]Lit *soul* [a]Job 8:13; 11:20 [b]Job 12:10
9 [a]Job 35:12, 13; Ps 18:41; Prov 1:28; Is 1:15; Jer 14:12; Mic 3:4 [b]Prov 1:27

10 "Will he take [a]delight in the Almighty?
Will he call on God at all times?
11 "I will instruct you in the [1]power of God;
What is with the Almighty I will not conceal.
12 "Behold, all of you have seen *it;*
Why then do you [1]act foolishly?

13 "This is [a]the portion of a wicked man from God,
And the inheritance *which* [b]tyrants receive from
the Almighty.
14 "Though his sons are many, [1]they are destined [a]for
the sword;
And his [b]descendants will not be satisfied with bread.
15 "His survivors will be buried because of the plague,
And [1]their [a]widows will not be able to weep.
16 "Though he piles up silver like dust
And prepares garments as *plentiful as* the clay,
17 He may prepare *it,* [a]but the just will wear *it*
And the innocent will divide the silver.
18 "He has built his [a]house like the [1]spider's web,
Or as a hut *which* the watchman has made.
19 "He lies down rich, but never [1]again;
He opens his eyes, and [a]it is no longer.
20 "[a]Terrors overtake him like a flood;
A tempest steals him away [b]in the night.
21 "The east [a]wind carries him away, and he is gone,
For it whirls him [b]away from his place.
22 "For it will hurl at him [a]without sparing;
He will surely try to [b]flee from its [1]power.
23 "*Men* will clap their hands at him
And will [a]hiss him from his place.

Chapter 28 Theme ______________________________

28 "Surely there is a [1]mine for silver
And a place [2]where they refine gold.
2 "Iron is taken from the dust,
And copper is smelted from rock.
3 "*Man* puts an end to darkness,
And [a]to the farthest limit he searches out
The rock in gloom and deep shadow.
4 "He [1]sinks a shaft far from [2]habitation,
Forgotten by the foot;
They hang and swing to and fro far from men.
5 "The earth, from it comes food,
And underneath it is turned up as fire.
6 "Its rocks are the [1]source of sapphires,
And its dust *contains* gold.
7 "The path no bird of prey knows,
Nor has the falcon's eye caught sight of it.
8 "The [1]proud beasts have not trodden it,
Nor has the *fierce* lion passed over it.

10 [a]Job 22:26, 27; Ps 37:4; Is 58:14
11 [1]Lit *hand*
12 [1]Or *speak vanity*
13 [a]Job 20:29 [b]Job 15:20
14 [1]Lit *the sword is for them* [a]Job 15:22; 18:19 [b]Job 20:10
15 [1]So ancient versions; Heb *his* [a]Ps 78:64
17 [a]Job 20:18-21
18 [1]So ancient versions; Heb *moth* [a]Job 8:15; 18:14
19 [1]So ancient versions; Heb *will be gathered* [a]Job 7:8, 21; 20:7
20 [a]Job 15:21 [b]Job 20:8; 34:20
21 [a]Job 21:18 [b]Job 7:10
22 [1]Lit *hand* [a]Jer 13:14; Ezek 5:11; 24:14 [b]Job 11:20
23 [a]Job 18:18; 20:8
28:1 [1]Or *source* [2]Lit *for gold they refine*
3 [a]Eccl 1:13
4 [1]Lit *breaks open* [2]Lit *sojourning*
6 [1]Or *place*
8 [1]Lit *sons of pride*

9 [1]Lit *roots*
11 [1]Lit *weeping*
12 [a]Job 28:23, 28; Eccl 7:24
13 [a]Matt 13:44-46
15 [a]Prov 3:13, 14; 8:10, 11; 16:16
17 [a]Prov 8:10; 16:16
18 [a]Prov 8:11
19 [a]Prov 8:19
20 [a]Job 28:23, 28
22 [1]I.e. Destruction [a]Job 26:6; Prov 8:32-36
23 [a]Job 9:4; Prov 8:22-36
24 [a]Ps 11:4; 33:13, 14; 66:7; Prov 15:3
25 [a]Ps 135:7 [b]Job 12:15; 38:8-11
26 [a]Job 37:6, 11, 12; 38:26-28 [b]Job 37:3; 38:25
28 [a]Ps 111:10; Prov 1:7; 9:10; Eccl 12:13
29:1 [a]Num 23:7; 24:3; Job 13:12; 27:1
2 [a]Jer 31:28
3 [a]Job 18:6 [b]Job 11:17
4 [1]Lit *the days of my autumn* [2]Lit *counsel* [a]Job 15:8; Ps 25:14; Prov 3:32

9 "He puts his hand on the flint;
He overturns the mountains at the [1]base.
10 "He hews out channels through the rocks,
And his eye sees anything precious.
11 "He dams up the streams from [1]flowing,
And what is hidden he brings out to the light.

12 "But [a]where can wisdom be found?
And where is the place of understanding?
13 "[a]Man does not know its value,
Nor is it found in the land of the living.
14 "The deep says, 'It is not in me';
And the sea says, 'It is not with me.'
15 "[a]Pure gold cannot be given in exchange for it,
Nor can silver be weighed as its price.
16 "It cannot be valued in the gold of Ophir,
In precious onyx, or sapphire.
17 "[a]Gold or glass cannot equal it,
Nor can it be exchanged for articles of fine gold.
18 "Coral and crystal are not to be mentioned;
And the acquisition of [a]wisdom is above *that of* pearls.
19 "The topaz of Ethiopia cannot equal it,
Nor can it be valued in [a]pure gold.
20 "[a]Where then does wisdom come from?
And where is the place of understanding?
21 "Thus it is hidden from the eyes of all living
And concealed from the birds of the sky.
22 "[1a]Abaddon and Death say,
'With our ears we have heard a report of it.'

23 "[a]God understands its way,
And He knows its place.
24 "For He [a]looks to the ends of the earth
And sees everything under the heavens.
25 "When He imparted [a]weight to the wind
And [b]meted out the waters by measure,
26 When He set a [a]limit for the rain
And a course for the [b]thunderbolt,
27 Then He saw it and declared it;
He established it and also searched it out.
28 "And to man He said, 'Behold, the [a]fear of the Lord, that is wisdom;
And to depart from evil is understanding.'"

Chapter 29 Theme ____________________

29 And Job again took up his [a]discourse and said,
2 "Oh that I were as in months gone by,
As in the days when God [a]watched over me;
3 When [a]His lamp shone over my head,
And [b]by His light I walked through darkness;
4 As I was in [1]the prime of my days,
When the [2a]friendship of God *was* over my tent;

5 When [1]the Almighty was yet with me,
And my children were around me;
6 When my steps were bathed in [a]butter,
And the [b]rock poured out for me streams of oil!
7 "When I went out to [a]the gate of the city,
When I [1]took my seat in the square,
8 The young men saw me and hid themselves,
And the old men arose *and* stood.
9 "The princes [a]stopped talking
And [b]put *their* hands on their mouths;
10 The voice of the nobles was [1a]hushed,
And their [b]tongue stuck to their palate.
11 "For when [a]the ear heard, it called me blessed,
And when the eye saw, it gave witness of me,
12 Because I delivered [a]the poor who cried for help,
And the [b]orphan who had no helper.
13 "The blessing of the one [a]ready to perish came upon me,
And I made the [b]widow's heart sing for joy.
14 "I [a]put on righteousness, and it clothed me;
My justice was like a robe and a turban.
15 "I was [a]eyes to the blind
And feet to the lame.
16 "I was a father to [a]the needy,
And I investigated the case which I did not know.
17 "I [a]broke the jaws of the wicked
And snatched the prey from his teeth.
18 "Then I [1]thought, 'I shall die [2]in my nest,
And I shall multiply *my* days as the sand.
19 'My [a]root is spread out to the waters,
And [b]dew lies all night on my branch.
20 'My glory is *ever* new with me,
And my [a]bow is renewed in my hand.'

21 "To me [a]they listened and waited,
And kept silent for my counsel.
22 "After my words they did not [a]speak again,
And [b]my speech dropped on them.
23 "They waited for me as for the rain,
And opened their mouth as for the spring rain.
24 "I smiled on them when they did not believe,
And the light of my face they did not cast down.
25 "I chose a way for them and sat as [a]chief,
And dwelt as a king among the troops,
As one who [b]comforted the mourners.

Chapter 30 Theme ________________

30 "But now those younger than I [a]mock me,
Whose fathers I disdained to put with the dogs of
my flock.
2 "Indeed, what *good was* the strength of their hands to me?
Vigor had perished from them.

5 [1]Heb *Shaddai*
6 [a]Deut 32:14; Job 20:17 [b]Deut 32:13; Ps 81:16
7 [1]Lit *set up* [a]Job 31:21
9 [a]Job 29:21 [b]Job 21:5
10 [1]Lit *hidden* [a]Job 29:22 [b]Ps 137:6
11 [a]Job 4:3, 4
12 [a]Job 24:4, 9; 34:28; Ps 72:12; Prov 21:13 [b]Job 31:17, 21
13 [a]Job 31:19 [b]Job 22:9
14 [a]Job 27:5, 6; Ps 132:9; Is 59:17; 61:10; Eph 6:14
15 [a]Num 10:31
16 [a]Job 24:4; Prov 29:7
17 [a]Ps 3:7
18 [1]Lit *said* [2]Lit *with*
19 [a]Jer 17:8 [b]Hos 14:5
20 [a]Gen 49:24; Ps 18:34
21 [a]Job 4:3; 29:9
22 [a]Job 29:10 [b]Deut 32:2
25 [a]Job 1:3; 31:37 [b]Job 4:4; 16:5
30:1 [a]Job 12:4

3 "From want and famine they are gaunt
Who gnaw the dry ground by night in waste
and desolation,
4 Who pluck [1]mallow by the bushes,
And whose food is the root of the broom shrub.
5 "They are driven from the community;
They shout against them as *against* a thief,
6 So that they dwell in dreadful [1]valleys,
In holes of the earth and of the rocks.
7 "Among the bushes they [1]cry out;
Under the nettles they are gathered together.
8 "[1]Fools, even [2]those without a name,
They were scourged from the land.

9 "And now I have become their [1a]taunt,
I have even become a [b]byword to them.
10 "They abhor me *and* stand aloof from me,
And they do not [1]refrain from [a]spitting at my face.
11 "Because [1]He has loosed [2]His [3]bowstring and [a]afflicted me,
They have cast off [b]the bridle before me.
12 "On the right hand their [1]brood arises;
They [a]thrust aside my feet [b]and build up against me their
ways of destruction.
13 "They [a]break up my path,
They profit [1]from my destruction;
No one restrains them.
14 "As *through* a wide breach they come,
[1]Amid the tempest they roll on.
15 "[a]Terrors are turned against me;
They pursue my [1]honor as the wind,
And my [2]prosperity has passed away [b]like a cloud.

16 "And now [a]my soul is poured out [1]within me;
Days of affliction have seized me.
17 "At night it pierces [a]my bones [1]within me,
And my gnawing *pains* take no rest.
18 "By a great force my garment is [a]distorted;
It binds me about as the collar of my coat.
19 "He has cast me into the [a]mire,
And I have become like dust and ashes.
20 "I [a]cry out to You for help, but You do not answer me;
I stand up, and You turn Your attention against me.
21 "You have [1]become cruel to me;
With the might of Your hand You [a]persecute me.
22 "You [a]lift me up to the wind *and* cause me to ride;
And You dissolve me in a storm.
23 "For I know that You [a]will bring me to death
And to the [b]house of meeting for all living.

24 "Yet does not one in a heap of ruins stretch out *his* hand,
Or in his disaster therefore [a]cry out for help?

4 [1]I.e. plant of the salt marshes
6 [1]Or *wadis*
7 [1]Or *bray*
8 [1]Lit *Sons of fools* [2]Lit *sons*
9 [1]Lit *song* [a]Job 12:4 [b]Job 17:6; Ps 69:11; Lam 3:14, 63
10 [1]Lit *withhold spit from my face* [a]Num 12:14; Deut 25:9; Job 17:6; Is 50:6; Matt 26:67
11 [1]Or *they* [2]Some mss read *my* [3]Or *cord* [a]Ruth 1:21; Ps 88:7 [b]Ps 32:9
12 [1]Possibly *sprout* or *offspring* [a]Ps 140:4, 5 [b]Job 19:12
13 [1]Lit *for* [a]Is 3:12
14 [1]Lit *Under*
15 [1]Or *nobility* [2]Or *welfare* [a]Job 3:25; 31:23; Ps 55:3-5 [b]Job 7:9; Hos 13:3
16 [1]Lit *upon* [a]1 Sam 1:15; Job 3:24; Ps 22:14; 42:4; Is 53:12
17 [1]Lit *from upon* [a]Job 30:30
18 [a]Job 2:7
19 [a]Ps 69:2, 14
20 [a]Job 19:7
21 [1]Lit *turned to be* [a]Job 10:3; 16:9, 14; 19:6, 22
22 [a]Job 9:17; 27:21
23 [a]Job 9:22; 10:8 [b]Job 3:19; Eccl 12:5
24 [a]Job 19:7

25 "Have I not [a]wept for the [1]one whose life is hard?
Was not my soul grieved for [b]the needy?
26 "When I [a]expected good, then evil came;
When I waited for light, [b]then darkness came.
27 "[1]I am seething [a]within and cannot relax;
Days of affliction confront me.
28 "I go about [1a]mourning without comfort;
I stand up in the assembly *and* [b]cry out for help.
29 "I have become a brother to [a]jackals
And a companion of ostriches.
30 "My [a]skin turns black [1]on me,
And my [b]bones burn with [2]fever.
31 "Therefore my [a]harp [1]is turned to mourning,
And my flute to the sound of those who weep.

Chapter 31 Theme ____

31 "I have made a covenant with my [a]eyes;
How then could I gaze at a virgin?
2 "And what is [a]the portion of God from above
Or the heritage of the Almighty from on high?
3 "Is it not [a]calamity to the unjust
And disaster to [b]those who work iniquity?
4 "Does He not [a]see my ways
And [b]number all my steps?

5 "If I have [a]walked with falsehood,
And my foot has hastened after deceit,
6 Let Him [a]weigh me with [1]accurate scales,
And let God know [b]my integrity.
7 "If my step has [a]turned from the way,
Or my heart [1]followed my eyes,
Or if any [b]spot has stuck to my hands,
8 Let me [a]sow and another eat,
And let my [1b]crops be uprooted.

9 "If my heart has been [a]enticed by a woman,
Or I have lurked at my neighbor's doorway,
10 May my wife [a]grind for another,
And let [b]others [1]kneel down over her.
11 "For that would be a [a]lustful crime;
Moreover, it would be [b]an iniquity *punishable by* judges.
12 "For it would be [a]fire that consumes to [1b]Abaddon,
And would [c]uproot all my [2]increase.

13 "If I have [a]despised the claim of my male or female slaves
When they filed a complaint against me,
14 What then could I do when God arises?
And when He calls me to account, what will I answer Him?
15 "Did not [a]He who made me in the womb make him,
And the same one fashion us in the womb?

25 [1]Lit *hard of day* [a]Ps 35:13, 14; Rom 12:15 [b]Job 24:4

26 [a]Job 3:25, 26; Jer 8:15 [b]Job 19:8

27 [1]Lit *My inward parts are boiling* [a]Lam 2:11

28 [1]Or *blackened, but not by the heat of the sun* [a]Job 30:31; Ps 38:6; 42:9; 43:2 [b]Job 19:7

29 [a]Ps 44:19; Mic 1:8

30 [1]Lit *from upon* [2]Lit *heat* [a]Job 2:7 [b]Ps 102:3

31 [1]Lit *becomes* [a]Is 24:8

31:1 [a]Matt 5:28

2 [a]Job 20:29

3 [a]Job 18:12; 21:30 [b]Job 34:22

4 [a]2 Chr 16:9; Job 24:23; 28:24; 34:21; 36:7; Prov 5:21; 15:3 [b]Job 14:16; 31:37

5 [a]Job 15:31; Mic 2:11

6 [1]Lit *just* [a]Job 6:2, 3 [b]Job 23:10; 27:5, 6

7 [1]Lit *walked after* [a]Job 23:11 [b]Job 9:30

8 [1]Or *offspring* [a]Lev 26:16; Job 20:18; Mic 6:15 [b]Job 31:12

9 [a]Job 24:15; 31:1

10 [1]I.e. sexual relations [a]Is 47:2 [b]Deut 28:30; Jer 8:10

11 [a]Lev 20:10; Deut 22:24 [b]Job 31:28

12 [1]I.e. place of destruction [2]Or *yield* [a]Job 15:30 [b]Job 26:6 [c]Job 20:28; 31:8

13 [a]Deut 24:14, 15

15 [a]Job 10:3

16 "If I have kept [a]the poor from *their* desire,
Or have caused the eyes of [b]the widow to fail,
17 Or have [a]eaten my morsel alone,
And [b]the orphan has not [1]shared it
18 (But from my youth he grew up with me as with a father,
And from [1]infancy I guided her),
19 If I have seen anyone perish [a]for lack of clothing,
Or that [b]the needy had no covering,
20 If his loins have not [1]thanked me,
And if he has not been warmed with the fleece of my sheep,
21 If I have lifted up my hand against [a]the orphan,
Because I saw [1]I had support [b]in the gate,
22 Let my shoulder fall from the [1]socket,
And my [a]arm be broken off [2]at the elbow.
23 "For [a]calamity from God is a terror to me,
And because of [b]His [1]majesty I can do nothing.

24 "If I have put my confidence *in* [a]gold,
And called fine gold my trust,
25 If I have [a]gloated because my wealth was great,
And because my hand had secured *so* much;
26 If I have [a]looked at the [1]sun when it shone
Or the moon going in splendor,
27 And my heart became secretly enticed,
And my hand [1]threw a kiss from my mouth,
28 That too would have been [a]an iniquity *calling for* [1]judgment,
For I would have [b]denied God above.

29 "Have I [a]rejoiced at the extinction of my enemy,
Or [1]exulted when evil befell him?
30 "[1]No, [a]I have not [2]allowed my mouth to sin
By asking for his life in [b]a curse.
31 "Have the men of my tent not said,
'Who can [1]find one who has not been [a]satisfied
with his meat'?
32 "The alien has not lodged outside,
For I have opened my doors to the [1]traveler.
33 "Have I [a]covered my transgressions like [1]Adam,
By hiding my iniquity in my bosom,
34 Because I [a]feared the great multitude,
And the contempt of families terrified me,
And kept silent and did not go out of doors?
35 "Oh that I had one to hear me!
Behold, here is my [1]signature;
[a]Let the Almighty answer me!
And the indictment which my [b]adversary has written,
36 Surely I would carry it on my shoulder,
I would bind it to myself like a crown.
37 "I would declare to Him [a]the number of my steps;
Like [b]a prince I would approach Him.

16 [a]Job 5:16; 20:19 [b]Ex 22:22-24; Job 22:9
17 [1]Lit *eaten from it* [a]Job 22:7 [b]Job 29:12
18 [1]Lit *my mother's womb*
19 [a]Job 22:6; 29:13 [b]Job 24:4
20 [1]Lit *blessed*
21 [1]Lit *my help* [a]Job 29:12; 31:17 [b]Job 29:7
22 [1]Lit *shoulder;* or *back* [2]Lit *from the bone of the upper arm* [a]Job 38:15
23 [1]Lit *exaltation* [a]Job 31:3 [b]Job 13:11
24 [a]Job 22:24; Mark 10:23-25
25 [a]Job 1:3, 10; Ps 62:10
26 [1]Lit *light* [a]Deut 4:19; 17:3; Ezek 8:16
27 [1]Lit *kissed my mouth*
28 [1]Lit *judges* [a]Deut 17:2-7; Job 31:11 [b]Josh 24:27; Is 59:13
29 [1]Lit *lifted myself up* [a]Prov 17:5; 24:17; Obad 12
30 [1]Lit *And* [2]Lit *given my palate* [a]Ps 7:4 [b]Job 5:3
31 [1]Lit *give* [a]Job 22:7
32 [1]M.T. *way*
33 [1]Or *mankind* [a]Gen 3:10; Prov 28:13
34 [a]Ex 23:2
35 [1]Lit *mark* [a]Job 19:7; 30:20, 24, 28; 35:14 [b]Job 27:7
37 [a]Job 31:4 [b]Job 1:3; 29:25

38 "If my [a]land cries out against me,
And its furrows weep together;
39 If I have [a]eaten its [1]fruit without money,
Or have [b]caused [2]its owners to lose their lives,
40 Let [a]briars [1]grow instead of wheat,
And stinkweed instead of barley."
The words of Job are ended.

Chapter 32 Theme ______________________________

32 Then these three men ceased answering Job, because he
was [a]righteous in his own eyes.
2 But the anger of Elihu the son of Barachel the [a]Buzite, of the
family of Ram burned; against Job his anger burned [b]because
he justified himself [1c]before God.
3 And his anger burned against his three friends because they
had found no answer, and yet had condemned Job.
4 Now Elihu had waited [1]to speak to Job because they were
years older than he.
5 And when Elihu saw that there was no answer in the mouth
of the three men his anger burned.
6 So Elihu the son of Barachel the Buzite [1]spoke out and said,
"I am young in years and you are [a]old;
Therefore I was shy and afraid to tell you [2]what I think.
7 "I [1]thought [2a]age should speak,
And [3]increased years should teach wisdom.
8 "But it is a spirit in man,
And the [a]breath of the Almighty gives them
[b]understanding.
9 "The [1]abundant *in years* may not be wise,
Nor may [a]elders understand justice.
10 "So I [1]say, 'Listen to me,
I too will tell [2]what I think.'

11 "Behold, I waited for your words,
I listened to your reasonings,
While you [1]pondered what to say.
12 "I even paid close attention to you;
[1]Indeed, there was no one who refuted Job,
Not one of you who answered his words.
13 "Do not say,
'[a]We have found wisdom;
God will [1]rout him, not man.'
14 "For he has not arranged *his* words against me,
Nor will I reply to him with your [1]arguments.

15 "They are dismayed, they no longer answer;
Words have [1]failed them.
16 "Shall I wait, because they do not speak,
Because they [1]stop *and* no longer answer?
17 "I too will answer my share,
I also will tell my opinion.

38 [a]Job 24:2

39 [1]Lit *strength* [2]Lit *the soul of its owners to expire* [a]Job 24:6, 10-12; James 5:4 [b]1 Kin 21:19

40 [1]Lit *come forth* [a]Job 32:13; Is 5:6

32:1 [a]Job 10:7; 13:18; 27:5, 6; 31:6

2 [1]Or *more than* [a]Gen 22:21 [b]Job 27:5, 6 [c]Job 30:21

4 [1]Lit *for Job with words;* or possibly *while they were speaking with Job*

6 [1]Lit *answered* [2]Lit *my knowledge* [a]Job 15:10

7 [1]Lit *said* [2]Lit *days* [3]Lit *many* [a]Job 8:8, 9

8 [a]Job 33:4 [b]Job 38:36

9 [1]Or *nobles* [a]Job 32:7

10 [1]Or *said* [2]Lit *my knowledge*

11 [1]Lit *searched out words*

12 [1]Lit *Behold*

13 [1]Lit *drive away* [a]Jer 9:23

14 [1]Lit *words*

15 [1]Lit *moved away from*

16 [1]Lit *stand*

18 "For I am full of words;
The spirit within me constrains me.
19 "Behold, my belly is like unvented wine,
Like new wineskins it is about to burst.
20 "Let me speak that I may get relief;
Let me open my lips and answer.
21 "Let me now [a]be partial to no one,
Nor flatter *any* man.
22 "For I do not know how to flatter,
Else my Maker would soon take me away.

Chapter 33 Theme ______________________

33

"However now, Job, please [a]hear my speech,
And listen to all my words.
2 "Behold now, I open my mouth,
My tongue in my [1]mouth speaks.
3 "My words are *from* the uprightness of my heart,
And my lips speak [a]knowledge sincerely.
4 "The [a]Spirit of God has made me,
And the [b]breath of [1]the Almighty gives me life.
5 "[a]Refute me if you can;
Array yourselves before me, take your stand.
6 "Behold, I belong to God like you;
I too have been [1]formed out of the [a]clay.
7 "Behold, [a]no fear of me should terrify you,
Nor should my pressure weigh heavily on you.

8 "Surely you have spoken in my hearing,
And I have heard the sound of *your* words:
9 'I am [a]pure, [b]without transgression;
I am innocent and there [c]is no guilt in me.
10 'Behold, He [1]invents pretexts against me;
He [a]counts me as His enemy.
11 'He [a]puts my feet in the stocks;
He watches all my paths.'
12 "Behold, let me [1]tell you, [a]you are not right in this,
For God is greater than man.

13 "Why do you [a]complain against Him
That He does not give an account of all His doings?
14 "Indeed [a]God speaks once,
Or twice, *yet* no one notices it.
15 "In a [a]dream, a vision of the night,
When sound sleep falls on men,
While they slumber in their beds,
16 Then [a]He opens the ears of men,
And seals their instruction,
17 That He may turn man aside *from his* conduct,
And [1]keep man from pride;
18 He [a]keeps back his soul from the pit,
And his life from [1]passing over [b]into Sheol.

21 [a]Lev 19:15; Job 13:8, 10; 34:19

33:1 [a]Job 13:6

2 [1]Lit *palate*

3 [a]Job 6:28; 27:4; 36:4

4 [1]Heb *Shaddai* [a]Gen 2:7; Job 10:3; 32:8 [b]Job 27:3

5 [a]Job 33:32

6 [1]Lit *cut out of* [a]Job 4:19

7 [a]Job 13:21

9 [a]Job 9:21; 10:7; 13:18; 16:17 [b]Job 7:21; 13:23; 14:17 [c]Job 10:14

10 [1]Lit *finds* [a]Job 13:24

11 [a]Job 13:27

12 [1]Lit *answer* [a]Eccl 7:20

13 [a]Job 40:2; Is 45:9

14 [a]Job 33:29; 40:5; Ps 62:11

15 [a]Job 4:12-17; 33:15-18

16 [a]Job 36:10, 15

17 [1]Lit *hide*

18 [1]M.T. *perishing by the sword* [a]Job 33:22, 24, 28, 30 [b]Job 15:22

19 "[1]Man is also chastened with [a]pain on his bed,
And with unceasing complaint in his bones;
20 So that his life [a]loathes bread,
And his soul favorite food.
21 "His [a]flesh wastes away from sight,
And his [b]bones which were not seen stick out.
22 "Then [a]his soul draws near to the pit,
And his life to those who bring death.

23 "If there is an angel *as* [a]mediator for him,
One out of a thousand,
To remind a man what is [1]right for him,
24 Then let him be gracious to him, and say,
'Deliver him from [a]going down to the pit,
I have found a [b]ransom';
25 Let his flesh become fresher than in youth,
Let him return to the days of his youthful vigor;
26 Then he will [a]pray to God, and He will accept him,
That [b]he may see His face with joy,
And He may restore His righteousness to man.
27 "He will sing to men and say,
'I [a]have sinned and perverted what is right,
And it is not [b]proper for me.
28 'He has redeemed my soul from going to the pit,
And my life shall [a]see the light.'

29 "Behold, God does [a]all these [1]oftentimes with men,
30 To [a]bring back his soul from the pit,
That he may be enlightened with the light of life.
31 "Pay attention, O Job, listen to me;
Keep silent, and let me speak.
32 "*Then* if [1]you have anything to say, answer me;
Speak, for I desire to justify you.
33 "If not, [a]listen to me;
Keep silent, and I will teach you wisdom."

Chapter 34 Theme ________________________

34 Then Elihu continued and said,
2 "Hear my words, you wise men,
And listen to me, you who know.
3 "For [a]the ear tests words
As the palate tastes food.
4 "Let us choose for ourselves what is right;
Let us know among ourselves what is good.
5 "For Job has said, '[a]I am righteous,
But [b]God has taken away my right;
6 [1]Should I lie concerning my right?
My [2a]wound is incurable, *though I am* without transgression.'
7 "What man is like Job,
Who [a]drinks up derision like water,

19 [1]Lit *He* [a]Job 30:17

20 [a]Job 3:24; 6:7; Ps 107:18

21 [a]Job 16:8 [b]Job 19:20; Ps 22:17; 102:5

22 [a]Job 33:18, 28

23 [1]Lit *his uprightness* [a]Gen 40:8

24 [a]Job 33:18, 28; Is 38:17 [b]Job 36:18; Ps 49:7

26 [a]Job 22:27; 34:28; Ps 50:14, 15 [b]Job 22:26

27 [a]2 Sam 12:13; Luke 15:21 [b]Rom 6:21

28 [a]Job 22:28

29 [1]Lit *twice, three times* [a]Eph 1:11; Phil 2:13

30 [a]Job 33:18; Zech 9:11

32 [1]Lit *there are words*

33 [a]Ps 34:11

34:3 [a]Job 12:11

5 [a]Job 13:18; 33:9 [b]Job 27:2

6 [1]Or *Although I am right I am accounted a liar* [2]Lit *arrow* [a]Job 6:4

7 [a]Job 15:16

8 Who goes [a]in company with the workers of iniquity,
And walks with wicked men?
9 "For he has said, '[a]It profits a man nothing
When he [1]is pleased with God.'

10 "Therefore, listen to me, you men of understanding.
Far be it from God to [a]do wickedness,
And from the Almighty to do wrong.
11 "For He pays a man according to [a]his work,
And makes [1]him find it according to his way.
12 "Surely, [a]God will not act wickedly,
And the Almighty will not pervert justice.
13 "Who [a]gave Him authority over the earth?
And who [b]has laid *on Him* the whole world?
14 "If He should [1]determine to do so,
If He should [a]gather to Himself His spirit and His breath,
15 All [a]flesh would perish together,
And man would [b]return to dust.

16 "But if *you have* understanding, hear this;
Listen to the sound of my words.
17 "Shall [a]one who hates justice rule?
And [b]will you condemn the righteous mighty One,
18 Who says to a king, 'Worthless one,'
To nobles, 'Wicked ones';
19 Who shows no [a]partiality to princes
Nor regards the rich above the poor,
For they all are the [b]work of His hands?
20 "In a moment they die, and [a]at midnight
People are shaken and pass away,
And [b]the mighty are taken away without a hand.

21 "For [a]His eyes are upon the ways of a man,
And He sees all his steps.
22 "There is [a]no darkness or deep shadow
Where the workers of iniquity may hide themselves.
23 "For He does not [a]*need to* consider a man further,
That he should go before God in judgment.
24 "He breaks in pieces [a]mighty men without inquiry,
And sets others in their place.
25 "Therefore He [a]knows their works,
And [b]He overthrows *them* in the night,
And they are crushed.
26 "He [a]strikes them like the wicked
[1]In a public place,
27 Because they [a]turned aside from following Him,
And [b]had no regard for any of His ways;
28 So that they caused [a]the cry of the poor to come to Him,
And that He might [b]hear the cry of the afflicted—
29 When He keeps quiet, who then can condemn?
And when He hides His face, who then can behold Him,
That is, in regard to both nation and man?—

8 [a]Job 22:15
9 [1]Or *takes delight in God* [a]Job 21:15; 35:3; Ps 50:18
10 [a]Gen 18:25; Deut 32:4; Job 8:3; 34:12; Rom 9:14
11 [1]Lit *a man* [a]Job 34:25; Ps 62:12; Prov 24:12; Jer 32:19; Ezek 33:20; Matt 16:27; Rom 2:6; 2 Cor 5:10; Rev 22:12
12 [a]Job 34:10
13 [a]Job 38:4 [b]Job 38:5
14 [1]Lit *set His mind on Himself* [a]Job 12:10; Ps 104:29; Eccl 12:7
15 [a]Gen 7:21; Job 9:22 [b]Gen 3:19; Job 10:9
17 [a]2 Sam 23:3; Job 34:30 [b]Job 40:8
19 [a]Lev 19:15; Deut 10:17; 2 Chr 19:7; Acts 10:34; Rom 2:11; Gal 2:6; Eph 6:9; Col 3:25; 1 Pet 1:17 [b]Job 10:3
20 [a]Ex 12:29; Job 34:25; 36:20 [b]Job 12:19
21 [a]Job 24:23; 31:4; Prov 5:21; 15:3; Jer 16:17
22 [a]Ps 139:11, 12; Amos 9:2, 3
23 [a]Job 11:11
24 [a]Job 12:19
25 [a]Job 34:11 [b]Job 34:20
26 [1]Lit *In the place of the ones seeing* [a]Ps 9:5; 11:5
27 [a]1 Sam 15:11 [b]Job 21:14
28 [a]Job 35:9; James 5:4 [b]Ex 22:23; Job 22:27

30 So that [a]godless men would not rule
Nor be snares of the people.

31 "For has anyone said to God,
'I have borne *chastisement;*
I will not offend *anymore;*
32 Teach me what I do not see;
If I have [a]done iniquity,
I will not do it again'?
33 "Shall He [a]recompense on your terms, because you have rejected *it?*
For you must choose, and not I;
Therefore declare what you know.
34 "Men of understanding will say to me,
And a wise man who hears me,
35 'Job [a]speaks without knowledge,
And his words are without wisdom.
36 'Job ought to be tried [1]to the limit,
Because he answers [a]like wicked men.
37 'For he adds [a]rebellion to his sin;
He [b]claps his hands among us,
And multiplies his words against God.'"

Chapter 35 Theme ____________________

35 Then Elihu continued and said,
2 "Do you think this is according to [a]justice?
Do you say, 'My righteousness is more than God's'?
3 "For you say, '[a]What advantage will it be to [1]You?
[b]What profit will I have, more than if I had sinned?'
4 "I will answer you,
And your friends with you.
5 "[a]Look at the heavens and see;
And behold [b]the clouds—they are higher than you.
6 "If you have sinned, [a]what do you accomplish against Him?
And if your transgressions are many, what do you do to Him?
7 "If you are righteous, [a]what do you give to Him,
Or what does He receive from your hand?
8 "Your wickedness is for a man like yourself,
And your righteousness is for a son of man.

9 "Because of the [a]multitude of oppressions they cry out;
They cry for help because of the arm [b]of the mighty.
10 "But [a]no one says, 'Where is God my Maker,
Who [b]gives songs in the night,
11 Who [a]teaches us more than the beasts of the earth
And makes us wiser than the birds of the heavens?'
12 "There [a]they cry out, but He does not answer
Because of the pride of evil men.
13 "Surely [a]God will not listen to [1]an empty *cry,*
Nor will the Almighty regard it.

30 [a]Job 5:15; 20:5; 34:17; Prov 29:2-12
32 [a]Job 33:27
33 [a]Job 41:11
35 [a]Job 35:16; 38:2
36 [1]Or *to the end* [a]Job 22:15
37 [a]Job 23:2 [b]Job 27:23
35:2 [a]Job 27:2
3 [1]Or *you* [a]Job 34:9 [b]Job 9:30, 31
5 [a]Gen 15:5; Ps 8:3 [b]Job 22:12
6 [a]Job 7:20; Prov 8:36; Jer 7:19
7 [a]Job 22:2, 3; Prov 9:12; Luke 17:10; Rom 11:35
9 [a]Ex 2:23 [b]Job 12:19
10 [a]Job 21:14; 27:10; 36:13; Is 51:13 [b]Job 8:21; Ps 42:8; 77:6; 149:5; Acts 16:25
11 [a]Job 36:22; Ps 94:12; Jer 32:33
12 [a]Prov 1:28
13 [1]Or *falsehood* [a]Job 27:9; Prov 15:29; Is 1:15; Jer 11:11; Mic 3:4

14 "How much less when [a]you say you do not behold Him,
The [b]case is before Him, and you must wait for Him!
15 "And now, because He has not visited *in* His anger,
Nor has He acknowledged [1]transgression well,
16 So Job opens his mouth [1]emptily;
He multiplies words [a]without knowledge."

Chapter 36 Theme ______________________________

36 Then Elihu continued and said,
2 "Wait for me a little, and I will show you
That there [1]is yet more to be said in God's behalf.
3 "I will fetch my knowledge from afar,
And I will ascribe [a]righteousness to my Maker.
4 "For truly [a]my words are not false;
One who is [b]perfect in knowledge is with you.
5 "Behold, God is mighty but does not [a]despise *any;*
He is [b]mighty in strength of understanding.
6 "He does not [a]keep the wicked alive,
But gives justice to [b]the afflicted.
7 "He does not [a]withdraw His eyes from the righteous;
But [b]with kings on the throne
He has seated them forever, and they are exalted.
8 "And if they are bound in fetters,
And are caught in the cords of [a]affliction,
9 Then He declares to them their work
And their transgressions, that they have
[a]magnified themselves.
10 "[a]He opens their ear to instruction,
And [b]commands that they return from evil.
11 "If they hear and serve *Him,*
They will [a]end their days in prosperity
And their years in [b]pleasures.
12 "But if they do not hear, they shall [1]perish [a]by the sword
And they will [b]die without knowledge.
13 "But the godless in heart lay up anger;
They do not cry for help when He binds them.
14 "[1]They die in youth,
And their life *perishes* among the [a]cult prostitutes.
15 "He delivers the afflicted in [1]their [a]affliction,
And [b]opens their ear [2]in *time of* oppression.
16 "Then indeed, He [a]enticed you from the mouth of distress,
Instead of it, a broad place with no constraint;
And that which was set on your table was full of [1]fatness.

17 "But you were full of [a]judgment on the wicked;
Judgment and justice take hold *of you.*
18 "*Beware* that [a]wrath does not entice you to scoffing;
And do not let the greatness of the [b]ransom turn you aside.
19 "Will your [1]riches keep you from distress,
Or all the forces of *your* strength?

---

14 [a]Job 9:11; 23:8, 9 [b]Job 31:35
15 [1]Or *arrogance*
16 [1]Lit *vainly* [a]Job 34:35; 38:2
36:2 [1]Lit *are yet words for God*
3 [a]Job 8:3; 37:23
4 [a]Job 33:3 [b]Job 37:16
5 [a]Ps 22:24; 69:33; 102:17 [b]Job 12:13
6 [a]Job 8:22; 34:26 [b]Job 5:15
7 [a]Ps 33:18; 34:15 [b]Job 5:11; Ps 113:8
8 [a]Job 36:15, 21
9 [a]Job 15:25
10 [a]Job 33:16; 36:15 [b]2 Kin 17:13; Job 36:21; Jon 3:8
11 [a]1 Tim 4:8 [b]Ps 16:11
12 [1]Lit *pass away* [a]Job 15:22 [b]Job 4:21
14 [1]Or *Their soul dies* [a]Deut 23:17
15 [1]Lit *his* [2]Or *in adversity* [a]Job 36:8, 21 [b]Job 36:10
16 [1]Or *rich food* [a]Hos 2:14
17 [a]Job 22:5, 10, 11
18 [a]Jon 4:4, 9 [b]Job 33:24
19 [1]Or *cry*

20 "Do not long for [a]the night,
When people [1]vanish in their place.
21 "Be careful, do [a]not turn to evil,
For you have preferred this to [b]affliction.
22 "Behold, God is exalted in His power;
Who is a [a]teacher like Him?
23 "Who has appointed Him His way,
And who has said, '[a]You have done wrong'?

24 "Remember that you should [a]exalt His work,
Of which men have [b]sung.
25 "All men have seen it;
Man beholds from afar.
26 "Behold, God is [a]exalted, and [b]we do not know *Him;*
The [c]number of His years is unsearchable.
27 "For [a]He draws up the drops of water,
They distill rain from [1]the [2]mist,
28 Which the clouds pour down,
They drip upon man abundantly.
29 "Can anyone understand the [a]spreading of the clouds,
The [b]thundering of His [1]pavilion?
30 "Behold, He spreads His [1]lightning about Him,
And He covers the depths of the sea.
31 "For by these He [a]judges peoples;
He [b]gives food in abundance.
32 "He covers *His* hands with the [1]lightning,
And [a]commands it to strike the mark.
33 "Its [a]noise declares [1]His presence;
The cattle also, concerning what is coming up.

Chapter 37 Theme ______________________

37 "At this also my heart trembles,
And leaps from its place.
2 "Listen closely to the [a]thunder of His voice,
And the rumbling that goes out from His mouth.
3 "Under the whole heaven He lets it loose,
And His [1]lightning to the [a]ends of the earth.
4 "After it, a voice roars;
He thunders with His majestic voice,
And He does not restrain [1]the lightnings when His voice
is heard.
5 "God [a]thunders with His voice wondrously,
Doing [b]great things which we cannot comprehend.
6 "For to [a]the snow He says, 'Fall on the earth,'
And to the [1b]downpour and the rain, 'Be strong.'
7 "He [a]seals the hand of every man,
That [b]all men may know His work.
8 "Then the beast goes into its [a]lair
And remains in its [1]den.
9 "Out of the [1a]south comes the storm,
And out of the [2]north the cold.

20 [1]Lit *go up* [a]Job 34:20, 25
21 [a]Job 36:10; Ps 31:6; 66:18 [b]Job 36:8, 15; Heb 11:25
22 [a]Job 35:11
23 [a]Deut 32:4; Job 8:3
24 [a]Ps 92:5; Rev 15:3 [b]Ex 15:1; Judg 5:1; 1 Chr 16:9; Ps 59:16; 138:5
26 [a]Job 11:7-9; 37:23 [b]1 Cor 13:12 [c]Job 10:5; Ps 90:2; 102:24, 27; Heb 1:12
27 [1]Lit *its* [2]Or *flood* [a]Job 5:10; 36:26-29; 37:6, 11; 38:28; Ps 147:8
29 [1]Lit *booth* [a]Job 37:11, 16 [b]Job 26:14
30 [1]Lit *light*
31 [a]Job 37:13 [b]Ps 104:27; 136:25; Acts 14:17
32 [1]Lit *light* [a]Job 37:11, 12, 15
33 [1]Lit *concerning Him* [a]Job 37:2
37:2 [a]Job 36:33; 37:4, 5; Ps 29:3-9
3 [1]Lit *light* [a]Job 28:24; 37:11, 12; 38:13
4 [1]Lit *them*
5 [a]Job 26:14 [b]Job 5:9; 37:14, 16, 23
6 [1]Lit *shower of rain and shower of rains* [a]Job 38:22 [b]Job 36:27
7 [a]Job 12:14 [b]Ps 111:2
8 [1]Lit *dens* [a]Job 38:40; Ps 104:21, 22
9 [1]Lit *chamber* [2]Lit *scattering winds* [a]Job 9:9

10 "From the breath of God [a]ice is made,
And the expanse of the waters is frozen.
11 "Also with moisture He [a]loads the thick cloud;
He [b]disperses [c]the cloud of His [1]lightning.
12 "It changes direction, turning around by His guidance,
That [1]it may do whatever He [a]commands [2]it
On the [b]face of the inhabited earth.
13 "Whether for [1a]correction, or for [b]His world,
Or for [c]lovingkindness, He causes it to [2]happen.

14 "Listen to this, O Job,
Stand and consider the wonders of God.
15 "Do you know how God establishes them,
And makes the [1]lightning of His cloud to shine?
16 "Do you know about the layers of the thick clouds,
The [a]wonders of one [b]perfect in knowledge,
17 You whose garments are hot,
When the land is still because of the south wind?
18 "Can you, with Him, [a]spread out the skies,
Strong as a molten mirror?
19 "Teach us what we shall say to Him;
We [a]cannot arrange *our case* because of darkness.
20 "Shall it be told Him that I would speak?
[1]Or should a man say that he would be swallowed up?

21 "Now [1]men do not see the light which is bright in the skies;
But the wind has passed and cleared them.
22 "Out of the north comes golden *splendor;*
Around God is awesome majesty.
23 "The Almighty—[a]we cannot find Him;
He is [b]exalted in power
And [c]He will not do violence [d]to justice and
abundant righteousness.
24 "Therefore men [a]fear Him;
He does not [b]regard any who are wise of heart."

Chapter 38 Theme ____________________

38 Then the LORD [a]answered Job out of the whirlwind and said,
2 "Who is this that [a]darkens counsel
By words without knowledge?
3 "Now [a]gird up your loins like a man,
And [b]I will ask you, and you instruct Me!
4 "Where were you [a]when I laid the foundation of the earth?
Tell *Me,* if you [1]have understanding,
5 Who set its [a]measurements? Since you know.
Or who stretched the line on it?
6 "On what [a]were its bases sunk?
Or who laid its cornerstone,
7 When the morning stars sang together
And all the [a]sons of God shouted for joy?

10 [a]Job 38:29; Ps 147:17
11 [1]Lit *light* [a]Job 36:27 [b]Job 36:29 [c]Job 37:15
12 [1]Lit *they* [2]Lit *them* [a]Job 36:32; Ps 148:8 [b]Is 14:21; 27:6
13 [1]Lit *the rod* [2]Lit *be found* [a]Ex 9:18, 23; 1 Sam 12:18, 19 [b]Job 38:26, 27 [c]1 Kin 18:41-46
15 [1]Lit *light*
16 [a]Job 37:5, 14, 23 [b]Job 36:4
18 [a]Job 9:8; Ps 104:2; Is 44:24; 45:12; Jer 10:12; Zech 12:1
19 [a]Job 9:14; Rom 8:26
20 [1]Or *If a man speak, surely he shall be swallowed up*
21 [1]Lit *they*
23 [a]Job 11:7, 8; Rom 11:33; 1 Tim 6:16 [b]Job 9:4; 36:5 [c]Is 63:9; Lam 3:33; Ezek 18:23, 32; 33:11 [d]Job 8:3
24 [a]Matt 10:28 [b]Job 5:13; Matt 11:25; 1 Cor 1:26
38:1 [a]Job 40:6
2 [a]Job 35:16; 42:3
3 [a]Job 40:7 [b]Job 42:4
4 [1]Lit *know understanding* [a]Job 15:7; Ps 104:5; Prov 8:29; 30:4
5 [a]Prov 8:29; Is 40:12
6 [a]Job 26:7
7 [a]Job 1:6

8 "Or *who* [a]enclosed the sea with doors
When, bursting forth, it went out from the womb;
9 When I made a cloud its garment
And thick darkness its swaddling band,
10 And I [1a]placed boundaries on it
And set a bolt and doors,
11 And I said, 'Thus far you shall come, but no farther;
And here shall your proud waves stop'?

12 "Have you [1]ever in your life commanded the morning,
And caused the dawn to know its place,
13 That it might take hold of [a]the ends of the earth,
And [b]the wicked be shaken out of it?
14 "It is changed like clay *under* the seal;
And they stand forth like a garment.
15 "[a]From the wicked their light is withheld,
And the [b]uplifted arm is broken.

16 "Have you entered into [a]the springs of the sea
Or walked [1]in the recesses of the deep?
17 "Have the gates of death been revealed to you,
Or have you seen the gates of [a]deep darkness?
18 "Have you understood the [1]expanse of [a]the earth?
Tell *Me,* if you know all this.

19 "Where is the way to the dwelling of light?
And darkness, where is its place,
20 That you may take it to [a]its territory
And that you may discern the paths to its [1]home?
21 "You know, for [a]you were born then,
And the number of your days is great!
22 "Have you entered the storehouses [a]of the snow,
Or have you seen the storehouses of the [b]hail,
23 Which I have reserved for the time of distress,
For the day of war and battle?
24 "Where is the way that [a]the light is divided,
Or the east wind scattered on the earth?

25 "Who has cleft a channel for the flood,
Or a way for the thunderbolt,
26 To bring [a]rain on a land without [1]people,
On a desert without a man in it,
27 To [a]satisfy the waste and desolate land
And to make the [1]seeds of grass to sprout?
28 "Has [a]the rain a father?
Or who has begotten the drops of dew?
29 "From whose womb has come the [a]ice?
And the frost of heaven, who has given it birth?
30 "Water [1]becomes hard like stone,
And the surface of the deep is imprisoned.

8 [a]Gen 1:9; Ps 104:6-9; Prov 8:29; Jer 5:22

10 [1]Lit *broke My decree on it* [a]Gen 1:9; Ps 33:7; 104:9; Prov 8:29; Jer 5:22

12 [1]Lit *from your days*

13 [a]Job 28:24; 37:3 [b]Job 34:25, 26; 36:6

15 [a]Job 5:14 [b]Num 15:30; Ps 10:15; 37:17

16 [1]Or *in search of* [a]Gen 7:11; 8:2; Prov 8:24, 28

17 [a]Job 10:21; 26:6; 34:22

18 [1]Or *width* [a]Job 28:24

20 [1]Lit *house* [a]Job 26:10

21 [a]Job 15:7

22 [a]Job 37:6 [b]Ex 9:18; Josh 10:11; Is 30:30; Ezek 13:11, 13; Rev 16:21

24 [a]Job 26:10

26 [1]Lit *man* [a]Job 36:27

27 [1]Or *growth* [a]Ps 104:13, 14; 107:35

28 [a]Job 36:27, 28; Ps 147:8; Jer 14:22

29 [a]Job 37:10; Ps 147:17

30 [1]Lit *hides itself*

31 "Can you bind the chains of the [a]Pleiades,
Or loose the cords of Orion?
32 "Can you lead forth a [1]constellation in its season,
And guide the Bear with her [2]satellites?
33 "Do you know the [a]ordinances of the heavens,
Or fix their rule over the earth?

34 "Can you lift up your voice to the clouds,
So that an [a]abundance of water will cover you?
35 "Can you [a]send forth lightnings that they may go
And say to you, 'Here we are'?
36 "Who has [a]put wisdom in the innermost being
Or given [b]understanding to the [1]mind?
37 "Who can count the clouds by wisdom,
Or [a]tip the water jars of the heavens,
38 When the dust hardens into a mass
And the clods stick together?

39 "Can you hunt the [a]prey for the lion,
Or satisfy the appetite of the young lions,
40 When they [a]crouch in *their* dens
And lie in wait in *their* lair?
41 "Who prepares for [a]the raven its nourishment
When its young cry to God
And wander about without food?

Chapter 39 Theme ____________________

39 "Do you know the time the [1a]mountain goats give birth?
Do you observe the calving of the [b]deer?
2 "Can you count the months they fulfill,
Or do you know the time they give birth?
3 "They kneel down, they bring forth their young,
They get rid of their labor pains.
4 "Their offspring become strong, they grow up in the open field;
They leave and do not return to them.

5 "Who sent out the [a]wild donkey free?
And who loosed the bonds of the swift donkey,
6 To whom I gave [a]the wilderness for a home
And the salt land for his dwelling place?
7 "He scorns the tumult of the city,
The shoutings of the driver he does not hear.
8 "He explores the mountains for his pasture
And searches after every green thing.
9 "Will the [a]wild ox consent to serve you,
Or will he spend the night at your manger?
10 "Can you bind the wild ox in a furrow with [1]ropes,
Or will he harrow the valleys after you?
11 "Will you trust him because his strength is great
And leave your labor to him?

31 [a]Job 9:9; Amos 5:8
32 [1]Heb *Mazzaroth* [2]Lit *sons*
33 [a]Ps 148:6; Jer 31:35, 36
34 [a]Job 22:11; 36:27, 28; 38:37
35 [a]Job 36:32; 37:3
36 [1]Or *rooster* [a]Job 9:4; Ps 51:6; Eccl 2:26 [b]Job 32:8
37 [a]Job 38:34
39 [a]Ps 104:21
40 [a]Job 37:8
41 [a]Ps 147:9; Matt 6:26; Luke 12:24
39:1 [1]Lit *goats of the rock* [a]Deut 14:5; 1 Sam 24:2; Ps 104:18 [b]Ps 29:9
5 [a]Job 6:5; 11:12; 24:5; Ps 104:11
6 [a]Job 24:5; Jer 2:24; Hos 8:9
9 [a]Num 23:22; Deut 33:17; Ps 22:21; 29:6; 92:10; Is 34:7
10 [1]Lit *his rope*

12 "Will you have faith in him that he will return your [1]grain
And gather *it from* your threshing floor?

13 "The ostriches' wings flap joyously
With the pinion and plumage of [1]love,
14 For she abandons her eggs to the earth
And warms them in the dust,
15 And she forgets that a foot may crush [1]them,
Or that a wild beast may trample [1]them.
16 "She treats her young [a]cruelly, as if *they* were not hers;
Though her labor be in vain, *she* is [1]unconcerned;
17 Because God has made her forget wisdom,
And has not given her a share of understanding.
18 "When she lifts herself [1]on high,
She laughs at the horse and his rider.

19 "Do you give the horse *his* might?
Do you clothe his neck with a mane?
20 "Do you make him [a]leap like the locust?
His majestic [b]snorting is terrible.
21 "[1]He paws in the valley, and rejoices in *his* strength;
He [a]goes out to meet the weapons.
22 "He laughs at fear and is not dismayed;
And he does not turn back from the sword.
23 "The quiver rattles against him,
The flashing spear and javelin.
24 "With shaking and rage he [1]races over the ground,
And he does not stand still at the voice of the trumpet.
25 "As often as the trumpet *sounds* he says, 'Aha!'
And he scents the battle from afar,
And the thunder of the captains and the war cry.

26 "Is it by your understanding that the hawk soars,
Stretching his wings toward the south?
27 "Is it at your [1]command that the eagle mounts up
And makes [a]his nest on high?
28 "On the cliff he dwells and lodges,
Upon the rocky crag, an inaccessible place.
29 "From there he [a]spies out food;
His eyes see *it* from afar.
30 "His young ones also suck up blood;
And [a]where the slain are, there is he."

Chapter 40 Theme

40 Then the LORD said to Job,
2 "Will the faultfinder [a]contend with the Almighty?
Let him who [b]reproves God answer it."

3 Then Job answered the LORD and said,
4 "Behold, I am insignificant; what can I reply to You?
I [a]lay my hand on my mouth.

12 [1]Lit *seed*

13 [1]Or *a stork*

15 [1]Lit *it*

16 [1]Lit *without fear*
[a]Lam 4:3

18 [1]Or *to flee*

20 [a]Joel 2:5
[b]Jer 8:16

21 [1]Lit *They paw*
[a]Jer 8:6

24 [1]Or *swallows up*

27 [1]Lit *mouth*
[a]Jer 49:16; Obad 4

29 [a]Job 9:26

30 [a]Matt 24:28; Luke 17:37

40:2 [a]Job 9:3; 10:2; 33:13; Is 45:9
[b]Job 13:3; 23:4; 31:35

4 [a]Job 21:5; 29:9

5 "Once I have spoken, and [a]I will not answer;
Even twice, and I will add nothing more."

6 Then the [a]LORD answered Job out of the storm and said,
7 "Now [a]gird up your loins like a man;
I will [b]ask you, and you instruct Me.
8 "Will you really [a]annul My judgment?
Will you [b]condemn Me [c]that you may be justified?
9 "Or do you have an arm like God,
And can you [a]thunder with a voice like His?

10 "[a]Adorn yourself with eminence and dignity,
And clothe yourself with honor and majesty.
11 "Pour out [a]the overflowings of your anger,
And look on everyone who is [b]proud, and make him low.
12 "Look on everyone who is proud, *and* [a]humble him,
And [b]tread down the wicked [1]where they stand.
13 "[a]Hide them in the dust together;
Bind [1]them in the hidden *place.*
14 "Then I will also [1]confess to you,
That your own right hand can save you.

15 "Behold now, [1]Behemoth, which [a]I made [2]as well as you;
He eats grass like an ox.
16 "Behold now, his strength in his loins
And his power in the muscles of his belly.
17 "He bends his tail like a cedar;
The sinews of his thighs are knit together.
18 "His bones are tubes of bronze;
His [1]limbs are like bars of iron.

19 "He is the [a]first of the ways of God;
Let his [b]maker bring near his sword.
20 "Surely the mountains [a]bring him food,
And all the beasts of the field [b]play there.
21 "Under the lotus plants he lies down,
In the covert of the reeds and the marsh.
22 "The lotus plants cover him with [1]shade;
The willows of the brook surround him.
23 "If a river [1]rages, he is not alarmed;
He is confident, though the [a]Jordan rushes to his mouth.
24 "Can anyone capture him [1]when he is on watch,
With [2]barbs can anyone pierce *his* nose?

Chapter 41 Theme ______________________

41

"[1]Can you draw out [2a]Leviathan with a fishhook?
Or press down his tongue with a cord?
2 "Can you [a]put a [1]rope in his nose
Or pierce his jaw with a [2]hook?
3 "Will he make many supplications to you,
Or will he speak to you soft words?

5 [a]Job 9:3, 15
6 [a]Job 38:1
7 [a]Job 38:3 [b]Job 38:3; 42:4
8 [a]Rom 3:4 [b]Job 10:3, 7; 16:11; 19:6; 27:2 [c]Job 13:18; 27:6
9 [a]Job 37:5; Ps 29:3
10 [a]Ps 93:1; 104:1
11 [a]Is 42:25; Nah 1:6, 8 [b]Is 2:12; Dan 4:37
12 [1]Lit *under them* [a]1 Sam 2:7; Is 2:12; 13:11; Dan 4:37 [b]Is 63:3
13 [1]Or *their faces* [a]Is 2:10-12
14 [1]Or *praise you*
15 [1]Or *the hippopotamus* [2]Lit *with* [a]Job 40:19
18 [1]Lit *bones*
19 [a]Job 41:33 [b]Job 40:15
20 [a]Ps 104:14 [b]Ps 104:26
22 [1]Lit *his shade*
23 [1]Or *oppresses* [a]Gen 13:10
24 [1]Lit *in his eyes* [2]Lit *snares*
41:1 [1]Ch 40:25 in Heb [2]Or *the crocodile* [a]Job 3:8; Ps 74:14; 104:26; Is 27:1
2 [1]Lit *rope of rushes* [2]Or *thorn* or *ring* [a]2 Kin 19:28; Is 37:29

4 "Will he make a covenant with you?
Will you take him for a servant forever?
5 "Will you play with him as with a bird,
Or will you bind him for your maidens?
6 "Will the [1]traders bargain over him?
Will they divide him among the merchants?
7 "Can you fill his skin with harpoons,
Or his head with fishing spears?
8 "Lay your hand on him;
Remember the battle; [1]you will not do it again!
9 "[1]Behold, [2]your expectation is false;
Will [3]you be laid low even at the sight of him?
10 "No one is so fierce that he dares to [a]arouse him;
Who then is he that can stand before Me?
11 "Who has [1a]given to Me that I should repay *him?*
Whatever is [b]under the whole heaven is Mine.

12 "I will not keep silence concerning his limbs,
Or his mighty strength, or his [1]orderly frame.
13 "Who can [1]strip off his outer armor?
Who can come within his double [2]mail?
14 "Who can open the doors of his face?
Around his teeth there is terror.
15 "*His* [1]strong scales are *his* pride,
Shut up *as with* a tight seal.
16 "One is so near to another
That no air can come between them.
17 "They are joined one to another;
They clasp each other and cannot be separated.
18 "His sneezes flash forth light,
And his eyes are like the [a]eyelids of the morning.
19 "Out of his mouth go burning torches;
Sparks of fire leap forth.
20 "Out of his nostrils smoke goes forth
As *from* a boiling pot and *burning* rushes.
21 "His breath kindles coals,
And a flame goes forth from his mouth.
22 "In his neck lodges strength,
And dismay leaps before him.
23 "The folds of his flesh are joined together,
Firm on him and immovable.
24 "His heart is as hard as a stone,
Even as hard as a lower millstone.
25 "When he raises himself up, the [1]mighty fear;
Because of the crashing they are bewildered.
26 "The sword that reaches him cannot avail,
Nor the spear, the dart or the javelin.
27 "He regards iron as straw,
Bronze as rotten wood.
28 "The [1]arrow cannot make him flee;
Slingstones are turned into stubble for him.

6 [1]Lit *partners*

8 [1]Lit *do not add*

9 [1]Ch 41:1 in Heb [2]Lit *his* [3]Lit *he*

10 [a]Job 3:8

11 [1]Lit *anticipated* [a]Rom 11:35 [b]Ex 19:5; Deut 10:14; Job 9:5-10; 26:6-14; 28:24; Ps 24:1; 50:12; 1 Cor 10:26

12 [1]Or *graceful*

13 [1]Lit *uncover the face of his garment* [2]So Gr; Heb *bridle*

15 [1]Lit *rows of shields*

18 [a]Job 3:9

25 [1]Or *gods*

28 [1]Lit *son of the bow*

29 "Clubs are regarded as stubble;
He laughs at the rattling of the javelin.
30 "His underparts are *like* sharp potsherds;
He [1]spreads out *like* a threshing sledge on the mire.
31 "He makes the depths boil like a pot;
He makes the sea like a jar of ointment.
32 "Behind him he makes a wake to shine;
One would think the deep to be gray-haired.
33 "[a]Nothing on [1]earth is like him,
One made without fear.
34 "[1]He looks on everything that is high;
He is king over all the [a]sons of pride."

Chapter 42 Theme ______________________________

42 Then Job answered the LORD and said,
2 "I know that [a]You can do all things,
And that no purpose of Yours can be thwarted.
3 'Who is this that [a]hides counsel without knowledge?'
"Therefore I have declared that which I did not understand,
Things [b]too wonderful for me, which I did not know."
4 'Hear, now, and I will speak;
I will [a]ask You, and You instruct me.'
5 "I have [a]heard of You by the hearing of the ear;
But now my [b]eye sees You;
6 Therefore I retract,
And I repent in dust and ashes."
7 It came about after the LORD had spoken these words to Job,
that the LORD said to Eliphaz the Temanite, "My wrath is kindled
against you and against your two friends, because you have not
spoken of Me what is right [a]as My servant Job has.
8 "Now therefore, take for yourselves [a]seven bulls and seven
rams, and go to My servant Job, and offer up a [b]burnt offering
for yourselves, and My servant Job will [c]pray for you. [d]For I will
[1]accept him so that I may not do with you *according to your*
folly, because you have not spoken of Me what is right, as My
servant Job has."
9 So Eliphaz the Temanite and Bildad the Shuhite *and* Zophar
the Naamathite went and did as the LORD told them; and the LORD
[1]accepted Job.
10 The LORD [a]restored the fortunes of Job when he prayed for
his friends, and the LORD increased all that Job had twofold.
11 Then all his [a]brothers and all his sisters and all who had
known him before came to him, and they ate bread with him
in his house; and they [b]consoled him and comforted him for all
the adversities that the LORD had brought on him. And each
one gave him one [1]piece of money, and each a ring of gold.
12 [a]The LORD blessed the latter *days* of Job more than his
beginning; [b]and he had 14,000 sheep and 6,000 camels and
1,000 yoke of oxen and 1,000 female donkeys.
13 [a]He had seven sons and three daughters.

30 [1]Or *moves across*
33 [1]Lit *dust* [a]Job 40:19
34 [1]Ch 41:26 in Heb [a]Job 28:8
42:2 [a]Gen 18:14; Matt 19:26
3 [a]Job 38:2 [b]Ps 40:5; 131:1; 139:6
4 [a]Job 38:3; 40:7
5 [a]Job 26:14; Rom 10:17 [b]Is 6:5; Eph 1:17, 18
7 [a]Job 40:3-5; 42:1-6
8 [1]Lit *lift up his face* [a]Num 23:1 [b]Job 1:5 [c]Gen 20:17; James 5:16; 1 John 5:16 [d]Job 22:30
9 [1]Lit *lifted up the face of*
10 [a]Deut 30:3; Job 1:2, 3; Ps 14:7; 85:1-3; 126:1-6
11 [1]Heb *qesitah* [a]Job 19:13 [b]Job 2:11
12 [a]Job 1:10; 8:7; James 5:11 [b]Job 1:3
13 [a]Job 1:2

14 He named the first Jemimah, and the second Keziah, and
the third Keren-happuch.
15 In all the land no women were found so fair as Job's
daughters; and their father gave them inheritance among their
brothers.
16 After this, Job lived 140 years, and saw his sons and his
grandsons, four generations.
17 [a]And Job died, an old man and full of days.

17 [a]Gen 15:15; 25:8; Job 5:26

INSIGHTS REGARDING SATAN

INSIGHTS REGARDING JOB

INSIGHTS REGARDING GOD

INSIGHTS REGARDING MAN

God's Power

Over Satan

Over Nature

INSIGHTS INTO LIFE AND DEATH

Over Man

Lessons I Learned About Dealing with Those in Pain

Theme of Job:

Author:

Date:

Purpose:

Key Words:

wisdom

sin (iniquity, transgression)

sons of God

righteous (right, righteousness)

SEGMENT DIVISIONS		CHAPTER THEMES
		1
		2
		3
		4
		5
		6
		7
		8
		9
		10
		11
		12
		13
		14
		15
		16
		17
		18
		19
		20
		21

SEGMENT DIVISIONS

		CHAPTER THEMES
		22
		23
		24
		25
		26
		27
		28
		29
		30
		31
		32
		33
		34
		35
		36
		37
		38
		39
		40
		41
		42

PSALMS תְּהִלִּים

TᵉHILIM

Man needs to pour out his heart to God, to come before Him and honestly present what is on his heart—whether it be distress or joy, confusion or confidence.

Man, in right relationship to God, was made to sing, to lift his voice in worship, to speak to God and to others in psalms and hymns and spiritual songs, singing and making melody with his heart to the Lord (see Ephesians 5:19).

Thus many of the psalms—praises, prayers, and songs—are to be accompanied on stringed instruments. Therefore, David, himself the writer of many psalms, appointed Levites over the service of song in the house of the Lord. They ministered with song before the tabernacle of the tent of meeting until Solomon built the house of the Lord in Jerusalem (see 1 Chronicles 6:31-32).

Psalms is a book of prayer and praise, written by men but inspired by God. "For from Him and through Him and to Him are all things. To Him be the glory forever. Amen" (Romans 11:36).

Things to Do

1. As you study Psalms, remember that the psalms are poetry whether they are prayers or songs. Hebrew poetry does not contain rhyme and meter. Rather, its distinctive feature is parallelism of some form, where one line relates to another in various ways. Usually the poetic lines are composed of two (or sometimes three) balanced segments in which the second is shorter than the first and repeats, contrasts, or completes the first segment.

   The psalms vary in design. Nine are alphabetical, with each stanza beginning with the next letter from the Hebrew alphabet. The alphabetical psalms are 9; 10; 25; 34; 37; 111; 112; 119; and 145.

2. The majority of the psalms have a superscription at the beginning, which designates one or several things: the composer, the occasion, who it is for, how it is to be accompanied, and what kind of psalm it is. If a psalm has a superscription, read it and consult the cross-references (if it is referenced). This will help put the psalm into context.

3. Watch for the theme of the psalm and how it is developed. Sometimes the theme will be stated at the very beginning of the psalm, while at other times the key thematic scheme will be found in the center of the psalm. Each will have a theme and will be developed in accordance with the author's design for the psalm.

   a. Some of the psalms give insights into the history of Israel, such as Psalm 78. Study these carefully. Note the events, God's intervention, and God's watchful care.

   b. If a psalm makes reference to a person or circumstance that is discussed in one of the historical books of the Bible, you might go back to that book and record the psalm that applies to that person or circumstance. For instance, in the margin of 2 Samuel 12, note "Psalm 51" as a cross-reference.

4. Key words bring out the theme of the psalm's song or prayer. Sometimes a key phrase will open and close the psalm. Watch for and mark these phrases. Also mark in a distinctive way the key words listed on the AT A GLANCE chart starting on page 1012. Write these words on an index card and use it as a bookmark when you study and meditate on the psalms.

5. Don't miss the central focus of these psalms—God. There is so much to be learned about Him, and then He is to be worshiped and adored. Observe His names, His titles, His attributes, and how man is to respond to Him.

a. Don't forget to look for Jesus, who is God, one with the Father, for He said, "All things which are written about Me in the Law of Moses and the Prophets and the Psalms must be fulfilled" (Luke 24:44).

b. The psalms are for the heart and soul, but they also address the mind. In the margin record your insights about God (use a △ as a heading). As you do this, meditate on what you learn. Spend time in praise and prayer. Let the book of Psalms help you love the Lord your God with all your heart, mind, body, soul, and strength.

6. When you finish each psalm, record the theme of that psalm in your Bible next to the number of the psalm and on the PSALMS AT A GLANCE chart starting on page 1012.

7. Psalms has five segments, which are marked on PSALMS AT A GLANCE.

   a. Give each segment a title or record its theme.

   b. Read Psalms 41:13; 72:18-19; 89:52; 106:48; and 150:6. Notice what is said and how each segment concludes.

   c. Complete PSALMS AT A GLANCE.

Things to Think About

1. When you are distressed, confused, afraid, or hurt, or when you need to talk with Someone who will understand, turn to Psalms. With the psalmist, be still (cease striving) and know that He is God.

2. Think about the practical value of Psalms and let it serve as your primary counselor when you need wisdom and understanding. Remember, blessed is the man who does not walk in the counsel of the wicked, but whose delight is in the law of the Lord, and who meditates in that law day and night (see Psalm 1).

3. Have you thought about ending each day as the book of Psalms ends—with a psalm of praise? "Let the godly ones exult in glory; let them sing for joy on their beds. Let the high praises of God be in their mouth.... Let everything that has breath praise the LORD. Praise the LORD!" (Psalm 149:5-6; 150:6). Try it and see what God does.

The following terms occur often in the Psalms:

Selah May mean *Pause, Crescendo,* or *Musical interlude*
Maskil Possibly *Contemplative,* or *Didactic,* or *Skillful Psalm*
Mikhtam Possibly *Epigrammatic Poem* or *Atonement Psalm*
Sheol The nether world

BOOK 1

Psalm 1 Theme ______________

1 How blessed is the man who [a]does not walk in the
[b]counsel of the wicked,
Nor stand in the [1c]path of sinners,
Nor [d]sit in the seat of scoffers!
2 But his [a]delight is [b]in the law of the LORD,
And in His law he meditates [c]day and [d]night.
3 He will be like [a]a tree *firmly* planted by [1]streams of water,

1:1 [1]Or *way* [a]Prov 4:14 [b]Ps 5:9, 10; 10:2-11; 36:1-4 [c]Ps 17:4; 119:104 [d]Ps 26:4, 5; Jer 15:17

2 [a]Ps 119:14, 16, 35 [b]Josh 1:8 [c]Ps 25:5 [d]Ps 63:5, 6

3 [1]Or *canals* [a]Ps 92:12-14; Jer 17:8; Ezek 19:10

Which yields its fruit in its season
And its [2]leaf does not wither;
And [3]in whatever he does, [b]he prospers.

4 The wicked are not so,
But they are like [a]chaff which the wind drives away.
5 Therefore [a]the wicked will not stand in the [b]judgment,
Nor sinners in [c]the assembly of the righteous.
6 For the LORD [1a]knows the way of the righteous,
But the way of [b]the wicked will perish.

Psalm 2 Theme ______________________

2 Why are [a]the [1]nations in an uproar
And the peoples [b]devising a vain thing?
2 The [a]kings of the earth take their stand
And the rulers take counsel together
[b]Against the LORD and against His [1c]Anointed, saying,
3 "Let us [a]tear their fetters apart
And cast away their cords from us!"

4 He who [1]sits in the heavens [a]laughs,
The Lord [b]scoffs at them.
5 Then He will speak to them in His [a]anger
And [b]terrify them in His fury, saying,
6 "But as for Me, I have [1]installed [a]My King
Upon Zion, [b]My holy mountain."

7 "I will surely tell of the [1]decree of the LORD:
He said to Me, 'You are [a]My Son,
Today I have begotten You.
8 'Ask of Me, and [a]I will surely give [b]the [1]nations as Your inheritance,
And the *very* [c]ends of the earth as Your possession.
9 'You shall [1a]break them with a [2]rod of iron,
You shall [b]shatter them like [3]earthenware.'"

10 Now therefore, O kings, [a]show discernment;
Take warning, O [1]judges of the earth.
11 [1]Worship the LORD with [2a]reverence
And rejoice with [b]trembling.
12 [1]Do homage to [a]the Son, that He not become angry, and you perish *in* the way,
For [b]His wrath may [2]soon be kindled.
How blessed are all who [c]take refuge in Him!

Psalm 3 Theme ______________________

A Psalm of David, when +he fled from Absalom his son.

3 O LORD, how [a]my adversaries have increased!
Many are rising up against me.

3 [2]Or *foliage* [3]Or *all that he does prospers* [b]Gen 39:2, 3, 23; Ps 128:2

4 [a]Job 21:18; Ps 35:5; Is 17:13

5 [a]Ps 5:5 [b]Ps 9:7, 8, 16 [c]Ps 89:5, 7

6 [1]Or *approves* or *has regard to* [a]Ps 37:18; Nah 1:7; John 10:14; 2 Tim 2:19 [b]Ps 9:5, 6; 11:6

2:1 [1]Or *Gentiles* [a]Ps 46:6; 83:2-5; Acts 4:25, 26 [b]Ps 21:11

2 [1]Or *Messiah* [a]Ps 48:4-6 [b]Ps 74:18, 23 [c]John 1:41

3 [a]Jer 5:5

4 [1]Or *is enthroned* [a]Ps 37:13 [b]Ps 59:8

5 [a]Ps 21:8, 9; 76:7 [b]Ps 78:49, 50

6 [1]Or *consecrated* [a]Ps 45:6 [b]Ps 48:1, 2

7 [1]Or *decree: The LORD said to Me* [a]Acts 13:33; Heb 1:5; 5:5

8 [1]Or *Gentiles* [a]Ps 21:1, 2 [b]Ps 22:27 [c]Ps 67:7

9 [1]Another reading is *rule* [2]Or *scepter* or *staff* [3]Lit *potter's ware* [a]Ps 89:23; 110:5, 6; Rev 2:26, 27; 12:5; 19:15 [b]Ps 28:5; 52:5; 72:4

10 [1]Or *leaders* [a]Prov 8:15; 27:11

11 [1]Or *Serve* [2]Or *fear* [a]Ps 5:7 [b]Ps 119:119, 120

12 [1]Lit *Kiss;* some ancient versions read *Do homage purely,* or, *Lay hold of instruction* [2]Or *quickly, suddenly, easily* [a]Ps 2:7 [b]Rev 6:16, 17 [c]Ps 5:11; 34:22

3:1 +2 Sam 15:13-17, 29 [a]2 Sam 15:12; Ps 69:4

2 Many are saying [1]of my soul,
"There is no [2a]deliverance for him in God." [3]Selah.

3 But You, O LORD, are [a]a shield about me,
My [b]glory, and the One who [c]lifts my head.
4 I was crying to the LORD with my voice,
And He [a]answered me from [b]His holy [1]mountain. Selah.
5 [1]I [a]lay down and slept;
I awoke, for the LORD sustains me.
6 I will [a]not be afraid of ten thousands of people
Who have [b]set themselves against me round about.

7 [a]Arise, O LORD; [b]save me, O my God!
For You [1]have [c]smitten all my enemies on the [2]cheek;
You [3]have [d]shattered the teeth of the wicked.
8 [1a]Salvation belongs to the LORD;
Your [b]blessing [2]*be* upon Your people! Selah.

Psalm 4 Theme ______________________

[+]For the choir director; on stringed instruments. A Psalm of David.

4 [a]Answer me when [b]I call, O God [1]of my righteousness!
You have [2c]relieved me in my distress;
Be [d]gracious to me and [e]hear my prayer.

2 O sons of men, how long will [a]my [1]honor become [b]a reproach?
How long will you love [c]what is worthless and aim at
[d]deception? [2]Selah.
3 But know that the LORD has [1a]set apart the [b]godly man for
Himself;
The LORD [c]hears when I call to Him.

4 [1a]Tremble, [2b]and do not sin;
[3c]Meditate in your heart upon your bed, and be still. Selah.
5 Offer [1]the [a]sacrifices of righteousness,
And [b]trust in the LORD.

6 Many are saying, "[a]Who will show us *any* good?"
[b]Lift up the light of Your countenance upon us, O LORD!
7 You have put [a]gladness in my heart,
More than when their grain and new wine abound.
8 In peace I will [1]both [a]lie down and sleep,
For You alone, O LORD, make me to [b]dwell in safety.

Psalm 5 Theme ______________________

For the choir director; for [+]flute accompaniment. A Psalm of David.

5 [a]Give ear to my words, O LORD,
Consider my [1b]groaning.
2 Heed [a]the sound of my cry for help, [b]my King and my God,
For to You I pray.

2 [1]Or *to* [2]Or *salvation* [3]*Selah* may mean: *Pause, Crescendo* or *Musical interlude* [a]Ps 22:7, 8; 71:11
3 [a]Ps 5:12; 28:7 [b]Ps 62:7 [c]Ps 9:13; 27:6
4 [1]Or *hill* [a]Ps 4:3; 34:4 [b]Ps 2:6; 15:1; 43:3
5 [1]Or *As for me, I* [a]Lev 26:6; Ps 4:8; Prov 3:24
6 [a]Ps 23:4; 27:3 [b]Ps 118:10-13
7 [1]Or *smite* [2]Or *jaw* [3]Or *shatter* [a]Ps 7:6 [b]Ps 6:4; 22:21 [c]Job 16:10 [d]Ps 57:4; 58:6
8 [1]Or *Deliverance* [2]Or *is* [a]Ps 28:8; 35:3; Is 43:11 [b]Ps 29:11
4:1 [+]I.e. Belonging to the choir director's anthology [1]I.e. who maintains my right [2]Lit *made room for* [a]Ps 3:4; 17:6 [b]Ps 18:6 [c]Ps 18:18, 19 [d]Ps 25:16 [e]Ps 17:6; 39:12
2 [1]Or *glory* [2]*Selah* may mean: *Pause, Crescendo* or *Musical interlude* [a]Ps 3:3 [b]Ps 69:7-10, 19, 20 [c]Ps 12:2; 31:6 [d]Ps 31:18
3 [1]Another reading is *dealt wonderfully with* [a]Ps 135:4 [b]Ps 31:23; 50:5; 79:2 [c]Ps 6:8, 9; 17:6
4 [1]I.e. with anger or fear [2]Or *but* [3]Lit *Speak* [a]Ps 99:1 [b]Ps 119:11; Eph 4:26 [c]Ps 77:6
5 [1]Or *righteous sacrifices* [a]Deut 33:19; Ps 51:19 [b]Ps 37:3, 5; 62:8
6 [a]Job 7:7; 9:25 [b]Num 6:26; Ps 80:3, 7, 19
7 [a]Ps 97:11, 12; Is 9:3; Acts 14:17
8 [1]Or *at the same time* [a]Job 11:19; Ps 3:5 [b]Lev 25:18; Deut 12:10; Ps 16:9
5:1 [+]Heb *Nehiloth* [1]Or *meditation* [a]Ps 54:2 [b]Ps 104:34
2 [a]Ps 140:6 [b]Ps 84:3

3 In the morning, O LORD, [1]You will hear my voice;
In the [a]morning I will order *my* [2]*prayer* to You and *eagerly* [b]watch.

4 For You are not a God [a]who takes pleasure in wickedness;
[b]No evil [1]dwells with You.
5 The [a]boastful shall not [b]stand before Your eyes;
You [c]hate all who do iniquity.
6 You [a]destroy those who speak falsehood;
The LORD abhors [b]the man of bloodshed and deceit.
7 But as for me, [a]by Your abundant lovingkindness I will enter Your house,
[1]At Your holy temple I will [b]bow in [c]reverence for You.

8 O LORD, [a]lead me [b]in Your righteousness [c]because of [1]my foes;
Make Your way [2]straight before me.
9 There is [a]nothing [1]reliable in [2]what they say;
Their [b]inward part is destruction *itself*.
Their [c]throat is an open grave;
They [3]flatter with their tongue.
10 Hold them guilty, O God;
[a]By their own devices let them fall!
In the multitude of their transgressions [b]thrust them out,
For they are [c]rebellious against You.

11 But let all who [a]take refuge in You [b]be glad,
Let them ever sing for joy;
And [1]may You [c]shelter them,
That those who [d]love Your name may exult in You.
12 For it is You who [a]blesses the righteous man, O LORD,
You [b]surround him with favor as with a shield.

Psalm 6 Theme ________________________

For the choir director; with stringed instruments, +upon an eight-string lyre. A Psalm of David.

6 O LORD, [a]do not rebuke me in Your anger,
Nor chasten me in Your wrath.
2 Be gracious to me, O LORD, for I *am* [a]pining away;
[b]Heal me, O LORD, for [c]my bones are dismayed.
3 And my [a]soul is greatly dismayed;
But You, O LORD—[b]how long?

4 Return, O LORD, [a]rescue my [1]soul;
Save me because of Your lovingkindness.
5 For [a]there is no [1]mention of You in death;
In [2]Sheol who will give You thanks?

6 I am [a]weary with my sighing;
Every night I make my bed swim,
I dissolve my couch with [b]my tears.

3 [1]Or *May You hear* [2]Or sacrifice [a]Ps 88:13 [b]Ps 130:5

4 [1]Lit *sojourns* [a]Ps 11:5; 34:16 [b]Ps 92:15

5 [a]Ps 73:3; 75:4 [b]Ps 1:5 [c]Ps 11:5; 45:7

6 [a]Ps 52:4, 5 [b]Ps 55:23

7 [1]Or *Toward* [a]Ps 69:13 [b]Ps 138:2 [c]Ps 115:11, 13

8 [1]Or *those who lie in wait for me* [2]Or *smooth* [a]Ps 31:3 [b]Ps 31:1 [c]Ps 27:11

9 [1]Or *true* [2]Lit *his mouth* [3]Or *make their tongue smooth* [a]Ps 52:3 [b]Ps 7:14 [c]Rom 3:13

10 [a]Ps 9:16 [b]Ps 36:12 [c]Ps 107:10, 11

11 [1]Or *You shelter* [a]Ps 2:12 [b]Ps 33:1; 64:10 [c]Ps 12:7 [d]Ps 69:36

12 [a]Ps 29:11 [b]Ps 32:7, 10

6:1 +Or *according to a lower octave* (Heb *Sheminith*) [a]Ps 38:1; 118:18

2 [a]Ps 102:4, 11 [b]Ps 41:4; 147:3; Hos 6:1 [c]Ps 22:14; 31:10

3 [a]Ps 88:3; John 12:27 [b]Ps 90:13

4 [1]Or *life* [a]Ps 17:13

5 [1]Or *remembrance* [2]I.e. the nether world [a]Ps 30:9; 88:10-12; 115:17; Eccl 9:10; Is 38:18

6 [a]Ps 69:3 [b]Ps 42:3

7 [a]Job 17:7; Ps 31:9; 38:10
8 [a]Ps 119:115; Matt 7:23; Luke 13:27 [b]Ps 3:4; 28:6
9 [a]Ps 116:1 [b]Ps 66:19, 20
10 [1]Or *again be ashamed suddenly* [a]Ps 71:13, 24 [b]Ps 73:19

7 My [a]eye has wasted away with grief;
It has become old because of all my adversaries.

8 [a]Depart from me, all you who do iniquity,
For the LORD [b]has heard the voice of my weeping.
9 The LORD [a]has heard my supplication,
The LORD [b]receives my prayer.
10 All my enemies will [a]be ashamed and greatly dismayed;
They shall [1]turn back, they will [b]suddenly be ashamed.

Psalm 7 Theme ____________________

7:1 +I.e. Dithyrambic rhythm; or wild passionate song •Or *concerning the words of* [a]Ps 31:1; 71:1 [b]Ps 31:15
2 [1]Or *me* [2]Or *Rending it in pieces, while* [a]Ps 57:4; Is 38:13
3 [a]1 Sam 24:11
4 [1]Lit *him who was at peace with me* [2]Or *my adversary without cause* [a]Ps 109:4, 5 [b]1 Sam 24:7; 26:9
5 [1]Or *me* [2]Or me [3]*Selah* may mean: *Pause, Crescendo* or *Musical interlude*

A +Shiggaion of David, which he sang to the LORD
•concerning Cush, a Benjamite.

7 O LORD my God, [a]in You I have taken refuge;
Save me from all those who pursue me, and [b]deliver me,
2 Or he will tear [1]my soul [a]like a lion,
[2]Dragging me away, while there is none to deliver.

3 O LORD my God, if I have done this,
If there is [a]injustice in my hands,
4 If I have [a]rewarded evil to [1]my friend,
Or have [b]plundered [2]him who without cause was my adversary,
5 Let the enemy pursue [1]my soul and overtake [2]*it;*
And let him trample my life down to the ground
And lay my glory in the dust. [3]Selah.

6 [1]One ancient version reads *O my God* [a]Ps 3:7 [b]Ps 94:2 [c]Ps 138:7 [d]Ps 35:23; 44:23
7 [1]Lit *it* [a]Ps 22:27
8 [1]Lit *Judge* [a]Ps 96:13; 98:9 [b]Ps 18:20; 26:1; 35:24; 43:1
9 [1]Lit *kidneys,* figurative for inner man [a]Ps 34:21; 94:23 [b]Ps 37:23; 40:2 [c]Ps 11:4, 5; Jer 11:20; Rev 2:23
10 [1]Lit *upon* [a]Ps 18:2, 30 [b]Ps 97:10, 11; 125:4
11 [a]Ps 50:6 [b]Ps 90:9
12 [1]Lit *he* [2]Lit *fixed it* [a]Ps 58:5 [b]Deut 32:41 [c]Ps 64:7
13 [1]Or *His deadly weapons* [a]Ps 18:14; 45:5
14 [a]Job 15:35; Is 59:4; James 1:15

6 [a]Arise, O LORD, in Your anger;
[b]Lift up Yourself against [c]the rage of my adversaries,
And [d]arouse Yourself [1]for me; You have appointed judgment.
7 Let the assembly of the [a]peoples encompass You,
And over [1]them return on high.
8 The LORD [a]judges the peoples;
[1b]Vindicate me, O LORD, according to my righteousness and my integrity that is in me.
9 O let [a]the evil of the wicked come to an end, but [b]establish the righteous;
For the righteous God [c]tries the hearts and [1]minds.
10 My [a]shield is [1]with God,
Who [b]saves the upright in heart.
11 God is a [a]righteous judge,
And a God who has [b]indignation every day.

12 If [1]a man [a]does not repent, He will [b]sharpen His sword;
He has [c]bent His bow and [2]made it ready.
13 He has also prepared [1]for Himself deadly weapons;
He makes His [a]arrows fiery shafts.
14 Behold, he travails with wickedness,
And he [a]conceives mischief and brings forth falsehood.

15 He has dug a pit and hollowed it out,
And has [a]fallen into the hole which he made.
16 His [a]mischief will return upon his own head,
And his [b]violence will descend upon [1]his own pate.

17 I will give thanks to the LORD [a]according to His righteousness
And will [b]sing praise to the name of the LORD Most High.

Psalm 8 Theme ____________________________

For the choir director; on the Gittith. A Psalm of David.

8 O LORD, our Lord,
How majestic is Your name in all the earth,
Who have [1a]displayed Your splendor above the heavens!
2 [a]From the mouth of infants and nursing babes You have established [1b]strength
Because of Your adversaries,
To make [c]the enemy and the revengeful cease.

3 When I [1a]consider [b]Your heavens, the work of Your fingers,
The [c]moon and the stars, which You have [2]ordained;
4 [a]What is man that You [1]take thought of him,
And the son of man that You care for him?
5 Yet You have made him a [a]little lower than [1]God,
And [b]You crown him with [c]glory and majesty!
6 You make him to [a]rule over the works of Your hands;
You have [b]put all things under his feet,
7 All sheep and oxen,
And also the [1]beasts of the field,
8 The birds of the heavens and the fish of the sea,
Whatever passes through the paths of the seas.

9 [a]O LORD, our Lord,
How majestic is Your name in all the earth!

Psalm 9 Theme ____________________________

For the choir director; on +Muth-labben. A Psalm of David.

9 I will give thanks to the LORD with all [a]my heart;
I will [b]tell of all Your [1]wonders.
2 I will be glad and [a]exult in You;
I will [b]sing praise to Your name, O [c]Most High.

3 When my enemies turn back,
They stumble and [a]perish before You.
4 For You have [a]maintained [1]my just cause;
You have sat on the throne [2b]judging righteously.
5 You have [a]rebuked the nations, You have destroyed the wicked;
You have [b]blotted out their name forever and ever.
6 [1]The enemy has come to an end in perpetual ruins,

15 [a]Job 4:8; Ps 57:6

16 [1]I.e. the crown of his own head [a]Esth 9:25; Ps 140:9 [b]Ps 140:11

17 [a]Ps 71:15, 16 [b]Ps 9:2; 66:1, 2, 4

8:1 [1]Or *set* [a]Ps 57:5, 11; 113:4; 148:13

2 [1]Or *a bulwark* [a]Matt 21:16; 1 Cor 1:27 [b]Ps 29:1; 118:14 [c]Ps 44:16

3 [1]Or *see* [2]Or *appointed, fixed* [a]Ps 111:2 [b]Ps 89:11; 144:5 [c]Ps 136:9

4 [1]Or *remember him* [a]Job 7:17; Ps 144:3; Heb 2:6-8

5 [1]Or *the angels;* Heb *Elohim* [a]Gen 1:26; Ps 82:6 [b]Ps 103:4 [c]Ps 21:5

6 [a]Gen 1:26, 28 [b]1 Cor 15:27; Eph 1:22; Heb 2:8

7 [1]Or *animals*

9 [a]Ps 8:1

9:1 +I.e. "Death to the Son" [1]Or *miracles* [a]Ps 86:12 [b]Ps 26:7

2 [a]Ps 5:11; 104:34 [b]Ps 66:2, 4 [c]Ps 83:18; 92:1

3 [a]Ps 27:2

4 [1]Lit *my right and my cause* [2]Or *a righteous Judge* [a]Ps 140:12 [b]Ps 50:6

5 [a]Ps 119:21 [b]Ps 69:28; Prov 10:7

6 [1]Or *O enemy, desolations are finished forever; And their cities You have plucked up*

And You have uprooted the cities;
The very [a]memory of them has perished.

7 But the [a]LORD [1]abides forever;
He has established His [b]throne for judgment,
8 And He will [a]judge the world in righteousness;
He will execute judgment for the peoples with equity.
9 [1]The LORD also will be a [a]stronghold for the oppressed,
A stronghold in times of trouble;
10 And [1]those who [a]know Your name will put their trust in You,
For You, O LORD, have not [b]forsaken those who seek You.

11 Sing praises to the LORD, who [a]dwells in Zion;
[b]Declare among the peoples His deeds.
12 For [a]He who [1]requires blood remembers them;
He does not forget [b]the cry of the afflicted.
13 Be gracious to me, O LORD;
See my affliction from those [a]who hate me,
You who [b]lift me up from the gates of death,
14 That I may tell of [a]all Your praises,
That in the gates of the daughter of Zion
I may [b]rejoice in Your [1]salvation.
15 The nations have sunk down [a]in the pit which they have made;
In the [b]net which they hid, their own foot has been caught.
16 The LORD has [a]made Himself known;
He has [b]executed judgment.
In the work of his own hands the wicked is snared. [1]Higgaion [2]Selah.

17 The wicked will [1a]return to [2]Sheol,
Even all the nations who [b]forget God.
18 For the [a]needy will not always be forgotten,
Nor the [b]hope of the afflicted perish forever.
19 [a]Arise, O LORD, do not let man prevail;
Let the nations be [b]judged before You.
20 Put them [a]in fear, O LORD;
Let the nations know that they are [b]but men. Selah.

Psalm 10 Theme ______________________________

10 Why [a]do You stand afar off, O LORD?
Why [b]do You hide [1]*Yourself* in times of trouble?
2 In [a]pride the wicked [1]hotly pursue the afflicted;
[2]Let them be [b]caught in the plots which they have devised.

3 For the wicked [a]boasts of his [b]heart's desire,
And [1]the greedy man curses *and* [c]spurns the LORD.
4 The wicked, in the haughtiness of his countenance, [a]does not seek *Him.*
All his [1]thoughts are, "[b]There is no God."

6 [a]Ps 34:16
7 [1]Or *sits* as king [a]Ps 10:16 [b]Ps 89:14
8 [a]Ps 96:13; 98:9
9 [1]Or *Let the LORD also be* [a]Ps 32:7; 59:9, 16, 17
10 [1]Or *let those . . . name put* [a]Ps 91:14 [b]Ps 37:28; 94:14
11 [a]Ps 76:2 [b]Ps 105:1; 107:22
12 [1]I.e. avenges bloodshed [a]Gen 9:5; Ps 72:14 [b]Ps 9:18
13 [a]Ps 38:19 [b]Ps 30:3; 86:13
14 [1]Or *deliverance* [a]Ps 106:2 [b]Ps 13:5; 20:5; 35:9; 51:12
15 [a]Ps 7:15, 16 [b]Ps 57:6
16 [1]Perhaps, resounding music or meditation [2]*Selah* may mean: *Pause, Crescendo* or *Musical interlude* [a]Ex 7:5 [b]Ps 9:4
17 [1]Or *turn* [2]I.e. the nether world [a]Ps 49:14 [b]Job 8:13; Ps 50:22
18 [a]Ps 9:12; 12:5 [b]Ps 62:5; 71:5; Prov 23:18
19 [a]Num 10:35 [b]Ps 9:5
20 [a]Ps 14:5 [b]Ps 62:9
10:1 [1]Or Your eyes [a]Ps 22:1 [b]Ps 13:1; 55:1
2 [1]Lit *burn* [2]Or *They will be caught* [a]Ps 73:6, 8 [b]Ps 7:16; 9:16
3 [1]Or *blesses the greedy man* [a]Ps 49:6; 94:3, 4 [b]Ps 112:10 [c]Ps 10:13
4 [1]Or *plots* [a]Ps 10:13; 36:2 [b]Ps 14:1; 36:1

5 His ways [1a]prosper at all times;
Your judgments are on high, [b]out of his sight;
As for all his adversaries, he snorts at them.
6 He says to himself, "[a]I will not be moved;
[1]Throughout all generations [b]I will not be in adversity."
7 His [a]mouth is full of curses and deceit and [b]oppression;
[c]Under his tongue is mischief and wickedness.
8 He sits in the [a]lurking places of the villages;
In the hiding places he [b]kills the innocent;
His eyes [1]stealthily watch for the [2c]unfortunate.
9 He lurks in a hiding place as [a]a lion in his [1]lair;
He [b]lurks to catch [c]the afflicted;
He catches the afflicted when he draws him into his [d]net.
10 He [1]crouches, he [2]bows down,
And the [3]unfortunate fall [4]by his mighty ones.
11 He [a]says to himself, "God has forgotten;
He has hidden His face; He will never see it."

12 Arise, O LORD; O God, [a]lift up Your hand.
[b]Do not forget the afflicted.
13 Why has the wicked [a]spurned God?
He has said to himself, "You will not require *it*."
14 You have seen *it*, for You have beheld [a]mischief and
vexation to [1]take it into Your hand.
The [2b]unfortunate commits *himself* to You;
You have been the [c]helper of the orphan.
15 [a]Break the arm of the wicked and the evildoer,
[1b]Seek out his wickedness until You find none.

16 The LORD is [a]King forever and ever;
[b]Nations have perished from His land.
17 O LORD, You have heard the [a]desire of the [1]humble;
You will [b]strengthen their heart, [c]You will incline Your ear
18 To [1]vindicate the [a]orphan and the [b]oppressed,
So that man who is of the earth will no longer cause [c]terror.

Psalm 11 Theme ____________________

For the choir director. *A Psalm* of David.

11 In the LORD I [a]take refuge;
How can you say to my soul, "Flee *as* a bird to your
[b]mountain;
2 For, behold, the wicked [a]bend the bow,
They [1b]make ready their arrow upon the string
To [c]shoot in darkness at the upright in heart.
3 If the [a]foundations are destroyed,
What can the righteous do?"

4 The LORD is in His [a]holy temple; the [1]LORD's [b]throne is in
heaven;
His [c]eyes behold, His eyelids test the sons of men.

5 [1]Lit *are strong* [a]Ps 52:7 [b]Ps 28:5

6 [1]Lit *To* [a]Ps 49:11; Eccl 8:11 [b]Rev 18:7

7 [a]Rom 3:14 [b]Ps 73:8 [c]Job 20:12; Ps 140:3

8 [1]Lit *lie in wait* [2]Or *poor* [a]Ps 11:2 [b]Ps 94:6 [c]Ps 72:12

9 [1]Or *thicket* [a]Ps 17:12 [b]Ps 59:3; Mic 7:2 [c]Ps 10:2 [d]Ps 140:5

10 [1]Or *is crushed* [2]Or *is bowed down* [3]Or *poor* [4]Or *into his claws*

11 [a]Ps 10:4

12 [a]Ps 17:7; Mic 5:9 [b]Ps 9:12

13 [a]Ps 10:3

14 [1]Lit *put, give* [2]Or *poor* [a]Ps 10:7 [b]Ps 22:11 [c]Ps 68:5

15 [1]Or *May You seek* [a]Ps 37:17 [b]Ps 140:11

16 [a]Ps 29:10 [b]Deut 8:20

17 [1]Or *afflicted* [a]Ps 9:18 [b]1 Chr 29:18 [c]Ps 34:15

18 [1]Lit *judge* [a]Ps 146:9 [b]Ps 9:9; 74:21 [c]Is 29:20

11:1 [a]Ps 2:12 [b]Ps 121:1

2 [1]Or *fixed* [a]Ps 7:12; 37:14 [b]Ps 64:3 [c]Ps 64:4

3 [a]Ps 82:5; 87:1; 119:152

4 [1]Lit *LORD*, His throne [a]Ps 18:6; Mic 1:2; Hab 2:20 [b]Ps 103:19; Is 66:1; Matt 5:34; Rev 4:2 [c]Ps 33:18; 34:15, 16

5 The LORD [a]tests the righteous and [b]the wicked,
And the one who loves violence His soul hates.
6 Upon the wicked He will [a]rain [1]snares;
[b]Fire and brimstone and [c]burning wind will be the portion of [d]their cup.
7 For the LORD is [a]righteous, [b]He loves [1]righteousness;
The upright will [c]behold His face.

Psalm 12 Theme ______________________________

For the choir director; +upon an eight-stringed lyre. A Psalm of David.

12 Help, LORD, for [a]the godly man ceases to be,
For the faithful disappear from among the sons of men.
2 They [a]speak [1]falsehood to one another;
With [b]flattering [2]lips and with a double heart they speak.
3 May the LORD cut off all flattering lips,
The tongue that [a]speaks great things;
4 Who [a]have said, "With our tongue we will prevail;
Our lips are [1]our own; who is lord over us?"
5 "Because of the [a]devastation of the afflicted, because of the groaning of the needy,
Now [b]I will arise," says the LORD; "I will [c]set him in the safety for which he longs."

6 The [a]words of the LORD are pure words;
As silver [b]tried in a furnace on the earth, refined seven times.
7 You, O LORD, will keep them;
You will [a]preserve him from this generation forever.
8 The [a]wicked strut about on every side
When [1b]vileness is exalted among the sons of men.

Psalm 13 Theme ______________________________

For the choir director. A Psalm of David.

13 How long, O LORD? Will You [a]forget me forever?
How long [b]will You hide Your face from me?
2 How long shall I [a]take counsel in my soul,
Having [b]sorrow in my heart all the day?
How long will my enemy be exalted over me?

3 [a]Consider *and* answer me, O LORD my God;
[b]Enlighten my eyes, or I will [c]sleep the *sleep of* death,
4 And my enemy will [a]say, "I have overcome him,"
And [b]my adversaries will rejoice when I am shaken.

5 But I have [a]trusted in Your lovingkindness;
My heart shall [b]rejoice in Your salvation.
6 I will [a]sing to the LORD,
Because He has [b]dealt bountifully with me.

5 [a]Gen 22:1; Ps 34:19; James 1:12 [b]Ps 5:5
6 [1]Or *coals of fire* [a]Ps 18:13, 14 [b]Gen 19:24; Ezek 38:22 [c]Jer 4:11, 12 [d]Ps 75:8
7 [1]Or *righteous deeds* [a]Ps 7:9, 11 [b]Ps 33:5; 45:7 [c]Ps 16:11; 17:15
12:1 +Or *according to a lower octave* (Heb *Sheminith*) [a]Is 57:1; Mic 7:2
2 [1]Or *emptiness* [2]Lit *lip* [a]Ps 10:7; 41:6 [b]Ps 28:3; 55:21; Jer 9:8; Rom 16:18
3 [a]Dan 7:8; Rev 13:5
4 [1]Lit *with us* [a]Ps 73:8, 9
5 [a]Ps 9:9; 10:18 [b]Is 33:10 [c]Ps 34:6; 35:10
6 [a]2 Sam 22:31; Ps 18:30; 19:8, 10; 119:140 [b]Prov 30:5
7 [a]Ps 37:28; 97:10
8 [1]Or *worthlessness* [a]Ps 55:10, 11 [b]Is 32:5
13:1 [a]Ps 44:24 [b]Job 13:24; Ps 89:46
2 [a]Ps 42:4 [b]Ps 42:9
3 [a]Ps 5:1 [b]1 Sam 14:29; Ezra 9:8; Job 33:30; Ps 18:28 [c]Jer 51:39
4 [a]Ps 12:4 [b]Ps 25:2; 38:16
5 [a]Ps 52:8 [b]Ps 9:14
6 [a]Ps 96:1, 2 [b]Ps 116:7; 119:17; 142:7

*Psalm 14 Theme*____________________

For the choir director. *A Psalm* of David.

14 The fool has [a]said in his heart, "There is no God."
They are corrupt, they have committed abominable [1]deeds;
There is [b]no one who does good.
2 The LORD has [a]looked down from heaven upon the sons of men
To see if there are any who [1b]understand,
Who [c]seek after God.
3 They have all [a]turned aside, together they have become corrupt;
There is [b]no one who does good, not even one.

4 Do all the workers of wickedness [a]not know,
Who [b]eat up my people *as* they eat bread,
And [c]do not call upon the Lord?
5 There they are in great dread,
For God is with the [a]righteous generation.
6 You would put to shame the counsel of the afflicted,
But the LORD is his [a]refuge.

7 Oh, that [a]the salvation of Israel [1]would come out of Zion!
When the LORD [2b]restores His captive people,
Jacob will rejoice, Israel will be glad.

*Psalm 15 Theme*____________________

A Psalm of David.

15 O LORD, who may [1]abide [a]in Your tent?
Who may dwell on Your [b]holy hill?
2 He who [a]walks with integrity, and works righteousness,
And [b]speaks truth in his heart.
3 He [a]does not slander [1]with his tongue,
Nor [b]does evil to his neighbor,
Nor [c]takes up a reproach against his friend;
4 In [1]whose eyes a reprobate is despised,
But [2]who [a]honors those who fear the LORD;
He [b]swears to his own hurt and does not change;
5 He [a]does not put out his money [1]at interest,
Nor [b]does he take a bribe against the innocent.
[c]He who does these things will never be shaken.

*Psalm 16 Theme*____________________

A +Mikhtam of David.

16 [a]Preserve me, O God, for [b]I take refuge in You.
2 [1]I said to the LORD, "You are [2]my Lord;
I [a]have no good besides You."
3 As for the [1a]saints who are in the earth,
[2]They are the majestic ones [b]in whom is all my delight.

14:1 [1]Lit *doings* [a]Ps 10:4; 53:1 [b]Ps 14:1-3; 130:3; Rom 3:10-12

2 [1]Or *act wisely* [a]Ps 33:13, 14; 102:19 [b]Ps 92:6 [c]1 Chr 22:19

3 [a]Ps 58:3 [b]Ps 143:2

4 [a]Ps 82:5 [b]Ps 27:2; Jer 10:25; Mic 3:3 [c]Ps 79:6; Is 64:7

5 [a]Ps 73:15; 112:2

6 [a]Ps 9:9; 40:17; 46:1; 142:5

7 [1]Lit *would be* [2]Or *restores the fortunes of His people* [a]Ps 53:6 [b]Ps 85:1, 2

15:1 [1]Lit *sojourn* [a]Ps 27:5, 6; 61:4 [b]Ps 24:3

2 [a]Ps 24:4; Is 33:15 [b]Zech 8:16; Eph 4:25

3 [1]Lit *according to* [a]Ps 50:20 [b]Ps 28:3 [c]Ex 23:1

4 [1]Lit *his* [2]Lit *he* [a]Acts 28:10 [b]Judg 11:35

5 [1]I.e. to a fellow Israelite [a]Ex 22:25; Lev 25:36; Deut 23:20; Ezek 18:8 [b]Ex 23:8; Deut 16:19 [c]2 Pet 1:10

16:1 +Possibly *Epigrammatic Poem* or *Atonement Psalm* [a]Ps 17:8 [b]Ps 7:1

2 [1]Or O my soul, *you said* [2]Or *the Lord* [a]Ps 73:25

3 [1]Lit *holy ones;* i.e. the godly [2]Lit *And the majestic ones . . . delight* [a]Ps 101:6 [b]Ps 119:63

4 The [1a]sorrows of those who have [2]bartered for another *god*
will be multiplied;
I shall not pour out their drink offerings of [b]blood,
Nor will I [c]take their names upon my lips.

5 The LORD is the [a]portion of my inheritance and my [b]cup;
You support my [c]lot.
6 The [a]lines have fallen to me in pleasant places;
Indeed, my heritage is [b]beautiful to me.

7 I will bless the LORD who has [a]counseled me;
Indeed, my [1b]mind instructs me in the night.
8 [a]I have [b]set the LORD continually before me;
Because He is [c]at my right hand, [d]I will not be shaken.
9 Therefore [a]my heart is glad and [b]my glory rejoices;
My flesh also will [c]dwell securely.
10 For You [a]will not abandon my soul to [1]Sheol;
Nor will You [2b]allow Your [3]Holy One to [4]undergo decay.
11 You will make known to me [a]the path of life;
In [b]Your presence is fullness of joy;
In Your right hand there are [c]pleasures forever.

Psalm 17 Theme ____________________

A Prayer of David.

17 Hear a [a]just cause, O LORD, [b]give heed to my cry;
[c]Give ear to my prayer, which is not from [d]deceitful lips.
2 Let [a]my [1]judgment come forth from Your presence;
Let Your eyes look with [b]equity.
3 You have [a]tried my heart;
You have visited *me* by night;
You have [b]tested me and [c]You find [1]nothing;
I have [d]purposed that my mouth will not transgress.
4 As for the deeds of men, [a]by the word of Your lips
I have kept from the [b]paths of the violent.
5 My [a]steps have held fast to Your [1]paths.
My [b]feet have not slipped.

6 I have [a]called upon You, for You will answer me, O God;
[b]Incline Your ear to me, hear my speech.
7 [a]Wondrously show Your lovingkindness,
O [b]Savior of those who take refuge [1]at Your right hand
From those who rise up *against them.*
8 Keep me as [1]the [a]apple of the eye;
Hide me [b]in the shadow of Your wings
9 From the [a]wicked who despoil me,
My [b]deadly enemies who surround me.
10 They have [a]closed their [1]unfeeling *heart,*
With their mouth they [b]speak proudly.
11 They have now [a]surrounded us in our steps;
They set their eyes [b]to cast *us* down to the ground.

4 [1]I.e. sorrows due to idolatry [2]Or *hastened to* [a]Ps 32:10 [b]Ps 106:37, 38 [c]Ex 23:13; Josh 23:7
5 [a]Ps 73:26; 119:57; 142:5; Lam 3:24 [b]Ps 23:5 [c]Ps 125:3 mg
6 [a]Ps 78:55 [b]Jer 3:19
7 [1]Lit *kidneys,* figurative for inner man [a]Ps 73:24 [b]Ps 77:6
8 [a]Ps 16:8-11; Acts 2:25-28 [b]Ps 27:8; 123:1, 2 [c]Ps 73:23; 110:5; 121:5 [d]Ps 112:6
9 [a]Ps 4:7; 13:5 [b]Ps 30:12; 57:8; 108:1 [c]Ps 4:8
10 [1]I.e. the nether world [2]Lit *give* [3]Or *godly one* [4]Or *see corruption* or *the pit* [a]Ps 49:15; 86:13 [b]Acts 13:35
11 [a]Ps 139:24; Matt 7:14 [b]Ps 21:6; 43:4 [c]Job 36:11; Ps 36:7, 8; 46:4
17:1 [a]Ps 9:4 [b]Ps 61:1; 142:6 [c]Ps 88:2 [d]Is 29:13
2 [1]I.e. vindication [a]Ps 103:6 [b]Ps 98:9; 99:4
3 [1]Or *no evil device in me; My mouth* [a]Ps 26:1, 2 [b]Job 23:10; Ps 66:10; Zech 13:9; 1 Pet 1:7 [c]Jer 50:20 [d]Ps 39:1
4 [a]Ps 119:9, 101 [b]Ps 10:5-11
5 [1]Lit *tracks* [a]Job 23:11; Ps 44:18; 119:133 [b]Ps 18:36; 37:31
6 [a]Ps 86:7; 116:2 [b]Ps 88:2
7 [1]Or *from those who rise up . . . at Your right hand* [a]Ps 31:21 [b]Ps 20:6
8 [1]Lit *the pupil, the daughter of the eye* [a]Deut 32:10; Zech 2:8 [b]Ruth 2:12; Ps 36:7; 57:1; 61:4; 63:7; 91:1, 4
9 [a]Ps 31:20 [b]Ps 27:12
10 [1]Lit *fat* [a]Job 15:27; Ps 73:7 [b]1 Sam 2:3; Ps 31:18; 73:8
11 [a]Ps 88:17 [b]Ps 37:14

12 He is [a]like a lion that is eager to tear,
And as a young lion [b]lurking in hiding places.

13 [a]Arise, O LORD, confront him, [b]bring him low;
[c]Deliver my soul from the wicked with [d]Your sword,
14 From men with [a]Your hand, O LORD,
From men [1]of the world, [b]whose portion is in *this* life,
And whose belly You [c]fill with Your treasure;
They are satisfied with children,
And leave their abundance to their babes.
15 As for me, I shall [a]behold Your face in righteousness;
[b]I will be satisfied [1]with Your [c]likeness when I awake.

Psalm 18 Theme ____________________

For the choir director. A *Psalm* of David the servant of the LORD, [+]who spoke to the LORD the words of this song in the day that the LORD delivered him from the hand of all his enemies and from the hand of Saul. And he said,

18 "I love You, O LORD, [a]my strength."
2 The LORD is [a]my [1]rock and [b]my fortress and my
[c]deliverer,
My God, my rock, in whom I take refuge;
My [d]shield and the [e]horn of my salvation, my [f]stronghold.
3 I call upon the LORD, who is [a]worthy to be praised,
And I am [b]saved from my enemies.

4 The [a]cords of death encompassed me,
And the [b]torrents of [1]ungodliness [2]terrified me.
5 The [a]cords of [1]Sheol surrounded me;
The snares of death confronted me.
6 In my [a]distress I called upon the LORD,
And cried to my God for help;
He heard my voice [b]out of His temple,
And my [c]cry for help before Him came into His ears.

7 Then the [a]earth shook and quaked;
And the [b]foundations of the mountains were trembling
And were shaken, because He was angry.
8 Smoke went up [1]out of His nostrils,
And [a]fire from His mouth devoured;
Coals were kindled by it.
9 He [a]bowed the heavens also, and came down
With thick [b]darkness under His feet.
10 He rode upon a [a]cherub and flew;
And He sped upon the [b]wings of the wind.
11 He made [a]darkness His hiding place, [b]His [1]canopy around
Him,
Darkness of waters, thick clouds of the skies.
12 From the [a]brightness before Him passed His thick clouds,
Hailstones and [b]coals of fire.

12 [a]Ps 7:2 [b]Ps 10:9

13 [a]Ps 3:7 [b]Ps 55:23 [c]Ps 22:20 [d]Ps 7:12

14 [1]Or *whose portion in life is of the world* [a]Ps 17:7 [b]Ps 73:3-7; Luke 16:25 [c]Ps 49:6

15 [1]Or *with* beholding [a]Ps 11:7; 16:11; 140:13; 1 John 3:2 [b]Ps 4:6, 7 [c]Num 12:8

18:1 [+]2 Sam 22:1-51 [a]Ps 59:17

2 [1]Or *crag* [a]Deut 32:18; 1 Sam 2:2; Ps 18:31, 46; 28:1; 31:3; 42:9; 71:3; 78:15 [b]Ps 144:2 [c]Ps 19:14 [d]Ps 28:7; 33:20; 59:11; 84:9, 11; Prov 30:5 [e]Ps 75:10 [f]Ps 59:9

3 [a]Ps 48:1; 96:4; 145:3 [b]Ps 34:6

4 [1]Or *destruction;* Heb *Belial* [2]Or *were assailing* or *terrifying* [a]Ps 116:3 [b]Ps 69:2; 124:3, 4

5 [1]I.e. the nether world [a]Ps 116:3

6 [a]Ps 50:15; 120:1 [b]Ps 3:4 [c]Ps 34:15

7 [a]Judg 5:4; Ps 68:7, 8; Is 13:13; Hag 2:6 [b]Ps 114:4, 6

8 [1]Or *in His wrath* [a]Ps 50:3

9 [a]Ps 144:5 [b]Ps 97:2

10 [a]Ps 80:1; 99:1 [b]Ps 104:3

11 [1]Or *pavilion* [a]Deut 4:11 [b]Ps 97:2

12 [a]Ps 104:2 [b]Ps 97:3; 140:10; Hab 3:4

13 The LORD also [a]thundered in the heavens,
And the Most High uttered His voice,
Hailstones and coals of fire.
14 He [a]sent out His arrows, and scattered them,
And lightning flashes in abundance, and [1]routed them.
15 Then the [a]channels of water appeared,
And the foundations of the world were [1]laid bare
At Your [b]rebuke, O LORD,
At the blast of the [c]breath of Your nostrils.

16 He [a]sent from on high, He took me;
He drew me out of [b]many waters.
17 He [a]delivered me from my strong enemy,
And from those who hated me, for they were [b]too mighty
for me.
18 They confronted me in [a]the day of my calamity,
But [b]the LORD was my stay.
19 He brought me forth also into a [a]broad place;
He rescued me, because [b]He delighted in me.

20 The LORD has [a]rewarded me according to my righteousness;
According to the [b]cleanness of my hands He has
recompensed me.
21 For I have [a]kept the ways of the LORD,
And have [b]not wickedly departed from my God.
22 For all [a]His ordinances were before me,
And I did not put away His [b]statutes from me.
23 I was also [1a]blameless with Him,
And I [b]kept myself from my iniquity.
24 Therefore the LORD has [a]recompensed me according to my
righteousness,
According to the cleanness of my hands in His eyes.

25 With [a]the kind You show Yourself kind;
With the [1]blameless [b]You show Yourself blameless;
26 With the pure You show Yourself [a]pure,
And with the crooked [b]You show Yourself [1]astute.
27 For You [a]save an afflicted people,
But [b]haughty eyes You abase.
28 For You [a]light my lamp;
The LORD my God [b]illumines my darkness.
29 For by You I can [1a]run upon a troop;
And by my God I can [b]leap over a wall.

30 As for God, His way is [1a]blameless;
The [b]word of the LORD is tried;
He is a [c]shield to all who take refuge in Him.
31 For [a]who is God, but the LORD?
And who is a [b]rock, except our God,
32 The God who [a]girds me with strength
And [1]makes my way [2b]blameless?

13 [a]Ps 29:3; 104:7
14 [1]Lit *confused* [a]Ps 144:6; Hab 3:11
15 [1]Or *uncovered* [a]Ps 106:9 [b]Ps 76:6 [c]Ps 18:8
16 [a]Ps 144:7 [b]Ps 32:6
17 [a]Ps 59:1 [b]Ps 35:10; 142:6
18 [a]Ps 59:16 [b]Ps 16:8
19 [a]Ps 4:1; 31:8; 118:5 [b]Ps 37:23; 41:11
20 [a]1 Sam 24:19; Job 33:26; Ps 7:8 [b]Job 22:30; Ps 24:4
21 [a]Ps 37:34; 119:33; Prov 8:32 [b]2 Chr 34:33; Ps 119:102
22 [a]Ps 119:30 [b]Ps 119:83
23 [1]Lit *complete;* or *having integrity;* or *perfect* [a]Ps 18:32 [b]Ps 19:12, 13; 25:11; 66:18
24 [a]1 Sam 26:23; Ps 18:20
25 [1]V 23, note 1 [a]1 Kin 8:32; Ps 62:12; Matt 5:7 [b]Ps 18:30
26 [1]Lit *twisted* [a]Job 25:5; Hab 1:13 [b]Lev 26:23, 24, 27, 28; Prov 3:34
27 [a]Ps 72:12 [b]Ps 101:5; Prov 6:17
28 [a]1 Kin 15:4; Job 18:6; Ps 132:17 [b]Ps 27:1
29 [1]Or *crush a troop* [a]Ps 118:10-12 [b]Ps 18:33; 40:2
30 [1]V 23, note 1 [a]Deut 32:4; Ps 19:7; 145:17; Rev 15:3 [b]Ps 12:6 [c]Ps 17:7; 91:4
31 [a]Deut 32:39; 1 Sam 2:2; Ps 86:8-10; Is 45:5 [b]Deut 32:31; Ps 18:2; 62:2
32 [1]Or *has made* [2]Lit *complete;* or *having integrity* [a]Ps 18:39; Is 45:5 [b]Ps 18:23

33 He [a]makes my feet like hinds' *feet,*
And [b]sets me upon my high places.
34 He [a]trains my hands for battle,
So that my arms can [b]bend a bow of bronze.
35 You have also given me [a]the shield of Your salvation,
And Your [b]right hand upholds me;
And [c]Your [1]gentleness makes me great.
36 You [a]enlarge my steps under me,
And my [1b]feet have not slipped.

37 I [a]pursued my enemies and overtook them,
And I did not turn back [b]until they were consumed.
38 I shattered them, so that they were [a]not able to rise;
They fell [b]under my feet.
39 For You have [a]girded me with strength for battle;
You have [1b]subdued under me those who rose up against
me.
40 You have also made my enemies [a]turn their backs to me,
And I [1b]destroyed those who hated me.
41 They cried for help, but there was [a]none to save,
Even to the LORD, but [b]He did not answer them.
42 Then I beat them fine as the [a]dust before the wind;
I emptied them out as the mire of the streets.

43 You have delivered me from the [a]contentions of the people;
You have placed me as [b]head of the nations;
A [c]people whom I have not known serve me.
44 As soon as they hear, they obey me;
Foreigners [1a]submit to me.
45 Foreigners [a]fade away,
And [b]come trembling out of their [1]fortresses.

46 The LORD [a]lives, and blessed be [b]my rock;
And exalted be [c]the God of my salvation,
47 The God who [a]executes vengeance for me,
And [b]subdues peoples under me.
48 He [a]delivers me from my enemies;
Surely You [b]lift me above those who rise up against me;
You rescue me from the [c]violent man.
49 Therefore I will [a]give thanks to You among the nations,
O LORD,
And I will [b]sing praises to Your name.
50 He gives great [1a]deliverance to His king,
And shows lovingkindness to [b]His anointed,
To David and [c]his [2]descendants forever.

Psalm 19 Theme ______________________________

For the choir director. A Psalm of David.

19 The [a]heavens are telling of the glory of God;
And their [b]expanse is declaring the work of His hands.

33 [a]Hab 3:19 [b]Deut 32:13

34 [a]Ps 144:1 [b]Job 29:20

35 [1]Or *condescension* [a]Ps 33:20 [b]Ps 63:8; 119:117 [c]Ps 138:6

36 [1]Lit *ankles* [a]Ps 18:33 [b]Ps 66:9; Prov 4:12

37 [a]Ps 44:5 [b]Ps 37:20

38 [a]Ps 36:12 [b]Ps 47:3

39 [1]Lit *caused to bow down* [a]Ps 18:32 [b]Ps 18:47

40 [1]Or *silenced* [a]Ps 21:12 [b]Ps 94:23

41 [a]Ps 50:22 [b]Job 27:9; Prov 1:28

42 [a]Ps 83:13

43 [a]2 Sam 3:1; 19:9; Ps 35:1 [b]2 Sam 8:1-18; Ps 89:27 [c]Is 55:5

44 [1]Lit *deceive me;* i.e. give feigned obedience [a]Ps 66:3

45 [1]Lit *fastnesses* [a]Ps 37:2 [b]Mic 7:17

46 [a]Job 19:25 [b]Ps 18:2 [c]Ps 51:14

47 [a]Ps 94:1 [b]Ps 18:43; 47:3; 144:2

48 [a]Ps 3:7 [b]Ps 27:6; 59:1 [c]Ps 11:5

49 [a]Rom 15:9 [b]Ps 108:1

50 [1]I.e. victories; lit *salvations* [2]Lit *seed* [a]Ps 21:1; 144:10 [b]Ps 28:8 [c]Ps 89:4

19:1 [a]Ps 8:1; 50:6; Rom 1:19, 20 [b]Gen 1:6, 7

2 Day to [a]day pours forth speech,
And [b]night to night reveals knowledge.
3 There is no speech, nor are there words;
Their voice is not heard.
4 Their [1a]line has gone out through all the earth,
And their utterances to the end of the world.
In them He has [b]placed a tent for the sun,
5 Which is as a bridegroom coming out of his chamber;
It rejoices as a strong man to run his course.
6 Its [a]rising is from [1]one end of the heavens,
And its circuit to the [2]other end of them;
And there is nothing hidden from its heat.

7 [a]The law of the LORD is [1b]perfect, [c]restoring the soul;
The testimony of the LORD is [d]sure, making [e]wise the simple.
8 The precepts of the LORD are [a]right, [b]rejoicing the heart;
The commandment of the LORD is [c]pure, [d]enlightening the eyes.
9 The fear of the LORD is clean, enduring forever;
The judgments of the LORD are [a]true; they are [b]righteous altogether.
10 They are more desirable than [a]gold, yes, than much fine gold;
[b]Sweeter also than honey and the drippings of the honeycomb.
11 Moreover, by them [a]Your servant is warned;
In keeping them there is great [b]reward.
12 Who can [a]discern *his* errors? [b]Acquit me of [c]hidden *faults*.
13 Also keep back Your servant [a]from presumptuous *sins;*
Let them not [b]rule over me;
Then I will be [1c]blameless,
And I shall be acquitted of [d]great transgression.
14 Let the words of my mouth and [a]the meditation of my heart
Be acceptable in Your sight,
O LORD, [b]my rock and my [c]Redeemer.

Psalm 20 Theme ________________________________

For the choir director. A Psalm of David.

20 May the LORD answer you [a]in the day of trouble!
May the [b]name of the [c]God of Jacob set you *securely* on high!
2 May He send you help [a]from the sanctuary
And [b]support you from Zion!
3 May He [a]remember all your meal offerings
And [b]find your burnt offering [1]acceptable! [2]Selah.

4 May He grant you your [a]heart's desire
And [b]fulfill all your [1]counsel!

2 [a]Ps 74:16 [b]Ps 139:12
4 [1]Another reading is *sound* [a]Rom 10:18 [b]Ps 104:2
6 [1]Lit *the* [2]Lit *the ends* [a]Ps 113:3; Eccl 1:5
7 [1]I.e. blameless [a]Ps 111:7 [b]Ps 119:160 [c]Ps 23:3 [d]Ps 93:5 [e]Ps 119:98-100
8 [a]Ps 119:128 [b]Ps 119:14 [c]Ps 12:6 [d]Ps 36:9
9 [a]Ps 119:142 [b]Ps 119:138
10 [a]Ps 119:72, 127 [b]Ps 119:103
11 [a]Ps 17:4 [b]Ps 24:5, 6; Prov 29:18
12 [a]Ps 40:12; 139:6 [b]Ps 51:1, 2 [c]Ps 90:8; 139:23, 24
13 [1]Lit *complete* [a]Num 15:30 [b]Ps 119:133 [c]Ps 18:32 [d]Ps 25:11
14 [a]Ps 104:34 [b]Ps 18:2 [c]Ps 31:5; Is 47:4
20:1 [a]Ps 50:15 [b]Ps 91:14 [c]Ps 46:7, 11
2 [a]Ps 3:4 [b]Ps 110:2
3 [1]Lit *fat* [2]*Selah* may mean: *Pause, Crescendo* or *Musical interlude* [a]Acts 10:4 [b]Ps 51:19
4 [1]Or *purpose* [a]Ps 21:2 [b]Ps 145:19

5 [1]We will [a]sing for joy over your [2]victory,
And in the name of our God we will [b]set up our banners.
May the LORD [c]fulfill all your petitions.

6 Now [a]I know that the LORD saves His anointed;
He will [b]answer him from His holy heaven
With the [1c]saving strength of His right hand.
7 Some [1]*boast* in chariots and some in [a]horses,
But [b]we [2]will boast in the name of the LORD, our God.
8 They have [a]bowed down and fallen,
But we have [b]risen and stood upright.
9 [1a]Save, O LORD;
May the [b]King answer us in the day we call.

Psalm 21 Theme ______________________

For the choir director. A Psalm of David.

21 O LORD, in Your strength the king will [a]be glad,
And in Your [1]salvation how greatly he will rejoice!
2 You have [a]given him his heart's desire,
And You have not withheld the request of his lips. [1]Selah.
3 For You [a]meet him with the blessings of good things;
You set a [b]crown of fine gold on his head.
4 He asked life of You,
You [a]gave it to him,
[b]Length of days forever and ever.
5 His [a]glory is great through Your [1]salvation,
[b]Splendor and majesty You place upon him.
6 For You make him [1]most [a]blessed forever;
You make him joyful [b]with gladness in Your presence.

7 For the king [a]trusts in the LORD,
And through the lovingkindness of the Most High [b]he will not be shaken.
8 Your hand will [a]find out all your enemies;
Your right hand will find out those who hate you.
9 You will make them [a]as a fiery oven in the time [1]of your anger;
The LORD will [b]swallow them up in His wrath,
And [c]fire will devour them.
10 Their [1]offspring You will destroy from the earth,
And their [2a]descendants from among the sons of men.
11 Though they [1a]intended evil against You
And [b]devised a plot,
They will not succeed.
12 For You will [a]make them turn their back;
You will [1]aim [b]with Your bowstrings at their faces.
13 Be exalted, O LORD, in Your strength;
We will [a]sing and praise Your power.

5 [1]Or *Let us sing* [2]Or *salvation* [a]Ps 9:14 [b]Ps 60:4 [c]1 Sam 1:17

6 [1]Or *mighty deeds of the victory of His right hand* [a]Ps 41:11 [b]Is 58:9 [c]Ps 28:8

7 [1]Or praise *chariots,* or trust, or are strong *through* [2]Lit *make mention of;* or *praise the name* [a]Ps 33:17 [b]2 Chr 32:8

8 [a]Is 2:11, 17 [b]Ps 37:24; Mic 7:8

9 [1]Or *O LORD,* save the king; answer us [a]Ps 3:7 [b]Ps 17:6

21:1 [1]Or *victory* [a]Ps 59:16, 17

2 [1]*Selah* may mean: *Pause, Crescendo* or *Musical interlude* [a]Ps 20:4; 37:4

3 [a]Ps 59:10 [b]2 Sam 12:30

4 [a]Ps 61:6; 133:3 [b]Ps 91:16

5 [1]Or *victory* [a]Ps 9:14; 20:5 [b]Ps 8:5; 96:6

6 [1]Lit *blessings* [a]1 Chr 17:27 [b]Ps 43:4

7 [a]Ps 125:1 [b]Ps 112:6

8 [a]Is 10:10

9 [1]Or *of your presence* [a]Mal 4:1 [b]Lam 2:2 [c]Ps 50:3

10 [1]Lit *fruit* [2]Lit *seed* [a]Ps 37:28

11 [1]Lit *stretched out* [a]Ps 2:1-3 [b]Ps 10:2

12 [1]Lit *make ready* [a]Ps 18:40 [b]Ps 7:12, 13

13 [a]Ps 59:16; 81:1

22:1 +Lit *the hind of the morning* [1]Or *Why are You so far from helping me, and from the words of my groaning?* [2]Lit *roaring* [a]Matt 27:46; Mark 15:34 [b]Ps 10:1 [c]Job 3:24; Ps 6:6; 32:3; 38:8
2 [1]Lit *there is no silence for me* [a]Ps 42:3; 88:1
3 [1]Or *inhabit the praises* [a]Ps 99:9 [b]Deut 10:21; Ps 148:14
4 [a]Ps 78:53 [b]Ps 107:6
5 [1]Or *ashamed* [a]Is 49:23
6 [a]Job 25:6; Is 41:14 [b]Ps 31:11 [c]Is 49:7; 53:3
7 [1]Or *mock me* [2]I.e. make mouths at me [a]Ps 79:4; Is 53:3; Luke 23:35 [b]Matt 27:39; Mark 15:29
8 [1]Lit *Roll;* another reading is *He committed* himself [a]Ps 91:14; Matt 27:43
9 [a]Ps 71:5, 6
10 [1]Lit *a womb* [a]Is 46:3; 49:1
11 [1]Or *distress* [a]Ps 71:12 [b]2 Kin 14:26; Ps 72:12; Is 63:5
12 [a]Ps 22:21; 68:30 [b]Deut 32:14; Amos 4:1
13 [a]Job 16:10; Ps 35:21; Lam 2:16; 3:46 [b]Ps 10:9; 17:12
14 [1]Lit *my inward parts* [a]Job 30:16 [b]Ps 31:10; Dan 5:6 [c]Josh 7:5; Job 23:16; Ps 73:26; Nah 2:10
15 [1]Lit *to* [a]Ps 38:10 [b]John 19:28 [c]Ps 104:29
16 [1]Or *An assembly* [2]Another reading is *Like a lion, my...* [a]Ps 59:6, 7 [b]Matt 27:35; John 20:25
17 [a]Luke 23:27, 35
18 [a]Matt 27:35; Mark 15:24; Luke 23:34; John 19:24
19 [a]Ps 22:11 [b]Ps 70:5
20 [1]Or *life* [2]Lit *paw* [a]Ps 37:14 [b]Ps 35:17

Psalm 22 Theme ____________________

For the choir director; upon +Aijeleth Hashshahar. A Psalm of David.

22

[a]My God, my God, why have You forsaken me?
[1b]Far from my deliverance are the words of my
[2c]groaning.
2 O my God, I [a]cry by day, but You do not answer;
And by night, but [1]I have no rest.
3 Yet [a]You are holy,
O You who [1]are enthroned upon [b]the praises of Israel.
4 In You our fathers [a]trusted;
They trusted and You [b]delivered them.
5 To You they cried out and were delivered;
[a]In You they trusted and were not [1]disappointed.

6 But I am a [a]worm and not a man,
A [b]reproach of men and [c]despised by the people.
7 All who see me [1a]sneer at me;
They [2]separate with the lip, they [b]wag the head, *saying,*
8 "[1]Commit *yourself* to the LORD; [a]let Him deliver him;
Let Him rescue him, because He delights in him."

9 Yet You are He who [a]brought me forth from the womb;
You made me trust *when* upon my mother's breasts.
10 Upon You I was cast [a]from [1]birth;
You have been my God from my mother's womb.

11 [a]Be not far from me, for [1]trouble is near;
For there is [b]none to help.
12 Many [a]bulls have surrounded me;
Strong *bulls* of [b]Bashan have encircled me.
13 They [a]open wide their mouth at me,
As a ravening and a roaring [b]lion.
14 I am [a]poured out like water,
And all my [b]bones are out of joint;
My [c]heart is like wax;
It is melted within [1]me.
15 My [a]strength is dried up like a potsherd,
And [b]my tongue cleaves to my jaws;
And You [c]lay me [1]in the dust of death.
16 For [a]dogs have surrounded me;
[1]A band of evildoers has encompassed me;
[2]They [b]pierced my hands and my feet.
17 I can count all my bones.
[a]They look, they stare at me;
18 They [a]divide my garments among them,
And for my clothing they cast lots.

19 But You, O LORD, [a]be not far off;
O You my help, [b]hasten to my assistance.
20 Deliver my [1]soul from [a]the sword,
My [b]only *life* from the [2]power of the dog.

21 Save me from the [a]lion's mouth;
From the horns of the [b]wild oxen You [c]answer me.

22 I will [a]tell of Your name to my brethren;
In the midst of the assembly I will praise You.
23 [a]You who fear the LORD, praise Him;
All you [1]descendants of Jacob, [b]glorify Him,
And [c]stand in awe of Him, all you [1]descendants of Israel.
24 For He has [a]not despised nor abhorred the affliction of the afflicted;
Nor has He [b]hidden His face from him;
But [c]when he cried to Him for help, He heard.

25 From You *comes* [a]my praise in the great assembly;
I shall [b]pay my vows before those who fear Him.
26 The [1]afflicted will eat and [a]be satisfied;
Those who seek Him will [b]praise the LORD.
Let your [c]heart live forever!
27 All the [a]ends of the earth will remember and turn to the LORD,
And all the [b]families of the nations will worship before [1]You.
28 For the [a]kingdom is the LORD'S
And He [b]rules over the nations.
29 All the [1a]prosperous of the earth will eat and worship,
All those who [b]go down to the dust will bow before Him,
Even he who [2c]cannot keep his soul alive.
30 [1a]Posterity will serve Him;
It will be told of the Lord to [b]the *coming* generation.
31 They will come and [a]will declare His righteousness
To a people [b]who will be born, that He has performed *it.*

Psalm 23 Theme ______________________

A Psalm of David.

23 The LORD is my [a]shepherd,
I [1]shall [b]not want.
2 He makes me lie down in [a]green pastures;
He [b]leads me beside [1c]quiet waters.
3 He [a]restores my soul;
He [b]guides me in the [1c]paths of righteousness
For His name's sake.

4 Even though I [a]walk through the [1]valley of the shadow of death,
I [b]fear no [2]evil, for [c]You are with me;
Your [d]rod and Your staff, they comfort me.
5 You [a]prepare a table before me in the presence of my enemies;
You [1]have [b]anointed my head with oil;
My [c]cup overflows.

21 [a]Ps 22:13 [b]Ps 22:12 [c]Ps 34:4; 118:5; 120:1

22 [a]Ps 40:10; Heb 2:12

23 [1]Lit *seed* [a]Ps 135:19, 20 [b]Ps 86:12 [c]Ps 33:8

24 [a]Ps 69:33 [b]Ps 27:9; 69:17; 102:2 [c]Ps 31:22; Heb 5:7

25 [a]Ps 35:18; 40:9, 10 [b]Ps 61:8; Eccl 5:4

26 [1]Or *poor* [a]Ps 107:9 [b]Ps 40:16 [c]Ps 69:32

27 [1]Some versions read *Him* [a]Ps 2:8; 82:8 [b]Ps 86:9

28 [a]Ps 47:7; Obad 21; Zech 14:9; Matt 6:13 [b]Ps 47:8

29 [1]Lit *fat ones* [2]Or *did not* [a]Ps 17:10; 45:12; Hab 1:16 [b]Ps 28:1; Is 26:19 [c]Ps 89:48

30 [1]Lit *A seed* [a]Ps 102:28 [b]Ps 102:18

31 [a]Ps 40:9; 71:18 [b]Ps 78:6

23:1 [1]Or *do* [a]Ps 78:52; 80:1; Is 40:11; Jer 31:10; Ezek 34:11-13; John 10:11; 1 Pet 2:25 [b]Ps 34:9, 10; Phil 4:19

2 [1]Lit *waters of rest* [a]Ps 65:11-13; Ezek 34:14 [b]Rev 7:17 [c]Ps 36:8; 46:4

3 [1]Lit *tracks* [a]Ps 19:7 [b]Ps 5:8; 31:3 [c]Ps 85:13; Prov 4:11; 8:20

4 [1]Or *valley of deep darkness* [2]Or *harm* [a]Job 10:21, 22; Ps 107:14 [b]Ps 3:6; 27:1 [c]Ps 16:8; Is 43:2 [d]Mic 7:14

5 [1]Or *anoint* [a]Ps 78:19 [b]Ps 92:10 Luke 7:46 [c]Ps 16:5

6 [1]Surely [a]goodness and lovingkindness will follow me all the
days of my life,
And I will [2b]dwell in the house of the LORD [3]forever.

Psalm 24 Theme ______________________________

A Psalm of David.

24 The [a]earth is the LORD's, and [1]all it contains,
The [b]world, and those who dwell in it.
2 For He has [a]founded it upon the seas
And established it upon the rivers.
3 Who may [a]ascend into the [b]hill of the LORD?
And who may stand in His holy [c]place?
4 He who has [a]clean hands and a [b]pure heart,
Who has not [c]lifted up his soul [1]to falsehood
And has not [d]sworn deceitfully.
5 He shall receive a [a]blessing from the LORD
And [1b]righteousness from the God of his salvation.
6 [1]This is the generation of those who [a]seek Him,
Who seek Your face—*even* Jacob. [2]Selah.

7 [a]Lift up your heads, O gates,
And be lifted up, O [1]ancient doors,
That the King of [b]glory may come in!
8 Who is the King of glory?
The LORD [a]strong and mighty,
The LORD [b]mighty in battle.
9 Lift up your heads, O gates,
And lift *them* up, O [1]ancient doors,
That the King of [a]glory may come in!
10 Who is this King of glory?
The LORD of [a]hosts,
He is the King of glory. Selah.

Psalm 25 Theme ______________________________

A Psalm of David.

25 To You, O LORD, I [a]lift up my soul.
2 O my God, in You [a]I trust,
Do not let me [b]be ashamed;
Do not let my [c]enemies exult over me.
3 Indeed, [a]none of those who wait for You will be
ashamed;
[1]Those who [b]deal treacherously without cause will be
ashamed.

4 [a]Make me know Your ways, O LORD;
Teach me Your paths.
5 Lead me in [a]Your truth and teach me,
For You are the [b]God of my salvation;
For You I [c]wait all the day.

6 [1]Or *Only* [2]Another reading is *return to* [3]Lit *for length of days* [a]Ps 25:7, 10 [b]Ps 27:4-6

24:1 [1]Lit *its fullness* [a]1 Cor 10:26 [b]Ps 89:11

2 [a]Ps 104:3, 5; 136:6

3 [a]Ps 15:1 [b]Ps 2:6 [c]Ps 65:4

4 [1]Or *in vain* [a]Job 17:9; Ps 22:30; 26:6 [b]Ps 51:10; 73:1; Matt 5:8 [c]Ezek 18:15 [d]Ps 15:4

5 [1]I.e. as vindicated [a]Ps 115:13 [b]Ps 36:10

6 [1]Or *Such* [2]*Selah* may mean: *Pause, Crescendo* or *Musical interlude* [a]Ps 27:4, 8

7 [1]Lit *everlasting* [a]Ps 118:20; Is 26:2 [b]Ps 29:2, 9; 97:6; Acts 7:2; 1 Cor 2:8

8 [a]Deut 4:34; Ps 96:7 [b]Ex 15:3, 6; Ps 76:3-6

9 [1]Lit *everlasting* [a]Ps 26:8; 57:11

10 [a]Gen 32:2; Josh 5:14; 2 Sam 5:10; Neh 9:6

25:1 [a]Ps 86:4; 143:8

2 [a]Ps 31:1 [b]Ps 25:20; 31:1 [c]Ps 13:4; 41:11

3 [1]Or *Let those . . . be ashamed* [a]Ps 37:9; 40:1; Is 49:23 [b]Ps 119:158; Is 21:2; Hab 1:13

4 [a]Ex 33:13; Ps 27:11; 86:11

5 [a]Ps 25:10; 43:3 [b]Ps 79:9 [c]Ps 40:1

6 [a]Remember, O LORD, Your compassion and Your
lovingkindnesses,
For they have been [1b]from of old.
7 Do not remember the [a]sins of my youth or my
transgressions;
[b]According to Your lovingkindness remember me,
For Your [c]goodness' sake, O LORD.

8 [a]Good and [b]upright is the LORD;
Therefore He [c]instructs sinners in the way.
9 He [a]leads the [1]humble in justice,
And He [b]teaches the [1]humble His way.
10 All the paths of the LORD are [a]lovingkindness and truth
To [b]those who keep His covenant and His testimonies.
11 For [a]Your name's sake, O LORD,
[b]Pardon my iniquity, for it is great.

12 Who is the man who [a]fears the LORD?
He will [b]instruct him in the way he should choose.
13 His soul will [a]abide in [1]prosperity,
And his [2]descendants will [b]inherit the [3]land.
14 The [1a]secret of the LORD is for those who fear Him,
[2]And He will [b]make them know His covenant.
15 My [a]eyes are continually toward the LORD,
For He will [1b]pluck my feet out of the net.

16 [a]Turn to me and be gracious to me,
For I am [b]lonely and afflicted.
17 [1]The [a]troubles of my heart are enlarged;
Bring me [b]out of my distresses.
18 [a]Look upon my affliction and my [1]trouble,
And [b]forgive all my sins.
19 Look upon my enemies, for they [a]are many,
And they [b]hate me with violent hatred.
20 [a]Guard my soul and deliver me;
Do not let me [b]be ashamed, for I take refuge in You.
21 Let [a]integrity and uprightness preserve me,
For [b]I wait for You.
22 [a]Redeem Israel, O God,
Out of all his troubles.

Psalm 26 Theme ____________________

A Psalm of David.

26 [1a]Vindicate me, O LORD, for I have [b]walked in
my integrity,
And I have [c]trusted in the LORD [2d]without wavering.
2 [a]Examine me, O LORD, and try me;
[b]Test my [1]mind and my heart.
3 For Your [a]lovingkindness is before my eyes,
And I have [b]walked in Your [1]truth.

6 [1]Or *everlasting* [a]Ps 98:3 [b]Ps 103:17

7 [a]Job 13:26; 20:11 [b]Ps 51:1 [c]Ps 31:19

8 [a]Ps 86:5 [b]Ps 92:15 [c]Ps 32:8

9 [1]Or *afflicted* [a]Ps 23:3 [b]Ps 27:11

10 [a]Ps 40:11 [b]Ps 103:18

11 [a]Ps 31:3; 79:9 [b]Ex 34:9

12 [a]Ps 31:19 [b]Ps 25:8; 37:23

13 [1]Lit *good* [2]Lit *seed* [3]Or *earth* [a]Prov 1:33; Jer 23:6 [b]Ps 37:11; 69:36; Matt 5:5

14 [1]Or *counsel* or *intimacy* [2]Or *And His covenant, to make them know it* [a]Prov 3:32; John 7:17 [b]Gen 17:1, 2

15 [1]Lit *bring out* [a]Ps 123:2; 141:8 [b]Ps 31:4; 124:7

16 [a]Ps 69:16 [b]Ps 143:4

17 [1]Some commentators read *Relieve the troubles of my heart* [a]Ps 40:12 [b]Ps 107:6

18 [1]Lit *toil* [a]2 Sam 16:12; Ps 31:7 [b]Ps 103:3

19 [a]Ps 3:1 [b]Ps 9:13

20 [a]Ps 86:2 [b]Ps 25:2

21 [a]Ps 41:12 [b]Ps 25:3

22 [a]Ps 130:8

26:1 [1]Lit *Judge* [2]Lit *I do not slide* [a]Ps 7:8 [b]2 Kin 20:3; Prov 20:7 [c]Ps 13:5; 28:7 [d]Heb 10:23

2 [1]Lit *kidneys,* figurative for inner man [a]Ps 17:3; 139:23 [b]Ps 7:9

3 [1]Or *faithfulness* [a]Ps 48:9 [b]2 Kin 20:3; Ps 86:11

4 I do not [a]sit with [1]deceitful men,
Nor will I go with [2b]pretenders.
5 I [a]hate the assembly of evildoers,
And I will not sit with the wicked.
6 I shall [a]wash my hands in innocence,
And I will go about [b]Your altar, O LORD,
7 That I may proclaim with the voice of [a]thanksgiving
And declare all Your [1]wonders.

8 O LORD, I [a]love the habitation of Your house
And the place [1]where Your [b]glory dwells.
9 [a]Do not [1]take my soul away *along* with sinners,
Nor my life with [b]men of bloodshed,
10 In whose hands is a [a]wicked scheme,
And whose right hand is full of [b]bribes.
11 But as for me, I shall [a]walk in my integrity;
[b]Redeem me, and be gracious to me.
12 [a]My foot stands on a [b]level place;
In the [c]congregations I shall bless the LORD.

Psalm 27 Theme

A Psalm of David.

27 The LORD is my [a]light and my [b]salvation;
Whom shall I fear?
The LORD is the [1c]defense of my life;
[d]Whom shall I dread?
2 When evildoers came upon me to [a]devour my flesh,
My adversaries and my enemies, they [b]stumbled and fell.
3 Though a [a]host encamp against me,
My heart will not fear;
Though war arise against me,
In *spite of* this I [1]shall be [b]confident.

4 [a]One thing I have asked from the LORD, that I shall seek:
That I may [b]dwell in the house of the LORD all the days of my life,
To behold [c]the [1]beauty of the LORD
And to [2d]meditate in His temple.
5 For in the [a]day of trouble He will [b]conceal me in His [1]tabernacle;
In the secret place of His tent He will [c]hide me;
He will [d]lift me up on a rock.
6 And now [a]my head will be lifted up above my enemies around me,
And I will offer in His tent [b]sacrifices [1]with shouts of joy;
I will [c]sing, yes, I will sing praises to the LORD.

7 [a]Hear, O LORD, when I cry with my voice,
And be gracious to me and [b]answer me.

4 [1]Or *worthless men;* lit *men of falsehood* [2]Or *dissemblers, hypocrites* [a]Ps 1:1 [b]Ps 28:3
5 [a]Ps 31:6; 139:21
6 [a]Ps 73:13 [b]Ps 43:3, 4
7 [1]Or *miracles* [a]Ps 9:1
8 [1]Lit *of the tabernacle of Your glory* [a]Ps 27:4 [b]Ps 24:7
9 [1]Lit *gather* [a]Ps 28:3 [b]Ps 139:19
10 [a]Ps 37:7 [b]Ps 15:5
11 [a]Ps 26:1 [b]Ps 44:26; 69:18
12 [a]Ps 40:2 [b]Ps 27:11 [c]Ps 22:22
27:1 [1]Or *refuge* [a]Ps 18:28; Is 60:20; Mic 7:8 [b]Ex 15:2; Ps 62:7; 118:14; Is 33:2; Jon 2:9 [c]Ps 28:8 [d]Ps 118:6
2 [a]Ps 14:4 [b]Ps 9:3
3 [1]Lit *am confident* [a]Ps 3:6 [b]Job 4:6
4 [1]Lit *delightfulness* [2]Lit *inquire* [a]Ps 26:8 [b]Ps 23:6 [c]Ps 90:17 [d]Ps 18:6
5 [1]Or *shelter* [a]Ps 50:15 [b]Ps 31:20 [c]Ps 17:8 [d]Ps 40:2
6 [1]Lit *of shouts* [a]Ps 3:3 [b]Ps 107:22 [c]Ps 13:6
7 [a]Ps 4:3; 61:1 [b]Ps 13:3

8 *When You said,* "[a]Seek My face," my heart said to You,
"Your face, O LORD, [b]I shall seek."
9 [a]Do not hide Your face from me,
Do not turn Your servant away in [b]anger;
You have been [c]my help;
[d]Do not abandon me nor [e]forsake me,
O God of my salvation!
10 [1]For my father and [a]my mother have forsaken me,
But [b]the LORD will take me up.

11 [a]Teach me Your way, O LORD,
And lead me in a [b]level path
Because of [1]my foes.
12 Do not deliver me over to the [1a]desire of my adversaries,
For [b]false witnesses have risen against me,
And such as [c]breathe out violence.
13 [1]*I would have despaired* unless I had believed that I would
see the [a]goodness of the LORD
In the [b]land of the living.
14 [a]Wait for the LORD;
Be [b]strong and let your heart take courage;
Yes, wait for the LORD.

Psalm 28 Theme ______________________

A Psalm of David.

28 To You, O LORD, I call;
My [a]rock, do not be deaf to me,
For if You [b]are silent to me,
I will become like those who [c]go down to the pit.
2 Hear the [a]voice of my supplications when I cry to You for
help,
When I [b]lift up my hands [c]toward [1]Your holy [d]sanctuary.
3 [a]Do not drag me away with the wicked
And with those who work iniquity,
Who [b]speak peace with their neighbors,
While evil is in their hearts.
4 Requite them [a]according to their work and according to the
evil of their practices;
Requite them according to the deeds of their hands;
Repay them their [1]recompense.
5 Because they [a]do not regard the works of the LORD
Nor the deeds of His hands,
He will tear them down and not build them up.

6 Blessed be the LORD,
Because He [a]has heard the voice of my supplication.
7 The LORD is my [a]strength and my [b]shield;
My heart [c]trusts in Him, and I am helped;
Therefore [d]my heart exults,
And with [e]my song I shall thank Him.

8 [a]Ps 105:4; Amos 5:6 [b]Ps 34:4
9 [a]Ps 69:17 [b]Ps 6:1 [c]Ps 40:17 [d]Ps 94:14 [e]Ps 37:28
10 [1]Or *If my father . . . forsake me, Then the LORD* [a]Is 49:15 [b]Is 40:11
11 [1]Or *those who lie in wait for me* [a]Ps 25:4; 86:11 [b]Ps 5:8; 26:12
12 [1]Lit *soul* [a]Ps 41:2 [b]Deut 19:18; Ps 35:11; Matt 26:60 [c]Acts 9:1
13 [1]Or *Surely I believed* [a]Ps 31:19 [b]Job 28:13; Ps 52:5; 116:9; 142:5; Is 38:11; Jer 11:19; Ezek 26:20
14 [a]Ps 25:3; 37:34; 40:1; 62:5; 130:5; Prov 20:22; Is 25:9 [b]Ps 31:24
28:1 [a]Ps 18:2 [b]Ps 35:22; 39:12; 83:1 [c]Ps 88:4; 143:7; Prov 1:12
2 [1]Lit *the innermost place of Your sanctuary* [a]Ps 140:6 [b]Ps 134:2; 141:2; Lam 2:19; 1 Tim 2:8 [c]Ps 5:7; 138:2 [d]1 Kin 6:5
3 [a]Ps 26:9 [b]Ps 12:2; 55:21; 62:4; Jer 9:8
4 [1]Or *dealings* [a]Ps 62:12; 2 Tim 4:14; Rev 18:6; 22:12
5 [a]Is 5:12
6 [a]Ps 28:2
7 [a]Ps 18:2; 59:17 [b]Ps 3:3 [c]Ps 13:5; 112:7 [d]Ps 16:9 [e]Ps 40:3; 69:30

8 [1]A few mss and ancient versions read *the strength of His people* [2]Or *refuge of salvation* [a]Ps 20:6; 89:17 [b]Ps 27:1; 140:7

9 [a]Ps 106:47 [b]Deut 9:29; 32:9; 1 Kin 8:51; Ps 33:12; 106:40 [c]Ps 80:1 [d]Deut 1:31; Is 40:11; 46:3; 63:9

29:1 [1]Or *sons of gods* [a]1 Chr 16:28, 29; Ps 96:7-9

2 [1]Lit *of His name* [2]Or *the majesty of holiness* [a]2 Chr 20:21; Ps 110:3

3 [1]Or *great* [a]Ps 104:7 [b]Job 37:4, 5; Ps 18:13 [c]Ps 18:16; 107:23

4 [a]Ps 68:33

5 [a]Judg 9:15; 1 Kin 5:6; Ps 104:16; Is 2:13; 14:8

6 [a]Ps 114:4, 6 [b]Deut 3:9

7 [1]I.e. lightning

8 [1]Or *causes... to whirl* [a]Num 13:26

9 [a]Job 39:1 [b]Ps 26:8

10 [a]Gen 6:17 [b]Ps 10:16

11 [1]Or *May the LORD give* [2]Or *May the LORD bless* [a]Ps 28:8; 68:35; Is 40:29 [b]Ps 37:11; 72:3

30:1 [a]Ps 118:28; 145:1 [b]Ps 3:3 [c]Ps 25:2; 35:19, 24

2 [a]Ps 88:13 [b]Ps 6:2; 103:3; Is 53:5

3 [1]I.e. the nether world [2]Some mss read *from among those who go down* [a]Ps 86:13 [b]Ps 28:1

4 [1]Lit *memorial* [a]Ps 149:1 [b]Ps 50:5 [c]Ps 97:12 [d]Ex 3:15; Ps 135:13; Hos 12:5

5 [a]Ps 103:9; Is 26:20; 54:7, 8 [b]Ps 118:1 [c]Ps 126:5; 2 Cor 4:17

8 The LORD is [1]their [a]strength,
And He is a [2b]saving defense to His anointed.
9 [a]Save Your people and bless [b]Your inheritance;
Be their [c]shepherd also, and [d]carry them forever.

Psalm 29 Theme ______________________

A Psalm of David.

29 [a]Ascribe to the LORD, O [1]sons of the mighty,
Ascribe to the LORD glory and strength.
2 Ascribe to the LORD the glory [1]due to His name;
Worship the LORD [a]in [2]holy array.

3 The [a]voice of the LORD is upon the waters;
The God of glory [b]thunders,
The LORD is over [1c]many waters.
4 The voice of the LORD is [a]powerful,
The voice of the LORD is majestic.
5 The voice of the LORD breaks the cedars;
Yes, the LORD breaks in pieces [a]the cedars of Lebanon.
6 He makes Lebanon [a]skip like a calf,
And [b]Sirion like a young wild ox.
7 The voice of the LORD hews out [1]flames of fire.
8 The voice of the LORD [1]shakes the wilderness;
The LORD shakes the wilderness of [a]Kadesh.
9 The voice of the LORD makes [a]the deer to calve
And strips the forests bare;
And [b]in His temple everything says, "Glory!"

10 The LORD sat *as King* at the [a]flood;
Yes, the LORD sits as [b]King forever.
11 [1]The LORD will give [a]strength to His people;
[2]The LORD will bless His people with [b]peace.

Psalm 30 Theme ______________________

A Psalm; a Song at the Dedication of the House. *A Psalm* of David.

30 I will [a]extol You, O LORD, for You have [b]lifted me up,
And have not let my [c]enemies rejoice over me.
2 O LORD my God,
I [a]cried to You for help, and You [b]healed me.
3 O LORD, You have [a]brought up my soul from [1]Sheol;
You have kept me alive, [2]that I would not [b]go down to the
pit.
4 [a]Sing praise to the LORD, you [b]His godly ones,
And [c]give thanks to His holy [1d]name.
5 For [a]His anger is but for a moment,
His [b]favor is for a lifetime;
Weeping may [c]last for the night,
But a shout of joy *comes* in the morning.

6 Now as for me, I said in my prosperity,
"I will [a]never be moved."
7 O LORD, by Your favor You have made my mountain to stand strong;
You [a]hid Your face, I was dismayed.
8 To You, O LORD, I called,
And to the Lord I made supplication:
9 "What profit is there in my blood, if I [a]go down to the pit?
Will the [b]dust praise You? Will it declare Your faithfulness?

10 "[a]Hear, O LORD, and be gracious to me;
O LORD, be my [b]helper."
11 You have turned for me [a]my mourning into dancing;
You have [b]loosed my sackcloth and girded me with [c]gladness,
12 That *my* [1a]soul may sing praise to You and not be silent.
O LORD my God, I will [b]give thanks to You forever.

Psalm 31 Theme ______________________

For the choir director. A Psalm of David.

31 [a]In You, O LORD, I have taken refuge;
Let me never [b]be ashamed;
[c]In Your righteousness deliver me.
2 [a]Incline Your ear to me, rescue me quickly;
Be to me a [b]rock of [1]strength,
A stronghold to save me.
3 For You are my [1]rock and [a]my fortress;
For [b]Your name's sake You will lead me and guide me.
4 You will [a]pull me out of the net which they have secretly laid for me,
For You are my [b]strength.
5 [a]Into Your hand I commit my spirit;
You have [b]ransomed me, O LORD, [c]God of [1]truth.

6 I hate those who [a]regard [1]vain idols,
But I [b]trust in the LORD.
7 I will [a]rejoice and be glad in Your lovingkindness,
Because You have [b]seen my affliction;
You have known the troubles of my soul,
8 And You have not [a]given me over into the hand of the enemy;
You have set my feet in a large place.

9 Be gracious to me, O LORD, for [a]I am in distress;
My [b]eye is wasted away from grief, [c]my soul and my body *also.*
10 For my life is spent with [a]sorrow
And my years with sighing;
My [b]strength has failed because of my iniquity,
And [c]my [1]body has wasted away.

6 [a]Ps 10:6; 62:2, 6
7 [a]Deut 31:17; Ps 104:29; 143:7
9 [a]Ps 28:1 [b]Ps 6:5
10 [a]Ps 4:1; 27:7 [b]Ps 27:9; 54:4
11 [a]Eccl 3:4; Jer 31:4, 13 [b]Is 20:2 [c]Ps 4:7
12 [1]Lit *glory* [a]Ps 16:9; 57:8; 108:1 [b]Ps 44:8
31:1 [a]Ps 31:1-3; 71:1-3 [b]Ps 25:2 [c]Ps 143:1
2 [1]Or *refuge, protection* [a]Ps 17:6; 71:2; 86:1; 102:2 [b]Ps 18:2; 71:3
3 [1]Or *crag* [a]Ps 18:2 [b]Ps 23:3; 25:11
4 [a]Ps 25:15 [b]Ps 46:1
5 [1]Or *faithfulness* [a]Luke 23:46; Acts 7:59 [b]Ps 55:18; 71:23 [c]Deut 32:4; Ps 71:22
6 [1]Lit *empty vanities* [a]Jon 2:8 [b]Ps 52:8
7 [a]Ps 90:14 [b]Ps 10:14
8 [a]Deut 32:30; Ps 37:33
9 [a]Ps 66:14; 69:17 [b]Ps 6:7 [c]Ps 63:1
10 [1]Or *bones, substance* [a]Ps 13:2 [b]Ps 39:11 [c]Ps 32:3; 38:3; 102:3

11 [a]Ps 69:19 [b]Job 19:13; Ps 38:11; 88:8, 18
12 [a]Ps 88:5
13 [1]Lit *whispering* [a]Ps 50:20; Jer 20:10 [b]Lam 2:22 [c]Ps 62:4; Matt 27:1 [d]Ps 41:7
14 [a]Ps 140:6
15 [a]Job 14:5; 24:1 [b]Ps 143:9
16 [a]Num 6:25; Ps 4:6; 80:3 [b]Ps 6:4
17 [1]I.e. the nether world [a]Ps 25:2, 20 [b]Ps 25:3 [c]1 Sam 2:9; Ps 94:17; 115:17
18 [a]Ps 109:2; 120:2 [b]1 Sam 2:3; Ps 94:4; Jude 15
19 [a]Ps 65:4; 145:7; Is 64:4; Rom 2:4; 11:22 [b]Ps 5:11 [c]Ps 23:5
20 [1]Or *pavilion* [a]Ps 27:5 [b]Ps 37:12 [c]Job 5:21; Ps 31:13
21 [a]Ps 28:6 [b]Ps 17:7 [c]1 Sam 23:7; Ps 87:5
22 [a]Ps 116:11 [b]Ps 88:5; Is 38:11, 12; Lam 3:54 [c]Ps 18:6; 66:19; 145:19
23 [a]Ps 30:4; 37:28; 50:5 [b]Ps 145:20; Rev 2:10 [c]Deut 32:41; Ps 94:2
24 [1]Or *wait for* [a]Ps 27:14
32:1 +Possibly *Contemplative*, or *Didactic*, or *Skillful Psalm* [a]Ps 85:2; 103:3; Rom 4:7, 8

11 Because of all my adversaries, I have become a [a]reproach,
Especially to my [b]neighbors,
And an object of dread to my acquaintances;
Those who see me in the street flee from me.
12 I am [a]forgotten as a dead man, out of mind;
I am like a broken vessel.
13 For I have heard the [1a]slander of many,
[b]Terror is on every side;
While they [c]took counsel together against me,
They [d]schemed to take away my life.

14 But as for me, I trust in You, O LORD,
I say, "[a]You are my God."
15 My [a]times are in Your hand;
[b]Deliver me from the hand of my enemies and from those who persecute me.
16 Make Your [a]face to shine upon Your servant;
[b]Save me in Your lovingkindness.
17 Let me not be [a]put to shame, O LORD, for I call upon You;
Let the [b]wicked be put to shame, let them [c]be silent in [1]Sheol.
18 Let the [a]lying lips be mute,
Which [b]speak arrogantly against the righteous
With pride and contempt.

19 How great is Your [a]goodness,
Which You have stored up for those who fear You,
Which You have wrought for those who [b]take refuge in You,
[c]Before the sons of men!
20 You hide them in the [a]secret place of Your presence from the [b]conspiracies of man;
You keep them secretly in a [1]shelter from the [c]strife of tongues.
21 [a]Blessed be the LORD,
For He has made [b]marvelous His lovingkindness to me in a besieged [c]city.
22 As for me, [a]I said in my alarm,
"I am [b]cut off from before Your eyes";
Nevertheless You [c]heard the voice of my supplications
When I cried to You.

23 O love the LORD, all you [a]His godly ones!
The LORD [b]preserves the faithful
And fully [c]recompenses the proud doer.
24 [a]Be strong and let your heart take courage,
All you who [1]hope in the LORD.

Psalm 32 Theme

A Psalm of David. A +Maskil.

32 [a]How blessed is he whose transgression is forgiven,
Whose sin is covered!

2 How blessed is the man to whom the LORD [a]does not
impute iniquity,
And in whose spirit there is [b]no deceit!

3 When [a]I kept silent *about my sin,* [b]my [1]body wasted away
Through my [2c]groaning all day long.
4 For day and night [a]Your hand was heavy upon me;
My [1b]vitality was drained away *as* with the fever heat of
summer. [2]Selah.
5 I [a]acknowledged my sin to You,
And my iniquity I [b]did not hide;
I said, "[c]I will confess my transgressions to the LORD";
And You [d]forgave the [1]guilt of my sin. Selah.
6 Therefore, let everyone who is godly pray to You [1a]in a
time when You may be found;
Surely [b]in a flood of great waters they will not reach him.
7 You are [a]my hiding place; You [b]preserve me from trouble;
You surround me with [1c]songs of deliverance. Selah.

8 I will [a]instruct you and teach you in the way which you
should go;
I will counsel you [b]with My eye upon you.
9 Do not be [a]as the horse or as the mule which have no
understanding,
Whose trappings include bit and bridle to hold them in check,
Otherwise they will not come near to you.
10 Many are the [a]sorrows of the wicked,
But [b]he who trusts in the LORD, lovingkindness shall
surround him.
11 Be [a]glad in the LORD and rejoice, you righteous ones;
And shout for joy, all you who are [b]upright in heart.

Psalm 33 Theme

33 [a]Sing for joy in the LORD, O you righteous ones;
Praise is [b]becoming to the upright.
2 Give thanks to the LORD with the [a]lyre;
Sing praises to Him with a [b]harp of ten strings.
3 Sing to Him a [a]new song;
Play skillfully with [b]a shout of joy.
4 For the word of the LORD [a]is upright,
And all His work is *done* [b]in faithfulness.
5 He [a]loves righteousness and justice;
The [b]earth is full of the lovingkindness of the LORD.

6 By the [a]word of the LORD the heavens were made,
And [b]by the breath of His mouth [c]all their host.
7 He gathers the [a]waters of the sea together [1]as a heap;
He lays up the deeps in storehouses.
8 Let [a]all the earth fear the LORD;
Let all the inhabitants of the world [b]stand in awe of Him.

2 [a]2 Cor 5:19 [b]John 1:47

3 [1]Or *bones, substance* [2]Lit *roaring* [a]Ps 39:2, 3 [b]Ps 31:10 [c]Ps 38:8

4 [1]Lit *life juices were turned into the drought of summer* [2]*Selah* may mean: *Pause, Crescendo* or *Musical interlude* [a]1 Sam 5:6; Job 23:2; 33:7; Ps 38:2; 39:10 [b]Ps 22:15

5 [1]Or *iniquity* [a]Lev 26:40 [b]Job 31:33 [c]Ps 38:18; Prov 28:13; 1 John 1:9 [d]Ps 103:12

6 [1]Lit *in a time of finding out* [a]Ps 69:13; Is 55:6 [b]Ps 46:1-3; 69:1; 124:5; 144:7; Is 43:2

7 [1]Or *shouts* [a]Ps 9:9; 31:20; 91:1; 119:114 [b]Ps 121:7 [c]Ex 15:1; Judg 5:1; Ps 40:3

8 [a]Ps 25:8 [b]Ps 33:18

9 [a]Prov 26:3

10 [a]Ps 16:4; Prov 13:21; Rom 2:9 [b]Ps 5:11, 12; Prov 16:20

11 [a]Ps 64:10; 68:3; 97:12 [b]Ps 7:10; 64:10

33:1 [a]Ps 32:11; Phil 3:1; 4:4 [b]Ps 92:1; 147:1

2 [a]Ps 71:22; 147:7 [b]Ps 144:9

3 [a]Ps 40:3; 96:1; 98:1; 144:9; Is 42:10; Rev 5:9 [b]Ps 98:4

4 [a]Ps 19:8 [b]Ps 119:90

5 [a]Ps 11:7; 37:28 [b]Ps 119:64

6 [a]Gen 1:6; Ps 148:5; Heb 11:3 [b]Ps 104:30 [c]Gen 2:1

7 [1]Some versions read *in a water skin;* i.e. container [a]Ex 15:8; Josh 3:16; Ps 78:13

8 [a]Ps 67:7 [b]Ps 96:9

9 For [a]He spoke, and it was done;
He commanded, and it [1]stood fast.
10 The LORD [a]nullifies the counsel of the nations;
He frustrates the plans of the peoples.
11 The [a]counsel of the LORD stands forever,
The [b]plans of His heart from generation to generation.
12 Blessed is the [a]nation whose God is the LORD,
The people whom He has [b]chosen for His own inheritance.

13 The LORD [a]looks from heaven;
He [b]sees all the sons of men;
14 From [a]His dwelling place He looks out
On all the inhabitants of the earth,
15 He who [a]fashions [1]the hearts of them all,
He who [b]understands all their works.
16 [a]The king is not saved by a mighty army;
A warrior is not delivered by great strength.
17 A [a]horse is a false hope for victory;
Nor does it deliver anyone by its great strength.

18 Behold, [a]the eye of the LORD is on those who fear Him,
On those who [1b]hope for His lovingkindness,
19 To [a]deliver their soul from death
And to keep them alive [b]in famine.
20 Our soul [a]waits for the LORD;
He is our [b]help and our shield.
21 For our [a]heart rejoices in Him,
Because we trust in His holy name.
22 Let Your lovingkindness, O LORD, be upon us,
According as we have [1]hoped in You.

Psalm 34 Theme ____________________________

A Psalm of David when he +feigned madness before •Abimelech, who drove him away and he departed.

34 I will [a]bless the LORD at all times;
His [b]praise shall continually be in my mouth.
2 My soul will [a]make its boast in the LORD;
The [b]humble will hear it and rejoice.
3 O [a]magnify the LORD with me,
And let us [b]exalt His name together.

4 I [a]sought the LORD, and He answered me,
And [b]delivered me from all my fears.
5 They [a]looked to Him and were radiant,
And their faces will [b]never be ashamed.
6 This [1]poor man cried, and [a]the LORD heard him
And saved him out of all his troubles.
7 The [a]angel of the LORD encamps around those who fear Him,
And rescues them.

9 [1]Or *stood forth* [a]Gen 1:3; Ps 148:5
10 [a]Ps 2:1-3; Is 8:10; 19:3
11 [a]Job 23:12; Prov 19:21 [b]Ps 40:5; 92:5; 139:17; Is 55:8
12 [a]Ps 144:15 [b]Ex 19:5; Deut 7:6; Ps 28:9
13 [a]Job 28:24; Ps 14:2 [b]Ps 11:4
14 [a]1 Kin 8:39, 43; Ps 102:19
15 [1]Or *their heart together* [a]Job 10:8; Ps 119:73 [b]2 Chr 16:9; Job 34:21; Jer 32:19
16 [a]Ps 44:6; 60:11
17 [a]Ps 20:7; 147:10; Prov 21:31
18 [1]Or *wait* [a]Job 36:7; Ps 32:8; 34:15; 1 Pet 3:12 [b]Ps 32:10; 147:11
19 [a]Ps 56:13; Acts 12:11 [b]Job 5:20; Ps 37:19
20 [a]Ps 62:1; 130:6; Is 8:17 [b]Ps 115:9
21 [a]Ps 13:5; 28:7; Zech 10:7; John 16:22
22 [1]Or *waited for*
34:1 +Or *changed his behavior* •Possibly a title of King Achish of Gath, see 1 Sam 21:10-15 [a]Eph 5:20; 1 Thess 5:18 [b]Ps 71:6
2 [a]Ps 44:8; Jer 9:24; 1 Cor 1:31 [b]Ps 69:32
3 [a]Ps 35:27; 69:30; Luke 1:46 [b]Ps 18:46
4 [a]2 Chr 15:2; Ps 9:10; Matt 7:7 [b]Ps 34:6, 17, 19
5 [a]Ps 36:9; Is 60:5 [b]Ps 25:3
6 [1]Or *afflicted* [a]Ps 34:4
7 [a]Ps 91:11; Dan 6:22

8 O [a]taste and see that the LORD is good;
How [b]blessed is the man who takes refuge in Him!
9 O fear the LORD, you [a]His saints;
For to those who fear Him there is [b]no want.
10 The young lions do lack and suffer hunger;
But they who seek the LORD shall [a]not be in want of any good thing.
11 [a]Come, you children, listen to me;
[b]I will teach you [c]the fear of the LORD.
12 [a]Who is the man who desires life
And loves *length of* days that he may [b]see good?
13 Keep [a]your tongue from evil
And your lips from speaking [b]deceit.
14 [a]Depart from evil and do good;
Seek peace and [b]pursue it.

15 The [a]eyes of the LORD are toward the righteous
And His ears are *open* to their cry.
16 The [a]face of the LORD is against evildoers,
To [b]cut off the memory of them from the earth.
17 *The righteous* [a]cry, and the LORD hears
And delivers them out of all their troubles.
18 The LORD [a]is near to the [b]brokenhearted
And saves those who are [1c]crushed in spirit.

19 [a]Many are the [b]afflictions of the righteous,
But the LORD [c]delivers him out of them all.
20 He keeps all his bones,
[a]Not one of them is broken.
21 [a]Evil shall slay the wicked,
And those who hate the righteous will be [1]condemned.
22 The LORD [a]redeems the soul of His servants,
And none of those who [b]take refuge in Him will be [1]condemned.

Psalm 35 Theme ______________________________

A Psalm of David.

35 Contend, O LORD, with those who [a]contend with me;
Fight against those who [b]fight against me.
2 Take hold of [1a]buckler and shield
And rise up for [b]my help.
3 Draw also the spear and [1]the battle-axe to meet those who pursue me;
Say to my soul, "I am [a]your salvation."
4 Let those be [a]ashamed and dishonored who seek my [1]life;
Let those be [b]turned back and humiliated who devise evil against me.
5 Let them be [a]like chaff before the wind,
With the angel of the LORD driving *them* on.

8 [a]Ps 119:103; Heb 6:5; 1 Pet 2:3 [b]Ps 2:12
9 [a]Ps 31:23 [b]Ps 23:1
10 [a]Ps 84:11
11 [a]Ps 66:16 [b]Ps 32:8 [c]Ps 111:10
12 [a]Ps 34:12-16; 1 Pet 3:10-12 [b]Eccl 3:13
13 [a]Ps 141:3; Prov 13:3; James 1:26 [b]1 Pet 2:22
14 [a]Ps 37:27; Is 1:16, 17 [b]Rom 14:19; Heb 12:14
15 [a]Job 36:7; Ps 33:18
16 [a]Lev 17:10; Jer 44:11; Amos 9:4 [b]Job 18:17; Ps 9:6; 109:15; Prov 10:7
17 [a]Ps 34:6; 145:19
18 [1]Or *contrite* [a]Ps 145:18 [b]Ps 147:3; Is 61:1 [c]Ps 51:17; Is 57:15
19 [a]Prov 24:16 [b]Ps 71:20; 2 Tim 3:11f [c]Ps 34:4, 6, 17
20 [a]John 19:33, 36
21 [1]Or *held guilty* [a]Ps 94:23; 140:11; Prov 24:16
22 [1]V 21, note 1 [a]1 Kin 1:29; Ps 71:23 [b]Ps 37:40
35:1 [a]Ps 18:43; Is 49:25 [b]Ps 56:2
2 [1]I.e. small shield [a]Ps 91:4 [b]Ps 44:26
3 [1]Or *close up the path against those* [a]Ps 62:2
4 [1]Or *soul* [a]Ps 70:2 [b]Ps 40:14; 129:5
5 [a]Job 21:18; Ps 83:13; Is 29:5

6 Let their way be dark and [a]slippery,
With the angel of the LORD pursuing them.
7 For [a]without cause they [b]hid their net for me;
Without cause they dug a [1]pit for my soul.
8 Let [a]destruction come upon him unawares,
And [b]let the net which he hid catch himself;
Into that very [c]destruction let him fall.

9 And my soul shall [a]rejoice in the LORD;
It shall [b]exult in His salvation.
10 All my [a]bones will say, "LORD, [b]who is like You,
Who delivers the afflicted from him [c]who is too strong for him,
And [d]the afflicted and the needy from him who robs him?"
11 [a]Malicious witnesses rise up;
They ask me of things that I do not know.
12 They [a]repay me evil for good,
To the bereavement of my soul.
13 But as for me, [a]when they were sick, my [b]clothing was sackcloth;
I [c]humbled my soul with fasting,
And my [d]prayer kept returning to my bosom.
14 I went about as though it were my friend or brother;
I [a]bowed down [1]mourning, as one who sorrows for a mother.
15 But [a]at my [1]stumbling they rejoiced and gathered themselves together;
The [2b]smiters whom I did not know gathered together against me,
They [3c]slandered me without ceasing.
16 Like godless jesters at a feast,
They [a]gnashed at me with their teeth.

17 Lord, [a]how long will You look on?
Rescue my soul [b]from their ravages,
My [c]only *life* from the lions.
18 I will [a]give You thanks in the great congregation;
I will [b]praise You among a mighty throng.
19 [a]Do not let those who are wrongfully [b]my enemies rejoice over me;
Nor let those [c]who hate me without cause [1d]wink maliciously.
20 For they do not speak peace,
But they devise [a]deceitful words against those who are quiet in the land.
21 They [a]opened their mouth wide against me;
They said, "[b]Aha, aha, our eyes have seen it!"

22 [a]You have seen it, O LORD, [b]do not keep silent;
O Lord, [c]do not be far from me.
23 [a]Stir up Yourself, and awake to my right
And to my cause, my God and my Lord.

6 [a]Ps 73:18; Jer 23:12
7 [1]*Pit* has been transposed from ine above [a]Ps 69:4; 109:3; 140:5 [b]Ps 9:15
8 [a]Ps 55:23; Is 47:11; 1 Thess 5:3 [b]Ps 9:15 [c]Ps 73:18
9 [a]Is 61:10 [b]Ps 9:14; 13:5; Luke 1:47
10 [a]Ps 51:8 [b]Ex 15:11; Ps 86:8; Mic 7:18 [c]Ps 18:17 [d]Ps 37:14; 109:16
11 [a]Ps 27:12
12 [a]Ps 38:20; 109:5; Jer 18:20; John 10:32
13 [a]Job 30:25 [b]Ps 69:11 [c]Ps 69:10 [d]Matt 10:13; Luke 10:6
14 [1]Or *dressed in black* [a]Ps 38:6
15 [1]Or *limping* [2]Or *smitten ones* [3]Lit *tore* [a]Obad 12 [b]Job 30:1, 8, 12 [c]Ps 7:2
16 [a]Job 16:9; Ps 37:12; Lam 2:16
17 [a]Ps 13:1; Hab 1:13 [b]Ps 35:7 [c]Ps 22:20, 21
18 [a]Ps 22:22 [b]Ps 22:25
9 [1]Or *wink the eye* [a]Ps 13:4; 30:1; 38:16 [b]Ps 38:19; 69:4 [c]John 15:25 [d]Prov 6:13; 10:10
20 [a]Ps 55:21; Jer 9:8; Mic 6:12
21 [a]Job 16:10; Ps 22:13 [b]Ps 40:15; 70:3
22 [a]Ex 3:7; Ps 10:14 [b]Ps 28:1 [c]Ps 10:1; 22:11; 38:21; 71:12
23 [a]Ps 7:6; 44:23; 59:4; 80:2

24 [a]Judge me, O LORD my God, according to Your
righteousness,
And [b]do not let them rejoice over me.
25 Do not let them say in their heart, "[a]Aha, our desire!"
Do not let them say, "We have [b]swallowed him up!"
26 Let [a]those be ashamed and humiliated altogether who
rejoice at my distress;
Let those be [b]clothed with shame and dishonor who
[c]magnify themselves over me.

27 Let them [a]shout for joy and rejoice, who favor [b]my
vindication;
And [c]let them say continually, "The LORD be magnified,
Who [d]delights in the prosperity of His servant."
28 And [a]my tongue shall declare Your righteousness
And Your praise all day long.

Psalm 36 Theme

For the choir director. *A Psalm* of David the servant of the LORD.

36 Transgression speaks to the ungodly within [1]his heart;
There is [a]no fear of God before his eyes.
2 For [1]it [a]flatters him in his *own* eyes
Concerning the discovery of his iniquity *and* the hatred
of it.
3 The [a]words of his mouth are wickedness and deceit;
He has [b]ceased to [1]be wise *and* to do good.
4 He [a]plans wickedness upon his bed;
He sets himself on a [b]path that is not good;
He [c]does not despise evil.

5 Your [a]lovingkindness, O LORD, [1]extends to the heavens,
Your faithfulness *reaches* to the skies.
6 Your [a]righteousness is like the [1]mountains of God;
Your [b]judgments are *like* a great deep.
O LORD, You [c]preserve man and beast.
7 How [a]precious is Your lovingkindness, O God!
And the children of men [b]take refuge in the shadow of
Your wings.
8 They [a]drink their fill of the [1]abundance of Your house;
And You give them to drink of the [b]river of Your delights.
9 For with You is the [a]fountain of life;
In Your light we see light.

10 O continue Your lovingkindness to [a]those who know You,
And Your [b]righteousness to the upright in heart.
11 Let not the foot of pride come upon me,
And let not the hand of the wicked drive me away.
12 There the doers of iniquity have fallen;
They have been thrust down and [a]cannot rise.

24 [a]Ps 9:4; 26:1; 43:1 [b]Ps 35:19

25 [a]Ps 35:21 [b]Ps 56:1; 124:3; Prov 1:12; Lam 2:16

26 [a]Ps 40:14 [b]Ps 109:29 [c]Job 19:5; Ps 38:16

27 [a]Ps 32:11 [b]Ps 9:4 [c]Ps 40:16; 70:4 [d]Ps 147:11; 149:4

28 [a]Ps 51:14; 71:15, 24

36:1 [1]Another reading is *my hea[rt]* [a]Rom 3:18

2 [1]Or *he flatters himself* [a]Deut 29:19; Ps 10:11; 49:18

3 [1]Or *understand to do good* [a]Ps 10:7; 12:2 [b]Ps 94:8; Jer 4:22

4 [a]Prov 4:16; Mic 2:1 [b]Is 65:2 [c]Ps 52:3; Rom 12:9

5 [1]Lit *is in* [a]Ps 57:10; 103:11; 108:4

6 [1]Or *mighty moun[tains]* [a]Ps 71:19 [b]Job 11:8; Ps 77:19; Rom 11:33 [c]Neh 9:6; Ps 104:14, 15; 145:16

7 [a]Ps 40:5; 139:17 [b]Ruth 2:12; Ps 17:8; 57:1; 91:4

8 [1]Lit *fatness* [a]Ps 63:5; 65:4; Is 25:6; Jer 31:12-14 [b]Job 20:17; Ps 46:4; Rev 22:1

9 [a]Jer 2:13

10 [a]Jer 22:16 [b]Ps 24:5

12 [a]Ps 140:10; Is 26:14

Psalm 37 Theme ____________________

A Psalm of David.

37 [a]Do not fret because of evildoers,
Be not [b]envious toward wrongdoers.
2 For they will [a]wither quickly like the grass
And [b]fade like the green herb.
3 [a]Trust in the LORD and do good;
[b]Dwell in the land and [1c]cultivate faithfulness.
4 [a]Delight yourself in the LORD;
And He will [b]give you the desires of your heart.
5 [a]Commit your way to the LORD,
Trust also in Him, and He will do it.
6 He will bring forth [a]your righteousness as the light
And your judgment [b]as the noonday.

7 [1]Rest in the LORD and [a]wait [2]patiently for Him;
[b]Do not fret because of him who [c]prospers in his way,
Because of the man who carries out wicked schemes.
8 Cease from anger and [a]forsake wrath;
Do not fret; *it leads* only to evildoing.
9 For [a]evildoers will be cut off,
But those who wait for the LORD, they will [b]inherit the land.
10 Yet [a]a little while and the wicked man will be no more;
And you will look carefully for [b]his place and he will not be *there.*
11 But [a]the humble will inherit the land
And will delight themselves in [b]abundant prosperity.

12 The wicked [a]plots against the righteous
And [b]gnashes at him with his teeth.
13 The Lord [a]laughs at him,
For He sees [b]his day is coming.
14 The wicked have drawn the sword and [a]bent their bow
To cast down the [b]afflicted and the needy,
To [c]slay those who are upright in conduct.
15 Their sword will enter their own heart,
And their [a]bows will be broken.

16 [a]Better is the little of the righteous
Than the abundance of many wicked.
17 For the [a]arms of the wicked will be broken,
But the LORD [b]sustains the righteous.
18 The LORD [a]knows the days of the [1]blameless,
And their [b]inheritance will be forever.
19 They will not be ashamed in the time of evil,
And [a]in the days of famine they will have abundance.
20 But the [a]wicked will perish;
And the enemies of the LORD will be like the [1]glory of the pastures,

37:1 [a]Prov 23:17; 24:19 [b]Ps 73:3; Prov 3:31
2 [a]Job 14:2; Ps 90:6; 92:7; James 1:11 [b]Ps 129:6
3 [1]Or *feed securely* or *feed on His faithfulness* [a]Ps 62:8 [b]Deut 30:20 [c]Is 40:11; Ezek 34:13, 14
4 [a]Job 22:26; Ps 94:19; Is 58:14 [b]Ps 21:2; 145:19; Matt 7:7, 8
5 [a]Ps 55:22; Prov 16:3; 1 Pet 5:7
6 [a]Ps 97:11; Is 58:8, 10; Mic 7:9 [b]Job 11:17
7 [1]Or *Be still* [2]Or *longingly* [a]Ps 40:1; 62:5; Lam 3:26 [b]Ps 37:1, 8 [c]Jer 12:1
8 [a]Eph 4:31; Col 3:8
9 [a]Ps 37:2, 22 [b]Ps 25:13; Prov 2:21; Is 57:13; 60:21; Matt 5:5
10 [a]Job 24:24 [b]Job 7:10; Ps 37:35, 36
11 [a]Matt 5:5 [b]Ps 72:7
12 [a]Ps 31:13, 20 [b]Ps 35:16
13 [a]Ps 2:4 [b]1 Sam 26:10; Job 18:20
14 [a]Ps 11:2; Lam 2:4 [b]Ps 35:10; 86:1 [c]Ps 11:2
15 [a]1 Sam 2:4; Ps 46:9
16 [a]Prov 15:16; 16:8
17 [a]Job 38:15; Ps 10:15; Ezek 30:21 [b]Ps 71:6; 145:14
18 [1]Lit *complete;* or *perfect* [a]Ps 1:6; 31:7 [b]Ps 37:27, 29
19 [a]Job 5:20; Ps 33:19
20 [1]I.e. flowers [a]Ps 73:27

They vanish—[b]like smoke they vanish away.
21 The wicked borrows and does not pay back,
But the righteous [a]is gracious and gives.
22 For [a]those blessed by Him will [b]inherit the land,
But those [c]cursed by Him will be cut off.

23 [a]The steps of a man are established by the LORD,
And He [b]delights in his way.
24 When [a]he falls, he will not be hurled headlong,
Because [b]the LORD is the One [1]who holds his hand.
25 I have been young and now I am old,
Yet [a]I have not seen the righteous forsaken
Or [b]his [1]descendants begging bread.
26 All day long [a]he is gracious and lends,
And [b]his [1]descendants are a blessing.

27 [a]Depart from evil and do good,
[1]So you will abide [b]forever.
28 For the LORD [a]loves [1]justice
And [b]does not forsake His godly ones;
They are [c]preserved forever,
But the [2d]descendants of the wicked will be cut off.
29 The righteous will [a]inherit the land
And [b]dwell in it forever.
30 The mouth of the righteous [a]utters wisdom,
And his tongue [b]speaks justice.
31 The [a]law of his God is in his heart;
His [b]steps do not slip.
32 The [a]wicked spies upon the righteous
And [b]seeks to kill him.
33 The LORD will [a]not leave him in his hand
Or [b]let him be condemned when he is judged.
34 [a]Wait for the LORD and keep His way,
And He will exalt you to inherit the land;
When the [b]wicked are cut off, you will see it.

35 I have [a]seen a wicked, violent man
Spreading himself like a [b]luxuriant [1]tree in its native soil.
36 Then [1]he passed away, and lo, he [a]was no more;
I sought for him, but he could not be found.
37 Mark the [1a]blameless man, and behold the [b]upright;
For the man of peace will have a [2c]posterity.
38 But transgressors will be altogether [a]destroyed;
The [1]posterity of the wicked will be [b]cut off.
39 But the [a]salvation of the righteous is from the LORD;
He is their strength [b]in time of trouble.
40 [a]The LORD helps them and delivers them;
He [b]delivers them from the wicked and saves them,
Because they [c]take refuge in Him.

20 [b]Ps 68:2; 102:3
21 [a]Ps 112:5, 9
22 [a]Prov 3:33 [b]Ps 37:9 [c]Job 5:3
23 [a]1 Sam 2:9; Ps 40:2; 66:9; 119:5 [b]Ps 147:11
24 [1]Or *who sustains him with His hand* [a]Ps 145:14; Prov 24:16; Mic 7:8 [b]Ps 147:6
25 [1]Lit *seed* [a]Ps 37:28; Is 41:17; Heb 13:5 [b]Ps 109:10
26 [1]Lit *seed* [a]Deut 15:8; Ps 37:21 [b]Ps 147:13
27 [1]Or *And dwell forever* [a]Ps 34:14 [b]Ps 37:18; 102:28
28 [1]Lit *judgment* [2]Lit *seed* [a]Ps 11:7; 33:5 [b]Ps 37:25 [c]Ps 31:23 [d]Ps 21:10; 37:9; Prov 2:22; Is 14:20
29 [a]Ps 37:9; Prov 2:21 [b]Ps 37:18
30 [a]Ps 49:3; Prov 10:13 [b]Ps 101:1; 119:13
31 [a]Deut 6:6; Ps 40:8; 119:11; Is 51:7; Jer 31:33 [b]Ps 26:1; 37:23
32 [a]Ps 10:8; 17:11 [b]Ps 37:14
33 [a]Ps 31:8; 2 Pet 2:9 [b]Ps 34:22; 109:31
34 [a]Ps 27:14; 37:9 [b]Ps 52:5, 6; 91:8
35 [1]Lit *native;* Heb obscure [a]Job 5:3; Jer 12:2 [b]Job 8:16
36 [1]Ancient versions read *I passed by* [a]Job 20:5; Ps 37:10
37 [1]Lit *complete;* or *perfect* [2]Lit *an end* [a]Ps 37:18 [b]Ps 7:10 [c]Is 57:1, 2
38 [1]Lit *end* [a]Ps 1:4-6; 37:20, 28 [b]Ps 37:9; 73:17
39 [a]Ps 3:8; 62:1 [b]Ps 9:9; 37:19
40 [a]Ps 54:4 [b]Ps 22:4; Is 31:5; Dan 3:17; 6:23 [c]1 Chr 5:20; Ps 34:22

Psalm 38 Theme ____________________

A Psalm of David, for a memorial.

38 O LORD, [a]rebuke me not in Your wrath,
And chasten me not in Your burning anger.
2 For Your [a]arrows have sunk deep into me,
And [b]Your hand has pressed down on me.
3 There is [a]no soundness in my flesh [b]because of Your indignation;
There is no health [c]in my bones because of my sin.
4 For my [a]iniquities are gone over my head;
As a heavy burden they weigh too much for me.
5 My [1]wounds grow foul *and* fester
Because of [a]my folly.
6 I am bent over and [a]greatly bowed down;
I [b]go mourning all day long.
7 For my loins are filled with [a]burning,
And there is [b]no soundness in my flesh.
8 I am [a]benumbed and [1]badly crushed;
I [2b]groan because of the [3]agitation of my heart.

9 Lord, all [a]my desire is [1]before You;
And my [b]sighing is not hidden from You.
10 My heart throbs, [a]my strength fails me;
And the [b]light of my eyes, even [1]that [2]has gone from me.
11 My [1a]loved ones and my friends stand aloof from my plague;
And my kinsmen [b]stand afar off.
12 Those who [a]seek my life [b]lay snares *for me;*
And those who [c]seek to injure me have [1]threatened destruction,
And they [d]devise treachery all day long.

13 But I, like a deaf man, do not hear;
And *I am* like a [a]mute man who does not open his mouth.
14 Yes, I am like a man who does not hear,
And in whose mouth are no arguments.
15 For [a]I [1]hope in You, O LORD;
You [b]will answer, O Lord my God.
16 For I said, "May they not rejoice over me,
Who, when my foot slips, [a]would magnify themselves against me."
17 For I am [a]ready to fall,
And [b]my [1]sorrow is continually before me.
18 For I [1a]confess my iniquity;
I am full of [b]anxiety because of my sin.
19 But my [a]enemies are vigorous *and* [1]strong,
And many are those who [b]hate me wrongfully.
20 And those who [a]repay evil for good,
They [b]oppose me, because I follow what is good.
21 Do not forsake me, O LORD;
O my God, [a]do not be far from me!

38:1 [a]Ps 6:1
2 [a]Job 6:4 [b]Ps 32:4
3 [a]Is 1:6 [b]Ps 102:10 [c]Job 33:19; Ps 6:2; 31:10
4 [a]Ezra 9:6; Ps 40:12
5 [1]Or *stripes* [a]Ps 69:5
6 [a]Ps 35:14 [b]Job 30:28; Ps 42:9; 43:2
7 [a]Ps 102:3 [b]Ps 38:3
8 [1]Or *greatly* [2]Lit *roar* [3]Lit *growling* [a]Lam 1:13, 20f; 2:11; 5:17 [b]Job 3:24; Ps 22:1; 32:3
9 [1]Or known *to You* [a]Ps 10:17 [b]Ps 6:6; 102:5
10 [1]Lit *they have* [2]Lit *is not with me* [a]Ps 31:10 [b]Ps 6:7; 69:3; 88:9
11 [1]Or *lovers* [a]Ps 31:11; 88:18 [b]Luke 23:49
12 [1]Lit *spoken* [a]Ps 54:3 [b]Ps 140:5 [c]Ps 35:4 [d]Ps 35:20
13 [a]Ps 39:2, 9
15 [1]Or *wait for* [a]Ps 39:7 [b]Ps 17:6
16 [a]Ps 35:26
17 [1]Lit *pain* [a]Ps 35:15 [b]Ps 13:2
18 [1]Or *declare* [a]Ps 32:5 [b]2 Cor 7:9, 10
19 [1]Or *numerous* [a]Ps 18:17 [b]Ps 35:19
20 [a]Ps 35:12 [b]Ps 109:5; 1 John 3:12
21 [a]Ps 22:19; 35:22

22 Make [a]haste to help me,
O Lord, [b]my salvation!

Psalm 39 Theme ______________________________

For the choir director, for +Jeduthun. A Psalm of David.

39 I said, "I will [a]guard my ways
That I [b]may not sin with my tongue;
I will guard [c]my mouth as with a muzzle
While the wicked are in my presence."
2 I was [a]mute [1]and silent,
I [2]refrained *even* from good,
And my [3]sorrow grew worse.
3 My [a]heart was hot within me,
While I was musing the fire burned;
Then I spoke with my tongue:
4 "LORD, make me to know [a]my end
And what is the extent of my days;
Let me know how [b]transient I am.
5 "Behold, You have made [a]my days *as* handbreadths,
And my [b]lifetime as nothing in Your sight;
Surely every man [1]at his best is [2]a mere [c]breath. [3]Selah.
6 "Surely every man [a]walks about as [1]a phantom;
Surely they make an [b]uproar for nothing;
He [c]amasses *riches* and does not know who will gather them.

7 "And now, Lord, for what do I wait?
My [a]hope is in You.
8 "[a]Deliver me from all my transgressions;
Make me not the [b]reproach of the foolish.
9 "I have become [a]mute, I do not open my mouth,
Because it is [b]You who have done *it.*
10 "[a]Remove Your plague from me;
Because of [b]the opposition of Your hand I am [1]perishing.
11 "With [a]reproofs You chasten a man for iniquity;
You [b]consume as a moth what is precious to him;
Surely [c]every man is a mere breath. Selah.

12 "[a]Hear my prayer, O LORD, and give ear to my cry;
Do not be silent [b]at my tears;
For I am [c]a stranger with You,
A [d]sojourner like all my fathers.
13 "[a]Turn Your gaze away from me, that I may [1]smile *again*
Before I depart and am no more."

Psalm 40 Theme ______________________________

For the choir director. A Psalm of David.

40 I [a]waited [1]patiently for the LORD;
And He inclined to me and [b]heard my cry.
2 He brought me up out of the [a]pit of destruction, out of the
[1]miry clay,

22 [a]Ps 40:13, 17 [b]Ps 27:1

39:1 +1 Chr 16:41 [a]1 Kin 2:4; 2 Kin 10:31; Ps 119:9 [b]Job 2:10; Ps 34:13; James 3:5-12 [c]Ps 141:3; James 3:2

2 [1]Lit *with silence* [2]Lit *kept silence* [3]Lit *pain* [a]Ps 38:13

3 [a]Ps 32:4; Jer 20:9; Luke 24:32

4 [a]Job 6:11; Ps 90:12; 119:84 [b]Ps 78:39; 103:14

5 [1]Lit *standing firm* [2]Or *altogether vanity* [3]*Selah* may mean: *Pause, Crescendo* or *Musical interlude* [a]Ps 89:47 [b]Ps 144:4 [c]Job 14:2; Ps 62:9; Eccl 6:12

6 [1]Lit *an image* [a]1 Cor 7:31; James 1:10, 11; 1 Pet 1:24 [b]Ps 127:2; Eccl 5:17 [c]Ps 49:10; Eccl 2:26; 5:14; Luke 12:20

7 [a]Ps 38:15

8 [a]Ps 51:9, 14; 79:9 [b]Ps 44:13; 79:4; 119:22

9 [a]Ps 39:2 [b]2 Sam 16:10; Job 2:10

10 [1]Or *wasting away* [a]Job 9:34; 13:21 [b]Ps 32:4

11 [a]Ezek 5:15; 2 Pet 2:16 [b]Job 13:28; Ps 90:7; Is 50:9 [c]Ps 39:5

12 [a]Ps 102:1; 143:1 [b]2 Kin 20:5; Ps 56:8 [c]Lev 25:23; 1 Chr 29:15; Ps 119:19; Heb 11:13; 1 Pet 2:11 [d]Gen 47:9

13 [1]Or *become cheerful* [a]Job 7:19; 10:20, 21; 14:6; Ps 102:24

40:1 [1]Or *intently* [a]Ps 25:5; 27:14; 37:7 [b]Ps 34:15

2 [1]Lit *mud of the mire* [a]Ps 69:2, 14; Jer 38:6

And [b]He set my feet upon a rock [c]making my footsteps firm.
3 He put a [a]new song in my mouth, a song of praise to our God;
Many will [b]see and fear
And will trust in the LORD.

4 How [a]blessed is the man who has made the LORD his trust,
And [b]has not [1]turned to the proud, nor to those who [c]lapse into falsehood.
5 Many, O LORD my God, are [a]the wonders which You have done,
And Your [b]thoughts toward us;
There is none to compare with You.
If I would declare and speak of them,
They [c]would be too numerous to count.

6 [1a]Sacrifice and meal offering You have not desired;
My ears You have [2]opened;
Burnt offering and sin offering You have not required.
7 Then I said, "Behold, I come;
In the scroll of the book it is [1]written of me.
8 [a]I delight to do Your will, O my God;
[b]Your Law is within my heart."

9 I have [a]proclaimed glad tidings of righteousness in the great congregation;
Behold, I will [b]not restrain my lips,
O LORD, [c]You know.
10 I have [a]not hidden Your righteousness within my heart;
I have [b]spoken of Your faithfulness and Your salvation;
I have not concealed Your lovingkindness and Your truth from the great congregation.

11 You, O LORD, will not withhold Your compassion from me;
[1]Your [a]lovingkindness and Your truth will continually preserve me.
12 For evils beyond number have [a]surrounded me;
My [b]iniquities have overtaken me, so that I am not able to see;
They are [c]more numerous than the hairs of my head,
And my [d]heart has [1]failed me.

13 [a]Be pleased, O LORD, to deliver me;
Make [b]haste, O LORD, to help me.
14 Let those be [a]ashamed and humiliated together
Who [b]seek my [1]life to destroy it;
Let those be turned back and dishonored
Who delight [2]in my hurt.
15 Let those [a]be [1]appalled because of their shame
Who [b]say to me, "Aha, aha!"
16 [a]Let all who seek You rejoice and be glad in You;
Let those who love Your salvation [b]say continually,
"The LORD be magnified!"

---

2 [b]Ps 27:5 [c]Ps 37:23

3 [a]Ps 32:7; 33:3 [b]Ps 52:6; 64:9

4 [1]Lit *regard* [a]Ps 34:8; 84:12 [b]Job 37:24 [c]Ps 125:5

5 [a]Job 5:9; Ps 136:4 [b]Ps 139:17; Is 55:8 [c]Ps 71:15; 139:18

6 [1]I.e. Blood sacrifice [2]Lit *dug;* or possibly *pierced* [a]1 Sam 15:22; Ps 51:16; Is 1:11; Jer 6:20; 7:22, 23; Amos 5:22; Mic 6:6-8; Heb 10:5-7

7 [1]Or *prescribed for*

8 [a]John 4:34 [b]Ps 37:31; Jer 31:33; 2 Cor 3:3

9 [a]Ps 22:22, 25 [b]Ps 119:13 [c]Josh 22:22; Ps 139:4

10 [a]Acts 20:20, 27 [b]Ps 89:1

11 [1]Or *May . . . preserve* [a]Ps 43:3; 57:3; 61:7; Prov 20:28

12 [1]Lit *forsaken* [a]Ps 18:5; 116:3 [b]Ps 38:4; 65:3 [c]Ps 69:4 [d]Ps 73:26

13 [a]Ps 70:1 [b]Ps 22:19; 71:12

14 [1]Or *soul* [2]Or *to injure me* [a]Ps 35:4, 26; 70:2; 71:13 [b]Ps 63:9

15 [1]Or *desolated* [a]Ps 70:3 [b]Ps 35:21; 70:3

16 [a]Ps 70:4 [b]Ps 35:27

17 Since [a]I am afflicted and needy,
[1b]Let the Lord be mindful of me.
You are my help and my deliverer;
Do not delay, O my God.

Psalm 41 Theme ____________________

For the choir director. A Psalm of David.

41 How blessed is he who [a]considers the [1]helpless;
The LORD will deliver him [b]in a day of [2]trouble.
2 The LORD will [a]protect him and keep him alive,
And he shall [1]be called [b]blessed upon the earth;
And [c]do not give him over to the desire of his enemies.
3 The LORD will sustain him upon his sickbed;
In his illness, You [1]restore him to health.

4 As for me, I said, "O LORD, be gracious to me;
[a]Heal my soul, for [b]I have sinned against You."
5 My enemies [a]speak evil against me,
"When will he die, and his name perish?"
6 And [1]when he comes to see *me,* he [a]speaks [2]falsehood;
His heart gathers wickedness to itself;
When he goes outside, he tells it.
7 All who hate me whisper together against me;
Against me they [a]devise my hurt, *saying,*
8 "A wicked thing is poured out [1]upon him,
That when he lies down, he will [a]not rise up again."
9 Even my [a]close friend in whom I trusted,
Who ate my bread,
Has lifted up his heel against me.

10 But You, O LORD, be gracious to me and [a]raise me up,
That I may repay them.
11 By this I know that [a]You are pleased with me,
Because [b]my enemy does not shout in triumph over me.
12 As for me, [a]You uphold me in my integrity,
And You set me [b]in Your presence forever.

13 [a]Blessed be the LORD, the God of Israel,
From everlasting to everlasting.
Amen and Amen.

BOOK 2

Psalm 42 Theme ____________________

For the choir director. A +Maskil of the sons of Korah.

42 As the deer [1]pants for the water brooks,
So my soul [1a]pants for You, O God.
2 My soul [a]thirsts for God, for the [b]living God;
When shall I come and [1c]appear before God?

17 [1]Or *The Lord is mindful* [a]Ps 70:5; 86:1; 109:22 [b]Ps 40:5; 1 Pet 5:7

41:1 [1]Or *poor* [2]Or *evil* [a]Ps 82:3, 4; Prov 14:21 [b]Ps 27:5; 37:19

2 [1]Or *be blessed* [a]Ps 37:28 [b]Ps 37:22 [c]Ps 27:12

3 [1]Lit *turn all his bed*

4 [a]Ps 6:2; 103:3; 147:3 [b]Ps 51:4

5 [a]Ps 38:12

6 [1]Or *if he* [2]Or *emptiness* [a]Ps 12:2; 62:4; Prov 26:24-26

7 [a]Ps 56:5

8 [1]Or *within* [a]Ps 71:10, 11

9 [a]2 Sam 15:12; Job 19:13, 19; Ps 55:12, 13, 20; Jer 20:10; Mic 7:5; Matt 26:23; Luke 22:21; John 13:18

10 [a]Ps 3:3

11 [a]Ps 37:23; 147:11 [b]Ps 25:2

12 [a]Ps 18:32; 37:17; 63:8 [b]Job 36:7; Ps 21:6

13 [a]Ps 72:18, 19; 89:52; 106:48; 150:6

42:1 +Possibly *Contemplative,* or *Didactic,* or *Skillful Psalm* [1]Lit *longs for* [a]Ps 119:131

2 [1]Some mss read *see the face of God* [a]Ps 63:1; 84:2; 143:6 [b]Josh 3:10; Ps 84:2; Jer 10:10; Dan 6:26; Matt 26:63; Rom 9:26; 1 Thess 1:9 [c]Ex 23:17; Ps 43:4; 84:7

3 My [a]tears have been my food day and night,
While *they* [b]say to me all day long, "Where is your God?"
4 These things I remember and I [a]pour out my soul within me.
For I [b]used to go along with the throng *and* [1]lead them in
procession to the house of God,
With the voice of [c]joy and thanksgiving, a multitude
keeping festival.

5 [a]Why are you [1b]in despair, O my soul?
And *why* have you become [c]disturbed within me?
[2d]Hope in God, for I shall [3]again praise [4]Him
For the [5e]help of His presence.
6 O my God, my soul is [1]in despair within me;
Therefore I [a]remember You from [b]the land of the Jordan
And the [2]peaks of [c]Hermon, from Mount Mizar.
7 Deep calls to deep at the sound of Your waterfalls;
All Your [a]breakers and Your waves have rolled over me.
8 The LORD will [a]command His lovingkindness in the daytime;
And His song will be with me [b]in the night,
A prayer to [c]the God of my life.

9 I will say to God [a]my rock, "Why have You forgotten me?
Why do I go [b]mourning [1]because of the [c]oppression of the
enemy?"
10 As a shattering of my bones, my adversaries revile me,
While they [a]say to me all day long, "Where is your God?"
11 [a]Why are you [1]in despair, O my soul?
And why have you become disturbed within me?
[2]Hope in God, for I shall yet praise Him,
The [3]help of my countenance and my God.

Psalm 43 Theme

43 [a]Vindicate me, O God, and [b]plead my case against
an ungodly nation;
[1]O deliver me from [c]the deceitful and unjust man!
2 For You are the [a]God of my strength; why have You
[b]rejected me?
Why do I go [c]mourning [1]because of the oppression of the
enemy?

3 O send out Your [a]light and Your truth, let them lead me;
Let them bring me to Your [b]holy hill
And to Your [c]dwelling places.
4 Then I will go to [a]the altar of God,
To God [1]my exceeding [b]joy;
And upon the [c]lyre I shall praise You, O God, my God.

5 [a]Why are you [1]in despair, O my soul?
And why are you disturbed within me?
[2]Hope in God, for I shall [3]again praise Him,
The [4]help of my countenance and my God.

---

3 [a]Ps 80:5; 102:9 [b]Ps 79:10; 115:2; Joel 2:17; Mic 7:10

4 [1]Or *move slowly with them* [a]1 Sam 1:15; Job 30:16; Ps 62:8; Lam 2:19 [b]Ps 55:14; 122:1; Is 30:29 [c]Ps 100:4

5 [1]Or *sunk down* [2]Or *Wait for* [3]Or *still* [4]Some ancient versions read *Him, the help of my countenance and my God* [5]Or *saving acts of* [a]Ps 42:11; 43:5 [b]Ps 38:6; Matt 26:38 [c]Ps 77:3 [d]Ps 71:14; Lam 3:24 [e]Ps 44:3

6 [1]Or *sunk down* [2]Lit *Hermons* [a]Ps 61:2 [b]2 Sam 17:22 [c]Deut 3:8

7 [a]Ps 69:1, 2; 88:7; Jon 2:3

8 [a]Ps 57:3; 133:3 [b]Job 35:10; Ps 16:7; 63:6; 77:6; 149:5 [c]Eccl 5:18; 8:15

9 [1]Or *while the enemy oppresses* [a]Ps 18:2 [b]Ps 38:6 [c]Ps 17:9

10 [a]Ps 42:3; Joel 2:17

11 [1]Or *sunk down* [2]Or *Wait for* [3]Or *saving acts of* [a]Ps 42:5; 43:5

43:1 [1]Or *May You* [a]Ps 26:1; 35:24 [b]1 Sam 24:15; Ps 35:1 [c]Ps 5:6; 38:12

2 [1]Or *while the enemy oppresses* [a]Ps 18:1; 28:7; 31:4 [b]Ps 44:9; 88:14 [c]Ps 42:9

3 [a]Ps 36:9 [b]Ps 2:6; 3:4; 42:4; 46:4 [c]Ps 84:1

4 [1]Lit *the gladness of my joy* [a]Ps 26:6 [b]Ps 21:6 [c]Ps 33:2; 49:4; 57:8; 71:22

5 [1]Or *sunk down* [2]Or *Wait for* [3]Or *still* [4]Or *saving acts of* [a]Ps 42:5, 11

Psalm 44 Theme ______________________________

For the choir director. A +Maskil of the sons of Korah.

44 O God, we have heard with our ears,
Our [a]fathers have told us
The [b]work that You did in their days,
In the [c]days of old.
2 You with Your own hand [a]drove out the nations;
Then You [b]planted them;
You [c]afflicted the peoples,
Then You [d]spread them abroad.
3 For by their own sword they [a]did not possess the land,
And their own arm did not save them,
But Your right hand and Your [b]arm and the [c]light of Your presence,
For You [d]favored them.

4 You are [a]my King, O God;
[b]Command [1]victories for Jacob.
5 Through You we will [a]push back our adversaries;
Through Your name we will [b]trample down those who rise up against us.
6 For I will [a]not trust in my bow,
Nor will my sword save me.
7 But You [a]have saved us from our adversaries,
And You have [b]put to shame those who hate us.
8 In God we have [a]boasted all day long,
And we will [b]give thanks to Your name forever. [1]Selah.

9 Yet You [a]have rejected *us* and brought us to [b]dishonor,
And [c]do not go out with our armies.
10 You cause us to [a]turn back from the adversary;
And those who hate us [b]have taken spoil for themselves.
11 You give us as [a]sheep [1]to be eaten
And have [b]scattered us among the nations.
12 You [a]sell Your people [1]cheaply,
And have not [2]profited by their sale.
13 You make us a [a]reproach to our neighbors,
A scoffing and a [b]derision to those around us.
14 You make us [a]a byword among the nations,
A [1][b]laughingstock among the peoples.
15 All day long my dishonor is before me
And [1]my [a]humiliation has overwhelmed me,
16 Because of the voice of him who [a]reproaches and reviles,
Because of the presence of the [b]enemy and the avenger.

17 All this has come upon us, but we have [a]not forgotten You,
And we have not [b]dealt falsely with Your covenant.
18 Our heart has not [a]turned back,
And our steps [b]have not deviated from Your way,
19 Yet You have [a]crushed us in a place of [b]jackals
And covered us with [c]the shadow of death.

44:1 +Possibly *Contemplative*, or *Didactic*, or *Skillful Psalm* [a]Ex 12:26, 27; Deut 6:20; Judg 6:13; Ps 78:3 [b]Ps 78:12 [c]Deut 32:7; Ps 77:5; Is 51:9; 63:9
2 [a]Josh 3:10; Neh 9:24; Ps 78:55; 80:8 [b]Ex 15:17; 2 Sam 7:10; Jer 24:6; Amos 9:15 [c]Ps 135:10-12 [d]Ps 80:9-11; Zech 2:6
3 [a]Deut 8:17, 18; Josh 24:12 [b]Ps 77:15 [c]Ps 4:6; 89:15 [d]Deut 4:37; 7:7, 8; 10:15; Ps 106:4
4 [1]Lit *salvation* [a]Ps 74:12 [b]Ps 42:8
5 [a]Deut 33:17; Ps 60:12; Dan 8:4 [b]Ps 108:13; Zech 10:5
6 [a]1 Sam 17:47; Ps 33:16; Hos 1:7
7 [a]Ps 136:24 [b]Ps 53:5
8 [1]*Selah* may mean: *Pause, Crescendo* or *Musical interlude* [a]Ps 34:2 [b]Ps 30:12
9 [a]Ps 43:2; 60:1, 10; 74:1; 89:38; 108:11 [b]Ps 69:19 [c]Ps 60:10; 108:11
10 [a]Lev 26:17; Josh 7:8, 12; Ps 89:43 [b]Ps 89:41
11 [1]Lit *for food* [a]Ps 44:22; Rom 8:36 [b]Lev 26:33; Deut 4:27; 28:64; Ps 106:27; Ezek 20:23
12 [1]Lit *for no wealth* [2]Or *set a high price on them* [a]Deut 32:30; Judg 2:14; 3:8; Is 52:3, 4; Jer 15:13
13 [a]Deut 28:37; Ps 79:4; 89:41 [b]Ps 80:6; Ezek 23:32
14 [1]Lit *shaking of the head* [a]Job 17:6; Ps 69:11; Jer 24:9 [b]2 Kin 19:21; Ps 109:25
15 [1]Lit *the shame of my face has covered me* [a]2 Chr 32:21; Ps 69:7
16 [a]Ps 74:10 [b]Ps 8:2
17 [a]Ps 78:7; 119:61, 83, 109, 141, 153, 176 [b]Ps 78:57
18 [a]Ps 78:57 [b]Job 23:11; Ps 119:51, 157
19 [a]Ps 51:8; 94:5 [b]Job 30:29; Is 13:22; Jer 9:11 [c]Job 3:5; Ps 23:4

20 [1]Lit *palms* [a]Ps 78:11 [b]Deut 6:14; Ps 81:9

21 [a]Ps 139:1, 2; Jer 17:10

22 [a]Rom 8:36 [b]Is 53:7; Jer 12:3

23 [a]Ps 7:6 [b]Ps 78:65 [c]Ps 77:7

24 [a]Job 13:24; Ps 88:14 [b]Ps 42:9; Lam 5:20

25 [a]Ps 119:25

26 [a]Ps 35:2 [b]Ps 6:4; 25:22

20 If we had [a]forgotten the name of our God
Or extended our [1]hands to [b]a strange god,
21 Would not God [a]find this out?
For He knows the secrets of the heart.
22 But [a]for Your sake we are killed all day long;
We are considered as [b]sheep to be slaughtered.
23 [a]Arouse Yourself, why [b]do You sleep, O Lord?
Awake, [c]do not reject us forever.
24 Why do You [a]hide Your face
And [b]forget our affliction and our oppression?
25 For our [a]soul has sunk down into the dust;
Our body cleaves to the earth.
26 [a]Rise up, be our help,
And [b]redeem us for the sake of Your lovingkindness.

Psalm 45 Theme ____

For the choir director; according to the +Shoshannim.
A •Maskil of the sons of Korah. A Song of Love.

45:1 +Or possibly *Lilies* •Possibly *Contemplative*, or *Didactic*, or *Skillful Psalm* [1]Lit *is astir* [2]Lit *am saying* [3]Lit *works* [4]Probably refers to Solomon as a type of Christ [a]Ezra 7:6

2 [1]Or *through* [a]Luke 4:22 [b]Ps 21:6

3 [1]Or *warrior* [a]Heb 4:12; Rev 1:16 [b]Is 9:6

4 [1]Or *fearful* [a]Zeph 2:3 [b]Ps 21:8

5 [a]Ps 18:14; 120:4; Is 5:28; 7:13 [b]Ps 92:9 [c]2 Sam 18:14

6 [a]Ps 93:2; Heb 1:8, 9 [b]Ps 98:9

7 [a]Ps 11:7; 33:5 [b]Ps 2:2

8 [a]Song 4:14; John 19:39 [b]Ps 150:4

9 [a]Song 6:8 [b]1 Kin 2:19 [c]1 Kin 9:28; Is 13:12

10 [a]Deut 21:13; Ruth 1:16, 17

11 [a]Gen 18:12; 1 Pet 3:6 [b]Eph 5:33

45 My heart [1]overflows with a good theme;
I [2]address my [3]verses to the [4]King;
My tongue is the pen of [a]a ready writer.
2 You are fairer than the sons of men;
[a]Grace is poured [1]upon Your lips;
Therefore God has [b]blessed You forever.

3 Gird [a]Your sword on *Your* thigh, O [1b]Mighty One,
In Your splendor and Your majesty!
4 And in Your majesty ride on victoriously,
For the cause of truth and [a]meekness *and* righteousness;
Let Your [b]right hand teach You [1]awesome things.
5 Your [a]arrows are sharp;
The [b]peoples fall under You;
Your arrows are [c]in the heart of the King's enemies.

6 [a]Your throne, O God, is forever and ever;
A scepter of [b]uprightness is the scepter of Your kingdom.
7 You have [a]loved righteousness and hated wickedness;
Therefore God, Your God, has [b]anointed You
With the oil of joy above Your fellows.
8 All Your garments are *fragrant with* [a]myrrh and aloes *and* cassia;
Out of ivory palaces [b]stringed instruments have made You glad.
9 Kings' daughters are among [a]Your noble ladies;
At Your [b]right hand stands the queen in [c]gold from Ophir.

10 Listen, O daughter, give attention and incline your ear:
[a]Forget your people and your father's house;
11 Then the King will desire your beauty.
Because He is your [a]Lord, [b]bow down to Him.

12 The daughter of [a]Tyre *will come* with a gift;
The [b]rich among the people will seek your favor.

13 The King's daughter is all glorious within;
Her clothing is [a]interwoven with gold.
14 She will be [a]led to the King [b]in embroidered work;
The [c]virgins, her companions who follow her,
Will be brought to You.
15 They will be led forth with gladness and rejoicing;
They will enter into the King's palace.

16 In place of your fathers will be your sons;
You shall make them princes in all the earth.
17 I will cause [a]Your name to be remembered in all generations;
Therefore the peoples [b]will give You thanks forever and ever.

Psalm 46 Theme

For the choir director. *A Psalm* of the sons of Korah, +set to Alamoth. A Song.

46 God is our [a]refuge and strength,
[1]A very [b]present help [c]in [2]trouble.
2 Therefore we will [a]not fear, though [b]the earth should change
And though [c]the mountains slip into the heart of the [1]sea;
3 Though its [a]waters roar *and* foam,
Though the mountains quake at its swelling pride. [1]Selah.

4 There is a [a]river whose streams make glad the [b]city of God,
The holy [c]dwelling places of the Most High.
5 God is [a]in the midst of her, she will not be moved;
God will [b]help her [1]when morning dawns.
6 The [1]nations [a]made an uproar, the kingdoms tottered;
He [2b]raised His voice, the earth [c]melted.
7 The LORD of hosts [a]is with us;
The God of Jacob is [b]our stronghold. Selah.

8 Come, [a]behold the works of the LORD,
[1]Who has wrought [b]desolations in the earth.
9 He [a]makes wars to cease to the end of the earth;
He [b]breaks the bow and cuts the spear in two;
He [c]burns the chariots with fire.
10 "[1]Cease *striving* and [a]know that I am God;
I will be [b]exalted among the [2]nations, I will be exalted in the earth."
11 The LORD of hosts is with us;
The God of Jacob is our stronghold. Selah.

12 [a]Ps 87:4 [b]Ps 22:29; 68:29; 72:10, 11; Is 49:23

13 [a]Ex 39:2, 3

14 [a]Song 1:4 [b]Judg 5:30; Ezek 16:10 [c]Ps 45:9

17 [a]Mal 1:11 [b]Ps 138:4

46:1 +Possibly *for soprano voices* [1]Or *Abundantly available for help* [2]Or *tight places* [a]Ps 14:6; 62:7, 8 [b]Deut 4:7; Ps 145:18 [c]Ps 9:9

2 [1]Lit *seas* [a]Ps 23:4; 27:1 [b]Ps 82:5 [c]Ps 18:7

3 [1]*Selah* may mean: *Pause, Crescendo* or *Musical interlude* [a]Ps 93:3, 4; Jer 5:22

4 [a]Ps 36:8; 65:9; Is 8:6; Rev 22:1 [b]Ps 48:1; 87:3; 101:8; Is 60:14; Rev 3:12 [c]Ps 43:3

5 [1]Lit *at the turning of the morning* [a]Deut 23:14; Is 12:6; Ezek 43:7, 9; Hos 11:9; Joel 2:27; Zech 2:5 [b]Ps 37:40; Is 41:14; Luke 1:54

6 [1]Or *Gentiles* [2]Lit *gave forth* [a]Ps 2:1, 2 [b]Ps 18:13; 68:33; Jer 25:30; Joel 2:11; Amos 1:2 [c]Amos 9:5; Mic 1:4; Nah 1:5

7 [a]Num 14:9; 2 Chr 13:12 [b]Ps 9:9; 48:3

8 [1]Or *Which He has wrought as desolations* [a]Ps 66:5 [b]Is 61:4; Jer 51:43

9 [a]Is 2:4; Mic 4:3 [b]1 Sam 2:4; Ps 76:3 [c]Is 9:5; Ezek 39:9

10 [1]Or *Let go, relax* [2]Or *Gentiles* [a]Ps 100:3 [b]Is 2:11, 17

47:1 [1]Or *a ringing cry* [a]Ps 98:8 [b]Ps 106:47
2 [a]Deut 7:21; Neh 1:5; Ps 66:3, 5; 68:35 [b]Mal 1:14
3 [a]Ps 18:47
4 [1]*Selah* may mean: *Pause, Crescendo* or *Musical interlude* [a]1 Pet 1:4 [b]Amos 6:8; 8:7; Nah 2:2
5 [1]Or *amid* [a]Ps 68:18 [b]Ps 98:6
6 [a]Ps 68:4 [b]Ps 89:18
7 [1]Heb *Maskil* [a]Zech 14:9 [b]1 Cor 14:15
8 [1]Or *has taken His seat* [a]1 Chr 16:31; Ps 22:28 [b]Ps 97:2
9 [1]Or *nobles* [2]Lit *has greatly exalted Himself* [a]Ps 72:11; 102:22; Is 49:7, 23 [b]Rom 4:11, 12 [c]Ps 89:18 [d]Ps 97:9

Psalm 47 Theme ____________________

For the choir director. A Psalm of the sons of Korah.

47 O [a]clap your hands, all peoples;
[b]Shout to God with the voice of [1]joy.
2 For the LORD Most High is to be [a]feared,
A [b]great King over all the earth.
3 He [a]subdues peoples under us
And nations under our feet.
4 He chooses our [a]inheritance for us,
The [b]glory of Jacob whom He loves. [1]Selah.

5 God has [a]ascended [1]with a shout,
The LORD, [1]with the [b]sound of a trumpet.
6 [a]Sing praises to God, sing praises;
Sing praises to [b]our King, sing praises.
7 For God is the [a]King of all the earth;
Sing praises [b]with a [1]skillful psalm.
8 God [a]reigns over the nations,
God [1]sits on [b]His holy throne.
9 The [1a]princes of the people have assembled themselves *as*
the [b]people of the God of Abraham,
For the [c]shields of the earth belong to God;
He [2]is [d]highly exalted.

48:1 [a]1 Chr 16:25; Ps 96:4; 145:3 [b]Ps 46:4 [c]Ps 2:6; 87:1; Is 2:3; Mic 4:1; Zech 8:3
2 [a]Ps 50:2 [b]Lam 2:15 [c]Matt 5:35
3 [a]Ps 46:7
4 [a]2 Sam 10:6-19
5 [1]Lit *were hurried away* [a]Ex 15:15
6 [1]Lit *Trembling* [a]Is 13:8
7 [a]Jer 18:17 [b]1 Kin 22:48 [c]1 Kin 10:22; Ezek 27:25
8 [1]*Selah* may mean: *Pause, Crescendo* or *Musical interlude* [a]Ps 87:5
9 [a]Ps 26:3; 40:10
10 [a]Deut 28:58; Josh 7:9; Mal 1:11 [b]Ps 65:1, 2; 100:1 [c]Is 41:10

Psalm 48 Theme ____________________

A Song; a Psalm of the sons of Korah.

48 [a]Great is the LORD, and greatly to be praised,
In the [b]city of our God, His [c]holy mountain.
2 [a]Beautiful in elevation, [b]the joy of the whole earth,
Is Mount Zion *in* the far north,
The [c]city of the great King.
3 God, in her palaces,
Has made Himself known as a [a]stronghold.

4 For, lo, the [a]kings assembled themselves,
They passed by together.
5 They saw *it,* then they were amazed;
They were [a]terrified, they [1]fled in alarm.
6 [1]Panic seized them there,
Anguish, as of [a]a woman in childbirth.
7 With the [a]east wind
You [b]break the [c]ships of Tarshish.
8 As we have heard, so have we seen
In the city of the LORD of hosts, in the city of our God;
God will [a]establish her forever. [1]Selah.

9 We have thought on [a]Your lovingkindness, O God,
In the midst of Your temple.
10 As is Your [a]name, O God,
So is Your [b]praise to the ends of the earth;
Your [c]right hand is full of righteousness.

11 Let Mount [a]Zion be glad,
Let the [a]daughters of Judah rejoice
Because of Your judgments.
12 Walk about Zion and go around her;
Count her [a]towers;
13 Consider her [a]ramparts;
Go through her palaces,
That you may [b]tell *it* to the next generation.
14 For [1]such is God,
Our God forever and ever;
He will [a]guide us [2]until death.

Psalm 49 Theme ____________________

For the choir director. A Psalm of the sons of Korah.

49 [a]Hear this, all peoples;
Give ear, all [b]inhabitants of the world,
2 Both [a]low and high,
Rich and poor together.
3 My mouth will [a]speak wisdom,
And the meditation of my heart *will be* [b]understanding.
4 I will incline my ear to [a]a proverb;
[b]I will [1]express my [c]riddle on the harp.

5 Why should I [a]fear in days of adversity,
When the iniquity of my [1]foes surrounds me,
6 Even those who [a]trust in their wealth
And boast in the abundance of their riches?
7 No man can by any means [a]redeem *his* brother
Or give to God a [b]ransom for him—
8 For [a]the redemption of [1]his soul is costly,
And he should cease *trying* forever—
9 That he should [a]live on eternally,
That he should not [1b]undergo decay.

10 For he sees *that even* [a]wise men die;
The [b]stupid and the senseless alike perish
And [c]leave their wealth to others.
11 Their [1a]inner thought is *that* their houses [b]are forever
And their dwelling places to all generations;
They have [c]called their lands after their own names.
12 But [a]man in *his* [1]pomp will not endure;
He is like the [2]beasts that [3]perish.

13 This is the [a]way of those who are foolish,
And of those after them who [b]approve their words. [1]Selah.
14 As sheep they are appointed [a]for [1]Sheol;
Death shall be their shepherd;
And the [b]upright shall rule over them in the morning,
And their form shall be for [1]Sheol [c]to consume
[2]So that they have no habitation.

11 [a]Ps 97:8

12 [a]Neh 3:1, 11, 25-27

13 [a]Ps 122:7 [b]Ps 78:5-7

14 [1]Lit *this* [2]Lit *upon;* some mss and the Gr read *forever* [a]Ps 23:4; Is 58:11

49:1 [a]Ps 78:1; Is 1:2; Mic 1:2 [b]Ps 33:8

2 [a]Ps 62:9

3 [a]Ps 37:30 [b]Ps 119:130

4 [1]Lit *open up* [a]Ps 78:2 [b]2 Kin 3:15 [c]Num 12:8

5 [1]Lit *supplanters* [a]Ps 23:4; 27:1

6 [a]Job 31:24; Ps 52:7; Prov 11:28; Mark 10:24

7 [a]Matt 25:8, 9 [b]Job 36:18, 19

8 [1]Lit *their* [a]Matt 16:26

9 [1]Or *see corruption* or *the pit* [a]Ps 22:29 [b]Ps 16:10; 89:48

10 [a]Eccl 2:16 [b]Ps 92:6; 94:8 [c]Ps 39:6; Eccl 2:18, 21; Luke 12:20

11 [1]Some versions read *graves are their houses* [a]Ps 64:6 [b]Ps 10:6 [c]Gen 4:17; Deut 3:14

12 [1]Lit *honor* [2]Or *animals* [3]Lit *are destroyed* [a]Ps 49:20

13 [1]*Selah* may mean: *Pause, Crescendo* or *Musical interlude* [a]Jer 17:11 [b]Ps 49:18

14 [1]I.e. the nether world [2]Lit *Away from his habitation* [a]Ps 9:17 [b]Dan 7:18; Mal 4:3; 1 Cor 6:2; Rev 2:26 [c]Job 24:19

15 [1]Lit *hand* [2]I.e. the nether world [a]Ps 16:10; 56:13; Hos 13:14 [b]Gen 5:24; Ps 16:11; 73:24

16 [1]Or *wealth* [a]Ps 37:7

17 [1]Or *wealth* [a]Ps 17:14; 1 Tim 6:7

18 [1]Lit *his soul* [a]Deut 29:19; Ps 10:3, 6; Luke 12:19

19 [1]Lit *You;* or *It* [a]Gen 15:15 [b]Job 33:30; Ps 56:13

20 [1]Lit *honor* [2]Or *animals* [3]Lit *are destroyed* [a]Ps 49:12 [b]Eccl 3:19

50:1 +1 Chr 15:17; 2 Chr 29:30 [a]Josh 22:22 [b]Ps 113:3

2 [a]Ps 48:2; Lam 2:15 [b]Deut 33:2; Ps 80:1; 94:1

3 [a]Ps 96:13 [b]Lev 10:2; Num 16:35; Ps 97:3; Dan 7:10 [c]Ps 18:12, 13

4 [a]Deut 4:26; 31:28; 32:1; Is 1:2

5 [a]Ps 30:4; 37:28; 52:9 [b]Ex 24:7; 2 Chr 6:11; Ps 25:10 [c]Ps 50:8

6 [1]*Selah* may mean: *Pause, Crescendo* or *Musical interlude* [a]Ps 89:5; 97:6 [b]Ps 75:7; 96:13

7 [1]Or *to* [a]Ps 49:1; 81:8 [b]Ex 20:2; Ps 48:14

8 [a]Ps 40:6; 51:16; Is 1:11; Hos 6:6

9 [a]Ps 69:31

10 [a]Ps 104:24

11 [1]Or *in My mind;* lit *with Me* [a]Matt 6:26

12 [1]Lit *its fullness* [a]Ex 19:5; Deut 10:14; Ps 24:1; 1 Cor 10:26

13 [1]Lit *strong ones* [a]Ps 50:9

14 [a]Ps 27:6; 69:30; 107:22; 116:17; Hos 14:2; Rom 12:1; Heb 13:15 [b]Num 30:2; Deut 23:21; Ps 22:25; 56:12; 61:8; 65:1; 76:11

15 [a]Ps 91:15; 107:6, 13; Zech 13:9 [b]Ps 81:7 [c]Ps 22:23

15 But God will [a]redeem my soul from the [1]power of [2]Sheol,
For [b]He will receive me. Selah.

16 Do not be afraid [a]when a man becomes rich,
When the [1]glory of his house is increased;
17 For when he dies he will [a]carry nothing away;
His [1]glory will not descend after him.
18 Though while he lives he [a]congratulates [1]himself—
And though *men* praise you when you do well for yourself—
19 [1]He shall [a]go to the generation of his fathers;
They will never see [b]the light.
20 [a]Man in *his* [1]pomp, yet without understanding,
Is [b]like the [2]beasts that [3]perish.

Psalm 50 Theme ______________________

A Psalm of +Asaph.

50 [a]The Mighty One, God, the LORD, has spoken,
And summoned the earth [b]from the rising of the sun
to its setting.
2 Out of Zion, [a]the perfection of beauty,
God [b]has shone forth.
3 May our God [a]come and not keep silence;
[b]Fire devours before Him,
And it is very [c]tempestuous around Him.
4 He [a]summons the heavens above,
And the earth, to judge His people:
5 "Gather My [a]godly ones to Me,
Those who have made a [b]covenant with Me by [c]sacrifice."
6 And the [a]heavens declare His righteousness,
For [b]God Himself is judge. [1]Selah.

7 "[a]Hear, O My people, and I will speak;
O Israel, I will testify [1]against you;
I am God, [b]your God.
8 "I do [a]not reprove you for your sacrifices,
And your burnt offerings are continually before Me.
9 "I shall take no [a]young bull out of your house
Nor male goats out of your folds.
10 "For [a]every beast of the forest is Mine,
The cattle on a thousand hills.
11 "I know every [a]bird of the mountains,
And everything that moves in the field is [1]Mine.
12 "If I were hungry I would not tell you,
For the [a]world is Mine, and [1]all it contains.
13 "Shall I eat the flesh of [1a]bulls
Or drink the blood of male goats?
14 "Offer to God [a]a sacrifice of thanksgiving
And [b]pay your vows to the Most High;
15 [a]Call upon Me in the day of trouble;
I shall [b]rescue you, and you will [c]honor Me."

16 But to the wicked God says,
"What right have you to tell of My statutes
And to take [a]My covenant in your mouth?
17 "For you [a]hate discipline,
And you [b]cast My words behind you.
18 "When you see a thief, you [1a]are pleased with him,
And [2]you [b]associate with adulterers.
19 "You [1a]let your mouth loose in evil
And your [b]tongue frames deceit.
20 "You sit and [a]speak against your brother;
You slander your own mother's son.
21 "These things you have done and [a]I kept silence;
You thought that I was just like you;
I will [b]reprove you and state *the case* in order before your eyes.

22 "Now consider this, you who [a]forget God,
Or I will [b]tear *you* in pieces, and there will be none to deliver.
23 "He who [a]offers a sacrifice of thanksgiving honors Me;
And to him who [1b]orders *his* way *aright*
I shall [c]show the salvation of God."

Psalm 51 Theme ____________

For the choir director. A Psalm of David, when +Nathan the prophet came to him, after he had gone in to Bathsheba.

51 [a]Be gracious to me, O God, according to Your lovingkindness;
According to the greatness of [b]Your compassion [c]blot out my transgressions.
2 [a]Wash me thoroughly from my iniquity
And [b]cleanse me from my sin.
3 For [1]I [a]know my transgressions,
And my sin is ever before me.
4 [a]Against You, You only, I have sinned
And done what is [b]evil in Your sight,
So that [c]You [1]are justified [2]when You speak
And [3]blameless when You judge.

5 Behold, I was [a]brought forth in iniquity,
And in sin my mother conceived me.
6 Behold, You desire [a]truth in the [1]innermost being,
And in the hidden part You will [b]make me know wisdom.
7 [1]Purify me [a]with hyssop, and I shall be clean;
[2]Wash me, and I shall be [b]whiter than snow.
8 [1]Make me to hear [a]joy and gladness,
Let the [b]bones which You have broken rejoice.
9 [a]Hide Your face from my sins
And blot out all my iniquities.

16 [a]Is 29:13

17 [a]Prov 5:12; 12:1; Rom 2:21, 22 [b]1 Kin 14:9; Neh 9:26

18 [1]Some ancient versions read *run together* [2]Lit *your part is with* [a]Rom 1:32 [b]1 Tim 5:22

19 [1]Lit *send* [a]Ps 10:7 [b]Ps 36:3; 52:2

20 [a]Job 19:18; Matt 10:21

21 [a]Eccl 8:11; Is 42:14; 57:11 [b]Ps 90:8

22 [a]Job 8:13; Ps 9:17 [b]Ps 7:2

23 [1]Lit *sets* [a]Ps 50:14 [b]Ps 85:13 [c]Ps 91:16

51:1 +2 Sam 12:1 [a]Ps 4:1; 109:26 [b]Ps 69:16; 106:45 [c]Ps 51:9; Is 43:25; 44:22; Acts 3:19; Col 2:14

2 [a]Ps 51:7; Is 1:16; 4:4; Jer 4:14; Acts 22:16; Rev 1:5 [b]Jer 33:8; Ezek 36:33; Heb 9:14; 1 John 1:7, 9

3 [1]Or *I myself know* [a]Is 59:12

4 [1]Or *may be in the right* [2]Many mss read *in Your words* [3]Lit *pure* [a]Gen 20:6; 39:9; 2 Sam 12:13; Ps 41:4 [b]Luke 15:21 [c]Rom 3:4

5 [a]Job 14:4; 15:14; Ps 58:3; Eph 2:3

6 [1]Or *inward parts* [a]Job 38:36; Ps 15:2 [b]Prov 2:6; Eccl 2:26; James 1:5

7 [1]Or *May You purify . . . that I may be clean* [2]Or *May You wash* [a]Ex 12:22; Lev 14:4; Num 19:18; Heb 9:19 [b]Is 1:18

8 [1]Or *May You make* [a]Is 35:10; Joel 1:16 [b]Ps 35:10

9 [a]Jer 16:17

10 [a]Create [1]in me a [b]clean heart, O God,
And renew [2]a [c]steadfast spirit within me.
11 [a]Do not cast me away from Your presence
And do not take Your [b]Holy Spirit from me.
12 Restore to me the [a]joy of Your salvation
And sustain me with a [b]willing spirit.
13 *Then* I will [a]teach transgressors Your ways,
And sinners will [1]be [b]converted to You.

14 Deliver me from [a]bloodguiltiness, O God, [b]the God of my salvation;
Then my [c]tongue will joyfully sing of Your righteousness.
15 O Lord, [1a]open my lips,
That my mouth may [b]declare Your praise.
16 For You [a]do not delight in sacrifice, otherwise I would give it;
You are not pleased with burnt offering.
17 The sacrifices of God are a [a]broken spirit;
A broken and a contrite heart, O God, You will not despise.

18 [a]By Your favor do good to Zion;
[1b]Build the walls of Jerusalem.
19 Then You will delight in [1a]righteous sacrifices,
In [b]burnt offering and whole burnt offering;
Then [2]young bulls will be offered on Your altar.

Psalm 52 Theme ______________________

For the choir director. A +Maskil of David, •when Doeg the Edomite came and told Saul and said to him, "David has come to the house of Ahimelech."

52 Why do you [a]boast in evil, O mighty man?
The [b]lovingkindness of God *endures* all day long.
2 Your tongue devises [a]destruction,
Like a [b]sharp razor, [c]O worker of deceit.
3 You [a]love evil more than good,
[b]Falsehood more than speaking what is right. [1]Selah.
4 You love all words that devour,
O [a]deceitful tongue.

5 [1]But God will break you down forever;
He will snatch you up and [a]tear you away from *your* tent,
And [b]uproot you from the [c]land of the living. Selah.
6 The righteous will [a]see and fear,
And will [b]laugh at him, *saying,*
7 "Behold, the man who would not make God his refuge,
But [a]trusted in the abundance of his riches
And [b]was strong in [1]his *evil* desire."

8 But as for me, I am like a [a]green olive tree in the house of God;
I [b]trust in the lovingkindness of God forever and ever.

10 [1]Lit *for* [2]Or *an upright* [a]Ezek 18:31; Eph 2:10 [b]Ps 24:4; Matt 5:8; Acts 15:9 [c]Ps 78:37
11 [a]2 Kin 13:23; 24:20; Jer 7:15 [b]Is 63:10, 11
12 [a]Ps 13:5 [b]Ps 110:3
13 [1]Or *turn back* [a]Acts 9:21, 22 [b]Ps 22:27
14 [a]2 Sam 12:9; Ps 26:9 [b]Ps 25:5 [c]Ps 35:28; 71:15
15 [1]Or *may You open* [a]Ex 4:15 [b]Ps 9:14
16 [a]1 Sam 15:22; Ps 40:6
17 [a]Ps 34:18
18 [1]Or *May You build* [a]Ps 69:35; Is 51:3 [b]Ps 102:16; 147:2
19 [1]Or *sacrifices of righteousness* [2]Lit *they will offer young bulls* [a]Ps 4:5 [b]Ps 66:13, 15
52:1 +Possibly *Contemplative,* or *Didactic,* or *Skillful Psalm* •1 Sam 22:9 [a]Ps 94:4 [b]Ps 52:8
2 [a]Ps 5:9 [b]Ps 57:4; 59:7 [c]Ps 101:7
3 [1]*Selah* may mean: *Pause, Crescendo* or *Musical interlude* [a]Ps 36:4 [b]Ps 58:3; Jer 9:5
4 [a]Ps 120:3
5 [1]Or *Also* [a]Is 22:18, 19 [b]Prov 2:22 [c]Ps 27:13
6 [a]Ps 37:34; 40:3 [b]Job 22:19
7 [1]Or *his destruction* [a]Ps 49:6 [b]Ps 10:6
8 [a]Ps 92:12; 128:3; Jer 11:16 [b]Ps 13:5

9 I will [a]give You thanks forever, because You have done *it,*
And I will wait on Your name, [b]for *it is* good, in the
presence of Your godly ones.

Psalm 53 Theme ____________________

For the choir director; according to +Mahalath. A •Maskil of David.

53 [a]The fool has said in his heart, "There is no God,"
They are corrupt, and have committed abominable
injustice;
[b]There is no one who does good.
2 God has looked down from heaven upon the sons of men
To see if there is [a]anyone who [1]understands,
Who [b]seeks after God.
3 [a]Every one of them has turned aside; together they have
become corrupt;
There is no one who does good, not even one.

4 Have the workers of wickedness [a]no knowledge,
Who eat up My people *as though* they ate bread
And have not called upon God?
5 There they were in great [1]fear [a]*where* no [1]fear had been;
For God [b]scattered the bones of [2]him who encamped
against you;
You [c]put *them* to shame, because [d]God had rejected them.
6 Oh, that [a]the salvation of Israel [1]would come out of Zion!
When God [2]restores His captive people,
[3]Let Jacob rejoice, let Israel be glad.

Psalm 54 Theme ____________________

For the choir director; on stringed instruments. A +Maskil of David, •when the Ziphites came and said to Saul, "Is not David hiding himself among us?"

54 Save me, O God, by [a]Your name,
And [1]vindicate me by [b]Your power.
2 [a]Hear my prayer, O God;
[b]Give ear to the words of my mouth.
3 For strangers have [a]risen against me
And [b]violent men have [c]sought my [1]life;
They have [d]not set God before them. [2]Selah.

4 Behold, [a]God is my helper;
The Lord is [1]the [b]sustainer of my soul.
5 [1]He will [a]recompense the evil to [2]my foes;
[3b]Destroy them [c]in Your [4]faithfulness.

6 [1a]Willingly I will sacrifice to You;
I will give [b]thanks to Your name, O LORD, for it is good.
7 For [1]He has [a]delivered me from all [2]trouble,
And my eye has [b]looked *with satisfaction* upon my enemies.

---

9 [a]Ps 30:12 [b]Ps 54:6

53:1 +I.e. sickness, a sad tone •Possibly *Contemplative,* or *Didactic,* or *Skillful Psalm* [a]Ps 10:4; 14:1-7; 53:1-6 [b]Rom 3:10

2 [1]Or *acts wisely* [a]Rom 3:11 [b]2 Chr 15:2

3 [a]Rom 3:12

4 [a]Jer 4:22

5 [1]Or *dread* [2]Or possibly *those* [a]Lev 26:17, 36; Prov 28:1 [b]Ps 141:7; Jer 8:1, 2; Ezek 6:5 [c]Ps 44:7 [d]2 Kin 17:20; Jer 6:30; Lam 5:22

6 [1]Lit *would be* [2]Or *restores the fortunes of His people* [3]Or *Jacob will rejoice, Israel will be glad* [a]Ps 14:7

54:1 +Possibly *Contemplative,* or *Didactic,* or *Skillful Psalm* •1 Sam 23:19; 26:1 [1]Lit *judge* [a]Ps 20:1 [b]2 Chr 20:6

2 [a]Ps 17:6; 55:1 [b]Ps 5:1

3 [1]Or *soul* [2]*Selah* may mean: *Pause, Crescendo* or *Musical interlude* [a]Ps 86:14 [b]Ps 18:48; 86:14; 140:1, 4, 11 [c]1 Sam 20:1; 25:29; Ps 40:14; 63:9; 70:2 [d]Ps 36:1

4 [1]Lit *as those who sustain* [a]Ps 30:10; 37:40; 118:7 [b]Ps 37:17, 24; 41:12; 51:12; 145:14; Is 41:10

5 [1]Lit *The evil will return* [2]Or *those who lie in wait for me* [3]Or *Put to silence* [4]Or *truth* [a]Ps 94:23 [b]Ps 143:12 [c]Ps 89:49; 96:13; Is 42:3

6 [1]Or *With a freewill offering* [a]Num 15:3; Ps 116:17 [b]Ps 50:14

7 [1]Or *it;* i.e. His name [2]Or *distress* [a]Ps 34:6 [b]Ps 59:10; 92:11; 112:8; 118:7

Psalm 55 Theme ______________________________

For the choir director; on stringed instruments.
A +Maskil of David.

55 [a]Give ear to my prayer, O God;
And [b]do not hide Yourself from my supplication.
2 Give [a]heed to me and answer me;
I am restless in my [b]complaint and [1c]am surely distracted,
3 Because of the voice of the enemy,
Because of the [a]pressure of the wicked;
For they [b]bring down [1]trouble upon me
And in anger they [c]bear a grudge against me.

4 My [a]heart is in anguish within me,
And the terrors of [b]death have fallen upon me.
5 Fear and [a]trembling come upon me,
And [1b]horror has overwhelmed me.
6 I said, "Oh, that I had wings like a dove!
I would fly away and [1a]be at rest.
7 "Behold, I would wander far away,
I would [a]lodge in the wilderness. [1]Selah.
8 "I would hasten to my place of refuge
From the [a]stormy wind *and* tempest."

9 [1]Confuse, O Lord, [a]divide their tongues,
For I have seen [b]violence and strife in the city.
10 Day and night they go around her upon her walls,
And iniquity and mischief are in her midst.
11 [a]Destruction is in her midst;
[b]Oppression and deceit do not depart from her [1]streets.

12 For it is [a]not an enemy who reproaches me,
Then I could bear *it;*
Nor is it one who hates me who [b]has exalted himself
against me,
Then I could hide myself from him.
13 But it is you, a man [1]my equal,
My [a]companion and my [2b]familiar friend;
14 We who had sweet [1]fellowship together
[a]Walked in the house of God in the throng.
15 Let [1]death come [a]deceitfully upon them;
Let them [b]go down alive to [2]Sheol,
For evil is in their dwelling, in their midst.

16 As for me, I shall [a]call upon God,
And the LORD will save me.
17 [a]Evening and [b]morning and at [c]noon, I will complain and
murmur,
And He will hear my voice.
18 He will [a]redeem my soul in peace [1]from the battle *which is*
against me,
For they are [b]many *who strive* with me.

55:1 +Possibly *Contemplative,* or *Didactic,* or *Skillful Psalm* [a]Ps 54:2; 61:1; 86:6 [b]Ps 27:9

2 [1]Or *I must moan* [a]Ps 66:19; 86:6, 7 [b]1 Sam 1:16; Job 9:27; Ps 64:1; 77:3; 142:2 [c]Is 38:14; 59:11; Ezek 7:16

3 [1]Or *wickedness* [a]Ps 17:9 [b]2 Sam 16:7, 8 [c]Ps 71:11; 143:3

4 [a]Ps 38:8 [b]Ps 18:4, 5; 116:3

5 [1]Lit *shuddering* [a]Ps 119:120 [b]Job 21:6; Is 21:4; Ezek 7:18

6 [1]Lit *settle down* [a]Job 3:13

7 [1]*Selah* may mean: *Pause, Crescendo* or *Musical interlude* [a]1 Sam 23:14

8 [a]Is 4:6; 25:4; 29:6

9 [1]Lit *Swallow up* [a]Gen 11:9 [b]Ps 11:5; Jer 6:7

11 [1]Or *plaza* [a]Ps 5:9 [b]Ps 10:7; 17:9

12 [a]Ps 41:9 [b]Ps 35:26

13 [1]Lit *according to my valuation* [2]Or *acquaintance* [a]2 Sam 15:12 [b]Job 19:14; Ps 41:9

14 [1]Lit *counsel;* or *intimacy* [a]Ps 42:4

15 [1]Another reading is *desolations be upon them* [2]I.e. the nether world [a]Ps 64:7; Prov 6:15; Is 47:11; 1 Thess 5:3 [b]Num 16:30, 33

16 [a]Ps 57:2, 3

17 [a]Ps 141:2; Dan 6:10; Acts 3:1; 10:3, 30 [b]Ps 5:3; 88:13; 92:2 [c]Acts 10:9

18 [1]Or *so that none may approach me* [a]Ps 103:4 [b]Ps 56:2

19 God will [a]hear and [1]answer them—
Even the one [b]who [2]sits enthroned from of old— Selah.
With whom there [3]is no change,
And who [c]do not fear God.
20 He has put forth his hands against [a]those who were at
peace with him;
He has [1b]violated his covenant.
21 His [1]speech was [a]smoother than butter,
But his heart was war;
His words were [a]softer than oil,
Yet they were drawn [b]swords.

22 [a]Cast [1]your burden upon the LORD and He will sustain you;
[b]He will never allow the righteous to [2c]be shaken.
23 But You, O God, will bring them down to the [1a]pit of
destruction;
[b]Men of bloodshed and deceit will [c]not live out half their days.
But I will [d]trust in You.

Psalm 56 Theme ____________________

For the choir director; according to +Jonath elem rehokim.
A •Mikhtam of David, ^when the Philistines seized him in Gath.

56 Be gracious to me, O God, for man has [1a]trampled
upon me;
[2]Fighting all day long he [b]oppresses me.
2 My foes have [1a]trampled upon me all day long,
For [2]they are many who [b]fight proudly against me.
3 [1]When I am [a]afraid,
[2]I will [b]put my trust in You.
4 [a]In God, whose word I praise,
In God I have put my trust;
I shall not be afraid.
[b]What can *mere* [1]man do to me?
5 All day long they [1a]distort my words;
All their [2b]thoughts are against me for evil.
6 They [1a]attack, they lurk,
They [b]watch my [2]steps,
As they have [c]waited *to take* my [3]life.
7 Because of wickedness, [1a]cast them forth,
In anger [b]put down the peoples, O God!

8 You [a]have taken account of my wanderings;
Put my [b]tears in Your bottle.
Are *they* not in [c]Your book?
9 Then my enemies will [a]turn back [b]in the day when I call;
This I know, [1]that [c]God is for me.
10 In God, *whose* word I praise,
In the LORD, *whose* word I praise,
11 In God I have put my [1]trust, I shall not be afraid.
What can man do to me?

19 [1]Or *afflict* [2]Or *abides from* [3]Lit *are no changes* [a]Ps 78:59 [b]Deut 33:27; Ps 90:2; 93:2 [c]Ps 36:1

20 [1]Lit *profaned* [a]Ps 7:4; 120:7 [b]Num 30:2; Ps 89:34

21 [1]Lit *mouth* [a]Ps 12:2; 28:3; Prov 5:3, 4 [b]Ps 57:4; 59:7

22 [1]Or *what He has given you* [2]Or *totter* [a]Ps 37:5; 1 Pet 5:7 [b]Ps 37:24 [c]Ps 15:5; 112:6

23 [1]Or *lowest pit* [a]Ps 73:18; Is 38:17; Ezek 28:8 [b]Ps 5:6 [c]Job 15:32; Prov 10:27 [d]Ps 25:2; 56:3

56:1 +Or *The silent dove of those who are far off*, or, *The dove of the distant terebinths* •Possibly *Epigrammatic Poem*, or *Atonement Psalm* ^1 Sam 21:10, 11 [1]Or *snapped at* [2]Or *A fighting man* [a]Ps 57:3 [b]Ps 17:9

2 [1]Or *snapped at* [2]Or *many are fighting* [a]Ps 35:25; 57:3; 124:3 [b]Ps 35:1

3 [1]Lit *In the day* [2]Or *I am one who puts* [a]Ps 55:4, 5 [b]Ps 11:1

4 [1]Lit *flesh* [a]Ps 56:10, 11 [b]Ps 118:6; Heb 13:6

5 [1]Or *trouble my affairs* [2]Or *purposes* [a]2 Pet 3:16 [b]Ps 41:7

6 [1]Or *stir up strife* [2]Lit *heels* [3]Lit *soul* [a]Ps 59:3; 140:2; Is 54:15 [b]Ps 17:11 [c]Ps 71:10

7 [1]Or *will they have escape?* [a]Ps 36:12; Prov 19:5; Ezek 17:15; Rom 2:3 [b]Ps 55:23

8 [a]Ps 139:3 [b]2 Kin 20:5; Ps 39:12 [c]Mal 3:16

9 [1]Or *because* [a]Ps 9:3 [b]Ps 102:2 [c]Ps 41:11; 118:6; Rom 8:31

11 [1]Or *trust without fear*

12 Your [a]vows are *binding* upon me, O God;
I will render thank offerings to You.
13 For You have [a]delivered my soul from death,
[1]Indeed [b]my feet from stumbling,
So that I may [c]walk before God
In the [d]light of the [2]living.

12 [a]Ps 50:14

13 [1]Or *have You* not *delivered* [2]Or *life* [a]Ps 33:19; 49:15; 86:13 [b]Ps 116:8 [c]Ps 116:9 [d]Job 33:30

Psalm 57 Theme ______________________________

For the choir director; *set to* +Al-tashheth. A •Mikhtam of David,
Δwhen he fled from Saul in the cave.

57 Be gracious to me, O God, be gracious to me,
For my soul [a]takes refuge in You;
And in the [b]shadow of Your wings I will take refuge
Until destruction [c]passes by.
2 I will cry to God Most High,
To God who [a]accomplishes *all things* for me.
3 He will [a]send from heaven and save me;
He reproaches him who [1b]tramples upon me. [2]Selah.
God will send forth His [c]lovingkindness and His [3]truth.

57:1 +Lit *Do Not Destroy* •Possibly, *Epigrammatic Poem* or *Atonement Psalm* Δ1 Sam 22:1; 24:3 [a]Ps 2:12; 34:22 [b]Ruth 2:12; Ps 17:8; 36:7; 63:7; 91:4 [c]Is 26:20

2 [a]Ps 138:8

3 [1]Or *snaps at* [2]*Selah* may mean: *Pause, Crescendo* or *Musical interlude* [3]Or *faithfulness* [a]Ps 18:16; 144:5, 7 [b]Ps 56:2 [c]Ps 25:10; 40:11

4 My soul is among [a]lions;
I must lie among those who breathe forth fire,
Even the sons of men, whose [b]teeth are spears and arrows
And their [c]tongue a sharp sword.
5 [a]Be exalted above the heavens, O God;
Let Your glory *be* above all the earth.
6 They have [1]prepared a [a]net for my steps;
My soul is [b]bowed down;
They [c]dug a pit before me;
They *themselves* have [d]fallen into the midst of it. Selah.

4 [a]Ps 35:17; 58:6 [b]Prov 30:14 [c]Ps 55:21; 59:7; 64:3; Prov 12:18

5 [a]Ps 57:11; 108:5

6 [1]Or *spread* [a]Ps 10:9; 31:4; 35:7; 140:5 [b]Ps 145:14 [c]Ps 7:15 [d]Prov 26:27; 28:10; Eccl 10:8

7 [a]My [b]heart is steadfast, O God, my heart is steadfast;
I will sing, yes, I will sing praises!
8 Awake, [a]my glory!
Awake, [b]harp and lyre!
I will awaken the dawn.
9 [a]I will give thanks to You, O Lord, among the peoples;
I will sing praises to You among the [1]nations.
10 For Your [a]lovingkindness is great to the heavens
And Your [1]truth to the clouds.
11 [a]Be exalted above the heavens, O God;
Let Your glory *be* above all the earth.

7 [a]Ps 57:7-11; 108:1-5 [b]Ps 112:7

8 [a]Ps 16:9; 30:12 [b]Ps 150:3

9 [1]Lit *peoples* [a]Ps 108:3

10 [1]Or *faithfulness* [a]Ps 36:5; 103:11; 108:4

11 [a]Ps 57:5; 108:5

Psalm 58 Theme ______________________________

For the choir director; *set to* +Al-tashheth. A •Mikhtam of David.

58 Do you indeed [1]speak righteousness, O [2]gods?
Do you [a]judge [3]uprightly, O sons of men?
2 No, in heart you [a]work unrighteousness;
On earth you [b]weigh out the violence of your hands.

58:1 +Lit *Do Not Destroy* •Possibly *Epigrammatic Poem* or *Atonement Psalm* [1]Another reading is *speak righteousness in silence* [2]Or *mighty ones* or *judges* [3]Or *uprightly the sons of men* [a]Ps 82:2

2 [a]Mal 3:15 [b]Ps 94:20; Is 10:1

3 The wicked are estranged [a]from the womb;
These who speak lies [b]go astray from [1]birth.
4 They have venom like the [a]venom of a serpent;
Like a deaf cobra that stops up its ear,
5 So that it [a]does not hear the voice of [1b]charmers,
Or a skillful caster of spells.

6 O God, [a]shatter their teeth in their mouth;
Break out the fangs of the young lions, O LORD.
7 Let them [a]flow away like water that runs off;
When he [1b]aims his arrows, let them be as [2]headless shafts.
8 *Let them be* as a snail which [1]melts away as it goes along,
Like the [a]miscarriages of a woman which never see the
sun.
9 Before your [a]pots can feel *the fire of* thorns
He will [b]sweep them away with a whirlwind, the [1]green
and the burning alike.

10 The [a]righteous will rejoice when he [b]sees the vengeance;
He will [c]wash his feet in the blood of the wicked.
11 And men will say, "Surely there is a [1a]reward for the
righteous;
Surely there is a God who [b]judges [2]on earth!"

Psalm 59 Theme ______________________________

For the choir director; *set to* [+]Al-tashheth. A [•]Mikhtam of David, [Δ]when Saul sent *men* and they watched the house in order to kill him.

59 [a]Deliver me from my enemies, O my God;
[1b]Set me *securely* on high away from those who rise
up against me.
2 Deliver me from [a]those who do iniquity
And save me from [b]men of bloodshed.
3 For behold, they [a]have [1]set an ambush for my [2]life;
[3]Fierce men [4a]launch an attack against me,
[b]Not for my transgression nor for my sin, O LORD,
4 [1a]For no guilt of *mine,* they run and set themselves against
me.
[b]Arouse Yourself to [2]help me, and see!
5 You, [a]O LORD God of hosts, the God of Israel,
Awake to [1b]punish all the nations;
[c]Do not be gracious to any *who are* treacherous in iniquity.
[2]Selah.

6 They [a]return at evening, they howl like a [b]dog,
And go around the city.
7 Behold, they [a]belch forth with their mouth;
[b]Swords are in their lips,
For, *they say,* "[c]Who hears?"
8 But You, O LORD, [a]laugh at them;
You [b]scoff at all the nations.

3 [1]Lit *the womb* [a]Ps 51:5; Is 48:8 [b]Ps 53:3

4 [a]Deut 32:33; Ps 140:3

5 [1]Or *whisperers* [a]Jer 8:17 [b]Eccl 10:11

6 [a]Job 4:10; Ps 3:7

7 [1]Lit *bends* [2]Lit *though they were cut off* [a]Josh 2:11; 7:5; Ps 112:10; Is 13:7; Ezek 21:7 [b]Ps 64:3

8 [1]I.e. secretes slime [a]Job 3:16; Eccl 6:3

9 [1]Lit *living* [a]Ps 118:12; Eccl 7:6 [b]Job 27:21; Ps 83:15; Prov 10:25

10 [a]Job 22:19; Ps 32:11; 64:10; 107:42 [b]Deut 32:43; Ps 91:8; Jer 11:20; 20:12 [c]Ps 68:23

11 [1]Lit *fruit* [2]Or *in* [a]Ps 18:20; 19:11; Is 3:10; Luke 6:23, 35 [b]Ps 9:8; 67:4; 75:7; 94:2

59:1 [+]Lit *Do Not Destroy* [•]Possibly *Epigrammatic Poem* or *Atonement Psalm* [Δ]1 Sam 19:11 [1]Or *May You put me in an inaccessibly high place* [a]Ps 143:9 [b]Ps 20:1; 69:29

2 [a]Ps 28:3; 36:12; 53:4; 92:7; 94:16 [b]Ps 26:9; 139:19; Prov 29:10

3 [1]Or *lain in wait* [2]Lit *soul* [3]Or *Strong* [4]Or *stir up strife* [a]Ps 56:6 [b]1 Sam 24:11; Ps 7:3, 4; 69:4

4 [1]Lit *Without guilt* [2]Lit *meet* [a]Ps 35:19 [b]Ps 7:6; 35:23

5 [1]Lit *visit* [2]*Selah* may mean: *Pause, Crescendo* or *Musical interlude* [a]Ps 69:6; 80:4; 84:8 [b]Ps 9:5; Is 26:14 [c]Is 2:9; Jer 18:23

6 [a]Ps 59:14 [b]Ps 22:16

7 [a]Ps 94:4; Prov 15:2, 28 [b]Ps 57:4; Prov 12:18 [c]Job 22:13; Ps 10:11; 73:11; 94:7

8 [a]Ps 37:13; Prov 1:26 [b]Ps 2:4

9 *Because of* [1]his [a]strength I will watch for You,
For God is my [b]stronghold.
10 [1]My God [a]in His lovingkindness will meet me;
God will let me [b]look *triumphantly* upon [2]my foes.
11 Do not slay them, [a]or my people will forget;
[1b]Scatter them by Your power, and bring them down,
O Lord, [c]our shield.
12 [1]*On account of* the [a]sin of their mouth *and* the words of
their lips,
Let them even be [b]caught in their pride,
And on account of [c]curses and [2]lies which they utter.
13 [1a]Destroy *them* in wrath, [1]destroy *them* that they may be
no more;
That *men* may [b]know that God [2]rules in Jacob
To the ends of the earth. Selah.
14 They [a]return at evening, they howl like a dog,
And go around the city.
15 They [a]wander about [1]for food
And [2]growl if they are not satisfied.

16 But as for me, I shall [a]sing of Your strength;
Yes, I shall [b]joyfully sing of Your lovingkindness in the
[c]morning,
For You have been my [d]stronghold
And a [e]refuge in the day of my distress.
17 [a]O my strength, I will sing praises to You;
For God is my [b]stronghold, the [1]God who shows me
lovingkindness.

Psalm 60 Theme ______________________________

For the choir director; according to [+]Shushan Eduth.
A [•]Mikhtam of David, to teach; [Δ]when he struggled with Aram-naharaim and with Aram-zobah, and Joab returned, and smote twelve thousand of Edom in the Valley of Salt.

60 O God, [a]You have rejected us. You have [1b]broken us;
You have been [c]angry; O, [d]restore us.
2 You have made the [1a]land quake, You have split it open;
[b]Heal its breaches, for it totters.
3 You have [1a]made Your people experience hardship;
You have given us [2]wine to [b]drink that makes us stagger.
4 You have given a [a]banner to those who fear You,
That it may be displayed because of the truth. [1]Selah.
5 [a]That Your [b]beloved may be delivered,
[c]Save with Your right hand, and answer [1]us!

6 God has spoken in His [1a]holiness:
"I will exult, I will portion out [b]Shechem and measure out
the valley of [c]Succoth.
7 "[a]Gilead is Mine, and Manasseh is Mine;
[b]Ephraim also is the [1]helmet of My head;
Judah is My [2c]scepter.

9 [1]Many mss and some ancient versions read *My strength* [a]Ps 18:17 [b]Ps 9:9; 62:2
10 [1]Many mss and some ancient versions read *The God of my lovingkindness* [2]Lit *those who lie in wait for me* [a]Ps 21:3 [b]Ps 54:7
11 [1]Or *Make them wander* [a]Deut 4:9; 6:12 [b]Ps 106:27; 144:6; Is 33:3 [c]Ps 84:9
12 [1]Or *The sin of their mouth is the word of their lips,* [2]Lit *lying* [a]Prov 12:13 [b]Zeph 3:11 [c]Ps 10:7
13 [1]Lit *Bring to an end* [2]Or *is Ruler* [a]Ps 104:35 [b]Ps 83:18
14 [a]Ps 59:6
15 [1]Or *to devour* [2]Another reading is *tarry all night* [a]Job 15:23
16 [a]Ps 21:13 [b]Ps 101:1 [c]Ps 5:3; 88:13 [d]Ps 59:9 [e]2 Sam 22:3; Ps 46:1
17 [1]Lit *God of my lovingkindness* [a]Ps 59:9 [b]Ps 59:10
60:1 [+]Lit *The lily of testimony* [•]Possibly, *Epigrammatic Poem* or *Atonement Psalm* [Δ]2 Sam 8:3, 13; 1 Chr 18:3, 12 [1]Or *broken out upon us* [a]Ps 44:9 [b]2 Sam 5:20 [c]Ps 79:5 [d]Ps 80:3
2 [1]Or *earth* [a]Ps 18:7 [b]2 Chr 7:14; Is 30:26
3 [1]Lit *caused Your people to see* [2]Lit *wine of staggering* [a]Ps 66:12; 71:20 [b]Ps 75:8; Is 51:17, 22; Jer 25:15
4 [1]*Selah* may mean: *Pause, Crescendo* or *Musical interlude* [a]Ps 20:5; Is 5:26; 11:12; 13:2
5 [1]Some authorities read *me* [a]Ps 60:5-12; 108:6-13 [b]Deut 33:12; Ps 127:2; Is 5:1; Jer 11:15 [c]Ps 17:7
6 [1]Or *sanctuary* [a]Ps 89:35 [b]Gen 12:6; 33:18; Josh 17:7 [c]Gen 33:17; Josh 13:27
7 [1]Lit *protection* [2]Or *lawgiver* [a]Josh 13:31 [b]Deut 33:17 [c]Gen 49:10

8 "[a]Moab is My washbowl;
Over [b]Edom I shall throw My shoe;
Shout loud, O [c]Philistia, because of Me!"

9 Who will bring me into the besieged city?
Who [1]will lead me to Edom?
10 Have not You Yourself, O God, [a]rejected us?
And [b]will You not go forth with our armies, O God?
11 O give us help against the adversary,
For [a]deliverance [1]by man is in vain.
12 [1]Through God we shall [a]do valiantly,
And it is He who will [b]tread down our adversaries.

Psalm 61 Theme ______________________

For the choir director; on a stringed instrument. *A Psalm* of David.

61 [a]Hear my cry, O God;
[b]Give heed to my prayer.
2 From the [a]end of the earth I call to You when my heart is [b]faint;
Lead me to [c]the rock that is higher than I.
3 For You have been a [a]refuge for me,
A [b]tower of strength [1]against the enemy.
4 Let me [1a]dwell in Your tent forever;
Let me [b]take refuge in the shelter of Your wings. [2]Selah.

5 For You have heard my [a]vows, O God;
You have given *me* the inheritance of those who [b]fear Your name.
6 You will [1a]prolong the king's [2]life;
His years will be as many generations.
7 He will [1]abide [a]before God forever;
Appoint [b]lovingkindness and truth that they may preserve him.
8 So I will [a]sing praise to Your name forever,
That I may [b]pay my vows day by day.

Psalm 62 Theme ______________________

For the choir director; +according to Jeduthun. A Psalm of David.

62 [a]My soul *waits* in silence for God only;
From Him [b]is my salvation.
2 He only is my [a]rock and my salvation,
My [b]stronghold; I shall not be greatly shaken.

3 How long will you assail a man,
That you may murder *him,* all of you,
Like a [a]leaning wall, like a tottering fence?
4 They have counseled only to thrust him down from his high position;
They [a]delight in falsehood;

8 [a]2 Sam 8:2 [b]2 Sam 8:14 [c]2 Sam 8:1

9 [1]Or *has led*

10 [a]Ps 60:1; 108:11 [b]Josh 7:12; Ps 44:9

11 [1]Lit *of* [a]Ps 146:3

12 [1]Or *In* or *With* [a]Num 24:18; Ps 118:16 [b]Ps 44:5; Is 63:3

61:1 [a]Ps 64:1 [b]Ps 86:6

2 [a]Ps 42:6 [b]Ps 77:3 [c]Ps 18:2; 94:22

3 [1]Lit *from* [a]Ps 62:7 [b]Ps 59:9; Prov 18:10

4 [1]Or *sojourn* [2]*Selah* may mean: *Pause, Crescendo* or *Musical interlude* [a]Ps 23:6; 27:4 [b]Ps 17:8; 91:4

5 [a]Job 22:27; Ps 56:12 [b]Deut 28:58; Neh 1:11; Ps 86:11; 102:15; Is 59:19; Mal 2:5; 4:2

6 [1]Lit *add days to* [2]Lit *days* [a]Ps 21:4

7 [1]Or *sit enthroned* [a]Ps 41:12 [b]Ps 40:11

8 [a]Judg 5:3; Ps 30:4; 33:2; 71:22 [b]Ps 65:1; Is 19:21

62:1 +Cf 1 Chr 16:41; 25:1; Ps 39 and 77 titles [a]Ps 33:20 [b]Ps 37:39

2 [a]Ps 89:26 [b]Ps 59:17; 62:6

3 [a]Is 30:13

4 [a]Ps 4:2

They [b]bless with [1]their mouth,
But inwardly they curse. [2]Selah.

5 My soul, [a]wait in silence for God only,
For my hope is from Him.
6 He only is [a]my rock and my salvation,
My stronghold; I shall not be shaken.
7 On God my [a]salvation and my glory *rest;*
The rock of my strength, my [b]refuge is in God.
8 [a]Trust in Him at all times, O people;
[b]Pour out your heart before Him;
God is a refuge for us. Selah.

9 Men of [a]low degree are only [b]vanity and men of rank are a
[c]lie;
In the [d]balances they go up;
They are together lighter than breath.
10 [a]Do not trust in oppression
And do not [1]vainly hope in [b]robbery;
If riches increase, [c]do not set *your* heart *upon them.*

11 [1]Once God has [a]spoken;
[2]Twice I have heard this:
That [b]power belongs to God;
12 And lovingkindness [a]is Yours, O Lord,
For You [b]recompense a man according to his work.

Psalm 63 Theme ______________________________

A Psalm of David, +when he was in the wilderness of Judah.

63 O God, [a]You are my God; I shall seek You [1]earnestly;
My soul [b]thirsts for You, my flesh [2]yearns for You,
In a [c]dry and weary land where there is no water.
2 Thus I have [a]seen You in the sanctuary,
To see Your power and Your glory.
3 Because Your [a]lovingkindness is better than life,
My lips will praise You.
4 So I will bless You [a]as long as I live;
I will [b]lift up my hands in Your name.
5 My soul is [a]satisfied as with [1]marrow and fatness,
And my mouth offers [b]praises with joyful lips.

6 When I remember You [a]on my bed,
I meditate on You in the [b]night watches,
7 For [a]You have been my help,
And in the [b]shadow of Your wings I sing for joy.
8 My soul [a]clings [1]to You;
Your [b]right hand upholds me.

9 But those who [a]seek my [1]life to destroy it,
Will go into the [2b]depths of the earth.

4 [1]Lit *his* [2]*Selah* may mean: *Pause, Crescendo* or *Musical interlude* [b]Ps 28:3; 55:21
5 [a]Ps 62:1
6 [a]Ps 62:2
7 [a]Ps 85:9; Jer 3:23 [b]Ps 46:1
8 [a]Ps 37:3, 5; 52:8; Is 26:4 [b]1 Sam 1:15; Ps 42:4; Lam 2:19
9 [a]Ps 49:2 [b]Job 7:16; Ps 39:5; Is 40:17 [c]Ps 116:11 [d]Is 40:15
10 [1]Lit *become vain in robbery* [a]Is 30:12 [b]Is 61:8; Ezek 22:29; Nah 3:1 [c]Job 31:25; Ps 49:6; 52:7; Mark 10:24; Luke 12:15; 1 Tim 6:10
11 [1]Or *One thing* [2]Or *These two things I have heard* [a]Job 33:14; 40:5 [b]Ps 59:17; Rev 19:1
12 [a]Ps 86:5; 103:8; 130:7 [b]Job 34:11; Ps 28:4; Jer 17:10; Matt 16:27; Rom 2:6; 1 Cor 3:8; Rev 2:23
63:1 +1 Sam 22:5; 23:14 [1]Lit *early* [2]Lit *faints* [a]Ps 118:28 [b]Ps 42:2; 84:2; Matt 5:6 [c]Ps 143:6
2 [a]Ps 27:4
3 [a]Ps 69:16
4 [a]Ps 104:33; 146:2 [b]Ps 28:2; 143:6
5 [1]Lit *fat* [a]Ps 36:8 [b]Ps 71:23
6 [a]Ps 4:4 [b]Ps 16:7; 42:8; 119:55
7 [a]Ps 27:9 [b]Ps 17:8
8 [1]Lit *after* [a]Num 32:12; Deut 1:36; Hos 6:3 [b]Ps 18:35; 41:12
9 [1]Lit *soul* [2]Lit *lowest places* [a]Ps 40:14 [b]Ps 55:15

10 [1]They will be [2a]delivered over to the power of the sword;
They will be a [3b]prey for foxes.
11 But the [a]king will rejoice in God;
Everyone who [b]swears by Him will glory,
For the [c]mouths of those who speak lies will be stopped.

Psalm 64 Theme ______________________

For the choir director. A Psalm of David.

64 Hear my voice, O God, in [a]my [1]complaint;
[b]Preserve my life from dread of the enemy.
2 Hide me from the [a]secret counsel of evildoers,
From the tumult of [b]those who do iniquity,
3 Who [a]have sharpened their tongue like a sword.
They [b]aimed bitter speech *as* their arrow,
4 To [a]shoot [1]from concealment at the blameless;
Suddenly they shoot at him, and [b]do not fear.
5 They [1]hold fast to themselves an evil purpose;
They [2]talk of [a]laying snares secretly;
They say, "[b]Who can see them?"
6 They [1]devise injustices, *saying,*
"We are [2]ready with a well-conceived plot";
For the [3a]inward thought and the heart of a man are [4]deep.

7 But [a]God [1]will shoot at them with an arrow;
Suddenly [2]they will be wounded.
8 So [1]they [2]will [a]make him stumble;
[b]Their own tongue is against them;
All who see them will [c]shake the head.
9 Then all men [1]will [a]fear,
And they [2]will [b]declare the work of God,
And [3]will consider [4]what He has done.
10 The righteous man will be [a]glad in the LORD and will [b]take refuge in Him;
And all the upright in heart will glory.

Psalm 65 Theme ______________________

For the choir director. A Psalm of David. A Song.

65 There will be silence [1]before You, *and* praise in Zion, O God,
And to You the [a]vow will be performed.
2 O You who hear prayer,
To You [a]all [1]men come.
3 [1a]Iniquities prevail against me;
As for our transgressions, You [2b]forgive them.
4 How [a]blessed is the one whom You [b]choose and bring near *to You*
To dwell in Your courts.
We will be [c]satisfied with the goodness of Your house,
Your holy temple.

10 [1]Lit *They will pour him out* [2]Lit *poured out by* [3]Lit *portion* [a]Jer 18:21; Ezek 35:5 [b]Lam 5:18

11 [a]Ps 21:1 [b]Deut 6:13; Is 45:23; 65:16 [c]Job 5:16; Ps 107:42; Rom 3:19

64:1 [1]Or *concern* [a]Ps 55:2 [b]Ps 140:1

2 [a]Ps 56:6 [b]Ps 59:2

3 [a]Ps 140:3 [b]Ps 58:7

4 [1]Lit *in* [a]Ps 10:8; 11:2 [b]Ps 55:19

5 [1]Lit *make firm* [2]Lit *tell of* [a]Ps 140:5 [b]Job 22:13; Ps 10:11

6 [1]Or *search out* [2]Lit *complete* [3]Or *inward part* [4]Or *unsearchable* [a]Ps 49:11

7 [1]Or *shot* [2]Or *they were wounded;* lit *their wounds occurred* [a]Ps 7:12, 13

8 [1]Or *they make their tongue a stumbling for themselves* [2]Or *made* [a]Ps 9:3 [b]Prov 12:13; 18:7 [c]Ps 22:7; 44:14; Jer 18:16; 48:27; Lam 2:15

9 [1]Or *feared* [2]Or *declared* [3]Or *considered* [4]Lit *His work* [a]Ps 40:3 [b]Jer 51:10

10 [a]Job 22:19; Ps 32:11 [b]Ps 11:1; 25:20

65:1 [1]Lit *to* [a]Ps 116:18

2 [1]Lit *flesh* [a]Ps 86:9; 145:21; Is 66:23

3 [1]Lit *Words of iniquities* [2]Lit *cover over, atone for* [a]Ps 38:4; 40:12 [b]Ps 79:9

4 [a]Ps 33:12; 84:4 [b]Ps 4:3 [c]Ps 36:8

5 By [a]awesome *deeds* You answer us in righteousness,
O [b]God of our salvation,
You who are the trust of all the [c]ends of the earth and of
the farthest [1d]sea;
6 Who [a]establishes the mountains by His strength,
Being [b]girded with might;
7 Who [a]stills the roaring of the seas,
The roaring of their waves,
And the [b]tumult of the peoples.
8 They who dwell in the [a]ends *of the earth* stand in awe of
Your signs;
You make the [1]dawn and the sunset shout for joy.

9 You visit the earth and [a]cause it to overflow;
You greatly [b]enrich it;
The [1c]stream of God is full of water;
You prepare their [d]grain, for thus You prepare [2]the earth.
10 You water its furrows abundantly,
You [1]settle its ridges,
You soften it [a]with showers,
You bless its growth.
11 You have crowned the year [1]with Your [2a]bounty,
And Your [3]paths [b]drip *with* fatness.
12 [a]The pastures of the wilderness drip,
And the [b]hills gird themselves with rejoicing.
13 The meadows are [a]clothed with flocks
And the valleys are [b]covered with grain;
They [c]shout for joy, yes, they sing.

*Psalm 66 Theme*______________________________

For the choir director. A Song. A Psalm.

66 [a]Shout joyfully to God, all the earth;
2 Sing the [a]glory of His name;
Make His [b]praise glorious.
3 Say to God, "How [a]awesome are Your works!
Because of the greatness of Your power Your enemies will
[1b]give feigned obedience to You.
4 "[a]All the earth will worship You,
And will [b]sing praises to You;
They will sing praises to Your name." [1]Selah.

5 [a]Come and see the works of God,
Who is [b]awesome in *His* deeds toward the sons of men.
6 He [a]turned the sea into dry land;
They passed through [b]the river on foot;
There let us [c]rejoice in Him!
7 He [a]rules by His might forever;
His [b]eyes keep watch on the nations;
Let not the rebellious [c]exalt themselves. Selah.

5 [1]Or *seas* [a]Ps 45:4; 66:3 [b]Ps 85:4 [c]Ps 22:27; 48:10 [d]Ps 107:23
6 [a]Ps 95:4 [b]Ps 93:1
7 [a]Ps 89:9; 93:3, 4; 107:29; Matt 8:26 [b]Ps 2:1; 74:23; Is 17:12, 13
8 [1]Lit *the outgoings of the morning and evening* [a]Ps 2:8; 139:9; Is 24:16
9 [1]Or *channel* [2]Lit *it* [a]Lev 26:4; Job 5:10; Ps 68:9; 104:13; 147:8; Jer 5:24 [b]Ps 104:24 [c]Ps 46:4 [d]Ps 104:14; 147:14
10 [1]Or *smooth* [a]Deut 32:2; Ps 72:6; 147:8
11 [1]Lit *of* [2]Or *goodness* [3]I.e. wagon tracks [a]Ps 104:28 [b]Job 36:28; Ps 147:14
12 [a]Job 38:26, 27; Joel 2:22 [b]Ps 98:8; Is 55:12
13 [a]Ps 144:13; Is 30:23 [b]Ps 72:16 [c]Ps 98:8; Is 44:23; 55:12
66:1 [a]Ps 81:1; 95:1; 98:4; 100:1
2 [a]Ps 79:9; Is 42:8 [b]Is 42:12
3 [1]Lit *deceive* [a]Ps 47:2; 65:5; 145:6 [b]Ps 18:44; 81:15
4 [1]*Selah* may mean: *Pause, Crescendo* or *Musical interlude* [a]Ps 22:27; 67:7; 86:9; 117:1; Zech 14:16 [b]Ps 67:4
5 [a]Ps 46:8 [b]Ps 106:22
6 [a]Ex 14:21; Ps 106:9 [b]Josh 3:16; Ps 114:3 [c]Ps 105:43
7 [a]Ps 145:13 [b]Ps 11:4 [c]Ps 140:8

8 Bless our God, O peoples,
And [1a]sound His praise abroad,
9 Who [1a]keeps us in life
And [b]does not allow our feet to [2]slip.
10 For You have [a]tried us, O God;
You have [b]refined us as silver is refined.
11 You [a]brought us into the net;
You laid an oppressive burden upon our loins.
12 You made men [a]ride over our heads;
We went through [b]fire and through water,
Yet You [c]brought us out into *a place of* abundance.
13 I shall [a]come into Your house with burnt offerings;
I shall [b]pay You my vows,
14 Which my lips uttered
And my mouth spoke when I was [a]in distress.
15 I shall [a]offer to You burnt offerings of fat beasts,
With the smoke of [b]rams;
I shall make *an offering of* [1]bulls with male goats. Selah.

16 [a]Come *and* hear, all who [1]fear God,
And I will [b]tell of what He has done for my soul.
17 I cried to Him with my mouth,
And [1]He was [a]extolled with my tongue.
18 If I [1a]regard wickedness in my heart,
The [b]Lord [2]will not [3]hear;
19 But certainly [a]God has heard;
He has given heed to the voice of my prayer.
20 [a]Blessed be God,
Who [b]has not turned away my prayer
Nor His lovingkindness from me.

8 [1]Lit *cause to hear the sound of His praise* [a]Ps 98:4

9 [1]Lit *puts our soul in life* [2]Or *dodder, stumble* [a]Ps 30:3 [b]Ps 121:3

10 [a]Job 23:10; Ps 7:9; 17:3; 26:2 [b]Is 48:10; Zech 13:9; Mal 3:3; 1 Pet 1:7

11 [a]Lam 1:13; Ezek 12:13

12 [a]Is 51:23 [b]Ps 78:21; Is 43:2 [c]Ps 18:19

13 [a]Ps 96:8; Jer 17:26 [b]Ps 22:25; 116:14; Eccl 5:4

14 [a]Ps 18:6

15 [1]Or *cattle* [a]Ps 51:19 [b]Num 6:14

16 [1]Or *revere* [a]Ps 34:11 [b]Ps 71:15, 24

17 [1]Or *praise was under my tongue* [a]Ps 30:1

18 [1]Or *had regarded* [2]Or *would* [3]Or *have heard* [a]Job 36:21; John 9:31 [b]Job 27:9; Ps 18:41; Prov 1:28; 28:9; Is 1:15; James 4:3

19 [a]Ps 18:6; 116:1, 2

20 [a]Ps 68:35 [b]Ps 22:24

Psalm 67 Theme ______________________________

For the choir director; with stringed instruments.
A Psalm. A Song.

67 God be gracious to us and [a]bless us,
And [b]cause His face to shine [1]upon us— [2]Selah.
2 That [a]Your way may be known on the earth,
[b]Your salvation among all nations.
3 Let the [a]peoples praise You, O God;
Let all the peoples praise You.
4 Let the [a]nations be glad and sing for joy;
For You will [b]judge the peoples with uprightness
And [c]guide the nations on the earth. Selah.
5 Let the [a]peoples praise You, O God;
Let all the peoples praise You.
6 The [a]earth has yielded its produce;
God, our God, [b]blesses us.
7 God blesses us,
[1]That [a]all the ends of the earth may fear Him.

67:1 [1]Lit *with* [2]*Selah* may mean: *Pause, Crescendo* or *Musical interlude* [a]Num 6:25 [b]Ps 4:6; 31:16; 80:3, 7, 19; 119:135

2 [a]Ps 98:2; Acts 18:25; Titus 2:11 [b]Is 52:10

3 [a]Ps 66:4

4 [a]Ps 100:1, 2 [b]Ps 9:8; 96:10, 13; 98:9 [c]Ps 47:8

5 [a]Ps 67:3

6 [a]Lev 26:4; Ps 85:12; Ezek 34:27; Zech 8:12 [b]Ps 29:11; 115:12

7 [1]Or *And let all . . . earth fear Him* [a]Ps 22:27; 33:8

Psalm 68 Theme ______________________

For the choir director. A Psalm of David. A Song.

68 [1]Let [a]God arise, [2]let His enemies be scattered,
And [3]let those who hate Him flee before Him.
2 As [a]smoke is driven away, *so* drive *them* away;
As [b]wax melts before the fire,
So let the [c]wicked perish before God.
3 But let the [a]righteous be glad; let them exult before God;
Yes, let them rejoice with gladness.
4 Sing to God, [a]sing praises to His name;
[1b]Lift up *a song* for Him who [c]rides through the deserts,
Whose [d]name is [2]the LORD, and exult before Him.

5 A [a]father of the fatherless and a [b]judge [1]for the widows,
Is God in His [c]holy habitation.
6 God [1a]makes a home for the lonely;
He [b]leads out the prisoners into prosperity,
Only [c]the rebellious dwell in a parched land.

7 O God, when You [a]went forth before Your people,
When You [b]marched through the wilderness, [1]Selah.
8 The [a]earth quaked;
The [b]heavens also dropped *rain* at the presence of God;
[1c]Sinai itself *quaked* at the presence of God, the God of Israel.
9 You [a]shed abroad a plentiful rain, O God;
You confirmed Your inheritance when it was [1]parched.
10 Your creatures settled in it;
You [a]provided in Your goodness for the poor, O God.

11 The Lord gives the [1]command;
The [a]women who proclaim the *good* tidings are a great host:
12 "[a]Kings of armies flee, they flee,
And she who remains at home will [b]divide the spoil!"
13 [1]When you lie down [a]among the [2]sheepfolds,
You are like the wings of a dove covered with silver,
And its pinions with glistening gold.
14 When the Almighty [a]scattered the kings [1]there,
It was snowing in [b]Zalmon.

15 A [1a]mountain of God is the mountain of Bashan;
A mountain *of many* peaks is the mountain of Bashan.
16 Why do you look with envy, O mountains with *many* peaks,
At the mountain which God has [a]desired for His abode?
Surely [b]the LORD will dwell *there* forever.
17 The [a]chariots of God are [1]myriads, [b]thousands upon thousands;
[2]The Lord is among them *as at* Sinai, in holiness.
18 You have [a]ascended on high, You have [b]led captive *Your* captives;

68:1 [1]Or *God shall* [2]Or *His enemies shall* [3]Or *those who hate Him shall* [a]Num 10:35; Ps 12:5; 132:8
2 [a]Ps 37:20; Is 9:18; Hos 13:3 [b]Ps 22:14; 97:5; Mic 1:4 [c]Ps 9:3; 37:20; 80:16
3 [a]Ps 32:11; 64:10; 97:12
4 [1]Or *Cast up a highway* [2]Heb YAH [a]Ps 66:2 [b]Is 57:14; 62:10 [c]Deut 33:26; Ps 18:10; 68:33; Is 40:3 [d]Ex 6:3; Ps 83:18
5 [1]Lit *of* [a]Ps 10:14; 146:9 [b]Deut 10:18 [c]Deut 26:15
6 [1]Lit *makes the solitary to dwell in a house* [a]Ps 107:4-7; 113:9 [b]Ps 69:33; 102:20; 107:10, 14; 146:7; Acts 12:7; 16:26 [c]Ps 78:17; 107:34, 40
7 [1]*Selah* may mean: *Pause, Crescendo* or *Musical interlude* [a]Ex 13:21; Ps 78:14; Hab 3:13 [b]Judg 5:4; Ps 78:52
8 [1]Lit *This is Sinai* which [a]Ex 19:18; Judg 5:4; 2 Sam 22:8; Ps 77:18; Jer 10:10 [b]Judg 5:4; Ps 18:9; Is 45:8 [c]Ex 19:18; Judg 5:5
9 [1]Lit *weary* [a]Lev 26:4; Deut 11:11; Job 5:10; Ezek 34:26
10 [a]Ps 65:9; 74:19; 78:20; 107:9
11 [1]Lit *word* [a]Ex 15:20; 1 Sam 18:6
12 [a]Josh 10:16; Judg 5:19; Ps 135:11 [b]Judg 5:30; 1 Sam 30:24
13 [1]Lit *If* [2]Or *cooking stones* or *saddle bags* [a]Gen 49:14; Judg 5:16
14 [1]Lit *in it* [a]Josh 10:10 [b]Judg 9:48
15 [1]Or *mighty mountain is* [a]Ps 36:6
16 [a]Deut 12:5; Ps 87:1, 2; 132:13 [b]Ps 132:14
17 [1]Lit *twice ten thousand* [2]Another reading is *The Lord came from Sinai into the sanctuary* [a]2 Kin 6:17; Hab 3:8 [b]Deut 33:2; Dan 7:10
18 [a]Ps 7:7; 47:5; [b]Judg 5:12

You have received gifts among men,
Even *among* the rebellious also, that [1]the LORD God may dwell *there.*

19 Blessed be the Lord, who daily [a]bears our burden,
[b]The God *who* is our salvation. Selah.
20 God is to us a [a]God of deliverances;
And [b]to [1]GOD the Lord belong escapes [2]from death.
21 Surely God will [a]shatter the head of His enemies,
The hairy crown of him who goes on in his guilty deeds.
22 The Lord [1]said, "[a]I will bring *them* back from Bashan.
I will bring *them* back from the depths of the sea;
23 That [1a]your foot may shatter *them* in blood,
The tongue of your [b]dogs *may have* its portion from *your* enemies."

24 They have seen [a]Your [1]procession, O God,
The [1]procession of my God, my King, [2b]into the sanctuary.
25 The [a]singers went on, the musicians after *them,*
[1]In the midst of the [b]maidens beating tambourines.
26 [a]Bless God in the congregations,
Even the LORD, *you who are* of the [b]fountain of Israel.
27 There is [a]Benjamin, the [1]youngest, [2]ruling them,
The princes of Judah *in* their throng,
The princes of [b]Zebulun, the princes of Naphtali.

28 [1]Your God has [a]commanded your strength;
Show Yourself strong, O God, [b]who have acted [2]on our behalf.
29 [1]Because of Your temple at Jerusalem
[a]Kings will bring gifts to You.
30 Rebuke the [a]beasts [1]in the reeds,
The herd of [b]bulls with the calves of the peoples,
Trampling under foot the pieces of silver;
He has [c]scattered the peoples who delight in war.
31 Envoys will come out of [a]Egypt;
[1b]Ethiopia will quickly stretch out her hands to God.

32 Sing to God, O [a]kingdoms of the earth,
[b]Sing praises to the Lord, Selah.
33 To Him who [a]rides upon the [1b]highest heavens, which are from ancient times;
Behold, [c]He [2]speaks forth with His voice, a [d]mighty voice.
34 [a]Ascribe strength to God;
His majesty is over Israel
And [b]His strength is in the [1]skies.
35 [1]O God, *You are* [a]awesome from Your [2]sanctuary.
The God of Israel Himself [b]gives strength and power to the people.
[c]Blessed be God!

18 [1]Heb YAH
19 [a]Ps 55:22; Is 46:4 [b]Ps 65:5
20 [1]Heb *YHWH,* usually rendered LORD [2]I.e. in view of; lit *for* [a]Ps 106:43 [b]Deut 32:39; Ps 49:15; 56:13
21 [a]Ps 110:6; Hab 3:13
22 [1]Or *says* [a]Num 21:33; Amos 9:1-3
23 [1]Some versions render, you may *bathe your foot in blood* [a]Ps 58:10 [b]1 Kin 21:19; Jer 15:3
24 [1]Lit *goings* [2]Lit *in the sanctuary;* or *in holiness* [a]Ps 77:13 [b]Ps 63:2
25 [1]Or *The maidens in the midst* [a]1 Chr 13:8; 15:6; Ps 47:6 [b]Ex 15:20; Judg 11:34
26 [a]Ps 22:22, 23; 26:12 [b]Deut 33:28; Is 48:1
27 [1]Or *smallest* [2]Or *their ruler* [a]Judg 5:14; 1 Sam 9:21 [b]Judg 5:18
28 [1]Some mss read *Command, God* [2]Lit *for us* [a]Ps 29:11; 44:4 [b]Is 26:12
29 [1]Or *From Your temple* [a]1 Kin 10:10, 25; 2 Chr 32:23; Ps 45:12; 72:10; Is 18:7
30 [1]Lit *of* [a]Job 40:21; Ezek 29:3 [b]Ps 22:12 [c]Ps 18:14; 89:10
31 [1]Lit *Cush* [a]Is 19:19, 21 [b]Is 45:14; Zeph 3:10
32 [a]Ps 102:22 [b]Ps 67:4
33 [1]Lit *heaven of heavens of old* [2]Lit *gives forth* [a]Deut 33:26; Ps 18:10; 104:3 [b]Deut 10:14; 1 Kin 8:27 [c]Ps 46:6 [d]Ps 29:4
34 [1]Lit *clouds* [a]Ps 29:1 [b]Ps 150:1
35 [1]Or *Awesome is God from your sanctuary* [2]Lit *holy places* [a]Deut 7:21; 10:17; Ps 47:2; 66:5 [b]Ps 29:11; Is 40:29 [c]Ps 66:20; 2 Cor 1:3

Psalm 69 Theme ______________________________

For the choir director; according to +Shoshannim. *A Psalm* of David.

69 Save me, O God,
For the [a]waters have [1]threatened my life.
2 I have sunk in deep [a]mire, and there is no foothold;
I have come into deep waters, and a [1b]flood overflows me.
3 I am [a]weary with my crying; my throat is parched;
My [b]eyes fail while I wait for my God.
4 Those [a]who hate me without a cause are more than the
hairs of my head;
Those who would [1]destroy me [b]are powerful, being
wrongfully my enemies;
[c]What I did not steal, I then have to restore.

5 O God, it is You who knows [a]my folly,
And [b]my wrongs are not hidden from You.
6 May those who wait for You not [a]be ashamed through me,
O Lord [1]GOD of hosts;
May those who seek You not be dishonored through me,
O God of Israel,
7 Because [a]for Your sake I have borne reproach;
[b]Dishonor has covered my face.
8 I have become [a]estranged [1]from my brothers
And an alien to my mother's sons.
9 For [a]zeal for Your house has consumed me,
And [b]the reproaches of those who reproach You have fallen
on me.
10 When I wept [a]in my soul with fasting,
It became my reproach.
11 When I made [a]sackcloth my clothing,
I became [b]a byword to them.
12 Those who [a]sit in the gate talk about me,
And I *am* the [1b]song of the drunkards.

13 But as for me, my prayer is to You, O LORD, [a]at an
acceptable time;
O God, in the [b]greatness of Your lovingkindness,
Answer me with [1]Your saving truth.
14 Deliver me from the [a]mire and do not let me sink;
May I be [b]delivered from [1]my foes and from the [2a]deep
waters.
15 May the [1a]flood of water not overflow me
Nor the deep swallow me up,
Nor the [b]pit shut its mouth on me.

16 Answer me, O LORD, for [a]Your lovingkindness is good;
[b]According to the greatness of Your compassion, [c]turn to
me,
17 And [a]do not hide Your face from Your servant,
For I am [b]in distress; answer me quickly.

69:1 +Or possibly *Lilies* [1]Lit *come to the soul* [a]Job 22:11; Ps 32:6; 42:7; 69:14, 15; Jon 2:5
2 [1]Lit *flowing stream* [a]Ps 40:2 [b]Jon 2:3
3 [a]Ps 6:6 [b]Deut 28:32; Ps 38:10; 119:82, 123; Is 38:14
4 [1]Or *silence* [a]Ps 35:19; John 15:25 [b]Ps 35:19; 38:19; 59:3 [c]Ps 35:11; Jer 15:10
5 [a]Ps 38:5 [b]Ps 44:21
6 [1]Heb *YHWH*, usually rendered *LORD* [a]2 Sam 12:14
7 [a]Jer 15:15 [b]Ps 44:15; Is 50:6; Jer 51:51
8 [1]Lit *to* [a]Job 19:13-15; Ps 31:11; 38:11
9 [a]Ps 119:139; John 2:17 [b]Ps 89:41, 50; Rom 15:3
10 [a]Ps 35:13
11 [a]1 Kin 20:31; Ps 35:13 [b]1 Kin 9:7; Job 17:6; Ps 44:14; Jer 24:9
12 [1]Lit *songs* [a]Gen 19:1; Ruth 4:1 [b]Job 30:9
13 [1]Or *the faithfulness of Your salvation* [a]Ps 32:6; Is 49:8; 2 Cor 6:2 [b]Ps 51:1
14 [1]Lit *those who hate me* [2]Lit *deep places of water* [a]Ps 69:2 [b]Ps 144:7
15 [1]Lit *stream* [a]Ps 124:4, 5 [b]Num 16:33; Ps 28:1; 141:7
16 [a]Ps 63:3; 109:21 [b]Ps 51:1; 106:45 [c]Ps 25:16; 86:16
17 [a]Ps 27:9; 102:2; 143:7 [b]Ps 31:9; 66:14

18 Oh draw near to my soul *and* [a]redeem it;
[b]Ransom me because of my enemies!
19 You know my [a]reproach and my shame and my dishonor;
All my adversaries are [1]before You.

20 Reproach has [a]broken my heart and I am so sick.
And [b]I looked for sympathy, but there was none,
And for [c]comforters, but I found none.
21 They also gave me [1a]gall [2]for my food
And for my thirst they [b]gave me vinegar to drink.

22 May [a]their table before them become a snare;
And [1b]when they are in peace, *may it become* a trap.
23 May their [a]eyes grow dim so that they cannot see,
And make their [b]loins shake continually.
24 [a]Pour out Your indignation on them,
And may Your burning anger overtake them.
25 May their [1a]camp be desolate;
May none dwell in their tents.
26 For they have [a]persecuted him whom [b]You Yourself have smitten,
And they tell of the pain of those whom [c]You have [1]wounded.
27 Add [a]iniquity to their iniquity,
And [b]may they not come into [c]Your righteousness.
28 May they be [a]blotted out of the [b]book of life
And may they not be [1c]recorded with the righteous.

29 But I am [a]afflicted and in pain;
[1]May Your salvation, O God, [b]set me *securely* on high.
30 I will [a]praise the name of God with song
And [b]magnify Him with [c]thanksgiving.
31 And it will [a]please the LORD better than an ox
Or a young bull with horns and hoofs.
32 The [a]humble [1]have seen *it and* are glad;
You who seek God, [b]let your heart [2]revive.
33 For [a]the LORD hears the needy
And [b]does not despise His *who are* prisoners.

34 Let [a]heaven and earth praise Him,
The seas and [b]everything that moves in them.
35 For God will [a]save Zion and [b]build the cities of Judah,
That they may dwell there and [c]possess it.
36 The [1a]descendants of His servants will inherit it,
And those who love His name [b]will dwell in it.

Psalm 70 Theme ____________________

For the choir director. *A Psalm* of David; for a memorial.

70 [a]O God, *hasten* to deliver me;
O LORD, hasten to my help!

18 [a]2 Sam 4:9; Ps 26:11; 49:15 [b]Ps 119:134

19 [1]Or known *to You* [a]Ps 22:6; 31:11

20 [a]Jer 23:9 [b]Ps 142:4; Is 63:5 [c]Job 16:2

21 [1]Or *poison* [2]Or *in* [a]Deut 29:18 [b]Matt 27:34, 48; Mark 15:23, 36; Luke 23:36; John 19:28-30

22 [1]Lit *for those who are secure* [a]Rom 11:9, 10 [b]1 Thess 5:3

23 [a]Is 6:10 [b]Dan 5:6

24 [a]Ps 79:6; Jer 10:25; Ezek 20:8; Hos 5:10

25 [1]Lit *encampment* [a]Matt 23:38; Luke 13:35; Acts 1:20

26 [1]Lit *pierced* [a]2 Chr 28:9; Zech 1:15 [b]Is 53:4 [c]Ps 109:22

27 [a]Neh 4:5; Ps 109:14; Rom 1:28 [b]Is 26:10 [c]Ps 103:17

28 [1]Lit *written* [a]Ex 32:32, 33; Rev 3:5 [b]Phil 4:3; Rev 13:8; 17:8; 20:15 [c]Ps 87:6; Ezek 13:9; Luke 10:20; Heb 12:23

29 [1]Or *Your salvation, O God, will set . . .* [a]Ps 70:5 [b]Ps 20:1; 59:1

30 [a]Ps 28:7 [b]Ps 34:3 [c]Ps 50:14

31 [a]Ps 50:13, 14; 51:16

32 [1]Some mss and ancient versions read *will see* [2]Or *live* [a]Ps 34:2 [b]Ps 22:26

33 [a]Ps 12:5 [b]Ps 68:6

34 [a]Ps 96:11; 98:7; 148:1-13; Is 44:23; 49:13 [b]Is 55:12

35 [a]Ps 46:5; 51:18 [b]Ps 147:2; Is 44:26 [c]Obad 17

36 [1]Lit *seed* [a]Ps 25:13; 102:28 [b]Ps 37:29

70:1 [a]Ps 40:13-17; 70:1-5

2 [1]Or *soul* [2]Or *to injure me* [a]Ps 35:4, 26

3 [1]Some mss read *appalled* [a]Ps 40:15

5 [a]Ps 40:17 [b]Ps 141:1

71:1 [a]Ps 25:2, 3; 31:1-3; 71:1-3

2 [a]Ps 31:1 [b]Ps 17:6

3 [1]Or *crag* [a]Ps 31:2, 3 [b]Deut 33:27; Ps 90:1; 91:9 [c]Ps 7:6; 42:8 [d]Ps 18:2

4 [1]Lit *palm* [a]Ps 140:1, 4

5 [1]Heb *YHWH*, usually rendered LORD [a]Ps 39:7; Jer 14:8; 17:7, 13, 17; 50:7 [b]Ps 22:9

6 [1]Lit *Upon You I have been supported* [2]Lit *in* [a]Ps 22:10; Is 46:3 [b]Job 10:18; Ps 22:9 [c]Ps 34:1

7 [a]Is 8:18; 1 Cor 4:9 [b]Ps 61:3

8 [a]Ps 35:28; 63:5 [b]Ps 96:6; 104:1

9 [a]Ps 71:18; 92:14; Is 46:4

10 [1]Lit *with reference to* [2]Lit *soul* [a]Ps 56:6 [b]Ps 31:13; 83:3; Matt 27:1

11 [a]Ps 3:2 [b]Ps 7:2

12 [a]Ps 10:1; 22:11; 35:22; 38:21 [b]Ps 38:22; 40:13; 70:1, 5

13 [1]Lit *my injury* [a]Ps 35:4, 26; 40:14 [b]Ps 109:29 [c]Esth 9:2; Ps 71:24

2 [a]Let those be ashamed and humiliated
Who seek my [1]life;
Let those be turned back and dishonored
Who delight [2]in my hurt.
3 [a]Let those be [1]turned back because of their shame
Who say, "Aha, aha!"

4 Let all who seek You rejoice and be glad in You;
And let those who love Your salvation say continually,
"Let God be magnified."
5 But [a]I am afflicted and needy;
[b]Hasten to me, O God!
You are my help and my deliverer;
O LORD, do not delay.

Psalm 71 Theme ______________________________

71 [a]In You, O LORD, I have taken refuge;
Let me never be ashamed.
2 [a]In Your righteousness deliver me and rescue me;
[b]Incline Your ear to me and save me.
3 [a]Be to me a rock of [b]habitation to which I may continually come;
You have given [c]commandment to save me,
For You are [d]my [1]rock and my fortress.
4 [a]Rescue me, O my God, out of the hand of the wicked,
Out of the [1]grasp of the wrongdoer and ruthless man,
5 For You are my [a]hope;
O Lord [1]GOD, *You are* my [b]confidence from my youth.
6 [1]By You I have been [a]sustained from *my* birth;
You are He who [b]took me from my mother's womb;
My [c]praise is continually [2]of You.

7 I have become a [a]marvel to many,
For You are [b]my strong refuge.
8 My [a]mouth is filled with Your praise
And with [b]Your glory all day long.
9 Do not cast me off in the [a]time of old age;
Do not forsake me when my strength fails.
10 For my enemies have spoken [1]against me;
And those who [a]watch for my [2]life [b]have consulted together,
11 Saying, "[a]God has forsaken him;
Pursue and seize him, for there is [b]no one to deliver."

12 O God, [a]do not be far from me;
O my God, [b]hasten to my help!
13 Let those who are adversaries of my soul be [a]ashamed *and* consumed;
Let them be [b]covered with reproach and dishonor, who [c]seek [1]to injure me.

14 But as for me, I will [a]hope continually,
And will [1b]praise You yet more and more.
15 My [a]mouth shall tell of Your righteousness
And of [b]Your salvation all day long;
For I [c]do not know the [1]sum *of them.*
16 I will come [a]with the mighty deeds of the Lord [1]GOD;
I will [b]make mention of Your righteousness, Yours alone.

17 O God, You [a]have taught me from my youth,
And I still [b]declare Your wondrous deeds.
18 And even when *I am* [a]old and gray, O God, do not forsake me,
Until I [b]declare Your [1]strength to *this* generation,
Your power to all who are to come.
19 [1]For Your [a]righteousness, O God, *reaches* to the [2]heavens,
You who have [b]done great things;
O God, [c]who is like You?
20 You who have [a]shown [1]me many troubles and distresses
Will [b]revive [1]me again,
And will bring [1]me up again [c]from the depths of the earth.
21 May You increase my [a]greatness
And turn *to* [b]comfort me.

22 I will also praise You with [1a]a harp,
Even Your [2]truth, O my God;
To You I will sing praises with the [b]lyre,
O [c]Holy One of Israel.
23 My lips will [a]shout for joy when I sing praises to You;
And my [b]soul, which You have redeemed.
24 My [a]tongue also will utter Your righteousness all day long;
For they are [b]ashamed, for they are humiliated who seek [1]my hurt.

Psalm 72 Theme ______________________

A Psalm of Solomon.

72 Give the king [a]Your judgments, O God,
And [b]Your righteousness to the king's son.
2 [1]May [2]he [a]judge Your people with righteousness
And [3b]Your afflicted with justice.
3 [1]Let the mountains bring [2a]peace to the people,
And the hills, in righteousness.
4 [1]May he [a]vindicate the [2]afflicted of the people,
Save the children of the needy
And crush the oppressor.

5 [1]Let them fear You [a]while the sun *endures,*
And [2]as long as the moon, throughout all generations.
6 [1]May he come down [a]like rain upon the mown grass,
Like [b]showers that water the earth.

14 [1]Lit *add upon all Your praise* [a]Ps 130:7 [b]Ps 71:8

15 [1]Lit *numbers* [a]Ps 35:28 [b]Ps 96:2 [c]Ps 40:5

16 [1]Heb *YHWH,* usually rendered *LORD* [a]Ps 106:2 [b]Ps 51:14

17 [a]Deut 4:5; 6:7 [b]Ps 26:7; 40:5; 119:27

18 [1]Lit *arm* [a]Ps 71:9 [b]Ps 22:31; 78:4, 6

19 [1]Or *And* [2]Lit *height* [a]Ps 36:6; 57:10 [b]Ps 126:2; Luke 1:49 [c]Deut 3:24; Ps 35:10

20 [1]Another reading is *us* [a]Ps 60:3 [b]Ps 80:18; 85:6; 119:25; 138:7; Hos 6:1, 2 [c]Ps 86:13

21 [a]Ps 18:35 [b]Ps 23:4; 86:17; Is 12:1; 49:13

22 [1]Lit *an instrument of a harp* [2]Or *faithfulness* [a]Ps 33:2; 81:2; 92:1-3; 144:9 [b]Ps 33:2; 147:7 [c]2 Kin 19:22; Ps 78:41; 89:18; Is 1:4

23 [a]Ps 5:11; 32:11; 132:9, 16 [b]Ps 34:22; 55:18; 103:4

24 [1]Or *to injure me* [a]Ps 35:28 [b]Ps 71:13

72:1 [a]1 Kin 3:9; 1 Chr 22:13 [b]Ps 24:5

2 [1]Or *He* will judge [2]Many of the pronouns in this Psalm may be rendered *He* since the typical reference is to the Messiah [3]Or *Your humble* [a]Is 9:7; 11:2-5; 32:1 [b]Ps 82:3

3 [1]Or *The mountains will bring* [2]Or *prosperity* [a]Is 2:4; 9:5, 6; Mic 4:3, 4; Zech 9:10

4 [1]Or *He will vindicate* [2]Or *humble* [a]Is 11:4

5 [1]Or *They will fear* [2]Lit *before the moon* [a]Ps 72:17; 89:36, 37

6 [1]Or *He will come down* [a]Deut 32:2; 2 Sam 23:4; Hos 6:3 [b]Ps 65:10

7 In his days [1]may the [a]righteous flourish,
And [b]abundance of peace till the moon is no more.

8 May he also rule [a]from sea to sea
And from the River to the ends of the earth.
9 [1]Let [a]the nomads of the desert [b]bow before him,
And his enemies [c]lick the dust.
10 [1]Let the kings of [a]Tarshish and of the [2b]islands bring presents;
The kings of [c]Sheba and [d]Seba [e]offer [3]gifts.
11 [1]And let all [a]kings bow down before him,
All [b]nations serve him.

12 For he will [a]deliver the needy when he cries for help,
The [1]afflicted also, and him who has no helper.
13 He will have [a]compassion on the poor and needy,
And the [1]lives of the needy he will save.
14 He will [1a]rescue their [2]life from oppression and violence,
And their blood will be [b]precious in his sight;
15 So may he live, and may the [a]gold of Sheba be given to him;
And let [1]them pray for him continually;
Let [1]them bless him all day long.

16 May there be abundance of grain in the earth on top of the mountains;
Its fruit will wave like *the cedars of* [a]Lebanon;
And may those from the city flourish like [b]vegetation of the earth.
17 May his [a]name endure forever;
May his name [1]increase [2b]as long as the sun *shines;*
And let *men* [c]bless themselves by him;
[d]Let all nations call him blessed.

18 [a]Blessed be the LORD God, the God of Israel,
Who alone [b]works wonders.
19 And blessed be His [a]glorious name forever;
And may the whole [b]earth be filled with His glory.
[c]Amen, and Amen.

20 The prayers of David the son of Jesse are ended.

BOOK 3

Psalm 73 Theme ______________________

A Psalm of Asaph.

73 Surely God is [a]good to Israel,
To those who are [b]pure in heart!
2 But as for me, [a]my feet came close to stumbling,
My steps [1]had almost slipped.

7 [1]Or *the righteous will flourish* [a]Ps 92:12 [b]Is 2:4

8 [a]Ex 23:31; Zech 9:10

9 [1]Or *The nomads . . . will bow* [a]Ps 74:14; Is 23:13 [b]Ps 22:29 [c]Is 49:23; Mic 7:17

10 [1]Or *The kings . . . will bring* [2]Or *coastlands* [3]Or *tribute* [a]2 Chr 9:21; Ps 48:7 [b]Ps 97:1; Is 42:4, 10; Zeph 2:11 [c]1 Kin 10:1; Job 6:19; Is 60:6 [d]Gen 10:7; Is 43:3 [e]Ps 45:12; 68:29

11 [1]Or *All kings will bow down* [a]Ps 138:4; Is 49:23 [b]Ps 86:9

12 [1]Or *humble* [a]Job 29:12; Ps 72:4

13 [1]Lit *souls* [a]Prov 19:17; 28:8

14 [1]Lit *redeem* [2]Lit *soul* [a]Ps 69:18 [b]1 Sam 26:21; Ps 116:15

15 [1]Lit *him* [a]Is 60:6

16 [a]Ps 104:16 [b]Job 5:25

17 [1]Or *sprout forth* [2]Lit *before the sun* [a]Ex 3:15; Ps 135:13 [b]Ps 89:36 [c]Gen 12:3; 22:18 [d]Luke 1:48

18 [a]1 Chr 29:10; Ps 41:13; 89:52; 106:48 [b]Ex 15:11; Job 5:9; Ps 77:14; 86:10; 136:4

19 [a]Neh 9:5; Ps 96:8 [b]Num 14:21 [c]Ps 41:13

73:1 [a]Ps 86:5 [b]Ps 24:4; 51:10; Matt 5:8

2 [1]Lit *were caused to slip* [a]Ps 94:18

3 For I was [a]envious of the [1]arrogant
As I saw the [b]prosperity of the wicked.
4 For there are no pains in their death,
And their [1]body is fat.
5 They are [a]not [1]in trouble *as other* [2]men,
Nor are they [b]plagued [3]like mankind.
6 Therefore pride is [a]their necklace;
The [b]garment of violence covers them.
7 Their eye [1]bulges from [a]fatness;
The imaginations of *their* heart [2]run riot.
8 They [a]mock and [1]wickedly speak of oppression;
They [b]speak from on high.
9 They have [a]set their mouth [1]against the heavens,
And their tongue [2]parades through the earth.

10 Therefore [1]his people return to this place,
And waters of [a]abundance are [2]drunk by them.
11 They say, "[a]How does God know?
And is there knowledge [1]with the Most High?"
12 Behold, [a]these are the wicked;
And always [b]at ease, they have increased *in* wealth.
13 Surely [a]in vain I have [1]kept my heart pure
And [b]washed my hands in innocence;
14 For I have been stricken [a]all day long
And [1b]chastened every morning.

15 If I had said, "I will speak thus,"
Behold, I would have betrayed the [a]generation of Your children.
16 When I [a]pondered to understand this,
It was [1]troublesome in my sight
17 Until I came into the [1a]sanctuary of God;
Then I perceived their [b]end.
18 Surely You set them in [a]slippery places;
You cast them down to [1b]destruction.
19 How they are [1a]destroyed in a moment!
They are utterly swept away by [b]sudden terrors!
20 Like a [a]dream when one awakes,
O Lord, when [b]aroused, You will [c]despise their [1]form.

21 When my [a]heart was embittered
And I was [b]pierced [1]within,
22 Then I was [a]senseless and ignorant;
I was *like* [1]a [b]beast [2]before You.
23 Nevertheless [a]I am continually with You;
You have taken hold of my right hand.
24 With Your counsel You will [a]guide me,
And afterward [b]receive me [1]to glory.

25 [a]Whom have I in heaven *but You?*
And [1]besides You, I desire nothing on earth.

3 [1]Or *boasters* [a]Ps 37:1; Prov 23:17 [b]Job 21:7; Ps 37:7; Jer 12:1

4 [1]Or *belly*

5 [1]Lit *in the trouble of men* [2]Or *mortals* [3]Lit *with* [a]Job 21:9; Ps 73:12 [b]Ps 73:14

6 [a]Gen 41:42; Prov 1:9 [b]Ps 109:18

7 [1]Lit *goes forth* [2]Lit *overflow* [a]Job 15:27; Ps 17:10; Jer 5:28

8 [1]Or *they speak in wickedness; From on high they speak of oppression* [a]Ps 1:1 [b]Ps 17:10; 2 Pet 2:18; Jude 16

9 [1]Or *in* [2]Lit *walks* [a]Rev 13:6

10 [1]Or *His* [2]Lit *drained out* [a]Ps 23:5

11 [1]Lit *in* [a]Job 22:13

12 [a]Ps 49:6; 52:7 [b]Jer 49:31; Ezek 23:42

13 [1]Or *cleansed my heart* [a]Job 21:15; 34:9; 35:3 [b]Ps 26:6

14 [1]Lit *my chastening* [a]Ps 38:6 [b]Job 33:19; Ps 118:18

15 [a]Ps 14:5

16 [1]Lit *labor, trouble* [a]Eccl 8:17

17 [1]Lit *sanctuaries* [a]Ps 27:4; 77:13 [b]Ps 37:38

18 [1]Lit *ruins* [a]Ps 35:6 [b]Ps 35:8; 36:12

19 [1]Lit *become a desolation* [a]Num 16:21; Is 47:11 [b]Job 18:11

20 [1]Or *image* [a]Job 20:8 [b]Ps 78:65 [c]1 Sam 2:30

21 [1]Lit *in my kidneys* [a]Judg 10:16 [b]Acts 2:37

22 [1]Or *an animal* [2]Lit *with You* [a]Ps 49:10; 92:6 [b]Job 18:3; Ps 49:20; Eccl 3:18

23 [a]Ps 16:8

24 [1]Or *with honor* [a]Ps 32:8; 48:14; Is 58:11 [b]Gen 5:24; Ps 49:15

25 [1]Or *with* [a]Ps 16:2; Phil 3:8

26 My [a]flesh and my heart may fail,
But God is the [1]strength of my heart and my [b]portion
forever.
27 For, behold, [a]those who are far from You will [b]perish;
You have [1]destroyed all those who [2c]are unfaithful to You.
28 But as for me, [a]the nearness of God is my good;
I have made the Lord [1]GOD my [b]refuge,
That I may [c]tell of all Your works.

Psalm 74 Theme ______________________________

A [+]Maskil of Asaph.

74 O God, why have You [a]rejected *us* forever?
Why does Your anger [b]smoke against the [c]sheep of
Your [1]pasture?
2 Remember Your congregation, which You have [a]purchased
of old,
Which You have [b]redeemed to be the [c]tribe of Your
inheritance;
And this Mount [d]Zion, where You have dwelt.
3 [1]Turn Your footsteps toward the [a]perpetual ruins;
The enemy [b]has damaged everything within the sanctuary.
4 Your adversaries have [a]roared in the midst of Your meeting
place;
They have set up their [b]own [1]standards [c]for signs.
5 It seems as if one had lifted up
His [1a]axe in a [2]forest of trees.
6 And now [1]all its [a]carved work
They smash with hatchet and [2]hammers.
7 They have [1a]burned Your sanctuary [2]to the ground;
They have [b]defiled the dwelling place of Your name.
8 They [a]said in their heart, "Let us [1]completely [2]subdue
them."
They have burned all the meeting places of God in the
land.
9 We do not see our [a]signs;
There is [b]no longer any prophet,
Nor is there any among us who knows [c]how long.
10 How long, O God, will the adversary [a]revile,
And the enemy [b]spurn Your name forever?
11 Why [a]do You withdraw Your hand, even Your right hand?
From within Your bosom, [b]destroy *them!*

12 Yet God is [a]my king from of old,
Who works deeds of deliverance in the midst of the earth.
13 [1]You [a]divided the sea by Your strength;
[1]You [b]broke the heads of the [c]sea monsters [2]in the waters.
14 [1]You crushed the heads of [2a]Leviathan;
[1]You gave him as food for the [3]creatures [b]of the wilderness.
15 [1]You [a]broke open springs and torrents;
[1]You [b]dried up ever-flowing streams.

26 [1]Lit *rock* [a]Ps 38:10; 40:12; 84:2; 119:81 [b]Ps 16:5

27 [1]Or *silenced* [2]Lit *go to a whoring from* [a]Ps 119:155 [b]Ps 37:20 [c]Ex 34:15; Num 15:39; Ps 106:39; Hos 4:12; 9:1

28 [1]Heb *YHWH,* usually rendered *LORD* [a]Ps 65:4; Heb 10:22; James 4:8 [b]Ps 14:6; 71:7 [c]Ps 40:5; 107:22; 118:17

74:1 [+]Possibly, *Contemplative,* or *Didactic,* or *Skillful Psalm* [1]Or *pasturing* [a]Ps 44:9; 77:7 [b]Deut 29:20; Ps 18:8; 89:46 [c]Ps 79:13; 95:7; 100:3

2 [a]Ex 15:16; Deut 32:6 [b]Ex 15:13; Ps 77:15; 106:10; Is 63:9 [c]Deut 32:9; Is 63:17; Jer 10:16; 51:19 [d]Ps 9:11; 68:16

3 [1]Lit *Lift up* [a]Is 61:4 [b]Ps 79:1

4 [1]Lit *signs* [a]Lam 2:7 [b]Num 2:2 [c]Ps 74:9

5 [1]Lit *axes* [2]Lit *thicket* [a]Jer 46:22

6 [1]Lit *altogether* [2]Or *axes* [a]1 Kin 6:18, 29, 32, 35

7 [1]Lit *set on fire* [2]Or *To the ground they...* [a]2 Kin 25:9 [b]Ps 89:39; Lam 2:2

8 [1]Lit *altogether* [2]Or *oppress* [a]Ps 83:4

9 [a]Ps 78:43 [b]1 Sam 3:1; Lam 2:9; Ezek 7:26; Amos 8:11 [c]Ps 6:3; 79:5; 80:4

10 [a]Ps 44:16; 79:12; 89:51 [b]Lev 24:16

11 [a]Lam 2:3 [b]Ps 59:13

12 [a]Ps 44:4

13 [1]Or *You Yourself* [2]Lit *on* [a]Ex 14:21; Ps 78:13 [b]Is 51:9 [c]Ps 148:7; Jer 51:34

14 [1]Or *You Yourself* [2]Or *sea monster* [3]Lit *people* [a]Job 41:1; Ps 104:26; Is 27:1 [b]Ps 72:9

15 [1]Or *You Yourself* [a]Ex 17:5, 6; Num 20:11; Ps 78:15; 105:41; 114:8; Is 48:21 [b]Ex 14:21, 22; Josh 2:10; 3:13; Ps 114:3

16 Yours is the day, Yours also is the night;
[1]You have [a]prepared the [2]light and the sun.
17 [1]You have [a]established all the boundaries of the earth;
[1]You have [2]made [b]summer and winter.

18 Remember this, [1]O LORD, that the enemy has [a]reviled,
And a [b]foolish people has spurned Your name.
19 Do not deliver the soul of Your [a]turtledove to the wild
beast;
[b]Do not forget the life of Your afflicted forever.
20 Consider the [a]covenant;
For the [b]dark places of the land are full of the habitations of
violence.
21 Let not the [a]oppressed return dishonored;
Let the [b]afflicted and needy praise Your name.

22 Arise, O God, *and* [a]plead Your own cause;
Remember [1]how the [b]foolish man reproaches You all day
long.
23 Do not forget the voice of Your [a]adversaries,
The [b]uproar of those who rise against You which ascends
continually.

Psalm 75 Theme ______________________

For the choir director; *set to* +Al-tashheth. A Psalm of Asaph, a Song.

75 We [a]give thanks to You, O God, we give thanks,
For Your name is [b]near;
Men declare [c]Your wondrous works.
2 "When I select an [a]appointed time,
It is I who [b]judge with equity.
3 "The [a]earth and all who dwell in it [1]melt;
It is I who have firmly set its [b]pillars. [2]Selah.
4 "I said to the boastful, 'Do not boast,'
And to the wicked, '[a]Do not lift up the horn;
5 Do not lift up your horn on high,
[a]Do not speak with insolent [1]pride.'"

6 For not from the east, nor from the west,
Nor from the [1a]desert *comes* exaltation;
7 But [a]God is the Judge;
He [b]puts down one and exalts another.
8 For a [a]cup is in the hand of the LORD, and the wine foams;
It is [1b]well mixed, and He pours out of this;
Surely all the wicked of the earth must drain *and* [c]drink
down its dregs.

9 But as for me, I will [a]declare *it* forever;
I will sing praises to the God of Jacob.
10 And all the [a]horns of the wicked [1]He will cut off,
But [b]the horns of the righteous will be lifted up.

16 [1]Or *You Yourself* [2]Or *luminary* [a]Gen 1:14-18; Ps 104:19; 136:7, 8

17 [1]Or *You Yourself* [2]Or *formed* [a]Deut 32:8; Acts 17:26 [b]Gen 8:22; Ps 147:16-18

18 [1]Or *that the enemy has reviled the LORD* [a]Ps 74:10 [b]Deut 32:6; Ps 14:1; 39:8; 53:1

19 [a]Song 2:14 [b]Ps 9:18

20 [a]Gen 17:7; Ps 106:45 [b]Ps 88:6; 143:3

21 [a]Ps 103:6 [b]Ps 35:10; Is 41:17

22 [1]Lit *Your reproach from the foolish man* [a]Ps 43:1; Is 3:13; 43:26; Ezek 20:35 [b]Ps 14:1; 53:1; 74:18

23 [a]Ps 74:10 [b]Ps 65:7

75:1 +Lit *Do Not Destroy* [a]Ps 79:13 [b]Ps 145:18 [c]Ps 26:7; 44:1; 71:17

2 [a]Ps 102:13 [b]Ps 9:8; 67:4; Is 11:4

3 [1]Or *totter* [2]*Selah* may mean: *Pause, Crescendo* or *Musical interlude* [a]Ps 46:6; Is 24:19 [b]1 Sam 2:8

4 [a]Zech 1:21

5 [1]Lit *neck* [a]1 Sam 2:3; Ps 94:4

6 [1]Or *mountainous desert* [a]Ps 3:3

7 [a]Ps 50:6 [b]1 Sam 2:7; Ps 147:6; Dan 2:21

8 [1]Lit *full of mixture* [a]Job 21:20; Ps 11:6; 60:3; Jer 25:15 [b]Prov 23:30 [c]Obad 16

9 [a]Ps 22:22; 40:10

10 [1]Heb *I* [a]Ps 101:8; Jer 48:25 [b]1 Sam 2:1; Ps 89:17; 92:10; 148:14

Psalm 76 Theme ______________________

For the choir director; on stringed instruments.
A Psalm of Asaph, a Song.

76 God is [a]known in Judah;
His name is [b]great in Israel.
2 His [1a]tabernacle is in [b]Salem;
His [c]dwelling place also is in Zion.
3 There He [a]broke the [1]flaming arrows,
The shield and the sword and the [2]weapons of war. [3]Selah.

4 You are resplendent,
[1]More majestic than the mountains of prey.
5 The [a]stouthearted were plundered,
[1]They sank into sleep;
And none of the [2]warriors could use his hands.
6 At Your [a]rebuke, O God of Jacob,
Both [1b]rider and horse were cast into a dead sleep.
7 You, even You, are [a]to be feared;
And [b]who may stand in Your presence when once [1]You are
angry?

8 You caused judgment to be heard from heaven;
The earth [a]feared and was still
9 When God [a]arose to judgment,
To save all the humble of the earth. Selah.
10 For the [1a]wrath of man shall praise You;
With a remnant of wrath You will gird Yourself.

11 [a]Make vows to the LORD your God and [b]fulfill *them;*
Let all who are around Him [c]bring gifts to Him who is to be
feared.
12 He will cut off the spirit of princes;
He is [1a]feared by the kings of the earth.

Psalm 77 Theme ______________________

For the choir director; +according to Jeduthun. A Psalm of Asaph.

77 My voice *rises* to God, and I will [a]cry aloud;
My voice *rises* to God, and He will hear me.
2 In the [a]day of my trouble I sought the Lord;
[b]In the night my [c]hand was stretched out [1]without
weariness;
My soul [d]refused to be comforted.
3 *When* I remember God, then I am [a]disturbed;
When I [b]sigh, then [c]my spirit grows faint. [1]Selah.
4 You have held my eyelids *open;*
I am so troubled that I [a]cannot speak.
5 I have considered the [a]days of old,
The years of long ago.
6 I will remember my [a]song in the night;
I [b]will meditate with my heart,
And my spirit [1]ponders:

76:1 [a]Ps 48:3 [b]Ps 99:3
2 [1]Lit *shelter* [a]Ps 27:5; Lam 2:6 [b]Gen 14:18 [c]Ps 9:11; 132:13; 135:21
3 [1]Lit *fiery shafts of the bow* [2]Lit *battle* [3]*Selah* may mean: *Pause, Crescendo* or *Musical interlude* [a]Ps 46:9
4 [1]Or *Majestic from the mountains*
5 [1]Lit *They slumbered their sleep* [2]Lit *men of might have found their hands* [a]Is 10:12; 46:12
6 [1]Lit *chariot* [a]Ps 80:16 [b]Ex 15:1, 21; Ps 78:53
7 [1]Lit *Your anger is* [a]1 Chr 16:25; Ps 89:7; 96:4 [b]Ezra 9:15; Ps 130:3; Nah 1:6; Mal 3:2; Rev 6:17
8 [a]1 Chr 16:30; 2 Chr 20:29, 30; Ps 33:8
9 [a]Ps 9:7, 8; 74:22; 82:8
10 [1]Lit *wraths* [a]Ex 9:16; Rom 9:17
11 [a]Eccl 5:4-6 [b]Ps 50:14 [c]2 Chr 32:23; Ps 68:29
12 [1]Lit *awesome to* [a]Ps 47:2
77:1 +1 Chr 16:41 [a]Ps 3:4; 142:1
2 [1]Lit *and did not grow numb* [a]Ps 50:15; 86:7 [b]Ps 63:6; Is 26:9 [c]Job 11:13; Ps 88:9 [d]Gen 37:35
3 [1]*Selah* may mean: *Pause, Crescendo* or *Musical interlude* [a]Ps 42:5, 11; 43:5 [b]Ps 55:2; 142:2 [c]Ps 61:2; 143:4
4 [a]Ps 39:9
5 [a]Deut 32:7; Ps 44:1; 143:5; Is 51:9
6 [1]Lit *searched* [a]Ps 42:8 [b]Ps 4:4

7 Will the Lord [a]reject forever?
And will He [b]never be favorable again?
8 Has His [a]lovingkindness ceased forever?
Has *His* [1b]promise come to an end [2]forever?
9 Has God [a]forgotten to be gracious,
Or has He in anger [1]withdrawn His [b]compassion? Selah.
10 Then I said, "[a]It is my [1]grief,
That the [b]right hand of the Most High has changed."

11 I shall remember the [a]deeds of [1]the LORD;
Surely I will [a]remember Your wonders of old.
12 I will [a]meditate on all Your work
And muse on Your deeds.
13 Your way, O God, is [a]holy;
[b]What god is great like our God?
14 You are the [a]God who works wonders;
You have [b]made known Your strength among the peoples.
15 You have by Your [1]power [a]redeemed Your people,
The sons of Jacob and [b]Joseph. Selah.

16 The [a]waters saw You, O God;
The waters saw You, they were in anguish;
The deeps also trembled.
17 The [a]clouds poured out water;
The skies [b]gave forth a sound;
Your [c]arrows [1]flashed here and there.
18 The [a]sound of Your thunder was in the whirlwind;
The [b]lightnings lit up the world;
The [c]earth trembled and shook.
19 Your [a]way was in the sea
And Your paths in the mighty waters,
And Your footprints may not be known.
20 You [a]led Your people like a flock
By the hand of [b]Moses and Aaron.

Psalm 78 Theme ______________________

A +Maskil of Asaph.

78 [a]Listen, O my people, to my [1]instruction;
[b]Incline your ears to the words of my mouth.
2 I will [a]open my mouth in a parable;
I will utter [b]dark sayings of old,
3 Which we have heard and known,
And [a]our fathers have told us.
4 We will [a]not conceal them from their children,
But [b]tell to the generation to come the praises of the LORD,
And His strength and His [c]wondrous works that He has done.

5 For He established a [a]testimony in Jacob
And appointed a [b]law in Israel,

7 [a]Ps 44:9 [b]Ps 85:1, 5

8 [1]Lit *word* [2]Lit *from generation to generation* [a]Ps 89:49 [b]2 Pet 3:9

9 [1]Lit *shut up* [a]Is 49:15 [b]Ps 25:6; 40:11; 51:1

10 [1]Or *infirmity, the years of the right hand of the Most High* [a]Ps 31:22; 73:14 [b]Ps 44:2, 3

11 [1]Heb YAH [a]Ps 105:5; 143:5

12 [a]Ps 145:5

13 [a]Ps 63:2; 73:17 [b]Ex 15:11; Ps 71:19; 86:8

14 [a]Ps 72:18 [b]Ps 106:8

15 [1]Lit *arm* [a]Ex 6:6; Deut 9:29; Ps 74:2; 78:42 [b]Ps 80:1

16 [a]Ex 14:21; Ps 114:3; Hab 3:8, 10

17 [1]Lit *went* [a]Judg 5:4 [b]Ps 68:33 [c]Ps 18:14

18 [a]Ps 18:13; 104:7 [b]Ps 97:4 [c]Judg 5:4; Ps 18:7

19 [a]Is 51:10; Hab 3:15

20 [a]Ex 13:21; 14:19; Ps 78:52; 80:1; Is 63:11-13 [b]Ex 6:26; Ps 105:26

78:1 +Possibly, *Contemplative,* or *Didactic,* or *Skillful Psalm* [1]Or *law, teaching* [a]Is 51:4 [b]Is 55:3

2 [a]Ps 49:4; Matt 13:35 [b]Prov 1:6

3 [a]Ps 44:1

4 [a]Ex 12:26; Deut 6:7; 11:19; Job 15:18; Ps 145:4; Is 38:19; Joel 1:3 [b]Ex 13:8, 14; Ps 22:30 [c]Job 37:16; Ps 26:7; 71:17

5 [a]Ps 19:7; 81:5; Is 8:20 [b]Ps 147:19

Which He [c]commanded our fathers
That they should [1d]teach them to their children,
6 [a]That the generation to come might know, *even* [b]the children *yet* to be born,
That they may arise and [c]tell *them* to their children,
7 That they should put their confidence in God
And [a]not forget the works of God,
But [b]keep His commandments,
8 And [a]not be like their fathers,
A [b]stubborn and rebellious generation,
A generation that [c]did not [1]prepare its heart
And whose spirit was not [d]faithful to God.

9 The sons of Ephraim [1]were [a]archers equipped with bows,
Yet [b]they turned back in the day of battle.
10 They [a]did not keep the covenant of God
And refused to [b]walk in His law;
11 They [a]forgot His deeds
And His [1]miracles that He had shown them.
12 [a]He wrought wonders before their fathers
In the land of Egypt, in the [b]field of Zoan.
13 He [a]divided the sea and caused them to pass through,
And He made the waters stand [b]up like a heap.
14 Then He led them with the cloud by [a]day
And all the night with a [b]light of fire.
15 He [a]split the rocks in the wilderness
And gave *them* abundant drink like the ocean depths.
16 He [a]brought forth streams also from the rock
And caused waters to run down like rivers.

17 Yet they still continued to sin against Him,
To [a]rebel against the Most High in the desert.
18 And in their heart they [a]put God to the test
By asking [b]food according to their desire.
19 Then they spoke against God;
They said, "[a]Can God prepare a table in the wilderness?
20 "Behold, He [a]struck the rock so that waters gushed out,
And streams were overflowing;
Can He give bread also?
Will He provide [1b]meat for His people?"

21 Therefore the LORD heard and [1]was [a]full of wrath;
And a fire was kindled against Jacob
And anger also mounted against Israel,
22 Because they [a]did not believe in God
And did not trust in His salvation.
23 Yet He commanded the clouds above
And [a]opened the doors of heaven;
24 He [a]rained down manna upon them to eat
And gave them [1b]food from heaven.

5 [1]Lit *make them known* [c]Deut 6:4-9 [d]Deut 4:9
6 [a]Ps 102:18 [b]Ps 22:31 [c]Deut 11:19
7 [a]Deut 4:9; 6:12; 8:14 [b]Deut 4:2; 5:1, 29; 27:1; Josh 22:5
8 [1]Or *put right* [a]2 Kin 17:14; 2 Chr 30:7; Ezek 20:18 [b]Ex 32:9; Deut 9:7, 24; 31:27; Judg 2:19; Is 30:9 [c]Job 11:13; Ps 78:37 [d]Ps 51:10
9 [1]Or *being* [a]1 Chr 12:2 [b]Judg 20:39; Ps 78:57
10 [a]Judg 2:20; 1 Kin 11:11; 2 Kin 17:15; 18:12 [b]Ps 119:1; Jer 32:23; 44:10, 23
11 [1]Or *wonderful works* [a]Ps 106:13
12 [a]Ex chs 7-12; Ps 106:22 [b]Num 13:22; Ps 78:43; Is 19:11; 30:4; Ezek 30:14
13 [a]Ex 14:21; Ps 74:13; 136:13 [b]Ex 15:8; Ps 33:7
14 [a]Ex 13:21; Ps 105:39 [b]Ex 14:24
15 [a]Ex 17:6; Num 20:11; Ps 105:41; 114:8; Is 48:21; 1 Cor 10:4
16 [a]Num 20:8, 10, 11
17 [a]Deut 9:22; Is 63:10; Heb 3:16
18 [a]Ex 17:6; Deut 6:16; Ps 78:41, 56; 95:9; 106:14; 1 Cor 10:9 [b]Num 11:4
19 [a]Ex 16:3; Num 11:4; 20:3; 21:5; Ps 23:5
20 [1]Lit *flesh* [a]Num 20:11; Ps 78:15, 16 [b]Num 11:18
21 [1]Or *became infuriated* [a]Num 11:1
22 [a]Deut 1:32; 9:23; Heb 3:18
23 [a]Gen 7:11; Mal 3:10
24 [1]Lit *grain* [a]Ex 16:4 [b]Ps 105:40; John 6:31

25 Man did eat the bread of [1]angels;
He sent them [2]food [3a]in abundance.
26 He [a]caused the east wind to blow in the heavens
And by His [1]power He directed the south wind.
27 When He rained [1]meat upon them like the dust,
Even [a]winged fowl like the sand of the seas,
28 Then He let *them* fall in the midst of [1]their camp,
Round about their dwellings.
29 So they [a]ate and were well filled,
And their desire He gave to them.
30 [1]Before they had satisfied their desire,
[a]While their food was in their mouths,
31 The [a]anger of God rose against them
And killed [1]some of their [b]stoutest ones,
And [2]subdued the choice men of Israel.
32 In spite of all this they [a]still sinned
And [b]did not believe in His wonderful works.
33 So He brought [a]their days to an end in [1]futility
And their years in sudden terror.

34 When He killed them, then they [a]sought Him,
And returned and searched [b]diligently for God;
35 And they remembered that God was their [a]rock,
And the Most High God their [b]Redeemer.
36 But they [a]deceived Him with their mouth
And [b]lied to Him with their tongue.
37 For their heart was not [a]steadfast toward Him,
Nor were they faithful in His covenant.
38 But He, being [a]compassionate, [1b]forgave *their* iniquity and did not destroy *them;*
And often He [2c]restrained His anger
And did not arouse all His wrath.
39 Thus [a]He remembered that they were but [b]flesh,
A [1c]wind that passes and does not return.

40 How often they [a]rebelled against Him in the wilderness
And [b]grieved Him in the [c]desert!
41 Again and again they [1a]tempted God,
And pained the [b]Holy One of Israel.
42 They [a]did not remember [b]His [1]power,
The day when He [c]redeemed them from the adversary,
43 When He performed His [a]signs in Egypt
And His [b]marvels in the field of Zoan,
44 And [a]turned their rivers to blood,
And their streams, they could not drink.
45 He sent among them swarms of [a]flies which devoured them,
And [b]frogs which destroyed them.
46 He gave also their crops to the [a]grasshopper
And the product of their labor to the [b]locust.
47 He [1]destroyed their vines with [a]hailstones
And their sycamore trees with frost.

25 [1]Lit *mighty ones* [2]Or *provision* [3]Lit *to satiation* [a]Ex 16:3
26 [1]Or *strength* [a]Num 11:31
27 [1]Lit *flesh* [a]Ex 16:13; Ps 105:40
28 [1]Lit *His*
29 [a]Num 11:19, 20
30 [1]Lit *They were not estranged from* [a]Num 11:33
31 [1]Lit *among their fat ones* [2]Lit *caused to bow down* [a]Num 11:33, 34; Job 20:23 [b]Is 10:16
32 [a]Num chs 14, 16, 17 [b]Num 14:11; Ps 78:11
33 [1]Lit *vanity, a mere breath* [a]Num 14:29, 35
34 [a]Num 21:7; Hos 5:15 [b]Ps 63:1
35 [a]Deut 32:4 [b]Ex 15:13; Deut 9:26; Ps 74:2; Is 41:14
36 [a]Ex 24:7, 8; Ezek 33:31 [b]Ex 32:7, 8; Is 57:11
37 [a]Ps 51:10; 78:8; Acts 8:21
38 [1]Lit *covered over, atoned for* [2]Lit *turned away* [a]Ex 34:6 [b]Num 14:18-20 [c]Is 48:9
39 [1]Or *breath* [a]Job 10:9; Ps 103:14 [b]Gen 6:3 [c]Job 7:7, 16; Ps 103:14; James 4:14
40 [a]Ps 95:8, 9; 106:43; 107:11; Heb 3:16 [b]Ps 95:10; Is 63:10; Eph 4:30 [c]Ps 106:14
41 [1]Or *put God to the test* [a]Num 14:22 [b]2 Kin 19:22; Ps 89:18
42 [1]Lit *hand* [a]Judg 8:34 [b]Ps 44:3 [c]Ps 106:10
43 [a]Ps 105:27 [b]Ex 4:21; 7:3
44 [a]Ex 7:20; Ps 105:29
45 [a]Ex 8:24; Ps 105:31 [b]Ex 8:6; Ps 105:30
46 [a]1 Kin 8:37; Ps 105:34 [b]Ex 10:14
47 [1]Lit *was killing* [a]Ex 9:23-25; Ps 105:32

48 He gave over their [a]cattle also to the hailstones
And their herds to bolts of lightning.
49 He [a]sent upon them His burning anger,
Fury and indignation and trouble,
[1]A band of destroying angels.
50 He leveled a path for His anger;
He did not spare their soul from death,
But [a]gave over their life to the plague,
51 And [a]smote all the firstborn in Egypt,
The [b]first *issue* of their virility in the tents of [c]Ham.
52 But He [a]led forth His own people like sheep
And guided them in the wilderness [b]like a flock;
53 He led them [a]safely, so that they did not fear;
But [b]the sea engulfed their enemies.

54 So [a]He brought them to His holy [1]land,
To this [2b]hill country [c]which His right hand had gained.
55 He also [a]drove out the nations before them
And [b]apportioned them for an inheritance by measurement,
And made the tribes of Israel dwell in their tents.
56 Yet they [1a]tempted and [b]rebelled against the Most High God
And did not keep His testimonies,
57 But turned back and [a]acted treacherously like their fathers;
They [b]turned aside like a treacherous bow.
58 For they [a]provoked Him with their [b]high places
And [c]aroused His jealousy with their [d]graven images.
59 When God heard, He [1]was filled with [a]wrath
And greatly [b]abhorred Israel;
60 So that He [a]abandoned the [b]dwelling place at Shiloh,
The tent [1]which He had pitched among men,
61 And gave up His [a]strength to captivity
And His glory [b]into the hand of the adversary.
62 He also [a]delivered His people to the sword,
And [1]was filled with wrath at His inheritance.
63 [a]Fire devoured [1]His young men,
And [1]His [b]virgins had no wedding songs.
64 [1]His [a]priests fell by the sword,
And [1]His [b]widows could not weep.

65 Then the Lord [a]awoke as *if from* sleep,
Like a [b]warrior [1]overcome by wine.
66 He [1a]drove His adversaries backward;
He put on them an everlasting reproach.
67 He also [a]rejected the tent of Joseph,
And did not choose the tribe of Ephraim,
68 But chose the tribe of Judah,
Mount [a]Zion which He loved.
69 And He [a]built His sanctuary like the heights,
Like the earth which He has founded forever.

48 [a]Ex 9:19
49 [1]Lit *A deputation of angels of evil* [a]Ex 15:7
50 [a]Ex 12:29, 30
51 [a]Ex 12:29; Ps 105:36; 135:8; 136:10 [b]Gen 49:3 [c]Ps 105:23, 27; 106:22
52 [a]Ex 15:22 [b]Ps 77:20
53 [a]Ex 14:19, 20 [b]Ex 14:27, 28; Ps 106:11
54 [1]Lit *border, territory* [2]Or *mountain* [a]Ex 15:17 [b]Ps 68:16; Is 11:9 [c]Ps 44:3
55 [a]Josh 11:16-23; Ps 44:2 [b]Josh 13:7; 23:4; Ps 105:11; 135:12
56 [1]Or *put to the test* [a]Ps 78:18 [b]Judg 2:11-13; Ps 78:40
57 [a]Ezek 20:27, 28 [b]Hos 7:16
58 [a]Deut 4:25; Judg 2:12; 1 Kin 14:9; Is 65:3 [b]Lev 26:30; 1 Kin 3:2; 2 Kin 16:4; Jer 17:3 [c]Deut 32:16, 21; 1 Kin 14:22 [d]Ex 20:4; Lev 26:1; Deut 4:25
59 [1]Or *became infuriated* [a]Deut 1:34; 9:19; Ps 106:40 [b]Lev 26:30; Deut 32:19; Amos 6:8
60 [1]Some ancient versions read *where He dwelt* [a]1 Sam 4:11; Ps 78:67; Jer 7:12, 14; 26:6 [b]Josh 18:1
61 [a]Ps 63:2; 132:8 [b]1 Sam 4:17
62 [1]Or *became infuriated* [a]Judg 20:21; 1 Sam 4:10
63 [1]Or *their* [a]Num 11:1; 21:28; Is 26:11; Jer 48:45 [b]Jer 7:34; 16:9; Lam 2:21
64 [1]Or *their* [a]1 Sam 4:17; 22:18 [b]Job 27:15; Ezek 24:23
65 [1]Or *sobered up from* [a]Ps 44:23; 73:20 [b]Is 42:13
66 [1]Lit *smote* [a]1 Sam 5:6
67 [a]Ps 78:60
68 [a]Ps 87:2; 132:13
69 [a]1 Kin 6:1-38

70 He also [a]chose David His servant
And took him from the sheepfolds;
71 From [1a]the care of the [2]ewes [b]with suckling lambs He brought him
To [c]shepherd Jacob His people,
And Israel [d]His inheritance.
72 So he shepherded them according to the [a]integrity of his heart,
And guided them with his skillful hands.

Psalm 79 Theme ______

A Psalm of Asaph.

79 O God, the [a]nations have [1]invaded [b]Your inheritance;
They have defiled Your [c]holy temple;
They have [d]laid Jerusalem in ruins.
2 They have given the [a]dead bodies of Your servants for food to the birds of the heavens,
The flesh of Your godly ones to the beasts of the earth.
3 They have poured out their blood like water round about Jerusalem;
And there was [a]no one to bury them.
4 We have become a [a]reproach to our neighbors,
A scoffing and derision to those around us.
5 [a]How long, O LORD? Will You be angry forever?
Will Your [b]jealousy [c]burn like fire?
6 [a]Pour out Your wrath upon the nations which [b]do not know You,
And upon the kingdoms which [c]do not call upon Your name.
7 For they have [a]devoured Jacob
And [b]laid waste his [1]habitation.

8 [a]Do not remember [1]the iniquities of *our* forefathers against us;
Let Your compassion come quickly to [b]meet us,
For we are [c]brought very low.
9 [a]Help us, O God of our salvation, for the glory of [b]Your name;
And deliver us and [1c]forgive our sins [d]for Your name's sake.
10 [a]Why should the nations say, "Where is their God?"
Let there be known among the nations in our sight,
[b]Vengeance for the blood of Your servants which has been shed.
11 Let [a]the groaning of the prisoner come before You;
According to the greatness of Your [1]power preserve [2]those who are [a]doomed to die.
12 And return to our neighbors [a]sevenfold [b]into their bosom
[1]The [c]reproach with which they have reproached You, O Lord.
13 So we Your people and the [a]sheep of Your [1]pasture
Will [b]give thanks to You forever;
To all generations we will [c]tell of Your praise.

70 [a]1 Sam 16:11, 12

71 [1]Lit *following* [2]Lit *ewes which gave suck, He . . .* [a]2 Sam 7:8; Is 40:11 [b]Gen 33:13 [c]2 Sam 5:2; 1 Chr 11:2; Ps 28:9 [d]1 Sam 10:1

72 [a]1 Kin 9:4

79:1 [1]Lit *come into* [a]Lam 1:10 [b]Ps 74:2 [c]Ps 74:3, 7 [d]2 Kin 25:9, 10; 2 Chr 36:17-19; Jer 26:18; 52:12-14; Mic 3:12

2 [a]Deut 28:26; Jer 7:33; 16:4; 19:7; 34:20

3 [a]Jer 14:16; 16:4

4 [a]Ps 44:13; 80:6; Dan 9:16

5 [a]Ps 13:1; 74:1, 9, 10; 85:5; 89:46 [b]Deut 29:20; Ezek 36:5; 38:19 [c]Ps 89:46; Zeph 3:8

6 [a]Ps 69:24; Jer 10:25; Ezek 21:31; Zeph 3:8 [b]1 Thess 4:5; 2 Thess 1:8 [c]Ps 14:4; 53:4

7 [1]Lit *pasture* [a]Ps 53:4 [b]2 Chr 36:19; Jer 39:8

8 [1]Or our *former iniquities* [a]Ps 106:6; Is 64:9 [b]Ps 21:3 [c]Deut 28:43; Ps 116:6; 142:6; Is 26:5

9 [1]Lit *cover over, atone for* [a]2 Chr 14:11 [b]Ps 31:3 [c]Ps 25:11; 65:3 [d]Jer 14:7

10 [a]Ps 42:10; 115:2 [b]Ps 94:1, 2

11 [1]Lit *arm* [2]Lit *the children of death* [a]Ps 102:20

12 [1]Lit *Their* [a]Gen 4:15; Lev 26:21, 28; Ps 12:6; 119:164; Prov 6:31; 24:16; Is 30:26 [b]Ps 35:13; Is 65:6, 7; Jer 32:18; Luke 6:38 [c]Ps 74:10, 18, 22

13 [1]Or *pasturing* [a]Ps 74:1; 95:7; 100:3 [b]Ps 44:8 [c]Ps 89:1; Is 43:21

Psalm 80 Theme ____________________

For the choir director; *set to* +El Shoshannim; •Eduth.
A Psalm of Asaph.

80 Oh, give ear, [a]Shepherd of Israel,
You who lead [b]Joseph like a flock;
You who [c]are enthroned *above* the cherubim, shine forth!
2 Before [a]Ephraim and Benjamin and Manasseh, [b]stir up Your
power
And come to save us!
3 O God, [a]restore us
And [b]cause Your face to shine *upon us,* [1]and we will be
saved.

4 O [a]LORD God *of* hosts,
[b]How long will You [1]be angry with the prayer of Your
people?
5 You have fed them with the [a]bread of tears,
And You have made them to drink tears in [1]large measure.
6 You make us [1]an object of contention [a]to our neighbors,
And our enemies laugh among themselves.
7 O God *of* hosts, restore us
And cause Your face to shine *upon us,* [1]and we will be
saved.

8 You removed a [a]vine from Egypt;
You [b]drove out the [1]nations and [c]planted it.
9 You [a]cleared *the ground* before it,
And it [b]took deep root and filled the land.
10 The mountains were covered with its shadow,
And [1]the cedars of God with its [a]boughs.
11 It was sending out its branches [a]to the sea
And its shoots to the River.
12 Why have You [a]broken down its [1]hedges,
So that all who pass *that* way pick its *fruit?*
13 A boar from the forest [a]eats it away
And whatever moves in the field feeds on it.

14 O God *of* hosts, [a]turn again now, we beseech You;
[b]Look down from heaven and see, and take care of this
vine,
15 Even the [1a]shoot which Your right hand has planted,
And on the [2]son whom You have [3]strengthened for
Yourself.
16 It is [a]burned with fire, it is cut down;
They perish at the [b]rebuke of Your countenance.
17 Let [a]Your hand be upon the man of Your right hand,
Upon the son of man whom You [b]made strong for Yourself.
18 Then we shall not [a]turn back from You;
[b]Revive us, and we will call upon Your name.
19 O LORD God of hosts, [a]restore us;
Cause Your face to shine *upon us,* [1]and we will be saved.

80:1 +Possibly, *to the Lilies* •Lit *A testimony* [a]Ps 23:1 [b]Ps 77:15; 78:67; Amos 5:15 [c]Ex 25:22; 1 Sam 4:4; 2 Sam 6:2; Ps 99:1

2 [a]Num 2:18-24 [b]Ps 35:23

3 [1]Or *that we may* [a]Ps 60:1; 80:7, 19; 85:4; 126:1; Lam 5:21 [b]Num 6:25; Ps 4:6; 31:16

4 [1]Lit *smoke against* [a]Ps 59:5; 84:8 [b]Ps 79:5; 85:5

5 [1]Lit *a third part of a* [a]Ps 42:3; 102:9; Is 30:20

6 [1]Lit *a strife to* [a]Ps 44:13; 79:4

7 [1]Or *that we may*

8 [1]Or *Gentiles* [a]Ps 80:15; Is 5:1, 2, 7; Jer 2:21; 12:10; Ezek 17:6; 19:10 [b]Josh 13:6; 2 Chr 20:7; Ps 44:2; Acts 7:45 [c]Jer 11:17; 32:41; Ezek 17:23; Amos 9:15

9 [a]Ex 23:28; Josh 24:12; Is 5:2 [b]Hos 14:5

10 [1]Or *its boughs are like the cedars of God* [a]Gen 49:22

11 [a]Ps 72:8

12 [1]Or *walls, fences* [a]Ps 89:40; Is 5:5

13 [a]Jer 5:6

14 [a]Ps 90:13 [b]Ps 102:19; Is 63:15

15 [1]Or *root* [2]Or figuratively: *branch* [3]Or *secured* [a]Ps 80:8

16 [a]2 Chr 36:19; Ps 74:8; Jer 52:13 [b]Ps 39:11; 76:6

17 [a]Ps 89:21 [b]Ps 80:15

18 [a]Is 50:5 [b]Ps 71:20

19 [1]Or *that we may* [a]Ps 80:3

Psalm 81 Theme ______________________

For the choir director; +on the Gittith. *A Psalm* of Asaph.

81 [a]Sing for joy to God our [b]strength;
Shout [c]joyfully to the [d]God of Jacob.
2 Raise a song, strike [a]the timbrel,
The sweet sounding [b]lyre with the [c]harp.
3 Blow the trumpet at the [a]new moon,
At the full moon, on our [b]feast day.
4 For it is a statute for Israel,
An ordinance of the God of Jacob.
5 He established it for a testimony in Joseph
When he [1a]went throughout the land of Egypt.
I heard a [b]language that I did not know:

6 "I [1a]relieved his shoulder of the burden,
His hands were freed from the [2]basket.
7 "You [a]called in trouble and I rescued you;
I [b]answered you in the hiding place of thunder;
I proved you at the [c]waters of Meribah. [1]Selah.
8 "[a]Hear, O My people, and I will [1]admonish you;
O Israel, if you [b]would listen to Me!
9 "Let there be no [a]strange god among you;
Nor shall you worship any foreign god.
10 "[a]I, the LORD, am your God,
Who brought you up from the land of Egypt;
[b]Open your mouth wide and I will [c]fill it.

11 "But My people [a]did not listen to My voice,
And Israel did not [1]obey Me.
12 "So I [a]gave [1]them over to the stubbornness of their heart,
To walk in their own devices.
13 "Oh that My people [a]would listen to Me,
That Israel would [b]walk in My ways!
14 "I would quickly [a]subdue their enemies
And [b]turn My hand against their adversaries.
15 "[a]Those who hate the LORD would [b]pretend obedience to Him,
And their time *of punishment* would be forever.
16 "[1]But I would feed you with the [2a]finest of the wheat,
And with [b]honey from the rock I would satisfy you."

Psalm 82 Theme ______________________

A Psalm of Asaph.

82 God takes His [a]stand in [1]His own congregation;
He [b]judges in the midst of the [2c]rulers.
2 How long will you [a]judge unjustly
And [b]show partiality to the wicked? [1]Selah.
3 [a]Vindicate the weak and fatherless;
Do justice to the afflicted and destitute.

81:1 +Or *according to* [a]Ps 51:14; 59:16; 95:1 [b]Ps 46:1 [c]Ps 66:1; 95:2; 98:4 [d]Ps 84:8

2 [a]Ex 15:20; Ps 149:3 [b]Ps 92:3; 98:5; 147:7 [c]Ps 108:2; 144:9

3 [a]Num 10:10 [b]Lev 23:24

5 [1]Lit *went out over* [a]Ex 11:4 [b]Deut 28:49; Ps 114:1; Jer 5:15

6 [1]Lit *removed his shoulder from* [2]Or *brick load* [a]Is 9:4; 10:27

7 [1]*Selah* may mean: *Pause, Crescendo* or *Musical interlude* [a]Ex 2:23; 14:10; Ps 50:15 [b]Ex 19:19; 20:18 [c]Ex 17:6, 7; Num 20:13; Ps 95:8

8 [1]Or *bear witness against* [a]Ps 50:7 [b]Ps 95:7

9 [a]Ex 20:3; Deut 5:7; 32:12; Ps 44:20; Is 43:12

10 [a]Ex 20:2; Deut 5:6 [b]Job 29:23 [c]Ps 37:4; 78:25; 107:9

11 [1]Lit *yield to* [a]Deut 32:15; Ps 106:25

12 [1]Lit *him* [a]Job 8:4; Acts 7:42; Rom 1:24, 26

13 [a]Deut 5:29; Ps 81:8; Is 48:18 [b]Ps 128:1; Is 42:24; Jer 7:23

14 [a]Ps 18:47; 47:3 [b]Amos 1:8

15 [a]Rom 1:30 [b]Ps 18:44; 66:3

16 [1]Lit *He would feed him* [2]Lit *fat* [a]Deut 32:14; Ps 147:14 [b]Deut 32:13

82:1 [1]Lit *the congregation of God* [2]Lit *gods* [a]Is 3:13 [b]2 Chr 19:6; Ps 58:11 [c]Ex 21:6; 22:8, 28

2 [1]*Selah* may mean: *Pause, Crescendo* or *Musical interlude* [a]Ps 58:1 [b]Deut 1:17; Prov 18:5

3 [a]Deut 24:17; Ps 10:18; Is 11:4; Jer 22:16

4 [a]Rescue the weak and needy;
Deliver *them* out of the hand of the wicked.
5 They [a]do not know nor do they understand;
They [b]walk about in darkness;
All the [c]foundations of the earth are shaken.
6 [1]I [a]said, “You are gods,
And all of you are [b]sons of the Most High.
7 “Nevertheless [a]you will die like men
And fall like *any* [b]one of the princes.”
8 [a]Arise, O God, [b]judge the earth!
For it is You who [c]possesses all the nations.

Psalm 83 Theme ____

A Song, a Psalm of Asaph.

83 O God, [a]do not remain quiet;
[b]Do not be silent and, O God, do not be still.
2 For behold, Your enemies [a]make an uproar,
And [b]those who hate You have [1c]exalted themselves.
3 They [a]make shrewd plans against Your people,
And [1]conspire together against [b]Your [2]treasured ones.
4 They have said, “Come, and [a]let us wipe them out [1]as a nation,
That the [b]name of Israel be remembered no more.”
5 For they have [1a]conspired together with one mind;
Against You they make a covenant:
6 The tents of [a]Edom and the [b]Ishmaelites,
[c]Moab and the [d]Hagrites;
7 [a]Gebal and [b]Ammon and [c]Amalek,
[d]Philistia with the inhabitants of [e]Tyre;
8 [a]Assyria also has joined with them;
They have become [1]a help to the [b]children of Lot. [2]Selah.

9 Deal with them [a]as with Midian,
As [b]with Sisera *and* Jabin at the torrent of Kishon,
10 Who were destroyed at En-dor,
Who [a]became as dung for the ground.
11 Make their nobles like [a]Oreb and Zeeb
And all their princes like [b]Zebah and Zalmunna,
12 Who said, “[a]Let us possess for ourselves
The [b]pastures of God.”

13 O my God, make them like the [1a]whirling dust,
Like [b]chaff before the wind.
14 Like [a]fire that burns the forest
And like a flame that [b]sets the mountains on fire,
15 So pursue them [a]with Your tempest
And terrify them with Your storm.
16 [a]Fill their faces with dishonor,
That they may seek Your name, O Lord.

4 [a]Job 29:12
5 [a]Ps 14:4; Jer 4:22; Mic 3:1 [b]Prov 2:13; Is 59:9; Jer 23:12 [c]Ps 11:3
6 [1]Lit *I, on my part* [a]Ps 82:1; John 10:34 [b]Ps 89:26
7 [a]Job 21:32; Ps 49:12; Ezek 31:14 [b]Ps 83:11
8 [a]Ps 12:5 [b]Ps 58:11; 96:13 [c]Ps 2:8; Rev 11:15
83:1 [a]Ps 28:1; 35:22 [b]Ps 109:1
2 [1]Lit *lifted up the head* [a]Ps 2:1; Is 17:12 [b]Ps 81:15 [c]Judg 8:28; Zech 1:21
3 [1]Or *consult* [2]Or *hidden ones* [a]Ps 64:2; Is 29:15 [b]Ps 27:5; 31:20
4 [1]Lit *from* [a]Esth 3:6; Ps 74:8; Jer 48:2 [b]Ps 41:5; Jer 11:19
5 [1]Or *consulted* [a]Ps 2:2; Dan 6:7
6 [a]2 Chr 20:10; Ps 137:7 [b]Gen 25:12-16 [c]2 Chr 20:10 [d]1 Chr 5:10
7 [a]Josh 13:5; Ezek 27:9 [b]2 Chr 20:10 [c]1 Sam 15:2 [d]1 Sam 4:1; 29:1 [e]Ezek 27:3; Amos 1:9
8 [1]Lit *an arm* [2]*Selah* may mean: *Pause, Crescendo* or *Musical interlude* [a]2 Kin 15:19 [b]Deut 2:9
9 [a]Judg 7:1-24 [b]Judg 4:7, 15, 21-24
10 [a]Zeph 1:17
11 [a]Judg 7:25 [b]Judg 8:12, 21
12 [a]2 Chr 20:11 [b]Ps 132:13
13 [1]Or *tumbleweed* [a]Is 17:13 [b]Job 21:18; Ps 35:5; Is 40:24; Jer 13:24
14 [a]Is 9:18 [b]Ex 19:18; Deut 32:22
15 [a]Job 9:17; Ps 58:9
16 [a]Job 10:15; Ps 109:29; 132:18

17 Let them be [a]ashamed and dismayed forever,
And let them be humiliated and perish,
18 That they may [a]know that [b]You alone, whose name is the LORD,
Are the [c]Most High over all the earth.

Psalm 84 Theme ____________________

For the choir director; +on the Gittith. A Psalm of the sons of Korah.

84 How lovely are Your [a]dwelling places,
O LORD of hosts!
2 My [a]soul longed and even yearned for the courts of the LORD;
My heart and my flesh sing for joy to the [b]living God.
3 The bird also has found a house,
And the swallow a nest for herself, where she may lay her young,
Even Your [a]altars, O LORD of hosts,
[b]My King and my God.
4 How [a]blessed are those who dwell in Your house!
They are [b]ever praising You. [1]Selah.

5 How blessed is the man whose [a]strength is in You,
In [1]whose heart are the [b]highways *to Zion!*
6 Passing through the valley of [1]Baca they make it a [2]spring;
The [a]early rain also covers it with blessings.
7 They [a]go from strength to strength,
[1]*Every one of them* [b]appears before God in Zion.

8 O [a]LORD God of hosts, hear my prayer;
Give ear, O [b]God of Jacob! Selah.
9 Behold our [a]shield, O God,
And look upon the face of [b]Your anointed.
10 For [a]a day in Your courts is better than a thousand *outside.*
I would rather stand at the threshold of the house of my God
Than dwell in the tents of wickedness.
11 For the LORD God is [a]a sun and [b]shield;
The LORD gives grace and [c]glory;
[d]No good thing does He withhold [1]from those who walk [2]uprightly.
12 O LORD of hosts,
How [a]blessed is the man who trusts in You!

Psalm 85 Theme ____________________

For the choir director. A Psalm of the sons of Korah.

85 O LORD, You showed [a]favor to Your land;
You [1b]restored the captivity of Jacob.
2 You [a]forgave the iniquity of Your people;
You [b]covered all their sin. [1]Selah.

17 [a]Ps 35:4; 70:2

18 [a]Ps 59:13 [b]Ps 86:10; Is 45:21 [c]Ps 9:2; 18:13; 97:9

84:1 +Or *according to* [a]Ps 43:3; 132:5

2 [a]Ps 42:1, 2; 63:1 [b]Ps 42:2

3 [a]Ps 43:4 [b]Ps 5:2

4 [1]*Selah* may mean: *Pause, Crescendo* or *Musical interlude* [a]Ps 65:4 [b]Ps 42:5, 11

5 [1]Lit *their* [a]Ps 81:1 [b]Ps 86:11; 122:1; Jer 31:6

6 [1]Probably, *Weeping;* or *Balsam trees* [2]Or *place of springs* [a]Ps 107:35; Joel 2:23

7 [1]Some ancient versions read *The God of gods will be seen in Zion* [a]Prov 4:18; Is 40:31; John 1:16; 2 Cor 3:18 [b]Ex 34:23; Deut 16:16; Ps 42:2

8 [a]Ps 59:5; 80:4; 84:1 [b]Ps 81:1

9 [a]Gen 15:1; Ps 3:3; 28:7; 59:11; 115:9-11 [b]1 Sam 16:6; 2 Sam 19:21; Ps 2:2; 132:17

10 [a]Ps 27:4

11 [1]Lit *with regard to* [2]Lit *with integrity* [a]Is 60:19, 20; Mal 4:2; Rev 21:23 [b]Gen 15:1 [c]Ps 85:9 [d]Ps 34:9, 10

12 [a]Ps 2:12; 40:4

85:1 [1]Or *restore the fortunes* [a]Ps 77:7; 106:4 [b]Ezra 1:11; Ps 14:7; 126:1; Jer 30:18; Ezek 39:25; Hos 6:11; Joel 3:1

2 [1]*Selah* may mean: *Pause, Crescendo* or *Musical interlude* [a]Num 14:19; 1 Kin 8:34; Ps 78:38; 103:3; Jer 31:34 [b]Ps 32:1

3 You [a]withdrew all Your fury;
You [b]turned away from Your burning anger.

4 [a]Restore us, O God of our salvation,
And [b]cause Your indignation toward us to cease.
5 Will [a]You be angry with us forever?
Will You prolong Your anger to [1]all generations?
6 Will You not Yourself [1a]revive us again,
That Your people may [b]rejoice in You?
7 Show us Your lovingkindness, O LORD,
And [a]grant us Your salvation.

8 [1]I will hear what God the LORD will say;
For He will [a]speak peace to His people, [2]to His godly ones;
But let them not [b]turn back to [3]folly.
9 Surely [a]His salvation is near to those who [1]fear Him,
That [b]glory may dwell in our land.
10 [a]Lovingkindness and [1]truth have met together;
[b]Righteousness and peace have kissed each other.
11 [1]Truth [a]springs from the earth,
And righteousness looks down from heaven.
12 Indeed, [a]the LORD will give what is good,
And our [b]land will yield its produce.
13 [a]Righteousness will go before Him
And will make His footsteps into a way.

Psalm 86 Theme ________________________

A Prayer of David.

86 [a]Incline Your ear, O LORD, *and* answer me;
For I am [b]afflicted and needy.
2 [a]Preserve my [1]soul, for I am a [b]godly man;
O You my God, save Your servant who [c]trusts in You.
3 Be [a]gracious to me, O Lord,
For [b]to You I cry all day long.
4 Make glad the soul of Your servant,
For to You, O Lord, [a]I lift up my soul.
5 For You, Lord, are [a]good, and [b]ready to forgive,
And [c]abundant in lovingkindness to all who call upon You.
6 [a]Give ear, O LORD, to my prayer;
And give heed to the voice of my supplications!
7 In [a]the day of my trouble I shall call upon You,
For [b]You will answer me.
8 There is [a]no one like You among the gods, O Lord,
Nor are there any works [b]like Yours.
9 [a]All nations whom You have made shall come and worship
before You, O Lord,
And they shall glorify Your name.
10 For You are [a]great and [b]do [1]wondrous deeds;
You alone [c]are God.

3 [a]Ps 78:38; 106:23 [b]Ex 32:12; Deut 13:17; Ps 106:23; Jon 3:9
4 [a]Ps 80:3,7 [b]Dan 9:16
5 [1]Lit *generation and generation* [a]Ps 74:1; 79:5; 80:4
6 [1]Or *bring to life* [a]Ps 71:20; 80:18 [b]Ps 33:1; 90:14; 149:2
7 [a]Ps 106:4
8 [1]Or *Let me hear* [2]Lit *even to* [3]Or *stupidity* [a]Ps 29:11; Hag 2:9; Zech 9:10 [b]Ps 78:57; 2 Pet 2:21
9 [1]Or *reverence* [a]Ps 34:18; Is 46:13 [b]Ps 84:11; Hag 2:7; Zech 2:5; John 1:14
10 [1]Or *faithfulness* [a]Ps 25:10; 89:14; Prov 3:3 [b]Ps 72:3; Is 32:17
11 [1]Or *Faithfulness* [a]Is 45:8
12 [a]Ps 84:11; James 1:17 [b]Lev 26:4; Ps 67:6; Ezek 34:27; Zech 8:12
13 [a]Ps 89:14
86:1 [a]Ps 17:6; 31:2; 71:2 [b]Ps 40:17; 70:5
2 [1]Or *life* [a]Ps 25:20 [b]Ps 4:3; 50:5 [c]Ps 25:2; 31:14; 56:4
3 [a]Ps 4:1; 57:1 [b]Ps 25:5; 88:9
4 [a]Ps 25:1; 143:8
5 [a]Ps 25:8 [b]Ps 130:4 [c]Ex 34:6; Neh 9:17; Ps 103:8; 145:8; Joel 2:13; Jon 4:2
6 [a]Ps 55:1
7 [a]Ps 50:15; 77:2 [b]Ps 17:6
8 [a]Ex 15:11; 2 Sam 7:22; 1 Kin 8:23; Ps 89:6; Jer 10:6 [b]Deut 3:24
9 [a]Ps 22:27; 66:4; Is 66:23; Rev 15:4
10 [1]Or *miracles* [a]Ps 77:13 [b]Ex 15:11; Ps 72:18; 77:14; 136:4 [c]Deut 6:4; 32:39; Ps 83:18; Is 37:16; 44:6, 8; Mark 12:29; 1 Cor 8:4

11 [a]Teach me Your way, O LORD;
I will walk in Your truth;
[b]Unite my heart to fear Your name.
12 I will [a]give thanks to You, O Lord my God, with all my
heart,
And will glorify Your name forever.
13 For Your lovingkindness toward me is great,
And You have [a]delivered my soul from the [1]depths of
[2]Sheol.

14 O God, arrogant men have [a]risen up against me,
And [1]a band of violent men have sought my [2]life,
And they have not set You before them.
15 But You, O Lord, are a God [a]merciful and gracious,
Slow to anger and abundant in lovingkindness and [1]truth.
16 [a]Turn to me, and be gracious to me;
Oh [b]grant Your strength to Your servant,
And save the [c]son of Your handmaid.
17 [a]Show me a sign for good,
That those who hate me may [b]see *it* and be ashamed,
Because You, O LORD, [c]have helped me and comforted me.

Psalm 87 Theme ____________________

A Psalm of the sons of Korah. A Song.

87 His [a]foundation is in the holy mountains.
2 The LORD [a]loves the gates of Zion
More than all the *other* dwelling places of Jacob.
3 [a]Glorious things are spoken of you,
O [b]city of God. [1]Selah.
4 "I shall mention [1a]Rahab and Babylon [2]among those who
know Me;
Behold, Philistia and [b]Tyre with [3c]Ethiopia:
'This one was born there.'"
5 But of Zion it shall be said, "This one and that one were
born in her";
And the Most High Himself will [a]establish her.
6 The LORD will count when He [a]registers the peoples,
"This one was born there." Selah.
7 Then those who [a]sing as well as those who [1b]play the flutes
shall say,
"All my [c]springs *of joy* are in you."

Psalm 88 Theme ____________________

A Song. A Psalm of the sons of Korah. For the choir director; according to Mahalath Leannoth. A +Maskil of Heman •the Ezrahite.

88 O LORD, the [a]God of my salvation,
I have [b]cried out by day and in the night before You.
2 Let my prayer [a]come before You;
[b]Incline Your ear to my cry!

11 [a]Ps 25:5 [b]Jer 32:39
12 [a]Ps 111:1
13 [1]Lit *lowest Sheol* [2]I.e. the nether world [a]Ps 30:3
14 [1]Or *an assembly* [2]Lit *soul* [a]Ps 54:3
15 [1]Or *faithfulness* [a]Ps 86:5
16 [a]Ps 25:16 [b]Ps 68:35 [c]Ps 116:16
17 [a]Judg 6:17; Ps 119:122 [b]Ps 112:10 [c]Ps 118:13
87:1 [a]Ps 78:69; Is 28:16
2 [a]Ps 78:67, 68
3 [1]*Selah* may mean: *Pause, Crescendo* or *Musical interlude* [a]Is 60:1 [b]Ps 46:4; 48:8
4 [1]I.e. Egypt [2]Or *as* [3]Lit *Cush* [a]Job 9:13; Ps 89:10; Is 19:23-25 [b]Ps 45:12 [c]Ps 68:31
5 [a]Ps 48:8
6 [a]Ps 69:28; Is 4:3; Ezek 13:9
7 [1]Or *dance* [a]Ps 68:25; 149:3 [b]2 Sam 6:14; Ps 30:11 [c]Ps 36:9
88:1 +Possibly *Contemplative,* or *Didactic,* or *Skillful Psalm* •1 Kin 4:31; 1 Chr 2:6; Ps 89: title [a]Ps 24:5; 27:9 [b]Ps 22:2; 86:3; Luke 18:7
2 [a]Ps 18:6 [b]Ps 31:2; 86:1

3 [1]Or *been satisfied with* [2]I.e. the nether world [a]Ps 107:26 [b]Ps 107:18; 116:3
4 [a]Ps 28:1; 143:7 [b]Job 29:12; Ps 22:11
5 [1]Lit *A freed one among the dead* [a]Ps 31:12 [b]Ps 31:22; Is 53:8
6 [a]Ps 86:13; Lam 3:55 [b]Ps 143:3 [c]Ps 69:15
7 [1]*Selah* may mean: *Pause, Crescendo* or *Musical interlude* [a]Ps 32:4; 39:10 [b]Ps 42:7
8 [1]Lit *abomination to them* [a]Job 19:13, 19; Ps 31:11; 142:4 [b]Job 30:10 [c]Ps 142:7; Jer 32:2; 36:5
9 [1]Lit *palms* [a]Ps 6:7; 31:9 [b]Ps 22:2; 86:3 [c]Job 11:13; Ps 143:6
10 [1]Or *ghosts, shades* [a]Ps 6:5; 30:9
11 [1]I.e. place of destruction
12 [1]I.e. faithfulness to His gracious promises [a]Job 10:21; Ps 88:6
13 [a]Ps 30:2 [b]Ps 5:3; 119:147
14 [a]Ps 43:2; 44:9 [b]Job 13:24; Ps 13:1; 44:24
15 [1]Or *embarrassed* [a]Prov 24:11 [b]Job 6:4; 31:23
16 [1]Or *silenced* [a]2 Chr 28:11; Is 13:13; Lam 1:12 [b]Lam 3:54; Ezek 37:11
17 [a]Ps 118:10-12 [b]Ps 124:4 [c]Ps 17:11; 22:12, 16
18 [a]Job 19:13; Ps 88:8; 31:11; 38:11
89:1 +Possibly *Contemplative*, or *Didactic*, or *Skillful Psalm* •1 Kin 4:31 ∆Ps 88: title [a]Ps 59:16; 101:1 [b]Ps 40:10 [c]Ps 36:5; 88:11; 89:5, 8, 24, 33, 49; 92:2; 119:90; Is 25:1; Lam 3:23
2 [a]Ps 103:17 [b]Ps 36:5; 119:90
3 [a]1 Kin 8:16 [b]Ps 132:11
4 [1]*Selah* may mean: *Pause, Crescendo* or *Musical interlude* [a]2 Sam 7:16 [b]2 Sam 7:13; Is 9:7; Luke 1:33

3 For my [a]soul has [1]had enough troubles,
And [b]my life has drawn near to [2]Sheol.
4 I am reckoned among those who [a]go down to the pit;
I have become like a man [b]without strength,
5 [1]Forsaken [a]among the dead,
Like the slain who lie in the grave,
Whom You remember no more,
And they are [b]cut off from Your hand.
6 You have put me in [a]the lowest pit,
In [b]dark places, in the [c]depths.
7 Your wrath [a]has rested upon me,
And You have afflicted me with [b]all Your waves. [1]Selah.
8 You have removed [a]my acquaintances far from me;
You have made me an [1b]object of loathing to them;
I am [c]shut up and cannot go out.
9 My [a]eye has wasted away because of affliction;
I have [b]called upon You every day, O LORD;
I have [c]spread out my [1]hands to You.

10 Will You perform wonders for the dead?
Will [a]the [1]departed spirits rise *and* praise You? Selah.
11 Will Your lovingkindness be declared in the grave,
Your faithfulness in [1]Abaddon?
12 Will Your wonders be made known in the [a]darkness?
And Your [1]righteousness in the land of forgetfulness?

13 But I, O LORD, have cried out [a]to You for help,
And [b]in the morning my prayer comes before You.
14 O LORD, why [a]do You reject my soul?
Why do You [b]hide Your face from me?
15 I was afflicted and [a]about to die from my youth on;
I suffer [b]Your terrors; I am [1]overcome.
16 Your [a]burning anger has passed over me;
Your terrors have [1b]destroyed me.
17 They have [a]surrounded me [b]like water all day long;
They have [c]encompassed me altogether.
18 You have removed [a]lover and friend far from me;
My acquaintances are *in* darkness.

Psalm 89 Theme ______________________

A +Maskil of •Ethan ∆the Ezrahite.

89 I will [a]sing of the lovingkindness of the LORD forever;
To all generations I will [b]make known Your
[c]faithfulness with my mouth.
2 For I have said, "[a]Lovingkindness will be built up forever;
In the heavens You will establish Your [b]faithfulness."
3 "I have made a covenant with [a]My chosen;
I have [b]sworn to David My servant,
4 I will establish your [a]seed forever
And build up your [b]throne to all generations." [1]Selah.

5 The [a]heavens will praise Your wonders, O LORD;
Your faithfulness also [b]in the assembly of the [c]holy ones.
6 For [a]who in the skies is comparable to the LORD?
Who among the [1b]sons of the mighty is like the LORD,
7 A God [a]greatly feared in the council of the [b]holy ones,
And [c]awesome above all those who are around Him?
8 O LORD God of hosts, [a]who is like You, O mighty [1]LORD?
Your faithfulness also surrounds You.
9 You rule the swelling of the sea;
When its waves rise, You [a]still them.
10 You Yourself crushed [1a]Rahab like one who is slain;
You [b]scattered Your enemies with [2]Your mighty arm.

11 The [a]heavens are Yours, the earth also is Yours;
The [b]world and [1]all it contains, You have founded them.
12 The [a]north and the south, You have created them;
[b]Tabor and [c]Hermon [d]shout for joy at Your name.
13 You have [1]a strong arm;
Your hand is mighty, Your [a]right hand is exalted.
14 [a]Righteousness and justice are the foundation of Your throne;
[b]Lovingkindness and [1]truth go before You.
15 How blessed are the people who know the [1a]joyful sound!
O LORD, they walk in the [b]light of Your countenance.
16 In [a]Your name they rejoice all the day,
And by Your righteousness they are exalted.
17 For You are the glory of [a]their strength,
And by Your favor [1]our [b]horn is exalted.
18 For our [a]shield belongs to the LORD,
[1]And our king to the [b]Holy One of Israel.

19 [1]Once You spoke in vision to Your godly [2]ones,
And said, "I have [3]given help to one who is [a]mighty;
I have exalted one [b]chosen from the people.
20 "I have [a]found David My servant;
With My holy [b]oil I have anointed him,
21 With whom [a]My hand will be established;
My arm also will [b]strengthen him.
22 "The enemy will not [1]deceive him,
Nor the [2a]son of wickedness afflict him.
23 "But I shall [a]crush his adversaries before him,
And strike those who hate him.
24 "My [a]faithfulness and My lovingkindness will be with him,
And in My name his [b]horn will be exalted.
25 "I shall also set his hand [a]on the sea
And his right hand on the rivers.
26 "He will cry to Me, 'You are [a]my Father,
My God, and the [b]rock of my salvation.'
27 "I also shall make him *My* [a]firstborn,
The [b]highest of the kings of the earth.
28 "My [a]lovingkindness I will keep for him forever,
And My [b]covenant shall be confirmed to him.

5 [a]Ps 19:1; 97:6 [b]Ps 149:1 [c]Job 5:1
6 [1]Or *sons of gods* [a]Ps 86:8; 113:5 [b]Ps 29:1; 82:1
7 [a]Ps 47:2; 68:35; 76:7, 11 [b]Ps 89:5 [c]Ps 96:4
8 [1]Heb *YAH* [a]Ps 35:10; 71:19
9 [a]Ps 65:7; 107:29
10 [1]I.e. Egypt [2]Lit *the arm of Your might* [a]Ps 87:4; Is 30:7; 51:9 [b]Ps 18:14; 68:1; 144:6
11 [1]Lit *its fullness* [a]Gen 1:1; 1 Chr 29:11; Ps 96:5 [b]Ps 24:1
12 [a]Job 26:7 [b]Josh 19:22; Judg 4:6; Jer 46:18 [c]Deut 3:8; Josh 11:17; 12:1; Ps 133:3; Song 4:8 [d]Ps 98:8
13 [1]Lit *an arm with strength* [a]Ps 98:1; 118:16
14 [1]Or *faithfulness* [a]Ps 97:2 [b]Ps 85:13
15 [1]Or *blast of the trumpet, shout of joy* [a]Lev 23:24; Num 10:10; Ps 98:6 [b]Ps 4:6; 44:3; 67:1; 80:3; 90:8
16 [a]Ps 105:3
17 [1]Another reading is *You exalt our horn* [a]Ps 28:8 [b]Ps 75:10; 92:10; 148:14
18 [1]Or *Even to the Holy One of Israel our King* [a]Ps 47:9 [b]Ps 71:22; 78:41
19 [1]Or *At that time* [2]Some mss read *one* [3]Lit *placed help upon* [a]2 Sam 17:10 [b]1 Kin 11:34; Ps 78:70
20 [a]1 Sam 13:14; 16:1-12; Acts 13:22 [b]1 Sam 16:13
21 [a]Ps 18:35; 80:17 [b]Ps 18:32
22 [1]Or *exact usury from him* [2]Or *wicked man* [a]2 Sam 7:10; Ps 125:3
23 [a]2 Sam 7:9; Ps 18:40
24 [a]Ps 89:1 [b]Ps 132:17
25 [a]Ps 72:8
26 [a]2 Sam 7:14; 1 Chr 22:10; Jer 3:19 [b]2 Sam 22:47; Ps 95:1
27 [a]Ex 4:22; Ps 2:7; Jer 31:9; Col 1:15, 18 [b]Num 24:7; Ps 72:11; Rev 19:16
28 [a]Ps 89:33 [b]Ps 89:3, 34

29 "So I will establish his [1a]descendants forever
And his [b]throne [c]as the days of heaven.

30 "If his sons [a]forsake My law
And do not walk in My judgments,
31 If they [1]violate My statutes
And do not keep My commandments,
32 Then I will punish their transgression with the [a]rod
And their iniquity with stripes.
33 "But I will not break off [a]My lovingkindness from him,
Nor deal falsely in My faithfulness.
34 "My [a]covenant I will not [1]violate,
Nor will I [b]alter [2]the utterance of My lips.
35 "[1]Once I have [a]sworn by My holiness;
I will not lie to David.
36 "His [1a]descendants shall endure forever
And his [b]throne [c]as the sun before Me.
37 "It shall be established forever [a]like the moon,
And the [b]witness in the sky is faithful." [1]Selah.

38 But You have [a]cast off and [b]rejected,
You have been full of wrath [1]against Your [c]anointed.
39 You have [a]spurned the covenant of Your servant;
You have [b]profaned [c]his crown [1]in the dust.
40 You have [a]broken down all his walls;
You have [b]brought his strongholds to ruin.
41 [a]All who pass along the way plunder him;
He has become a [b]reproach to his neighbors.
42 You have [a]exalted the right hand of his adversaries;
You have [b]made all his enemies rejoice.
43 You also turn back the edge of his sword
And have [a]not made him stand in battle.
44 You have made his [1a]splendor to cease
And cast his throne to the ground.
45 You have [a]shortened the days of his youth;
You have [b]covered him with shame. Selah.

46 [a]How long, O LORD?
Will You hide Yourself forever?
Will Your [b]wrath burn like fire?
47 [a]Remember [1]what my span of life is;
For what [b]vanity [2]You have created all the sons of men!
48 What man can live and not [a]see death?
Can he [b]deliver his soul from the [1]power of
[2]Sheol? Selah.

49 Where are Your former lovingkindnesses, O Lord,
Which You [a]swore to David in Your faithfulness?
50 Remember, O Lord, the [a]reproach of Your servants;
[1]How I bear in my bosom *the reproach of* all the many
peoples,

29 [1]Lit *seed* [a]Ps 18:50; 89:4, 36 [b]1 Kin 2:4; Ps 89:4; 132:12; Is 9:7; Jer 33:17 [c]Deut 11:21
30 [a]2 Sam 7:14; Ps 119:53
31 [1]Lit *profane*
32 [a]Job 9:34; 21:9
33 [a]2 Sam 7:15
34 [1]Lit *profane* [2]Lit *that which goes forth* [a]Deut 7:9; Jer 33:20, 21 [b]Num 23:19
35 [1]Or *One thing* [a]Ps 60:6; Amos 4:2
36 [1]Lit *seed* [a]Ps 89:29; Luke 1:33 [b]Ps 72:5 [c]Ps 72:17
37 [1]*Selah* may mean: *Pause, Crescendo* or *Musical interlude* [a]Ps 72:5 [b]Job 16:19
38 [1]Lit *with* [a]Ps 44:9 [b]Deut 32:19; 1 Chr 28:9 [c]Ps 20:6; 89:20, 51
39 [1]Lit *to the ground* [a]Ps 78:59; Lam 2:7 [b]Ps 74:7 [c]Lam 5:16
40 [a]Ps 80:12 [b]Lam 2:2, 5
41 [a]Ps 80:12 [b]Ps 44:13; 69:9, 19; 79:4
42 [a]Ps 13:2 [b]Ps 80:6
43 [a]Ps 44:10
44 [1]Lit *clearness, luster* [a]Ezek 28:7
45 [a]Ps 102:23 [b]Ps 44:15; 71:13; 109:29
46 [a]Ps 13:1; 44:24 [b]Ps 79:5; 80:4
47 [1]Lit *of what duration I am* [2]Or *have You . . . men?* [a]Job 7:7; 10:9; 14:1 [b]Ps 39:5; 62:9; Eccl 1:2; 2:11
48 [1]Lit *hand* [2]I.e. the nether world [a]Ps 22:29; 49:9 [b]Ps 49:15
49 [a]2 Sam 7:15; Jer 30:9; Ezek 34:23
50 [1]Lit *My bearing in my bosom* [a]Ps 69:9; 74:18, 22

51 With which [a]Your enemies have reproached, O LORD,
With which they have reproached the footsteps of [b]Your anointed.

52 [a]Blessed be the LORD forever!
Amen and Amen.

BOOK 4

Psalm 90 Theme ______________________________

A Prayer of +Moses, the man of God.

90 Lord, You have been our [1a]dwelling place in all generations.
2 Before [a]the mountains were born
[1]Or You [b]gave birth to the earth and the world,
Even [c]from everlasting to everlasting, You are God.

3 You [a]turn man back into dust
And say, "Return, O children of men."
4 For [a]a thousand years in Your sight
Are like [b]yesterday when it passes by,
[1]Or *as* a [c]watch in the night.
5 You [a]have [1]swept them away like a flood, they [2b]fall asleep;
In the morning they are like [c]grass which [3]sprouts anew.
6 In the morning it [a]flourishes and [1]sprouts anew;
Toward evening it [b]fades and [c]withers away.

7 For we have been [a]consumed by Your anger
And by Your wrath we have been [1]dismayed.
8 You have [a]placed our iniquities before You,
Our [b]secret *sins* in the light of Your presence.
9 For [a]all our days have declined in Your fury;
We have finished our years like a [1]sigh.
10 As for the days of our [1]life, [2]they contain seventy years,
Or if due to strength, [a]eighty years,
Yet their pride is *but* [b]labor and sorrow;
For soon it is gone and we [c]fly away.
11 Who [1]understands the [a]power of Your anger
And Your fury, according to the [b]fear [2]that is due You?
12 So [a]teach us to number our days,
That we may [1b]present to You a heart of wisdom.

13 Do [a]return, O LORD; [b]how long *will it be?*
And [1]be [c]sorry for Your servants.
14 O [a]satisfy us in the morning with Your lovingkindness,
That we may [b]sing for joy and be glad all our days.
15 [a]Make us glad [1]according to the days You have afflicted us,
And the [b]years we have seen [2]evil.
16 Let Your [a]work appear to Your servants
And Your [b]majesty [1]to their children.

51 [a]Ps 74:10, 18, 22 [b]Ps 89:38
52 [a]Ps 41:13; 72:19; 106:48
90:1 +Deut 33:1 [1]Or *hiding place;* some ancient mss read *place of refuge* [a]Deut 33:27; Ps 71:3; 91:1; Ezek 11:16
2 [1]Or *And* [a]Job 15:7; Prov 8:25 [b]Gen 1:1; Ps 102:25; 104:5 [c]Ps 93:2; 102:24, 27; Jer 10:10
3 [a]Gen 3:19; Job 34:14, 15; Ps 104:29
4 [1]Or *And* [a]2 Pet 3:8 [b]Ps 39:5 [c]Ex 14:24; Judg 7:19
5 [1]Or *flooded* [2]Lit *become asleep* [3]Or *passes away* [a]Job 22:16; 27:20 [b]Job 14:12; 20:8; Ps 76:5 [c]Ps 103:15; Is 40:6
6 [1]Or *passes away* [a]Job 14:2 [b]Ps 92:7; Matt 6:30 [c]James 1:11
7 [1]Or *terrified* [a]Ps 39:11
8 [a]Ps 50:21; Jer 16:17 [b]Ps 19:12; Eccl 12:14
9 [1]Or *whisper* [a]Ps 78:33
10 [1]Lit *years* [2]Lit *in them are* [a]2 Kin 19:35 [b]Eccl 12:2-7; Jer 20:18 [c]Job 20:8; Ps 78:39
11 [1]Or *knows* [2]Lit *of You* [a]Ps 76:7 [b]Neh 5:9
12 [1]Or *gain, bring in* [a]Deut 32:29; Ps 39:4 [b]Prov 2:1-6
13 [1]Or *repent in regard to* [a]Ps 6:4; 80:14 [b]Ps 6:3; 74:10 [c]Ex 32:12; Deut 32:36; Ps 106:45; 135:14; Amos 7:3, 6; Jon 3:9
14 [a]Ps 36:8; 65:4; 103:5; Jer 31:14 [b]Ps 31:7; 85:6
15 [1]Or *as many days as* [2]Or *trouble* [a]Ps 86:4 [b]Deut 2:14-16; Ps 31:10
16 [1]Or *upon* [a]Deut 32:4; Ps 44:1; 77:12; 92:4; Hab 3:2 [b]1 Kin 8:11; Is 6:3

17 [1]Or *give permanence to* [a]Ps 27:4 [b]Ps 37:23; Is 26:12; 1 Cor 3:7

91:1 [a]Ps 27:5; 31:20; 32:7 [b]Ps 17:8; 121:5; Is 25:4; 32:2

2 [a]Ps 14:6; 91:9; 94:22; 142:5 [b]Ps 18:2; 31:3; Jer 16:19 [c]Ps 25:2; 56:4

3 [a]Ps 124:7; Prov 6:5 [b]1 Kin 8:37; 2 Chr 20:9; Ps 91:6

4 [a]Is 51:16 [b]Ps 17:8; 36:7; 57:1; 63:7 [c]Ps 40:11 [d]Ps 35:2

5 [a]Job 5:19-23; Ps 23:4; 27:1 [b]Song 3:8 [c]Ps 64:4

6 [1]Or *walks* [a]2 Kin 19:35; Ps 91:10 [b]Job 5:22

7 [a]Gen 7:23; Josh 14:10

8 [a]Ps 37:34; 58:10

9 [1]Or *For You O LORD are my Refuge; You have made the Most High your dwelling place* [a]Ps 91:2 [b]Ps 90:1

10 [1]Or *dwelling* [a]Prov 12:21

11 [a]Ps 34:7; Matt 4:6; Luke 4:10, 11; Heb 1:14

12 [a]Matt 4:6; Luke 4:11

13 [1]Or *dragon* [a]Judg 14:6; Dan 6:22; Luke 10:19

14 [a]Ps 145:20 [b]Ps 59:1 [c]Ps 9:10

15 [1]Or *distress* [a]Job 12:4; Ps 50:15 [b]1 Sam 2:30; John 12:26

16 [1]Lit *length of days* [2]Or *cause him to feast his eyes on* [a]Deut 6:2; Ps 21:4; Prov 3:1, 2 [b]Ps 50:23

92:1 [a]Ps 147:1 [b]Ps 135:3

17 Let the [a]favor of the Lord our God be upon us;
And [1b]confirm for us the work of our hands;
Yes, [1]confirm the work of our hands.

Psalm 91 Theme ______________________________

91 He who dwells in the [a]shelter of the Most High
Will abide in the [b]shadow of the Almighty.
2 I will say to the LORD, "My [a]refuge and my [b]fortress,
My God, in whom I [c]trust!"
3 For it is He who delivers you from the [a]snare of the trapper
And from the deadly [b]pestilence.
4 He will [a]cover you with His pinions,
And [b]under His wings you may seek refuge;
His [c]faithfulness is a [d]shield and bulwark.

5 You [a]will not be afraid of the [b]terror by night,
Or of the [c]arrow that flies by day;
6 Of the [a]pestilence that [1]stalks in darkness,
Or of the [b]destruction that lays waste at noon.
7 A thousand may fall at your side
And ten thousand at your right hand,
But [a]it shall not approach you.
8 You will only look on with your eyes
And [a]see the recompense of the wicked.
9 [1]For you have made the LORD, [a]my refuge,
Even the Most High, [b]your dwelling place.
10 [a]No evil will befall you,
Nor will any plague come near your [1]tent.

11 For He will give [a]His angels charge concerning you,
To guard you in all your ways.
12 They will [a]bear you up in their hands,
That you do not strike your foot against a stone.
13 You will [a]tread upon the lion and cobra,
The young lion and the [1]serpent you will trample down.

14 "[a]Because he has loved Me, therefore I will deliver him;
I will [b]set him *securely* on high, because he has [c]known
My name.
15 "He will [a]call upon Me, and I will answer him;
I will be with him in [1]trouble;
I will rescue him and [b]honor him.
16 "With [1]a [a]long life I will satisfy him
And [2b]let him see My salvation."

Psalm 92 Theme ______________________________

A Psalm, a Song for the Sabbath day.

92 It is [a]good to give thanks to the LORD
And to [b]sing praises to Your name, O Most High;

2 To [a]declare Your lovingkindness in the morning
And Your [b]faithfulness [1]by night,
3 [1]With the [a]ten-stringed lute and [1]with the [a]harp,
[1]With resounding music [2]upon the [a]lyre.
4 For You, O LORD, have made me glad by [1]what You [a]have done,
I will [b]sing for joy at the [c]works of Your hands.

5 How [a]great are Your works, O LORD!
Your [1b]thoughts are very [c]deep.
6 A [a]senseless man has no knowledge,
Nor does a [a]stupid man understand this:
7 That when the wicked [a]sprouted up like grass
And all [b]who did iniquity flourished,
It *was only* that they might be [c]destroyed forevermore.
8 But You, O LORD, are [a]on high forever.
9 For, behold, Your enemies, O LORD,
For, behold, [a]Your enemies will perish;
All who do iniquity will be [b]scattered.

10 But You have exalted my [a]horn like *that of* the wild ox;
I have [1]been [b]anointed with fresh oil.
11 And my eye has [a]looked *exultantly* upon [1]my foes,
My ears hear of the evildoers who rise up against me.
12 The [a]righteous man will [1]flourish like the palm tree,
He will grow like a [b]cedar in Lebanon.
13 [a]Planted in the house of the LORD,
They will flourish [b]in the courts of our God.
14 They will still [1a]yield fruit in old age;
They shall be [2]full of sap and very green,
15 To [1]declare that [a]the LORD is upright;
He is my [b]rock, and there is [c]no unrighteousness in Him.

Psalm 93 Theme ______________________

93 [a]The LORD [1]reigns, He is [b]clothed with majesty;
The LORD has [c]clothed and girded Himself with strength;
Indeed, the [d]world is firmly established, it will not be moved.
2 Your [a]throne is established from of old;
You [b]are from everlasting.

3 The [a]floods have lifted up, O LORD,
The floods have lifted up their voice,
The floods lift up their pounding waves.
4 More than the sounds of many waters,
Than the mighty breakers of the sea,
The LORD [a]on high is mighty.
5 Your [a]testimonies are fully confirmed;
[b]Holiness befits Your house,
O LORD, [1]forevermore.

2 [1]Lit *nights* [a]Ps 59:16 [b]Ps 89:1

3 [1]Lit *Upon* [2]Lit *by means of* [a]1 Sam 10:5; 1 Chr 13:8; Neh 12:27; Ps 33:2

4 [1]Lit *Your working* [a]Ps 40:5; 90:16 [b]Ps 106:47 [c]Ps 8:6; 111:7; 143:5

5 [1]Or *purposes* [a]Ps 40:5; 111:2; Rev 15:3 [b]Ps 33:11; 40:5; 139:17 [c]Ps 36:6; Rom 11:33

6 [a]Ps 49:10; 73:22; 94:8

7 [a]Job 12:6; Ps 90:5 [b]Ps 94:4 [c]Ps 37:38

8 [a]Ps 83:18; 93:4; 113:5

9 [a]Ps 37:20 [b]Ps 68:1; 89:10

10 [1]Or *become moist* [a]Ps 75:10; 89:17; 112:9 [b]Ps 23:5; 45:7

11 [1]Or *those who lie in wait for me* [a]Ps 54:7; 91:8

12 [1]Lit *sprout* [a]Num 24:6; Ps 1:3; 52:8; 72:7; Jer 17:8; Hos 14:5, 6 [b]Ps 104:16; Ezek 31:3

13 [a]Ps 80:15; Is 60:21 [b]Ps 100:4; 116:19

14 [1]Or *thrive in* [2]Lit *fat and* [a]Prov 11:30; Is 37:31; John 15:2; James 3:18

15 [1]Or *show forth* [a]Job 34:10; Ps 25:8 [b]Deut 32:4; Ps 18:2; 94:22 [c]Rom 9:14

93:1 [1]Or *has assumed kingship* [a]Ps 96:10; 97:1; 99:1 [b]Ps 104:1 [c]Ps 65:6; Is 51:9 [d]Ps 96:10

2 [a]Ps 45:6; Lam 5:19 [b]Ps 90:2

3 [a]Ps 96:11; 98:7, 8

4 [a]Ps 65:7; 89:6, 9; 92:8

5 [1]Lit *for length of days* [a]Ps 19:7 [b]Ps 29:2; 96:9; 1 Cor 3:17

Psalm 94 Theme ________________

94 O LORD, God of [1a]vengeance,
God of [1]vengeance, [2b]shine forth!
2 [a]Rise up, O [b]Judge of the earth,
Render recompense [c]to the proud.
3 How long shall the wicked, O LORD,
How long shall the [a]wicked exult?
4 They pour forth *words,* they [a]speak arrogantly;
All who do wickedness [b]vaunt themselves.
5 They [a]crush Your people, O LORD,
And [b]afflict Your heritage.
6 They [a]slay the widow and the [1]stranger
And murder the orphans.
7 [a]They have said, "[1]The LORD does not see,
Nor does the God of Jacob pay heed."

8 Pay heed, you [a]senseless among the people;
And when will you understand, [a]stupid ones?
9 He who [a]planted the ear, [1]does He not hear?
He who formed the eye, [1]does He not see?
10 He who [1a]chastens the nations, will He not rebuke,
Even He who [b]teaches man knowledge?
11 The LORD [a]knows the thoughts of man,
[1]That they are a *mere* breath.

12 Blessed is the man whom [a]You chasten, O [1]LORD,
And [b]whom You teach out of Your law;
13 That You may grant him [a]relief from the [b]days of adversity,
Until [c]a pit is dug for the wicked.
14 For [a]the LORD will not abandon His people,
Nor will He [b]forsake His inheritance.
15 For [1a]judgment [2]will again be righteous,
And all the upright in heart [3]will follow it.
16 Who will [a]stand up for me against evildoers?
Who will take his stand for me [b]against those who do wickedness?

17 If [a]the LORD had not been my help,
My soul would soon have dwelt in *the abode of* silence.
18 If I should say, "[a]My foot has slipped,"
Your lovingkindness, O LORD, will hold me up.
19 When my anxious thoughts [1]multiply within me,
Your [a]consolations delight my soul.
20 Can a [1a]throne of destruction be allied with You,
One [b]which devises [2]mischief by decree?
21 They [a]band themselves together against the [1]life of the righteous
And [b]condemn [2]the innocent to death.
22 But the LORD has been my [a]stronghold,
And my God the [b]rock of my refuge.

94:1 [1]Or *avenging acts* [2]Or *has shone forth* [a]Deut 32:35; Is 35:4; Nah 1:2; Rom 12:19 [b]Ps 50:2; 80:1
2 [a]Ps 7:6 [b]Gen 18:25 [c]Ps 31:23
3 [a]Job 20:5
4 [a]Ps 31:18; 75:5 [b]Ps 10:3; 52:1
5 [a]Is 3:15 [b]Ps 79:1
6 [1]Or *sojourner* [a]Is 10:2
7 [1]Heb *YAH* [a]Job 22:13; Ps 10:11
8 [a]Ps 92:6
9 [1]Or *can* [a]Ex 4:11; Prov 20:12
10 [1]Or *instructs* [a]Ps 44:2 [b]Job 35:11; Is 28:26
11 [1]Or *For* [a]Job 11:11; 1 Cor 3:20
12 [1]Heb *YAH* [a]Deut 8:5; Job 5:17; Ps 119:71; Prov 3:11, 12; Heb 12:5, 6 [b]Ps 119:171
13 [a]Job 34:29; Hab 3:16 [b]Ps 49:5 [c]Ps 9:15; 55:23
14 [a]1 Sam 12:22; Lam 3:31; Rom 11:2 [b]Ps 37:28
15 [1]I.e. administration of justice [2]Lit *will return to righteousness* [3]Lit *will be after it* [a]Ps 97:2; Is 42:3; Mic 7:9
16 [a]Num 10:35; Is 28:21; 33:10 [b]Ps 17:13; 59:2
17 [a]Ps 124:1, 2
18 [a]Ps 38:16; 73:2
19 [1]Or *are many* [a]Is 57:18; 66:13
20 [1]Or *tribunal* [2]Or *trouble, misfortune* [a]Amos 6:3 [b]Ps 50:16; 58:2
21 [1]Or *soul* [2]Lit *innocent blood* [a]Ps 56:6; 59:3 [b]Ex 23:7; Ps 106:38; Prov 17:15; Matt 27:4
22 [a]Ps 9:9; 59:9 [b]Ps 18:2; 71:7

23 He has [a]brought back their wickedness upon them
And will [1b]destroy them in their evil;
The LORD our God will [1]destroy them.

Psalm 95 Theme ______________________

95 O come, let us [a]sing for joy to the LORD,
Let us shout joyfully to [b]the rock of our salvation.
2 Let us [a]come before His presence [b]with [1]thanksgiving,
Let us shout joyfully to Him [c]with [2]psalms.
3 For the LORD is a [a]great God
And a great King [b]above all gods,
4 In whose hand are the [a]depths of the earth,
The peaks of the mountains are His also.
5 [1]The sea is His, for it was He [a]who made it,
And His hands formed the dry land.

6 Come, let us [a]worship and bow down,
Let us [b]kneel before the LORD our [c]Maker.
7 For He is our God,
And [a]we are the people of His [1b]pasture and the sheep of His hand.
[c]Today, [2]if you would hear His voice,
8 Do not harden your hearts, as at [1a]Meribah,
As in the day of [2b]Massah in the wilderness,
9 "When your fathers [a]tested Me,
They tried Me, though they had seen My work.
10 "For [a]forty years I loathed *that* generation,
And said they are a people who err in their heart,
And they do not know My ways.
11 "Therefore I [a]swore in My anger,
Truly they shall not enter into My [b]rest."

Psalm 96 Theme ______________________

96 [a]Sing to the LORD a [b]new song;
Sing to the LORD, all the earth.
2 Sing to the LORD, bless His name;
[a]Proclaim good tidings of His salvation from day to day.
3 Tell of [a]His glory among the nations,
His wonderful deeds among all the peoples.
4 For [a]great is the LORD and [b]greatly to be praised;
He is to be [c]feared [d]above all gods.
5 For [a]all the gods of the peoples are [1]idols,
But [b]the LORD made the heavens.
6 [a]Splendor and majesty are before Him,
Strength and beauty are in His sanctuary.

7 [1]Ascribe to the LORD, O [a]families of the peoples,
[1b]Ascribe to the LORD glory and strength.
8 [1]Ascribe to the LORD the [a]glory of His name;
Bring an [2b]offering and come into His courts.

---

23 [1]Or *silence* [a]Ps 7:16; 140:9, 11 [b]Gen 19:15

95:1 [a]Ps 66:1; 81:1 [b]Ps 89:26

2 [1]Or *a song of thanksgiving* [2]Or *songs* (with instrumental accompaniment) [a]Mic 6:6 [b]Ps 100:4; 147:7; Jon 2:9 [c]Ps 81:2; Eph 5:19; James 5:13

3 [a]Ps 48:1; 135:5; 145:3 [b]Ps 96:4; 97:9

4 [a]Ps 135:6

5 [1]Lit *Who has the sea* [a]Gen 1:9, 10; Ps 146:6; Jon 1:9

6 [a]Ps 96:9; 99:5, 9 [b]2 Chr 6:13; Dan 6:10; Phil 2:10 [c]Ps 100:3; 149:2; Is 17:7; Hos 8:14

7 [1]Lit *pasturing* [2]Or *O that you would obey* [a]Ps 79:13 [b]Ps 74:1 [c]Heb 3:7-11, 15; 4:7

8 [1]Or *place of strife* [2]Or *temptation* [a]Ex 17:2-7; Num 20:13 [b]Ex 17:7; Deut 6:16

9 [a]Num 14:22; Ps 78:18; 1 Cor 10:9

10 [a]Acts 7:36; 13:18; Heb 3:10, 17

11 [a]Num 14:23, 28-30; Deut 1:35; Heb 4:3, 5 [b]Deut 12:9

96:1 [a]1 Chr 16:23-33 [b]Ps 40:3

2 [a]Ps 71:15

3 [a]Ps 145:12

4 [a]Ps 48:1; 145:3 [b]Ps 18:3 [c]Ps 89:7 [d]Ps 95:3

5 [1]Or *non-existent things* [a]1 Chr 16:26; Jer 10:11 [b]Ps 115:15; Is 42:5

6 [a]Ps 104:1

7 [1]Lit *Give* [a]Ps 22:27 [b]1 Chr 16:28, 29; Ps 29:1, 2

8 [1]Lit *Give* [2]Or *meal offering* [a]Ps 79:9; 115:1 [b]Ps 45:12; 72:10

9 [a]Worship the LORD in [1]holy attire;
[b]Tremble before Him, all the earth.
10 Say among the nations, "[a]The LORD reigns;
Indeed, the [a]world is firmly established, it will not be moved;
He will [b]judge the peoples with [1]equity."

11 Let the [a]heavens be glad, and let the [b]earth rejoice;
Let [c]the sea [1]roar, and [2]all it contains;
12 Let the [a]field exult, and all that is in it.
Then all the [b]trees of the forest will sing for joy
13 Before the LORD, [a]for He is coming,
For He is coming to judge the earth.
[b]He will judge the world in righteousness
And the peoples in His faithfulness.

Psalm 97 Theme ______________________

97 [a]The LORD [1]reigns, let the [b]earth rejoice;
Let the many [2c]islands be glad.
2 [a]Clouds and thick darkness surround Him;
[b]Righteousness and justice are the foundation of His throne.
3 [a]Fire goes before Him
And [b]burns up His adversaries round about.
4 His [a]lightnings lit up the world;
The earth saw and [b]trembled.
5 The mountains [a]melted like wax at the presence of the LORD,
At the presence of the [b]Lord of the whole earth.
6 The [a]heavens declare His righteousness,
And [b]all the peoples have seen His glory.

7 Let all those be ashamed who serve [a]graven images,
Who boast themselves of [b]idols;
[1c]Worship Him, all you [2]gods.
8 Zion [1]heard *this* and [a]was glad,
And the daughters of Judah have rejoiced
Because of Your judgments, O LORD.
9 For You are the LORD [a]Most High over all the earth;
You are exalted far [b]above all [1]gods.

10 [a]Hate evil, you who love the LORD,
Who [b]preserves the souls of His godly ones;
He [c]delivers them from the hand of the wicked.
11 [a]Light is sown *like seed* for the righteous
And [b]gladness for the upright in heart.
12 Be [a]glad in the LORD, you righteous ones,
And [b]give thanks [1]to His holy name.

Psalm 98 Theme ______________________

A Psalm.

98 O sing to the LORD a [a]new song,
For He has done [b]wonderful things,

---

9 [1]Or *the splendor of holiness* [a]1 Chr 16:29; 2 Chr 20:21; Ps 29:2; 110:3 [b]Ps 33:8; 114:7
10 [1]Or *uprightness* [a]Ps 93:1; 97:1 [b]Ps 9:8; 58:11; 67:4; 98:9
11 [1]Or *thunder* [2]Lit *its fullness* [a]Ps 69:34; Is 49:13 [b]Ps 97:1 [c]Ps 98:7
12 [a]Ps 65:13; Is 35:1; 55:12, 13 [b]Is 44:23
13 [a]Ps 98:9 [b]Rev 19:11
97:1 [1]Or *has assumed Kingship* [2]Or *coastlands* [a]Ps 96:10 [b]Ps 96:11 [c]Is 42:10, 12
2 [a]Ex 19:9; Deut 4:11; 1 Kin 8:12; Ps 18:11 [b]Ps 89:14
3 [a]Ps 18:8; 50:3; Dan 7:10; Hab 3:5 [b]Mal 4:1; Heb 12:29
4 [a]Ex 19:16; Ps 77:18 [b]Ps 96:9; 104:32
5 [a]Ps 46:6; Amos 9:5; Mic 1:4; Nah 1:5 [b]Josh 3:11
6 [a]Ps 19:1; 50:6 [b]Ps 98:2; Is 6:3; 40:5; 66:18
7 [1]Or *All the gods have worshiped Him* [2]Or *supernatural powers* [a]Ps 78:58; Is 42:17; 44:9, 11; Jer 10:14 [b]Ps 106:36; Jer 50:2; Hab 2:18 [c]Heb 1:6
8 [1]Or possibly *hears and is glad* [a]Ps 48:11; Zeph 3:14
9 [1]Or *supernatural powers* [a]Ps 83:18 [b]Ex 18:11; Ps 95:3; 96:4; 135:5
10 [a]Ps 34:14; Prov 8:13; Amos 5:15; Rom 12:9 [b]Ps 31:23; 145:20; Prov 2:8 [c]Ps 37:40; Jer 15:21; Dan 3:28
11 [a]Job 22:28; Ps 112:4; Prov 4:18 [b]Ps 64:10
12 [1]Lit *for the memory of His holiness* [a]Ps 32:11 [b]Ps 30:4
98:1 [a]Ps 33:3 [b]Ps 40:5; 96:3

His [c]right hand and His [d]holy arm have [1]gained the victory for Him.
2 [a]The LORD has made known His salvation;
He has [b]revealed His [1]righteousness in the sight of the nations.
3 He has [a]remembered His lovingkindness and His faithfulness to the house of Israel;
[b]All the ends of the earth have seen the salvation of our God.

4 [a]Shout joyfully to the LORD, all the earth;
[b]Break forth and sing for joy and sing praises.
5 Sing praises to the LORD with the [a]lyre,
With the lyre and the [1b]sound of melody.
6 With [a]trumpets and the sound of the horn
[b]Shout joyfully before [c]the King, the LORD.

7 Let the [a]sea roar and [1]all it contains,
The [b]world and those who dwell in it.
8 Let the [a]rivers clap their hands,
Let the [b]mountains sing together for joy
9 Before the LORD, for He is coming to [a]judge the earth;
He will judge the world with righteousness
And [b]the peoples with [1]equity.

Psalm 99 Theme

99 [a]The LORD reigns, let the peoples tremble;
He [1b]is enthroned *above* the cherubim, let the earth shake!
2 The LORD [1]is [a]great in Zion,
And He is [b]exalted above all the peoples.
3 Let them praise Your [a]great and awesome name;
[b]Holy is [1]He.
4 The [1]strength of the King [a]loves [2]justice;
You have established [3b]equity;
You have [c]executed [2]justice and righteousness in Jacob.
5 [1a]Exalt the LORD our God
And [b]worship at His footstool;
[c]Holy is He.

6 [a]Moses and Aaron were among His [b]priests,
And [a]Samuel was among those who [c]called on His name;
They [d]called upon the LORD and He answered them.
7 He [a]spoke to them in the pillar of cloud;
They [b]kept His testimonies
And the statute that He gave them.
8 O LORD our God, You [a]answered them;
You were a [b]forgiving God to them,
And *yet* an [c]avenger of their *evil* deeds.
9 Exalt the LORD our God
And worship at His holy hill,
For holy is the LORD our God.

98:1 [1]Or *accomplished salvation* [c]Ex 15:6 [d]Is 52:10
2 [1]I.e. faithfulness to His gracious promises [a]Is 52:10 [b]Is 62:2; Rom 3:25
3 [a]Luke 1:54, 72 [b]Ps 22:27
4 [a]Ps 100:1 [b]Is 44:23
5 [1]Or *voice of song* (accompanied by music) [a]Ps 92:3 [b]Is 51:3
6 [a]Num 10:10; 2 Chr 15:14 [b]Ps 66:1 [c]Ps 47:7
7 [1]Lit *its fullness* [a]Ps 96:11 [b]Ps 24:1
8 [a]Ps 93:3; Is 55:12 [b]Ps 65:12; 89:12
9 [1]Or *uprightness* [a]Ps 96:13 [b]Ps 96:10
99:1 [1]Lit *sits* [a]Ps 97:1 [b]Ex 25:22; 1 Sam 4:4; Ps 80:1
2 [1]Or *in Zion is great* [a]Ps 48:1; Is 12:6 [b]Ps 97:9; 113:4
3 [1]Or *it* [a]Deut 28:58; Ps 76:1 [b]Lev 19:2; Josh 24:19; 1 Sam 2:2; Ps 22:3; Is 6:3
4 [1]Or *You have established in equity the strength of the King who loves justice* [2]Or *judgment* [3]Or *uprightness* [a]Ps 11:7; 33:5 [b]Ps 17:2; 98:9 [c]Ps 103:6; 146:7; Jer 23:5
5 [1]The verb is plural [a]Ps 34:3; 107:32; 118:28 [b]Ps 132:7 [c]Ps 99:3
6 [a]Jer 15:1 [b]Ex 24:6-8; 29:26; 40:23-27; Lev 8:1-30 [c]1 Sam 7:9; 12:18; Ps 22:4, 5 [d]Ex 15:25; 32:30-34
7 [a]Ex 33:9; Num 12:5 [b]Ps 105:28
8 [a]Ps 106:44 [b]Num 14:20; Ps 78:38 [c]Ex 32:28; Num 20:12; Ps 95:11; 107:12

*Psalm 100 Theme*________________________

A Psalm for +Thanksgiving.

100 [a]Shout joyfully to the LORD, all the earth.
2 [a]Serve the LORD with gladness;
[b]Come before Him with joyful singing.
3 Know that [a]the LORD [1]Himself is God;
It is He who has [b]made us, and [2]not we ourselves;
We are [c]His people and the sheep of His pasture.

4 Enter His gates [a]with [1]thanksgiving
And His courts with praise.
Give thanks to Him, [b]bless His name.
5 For [a]the LORD is good;
[b]His lovingkindness is everlasting
And His [c]faithfulness to all generations.

*Psalm 101 Theme*________________________

A Psalm of David.

101 I will [a]sing of lovingkindness and [1]justice,
To You, O LORD, I will sing praises.
2 I will [1a]give heed to the [2]blameless way.
When will You come to me?
I will walk within my house in the [3b]integrity of my heart.
3 I will set no [a]worthless thing before my eyes;
I hate the [1]work of those who [b]fall away;
It shall not fasten its grip on me.
4 A [a]perverse heart shall depart from me;
I will know no evil.
5 Whoever secretly [a]slanders his neighbor, him I will
[1]destroy;
No one who has a [b]haughty look and an arrogant heart will
I endure.

6 My eyes shall be upon the faithful of the land, that they
may dwell with me;
He who walks in a [1a]blameless way is the one who will
minister to me.
7 He who [a]practices deceit shall not dwell within my house;
He who speaks falsehood [b]shall not [1]maintain his position
before me.
8 [a]Every morning I will [1b]destroy all the wicked of the land,
So as to [c]cut off from the [d]city of the LORD all those who do
iniquity.

*Psalm 102 Theme*________________________

A Prayer of the Afflicted when he is faint and +pours out his complaint before the LORD.

102 [a]Hear my prayer, O LORD!
And let my cry for help [b]come to You.

100:1 +Or *thank offering* [a]Ps 95:1; 98:4, 6

2 [a]Deut 12:11, 12; 28:47 [b]Ps 95:2

3 [1]Or *He* [2]Some mss read *His we are* [a]Deut 4:35; 1 Kin 18:39; Ps 46:10 [b]Job 10:3, 8; Ps 95:6; 119:73 [c]Ps 74:1, 2; 95:7; Is 40:11; Ezek 34:30, 31

4 [1]Or *a thank offering* [a]Ps 95:2; 116:17 [b]Ps 96:2

5 [a]1 Chr 16:34; 2 Chr 5:13; 7:3; Ezra 3:11; Ps 25:8; 86:5; 106:1; 107:1; 118:1; Jer 33:11; Nah 1:7 [b]Ps 136:1 [c]Ps 119:90

101:1 [1]Or *judgment* [a]Ps 51:14; 89:1; 145:7

2 [1]Or *behave prudently in* [2]Or *way of integrity* [3]Or *blamelessness* [a]1 Sam 18:5, 14 [b]1 Kin 9:4

3 [1]Or *practice of apostasy* [a]Deut 15:9 [b]Josh 23:6; Ps 40:4

4 [a]Prov 11:20

5 [1]Or *silence* [a]Ps 50:20; Jer 9:4 [b]Ps 10:4; 18:27; Prov 6:17

6 [1]Or *way of integrity* [a]Ps 119:1

7 [1]Lit *be established before my eyes* [a]Ps 43:1; 52:2 [b]Ps 52:4, 5

8 [1]Or *silence* [a]Jer 21:12 [b]Ps 75:10 [c]Ps 118:10-12 [d]Ps 46:4; 48:2, 8

102:1 +Ps 142:2 [a]Ps 39:12; 61:1 [b]Ex 2:23; 1 Sam 9:16

2 [a]Do not hide Your face from me in the day of my distress;
[b]Incline Your ear to me;
In the day when I call [a]answer me quickly.
3 For my days [a]have been [1]consumed in smoke,
And my [b]bones have been scorched like a hearth.
4 My heart [a]has been smitten like [1]grass and has [b]withered away,
Indeed, I [c]forget to eat my bread.
5 Because of the [1]loudness of my groaning
My [a]bones [2]cling to my flesh.
6 I [1]resemble a [a]pelican of the wilderness;
I have become like an owl of the waste places.
7 I [a]lie awake,
I have become like a lonely bird on a housetop.

8 My enemies [a]have reproached me all day long;
Those who [1b]deride me [2]have used my *name* as a [c]curse.
9 For I have eaten ashes like bread
And [a]mingled my drink with weeping
10 [a]Because of Your indignation and Your wrath,
For You have [b]lifted me up and cast me away.
11 My days are like a [1a]lengthened shadow,
And [2]I [b]wither away like [3]grass.

12 But You, O LORD, [1a]abide forever,
And Your [2b]name to all generations.
13 You will [a]arise *and* have [b]compassion on Zion;
For [c]it is time to be gracious to her,
For the [d]appointed time has come.
14 Surely Your servants [1]find pleasure in her stones
And feel pity for her dust.
15 [1]So the [2a]nations will fear the name of the LORD
And [b]all the kings of the earth Your glory.
16 For the LORD has [a]built up Zion;
He has [b]appeared in His glory.
17 He has [a]regarded the prayer of the [1]destitute
And has not despised their prayer.

18 [1]This will be [a]written for the [b]generation to come,
[2]That [c]a people yet to be created [3]may praise [4]the LORD.
19 For He [a]looked down from His holy height;
[b]From heaven the LORD gazed [1]upon the earth,
20 To hear the [a]groaning of the prisoner,
To [b]set free [1]those who were doomed to death,
21 That *men* may [a]tell of the name of the LORD in Zion
And His praise in Jerusalem,
22 When [a]the peoples are gathered together,
And the kingdoms, to serve the LORD.

23 He has weakened my strength in the way;
He has [a]shortened my days.

2 [a]Ps 69:17 [b]Ps 31:2
3 [1]Or *finished* [a]Ps 37:20; James 4:14 [b]Job 30:30; Lam 1:13
4 [1]Lit *herbage* [a]Ps 90:5, 6 [b]Ps 37:2; Is 40:7 [c]1 Sam 1:7; 2 Sam 12:17; Ezra 10:6; Job 33:20
5 [1]Lit *voice* [2]Lit *have cleaved* [a]Job 19:20; Lam 4:8
6 [1]Lit *have become similar to* [a]Is 34:11; Zeph 2:14
7 [a]Ps 77:4
8 [1]Or *made a fool of* [2]Lit *have sworn by me* [a]Ps 31:11 [b]Acts 26:11 [c]2 Sam 16:5; Is 65:15; Jer 29:22
9 [a]Ps 42:3; 80:5
10 [a]Ps 38:3 [b]Job 27:21; 30:22
11 [1]Lit *stretched out* [2]Or *as for me, I* [3]Lit *herbage* [a]Job 14:2; Ps 109:23 [b]Ps 102:4
12 [1]Or *sit enthroned* [2]Lit *memorial* [a]Ps 9:7; 10:16; Lam 5:19 [b]Ex 3:15; Ps 135:13
13 [a]Ps 12:5; 44:26 [b]Is 60:10; Zech 1:12 [c]Ps 119:126 [d]Ps 75:2; Dan 8:19
14 [1]Or *have found*
15 [1]Or *And* [2]Or *Gentiles, heathen* [a]1 Kin 8:43; Ps 67:7 [b]Ps 138:4
16 [a]Ps 147:2 [b]Is 60:1, 2
17 [1]Or *naked* [a]Neh 1:6; Ps 22:24
18 [1]Or *Let this be written* [2]Or *And* [3]Or *will* [4]Heb *YAH* [a]Deut 31:19; Rom 15:4; 1 Cor 10:11 [b]Ps 22:30; 48:13 [c]Ps 22:31; 78:6f
19 [1]Lit *toward* [a]Deut 26:15; Ps 14:2; 53:2 [b]Ps 33:13
20 [1]Lit *the sons of death* [a]Ps 79:11 [b]Ps 146:7
21 [a]Ps 22:22
22 [a]Ps 22:27; 86:9; Is 49:22, 23; 60:3; Zech 8:20-23
23 [a]Ps 39:5

24 I say, "O my God, [a]do not take me away in the [1]midst of
my days,
Your [b]years are throughout all generations.
25 "Of old You [a]founded the earth,
And the [b]heavens are the work of Your hands.
26 "[1]Even they will [a]perish, but You endure;
And all of them will wear out like a garment;
Like clothing You will change them and they will be
changed.
27 "But You are [1a]the same,
And Your years will not come to an end.
28 "The [a]children of Your servants will continue,
And their [1b]descendants will be established before You."

Psalm 103 Theme ______________________________

A Psalm of David.

103 [a]Bless the LORD, O my soul,
And all that is within me, *bless* His [b]holy name.
2 Bless the LORD, O my soul,
And [a]forget none of His benefits;
3 Who [a]pardons all your iniquities,
Who [b]heals all your diseases;
4 Who [a]redeems your life from the pit,
Who [b]crowns you with lovingkindness and compassion;
5 Who [a]satisfies your [1]years with good things,
So that your youth is [b]renewed like the eagle.

6 The LORD [a]performs [1]righteous deeds
And judgments for all who are [b]oppressed.
7 He [a]made known His ways to Moses,
His [b]acts to the sons of Israel.
8 The LORD is [a]compassionate and gracious,
[b]Slow to anger and abounding in lovingkindness.
9 He [a]will not always strive *with us,*
Nor will He [b]keep *His anger* forever.
10 He has [a]not dealt with us according to our sins,
Nor rewarded us according to our iniquities.
11 For as high [a]as the heavens are above the earth,
So great is His lovingkindness toward those who [1]fear Him.
12 As far as the east is from the west,
So far has He [a]removed our transgressions from us.
13 Just [a]as a father has compassion on *his* children,
So the LORD has compassion on those who [1]fear Him.
14 For [a]He Himself knows [1]our frame;
He [b]is mindful that we are *but* [c]dust.

15 As for man, his days are [a]like grass;
As a [b]flower of the field, so he flourishes.
16 When the [a]wind has passed over it, it is no more,
And its [b]place acknowledges it no longer.

24 [1]Lit *half* [a]Ps 39:13; Is 38:10 [b]Job 36:26; Ps 90:2; 102:12; Hab 1:12
25 [a]Gen 1:1; Neh 9:6; Heb 1:10-12 [b]Ps 96:5
26 [1]Lit *They themselves* [a]Is 34:4; 51:6; Matt 24:35; 2 Pet 3:10; Rev 20:11
27 [1]Lit *He* [a]Is 41:4; 43:10; Mal 3:6; James 1:17
28 [1]Lit *seed* [a]Ps 69:36 [b]Ps 89:4
103:1 [a]Ps 104:1, 35 [b]Ps 33:21; 105:3; 145:21; Ezek 36:21; 39:7
2 [a]Deut 6:12; 8:11
3 [a]Ex 34:7; Ps 86:5; 130:8; Is 43:25 [b]Ex 15:26; Ps 30:2; Jer 30:17
4 [a]Ps 49:15 [b]Ps 5:12
5 [1]Or *desire* [a]Ps 107:9; 145:16 [b]Is 40:31
6 [1]Or *deeds of vindication* [a]Ps 99:4; 146:7 [b]Ps 12:5
7 [a]Ex 33:13; Ps 99:7; 147:19 [b]Ps 78:11; 106:22
8 [a]Ex 34:6; Num 14:18; Neh 9:17; Ps 86:15; Jon 4:2; James 5:11 [b]Ps 145:8; Joel 2:13; Nah 1:3
9 [a]Ps 30:5; Is 57:16 [b]Jer 3:5, 12; Mic 7:18
10 [a]Ezra 9:13; Lam 3:22
11 [1]Or *revere* [a]Ps 36:5; 57:10
12 [a]2 Sam 12:13; Is 38:17; 43:25; Zech 3:9; Heb 9:26
13 [1]Or *revere* [a]Mal 3:17
14 [1]I.e. what we are made of [a]Is 29:16 [b]Ps 78:39 [c]Gen 3:19; Eccl 12:7
15 [a]Ps 90:5; Is 40:6; 1 Pet 1:24 [b]Job 14:2; James 1:10, 11
16 [a]Is 40:7 [b]Job 7:10; 8:18; 20:9

17 But the [a]lovingkindness of the LORD is from everlasting to
everlasting on those who [1]fear Him,
And His [2]righteousness [b]to children's children,
18 To [a]those who keep His covenant
And remember His precepts to do them.

19 The LORD has established His [a]throne in the heavens,
And His [1b]sovereignty rules over [2]all.
20 Bless the LORD, you [a]His angels,
[b]Mighty in strength, who [c]perform His word,
[d]Obeying the voice of His word!
21 Bless the LORD, all you [a]His hosts,
You [b]who serve Him, doing His will.
22 Bless the LORD, [a]all you works of His,
In all places of His dominion;
Bless the LORD, O my soul!

*Psalm 104 Theme*____________________________________

104 [a]Bless the LORD, O my soul!
O LORD my God, You are very great;
You are [b]clothed with splendor and majesty,
2 Covering Yourself with [a]light as with a cloak,
[b]Stretching out heaven like a *tent* curtain.
3 [1]He [a]lays the beams of His upper chambers in the
waters;
[1]He makes the [b]clouds His chariot;
[1]He walks upon the [c]wings of the wind;
4 [1]He makes [2a]the winds His messengers,
[3]Flaming [b]fire His ministers.

5 He [a]established the earth upon its foundations,
So that it will not [1]totter forever and ever.
6 You [a]covered it with the deep as with a garment;
The waters were standing above the mountains.
7 At Your [a]rebuke they fled,
At the [b]sound of Your thunder they hurried away.
8 The mountains rose; the valleys sank down
To the [a]place which You established for them.
9 You set a [a]boundary that they may not pass over,
So that they will not return to cover the earth.

10 [1]He sends forth [a]springs in the valleys;
They flow between the mountains;
11 They [a]give drink to every beast of the field;
The [b]wild donkeys quench their thirst.
12 [1]Beside them the birds of the heavens [a]dwell;
They [2]lift up *their* voices among the branches.
13 [1]He [a]waters the mountains from His upper chambers;
[b]The earth is satisfied with the fruit of His works.

17 [1]Or *revere* [2]I.e. faithfulness to His gracious promises [a]Ps 25:6 [b]Ex 20:6; Deut 5:10; Ps 105:8

18 [a]Deut 7:9; Ps 25:10

19 [1]Or *kingdom* [2]I.e. the universe [a]Ps 11:4 [b]Ps 47:2, 8; Dan 4:17, 25

20 [a]Ps 148:2 [b]Ps 29:1; 78:25 [c]Matt 6:10 [d]Ps 91:11; Heb 1:14

21 [a]1 Kin 22:19; Neh 9:6; Ps 148:2; Luke 2:13 [b]Ps 104:4

22 [a]Ps 145:10

104:1 [a]Ps 103:22 [b]Ps 93:1

2 [a]Dan 7:9 [b]Is 40:22

3 [1]Lit *The one who* [a]Amos 9:6 [b]Is 19:1 [c]Ps 18:10

4 [1]Lit *Who* [2]Or *His angels, spirits* [3]Or *His ministers flames of fire* [a]Ps 148:8; Heb 1:7 [b]2 Kin 2:11; 6:17

5 [1]Or *move out of place* [a]Job 38:4; Ps 24:2

6 [a]Gen 1:2

7 [a]Ps 18:15; 106:9; Is 50:2 [b]Ps 29:3; 77:18

8 [a]Ps 33:7

9 [a]Job 38:10, 11; Jer 5:22

10 [1]Lit *The one who sends* [a]Ps 107:35; Is 41:18

11 [a]Ps 104:13 [b]Job 39:5

12 [1]Or *Over,* Above [2]Lit *give forth* [a]Matt 8:20

13 [1]Lit *Who* [a]Ps 65:9; 147:8 [b]Jer 10:13

14 [1]He causes the [a]grass to grow for the [2]cattle,
And [b]vegetation for the [3]labor of man,
So that [4]he may bring forth [5]food [c]from the earth,
15 And [a]wine which makes man's heart glad,
[b]So that he may make *his* face glisten with oil,
And [1]food which [c]sustains man's heart.
16 The trees of the LORD [1]drink their fill,
The cedars of Lebanon which He planted,
17 Where the [a]birds build their nests,
And the [b]stork, whose home is the [1]fir trees.

18 The high mountains are for the [a]wild goats;
The [b]cliffs are a refuge for the [1c]shephanim.
19 He made the moon [a]for the seasons;
The [b]sun knows the place of its setting.
20 You [a]appoint darkness and it becomes night,
In which all the [b]beasts of the forest [1]prowl about.
21 The [a]young lions roar after their prey
[1]And [b]seek their food from God.
22 *When* the sun rises they withdraw
And lie down in their [a]dens.
23 Man goes forth to [a]his work
And to his labor until evening.

24 O LORD, how [a]many are Your works!
[1]In [b]wisdom You have made them all;
The [c]earth is full of Your [2]possessions.
25 [1]There is the [a]sea, great and [2]broad,
In which are swarms without number,
Animals both small and great.
26 There the [a]ships move along,
And [1b]Leviathan, which You have formed to sport in it.

27 They all [a]wait for You
To [b]give them their food in [1]due season.
28 You give to them, they gather *it* up;
You [a]open Your hand, they are satisfied with good.
29 You [a]hide Your face, they are dismayed;
You [b]take away their [1]spirit, they expire
And [c]return to their dust.
30 You send forth Your [1a]Spirit, they are created;
And You renew the face of the ground.

31 Let the [a]glory of the LORD endure forever;
Let the LORD [b]be glad in His works;
32 [1]He [a]looks at the earth, and it [b]trembles;
He [c]touches the mountains, and they smoke.
33 [1]I will sing to the LORD [2a]as long as I live;
[1]I will [b]sing praise to my God [3]while I have my being.
34 Let my [a]meditation be pleasing to Him;
As for me, I shall [b]be glad in the LORD.

14 [1]Lit *Who* [2]Or *beasts* [3]Or *cultivation by* or *service of* [4]Or *He* [5]Lit *bread* [a]Job 38:27; Ps 147:8 [b]Gen 1:29 [c]Job 28:5
15 [1]Lit *bread* [a]Judg 9:13; Prov 31:6; Eccl 10:19 [b]Ps 23:5; 92:10; 141:5; Luke 7:46 [c]Gen 18:5; Judg 19:5, 8
16 [1]Lit *are satisfied*
17 [1]Or *cypress* [a]Ps 104:12 [b]Lev 11:19
18 [1]Small, shy, furry animals *(Hyrax syriacus)* found in the peninsula of the Sinai, northern Israel, and the region round the Dead Sea; KJV *coney,* orig NASB *rock badgers* [a]Job 39:1 [b]Prov 30:26 [c]Lev 11:5
19 [a]Gen 1:14 [b]Ps 19:6
20 [1]Lit *creep* [a]Ps 74:16; Is 45:7 [b]Ps 50:10; Is 56:9; Mic 5:8
21 [1]Lit *And to seek* [a]Job 38:39 [b]Ps 145:15; Joel 1:20
22 [a]Job 37:8
23 [a]Gen 3:19
24 [1]Or *With* [2]Or *creatures* [a]Ps 40:5 [b]Ps 136:5; Prov 3:19; Jer 10:12; 51:15 [c]Ps 65:9
25 [1]Or *This* [2]Or *broad of dimensions* (lit *hands*) [a]Ps 8:8; 69:34
26 [1]Or *a sea monster* [a]Ps 107:23; Ezek 27:9 [b]Job 41:1; Ps 74:14; Is 27:1
27 [1]Lit *its appointed time* [a]Ps 145:15 [b]Job 36:31; 38:41; Ps 136:25; 147:9
28 [a]Ps 145:16
29 [1]Or *breath* [a]Deut 31:17; Ps 30:7 [b]Job 34:14, 15; Ps 146:4; Eccl 12:7 [c]Gen 3:19; Job 10:9; Ps 90:3
30 [1]Or *breath* [a]Job 33:4; Ezek 37:9
31 [a]Ps 86:12; 111:10 [b]Gen 1:31
32 [1]Lit *The one who* [a]Judg 5:5; Ps 97:4, 5; 114:7 [b]Hab 3:10 [c]Ex 19:18; Ps 144:5
33 [1]Or *Let me sing* [2]Lit *in my lifetime* [3]Lit *while I still am* [a]Ps 63:4 [b]Ps 146:2
34 [a]Ps 19:14 [b]Ps 9:2

35 Let sinners be [a]consumed from the earth
And let the [b]wicked be no more.
[c]Bless the LORD, O my soul.
[1d]Praise [2]the LORD!

*Psalm 105 Theme*______________________________

105 Oh [a]give thanks to the LORD, [b]call upon His name;
[c]Make known His deeds among the peoples.
2 Sing to Him, [a]sing praises to Him;
[1b]Speak of all His [2]wonders.
3 [1]Glory in His holy name;
Let the [a]heart of those who seek the LORD be glad.
4 Seek the LORD and [a]His strength;
[b]Seek His face continually.
5 Remember His [1a]wonders which He has done,
His marvels and the [b]judgments [2]uttered by His mouth,
6 O seed of [a]Abraham, His servant,
O sons of [b]Jacob, His [c]chosen ones!
7 He is the LORD our God;
His [a]judgments are in all the earth.

8 He has [a]remembered His covenant forever,
The word which He commanded to a [b]thousand generations,
9 *The* [a]*covenant* which He made with Abraham,
And His [b]oath to Isaac.
10 Then He [a]confirmed it to Jacob for a statute,
To Israel as an everlasting covenant,
11 Saying, "[a]To you I will give the land of Canaan
As the [1b]portion of your inheritance,"
12 When they were only a [a]few men in number,
Very few, and [b]strangers in it.
13 And they wandered about from nation to nation,
From *one* kingdom to another people.
14 He [a]permitted no man to oppress them,
And He [b]reproved kings for their sakes:
15 "[a]Do not touch My anointed ones,
And do My prophets no harm."

16 And He [a]called for a famine upon the land;
He [b]broke the whole staff of bread.
17 He [a]sent a man before them,
Joseph, *who* was [b]sold as a slave.
18 They afflicted his [a]feet with fetters,
[1]He himself was laid in irons;
19 Until the time that his [a]word came to pass,
The word of the LORD [1b]tested him.
20 The [a]king sent and released him,
The ruler of peoples, and set him free.
21 He [a]made him lord of his house
And ruler over all his possessions,

35 [1]Or *Hallelujah!* [2]Heb *YAH* [a]Ps 59:13 [b]Ps 37:10 [c]Ps 104:1 [d]Ps 105:45; 106:48

105:1 [a]1 Chr 16:8-22, 34; Ps 106:1; Is 12:4 [b]Ps 99:6 [c]Ps 145:12

2 [1]Or *Meditate on* [2]I.e. wonderful acts [a]Ps 96:1; 98:5 [b]Ps 77:12; 119:27; 145:5

3 [1]Or *Boast* [a]Ps 33:21

4 [a]Ps 63:2 [b]Ps 27:8

5 [1]I.e. wonderful acts [2]Lit *of His mouth* [a]Ps 40:5; 77:11 [b]Ps 119:13

6 [a]Ps 105:42 [b]Ps 135:4 [c]1 Chr 16:13; Ps 106:5; 135:4

7 [a]Is 26:9

8 [a]Ps 105:42; 106:45; Luke 1:72 [b]Deut 7:9

9 [a]Gen 12:7; 17:2, 8; 22:16-18; Gal 3:17 [b]Gen 26:3

10 [a]Gen 28:13-15

11 [1]Lit *measuring line* [a]Gen 13:15; 15:18 [b]Josh 23:4; Ps 78:55

12 [a]Gen 34:30; Deut 7:7 [b]Gen 23:4; Heb 11:9

14 [a]Gen 20:7; 35:5 [b]Gen 12:17; 20:3, 7

15 [a]Gen 26:11

16 [a]Gen 41:54 [b]Lev 26:26; Is 3:1; Ezek 4:16

17 [a]Gen 45:5 [b]Gen 37:28, 36; Acts 7:9

18 [1]Lit *His soul came into* [a]Gen 39:20; 40:15

19 [1]Or *refined* [a]Gen 40:20, 21 [b]Ps 66:10

20 [a]Gen 41:14

21 [a]Gen 41:40-44

22 To [1]imprison his princes [2a]at will,
That he might teach his elders wisdom.
23 [a]Israel also came into Egypt;
Thus Jacob [b]sojourned in the land of Ham.
24 And He [a]caused His people to be very fruitful,
And made them stronger than their adversaries.

25 He [a]turned their heart to hate His people,
To [b]deal craftily with His servants.
26 He [a]sent Moses His servant,
And [b]Aaron, whom He had chosen.
27 They [1a]performed His wondrous acts among them,
And miracles in the land of Ham.
28 He [a]sent darkness and made *it* dark;
And they did not [b]rebel against His words.
29 He [a]turned their waters into blood
And caused their fish to die.
30 Their land swarmed with [a]frogs
Even in the [b]chambers of their kings.
31 He spoke, and there came a [a]swarm of flies
And [b]gnats in all their territory.
32 He [1]gave them [a]hail for rain,
And flaming fire in their land.
33 He [a]struck down their vines also and their fig trees,
And shattered the trees of their territory.
34 He spoke, and [a]locusts came,
And young locusts, even without number,
35 And ate up all vegetation in their land,
And ate up the fruit of their ground.
36 He also [a]struck down all the firstborn in their land,
The [b]first fruits of all their vigor.

37 Then He brought them out with [a]silver and gold,
And among His tribes there was not one who stumbled.
38 Egypt was [a]glad when they departed,
For the [b]dread of them had fallen upon them.
39 He spread a [a]cloud for a [1]covering,
And [b]fire to illumine by night.
40 [1]They [a]asked, and He brought [b]quail,
And satisfied them with the [2c]bread of heaven.
41 He opened the [1]rock and [a]water flowed out;
[2]It ran in the dry places *like* a river.
42 For He [a]remembered His holy word
With Abraham His servant;
43 And He brought forth His people with joy,
His chosen ones with a joyful [a]shout.
44 He [a]gave them also the lands of the [1]nations,
That they [b]might take possession of *the fruit of* the peoples'
labor,
45 So that they might [a]keep His statutes
And observe His laws,
[1]Praise [2]the LORD!

22 [1]Lit *bind* [2]Lit *at his* [a]Gen 41:44
23 [a]Gen 46:6; Acts 7:15 [b]Acts 13:17
24 [a]Ex 1:7, 9
25 [a]Ex 1:8; 4:21 [b]Ex 1:10; Acts 7:19
26 [a]Ex 3:10; 4:12 [b]Ex 4:14; Num 16:5; 17:5-8
27 [1]Lit *set the words of His signs* [a]Ps 78:43-51; 105:27-36
28 [a]Ex 10:21, 22 [b]Ps 99:7
29 [a]Ex 7:20, 21
30 [a]Ex 8:6 [b]Ex 8:3
31 [a]Ex 8:21 [b]Ex 8:16, 17
32 [1]Or *made their rain hail* [a]Ex 9:23-25
33 [a]Ps 78:47
34 [a]Ex 10:12-15
36 [a]Ex 12:29; 13:15; Ps 135:8; 136:10 [b]Gen 49:3
37 [a]Ex 12:35, 36
38 [a]Ex 12:33 [b]Ex 15:16
39 [1]Or *curtain* [a]Ex 13:21; Neh 9:12; Ps 78:14; Is 4:5 [b]Ex 40:38
40 [1]Or *One* [2]Or *food* [a]Ex 16:12; Ps 78:18 [b]Ex 16:13; Num 11:31; Ps 78:27 [c]Ex 16:15; Neh 9:15; Ps 78:24; John 6:31
41 [1]Or *boulder* [2]Lit *They went* [a]Ex 17:6; Num 20:11; Ps 78:15; 114:8; Is 48:21; 1 Cor 10:4
42 [a]Gen 15:13, 14; Ps 105:8
43 [a]Ex 15:1; Ps 106:12
44 [1]Or *Gentiles* [a]Josh 11:16-23; 13:7; Ps 78:55 [b]Deut 6:10, 11
45 [1]Or *Hallelujah!* [2]Heb YAH [a]Deut 4:1, 40

Psalm 106 Theme ____________________

106 [1]Praise [2]the LORD!
Oh [a]give thanks to the LORD, for He [b]is good;
For [c]His lovingkindness is everlasting.
2 Who can speak of the [a]mighty deeds of the LORD,
Or can show forth all His praise?
3 How blessed are those who keep [1]justice,
[2]Who [a]practice righteousness at all times!

4 Remember me, O LORD, in *Your* [a]favor [1]toward Your people;
Visit me with Your salvation,
5 That I may see the [a]prosperity of Your chosen ones,
That I may [b]rejoice in the gladness of Your nation,
That I may [c]glory with Your [1]inheritance.

6 [a]We have sinned [1b]like our fathers,
We have committed iniquity, we have behaved wickedly.
7 Our fathers in Egypt did not understand Your [1]wonders;
They [a]did not remember [2]Your abundant kindnesses,
But [b]rebelled by the sea, at the [3]Red Sea.
8 Nevertheless He saved them [a]for the sake of His name,
That He might [b]make His power known.
9 Thus He [a]rebuked the [1]Red Sea and it [b]dried up,
And He [c]led them through the deeps, as through the wilderness.
10 So He [a]saved them from the [1]hand of the one who hated *them,*
And [b]redeemed them from the [1]hand of the enemy.
11 [a]The waters covered their adversaries;
Not one of them was left.
12 Then they [a]believed His words;
They [b]sang His praise.

13 They quickly [a]forgot His works;
They [b]did not wait for His counsel,
14 But [a]craved intensely in the wilderness,
And [1b]tempted God in the desert.
15 So He [a]gave them their request,
But [b]sent a [1]wasting disease among them.

16 When they became [a]envious of Moses in the camp,
And of Aaron, the holy one of the LORD,
17 The [a]earth opened and swallowed up Dathan,
And engulfed the [1]company of Abiram.
18 And a [a]fire blazed up in their [1]company;
The flame consumed the wicked.

19 They [a]made a calf in Horeb
And worshiped a molten image.
20 Thus they [a]exchanged their glory
For the image of an ox that eats grass.

106:1 [1]Or *Hallelujah!* [2]Heb YAH [a]Ps 105:1; 107:1; 118:1; 136:1; Jer 33:11 [b]2 Chr 5:13; 7:3; Ezra 3:11; Ps 100:5 [c]1 Chr 16:34, 41

2 [a]Ps 145:4, 12; 150:2

3 [1]Or *judgment* [2]Many Heb mss read *The one who performs* [a]Ps 15:2

4 [1]Lit *of* [a]Ps 44:3; 119:132

5 [1]I.e. people [a]Ps 1:3 [b]Ps 118:15 [c]Ps 105:3

6 [1]Lit *with* [a]1 Kin 8:47; Ezra 9:7; Neh 1:7; Jer 3:25; Dan 9:5 [b]2 Chr 30:7; Neh 9:2; Ps 78:8, 57; Zech 1:4

7 [1]I.e. wonderful acts [2]Lit *the multitude of Your lovingkindnesses* [3]Lit *Sea of Reeds* [a]Judg 3:7; Ps 78:11, 42 [b]Ex 14:11, 12; Ps 78:17

8 [a]Ezek 20:9 [b]Ex 9:16

9 [1]Lit *Sea of Reeds* [a]Ps 18:15; 78:13; Is 50:2; Nah 1:4 [b]Ex 14:21; Is 51:10 [c]Is 63:11-13

10 [1]Or *power* [a]Ex 14:30 [b]Ps 78:42; 107:2

11 [a]Ex 14:27, 28; 15:5; Ps 78:53

12 [a]Ex 14:31 [b]Ex 15:1-21; Ps 105:43

13 [a]Ex 15:24; 16:2; 17:2 [b]Ps 107:11

14 [1]Or *put God to the test* [a]Num 11:4; Ps 78:18; 1 Cor 10:6 [b]Ex 17:2; 1 Cor 10:9

15 [1]Or *leanness into their soul* [a]Num 11:31; Ps 78:29 [b]Is 10:16

16 [a]Num 16:1-3

17 [1]Or *assembly, band* [a]Num 16:32; Deut 11:6

18 [1]Or *assembly, band* [a]Num 16:35

19 [a]Ex 32:4; Deut 9:8; Acts 7:41

20 [a]Jer 2:11; Rom 1:23

21 [a]Ps 78:11; 106:7, 13 [b]Deut 10:21
22 [1]I.e. Wonderful acts [2]Lit *Sea of Reeds* [a]Ps 105:27
23 [a]Ex 32:10; Deut 9:14; Ezek 20:8, 13 [b]Ex 32:11-14; Deut 9:25-29
24 [a]Num 14:31 [b]Deut 8:7; Jer 3:19; Ezek 20:6 [c]Deut 1:32; 9:23; Heb 3:19
25 [a]Num 14:2; Deut 1:27
26 [1]Lit *lifted up His hand* [a]Num 14:28-35; Ps 95:11; Ezek 20:15; Heb 3:11
27 [a]Deut 4:27 [b]Lev 26:33; Ps 44:11
28 [1]Or *Baal of Peor* [a]Num 25:3; Deut 4:3; Hos 9:10 [b]Num 25:2
29 [a]Num 25:4
30 [a]Num 25:7 [b]Num 25:8
31 [a]Gen 15:6; Num 25:11-13
32 [1]Lit *strife* [a]Num 20:2-13; Ps 81:7; 95:9 [b]Num 20:12
33 [1]Or *his spirit* [a]Num 20:3, 10; Ps 78:40; 107:11
34 [a]Judg 1:21, 27-36 [b]Deut 7:2, 16
35 [1]Lit *works* [a]Judg 3:5, 6
36 [a]Judg 2:12 [b]Deut 7:16
37 [a]Deut 12:31; 32:17; 2 Kin 16:3; 17:17; Ezek 16:20, 21; 1 Cor 10:20 [b]Lev 17:7
38 [a]Ps 94:21 [b]Deut 18:10 [c]Num 35:33; Is 24:5; Jer 3:1, 2
39 [1]Lit *works* [a]Lev 18:24; Ezek 20:18 [b]Lev 17:7; Num 15:39; Judg 2:17; Hos 4:12
40 [1]I.e. people [a]Judg 2:14; Ps 78:59 [b]Lev 26:30; Deut 32:19 [c]Deut 9:29; 32:9
41 [1]Or *Gentiles* [a]Judg 2:14; Neh 9:27

21 They [a]forgot God their Savior,
Who had done [b]great things in Egypt,
22 [1a]Wonders in the land of Ham
And awesome things by the [2]Red Sea.
23 Therefore [a]He said that He would destroy them,
Had not [b]Moses His chosen one stood in the breach before Him,
To turn away His wrath from destroying *them.*
24 Then they [a]despised the [b]pleasant land;
They [c]did not believe in His word,
25 But [a]grumbled in their tents;
They did not listen to the voice of the LORD.
26 Therefore He [1a]swore to them
That He would cast them down in the wilderness,
27 And that He would [a]cast their seed among the nations
And [b]scatter them in the lands.

28 They [a]joined themselves also to [1]Baal-peor,
And ate [b]sacrifices offered to the dead.
29 Thus they [a]provoked *Him* to anger with their deeds,
And the plague broke out among them.
30 Then Phinehas [a]stood up and interposed,
And so the [b]plague was stayed.
31 And it was [a]reckoned to him for righteousness,
To all generations forever.

32 They also [a]provoked *Him* to wrath at the waters of [1]Meribah,
So that it [b]went hard with Moses on their account;
33 Because they [a]were rebellious against [1]His Spirit,
He spoke rashly with his lips.

34 They [a]did not destroy the peoples,
As [b]the LORD commanded them,
35 But [a]they mingled with the nations
And learned their [1]practices,
36 And [a]served their idols,
[b]Which became a snare to them.
37 They even [a]sacrificed their sons and their daughters to the [b]demons,
38 And shed [a]innocent blood,
The blood of their [b]sons and their daughters,
Whom they sacrificed to the idols of Canaan;
And the land was [c]polluted with the blood.
39 Thus they became [a]unclean in their [1]practices,
And [b]played the harlot in their deeds.

40 Therefore the [a]anger of the LORD was kindled against His people
And He [b]abhorred His [1c]inheritance.
41 Then [a]He gave them into the hand of the [1]nations,
And those who hated them ruled over them.

42 Their enemies also [a]oppressed them,
And they were subdued under their [1]power.
43 Many times He would [a]deliver them;
They, however, were rebellious in their [b]counsel,
And *so* [c]sank down in their iniquity.

44 Nevertheless He looked upon their distress
When He [a]heard their cry;
45 And He [a]remembered His covenant for their sake,
And [1b]relented [c]according to the greatness of His
lovingkindness.
46 He also made them [a]*objects* of compassion
In the presence of all their captors.

47 [a]Save us, O LORD our God,
And [b]gather us from among the nations,
To give thanks to Your holy name
And [1c]glory in Your praise.
48 [a]Blessed be the LORD, the God of Israel,
From everlasting even to everlasting.
And let all the people say, "Amen."
[1]Praise [2]the LORD!

BOOK 5

*Psalm 107 Theme*______________________________

107 Oh [a]give thanks to the LORD, for [b]He is good,
For His lovingkindness is everlasting.
2 Let [a]the redeemed of the LORD say *so,*
Whom He has [b]redeemed from the hand of the adversary
3 And [a]gathered from the lands,
From the east and from the west,
From the north and from the [1]south.

4 They [a]wandered in the wilderness in a [1]desert region;
They did not find a way to [2]an inhabited [b]city.
5 *They were* hungry [1]and thirsty;
Their [a]soul fainted within them.
6 Then they [a]cried out to the LORD in their trouble;
He delivered them out of their distresses.
7 He led them also by a [1a]straight way,
To go to [2b]an inhabited city.
8 [a]Let them give thanks to the LORD for His lovingkindness,
And for His [1]wonders to the sons of men!
9 For He has [a]satisfied the [1]thirsty soul,
And the [b]hungry soul He has filled with what is good.

10 There were those who [a]dwelt in darkness and in the
shadow of death,
[b]Prisoners in [1]misery and [2]chains,

42 [1]Lit *hand* [a]Judg 4:3; 10:12

43 [a]Judg 2:16-18 [b]Ps 81:12 [c]Judg 6:6

44 [a]Judg 3:9; 6:7; 10:10

45 [1]Lit *was sorry* [a]Lev 26:42; Ps 105:8 [b]Judg 2:18 [c]Ps 69:16

46 [a]1 Kin 8:50; 2 Chr 30:9; Ezra 9:9; Neh 1:11; Jer 42:12

47 [1]Lit *boast* [a]1 Chr 16:35, 36 [b]Ps 147:2 [c]Ps 47:1

48 [1]Or *Hallelujah!* [2]Heb YAH [a]Ps 41:13; 72:18; 89:52

107:1 [a]1 Chr 16:34; Ps 106:1; 118:1; 136:1; Jer 33:11 [b]2 Chr 5:13; 7:3; Ezra 3:11; Ps 100:5

2 [a]Is 35:9, 10; 62:12; 63:4 [b]Ps 78:42; 106:10

3 [1]Lit *sea* [a]Deut 30:3; Neh 1:9; Ps 106:47; Is 11:12; 43:5; 56:8; Ezek 11:17; 20:34

4 [1]Lit *waste* [2]Or *a habitable city;* lit *a city of habitation* [a]Num 14:33; 32:13; Deut 2:7; 32:10; Josh 5:6; 14:10 [b]Ps 107:7, 36

5 [1]Lit *also* [a]Ps 77:3

6 [a]Ps 50:15; 107:13, 19, 28

7 [1]Or *level* [2]Or *a habitable city;* lit *a city of habitation* [a]Ezra 8:21; Ps 5:8; Jer 31:9 [b]Ps 107:4, 36

8 [1]I.e. wonderful acts [a]Ps 107:15, 21, 31

9 [1]Or *parched* [a]Ps 22:26; 34:10; 63:5; 103:5 [b]Ps 146:7; Matt 5:6; Luke 1:53

10 [1]Lit *affliction* [2]Lit *irons* [a]Ps 143:3; Is 42:7; Mic 7:8; Luke 1:79 [b]Job 36:8; Ps 102:20

11 [a]Ps 78:40; 106:7; Lam 3:42 [b]Num 15:31; 2 Chr 36:16; Prov 1:25; Is 5:24 [c]Ps 73:24
12 [a]Ps 22:11; 72:12
13 [a]Ps 107:6
14 [a]Ps 86:13; 107:10 [b]Ps 116:16; Jer 2:20; 30:8; Nah 1:13; Luke 13:16; Acts 12:7
15 [1]I.e. wonderful acts [a]Ps 107:8, 21, 31
16 [a]Is 45:1, 2
17 [1]Lit *the way of their transgression* [a]Is 65:6, 7; Jer 30:14, 15; Lam 3:39; Ezek 24:23
18 [a]Job 33:20; Ps 102:4 [b]Job 33:22; Ps 88:3 [c]Job 38:17; Ps 9:13
20 [1]Or *pits* [a]Ps 147:15, 18; Matt 8:8 [b]2 Kin 20:5; Ps 30:2; 103:3; 147:3 [c]Job 33:28, 30; Ps 30:3; 49:15; 56:13; 103:4
21 [1]I.e. wonderful acts [a]Ps 107:8, 15, 31
22 [a]Lev 7:12; Ps 50:14; 116:17 [b]Ps 9:11; 73:28; 118:17
23 [a]Is 42:10; Jon 1:3
24 [1]I.e. wonderful acts
25 [1]Lit *of it* [a]Ps 105:31, 34 [b]Ps 148:8; Jon 1:4 [c]Ps 93:3, 4
26 [a]Ps 22:14; 119:28
27 [1]Lit *all their wisdom was swallowed up* [a]Job 12:25; Is 24:20
29 [1]Lit *of it* [a]Ps 65:7; 89:9; Matt 8:26; Luke 8:24
31 [1]I.e. wonderful acts [a]Ps 107:8, 15, 21 [b]Ps 78:4; 111:4
32 [a]Ps 34:3; 99:5; Is 25:1 [b]Ps 22:22, 25 [c]Ps 35:18
33 [1]Or *turns* [2]Or *desert* [a]1 Kin 17:1, 7; Ps 74:15; Is 42:15; 50:2

11 Because they had [a]rebelled against the words of God
And [b]spurned the [c]counsel of the Most High.
12 Therefore He humbled their heart with labor;
They stumbled and there was [a]none to help.
13 Then they [a]cried out to the LORD in their trouble;
He saved them out of their distresses.
14 He [a]brought them out of darkness and the shadow of death
And [b]broke their bands apart.
15 [a]Let them give thanks to the LORD for His lovingkindness,
And for His [1]wonders to the sons of men!
16 For He has [a]shattered gates of bronze
And cut bars of iron asunder.

17 Fools, because of [1]their rebellious way,
And [a]because of their iniquities, were afflicted.
18 Their [a]soul abhorred all kinds of food,
And they [b]drew near to the [c]gates of death.
19 Then they cried out to the LORD in their trouble;
He saved them out of their distresses.
20 He [a]sent His word and [b]healed them,
And [c]delivered *them* from their [1]destructions.
21 [a]Let them give thanks to the LORD for His lovingkindness,
And for His [1]wonders to the sons of men!
22 Let them also offer [a]sacrifices of thanksgiving,
And [b]tell of His works with joyful singing.

23 Those who [a]go down to the sea in ships,
Who do business on great waters;
24 They have seen the works of the LORD,
And His [1]wonders in the deep.
25 For He [a]spoke and raised up a [b]stormy wind,
Which [c]lifted up the waves [1]of the sea.
26 They rose up to the heavens, they went down to the depths;
Their soul [a]melted away in *their* misery.
27 They reeled and [a]staggered like a drunken man,
And [1]were at their wits' end.
28 Then they cried to the LORD in their trouble,
And He brought them out of their distresses.
29 He [a]caused the storm to be still,
So that the waves [1]of the sea were hushed.
30 Then they were glad because they were quiet,
So He guided them to their desired haven.
31 [a]Let them give thanks to the LORD for His lovingkindness,
And for His [1b]wonders to the sons of men!
32 Let them [a]extol Him also [b]in the congregation of the people,
And [c]praise Him at the seat of the elders.

33 He [1a]changes rivers into a [2]wilderness
And springs of water into a thirsty ground;

34 A [a]fruitful land into a [b]salt waste,
Because of the wickedness of those who dwell in it.
35 He [1a]changes a [2]wilderness into a pool of water
And a dry land into springs of water;
36 And there He makes the hungry to dwell,
So that they may establish [1a]an inhabited city,
37 And sow fields and [a]plant vineyards,
And [1]gather a fruitful harvest.
38 Also He blesses them and they [a]multiply greatly,
And He [b]does not let their cattle decrease.

39 When they are [a]diminished and [b]bowed down
Through oppression, misery and sorrow,
40 He [a]pours contempt upon [1]princes
And [b]makes them wander [c]in a pathless waste.
41 But He [a]sets the needy [1]securely on high away from affliction,
And [b]makes *his* families like a flock.
42 The [a]upright see it and are glad;
But all [b]unrighteousness shuts its mouth.
43 Who is [a]wise? Let him give heed to these things,
And consider the [b]lovingkindnesses of the LORD.

*Psalm 108 Theme*____________________

A Song, a Psalm of David.

108 [a]My heart is steadfast, O God;
I will sing, I will sing praises, even with my [1]soul.
2 Awake, harp and lyre;
I will awaken the dawn!
3 I will give thanks to You, O LORD, among the peoples,
And I will sing praises to You among the nations.
4 For Your [a]lovingkindness is great [b]above the heavens,
And Your truth *reaches* to the skies.
5 [a]Be exalted, O God, above the heavens,
And Your glory above all the earth.
6 [a]That Your beloved may be delivered,
Save with Your right hand, and answer me!

7 God has spoken in His [1]holiness:
"I will exult, I will portion out Shechem
And measure out the valley of Succoth.
8 "Gilead is Mine, Manasseh is Mine;
Ephraim also is the [1]helmet of My head;
[a]Judah is My [2]scepter.
9 "Moab is My washbowl;
Over Edom I shall throw My shoe;
Over Philistia I will shout aloud."

10 [a]Who will bring me into the besieged city?
Who [1]will lead me to Edom?

34 [a]Gen 13:10; 14:3; 19:24, 25; Deut 29:23 [b]Job 39:6; Jer 17:6

35 [1]Or *turns* [2]Or *desert* [a]Ps 105:41; 114:8; Is 35:6, 7; 41:18

36 [1]Or *a habitable city;* lit *a city of habitation* [a]Ps 107:4, 7

37 [1]Lit *acquire fruits of yield* [a]2 Kin 19:29; Is 65:21; Amos 9:14

38 [a]Gen 12:2; 17:20; Ex 1:7; Deut 1:10 [b]Deut 7:14

39 [a]2 Kin 10:32; Ezek 5:11; 29:15 [b]Ps 38:6; 44:25; 57:6

40 [1]Or *nobles* [a]Job 12:21 [b]Job 12:24 [c]Deut 32:10

41 [1]Lit *in an inaccessibly high place* [a]1 Sam 2:8; Ps 59:1; 113:7, 8 [b]Job 21:11; Ps 78:52; 113:9

42 [a]Job 22:19; Ps 52:6 [b]Job 5:16; Ps 63:11; Rom 3:19

43 [a]Ps 64:9; Jer 9:12; Hos 14:9 [b]Ps 107:1

108:1 [1]Lit *glory* [a]Ps 57:7-11; 108:1-5

4 [a]Num 14:18; Deut 7:9; Ps 36:5; 100:5; Mic 7:18-20 [b]Ps 113:4

5 [a]Ps 57:5

6 [a]Ps 60:5-12; 108:6-13

7 [1]Or *sanctuary*

8 [1]Lit *protection* [2]Or *lawgiver* [a]Gen 49:10

10 [1]Or *has led* [a]Ps 60:9

11 Have not You Yourself, O God, [a]rejected us?
And will You not go forth with our armies, O God?
12 Oh give us help against the adversary,
For [a]deliverance [1]by man is in vain.
13 [1]Through God we will do valiantly,
And [a]it is He who shall tread down our adversaries.

Psalm 109 Theme ______________________________

For the choir director. A Psalm of David.

109 O [a]God of my praise,
[b]Do not be silent!
2 For they have opened the [1]wicked and [a]deceitful mouth
against me;
They have spoken [2]against me with a [b]lying tongue.
3 They have also surrounded me with words of hatred,
And fought against me [a]without cause.
4 In return [a]for my love they act as my accusers;
But [b]I am *in* prayer.
5 Thus they have [1a]repaid me evil for good
And [b]hatred for my love.

6 Appoint a wicked man over him,
And let an [1a]accuser stand at his right hand.
7 When he is judged, let him [a]come forth guilty,
And let his [b]prayer become sin.
8 Let [a]his days be few;
Let [b]another take his office.
9 Let his [a]children be fatherless
And his [b]wife a widow.
10 Let his [a]children wander about and beg;
And let them [b]seek *sustenance* [1]far from their ruined homes.
11 Let [a]the creditor [1]seize all that he has,
And let [b]strangers plunder the product of his labor.
12 Let there be none to [1a]extend lovingkindness to him,
Nor [b]any to be gracious to his fatherless children.
13 Let his [a]posterity be [1]cut off;
In a following generation let their [b]name be blotted out.

14 Let [a]the iniquity of his fathers be remembered [1]before the LORD,
And do not let the sin of his mother be [b]blotted out.
15 Let [a]them be before the LORD continually,
That He may [b]cut off their memory from the earth;
16 Because he did not remember to show lovingkindness,
But persecuted the [a]afflicted and needy man,
And the [b]despondent in heart, to [c]put *them* to death.
17 He also loved cursing, so [a]it came to him;
And he did not delight in blessing, so it was far from him.
18 But he [a]clothed himself with cursing as with his garment,
And it [b]entered into [1]his body like water
And like oil into his bones.

11 [a]Ps 44:9
12 [1]Lit *of* [a]Is 30:3
13 [1]Or *In* or *With* [a]Is 60:12; 63:1-4
109:1 [a]Deut 10:21 [b]Ps 28:1; 83:1
2 [1]Lit *wicked mouth and the deceitful* [2]Lit *with* [a]Ps 10:7; 52:4 [b]Ps 120:2
3 [a]Ps 35:7; 69:4; John 15:25
4 [a]Ps 38:20 [b]Ps 69:13; 141:5
5 [1]Lit *laid upon me* [a]Ps 35:12; 38:20 [b]John 7:7; 10:32
6 [1]Or *adversary, Satan* [a]Zech 3:1
7 [a]Ps 1:5 [b]Prov 28:9
8 [a]Ps 55:23 [b]Acts 1:20
9 [a]Ex 22:24 [b]Jer 18:21
10 [1]Or *out of their desolate places* [a]Gen 4:12; Job 30:5-8; Ps 59:15 [b]Ps 37:25
11 [1]Lit *ensnare, strike at* [a]Neh 5:7; Job 5:5; 20:15 [b]Is 1:7; Lam 5:2; Ezek 7:21
12 [1]Lit *continue* [a]Ezra 7:28; 9:9 [b]Job 5:4; Is 9:17
13 [1]Lit *for cutting off* [a]Job 18:19; Ps 21:10; 37:28 [b]Ps 9:5; Prov 10:7
14 [1]Lit *to* [a]Ex 20:5; Num 14:18; Is 65:6, 7; Jer 32:18 [b]Neh 4:5; Jer 18:23
15 [a]Ps 90:8; Jer 16:17 [b]Job 18:17; Ps 34:16
16 [a]Ps 37:14 [b]Ps 34:18 [c]Ps 37:32; 94:6
17 [a]Prov 14:14; Ezek 35:9; Matt 7:2
18 [1]Lit *his inward parts* [a]Ps 73:6; 109:29; Ezek 7:27 [b]Num 5:22

19 Let it be to him as [a]a garment with which he covers
himself,
And for a belt with which he constantly [b]girds himself.
20 [1]Let this be the [a]reward of my accusers from the LORD,
And of those who [b]speak evil against my soul.

21 But You, O [1]GOD, the Lord, deal *kindly* with me [a]for Your
name's sake;
Because [b]Your lovingkindness is good, deliver me;
22 For [a]I am afflicted and needy,
And [1]my heart is [b]wounded within me.
23 I am passing [a]like a shadow when it lengthens;
I am shaken off [b]like the locust.
24 My [a]knees [1]are weak from [b]fasting,
And my flesh has grown lean, without fatness.
25 I also have become a [a]reproach to them;
When they see me, they [b]wag their head.

26 [a]Help me, O LORD my God;
Save me according to Your lovingkindness.
27 [1]And let them [a]know that this is Your hand;
You, LORD, have done it.
28 [a]Let them curse, but You bless;
When they arise, they shall be ashamed,
But Your [b]servant shall be glad.
29 [1]Let [a]my accusers be clothed with dishonor,
And [2]let them [b]cover themselves with their own shame as
with a robe.

30 With my mouth I will give thanks abundantly to the LORD;
And in the midst of many [a]I will praise Him.
31 For He stands [a]at the right hand of the needy,
To save him from those who [b]judge his soul.

*Psalm 110 Theme*____________________

A Psalm of David.

110 [a]The LORD says to my Lord:
"[b]Sit at My right hand
Until I make [c]Your enemies a footstool for Your feet."
2 The LORD will stretch forth Your strong [a]scepter from Zion,
saying,
"[b]Rule in the midst of Your enemies."
3 Your [a]people [1]will volunteer freely in the day of Your
[2]power;
[b]In [3]holy array, from the womb of the dawn,
[4]Your youth are to You *as* the [c]dew.

4 [a]The LORD has sworn and will [b]not [1]change His mind,
"You are a [c]priest forever
According to the order of Melchizedek."

19 [a]Ps 73:6; 109:29; Ezek 7:27 [b]2 Sam 22:40; Ps 30:11; Is 11:5

20 [1]Lit *This is* [a]Ps 54:5; 94:23; Is 3:11; 2 Tim 4:14 [b]Ps 41:5; 71:10

21 [1]Heb *YHWH,* usually rendered *LORD* [a]Ps 23:3; 25:11; 79:9; 106:8; Ezek 36:22 [b]Ps 69:16

22 [1]Lit *one has pierced my heart within me* [a]Ps 40:17; 86:1 [b]Job 24:12; Ps 143:4; Prov 18:14

23 [a]Ps 102:11 [b]Ex 10:19; Job 39:20

24 [1]Or *totter* [a]Heb 12:12 [b]Ps 35:13

25 [a]Ps 22:6 [b]Ps 22:7; Jer 18:16; Lam 2:15; Matt 27:39; Mark 15:29

26 [a]Ps 119:86

27 [1]Or *That they may know* [a]Job 37:7

28 [a]2 Sam 16:11, 12 [b]Is 65:14

29 [1]Or *My accusers will be* [2]Or *they will cover* [a]Job 8:22; Ps 132:18 [b]Job 8:22; Ps 35:26

30 [a]Ps 22:22; 35:18; 111:1

31 [a]Ps 16:8; 73:23; 110:5; 121:5 [b]Ps 37:33

110:1 [a]Matt 22:44; Mark 12:36; Luke 20:42, 43; Acts 2:34, 35; Heb 1:13 [b]Matt 26:64; Eph 1:20; Col 3:1; Heb 1:3; 8:1; 10:12; 12:2 [c]1 Cor 15:25; Eph 1:22

2 [a]Ps 45:6; Jer 48:17; Ezek 19:14 [b]Ps 2:9; 72:8; Dan 7:13, 14

3 [1]Lit *will be freewill offerings* [2]Or *army* [3]Or *the splendor of holiness* [4]Or *The dew of Your youth is Yours* [a]Judg 5:2; Neh 11:2 [b]1 Chr 16:29; Ps 96:9 [c]2 Sam 17:12; Mic 5:7

4 [1]Lit *be sorry* [a]Heb 7:21 [b]Num 23:19 [c]Zech 6:13; Heb 5:6, 10; 6:20; 7:17, 21

5 The Lord is [a]at Your right hand;
He [1]will [b]shatter kings in the [c]day of His wrath.
6 He will [a]judge among the nations,
He [1]will fill *them* with [b]corpses,
He [2]will [c]shatter the [3]chief men over a broad country.
7 He will [a]drink from the brook by the wayside;
Therefore He will [b]lift up *His* head.

*Psalm 111 Theme*________________________

111 [1]Praise [2]the LORD!
I [a]will give thanks to the LORD with all *my* heart,
In the [b]company of the upright and in the assembly.
2 [a]Great are the works of the LORD;
They are [1b]studied by all who delight in them.
3 [1a]Splendid and majestic is His work,
And [b]His righteousness endures forever.
4 He has made His [1]wonders [2]to be remembered;
The LORD is [a]gracious and compassionate.
5 He has [a]given [1]food to those who [2]fear Him;
He will [b]remember His covenant forever.
6 He has made known to His people the power of His works,
In giving them the heritage of the nations.

7 The works of His hands are [1a]truth and justice;
All His precepts [b]are [2]sure.
8 They are [a]upheld forever and ever;
They are performed in [1b]truth and uprightness.
9 He has sent [a]redemption to His people;
He has [1]ordained His covenant forever;
[b]Holy and [2]awesome is His name.
10 The [1a]fear of the LORD is the beginning of wisdom;
A [b]good understanding have all those who [2]do *His commandments;*
His [c]praise endures forever.

*Psalm 112 Theme*________________________

112 [1]Praise [2]the LORD!
How [a]blessed is the man who [3]fears the LORD,
Who greatly [b]delights in His commandments.
2 His [1a]descendants will be mighty [2]on earth;
The generation of the [b]upright will be blessed.
3 [a]Wealth and riches are in his house,
And his righteousness endures forever.
4 Light arises in the darkness [a]for the upright;
He is [b]gracious and compassionate and righteous.
5 It is well with the man who [a]is gracious and lends;
He will [1]maintain his cause in judgment.
6 For he will [a]never be shaken;
The [b]righteous will be [1]remembered forever.

5 [1]Or *has shattered* [a]Ps 16:8; 109:31 [b]Ps 68:14; 76:12 [c]Ps 2:5, 12; Rom 2:5; Rev 6:17

6 [1]Or *has filled* [2]Or *has shattered* [3]Lit *head over* [a]Is 2:4; Joel 3:12; Mic 4:3 [b]Is 66:24 [c]Ps 68:21

7 [a]Judg 7:5, 6 [b]Ps 27:6

111:1 [1]Or *Hallelujah! I will* [2]Heb YAH [a]Ps 35:18; 138:1 [b]Ps 89:7; 149:1

2 [1]Lit *sought out* [a]Ps 92:5 [b]Ps 143:5

3 [1]Lit *Splendor and majesty* [a]Ps 96:6; 145:5 [b]Ps 112:3, 9; 119:142

4 [1]I.e. wonderful acts [2]Lit *a memorial* [a]Ps 86:5, 15; 103:8; 145:8

5 [1]Lit *prey* [2]Or *revere* [a]Matt 6:31-33 [b]Ps 105:8

7 [1]Or *faithfulness* [2]Or *trustworthy* [a]Rev 15:3 [b]Ps 19:7; 93:5

8 [1]Or *faithfulness* [a]Ps 119:160; Is 40:8; Matt 5:18 [b]Ps 19:9

9 [1]Lit *commanded* [2]I.e. inspiring reverence [a]Luke 1:68 [b]Ps 99:3; Luke 1:49

10 [1]Or *reverence for* [2]Lit *do* them [a]Job 28:28; Prov 1:7; 9:10; Eccl 12:13 [b]Ps 119:98; Prov 3:4 [c]Ps 145:2

112:1 [1]Or *Hallelujah! Blessed* [2]Heb YAH [3]Or *reveres* [a]Ps 128:1 [b]Ps 1:2; 119:14, 16

2 [1]Lit *seed* [2]Or *in the land* [a]Ps 102:28; 127:4 [b]Ps 128:4

3 [a]Prov 3:16; 8:18; Matt 6:33

4 [a]Job 11:17; Ps 97:11 [b]Ps 37:26

5 [1]Or *conduct his affairs with justice* [a]Ps 37:21

6 [1]Lit *for an eternal remembrance* [a]Ps 15:5; 55:22 [b]Prov 10:7

7 He will not fear [a]evil tidings;
His [b]heart is steadfast, [c]trusting in the LORD.
8 His [a]heart is upheld, he [b]will not fear,
Until he [c]looks *with satisfaction* on his adversaries.
9 [1]He [a]has given freely to the poor,
His righteousness endures forever;
His [b]horn will be exalted in honor.

10 The [a]wicked will see it and be [1]vexed,
He will [b]gnash his teeth and [c]melt away;
The [d]desire of the wicked will perish.

*Psalm 113 Theme*____

113

[1]Praise [2]the LORD!
[a]Praise, O [b]servants of the LORD,
Praise the name of the LORD.
2 [a]Blessed be the name of the LORD
From this time forth and forever.
3 [a]From the rising of the sun to its setting
The [b]name of the LORD is to be praised.
4 The LORD is [a]high above all nations;
His [b]glory is above the heavens.

5 [a]Who is like the LORD our God,
Who [b]is enthroned on high,
6 Who [1a]humbles Himself to behold
The things that are in heaven and in the earth?
7 He [a]raises the poor from the dust
And lifts the needy from the ash heap,
8 To make *them* [a]sit with [1]princes,
With the [1]princes of His people.
9 He [a]makes the barren woman abide in the house
As a joyful mother of children.
[1]Praise [2]the LORD!

*Psalm 114 Theme*____

114

When Israel went forth [a]from Egypt,
The house of Jacob from a people of [b]strange language,
2 Judah became [a]His sanctuary,
Israel, [b]His dominion.

3 The [a]sea looked and fled;
The [b]Jordan turned back.
4 The mountains [a]skipped like rams,
The hills, like lambs.
5 What [a]ails you, O sea, that you flee?
O Jordan, that you turn back?
6 O mountains, that you skip like rams?
O hills, like lambs?

7 [a]Prov 1:33 [b]Ps 57:7; 108:1 [c]Ps 56:4

8 [a]Heb 13:9 [b]Ps 27:1; 56:11; Prov 1:33; 3:24; Is 12:2 [c]Ps 54:7; 59:10

9 [1]Lit *He has scattered, he has given to . . .* [a]2 Cor 9:9 [b]Ps 75:10; 89:17; 92:10; 148:14

10 [1]Or *angry* [a]Ps 86:17 [b]Ps 35:16; 37:12; Matt 8:12; 25:30; Luke 13:28 [c]Ps 58:7 [d]Job 8:13; Prov 10:28; 11:7

113:1 [1]Or *Hallelujah! Praise* [2]Heb YAH [a]Ps 135:1 [b]Ps 34:22; 69:36; 79:10; 90:13

2 [a]Ps 145:21; Dan 2:20

3 [a]Ps 50:1; Is 59:19; Mal 1:11 [b]Ps 18:3; 48:1, 10

4 [a]Ps 97:9; 99:2 [b]Ps 8:1; 57:11; 148:13

5 [a]Ex 15:11; Ps 35:10; 89:6 [b]Ps 103:19

6 [1]Or *looks far below in the heavens and on the earth?* [a]Ps 11:4; 138:6; Is 57:15

7 [a]1 Sam 2:8; Ps 107:41

8 [1]Or *nobles* [a]Job 36:7

9 [1]Or *Hallelujah!* [2]Heb YAH [a]1 Sam 2:5; Ps 68:6; Is 54:1

114:1 [a]Ex 12:51; 13:3 [b]Ps 81:5

2 [a]Ex 15:17; 29:45, 46; Ps 78:68, 69 [b]Ex 19:6

3 [a]Ex 14:21; Ps 77:16 [b]Josh 3:13, 16

4 [a]Ex 19:18; Judg 5:5; Ps 18:7; 29:6; Hab 3:6

5 [a]Hab 3:8

7 [a]Tremble, O earth, before the Lord,
Before the God of Jacob,
8 Who [a]turned the rock into a [b]pool of water,
The [c]flint into a fountain of water.

*Psalm 115 Theme*______________________________

115 [a]Not to us, O LORD, not to us,
But [b]to Your name give glory
Because of Your lovingkindness, because of Your [1]truth.
2 [a]Why should the nations say,
"[b]Where, now, is their God?"
3 But our [a]God is in the heavens;
He [b]does whatever He pleases.
4 Their [a]idols are silver and gold,
The [b]work of man's hands.
5 They have mouths, but they [a]cannot speak;
They have eyes, but they cannot see;
6 They have ears, but they cannot hear;
They have noses, but they cannot smell;
7 [1]They have hands, but they cannot feel;
[2]They have feet, but they cannot walk;
They cannot make a sound with their throat.
8 [a]Those who make them [1]will become like them,
Everyone who trusts in them.

9 O [a]Israel, [b]trust in the LORD;
He is their [c]help and their shield.
10 O house of [a]Aaron, trust in the LORD;
He is their help and their shield.
11 You who [1a]fear the LORD, trust in the LORD;
He is their help and their shield.
12 The LORD [a]has been mindful of us; He will bless *us;*
He will bless the house of Israel;
He will bless the house of Aaron.
13 He will [a]bless those who [1]fear the LORD,
[b]The small together with the great.
14 May the LORD [a]give you increase,
You and your children.
15 May you be blessed of the LORD,
[a]Maker of heaven and earth.

16 The heavens are [a]the heavens of the LORD,
But [b]the earth He has given to the sons of men.
17 The [a]dead do not praise [1]the LORD,
Nor *do* any who go down into [b]silence;
18 But as for us, we will [a]bless [1]the LORD
From this time forth and forever.
[2]Praise [1]the LORD!

7 [a]Ps 96:9
8 [a]Ex 17:6; Num 20:11; Ps 78:15; 105:41 [b]Ps 107:35 [c]Deut 8:15
115:1 [1]Or *faithfulness* [a]Is 48:11; Ezek 36:22 [b]Ps 29:2; 96:8
2 [a]Ps 79:10 [b]Ps 42:3, 10
3 [a]Ps 103:19 [b]Ps 135:6; Dan 4:35
4 [a]Ps 115:4-8; 135:15-18; Jer 10:4 [b]Deut 4:28; 2 Kin 19:18; Is 37:19; 44:10, 20; Jer 10:3
5 [a]Jer 10:5
7 [1]Lit *Their hands* [2]Lit *Their feet*
8 [1]Or *are like them* [a]Ps 135:18; Is 44:9-11
9 [a]Ps 118:2; 135:19 [b]Ps 37:3; 62:8 [c]Ps 33:20
10 [a]Ps 118:3; 135:19
11 [1]Or *revere* [a]Ps 22:23; 103:11; 135:20
12 [a]Ps 98:3
13 [1]Or *revere* [a]Ps 103:11; 112:1; 128:1 [b]Rev 11:18; 19:5
14 [a]Deut 1:11
15 [a]Gen 1:1; Neh 9:6; Ps 96:5; 102:25; 121:2; 124:8; 134:3; 146:6; Acts 14:15; Rev 14:7
16 [a]Ps 89:11 [b]Ps 8:6
17 [1]Heb YAH [a]Ps 6:5; 88:10-12; Is 38:18 [b]Ps 31:17
18 [1]Heb YAH [2]Or *Hallelujah!* [a]Ps 113:2; Dan 2:20

*Psalm 116 Theme*________________________________

116 [a]I love the LORD, because He [b]hears
My voice *and* my supplications.
2 Because He has [a]inclined His ear to me,
Therefore I shall call *upon Him* as long as I live.
3 The [a]cords of death encompassed me
And the [1]terrors of [2]Sheol [3]came upon me;
I found distress and sorrow.
4 Then [a]I called upon the name of the LORD:
"O LORD, I beseech You, [1b]save my life!"

5 [a]Gracious is the LORD, and [b]righteous;
Yes, our God is [c]compassionate.
6 The LORD preserves [a]the simple;
I was [b]brought low, and He saved me.
7 Return to your [a]rest, O my soul,
For the LORD has [b]dealt bountifully with you.
8 For You have [a]rescued my soul from death,
My eyes from tears,
My feet from stumbling.
9 I shall walk before the LORD
In the [1a]land of the living.
10 I [a]believed when I said,
"I am [b]greatly afflicted."
11 I [a]said in my alarm,
"[b]All men are liars."

12 What shall I [a]render to the LORD
For all His [b]benefits [1]toward me?
13 I shall lift up the [a]cup of salvation
And [b]call upon the name of the LORD.
14 I shall [a]pay my vows to the LORD,
Oh *may it be* [b]in the presence of all His people.
15 [a]Precious in the sight of the LORD
Is the death of His godly ones.
16 O LORD, [1]surely I am [a]Your servant,
I am Your servant, the [b]son of Your handmaid,
You have [c]loosed my bonds.
17 To You I shall offer [a]a sacrifice of thanksgiving,
And [b]call upon the name of the LORD.
18 I shall [a]pay my vows to the LORD,
Oh *may it be* in the presence of all His people,
19 In the [a]courts of the LORD's house,
In the midst of you, O [b]Jerusalem.
[1]Praise [2]the LORD!

*Psalm 117 Theme*________________________________

117 [a]Praise the LORD, all nations;
Laud Him, all peoples!

116:1 [a]Ps 18:1 [b]Ps 6:8; 66:19; Is 37:17; Dan 9:18
2 [a]Ps 17:6; 31:2; 40:1
3 [1]Lit *straits* [2]I.e. the nether world [3]Lit *found me* [a]Ps 18:4, 5
4 [1]Or *deliver my soul* [a]Ps 18:6; 118:5 [b]Ps 17:13; 22:20
5 [a]Ps 86:15; 103:8 [b]Ezra 9:15; Neh 9:8; Ps 119:137; 145:17; Jer 12:1; Dan 9:14 [c]Ex 34:6
6 [a]Ps 19:7; Prov 1:4 [b]Ps 79:8; 142:6
7 [a]Jer 6:16; Matt 11:29 [b]Ps 13:6; 142:7
8 [a]Ps 49:15; 56:13; 86:13
9 [1]Lit *lands* [a]Ps 27:13
10 [a]2 Cor 4:13 [b]Ps 88:7
11 [a]Ps 31:22 [b]Ps 62:9; Rom 3:4
12 [1]Lit *upon* [a]2 Chr 32:25; 1 Thess 3:9 [b]Ps 103:2
13 [a]Ps 16:5 [b]Ps 80:18; 105:1
14 [a]Ps 50:14; 116:18 [b]Ps 22:25
15 [a]Ps 72:14
16 [1]Or *because* [a]Ps 86:16; 119:125; 143:12 [b]Ps 86:16 [c]Ps 107:14
17 [a]Lev 7:12; Ps 50:14 [b]Ps 116:13
18 [a]Ps 116:14
19 [1]Or *Hallelujah!* [2]Heb YAH [a]Ps 92:13; 96:8; 135:2 [b]Ps 102:21
117:1 [a]Rom 15:11

2 For His [a]lovingkindness [1]is great toward us,
And the [2b]truth of the LORD is everlasting.
[3]Praise [4]the LORD!

Psalm 118 Theme ______________________

118 [a]Give thanks to the LORD, for [b]He is good;
For His lovingkindness is everlasting.
2 Oh let [a]Israel say,
"His lovingkindness is everlasting."
3 Oh let the [a]house of Aaron say,
"His lovingkindness is everlasting."
4 Oh let those [a]who [1]fear the LORD say,
"His lovingkindness is everlasting."

5 From *my* [a]distress I called upon [1]the LORD;
[1]The LORD answered me *and* [b]*set me* in a large place.
6 The LORD is [a]for me; I will [b]not fear;
[c]What can man do to me?
7 The LORD is for me [a]among those who help me;
Therefore I will [b]look *with satisfaction* on those who hate
me.
8 It is [a]better to take refuge in the LORD
Than to trust in man.
9 It is [a]better to take refuge in the LORD
Than to trust in princes.

10 All nations [a]surrounded me;
In the name of the LORD I will surely [b]cut them off.
11 They [a]surrounded me, yes, they surrounded me;
In the name of the LORD I will surely cut them off.
12 They surrounded me [a]like bees;
They were extinguished as a [b]fire of thorns;
In the name of the LORD I will surely cut them off.
13 You [a]pushed me violently so that I [1]was falling,
But the LORD [b]helped me.
14 [1a]The LORD is my strength and song,
And He has become [b]my salvation.

15 The sound of [a]joyful shouting and salvation is in the tents of
the righteous;
The [b]right hand of the LORD does valiantly.
16 The [a]right hand of the LORD is exalted;
The right hand of the LORD does valiantly.
17 I [a]will not die, but live,
And [b]tell of the works of [1]the LORD.
18 [1]The LORD has [a]disciplined me severely,
But He has [b]not given me over to death.

19 [a]Open to me the gates of righteousness;
I shall enter through them, I shall give thanks to [1]the LORD.

2 [1]Lit *prevails over us* [2]Or *faithfulness* [3]Or *Hallelujah!* [4]Heb YAH [a]Ps 103:11 [b]Ps 100:5; 146:6
118:1 [a]1 Chr 16:8, 34; Ps 106:1; 107:1; Jer 33:11 [b]2 Chr 5:13; 7:3; Ezra 3:11; Ps 100:5; 136:1-26
2 [a]Ps 115:9
3 [a]Ps 115:10
4 [1]Or *revere* [a]Ps 115:11
5 [1]Heb YAH [a]Ps 18:6; 86:7; 120:1 [b]Ps 18:19
6 [a]Job 19:27; Ps 56:9; Heb 13:6 [b]Ps 23:4; 27:1 [c]Ps 56:4, 11
7 [a]Ps 54:4 [b]Ps 54:7; 59:10
8 [a]2 Chr 32:7, 8; Ps 40:4; 108:12; Is 31:1, 3; 57:13; Jer 17:5
9 [a]Ps 146:3
10 [a]Ps 3:6; 88:17 [b]Ps 18:40
11 [a]Ps 88:17
12 [a]Deut 1:44 [b]Ps 58:9; Nah 1:10
13 [1]Or *fell* [a]Ps 140:4 [b]Ps 86:17
14 [1]Heb YAH [a]Ex 15:2; Is 12:2 [b]Ps 27:1
15 [a]Ps 68:3 [b]Ex 15:6; Ps 89:13; Luke 1:51
16 [a]Ex 15:6; Ps 89:13
17 [1]Heb YAH [a]Ps 6:5; 116:8, 9; Hab 1:12 [b]Ps 73:28; 107:22
18 [1]Heb YAH [a]Ps 73:14; Jer 31:18; 1 Cor 11:32; 2 Cor 6:9 [b]Ps 86:13
19 [1]Heb YAH [a]Is 26:2

20 This is the gate of the LORD;
The [a]righteous will enter through it.
21 I shall give thanks to You, for You have [a]answered me,
And You have [b]become my salvation.

22 The [a]stone which the builders rejected
Has become the chief corner *stone.*
23 This is [1]the LORD's doing;
It is marvelous in our eyes.
24 This is the day which the LORD has made;
Let us [a]rejoice and be glad in it.
25 O LORD, [a]do save, we beseech You;
O LORD, we beseech You, do send [b]prosperity!
26 [a]Blessed is the one who comes in the name of the LORD;
We have [b]blessed you from the house of the LORD.
27 [a]The LORD is God, and He has given us [b]light;
Bind the festival sacrifice with cords [1]to the [c]horns of the altar.
28 [a]You are my God, and I give thanks to You;
You are my God, [b]I extol You.
29 [a]Give thanks to the LORD, for He is good;
For His lovingkindness is everlasting.

*Psalm 119 Theme*________________________

א Aleph.

119 How blessed are those whose way is [1a]blameless,
Who [b]walk in the law of the LORD.
2 How blessed are those who [a]observe His testimonies,
Who [b]seek Him [c]with all *their* heart.
3 They also [a]do no unrighteousness;
They walk in His ways.
4 You have [1a]ordained Your precepts,
[2]That we should keep *them* diligently.
5 Oh that my [a]ways may be established
To [b]keep Your statutes!
6 Then I [a]shall not be ashamed
When I look [1]upon all Your commandments.
7 I shall [a]give thanks to You with uprightness of heart,
When I learn Your righteous judgments.
8 I shall keep Your statutes;
Do not [a]forsake me utterly!

ב Beth.

9 How can a young man keep his way pure?
By [a]keeping *it* according to Your word.
10 With [a]all my heart I have sought You;
Do not let me [b]wander from Your commandments.

20 [a]Ps 15:1, 2; 24:3-6; 140:13; Is 35:8; Rev 22:14

21 [a]Ps 116:1; 118:5 [b]Ps 118:14

22 [a]Matt 21:42; Mark 12:10, 11; Luke 20:17; Acts 4:11; Eph 2:20; 1 Pet 2:7

23 [1]Lit *from the LORD*

24 [a]Ps 31:7

25 [a]Ps 106:47 [b]Ps 122:6, 7

26 [a]Matt 21:9; 23:39; Mark 11:9; Luke 13:35; 19:38; John 12:13 [b]Ps 129:8

27 [1]Lit *unto* [a]1 Kin 18:39 [b]Esth 8:16; Ps 18:28; 27:1; 1 Pet 2:9 [c]Ex 27:2

28 [a]Ps 63:1; 140:6 [b]Ex 15:2; Is 25:1

29 [a]Ps 118:1

119:1 [1]Lit *complete;* or *having integrity* [a]Ps 101:2, 6; Prov 11:20; 13:6 [b]Ps 128:1; Ezek 11:20; 18:17; Mic 4:2

2 [a]Ps 25:10; 99:7; 119:22, 168 [b]Deut 4:29; Ps 119:10 [c]Deut 6:5; 10:12; 11:13; 13:3; 30:2

3 [a]1 John 3:9; 5:18

4 [1]Lit *commanded* [2]Lit *To keep* [a]Deut 4:13; Neh 9:13

5 [a]Ps 40:2; Prov 4:26 [b]Deut 12:1; 2 Chr 7:17

6 [1]Lit *to* [a]Job 22:26; Ps 119:80

7 [a]Ps 119:62

8 [a]Ps 38:21; 71:9, 18

9 [a]1 Kin 2:4; 8:25; 2 Chr 6:16

10 [a]2 Chr 15:15; Ps 119:2, 145 [b]Ps 119:21, 118

11 [a]Ps 37:31; 40:8; Luke 2:19, 51
12 [a]Ps 119:26, 64, 108, 124, 135, 171
13 [a]Ps 40:9 [b]Ps 119:72
14 [1]Lit *As over all* [a]Ps 119:111, 162
15 [1]Or *look upon* [a]Ps 1:2; 119:23, 48, 78, 97, 148 [b]Ps 25:4; 27:11; Is 58:2
16 [1]Lit *delight myself* [a]Ps 1:2; 119:24, 35, 47, 70, 77, 92, 143, 174 [b]Ps 119:93
17 [a]Ps 13:6; 116:7
19 [a]Gen 47:9; Lev 25:23; 1 Chr 29:15; Ps 39:12; 119:54; Heb 11:13
20 [1]Lit *for* [a]Ps 42:1, 2; 63:1; 84:2; 119:40, 131
21 [1]Or *Cursed are those who wander...* [a]Ps 68:30 [b]Deut 27:26; Ps 37:22 [c]Ps 119:10, 118
22 [a]Ps 39:8; 119:39 [b]Ps 119:2
23 [a]Ps 119:161 [b]Ps 119:15
24 [1]Lit *the men of my counsel* [a]Ps 119:16
25 [a]Ps 44:25 [b]Ps 119:37, 40, 88, 93, 107, 149, 154, 156, 159; 143:11 [c]Ps 119:65
26 [a]Ps 25:4; 27:11; 86:11; 119:12
27 [a]Ps 105:2; 145:5
28 [1]Lit *drops* [a]Ps 22:14; 107:26 [b]Ps 20:2; 1 Pet 5:10
30 [1]Or *accounted Your ordinances worthy*
31 [a]Deut 11:22
32 [a]1 Kin 4:29; Is 60:5; 2 Cor 6:11, 13

11 Your word I have [a]treasured in my heart,
That I may not sin against You.
12 Blessed are You, O LORD;
[a]Teach me Your statutes.
13 With my lips I have [a]told of
All the [b]ordinances of Your mouth.
14 I have [a]rejoiced in the way of Your testimonies,
[1]As much as in all riches.
15 I will [a]meditate on Your precepts
And [1]regard [b]Your ways.
16 I shall [1a]delight in Your statutes;
I shall [b]not forget Your word.

ג Gimel.

17 [a]Deal bountifully with Your servant,
That I may live and keep Your word.
18 Open my eyes, that I may behold
Wonderful things from Your law.
19 I am a [a]stranger in the earth;
Do not hide Your commandments from me.
20 My soul is crushed [1a]with longing
After Your ordinances at all times.
21 You [a]rebuke the arrogant, [1]the [b]cursed,
Who [c]wander from Your commandments.
22 [a]Take away reproach and contempt from me,
For I [b]observe Your testimonies.
23 Even though [a]princes sit *and* talk against me,
Your servant [b]meditates on Your statutes.
24 Your testimonies also are my [a]delight;
They are [1]my counselors.

ד Daleth.

25 My [a]soul cleaves to the dust;
[b]Revive me [c]according to Your word.
26 I have told of my ways, and You have answered me;
[a]Teach me Your statutes.
27 Make me understand the way of Your precepts,
So I will [a]meditate on Your wonders.
28 My [a]soul [1]weeps because of grief;
[b]Strengthen me according to Your word.
29 Remove the false way from me,
And graciously grant me Your law.
30 I have chosen the faithful way;
I have [1]placed Your ordinances *before me.*
31 I [a]cling to Your testimonies;
O LORD, do not put me to shame!
32 I shall run the way of Your commandments,
For You will [a]enlarge my heart.

ה He.

33 [a]Teach me, O LORD, the way of Your statutes,
And I shall observe it to the end.
34 [a]Give me understanding, that I may [b]observe Your law
And keep it [c]with all *my* heart.
35 Make me walk in the [a]path of Your commandments,
For I [b]delight in it.
36 [a]Incline my heart to Your testimonies
And not to [b]*dishonest* gain.
37 Turn away my [a]eyes from looking at vanity,
And [b]revive me in Your ways.
38 [a]Establish Your [1]word to Your servant,
[2]As that which produces reverence for You.
39 [a]Turn away my reproach which I dread,
For Your ordinances are good.
40 Behold, I [a]long for Your precepts;
Revive me through Your righteousness.

ו Vav.

41 May Your [a]lovingkindnesses also come to me, O LORD,
Your salvation [b]according to Your [1]word;
42 So I will have an [a]answer for him who [b]reproaches me,
For I trust in Your word.
43 And do not take the word of truth utterly out of my mouth,
For I [1a]wait for Your ordinances.
44 So I will [a]keep Your law continually,
Forever and ever.
45 And I will [a]walk [1]at liberty,
For I [b]seek Your precepts.
46 I will also speak of Your testimonies [a]before kings
And shall not be ashamed.
47 I shall [1a]delight in Your commandments,
Which I [b]love.
48 And I shall lift up my hands to Your commandments,
Which I [a]love;
And I will [b]meditate on Your statutes.

ז Zayin.

49 Remember the word to Your servant,
[1]In which You have made me hope.
50 This is my [a]comfort in my affliction,
That Your word has [1]revived me.
51 The arrogant [a]utterly deride me,
Yet I do not [b]turn aside from Your law.
52 I have [a]remembered Your ordinances from [1]of old, O LORD,
And comfort myself.

33 [a]Ps 119:5, 12

34 [a]Ps 119:27, 73, 125, 144, 169 [b]1 Chr 22:12; Ezek 44:24 [c]Ps 119:2, 69

35 [a]Ps 25:4; Is 40:14 [b]Ps 112:1; 119:16

36 [a]1 Kin 8:58 [b]Ezek 33:31; Mark 7:21, 22; Luke 12:15; Heb 13:5

37 [a]Is 33:15 [b]Ps 71:20; 119:25

38 [1]Or *promise* [2]Lit *Which is for the fear of You* [a]2 Sam 7:25

39 [a]Ps 119:22

40 [a]Ps 119:20

41 [1]Or *promise* [a]Ps 119:77 [b]Ps 119:58, 76, 116, 170

42 [a]Prov 27:11 [b]Ps 102:8; 119:39

43 [1]Or *hope in* [a]Ps 119:49, 74, 81, 114, 147

44 [a]Ps 119:33

45 [1]Lit *in a wide place* [a]Prov 4:12 [b]Ps 119:94, 155

46 [a]Matt 10:18; Acts 26:1, 2

47 [1]Lit *delight myself* [a]Ps 119:16 [b]Ps 119:97, 127, 159

48 [a]Ps 119:97, 127, 159 [b]Ps 119:15

49 [1]Lit *On*

50 [1]Or *preserved me alive* [a]Job 6:10; Rom 15:4

51 [a]Job 30:1; Jer 20:7 [b]Job 23:11; Ps 44:18; 119:157

52 [1]Or *everlasting* [a]Ps 103:18

53 Burning [a]indignation has seized me because of the
wicked,
Who [b]forsake Your law.
54 Your statutes are my songs
In the house of my [a]pilgrimage.
55 O LORD, I [a]remember Your name [b]in the night,
And keep Your law.
56 This has become mine,
[1]That I [a]observe Your precepts.

ח Heth.

57 The LORD is my [a]portion;
I have [1]promised to [b]keep Your words.
58 I [a]sought Your favor [b]with all *my* heart;
[c]Be gracious to me [d]according to Your [1]word.
59 I [a]considered my ways
And turned my feet to Your testimonies.
60 I hastened and did not delay
To keep Your commandments.
61 The [a]cords of the wicked have encircled me,
But I have [b]not forgotten Your law.
62 At [a]midnight I shall rise to give thanks to You
Because of Your [b]righteous ordinances.
63 I am a [a]companion of all those who [1]fear You,
And of those who keep Your precepts.
64 [a]The earth is full of Your lovingkindness, O LORD;
[b]Teach me Your statutes.

ט Teth.

65 You have dealt well with Your servant,
O LORD, according to Your word.
66 Teach me good [1a]discernment and knowledge,
For I believe in Your commandments.
67 [a]Before I was afflicted I went astray,
But now I keep Your word.
68 You are [a]good and [b]do good;
[c]Teach me Your statutes.
69 The arrogant [1]have [a]forged a lie against me;
With all *my* heart I will [b]observe Your precepts.
70 Their heart is [1a]covered with fat,
But I [b]delight in Your law.
71 It is [a]good for me that I was afflicted,
That I may learn Your statutes.
72 The [a]law of Your mouth is better to me
Than thousands of gold and silver *pieces.*

53 [a]Ex 32:19; Ezra 9:3; Neh 13:25; Ps 119:158 [b]Ps 89:30
54 [a]Gen 47:9; Ps 119:19
55 [a]Ps 63:6 [b]Ps 42:8; 92:2; 119:62; Is 26:9; Acts 16:25
56 [1]Or *Because* [a]Ps 119:22, 69, 100
57 [1]Lit *said that I would keep* [a]Ps 16:5; Lam 3:24 [b]Deut 33:9
58 [1]Or *promise* [a]1 Kin 13:6 [b]Ps 119:2 [c]Ps 41:4; 56:1; 57:1 [d]Ps 119:41
59 [a]Mark 14:72; Luke 15:17
61 [a]Job 36:8; Ps 140:5 [b]Ps 119:83, 141, 153, 176
62 [a]Ps 119:55 [b]Ps 119:7
63 [1]Or *revere* [a]Ps 101:6
64 [a]Ps 33:5 [b]Ps 119:12
66 [1]Or *judgment* [a]Phil 1:9
67 [a]Ps 119:71, 75; Jer 31:18, 19; Heb 12:5-11
68 [a]Ps 86:5; 100:5; 106:1; 107:1; Matt 19:17 [b]Deut 8:16; 28:63; 30:5; Ps 125:4 [c]Ps 119:12
69 [1]Lit *besmear me with lies* [a]Job 13:4; Ps 109:2 [b]Ps 119:56
70 [1]Lit *gross like fat* [a]Deut 32:15; Job 15:27; Ps 17:10; Is 6:10; Jer 5:28; Acts 28:27 [b]Ps 119:16
71 [a]Ps 119:67, 75
72 [a]Ps 19:10; 119:127; Prov 8:10, 11, 19

י Yodh.

73 [a]Your hands made me and [1]fashioned me;
[b]Give me understanding, that I may learn Your commandments.
74 May those who [1]fear You [a]see me and be glad,
Because I [2b]wait for Your word.
75 I know, O LORD, that Your judgments are [a]righteous,
And that [b]in faithfulness You have afflicted me.
76 O may Your lovingkindness [1]comfort me,
According to Your [2]word to Your servant.
77 May [a]Your compassion come to me that I may live,
For Your law is my [b]delight.
78 May [a]the arrogant be ashamed, for they subvert me [b]with a lie;
But I shall [c]meditate on Your precepts.
79 May those who [1]fear You turn to me,
Even those who know Your testimonies.
80 May my heart be [1a]blameless in Your statutes,
So that I will not [b]be ashamed.

כ Kaph.

81 My [a]soul languishes for Your salvation;
I [1b]wait for Your word.
82 My [a]eyes fail *with longing* for Your [1]word,
[2]While I say, "When will You comfort me?"
83 Though I have [a]become like a wineskin in the smoke,
I do [b]not forget Your statutes.
84 How many are the [a]days of Your servant?
When will You [b]execute judgment on those who persecute me?
85 The arrogant have [a]dug pits for me,
Men who are not [1]in accord with Your law.
86 All Your commandments are [a]faithful;
They have [b]persecuted me with a lie; [c]help me!
87 They almost destroyed me [1]on earth,
But as for me, I [a]did not forsake Your precepts.
88 Revive me according to Your lovingkindness,
So that I may keep the testimony of Your mouth.

ל Lamedh.

89 [a]Forever, O LORD,
Your word [1]is settled in heaven.
90 Your [a]faithfulness *continues* [1]throughout all generations;
You [b]established the earth, and it [c]stands.
91 They stand this day according to Your [a]ordinances,
For [b]all things are Your servants.

73 [1]Lit *established* [a]Job 10:8; 31:15; Ps 100:3; 138:8; 139:15, 16 [b]Ps 119:34

74 [1]Or *revere* [2]Or *hope in* [a]Ps 34:2; 35:27; 107:42 [b]Ps 119:43

75 [a]Ps 119:138 [b]Heb 12:10

76 [1]Lit *be for my comfort* [2]Or *promise*

77 [a]Ps 119:41 [b]Ps 119:16

78 [a]Jer 50:32 [b]Ps 119:86 [c]Ps 119:15

79 [1]Or *revere*

80 [1]Lit *complete;* or *having integrity* [a]Ps 119:1 [b]Ps 119:46

81 [1]Or *hope in* [a]Ps 84:2 [b]Ps 119:43

82 [1]Or *promise* [2]Lit *Saying* [a]Ps 69:3; 119:123; Is 38:14; Lam 2:11

83 [a]Job 30:30 [b]Ps 119:61

84 [a]Ps 39:4 [b]Rev 6:10

85 [1]Lit *according to Your law* [a]Ps 7:15; 35:7; 57:6; Jer 18:22

86 [a]Ps 119:138 [b]Ps 35:19; 119:78, 161 [c]Ps 109:26

87 [1]Lit *in the earth* [a]Is 58:2

89 [1]Lit *stands firm* [a]Ps 89:2; 119:160; Is 40:8; Matt 24:35; 1 Pet 1:25

90 [1]Lit *to* [a]Ps 36:5; 89:1, 2 [b]Ps 148:6 [c]Eccl 1:4

91 [a]Jer 31:35; 33:25 [b]Ps 104:2-4

92 If Your law had not been my [a]delight,
Then I would have perished [b]in my affliction.
93 I will [a]never forget Your precepts,
For by them You have [1b]revived me.
94 I am Yours, [a]save me;
For I have [b]sought Your precepts.
95 The wicked [a]wait for me to destroy me;
I shall diligently consider Your testimonies.
96 I have seen [1]a limit to all perfection;
Your commandment is exceedingly broad.

מ Mem.

97 O how I [a]love Your law!
It is my [b]meditation all the day.
98 Your [a]commandments make me wiser than my enemies,
For they are ever [1]mine.
99 I have more insight than all my teachers,
For Your testimonies are my [a]meditation.
100 I understand [a]more than the aged,
Because I have [b]observed Your precepts.
101 I have [a]restrained my feet from every evil way,
That I may keep Your word.
102 I have not [a]turned aside from Your ordinances,
For You Yourself have taught me.
103 How [a]sweet are Your [1]words to my [2]taste!
Yes, sweeter than honey to my mouth!
104 From Your precepts I [a]get understanding;
Therefore I [b]hate every false way.

נ Nun.

105 Your word is a [a]lamp to my feet
And a light to my path.
106 I have [a]sworn and I will confirm it,
That I will keep Your righteous ordinances.
107 I am exceedingly [a]afflicted;
[1b]Revive me, O LORD, according to Your word.
108 O accept the [a]freewill offerings of my mouth, O LORD,
And [b]teach me Your ordinances.
109 My [1a]life is continually [2]in my hand,
Yet I do not [b]forget Your law.
110 The wicked have [a]laid a snare for me,
Yet I have not [b]gone astray from Your precepts.
111 I have [a]inherited Your testimonies forever,
For they are the [b]joy of my heart.
112 I have [a]inclined my heart to perform Your statutes
Forever, *even* [b]to the end.

92 [a]Ps 119:16 [b]Ps 119:50
93 [1]Or *kept me alive* [a]Ps 119:16, 83 [b]Ps 119:25
94 [a]Ps 119:146 [b]Ps 119:45
95 [a]Ps 40:14; Is 32:7
96 [1]Lit *an end of*
97 [a]Ps 119:47, 48, 127, 163, 165 [b]Ps 1:2; 119:15
98 [1]Or *with me* [a]Deut 4:6; Ps 119:130
99 [a]Ps 119:15
100 [a]Job 32:7-9 [b]Ps 119:22, 56
101 [a]Prov 1:15
102 [a]Deut 17:20; Josh 23:6; 1 Kin 15:5
103 [1]Or *promises* [2]Lit *palate* [a]Ps 19:10; Prov 8:11; 24:13, 14
104 [a]Ps 119:130 [b]Ps 119:128
105 [a]Prov 6:23
106 [a]Neh 10:29
107 [1]Or *Keep me alive* [a]Ps 119:25, 50 [b]Ps 119:25
108 [a]Hos 14:2; Heb 13:15 [b]Ps 119:12
109 [1]Lit *soul* [2]I.e. in danger [a]Judg 12:3; Job 13:14 [b]Ps 119:16
110 [a]Ps 91:3; 140:5; 141:9 [b]Ps 119:10
111 [a]Deut 33:4 [b]Ps 119:14, 162
112 [a]Ps 119:36 [b]Ps 119:33

ס Samekh.

113 I hate those who are [a]double-minded,
But I love Your [b]law.
114 You are my [a]hiding place and my [b]shield;
I [1c]wait for Your word.
115 [a]Depart from me, evildoers,
That I may [b]observe the commandments of my God.
116 [a]Sustain me according to Your [1]word, that I may live;
And [b]do not let me be [2]ashamed of my hope.
117 Uphold me that I may be [a]safe,
That I may [b]have regard for Your statutes continually.
118 You have [1]rejected all those [a]who wander from Your statutes,
For their deceitfulness is [2]useless.
119 You have [1]removed all the wicked of the earth *like*
[a]dross;
Therefore I [b]love Your testimonies.
120 My flesh [1a]trembles for fear of You,
And I am [b]afraid of Your judgments.

ע Ayin.

121 I have [a]done justice and righteousness;
Do not leave me to my oppressors.
122 Be [a]surety for Your servant for good;
Do not let the arrogant [b]oppress me.
123 My [a]eyes fail *with longing* for Your salvation
And for Your righteous [1]word.
124 Deal with Your servant [a]according to Your
lovingkindness
And [b]teach me Your statutes.
125 [a]I am Your servant; [b]give me understanding,
That I may know Your testimonies.
126 It is time for the LORD to [a]act,
For they have broken Your law.
127 Therefore I [a]love Your commandments
Above gold, yes, above fine gold.
128 Therefore I esteem right all *Your* [a]precepts concerning
everything,
I [b]hate every false way.

פ Pe.

129 Your testimonies are [a]wonderful;
Therefore my soul [b]observes them.
130 The [a]unfolding of Your words gives light;
It gives [b]understanding to the simple.
131 I [a]opened my mouth wide and [b]panted,
For I [c]longed for Your commandments.

113 [a]1 Kin 18:21; James 1:8; 4:8 [b]Ps 119:47

114 [1]Or *hope in* [a]Ps 31:20; 32:7; 61:4; 91:1 [b]Ps 84:9 [c]Ps 119:74

115 [a]Ps 6:8; 139:19; Matt 7:23 [b]Ps 119:22

116 [1]Or *promise* [2]Lit *put to shame because of* [a]Ps 37:17, 24; 54:4 [b]Ps 25:2, 20; 31:1, 17; Rom 5:5; 9:33; Phil 1:20

117 [a]Ps 12:5; Prov 29:25 [b]Ps 119:6, 15

118 [1]Lit *made light of* [2]Lit *falsehood* [a]Ps 119:10, 21

119 [1]Lit *caused to cease* [a]Is 1:22, 25; Ezek 22:18, 19 [b]Ps 119:47

120 [1]Lit *bristles up from* [a]Job 4:14; Hab 3:16 [b]Ps 119:161

121 [a]2 Sam 8:15; Job 29:14

122 [a]Job 17:3; Heb 7:22 [b]Ps 119:134

123 [1]Or *promise* [a]Ps 119:82

124 [a]Ps 51:1; 106:45; 109:26; 119:88, 149, 159 [b]Ps 119:12

125 [a]Ps 116:16 [b]Ps 119:27

126 [a]Jer 18:23; Ezek 31:11

127 [a]Ps 19:10; 119:47

128 [a]Ps 19:8 [b]Ps 119:104

129 [a]Ps 119:18 [b]Ps 119:22

130 [a]Prov 6:23 [b]Ps 19:7

131 [a]Job 29:23; Ps 81:10 [b]Ps 42:1 [c]Ps 119:20

132 [a]Turn to me and be gracious to me,
After Your manner [1]with those who love Your name.
133 Establish my [a]footsteps in Your [1]word,
And do not let any iniquity [b]have dominion over me.
134 [a]Redeem me from the oppression of man,
That I may keep Your precepts.
135 [a]Make Your face shine upon Your servant,
And [b]teach me Your statutes.
136 My eyes [1]shed [a]streams of water,
Because they [b]do not keep Your law.

צ Tsadhe.

137 [a]Righteous are You, O LORD,
And upright are Your judgments.
138 You have commanded Your testimonies in
[a]righteousness
And exceeding [b]faithfulness.
139 My [a]zeal has [1]consumed me,
Because my adversaries have forgotten Your words.
140 Your [1a]word is very [2]pure,
Therefore Your servant [b]loves it.
141 I am small and [a]despised,
Yet I do not [b]forget Your precepts.
142 Your righteousness is an everlasting righteousness,
And [a]Your law is truth.
143 Trouble and anguish have [1]come upon me,
Yet Your commandments are my [a]delight.
144 Your [a]testimonies are righteous forever;
[b]Give me understanding that I may live.

ק Qoph.

145 I cried [a]with all my heart; answer me, O LORD!
I will [b]observe Your statutes.
146 I cried to You; [a]save me
And I shall keep Your testimonies.
147 I [1a]rise before dawn and cry for help;
I [2]wait for Your words.
148 My eyes anticipate the [a]night watches,
That I may [b]meditate on Your [1]word.
149 Hear my voice [a]according to Your lovingkindness;
[b]Revive me, O LORD, according to Your ordinances.
150 Those who follow after wickedness draw near;
They are far from Your law.
151 You are [a]near, O LORD,
And all Your commandments are [b]truth.
152 Of old I have [a]known from Your testimonies
That You have founded them [b]forever.

132 [1]Lit *to* [a]Ps 25:16; 106:4
133 [1]Or *promise* [a]Ps 17:5 [b]Ps 19:13; Rom 6:12
134 [a]Ps 119:84; 142:6; Luke 1:74
135 [a]Num 6:25; Ps 4:6; 31:16; 67:1; 80:3, 7, 19 [b]Ps 119:12
136 [1]Lit *run down* [a]Jer 9:1, 18; 14:17; Lam 3:48 [b]Ps 119:158
137 [a]Ezra 9:15; Neh 9:33; Ps 116:5; 129:4; 145:17; Jer 12:1; Lam 1:18; Dan 9:7, 14
138 [a]Ps 19:7-9; 119:144, 172 [b]Ps 119:86, 90
139 [1]Lit *put an end to* [a]Ps 69:9; John 2:17
140 [1]Or *promise* [2]Lit *refined* [a]Ps 12:6; 19:8 [b]Ps 119:47
141 [a]Ps 22:6 [b]Ps 119:61
142 [a]Ps 19:9; 119:151, 160
143 [1]Lit *found me* [a]Ps 119:24
144 [a]Ps 19:9 [b]Ps 119:27
145 [a]Ps 119:10 [b]Ps 119:22, 55
146 [a]Ps 3:7
147 [1]Lit *anticipate the dawn* [2]Or *hope in* [a]Ps 5:3; 57:8; 108:2
148 [1]Or *promise* [a]Ps 63:6 [b]Ps 119:15
149 [a]Ps 119:124 [b]Ps 119:25
151 [a]Ps 34:18; 145:18; Is 50:8 [b]Ps 119:142
152 [a]Ps 119:125 [b]Ps 119:89; Luke 21:33

ר Resh.

153 [a]Look upon my [b]affliction and rescue me,
For I do not [c]forget Your law.
154 [a]Plead my cause and [b]redeem me;
Revive me according to Your [1]word.
155 Salvation is [a]far from the wicked,
For they [b]do not seek Your statutes.
156 [1a]Great are Your mercies, O LORD;
Revive me according to Your ordinances.
157 Many are my [a]persecutors and my adversaries,
Yet I do not [b]turn aside from Your testimonies.
158 I behold the [a]treacherous and [b]loathe *them,*
Because they do not keep Your [1]word.
159 Consider how I [a]love Your precepts;
[b]Revive me, O LORD, according to Your lovingkindness.
160 The [a]sum of Your word is [b]truth,
And every one of Your righteous ordinances [c]is
everlasting.

ש Shin.

161 [a]Princes persecute me without cause,
But my heart [b]stands in awe of Your words.
162 I [a]rejoice at Your [1]word,
As one who [b]finds great spoil.
163 I [a]hate and despise falsehood,
But I [b]love Your law.
164 Seven times a day I praise You,
Because of Your [a]righteous ordinances.
165 Those who love Your law have [a]great peace,
And [1b]nothing causes them to stumble.
166 I [a]hope for Your salvation, O LORD,
And do Your commandments.
167 My [a]soul keeps Your testimonies,
And I [b]love them exceedingly.
168 I [a]keep Your precepts and Your testimonies,
For all my [b]ways are before You.

ת Tav.

169 Let my [a]cry [1]come before You, O LORD;
[b]Give me understanding [c]according to Your word.
170 Let my [a]supplication come before You;
[b]Deliver me according to Your [1]word.
171 Let my [a]lips utter praise,
For You [b]teach me Your statutes.
172 Let my [a]tongue sing of Your [1]word,
For all Your [b]commandments are righteousness.

153 [a]Lam 5:1 [b]Ps 119:50 [c]Ps 119:16; Prov 3:1; Hos 4:6

154 [1]Or *promise* [a]1 Sam 24:15; Ps 35:1; Mic 7:9 [b]Ps 119:134

155 [a]Job 5:4 [b]Ps 119:45, 94

156 [1]Or *Many* [a]2 Sam 24:14

157 [a]Ps 7:1; 119:86, 161 [b]Ps 119:51

158 [1]Or *promise* [a]Is 21:2; 24:16 [b]Ps 139:21

159 [a]Ps 119:47 [b]Ps 119:25

160 [a]Ps 139:17 [b]Ps 119:142 [c]Ps 119:89, 152

161 [a]1 Sam 24:11; 26:18; Ps 119:23 [b]Ps 119:120

162 [1]Or *promise* [a]Ps 119:14, 111 [b]1 Sam 30:16; Is 9:3

163 [a]Ps 31:6; 119:104, 128; Prov 13:5 [b]Ps 119:47

164 [a]Ps 119:7, 160

165 [1]Lit *they have no stumbling block* [a]Ps 37:11; Prov 3:2; Is 26:3; 32:17 [b]Prov 3:23; Is 63:13; 1 John 2:10

166 [a]Gen 49:18; Ps 119:81, 174

167 [a]Ps 119:129 [b]Ps 119:47

168 [a]Ps 119:22 [b]Job 24:23; Ps 139:3; Prov 5:21

169 [1]Lit *come near before* [a]Job 16:18; Ps 18:6; 102:1 [b]Ps 119:27, 144 [c]Ps 119:65, 154

170 [1]Or *promise* [a]Ps 28:2; 130:2; 140:6; 143:1 [b]Ps 22:20; 31:2; 59:1

171 [a]Ps 51:15; 63:3 [b]Ps 94:12; 119:12; Is 2:3; Mic 4:2

172 [1]Or *promise* [a]Ps 51:14 [b]Ps 119:138

173 Let Your [a]hand be [1]ready to help me,
For I have [b]chosen Your precepts.
174 I [a]long for Your salvation, O LORD,
And Your law is my [b]delight.
175 Let my [a]soul live that it may praise You,
And let Your ordinances help me.
176 I have [a]gone astray like a lost sheep; seek Your servant,
For I do [b]not forget Your commandments.

*Psalm 120 Theme*________________________

A Song of +Ascents.

120 [a]In my trouble I cried to the LORD,
And He answered me.
2 Deliver my soul, O LORD, from [a]lying lips,
From a [b]deceitful tongue.
3 What shall be given to you, and what more shall be done to you,
You [a]deceitful tongue?
4 [a]Sharp arrows of the warrior,
With the *burning* [b]coals of the broom tree.

5 Woe is me, for I sojourn in [a]Meshech,
For I dwell among the [b]tents of [c]Kedar!
6 Too long has my soul had its dwelling
With those who [a]hate peace.
7 I [a]am *for* peace, but when I speak,
They are [b]for war.

*Psalm 121 Theme*________________________

A Song of Ascents.

121 I will [a]lift up my eyes to [b]the mountains;
From where shall my help come?
2 My [a]help *comes* from the LORD,
Who [b]made heaven and earth.
3 He will not [a]allow your foot to slip;
He who [b]keeps you will not slumber.
4 Behold, He who keeps Israel
Will neither slumber nor sleep.

5 The LORD is your [a]keeper;
The LORD is your [b]shade on your right hand.
6 The [a]sun will not smite you by day,
Nor the moon by night.
7 The LORD will [1a]protect you from all evil;
He will keep your soul.
8 The LORD will [1a]guard your going out and your coming in
[b]From this time forth and forever.

---

173 [1]Lit *to help me* [a]Ps 37:24; 73:23 [b]Josh 24:22; Luke 10:42
174 [a]Ps 119:166 [b]Ps 119:16, 24
175 [a]Is 55:3
176 [a]Is 53:6; Jer 50:6; Matt 18:12; Luke 15:4 [b]Ps 119:16
120:1 +Ex 34:24; 1 Kin 12:27 [a]Ps 18:6; 66:14; 102:2; Jon 2:2
2 [a]Ps 109:2; Prov 12:22 [b]Ps 52:4; Zeph 3:13
3 [a]Ps 52:4; Zeph 3:13
4 [a]Ps 45:5; Prov 25:18; Is 5:28 [b]Ps 140:10
5 [a]Gen 10:2; 1 Chr 1:5; Ezek 27:13; 38:2, 3; 39:1 [b]Song 1:5 [c]Gen 25:13; Is 21:16; 60:7; Jer 2:10; 49:28; Ezek 27:21
6 [a]Ps 35:20
7 [a]Ps 109:4 [b]Ps 55:21
121:1 [a]Ps 123:1; Is 40:26 [b]Ps 87:1
2 [a]Ps 124:8 [b]Ps 115:15
3 [a]1 Sam 2:9; Ps 66:9 [b]Ps 41:2; 127:1; Is 27:3
5 [a]Ps 91:4 [b]Ps 16:8; 91:1; Is 25:4
6 [a]Ps 91:5; Is 49:10; Jon 4:8; Rev 7:16
7 [1]Or *keep* [a]Ps 41:2; 91:10-12
8 [1]Or *keep* [a]Deut 28:6 [b]Ps 113:2; 115:18

*Psalm 122 Theme*______________________________

A Song of Ascents, of David.

122 I was glad when they said to me,
"Let us [a]go to the house of the LORD."
2 Our feet are standing
Within your [a]gates, O Jerusalem,
3 Jerusalem, that is [a]built
As a city that is [b]compact together;
4 To which the tribes [a]go up, even the tribes of [1]the LORD—
[2]An ordinance for Israel—
To give thanks to the name of the LORD.
5 For there [a]thrones were set for judgment,
The thrones of the house of David.

6 Pray for the [a]peace of Jerusalem:
"May they prosper who [b]love you.
7 "May peace be within your [a]walls,
And prosperity within your [b]palaces."
8 For the sake of my [a]brothers and my friends,
I will now say, "[b]May peace be within you."
9 For the sake of the house of the LORD our God,
I will [a]seek your good.

*Psalm 123 Theme*______________________________

A Song of Ascents.

123 To You I [a]lift up my eyes,
O You who [b]are enthroned in the heavens!
2 Behold, as the eyes of [a]servants *look* to the hand of their master,
As the eyes of a maid to the hand of her mistress,
So our [b]eyes *look* to the LORD our God,
Until He is gracious to us.

3 [a]Be gracious to us, O LORD, be gracious to us,
For we are greatly filled [b]with contempt.
4 Our soul is greatly filled
With the [a]scoffing of [b]those who are at ease,
And with the [c]contempt of the proud.

*Psalm 124 Theme*______________________________

A Song of Ascents, of David.

124 "[a]Had it not been the LORD who was on our side,"
[b]Let Israel now say,
2 "Had it not been the LORD who was on our side
When men rose up against us,
3 Then they would have [a]swallowed us alive,
When their [b]anger was kindled against us;
4 Then the [a]waters would have engulfed us,
The stream would have [1]swept over our soul;

122:1 [a]Ps 42:4; Is 2:3; Mic 4:2; Zech 8:21
2 [a]Ps 9:14; 87:2; 116:19; Jer 7:2
3 [a]Ps 48:13; 147:2 [b]2 Sam 5:9; Neh 4:6
4 [1]Heb *YAH* [2]Or *A testimony* [a]Ex 23:17; Deut 16:16; Ps 84:5
5 [a]Deut 17:8; 2 Chr 19:8; Ps 89:29
6 [a]Ps 29:11; Jer 29:7 [b]Ps 102:14
7 [a]Ps 51:18; Is 62:6 [b]Ps 48:3, 13; Jer 17:27
8 [a]Ps 133:1 [b]1 Sam 25:6; John 20:19
9 [a]Neh 2:10; Esth 10:3
123:1 [a]Ps 121:1; 141:8 [b]Ps 2:4; 11:4
2 [a]Prov 27:18; Mal 1:6 [b]Ps 25:15
3 [a]Ps 4:1; 51:1 [b]Neh 4:4; Ps 119:22
4 [a]Neh 2:19; Ps 79:4 [b]Job 12:5; Is 32:9, 11; Amos 6:1 [c]Neh 4:4; Ps 119:22
124:1 [a]Ps 94:17 [b]Ps 129:1
3 [a]Num 16:30; Ps 35:25; 56:1; 57:3; Prov 1:12 [b]Gen 39:19; Ps 138:7
4 [1]Or *passed over* [a]Job 22:11; Ps 18:16; 32:6; 69:2; 144:7

5 [1]Or *passed over* [a]Job 38:11

6 [1]Lit *as a prey to* [a]Ps 27:2; Prov 30:14

7 [a]Ps 141:10; 2 Cor 11:33; Heb 11:34 [b]Prov 6:5 [c]Ps 91:3; Hos 9:8

8 [a]Ps 121:2 [b]Gen 1:1; Ps 134:3

125:1 [a]Ps 46:5 [b]Ps 61:7; Eccl 1:4

2 [a]Zech 2:5 [b]Ps 121:8

3 [1]Lit *lot* [a]Ps 89:22; Prov 22:8; Is 14:5 [b]1 Sam 24:10; Ps 55:20; Acts 12:1

4 [a]Ps 119:68 [b]Ps 7:10; 11:2; 32:11; 36:10; 94:15

5 [a]Job 23:11; Ps 40:4; 101:3 [b]Prov 2:15; Is 59:8 [c]Ps 92:7; 94:4 [d]Ps 128:6; Gal 6:16

126:1 [1]Or *those who returned to* [a]Ps 85:1; Jer 29:14; Hos 6:11 [b]Acts 12:9

2 [a]Job 8:21 [b]Ps 51:14; Is 35:6 [c]1 Sam 12:24; Ps 71:19; Luke 1:49

3 [a]Is 25:9; Zeph 3:14

4 [1]Lit *stream-beds* [2]Heb *Negev* [a]Is 35:6; 43:19

5 [a]Ps 80:5; Jer 31:9, 16; Lam 1:2 [b]Is 35:10; 51:11; 61:7; Gal 6:9

5 Then the [a]raging waters would have [1]swept over our soul."

6 Blessed be the LORD,
Who has not given us [1]to be [a]torn by their teeth.
7 Our soul has [a]escaped [b]as a bird out of the [c]snare of the trapper;
The snare is broken and we have escaped.
8 Our [a]help is in the name of the LORD,
Who [b]made heaven and earth.

Psalm 125 Theme ______________________

A Song of Ascents.

125 Those who trust in the LORD
Are as Mount Zion, which [a]cannot be moved but [b]abides forever.
2 As the mountains surround Jerusalem,
So [a]the LORD surrounds His people
[b]From this time forth and forever.
3 For the [a]scepter of wickedness shall not rest upon the [1]land of the righteous,
So that the righteous [b]will not put forth their hands to do wrong.

4 [a]Do good, O LORD, to those who are good
And to those who are [b]upright in their hearts.
5 But as for those who [a]turn aside to their [b]crooked ways,
The LORD will lead them away with the [c]doers of iniquity.
[d]Peace be upon Israel.

Psalm 126 Theme ______________________

A Song of Ascents.

126 When the LORD [a]brought back [1]the captive ones of Zion,
We were [b]like those who dream.
2 Then our [a]mouth was filled with laughter
And our [b]tongue with joyful shouting;
Then they said among the nations,
"The LORD has [c]done great things for them."
3 The LORD has done great things for us;
We are [a]glad.

4 Restore our captivity, O LORD,
As the [1a]streams in the [2]South.
5 Those who sow in [a]tears shall reap with [b]joyful shouting.
6 He who goes to and fro weeping, carrying *his* bag of seed,
Shall indeed come again with a shout of joy, bringing his sheaves *with him.*

*Psalm 127 Theme*____________________________________

A Song of Ascents, of Solomon.

127 Unless the LORD [a]builds the house,
They labor in vain who build it;
Unless the LORD [b]guards the city,
The watchman keeps awake in vain.
2 It is vain for you to rise up early,
To [1]retire late,
To [a]eat the bread of [2]painful labors;
For He gives to His [b]beloved [c]*even in his* sleep.

3 Behold, [a]children are a [1]gift of the LORD,
The [b]fruit of the womb is a reward.
4 Like arrows in the hand of a [a]warrior,
So are the children of one's youth.
5 How [a]blessed is the man whose quiver is full of them;
[b]They will not be ashamed
When they [c]speak with their enemies [d]in the gate.

*Psalm 128 Theme*____________________________________

A Song of Ascents.

128 [a]How blessed is everyone who fears the LORD,
Who [b]walks in His ways.
2 When you shall [a]eat of the [1b]fruit of your hands,
You will be happy and [c]it will be well with you.
3 Your wife shall be like a [a]fruitful vine
[1]Within your house,
Your children like [b]olive plants
Around your table.
4 Behold, for thus shall the man be blessed
Who fears the LORD.

5 [a]The LORD bless you [b]from Zion,
And may you see the prosperity of Jerusalem all the days of your life.
6 Indeed, may you see your [a]children's children.
[b]Peace be upon Israel!

*Psalm 129 Theme*____________________________________

A Song of Ascents.

129 "[1]Many times they have [2a]persecuted me from my [b]youth up,"
[c]Let Israel now say,
2 "[1]Many times they have [2]persecuted me from my youth up;
Yet they have [a]not prevailed against me.
3 "The plowers plowed upon my back;
They lengthened their furrows."
4 The LORD [a]is righteous;
He has cut in two the [b]cords of the wicked.

127:1 [a]Ps 78:69 [b]Ps 121:4

2 [1]Lit *delay sitting* [2]Lit *toils* [a]Gen 3:17, 19 [b]Ps 60:5 [c]Job 11:18, 19; Prov 3:24; Eccl 5:12

3 [1]Or *heritage* [a]Gen 33:5; 48:4; Josh 24:3, 4; Ps 113:9 [b]Deut 7:13; 28:4; Is 13:18

4 [a]Ps 112:2; 120:4

5 [a]Ps 128:2, 3 [b]Prov 27:11 [c]Is 29:21; Amos 5:12 [d]Gen 34:20

128:1 [a]Ps 112:1; 119:1 [b]Ps 119:3

2 [1]Lit *labor* [a]Is 3:10 [b]Ps 109:11; Hag 2:17 [c]Eccl 8:12; Eph 6:3

3 [1]Lit *In the innermost parts of* [a]Ezek 19:10 [b]Ps 52:8; 144:12

5 [a]Ps 134:3 [b]Ps 20:2; 135:21

6 [a]Gen 48:11; 50:23; Job 42:16; Ps 103:17; Prov 17:6 [b]Ps 125:5

129:1 [1]Lit *Much* [2]Lit *showed hostility toward* [a]Ex 1:11; Judg 3:8; Ps 88:15 [b]Is 47:12; Jer 2:2; 22:21; Ezek 16:22; Hos 2:15; 11:1 [c]Ps 124:1

2 [1]Lit *Much* [2]Lit *showed hostility toward* [a]Jer 1:19; 15:20; 20:11; Matt 16:18; 2 Cor 4:8, 9

4 [a]Ps 119:137 [b]Ps 140:5

5 May all who [a]hate Zion
Be [b]put to shame and turned backward;
6 Let them be like [a]grass upon the housetops,
Which withers before it [1]grows up;
7 With which the reaper does not fill his [1]hand,
Or the binder of sheaves his [a]bosom;
8 Nor do those who pass by say,
"The [a]blessing of the LORD be upon you;
We bless you in the name of the LORD."

Psalm 130 Theme ______________________

A Song of Ascents.

130 Out of the [a]depths I have cried to You, O LORD.
2 Lord, [a]hear my voice!
Let [b]Your ears be attentive
To the [c]voice of my supplications.
3 If You, [1]LORD, should mark iniquities,
O Lord, who could [a]stand?
4 But there is [a]forgiveness with You,
That You may be [b]feared.

5 I wait for the LORD, my [a]soul does wait,
And [1b]in His word do I hope.
6 My soul *waits* for the Lord
More than the watchmen [a]for the morning;
Indeed, more than the watchmen for the morning.
7 O Israel, [a]hope in the LORD;
For with the LORD there is [b]lovingkindness,
And with Him is [c]abundant redemption.
8 And He will [a]redeem Israel
From all his iniquities.

Psalm 131 Theme ______________________

A Song of Ascents, of David.

131 O LORD, my heart is not [a]proud, nor my eyes [1b]haughty;
Nor do I [2]involve myself in [c]great matters,
Or in things [d]too [3]difficult for me.
2 Surely I have [a]composed and quieted my soul;
Like a weaned [b]child *rests* [1]against his mother,
My soul is like a weaned child [1]within me.
3 O Israel, [a]hope in the LORD
[b]From this time forth and forever.

Psalm 132 Theme ______________________

A Song of Ascents.

132 Remember, O LORD, on David's behalf,
All [a]his affliction;
2 How he swore to the LORD
And vowed to [a]the Mighty One of Jacob,

5 [a]Mic 4:11 [b]Ps 70:3; 71:13
6 [1]Lit *draws out* [a]2 Kin 19:26; Ps 37:2; Is 37:27
7 [1]Lit *palm* [a]Ps 79:12
8 [a]Ruth 2:4; Ps 118:26
130:1 [a]Ps 42:7; 69:2; Lam 3:55
2 [a]Ps 64:1; 119:149 [b]2 Chr 6:40; Neh 1:6, 11 [c]Ps 28:2; 140:6
3 [1]Heb YAH [a]Ps 76:7; 143:2; Nah 1:6; Mal 3:2; Rev 6:17
4 [a]Ex 34:7; Neh 9:17; Ps 86:5; Is 55:7; Dan 9:9 [b]1 Kin 8:39, 40; Jer 33:8, 9
5 [1]Lit *for* [a]Ps 27:14; 33:20; 40:1; 62:1, 5; Is 8:17; 26:8 [b]Ps 119:74, 81
6 [a]Ps 63:6; 119:147
7 [a]Ps 131:3 [b]Ps 86:5; 103:4 [c]Ps 111:9; Rom 3:24; Eph 1:7
8 [a]Ps 103:3, 4; Luke 1:68; Titus 2:14
131:1 [1]Or *lofty* [2]Lit *go after,* walk [3]Or *marvelous* [a]2 Sam 22:28; Ps 101:5; Is 2:12; Zeph 3:11 [b]Prov 30:13; Is 5:15 [c]Jer 45:5; Rom 12:16 [d]Job 42:3; Ps 139:6
2 [1]Or *upon* [a]Ps 62:1 [b]Matt 18:3; 1 Cor 14:20
3 [a]Ps 130:7 [b]Ps 113:2
132:1 [a]Gen 49:24; 2 Sam 16:12
2 [a]Gen 49:24; Is 49:26; 60:16

3 "Surely I will not [1]enter [a]my house,
Nor [2]lie on my bed;
4 I will not [a]give sleep to my eyes
Or slumber to my eyelids,
5 Until I find a [a]place for the LORD,
[1]A dwelling place for [b]the Mighty One of Jacob."

6 Behold, we heard of it in [a]Ephrathah,
We found it in the [b]field of [1]Jaar.
7 Let us go into His [1a]dwelling place;
Let us [b]worship at His [c]footstool.
8 [a]Arise, O LORD, to Your [b]resting place,
You and the ark of Your [c]strength.
9 Let Your priests be [a]clothed with righteousness,
And let Your [b]godly ones sing for joy.

10 For the sake of David Your servant,
Do not turn away the face of Your [a]anointed.
11 The LORD has [a]sworn to David
A truth from which He will not turn back:
"[b]Of the fruit of your body I will set upon your throne.
12 "If your sons will keep My covenant
And My testimony which I will teach them,
Their sons also shall [a]sit upon your throne forever."

13 For the LORD has [a]chosen Zion;
He has [b]desired it for His habitation.
14 "This is My [a]resting place forever;
Here I will [b]dwell, for I have desired it.
15 "I will abundantly [a]bless her provision;
I will [b]satisfy her needy with bread.
16 "Her [a]priests also I will clothe with salvation,
And her [a]godly ones will sing aloud for joy.
17 "There I will cause the [a]horn of David to spring forth;
I have prepared a [b]lamp for Mine anointed.
18 "His enemies I will [a]clothe with shame,
But upon himself his [b]crown shall shine."

Psalm 133 Theme ________________

A Song of Ascents, of David.

133 Behold, how good and how pleasant it is
For [a]brothers to dwell together in unity!
2 It is like the precious [a]oil upon the head,
Coming down upon the beard,
Even Aaron's beard,
Coming down upon the [b]edge of his robes.
3 It is like the [a]dew of [b]Hermon
Coming down upon the [c]mountains of Zion;
For there the LORD [d]commanded the blessing—[e]life forever.

3 [1]Lit *come into the tabernacle of* [2]Lit *go up into the couch of* [a]Job 21:28
4 [a]Prov 6:4
5 [1]Lit *Dwelling places* [a]1 Kin 8:17; 1 Chr 22:7; Ps 26:8; Acts 7:46 [b]Ps 132:2
6 [1]Or *the wood* [a]Gen 35:19; 1 Sam 17:12 [b]1 Sam 7:1
7 [1]Lit *dwelling places* [a]Ps 43:3 [b]Ps 5:7; 99:5 [c]1 Chr 28:2
8 [a]Num 10:35; 2 Chr 6:41; Ps 68:1 [b]Ps 132:14 [c]Ps 78:61
9 [a]Job 29:14 [b]Ps 30:4; 132:16; 149:5
10 [a]Ps 2:2; 132:17
11 [a]Ps 89:3, 35 [b]2 Sam 7:12-16; 1 Chr 17:11-14; 2 Chr 6:16; Ps 89:4; Acts 2:30
12 [a]Luke 1:32; Acts 2:30
13 [a]Ps 48:1, 2; 78:68 [b]Ps 68:16
14 [a]Ps 132:8 [b]Ps 68:16; Matt 23:21
15 [a]Ps 147:14 [b]Ps 107:9
16 [a]2 Chr 6:41; Ps 132:9
17 [a]Ezek 29:21; Luke 1:69 [b]1 Kin 11:36; 15:4; 2 Kin 8:19; 2 Chr 21:7; Ps 18:28
18 [a]Job 8:22; Ps 35:26; 109:29 [b]Ps 21:3
133:1 [a]Gen 13:8; Heb 13:1
2 [a]Ex 29:7; 30:25, 30; Lev 8:12 [b]Ex 28:33; 39:24
3 [a]Prov 19:12; Hos 14:5; Mic 5:7 [b]Deut 3:9; 4:48 [c]Ps 48:2; 74:2; 78:68 [d]Lev 25:21; Deut 28:8; Ps 42:8 [e]Ps 21:4

*Psalm 134 Theme*____________________

A Song of Ascents.

134 Behold, [a]bless the LORD, all [b]servants of the LORD,
Who [1c]serve [d]by night in the house of the LORD!
2 [a]Lift up your hands to the [b]sanctuary
And bless the LORD.
3 May the LORD [a]bless you from Zion,
He who [b]made heaven and earth.

*Psalm 135 Theme*____________________

135 [1a]Praise [2]the LORD!
Praise the name of the LORD;
Praise *Him,* O [b]servants of the LORD,
2 You who stand in the house of the LORD,
In the [a]courts of the house of our God!
3 [1]Praise [2]the LORD, for [a]the LORD is good;
[b]Sing praises to His name, [c]for it is lovely.
4 For [1]the LORD has [a]chosen Jacob for Himself,
Israel for His [2b]own possession.

5 For I know that [a]the LORD is great
And that our Lord is [b]above all gods.
6 [a]Whatever the LORD pleases, He does,
In heaven and in earth, in the seas and in all deeps.
7 [1]He [a]causes the [2]vapors to ascend from the ends of the earth;
Who [b]makes lightnings for the rain,
Who [a]brings forth the wind from His treasuries.

8 [1]He [a]smote the firstborn of Egypt,
[2]Both of man and beast.
9 [1]He sent [a]signs and wonders into your midst, O Egypt,
Upon [b]Pharaoh and all his servants.
10 [1a]He [b]smote many nations
And slew mighty kings,
11 [a]Sihon, king of the Amorites,
And [b]Og, king of Bashan,
And [c]all the kingdoms of Canaan;
12 And He [a]gave their land as a heritage,
A heritage to Israel His people.
13 Your [a]name, O LORD, is everlasting,
Your [1]remembrance, O LORD, [2]throughout all generations.
14 For the LORD will [a]judge His people
And [b]will have compassion on His servants.
15 The [a]idols of the nations are *but* silver and gold,
The work of man's hands.
16 They have mouths, but they do not speak;
They have eyes, but they do not see;
17 They have ears, but they do not hear,
Nor is there any breath at all in their mouths.

134:1 [1]Lit *stand* [a]Ps 103:21 [b]Ps 135:1, 2 [c]Deut 10:8; 1 Chr 23:30; 2 Chr 29:11 [d]1 Chr 9:33
2 [a]Ps 28:2; 1 Tim 2:8 [b]Ps 63:2
3 [a]Ps 128:5 [b]Ps 124:8
135:1 [1]Or *Hallelujah!* [2]Heb *YAH* [a]Ps 113:1 [b]Ps 134:1
2 [a]Ps 92:13; 116:19
3 [1]Or *Hallelujah!* [2]Heb *YAH* [a]Ps 100:5; 119:68 [b]Ps 68:4 [c]Ps 147:1
4 [1]Heb *YAH* [2]Or *special treasure* [a]Deut 7:6; 10:15; Ps 105:6 [b]Ex 19:5; Mal 3:17; Titus 2:14; 1 Pet 2:9
5 [a]Ps 48:1; 95:3; 145:3 [b]Ps 97:9
6 [a]Ps 115:3
7 [1]Lit *The one who* [2]I.e. clouds [a]Jer 10:13; 51:16 [b]Job 28:25, 26; 38:25, 26; Zech 10:1
8 [1]Lit *The one who* [2]Lit *From man to beast* [a]Ex 12:12; Ps 78:51; 105:36
9 [1]Lit *The one who* [a]Ex 7:10; Deut 6:22; Ps 78:43 [b]Ps 136:15
10 [1]Lit *The one who* [a]Num 21:24; Ps 135:10-12; 136:17-21 [b]Ps 44:2
11 [a]Num 21:21-26; Deut 29:7 [b]Num 21:33-35 [c]Josh 12:7-24
12 [a]Deut 29:8; Ps 78:55; 136:21, 22
13 [1]Or *memorial* [2]Lit *to* [a]Ex 3:15; Ps 102:12
14 [a]Deut 32:36; Ps 50:4 [b]Ps 90:13; 106:46
15 [a]Ps 115:4-8; 135:15-18

18 Those who make them will be like them,
Yes, everyone who trusts in them.

19 O house of [a]Israel, bless the LORD;
O house of Aaron, bless the LORD;
20 O house of Levi, bless the LORD;
You [a]who [1]revere the LORD, bless the LORD.
21 Blessed be the LORD [a]from Zion,
Who [b]dwells in Jerusalem.
[1]Praise [2]the LORD!

*Psalm 136 Theme*________________________

136 [a]Give thanks to the LORD, for [b]He is good,
For [c]His lovingkindness is everlasting.
2 Give thanks to the [a]God of gods,
For His lovingkindness is everlasting.
3 Give thanks to the [a]Lord of lords,
For His lovingkindness is everlasting.
4 To Him who [a]alone does great [1]wonders,
For His lovingkindness is everlasting;
5 To Him who [a]made the heavens [1b]with skill,
For His lovingkindness is everlasting;
6 To Him who [a]spread out the earth above the waters,
For His lovingkindness is everlasting;
7 To Him who [a]made *the* great lights,
For His lovingkindness is everlasting:
8 The [a]sun to rule [1]by day,
For His lovingkindness is everlasting,
9 The [a]moon and stars to rule [1]by night,
For His lovingkindness is everlasting.

10 To Him who [a]smote [1]the Egyptians in their firstborn,
For His lovingkindness is everlasting,
11 And [a]brought Israel out from their midst,
For His lovingkindness is everlasting,
12 With a [a]strong hand and an [b]outstretched arm,
For His lovingkindness is everlasting.
13 To Him who [a]divided the [1]Red Sea [2]asunder,
For His lovingkindness is everlasting,
14 And [a]made Israel pass through the midst of it,
For His lovingkindness is everlasting;
15 But [a]He [1]overthrew Pharaoh and his army in the [2]Red Sea,
For His lovingkindness is everlasting.
16 To Him who [a]led His people through the wilderness,
For His lovingkindness is everlasting;
17 To Him who [a]smote great kings,
For His lovingkindness is everlasting,
18 And [a]slew [1]mighty kings,
For His lovingkindness is everlasting:
19 [a]Sihon, king of the Amorites,
For His lovingkindness is everlasting,

19 [a]Ps 115:9

20 [1]Lit *fear* [a]Ps 118:4

21 [1]Or *Hallelujah!* [2]Heb *YAH* [a]Ps 128:5; 134:3 [b]Ps 132:14

136:1 [a]1 Chr 16:34; Ps 106:1; 107:1; 118:1; Jer 33:11 [b]2 Chr 5:13; 7:3; Ezra 3:11; Ps 100:5 [c]1 Chr 16:41; 2 Chr 20:21; Ps 118:1-4

2 [a]Deut 10:17

3 [a]Deut 10:17

4 [1]I.e. wonderful acts [a]Deut 6:22; Job 9:10; Ps 72:18

5 [1]Lit *with understanding* [a]Gen 1:1 [b]Ps 104:24; Prov 3:19; Jer 10:12; 51:15

6 [a]Gen 1:2, 6, 9; Ps 24:2; Is 42:5; 44:24; Jer 10:12

7 [a]Gen 1:14-18; Ps 74:16

8 [1]Or *over the* [a]Gen 1:16

9 [1]Or *over the* [a]Gen 1:16

10 [1]Lit *Egypt* [a]Ex 12:29; Ps 78:51; 135:8

11 [a]Ex 12:51; 13:3; Ps 105:43

12 [a]Ex 6:1; 13:9; 1 Kin 8:42; Neh 1:10; Ps 44:3; Jer 32:21 [b]Ex 6:6; Deut 4:34; 5:15; 7:19; 9:29; 11:2; 2 Kin 17:36; 2 Chr 6:32; Jer 32:17

13 [1]Lit *Sea of Reeds* [2]Lit *in parts* [a]Ex 14:21; Ps 66:6; 78:13

14 [a]Ex 14:22; Ps 106:9

15 [1]Lit *shook off* [2]Lit *Sea of Reeds* [a]Ex 14:27; Ps 78:53; 106:11

16 [a]Ex 13:18; 15:22; Deut 8:15; Ps 78:52

17 [a]Ps 135:10-12; 136:17-22

18 [1]Lit *majestic* [a]Deut 29:7

19 [a]Num 21:21-24

20 And [a]Og, king of Bashan,
For His lovingkindness is everlasting,
21 And [a]gave their land as a heritage,
For His lovingkindness is everlasting,
22 Even a heritage to Israel His [a]servant,
For His lovingkindness is everlasting.

23 Who [a]remembered us in our low estate,
For His lovingkindness is everlasting,
24 And has [a]rescued us from our adversaries,
For His lovingkindness is everlasting;
25 Who [a]gives food to all flesh,
For His lovingkindness is everlasting.
26 Give thanks to the [a]God of heaven,
For His lovingkindness is everlasting.

*Psalm 137 Theme*____________________

137 By the [a]rivers of Babylon,
There we sat down and [b]wept,
When we remembered Zion.
2 Upon the [1a]willows in the midst of it
We [b]hung our [2]harps.
3 For there our captors [1a]demanded of us [2]songs,
And [b]our tormentors mirth, *saying,*
"Sing us one of the songs of Zion."

4 How can we sing [a]the LORD's song
In a foreign land?
5 If I [a]forget you, O Jerusalem,
May my right hand [1]forget *her skill.*
6 May my [a]tongue cling to the roof of my mouth
If I do not remember you,
If I do not [1b]exalt Jerusalem
Above my chief joy.

7 Remember, O LORD, against the sons of [a]Edom
The day of Jerusalem,
Who said, "Raze it, raze it
[b]To its very foundation."
8 O daughter of Babylon, you [1a]devastated one,
How blessed will be the one who [b]repays you
With [2]the recompense with which you have repaid us.
9 How blessed will be the one who seizes and [a]dashes your
little ones
Against the rock.

*Psalm 138 Theme*____________________

A Psalm of David.

138 [a]I will give You thanks with all my heart;
I will sing praises to You before the [b]gods.

20 [a]Num 21:33-35
21 [a]Josh 12:1
22 [a]Ps 105:6; Is 41:8; 44:1; 45:4
23 [a]Ps 9:12; 103:14; 106:45
24 [a]Judg 6:9; Neh 9:28; Ps 107:2
25 [a]Ps 104:27; 145:15
26 [a]Gen 24:3, 7; 2 Chr 36:23; Ezra 1:2; 5:11; Neh 1:4
137:1 [a]Ezek 1:1, 3 [b]Neh 1:4
2 [1]Or *poplars* [2]Lit *lyres* [a]Lev 23:40; Is 44:4 [b]Job 30:31; Is 24:8; Ezek 26:13
3 [1]Lit *asked* [2]Lit *words of song* [a]Ps 80:6 [b]Is 49:17
4 [a]2 Chr 29:27; Neh 12:46
5 [1]I.e. become lame [a]Is 65:11
6 [1]Lit *cause to ascend* [a]Job 29:10; Ps 22:15; Ezek 3:26 [b]Neh 2:3
7 [a]Ps 83:4-8; Is 34:5, 6; Jer 49:7-22; Lam 4:21; Ezek 25:12-14; 35:2; Amos 1:11; Obad 10-14 [b]Ps 74:7; Hab 3:13
8 [1]Or *devastator* [2]Lit *your recompense* [a]Is 13:1-22; 47:1-15; Jer 25:12; 50:1-46; 51:1-64 [b]Jer 50:15; 51:24, 35, 36, 49; Rev 18:6
9 [a]2 Kin 8:12; Is 13:16; Hos 13:16; Nah 3:10
138:1 [a]Ps 111:1 [b]Ps 95:3; 96:4; 97:7

2 I will bow down [a]toward Your holy temple
And [b]give thanks to Your name for Your lovingkindness and Your [1]truth;
For You have [c]magnified Your [2]word [3]according to all Your name.
3 On the day I [a]called, You answered me;
You made me bold with [b]strength in my soul.

4 [a]All the kings of the earth will give thanks to You, O LORD,
When they have heard the words of Your mouth.
5 And they will [a]sing of the ways of the LORD,
For [b]great is the glory of the LORD.
6 For [a]though the LORD is exalted,
Yet He [b]regards the lowly,
But the [c]haughty He knows from afar.

7 Though I [a]walk in the midst of trouble, You will [1b]revive me;
You will [c]stretch forth Your hand against the wrath of my enemies,
And Your right hand will [d]save me.
8 The LORD will [a]accomplish what concerns me;
Your [b]lovingkindness, O LORD, is everlasting;
[c]Do not forsake the [d]works of Your hands.

*Psalm 139 Theme*_______________________________

For the choir director. A Psalm of David.

139 O LORD, You have [a]searched me and known *me.*
2 You [a]know [1]when I sit down and [2]when I rise up;
You [b]understand my thought from afar.
3 You [1a]scrutinize my [2]path and my lying down,
And are intimately acquainted with all my ways.
4 [1]Even before there is a word on my tongue,
Behold, O LORD, You [a]know it all.
5 You have [a]enclosed me behind and before,
And [b]laid Your hand upon me.
6 *Such* [a]knowledge is [b]too wonderful for me;
It is *too* high, I cannot attain to it.

7 [a]Where can I go from Your Spirit?
Or where can I flee from Your presence?
8 [a]If I ascend to heaven, You are there;
If I make my bed in [1]Sheol, behold, [b]You are there.
9 If I take the wings of the dawn,
If I dwell in the remotest part of the sea,
10 Even there Your hand will [a]lead me,
And Your right hand will lay hold of me.
11 If I say, "Surely the [a]darkness will [1]overwhelm me,
And the light around me will be night,"
12 Even the [a]darkness is not dark [1]to You,
And the night is as bright as the day.
[b]Darkness and light are alike *to You.*

2 [1]Or *faithfulness* [2]Or *promise* [3]Or *together with* [a]1 Kin 8:29; Ps 5:7; 28:2 [b]Ps 140:13 [c]Is 42:21

3 [a]Ps 118:5 [b]Ps 28:7; 46:1

4 [a]Ps 72:11; 102:15

5 [a]Ps 145:7 [b]Ps 21:5

6 [a]Ps 113:4-7 [b]Prov 3:34; Is 57:15; Luke 1:48; James 4:6; 1 Pet 5:5 [c]Ps 40:4; 101:5

7 [1]Or *keep me alive* [a]Ps 23:4; 143:11 [b]Ezra 9:8, 9; Ps 71:20; Is 57:15 [c]Ex 7:5; 15:12; Is 5:25; Jer 51:25; Ezek 6:14; 25:13 [d]Ps 20:6; 60:5

8 [a]Ps 57:2; Phil 1:6 [b]Ps 136:1 [c]Job 10:8; Ps 27:9; 71:9; 119:8 [d]Job 10:3; 14:15; Ps 100:3

139:1 [a]Ps 17:3; 44:21; Jer 12:3

2 [1]Lit *my sitting* [2]Lit *my rising* [a]2 Kin 19:27 [b]Ps 94:11; Is 66:18; Matt 9:4

3 [1]Lit *winnow* [2]Or *journeying* [a]Job 14:16; 31:4

4 [1]Lit *For there is not* [a]Heb 4:13

5 [a]Ps 34:7; 125:2 [b]Job 9:33

6 [a]Rom 11:33 [b]Job 42:3

7 [a]Jer 23:24

8 [1]I.e. the nether world [a]Amos 9:2-4 [b]Job 26:6; Prov 15:11

10 [a]Ps 23:2, 3

11 [1]Lit *bruise;* some commentators read *cover* [a]Job 22:13

12 [1]Lit *from* [a]Job 34:22; Dan 2:22 [b]1 John 1:5

13 [1]Lit *kidneys* [a]Ps 119:73; Is 44:24 [b]Job 10:11

14 [1]Some ancient versions read *You are fearfully wonderful* [a]Ps 40:5

15 [1]Lit *bones were* [a]Job 10:8-10; Eccl 11:5 [b]Ps 63:9

16 [a]Job 10:8-10; Eccl 11:5 [b]Ps 56:8 [c]Job 14:5

17 [a]Ps 40:5; 92:5

18 [a]Ps 40:5 [b]Ps 3:5

19 [a]Is 11:4 [b]Ps 6:8; 119:115 [c]Ps 5:6; 26:9

20 [1]Or *of* [2]Some mss read *lift themselves up* against You [a]Jude 15 [b]Ex 20:7; Deut 5:11

21 [a]2 Chr 19:2; Ps 26:5; 31:6 [b]Ps 119:158

23 [a]Job 31:6; Ps 26:2 [b]Ps 7:9; Prov 17:3; Jer 11:20; 1 Thess 2:4

24 [1]Lit *way of pain* [a]Ps 146:9; Prov 15:9; 28:10; Jer 25:5; 36:3 [b]Ps 5:8; 143:10 [c]Ps 16:11

140:1 [a]Ps 17:13; 59:2; 71:4 [b]Ps 18:48; 86:14; 140:11

2 [a]Ps 7:14; 36:4; 52:2; Prov 6:14; Is 59:4; Hos 7:15 [b]Ps 56:6

3 [1]*Selah* may mean: *Pause, Crescendo* or *Musical interlude* [a]Ps 57:4; 64:3 [b]Ps 58:4; Rom 3:13; James 3:8

4 [1]Or *devised* [2]Lit *push violently* [a]Ps 71:4 [b]Ps 140:1 [c]Ps 36:11

5 [1]Lit *track* [a]Job 18:9; Ps 35:7; 141:9; 142:3 [b]Ps 31:4; 57:6; Lam 1:13 [c]Ps 141:9; Is 8:14; Amos 3:5

6 [a]Ps 16:2; 31:14 [b]Ps 143:1 [c]Ps 116:1; 130:2

13 For You [a]formed my [1]inward parts;
You [b]wove me in my mother's womb.
14 I will give thanks to You, for [1]I am fearfully and wonderfully made;
[a]Wonderful are Your works,
And my soul knows it very well.
15 My [1a]frame was not hidden from You,
When I was made in secret,
And skillfully wrought in the [b]depths of the earth;
16 Your [a]eyes have seen my unformed substance;
And in [b]Your book were all written
The [c]days that were ordained *for me,*
When as yet there was not one of them.

17 How precious also are Your [a]thoughts to me, O God!
How vast is the sum of them!
18 If I should count them, they would [a]outnumber the sand.
When [b]I awake, I am still with You.

19 O that You would [a]slay the wicked, O God;
[b]Depart from me, therefore, [c]men of bloodshed.
20 For they [a]speak [1]against You wickedly,
And Your enemies [2b]take *Your name* in vain.
21 Do I not [a]hate those who hate You, O LORD?
And do I not [b]loathe those who rise up against You?
22 I hate them with the utmost hatred;
They have become my enemies.

23 [a]Search me, O God, and know my heart;
[b]Try me and know my anxious thoughts;
24 And see if there be any [1a]hurtful way in me,
And [b]lead me in the [c]everlasting way.

*Psalm 140 Theme*________________________________

For the choir director. A Psalm of David.

140 [a]Rescue me, O LORD, from evil men;
Preserve me from [b]violent men
2 Who [a]devise evil things in *their* hearts;
They [b]continually stir up wars.
3 They [a]sharpen their tongues as a serpent;
[b]Poison of a viper is under their lips. [1]Selah.

4 [a]Keep me, O LORD, from the hands of the wicked;
[b]Preserve me from violent men
Who have [1]purposed to [2c]trip up my feet.
5 The proud have [a]hidden a trap for me, and cords;
They have spread a [b]net by the [1]wayside;
They have set [c]snares for me. Selah.

6 I [a]said to the LORD, "You are my God;
[b]Give ear, O LORD, to the [c]voice of my supplications.

7 "O [1]GOD the Lord, [a]the strength of my salvation,
You have [b]covered my head in the day of [2]battle.
8 "Do not grant, O LORD, the [a]desires of the wicked;
Do not promote [b]his *evil* device, *that* they *not* be
exalted. Selah.

9 "As for the head of those who surround me,
May the [a]mischief of their lips cover them.
10 "May [a]burning coals fall upon them;
May they be [b]cast into the fire,
Into [1]deep pits from which they [c]cannot rise.
11 "May a [1]slanderer not be established in the earth;
[a]May evil hunt the violent man [2]speedily."

12 I know that the LORD will [a]maintain the cause of the
afflicted
And [b]justice for the poor.
13 Surely the [a]righteous will give thanks to Your name;
The [b]upright will dwell in Your presence.

Psalm 141 Theme ______________________

A Psalm of David.

141 O LORD, I call upon You; [a]hasten to me!
[b]Give ear to my voice when I call to You!
2 May my prayer be [1]counted as [a]incense before You;
The [b]lifting up of my hands as the [c]evening offering.
3 Set a [a]guard, O LORD, [1]over my mouth;
Keep watch over the [b]door of my lips.
4 [a]Do not incline my heart to any evil thing,
To practice deeds [1]of wickedness
With men who [b]do iniquity;
And [c]do not let me eat of their delicacies.

5 Let the [a]righteous smite me [1]in kindness and reprove me;
It is [b]oil upon the head;
Do not let my head refuse it,
[2]For still my prayer [c]is [3]against their wicked deeds.
6 Their judges are [a]thrown down by the sides of the rock,
And they hear my words, for they are pleasant.
7 As when one [a]plows and breaks open the earth,
Our [b]bones have been scattered at the [c]mouth of [1]Sheol.

8 For my [a]eyes are toward You, O [1]GOD, the Lord;
In You I [b]take refuge; [c]do not [2]leave me defenseless.
9 Keep me from the [1a]jaws of the trap which they have set
for me,
And from the [b]snares of those who do iniquity.
10 Let the wicked [a]fall into their own nets,
While I pass by [1b]safely.

7 [1]Heb *YHWH*, usually rendered *LORD* [2]Lit *weapons* [a]Ps 28:8; 118:14 [b]Ps 144:10

8 [a]Ps 112:10 [b]Esth 9:25; Ps 10:2, 3

9 [a]Ps 7:16; Prov 18:7

10 [1]Lit *watery* [a]Ps 11:6 [b]Ps 21:9; Matt 3:10 [c]Ps 36:12

11 [1]Lit *man of tongue* [2]Lit *thrust upon thrust* [a]Ps 34:21

12 [a]1 Kin 8:45, 49; Ps 9:4; 18:27; 82:3 [b]Ps 12:5; 35:10

13 [a]Ps 97:12 [b]Ps 11:7; 16:11; 17:15

141:1 [a]Ps 22:19; 38:22; 70:5 [b]Ps 5:1; 143:1

2 [1]Lit *fixed* [a]Ex 30:8; Luke 1:10; Rev 5:8; 8:3, 4 [b]1 Tim 2:8 [c]Ex 29:39, 41; 1 Kin 18:29, 36; Dan 9:21

3 [1]Lit *to* [a]Ps 34:13; 39:1; Prov 13:3; 21:23 [b]Mic 7:5

4 [1]Lit *in* [a]Ps 119:36 [b]Is 32:6; Hos 6:8; Mal 3:15 [c]Prov 23:6

5 [1]Or *lovingly* [2]Lit *And my prayer* [3]Or *in spite of their calamities* [a]Prov 9:8; 19:25; 25:12; 27:6; Eccl 7:5; Gal 6:1 [b]Ps 23:5; 133:2 [c]Ps 35:14

6 [a]2 Chr 25:12

7 [1]I.e. the nether world [a]Ps 129:3 [b]Ps 53:5 [c]Num 16:32, 33; Ps 88:3-5

8 [1]Heb *YHWH*, usually rendered *LORD* [2]Lit *pour out my soul* [a]Ps 25:15; 123:2 [b]Ps 2:12; 11:1 [c]Ps 27:9

9 [1]Lit *hands of the trap* [a]Ps 38:12; 64:5; 91:3; 119:110 [b]Ps 140:5

10 [1]Lit *altogether* [a]Ps 7:15; 35:8; 57:6 [b]Ps 124:7

Psalm 142 Theme ____________________

[+]Maskil of David, when he was [•]in the cave. A Prayer.

142
I [a]cry aloud with my voice to the LORD;
I [b]make supplication with my voice to the LORD.
2 I [a]pour out my complaint before Him;
I declare my [b]trouble before Him.
3 When [a]my spirit [1]was overwhelmed within me,
You knew my path.
In the way where I walk
They have [b]hidden a trap for me.
4 Look to the right and see;
For there is [a]no one who regards me;
[1]There is no [b]escape for me;
[c]No one cares for my soul.

5 I cried out to You, O LORD;
I said, "You are [a]my refuge,
My [b]portion in the [c]land of the living.
6 "[a]Give heed to my cry,
For I am [b]brought very low;
Deliver me from my persecutors,
For they are too [c]strong for me.
7 "[a]Bring my soul out of prison,
So that I may give thanks to Your name;
The righteous will surround me,
For You will [b]deal bountifully with me."

Psalm 143 Theme ____________________

A Psalm of David.

143
Hear my prayer, O LORD,
[a]Give ear to my supplications!
Answer me in Your [b]faithfulness, in Your [c]righteousness!
2 And [a]do not enter into judgment with Your servant,
For in Your sight [b]no man living is righteous.
3 For the enemy has persecuted my soul;
He has crushed my life [a]to the ground;
He [b]has made me dwell in dark places, like those who have long been dead.
4 Therefore [a]my spirit [1]is overwhelmed within me;
My heart is [2b]appalled within me.

5 I [a]remember the days of old;
I [b]meditate on all Your doings;
I [c]muse on the work of Your hands.
6 I [a]stretch out my hands to You;
My [b]soul *longs* for You, as a [1]parched land. [2]Selah.

7 [a]Answer me quickly, O LORD, my [b]spirit fails;
[c]Do not hide Your face from me,
Or I will become like [d]those who go down to the pit.

142:1 [+]Possibly *Contemplative,* or *Didactic,* or *Skillful Psalm* [•]1 Sam 22:1; 24:3 [a]Ps 77:1 [b]Ps 30:8
2 [a]Ps 102: title [b]Ps 77:2
3 [1]Lit *fainted* [a]Ps 77:3; 143:4 [b]Ps 140:5
4 [1]Lit *Escape has perished from me* [a]Ps 31:11; 88:8, 18 [b]Job 11:20; Jer 25:35 [c]Jer 30:17
5 [a]Ps 91:2, 9 [b]Ps 16:5; 73:26 [c]Ps 27:13
6 [a]Ps 17:1 [b]Ps 79:8; 116:6 [c]Ps 18:17
7 [a]Ps 143:11; 146:7 [b]Ps 13:6
143:1 [a]Ps 140:6 [b]Ps 89:1, 2 [c]Ps 71:2
2 [a]Job 14:3; 22:4 [b]1 Kin 8:46; Job 4:17; 9:2; 25:4; Ps 130:3; Eccl 7:20; Rom 3:10, 20; Gal 2:16
3 [a]Ps 44:25 [b]Ps 88:6; Lam 3:6
4 [1]Lit *faints* [2]Or *desolate* [a]Ps 77:3; 142:3 [b]Lam 3:11
5 [a]Ps 77:5, 10, 11 [b]Ps 77:12 [c]Ps 105:2
6 [1]Lit *weary* [2]*Selah* may mean: *Pause, Crescendo* or *Musical interlude* [a]Job 11:13; Ps 88:9 [b]Ps 42:2; 63:1
7 [a]Ps 69:17 [b]Ps 73:26; 84:2; Jer 8:18; Lam 1:22 [c]Ps 27:9; 69:17; 102:2 [d]Ps 28:1; 88:4

8 Let me hear Your [a]lovingkindness [b]in the morning;
For I trust [c]in You;
Teach me the [d]way in which I should walk;
For to You I [e]lift up my soul.
9 [a]Deliver me, O LORD, from my enemies;
[1]I take refuge in You.

10 [a]Teach me to do Your will,
For You are my God;
Let [b]Your good Spirit [c]lead me on level [1]ground.
11 [a]For the sake of Your name, O LORD, [b]revive me.
[c]In Your righteousness bring my soul out of trouble.
12 And in Your lovingkindness, [1a]cut off my enemies
And [b]destroy all those who afflict my soul,
For [c]I am Your servant.

Psalm 144 Theme ______________________________

A Psalm of David.

144 Blessed be the LORD, [a]my rock,
Who [b]trains my hands for war,
And my fingers for battle;
2 My lovingkindness and [a]my fortress,
My [b]stronghold and my deliverer,
My [c]shield and He in whom I take refuge,
Who [d]subdues [1]my people under me.
3 O LORD, [a]what is man, that You take knowledge of him?
Or the son of man, that You think of him?
4 [a]Man is like a mere breath;
His [b]days are like a passing shadow.

5 [a]Bow Your heavens, O LORD, and [b]come down;
[c]Touch the mountains, that they may smoke.
6 Flash forth [a]lightning and scatter them;
Send out Your [b]arrows and confuse them.
7 Stretch forth Your hand [a]from on high;
Rescue me and [b]deliver me out of great waters,
Out of the hand of [c]aliens
8 Whose mouths [a]speak deceit,
And whose [b]right hand is a right hand of falsehood.

9 I will sing a [a]new song to You, O God;
Upon a [b]harp of ten strings I will sing praises to You,
10 Who [a]gives salvation to kings,
Who [b]rescues David His servant from the evil sword.
11 Rescue me and deliver me out of the hand of [a]aliens,
Whose mouth [b]speaks deceit
And whose [c]right hand is a right hand of falsehood.

12 Let our sons in their youth be as [a]grown-up plants,
And our daughters as [b]corner pillars [1]fashioned as for a palace;

8 [a]Ps 90:14 [b]Ps 46:5 [c]Ps 25:2 [d]Ps 27:11; 32:8; 86:11 [e]Ps 25:1; 86:4

9 [1]Lit *To You have I hidden* [a]Ps 31:15; 59:1

10 [1]Lit *land* [a]Ps 25:4, 5; 119:12 [b]Neh 9:20 [c]Ps 23:3

11 [a]Ps 25:11 [b]Ps 119:25 [c]Ps 31:1; 71:2

12 [1]Or *silence* [a]Ps 54:5 [b]Ps 52:5 [c]Ps 116:16

144:1 [a]Ps 18:2 [b]2 Sam 22:35; Ps 18:34

2 [1]Another reading is *peoples* [a]Ps 18:2; 91:2 [b]Ps 59:9 [c]Ps 3:3; 28:7; 84:9 [d]Ps 18:39

3 [a]Job 7:17; Ps 8:4; Heb 2:6

4 [a]Ps 39:11 [b]Job 8:9; 14:2; Ps 102:11; 109:23

5 [a]Ps 18:9 [b]Is 64:1 [c]Ps 104:32

6 [a]Ps 18:14 [b]Ps 7:13; 58:7; Hab 3:11; Zech 9:14

7 [a]Ps 18:16 [b]Ps 69:1, 14 [c]Ps 18:44; 54:3

8 [a]Ps 12:2; 41:6 [b]Gen 14:22; Deut 32:40; Ps 106:26; Is 44:20

9 [a]Ps 33:3; 40:3 [b]Ps 33:2

10 [a]Ps 18:50 [b]2 Sam 18:7; Ps 140:7

11 [a]Ps 18:44; 54:3 [b]Ps 12:2; 41:6 [c]Gen 14:22; Deut 32:40; Ps 106:26; Is 44:20

12 [1]Lit *cut after the pattern of* [a]Ps 92:12-14; 128:3 [b]Song 4:4; 7:4

13 Let our [a]garners be full, furnishing every kind of produce,
And our flocks bring forth thousands and ten thousands in
our [1]fields;
14 Let our [a]cattle [1]bear
Without [2b]mishap and without [3c]loss,
Let there be no [d]outcry in our streets!
15 How blessed are the people who are so situated;
How [a]blessed are the people whose God is the LORD!

*Psalm 145 Theme*____

A Psalm of Praise, of David.

145 I will [a]extol You, [b]my God, O King,
And I will [c]bless Your name forever and ever.
2 Every day I will bless You,
And I will [a]praise Your name forever and ever.
3 [a]Great is the LORD, and highly to be praised,
And His [b]greatness is unsearchable.
4 One [a]generation shall praise Your works to another,
And shall declare Your mighty acts.
5 On the [a]glorious [1]splendor of Your majesty
And [b]on Your wonderful works, I will meditate.
6 Men shall speak of the [1]power of Your [a]awesome acts,
And I will [b]tell of Your greatness.
7 They shall [1]eagerly utter the memory of Your [a]abundant
goodness
And will [b]shout joyfully of Your righteousness.

8 The LORD is [a]gracious and merciful;
Slow to anger and great in lovingkindness.
9 The LORD is [a]good to all,
And His [b]mercies are over all His works.
10 [a]All Your works shall give thanks to You, O LORD,
And Your [b]godly ones shall bless You.
11 They shall speak of the [a]glory of Your kingdom
And talk of Your power;
12 To [a]make known to the sons of men [1]Your mighty acts
And the [b]glory of the majesty of [1]Your kingdom.
13 Your kingdom is [1]an [a]everlasting kingdom,
And Your dominion *endures* throughout all generations.

14 The LORD [a]sustains all who fall
And [b]raises up all who are bowed down.
15 The eyes of all [1]look to You,
And You [a]give them their food in due time.
16 You [a]open Your hand
And satisfy the desire of every living thing.

17 The LORD is [a]righteous in all His ways
And kind in all His deeds.
18 The LORD is [a]near to all who call upon Him,
To all who call upon Him [b]in truth.

13 [1]Lit *outside* [a]Prov 3:9, 10
14 [1]Lit *be laden* [2]Lit *bursting forth* [3]Lit *going out* [a]Prov 14:4 [b]2 Kin 25:10, 11 [c]Amos 5:3 [d]Is 24:11; Jer 14:2
15 [a]Ps 33:12
145:1 [a]Ps 30:1; 66:17 [b]Ps 5:2 [c]Ps 34:1
2 [a]Ps 71:6
3 [a]Ps 48:1; 86:10; 147:5 [b]Job 5:9; 9:10; 11:7; Is 40:28; Rom 11:33
4 [a]Ps 22:30, 31; Is 38:19
5 [1]Or *majesty of Your splendor* [a]Ps 145:12 [b]Ps 119:27
6 [1]Or *strength* [a]Deut 10:21; Ps 66:3; 106:22 [b]Deut 32:3
7 [1]Or *bubble over with* [a]Ps 31:19; Is 63:7 [b]Ps 51:14
8 [a]Ex 34:6; Num 14:18; Ps 86:5, 15; 103:8
9 [a]Ps 100:5; 136:1; Jer 33:11; Nah 1:7; Matt 19:17; Mark 10:18 [b]Ps 145:15
10 [a]Ps 19:1; 103:22 [b]Ps 68:26
11 [a]Jer 14:21
12 [1]Lit *His* [a]Ps 105:1 [b]Ps 145:5; Is 2:10, 19, 21
13 [1]Lit *a kingdom of all ages* [a]Ps 10:16; 29:10; 1 Tim 1:17; 2 Pet 1:11
14 [a]Ps 37:24 [b]Ps 146:8
15 [1]Lit *wait;* or *hope for* [a]Ps 104:27; 136:25
16 [a]Ps 104:28
17 [a]Ps 116:5
18 [a]Deut 4:7; Ps 34:18; 119:151 [b]John 4:24

19 He will [a]fulfill the desire of those who fear Him;
He will also [b]hear their cry and will save them.
20 The LORD [a]keeps all who love Him,
But all the [b]wicked He will destroy.
21 My [a]mouth will speak the praise of the LORD,
And [b]all flesh will [c]bless His holy name forever and ever.

Psalm 146 Theme ______________________

146 [1]Praise [2]the LORD!
[a]Praise the LORD, O my soul!
2 I will praise the LORD [a]while I live;
I will [b]sing praises to my God while I have my being.
3 [a]Do not trust in princes,
In [1]mortal [b]man, in whom there is [c]no salvation.
4 His [a]spirit departs, he [b]returns to [1]the earth;
In that very day his [c]thoughts perish.
5 How [a]blessed is he whose help is the God of Jacob,
Whose [b]hope is in the LORD his God,
6 Who [a]made heaven and earth,
The [b]sea and all that is in them;
Who [c]keeps [1]faith forever;
7 Who [a]executes justice for the oppressed;
Who [b]gives food to the hungry.
The LORD [c]sets the prisoners free.

8 The LORD [a]opens *the eyes of* the blind;
The LORD [b]raises up those who are bowed down;
The LORD [c]loves the righteous;
9 The LORD [1a]protects the [2]strangers;
He [3b]supports the fatherless and the widow,
But He [4]thwarts [c]the way of the wicked.
10 The LORD will [a]reign forever,
Your God, O Zion, to all generations.
[1]Praise [2]the LORD!

Psalm 147 Theme ______________________

147 [1]Praise [2]the LORD!
For [a]it is good to sing praises to our God;
For [3]it is pleasant *and* praise is [b]becoming.
2 The LORD [a]builds up Jerusalem;
He [b]gathers the outcasts of Israel.
3 He heals the [a]brokenhearted
And [b]binds up their [1]wounds.
4 He [a]counts the number of the stars;
He [1b]gives names to all of them.
5 [a]Great is our Lord and abundant in strength;
His [b]understanding is [1]infinite.
6 The LORD [1a]supports the afflicted;
He brings down the wicked to the ground.

19 [a]Ps 21:2; 37:4 [b]Ps 10:17; Prov 15:29; 1 John 5:14

20 [a]Ps 31:23; 91:14; 97:10 [b]Ps 9:5; 37:38

21 [a]Ps 71:8 [b]Ps 65:2; 150:6 [c]Ps 145:1, 2

146:1 [1]Or *Hallelujah!* [2]Heb YAH [a]Ps 103:1

2 [a]Ps 63:4 [b]Ps 104:33

3 [1]Lit *a son of a man* [a]Ps 118:9 [b]Ps 118:8; Is 2:22 [c]Ps 60:11; 108:12

4 [1]Lit *his earth* [a]Ps 104:29 [b]Eccl 12:7 [c]Ps 33:10; 1 Cor 2:6

5 [a]Ps 144:15; Jer 17:7 [b]Ps 71:5

6 [1]Or *truth* [a]Ps 115:15; Rev 14:7 [b]Acts 14:15 [c]Ps 117:2

7 [a]Ps 103:6 [b]Ps 107:9; 145:15 [c]Ps 68:6; Is 61:1

8 [a]Matt 9:30; John 9:7 [b]Ps 145:14 [c]Ps 11:7

9 [1]Or *keeps* [2]Or *sojourners* [3]Or *relieves* [4]Lit *makes crooked* [a]Ex 22:21; Lev 19:34 [b]Deut 10:18; Ps 68:5 [c]Ps 147:6

10 [1]Or *Hallelujah!* [2]Heb YAH [a]Ex 15:18; Ps 10:16

147:1 [1]Or *Hallelujah!* [2]Heb YAH [3]Or *He is gracious* [a]Ps 92:1; 135:3 [b]Ps 33:1

2 [a]Ps 51:18; 102:16 [b]Deut 30:3; Ps 106:47; Is 11:12; 56:8; Ezek 39:28

3 [1]Lit *sorrows* [a]Ps 34:18; 51:17; Is 61:1 [b]Job 5:18; Is 30:26; Ezek 34:16

4 [1]Or *calls them all by their names* [a]Gen 15:5 [b]Is 40:26

5 [1]Lit *innumerable* [a]Ps 48:1; 145:3 [b]Is 40:28

6 [1]Or *relieves* [a]Ps 37:24; 146:8, 9

7 [a]Sing to the LORD with thanksgiving;
Sing praises to our God on the lyre,
8 Who [a]covers the heavens with clouds,
Who [b]provides rain for the earth,
Who [c]makes grass to [1]grow on the mountains.
9 He [a]gives to the beast its food,
And to the [b]young ravens which cry.
10 He does not delight in the strength of the [a]horse;
He [b]does not take pleasure in the legs of a man.
11 The LORD [a]favors those who fear Him,
[b]Those who wait for His lovingkindness.

12 Praise the LORD, O Jerusalem!
Praise your God, O Zion!
13 For He has strengthened the [a]bars of your gates;
He has [b]blessed your sons within you.
14 He [a]makes [1]peace in your borders;
He [b]satisfies you with [c]the [2]finest of the wheat.
15 He sends forth His [a]command to the earth;
His [b]word runs very swiftly.
16 He gives [a]snow like wool;
He scatters the [b]frost like ashes.
17 He casts forth His [a]ice as fragments;
Who can stand before His [b]cold?
18 He [a]sends forth His word and melts them;
He [b]causes His wind to blow and the waters to flow.
19 He [a]declares His words to Jacob,
His [b]statutes and His ordinances to Israel.
20 He [a]has not dealt thus with any nation;
And as for His ordinances, they have [b]not known them.
[1]Praise [2]the LORD!

*Psalm 148 Theme*____________________

148

[1]Praise [2]the LORD!
Praise the LORD [a]from the heavens;
Praise Him [b]in the heights!
2 Praise Him, [a]all His angels;
Praise Him, [b]all His hosts!
3 Praise Him, sun and moon;
Praise Him, all stars of light!
4 Praise Him, [1a]highest heavens,
And the [b]waters that are above the heavens!
5 Let them praise the name of the LORD,
For [a]He commanded and they were created.
6 He has also [a]established them forever and ever;
He has made a [b]decree which will not pass away.

7 Praise the LORD from the earth,
[a]Sea monsters and all [b]deeps;
8 [a]Fire and hail, [b]snow and [c]clouds;
[d]Stormy wind, [e]fulfilling His word;

7 [a]Ps 33:2; 95:1, 2
8 [1]Lit *spring forth* [a]Job 26:8 [b]Job 5:10; 38:26; Ps 104:13 [c]Job 38:27; Ps 104:14
9 [a]Ps 104:27, 28; 145:15 [b]Job 38:41; Matt 6:26
10 [a]Ps 33:17 [b]1 Sam 16:7
11 [a]Ps 149:4 [b]Ps 33:18
13 [a]Neh 3:3; 7:3 [b]Ps 37:26
14 [1]Lit *your borders peace* [2]Lit *fat* [a]Ps 29:11; Is 54:13; 60:17, 18 [b]Ps 132:15 [c]Deut 32:14; Ps 81:16
15 [a]Job 37:12; Ps 148:5 [b]Ps 104:4
16 [a]Job 37:6; Ps 148:8 [b]Job 38:29
17 [a]Job 37:10 [b]Job 37:9
18 [a]Ps 33:9; 107:20; 147:15 [b]Ps 107:25
19 [a]Deut 33:3, 4 [b]Mal 4:4
20 [1]Or *Hallelujah!* [2]Heb YAH [a]Deut 4:7, 8, 32-34; Rom 3:1, 2 [b]Ps 79:6; Jer 10:25
148:1 [1]Or *Hallelujah!* [2]Heb YAH [a]Ps 69:34 [b]Job 16:19; Ps 102:19; Matt 21:9
2 [a]Ps 103:20 [b]Ps 103:21
4 [1]Lit *heavens of heavens* [a]Deut 10:14; 1 Kin 8:27; Neh 9:6; Ps 68:33 [b]Gen 1:7
5 [a]Gen 1:1; Ps 33:6, 9
6 [a]Ps 89:37; Jer 31:35, 36; 33:20, 25 [b]Job 38:33
7 [a]Gen 1:21; Ps 74:13 [b]Gen 1:2; Deut 33:13; Hab 3:10
8 [a]Ps 18:12 [b]Ps 147:16 [c]Ps 135:7 [d]Ps 107:25 [e]Job 37:12; Ps 103:20

9 [a]Mountains and all hills;
Fruit [b]trees and all cedars;
10 [a]Beasts and all cattle;
[b]Creeping things and winged fowl;
11 [a]Kings of the earth and all peoples;
Princes and all judges of the earth;
12 Both young men and virgins;
Old men and children.

13 Let them praise the name of the LORD,
For His [a]name alone is exalted;
His [b]glory is above earth and heaven.
14 And He has [a]lifted up a horn for His people,
[b]Praise for all His godly ones;
Even for the sons of Israel, a people [c]near to Him.
[1]Praise [2]the LORD!

Psalm 149 Theme ____________________

149 [1]Praise [2]the LORD!
Sing to the LORD a [a]new song,
And His praise [b]in the congregation of the godly ones.
2 Let Israel be glad in [a]his Maker;
Let the sons of Zion rejoice in their [b]King.
3 Let them praise His name with [a]dancing;
Let them sing praises to Him with [b]timbrel and lyre.
4 For the LORD [a]takes pleasure in His people;
He will [b]beautify the afflicted ones with salvation.

5 Let the [a]godly ones exult in glory;
Let them [b]sing for joy on their beds.
6 *Let* the [a]high praises of God *be* in their [1]mouth,
And a [b]two-edged [c]sword in their hand,
7 To [a]execute vengeance on the nations
And punishment on the peoples,
8 To bind their kings [a]with chains
And their [b]nobles with fetters of iron,
9 To [a]execute on them the judgment written;
This is an [b]honor for all His godly ones.
[1]Praise [2]the LORD!

Psalm 150 Theme ____________________

150 [1]Praise [2]the LORD!
Praise God in His [a]sanctuary;
Praise Him in His mighty [3b]expanse.
2 Praise Him for His [a]mighty deeds;
Praise Him according to His excellent [b]greatness.

3 Praise Him with [a]trumpet sound;
Praise Him with [b]harp and lyre.

9 [a]Is 44:23; 49:13 [b]Is 55:12
10 [a]Is 43:20 [b]Hos 2:18
11 [a]Ps 102:15
13 [a]Is 12:4 [b]Ps 8:1; 113:4
14 [1]Or *Hallelujah!* [2]Heb YAH [a]1 Sam 2:1; Ps 75:10 [b]Deut 10:21; Ps 109:1; Jer 17:14 [c]Lev 10:3; Eph 2:17
149:1 [1]Or *Hallelujah!* [2]Heb YAH [a]Ps 33:3 [b]Ps 35:18; 89:5
2 [a]Ps 95:6 [b]Judg 8:23; Ps 47:6; Zech 9:9
3 [a]2 Sam 6:14; Ps 150:4 [b]Ex 15:20; Ps 81:2
4 [a]Job 36:11; Ps 16:11; 35:27; 147:11 [b]Ps 132:16; Is 61:3
5 [a]Ps 132:16 [b]Job 35:10; Ps 42:8
6 [1]Lit *throat* [a]Ps 66:17 [b]Heb 4:12 [c]Neh 4:17
7 [a]Ezek 25:17; Mic 5:15
8 [a]Job 36:8 [b]Nah 3:10
9 [1]Or *Hallelujah!* [2]Heb YAH [a]Deut 7:12; Ezek 28:26 [b]Ps 112:9; 148:14
150:1 [1]Or *Hallelujah!* [2]Heb YAH [3]Or *firmament* [a]Ps 73:17; 102:19 [b]Ps 19:1
2 [a]Ps 145:12 [b]Deut 3:24; Ps 145:3
3 [a]Ps 98:6 [b]Ps 33:2

4 [a]Ps 149:3 [b]Ps 45:8; Is 38:20 [c]Gen 4:21; Job 21:12
5 [a]2 Sam 6:5; 1 Chr 13:8; 15:16; Ezra 3:10; Neh 12:27
6 [1]Heb *YAH* [2]Or *Hallelujah!* [a]Ps 103:22; 145:21

4 Praise Him with [a]timbrel and dancing;
Praise Him with [b]stringed instruments and [c]pipe.
5 Praise Him with loud [a]cymbals;
Praise Him with resounding cymbals.
6 Let [a]everything that has breath praise [1]the LORD.
[2]Praise [1]the LORD!

Theme of Psalms:

SEGMENT DIVISIONS

		CHAPTER THEMES
		1
		2
		3
		4
		5
		6
		7
		8
		9
		10
		11
		12
		13
		14
		15
		16
		17
		18
		19
		20
		21
		22
		23
		24
		25

Author:

Date:

Geographical Location:

Purpose:

Key Words (and their synonyms):

affliction

take refuge

righteous

wicked

sin (iniquity)

prayer

praise

sing

fear

hope

save

cry

SEGMENT DIVISIONS

		CHAPTER THEMES
		26
		27
		28
		29
		30
		31
		32
		33
		34
		35
		36
		37
		38
		39
		40
		41
		42
		43
		44
		45
		46
		47
		48
		49
		50

SEGMENT DIVISIONS

		CHAPTER THEMES
		51
		52
		53
		54
		55
		56
		57
		58
		59
		60
		61
		62
		63
		64
		65
		66
		67
		68
		69
		70
		71
		72
		73
		74
		75

Segment Divisions

		Chapter Themes
		76
		77
		78
		79
		80
		81
		82
		83
		84
		85
		86
		87
		88
		89
		90
		91
		92
		93
		94
		95
		96
		97
		98
		99
		100

SEGMENT DIVISIONS

		CHAPTER THEMES
		101
		102
		103
		104
		105
		106
		107
		108
		109
		110
		111
		112
		113
		114
		115
		116
		117
		118
		119
		120
		121
		122
		123
		124
		125

SEGMENT DIVISIONS

		CHAPTER THEMES
		126
		127
		128
		129
		130
		131
		132
		133
		134
		135
		136
		137
		138
		139
		140
		141
		142
		143
		144
		145
		146
		147
		148
		149
		150

PROVERBS

MISHLE

When God appeared to King Solomon in a dream, He said, "Ask what you wish me to give you." Solomon asked for an understanding heart so that he could lead the nation of Israel (see 1 Kings 3). In response to that prayer "God gave Solomon wisdom and very great discernment and breadth of mind, like the sand that is on the seashore. Solomon's wisdom surpassed the wisdom of all the sons of the east and all the wisdom of Egypt. For he was wiser than all men.... He also spoke 3,000 proverbs" (1 Kings 4:29-32).

Many of Solomon's wise sayings have been preserved for us in the book of Proverbs. A proverb is usually a short saying or maxim that gives insight on life and human behavior.

The book of Proverbs is a compilation of true sayings that give wisdom and instruction. However, these maxims should not be interpreted as prophecies, nor can they be held as absolute doctrines. For example, Proverbs says a man's enemies will be at peace with him when his ways please the Lord. We can accept this as a valid proverb which generally proves to be true, though not always. Our Lord's enemies were not at peace with Him even though He did only those things that pleased the Father.

The Proverbs are inspired by God; don't rush through them. Give yourself time for meditation and application. Although Proverbs was written between 971 and 686 B.C., these sayings are timeless. They can equip you for life in the home and the marketplace.

THINGS TO DO

1. Proverbs uses figurative language—similes and metaphors. Read the section called "Figures of Speech" on page 2103 before you study Proverbs.

2. Read Proverbs 1:1-7 and note the author, purpose, and theme of the book in the margin of chapter 1. As you look for the purpose, watch the repeated use of *to*. The theme is also repeated in 9:10. Record these insights on the PROVERBS AT A GLANCE chart on page 1061.

3. A wise person appreciates the wisdom of others. Look at PROVERBS AT A GLANCE and note the major segment divisions of this book. You will see that Solomon respected the wisdom of others. Look up the following verses and note whose words or proverbs follow: Proverbs 10:1; 22:17; 25:1; 30:1; 31:1.

4. Mark the key words listed on PROVERBS AT A GLANCE along with their synonyms. Keep a list of what you learn about wisdom, especially in the first nine chapters. Note how wisdom is personified. (An abstraction, such as wisdom, is personified when it takes on the characteristics of a person. Proverbs 1:20 is an example.)

5. Watch for and mark the phrase *my son (O son)*. Then listen as if it is God the Father speaking to you, His own dear child whom He wants to show the path of life.

6. Develop a code for marking the subjects covered throughout Proverbs: sexual morality, finances, discipline, the heart, the tongue, the company we keep, etc. As you read through Proverbs repeatedly you will learn more and more about mankind and will find yourself much wiser when it comes to living in the "fear of the Lord." You will have a collection of insights on the critical issues of life.

7. Record the theme or themes of each chapter on PROVERBS AT A GLANCE and in your Bible. You may find this difficult between chapters 10 and 29 because the proverbs are short and varied. However, simply listing the major topics of each chapter will help you find the major topics at a glance. Color-coding or marking each topic throughout the book will help you easily spot what Proverbs teaches about a particular subject. This will be a great help as you share these truths with others or need wisdom on a specific topic.

Things to Think About

1. Are you walking in the fear of the Lord? To fear God is to have an awesome respect of who He is and a reverential trust in His Word and His character, and to live accordingly.

2. The wisdom of the world is different from the wisdom that comes from God. Which is of more value to you? How quick are you, beloved, to seek God's wisdom in the matters of everyday life?

3. What do you need to do or change in light of the insight and wisdom you have learned from these proverbs?

4. Since there are 31 chapters in Proverbs, some people read a chapter a day, month after month. This is good as long as you do not neglect other portions of the Word and as long as you give yourself adequate time to meditate on these proverbs.

   a. After chapter 9, many proverbs are only two to four lines long. You may want to choose one or two proverbs a day, evaluating your life and relationships in the light of them.

   b. Or you may want to select a theme you marked throughout Proverbs, list what you learned from the book as a whole, and then meditate on that theme. For example, you might meditate on what you learned about diligence versus laziness, or about the tongue.

Chapter 1 Theme ____________________

1 The [a]proverbs of Solomon [b]the son of David, king of Israel:
2 To know [a]wisdom and instruction,
To discern the sayings of [b]understanding,
3 To [a]receive instruction in wise behavior,
[b]Righteousness, justice and equity;
4 To give [a]prudence to the [1]naive,
To the youth [b]knowledge and discretion,
5 A wise man will hear and [a]increase in learning,
And a [b]man of understanding will acquire wise counsel,
6 To understand a proverb and a figure,
The words of the wise and their [a]riddles.

7 [a]The fear of the LORD is the beginning of knowledge;
Fools despise wisdom and instruction.

8 [a]Hear, my son, your father's instruction
And [b]do not forsake your mother's teaching;
9 Indeed, they are a [a]graceful wreath to your head
And [1b]ornaments about your neck.
10 My son, if sinners [a]entice you,
[b]Do not consent.
11 If they say, "Come with us,
Let us [a]lie in wait for blood,
Let us [b]ambush the innocent without cause;

INSIGHT

To have ***knowledge*** is to have understanding or information about something. To have ***wisdom*** is to have the ability to apply knowledge to daily life.

1:1 [a]1 Kin 4:32; Prov 10:1; 25:1; Eccl 12:9 [b]Eccl 1:1
2 [a]Prov 15:33 [b]Prov 4:1
3 [a]Prov 2:1; 19:20 [b]Prov 2:9
4 [1]Lit *simple ones* [a]Prov 8:5, 12 [b]Prov 2:10, 11; 3:21
5 [a]Prov 9:9 [b]Prov 14:6; Eccl 9:11
6 [a]Num 12:8; Ps 49:4; 78:2; Dan 8:23
7 [a]Job 28:28; Ps 111:10; Prov 9:10; 15:33; Eccl 12:13
8 [a]Prov 4:1 [b]Prov 6:20
9 [1]Lit *necklaces* [a]Prov 4:9 [b]Gen 41:42; Dan 5:29
10 [a]Prov 16:29 [b]Gen 39:7-10; Deut 13:8; Ps 50:18; Eph 5:11
11 [a]Prov 12:6; Jer 5:26 [b]Ps 10:8; Prov 1:18

12 Let us [a]swallow them alive like Sheol,
Even whole, as those who [b]go down to the pit;
13 We will find all *kinds* of precious wealth,
We will fill our houses with spoil;
14 Throw in your lot [1]with us,
We shall all have one purse,"
15 My son, [a]do not walk in the way with them.
[b]Keep your feet from their path,
16 For [a]their feet run to evil
And they hasten to shed blood.
17 Indeed, it is [1]useless to spread the *baited* net
In the sight of any [2]bird;
18 But they [a]lie in wait for their own blood;
They ambush their own lives.
19 So are the ways of everyone who [a]gains by violence;
It takes away the life of its possessors.

20 [a]Wisdom shouts in the street,
She [1]lifts her voice in the square;
21 At the head of the noisy *streets* she cries out;
At the entrance of the gates in the city she utters her sayings:
22 "How long, O [1a]naive ones, will you love [2]being simple-minded?
And [b]scoffers delight themselves in scoffing
And fools [c]hate knowledge?
23 "Turn to my reproof,
Behold, I will [a]pour out my spirit on you;
I will make my words known to you.
24 "Because [a]I called and you [b]refused,
I [c]stretched out my hand and no one paid attention;
25 And you [a]neglected all my counsel
And did not [b]want my reproof;
26 I will also [a]laugh at your [b]calamity;
I will mock when your [c]dread comes,
27 When your dread comes like a storm
And your calamity comes like a [a]whirlwind,
When distress and anguish come upon you.
28 "Then they will [a]call on me, but I will not answer;
They will [b]seek me diligently but they will not find me,
29 Because they [a]hated knowledge
And did not choose the fear of the LORD.
30 "They [a]would not accept my counsel,
They spurned all my reproof.
31 "So they shall [a]eat of the fruit of their own way
And be [b]satiated with their own devices.
32 "For the [a]waywardness of the [1]naive will kill them,
And the complacency of fools will destroy them.
33 "But [a]he who listens to me shall [1]live securely
And will be at ease from the dread of evil."

12 [a]Ps 124:3 [b]Ps 28:1

14 [1]Lit *in the midst of us*

15 [a]Ps 1:1; Prov 4:14 [b]Ps 119:101

16 [a]Prov 6:17, 18; Is 59:7

17 [1]Lit *in vain* [2]Lit *possessor of wing*

18 [a]Prov 11:19

19 [a]Prov 15:27

20 [1]Lit *gives* [a]Prov 8:1-3; 9:3

22 [1]Lit *simple ones* [2]Or *naivete* [a]Prov 1:4, 32; 8:5; 9:4; 22:3 [b]Ps 1:1 [c]Prov 1:29; 5:12

23 [a]Is 32:15; Joel 2:28; John 7:39

24 [a]Is 65:12; 66:4; Jer 7:13 [b]Zech 7:11 [c]Is 65:2; Rom 10:21

25 [a]Ps 107:11; Luke 7:30 [b]Prov 15:10

26 [a]Ps 2:4 [b]Prov 6:15 [c]Prov 10:24

27 [a]Prov 10:25

28 [a]1 Sam 8:18; Job 27:9; 35:12; Ps 18:41; Is 1:15; Jer 11:11; 14:12; Ezek 8:18; Mic 3:4; Zech 7:13; James 4:3 [b]Prov 8:17

29 [a]Job 21:14; Prov 1:22

30 [a]Ps 81:11; Prov 1:25

31 [a]Job 4:8; Prov 5:22, 23; 22:8; Is 3:11; Jer 6:19 [b]Prov 14:14

32 [1]Lit *simple ones* [a]Jer 2:19

33 [1]Lit *dwell* [a]Ps 25:12, 13; Prov 3:24-26

Chapter 2 Theme ____________________________

2 My son, if you will [a]receive my words
And [b]treasure my commandments within you,
2 [a]Make your ear attentive to wisdom,
Incline your heart to understanding;
3 For if you cry for discernment,
[1]Lift your voice for understanding;
4 If you seek her as [a]silver
And search for her as for [b]hidden treasures;
5 Then you will discern the [a]fear of the LORD
And discover the knowledge of God.
6 For [a]the LORD gives wisdom;
From His mouth *come* knowledge and understanding.
7 He stores up sound wisdom for the upright;
He is a [a]shield to those who walk in integrity,
8 Guarding the paths of justice,
And He [a]preserves the way of His godly ones.
9 Then you will discern [a]righteousness and justice
And equity *and* every [b]good course.
10 For [a]wisdom will enter your heart
And [b]knowledge will be pleasant to your soul;
11 Discretion will [a]guard you,
Understanding will watch over you,
12 To [a]deliver you from the way of evil,
From the man who speaks [b]perverse things;
13 From those who [a]leave the paths of uprightness
To walk in the [b]ways of darkness;
14 Who [a]delight in doing evil
And rejoice in the perversity of evil;
15 Whose paths are [a]crooked,
And who are devious in their ways;
16 To [a]deliver you from the strange woman,
From the [1b]adulteress who flatters with her words;
17 That leaves the [a]companion of her youth
And forgets the [b]covenant of her God;
18 For [a]her house [1]sinks down to death
And her tracks *lead* to the [2]dead;
19 None [a]who go to her return again,
Nor do they reach the [b]paths of life.
20 So you will [a]walk in the way of good men
And keep to the [b]paths of the righteous.
21 For [a]the upright will [1]live in the land
And [b]the blameless will remain in it;
22 But [a]the wicked will be cut off from the land
And [b]the treacherous will be [c]uprooted from it.

Chapter 3 Theme ____________________________

3 My son, [a]do not forget my [1]teaching,
But let your heart [b]keep my commandments;
2 For [a]length of days and years of life

2:1 [a]Prov 4:10 [b]Prov 3:1
2 [a]Prov 22:17
3 [1]Lit *Give*
4 [a]Prov 3:14 [b]Job 3:21; Matt 13:44
5 [a]Prov 1:7
6 [a]1 Kin 3:12; Job 32:8; James 1:5
7 [a]Ps 84:11; Prov 30:5
8 [a]1 Sam 2:9; Ps 66:9
9 [a]Prov 8:20 [b]Prov 4:18
10 [a]Prov 14:33 [b]Prov 22:18
11 [a]Prov 4:6; 6:22
12 [a]Prov 28:26 [b]Prov 6:12
13 [a]Prov 21:16 [b]Ps 82:5; Prov 4:19; John 3:19, 20
14 [a]Prov 10:23; Jer 11:15
15 [a]Ps 125:5; Prov 21:8
16 [1]Lit *strange woman* [a]Prov 6:24; 7:5 [b]Prov 23:27
17 [a]Mal 2:14, 15 [b]Gen 2:24
18 [1]Lit *bows down* [2]Lit *departed spirits* [a]Prov 7:27
19 [a]Eccl 7:26 [b]Ps 16:11; Prov 5:6
20 [a]Heb 6:12 [b]Prov 4:18
21 [1]Or *dwell* [a]Ps 37:9, 29; Prov 10:30 [b]Prov 28:10
22 [a]Ps 37:38; Prov 10:30 [b]Prov 11:3 [c]Deut 28:63; Ps 52:5
3:1 [1]Or *law* [a]Ps 119:61; Prov 4:5 [b]Ex 20:6; Deut 30:16
2 [a]Ps 91:16; Prov 3:16; 4:10; 9:11; 10:27

And peace they will add to you.
3 Do not let [a]kindness and truth leave you;
[b]Bind them around your neck,
[c]Write them on the tablet of your heart.
4 So you will [a]find favor and [b]good [1]repute
In the sight of God and man.
5 [a]Trust in the LORD with all your heart
And [b]do not lean on your own understanding.
6 In all your ways [a]acknowledge Him,
And He will [b]make your paths straight.
7 [a]Do not be wise in your own eyes;
[b]Fear the LORD and turn away from evil.
8 It will be [a]healing to your [1]body
And [b]refreshment to your bones.
9 [a]Honor the LORD from your wealth
And from the [b]first of all your produce;
10 So your [a]barns will be filled with plenty
And your [b]vats will overflow with new wine.
11 [a]My son, do not reject the [1]discipline of the LORD
Or loathe His reproof,
12 For [a]whom the LORD loves He reproves,
Even [b]as a father *corrects* the son in whom he delights.

13 [a]How blessed is the man who finds wisdom
And the man who gains understanding.
14 For her [a]profit is better than the profit of silver
And her gain better than fine gold.
15 She is [a]more precious than [1]jewels;
And nothing you desire compares with her.
16 [1a]Long life is in her right hand;
In her left hand are [b]riches and honor.
17 Her [a]ways are pleasant ways
And all her paths are [b]peace.
18 She is a [a]tree of life to those who take hold of her,
And happy are all who hold her fast.
19 The LORD [a]by wisdom founded the earth,
By understanding He [b]established the heavens.
20 By His knowledge the [a]deeps were broken up
And the [b]skies drip with dew.
21 My son, [a]let them not [1]vanish from your sight;
Keep sound wisdom and discretion,
22 So they will be [a]life to your soul
And [b]adornment to your neck.
23 Then you will [a]walk in your way securely
And your foot will not [b]stumble.
24 When you [a]lie down, you will not be afraid;
When you lie down, your sleep will be sweet.
25 [a]Do not be afraid of sudden fear
Nor of the [1b]onslaught of the wicked when it comes;
26 For the LORD will be [1]your confidence
And will [a]keep your foot from being caught.

3 [a]2 Sam 15:20; Prov 14:22 [b]Deut 6:8; 11:18; Prov 1:9; 6:21 [c]Prov 7:3; Jer 17:1; 2 Cor 3:3
4 [1]Lit *understanding* [a]1 Sam 2:26; Prov 8:35; Luke 2:52 [b]Ps 111:10
5 [a]Ps 37:3, 5; Prov 22:19 [b]Prov 23:4; Jer 9:23
6 [a]1 Chr 28:9; Prov 16:3; Phil 4:6; James 1:5 [b]Is 45:13; Jer 10:23
7 [a]Rom 12:16 [b]Job 1:1; 28:28; Prov 8:13; 16:6
8 [1]Lit *navel* [a]Prov 4:22 [b]Job 21:24
9 [a]Is 43:23 [b]Ex 23:19; Deut 26:2; Mal 3:10
10 [a]Deut 28:8 [b]Joel 2:24
11 [1]Or *instruction* [a]Job 5:17; Heb 12:5, 6
12 [a]Rev 3:19 [b]Deut 8:5; Prov 13:24
13 [a]Prov 8:32, 34
14 [a]Job 28:15-19; Prov 8:10, 19; 16:16
15 [1]Lit *corals* [a]Job 28:18; Prov 8:11
16 [1]Lit *Length of days* [a]Prov 3:2 [b]Prov 8:18; 22:4
17 [a]Matt 11:29 [b]Ps 119:165; Prov 16:7
18 [a]Gen 2:9; Prov 11:30; 13:12; 15:4; Rev 2:7
19 [a]Ps 104:24; Prov 8:27 [b]Prov 8:27, 28
20 [a]Gen 7:11 [b]Deut 33:28; Job 36:28
21 [1]Lit *depart* [a]Prov 4:21
22 [a]Deut 32:47; Prov 4:22; 8:35; 16:22; 21:21 [b]Prov 1:9
23 [a]Prov 4:12; 10:9 [b]Ps 91:12; Is 5:27; 63:13
24 [a]Job 11:19; Ps 3:5; Prov 1:33; 6:22
25 [1]Lit *storm* [a]Ps 91:5; 1 Pet 3:14 [b]Job 5:21
26 [1]Or *at your side* [a]1 Sam 2:9

27 [a]Do not withhold good from [1]those to whom it is due,
When it is in your power to do *it.*
28 [a]Do not say to your neighbor, "Go, and come back,
And tomorrow I will give *it,*"
When you have it with you.
29 [a]Do not devise harm against your neighbor,
While he lives securely beside you.
30 [a]Do not contend with a man without cause,
If he has done you no harm.
31 [a]Do not envy a man of violence
And do not choose any of his ways.
32 For the [a]devious are an abomination to the LORD;
But [1]He is [b]intimate with the upright.
33 The [a]curse of the LORD is on the house of the wicked,
But He [b]blesses the dwelling of the righteous.
34 Though [a]He scoffs at the scoffers,
Yet [b]He gives grace to the afflicted.
35 [a]The wise will inherit honor,
But fools [1]display dishonor.

Chapter 4 Theme ______________________

4 Hear, *O* sons, the [a]instruction of a father,
And [b]give attention that you may [1]gain understanding,
2 For I give you [1]sound [a]teaching;
[b]Do not abandon my [2]instruction.
3 When I was a son to my father,
[a]Tender and [b]the only son in the sight of my mother,
4 Then he [a]taught me and said to me,
"Let your heart [b]hold fast my words;
[c]Keep my commandments and live;
5 [a]Acquire wisdom! [b]Acquire understanding!
Do not forget nor turn away from the words of my mouth.
6 "Do not forsake her, and she will guard you;
[a]Love her, and she will watch over you.
7 "[a]The [1]beginning of wisdom *is:* [b]Acquire wisdom;
And with all your acquiring, get understanding.
8 "[a]Prize her, and she will exalt you;
She will honor you if you embrace her.
9 "She will place [a]on your head a garland of grace;
She will present you with a crown of beauty."

10 Hear, my son, and [a]accept my sayings
And the [b]years of your life will be many.
11 I have [a]directed you in the way of wisdom;
I have led you in upright paths.
12 When you walk, your [a]steps will not be impeded;
And if you run, you [b]will not stumble.
13 [a]Take hold of instruction; do not let go.
Guard her, for she is your [b]life.

27 [1]Lit *its owners* [a]Rom 13:7; Gal 6:10
28 [a]Lev 19:13; Deut 24:15
29 [a]Prov 6:14; 14:22
30 [a]Prov 26:17; Rom 12:18
31 [a]Ps 37:1; Prov 24:1
32 [1]Lit *His private counsel is* [a]Prov 11:20 [b]Job 29:4; Ps 25:14
33 [a]Lev 26:14, 16; Deut 11:28; Zech 5:3, 4; Mal 2:2 [b]Job 8:6; Ps 1:3
34 [a]James 4:6 [b]1 Pet 5:5
35 [1]Lit *raise high* [a]Dan 12:3
4:1 [1]Lit *know* [a]Ps 34:11; Prov 1:8 [b]Prov 1:2; 2:2
2 [1]Lit *good* [2]Or *law* [a]Deut 32:2; Job 11:4 [b]Ps 89:30; 119:87; Prov 3:1
3 [a]1 Chr 22:5; 29:1 [b]Zech 12:10
4 [a]Eph 6:4 [b]Ps 119:168 [c]Prov 7:2
5 [a]Prov 4:7 [b]Prov 16:16
6 [a]2 Thess 2:10
7 [1]Or *the primary thing is wisdom* [a]Prov 8:23 [b]Prov 23:23
8 [a]1 Sam 2:30
9 [a]Prov 1:9
10 [a]Prov 2:1 [b]Prov 3:2
11 [a]1 Sam 12:23
12 [a]Job 18:7; Ps 18:36 [b]Ps 91:11; Prov 3:23
13 [a]Prov 3:18 [b]Prov 3:22; John 6:63

14 [a]Do not enter the path of the wicked
And do not proceed in the way of evil men.
15 Avoid it, do not pass by it;
Turn away from it and pass on.
16 For they [a]cannot sleep unless they do evil;
And [1]they are robbed of sleep unless they make *someone*
stumble.
17 For they [a]eat the bread of wickedness
And drink the wine of violence.
18 But the [a]path of the righteous is like the [b]light of dawn,
That [c]shines brighter and brighter until the [d]full day.
19 The [a]way of the wicked is like darkness;
They do not know over what they [1b]stumble.

20 My son, [a]give attention to my words;
[b]Incline your ear to my sayings.
21 [a]Do not let them depart from your sight;
[b]Keep them in the midst of your heart.
22 For they are [a]life to those who find them
And [b]health to all [1]their body.
23 Watch over your heart with all diligence,
For [a]from it *flow* the springs of life.
24 Put away from you a [a]deceitful mouth
And [b]put devious [1]speech far from you.
25 Let your eyes look directly ahead
And let your [1]gaze be fixed straight in front of you.
26 [a]Watch the path of your feet
And all your [b]ways will be established.
27 [a]Do not turn to the right nor to the left;
[b]Turn your foot from evil.

Chapter 5 Theme ______________________________

5 My son, [a]give attention to my wisdom,
[b]Incline your ear to my understanding;
2 That you may [a]observe discretion
And your [b]lips may reserve knowledge.
3 For the lips of an [1a]adulteress [b]drip honey
And [c]smoother than oil is her [2]speech;
4 But in the end she is [a]bitter as wormwood,
[b]Sharp as a two-edged sword.
5 Her feet [a]go down to death,
Her steps take hold of Sheol.
6 [1]She does not ponder the [a]path of life;
Her ways are [b]unstable, she [c]does not know *it.*

7 [a]Now then, *my* sons, listen to me
And [b]do not depart from the words of my mouth.
8 [a]Keep your way far from her
And do not go near the [b]door of her house,

14 [a]Ps 1:1; Prov 1:15

16 [1]Lit *their sleep is robbed* [a]Ps 36:4; Mic 2:1

17 [a]Prov 13:2

18 [a]Is 26:7; Matt 5:14; Phil 2:15 [b]2 Sam 23:4 [c]Dan 12:3 [d]Job 11:17

19 [1]Or *may stumble* [a]Job 18:5, 6; Prov 2:13; Is 59:9, 10; Jer 23:12; John 12:35 [b]John 11:10

20 [a]Prov 5:1 [b]Prov 2:2

21 [a]Prov 3:21 [b]Prov 7:1, 2

22 [1]Lit *his* [a]Prov 3:22 [b]Prov 3:8; 12:18

23 [a]Matt 12:34; 15:18, 19; Mark 7:21; Luke 6:45

24 [1]Or *lips* [a]Prov 6:12; 10:32 [b]Prov 19:1

25 [1]Or *eyelids*

26 [a]Prov 5:21; Heb 12:13 [b]Ps 119:5

27 [a]Deut 5:32; 28:14 [b]Prov 1:15; Is 1:16

5:1 [a]Prov 4:20 [b]Prov 22:17

2 [a]Prov 3:21 [b]Mal 2:7

3 [1]Lit *strange woman* [2]Lit *palate* [a]Prov 2:16; 5:20; 7:5; 22:14 [b]Song 4:11 [c]Ps 55:21

4 [a]Eccl 7:26 [b]Ps 57:4; Heb 4:12

5 [a]Prov 7:27

6 [1]Lit *That she not watch* [a]Prov 4:26; 5:21 [b]2 Pet 2:14 [c]Prov 30:20

7 [a]Prov 7:24 [b]Ps 119:102

8 [a]Prov 7:25 [b]Prov 9:14

11 [1]Or *latter*

12 [a]Prov 1:7, 22, 29 [b]Prov 1:25; 12:1

13 [a]Prov 1:8

15 [1]Lit *flowing*

16 [a]Prov 5:18; 9:17; Song 4:12, 15

18 [a]Prov 9:17; Song 4:12, 15 [b]Eccl 9:9 [c]Mal 2:14

19 [1]Lit *intoxicated* [a]Song 2:9, 17; 4:5; 7:3

20 [1]Lit *strange woman* [a]Prov 5:3 [b]Prov 2:16; 6:24; 7:5; 23:27

21 [a]Job 14:16; 31:4; 34:21; Ps 119:168; Prov 15:3; Jer 16:17; 32:19; Hos 7:2; Heb 4:13 [b]Prov 4:26

22 [a]Num 32:23; Ps 7:15; 9:15; 40:12; Prov 1:31, 32

23 [a]Job 4:21; 36:12

6:1 [1]Lit *clapped your palms* [a]Prov 11:15; 17:18; 20:16; 22:26; 27:13

3 [1]Lit *palm*

4 [a]Ps 132:4

5 [a]Ps 91:3; 124:7

6 [a]Prov 30:24, 25 [b]Prov 6:9; 10:26; 13:4; 20:4; 26:16

9 Or you will give your vigor to others
And your years to the cruel one;
10 And strangers will be filled with your strength
And your hard-earned goods *will go* to the house of an alien;
11 And you groan at your [1]final end,
When your flesh and your body are consumed;
12 And you say, "How I have [a]hated instruction!
And my heart [b]spurned reproof!
13 "I have not listened to the voice of my [a]teachers,
Nor inclined my ear to my instructors!
14 "I was almost in utter ruin
In the midst of the assembly and congregation."

15 Drink water from your own cistern
And [1]fresh water from your own well.
16 Should your [a]springs be dispersed abroad,
Streams of water in the streets?
17 Let them be yours alone
And not for strangers with you.
18 Let your [a]fountain be blessed,
And [b]rejoice in the [c]wife of your youth.
19 *As* a loving [a]hind and a graceful doe,
Let her breasts satisfy you at all times;
Be [1]exhilarated always with her love.
20 For why should you, my son, be exhilarated with an [1a]adulteress
And embrace the bosom of a [b]foreigner?
21 For the [a]ways of a man are before the eyes of the LORD,
And He [b]watches all his paths.
22 His [a]own iniquities will capture the wicked,
And he will be held with the cords of his sin.
23 He will [a]die for lack of instruction,
And in the greatness of his folly he will go astray.

Chapter 6 Theme ______________________

6 My son, if you have become [a]surety for your neighbor,
Have [1]given a pledge for a stranger,
2 *If* you have been snared with the words of your mouth,
Have been caught with the words of your mouth,
3 Do this then, my son, and deliver yourself;
Since you have come into the [1]hand of your neighbor,
Go, humble yourself, and importune your neighbor.
4 Give no [a]sleep to your eyes,
Nor slumber to your eyelids;
5 Deliver yourself like a gazelle from *the hunter's* hand
And like a [a]bird from the hand of the fowler.

6 Go to the [a]ant, O [b]sluggard,
Observe her ways and be wise,

7 Which, having [a]no chief,
Officer or ruler,
8 Prepares her food [a]in the summer
And gathers her provision in the harvest.
9 How long will you lie down, O sluggard?
When will you arise from your sleep?
10 "[a]A little sleep, a little slumber,
A little folding of the hands to [1]rest"—
11 [a]Your poverty will come in like a [1]vagabond
And your need like [2]an armed man.

12 A [a]worthless person, a wicked man,
Is the one who walks with a [b]perverse mouth,
13 Who [a]winks with his eyes, who [1]signals with his feet,
Who [2]points with his fingers;
14 Who *with* [a]perversity in his heart continually [b]devises evil,
Who [1c]spreads strife.
15 Therefore [a]his calamity will come suddenly;
[b]Instantly he will be broken and there will be [c]no healing.

16 There are six things which the LORD hates,
Yes, seven which are an abomination [1]to Him:
17 [a]Haughty eyes, a [b]lying tongue,
And hands that [c]shed innocent blood,
18 A heart that devises [a]wicked plans,
[b]Feet that run rapidly to evil,
19 A [a]false witness *who* utters lies,
And one who [1b]spreads strife among brothers.

20 [a]My son, observe the commandment of your father
And do not forsake the [1]teaching of your mother;
21 [a]Bind them continually on your heart;
Tie them around your neck.
22 When you [a]walk about, [1]they will guide you;
When you sleep, [1]they will watch over you;
And when you awake, [1]they will talk to you.
23 For [a]the commandment is a lamp and the [1]teaching is light;
And reproofs for discipline are the way of life
24 To [a]keep you from the evil woman,
From the smooth tongue of the [1]adulteress.
25 [a]Do not desire her beauty in your heart,
Nor let her capture you with her [b]eyelids.
26 For [a]on account of a harlot *one is reduced* to a loaf of bread,
And [1]an adulteress [b]hunts for the precious life.
27 Can a man [1]take fire in his bosom
And his clothes not be burned?
28 Or can a man walk on hot coals
And his feet not be scorched?
29 So is the one who [a]goes in to his neighbor's wife;
Whoever touches her [b]will not [1]go unpunished.

7 [a]Prov 30:27

8 [a]Prov 10:5

10 [1]Lit *lie down* [a]Prov 24:33

11 [1]Lit *one who walks* [2]Lit *a man with a shield* [a]Prov 24:34

12 [a]Prov 16:27 [b]Prov 4:24; 10:32

13 [1]Lit *scrapes* [2]Lit *instructs with* [a]Job 15:12; Ps 35:19; Prov 10:10

14 [1]Lit *sends out* [a]Prov 17:20 [b]Prov 3:29; Mic 2:1 [c]Prov 6:19; 16:28

15 [a]Prov 24:22 [b]Is 30:13, 14; Jer 19:11 [c]2 Chr 36:16

16 [1]Lit *of His soul*

17 [a]Ps 18:27; 101:5; Prov 21:4; 30:13 [b]Ps 31:18; 120:2; Prov 12:22; 17:7 [c]Deut 19:10; Prov 28:17; Is 1:15; 59:7

18 [a]Gen 6:5; Prov 24:2 [b]Prov 1:16; Is 59:7; Rom 3:15

19 [1]Lit *sends out* [a]Ps 27:12; Prov 12:17; 19:5, 9; 21:28 [b]Prov 6:14

20 [1]Or *law* [a]Eph 6:1

21 [a]Prov 3:3

22 [1]Lit *she* [a]Prov 3:23

23 [1]Or *law* [a]Ps 19:8; 119:105

24 [1]Lit *foreign woman* [a]Prov 5:3; 7:5, 21

25 [a]Matt 5:28 [b]2 Kin 9:30; Jer 4:30; Ezek 23:40

26 [1]Lit *a man's wife* [a]Prov 5:9, 10; 29:3 [b]Prov 7:23; Ezek 13:18

27 [1]Lit *snatch up*

29 [1]Lit *be innocent* [a]Ezek 18:6; 33:26 [b]Prov 16:5

30 [1]Men do not despise a thief if he steals
To [a]satisfy [2]himself when he is hungry;
31 But when he is found, he must [a]repay sevenfold;
He must give all the [1]substance of his house.
32 The one who commits adultery with a woman is [a]lacking
[1]sense;
He who would [b]destroy [2]himself does it.
33 Wounds and disgrace he will find,
And his reproach will not be blotted out.
34 For [a]jealousy [1]enrages a man,
And he will not spare in the [b]day of vengeance.
35 He will not [1]accept any ransom,
Nor will he be [2]satisfied though you give many [3]gifts.

Chapter 7 Theme ______________________

7 My son, [a]keep my words
And treasure my commandments within you.
2 [a]Keep my commandments and live,
And my [1]teaching [b]as the [2]apple of your eye.
3 [a]Bind them on your fingers;
[b]Write them on the tablet of your heart.
4 Say to wisdom, "You are my sister,"
And call understanding *your* intimate friend;
5 That they may keep you from an [1]adulteress,
From the foreigner who [2]flatters with her words.

6 For [a]at the window of my house
I looked out [b]through my lattice,
7 And I saw among the [1][a]naive,
And discerned among the [2]youths
A young man [b]lacking [3]sense,
8 Passing through the street near [a]her corner;
And he [1]takes the way to [b]her house,
9 In the [a]twilight, in the [1]evening,
In the [2]middle of the night and *in* the darkness.
10 And behold, a woman *comes* to meet him,
[a]Dressed as a harlot and cunning of heart.
11 She is [a]boisterous and rebellious,
Her [b]feet do not remain at home;
12 *She is* now in the streets, now [a]in the squares,
And [b]lurks by every corner.
13 So she seizes him and kisses him
[1]And with a [a]brazen face she says to him:
14 "[1]I was due to offer [a]peace offerings;
Today I have [b]paid my vows.
15 "Therefore I have come out to meet you,
To seek your presence earnestly, and I have found you.
16 "I have spread my couch with [a]coverings,
With colored [b]linens of Egypt.

30 [1]Lit *They do not;* or *Do not men...?* [2]Lit *his soul* [a]Job 38:39
31 [1]Or *wealth* [a]Ex 22:1-4
32 [1]Lit *heart* [2]Lit *his soul* [a]Prov 7:7; 9:4, 16; 10:13, 21; 11:12; 12:11 [b]Prov 7:22, 23
34 [1]Lit *is the rage of* [a]Prov 27:4; Song 8:6 [b]Prov 11:4
35 [1]Lit *lift up the face of any* [2]Lit *willing* [3]Or *bribes*
7:1 [a]Prov 2:1; 6:20
2 [1]Or *law* [2]Lit *pupil* [a]Prov 4:4 [b]Deut 32:10; Ps 17:8; Zech 2:8
3 [a]Deut 6:8; 11:18; Prov 6:21 [b]Prov 3:3
5 [1]Lit *strange woman* [2]Lit *is smooth*
6 [a]Judg 5:28 [b]Song 2:9
7 [1]Lit *simple ones* [2]Lit *sons* [3]Lit *heart* [a]Prov 1:22 [b]Prov 6:32; 9:4
8 [1]Lit *steps* [a]Prov 7:12 [b]Prov 7:27
9 [1]Lit *evening of the day* [2]Lit *pupil* (of the eye) [a]Job 24:15
10 [a]Gen 38:14, 15; 1 Tim 2:9
11 [a]Prov 9:13 [b]1 Tim 5:13; Titus 2:5
12 [a]Prov 9:14 [b]Prov 23:28
13 [1]Lit *She makes bold her face and says* [a]Prov 21:29
14 [1]Lit *Sacrifices of peace offerings are with me* [a]Lev 7:11 [b]Lev 7:16
16 [a]Prov 31:22 [b]Is 19:9; Ezek 27:7

17 "I have sprinkled my bed
With [a]myrrh, aloes and [b]cinnamon.
18 "Come, let us drink our fill of love until morning;
Let us delight ourselves with caresses.
19 "For [1]my husband is not at home,
He has gone on a long journey;
20 He has taken a [a]bag of money [1]with him,
At the full moon he will come home."
21 With her many persuasions she entices him;
With her [1a]flattering lips she seduces him.
22 Suddenly he follows her
As an ox goes to the slaughter,
Or as [1]*one in* fetters to the discipline of a fool,
23 Until an arrow pierces through his liver;
As a [a]bird hastens to the snare,
So he does not know that it *will cost him* his life.

24 Now therefore, *my* sons, [a]listen to me,
And pay attention to the words of my mouth.
25 Do not let your heart [a]turn aside to her ways,
Do not stray into her paths.
26 For many are the [1]victims she has cast down,
And [a]numerous are all her slain.
27 Her [a]house is the way to Sheol,
Descending to the chambers of death.

Chapter 8 Theme ______________________

8 Does not [a]wisdom call,
And understanding [1]lift up her voice?
2 On top of [a]the heights beside the way,
Where the paths meet, she takes her stand;
3 Beside the [a]gates, at the opening to the city,
At the entrance of the doors, she cries out:
4 "To you, O men, I call,
And my voice is to the sons of men.
5 "O [1a]naive ones, understand prudence;
And, O [b]fools, understand [2]wisdom.
6 "Listen, for I will speak [a]noble things;
And the opening of my lips *will reveal* [b]right things.
7 "For my [a]mouth will utter truth;
And wickedness is an abomination to my lips.
8 "All the utterances of my mouth are in righteousness;
There is nothing [a]crooked or perverted in them.
9 "They are all [a]straightforward to him who understands,
And right to those who [b]find knowledge.
10 "Take my [a]instruction and not silver,
And knowledge rather than choicest gold.
11 "For wisdom is [a]better than [1]jewels;
And [b]all desirable things cannot compare with her.

17 [a]Ps 45:8 [b]Ex 30:23
19 [1]Lit *the man*
20 [1]Lit *in his hand* [a]Gen 42:35
21 [1]Lit *smooth* [a]Prov 5:3; 6:24
22 [1]Or *as a stag goes into a trap;* so some ancient versions
23 [a]Eccl 9:12
24 [a]Prov 5:7
25 [a]Prov 5:8
26 [1]Lit *mortally wounded* [a]Prov 9:18
27 [a]Prov 2:18; 5:5; 9:18; 1 Cor 6:9, 10; Rev 22:15
8:1 [1]Lit *give* [a]Prov 1:20, 21; 8:1-3; 9:3; 1 Cor 1:24
2 [a]Prov 9:3, 14
3 [a]Job 29:7
5 [1]Lit *simple* [2]Lit *heart* [a]Prov 1:4 [b]Prov 1:22, 32; 3:35
6 [a]Prov 22:20 [b]Prov 23:16
7 [a]Ps 37:30; John 8:14; Rom 15:8
8 [a]Deut 32:5; Prov 2:15; Phil 2:15
9 [a]Prov 14:6 [b]Prov 3:13
10 [a]Prov 3:14, 15; 8:19
11 [1]Lit *corals* [a]Job 28:15, 18; Ps 19:10 [b]Prov 3:15

12 "I, wisdom, [a]dwell with prudence,
And I find [b]knowledge *and* discretion.
13 "The [a]fear of the LORD is to hate evil;
[b]Pride and arrogance and [c]the evil way
And the [d]perverted mouth, I hate.
14 "[a]Counsel is mine and [b]sound wisdom;
I am understanding, [c]power is mine.
15 "By me [a]kings reign,
And rulers decree justice.
16 "By me princes rule, and nobles,
All who judge rightly.
17 "I [a]love those who love me;
And [b]those who diligently seek me will find me.
18 "[a]Riches and honor are with me,
Enduring [b]wealth and righteousness.
19 "My fruit is [a]better than gold, even pure gold,
And my yield *better* than [b]choicest silver.
20 "I walk in the way of righteousness,
In the midst of the paths of justice,
21 To endow those who love me with wealth,
That I may [a]fill their treasuries.

22 "The LORD possessed me [a]at the beginning of His way,
Before His works [1]of old.
23 "From everlasting I was [1a]established,
From the beginning, [b]from the earliest times of the earth.
24 "When there were no [a]depths I was [1]brought forth,
When there were no springs abounding with water.
25 "[a]Before the mountains were settled,
Before the hills I was [1]brought forth;
26 While He had not yet made the earth and the [1]fields,
Nor the first dust of the world.
27 "When He [a]established the heavens, I was there,
When [b]He inscribed a circle on the face of the deep,
28 When He made firm the skies above,
When the springs of the deep became [1]fixed,
29 When [a]He set for the sea its boundary
So that the water would not transgress His [1]command,
When He marked out [b]the foundations of the earth;
30 Then [a]I was beside Him, *as* a master workman;
And I was daily *His* delight,
[1]Rejoicing always before Him,
31 [1]Rejoicing in the world, His earth,
And *having* [a]my delight in the sons of men.

32 "Now therefore, *O* sons, [a]listen to me,
For [b]blessed are they who keep my ways.
33 "[a]Heed instruction and be wise,
And do not neglect *it.*
34 "[a]Blessed is the man who listens to me,
Watching daily at my gates,

12 [a]Prov 8:5 [b]Prov 1:4
13 [a]Prov 3:7; 16:6 [b]1 Sam 2:3; Prov 16:18; Is 13:11 [c]Prov 15:9 [d]Prov 6:12
14 [a]Prov 1:25; 19:20; Is 28:29; Jer 32:19 [b]Prov 2:7; 3:21; 18:1 [c]Eccl 7:19; 9:16
15 [a]2 Chr 1:10; Prov 29:4; Dan 2:21; Matt 28:18; Rom 13:1
17 [a]1 Sam 2:30; Prov 4:6; John 14:21 [b]Prov 2:4, 5; John 7:37; James 1:5
18 [a]Prov 3:16 [b]Ps 112:3; Matt 6:33
19 [a]Job 28:15; Prov 3:14 [b]Prov 10:20
21 [a]Prov 24:4
22 [1]Lit *from then* [a]Job 28:26-28; Ps 104:24; Prov 3:19
23 [1]Or *consecrated* [a]John 1:1-3 [b]John 17:5
24 [1]Or *born* [a]Gen 1:2; Ex 15:5; Job 38:16; Prov 3:20
25 [1]Or *born* [a]Job 15:7; Ps 90:2
26 [1]Lit *outside places*
27 [a]Prov 3:19 [b]Job 26:10
28 [1]Lit *strong*
29 [1]Lit *mouth* [a]Job 38:10; Ps 104:9 [b]Job 38:6; Ps 104:5
30 [1]Or *Playing* [a]John 1:2, 3
31 [1]Or *Playing* [a]Ps 16:3; John 13:1
32 [a]Prov 5:7; 7:24 [b]Ps 119:1, 2; 128:1; Prov 29:18; Luke 11:28
33 [a]Prov 4:1
34 [a]Prov 3:13, 18

Waiting at my doorposts.
35 "For [a]he who finds me finds life
And [b]obtains favor from the LORD.
36 "But he who [1]sins against me [a]injures himself;
All those who [b]hate me [c]love death."

Chapter 9 Theme ________________________

9 Wisdom has [a]built her house,
She has hewn out her seven pillars;
2 She has [1a]prepared her food, she has [b]mixed her wine;
She has also [c]set her table;
3 She has [a]sent out her maidens, she [b]calls
From the [c]tops of the heights of the city:
4 "[a]Whoever is [1]naive, let him turn in here!"
To him who [b]lacks [2]understanding she says,
5 "Come, [a]eat of my food
And drink of the wine I have mixed.
6 "[1]Forsake *your* folly and [a]live,
And [b]proceed in the way of understanding."

7 He who [a]corrects a scoffer gets dishonor for himself,
And he who reproves a wicked man *gets* [1]insults for himself.
8 [a]Do not reprove a scoffer, or he will hate you,
[b]Reprove a wise man and he will love you.
9 Give *instruction* to a wise man and he will be still wiser,
Teach a righteous man and he will [a]increase *his* learning.
10 The [a]fear of the LORD is the beginning of wisdom,
And the knowledge of the Holy One is understanding.
11 For [a]by me your days will be multiplied,
And years of life will be added to you.
12 If you are wise, you are wise [a]for yourself,
And if you [b]scoff, you alone will bear it.

13 The [1]woman of folly is [a]boisterous,
She is [2]naive and [b]knows nothing.
14 She sits at the doorway of her house,
On a seat by [a]the high places of the city,
15 Calling to those who pass by,
Who are making their paths straight:
16 "[a]Whoever is [1]naive, let him turn in here,"
And to him who lacks [2]understanding she says,
17 "Stolen water is sweet;
And [a]bread *eaten* in secret is pleasant."
18 But he does not know that the [1]dead are there,
That her guests are in the [a]depths of Sheol.

Chapter 10 Theme ________________________

10 The [a]proverbs of Solomon.
[b]A wise son makes a father glad,
But [c]a foolish son is a grief to his mother.

35 [a]Prov 4:22; John 17:3 [b]Prov 3:4; 12:2

36 [1]Or *misses me* [a]Prov 1:31, 32; 15:32 [b]Prov 5:12; 12:1 [c]Prov 21:6

9:1 [a]1 Cor 3:9, 10; Eph 2:20-22; 1 Pet 2:5

2 [1]Lit *slaughtered her slaughter* [a]Matt 22:4 [b]Song 8:2 [c]Luke 14:16, 17

3 [a]Ps 68:11; Matt 22:3 [b]Prov 8:1, 2 [c]Prov 9:14

4 [1]Lit *simple* [2]Lit *heart* [a]Prov 8:5; 9:16 [b]Prov 6:32

5 [a]Song 5:1; Is 55:1; John 6:27

6 [1]Or *Forsake the simple ones* [a]Prov 8:35; 9:11 [b]Ezek 11:20; 37:24

7 [1]Lit *a blemish* [a]Prov 23:9

8 [a]Prov 15:12; Matt 7:6 [b]Ps 141:5; Prov 10:8

9 [a]Prov 1:5

10 [a]Job 28:28; Ps 111:10; Prov 1:7

11 [a]Prov 3:16; 10:27

12 [a]Job 22:2; Prov 14:14 [b]Prov 19:29

13 [1]Or *foolish woman* [2]Lit *simple* [a]Prov 7:11 [b]Prov 5:6

14 [a]Prov 9:3

16 [1]Lit *simple* [2]Lit *heart* [a]Prov 9:4

17 [a]Prov 20:17

18 [1]Lit *departed spirits* [a]Prov 7:27

10:1 [a]Prov 1:1 [b]Prov 15:20; 29:3 [c]Prov 17:25; 29:15

2 [1a]Ill-gotten gains do not profit,
But righteousness delivers from death.
3 The LORD [a]will not allow the [1]righteous to hunger,
But He [b]will [2]reject the craving of the wicked.
4 Poor is he who works with a negligent hand,
But the [a]hand of the diligent makes rich.
5 He who gathers in summer is a son who acts wisely,
But he who sleeps in harvest is a son who acts shamefully.
6 [a]Blessings are on the head of the righteous,
But [b]the mouth of the wicked conceals violence.
7 The [a]memory of the righteous is blessed,
But [b]the name of the wicked will rot.
8 The [a]wise of heart will receive commands,
But [1]a babbling fool will be [2]ruined.
9 He [a]who walks in integrity walks securely,
But [b]he who perverts his ways will be found out.
10 He [a]who winks the eye causes trouble,
And [1b]a babbling fool will be [2]ruined.
11 The [a]mouth of the righteous is a fountain of life,
But [b]the mouth of the wicked conceals violence.
12 Hatred stirs up strife,
But [a]love covers all transgressions.
13 On [a]the lips of the discerning, wisdom is found,
But [b]a rod is for the back of him who lacks [1]understanding.
14 Wise men [a]store up knowledge,
But with [b]the mouth of the foolish, ruin is at hand.
15 The [a]rich man's wealth is his [1]fortress,
The [b]ruin of the poor is their poverty.
16 The [1a]wages of the righteous is life,
The income of the wicked, punishment.
17 He [a]is *on* the path of life who heeds instruction,
But he who ignores reproof goes astray.
18 He [a]who conceals hatred *has* lying lips,
And he who spreads slander is a fool.
19 When there are [a]many words, transgression is unavoidable,
But [b]he who restrains his lips is wise.
20 The tongue of the righteous is *as* [a]choice silver,
The heart of the wicked is *worth* little.
21 The [a]lips of the righteous feed many,
But fools [b]die for lack of [1]understanding.
22 It is the [a]blessing of the LORD that makes rich,
And He adds no sorrow to it.
23 Doing wickedness is like [a]sport to a fool,
And *so is* wisdom to a man of understanding.
24 What [a]the wicked fears will come upon him,
But the [b]desire of the righteous will be granted.
25 When the [a]whirlwind passes, the wicked is no more,
But the [b]righteous *has* an everlasting foundation.

2 [1]Lit *Treasures of wickedness* [a]Ps 49:7; Prov 11:4; 21:6; Ezek 7:19; Luke 12:19, 20
3 [1]Lit *soul of the righteous* [2]Lit *thrust away* [a]Ps 34:9, 10; 37:25; Prov 28:25; Matt 6:33 [b]Ps 112:10; Prov 28:9
4 [a]Prov 13:4; 21:5
6 [a]Prov 28:20 [b]Prov 10:11; Obad 10
7 [a]Ps 112:6 [b]Ps 9:5, 6; 109:13; Eccl 8:10
8 [1]Lit *the foolish of lips* [2]Lit *thrust down* [a]Prov 9:8; Matt 7:24
9 [a]Ps 23:4; Prov 3:23; 28:18; Is 33:15, 16 [b]Prov 26:26; Matt 10:26; 1 Tim 5:25
10 [1]Lit *the foolish of lips* [2]Lit *thrust down* [a]Ps 35:19; Prov 6:13 [b]Prov 10:8
11 [a]Ps 37:30; Prov 13:14; 18:4 [b]Prov 10:6
12 [a]Prov 17:9; 1 Cor 13:4-7; James 5:20; 1 Pet 4:8
13 [1]Lit *heart* [a]Prov 10:31 [b]Prov 19:29; 26:3
14 [a]Prov 9:9 [b]Prov 10:8, 10; 13:3; 18:7
15 [1]Lit *strong city* [a]Job 31:24; Ps 52:7; Prov 18:11 [b]Prov 19:7
16 [1]Or *work* [a]Prov 11:18, 19
17 [a]Prov 6:23
18 [a]Prov 26:24
19 [a]Job 11:2; Prov 18:21; Eccl 5:3 [b]Prov 17:27; James 1:19; 3:2
20 [a]Prov 8:19
21 [1]Lit *heart* [a]Prov 10:11 [b]Prov 5:23; Hos 4:6
22 [a]Gen 24:35; 26:12; Deut 8:18; Prov 8:21
23 [a]Prov 2:14; 15:21
24 [a]Job 15:21; Prov 1:27; Is 66:4 [b]Ps 145:19; Prov 15:8; Matt 5:6; 1 John 5:14, 15
25 [a]Job 21:18; Ps 58:9; Prov 12:7 [b]Ps 15:5; Prov 12:3; Matt 7:24, 25

26 Like vinegar to the teeth and smoke to the eyes,
So is the [a]lazy one to those who send him.
27 The [a]fear of the LORD prolongs [1]life,
But the [b]years of the wicked will be shortened.
28 The [a]hope of the righteous is gladness,
But the [b]expectation of the wicked perishes.
29 The [a]way of the LORD is a stronghold to the upright,
But [b]ruin to the workers of iniquity.
30 The [a]righteous will never be shaken,
But [b]the wicked will not dwell in the land.
31 The [a]mouth of the righteous flows with wisdom,
But the [b]perverted tongue will be cut out.
32 The lips of the righteous bring forth [a]what is acceptable,
But the [b]mouth of the wicked what is perverted.

Chapter 11 Theme ______________________

11 A [a]false balance is an abomination to the LORD,
But a [b]just weight is His delight.
2 When [a]pride comes, then comes dishonor,
But with the humble is wisdom.
3 The [a]integrity of the upright will guide them,
But the [b]crookedness of the treacherous will destroy them.
4 [a]Riches do not profit in the day of wrath,
But [b]righteousness delivers from death.
5 The [a]righteousness of the blameless will smooth his way,
But [b]the wicked will fall by his own wickedness.
6 The righteousness of the upright will deliver them,
But the treacherous will [a]be caught by *their own* greed.
7 When a wicked man dies, *his* [a]expectation will perish,
And the [b]hope of strong men perishes.
8 The righteous is delivered from trouble,
But the wicked [1]takes his place.
9 With *his* [a]mouth the godless man destroys his neighbor,
But through knowledge the [b]righteous will be delivered.
10 When it [a]goes well with the righteous, the city rejoices,
And when the wicked perish, there is joyful shouting.
11 By the blessing of the upright a city is exalted,
But by the mouth of the wicked it is torn down.
12 He who despises his neighbor lacks [1]sense,
But a man of understanding keeps silent.
13 He [a]who goes about as a talebearer reveals secrets,
But he who is [1]trustworthy [b]conceals a matter.
14 Where there is no [a]guidance the people fall,
But in abundance of counselors there is [1]victory.
15 He who is [a]guarantor for a stranger will surely suffer for it,
But he who hates [1]being a guarantor is secure.
16 A [a]gracious woman attains honor,
And ruthless men attain riches.

26 [a]Prov 26:6
27 [1]Lit *days* [a]Prov 3:2; 9:11; 14:27 [b]Job 15:32, 33; 22:16; Ps 55:23
28 [a]Prov 11:23 [b]Job 8:13; 11:20; Prov 11:7
29 [a]Prov 13:6 [b]Prov 21:15
30 [a]Ps 37:29; 125:1; Prov 2:21 [b]Prov 2:22
31 [a]Ps 37:30; Prov 10:13 [b]Prov 17:20
32 [a]Eccl 12:10 [b]Prov 2:12; 6:12
11:1 [a]Lev 19:35, 36; Deut 25:13-16; Prov 20:10, 23; Mic 6:11 [b]Prov 16:11
2 [a]Prov 16:18; 18:12; 29:23
3 [a]Prov 13:6 [b]Prov 19:3; 22:12
4 [a]Prov 10:2; Ezek 7:19; Zeph 1:18 [b]Gen 7:1
5 [a]Prov 3:6 [b]Prov 5:22
6 [a]Ps 7:15, 16; 9:15; Eccl 10:8
7 [a]Prov 10:28 [b]Job 8:13, 14
8 [1]Lit *enters*
9 [a]Prov 16:29 [b]Prov 11:6
10 [a]Prov 28:12
12 [1]Lit *heart*
13 [1]Lit *faithful of spirit* [a]Lev 19:16; Prov 20:19; 1 Tim 5:13 [b]Prov 19:11
14 [1]Lit *deliverance* [a]Prov 15:22; 20:18; 24:6
15 [1]Lit *those who strike hands* [a]Prov 6:1; 27:13
16 [a]Prov 31:28, 30

17 The [a]merciful man does [1]himself good,
But the cruel man [2]does himself harm.
18 The wicked earns deceptive wages,
But he who [a]sows righteousness *gets* a true reward.
19 He who is steadfast in [a]righteousness *will attain* to life,
And [b]he who pursues evil *will bring about* his own death.
20 The perverse in heart are an abomination to the LORD,
But the [a]blameless in *their* [1]walk are His [b]delight.
21 [1]Assuredly, the evil man will not go unpunished,
But the [2]descendants of the righteous will be delivered.
22 *As* a [a]ring of gold in a swine's snout
So is a beautiful woman who lacks [1]discretion.
23 The desire of the righteous is only good,
But the [a]expectation of the wicked is wrath.
24 There is one who scatters, and *yet* increases all the more,
And there is one who withholds what is justly due, *and yet it results* only in want.
25 The [1a]generous man will be [2]prosperous,
And he who [b]waters will himself be watered.
26 He who withholds grain, the [a]people will curse him,
But [b]blessing will be on the head of him who [c]sells *it.*
27 He who diligently seeks good seeks favor,
But [a]he who seeks evil, evil will come to him.
28 He who [a]trusts in his riches will fall,
But [b]the righteous will flourish like the *green* leaf.
29 He who [a]troubles his own house will [b]inherit wind,
And [c]the foolish will be servant to the wisehearted.
30 The fruit of the righteous is [a]a tree of life,
And [b]he who is wise [1]wins souls.
31 If [a]the righteous will be rewarded in the earth,
How much more the wicked and the sinner!

Chapter 12 Theme ______________________

12 Whoever loves [1]discipline loves knowledge,
But he who hates reproof is stupid.
2 A [a]good man will obtain favor from the LORD,
But He will condemn a man [1]who devises evil.
3 A man will [a]not be established by wickedness,
But the root of the [b]righteous will not be moved.
4 An [1a]excellent wife is the crown of her husband,
But she who shames *him* is like [b]rottenness in his bones.
5 The thoughts of the righteous are just,
But the counsels of the wicked are deceitful.
6 The [a]words of the wicked lie in wait for blood,
But the [b]mouth of the upright will deliver them.
7 The [a]wicked are overthrown and are no more,
But the [b]house of the righteous will stand.

17 [1]Lit *good to his own soul* [2]Lit *troubles his flesh* [a]Matt 5:7; 25:34-36
18 [a]Hos 10:12; Gal 6:8, 9; James 3:18
19 [a]Prov 10:16; 12:28; 19:23 [b]Prov 21:16; Rom 6:23; James 1:15
20 [1]Lit *way* [a]Ps 119:1; Prov 13:6 [b]1 Chr 29:17
21 [1]Lit *Hand to hand* [2]Lit *seed*
22 [1]Lit *taste* [a]Gen 24:47
23 [a]Prov 10:28; Rom 2:8, 9
25 [1]Lit *soul of blessing* [2]Lit *made fat* [a]Prov 3:9, 10; 2 Cor 9:6, 7 [b]Matt 5:7
26 [a]Prov 24:24 [b]Job 29:13 [c]Gen 42:6
27 [a]Esth 7:10; Ps 7:15, 16; 57:6
28 [a]Ps 49:6; Mark 10:25; 1 Tim 6:17 [b]Ps 1:3; 92:12; Jer 17:8
29 [a]Prov 15:27 [b]Eccl 5:16 [c]Prov 14:19
30 [1]Lit *takes* [a]Prov 3:18 [b]Prov 14:25; Dan 12:3; 1 Cor 9:19-22; James 5:20
31 [a]2 Sam 22:21, 25; Prov 13:21; 1 Pet 4:18
12:1 [1]Or *instruction*
2 [1]Lit *of evil devices* [a]Prov 3:4; 8:35
3 [a]Prov 11:5 [b]Prov 10:25
4 [1]Or *virtuous* [a]Prov 31:11; 1 Cor 11:7 [b]Prov 14:30; Hab 3:16
6 [a]Prov 1:11, 16 [b]Prov 14:3
7 [a]Job 34:25; Prov 10:25 [b]Matt 7:24-27

8 A man will be praised according to his insight,
But one of perverse [1]mind will be despised.
9 Better is he who is lightly esteemed and has a servant
Than he who honors himself and lacks bread.
10 A [a]righteous man has regard for the life of his animal,
But *even* the compassion of the wicked is cruel.
11 He [a]who tills his land will have plenty of bread,
But he who pursues worthless *things* lacks [1]sense.
12 The [a]wicked man desires the [1]booty of evil men,
But the root of the righteous [b]yields *fruit.*
13 [1]An evil man is ensnared by the transgression of his lips,
But the [a]righteous will escape from trouble.
14 A man will be [a]satisfied with good by the fruit of his [1]words,
And the [b]deeds of a man's hands will return to him.
15 The [a]way of a fool is right in his own eyes,
But a wise man is he who listens to counsel.
16 A [a]fool's anger is known at once,
But a prudent man conceals dishonor.
17 He who [1]speaks truth tells what is right,
But a false witness, deceit.
18 There is one who [a]speaks rashly like the thrusts of a sword,
But the [b]tongue of the wise brings healing.
19 Truthful lips will be established forever,
But a [a]lying tongue is only for a moment.
20 Deceit is in the heart of those who devise evil,
But counselors of peace have joy.
21 [a]No harm befalls the righteous,
But the wicked are filled with trouble.
22 [a]Lying lips are an abomination to the LORD,
But those who deal faithfully are His delight.
23 A [a]prudent man conceals knowledge,
But the heart of fools proclaims folly.
24 The hand of the diligent will rule,
But the [1]slack *hand* will be [a]put to forced labor.
25 [a]Anxiety in a man's heart weighs it down,
But a [b]good word makes it glad.
26 The righteous is a guide to his neighbor,
But the way of the wicked leads them astray.
27 A [1]lazy man does not [2]roast his prey,
But the [a]precious possession of a man *is* diligence.
28 [a]In the way of righteousness is life,
And in *its* pathway there is no death.

Chapter 13 Theme ____________________

13 A [a]wise son *accepts his* father's discipline,
But a [b]scoffer does not listen to rebuke.
2 From the fruit of a man's mouth he [1a]enjoys good,
But the [2]desire of the treacherous is [b]violence.

8 [1]Lit *heart*
10 [a]Deut 25:4
11 [1]Lit *heart* [a]Prov 28:19
12 [1]Lit *net* [a]Prov 21:10 [b]Prov 11:30
13 [1]Lit *In the transgression of the lips is an evil snare* [a]Prov 11:8; 21:23; 2 Pet 2:9
14 [1]Lit *mouth* [a]Prov 13:2; 15:23; 18:20 [b]Job 34:11; Prov 1:31; 24:12; Is 3:10, 11; Hos 4:9
15 [a]Prov 14:12; 16:2; 21:2
16 [a]Prov 14:33; 27:3; 29:11
17 [1]Lit *breathes*
18 [a]Ps 57:4 [b]Prov 4:22; 15:4
19 [a]Ps 52:4, 5; Prov 19:9
21 [a]Ps 91:10; 121:7; Prov 1:33; 1 Pet 3:13
22 [a]Rev 22:15
23 [a]Prov 10:14; 11:13; 13:16; 15:2; 29:11
24 [1]Lit *slackness* [a]Gen 49:15; Judg 1:28; 1 Kin 9:21
25 [a]Prov 15:13 [b]Is 50:4
27 [1]Lit *slackness* [2]Or *catch* [a]Prov 10:4; 13:4
28 [a]Deut 30:15f; 32:46f; Jer 21:8
13:1 [a]Prov 10:1; 15:20 [b]Prov 9:7, 8; 15:12
2 [1]Lit *eats* [2]Lit *soul* [a]Prov 12:14 [b]Prov 1:31; Hos 10:13

3 The one who [a]guards his mouth preserves his life;
The one who [b]opens wide his lips [1]comes to ruin.
4 The soul of the sluggard craves and *gets* nothing,
But the soul of the diligent is made fat.
5 A righteous man [a]hates falsehood,
But a wicked man [1b]acts disgustingly and shamefully.
6 Righteousness [a]guards the [1]one whose way is blameless,
But wickedness subverts the [2]sinner.
7 There is one who [a]pretends to be rich, but has nothing;
Another [1]pretends to be [b]poor, but has great wealth.
8 The ransom of a man's life is his wealth,
But the poor hears no rebuke.
9 The [a]light of the righteous [1]rejoices,
But the [b]lamp of the wicked goes out.
10 Through insolence [1]comes nothing but strife,
But wisdom is with those who receive counsel.
11 Wealth *obtained* by [1]fraud dwindles,
But the one who gathers [2]by labor increases *it.*
12 Hope deferred makes the heart sick,
But desire [1]fulfilled is a tree of life.
13 The one who [a]despises the word will be [1]in debt to it,
But the one who fears the commandment will be
[b]rewarded.
14 The [1]teaching of the wise is a [a]fountain of life,
To turn aside from the [b]snares of death.
15 [a]Good understanding produces favor,
But the way of the treacherous is hard.
16 Every [a]prudent man acts with knowledge,
But a fool [1]displays folly.
17 A wicked messenger falls into adversity,
But [a]a faithful envoy *brings* healing.
18 Poverty and shame *will come* to him who [a]neglects
[1]discipline,
But he who regards reproof will be honored.
19 Desire realized is sweet to the soul,
But it is an abomination to fools to turn away from evil.
20 [a]He who walks with wise men will be wise,
But the companion of fools will suffer harm.
21 [a]Adversity pursues sinners,
But the [b]righteous will be rewarded with prosperity.
22 A good man [a]leaves an inheritance to his [1]children's
children,
And the [b]wealth of the sinner is stored up for the
righteous.
23 [a]Abundant food *is in* the fallow ground of the poor,
But [1]it is swept away by injustice.
24 He who [a]withholds his [1]rod hates his son,
But he who loves him [2b]disciplines him diligently.
25 The [a]righteous [1]has enough to satisfy his appetite,
But the stomach of the [b]wicked is in need.

3 [1]Lit *ruin is his* [a]Prov 18:21; 21:23; James 3:2 [b]Prov 18:7; 20:19
5 [1]Lit *causes a bad odor and causes shame* [a]Col 3:9 [b]Prov 3:35
6 [1]Lit *blamelessness of way* [2]Lit *sin* [a]Prov 11:3
7 [1]Lit *impoverishes himself* [a]Prov 11:24; Luke 12:20, 21 [b]Luke 12:33; 2 Cor 6:10; James 2:5
9 [1]I.e. shines brightly [a]Job 29:3; Prov 4:18 [b]Job 18:5; Prov 24:20
10 [1]Lit *gives*
11 [1]Lit *vanity* [2]Or *gradually;* lit *on the hand*
12 [1]Lit *coming*
13 [1]Lit *pledged to it* [a]Num 15:31; 2 Chr 36:16 [b]Prov 13:21
14 [1]Or *law* [a]Prov 10:11; 14:27 [b]Ps 18:5
15 [a]Ps 111:10; Prov 3:4
16 [1]Lit *spreads out* [a]Prov 12:23
17 [a]Prov 25:13
18 [1]Or *instruction* [a]Prov 15:5, 32
20 [a]Prov 2:20; 15:31
21 [a]Ps 32:10; 54:5; Is 47:11 [b]Prov 11:31; 13:13; Is 3:10
22 [1]Lit *sons' sons* [a]Ezra 9:12; Ps 37:25 [b]Job 27:16, 17; Prov 28:8; Eccl 2:26
23 [1]Lit *there is what is swept* [a]Prov 12:11
24 [1]I.e. correction or discipline [2]Lit *seeks him diligently with discipline* [a]Prov 19:18; 22:15; 23:13, 14; 29:15, 17 [b]Deut 8:5; Prov 3:12; Heb 12:7
25 [1]Lit *eats to the satisfaction of his soul* [a]Ps 34:10; 103:5; 132:15; Prov 10:3 [b]Prov 13:18; Luke 15:14

Chapter 14 Theme ______________________

14 The [a]wise woman builds her house,
But the foolish tears it down with her own hands.
2 He who [a]walks in his uprightness fears the LORD,
But he who is [b]devious in his ways despises Him.
3 In the mouth of the foolish is a rod [1]for *his* back,
But [a]the lips of the wise will protect them.
4 Where no oxen are, the manger is clean,
But much revenue *comes* by the strength of the ox.
5 A [a]trustworthy witness will not lie,
But a [b]false witness [1c]utters lies.
6 A scoffer seeks wisdom and *finds* none,
But knowledge is easy to one who has understanding.
7 Leave the [a]presence of a fool,
Or you will not [1]discern [2]words of knowledge.
8 The wisdom of the sensible is to understand his way,
But [a]the foolishness of fools is deceit.
9 Fools mock at [1]sin,
But [a]among the upright there is [2]good will.
10 The heart knows its own [a]bitterness,
And a stranger does not share its joy.
11 The [a]house of the wicked will be destroyed,
But the tent of the upright will flourish.
12 There [a]is a way *which seems* right to a man,
But its [b]end is the way of death.
13 Even in laughter the heart may be in pain,
And the [a]end of joy may be grief.
14 The backslider in heart will have his [a]fill of his own ways,
But a good man will [b]*be satisfied* [1]with his.
15 The [1]naive believes everything,
But the sensible man considers his steps.
16 A wise man [1]is cautious and [a]turns away from evil,
But a fool is arrogant and careless.
17 A quick-tempered man acts foolishly,
And a man of evil devices is hated.
18 The [1]naive inherit foolishness,
But the sensible are crowned with knowledge.
19 The [a]evil will bow down before the good,
And the wicked at the gates of the righteous.
20 The [a]poor is hated even by his neighbor,
But those who love the rich are many.
21 He who [a]despises his neighbor sins,
But [b]happy is he who is gracious to the [1]poor.
22 Will they not go astray who [a]devise evil?
But kindness and truth *will be to* those who devise good.
23 In all labor there is profit,
But [1]mere talk *leads* only to poverty.
24 The [a]crown of the wise is their riches,
But the folly of fools is foolishness.
25 A truthful witness saves lives,
But he who [1a]utters lies is [2]treacherous.

14:1 [a]Ruth 4:11; Prov 31:10-27
2 [a]Prov 19:1; 28:6 [b]Prov 2:15
3 [1]Lit *of pride* [a]Prov 12:6
5 [1]Lit *breathes out* [a]Rev 1:5; 3:14 [b]Ex 23:1; Deut 19:16; Prov 6:19; 12:17 [c]Prov 19:5
7 [1]Lit *know* [2]Lit *lips* [a]Prov 23:9
8 [a]1 Cor 3:19
9 [1]Lit *guilt* [2]Or the *favor* of God [a]Prov 3:34; 11:20
10 [a]1 Sam 1:10; Job 21:25
11 [a]Job 8:15
12 [a]Prov 12:15; 16:25 [b]Rom 6:21
13 [a]Eccl 2:1, 2
14 [1]Lit *from himself* [a]Prov 1:31; 12:21 [b]Prov 12:14; 18:20
15 [1]Lit *simple*
16 [1]Lit *fears* [a]Job 28:28; Ps 34:14; Prov 3:7; 22:3
18 [1]Lit *simple*
19 [a]1 Sam 2:36; Prov 11:29
20 [a]Prov 19:7
21 [1]Or *afflicted* [a]Prov 11:12 [b]Ps 41:1; Prov 19:17; 28:8
22 [a]Ps 36:4; Prov 3:29; 12:2; Mic 2:1
23 [1]Lit *word of lips*
24 [a]Prov 10:22; 13:8; 21:20
25 [1]Lit *breathes out* [2]Lit *treachery* [a]Prov 14:5

26 In the [1a]fear of the LORD there is strong confidence,
And [2]his children will have refuge.
27 The [1]fear of the LORD is a fountain of life,
That one may avoid the snares of death.
28 In a multitude of people is a king's glory,
But in the dearth of people is a prince's ruin.
29 He who is [a]slow to anger has great understanding,
But he who is [1]quick-tempered exalts folly.
30 A [a]tranquil heart is life to the body,
But passion is [b]rottenness to the bones.
31 He [a]who oppresses the poor taunts [b]his Maker,
But he who is gracious to the needy honors Him.
32 The wicked is [a]thrust down by his [1]wrongdoing,
But the [b]righteous has a refuge when he dies.
33 Wisdom rests in the heart of one who has understanding,
But in the [1]hearts of fools it is made known.
34 Righteousness exalts a nation,
But sin is a disgrace to *any* people.
35 The king's favor is toward a [a]servant who acts wisely,
But his anger is toward him who acts shamefully.

Chapter 15 Theme __________________________

15 A [a]gentle answer turns away wrath,
But a [1b]harsh word stirs up anger.
2 The [a]tongue of the wise makes knowledge [1]acceptable,
But the [b]mouth of fools spouts folly.
3 The [a]eyes of the LORD are in every place,
Watching the evil and the good.
4 A [1]soothing tongue is a tree of life,
But perversion in it [2]crushes the spirit.
5 A fool [1]rejects his father's discipline,
But he who regards reproof is sensible.
6 Great wealth is *in* the house of the [a]righteous,
But trouble is in the income of the wicked.
7 The lips of the wise spread knowledge,
But the hearts of fools are not so.
8 The [a]sacrifice of the wicked is an abomination to the LORD,
But [b]the prayer of the upright is His delight.
9 The way of the wicked is an abomination to the LORD,
But He loves one who [a]pursues righteousness.
10 Grievous punishment is for him who forsakes the way;
He who hates reproof will die.
11 [1a]Sheol and [2]Abaddon *lie open* before the LORD,
How much more the [b]hearts of [3]men!
12 A [a]scoffer does not love one who reproves him,
He will not go to the wise.
13 A [a]joyful heart makes a [1]cheerful face,
But [2]when the heart is [b]sad, the [c]spirit is broken.
14 The [a]mind of the intelligent seeks knowledge,
But the mouth of fools feeds on folly.

26 [1]Or *reverence* [2]Or *His* [a]Prov 18:10; 19:23; Is 33:6
27 [1]Or *reverence*
29 [1]Lit *short of spirit* [a]Prov 16:32; 19:11; Eccl 7:9; James 1:19
30 [a]Prov 15:13 [b]Prov 12:4; Hab 3:16
31 [a]Prov 17:5; Matt 25:40; 1 John 3:17 [b]Job 31:15; Prov 22:2
32 [1]Or *calamity* [a]Prov 6:15; 24:16 [b]Gen 49:18; Ps 16:11; 17:15; 37:37; 73:24; 2 Cor 1:9; 5:8; 2 Tim 4:18
33 [1]Lit *inward part*
35 [a]Matt 24:45, 47; 25:21, 23
15:1 [1]Lit *painful* [a]Judg 8:1-3; Prov 15:18; 25:15 [b]1 Sam 25:10-13
2 [1]Lit *good* [a]Prov 15:7 [b]Prov 12:23; 13:16; 15:28
3 [a]2 Chr 16:9; Job 31:4; Jer 16:17; Zech 4:10; Heb 4:13
4 [1]Lit *healing* [2]Lit *is the crushing of the spirit*
5 [1]Or *despises*
6 [a]Prov 8:21
8 [a]Prov 21:27; Eccl 5:1; Is 1:11; Jer 6:20; Mic 6:7 [b]Prov 15:29
9 [a]1 Tim 6:11
11 [1]I.e. the nether world [2]I.e. place of destruction [3]Lit *sons of Adam* [a]Job 26:6; Ps 139:8 [b]1 Sam 16:7; 2 Chr 6:30; Ps 44:21; Acts 1:24
12 [a]Prov 13:1; Amos 5:10
13 [1]Lit *good* [2]Lit *in sadness of heart* [a]Prov 17:22 [b]Prov 12:25 [c]Prov 17:22; 18:14
14 [a]Prov 18:15

15 All the days of the afflicted are bad,
But a [1]cheerful heart *has* a continual feast.
16 [a]Better is a little with the [1]fear of the LORD
Than great treasure and turmoil with it.
17 [a]Better is a [1]dish of [2]vegetables where love is
Than a [b]fattened ox *served* with hatred.
18 A [a]hot-tempered man stirs up strife,
But the [b]slow to anger [c]calms a dispute.
19 The way of the lazy is as a hedge of thorns,
But the path of the upright is a highway.
20 A [a]wise son makes a father glad,
But a foolish man [b]despises his mother.
21 Folly is joy to him who lacks [1]sense,
But a man of understanding [a]walks straight.
22 Without consultation, plans are frustrated,
But with many counselors they [1]succeed.
23 A [a]man has joy in an [1]apt answer,
And how delightful is a timely [b]word!
24 The [a]path of life *leads* upward for the wise
That he may keep away from [1]Sheol below.
25 The LORD will [a]tear down the house of the proud,
But He will [b]establish the boundary of the [c]widow.
26 Evil plans are an abomination to the LORD,
But pleasant words are pure.
27 He who [a]profits illicitly troubles his own house,
But he who [b]hates bribes will live.
28 The heart of the righteous [a]ponders how to answer,
But the [b]mouth of the wicked pours out evil things.
29 The LORD is [a]far from the wicked,
But He [b]hears the prayer of the righteous.
30 [1]Bright eyes gladden the heart;
Good news puts fat on the bones.
31 He whose ear listens to the life-giving reproof
Will dwell among the wise.
32 He who [a]neglects discipline [b]despises himself,
But he who [c]listens to reproof acquires [1]understanding.
33 The [1]fear of the LORD is the instruction for wisdom,
And before honor *comes* humility.

Chapter 16 Theme ______________________

16 The [a]plans of the heart belong to man,
But the answer of the tongue is from the LORD.
2 All the ways of a man are clean in his own sight,
But the [a]LORD weighs the [1]motives.
3 [1a]Commit your works to the LORD
And your plans will be established.
4 The LORD [a]has made everything for [1]its own purpose,
Even the [b]wicked for the day of evil.
5 Everyone who is proud in heart is an abomination to the
LORD;

15 [1]Lit *good*

16 [1]Or *reverence* [a]Ps 37:16; Prov 16:8; Eccl 4:6; 1 Tim 6:6

17 [1]Or *portion* [2]Or *herbs* [a]Prov 17:1 [b]Matt 22:4; Luke 15:23

18 [a]Prov 16:28; 26:21; 29:22 [b]Prov 14:29 [c]Gen 13:8; Prov 16:14; Eccl 10:4

20 [a]Prov 10:1; 29:3 [b]Prov 30:17

21 [1]Lit *heart* [a]Prov 14:8; Eph 5:15

22 [1]Or *are established*

23 [1]Lit *answer of his mouth* [a]Prov 12:14 [b]Prov 25:11; Is 50:4

24 [1]I.e. the nether world [a]Prov 4:18

25 [a]Prov 12:7; 14:11 [b]Deut 19:14; Prov 23:10 [c]Ps 68:5; 146:9

27 [a]Prov 1:19; 28:25; 1 Tim 6:10 [b]Ex 23:8; Deut 16:19; 1 Sam 12:3; Is 33:15

28 [a]1 Pet 3:15 [b]Prov 10:32; 15:2

29 [a]Ps 18:41; Prov 1:28 [b]Ps 145:18, 19

30 [1]Lit *The light of the eyes gladdens*

32 [1]Lit *heart* [a]Prov 1:7; 8:33 [b]Prov 8:36 [c]Prov 15:5

33 [1]Or *reverence*

16:1 [a]Prov 16:9; 19:21

2 [1]Lit *spirits* [a]1 Sam 16:7; Dan 5:27

3 [1]Lit *Roll* [a]Ps 37:5; 55:22; Prov 3:6; 1 Pet 5:7

4 [1]Or *His* [a]Gen 1:31; Eccl 3:11 [b]Rom 9:22

Assuredly, he will not be unpunished.
6 By [a]lovingkindness and truth iniquity is atoned for,
And by the [1b]fear of the LORD one keeps away from evil.
7 When a man's ways are pleasing to the LORD,
He [a]makes even his enemies to be at peace with him.
8 Better is a little with righteousness
Than great income with injustice.
9 The mind of [a]man plans his way,
But [b]the LORD directs his steps.
10 A divine [a]decision is in the lips of the king;
His mouth should not [1]err in judgment.
11 A [a]just balance and scales belong to the LORD;
All the [1]weights of the bag are His [2]concern.
12 It is an abomination for kings to commit wicked acts,
For a [a]throne is established on righteousness.
13 Righteous lips are the delight of kings,
And he who speaks right is loved.
14 The fury of a king is *like* messengers of death,
But a wise man will appease it.
15 In the light of a king's face is life,
And his favor is like a cloud with the [1a]spring rain.
16 How much [a]better it is to get wisdom than gold!
And to get understanding is to be chosen above silver.
17 The [a]highway of the upright is to depart from evil;
He who watches his way preserves his [1]life.
18 [a]Pride *goes* before destruction,
And a haughty spirit before stumbling.
19 It is better to be [a]humble in spirit with the lowly
Than to [b]divide the spoil with the proud.
20 He who gives attention to the word will [a]find good,
And [b]blessed is he who trusts in the LORD.
21 The [a]wise in heart will be called understanding,
And sweetness of [1]speech [b]increases [2]persuasiveness.
22 Understanding is a fountain of life to one who has it,
But the discipline of fools is folly.
23 The [a]heart of the wise instructs his mouth
And adds [1]persuasiveness to his lips.
24 [a]Pleasant words are a honeycomb,
Sweet to the soul and [b]healing to the bones.
25 [a]There is a way *which seems* right to a man,
But its end is the way of death.
26 A worker's appetite works for him,
For his [1]hunger urges him *on*.
27 A [a]worthless man digs up evil,
While [1]his words are like [b]scorching fire.
28 A perverse man spreads strife,
And a slanderer separates intimate friends.
29 A man of violence [a]entices his neighbor
And leads him in a way that is not good.
30 He who winks his eyes *does so* to devise perverse
things;

6 [1]Or *reverence* [a]Dan 4:27; Luke 11:41 [b]Prov 8:13; 14:16
7 [a]Gen 33:4; 2 Chr 17:10
9 [a]Prov 16:1; 19:21 [b]Ps 37:23; Prov 20:24; Jer 10:23
10 [1]Lit *be unfaithful* [a]1 Kin 3:28
11 [1]Lit *stones* [2]Lit *work* [a]Prov 11:1
12 [a]Prov 25:5
15 [1]Lit *latter* [a]Job 29:23
16 [a]Prov 8:10, 19
17 [1]Lit *soul* [a]Is 35:8
18 [a]Prov 11:2; 18:12; Jer 49:16; Obad 3, 4
19 [a]Prov 3:34; 29:23; Is 57:15 [b]Ex 15:9; Judg 5:30; Prov 1:13, 14
20 [a]Prov 19:8 [b]Ps 2:12; 34:8; Jer 17:7
21 [1]Lit *lips* [2]Or *learning* [a]Hos 14:9 [b]Prov 16:23
23 [1]Or *learning* [a]Ps 37:30; Prov 15:28; Matt 12:34
24 [a]Ps 19:10; Prov 15:26; 24:13, 14 [b]Prov 4:22; 17:22
25 [a]Prov 12:15; 14:12
26 [1]Lit *mouth*
27 [1]Lit *on his lips* [a]Prov 6:12, 14, 18 [b]James 3:6
29 [a]Prov 1:10; 12:26

He who compresses his lips brings evil to pass.
31 A [a]gray head is a crown of glory;
It [b]is found in the way of righteousness.
32 He who is slow to anger is better than the mighty,
And he who rules his spirit, than he who captures a city.
33 The [a]lot is cast into the lap,
But its every [b]decision is from the LORD.

Chapter 17 Theme ____________________

17 [a]Better is a dry morsel and quietness with it
Than a house full of [1]feasting with strife.
2 A servant who acts wisely will rule over a son who acts shamefully,
And will share in the inheritance among brothers.
3 The [a]refining pot is for silver and the furnace for gold,
But [b]the LORD tests hearts.
4 An [a]evildoer listens to wicked lips;
A [1]liar pays attention to a destructive tongue.
5 He who mocks the [a]poor taunts his Maker;
He who [b]rejoices at calamity will not go unpunished.
6 [a]Grandchildren are the crown of old men,
And the [b]glory of sons is their fathers.
7 [1a]Excellent speech is not fitting for a fool,
Much less are [b]lying lips to a prince.
8 A [a]bribe is a [1]charm in the sight of its owner;
Wherever he turns, he prospers.
9 He who [a]conceals a transgression seeks love,
But he who repeats a matter [b]separates intimate friends.
10 A rebuke goes deeper into one who has understanding
Than a hundred blows into a fool.
11 A rebellious man seeks only evil,
So a cruel messenger will be sent against him.
12 Let a [a]man meet a [b]bear robbed of her cubs,
Rather than a fool in his folly.
13 He who [a]returns evil for good,
[b]Evil will not depart from his house.
14 The beginning of strife is *like* letting out water,
So [a]abandon the quarrel before it breaks out.
15 He who [a]justifies the wicked and he who condemns the righteous,
Both of them alike are an abomination to the LORD.
16 Why is there a price in the hand of a fool to [a]buy wisdom,
When [1]he has no sense?
17 A [a]friend loves at all times,
And a brother is born for adversity.
18 A man lacking in [1]sense [2a]pledges
And becomes guarantor in the presence of his neighbor.
19 He who [a]loves transgression loves strife;
He who [b]raises his door seeks destruction.

31 [a]Prov 20:29 [b]Prov 3:1, 2
33 [a]Prov 18:18 [b]Prov 29:26
17:1 [1]Lit *sacrifices of strife* [a]Prov 15:17
3 [a]Prov 27:21 [b]1 Chr 29:17; Ps 26:2; Prov 15:11; Jer 17:10; Mal 3:3
4 [1]Lit *falsehood* [a]Prov 14:15
5 [a]Prov 14:31 [b]Job 31:29; Prov 24:17; Obad 12
6 [a]Gen 48:11; Prov 13:22 [b]Ex 20:12; Mal 1:6
7 [1]Lit *A lip of abundance* [a]Prov 24:7 [b]Ps 31:18; Prov 12:22
8 [1]Lit *stone of favor* [a]Prov 21:14; Is 1:23; Amos 5:12
9 [a]Prov 10:12; James 5:20; 1 Pet 4:8 [b]Prov 16:28
12 [a]Prov 29:9 [b]2 Sam 17:8; Hos 13:8
13 [a]Ps 35:12; 109:5; Jer 18:20 [b]2 Sam 12:10; 1 Kin 21:22; Prov 13:21
14 [a]Prov 20:3; 25:8; 1 Thess 4:11
15 [a]Ex 23:7; Prov 18:5; 24:24; Is 5:23
16 [1]Lit *there is no heart* [a]Prov 23:23
17 [a]Ruth 1:16; Prov 18:24
18 [1]Lit *heart* [2]Lit *shakes hands* [a]Prov 6:1; 11:15; 22:26
19 [a]Prov 29:22 [b]Prov 16:18; 29:23

20 He who has a crooked [1]mind [a]finds no good,
And he who is [b]perverted in his language falls into evil.
21 He who [a]sires a fool *does so* to his sorrow,
And the father of a fool has no joy.
22 A [a]joyful heart [1]is good medicine,
But a broken spirit [b]dries up the bones.
23 A wicked man receives a [a]bribe from the bosom
To [b]pervert the ways of justice.
24 Wisdom is in the presence of the one who has understanding,
But the [a]eyes of a fool are on the ends of the earth.
25 A [a]foolish son is a grief to his father
And [b]bitterness to her who bore him.
26 It is also not good to [a]fine the righteous,
Nor to strike the noble for *their* uprightness.
27 He who [a]restrains his words [1]has knowledge,
And he who has a [b]cool spirit is a man of understanding.
28 Even a fool, when he [a]keeps silent, is considered wise;
When he closes his lips, he is *considered* prudent.

Chapter 18 Theme ______________________

18 He who separates himself seeks *his own* desire,
He [1a]quarrels against all sound wisdom.
2 A fool does not delight in understanding,
But only [a]in revealing his own [1]mind.
3 When a wicked man comes, contempt also comes,
And with dishonor *comes* scorn.
4 The words of a man's mouth are [a]deep waters;
[1]The fountain of wisdom is a bubbling brook.
5 To [a]show partiality to the wicked is not good,
Nor to [b]thrust aside the righteous in judgment.
6 A fool's lips [1]bring strife,
And his mouth calls for [a]blows.
7 A [a]fool's mouth is his ruin,
And his lips are the snare of his soul.
8 The words of a whisperer are like dainty morsels,
And they go down into the [1]innermost parts of the body.
9 He also who is [a]slack in his work
[b]Is brother to him who destroys.
10 The [a]name of the LORD is a [b]strong tower;
The righteous runs into it and [c]is [1]safe.
11 A [a]rich man's wealth is his strong city,
And like a high wall in his own imagination.
12 [a]Before destruction the heart of man is haughty,
But [b]humility *goes* before honor.
13 He who [a]gives an answer before he hears,
It is folly and shame to him.
14 The [a]spirit of a man can endure his sickness,
But *as for* a [b]broken spirit who can bear it?
15 The [1a]mind of the prudent acquires knowledge,

20 [1]Lit *heart* [a]Prov 24:20 [b]James 3:8
21 [a]Prov 10:1; 17:25; 19:13
22 [1]Lit *causes good healing* [a]Prov 15:13 [b]Ps 22:15
23 [a]Prov 17:8 [b]Ex 23:8; Mic 3:11; 7:3
24 [a]Eccl 2:14
25 [a]Prov 19:13 [b]Prov 10:1
26 [a]Prov 17:15; 18:5
27 [1]Lit *knows* [a]Prov 10:19; James 1:19 [b]Prov 14:29
28 [a]Job 13:5
18:1 [1]Lit *breaks out* [a]Prov 3:21; 8:14
2 [1]Lit *heart* [a]Prov 12:23; 13:16; Eccl 10:3
4 [1]Or *A bubbling brook, a fountain of wisdom* [a]Prov 20:5
5 [a]Lev 19:15; Deut 1:17; 16:19; Ps 82:2; Prov 17:15; 24:23; 28:21 [b]Ex 23:2, 6; Prov 17:26; 31:5; Mic 3:9
6 [1]Lit *come with* [a]Prov 19:29
7 [a]Ps 64:8; 140:9; Prov 10:14; 12:13; 13:3; Eccl 10:12
8 [1]Lit *chambers of the belly*
9 [a]Prov 10:4 [b]Prov 28:24
10 [1]Lit *set on high* [a]Ex 3:15 [b]2 Sam 22:2, 3, 33; Ps 18:2; 61:3; 91:2; 144:2 [c]Prov 29:25
11 [a]Prov 10:15
12 [a]Prov 11:2; 16:18; 29:23 [b]Prov 15:33
13 [a]Prov 20:25; John 7:51
14 [a]Prov 17:22 [b]Prov 15:13
15 [1]Lit *heart* [a]Prov 15:14; Eph 1:17

And the [b]ear of the wise seeks knowledge.
16 A man's [a]gift makes room for him
And brings him before great men.
17 The first [1]to plead his case *seems* right,
Until [2]another comes and examines him.
18 The *cast* [a]lot puts an end to strife
And [1]decides between the mighty ones.
19 A brother offended *is harder to be won* than a strong city,
And contentions are like the bars of a citadel.
20 With the [1a]fruit of a man's mouth his stomach will be
satisfied;
[b]He will be satisfied *with* the product of his lips.
21 [a]Death and life are in the [1]power of the tongue,
And those who love it will eat its [b]fruit.
22 He who finds a [a]wife finds a good thing
And [b]obtains favor from the LORD.
23 The [a]poor man utters supplications,
But the [b]rich man [c]answers roughly.
24 A man of *too many* friends *comes* to [1]ruin,
But there is [a]a [2]friend who sticks closer than a brother.

Chapter 19 Theme ______________________

19 [a]Better is a poor man who [b]walks in his integrity
Than he who is perverse in [1]speech and is a fool.
2 Also it is not good for a person to be without knowledge,
And he who hurries [1a]his footsteps [2]errs.
3 The [a]foolishness of man ruins his way,
And his heart [b]rages against the LORD.
4 [a]Wealth adds many friends,
But a poor man is separated from his friend.
5 A [a]false witness will not go unpunished,
And he who [1b]tells lies will not escape.
6 [a]Many will seek the favor of a [1]generous man,
And every man is a friend to him who [b]gives gifts.
7 All the brothers of a poor man hate him;
How much more do his [a]friends abandon him!
He [b]pursues *them with* words, *but* they are [1]gone.
8 He who gets [1]wisdom loves his own soul;
He who keeps understanding will [a]find good.
9 A [a]false witness will not go unpunished,
And he who [1]tells lies will perish.
10 Luxury is [a]not fitting for a fool;
Much less for a [b]slave to rule over princes.
11 A man's [a]discretion makes him slow to anger,
And it is his glory [b]to overlook a transgression.
12 The [a]king's wrath is like the roaring of a lion,
But his favor is like [b]dew on the grass.
13 A [a]foolish son is destruction to his father,
And the [b]contentions of a wife are a constant dripping.
14 House and wealth are an [a]inheritance from fathers,

15 [b]Prov 15:31

16 [a]Gen 32:20; 1 Sam 25:27

17 [1]Lit *in his plea* [2]Lit *his neighbor*

18 [1]Lit *makes a division* [a]Prov 16:33

20 [1]I.e. speech [a]Prov 12:14 [b]Prov 14:14

21 [1]Lit *hand* [a]Prov 12:13; 13:3; Matt 12:37 [b]Prov 13:2; Is 3:10; Hos 10:13

22 [a]Gen 2:18; Prov 12:4; 19:14; 31:10-31 [b]Prov 8:35

23 [a]Prov 19:7 [b]James 2:3, 6 [c]1 Kin 12:13; 2 Chr 10:13

24 [1]Lit *be broken in pieces* [2]Or *lover* [a]Prov 17:17; John 15:14, 15

19:1 [1]Lit *his lips* [a]Prov 28:6 [b]Ps 26:11; Prov 14:2; 20:7

2 [1]Lit *with his feet* [2]Lit *sins* [a]Prov 21:5; 28:20; 29:20

3 [a]Prov 11:3 [b]Is 8:21

4 [a]Prov 14:20

5 [1]Lit *breathes* [a]Ex 23:1; Deut 19:16-19; Prov 19:9; 21:28 [b]Prov 6:19

6 [1]Or *noble* [a]Prov 29:26 [b]Prov 18:16; 21:14

7 [1]Lit *not* [a]Ps 38:11 [b]Prov 18:23

8 [1]Lit *heart* [a]Prov 16:20

9 [1]Lit *breathes* [a]Prov 19:5; Dan 6:24

10 [a]Prov 17:7; 26:1; Eccl 10:6, 7 [b]Prov 30:22

11 [a]Prov 14:29; 16:32 [b]Matt 5:44; Eph 4:32; Col 3:13

12 [a]Prov 16:14 [b]Gen 27:28; Deut 33:28; Ps 133:3; Hos 14:5; Mic 5:7

13 [a]Prov 17:25 [b]Prov 21:9, 19; 27:15

14 [a]2 Cor 12:14

But a prudent wife is from the LORD.
15 [a]Laziness casts into a deep sleep,
And an idle [1]man will suffer hunger.
16 He who [a]keeps the commandment keeps his soul,
But he who [1]is careless of [2]conduct will die.
17 One who [a]is gracious to a poor man lends to the LORD,
And He will repay him for his [1b]good deed.
18 [a]Discipline your son while there is hope,
And do not desire [1]his death.
19 *A man of* great anger will bear the penalty,
For if you rescue *him,* you will only have to do it again.
20 [a]Listen to counsel and accept discipline,
That you may be wise [1]the rest of your days.
21 Many [a]plans are in a man's heart,
But the [b]counsel of the LORD will stand.
22 What is desirable in a man is his [1]kindness,
And *it is* better to be a poor man than a liar.
23 The [1a]fear of the LORD *leads* to life,
So that one may sleep [b]satisfied, [2c]untouched by evil.
24 The [a]sluggard buries his hand [b]in the dish,
But will not even bring it back to his mouth.
25 [a]Strike a scoffer and the [1]naive may become shrewd,
But [b]reprove one who has understanding and he will [2]gain knowledge.
26 He [a]who assaults *his* father *and* drives *his* mother away
Is a shameful and disgraceful son.
27 Cease listening, my son, to discipline,
And you will stray from the words of knowledge.
28 A rascally witness makes a mockery of justice,
And the mouth of the wicked [1a]spreads iniquity.
29 [1]Judgments are prepared for [a]scoffers,
And [b]blows for the back of fools.

Chapter 20 Theme ____________________

20 [a]Wine is a mocker, [b]strong drink a brawler,
And whoever [1]is intoxicated by it is not wise.
2 The terror of a king is like the growling of a lion;
He who provokes him to anger [1a]forfeits his own life.
3 [1a]Keeping away from strife is an honor for a man,
But any fool will [2]quarrel.
4 The [a]sluggard does not plow after the autumn,
So he [1]begs during the harvest and has nothing.
5 A plan in the heart of a man is *like* deep water,
But a man of understanding draws it out.
6 Many a man [a]proclaims his own loyalty,
But who can find a [b]trustworthy man?
7 A righteous man who [a]walks in his integrity—
[b]How blessed are his sons after him.
8 [a]A king who sits on the throne of justice
[1]Disperses all evil with his eyes.

15 [1]Lit *soul* [a]Prov 6:9, 10; 24:33
16 [1]Lit *despises* [2]Lit *ways* [a]Prov 13:13; 16:17; Luke 10:28; 11:28
17 [1]Or *benefits* [a]Deut 15:7, 8; Prov 14:31; 28:27; Eccl 11:1, 2; Matt 10:42; 25:40; 2 Cor 9:6-8; Heb 6:10 [b]Prov 12:14; Luke 6:38
18 [1]Lit *causing him to die* [a]Prov 13:24; 23:13; 29:15, 17
20 [1]Lit *in your latter end* [a]Prov 4:1; 8:33; 12:15
21 [a]Prov 16:1, 9 [b]Ps 33:10, 11; Is 14:26, 27
22 [1]Or *loyalty*
23 [1]Or *reverence* [2]Lit *not visited* [a]Prov 14:27; 1 Tim 4:8 [b]Ps 25:13 [c]Ps 91:10; Prov 12:21
24 [a]Prov 26:15 [b]Matt 26:23; Mark 14:20
25 [1]Lit *simple* [2]Lit *discern* [a]Prov 21:11 [b]Prov 9:8
26 [a]Prov 28:24
28 [1]Or *swallows* [a]Job 15:16; 20:12, 13; 34:7
29 [1]Gr *Rods* [a]Ps 1:1; Prov 9:12 [b]Prov 10:13; 18:6; 26:3
20:1 [1]Lit *errs* [a]Gen 9:21; Prov 23:29, 30; Is 28:7; Hos 4:11 [b]Prov 31:4; Is 5:22; 56:12
2 [1]Lit *sins against* [a]Num 16:38; 1 Kin 2:23; Prov 8:36; Hab 2:10
3 [1]Lit *Ceasing* [2]Lit *burst out* [a]Gen 13:7f; Prov 17:14
4 [1]Lit *asks* [a]Prov 13:4; 21:25
6 [a]Prov 25:14; Matt 6:2; Luke 18:11 [b]Ps 12:1; Luke 18:8
7 [a]Prov 19:1 [b]Ps 37:26; 112:2
8 [1]Or *Sifts* [a]Prov 20:26; 25:5

9 [a]Who can say, "I have cleansed my heart,
I am pure from my sin"?
10 [1a]Differing weights and differing measures,
Both of them are abominable to the LORD.
11 It is by his deeds that a lad [1a]distinguishes himself
If his conduct is pure and right.
12 The hearing [a]ear and the seeing eye,
The LORD has made both of them.
13 [a]Do not love sleep, or you will become poor;
Open your eyes, *and* you will be satisfied with [1]food.
14 "Bad, bad," says the buyer,
But when he goes his way, then he boasts.
15 There is gold, and an abundance of [1]jewels;
But the lips of knowledge are a more precious thing.
16 Take his garment when he becomes surety for
a stranger;
And for foreigners, hold him in pledge.
17 [a]Bread obtained by falsehood is sweet to a man,
But afterward his mouth will be filled with gravel.
18 Prepare [a]plans by consultation,
And [b]make war by wise guidance.
19 He who [a]goes about as a slanderer reveals secrets,
Therefore do not associate with [1b]a gossip.
20 He who [a]curses his father or his mother,
His [b]lamp will go out in [1]time of darkness.
21 An inheritance gained hurriedly at the beginning
Will not be blessed in the end.
22 [a]Do not say, "I will repay evil";
[b]Wait for the LORD, and He will save you.
23 [1a]Differing weights are an abomination to the LORD,
And a [2b]false scale is not good.
24 [a]Man's steps are *ordained* by the LORD,
How then can man understand his way?
25 It is a trap for a man to say rashly, "It is holy!"
And [a]after the vows to make inquiry.
26 A [a]wise king winnows the wicked,
And [1]drives the [b]*threshing* wheel over them.
27 The [1a]spirit of man is the lamp of the LORD,
Searching all the [2]innermost parts of his being.
28 [1]Loyalty and [a]truth preserve the king,
And he upholds his throne by [1]righteousness.
29 The glory of young men is their strength,
And the [1a]honor of old men is their gray hair.
30 [a]Stripes that wound scour away evil,
And strokes *reach* the [1]innermost parts.

Chapter 21 Theme ______________________

21 The king's heart is *like* channels of water in the hand
of the LORD;
He [a]turns it wherever He wishes.

9 [a]1 Kin 8:46; 2 Chr 6:36; Job 14:4; Eccl 7:20; Rom 3:9; 1 John 1:8
10 [1]Lit *A stone and a stone, an ephah and an ephah* [a]Prov 11:1; 20:23
11 [1]Or *makes himself known* [a]Matt 7:16
12 [a]Ex 4:11; Ps 94:9
13 [1]Lit *bread* [a]Prov 6:9, 10; 19:15; 24:33
15 [1]Or *corals*
17 [a]Prov 9:17
18 [a]Prov 11:14; 15:22 [b]Prov 24:6; Luke 14:31
19 [1]Lit *one who opens his lips* [a]Prov 11:13 [b]Prov 13:3
20 [1]Lit *pupil* (of eye) [a]Ex 21:17; Lev 20:9; Prov 30:11; Matt 15:4 [b]Job 18:5; Prov 13:9; 24:20
22 [a]Prov 24:29; Matt 5:39; Rom 12:17, 19; 1 Thess 5:15; 1 Pet 3:9 [b]Ps 27:14
23 [1]Lit *A stone and a stone* [2]Lit *balance of deceit* [a]Prov 20:10 [b]Prov 11:1
24 [a]Prov 16:9
25 [a]Eccl 5:4, 5
26 [1]Lit *turns* [a]Prov 20:8 [b]Is 28:27
27 [1]Lit *breath* [2]Lit *chambers of the body* [a]1 Cor 2:11
28 [1]Lit *Covenant loyalty* [a]Prov 29:14
29 [1]Or *splendor* [a]Prov 16:31
30 [1]Lit *chambers of the body* [a]Ps 89:32; Prov 22:15; Is 53:5; 1 Pet 2:24
21:1 [a]Ezra 6:22

2 [a]Every man's way is right in his own eyes,
But the LORD [b]weighs the hearts.
3 To do [a]righteousness and justice
Is desired by the LORD more than sacrifice.
4 Haughty eyes and a proud heart,
The [a]lamp of the wicked, is sin.
5 The plans of the [a]diligent *lead* surely to advantage,
But everyone [b]who is hasty *comes* surely to poverty.
6 The [a]acquisition of treasures by a lying tongue
Is a fleeting vapor, the [1]pursuit of [b]death.
7 The violence of the wicked will drag them away,
Because they [a]refuse to act with justice.
8 The way of a guilty man is [a]crooked,
But as for the pure, his conduct is upright.
9 It is better to live in a corner of a roof
Than [1]in a house shared with a contentious woman.
10 The soul of the wicked desires evil;
His [a]neighbor finds no favor in his eyes.
11 When the [a]scoffer is punished, the [1]naive becomes wise;
But when the wise is instructed, he receives knowledge.
12 The righteous one considers the house of the wicked,
Turning the [a]wicked to ruin.
13 He who [a]shuts his ear to the cry of the poor
Will also cry himself and not be [b]answered.
14 A [a]gift in secret subdues anger,
And a bribe in the bosom, strong wrath.
15 The exercise of justice is joy for the righteous,
But is [a]terror to the workers of iniquity.
16 A man who wanders from the way of understanding
Will [a]rest in the assembly of the [1]dead.
17 He who [a]loves pleasure *will become* a poor man;
He who loves wine and oil will not become rich.
18 The wicked is a [a]ransom for the righteous,
And the [b]treacherous is in the place of the upright.
19 [a]It is better to live in a desert land
Than with a contentious and vexing woman.
20 There is precious [a]treasure and oil in the dwelling of the wise,
But a foolish man [b]swallows it up.
21 He who [a]pursues righteousness and loyalty
Finds life, righteousness and honor.
22 A [a]wise man scales the city of the mighty
And brings down the [1]stronghold in which they trust.
23 He who [a]guards his mouth and his tongue,
Guards his soul from troubles.
24 "Proud," "Haughty," "[a]Scoffer," are his names,
Who acts with [b]insolent pride.
25 The [a]desire of the sluggard puts him to death,
For his hands refuse to work;
26 All day long he [1]is craving,
While the righteous [a]gives and does not hold back.

2 [a]Prov 16:2 [b]Prov 16:2; 24:12; Luke 16:15
3 [a]1 Sam 15:22; Prov 15:8; Is 1:11, 16, 17; Hos 6:6; Mic 6:7, 8
4 [a]Prov 24:20; Luke 11:34
5 [a]Prov 10:4; 13:4 [b]Prov 28:22
6 [1]Lit *seekers* [a]Prov 13:11; 20:21 [b]Prov 8:36
7 [a]Amos 5:7; Mic 3:9
8 [a]Prov 2:15
9 [1]Lit *with a woman of contentions and a house of association*
10 [a]Ps 52:3; Prov 2:14; 14:21
11 [1]Lit *simple* [a]Prov 19:25
12 [a]Prov 14:11
13 [a]Matt 18:30-34; 1 John 3:17 [b]James 2:13
14 [a]Prov 18:16; 19:6
15 [a]Prov 10:29
16 [1]Lit *departed spirits* [a]Ps 49:14
17 [a]Prov 23:21
18 [a]Is 43:3 [b]Prov 11:8
19 [a]Prov 21:9
20 [a]Ps 112:3; Prov 8:21; 22:4 [b]Job 20:15, 18
21 [a]Prov 15:9; Matt 5:6; 1 Cor 15:58
22 [1]Lit *strength of trust* [a]2 Sam 5:6-9; Prov 24:5; Eccl 7:19; 9:15, 16
23 [a]Prov 12:13; 13:3; 18:21; James 3:2
24 [a]Ps 1:1; Prov 1:22; 3:34; 24:9; Is 29:20 [b]Is 16:6; Jer 48:29
25 [a]Prov 13:4
26 [1]Lit *desires desire* [a]Ps 37:26; 112:5, 9; Matt 5:42; Eph 4:28

27 The [a]sacrifice of the wicked is an abomination,
How much more when he brings it with evil intent!
28 A [a]false witness will perish,
But the man who listens *to the truth* will speak forever.
29 A wicked man [1a]displays a bold face,
But as for the [b]upright, he makes his way sure.
30 There is [a]no wisdom and no understanding
And no counsel against the LORD.
31 The [a]horse is prepared for the day of battle,
But [b]victory belongs to the LORD.

Chapter 22 Theme ______________________

22 A [a]*good* name is to be more desired than great wealth,
Favor is better than silver and gold.
2 The rich and the poor [1]have a common bond,
The LORD is the [a]maker of them all.
3 The [a]prudent sees the evil and hides himself,
But the [1]naive go on, and are punished for it.
4 The reward of humility *and* the [1]fear of the LORD
Are riches, honor and life.
5 [a]Thorns *and* snares are in the way of the perverse;
He who guards himself will be far from them.
6 [a]Train up a child [1]in the way he should go,
Even when he is old he will not depart from it.
7 The [a]rich rules over the poor,
And the borrower *becomes* the lender's slave.
8 He who [a]sows iniquity will reap vanity,
And the [b]rod of his fury will perish.
9 He who [1]is [a]generous will be blessed,
For he [b]gives some of his food to the poor.
10 [a]Drive out the scoffer, and contention will go out,
Even strife and dishonor will cease.
11 He who loves [a]purity of heart
And [1]whose speech is [b]gracious, the king is his friend.
12 The eyes of the LORD preserve knowledge,
But He overthrows the words of the treacherous man.
13 The [a]sluggard says, "There is a lion outside;
I will be killed in the streets!"
14 The mouth of [1a]an adulteress is a deep pit;
He who is [b]cursed of the LORD will fall [2]into it.
15 Foolishness is bound up in the heart of a child;
The [a]rod of discipline will remove it far from him.
16 He [a]who oppresses the poor to make [1]more for himself
Or who gives to the rich, [b]*will* only *come to* poverty.

17 [a]Incline your ear and hear the words of the wise,
And apply your mind to my knowledge;
18 For it will be [a]pleasant if you keep them within you,
[1]That they may be ready on your lips.

27 [a]Prov 15:8; Is 66:3; Jer 6:20; Amos 5:22
28 [a]Prov 19:5, 9
29 [1]Lit *makes firm with his face* [a]Eccl 8:1 [b]Ps 119:5; Prov 11:5
30 [a]Jer 9:23; Acts 5:38, 39; 1 Cor 3:19, 20
31 [a]Ps 20:7; 33:17; Is 31:1 [b]Ps 3:8; Jer 3:23; 1 Cor 15:57
22:1 [a]Prov 10:7; Eccl 7:1
2 [1]Lit *meet together* [a]Job 31:15; Prov 14:31
3 [1]Lit *simple* [a]Prov 14:16; 27:12; Is 26:20
4 [1]Or *reverence*
5 [a]Prov 15:19
6 [1]Lit *according to his way* [a]Eph 6:4
7 [a]Prov 18:23; James 2:6
8 [a]Job 4:8 [b]Ps 125:3
9 [1]Lit *has a good eye* [a]Prov 19:17; 2 Cor 9:6 [b]Luke 14:13
10 [a]Gen 21:9, 10; Prov 18:6; 26:20
11 [1]Lit *has grace on his lips* [a]Ps 24:4; Matt 5:8 [b]Prov 14:35; 16:13
13 [a]Prov 26:13
14 [1]Lit *strange woman* [2]Lit *there* [a]Prov 2:16; 5:3; 7:5; 23:27 [b]Eccl 7:26
15 [a]Prov 13:24; 23:14
16 [1]Lit *much* [a]Eccl 5:8; James 2:13 [b]Prov 28:22
17 [a]Prov 5:1
18 [1]Lit *They together* [a]Prov 2:10

19 [1]Lit *made you know* [a]Prov 3:5

20 [1]Or *previous* [a]Prov 8:6

21 [1]Lit *truth* [2]Lit *return to words of truth* [a]Luke 1:3, 4 [b]Prov 25:13; 1 Pet 3:15

22 [a]Ex 23:6; Job 31:16; Prov 22:16 [b]Zech 7:10; Mal 3:5

23 [1]Lit *rob the soul* [a]1 Sam 25:39; Ps 12:5; 35:10; 140:12; Prov 23:11; Jer 51:36

24 [a]Prov 29:22

25 [1]Lit *take* [a]1 Cor 15:33

26 [1]Lit *strike hands* [a]Prov 17:18

27 [a]Ex 22:26; Prov 20:16

28 [a]Deut 19:14; 27:17; Job 24:2; Prov 23:10

29 [a]Gen 41:46; 1 Kin 10:8

23:1 [1]Or *who*

2 [a]Prov 23:20

3 [a]Ps 141:4; Prov 23:6; Dan 1:5, 8, 13, 15, 16

4 [1]Or *understanding* [a]Prov 15:27; 28:20; Matt 6:19; 1 Tim 6:9; Heb 13:5 [b]Prov 3:5, 7

5 [1]Lit *Will your eyes fly upon it and it is not?* [a]Prov 27:24; 1 Tim 6:17

6 [1]Lit *an evil eye* [a]Ps 141:4 [b]Deut 15:9; Prov 28:22

7 [1]Lit *reckons in his soul* [a]Prov 26:24, 25

8 [1]Lit *your* [2]Lit *pleasant words* [a]Prov 25:16

19 So that your [a]trust may be in the LORD,
I have [1]taught you today, even you.
20 Have I not written to you [1a]excellent things
Of counsels and knowledge,
21 To make you [a]know the [1]certainty of the words of truth
That you may [2b]correctly answer him who sent you?

22 [a]Do not rob the poor because he is poor,
Or [b]crush the afflicted at the gate;
23 For the LORD will [a]plead their case
And [1]take the life of those who rob them.

24 Do not associate with a man *given* to anger;
Or go with a [a]hot-tempered man,
25 Or you will [a]learn his ways
And [1]find a snare for yourself.

26 Do not be among those who [a]give [1]pledges,
Among those who become guarantors for debts.
27 If you have nothing with which to pay,
Why should he [a]take your bed from under you?

28 [a]Do not move the ancient boundary
Which your fathers have set.

29 Do you see a man skilled in his work?
He will [a]stand before kings;
He will not stand before obscure men.

Chapter 23 Theme ____________________

23 When you sit down to dine with a ruler,
Consider carefully [1]what is before you,
2 And put a knife to your throat
If you are a [a]man of *great* appetite.
3 Do not [a]desire his delicacies,
For it is deceptive food.

4 [a]Do not weary yourself to gain wealth,
[b]Cease from your [1]consideration *of it.*
5 [1]When you set your eyes on it, it is gone.
For [a]*wealth* certainly makes itself wings
Like an eagle that flies *toward* the heavens.

6 [a]Do not eat the bread of [1]a [b]selfish man,
Or desire his delicacies;
7 For as he [1]thinks within himself, so he is.
He says to you, "Eat and drink!"
But [a]his heart is not with you.
8 You will [a]vomit up [1]the morsel you have eaten,
And waste your [2]compliments.

9 [a]Do not speak in the [1]hearing of a fool,
For he will [b]despise the wisdom of your words.

10 Do not move the ancient boundary
Or [a]go into the fields of the fatherless,
11 For their [a]Redeemer is strong;
[b]He will plead their case against you.
12 Apply your heart to discipline
And your ears to words of knowledge.

13 [a]Do not hold back discipline from the child,
Although you [1]strike him with the rod, he will not die.
14 You shall [1]strike him with the rod
And [a]rescue his soul from Sheol.

15 My son, if your heart is [a]wise,
My own heart also will be glad;
16 And my [1]inmost being will rejoice
When your lips speak [a]what is right.

17 [a]Do not let your heart envy sinners,
But *live* in the [1b]fear of the LORD [2]always.
18 Surely there is a [1a]future,
And your [b]hope will not be cut off.
19 Listen, my son, and [a]be wise,
And [b]direct your heart in the way.
20 Do not be with [a]heavy drinkers of wine,
Or with [b]gluttonous eaters of meat;
21 For the [a]heavy drinker and the glutton will come to poverty,
And [b]drowsiness will clothe *one* with rags.

22 [a]Listen to your father who begot you,
And [b]do not despise your mother when she is old.
23 [a]Buy truth, and do not sell *it,*
Get wisdom and instruction and understanding.

24 The father of the righteous will greatly rejoice,
And [a]he who sires a wise son will be glad in him.
25 Let your [a]father and your mother be glad,
And let her rejoice who gave birth to you.

26 [a]Give me your heart, my son,
And let your eyes [1b]delight in my ways.
27 For a harlot is a [a]deep pit
And an [1b]adulterous woman is a narrow well.
28 Surely she [a]lurks as a robber,
And increases the [1]faithless among men.

29 Who has [a]woe? Who has sorrow?
Who has contentions? Who has complaining?

9 [1]Lit *ears* [a]Matt 7:6 [b]Prov 1:7

10 [a]Jer 22:3; Zech 7:10

11 [a]Job 19:25; Jer 50:34 [b]Prov 22:23

13 [1]Lit *smite* [a]Prov 13:24; 19:18

14 [1]Lit *smite* [a]1 Cor 5:5

15 [a]Prov 23:24f; 27:11; 29:3

16 [1]Lit *kidneys* [a]Prov 8:6

17 [1]Or *reverence* [2]Lit *all the day* [a]Ps 37:1; Prov 24:1, 19 [b]Prov 28:14

18 [1]Lit *latter end* [a]Ps 19:11; 58:11; Prov 24:14 [b]Ps 9:18

19 [a]Prov 6:6 [b]Prov 4:23; 9:6

20 [a]Prov 20:1; 23:29, 30; Is 5:22; Matt 24:49; Luke 21:34; Rom 13:13; Eph 5:18 [b]Deut 21:20; Prov 28:7

21 [a]Prov 21:17 [b]Prov 6:10, 11

22 [a]Prov 1:8; Eph 6:1 [b]Prov 15:20; 30:17

23 [a]Prov 4:7; 18:15; Matt 13:44

24 [a]Prov 10:1; 15:20; 29:3

25 [a]Prov 27:11

26 [1]Another reading is *observe* [a]Prov 3:1; 4:4 [b]Ps 1:2; 119:24

27 [1]Lit *strange* [a]Prov 22:14 [b]Prov 5:20

28 [1]Lit *treacherous* [a]Prov 6:26; 7:12; Eccl 7:26

29 [a]Is 5:11, 22

30 [1]Or *search out* [a]1 Sam 25:36; Prov 20:1; Is 5:11; 28:7; Eph 5:18 [b]Ps 75:8

31 [1]Lit *gives its eye* [a]Song 7:9

32 [a]Job 20:16; Prov 20:1; Eph 5:18 [b]Ps 91:13; Is 11:8

33 [1]Lit *heart* [a]Prov 2:12

34 [1]Lit *heart* [2]Or *lookout*

35 [1]I.e. from the effect of wounds [2]Lit *it yet again* [a]Prov 27:22; Jer 5:3 [b]Prov 26:11; Is 56:12

24:1 [a]Ps 37:1; Prov 3:31; 23:17; 24:19 [b]Ps 1:1; Prov 1:15

2 [1]Lit *hearts* [a]Is 30:12; Jer 22:17 [b]Job 15:35; Ps 10:7; 38:12

3 [a]Prov 9:1; 14:1

4 [a]Prov 8:21

5 [1]Lit *in strength* [2]Lit *strengthens power* [a]Prov 21:22

6 [1]Lit *make battle for yourself* [a]Prov 20:18 [b]Prov 11:14

7 [a]Ps 10:5; Prov 14:6; 17:16 [b]Job 5:4; Ps 127:5

8 [1]Or *deviser of evil* [a]Prov 6:14; 14:22; Rom 1:30

9 [a]Matt 15:19; Acts 8:22

10 [a]Deut 20:8; Job 4:5; Jer 51:46; Heb 12:3

11 [a]Ps 82:4; Is 58:6, 7

Who has wounds without cause?
Who has redness of eyes?
30 Those who [a]linger long over wine,
Those who go to [1]taste [b]mixed wine.
31 Do not look on the wine when it is red,
When it [1]sparkles in the cup,
When it [a]goes down smoothly;
32 At the last it [a]bites like a serpent
And stings like a [b]viper.
33 Your eyes will see strange things
And your [1]mind will [a]utter perverse things.
34 And you will be like one who lies down in the [1]middle of the sea,
Or like one who lies down on the top of a [2]mast.
35 "They [a]struck me, *but* I did not become [1]ill;
They beat me, *but* I did not know *it.*
When shall I awake?
I will [b]seek [2]another drink."

Chapter 24 Theme ______________________

24 Do not be [a]envious of evil men,
Nor desire to [b]be with them;
2 For their [1]minds devise [a]violence,
And their lips [b]talk of trouble.

3 [a]By wisdom a house is built,
And by understanding it is established;
4 And by knowledge the rooms are [a]filled
With all precious and pleasant riches.

5 A [a]wise man is [1]strong,
And a man of knowledge [2]increases power.
6 For [a]by wise guidance you will [1]wage war,
And [b]in abundance of counselors there is victory.

7 Wisdom is [a]*too* exalted for a fool,
He does not open his mouth [b]in the gate.

8 One who [a]plans to do evil,
Men will call a [1]schemer.
9 The [a]devising of folly is sin,
And the scoffer is an abomination to men.

10 If you [a]are slack in the day of distress,
Your strength is limited.

11 [a]Deliver those who are being taken away to death,
And those who are staggering to slaughter, Oh hold *them* back.

12 If you say, "See, we did not know this,"
Does He not [a]consider *it* [b]who weighs the hearts?
And [c]does He not know *it* who [d]keeps your soul?
And will He not [1e]render to man according to his work?

13 My son, eat [a]honey, for it is good,
Yes, the [b]honey from the comb is sweet to your taste;
14 Know *that* [a]wisdom is thus for your soul;
If you find *it,* then there will be a [1b]future,
And your hope will not be cut off.

15 [a]Do not lie in wait, O wicked man, against the dwelling of the righteous;
Do not destroy his resting place;
16 For a [a]righteous man falls seven times, and rises again,
But the [b]wicked stumble in *time of* calamity.

17 [a]Do not rejoice when your enemy falls,
And do not let your heart be glad when he stumbles;
18 Or the LORD will see *it* and [1]be displeased,
And turn His anger away from him.

19 [a]Do not fret because of evildoers
Or be [b]envious of the wicked;
20 For [a]there will be no [1b]future for the evil man;
The [c]lamp of the wicked will be put out.

21 My son, [1a]fear the LORD and the king;
Do not associate with those who are given to change,
22 For their [a]calamity will rise suddenly,
And who knows the ruin *that comes* from both of them?

23 These also are [a]sayings of the wise.
To [1b]show partiality in judgment is not good.
24 He [a]who says to the wicked, "You are righteous,"
[b]Peoples will curse him, nations will abhor him;
25 But [a]to those who rebuke the *wicked* will be delight,
And a good blessing will come upon them.
26 He kisses the lips
Who gives [1]a right answer.

27 Prepare your work outside
And [a]make it ready for yourself in the field;
Afterwards, then, build your house.

28 Do not be a [a]witness against your neighbor without cause,
And [b]do not deceive with your lips.
29 [a]Do not say, "Thus I shall do to him as he has done to me;
I will [1]render to the man according to his work."

12 [1]Lit *bring back* [a]Eccl 5:8 [b]1 Sam 16:7; Prov 21:2 [c]Ps 94:9-11 [d]Ps 121:3-8 [e]Job 34:11; Prov 12:14

13 [a]Ps 19:10; 119:103; Prov 25:16; Song 5:1 [b]Prov 16:24; 27:7; Song 4:11

14 [1]Lit *latter end* [a]Prov 2:10 [b]Prov 23:18

15 [a]Ps 10:9, 10

16 [a]Job 5:19; Ps 37:24; Mic 7:8 [b]Prov 6:15; 14:32; 24:22; Jer 18:17

17 [a]Job 31:29; Ps 35:15, 19; Prov 17:5; Obad 12

18 [1]Lit it *is evil in His eyes*

19 [a]Ps 37:1 [b]Prov 23:17; 24:1

20 [1]Lit *latter end* [a]Job 15:31 [b]Prov 23:18 [c]Job 18:5, 6; 21:17; Prov 13:9; 20:20

21 [1]Or *reverence* [a]Rom 13:1-7; 1 Pet 2:17

22 [a]Prov 24:16

23 [1]Lit *regard the face* [a]Prov 1:6; 22:17 [b]Prov 18:5; 28:21

24 [a]Prov 17:15; Is 5:23 [b]Prov 11:26

25 [a]Prov 28:23

26 [1]Or *an honest*

27 [a]Prov 27:23-27

28 [a]Prov 25:18 [b]Lev 6:2, 3; 19:11; Eph 4:25

29 [1]Lit *bring back* [a]Prov 20:22; Matt 5:39; Rom 12:17

30 I passed by the field of the sluggard
And by the vineyard of the man [a]lacking [1]sense,
31 And behold, it was completely [a]overgrown with thistles;
Its surface was covered with [1b]nettles,
And its stone [c]wall was broken down.
32 When I saw, I [1]reflected upon it;
I looked, *and* received instruction.
33 "[a]A little sleep, a little slumber,
A little folding of the hands to rest,"
34 Then your poverty will come *as* [1]a robber
And your want like [2]an armed man.

Chapter 25 Theme ______________________

25 These also are [a]proverbs of Solomon which the men of
Hezekiah, king of Judah, transcribed.
2 It is the glory of God to [a]conceal a matter,
But the glory of [b]kings is to search out a matter.
3 *As* the heavens for height and the earth for depth,
So the heart of kings is unsearchable.
4 Take away the [a]dross from the silver,
And there comes out a vessel for the [b]smith;
5 Take away the [a]wicked before the king,
And his [b]throne will be established in righteousness.
6 Do not claim honor in the presence of the king,
And do not stand in the place of great men;
7 For [a]it is better that it be said to you, "Come up here,"
Than for you to be placed lower in the presence of the
prince,
Whom your eyes have seen.

8 Do not go out [a]hastily to [1]argue *your case;*
[2]Otherwise, what will you do in [3]the end,
When your neighbor humiliates you?
9 [1a]Argue your case with your neighbor,
And [b]do not reveal the secret of another,
10 Or he who hears *it* will reproach you,
And the evil report about you will not [1]pass away.

11 *Like* apples of gold in settings of silver
Is a [a]word spoken in [1]right circumstances.
12 *Like* [1]an [a]earring of gold and an [b]ornament of [c]fine gold
Is a wise reprover to a [d]listening ear.
13 Like the cold of snow in the [1]time of harvest
Is a [a]faithful messenger to those who send him,
For he refreshes the soul of his masters.
14 *Like* [a]clouds and [b]wind without rain
Is a man who boasts [1]of his gifts falsely.
15 By [1a]forbearance a ruler may be persuaded,
And a soft tongue breaks the bone.

30 [1]Lit *heart* [a]Prov 6:32
31 [1]I.e. a kind of weed [a]Gen 3:18 [b]Job 30:7 [c]Is 5:5
32 [1]Lit *set my heart*
33 [a]Prov 6:10
34 [1]Or *a vagabond;* lit *one who walks* [2]Lit *a man with a shield*
25:1 [a]Prov 1:1
2 [a]Deut 29:29; Rom 11:33 [b]Ezra 6:1
4 [a]Prov 26:23; Ezek 22:18 [b]Mal 3:2, 3
5 [a]Prov 20:8 [b]Prov 16:12
7 [a]Luke 14:7-11
8 [1]Lit *contend* [2]Lit *Lest* [3]Lit *its* [a]Prov 17:14; Matt 5:25
9 [1]Lit *Contend* [a]Matt 18:15 [b]Prov 11:13
10 [1]Lit *return*
11 [1]Lit *its* [a]Prov 15:23
12 [1]Or *a nose ring* [a]Ex 32:2; 35:22; Ezek 16:12 [b]2 Sam 1:24 [c]Job 28:17 [d]Prov 15:31; 20:12
13 [1]Lit *day* [a]Prov 13:17
14 [1]Lit *in a gift of falsehood* [a]Jude 12 [b]Jer 5:13; Mic 2:11
15 [1]Lit *length of anger* [a]Gen 32:4; 1 Sam 25:24; Eccl 10:4

16 Have you [a]found honey? Eat *only* [1]what you need,
That you not have it in excess and vomit it.
17 Let your foot rarely be in your neighbor's house,
Or he will become [1]weary of you and hate you.
18 *Like* a club and a [a]sword and a sharp [b]arrow
Is a man who bears [c]false witness against his neighbor.
19 *Like* a bad tooth and [1]an unsteady foot
Is confidence in a [a]faithless man in time of trouble.
20 *Like* one who takes off a garment on a cold day, *or like* vinegar on [1]soda,
Is he who sings songs to [2]a troubled heart.
21 [a]If [1]your enemy is hungry, give him food to eat;
And if he is thirsty, give him water to drink;
22 For you will [1]heap burning coals on his head,
And [a]the LORD will reward you.
23 The north wind brings forth rain,
And a [1a]backbiting tongue, an angry countenance.
24 It is [a]better to live in a corner of the roof
Than [1]in a house shared with a contentious woman.
25 *Like* cold water to a weary soul,
So is [a]good news from a distant land.
26 *Like* a [a]trampled spring and a [1]polluted well
Is a righteous man who gives way before the wicked.
27 It is not good to eat much honey,
Nor is it glory to [a]search out [1]one's own glory.
28 *Like* a [a]city that is broken into *and* without walls
Is a man [b]who has no control over his spirit.

Chapter 26 Theme ____________________

26 Like snow in summer and like [a]rain in harvest,
So honor is not [b]fitting for a fool.
2 Like a [a]sparrow in *its* [1]flitting, like a swallow in *its* flying,
So a [b]curse without cause does not [2]alight.
3 A [a]whip is for the horse, a bridle for the donkey,
And a [b]rod for the back of fools.
4 [a]Do not answer a fool according to his folly,
Or you will also be like him.
5 [a]Answer a fool as his folly *deserves,*
That he not be [b]wise in his own eyes.
6 He cuts off *his own* feet *and* drinks violence
Who sends a message by the hand of a fool.
7 *Like* the legs *which* [1]are useless to the lame,
So is a proverb in the mouth of fools.
8 Like [1]one who binds a stone in a sling,
So is he who gives honor to a fool.
9 *Like* a thorn *which* [1]falls into the hand of a drunkard,
So is a proverb in the mouth of fools.
10 [1]*Like* an archer who wounds everyone,
So is he who hires a fool or who hires those who pass by.

16 [1]Lit *your sufficiency* [a]Judg 14:8; 1 Sam 14:25

17 [1]Lit *surfeited with*

18 [a]Ps 57:4; Prov 12:18 [b]Jer 9:8 [c]Ex 20:16; Prov 24:28

19 [1]Lit *a slipping foot* [a]Job 6:15; Is 36:6

20 [1]I.e. natron [2]Lit *an evil*

21 [1]Lit *one who hates you* [a]Ex 23:4, 5; 2 Kin 6:22; 2 Chr 28:15; Matt 5:44; Rom 12:20

22 [1]Lit *snatch up* [a]2 Sam 16:12; Matt 6:4, 6

23 [1]Lit *tongue of secrecy* [a]Ps 101:5

24 [1]Lit *with a woman of contentions and a house of association* [a]Prov 21:9

25 [a]Prov 15:30

26 [1]Lit *ruined* [a]Ezek 32:2; 34:18, 19

27 [1]Lit *their* [a]Prov 27:2; Luke 14:11

28 [a]Prov 16:32 [b]2 Chr 32:5; Neh 1:3

26:1 [a]1 Sam 12:17 [b]Prov 17:7

2 [1]Lit *wandering* [2]Lit *come* [a]Prov 27:8; Is 16:2 [b]Num 23:8; Deut 23:5; 2 Sam 16:12

3 [a]Ps 32:9 [b]Prov 10:13; 19:29

4 [a]Prov 23:9; 29:9; Is 36:21; Matt 7:6

5 [a]Matt 16:1-4; 21:24-27 [b]Prov 3:7; 28:11; Rom 12:16

7 [1]Lit *hang down from*

8 [1]Lit *the binding of*

9 [1]Lit *goes up*

10 [1]Or *A master* workman *produces all things, But he who hires a fool is* like *one who hires those who pass by*

11 Like [a]a dog that returns to its vomit
Is a fool who [b]repeats [1]his folly.
12 Do you see a man [a]wise in his own eyes?
[b]There is more hope for a fool than for him.
13 The [a]sluggard says, "There is a lion in the road!
A lion is [1]in the open square!"
14 *As* the door turns on its hinges,
So *does* the [a]sluggard on his bed.
15 The [a]sluggard buries his hand in the dish;
He is weary of bringing it to his mouth again.
16 The sluggard is [a]wiser in his own eyes
Than seven men who can [1]give a discreet answer.
17 *Like* one who takes a dog by the ears
Is he who passes by *and* [1]meddles with [a]strife not belonging to him.
18 Like a madman who throws
[a]Firebrands, arrows and death,
19 So is the man who [a]deceives his neighbor,
And says, "[b]Was I not joking?"
20 For lack of wood the fire goes out,
And where there is no [a]whisperer, [b]contention quiets down.
21 *Like* charcoal to hot embers and wood to fire,
So is a [a]contentious man to kindle strife.
22 The [a]words of a whisperer are like dainty morsels,
And they go down into the [1]innermost parts of the body.
23 *Like* an earthen [a]vessel overlaid with silver [b]dross
Are burning lips and a wicked heart.
24 He who [a]hates disguises *it* with his lips,
But he lays up [b]deceit in his [1]heart.
25 When [1]he [a]speaks graciously, do not believe him,
For there are seven abominations in his heart.
26 *Though his* hatred [a]covers itself with guile,
His wickedness will be [b]revealed before the assembly.
27 He who [a]digs a pit will fall into it,
And he who rolls a stone, it will come back on him.
28 A lying tongue hates [1]those it crushes,
And a [a]flattering mouth works ruin.

Chapter 27 Theme ______________________

27 [a]Do not boast about tomorrow,
For you [b]do not know what a day may bring forth.
2 Let [a]another praise you, and not your own mouth;
A stranger, and not your own lips.
3 A stone is heavy and the sand weighty,
But the provocation of a fool is heavier than both of them.
4 Wrath is fierce and anger is a flood,
But [a]who can stand before jealousy?
5 Better is [a]open rebuke
Than love that is concealed.

11 [1]Lit *with his* [a]2 Pet 2:22 [b]Ex 8:15
12 [a]Prov 3:7; 26:5 [b]Prov 29:20
13 [1]Lit *within* [a]Prov 22:13
14 [a]Prov 6:9
15 [a]Prov 19:24
16 [1]Lit *return discreetly* [a]Prov 27:11
17 [1]Lit *infuriates himself* [a]Prov 3:30
18 [a]Is 50:11
19 [a]Prov 24:28 [b]Eph 5:4
20 [a]Prov 16:28 [b]Prov 22:10
21 [a]Prov 15:18; 29:22
22 [1]Lit *chambers of the belly* [a]Prov 18:8
23 [a]Matt 23:27; Luke 11:39 [b]Prov 25:4
24 [1]Lit *inward part* [a]Ps 41:6; Prov 10:18 [b]Prov 12:20
25 [1]Lit *his voice is gracious* [a]Ps 28:3; Prov 26:23; Jer 9:8
26 [a]Matt 23:28 [b]Luke 8:17
27 [a]Esth 7:10; Prov 28:10
28 [1]Lit *its crushed ones* [a]Prov 29:5
27:1 [a]James 4:13-16 [b]Luke 12:19, 20; James 4:14
2 [a]Prov 25:27; 2 Cor 10:12, 18; 12:11
4 [a]Prov 6:34; 1 John 3:12
5 [a]Prov 28:23; Gal 2:14

6 Faithful are the [a]wounds of a friend,
But [1]deceitful are the [b]kisses of an enemy.
7 A sated [1]man [2]loathes honey,
But to a famished [1]man any bitter thing is sweet.
8 Like a [a]bird that wanders from her nest,
So is a man who [b]wanders from his [1]home.
9 [a]Oil and perfume make the heart glad,
So a [1]man's counsel is sweet to his friend.
10 Do not forsake your own [a]friend or [b]your father's friend,
And do not go to your brother's house in the day of your calamity;
Better is a neighbor who is near than a brother far away.
11 [a]Be wise, my son, and make my heart glad,
That I may [b]reply to him who reproaches me.
12 A prudent man sees evil *and* hides himself,
The [1]naive proceed *and* pay the penalty.
13 [a]Take his garment when he becomes surety for a stranger;
And for an [1]adulterous woman hold him in pledge.
14 [a]He who blesses his friend with a loud voice early in the morning,
It will be reckoned a curse to him.
15 A [a]constant dripping on a day of steady rain
And a contentious woman are alike;
16 He who would [1]restrain her [1]restrains the wind,
And [2]grasps oil with his right hand.
17 Iron sharpens iron,
So one man sharpens another.
18 He who tends the [a]fig tree will eat its fruit,
And he who [b]cares for his master will be honored.
19 As in water face *reflects* face,
So the heart of man *reflects* man.
20 [1a]Sheol and [2]Abaddon are [b]never satisfied,
Nor are the [c]eyes of man ever satisfied.
21 The [a]crucible is for silver and the furnace for gold,
And each [b]*is tested* by the praise accorded him.
22 Though you [a]pound a fool in a mortar with a pestle along with crushed grain,
Yet his foolishness will not depart from him.

23 [a]Know well the [1]condition of your flocks,
And pay attention to your herds;
24 For riches are not forever,
Nor does a [a]crown *endure* to all generations.
25 *When* the grass disappears, the new growth is seen,
And the herbs of the mountains are [a]gathered in,
26 The lambs *will be* for your clothing,
And the goats *will bring* the price of a field,
27 And *there will be* goats' milk enough for your food,
For the food of your household,
And sustenance for your maidens.

6 [1]Or *excessive* [a]Ps 141:5; Prov 20:30 [b]Matt 26:49

7 [1]Lit *soul* [2]Lit *tramples on*

8 [1]Lit *place* [a]Prov 26:2; Is 16:2 [b]Gen 21:14

9 [1]Lit *soul's* [a]Ps 23:5; 141:5

10 [a]Prov 18:24 [b]1 Kin 12:6-8; 2 Chr 10:6-8

11 [a]Prov 10:1; 23:15; 29:3 [b]Ps 119:42

12 [1]Lit *simple*

13 [1]Lit *strange* [a]Prov 20:16

14 [a]Ps 12:2

15 [a]Prov 19:13

16 [1]Lit *hide(s)* [2]Lit *encounters*

18 [a]2 Kin 18:31; Song 8:12; Is 36:16; 1 Cor 3:8; 9:7; 2 Tim 2:6 [b]Luke 12:42-44; 19:17

20 [1]I.e. The nether world [2]I.e. the place of destruction [a]Job 26:6; Prov 15:11 [b]Prov 30:15, 16; Hab 2:5 [c]Eccl 1:8; 4:8

21 [a]Prov 17:3 [b]Luke 6:26

22 [a]Prov 23:35; 26:11; Jer 5:3

23 [1]Lit *face* [a]Jer 31:10; Ezek 34:12; John 10:3

24 [a]Job 19:9; Ps 89:39; Jer 13:18; Lam 5:16; Ezek 21:26

25 [a]Is 17:5; Jer 40:10, 12

Chapter 28 Theme ________________________

28 The wicked [a]flee when no one is pursuing,
But the righteous are [1]bold as a lion.
2 By the transgression of a land [a]many are its princes,
But [b]by a man of understanding *and* knowledge, so it
endures.
3 A [a]poor man who oppresses the lowly
Is *like* a driving rain [1]which leaves no food.
4 Those who forsake the law [a]praise the wicked,
But those who keep the law [b]strive with them.
5 Evil men [a]do not understand justice,
But those who seek the LORD [b]understand all things.
6 [a]Better is the poor who walks in his integrity
Than he who is [1]crooked though he be rich.
7 He who keeps the law is a discerning son,
But he who is a companion of [a]gluttons humiliates his
father.
8 He who increases his wealth by [a]interest and usury
Gathers it [b]for him who is gracious to the poor.
9 He who turns away his ear from listening to the law,
Even his [a]prayer is an abomination.
10 He who leads the upright astray in an evil way
Will [a]himself fall into his own pit,
But the [b]blameless will inherit good.
11 The rich man is [a]wise in his own eyes,
But the poor who has understanding [1]sees through him.
12 When the [a]righteous triumph, there is great glory,
But [b]when the wicked rise, men [1]hide themselves.
13 He who [a]conceals his transgressions will not prosper,
But he who [b]confesses and forsakes *them* will find
compassion.
14 How blessed is the man who [a]fears always,
But he who [b]hardens his heart will fall into calamity.
15 *Like* a [a]roaring lion and a rushing bear
Is a [b]wicked ruler over a poor people.
16 A [a]leader who is a great oppressor lacks understanding,
But he who hates unjust gain will prolong *his* days.
17 A man who is [a]laden with the guilt of human blood
Will [1]be a fugitive until death; let no one support him.
18 He who walks blamelessly will be delivered,
But he who is [1a]crooked will fall all at once.
19 [a]He who tills his land will [b]have plenty of food,
But he who follows empty *pursuits* will have poverty in
plenty.
20 A [a]faithful man will abound with blessings,
But he who [b]makes haste to be rich will not go
unpunished.
21 To [1a]show partiality is not good,
[b]Because for a piece of bread a man will transgress.
22 A man with an [a]evil eye [b]hastens after wealth
And does not know that want will come upon him.

28:1 [1]Lit *confident* [a]Lev 26:17, 36; Ps 53:5
2 [a]1 Kin 16:8-28; 2 Kin 15:8-15 [b]Prov 11:11
3 [1]Lit *and there is no bread* [a]Matt 18:28
4 [a]Ps 49:18; Rom 1:32 [b]1 Kin 18:18; Neh 13:11, 15; Matt 3:7; 14:4; Eph 5:11
5 [a]Ps 92:6; Is 6:9; 44:18 [b]Ps 119:100; Prov 2:9; John 7:17; 1 Cor 2:15; 1 John 2:20, 27
6 [1]Lit *perverse of two ways* [a]Prov 19:1
7 [a]Prov 23:20
8 [a]Ex 22:25; Lev 25:36 [b]Job 27:17; Prov 13:22; 14:31
9 [a]Ps 66:18; 109:7; Prov 15:8; 21:27
10 [a]Ps 7:15; Prov 26:27 [b]Matt 6:33; Heb 6:12; 1 Pet 3:9
11 [1]Lit *examines him* [a]Prov 3:7; 26:5, 12
12 [1]Lit *will be searched for* [a]Prov 11:10; 29:2 [b]Prov 28:28; Eccl 10:5, 6
13 [a]Job 31:33; Ps 32:3 [b]Ps 32:5; 1 John 1:9
14 [a]Prov 23:17 [b]Ps 95:8; Rom 2:5
15 [a]Prov 19:12; 1 Pet 5:8 [b]Ex 1:14; Prov 29:2; Matt 2:16
16 [a]Eccl 10:16; Is 3:12
17 [1]Lit *flee to the pit* [a]Gen 9:6; Ex 21:14
18 [1]Lit *perverse of two ways* [a]Prov 10:27
19 [a]Prov 12:11 [b]Prov 20:13
20 [a]Prov 10:6; Matt 24:45; 25:21 [b]Prov 20:21; 28:22; 1 Tim 6:9
21 [1]Lit *regard the face* [a]Prov 24:23 [b]Ezek 13:19
22 [a]Prov 23:6 [b]Prov 21:5

23 He who [a]rebukes a man will afterward find *more* favor
Than he who [b]flatters with the tongue.
24 He who [a]robs his father or his mother
And says, "It is not a transgression,"
Is the [b]companion of a man who destroys.
25 An [1]arrogant man [a]stirs up strife,
But he who [b]trusts in the LORD [c]will [2]prosper.
26 He who [a]trusts in his own heart is a fool,
But he who walks wisely will be delivered.
27 He who [a]gives to the poor will never want,
But he who [1]shuts his eyes will have many curses.
28 When the wicked rise, men hide themselves;
But when they perish, the righteous increase.

Chapter 29 Theme ____________________

29 A man who hardens *his* neck after [a]much reproof
Will [b]suddenly be broken [1]beyond remedy.
2 When the [a]righteous [1]increase, the people rejoice,
But when a wicked man rules, people groan.
3 A man who [a]loves wisdom makes his father glad,
But he who [b]keeps company with harlots wastes *his* wealth.
4 The [a]king gives stability to the land by justice,
But a man who takes bribes overthrows it.
5 A man who [a]flatters his neighbor
Is spreading a net for his steps.
6 By transgression an evil man is [a]ensnared,
But the righteous [b]sings and rejoices.
7 The [a]righteous [1]is concerned for the rights of the poor,
The wicked does not understand *such* [2]concern.
8 Scorners [a]set a city aflame,
But [b]wise men turn away anger.
9 When a wise man has a controversy with a foolish man,
[1]The foolish man either rages or laughs, and there is no rest.
10 Men of [a]bloodshed hate the blameless,
But the upright [1]are concerned for his life.
11 A [a]fool [1]always loses his temper,
But a [b]wise man holds it back.
12 If a [a]ruler pays attention to falsehood,
All his ministers *become* wicked.
13 The [a]poor man and the oppressor [1]have this in common:
The LORD gives [b]light to the eyes of both.
14 If a [a]king judges the poor with truth,
His [b]throne will be established forever.
15 The [a]rod and reproof give wisdom,
But a child [1]who gets his own way [b]brings shame to his mother.
16 When the wicked [1]increase, transgression increases;
But the [a]righteous will see their fall.

23 [a]Prov 27:5, 6 [b]Prov 29:5

24 [a]Prov 19:26 [b]Prov 18:9

25 [1]Lit *broad soul* [2]Lit *be made fat* [a]Prov 15:18 [b]Prov 29:25; 1 Tim 6:6 [c]Prov 11:25

26 [a]Prov 3:5

27 [1]Lit *hides* [a]Prov 11:24; 19:17

29:1 [1]Lit *and there is no remedy* [a]1 Sam 2:25; 2 Chr 36:16; Prov 1:24-31 [b]Prov 6:15

2 [1]Or *become great* [a]Esth 8:15; Prov 11:10; 28:12

3 [a]Prov 10:1; 15:20; 27:11; 28:7 [b]Prov 5:10; 6:26; Luke 15:30

4 [a]2 Chr 9:8; Prov 8:15; 29:14

5 [a]Ps 5:9

6 [a]Prov 22:5; Eccl 9:12 [b]Ex 15:1

7 [1]Lit *knows the cause* [2]Lit *knowledge* [a]Job 29:16; Ps 41:1; Prov 31:8, 9

8 [a]Prov 11:11 [b]Prov 16:14

9 [1]Lit *He*

10 [1]Lit *seek his soul* [a]Gen 4:5-8; 1 John 3:12

11 [1]Lit *sends forth all his spirit* [a]Prov 12:16; 14:33 [b]Prov 19:11

12 [a]1 Kin 12:14

13 [1]Lit *meet together* [a]Prov 22:2 [b]Ezra 9:8; Ps 13:3

14 [a]Ps 72:4; Is 11:4 [b]Prov 16:12; 25:5

15 [1]Lit *left to himself* [a]Prov 13:24; 22:15 [b]Prov 10:1; 17:25

16 [1]Or *become great* [a]Ps 37:34, 36; 58:10; 91:8; 92:11; Prov 21:12

17 [a]Correct your son, and he will give you comfort;
He will also [1b]delight your soul.
18 Where there is [a]no [1]vision, the people [b]are unrestrained,
But [c]happy is he who keeps the law.
19 A slave will not be instructed by words *alone;*
For though he understands, there will be no response.
20 Do you see a man who is [a]hasty in his words?
There is [b]more hope for a fool than for him.
21 He who pampers his slave from childhood
Will in the end find him to be a son.
22 An [a]angry man stirs up strife,
And a hot-tempered man abounds in transgression.
23 A man's [a]pride will bring him low,
But a [b]humble spirit will obtain honor.
24 He who is a partner with a thief hates his own life;
He [a]hears the oath but tells nothing.
25 The [a]fear of man [1]brings a snare,
But he who [b]trusts in the LORD will be exalted.
26 [a]Many seek the ruler's [1]favor,
But [b]justice for man *comes* from the LORD.
27 An [a]unjust man is abominable to the righteous,
And he who is [b]upright in the way is abominable to the wicked.

Chapter 30 Theme ____________________

30 The words of Agur the son of Jakeh, the [1]oracle.
The man declares to Ithiel, to Ithiel and Ucal:
2 Surely I am more [a]stupid than any man,
And I do not have the understanding of a man.
3 Neither have I learned wisdom,
Nor do I have the [a]knowledge of the Holy One.
4 Who has [a]ascended into heaven and descended?
Who has gathered the [b]wind in His fists?
Who has [c]wrapped the waters in [1]His garment?
Who has [d]established all the ends of the earth?
What is His [e]name or His son's name?
Surely you know!

5 Every [a]word of God is tested;
He is a [b]shield to those who take refuge in Him.
6 [a]Do not add to His words
Or He will reprove you, and you will be proved a liar.

7 Two things I asked of You,
Do not refuse me before I die:
8 Keep deception and [1]lies far from me,
Give me neither poverty nor riches;
Feed me with the [a]food that is my portion,
9 That I not be [a]full and deny [b]*You* and say, "Who is the LORD?"

17 [1]Lit *give delight to* [a]Prov 13:24; 29:15 [b]Prov 10:1

18 [1]Or *revelation* [a]1 Sam 3:1; Ps 74:9; Amos 8:11, 12 [b]Ex 32:25 [c]Ps 1:1, 2; 106:3; 119:2; Prov 8:32; John 13:17

20 [a]James 1:19 [b]Prov 26:12

22 [a]Prov 15:18; 26:21

23 [a]Prov 11:2; 16:18; Dan 4:30, 31; Matt 23:12; James 4:6 [b]Prov 15:33; 18:12; 22:4; Is 66:2; Luke 14:11; 18:14; James 4:10

24 [a]Lev 5:1

25 [1]Lit *gives* [a]Gen 12:12; 20:2; Luke 12:4; John 12:42, 43 [b]Ps 91:1-16; Prov 18:10; 28:25

26 [1]Lit *face* [a]Prov 19:6 [b]Is 49:4; 1 Cor 4:4

27 [a]Ps 6:8; 139:21, 22; Prov 12:8 [b]Ps 69:4; Prov 29:10; Matt 10:22; 24:9; John 15:18; 17:14; 1 John 3:13

30:1 [1]Or *burden*

2 [a]Ps 49:10; 73:22; Prov 12:1

3 [a]Prov 9:10

4 [1]Lit *the* [a]Ps 68:18; John 3:13; Eph 4:8 [b]Ex 15:10; Ps 135:7 [c]Job 26:8; 38:8, 9 [d]Ps 24:2; Is 45:18 [e]Rev 19:12

5 [a]Ps 12:6; 18:30 [b]Ps 3:3; 84:11; Prov 2:7

6 [a]Deut 4:2; 12:32; Rev 22:18

8 [1]Lit *words of falsehood* [a]Job 23:12; Matt 6:11

9 [a]Deut 8:12; 31:20; Neh 9:25; Hos 13:6 [b]Josh 24:27; Job 31:28

Or that I not be [c]in want and steal,
And [d]profane the name of my God.

10 Do not slander a slave to his master,
Or he will [a]curse you and you will be found guilty.

11 There is a [1]kind of *man* who [a]curses his father
And does not bless his mother.
12 There is a [1]kind who is [a]pure in his own eyes,
Yet is not washed from his filthiness.
13 There is a [1]kind—oh how [a]lofty are his eyes!
And his eyelids are raised *in arrogance.*
14 There is a [1]kind of *man* whose [a]teeth are *like* swords
And his [b]jaw teeth *like* knives,
To [c]devour the afflicted from the earth
And the needy from among men.

15 The leech has two daughters,
"Give," "Give."
There are three things that will not be satisfied,
Four that will not say, "Enough":
16 [1a]Sheol, and the [b]barren womb,
Earth that is never satisfied with water,
And fire that never says, "Enough."
17 The eye that [a]mocks a father
And [1b]scorns a mother,
The [c]ravens of the valley will pick it out,
And the young [c]eagles will eat it.

18 There are three things which are too wonderful for me,
Four which I do not understand:
19 The way of an [a]eagle in the sky,
The way of a serpent on a rock,
The way of a ship in the middle of the sea,
And the way of a man with a maid.
20 This is the way of an [a]adulterous woman:
She eats and wipes her mouth,
And says, "I have done no wrong."

21 Under three things the earth quakes,
And under four, it cannot bear up:
22 Under a [a]slave when he becomes king,
And a fool when he is satisfied with food,
23 Under an unloved woman when she gets a husband,
And a maidservant when she supplants her mistress.

24 Four things are small on the earth,
But they are exceedingly wise:
25 The [a]ants are not a strong people,
But they prepare their food in the summer;

9 [c]Prov 6:30 [d]Ex 20:7

10 [a]Eccl 7:21

11 [1]Or *generation* [a]Ex 21:17; Prov 20:20

12 [1]Or *generation* [a]Prov 16:2; Is 65:5; Luke 18:11; Titus 1:15, 16

13 [1]Or *generation* [a]Prov 6:17; Is 2:11; 5:15

14 [1]Or *generation* [a]Ps 57:4 [b]Job 29:17 [c]Ps 14:4; Amos 8:4

16 [1]I.e. The nether world [a]Prov 27:20 [b]Gen 30:1

17 [1]Lit *despises to obey* [a]Gen 9:22 [b]Prov 15:20 [c]Deut 28:26

19 [a]Deut 28:49; Jer 48:40; 49:22

20 [a]Prov 5:6

22 [a]Prov 19:10; Eccl 10:7

25 [a]Prov 6:6

26 The [1a]shephanim are not mighty people,
Yet they make their houses in the rocks;
27 The locusts have no king,
Yet all of them go out in [a]ranks;
28 The lizard you may grasp with the hands,
Yet it is in kings' palaces.

29 There are three things which are stately in *their* march,
Even four which are stately when they walk:
30 The lion *which* is [a]mighty among beasts
And does not [1b]retreat before any,
31 The [1]strutting rooster, the male goat also,
And a king *when his* army is with him.

32 If you have been foolish in exalting yourself
Or if you have plotted *evil,* [a]*put your* hand on your mouth.
33 For the [1]churning of milk produces butter,
And pressing the nose brings forth blood;
So the [1]churning of [a]anger produces strife.

Chapter 31 Theme ____________________

31 The words of King Lemuel, the [1]oracle which his mother taught him:
2 What, O my son?
And what, O [a]son of my womb?
And what, O son of my [b]vows?
3 [a]Do not give your strength to women,
Or your ways to that which [b]destroys kings.
4 It is not for [a]kings, O Lemuel,
It is not for kings to [b]drink wine,
Or for rulers to desire strong drink,
5 For they will drink and forget what is decreed,
And [a]pervert the [1]rights of all the [2]afflicted.
6 Give strong drink to him who is [a]perishing,
And wine to him [1b]whose life is bitter.
7 Let him drink and forget his poverty
And remember his trouble no more.
8 [a]Open your mouth for the mute,
For the [1]rights of all the [2]unfortunate.
9 Open your mouth, [a]judge righteously,
And [1]defend the [b]rights of the afflicted and needy.

10 An [a]excellent wife, who can find?
For her worth is far [b]above jewels.
11 The heart of her husband trusts in her,
And he will have no lack of gain.
12 She does him good and not evil
All the days of her life.

26 [1]Small, shy, furry animals *(Hyrax syriacus)* found in the peninsula of the Sinai, northern Israel, and the region round the Dead Sea; KJV *coney,* orig NASB *badgers* [a]Lev 11:5; Ps 104:18
27 [a]Joel 2:7
30 [1]Lit *turn back* [a]Judg 14:18; 2 Sam 1:23 [b]Mic 5:8
31 [1]Lit *girt in the loins*
32 [a]Job 21:5; 40:4; Mic 7:16
33 [1]Lit *pressing* [a]Prov 10:12; 29:22
31:1 [1]Or *burden*
2 [a]Is 49:15 [b]1 Sam 1:11
3 [a]Prov 5:9 [b]Deut 17:17; 1 Kin 11:1; Neh 13:26
4 [a]Eccl 10:17 [b]Prov 20:1; Is 5:22; Hos 4:11
5 [1]Lit *judgment* [2]Lit *sons of affliction* [a]Ex 23:6; Deut 16:19; Prov 17:15
6 [1]Lit *bitter of soul* [a]Job 29:13 [b]Job 3:20; Is 38:15
8 [1]Lit *judgment* [2]Lit *sons of passing away* [a]Job 29:12-17; Ps 82
9 [1]Lit *judge the afflicted* [a]Lev 19:15; Deut 1:16 [b]Is 1:17; Jer 22:16
10 [a]Ruth 3:11; Prov 12:4; 19:14 [b]Job 28:18; Prov 8:11

13 She looks for wool and flax
And works with her [1]hands [2]in delight.
14 She is like [a]merchant ships;
She brings her food from afar.
15 She [a]rises also while it is still night
And [b]gives food to her household
And [1]portions to her maidens.
16 She considers a field and buys it;
From [1]her earnings she plants a vineyard.
17 She [a]girds [1]herself with strength
And makes her arms strong.
18 She senses that her gain is good;
Her lamp does not go out at night.
19 She stretches out her hands to the distaff,
And her [1]hands grasp the spindle.
20 She [1a]extends her hand to the poor,
And she stretches out her hands to the needy.
21 She is not afraid of the snow for her household,
For all her household are [a]clothed with scarlet.
22 She makes [a]coverings for herself;
Her clothing is [b]fine linen and [c]purple.
23 Her husband is known [a]in the gates,
When he sits among the elders of the land.
24 She makes [a]linen garments and sells *them,*
And [1]supplies belts to the [2]tradesmen.
25 Strength and [a]dignity are her clothing,
And she smiles at the [1]future.
26 She [a]opens her mouth in wisdom,
And the [1]teaching of kindness is on her tongue.
27 She looks well to the ways of her household,
And does not eat the [a]bread of idleness.
28 Her children rise up and bless her;
Her husband *also,* and he praises her, *saying:*
29 "Many daughters have done nobly,
But you excel them all."
30 Charm is deceitful and beauty is vain,
But a woman who [1a]fears the LORD, she shall be praised.
31 Give her the [1]product of her hands,
And let her works praise her in the gates.

13 [1]Lit *palms* [2]Or *willingly*

14 [a]Ezek 27:25

15 [1]Or *prescribed tasks* [a]Prov 20:13; Rom 12:11 [b]Luke 12:42

16 [1]Lit *the fruit of her palms*

17 [1]Lit *her loins* [a]1 Kin 18:46; 2 Kin 4:29; Job 38:3

19 [1]Lit *palms*

20 [1]Lit *spreads out her palm* [a]Deut 15:11; Job 31:16-20; Prov 22:9; Rom 12:13; Eph 4:28

21 [a]2 Sam 1:24

22 [a]Prov 7:16 [b]Gen 41:42; Rev 19:8, 14 [c]Judg 8:26; Luke 16:19

23 [a]Deut 16:18; Ruth 4:1, 11

24 [1]Lit *gives* [2]Lit *Canaanite* [a]Judg 14:12

25 [1]Lit *latter days* [a]1 Tim 2:9, 10

26 [1]Or *law* [a]Prov 10:31

27 [a]Prov 19:15

30 [1]Or *reverences* [a]Ps 112:1; Prov 22:4

31 [1]Lit *fruit*

Theme of Proverbs:

SEGMENT DIVISIONS

	MAIN DIVISIONS		CHAPTER THEMES
	THE CRY OF WISDOM, KNOWLEDGE, AND UNDERSTANDING	1	
		2	
		3	
		4	
		5	
		6	
		7	
		8	
		9	
	THE PROVERBS OF SOLOMON AND WISDOM OF WISE MEN	10	
		11	
		12	
		13	
		14	
		15	
		16	
		17	
		18	
		19	
		20	
		21	
		22	
		23	
		24	
	SOLOMON'S PROVERBS TRANSCRIBED	25	
		26	
		27	
		28	
		29	
	WORDS & COUNSEL OF OTHERS	30	
		31	

Author:

Date:

Purpose:

Key Words:

my son

wisdom (wise)

knowledge

understanding

fear

commandment(s)

instruction

tongue

fool (folly)

righteous

evil

wicked

ECCLESIASTES קוהלת QOHELET

*L*ife seems inconsistent, unpredictable, and unfair at times. Regardless of the generation, regardless of the time in history, the righteous and the wicked have the same experiences, face the same trials, grapple with the same problems—and all end up in the grave!

As people grow older they look back and see that life is but a breath, a vapor. It passes so quickly. What is its purpose? Have we sought after the right things? Have we lived as we should?

"What advantage does man have in all his work which he does under the sun?" (Ecclesiastes 1:3). And what is the conclusion of it all? Ecclesiastes not only asks questions, it also points toward the answers.

Things to Do

General Instructions

1. A careful observation of Ecclesiastes gives insight into why this book is included in the Bible. So as you begin your study of this book, do the following:
   a. Remember that all you read must be considered in the context of the whole counsel of God.
   b. Read 1:1-3 and 12:13-14 to see how Ecclesiastes begins and ends. Keep these verses in mind as you study.

2. As you read Ecclesiastes, mark every reference to the author in a distinctive way:
   a. Who and/or what he is; how he describes himself; what he pursued, had, or experienced, and what gain it was to him. This is important. You may want to list your insights in your notebook as you go through Ecclesiastes.
   b. As you read the book, observe what the author has seen, come to know, commends, and concludes. Mark or note these insights in a special way, since these usually include important key repeated phrases.
   c. After chapter 4, mark or list in the margin the author's commands and warnings. For example, in 5:1 he tells us to guard our steps when we go into the house of God.

3. As you read each chapter, mark in a distinctive way the key words listed on the ECCLESIASTES AT A GLANCE chart on page 1077. List these key words on an index card that you can use as a bookmark while observing this book.

4. When you finish observing each chapter:
   a. Look at every reference to God that you marked in the text. In your notebook, list all you learn about Him, what He does, and what we are to do in respect to Him.
   b. Mark the contrasting groups of people: the righteous and the wicked, the wise and the foolish. In your notebook, list what you learn about these persons from each chapter.
   c. Also make a list of what you learn about *riches (wealth)* and *labor*.
   d. When you have completed your study of the book, you may want to summarize in your notebook what you learned from compiling the above lists.

5. Record the theme of each chapter on ECCLESIASTES AT A GLANCE and in your Bible.

Chapters 1–8: Exploring Life's Inconsistencies

1. As you read, mark the key words listed on ECCLESIASTES AT A GLANCE. Also watch for and mark these words: *explore (explored), discover (discovered),* and *directed.*

2. The words *vanity, futile,* and *futility* are all from the Hebrew word *hebel,* which means "vapor" or "breath."

   a. *Hebel* appears more in Ecclesiastes than in any other book of the Bible; half of all its occurrences are in Ecclesiastes.

   b. Except for 11:8 and 12:8, all the occurrences of *vanity* and *futility* appear in this first segment of Ecclesiastes. Therefore after you finish marking in a distinctive way each occurrence of these words, you might want to record in your notebook everything you learn from the text about vanity and futility. Remember that although they are translated two different ways, they are the same Hebrew word.

Chapters 9–12: Explaining Life's Inconsistencies

1. Read 9:1 and mark the word *explain.* Do you see how this verse might be used as a pivotal point in the book? If so, watch for any explanations the author might give to life's inconsistencies.

2. When you finish observing chapter 10, review each reference to wisdom that you have marked and summarize everything you learned about wisdom from Ecclesiastes.

3. As you read 12:1-7, think of the human body and the effects of age on its members. See if you find any "pictorial descriptions" of the body and what happens as you get old (e.g., "the grinding ones which are few" might be a picture of losing some teeth).

4. Complete ECCLESIASTES AT A GLANCE.

Things to Think About

1. Where have you been searching for the meaning of life? Reflect on what you've been pursuing in order to find fulfillment or happiness. Has it worked?

2. According to God, where can the meaning of life be found? Where can't it be found?

3. The author of Ecclesiastes is Solomon, David's son, who was the richest and wisest of men. What can you learn from his experience that can help you?

4. Review all you have learned about God from this book. Since God is going to bring every act to judgment, even those of Christians (2 Corinthians 5:10; Romans 14:10), what are you doing that you should continue to do and what do you need to stop doing? Will you?

Chapter 1 Theme ______________________

1 The words of the [a]Preacher, the son of David, king in Jerusalem.
2 "[1a]Vanity of vanities," says the Preacher,
"[1]Vanity of vanities! All is [2]vanity."

3 [a]What advantage does man have in all his work
Which he does under the sun?
4 A generation goes and a generation comes,
But the [a]earth [1]remains forever.
5 Also, [a]the sun rises and the sun sets;
And [1]hastening to its place it rises there *again.*

1:1 [a]Eccl 1:12; 7:27; 12:8-10

2 [1]Or *Futility of futilities* [2]Or *futile* [a]Ps 39:5, 6; 62:9; 144:4; Eccl 12:8; Rom 8:20

3 [a]Eccl 2:11; 3:9; 5:16

4 [1]Lit *stands* [a]Ps 104:5; 119:90

5 [1]Lit *panting* [a]Ps 19:6

6 [1a]Blowing toward the south,
Then turning toward the north,
The wind continues [2]swirling along;
And on its circular courses the wind returns.
7 All the rivers [1]flow into the sea,
Yet the sea is not full.
To the place where the rivers [1]flow,
There they [1]flow again.
8 All things are wearisome;
Man is not able to tell *it.*
[a]The eye is not satisfied with seeing,
Nor is the ear filled with hearing.
9 [a]That which has been is that which will be,
And that which has been done is that which will be done.
So there is nothing new under the sun.
10 Is there anything of which one might say,
"See this, it is new"?
Already it has existed for ages
Which were before us.
11 There is [a]no remembrance of [1]earlier things;
And also of the [2]later things which will occur,
There will be for them no remembrance
Among those who will come [2]later *still.*
12 I, the [a]Preacher, have been king over Israel in Jerusalem.
13 And I [a]set my [1]mind to seek and [b]explore by wisdom
concerning all that has been done under heaven. *It* is [2]a grievous
[c]task *which* God has given to the sons of men to be afflicted with.
14 I have seen all the works which have been done under the
sun, and behold, all is [1a]vanity and striving after wind.
15 What is [a]crooked cannot be straightened and what is lacking
cannot be counted.
16 I [1]said to myself, "Behold, I have magnified and increased
[a]wisdom more than all who were over Jerusalem before me; and
my [2]mind has observed [3]a wealth of wisdom and knowledge."
17 And I [a]set my [1]mind to know wisdom and to [b]know madness
and folly; I realized that this also is [c]striving after wind.
18 Because [a]in much wisdom there is much grief, and increasing
knowledge *results in* increasing pain.

Chapter 2 Theme ________________________________

2 I said [1]to myself, "Come now, I will test you with [a]plea-
sure. So [2]enjoy yourself." And behold, it too was futility.
2 [a]I said of laughter, "It is madness," and of pleasure, "What
does it accomplish?"
3 I explored with my [1]mind *how* to [a]stimulate my body with
wine while my [1]mind was guiding *me* wisely, and how to take
hold of [b]folly, until I could see [c]what good there is for the sons
of men [2]to do under heaven the few [3]years of their lives.
4 I enlarged my works: I [a]built houses for myself, I planted
[b]vineyards for myself;

6 [1]Lit *Going* [2]Lit *turning* [a]Eccl 11:5; John 3:8
7 [1]Lit *go*
8 [a]Prov 27:20; Eccl 4:8
9 [a]Eccl 1:10; 2:12; 3:15; 6:10
11 [1]Lit *first* or *former* [2]Lit *latter* or *after* [a]Eccl 2:16; 9:5
12 [a]Eccl 1:1; 7:27; 12:8-10
13 [1]Lit *heart* [2]Lit *an evil* [a]Eccl 1:17 [b]Eccl 3:10, 11; 7:25; 8:17 [c]Eccl 2:23, 26; 3:10; 4:8
14 [1]Or *futility* [a]Eccl 2:11, 17; 4:4; 6:9
15 [a]Eccl 7:13
16 [1]Lit *spoke with my heart, saying* [2]Lit *heart* [3]Lit *an abundance* [a]1 Kin 3:12; 4:30; 10:23; Eccl 2:9
17 [1]Lit *heart* [a]Eccl 1:13; 7:25 [b]Eccl 2:12; 7:25 [c]Eccl 1:14; 2:11, 17; 4:4, 6, 16; 6:9
18 [a]Eccl 2:23; 12:12
2:1 [1]Lit *in my heart* [2]Lit *consider with goodness* [a]Eccl 7:4; 8:15
2 [a]Prov 14:13; Eccl 7:3, 6
3 [1]Lit *heart* [2]Lit *which they do* [3]Lit *days* [a]Judg 9:13; Ps 104:15; Eccl 10:19 [b]Eccl 7:25 [c]Eccl 2:24; 3:12, 13; 5:18; 6:12; 8:15; 12:13
4 [a]1 Kin 7:1-12 [b]Song 8:11

5 I made [a]gardens and [b]parks for myself and I planted in
them all kinds of fruit trees;
6 I made [a]ponds of water for myself from which to irrigate a
forest of growing trees.
7 I bought male and female slaves and I had [1a]homeborn
slaves. Also I possessed flocks and [b]herds larger than all who
preceded me in Jerusalem.
8 Also, I collected for myself silver and [a]gold and the treasure
of kings and provinces. I provided for myself [b]male and female
singers and the pleasures of men—many concubines.
9 Then I became [a]great and increased more than all who
preceded me in Jerusalem. My wisdom also stood by me.
10 [a]All that my eyes desired I did not refuse them. I did not
withhold my heart from any pleasure, for my heart was pleased
because of all my labor and this was my [b]reward for all my labor.
11 Thus I considered all my activities which my hands had
done and the labor which I had [1]exerted, and behold all was
[2a]vanity and striving after wind and there was [b]no profit under
the sun.
12 So I turned to [a]consider wisdom, madness and folly; for what
will the man *do* who will come after the king *except* [b]what has
already been done?
13 And I saw that [a]wisdom excels folly as light excels darkness.
14 The wise man's eyes are in his head, but the [a]fool walks in
darkness. And yet I know that [b]one fate befalls them both.
15 Then I said [1]to myself, "[a]As is the fate of the fool, it will
also befall me. [b]Why then have I been extremely wise?" So [2]I
said to myself, "This too is vanity."
16 For there is [a]no [1]lasting remembrance of the wise man *as*
with the fool, inasmuch as *in* the coming days all will be
forgotten. And [b]how the wise man and the fool alike die!
17 So I [a]hated life, for the work which had been done under
the sun was [1]grievous to me; because everything is futility and
striving after wind.
18 Thus I hated [a]all the fruit of my labor for which I had
labored under the sun, for I must [b]leave it to the man who will
come after me.
19 And who knows whether he will be a wise man or [a]a fool?
Yet he will have [1]control over all the fruit of my labor for which
I have labored by acting wisely under the sun. This too is
[b]vanity.
20 Therefore I [1]completely despaired of all the fruit of my labor
for which I had labored under the sun.
21 When there is a man who has labored with wisdom,
knowledge and [a]skill, then he [b]gives his [1]legacy to one who has
not labored with them. This too is vanity and a great evil.
22 For what does a man get in [a]all his labor and in [1]his
striving with which he labors under the sun?
23 Because all his days his task is painful and [a]grievous; even
at night his [1]mind [b]does not rest. This too is vanity.
24 There is [a]nothing better for a man *than* to eat and drink

5 [a]Song 4:16; 5:1 [b]Neh 2:8
6 [a]Neh 2:14; 3:15, 16
7 [1]Lit *sons of the house* [a]Gen 14:14; 15:3 [b]1 Kin 4:23
8 [a]1 Kin 9:28; 10:10, 14, 21 [b]2 Sam 19:35
9 [a]1 Chr 29:25; Eccl 1:16
10 [a]Eccl 6:2 [b]Eccl 3:22; 5:18; 9:9
11 [1]Lit *labored to do* [2]Or *futility,* and so throughout the ch [a]Eccl 1:14; 2:22, 23 [b]Eccl 1:3; 3:9; 5:16
12 [a]Eccl 1:17 [b]Eccl 1:9, 10; 3:15
13 [a]Eccl 7:11, 12, 19; 9:18; 10:10
14 [a]1 John 2:11 [b]Ps 49:10; Eccl 3:19; 6:6; 7:2; 9:2, 3
15 [1]Lit *in my heart* [2]Lit *I spoke in my heart* [a]Eccl 2:16 [b]Eccl 6:8, 11
16 [1]Lit *forever* [a]Eccl 1:11; 9:5 [b]Eccl 2:14
17 [1]Lit *evil* [a]Eccl 4:2, 3
18 [a]Eccl 1:3; 2:11 [b]Ps 39:6; 49:10
19 [1]Lit *dominion* [a]1 Kin 12:13 [b]1 Tim 6:10
20 [1]Lit *turned aside my heart to despair*
21 [1]Lit *share* [a]Eccl 4:4 [b]Eccl 2:18
22 [1]Lit *the striving of his heart* [a]Eccl 1:3; 2:11
23 [1]Lit *heart* [a]Job 5:7; 14:1; Eccl 1:18; 5:17 [b]Ps 127:2
24 [a]Eccl 2:3; 3:12, 13, 22; 5:18; 6:12; 8:15; 9:7; Is 56:12; Luke 12:19; 1 Cor 15:32; 1 Tim 6:17

and [1]tell himself that his labor is good. This also I have seen
that it is [b]from the hand of God.
25 For who can eat and who can have enjoyment without [1]Him?
26 For to a person who is good in His sight [a]He has given
wisdom and knowledge and joy, while to the sinner He has
given the task of gathering and collecting so that he may [b]give
to one who is good in God's sight. This too is [c]vanity and
striving after wind.

Chapter 3 Theme ______________________

3 There is an appointed time for everything. And there is a
[a]time for every [1]event under heaven—
2 A time to give birth and a [a]time to die;
A time to plant and a time to uproot what is planted.
3 A [a]time to kill and a time to heal;
A time to tear down and a time to build up.
4 A time to [a]weep and a time to [b]laugh;
A time to mourn and a time to [c]dance.
5 A time to throw stones and a time to gather stones;
A time to embrace and a time to shun embracing.
6 A time to search and a time to give up as lost;
A time to keep and a time to throw away.
7 A time to tear apart and a time to sew together;
A time to [a]be silent and a time to speak.
8 A time to love and a time to [a]hate;
A time for war and a time for peace.
9 [a]What profit is there to the worker from that in which he
toils?
10 I have seen the [a]task which God has given the sons of men
with which to occupy themselves.
11 He has [a]made everything [1]appropriate in its time. He has also
set eternity in their heart, [2]yet so that man [b]will not find out the
work which God has done from the beginning even to the end.
12 I know that there is [a]nothing better for them than to
rejoice and to do good in one's lifetime;
13 moreover, that every man who eats and drinks sees good in
all his labor—it is the [a]gift of God.
14 I know that everything God does will remain forever; there
is nothing to add to it and there is nothing to take from it, for
God has *so* worked that men should [1a]fear Him.
15 That [a]which is has been already and that which will be has
already been, for God seeks what has passed by.
16 Furthermore, I have seen under the sun *that* in the place of
justice there is [a]wickedness and in the place of righteousness
there is wickedness.
17 I said [1]to myself, "[a]God will judge both the righteous man
and the wicked man," for a [b]time for every [2]matter and for
every deed is there.
18 I said [1]to myself concerning the sons of men, "God has surely
tested them in order for them to see that they are but [a]beasts."

24 [1]Lit *cause his soul to see good in his labor* [b]Eccl 3:13
25 [1]So Gr; Heb *me*
26 [a]Job 32:8; Prov 2:6 [b]Job 27:16, 17; Prov 13:22 [c]Eccl 1:14
3:1 [1]Lit *delight* [a]Eccl 3:17; 8:6
2 [a]Job 14:5; Heb 9:27
3 [a]Gen 9:6; 1 Sam 2:6; Hos 6:1, 2
4 [a]Rom 12:15 [b]Ps 126:2 [c]Ex 15:20
7 [a]Amos 5:13
8 [a]Ps 101:3; Prov 13:5
9 [a]Eccl 1:3; 2:11; 5:16
10 [a]Eccl 1:13; 2:26
11 [1]Lit *beautiful* [2]Or *without which man* [a]Gen 1:31 [b]Job 5:9; Eccl 7:23; 8:17; Rom 11:33
12 [a]Eccl 2:24
13 [a]Eccl 2:24; 5:19
14 [1]Or *be in awe before Him* [a]Eccl 5:7; 7:18; 8:12, 13; 12:13
15 [a]Eccl 1:9; 6:10
16 [a]Eccl 4:1; 5:8; 8:9
17 [1]Lit *in my heart* [2]Or *delight* [a]Gen 18:25; Ps 96:13; 98:9; Eccl 11:9; Matt 16:27; Rom 2:6-10; 2 Thess 1:6-9 [b]Eccl 3:1; 8:6
18 [1]Lit *in my heart* [a]Ps 49:12, 20; 73:22

19 [a]For the fate of the sons of men and the fate of beasts [1]is
the same. As one dies so dies the other; indeed, they all have
the same breath and there is no advantage for man over beast,
for all is [2]vanity.
20 All go to the same place. All came from the [a]dust and all
return to the dust.
21 Who knows that the [a]breath of man ascends upward and
the breath of the beast descends downward to the earth?
22 I have seen that [a]nothing is better than that man should be
happy in his activities, for that is his lot. For who will bring
him to see [b]what will occur after him?

Chapter 4 Theme ______________________

4 Then I looked again at all the acts of [a]oppression which
were being done under the sun. And behold *I saw* the tears
of the oppressed and *that* they had [b]no one to comfort *them;*
and on the side of their oppressors was power, but they had no
one to comfort *them.*
2 So [a]I congratulated the dead who are already dead more
than the living who are still living.
3 But [a]better *off* than both of them is the one who has never
existed, who has never seen the evil activity that is done under
the sun.
4 I have seen that every labor and every [a]skill which is done
is *the result of* rivalry between a man and his neighbor. This
too is [1b]vanity and striving after wind.
5 The fool [a]folds his hands and [b]consumes his own flesh.
6 One hand full of rest is [a]better than two fists full of labor
and striving after wind.
7 Then I looked again at vanity under the sun.
8 There was a certain man without a [1]dependent, having
neither a son nor a brother, yet there was no end to all his labor.
Indeed, [a]his eyes were not satisfied with riches *and he never
asked,* "And [b]for whom am I laboring and depriving myself of
pleasure?" This too is vanity and it is a [c]grievous task.
9 Two are better than one because they have a good return
for their labor.
10 For if [1]either of them falls, the one will lift up his companion.
But woe to the one who falls when there is not [2]another to lift
him up.
11 Furthermore, if two lie down together they [1]keep warm,
but [a]how can one be warm *alone?*
12 And if [1]one can overpower him who is alone, two can
resist him. A cord of three *strands* is not quickly torn apart.
13 A [a]poor yet wise lad is better than an old and foolish king
who no longer knows *how* to receive [1]instruction.
14 For he has come [a]out of prison to become king, even
though he was born poor in his kingdom.
15 I have seen all the living under the sun throng to the side
of the second lad who [1]replaces him.

19 [1]Lit *and they have one fate* [2]Or *futility* [a]Ps 49:12; Eccl 9:12

20 [a]Gen 3:19; Ps 103:14; Eccl 12:7

21 [a]Eccl 12:7

22 [a]Eccl 2:24 [b]Eccl 2:18; 6:12; 8:7; 10:14

4:1 [a]Job 35:9; Ps 12:5; Eccl 3:16; 5:8; Is 5:7 [b]Jer 16:7; Lam 1:9

2 [a]Job 3:11-26; Eccl 2:17; 7:1

3 [a]Job 3:11-22; Eccl 6:3; Luke 23:29

4 [1]Or *futility,* and so throughout the ch [a]Eccl 2:21 [b]Eccl 1:14

5 [a]Prov 6:10; 24:33 [b]Is 9:20

6 [a]Prov 15:16, 17; 16:8

8 [1]Lit *second* [a]Prov 27:20; Eccl 1:8; 5:10 [b]Eccl 2:21 [c]Eccl 1:13

10 [1]Lit *they fall* [2]Lit *a second*

11 [1]Lit *have warmth* [a]1 Kin 1:1-4

12 [1]Lit *he*

13 [1]Or *warning* [a]Eccl 7:19; 9:15

14 [a]Gen 41:14, 41-43

15 [1]Lit *stands in his stead*

16 There is no end to all the people, to all who were before
them, and even the ones who will come later will not be happy
with him, for this too is [a]vanity and striving after wind.

Chapter 5 Theme ______________________________

5 [1a]Guard your steps as you go to the house of God and draw
near to listen rather than to offer the [b]sacrifice of fools; for
they do not know they are doing evil.
2 [1]Do not be [a]hasty [2]in word or [3]impulsive in thought to
bring up a matter in the presence of God. For God is in heaven
and you are on the earth; therefore let your [b]words be few.
3 For the dream comes through much [1]effort and the voice of
a [a]fool through many words.
4 When you [a]make a vow to God, do not be late in paying it;
for *He takes* no delight in fools. [b]Pay what you vow!
5 It is [a]better that you should not vow than that you should
vow and not pay.
6 Do not let your [1]speech cause [2]you to sin and do not say in
the presence of the messenger *of God* that it was a [a]mistake.
Why should God be angry on account of your voice and destroy
the work of your hands?
7 For in many dreams and in many words there is [1]emptiness.
Rather, [2a]fear God.
8 If you see [a]oppression of the poor and [b]denial of justice and
righteousness in the province, do not be [c]shocked at the [1]sight;
for one [2]official watches over another [2]official, and there are
higher [3]officials over them.
9 After all, a king who cultivates the field is an advantage to
the land.
10 [a]He who loves money will not be satisfied with money, nor
he who loves abundance *with its* income. This too is [1]vanity.
11 [a]When good things increase, those who consume them
increase. So what is the advantage to their owners except to
[1]look on?
12 The sleep of the working man is [a]pleasant, whether he eats
little or much; but the [1]full stomach of the rich man does not
allow him to sleep.
13 There is a grievous evil *which* I have seen under the sun:
[a]riches being [1]hoarded by their owner to his hurt.
14 When those riches were lost through [1]a bad investment
and he had fathered a son, then there was nothing [2]to support
him.
15 [a]As he had come naked from his mother's womb, so will
he return as he came. He will [b]take nothing from the fruit of
his labor that he can carry in his hand.
16 This also is a grievous evil—exactly as a man [1]is born, thus
will he [2]die. So [a]what is the advantage to him who [b]toils for the
wind?
17 Throughout his life [a]*he* also eats in darkness with [b]great
vexation, sickness and anger.

16 [a]Eccl 1:14
5:1 [1]Ch 4:17 in Heb [a]Ex 3:5; 30:18-20; Is 1:12 [b]1 Sam 15:22; Prov 15:8; 21:27
2 [1]Ch 5:1 in Heb [2]Lit *with your mouth* [3]Lit *hurry your heart* [a]Prov 20:25 [b]Prov 10:19; Matt 6:7
3 [1]Lit *task* [a]Job 11:2; Prov 15:2; Eccl 10:14
4 [a]Num 30:2; Ps 50:14; 76:11 [b]Ps 66:13, 14
5 [a]Prov 20:25; Acts 5:4
6 [1]Lit *mouth* [2]Lit *your body* [a]Lev 4:2, 22; Num 15:25
7 [1]Lit *vanity* [2]Or *revere* [a]Eccl 3:14; 7:18; 8:12, 13; 12:13
8 [1]Lit *delight* [2]Lit *high one* [3]Lit *ones* [a]Eccl 4:1 [b]Ezek 18:18 [c]1 Pet 4:12
10 [1]Or *futility* [a]Eccl 1:8; 2:10, 11; 4:8
11 [1]Lit *see with their eyes* [a]Eccl 2:9
12 [1]Lit *satiety* [a]Prov 3:24
13 [1]Lit *guarded* [a]Eccl 6:2
14 [1]Lit *an evil task* [2]Lit *in his hand*
15 [a]Job 1:21 [b]Ps 49:17; 1 Tim 6:7
16 [1]Lit *comes* [2]Lit *go* [a]Eccl 1:3; 2:11; 3:9 [b]Prov 11:29
17 [a]Ps 127:2 [b]Eccl 2:23

18 Here is what I have seen to be [a]good and [1]fitting: to eat, to
drink and [2]enjoy oneself in all one's labor in which he toils
under the sun *during* the few [3]years of his life which God has
given him; for this is his [4b]reward.
19 Furthermore, as for every man to whom [a]God has given
riches and wealth, He has also [b]empowered him to eat from
them and to receive his [1]reward and rejoice in his labor; this is
the [c]gift of God.
20 For he will not often [1]consider the [2]years of his life, because
[a]God keeps [3]him occupied with the gladness of his heart.

Chapter 6 Theme ______________________________

6 There is an [a]evil which I have seen under the sun and it is
prevalent [1]among men—
2 a man to whom God has [a]given riches and wealth and
honor so that his soul [b]lacks nothing of all that he desires; yet
God has not empowered him to eat from them, for a foreigner
[1]enjoys them. This is [2]vanity and a severe affliction.
3 If a man fathers a hundred *children* and lives many years,
however many [1]they be, but his soul is not satisfied with good
things and he does not even have a *proper* [a]burial, *then* I say,
"Better [b]the miscarriage than he,
4 for it comes in futility and goes into obscurity; and its name
is covered in obscurity.
5 "It never sees the sun and it never knows *anything;* [1]it is
better off than he.
6 "Even if the *other* man lives a thousand years twice and
does not [1]enjoy good things—[a]do not all go to one place?"
7 [a]All a man's labor is for his mouth and yet the [1]appetite is
not [2]satisfied.
8 For [a]what advantage does the wise man have over the fool?
What *advantage* does the poor man have, knowing *how* to
walk before the living?
9 What the eyes [a]see is better than what the soul [1]desires.
This too is [b]futility and a striving after wind.
10 Whatever [a]exists has already been named, and it is known
what man is; for he [b]cannot dispute with him who is stronger
than he is.
11 For there are many words which increase futility. What
then is the advantage to a man?
12 For who knows what is good for a man during *his* lifetime,
during the few [1]years of his futile life? He will [2]spend them like
a shadow. For who can tell a man [a]what will be after him under
the sun?

Chapter 7 Theme ______________________________

7 A [a]good name is better than a good ointment,
And the [b]day of *one's* death is better than the day of
one's birth.

18 [1]Lit *beautiful* [2]Lit *see good* [3]Or *days* [4]Or *share* [a]Eccl 2:24 [b]Eccl 2:10

19 [1]Or *share* [a]2 Chr 1:12; Eccl 6:2 [b]Eccl 6:2 [c]Eccl 3:13

20 [1]Lit *remember* [2]Or *days* [3]So with Gr [a]Ex 23:25

6:1 [1]Lit *upon* [a]Eccl 5:13

2 [1]Lit *eats from them* [2]Or *futility* [a]1 Kin 3:13 [b]Ps 17:14; 73:7; Eccl 2:10

3 [1]Lit *the days of his years* [a]Is 14:20; Jer 8:2; 22:19 [b]Job 3:16; Eccl 4:3

5 [1]Lit *more rest has this one than that*

6 [1]Lit *see* [a]Eccl 2:14

7 [1]Lit *soul* [2]Lit *filled* [a]Prov 16:26

8 [a]Eccl 2:15

9 [1]Lit *goes after* [a]Eccl 11:9 [b]Eccl 1:14

10 [a]Eccl 1:9; 3:15 [b]Job 9:32; 40:2; Prov 21:30; Is 45:9

12 [1]Lit *days* [2]Lit *do* [a]Eccl 3:22

7:1 [a]Prov 22:1 [b]Eccl 4:2; 7:8

2 It is better to go to a house of mourning
Than to go to a house of feasting,
Because [1]that is the [a]end of every man,
And the living [2b]takes *it* to [3]heart.
3 [a]Sorrow is better than laughter,
For [b]when a face is sad a heart may be happy.
4 The [1]mind of the wise is in the house of mourning,
While the [1]mind of fools is in the house of pleasure.
5 It is better to [a]listen to the rebuke of a wise man
Than for one to listen to the song of fools.
6 For as the [1]crackling of [a]thorn bushes under a pot,
So is the [b]laughter of the fool;
And this too is futility.
7 For [a]oppression makes a wise man mad,
And a [b]bribe [1]corrupts the heart.
8 The [a]end of a matter is better than its beginning;
[b]Patience of spirit is better than haughtiness of spirit.
9 Do not be [1a]eager in your heart to be angry,
For anger resides in the bosom of fools.
10 Do not say, "Why is it that the former days were better
than these?"
For it is not from wisdom that you ask about this.
11 Wisdom along with an inheritance is good
And an [a]advantage to those who see the sun.
12 For [a]wisdom is [1]protection *just as* money is [1]protection,
But the advantage of knowledge is that [b]wisdom preserves
the lives of its possessors.
13 Consider the [a]work of God,
For who is [b]able to straighten what He has bent?
14 [a]In the day of prosperity be happy,
But [b]in the day of adversity consider—
God has made the one as well as the other
So that man will [c]not discover anything *that will be* after him.
15 I have seen everything during my [1a]lifetime of futility; there
is [b]a righteous man who perishes in his righteousness and
there is [c]a wicked man who prolongs *his life* in his wickedness.
16 Do not be excessively [a]righteous and do not [b]be overly
wise. Why should you ruin yourself?
17 Do not be excessively wicked and do not be a fool. Why
should you [a]die before your time?
18 It is good that you grasp one thing and also not [1]let go of
the other; for the one who [a]fears God comes forth with [2]both
of them.
19 [a]Wisdom strengthens a wise man more than ten rulers who
are in a city.
20 Indeed, [a]there is not a righteous man on earth who
continually does good and who never sins.
21 Also, do not [1]take seriously all words which are spoken, so
that you will not hear your servant [a]cursing you.
22 For [1]you also have realized that you likewise have many
times cursed others.

2 [1]I.e. death [2]Lit *gives* [3]Lit *his heart* [a]Eccl 2:14, 16; 3:19, 20; 6:6; 9:2, 3 [b]Ps 90:12
3 [a]Eccl 2:2 [b]2 Cor 7:10
4 [1]Lit *heart*
5 [a]Ps 141:5; Prov 6:23; 13:18; 15:31, 32; 25:12; Eccl 9:17
6 [1]Lit *voice* [a]Ps 58:9; 118:12 [b]Eccl 2:2
7 [1]Lit *destroys* [a]Eccl 4:1; 5:8 [b]Ex 23:8; Deut 16:19; Prov 17:8, 23
8 [a]Eccl 7:1 [b]Prov 14:29; 16:32; Gal 5:22; Eph 4:2
9 [1]Lit *hasty in your spirit* [a]Prov 14:17; James 1:19
11 [a]Prov 8:10, 11; Eccl 2:13
12 [1]Lit *in a shadow* [a]Eccl 7:19; 9:18 [b]Prov 3:18; 8:35
13 [a]Eccl 3:11; 8:17 [b]Eccl 1:15
14 [a]Deut 26:11; Eccl 3:22; 9:7; 11:9 [b]Deut 8:5; Job 2:10 [c]Eccl 3:22
15 [1]Lit *days* [a]Eccl 6:12; 9:9 [b]Eccl 8:14 [c]Eccl 8:12, 13
16 [a]Prov 25:16; Phil 3:6 [b]Rom 12:3
17 [a]Job 22:16; Ps 55:23; Prov 10:27
18 [1]Lit *rest your hand* [2]Lit *all* [a]Eccl 3:14; 5:7; 8:12, 13; 12:13
19 [a]Eccl 7:12; 9:13-18
20 [a]1 Kin 8:46; 2 Chr 6:36; Ps 143:2; Prov 20:9; Rom 3:23
21 [1]Lit *give your heart to* [a]Prov 30:10
22 [1]Lit *your heart knows also*

23 I tested all this with wisdom, *and* I said, "I will be wise,"
[a]but it was far from me.
24 What has been is remote and [a]exceedingly [1]mysterious.
[b]Who can discover it?
25 I [1a]directed my [2]mind to know, to investigate and to seek
wisdom and an explanation, and to know the evil of folly and
the foolishness of madness.
26 And I discovered more [a]bitter than death the woman
whose heart is [b]snares and nets, whose hands are chains. [c]One
who is pleasing to God will escape from her, but [d]the sinner
will be captured by her.
27 "Behold, I have discovered this," says the Preacher, "*adding*
one thing to another to find an explanation,
28 which [1]I am still seeking but have not found. I have found
one man among a thousand, but I have not found a [a]woman
among all these.
29 "Behold, I have found only this, that [a]God made men upright,
but they have sought out many devices."

Chapter 8 Theme ______________________________

8 Who is like the wise man and who knows the interpretation
of a matter? A man's wisdom [a]illumines [1]him and causes
his [b]stern face to [2]beam.
2 I say, "Keep the [1]command of the king because of the [a]oath
[2]before God.
3 "Do not be in a hurry [1a]to leave him. Do not join in an evil
matter, for he will do whatever he pleases."
4 Since the word of the king is authoritative, [a]who will say to
him, "What are you doing?"
5 He who [a]keeps a *royal* command [b]experiences no [1]trouble,
for a wise heart knows the proper time and procedure.
6 For [a]there is a proper time and procedure for every delight,
though a man's trouble is heavy upon him.
7 If no one [a]knows what will happen, who can tell him when
it will happen?
8 [a]No man has authority to restrain the wind with the wind,
or authority over the day of death; and there is no discharge in
the time of war, and [b]evil will not deliver [1]those who practice it.
9 All this I have seen and applied my [1]mind to every deed
that has been done under the sun wherein a man has exercised
[a]authority over *another* man to his hurt.
10 So then, I have seen the wicked buried, those who used to
go in and out from the holy place, and they are [a]*soon* forgotten
in the city where they did thus. This too is futility.
11 Because the [a]sentence against an evil deed is not executed
quickly, therefore [b]the hearts of the sons of men among them
are given fully to do evil.
12 Although a sinner does evil a hundred *times* and may
[a]lengthen his *life,* still I know that it will be [b]well for those who
fear God, who fear [1]Him openly.

23 [a]Eccl 3:11; 8:17

24 [1]Lit *deep* [a]Rom 11:33 [b]Job 11:7; 37:23; Eccl 8:17

25 [1]Lit *turned about* [2]Lit *heart* [a]Eccl 1:15, 17; 10:13

26 [a]Prov 5:4 [b]Prov 7:23 [c]Prov 6:23, 24 [d]Prov 22:14

28 [1]Lit *my soul still seeks* [a]1 Kin 11:3

29 [a]Gen 1:27

8:1 [1]Lit *his face* [2]Or *change* [a]Ex 34:29, 30 [b]Deut 28:50

2 [1]Lit *mouth* [2]Lit *of* [a]Ex 22:11; 2 Sam 21:7; Ezek 17:18

3 [1]Lit *to go out from his presence* [a]Eccl 10:4

4 [a]Job 9:12; Dan 4:35

5 [1]Lit *evil thing* [a]Eccl 12:13 [b]Prov 12:21

6 [a]Eccl 3:1, 17

7 [a]Eccl 3:22; 6:12; 7:14; 9:12

8 [1]Lit *its possessors* [a]Ps 49:7 [b]Eccl 8:13

9 [1]Lit *heart* [a]Eccl 4:1; 5:8; 7:7

10 [a]Eccl 1:11; 2:16; 9:5, 15

11 [a]Ex 34:6; Ps 86:15; Rom 2:4; 2 Pet 3:9 [b]Eccl 9:3

12 [1]Lit *before Him* [a]Eccl 7:15 [b]Deut 4:40; 12:25; Ps 37:11; Prov 1:33; Is 3:10

13 But it will [a]not be well for the evil man and he will not lengthen his days like a [b]shadow, because he does not fear God.

13 [a]Eccl 8:8; Is 3:11 [b]Job 14:2; Eccl 6:12

14 There is futility which is done on the earth, that is, there are [a]righteous men to whom it [1]happens according to the deeds of the wicked. On the other hand, there are [b]evil men to whom it [1]happens according to the deeds of the righteous. I say that this too is futility.

14 [1]Lit *strikes* [a]Ps 73:14; Eccl 7:15 [b]Job 21:7; Ps 73:3, 12; Jer 12:1; Mal 3:15

15 So I commended pleasure, for there is nothing good for [a]a man under the sun except to eat and to drink and to be merry, and this will stand by him in his [1]toils *throughout* the days of his life which God has given him under the sun.

15 [1]Lit *labor* [a]Eccl 2:24; 3:12, 13; 5:18; 9:7

16 When I [a]gave my heart to know wisdom and to see the task which has been done on the earth (even though one should [1b]never sleep day or night),

16 [1]Lit *see no sleep in his eyes* [a]Eccl 1:13, 14 [b]Eccl 2:23

17 and I saw every work of God, *I concluded* that [a]man cannot discover the work which has been done under the sun. Even though man should seek laboriously, he will not discover; and [b]though the wise man should say, "I know," he cannot discover.

17 [a]Eccl 3:11 [b]Ps 73:16; Eccl 7:23; Rom 11:33

Chapter 9 Theme ______________________________

9 For I have taken all this to my heart and explain [1]it that righteous men, wise men, and their deeds are [a]in the hand of God. [b]Man does not know whether *it will be* [c]love or hatred; anything [2]awaits him.

9:1 [1]Lit *all this* [2]Lit *is before them* [a]Deut 33:3; Job 12:10; Ps 119:109 [b]Eccl 10:14 [c]Eccl 9:6

RETURN TO INSTRUCTIONS

2 [a]It is the same for all. There is [b]one fate for the righteous and for the wicked; for the good, for the clean and for the unclean; for the man who offers a sacrifice and for the one who does not sacrifice. As the good man is, so is the sinner; as the swearer is, so is the one who [1]is afraid to swear.

2 [1]Lit *fears an oath* [a]Job 9:22; Eccl 9:11 [b]Eccl 2:14; 3:19; 6:6; 7:2

3 This is an evil in all that is done under the sun, that there is [a]one fate for all men. Furthermore, [b]the hearts of the sons of men are full of evil and [c]insanity is in their hearts throughout their lives. Afterwards they *go* to the dead.

3 [a]Eccl 9:2; Jer 17:10 [b]Eccl 8:11 [c]Eccl 1:17

4 For whoever is joined with all the living, there is hope; surely a live dog is better than a dead lion.

5 For the living know they will die; but the dead [a]do not know anything, nor have they any longer a reward, for their [b]memory is forgotten.

5 [a]Job 14:21 [b]Ps 88:12; Eccl 1:11; 2:16; 8:10; Is 26:14

6 Indeed their love, their hate and their zeal have already perished, and they will no longer have a [a]share in all that is done under the sun.

6 [a]Eccl 2:10; 3:22

7 Go *then,* [a]eat your bread in happiness and drink your wine with a cheerful heart; for God has already approved your works.

7 [a]Eccl 2:24; 8:15

8 Let your [a]clothes be white all the time, and let not [b]oil be lacking on your head.

8 [a]Rev 3:4 [b]Ps 23:5

9 Enjoy life with the woman whom you love all the days of your [1a]fleeting life which He has given to you under the sun[2]; for this is your [b]reward in life and in your toil in which you have labored under the sun.

9 [1]Lit *life of vanity* [2]Heb adds *all the days of your vanity* [a]Eccl 6:12; 7:15 [b]Eccl 2:10

10 Whatever your hand finds to do, [a]do *it* with *all* your might;
for there is no [b]activity or planning or knowledge or wisdom in
[c]Sheol where you are going.
11 I again saw under the sun that the [a]race is not to the swift
and the [b]battle is not to the warriors, and neither is bread to
the wise nor [c]wealth to the discerning nor favor to men of
ability; for time and [d]chance overtake them all.
12 Moreover, man does not [a]know his time: like fish caught in a
treacherous net and [b]birds trapped in a snare, so the sons of men
are [c]ensnared at an evil time when it [d]suddenly falls on them.
13 Also this I came to see as wisdom under the sun, and [1]it
impressed me.
14 There [a]was a small city with few men in it and a great king
came to it, surrounded it and constructed large siegeworks
against it.
15 But there was found in it a [a]poor wise man and he [1]delivered
the city [b]by his wisdom. Yet [c]no one remembered that poor man.
16 So I said, "[a]Wisdom is better than strength." But the wisdom
of the poor man is despised and his words are not heeded.
17 The [a]words of the wise heard in quietness are *better* than
the shouting of a ruler among fools.
18 [a]Wisdom is better than weapons of war, but [b]one sinner
destroys much good.

Chapter 10 Theme ______________________

10 Dead flies make a [a]perfumer's oil stink, so a little foolishness is weightier than wisdom *and* honor.
2 A wise man's heart *directs him* toward the right, but the
foolish [a]man's heart *directs him* toward the left.
3 Even when the fool walks along the road, his [1]sense is
lacking and he [2a]demonstrates to everyone *that* he is a fool.
4 If the ruler's [1]temper rises against you, [a]do not abandon
your position, because [b]composure allays great offenses.
5 There is an evil I have seen under the sun, like an error
which goes forth from the ruler—
6 [a]folly is set in many exalted places while rich men sit in
humble places.
7 I have seen [a]slaves *riding* [b]on horses and princes walking
like slaves on the land.
8 [a]He who digs a pit may fall into it, and a [b]serpent may bite
him who breaks through a wall.
9 He who quarries stones may be hurt by them, and he who
splits logs may be endangered by them.
10 If the [1]axe is dull and he does not sharpen *its* edge, then he
must [2]exert more strength. Wisdom has the advantage of
giving success.
11 If the serpent bites [1a]before being charmed, there is no
profit for the charmer.
12 [a]Words from the mouth of a wise man are gracious, while
the lips of a [b]fool consume him;

10 [a]Eccl 11:6; Rom 12:11; Col 3:23 [b]Eccl 9:5 [c]Gen 37:35; Job 21:13; Is 38:10
11 [a]Amos 2:14, 15 [b]2 Chr 20:15; Ps 76:5; Zech 4:6 [c]Deut 8:17, 18 [d]1 Sam 6:9
12 [a]Eccl 8:7 [b]Prov 7:23 [c]Prov 29:6; Is 24:18; Hos 9:8 [d]Luke 21:34, 35
13 [1]Lit *great it was to me*
14 [a]2 Sam 20:16-22
15 [1]Or *might have delivered* [a]Eccl 4:13 [b]2 Sam 20:22 [c]Eccl 2:16; 8:10
16 [a]Prov 21:22; Eccl 7:12, 19
17 [a]Eccl 7:5; 10:12
18 [a]Eccl 9:16 [b]Josh 7:1-26; 2 Kin 21:2-17
10:1 [a]Ex 30:25
2 [a]Matt 6:33; Col 3:1
3 [1]Lit *heart* [2]Lit *says* [a]Prov 13:16; 18:2
4 [1]Lit *spirit* [a]Eccl 8:3 [b]1 Sam 25:24-33; Prov 25:15
6 [a]Esth 3:1, 5f; Prov 28:12; 29:2
7 [a]Prov 19:10 [b]Esth 6:8-10
8 [a]Ps 7:15; Prov 26:27 [b]Amos 5:19
10 [1]Lit *iron* [2]Lit *strengthen*
11 [1]Lit *without enchantment* [a]Ps 58:4, 5; Jer 8:17
12 [a]Prov 10:32; 22:11; Luke 4:22 [b]Prov 10:14; 18:7; Eccl 4:5

13 the beginning of [1]his talking is folly and the end of [2]it is
wicked [a]madness.
14 Yet the [a]fool multiplies words. No man knows what will
happen, and who can tell him [b]what will come after him?
15 The toil of [1]a fool *so* wearies him that he does not *even*
know how to go to a city.
16 Woe to you, O land, whose [a]king is a lad and whose
princes [1]feast in the morning.
17 Blessed are you, O land, whose king is of nobility and
whose princes eat at the appropriate time—for strength and
not for [a]drunkenness.
18 Through [a]indolence the rafters sag, and through slackness
the house leaks.
19 *Men* prepare a meal for enjoyment, and [a]wine makes life
merry, and [b]money [1]is the answer to everything.
20 Furthermore, [a]in your bedchamber do not [b]curse a king,
and in your sleeping rooms do not curse a rich man, for a bird
of the heavens will carry the sound and the winged creature
will make the matter known.

Chapter 11 Theme ______________________

11 [a]Cast your bread on the surface of the waters, for you
[a]will find it [1]after many days.
2 [a]Divide your portion to seven, or even to eight, for you do
not know what [b]misfortune may occur on the earth.
3 If the clouds are full, they pour out rain upon the earth;
and whether a tree falls toward the south or toward the north,
wherever the tree falls, there it [1]lies.
4 He who watches the wind will not sow and he who looks
at the clouds will not reap.
5 Just as you do not [a]know [1]the path of the wind and [b]how
bones *are formed* in the womb of the [2]pregnant woman, so you
do not [c]know the activity of God who makes all things.
6 Sow your seed [a]in the morning and do not [1]be idle in the
evening, for you do not know whether [2]morning or evening
sowing will succeed, or whether both of them alike will be
good.
7 The light is pleasant, and *it is* good for the eyes to [a]see the
sun.
8 Indeed, if a man should live many years, let him [a]rejoice in
them all, and let him remember the [b]days of darkness, for they
will be many. Everything that is to come *will be* futility.
9 Rejoice, young man, during your childhood, and let your
heart be pleasant during the days of young manhood. And
follow the [1]impulses of your heart and the [2a]desires of your
eyes. Yet know that [b]God will bring you to judgment for all
these things.
10 So, remove grief and anger from your heart and put away
[1a]pain from your body, because childhood and the prime of life
are fleeting.

13 [1]Lit *the words of his mouth* [2]Lit *his mouth* [a]Eccl 7:25
14 [a]Prov 15:2; Eccl 5:3 [b]Eccl 3:22; 6:12; 7:14; 8:7
15 [1]Lit *fools*
16 [1]Lit *eat* [a]Is 3:4, 12
17 [a]Prov 31:4; Is 5:11
18 [a]Prov 24:30-34
19 [1]Lit *answers all* [a]Judg 9:13; Ps 104:15; Eccl 2:3 [b]Eccl 7:12
20 [a]2 Kin 6:12; Luke 12:3 [b]Ex 22:28; Acts 23:5
11:1 [1]Lit *in, within* [a]Deut 15:10; Prov 19:17; Matt 10:42; Gal 6:9; Heb 6:10
2 [a]Ps 112:9; Matt 5:42; Luke 6:30; 1 Tim 6:18, 19 [b]Eccl 11:8; 12:1
3 [1]Lit *is*
5 [1]Or with many mss *how the spirit enters the bones in the womb* [2]Lit *full* [a]John 3:8 [b]Ps 139:13-16 [c]Eccl 1:13; 3:10, 11; 8:17
6 [1]Lit *let down your hand* [2]Lit *this or that* [a]Eccl 9:10
7 [a]Eccl 6:5; 7:11
8 [a]Eccl 9:7 [b]Eccl 12:1
9 [1]Lit *ways* [2]Lit *sights* [a]Num 15:39; Job 31:7; Eccl 2:10 [b]Eccl 3:17; 12:14; Rom 14:10
10 [1]Lit *evil* [a]2 Cor 7:1; 2 Tim 2:22

Chapter 12 Theme ______________________________

12 [a]Remember also your Creator in the days of your youth,
before the [b]evil days come and the years draw near
when you will say, "I have no delight in them";
2 before the [a]sun and the light, the moon and the stars are
darkened, and clouds return after the rain;
3 in the day that the watchmen of the house tremble, and
mighty men [a]stoop, the grinding ones stand idle because they
are few, and [b]those who look through [1]windows grow dim;
4 and the doors on the street are shut as the [a]sound of the
grinding mill is low, and one will arise at the sound of the bird,
and all the [b]daughters of song will [1]sing softly.
5 Furthermore, [1]men are afraid of a high place and of terrors
on the road; the almond tree blossoms, the grasshopper drags
himself along, and the caperberry is ineffective. For man goes
to his eternal [a]home while [b]mourners go about in the street.
6 *Remember Him* before the silver cord is [1]broken and the
[a]golden bowl is crushed, the pitcher by the well is shattered
and the wheel at the cistern is crushed;
7 then the [a]dust will return to the earth as it was, and the
[1b]spirit will return to [c]God who gave it.
8 "[a]Vanity of vanities," says the Preacher, "all is vanity!"
9 In addition to being a wise man, the Preacher also taught
the people knowledge; and he pondered, searched out and
arranged [a]many proverbs.
10 The Preacher sought to find [a]delightful words and to write
[b]words of truth correctly.
11 The [a]words of wise men are like [b]goads, and masters of
these collections are like [1]well-driven [c]nails; they are given by
one Shepherd.
12 But beyond this, my son, be warned: the [1]writing of [a]many
books is endless, and excessive [b]devotion *to books* is wearying
to the body.
13 The conclusion, when all has been heard, *is:* [a]fear God and
[b]keep His commandments, because this *applies to* [c]every person.
14 For [a]God will bring every act to judgment, everything which
is hidden, whether it is good or evil.

12:1 [a]Deut 8:18; Neh 4:14; Ps 63:6; 119:55 [b]Eccl 11:8
2 [a]Is 5:30; 13:10; Ezek 32:7, 8; Joel 3:15; Matt 24:29
3 [1]Or *holes* [a]Ps 35:14; 38:6 [b]Gen 27:1; 48:10; 1 Sam 3:2
4 [1]Lit *be brought low* [a]Jer 25:10; Rev 18:22 [b]2 Sam 19:35
5 [1]Lit *they* [a]Job 17:13; 30:23 [b]Gen 50:10; Jer 9:17
6 [1]So with Gr; Heb *removed* [a]Zech 4:2, 3
7 [1]Or *breath* [a]Gen 3:19; Job 34:15; Ps 104:29; Eccl 3:20 [b]Job 34:14; Eccl 3:21; Luke 23:46; Acts 7:59 [c]Num 16:22; 27:16; Is 57:16; Zech 12:1
8 [a]Eccl 1:2
9 [a]1 Kin 4:32
10 [a]Prov 10:32 [b]Prov 22:20, 21
11 [1]Lit *planted* [a]Prov 1:6; 22:17; Eccl 7:5; 10:12 [b]Acts 2:37 [c]Ezra 9:8; Is 22:23
12 [1]Lit *making* [a]1 Kin 4:32 [b]Eccl 1:18
13 [a]Eccl 3:14; 5:7; 7:18; 8:12 [b]Deut 4:2; Eccl 8:5 [c]Deut 10:12; Mic 6:8
14 [a]Eccl 3:17; 11:9; Matt 10:26; Rom 2:16; 1 Cor 4:5

Ecclesiastes at a Glance

Theme of Ecclesiastes:

Author:

Date:

Purpose:

Key Words:

God

vanity
(futile, futility)

under the sun
(under heaven)

wisdom

righteous
(righteousness)

wicked
(wickedness)

wise

fool

evil

labor (labored)

riches (wealth)

Segment Divisions		Chapter Themes
		1
		2
		3
		4
		5
		6
		7
		8
		9
		10
		11
		12

SONG OF SOLOMON שִׁיר הַשִּׁירִים
SHIR HASHIRI

Song of Solomon is a love story included in the canon of Scripture. On the eighth day of Passover the Jews would sing portions of the Song of Solomon, a book they compared to the most holy place in the temple.

Song of Solomon is a book never quoted by our Lord, but one from which many Christians sing, "I am my Beloved's, and He is mine" and "His banner over me is love."

Many waters cannot quench love,
    Nor will rivers overflow it;
If a man were to give all the riches of his house for love,
    It would be utterly despised (8:7).

Things to Do

1. The Song of Solomon is a unified lyrical poem composed of a variety of songs. There is no other book like it in Scripture. Before you begin to analyze its content, sit down and read it through slowly without stopping. Remember, the phrases may seem different or unusual because of the culture of the Eastern people.

2. As you read Song of Solomon, notice who is speaking when. The reference notes of the NASB identify who speaks. If you prefer to identify the speaker yourself, do the following:

   a. Read the book again and mark every time the woman (bride) speaks and also when the man (bridegroom) speaks. Watch for the pronouns *he* and *she* and mark them in distinctive colors.

   b. As you read, you will notice there is a third party referred to in the text as "the daughters of Jerusalem" and in the reference notes in the margin as "Chorus." Note when "the daughters of Jerusalem" (the chorus) intervenes. When you see any other parties speaking, mark these as well. Note these under "Segment Divisions" on the SONG OF SOLOMON AT A GLANCE chart on page 1088.

3. Now read through the Song of Solomon again. This time do the following:

   a. As you read, mark the key words listed on SONG OF SOLOMON AT A GLANCE.

   b. Watch for details about the bride and the bridegroom—their position, family, how they met, where they met, etc. A careful reading of the book as a whole can help you piece together these facts. You might want to write your observations on a piece of paper and then transfer them to the margin of the text.

   c. Watch for other segment divisions in the book. For instance, note when the courtship ends, when the wedding takes place, and what occurs in the marriage and why. (Watch for the word *wedding*.) Record these divisions on SONG OF SOLOMON AT A GLANCE.

   d. Record the theme of each chapter on SONG OF SOLOMON AT A GLANCE and then in your Bible. Complete the chart.

Things to Think About

1. There are many different interpretations in respect to the meaning of this book. Does Song of Solomon speak only about the emotional and physical relationship of love and marriage? Or does it symbolize something such as Israel's relationship to God, or the

church's relationship to Jesus, their heavenly bridegroom, or the individual's devotion to Christ? If it goes beyond the natural to the spiritual, what would you see that you might apply to your relationship with the Lord Jesus Christ?

2. If this book speaks merely of the physical and emotional bonds of marriage, what do you learn from it that you might apply to your relationship with your mate? Think about the way the bride and bridegroom communicated with each other, what they shared, what their physical relationship was like, what caused problems, and how they solved them.

3. What can you learn from Song of Solomon that would help you prepare for marriage? For instance, what can you learn from this book about understanding yourself, your future mate, and the importance of intimacy, purity, and physical oneness?

4. What do you think an adulterous relationship would do to the intimacy between the bride and the bridegroom? James 4:4 tells us that when we become friends with the world (the world system) we are committing spiritual adultery. What does this do to our intimacy with God? Read 2 Corinthians 11:2-3 and think about it.

Chapter 1 Theme ______________________________

1 The [1]Song of [a]Songs, which is Solomon's.
2 "[1]May he kiss me with the kisses of his mouth!
For your [a]love is better than wine.
3 "Your [a]oils have a pleasing fragrance,
Your [b]name is *like* [1]purified oil;
Therefore the [2c]maidens love you.
4 "Draw me after you *and* let us run *together!*
The [a]king has brought me into his chambers."

"[1]**W**e will rejoice in you and be glad;
We will [2]extol your [b]love more than wine.
Rightly do they love you."

5 "[1]I am black but [a]lovely,
O [b]daughters of Jerusalem,
Like the [c]tents of [d]Kedar,
Like the curtains of Solomon.
6 "Do not stare at me because I am [1]swarthy,
For the sun has burned me.
My [a]mother's sons were angry with me;
They made me [b]caretaker of the vineyards,
But I have not taken care of my own vineyard.
7 "Tell me, O you [a]whom my soul loves,
Where do you [b]pasture *your flock,*
Where do you make *it* [c]lie down at noon?
For why should I be like one who [1]veils herself
Beside the flocks of your [d]companions?"

8 "[1]If you yourself do not know,
[a]Most beautiful among women,
Go forth on the trail of the flock

1:1 [1]Or *Best of the Songs* [a]1 Kin 4:32
2 [1]BRIDE [a]Song 1:4; 4:10
3 [1]Lit *oil which is emptied* (from one vessel to another) [2]Or *virgins* [a]Song 4:10; John 12:3 [b]Eccl 7:1 [c]Ps 45:14
4 [1]CHORUS [2]Lit *mention with praise* [a]Ps 45:14, 15 [b]Song 1:4; 4:10
5 [1]BRIDE [a]Song 2:14; 4:3; 6:4 [b]Song 2:7; 3:5, 10; 5:8, 16; 8:4 [c]Ps 120:5 [d]Is 60:7
6 [1]Or *black* [a]Ps 69:8 [b]Song 8:11
7 [1]Some versions read *wanders* [a]Song 3:1-4 [b]Song 2:16; 6:3 [c]Is 13:20; Jer 33:12 [d]Song 8:13
8 [1]BRIDEGROOM [a]Song 5:9; 6:1

And pasture your young goats
By the tents of the shepherds.

9 "[1]To me, [a]my darling, you are like
My [b]mare among the chariots of Pharaoh.
10 "Your [a]cheeks are lovely with ornaments,
Your neck with strings of [b]beads."

11 "[1]We will make for you ornaments of gold
With beads of silver."

12 "[1]While the king was at his [2]table,
My [3a]perfume gave forth its fragrance.
13 "My beloved is to me a pouch of [a]myrrh
Which lies all night between my breasts.
14 "My beloved is to me a cluster of [a]henna blossoms
In the vineyards of [b]Engedi."

15 "[1,2a]How beautiful you are, my darling,
[2]How beautiful you are!
Your [b]eyes are *like* doves."

16 "[1,2]How handsome you are, [a]my beloved,
And so pleasant!
Indeed, our couch is luxuriant!
17 "The beams of our houses are [a]cedars,
Our rafters, [1b]cypresses.

Chapter 2 Theme ______________________________

2 "[1]I am the [2a]rose of [b]Sharon,
The [c]lily of the valleys."

2 "[1]Like a lily among the thorns,
So is [a]my darling among the [2]maidens."

3 "[1]Like an [2a]apple tree among the trees of the forest,
So is my beloved among the [3]young men.
In his shade I took great delight and sat down,
And his [b]fruit was sweet to my [4]taste.
4 "He has [a]brought me to *his* [1]banquet hall,
And his [b]banner over me is love.
5 "Sustain me with [a]raisin cakes,
Refresh me with [1b]apples,
Because [c]I am lovesick.
6 "Let [a]his left hand be under my head
And [a]his right hand [b]embrace me."

7 "[1]I [a]adjure you, O [b]daughters of Jerusalem,
By the [c]gazelles or by the [d]hinds of the field,
[a]That you do not arouse or awaken *my* love
Until [2]she pleases."

9 [1]Lit *I have compared you to* [a]Song 1:15; 2:2, 10, 13 [b]2 Chr 1:16, 17

10 [a]Song 5:13 [b]Gen 24:53; Is 61:10

11 [1]CHORUS

12 [1]BRIDE [2]Or *couch* [3]Lit *nard* [a]Song 4:14; Mark 14:3; John 12:3

13 [a]Ps 45:8; John 19:39

14 [a]Song 4:13 [b]1 Sam 23:29

15 [1]BRIDEGROOM [2]Lit *Behold* [a]Song 1:16; 2:10, 13; 4:1, 7; 6:4, 10 [b]Song 4:1; 5:12

16 [1]BRIDE [2]Lit *Behold* [a]Song 2:3, 9, 17; 5:2, 5, 6, 8

17 [1]Or *junipers* [a]1 Kin 6:9, 10; Jer 22:14 [b]2 Chr 3:5

2:1 [1]BRIDE [2]Lit *crocus* [a]Is 35:1 [b]Is 33:9; 35:2 [c]Song 5:13; 7:2; Hos 14:5

2 [1]BRIDEGROOM [2]Lit *daughters* [a]Song 1:9

3 [1]BRIDE [2]Or *apricot* [3]Lit *sons* [4]Lit *palate* [a]Song 8:5 [b]Song 4:13, 16; 8:11, 12

4 [1]Lit *house of wine* [a]Song 1:4 [b]Ps 20:5

5 [1]Or *apricots* [a]2 Sam 6:19; 1 Chr 16:3; Hos 3:1 [b]Song 7:8 [c]Song 5:8

6 [a]Song 8:3 [b]Prov 4:8

7 [1]BRIDEGROOM [2]Or *it* [a]Song 3:5; 5:8, 9; 8:4 [b]Song 1:5 [c]Prov 6:5; Song 2:9, 17; 3:5; 8:14 [d]Gen 49:21; Ps 18:33; Hab 3:19

8 “[1]Listen! My beloved!
Behold, he is coming,
Climbing [a]on the mountains,
Leaping on the hills!
9 “My beloved is like a [a]gazelle or a [b]young [1]stag.
Behold, he is standing behind our wall,
He is looking through the windows,
He is peering [c]through the lattice.

10 “My beloved responded and said to me,
‘[a]Arise, my darling, my beautiful one,
And come along.
11 ‘For behold, the winter is past,
The rain is over *and* gone.
12 ‘The flowers have *already* appeared in the land;
The time has arrived for [1]pruning *the vines,*
And the voice of the [a]turtledove has been heard in
our land.
13 ‘The [a]fig tree has ripened its figs,
And the [b]vines in blossom have given forth
their fragrance.
Arise, my darling, my beautiful one,
And come along!’”

14 “[1]O [a]my dove, [b]in the clefts of the [2]rock,
In the secret place of the steep [3]pathway,
Let me see your [4]form,
[c]Let me hear your voice;
For your voice is sweet,
And your [4]form is [d]lovely.”

15 “[1][a]Catch the foxes for us,
The [2]little foxes that are ruining the vineyards,
While our [b]vineyards are in blossom.”

16 “[1][a]My beloved is mine, and I am his;
He [b]pastures *his flock* among the lilies.
17 “[a]Until [1]the cool of the day when the shadows flee away,
Turn, my beloved, and be like a [b]gazelle
Or a young stag [c]on the mountains of [2]Bether.”

Chapter 3 Theme ____________________

3 “[1]On my bed night after night I sought him
[a]Whom my soul loves;
I [b]sought him but did not find him.
2 ‘[1]I must arise now and [1]go about the city;
In the [a]streets and in the squares
[2]I must seek him whom my soul loves.’
I sought him but did not find him.
3 “[a]The watchmen who make the rounds in the city found me,
And I said, ‘Have you seen him whom my soul loves?’

8 [1]BRIDE [a]Song 2:17; Is 52:7
9 [1]Lit *of the stags* [a]Prov 6:5; Song 2:17; 3:5; 8:14 [b]Song 2:17; 8:14 [c]Judg 5:28
10 [a]Song 2:13
12 [1]Or *singing* [a]Gen 15:9; Ps 74:19; Jer 8:7
13 [a]Matt 24:32 [b]Song 7:12
14 [1]BRIDEGROOM [2]Or *crag* [3]Or *cliff* [4]Lit *appearance* [a]Song 5:2; 6:9 [b]Jer 48:28 [c]Song 8:13 [d]Song 1:5
15 [1]CHORUS [2]Or *young* [a]Ezek 13:4; Luke 13:32 [b]Song 2:13
16 [1]BRIDE [a]Song 6:3; 7:10 [b]Song 4:5; 6:2, 3
17 [1]Lit *the day blows* [2]Or *cleavage* or *a kind of spice* [a]Song 4:6 [b]Song 2:9 [c]Song 2:8
3:1 [1]BRIDE [a]Song 1:7 [b]Song 5:6
2 [1]Or *Let me arise* [2]Or *Let me seek* [a]Jer 5:1
3 [a]Song 5:7; Is 21:6-8, 11, 12

4 "[a]Scarcely had I [1]left them
When I found him whom my soul loves;
I [b]held on to him and would not let him go
Until I had [c]brought him to my mother's house,
And into the room of her who conceived me."

5 "[1]I [a]adjure you, O daughters of Jerusalem,
By the [b]gazelles or by the hinds of the field,
That you will not arouse or awaken *my* love
Until [2]she pleases."

6 "[1,2a]What is this coming up from the wilderness
Like [b]columns of smoke,
Perfumed with [c]myrrh and [d]frankincense,
With all scented powders of the merchant?
7 "Behold, it is the *traveling* couch of Solomon;
Sixty mighty men around it,
Of the mighty men of Israel.
8 "All of them are wielders of the sword,
[a]Expert in war;
Each man has his [b]sword at his side,
Guarding against the [1c]terrors of the night.
9 "King Solomon has made for himself a sedan chair
From the timber of Lebanon.
10 "He made its posts of silver,
Its [1]back of gold
And its seat of purple fabric,
With its interior lovingly fitted out
By the [a]daughters of Jerusalem.
11 "Go forth, O [a]daughters of Zion,
And gaze on King Solomon with the [1]crown
With which his mother has crowned him
On the [b]day of his wedding,
And on the day of his gladness of heart."

Chapter 4 Theme ____________________

4 "[1,2]How beautiful [a]you are, my darling,
[2]How beautiful you are!
Your [b]eyes are *like* doves [c]behind your veil;
Your [d]hair is like a flock of goats
That have descended from Mount [e]Gilead.
2 "Your [a]teeth are like a flock of *newly* shorn ewes
Which have come up from *their* washing,
All of which bear twins,
And not one among them has [1]lost her young.
3 "Your lips are like a [a]scarlet thread,
And your [b]mouth is lovely.
Your [c]temples are like a slice of a pomegranate
Behind your veil.
4 "Your [a]neck is like the tower of David,
Built [1]with rows of stones

4 [1]Lit *passed* [a]Prov 8:17 [b]Prov 4:13; Rom 8:35, 39 [c]Song 8:2

5 [1]BRIDEGROOM [2]Or *it* [a]Song 2:7; 5:8; 8:4 [b]Song 2:7

6 [1]CHORUS [2]Lit *Who* [a]Song 8:5 [b]Ex 13:21; Joel 2:30 [c]Song 1:13; 4:6, 14; Matt 2:11 [d]Ex 30:34; Rev 18:13

8 [1]Lit *terror in the nights* [a]Jer 50:9 [b]Ps 45:3 [c]Ps 91:5

10 [1]Or *support* [a]Song 1:5

11 [1]Or *wreath* [a]Is 3:16, 17; 4:4 [b]Is 62:5

4:1 [1]BRIDEGROOM [2]Lit *Behold* [a]Song 1:15 [b]Song 1:15; 5:12 [c]Song 6:7 [d]Song 6:5 [e]Mic 7:14

2 [1]Or *miscarried* [a]Song 6:6

3 [a]Josh 2:18 [b]Song 5:16 [c]Song 6:7

4 [1]Or *for an arsenal* [a]Song 7:4

On which are [b]hung a thousand shields,
All the round [c]shields of the mighty men.
5 "Your [a]two breasts are like two fawns,
Twins of a gazelle
Which [b]feed among the lilies.
6 "[a]Until [1]the cool of the day
When the shadows flee away,
I will go my way to the mountain of [b]myrrh
And to the hill of [b]frankincense.

7 "[a]You are altogether beautiful, my darling,
And there is no blemish in you.
8 "*Come* with me from [a]Lebanon, *my* [b]bride,
May you come with me from Lebanon.
[1]Journey down from the summit of [c]Amana,
From the summit of [d]Senir and Hermon,
From the dens of lions,
From the mountains of leopards.
9 "You have made my heart beat faster, [a]my sister, *my* bride;
You have made my heart beat faster with a single *glance* of your eyes,
With a single strand of your [b]necklace.
10 "[a]How beautiful is your love, my sister, *my* bride!
How much [b]better is your love than wine,
And the [c]fragrance of your oils
Than all *kinds* of [1]spices!
11 "Your lips, *my* bride, [a]drip [b]honey;
Honey and milk are under your tongue,
And the fragrance of your garments is like the [c]fragrance of Lebanon.
12 "A garden locked is my sister, *my* bride,
A [1]rock garden locked, a [a]spring [b]sealed up.
13 "Your shoots are an [1a]orchard of [b]pomegranates
With [c]choice fruits, [d]henna with nard plants,
14 [a]Nard and saffron, calamus and [b]cinnamon,
With all the trees of [c]frankincense,
[d]Myrrh and aloes, along with all the finest [1]spices.
15 "*You are* a garden spring,
A well of [1a]fresh water,
And streams *flowing* from Lebanon."

16 "[1]Awake, O north *wind*,
And come, *wind of* the south;
Make my [a]garden breathe out *fragrance,*
Let its [2]spices [3]be wafted abroad.
May [b]my beloved come into his garden
And eat its [c]choice fruits!"

Chapter 5 Theme ______________________

5 "[1]I have [a]come into my garden, [b]my sister, *my* bride;
I have gathered my [c]myrrh along with my balsam.

4 [b]Ezek 27:10, 11 [c]2 Sam 1:21

5 [a]Song 7:3 [b]Song 2:16; 6:2, 3

6 [1]Lit *the day blows* [a]Song 2:17 [b]Song 4:14

7 [a]Song 1:15; Eph 5:27

8 [1]Or *Look* [a]1 Kin 4:33; Ps 72:16 [b]Song 5:1; Is 62:5 [c]2 Kin 5:12 [d]Deut 3:9; 1 Chr 5:23; Ezek 27:5

9 [a]Song 4:10, 12; 5:1, 2 [b]Gen 41:42; Prov 1:9; Ezek 16:11; Dan 5:7

10 [1]Or *balsam odors* [a]Song 7:6 [b]Song 1:2, 4 [c]Song 1:3

11 [a]Prov 5:3 [b]Ps 19:10; Prov 24:13 [c]Gen 27:27; Hos 14:6

12 [1]Lit *stone heap* [a]Prov 5:15-18 [b]Gen 29:3

13 [1]Or *park* or *paradise* [a]Eccl 2:5 [b]Song 6:11; 7:12 [c]Song 2:3; 4:16; 7:13 [d]Song 1:14

14 [1]Or *balsam odors* [a]Song 1:12 [b]Ex 30:23 [c]Song 4:6 [d]Ps 45:8; Song 3:6; John 19:39

15 [1]Lit *living* [a]Zech 14:8; John 4:10

16 [1]BRIDE [2]Or *balsam odors* [3]Lit *flow forth* [a]Song 5:1; 6:2 [b]Song 1:13; 2:3, 8; 6:2 [c]Song 4:13

5:1 [1]BRIDEGROOM [a]Song 6:2 [b]Song 4:9 [c]Song 1:13; 4:14

I have eaten my honeycomb [2]and my [d]honey;
I have [e]drunk my wine [2]and my milk.
Eat, [f]friends;
Drink and [3]imbibe deeply, O lovers."

2 "[1]I was asleep but my heart was awake.
A voice! My beloved was knocking:
'Open to me, [a]my sister, my darling,
[b]My dove, my perfect one!
For my head is [2]drenched with dew,
My [c]locks with the [3]damp of the night.'
3 "I have [a]taken off my dress,
How can I put it on *again?*
I have [b]washed my feet,
How can I dirty them *again?*
4 "My beloved extended his hand through the opening,
And my [1a]feelings were aroused for him.
5 "I arose to open to my beloved;
And my hands [a]dripped with myrrh,
And my fingers with [1]liquid myrrh,
On the handles of the bolt.
6 "I opened to my beloved,
But my beloved had [a]turned away *and* had gone!
My [1]heart went out *to him* as he [b]spoke.
I [c]searched for him but I did not find him;
I [d]called him but he did not answer me.
7 "The [a]watchmen who make the rounds in the city found me,
They struck me *and* wounded me;
The guardsmen of the walls took away my shawl from me.
8 "I [a]adjure you, O daughters of Jerusalem,
If you find my beloved,
As to what you will tell him:
For [b]I am lovesick."

9 "[1,2]What kind of beloved is your beloved,
O [a]most beautiful among women?
[2]What kind of beloved is your beloved,
That thus you adjure us?"

10 "[1]My beloved is dazzling and [a]ruddy,
[2b]Outstanding among ten thousand.
11 "His head is *like* gold, pure gold;
His [a]locks are *like* clusters of dates
And black as a raven.
12 "His [a]eyes are like doves
Beside streams of water,
Bathed in milk,
And [1]reposed in *their* [b]setting.
13 "His cheeks are like a [a]bed of balsam,
Banks of sweet-scented herbs;
His lips are [b]lilies
[c]Dripping with liquid myrrh.

1 [2]Lit *with* [3]Or *become drunk* [d]Song 4:11 [e]Prov 9:5; Is 55:1 [f]Judg 14:11, 20; John 3:29
2 [1]BRIDE [2]Lit *filled* [3]Lit *drops* [a]Song 4:9 [b]Song 2:14; 6:9 [c]Song 5:11
3 [a]Luke 11:7 [b]Gen 19:2
4 [1]Lit *bowels* [a]Jer 31:20
5 [1]Lit *passing* [a]Song 5:13
6 [1]Lit *soul* [a]Song 6:1 [b]Song 5:2 [c]Song 3:1 [d]Prov 1:28
7 [a]Song 3:3
8 [a]Song 2:7; 3:5 [b]Song 2:5
9 [1]CHORUS [2]Or *What is your beloved more than another beloved* [a]Song 1:8; 6:1
10 [1]BRIDE [2]Lit *Lifted up banner* [a]1 Sam 16:12 [b]Ps 45:2
11 [a]Song 5:2
12 [1]Lit *sitting upon* [a]Song 1:15; 4:1 [b]Ex 25:7
13 [a]Song 6:2 [b]Song 2:1 [c]Song 5:5

14 [1]Lit *lapis lazuli* [a]Ex 28:20; 39:13; Ezek 1:16; Dan 10:6 [b]Ex 24:10; 28:18; Job 28:16; Is 54:11

15 [a]Song 7:4 [b]1 Kin 4:33; Ps 80:10; Ezek 17:23; 31:8

16 [1]Lit *palate* [a]Song 7:9 [b]2 Sam 1:23

6:1 [1]CHORUS [a]Song 5:6 [b]Song 1:8

2 [1]BRIDE [a]Song 4:16; 5:1 [b]Song 5:13 [c]Song 1:7 [d]Song 2:1; 5:13

3 [a]Song 2:16; 7:10 [b]Song 2:16; 4:5

4 [1]BRIDEGROOM [2]Lit *bannered ones* [a]Song 1:15 [b]1 Kin 14:17 [c]Song 1:5 [d]Ps 48:2; 50:2 [e]Song 6:10

5 [a]Song 4:1

6 [1]Or *miscarried* [a]Song 4:2

7 [a]Song 4:3

8 [1]Or *virgins* [a]1 Kin 11:3 [b]Song 1:3

9 [1]Lit *one* [2]Lit *daughters* [a]Song 2:14; 5:2 [b]Gen 30:13 [c]1 Kin 11:3

10 [1]Lit *looks down* [a]Job 31:26

14 "His hands are rods of gold
Set with [a]beryl;
His abdomen is carved ivory
Inlaid with [1b]sapphires.
15 "His legs are pillars of alabaster
Set on pedestals of pure gold;
His appearance is like [a]Lebanon
Choice as the [b]cedars.
16 "His [1a]mouth is *full of* sweetness.
And he is wholly [b]desirable.
This is my beloved and this is my friend,
O daughters of Jerusalem."

Chapter 6 Theme ________________________

6 "[1a]Where has your beloved gone,
O [b]most beautiful among women?
Where has your beloved turned,
That we may seek him with you?"

2 "[1]My beloved has gone down to his [a]garden,
To the [b]beds of balsam,
To [c]pasture *his flock* in the gardens
And gather [d]lilies.
3 "[a]I am my beloved's and my beloved is mine,
He who [b]pastures *his flock* among the lilies."

4 "[1a]You are as beautiful as [b]Tirzah, my darling,
As [c]lovely as [d]Jerusalem,
As [e]awesome as [2]an army with banners.
5 "Turn your eyes away from me,
For they have confused me;
[a]Your hair is like a flock of goats
That have descended from Gilead.
6 "[a]Your teeth are like a flock of ewes
Which have come up from *their* washing,
All of which bear twins,
And not one among them has [1]lost her young.
7 "[a]Your temples are like a slice of a pomegranate
Behind your veil.
8 "There are sixty [a]queens and eighty concubines,
And [1b]maidens without number;
9 *But* [a]my dove, my perfect one, is [1]unique:
She is her mother's [1]only *daughter;*
She is the pure *child* of the one who bore her.
The [2b]maidens saw her and called her blessed,
The [c]queens and the concubines *also,* and they praised
her, *saying,*

10 'Who is this that [1]grows like the dawn,
As beautiful as the full [a]moon,

As pure [b]as the sun,
As [c]awesome as [2]an army with banners?'
11 "I went down to the orchard of nut trees
To see the blossoms of the valley,
To see whether [a]the vine had budded
Or the [b]pomegranates had bloomed.
12 "Before I was aware, my soul set me
Over the chariots of [1]my noble people."

13 "[1,2]Come back, come back, O Shulammite;
Come back, come back, that we may gaze at you!"

"[3]**W**hy should you gaze at the Shulammite,
As at the [a]dance of [4b]the two companies?

Chapter 7 Theme ____________________

7 "[1]How beautiful are your [2]feet in sandals,
O [3a]prince's daughter!
The curves of your hips are like [4]jewels,
The work of the hands of an artist.
2 "Your navel is *like* a round goblet
Which never lacks mixed wine;
Your belly is like a heap of wheat
Fenced about with lilies.
3 "Your [a]two breasts are like two fawns,
Twins of a gazelle.
4 "Your [a]neck is like a tower of ivory,
Your eyes *like* the pools in [b]Heshbon
By the gate of Bath-rabbim;
Your nose is like the tower of Lebanon,
Which faces toward Damascus.
5 "Your head [1]crowns you like [a]Carmel,
And the flowing locks of your head are like purple threads;
The king is captivated by *your* tresses.
6 "How [a]beautiful and how delightful you are,
[1]*My* love, with *all* your charms!
7 "[1]Your stature is like a palm tree,
And your breasts are *like its* clusters.
8 "I said, 'I will climb the palm tree,
I will take hold of its fruit stalks.'
Oh, may your breasts be like clusters of the vine,
And the fragrance of your [1]breath like [2a]apples,
9 And your [1a]mouth like the best wine!"

"[2]**I**t [b]goes *down* smoothly for my beloved,
Flowing gently *through* the lips of those who fall asleep.

10 "[a]I am my beloved's,
And his [b]desire is for me.

---

10 [2]Lit *bannered ones* [b]Matt 17:2; Rev 1:16 [c]Song 6:4

11 [a]Song 7:12 [b]Song 4:13

12 [1]Another reading is *Ammi-nadib*

13 [1]CHORUS [2]Ch 7:1 in Heb [3]BRIDEGROOM [4]Or *Mahanaim* [a]Judg 21:21 [b]Gen 32:2; 2 Sam 17:24

7:1 [1]Ch 7:2 in Heb [2]Lit *footsteps* [3]Or *nobleman's* [4]Or *ornaments* [a]Ps 45:13

3 [a]Song 4:5

4 [a]Song 4:4 [b]Num 21:26

5 [1]Lit *is upon* [a]Is 35:2

6 [1]Or With *love among your delights* [a]Song 1:15, 16; 4:10

7 [1]Lit *This stature of yours*

8 [1]Lit *nose* [2]Or *apricots* [a]Song 2:5

9 [1]Lit *palate* [2]BRIDE [a]Song 5:16 [b]Prov 23:31

10 [a]Song 2:16; 6:3 [b]Ps 45:11; Gal 2:20

11 "Come, my beloved, let us go out into the [1]country,
Let us spend the night in the villages.
12 "Let us rise early *and go* to the vineyards;
Let us [a]see whether the vine has budded
And its blossoms have opened,
And whether the pomegranates have bloomed.
There I will give you my love.
13 "The [a]mandrakes have given forth fragrance;
And over our doors are all [b]choice *fruits,*
Both new and old,
Which I have saved up for you, my beloved.

Chapter 8 Theme ______________________________

8 "Oh that you were like a brother to me
Who nursed at my mother's breasts.
If I found you outdoors, I would kiss you;
No one would despise me, either.
2 "I would lead you *and* [a]bring you
Into the house of my mother, who used to instruct me;
I would give you spiced wine to drink from the juice of
my pomegranates.
3 "Let [a]his left hand be under my head
And his right hand embrace me."

4 "[1a]I want you to swear, O daughters of Jerusalem,
[2]Do not arouse or awaken *my* love
Until [3]she pleases."

5 "[1a]Who is this coming up from the wilderness
Leaning on her beloved?"

"[2]**B**eneath the [3b]apple tree I awakened you;
There your mother was in labor with you,
There she was in labor *and* gave you birth.
6 "Put me like a [1]seal over your heart,
Like a [a]seal on your arm.
For love is as strong as death,
[2b]Jealousy is as severe as Sheol;
Its flashes are flashes of fire,
[3]The *very* flame of the LORD.
7 "Many waters cannot quench love,
Nor will rivers overflow it;
[a]If a man were to give all the riches of his house for love,
It would be utterly despised."

8 "[1]We have a little sister,
And she [a]has no breasts;
What shall we do for our sister
On the day when she is spoken for?
9 "If she is a wall,
We will build on her a battlement of silver;

11 [1]Lit *field*
12 [a]Song 6:11
13 [a]Gen 30:14 [b]Song 2:3; 4:13, 16; Matt 13:52
8:2 [a]Song 3:4
3 [a]Song 2:6
4 [1]BRIDEGROOM [2]Or *Why should you arouse* [3]Or *it* [a]Song 2:7; 3:5
5 [1]CHORUS [2]BRIDE [3]Or *apricot* [a]Song 3:6 [b]Song 2:3
6 [1]Or *signet* [2]Or Its *ardor is as inflexible* [3]Another reading is *A vehement flame* [a]Is 49:16; Jer 22:24; Hag 2:23 [b]Prov 6:34
7 [a]Prov 6:35
8 [1]CHORUS [a]Ezek 16:7

But if she is a door,
We will barricade her with [a]planks of cedar."

10 "[1]I was a wall, and [a]my breasts were like towers;
Then I became in his eyes as one who finds peace.
11 "Solomon had a [a]vineyard at Baal-hamon;
He [b]entrusted the vineyard to [c]caretakers.
Each one was to bring a [d]thousand *shekels* of silver for
its [e]fruit.
12 "My very own vineyard is [1]at my disposal;
The thousand *shekels* are for you, Solomon,
And two hundred are for those who take care of its fruit."

13 "[1]O you who sit in the gardens,
My [a]companions are listening for your voice—
[b]Let me hear it!"

14 "[1,2]Hurry, my beloved,
And be [a]like a gazelle or a young [3]stag
On the [b]mountains of spices."

9 [a]1 Kin 6:15

10 [1]BRIDE [a]Ezek 16:7

11 [a]Eccl 2:4 [b]Matt 21:33 [c]Song 1:6 [d]Is 7:23 [e]Song 2:3; 8:12

12 [1]Lit *before me*

13 [1]BRIDEGROOM [a]Song 1:7 [b]Song 2:14

14 [1]BRIDE [2]Lit *Flee* [3]Lit *of the stags* [a]Song 2:7, 9, 17 [b]Song 4:6

Song of Solomon at a Glance

Theme of Song of Solomon:

Segment Divisions

		Chapter Themes
		1
		2
		3
		4
		5
		6
		7
		8

Author:

Date:

Purpose:

Key Words:

love

beloved

come (coming)

beautiful

ISAIAH ישעיהו

YESHA'YAHU

The messages of the Old Testament prophets addressed the people of Israel and Judah who lived between the years of 840 and 420 B.C. Isaiah is the first of the major prophets. Isaiah's name, *Yesha'yahu*, means "Jehovah Saves" or "Salvation of Jehovah." No other prophet offers more prophecies regarding the coming Messiah. Isaiah reveals the Messiah (Christ) as the Suffering Servant and the Conquering King. Under divine inspiration, Isaiah announces the things that will occur in the future so that God's people might know there is no God besides Him.

From Isaiah 37:37-38 we know Isaiah lived until at least 681 B.C., the year Esarhaddon, the son of Sennacherib, became king of Assyria after his father's death. Tradition says Isaiah died a martyr, sawn in two by Manasseh, the king of Judah who reigned after Hezekiah (2 Kings 21:16). If tradition is correct, Isaiah may be one of the heroes of faith referred to in Hebrews 11:37.

THINGS TO DO

The basic structure of Isaiah is easy to remember if it is compared to the Bible's structure. The Bible is comprised of 66 books, 39 in the Old Testament and 27 in the New Testament. Isaiah, which focuses on the Holy One of Israel, has 66 chapters, which fall into two main divisions: Isaiah 1 through 39 reveals God's character and judgment, and Isaiah 40 through 66 shows God's comfort and redemption. Because Isaiah is a long book filled with discourses and songs, it needs to be studied segment by segment so that you don't miss the wonder of its promises and prophecies. Ask God to help you understand the important message of this book.

General Instructions

1. As you read through Isaiah one chapter at a time, observe each chapter in the light of the "5 W's and an H." Ask general questions such as: Who does this chapter focus on? What happens or what is this about? When is this happening? Where will it happen? Why is this going to happen and how?

2. Mark any reference to God with a △ and observe any insights into His character, His power, His ways. Note these in the margin. If the verse mentions the sovereignty of God, note it in the margin with "△ Sovereignty." Also, watch for and mark any references to God as the Creator. Note these in the margin with "△ Creator."

3. Isaiah is a set of discourses, songs, or oracles rather than a historical chronology of events in the life of Israel. Periodically there are historical interludes, which are very important. In these interludes God often will tell Isaiah to do something that will act as a sign to the people. For instance, in Isaiah 8:3 Isaiah is to name his son *Maher-shalal-hash-baz*, which means "swift is the booty, speedy is the prey." His name pointed the people to the Assyrian invasion, which would come before Maher-shalal-hash-baz would learn to say Momma or Daddy. Observe these interludes carefully.

4. Isaiah recorded many prophecies regarding future events, including the captivity, the birth of Messiah, the reign of Messiah, and the last days. Watch for these prophecies and mark them in a significant way.

   a. As you read some of these prophecies, you will see that the first and second comings of Messiah (Christ) are prophesied without any indication that there is an interval of time between these comings. For instance, Isaiah 61:1-2a covers the first coming of Jesus Christ. In fact, Jesus read this passage in the synagogue in Nazareth and stopped at this point (Luke 4:18-19). Why? Because the next part of the verse, "And the day of vengeance of our God," skips to the day of the Lord, which encompasses Christ's judgment and His second coming.

b. You will find it beneficial to read the section entitled "Guidelines for Interpreting Predictive Prophecy" on page 2101.

c. On page 1094 is a chart called THE PROPHETIC POINTS OF HISTORY. This will help you distinguish the time periods to which Isaiah refers. Watch for and mark any references to the Lord's coming. Note which coming it is and the circumstances associated with it.

5. On the ISAIAH AT A GLANCE chart are key words to mark in a distinctive way. Put these on an index card now and use it as a bookmark. As you mark *in that day,* carefully observe what day it is referring to. List observations on the *day of the Lord* on the chart on page 2076.

6. Babylon plays a significant prophetic role throughout Scripture, even in the day of the Lord. List what you learn about Babylon on the chart on page 2074. Note the reference (book, chapter, and verse) from which you took your information. You will want this for future reference.

7. Note any references to time with a clock ⏲.

8. Finally, there's much you can learn about Isaiah himself. Mark in a distinctive color every reference to Isaiah that tells you something about him. You may want to record these insights at the end of Isaiah 66 (page 1192).

Isaiah 1–39: God's Character and Judgment

Chapters 1–12: Discourses Regarding Judah and Jerusalem

1. Read Isaiah 1 to get the spiritual and moral condition and the historical setting of this book.
   a. Read Isaiah 1 and color in a distinctive way every reference to God's people, Israel. Then on a separate piece of paper list what you learn about Israel just from this chapter.
   b. There is much to learn about Israel as a society around 700 B.C. Mark any reference that will give you insight into this nation's status or condition at this time.
   c. To put the book into its chronological setting, compare Isaiah 1:1 with the historical chart on page 1095. Record your insights under "Author" and "Date" on the ISAIAH AT A GLANCE chart on pages 1193, 1194.
2. As you read Isaiah 2–12 one chapter at a time:
   a. Add the following key words and mark them through Isaiah 39: *Samaria*, *Assyria*, *woe* (also 45:9-10), and *remnant* (also in 46:3).
   b. Mark references to time with a clock ⏲.
3. As you read each chapter observe the following:
   a. Note to whom God is speaking and what He says about their behavior.
   b. Observe the consequences of the behavior.
   c. See if there is an exhortation or plea followed by a promise of how God will cleanse them, bless them, or move on their behalf.
4. Isaiah 6 is a strategic chapter. It records Isaiah's call and commission from the Lord.
   a. To get the historical setting of this chapter, read 2 Kings 15. Uzziah is called Azariah in 2 Kings 15:1 (see 2 Chronicles 26:1). The reigns of Uzziah and Jotham overlapped because they served as co-regents for a time (see chart, page 1095).
   b. Observe the progression of events in this chapter and note them in the margin.

5. As you study each chapter, don't forget the "General Instructions." These are an important part of the process of carefully observing the text.

6. When you finish observing each chapter, record the theme of that chapter on ISAIAH AT A GLANCE and in your Bible.

Chapters 13–23: Oracles Against Various Nations

1. As you read this section chapter by chapter, watch for and mark in a distinctive way the key repeated phrase, *the oracle concerning* _______________. Note who the oracle concerns and locate each of these on a map.

2. As you observe each chapter, note the following in the margin or mark it in the text:
   a. Observe if there is any judgment connected with those to whom the oracle is given and why.
   b. Watch where the judgment comes and if there is any effect on Israel.
   c. Watch for *when* something happens. Note this with the symbol of a clock.
   d. Notice how God's purposes are being worked out in history.
   e. Mark references to the day of the Lord.

3. Record the theme of each chapter in the same way you did previously. However, remember that this will not always be easy. The chapter divisions in the Bible are not part of the original Scriptures. Therefore, if you have a hard time summarizing the theme of each chapter, don't be discouraged. When it is not easy to settle on a chapter theme, pick a key verse that the truths of the chapter seem to pivot around, or simply choose some words from the first verse and record these on ISAIAH AT A GLANCE.

Chapters 24–27: Discourses Regarding "That Day"

1. As you read this segment, add *covenant* to your key words list.

2. As you read each chapter observe the following:
   a. What happens to the earth and its inhabitants (humans and animals)
   b. What the Lord of hosts will do and where He will be
   c. What the people's response will be

3. Record the theme of each chapter on ISAIAH AT A GLANCE and in the text.

Chapters 28–33: Six Woes

1. Mark the key words, and add *the* (or *My*) *Spirit* to your list. It is also used in Isaiah 11:2, so go back and mark it.

2. As you read each of these chapters, mark in the text the following:
   a. To whom the woe is given
   b. What was done to cause the woe
   c. What the Lord will do and what the result will be

3. Record the chapter themes on ISAIAH AT A GLANCE and in your Bible.

Chapters 34–35: God's Recompense and Ransom for Zion

1. As you read these two chapters, add the following key words and watch for them from this point onward: *sword*, *recompense*, *glory (the Lord's)*, and *ransomed*.

2. Look for and record in your notebook on whom God's recompense will come, what it will be, and what will follow. Make sure you note what happens to the ransomed and the redeemed. Also note what this will mean to Zion.

3. Record the chapter themes on ISAIAH AT A GLANCE and in your Bible.

Chapters 36–39: Historical Account from the Threat of Assyria to the Threat of Babylon

1. Read these chapters and mark the following words: *Assyria*, *Sennacherib*, *Rabshakeh*, *Hezekiah*, *Isaiah*, *Babylon*, *remnant*, *Lord of hosts*, and *prayer (prayed)*.

2. Now read the chapters again, observing the words you marked. In your notebook, note what you learn about each of the characters and what they do, what happens as a result, and how God intervenes. List what you learn about God from these chapters. Don't miss what happens to Assyria and Babylon. This is a pivotal point in respect to these two powers and the nation of Israel.

3. For additional insight into Hezekiah, read 2 Kings 18–20 and 2 Chronicles 29–32.

4. Record the chapter themes on ISAIAH AT A GLANCE and in your Bible.

Isaiah 40–66: God's Comfort and Redemption

Chapters 40–48: Behold the Lord, Your Redeemer

1. Continue to mark any key words on your list. Also mark the following references to God in a distinctive way: *I am the Lord (God), no one besides Me* (*no other God*), and *Redeemer*. Then list in your notebook all you see about God that you want to remember for future reference. Note God's character, what He does, and to what or whom He is compared.

2. As you do all this don't simply mark these and move on. Meditate on what you see. Think of what these insights can do for your relationship with God. Remember, He is not only Israel's Redeemer but yours also if you have repented and believed in the Lord Jesus Christ.

3. Also add and mark *servant*. As you read each chapter, check the context (the surrounding verses) in which *servant* is used. This is vital. Note whether *servant* refers to Israel (Jacob) or to the Lord Jesus Christ. Record your insights in your notebook. If it seems to be a prophetic reference to Jesus, check your Bible's reference notes and see if the New Testament verses show how this prophecy was fulfilled by Jesus. When you make your list in the margin put it under "Israel the Servant" or "Messiah the Servant."

4. Once again mark *remnant* (used only one time in this segment), *glory of the Lord, salvation, nation (nations),* and *Babylon*. Record in your notebook what you learn about each.

5. Record your chapter themes as before. Fill in the second line of the segment division for these chapters: Discourses Regarding ______________________.

Chapters 49–57: Your Redeemer Will Save

1. Do everything you did under numbers 1 through 4 in the previous segment. Watch carefully all that the Lord can and will do; you might want to note it in your notebook. Observe the text carefully to see why this segment is titled "Your Redeemer Will Save." Watch for God's instructions and take them to heart.

2. Watch for prophetic verses that come in the midst of what Isaiah is saying. Give special attention to 50:6 and 52:13–53:12. After you observe Isaiah 53, read it through on your knees and substitute your name every time you see *we* or *us*. Mark every reference to *He* and *Him* from verse 2 onward. Then list all that the text tells you about Him.

3. Look for and record the theme of each chapter. If you think it will be helpful, summarize and list in the margin the subpoints covered in the chapter. Fill in the second line of the segment division for these chapters.

Chapters 58–66: Your Redeemer Will Come

1. Once again mark the key words on your bookmark. Also mark *redemption* and the references to fasting. *Servant* becomes *servants* in this segment; don't miss it.

2. There is much in this segment about the events that surround or accompany the Lord's coming to reign and what will follow, even in regard to the new heaven and new earth. In your notebook list what you observe. Also watch for practical lessons and list what you learn. For instance, in Isaiah 58 you will gain insights on fasting.

3. Once again continue marking everything as you did under steps 1 through 4 (Isaiah 40–48).

4. Record your chapter themes and then complete ISAIAH AT A GLANCE. Fill in the second line of the segment division for these chapters. Write in any new segment divisions you have seen.

Things to Think About

1. God's character never changes; therefore what distressed Him in the days of Isaiah still distresses Him today. And what He had to judge then, He cannot overlook now. Is there anything in your life you must confess and forsake? And what if you are not willing to do so? Will God be able to overlook it? Think about what you learned about God and His ways.

2. God is sovereign. He ruled over the nations in the days of Israel. Does He do the same today? What, then, can you know? How might your nation fit into all this?

3. Amos says God doesn't do anything without first revealing it to His servants, the prophets (Amos 3:7). Therefore, from studying Isaiah, what do you know with an absolute certainty is going to come to pass? If the prophecies regarding the first coming of Jesus Christ literally came to pass (and they did), won't the prophecies regarding His second coming be literally fulfilled? How, then, are you to live?

Chapter 1 Theme ______________________________

1 The vision of Isaiah the son of Amoz concerning [a]Judah and
Jerusalem, which he saw during the [1]reigns of [b]Uzziah,
[c]Jotham, [d]Ahaz *and* [e]Hezekiah, kings of Judah.

2 [a]Listen, O heavens, and hear, O [b]earth;
For the LORD speaks,
"[c]Sons I have reared and brought up,
But they have [d]revolted against Me.

3 "An ox knows its owner,
And a donkey its master's manger,
But Israel [a]does not know,
My people [b]do not understand."

4 Alas, sinful nation,
People weighed down with iniquity,
[1a]Offspring of evildoers,
Sons who [b]act corruptly!
They have [c]abandoned the LORD,

1:1 [1]Lit *days*
[a]Is 2:1; 40:9
[b]2 Kin 15:1-7, 13; 2 Chr 26:1-23
[c]2 Kin 15:32-38; 2 Chr 27:1-9
[d]2 Kin 16:1-20; 2 Chr 28:1-27; Is 7:1
[e]2 Kin 18:1-20:21; 2 Chr 29:1-32:33

2 [a]Deut 32:1
[b]Mic 1:2
[c]Jer 3:22
[d]Is 30:1, 9; 65:2

3 [a]Jer 9:3, 6
[b]Is 44:18

4 [1]Lit *Seed*
[a]Is 14:20
[b]Neh 1:7
[c]Is 1:28

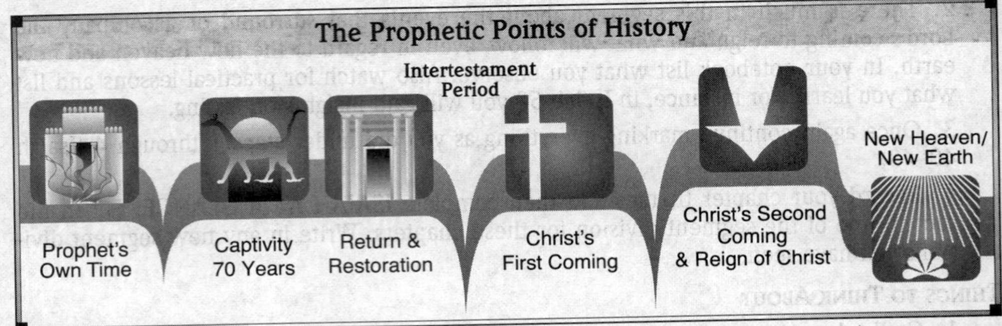

They have [d]despised the Holy One of Israel,
They have turned away [2]from Him.

5 Where will you be stricken again,
As you [a]continue in *your* rebellion?
The whole head is [b]sick
And the whole heart is faint.
6 [a]From the sole of the foot even to the head
There is [b]nothing sound in it,
Only bruises, welts and raw wounds,
[c]Not pressed out or bandaged,
Nor softened with oil.

7 Your [a]land is desolate,
Your cities are burned with fire,
Your fields—strangers are devouring them in your presence;
It is desolation, as overthrown by strangers.
8 The daughter of Zion is left like a shelter in a vineyard,
Like a watchman's hut in a cucumber field, like a
besieged city.
9 [a]Unless the LORD of hosts
Had left us a few [b]survivors,
We would be like [c]Sodom,
We would be like Gomorrah.

10 Hear [a]the word of the LORD,
You rulers of [b]Sodom;
Give ear to the instruction of our God,
You people of Gomorrah.
11 "[a]What are your multiplied sacrifices to Me?"
Says the LORD.
"I [1]have had enough of burnt offerings of rams
And the fat of fed cattle;
And I take no pleasure in the blood of bulls, lambs or goats.
12 "When you come [a]to appear before Me,
Who requires [1]of you this trampling of My courts?
13 "Bring your worthless offerings no longer,
[a]Incense is an abomination to Me.
[b]New moon and sabbath, the [c]calling of assemblies—
I cannot [d]endure iniquity and the solemn assembly.

4 [2]Lit *backward* [d]Is 5:24

5 [a]Is 31:6 [b]Is 33:24; Ezek 34:4, 16

6 [a]Job 2:7 [b]Ps 38:3 [c]Jer 8:22

7 [a]Lev 26:33; Jer 44:6

9 [a]Rom 9:29 [b]Is 10:20-22; 11:11, 16; 37:4, 31, 32; 46:3 [c]Gen 19:24

10 [a]Is 8:20; 28:14 [b]Is 3:9; Ezek 16:49; Rom 9:29; Rev 11:8

11 [1]Or *am sated with* [a]Ps 50:8; Jer 6:20; Amos 5:21, 22; Mal 1:10

12 [1]Lit *of your hand* [a]Ex 23:17

13 [a]Is 66:3 [b]1 Chr 23:31 [c]Ex 12:16 [d]Jer 7:9, 10

14 “I hate your new moon *festivals* and your [a]appointed feasts,
They have become a burden to Me;
I am [b]weary of bearing *them.*
15 “So when you [a]spread out your hands *in prayer,*
[b]I will hide My eyes from you;
Yes, even though you [c]multiply prayers,
I will not listen.
[d]Your hands are [1]covered with blood.

16 “[a]Wash yourselves, [b]make yourselves clean;
[c]Remove the evil of your deeds from My sight.
[d]Cease to do evil,
17 Learn to do good;
[a]Seek justice,
Reprove the ruthless,
[1b]Defend the orphan,
Plead for the widow.

18 “Come now, and [a]let us reason together,”
Says the LORD,
“[b]Though your sins are as scarlet,
They will be as white as snow;
Though they are red like crimson,
They will be like wool.
19 “[a]If you consent and obey,
You will [b]eat the best of the land;
20 “But if you refuse and rebel,
You will be [a]devoured by the sword.”
Truly, [b]the mouth of the LORD has spoken.

21 How the faithful city has become a [a]harlot,
She *who* was full of justice!

14 [a]Is 29:1, 2 [b]Is 7:13; 43:24

15 [1]Lit *full of* [a]1 Kin 8:22; Lam 1:17 [b]Is 8:17; 59:2 [c]Mic 3:4 [d]Is 59:3

16 [a]Ps 26:6 [b]Is 52:11 [c]Is 55:7 [d]Jer 25:5

17 [1]Or *Vindicate the fatherless* [a]Jer 22:3; Zeph 2:3 [b]Ps 82:3

18 [a]Is 41:1, 21; 43:26; Mic 6:2 [b]Ps 51:7; Is 43:25; 44:22; Rev 7:14

19 [a]Deut 28:1; 30:15, 16 [b]Is 55:2

20 [a]Is 3:25; 65:12 [b]Is 40:5; 58:14; Mic 4:4; Titus 1:2

21 [a]Is 57:3-9; Jer 2:20

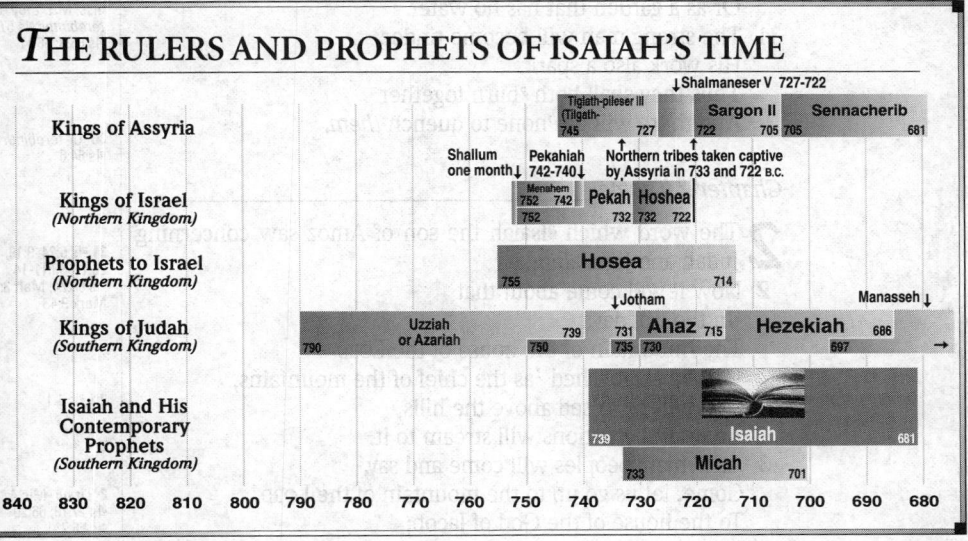

THE RULERS AND PROPHETS OF ISAIAH'S TIME

Righteousness once lodged in her,
But now murderers.
22 Your silver has become dross,
Your drink diluted with water.
23 Your [a]rulers are rebels
And companions of thieves;
Everyone [b]loves a bribe
And chases after rewards.
They [c]do not [1]defend the [2]orphan,
Nor does the widow's plea come before them.

24 Therefore the Lord [1]GOD of hosts,
The [a]Mighty One of Israel, declares,
"Ah, I will be relieved of My adversaries
And [b]avenge Myself on My foes.
25 "I will also turn My hand against you,
And will [a]smelt away your dross as with lye
And will remove all your alloy.
26 "Then I will restore your [a]judges as at the first,
And your counselors as at the beginning;
After that you will be called the [b]city of righteousness,
A faithful city."

27 Zion will be [a]redeemed with justice
And her [1]repentant ones with righteousness.
28 But [1]transgressors and sinners will be [a]crushed together,
And those who forsake the LORD will come to an end.
29 Surely [1]you will be ashamed of the [2a]oaks which you have desired,
And you will be embarrassed at the [b]gardens which you have chosen.
30 For you will be like an [1]oak whose [a]leaf fades away
Or as a garden that has no water.
31 The strong man will become tinder,
His work also a spark.
Thus they shall both [a]burn together
And there will be [b]none to quench *them.*

Chapter 2 Theme ____________________________

2 The word which [a]Isaiah the son of Amoz saw concerning Judah and Jerusalem.
2 Now it will come about that
[a]In the last days
The [b]mountain of the house of the LORD
Will be established [1]as the chief of the mountains,
And will be raised above the hills;
And [c]all the nations will stream to it.
3 And many peoples will come and say,
"Come, let us go up to the mountain of the LORD,
To the house of the God of Jacob;

23 [1]Or *vindicate* [2]Or *fatherless* [a]Hos 5:10; Mic 7:3 [b]Ex 23:8; Mic 7:3 [c]Is 10:2; Jer 5:28; Ezek 22:7; Zech 7:10

24 [1]Heb *YHWH,* usually rendered *LORD* [a]Ps 132:2; Is 49:26; 60:16 [b]Deut 28:63; Is 35:4; 59:18; 61:2; 63:4

25 [a]Ezek 22:19-22; Mal 3:3

26 [a]Is 60:17 [b]Is 33:5; 60:14; 62:1, 2; Zech 8:3

27 [1]Or *returnees* [a]Is 35:9f; 62:12; 63:4

28 [1]Lit *crushing of transgressors and sinners shall be together* [a]Ps 9:5; Is 66:24; 2 Thess 1:8, 9

29 [1]So with some mss; M.T. *they* [2]Or *terebinths* [a]Is 57:5 [b]Is 65:3; 66:17

30 [1]Or *terebinth* [a]Is 64:6

31 [a]Is 5:24; 9:19; 26:11; 33:11-14 [b]Is 66:24; Matt 3:12; Mark 9:43

2:1 [a]Is 1:1

2 [1]Lit *on* [a]Mic 4:1-3 [b]Is 27:13; 66:20 [c]Is 56:7

That He may teach us [1]concerning His ways
And that we may walk in His paths."
For the [2]law will go forth [a]from Zion
And the word of the LORD from Jerusalem.
4 And He will judge between the nations,
And will [1]render decisions for many peoples;
And [a]they will hammer their swords into plowshares and
their spears into pruning hooks.
[b]Nation will not lift up sword against nation,
And never again will they learn war.

5 Come, [a]house of Jacob, and let us walk in the [b]light of
the LORD.
6 For You have [a]abandoned Your people, the house of Jacob,
Because they are filled *with influences* from the east,
And *they are* soothsayers [b]like the Philistines,
And they [c]strike *bargains* with the children of foreigners.
7 Their land has also been filled with silver and gold
And there is no end to their treasures;
Their land has also been filled with [a]horses
And there is no end to their chariots.
8 Their land has also been [a]filled with idols;
They worship the [b]work of their hands,
That which their fingers have made.
9 So [a]the *common* man has been humbled
And the man *of importance* has been abased,
But [b]do not forgive them.
10 [a]Enter the rock and hide in the dust
[b]From the terror of the LORD and from the splendor of
His majesty.
11 The [1a]proud look of man will be abased
And the [b]loftiness of man will be humbled,
And the LORD alone will be exalted in that day.

12 For the LORD of hosts will have a day *of reckoning*
Against [a]everyone who is proud and lofty
And against everyone who is lifted up,
That he may be abased.
13 And *it will be* against all the cedars of Lebanon that are
lofty and lifted up,
Against all the [a]oaks of Bashan,
14 Against all the [a]lofty mountains,
Against all the hills that are lifted up,
15 Against every [a]high tower,
Against every fortified wall,
16 Against all the [a]ships of Tarshish
And against all the beautiful craft.
17 The pride of man will be humbled
And the loftiness of men will be abased;
And the LORD alone will be exalted in that day,
18 But the [a]idols will completely vanish.

3 [1]Or *some of* [2]Or *instruction* [a]Is 51:4, 5; Luke 24:47

4 [1]Or *reprove many* [a]Is 32:17, 18; Joel 3:10 [b]Is 9:5, 7; 11:6-9; Hos 2:18; Zech 9:10

5 [a]Is 58:1 [b]Is 60:1, 2, 19, 20; 1 John 1:5

6 [a]Deut 31:17 [b]2 Kin 1:2 [c]2 Kin 16:7, 8; Prov 6:1

7 [a]Deut 17:16; Is 30:16; 31:1; Mic 5:10

8 [a]Is 10:11 [b]Ps 115:4-8; Is 17:8; 37:19; 40:19; 44:17

9 [a]Ps 49:2; 62:9; Is 5:15 [b]Neh 4:5

10 [a]Is 2:19, 21; Rev 6:15, 16 [b]2 Thess 1:9

11 [1]Lit *eyes of the loftiness of men* [a]Is 5:15; 37:23 [b]Ps 18:27; Is 13:11; 23:9; 2 Cor 10:5

12 [a]Job 40:11, 12; Is 24:4, 21; Mal 4:1

13 [a]Zech 11:2

14 [a]Is 40:4

15 [a]Is 25:12

16 [a]1 Kin 10:22; Is 23:1, 14; 60:9

18 [a]Is 21:9; Mic 1:7

19 *Men* will [a]go into caves of the rocks
And into holes of the [1]ground
Before the terror of the LORD
And the splendor of His majesty,
When He arises [b]to make the earth tremble.
20 In that day men will [a]cast away to the moles and the [b]bats
Their idols of silver and their idols of gold,
Which they made for themselves to worship,
21 In order to [a]go into the caverns of the rocks and the clefts of the cliffs
Before the terror of the LORD and the splendor of His majesty,
When He arises to make the earth tremble.
22 [1a]Stop regarding man, whose breath *of life* is in his nostrils;
For [2b]why should he be esteemed?

Chapter 3 Theme ______________________

3 For behold, the Lord [1]GOD of hosts [a]is going to remove from Jerusalem and Judah
Both [2]supply and support, the whole [2]supply of bread
And the whole [2]supply of water;
2 [a]The mighty man and the warrior,
The judge and the prophet,
The diviner and the elder,
3 The captain of fifty and the honorable man,
The counselor and the expert artisan,
And the skillful enchanter.
4 And I will make mere [a]lads their princes,
And [1]capricious children will rule over them,
5 And the people will be [a]oppressed,
Each one by another, and each one by his [b]neighbor;
The youth will storm against the elder
And the inferior against the honorable.
6 When a man [a]lays hold of his brother in his father's house, *saying,*
"You have a cloak, you shall be our ruler,
And these ruins will be under your [1]charge,"
7 He will [1]protest on that day, saying,
"I will not be *your* [2a]healer,
For in my house there is neither bread nor cloak;
You should not appoint me ruler of the people."
8 For [a]Jerusalem has stumbled and Judah has fallen,
Because their [1b]speech and their actions are against the LORD,
To [c]rebel against [2]His glorious presence.
9 [1]The expression of their faces bears witness against them,
And they display their sin like [a]Sodom;
They do not *even* conceal *it.*
Woe to [2]them!
For they have [b]brought evil on themselves.

19 [1]Lit *dust* [a]Is 2:10 [b]Ps 18:7; Is 2:21; 13:13; 24:1, 19, 20; Hag 2:6, 7; Heb 12:26

20 [a]Is 30:22; 31:7 [b]Lev 11:19

21 [a]Is 2:19

22 [1]Lit *Cease from man* [2]Lit *in what* [a]Ps 146:3; Jer 17:5 [b]Ps 8:4; 144:3, 4; Is 40:15, 17; James 4:14

3:1 [1]Heb *YHWH,* usually rendered LORD [2]Lit *staff* [a]Lev 26:26; Is 5:13; 9:20; Ezek 4:16

2 [a]2 Kin 24:14; Is 9:14, 15; Ezek 17:12, 13

4 [1]Lit *arbitrary power will rule* [a]Eccl 10:16

5 [a]Mic 7:3-6 [b]Is 9:19; Jer 9:3-8

6 [1]Lit *hand* [a]Is 4:1

7 [1]Lit *lift up his voice* [2]Lit *binder of wounds* [a]Ezek 34:4; Hos 5:13

8 [1]Lit *tongue* [2]Lit *the eyes of His glory* [a]Is 1:7; 6:11 [b]Ps 73:9-11; Is 9:17; 59:3 [c]Is 65:3

9 [1]Or *Their partiality bears* [2]Lit *their soul* [a]Gen 13:13; Is 1:10-15 [b]Prov 8:36; 15:32; Rom 6:23

10 [a]Deut 28:1-14; Eccl 8:12; Is 54:17

11 [1]Lit *the dealing of his hands* [a]Deut 28:15-68; Is 65:6, 7

12 [1]Or *deal severely* [a]Is 3:4 [b]Is 9:16; 28:14, 15

13 [a]Is 66:16; Hos 4:1; Mic 6:2

14 [a]Job 22:4; Ps 143:2; Ezek 20:35, 36 [b]Ps 14:4; Mic 3:3 [c]Job 24:9, 14; Ps 10:9; Prov 30:14; Is 10:1, 2; Ezek 18:12; James 2:6

15 [1]Heb *YHWH,* usually rendered *LORD* [a]Ps 94:5

16 [1]Lit *outstretched necks* [a]Song 3:11; Is 3:16-4:1, 4; 32:9-15

18 [a]Judg 8:21, 26

20 [a]Ex 39:28

21 [1]Or *signet rings* [a]Gen 24:47; Ezek 16:12

24 [1]Or *balsam oil* [a]Esth 2:12 [b]1 Pet 3:3 [c]Is 22:12; Ezek 27:31; Amos 8:10 [d]Is 15:3; Lam 2:10

25 [1]Lit *strength* [a]Is 1:20; 65:12

26 [1]Lit *entrances* [a]Jer 14:2; Lam 1:4 [b]Lam 2:10

4:1 [a]Is 13:12 [b]Gen 30:23; Is 54:4

2 [a]Is 11:1; 53:2; Jer 23:5; 33:15; Zech 3:8; 6:12

10 Say to the [a]righteous that *it will go* well *with them,*
For they will eat the fruit of their actions.
11 Woe to the wicked! *It will go* badly *with him,*
For [1a]what he deserves will be done to him.
12 O My people! Their oppressors [1]are [a]children,
And women rule over them.
O My people! [b]Those who guide you lead *you* astray
And confuse the direction of your paths.

13 [a]The LORD arises to contend,
And stands to judge the people.
14 The LORD [a]enters into judgment with the elders and princes of His people,
"It is you who have [b]devoured the vineyard;
The [c]plunder of the poor is in your houses.
15 "What do you mean by [a]crushing My people
And grinding the face of the poor?"
Declares the Lord [1]GOD of hosts.

16 Moreover, the LORD said, "Because the [a]daughters of Zion are proud
And walk with [1]heads held high and seductive eyes,
And go along with mincing steps
And tinkle the bangles on their feet,
17 Therefore the Lord will afflict the scalp of the daughters of Zion with scabs,
And the LORD will make their foreheads bare."
18 In that day the Lord will take away the beauty of *their* anklets,
headbands, [a]crescent ornaments,
19 dangling earrings, bracelets, veils,
20 [a]headdresses, ankle chains, sashes, perfume boxes, amulets,
21 [1]finger rings, [a]nose rings,
22 festal robes, outer tunics, cloaks, money purses,
23 hand mirrors, undergarments, turbans and veils.
24 Now it will come about that instead of [1]sweet [a]perfume there will be putrefaction;
Instead of a belt, a rope;
Instead of [b]well-set hair, a [c]plucked-out scalp;
Instead of fine clothes, a [d]donning of sackcloth;
And branding instead of beauty.
25 Your men will [a]fall by the sword
And your [1]mighty ones in battle.
26 And her [1a]gates will lament and mourn,
And deserted she will [b]sit on the ground.

Chapter 4 Theme ____________________________

4 For seven women will take hold of [a]one man in that day, saying, "We will eat our own bread and wear our own clothes, only let us be called by your name; [b]take away our reproach!"
2 In that day the [a]Branch of the LORD will be beautiful and

glorious, and the [b]fruit of the earth *will be* the pride and the
adornment of the [c]survivors of Israel.
3 It will come about that he who is [a]left in Zion and remains in
Jerusalem will be called [b]holy—everyone who is [c]recorded for
life in Jerusalem.
4 When the Lord has washed away the filth of the [a]daughters
of Zion and [1]purged the [b]bloodshed of Jerusalem from her midst,
by the [c]spirit of judgment and the [d]spirit of burning,
5 then the LORD will create over the whole area of Mount
Zion and over her assemblies [a]a cloud by day, even smoke, and
the brightness of a flaming fire by night; for over all the [b]glory
will be a canopy.
6 There will be a [a]shelter to *give* shade from the heat by day,
and refuge and [1]protection from the storm and the rain.

Chapter 5 Theme ______________________________

5 Let me sing now for my well-beloved
A song of my beloved concerning His vineyard.
My well-beloved had a [a]vineyard on [1]a fertile hill.
2 He dug it all around, removed its stones,
And planted it with [1]the [a]choicest vine.
And He built a tower in the middle of it
And also hewed out a [2]wine vat in it;
Then He [b]expected *it* to produce *good* grapes,
But it produced *only* [3]worthless ones.

3 "And now, O inhabitants of Jerusalem and men of Judah,
[a]Judge between Me and My vineyard.
4 "[a]What more was there to do for My vineyard [1]that I have
not done in it?
Why, when I expected *it* to produce *good* grapes did it
produce [2]worthless ones?
5 "So now let Me tell you what I am going to do to
My vineyard:
I will [a]remove its hedge and it will be consumed;
I will [b]break down its wall and it will become
[c]trampled ground.
6 "I will [a]lay it waste;
It will not be pruned or hoed,
But briars and thorns will come up.
I will also charge the clouds to [b]rain no rain on it."

7 For the [a]vineyard of the LORD of hosts is the house of Israel
And the men of Judah His delightful plant.
Thus He looked for justice, but behold, [b]bloodshed;
For righteousness, but behold, a cry of distress.

8 Woe to those who [a]add house to house *and* join field
to field,
Until there is no more room,
So that you have to live alone in the midst of the land!

2 [b]Ps 72:16 [c]Is 10:20; 37:31, 32; Joel 2:32; Obad 17

3 [a]Is 28:5; 46:3; Rom 11:4, 5 [b]Is 52:1; 62:12 [c]Ex 32:32; Ps 69:28; Luke 10:20

4 [1]Lit *rinsed away* [a]Is 3:16 [b]Is 1:15 [c]Is 28:6 [d]Is 1:31; 9:19; Matt 3:11

5 [a]Ex 13:21, 22; 24:16; Num 9:15-23 [b]Is 60:1, 2

6 [1]Lit *a hiding place* [a]Ps 27:5; Is 25:4; 32:1, 2

5:1 [1]Lit *a horn, the son of fatness* [a]Ps 80:8; Jer 12:10; Matt 21:33; Mark 12:1; Luke 20:9

2 [1]Lit *a bright red grape* [2]Or *wine press* [3]Or *wild grapes* [a]Jer 2:21 [b]Matt 21:19; Mark 11:13; Luke 13:6

3 [a]Matt 21:40

4 [1]Lit *and I have not done* [2]Or *wild grapes* [a]2 Chr 36:16; Jer 2:5; 7:25, 26; Mic 6:3; Matt 23:37

5 [a]Ps 89:40 [b]Ps 80:12 [c]Is 10:6; 28:18; Lam 1:15; Luke 21:24; Rev 11:2

6 [a]2 Chr 36:19-21; Is 7:19-25; 24:1, 3; Jer 25:11 [b]1 Kin 8:35; 17:1; Jer 14:1-22

7 [a]Ps 80:8-11 [b]Is 3:14, 15; 30:12; 59:13

8 [a]Jer 22:13-17; Mic 2:2; Hab 2:9-12

9 In my ears the LORD of hosts *has sworn,* "Surely, [a]many
houses shall become [b]desolate,
Even great and fine ones, without occupants.
10 "For [a]ten acres of vineyard will yield *only* one [1]bath *of wine,*
And a [b]homer of seed will yield *but* an [2]ephah of grain."
11 Woe to those who rise early in the morning that they may
pursue [a]strong drink,
Who stay up late in the evening that wine may
inflame them!
12 Their banquets are *accompanied* by lyre and [a]harp, by
tambourine and flute, and by wine;
But they [b]do not pay attention to the deeds of the LORD,
Nor do they consider the work of His hands.

13 Therefore My people go into exile for their [a]lack
of knowledge;
And [1]their [b]honorable men are famished,
And their multitude is parched with thirst.
14 Therefore [a]Sheol has enlarged its [1]throat and opened its
mouth without measure;
And [2]Jerusalem's splendor, her multitude, her din *of revelry*
and the jubilant within her, descend *into it.*
15 So the *common* man will be humbled and the man of
importance abased,
[a]The eyes of the proud also will be abased.
16 But the [a]LORD of hosts will be [b]exalted in judgment,
And the holy God will show Himself [c]holy
in righteousness.
17 [a]Then the lambs will graze as in their pasture,
And strangers will eat in the waste places of the [1]wealthy.

18 Woe to those who drag [a]iniquity with the cords
of [1]falsehood,
And sin as if with cart ropes;
19 [a]Who say, "Let Him make speed, let Him hasten His work,
that we may see *it;*
And let the purpose of the Holy One of Israel draw near
And come to pass, that we may know *it!*"
20 Woe to those who [a]call evil good, and good evil;
Who [1b]substitute darkness for light and light for darkness;
Who [1]substitute bitter for sweet and sweet for bitter!
21 Woe to those who are [a]wise in their own eyes
And clever in their own sight!
22 [a]Woe to those who are heroes in drinking wine
And valiant men in mixing strong drink,
23 [a]Who justify the wicked for a bribe,
And [b]take away the [1]rights of the ones who are in
the right!

24 Therefore, [a]as a tongue of fire consumes stubble
And dry grass collapses into the flame,

9 [a]Is 6:11, 12 [b]Matt 23:38

10 [1]I.e. Approx 10 1/2 gal. [2]I.e. Approx one bu [a]Lev 26:26; Is 7:23; Hag 1:6; 2:16 [b]Ezek 45:11

11 [a]Prov 23:29, 30; Eccl 10:16, 17; Is 5:22; 22:13; 28:1, 3, 7, 8

12 [a]Amos 6:5, 6 [b]Job 34:27; Ps 28:5

13 [1]Lit *their glory are men of famine* [a]Is 1:3; 27:11; Hos 4:6 [b]Is 3:3

14 [1]Or *appetite* [2]Lit *her* [a]Prov 30:16; Hab 2:5

15 [a]Is 2:11; 10:33

16 [a]Is 28:17; 30:18; 61:8 [b]Is 2:11, 17; 33:5, 10 [c]Is 8:13; 29:23; 1 Pet 3:15

17 [1]Lit *the fat* [a]Is 7:25; Mic 2:12; Zeph 2:6

18 [1]Or *worthlessness* [a]Is 59:4-8; Jer 23:10-14

19 [a]Ezek 12:22; 2 Pet 3:4

20 [1]Lit *set* [a]Prov 17:15; Amos 5:7 [b]Job 17:12; Matt 6:22, 23; Luke 11:34, 35

21 [a]Prov 3:7; Rom 12:16; 1 Cor 3:18-20

22 [a]Prov 23:20; Is 5:11; 56:12; Hab 2:15

23 [1]Lit *righteousness* [a]Ex 23:8; Is 1:23; 10:1, 2; Mic 3:11; 7:3 [b]Ps 94:21; James 5:6

24 [a]Is 9:18, 19; Joel 2:5

So their [b]root will become [c]like rot and their blossom
[1]blow away as dust;
For they have [d]rejected the law of the LORD of hosts
And despised the word of the Holy One of Israel.
25 On this account the [a]anger of the LORD has burned against
His people,
And He has stretched out His hand against them and
struck them down.
And the [b]mountains quaked, and their [c]corpses [1]lay like
refuse in the middle of the streets.
[d]For all this His anger [2]is not spent,
But His [e]hand is still stretched out.

26 He will also lift up a [a]standard to the [1]distant nation,
And will [b]whistle for it [c]from the ends of the earth;
And behold, it will [d]come with speed swiftly.
27 [a]No one in it is weary or stumbles,
None slumbers or sleeps;
Nor is the [b]belt at its waist undone,
Nor its sandal strap broken.
28 [1a]Its arrows are sharp and all its bows are bent;
The hoofs of its horses [2]seem like flint and its *chariot*
[b]wheels like a whirlwind.
29 Its [a]roaring is like a lioness, and it roars like young lions;
It growls as it [b]seizes the prey
And carries *it* off with [c]no one to deliver *it*.
30 And it will [a]growl over it in that day like the roaring of
the sea.
If one [b]looks to the land, behold, there is darkness
and distress;
Even the light is darkened by its clouds.

Chapter 6 Theme ______________________________

6 In the year of [a]King Uzziah's death [b]I saw the Lord sitting on
a throne, lofty and exalted, with the train of His robe filling
the temple.
2 Seraphim stood above Him, [a]each having six wings: with
two he covered his face, and with two he covered his feet, and
with two he flew.
3 And one called out to another and said,
"[a]Holy, Holy, Holy, is the LORD of hosts,
The [1b]whole earth is full of His glory."
4 And the [1]foundations of the thresholds trembled at the
voice of him who called out, while the [2a]temple was filling
with smoke.
5 Then I said,
"[a]Woe is me, for I am ruined!
Because I am a man of [b]unclean lips,
And I live among a [c]people of unclean lips;
For my eyes have seen the [d]King, the LORD of hosts."

INSIGHT

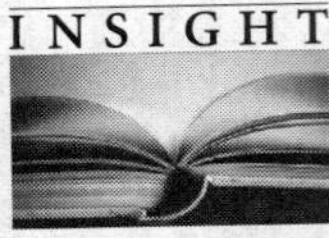

For the historical background of King Uzziah (also called Azariah), read 2 Kings 15 and 2 Chronicles 26.

24 [1]Lit *ascend* [b]Job 18:16 [c]Hos 5:12 [d]Is 8:6; 30:9, 12; Acts 13:41

25 [1]Lit *were* [2]Lit *has not turned away* [a]2 Kin 22:13, 17; Is 66:15 [b]Ps 18:7; Is 64:3; Jer 4:24; Nah 1:5 [c]2 Kin 9:37; Is 14:19; Jer 16:4 [d]Is 9:12, 17, 19, 21; 10:4; Jer 4:8; Dan 9:16 [e]Ex 7:19; Is 23:11

26 [1]Lit *nations;* probably Assyria [a]Is 13:2, 3 [b]Is 7:18; Zech 10:8 [c]Deut 28:49 [d]Is 13:4, 5

27 [a]Joel 2:7, 8 [b]Job 12:18

28 [1]Lit *Which, its arrows* [2]Lit *are regarded as* [a]Ps 7:12, 13; 45:5; Is 13:18 [b]Is 21:1; Jer 4:13

29 [a]Jer 51:38; Zeph 3:3; Zech 11:3 [b]Is 10:6; 49:24, 25; Mic 5:8 [c]Is 42:22

30 [a]Is 17:12; Jer 6:23; Luke 21:25 [b]Is 8:22; Jer 4:23-28; Joel 2:10; Luke 21:25, 26

6:1 [a]2 Kin 15:7; 2 Chr 26:23; Is 1:1 [b]John 12:41; Rev 4:2, 3; 20:11

2 [a]Rev 4:8

3 [1]Lit *fullness of the whole earth is His glory* [a]Rev 4:8 [b]Num 14:21; Ps 72:19

4 [1]Lit *door sockets* [2]Lit *house* [a]Rev 15:8

5 [a]Ex 33:20; Luke 5:8 [b]Ex 6:12, 30 [c]Is 59:3; Jer 9:3-8 [d]Jer 51:57

6 Then one of the seraphim flew to me with a burning coal
in his hand, which he had taken from the [a]altar with tongs.
7 He [a]touched my mouth *with it* and said, "Behold, this has
touched your lips; and [b]your iniquity is taken away and your
sin is [1]forgiven."
8 Then I heard the [a]voice of the Lord, saying, "Whom shall I
send, and who will go for Us?" Then [b]I said, "Here am I. Send
me!"
9 He said, "Go, and tell this people:
'Keep on [a]listening, but do not perceive;
Keep on looking, but do not understand.'
10 "[a]Render the hearts of this people [1b]insensitive,
Their ears [2]dull,
And their eyes [3]dim,
[c]Otherwise they might see with their eyes,
Hear with their ears,
Understand with their hearts,
And return and be healed."
11 Then I said, "Lord, [a]how long?" And He answered,
"Until [b]cities are devastated *and* without inhabitant,
Houses are without people
And the land is utterly desolate,
12 "The LORD has [a]removed men far away,
And the [1b]forsaken places are many in the midst of
the land.
13 "Yet there will be a tenth portion in it,
And it will again be *subject* to burning,
Like a terebinth or an [a]oak
Whose stump remains when it is felled.
The [b]holy seed is its stump."

Chapter 7 Theme

7 Now it came about in the days of [a]Ahaz, the son of Jotham,
the son of Uzziah, king of Judah, that [b]Rezin the king of
Aram and [c]Pekah the son of Remaliah, king of Israel, went up to
Jerusalem to *wage* war against it, but [d]could not [1]conquer it.
2 When it was reported to the [a]house of David, saying, "The
Arameans [1b]have camped in [c]Ephraim," his heart and the
hearts of his people shook as the trees of the forest shake [2]with
the wind.
3 Then the LORD said to Isaiah, "Go out now to meet Ahaz, you
and your son [1]Shear-jashub, at the end of the [a]conduit of the
upper pool, on the highway to the [2]fuller's field,
4 and say to him, 'Take care and be [a]calm, have no [b]fear and
[c]do not be fainthearted because of these two stubs of smoldering
[d]firebrands, on account of the fierce anger of Rezin and Aram
and the [e]son of Remaliah.
5 'Because [a]Aram, *with* Ephraim and the son of Remaliah, has
planned evil against you, saying,
6 "Let us go up against Judah and [1]terrorize it, and make for

6 [a]Rev 8:3

7 [1]Lit *atoned for* [a]Jer 1:9; Dan 10:16 [b]Is 40:2; 53:5, 6, 11; 1 John 1:7

8 [a]Ezek 10:5; Acts 9:4 [b]Acts 26:19

9 [a]Is 43:8; Matt 13:14; Mark 4:12; Luke 8:10; John 12:40; Acts 28:26; Rom 11:8

10 [1]Lit *fat* [2]Lit *heavy* [3]Lit *besmeared* [a]Matt 13:15 [b]Deut 31:20; 32:15 [c]Jer 5:21

11 [a]Ps 79:5 [b]Lev 26:31; Is 1:7; 3:8, 26

12 [1]Or *forsakenness will be great* [a]Deut 28:64 [b]Jer 4:29

13 [a]Job 14:7 [b]Deut 7:6; Ezra 9:2

7:1 [1]Lit *fight against* [a]2 Kin 16:1; Is 1:1 [b]2 Kin 15:37 [c]2 Kin 15:25; 2 Chr 28:6 [d]Is 7:6, 7

2 [1]Lit *has settled down on* [2]Lit *from before* [a]Is 7:13; 22:22 [b]Is 8:12 [c]Is 9:9

3 [1]I.e. a remnant shall return [2]I.e. laundryman's [a]2 Kin 18:17; Is 36:2

4 [a]Ex 14:13; Is 30:15; Lam 3:26 [b]Is 10:24; Matt 24:6 [c]Deut 20:3; 1 Sam 17:32; Is 35:4 [d]Amos 4:11; Zech 3:2 [e]Is 7:1, 9

5 [a]Is 7:2

6 [1]Lit *cause it a sickening dread*

ourselves a breach in [2]its walls and set up the son of Tabeel as
king in the midst of it,"
7 thus says the Lord [1]GOD: "[a]It shall not stand nor shall it come
to pass.
8 "For the head of Aram is [a]Damascus and the head of Damascus
is Rezin (now within another 65 years Ephraim will be shattered,
so that it is no longer a people),
9 and the head of Ephraim is Samaria and the head of Samaria
is the son of Remaliah. [a]If you will not believe, you surely shall
not [1]last."'"
10 Then the LORD spoke again to Ahaz, saying,
11 "Ask a [a]sign for yourself from the LORD your God; [1]make *it*
deep as Sheol or high as [2]heaven."
12 But Ahaz said, "I will not ask, nor will I test the LORD!"
13 Then he said, "Listen now, O [a]house of David! Is it too
slight a thing for you to try the patience of men, that you will
[b]try the patience of [c]my God as well?
14 "Therefore the Lord Himself will give you a sign: Behold, [a]a
[1]virgin will be with child and bear a son, and she will call His
name [2b]Immanuel.
15 "He will eat [a]curds and honey [1]at the time He knows *enough*
to refuse evil and choose good.
16 "[a]For before the boy will know *enough* to refuse evil and
choose good, [b]the land whose two kings you dread will be
forsaken.
17 "The LORD will bring on you, on your people, and on your
father's house such days as have never come since the day that
[a]Ephraim separated from Judah, the [b]king of Assyria."
18 In that day the LORD will [a]whistle for the fly that is in the
[1b]remotest part of the rivers of Egypt and for the bee that is in
the land of Assyria.
19 They will all come and settle on the steep [1]ravines, on the
[a]ledges of the cliffs, [b]on all the thorn bushes and on all the
[2]watering places.
20 In that day the Lord will [a]shave with a [b]razor, [c]hired from
regions beyond [d]the [1]Euphrates (*that is,* with the king of
Assyria), the head and the hair of the legs; and it will also
remove the beard.
21 Now in that day a man may keep alive a [a]heifer and a pair
of sheep;
22 and because of the abundance of the milk produced he will
eat curds, for everyone that is left within the land will eat
[a]curds and honey.
23 And it will come about in that day, [a]that every place where
there used to be a thousand vines, *valued* at a thousand *shekels*
of silver, will become [b]briars and thorns.
24 *People* will come there with bows and arrows because all
the land will be briars and thorns.
25 As for all the hills which used to be cultivated with the hoe,
you will not go there for fear of briars and thorns; but they will
become a place for [1a]pasturing oxen and for sheep to trample.

6 [2]Lit *it*

7 [1]Heb *YHWH,* usually rendered *LORD* [a]Is 8:10; 28:18; Acts 4:25, 26

8 [a]Gen 14:15; Is 17:1-3

9 [1]Or *be established* [a]2 Chr 20:20; Is 5:24; 8:6-8; 30:12-14

11 [1]So with the versions; M.T. *make the request deep or high* [2]Lit *heights* [a]2 Kin 19:29; Is 37:30; 38:7, 8; 55:13

13 [a]Is 7:2 [b]Is 1:14; 43:24 [c]Is 25:1

14 [1]Or *maiden* [2]I.e. God is with us [a]Matt 1:23 [b]Is 8:8, 10

15 [1]Lit *with respect to his knowing* [a]Is 7:22

16 [a]Is 8:4 [b]Is 8:14; 17:3; Jer 7:15; Hos 5:3, 9, 14; Amos 1:3-5

17 [a]1 Kin 12:16 [b]2 Chr 28:20; Is 8:7, 8; 10:5, 6

18 [1]Or *mouth of the rivers;* i.e. the Nile Delta [a]Is 5:26 [b]Is 13:5

19 [1]Or *wadis* [2]Or *pastures* [a]Is 2:19; Jer 16:16 [b]Is 7:24, 25

20 [1]Lit *River* [a]2 Kin 18:13-16; Is 24:1 [b]Ezek 5:1-4 [c]Is 10:5, 15 [d]Is 8:7; 11:15; Jer 2:18

21 [a]Is 14:30; 27:10; Jer 39:10

22 [a]Is 8:15

23 [a]Is 5:10; 32:13, 14 [b]Is 5:6

25 [1]Lit *sending* [a]Is 5:17

Chapter 8 Theme ______________________________

8 Then the LORD said to me, "Take for yourself a large tablet
and [a]write on it [1]in ordinary letters: [2b]Swift is the booty,
speedy is the prey.
2 "And [1]I will take to Myself faithful witnesses for testimony,
[a]Uriah the priest and Zechariah the son of Jeberechiah."
3 So I approached the prophetess, and she conceived and
gave birth to a son. Then the LORD said to me, "Name him
[1a]Maher-shalal-hash-baz;
4 for [a]before the boy knows how to cry out 'My father' or
'My mother,' the wealth of [b]Damascus and the spoil of Samaria
will be carried away before the king of Assyria."
5 Again the LORD spoke to me further, saying,
6 "Inasmuch as these people have [a]rejected the gently flowing
waters of Shiloah
And rejoice in [b]Rezin and the son of Remaliah;
7 "Now therefore, behold, the Lord is about to bring on them
the [a]strong and abundant waters of the [1b]Euphrates,
Even the [c]king of Assyria and all his glory;
And it will [d]rise up over all its channels and go over all
its banks.
8 "Then [a]it will sweep on into Judah, it will overflow and
pass through,
It will [b]reach even to the neck;
And the spread of its wings will [1]fill the breadth of [2]your
land, O [c]Immanuel.

9 "[a]Be broken, O peoples, and be [1b]shattered;
And give ear, all remote places of the earth.
Gird yourselves, yet be [1]shattered;
Gird yourselves, yet be [1]shattered.
10 "[a]Devise a plan, but it will be thwarted;
State a [1]proposal, but [b]it will not stand,
For [2c]God is with us."
11 For thus the LORD spoke to me [1]with [a]mighty power and
instructed me [b]not to walk in the way of this people, saying,
12 "You are not to say, '*It is* a [a]conspiracy!'
In regard to all that this people call a conspiracy,
And [b]you are not to fear [1]what they fear or be in dread
of *it.*
13 "It is the [a]LORD of hosts [b]whom you should regard as holy.
And He shall be your fear,
And He shall be your dread.
14 "Then He shall become a [a]sanctuary;
But to both the houses of Israel, a [b]stone to strike and a
rock to stumble over,
And a snare and a [c]trap for the inhabitants of Jerusalem.
15 "Many [a]will stumble over them,
Then they will fall and be broken;
They will even be snared and caught."
16 [a]Bind up the testimony, [b]seal the [1]law among [c]my disciples.

8:1 [1]Lit *with the stylus of man* [2]Heb *Maher-shalal-hash-baz* [a]Is 30:8; Hab 2:2 [b]Is 8:3
2 [1]Another reading is *take for me* [a]2 Kin 16:10, 11, 15, 16
3 [1]I.e. swift is the booty, speedy is the prey [a]Is 8:1
4 [a]Is 7:16 [b]Is 7:8, 9
6 [a]Is 1:20; 5:24; 7:9; 30:12 [b]Is 7:1
7 [1]Lit *River* [a]Is 17:12, 13 [b]Is 7:20; 11:15 [c]Is 7:17; 10:5 [d]Amos 8:8; 9:5
8 [1]Lit *be the fullness of* [2]Or *Your* [a]Is 10:6 [b]Is 30:28 [c]Is 7:14
9 [1]Or *dismayed* [a]Is 17:12-14 [b]Dan 2:34, 35
10 [1]Lit *word* [2]Heb *Immanu-el* [a]Job 5:12; Is 28:18 [b]Is 7:7 [c]Is 8:8; Rom 8:31
11 [1]Lit *with strength of the hand* [a]Ezek 3:14 [b]Ezek 2:8
12 [1]Lit *their fear* [a]Is 7:2; 30:1 [b]1 Pet 3:14, 15
13 [a]Is 5:16; 29:23 [b]Num 20:12
14 [a]Is 4:6; 25:4; Ezek 11:16 [b]Luke 2:34; Rom 9:33; 1 Pet 2:8 [c]Is 24:17, 18
15 [a]Is 28:13; 59:10; Luke 20:18; Rom 9:32
16 [1]Or *teaching* [a]Is 8:1, 2; 29:11, 12 [b]Dan 12:4 [c]Is 50:4

17 And I will [a]wait for the LORD [b]who is hiding His face from
the house of Jacob; I will even look eagerly for Him.
18 [a]Behold, I and the children whom the LORD has given me
are for [b]signs and wonders in Israel from the LORD of hosts,
who [c]dwells on Mount Zion.
19 When they say to you, "[a]Consult the mediums and the
spiritists who whisper and mutter," should not a people [b]consult
their God? *Should they* [c]*consult* the dead on behalf of the living?
20 To the [1a]law and to the testimony! If they do not speak
according to this word, it is because [b]they have no dawn.
21 They will pass through [1]the land [a]hard-pressed and
famished, and it will turn out that when they are hungry, they
will be enraged and curse [2]their king and their God as they
face upward.
22 Then they will [a]look to the earth, and behold, distress and
darkness, the gloom of anguish; and *they will be* [b]driven away
into darkness.

Chapter 9 Theme ______________________________

9 [1]But there will be no *more* [a]gloom for her who was in
anguish; in earlier times He [b]treated the [c]land of Zebulun
and the land of Naphtali with contempt, but later on He shall
make *it* glorious, by the way of the sea, on the other side of
Jordan, Galilee of the [2]Gentiles.

2 [1a]The people who walk in darkness
Will see a great light;
Those who live in a dark land,
The light will shine on them.
3 [a]You shall multiply the nation,
You [b]shall [1]increase [2]their gladness;
They will be glad in Your presence
As with the gladness [3]of harvest,
As [4c]men rejoice when they divide the spoil.
4 For [a]You shall break the yoke of their burden and the staff
on their shoulders,
The rod of their [b]oppressor, as [1]at the battle of [c]Midian.
5 For every boot of the booted warrior in the *battle* tumult,
And cloak rolled in blood, will be for burning, fuel for
the fire.
6 For a [a]child will be born to us, a [b]son will be given to us;
And the [c]government will [1]rest [d]on His shoulders;
And His name will be called [e]Wonderful Counselor,
[f]Mighty God,
Eternal [g]Father, Prince of [h]Peace.
7 There will be [a]no end to the increase of *His* government or
of peace,
On the [b]throne of David and over his kingdom,
To establish it and to uphold it with [c]justice
and righteousness
From then on and forevermore.
[d]The zeal of the LORD of hosts will accomplish this.

17 [a]Is 25:9; 30:18; Hab 2:3 [b]Deut 31:17; Is 1:15; 45:15; 54:8

18 [a]Heb 2:13 [b]Luke 2:34 [c]Ps 9:11; Zech 8:3

19 [a]Lev 20:6; 2 Kin 21:6; 23:24; Is 19:3; 29:4; 47:12, 13 [b]Is 30:2; 45:11 [c]1 Sam 28:8-11

20 [1]Or *teaching* [a]Is 1:10; 8:16; Luke 16:29 [b]Is 8:22; Mic 3:6

21 [1]Lit *it* [2]Or *by their king* [a]Is 9:20, 21

22 [a]Is 5:30; 59:9; Jer 13:16; Amos 5:18, 20; Zeph 1:14, 15 [b]Is 8:20

9:1 [1]Ch 8:23 in Heb [2]Or *nations* [a]Is 8:22 [b]2 Kin 15:29; 2 Chr 16:4 [c]Matt 4:15, 16

2 [1]Ch 9:1 in Heb [a]Matt 4:16; Luke 1:79; Eph 5:8

3 [1]Another reading is *not increase* [2]Lit *the* [3]Lit *in* [4]Lit *they* [a]Is 26:15 [b]Is 35:10; 65:14, 18, 19; 66:10 [c]1 Sam 30:16

4 [1]Lit *in the day of Midian* [a]Is 10:27; 14:25 [b]Is 14:4; 49:26; 51:13; 54:14 [c]Judg 7:25; Is 10:26

6 [1]Lit *be* [a]Is 7:14; 11:1, 2; 53:2; Luke 2:11 [b]John 3:16 [c]Matt 28:18; 1 Cor 15:25 [d]Is 22:22 [e]Is 28:29 [f]Deut 10:17; Neh 9:32; Is 10:21 [g]Is 63:16; 64:8 [h]Is 26:3, 12; 54:10; 66:12

7 [a]Dan 2:44; Luke 1:32, 33 [b]Is 16:5 [c]Is 11:4, 5; 32:1; 42:3, 4; 63:1 [d]Is 37:32; 59:17

8 The Lord sends a [1]message against Jacob,
And it falls on Israel.
9 And all the people know *it,*
That is, [a]Ephraim and the inhabitants of Samaria,
Asserting in pride and in [b]arrogance of heart:
10 "The bricks have fallen down,
But we will [a]rebuild with smooth stones;
The sycamores have been cut down,
But we will replace *them* with cedars."
11 Therefore the LORD raises against them adversaries
from [a]Rezin
And spurs their enemies on,
12 The Arameans on the east and the [a]Philistines on the west;
And they [b]devour Israel with [1]gaping jaws.
[c]In *spite of* all this, His anger does not turn away
And His hand is still stretched out.

13 Yet the people [a]do not turn back to Him who struck them,
Nor do they [b]seek the LORD of hosts.
14 So the LORD cuts off [a]head and tail from Israel,
Both palm branch and bulrush [b]in a single day.
15 The head is [a]the elder and honorable man,
And the prophet who teaches [b]falsehood is the tail.
16 [a]For those who guide this people are leading *them* astray;
And those who are guided by them are [1]brought
to confusion.
17 Therefore the Lord does [a]not take pleasure in their
young men,
[b]Nor does He have pity on their [1]orphans or their widows;
For every one of them is [c]godless and an [d]evildoer,
And every [e]mouth is speaking foolishness.
[f]In *spite of* all this, His anger does not turn away
And His hand is still stretched out.

18 [a]For wickedness burns like a fire;
It consumes briars and thorns;
It even sets the thickets of the forest aflame
And they roll upward in a column of smoke.
19 By the [a]fury of the LORD of hosts the [b]land is burned up,
And the [c]people are like fuel for the fire;
No [d]man spares his brother.
20 [1]They slice off *what is* on the right hand but *still*
are [a]hungry,
And [2]they eat *what is* on the left hand but they are
not satisfied;
Each of them eats the [b]flesh of his own arm.
21 Manasseh *devours* Ephraim, and Ephraim Manasseh,
[a]*And* together they are against Judah.
[b]In *spite of* all this, His anger does not turn away
And His hand is still stretched out.

8 [1]Lit *word*
9 [a]Is 7:8, 9; 28:1, 3 [b]Is 46:12
10 [a]Mal 1:4
11 [a]Is 7:1, 8
12 [1]Lit *the whole mouth* [a]2 Chr 28:18 [b]Ps 79:7; Jer 10:25 [c]Is 5:25
13 [a]Jer 5:3; Hos 7:10 [b]Is 31:1; Hos 3:5
14 [a]Is 19:15 [b]Rev 18:8
15 [a]Is 3:2, 3 [b]Is 28:15; 59:3, 4; Jer 23:14, 32; Matt 24:24
16 [1]Or *swallowed up* [a]Is 3:12; Matt 15:14; 23:16, 24
17 [1]Or *fatherless* [a]Jer 18:21; Amos 4:10; 8:13 [b]Is 27:11 [c]Is 10:6; 32:6 [d]Is 1:4; 14:20; 31:2 [e]Matt 12:34 [f]Is 5:25
18 [a]Ps 83:14; Is 1:7; Nah 1:10; Mal 4:1
19 [a]Is 10:6; 13:9, 13; 42:25 [b]Joel 2:3 [c]Is 1:31; 24:6 [d]Mic 7:2, 6
20 [1]Lit *he slices* [2]Lit *he eats* [a]Is 8:21, 22 [b]Is 49:26
21 [a]2 Chr 28:6, 8; Is 11:13 [b]Is 5:25

Chapter 10 Theme ______________________

10 Woe to those who [a]enact evil statutes
And to those who constantly record [1]unjust decisions,
2 So as [a]to [1]deprive the needy of justice
And rob the poor of My people of *their* rights,
So [b]that widows may be their spoil
And that they may plunder the [2]orphans.
3 Now [a]what will you do in the [b]day of punishment,
And in the devastation which will come [c]from afar?
[d]To whom will you flee for help?
And where will you leave your [1]wealth?
4 Nothing *remains* but to crouch [1]among the [a]captives
Or fall [1]among the [b]slain.
[c]In *spite of* all this, His anger does not turn away
And His hand is still stretched out.

5 Woe to [a]Assyria, the [b]rod of My anger
And the staff in whose hands is [c]My indignation,
6 I send it against a [a]godless nation
And commission it against the [b]people of My fury
To capture booty and [c]to seize plunder,
And to [1]trample them down like [d]mud in the streets.
7 Yet it [a]does not so intend,
Nor does [1]it plan so in its heart,
But rather it is [2]its purpose to destroy
And to cut off [3]many nations.
8 For it says, "Are not my princes [1]all kings?
9 "Is not [a]Calno like [b]Carchemish,
Or [c]Hamath like Arpad,
Or [d]Samaria like [e]Damascus?
10 "As my hand has reached to the [a]kingdoms of the idols,
Whose graven images *were* greater than those of Jerusalem
and Samaria,
11 Shall I not [1]do to Jerusalem and her images
Just as I have done to Samaria and [a]her idols?"
12 So it will be that when the Lord has completed all His
[a]work on Mount Zion and on Jerusalem, *He will say,* "I will
[1]punish the fruit of the arrogant heart of the king of Assyria
and [b]the pomp of [2]his haughtiness."
13 For [a]he has said,
"By the power of my hand and by my wisdom I did *this,*
For I have understanding;
And I [b]removed the boundaries of the peoples
And plundered their treasures,
And like a mighty man I brought down [1]*their* inhabitants,
14 And my hand reached to the riches of the peoples like
a [a]nest,
And as one gathers abandoned eggs, I gathered all
the earth;
And there was not one that flapped its wing or opened *its*
beak or chirped."

10:1 [1]Lit *mischief or misfortune* [a]Ps 94:20; Is 29:21; 59:4, 13

2 [1]Lit *turn aside from* [2]Or *fatherless* [a]Is 5:23 [b]Is 1:23; 3:14, 15

3 [1]Lit *glory* [a]Job 31:14 [b]Is 13:6; 26:14, 21; 29:6; Jer 9:9; Hos 9:7; Luke 19:44 [c]Is 5:26 [d]Is 20:6; 30:5, 7; 31:3

4 [1]Lit *under* [a]Is 24:22 [b]Is 22:2; 34:3; 66:16 [c]Is 5:25

5 [a]Is 7:17; 8:7; 14:24-27; Zeph 2:13-15 [b]Jer 51:20 [c]Is 13:5; 30:30; 34:2; 66:14

6 [1]Lit *make them a trampled place* [a]Is 9:17 [b]Is 9:19 [c]Is 5:29 [d]Is 5:25

7 [1]Lit *its heart so plan* [2]Lit *in its heart* [3]Lit *not a few* [a]Gen 50:20; Mic 4:11, 12; Acts 2:23, 24

8 [1]Lit *altogether*

9 [a]Gen 10:10; Amos 6:2 [b]2 Chr 35:20 [c]Num 34:8 [d]2 Kin 17:6 [e]2 Kin 16:9

10 [a]2 Kin 19:17, 18

11 [1]Lit *do thus* [a]Is 2:8

12 [1]Lit *visit* [2]Lit *haughtiness of his eyes* [a]2 Kin 19:31; Is 28:21, 22; 29:14; 65:7 [b]Is 37:23

13 [1]Or *those who sit* on thrones [a]2 Kin 19:22-24; Is 37:24-27; Ezek 28:4; Dan 4:30 [b]Hab 2:6-11

14 [a]Jer 49:16; Obad 4

15 [1]Lit *staff* [a]Jer 51:20 [b]Is 29:16; 45:9; Rom 9:20, 21 [c]Is 10:5
16 [1]Heb *YHWH,* usually rendered LORD [a]Ps 106:15 [b]Is 17:4 [c]Is 8:7; 10:18
17 [a]Is 30:33; 31:9 [b]Is 37:23 [c]Num 11:1-3; Is 27:4; 33:12; Jer 4:4; 7:20
18 [a]Is 10:33, 34
19 [a]Is 21:17
20 [a]Is 1:9; 11:11, 16; 46:3 [b]Is 4:2; 37:31, 32 [c]2 Chr 14:11; Is 17:7, 8; 50:10
21 [a]Is 7:3 [b]Is 9:6
22 [a]Rom 9:27, 28 [b]Is 28:22; Dan 9:27; Rom 9:28
23 [1]Heb *YHWH,* usually rendered LORD [a]Is 28:22; Dan 9:27; Rom 9:28
24 [1]Heb *YHWH,* usually rendered LORD [2]Lit *he* [a]Ps 87:5, 6 [b]Is 7:4; 12:2; 37:6 [c]Ex 5:14-16
25 [a]Is 17:14; Hag 2:6 [b]Is 10:5; 26:20; Dan 11:36
26 [a]Is 37:36-38 [b]Judg 7:25; Is 9:4 [c]Ex 14:16 [d]Ex 14:27
27 [1]I.e. the Assyrian [a]Is 9:4; 14:25 [b]Is 30:23; 55:2
28 [a]1 Sam 14:2 [b]1 Sam 13:2, 5 [c]Judg 18:21; 1 Sam 17:22
29 [a]1 Sam 13:23 [b]Josh 21:17; 1 Sam 13:16 [c]Josh 18:25; 1 Sam 7:17 [d]1 Sam 10:26
30 [1]An ancient version reads *Answer her, O Anathoth* [a]1 Sam 25:44 [b]Josh 21:18; Jer 1:1

15 Is the [a]axe to [b]boast itself over the one who chops with it?
Is the saw to exalt itself over the one who wields it?
That would be like [c]a [1]club wielding those who lift it,
Or like [c]a rod lifting *him who* is not wood.
16 Therefore the Lord, the [1]GOD of hosts, will send a [a]wasting disease among his [b]stout warriors;
And under his [c]glory a fire will be kindled like a burning flame.
17 And the [a]light of Israel will become a fire and his [b]Holy One a flame,
And it will [c]burn and devour his thorns and his briars in a single day.
18 And He will [a]destroy the glory of his forest and of his fruitful garden, both soul and body,
And it will be as when a sick man wastes away.
19 And the [a]rest of the trees of his forest will be so small in number
That a child could write them down.
20 Now in that day the [a]remnant of Israel, and those of the
house of Jacob [b]who have escaped, will never again rely on the
one who struck them, but will truly [c]rely on the LORD, the Holy
One of Israel.
21 A [a]remnant will return, the remnant of Jacob, to the [b]mighty God.
22 For [a]though your people, O Israel, may be like the sand of the sea,
Only a remnant within them will return;
A [b]destruction is determined, overflowing with righteousness.
23 For a complete destruction, one that is decreed, [a]the Lord
[1]GOD of hosts will execute in the midst of the whole land.
24 Therefore thus says the Lord [1]GOD of hosts, "O My people
who dwell in [a]Zion, [b]do not fear the Assyrian [2]who [c]strikes you
with the rod and lifts up his staff against you, the way Egypt
did.
25 "For in a very [a]little while [b]My indignation *against you* will
be spent and My anger *will be directed* to their destruction."
26 The LORD of hosts will [a]arouse a scourge against him like
the slaughter of [b]Midian at the rock of Oreb; and His [c]staff will
be over the sea and He will lift it up [d]the way *He did* in Egypt.
27 So it will be in that day, that [1]his [a]burden will be removed
from your shoulders and his yoke from your neck, and the yoke
will be broken because [b]of fatness.
28 He has come against Aiath,
He has passed through [a]Migron;
At [b]Michmash he deposited his [c]baggage.
29 They have gone through [a]the pass, *saying,*
"[b]Geba will be our lodging place."
[c]Ramah is terrified, and [d]Gibeah of Saul has fled away.
30 Cry aloud with your voice, O daughter of [a]Gallim!
Pay attention, Laishah *and* [1]wretched [b]Anathoth!

31 Madmenah has fled.
The inhabitants of Gebim have sought refuge.
32 Yet today he will halt at [a]Nob;
He [b]shakes his fist at the mountain of the [1c]daughter of
Zion, the hill of Jerusalem.

33 Behold, the Lord, the [1]GOD of hosts, will lop off the boughs
with a terrible crash;
Those also who are [a]tall in stature will be cut down
And those who are lofty will be abased.
34 He will cut down the thickets of the forest with an iron *axe,*
And [a]Lebanon will fall [1]by the Mighty One.

Chapter 11 Theme

11 Then a [a]shoot will spring from the [b]stem of Jesse,
And a [c]branch from [d]his roots will bear fruit.
2 The [a]Spirit of the LORD will rest on Him,
The spirit of [b]wisdom and understanding,
The spirit of counsel and [c]strength,
The spirit of knowledge and the fear of the LORD.
3 And He will delight in the fear of the LORD,
And He will not judge by what His eyes [a]see,
Nor make a decision by what His ears hear;
4 But with [a]righteousness He will judge the [b]poor,
And decide with fairness for the [c]afflicted of the earth;
And He will strike the earth with the [d]rod of His mouth,
And with the [e]breath of His lips He will slay the wicked.
5 Also [a]righteousness will be the belt about His loins,
And [b]faithfulness the belt about His waist.

6 And the [a]wolf will dwell with the lamb,
And the leopard will lie down with the young goat,
And the calf and the young lion [1]and the fatling together;
And a little boy will lead them.
7 Also the cow and the bear will graze,
Their young will lie down together,
And the [a]lion will eat straw like the ox.
8 The nursing child will play by the hole of the cobra,
And the weaned child will put his hand on the viper's den.
9 They will [a]not hurt or destroy in all My holy mountain,
For the [b]earth will be full of the knowledge of the LORD
As the waters cover the sea.

10 Then in that day
The [a]nations will resort to the [b]root of Jesse,
Who will stand as a [1c]signal for the peoples;
And His [d]resting place will be [2]glorious.

11 Then it will happen on that day that the Lord
Will again recover the second time with His hand

32 [1]Another reading is *house of* [a]1 Sam 21:1; 22:9 [b]Is 19:16; Zech 2:9 [c]Is 1:8; Jer 6:23

33 [1]Heb *YHWH,* usually rendered *LORD* [a]Is 37:24, 36-38; Ezek 31:3; Amos 2:9

34 [1]Or *as a mighty one* [a]Is 2:13; 33:9; 37:24

11:1 [a]Is 4:2; 53:2 [b]Is 9:7; 11:10; Acts 13:23 [c]Is 6:13; Jer 23:5; Zech 3:8 [d]Rev 5:5; 22:16

2 [a]Is 42:1; 48:16; 61:1; Matt 3:16; John 1:32 [b]John 16:13; 1 Cor 1:30; Eph 1:17, 18 [c]2 Tim 1:7

3 [a]John 2:25; 7:24

4 [a]Is 9:7; 16:5; 32:1 [b]Ps 72:2, 13, 14; Is 3:14 [c]Is 29:19; 32:7; 61:1 [d]Ps 2:9; Is 49:2; Mal 4:6 [e]Job 4:9; Is 30:28, 33; 2 Thess 2:8

5 [a]Eph 6:14 [b]Is 25:1

6 [1]Some versions read *will feed together* [a]Is 65:25

7 [a]Is 65:25

9 [a]Job 5:23; Is 65:25; Ezek 34:25; Hos 2:18 [b]Ps 98:2, 3; Is 45:6; 52:10; 66:18-23; Hab 2:14

10 [1]Or *standard* [2]Lit *glory* [a]Luke 2:32; Acts 11:18 [b]Is 11:1; Rom 15:12 [c]Is 11:12; 49:22; 62:10; John 3:14, 15; 12:32 [d]Is 14:3; 28:12; 32:17, 18

The [a]remnant of His people, who will remain,
From [b]Assyria, [c]Egypt, Pathros, Cush, [d]Elam,
Shinar, Hamath,
And from the [1][e]islands of the sea.
12 And He will lift up a [a]standard for the nations
And [b]assemble the banished ones of Israel,
And will gather the dispersed of Judah
From the four corners of the earth.
13 Then the [a]jealousy of Ephraim will depart,
And those who harass Judah will be cut off;
Ephraim will not be jealous of Judah,
And Judah will not harass Ephraim.
14 They will [a]swoop down on the slopes of the Philistines on
the [b]west;
Together they will [c]plunder the sons of the east;
[1]They will possess [d]Edom and [e]Moab,
And the sons of Ammon will be [2]subject to them.
15 And the LORD will [1][a]utterly destroy
The tongue of the [2]Sea of Egypt;
And He will [b]wave His hand over the [3][c]River
With His scorching wind;
And He will strike it into seven streams
And make *men* walk over [4]dry-shod.
16 And there will be a [a]highway from Assyria
For the [b]remnant of His people who will be left,
Just as there was for Israel
In [c]the day that they came up out of the land
of Egypt.

Chapter 12 Theme ______________________________

12 Then you will say on that day,
"[a]I will give thanks to You, O LORD;
For [b]although You were angry with me,
Your anger is turned away,
And You comfort me.
2 "Behold, [a]God is my salvation,
I will [b]trust and not be afraid;
For [c]the LORD GOD is my strength and song,
And He has become my salvation."
3 Therefore you will joyously [a]draw water
From the [b]springs of salvation.
4 And in that day you will [a]say,
"[b]Give thanks to the LORD, call on His name.
[c]Make known His deeds among the peoples;
[1]Make *them* remember that His name is exalted."
5 [a]Praise the LORD in song, for He has done [1]excellent things;
Let this be known throughout the earth.
6 [a]Cry aloud and shout for joy, O inhabitant of Zion,
For [b]great in your midst is the Holy One of Israel.

11 [1]Or *coastlands* [a]Is 10:20-22; 37:4, 31, 32; 46:3 [b]Is 19:23-25; Hos 11:11; Zech 10:10 [c]Is 19:21, 22; Mic 7:12 [d]Gen 10:22; 14:1 [e]Is 24:15; 42:4, 10, 12; 49:1; 51:5; 60:9; 66:19

12 [a]Is 11:10 [b]Is 56:8; Zeph 3:10; Zech 10:6

13 [a]Is 9:21; Jer 3:18; Ezek 37:16, 17, 22; Hos 1:11

14 [1]Lit *Edom and Moab will be the outstretching of their hand* [2]Lit *their obedience* [a]Jer 48:40; 49:22; Hab 1:8 [b]Is 9:12 [c]Jer 49:28 [d]Is 63:1; Dan 11:41; Joel 3:19; Amos 9:12 [e]Is 16:14; 25:10

15 [1]Another reading is *dry up the tongue* [2]Perhaps the Red Sea [3]I.e. Euphrates [4]Lit *in sandals* [a]Is 43:16; 44:27; 50:2; 51:10, 11 [b]Is 19:16 [c]Is 7:20; 8:7; Rev 16:12

16 [a]Is 19:23; 35:8; 40:3; 62:10 [b]Is 11:11 [c]Ex 14:26-29

12:1 [a]Ps 9:1; Is 25:1 [b]Ps 30:5; Is 40:1, 2; 54:7-10

2 [a]Is 32:2; 45:17; 62:11 [b]Is 26:3 [c]Ex 15:2; Ps 118:14

3 [a]John 4:10; 7:37, 38 [b]Is 41:18; Jer 2:13

4 [1]Or *Proclaim* to them *that* [a]Is 24:15; 42:12; 48:20 [b]Ps 105:1 [c]Ps 145:4

5 [1]Or *gloriously* [a]Ex 15:1; Ps 98:1; Is 24:14; 42:10, 11; 44:23

6 [a]Is 52:9; 54:1; Zeph 3:14 [b]Is 1:24; 49:26; 60:16; Zeph 3:15-17; Zech 2:5, 10, 11

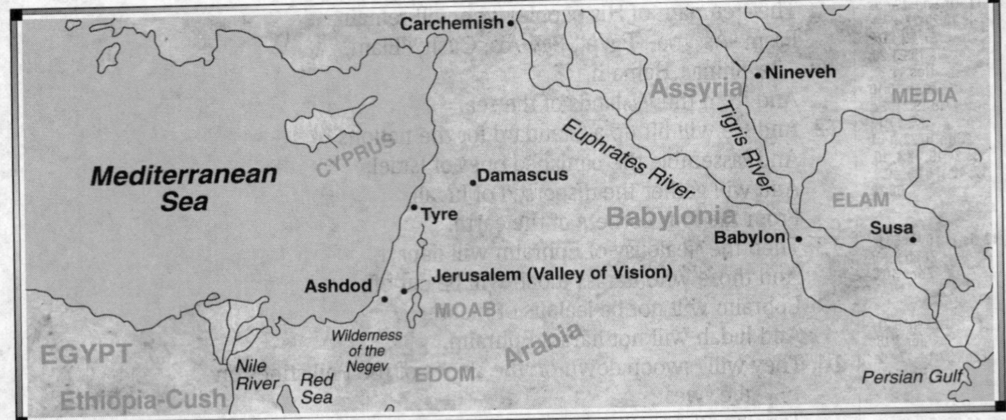

The Nations That Received the Oracles

RETURN TO INSTRUCTIONS

Chapter 13 Theme ______________________________

13 The [1a]oracle concerning [b]Babylon which [c]Isaiah the son of Amoz saw.

2 [a]Lift up a standard on the [1b]bare hill,
Raise your voice to them,
[c]Wave the hand that they may [d]enter the doors of the nobles.
3 I have commanded My consecrated ones,
I have even called My [a]mighty warriors,
My proudly exulting ones,
To *execute* My anger.
4 A [a]sound of tumult on the mountains,
Like that of many people!
A sound of the uproar of kingdoms,
Of nations gathered together!
The LORD of hosts is mustering the army for battle.
5 They are coming from a far country,
From the [1a]farthest horizons,
The LORD and His instruments of [b]indignation,
To [c]destroy the whole land.
6 Wail, for the [a]day of the LORD is near!
It will come as [b]destruction from [1]the Almighty.
7 Therefore [a]all hands will fall limp,
And every man's [b]heart will melt.
8 They will be [a]terrified,
Pains and anguish will take hold of *them;*
They will [b]writhe like a woman in labor,
They will look at one another in astonishment,
Their faces aflame.
9 Behold, [a]the day of the LORD is coming,
Cruel, with fury and burning anger,
To make the land a desolation;
And He will exterminate its sinners from it.
10 For the [a]stars of heaven and their constellations
Will not flash forth their light;

13:1 [1]Or *burden of* [a]Is 14:28; 15:1 [b]Is 13:19; 14:4; 47:1-15; Jer 24:1; 50:1-51:64; Matt 1:11; Rev 14:8 [c]Is 1:1

2 [1]Or *wind-swept mountain* [a]Is 5:26; Jer 50:2 [b]Jer 51:25 [c]Is 10:32; 19:16 [d]Is 45:1-3; Jer 51:58

3 [a]Joel 3:11

4 [a]Is 5:30; 17:12; Joel 3:14

5 [1]Lit *end of heaven* [a]Is 5:26; 7:18 [b]Is 10:5 [c]Is 24:1

6 [1]Heb *Shaddai* [a]Is 2:12; 10:3; 13:9; 34:2, 8; 61:2; Ezek 30:3; Amos 5:18; Zeph 1:7 [b]Is 10:25; 14:23; Joel 1:15

7 [a]Ezek 7:17 [b]Is 19:1; Ezek 21:7; Nah 2:10

8 [a]2 Kin 19:26; Is 21:3; Jer 46:5 [b]Is 26:17; Jer 4:31; John 16:21

9 [a]Is 13:6

10 [a]Is 5:30; Ezek 32:7; Joel 2:10; Matt 24:29; Mark 13:24; Luke 21:25; Rev 6:13; 8:12

The [b]sun will be dark when it rises
And the moon will not shed its light.
11 Thus I will [a]punish the world for its evil
And the [b]wicked for their iniquity;
I will also put an end to the [c]arrogance of the proud
And abase the [d]haughtiness of the [1e]ruthless.
12 I will make mortal man [1a]scarcer than pure gold
And mankind than the [b]gold of Ophir.
13 Therefore I will make the [a]heavens tremble,
And [b]the earth will be shaken from its place
At the fury of the LORD of hosts
In [c]the day of His burning anger.
14 And it will be that like a hunted gazelle,
Or like [a]sheep with none to gather *them,*
They will each turn to his own people,
And each one flee to his own land.
15 Anyone who is found will be [a]thrust through,
And anyone who is captured will fall by the sword.
16 Their [a]little ones also will be dashed to pieces
Before their eyes;
Their houses will be plundered
And their wives ravished.

17 Behold, I am going to [a]stir up the Medes against them,
Who will not value silver or [b]take pleasure in gold.
18 And *their* bows will [1]mow down the [a]young men,
They will not even have compassion on the fruit of the womb,
Nor will their [b]eye pity [2]children.
19 And [a]Babylon, the [b]beauty of kingdoms, the glory of the Chaldeans' pride,
Will be as when God [c]overthrew Sodom and Gomorrah.
20 It will [a]never be inhabited or lived in from generation to generation;
Nor will the [b]Arab pitch *his* tent there,
Nor will shepherds make *their flocks* lie down there.
21 But [a]desert creatures will lie down there,
And their houses will be full of [1]owls;
Ostriches also will live there, and [2]shaggy goats will frolic there.
22 [1]Hyenas will howl in their fortified towers
And jackals in their luxurious [a]palaces.
Her *fateful* time also [2]will soon come
And her days will not be prolonged.

Chapter 14 Theme ____________________

14 When the LORD will [a]have compassion on Jacob and again [b]choose Israel, and settle them in their own land, then [c]strangers will join them and attach themselves to the house of Jacob.

10 [b]Is 24:23; 50:3; Ezek 32:7; Acts 2:20; Rev 6:12

11 [1]Or *tyrants, despots* [a]Is 26:21 [b]Is 3:11; 11:4; 14:5 [c]Is 2:11; 23:9; Dan 5:22, 23 [d]Jer 48:29 [e]Is 25:3; 29:5, 20

12 [1]Lit *more precious* [a]Is 4:1; 6:11, 12 [b]1 Kin 9:28; Job 28:16; Ps 45:9

13 [a]Is 34:4; 51:6 [b]Ps 18:7; Is 2:19; 24:1, 19, 20; Hag 2:6 [c]Lam 1:12

14 [a]1 Kin 22:17; Matt 9:36; Mark 6:34; 1 Pet 2:25

15 [a]Is 14:19; Jer 50:25; 51:3, 4

16 [a]Ps 137:8, 9; Is 13:18; 14:21; Hos 10:14; Nah 3:10

17 [a]Jer 51:11; Dan 5:28 [b]Prov 6:34, 35

18 [1]Lit *dash in pieces* [2]Lit *sons* [a]2 Kin 8:12; 2 Chr 36:17 [b]Ezek 9:5, 10

19 [a]Is 21:9; 48:14 [b]Dan 4:30; Rev 18:11-16, 19, 21 [c]Gen 19:24; Deut 29:23; Jer 49:18; Amos 4:11

20 [a]Is 14:23; 34:10-15; Jer 51:37-43 [b]2 Chr 17:11

21 [1]Or *howling creatures* [2]Or *goat demons* [a]Is 34:11-15; Zeph 2:14; Rev 18:2

22 [1]Or *howling creatures* [2]Lit *is near to come* [a]Is 25:2; 32:14; 34:13

14:1 [a]Ps 102:13; Is 49:13, 15; 54:7, 8 [b]Is 41:8, 9; 44:1; 49:7; Zech 1:17; 2:12 [c]Is 56:3, 6; Eph 2:12-19

INSIGHT

From 729 B.C. Babylon was part of the Assyrian Empire. The ruler of Assyria assumed the title "King of Babylon." Babylon then became the capital of the Neo-Babylonian Empire which Nebuchadnezzar ruled after the death of his father, Nabopolassar. Nebuchadnezzar first besieged Jerusalem in 605 B.C. In 586 B.C. he destroyed Jerusalem and the temple.

2 The peoples will take them along and bring them to their
place, and the [a]house of Israel will possess them as an inheritance
in the land of the LORD [b]as male servants and female servants; and
[1]they will take their captors captive and will rule over their
oppressors.
3 And it will be in the day when the LORD gives you [a]rest from
your pain and turmoil and harsh service in which you have
been enslaved,
4 that you will [a]take up this [1]taunt against the king of Babylon,
and say,

"How [b]the oppressor has ceased,
And how [2]fury has ceased!
5 "The LORD has broken the staff of the wicked,
The scepter of rulers
6 [a]Which used to strike the peoples in fury with
unceasing strokes,
Which [1]subdued the nations in anger with
unrestrained persecution.
7 "The whole earth is at rest *and* is quiet;
They [a]break forth into shouts of joy.
8 "Even the [a]cypress trees rejoice over you, *and* the cedars of
Lebanon, *saying,*
'Since you were laid low, no *tree* cutter comes up
against us.'
9 "[a]Sheol from beneath is excited over you to meet you when
you come;
It arouses for you the [1]spirits of the dead, all the [2]leaders of
the earth;
It raises all the kings of the nations from their thrones.
10 "[a]They will all respond and say to you,
'Even you have been made weak as we,
You have become like us.
11 'Your [a]pomp *and* the music of your harps
Have been brought down to Sheol;
Maggots are spread out *as your bed* beneath you
And worms are your covering.'
12 "How you have [a]fallen from heaven,
O [1b]star of the morning, son of the dawn!
You have been cut down to the earth,
You who have weakened the nations!
13 "But you said in your heart,
'I will [a]ascend to heaven;
I will [b]raise my throne above the stars of God,
And I will sit on the mount of assembly
In the recesses of the north.
14 'I will ascend above the heights of the clouds;
[a]I will make myself like the Most High.'
15 "Nevertheless you [a]will be thrust down to Sheol,
To the recesses of the pit.
16 "Those who see you will gaze at you,
They will [1]ponder over you, *saying,*

2 [1]Lit *the captors will become their captives* [a]Is 45:14; 49:23; 54:3 [b]Is 60:10; 61:5; Dan 7:18, 27

3 [a]Ezra 9:8, 9; Is 11:10; 40:2; Jer 30:10; 46:27

4 [1]Or *proverb* [2]Amended from the meaningless *medhebah* to *marhebah* [a]Hab 2:6 [b]Is 9:4; 16:4; 49:26; 51:13; 54:14

6 [1]Or *ruled* [a]Is 10:14; 47:6

7 [a]Ps 47:1-3; 98:1-9; 126:1-3

8 [a]Is 55:12; Ezek 31:16

9 [1]Or *shades* (Heb *Repha'im*) [2]Lit *male goats* [a]Is 5:14

10 [a]Ezek 32:21

11 [a]Is 5:14

12 [1]Heb *Helel;* i.e. shining one [a]Is 34:4; Luke 10:18; Rev 8:10; 9:1 [b]2 Pet 1:19; Rev 2:28; 22:16

13 [a]Ezek 28:2 [b]Dan 5:22, 23; 8:10; 2 Thess 2:4

14 [a]Is 47:8; 2 Thess 2:4

15 [a]Ezek 28:8; Matt 11:23; Luke 10:15

16 [1]Lit *show themselves attentive to*

'Is this the man who made the earth tremble,
Who shook kingdoms,
17 Who made the world like a [a]wilderness
And overthrew its cities,
Who [b]did not [1]allow his prisoners to *go* home?'
18 "All the kings of the nations lie in glory,
Each in his own [1]tomb.
19 "But you have been [a]cast out of your tomb
Like [1]a rejected branch,
[2]Clothed with the slain who are pierced with
a sword,
Who go down to the stones of the [b]pit
Like a [c]trampled corpse.
20 "You will not be united with them in burial,
Because you have ruined your country,
You have slain your people.
May the [a]offspring of evildoers not be mentioned forever.
21 "Prepare for his sons a place of slaughter
Because of the [a]iniquity of their fathers.
They must not arise and take possession of the earth
And fill the face of the world with cities."
22 "I will rise up against them," declares the LORD of hosts, "and
will cut off from Babylon [a]name and survivors, [b]offspring and
posterity," declares the LORD.
23 "I will also make it a possession for the [a]hedgehog and swamps
of water, and I will sweep it with the broom of [b]destruction,"
declares the LORD of hosts.
24 The LORD of hosts has sworn saying, "Surely, [a]just as I have
intended so it has happened, and just as I have planned so it will
stand,
25 to [a]break Assyria in My land, and I will trample him on My
mountains. Then his [b]yoke will be removed from them and his
burden removed from their shoulder.
26 "This is the [a]plan [1]devised against the whole earth; and this
is the [b]hand that is stretched out against all the nations.
27 "For [a]the LORD of hosts has planned, and who can frustrate
it? And as for His stretched-out hand, who can turn it back?"
28 In the [a]year that King Ahaz died this [1b]oracle came:
29 "Do not rejoice, O [a]Philistia, all of you,
Because the rod that [b]struck you is broken;
For from the serpent's root a [c]viper will come out,
And its fruit will be a [d]flying serpent.
30 "[1]Those who are most [a]helpless will eat,
And the needy will lie down in security;
I will [2]destroy your root with [b]famine,
And it will kill off your survivors.
31 "Wail, O [a]gate; cry, O city;
[1]Melt away, O [b]Philistia, all of you;
For smoke comes from the [c]north,
And [d]there is no straggler in his ranks.
32 "How then will one answer the [a]messengers of the nation?

17 [1]Lit *open* [a]Joel 2:3 [b]Is 45:13
18 [1]Lit *house*
19 [1]Lit *an abhorred branch* [2]Or *As the clothing of those who are slain* [a]Is 22:16-18 [b]Jer 41:7, 9 [c]Is 5:25
20 [a]Job 18:16, 19; Ps 21:10; 37:28; Is 1:4; 31:2
21 [a]Ex 20:5; Lev 26:39; Is 13:16; Matt 23:35
22 [a]Prov 10:7 [b]Job 18:19; Is 47:9
23 [a]Is 34:11; Zeph 2:14 [b]1 Kin 14:10; Is 13:6
24 [a]Job 23:13; Is 46:11; 55:8, 9; Acts 4:28
25 [a]Is 10:12; 30:31; 31:8 [b]Is 9:4; 10:27; Nah 1:13
26 [1]Lit *planned* [a]Is 23:9; Zeph 3:6, 8 [b]Ex 15:12
27 [a]2 Chr 20:6; Is 43:13; Dan 4:31, 35
28 [1]Or *burden* [a]2 Kin 16:20; 2 Chr 28:27 [b]Is 13:1
29 [a]Is 2:6; 11:14; Jer 47:1-7; Ezek 25:15-17; Joel 3:4-8; Amos 1:6-8; Zeph 2:4-7; Zech 9:5-7 [b]2 Chr 26:6 [c]Is 11:8 [d]Is 30:6
30 [1]Lit *the firstborn of the helpless* [2]Lit *put to death* [a]Is 3:14, 15; 7:21, 22; 11:4 [b]Is 8:21; 9:20; 51:19
31 [1]Or *Become demoralized* [a]Is 3:26; 24:12; 45:2 [b]Is 14:29 [c]Jer 1:14 [d]Is 34:16
32 [a]Is 37:9

That [b]the LORD has founded Zion,
And [c]the afflicted of His people will seek refuge in it."

Chapter 15 Theme ______________________

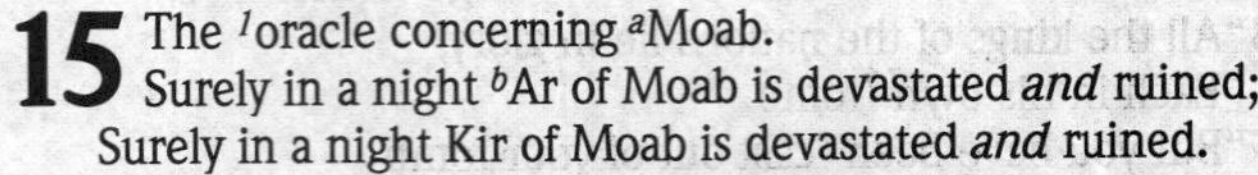

15 The [1]oracle concerning [a]Moab.
Surely in a night [b]Ar of Moab is devastated *and* ruined;
Surely in a night Kir of Moab is devastated *and* ruined.
2 They have go up to the [1]temple and *to* [a]Dibon, *even* to
the high places to weep.
Moab wails over Nebo and Medeba;
Everyone's head is [b]bald *and* every beard is cut off.
3 In their streets they have girded themselves with
[a]sackcloth;
[b]On their housetops and in their squares
Everyone is wailing, [1c]dissolved in tears.
4 [a]Heshbon and Elealeh also cry out,
Their voice is heard all the way to Jahaz;
Therefore the [1]armed men of Moab cry aloud;
His soul trembles within him.
5 My heart cries out for Moab;
His fugitives are as far as [a]Zoar *and* Eglath-shelishiyah,
For they go up the [b]ascent of Luhith weeping;
Surely on the road to Horonaim they raise a cry of distress
[c]over *their* ruin.
6 For the [a]waters of Nimrim are [1]desolate.
Surely the grass is withered, the tender grass [2]died out,
There is [b]no green thing.
7 Therefore the [a]abundance *which* they have acquired and
stored up
They carry off over the brook of [1]Arabim.
8 For the cry of distress has gone around the territory
of Moab,
Its wail *goes* as far as Eglaim and its wailing even to
Beer-elim.
9 For the waters of Dimon are full of [1]blood;
Surely I will bring added *woes* upon Dimon,
A [a]lion upon the fugitives of Moab and upon the remnant
of the land.

INSIGHT

Moab was a narrow strip of land directly east of the Dead (Salt) Sea. Its inhabitants were called Moabites and were neighbors to the Israelites. Moab, the father of the Moabites, was the son of Lot by his firstborn daughter. Ruth, who is in the genealogy of King David, was a Moabitess.

Chapter 16 Theme ______________________

16 [a]Send the *tribute* lamb to the ruler of the land,
From [1b]Sela by way of the wilderness to the [c]mountain of
the daughter of Zion.
2 Then, like [1a]fleeing birds *or* scattered [2]nestlings,
The daughters of [b]Moab will be at the fords of the [c]Arnon.
3 "[1]Give *us* advice, make a decision;
[2]Cast your [a]shadow like night [3]at high noon;
[b]Hide the outcasts, do not betray the fugitive.
4 "Let the [1]outcasts of Moab stay with you;

32 [b]Ps 87:1, 5; 102:16; Is 28:16; 44:28; 54:11 [c]Is 4:6; 25:4; 57:13; Zeph 3:12; Heb 11:10; James 2:5

15:1 [1]Or *burden of* [a]Is 11:14; 25:10; Jer 48:1; Ezek 25:8-11; Amos 2:1-3; Zeph 2:8-11 [b]Num 21:28

2 [1]Lit *house* [a]Jer 48:18, 22 [b]Lev 21:5; Jer 48:37

3 [1]Lit *going down in weeping* [a]Jon 3:6-8 [b]Jer 48:38 [c]Is 22:4

4 [1]Another reading is *the loins of* [a]Num 21:28; 32:3; Jer 48:34

5 [a]Jer 48:34 [b]Jer 48:5 [c]Is 59:7; Jer 4:20

6 [1]Lit *desolations* [2]Lit *come to an end* [a]Is 19:5-7; Jer 48:34 [b]Joel 1:10-12; 2:3

7 [1]Or *the poplars* [a]Is 30:6; Jer 48:36

9 [1]Heb *dam* (a wordplay) [a]2 Kin 17:25; Jer 50:17

16:1 [1]I.e. Petra in Edom [a]2 Kin 3:4; Ezra 7:17 [b]2 Kin 14:7; Is 42:11 [c]Is 10:32

2 [1]Or *fluttering* [2]Lit *nest* [a]Prov 27:8 [b]Jer 48:20, 46 [c]Num 21:13, 14

3 [1]Lit *Bring* [2]Lit *Set* [3]Lit *in the midst of the noon* [a]Is 25:4; 32:2 [b]1 Kin 18:4

4 [1]So the versions; M.T. *My outcasts, as for Moab*

Be a hiding place to them from the destroyer."
For the extortioner has come to an end, destruction
has ceased,
[a]Oppressors have completely *disappeared* from the land.
5 A [a]throne will even be established in lovingkindness,
And a judge will sit on it in faithfulness in the tent
of [b]David;
Moreover, he will seek justice
And be prompt in righteousness.

6 [a]We have heard of the pride of Moab, an excessive pride;
Even of his arrogance, pride, and fury;
[b]His idle boasts are [1]false.
7 Therefore Moab will wail; everyone of Moab will wail.
You will moan for the [a]raisin cakes of [b]Kir-hareseth
As those who are utterly stricken.
8 For the fields of [a]Heshbon have [1]withered, the vines of
[b]Sibmah *as well;*
The lords of the nations have trampled down its
choice clusters
Which reached as far as Jazer *and* wandered to the deserts;
[c]Its tendrils spread themselves out *and* passed over the sea.
9 Therefore I will [a]weep bitterly for Jazer, for the vine
of Sibmah;
I will drench you with my tears, O [b]Heshbon and Elealeh;
For the shouting over your [c]summer fruits and your harvest
has fallen away.
10 [a]Gladness and joy are taken away from the fruitful field;
In the [b]vineyards also there will be no cries of joy or
jubilant shouting,
No [c]treader treads out wine in the presses,
For I have made the shouting to cease.
11 Therefore my [1a]heart intones like a harp for Moab
And my [2]inward feelings for Kir-hareseth.
12 So it will come about when Moab [a]presents himself,
When he [b]wearies himself upon *his* [c]high place
And comes to his sanctuary to pray,
That he will not prevail.
13 This is the word which the LORD spoke earlier concerning
Moab.
14 But now the LORD speaks, saying, "Within three years, as
[1a]a hired man would count them, the glory of [b]Moab will be
degraded along with all *his* great population, and *his* remnant
will be very small *and* [2]impotent."

Chapter 17 Theme ____________________

17 The [1a]oracle concerning [b]Damascus.
"Behold, Damascus is about to be [c]removed from being
a city
And will become a [d]fallen ruin.

4 [a]Is 9:4; 14:4; 49:26; 51:13; 54:14
5 [a]Is 9:6, 7; 32:1; 55:4; Dan 7:14; Mic 4:7; Luke 1:33 [b]Is 9:7
6 [1]Lit *not so* [a]Jer 48:29; Amos 2:1; Obad 3, 4; Zeph 2:8, 10 [b]Jer 48:30
7 [a]1 Chr 16:3 [b]2 Kin 3:25; Jer 48:31
8 [1]Or *languished* [a]Is 15:4 [b]Num 32:38 [c]Jer 48:32
9 [a]Jer 48:32 [b]Is 15:4 [c]Jer 40:10, 12; 48:32
10 [a]Is 24:8; Jer 48:33 [b]Judg 9:27; Is 24:7; Amos 5:11, 17 [c]Job 24:11; Amos 9:13
11 [1]Lit *entrails murmur* [2]Lit *inward part* [a]Is 15:5; 63:15; Jer 48:36; Hos 11:8; Phil 2:1
12 [a]Num 22:39-41; Jer 48:35 [b]1 Kin 18:29 [c]Is 15:2
14 [1]Lit *the years of a hireling* [2]Lit *not mighty* [a]Job 7:1; 14:6; Is 21:16 [b]Is 25:10; Jer 48:42
17:1 [1]Or *burden of* [a]Is 13:1 [b]Gen 14:15; 15:2; 2 Kin 16:9; Jer 49:23; Amos 1:3-5; Zech 9:1; Acts 9:2 [c]Is 7:16; 8:4; 10:9 [d]Is 25:2; Jer 49:2; Mic 1:6

2 "The cities [1]of [a]Aroer are forsaken;
They will be for [b]flocks [2]to lie down in,
And there will be [c]no one to frighten *them.*
3 "The [1a]fortified city will disappear from Ephraim,
And [2]sovereignty from Damascus
And the remnant of Aram;
They will be like the [b]glory of the sons of Israel,"
Declares the LORD of hosts.

INSIGHT

Damascus is the capital of Aram (or Syria).

4 Now in that day the [a]glory of Jacob will [1]fade,
And [b]the fatness of his flesh will become lean.
5 It will be [a]even like the [1]reaper gathering the standing grain,
As his arm harvests the ears,
Or it will be like one gleaning ears of grain
In the [b]valley of Rephaim.
6 Yet [a]gleanings will be left in it like the [1]shaking of an olive tree,
Two *or* three olives on the topmost bough,
Four *or* five on the branches of a fruitful tree,
Declares the LORD, the God of Israel.
7 In that day man will [a]have regard for his Maker
And his eyes will look to the Holy One of Israel.
8 He will not have regard for the [a]altars, the work of his hands,
Nor will he look to that which his [b]fingers have made,
Even the [1c]Asherim and [2]incense stands.
9 In that day [1]their strong cities will be like [2]forsaken places in the forest,
Or like [3]branches which they abandoned before the sons of Israel;
And [4]the land will be a desolation.
10 For [a]you have forgotten the [b]God of your salvation
And have not remembered the [c]rock of your refuge.
Therefore you plant delightful plants
And set them with vine slips of a strange *god.*
11 In the day that you plant *it* you carefully fence *it* in,
And in the [a]morning you bring your seed to blossom;
But the harvest will [b]*be* a heap
In a day of sickliness and incurable pain.

12 Alas, the uproar of many peoples
[a]Who roar like the roaring of the seas,
And the rumbling of nations
Who rush on like the [b]rumbling of mighty waters!
13 The [a]nations rumble on like the rumbling of many waters,
But He will [b]rebuke them and they will flee far away,
And be chased [c]like chaff in the mountains before the wind,
Or like whirling dust before a gale.
14 At evening time, behold, *there is* terror!
Before morning [a]they are no more.
[1]Such *will be* the portion of those who plunder us
And the lot of those who pillage us.

2 [1]Gr reads *forever and ever* [2]Lit *and they will lie down* [a]Num 32:34 [b]Is 7:21, 22; Ezek 25:5; Zeph 2:6 [c]Mic 4:4

3 [1]Or *fortification* [2]Or *royal power, kingdom* [a]Is 7:8, 16; 8:4 [b]Is 17:4; Hos 9:11

4 [1]Lit *become thin* [a]Is 10:3 [b]Is 10:16

5 [1]Lit *gathering of the harvest, the standing grain* [a]Is 17:11; Jer 51:33; Joel 3:13; Matt 13:30 [b]2 Sam 5:18, 22

6 [1]Lit *striking* [a]Deut 4:27; Is 24:13; 27:12; Obad 5

7 [a]Is 10:20; Hos 3:5; 6:1; Mic 7:7

8 [1]I.e. wooden symbols of a female deity [2]Or *sun pillars* [a]2 Chr 34:7; Is 27:9 [b]Is 2:8, 20; 30:22; 31:7 [c]Ex 34:13; Deut 7:5; Mic 5:14

9 [1]I.e. man's [2]Gr reads *the deserted places of the Amorites and the Hivites which they abandoned* [3]Or *the treetop* [4]Lit *it*

10 [a]Is 51:13 [b]Ps 68:19; Is 12:2; 33:2; 61:10; 62:11 [c]Deut 32:4, 18, 31; Is 26:4; 30:29; 44:8

11 [a]Ps 90:6 [b]Job 4:8; Hos 8:7; 10:13

12 [a]Is 5:30; Jer 6:23; Ezek 43:2; Luke 21:25 [b]Ps 18:4

13 [a]Is 33:3 [b]Ps 9:5; Is 41:11 [c]Job 21:18; Ps 1:4; 83:13; Is 29:5; 41:15, 16

14 [1]Lit *This* [a]2 Kin 19:35; Is 41:12

Chapter 18 Theme ________________________

18 Alas, oh land of whirring wings
Which lies beyond the rivers of [1a]Cush,
2 Which sends envoys by the sea,
Even in [a]papyrus vessels on the surface of the waters.
Go, swift messengers, to a nation [1b]tall and smooth,
To a people [c]feared [2]far and wide,
A powerful and oppressive nation
Whose land the rivers divide.
3 [a]All you inhabitants of the world and dwellers on earth,
As soon as a standard is raised on the mountains, [b]you will
see *it*,
And as soon as the trumpet is blown, you will hear *it*.
4 For thus the LORD has told me,
"I will look [1]from My [a]dwelling place quietly
Like dazzling heat in the [2b]sunshine,
Like a cloud of [c]dew in the heat of harvest."
5 For [a]before the harvest, as soon as the bud [1]blossoms
And the flower becomes a ripening grape,
Then He will cut off the sprigs with pruning knives
And remove *and* cut away the spreading branches.
6 They will be left together for mountain birds [a]of prey,
And for the beasts of the earth;
And the birds of prey will spend the summer *feeding*
on them,
And all the beasts of the earth will spend harvest time
on them.
7 At that time a gift of homage will be brought to the LORD
of hosts
[1]From a [a]people [2]tall and smooth,
Even from a people feared [3]far and wide,
A powerful and oppressive nation,
Whose land the rivers divide—
To the [b]place of the name of the LORD of hosts, *even*
Mount Zion.

Chapter 19 Theme ________________________

19 The [1a]oracle concerning [b]Egypt.
Behold, the LORD is [c]riding on a swift cloud and is about
to come to Egypt;
The [d]idols of Egypt will tremble at His presence,
And the [e]heart of the Egyptians will melt within them.
2 "So I will incite Egyptians against Egyptians;
And they will [a]each fight against his brother and each
against his neighbor,
City against city *and* kingdom against kingdom.
3 "Then the spirit of the Egyptians will be demoralized
within them;
And I will confound their strategy,

18:1 [1]Or *Ethiopia* [a]2 Kin 19:9; Is 20:3-5; Ezek 30:4, 5, 9; Zeph 2:12; 3:10
2 [1]Lit *drawn out* [2]Lit *from it and beyond* [a]Ex 2:3 [b]Is 18:7 [c]Gen 10:8, 9; 2 Chr 12:2-4; 14:9; 16:8
3 [a]Ps 49:1; Mic 1:2 [b]Is 26:11
4 [1]Lit *in* [2]Lit *light* [a]Is 26:21; Hos 5:15 [b]2 Sam 23:4 [c]Prov 19:12; Is 26:19; Hos 14:5
5 [1]Lit *is finished* [a]Is 17:10, 11; Ezek 17:6-10
6 [a]Is 46:11; 56:9; Jer 7:33; Ezek 32:4-6; 39:17-20
7 [1]So with some ancient versions and DSS; M.T. implies *Consisting of a people* [2]Lit *drawn out* [3]Lit *from it and beyond* [a]Ps 68:31; Is 45:14; Zeph 3:10; Acts 8:27-38 [b]Zech 14:16, 17
19:1 [1]Or *burden of* [a]Is 13:1 [b]Joel 3:19 [c]Ps 18:9, 10; 104:3; Matt 26:64; Rev 1:7 [d]Ex 12:12; Jer 43:12; 44:8 [e]Josh 2:11; Is 13:7
2 [a]Judg 7:22; 1 Sam 14:20; 2 Chr 20:23; Matt 10:21, 36

So that [a]they will resort to idols and ghosts of the dead
And to [1]mediums and spiritists.
4 "Moreover, I will deliver the Egyptians into the hand of a
[a]cruel master,
And a [1]mighty king will rule over them," declares the Lord
[2]GOD of hosts.

5 [a]The waters from the sea will dry up,
And the river will be parched and dry.
6 The [1a]canals will emit a stench,
The [2b]streams of Egypt will thin out and dry up;
[c]The reeds and rushes will rot away.
7 The bulrushes by the [a]Nile, by the [1]edge of the Nile
And all the sown fields by the Nile
Will become dry, be driven away, and be no more.
8 And the [a]fishermen will lament,
And all those who cast a [1]line into the Nile will mourn,
And those who spread nets on the waters will [2]pine away.
9 Moreover, the manufacturers of linen made from
combed flax
And the weavers of white [a]cloth will be [1]utterly dejected.
10 And [1]the [a]pillars *of Egypt* will be crushed;
All the hired laborers will be grieved in soul.

11 The princes of [1a]Zoan are mere fools;
The advice of Pharaoh's wisest advisers has become
[2]stupid.
How can you *men* say to Pharaoh,
"I am a son of the [b]wise, a son of ancient kings"?
12 Well then, where are your wise men?
Please let them tell you,
And let them [1]understand what the LORD of hosts
Has [a]purposed against Egypt.
13 The princes of [1]Zoan have acted foolishly,
The princes of [a]Memphis are deluded;
Those who are the [b]cornerstone of her tribes
Have [2]led Egypt astray.
14 The LORD has mixed within her a spirit of [a]distortion;
[b]They have led Egypt astray in all [1]that it does,
As a [c]drunken man [2]staggers in his vomit.
15 There will be no work for Egypt
[a]Which *its* head or tail, *its* palm branch or bulrush, may do.

16 In that day the Egyptians will become like women, and they
will tremble and be in [a]dread because of the [b]waving of the
hand of the LORD of hosts, which He is going to wave over
them.
17 The land of Judah will become a [1]terror to Egypt; everyone
[2]to whom it is mentioned will be in dread of it, because of the
[a]purpose of the LORD of hosts which He is purposing against
them.
18 In that day five cities in the land of Egypt will be speaking

3 [1]Or *ghosts and spirits* [a]1 Chr 10:13; Is 8:19; Dan 2:2

4 [1]Or *fierce* [2]Heb *YHWH,* usually rendered *LORD* [a]Is 20:4; Jer 46:26; Ezek 29:19

5 [a]Is 50:2; Jer 51:36; Ezek 30:12

6 [1]Lit *rivers* [2]Or *Nile branches;* i.e. the delta [a]Ex 7:18 [b]Is 37:25 [c]Ex 2:3; Job 8:11; Is 15:6

7 [1]Or *mouth* [a]Is 23:3, 10

8 [1]Lit *hook* [2]Or *languish* [a]Ezek 47:10; Hab 1:15

9 [1]Lit *ashamed* [a]Prov 7:16; Ezek 27:7

10 [1]Lit *her pillars* or, *her weavers* [a]Ps 11:3

11 [1]Or *Tanis* [2]Or *brutish* [a]Num 13:22; Ps 78:12, 43; Is 30:4 [b]Gen 41:38, 39; 1 Kin 4:30; Acts 7:22

12 [1]Or *know* [a]Is 14:24; Rom 9:17

13 [1]Or *Tanis* [2]Or *have caused Egypt to stagger* [a]Jer 2:16; 46:14, 19; Ezek 30:13 [b]Zech 10:4

14 [1]Lit *its work* [2]Or *goes astray* [a]Prov 12:8; Matt 17:17 [b]Is 3:12; 9:16 [c]Is 28:7

15 [a]Is 9:14, 15

16 [a]2 Cor 5:11; Heb 10:31 [b]Is 11:15

17 [1]Or *cause of shame* [2]Lit *who mentions it will be in dread to it* [a]Is 14:24; Dan 4:35

the language of Canaan and [a]swearing *allegiance* to the LORD of
hosts; one will be called the City of [1]Destruction.
19 In that day there will be an [a]altar to the LORD in the midst
of the land of Egypt, and a [b]pillar to the LORD near its border.
20 It will become a sign and a witness to the LORD of hosts in
the land of Egypt; for they will cry to the LORD because of
oppressors, and He will send them a [a]Savior and a [1b]Champion,
and He will deliver them.
21 Thus the LORD will make Himself known to Egypt, and the
Egyptians will know the LORD in that day. They will even
worship with [a]sacrifice and offering, and will make a vow to
the LORD and perform it.
22 The LORD will strike Egypt, striking but [a]healing; so they
will [b]return to the LORD, and He will respond to them and will
heal them.
23 In that day there will be a [a]highway from Egypt to Assyria,
and the Assyrians will come into Egypt and the Egyptians into
Assyria, and the Egyptians will [b]worship with the Assyrians.
24 In that day Israel will be the third *party* with Egypt and
Assyria, a blessing in the midst of the earth,
25 whom the LORD of hosts has blessed, saying, "Blessed is
[a]Egypt My people, and Assyria [b]the work of My hands, and
Israel My inheritance."

Chapter 20 Theme ______________________________

20 In the year that the [1a]commander came to [b]Ashdod,
when Sargon the king of Assyria sent him and he
fought against Ashdod and captured it,
2 at that time the LORD spoke through [a]Isaiah the son of Amoz,
saying, "Go and loosen the [b]sackcloth from your hips and take
your [c]shoes off your feet." And he did so, going [d]naked and
barefoot.
3 And the LORD said, "Even as My servant Isaiah has gone
naked and barefoot three years as a [1a]sign and token against
Egypt and [2b]Cush,
4 so the [a]king of Assyria will lead away the captives of Egypt
and the exiles of Cush, [b]young and old, naked and barefoot with
buttocks uncovered, to the [1]shame of Egypt.
5 "Then they will be [a]dismayed and ashamed because of Cush
their hope and Egypt their [b]boast.
6 "So the inhabitants of this coastland will say in that day,
'Behold, such is our hope, where we fled [a]for help to be
delivered from the king of Assyria; and we, [b]how shall we
escape?'"

Chapter 21 Theme ______________________________

21 The [1a]oracle concerning the [2b]wilderness of the sea.
As [c]windstorms in the [3]Negev sweep on,
It comes from the wilderness, from a terrifying land.

18 [1]Some ancient mss and versions read *the Sun* [a]Is 45:23; 65:16

19 [a]Is 56:7; 60:7 [b]Gen 28:18; Ex 24:4; Josh 22:10, 26, 27

20 [1]Lit *Mighty One* [a]Is 43:3, 11; 45:15, 21; 49:26; 60:16; 63:8 [b]Is 49:25

21 [a]Is 56:7; 60:7; Zech 14:16-18

22 [a]Deut 32:39; Is 30:26; 57:18; Heb 12:11 [b]Is 27:13; 45:14; Hos 14:1

23 [a]Is 11:16; 35:8; 49:11; 62:10 [b]Is 27:13

25 [a]Is 45:14 [b]Ps 100:3; Is 29:23; 45:11; 60:21; 64:8; Eph 2:10

20:1 [1]Heb *Tartan* [a]2 Kin 18:17 [b]1 Sam 5:1

2 [a]Is 1:1; 13:1 [b]Zech 13:4; Matt 3:4 [c]Ezek 24:17, 23 [d]1 Sam 19:24; Mic 1:8

3 [1]Or *wonder* [2]Or *Ethiopia,* so in vv 4, 5 [a]Is 8:18 [b]Is 37:9; 43:3

4 [1]Lit *nakedness* [a]Is 19:4 [b]Is 47:2, 3

5 [a]2 Kin 18:21; Is 30:3-5; 31:1; Ezek 29:6, 7 [b]Jer 9:23, 24; 17:5; 1 Cor 3:21

6 [a]Is 10:3; 30:7; 31:3; Jer 30:1, 7, 15-17; 31:1-3 [b]Matt 23:33; 1 Thess 5:3; Heb 2:3

21:1 [1]Or *burden of* [2]Or *sandy wastes, sea country* [3]I.e. South country [a]Is 13:1 [b]Is 13:20-22; 14:23; Jer 51:42 [c]Zech 9:14

2 A [a]harsh vision has been shown to me;
The [b]treacherous one *still* deals treacherously, and the
destroyer *still* destroys.
Go up, [c]Elam, lay siege, Media;
I have made an end of all [1]the groaning she has caused.
3 For this reason my [a]loins are full of anguish;
Pains have seized me like the pains of a [b]woman in labor.
I am so bewildered I cannot hear, so terrified I cannot see.
4 My [1]mind reels, [2]horror overwhelms me;
The twilight I longed for has been [a]turned for me into
trembling.
5 They [a]set the table, they [1]spread out the cloth, they eat,
they drink;
"Rise up, captains, oil the shields,"
6 For thus the Lord says to me,
"Go, station the lookout, let him [a]report what he sees.
7 "When he sees [a]riders, horsemen in pairs,
A train of donkeys, a train of camels,
Let him pay close attention, very close attention."
8 Then [1]the lookout called,
"[a]O Lord, I stand continually by day on the watchtower,
And I am stationed every night at my guard post.
9 "Now behold, here comes a troop of riders, horsemen in pairs."
And one said, "[a]Fallen, fallen is Babylon;
And all the [b]images of her gods [1]are shattered on
the ground."
10 O my [a]threshed *people,* and my [1]afflicted of the
threshing floor!
What I have heard from the LORD of hosts,
The God of Israel, I make known to you.

11 The [1]oracle concerning [2a]Edom.
One keeps calling to me from [b]Seir,
"Watchman, [3]how far gone is the night?
Watchman, [3]how far gone is the night?"
12 The watchman says,
"Morning comes but also night.
If you would inquire, inquire;
Come back again."

13 The [1]oracle about [a]Arabia.
In the thickets of Arabia you [2]must spend the night,
O caravans of [b]Dedanites.
14 Bring water [1]for the thirsty,
O inhabitants of the land of [a]Tema,
Meet the fugitive with bread.
15 For they have [a]fled from the swords,
From the drawn sword, and from the bent bow
And from the press of battle.
16 For thus the Lord said to me, "In a [a]year, as [1]a hired man
would count it, all the splendor of [b]Kedar will terminate;

2 [1]Lit *her groaning* [a]Ps 60:3 [b]Is 24:16; 33:1 [c]Is 22:6; Jer 49:34

3 [a]Is 13:8; 16:11 [b]Ps 48:6; Is 13:8; 26:17; 1 Thess 5:3

4 [1]Lit *heart has wandered* [2]Lit *shuddering* [a]Deut 28:67

5 [1]Or *spread out the rugs* or possibly *they arranged the seating* [a]Jer 51:39, 57; Dan 5:1-4

6 [a]2 Kin 9:17-20

7 [a]Is 21:9

8 [1]So DSS; M.T. *he called* like *a lion* [a]Hab 2:1

9 [1]Lit *he has shattered to the earth* [a]Is 13:19; 47:5, 9; 48:14; Jer 51:8; Rev 14:8; 18:2 [b]Is 46:1; Jer 50:2; 51:44

10 [1]Lit *son* [a]Jer 51:33; Mic 4:13

11 [1]Or *burden* [2]So the Gr; Heb *Dumah, silence* [3]Lit *what* is the time *of the night?* [a]Gen 25:14 [b]Gen 32:3

13 [1]Or *burden* [2]Or *will spend* [a]Jer 25:23, 24; 49:28 [b]Gen 10:7; Ezek 27:15

14 [1]Lit *to meet* [a]Gen 25:15; Job 6:19

15 [a]Is 13:14, 15; 17:13

16 [1]Lit *the years of a hireling* [a]Is 16:14 [b]Ps 120:5; Song 1:5; Is 42:11; 60:7; Ezek 27:21

17 [a]Is 10:19 [b]Num 23:19; Zech 1:6

17 and the [a]remainder of the number of bowmen, the mighty
men of the sons of Kedar, will be few; for the LORD God of
Israel [b]has spoken."

22:1 [1]Or *burden of* [a]Ps 125:2; Jer 21:13; Joel 3:12, 14 [b]Is 15:3

2 [1]Lit *dead in battle* [a]Is 23:7; 32:13 [b]Jer 14:18; Lam 2:20

3 [1]Lit *from a bow* [2]So with ancient versions; Heb *They fled far away* [a]Is 21:15

4 [1]Lit *insist* [a]Is 15:3; Jer 9:1; Luke 19:41

5 [1]Heb *YHWH*, usually rendered LORD [2]Or *against* [a]Lam 1:5; 2:2 [b]Is 37:3 [c]Is 10:6; 63:3 [d]Is 22:1

6 [1]Lit *man* [a]Is 21:2; Jer 49:35 [b]2 Kin 16:9; Amos 1:5; 9:7

8 [1]Lit *screen, covering* [2]Or *looked to, considered* [a]1 Kin 7:2; 10:17

9 [a]2 Kin 20:20; Neh 3:16

11 [1]Or *look to, consider* [2]Lit *see . . . Him* [a]2 Kin 25:4; Jer 39:4 [b]2 Kin 20:20; 2 Chr 32:3, 4

12 [1]Heb *YHWH*, usually rendered LORD [a]Is 32:11; Joel 1:13; 2:17 [b]Mic 1:16

13 [a]Is 5:11, 22; 28:7, 8; Luke 17:26-29 [b]Is 56:12; 1 Cor 15:32

Chapter 22 Theme ____________________

22 The [1]oracle concerning the [a]valley of vision.
What is the matter with you now, that you have all
gone up to the [b]housetops?
2 You who were full of noise,
You boisterous town, you [a]exultant city;
Your slain were [b]not slain with the sword,
Nor [1]did they die in battle.
3 [a]All your rulers have fled together,
And have been captured [1]without the bow;
All of you who were found were taken captive together,
[2]Though they had fled far away.
4 Therefore I say, "Turn your eyes away from me,
Let me [a]weep bitterly,
Do not [1]try to comfort me concerning the destruction of
the daughter of my people."
5 [a]For the Lord [1]GOD of hosts has a [b]day of panic,
[c]subjugation and confusion
[d]In the valley of vision,
A breaking down of walls
And a crying [2]to the mountain.
6 [a]Elam took up the quiver
With the chariots, [1]infantry *and* horsemen;
And [b]Kir uncovered the shield.
7 Then your choicest valleys were full of chariots,
And the horsemen took up fixed positions at the gate.
8 And He removed the [1]defense of Judah.
In that day you [2]depended on the weapons of the [a]house of
the forest,
9 And you saw that the breaches
In the *wall* of the city of David were many;
And you [a]collected the waters of the lower pool.
10 Then you counted the houses of Jerusalem
And tore down houses to fortify the wall.
11 And you made a reservoir [a]between the two walls
For the waters of the [b]old pool.
But you did not [1]depend on Him who made it,
Nor did you [2]take into consideration Him who planned it
long ago.

12 Therefore in that day the Lord [1]GOD of hosts called *you* to
[a]weeping, to wailing,
To [b]shaving the head and to wearing sackcloth.
13 Instead, there is [a]gaiety and gladness,
Killing of cattle and slaughtering of sheep,
Eating of meat and drinking of wine:
"[b]Let us eat and drink, for tomorrow we may die."

14 But the LORD of hosts revealed Himself [1]to me,
"Surely this [a]iniquity [b]shall not be [2]forgiven you
[c]Until you die," says the Lord [3]GOD of hosts.

15 Thus says the Lord [1]GOD of hosts,
"Come, go to this steward,
To [a]Shebna, who is in charge of the *royal* household,
16 'What right do you have here,
And whom do you have here,
That you have [a]hewn a tomb for yourself here,
You who hew a tomb on the height,
You who carve a resting place for [1]yourself in the rock?
17 'Behold, the LORD is about to hurl you headlong, O man.
And He is about to grasp you firmly
18 *And* roll you tightly like a ball,
To be [a]*cast* into a vast country;
There you will die
And there your splendid chariots will be,
You shame of your master's house.'
19 "I will [a]depose you from your office,
And [1]I will pull you down from your station.
20 "Then it will come about in that day,
That I will summon My servant [a]Eliakim the son of Hilkiah,
21 And I will clothe him with your tunic
And tie your sash securely about him.
I will entrust him with your [1]authority,
And he will become a [a]father to the inhabitants of Jerusalem and to the house of Judah.
22 "Then I will set [a]the key of the [b]house of David on his shoulder,
When he opens no one will shut,
When he shuts no one will [c]open.
23 "I will drive him *like* a [a]peg in a firm place,
And he will become a [b]throne of glory to his father's house.
24 "So they will hang on him all the glory of his father's house,
offspring and [1]issue, all the least of vessels, from bowls to all
the jars.
25 "In that day," declares the LORD of hosts, "the [a]peg driven in
a firm place will give way; it will even [b]break off and fall, and the
load hanging on it will be cut off, for the [c]LORD has spoken."

Chapter 23 Theme ____________________

23

The [1]oracle concerning [a]Tyre.
Wail, O [b]ships of [c]Tarshish,
For *Tyre* is destroyed, without house *or* [2d]harbor;
It is reported to them from the land of [3e]Cyprus.
2 [a]Be silent, you inhabitants of the coastland,
You merchants of Sidon;
[1]Your messengers crossed the sea

14 [1]Lit *in my ears* [2]Lit *atoned for* [3]Heb *YHWH*, usually rendered *LORD* [a]Is 13:11; 26:21; 30:13; 65:7 [b]1 Sam 3:14; Ezek 24:13 [c]Is 65:20

15 [1]Heb *YHWH*, usually rendered *LORD* [a]2 Kin 18:18, 26, 37; Is 36:3, 11, 22; 37:2

16 [1]Lit *himself* [a]2 Sam 18:18; 2 Chr 16:14; Matt 27:60

18 [a]Job 18:18; Is 17:13

19 [1]So with many ancient versions; Heb *He* [a]Job 40:11, 12; Ezek 17:24

20 [a]2 Kin 18:18; Is 36:3, 22; 37:2

21 [1]Lit *rule* [a]Gen 45:8; Job 29:16

22 [a]Rev 3:7 [b]Is 7:2, 13 [c]Job 12:14

23 [a]Ezra 9:8; Zech 10:4 [b]1 Sam 2:8; Job 36:7

24 [1]Or perhaps, *leaf*

25 [a]Is 22:23 [b]Esth 9:24, 25 [c]Is 46:11; Mic 4:4

23:1 [1]Or *burden of* [2]Lit *entering* [3]Heb *Kittim* [a]Josh 19:29; 1 Kin 5:1; Jer 25:22; 47:4; Ezek 26:1-27:36; Joel 3:4-8; Amos 1:9; Zech 9:2-4 [b]Is 2:16 [c]Gen 10:4; 1 Kin 10:22 [d]Is 24:10 [e]Gen 10:4; Is 23:12; Ezek 27:6

2 [1]So DSS; M.T. *Who passed over the sea, they replenished you* [a]Is 47:5

3 And *were* on many waters.
[a]The grain of the [1b]Nile, the harvest of the River was
her revenue;
And she was the [c]market of nations.
4 Be ashamed, O [a]Sidon;
For the sea speaks, the stronghold of the sea, saying,
"I have neither travailed nor given birth,
I have neither brought up young men *nor* reared virgins."
5 When the report *reaches* Egypt,
They will be in [a]anguish at the report of Tyre.
6 Pass over to [a]Tarshish;
Wail, O inhabitants of the coastland.
7 Is this your [a]jubilant *city,*
Whose origin is from antiquity,
Whose feet used to carry her to [1]colonize distant places?

8 Who has planned this against Tyre, [a]the bestower
of crowns,
Whose merchants were princes, whose traders were the
honored of the earth?
9 [a]The LORD of hosts has planned it, to [b]defile the pride of
all beauty,
To despise all the [c]honored of the earth.
10 [1]Overflow your land like the Nile, O daughter of Tarshish,
There is no more [2]restraint.
11 He has [a]stretched His hand out [b]over the sea,
He has [c]made the kingdoms tremble;
The LORD has given a command concerning Canaan to
[d]demolish its strongholds.

12 He has said, "[a]You shall exult no more, O crushed virgin
daughter of Sidon.
Arise, pass over to [1b]Cyprus; even there you will find
no rest."
13 Behold, the land of the Chaldeans—this is the people
which was not; [a]Assyria appointed it for [b]desert creatures—
they erected their siege towers, they stripped its palaces, [c]they
made it a ruin.
14 Wail, O [a]ships of Tarshish,
For your stronghold is destroyed.
15 Now in that day Tyre will be forgotten for [a]seventy years
like the days of one king. At the end of seventy years it will
happen to Tyre as *in* the song of the harlot:
16 Take *your* harp, walk about the city,
O forgotten harlot;
Pluck the strings skillfully, sing many songs,
That you may be remembered.
17 It will come about at [a]the end of seventy years that the
LORD will visit Tyre. Then she will go back to her harlot's wages
and will [b]play the harlot with all the kingdoms [1]on the face of
the earth.

3 [1]Heb *Shihor* [a]Is 19:7-9 [b]Josh 13:3; 1 Chr 13:5; Jer 2:18 [c]Ezek 27:3-23
4 [a]Gen 10:15, 19; Josh 11:8; Judg 10:6; Jer 25:22; 27:3; 47:4; Ezek 28:21, 22
5 [a]Ex 15:14-16; Josh 2:9-11
6 [a]Is 23:1
7 [1]Lit *sojourn afar off* [a]Is 22:2; 32:13
8 [a]Ezek 28:2
9 [a]Is 2:11; 13:11 [b]Job 40:11, 12; Dan 4:37 [c]Is 5:13; 9:15
10 [1]Lit *Pass over* [2]Perhaps *girdle* or *shipyard*
11 [a]Ex 14:21; Is 14:26 [b]Is 19:5; 50:2 [c]Is 13:13 [d]Is 25:2; Zech 9:3, 4
12 [1]Heb *Kittim* [a]Ezek 26:13, 14; Rev 18:22 [b]Is 23:1
13 [a]Is 10:5 [b]Is 13:21; 18:6 [c]Is 10:7
14 [a]Is 2:16; Ezek 27:25, 26
15 [a]Jer 25:11, 22
17 [1]Lit *of the earth on the face of the land* [a]Is 23:15 [b]Ezek 16:25-29; Nah 3:4

18 Her [a]gain and her harlot's wages will be [b]set apart to the
LORD; it will not be stored up or hoarded, but her gain will
become sufficient food and choice attire for those who dwell in
the presence of the LORD.

Chapter 24 Theme ______________________

RETURN TO INSTRUCTIONS

24 Behold, the LORD [a]lays the earth waste, devastates it,
distorts its surface and scatters its inhabitants.
2 And the people will be like the priest, the servant like his
master, the maid like her mistress, the buyer like the seller, the
lender like the borrower, the [a]creditor like the debtor.
3 The earth will be completely laid waste and completely
despoiled, for the LORD has spoken this word.
4 The [a]earth mourns *and* withers, the world fades *and*
withers, the [b]exalted of the people of the earth fade away.
5 The earth is also [a]polluted [1]by its inhabitants, for they
transgressed laws, violated statutes, [b]broke the everlasting
covenant.
6 Therefore, a [a]curse devours the earth, and those who live
in it are held guilty. Therefore, the [b]inhabitants of the earth are
burned, and few men are left.

7 The [a]new wine mourns,
The vine decays,
All the merry-hearted sigh.
8 The [a]gaiety of tambourines ceases,
The noise of revelers stops,
The gaiety of the harp ceases.
9 They do not drink wine with song;
[a]Strong drink is [b]bitter to those who drink it.
10 The [a]city of chaos is broken down;
[b]Every house is shut up so that none may enter.
11 There is an [a]outcry in the streets concerning the wine;
[b]All joy [1]turns to gloom.
The gaiety of the earth is banished.
12 Desolation is left in the city
And the [a]gate is battered to ruins.
13 For [a]thus it will be in the midst of the earth among the peoples,
As the [1]shaking of an olive tree,
As the gleanings when the grape harvest is over.
14 [a]They raise their voices, they shout for joy;
They cry out from the [1]west concerning the majesty of the LORD.
15 Therefore [a]glorify the LORD in the [1]east,
The [b]name of the LORD, the God of Israel,
In the [2c]coastlands of the sea.
16 From the [a]ends of the earth we hear songs, "[b]Glory to the Righteous One,"
But I say, "[1c]Woe to me! [1]Woe to me! Alas for me!
The [d]treacherous deal treacherously,
And the treacherous deal very treacherously."

18 [a]Ps 72:10, 11; Is 60:5-9; Mic 4:13 [b]Ex 28:36; Zech 14:20

24:1 [a]Is 2:19; 13:13; 24:19, 20; 30:32; 33:9

2 [a]Lev 25:36, 37; Deut 23:19, 20

4 [a]Is 33:9 [b]Is 2:12; 24:21

5 [1]Lit *under* [a]Gen 3:17; Num 35:33; Is 9:17; 10:6 [b]Is 33:8

6 [a]Josh 23:15; Is 34:5; 43:28; Zech 5:3, 4 [b]Is 1:31; 5:24; 9:19

7 [a]Is 16:10; Joel 1:10, 12

8 [a]Is 5:12, 14; Ezek 26:13; Hos 2:11; Rev 18:22

9 [a]Is 5:11, 22 [b]Is 5:20

10 [a]Is 34:11 [b]Is 23:1

11 [1]Lit is *darkened* [a]Jer 14:2; 46:12 [b]Is 16:10; 32:13

12 [a]Is 14:31; 45:2

13 [1]Lit *striking* [a]Is 17:6; 27:12

14 [1]Lit *sea* [a]Is 12:6; 48:20; 52:8; 54:1

15 [1]Lit *region of light* [2]Or *islands* [a]Is 25:3 [b]Mal 1:11 [c]Is 11:11; 42:4, 10, 12; 49:1; 51:5; 60:9; 66:19

16 [1]Lit *Wasting to me!* [a]Is 11:12; 42:10 [b]Is 28:5; 60:21 [c]Lev 26:39 [d]Is 21:2; 33:1; Jer 3:20; 5:11

17 [a]Terror and pit and snare
[1]Confront you, O inhabitant of the earth.
18 Then it will be that he who flees the [1]report of disaster will
fall into the pit,
And he who [2]climbs out of the pit will be caught in
the snare;
For the [a]windows [3]above are opened, and the [b]foundations
of the earth shake.
19 [a]The earth is broken asunder,
The earth is [b]split through,
The earth is shaken violently.
20 The earth [a]reels to and fro like a drunkard
And it totters like a [1]shack,
For its [b]transgression is heavy upon it,
And it will fall, [c]never to rise again.
21 So it will happen in that day,
That the LORD will [a]punish the host of [1]heaven on high,
And the [b]kings of the earth on earth.
22 They will be gathered together
Like [a]prisoners in the [1]dungeon,
And will be confined in prison;
And after many days they *will* [b]*be* punished.
23 Then the [a]moon will be abashed and the sun ashamed,
For the [b]LORD of hosts will reign on [c]Mount Zion and
in Jerusalem,
And *His* glory will be before His elders.

Chapter 25 Theme ______________________________

25 O LORD, You are [a]my God;
I will exalt You, I will give thanks to Your name;
For You have [b]worked wonders,
[c]Plans *formed* long ago, with perfect faithfulness.
2 For You have made a city into a [a]heap,
A [b]fortified city into a ruin;
A [c]palace of strangers is a city no more,
It will never be rebuilt.
3 Therefore a strong people will [a]glorify You;
[b]Cities of ruthless nations will revere You.
4 For You have been a [a]defense for the helpless,
A defense for the needy in his distress,
A [b]refuge from the storm, a shade from the heat;
For the breath of the [c]ruthless
Is like a *rain* storm *against* a wall.
5 Like heat in drought, You subdue the [a]uproar of aliens;
Like heat by the shadow of a cloud, the song of the ruthless
is [1]silenced.

6 [a]The LORD of hosts will prepare a [1]lavish banquet for [b]all
peoples on this mountain;
A banquet of [2]aged wine, [3]choice pieces with marrow,
And [4]refined, aged wine.

17 [1]Lit *Are upon you* [a]Jer 48:43; Amos 5:19

18 [1]Lit *sound of terror* [2]Lit *goes up from the midst of* [3]Lit *from the height;* i.e. heaven [a]Gen 7:11 [b]Ps 18:7; 46:2; Is 2:19, 21; 13:13

19 [a]Is 24:1 [b]Num 16:31, 32; Deut 11:6

20 [1]Or *hut* [a]Is 19:14; 24:1; 28:7 [b]Is 1:28; 43:27; 66:24 [c]Dan 11:19; Amos 8:14

21 [1]Lit *the height in the height* [a]Is 10:12; 13:11 [b]Ps 76:12

22 [1]Lit *pit* [a]Is 10:4; 42:22 [b]Ezek 38:8; Zech 9:11, 12

23 [a]Is 13:10 [b]Is 60:19, 20; Zech 14:6, 7; Rev 21:23; 22:5 [c]Mic 4:7; Heb 12:22

25:1 [a]Ex 15:2; Ps 118:28; Is 7:13; 49:4, 5; 61:10 [b]Ps 40:5; 98:1 [c]Eph 1:11

2 [a]Is 17:1; 26:5; 27:10; 32:19 [b]Is 17:3; 25:12 [c]Is 13:22; 32:14; 34:13

3 [a]Is 24:15 [b]Is 13:11

4 [a]Is 14:32; 17:10; 27:5; 33:16 [b]Is 4:6; 32:2 [c]Is 29:5, 20; 49:25

5 [1]Lit *humbled* [a]Jer 51:54-56

6 [1]Lit *feast of fat things;* i.e. abundance [2]Lit *wine on the lees* [3]Lit *fat pieces* [4]Lit *wine refined on the lees* [a]Is 1:19 [b]Is 2:2-4; 56:7

7 And on this mountain He will swallow up the [1a]covering
which is over all peoples,
Even the veil which is [2]stretched over all nations.
8 He will [a]swallow up death for all time,
And the Lord [1]GOD will [b]wipe tears away from all faces,
And He will remove the [c]reproach of His people from all
the earth;
For the LORD has spoken.
9 And it will be said in that day,
"Behold, [a]this is our God for whom we have [b]waited that
[c]He might save us.
This is the LORD for whom we have waited;
[d]Let us rejoice and be glad in His salvation."
10 For the hand of the LORD will rest on this mountain,
And [a]Moab will be trodden down in his place
As straw is trodden down in the water of a manure pile.
11 And he will [a]spread out his hands in the middle of it
As a swimmer spreads out *his hands* to swim,
But *the Lord* will [b]lay low his pride together with the
trickery of his hands.
12 The [a]unassailable fortifications of your walls He will
bring down,
Lay low *and* cast to the ground, even to the dust.

Chapter 26 Theme ____________________

26

[a]In that day this song will be sung in the land of Judah:
"We have a [b]strong city;
He sets up walls and ramparts for [1c]security.
2 "Open the [a]gates, that the [b]righteous nation may enter,
The one that [1]remains faithful.
3 "The steadfast of mind You will keep in perfect [a]peace,
Because he trusts in You.
4 "[a]Trust in the LORD forever,
For in [1]GOD the LORD, *we have* an everlasting [b]Rock.
5 "For He has brought low those who dwell on high, the
[a]unassailable city;
[b]He lays it low, He lays it low to the ground, He casts it to
the dust.
6 "[a]The foot will trample it,
The feet of the [b]afflicted, the steps of the helpless."

7 The [a]way of the righteous is smooth;
O Upright One, [b]make the path of the righteous level.
8 Indeed, *while following* the way of [a]Your judgments, O LORD,
We have waited for You eagerly;
[b]Your name, even Your [c]memory, is the desire of *our* souls.
9 [a]At night [1]my soul longs for You,
Indeed, [2]my spirit within me [b]seeks You diligently;
For when the earth [3]experiences Your judgments
The inhabitants of the world [c]learn righteousness.
10 *Though* the wicked is shown favor,

7 [1]Lit *face of the covering* [2]Lit *woven* [a]2 Cor 3:15, 16; Eph 4:18

8 [1]Heb *YHWH,* usually rendered *LORD* [a]Hos 13:14; 1 Cor 15:54 [b]Is 30:19; 35:10; 51:11; 65:19; Rev 7:17; 21:4 [c]Ps 69:9; 89:50, 51; Is 51:7; 54:4; Matt 5:11; 1 Pet 4:14

9 [a]Is 35:2; 40:9; 52:10 [b]Is 8:17; 30:18; 33:2 [c]Is 33:22; 35:4; 49:25, 26; 60:16 [d]Ps 20:5; Is 35:1, 2, 10; 65:18; 66:10

10 [a]Is 16:14; Jer 48:1-47; Ezek 25:8-11; Amos 2:1-3; Zeph 2:9

11 [a]Is 5:25; 14:26 [b]Job 40:11; Is 2:10-12, 15-17; 16:6, 14

12 [a]Is 15:1; 25:2; 26:5

26:1 [1]Or *salvation* [a]Is 4:2; 12:1 [b]Is 14:31; 31:5, 9; 33:5, 6, 20-24 [c]Is 60:18

2 [1]Lit *keeps faithfulness* [a]Is 60:11, 18; 62:10 [b]Is 45:25; 54:14, 17; 58:8; 60:21; 61:3; 62:1, 2

3 [a]Is 26:12; 27:5; 57:19; 66:12

4 [1]Heb *YAH,* usually rendered *LORD* [a]Is 12:2; 50:10; 51:5 [b]Is 17:10; 30:29; 44:8

5 [a]Is 25:12 [b]Job 40:11-13

6 [a]Is 28:3 [b]Is 3:14, 15; 11:4; 29:19

7 [a]Is 57:2 [b]Ps 25:4, 5; 27:11; Is 42:16; 52:12

8 [a]Is 51:4; 56:1 [b]Is 12:4; 24:15; 25:1; 26:13 [c]Ex 3:15

9 [1]Lit with *my soul I long* [2]Lit with *my spirit . . . I seek* [3]Lit *has* [a]Ps 63:5, 6; 77:2; 119:62; Is 50:10; Luke 6:12 [b]Ps 63:1; 78:34; Matt 6:33 [c]Is 55:6; Hos 5:15

He does not [a]learn righteousness;
He [b]deals unjustly in the land of uprightness,
And does not perceive the majesty of the LORD.

11 O LORD, Your hand is lifted up *yet* they [a]do not see it.
[1]They see [b]*Your* zeal for the people and are put to shame;
Indeed, [2c]fire will devour Your enemies.
12 LORD, You will establish [a]peace for us,
Since You have also performed for us all our works.
13 O LORD our God, [a]other masters besides You have ruled us;
But through You alone we [1b]confess Your name.
14 [a]The dead will not live, the [1]departed spirits will not rise;
Therefore You have [b]punished and destroyed them,
And You have wiped out all remembrance of them.
15 [a]You have increased the nation, O LORD,
You have increased the nation, You are glorified;
You have [b]extended all the borders of the land.
16 O LORD, they sought You [a]in distress;
They [1]could only whisper a prayer,
Your chastening was upon them.
17 [a]As the pregnant woman approaches *the time* to give birth,
She writhes *and* cries out in her labor pains,
Thus were we before You, O LORD.
18 We were pregnant, we writhed *in labor,*
We [a]gave birth, as it seems, *only* to wind.
We could not accomplish deliverance for the earth,
Nor were [b]inhabitants of the world [1]born.
19 Your [a]dead will live;
[1]Their corpses will rise.
You who lie in the dust, [b]awake and shout for joy,
For your dew *is as* the dew of the [2]dawn,
And the earth will [3]give birth to the [4]departed spirits.

20 Come, my people, [a]enter into your rooms
And close your doors behind you;
Hide for a little [1b]while
Until [c]indignation [2]runs *its* course.
21 For behold, the LORD is about to [a]come out from His place
To [b]punish the inhabitants of the earth for their iniquity;
And the earth will [c]reveal her bloodshed
And will no longer cover her slain.

Chapter 27 Theme ______________________

27 In that day [a]the LORD will punish [1b]Leviathan the
fleeing serpent,
With His fierce and great and mighty sword,
Even [1]Leviathan the twisted serpent;
And [c]He will kill the dragon who *lives* in the sea.

2 In that day,
"A [1a]vineyard of wine, sing of it!

10 [a]Is 22:12, 13; 32:6, 7 [b]Hos 11:7; John 5:37, 38

11 [1]Or *Let them see . . . and be* [2]Or *let the fire for Your adversaries devour them* [a]Is 44:9, 18 [b]Is 9:7; 37:32; 59:17 [c]Is 5:24; 9:18, 19; 10:17; 66:15, 24; Heb 10:27

12 [a]Is 26:3

13 [1]Or *cause to be remembered* [a]Is 2:8; 10:11 [b]Is 63:7

14 [1]Or *shades* [a]Deut 4:28; Ps 135:17; Is 8:19; Hab 2:19 [b]Is 10:3

15 [a]Is 9:3 [b]Is 33:17; 54:2, 3

16 [1]Lit *sound forth a whisper* [a]Is 37:3; Hos 5:15

17 [a]Is 13:8; 21:3; John 16:21

18 [1]Lit *fallen* [a]Is 33:11; 59:4 [b]Ps 17:14

19 [1]So with some ancient versions; Heb *My* [2]Lit *lights* [3]Lit *cause to fall* [4]Or *shades* [a]Is 25:8; Ezek 37:1-14; Dan 12:2; Hos 13:14 [b]Eph 5:14

20 [1]Lit *moment* [2]Lit *passes over* [a]Ex 12:22, 23; Ps 91:1, 4 [b]Ps 30:5; Is 54:7, 8; 2 Cor 4:17 [c]Is 10:5, 25; 13:5; 34:2; 66:14

21 [a]Mic 1:3; Jude 14 [b]Is 13:11; 30:12-14; 65:6, 7 [c]Job 16:18; Luke 11:50

27:1 [1]Or *sea monster* [a]Is 66:16 [b]Job 3:8; 41:1; Ps 74:14; 104:26 [c]Is 51:9

2 [1]Some mss read *a vineyard of delight* [a]Ps 80:8; Is 5:7; Jer 2:21

3 "I, the LORD, am its keeper;
[a]I water it every moment.
So that no one will [1]damage it,
I [b]guard it night and day.
4 "I have no wrath.
Should [1]someone give Me [a]briars *and* thorns in battle,
Then I would step on them, [b]I would burn them [2]completely.
5 "Or let him [1][a]rely on My protection,
Let him make peace with Me,
Let him [b]make peace with Me."
6 [1]In the days to come Jacob [a]will take root,
Israel will [b]blossom and sprout,
And they will fill the [2]whole world with [c]fruit.

7 Like the striking of Him who has struck them, has [a]He struck them?
Or like the slaughter of His slain, [1]have they been slain?
8 You contended with them [1]by banishing them, by [a]driving them away.
With His fierce wind He has expelled *them* on the day of the [b]east wind.
9 Therefore through this Jacob's iniquity will be [a]forgiven;
And this will be [1]the full price of the [2][b]pardoning of his sin:
When he makes all the [c]altar stones like pulverized chalk stones;
When [3]Asherim and incense altars will not stand.
10 For the fortified city is [a]isolated,
A [1]homestead forlorn and forsaken like the desert;
[b]There the calf will graze,
And there it will lie down and [2]feed on its branches.
11 When its [a]limbs are dry, they are broken off;
Women come *and* make a fire with them,
For they are not a people of [b]discernment,
Therefore [c]their Maker [d]will not have compassion on them.
And their Creator will not be gracious to them.
12 In that day the LORD [a]will start *His* threshing from the
flowing stream of the [b]Euphrates to the brook of Egypt, and you
will be [c]gathered up one by one, O sons of Israel.
13 It will come about also in that day that a great [a]trumpet will
be blown, and those who were perishing in the land of [b]Assyria
and who were scattered in the land of Egypt will come and
[c]worship the LORD in the holy mountain at Jerusalem.

Chapter 28 Theme ______________________________

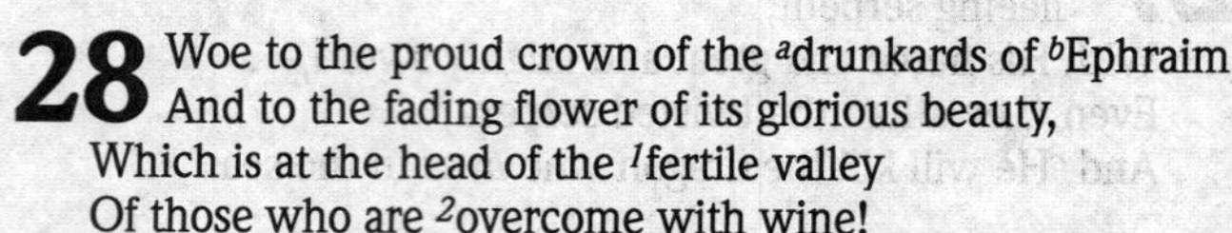

28 Woe to the proud crown of the [a]drunkards of [b]Ephraim,
And to the fading flower of its glorious beauty,
Which is at the head of the [1]fertile valley
Of those who are [2]overcome with wine!
2 Behold, the Lord has a strong and [a]mighty *agent;*
As a storm of [b]hail, a tempest of destruction,

3 [1]Lit *punish* [a]Is 58:11 [b]1 Sam 2:9; Is 31:5; John 10:28

4 [1]Lit *who* [2]Lit *altogether* [a]2 Sam 23:6; Is 10:17 [b]Is 33:12; Matt 3:12; Heb 6:8

5 [1]Lit *take hold of* [a]Is 12:2; 25:4 [b]Job 22:21; Is 26:3, 12; Rom 5:1; 2 Cor 5:20

6 [1]Lit *Those coming* [2]Lit *face of* [a]Is 37:31 [b]Is 35:1, 2; Hos 14:5, 6 [c]Is 4:2

7 [1]Lit *he was slain* [a]Is 10:12, 17; 30:31-33; 31:8, 9; 37:36-38

8 [1]Some ancient versions read *by exact measure* [a]Is 50:1; 54:7 [b]Jer 4:11; Ezek 19:12; Hos 13:15

9 [1]Lit *all the fruit* [2]Lit *removing* [3]I.e. wooden symbols of a female deity [a]Is 1:25; 48:10; Dan 11:35 [b]Rom 11:27 [c]Ex 34:13; Deut 12:3; 2 Kin 10:26; Is 17:8

10 [1]Lit *pasture* [2]Lit *consume* [a]Is 32:13, 14 [b]Is 17:2

11 [a]Is 18:5 [b]Deut 32:28; Is 1:3; 5:13; Jer 8:7 [c]Deut 32:18; Is 43:1, 7; 44:2, 21, 24 [d]Is 9:17

12 [a]Is 11:11; 17:6; 24:13; 56:8 [b]Gen 15:18 [c]Deut 30:3, 4; Neh 1:9

13 [a]Lev 25:9; 1 Chr 15:24; Matt 24:31; Rev 11:15 [b]Is 19:24, 25 [c]Is 19:21, 23; 49:7; 66:23; Zech 14:16; Heb 12:22

28:1 [1]Lit *valley of fatness* [2]Lit *smitten* [a]Is 28:7; Hos 7:5 [b]Is 9:9

2 [a]Is 8:7; 40:10 [b]Is 28:17; 30:30; 32:19; Ezek 13:11

Like a storm of [c]mighty overflowing waters,
He has cast *it* down to the earth with *His* hand.
3 The proud crown of the drunkards of Ephraim is [a]trodden under foot.
4 And the fading flower of its glorious beauty,
Which is at the head of the [1]fertile valley,
Will be like the [a]first-ripe fig prior to summer,
Which [2]one sees,
And [3]as soon as it is in his [4]hand,
He swallows it.
5 In that day the [a]LORD of hosts will become a beautiful [b]crown
And a glorious diadem to the remnant of His people;
6 A [a]spirit of justice for him who sits in judgment,
A [b]strength to those who repel the [1]onslaught at the gate.
7 And these also [a]reel with wine and stagger from strong drink:
[b]The priest and [c]the prophet reel with strong drink,
They are confused by wine, they stagger from [d]strong drink;
They reel while [1]having [e]visions,
They totter *when rendering* judgment.
8 For all the tables are full of filthy [a]vomit, without a *single clean* place.

9 "To [a]whom would He teach knowledge,
And to whom would He interpret the message?
Those *just* [b]weaned from milk?
Those *just* taken from the breast?
10 "For *He says,*
'[1a]Order on order, order on order,
Line on line, line on line,
A little here, a little there.'"
11 Indeed, He will speak to this people
Through [a]stammering lips and a foreign tongue,
12 He who said to them, "Here is [a]rest, give rest to the weary,"
And, "Here is repose," but they would not listen.
13 So the word of the LORD to them will be,
"[1]Order on order, order on order,
Line on line, line on line,
A little here, a little there,"
That they may go and [a]stumble backward, be broken, snared and taken captive.
14 Therefore, [a]hear the word of the LORD, O [b]scoffers,
Who rule this people who are in Jerusalem,
15 Because you have said, "We have made a [a]covenant with death,
And with [1]Sheol we have made a [2]pact.
[b]The overwhelming [3]scourge will not reach us when it passes by,
For we have made [c]falsehood our refuge and we have [d]concealed ourselves with deception."
16 Therefore thus says the Lord [1]GOD,
"[a]Behold, I am laying in Zion a stone, a tested [b]stone,

2 [c]Is 8:6, 7; 30:28; Nah 1:8

3 [a]Is 26:6; 28:18

4 [1]Lit *valley of fatness* [2]Lit *the one seeing sees* [3]Lit *while it is yet* [4]Lit *palm* [a]Hos 9:10; Mic 7:1; Nah 3:12

5 [a]Is 41:16; 45:25; 60:1, 19 [b]Is 62:3

6 [1]Lit *battle* [a]1 Kin 3:28; Is 11:2; 32:15, 16; John 5:30 [b]2 Chr 32:6-8; Is 25:4

7 [1]Lit *seeing* [a]Is 5:11, 22; 22:13; 56:12; Hos 4:11 [b]Is 24:2 [c]Is 9:15 [d]Hab 2:15, 16 [e]Is 29:11

8 [a]Jer 48:26

9 [a]Is 2:3; 28:26; 30:20; 48:17; 50:4; 54:13 [b]Ps 131:2

10 [1]Heb *Sav lasav, sav lasav, Kav lakav, kav lakav, Ze' er sham, ze' er sham* These Hebrew monosyllables, imitating the babbling of a child, mock the prophet's preaching [a]2 Chr 36:15; Neh 9:30

11 [a]Is 33:19; 1 Cor 14:21

12 [a]Is 11:10; 30:15; 32:17, 18; Jer 6:16; Matt 11:28, 29

13 [1]V 10, note 1 The LORD responds to their scoffing by imitating their mockery, to represent the unintelligible language of a conqueror [a]Is 8:15; Matt 21:44

14 [a]Is 1:10; 28:22 [b]Is 29:20

15 [1]I.e. the nether world [2]So some ancient versions; Heb *seer* [3]Or *flood* [a]Is 28:18 [b]Is 8:8; 28:2; 30:28; Dan 11:22 [c]Is 9:15; 30:9; 44:20; 59:3, 4; Ezek 13:22 [d]Is 29:15

16 [1]Heb *YHWH,* usually rendered *LORD* [a]Rom 9:33; 10:11; 1 Pet 2:6 [b]Ps 118:22; Is 8:14, 15; Matt 21:42; Mark 12:10; Luke 20:17; Acts 4:11; Eph 2:20

A costly cornerstone *for* the foundation, [2]firmly placed.
He who believes *in it* will not be [3]disturbed.
17 "I will make [a]justice the measuring line
And righteousness the level;
Then [b]hail will sweep away the refuge of lies
And the waters will overflow the secret place.
18 "Your [a]covenant with death will be [1b]canceled,
And your pact with Sheol will not stand;
When the [a]overwhelming scourge passes through,
Then you become its [c]trampling *place.*
19 "As [a]often as it passes through, it will [1]seize you;
For [b]morning after morning it will pass through, *anytime*
during the day or night,
And it will be [2]sheer [c]terror to understand [3]what it means."
20 The bed is too short on which to stretch out,
And the [a]blanket is too [1]small to wrap oneself in.
21 For the LORD will rise up as *at* Mount [a]Perazim,
He will be stirred up as in the valley of [b]Gibeon,
To do His [c]task, His [1d]unusual task,
And to work His work, His [2]extraordinary work.
22 And now do not carry on as [a]scoffers,
Or your fetters will be made stronger;
For I have heard from the Lord [1]GOD of hosts
Of decisive [b]destruction on all the earth.

23 Give ear and hear my voice,
Listen and hear my words.
24 Does the [1]farmer plow [2]continually to plant seed?
Does he *continually* [3]turn and harrow the ground?
25 Does he not level its surface
And sow dill and scatter [a]cummin
And [1]plant [b]wheat in rows,
Barley in its place and rye within its [2]area?
26 For his God instructs and teaches him properly.
27 For dill is not threshed with a [a]threshing sledge,
Nor is the cartwheel [1]driven over cummin;
But dill is beaten out with a rod, and cummin with a club.
28 *Grain for* bread is crushed,
Indeed, he does not continue to thresh it forever.
Because the wheel of *his* cart and his horses *eventually*
[1]damage *it,*
He does not thresh it longer.
29 This also comes from the LORD of hosts,
Who has made *His* counsel [a]wonderful and *His* wisdom [b]great.

Chapter 29 Theme ______________________

29 Woe, O [1]Ariel, [1]Ariel the city *where* David *once* [a]camped!
Add year to year, [2b]observe *your* feasts on schedule.
2 I will bring distress to Ariel,
And she will be *a city of* lamenting and [a]mourning;
And she will be like an Ariel to me.

16 [2]Lit *well-laid* [3]Lit *in a hurry*

17 [a]2 Kin 21:13; Is 5:16; 30:18; 61:8; Amos 7:7-9 [b]Is 28:2

18 [1]Lit *covered over* [a]Is 28:15 [b]Is 7:7; 8:10 [c]Is 28:3; Dan 8:13

19 [1]Lit *take* [2]Lit *only* [3]Lit *the report*, or, *the message* [a]2 Kin 24:2 [b]Is 50:4 [c]Job 6:4; 18:11; 24:17; Ps 55:4; 88:15; Lam 2:22

20 [1]Lit *narrow* [a]Is 59:6

21 [1]Lit *task is strange* [2]Lit *work is alien* [a]2 Sam 5:20; 1 Chr 14:11 [b]Josh 10:10, 12; 2 Sam 5:25; 1 Chr 14:16 [c]Is 10:12; 29:14; 65:7 [d]Lam 2:15; 3:33; Luke 19:41-44

22 [1]Heb *YHWH*, usually rendered LORD [a]Is 28:14 [b]Is 10:22, 23

24 [1]Lit *plowman* [2]Lit *all day* [3]Lit *open*

25 [1]Lit *put* [2]Lit *region* [a]Matt 23:23 [b]Ex 9:32

27 [1]Lit *rolled* [a]Amos 1:3

28 [1]Lit *discomfit*

29 [a]Is 9:6 [b]Is 31:2; Rom 11:33

29:1 [1]I.e. Lion of God, or Jerusalem [2]Lit *let your feasts run their round* [a]2 Sam 5:9 [b]Is 1:14; 5:12; 22:12, 13; 29:9, 13

2 [a]Is 3:26; Lam 2:5

3 [1]Lit *like a circle* [a]Luke 19:43, 44

4 [1]Or *ghost* [a]Is 8:19

5 [1]Lit *strangers* [2]Lit *passes away* [a]Is 17:13; 41:15, 16 [b]Is 13:11; 25:3; 29:20 [c]Is 17:14; 30:13; 47:11; 1 Thess 5:3

6 [a]Is 10:3; 26:14, 21 [b]1 Sam 2:10; Matt 24:7; Mark 13:8; Luke 21:11; Rev 11:13, 19; 16:18

7 [1]V 1, note 1 [a]Mic 4:11, 12; Zech 12:9 [b]Job 20:8; Ps 73:20; Is 17:14

8 [1]Lit *soul* [a]Is 54:17

9 [a]Is 29:1 [b]Is 51:17, 21, 22; 63:6

10 [a]Ps 69:23; Is 6:9, 10; Mic 3:6; Rom 11:8 [b]Is 44:18; 2 Thess 2:9-12

11 [1]Or *scroll* [2]Lit *knows books* [a]Is 8:16; Dan 12:4, 9; Matt 13:11

12 [1]Or *scroll* [2]Lit *does not know books* [3]Lit *do not know books*

13 [1]Lit *mouth* [2]Lit *lips* [3]Lit *fear of Me* [4]Lit *is* [5]Lit *commandment of rulers* [a]Ezek 33:31; Matt 15:8, 9; Mark 7:6, 7

3 I will [a]camp against you [1]encircling *you,*
And I will set siegeworks against you,
And I will raise up battle towers against you.
4 Then you will [a]be brought low;
From the earth you will speak,
And from the dust *where* you are prostrate
Your words *will come.*
Your voice will also be like that of a [1]spirit from the ground,
And your speech will whisper from the dust.

5 But the multitude of your [1]enemies will become like
fine [a]dust,
And the multitude of the [b]ruthless ones like the chaff
which [2]blows away;
And it will happen [c]instantly, suddenly.
6 From the LORD of hosts you will be [a]punished with
[b]thunder and earthquake and loud noise,
With whirlwind and tempest and the flame of a
consuming fire.
7 And the [a]multitude of all the nations who wage war
against [1]Ariel,
Even all who wage war against her and her stronghold, and
who distress her,
Will be like a dream, a [b]vision of the night.
8 It will be as when a hungry man dreams—
And behold, he is eating;
But when he awakens, his [1]hunger is not satisfied,
Or as when a thirsty man dreams—
And behold, he is drinking,
But when he awakens, behold, he is faint
And his [1]thirst is not quenched.
[a]Thus the multitude of all the nations will be
Who wage war against Mount Zion.

9 [a]Be delayed and wait,
Blind yourselves and be blind;
They [b]become drunk, but not with wine,
They stagger, but not with strong drink.
10 For the LORD has poured over you a spirit of deep [a]sleep,
He has [b]shut your eyes, the prophets;
And He has covered your heads, the seers.
11 The entire vision will be to you like the words of a sealed
[1a]book, which when they give it to the one who [2]is literate,
saying, "Please read this," he will say, "I cannot, for it is sealed."
12 Then the [1]book will be given to the one who [2]is illiterate,
saying, "Please read this." And he will say, "I [3]cannot read."
13 Then the Lord said,
"Because [a]this people draw near with their [1]words
And honor Me with their [2]lip service,
But they remove their hearts far from Me,
And their [3]reverence for Me [4]consists of [5]tradition learned
by rote,

14 Therefore behold, I will once again deal [a]marvelously with
this people, wondrously marvelous;
And [b]the wisdom of their wise men will perish,
And the discernment of their discerning men will
be concealed."

15 Woe to those who deeply [a]hide their [1]plans from the LORD,
And whose [b]deeds are *done* in a dark place,
And they say, "[c]Who sees us?" or "Who knows us?"
16 You turn *things* around!
Shall the potter be considered [1]as equal with the clay,
That [a]what is made would say to its maker, "He did not
make me";
Or what is formed say to him who formed it, "He has no
understanding"?

17 Is it not yet just a little while
[1]Before Lebanon will be turned into a [a]fertile field,
And the fertile field will be considered as a forest?
18 On that day the [a]deaf will hear [b]words of a book,
And out of *their* gloom and darkness the [c]eyes of the blind
will see.
19 The [a]afflicted also will increase their gladness in the LORD,
And the [b]needy of mankind will rejoice in the Holy One
of Israel.
20 For the [a]ruthless will come to an end and the [b]scorner will
be finished,
Indeed [c]all who [1]are intent on doing evil will be cut off;
21 Who [1]cause a person to be indicted by a word,
And [a]ensnare him who adjudicates at the gate,
And [2b]defraud the one in the right with [3]meaningless
arguments.
22 Therefore thus says the LORD, who redeemed [a]Abraham,
concerning the house of Jacob:
"Jacob [b]shall not now be ashamed, nor shall his face now
turn pale;
23 But when [1]he sees his [a]children, the [b]work of My hands, in
his midst,
They will sanctify My name;
Indeed, they will [c]sanctify the Holy One of Jacob
And will stand in awe of the God of Israel.
24 "Those who [a]err in [1]mind will [b]know [2]the truth,
And those who [3]criticize will [4c]accept instruction.

Chapter 30 Theme ______________________

30

"Woe to the [a]rebellious children," declares the LORD,
"Who [b]execute a plan, but not Mine,
And [1c]make an alliance, but not of My Spirit,
In order to add sin to sin;
2 Who [a]proceed down to Egypt
Without [b]consulting [1]Me,

14 [a]Is 6:9, 10; 28:21; 65:7; Hab 1:5 [b]Is 44:25; Jer 8:9; 49:7; 1 Cor 1:19

15 [1]Lit *counsel* [a]Ps 10:11, 13; Is 28:15; 30:1 [b]Job 22:13; Is 57:12; Ezek 8:12 [c]Ps 94:7; Is 47:10; Mal 2:17

16 [1]Lit *like* [a]Is 45:9; 64:8; Jer 18:1-6; Rom 9:19-21

17 [1]Lit *And* [a]Ps 84:6; 107:33, 35; Is 32:15

18 [a]Is 35:5; 42:18, 19; 43:8; Matt 11:5; Mark 7:37 [b]Is 29:11 [c]Ps 119:18; Prov 20:12; Is 32:3

19 [a]Ps 25:9; 37:11; Is 11:4; 61:1; Matt 5:5; 11:29 [b]Is 3:14, 15; 11:4; 14:30, 32; 25:4; 26:6; Matt 11:5; James 1:9; 2:5

20 [1]Lit *watch evil* [a]Is 29:5 [b]Is 28:14 [c]Is 59:4; Mic 2:1

21 [1]Lit *bring a person under condemnation* [2]Lit *turn aside* [3]Lit *confusion* [a]Amos 5:10 [b]Is 32:7; Amos 5:12

22 [a]Is 41:8; 51:2; 63:16 [b]Is 45:17; 49:23; 50:7; 54:4

23 [1]Or *his children see* [a]Is 49:20-26 [b]Is 26:12; 45:11; Eph 2:10 [c]Is 5:16; 8:13

24 [1]Lit *spirit* [2]Lit *understanding* [3]Lit *murmur* [4]Lit *learn* [a]Is 30:21; Heb 5:2 [b]Is 41:20; 60:16 [c]Is 54:13

30:1 [1]Lit *pour out a drink offering* [a]Is 1:2, 23; 30:9; 65:2 [b]Is 29:15 [c]Is 8:11, 12

2 [1]Lit *My mouth* [a]Is 31:1; Jer 43:7 [b]Is 8:19

[c]To take refuge in the safety of Pharaoh
And to seek shelter in the shadow of Egypt!
3 "Therefore the safety of Pharaoh will be [a]your shame
And the shelter in the shadow of Egypt, your humiliation.
4 "For [a]their princes are at Zoan
And their ambassadors arrive at Hanes.
5 "Everyone will be [a]ashamed because of a people who cannot profit them,
Who are [b]not for help or profit, but for shame and also for reproach."

6 The [1]oracle concerning the [a]beasts of the [b]Negev.
Through a land of [c]distress and anguish,
From [2]where *come* lioness and lion, viper and [d]flying serpent,
They [e]carry their riches on the [3]backs of young donkeys
And their treasures on [f]camels' humps,
To a people who cannot profit *them;*
7 Even Egypt, whose [a]help is vain and empty.
Therefore, I have called [1]her
"[2][b]Rahab who has been exterminated."
8 Now go, [a]write it on a tablet before them
And inscribe it on a scroll,
That it may [1]serve in the time to come
[2]As a witness forever.
9 For this is a [a]rebellious people, [b]false sons,
Sons who [1]refuse to [c]listen
To the [2]instruction of the LORD;
10 Who say to the [a]seers, "You must not see *visions";*
And to the prophets, "You must not [b]prophesy to us what is right,
[c]Speak to us [1]pleasant words,
Prophesy illusions.
11 "Get out of the way, [a]turn aside from the path,
[1][b]Let us hear no more about the Holy One of Israel."
12 Therefore thus says the Holy One of Israel,
"[a]Since you have rejected this word
And have put your trust in [b]oppression and guile, and have relied on them,
13 Therefore this [a]iniquity will be to you
Like a [b]breach about to fall,
A bulge in a high wall,
Whose collapse comes [c]suddenly in an instant,
14 Whose collapse is like the smashing of a [a]potter's jar,
[1]So ruthlessly shattered
That a sherd will not be found among its pieces
To [2]take fire from a hearth
Or to scoop water from a cistern."
15 For thus the Lord [1]GOD, the Holy One of Israel, has said,
"In [2]repentance and [a]rest you will be saved,
In [b]quietness and trust is your strength."
But you were not willing,

2 [c]Is 36:9

3 [a]Is 20:5, 6; 36:6; Jer 42:18, 22

4 [a]Is 19:11

5 [a]Jer 2:36 [b]Is 10:3; 30:7; 31:3

6 [1]Or *burden of* [2]Lit *them* [3]Lit *shoulders* [a]Is 46:1, 2 [b]Gen 12:9 [c]Ex 5:10, 21; Deut 4:20; 8:15; Is 5:30; 8:22; Jer 11:4 [d]Deut 8:15; Is 14:29 [e]Is 15:7; 46:1, 2 [f]1 Kin 10:2

7 [1]Lit *this* one [2]M.T. reads *They are Rahab* (or *arrogance*), *to remain* [a]Is 30:5 [b]Job 9:13; Ps 87:4; 89:10; Is 51:9

8 [1]Lit *be* [2]So the versions; Heb *Forever and ever* [a]Is 8:1

9 [1]Lit *are not willing* [2]Or *law* [a]Is 30:1 [b]Is 28:15; 59:3, 4 [c]Is 1:10; 5:24; 24:5

10 [1]Lit *smooth things* [a]Is 29:10 [b]Is 5:20; Jer 11:21; Amos 2:12; 7:13 [c]1 Kin 22:8, 13; Jer 6:14; 23:17, 26; Ezek 13:7; Rom 16:18; 2 Tim 4:3, 4

11 [1]Lit *Cause to cease from our presence* the [a]Acts 13:8 [b]Job 21:14

12 [a]Is 5:24; 7:9; 8:6 [b]Is 3:14, 15; 5:7; 59:13

13 [a]Is 26:21 [b]1 Kin 20:30; Ps 62:4; Is 58:12 [c]Is 29:5; 47:11

14 [1]Lit *Crushed, it will not be spared* [2]Lit *snatch up* [a]Ps 2:9; Jer 19:10, 11

15 [1]Heb *YHWH,* usually rendered LORD [2]Lit *returning* [a]Ps 116:7; Is 28:12 [b]Is 7:4; 32:17

16 And you said, “No, for we will flee on [a]horses,”
Therefore you shall flee!
“And we will ride on swift *horses,*”
Therefore those who pursue you shall be swift.
17 [a]One thousand *will flee* at the threat of one *man;*
You will flee at the threat of five,
Until you are left as a [1]flag on a mountain top
And as a signal on a hill.

18 Therefore the LORD [1][a]longs to be gracious to you,
And therefore He [2]waits on [b]high to have compassion on you.
For the LORD is a [c]God of justice;
How blessed are all those who [3][d]long for Him.
19 [1]O people in Zion, [a]inhabitant in Jerusalem, you will [b]weep
no longer. He will surely be gracious to you at the sound of
your cry; when He hears it, He will [c]answer you.
20 Although the Lord has given you [a]bread of privation and
water of oppression, *He,* your Teacher will no longer [b]hide
Himself, but your eyes will behold your Teacher.
21 Your ears will hear a word behind you, “[1]This is the [a]way,
walk in it,” whenever you [b]turn to the right or to the left.
22 And you will defile your graven [a]images overlaid with
silver, and your molten [a]images plated with gold. You will
scatter them as an impure thing, *and* say to [1]them, “[b]Be gone!”
23 Then He will [a]give *you* rain for [1]the seed which you will
sow in the ground, and bread *from* the yield of the ground, and
it will be [2]rich and [3]plenteous; on that day [b]your livestock will
graze in a roomy pasture.
24 Also the oxen and the donkeys which work the ground will eat
salted fodder, which [1]has been [a]winnowed with shovel and fork.
25 On every lofty mountain and on [a]every high hill there will
be [1]streams running with water on the day of the great
[b]slaughter, when the towers fall.
26 [a]The light of the moon will be as the light of the sun, and
the light of the sun will be seven times *brighter,* like the light of
seven days, on the day [b]the LORD binds up the [c]fracture of His
people and [d]heals the bruise [1]He has inflicted.
27 Behold, [a]the name of the LORD comes from a [1]remote place;
[b]Burning is His anger and [2]dense is *His* [3]smoke;
His lips are filled with [c]indignation
And His tongue is like a [d]consuming fire;
28 His [a]breath is like an overflowing torrent,
Which [b]reaches to the neck,
To [c]shake the nations back and forth in a [1]sieve,
And to *put* in the jaws of the peoples [d]the bridle which
[2]leads to ruin.
29 You will have [1]songs as in the night when you keep the
festival,
And gladness of heart as when one marches to *the sound
of* the flute,
To go to the mountain of the LORD, to the Rock of Israel.

16 [a]Is 2:7; 31:1, 3

17 [1]Lit *pole* [a]Lev 26:36; Deut 28:25; 32:30; Josh 23:10; Prov 28:1

18 [1]Lit *waits* [2]Lit *is on high* [3]Lit *wait* [a]Is 42:14, 16; 48:9; Jon 3:4, 10; 2 Pet 3:9, 15 [b]Is 2:11, 17; 33:5 [c]Is 5:16; 28:17; 61:8 [d]Is 8:17; 25:9; 26:8; 33:2

19 [1]M.T. reads *A people will inhabit Zion, Jerusalem* [a]Is 65:9; Ezek 37:25, 28 [b]Is 25:8; 60:20; 61:1-3 [c]Ps 50:15; Is 58:9; 65:24; Matt 7:7-11

20 [a]1 Kin 22:27; Ps 80:5 [b]Ps 74:9; Amos 8:11

21 [1]Lit *saying, "This* [a]Ps 25:8, 9; Prov 3:6; Is 35:8, 9; 42:16 [b]Is 29:24

22 [1]Lit *it "Go out"* [a]Ex 32:2, 4; Judg 17:3, 4; Is 46:6 [b]Matt 4:10

23 [1]Lit *your* [2]Lit *fatness* [3]Lit *fat* [a]Ps 65:9-13; 104:13, 14 [b]Ps 144:13; Is 32:20; Hos 4:16

24 [1]Lit *one winnows* [a]Matt 3:12; Luke 3:17

25 [1]Lit *canals, streams of water* [a]Is 35:6, 7; 41:18; 43:19, 20 [b]Is 34:2

26 [1]Lit *of His blow* [a]Is 24:23; 60:19, 20; Rev 21:23; 22:5 [b]Is 61:1 [c]Is 1:6; 30:13, 14 [d]Deut 32:39; Job 5:18; Is 33:24; Jer 33:6; Hos 6:1, 2

27 [1]Lit *distance* [2]Lit *heaviness* [3]Lit *uplifting* [a]Is 59:19 [b]Is 10:17 [c]Is 10:5; 13:5; 66:14 [d]Is 66:15

28 [1]Lit *sifting of the worthless* [2]Lit *misleads* [a]Is 11:4; 30:33; 2 Thess 2:8 [b]Is 8:8 [c]Amos 9:9 [d]2 Kin 19:28; Is 37:29

29 [1]Lit *the song*

30 And the LORD will cause [1]His voice of authority to be heard,
And the [2]descending of His arm to be seen in fierce anger,
And *in* the flame of a consuming fire
In cloudburst, downpour and hailstones.
31 For [a]at the voice of the LORD [b]Assyria will be terrified,
When He strikes with the [c]rod.
32 And every [1]blow of the [2a]rod of punishment,
Which the LORD will lay on him,
Will be with *the music of* [b]tambourines and lyres;
And in battles, [c]brandishing weapons, He will fight them.
33 For [1a]Topheth has long been ready,
Indeed, it has been prepared for the king.
He has made it deep and large,
[2]A pyre of fire with plenty of wood;
The [b]breath of the LORD, like a torrent of [c]brimstone, sets
it afire.

Chapter 31 Theme ______

31 Woe to those who go down to [a]Egypt for help
And [b]rely on horses,
And trust in chariots because they are many
And in horsemen because they are very strong,
But they do not [c]look to the [d]Holy One of Israel, nor seek
the LORD!
2 Yet He also is [a]wise and will [b]bring disaster
And does [c]not retract His words,
But will arise against the house of [d]evildoers
And against the help of the [e]workers of iniquity.
3 Now the Egyptians are [a]men and not God,
And their [b]horses are flesh and not spirit;
So the LORD will [c]stretch out His hand,
And [d]he who helps will stumble
And he who is helped will fall,
And all of them will come to an end together.

4 For thus says the LORD to me,
"As the [a]lion or the young lion growls over his prey,
Against which a band of shepherds is called out,
And he will not be terrified at their voice nor disturbed at
their noise,
So will the LORD of hosts come down to wage [b]war on
Mount Zion and on its hill."
5 Like [1]flying [a]birds so the LORD of hosts will protect Jerusalem.
He will [b]protect and deliver *it;*
He will pass over and rescue *it.*
6 [a]Return to Him from whom [1]you have [b]deeply defected,
O sons of Israel.
7 For in that day every man will [a]cast away his silver idols
and his gold idols, which your [b]sinful hands have made for you
as [b]a sin.

30 [1]Lit *the majesty of His voice* [2]Lit *descent*

31 [a]Is 11:4 [b]Is 10:12; 14:25; 31:8 [c]Is 10:26; 11:4

32 [1]Lit *passing* [2]Lit *staff of foundation* [a]Is 10:24 [b]1 Sam 18:6; Jer 31:4 [c]Ezek 32:10

33 [1]I.e. the place of human sacrifice to Molech [2]Lit *Its pile* [a]2 Kin 23:10; Jer 7:31; 19:6 [b]Is 11:4; 30:28 [c]Gen 19:24; Is 34:9

31:1 [a]Is 30:2, 7; 36:6 [b]Deut 17:16; Ps 20:7; 33:17; Is 2:7; 30:16 [c]Is 9:13; Dan 9:13; Amos 5:4-8 [d]Is 10:17; 43:15; Hos 11:9; Hab 1:12; 3:3

2 [a]Is 28:29; Rom 16:27 [b]Is 45:7 [c]Num 23:19; Jer 44:29 [d]Is 1:4; 9:17; 14:20 [e]Is 22:14; 32:6

3 [a]Ezek 28:9; 2 Thess 2:4 [b]Is 36:9 [c]Is 9:17; Jer 15:6; Ezek 20:33, 34 [d]Is 30:5, 7; Matt 15:14

4 [a]Num 24:9; Hos 11:10; Amos 3:8 [b]Is 42:13; Zech 12:8

5 [1]Or *hovering* [a]Deut 32:11; Ps 91:4 [b]Is 37:35; 38:6

6 [1]Lit *they* [a]Is 44:22; 55:7; Jer 3:10, 14, 22; Ezek 18:31, 32 [b]Is 1:2, 5

7 [a]Is 2:20; 30:22 [b]1 Kin 12:30

8 And the [a]Assyrian will fall by a sword not of man,
And a [b]sword not of man will devour him.
So he will [1c]not escape the sword,
And his young men will become [d]forced laborers.
9 "His [a]rock will pass away because of panic,
And his princes will be terrified at the [b]standard,"
Declares the LORD, whose [c]fire is in Zion and whose
furnace is in Jerusalem.

Chapter 32 Theme ______________________________

32 Behold, a [a]king will reign righteously
And princes will rule justly.
2 Each will be like a [a]refuge from the wind
And a shelter from the storm,
Like [1b]streams of water in a dry country,
Like the [a]shade of a [2]huge rock in [3]a parched land.
3 Then [a]the eyes of those who see will not be [1]blinded,
And the ears of those who hear will listen.
4 The [1]mind of the [a]hasty will discern the [2]truth,
And the tongue of the stammerers will hasten to
speak clearly.
5 No longer will the [a]fool be called noble,
Or the rogue be spoken of *as* generous.
6 For a fool speaks nonsense,
And his heart [1a]inclines toward wickedness:
To practice [b]ungodliness and to speak error against the LORD,
To [2c]keep the hungry person unsatisfied
And [3]to withhold drink from the thirsty.
7 As for a rogue, his weapons are evil;
He [a]devises wicked schemes
To [b]destroy *the* afflicted with [1]slander,
[c]Even though *the* needy one speaks [2]what is right.
8 But [a]the noble man devises noble plans;
And by noble plans he stands.

9 Rise up, you [a]women who are at ease,
And hear my voice;
[b]Give ear to my word,
You complacent daughters.
10 Within a year and *a few* days
You will be troubled, O complacent *daughters;*
[a]For the vintage is ended,
And the *fruit* gathering will not come.
11 Tremble, you *women* who are at ease;
[a]Be troubled, you complacent *daughters;*
[b]Strip, undress and put *sackcloth* on *your* waist,
12 [a]Beat your breasts for the pleasant fields, for the fruitful vine,
13 [a]For the land of my people *in which* thorns *and* briars shall
come up;
Yea, for all the joyful houses *and for* the [b]jubilant city.

8 [1]Lit *flee* [a]Is 10:12; 14:25; 30:31-33; 37:7, 36-38 [b]Is 66:16 [c]Is 21:15 [d]Gen 49:15; Is 14:2

9 [a]Deut 32:31, 37 [b]Is 5:26; 13:2; 18:3 [c]Is 10:16, 17; 30:33; Zech 2:5

32:1 [a]Ps 72:1-4; Is 9:6, 7; 11:4, 5; Jer 23:5; 33:15; Ezek 37:24; Zech 9:9

2 [1]Lit *canals* [2]Lit *heavy* [3]Lit *an exhausted* [a]Is 4:6; 25:4 [b]Is 35:6; 41:18; 43:19, 20

3 [1]Or *turned away* [a]Is 29:18

4 [1]Lit *heart* [2]Lit *knowledge* [a]Is 29:24

5 [a]1 Sam 25:25

6 [1]Or *does* [2]Lit *make empty the hungry soul* [3]Lit *he causes to lack* [a]Prov 19:3; 24:7-9; Is 59:7, 13 [b]Is 9:17; 10:6 [c]Is 3:15; 10:2

7 [1]Lit *words of falsehood* [2]Lit *justly* [a]Jer 5:26-28; Mic 7:3 [b]Is 11:4; 61:1 [c]Is 5:23

8 [a]Prov 11:25

9 [a]Is 47:8; Amos 6:1; Zeph 2:15 [b]Is 28:23

10 [a]Is 5:5, 6; 7:23; 24:7

11 [a]Is 22:12 [b]Is 47:2

12 [a]Nah 2:7

13 [a]Is 5:6, 10, 17; 27:10 [b]Is 22:2; 23:9

14 Because [a]the palace has been abandoned, the [1]populated
[b]city forsaken.
[2]Hill and watch-tower have become [c]caves forever,
A delight for [d]wild donkeys, a pasture for flocks;
15 Until the [a]Spirit is poured out upon us from on high,
And the wilderness becomes a [b]fertile field,
And the fertile field is considered as a forest.
16 Then [a]justice will dwell in the wilderness
And righteousness will abide in the fertile field.
17 And the [a]work of righteousness will be peace,
And the service of righteousness, [b]quietness and
[1]confidence forever.
18 Then my people will live in a [a]peaceful habitation,
And in secure dwellings and in undisturbed [b]resting places;
19 And it will [a]hail when the [b]forest comes down,
And [c]the city will be utterly laid low.
20 How [a]blessed will you be, you who sow beside all waters,
Who [1]let out freely the ox and the donkey.

Chapter 33 Theme ____________________

33 Woe [a]to you, O destroyer,
While you were not destroyed;
And he [b]who is treacherous, while *others* did not deal
treacherously with him.
As soon as you finish destroying, [c]you will be destroyed;
As soon as you cease to deal treacherously, *others* will [d]deal
treacherously with you.
2 O LORD, [a]be gracious to us; we have [b]waited for You.
Be [1]their [2c]strength every morning,
Our salvation also in the [d]time of distress.
3 At the sound of the tumult [a]peoples flee;
At the [b]lifting up of Yourself nations disperse.
4 Your spoil is gathered *as* the caterpillar gathers;
As locusts rushing about men rush about on it.
5 The LORD is [a]exalted, for He dwells on high;
He has [b]filled Zion with justice and righteousness.
6 And He will be the [1a]stability of your times,
A [b]wealth of salvation, wisdom and [c]knowledge;
The [d]fear of the LORD is his treasure.
7 Behold, their brave men cry in [1]the streets,
The [2a]ambassadors of peace weep bitterly.
8 The highways are desolate, [1]the [a]traveler has ceased,
He has [b]broken the covenant, he has despised the cities,
He has no regard for man.
9 [a]The land mourns *and* pines away,
[b]Lebanon is shamed *and* withers;
[c]Sharon is like a desert plain,
And Bashan and Carmel [1]lose *their foliage.*
10 "Now [a]I will arise," says the LORD,
"Now I will be exalted, now I will be lifted up.

14 [1]Lit *multitude of the* [2]Or *Ophel* [a]Is 13:22; 25:2; 34:13 [b]Is 6:11; 22:2; 24:10, 12 [c]Is 13:21; 34:13 [d]Ps 104:11; Jer 14:6

15 [a]Is 11:2; 44:3; 59:21; Ezek 39:29; Joel 2:28 [b]Ps 107:35; Is 29:17; 35:1, 2

16 [a]Is 33:5; Zech 8:3

17 [1]Or *security* [a]Ps 72:2, 3; 85:8; 119:165; Is 2:4; Rom 14:17; James 3:18 [b]Is 30:15

18 [a]Is 26:3, 12 [b]Is 11:10; 14:3; 30:15; Hos 2:18-23; Zech 2:5; 3:10

19 [a]Is 28:2, 17; 30:30 [b]Is 10:18, 19, 34 [c]Is 24:10, 12; 26:5; 27:10; 29:4

20 [1]Lit *send out the foot of the ox* [a]Eccl 11:1; Is 30:23, 24

33:1 [a]Is 10:6; 21:2 [b]Is 24:16; 48:8 [c]Is 10:12; 14:25; 31:8; Hab 2:8 [d]Jer 25:12-14; Matt 7:2

2 [1]Some versions read *our* [2]Lit *arm* [a]Is 30:18, 19 [b]Is 25:9 [c]Is 40:10; 51:5; 59:16 [d]Is 37:3

3 [a]Is 17:13; 21:15 [b]Is 10:33; 17:13; 59:16-18; Jer 25:30, 31

5 [a]Ps 97:9 [b]Is 1:26; 28:6; 32:16

6 [1]Or *faithfulness* [a]Is 33:20 [b]Is 45:17; 51:6 [c]Is 11:9 [d]2 Kin 18:7; Ps 112:1-3; Is 11:3; Matt 6:33

7 [1]Lit *the outside* [2]Lit *messengers* [a]2 Kin 18:18, 37

8 [1]Lit *he who passes along the way* [a]Is 35:8 [b]Is 24:5

9 [1]Lit *shake off* [a]Is 3:26; 24:4; 29:2 [b]Is 2:13; 10:34 [c]Is 35:2; 65:10

10 [a]Ps 12:5; Is 2:19, 21

11 "You have [a]conceived [1]chaff, you will give birth to stubble;
[2]My [b]breath will consume you like a fire.
12 "The peoples will be burned to lime,
[a]Like cut thorns which are burned in the fire.

13 "You who are far away, [a]hear what I have done;
And you who are near, [1]acknowledge My might."
14 [a]Sinners in Zion are terrified;
[b]Trembling has seized the godless.
"Who among us can live with [c]the consuming fire?
Who among us can live with [1]continual [d]burning?"
15 He who [a]walks righteously and speaks with sincerity,
He who rejects [1]unjust gain
And shakes his hands so that they hold no bribe;
He who stops his ears from hearing about bloodshed
And [b]shuts his eyes from looking upon evil;
16 He will dwell on the heights,
[a]His refuge will be the [1]impregnable rock;
[b]His bread will be given *him,*
His water will be sure.

17 Your eyes will see [a]the King in His beauty;
They will behold [b]a far-distant land.
18 Your heart will meditate on [a]terror:
"Where is [b]he who counts?
Where is he who weighs?
Where is he who counts the towers?"
19 You will no longer see a fierce people,
A people of [1a]unintelligible speech [2]which no one
comprehends,
Of a stammering tongue [3]which no one understands.
20 [a]Look upon Zion, the city of our appointed feasts;
Your eyes will see Jerusalem, an [b]undisturbed habitation,
[c]A tent which will not be folded;
Its stakes will never be pulled up,
Nor any of its cords be torn apart.
21 But there the majestic *One,* the LORD, will be for us
A place of [a]rivers *and* wide canals
On which no boat with oars will go,
And on which no mighty ship will pass—
22 For the LORD is our [a]judge,
The LORD is [b]our lawgiver,
The LORD is [c]our king;
[d]He will save us—
23 Your tackle hangs slack;
It cannot hold the base of its mast firmly,
Nor spread out the sail.
Then the [a]prey of an abundant spoil will be divided;
[b]The lame will take the plunder.
24 And no resident will say, "I am [a]sick";
The people who dwell [1]there will be [b]forgiven *their* iniquity.

11 [1]Lit *dry grass* [2]So one ancient version; M.T. reads *Your breath will* [a]Ps 7:14; Is 26:18; 59:4; James 1:15 [b]Is 1:31

12 [a]2 Sam 23:6, 7; Is 10:17; 27:4

13 [1]Lit *know* [a]Ps 48:10; Is 49:1

14 [1]Lit *everlasting* [a]Is 1:28 [b]Is 32:11 [c]Is 30:27, 30; Heb 12:29 [d]Is 9:18, 19; 10:16; 47:14

15 [1]Lit *gain of extortioners* [a]Ps 15:2; 24:4; Is 58:6-11 [b]Ps 119:37

16 [1]Lit *stronghold of rock* [a]Is 25:4 [b]Is 49:10

17 [a]Is 6:5; 24:23; 33:21, 22 [b]Is 26:15

18 [a]Is 17:14 [b]1 Cor 1:20

19 [1]Lit *deepness of lip* [2]Lit *from hearing* [3]Lit *there is no understanding* [a]Deut 28:49, 50; Is 28:11; Jer 5:15

20 [a]Ps 48:12 [b]Ps 46:5; 125:1, 2; Is 32:18 [c]Is 54:2

21 [a]Is 41:18; 43:19, 20; 48:18; 66:12

22 [a]Is 2:4; 11:4; 16:5; 51:5 [b]Is 1:10; 51:4, 7; James 4:12 [c]Ps 89:18; Is 33:17; Zech 9:9 [d]Is 25:9; 35:4; 49:25, 26; 60:16

23 [a]2 Kin 7:16 [b]2 Kin 7:8; Is 35:6

24 [1]Lit *in it* [a]Is 30:26; 58:8; Jer 30:17 [b]Is 40:2; 44:22; Jer 50:20; Mic 7:18, 19; 1 John 1:7-9

Chapter 34 Theme ______________________

34 Draw near, [a]O nations, to hear; and listen, O peoples!
[b]Let the earth and [1]all it contains hear, and the world
and all that springs from it.
2 For the LORD'S [a]indignation is against all the nations,
And *His* wrath against all their armies;
He has [1b]utterly destroyed them,
He has given them over to [c]slaughter.
3 So their slain will be [a]thrown out,
And their corpses [1]will give off their [b]stench,
And the mountains will [2]be drenched with their [c]blood.
4 And [a]all the host of heaven will [1]wear away,
And the [b]sky will be rolled up like a scroll;
All their hosts will also wither away
As a leaf withers from the vine,
Or as *one* withers from the fig tree.
5 For [a]My sword is satiated in heaven,
Behold it shall descend for judgment upon [b]Edom
And upon the people whom I have [c]devoted
to destruction.
6 The sword of the LORD is filled with blood,
It is [1]sated with fat, with the blood of lambs and goats,
With the fat of the kidneys of rams.
For the LORD has a sacrifice in [a]Bozrah
And a great slaughter in the land of [b]Edom.
7 [a]Wild oxen will also [1]fall with them
And [b]young bulls with strong ones;
Thus their land will be [c]soaked with blood,
And their dust [2]become greasy with fat.
8 For the LORD has a day of [a]vengeance,
A year of recompense for the [1]cause of Zion.
9 [1]Its streams will be turned into pitch,
And its loose earth into [a]brimstone,
And its land will become burning pitch.
10 It will [a]not be quenched night or day;
Its [b]smoke will go up forever.
From [c]generation to generation it will be desolate;
[d]None will pass through it forever and ever.
11 But [1a]pelican and hedgehog will possess it,
And [2]owl and raven will dwell in it;
And He will stretch over it the [b]line of [3]desolation
And the [4]plumb line of emptiness.
12 Its nobles—there is [a]no one there
Whom they may proclaim king—
And all its princes will be [b]nothing.
13 Thorns will come up in its [a]fortified towers,
Nettles and thistles in its fortified cities;
It will also be a haunt of [b]jackals
And an abode of ostriches.
14 The desert [a]creatures will meet with the [1]wolves,
The [2a]hairy goat also will cry to its kind;

34:1 [1]Lit *its fullness* [a]Ps 49:1; Is 41:1; 43:9 [b]Deut 32:1; Is 1:2
2 [1]Lit *put under the ban* [a]Is 26:20 [b]Is 13:5; 24:1 [c]Is 30:25; 63:6; 65:12
3 [1]Lit *their stench will go up* [2]Lit *dissolve* [a]Is 14:19 [b]Joel 2:20; Amos 4:10 [c]Ezek 14:19; 35:6; 38:22
4 [1]Lit *rot* [a]Is 13:13; 51:6; Ezek 32:7, 8; Joel 2:31; Matt 24:29; 2 Pet 3:10 [b]Rev 6:12-14
5 [a]Deut 32:41, 42; Jer 46:10; Ezek 21:3-5 [b]Is 63:1; Jer 49:7, 8, 20; Ezek 25:12-14; 35:1-15; Amos 1:11, 12; Obad 1-14; Mal 1:4 [c]Is 24:6; 43:28
6 [1]Lit *made fat* [a]Is 63:1; Jer 49:13 [b]Is 63:1
7 [1]Lit *go down* [2]Lit *made fat* [a]Num 23:22; Ps 22:21 [b]Ps 68:30; Jer 50:27 [c]Is 63:6
8 [1]Or *controversy* [a]Is 13:6; 35:4; 47:3; 61:2; 63:4
9 [1]I.e. Edom's [a]Deut 29:23; Ps 11:6; Is 30:33
10 [a]Is 1:31; 66:24 [b]Rev 14:11; 19:3 [c]Is 13:20-22; 24:1; 34:10-15; Mal 1:3, 4 [d]Ezek 29:11
11 [1]Or *owl* or *jackdaw* [2]Or *great horned owl* [3]Or *formlessness* [4]Lit *stones of void* [a]Zeph 2:14 [b]2 Kin 21:13; Is 24:10; Lam 2:8
12 [a]Jer 27:20; 39:6 [b]Is 41:11, 12
13 [a]Is 13:22; 25:2; 32:13 [b]Ps 44:19; Jer 9:11; 10:22
14 [1]Or *howling creatures* [2]Or *demon* [a]Is 13:21

Yes, the [3]night monster will settle there
And will find herself a resting place.
15 The tree snake will make its nest and lay *eggs* there,
And it will hatch and gather *them* under its [1]protection.
Yes, [a]the [2]hawks will be gathered there,
Every one with its kind.

16 Seek from the [a]book of the LORD, and read:
Not one of these will be missing;
None will lack its mate.
For [1b]His mouth has commanded,
And His Spirit has gathered them.
17 He has cast the [a]lot for them,
And His hand has divided it to them by [b]line.
They shall possess it forever;
From [c]generation to generation they will dwell in it.

Chapter 35 Theme ________________________________

35 The [a]wilderness and the desert will be glad,
And the [1b]Arabah will rejoice and blossom;
Like the crocus
2 It will [a]blossom profusely
And [b]rejoice with rejoicing and shout of joy.
The [c]glory of Lebanon will be given to it,
The majesty of [d]Carmel and Sharon.
They will see the [e]glory of the LORD,
The majesty of our God.
3 [a]Encourage the [1]exhausted, and strengthen the [2]feeble.
4 Say to those with [a]anxious heart,
"Take courage, fear not.
Behold, your God will come *with* [b]vengeance;
The [c]recompense of God will come,
But He will [d]save you."
5 Then the [a]eyes of the blind will be opened
And the ears of the deaf will be unstopped.
6 Then the [a]lame will leap like a deer,
And the [b]tongue of the mute will shout for joy.
For waters will break forth in the [c]wilderness
And streams in the [1]Arabah.
7 The [1]scorched land will become a pool
And the thirsty ground [a]springs of water;
In the [b]haunt of jackals, its resting place,
Grass *becomes* reeds and rushes.
8 [a]A highway will be there, [b]a roadway,
And it will be called the Highway of [c]Holiness.
The unclean will not travel on it,
But it *will* be for him who walks *that* way,
And [d]fools will not wander *on it.*
9 No [a]lion will be there,
Nor will any vicious beast go up on it;

14 [3]Heb *Lilith*

15 [1]Lit *shade* [2]Or *kites* [a]Deut 14:13

16 [1]So DSS; M.T. *My* [a]Is 30:8 [b]Is 1:20; 40:5; 58:14

17 [a]Is 17:13, 14; Jer 13:25 [b]Is 34:11 [c]Is 34:10

35:1 [1]Or *desert* [a]Is 6:11; 7:21-25; 27:10; 41:18; 55:12, 13 [b]Is 41:19; 51:3

2 [a]Is 27:6; 32:15 [b]Is 25:9; 35:10; 55:12, 13; 66:10, 14 [c]Is 60:13 [d]Song 7:5 [e]Is 25:9

3 [1]Lit *slack hands* [2]Lit *tottering knees* [a]Job 4:3, 4; Heb 12:12

4 [a]Is 32:4 [b]Is 1:24; 47:3; 61:2; 63:4 [c]Is 34:8; 59:18 [d]Ps 145:19; Is 33:22; 35:4

5 [a]Is 29:18; 32:3, 4; 42:7, 16; 50:4; Matt 11:5; John 9:6, 7

6 [1]Or *desert* [a]Matt 15:30; John 5:8, 9; Acts 3:8 [b]Matt 9:32; Luke 11:14 [c]Is 35:1; 41:18; 43:19; 49:10; 51:3; John 7:38

7 [1]Or *mirage* [a]Is 49:10 [b]Is 13:22; 34:13

8 [a]Is 11:16; 19:23; 40:3; 49:11; 62:10 [b]Is 30:21; 51:10 [c]Is 4:3; 52:1; Matt 7:13, 14; 1 Pet 1:15, 16 [d]Is 33:8

9 [a]Is 5:29; 30:6

[1]These will not be found there.
But [b]the redeemed will walk *there,*
10 And [a]the ransomed of the LORD will return
And come with joyful shouting to Zion,
With everlasting joy upon their heads.
They will [1]find gladness and joy,
And [b]sorrow and sighing will flee away.

Chapter 36 Theme ______________________________

36 [a]Now in the fourteenth year of King Hezekiah,
[b]Sennacherib king of Assyria came up against all the
fortified cities of Judah and seized them.
2 And the [a]king of Assyria sent Rabshakeh from Lachish to
Jerusalem to King Hezekiah with a large army. And he stood by
the [b]conduit of the upper pool on the highway of the [1]fuller's field.
3 Then [a]Eliakim the son of Hilkiah, who was over the household, and [b]Shebna the scribe, and Joah the son of Asaph, the
recorder, came out to him.
4 Then [a]Rabshakeh said to them, "Say now to Hezekiah, 'Thus
says the great king, the king of Assyria, "What is this confidence
that you [1]have?
5 "I say, 'Your counsel and strength for the war are only [1]empty
words.' Now on whom do you rely, that [a]you have rebelled
against me?
6 "Behold, you rely on the [a]staff of this crushed reed, *even* on
Egypt, on which if a man leans, it will go into his [1]hand and
pierce it. [b]So is Pharaoh king of Egypt to all who rely on him.
7 "But if you say to me, 'We trust in the LORD our God,' is it
not He [a]whose high places and whose altars Hezekiah has
taken away and has said to Judah and to Jerusalem, 'You shall
worship before this altar'?
8 "Now therefore, [1]come make a bargain with my master the
king of Assyria, and I will give you two thousand horses, if you
are able on your part to set riders on them.
9 "How then can you [1]repulse one [2]official of the least of my
master's servants and [3a]rely on Egypt for chariots and for
horsemen?
10 "Have I now come up [1]without the LORD's approval against
this land to destroy it? [a]The LORD said to me, 'Go up against
this land and destroy it.'"'"
11 Then Eliakim and Shebna and Joah said to Rabshakeh,
"Speak now to your servants in [a]Aramaic, for we [1]understand
it; and do not speak with us in [2b]Judean in the hearing of the
people who are on the wall."
12 But Rabshakeh said, "Has my master sent me only to your
master and to you to speak these words, *and* not to the men
who sit on the wall, *doomed* to eat their own dung and drink
their own urine with you?"
13 Then Rabshakeh stood and [a]cried with a loud voice in Judean
and said, "Hear the words of the great king, the king of Assyria.

9 [1]Lit *It* [b]Is 51:10; 62:12; 63:4
10 [1]Lit *overtake* [a]Is 1:27; 51:11 [b]Is 25:8; 30:19; 65:19; Rev 7:17; 21:4
36:1 [a]2 Kin 18:13 [b]2 Chr 32:1
2 [1]I.e. launderer's [a]2 Kin 18:17-20:11; 2 Chr 32:9-24; Is 36:2-38:8 [b]Is 7:3
3 [a]Is 22:20 [b]Is 22:15
4 [1]Lit *trust* [a]2 Kin 18:19
5 [1]Lit *words of lips* [a]2 Kin 18:7
6 [1]Lit *palm* [a]Ezek 29:6, 7 [b]Ps 146:3; Is 30:3, 5, 7
7 [a]Deut 12:2-5; 2 Kin 18:4, 5
8 [1]Lit *please exchange pledges*
9 [1]Lit *turn away the face of* [2]Or *governor* [3]Lit *rely on for yourself* [a]Is 20:5; 30:2-5, 7; 31:3
10 [1]Lit *without the LORD* [a]1 Kin 13:18; 22:6, 12
11 [1]Lit *hear* [2]I.e. Hebrew [a]Ezra 4:7; Dan 2:4 [b]Is 36:13
13 [a]2 Chr 32:18

RETURN TO INSTRUCTIONS

2 Kings 18
2 Chronicles 32

14 "Thus says the king, 'Do not let Hezekiah [a]deceive you, for
he will not be able to deliver you;
15 nor let Hezekiah make you [a]trust in the LORD, saying, "The
LORD will surely deliver us, this city will not be given into the
hand of the king of Assyria."
16 'Do not listen to Hezekiah,' for thus says the king of
Assyria, '[1]Make your peace with me and come out to me, and
eat each of his [a]vine and each of his fig tree and drink each of
the [b]waters of his own cistern,
17 until I come and take you away to a land like your own land,
a land of grain and new wine, a land of bread and vineyards.
18 '*Beware* that Hezekiah does not mislead you, saying, "[a]The
LORD will deliver us." Has any one of the gods of the nations
delivered his land from the hand of the king of Assyria?
19 'Where are the gods of [a]Hamath and Arpad? Where are the
gods of [a]Sepharvaim? And when have they [b]delivered Samaria
from my hand?
20 'Who among all the [a]gods of these lands have delivered
their land from my hand, that the [b]LORD would deliver
Jerusalem from my hand?'"
21 But they were silent and [a]answered him not a word; for the
king's commandment was, "Do not answer him."
22 Then [a]Eliakim the son of Hilkiah, who was over the
household, and [b]Shebna the scribe and Joah the son of Asaph,
the recorder, came to Hezekiah with their clothes torn and told
him the words of Rabshakeh.

Chapter 37 Theme ____________________

2 Kings 19

37 And [a]when King Hezekiah heard *it,* he tore his clothes,
covered himself with sackcloth and entered the house
of the LORD.
2 Then he sent [a]Eliakim who was over the household with
[b]Shebna the scribe and the elders of the priests, covered with
sackcloth, to [c]Isaiah the prophet, the son of Amoz.
3 They said to him, "Thus says Hezekiah, 'This day is a [a]day
of distress, rebuke and rejection; for [b]children have come to
birth, and there is no strength to [1]deliver.
4 'Perhaps the LORD your God will hear the words of
Rabshakeh, whom his master the king of Assyria has sent to
[a]reproach the living God, and will rebuke the words which the
LORD your God has heard. Therefore, offer a prayer for [b]the
remnant that is left.'"
5 So the servants of King Hezekiah came to Isaiah.
6 Isaiah said to them, "Thus you shall say to your master,
'Thus says the LORD, "[a]Do not be afraid because of the words
that you have heard, with which the servants of the king of
Assyria have blasphemed Me.
7 "Behold, I will put a spirit in him so that he will [a]hear a
rumor and [b]return to his own land. And I will make him fall by
the sword in his own land."'"

14 [a]Is 37:10
15 [a]Is 36:18, 20; 37:10, 11
16 [1]Lit *Make with me a blessing* [a]1 Kin 4:25; Mic 4:4; Zech 3:10 [b]Prov 5:15
18 [a]Is 36:15
19 [a]Is 10:9-11; 37:11-13; Jer 49:23 [b]2 Kin 17:6
20 [a]1 Kin 20:23, 28 [b]Is 36:15
21 [a]Prov 9:7, 8; 26:4
22 [a]Is 22:20; 36:3 [b]Is 22:15
37:1 [a]2 Kin 19:1-37; Is 37:1-38
2 [a]Is 22:20 [b]Is 22:15 [c]Is 1:1; 20:2
3 [1]Lit *give birth* [a]Is 22:5; 26:16; 33:2 [b]Is 26:17, 18; 66:9; Hos 13:13
4 [a]Is 36:13-15, 18, 20 [b]Is 1:9; 10:20-22; 37:31, 32; 46:3
6 [a]Is 7:4; 35:4
7 [a]Is 37:9 [b]Is 37:37, 38

8 Then Rabshakeh returned and found the king of Assyria
fighting against [a]Libnah, for he had heard that [1]the king had
left [b]Lachish.
9 When he [a]heard *them* say concerning Tirhakah king of
[1b]Cush, "He has come out to fight against you," and when he
heard *it* he sent messengers to Hezekiah, saying,
10 "Thus you shall say to Hezekiah king of [1]Judah, '[a]Do not let
your God in whom you trust deceive you, saying, "Jerusalem
will not be given into the hand of the king of Assyria."
11 '[a]Behold, you have heard what the kings of Assyria have
done to all the lands, destroying them completely. So will you
be [1]spared?
12 'Did the gods of [1]those nations which my fathers have
destroyed deliver them, *even* [a]Gozan and [b]Haran and Rezeph
and the sons of Eden who *were* in Telassar?
13 'Where is the king of Hamath, the king of Arpad, the king
of the city of Sepharvaim, *and of* Hena and Ivvah?'"
14 Then Hezekiah took the [1]letter from the hand of the
messengers and read it, and he went up to the house of the
LORD and [2]spread it out before the LORD.
15 Hezekiah prayed to the LORD saying,
16 "O LORD of hosts, the God of Israel, [a]who is enthroned
above the cherubim, You are the [b]God, You alone, of all the
kingdoms of the earth. [c]You have made heaven and earth.
17 "[a]Incline Your ear, O LORD, and hear; open Your eyes, O
LORD, and see; and [b]listen to all the words of Sennacherib, who
sent *them* to [c]reproach the living God.
18 "Truly, O LORD, the [a]kings of Assyria have devastated all the
countries and their lands,
19 and have cast their gods into the fire, for they were not gods
but the [a]work of men's hands, wood and stone. So they have
[b]destroyed them.
20 "Now, O LORD our God, [a]deliver us from his hand that [b]all
the kingdoms of the earth may know that You alone, LORD,
[1]are God."
21 Then [a]Isaiah the son of Amoz sent *word* to Hezekiah,
saying, "Thus says the LORD, the God of Israel, 'Because you
have prayed to Me about Sennacherib king of Assyria,
22 this is the word that the LORD has spoken against him:
"She has despised you and mocked you,
The [a]virgin [b]daughter of Zion;
She has [c]shaken *her* head behind you,
The daughter of Jerusalem!
23 "Whom have you [a]reproached and blasphemed?
And against whom have you raised *your* voice
And [1]haughtily [b]lifted up your eyes?
Against the [c]Holy One of Israel!
24 "Through your servants you have reproached the Lord,
And you have said, 'With my many chariots I came up to
the heights of the mountains,
To the remotest parts of [a]Lebanon;

8 [1]Lit *he* [a]Num 33:20; Josh 10:29 [b]Josh 10:31, 32
9 [1]Or *Ethiopia* [a]Is 37:7 [b]Is 18:1; 20:5
10 [1]Lit *Judah, saying* [a]Is 36:15
11 [1]Lit *delivered* [a]Is 10:9-11; 36:18-20
12 [1]Lit *the* [a]2 Kin 17:6; 18:11 [b]Gen 11:31; 12:1-4; Acts 7:2
14 [1]Lit *letters* [2]Lit *Hezekiah spread*
16 [a]Ex 25:22; 1 Sam 4:4; Ps 80:1; 99:1 [b]Deut 10:17; Ps 86:10; 136:2, 3 [c]Is 42:5; 45:12; Jer 10:12
17 [a]2 Chr 6:40; Ps 17:6; Dan 9:18 [b]Ps 74:22 [c]Is 37:4
18 [a]2 Kin 15:29; 16:9; 17:6, 24; 1 Chr 5:26
19 [a]Is 2:8; 17:8; 41:24, 29 [b]Is 26:14
20 [1]So DSS and 2 Kin 19:19; M.T. omits *God* [a]Is 25:9; 33:22; 35:4 [b]1 Kin 18:36, 37; Ps 46:10; Is 37:16; Ezek 36:23
21 [a]Is 37:2
22 [a]Jer 14:17; Lam 2:13 [b]Ps 9:14; Zeph 3:14; Zech 2:10 [c]Job 16:4
23 [1]Lit *on high* [a]Is 37:4 [b]Is 2:11; 5:15, 21 [c]Ezek 39:7; Hab 1:12
24 [a]Is 10:33, 34

And I cut down its tall [b]cedars *and* its choice cypresses.
And I will go to its [1]highest peak, its thickest [c]forest.
25 'I dug *wells* and drank waters,
And [a]with the sole of my feet I dried up
All the rivers of [1]Egypt.'
26 "[a]Have you not heard?
Long ago I did it,
From ancient times I [b]planned it.
Now [c]I have brought it to pass,
That [d]you should turn fortified cities into [e]ruinous heaps.
27 "Therefore their inhabitants were short of strength,
They were dismayed and put to shame;
They were *as* the [a]vegetation of the field and *as* the
green herb,
As [b]grass on the housetops [1]is scorched before it is
grown up.
28 "But I [a]know your sitting down
And your going out and your coming in
And your raging against Me.
29 "Because of your raging against Me
And because your [1a]arrogance has come up to My ears,
Therefore I will put My [b]hook in your nose
And My [c]bridle in your lips,
And I will turn you back [d]by the way which you came.

30 "Then this shall be the sign for you: [1]you will eat this year
what [a]grows of itself, in the second year what springs from the
same, and in the third year sow, reap, plant vineyards and eat
their fruit.
31 "The [a]surviving [b]remnant of the house of Judah will again
[c]take root downward and bear fruit upward.
32 "For out of Jerusalem will go forth a [a]remnant and out of
Mount Zion [1]survivors. The [b]zeal of the LORD of hosts will
perform this."'
33 "Therefore, thus says the LORD concerning the king of
Assyria, 'He will not come to this city or shoot an arrow there;
and he will not come before it with a shield, or throw up a
[a]siege ramp against it.
34 '[a]By the way that he came, by the same he will return, and
he will not come to this city,' declares the LORD.
35 'For I will [a]defend this city to save it [b]for My own sake and
for My servant David's sake.'"
36 Then the [a]angel of the LORD went out and struck 185,000
in the camp of the Assyrians; and when [1]men arose early in the
morning, behold, all of these were [2]dead.
37 So Sennacherib king of Assyria departed and [1]returned
home and lived at [a]Nineveh.
38 It came about as he was worshiping in the house of Nisroch
his god, that Adrammelech and Sharezer his sons killed him
with the sword; and they escaped into the land of [a]Ararat. And
[b]Esarhaddon his son became king in his place.

24 [1]Lit *farthest height* [b]Is 14:8 [c]Is 10:18

25 [1]Or *the besieged place* [a]Deut 11:10; 1 Kin 20:10

26 [a]Is 40:21, 28 [b]Acts 2:23; 4:27, 28; 1 Pet 2:8 [c]Is 46:11 [d]Is 10:6 [e]Is 17:1; 25:2

27 [1]So DSS and 2 Kin 19:26; M.T. as *a plowed field* [a]Is 40:7 [b]Ps 129:6

28 [a]Ps 139:1

29 [1]Lit *complacency* [a]Is 10:12 [b]Ezek 29:4; 38:4 [c]Is 30:28 [d]Is 37:34

30 [1]Lit *eating* [a]Lev 25:5, 11

31 [a]Is 4:2; 10:20 [b]Is 37:4 [c]Is 27:6

32 [1]Lit *those who escape* [a]Is 37:4 [b]2 Kin 19:31; Is 9:7; 59:17; Joel 2:18; Zech 1:14

33 [a]Jer 6:6; 32:24

34 [a]Is 37:29

35 [a]2 Kin 20:6; Is 31:5; 38:6 [b]Is 43:25; 48:9, 11

36 [1]Lit *they* [2]Lit *dead bodies* [a]2 Kin 19:35; Is 10:12, 33, 34

37 [1]Lit *went and returned* [a]Gen 10:11; Jon 1:2; 3:3; 4:11; Zeph 2:13

38 [a]Gen 8:4; Jer 51:27 [b]Ezra 4:2

Chapter 38 Theme ______________________

2 Kings 20

38 [a]In those days Hezekiah became [1]mortally ill. And
[b]Isaiah the prophet the son of Amoz came to him and
said to him, "Thus says the LORD, '[c]Set your house in order, for
you shall die and not live.'"
2 Then Hezekiah turned his face to the wall and prayed to
the LORD,
3 and said, "[a]Remember now, O LORD, I beseech You, how I have
[b]walked before You in truth and with a [c]whole heart, and [d]have
done what is good in Your sight." And Hezekiah [e]wept [1]bitterly.
4 Then the word of the LORD came to Isaiah, saying,
5 "Go and say to Hezekiah, 'Thus says the LORD, the God of
your father David, "I have heard your prayer, I have seen your
tears; behold, I will add [a]fifteen years to your [1]life.
6 "I will [a]deliver you and this city from the hand of the king of
Assyria; and I will defend this city."'
7 "This shall be the [a]sign to you from the LORD, that the LORD
will do this thing that He has spoken:
8 "Behold, I will [a]cause the shadow on the stairway, which
has gone down with the sun on the stairway of Ahaz, to go
back ten steps." So the [b]sun's *shadow* went back ten steps on
the stairway on which it had gone down.
9 A writing of Hezekiah king of Judah after his illness and
[1]recovery:

10 I said, "[a]In the middle of my [1]life
I am to enter the [b]gates of Sheol;
I am to be [c]deprived of the rest of my years."
11 I said, "I will not see the LORD,
The LORD [a]in the land of the living;
I will look on man no more among the inhabitants of the
world.
12 "Like a shepherd's [a]tent my dwelling is pulled up and
removed from me;
As a [b]weaver I [c]rolled up my life.
He [d]cuts me off from the loom;
From [e]day until night You make an end of me.
13 "I composed *my soul* until morning.
[a]Like a lion—so He [b]breaks all my bones,
From [c]day until night You make an end of me.
14 "[a]Like a swallow, *like* a crane, so I twitter;
I [b]moan like a dove;
My [c]eyes look wistfully to the heights;
O Lord, I am oppressed, be my [d]security.

15 "[a]What shall I say?
[1]For He has spoken to me, and He Himself has done it;
I will [b]wander about all my years because of the
[c]bitterness of my soul.
16 "O Lord, [a]by *these* things *men* live,
And in all these is the life of my spirit;
[1][b]O restore me to health and [c]let me live!

38:1 [1]Lit *sick to the point of death* [a]2 Kin 20:1-6, 9-11; 2 Chr 32:24; Is 38:1-8 [b]Is 1:1; 37:2 [c]2 Sam 17:23

3 [1]Lit *great weeping* [a]Neh 13:14 [b]2 Kin 18:5, 6; Ps 26:3 [c]1 Chr 28:9; 29:19 [d]Deut 6:18 [e]Ps 6:6-8

5 [1]Lit *days* [a]2 Kin 18:2, 13

6 [a]Is 31:5; 37:35

7 [a]Judg 6:17, 21, 36-40; Is 7:11, 14; 37:30

8 [a]2 Kin 20:9-11 [b]Josh 10:12-14

9 [1]Lit *he lived after his illness*

10 [1]Lit *days* [a]Ps 102:24 [b]Ps 107:18 [c]Job 17:11, 15; 2 Cor 1:9

11 [a]Ps 27:13; 116:9

12 [a]2 Cor 5:1, 4; 2 Pet 1:13, 14 [b]Job 7:6 [c]Heb 1:12 [d]Job 6:9 [e]Job 4:20; Ps 73:14

13 [a]Job 10:16 [b]Ps 51:8; Dan 6:24 [c]Ps 32:4

14 [a]Job 30:29; Ps 102:6 [b]Is 59:11; Ezek 7:16; Nah 2:7 [c]Ps 119:123 [d]Job 17:3; Ps 119:122

15 [1]Targum and DSS read *And what shall I say for He* [a]Ps 39:9 [b]1 Kin 21:27 [c]Job 7:11; 10:1; Is 38:17

16 [1]Lit *You will* [a]Ps 119:71, 75 [b]Ps 39:13 [c]Ps 119:25

17 "Lo, for *my own* welfare I had great bitterness;
It is You who has [1a]kept my soul from the pit of [2]nothingness,
For You have [b]cast all my sins behind Your back.
18 "For [a]Sheol cannot thank You,
Death cannot praise You;
Those who go down [b]to the pit cannot hope for
Your faithfulness.
19 "It is the [a]living who give thanks to You, as I do today;
A [b]father tells his sons about Your faithfulness.
20 "The LORD will surely save me;
So we will [a]play my songs on stringed instruments
[b]All *the* days of our life [c]at the house of the LORD."
21 Now [a]Isaiah had said, "Let them take a cake of figs and
apply it to the boil, that he may recover."
22 Then Hezekiah had said, "What is the [a]sign that I shall go
up to the house of the LORD?"

Chapter 39 Theme ____________________

2 Kings 20

39 [a]At that time Merodach-baladan son of Baladan, king of
Babylon, sent letters and a present to Hezekiah, for he
heard that he had been sick and had recovered.
2 Hezekiah [1]was [a]pleased, and showed them *all* his treasure
house, the [b]silver and the gold and the spices and the precious
oil and his whole armory and all that was found in his treasuries.
There was nothing in his house nor in all his dominion that
Hezekiah did not show them.
3 Then Isaiah the [a]prophet came to King Hezekiah and said
to him, "What did these men say, and from where have they
come to you?" And Hezekiah said, "They have come to me
from a far [b]country, from Babylon."
4 He said, "What have they seen in your house?" So Hezekiah
[1]answered, "They have seen all that is in my house; there is
nothing among my treasuries that I have not shown them."
5 Then Isaiah said to Hezekiah, "Hear the [a]word of the LORD
of hosts,
6 'Behold, the days are coming when [a]all that is in your house
and all that your fathers have laid up in store to this day will be
carried to Babylon; nothing will be left,' says the LORD.
7 'And *some* of your sons who will issue from you, whom you
will beget, [a]will be taken away, and [b]they will become officials
in the palace of the king of Babylon.'"
8 [a]Then Hezekiah said to Isaiah, "The word of the LORD
which you have spoken is good." For he [1]thought, "For there
will be peace and truth [b]in my days."

Chapter 40 Theme ____________________

40 "[a]Comfort, O comfort My people," says your God.
2 "[a]Speak [1]kindly to Jerusalem;
And call out to her, that her [2b]warfare has ended,
That her [3c]iniquity has been removed,

17 [1]So some versions; Heb *loved* [2]Or *destruction* [a]Ps 30:3; 86:13; Jon 2:6 [b]Is 43:25; Jer 31:34; Mic 7:19

18 [a]Ps 6:5; 30:9; 88:11; Eccl 9:10 [b]Num 16:33; Ps 28:1

19 [a]Ps 118:17; 119:175 [b]Deut 6:7; 11:19; Ps 78:5-7

20 [a]Ps 33:1-3; 68:24-26 [b]Ps 104:33; 116:2; 146:2 [c]Ps 116:17-19

21 [a]2 Kin 20:7, 8

22 [a]Is 38:7

39:1 [a]2 Kin 20:12-19; 2 Chr 32:31; Is 39:1-8

2 [1]Lit *rejoiced over them* [a]2 Chr 32:25, 31; Job 31:25 [b]2 Kin 18:15, 16

3 [a]2 Sam 12:1; 2 Chr 16:7 [b]Deut 28:49; Jer 5:15

4 [1]Lit *said*

5 [a]1 Sam 13:13, 14; 15:16

6 [a]2 Kin 24:13; 25:13-15; Jer 20:5

7 [a]2 Kin 24:10-16; 2 Chr 36:10 [b]Dan 1:1-7

8 [1]Lit *said* [a]2 Chr 32:26 [b]2 Chr 34:28

40:1 [a]Is 12:1; 49:13; 51:3, 12; 52:9; 61:2; 66:13; Jer 31:10-14; Zeph 3:14-17; 2 Cor 1:4

2 [1]Lit *to the heart of* [2]Or *hard service* [3]Or *penalty of iniquity accepted as paid off* [a]Is 35:4; Zech 1:13 [b]Is 41:11-13; 49:25; 54:15, 17 [c]Is 33:24; 53:5, 6, 11

RETURN TO INSTRUCTIONS

That she has received of the LORD's hand
[d]Double for all her sins."

3 [a]A voice [1]is calling,
"[b]Clear the way for the LORD in the wilderness;
Make smooth in the desert a highway for our God.
4 "Let every valley be lifted up,
And every mountain and hill be made low;
And let the rough ground become a plain,
And the rugged terrain a broad valley;
5 [1]Then the [a]glory of the LORD will be revealed,
And [b]all flesh will see *it* together;
For the [c]mouth of the LORD has spoken."
6 A voice says, "Call out."
Then [1]he answered, "What shall I call out?"
[a]All flesh is grass, and all its [2]loveliness is like the flower
of the field.
7 The [a]grass withers, the flower fades,
[1]When the [b]breath of the LORD blows upon it;
Surely the people are grass.
8 The grass withers, the flower fades,
But [a]the word of our God stands forever.

9 Get yourself up on a [a]high mountain,
O Zion, bearer of [b]good news,
Lift up your voice mightily,
O Jerusalem, bearer of good news;
Lift *it* up, do not fear.
Say to the [c]cities of Judah,
"[d]Here is your God!"
10 Behold, the Lord [1]GOD will come [a]with might,
With His [b]arm ruling for Him.
Behold, His [c]reward is with Him
And His recompense before Him.
11 Like a shepherd He will [a]tend His flock,
In His arm He will gather the lambs
And carry *them* in His bosom;
He will gently lead the nursing *ewes.*

12 Who has [a]measured the [1]waters in the hollow of His hand,
And marked off the heavens by the [2]span,
And [3]calculated the dust of the earth by the measure,
And weighed the mountains in a balance
And the hills in a pair of scales?
13 [a]Who has [1]directed the Spirit of the LORD,
Or as His [b]counselor has informed Him?
14 [a]With whom did He consult and *who* [b]gave Him
understanding?
And *who* taught Him in the path of justice and taught Him
knowledge
And informed Him of the way of understanding?

2 [d]Jer 16:18; Zech 9:12; Rev 18:6

3 [1]Or *of one calling out* [a]Matt 3:3; Mark 1:3; Luke 3:4-6; John 1:23 [b]Mal 3:1; 4:5, 6

5 [1]Or *In order that the* [a]Is 6:3; Hab 2:14 [b]Is 52:10; Joel 2:28 [c]Is 1:20; 34:16; 58:14

6 [1]Another reading is *I said* [2]Or *constancy* [a]Job 14:2; Ps 102:11; 103:15; 1 Pet 1:24, 25

7 [1]Or *Because* [a]Ps 90:5, 6; James 1:10, 11 [b]Job 4:9; 41:21; Is 11:4; 40:24

8 [a]Is 55:11; 59:21; Matt 5:18

9 [a]Is 52:7 [b]Is 61:1 [c]Is 44:26 [d]Is 25:9; 35:2

10 [1]Heb *YHWH,* usually rendered *LORD* [a]Is 9:6, 7 [b]Is 59:16, 18 [c]Is 62:11; Rev 22:12

11 [a]Jer 31:10; Ezek 34:12-14, 23, 31; Mic 5:4; John 10:11, 14-16

12 [1]DSS reads *waters of the sea* [2]Or *half cubit;* i.e. 9 in. [3]Lit *contained* or *comprehended* [a]Job 38:8-11; Ps 102:25, 26; Is 48:13; Heb 1:10-12

13 [1]Or *measured, marked off* [a]Rom 11:34; 1 Cor 2:16 [b]Is 41:28

14 [a]Job 38:4 [b]Job 21:22; Col 2:3

15 Behold, the [a]nations are like a drop from a bucket,
And are regarded as a speck of [b]dust on the scales;
Behold, He lifts up the [1]islands like fine dust.
16 Even Lebanon is not enough to burn,
Nor its [a]beasts enough for a burnt offering.
17 [a]All the nations are as nothing before Him,
They are regarded by Him as less than nothing and
[1]meaningless.

18 [a]To whom then will you liken God?
Or what likeness will you compare with Him?
19 *As for* the [1a]idol, a craftsman casts it,
A goldsmith [b]plates it with gold,
And a silversmith *fashions* chains of silver.
20 He who is too impoverished for *such* an offering
Selects a [a]tree that does not rot;
He seeks out for himself a skillful craftsman
To [1]prepare [2]an idol that [b]will not totter.

21 [a]Do you not know? Have you not heard?
Has it not been declared to you from the beginning?
Have you not understood [b]from the foundations of
the earth?
22 It is He who [1]sits above the [2a]circle of the earth,
And its inhabitants are like [b]grasshoppers,
Who [c]stretches out the heavens like a [d]curtain
And spreads them out like a [e]tent to dwell in.
23 He *it is* who reduces [a]rulers to nothing,
Who [b]makes the judges of the earth [1]meaningless.
24 [1]Scarcely have they been planted,
[1]Scarcely have they been sown,
[1]Scarcely has their stock taken root in the earth,
But He merely blows on them, and they wither,
And the [a]storm carries them away like stubble.
25 "[a]To whom then will you liken Me
That I would be *his* equal?" says the Holy One.
26 [a]Lift up your eyes on high
And see [b]who has created these *stars*,
The [c]One who leads forth their host by number,
He calls them all by name;
Because of the [d]greatness of His might and the [1]strength
of *His* power,
[e]Not one *of them* is missing.

27 [a]Why do you say, O Jacob, and assert, O Israel,
"My way is [b]hidden from the LORD,
And the [c]justice due me [1]escapes the notice of
[d]my God"?
28 [a]Do you not know? Have you not heard?
The [b]Everlasting God, the LORD, the Creator of the ends
of the earth

15 [1]Or *coastlands* [a]Jer 10:10 [b]Is 17:13; 29:5

16 [a]Ps 50:9-11; Mic 6:6, 7; Heb 10:5-9

17 [1]Or *void* [a]Is 29:7

18 [a]Ex 8:10; 15:11; 1 Sam 2:2; Is 40:25; 46:5; Mic 7:18; Acts 17:29

19 [1]Or *graven image* [a]Ps 115:4-8; Is 41:7; 44:10; Hab 2:18, 19 [b]Is 2:20; 30:22

20 [1]Or *set up* [2]Or *a graven image* [a]Is 44:14 [b]1 Sam 5:3, 4; Is 41:7; 46:7

21 [a]Ps 19:1; 50:6; Is 37:26; Acts 14:17; Rom 1:19 [b]Is 48:13; 51:13

22 [1]Or *is enthroned* [2]Or *vault* [a]Job 22:14; Prov 8:27 [b]Num 13:33 [c]Job 9:8; Is 37:16; 42:5; 44:24 [d]Ps 104:2 [e]Job 36:29; Ps 18:11; 19:4

23 [1]Or *void* [a]Job 12:21; Ps 107:40; Is 34:12 [b]Is 5:21; Jer 25:18-27

24 [1]Or *Not even* [a]Is 17:13; 41:16

25 [a]Is 40:18

26 [1]So DSS and ancient versions; M.T. *strong* [a]Is 51:6 [b]Is 42:5; 48:12, 13 [c]Ps 147:4 [d]Ps 89:11-13 [e]Is 34:16; 48:13

27 [1]Lit *passes by my God* [a]Is 49:4, 14 [b]Is 54:8 [c]Job 27:2; 34:5; Luke 18:7, 8 [d]Is 25:1

28 [a]Is 40:21 [b]Gen 21:33; Ps 90:2

Does not become weary or tired.
His understanding is [c]inscrutable.
29 He gives strength to the [a]weary,
And to *him who* lacks might He [b]increases power.
30 Though [a]youths grow weary and tired,
And vigorous [b]young men stumble badly,
31 Yet those who [1]wait for the LORD
Will [a]gain new strength;
They will [2b]mount up *with* [3]wings like eagles,
They will run and not get tired,
They will walk and not become weary.

Chapter 41 Theme ____________________

41 "[a]Coastlands, listen to Me [b]in silence,
And let the peoples [c]gain new strength;
[d]Let them come forward, then let them speak;
[e]Let us come together for judgment.
2 "[a]Who has aroused one from the east
Whom He [b]calls in righteousness to His [1]feet?
He [c]delivers up nations before him
And subdues kings.
He makes them like [d]dust with his sword,
As the wind-driven [e]chaff with his bow.
3 "He pursues them, passing on in safety,
By a way he had not been [1]traversing with his feet.
4 "[a]Who has performed and accomplished *it*,
Calling forth the generations from the beginning?
'[b]I, the LORD, am the first, and with the last.
[c]I am He.'"

5 The [a]coastlands have seen and are afraid;
The [b]ends of the earth tremble;
They have drawn near and have come.
6 Each one helps his neighbor
And says to his brother, "Be strong!"
7 So the [a]craftsman encourages the [b]smelter,
And he who smooths *metal* with the hammer *encourages*
him who beats the anvil,
Saying of the soldering, "It is good";
And he fastens it with nails,
[c]*So that* it will not totter.
8 "But you, Israel, [a]My servant,
Jacob whom I have chosen,
Descendant of [b]Abraham My [c]friend,
9 You whom I have [1a]taken from the ends of the earth,
And called from its [b]remotest parts
And said to you, 'You are [c]My servant,
I have [d]chosen you and not rejected you.
10 'Do not [a]fear, for I am with you;
Do not anxiously look about you, for I am your God.

28 [c]Ps 147:5; Rom 11:33

29 [a]Is 50:4; Jer 31:25 [b]Is 41:10

30 [a]Jer 6:11; 9:21 [b]Is 9:17

31 [1]Or *hope in* [2]Or *sprout wings* [3]Or *pinions* [a]Job 17:9; Ps 103:5; 2 Cor 4:8-10, 16 [b]Ex 19:4; Deut 32:11; Luke 18:1; 2 Cor 4:1, 16; Gal 6:9; Heb 12:3

41:1 [a]Is 11:11 [b]Hab 2:20; Zech 2:13 [c]Is 40:31 [d]Is 34:1; 48:16 [e]Is 1:18; 43:26; 50:8

2 [1]Lit *foot* [a]Is 41:25; 45:1-3; 46:11 [b]Is 42:6 [c]2 Chr 36:23; Ezra 1:2 [d]2 Sam 22:43 [e]Is 40:24

3 [1]Lit *going*

4 [a]Is 41:26; 44:7; 46:10 [b]Is 43:10; 44:6; Rev 1:8, 17; 22:13 [c]Is 43:13; 46:4; 48:12

5 [a]Is 41:1; Ezek 26:15, 16 [b]Josh 5:1; Ps 67:7

7 [a]Is 44:12, 13 [b]Is 40:19 [c]Is 40:20; 46:7

8 [a]Is 42:19; 43:10; 44:1, 2, 21 [b]Is 29:22; 51:2; 63:16 [c]2 Chr 20:7; James 2:23

9 [1]Or *taken hold of* [a]Is 11:11 [b]Is 43:5-7 [c]Is 42:1; 44:1 [d]Deut 7:6; 14:2; Ps 135:4

10 [a]Deut 20:1; 31:6; Josh 1:9; Ps 27:1; Is 41:13, 14; 43:2, 5; Rom 8:31

I will strengthen you, surely [b]I will help you,
Surely I will uphold you with My righteous [c]right hand.'
11 "Behold, [a]all those who are angered at you will be shamed and dishonored;
[b]Those who contend with you will be as nothing and will perish.
12 "[a]You will seek those who quarrel with you, but will not find them,
Those who war with you will be as nothing and non-existent.
13 "For I am the LORD your God, [a]who upholds your right hand,
Who says to you, '[b]Do not fear, I will help you.'
14 "Do not fear, you [a]worm Jacob, you men of Israel;
I will help you," declares the LORD, "[1]and [b]your Redeemer is the Holy One of Israel.
15 "Behold, I have made you a new, sharp threshing sledge with double edges;
[a]You will thresh the [b]mountains and pulverize *them,*
And will make the hills like chaff.
16 "You will [a]winnow them, and the wind will carry them away,
And the storm will scatter them;
But you will [b]rejoice in the LORD,
You will glory in the Holy One of Israel.

17 "The [1]afflicted and needy are seeking [a]water, but there is none,
And their tongue is parched with thirst;
I, the LORD, [b]will answer them Myself,
As the God of Israel I [c]will not forsake them.
18 "I will open [a]rivers on the bare heights
And springs in the midst of the valleys;
I will make [b]the wilderness a pool of water
And the dry land fountains of water.
19 "I will put the cedar in the wilderness,
The acacia and the [a]myrtle and the [1]olive tree;
I will place the [a]juniper in the desert
Together with the box tree and the cypress,
20 That [a]they may see and recognize,
And consider and gain insight as well,
That the [b]hand of the LORD has done this,
And the Holy One of Israel has created it.

21 "[1]Present your case," the LORD says.
"Bring forward your strong *arguments,*"
The [a]King of Jacob says.
22 [a]Let them bring forth and declare to us what is going to take place;
As for the [b]former *events,* declare what they *were,*
That we may consider them and know their outcome.
Or announce to us what is coming;
23 [a]Declare the things that are going to come afterward,
That we may know that you are gods;

10 [b]Is 41:14; 44:2; 49:8 [c]Ps 89:13, 14
11 [a]Is 45:24 [b]Is 17:13; 29:5, 7, 8
12 [a]Job 20:7-9; Ps 37:35, 36; Is 17:14
13 [a]Is 42:6; 45:1 [b]Is 41:10
14 [1]Or *even your Redeemer, the Holy One* [a]Job 25:6; Ps 22:6 [b]Is 35:10; 43:14; 44:6, 22-24
15 [a]Mic 4:13; Hab 3:12 [b]Is 42:15; 64:1; Jer 9:10; Ezek 33:28
16 [a]Jer 51:2 [b]Is 25:9; 35:10; 51:3; 61:10
17 [1]Or *poor* [a]Is 43:20; 44:3; 49:10; 55:1 [b]Is 30:19; 65:24 [c]Is 42:16; 62:12
18 [a]Is 30:25; 43:19 [b]Ps 107:35; Is 35:6, 7
19 [1]Or *oleaster* [a]Is 35:1; 55:13; 60:13
20 [a]Is 40:5; 43:10 [b]Job 12:9; Is 66:14
21 [1]Lit *Bring near* [a]Is 44:6
22 [a]Is 44:7; 45:21; 46:10 [b]Is 43:9
23 [a]Is 42:9; 44:7, 8; 45:3; John 13:19

Indeed, [b]do good or evil, that we may anxiously look about
us and fear together.
24 Behold, [a]you are of [1]no account,
And [b]your work amounts to nothing;
He who chooses you is an [c]abomination.

25 "I have aroused [a]one from the north, and he has come;
From the rising of the sun he will call on My name;
And he will come upon rulers as *upon* [b]mortar,
Even as the potter treads clay."
26 Who has [a]declared *this* from the beginning, that we
might know?
Or from former times, that we may say, "*He is* right!"?
Surely there was [b]no one who declared,
Surely there was no one who proclaimed,
Surely there was no one who heard your words.
27 "[a]Formerly *I said* to Zion, 'Behold, here they are.'
And to Jerusalem, 'I will give a [b]messenger of good news.'
28 "But [a]when I look, there is no one,
And there is no [b]counselor [1]among them
Who, if I ask, can [c]give an answer.
29 "Behold, all of them are [1]false;
Their [a]works are [b]worthless,
Their molten images are [c]wind and emptiness.

Chapter 42 Theme ______________________

42 "[a]Behold, My [b]Servant, whom I [1]uphold;
My [c]chosen one *in whom* My [d]soul delights.
I have put My [e]Spirit upon Him;
He will bring forth [f]justice to the [2]nations.
2 "He will not cry out or raise *His voice,*
Nor make His voice heard in the street.
3 "A bruised reed He will not break
And a dimly burning wick He will not extinguish;
He will faithfully bring forth [a]justice.
4 "He will not be [a]disheartened or crushed
Until He has established justice in the earth;
And the [b]coastlands will wait expectantly for His [1]law."

5 Thus says God the LORD,
Who [a]created the heavens and [b]stretched them out,
Who spread out the [c]earth and its [1]offspring,
Who [d]gives breath to the people on it
And spirit to those who walk in it,
6 "I am the LORD, I have [a]called You in righteousness,
I will also [b]hold You by the hand and [c]watch over You,
And I will appoint You as a [d]covenant to the people,
As a [e]light to the nations,
7 To [a]open blind eyes,
To [b]bring out prisoners from the dungeon
And those who dwell in darkness from the prison.

23 [b]Jer 10:5

24 [1]Lit *nothing* [a]Ps 115:8; Is 44:9; 1 Cor 8:4 [b]Is 37:19; 41:29 [c]Prov 3:32; 28:9

25 [a]Is 41:2; Jer 50:3 [b]2 Sam 22:43; Is 10:6; Mic 7:10; Zech 10:5

26 [a]Is 41:22; 44:7; 45:21 [b]Hab 2:18, 19

27 [a]Is 48:3-8 [b]Is 40:9; 44:28; 52:7; Nah 1:15

28 [1]Lit *out of those* [a]Is 50:2; 59:16; 63:5 [b]Is 40:13, 14 [c]Is 46:7

29 [1]Another reading is *nothing* [a]Is 2:8; 17:8; 41:24 [b]Is 44:9 [c]Jer 5:13

42:1 [1]Or *hold fast* [2]Or *Gentiles* [a]Matt 12:18-21 [b]Is 41:8; 43:10; 49:3-6; 52:13; 53:11; Matt 12:18-21; Phil 2:7 [c]Luke 9:35; 1 Pet 2:4, 6 [d]Matt 3:17; 17:5; Mark 1:11; Luke 3:22 [e]Is 11:2; 59:21; 61:1; Matt 3:16; Luke 4:18, 19, 21 [f]Is 2:4

3 [a]Ps 72:2, 4; 96:13

4 [1]Or *instruction* [a]Is 40:28 [b]Is 11:11; 24:15; 42:10, 12; 49:1; 51:5; 60:9; 66:19

5 [1]Or *vegetation* [a]Ps 102:25, 26; Is 45:18 [b]Ps 104:2; Is 40:22 [c]Ps 24:1, 2; 136:6 [d]Job 12:10; 33:4; Is 57:16; Dan 5:23; Acts 17:25

6 [a]Is 41:2; Jer 23:5, 6 [b]Is 41:13; 45:1 [c]Is 26:3; 27:3 [d]Is 49:8 [e]Is 49:6; 51:4; 60:1, 3; Luke 2:32; Acts 13:47; 26:23

7 [a]Is 29:18; 35:5 [b]Is 49:9; 61:1

8 "[a]I am the LORD, that is [b]My name;
I will not give My [c]glory to another,
Nor My praise to [1]graven images.
9 "Behold, the [a]former things have come to pass,
Now I declare [b]new things;
Before they spring forth I proclaim *them* to you."

10 Sing to the LORD a [a]new song,
Sing His praise from the [b]end of the earth!
[c]You who go down to the sea, and [d]all that is in it.
You [e]islands, and those who dwell on them.
11 Let the [a]wilderness and its cities lift up *their voices,*
The settlements where [b]Kedar inhabits.
Let the inhabitants of [c]Sela sing aloud,
Let them shout for joy from the tops of the [d]mountains.
12 Let them [a]give glory to the LORD
And declare His praise in the [b]coastlands.
13 [a]The LORD will go forth like a warrior,
He will arouse *His* [b]zeal like a man of war.
He will utter a shout, yes, He will raise a war cry.
He will [c]prevail against His enemies.

14 "[a]I have kept silent for a long time,
I have kept still and restrained Myself.
Now like a woman in labor I will groan,
I will both gasp and pant.
15 "I will [a]lay waste the mountains and hills
And wither all their vegetation;
I will [b]make the rivers into coastlands
And dry up the ponds.
16 "I will [a]lead the blind by a way they do not know,
In paths they do not know I will guide them.
I will [b]make darkness into light before them
And [c]rugged places into plains.
These are the things I will do,
And I will [d]not leave them undone."
17 They will be turned back *and* be [a]utterly put to shame,
Who trust in [1]idols,
Who say to molten images,
"You are our gods."

18 [a]Hear, you deaf!
And look, you blind, that you may see.
19 Who is blind but My [a]servant,
Or so deaf as My [b]messenger whom I send?
Who is so blind as he that is [1c]at peace *with Me,*
Or so blind as the servant of the LORD?
20 [a]You have seen many things, but you do not observe *them;*
Your ears are open, but none hears.
21 The LORD was pleased for His righteousness' sake
To make the law [a]great and glorious.

8 [1]Or *idols* [a]Is 43:3, 11, 15 [b]Ex 3:15; Ps 83:18 [c]Ex 20:3-5; Is 48:11

9 [a]Is 48:3 [b]Is 43:19; 48:6

10 [a]Ps 33:3; 40:3; 98:1 [b]Is 49:6; 62:11 [c]Ps 65:5; 107:23 [d]Ex 20:11; 1 Chr 16:32; Ps 96:11 [e]Is 42:4

11 [a]Is 32:16; 35:1, 6 [b]Is 21:16; 60:7 [c]Is 16:1 [d]Is 52:7; Nah 1:15

12 [a]Is 24:15 [b]Is 42:4

13 [a]Ex 15:3 [b]Is 9:7; 26:11; 37:32; 59:17 [c]Is 66:14-16

14 [a]Ps 50:21; Is 57:11

15 [a]Is 2:12-16; Ezek 38:19, 20 [b]Is 44:27; 50:2; Nah 1:4-6

16 [a]Is 29:18; 30:21; 32:3; Jer 31:8, 9; Luke 1:78, 79 [b]Is 29:18; Eph 5:8 [c]Is 40:4; Luke 3:5 [d]Josh 1:5; Ps 94:14; Is 41:17; Heb 13:5

17 [1]Or *graven images* [a]Ps 97:7; Is 1:29; 44:9, 11; 45:16

18 [a]Is 29:18; 35:5

19 [1]Or *the devoted one* [a]Is 41:8 [b]Is 44:26 [c]Is 26:3; 27:5

20 [a]Rom 2:21

21 [a]Is 42:4; 51:4

22 But this is a people plundered and despoiled;
All of them are [a]trapped in [1]caves,
Or are [b]hidden away in prisons;
They have become a prey with none to deliver *them,*
And a spoil, with none to say, "Give *them* back!"

23 Who among you will give ear to this?
Who will give heed and listen hereafter?
24 Who gave Jacob up for spoil, and Israel to plunderers?
Was it not the LORD, against whom we have sinned,
And in whose ways they [a]were not willing to walk,
And whose law they did not [b]obey?
25 So He poured out on him the heat of His anger
And the [a]fierceness of battle;
And it set him aflame all around,
Yet he did not recognize *it;*
And it burned him, but he [1b]paid no attention.

Chapter 43 Theme ________________________

43 But now, thus says the LORD, your [a]Creator, O Jacob,
And He who [b]formed you, O Israel,
"Do not [c]fear, for I have [d]redeemed you;
I have [e]called you by name; you are [f]Mine!
2 "When you [a]pass through the waters, [b]I will be with you;
And through the rivers, they will not overflow you.
When you [c]walk through the fire, you will not be scorched,
Nor will the flame burn you.
3 "For [a]I am the LORD your God,
The Holy One of Israel, your [b]Savior;
I have given Egypt as your ransom,
[1c]Cush and Seba in your place.
4 "Since you are [a]precious in My sight,
Since you are [b]honored and I [c]love you,
I will give *other* men in your place and *other* peoples in exchange for your life.
5 "Do not fear, for [a]I am with you;
I will bring [b]your offspring from the east,
And [c]gather you from the west.
6 "I will say to the [a]north, 'Give *them* up!'
And to the south, 'Do not hold *them* back.'
Bring My [b]sons from afar
And My daughters from the [c]ends of the earth,
7 Everyone who is [a]called by My name,
And whom I have [b]created for My [c]glory,
[d]Whom I have formed, even whom I have made."

8 Bring out the people who are [a]blind, even though they have eyes,
And the deaf, even though they have ears.
9 All the nations have [a]gathered together

22 [1]Or *holes* [a]Is 24:18 [b]Is 24:22
24 [a]Is 30:15 [b]Is 48:18; 57:17
25 [1]Lit *did not lay* it *to heart* [a]Is 5:25; 9:19 [b]Is 29:13; 47:7; 57:1; Hos 7:9
43:1 [a]Is 43:15 [b]Is 43:7, 21; 44:2, 21, 24 [c]Is 43:5 [d]Is 44:22, 23; 48:20 [e]Gen 32:28; Is 43:7; 45:3, 4 [f]Is 43:21
2 [a]Ps 66:12; Is 8:7, 8 [b]Deut 31:6, 8 [c]Is 29:6; 30:27-29; Dan 3:25, 27
3 [1]Or *Ethiopia* [a]Ex 20:2 [b]Is 19:20; 43:11; 45:15, 21; 49:26; 60:16; 63:8 [c]Is 20:3-5
4 [a]Ex 19:5, 6 [b]Is 49:5 [c]Is 63:9
5 [a]Is 8:10; 43:2 [b]Is 41:8; 49:12; 61:9 [c]Is 49:12
6 [a]Ps 107:3 [b]2 Cor 6:18 [c]Is 45:22
7 [a]Is 56:5; 62:2; James 2:7 [b]Ps 100:3; Is 29:23; Eph 2:10 [c]Is 44:23; 46:13 [d]Is 43:1
8 [a]Is 6:9; 42:19; Ezek 12:2
9 [a]Is 34:1; 41:1

So that the peoples may be assembled.
Who among them can [b]declare this
And proclaim to us the former things?
Let them present [c]their witnesses [d]that they may be justified,
Or let them hear and say, "It is true."
10 "You are [a]My witnesses," declares the LORD,
"And [b]My servant whom I have chosen,
So that you may know and believe Me
And understand that [c]I am He.
[d]Before Me there was no God formed,
And there will be none after Me.
11 "I, even I, am the LORD,
And there is no [a]savior [b]besides Me.
12 "It is I who have declared and saved and proclaimed,
And there was no [a]strange *god* among you;
So you are My witnesses," declares the LORD,
"And I am God.
13 "Even [1a]from eternity [b]I am He,
And there is [c]none who can deliver out of My hand;
[d]I act and who can reverse it?"

14 Thus says the LORD your [a]Redeemer, the Holy One of Israel,
"For your sake I have sent to Babylon,
And will bring them all down as fugitives,
[1]Even the [b]Chaldeans, into the [c]ships [2]in which they rejoice.
15 "I am the LORD, your Holy One,
[a]The Creator of Israel, your [b]King."
16 Thus says the LORD,
Who [a]makes a way through the sea
And a path through the mighty waters,
17 Who brings forth the [a]chariot and the horse,
The army and the mighty man
(They will lie down together *and* not rise again;
They have been [b]quenched *and* extinguished like a wick):
18 "[a]Do not call to mind the former things,
Or ponder things of the past.
19 "Behold, I will do something [a]new,
Now it will spring forth;
Will you not be aware of it?
I will even [b]make a roadway in the wilderness,
Rivers in the desert.
20 "The beasts of the field will glorify Me,
The [a]jackals and the ostriches,
Because I have [b]given waters in the wilderness
And rivers in the desert,
To give drink to My chosen people.
21 "The people whom [a]I formed for Myself
[b]Will declare My praise.

22 "Yet you have not called on Me, O Jacob;
But you have become [a]weary of Me, O Israel.

9 [b]Is 41:22, 23, 26 [c]Is 44:9 [d]Is 43:26
10 [a]Is 44:8 [b]Is 41:8 [c]Is 41:4 [d]Is 45:5, 6
11 [a]Is 43:3; 45:21; Hos 13:4 [b]Is 44:6, 8
12 [a]Deut 32:16; Ps 81:9
13 [1]So with Gr; Heb *from the day* [a]Ps 90:2; Is 48:16 [b]Is 41:4 [c]Ps 50:22 [d]Job 9:12; Is 14:27
14 [1]Another reading is *As for the Chaldeans, their rejoicing* is turned *into lamentations* [2]Lit *of their rejoicing* [a]Is 41:14 [b]Is 23:13 [c]Jer 51:13
15 [a]Is 43:1 [b]Is 41:20; 44:6
16 [a]Ex 14:21, 22; Ps 77:19; Is 11:15; 44:27; 50:2; 51:10; 63:11, 12
17 [a]Ex 15:19 [b]Ps 118:12; Is 1:31
18 [a]Is 65:17; Jer 23:7
19 [a]Is 42:9; 48:6; 2 Cor 5:17 [b]Ex 17:6; Num 20:11; Deut 8:15; Ps 78:16; Is 35:1, 6; 41:18, 19; 49:10; 51:3
20 [a]Is 13:22; 35:7 [b]Is 41:17, 18; 48:21
21 [a]Is 43:1 [b]Ps 102:18; Is 42:12; Luke 1:74, 75; 1 Pet 2:9
22 [a]Mic 6:3; Mal 1:13; 3:14

23 "You have [a]not brought to Me the sheep of your
burnt offerings,
Nor have you [b]honored Me with your sacrifices.
I have not [c]burdened you with [1]offerings,
Nor wearied you with [d]incense.
24 "You have bought Me not [1a]sweet cane with money,
Nor have you [2]filled Me with the fat of your sacrifices;
Rather you have burdened Me with your sins,
You have [b]wearied Me with your iniquities.

25 "I, even I, am the one who [a]wipes out your transgressions
[b]for My own sake,
And I will [c]not remember your sins.
26 "[1]Put Me in remembrance, [a]let us argue our case together;
State your *cause,* [b]that you may be proved right.
27 "Your [a]first [1]forefather sinned,
And your [2b]spokesmen have [3]transgressed against Me.
28 "So I will [1]pollute the [2]princes of the sanctuary,
And I will consign Jacob to the [a]ban and Israel
to [b]revilement.

Chapter 44 Theme ______________________

44 "But now listen, O Jacob, My [a]servant,
And Israel, whom I have chosen:
2 Thus says the LORD who made you
And [a]formed you from the womb, who [b]will help you,
'[c]Do not fear, O Jacob My servant;
And you [d]Jeshurun whom I have chosen.
3 'For [a]I will pour out water on [1]the thirsty *land*
And streams on the dry ground;
I will [b]pour out My Spirit on your [c]offspring
And My blessing on your descendants;
4 And they will spring up [1]among the grass
Like [a]poplars by streams of water.'
5 "This one will say, 'I am the LORD'S';
And that one [1]will call on the name of Jacob;
And another will [a]write [2]*on* his hand, 'Belonging to the LORD,'
And will name Israel's name with honor.

6 "Thus says the LORD, the [a]King of Israel and his [b]Redeemer,
the LORD of hosts:
'I am the [c]first and I am the last,
And there is no God [d]besides Me.
7 'Who is like Me? [a]Let him proclaim and declare it;
Yes, let him recount it to Me in order,
[1]From the time that I established the ancient [2]nation.
And let them declare to them the things that are coming
And the events that are going to take place.
8 'Do not tremble and do not be afraid;
[a]Have I not long since announced *it* to you and declared *it?*

23 [1]Or *a meal offering* [a]Amos 5:25 [b]Zech 7:5, 6; Mal 1:6-8 [c]Jer 7:21-26 [d]Ex 30:34; Lev 2:1; 24:7

24 [1]Or *calamus* [2]Or *saturated* [a]Ex 30:23; Jer 6:20 [b]Ps 95:10; Is 1:14; 7:13; Ezek 6:9; Mal 2:17

25 [a]Is 44:22; 55:7; Jer 50:20 [b]Is 37:35; 48:9, 11; Ezek 36:22 [c]Is 38:17; Jer 31:34

26 [1]Or *Report to Me* [a]Is 1:18; 41:1; 50:8 [b]Is 43:9

27 [1]Lit *father* [2]Or *interpreters* [3]Or *rebelled* [a]Is 51:2; Ezek 16:3 [b]Is 9:15; 28:7; 29:10; Jer 5:31

28 [1]Or *pierce through* [2]Or *holy princes* [a]Is 24:6; 34:5; Jer 24:9; Dan 9:11; Zech 8:13 [b]Ps 79:4; Ezek 5:15

44:1 [a]Is 41:8; Jer 30:10; 46:27, 28

2 [a]Is 44:21, 24 [b]Is 41:10 [c]Is 43:5 [d]Deut 32:15; 33:5, 26

3 [1]Or *him who is thirsty* [a]Is 41:17; Ezek 34:26; Joel 3:18 [b]Is 32:15; Joel 2:28 [c]Is 61:9; 65:23

4 [1]Another reading is *like grass among the waters* [a]Lev 23:40; Job 40:22

5 [1]Another reading is *will be called by the name of Jacob* [2]Or *with* [a]Ex 13:9; Neh 9:38

6 [a]Is 41:21; 43:15 [b]Is 41:14; 43:1, 14 [c]Is 41:4; 43:10; 48:12; Rev 1:8, 17; 22:13 [d]Is 43:11; 44:8; 45:5, 6, 21

7 [1]Lit *From My establishing of* [2]Or *people* [a]Is 41:22, 26

8 [a]Is 42:9; 48:5

And [b]you are My witnesses.
Is there any God [c]besides Me,
Or is there any *other* [d]Rock?
I know of none.'"

9 Those who fashion [1]a graven image are all of them futile, and their precious things are of no profit; even their own witnesses fail to see or know, so that they will be [a]put to shame.

10 Who has fashioned a god or cast [1]an idol to [a]no profit?

11 Behold, all his companions will be [a]put to shame, for the craftsmen themselves are mere men. Let them all assemble themselves, let them stand up, let them tremble, let them together be put to shame.

12 The [a]man shapes iron into a cutting tool and does his work over the coals, [1]fashioning it with hammers and working it with his strong arm. He also gets hungry and [2]his strength fails; he drinks no water and becomes weary.

13 [a]*Another* shapes wood, he extends a measuring line; he outlines it with red chalk. He works it with planes and outlines it with a compass, and makes it like the form of a man, like the beauty of [b]man, so that it may sit in a [c]house.

14 Surely he cuts cedars for himself, and takes a [1]cypress or an oak and [2]raises *it* for himself among the trees of the forest. He plants a fir, and the rain makes it grow.

15 Then it becomes *something* for a man to burn, so he takes one of them and warms himself; he also makes a fire to bake bread. He also [a]makes a god and worships it; he makes it a graven image and [b]falls down before it.

16 Half of it he burns in the fire; over *this* half he eats meat as he roasts a roast and is satisfied. He also warms himself and says, "Aha! I am warm, I have seen the fire."

17 But the rest of it he [a]makes into a god, his graven image. He falls down before it and worships; he also [b]prays to it and says, "Deliver me, for you are my god."

18 They do not [a]know, nor do they understand, for He has [b]smeared over their eyes so that they cannot see and their hearts so that they cannot comprehend.

19 No one [1]recalls, nor is there [a]knowledge or understanding to say, "I have burned half of it in the fire and also have baked bread over its coals. I roast meat and eat *it*. Then [2]I make the rest of it into an [b]abomination, [3]I fall down before a block of wood!"

20 He [1a]feeds on ashes; a [b]deceived heart has turned him aside. And he cannot deliver [2]himself, nor say, "[c]Is there not a lie in my right hand?"

21 "[a]Remember these things, O Jacob,
And Israel, for you are [b]My servant;
I have formed you, you are My servant,
O Israel, you will [c]not be forgotten by Me.

22 "I have [a]wiped out your transgressions like a thick cloud
And your sins like a [1]heavy mist.
[b]Return to Me, for I have [c]redeemed you."

8 [b]Is 43:10 [c]Deut 4:35, 39; 1 Sam 2:2; Is 45:5; Joel 2:27 [d]Is 17:10; 26:4; 30:29

9 [1]Or *an idol* [a]Ps 97:7; Is 42:17; 44:11; 45:16

10 [1]Or *a graven image* [a]Is 41:29; Jer 10:5; Hab 2:18; Acts 19:26

11 [a]Ps 97:7; Is 42:17; 44:9; 45:16

12 [1]Lit *and fashions* [2]Lit *there is no strength* [a]Is 40:19, 20; 41:6, 7; 46:6, 7; Jer 10:3-5; Hab 2:18

13 [a]Is 41:7 [b]Ps 115:5-7 [c]Judg 17:4, 5; Ezek 8:10, 11

14 [1]Or *holm-oak* [2]Lit *makes strong*

15 [a]Is 44:17 [b]2 Chr 25:14

17 [a]Is 44:15 [b]1 Kin 18:26, 28; Is 45:20

18 [a]Is 1:3; Jer 10:8, 14 [b]Ps 81:12; Is 6:9, 10; 29:10

19 [1]Lit *returns to his heart* [2]Or *shall I make?* [3]Or *shall I fall . . . ?* [a]Is 5:13; 44:18, 19; 45:20 [b]Deut 27:15; 1 Kin 11:5, 7; 2 Kin 23:13, 14

20 [1]Or *is a companion of ashes* [2]Lit *his soul* [a]Ps 102:9 [b]Job 15:31; Hos 4:12; Rom 1:21, 22; 2 Thess 2:11; 2 Tim 3:13 [c]Is 57:11; 59:3, 4, 13; Rom 1:25

21 [a]Is 46:8; Zech 10:9 [b]Is 44:1, 2 [c]Is 49:15

22 [1]Or *cloud* [a]Ps 51:1, 9; Is 43:25; Acts 3:19 [b]Is 31:6; 55:7 [c]Is 43:1; 48:20; 1 Cor 6:20; 1 Pet 1:18, 19

23 [a]Ps 69:34; 96:11, 12; Is 42:10; 49:13 [b]Ps 98:7, 8; 148:7, 9; Is 55:12 [c]Is 43:1 [d]Is 49:3; 61:3

23 [a]Shout for joy, O heavens, for the LORD has done *it!*
Shout joyfully, you lower parts of the earth;
[b]Break forth into a shout of joy, you mountains,
O forest, and every tree in it;
For [c]the LORD has redeemed Jacob
And in Israel He [d]shows forth His glory.

24 [1]Or *who was with Me?* [a]Is 41:14; 43:14 [b]Is 44:2 [c]Is 40:22; 42:5; 45:12, 18; 51:13

24 Thus says the LORD, your [a]Redeemer, and the one who
[b]formed you from the womb,
"I, the LORD, am the maker of all things,
[c]Stretching out the heavens by Myself
And spreading out the earth [1]all alone,

25 [1]Lit *signs* [2]Lit *He makes* [3]Lit *He turns* [a]Is 47:13 [b]2 Sam 15:31; Job 5:12-14; Ps 33:10; Is 29:14; Jer 51:57; 1 Cor 1:20, 27

25 [a]Causing the [1]omens of boasters to fail,
[2]Making fools out of diviners,
[b]Causing wise men to draw back
And [3]turning their knowledge into foolishness,

26 [1]Lit *He performs* [a]Zech 1:6; Matt 5:18 [b]Is 40:9 [c]Jer 32:15, 44

26 [a]Confirming the word of His servant
And [1]performing the purpose of His messengers.
It is I who says of Jerusalem, 'She shall be inhabited!'
And of the [b]cities of Judah, '[c]They shall be built.'
And I will raise up her ruins *again.*

27 [a]Is 42:15; 50:2; Jer 50:38; 51:36

27 "*It is I* who says to the depth of the sea, 'Be dried up!'
And I will make your rivers [a]dry.

28 [1]Lit *to say* [2]Lit *You will be founded* [a]Is 45:1 [b]2 Chr 36:22, 23; Ezra 1:1; Is 14:32; 45:13; 54:11

28 "*It is I* who says of [a]Cyrus, '*He is* My shepherd!
And he will perform all My desire.'
And [1]he declares of Jerusalem, '[b]She will be built,'
And of the temple, '[2]Your foundation will be laid.'"

Chapter 45 Theme ______________________________

45:1 [1]Lit *I will loose* [a]Is 44:28 [b]Ps 73:23; Is 41:13; 42:6 [c]Is 41:2, 25; Jer 50:3, 35; 51:11, 20, 24 [d]Job 12:21; Is 45:5

45 Thus says the LORD to [a]Cyrus His anointed,
Whom I have taken by the right [b]hand,
To [c]subdue nations before him
And [1]to [d]loose the loins of kings;
To open doors before him so that gates will not be shut:

2 [1]Another reading is *mountains* [a]Is 40:4 [b]Ps 107:16 [c]Jer 51:30

2 "I will go before you and [a]make the [1]rough places smooth;
I will [b]shatter the doors of bronze and cut through their
iron [c]bars.

3 [1]Or *hoarded treasures* [a]Jer 41:8; 50:37 [b]Ex 33:12, 17; Is 43:1; 49:1

3 "I will give you the [1a]treasures of darkness
And hidden wealth of secret places,
So that you may know that it is I,
The LORD, the God of Israel, who [b]calls you by your name.

4 [a]Is 41:8, 9; 44:1 [b]Is 43:1 [c]Acts 17:23

4 "For the sake of [a]Jacob My servant,
And Israel My chosen *one,*
I have also [b]called you by your name;
I have given you a title of honor
Though you have [c]not known Me.

5 [1]Or *arm* [a]Is 45:6, 14, 18, 21; 46:9 [b]Is 44:6, 8 [c]Ps 18:39

5 "I am the LORD, and [a]there is no other;
[b]Besides Me there is no God.
I will [1c]gird you, though you have not known Me;

6 [1]Lit *they* [a]Ps 102:15; Mal 1:11

6 That [1a]men may know from the rising to the setting of
the sun

INSIGHT

This prophecy regarding Cyrus was given over 100 years before his birth. In 539 B.C. Babylon was conquered by Cyrus and Darius of the Medo-Persian Empire.

That there is [b]no one besides Me.
I am the LORD, and there is no other,
7 The One [a]forming light and [b]creating darkness,
Causing [1]well-being and [c]creating calamity;
I am the LORD who does all these.

8 "[a]Drip down, O heavens, from above,
And let the clouds pour down righteousness;
Let the [b]earth open up and salvation bear fruit,
[c]And righteousness spring up with it.
I, the LORD, have created it.

9 "Woe to *the one* who [a]quarrels with his [1]Maker—
An earthenware vessel [2]among the vessels of earth!
Will the [b]clay say to the [1]potter, 'What are you doing?'
Or the thing you are making *say,* 'He has no hands'?
10 "Woe to him who says to a father, 'What are you begetting?'
Or to a woman, 'To what are you [1]giving birth?'"

11 Thus says the [a]LORD, the Holy One of Israel, and his [1b]Maker:
"[2c]Ask Me about the things to come [3]concerning My [d]sons,
And you shall commit to Me [e]the work of My hands.
12 "It is I who [a]made the earth, and created man upon it.
I [b]stretched out the heavens with My hands
And I [1]ordained [c]all their host.
13 "I have aroused him in [a]righteousness
And I will [b]make all his ways smooth;
He will [c]build My city and will let My exiles go [d]free,
Without any payment or reward," says the LORD of hosts.

14 Thus says the LORD,
"The [1]products of [a]Egypt and the merchandise of [2b]Cush
And the Sabeans, men of stature,
Will [c]come over to you and will be yours;
They will walk behind you, they will come over in [d]chains
And will [e]bow down to you;
They will make supplication to you:
'[3]Surely, [f]God is [4]with you, and [g]there is none else,
No other God.'"
15 Truly, You are a God who [a]hides Himself,
O God of Israel, [b]Savior!
16 They will be [a]put to shame and even humiliated, all of them;
The [b]manufacturers of idols will go away together
in humiliation.
17 Israel has been saved by the LORD
With an [a]everlasting salvation;
You [b]will not be put to shame or humiliated
To all eternity.
18 For thus says the LORD, who [a]created the heavens (He is the
God who [b]formed the earth and made it, He established it *and* did
not create it [1]a [c]waste place, *but* formed it to be [d]inhabited),
"I am the LORD, and [e]there is none else.

6 [b]Is 45:5

7 [1]Or *peace* [a]Is 42:16 [b]Ps 104:20; 105:28 [c]Is 31:2; 47:11; Amos 3:6

8 [a]Ps 72:6; Hos 10:12; 14:5; Joel 3:18 [b]Ps 85:11 [c]Is 60:21; 61:11

9 [1]Lit *Fashioner* [2]Lit *with* [a]Job 15:25; 40:8, 9; Ps 2:2, 3; Prov 21:30; Jer 50:24 [b]Is 29:16; 64:8; Jer 18:6; Rom 9:20, 21

10 [1]Lit *in labor pains with*

11 [1]Lit *Fashioner* [2]Or *Will you ask* [3]Or *upon* [a]Is 43:15; 48:17; Ezek 39:7 [b]Is 44:2; 54:5 [c]Is 8:19 [d]Jer 31:9 [e]Is 19:25; 29:23; 60:21; 64:8

12 [1]Or *commanded* [a]Is 42:5; 45:18; Jer 27:5 [b]Ps 104:2; Is 42:5; 44:24 [c]Gen 2:1; Neh 9:6

13 [a]Is 41:2 [b]Is 45:2 [c]2 Chr 36:22, 23; Is 44:28 [d]Is 52:3

14 [1]Lit *labor* [2]Or *Ethiopia* [3]Or *God is with you alone* [4]Or *in* [a]Ps 68:31; Is 19:21 [b]Is 18:1; 43:3 [c]Is 14:1, 2; 49:23; 54:3 [d]Ps 149:8 [e]Is 49:23; 60:14 [f]Jer 16:19; Zech 8:20-23; 1 Cor 14:25 [g]Is 45:5

15 [a]Ps 44:24; Is 1:15; 8:17; 57:17 [b]Is 43:3

16 [a]Is 42:17; 44:9 [b]Is 44:11

17 [a]Is 26:4; 51:6; Rom 11:26 [b]Is 49:23; 50:7; 54:4

18 [1]Or *in vain* [a]Is 42:5 [b]Is 45:12 [c]Gen 1:2 [d]Gen 1:26; Ps 115:16 [e]Is 45:5

19 "[a]I have not spoken in secret,
In [1]some dark land;
I did not say to the [2b]offspring of Jacob,
'[c]Seek Me in [3]a waste place';
I, the LORD, [d]speak righteousness,
[e]Declaring things that are upright.

20 "[a]Gather yourselves and come;
Draw near together, you fugitives of the nations;
[b]They have no knowledge,
Who [c]carry about [1]their wooden idol
And [d]pray to a god who cannot save.
21 "[a]Declare and set forth *your case;*
Indeed, let them consult together.
[b]Who has announced this from of old?
Who has long since declared it?
Is it not I, the LORD?
And there is [c]no other God besides Me,
A righteous God and a [d]Savior;
There is none except Me.
22 "[a]Turn to Me and [b]be saved, all the ends of the earth;
For I am God, and there is no other.
23 "[a]I have sworn by Myself,
The [b]word has gone forth from My mouth
in righteousness
And will not turn back,
That to Me [c]every knee will bow, every tongue will
[d]swear *allegiance.*
24 "They will say of Me, 'Only [a]in the LORD are righteousness
and strength.'
Men will come to Him,
And [b]all who were angry at Him will be put to shame.
25 "In the LORD all the offspring of Israel
Will be [a]justified and will [b]glory."

Chapter 46 Theme ______________________

46 [a]Bel has bowed down, Nebo stoops over;
Their images are *consigned* to the beasts and the cattle.
The things [1]that you carry are burdensome,
A load for the weary *beast.*
2 They stooped over, they have bowed down together;
They could not rescue the burden,
But [1]have themselves [a]gone into captivity.

3 "[a]Listen to Me, O house of Jacob,
And all [b]the remnant of the house of Israel,
You who have been [c]borne by Me from [1]birth
And have been carried from the womb;
4 Even to *your* old age [a]I [1]will be the same,
And even to *your* [2b]graying years I will bear *you!*

19 [1]Lit *a place of a land of darkness* [2]Lit *seed* [3]Or *vain* [a]Is 48:16 [b]Is 45:25; 65:9 [c]2 Chr 15:2; Ps 78:34; Jer 29:13, 14 [d]Ps 19:8; Is 45:23; 63:1 [e]Is 43:12; 44:8

20 [1]Lit *the wood of their graven image* [a]Is 43:9 [b]Is 44:18, 19; 48:5-7 [c]Is 46:1, 7; Jer 10:5 [d]Is 44:17; 46:6, 7

21 [a]Is 41:23; 43:9 [b]Is 41:26; 44:7; 48:14 [c]Is 45:5 [d]Is 43:3, 11

22 [a]Num 21:8, 9; 2 Chr 20:12; Mic 7:7; Zech 12:10 [b]Is 30:15; 49:6, 12; 52:10

23 [a]Gen 22:16; Is 62:8; Heb 6:13 [b]Is 55:11 [c]Rom 14:11; Phil 2:10 [d]Deut 6:13; Ps 63:11; Is 19:18; 65:16

24 [a]Jer 33:16 [b]Is 41:11

25 [a]1 Kin 8:32; Is 53:11 [b]Is 41:16; 60:19

46:1 [1]Lit *carried by you* [a]Is 2:18; 21:9; Jer 50:2-4; 51:44

2 [1]Or *their soul has* [a]Judg 18:17, 18, 24; 2 Sam 5:21; Jer 43:12, 13; 48:7; Hos 10:5, 6

3 [1]Lit *the belly* [a]Is 46:12 [b]Is 10:21, 22 [c]Ps 71:6; Is 49:1

4 [1]Lit *I am He* [2]Lit *gray hairs* [a]Is 41:4; 43:13; 48:12 [b]Ps 71:18

I have [3]done *it,* and I will carry *you;*
And I will bear *you* and I will deliver *you.*

5 "[a]To whom would you liken Me
And make Me equal and compare Me,
That we would be alike?
6 "Those who [a]lavish gold from the purse
And weigh silver on the scale
Hire a goldsmith, and he makes it *into* a god;
They [b]bow down, indeed they worship it.
7 "They [a]lift it upon the shoulder *and* carry it;
They set it in its place and it stands *there.*
[b]It does not move from its place.
Though one may cry to it, it [c]cannot answer;
It [d]cannot deliver him from his distress.

8 "[a]Remember this, and be [1]assured;
[b]Recall it to [2]mind, you [c]transgressors.
9 "Remember the [a]former things long past,
For I am God, and there is [b]no other;
I am God, and there is [c]no one like Me,
10 Declaring the end from the beginning,
And from ancient times things which have not been done,
Saying, '[a]My purpose will be established,
And I will accomplish all My good pleasure';
11 Calling a [a]bird of prey from the [b]east,
The man of [1]My purpose from a far country.
Truly I have [c]spoken; truly I will bring it to pass.
I have planned *it, surely* I will do it.

12 "[a]Listen to Me, you [b]stubborn-minded,
Who are [c]far from righteousness.
13 "I [a]bring near My righteousness, it is not far off;
And My salvation will not delay.
And I will grant [b]salvation in Zion,
And My [c]glory for Israel.

Chapter 47 Theme ____________________

47

"[a]Come down and sit in the dust,
O [b]virgin [c]daughter of Babylon;
Sit on the ground without a throne,
O daughter of the Chaldeans!
For you shall no longer be called [d]tender and delicate.
2 "Take the [a]millstones and [b]grind meal.
Remove your [c]veil, [d]strip off the skirt,
Uncover the leg, cross the rivers.
3 "Your [a]nakedness will be uncovered,
Your shame also will be exposed;
I will [b]take vengeance and will not [1]spare a man."

4 [3]Or *made* you

5 [a]Is 40:18, 25

6 [a]Is 40:19; 41:7; 44:12-17; Jer 10:4 [b]Is 44:15, 17

7 [a]Is 45:20; 46:1; Jer 10:5 [b]Is 40:20; 41:7 [c]Is 41:28 [d]Is 45:20

8 [1]Lit *firm* [2]Lit *heart* [a]Is 44:21 [b]Is 44:19 [c]Is 50:1

9 [a]Deut 32:7; Is 42:9; 65:17 [b]Is 45:5, 21 [c]Is 41:26, 27

10 [a]Ps 33:11; Prov 19:21; Is 14:24; 25:1; 40:8; Acts 5:39

11 [1]Lit *His* [a]Is 18:6 [b]Is 41:2 [c]Num 23:19; Is 14:24; 37:26

12 [a]Is 46:3 [b]Ps 76:5; Is 48:4; Zech 7:11, 12; Mal 3:13 [c]Ps 119:150; Is 48:1; Jer 2:5

13 [a]Is 51:5; 61:11; Rom 3:21 [b]Is 61:3; 62:11; Joel 3:17; 1 Pet 2:6 [c]Is 43:7; 44:23

47:1 [a]Is 3:26; Jer 48:18 [b]Is 23:12; 37:22; Jer 46:11 [c]Ps 137:8; Jer 50:42; 51:33; Zech 2:7 [d]Deut 28:56

2 [a]Ex 11:5; Jer 25:10 [b]Job 31:10; Eccl 12:4; Matt 24:41 [c]Gen 24:65; Is 3:23; 1 Cor 11:5 [d]Is 32:11

3 [1]Lit *meet* [a]Ezek 16:37; Nah 3:5 [b]Is 34:8; 63:4

4 Our [a]Redeemer, the LORD of hosts is His name,
The Holy One of Israel.
5 "[a]Sit silently, and go into [b]darkness,
O daughter of the Chaldeans,
For you will no longer be called
The [c]queen of [d]kingdoms.
6 "I was angry with My people,
I profaned My heritage
And gave them into your hand.
You did not show mercy to them,
On the [a]aged you made your yoke very heavy.
7 "Yet you said, 'I will be a [a]queen forever.'
These things you did not [b]consider
Nor remember the [c]outcome of [1]them.

8 "Now, then, hear this, you [a]sensual one,
Who [b]dwells securely,
Who says in [1]your heart,
'[c]I am, and there is no one besides me.
I will [d]not sit as a widow,
Nor know loss of children.'
9 "But these [a]two things will come on you [b]suddenly in
one day:
Loss of children and widowhood.
They will come on you in full measure
In spite of your many [c]sorceries,
In spite of the great power of your spells.
10 "You felt [a]secure in your wickedness and said,
'[b]No one sees me,'
Your [c]wisdom and your knowledge, [1]they have
deluded you;
For you have said in your heart,
'[d]I am, and there is no one besides me.'
11 "But [a]evil will come on you
Which you will not know how to charm away;
And disaster will fall on you
For which you cannot atone;
And [b]destruction about which you do not know
Will come on you [c]suddenly.

12 "Stand *fast* now in your [a]spells
And in your many sorceries
With which you have labored from your youth;
Perhaps you will be able to profit,
Perhaps you may cause trembling.
13 "You are [a]wearied with your many counsels;
Let now the [b]astrologers,
Those who prophesy by the stars,
Those who predict by the new moons,
Stand up and [c]save you from what will come upon you.
14 "Behold, they have become [a]like stubble,

4 [a]Is 41:14
5 [a]Is 23:2; Jer 8:14; Lam 2:10 [b]Is 13:10 [c]Is 47:7 [d]Is 13:19; Dan 2:37
6 [a]Deut 28:50
7 [1]Lit *it* [a]Is 47:5 [b]Is 42:25; 57:11 [c]Deut 32:29; Jer 5:31; Ezek 7:2, 3
8 [1]Lit *her* [a]Is 22:13; 32:9; Jer 50:11 [b]Is 32:9, 11; Zeph 2:15 [c]Is 45:5, 6, 18; 47:10; Zeph 2:15 [d]Rev 18:7
9 [a]Is 13:16, 18; 14:22 [b]Ps 73:19; 1 Thess 5:3; Rev 18:8, 10 [c]Is 47:13; Nah 3:4; Rev 18:23
10 [1]Lit *it has* [a]Ps 52:7; 62:10; Is 59:4 [b]Is 29:15; Ezek 8:12; 9:9 [c]Is 5:21; 44:20 [d]Is 47:8
11 [a]Is 57:1 [b]Is 13:6; Jer 51:8, 43; Luke 17:27; 1 Thess 5:3 [c]Is 47:9
12 [a]Is 47:9
13 [a]Jer 51:58, 64 [b]Is 8:19; 44:25; 47:9; Dan 2:2, 10 [c]Is 47:15
14 [a]Is 5:24; Nah 1:10; Mal 4:1

[b]Fire burns them;
They cannot deliver themselves from the power of
the flame;
There will be [c]no coal to warm by
Nor a fire to sit before!
15 "So have those become to you with whom you
have labored,
Who have [a]trafficked with you from your youth;
Each has wandered in his own [1]way;
There is [b]none to save you.

Chapter 48 Theme _____________________________

48

"[a]Hear this, O house of Jacob, who are named Israel
And who came forth from the [1b]loins of Judah,
Who [c]swear by the name of the LORD
And invoke the God of Israel,
But not in truth nor in [d]righteousness.
2 "For they call themselves after the [a]holy city
And [b]lean on the God of Israel;
The LORD of hosts is His name.
3 "I [a]declared the former things long ago
And they went forth from My mouth, and I
proclaimed them.
[b]Suddenly I acted, and they [c]came to pass.
4 "Because I know that you are [1a]obstinate,
And your [b]neck is an iron sinew
And your [c]forehead bronze,
5 Therefore I declared *them* to you long ago,
Before [1]they took place I proclaimed *them* to you,
So that you would not say, 'My [a]idol has
done them,
And my graven image and my molten image have
commanded them.'
6 "You have heard; look at all this.
And you, will you not declare it?
I proclaim to you [a]new things from this time,
Even hidden things which you have not known.
7 "They are created now and not long ago;
And before today you have not heard them,
So that you will not say, 'Behold, I knew them.'
8 "You have not [a]heard, you have not known.
Even from long ago your ear has not been open,
Because I knew that you would deal
very treacherously;
And you have been called a [1b]rebel from [2]birth.
9 "[a]For the sake of My name I [b]delay My wrath,
And *for* My praise I restrain *it* for you,
In order not to cut you off.
10 "Behold, I have refined you, but [a]not as silver;
I have tested you in the [b]furnace of affliction.
11 "[a]For My own sake, for My own sake, I will act;

14 [b]Is 10:17; Jer 51:30, 32, 58 [c]Is 44:16

15 [1]Lit *side, region* [a]Rev 18:11 [b]Is 5:29; 43:13; 46:7

48:1 [1]Lit *waters* [a]Is 46:12 [b]Num 24:7; Deut 33:28; Ps 68:26 [c]Deut 6:13; Is 45:23; 65:16 [d]Is 58:2; Jer 4:2

2 [a]Is 52:1; 64:10 [b]Is 10:20; Jer 7:4; 21:2; Mic 3:11; Rom 2:17

3 [a]Is 41:22; 42:9; 43:9; 44:7, 8; 45:21; 46:10 [b]Is 29:5; 30:13 [c]Josh 21:45; Is 42:9

4 [1]Or *harsh* [a]Ex 32:9; Deut 31:27; Ezek 2:4; 3:7 [b]2 Chr 36:13; Prov 29:1; Acts 7:51 [c]Ezek 3:7-9

5 [1]Lit *it* [a]Jer 44:15-18

6 [a]Is 42:9; 43:19

8 [1]Or *transgressor* [2]Lit *the belly* [a]Is 42:25; 47:11; Hos 7:9 [b]Deut 9:7, 24; Ps 58:3; Is 46:8

9 [a]Is 48:11 [b]Neh 9:30, 31; Ps 78:38; 103:8-10; Is 30:18; 65:8

10 [a]Jer 9:7; Ezek 22:18-22 [b]Deut 4:20; 1 Kin 8:51; Jer 11:4

11 [a]1 Sam 12:22; Ps 25:11; 106:8; Is 37:35; 43:25; Jer 14:7; Ezek 20:9, 14, 22, 44; Dan 9:17-19

For how can *My name* be profaned?
And My [b]glory I will not give to another.

12 "Listen to Me, O Jacob, even Israel [1]whom I called;
[a]I am He, [b]I am the first, I am also the last.
13 "Surely My hand [a]founded the earth,
And My right hand spread out the heavens;
When I [b]call to them, they stand together.
14 "[a]Assemble, all of you, and listen!
[b]Who among them has declared these things?
The LORD loves him; he will [c]carry out His good pleasure
on [d]Babylon,
And His arm *will be against* the Chaldeans.
15 "I, even I, have spoken; indeed I have [a]called him,
I have brought him, and He will make his
ways successful.
16 "[a]Come near to Me, listen to this:
From the first I have [b]not spoken in secret,
[c]From the time it took place, I was there.
And now [d]the Lord [1]GOD has sent Me, and His Spirit."

17 Thus says the LORD, your [a]Redeemer, the Holy One of Israel,
"I am the LORD your God, who teaches you to profit,
Who [b]leads you in the way you should go.
18 "If only you had [a]paid attention to My commandments!
Then your [1b]well-being would have been like a river,
And your [c]righteousness like the waves of the sea.
19 "Your [1a]descendants would have been like the sand,
And [2]your offspring like its grains;
[b]Their name would never be cut off or destroyed from
My presence."

20 [a]Go forth from Babylon! Flee from the Chaldeans!
Declare with the sound of [b]joyful shouting, proclaim this,
[c]Send it out to the end of the earth;
Say, "[d]The LORD has redeemed His servant Jacob."
21 They did not [a]thirst when He led them through
the deserts.
He [b]made the water flow out of the rock for them;
He split the rock and [c]the water gushed forth.
22 "[a]There is no peace for the wicked," says the LORD.

Chapter 49 Theme ______________________

49 Listen to Me, O [a]islands,
And pay attention, you peoples from afar.
[b]The LORD called Me from the womb;
From the [1]body of My mother He named Me.
2 He has made My [a]mouth like a sharp sword,
In the [b]shadow of His hand He has concealed Me;
And He has also made Me a [1]select [c]arrow,

11 [b]Deut 32:26, 27; Is 42:8

12 [1]Lit *My called one* [a]Is 41:4; 43:10-13; 46:4 [b]Is 44:6; Rev 1:17; 22:13

13 [a]Ex 20:11; Ps 102:25; Is 42:5; 45:12, 18; Heb 1:10-12 [b]Is 40:26

14 [a]Is 43:9; 45:20 [b]Is 45:21 [c]Is 46:10, 11 [d]Is 13:4, 5, 17-19; Jer 50:21-29; 51:24

15 [a]Is 41:2; 45:1, 2

16 [1]Heb *YHWH,* usually rendered *LORD* [a]Is 34:1; 41:1; 57:3 [b]Is 45:19 [c]Is 43:13 [d]Zech 2:9, 11

17 [a]Is 41:14; 43:14; 49:7, 26; 54:5, 8 [b]Ps 32:8; Is 30:21; 49:9, 10

18 [1]Or *peace* [a]Deut 5:29; 32:29; Ps 81:13-16 [b]Ps 119:165; Is 32:16-18; 66:12 [c]Is 45:8; 61:10, 11; 62:1; Hos 10:12; Amos 5:24

19 [1]Lit *seed* [2]Lit *the offspring of your inward parts* [a]Gen 22:17; Is 10:22; 44:3, 4; 54:3; Jer 33:22 [b]Is 56:5; 66:22

20 [a]Jer 50:8; 51:6, 45; Zech 2:6, 7; Rev 18:4 [b]Is 42:10; 49:13; 52:9 [c]Is 62:11; Jer 31:10; 50:2 [d]Is 43:1; 52:9; 63:9

21 [a]Is 30:25; 35:6, 7; 41:17, 18; 43:19, 20; 49:10 [b]Ex 17:6; Ps 78:15, 16 [c]Ps 78:20; 105:41

22 [a]Is 57:21

49:1 [1]Lit *inward parts* [a]Is 42:4 [b]Is 44:2, 24; 46:3; Jer 1:5

2 [1]Or *sharpened* [a]Is 11:4; Heb 4:12; Rev 1:16; 2:12, 16 [b]Is 51:16 [c]Hab 3:11

He has hidden Me in His quiver.
3 He said to Me, "[a]You are My Servant, Israel,
[b]In Whom I will [1]show My glory."
4 But I said, "I have [a]toiled in vain,
I have spent My strength for nothing and vanity;
Yet surely the justice *due* to Me is with the LORD,
And My [b]reward with My God."

5 And now says [a]the LORD, who formed Me from the womb
to be His Servant,
To bring Jacob back to Him, so that [b]Israel might be
gathered to Him
(For I am [c]honored in the sight of the LORD,
And My God is My [d]strength),
6 He says, "It is too [1]small a thing that You should be
My Servant
To raise up the tribes of Jacob and to restore the [a]preserved
ones of Israel;
I will also make You a [b]light [2]of the nations
So that My salvation may [3]reach to the [c]end of the earth."
7 Thus says the LORD, the [a]Redeemer of Israel *and* its
Holy One,
To the [b]despised One,
To the One abhorred by the nation,
To the Servant of rulers,
"[c]Kings will see and arise,
Princes will also [d]bow down,
Because of the LORD who is faithful, the Holy One of Israel
who has chosen You."

8 Thus says the LORD,
"In a [a]favorable time I have answered You,
And in a day of salvation I have helped You;
And I will [b]keep You and [c]give You for a covenant of
the people,
To [1][d]restore the land, to make *them* inherit the
desolate heritages;
9 Saying to those who are [a]bound, 'Go forth,'
To those who are in darkness, 'Show yourselves.'
Along the roads they will feed,
And their pasture *will be* on all [b]bare heights.
10 "They will [a]not hunger or thirst,
Nor will the scorching [b]heat or sun strike them down;
For [c]He who has compassion on them will [d]lead them
And will guide them to [e]springs of water.
11 "I will make all [a]My mountains a road,
And My [b]highways will be raised up.
12 "Behold, these will come [a]from afar;
And lo, these *will come* from the [b]north and from
the west,
And these from the land of Sinim."

3 [1]Or *glorify Myself* [a]Zech 3:8 [b]Is 44:23

4 [a]Is 65:23 [b]Is 35:4; 59:18

5 [a]Is 44:2 [b]Is 11:12; 27:12 [c]Is 43:4 [d]Is 12:2

6 [1]Lit *light* [2]Or *to* [3]Lit *be* [a]Ps 37:28; 97:10 [b]Is 42:6; 51:4; Luke 2:32; Acts 13:47; 26:23 [c]Is 48:20

7 [a]Is 48:17 [b]Ps 22:6-8; 69:7-9; Is 53:3 [c]Is 52:15 [d]Is 19:21, 23; 27:13; 66:23

8 [1]Lit *establish* [a]Ps 69:13; 2 Cor 6:2 [b]Is 26:3; 27:3; 42:6 [c]Is 42:6 [d]Is 44:26

9 [a]Is 42:7; 61:1; Luke 4:18 [b]Is 41:18

10 [a]Is 33:16; 48:21; Rev 7:16 [b]Ps 121:6 [c]Is 14:1 [d]Ps 23:2; Is 40:11 [e]Is 35:7; 41:17

11 [a]Is 40:4 [b]Is 11:16; 19:23; 35:8; 62:10

12 [a]Is 49:1; 60:4 [b]Is 43:5, 6

13 [a]Is 44:23 [b]Is 40:1; 51:3, 12 [c]Is 54:7, 8, 10

13 [a]Shout for joy, O heavens! And rejoice, O earth!
Break forth into joyful shouting, O mountains!
For the [b]LORD has comforted His people
And will [c]have compassion on His afflicted.

15 [a]Is 44:21

14 But Zion said, "The LORD has forsaken me,
And the Lord has forgotten me."

16 [a]Song 8:6; Hag 2:23 [b]Ps 48:12, 13; Is 62:6, 7

15 "Can a woman forget her nursing child
And have no compassion on the son of her womb?
Even these may forget, but [a]I will not forget you.
16 "Behold, I have [a]inscribed you on the palms *of My hands;*
Your [b]walls are continually before Me.

17 [1]So ancient versions and DSS; M.T. reads *sons* [a]Is 10:6; 37:18

17 "Your [1]builders hurry;
Your [a]destroyers and devastators
Will depart from you.

18 [1]Lit *an ornament* [a]Is 60:4; John 4:35 [b]Is 43:5; 54:7; 60:4 [c]Is 49:12 [d]Is 45:23; 54:9 [e]Is 52:1; 61:10

18 "[a]Lift up your eyes and look around;
[b]All of them gather together, [c]they come to you.
[d]As I live," declares the LORD,
"You will surely [e]put on all of them as [1]jewels and bind
them on as a bride.

19 [a]Is 1:7; 3:8; 5:6; 51:3 [b]Is 54:1, 2; Zech 10:10 [c]Ps 56:1, 2

19 "For [a]your waste and desolate places and your
destroyed land—
Surely now you will be [b]too cramped for
the inhabitants,
And those who [c]swallowed you will be far away.

20 [1]Lit *your bereavement* [a]Is 54:1-3

20 "The [a]children of [1]whom you were bereaved will yet say
in your ears,
'The place is too cramped for me;
Make room for me that I may live *here.*'

21 [1]Lit *These, where are they?* [a]Is 29:23; 54:6, 7 [b]Is 27:10; Lam 1:1 [c]Is 5:13 [d]Is 1:8 [e]Is 60:8

21 "Then you will [a]say in your heart,
'Who has begotten these for me,
Since I have been bereaved of my children
And am [b]barren, an [c]exile and a wanderer?
And who has reared these?
Behold, I was [d]left alone;
[1e]From where did these come?'"

22 [1]Heb *YHWH,* usually rendered *LORD* [a]Is 11:10, 12; 18:3; 62:10 [b]Is 14:2; 43:6; 60:4

22 Thus says the Lord [1]GOD,
"Behold, I will lift up My hand to the nations
And set up My [a]standard to the peoples;
And they will [b]bring your sons in *their* bosom,
And your daughters will be carried on *their* shoulders.

23 [a]Is 14:1, 2; 60:3, 10, 11 [b]Is 45:14; 60:14 [c]Ps 72:9; Mic 7:17 [d]Is 41:20; 43:10; 60:16 [e]Ps 37:9; Is 25:9; 26:8 [f]Ps 25:3; Is 45:17; Joel 2:27

23 "[a]Kings will be your guardians,
And their princesses your nurses.
They will [b]bow down to you with their faces to the earth
And [c]lick the dust of your feet;
And *you* will [d]know that I am the LORD;
Those who hopefully [e]wait for Me will [f]not be put to shame.

24 [1]So ancient versions and DSS; M.T. reads *the righteous,* cf v 25 [a]Matt 12:29; Luke 11:21

24 "[a]Can the prey be taken from the mighty man,
Or the captives of [1]a tyrant be rescued?"

25 Surely, thus says the LORD,
"Even the [a]captives of the mighty man will be taken away,
And the prey of the tyrant will be rescued;
For I will contend with the one who contends with you,
And I will [b]save your sons.
26 "I will feed your [a]oppressors with their [b]own flesh,
And they will become drunk with their own blood as with sweet wine;
And [c]all flesh will know that I, the LORD, am your [d]Savior
And your [e]Redeemer, the Mighty One of Jacob."

Chapter 50 Theme ______________________

50 Thus says the LORD,
"Where is the [a]certificate of divorce
By which I have [b]sent your mother away?
Or to whom of My creditors did I [c]sell you?
Behold, you were sold for your [d]iniquities,
And for your [e]transgressions your mother [f]was sent away.
2 "Why was there [a]no man when I came?
When I called, *why* was there none to answer?
Is My [b]hand so short that it cannot ransom?
Or have I no power to deliver?
Behold, I [c]dry up the sea with My rebuke,
I [d]make the rivers a wilderness;
Their fish stink for lack of water
And die of thirst.
3 "I [a]clothe the heavens with blackness
And make sackcloth their covering."

4 The Lord [1]GOD has given Me the tongue of [a]disciples,
That I may know how to [b]sustain the weary one with a word.
He awakens *Me* [c]morning by morning,
He awakens My ear to listen as a disciple.
5 The Lord GOD has [a]opened My ear;
And I was [b]not disobedient
Nor did I turn back.
6 I [a]gave My back to those who strike *Me,*
And My cheeks to those who pluck out the beard;
I did not cover My face from humiliation and spitting.
7 For the Lord GOD [a]helps Me,
Therefore, I am [b]not disgraced;
Therefore, I have set My face like [c]flint,
And I know that I will not be ashamed.
8 He who [a]vindicates Me is near;
Who will contend with Me?
Let us [b]stand up to each other;
Who has a case against Me?
Let him draw near to Me.
9 Behold, [a]the Lord GOD helps Me;

25 [a]Is 10:6; 14:1, 2; Jer 50:33, 34 [b]Is 25:9; 33:22; 35:4

26 [a]Is 9:4; 14:4; 16:4; 51:13; 54:14 [b]Is 9:20 [c]Is 45:6; Ezek 39:7 [d]Is 43:3 [e]Is 49:7

50:1 [a]Deut 24:1, 3; Jer 3:8 [b]Is 54:6, 7 [c]Deut 32:30; 2 Kin 4:1; Neh 5:5 [d]Is 52:3; 59:2 [e]Is 1:28; 43:27 [f]Jer 3:8

2 [a]Is 41:28; 59:16; 66:4 [b]Gen 18:14; Num 11:23; Is 59:1 [c]Ex 14:21; Is 19:5; 43:16; 44:27 [d]Josh 3:16; Is 42:15

3 [a]Is 13:10; Rev 6:12

4 [1]Heb *YHWH,* usually rendered *LORD,* and so throughout the ch [a]Is 8:16; 54:13 [b]Is 57:19; Jer 31:25 [c]Ps 5:3; 88:13; 119:147; 143:8

5 [a]Ps 40:6; Is 35:5 [b]Matt 26:39; John 8:29; 14:31; 15:10; Acts 26:19; Phil 2:8; Heb 5:8; 10:7

6 [a]Matt 26:67; 27:30; Mark 14:65; 15:19; Luke 22:63

7 [a]Is 42:1; 49:8 [b]Is 45:17; 54:4 [c]Ezek 3:8, 9

8 [a]Is 45:25; Rom 8:33, 34 [b]Is 1:18; 41:1; 43:26

9 [a]Is 41:10

9 [b]Is 54:17 [c]Job 13:28; Is 51:8

[b]Who is he who condemns Me?
Behold, [c]they will all wear out like a garment;
The moth will eat them.

10 [a]Is 49:2, 3; 50:4 [b]Is 9:2; 26:9; Eph 5:8 [c]Is 12:2; 26:4

10 Who is among you that fears the LORD,
That obeys the voice of His [a]servant,
That [b]walks in darkness and has no light?
Let him [c]trust in the name of the LORD and rely
on his God.

11 [1]Lit *gird* [a]Prov 26:18; Is 9:18; James 3:6 [b]Is 8:22; 65:13-15; Amos 4:9, 10

11 Behold, all you who [a]kindle a fire,
Who [1]encircle yourselves with firebrands,
Walk in the light of your fire
And among the brands you have set ablaze.
This you will have from My hand:
You will [b]lie down in torment.

Chapter 51 Theme ______________________________

51:1 [1]Lit *excavation of a pit* [a]Is 46:3; 48:12; 51:7 [b]Ps 94:15; Prov 15:9 [c]Gen 17:15-17

51 "[a]Listen to me, you who [b]pursue righteousness,
Who seek the LORD:
Look to the [c]rock from which you were hewn
And to the [1]quarry from which you were dug.

2 [a]Is 29:22; 41:8; 63:16 [b]Gen 12:1; 15:5; Deut 1:10; Ezek 33:24

2 "Look to [a]Abraham your father
And to Sarah who gave birth to you in pain;
When *he* [b]*was but* one I called him,
Then I blessed him and multiplied him."

3 [a]Is 40:1; 49:13 [b]Is 52:9 [c]Is 35:1; 41:19 [d]Gen 2:8; Joel 2:3 [e]Gen 13:10 [f]Is 25:9; 41:16; 65:18; 66:10

3 Indeed, [a]the LORD will comfort Zion;
He will comfort all her [b]waste places.
And her [c]wilderness He will make like [d]Eden,
And her desert like the [e]garden of the LORD;
[f]Joy and gladness will be found in her,
Thanksgiving and sound of a melody.

4 [1]Or *people* [2]Lit *cause to rest* [a]Ps 50:7; 78:1 [b]Deut 18:18; Is 2:3; Mic 4:2 [c]Is 1:27; 42:4 [d]Is 42:6; 49:6

4 "[a]Pay attention to Me, O My people,
And give ear to Me, O My [1]nation;
For a [b]law will go forth from Me,
And I will [2]set My [c]justice for a [d]light of
the peoples.

5 [a]Is 46:13; 54:17 [b]Is 40:10 [c]Is 42:4; 60:9 [d]Is 59:16; 63:5

5 "My [a]righteousness is near, My salvation has
gone forth,
And My [b]arms will judge the peoples;
The [c]coastlands will wait for Me,
And for My [d]arm they will wait expectantly.

6 [1]Or *like gnats* [2]Lit *be broken* [a]Is 40:26 [b]Ps 102:25, 26; Is 13:13; 34:4; Matt 24:35; Heb 1:10-12; 2 Pet 3:10 [c]Is 45:17; 51:8

6 "[a]Lift up your eyes to the sky,
Then look to the earth beneath;
For the [b]sky will vanish like smoke,
And the [b]earth will wear out like a garment
And its inhabitants will die [1]in like manner;
But My [c]salvation will be forever,
And My righteousness will not [2]wane.

7 [a]Is 51:1 [b]Ps 37:31

7 "[a]Listen to Me, you who know righteousness,
A people in whose [b]heart is My law;

Do not fear the [c]reproach of man,
Nor be dismayed at their revilings.
8 "For the [a]moth will eat them like a garment,
And the [b]grub will eat them like wool.
But My [c]righteousness will be forever,
And My salvation to all generations."

9 [a]Awake, awake, put on strength, O arm of the LORD;
Awake as in the [b]days of old, the generations of long ago.
[c]Was it not You who cut Rahab in pieces,
Who pierced the [d]dragon?
10 Was it not You who [a]dried up the sea,
The waters of the great deep;
Who made the depths of the sea a pathway
For the [b]redeemed to cross over?
11 So the [a]ransomed of the LORD will return
And come with joyful shouting to Zion,
And [b]everlasting joy *will be* on their heads.
They will obtain gladness and joy,
And [c]sorrow and sighing will flee away.

12 "I, even I, am He who [a]comforts you.
Who are you that you are afraid of [b]man who dies
And of the son of man who is made [c]like grass,
13 That you have [a]forgotten the LORD your Maker,
Who [b]stretched out the heavens
And laid the foundations of the earth,
That you [c]fear continually all day long because of the fury
of the oppressor,
As he makes ready to destroy?
But where is the fury of the [d]oppressor?
14 "The [1a]exile will soon be set free, and will not die in the
dungeon, [b]nor will his bread be lacking.
15 "For I am the LORD your God, who [a]stirs up the sea and its
waves roar (the LORD of hosts is His name).
16 "I have [a]put My words in your mouth and have [b]covered
you with the shadow of My hand, to [1c]establish the heavens, to
found the earth, and to say to Zion, 'You are My people.'"
17 [a]Rouse yourself! Rouse yourself! Arise, O Jerusalem,
You who have [b]drunk from the LORD's hand the cup of
His anger;
The [1]chalice of reeling you have [2]drained to the dregs.
18 There is [a]none to guide her among all the sons she has
borne,
Nor is there one to take her by the hand among all the
sons she has reared.
19 These two things have befallen you;
Who will mourn for you?
The [a]devastation and destruction, famine and sword;
How shall I comfort you?
20 Your sons have fainted,

7 [c]Is 25:8; 54:4; Matt 5:11; Acts 5:41

8 [a]Is 50:9 [b]Is 14:11; 66:24 [c]Is 51:6

9 [a]Is 51:17; 52:1 [b]Ex 6:6; Deut 4:34 [c]Job 26:12; Ps 89:10; Is 30:7 [d]Ps 74:13; Is 27:1

10 [a]Is 11:15, 16; 50:2; 63:11, 12 [b]Ex 15:13; Ps 106:10; Is 63:9

11 [a]Is 35:10; Jer 31:11, 12 [b]Is 60:19; 61:7 [c]Is 25:8; 60:20; 65:19; Rev 7:17; 21:1, 4; 22:3

12 [a]Is 51:3 [b]Ps 118:6; Is 2:22 [c]Is 40:6, 7; 1 Pet 1:24

13 [a]Deut 6:12; 8:11; Is 17:10 [b]Job 9:8; Ps 104:2; Is 40:22; 45:12, 18; 48:13 [c]Is 7:4; 10:24 [d]Is 49:26; 54:14

14 [1]Lit *one in chains* [a]Is 48:20; 52:2 [b]Is 33:6; 49:10

15 [a]Ps 107:25; Jer 31:35

16 [1]Lit *plant* [a]Deut 18:18; Is 59:21 [b]Ex 33:22; Is 49:2 [c]Is 66:22

17 [1]Lit *bowl of the cup of reeling* [2]Lit *drunk* [a]Is 51:9; 52:1 [b]Job 21:20; Is 29:9; 63:6; Jer 25:15; Rev 14:10; 16:19

18 [a]Ps 88:18; 142:4; Is 49:21

19 [a]Is 8:21; 9:20; 14:30

They [a]lie *helpless* at the head of every street,
Like an [b]antelope in a net,
Full of the wrath of the LORD,
The [c]rebuke of your God.

21 Therefore, please hear this, you [a]afflicted,
Who are [b]drunk, but not with wine:
22 Thus says your Lord, the LORD, even your God
Who [a]contends for His people,
"Behold, I have taken out of your hand the [b]cup of reeling,
The [1]chalice of My anger;
You will never drink it again.
23 "I will [a]put it into the hand of your tormentors,
Who have said to [1]you, '[b]Lie down that we may walk
over *you.*'
You have even made your back like the ground
And like the street for those who walk over *it.*"

Chapter 52 Theme ______________________

52

[a]Awake, awake,
Clothe yourself in your strength, O Zion;
Clothe yourself in your [b]beautiful garments,
O Jerusalem, the [c]holy city;
For the uncircumcised and the [d]unclean
Will no longer come into you.
2 Shake yourself [a]from the dust, [b]rise up,
O captive Jerusalem;
[c]Loose yourself from the chains around your neck,
O captive daughter of Zion.
3 For thus says the LORD, "You were [a]sold for nothing and
you will be [b]redeemed [c]without money."
4 For thus says the Lord [1]GOD, "My people [a]went down at
the first into Egypt to reside there; then the Assyrian oppressed
them without cause.
5 "Now therefore, what do I have here," declares the LORD,
"seeing that My people have been taken away without cause?"
Again the LORD declares, "Those who rule over them howl,
and My [a]name is continually blasphemed all day long.
6 "Therefore My people shall [a]know My name; therefore in
that day I am the one who is speaking, 'Here I am.'"
7 How lovely on the mountains
Are the feet of him who brings [a]good news,
Who announces [1]peace
And brings good news of [2]happiness,
Who announces salvation,
And says to Zion, "Your [b]God [3]reigns!"
8 Listen! Your watchmen lift up *their* [a]voices,
They shout joyfully together;
For they will see [1]with their own eyes
When the LORD restores Zion.

20 [a]Is 5:25; Jer 14:16 [b]Deut 14:5 [c]Is 66:15

21 [a]Is 54:11 [b]Is 29:9; 51:17; 63:6

22 [1]Lit *bowl of the cup of* [a]Is 3:12, 13; 49:25; Jer 50:34 [b]Is 51:17

23 [1]Lit *your soul* [a]Is 49:26; Jer 25:15-17, 26, 28; Zech 12:2 [b]Josh 10:24

52:1 [a]Is 51:9, 17 [b]Ex 28:2, 40; 1 Chr 16:29; Ps 110:3; Is 49:18; 61:3, 10; Zech 3:4 [c]Neh 11:1; Is 48:2; 64:10; Zech 14:20, 21; Matt 4:5; Rev 21:2-27 [d]Is 35:8

2 [a]Is 29:4 [b]Is 60:1 [c]Is 9:4; 10:27; 14:25; Zech 2:7

3 [a]Ps 44:12; Jer 15:13 [b]Is 1:27; 62:12; 63:4 [c]Is 45:13

4 [1]Heb *YHWH,* usually rendered *LORD* [a]Gen 46:6

5 [a]Ezek 36:20, 23; Rom 2:24

6 [a]Is 49:23

7 [1]Or *well-being* [2]Lit *good* [3]Or *is King* [a]Is 40:9; 61:1; Nah 1:15; Rom 10:15; Eph 6:15 [b]Ps 93:1; Is 24:23

8 [1]Lit *eye to eye* [a]Is 62:6

9 [a]Break forth, shout joyfully together,
You [b]waste places of Jerusalem;
For the LORD has comforted His people,
He has [c]redeemed Jerusalem.
10 The LORD has bared His holy [a]arm
In the sight of all the nations,
[1]That [b]all the ends of the earth may see
The salvation of our God.

11 [a]Depart, depart, go out from there,
[b]Touch nothing unclean;
Go out of the midst of her, [c]purify yourselves,
You who carry the vessels of the LORD.
12 But you will not go out in [a]haste,
Nor will you go [1]as fugitives;
For the [b]LORD will go before you,
And [c]the God of Israel *will be* your rear guard.

13 Behold, My [a]servant will prosper,
He will be high and lifted up and [1]greatly [b]exalted.
14 Just as many were astonished at you, *My people,*
So His [a]appearance was marred more than any man
And His form more than the sons of men.
15 Thus He will [a]sprinkle many nations,
Kings will [b]shut their mouths on account of Him;
For [c]what had not been told them they will see,
And what they had not heard they will understand.

Chapter 53 Theme ______________________

53 [a]Who has believed our message?
And to whom has the arm of the LORD been revealed?
2 For He grew up before Him like a [a]tender [1]shoot,
And like a root out of parched ground;
He has [b]no *stately* form or majesty
That we should look upon Him,
Nor appearance that we should [2]be attracted to Him.
3 He was [a]despised and forsaken of men,
A man of [1]sorrows and [b]acquainted with [2]grief;
And like one from whom men hide their face
He was [c]despised, and we did not [d]esteem Him.

4 Surely our [1]griefs He Himself [a]bore,
And our [2]sorrows He carried;
Yet we ourselves esteemed Him stricken,
[3]Smitten of [b]God, and afflicted.
5 But He was [1]pierced through for [a]our transgressions,
He was crushed for [b]our iniquities;
The [c]chastening for our [2]well-being *fell* upon Him,
And by [d]His scourging we are healed.

9 [a]Ps 98:4; Is 44:23 [b]Is 44:26; 51:3; 61:4 [c]Is 43:1; 48:20

10 [1]Lit *And . . . earth will see* [a]Ps 98:1-3; Is 51:9; 66:18, 19 [b]Is 45:22; 48:20

11 [a]Is 48:20; Jer 50:8; Zech 2:6, 7; 2 Cor 6:17 [b]Num 19:11, 16 [c]Lev 22:2; Is 1:16

12 [1]Lit *in flight* [a]Ex 12:11, 33; Deut 16:3 [b]Is 26:7; 42:16; 49:10, 11 [c]Ex 14:19, 20; Is 58:8

13 [1]Or *very high* [a]Is 42:1; 49:1-7; 53:11 [b]Is 57:15; Phil 2:9

14 [a]Is 53:2, 3

15 [a]Num 19:18-21; Ezek 36:25 [b]Job 21:5 [c]Rom 15:21; Eph 3:5

53:1 [a]John 12:38; Rom 10:16

2 [1]Lit *suckling* [2]Lit *desire* [a]Is 11:1 [b]Is 52:14

3 [1]Or *pains* [2]Or *sickness* [a]Ps 22:6; Is 49:7; Luke 18:31-33 [b]Is 53:10 [c]Mark 10:33, 34 [d]John 1:10, 11

4 [1]Or *sickness* [2]Or *pains* [3]Or *Struck down by* [a]Matt 8:17 [b]John 19:7

5 [1]Or *wounded* [2]Or *peace* [a]Is 53:8; Heb 9:28 [b]Is 53:10; Rom 4:25; 1 Cor 15:3 [c]Deut 11:2; Heb 5:8 [d]1 Pet 2:24, 25

6 [1]Lit *encounter Him*

7 [a]Matt 26:63; 27:12-14; Mark 14:61; 15:5; Luke 23:9; John 19:9 [b]Acts 8:32, 33; Rev 5:6

8 [1]Or *life* [a]Is 53:5, 12

9 [a]Matt 27:57-60 [b]Is 42:1-3 [c]1 Pet 2:22

10 [1]Lit *He made Him sick* [2]Lit *His soul* [3]Lit *seed* [4]Or *will of* [a]Is 53:5 [b]Is 53:3, 4 [c]Is 53:6, 12; John 1:29 [d]Ps 22:30; Is 54:3; 61:9; 66:22 [e]Is 46:10

11 [1]Or *toilsome labor* [2]Another reading is *light* [a]John 10:14-18 [b]Is 45:25; Rom 5:18, 19 [c]Is 53:5, 6

12 [1]Lit *His soul* [a]Is 52:13; Phil 2:9-11 [b]Matt 26:38, 39, 42 [c]Mark 15:28; Luke 22:37 [d]Is 53:6, 11; 2 Cor 5:21

54:1 [a]Gal 4:27 [b]Is 62:4 [c]1 Sam 2:5; Is 49:20

2 [1]Lit *Let them stretch out* [a]Is 33:20; 49:19, 20 [b]Ex 35:18; 39:40

6 All of us like sheep have gone astray,
Each of us has turned to his own way;
But the LORD has caused the iniquity of us all
To [1]fall on Him.

7 He was oppressed and He was afflicted,
Yet He did not [a]open His mouth;
[b]Like a lamb that is led to slaughter,
And like a sheep that is silent before its shearers,
So He did not open His mouth.
8 By oppression and judgment He was taken away;
And as for His generation, who considered
That He was cut off out of the land of the [1]living
[a]For the transgression of my people, to whom the stroke *was due?*
9 His grave was assigned with wicked men,
Yet He was with a [a]rich man in His death,
[b]Because He had [c]done no violence,
Nor was there any deceit in His mouth.

10 But the LORD was pleased
To [a]crush Him, [1b]putting *Him* to grief;
If [2]He would render Himself *as* a guilt [c]offering,
He will see [d]*His* [3]offspring,
He will prolong *His* days,
And the [4]good [e]pleasure of the LORD will prosper in His hand.
11 As a result of the [1]anguish of His soul,
He will [a]see [2]*it and* be satisfied;
By His [b]knowledge the Righteous One,
My Servant, will justify the many,
As He will [c]bear their iniquities.
12 Therefore, I will allot Him a [a]portion with the great,
And He will divide the booty with the strong;
Because He poured out [1b]Himself to death,
And was [c]numbered with the transgressors;
Yet He Himself [d]bore the sin of many,
And interceded for the transgressors.

Chapter 54 Theme ______________________

54

"[a]Shout for joy, O barren one, you who have borne no *child;*
Break forth into joyful shouting and cry aloud, you who have not travailed;
For the sons of the [b]desolate one *will be* [c]more numerous
Than the sons of the married woman," says the LORD.
2 "[a]Enlarge the place of your tent;
[1]Stretch out the curtains of your dwellings, spare not;
Lengthen your [b]cords
And strengthen your [b]pegs.

3 "For you will [a]spread abroad to the right and to the left.
And your [1]descendants will [b]possess nations
And will [c]resettle the desolate cities.

4 "Fear not, for you will [a]not be put to shame;
And do not feel humiliated, for you will not be disgraced;
But you will forget the [b]shame of your youth,
And the [c]reproach of your widowhood you will remember
no more.
5 "For your [a]husband is your Maker,
Whose name is the LORD of hosts;
And your [b]Redeemer is the Holy One of Israel,
Who is called the [c]God of all the earth.
6 "For the LORD has called you,
Like a wife [a]forsaken and grieved in spirit,
Even like a wife of *one's* youth when she is rejected,"
Says your God.
7 "[1]For a [a]brief moment I forsook you,
But with great compassion I will [b]gather you.
8 "In an [1a]outburst of anger
I hid My face from you for a moment,
But with everlasting [b]lovingkindness I will [c]have
compassion on you,"
Says the LORD your [d]Redeemer.

9 "For [1]this is like the days of Noah to Me,
When I swore that the waters of Noah
Would [a]not [2]flood the earth again;
So I have sworn that I will [b]not be angry with you
Nor will I rebuke you.
10 "For the [a]mountains may be removed and the hills
may shake,
But My lovingkindness will not be removed from you,
And My [b]covenant of peace will not be shaken,"
Says [c]the LORD who has compassion on you.

11 "O [a]afflicted one, storm-tossed, *and* [b]not comforted,
Behold, I will set your stones in antimony,
And your foundations I will [c]lay in [1d]sapphires.
12 "Moreover, I will make your battlements of [1]rubies,
And your gates of [2]crystal,
And your entire [3]wall of precious stones.
13 "[a]All your sons will be [1]taught of the LORD;
And the well-being of your sons will be [b]great.
14 "In [a]righteousness you will be established;
You will be far from [b]oppression, for you will [c]not fear;
And from [d]terror, for it will not come near you.
15 "If anyone fiercely assails *you* it will not be from Me.
[a]Whoever assails you will fall because of you.
16 "Behold, I Myself have created the smith who blows
the fire of coals

3 [1]Lit *seed* [a]Gen 28:14; Is 43:5, 6; 60:3 [b]Is 14:1, 2 [c]Is 49:19

4 [a]Is 45:17 [b]Jer 31:19 [c]Is 4:1; 25:8; 51:7

5 [a]Jer 3:14; Hos 2:19 [b]Is 43:14; 48:17 [c]Is 6:3; 11:9; 65:16

6 [a]Is 49:14-21; 50:1, 2; 62:4

7 [1]Lit *In* [a]Is 26:20 [b]Is 11:12; 43:5; 49:18

8 [1]Lit *overflowing* [a]Is 60:10 [b]Is 54:10; 63:7 [c]Is 49:10, 13 [d]Is 54:5

9 [1]Some mss read *the waters of Noah this is to Me* [2]Lit *cross over* [a]Gen 9:11 [b]Is 12:1; Ezek 39:29

10 [a]Ps 102:26; Is 51:6 [b]2 Sam 23:5; Ps 89:34; Is 55:3; 59:21; 61:8 [c]Is 54:8

11 [1]Or *lapis lazuli* [a]Is 51:21 [b]Is 51:18, 19 [c]Is 14:32; 28:16; 44:28 [d]Job 28:16; Rev 21:19

12 [1]I.e. bright red [2]Or *carbuncles* [3]Lit *border, boundary*

13 [1]Or *disciples* [a]John 6:45 [b]Is 48:18; 66:12

14 [a]Is 1:26, 27; 9:7; 62:1 [b]Is 9:4; 14:4 [c]Is 54:4 [d]Is 33:18

15 [a]Is 41:11-16

And brings out a weapon for its work;
And I have created the destroyer to ruin.
17 “[a]No weapon that is formed against you will prosper;
And [b]every tongue that [1]accuses you in judgment you
will condemn.
This is the heritage of the servants of the LORD,
And their [c]vindication is from Me,” declares the LORD.

Chapter 55 Theme ____

55 “Ho! Every one who [a]thirsts, come to the waters;
And you who have [b]no [1]money come, buy and eat.
Come, buy [c]wine and milk
[d]Without money and without cost.
2 “Why do you [1]spend money for what is [a]not bread,
And your wages for what does not satisfy?
Listen carefully to Me, and [b]eat what is good,
And [c]delight yourself in abundance.
3 “[a]Incline your ear and come to Me.
Listen, that [1]you may [b]live;
And I will make [c]an everlasting covenant with you,
According to the [d]faithful mercies [2]shown to David.
4 “Behold, I have made [a]him a witness to the peoples,
A [b]leader and commander for the peoples.
5 “Behold, you will call a [a]nation you do not know,
And a nation which knows you not will [b]run to you,
Because of the LORD your God, even the Holy One
of Israel;
For He has [c]glorified you.”

6 [a]Seek the LORD while He may be found;
[b]Call upon Him while He is near.
7 [a]Let the wicked forsake his way
And the unrighteous man his [b]thoughts;
And let him [c]return to the LORD,
And He will have [d]compassion on him,
And to our God,
For He will [e]abundantly pardon.
8 “For My thoughts are not [a]your thoughts,
Nor are [b]your ways My ways,” declares the LORD.
9 “For [a]*as* the heavens are higher than the earth,
So are My ways higher than your ways
And My thoughts than your thoughts.
10 “For as the [a]rain and the snow come down from heaven,
And do not return there without watering the earth
And making it bear and sprout,
And furnishing [b]seed to the sower and bread
to the eater;
11 So will My [a]word be which goes forth from My mouth;
It will [b]not return to Me empty,
Without [c]accomplishing what I desire,

17 [1]Lit *rises against* [a]Is 17:12-14; 29:8 [b]Is 50:8, 9 [c]Is 45:24; 46:13

55:1 [1]Lit *silver* [a]Ps 42:1, 2; 63:1; 143:6; Is 41:17; 44:3; John 4:14; 7:37; Rev 21:6 [b]Lam 5:4 [c]Song 5:1; Joel 3:18 [d]Hos 14:4; Matt 10:8

2 [1]Lit *weigh out silver* [a]Eccl 6:2; Hos 8:7 [b]Ps 22:26; Is 1:19; 62:8, 9 [c]Is 25:6; Jer 31:14

3 [1]Lit *your soul* [2]Lit *of David* [a]Is 51:4 [b]Lev 18:5; Rom 10:5 [c]Is 61:8 [d]Acts 13:34

4 [a]Ps 18:43; Jer 30:9; Hos 3:5 [b]Ezek 34:24; 37:24, 25; Dan 9:25; Mic 5:2

5 [a]Is 45:14, 22-24; 49:6, 12, 23 [b]Zech 8:22 [c]Is 60:9

6 [a]Ps 32:6; Is 45:19, 22; 49:8; Amos 5:6 [b]Is 58:9; 65:24

7 [a]Is 1:16, 19; 58:6 [b]Is 32:7; 59:7 [c]Is 31:6; 44:22 [d]Is 14:1; 54:8, 10 [e]Is 1:18; 40:2; 43:25; 44:22

8 [a]Is 65:2; 66:18 [b]Is 53:6

9 [a]Ps 103:11

10 [a]Is 30:23 [b]2 Cor 9:10

11 [a]Is 45:23; Matt 24:35 [b]Is 44:26; 59:21 [c]Is 46:10; 53:10

And without succeeding *in the matter* for which I sent it.
12 "For you will go out with [a]joy
And be led forth with [b]peace;
The [c]mountains and the hills will break forth into shouts of joy before you,
And all the [d]trees of the field will clap *their* hands.
13 "Instead of the [a]thorn bush the [b]cypress will come up,
And instead of the [c]nettle the myrtle will come up,
And [1]it will be a [2d]memorial to the LORD,
For an everlasting [e]sign which [f]will not be cut off."

12 [a]Ps 105:43; Is 51:11; 52:9 [b]Is 54:10, 13; Jer 29:11 [c]Is 44:23; 49:13 [d]1 Chr 16:33

13 [1]I.e. the transformation of the desert [2]Lit *name* [a]Is 7:19 [b]Is 60:13 [c]Is 5:6; 7:24; 32:13 [d]Is 63:12, 14; Jer 33:9 [e]Is 19:20 [f]Is 56:5

Chapter 56 Theme ____________________

56 Thus says the LORD,
"[a]Preserve justice and do righteousness,
For My [b]salvation is about to come
And My righteousness to be revealed.
2 "How [a]blessed is the man who does this,
And the son of man who [b]takes hold of it;
Who [c]keeps from profaning the sabbath,
And keeps his hand from doing any evil."
3 Let not the [a]foreigner who has joined himself to the LORD say,
"The LORD will surely separate me from His people."
Nor let the [b]eunuch say, "Behold, I am a dry tree."
4 For thus says the LORD,
"To the eunuchs who [a]keep My sabbaths,
And choose what pleases Me,
And [b]hold fast My covenant,
5 To them I will give in My [a]house and within My [b]walls a memorial,
And a name better than that of sons and daughters;
I will give [1]them an everlasting [c]name which [d]will not be cut off.

6 "Also the [a]foreigners who join themselves to the LORD,
To minister to Him, and to love the name of the LORD,
To be His servants, every one who [b]keeps from profaning the sabbath
And holds fast My covenant;
7 Even [a]those I will bring to My [b]holy mountain
And [c]make them joyful in My house of prayer.
Their burnt offerings and their sacrifices will be acceptable on [d]My altar;
For [e]My house will be called a house of prayer for all the peoples."
8 The Lord [1]GOD, who [a]gathers the dispersed of Israel, declares,
"Yet [b]*others* I will gather to [2]them, to those *already* gathered."

56:1 [a]Is 1:17; 33:5; 61:8 [b]Ps 85:9; Is 46:13; 51:5

2 [a]Ps 112:1; 119:1, 2 [b]Is 56:4, 6 [c]Ex 20:8-11; 31:13-17; Is 56:6; 58:13; Jer 17:21, 22; Ezek 20:12, 20

3 [a]Is 14:1; 56:6 [b]Deut 23:1; Jer 38:7; Acts 8:27

4 [a]Is 56:2, 6 [b]Is 56:6

5 [1]So DSS; M.T. reads *him* [a]Is 2:2, 3; 56:7; 66:20 [b]Is 26:1; 60:18 [c]Is 62:2 [d]Is 48:19; 55:13

6 [a]Is 56:3; 60:10; 61:5 [b]Is 56:2, 4

7 [a]Is 2:2, 3; 60:11; Mic 4:1, 2 [b]Is 11:9; 65:25 [c]Is 61:10 [d]Is 60:7 [e]Matt 21:13; Mark 11:17; Luke 19:46

8 [1]Heb *YHWH,* usually rendered LORD [2]Lit *him* [a]Is 11:12 [b]Is 60:3-11; 66:18-21; John 10:16

9 All you [a]beasts of the field,
All you beasts in the forest,
Come to eat.
10 His [a]watchmen are [b]blind,
All of them know nothing.
All of them are mute dogs unable to bark,
[1]Dreamers lying down, who love to slumber;
11 And the dogs are [1a]greedy, they [2]are not satisfied.
And they are shepherds who have [b]no understanding;
They have all [c]turned to their own way,
Each one to his unjust gain, to the last one.
12 "Come," *they say*, "let [1]us get [a]wine, and let us drink
heavily of strong drink;
And [b]tomorrow will be like today, only more so."

Chapter 57 Theme ______

57 The righteous man perishes, and no man [a]takes it
to heart;
And devout men are taken away, while no one
understands.
For the righteous man is taken away from [b]evil,
2 He enters into peace;
They rest in their [1]beds,
Each one who [a]walked in his upright way.
3 "But come here, you sons of a [a]sorceress,
[b]Offspring of an adulterer and [1]a [c]prostitute.
4 "Against whom do you jest?
Against whom do you open wide your mouth
And stick out your tongue?
Are you not children of [a]rebellion,
Offspring of deceit,
5 *Who* inflame yourselves among the [1a]oaks,
[b]Under every luxuriant tree,
Who [c]slaughter the children in the [2]ravines,
Under the clefts of the crags?
6 "Among the [1a]smooth *stones* of the [2]ravine
Is your portion, [3]they are your lot;
Even to them you have [b]poured out a drink offering,
You have made a grain offering.
Shall I [4c]relent concerning these things?
7 "Upon a [a]high and lofty mountain
You have [b]made your bed.
You also went up there to offer sacrifice.
8 "Behind the door and the doorpost
You have set up your sign;
Indeed, far removed from Me, you have
[a]uncovered yourself,
And have gone up and made your bed wide.
And you have made an agreement for yourself
with them,

9 [a]Is 18:6; 46:11

10 [1]So DSS; M.T. *Ravers* [a]Ezek 3:17 [b]Is 29:9-14; Jer 14:13, 14

11 [1]Lit *strong of soul/appetite* [2]Lit *do not know satisfaction* [a]Is 28:7; Ezek 13:19; Mic 3:5, 11 [b]Is 1:3 [c]Is 57:17; Jer 22:17

12 [1]So DSS and many versions; M.T. *me* [a]Is 5:11, 12, 22 [b]Ps 10:6; Luke 12:19, 20

57:1 [a]Is 42:25; 47:7 [b]2 Kin 22:20; Is 47:11; Jer 18:11

2 [1]I.e. graves [a]Is 26:7

3 [1]So ancient versions; Heb *she prostitutes herself* [a]Mal 3:5 [b]Is 1:4; Matt 16:4 [c]Is 1:21; 57:7-9

4 [a]Is 48:8

5 [1]Or *terebinths* [2]Or *wadis* [a]Is 1:29 [b]2 Kin 16:4; Jer 2:20; 3:13 [c]2 Kin 23:10; Ps 106:37, 38; Jer 7:31

6 [1]I.e. symbols of fertility gods [2]Or *wadi* [3]Lit *they, they* [4]Or *repent* [a]Jer 3:9; Hab 2:19 [b]Jer 7:18 [c]Jer 5:9, 29; 9:9

7 [a]Jer 3:6; Ezek 16:16 [b]Ezek 23:41

8 [a]Ezek 23:18

You have loved their [1]bed,
You have looked on *their* [2]manhood.
9 "You have journeyed to the king with oil
And increased your perfumes;
You have [a]sent your envoys a great distance
And made *them* go down to [1]Sheol.
10 "You were tired out by the length of your road,
Yet you did not say, '[a]It is hopeless.'
You found [1]renewed strength,
Therefore you did not [2]faint.

11 "Of [a]whom were you worried and fearful
When you lied, and did [b]not remember Me
[1]Nor [c]give *Me* a thought?
Was I not silent even for a long time
So you do not fear Me?
12 "I will [a]declare your righteousness and your [b]deeds,
But they will not profit you.
13 "When you cry out, [a]let your collection *of idols* deliver you.
But the wind will carry all of them up,
And a breath will take *them away.*
But he who [b]takes refuge in Me will [c]inherit the land
And will [d]possess My holy mountain."

14 And it will be said,
"[a]Build up, build up, prepare the way,
Remove *every* obstacle out of the way of My people."
15 For thus says the [a]high and exalted One
Who [1b]lives forever, whose name is Holy,
"I [c]dwell *on* a high and holy place,
And *also* with the [d]contrite and lowly of spirit
In order to [e]revive the spirit of the lowly
And to revive the heart of the contrite.
16 "For I will [a]not contend forever,
[b]Nor will I always be angry;
For the spirit would grow faint before Me,
And the [c]breath *of those whom* I have made.
17 "Because of the iniquity of his [a]unjust gain I was angry
and struck him;
I hid *My face* and was angry,
And he went on [b]turning away, in the way of his heart.
18 "I have seen his ways, but I will [a]heal him;
I will [b]lead him and [c]restore comfort to him and to
his mourners,
19 Creating the [1a]praise of the lips.
[b]Peace, peace to him who is [c]far and to him who is near,"
Says the LORD, "and I will heal him."
20 But the [a]wicked are like the tossing sea,
For it cannot be quiet,
And its waters toss up refuse and mud.
21 "[a]There is no peace," says [b]my God, "for the wicked."

8 [1]Or *lying down* [2]Lit *hand*

9 [1]I.e. the nether world [a]Ezek 23:16, 40

10 [1]Lit *the life of your hand* [2]Or *become sick* [a]Jer 2:25; 18:12

11 [1]Lit *You did not set it upon your heart* [a]Prov 29:25; Is 51:12, 13 [b]Jer 2:32; 3:21 [c]Ps 50:21; Is 42:14

12 [a]Is 58:1, 2 [b]Is 29:15; 59:6; 65:7; 66:18; Mic 3:2-4

13 [a]Jer 22:20; 30:14 [b]Ps 37:3, 9; Is 25:4 [c]Is 49:8; 60:21 [d]Is 65:9

14 [a]Is 62:10; Jer 18:15

15 [1]Or *dwells in eternity* [a]Is 52:13 [b]Deut 33:27; Is 40:28 [c]Is 33:5; 66:1 [d]Ps 34:18; 51:17; Is 66:2 [e]Ps 147:3; Is 61:1-3

16 [a]Gen 6:3 [b]Ps 85:5; 103:9; Mic 7:18 [c]Is 42:5

17 [a]Is 2:7; 56:11; Jer 6:13 [b]Is 1:4; Jer 3:14, 22

18 [a]Is 19:22; 30:26; 53:5 [b]Is 52:12 [c]Is 61:1-3

19 [1]Lit *fruit of the lips* [a]Is 6:7; 51:16; 59:21; Heb 13:15 [b]Is 26:12; 32:17 [c]Acts 2:39; Eph 2:17

20 [a]Job 18:5-14; Is 3:9, 11

21 [a]Is 48:22; 59:8 [b]Is 49:4

RETURN TO INSTRUCTIONS

Chapter 58 Theme ____________________

58 "[a]Cry loudly, do not hold back;
Raise your voice like a trumpet,
And declare to My people their [b]transgression
And to the house of Jacob their sins.
2 "Yet they [a]seek Me day by day and delight to know
My ways,
As a nation that has done [b]righteousness
And [c]has not forsaken the ordinance of their God.
They ask Me *for* just decisions,
They delight [d]in the nearness of God.
3 'Why have we [a]fasted and You do not see?
Why have we humbled ourselves and You do not [1]notice?'
Behold, on the [b]day of your fast you find *your* desire,
And drive hard all your workers.
4 "Behold, you fast for contention and [a]strife and to strike
with a wicked fist.
You do not fast like *you do* today to [b]make your voice heard
on high.
5 "Is it a fast like this which I choose, a day for a man to
humble himself?
Is it for bowing [1]one's head like a reed
And for spreading out [a]sackcloth and ashes as a bed?
Will you call this a fast, even an [b]acceptable day to
the LORD?
6 "Is this not the fast which I choose,
To [a]loosen the bonds of wickedness,
To undo the bands of the yoke,
And to [b]let the oppressed go free
And [c]break every yoke?
7 "Is it not to [a]divide your bread [1]with the hungry
And [b]bring the homeless poor into the house;
When you see the [c]naked, to cover him;
And not to [d]hide yourself from your own flesh?
8 "Then your [a]light will break out like the dawn,
And your [b]recovery will speedily spring forth;
And your [c]righteousness will go before you;
The glory of the [d]LORD will be your rear guard.
9 "Then you will [a]call, and the LORD will answer;
You will cry, and He will say, 'Here I am.'
If you [b]remove the yoke from your midst,
The [1c]pointing of the finger and [d]speaking wickedness,
10 And if you [1a]give yourself to the hungry
And satisfy the [2]desire of the afflicted,
Then your [b]light will rise in darkness
And your gloom *will become* like midday.
11 "And the [a]LORD will continually guide you,
And [b]satisfy your [1]desire in scorched places,
And [c]give strength to your bones;
And you will be like a [d]watered garden,
And like a [e]spring of water whose waters do not [2]fail.

58:1 [a]Is 40:6 [b]Is 43:27; 50:1; 59:12
2 [a]Is 1:11; Titus 1:16 [b]Is 48:1; Jer 7:9, 10 [c]Is 1:4, 28; 59:13 [d]Ps 119:151; Is 29:13; 57:3; James 4:8
3 [1]Lit *know* [a]Mal 3:14; Luke 18:12 [b]Is 22:12, 13; Zech 7:5, 6
4 [a]Is 3:14, 15; 59:6 [b]Is 1:15; 59:2; Joel 2:12-14
5 [1]Lit *his* [a]1 Kin 21:27 [b]Is 49:8; 61:2
6 [a]Neh 5:10-12; Jer 34:8 [b]Is 1:17 [c]Is 58:9
7 [1]Lit *for* [a]Job 31:19, 20; Is 58:10; Ezek 18:7, 16 [b]Is 16:3, 4; Heb 13:2 [c]Matt 25:35, 36; Luke 3:11 [d]Deut 22:1-4; Luke 10:31, 32
8 [a]Is 58:10 [b]Is 30:26; 33:24; Jer 30:17; 33:6 [c]Ps 85:13; Is 62:1 [d]Ex 14:19; Is 52:12
9 [1]Lit *sending out* [a]Ps 50:15; Is 55:6; 65:24 [b]Is 58:6 [c]Prov 6:13 [d]Ps 12:2; Is 59:13
10 [1]Lit *furnish* [2]Or *soul* [a]Deut 15:7; Is 58:7 [b]Job 11:17; Ps 37:6; Is 42:16; 58:8
11 [1]Or *soul* [2]Or *deceive* [a]Is 49:10; 57:18 [b]Ps 107:9; Is 41:17 [c]Is 66:14 [d]Song 4:15; Is 27:3; Jer 31:12 [e]John 4:14; 7:38

12 "Those from among you will [a]rebuild the ancient ruins;
You will [b]raise up the age-old foundations;
And you will be called the repairer of the [c]breach,
The restorer of the [1]streets in which to dwell.

13 "If because of the sabbath, you [a]turn your foot
From doing your *own* pleasure on My holy day,
And call the sabbath a [b]delight, the holy *day* of the LORD honorable,
And honor it, desisting from your [c]*own* ways,
From seeking your *own* pleasure
And [d]speaking *your own* word,
14 Then you will take [a]delight in the LORD,
And I will make you ride [b]on the heights of the earth;
And I will feed you *with* the heritage of Jacob your father,
For the [c]mouth of the LORD has spoken."

Chapter 59 Theme ______________________________

59 Behold, [a]the LORD's hand is not so short
That it cannot save;
[b]Nor is His ear so dull
That it cannot hear.
2 But your [a]iniquities have made a separation between you and your God,
And your sins have hidden *His* [1]face from you so that He does [b]not hear.
3 For your [a]hands are defiled with blood
And your fingers with iniquity;
Your lips have spoken [b]falsehood,
Your tongue mutters wickedness.
4 [a]No one sues righteously and [b]no one pleads [1]honestly.
They [c]trust in confusion and speak lies;
They [d]conceive mischief and bring forth iniquity.
5 They hatch adders' eggs and [a]weave the spider's web;
He who eats of their eggs dies,
And *from* that which is crushed a snake breaks forth.
6 Their webs will not become clothing,
Nor will they [a]cover themselves with their works;
Their [b]works are works of iniquity,
And an [c]act of violence is in their [1]hands.
7 [a]Their feet run to evil,
And they hasten to shed innocent blood;
[b]Their thoughts are thoughts of iniquity,
Devastation and destruction are in their highways.
8 They do not know the [a]way of peace,
And there is [b]no justice in their tracks;
They have made their paths crooked,
[c]Whoever treads on [1]them does not know peace.

9 Therefore [a]justice is far from us,

12 [1]Lit *paths* [a]Is 49:8; 61:4; Ezek 36:10 [b]Is 44:28 [c]Is 30:13; Amos 9:11

13 [a]Ex 31:16, 17; 35:2, 3; Is 56:2, 4, 6; Jer 17:21-27 [b]Ps 27:4; 42:4; 84:2, 10 [c]Is 55:8 [d]Is 59:13

14 [a]Job 22:26; Is 61:10 [b]Deut 32:13; 33:29; Is 33:16; Hab 3:19 [c]Is 1:20; 40:5

59:1 [a]Num 11:23; Is 50:2; Jer 32:17 [b]Is 58:9; 65:24; Ezek 8:18

2 [1]So versions; M.T. *faces* [a]Is 1:15; 50:1 [b]Is 58:4

3 [a]Is 1:15, 21; Jer 2:30, 34; Ezek 7:23; Hos 4:2 [b]Is 28:15; 30:9; 59:13

4 [1]Lit *in truth* [a]Is 5:7; 59:14 [b]Is 59:14, 15 [c]Is 30:12; Jer 7:4, 8 [d]Job 15:35; Ps 7:14; Is 33:11

5 [a]Job 8:14

6 [1]Lit *palms* [a]Is 28:20 [b]Is 57:12; Jer 6:7 [c]Is 58:4; Ezek 7:11

7 [a]Prov 1:16; 6:17; Rom 3:15-17 [b]Is 65:2; 66:18; Mark 7:21, 22

8 [1]Lit *it* [a]Luke 1:79 [b]Is 59:9, 11; Hos 4:1 [c]Is 57:20, 21

9 [a]Is 59:14

And righteousness does not overtake us;
We [b]hope for light, but behold, darkness,
For brightness, but we walk in gloom.
10 We [a]grope along the wall like blind men,
We grope like those who have no eyes;
We [b]stumble at midday as in the twilight,
Among those who are vigorous *we are* [c]like dead men.
11 All of us growl like bears,
And [a]moan sadly like doves;
We hope for [b]justice, but there is none,
For salvation, *but* it is far from us.
12 For our [a]transgressions are multiplied before You,
And our [b]sins [1]testify against us;
For our transgressions are with us,
And [2]we know our iniquities:
13 Transgressing and [a]denying the LORD,
And turning away from our God,
Speaking [b]oppression and revolt,
Conceiving *in* and [c]uttering from the heart lying words.
14 [a]Justice is turned back,
And [b]righteousness stands far away;
For truth has stumbled in the street,
And uprightness cannot enter.

15 Yes, truth is lacking;
And he who turns aside from evil [a]makes himself a prey.
Now the LORD saw,
And it was [1]displeasing in His sight [b]that there was no justice.
16 And He saw that there was [a]no man,
And was astonished that there was no one to intercede;
Then His [b]own arm brought salvation to Him,
And His righteousness upheld Him.
17 He put on [a]righteousness like a breastplate,
And a [b]helmet of salvation on His head;
And He put on [c]garments of vengeance for clothing
And wrapped Himself with [d]zeal as a mantle.
18 [a]According to *their* [1]deeds, [2]so He will repay,
Wrath to His adversaries, recompense to His enemies;
To the coastlands He will [3]make recompense.
19 So they will fear the name of the LORD from the [a]west
And His glory from the [b]rising of the sun,
For He will [c]come like a [1]rushing stream
Which the wind of the LORD drives.
20 "A [a]Redeemer will come to Zion,
And to those who [b]turn from transgression in Jacob,"
declares the LORD.

21 "As for Me, this is My [a]covenant with them," says the LORD:
"My [b]Spirit which is upon you, and My [c]words which I have
put in your mouth shall not depart from your mouth, nor from
the mouth of your [1]offspring, nor from the mouth of your
[1]offspring's offspring," says the LORD, "from now and forever."

9 [b]Is 5:30; 8:21, 22
10 [a]Deut 28:29; Job 5:14 [b]Is 8:14, 15; 28:13 [c]Lam 3:6
11 [a]Is 38:14; Ezek 7:16 [b]Is 59:9, 14
12 [1]Lit *answer* [2]Lit *our iniquities we know them* [a]Ezra 9:6; Is 58:1 [b]Is 3:9; Jer 14:7; Hos 5:5
13 [a]Josh 24:27; Prov 30:9; Matt 10:33; Titus 1:16 [b]Is 5:7; 30:12; Jer 9:3, 4 [c]Is 59:3, 4; Mark 7:21, 22
14 [a]Is 1:21; 5:7 [b]Is 46:12; Hab 1:4
15 [1]Or *evil* [a]Is 5:23; 10:2; 29:21; 32:7 [b]Is 1:21-23
16 [a]Is 41:28; 63:5; Ezek 22:30 [b]Ps 98:1; Is 52:10; 63:5
17 [a]Eph 6:14 [b]Eph 6:17; 1 Thess 5:8 [c]Is 63:2, 3 [d]Is 9:7; 37:32; Zech 1:14
18 [1]Lit *recompense* [2]Lit *accordingly* [3]Lit *repay* [a]Job 34:11; Is 65:6, 7; 66:6; Jer 17:10
19 [1]Lit *narrow* [a]Is 49:12 [b]Ps 113:3 [c]Is 30:28; 66:12
20 [a]Rom 11:26 [b]Ezek 18:30, 31; Acts 2:38, 39
21 [1]Lit *seed* [a]Jer 31:31-34; Rom 11:27 [b]Is 11:2; 32:15; 44:3 [c]Is 55:11

Chapter 60 Theme ______________________

60 "[a]Arise, shine; for your [b]light has come,
And the [c]glory of the LORD has risen upon you.
2 "For behold, [a]darkness will cover the earth
And deep darkness the peoples;
But the LORD will rise upon you
And His [b]glory will appear upon you.
3 "[a]Nations will come to your light,
And kings to the brightness of your rising.

4 "[a]Lift up your eyes round about and see;
They all gather together, they [b]come to you.
Your sons will come from afar,
And your [c]daughters will be [1]carried in the arms.
5 "Then you will see and be [a]radiant,
And your heart will [1]thrill and rejoice;
Because the [b]abundance of the sea will be turned
to you,
The [c]wealth of the nations will come to you.
6 "A multitude of camels will cover you,
The young camels of Midian and [a]Ephah;
All those from [b]Sheba will come;
They will bring [c]gold and frankincense,
And will [d]bear good news of the praises of the LORD.
7 "All the flocks of [a]Kedar will be gathered together
to you,
The rams of Nebaioth will minister to you;
They will go up with acceptance on My [b]altar,
And I shall [1c]glorify My [2]glorious house.
8 "[a]Who are these who fly like a cloud
And like the doves to their [1]lattices?
9 "Surely the [a]coastlands will wait for Me;
And the [b]ships of Tarshish *will come* first,
To [c]bring your sons from afar,
Their silver and their gold with them,
For the name of the LORD your God,
And for the Holy One of Israel because He has
[1d]glorified you.

10 "[a]Foreigners will build up your walls,
And their [b]kings will minister to you;
For in My [c]wrath I struck you,
And in My favor I have had compassion on you.
11 "Your [a]gates will be open continually;
They will not be closed day or night,
So that *men* may [b]bring to you the wealth of the nations,
With [c]their kings led in procession.
12 "For the [a]nation and the kingdom which will not serve
you will perish,
And the nations will be utterly ruined.
13 "The [a]glory of Lebanon will come to you,

60:1 [a]Is 52:2 [b]Is 60:19, 20 [c]Is 24:23; 35:2; 58:8

2 [a]Is 58:10; Jer 13:16; Col 1:13 [b]Is 4:5

3 [a]Is 2:3; 45:14, 22-25; 49:23

4 [1]Lit *nursed upon the side* [a]Is 11:12; 49:18 [b]Is 49:20-22 [c]Is 43:6; 49:22

5 [1]Lit *tremble and be enlarged* [a]Ps 34:5 [b]Is 23:18; 24:14 [c]Is 61:6

6 [a]Gen 25:4 [b]Gen 25:3; Ps 72:10 [c]Is 60:9; Matt 2:11 [d]Is 42:10

7 [1]Or *beautify* [2]Or *beautiful* [a]Gen 25:13 [b]Is 19:19; 56:7 [c]Is 60:13; Hag 2:7, 9

8 [1]Or *dovecotes, windows* [a]Is 49:21

9 [1]Lit *beautified* [a]Is 11:11; 24:15; 42:4, 10, 12; 49:1; 51:5; 66:19 [b]Ps 48:7; Is 2:16 [c]Is 14:2; 43:6; 49:22 [d]Is 55:5

10 [a]Is 14:1, 2; 61:5; Zech 6:15 [b]Is 49:23; Rev 21:24 [c]Is 54:8

11 [a]Is 26:2; 60:18; 62:10; Rev 21:25, 26 [b]Is 60:5 [c]Ps 149:8; Is 24:21

12 [a]Is 14:2; Zech 14:17

13 [a]Is 35:2

The [b]juniper, the box tree and the cypress together,
To beautify the place of My sanctuary;
And I shall make the [c]place of My feet glorious.

13 [b]Is 41:19 [c]1 Chr 28:2; Ps 99:5; 132:7

14 "The [a]sons of those who afflicted you will come bowing
to you,
And all those who despised you will bow themselves at the
soles of your feet;
And they will call you the [b]city of the LORD,
The [c]Zion of the Holy One of Israel.

14 [a]Is 14:1, 2; 45:14, 23; 49:23; Rev 3:9 [b]Is 1:26 [c]Heb 12:22

15 "Whereas you have been [a]forsaken and [b]hated
With no one passing through,
I will make you an everlasting [c]pride,
A joy from generation to generation.

15 [a]Is 1:7-9; 6:11-13; Jer 30:17 [b]Is 66:5 [c]Is 4:2; 65:18

16 "You will also [a]suck the milk of nations
And suck the breast of kings;
Then you will know that I, the LORD, am your [b]Savior
And your [c]Redeemer, the Mighty One of Jacob.

16 [a]Is 66:11 [b]Is 19:20; 43:3, 11; 45:15, 21; 63:8 [c]Is 59:20; 63:16

17 "Instead of bronze I will bring gold,
And instead of iron I will bring silver,
And instead of wood, bronze,
And instead of stones, iron.
And I will make peace your administrators
And righteousness your overseers.

18 "[a]Violence will not be heard again in your land,
Nor [b]devastation or destruction within your borders;
But you will call your [c]walls salvation, and your
[d]gates praise.

18 [a]Is 54:14 [b]Is 51:19 [c]Is 26:1 [d]Is 60:11

19 "No longer will you have the [a]sun for light by day,
Nor for brightness will the moon give you light;
But you will have the [b]LORD for an everlasting light,
And your [c]God for your [1]glory.

19 [1]Or *beauty* [a]Rev 21:23; 22:5 [b]Is 2:5; 9:2 [c]Is 41:16; 45:25; Zech 2:5

20 "Your [a]sun will no longer set,
Nor will your moon wane;
For you will have the LORD for an everlasting light,
And the days of your [b]mourning will be over.

20 [a]Is 30:26 [b]Is 35:10; 65:19; Rev 21:4

21 "Then all your [a]people *will be* righteous;
They will [b]possess the land forever,
The branch of [1]My planting,
The [c]work of My hands,
That I may be [d]glorified.

21 [1]Lit *His* [a]Is 45:24, 25; 52:1 [b]Ps 37:11, 22; Is 57:13; 61:7 [c]Is 19:25; 29:23; 45:11; 64:8 [d]Is 61:3

22 "The [a]smallest one will become a [1]clan,
And the least one a mighty nation.
I, the LORD, will hasten it in its time."

22 [1]Or *thousand* [a]Is 10:22; 51:2

Chapter 61 Theme ________________________

61 The [a]Spirit of the Lord [1]GOD is upon me,
Because the LORD has anointed me
To [b]bring good news to the [2c]afflicted;
He has sent me to [d]bind up the brokenhearted,

61:1 [1]Heb *YHWH,* usually rendered *LORD* [2]Or *humble* [a]Is 11:2; 48:16; Luke 4:18 [b]Matt 11:5; Luke 7:22 [c]Is 11:4; 29:19; 32:7 [d]Is 57:15

To [e]proclaim liberty to captives
And [3]freedom to prisoners;
2 To [a]proclaim the favorable year of the LORD
And the [b]day of vengeance of our God;
To [c]comfort all who mourn,
3 To [a]grant those who mourn *in* Zion,
Giving them a garland instead of ashes,
The [b]oil of gladness instead of mourning,
The mantle of praise instead of a spirit of fainting.
So they will be called [1c]oaks of righteousness,
The planting of the LORD, that He may be glorified.

4 Then they will [a]rebuild the ancient ruins,
They will raise up the former devastations;
And they will repair the ruined cities,
The desolations of many generations.
5 [a]Strangers will stand and pasture your flocks,
And [1]foreigners will be your farmers and your
vinedressers.
6 But you will be called the [a]priests of the LORD;
You will be spoken of *as* [b]ministers of our God.
You will eat the [c]wealth of nations,
And in their [1]riches you will boast.
7 Instead of your [a]shame *you will have a* [b]double *portion,*
And *instead of* humiliation they will shout for joy over
their portion.
Therefore they will possess a double *portion* in
their land,
[c]Everlasting joy will be theirs.
8 For I, the LORD, [a]love justice,
I hate robbery [1]in the burnt offering;
And I will faithfully give them their recompense
And make an [b]everlasting covenant with them.
9 Then their offspring will be known among the nations,
And their descendants in the midst of the peoples.
All who see them will recognize them
Because they are the [a]offspring *whom* the LORD
has blessed.

10 I will [a]rejoice greatly in the LORD,
My soul will exult in [b]my God;
For He has [c]clothed me with garments of salvation,
He has wrapped me with a robe of righteousness,
As a bridegroom decks himself with a garland,
And [d]as a bride adorns herself with her jewels.
11 For as the [a]earth brings forth its sprouts,
And as a garden causes the things sown in it to
spring up,
So the Lord [1]GOD will [b]cause [c]righteousness and praise
To spring up before all the nations.

1 [3]Lit *opening to those who are bound* [e]Is 42:7; 49:9

2 [a]Is 49:8; 60:10 [b]Is 2:12; 13:6; 34:2, 8 [c]Is 57:18; Jer 31:13; Matt 5:4

3 [1]Or *terebinths* [a]Is 60:20 [b]Ps 23:5; 45:7; 104:15 [c]Is 60:21; Jer 17:7, 8

4 [a]Is 49:8; 58:12; Ezek 36:33; Amos 9:14

5 [1]Lit *sons of the foreigner* [a]Is 14:2; 60:10

6 [1]Or *glory* [a]Is 66:21 [b]Is 56:6 [c]Is 60:5, 11

7 [a]Is 54:4 [b]Is 40:2; Zech 9:12 [c]Ps 16:11

8 [1]Or *with iniquity* [a]Is 5:16; 28:17; 30:18 [b]Gen 17:7; Ps 105:10; Is 55:3; Jer 32:40

9 [a]Is 44:3

10 [a]Is 12:1, 2; 25:9; 41:16; 51:3 [b]Is 49:4 [c]Is 49:18; 52:1 [d]Rev 21:2

11 [1]Heb *YHWH,* usually rendered LORD [a]Is 4:2; 55:10 [b]Is 45:23, 24; 60:18, 21 [c]Ps 72:3; 85:11

62:1 [a]Is 1:26; 58:8; 61:11 [b]Is 46:13; 52:10
2 [a]Is 60:3 [b]Is 56:5; 62:4, 12; 65:15
3 [1]Lit *turban* [a]Is 28:5; Zech 9:16; 1 Thess 2:19
4 [1]I.e. Azubah [2]I.e. Shemamah [3]I.e. Hephzibah [4]I.e. Beulah [a]Is 54:6, 7; 60:15, 18 [b]Hos 2:19, 20 [c]Jer 32:41; Zeph 3:17
5 [1]Lit *exultation of the bridegroom* [a]Is 65:19
6 [a]Is 52:8; Jer 6:17; Ezek 3:17; 33:7 [b]Ps 74:2; Jer 14:21; Lam 5:1, 20
7 [a]Luke 18:1-8 [b]Is 60:18; Jer 33:9; Zeph 3:19, 20
8 [1]Lit *sons of foreigners* [a]Is 45:23; 54:9 [b]Lev 26:16; Deut 28:31, 33; Judg 6:3-6; Is 1:7; Jer 5:17
9 [a]Is 65:13, 21-23
10 [1]Lit *of* [a]Is 26:1; 60:11, 18 [b]Is 57:14 [c]Is 11:16; 19:23; 35:8; 49:11 [d]Is 11:10, 12; 49:22
11 [a]Is 42:10; 49:6 [b]Matt 21:5; Zech 9:9 [c]Is 51:5 [d]Is 40:10; Rev 22:12
12 [a]Deut 7:6; Is 4:3; 1 Pet 2:9 [b]Is 35:9; 51:10 [c]Is 41:17; 42:16; 62:4

Chapter 62 Theme ____________________

62 For Zion's sake I will not keep silent,
And for Jerusalem's sake I will not keep quiet,
Until her [a]righteousness goes forth like brightness,
And her [b]salvation like a torch that is burning.
2 The [a]nations will see your righteousness,
And all kings your glory;
And you will be called by a new [b]name
Which the mouth of the LORD will designate.
3 You will also be a [a]crown of beauty in the hand
of the LORD,
And a royal [1]diadem in the hand of your God.
4 It will no longer be said to you, "[1a]Forsaken,"
Nor to your land will it any longer be said, "[2]Desolate";
But you will be called, "[3]My delight is in her,"
And your land, "[4b]Married";
For the [c]LORD delights in you,
And *to Him* your land will be married.
5 For *as* a young man marries a virgin,
So your sons will marry you;
And *as* the [1]bridegroom rejoices over the bride,
So your [a]God will rejoice over you.

6 On your walls, O Jerusalem, I have appointed
[a]watchmen;
All day and all night they will never keep silent.
You who [b]remind the LORD, take no rest for
yourselves;
7 And [a]give Him no rest until He establishes
And makes [b]Jerusalem a praise in the earth.
8 [a]The LORD has sworn by His right hand and by
His strong arm,
"I will [b]never again give your grain *as* food for your
enemies;
Nor will [1]foreigners drink your new wine for which you
have labored."
9 But those who [a]garner it will eat it and praise the LORD;
And those who gather it will drink it in the courts of
My sanctuary.

10 Go through, [a]go through the gates,
Clear the way [1]for the people;
[b]Build up, build up the [c]highway,
Remove the stones, lift up a [d]standard over the peoples.
11 Behold, the LORD has proclaimed to the [a]end of the earth,
[b]Say to the daughter of Zion, "Lo, your [c]salvation comes;
[d]Behold His reward is with Him, and His recompense
before Him."
12 And they will call them, "[a]The holy people,
The [b]redeemed of the LORD";
And you will be called, "Sought out, a city [c]not forsaken."

Chapter 63 Theme ______________________

63 Who is this who comes from [a]Edom,
With [b]garments of [1]glowing colors from [c]Bozrah,
This One who is majestic in His apparel,
[2]Marching in the greatness of His strength?
"It is I who speak in righteousness, [d]mighty to save."
2 Why is Your apparel red,
And Your garments like the one who [a]treads in the
wine press?
3 "[a]I have trodden the wine trough alone,
And from the peoples there was no man with Me.
I also [b]trod them in My anger
And [c]trampled them in My wrath;
And [d]their [1]lifeblood is sprinkled on My garments,
And I [2]stained all My raiment.
4 "For the [a]day of vengeance was in My heart,
And My year of redemption has come.
5 "I looked, and there was [a]no one to help,
And I was astonished and there was no one to uphold;
So My [b]own arm brought salvation to Me,
And My wrath upheld Me.
6 "I [a]trod down the peoples in My anger
And made them [b]drunk in My wrath,
And I [1]poured out their lifeblood on the earth."

7 I shall make mention of the [a]lovingkindnesses of the LORD,
the praises of the LORD,
According to all that the LORD has granted us,
And the great [b]goodness toward the house of Israel,
Which He has granted them according to His [c]compassion
And according to the abundance of His lovingkindnesses.
8 For He said, "Surely, they are [a]My people,
Sons who will not deal falsely."
So He became their [b]Savior.
9 In all their affliction [1a]He was afflicted,
And the [b]angel of His presence saved them;
In His [c]love and in His mercy He [d]redeemed them,
And He [e]lifted them and carried them all the days of old.
10 But they [a]rebelled
And grieved His [b]Holy Spirit;
Therefore He turned Himself to become their enemy,
He fought against them.
11 Then [a]His people remembered the days of old, of Moses.
Where is [b]He who brought them up out of the sea with the
[1]shepherds of His flock?
Where is He who [c]put His Holy Spirit in the midst
of [2]them,
12 Who caused His [a]glorious arm to go at the right hand
of Moses,
Who [b]divided the waters before them to make for Himself
an everlasting name,

63:1 [1]Or *crimson* [2]Lit *Inclining* [a]Ps 137:7; Is 34:5, 6; Ezek 25:12-14; 35:1-15; Obad 1-14; Mal 1:2-5 [b]Is 63:2 [c]Is 34:6; Jer 49:13; Amos 1:12 [d]Zeph 3:17

2 [a]Rev 19:13, 15

3 [1]Lit *juice* [2]Lit *defiled* [a]Rev 14:20; 19:15 [b]Is 22:5; 28:3 [c]Mic 7:10 [d]Rev 19:13

4 [a]Is 34:8; 35:4; 61:2; Jer 51:6

5 [a]Is 59:16 [b]Ps 44:3; Is 40:10; 52:10

6 [1]Lit *brought down their juice to the earth* [a]Is 22:5; 34:2; 65:12 [b]Is 29:9; 51:17, 21

7 [a]Ps 25:6; 92:2; Is 54:8, 10 [b]1 Kin 8:66; Neh 9:25, 35 [c]Ps 51:1; 86:5, 15; Is 54:7, 8; Eph 2:4

8 [a]Ex 6:7; Is 3:15; 51:4 [b]Is 60:16

9 [1]Another reading is *He was not an adversary* [a]Judg 10:16 [b]Ex 23:20-23; 33:14, 15 [c]Deut 7:7, 8 [d]Is 43:1; 52:9 [e]Deut 1:31; 32:10-12; Is 46:3

10 [a]Ps 78:40; 106:33; Acts 7:51; Eph 4:30 [b]Ps 51:11; Is 63:11

11 [1]Some mss read *shepherd* [2]Lit *him* [a]Ps 106:44, 45 [b]Is 51:10 [c]Num 11:17, 25, 29; Hag 2:5

12 [a]Ex 6:6; 15:16 [b]Ex 14:21, 22; Is 11:15; 51:10

13 [a]Jer 31:9

13 Who led them through the depths?
Like the horse in the wilderness, they did not [a]stumble;

14 [1]Lit *him* [a]Josh 21:44; 23:1 [b]Deut 32:12

14 As the cattle which go down into the valley,
The Spirit of the [a]LORD gave [1]them rest.
So You [b]led Your people,
To make for Yourself a glorious name.

15 [a]Deut 26:15; Ps 80:14 [b]Ps 68:5; 123:1 [c]Is 9:7; 26:11; 37:32; 42:13; 59:17 [d]Jer 31:20; Hos 11:8

15 [a]Look down from heaven and see from Your holy and
glorious [b]habitation;
Where are Your [c]zeal and Your mighty deeds?
The [d]stirrings of Your heart and Your compassion are
restrained toward me.

16 [a]Is 1:2; 64:8 [b]Is 29:22; 41:8; 51:2 [c]Is 41:14; 44:6; 60:16

16 For You are our [a]Father, though [b]Abraham does not
know us
And Israel does not recognize us.
You, O LORD, are our Father,
Our [c]Redeemer from of old is Your name.

17 [a]Is 30:28; Ezek 14:7-9 [b]Is 29:13, 14 [c]Num 10:36

17 Why, O LORD, do You [a]cause us to stray from Your ways
And [b]harden our heart from fearing You?
[c]Return for the sake of Your servants, the tribes of
Your heritage.

18 [a]Ps 74:3-7; Is 64:11

18 Your holy people possessed Your sanctuary for a
little while,
Our adversaries have [a]trodden *it* down.

19 We have become *like* those over whom You have
never ruled,
Like those who were not called by Your name.

Chapter 64 Theme ____________

64:1 [1]Ch 63:19b in Heb [a]Ex 19:18; Ps 18:9; 144:5; Mic 1:3, 4; Hab 3:13 [b]Judg 5:5; Ps 68:8; Nah 1:5

64 [1]Oh, that You would rend the heavens *and* [a]come down,
That the mountains might [b]quake at Your presence—

2 [1]Ch 64:1 in Heb [a]Ps 99:1; Jer 5:22; 33:9

2 [1]As fire kindles the brushwood, *as* fire causes water
to boil—
To make Your name known to Your adversaries,
That the [a]nations may tremble at Your presence!

3 [a]Ps 65:5; 66:3, 5; 106:22

3 When You did [a]awesome things which we did not expect,
You came down, the mountains quaked at Your presence.

4 [a]1 Cor 2:9 [b]Is 25:9; 30:18; 40:31

4 For from days of old [a]they have not heard or perceived
by ear,
Nor has the eye seen a God besides You,
Who acts in behalf of the one who [b]waits for Him.

5 [a]Ex 20:24 [b]Is 56:1 [c]Is 26:13; 63:7 [d]Is 12:1

5 You [a]meet him who rejoices in [b]doing righteousness,
Who [c]remembers You in Your ways.
Behold, [d]You were angry, for we sinned,
We continued in them a long time;
And shall we be saved?

6 [a]Is 6:5 [b]Is 46:12; 48:1 [c]Ps 90:5, 6; Is 1:30 [d]Is 50:1

6 For all of us have become like one who is [a]unclean,
And all our [b]righteous deeds are like a filthy garment;
And all of us [c]wither like a leaf,
And our [d]iniquities, like the wind, take us away.

7 There is [a]no one who calls on Your name,
Who arouses himself to take hold of You;
For You have [b]hidden Your face from us
And have [1]delivered us into the power of our iniquities.

8 But now, O LORD, [a]You are our Father,
We are the [b]clay, and You our potter;
And all of us are the [c]work of Your hand.
9 Do not be [a]angry beyond measure, O LORD,
[b]Nor remember iniquity forever;
Behold, look now, all of us are [c]Your people.
10 Your [a]holy cities have become a [b]wilderness,
Zion has become a wilderness,
Jerusalem a desolation.
11 Our holy and beautiful [a]house,
Where our fathers praised You,
Has been burned *by* fire;
And [b]all our precious things have become a ruin.
12 Will You [a]restrain Yourself at these things, O LORD?
Will You keep silent and afflict us beyond measure?

Chapter 65 Theme ______________________________

65 "I permitted Myself to be sought by [a]those who did not ask *for Me;*
I permitted Myself to be found by those who did not seek Me.
I said, 'Here am I, here am I,'
To a nation which [b]did not call on My name.
2 "[a]I have spread out My hands all day long to a [b]rebellious people,
Who walk *in* the way which is not good, [1]following their own [c]thoughts,
3 A people who continually [a]provoke Me to My face,
Offering sacrifices in [b]gardens and [c]burning incense on bricks;
4 Who sit among graves and spend the night in secret places;
Who [a]eat swine's flesh,
And the broth of unclean meat is *in* their pots.
5 "Who say, '[a]Keep to yourself, do not come near me,
For I am holier than you!'
These are smoke in My [1]nostrils,
A fire that burns all the day.
6 "Behold, it is written before Me,
I will [a]not keep silent, but [b]I will repay;
I will even repay into their bosom,
7 Both [1]their own [a]iniquities and the iniquities of their fathers together," says the LORD.
"Because they have [b]burned incense on the mountains
And [c]scorned Me on the hills,

7 [1]Reading with the DSS and versions; M.T. *melted* [a]Is 59:4; Ezek 22:30 [b]Deut 31:18; Is 1:15; 54:8

8 [a]Is 63:16 [b]Is 29:16; 45:9 [c]Ps 100:3; Is 60:21

9 [a]Is 57:17; 60:10 [b]Is 43:25; Mic 7:18 [c]Ps 79:13; Is 63:8

10 [a]Is 48:2; 52:1 [b]Is 1:7; 6:11

11 [a]2 Kin 25:9; Ps 74:5-7; Is 63:18 [b]Lam 1:7, 10, 11

12 [a]Ps 74:10, 11, 18, 19; Is 42:14; 63:15

65:1 [a]Rom 9:24-26; 10:20 [b]Is 63:19; Hos 1:10

2 [1]Lit *after* [a]Rom 10:21 [b]Is 1:2, 23; 30:1, 9 [c]Ps 81:11, 12; Is 59:7; 66:18

3 [a]Job 1:11; 2:5; Is 3:8 [b]Is 1:29; 66:17 [c]Is 66:3

4 [a]Lev 11:7; Is 66:3, 17

5 [1]Lit *nose* [a]Matt 9:11; Luke 7:39; 18:9-12

6 [a]Ps 50:3, 21; Is 42:14; 64:12 [b]Jer 16:18

7 [1]Lit *your* [a]Is 13:11; 22:14; 26:21; 30:13, 14 [b]Is 57:7; Hos 2:13 [c]Ezek 20:27, 28

Therefore I will [d]measure their former work into
their bosom."

8 Thus says the LORD,
"As the new wine is found in the cluster,
And one says, 'Do not destroy it, for there is
[1]benefit in it,'
So I will act on behalf of My servants
In order [a]not to destroy [2]all of them.
9 "I will bring forth [a]offspring from Jacob,
And an [b]heir of My mountains from Judah;
Even [c]My chosen ones shall inherit it,
And [d]My servants will dwell there.
10 "[a]Sharon will be a pasture land for flocks,
And the [b]valley of Achor a resting place for herds,
For My people who [c]seek Me.
11 "But you who [a]forsake the LORD,
Who forget My [b]holy mountain,
Who set a table for [1]Fortune,
And who fill *cups* with mixed wine for [2]Destiny,
12 I will destine you for the [a]sword,
And all of you will bow down to the [b]slaughter.
Because I called, but you [c]did not answer;
I spoke, but you did not hear.
And you did evil in My sight
And chose that in which I did not delight."

13 Therefore, thus says the Lord [1]GOD,
"Behold, My servants will [a]eat, but you will be [b]hungry.
Behold, My servants will [c]drink, but you will be [d]thirsty.
Behold, My servants will [e]rejoice, but you will be [f]put
to shame.
14 "Behold, My servants will [a]shout joyfully with a glad heart,
But you will [b]cry out with a [1]heavy heart,
And you will wail with a broken spirit.
15 "You will leave your name for a [a]curse to My chosen ones,
And the Lord [1]GOD will slay you.
But [2]My servants will be called by [b]another name.
16 "Because he who [1]is blessed in the earth
Will [1]be blessed by the [a]God of truth;
And he who swears in the earth
Will [b]swear by the God of truth;
Because the former troubles are forgotten,
And because they are hidden from My sight!

17 "For behold, I create [a]new heavens and a new earth;
And the [b]former things will not be remembered or come to
[1]mind.
18 "But be [a]glad and rejoice forever in what I create;
For behold, I create Jerusalem *for* rejoicing
And her people *for* gladness.

7 [d]Jer 5:29; 13:25

8 [1]Lit *blessing* [2]Lit *the whole* [a]Is 1:9; 10:21, 22; 48:9

9 [a]Is 45:19, 25; Jer 31:36, 37 [b]Is 49:8; 60:21; Amos 9:11-15 [c]Is 57:13 [d]Is 32:18

10 [a]Is 33:9; 35:2 [b]Josh 7:24, 26; Hos 2:15 [c]Is 51:1; 55:6

11 [1]Heb *Gad* [2]Heb *Meni* [a]Deut 29:24, 25; Is 1:4, 28 [b]Is 2:2, 3; 66:20

12 [a]Is 27:1; 34:5, 6; 66:16 [b]Is 63:6 [c]2 Chr 36:15, 16; Prov 1:24; Is 41:28; 50:2; 66:4; Jer 7:13

13 [1]Heb *YHWH,* usually rendered *LORD* [a]Is 1:19 [b]Is 8:21 [c]Is 41:17, 18; 49:10 [d]Is 5:13 [e]Is 61:7; 66:14 [f]Is 42:17; 44:9, 11; 66:5

14 [1]Lit *pain of* [a]Ps 66:4; Is 51:11; James 5:13 [b]Is 13:6; Matt 8:12

15 [1]Heb *YHWH,* usually rendered *LORD* [2]So with Gr; Heb *He will call His servants* [a]Jer 24:9; 25:18; Zech 8:13 [b]Is 62:2

16 [1]Or *bless(es) himself* [a]Ex 34:6; Ps 31:5 [b]Is 19:18; 45:23

17 [1]Lit *heart* [a]Is 66:22; 2 Pet 3:13; Rev 21:1 [b]Is 43:18; Jer 3:16

18 [a]Ps 98; Is 12:1, 2; 25:9; 35:10; 41:16; 51:3; 61:10

19 "I will also [a]rejoice in Jerusalem and be glad in My people;
And there will no longer be heard in her
The voice of [b]weeping and the sound of crying.
20 "No longer will there be [1]in it an infant *who lives but a few* days,
Or an old man who does [a]not [2]live out his days;
For the youth will die at the age of one hundred
And the [3b]one who does not reach the age of one hundred
Will be *thought* accursed.
21 "They will [a]build houses and inhabit *them;*
They will also [b]plant vineyards and eat their fruit.
22 "They will not build and [a]another inhabit,
They will not plant and another eat;
For [b]as the [1]lifetime of a tree, *so will be* the days of My people,
And My chosen ones will [c]wear out the work of their hands.
23 "They will [a]not labor in vain,
Or bear *children* for calamity;
For they are the [1b]offspring of those blessed by the LORD,
And their descendants with them.
24 "It will also come to pass that before they call, I will [a]answer;
and while they are still speaking, I will hear.
25 "The [a]wolf and the lamb will graze together, and the [b]lion
will eat straw like the ox; and [c]dust will be the serpent's food.
They will [d]do no evil or harm in all My [e]holy mountain," says
the LORD.

Chapter 66 Theme ______________________________

66

Thus says the LORD,
"[a]Heaven is My throne and the earth is My footstool.
Where then is a [b]house you could build for Me?
And where is a place that [1]I may rest?
2 "For [a]My hand made all these things,
Thus all these things came into being," declares the LORD.
"But to this one I will look,
To him who is humble and [b]contrite of spirit, and who [c]trembles at My word.

3 "*But* he who kills an ox is *like* one who slays a man;
He who sacrifices a lamb is *like* the one who breaks a dog's neck;
He who offers a grain offering *is like one who offers* [a]swine's blood;
He who [1b]burns incense is *like* the one who blesses an idol.
As they have chosen their [c]*own* ways,
And their soul delights in their [d]abominations,
4 So I will [a]choose their [1]punishments
And will [b]bring on them what they dread.
Because I called, but [c]no one answered;
I spoke, but they did not listen.
And they did [d]evil in My sight
And chose that in which I did not delight."

19 [a]Is 62:4, 5; Jer 32:41 [b]Is 25:8; 30:19; 35:10; 51:11; Rev 7:17; 21:4

20 [1]Lit *from there* [2]Lit *fill out* [3]Lit *one who misses the mark* [a]Deut 4:40; Job 5:26; Ps 34:12 [b]Eccl 8:12, 13; Is 3:11; 22:14

21 [a]Is 32:18; Amos 9:14 [b]Is 30:23; 37:30; Jer 31:5

22 [1]Lit *days* [a]Is 62:8, 9 [b]Ps 92:12-14 [c]Ps 21:4; 91:16

23 [1]Lit *seed* [a]Deut 28:3-12; Is 55:2 [b]Is 61:9; Jer 32:38, 39; Acts 2:39

24 [a]Ps 91:15; Is 55:6; 58:9; Dan 9:20-23; 10:12

25 [a]Is 11:6 [b]Is 11:7 [c]Gen 3:14; Mic 7:17 [d]Is 11:9; Mic 4:3 [e]Is 65:11

66:1 [1]Lit *is My resting place?* [a]1 Kin 8:27; Ps 11:4; Matt 5:34, 35; 23:22 [b]2 Sam 7:5-7; Jer 7:4; John 4:20, 21; Acts 7:48-50

2 [a]Is 40:26 [b]Ps 34:18; Is 57:15; Matt 5:3, 4; Luke 18:13, 14 [c]Ps 119:120; Is 66:5

3 [1]Lit *offers a memorial of incense* [a]Is 65:4 [b]Lev 2:2; Is 1:13 [c]Is 57:17; 65:2 [d]Is 44:19

4 [1]Lit *ill treatments* [a]Prov 1:31, 32; Is 65:7 [b]Prov 10:24 [c]Prov 1:24; Is 65:12; Jer 7:13 [d]2 Kin 21:2, 6; Is 59:7; 65:12; Jer 7:30

5 Hear the word of the LORD, you who [a]tremble at His word:
"Your brothers who [b]hate you, who [c]exclude you for My
name's sake,
Have said, 'Let the LORD be glorified, that we may see
your joy.'
But [d]they will be put to shame.
6 "A voice of uproar from the city, a voice from the temple,
The voice of the LORD who is [a]rendering recompense to
His enemies.

7 "Before she travailed, [a]she brought forth;
Before her pain came, [b]she gave birth to a boy.
8 "[a]Who has heard such a thing? Who has seen such things?
Can a land be [1]born in one day?
Can a nation be brought forth all at once?
As soon as Zion travailed, she also brought forth her sons.
9 "Shall I bring to the point of birth and [a]not give delivery?"
says the LORD.
"Or shall I who gives delivery shut *the womb?*" says
your God.
10 "Be [a]joyful with Jerusalem and rejoice for her, all you who
[b]love her;
Be exceedingly [c]glad with her, all you who mourn over her,
11 That you may nurse and [a]be satisfied with her
comforting breasts,
That you may suck and be delighted with her
[b]bountiful bosom."
12 For thus says the LORD, "Behold, I extend [a]peace to her
like a river,
And the [b]glory of the nations like an overflowing stream;
And you will [1]be nursed, you will be [c]carried on the [2]hip
and fondled on the knees.
13 "As one whom his mother comforts, so I will [a]comfort you;
And you will be comforted in Jerusalem."
14 Then you will [a]see *this,* and your [b]heart will be glad,
And your [c]bones will flourish like the new grass;
And the [d]hand of the LORD will be made known to
His servants,
But He will be [e]indignant toward His enemies.
15 For behold, the LORD will come in [a]fire
And His [b]chariots like the whirlwind,
To render His anger with fury,
And His rebuke with flames of fire.
16 For the LORD will execute judgment by [a]fire
And by His [b]sword on all flesh,
And those slain by the LORD will be many.
17 "Those who sanctify and purify themselves *to go* to
the [a]gardens,
[1]Following one in the center,
Who eat [b]swine's flesh, detestable things and mice,
Will [c]come to an end altogether," declares the LORD.

5 [a]Is 66:2 [b]Ps 38:20; Is 60:15 [c]Matt 5:10-12; 10:22; John 9:34; 15:18-20 [d]Luke 13:17
6 [a]Is 59:18; 65:6; Joel 3:7
7 [a]Is 37:3; 54:1 [b]Rev 12:5
8 [1]Lit *travailed with* [a]Is 64:4
9 [a]Is 37:3
10 [a]Deut 32:43; Is 65:18; Rom 15:10 [b]Ps 26:8; 122:6 [c]Ps 137:6
11 [a]Is 49:23; 60:16; Joel 3:18 [b]Is 60:1, 2; 62:2
12 [1]Lit *nurse* [2]Lit *side* [a]Ps 72:3, 7; Is 48:18 [b]Is 60:5; 61:6 [c]Is 60:4
13 [a]Is 12:1; 40:1, 2; 49:13; 51:3; 2 Cor 1:3, 4
14 [a]Is 33:20 [b]Zech 10:7 [c]Prov 3:8; Is 58:11 [d]Ezra 7:9; 8:31 [e]Is 10:5; 13:5; 34:2
15 [a]Is 10:17; 30:27, 33; 31:9 [b]Ps 68:17; Is 5:28; Hab 3:8
16 [a]Is 30:30; Ezek 38:22 [b]Is 65:12; Ezek 38:21
17 [1]Lit *After* [a]Is 1:29; 65:3 [b]Lev 11:7; Is 65:4 [c]Is 1:28, 31

18 "For I [1]know their works and their [a]thoughts; [2]the time is
coming to [b]gather all nations and tongues. And they shall come
and see My glory.
19 "I will set a [a]sign among them and will send survivors from
them to the nations: [b]Tarshish, [1]Put, [c]Lud, [2]Meshech, [d]Tubal
and [3]Javan, to the distant [e]coastlands that have neither heard
My fame nor seen My glory. And they will [f]declare My glory
among the nations.
20 "Then they shall [a]bring all your brethren from all the
nations as a grain offering to the LORD, on horses, in chariots,
in litters, on mules and on camels, to My [b]holy mountain
Jerusalem," says the LORD, "just as the sons of Israel bring their
grain offering in a [c]clean vessel to the house of the LORD.
21 "I will also take some of them for [a]priests *and* for Levites,"
says the LORD.
22 "For just as the [a]new heavens and the new earth
Which I make will endure before Me," declares the LORD,
"So your [b]offspring and your [c]name will endure.
23 "And it shall be from [a]new moon to new moon
And from sabbath to sabbath,
All [1]mankind will come to [b]bow down before Me," says
the LORD.
24 "Then they will go forth and look
On the [a]corpses of the men
Who have [1b]transgressed against Me.
For their [c]worm will not die
[d]And their fire will not be quenched;
And they will be an [e]abhorrence to all [2]mankind."

18 [1]So with Gr; Heb omits *know* [2]Lit *it is coming* [a]Is 59:7; 65:2 [b]Is 45:22-25; Jer 3:17

19 [1]So with Gr; Heb *Pul* [2]So with Gr; Heb *those who draw the bow* [3]I.e. Greece [a]Is 11:10, 12; 49:22; 62:10 [b]Is 2:16; 60:9 [c]Ezek 27:10 [d]Gen 10:2 [e]Is 11:11; 24:15; 60:9 [f]1 Chr 16:24; Is 42:12

20 [a]Is 43:6; 49:22; 60:4 [b]Is 2:2, 3; 11:9; 56:7; 65:11, 25 [c]Is 52:11

21 [a]Ex 19:6; Is 61:6; 1 Pet 2:5, 9

22 [a]Is 65:17; Heb 12:26, 27; 2 Pet 3:13; Rev 21:1 [b]Is 61:8, 9; 65:22, 23; John 10:27-29; 1 Pet 1:4, 5 [c]Is 56:5

23 [1]Lit *flesh* [a]Is 1:13, 14; Ezek 46:1, 6 [b]Is 19:21, 23; 27:13; 49:7

24 [1]Or *rebelled* [2]Lit *flesh* [a]Is 5:25; 34:3 [b]Is 1:28; 24:20 [c]Is 14:11; Mark 9:48 [d]Is 1:31; Matt 3:12 [e]Dan 12:2

Isaiah at a Glance

Theme of Isaiah:

Author:

Date:

Purpose:

Key Words:

in that day

Lord of hosts

Holy One of Israel

earth

Babylon (Babylonians, Chaldeans)

nations (other than Israel)

Israel (Jacob)

Judah

covenant

Zion (Jerusalem)

sin (sinners, evil, iniquity, transgressions, transgressed)

every reference to the Lord's coming

Segment Divisions

				Chapter Themes
	Discourses Regarding Jerusalem	God's Character and Judgment	1	
			2	
			3	
			4	
			5	
			6	
			7	
			8	
			9	
			10	
			11	
			12	
	Oracles		13	
			14	
			15	
			16	
			17	
			18	
			19	
			20	
			21	
			22	
			23	
	Discourses Regarding That Day		24	
			25	
			26	
			27	
	Woes		28	
			29	
			30	
			31	
			32	
			33	

SEGMENT DIVISIONS

			CHAPTER THEMES
	GOD'S RANSOM	GOD'S CHARACTER AND JUDGMENT	34
			35
	HISTORICAL INTERLUDE		36
			37
			38
			39
	DISCOURSES REGARDING:	GOD'S COMFORT AND REDEMPTION	40
			41
			42
			43
			44
			45
			46
			47
			48
	DISCOURSES REGARDING:		49
			50
			51
			52
			53
			54
			55
			56
			57
	DISCOURSES REGARDING:		58
			59
			60
			61
			62
			63
			64
			65
			66

JEREMIAH יִרְמְיָהוּ
YIRMEYAHU

Isaiah lived and prophesied one hundred years before the Babylonian captivity; Jeremiah prophesied just before and during Babylon's three sieges of Judah. Between these two great prophets there was about a 30-year period when God didn't speak. While the true prophets were silent, false prophets were very vocal, proclaiming peace rather than judgment—and the people loved it. This occurred during Manasseh's reign, a reign noted for its blasphemy and bloodshed.

Although Jeremiah was living at this time, his ministry as a prophet didn't begin until about 627 B.C., the same time that Nabopolassar began his rule of the Neo-Babylonian Empire. Josiah succeeded Manasseh as ruler over Judah, and when the Word of the Lord was found in the house of God, Josiah called the people to repentance, bringing about a revival.

Then, in 612 B.C., Nineveh, the capital of Assyria, fell to the Babylonians. In 609 B.C., as Egypt went to aid Assyria against Babylon at Carchemish, Josiah intercepted Neco, king of Egypt, on the plain of Megiddo. Although Neco had warned Josiah not to try to stop him, Josiah tried anyway, and as a result he was killed in battle (see 2 Chronicles 35:20-27).

The revival came to an end, and like her sister Israel, Judah played the harlot again. In 605 B.C., Egypt was defeated by Babylon at Carchemish, leaving Babylon the dominant world power, God's rod of judgment for His adulterous wife and the surrounding nations. And Jeremiah the prophet wept.

THINGS TO DO

Chapter 1: Understanding Jeremiah's Message

To understand Jeremiah's message you must understand Jeremiah's call and commission from the Lord. To do so, become thoroughly familiar with Jeremiah 1 before reading the instructions for Jeremiah 2 through 38.

1. Read the chapter, asking God for insight and understanding. Then read the chapter and mark any of the key words listed on JEREMIAH AT A GLANCE on page 1301.
2. The first three verses give the historical setting of Jeremiah.
   a. The exile (1:3) refers to the final siege and destruction of Jerusalem by Nebuchadnezzar, king of Babylon, in 586 B.C. See "Israel's Division and Captivity" on page 649.
   b. Jeremiah contains many references to time, such as in Jeremiah 1:1-3. When you read one, try to determine who was reigning at the time and what his relationship was to the other kings. The book of Jeremiah is not chronological, so this will help you keep the timing of events in perspective. Mark every reference to time with a clock ⌚ and color it green for easy reference.
   c. Fill in "Author" and "Date" on the JEREMIAH AT A GLANCE chart.
3. Read Jeremiah 1 again. As you do, ask the "5 W's and an H." Ask questions such as: Who was Jeremiah? What was Jeremiah called to do or be? To whom was he appointed and by whom? When was he called and why? How did he respond? How will he be able to fulfill his appointment? What was he to say? How would the people respond? What was Jeremiah to do? What if the people didn't respond? What would God do?
   a. In your notebook, jot down your answers to these questions and any others you think of while observing the text. Don't read anything into the text; simply let it speak for itself.

b. In your notebook, you may want to list the main points about Jeremiah, his call, and the specifics of his commission. Record what you observed from examining the chapter in light of the "5 W's and an H." Be as specific as possible.

4. Mark references to God with a △, and note insights into His character, sovereignty, power, and ways. Draw a △ in the margin so you can note what the text tells you about Him.

5. Record the theme of this chapter on JEREMIAH AT A GLANCE and in your Bible.

6. The rest of Jeremiah revolves around Jeremiah's call and commission as a prophet to the nations. Everything Jeremiah says and does is rooted in chapter 1. Remember this as you study!

Jeremiah's critical and passionate message consists of discourses and narrative accounts of events in Jeremiah's life and in the history of Israel, Judah, and the nations.

Chapters 2–38: Judah's Sin and God's Warning to Return

Read all the instructions before you begin. Every now and then refresh your memory, since Jeremiah is a long book.

1. Study this segment chapter by chapter, doing the following:

a. When Jeremiah spoke he was to do two things—one negative and one positive. First, in respect to the nations, he was to pluck up, break down, destroy, and overthrow. Second, he was to build and plant. As you read, observe how Jeremiah does these in regard to Judah.

1) In your notebook, list their sins, their "wickedness" (1:16), which God has to deal with by plucking up, breaking down, destroying, and overthrowing.

2) Also note any promise of building and planting—restoration. Record what God will do on their behalf, when He will do it, and why.

b. Jeremiah had the assurance that God would perform His word (1:12). As you read, note what God says will happen to Judah in the way of judgment.

1) Watch for how God will bring about this judgment. In several places God has Jeremiah do some symbolic acts in order to get His point across to the people. Watch for these.

2) Watch for any verse that shows that God performed (accomplished or carried out) what He said He would do. Also note what God has to do because of the covenant (the law) He made with them.

2. Jeremiah was told to speak all God commanded him and that he would be opposed by kings, princes, priests, and people.

a. When you see Jeremiah encountering any opposition, write the word "opposition" in the margin. Observe Jeremiah's struggles and how he handles these. Also note how God delivers Jeremiah as He said He would in 1:8,18-19. (The height of Jeremiah's physical suffering is described in chapters 37–38.)

b. Also note what you learn about the leaders, the shepherds (spiritual), and the prophets.

3. In chapter 20 the king of Babylon appears on the scene, for "out of the north the evil will break forth on all the inhabitants of the land" (1:14). From this point on, Babylon and Nebuchadnezzar are prominent. You might want to mark every reference to *Babylon (Chaldeans)* from this point onward and summarize your insights about them in the margin under the heading "Babylon."

4. Make a list of the key words on the AT A GLANCE chart, writing them on an index card. On the card, mark the words the same way as you will mark them in the text. Mark references to time with a clock 🕒 and color them green for consistency and easy identification.

a. As you mark every reference to *nation* or *nations* (except Babylon), observe which nation it is and record it.

b. Watch for any words or synonyms that have to do with plucking up, uprooting, destroying, building, planting, or restoring. Mark these in a distinctive way or underline them in the text.

5. As you finish observing each chapter, marking its key words and putting notes in the margin, record the theme of that chapter on JEREMIAH AT A GLANCE. Also record it in your Bible next to the chapter number.

Chapters 39–45: Jerusalem's Fall and Judah's Uprooting

1. Except for chapter 45, this section is narrative. Therefore, as you read each chapter:

a. Note what happens, when it happens (mark references to time), where it happens, and why. Double-underline in green all the geographical references.

b. Note who is involved. Mark in a distinctive way the main characters in each chapter. Then you might want to record who they are and anything significant you want to remember about them.

2. Record the theme of each chapter as you have done before.

Chapters 46–51: Jeremiah's Prophecy Concerning the Nations

1. As you read, note what the Lord says will happen and why. Also note the end result and if the Lord gives any hope for the future. Watch for and mark time phrases.

2. Pay attention to the references to the *north* and to the *Medes*. Also observe what you learn about Israel from these chapters.

3. These chapters contain critical information about Babylon that will help when you study prophecy and/or the book of Revelation. In your notebook, list what you learn about Babylon. Also list your insights on the chart on page 2074.

Chapter 52: Judah's Final Days of Exile

1. As you observe this chapter, mark the time phrases and note what was done to the kings, the city, the temple vessels, and who did it.

2. Record the theme of this chapter on JEREMIAH AT A GLANCE and then complete the chart. Record the segment divisions of Jeremiah.

Things to Think About

1. Judah played the harlot. How have you behaved as the bride of Christ? Do you relate to any of Judah's sins? In James 4:4 God calls those who are friends with the world adulteresses. What would He call you?

2. How faithful are you to proclaim God's Word to others? What can you learn from Jeremiah's life in this respect? Do you hesitate to share God's Word with others because of fear or because you think they wouldn't listen? Are you dismayed by their faces? What should you do? Think about all the times you marked *listened* and *hear* in Jeremiah. Judah didn't listen to God—only to those prophets who tickled her ears. How carefully do you listen to God's Word?

3. Would God have relented of the calamity He was about to bring on Judah? Why? What do you learn from this?

4. God uses nations as His rod of judgment, and yet He holds them accountable for their actions. What does this tell you about God and about your accountability before Him?

Chapter 1 Theme ______________________________

1 The words of [a]Jeremiah the son of Hilkiah, of the priests
who were in [b]Anathoth in the land of Benjamin,
2 to whom the word of the LORD came in the days of [a]Josiah the
son of [b]Amon, king of Judah, in the [c]thirteenth year of his reign.
3 It came also in the days of [a]Jehoiakim the son of Josiah,
king of Judah, until the end of the eleventh year of [b]Zedekiah
the son of Josiah, king of Judah, until the exile of Jerusalem in
the fifth month.
4 Now the word of the LORD came to me saying,
5 "Before I [a]formed you in the womb I knew you,
And [b]before you were born I consecrated you;
I have [c]appointed you a prophet to the nations."
6 Then [a]I said, "Alas, Lord [1]GOD!
Behold, I do not know how to speak,
Because [b]I am a youth."
7 But the LORD said to me,
"Do not say, 'I am a youth,'
[a]Because everywhere I send you, you shall go,
And [b]all that I command you, you shall speak.
8 "[a]Do not be afraid of them,
For [b]I am with you to deliver you," declares the LORD.
9 Then the LORD stretched out His hand and [a]touched my
mouth, and the LORD said to me,
"Behold, I have [b]put My words in your mouth.
10 "See, [a]I have appointed you this day over the nations and
over the kingdoms,
[b]To pluck up and to break down,
To destroy and to overthrow,
[c]To build and to plant."
11 The word of the LORD came to me saying, "What do you see,
[a]Jeremiah?" And I said, "I see a rod of an [1]almond tree."
12 Then the LORD said to me, "You have seen well, for [a]I am
[1]watching over My word to perform it."
13 The word of the LORD came to me a second time saying,
"[a]What do you see?" And I said, "I see a boiling [b]pot, facing away
from the north."
14 Then the LORD said to me, "[a]Out of the north the evil [1]will
break forth on all the inhabitants of the land.
15 "For, behold, I am calling [a]all the families of the kingdoms of
the north," declares the LORD; "and they will come and they
will [b]set each one his throne at the entrance of the gates of
Jerusalem, and against all its walls round about and against all
the [c]cities of Judah.
16 "I will [1]pronounce My judgments on them concerning all
their wickedness, whereby they have [a]forsaken Me and have
[2b]offered sacrifices to other gods, and worshiped the [c]works of
their own hands.
17 "Now, [a]gird up your loins and arise, and speak to them all
which I command you. [b]Do not be dismayed before them, or I
will dismay you before them.

INSIGHT

The Last Kings of Judah

Josiah
640-609 B.C.

Jehoahaz
(also called Joahaz or Shallum)
609 B.C.

Jehoiakim
(also called Eliakim)
609-597 B.C.

Jehoiachin
(also called Coniah or Jeconiah)
597 B.C.

Zedekiah
(also called Mattaniah)
597-586 B.C.

1:1 [a]2 Chr 35:25; 36:12, 21, 22; Ezra 1:1; Dan 9:2; Matt 2:17; 16:14; 27:9 [b]Josh 21:18; 1 Kin 2:26; 1 Chr 6:60; Is 10:30; Jer 11:21; 32:7

2 [a]1 Kin 13:2; 2 Kin 21:24; 22:3; 2 Chr 34:1; Jer 3:6; 36:2 [b]2 Kin 21:18, 24 [c]Jer 25:3

3 [a]2 Kin 23:34; 1 Chr 3:15; 2 Chr 36:5-8; Jer 25:1 [b]2 Kin 24:17; 1 Chr 3:15; 2 Chr 36:11-13; Jer 39:2

5 [a]Ps 139:15, 16 [b]Is 49:1, 5; Luke 1:15 [c]Jer 1:10; 25:15-26

6 [1]Heb *YHWH,* usually rendered *LORD* [a]Ex 4:10 [b]1 Kin 3:7

7 [a]Ezek 2:3, 4 [b]Num 22:20; Jer 1:17

8 [a]Ex 3:12; Deut 31:6; Josh 1:5; Jer 15:20 [b]Ezek 2:6

9 [a]Is 6:7; Mark 7:33-35 [b]Ex 4:11-16; Deut 18:18; Is 51:16

10 [a]Rev 11:3-6 [b]Jer 18:7-10; Ezek 32:18; 2 Cor 10:4 [c]Is 44:26-28; Jer 24:6; 31:28, 40

11 [1]Heb *shaqed* [a]Jer 24:3; Amos 7:8

12 [1]Heb *shoqed* [a]Jer 31:28

13 [a]Zech 4:2 [b]Ezek 11:3, 7

14 [1]Lit *will be opened* [a]Is 41:25; Jer 4:6; 10:22

15 [a]Jer 25:9 [b]Is 22:7; Jer 39:3 [c]Jer 4:16; 9:11

16 [1]Lit *speak* [2]Or *burned incense* [a]Deut 28:20 [b]Jer 7:9; 19:4; 44:17 [c]Is 2:8; 37:19; Jer 10:3-5

17 [a]1 Kin 18:46; Job 38:3 [b]Ezek 2:6; 3:16-18

THE RULERS AND PROPHETS OF JEREMIAH'S TIME

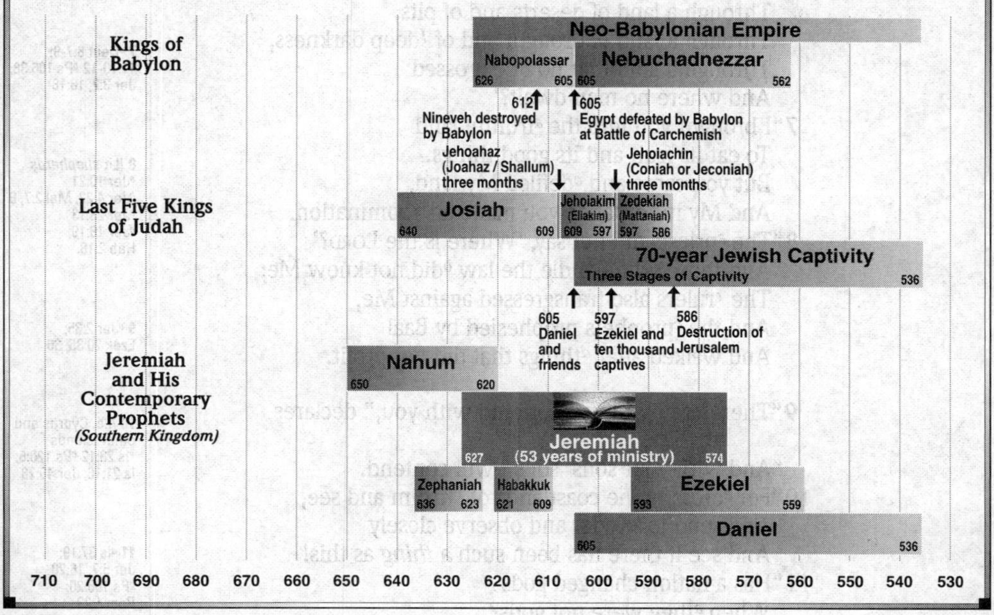

Kings of Babylon

Neo-Babylonian Empire

Nabopolassar 626 605

Nebuchadnezzar 605 562

612 Nineveh destroyed by Babylon

605 Egypt defeated by Babylon at Battle of Carchemish

Last Five Kings of Judah

Jehoahaz (Joahaz / Shallum) three months

Jehoiachin (Coniah or Jeconiah) three months

Josiah 640 609

Jehoiakim (Eliakim) 609 597

Zedekiah (Mattaniah) 597 586

70-year Jewish Captivity

Three Stages of Captivity 536

605 Daniel and friends

597 Ezekiel and ten thousand captives

586 Destruction of Jerusalem

Jeremiah and His Contemporary Prophets *(Southern Kingdom)*

Nahum 650 620

Jeremiah 627 (53 years of ministry) 574

Zephaniah 636 623

Habakkuk 621 609

Ezekiel 593 559

Daniel 605 536

710 700 690 680 670 660 650 640 630 620 610 600 590 580 570 560 550 540 530

19 [a]Num 14:9; Jer 1:8; 20:11

18 "Now behold, I have made you today as a fortified city and
as a pillar of iron and as walls of bronze against the whole land,
to the kings of Judah, to its princes, to its priests and to the
people of the land.
19 "They will fight against you, but they will not overcome you,
for [a]I am with you to deliver you," declares the LORD.

2:2 [1]Or *lovingkindness* [a]Is 58:1; Jer 7:2; 11:6 [b]Ezek 16:8; Hos 2:15 [c]Deut 2:7; Jer 2:6

Chapter 2 Theme ____________________

2 Now the word of the LORD came to me saying,
2 "Go and [a]proclaim in the ears of Jerusalem, saying, 'Thus
says the LORD,

"I remember concerning you the [1b]devotion of your youth,
The love of your betrothals,
[c]Your following after Me in the wilderness,
Through a land not sown.

3 [a]Ex 19:5, 6; Deut 7:6; 14:2 [b]James 1:18; Rev 14:4 [c]Is 41:11; Jer 30:16; 50:7

3 "Israel was [a]holy to the LORD,
The [b]first of His harvest.
[c]All who ate of it became guilty;
Evil came upon them," declares the LORD.'"

4 Hear the word of the LORD, O house of Jacob, and all the
families of the house of Israel.

5 Thus says the LORD,
"[a]What injustice did your fathers find in Me,
That they went far from Me
And walked after [b]emptiness and became empty?

5 [a]Is 5:4; Mic 6:3 [b]2 Kin 17:15; Jer 8:19; Rom 1:21

RETURN TO INSTRUCTIONS

6 "They did not say, 'Where is the LORD
Who [a]brought us up out of the land of Egypt,
Who [b]led us through the wilderness,
Through a land of deserts and of pits,
Through a land of drought and of [1]deep darkness,
Through a land that no one crossed
And where no man dwelt?'
7 "I brought you into the [a]fruitful land
To eat its fruit and its good things.
But you came and [b]defiled My land,
And My inheritance you made an abomination.
8 "The [a]priests did not say, 'Where is the LORD?'
And those who handle the law [b]did not know Me;
The [1]rulers also transgressed against Me,
And the [c]prophets prophesied by Baal
And walked after [d]things that did not profit.

9 "Therefore I will yet [a]contend with you," declares the LORD,
"And with your sons' sons I will contend.
10 "For [a]cross to the coastlands of [1]Kittim and see,
And send to [b]Kedar and observe closely
And see if there has been such *a thing* as this!
11 "Has a nation changed gods
When [a]they were not gods?
But My people have [b]changed their glory
For that which does not profit.
12 "Be appalled, [a]O heavens, at this,
And shudder, be very desolate," declares the LORD.
13 "For My people have committed two evils:
They have forsaken Me,
The [a]fountain of living waters,
To hew for themselves [b]cisterns,
Broken cisterns
That can hold no water.

14 "Is Israel [a]a slave? Or is he a homeborn servant?
Why has he become a prey?
15 "The young [a]lions have roared at him,
They have [1]roared loudly.
And they have [b]made his land a waste;
His cities have been destroyed, without inhabitant.
16 "Also the [1]men of [a]Memphis and Tahpanhes
Have [2]shaved the [b]crown of your head.
17 "Have you not [a]done this to yourself
By your forsaking the LORD your God
When He [a]led you in the way?
18 "But now what are you doing [a]on the road to Egypt,
To drink the waters of the [1b]Nile?
Or what are you doing on the road to Assyria,
To drink the waters of the [2]Euphrates?

6 [1]Or *the shadow of death* [a]Ex 20:2; Is 63:11 [b]Deut 8:15; 32:10

7 [a]Deut 8:7-9; 11:10-12 [b]Ps 106:38; Jer 3:2; 16:18

8 [1]Lit *shepherds* [a]Jer 10:21 [b]Jer 4:22; Mal 2:7, 8 [c]Jer 23:13 [d]Jer 16:19; Hab 2:18

9 [a]Jer 2:35; Ezek 20:35, 36

10 [1]I.e. Cyprus and other islands [a]Is 23:12 [b]Ps 120:5; Is 21:16; Jer 49:28

11 [a]Is 37:19; Jer 5:7; 16:20 [b]Ps 106:20; Rom 1:23

12 [a]Is 1:2; Jer 4:23

13 [a]Ps 36:9; Jer 17:13; John 4:14 [b]Jer 14:3

14 [a]Jer 5:19; 17:4

15 [1]Lit *given their voice* [a]Jer 50:17 [b]Jer 4:7

16 [1]Or *sons* [2]Lit *grazed* [a]Is 19:13; Jer 44:1; Hos 9:6 [b]Deut 33:20; Jer 48:45

17 [a]Deut 32:10; Jer 4:18

18 [1]Heb *Shihor* [2]Lit *River* [a]Is 30:2 [b]Josh 13:3

19 "[a]Your own wickedness will correct you,
And your [b]apostasies will reprove you;
Know therefore and see that it is evil and [c]bitter
For you to forsake the LORD your God,
And [d]the dread of Me is not in you," declares the Lord
[1]GOD of hosts.

20 "For long ago [1a]I broke your yoke
And tore off your bonds;
But you said, 'I will not serve!'
For on every [b]high hill
And under every green tree
You have lain down as a harlot.
21 "Yet I [a]planted you a choice vine,
A completely faithful seed.
How then have you turned yourself before Me
Into the [b]degenerate shoots of a foreign vine?
22 "Although you [a]wash yourself with lye
And [1]use much soap,
The [b]stain of your iniquity is before Me," declares the
Lord [2]GOD.
23 "[a]How can you say, 'I am not defiled,
I have not gone after the [b]Baals'?
Look at your way in the [c]valley!
Know what you have done!
You are a swift young camel [d]entangling her ways,
24 A [a]wild donkey accustomed to the wilderness,
That sniffs the wind in her passion.
In *the time of* her [1]heat who can turn her away?
All who seek her will not become weary;
In her month they will find her.
25 "Keep your feet from being unshod
And your throat from thirst;
But you said, '[a]It is [1]hopeless!
No! For I have [b]loved strangers,
And after them I will walk.'

26 "As the [a]thief is shamed when he is discovered,
So the house of Israel is shamed;
They, their kings, their princes
And their priests and their prophets,
27 Who say to a tree, 'You are my father,'
And to a stone, 'You gave me birth.'
For they have turned *their* [a]back to Me,
And not *their* face;
But in the [b]time of their [1]trouble they will say,
'Arise and save us.'
28 "But where are your [a]gods
Which you made for yourself?
Let them arise, if they can [b]save you
In the time of your [1]trouble;

19 [1]Heb *YHWH,* usually rendered LORD [a]Is 3:9; Jer 4:18; Hos 5:5 [b]Jer 3:6, 8, 11, 14; Hos 11:7 [c]Job 20:12-16; Amos 8:10 [d]Ps 36:1; Jer 5:24

20 [1]Or *you* [a]Lev 26:13 [b]Deut 12:2; Is 57:5, 7; Jer 3:2, 6; 17:2

21 [a]Ex 15:17; Ps 44:2; 80:8; Is 5:2 [b]Is 5:4

22 [1]Lit *cause to be great to you* [2]Heb *YHWH,* usually rendered LORD [a]Jer 4:14 [b]Job 14:17; Hos 13:12

23 [a]Prov 30:12 [b]Jer 9:14 [c]Jer 7:31 [d]Jer 2:33, 36; 31:22

24 [1]Lit *occasion* [a]Jer 14:6

25 [1]Or *desperate* [a]Jer 18:12 [b]Deut 32:16; Jer 14:10

26 [a]Jer 48:27

27 [1]Or *evil* [a]Jer 18:17; 32:33 [b]Judg 10:10; Is 26:16

28 [1]Or *evil* [a]Deut 32:37; Judg 10:14; Is 45:20; Jer 1:16 [b]Jer 11:12

For [c]*according to* the number of your cities
Are your gods, O Judah.

29 "Why do you contend with Me?
You have [a]all transgressed against Me," declares the LORD.
30 "[a]In vain I have struck your sons;
They accepted no chastening.
Your [b]sword has devoured your prophets
Like a destroying lion.
31 "O generation, heed the word of the LORD.
Have I been a wilderness to Israel,
Or a [a]land of thick darkness?
Why do My people say, '[b]We *are free to* roam;
We will no longer come to You'?
32 "Can a virgin forget her ornaments,
Or a bride her attire?
Yet My people have [a]forgotten Me
Days without number.
33 "How well you prepare your way
To seek love!
Therefore even [1]the wicked women
You have taught your ways.
34 "Also on your skirts is found
The [a]lifeblood of the innocent poor;
You did not find them [b]breaking in.
But in spite of all these things,
35 Yet you said, 'I am innocent;
Surely His anger is turned away from me.'
Behold, I will [a]enter into judgment with you
Because you [b]say, 'I have not sinned.'
36 "Why do you [a]go around so much
Changing your way?
Also, [b]you will be put to shame by Egypt
As you were put to shame by [c]Assyria.
37 "From this *place* also you will go out
With [a]your hands on your head;
For the LORD has rejected [b]those in whom you trust,
And you will not prosper with them."

Chapter 3 Theme ____________________

3 *God* [1]says, "[a]If a husband divorces his wife
And she goes from him
And belongs to another man,
Will he still return to her?
Will not that land be completely [2]polluted?
But you [b]are a harlot *with* many [3]lovers;
Yet you [c]turn to Me," declares the LORD.
2 "Lift up your eyes to the [a]bare heights and see;
Where have you not been violated?
By the roads you have [b]sat for them
Like an Arab in the desert,

28 [c]2 Kin 17:30, 31; Jer 11:13

29 [a]Jer 5:1; 6:13; Dan 9:11

30 [a]Is 1:5; Jer 5:3; 7:28 [b]Neh 9:26; Jer 26:20-24; Acts 7:52; 1 Thess 2:15

31 [a]Is 45:19 [b]Deut 32:15; Jer 2:20, 25

32 [a]Ps 106:21; Is 17:10; Jer 3:21; 13:25; Hos 8:14

33 [1]Or *in wickedness*

34 [a]2 Kin 21:16; 24:4; Ps 106:38; Jer 7:6; 19:4 [b]Ex 22:2

35 [a]Jer 25:31 [b]Prov 28:13; 1 John 1:8, 10

36 [a]Jer 2:23; 31:22; Hos 12:1 [b]Is 30:3 [c]2 Chr 28:16, 20, 21

37 [a]2 Sam 13:19; Jer 14:3, 4 [b]Jer 37:7-10

3:1 [1]Lit *saying* [2]Or *alienated* [3]Lit *companions* [a]Deut 24:1-4 [b]Jer 2:20; Ezek 16:26, 28, 29 [c]Jer 4:1; Zech 1:3

2 [a]Deut 12:2; Jer 2:20; 3:21; 7:29 [b]Gen 38:14; Ezek 16:25

And you have [c]polluted a land
With your harlotry and with your wickedness.
3 "Therefore the [a]showers have been withheld,
And there has been no spring rain.
Yet you had a [b]harlot's forehead;
You refused to be ashamed.
4 "Have you not just now called to Me,
'[a]My Father, You are the [1b]friend of my [c]youth?
5 '[a]Will He be angry forever?
Will He [1]be indignant to the end?'
Behold, you have spoken
And have done evil things,
And you have [2]had your way."

6 Then the LORD said to me in the days of Josiah the king,
"Have you seen what faithless Israel did? She [a]went up on every
high hill and under every green tree, and she was a harlot there.
7 "[a]I [1]thought, 'After she has done all these things she will
return to Me'; but she did not return, and her [b]treacherous
sister Judah saw it.
8 "And I saw that for all the adulteries of faithless Israel, I had
sent her away and [a]given her a writ of divorce, yet her
[b]treacherous sister Judah did not fear; but she went and was a
harlot also.
9 "Because of the lightness of her harlotry, she [a]polluted the
land and committed adultery with [b]stones and trees.
10 "Yet in spite of all this her treacherous sister Judah did not
return to Me with all her heart, but rather in [a]deception,"
declares the LORD.
11 And the LORD said to me, "[a]Faithless Israel has proved herself
more righteous than treacherous Judah.
12 "Go and proclaim these words toward the north and say,
'[a]Return, faithless Israel,' declares the LORD;
'[b]I will not [1]look upon you in anger.
For I am [c]gracious,' declares the LORD;
'I will not be angry forever.
13 'Only [1a]acknowledge your iniquity,
That you have transgressed against the LORD your God
And have [b]scattered your [2]favors to the strangers [c]under every green tree,
And you have not obeyed My voice,' declares the LORD.
14 'Return, O faithless sons,' declares the LORD;
'For I am a [a]master to you,
And I will take you one from a city and two from a family,
And [b]I will bring you to Zion.'
15 "Then I will give you [a]shepherds after My own heart, who
will [b]feed you on knowledge and understanding.
16 "It shall be in those days when you are multiplied and
increased in the land," declares the LORD, "they will [a]no longer
say, 'The ark of the covenant of the LORD.' And it will not come
to mind, nor will they remember it, nor will they miss *it,* nor
will it be made again.

2 [c]Jer 2:7
3 [a]Lev 26:19; Jer 14:3-6 [b]Jer 6:15; 8:12
4 [1]Lit *leader* [a]Jer 3:19; 31:9 [b]Ps 71:17; Prov 2:17 [c]Jer 2:2; Hos 2:15
5 [1]Lit *keep it* [2]Lit *been able* [a]Ps 103:9; Is 57:16; Jer 3:12
6 [a]Jer 17:2; Ezek 23:4-10
7 [1]Lit *said* [a]2 Kin 17:13 [b]Jer 3:11; Ezek 16:47
8 [a]Deut 24:1, 3; Is 50:1 [b]Ezek 16:46, 47; 23:11
9 [a]Jer 2:7; 3:2 [b]Is 57:6; Jer 2:27; 10:8
10 [a]Jer 12:2; Hos 7:14
11 [a]Ezek 16:51, 52; 23:11
12 [1]Lit *cause My countenance to fall* [a]Jer 3:14, 22; Ezek 33:11 [b]Jer 3:5 [c]Ps 86:15; Jer 12:15; 31:20; 33:26
13 [1]Lit *know* [2]Lit *ways* [a]Deut 30:1-3; Jer 3:25; 14:20; 1 John 1:9 [b]Jer 2:20, 25; 3:2, 6 [c]Deut 12:2
14 [a]Jer 31:32; Hos 2:19 [b]Jer 31:6, 12
15 [a]Jer 23:4; 31:10; Ezek 34:23; Eph 4:11 [b]Acts 20:28
16 [a]Is 65:17

17 "At that time they will call Jerusalem 'The [a]Throne of the
LORD,' and [b]all the nations will be gathered to it, to Jerusalem,
for the [c]name of the LORD; nor will they [d]walk anymore after
the stubbornness of their evil heart.
18 "[a]In those days the house of Judah will walk with the house
of Israel, and they will come together [b]from the land of the
north to the [c]land that I gave your fathers as an inheritance.
19 "Then I said,
'How I would set you among [1]My sons
And give you a pleasant land,
The most [a]beautiful inheritance of the nations!'
And I said, 'You shall call Me, [b]My Father,
And not turn away from following Me.'
20 "Surely, as a woman treacherously departs from her [1]lover,
So you have [a]dealt treacherously with Me,
O house of Israel," declares the LORD.

21 A voice is heard on the [a]bare heights,
The weeping *and* the supplications of the sons of Israel;
Because they have perverted their way,
They have [b]forgotten the LORD their God.
22 "Return, O faithless sons,
[a]I will heal your faithlessness."
"Behold, we come to You;
For You are the LORD our God.
23 "Surely, [a]the hills are a deception,
A tumult *on* the mountains.
Surely in the [b]LORD our God
Is the salvation of Israel.
24 "But [a]the shameful thing has consumed the labor of our
fathers since our youth, their flocks and their herds, their sons
and their daughters.
25 "Let us lie down in our [a]shame, and let our humiliation
cover us; for we have sinned against the LORD our God, we and
our fathers, [b]from our youth even to this day. And we have not
obeyed the voice of the LORD our God."

INSIGHT

The people set up their idols on hills (see 1 Kings 14:23).

Chapter 4 Theme ______________________

4 "If you will [a]return, O Israel," declares the LORD,
"*Then* you should return to Me.
And [b]if you will put away your detested things from My presence,
And will not waver,
2 And you will [a]swear, 'As the LORD lives,'
[b]In truth, in justice and in righteousness;
Then the [c]nations will bless themselves in Him,
And [d]in Him they will glory."

3 For thus says the LORD to the men of Judah and to Jerusalem,
"[1a]Break up your fallow ground,
And [b]do not sow among thorns.

17 [a]Jer 17:12; Ezek 43:7 [b]Jer 3:19; 4:2; 12:15, 16; 16:19 [c]Is 60:9 [d]Jer 11:8

18 [a]Is 11:13; Jer 50:4, 5; Hos 1:11 [b]Jer 16:15; 31:8 [c]Amos 9:15

19 [1]Lit *the* [a]Ps 16:6 [b]Is 63:16; Jer 3:4

20 [1]Or *companion* [a]Is 48:8

21 [a]Is 15:2; Jer 3:2; 7:29 [b]Is 17:10; Jer 2:32; 13:25

22 [a]Jer 30:17; 33:6; Hos 6:1; 14:4

23 [a]Jer 17:2 [b]Ps 3:8; Jer 17:14; 31:7

24 [a]Hos 9:10

25 [a]Ezra 9:6, 7 [b]Jer 22:21

4:1 [a]Jer 3:22; 15:19; Joel 2:12 [b]Jer 7:3, 7; 35:15

2 [a]Deut 10:20; Is 45:23; 65:16; Jer 12:16 [b]Is 48:1 [c]Gen 22:18; Jer 3:17; 12:15, 16; Gal 3:8 [d]Is 45:25; Jer 9:24; 1 Cor 1:31

3 [1]Lit *Plow for yourselves plowed ground* [a]Hos 10:12 [b]Matt 13:7

4 "[a]Circumcise yourselves to the LORD
And remove the foreskins of your heart,
Men of Judah and inhabitants of Jerusalem,
Or else My [b]wrath will go forth like fire
And burn with [c]none to quench it,
Because of the evil of your deeds."

5 Declare in Judah and proclaim in Jerusalem, and say,
"[a]Blow the trumpet in the land;
Cry aloud and say,
'[b]Assemble yourselves, and let us go
Into the fortified cities.'
6 "Lift up a [a]standard toward Zion!
Seek refuge, do not stand *still,*
For I am bringing [b]evil from the north,
And great destruction.
7 "A [a]lion has gone up from his thicket,
And a [b]destroyer of nations has set out;
He has gone out from his place
To [c]make your land a waste.
Your cities will be ruins
Without inhabitant.
8 "For this, [a]put on sackcloth,
Lament and wail;
For the [b]fierce anger of the LORD
Has not turned back from us."
9 "It shall come about in that day," declares the LORD, "that the
[a]heart of the king and the heart of the princes will fail; and the
priests will be appalled and the [b]prophets will be astounded."
10 Then I said, "Ah, Lord [1]GOD! Surely You have utterly [a]de-
ceived this people and Jerusalem, saying, '[b]You will have peace';
whereas a sword touches the [2]throat."
11 In that time it will be said to this people and to Jerusalem,
"A [a]scorching wind from the bare heights in the wilderness in
the direction of the daughter of My people—not to winnow
and not to cleanse,
12 a wind too strong for [1]this—will come [2]at My command;
now I will also pronounce judgments against them.
13 "Behold, he [a]goes up like clouds,
And his [b]chariots like the whirlwind;
His horses are [c]swifter than eagles.
Woe to us, for [d]we are ruined!"

14 Wash your heart from evil, O Jerusalem,
That you may be saved.
How long will your [a]wicked thoughts
Lodge within you?
15 For a voice declares from [a]Dan,
And proclaims wickedness from Mount Ephraim.
16 "Report *it* to the nations, now!
Proclaim over Jerusalem,

4 [a]Deut 10:16; 30:6; Jer 9:25, 26; Rom 2:28, 29; Col 2:11 [b]Is 30:27, 33; Jer 21:12; Zeph 2:2 [c]Amos 5:6; Mark 9:43, 48

5 [a]Jer 6:1; Hos 8:1 [b]Josh 10:20; Jer 8:14

6 [a]Is 62:10; Jer 4:21; 50:2 [b]Jer 1:14, 15; 6:1, 22

7 [a]Jer 5:6; 25:38; 50:17 [b]Jer 25:9; Ezek 26:7-10 [c]Is 1:7; 6:11; Jer 2:15

8 [a]Is 22:12; Jer 6:26 [b]Is 5:25; 10:4; Jer 30:24

9 [a]Is 22:3-5; Jer 48:41 [b]Is 29:9, 10; Ezek 13:9-16

10 [1]Heb *YHWH,* usually rendered LORD [2]Or *life* [a]Ezek 14:9; 2 Thess 2:11 [b]Jer 5:12; 14:13

11 [a]Jer 13:24; 51:1; Ezek 17:10; Hos 13:15

12 [1]Lit *these* [2]Lit *for Me*

13 [a]Is 19:1; Nah 1:3 [b]Is 5:28; 66:15 [c]Lam 4:19; Hab 1:8 [d]Is 3:8

14 [a]Prov 1:22; Jer 6:19; 13:27; James 4:8

15 [a]Jer 8:16

'Besiegers come from a [a]far country,
And [b]lift their voices against the cities of Judah.
17 'Like watchmen of a field they are [a]against her round about,
Because she has [b]rebelled against Me,' declares the LORD.
18 "Your [a]ways and your deeds
Have [1]brought these things to you.
This is your evil. How [b]bitter!
How it has touched your heart!"

19 [a]My [1]soul, my [1]soul! I am in anguish! [2]Oh, my heart!
My [b]heart is pounding in me;
I cannot be silent,
Because [3]you have heard, O my soul,
The [c]sound of the trumpet,
The alarm of war.
20 [a]Disaster on disaster is proclaimed,
For the [b]whole land is devastated;
Suddenly my [c]tents are devastated,
My curtains in an instant.
21 How long must I see the standard
And hear the sound of the trumpet?
22 "[a]For My people are foolish,
They know Me not;
They are stupid children
And have no understanding.
They are shrewd to [b]do evil,
But to do good they do not know."

23 I looked on the earth, and behold, *it was* [1a] formless
and void;
And to the heavens, and they had no light.
24 I looked on the mountains, and behold, they were [a]quaking,
And all the hills [1]moved to and fro.
25 I looked, and behold, there was no man,
And all the [a]birds of the heavens had fled.
26 I looked, and behold, [1]the [a]fruitful land was a wilderness,
And all its cities were pulled down
Before the LORD, before His fierce anger.

27 For thus says the LORD,
"The [a]whole land shall be a desolation,
Yet I will [b]not execute a complete destruction.
28 "For this the [a]earth shall mourn
And the [b]heavens above be dark,
Because I have [c]spoken, I have purposed,
And I will not [1]change My mind, nor will I turn from it."
29 At the sound of the horseman and bowman
[a]every city flees;
They [b]go into the thickets and climb among the rocks;
[c]Every city is forsaken,
And no man dwells in them.

16 [a]Is 39:3; Jer 5:15 [b]Ezek 21:22

17 [a]2 Kin 25:1, 4 [b]Is 1:20, 23; Jer 5:23

18 [1]Lit *done* [a]Ps 107:17; Is 50:1; Jer 2:17, 19 [b]Jer 2:19

19 [1]Lit *inward parts* [2]Lit *The walls of my heart* [3]Or *I, my soul, heard* [a]Is 15:5; 16:11; 21:3; 22:4; Jer 9:1, 10; 20:9 [b]Hab 3:16 [c]Num 10:9

20 [a]Ps 42:7; Ezek 7:26 [b]Jer 4:27 [c]Jer 10:20

22 [a]Jer 5:4, 21; 10:8; Rom 1:22 [b]Jer 9:3; 13:23; Rom 16:19; 1 Cor 14:20

23 [1]Or *a waste and emptiness* [a]Gen 1:2; Is 24:19

24 [1]Lit *moved lightly* [a]Is 5:25; Jer 10:10; Ezek 38:20

25 [a]Jer 9:10; 12:4; Zeph 1:3

26 [1]Or *Carmel* [a]Jer 9:10

27 [a]Jer 12:11, 12; 25:11 [b]Jer 5:10, 18; 30:11; 46:28

28 [1]Lit *be sorry* [a]Jer 12:4, 11; 14:2; Hos 4:3 [b]Is 5:30; 50:3; Joel 2:30, 31 [c]Num 23:19; Jer 23:20; 30:24

29 [a]2 Kin 25:4 [b]Is 2:19-21; Jer 16:16 [c]Jer 4:7

30 [1]Lit *paramours* [a]Is 10:3; 20:6; Jer 13:21 [b]2 Kin 9:30; Ezek 23:40 [c]Jer 22:20, 22; Lam 1:2, 19; Ezek 23:9, 10, 22

30 And you, O desolate one, [a]what will you do?
Although you dress in scarlet,
Although you decorate *yourself with* ornaments of gold,
Although you [b]enlarge your eyes with paint,
In vain you make yourself beautiful.
Your [1c]lovers despise you;
They seek your life.

31 [1]Lit *sound* [2]Lit *palms* [3]Lit *my soul faints* [a]Is 42:14 [b]Is 1:15; Lam 1:17

31 For I heard a [1]cry as of a woman in labor,
The anguish as of one giving birth to her first child,
The [1]cry of the daughter of Zion [a]gasping for breath,
[b]Stretching out her [2]hands, *saying,*
"Ah, woe is me, for [3]I faint before murderers."

Chapter 5 Theme

5:1 [1]Lit *faithfulness* [a]2 Chr 16:9; Dan 12:4 [b]Ezek 22:30 [c]Gen 18:26, 32

5 "[a]Roam to and fro through the streets of Jerusalem,
And look now and take note.
And seek in her open squares,
If you can [b]find a man,
[c]If there is one who does justice, who seeks [1]truth,
Then I will pardon her.

2 [a]Is 48:1; Titus 1:16

2 "And [a]although they say, 'As the LORD lives,'
Surely they swear falsely."

3 [1]Lit *faithfulness* [2]Or *become sick* [a]2 Chr 16:9 [b]Is 1:5; 9:13; Jer 2:30 [c]Jer 7:28; 8:5; Zeph 3:2 [d]Jer 7:26; 19:15; Ezek 3:8

3 O LORD, do not [a]Your eyes *look* for [1]truth?
You have [b]smitten them,
But they did not [2]weaken;
You have consumed them,
But they [c]refused to take correction.
They have [d]made their faces harder than rock;
They have refused to repent.

4 [a]Is 27:11; Jer 8:7; Hos 4:6

4 Then I said, "They are only the poor,
They are foolish;
For they [a]do not know the way of the LORD
Or the ordinance of their God.

5 [a]Mic 3:1 [b]Ex 32:25; Ps 2:3; Jer 2:20

5 "I will go to the great
And will speak to them,
For [a]they know the way of the LORD
And the ordinance of their God."
But they too, with one accord, have [b]broken the yoke
And burst the bonds.

6 [a]Jer 4:7 [b]Ezek 22:27; Hab 1:8; Zeph 3:3 [c]Hos 13:7 [d]Jer 30:14, 15

6 Therefore [a]a lion from the forest will slay them,
A [b]wolf of the deserts will destroy them,
A [c]leopard is watching their cities.
Everyone who goes out of them will be torn in pieces,
Because their [d]transgressions are many,
Their apostasies are numerous.

7 [a]Josh 23:7; Jer 12:16; Zeph 1:5 [b]Deut 32:21; Jer 2:11; Gal 4:8

7 "Why should I pardon you?
Your sons have forsaken Me
And [a]sworn by those who are [b]not gods.

When I had fed them to the full,
They [c]committed adultery
And trooped to the harlot's house.
8 "They were well-fed lusty horses,
Each one neighing after his [a]neighbor's wife.
9 "Shall I not punish [1]these *people*," declares the LORD,
"And on a nation such as this
[a]Shall I not avenge Myself?

10 "Go up through her vine rows and destroy,
But do not execute a complete destruction;
Strip away her branches,
For they are not the LORD'S.
11 "For the [a]house of Israel and the house of Judah
Have dealt very treacherously with Me," declares
the LORD.
12 They have [a]lied about the LORD
And said, "[1b]Not He;
Misfortune will [c]not come on us,
And we [d]will not see sword or famine.
13 "The [a]prophets are *as* wind,
And the word is not in them.
Thus it will be done to them!"

14 Therefore, thus says the LORD, the God of hosts,
"Because you have spoken this word,
Behold, I am [a]making My words in your mouth fire
And this people wood, and it will consume them.
15 "Behold, I am [a]bringing a nation against you from afar,
O house of Israel," declares the LORD.
"It is an enduring nation,
It is an ancient nation,
A nation whose [b]language you do not know,
Nor can you understand what they say.
16 "Their [a]quiver is like an [b]open grave,
All of them are mighty men.
17 "They will [a]devour your harvest and your food;
They will devour your sons and your daughters;
They will devour your flocks and your herds;
They will devour your [b]vines and your fig trees;
They will demolish with the sword your [c]fortified cities in
which you trust.
18 "Yet even in those days," declares the LORD, "I will not make
you a complete destruction.
19 "It shall come about [a]when [1]they say, 'Why has the LORD our
God done all these things to us?' then you shall say to them,
'As you have forsaken Me and served foreign gods in your land,
so you will [b]serve strangers in a land that is not yours.'
20 "Declare this in the house of Jacob
And proclaim it in Judah, saying,

7 [c]Jer 7:9
8 [a]Jer 13:27; 29:23; Ezek 22:11
9 [1]Or *for these things* [a]Jer 9:9
11 [a]Jer 3:6, 7, 20
12 [1]Lit *He is not* [a]2 Chr 36:16 [b]Prov 30:9; Jer 14:22; 43:1-4 [c]Jer 23:17 [d]Jer 14:13
13 [a]Job 8:2; Jer 14:13, 15; 22:22
14 [a]Is 24:6; Jer 1:9; 23:29; Hos 6:5; Zech 1:6
15 [a]Deut 28:49; Is 5:26; Jer 4:16 [b]Is 28:11
16 [a]Is 5:28; 13:18 [b]Ps 5:9
17 [a]Lev 26:16; Deut 28:31, 33; Jer 8:16; 50:7, 17 [b]Jer 8:13 [c]Hos 8:14
19 [1]Or *you* [a]Deut 29:24-26; 1 Kin 9:8, 9; Jer 13:22; 16:10-13 [b]Deut 28:48; Jer 16:13

21 'Now hear this, O foolish and [1]senseless people,
Who have [a]eyes but do not see;
Who have ears but do not hear.
22 'Do you not [a]fear Me?' declares the LORD.
'Do you not tremble in My presence?
For I have [b]placed the sand as a boundary for the sea,
An eternal decree, so it cannot cross over it.
Though the waves toss, yet they cannot prevail;
Though they roar, yet they cannot cross over it.
23 'But this people has a [a]stubborn and rebellious heart;
They have turned aside and departed.
24 'They do not say in their heart,
"Let us now fear the LORD our God,
Who [a]gives rain in its season,
Both [b]the autumn rain and the spring rain,
Who keeps for us
The [c]appointed weeks of the harvest."
25 'Your [a]iniquities have turned these away,
And your sins have withheld good from you.
26 'For wicked men are found among My people,
They [a]watch like fowlers [1]lying in wait;
They set a trap,
They catch men.
27 'Like a cage full of birds,
So their houses are full of [a]deceit;
Therefore they have become great and rich.
28 'They are [a]fat, they are sleek,
They also [1]excel in deeds of wickedness;
They do not plead the cause,
The cause of the [2b]orphan, that they may prosper;
And they do not [3]defend the rights of the poor.
29 '[a]Shall I not punish [1]these *people?*' declares the LORD,
'On a nation such as this
Shall I not avenge Myself?'

30 "An appalling and [a]horrible thing
Has happened in the land:
31 The [a]prophets prophesy falsely,
And the priests rule [1]on their *own* authority;
And My people [b]love it so!
But what will you do at the end of it?

Chapter 6 Theme ____________________

6 "Flee for safety, O sons of [a]Benjamin,
From the midst of Jerusalem!
Now blow a trumpet in Tekoa
And raise a signal over [1b]Beth-haccerem;
For evil looks down from the [c]north,
And a great destruction.
2 "The comely and [a]dainty one, [b]the daughter of Zion,
I will cut off.

21 [1]Lit *without heart* [a]Is 6:9; 43:8; Ezek 12:2; Matt 13:14; Mark 8:18; John 12:40; Acts 28:26; Rom 11:8
22 [a]Deut 28:58; Ps 119:120; Jer 2:19; 10:7; Rev 15:4 [b]Job 38:8-11; Ps 104:9; Prov 8:29
23 [a]Deut 21:18; Ps 78:8; Jer 4:17; 6:28
24 [a]Ps 147:8; Jer 3:3; Matt 5:45; Acts 14:17 [b]Joel 2:23 [c]Gen 8:22
25 [a]Jer 2:17; 4:18
26 [1]Perhaps, *crouching down* [a]Ps 10:9; Prov 1:11; Jer 18:22; Hab 1:15
27 [a]Jer 9:6
28 [1]Lit *pass over,* or, *overlook deeds* [2]Or *fatherless* [3]Lit *judge* [a]Deut 32:15 [b]Is 1:23; Jer 7:6; 22:3; Zech 7:10
29 [1]Or *for these things* [a]Jer 5:9; Mal 3:5
30 [a]Jer 23:14; Hos 6:10
31 [1]Lit *over their own hands* [a]Ezek 13:6 [b]Mic 2:11
6:1 [1]I.e. house of the vineyard [a]Josh 18:28 [b]Neh 3:14 [c]Jer 1:14; 4:6; 6:22
2 [a]Deut 28:56 [b]Is 1:8; Jer 4:31

3 "[a]Shepherds and their flocks will come to her,
They will [b]pitch *their* tents [1]around her,
They will pasture each in his [2]place.
4 "[1a]Prepare war against her;
Arise, and let us [2]attack at [b]noon.
Woe to us, for the day declines,
For the shadows of the evening lengthen!
5 "Arise, and let us [1]attack by night
And [a]destroy her [2]palaces!"
6 For thus says the LORD of hosts,
"[a]Cut down her trees
And cast up a [b]siege against Jerusalem.
This is the city to be punished,
In whose midst there is only [c]oppression.
7 "[a]As a well [1]keeps its waters fresh,
So she [1]keeps fresh her wickedness.
[b]Violence and destruction are heard in her;
[c]Sickness and wounds are ever before Me.
8 "[a]Be warned, O Jerusalem,
Or [1b]I shall be alienated from you,
And make you a desolation,
A land not inhabited."

9 Thus says the LORD of hosts,
"They will [a]thoroughly glean as the vine the [b]remnant of Israel;
Pass your hand again like a grape gatherer
Over the branches."
10 To whom shall I speak and give warning
That they may hear?
Behold, their [a]ears are [1]closed
And they cannot listen.
Behold, [b]the word of the LORD has become a reproach to them;
They have no delight in it.
11 But I am [a]full of the wrath of the LORD;
I am [b]weary with holding *it* in.
"[c]Pour *it* out on the children in the street
And on the [1]gathering of young men together;
For both husband and wife shall be taken,
The aged [2]and the very old.
12 "Their [a]houses shall be turned over to others,
Their fields and their wives together;
For I will [b]stretch out My hand
Against the inhabitants of the land," declares the LORD.
13 "For [a]from the least of them even to the greatest of them,
Everyone is [b]greedy for gain,
And from the prophet even to the priest
Everyone [1]deals falsely.
14 "They have [a]healed the brokenness of My people superficially,
Saying, 'Peace, peace,'

3 [1]Lit *against her round about* [2]Lit *hand* [a]Jer 12:10 [b]2 Kin 25:1; Jer 4:17; Luke 19:43

4 [1]Lit *Sanctify* [2]Lit *go up* [a]Jer 6:23; Joel 3:9 [b]Jer 15:8; Zeph 2:4

5 [1]Lit *go up* [2]Or *fortified towers* [a]Is 32:14; Jer 52:13

6 [a]Deut 20:19, 20 [b]Jer 32:24; 33:4 [c]Jer 22:17

7 [1]Lit *keeps cold* [a]James 3:11f [b]Jer 20:8; Ezek 7:11, 23 [c]Jer 30:12, 13

8 [1]Lit *my soul* [a]Jer 7:28; 17:23 [b]Ezek 23:18; Hos 9:12

9 [a]Jer 16:16; 49:9; Obad 5, 6 [b]Jer 8:3; 11:23

10 [1]Lit *uncircumcised* [a]Jer 5:21; 7:26; Acts 7:51 [b]Jer 20:8

11 [1]Lit *council* [2]Lit *with fullness of days* [a]Job 32:18, 19; Mic 3:8 [b]Jer 15:6; 20:9 [c]Jer 7:20; 9:21

12 [a]Deut 28:30; Jer 8:10; 38:22, 23 [b]Jer 15:6

13 [1]Or *makes lies* [a]Jer 8:10 [b]Is 56:11; 57:17; Jer 8:10; 22:17

14 [a]Jer 8:11; Ezek 13:10

15 [a]Jer 3:3; 8:12
16 [a]Is 8:20; Jer 12:16; 18:15; 31:21; Mal 4:4; Luke 16:29 [b]Matt 11:29
17 [a]Is 21:11; 58:1; Jer 25:4; Ezek 3:17; Hab 2:1
19 [1]Or *devices* [a]Is 1:2; Jer 19:3, 15; 22:29 [b]Prov 1:31 [c]Jer 8:9
20 [1]Lit *good* [a]Ps 50:7-9; Is 1:11; 66:3; Mic 6:6 [b]Is 60:6 [c]Ex 30:23 [d]Ps 40:6; Amos 5:22
21 [1]Lit *giving* [2]Lit *his friend* [a]Is 8:14; Jer 13:16 [b]Is 9:14-17; Jer 9:21, 22
22 [a]Jer 1:15; 10:22; 50:41-43 [b]Neh 1:9
23 [a]Is 13:18; Jer 4:29 [b]Jer 50:42 [c]Is 5:30
24 [a]Is 28:19; Jer 4:19-21 [b]Is 21:3; Jer 4:31; 13:21; 30:6; 49:24; 50:43

But there is no peace.
15 "Were they [a]ashamed because of the abomination
they have done?
They were not even ashamed at all;
They did not even know how to blush.
Therefore they shall fall among those who fall;
At the time that I punish them,
They shall be cast down," says the LORD.

16 Thus says the LORD,
"Stand by the ways and see and ask for the [a]ancient paths,
Where the good way is, and walk in it;
And [b]you will find rest for your souls.
But they said, 'We will not walk *in it.*'
17 "And I set [a]watchmen over you, *saying,*
'Listen to the sound of the trumpet!'
But they said, 'We will not listen.'
18 "Therefore hear, O nations,
And know, O congregation, what is among them.
19 "[a]Hear, O earth: behold, I am bringing disaster
on this people,
The [b]fruit of their [1]plans,
Because they have not listened to My words,
And as for My law, they have [c]rejected it also.
20 "[a]For what purpose does [b]frankincense come to Me
from Sheba
And the [1c]sweet cane from a distant land?
[d]Your burnt offerings are not acceptable
And your sacrifices are not pleasing to Me."
21 Therefore, thus says the LORD,
"Behold, [a]I am [1]laying stumbling blocks before
this people.
And they will stumble against them,
[b]Fathers and sons together;
Neighbor and [2]friend will perish."

22 Thus says the LORD,
"Behold, [a]a people is coming from the north land,
And a great nation will be aroused from the [b]remote parts
of the earth.
23 "They seize [a]bow and spear;
They are [b]cruel and have no mercy;
Their voice [c]roars like the sea,
And they ride on horses,
Arrayed as a man for the battle
Against you, O daughter of Zion!"
24 We have [a]heard the report of it;
Our hands are limp.
[b]Anguish has seized us,
Pain as of a woman in childbirth.

25 [a]Do not go out into the field
And [b]do not walk on the road,
For the enemy has a sword,
[c]Terror is on every side.
26 O daughter of my people, [a]put on sackcloth
And [b]roll in ashes;
[1c]Mourn as for an only son,
A lamentation most bitter.
For suddenly the destroyer
Will come upon us.

27 "I have [a]made you an assayer *and* a tester among
My people,
That you may know and assay their way."
28 All of them are stubbornly rebellious,
[a]Going about as a talebearer.
They are [b]bronze and iron;
They, all of them, are corrupt.
29 The bellows blow fiercely,
The lead is consumed by the fire;
In vain the refining goes on,
But the [a]wicked are not [1]separated.
30 [a]They call them rejected silver,
Because the [b]LORD has rejected them.

Chapter 7 Theme ____________________________

7 The word that came to Jeremiah from the LORD, saying,
2 "[a]Stand in the gate of the LORD's house and proclaim
there this word and say, 'Hear the word of the LORD, all you of
Judah, who enter by these gates to worship the LORD!'"
3 Thus says the LORD of hosts, the God of Israel, "[a]Amend
your ways and your deeds, and I will let you dwell in this place.
4 "[a]Do not trust in deceptive words, saying, '[1]This is the temple
of the LORD, the temple of the LORD, the temple of the LORD.'
5 "For [a]if you truly amend your ways and your deeds, if you
truly [b]practice justice between a man and his neighbor,
6 *if* you do not oppress the alien, the [1a]orphan, or the widow,
and do not shed [b]innocent blood in this place, nor [c]walk after
other gods to your own ruin,
7 then I will let you [a]dwell in this place, in the [b]land that I
gave to your fathers forever and ever.
8 "Behold, you are trusting in [a]deceptive words to no avail.
9 "Will you steal, murder, and commit adultery and swear
falsely, and [1a]offer sacrifices to Baal and walk after [b]other gods
that you have not known,
10 then [a]come and stand before Me in [b]this house, which is
called by My name, and say, 'We are delivered!'—that you may
do all these abominations?
11 "Has [a]this house, which is called by My name, become a
[b]den of robbers in your sight? Behold, [c]I, even I, have seen *it*,"
declares the LORD.

25 [a]Jer 14:18 [b]Judg 5:6 [c]Jer 20:10; 46:5; 49:29

26 [1]Lit *Make for yourself mourning* [a]Jer 4:8 [b]Jer 25:34; Mic 1:10 [c]Amos 8:10; Zech 12:10

27 [a]Jer 1:18; 15:20

28 [a]Jer 9:4 [b]Ezek 22:18

29 [1]Or *drawn off* [a]Jer 15:19

30 [a]Ps 119:119; Is 1:22 [b]Jer 7:29; Hos 9:17; Zech 11:8

7:2 [a]Jer 17:19; 26:2

3 [a]Jer 4:1; 7:5; 18:11; 26:13

4 [1]Lit *They are* [a]Jer 7:8; Mic 3:11

5 [a]Is 1:19; Jer 4:1, 2 [b]1 Kin 6:12; Jer 21:12; 22:3

6 [1]Or *fatherless* [a]Ex 22:21-24; Jer 5:28 [b]Jer 2:34; 19:4 [c]Deut 6:14, 15; 8:19; 11:28; Jer 13:10

7 [a]Deut 4:40 [b]Jer 3:18

8 [a]Jer 7:4; 28:15

9 [1]Or *burn incense* [a]Jer 11:13, 17 [b]Ex 20:3; Jer 7:6; 19:4

10 [a]Ezek 23:39 [b]Jer 7:11, 14, 30; 32:34

11 [a]Is 56:7 [b]Matt 21:13; Mark 11:17; Luke 19:46 [c]Jer 29:23

12 "But go now to My place which was in [a]Shiloh, where I
[b]made My name dwell at the first, and [c]see what I did to it
because of the wickedness of My people Israel.
13 "And now, because you have done all these things," declares
the LORD, "and I spoke to you, [a]rising up early and [b]speaking,
but you did not hear, and I [c]called you but you did not answer,
14 therefore, I will do to the [a]house which is called by My
name, [b]in which you trust, and to the place which I gave you
and your fathers, as I [c]did to Shiloh.
15 "I will [a]cast you out of My sight, as I have cast out all your
brothers, all the [1]offspring of [b]Ephraim.
16 "As for you, [a]do not pray for this people, and do not lift up
cry or prayer for them, and do not intercede with Me; for I do
not hear you.
17 "Do you not see what they are doing in the cities of Judah
and in the streets of Jerusalem?
18 "The [1]children gather wood, and the fathers kindle the fire,
and the women knead dough to make cakes for the queen of
heaven; and *they* [a]pour out drink offerings to other gods in
order to [b]spite Me.
19 "[a]Do they spite Me?" declares the LORD. "Is it not themselves
they spite, to [1]their own [b]shame?"
20 Therefore thus says the Lord [1]GOD, "Behold, My [a]anger
and My wrath will be poured out on this place, on man and on
beast and on the [b]trees of the field and on the fruit of the
ground; and it will burn and not be quenched."
21 Thus says the LORD of hosts, the God of Israel, "Add your
[a]burnt offerings to your sacrifices and [b]eat flesh.
22 "For I did not [a]speak to your fathers, or command them in the
day that I brought them out of the land of Egypt, concerning
burnt offerings and sacrifices.
23 "But this is [1]what I commanded them, saying, '[a]Obey My
voice, and [b]I will be your God, and you will be My people; and
you will walk in all the way which I command you, that it may
[c]be well with you.'
24 "Yet they [a]did not obey or incline their ear, but walked in
their own counsels *and* in the stubbornness of their evil heart,
and [1][b]went backward and not forward.
25 "Since the day that your fathers came out of the land of Egypt
until this day, I have [a]sent you all My servants the prophets,
daily rising early and sending *them.*
26 "Yet they did not listen to Me or incline their ear, but
[a]stiffened their neck; they [b]did more evil than their fathers.
27 "You shall [a]speak all these words to them, but they will not
listen to you; and you shall call to them, but they will [b]not
answer you.
28 "You shall say to them, 'This is the nation that [a]did not obey
the voice of the LORD their God or accept correction; [1][b]truth
has perished and has been cut off from their mouth.
29 '[a]Cut off [1]your hair and cast *it* away,
And [b]take up a lamentation on the bare heights;

INSIGHT

Shiloh, the home of the tabernacle, was Israel's religious center for about 400 years after the conquest of Canaan under Joshua. When they took the ark of the covenant from Shiloh, the Philistines slaughtered 30,000 of Israel's foot soldiers (1 Samuel 4:1-11).

12 [a]Judg 18:31; Jer 26:6 [b]Josh 18:1, 10 [c]1 Sam 4:10, 11, 22; Ps 78:60-64

13 [a]Jer 7:25 [b]Jer 35:17 [c]Prov 1:24; Is 65:12; 66:4

14 [a]Deut 12:5; 1 Kin 9:7 [b]Jer 7:4 [c]Jer 7:12

15 [1]Lit *seed* [a]Jer 15:1; 52:3 [b]Ps 78:67; Hos 7:13; 9:13; 12:1

16 [a]Ex 32:10; Deut 9:14; Jer 11:14

18 [1]Lit *sons* [a]Jer 19:13 [b]Deut 32:16, 21; 1 Kin 14:9; 16:2; Jer 11:17; Ezek 8:17

19 [1]Lit *their faces'* [a]Job 35:6; 1 Cor 10:22 [b]Jer 9:19; 15:9; 22:22

20 [1]Heb *YHWH,* usually rendered *LORD* [a]Is 42:25; Jer 6:11, 12; 42:18; Lam 2:3-5; 4:11 [b]Jer 8:13; 11:16

21 [a]Is 1:11; Jer 6:20; 14:12; Amos 5:22 [b]Ezek 33:25; Hos 8:13

22 [a]1 Sam 15:22; Ps 51:16; Hos 6:6

23 [1]Lit *the word which* [a]Ex 15:26; 16:32; Deut 6:3 [b]Ex 19:5, 6; Lev 26:12; Jer 11:4; 13:11 [c]Is 3:10; Jer 38:20; 42:6

24 [1]Lit *they were* [a]Deut 29:19; Ps 81:11; Jer 11:8; Ezek 20:8, 13, 16, 21 [b]Jer 15:6

25 [a]2 Chr 36:15; Jer 25:4; 29:19; Luke 11:49

26 [a]Neh 9:16; Jer 17:23; 19:15 [b]Jer 16:12; Matt 23:32

27 [a]Jer 1:7; 26:2; Ezek 2:7 [b]Is 50:2; 65:12; Zech 7:13

28 [1]Lit *faithfulness* [a]Jer 6:17; 11:10 [b]Is 59:14, 15; Jer 9:5

29 [1]Lit *your crown* [a]Job 1:20; Is 15:2; 22:12; Jer 16:6; Mic 1:16 [b]Jer 3:21; 9:17, 18

For the LORD has [c]rejected and forsaken
The generation of His wrath.'
30 "For the sons of Judah have done that which is evil in My
sight," declares the LORD, "they have [a]set their detestable
things in the house which is called by My name, to defile it.
31 "They have [a]built the high places of Topheth, which is in
the valley of the son of Hinnom, to [b]burn their sons and their
daughters in the fire, which I [c]did not command, and it did not
come into My [1]mind.
32 "[a]Therefore, behold, days are coming," declares the LORD,
"when it will no longer be called Topheth, or the valley of the
son of Hinnom, but the valley of the Slaughter; for they will
[b]bury in Topheth [1]because there is no *other* place.
33 "The [a]dead bodies of this people will be food for the birds of
the sky and for the beasts of the earth; and no one will frighten
them away.
34 "Then I will make to [a]cease from the cities of Judah and from
the streets of Jerusalem the voice of joy and the voice of
gladness, the voice of the bridegroom and the voice of the
bride; for the [b]land will become a ruin.

Chapter 8 Theme

8 "At that time," declares the LORD, "they will [a]bring out the
bones of the kings of Judah and the bones of its princes,
and the bones of the priests and the bones of the prophets, and
the bones of the inhabitants of Jerusalem from their graves.
2 "They will spread them out to the sun, the moon and to all
the [a]host of heaven, which they have loved and which they
have served, and which they have gone after and which they
have sought, and which they have worshiped. They will not be
gathered [b]or buried; [c]they will be as dung on the face of the
ground.
3 "And [a]death will be chosen rather than life by all the remnant
that remains of this evil family, that remains in all the [b]places to
which I have driven them," declares the LORD of hosts.
4 "You shall say to them, 'Thus says the LORD,
"Do *men* [a]fall and not get up again?
Does one turn away and not [1]repent?
5 "Why then has this people, Jerusalem,
[a]Turned away in continual apostasy?
They [b]hold fast to deceit,
They [c]refuse to return.
6 "I [a]have listened and heard,
They have spoken what is not right;
[b]No man repented of his wickedness,
Saying, 'What have I done?'
Everyone turned to his course,
Like a [c]horse charging into the battle.
7 "Even the stork in the sky
[a]Knows her seasons;

29 [c]Jer 6:30; 14:19

30 [a]2 Kin 21:3f; 2 Chr 33:3-5, 7; Jer 32:34, 35; Ezek 7:20; Dan 9:27; 11:31

31 [1]Lit *heart* [a]2 Kin 23:10; Jer 19:5; 32:35 [b]Lev 18:21; 2 Kin 17:17; Ps 106:38 [c]Deut 17:3

32 [1]Or *until there is no place left* [a]Jer 19:6, 11 [b]2 Kin 23:10

33 [a]Deut 28:26; Ps 79:2; Jer 12:9; 19:7

34 [a]Is 24:7, 8; Jer 16:9; 25:10; Ezek 26:13; Hos 2:11; Rev 18:23 [b]Lev 26:33; Is 1:7; Jer 4:27

8:1 [a]Ezek 6:5

2 [a]2 Kin 23:5; Jer 19:13; Zeph 1:5; Acts 7:42 [b]Jer 22:19; 36:30 [c]2 Kin 9:37; Ps 83:10; Jer 9:22

3 [a]Job 3:21, 22; 7:15, 16; Jon 4:3; Rev 9:6 [b]Deut 30:1, 4; Jer 23:3, 8; 29:14

4 [1]Lit *turn back* [a]Prov 24:16; Amos 5:2; Mic 7:8

5 [a]Jer 5:6; 7:24 [b]Jer 5:27; 9:6 [c]Jer 5:3

6 [a]Ps 14:2; Mal 3:16 [b]Ezek 22:30; Mic 7:2; Rev 9:20 [c]Job 39:21-25

7 [a]Prov 6:6-8; Is 1:3

And the [b]turtledove and the swift and the thrush
Observe the time of their [1]migration;
But [c]My people do not know
The ordinance of the LORD.

8 "[a]How can you say, 'We are wise,
And the law of the LORD is with us'?
But behold, the lying pen of the scribes
Has made *it* into a lie.
9 "The wise men are [a]put to shame,
They are dismayed and caught;
Behold, they have [b]rejected the word of the LORD,
And what kind of wisdom do they have?
10 "Therefore I will [a]give their wives to others,
Their fields to [1]new owners;
Because from the least even to the greatest
Everyone is [b]greedy for gain;
From the prophet even to the priest
Everyone practices deceit.
11 "They [a]heal the brokenness of the daughter of My people
superficially,
Saying, 'Peace, peace,'
But there is no peace.
12 "Were they [a]ashamed because of the abomination
they had done?
They certainly were not ashamed,
And they did not know how to blush;
Therefore they shall [b]fall among those who fall;
At the [c]time of their punishment they shall be
brought down,"
Says the LORD.

13 "I will [a]surely snatch them away," declares the LORD;
"There will be [b]no grapes on the vine
And [c]no figs on the fig tree,
And the leaf will wither;
And what I have given them will pass away.""
14 Why are we sitting still?
[a]Assemble yourselves, and let us [b]go into the
fortified cities
And let us perish there,
Because the LORD our God has doomed us
And given us [c]poisoned water to drink,
For [d]we have sinned against the LORD.
15 *We* [a]waited for peace, but no good *came;*
For a time of healing, but behold, terror!
16 From [a]Dan is heard the snorting of his horses;
At the sound of the neighing of his [b]stallions
The whole land quakes;
For they come and [c]devour the land and its fullness,
The city and its inhabitants.

7 [1]Lit *coming* [b]Song 2:12 [c]Jer 5:4
8 [a]Job 5:12, 13; Jer 4:22; Rom 1:22
9 [a]Is 19:11; Jer 6:15; 1 Cor 1:27 [b]Jer 6:19
10 [1]Lit *possessing ones* [a]Deut 28:30; Jer 6:12, 13; 38:22f [b]Is 56:11; 57:17; Jer 6:13
11 [a]Jer 6:14; 14:13, 14; Lam 2:14; Ezek 13:10
12 [a]Ps 52:1, 7; Is 3:9; Jer 3:3; 6:15; Zeph 3:5 [b]Is 9:14; Jer 6:21; Hos 4:5 [c]Deut 32:35; Jer 10:15
13 [a]Jer 14:12; Ezek 22:20, 21 [b]Jer 5:17; 7:20; Joel 1:7 [c]Matt 21:19; Luke 13:6
14 [a]Jer 4:5 [b]2 Sam 20:6; Jer 35:11 [c]Deut 29:18; Ps 69:21; Jer 9:15; 23:15; Lam 3:19; Matt 27:34 [d]Jer 3:25; 14:20
15 [a]Jer 8:11; 14:19
16 [a]Judg 18:29; Jer 4:15 [b]Judg 5:22 [c]Jer 3:24; 10:25

17 "For behold, I am [a]sending serpents against you,
Adders, for which there is [b]no charm,
And they will bite you," declares the LORD.

18 [1]My [a]sorrow is beyond healing,
My [b]heart is faint *within me!*
19 Behold, listen! The cry of the daughter of my people
from a [a]distant land:
"Is the LORD not in Zion? Is her King not within her?"
"Why have they [b]provoked Me with their graven images,
with foreign [1c]idols?"
20 "Harvest is past, summer is ended,
And we are not saved."
21 For the [a]brokenness of the daughter of my people
I am broken;
I [b]mourn, dismay has taken hold of me.
22 Is there no [a]balm in Gilead?
Is there no physician there?
[b]Why then has not the [1]health of the daughter of my people
[2]been restored?

Chapter 9 Theme ____________________

9 [1a]Oh that my head were waters
And my eyes a fountain of tears,
That I might weep day and night
For the slain of the [b]daughter of my people!
2 [1a]Oh that I had in the desert
A wayfarers' lodging place;
That I might leave my people
And go from them!
For all of them are [b]adulterers,
An assembly of [c]treacherous men.
3 "They [a]bend their tongue *like* their bow;
Lies and not truth prevail in the land;
For they [b]proceed from evil to evil,
And they [c]do not know Me," declares the LORD.
4 "Let everyone [a]be on guard against his neighbor,
And [b]do not trust any brother;
Because every [c]brother deals [1]craftily,
And every neighbor [d]goes about as a slanderer.
5 "Everyone [a]deceives his neighbor
And does not speak the truth,
They have taught their tongue to speak lies;
They [b]weary themselves committing iniquity.
6 "Your [a]dwelling is in the midst of deceit;
Through deceit they [b]refuse to know Me," declares the LORD.

7 Therefore thus says the LORD of hosts,
"Behold, I will refine them and [a]assay them;
For [b]what *else* can I do, because of the daughter of My people?

17 [a]Num 21:6; Deut 32:24 [b]Ps 58:4, 5

18 [1]So Gr and versions [a]Is 22:4; Lam 1:16, 17 [b]Jer 23:9; Lam 5:17

19 [1]Lit *vanities* [a]Is 13:5; 39:3; Jer 4:16; 9:16 [b]Deut 32:21; Jer 7:19 [c]Ps 31:6

21 [a]Jer 4:19; 9:1; 14:17 [b]Jer 14:2; Joel 2:6; Nah 2:10

22 [1]Or *healing* [2]Lit *gone up* [a]Gen 37:25; Jer 46:11 [b]Jer 14:19; 30:13

9:1 [1]Ch 8:23 in Heb [a]Is 22:4; Jer 8:18; 13:17; Lam 2:18 [b]Jer 6:26; 8:21, 22

2 [1]Ch 9:1 in Heb [a]Ps 55:6, 7; 120:5, 6 [b]Jer 5:7, 8; 23:10; Hos 4:2 [c]Jer 5:11; 12:1, 6

3 [a]Ps 64:3; Is 59:4; Jer 9:8 [b]Jer 4:22 [c]Judg 2:10; 1 Sam 2:12; Jer 4:22; 5:4, 5; Hos 4:1; 1 Cor 15:34

4 [1]I.e. like Jacob (a play on words) [a]Ps 12:2; Prov 26:24, 25; Jer 9:8; Mic 7:5, 6 [b]Jer 12:6 [c]Gen 27:35 [d]Ps 15:3; Prov 10:18; Jer 6:28

5 [a]Mic 6:12 [b]Jer 12:13; 51:58, 64

6 [a]Ps 120:5, 6; Jer 5:27; 8:5 [b]Job 21:14, 15; Prov 1:24; Jer 11:10; 13:10; John 3:19, 20

7 [a]Is 1:25; Jer 6:27; Mal 3:3 [b]Hos 11:8

8 "Their [a]tongue is a deadly arrow;
It speaks deceit;
With his mouth one [b]speaks peace to his neighbor,
But inwardly he [c]sets an ambush for him.
9 "[a]Shall I not punish them for these things?" declares
the LORD.
"On a nation such as this
Shall I not avenge Myself?

10 "For the [a]mountains I will take up a weeping and wailing,
And for the pastures of the [b]wilderness a dirge,
Because they are [c]laid waste so that no one
passes through,
And the lowing of the cattle is not heard;
Both the [d]birds of the sky and the beasts have fled;
they are gone.
11 "I will make Jerusalem a [a]heap of ruins,
A haunt of [b]jackals;
And I will make the cities of Judah a [c]desolation,
without inhabitant."

12 Who is the [a]wise man that may understand this? And *who*
is he to whom [b]the mouth of the LORD has spoken, that he may
declare it? [c]Why is the land ruined, laid waste like a desert, so
that no one passes through?
13 The LORD said, "Because they have [a]forsaken My law which
I set before them, and have not obeyed My voice nor walked
according to it,
14 but have [a]walked after the stubbornness of their heart and
after the [b]Baals, as their [c]fathers taught them,"
15 therefore thus says the LORD of hosts, the God of Israel,
"behold, [a]I will feed them, this people, with wormwood and
give them [b]poisoned water to drink.
16 "I will [a]scatter them among the nations, whom neither they
nor their fathers have known; and I will send the [b]sword after
them until I have annihilated them."

17 Thus says the LORD of hosts,
"Consider and call for the [a]mourning women,
that they may come;
And send for the [1b]wailing women, that they may come!
18 "Let them make haste and take up a wailing for us,
That our [a]eyes may shed tears
And our eyelids flow with water.
19 "For a voice of [a]wailing is heard from Zion,
'[b]How are we ruined!
We are put to great shame,
For we have [c]left the land,
Because they have cast down our dwellings.'"
20 Now hear the word of the LORD, O you [a]women,
And let your ear receive the word of His mouth;
Teach your daughters wailing,
And everyone her neighbor a dirge.

8 [a]Jer 9:3 [b]Ps 28:3 [c]Jer 5:26
9 [a]Is 1:24; Jer 5:9, 29
10 [a]Jer 4:24; 7:29 [b]Jer 4:26; Hos 4:3 [c]Jer 12:4, 10; Ezek 14:15; 29:11; 33:28 [d]Jer 4:25; 12:4; Hos 4:3
11 [a]Is 25:2; Jer 51:37 [b]Is 13:22; 34:13 [c]Jer 4:27; 26:9
12 [a]Ps 107:43; Is 42:23; Hos 14:9 [b]Jer 9:20; 23:16 [c]Ps 107:34; Jer 23:10
13 [a]2 Chr 7:19; Ps 89:30; Jer 5:19; 22:9
14 [a]Jer 7:24; 11:8; Rom 1:21-24 [b]Jer 2:8, 23; 23:27 [c]Gal 1:14; 1 Pet 1:18
15 [a]Ps 80:5 [b]Deut 29:18; Jer 8:14; 23:15; Lam 3:15
16 [a]Lev 26:33; Deut 28:64; Jer 13:24 [b]Jer 44:27; Ezek 5:2, 12
17 [1]Lit *skilled* [a]2 Chr 35:25; Eccl 12:5 [b]Amos 5:16
18 [a]Is 22:4; Jer 9:1; 14:17
19 [a]Jer 7:29; Ezek 7:16-18 [b]Deut 28:29; Jer 4:13 [c]Jer 7:15; 15:1
20 [a]Is 32:9

21 For [a]death has come up through our windows;
It has entered our palaces
To cut off the [b]children from the streets,
The young men from the town squares.
22 Speak, "Thus says the LORD,
'The corpses of men will fall [a]like dung on the
open field,
And like the sheaf after the reaper,
But no one will gather *them.*'"

23 Thus says the LORD, "[a]Let not a wise man boast of his
wisdom, and let not the [b]mighty man boast of his might, let not
a [c]rich man boast of his riches;
24 but let him who boasts [a]boast of this, that he understands and
knows Me, that I am the LORD who [b]exercises lovingkindness,
justice and righteousness on earth; for I [c]delight in these things,"
declares the LORD.
25 "Behold, the days are coming," declares the LORD, "that I
will punish all who are circumcised and yet [a]uncircumcised—
26 Egypt and Judah, and Edom and the sons of Ammon, and
Moab and [a]all those inhabiting the desert who clip the hair on
their temples; for all the nations are uncircumcised, and all the
house of Israel are [b]uncircumcised of heart."

Chapter 10 Theme ______________________

10 Hear the word which the LORD speaks to you, O house of Israel.

2 Thus says the LORD,
"[a]Do not learn the way of the nations,
And do not be terrified by the signs of the heavens
Although the nations are terrified by them;
3 For the customs of the peoples are [1a]delusion;
Because [b]it is wood cut from the forest,
The work of the hands of a craftsman with a cutting tool.
4 "They [a]decorate *it* with silver and with gold;
They [b]fasten it with nails and with hammers
So that it will not totter.
5 "Like a scarecrow in a cucumber field are they,
And they [a]cannot speak;
They must be [b]carried,
Because they cannot walk!
Do not fear them,
For they [c]can do no harm,
Nor can they do any good."

6 [a]There is none like You, O LORD;
You are [b]great, and great is Your name in might.
7 [a]Who would not fear You, O [b]King of the nations?
Indeed it is Your due!
For among all the [c]wise men of the nations
And in all their kingdoms,
There is none like You.

21 [a]2 Chr 36:17; Jer 15:7; 18:21; Ezek 9:5, 6; Amos 6:9, 10 [b]Jer 6:11

22 [a]Ps 83:10; Is 5:25; Jer 8:2; 16:4; 25:33

23 [a]Eccl 9:11; Is 47:10; Ezek 28:3-7 [b]1 Kin 20:10, 11; Is 10:8-12 [c]Job 31:24, 25; Ps 49:6-9

24 [a]Ps 20:7; 44:8; Is 41:16; Jer 4:2; 1 Cor 1:31; 2 Cor 10:17; Gal 6:14 [b]Ex 34:6, 7; Ps 36:5, 7; 51:1 [c]Is 61:8; Mic 7:18

25 [a]Jer 4:4; Rom 2:28, 29

26 [a]Jer 25:23 [b]Lev 26:41; Jer 4:4; 6:10; Ezek 44:7; Rom 2:28

10:2 [a]Lev 18:3; 20:23; Deut 12:30

3 [1]Lit *vanity* [a]Jer 14:22 [b]Is 44:9-20

4 [a]Is 40:19 [b]Is 40:20; 41:7

5 [a]Ps 115:5; Is 46:7; Jer 10:14; 1 Cor 12:2 [b]Ps 115:7; Is 46:1, 7 [c]Is 41:23, 24

6 [a]Ex 15:11; Deut 33:26; Ps 86:8, 10; Jer 10:16 [b]Ps 48:1; 96:4; Is 12:6; Jer 32:18

7 [a]Rev 15:4 [b]Ps 22:28 [c]Dan 2:27, 28; 1 Cor 1:19, 20

8 But they are altogether [a]stupid and foolish
In their discipline of [1]delusion—[2]their idol is wood!
9 Beaten [a]silver is brought from [b]Tarshish,
And [c]gold from Uphaz,
The work of a craftsman and of the hands of a goldsmith;
Violet and purple are their clothing;
They are all the [d]work of skilled men.
10 But the LORD is the [a]true God;
He is the [b]living God and the [c]everlasting King.
At His wrath the [d]earth quakes,
And the nations cannot [e]endure His indignation.
11 [1]Thus you shall say to them, "The [a]gods that did not make
the heavens and the earth will [b]perish from the earth and from
under the [2]heavens."
12 *It is* [a]He who made the earth by His power,
Who [b]established the world by His wisdom;
And by His understanding He has [c]stretched out the
heavens.
13 When He utters His [a]voice, *there is* a tumult of waters
in the heavens,
And He causes the [b]clouds to ascend from the end
of the earth;
He makes lightning for the rain,
And brings out the [c]wind from His storehouses.
14 Every man is [a]stupid, devoid of knowledge;
Every goldsmith is put to shame by his [1]idols;
For his molten images are deceitful,
And there is no breath in them.
15 They are [a]worthless, a work of mockery;
In the [b]time of their punishment they will perish.
16 The [a]portion of Jacob is not like these;
For the [1b]Maker of all is He,
And [c]Israel is the tribe of His inheritance;
The [d]LORD of hosts is His name.

17 [a]Pick up your bundle from the ground,
You who dwell under siege!
18 For thus says the LORD,
"Behold, I am [a]slinging out the inhabitants of the land
At this time,
And will cause them distress,
That they may [1]be found."

19 [a]Woe is me, because of my [1]injury!
My [b]wound is incurable.
But I said, "Truly this is a sickness,
And I [c]must bear it."
20 My [a]tent is destroyed,
And all my ropes are broken;
My [b]sons have gone from me and are no more.

8 [1]Lit *vanities, or idols* [2]Lit *it is* [a]Jer 4:22; 5:4; 10:14

9 [a]Is 40:19 [b]Ps 72:10; Is 23:6 [c]Dan 10:5 [d]Ps 115:4

10 [a]Is 65:16 [b]Jer 4:2 [c]Ps 10:16; 29:10 [d]Jer 4:24; 50:46 [e]Ps 76:7

11 [1]This verse is in Aram [2]Or *these heavens* [a]Ps 96:5 [b]Is 2:18; Zeph 2:11

12 [a]Gen 1:1, 6; Job 38:4-7; Ps 136:5; 148:4, 5; Jer 51:15, 19 [b]Ps 78:69; Is 45:18 [c]Job 9:8; Is 40:22

13 [a]Ps 29:3-9 [b]Job 36:27-29 [c]Ps 135:7

14 [1]Or *graven image* [a]Jer 10:8; 51:17, 18

15 [a]Is 41:24; Jer 8:19; 14:22 [b]Jer 8:12; 51:18

16 [1]Lit *Fashioner* [a]Ps 16:5; 73:26; 119:57; Jer 51:19; Lam 3:24 [b]Is 45:7; Jer 10:12 [c]Deut 32:9; Ps 74:2 [d]Jer 31:35; 32:18

17 [a]Ezek 12:3-12

18 [1]Lit *find* [a]1 Sam 25:29

19 [1]Lit *breaking* [a]Jer 4:31 [b]Jer 14:17 [c]Mic 7:9

20 [a]Jer 4:20; Lam 2:4 [b]Jer 31:15; Lam 1:5

There is [c]no one to stretch out my tent again
Or to set up my curtains.
21 For the shepherds have become stupid
And [a]have not sought the LORD;
Therefore they have not prospered,
And [b]all their flock is scattered.
22 The sound of a [a]report! Behold, it comes—
A great commotion [b]out of the land of the north—
To [c]make the cities of Judah
A desolation, a haunt of jackals.

23 I know, O LORD, that [a]a man's way is not in himself,
[b]Nor is it in a man who walks to direct his steps.
24 [a]Correct me, O LORD, but with justice;
Not with Your anger, or You will [1]bring me to nothing.
25 [a]Pour out Your wrath on the nations that [b]do not
know You
And on the families that [c]do not call Your name;
For they have devoured Jacob;
They have [d]devoured him and consumed him
And have laid waste his [1]habitation.

Chapter 11 Theme ________________

11 The word which came to Jeremiah from the LORD, saying,
2 "[a]Hear the words of this [b]covenant, and speak to the
men of Judah and to the inhabitants of Jerusalem;
3 and say to them, 'Thus says the LORD, the God of Israel,
"[a]Cursed is the man who does not heed the words of this
covenant
4 which I commanded your forefathers in the [a]day that I
brought them out of the land of Egypt, from the [b]iron furnace,
saying, '[c]Listen to My voice, and [1]do according to all which I
command you; so you shall be [d]My people, and I will be your
God,'
5 in order to confirm the [a]oath which I swore to your forefathers, to give them a land flowing with milk and honey, as *it*
is this day."'" Then I said, "[b]Amen, O LORD."
6 And the LORD said to me, "[a]Proclaim all these words in the
cities of Judah and in the streets of Jerusalem, saying, '[b]Hear
the words of this covenant and [c]do them.
7 'For I solemnly [a]warned your fathers in the [b]day that I
brought them up from the land of Egypt, even to this day,
[1c]warning persistently, saying, "[d]Listen to My voice."
8 'Yet they [a]did not obey or incline their ear, but walked, each
one, in the stubbornness of his evil heart; therefore I brought
on them all the [b]words of this covenant, which I commanded
them to do, but they did not.'"
9 Then the LORD said to me, "A [a]conspiracy has been found
among the men of Judah and among the inhabitants of
Jerusalem.

20 [c]Is 51:18
21 [a]Jer 2:8 [b]Jer 23:2
22 [a]Jer 4:15 [b]Jer 1:14; 25:9 [c]Jer 9:11; 49:33
23 [a]Prov 16:1; 20:24 [b]Is 26:7
24 [1]Lit *diminish me* [a]Ps 6:1; 38:1
25 [1]Or *pasture* [a]Ps 79:6, 7; Zeph 3:8 [b]Job 18:21; 1 Thess 4:5; 2 Thess 1:8 [c]Zeph 1:6 [d]Jer 8:16; 50:7, 17
11:2 [a]Jer 11:6 [b]Ex 19:5
3 [a]Deut 27:26; Jer 17:5; Gal 3:10
4 [1]Lit *do them* [a]Ex 24:3-8; Jer 31:32 [b]Deut 4:20; 1 Kin 8:51 [c]Lev 26:3; Deut 11:27; Jer 7:23; 26:13 [d]Jer 24:7; Zech 8:8
5 [a]Ex 13:5; Deut 7:12; Ps 105:9; Jer 32:22 [b]Jer 28:6
6 [a]Jer 3:12; 7:2 [b]Jer 11:2 [c]John 13:17; Rom 2:13; James 1:22
7 [1]Lit *rising early and warning* [a]1 Sam 8:9 [b]Jer 11:4 [c]Ex 15:26; 2 Chr 36:15; Jer 7:25 [d]Jer 11:7
8 [a]Jer 7:24; 9:14; 35:15; Ezek 20:8 [b]Lev 26:14-43
9 [a]Ezek 22:25; Hos 6:9

10 "They have [a]turned back to the iniquities of their [1]ancestors
who [b]refused to hear My words, and they [c]have gone after
other gods to serve them; the house of Israel and the house of
Judah have [d]broken My covenant which I made with their
fathers."
11 Therefore thus says the LORD, "Behold I am [a]bringing disaster on them which they will [b]not be able to escape; though they
will [c]cry to Me, yet I will not listen to them.
12 "Then the cities of Judah and the inhabitants of Jerusalem
will [a]go and cry to the gods to whom they burn incense, but
they surely will not save them in the time of their disaster.
13 "For your gods are [1a]as many as your cities, O Judah; and [1]as
many as the streets of Jerusalem are the altars you have set up
to the [b]shameful thing, altars to [c]burn incense to Baal.
14 "Therefore [a]do not pray for this people, nor lift up a cry or
prayer for them; for I will [b]not listen when they call to Me
because of their disaster.
15 "What right has My [a]beloved in My house
When [b]she has done many vile deeds?
Can the sacrificial flesh take away from you your disaster,
[1]So *that* you can rejoice?"
16 The LORD called your name,
"A [a]green olive tree, beautiful in fruit and form";
With the [b]noise of a great tumult
He has [c]kindled fire on it,
And its branches are worthless.
17 The LORD of hosts, who [a]planted you, has [b]pronounced evil
against you because of the evil of the house of Israel and of the
house of Judah, which they have [1]done to provoke Me by
[2c]offering up sacrifices to Baal.
18 Moreover, the LORD [a]made it known to me and I knew it;
Then You showed me their deeds.
19 But I was like a gentle [a]lamb led to the slaughter;
And I did not know that they had [b]devised plots against
me, *saying,*
"Let us destroy the tree with its [1]fruit,
And [c]let us cut him off from the [d]land of the living,
That his [e]name be remembered no more."
20 But, O LORD of hosts, who [a]judges righteously,
Who [b]tries the [1]feelings and the heart,
Let me see Your vengeance on them,
For to You have I [2]committed my cause.
21 Therefore thus says the LORD concerning the men of
[a]Anathoth, who [b]seek your life, saying, "[c]Do not prophesy in
the name of the LORD, so that you will not [d]die at our hand";
22 therefore, thus says the LORD of hosts, "Behold, I am about
to [a]punish them! The [b]young men will die by the sword, their
sons and daughters will die by famine;
23 and a remnant [a]will not be left to them, for I will [b]bring
disaster on the men of Anathoth—[c]the year of their punishment."

10 [1]Lit *former fathers* [a]1 Sam 15:11; Jer 3:10, 11; Ezek 20:18 [b]Deut 9:7; Ps 78:8-10; Jer 13:10 [c]Judg 2:11-13 [d]Jer 3:6-11; Ezek 16:59

11 [a]2 Kin 22:16; Jer 6:19; 11:17 [b]Is 24:17; Jer 25:35 [c]Ps 18:41; Prov 1:28; Is 1:15; Jer 11:14; 14:12; Ezek 8:18; Mic 3:4; Zech 7:13

12 [a]Deut 32:37; Jer 44:17

13 [1]Lit *the number of* [a]2 Kin 23:13; Jer 2:28 [b]Jer 3:24 [c]Jer 7:9

14 [a]Ex 32:10; Jer 7:16; 14:11; 1 John 5:16 [b]Ps 66:18; Jer 11:11; Hos 5:6

15 [1]Lit *Then* [a]Jer 13:27 [b]Ezek 16:25

16 [a]Ps 52:8; Rom 11:17 [b]Ps 83:2 [c]Ps 80:16; Is 27:11; Jer 21:14

17 [1]Or *done for themselves* [2]Or *burning incense* [a]Is 5:2; Jer 2:21; 12:2 [b]Jer 1:14; 16:10; 19:15 [c]Jer 7:9; 11:13; 32:29

18 [a]1 Sam 23:11, 12; 2 Kin 6:9, 10; Ezek 8:6

19 [1]Lit *bread* [a]Is 53:7 [b]Jer 18:18; 20:10 [c]Ps 83:4; Is 53:8 [d]Job 28:13; Ps 52:5 [e]Ps 109:13

20 [1]Lit *kidneys* [2]Lit *revealed* [a]Gen 18:25; Ps 7:8; Jer 20:12 [b]1 Sam 16:7; Ps 7:9; Jer 17:10

21 [a]Jer 1:1 [b]Jer 12:5, 6; 20:10 [c]Amos 2:12 [d]Jer 26:8; 38:4

22 [a]Jer 21:14 [b]2 Chr 36:17; Jer 18:21

23 [a]Jer 6:9 [b]Jer 23:12; Hos 9:7; Mic 7:4 [c]Luke 19:44

Chapter 12 Theme ______________________________

12 [a]Righteous are You, O LORD, that I would plead *my* case
with You;
Indeed I would [b]discuss matters of justice with You:
Why has the [c]way of the wicked prospered?
Why are all those who [d]deal in treachery at ease?
2 You have [a]planted them, they have also taken root;
They grow, they have even produced fruit.
You are [b]near [1]to their lips
But far from their [2]mind.
3 But You [a]know me, O LORD;
You see me;
And You [b]examine my heart's *attitude* toward You.
Drag them off like sheep for the slaughter
And [1]set them apart for a [c]day of carnage!
4 How long is the [a]land to mourn
And the [b]vegetation of the countryside to wither?
For the [c]wickedness of those who dwell in it,
[d]Animals and birds have been snatched away,
Because *men* have said, "He will not see our
latter [e]ending."

5 "If you have run with footmen and they have tired
you out,
Then how can you compete with horses?
If you fall down in a land of peace,
How will you do in the [1a]thicket of the Jordan?
6 "For even your [a]brothers and the household of your father,
Even they have dealt treacherously with you,
Even they have cried aloud after you.
Do not believe them, although they may say [b]nice things
to you."

7 "I have [a]forsaken My house,
I have abandoned My inheritance;
I have given the [b]beloved of My soul
Into the hand of her enemies.
8 "My inheritance has become to Me
Like a lion in the forest;
She has [1a]roared against Me;
Therefore I have come to [b]hate her.
9 "Is My inheritance like a speckled bird of prey to Me?
Are the [a]birds of prey against her on every side?
Go, gather all the [b]beasts of the field,
Bring them to devour!
10 "Many [a]shepherds have ruined My [b]vineyard,
They have [c]trampled down My field;
They have made My [d]pleasant field
A desolate wilderness.
11 "[1]It has been made a desolation,
Desolate, it [a]mourns [2]before Me;

12:1 [a]Ezra 9:15; Ps 51:4; 129:4; Jer 11:20 [b]Job 13:3 [c]Job 12:6; Jer 5:27, 28; Hab 1:4; Mal 3:15 [d]Jer 3:7, 20; 5:11

2 [1]Lit *in their mouth* [2]Lit *kidneys* [a]Jer 11:17; 45:4; Ezek 17:5-10 [b]Is 29:13; Jer 3:10; Ezek 33:31; Titus 1:16

3 [1]Lit *sanctify them* [a]Ps 139:1-4 [b]Ps 7:9; 11:5; Jer 11:20 [c]Jer 17:18; 50:27; James 5:5

4 [a]Jer 4:28; 9:10; 23:10 [b]Joel 1:10-17 [c]Ps 107:34 [d]Jer 4:25; 7:20; 9:10; Hos 4:3; Hab 3:17 [e]Jer 5:31; Ezek 7:2

5 [1]Lit *pride* [a]Jer 49:19; 50:44

6 [a]Gen 37:4-11; Job 6:15; Ps 69:8; Jer 9:4, 5 [b]Ps 12:2; Prov 26:25

7 [a]Is 2:6; Jer 7:29; 23:39 [b]Jer 11:15; Hos 11:1-8

8 [1]Lit *raised her voice* [a]Is 59:13 [b]Hos 9:15; Amos 6:8

9 [a]2 Kin 24:2; Ezek 23:22-25 [b]Is 56:9; Jer 7:33; 15:3; 34:20

10 [a]Jer 6:3; 23:1 [b]Ps 80:8-16; Is 5:1-7 [c]Is 63:18 [d]Jer 3:19

11 [1]Lit *One has made it* [2]Or *upon* [a]Jer 12:4; 14:2; 23:10

The [b]whole land has been made desolate,
Because no man [c]lays it to heart.
12 "On all the [1a]bare heights in the wilderness
Destroyers have come,
For a [b]sword of the LORD is devouring
From one end of the land even to the [2]other;
There is [c]no peace for [3]anyone.
13 "They have [a]sown wheat and have reaped thorns,
They have [b]strained themselves [1]to no profit.
But be ashamed of your [2c]harvest
Because of the [d]fierce anger of the LORD."
14 Thus says the LORD concerning all My [a]wicked neighbors
who [b]strike at the inheritance with which I have endowed My
people Israel, "Behold I am about to uproot them from their
land and will [c]uproot the house of Judah from among them.
15 "And it will come about that after I have uprooted them, I will
[a]again have compassion on them; and I will [b]bring them back,
each one to his inheritance and each one to his land.
16 "Then if they will really [a]learn the ways of My people, to
[b]swear by My name, 'As the LORD lives,' even as they taught My
people to [c]swear by Baal, they will be [d]built up in the midst of
My people.
17 "But if they will not listen, then I will [a]uproot that nation,
uproot and destroy it," declares the LORD.

Chapter 13 Theme ______________________

13 Thus the LORD said to me, "Go and [a]buy yourself a linen
waistband and put it around your waist, but do not put it
in water."
2 So I bought the waistband in accordance with the [a]word of
the LORD and put it around my waist.
3 Then the word of the LORD came to me a second time, saying,
4 "Take the waistband that you have bought, which is around
your waist, and arise, go to [1]the [a]Euphrates and hide it there in
a crevice of the rock."
5 So I went and hid it by the Euphrates, [a]as the LORD had
commanded me.
6 After many days the LORD said to me, "Arise, go to the
Euphrates and take from there the waistband which I commanded you to hide there."
7 Then I went to the Euphrates and dug, and I took the
waistband from the place where I had hidden it; and lo, the
waistband was ruined, it was totally worthless.
8 Then the word of the LORD came to me, saying,
9 "Thus says the LORD, 'Just so will I destroy the [a]pride of
Judah and the great pride of Jerusalem.
10 'This wicked people, who [a]refuse to listen to My words,
who [b]walk in the stubbornness of their hearts and have gone
after other gods to serve them and to bow down to them, let
them be just like this waistband which is totally worthless.

11 [b]Jer 4:20, 27; 25:11 [c]Is 42:25

12 [1]Or *caravan trails* [2]Lit *other end of the land* [3]Lit *all flesh* [a]Jer 3:2, 21 [b]Is 34:6; Jer 47:6; Amos 9:4 [c]Jer 16:5; 30:5

13 [1]Lit *they do not profit* [2]Lit *products* [a]Lev 26:16; Deut 28:38; Mic 6:15; Hag 1:6 [b]Is 55:2; Jer 9:5 [c]Jer 17:10 [d]Jer 4:26; 25:37, 38

14 [a]Jer 49:1, 7; Zeph 2:8-10 [b]Jer 2:3; 50:11, 12; Zech 2:8 [c]Deut 30:3; Ps 106:47; Is 11:11-16

15 [a]Jer 48:47; 49:6, 39 [b]Amos 9:14

16 [a]Is 42:6; 49:6 [b]Jer 4:2; Zeph 1:5 [c]Josh 23:7; Jer 5:7 [d]Jer 3:17; 4:2; 16:19

17 [a]Ps 2:8-12; Is 60:12

13:1 [a]Jer 13:11

2 [a]Is 20:2; Ezek 2:8

4 [1]Or *Parah*, cf Josh 18:23; so through v 7 [a]Jer 51:63

5 [a]Ex 39:42, 43; 40:16

9 [a]Lev 26:19; Is 2:10-17; 23:9; Jer 13:15-17; Zeph 3:11

10 [a]Num 14:11; 2 Chr 36:15, 16; Jer 11:10 [b]Jer 9:14; 11:8; 16:12

11 'For as the waistband clings to the waist of a man, so I made
the whole household of Israel and the whole household of Judah
[a]cling to Me,' declares the LORD, 'that they might be for Me a
people, for [1b]renown, for [c]praise and for glory; but they [d]did
not listen.'
12 "Therefore you are to speak this word to them, 'Thus says
the LORD, the God of Israel, "Every jug is to be filled with wine."'
And when they say to you, 'Do we not very well know that
every jug is to be filled with wine?'
13 then say to them, 'Thus says the LORD, "Behold I am about
to fill all the inhabitants of this land—the kings that sit for
David on his throne, the priests, the prophets and all the
inhabitants of Jerusalem—with [a]drunkenness!
14 "I will [a]dash them against each other, both the [b]fathers and
the sons together," declares the LORD. "I will [c]not show pity nor
be sorry nor have compassion so as not to destroy them."'"

15 Listen and give heed, do not be [a]haughty,
For the LORD has spoken.
16 [a]Give glory to the LORD your God,
Before He brings [b]darkness
And before your [c]feet stumble
On the dusky mountains,
And while you are hoping for light
He makes it into [d]deep darkness,
And turns *it* into gloom.
17 But [a]if you will not listen to it,
My soul will [b]sob in secret for *such* pride;
And my eyes will bitterly weep
And flow down with tears,
Because the [c]flock of the LORD has been taken captive.
18 Say to the [a]king and the queen mother,
"[b]Take a lowly seat,
For your beautiful [c]crown
Has come down from your head."
19 The [a]cities of the Negev have been locked up,
And there is no one to open *them;*
All [b]Judah has been carried into exile,
Wholly carried into exile.

20 "Lift up your eyes and see
Those coming [a]from the north.
Where is the [b]flock that was given you,
Your beautiful sheep?
21 "What will you say when He appoints over you—
And you yourself had taught them—
Former [1a]companions to be head over you?
Will not [b]pangs take hold of you
Like a woman in childbirth?
22 "If you [a]say in your heart,
'[b]Why have these things happened to me?'

11 [1]Lit *a name* [a]Ex 19:5, 6; Deut 32:10, 11 [b]Jer 32:20 [c]Is 43:21; Jer 33:9 [d]Ps 81:11; Jer 7:13, 24, 26

13 [a]Ps 60:3; 75:8; Is 51:17; 63:6; Jer 25:27; 51:7, 57

14 [a]Is 9:20, 21; Jer 19:9-11 [b]Jer 6:21; Ezek 5:10 [c]Deut 29:20; Is 27:11; Jer 16:5; 21:7

15 [a]Prov 16:5; Is 28:14-22

16 [a]Josh 7:19; Ps 96:8 [b]Is 5:30; 8:22; 59:9; Amos 5:18; 8:9 [c]Prov 4:19; Jer 23:12 [d]Ps 44:19; 107:10, 14; Jer 2:6

17 [a]Mal 2:2 [b]Ps 119:136; Jer 9:1; 14:17; Luke 19:41, 42 [c]Ps 80:1; Jer 23:1, 2

18 [a]2 Kin 24:12, 15; Jer 22:26 [b]2 Chr 33:12, 19 [c]Ex 39:28; Is 3:20; Ezek 24:17, 23; 44:18

19 [a]Jer 32:44 [b]Jer 20:4; 52:27-30

20 [a]Jer 1:15; 6:22; Hab 1:6 [b]Jer 13:17; 23:2

21 [1]Or *chieftains* [a]Jer 2:25; 38:22 [b]Is 13:8; Jer 4:31

22 [a]Deut 7:17 [b]Jer 5:19; 16:10

Because of the [c]magnitude of your iniquity
[d]Your skirts have been removed
And your heels have [1]been exposed.
23 "[a]Can the Ethiopian change his skin
Or the leopard his spots?
Then you also can [b]do good
Who are accustomed to doing evil.
24 "Therefore I will [a]scatter them like drifting straw
To the desert [b]wind.
25 "This is your [a]lot, the portion measured to you
From Me," declares the LORD,
"Because you have [b]forgotten Me
And trusted in falsehood.
26 "So I Myself have also [a]stripped your skirts off over
your face,
That your shame may be seen.
27 "As for your [a]adulteries and your *lustful* neighings,
The [b]lewdness of your prostitution
On the [c]hills in the field,
I have seen your abominations.
Woe to you, O Jerusalem!
[d]How long will you remain unclean?"

Chapter 14 Theme ____________________

14 That which came as the word of the LORD to Jeremiah in regard to the [a]drought:
2 "Judah mourns
And [a]her gates languish;
They sit on the ground [b]in mourning,
And the [c]cry of Jerusalem has ascended.
3 "Their nobles have [a]sent their [1]servants for water;
They have come to the [b]cisterns and found no water.
They have returned with their vessels empty;
They have been [c]put to shame and humiliated,
And they [d]cover their heads.
4 "Because the [a]ground is [1]cracked,
For there has been [b]no rain on the land;
The [c]farmers have been put to shame,
They have covered their heads.
5 "For even the doe in the field has given birth only to
abandon *her young,*
Because there is [a]no grass.
6 "The [a]wild donkeys stand on the bare heights;
They pant for air like jackals,
Their eyes fail
For there is [b]no vegetation.
7 "Although our [a]iniquities testify against us,
O LORD, act [b]for Your name's sake!
Truly our [c]apostasies have been many,
We have [d]sinned against You.

22 [1]Or *suffered violence* [c]Jer 2:17-19; 9:2-9 [d]Is 47:2; Ezek 16:37; Nah 3:5

23 [a]Prov 27:22; Is 1:5 [b]Jer 4:22; 9:5

24 [a]Lev 26:33; Jer 9:16; Ezek 5:2, 12 [b]Jer 4:11; 18:17

25 [a]Job 20:29; Ps 11:6; Matt 24:51 [b]Ps 9:17; Jer 2:32; 3:21

26 [a]Lam 1:8; Ezek 23:29; Hos 2:10

27 [a]Jer 5:7, 8 [b]Jer 11:15 [c]Is 65:7; Jer 2:20; Ezek 6:13 [d]Prov 1:22; Hos 8:5

14:1 [a]Jer 17:8

2 [a]Is 3:26 [b]Jer 8:21 [c]1 Sam 5:12; Jer 11:11; 46:12; Zech 7:13

3 [1]Lit *little ones* [a]1 Kin 18:5 [b]2 Kin 18:31; Jer 2:13 [c]Job 6:20; Ps 40:14 [d]2 Sam 15:30

4 [1]Lit *shattered* [a]Joel 1:19, 20 [b]Jer 3:3 [c]Joel 1:11

5 [a]Is 15:6

6 [a]Job 39:5, 6; Jer 2:24 [b]Joel 1:18

7 [a]Is 59:12; Hos 5:5 [b]Ps 25:11; Jer 14:21 [c]Jer 5:6; 8:5 [d]Jer 3:25; 8:14; 14:20

8 "O [a]Hope of Israel,
Its [b]Savior in [c]time of distress,
Why are You like a stranger in the land
Or like a traveler who has pitched his *tent* for the night?
9 "Why are You like a man dismayed,
Like a mighty man who [a]cannot save?
Yet [b]You are in our midst, O LORD,
And we are [c]called by Your name;
Do not forsake us!"

10 Thus says the LORD to this people, "Even so they have
[a]loved to wander; they have not [b]kept their feet in check.
Therefore the LORD does [c]not accept them; now He will
[d]remember their iniquity and call their sins to account."
11 So the LORD said to me, "[a]Do not pray for the welfare of
this people.
12 "When they fast, I am [a]not going to listen to their cry; and
when they offer [b]burnt offering and grain offering, I am not
going to accept them. Rather I am going to [c]make an end of
them by the [d]sword, famine and pestilence."
13 But, "Ah, Lord [1]GOD!" I said, "Look, the prophets are telling
them, 'You [a]will not see the sword nor will you have famine,
but I will give you [2]lasting [b]peace in this place.'"
14 Then the LORD said to me, "The [a]prophets are prophesying
falsehood in My name. [b]I have neither sent them nor
commanded them nor spoken to them; they are prophesying to
you a [c]false vision, divination, futility and the deception of their
own [1]minds.
15 "Therefore thus says the LORD concerning the prophets who
are prophesying in My name, although it was not I who sent
them—yet they keep saying, 'There will be no sword or famine
in this land'—[a]by sword and famine those prophets shall [1]meet
their end!
16 "The people also to whom they are prophesying will be
[a]thrown out into the streets of Jerusalem because of the famine
and the sword; and there will be no one to [b]bury them—*neither*
them, *nor* their wives, nor their sons, nor their daughters—for
I will [c]pour out their *own* wickedness on them.
17 "You will say this word to them,

'[a]Let my eyes flow down with tears night and day,
And let them not cease;
For the virgin [b]daughter of my people has been crushed
with a mighty blow,
With a sorely [c]infected wound.
18 'If I [a]go out to the country,
Behold, those [1]slain with the sword!
Or if I enter the city,
Behold, diseases of famine!
For [b]both prophet and priest
Have [2]gone roving about in the land that they
do not know.'"

8 [a]Jer 17:13 [b]Is 43:3; 63:8 [c]Ps 9:9; 50:15

9 [a]Num 11:23; Is 50:2; 59:1 [b]Ex 29:45; Ps 46:5; Jer 8:19 [c]Is 63:19; Jer 15:16

10 [a]Jer 2:25; 3:13 [b]Ps 119:101 [c]Jer 6:20; Amos 5:22 [d]Jer 44:21-23; Hos 8:13; 9:9

11 [a]Ex 32:10; Jer 7:16; 11:14

12 [a]Prov 1:28; Is 1:15; Jer 11:11; Ezek 8:18; Mic 3:4; Zech 7:13 [b]Jer 6:20; 7:21 [c]Jer 8:13 [d]Jer 21:9

13 [1]Heb *YHWH,* usually rendered LORD [2]Lit *peace of truth* [a]Jer 5:12; 23:17 [b]Jer 6:14; 8:11

14 [1]Lit *hearts* [a]Jer 5:31; 23:25 [b]Jer 23:21 [c]Jer 23:16, 26; 27:9, 10; Ezek 12:24

15 [1]Lit *be finished* [a]Jer 23:15; Ezek 14:10

16 [a]Ps 79:2, 3; Jer 7:33; 15:2, 3 [b]Jer 8:1, 2 [c]Prov 1:31; Jer 13:22-25

17 [a]Jer 9:1; 13:17; Lam 1:16 [b]Is 37:22; Jer 8:21; Lam 1:15; 2:13 [c]Jer 10:19; 30:14

18 [1]Lit *pierced* [2]Or *gone around trading* [a]Jer 6:25; Lam 1:20; Ezek 7:15 [b]Jer 6:13; 8:10

19 Have You completely [a]rejected Judah?
Or have [1]You loathed Zion?
Why have You stricken us so that we [b]are beyond healing?
We [c]waited for peace, but nothing good *came;*
And for a time of healing, but behold, terror!
20 We [a]know our wickedness, O LORD,
The iniquity of our fathers, for [b]we have sinned
against You.
21 Do not despise *us,* [a]for Your own name's sake;
Do not disgrace the [b]throne of Your glory;
Remember *and* do not annul Your covenant with us.
22 Are there any among the [1a]idols of the nations who
[b]give rain?
Or can the heavens grant showers?
Is it not You, O LORD our God?
Therefore we [2c]hope in You,
For You are the one who has done all these things.

Chapter 15 Theme __________________________

15 Then the LORD said to me, "Even [a]though [b]Moses and
[c]Samuel were to [d]stand before Me, My [1]heart would not
be [2]with this people; [e]send them away from My presence and
let them go!
2 "And it shall be that when they say to you, 'Where should
we go?' then you are to tell them, 'Thus says the LORD:
"Those *destined* [a]for death, to death;
And those *destined* for the sword, to the sword;
And those *destined* for famine, to famine;
And those *destined* for captivity, to captivity."'
3 "I will [a]appoint over them four kinds *of doom,*" declares the
LORD: "the sword to slay, the [b]dogs to drag off, and the [c]birds of
the sky and the beasts of the earth to devour and destroy.
4 "I will [a]make them an object of horror among all the kingdoms
of the earth because of [b]Manasseh, the son of Hezekiah, the
king of Judah, for what he did in Jerusalem.
5 "Indeed, who will have [a]pity on you, O Jerusalem,
Or who will [b]mourn for you,
Or who will turn aside to ask about your welfare?
6 "You who have [a]forsaken Me," declares the LORD,
"You keep [b]going backward.
So I will [c]stretch out My hand against you and
destroy you;
I am [d]tired of relenting!
7 "I will [a]winnow them with a winnowing fork
At the gates of the land;
I will [b]bereave *them* of children, I will destroy My people;
[c]They did not [1]repent of their ways.
8 "Their [a]widows will be more numerous before Me
Than the sand of the seas;

INSIGHT

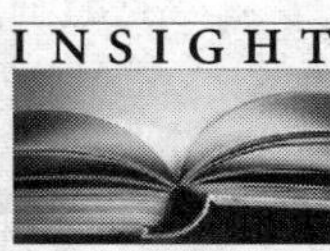

Read 2 Chronicles 33:1-13 to see what Manasseh did.

19 [1]Lit *Your soul* [a]Jer 6:30; 7:29; 12:7; Lam 5:22 [b]Jer 30:13 [c]Job 30:26; Jer 8:15; 1 Thess 5:3
20 [a]Neh 9:2; Ps 32:5; Jer 3:25 [b]Jer 8:14; 14:7; Dan 9:8
21 [a]Ps 25:11; Jer 14:7 [b]Jer 3:17; 17:12
22 [1]Lit *vanities* [2]Or *wait for* [a]Is 41:29; Jer 10:3 [b]1 Kin 17:1; Jer 5:24 [c]Lam 3:26
15:1 [1]Lit *soul* [2]Lit *toward* [a]Ps 99:6; Ezek 14:14, 20 [b]Ex 32:11-14; Num 14:13-20; Ps 99:6; 106:23 [c]1 Sam 7:9; 12:23 [d]Jer 15:19; 18:20; 35:19 [e]2 Kin 17:20; Jer 7:15; 10:18; 52:3
2 [a]Jer 14:12; 24:10; 43:11; Ezek 5:2, 12; Zech 11:9; Rev 13:10
3 [a]Lev 26:16, 22, 25; Ezek 14:21 [b]1 Kin 21:23, 24 [c]Deut 28:26; Is 18:6; Jer 7:33
4 [a]Lev 26:33; Jer 24:9; 29:18; Ezek 23:46 [b]2 Kin 21:1-18; 23:26, 27; 24:3, 4; 2 Chr 33:1-9
5 [a]Ps 69:20; Is 51:19; Jer 13:14; 21:7 [b]Nah 3:7
6 [a]Jer 6:19; 8:9 [b]Is 1:4; Jer 7:24 [c]Jer 6:12; Zeph 1:4 [d]Jer 6:11; 7:16
7 [1]Lit *turn back from* [a]Ps 1:4; Jer 51:2 [b]Jer 18:21; Hos 9:12-16 [c]Is 9:13
8 [a]Is 3:25, 26; 4:1

I will bring against them, against the mother of
a young man,
A [b]destroyer at noonday;
I will suddenly bring down on her
Anguish and dismay.
9 "She who [a]bore seven *sons* pines away;
[1]Her breathing is labored.
Her [b]sun has set while it was yet day;
She has been [c]shamed and humiliated.
So I will [d]give over their survivors to the sword
Before their enemies," declares the LORD.

10 [a]Woe to me, my mother, that you have borne me
As a [b]man of strife and a man of contention to all the land!
I have not [c]lent, nor have men lent money to me,
Yet everyone curses me.
11 The LORD said, "Surely I will [a]set you free for *purposes of* good;
Surely I will cause the [b]enemy to make supplication to you
In a time of disaster and a time of distress.

12 "Can anyone smash iron,
[a]Iron from the north, or bronze?
13 "Your [a]wealth and your treasures
I will give for booty [b]without cost,
Even for all your sins
And within all your borders.
14 "Then I will cause your enemies to bring [1]*it*
Into a [a]land you do not know;
For a [b]fire has been kindled in My anger,
It will burn upon you."

15 [a]You who know, O LORD,
Remember me, take notice of me,
And [b]take vengeance for me on my persecutors.
Do not, in view of Your patience, take me away;
Know that [c]for Your sake I endure reproach.
16 Your words were found and I [a]ate them,
And Your [b]words became for me a joy and the delight of my heart;
For I have been [c]called by Your name,
O LORD God of hosts.
17 I [a]did not sit in the circle of merrymakers,
Nor did I exult.
Because of Your hand *upon me* I sat [b]alone,
For You [c]filled me with indignation.
18 Why has my pain been perpetual
And my [a]wound incurable, refusing to be healed?
Will You indeed be to me [b]like a deceptive *stream*
With water that is unreliable?

8 [b]Jer 22:7

9 [1]Or *She has breathed out her soul* [a]1 Sam 2:5; Is 47:9 [b]Jer 6:4; Amos 8:9 [c]Jer 50:12 [d]Jer 21:7

10 [a]Job 3:1, 3; Jer 20:14 [b]Jer 1:18, 19; 15:20; 20:7, 8 [c]Ex 22:25; Lev 25:36, 37; Deut 23:19

11 [a]Ps 138:3; Is 41:10 [b]Jer 21:2; 37:3; 38:14; 42:2

12 [a]Jer 28:14

13 [a]Jer 17:3; 20:5 [b]Ps 44:12; Is 52:3

14 [1]I.e. your possessions [a]Deut 28:36, 64; Jer 16:13 [b]Deut 32:22; Ps 21:9; Jer 17:4

15 [a]Jer 12:3 [b]Jer 11:20 [c]Ps 44:22; 69:7-9; Jer 20:8

16 [a]Ezek 3:3 [b]Job 23:12; Ps 119:103 [c]Jer 14:9

17 [a]Ps 1:1; Jer 16:8; 2 Cor 6:17 [b]Ps 102:7; Jer 13:17; Lam 3:28; Ezek 3:24, 25 [c]Jer 6:11

18 [a]Job 34:6; Jer 30:12, 15; Mic 1:9 [b]Job 6:15, 20; Jer 14:3

19 Therefore, thus says the LORD,
"[a]If you return, then I will restore you—
[b]Before Me you will stand;
And [c]if you extract the precious from the worthless,
You will become [1]My spokesman.
They for their part may turn to you,
But as for you, you must not turn to them.
20 "Then I will [a]make you to this people
A fortified wall of bronze;
And though they fight against you,
They will not prevail over you;
For [b]I am with you to save you
And deliver you," declares the LORD.
21 "So I will [a]deliver you from the hand of the wicked,
And I will [b]redeem you from the [1]grasp of the violent."

Chapter 16 Theme ________________________________

16 The word of the LORD also came to me saying,
2 "You shall not take a wife for yourself nor have sons or daughters in this place."

3 For thus says the LORD concerning the sons and daughters born in this place, and concerning their [a]mothers who bear them, and their [b]fathers who beget them in this land:

4 "They will [a]die of deadly diseases, they [b]will not be lamented or buried; they will be as [c]dung on the surface of the ground and come to an end by sword and famine, and their carcasses will become food for the [d]birds of the sky and for the beasts of the earth."

5 For thus says the LORD, "Do not enter a house of [1a]mourning, or go to lament or to console them; for I have [b]withdrawn My peace from this people," declares the LORD, "*My* [c]lovingkindness and compassion.

6 "Both [a]great men and small will die in this land; they will not be buried, they will not be lamented, nor will anyone [b]gash himself or [c]shave his head for them.

7 "Men will not [a]break *bread* in mourning for them, to comfort anyone for the dead, nor give them a cup of consolation to drink for anyone's father or mother.

8 "Moreover you shall [a]not go into a house of feasting to sit with them to eat and drink."

9 For thus says the LORD of hosts, the God of Israel: "Behold, I am going to [1a]eliminate from this place, before your eyes and in your time, the voice of rejoicing and the voice of gladness, the voice of the groom and the voice of the bride.

10 "Now when you tell this people all these words, they will say to you, '[a]For what reason has the LORD declared all this great calamity against us? And what is our iniquity, or what is our sin which we have committed against the LORD our God?'

11 "Then you are to say to them, '*It is* [a]because your forefathers have forsaken Me,' declares the LORD, 'and have followed

19 [1]Lit *as My mouth* [a]Jer 4:1; Zech 3:7 [b]1 Kin 17:1; Jer 15:1; 35:19 [c]Jer 6:29; Ezek 22:26; 44:23

20 [a]Jer 1:18, 19; Ezek 3:9 [b]Ps 46:7; Is 41:10; Jer 1:8, 19; 15:15; 20:11

21 [1]Lit *palm* [a]Ps 37:40; Is 49:25; Jer 20:13; 39:11, 12 [b]Gen 48:16; Is 49:26; 60:16; Jer 31:11; 50:34

16:3 [a]Jer 15:8 [b]Jer 6:21

4 [a]Jer 15:2 [b]Jer 25:33 [c]Ps 83:10; Jer 9:22; 25:33 [d]Ps 79:2; Is 18:6; Jer 15:3; 34:20

5 [1]Or *banqueting* [a]Ezek 24:16-23 [b]Jer 12:12; 15:1-4 [c]Ps 25:6; Is 27:11; Jer 13:14

6 [a]2 Chr 36:17; Ezek 9:6 [b]Deut 14:1; Jer 41:5; 47:5 [c]Is 22:12

7 [a]Deut 26:14; Ezek 24:17; Hos 9:4

8 [a]Eccl 7:2-4; Is 22:12-14; Jer 15:17; Amos 6:4-6

9 [1]Lit *cause to cease* [a]Jer 7:34; 25:10; Ezek 26:13; Hos 2:11; Rev 18:23

10 [a]Deut 29:24; 1 Kin 9:8; Jer 5:19; 13:22; 22:8

11 [a]Deut 29:25; 1 Kin 9:9; 2 Chr 7:22; Neh 9:26-29; Jer 22:9

[b]other gods and served them and bowed down to them; but
Me they have forsaken and have not kept My law.
12 'You too have done evil, *even* [a]more than your forefathers;
for behold, you are each one walking according to the [b]stubborn-
ness of his own [c]evil heart, without listening to Me.
13 'So I will [a]hurl you out of this land into the [b]land which you
have not known, neither you nor your fathers; and there you will
[c]serve other gods day and night, for I will grant you no favor.'
14 "[a]Therefore behold, days are coming," declares the LORD,
"when it will no longer be said, 'As the LORD lives, who
[b]brought up the sons of Israel out of the land of Egypt,'
15 but, 'As the LORD lives, who brought up the sons of Israel
from the [a]land of the north and from all the countries where
He had banished them.' For I will restore them to their own
land which I gave to their fathers.
16 "Behold, I am going to send for many [a]fishermen," declares
the LORD, "and they will fish for them; and afterwards I will
send for many hunters, and they will [b]hunt them [c]from every
mountain and every hill and from the clefts of the rocks.
17 "[a]For My eyes are on all their ways; they are not hidden
from My face, [b]nor is their iniquity concealed from My eyes.
18 "I will first [a]doubly repay their iniquity and their sin, because
they have [b]polluted My land; they have filled My inheritance
with the carcasses of their [c]detestable idols and with their
abominations."

19 O LORD, my [a]strength and my stronghold,
And my [b]refuge in the day of distress,
To You the [c]nations will come
From the ends of the earth and say,
"Our fathers have inherited nothing but [d]falsehood,
Futility and [1e]things of no profit."
20 Can man make gods for himself?
Yet they are [a]not gods!

21 "Therefore behold, I am going to make them know—
This time I will [a]make them know
My [1]power and My might;
And they shall [b]know that My name is the LORD."

Chapter 17 Theme ______________________________

17

The [a]sin of Judah is written down with an [b]iron stylus;
With a diamond point it is [c]engraved upon the tablet
of their heart
And on the horns of [1]their altars,
2 As they remember their [a]children,
So they *remember* their altars and their [1b]Asherim
By [c]green trees on the high hills.
3 O [a]mountain of Mine in the countryside,
I will [b]give over your wealth and all your treasures
for booty,

11 [b]Deut 29:26; 1 Kin 9:9; Ps 106:35-41; Jer 5:7-9; 8:2; Ezek 11:21; 1 Pet 4:3

12 [a]Jer 7:26 [b]1 Sam 15:23; Jer 7:24; 9:14; 13:10 [c]Eccl 9:3; Mark 7:21

13 [a]Deut 4:26, 27; 2 Chr 7:20; Jer 15:1 [b]Jer 15:14; 17:4 [c]Deut 4:28; 28:36; Jer 5:19

14 [a]Is 43:18; Jer 23:7 [b]Ex 20:2; Deut 15:15

15 [a]Ps 106:47; Is 11:11-16; 14:1; Jer 3:18; 23:8; 24:6

16 [a]Amos 4:2; Hab 1:14, 15 [b]1 Sam 26:20; Mic 7:2 [c]Is 2:21; Amos 9:3

17 [a]2 Chr 16:9; Job 34:21; Ps 90:8; Prov 5:21; 15:3; Jer 23:24; 32:19; Zech 4:10; Luke 12:2; 1 Cor 4:5; Heb 4:13 [b]Jer 2:22

18 [a]Jer 17:18; Rev 18:6 [b]Num 35:33, 34; Jer 2:7; 3:9 [c]Jer 7:30; Ezek 11:18, 21

19 [1]Lit *there is nothing profitable in them* [a]Ps 18:1, 2; Is 25:4 [b]Nah 1:7 [c]Ps 22:27; Is 2:2; Jer 3:17; 4:2 [d]Is 44:20; Hab 2:18 [e]Is 44:10

20 [a]Ps 115:4-8; Is 37:19; Jer 2:11; 5:7; Hos 8:4-6; Gal 4:8

21 [1]Lit *hand* [a]Ps 9:16 [b]Ps 83:18; Is 43:3; Jer 33:2; Amos 5:8

17:1 [1]So ancient versions; M.T. *your* [a]Jer 2:22; 4:14 [b]Job 19:24 [c]Prov 3:3; 7:3; Is 49:16; 2 Cor 3:3

2 [1]I.e. wooden symbols of a female deity [a]Jer 7:18 [b]Ex 34:13; 2 Chr 24:18; 33:3; Is 17:8 [c]Jer 3:6

3 [a]Jer 26:18; Mic 3:12 [b]2 Kin 24:13; Is 39:4-6; Jer 15:13; 20:5

Your high places for sin throughout your borders.
4 And you will, even of yourself, [a]let go of your
inheritance
That I gave you;
And I will make you serve your [b]enemies
In the [c]land which you do not know;
For you have [d]kindled a fire in My anger
Which will burn forever.

5 Thus says the LORD,
"[a]Cursed is the man who trusts in mankind
And makes [b]flesh his [1]strength,
And whose heart turns away from the LORD.
6 "For he will be like a [a]bush in the desert
And will not see when prosperity comes,
But will live in stony wastes in the wilderness,
A [b]land of salt [1]without inhabitant.
7 "[a]Blessed is the man who trusts in the LORD
And whose [b]trust is the LORD.
8 "For he will be like a [a]tree planted by the water,
That extends its roots by a stream
And will not fear when the heat comes;
But its leaves will be green,
And it will not be anxious in a year of [b]drought
Nor cease to yield fruit.

9 "The [a]heart is more [b]deceitful than all else
And is desperately [c]sick;
Who can understand it?
10 "I, the LORD, [a]search the heart,
I test the [1]mind,
Even [b]to give to each man according to his ways,
According to the [2]results of his deeds.
11 "As a partridge that hatches eggs which it has not laid,
So is he who [a]makes a fortune, but unjustly;
In the midst of his days it will forsake him,
And in [1]the end he will be a [b]fool."

12 [a]A glorious throne on high from the beginning
Is the place of our sanctuary.
13 O LORD, the [a]hope of Israel,
All who [b]forsake You will be put to shame.
Those who turn [1]away on earth will be [c]written down,
Because they have forsaken the fountain of living water,
even the LORD.
14 [a]Heal me, O LORD, and I will be healed;
[b]Save me and I will be saved,
For You are my [c]praise.
15 Look, they keep [a]saying to me,
"Where is the word of the LORD?
Let it come now!"

4 [a]Jer 12:7; Lam 5:2 [b]Deut 28:48; Is 14:3; Jer 15:14; 27:12, 13 [c]Jer 16:13 [d]Is 5:25; Jer 7:20; 15:14

5 [1]Lit *arm* [a]Ps 146:3; Is 2:22; 30:1; Ezek 29:7 [b]2 Chr 32:8; Is 31:3

6 [1]Lit *and is not inhabited* [a]Jer 48:6 [b]Deut 29:23; Job 39:6

7 [a]Ps 2:12; 34:8; 84:12; Prov 16:20 [b]Ps 40:4

8 [a]Ps 1:3; 92:12-14; Ezek 31:3-9 [b]Jer 14:1-6

9 [a]Eccl 9:3; Mark 7:21, 22 [b]Rom 7:11; Eph 4:22 [c]Is 1:5, 6; 6:10; Matt 13:15; Mark 2:17; Rom 1:21

10 [1]Lit *kidneys* [2]Lit *fruit* [a]1 Sam 16:7; 1 Chr 28:9; Ps 139:23; Prov 17:3; Jer 11:20; 20:12; Rom 8:27; Rev 2:23 [b]Ps 62:12; Jer 32:19; Rom 2:6

11 [1]Lit *his* [a]Jer 6:13; 8:10; 22:13, 17 [b]Luke 12:20

12 [a]Jer 3:17; 14:21

13 [1]Lit *away from Me* [a]Jer 14:8; 50:7 [b]Is 1:28 [c]Luke 10:20

14 [a]Jer 30:17; 33:6 [b]Ps 54:1; 60:5 [c]Deut 10:21; Ps 109:1

15 [a]Is 5:19; 2 Pet 3:4

16 But as for me, I have not hurried away from *being* a
shepherd after You,
Nor have I longed for the woeful day;
[a]You Yourself know that the utterance of my lips
Was in Your presence.
17 Do not be a [a]terror to me;
You are my [b]refuge in the day of disaster.
18 Let those who persecute me be [a]put to shame, but as for
me, [b]let me not be put to shame;
Let them be dismayed, but let me not be dismayed.
[c]Bring on them a day of disaster,
And crush them with twofold destruction!

19 Thus the LORD said to me, "Go and stand in the [1]public
gate, through which the kings of Judah come in and go out, as
well as in all the gates of Jerusalem;
20 and say to them, '[a]Listen to the word of the LORD, [b]kings of
Judah, and all Judah and all inhabitants of Jerusalem who come
in through these gates:
21 'Thus says the LORD, "[a]Take heed for yourselves, and [b]do not
carry any load on the sabbath day or bring anything in through
the gates of Jerusalem.
22 "You shall not bring a load out of your houses on the sabbath
day [a]nor do any work, but keep the sabbath day holy, as I
[b]commanded your [1]forefathers.
23 "Yet they [a]did not listen or incline their ears, but [b]stiffened
their necks in order not to listen or take correction.
24 "But it will come about, if you [a]listen attentively to Me,"
declares the LORD, "to [b]bring no load in through the gates of
this city on the sabbath day, [c]but to keep the sabbath day holy
by doing no work on it,
25 [a]then there will come in through the gates of this city kings
and princes [b]sitting on the throne of David, riding in chariots
and on horses, they and their princes, the men of Judah and
the inhabitants of Jerusalem, and this [c]city will be inhabited
forever.
26 "They will come in from the [a]cities of Judah and from the
environs of Jerusalem, from the land of Benjamin, from the
[b]lowland, from the hill country and from the [c]Negev, bringing
burnt offerings, sacrifices, grain offerings and incense, and
bringing sacrifices of thanksgiving to the house of the LORD.
27 "But [a]if you do not listen to Me to keep the sabbath day holy
by not carrying a load and coming in through the gates of
Jerusalem on the sabbath day, then [b]I will kindle a fire in its
gates and it will [c]devour the palaces of Jerusalem and [d]not be
quenched."'"

Chapter 18 Theme ______________________________

18 The word which came to Jeremiah from the LORD saying,
2 "Arise and [a]go down to the potter's house, and there I
will announce My words to you."

16 [a]Jer 12:3
17 [a]Ps 88:15 [b]Jer 16:19; Nah 1:7
18 [a]Ps 35:4, 26; Jer 17:13; 20:11 [b]Jer 1:17 [c]Ps 35:8
19 [1]Lit *gate of the sons of the people*
20 [a]Ezek 2:7 [b]Ps 49:1, 2; Jer 19:3, 4
21 [a]Deut 4:9, 15, 23; Mark 4:24 [b]Num 15:32-36; Neh 13:15-21; John 5:9-12
22 [1]Lit *fathers* [a]Ex 16:23-29; 20:8-10; Deut 5:12-14; Is 56:2-6; 58:13 [b]Ex 31:13-17; Ezek 20:12; Zech 1:4
23 [a]Jer 7:24, 28; 11:10 [b]Prov 29:1; Jer 7:26; 19:15
24 [a]Ex 15:26; Deut 11:13; Is 21:7; 55:2 [b]Jer 17:21, 22 [c]Ex 20:8-11; Ezek 20:20
25 [a]Jer 22:4 [b]2 Sam 7:16; Is 9:7; Jer 33:15, 17, 21; Luke 1:32 [c]Ps 132:13, 14; Heb 12:22
26 [a]Jer 32:44; 33:13 [b]Zech 7:7 [c]Ps 107:22; Jer 33:11
27 [a]Is 1:20; Jer 22:5; 26:4; Zech 7:11-14 [b]Lam 4:11 [c]2 Kin 25:9; Jer 39:8; Amos 2:5 [d]Jer 7:20; Ezek 20:47
18:2 [a]Jer 19:1, 2

3 Then I went down to the potter's house, and there he was,
making something on the [1]wheel.
4 But the vessel that he was making of clay was spoiled in
the hand of the potter; so he remade it into another vessel, as it
pleased the potter to make.
5 Then the word of the LORD came to me saying,
6 "Can I not, O house of Israel, deal with you as this potter
does?" declares the LORD. "Behold, like the [a]clay in the potter's
hand, so are you in My hand, O house of Israel.
7 "At one moment I might speak concerning a nation or
concerning a kingdom to [a]uproot, to pull down, or to destroy *it;*
8 [a]if that nation against which I have spoken turns from its
evil, I will [1b]relent concerning the calamity I planned to bring
on it.
9 "Or at another moment I might speak concerning a nation
or concerning a kingdom to [a]build up or to plant *it;*
10 if it does [a]evil in My sight by not obeying My voice, then I
will [1b]think better of the good with which I had promised to
[2]bless it.
11 "So now then, speak to the men of Judah and against the
inhabitants of Jerusalem saying, 'Thus says the LORD, "Behold, I
am [a]fashioning calamity against you and devising a plan against
you. Oh [b]turn back, each of you from his evil way, and [1]reform
your ways and your deeds."'
12 "But [a]they will say, 'It's hopeless! For we are going to follow
our own plans, and each of us will act according to the [b]stub-
bornness of his evil heart.'
13 "Therefore thus says the LORD,
'[a]Ask now among the nations,
Who ever heard the like of [1]this?
The [b]virgin of Israel
Has done a most [c]appalling thing.
14 'Does the snow of Lebanon forsake the rock of the
open country?
Or is the cold flowing water *from* a foreign *land* ever
snatched away?
15 'For [a]My people have forgotten Me,
[b]They burn incense [1]to worthless gods
And they [2]have stumbled [3]from their ways,
[3]From the [c]ancient paths,
To walk in bypaths,
Not on a [d]highway,
16 To make their land a [a]desolation,
An object of perpetual [b]hissing;
Everyone who passes by it will be astonished
And [c]shake his head.
17 'Like an [a]east wind I will [b]scatter them
Before the enemy;
I will [1]show them [c]My back and not *My* face
[d]In the day of their calamity.'"

3 [1]Lit *pair of stone discs*
6 [a]Is 45:9; 64:8; Matt 20:15; Rom 9:21
7 [a]Jer 1:10
8 [1]Lit *repent of* [a]Jer 7:3-7; 12:16; Ezek 18:21 [b]Ps 106:45; Jer 26:3, 13, 19; Hos 11:8; Joel 2:13, 14; Jon 3:10
9 [a]Jer 1:10; 31:28; Amos 9:11-15
10 [1]Lit *repent* [2]Lit *do it good* [a]Ps 125:5; Jer 7:24-28; Ezek 33:18 [b]1 Sam 2:30; 13:13
11 [1]Lit *make good* [a]Is 5:5; Jer 4:6; 11:11 [b]2 Kin 17:13; Is 1:16-19; Jer 4:1; Acts 26:20
12 [a]Is 57:10; Jer 2:25 [b]Deut 29:19; Jer 7:24; 16:12
13 [1]Lit *these* [a]Is 66:8; Jer 2:10, 11 [b]Jer 14:17; 31:4 [c]Jer 5:30; 23:14; Hos 6:10
15 [1]Lit *to worthlessness* [2]So ancient versions; Heb *caused them to* [3]Or *in* [a]Jer 2:32; 3:21 [b]Is 65:7; Jer 7:9; 10:15; 44:17 [c]Jer 6:16 [d]Is 57:14; 62:10
16 [a]Jer 25:9; 49:13; 50:13; Ezek 33:28, 29 [b]1 Kin 9:8; Lam 2:15; Mic 6:16 [c]Ps 22:7; Is 37:22; Jer 48:27
17 [1]So ancient versions; M.T. reads *look them in the back and not in the face* [a]Ps 48:7 [b]Job 27:21; Jer 13:24 [c]Jer 2:27; 32:33 [d]Jer 46:21

18 Then they said, "Come and let us [a]devise plans against
Jeremiah. Surely the [b]law is not going to be lost to the priest,
nor [c]counsel to the sage, nor the *divine* [d]word to the prophet!
Come on and let us [e]strike at him with *our* tongue, and let us
[f]give no heed to any of his words."

19 Do give heed to me, O LORD,
And listen to [1]what my opponents are saying!
20 [a]Should good be repaid with evil?
For they have [b]dug a pit for [1]me.
Remember how I [c]stood before You
To speak good on their behalf,
So as to turn away Your wrath from them.
21 Therefore, [a]give their children over to famine
And deliver them up to the [1]power of the sword;
And let their wives become [b]childless and [c]widowed.
Let their men also be smitten to death,
Their [d]young men struck down by the sword in battle.
22 May an [a]outcry be heard from their houses,
When You suddenly bring raiders upon them;
[b]For they have dug a pit to capture me
And [c]hidden snares for my feet.
23 Yet You, O LORD, know
All their [1]deadly designs against me;
[a]Do not [2]forgive their iniquity
Or blot out their sin from Your sight.
But may they be [3b]overthrown before You;
Deal with them in the [c]time of Your anger!

Chapter 19 Theme ________________

19 Thus says the LORD, "Go and buy a [a]potter's earthenware
[b]jar, and *take* some of the [c]elders of the people and some
of the [1d]senior priests.
2 "Then go out to the [a]valley of Ben-hinnom, which is by the
entrance of the potsherd gate, and [b]proclaim there the words that
I tell you,
3 and say, 'Hear the word of the LORD, O [a]kings of Judah and
inhabitants of Jerusalem: thus says the LORD of hosts, the God
of Israel, "Behold I am about to bring a [b]calamity upon this
place, at which the [c]ears of everyone that hears of it will tingle.
4 "Because they have [a]forsaken Me and have [b]made this an
alien place and have burned [1]sacrifices in it to [c]other gods, that
neither they nor their forefathers nor the kings of Judah had
ever known, and *because* they have filled this place with the
[d]blood of the innocent
5 and have built the [a]high places of Baal to burn their [b]sons
in the fire as burnt offerings to Baal, a thing which I never
commanded or spoke of, nor did it *ever* enter My [1]mind;
6 therefore, behold, [a]days are coming," declares the LORD,
"when this place will no longer be called [b]Topheth or [c]the
valley of Ben-hinnom, but rather the valley of Slaughter.

18 [a]Jer 11:19; 18:11 [b]Jer 2:8; Mal 2:7 [c]Job 5:13; Jer 8:8 [d]Jer 5:13 [e]Ps 52:2; Jer 20:10 [f]Jer 43:2

19 [1]Lit *the voice of my opponents*

20 [1]Lit *my soul* [a]Ps 109:4 [b]Ps 35:7; 57:6; Jer 5:26; 18:22 [c]Ps 106:23

21 [1]Lit *hands of* [a]Ps 109:9-20; Jer 11:22; 14:16 [b]1 Sam 15:33; Is 13:18 [c]Jer 15:8; Ezek 22:25 [d]Jer 9:21; 11:22

22 [a]Jer 6:26; 25:34, 36 [b]Jer 18:20 [c]Ps 140:5

23 [1]Lit *unto death* [2]Lit *cover over, atone for* [3]Lit *ones made to stumble* [a]Neh 4:5; Ps 109:14; Is 2:9 [b]Jer 6:15, 21 [c]Jer 7:20; 17:4

19:1 [1]Or *elders of* [a]Jer 18:2 [b]Jer 19:10 [c]Num 11:16 [d]2 Kin 19:2; Ezek 8:11

2 [a]Josh 15:8; 2 Kin 23:10; Jer 7:31, 32; 32:35 [b]Prov 1:20

3 [a]Jer 17:20 [b]Jer 6:19; 19:15 [c]1 Sam 3:11

4 [1]Or *incense* [a]Deut 28:20; Is 65:11; Jer 2:13, 17, 19; 17:13 [b]Ezek 7:22; Dan 11:31 [c]Jer 7:9; 11:13 [d]2 Kin 21:6, 16; Jer 2:34; 7:6

5 [1]Lit *heart* [a]Num 22:41; Jer 32:35 [b]Lev 18:21; 2 Kin 17:17; Ps 106:37, 38

6 [a]Jer 7:32 [b]Is 30:33 [c]Josh 15:8

7 "I will [a]make void the counsel of Judah and Jerusalem in this
place, and [b]I will cause them to fall by the sword before their
enemies and by the hand of those who seek their life; and I
will give over their [c]carcasses as food for the birds of the sky
and the beasts of the earth.
8 "I will also make this city a [a]desolation and an *object of*
hissing; [b]everyone who passes by it will be astonished and hiss
because of all its [1]disasters.
9 "I will make them [a]eat the flesh of their sons and the flesh
of their daughters, and they will eat one another's flesh in the
siege and in the distress with which their enemies and those
who seek their life will distress them."'
10 "Then you are to break the [a]jar in the sight of the men who
accompany you
11 and say to them, 'Thus says the LORD of hosts, "Just so will
I [a]break this people and this city, even as one breaks a potter's
vessel, which cannot again be repaired; and they will [b]bury in
Topheth [1]because there is no *other* place for burial.
12 "This is how I will treat this place and its inhabitants," declares
the LORD, "so as to make this city like Topheth.
13 "The [a]houses of Jerusalem and the houses of the kings of
Judah will be [b]defiled like the place Topheth, because of all the
[c]houses on whose rooftops they burned [1]sacrifices to [d]all the
heavenly host and [e]poured out drink offerings to other gods."'"
14 Then Jeremiah came from Topheth, where the LORD had
sent him to prophesy; and he stood in the [a]court of the LORD'S
house and said to all the people:
15 "Thus says the LORD of hosts, the God of Israel, 'Behold, I
am about to bring on this city and all its towns the entire
calamity that I have declared against it, because they have
[a]stiffened their necks so [b]as not to heed My words.'"

Chapter 20 Theme ______________

20 When Pashhur the priest, the son of [a]Immer, who was
[b]chief officer in the house of the LORD, heard Jeremiah
prophesying these things,
2 Pashhur had Jeremiah the prophet [a]beaten and put him in
the [b]stocks that were at the upper [c]Benjamin Gate, which was
by the house of the LORD.
3 On the next day, when Pashhur released Jeremiah from the
stocks, Jeremiah said to him, "Pashhur is not the name the
LORD has [a]called you, but rather [1b]Magor-missabib.
4 "For thus says the LORD, 'Behold, I am going to make you a
[a]terror to yourself and to all your friends; and while [b]your eyes
look on, they will fall by the sword of their enemies. So I will
[c]give over all Judah to the hand of the king of Babylon, and he
will carry them away as [d]exiles to Babylon and will slay them
with the sword.
5 'I will also give over all the [a]wealth of this city, all its
produce and all its costly things; even all the treasures of the

7 [a]Ps 33:10, 11; Is 28:17, 18; Jer 8:8, 9 [b]Lev 26:17; Deut 28:25; Jer 15:2, 9 [c]Ps 79:2; Jer 16:4

8 [1]Lit *blows* [a]Jer 18:16; 49:13; 50:13 [b]1 Kin 9:8; 2 Chr 7:21

9 [a]Lev 26:29; Deut 28:53, 55; Is 9:20; Lam 4:10; Ezek 5:10

10 [a]Jer 19:1

11 [1]Or *until there is no place* left *to bury* [a]Ps 2:9; Is 30:14; Lam 4:2; Rev 2:27 [b]Jer 7:32

13 [1]Or *incense* [a]Jer 52:13 [b]2 Kin 23:10; Ps 74:7; 79:1; Ezek 7:21, 22 [c]Jer 32:29; Zeph 1:5 [d]Deut 4:19; 2 Kin 17:16; Jer 8:2 [e]Jer 7:18; 44:18; Ezek 20:28

14 [a]2 Chr 20:5; Jer 26:2

15 [a]Neh 9:17, 29; Jer 7:26; 17:23 [b]Ps 58:4

20:1 [a]1 Chr 24:14; Ezra 2:37, 38 [b]2 Kin 25:18

2 [a]1 Kin 22:27; 2 Chr 16:10; 24:21; Jer 1:19; Amos 7:10-13 [b]Job 13:27; 33:11 [c]Jer 37:13; 38:7; Zech 14:10

3 [1]I.e. terror on every side [a]Is 8:3; Hos 1:4, 9 [b]Jer 6:25; 20:10

4 [a]Job 18:11-21; Jer 6:25; 46:5; Ezek 26:21 [b]Jer 29:21; 39:6, 7 [c]Jer 21:4-10; 25:9 [d]Jer 13:10; 52:27

5 [a]Jer 15:13; 17:3

kings of Judah I will give over to the [b]hand of their enemies,
and they will plunder them, take them away and bring them to
Babylon.
6 'And you, [a]Pashhur, and all who live in your house will go
into captivity; and you will enter Babylon, and there you will
die and there you will be buried, you and all your [b]friends to
whom you have [c]falsely prophesied.'"

7 O LORD, You have deceived me and I was deceived;
You have [a]overcome me and prevailed.
I have become a [b]laughingstock all day long;
Everyone [c]mocks me.
8 For each time I speak, I cry aloud;
I [a]proclaim violence and destruction,
Because for me the [b]word of the LORD has [1]resulted
In reproach and derision all day long.
9 But if I say, "I will not [a]remember Him
Or speak anymore in His name,"
Then in [b]my heart it becomes like a burning fire
Shut up in my bones;
And I am weary of holding *it* in,
And [c]I cannot endure *it*.
10 For [a]I have heard the whispering of many,
"[b]Terror on every side!
[c]Denounce *him;* yes, let us denounce him!"
[1]All my [d]trusted friends,
Watching for my fall, say:
"Perhaps he will be [2]deceived, so that we may [e]prevail
against him
And take our revenge on him."
11 But the [a]LORD is with me like a dread champion;
Therefore my [b]persecutors will stumble and not prevail.
They will be utterly ashamed, because they have [1]failed,
With an [c]everlasting disgrace that will not be forgotten.
12 Yet, O LORD of hosts, You who [a]test the righteous,
Who see the [1]mind and the heart;
Let me [b]see Your vengeance on them;
For [c]to You I have set forth my cause.
13 [a]Sing to the LORD, praise the LORD!
For He has [b]delivered the soul of the needy one
From the hand of evildoers.

14 Cursed be the [a]day when I was born;
Let the day not be blessed when my mother bore me!
15 Cursed be the man who brought the news
To my father, saying,
"A [1a]baby boy has been born to you!"
And made him very happy.
16 But let that man be like the cities
Which the LORD [a]overthrew without [1]relenting,
And let him hear an [b]outcry in the morning
And a [2]shout of alarm at noon;

5 [b]2 Kin 20:17, 18; 2 Chr 36:10; Jer 27:21, 22

6 [a]Jer 20:1 [b]Jer 20:4; 29:21 [c]Jer 14:14, 15; Lam 2:14

7 [a]Ezek 3:14 [b]Job 12:4; Lam 3:14 [c]Ps 22:7; Jer 38:19

8 [1]Lit *become* [a]Jer 6:7 [b]2 Chr 36:16; Jer 6:10

9 [a]1 Kin 19:3, 4; Jon 1:2, 3 [b]Job 32:18-20; Ps 39:3; Jer 4:19; 23:9; Ezek 3:14; Acts 4:20 [c]Job 32:18-20

10 [1]Lit *Every man of my peace* [2]Or *persuaded* [a]Ps 31:13 [b]Jer 6:25 [c]Neh 6:6-13; Is 29:21; Jer 18:18 [d]Ps 41:9 [e]1 Kin 19:2

11 [1]Lit *not succeeded;* or *not acted wisely* [a]Jer 1:8; 15:20; Rom 8:31 [b]Deut 32:35, 36; Jer 15:15, 20; 17:18 [c]Jer 23:40

12 [1]Lit *kidneys* [a]Ps 7:9; 11:5; 17:3; 139:23; Jer 11:20; 17:10 [b]Ps 54:7; 59:10; Jer 11:20 [c]Ps 62:8

13 [a]Jer 31:7 [b]Ps 34:6; 69:33; Jer 15:21

14 [a]Job 3:3-6; Jer 15:10

15 [1]Lit *male child* [a]Gen 21:6, 7

16 [1]Lit *being sorry* [2]Or *trumpet blast* [a]Gen 19:25 [b]Jer 18:22; 48:3, 4

17 Because he did not [a]kill me [1]before birth,
So that my mother would have been my grave,
And her womb ever pregnant.
18 Why did I ever come forth from the womb
To [a]look on trouble and sorrow,
So that my [b]days have been spent in [c]shame?

Chapter 21 Theme ____________________

21 The word which came to Jeremiah from the LORD when
[a]King Zedekiah sent to him [b]Pashhur the son of Malchijah,
and [c]Zephaniah the priest, the son of Maaseiah, saying,
2 "Please [a]inquire of the LORD on our behalf, for [b]Nebuchad-
nezzar king of [c]Babylon is warring against us; perhaps the LORD
will deal with us [d]according to all His [1]wonderful acts, so that
the enemy will withdraw from us."
3 Then Jeremiah said to them, "You shall say to Zedekiah as
follows:
4 'Thus says the LORD God of Israel, "Behold, I am about to
[a]turn back the weapons of war which are in your hands, with
which you are warring against the king of Babylon and the
Chaldeans who are besieging you outside the wall; and I will
[b]gather them into the center of this city.
5 "I [a]Myself will war against you with an [b]outstretched hand and
a mighty arm, even in [c]anger and wrath and great indignation.
6 "I will also strike down the inhabitants of this city, both man
and beast; they will die of a great [a]pestilence.
7 "Then afterwards," declares the LORD, "[a]I will give over
Zedekiah king of Judah and his servants and the people, even
those who survive in this city from the pestilence, the sword
and the famine, into the hand of Nebuchadnezzar king of
Babylon, and into the hand of their foes and into the hand of
those who seek their lives; and he will strike them down with
the edge of the sword. He [b]will not spare them nor have pity
nor compassion."'
8 "You shall also say to this people, 'Thus says the LORD,
"Behold, I [a]set before you the way of life and the way of death.
9 "He who [a]dwells in this city will die by the [b]sword and by
famine and by pestilence; but he who goes out and falls away
to the Chaldeans who are besieging you will live, and he will
have his own life as booty.
10 "For I have [a]set My face against this city for [1]harm and not
for good," declares the LORD. "It will be [b]given into the hand of
the king of Babylon and he will [c]burn it with fire."'
11 "Then *say* to the household of the [a]king of Judah, 'Hear the
word of the LORD,
12 O [a]house of David, thus says the LORD:
"[b]Administer justice [1]every [c]morning;
And deliver the *person* who has been robbed from
the [2]power of *his* oppressor,
[d]That My wrath may not go forth like fire

17 [1]Lit *from the womb* [a]Job 3:10, 11, 16; 10:18, 19
18 [a]Job 3:20; 5:7; 14:1; Jer 15:10; Lam 3:1 [b]Ps 90:9; 102:3 [c]Ps 69:19; Jer 3:25; 1 Cor 4:9-13
21:1 [a]2 Kin 24:17, 18; Jer 32:1-3; 37:1; 52:1-3 [b]1 Chr 9:12; Jer 38:1 [c]2 Kin 25:18; Jer 29:25, 29; 37:3; 52:24
2 [1]Or *miracles* [a]Ex 9:28; Jer 37:3, 17; Ezek 14:7; 20:1-3 [b]2 Kin 25:1 [c]Gen 10:10; 2 Kin 17:24 [d]Ps 44:1-3; Jer 32:17
4 [a]Jer 32:5; 33:5; 37:8-10; 38:2, 3, 17, 18 [b]Is 5:5; 13:4; Jer 39:3; Lam 2:5, 7; Zech 14:2
5 [a]Is 63:10 [b]Ex 6:6; Deut 4:34; Jer 6:12 [c]Is 5:25; Jer 32:37
6 [a]Jer 14:12; 32:24
7 [a]2 Kin 25:5-7, 18-21; Jer 37:17; 39:5-9; 52:9 [b]2 Chr 36:17; Jer 13:14; Ezek 7:9; Hab 1:6-10
8 [a]Deut 30:15, 19; Is 1:19, 20
9 [a]Jer 38:2, 17-23; 39:18; 45:5 [b]Jer 14:12; 24:10
10 [1]Lit *evil* [a]Lev 17:10; Jer 44:11, 27; Amos 9:4 [b]Jer 32:28, 29; 38:3 [c]2 Chr 36:19; Jer 34:2; 37:10; 38:18; 39:8; 52:13
11 [a]Jer 17:20
12 [1]Or *in the* [2]Lit *hand* [a]Is 7:2, 13 [b]Ps 72:1; Is 1:17; Jer 7:5; 22:3; Zech 7:9, 10 [c]Ps 101:8; Zeph 3:5 [d]Jer 4:4; 17:4; Ezek 20:47, 48; Nah 1:6

And [e]burn with none to extinguish *it,*
Because of the evil of their deeds.

13 "Behold, [a]I am against you, O [b]valley dweller,
O [1]rocky plain," declares the LORD,
"You men who say, '[c]Who will come down against us?
Or who will enter into our habitations?'
14 "But I will punish you [a]according to the [1]results of your deeds," declares the LORD,
"And I will [b]kindle a fire in its forest
That it may devour all its environs."'"

Chapter 22 Theme ________________________________

22 Thus says the LORD, "Go down to the house of the king
of Judah, and there speak this word
2 and say, 'Hear the word of the LORD, O king of Judah, who
[a]sits on David's throne, you and your servants and your people
who enter these gates.
3 'Thus says the LORD, "[a]Do justice and righteousness, and
deliver the one who has been robbed from the power of *his*
[b]oppressor. Also [c]do not mistreat *or* do violence to the stranger,
the orphan, or the widow; and do not [d]shed innocent blood in
this place.
4 "For if you men will indeed perform this thing, then [a]kings
will enter the gates of this house, sitting [1]in David's place on his
throne, riding in chariots and on horses, *even the king* himself
and his servants and his people.
5 "[a]But if you will not obey these words, I [b]swear by Myself,"
declares the LORD, "that this house will become a desolation."'"
6 For thus says the LORD concerning the house of the king of
Judah:
"You are *like* [a]Gilead to Me,
Like the summit of Lebanon;
Yet most assuredly I will make you like a [b]wilderness,
Like cities which are not inhabited.
7 "For I will set apart [a]destroyers against you,
Each with his weapons;
And they will [b]cut down your choicest cedars
And [c]throw *them* on the fire.
8 "Many nations will pass by this city; and they will [a]say to
one another, 'Why has the LORD done thus to this great city?'
9 "Then they will [1]answer, 'Because they [a]forsook the covenant
of the LORD their God and bowed down to other gods and
served them.'"
10 [a]Do not weep for the dead or mourn for him,
But weep continually for the one who goes away;
For [b]he will never return
Or see his native land.
11 For thus says the LORD in regard to [1a]Shallum the son of
Josiah, king of Judah, who became king in the place of Josiah his

12 [e]Is 1:31; Jer 7:20

13 [1]Lit *rock of the level place* [a]Jer 23:30-32; Ezek 13:8 [b]Ps 125:2; Is 22:1 [c]2 Sam 5:6, 7; Jer 49:4; Lam 4:12; Obad 3, 4

14 [1]Lit *fruit* [a]Is 3:10, 11; Jer 17:10; 32:19 [b]2 Chr 36:19; Is 10:16, 18; Jer 11:16; 17:27; 52:13; Ezek 20:47, 48

22:2 [a]Is 9:7; Jer 17:25; 22:4, 30; Luke 1:32

3 [a]Is 58:6, 7; Jer 7:5, 23; 21:12; Mic 6:8; Zech 7:9; 8:16; Matt 23:23 [b]Ps 72:4 [c]Ex 22:21-24 [d]Jer 7:6; 19:4; 22:17

4 [1]Lit *for David* [a]Jer 17:25

5 [a]Jer 17:27; 26:4 [b]Gen 22:16; Amos 6:8; Heb 6:13

6 [a]Gen 37:25; Num 32:1; Song 4:1 [b]Ps 107:34; Is 6:11; Jer 7:34; Mic 3:12

7 [a]Is 10:3-6; Jer 4:6, 7 [b]Is 10:33, 34; 37:24 [c]Jer 21:14

8 [a]Deut 29:24-26; 1 Kin 9:8, 9; 2 Chr 7:20-22; Jer 16:10

9 [1]Lit *say* [a]2 Kin 22:17; 2 Chr 34:25; Jer 11:3

10 [a]Eccl 4:2; Is 57:1; Jer 16:7; 22:18 [b]Jer 25:27; 44:14

11 [1]I.e. Jehoahaz [a]2 Kin 23:30-34; 1 Chr 3:15; 2 Chr 36:1-4

12 [a]2 Kin 23:34; Jer 22:18

father, who went forth from this place, "He will never return
there;
12 but in the place where they led him captive, there he will
[a]die and not see this land again.

13 [1]Or *roof chambers* [a]Jer 17:11; Mic 3:10; Hab 2:9 [b]Lev 19:13; James 5:4

13 "Woe to him who builds his house [a]without righteousness
And his [1]upper rooms without justice,
Who uses his neighbor's services without pay
And [b]does not give him his wages,

14 [1]Or *roof chambers* [2]Or *Paneled* [3]Or *vermilion* [a]Is 5:8 [b]2 Sam 7:2; Hag 1:4

14 Who says, 'I will [a]build myself a roomy house
With spacious [1]upper rooms,
And cut out its windows,
[2]Paneling *it* with [b]cedar and painting *it* [3]bright red.'

15 [a]2 Kin 23:25; Jer 7:5; 21:12 [b]Ps 128:2; Is 3:10; Jer 42:6

15 "Do you become a king because you are competing in cedar?
Did not your father eat and drink
And [a]do justice and righteousness?
Then it was [b]well with him.

16 [a]Ps 72:1-4, 12, 13 [b]1 Chr 28:9; Jer 9:24

16 "He pled the cause of the [a]afflicted and needy;
Then it was well.
[b]Is not that what it means to know Me?"
Declares the LORD.

17 [a]Jer 6:13; 8:10; Luke 12:15-20 [b]2 Kin 24:4; Jer 22:3

17 "But your eyes and your heart
Are *intent* only upon your own [a]dishonest gain,
And on [b]shedding innocent blood
And on practicing oppression and extortion."

18 [a]2 Kin 23:36-24:6; 2 Chr 36:5 [b]Jer 22:10; 34:5 [c]1 Kin 13:30

18 Therefore thus says the LORD in regard to [a]Jehoiakim the
son of Josiah, king of Judah,
"They will not [b]lament for him:
'[c]Alas, my brother!' or, 'Alas, sister!'
They will not lament for him:
'Alas for the master!' or, 'Alas for his splendor!'

19 [a]1 Kin 21:23, 24; Jer 36:30

19 "He will be [a]buried with a donkey's burial,
Dragged off and thrown out beyond the gates of Jerusalem.

20 [a]Num 27:12; Deut 32:49 [b]Jer 2:25; 3:1

20 "Go up to Lebanon and cry out,
And lift up your voice in Bashan;
Cry out also from [a]Abarim,
For all your [b]lovers have been crushed.

21 [a]Jer 13:10; 19:15 [b]Jer 3:25 [c]Jer 3:24; 32:30

21 "I spoke to you in your prosperity;
But [a]you said, 'I will not listen!'
[b]This has been your practice [c]from your youth,
That you have not obeyed My voice.

22 [a]Jer 23:1 [b]Jer 30:14 [c]Is 65:13; Jer 20:11

22 "The wind will sweep away all your [a]shepherds,
And your [b]lovers will go into captivity;
Then you will surely be [c]ashamed and humiliated
Because of all your wickedness.

23 [a]Jer 4:31; 6:24

23 "You who dwell in Lebanon,
Nested in the cedars,
How you will groan when pangs come upon you,
[a]Pain like a woman in childbirth!

24 [1]I.e. Jehoiachin [2]Lit *off from there* [a]2 Kin 24:6; 1 Chr 3:16; 2 Chr 36:9; Jer 37:1 [b]Song 8:6; Is 49:16; Hag 2:23

24 "As I live," declares the LORD, "even though [1a]Coniah the son
of Jehoiakim king of Judah were a [b]signet *ring* on My right hand,
yet I would pull [1]you [2]off;

25 and I will [a]give you over into the hand of those who are
seeking your life, yes, into the hand of those whom you dread,
even into the hand of Nebuchadnezzar king of Babylon and
into the hand of the Chaldeans.
26 "I will [a]hurl you and your [b]mother who bore you into another
country where you were not born, and there you will die.
27 "But as for the land to which they desire to return, they will
not return to it.
28 "Is this man Coniah a despised, shattered jar?
Or is he an [a]undesirable vessel?
Why have he and his descendants been [b]hurled out
And cast into a [c]land that they had not known?
29 "[a]O land, land, land,
Hear the word of the LORD!
30 "Thus says the LORD,
'Write this man down [a]childless,
A man who will [b]not prosper in his days;
For no man of his [c]descendants will prosper
Sitting on the throne of David
Or ruling again in Judah.'"

Chapter 23 Theme ____________________

23 "[a]Woe to the shepherds who are [b]destroying and scattering the [c]sheep of My pasture!" declares the LORD.
2 Therefore thus says the LORD God of Israel concerning the
shepherds who are [1]tending My people: "You have scattered
My flock and driven them away, and have not attended to
them; behold, I am about to [a]attend to you for the [b]evil of your
deeds," declares the LORD.
3 "Then I Myself will [a]gather the remnant of My flock out of
all the countries where I have driven them and bring them
back to their pasture, and they will be fruitful and multiply.
4 "I will also raise up [a]shepherds over them and they will
[1]tend them; and they will [b]not be afraid any longer, nor be
terrified, [c]nor will any be missing," declares the LORD.
5 "Behold, *the* [a]days are coming," declares the LORD,
"When I will raise up for David a righteous [1b]Branch;
And He will [c]reign as king and [2]act wisely
And [d]do justice and righteousness in the land.
6 "In His days Judah will be saved,
And [a]Israel will dwell securely;
And this is His [b]name by which He will be called,
'The [c]LORD our righteousness.'
7 "[a]Therefore behold, *the* days are coming," declares the LORD,
"when they will no longer say, 'As the LORD lives, who brought
up the sons of Israel from the land of Egypt,'
8 [a]but, 'As the LORD lives, who [b]brought up and led back the
descendants of the household of Israel from *the* north land and
from all the countries where I had driven them.' Then they
will live on their own soil."

25 [a]2 Kin 24:15, 16; Jer 21:7; 34:20, 21

26 [a]2 Kin 24:15; Jer 10:18; 16:13 [b]2 Kin 24:8

28 [a]Ps 31:12; Jer 48:38; Hos 8:8 [b]Jer 15:1 [c]Jer 17:4

29 [a]Deut 4:26; Jer 6:19; Mic 1:2

30 [a]1 Chr 3:17; Matt 1:12 [b]Jer 2:37; 10:21 [c]Ps 94:20; Jer 36:30

23:1 [a]Ezek 13:3; 34:2; Zech 11:17 [b]Is 56:9-12; Jer 10:21; 50:6 [c]Ezek 34:31

2 [1]Lit *shepherding* [a]Ex 32:34 [b]Jer 21:12; 44:22

3 [a]Is 11:11, 12, 16; Jer 31:7, 8; 32:37

4 [1]Or *shepherd* [a]Jer 3:15; 31:10; Ezek 34:23 [b]Jer 30:10; 46:27, 28 [c]John 6:39; 10:28; 1 Pet 1:5

5 [1]Lit *Sprout* [2]Or *succeed* [a]Jer 33:14 [b]Is 4:2; 11:1-5; 53:2; Jer 30:9; 33:15, 16; Zech 3:8; 6:12, 13 [c]Is 9:7; 52:13; Luke 1:32, 33 [d]Ps 72:2; Is 9:7; 32:1; Dan 9:24

6 [a]Deut 33:28; Jer 30:10; Zech 14:11 [b]Is 7:14; 9:6; Matt 1:21-23 [c]Is 45:24; Jer 33:16; Dan 9:24; Rom 3:22; 1 Cor 1:30

7 [a]Is 43:18, 19; Jer 16:14, 15

8 [a]Jer 16:15 [b]Is 43:5, 6; Ezek 34:13; Amos 9:14, 15

9 As for the prophets:
My [a]heart is broken within me,
All my bones tremble;
I have become like a drunken man,
Even like a man overcome with wine,
Because of the LORD
And because of His holy words.
10 For the land is full of [a]adulterers;
For the land [b]mourns because of the curse.
The [c]pastures of the wilderness have dried up.
Their course also is evil
And their might is not right.
11 "For [a]both prophet and priest are polluted;
Even in My house I have found their wickedness,"
declares the LORD.
12 "Therefore their way will be like [a]slippery paths to them,
They will be driven away into the [b]gloom and fall
down in it;
For I will bring [c]calamity upon them,
The year of their punishment," declares the LORD.

13 "Moreover, among the prophets of Samaria I saw an
[a]offensive thing:
They [b]prophesied by Baal and [c]led My people Israel astray.
14 "Also among the prophets of Jerusalem I have seen a
[a]horrible thing:
The committing of [b]adultery and walking in falsehood;
And they strengthen the hands of [c]evildoers,
So that no one has turned back from his wickedness.
All of them have become to Me like [d]Sodom,
And her inhabitants like Gomorrah.
15 "Therefore thus says the LORD of hosts concerning the prophets,
'Behold, I am going to [a]feed them wormwood
And make them drink poisonous water,
For from the prophets of Jerusalem
Pollution has gone forth into all the land.'"

16 Thus says the LORD of hosts,
"[a]Do not listen to the words of the prophets who are
prophesying to you.
They are [b]leading you into futility;
They speak a [c]vision of their own [1]imagination,
Not [d]from the mouth of the LORD.
17 "They keep saying to those who [a]despise Me,
'The LORD has said, "[b]You will have peace"';
And as for everyone who walks in the [c]stubbornness
of his own heart,
They say, '[d]Calamity will not come upon you.'
18 "But [a]who has stood in the council of the LORD,
That he should see and hear His word?
Who has given [b]heed to [1]His word and listened?

9 [a]Jer 8:18; Hab 3:16
10 [a]Jer 9:2; Hos 4:2, 3; Mal 3:5 [b]Jer 12:4 [c]Ps 107:34; Jer 9:10
11 [a]Jer 6:13; Zeph 3:4
12 [a]Ps 35:6; Prov 4:19; Jer 13:16 [b]Is 8:22; John 12:35 [c]Jer 11:23
13 [a]Hos 9:7, 8 [b]1 Kin 18:18-21; Jer 2:8; 23:32 [c]Is 9:16
14 [a]Jer 5:30 [b]Jer 29:23 [c]Jer 23:22; Ezek 13:22, 23 [d]Gen 18:20; Deut 32:32; Is 1:9, 10; Jer 20:16; 49:18; Matt 11:24
15 [a]Deut 29:18; Jer 8:14; 9:15
16 [1]Lit *heart* [a]Jer 27:9, 10, 14-17; 1 John 4:1 [b]Matt 7:15; 2 Cor 11:13-15; Gal 1:8, 9 [c]Jer 14:14; Ezek 13:3, 6 [d]Jer 9:12, 20
17 [a]Mic 2:11 [b]Jer 8:11; Ezek 13:10 [c]Jer 13:10; 18:12 [d]Jer 5:12; Amos 9:10; Mic 3:11
18 [1]Another reading is *My* [a]Job 15:8, 9; Jer 23:22; 1 Cor 2:16 [b]Job 33:31

19 "Behold, the [a]storm of the LORD has gone forth in wrath,
Even a whirling tempest;
It will swirl down on the head of the wicked.
20 "The [a]anger of the LORD will not turn back
Until He has [b]performed and carried out the purposes
of His heart;
[c]In the last days you will clearly understand it.
21 "[a]I did not send *these* prophets,
But they ran.
I did not speak to them,
But they prophesied.
22 "But if they had [a]stood in My council,
Then they would have [b]announced My words
to My people,
And would have turned them back from their evil way
And from the evil of their deeds.

23 "Am I a God who is [a]near," declares the LORD,
"And not a God far off?
24 "Can a man [a]hide himself in hiding places
So I do not see him?" declares the LORD.
"[b]Do I not fill the heavens and the earth?"
declares the LORD.
25 "I have [a]heard what the prophets have said who [b]prophesy
falsely in My name, saying, 'I had a [c]dream, I had a dream!'
26 "How long? Is there *anything* in the hearts of the prophets
who prophesy falsehood, even *these* prophets of the [a]deception
of their own heart,
27 who intend to [a]make My people forget My name by their
dreams which they relate to one another, just as their fathers
[b]forgot My name because of Baal?
28 "The prophet who has a dream may relate *his* dream, but let
him who has [a]My word speak My word in truth. [b]What does
straw have *in common* with grain?" declares the LORD.
29 "Is not My word like [a]fire?" declares the LORD, "and like a
[b]hammer which shatters a rock?
30 "Therefore behold, [a]I am against the prophets," declares the
LORD, "who steal My words from each other.
31 "Behold, I am against the prophets," declares the LORD,
"who use their tongues and declare, '*The Lord* declares.'
32 "Behold, I am against those who have prophesied [a]false
dreams," declares the LORD, "and related them and led My
people astray by their falsehoods and [b]reckless boasting; yet [c]I
did not send them or command them, nor do they [d]furnish this
people the slightest benefit," declares the LORD.
33 "Now when this people or the prophet or a priest asks you
saying, 'What is the [1a]oracle of the LORD?' then you shall say to
them, 'What [1]oracle?' The LORD declares, 'I will [b]abandon you.'
34 "Then as for the prophet or the priest or the people who
say, 'The [a]oracle of the LORD,' I will bring punishment upon
that man and his household.

19 [a]Jer 25:32; 30:23; Amos 1:14

20 [a]2 Kin 23:26, 27; Jer 30:24 [b]Is 55:11; Zech 1:6 [c]Gen 49:1

21 [a]Jer 14:14; 23:32; 27:15

22 [a]Jer 9:12; 23:18 [b]Jer 35:15; Zech 1:4

23 [a]Ps 139:1-10

24 [a]Job 22:13, 14; 34:21, 22; Ps 139:7-12; Is 29:15; Jer 49:10; Heb 4:13 [b]1 Kin 8:27; 2 Chr 2:6; Is 66:1

25 [a]Jer 8:6; 1 Cor 4:5 [b]Jer 14:14 [c]Num 12:6; Jer 23:28, 32; 29:8; Joel 2:28

26 [a]1 Tim 4:1, 2

27 [a]Deut 13:1-3; Jer 29:8 [b]Judg 3:7; 8:33, 34

28 [a]Jer 9:12, 20 [b]1 Cor 3:12, 13

29 [a]Jer 5:14; 20:9 [b]2 Cor 10:4, 5

30 [a]Deut 18:20; Ps 34:16; Jer 14:14, 15; Ezek 13:8

32 [a]Deut 13:1, 2; Jer 23:25 [b]Zeph 3:4 [c]Jer 23:21; Lam 3:37 [d]Jer 7:8; Lam 2:14

33 [1]Or *burden,* and so throughout the ch [a]Is 13:1; Nah 1:1; Hab 1:1; Zech 9:1; Mal 1:1 [b]Jer 12:7; 23:39

34 [a]Lam 2:14; Zech 13:3

35 "Thus will each of you say to his neighbor and to his brother, '[a]What has the LORD answered?' or, 'What has the LORD spoken?'

36 "For you will no longer remember the oracle of the LORD, because every man's own word will become the oracle, and you have [a]perverted the words of the [b]living God, the LORD of hosts, our God.

37 "Thus you will say to *that* prophet, 'What has the LORD answered you?' and, 'What has the LORD spoken?'

38 "For if you say, 'The oracle of the LORD!' surely thus says the LORD, 'Because you said this word, "The oracle of the LORD!" I have also sent to you, saying, "You shall not say, 'The oracle of the LORD!'"'

39 "Therefore behold, [a]I will surely forget you and cast you away from My presence, along with the city which I gave you and your fathers.

40 "I will put an everlasting [a]reproach on you and an everlasting humiliation which will not be forgotten."

Chapter 24 Theme ________________________________

24 After [a]Nebuchadnezzar king of Babylon had carried away captive Jeconiah the son of Jehoiakim, king of Judah, and the officials of Judah with the craftsmen and smiths from Jerusalem and had brought them to Babylon, the LORD showed me: behold, two [b]baskets of figs set before the temple of the LORD!

2 One basket had very good figs, like [a]first-ripe figs, and the other basket had [b]very bad figs which could not be eaten due to rottenness.

3 Then the LORD said to me, "[a]What do you see, Jeremiah?" And I said, "Figs, the good figs, very good; and the bad *figs,* very bad, which cannot be eaten due to rottenness."

4 Then the word of the LORD came to me, saying,

5 "Thus says the LORD God of Israel, 'Like these good figs, so I will regard [a]as good the captives of Judah, whom I have sent out of this place *into* the land of the Chaldeans.

6 'For I will set My eyes on them for good, and I will [a]bring them again to this land; and I will [b]build them up and not overthrow them, and I will [c]plant them and not pluck them up.

7 'I will give them a [a]heart to know Me, for I am the LORD; and they will be [b]My people, and I will be their God, for they will [c]return to Me with their whole heart.

8 'But like the [a]bad figs which cannot be eaten due to rottenness—indeed, thus says the LORD—so I will [1]abandon [b]Zedekiah king of Judah and his officials, and the [c]remnant of Jerusalem who remain in this land and the ones who dwell in the land of [d]Egypt.

9 'I will [a]make them a terror *and an* evil for all the kingdoms of the earth, as a [b]reproach and a proverb, a taunt and a [c]curse in all places where I will scatter them.

INSIGHT

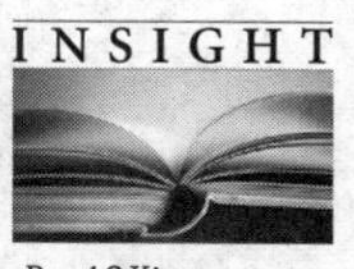

Read 2 Kings 24:10-17 for the historical account of this time. Jehoiachin is also called Jeconiah.

35 [a]Jer 33:3; 42:4
36 [a]Gal 1:7, 8; 2 Pet 3:16 [b]2 Kin 19:4; Jer 10:10
39 [a]Jer 7:14, 15; 23:33; Ezek 8:18
40 [a]Jer 20:11; 42:18; Ezek 5:14, 15
24:1 [a]2 Kin 24:10-16; 2 Chr 36:10; Jer 27:20; 29:1, 2 [b]Amos 8:1
2 [a]Mic 7:1; Nah 3:12 [b]Is 5:4, 7; Jer 29:17
3 [a]Jer 1:11, 13; Amos 8:2; Zech 4:2
5 [a]Nah 1:7; Zech 13:9
6 [a]Jer 12:15; 29:10; 32:37; Ezek 11:17 [b]Jer 31:4; 32:41; 33:7; 42:10 [c]Jer 32:41
7 [a]Deut 30:6; Jer 31:33; 32:40; Ezek 11:19; 36:26 [b]Is 51:16; Jer 7:23; 30:22; 31:33; 32:38; Ezek 14:11; Zech 8:8; Heb 8:10 [c]1 Sam 7:3; Ps 119:2; Jer 29:13
8 [1]Lit *give up* [a]Jer 29:17 [b]Jer 39:5; Ezek 12:12, 13 [c]Jer 39:9 [d]Jer 44:1, 26-30
9 [a]Jer 15:4; 29:18; 34:17 [b]1 Kin 9:7; Ps 44:13, 14 [c]Is 65:15

10 'I will send the [a]sword, the famine and the pestilence upon
them until they are destroyed from the land which I gave to
them and their forefathers.'"

Chapter 25 Theme ______________________________________

25 The word that came to Jeremiah concerning all the people of Judah, in the [a]fourth year of [b]Jehoiakim the son of
Josiah, king of Judah (that was the [c]first year of Nebuchadnezzar
king of Babylon),
2 which Jeremiah the prophet spoke to all the [a]people of
Judah and to all the inhabitants of Jerusalem, saying,
3 "From the [a]thirteenth year of [b]Josiah the son of Amon, king
of Judah, even to this day, [1]these [c]twenty-three years the word
of the LORD has come to me, and I have spoken to you [2d]again
and again, but you have not listened.
4 "And the LORD has sent to you all His [a]servants the prophets
[1]again and again, but you have not listened nor inclined your
ear to hear,
5 saying, '[a]Turn now everyone from his evil way and from the
evil of your deeds, and dwell on the land which the LORD has
given to you and your forefathers [b]forever and ever;
6 and [a]do not go after other gods to [1]serve them and to
[2]worship them, and do not provoke Me to anger with the work
of your hands, and I will do you no harm.'
7 "Yet you have not listened to Me," declares the LORD, "in
order that you might [a]provoke Me to anger with the work of
your hands to your own harm.
8 "Therefore thus says the LORD of hosts, 'Because you have
not obeyed My words,
9 behold, I will [a]send and take all the families of the north,'
declares the LORD, 'and *I will send* to Nebuchadnezzar king of
Babylon, [b]My servant, and will bring them against this land and
against its inhabitants and against all these nations round about;
and I will [1]utterly destroy them and [c]make them a horror and a
hissing, and an everlasting desolation.
10 'Moreover, I will [1a]take from them the voice of joy and the
voice of gladness, the voice of the bridegroom and the voice of
the bride, the [b]sound of the millstones and the light of the lamp.
11 '[a]This whole land will be a desolation and a horror, and
these nations will serve the king of Babylon [b]seventy years.
12 'Then it will be [a]when seventy years are completed I will
[b]punish the king of Babylon and that nation,' declares the LORD,
'for their iniquity, and the land of the Chaldeans; and [c]I will
make it an everlasting desolation.
13 'I will bring upon that land all My words which I have
pronounced against it, all that is written in [a]this book which
Jeremiah has prophesied against [b]all the nations.
14 '([1]For [a]many nations and great kings will make slaves of
them, even them; and I will [b]recompense them according to
their deeds and according to the work of their hands.)'"

10 [a]Is 51:19; Jer 21:9; 27:8; Ezek 5:12-17

25:1 [a]Jer 36:1; 46:2 [b]2 Kin 24:1, 2; 2 Chr 36:4-6; Dan 1:1, 2 [c]Jer 32:1

2 [a]Jer 18:11

3 [1]Lit *this* [2]Lit *rising early and speaking* [a]Jer 1:2 [b]2 Chr 34:1-3, 8 [c]Jer 36:2 [d]Jer 7:25; 11:7; 26:5

4 [1]Lit *rising early and sending* [a]2 Chr 36:15; Jer 26:5

5 [a]2 Kin 17:13; Is 55:6, 7; Jer 4:1; 35:15; Ezek 18:30; Jon 3:8-10 [b]Gen 17:8; Jer 7:7; 17:25

6 [1]Or *worship* [2]Or *bow down to* [a]Deut 6:14; 8:19; 2 Kin 17:35; Jer 35:15

7 [a]2 Kin 17:17; 21:15; Jer 7:19; 32:30-33

9 [1]Or *put them under the ban* [a]Jer 1:15; 6:22, 23 [b]Is 13:3; Jer 27:6; 43:10 [c]1 Kin 9:7, 8; Jer 18:16; 25:18

10 [1]Lit *cause to perish* [a]Is 24:8-11; Jer 7:34; 16:9; Ezek 26:13; Rev 18:23 [b]Eccl 12:4; Is 47:2

11 [a]Jer 4:27; 12:11, 12 [b]2 Chr 36:21; Jer 29:10; Dan 9:2; Zech 7:5

12 [a]Ezra 1:1; Jer 29:10; Dan 9:2 [b]Is 13:14; Jer ch 50, 51 [c]Is 13:19

13 [a]Jer 36:4, 29, 32 [b]Jer 1:5, 10; 36:2

14 [1]Or *For they have served many nations and great kings* [a]Jer 27:7; 50:9, 41; 51:27, 28 [b]Jer 51:6, 24, 56

15 For thus the LORD, the God of Israel, says to me, "Take this
[a]cup of the wine of wrath from My hand and cause all the
nations to whom I send you to drink it.
16 "They will [a]drink and stagger and go mad because of the
sword that I will send among them."
17 Then I took the cup from the LORD's hand and [a]made all the
nations to whom the LORD sent me drink it:
18 [a]Jerusalem and the cities of Judah and its kings *and* its
princes, to make them a ruin, a horror, a hissing and a curse, as
it is this day;
19 [a]Pharaoh king of Egypt, his servants, his princes and all his
people;
20 and all the [1a]foreign people, all the kings of the [b]land of Uz,
all the kings of the land of the [c]Philistines (even Ashkelon,
Gaza, Ekron and the remnant of [d]Ashdod);
21 [a]Edom, [b]Moab and the sons of [c]Ammon;
22 and all the kings of [a]Tyre, all the kings of Sidon and the kings
of [b]the coastlands which are beyond the sea;
23 and [a]Dedan, Tema, [b]Buz and all who [c]cut the corners *of their
hair;*
24 and all the kings of [a]Arabia and all the kings of the
[1b]foreign people who dwell in the desert;
25 and all the kings of Zimri, all the kings of [a]Elam and all the
kings of [b]Media;
26 and all the kings of the north, near and far, one with another;
and [a]all the kingdoms of the earth which are upon the face of
the ground, and the king of [1b]Sheshach shall drink after them.
27 "You shall say to them, 'Thus says the LORD of hosts, the God
of Israel, "[a]Drink, be drunk, vomit, fall and rise no more because
of the [b]sword which I will send among you."'
28 "And it will be, if they [a]refuse to take the cup from your
hand to drink, then you will say to them, 'Thus says the LORD
of hosts: "[b]You shall surely drink!
29 "For behold, I am [a]beginning to work calamity in *this* city
which is [b]called by My name, and shall you be completely free
from punishment? You will not be free from punishment; for [c]I
am summoning a sword against all the inhabitants of the
earth," declares the LORD of hosts.'
30 "Therefore you shall prophesy against them all these words,
and you shall say to them,

'The [a]LORD will [b]roar from on high
And utter His voice from His holy habitation;
He will roar mightily against His [1]fold.
He will shout like those who tread *the grapes,*
Against all the inhabitants of the earth.
31 'A clamor has come to the end of the earth,
Because the LORD has [a]a controversy with the nations.
He is entering into [b]judgment with all flesh;
As for the wicked, He has given them to the sword,'
declares the LORD."

15 [a]Job 21:20; Ps 75:8; Is 51:17, 22; Jer 51:7
16 [a]Nah 3:11
17 [a]Jer 1:10; 25:28
18 [a]Ps 60:3; Is 51:17
19 [a]Jer 46:2-28; Nah 3:8-10
20 [1]Or *mixed multitude* [a]Jer 25:24; 50:37; Ezek 30:5 [b]Job 1:1; Lam 4:21 [c]Jer 47:1-7 [d]Is 20:1
21 [a]Ps 137:7; Jer 49:7-22 [b]Jer 48:1-47; Amos 2:1-3 [c]Jer 49:1-6; Amos 1:13-15
22 [a]Jer 47:4; Zech 9:2-4 [b]Jer 31:10
23 [a]Is 21:13; Jer 49:7, 8 [b]Gen 22:21 [c]Jer 9:26; 49:32
24 [1]Or *mixed multitude* [a]2 Chr 9:14 [b]Jer 25:20; 50:37; Ezek 30:5
25 [a]Gen 10:22; Is 11:11; Jer 49:34 [b]Is 13:17; Jer 51:11, 28
26 [1]Cryptic name for Babylon [a]Jer 25:9; 50:9 [b]Jer 51:41
27 [a]Jer 25:16; Hab 2:16 [b]Ezek 21:4, 5
28 [a]Job 34:33 [b]Jer 49:12
29 [a]Prov 11:31; Is 10:12; Jer 13:13; Ezek 9:6; 1 Pet 4:17 [b]1 Kin 8:43 [c]Ezek 38:21
30 [1]Or *pasture* [a]Is 42:13; Jer 25:38 [b]Joel 2:11; 3:16; Amos 1:2
31 [a]Hos 4:1; Mic 6:2 [b]Is 66:16; Ezek 20:35, 36; Joel 3:2

32 Thus says the LORD of hosts,
"Behold, evil is going forth
From [a]nation to nation,
And a great [b]storm is being stirred up
From the remotest parts of the earth.

33 "Those [a]slain by the LORD on that day will be from one end of the earth to the [1]other. They will [b]not be lamented, gathered or buried; they will be like [c]dung on the face of the ground.

34 "Wail, you shepherds, and cry;
And [a]wallow *in ashes,* you masters of the flock;
For the days of your [b]slaughter and your dispersions
[1]have come,
And you will fall like a choice vessel.
35 "[a]Flight will perish from the shepherds,
And escape from the masters of the flock.
36 "*Hear* the sound of the cry of the shepherds,
And the wailing of the masters of the flock!
For the LORD is destroying their pasture,
37 "And the peaceful [1a]folds are made silent
Because of the [b]fierce anger of the LORD.
38 "He has left His hiding place [a]like the lion;
For their land has become a horror
Because of the fierceness of the [1]oppressing *sword*
And because of His fierce anger."

Chapter 26 Theme ________________________

26 In the beginning of the reign of [a]Jehoiakim the son of Josiah, king of Judah, this word came from the LORD, saying,

2 "Thus says the LORD, '[a]Stand in the court of the LORD's house, and speak to all the cities of Judah who have [b]come to worship *in* the LORD's house [c]all the words that I have commanded you to speak to them. [d]Do not omit a word!

3 '[a]Perhaps they will listen and everyone will turn from his evil way, that [b]I may repent of the calamity which I am planning to do to them because of the evil of their deeds.'

4 "And you will say to them, 'Thus says the LORD, "[a]If you will not listen to Me, to [b]walk in My law which I have set before you,

5 to listen to the words of [a]My servants the prophets, whom I have been sending to you [1]again and again, but you have not listened;

6 then I will make this house like [a]Shiloh, and this city I will make a [b]curse to all the nations of the earth."'"

7 The [a]priests and the prophets and all the people heard Jeremiah speaking these words in the house of the LORD.

8 When Jeremiah finished speaking all that the LORD had commanded *him* to speak to all the people, the priests and the prophets and all the people seized him, saying, "[a]You must die!

32 [a]2 Chr 15:6; Is 34:2 [b]Is 30:30; Jer 23:19

33 [1]Lit *other end of the earth* [a]Is 34:2, 3; 66:16 [b]Ps 79:3; Jer 16:4; Ezek 39:4, 17 [c]Is 5:25

34 [1]Lit *are full* [a]Jer 6:26; Ezek 27:30 [b]Is 34:6, 7; Jer 50:27

35 [a]Job 11:20; Jer 11:11; Amos 2:14

37 [1]Or *pastures* [a]Is 27:10, 11; Jer 5:17; 13:20 [b]Ps 97:1-3; Is 66:15; Heb 12:29

38 [1]Or *oppressor* [a]Jer 4:7; 5:6; Hos 5:14; 13:7, 8

26:1 [a]2 Kin 23:36; 2 Chr 36:4, 5

2 [a]2 Chr 24:20, 21; Jer 7:2; 19:14 [b]Deut 12:5 [c]Jer 1:17; 42:4; Matt 28:20; Acts 20:20, 27 [d]Deut 4:2

3 [a]Is 1:16-19; Jer 36:3-7 [b]Jer 18:8; Jon 3:8

4 [a]Lev 26:14; 1 Kin 9:6; Is 1:20; Jer 17:27; 22:5 [b]Jer 32:23; 44:10, 23

5 [1]Lit *rising early and sending* [a]2 Kin 9:7; Ezra 9:11; Jer 7:13; 25:3, 4

6 [a]Josh 18:1; 1 Sam 4:12; Ps 78:60, 61; Jer 7:12, 14 [b]2 Kin 22:19; Is 65:15; Jer 24:9; 25:18

7 [a]Jer 5:31; Mic 3:11

8 [a]Jer 11:19; 18:23; Lam 4:13, 14; Matt 21:35, 36; 23:34, 35; 27:20

9 "Why have you prophesied in the name of the LORD saying,
'This house will be like Shiloh and this city will be [a]desolate,
without inhabitant'?" And [b]all the people gathered about Jeremiah in the house of the LORD.
10 When the [a]officials of Judah heard these things, they came
up from the king's house to the house of the LORD and sat in
the [b]entrance of the New Gate of the LORD's *house.*
11 Then the priests and the prophets [a]spoke to the officials and
to all the people, saying, "A [b]death sentence for this man! For
he has prophesied [c]against this city as you have heard in your
hearing."
12 Then Jeremiah spoke to all the officials and to all the people,
saying, "[a]The LORD sent me to prophesy against this house and
against this city all the words that you have heard.
13 "Now therefore [a]amend your ways and your deeds and obey
the voice of the LORD your God; and the LORD will [1]change His
mind about the misfortune which He has pronounced against
you.
14 "But as for me, behold, [a]I am in your hands; do with me as
is good and right in your sight.
15 "Only know for certain that if you put me to death, you will
bring [a]innocent blood on yourselves, and on this city and on its
inhabitants; for truly the LORD has sent me to you to speak all
these words in your hearing."
16 Then the officials and all the people [a]said to the priests and
to the prophets, "No [b]death sentence for this man! For he has
spoken to us in the name of the LORD our God."
17 Then [a]some of the elders of the land rose up and spoke to
all the assembly of the people, saying,
18 "[1][a]Micah of Moresheth prophesied in the days of Hezekiah
king of Judah; and he spoke to all the people of Judah, saying,
'Thus the LORD of hosts has said,

"[b]Zion will be plowed *as* a field,
And Jerusalem will become ruins,
And the [c]mountain of the house as the [2]high places
of a forest."'

19 "Did Hezekiah king of Judah and all Judah put him to death?
Did he not [a]fear the LORD and entreat the favor of the LORD,
and [b]the LORD [1]changed His mind about the misfortune which
He had pronounced against them? But we are [c]committing a
great evil against ourselves."
20 Indeed, there was also a man who prophesied in the name
of the LORD, Uriah the son of Shemaiah from [a]Kiriath-jearim;
and he prophesied against this city and against this land words
similar to all those of Jeremiah.
21 When King Jehoiakim and all his mighty men and all the
officials heard his words, then the [a]king sought to put him to
death; but Uriah heard *it,* and he was afraid and [b]fled and went
to Egypt.
22 Then King Jehoiakim sent men to Egypt: [a]Elnathan the son
of Achbor and *certain* men with him *went* into Egypt.

9 [a]Jer 9:11; 33:10 [b]Acts 3:11; 5:12
10 [a]Jer 26:21 [b]Jer 36:10
11 [a]Jer 18:23 [b]Deut 18:20; Matt 26:66 [c]Jer 38:4; Acts 6:11-14
12 [a]Jer 1:17, 18; 26:15; Amos 7:15; Acts 4:19; 5:29
13 [1]Lit *be sorry for* [a]Jer 7:3, 5; 18:8, 11; 26:3; 35:15; Joel 2:14; Jon 3:9; 4:2
14 [a]Jer 38:5
15 [a]Num 35:33; Prov 6:16, 17; Jer 7:6
16 [a]Jer 26:11; 36:19, 25; 38:7, 13 [b]Acts 5:34-39; 23:9, 29; 25:25; 26:31
17 [a]Acts 5:34
18 [1]Lit *Micaiah the Morasthite* [2]Or *a wooded height* [a]Mic 1:1 [b]Neh 4:2; Ps 79:1; Jer 9:11; Mic 3:12 [c]Is 2:2, 3; Jer 17:3; Mic 4:1; Zech 8:3
19 [1]Lit *was sorry for* [a]2 Chr 29:6-11; 32:26; Is 37:1, 4, 15-20 [b]Ex 32:14; 2 Sam 24:16 [c]Jer 44:7; Hab 2:10
20 [a]Josh 9:17; 1 Sam 6:21; 7:2
21 [a]2 Chr 16:10; 24:21; Jer 36:26; Matt 14:5 [b]1 Kin 19:2-4; Matt 10:23
22 [a]Jer 36:12

23 And they brought Uriah from Egypt and led him to King
Jehoiakim, who [a]slew him with a sword and cast his dead body
into the [1]burial place of the [2]common people.
24 But the hand of [a]Ahikam the son of Shaphan was with
Jeremiah, so that he was [b]not given into the hands of the people
to put him to death.

Chapter 27 Theme ____________________________

27 In the beginning of the reign of [1a]Zedekiah the son of
Josiah, king of Judah, this word came to Jeremiah from
the LORD, saying—
2 thus says the LORD to me—"Make for yourself [a]bonds and
[b]yokes and put them on your neck,
3 and send [1]word to the king of [a]Edom, to the king of [a]Moab,
to the king of the sons of [a]Ammon, to the king of [a]Tyre and to
the king of [a]Sidon [2]by the messengers who come to Jerusalem
to Zedekiah king of Judah.
4 "Command them *to go* to their masters, saying, 'Thus says
the LORD of hosts, the God of Israel, thus you shall say to your
masters,
5 "[a]I have made the earth, the men and the beasts which are
on the face of the earth [b]by My great power and by My outstretched arm, and I will [c]give it to the one who is [1]pleasing in
My sight.
6 "Now I [a]have given all these lands into the hand of
Nebuchadnezzar king of Babylon, [b]My servant, and I have
given him also the [c]wild animals of the field to serve him.
7 "[a]All the nations shall serve him and his son and his
grandson [b]until the time of his own land comes; then [c]many
nations and great kings will [1]make him their servant.
8 "It will be, *that* the nation or the kingdom which [a]will not
serve him, Nebuchadnezzar king of Babylon, and which will not
put its neck under the yoke of the king of Babylon, I will punish
that nation with the [b]sword, with famine and with pestilence,"
declares the LORD, "until I have destroyed [1]it by his hand.
9 "But as for you, [a]do not listen to your prophets, your
diviners, your [1]dreamers, your soothsayers or your sorcerers
who speak to you, saying, 'You will not serve the king of
Babylon.'
10 "For they prophesy a [a]lie to you in order to [b]remove you far
from your land; and I will drive you out and you will perish.
11 "But the nation which will [a]bring its neck under the yoke of
the king of Babylon and serve him, I will [b]let remain on its
land," declares the LORD, "and they will till it and dwell in it."'"
12 I spoke words like all these to [a]Zedekiah king of Judah,
saying, "Bring your necks under the yoke of the king of Babylon
and serve him and his people, and live!
13 "Why will you [a]die, you and your people, by the sword,
famine and pestilence, as the LORD has spoken to that nation
which will not serve the king of Babylon?

23 [1]Lit *graves* [2]Lit *sons of the people* [a]Jer 2:30
24 [a]2 Kin 22:12-14; Jer 39:14; 40:5-7 [b]1 Kin 18:4; Jer 1:18, 19
27:1 [1]Many mss read *Jehoiakim* [a]2 Kin 24:18-20; 2 Chr 36:11-13
2 [a]Jer 30:8 [b]Jer 28:10, 13
3 [1]Lit *them* [2]Lit *by the hand of* [a]Jer 25:21, 22
5 [1]Or *upright* [a]Ps 96:5; 146:5, 6; Is 42:5; 45:12; Jer 10:12; 51:15 [b]Deut 9:29; Jer 32:17; Dan 4:17 [c]Ps 115:15, 16; Acts 17:26
6 [a]Jer 21:7; 22:25; Ezek 29:18-20 [b]Is 44:28; Jer 25:9; 43:10 [c]Jer 28:14; Dan 2:38
7 [1]Or *enslave him* [a]2 Chr 36:20; Jer 44:30; 46:13 [b]Dan 5:26; Zech 2:8, 9 [c]Is 14:4-6; Jer 25:12
8 [1]Lit *them* [a]Jer 38:17-19; 42:15, 16; Ezek 17:19-21 [b]Jer 24:10; 27:13; 29:17, 18; Ezek 14:21
9 [1]Lit *dreams* [a]Ex 22:18; Deut 18:10; Prov 19:27; Is 8:19; Mal 3:5; Eph 5:6
10 [a]Jer 23:25 [b]Jer 8:19; 32:31
11 [a]Jer 27:2, 8, 12 [b]Jer 21:9; 38:2; 40:9-12; 42:10, 11
12 [a]Jer 27:3; 28:1; 38:17
13 [a]Prov 8:36; Jer 27:8; 38:23; Ezek 18:31

14 "So [a]do not listen to the words of the prophets who speak to
you, saying, 'You will not serve the king of Babylon,' for they
prophesy a [b]lie to you;
15 for [a]I have not sent them," declares the LORD, "but they
[b]prophesy falsely in My name, in order that I may [c]drive you out
and that you may perish, [d]you and the prophets who prophesy
to you."
16 *Then* I spoke to the priests and to all this people, saying,
"Thus says the LORD: Do not listen to the words of your
prophets who prophesy to you, saying, 'Behold, the [a]vessels of
the LORD'S house will now shortly be brought again from
Babylon'; for they are prophesying a [b]lie to you.
17 "Do not listen to them; serve the king of Babylon, and live!
Why should this city [a]become a ruin?
18 "But [a]if they are prophets, and if the word of the LORD is
with them, let them now [b]entreat the LORD of hosts that the
vessels which are left in the house of the LORD, in the house of
the king of Judah and in Jerusalem may not go to Babylon.
19 "For thus says the LORD of hosts concerning the [a]pillars,
concerning the sea, concerning the stands and concerning the
rest of the vessels that are left in this city,
20 which Nebuchadnezzar king of Babylon did not take when
he [a]carried into exile Jeconiah the son of Jehoiakim, king of
Judah, from Jerusalem to Babylon, and all the nobles of Judah
and Jerusalem.
21 "Yes, thus says the LORD of hosts, the God of Israel, concerning
the vessels that are left in the house of the LORD and in the
house of the king of Judah and in Jerusalem,
22 'They will be [a]carried to Babylon and they will be there until
the [b]day I visit them,' declares the LORD. 'Then I will [c]bring
them [1]back and restore them to this place.'"

Chapter 28 Theme ______________________

28 Now in the same year, [a]in the beginning of the reign of
[b]Zedekiah king of Judah, in the fourth year, in the fifth
month, [c]Hananiah the son of Azzur, the prophet, who was
from [d]Gibeon, spoke to me in the house of the LORD in the
presence of the priests and all the people, saying,
2 "[a]Thus says the LORD of hosts, the God of Israel, 'I have
broken the yoke of the king of Babylon.
3 'Within two years I am going to bring back to this place [a]all
the vessels of the LORD'S house, which Nebuchadnezzar king of
Babylon took away from this place and carried to Babylon.
4 'I am [a]also going to bring back to this place [b]Jeconiah the
son of Jehoiakim, king of Judah, and all the [c]exiles of Judah
who went to Babylon,' declares the LORD, 'for I will break the
[d]yoke of the king of Babylon.'"
5 Then the prophet Jeremiah spoke to the prophet Hananiah
in the presence of the priests and in the presence of all the
people who were standing in the [a]house of the LORD,

14 [a]Jer 27:9; 2 Cor 11:13-15 [b]Jer 14:14; 23:21; 27:10; 29:8, 9; Ezek 13:22
15 [a]Jer 23:21; 29:9 [b]Jer 23:25 [c]2 Chr 25:16; Jer 27:10 [d]Jer 6:13-15; 14:15, 16
16 [a]2 Kin 24:13; 2 Chr 36:7, 10; Jer 28:3; Dan 1:2 [b]Jer 27:10
17 [a]Jer 7:34
18 [a]1 Kin 18:24 [b]1 Sam 7:8; 12:19, 23; Jer 18:20
19 [a]1 Kin 7:15; 2 Kin 25:13, 17; Jer 52:17-23
20 [a]2 Kin 24:12, 14-16; 2 Chr 36:10, 18; Jer 22:28; 24:1
22 [1]Lit *up* [a]Jer 34:2, 3 [b]Jer 25:11, 12; 27:7; 29:10; 32:5 [c]Ezra 1:7-11; 5:13-15; 7:19
28:1 [a]Jer 27:1; 49:34 [b]2 Kin 24:18-20; 2 Chr 36:11-13; Jer 27:3, 12 [c]Jer 28:17 [d]Josh 9:3; 10:12; 1 Kin 3:4
2 [a]Jer 27:12; 28:11
3 [a]2 Kin 24:13; 2 Chr 36:10; Jer 27:16; Dan 1:2
4 [a]Jer 22:26, 27 [b]2 Kin 25:27; Jer 22:24; 24:1 [c]Jer 22:10 [d]Jer 27:8
5 [a]Jer 28:1

6 and the prophet Jeremiah said, "[a]Amen! May the LORD do
so; may the LORD [1]confirm your words which you have
prophesied to bring back the vessels of the LORD's house and all
the exiles, from Babylon to this place.
7 "Yet [a]hear now this word which I am about to speak in your
hearing and in the hearing of all the people!
8 "The prophets who were before me and before you from
ancient times [a]prophesied against many lands and against great
kingdoms, of war and of calamity and of pestilence.
9 "The prophet who prophesies of peace, [a]when the word of
the prophet comes to pass, then that prophet will be known *as*
one whom the LORD has truly sent."
10 Then Hananiah the prophet took the [a]yoke from the neck
of Jeremiah the prophet and broke it.
11 Hananiah spoke in the presence of all the people, saying,
"[a]Thus says the LORD, 'Even so will I break within two full years
the yoke of Nebuchadnezzar king of Babylon from the neck of
all the nations.'" Then the prophet Jeremiah went his way.
12 The [a]word of the LORD came to Jeremiah after Hananiah the
prophet had broken the yoke from off the neck of the prophet
Jeremiah, saying,
13 "Go and speak to Hananiah, saying, 'Thus says the LORD, "You
have broken the yokes of wood, but you have made instead of
them [a]yokes of iron."
14 'For thus says the LORD of hosts, the God of Israel, "I have
put a [a]yoke of iron on the neck of all these nations, that they may
serve Nebuchadnezzar king of Babylon; and they will [b]serve
him. And [c]I have also given him the beasts of the field."'"
15 Then Jeremiah the prophet said to Hananiah the prophet,
"Listen now, Hananiah, the LORD has not sent you, and [a]you
have made this people trust in a lie.
16 "Therefore thus says the LORD, '[a]Behold, I am about to
[1]remove you from the face of the earth. This year you are going to
[b]die, because you have [2c]counseled rebellion against the LORD.'"
17 So Hananiah the prophet died in the same year in the
seventh month.

INSIGHT

Read 2 Chronicles 36:11-13 and 2 Kings 24:18–25:7 to see whose prophecy came to pass.

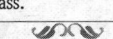

Chapter 29 Theme ________________________

29 Now these are the words of the [a]letter which Jeremiah
the prophet sent from Jerusalem to the rest of the elders
of the exile, the priests, the prophets and all the people whom
Nebuchadnezzar had taken into exile from Jerusalem to Babylon.
2 (This was after King [a]Jeconiah and the [b]queen mother, the
court officials, the princes of Judah and Jerusalem, the craftsmen
and the smiths had departed from Jerusalem.)
3 *The letter was sent* by the hand of Elasah the son of
Shaphan, and Gemariah the son of [a]Hilkiah, whom Zedekiah
king of Judah sent to Babylon to Nebuchadnezzar king of
Babylon, saying,

6 [1]Or *fulfill* [a]1 Kin 1:36; Ps 41:13; Jer 11:5
7 [a]1 Kin 22:28
8 [a]Lev 26:14-39; 1 Kin 14:15; 17:1; 22:17; Is 5:5-7; Joel 1:20; Amos 1:2; Nah 1:2
9 [a]Deut 18:22
10 [a]Jer 27:2
11 [a]Jer 14:14; 27:10; 28:15
12 [a]Jer 1:2
13 [a]Ps 107:16; Is 45:2
14 [a]Deut 28:48; Jer 27:8 [b]Jer 25:11 [c]Jer 27:6
15 [a]Jer 20:6; 29:31; Lam 2:14; Ezek 13:2, 3, 22; 22:28; Zech 13:3
16 [1]Lit *send you away* [2]Lit *spoken* [a]Gen 7:4; Ex 32:12; Deut 6:15; 1 Kin 13:34 [b]Jer 20:6 [c]Deut 13:5; Jer 29:32
29:1 [a]2 Chr 30:1, 6; Esth 9:20; Jer 29:25, 29
2 [a]2 Kin 24:12-16; 2 Chr 36:9, 10; Jer 22:24-28; 24:1; 27:20 [b]2 Kin 24:12, 15; Jer 13:18; 22:26
3 [a]1 Chr 6:13

4 "Thus says the LORD of hosts, the God of Israel, to all the
exiles whom I have [a]sent into exile from Jerusalem to Babylon,
5 '[a]Build houses and live *in them;* and plant gardens and eat
their [1]produce.
6 'Take [a]wives and [1]become the fathers of sons and daughters,
and take wives for your sons and give your daughters to
husbands, that they may bear sons and daughters; and multiply
there and do not decrease.
7 '[a]Seek the [1]welfare of the city where I have sent you into
exile, and [b]pray to the LORD on its behalf; for in its [1]welfare you
will have [1]welfare.'
8 "For thus says the LORD of hosts, the God of Israel, 'Do not
let your [a]prophets who are in your midst and your diviners
[b]deceive you, and do not listen to [1c]the dreams which [2]they
dream.
9 'For they [a]prophesy falsely to you in My name; [b]I have not
sent them,' declares the LORD.
10 "For thus says the LORD, 'When [a]seventy years have been
completed for Babylon, I will visit you and fulfill My [b]good
word to you, to bring you back to this place.
11 'For I know the [a]plans that I [1]have for you,' declares the
LORD, 'plans for [b]welfare and not for calamity to give you a
future and a [c]hope.
12 'Then you will [a]call upon Me and come and pray to Me, and
I will [b]listen to you.
13 'You will [a]seek Me and find *Me* when you [b]search for Me
with all your heart.
14 'I will be [a]found by you,' declares the LORD, 'and I will
[b]restore your [1]fortunes and will [c]gather you from all the nations
and from all the places where I have driven you,' declares the
LORD, 'and I will [d]bring you back to the place from where I sent
you into exile.'
15 "Because you have said, 'The LORD has raised up [a]prophets
for us in Babylon'—
16 for thus says the LORD concerning the king who sits on the
throne of David, and concerning all the people who dwell in
this city, your brothers who did [a]not go with you into exile—
17 thus says the LORD of hosts, 'Behold, I am sending upon
them the [a]sword, famine and pestilence, and I will make them
like [b]split-open figs that cannot be eaten due to rottenness.
18 'I will pursue them with the sword, with famine and with
pestilence; and I will [a]make them a terror to all the kingdoms
of the earth, to be a [b]curse and a horror and a [c]hissing, and a
reproach among all the nations where I have driven them,
19 because they have [a]not listened to My words,' declares the
LORD, 'which I sent to them again and again by [b]My servants
the prophets; but you did not listen,' declares the LORD.
20 "You, therefore, hear the word of the LORD, all you exiles,
whom I have [a]sent away from Jerusalem to Babylon.
21 "Thus says the LORD of hosts, the God of Israel, concerning
Ahab the son of Kolaiah and concerning Zedekiah the son of

4 [a]Jer 24:5
5 [1]Lit *fruit* [a]Jer 29:28
6 [1]Lit *beget* [a]Jer 16:2-4
7 [1]Or *peace* [a]Dan 4:27; 6:4, 5 [b]Ezra 6:10; 7:23; Dan 4:19; 1 Tim 2:1, 2
8 [1]Lit *your* [2]Lit *you* [a]Jer 27:9; 29:1 [b]Jer 14:14; 23:21; 27:14, 15; 28:15; Eph 5:6 [c]Jer 23:25, 27
9 [a]Jer 27:15; 29:21 [b]Jer 29:31
10 [a]2 Chr 36:21-23; Jer 25:12; 27:22; Dan 9:2; Zech 7:5 [b]Jer 24:6, 7; Zeph 2:7
11 [1]Lit *am planning* [a]Ps 40:5; Jer 23:5, 6; 30:9, 10 [b]Is 40:9-11; Jer 30:18-22 [c]Jer 31:17; Hos 2:15
12 [a]Ps 50:15; Jer 33:3; Dan 9:3 [b]Ps 145:19
13 [a]Deut 4:29; Ps 32:6; Matt 7:7 [b]1 Chr 22:19; 2 Chr 22:9; Jer 24:7
14 [1]Or *captivity* [a]Deut 30:1-10; Ps 32:6; Is 55:6 [b]Jer 30:3; 32:37-41 [c]Is 43:5, 6; Jer 23:8; 32:37 [d]Jer 3:14; 12:15; 16:15
15 [a]Jer 29:21, 24
16 [a]Jer 38:2, 3, 17-23
17 [a]Jer 27:8; 29:18; 32:24 [b]Jer 24:3, 8-10
18 [a]Deut 28:25; 2 Chr 29:8; Jer 15:4; 24:9; 34:17; Ezek 12:15 [b]Is 65:15; Jer 42:18 [c]Jer 25:9; Lam 2:15, 16
19 [a]Jer 6:19 [b]Jer 25:4; 26:5; 35:15
20 [a]Jer 24:5; Ezek 11:9; Mic 4:10

INSIGHT

Why 70 years of captivity? Because for 490 years Israel had not given the land its Sabbath rest. See Leviticus 25:1-7; 26:27-35, 40-43; 2 Chronicles 36:20, 21.

Maaseiah, who are [a]prophesying to you falsely in My name,
'Behold, I will deliver them into the hand of Nebuchadnezzar
king of Babylon, and he will slay them before your eyes.
22 'Because of them a [a]curse will be [1]used by all the exiles
from Judah who are in Babylon, saying, "May the LORD make
you like Zedekiah and like Ahab, whom the king of Babylon
[b]roasted in the fire,
23 because they have [a]acted foolishly in Israel, and [b]have
committed adultery with their neighbors' wives and have [c]spoken
words in My name falsely, which I did not command them; and
I am He who [d]knows and am a witness," declares the LORD.'"
24 To [a]Shemaiah the Nehelamite you shall speak, saying,
25 "Thus says the LORD of hosts, the God of Israel, 'Because you
have sent [a]letters in your own name to all the people who are
in Jerusalem, and to [b]Zephaniah the son of Maaseiah, the
priest, and to all the priests, saying,
26 "The LORD has made you priest instead of Jehoiada the priest,
to be the [1a]overseer in the house of the LORD over every
[b]madman who [c]prophesies, to [d]put him in the stocks and in the
iron collar,
27 now then, why have you not rebuked Jeremiah of [a]Anathoth
who prophesies to you?
28 "For he has [a]sent to us in Babylon, saying, '*The exile* will be
[b]long; [c]build houses and live *in them* and plant gardens and eat
their [1]produce.'"'"
29 [a]Zephaniah the priest read this letter [1]to Jeremiah the
prophet.
30 Then came the word of the LORD to Jeremiah, saying,
31 "Send to [a]all the exiles, saying, 'Thus says the LORD
concerning [b]Shemaiah the Nehelamite, "Because Shemaiah has
[c]prophesied to you, although I did not send him, and he has
[d]made you trust in a lie,"
32 therefore thus says the LORD, "Behold, I am about to
[a]punish Shemaiah the Nehelamite and his [1]descendants; he
will [b]not have anyone living among this people, [c]and he will
not see the good that I am about to do to My people," declares
the LORD, "because he has [2d]preached rebellion against the
LORD."'"

Chapter 30 Theme ____________________

30 The word which came to Jeremiah from the LORD, saying,
2 "Thus says the LORD, the God of Israel, '[a]Write all the
words which I have spoken to you in a book.

3 'For behold, [a]days are coming,' declares the LORD, 'when I
will [b]restore the [1]fortunes of My people [c]Israel and Judah.' The
LORD says, 'I will also [d]bring them back to the land that I gave
to their forefathers and they shall possess it.'"

4 Now these are the words which the LORD spoke concerning
Israel and concerning Judah:

21 [a]Jer 14:14, 15; 29:8, 9; Lam 2:14; 2 Pet 2:1

22 [1]Lit *taken* [a]Is 65:15 [b]Dan 3:6, 21

23 [a]Gen 34:7; 2 Sam 13:12 [b]Jer 5:8; 23:14 [c]Jer 29:8, 9, 21 [d]Prov 5:21; Jer 7:11; 16:17; Mal 3:5; Heb 4:13

24 [a]Jer 29:31, 32

25 [a]Jer 29:1 [b]2 Kin 25:18; Jer 21:1; 29:29; 37:3; 52:24

26 [1]Lit *overseers* [a]Jer 20:1 [b]2 Kin 9:11; Hos 9:7; Mark 3:21; John 10:20; Acts 26:24, 25; 2 Cor 5:13 [c]Deut 13:1-5; Zech 13:1-5 [d]Jer 20:1, 2; Acts 16:24

27 [a]Jer 1:1

28 [1]Lit *fruit* [a]Jer 29:1 [b]Jer 29:10 [c]Jer 29:5

29 [1]Lit *in the ears of* [a]Jer 29:25

31 [a]Jer 29:20 [b]Jer 29:24 [c]Jer 14:14, 15; 29:9, 23; Ezek 13:8-16, 22, 23 [d]Jer 28:15

32 [1]Lit *seed* [2]Lit *spoken* [a]Jer 36:31 [b]1 Sam 2:30-34; Jer 22:30 [c]2 Kin 7:2, 19, 20; Jer 17:6; 29:10 [d]Deut 13:5; Jer 28:16

30:2 [a]Is 30:8; Jer 25:13; 36:4, 28, 32; Hab 2:2

3 [1]Or *captivity* [a]Jer 29:10 [b]Ps 53:6; Jer 29:14; 30:18; 32:44; Ezek 39:25; Amos 9:14; Zeph 3:20 [c]Jer 3:18 [d]Jer 16:15; 23:7, 8; Ezek 20:42; 36:24

5 "For thus says the LORD,
'[1]I have heard a sound of [a]terror,
Of dread, and there is no peace.
6 'Ask now, and see
If a male can give birth.
Why do I see every man
With his hands on his loins, [a]as a woman in childbirth?
And *why* have all faces turned pale?
7 'Alas! for that [a]day is great,
There is [b]none like it;
And it is the time of Jacob's [c]distress,
But he will be [d]saved from it.
8 'It shall come about on that day,' declares the LORD of hosts,
'that I will [a]break his yoke from off [1]their neck and will tear off
[1]their [b]bonds; and strangers will no longer [c]make [2]them their
slaves.
9 'But they shall serve the LORD their God and [a]David their
king, whom I will raise up for them.
10 '[a]Fear not, O Jacob My servant,' declares the LORD,
'And do not be dismayed, O Israel;
For behold, I will save you [b]from afar
And your [1]offspring from the land of their captivity.
And Jacob will return and will be [c]quiet and at ease,
And [d]no one will make him afraid.
11 'For [a]I am with you,' declares the LORD, 'to save you;
For I will [b]destroy completely all the nations where I have
scattered you,
Only I will [c]not destroy you completely.
But I will [d]chasten you justly
And will by no means leave you unpunished.'

12 "For thus says the LORD,
'Your wound is incurable
And your [a]injury is serious.
13 'There is no one to plead your cause;
No healing for *your* sore,
[a]No recovery for you.
14 'All your [a]lovers have forgotten you,
They do not seek you;
For I have [b]wounded you with the wound of an enemy,
With the [c]punishment of a [d]cruel one,
Because your [e]iniquity is great
And your [f]sins are numerous.
15 'Why do you cry out over your injury?
Your pain is incurable.
Because your iniquity is great
And your sins are numerous,
I have done these things to you.
16 'Therefore all who [a]devour you will be devoured;
And all your adversaries, every one of them, [b]will go into
captivity;

5 [1]Lit *We* [a]Is 5:30; Jer 6:25; 8:16; Amos 5:16-18
6 [a]Jer 4:31; 6:24; 22:23
7 [a]Is 2:12; Hos 1:11; Joel 2:11; Amos 5:18; Zeph 1:14 [b]Lam 1:12; Dan 9:12; 12:1 [c]Jer 2:27, 28; 14:8 [d]Jer 30:10; 50:19
8 [1]So Gr; Heb *your* [2]Lit *him their slave* [a]Is 9:4; Jer 2:20; Ezek 34:27 [b]Jer 27:2 [c]Ezek 34:27
9 [a]Is 55:3-5; Ezek 34:23, 24; 37:24, 25; Hos 3:5; Luke 1:69; Acts 2:30; 13:23, 34
10 [1]Lit *seed* [a]Is 41:13; 43:5; 44:2; Jer 46:27, 28 [b]Is 60:4; Jer 23:3, 8; 29:14 [c]Is 35:9; Jer 33:16; Hos 2:18 [d]Mic 4:4
11 [a]Jer 1:8, 19 [b]Jer 46:28; Amos 9:8 [c]Jer 4:27; 5:10, 18 [d]Ps 6:1; Jer 10:24
12 [a]2 Chr 36:16; Jer 15:18; 30:15
13 [a]Jer 14:19; 46:11
14 [a]Jer 22:20, 22; Lam 1:2 [b]Lam 2:4, 5 [c]Job 30:21 [d]Jer 6:23; 50:42 [e]Jer 32:30-35; 44:22 [f]Jer 5:6
16 [a]Jer 2:3; 8:16; 10:25 [b]Is 14:2; Joel 3:8

And those who plunder you will be for plunder,
And all who prey upon you I will give for prey.
17 'For I will [1]restore you to [2a]health
And I will heal you of your wounds,' declares the LORD,
'Because they have called you an [b]outcast, saying:
"It is Zion; no one [3]cares for her."'

18 "Thus says the LORD,
'Behold, I will [a]restore the [1]fortunes of the tents
of Jacob
And [b]have compassion on his dwelling places;
And the [c]city will be rebuilt on its ruin,
And the [d]palace will stand on its rightful place.
19 'From them will proceed [a]thanksgiving
And the voice of those who [1b]celebrate;
And I will [c]multiply them and they will not be
diminished;
I will also [d]honor them and they will not be insignificant.
20 '[1]Their children also will be as formerly,
And [2]their congregation shall be [a]established before Me;
And I will punish all [2]their oppressors.
21 '[1]Their [a]leader shall be one of them,
And [1]their ruler shall come forth from [1]their midst;
And I will [b]bring him near and he shall approach Me;
For [2]who would dare to risk his life to [c]approach Me?'
declares the LORD.
22 'You shall be [a]My people,
And I will be your God.'"

23 Behold, the [a]tempest of the LORD!
Wrath has gone forth,
A [1]sweeping tempest;
It will burst on the head of the wicked.
24 The [a]fierce anger of the LORD will not turn back
Until He has performed and until He has accomplished
The intent of His heart;
In the [b]latter days you will understand this.

Chapter 31 Theme ____________________

31 "At that time," declares the LORD, "I will be the [a]God of
all the [b]families of Israel, and they shall be My people."
2 Thus says the LORD,
"The people who survived the sword
[a]Found grace in the wilderness—
Israel, when it went to [b]find its rest."
3 The LORD appeared to [1]him from afar, *saying*,
"I have [a]loved you with an everlasting love;
Therefore I have drawn you with [b]lovingkindness.
4 "[a]Again I will build you and you will be rebuilt,
O virgin of Israel!

17 [1]Lit *cause to go up* [2]Or *healing* [3]Lit *is seeking* [a]Ex 15:26; Ps 107:20; Is 30:26; Jer 8:22; 33:6 [b]Is 11:12; 56:8; Jer 33:24

18 [1]Or *captivity* [a]Jer 30:3; 31:23 [b]Ps 102:13 [c]Jer 31:4, 38-40 [d]1 Chr 29:1, 19; Ps 48:3, 13; 122:7

19 [1]Or *dance* [a]Is 12:1; 35:10; 51:3; Jer 17:26; 33:11 [b]Ps 126:1, 2; Is 51:11; Jer 31:4; Zeph 3:14 [c]Jer 33:22 [d]Is 55:5; 60:9

20 [1]Lit *His* [2]Lit *his* [a]Is 54:14

21 [1]Lit *his* [2]Lit *who is he that gives his heart in pledge* [a]Jer 30:9; Ezek 34:23, 24; 37:24 [b]Num 16:5; Ps 65:4 [c]Ex 3:5; Jer 50:44

22 [a]Ex 6:7; Jer 32:38; Ezek 36:28; Hos 2:23; Zech 13:9

23 [1]Or *raging* [a]Jer 23:19

24 [a]Jer 4:8 [b]Jer 23:20

31:1 [a]Jer 30:22 [b]Gen 17:7, 8; Is 41:10; Rom 11:26-28

2 [a]Num 14:20 [b]Ex 33:14; Num 10:33; Deut 1:33; Josh 1:13

3 [1]Lit *me* [a]Deut 4:37; 7:8; Mal 1:2 [b]Ps 25:6

4 [a]Jer 24:6; 33:7

Again you will [1]take up your [b]tambourines,
And go forth to the dances of the [c]merrymakers.
5 "Again you will [a]plant vineyards
On the [1]hills of Samaria;
The planters will plant
And will [2]enjoy *them.*
6 "For there will be a day when watchmen
On the hills of Ephraim call out,
'Arise, and [a]let us go up *to* Zion,
To the LORD our God.'"

7 For thus says the LORD,
"[a]Sing aloud with gladness for Jacob,
And shout among the [1b]chief of the nations;
Proclaim, give praise and say,
'O LORD, [c]save Your people,
The [d]remnant of Israel.'
8 "Behold, I am [a]bringing them from the north country,
And I will [b]gather them from the remote parts of the earth,
Among them the [c]blind and the [d]lame,
The woman with child and she who is in labor with child,
together;
A great [1]company, they will return here.
9 "[a]With weeping they will come,
And by supplication I will lead them;
I will make them walk by [b]streams of waters,
On a straight path in which they will [c]not stumble;
For I am a [d]father to Israel,
And Ephraim is [e]My firstborn."

10 Hear the word of the LORD, O nations,
And declare in the [a]coastlands afar off,
And say, "He who scattered Israel will [b]gather him
And keep him as a [c]shepherd keeps his flock."
11 For the LORD has [a]ransomed Jacob
And redeemed him from the hand of him who was
[b]stronger than he.
12 "They will [a]come and shout for joy on the [b]height of Zion,
And they will be [c]radiant over the [1]bounty of the LORD—
Over the [d]grain and the new wine and the oil,
And over the young of the [e]flock and the herd;
And their life will be like a [f]watered garden,
And they will [g]never languish again.
13 "Then the virgin will rejoice in the [a]dance,
And the young men and the old, together,
For I will [b]turn their mourning into joy
And will comfort them and give them [c]joy for
their sorrow.
14 "I will [1]fill the soul of the priests with [2]abundance,
And My people will be [a]satisfied with My goodness,"
declares the LORD.

4 [1]Or *be adorned with* [b]Is 30:32 [c]Jer 30:19

5 [1]Or *mountains* [2]Lit *defile* [a]Ps 107:37; Is 65:21; Ezek 28:26; Amos 9:14

6 [a]Is 2:3; Jer 31:12; 50:4, 5; Mic 4:2

7 [1]Lit *head* [a]Ps 14:7; Jer 20:13 [b]Deut 28:13; Is 61:9 [c]Ps 28:9 [d]Is 37:31; Jer 23:3

8 [1]Or *assembly* [a]Jer 3:18; 23:8 [b]Deut 30:4; Is 43:6; Ezek 34:13 [c]Is 42:16 [d]Is 40:11; Ezek 34:16; Mic 4:6

9 [a]Ps 126:5; Jer 50:4 [b]Is 43:20; 49:10 [c]Is 63:13 [d]Is 64:8; Jer 3:4, 19 [e]Ex 4:22

10 [a]Is 66:19; Jer 25:22 [b]Jer 50:19 [c]Is 40:11; Ezek 34:12

11 [a]Is 44:23; 48:20; Jer 15:21; 50:34 [b]Ps 142:6

12 [1]Lit *goodness* [a]Jer 31:6, 7 [b]Ezek 17:23 [c]Is 2:2; Mic 4:1 [d]Hos 2:22; Joel 3:18 [e]Jer 31:24; 33:12, 13 [f]Is 58:11 [g]Is 35:10; 60:20; 65:19; John 16:22; Rev 21:4

13 [a]Judg 21:21; Ps 30:11; Zech 8:4, 5 [b]Is 61:3 [c]Is 51:11

14 [1]Lit *saturate* [2]Lit *fatness* [a]Jer 50:19

15 Thus says the LORD,
"[a]A voice is heard in [b]Ramah,
Lamentation *and* bitter weeping.
Rachel is weeping for her children;
She [c]refuses to be comforted for her children,
Because [d]they are no more."
16 Thus says the LORD,
"[a]Restrain your voice from weeping
And your eyes from tears;
For your [b]work will be rewarded," declares the LORD,
"And they will [c]return from the land of the enemy.
17 "There is [a]hope for your future," declares the LORD,
"And *your* children will return to their own territory.
18 "I have surely heard Ephraim [a]grieving,
'You have [b]chastised me, and I was chastised,
Like an untrained [c]calf;
[d]Bring me back that I may be restored,
For You are the LORD my God.
19 'For after I turned back, I [a]repented;
And after I was instructed, I [b]smote on *my* thigh;
I was [c]ashamed and also humiliated
Because I bore the reproach of my youth.'
20 "Is [a]Ephraim My dear son?
Is he a delightful child?
Indeed, as often as I have spoken against him,
I certainly *still* remember him;
Therefore My [1b]heart yearns for him;
I will surely [c]have mercy on him," declares the LORD.

21 "Set up for yourself roadmarks,
Place for yourself guideposts;
[a]Direct your [1]mind to the highway,
The way by which you went.
[b]Return, O virgin of Israel,
Return to these your cities.
22 "How long will you go here and there,
O [a]faithless daughter?
For the LORD has created a new thing in the earth—
A woman will encompass a man."
23 Thus says the LORD of hosts, the God of Israel, "Once again
they will speak this word in the land of Judah and in its cities
when I [a]restore their [1]fortunes,
'The LORD bless you, O [b]abode of righteousness,
O [c]holy hill!'
24 "Judah and all its cities will [a]dwell together in it, the farmer
and they who go about with flocks.
25 "[a]For I satisfy the weary ones and [1]refresh everyone who
languishes."
26 At this I [a]awoke and looked, and my [b]sleep was pleasant to
me.
27 "Behold, days are coming," declares the LORD, "when I will

15 [a]Matt 2:18 [b]Josh 18:25; Judg 4:5; Is 10:29; Jer 40:1 [c]Gen 37:35; Ps 77:2 [d]Gen 5:24; 42:13, 36; Jer 10:20

16 [a]Is 25:8; 30:19 [b]Ruth 2:12; Heb 6:10 [c]Jer 30:3; Ezek 11:17

17 [a]Jer 29:11

18 [a]Jer 3:21 [b]Job 5:17; Ps 94:12 [c]Hos 4:16 [d]Ps 80:3, 7, 19; Jer 17:14; Lam 5:21; Acts 3:26

19 [a]Ezek 36:31; Zech 12:10 [b]Ezek 21:12; Luke 18:13 [c]Jer 3:25

20 [1]Lit *inward parts* [a]Hos 11:8 [b]Gen 43:30; Judg 10:16; Is 63:15; Hos 11:8 [c]Is 55:7; 57:18; Hos 14:4; Mic 7:18

21 [1]Lit *heart* [a]Jer 50:5 [b]Is 48:20; 52:11

22 [a]Jer 3:6; 49:4

23 [1]Or *captivity* [a]Jer 30:18; 32:44 [b]Is 1:26; Jer 50:7 [c]Ps 48:1; 87:1; Zech 8:3

24 [a]Jer 31:12; Ezek 36:10; Zech 8:4-8

25 [1]Lit *fill* [a]Ps 107:9; Jer 31:12, 14; Matt 5:6; John 4:14

26 [a]Zech 4:1 [b]Prov 3:24

[a]sow the house of Israel and the house of Judah with the seed
of man and with the seed of beast.
28 "As I have [a]watched over them to [b]pluck up, to break down,
to overthrow, to destroy and to bring disaster, so I will watch
over them to [c]build and to plant," declares the LORD.
29 "In those days they will not say again,
'[a]The fathers have eaten sour grapes,
And the children's teeth are [1]set on edge.'
30 "But [a]everyone will die for his own iniquity; each man who
eats the sour grapes, his teeth will be [1]set on edge.
31 "[a]Behold, days are coming," declares the LORD, "when I will
make a [b]new covenant with the house of Israel and with the
house of Judah,
32 not like the [a]covenant which I made with their fathers in
the day I [b]took them by the hand to bring them out of the land
of Egypt, My [c]covenant which they broke, although I was a
husband to them," declares the LORD.
33 "But [a]this is the covenant which I will make with the house
of Israel after those days," declares the LORD, "[b]I will put My
law within them and on their heart I will write it; and [c]I will
be their God, and they shall be My people.
34 "They will [a]not teach again, each man his neighbor and each
man his brother, saying, 'Know the LORD,' for they will all [b]know
Me, from the least of them to the greatest of them," declares
the LORD, "for I will [c]forgive their iniquity, and their [d]sin I will
remember no more."
35 Thus says the LORD,
Who [a]gives the sun for light by day
And the [1]fixed order of the moon and the stars for light
by night,
Who [b]stirs up the sea so that its waves roar;
[c]The LORD of hosts is His name:
36 "[a]If [1]this fixed order departs
From before Me," declares the LORD,
"Then the offspring of Israel also will [b]cease
From being a nation before Me [2]forever."
37 Thus says the LORD,
"[a]If the heavens above can be measured
And the foundations of the earth searched out below,
Then I will also [b]cast off all the offspring of Israel
For all that they have done," declares the LORD.
38 "Behold, days are coming," declares the LORD, "when the [a]city
will be rebuilt for the LORD from the [b]Tower of Hananel to the
[c]Corner Gate.
39 "The [a]measuring line will go out farther straight ahead to
the hill Gareb; then it will turn to Goah.
40 "And [a]the whole valley of the dead bodies and of the ashes,
and all the fields as far as the brook [b]Kidron, to the corner of
the [c]Horse Gate toward the east, shall be [d]holy to the LORD; it
will not be plucked up or overthrown anymore forever."

27 [a]Ezek 36:9, 11; Hos 2:23
28 [a]Jer 44:27; Dan 9:14 [b]Jer 1:10; 18:7 [c]Jer 24:6
29 [1]Or *dull* [a]Lam 5:7; Ezek 18:2
30 [1]Or *dull* [a]Deut 24:16; Is 3:11; Ezek 18:4, 20
31 [a]Jer 31:31-34; Heb 8:8-12 [b]Jer 32:40; 33:14; Ezek 37:26; Luke 22:20; 1 Cor 11:25; 2 Cor 3:6; Heb 8:8-12; 10:16, 17
32 [a]Ex 19:5; 24:6-8; Deut 5:2, 3 [b]Deut 1:31; Is 63:12 [c]Jer 11:7, 8
33 [a]Jer 32:40; Heb 10:16 [b]Ps 40:8; 2 Cor 3:3 [c]Jer 24:7; 30:22; 32:38
34 [a]1 Thess 4:9; 1 John 2:27 [b]Is 11:9; 54:13; Jer 24:7; Hab 2:14; John 6:45; 1 John 2:20 [c]Jer 33:8; 50:20; Mic 7:18; Rom 11:27 [d]Is 43:25; Heb 10:17
35 [1]Lit *statutes* [a]Gen 1:14-18; Deut 4:19; Ps 19:1-6; 136:7-9 [b]Is 51:15 [c]Jer 10:16; 32:18; 50:34
36 [1]Lit *these statutes* [2]Lit *all the days* [a]Ps 89:36, 37; 148:6; Is 54:9, 10; Jer 33:20-26 [b]Amos 9:8, 9
37 [a]Is 40:12; Jer 33:22 [b]Jer 33:24-26; Rom 11:2-5, 26, 27
38 [a]Jer 30:18; 31:4 [b]Neh 3:1; 12:39; Zech 14:10 [c]2 Kin 14:13; 2 Chr 26:9
39 [a]Zech 2:1
40 [a]Jer 7:32; 8:2 [b]2 Sam 15:23; 2 Kin 23:6, 12; John 18:1 [c]2 Kin 11:16; 2 Chr 23:15; Neh 3:28 [d]Joel 3:17; Zech 14:20

Chapter 32 Theme ____________________

32 The word that came to Jeremiah from the LORD in the
[a]tenth year of Zedekiah king of Judah, which was the
eighteenth year of Nebuchadnezzar.
2 Now at that time the army of the king of Babylon was
besieging Jerusalem, and Jeremiah the prophet was shut up in
the [a]court of the guard, which *was in* the house of the king of
Judah,
3 because Zedekiah king of Judah had [a]shut him up, saying,
"Why do you [b]prophesy, saying, '[c]Thus says the LORD, "Behold, I
am about to [d]give this city into the hand of the king of Babylon,
and he will take it;
4 and Zedekiah king of Judah will [a]not escape out of the hand
of the Chaldeans, but he will surely be given into the hand of
the king of Babylon, and he will [b]speak with him [1]face to face
and see him eye to eye;
5 and he will [a]take Zedekiah to Babylon, and he will be there
until I visit him," declares the LORD. "If you fight against the
Chaldeans, you will [b]not succeed"'?"
6 And Jeremiah said, "The word of the LORD came to me,
saying,
7 'Behold, Hanamel the son of Shallum your uncle is coming
to you, saying, "Buy for yourself my field which is at [a]Anathoth,
for you have the [b]right of redemption to buy *it*."'
8 "Then Hanamel my uncle's son came to me in the [a]court of
the guard according to the word of the LORD and said to me,
'Buy my field, please, that is at [b]Anathoth, which is in the land
of Benjamin; for you have the right of possession and the
redemption is yours; buy *it* for yourself.' Then I knew that this
was the [c]word of the LORD.
9 "I bought the field which was at Anathoth from Hanamel my
uncle's son, and I [a]weighed out the silver for him, seventeen
[b]shekels of silver.
10 "I [1a]signed and [b]sealed the deed, and [c]called in witnesses,
and weighed out the silver on the scales.
11 "Then I took the deeds of purchase, both the sealed *copy*
containing the [a]terms and conditions and the open *copy;*
12 and I gave the deed of purchase to [a]Baruch the son of
[b]Neriah, the son of Mahseiah, in the sight of Hanamel my
uncle's *son* and in the sight of the witnesses who signed the
deed of purchase, before all the Jews who were sitting in the
court of the guard.
13 "And I commanded Baruch in their presence, saying,
14 'Thus says the LORD of hosts, the God of Israel, "Take these
deeds, this sealed deed of purchase and this open deed, and
put them in an earthenware jar, that they may [1]last a long
time."
15 'For thus says the LORD of hosts, the God of Israel, "[a]Houses
and fields and vineyards will again be bought in this land."'
16 "After I had given the deed of purchase to Baruch the son of
Neriah, then I [a]prayed to the LORD, saying,

INSIGHT

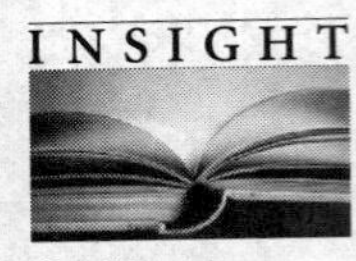

Read Leviticus 25:23-28 in regard to redeeming the land.

32:1 [a]2 Kin 25:1, 2; Jer 39:1, 2
2 [a]Neh 3:25; Jer 33:1; 37:21; 38:6; 39:14
3 [a]2 Kin 6:32 [b]Jer 26:8, 9 [c]Jer 21:3-7; 34:2, 3 [d]Jer 21:4-7; 32:28, 29; 34:2, 3
4 [1]Lit *mouth to mouth* [a]2 Kin 25:4-7; Jer 37:17; 38:18, 23; 39:4-7 [b]Jer 39:5
5 [a]Jer 27:22; 39:7; Ezek 12:12, 13 [b]Ezek 17:9, 10, 15
7 [a]Jer 1:1; 11:21 [b]Lev 25:25; Ruth 4:3, 4
8 [a]Jer 32:2; 33:1 [b]Jer 1:1; 32:7 [c]1 Sam 9:16, 17; 10:3-7; 1 Kin 22:25; Jer 32:25
9 [a]Gen 23:16; Zech 11:12 [b]Gen 24:22; Ex 21:32; Neh 5:15; Ezek 4:10
10 [1]Or *wrote . . . on the document* [a]Is 44:5; Jer 32:44 [b]Deut 32:34; Job 14:17 [c]Ruth 4:1, 9; Is 8:2
11 [a]Luke 2:27
12 [a]Jer 32:16; 36:4, 5, 32; 43:3; 45:1 [b]Jer 51:59
14 [1]Lit *stand many days*
15 [a]Jer 30:18; 31:5, 12, 24; 32:37, 43, 44; 33:12, 13; Amos 9:14, 15; Zech 3:10
16 [a]Gen 32:9-12; Jer 12:1; Phil 4:6, 7

17 '[a]Ah Lord [1]GOD! Behold, You have [b]made the heavens and
the earth by Your great power and by Your outstretched arm!
[c]Nothing is too difficult for You,
18 who [a]shows lovingkindness to thousands, but [b]repays the
iniquity of fathers into the bosom of their children after them,
O [c]great and [d]mighty God. The [e]LORD of hosts is His name;
19 [a]great in counsel and mighty in deed, whose [b]eyes are open
to all the ways of the sons of men, [c]giving to everyone according
to his ways and according to the fruit of his deeds;
20 who has [a]set signs and wonders in the land of Egypt, *and*
even to this day both in Israel and among mankind; and You
have [b]made a name for Yourself, as at this day.
21 'You [a]brought Your people Israel out of the land of Egypt
with signs and with wonders, and with a strong hand and with
an outstretched arm and with great terror;
22 and gave them this land, which You [a]swore to their forefathers to give them, a land flowing with milk and honey.
23 'They [a]came in and took possession of it, but they [b]did not
obey Your voice or [c]walk in Your law; they have done nothing
of all that You commanded them to do; therefore You have
made [d]all this calamity come upon them.
24 'Behold, the [a]siege ramps have reached the city to take it;
and the city is [b]given into the hand of the Chaldeans who fight
against it, because of the [c]sword, the famine and the pestilence;
and what You have spoken has [d]come to pass; and behold, You
see *it*.
25 'You have said to me, O Lord [1]GOD, "Buy for yourself the
field with money and call in witnesses"—although the city is
given into the hand of the Chaldeans.'"
26 Then the word of the LORD came to Jeremiah, saying,
27 "Behold, I am the LORD, the [a]God of all flesh; is anything
[b]too difficult for Me?"
28 Therefore thus says the LORD, "Behold, I am about to [a]give
this city into the hand of the Chaldeans and into the hand of
Nebuchadnezzar king of Babylon, and he will take it.
29 "The Chaldeans who are fighting against this city will enter
and [a]set this city on fire and burn it, with the [b]houses where
people have offered incense to Baal on their roofs and poured
out drink offerings to other gods to provoke Me to anger.
30 "Indeed the sons of Israel and the sons of Judah have been
doing only [a]evil in My sight from their youth; for the sons of
Israel have been only [b]provoking Me to anger by the work of
their hands," declares the LORD.
31 "Indeed this city has been to Me *a* [a]*provocation of* My anger
and My wrath from the day that they built it, even to this day,
so that it should be [b]removed from before My face,
32 because of all the evil of the sons of Israel and the sons of
Judah which they have done to provoke Me to anger—they,
their [a]kings, their leaders, their priests, their prophets, the men
of Judah and the inhabitants of Jerusalem.
33 "They have turned *their* back to Me and not *their* face;

17 [1]Heb *YHWH,* usually rendered *LORD* [a]Jer 1:6; 4:10 [b]2 Kin 19:15; Ps 102:25; Is 40:26-29; Jer 27:5 [c]Gen 18:14; Jer 32:27; Zech 8:6; Matt 19:26; Mark 10:27; Luke 1:37; 18:27
18 [a]Ex 20:6; 34:6, 7; Deut 5:9, 10; 7:9, 10 [b]1 Kin 14:9, 10; 16:1-3; Matt 23:32-36 [c]Ps 145:3 [d]Ps 50:1; Is 9:6; Jer 20:11 [e]Jer 10:16; 31:35
19 [a]Is 9:6; 28:29 [b]Job 34:21; Jer 23:24 [c]Ps 62:12; Jer 17:10; 21:14; Matt 16:27; John 5:29
20 [a]Ps 78:43; 105:27 [b]Ex 9:16; Is 63:12, 14; Dan 9:15
21 [a]Ex 6:6; Deut 4:34; 7:19; 26:8; 2 Sam 7:23; 1 Chr 17:21; Ps 136:11
22 [a]Ex 3:8, 17; 13:5; Deut 1:8; Ps 105:9-11; Jer 11:5
23 [a]Ps 44:2, 3; 78:54, 55; Jer 2:7 [b]Neh 9:26; Jer 11:8; Dan 9:10-14 [c]Ezra 9:7; Jer 26:4; 44:10 [d]Lam 1:18; Dan 9:11, 12
24 [a]Jer 33:4; Ezek 21:22 [b]Jer 20:5; 21:4-7; 32:5 [c]Jer 14:12; 29:17, 18; 32:36; 34:17; Ezek 14:21 [d]Deut 4:26; Josh 23:15, 16; Zech 1:6
25 [1]Heb *YHWH,* usually rendered *LORD*
27 [a]Num 16:22; 27:16 [b]Jer 32:17; Matt 19:26
28 [a]2 Kin 25:11; 2 Chr 36:17-21; Jer 19:7-12; 32:3, 24, 36; 34:2, 3
29 [a]2 Chr 36:19; Jer 21:10; 37:8, 10; 39:8 [b]Jer 19:13; 44:17-19, 25; 52:13
30 [a]Deut 9:7-12; Is 63:10; Jer 2:7; 7:22-26 [b]Jer 8:19; 11:17; 25:7
31 [a]1 Kin 11:7, 8; 2 Kin 21:4-7, 16; Jer 5:9-11; 6:6, 7; Matt 23:37 [b]2 Kin 23:27; 24:3, 4; Jer 27:10
32 [a]Ezra 9:7; Is 1:4-6, 23; Jer 2:26; 44:17, 21; Dan 9:8

though *I* taught them, [1a]teaching again and again, they would
not listen [2]and receive instruction.
34 "But they [a]put their detestable things in the house which is
called by My name, to defile it.
35 "They built the [a]high places of Baal that are in the valley of
Ben-hinnom to cause their sons and their daughters to pass
through *the fire* to [b]Molech, which I had not commanded them
nor had it [1]entered My mind that they should do this
abomination, to cause Judah to sin.
36 "Now therefore thus says the LORD God of Israel concerning
this city of which you say, 'It is [a]given into the hand of the king
of Babylon by sword, by famine and by pestilence.'
37 "Behold, I will [a]gather them out of all the lands to which I
have driven them in My anger, in My wrath and in great
indignation; and I will bring them back to this place and [b]make
them dwell in safety.
38 "They shall be [a]My people, and I will be their God;
39 and I will [a]give them one heart and one way, that they may
fear Me always, for their own [b]good and for *the good of* their
children after them.
40 "I will make an [a]everlasting covenant with them that I will [b]not
turn away from them, to do them good; and I will [c]put the fear
of Me in their hearts so that they will not turn away from Me.
41 "I will [a]rejoice over them to do them good and will [1]faith-
fully [b]plant them in this land with [c]all My heart and with all
My soul.
42 "For thus says the LORD, '[a]Just as I brought all this great
disaster on this people, so I am going to [b]bring on them all the
good that I am promising them.
43 '[a]Fields will be bought in this land of which you say, "[b]It is a
desolation, without man or beast; it is given into the hand of
the Chaldeans."
44 'Men will buy fields for money, [1a]sign and seal deeds, and call
in witnesses in the [b]land of Benjamin, in the environs of
Jerusalem, in the cities of Judah, in the cities of the hill
country, in the cities of the lowland and in the cities of the
[2]Negev; for I will [c]restore their [3]fortunes,' declares the LORD."

Chapter 33 Theme ______________________

33 Then the word of the LORD came to Jeremiah the second time, while he was still [1a]confined in the court of
the guard, saying,
2 "Thus says [a]the LORD who made [1]*the earth,* the LORD who
formed it to establish it, the [b]LORD is His name,
3 '[a]Call to Me and I will answer you, and I will tell you [b]great
and mighty things, [c]which you do not know.'
4 "For thus says the LORD God of Israel concerning the
[a]houses of this city, and concerning the houses of the kings of
Judah which are broken down *to make a defense* against the
[b]siege ramps and against the sword,

33 [1]Lit *rising up early and teaching* [2]Lit *to* [a]2 Chr 36:15, 16; Jer 7:13; 25:3; 26:5; 35:15; John 8:2

34 [a]2 Kin 21:1-7; Jer 7:30; 19:4-6; Ezek 8:5

35 [1]Lit *come up into My heart* [a]2 Chr 28:2, 3; 33:6; Jer 7:31; 19:5 [b]Lev 18:21; 20:2-5; 1 Kin 11:7; 2 Kin 23:10; Acts 7:43

36 [a]Jer 32:24

37 [a]Deut 30:3; Ps 106:47; Is 11:11-16; Jer 16:14, 15; 23:3, 8; Ezek 11:17; Hos 1:11; Amos 9:14, 15 [b]Jer 23:6; Ezek 34:25, 28; Zech 14:11

38 [a]Jer 24:7

39 [a]2 Chr 30:12; Jer 31:33; Ezek 11:19; John 17:21; Acts 4:32 [b]Deut 11:18-21; Ezek 37:25

40 [a]Is 55:3; Jer 31:33, 34; 50:5; Ezek 37:26 [b]Deut 31:6, 8; Ezek 39:29 [c]Jer 24:7; 31:33

41 [1]Or *truly* [a]Deut 30:9; Is 62:5; 65:19 [b]Jer 24:6; 31:28; Amos 9:15 [c]Hos 2:19, 20

42 [a]Jer 31:28; Zech 8:14, 15 [b]Jer 33:14

43 [a]Jer 32:15, 25; Ezek 37:11-14 [b]Jer 33:10

44 [1]Or *write . . . on the document* [2]I.e. South country [3]Or *captivity* [a]Jer 32:10 [b]Jer 17:26; 33:13 [c]Jer 31:23; 33:7, 11, 26

33:1 [1]Lit *shut up* [a]Jer 32:2, 8; 37:21; 38:28

2 [1]Lit *it* [a]Jer 51:19 [b]Ex 3:15; 6:3; 15:3; Jer 10:16

3 [a]Ps 50:15; 91:15; Is 55:6, 7; Jer 29:12 [b]Jer 32:17, 27 [c]Is 48:6

4 [a]Is 32:13, 14 [b]Jer 32:24; Ezek 4:2; 21:22; Hab 1:10

5 'While *they* are coming to [a]fight with the Chaldeans and to
fill them with the corpses of men whom I have slain in My
anger and in My wrath, and I have [b]hidden My face from this
city because of all their wickedness:
6 'Behold, I will bring to it [a]health and healing, and I will heal
them; and I will reveal to them an [b]abundance of peace and truth.
7 'I will [a]restore the [1]fortunes of Judah and the fortunes of
Israel and will [b]rebuild them as they were at first.
8 'I will [a]cleanse them from all their iniquity by which they
have sinned against Me, and I will pardon all their iniquities by
which they have sinned against Me and by which they have
transgressed against Me.
9 '[1]It will be to Me a [a]name of joy, praise and glory before [b]all
the nations of the earth which will hear of all the [c]good that I
do for them, and they will [d]fear and tremble because of all the
good and all the peace that I make for it.'
10 "Thus says the LORD, 'Yet again there will be heard in this
place, of which you say, "It is a [a]waste, without man and without
beast," *that is,* in the cities of Judah and in the streets of Jerusalem that are [b]desolate, without man and without inhabitant
and without beast,
11 the voice of [a]joy and the voice of gladness, the voice of the
bridegroom and the voice of the bride, the voice of those who say,
"[b]Give thanks to the LORD of hosts,
For the LORD is good,
For His lovingkindness is everlasting";
and of those who bring a [c]thank offering into the house of the
LORD. For I will restore the [1]fortunes of the land as they were
at first,' says the LORD.
12 "Thus says the LORD of hosts, 'There will again be in this
place which is waste, [a]without man or beast, and in all its
cities, a [1]habitation of shepherds who rest their [b]flocks.
13 'In the [a]cities of the hill country, in the cities of the
lowland, in the cities of the Negev, in the land of Benjamin, in
the environs of Jerusalem and in the cities of Judah, the flocks
will again [b]pass under the hands of the one who numbers
them,' says the LORD.
14 'Behold, [a]days are coming,' declares the LORD, 'when I will
[b]fulfill the good word which I have spoken concerning the
house of Israel and the house of Judah.
15 'In those days and at that time I will cause a [a]righteous
Branch of David to spring forth; and He shall execute [b]justice
and righteousness on the earth.
16 'In those days [a]Judah will be saved and Jerusalem will dwell
in safety; and this is *the name* by which she will be called: the
[b]LORD is our righteousness.'
17 "For thus says the LORD, '[1]David shall [a]never lack a man to
sit on the throne of the house of Israel;
18 [1]and the [a]Levitical priests shall never lack a man before Me
to offer burnt offerings, to burn grain offerings and to [b]prepare
sacrifices [2]continually.'"

5 [a]Jer 21:4-7; 32:5 [b]Is 8:17; Jer 21:10; Mic 3:4
6 [a]Jer 17:14; 30:17; Hos 6:1 [b]Is 66:12; Gal 5:22, 23
7 [1]Or *captivity* [a]Ps 85:1; Jer 30:18; 32:44; 33:26; Amos 9:14 [b]Is 1:26; Jer 30:18; 31:4, 38; Amos 9:14, 15
8 [a]Ps 51:2; Is 44:22; Jer 50:20; Ezek 36:25, 33; Mic 7:18, 19; Zech 13:1; Heb 9:11-14
9 [1]I.e. This city [a]Is 62:2, 4, 7; Jer 13:11 [b]Jer 3:17, 19; 4:2; 16:19 [c]Jer 24:6; 32:42 [d]Neh 6:16; Ps 40:3; Is 60:5; Hos 3:5
10 [a]Jer 32:43 [b]Jer 26:9; 34:22
11 [1]Or *captivity* [a]Is 35:10; 51:3, 11 [b]1 Chr 16:8, 34; 2 Chr 5:13; 7:3; Ezra 3:11; Ps 100:4, 5; 106:1; 107:1; 118:1; 136:1 [c]Lev 7:12, 13; Ps 107:22; 116:17; Jer 17:26; Heb 13:15
12 [1]Or *pasture* [a]Jer 32:43; 36:29; 51:62 [b]Is 65:10; Jer 31:12; Ezek 34:12-15; Zeph 2:6, 7
13 [a]Jer 17:26; 32:44 [b]Lev 27:32; Luke 15:4
14 [a]Jer 23:5 [b]Is 32:1, 2; Jer 29:10; 32:42; 33:9; Ezek 34:23-25; Hag 2:6-9
15 [a]Is 4:2; 11:1-5; Jer 23:5, 6; 30:9; Zech 3:8; 6:12, 13 [b]Ps 72:1-5
16 [a]Is 45:17, 22; Jer 23:6 [b]Is 45:24, 25; Jer 23:6; 1 Cor 1:30; 2 Cor 5:21; Phil 3:9
17 [1]Lit *There shall not be cut off for David* [a]2 Sam 7:16; 1 Kin 2:4; 8:25; 1 Chr 17:11-14; Ps 89:29-37
18 [1]Lit *there shall not be cut off for the Levitical priests* [2]Lit *all the days* [a]Num 3:5-10; Deut 18:1; 24:8; Josh 3:3; Ezek 44:15 [b]Ezra 3:5; Heb 13:15

19 The word of the LORD came to Jeremiah, saying,
20 "Thus says the LORD, 'If you can [a]break My covenant for the
day and My covenant for the night, so that day and night will
not be at their appointed time,
21 then [a]My covenant may also be broken with David My
servant so that he will not have a son to reign on his throne,
and with the Levitical priests, My ministers.
22 'As the [a]host of heaven cannot be counted and the [b]sand of
the sea cannot be measured, so I will [c]multiply the [1]descendants
of David My servant and the [d]Levites who minister to Me.'"
23 And the word of the LORD came to Jeremiah, saying,
24 "Have you not observed what this people have spoken, saying,
'The [a]two families which the LORD chose, He has [b]rejected them'?
Thus they [c]despise My people, no longer are they as a nation
[1]in their sight.
25 "Thus says the LORD, 'If My [a]covenant *for* day and night
stand not, *and* the [1]fixed patterns of heaven and earth I have
[b]not established,
26 then I would [a]reject the [1]descendants of Jacob and David My
servant, [2]not taking from his [1]descendants [b]rulers over the
[1]descendants of Abraham, Isaac and Jacob. But I will [c]restore
their [3]fortunes and will have [d]mercy on them.'"

Chapter 34 Theme ______________________

34 The word which came to Jeremiah from the LORD, when
[a]Nebuchadnezzar king of Babylon and all his army, with
[b]all the kingdoms of the earth that were under his dominion
and all the peoples, were fighting against Jerusalem and against
all its cities, saying,
2 "Thus says the LORD God of Israel, '[a]Go and speak to
Zedekiah king of Judah and say to him: "Thus says the LORD,
'Behold, [b]I am giving this city into the hand of the king of
Babylon, and [c]he will burn it with fire.
3 '[a]You will not escape from his hand, for you will surely be
captured and delivered into his hand; and you will [b]see the
king of Babylon eye to eye, and he will speak with you [1]face to
face, and you will go to Babylon.'"'
4 "Yet hear the word of the LORD, O Zedekiah king of Judah!
Thus says the LORD concerning you, 'You will not die by the
sword.
5 'You will die in peace; and as *spices* were burned for your
fathers, the former kings who were before you, so they will
[a]burn *spices* for you; and [b]they will lament for you, "Alas,
lord!"' For I have spoken the word," declares the LORD.
6 Then Jeremiah the prophet spoke [a]all these words to
Zedekiah king of Judah in Jerusalem
7 when the army of the king of Babylon was fighting against
Jerusalem and against all the remaining cities of Judah, *that is,*
[a]Lachish and [b]Azekah, for they *alone* remained as [c]fortified
cities among the cities of Judah.

20 [a]Ps 89:37; 104:19-23; Is 54:9, 10; Jer 31:35-37; 33:25

21 [a]2 Sam 23:5; 2 Chr 7:18; 21:7

22 [1]Lit *seed* [a]Gen 15:5; Jer 31:37 [b]Gen 22:17 [c]Ezek 37:24-27 [d]Is 66:21; Jer 33:18

24 [1]Lit *to their faces* [a]Is 7:17; 11:13; Jer 3:7, 8, 10, 18; 33:26; Ezek 37:22 [b]Jer 30:17 [c]Neh 4:2-4; Esth 3:6, 8, 9; Ps 44:13, 14; 83:4

25 [1]Lit *statutes* [a]Gen 8:22; Jer 31:35, 36; 33:20 [b]Ps 74:16, 17

26 [1]Lit *seed* [2]Lit *from taking* [3]Or *captivity* [a]Jer 31:37 [b]Gen 49:10 [c]Jer 33:7 [d]Is 14:1; 54:8; Jer 31:20; Ezek 39:25; Hos 1:7; 2:23

34:1 [a]2 Kin 25:1; Jer 32:2; 39:1; 52:4 [b]Jer 1:15; 27:7; Dan 2:37, 38

2 [a]2 Chr 36:11, 12; Jer 22:1, 2; 37:1, 2 [b]Jer 21:10; 32:3; 34:22; 37:8-10 [c]Jer 32:29

3 [1]Lit *mouth to mouth* [a]2 Kin 25:4, 5; Jer 21:7; 32:4; 34:21 [b]2 Kin 25:6, 7; Jer 39:6, 7

5 [a]2 Chr 16:14; 21:19 [b]Jer 22:18

6 [a]1 Sam 3:18; 15:16-24

7 [a]Josh 10:3, 5; 2 Kin 14:19; 18:14; Is 36:2 [b]Josh 10:10; 2 Chr 11:9 [c]2 Chr 11:5-10

8 The word which came to Jeremiah from the LORD after King Zedekiah had [a]made a covenant with all the people who were in Jerusalem to [b]proclaim [1]release to them:

9 that each man should set free his male servant and each man his female servant, a [a]Hebrew man or a Hebrew woman; so that [b]no one should keep them, a Jew his brother, in bondage.

10 And all the [a]officials and all the people obeyed who had entered into the covenant that each man should set free his male servant and each man his female servant, so that no one should keep them any longer in bondage; they obeyed, and set *them free.*

11 But afterward they turned around and took back the male servants and the female servants whom they had set free, and brought them into subjection for male servants and for female servants.

12 Then the word of the LORD came to Jeremiah from the LORD, saying,

13 "Thus says the LORD God of Israel, 'I [a]made a covenant with your forefathers in the day that I [b]brought them out of the land of Egypt, from the house of bondage, saying,

14 "[a]At the end of seven years each of you shall set free his Hebrew brother who [1]has been sold to you and has served you six years, you shall send him out free from you; but your forefathers [b]did not obey Me or incline their ear to Me.

15 "Although recently you *had* turned and [a]done what is right in My sight, each man proclaiming [1]release to his neighbor, and you had [b]made a covenant before Me [c]in the house which is called by My name.

16 "Yet you [a]turned and [b]profaned My name, and each man [1]took back his male servant and each man his female servant whom you had set free according to their desire, and you brought them into subjection to be your male servants and female servants."'

17 "Therefore thus says the LORD, 'You have not obeyed Me in proclaiming [1]release each man to his brother and each man to his neighbor. Behold, I am [a]proclaiming a [1]release to you,' declares the LORD, 'to the [b]sword, to the pestilence and to the famine; and I will make you a [c]terror to all the kingdoms of the earth.

18 'I will give the men who have [a]transgressed My covenant, who have not fulfilled the words of the covenant which they made before Me, *when* they [b]cut the calf in two and passed between its parts—

19 the [a]officials of Judah and the officials of Jerusalem, the court officers and the priests and all the people of the land who passed between the parts of the calf—

20 I will give them into the hand of their enemies and into the hand of those who [a]seek their life. And their [b]dead bodies will be food for the birds of the sky and the beasts of the earth.

21 '[a]Zedekiah king of Judah and his officials I will give into the hand of their enemies and into the hand of those who seek their life, and into the hand of the army of the king of Babylon which has [b]gone away from you.

8 [1]Or *liberty* [a]2 Kin 11:17; 23:2, 3 [b]Ex 21:2; Lev 25:10, 39-46; Neh 5:1-13; Is 58:6; Jer 34:14, 17

9 [a]Gen 14:13; Ex 2:6 [b]Lev 25:39

10 [a]Jer 26:10, 16

13 [a]Ex 24:3, 7, 8; Deut 5:2, 3, 27; Jer 31:32 [b]Ex 20:2

14 [1]Or *has sold himself* [a]Ex 21:2; Deut 15:12; 1 Kin 9:22 [b]1 Sam 8:7, 8; 2 Kin 17:13, 14

15 [1]Or *liberty* [a]Jer 34:8 [b]2 Kin 23:3; Neh 10:29 [c]Jer 7:10f; 32:34

16 [1]Lit *caused them to return* [a]1 Sam 15:11; Jer 34:11; Ezek 3:20; 18:24 [b]Ex 20:7; Lev 19:12

17 [1]Or *liberty* [a]Lev 26:34, 35; Esth 7:10; Dan 6:24; Matt 7:2 [b]Jer 32:24; 38:2 [c]Deut 28:25; Jer 29:18

18 [a]Deut 17:2; Hos 6:7; 8:1; Rom 2:8 [b]Gen 15:10

19 [a]Jer 34:10; Ezek 22:27; Zeph 3:3, 4

20 [a]Jer 11:21; 21:7; 22:25 [b]Deut 28:26; 1 Sam 17:44, 46; 1 Kin 14:11; 16:4; Ps 79:2; Jer 7:33; 16:4; 19:7

21 [a]2 Kin 25:18-21; Jer 32:3, 4; 39:6; 52:10, 24-27; Ezek 17:16 [b]Jer 37:5-11

22 'Behold, I am going to command,' declares the LORD, 'and I
will bring them back to this city; and they will fight against it
and [a]take it and burn it with fire; and I will make the cities of
Judah a [b]desolation [c]without inhabitant.'"

Chapter 35 Theme ______________________________

35 The word which came to Jeremiah from the LORD in
the days of [a]Jehoiakim the son of Josiah, king of Judah,
saying,
2 "Go to the house of the [a]Rechabites and speak to them, and
bring them into the house of the LORD, into one of the [b]chambers,
and give them wine to drink."
3 Then I took Jaazaniah the son of Jeremiah, son of Habazziniah, and his brothers and all his sons and the whole house
of the Rechabites,
4 and I brought them into the house of the LORD, into the
chamber of the sons of Hanan the son of Igdaliah, the [a]man of
God, which was near the chamber of the officials, which was
above the chamber of Maaseiah the son of Shallum, [b]the
doorkeeper.
5 Then I set before the [1]men of the house of the Rechabites
pitchers full of wine and cups; and I said to them, "[a]Drink wine!"
6 But they said, "We will not drink wine, for [a]Jonadab the
son of [b]Rechab, our father, commanded us, saying, 'You shall
[c]not drink wine, you or your sons, forever.
7 'You shall not build a house, and you shall not sow seed and
you shall not plant a vineyard or own one; but in [a]tents you
shall dwell all your days, that you may live [b]many days in the
land where you [c]sojourn.'
8 "We have [a]obeyed the voice of Jonadab the son of Rechab,
our father, in all that he commanded us, not to drink wine all
our days, we, our wives, our sons or our daughters,
9 nor to build ourselves houses to dwell in; and we [a]do not
have vineyard or field or seed.
10 "We have only [a]dwelt in tents, and have obeyed and have
done according to all that [b]Jonadab our father commanded us.
11 "But when [a]Nebuchadnezzar king of Babylon came up
against the land, we said, 'Come and let us [b]go to Jerusalem
before the army of the Chaldeans and before the army of the
Arameans.' So we have dwelt in Jerusalem."
12 Then the word of the LORD came to Jeremiah, saying,
13 "Thus says the LORD of hosts, the God of Israel, 'Go and say
to the men of Judah and the inhabitants of Jerusalem, "[a]Will
you not receive instruction by listening to My words?" declares
the LORD.
14 "The [a]words of Jonadab the son of Rechab, which he
commanded his sons not to drink wine, are observed. So they
do not drink *wine* to this day, for they have obeyed their
father's command. But I have spoken to you [1][b]again and again;
yet you have [c]not listened to Me.

22 [a]Jer 34:2; 39:1, 2, 8; 52:7, 13 [b]Jer 4:7; 9:11 [c]Jer 33:10; 44:22

35:1 [a]2 Kin 23:34-36; 24:1; 2 Chr 36:5-7; Jer 1:3; 27:20; Dan 1:1

2 [a]2 Kin 10:15; 1 Chr 2:55 [b]1 Kin 6:5, 8; 1 Chr 9:26, 33

4 [a]Deut 33:1; Josh 14:6; 1 Kin 12:22; 2 Kin 1:9-13 [b]1 Chr 9:18f

5 [1]Lit *sons* [a]Amos 2:12

6 [a]2 Kin 10:15, 23 [b]1 Chr 2:55 [c]Lev 10:9; Num 6:2-4; Judg 13:7, 14; Luke 1:15

7 [a]Gen 25:27; Heb 11:9 [b]Ex 20:12; Eph 6:2, 3 [c]Gen 36:7

8 [a]Prov 1:8, 9; 4:1, 2, 10; 6:20; Eph 6:1; Col 3:20

9 [a]Ps 37:16; Jer 35:7; 1 Tim 6:6

10 [a]Jer 35:7 [b]Jer 35:6

11 [a]2 Kin 24:1, 2; Dan 1:1, 2 [b]Jer 4:5-7; 8:14

13 [a]Is 28:9-12; Jer 5:3; 6:8-10; 32:33

14 [1]Lit *rising early and speaking* [a]Jer 35:6-10 [b]2 Chr 36:15; Jer 7:13, 25; 11:7; 25:3, 4 [c]Is 30:9; 50:2

15 "Also I have sent to you all My [a]servants the prophets,
sending *them* [1]again and again, saying: '[b]Turn now every man
from his evil way and amend your deeds, and [c]do not go after
other gods to worship them. Then you will [d]dwell in the land
which I have given to you and to your forefathers; but you have
not [e]inclined your ear or listened to Me.
16 'Indeed, the sons of Jonadab the son of Rechab have
[a]observed the command of their father which he commanded
them, but this people has not listened to Me.'"'
17 "Therefore thus says the LORD, the God of hosts, the God of
Israel, 'Behold, [a]I am bringing on Judah and on all the
inhabitants of Jerusalem all the disaster that I have pronounced
against them; because I [b]spoke to them but they did not listen,
and I have called them but they did not answer.'"
18 Then Jeremiah said to the house of the Rechabites, "Thus
says the LORD of hosts, the God of Israel, 'Because you have
[a]obeyed the command of Jonadab your father, kept all his
commands and done according to all that he commanded you;
19 therefore thus says the LORD of hosts, the God of Israel,
"Jonadab the son of Rechab [a]shall not lack a man to [b]stand
before Me [1]always."'"

Chapter 36 Theme ____________________

36 In the [a]fourth year of Jehoiakim the son of Josiah, king of
Judah, this word came to Jeremiah from the LORD, saying,
2 "Take a [1a]scroll and write on it all the [b]words which I have
spoken to you concerning [c]Israel and concerning Judah, and
concerning all the [d]nations, from the [e]day I *first* spoke to you,
from the days of Josiah, even to this day.
3 "[a]Perhaps the house of Judah will hear all the calamity which
I plan to bring on them, in order that every man will [b]turn from
his evil way; then I will [c]forgive their iniquity and their sin."
4 Then Jeremiah called [a]Baruch the son of Neriah, and
Baruch wrote on a [1b]scroll [2]at the dictation of Jeremiah all the
words of the LORD which He had spoken to him.
5 Jeremiah commanded Baruch, saying, "I am [1a]restricted; I
cannot go into the house of the LORD.
6 "So you go and [a]read from the scroll which you have [b]written
[1]at my dictation the words of the LORD [2]to the people in the
LORD'S house on a [c]fast day. And also you shall read them [2]to all
the people of Judah who come from their cities.
7 "[a]Perhaps their supplication will [1]come before the LORD, and
everyone will turn from his evil way, for [b]great is the anger and
the wrath that the LORD has pronounced against this people."
8 Baruch the son of Neriah did according to all that Jeremiah
the prophet commanded him, [a]reading from the book the
words of the LORD in the LORD'S house.
9 Now in the [a]fifth year of Jehoiakim the son of Josiah, king
of Judah, in the [b]ninth month, all the people in Jerusalem and
all the people who [c]came from the cities of Judah to Jerusalem
proclaimed a [d]fast before the LORD.

15 [1]Lit *rising early and speaking* [a]Jer 7:25; 25:4; 26:5; 29:19; 32:33 [b]Is 1:16, 17; Jer 4:1; 18:11; 25:5f; Ezek 18:30-32; Acts 26:20 [c]Deut 6:14; Jer 7:6; 13:10; 25:6 [d]Jer 7:7; 25:5, 6 [e]Jer 7:24, 26; 11:8; 17:23; 34:14
16 [a]Jer 35:14; Mal 1:6
17 [a]Josh 23:15; Jer 19:3, 15; 21:4-10; Mic 3:12 [b]Prov 1:24, 25; Is 65:12; 66:4; Jer 7:13, 26, 27; 26:5; Luke 13:34, 35; Rom 10:21
18 [a]Ex 20:12; Eph 6:1-3
19 [1]Lit *all the days* [a]1 Chr 2:55; Jer 33:17 [b]Jer 15:19; Luke 21:36
36:1 [a]2 Kin 24:1; 2 Chr 36:5-7; Jer 25:1, 3; 45:1; 46:2; Dan 1:1
2 [1]Lit *scroll of a book* [a]Ex 17:14; Is 8:1; Jer 36:6, 23, 28; Zech 5:1, 2 [b]Jer 1:9, 10; 30:2; Hab 2:2 [c]Jer 3:3-10; 23:13, 14; 32:30-32 [d]Jer 1:5, 10; 25:9-29; chs 47-51 [e]Jer 1:2, 3; 25:3
3 [a]Jer 26:3; 36:7; Ezek 12:3 [b]Deut 30:2, 8; 1 Sam 7:3; Is 55:7; Jer 18:8, 11; 35:15; Jon 3:8 [c]Jon 3:10; Mark 4:12; Acts 3:19
4 [1]Lit *scroll of a book* [2]Lit *from the mouth of* [a]Jer 32:12; 36:18; 43:3; 45:1 [b]Jer 36:14; Ezek 2:9
5 [1]Lit *shut up* [a]Jer 32:2; 33:1; 2 Cor 11:23
6 [1]Lit *from my mouth* [2]Lit *in the ears of,* and so throughout this context [a]Jer 36:8 [b]Jer 36:4 [c]Jer 36:9; Zech 8:19
7 [1]Lit *fall* [a]1 Kin 8:33; 2 Chr 33:12, 13; Jer 26:3; 36:3 [b]Deut 28:15; 31:16, 17; 2 Kin 22:13, 17; Jer 4:4; 21:5; Lam 4:11
8 [a]Jer 1:17; 36:6
9 [a]Jer 36:1 [b]Jer 36:22 [c]Jer 36:6 [d]Judg 20:26; 1 Sam 7:6; 2 Chr 20:3; Esth 4:16; Joel 1:14; 2:15; Jon 3:5

10 Then Baruch read from the book the words of Jeremiah in
the house of the LORD in the [a]chamber of [b]Gemariah the son of
Shaphan the [c]scribe, in the upper court, at the [d]entry of the
New Gate of the LORD's house, to all the people.
11 Now when [a]Micaiah the son of Gemariah, the son of
Shaphan, had heard all the words of the LORD from the book,
12 he went down to the king's house, into the scribe's chamber.
And behold, all the officials were sitting there—[a]Elishama the
scribe, and [b]Delaiah the son of Shemaiah, and [c]Elnathan the
son of Achbor, and Gemariah the son of Shaphan, and
Zedekiah the son of Hananiah, and all the *other* officials.
13 Micaiah [a]declared to them all the words that he had heard
when Baruch read from the book to the people.
14 Then all the officials sent [a]Jehudi the son of Nethaniah, the
son of Shelemiah, the son of Cushi, to Baruch, saying, "Take in
your hand the scroll from which you have read to the people
and come." So Baruch the son of Neriah [b]took the scroll in his
hand and went to them.
15 They said to him, "Sit down, please, and read it to us." So
Baruch [a]read it to them.
16 When they had heard all the words, they turned in [a]fear
one to another and said to Baruch, "We will surely [b]report all
these words to the king."
17 And they asked Baruch, saying, "Tell us, please, [a]how did
you write all these words? *Was it* [1]at his dictation?"
18 Then Baruch said to them, "He [a]dictated all these words to
me, and I wrote them with ink on the book."
19 Then the officials said to Baruch, "Go, [a]hide yourself, you
and Jeremiah, and do not let anyone know where you are."
20 So they went to the [a]king in the court, but they had
deposited the scroll in the chamber of [a]Elishama the scribe,
and they reported all the words to the king.
21 Then the king sent Jehudi to get the scroll, and he took it
out of the chamber of Elishama the scribe. And Jehudi [a]read it to
the king as well as to all the officials who stood beside the king.
22 Now the king was sitting in the [a]winter house in the
[b]ninth month, with *a fire* burning in the brazier before him.
23 When Jehudi had read three or four columns, *the king* cut
it with a scribe's knife and [a]threw *it* into the fire that was in
the brazier, until all the scroll was consumed in the fire that
was in the brazier.
24 Yet the king and all his servants who heard all these words
were [a]not afraid, nor did they [b]rend their garments.
25 Even though Elnathan and Delaiah and Gemariah [a]pleaded
with the king not to burn the scroll, he would not listen to them.
26 And the king commanded Jerahmeel the king's son, Seraiah
the son of Azriel, and Shelemiah the son of Abdeel to [a]seize Baruch
the scribe and Jeremiah the prophet, but the [b]LORD hid them.
27 Then the word of the LORD came to Jeremiah after the king
had [a]burned the scroll and the words which [b]Baruch had
written at the dictation of Jeremiah, saying,

10 [a]Jer 35:4 [b]Jer 36:11, 25 [c]2 Sam 8:17; Jer 52:25 [d]Jer 26:10
11 [a]Jer 36:13
12 [a]Jer 36:20 [b]Jer 36:25 [c]Jer 26:22
13 [a]2 Kin 22:10
14 [a]Jer 36:21 [b]Jer 36:2; Ezek 2:7-10
15 [a]Jer 36:21
16 [a]Jer 36:24; Acts 24:25 [b]Jer 13:18; Amos 7:10, 11
17 [1]Lit *from his mouth,* and so throughout this context [a]John 9:10, 15, 26
18 [a]Jer 36:4
19 [a]1 Kin 17:3; 18:4, 10; Jer 26:20-24; 36:26
20 [a]Jer 36:12
21 [a]2 Kin 22:10; 2 Chr 34:18; Ezek 2:4, 5
22 [a]Judg 3:20; Amos 3:15 [b]Jer 36:9
23 [a]1 Kin 22:8, 27; Prov 1:30; Is 5:18, 19; 28:14, 22; Jer 36:29
24 [a]Ps 36:1; 64:5; Jer 36:16 [b]Gen 37:29, 34; 2 Sam 1:11; 1 Kin 21:27; 2 Kin 19:1, 2; 22:11, 19; Is 36:22; 37:1; Jon 3:6
25 [a]Gen 37:22, 26, 27; Acts 5:34-39
26 [a]1 Kin 19:1-3, 10, 14; Matt 23:34, 37 [b]Ps 91:1
27 [a]Jer 36:23 [b]Jer 36:4, 18

28 [a]Zech 1:5, 6 [b]Jer 36:4, 23

28 "[a]Take again another scroll and write on it all the former words that were [b]on the first scroll which Jehoiakim the king of Judah burned.

29 [1]Lit *saying* [a]Deut 29:19; Job 15:24, 25; Is 45:9 [b]Is 29:21; 30:10; Jer 26:9; 32:3 [c]Jer 25:9-11

29 "And concerning Jehoiakim king of Judah you shall say, 'Thus says the LORD, "You have [a]burned this scroll, saying, '[b]Why have you written on it [1]that the [c]king of Babylon will certainly come and destroy this land, and will make man and beast to cease from it?'"

30 [a]2 Kin 24:12-15; Jer 22:30 [b]Jer 22:19

30 'Therefore thus says the LORD concerning Jehoiakim king of Judah, "He shall have [a]no one to sit on the throne of David, and his [b]dead body shall be cast out to the heat of the day and the frost of the night.

31 [1]Lit *seed* [a]Jer 23:34 [b]Deut 28:15; Prov 29:1; Jer 19:15; 35:17

31 "I will also [a]punish him and his [1]descendants and his servants for their iniquity, and I will [b]bring on them and the inhabitants of Jerusalem and the men of Judah all the calamity that I have declared to them—but they did not listen."'"

32 [1]Lit *like those* [a]Ex 4:15, 16; 34:1; Jer 36:4, 18, 23

32 Then Jeremiah took another scroll and gave it to Baruch the son of Neriah, the scribe, and he [a]wrote on it at the dictation of Jeremiah all the words of the book which Jehoiakim king of Judah had burned in the fire; and many [1]similar words were added to them.

37:1 [a]2 Kin 24:17; 1 Chr 3:15; 2 Chr 36:10 [b]Ezek 17:12-21 [c]2 Kin 24:12; 1 Chr 3:16; 2 Chr 36:9, 10; Jer 22:24, 28; 24:1; 52:31

Chapter 37 Theme ________________________

37 Now [a]Zedekiah the son of Josiah whom Nebuchadnezzar king of Babylon had [b]made king in the land of Judah, reigned as king in place of [c]Coniah the son of Jehoiakim.

2 [a]2 Kin 24:19, 20; 2 Chr 36:12-16; Prov 29:12

2 But [a]neither he nor his servants nor the people of the land listened to the words of the LORD which He spoke through Jeremiah the prophet.

3 [a]Jer 21:1, 2 [b]Jer 29:25; 52:24 [c]1 Kin 13:6; Jer 2:27; 15:11; 21:1, 2; 42:1-4, 20; Acts 8:24

3 Yet [a]King Zedekiah sent Jehucal the son of Shelemiah, and [b]Zephaniah the son of Maaseiah, the priest, to Jeremiah the prophet, saying, "[c]Please pray to the LORD our God on our behalf."

4 [a]Jer 32:2, 3; 37:15

4 Now Jeremiah was *still* coming in and going out among the people, for they had not *yet* [a]put him in the prison.

5 [a]2 Kin 24:7; Jer 37:7; Ezek 17:15 [b]Jer 37:11

5 Meanwhile, [a]Pharaoh's army had set out from Egypt; and when the Chaldeans who had been besieging Jerusalem heard the report about them, they [b]lifted the *siege* from Jerusalem.

6 Then the word of the LORD came to Jeremiah the prophet, saying,

7 [a]2 Kin 22:18; Jer 21:1, 2; 37:3 [b]Is 30:1-3; 31:1-3; Jer 2:18, 36; Lam 4:17; Ezek 17:17

7 "Thus says the LORD God of Israel, '[a]Thus you are to say to the king of Judah, who sent you to Me to inquire of Me: "Behold, [b]Pharaoh's army which has come out for your assistance is going to return to its own land of Egypt.

8 [a]Jer 34:22; 38:23; 39:2-8

8 "The Chaldeans will also [a]return and fight against this city, and they will capture it and burn it with fire."'

9 [a]Jer 29:8; Obad 3; Matt 24:4, 5; Eph 5:6

9 "Thus says the LORD, 'Do not [a]deceive yourselves, saying, "The Chaldeans will surely go away from us," for they will not go.

10 [a]Lev 26:36-38; Is 30:17; Jer 21:4, 5

10 'For [a]even if you had defeated the entire army of Chaldeans who were fighting against you, and there were *only* wounded

men left among them, each man in his tent, they would rise up
and [b]burn this city with fire.'"
11 Now it happened when the army of the Chaldeans had
lifted *the siege* from Jerusalem because of Pharaoh's army,
12 that Jeremiah went out from Jerusalem to go to the land of
Benjamin in order to [a]take [1]possession of *some* property there
among the people.
13 While he was at the [a]Gate of Benjamin, a captain of the
guard whose name was Irijah, the son of Shelemiah the son of
Hananiah was there; and he [b]arrested Jeremiah the prophet,
saying, "You are [1]going over to the Chaldeans!"
14 But Jeremiah said, "[a]A lie! I am not [1]going over to the
Chaldeans"; yet he would not listen to him. So Irijah arrested
Jeremiah and brought him to the officials.
15 Then the officials were [a]angry at Jeremiah and beat him,
and they [b]put him in jail in the house of Jonathan the scribe,
which they had made into the prison.
16 For Jeremiah had come into the [1a]dungeon, that is, the
vaulted cell; and Jeremiah stayed there many days.
17 Now King Zedekiah sent and took him *out;* and in his
palace the king [a]secretly asked him and said, "Is there a [b]word
from the LORD?" And Jeremiah said, "There is!" Then he said,
"You will be [c]given into the hand of the king of Babylon!"
18 Moreover Jeremiah said to King Zedekiah, "[a]*In* what *way*
have I sinned against you, or against your servants, or against
this people, that you have put me in prison?
19 "[a]Where then are your prophets who prophesied to you,
saying, 'The [b]king of Babylon will not come against you or
against this land'?
20 "But now, please listen, O my lord the king; please let my
[a]petition [1]come before you and do not make me return to the
house of Jonathan the scribe, that I may not die there."
21 Then King Zedekiah gave commandment, and they
committed Jeremiah to the [a]court of the guardhouse and gave
him a loaf of [b]bread daily from the bakers' street, until all the
bread in the city was [c]gone. So Jeremiah remained in the court
of the guardhouse.

Chapter 38 Theme

38 Now Shephatiah the son of Mattan, and Gedaliah the
son of Pashhur, and Jucal the [a]son of Shelemiah, and
[b]Pashhur the son of Malchijah heard the words that Jeremiah
was speaking to all the people, saying,
2 "Thus says the LORD, 'He who [a]stays in this city will die by
the [b]sword and by famine and by pestilence, but he who goes
out to the Chaldeans will live and have his *own* [c]life as booty
and stay alive.'
3 "Thus says the LORD, 'This city will certainly be [a]given into the
hand of the army of the king of Babylon and he will capture it.'"
4 Then the [a]officials said to the king, "Now let this man be
put to death, inasmuch as he is [1b]discouraging the men of war

10 [b]Jer 37:8

12 [1]Or *part in a dividing* [a]Jer 32:8

13 [1]Lit *falling* [a]Jer 38:7; Zech 14:10 [b]Jer 18:18; 20:10; Luke 23:2; Acts 6:11; 24:5-9, 13

14 [1]Lit *falling* [a]Ps 27:12; 52:1, 2; Jer 40:4-6; Matt 5:11, 12

15 [a]Jer 18:23; 20:1-3; 26:16; Matt 21:35 [b]Gen 39:20; 2 Chr 16:10; 18:26; Jer 38:26; Acts 5:18

16 [1]Lit *house of the cistern-pit* [a]Jer 38:6

17 [a]1 Kin 14:1-4; Jer 38:5, 14-16, 24-27 [b]1 Kin 22:15, 16; 2 Kin 3:11, 12; Jer 15:11; 21:1, 2; 37:3 [c]Jer 21:7; 24:8; Ezek 12:12, 13; 17:19, 20

18 [a]1 Sam 24:9; 26:18; Dan 6:22; John 10:32; Acts 25:8, 11, 25

19 [a]Deut 32:37, 38; 2 Kin 3:13; Jer 2:28 [b]Jer 27:14; 28:1-4, 10-17

20 [1]Lit *fall* [a]Jer 36:7; 38:26

21 [a]Jer 32:2; 38:13, 28 [b]1 Kin 17:6; Job 5:20; Ps 33:18, 19; Is 33:16 [c]2 Kin 25:3; Jer 38:9; 52:6

38:1 [a]Jer 37:3 [b]Jer 21:1

2 [a]Jer 21:9 [b]Jer 34:17; 42:17 [c]Jer 21:9; 39:18; 45:5

3 [a]Jer 21:10; 32:3-5

4 [1]Lit *weakening the hands of* [a]Jer 18:23; 26:11, 21; 36:12 [b]Ex 5:4; 1 Kin 18:17, 18; 21:20; Neh 6:9; Amos 7:10; Acts 16:20

who are left in this city and [2]all the people, by speaking such
words to them; for this man [c]is not seeking the well-being of
this people but rather their harm."
5 So King Zedekiah said, "Behold, he is in your [1]hands; for
the king [a]can *do* nothing against you."
6 Then they took Jeremiah and cast him into the [a]cistern *of*
Malchijah the king's son, which was in the court of the
guardhouse; and they let Jeremiah down with ropes. Now in
the cistern there was no water but only [b]mud, and Jeremiah
sank into the mud.
7 But [a]Ebed-melech the Ethiopian, [1]a [b]eunuch, while he was
in the king's palace, heard that they had put Jeremiah into the
cistern. Now the king was sitting in the [c]Gate of Benjamin;
8 and Ebed-melech went out from the king's palace and
spoke to the king, saying,
9 "My lord the king, these men have acted wickedly in all that
they have done to Jeremiah the prophet whom they have cast
into the cistern; and he [1]will die right where he is because of
the famine, for there is [a]no more bread in the city."
10 Then the king commanded Ebed-melech the Ethiopian,
saying, "Take thirty men from here [1]under your authority and
bring up Jeremiah the prophet from the cistern before he dies."
11 So Ebed-melech took the men under his [1]authority and
went into the king's palace to *a place* beneath the storeroom
and took from there worn-out clothes and worn-out rags and let
them down by ropes into the cistern to Jeremiah.
12 Then Ebed-melech the Ethiopian said to Jeremiah, "Now
put these worn-out clothes and rags under your armpits under
the ropes"; and Jeremiah did so.
13 So they pulled Jeremiah up with the ropes and lifted him
out of the cistern, and Jeremiah stayed in the [a]court of the
guardhouse.
14 Then King Zedekiah [a]sent and [1]had Jeremiah the prophet
brought to him at the third entrance that is in the house of the
LORD; and the king said to Jeremiah, "I am going to [b]ask you
something; do not hide anything from me."
15 Then Jeremiah said to Zedekiah, "[a]If I tell you, will you not
certainly put me to death? Besides, if I give you advice, you will
not listen to me."
16 But King Zedekiah swore to Jeremiah in [a]secret saying, "As
the LORD lives, who made this [1b]life for us, surely I will not put
you to death nor will I give you over to the hand of [c]these men
who are seeking your [1]life."
17 Then Jeremiah said to Zedekiah, "Thus says the LORD [a]God of
hosts, the [b]God of Israel, 'If you will indeed [c]go out to the officers
of the king of Babylon, then [1]you will live, this city will not be
burned with fire, and you and your household will [2]survive.
18 'But if you will [a]not go out to the officers of the king of
Babylon, then this city [b]will be given over to the hand of the
Chaldeans; and they will burn it with fire, and [c]you yourself
will not escape from their hand.'"

4 [2]Lit *the hands of all* [c]Jer 29:7
5 [1]Lit *hand* [a]2 Sam 3:39
6 [a]Jer 37:16, 21; Acts 16:24 [b]Ps 40:2; 69:2, 14, 15; Jer 38:22; Zech 9:11
7 [1]Or *an official* [a]Jer 39:16 [b]Jer 29:2; Acts 8:27 [c]Deut 21:19; Job 29:7; Jer 37:13; Amos 5:10
9 [1]M.T. reads *has died* [a]Jer 37:21; 52:6
10 [1]Lit *in your hand*
11 [1]Lit *hand*
13 [a]Neh 3:25; Jer 32:2; 37:21; 38:6; 39:14, 15; Acts 23:35; 24:27; 28:16, 30
14 [1]Lit *took Jeremiah the prophet to him* [a]Jer 21:1, 2; 37:17 [b]1 Sam 3:17, 18; 1 Kin 22:16; Jer 15:11; 42:2-5, 20
15 [a]Luke 22:67, 68
16 [1]Lit *soul* [a]Jer 37:17; John 3:2 [b]Num 16:22; 27:16; Is 42:5; 57:16; Zech 12:1; Acts 17:25, 28 [c]Jer 34:20; 38:4-6
17 [1]Lit *your soul* [2]Lit *live* [a]Ps 80:7, 14; Amos 5:27 [b]1 Chr 17:24; Ezek 8:4 [c]2 Kin 24:12; 25:27-30; Jer 21:8-10; 27:12, 17; 38:2; 39:3
18 [a]Jer 27:8 [b]2 Kin 25:4-10; Jer 24:8-10; 32:3-5; 37:8; 38:3 [c]Jer 32:4; 34:3

19 Then King Zedekiah said to Jeremiah, "I [a]dread the Jews
who have [1b]gone over to the Chaldeans, for they may give me
over into their hand and they will [c]abuse me."
20 But Jeremiah said, "They will not give you over. Please
[1a]obey the LORD in what I am saying to you, that it may go [b]well
with you and [2c]you may live.
21 "But if you keep refusing to go out, this is the word which
the LORD has shown me:
22 'Then behold, all of the [a]women who have been left in the
palace of the king of Judah are going to be brought out to the
[1]officers of the king of Babylon; and those women will say,

"[2]Your close friends
Have misled and overpowered you;
While your feet were sunk in the mire,
They turned back."

23 'They will also bring out all your wives and your [a]sons to
the Chaldeans, and [b]you yourself will not escape from their
hand, but will be seized by the hand of the king of Babylon,
and [b]this city will be burned with fire.'"
24 Then Zedekiah said to Jeremiah, "Let no man know about
these words and you will not die.
25 "But if the [a]officials hear that I have talked with you and
come to you and say to you, 'Tell us now what you said to the
king and what the king said to you; do not hide *it* from us and
we will not put you to death,'
26 then you are to say to them, 'I was [a]presenting my petition
before the king, not to make me return to the house of Jonathan
to die there.'"
27 Then all the officials came to Jeremiah and questioned him.
So he reported to them in accordance with all these words
which the king had commanded; and they ceased speaking
with him, since the [1]conversation had not been overheard.
28 So Jeremiah [a]stayed in the court of the guardhouse until
the day that Jerusalem was captured.

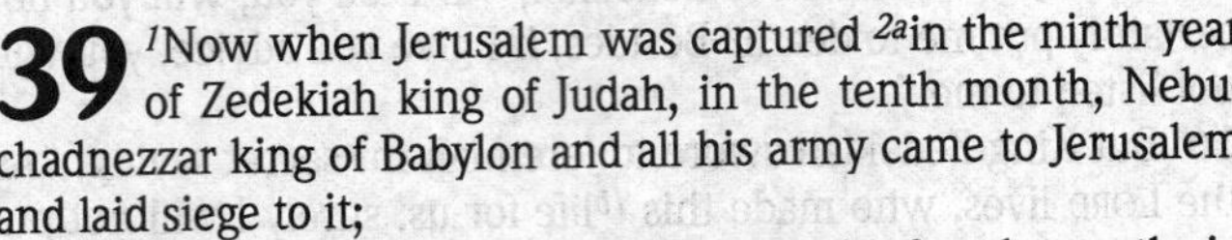

Chapter 39 Theme ____________________

39 [1]Now when Jerusalem was captured [2a]in the ninth year
of Zedekiah king of Judah, in the tenth month, Nebuchadnezzar king of Babylon and all his army came to Jerusalem
and laid siege to it;
2 in the eleventh year of Zedekiah, in the fourth month, in
the ninth *day* of the month, the city *wall* was [a]breached.
3 Then all the [a]officials of the king of Babylon came in and
sat down at the [b]Middle Gate: Nergal-sar-ezer, Samgar-nebu,
Sar-sekim the [1]Rab-saris, Nergal-sar-ezer *the* [2]Rab-mag, and all
the rest of the officials of the king of Babylon.
4 When Zedekiah the king of Judah and all the men of war
saw them, they [a]fled and went out of the city at night by way of
the king's garden through the gate [b]between the two walls; and
he went out toward the [1]Arabah.

19 [1]Lit *fallen* [a]Is 51:12, 13; 57:11; John 12:42; 19:12, 13 [b]Jer 39:9 [c]2 Chr 30:10; Neh 4:1; Jer 38:22

20 [1]Lit *listen to the voice of* [2]Lit *your soul* [a]2 Chr 20:20; Jer 11:4, 8; 26:13; Dan 4:27; Acts 26:29 [b]Jer 7:23 [c]Gen 19:20; Is 55:3

22 [1]Or *princes* [2]Lit *The men of your peace* [a]Jer 6:12; 8:10; 43:6

23 [a]2 Kin 25:7; Jer 39:6; 41:10 [b]Jer 38:18

25 [a]Jer 38:4-6, 27

26 [a]Jer 37:20

27 [1]Lit *word*

28 [a]Ps 23:4; Jer 15:20, 21; 37:20, 21; 38:13; 39:13, 14

39:1 [1]Ch 38:28-b in Heb [2]Ch 39:1 in Heb [a]2 Kin 25:1-12; Jer 52:4; Ezek 24:1, 2

2 [a]2 Kin 25:4; Jer 52:7

3 [1]I.e. chief official [2]I.e. title of a high official [a]Jer 38:17 [b]Jer 21:4

4 [1]I.e. Jordan valley [a]2 Kin 25:4; Is 30:16; Jer 52:7; Amos 2:14 [b]2 Chr 32:5

5 But the army of the [a]Chaldeans pursued them and overtook
Zedekiah in the [b]plains of Jericho; and they seized him and
brought him up to Nebuchadnezzar king of Babylon at [c]Riblah
in the land of Hamath, and he passed sentence on him.
6 Then the [a]king of Babylon slew the sons of Zedekiah
[b]before his eyes at Riblah; the king of Babylon also slew all the
[c]nobles of Judah.
7 He then [a]blinded Zedekiah's eyes and bound him in [b]fetters
of bronze to bring him to [c]Babylon.
8 The Chaldeans also [a]burned with fire the king's palace and
the houses of the people, and they [b]broke down the walls of
Jerusalem.
9 As for the rest of the people who were left in the city, the
[1a]deserters who had gone over to him and [b]the rest of the
people who remained, [c]Nebuzaradan the [d]captain of the bodyguard carried *them* into exile in Babylon.
10 But some of the [a]poorest people who had nothing,
[a]Nebuzaradan the captain of the bodyguard left behind in the
land of Judah, and gave them vineyards and fields [1]at that time.
11 Now Nebuchadnezzar king of Babylon gave orders about
[a]Jeremiah through Nebuzaradan the captain of the bodyguard,
saying,
12 "Take him and [1]look after him, and [a]do nothing harmful to
him, but rather deal with him just as he tells you."
13 So Nebuzaradan the captain of the bodyguard sent *word,*
along with Nebushazban the [1]Rab-saris, and Nergal-sar-ezer the
[2]Rab-mag, and all the leading officers of the king of Babylon;
14 they even sent and [a]took Jeremiah out of the court of the
guardhouse and entrusted him to [b]Gedaliah, the son of [c]Ahikam,
the son of Shaphan, to take him home. So he stayed among the
people.
15 Now the word of the LORD had come to Jeremiah while he
was [a]confined in the court of the guardhouse, saying,
16 "Go and speak to [a]Ebed-melech the Ethiopian, saying, 'Thus
says the LORD of hosts, the God of Israel, "Behold, I am about
to bring My words on this city [b]for disaster and not for
[1]prosperity; and they will [c]take place before you on that day.
17 "But I will [a]deliver you on that day," declares the LORD, "and
you will not be given into the hand of the men whom you
dread.
18 "For I will certainly rescue you, and you will not fall by the
sword; but you will have your *own* [a]life as booty, because you
have [b]trusted in Me," declares the LORD.'"

Chapter 40 Theme ____________________

40 The word which came to Jeremiah from the LORD after
[a]Nebuzaradan captain of the bodyguard had released
him from [b]Ramah, when he had taken him bound in [c]chains
among all the exiles of Jerusalem and Judah who were being
exiled to Babylon.

5 [a]Jer 32:4, 5; 38:18, 23; 52:8 [b]Josh 4:13; 5:10 [c]2 Kin 23:33; Jer 52:9, 26, 27

6 [a]2 Kin 25:7; Jer 52:10 [b]Deut 28:34 [c]Jer 21:7; 24:8-10; 34:19-21

7 [a]2 Kin 25:7; Jer 52:11; Ezek 12:13 [b]Judg 16:21 [c]Jer 32:5

8 [a]2 Kin 25:9; Jer 21:10; 38:18; 52:13 [b]2 Kin 25:10; Neh 1:3; Jer 52:14

9 [1]Lit *fallers who had fallen* [a]Jer 38:19; 52:15 [b]Jer 24:8 [c]2 Kin 25:11, 20; Jer 39:13; 40:1; 52:12-16, 26 [d]Gen 37:36

10 [1]Lit *on that day* [a]2 Kin 25:12; Jer 52:16

11 [a]Job 5:15, 16; Jer 1:8; 15:20, 21; Acts 24:23

12 [1]Lit *set your eyes on* [a]Ps 105:14, 15; Prov 16:7; 21:1; 1 Pet 3:13

13 [1]I.e. chief official [2]I.e. title of a high official

14 [a]Jer 38:28; 40:1-6 [b]Jer 40:5 [c]2 Kin 22:12, 14; 2 Chr 34:20; Jer 26:24

15 [a]Jer 38:28

16 [1]Lit *good* [a]Jer 38:7 [b]Jer 21:10; Dan 9:12; Zech 1:6 [c]Ps 91:8

17 [a]Ps 41:1, 2; 50:15

18 [a]Jer 21:9; 38:2; 45:5 [b]Ps 34:22; Jer 17:7, 8

40:1 [a]Jer 39:9, 11 [b]Jer 31:15 [c]Acts 12:6, 7; 21:13; 28:20; Eph 6:20

2 Now the captain of the bodyguard had taken Jeremiah and
said to him, "The [a]LORD your God promised this calamity
against this place;
3 and the LORD has brought *it* on and done just as He
promised. Because you *people* [a]sinned against the LORD and did
not listen to His voice, therefore this thing has happened to you.
4 "But now, behold, I am [a]freeing you today from the chains
which are on your hands. If [1]you would prefer to come with
me to Babylon, come *along,* and I will [2]look after you; but if
[3]you would prefer not to come with me to Babylon, [4]never
mind. Look, the [b]whole land is before you; go wherever it
seems good and right for you to go."
5 As [1]Jeremiah was still not going back, [2]*he said,* "Go on
back then to [a]Gedaliah the son of Ahikam, the son of Shaphan,
whom the king of Babylon has [b]appointed over the cities of Judah,
and stay with him among the people; or else go anywhere it
seems right for you to go." So the captain of the bodyguard
gave him a [c]ration and a [d]gift and let him go.
6 Then Jeremiah went to [a]Mizpah to [b]Gedaliah the son of
Ahikam and stayed with him among the people who were left
in the land.
7 [a]Now all the [1]commanders of the forces that were in the
field, they and their men, heard that the king of Babylon had
appointed Gedaliah the son of Ahikam over the land and that
he had put him in charge of the men, women and [2]children,
those of the [b]poorest of the land who had not been exiled to
Babylon.
8 So they came to Gedaliah at Mizpah, along with [a]Ishmael
the son of Nethaniah, and [b]Johanan and Jonathan the sons of
Kareah, and Seraiah the son of Tanhumeth, and the sons of Ephai
the [c]Netophathite, and [d]Jezaniah the son of the [e]Maacathite,
both they and their men.
9 Then Gedaliah the son of Ahikam, the son of Shaphan,
[a]swore to them and to their men, saying, "[b]Do not be afraid of
serving the Chaldeans; stay in the land and serve the king of
Babylon, that it may go well with you.
10 "Now as for me, behold, I am going to stay at Mizpah to [a]stand
for you before the Chaldeans who come to us; but as for you,
[b]gather in wine and [c]summer fruit and oil and put *them* in your
storage vessels, and live in your cities that you have taken over."
11 Likewise, also all the Jews who were in [a]Moab and among
the sons of [b]Ammon and in [c]Edom and who were in all the *other*
countries, heard that the king of Babylon had left a remnant for
Judah, and that he had appointed over them Gedaliah the son
of Ahikam, the son of Shaphan.
12 Then all the Jews [a]returned from all the places to which
they had been driven away and came to the land of Judah, to
Gedaliah at Mizpah, and gathered in wine and summer fruit in
great abundance.
13 Now Johanan the son of Kareah and all the commanders of
the forces that were in the field came to Gedaliah at Mizpah

2 [a]Lev 26:14-38; Deut 28:15-68; 29:24-28; 31:17; 32:19-25; Jer 22:8, 9

3 [a]Jer 50:7; Dan 9:11; Rom 2:5

4 [1]Lit *it is good in your eyes* [2]Lit *set my eyes on* [3]Lit *it is evil in your eyes* [4]Lit *refrain!* [a]Jer 39:11, 12 [b]Gen 13:9; 20:15; 47:6

5 [1]Lit *he* [2]I.e. Nebuzaradan [a]Jer 39:14 [b]2 Kin 25:23 [c]Jer 52:34 [d]2 Kin 8:7-9

6 [a]Judg 20:1; 21:1; 1 Sam 7:5; 2 Chr 16:6 [b]Jer 39:14

7 [1]Or *princes* [2]Lit *infants* [a]2 Kin 25:23 [b]Jer 39:10; 52:16

8 [a]Jer 40:14; 41:2 [b]Jer 40:13, 15; 42:1; 43:2 [c]2 Sam 23:28, 29; Ezra 2:22; Neh 7:26 [d]Jer 42:1 [e]Deut 3:14; Josh 12:5; 2 Sam 10:6, 8

9 [a]1 Sam 20:16, 17; 2 Kin 25:24 [b]Jer 27:11; 38:17-20

10 [a]Deut 1:38; 1 Kin 10:8; Jer 35:19 [b]Deut 16:13; Jer 39:10 [c]Is 16:9; Jer 40:12; 48:32

11 [a]Num 22:1; 25:1, 2; Is 16:4; Jer 9:26 [b]1 Sam 11:1; 12:12 [c]Gen 36:8; Is 11:14

12 [a]Jer 43:5

14 and said to him, "Are you well aware that Baalis the king of
the sons of [a]Ammon has sent Ishmael the son of Nethaniah to
take your life?" But Gedaliah the son of Ahikam did not believe
them.
15 Then Johanan the son of Kareah spoke secretly to Gedaliah
in Mizpah, saying, "[a]Let me go and kill Ishmael the son of
Nethaniah, and not a man will know! Why should he [b]take
your life, so that all the Jews who are gathered to you would be
scattered and the [c]remnant of Judah would perish?"
16 But Gedaliah the son of Ahikam said to Johanan the son of
Kareah, "[a]Do not do this thing, for you are telling a lie about
Ishmael."

Chapter 41 Theme ____________________

41 [a]In the seventh month [b]Ishmael the son of Nethaniah,
the son of Elishama, of the royal [1]family and *one* of the
chief officers of the king, along with ten men, came to Mizpah
to [c]Gedaliah the son of Ahikam. While they [d]were eating bread
together there in Mizpah,
2 Ishmael the son of Nethaniah and the ten men who were
with him arose and [a]struck down Gedaliah the son of Ahikam,
the son of Shaphan, with the sword and [b]put to death the one
[c]whom the king of Babylon had appointed over the land.
3 Ishmael also struck down all the Jews who were with him,
that is with Gedaliah at Mizpah, and the Chaldeans who were
found there, the men of war.
4 Now it happened on the [1]next day after the killing of
Gedaliah, when no one knew about *it,*
5 that eighty men [a]came from [b]Shechem, from [c]Shiloh, and
from [d]Samaria with [e]their beards shaved off and their clothes
torn and [1]their bodies [f]gashed, having grain offerings and
incense in their hands to bring to the [g]house of the LORD.
6 Then Ishmael the son of Nethaniah went out from Mizpah
to meet them, [a]weeping as he went; and as he met them, he
said to them, "Come to Gedaliah the son of Ahikam!"
7 Yet it turned out that as soon as they came inside the city,
Ishmael the son of Nethaniah and the men that were with him
[a]slaughtered them *and cast them* into the cistern.
8 But ten men who were found among them said to Ishmael,
"Do not put us to death; for we have [a]stores of wheat, barley,
oil and honey hidden in the field." So he refrained and did not
put them to death along with their companions.
9 Now as for the cistern where Ishmael had cast all the corpses
of the men whom he had struck down [1]because of Gedaliah, it
was the [a]one that King Asa had made on [b]account of Baasha, king
of Israel; Ishmael the son of Nethaniah filled it with the slain.
10 Then Ishmael took captive all the [a]remnant of the people
who were in Mizpah, the [b]king's daughters and all the people
who were left in Mizpah, whom Nebuzaradan the captain of
the bodyguard had put under the charge of Gedaliah the son of

14 [a]1 Sam 11:1-3; 2 Sam 10:1-6; Jer 25:21; 41:10
15 [a]1 Sam 26:8 [b]2 Sam 21:17 [c]Jer 42:2
16 [a]Matt 10:16; 1 Cor 13:5
41:1 [1]Lit *seed* [a]2 Kin 25:25 [b]Jer 40:8, 14 [c]Jer 39:14; 40:5, 6 [d]Ps 41:9; Jer 40:13, 14
2 [a]2 Sam 3:27; 20:9, 10; 2 Kin 25:25; Ps 41:9; 109:5; John 13:18 [b]2 Kin 25:25 [c]Jer 40:5
4 [1]Or *second*
5 [1]Lit *having cut themselves* [a]2 Kin 10:13, 14 [b]Gen 33:18; 37:12; Judg 9:1; 1 Kin 12:1, 25 [c]Josh 18:1; Judg 18:31; 1 Sam 3:21; Ps 78:60 [d]1 Kin 16:24, 29 [e]Lev 19:27; Deut 14:1 [f]Deut 14:1; Jer 16:6 [g]1 Sam 1:7; 2 Kin 25:9
6 [a]2 Sam 3:16; Jer 50:4
7 [a]Ps 55:23; Is 59:7; Ezek 22:27; 33:24, 26
8 [a]Is 45:3
9 [1]Or *by the side of* [a]1 Kin 15:17-22; 2 Chr 16:1-6 [b]Judg 6:2; 1 Sam 13:6; 2 Sam 17:9; Heb 11:38
10 [a]Jer 40:11, 12 [b]Jer 43:6

Ahikam; thus Ishmael the son of Nethaniah took them captive
and proceeded to cross over to the sons of [c]Ammon.
11 But Johanan the son of Kareah and all the [a]commanders of
the forces that were with him heard of all the evil that Ishmael
the son of Nethaniah had done.
12 So they took all the men and went to [a]fight with Ishmael
the son of Nethaniah and they found him by the [b]great [1]pool
that is in Gibeon.
13 Now as soon as all the people who were with Ishmael saw
Johanan the son of Kareah and the commanders of the forces
that were with him, they were glad.
14 So all the people whom Ishmael had taken captive from
Mizpah turned around and came back, and went to Johanan
the son of Kareah.
15 But Ishmael the son of Nethaniah [a]escaped from Johanan
with eight men and went to the sons of Ammon.
16 Then Johanan the son of Kareah and all the commanders of
the forces that were with him took from Mizpah [a]all the remnant
of the people whom he had [1]recovered from Ishmael the son of
Nethaniah, after he had struck down Gedaliah the son of Ahikam,
that is, the men who were [2]soldiers, *the* women, *the* [3]children,
and *the* eunuchs, whom he had brought back from Gibeon.
17 And they went and stayed in [1a]Geruth Chimham, which is
beside Bethlehem, in order to [b]proceed into Egypt
18 because of the Chaldeans; for they were [a]afraid of them,
since Ishmael the son of Nethaniah had struck down Gedaliah
the son of Ahikam, whom [b]the king of Babylon had appointed
over the land.

Chapter 42 Theme __________________________

42 Then all the [1]commanders of the forces, [a]Johanan the
son of Kareah, Jezaniah the son of Hoshaiah, and all the
people [b]both small and great approached
2 and said to Jeremiah the prophet, "Please let our [a]petition
[1]come before you, and [b]pray for us to the LORD your God, *that*
is for all this remnant; because we are left *but* a [c]few out of
many, as your own eyes *now* see us,
3 that the LORD your God may tell us the [a]way in which we
should walk and the thing that we should do."
4 Then Jeremiah the prophet said to them, "I have heard
you. Behold, I am going to [a]pray to the LORD your God in
accordance with your words; and I will tell you the whole
[1]message which the [b]LORD will answer you. I will [c]not keep
back a word from you."
5 Then they said to Jeremiah, "May the [a]LORD be a true and
faithful witness against us if we do not act in accordance with
the whole [1]message with which the LORD your God will send
you to us.
6 "Whether *it* is [1]pleasant or [2]unpleasant, we will [a]listen to
the voice of the LORD our God to whom we are sending you, so

10 [c]Neh 2:10, 19; 4:7; Jer 40:14

11 [a]Jer 40:7, 8, 13-16

12 [1]Lit *waters* [a]Gen 14:14-16; 1 Sam 30:1-8, 18, 20 [b]2 Sam 2:13

15 [a]1 Sam 30:17; 1 Kin 20:20; Job 21:30; Prov 28:17

16 [1]Lit *brought back* [2]Lit *men of war* [3]Lit *infants* [a]Jer 42:8; 43:4-7

17 [1]Or *the lodging place of Chimham* [a]2 Sam 19:37, 38, 40 [b]Jer 42:14

18 [a]Is 51:12, 13; 57:11; Jer 42:11, 16; 43:2, 3; Luke 12:4, 5 [b]Jer 40:5

42:1 [1]Or *princes* [a]Jer 40:8, 13; 41:11, 18 [b]Jer 6:13; 8:10; 42:8; 44:12; Acts 8:10

2 [1]Lit *fall* [a]Jer 36:7; 37:20 [b]Ex 8:28; 1 Sam 7:8; 12:19; 1 Kin 13:6; Is 37:4; Jer 37:3; 42:20; Acts 8:24; James 5:16 [c]Lev 26:22; Deut 28:62; Is 1:9; Lam 1:1

3 [a]Ps 86:11; Prov 3:6; Jer 6:16; Mic 4:2

4 [1]Lit *word* [a]Ex 8:29; 1 Sam 12:23 [b]1 Kin 22:14; Jer 23:28 [c]1 Sam 3:17, 18; Ps 40:10; Acts 20:20

5 [1]Lit *word* [a]Gen 31:50; Judg 11:10; Jer 43:2; Mic 1:2; Mal 2:14; 3:5

6 [1]Lit *good* [2]Lit *evil* [a]Ex 24:7; Deut 5:27; Josh 24:24

that it may go [b]well with us when we listen to the voice of the
LORD our God."
7 Now at the [a]end of ten days the word of the LORD came to
Jeremiah.
8 Then he called for Johanan the son of Kareah and all the
[1]commanders of the forces that were with him, and for all the
people both small and great,
9 and said to them, "Thus [a]says the LORD the God of Israel, to
whom you sent me to present your petition before Him:
10 'If you will indeed stay in this land, then I will [a]build you up
and not tear you down, and I will plant you and not uproot you;
for I [1]will [b]relent concerning the calamity that I have inflicted
on you.
11 '[a]Do not be afraid of the king of Babylon, whom you are
now fearing; do not be afraid of him,' declares the LORD, 'for [b]I
am with you to save you and deliver you from his hand.
12 'I will also show you compassion, so that [a]he will have
compassion on you and restore you to your own soil.
13 'But if you are going to say, "We will [a]not stay in this land,"
so as not to listen to the voice of the LORD your God,
14 saying, "No, but we will [a]go to the land of Egypt, where we
will not see war or [b]hear the sound of a trumpet or hunger for
bread, and we will stay there";
15 then [1]in that case listen to the word of the LORD, O remnant
of Judah. Thus says the LORD of hosts, the God of Israel, "If you
really set your [2]mind to enter [a]Egypt and go in to reside there,
16 then the [a]sword, which you are afraid of, will overtake you
there in the land of Egypt; and the famine, about which you are
anxious, will follow closely after you there *in* Egypt, and you
will die there.
17 "So all the men who set their [1]mind to go to Egypt to reside
there will die by the [a]sword, by famine and by pestilence; and
they will [b]have no survivors or refugees from the calamity that
I am going to bring on them."'"
18 For thus says the LORD of hosts, the God of Israel, "As My
[a]anger and wrath have been poured out on the inhabitants of
Jerusalem, so My wrath will be poured out on you when you
enter Egypt. And you will become a [b]curse, an object of horror,
an imprecation and a reproach; and [c]you will see this place no
more."
19 The LORD has spoken to you, O remnant of Judah, "Do not
[a]go into Egypt!" You should clearly [b]understand that today I
have [c]testified against you.
20 For you have *only* [1a]deceived yourselves; for it is you who
sent me to the LORD your God, saying, "Pray for us to the LORD
our God; and whatever the LORD our God says, tell us so, and
we will do it."
21 So I have [a]told you today, but you have [b]not [1]obeyed the
LORD your God, even in whatever He has sent me to *tell* you.
22 Therefore you should now clearly understand that you will
[a]die by the sword, by famine and by pestilence, in the [b]place
where you wish to go to reside.

6 [b]Deut 5:29, 33; 6:3; Jer 7:23
7 [a]Ps 27:14; Is 30:18
8 [1]Or *princes*
9 [a]2 Kin 19:4, 6, 20; 22:15
10 [1]Or *shall have changed my mind about* [a]Jer 24:6; 31:28; 33:7; Ezek 36:36 [b]Jer 18:7, 8; Hos 11:8; Joel 2:13; Amos 7:3, 6; Jon 3:10; 4:2
11 [a]Jer 1:8; 27:12, 17; 41:18 [b]Num 14:9; 2 Chr 32:7, 8; Ps 46:7, 11; 118:6; Is 8:9, 10; 43:2, 5; Jer 1:19; 15:20; Rom 8:31
12 [a]Neh 1:11; Ps 106:46; Prov 16:7
13 [a]Ex 5:2; Jer 44:16
14 [a]Is 31:1; Jer 41:17 [b]Ex 16:3; Num 11:4; Jer 4:19, 21
15 [1]Lit *now therefore* [2]Lit *face* [a]Deut 17:16; Jer 42:17; 44:12-14
16 [a]Jer 44:13, 27; Ezek 11:8; Amos 9:1-4
17 [1]Lit *face* [a]Jer 24:10; 38:2; 42:22; 44:13 [b]Jer 44:14, 28
18 [a]2 Chr 36:16-19; Jer 7:20; 33:5; 39:1-9 [b]Deut 29:21; Is 65:15; Jer 18:16; 24:9; 29:18; 44:12 [c]Jer 22:10, 27
19 [a]Deut 17:16; Is 30:1-7 [b]Ezek 2:5 [c]Neh 9:26, 29, 30
20 [1]Or *acted errantly in your souls* [a]Jer 43:2; Ezek 14:3
21 [1]Lit *listened to the voice of* [a]Deut 11:26; Jer 43:1; Ezek 2:7; Zech 7:11; Acts 20:26, 27 [b]Jer 43:4
22 [a]Jer 43:11; Ezek 6:11 [b]Hos 9:6

Chapter 43 Theme ______________________________

43 But as soon as Jeremiah, whom the LORD their God had
sent, had [a]finished telling all the people all the words of
the LORD their God—that is, all these words—
2 Azariah the [a]son of Hoshaiah, and Johanan the son of
Kareah, and all the arrogant men said to Jeremiah, "You are
[b]telling a lie! The LORD our God has not sent you to say, 'You
are not to enter Egypt to reside there';
3 but [a]Baruch the son of Neriah is inciting you against us to
give us over into the hand of the Chaldeans, so they will put us
to death or exile us to Babylon."
4 So [a]Johanan the son of Kareah and all the [1]commanders of
the forces, and all the people, [b]did not obey the voice of the
LORD to [c]stay in the land of Judah.
5 But Johanan the son of Kareah and all the [1]commanders of
the forces took the [a]entire remnant of Judah who had returned
from all the nations to which they had been driven away, in
order to reside in the land of Judah—
6 the men, the women, the [1]children, the [a]king's daughters
and [b]every person that Nebuzaradan the captain of the
bodyguard had left with Gedaliah the son of Ahikam [2]and
grandson of Shaphan, together with [c]Jeremiah the prophet and
Baruch the son of Neriah—
7 and they entered the land of Egypt (for they did not obey
the voice of the LORD) and went in as far as [a]Tahpanhes.
8 Then the word of the LORD came to Jeremiah in [a]Tahpanhes,
saying,
9 "Take *some* large stones in your [1]hands and hide them in
the mortar in the [2]brick *terrace* which is at the entrance of
Pharaoh's [3]palace in Tahpanhes, in the sight of [4]some *of the* Jews;
10 and say to them, 'Thus says the LORD of hosts, the God of
Israel, "Behold, I am going to send and get [a]Nebuchadnezzar
the king of Babylon, [b]My servant, and I am going to set his
throne *right* over these stones that I have hidden; and he will
spread his [c]canopy over them.
11 "He will also come and [a]strike the land of Egypt; those who
are *meant* for death *will be given over* to death, and those for
captivity to captivity, and [b]those for the sword to the sword.
12 "And [1]I shall set fire to the temples of the [a]gods of Egypt,
and he will burn them and take them captive. So he will [b]wrap
himself with the land of Egypt as a shepherd wraps himself
with his garment, and he will depart from there safely.
13 "He will also shatter the [1]obelisks of [2]Heliopolis, which is in
the land of Egypt; and the temples of the gods of Egypt he will
burn with fire."'"

INSIGHT

Jeremiah's ministry ended sometime after 586 B.C., possibly about 574 B.C., when, according to tradition, he was stoned to death in Egypt. Jeremiah 43:6, 7 tells us that Jeremiah's last days were spent in Egypt.

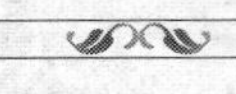

Chapter 44 Theme ______________________________

44 The word that came to Jeremiah for all the Jews living
in the land of Egypt, those who were living in [a]Migdol,
[b]Tahpanhes, [c]Memphis, and the land of [d]Pathros, saying,

43:1 [a]Jer 26:8; 51:63
2 [a]Jer 42:1 [b]2 Chr 36:13; Is 7:9; Jer 5:12, 13; 42:5
3 [a]Jer 36:4, 10, 26, 32; 43:6; 45:1-3
4 [1]Or *princes* [a]Jer 42:8 [b]2 Chr 25:16; Jer 42:5, 6; 44:5 [c]Ps 37:3; Jer 42:10-12
5 [1]Or *princes* [a]Jer 40:11
6 [1]Lit *infants* [2]Lit *the son* [a]Jer 41:10 [b]Jer 39:10; 40:7 [c]Eccl 9:1, 2; Lam 3:1
7 [a]Jer 2:16; 44:1
8 [a]Jer 2:16; 44:1; 46:14; Ezek 30:18
9 [1]Lit *hand* [2]Or *brickwork* [3]Lit *house* [4]Lit *men*
10 [a]Jer 25:9, 11 [b]Is 44:28; 45:1; Jer 25:9; 27:6 [c]Ps 18:11; 27:5; 31:20
11 [a]Is 19:1-25; Jer 25:15-19; 44:13; 46:1, 2, 13-26; Ezek 29:19, 20 [b]Jer 15:2
12 [1]Some ancient versions read *He will set* [a]Ex 12:12; Is 19:1; Jer 46:25; Ezek 30:13 [b]Ps 104:2; 109:18, 19; Is 49:18
13 [1]Or *stone pillars* [2]Heb *Beth-shemesh;* i.e. the house of the sun-god
44:1 [a]Ex 14:2; Jer 46:14 [b]Jer 43:7; Ezek 30:18 [c]Is 19:13; Jer 2:16; 46:14; Ezek 30:13, 16; Hos 9:6 [d]Is 11:11; Ezek 29:14; 30:14

2 "Thus says the LORD of hosts, the God of Israel, 'You yourselves have seen all the calamity that I have brought on
Jerusalem and all the cities of Judah; and behold, this day they
are in [a]ruins and no one lives in them,
3 [a]because of their wickedness which they committed so as
to [b]provoke Me to anger by continuing to [c]burn [1]sacrifices *and*
to [d]serve other gods whom they had not known, *neither* they,
you, nor your fathers.
4 'Yet I [a]sent you all My servants the prophets, [1]again and again,
saying, "Oh, do not do this [b]abominable thing which I hate."
5 'But [a]they did not listen or incline their ears to turn from
their wickedness, so as not to burn [1]sacrifices to other gods.
6 'Therefore My [a]wrath and My anger were poured out and
burned in the [b]cities of Judah and in the streets of Jerusalem, so
they have become a ruin and a [c]desolation as it is this day.
7 'Now then thus says the LORD God of hosts, the God of
Israel, "Why are you [a]doing great harm to yourselves, so as to
[b]cut off from you man and woman, child and infant, from
among Judah, leaving yourselves without remnant,
8 [a]provoking Me to anger with the works of your hands,
[b]burning [1]sacrifices to other gods in the land of Egypt, where you
are entering to reside, so that you might be cut off and become
a [c]curse and a reproach among all the nations of the earth?
9 "Have you forgotten the [a]wickedness of your fathers, the
wickedness of the kings of Judah, and the wickedness of their
wives, your own wickedness, and the wickedness of your
wives, which they committed in the land of Judah and in the
streets of Jerusalem?
10 "But they [a]have not become [1]contrite even to this day, nor
have they feared nor [b]walked in My law or My statutes, which
I have set before you and before your fathers."'
11 "Therefore thus says the LORD of hosts, the God of Israel,
'Behold, I am going to [a]set My face against you for [1]woe, even
to cut off all Judah.
12 'And I will [a]take away the remnant of Judah who have set
their [1]mind on entering the land of Egypt to reside there, and
they will all [2b]meet their end in the land of Egypt; they will fall
by the sword *and* meet their end by famine. Both small and
great will die by the sword and famine; and they will become a
[c]curse, an object of horror, an imprecation and a reproach.
13 'And I will [a]punish those who live in the land of Egypt, as I
have punished Jerusalem, with the sword, with famine and
with pestilence.
14 'So there will be [a]no refugees or survivors for the remnant
of Judah who have entered the land of Egypt to reside there
and then to return to the land of Judah, to which they are
[1b]longing to return and live; for none will [c]return except *a few*
refugees.'"
15 Then [a]all the men who were aware that their wives were
burning [1]sacrifices to other gods, along with all the women
who were standing by, *as* a large assembly, [2]including all the

2 [a]Is 6:11; Jer 4:7; 9:11; 34:22; Mic 3:12
3 [1]Or *incense* [a]Neh 9:33; Jer 2:17-19; 44:23; Ezek 8:17, 18; Dan 9:5 [b]Is 3:8; Jer 7:19; 32:30-32; 44:8 [c]Jer 19:4 [d]Deut 13:6; 29:26; 32:17
4 [1]Lit *rising early and sending* [a]Jer 7:13, 25; 25:4; 26:5; 29:19; 35:15; Zech 7:7 [b]Jer 16:18; 32:34, 35; Ezek 8:10
5 [1]Or *incense* [a]Jer 11:8, 10; 13:10
6 [a]Is 51:17-20; Jer 42:18; Ezek 8:18 [b]Jer 7:17, 34 [c]Jer 4:27; 34:22
7 [a]Num 16:38; Jer 26:19; Ezek 33:11; Hab 2:10 [b]Jer 3:24; 9:21; 51:22
8 [1]Or *incense* [a]2 Kin 17:15-17; Jer 25:6, 7; 44:3; 1 Cor 10:21, 22 [b]Jer 7:9; 11:12, 17; 44:3; Hos 4:13; Hab 1:16 [c]1 Kin 9:7, 8; 2 Chr 7:20; Jer 42:18
9 [a]Jer 7:9, 10, 17, 18; 44:17, 21
10 [1]Lit *crushed* [a]Jer 6:15; 8:12 [b]Jer 26:4; 32:23; 44:23
11 [1]Lit *evil* [a]Lev 17:10; 20:5, 6; 26:17; Jer 21:10; Amos 9:4
12 [1]Lit *face* [2]Lit *be finished* [a]Jer 42:15-18, 22 [b]Is 1:28; Jer 16:4; 44:7 [c]Is 65:15; Jer 18:16; 24:9; 26:6; 29:18; 42:18; Zech 8:13
13 [a]Jer 11:22; 44:27, 28
14 [1]Lit *lifting up their soul* [a]Jer 22:10; 44:27 [b]Jer 22:26, 27 [c]Is 4:2; 10:20; Jer 44:28; Rom 9:27
15 [1]Or *incense* [2]Lit *and* [a]Prov 11:21; Is 1:5; Jer 5:1-5

people who were living in Pathros in the land of Egypt,
responded to Jeremiah, saying,
16 "As for the [1a]message that you have spoken to us in the
name of the LORD, [b]we are not going to listen to you!
17 "But rather we will certainly [a]carry out every word that has
proceeded from our mouths, [1]by burning [2]sacrifices to the
[b]queen of heaven and pouring out drink offerings to her, just as
[c]we ourselves, our forefathers, our kings and our princes did in
the cities of Judah and in the streets of Jerusalem; for *then* we
had [d]plenty of [3]food and were well off and saw no [4]misfortune.
18 "But since we stopped burning [1]sacrifices to the queen of
heaven and pouring out drink offerings to her, we have [a]lacked
everything and have [2]met our end by the sword and by famine."
19 "And," *said the women,* "when we were [a]burning [1]sacrifices
to the queen of heaven and [2]were pouring out drink offerings to
her, was it [b]without our husbands that we made for her *sacrificial*
cakes [3]in her image and poured out drink offerings to her?"
20 Then Jeremiah said to all the people, to the men and
women—even to all the people who were giving him *such* an
answer—saying,
21 "As for the [1a]smoking sacrifices that you burned in the cities
of Judah and in the [b]streets of Jerusalem, you and your
forefathers, your kings and your princes, and the people of the
land, did not the LORD [c]remember them and did not *all this*
come into His [2]mind?
22 "So the LORD was [a]no longer able to endure *it,* [b]because of
the evil of your deeds, because of the abominations which you
have committed; thus your land has become a [c]ruin, an object
of horror and a curse, without an inhabitant, as *it is* this day.
23 "Because you have burned [1]sacrifices and have sinned
against the LORD and [a]not obeyed the voice of the LORD or
[b]walked in His law, His statutes or His testimonies, therefore
this [c]calamity has befallen you, as *it has* this day."
24 Then Jeremiah said to all the people, including all the
women, "[a]Hear the word of the LORD, all Judah who are [b]in the
land of Egypt,
25 thus says the LORD of hosts, the God of Israel, as follows:
'As for you and your wives, you have spoken with your mouths
and fulfilled *it* with your hands, saying, "We will [a]certainly
perform our vows that we have vowed, to burn [1]sacrifices to
the queen of heaven and pour out drink offerings to her." [2b]Go
ahead and confirm your vows, and certainly perform your vows!'
26 "[1]Nevertheless hear the word of the LORD, all Judah who are
living in the land of Egypt, 'Behold, I have [a]sworn by My great
name,' says the LORD, '[b]never shall My name be invoked again
by the mouth of any man of Judah in all the land of Egypt,
saying, "[c]As the Lord [2]GOD lives."
27 'Behold, I am watching over them [a]for harm and not for
good, and [b]all the men of Judah who are in the land of Egypt
will [1]meet their end by the sword and by famine until they
[2]are completely gone.

16 [1]Lit *word* [a]Jer 43:2 [b]Prov 1:24-27; Jer 11:8, 10; 13:10

17 [1]Or *so as to burn* [2]Or *incense* [3]Lit *bread* [4]Lit *evil* [a]Num 30:12; Deut 23:23 [b]2 Kin 17:16; Jer 7:18 [c]Neh 9:34; Jer 32:32; 44:21 [d]Ex 16:3; Hos 2:5-9; Phil 3:19

18 [1]Or *incense* [2]Lit *been finished* [a]Num 11:5, 6; Jer 40:12; Mal 3:13-15

19 [1]Or *incense* [2]Lit *to pour* [3]Lit *to make an image of her* [a]Jer 7:18 [b]Num 30:6, 7; Jer 44:15

21 [1]Or *incense* [2]Lit *heart* [a]Ezek 8:10, 11 [b]Jer 11:13; 44:9, 17 [c]Ps 79:8; Is 64:9; Jer 14:10; Hos 7:2; Amos 8:7

22 [a]Is 7:13; 43:24; Mal 2:17 [b]Jer 4:4; 21:12; 30:14 [c]Gen 19:13; Ps 107:33, 34; Jer 25:11, 18, 38; 29:18; 42:18; 44:12

23 [1]Or *incense* [a]Jer 7:13-15; 40:3 [b]Jer 44:10; Ps 119:136, 150 [c]1 Kin 9:9; Neh 13:18; Jer 44:2; Dan 9:11, 12

24 [a]Jer 42:15; 44:16 [b]Jer 43:7; 44:15, 26

25 [1]Or *incense* [2]Lit *Surely cause to stand* [a]Jer 44:17; Matt 14:9; Acts 23:12 [b]Ezek 20:39

26 [1]Lit *Therefore* [2]Heb *YHWH,* usually rendered LORD [a]Gen 22:16; Deut 32:40, 41; Jer 22:5; Amos 6:8; Heb 6:13 [b]Ps 50:16; Ezek 20:39 [c]Is 48:1, 2; Jer 5:2

27 [1]Lit *be finished* [2]Lit *come to an end* [a]Jer 1:10; 31:28; 39:16 [b]2 Kin 21:14; Jer 44:14

28 [1]Lit *men of number* [a]Jer 44:14 [b]Is 10:19; 27:12, 13 [c]Ps 33:11; Is 14:27; 46:10, 11; Zech 1:6

29 [a]Is 7:11, 14; 8:18; Jer 44:30; Matt 24:15, 16, 32 [b]Prov 19:21; Is 40:8

30 [a]Jer 43:9-13; 46:25; Ezek 29:3; 30:21 [b]2 Kin 25:4-7; Jer 34:21; 39:5-7

45:1 [1]Lit *from the mouth of Jeremiah* [a]Jer 32:12, 16; 43:3, 6 [b]Jer 36:4, 18, 32 [c]2 Kin 24:1; 2 Chr 36:5-7; Jer 25:1; 36:1; 46:2; Dan 1:1

3 [a]Ps 6:6; 69:3; 2 Cor 4:1, 16; Gal 6:9

28 '[a]Those who escape the sword will return out of the land of
Egypt to the land of Judah [1b]few in number. Then all the
remnant of Judah who have gone to the land of Egypt to reside
there will know [c]whose word will stand, Mine or theirs.
29 'This will be the [a]sign to you,' declares the LORD, 'that I am
going to punish you in this place, so that you may know that
[b]My words will surely stand against you for harm.'
30 "Thus says the LORD, 'Behold, I am going to give over
[a]Pharaoh Hophra king of Egypt to the hand of his enemies, to
the hand of those who seek his life, just as I gave over
[b]Zedekiah king of Judah to the hand of Nebuchadnezzar king of
Babylon, *who was* his enemy and was seeking his life.'"

Chapter 45 Theme ______________________

45 *This is* the message which Jeremiah the prophet spoke
to [a]Baruch the son of Neriah, when he had [b]written
down these words in a book [1]at Jeremiah's dictation, in the
[c]fourth year of Jehoiakim the son of Josiah, king of Judah, saying:
2 "Thus says the LORD the God of Israel to you, O Baruch:
3 'You said, "Ah, woe is me! For the LORD has added sorrow to
my pain; I am [a]weary with my groaning and have found no rest."'

The Nations of Jeremiah's Prophecy

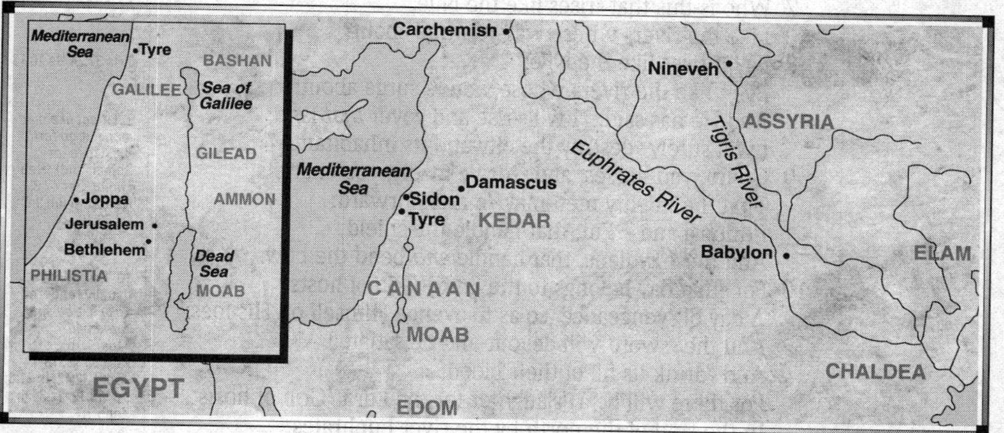

4 [a]Is 5:5; Jer 1:10; 11:17; 18:7-10; 31:28

5 [a]1 Kin 3:9, 11; 2 Kin 5:26; Matt 6:25, 32; Rom 12:16 [b]Is 66:16; Jer 25:31 [c]Jer 21:9; 38:2; 39:18

46:1 [a]Jer 1:10; 25:15-38

4 "Thus you are to say to him, 'Thus says the LORD, "Behold,
[a]what I have built I am about to tear down, and what I have
planted I am about to uproot, that is, the whole land."
5 'But you, are you [a]seeking great things for yourself? Do not
seek *them;* for behold, I am going to [b]bring disaster on all
flesh,' declares the LORD, 'but I will [c]give your life to you as
booty in all the places where you may go.'"

Chapter 46 Theme ______________________

46 That which came as the word of the LORD to Jeremiah
the prophet [a]concerning the nations.

2 To [a]Egypt, concerning the army of [b]Pharaoh Neco king of
Egypt, which was by the Euphrates River at [c]Carchemish, which
Nebuchadnezzar king of Babylon defeated in the [d]fourth year of
Jehoiakim the son of Josiah, king of Judah:

3 "[a]Line up the shield and [1]buckler,
And draw near for the battle!
4 "Harness the horses,
And [1]mount the steeds,
And take your stand with helmets *on!*
[a]Polish the spears,
Put on the [b]scale-armor!
5 "Why have I seen *it?*
They are terrified,
They are [a]drawing back,
And their [b]mighty men are defeated
And have taken refuge in flight,
Without facing back;
[1c]Terror is on every side!"
Declares the LORD.
6 Let not the [a]swift man flee,
Nor the mighty man escape;
In the north beside the river Euphrates
They have [b]stumbled and fallen.
7 Who is this that [a]rises like the Nile,
Like the rivers whose waters surge about?
8 Egypt rises like the Nile,
Even like the rivers whose waters surge about;
And He has said, "I will [a]rise and cover *that* land;
I will surely [b]destroy the city and its inhabitants."
9 Go up, you horses, and [1a]drive madly, you chariots,
That the mighty men may [2]march forward:
Ethiopia and [3b]Put, that handle the shield,
And the [4c]Lydians, that handle *and* bend the bow.
10 For [a]that day belongs to the Lord [1]GOD of hosts,
A day of [b]vengeance, so as to avenge Himself on His foes;
And the [c]sword will devour and be satiated
And [2]drink its fill of their blood;
For there will be a [d]slaughter for the Lord [1]GOD of hosts,
In the land of the north by the river Euphrates.
11 Go [a]up to Gilead and obtain balm,
[b]O virgin daughter of Egypt!
In vain have you multiplied [1]remedies;
There is [c]no healing for you.
12 The nations have heard of your [a]shame,
And the earth is full of your [b]cry *of distress;*
For one [c]warrior has stumbled over [1]another,
And both of them have fallen down together.

13 *This is* the [1]message which the LORD spoke to Jeremiah the
prophet about the [a]coming of Nebuchadnezzar king of Babylon
to [b]smite the land of Egypt:

14 "Declare in Egypt and proclaim in [a]Migdol,
Proclaim also in Memphis and [b]Tahpanhes;

2 [a]Jer 46:14; Ezek chs 29-32 [b]2 Kin 18:21; 23:29, 33-35; Jer 25:19 [c]2 Chr 35:20; Is 10:9 [d]Jer 45:1

3 [1]I.e. small shield [a]Is 21:5; Jer 51:11; Joel 3:9; Nah 2:1; 3:14

4 [1]Or *go up, you horsemen* [a]Ezek 21:9-11 [b]1 Sam 17:5, 38; 2 Chr 26:14; Neh 4:16; Jer 51:3

5 [1]Heb *Magor-missabib;* i.e. Terror is on every side [a]Is 42:17; Jer 46:21 [b]Is 5:25; Ezek 39:18 [c]Jer 6:25; 20:3; 49:29

6 [a]Is 30:16 [b]Jer 46:12, 16; Dan 11:19

7 [a]Jer 47:2

8 [a]Is 37:24 [b]Is 10:13

9 [1]Lit *act like madmen* [2]Lit *go forth* [3]I.e. Libya (or Somaliland) [4]Heb *Ludim* [a]Jer 47:3; Nah 2:4 [b]Nah 3:9 [c]Is 66:19

10 [1]Heb *YHWH,* usually rendered LORD [2]Lit *be saturated with* [a]Joel 1:15 [b]Jer 50:15, 18 [c]Deut 32:42; Is 31:8; Jer 12:12 [d]Is 34:6; Zeph 1:7

11 [1]Lit *healings* [a]Jer 8:22 [b]Is 47:1; Jer 31:4, 21 [c]Jer 30:13; Mic 1:9; Nah 3:19

12 [1]Lit *warrior* [a]Jer 2:36; Nah 3:8-10 [b]Jer 14:2 [c]Is 19:2

13 [1]Lit *word* [a]Jer 43:10-13 [b]Is 19:1

14 [a]Jer 44:1 [b]Jer 43:8

Say, ‘Take your stand and get yourself ready,
For the [c]sword has devoured those around you.’
15 “Why have your [a]mighty ones become prostrate?
They do not stand because the LORD has [b]thrust them down.
16 “They have repeatedly [a]stumbled;
Indeed, they have fallen one against another.
Then they said, ‘Get up! And [b]let us go back
To our own people and our native land
Away from the [1c]sword of the oppressor.’
17 “[1]They cried there, ‘Pharaoh king of Egypt *is but* [a]a
big noise;
He has let the appointed time pass by!’
18 “As I live,” declares the [a]King
Whose name is the LORD of hosts,
“Surely one shall come *who looms up* like [b]Tabor
among the mountains,
Or like [c]Carmel by the sea.
19 “Make your baggage ready for [a]exile,
O [b]daughter dwelling in Egypt,
For [c]Memphis will become a desolation;
It will even be burned down *and* [1]bereft of inhabitants.
20 “Egypt is a pretty [a]heifer,
But a [1]horsefly is coming [b]from the north—it is coming!
21 “Also her [a]mercenaries in her midst
Are like [1]fattened [b]calves,
For even they too have turned back *and* have fled
away together;
They did not stand *their ground.*
For the day of their calamity has come upon them,
The time of their [c]punishment.
22 “Its sound moves along like a serpent;
For they move on [1]like an army
And come to her as woodcutters with axes.
23 “They have cut down her [a]forest,” declares the LORD;
“Surely it will no *more* be found,
Even though [1]they are *now* more numerous than [b]locusts
And are without number.
24 “The daughter of Egypt has been put to shame,
Given over to the [1]power of the [a]people of the north.”

25 The LORD of hosts, the God of Israel, says, “Behold, I am
going to punish Amon of [a]Thebes, and [b]Pharaoh, and Egypt
along with her [c]gods and her kings, even Pharaoh and those
who [d]trust in him.
26 “I shall give them over to the [1]power of those who are [a]seeking
their lives, even into the hand of Nebuchadnezzar king of
Babylon and into the hand of his [2]officers. [b]Afterwards, however,
it will be inhabited as in the days of old,” declares the LORD.

27 “But as for you, O Jacob My servant, [a]do not fear,
Nor be dismayed, O Israel!
For, see, I am going to [b]save you from afar,
And your descendants from the land of their captivity;

14 [c]Is 1:20; Jer 2:30; 46:10; Nah 2:13

15 [a]Is 66:15, 16; Jer 46:5 [b]Ps 18:14, 39; 68:1, 2

16 [1]Lit *oppressing sword* [a]Lev 26:36, 37; Jer 46:6 [b]Jer 51:9 [c]Jer 50:16

17 [1]Some ancient versions read *Call the name of Pharaoh a big noise* [a]Ex 15:9, 10; 1 Kin 20:10, 11; Is 19:11-16

18 [a]Jer 48:15; Mal 1:14 [b]Josh 19:22; Judg 4:6; Ps 89:12 [c]Josh 12:22; 1 Kin 18:42

19 [1]Lit *without* [a]Is 20:4 [b]Jer 48:18 [c]Jer 46:14; Ezek 30:13

20 [1]Or possibly *mosquito* [a]Hos 10:11 [b]Jer 1:14; 47:2

21 [1]Lit *of the stall* [a]2 Sam 10:6; 2 Kin 7:6; Jer 46:5 [b]Is 34:7 [c]Jer 48:44; Hos 9:7; Obad 13; Mic 7:4

22 [1]Or *in force*

23 [1]I.e. trees of the forest, the Egyptians [a]Jer 21:14 [b]Judg 6:5; 7:12; Joel 2:25

24 [1]Lit *hand* [a]Jer 1:15

25 [a]Ezek 30:14-16; Nah 3:8 [b]Jer 44:30 [c]Ex 12:12; Jer 43:12, 13; Ezek 30:13; Zeph 2:11 [d]Is 20:5

26 [1]Lit *hand* [2]Lit *servants* [a]Jer 44:30; Ezek 32:11 [b]Ezek 29:8-14

27 [a]Is 41:13, 14; Jer 30:10, 11 [b]Is 11:11; Jer 23:3, 4; 29:14; Mic 7:12

And Jacob will return and be [c]undisturbed
And secure, with no one making *him* tremble.
28 "O Jacob My servant, do not fear," declares the LORD,
"For [a]I am with you.
For I will make a full end of all the nations
Where I have driven you,
Yet I will [b]not make a full end of you;
But I will [c]correct you properly
And by no means leave you unpunished."

Chapter 47 Theme ____________

47

That which came as the word of the LORD to Jeremiah the prophet concerning the [a]Philistines, before Pharaoh [1]conquered [b]Gaza.

2 Thus says the LORD:
"Behold, waters are going to rise from [a]the north
And become an overflowing torrent,
And [b]overflow the land and all its fullness,
The city and those who live in it;
And the men will [c]cry out,
And every inhabitant of the land will wail.
3 "Because of the noise of the [1a]galloping hoofs of his [2]stallions,
The tumult of his chariots, *and* the rumbling of his wheels,
The fathers have not turned back for *their* children,
Because of the limpness of *their* hands,
4 On account of the day that is coming
To [a]destroy all the Philistines,
To cut off from [b]Tyre and Sidon
Every ally that is left;
For the LORD is going to destroy the Philistines,
The remnant of the coastland of [c]Caphtor.
5 "[a]Baldness has come upon Gaza;
[b]Ashkelon has been ruined.
O remnant of their valley,
How long will you [c]gash yourself?
6 "Ah, [a]sword of the LORD,
How long will you not be quiet?
Withdraw into your sheath;
Be at rest and stay still.
7 "How can [1]it be quiet,
When the LORD has [a]given it an order?
Against Ashkelon and against the seacoast—
There He has [b]assigned it."

Chapter 48 Theme ____________

48

Concerning [a]Moab. Thus says the LORD of hosts, the God of Israel,

27 [c]Jer 23:6; 50:19

28 [a]Ps 46:7, 11; Is 8:10; 43:2; Jer 1:19 [b]Jer 4:27; Amos 9:8, 9 [c]Jer 10:24; Hab 3:2

47:1 [1]Lit *smote* [a]Jer 25:20; Zech 9:6 [b]Gen 10:19; 1 Kin 4:24; Jer 25:20; Amos 1:6; Zeph 2:4

2 [a]Is 14:31; Jer 1:14; 6:22; 46:20, 24 [b]Is 8:7, 8 [c]Is 15:2-5; Jer 46:12

3 [1]Lit *stamping of the* [2]Lit *mighty ones* [a]Judg 5:22; Jer 8:16; Nah 3:2

4 [a]Is 14:31 [b]Is 23:5; Jer 25:22; Joel 3:4; Amos 1:9, 10; Zech 9:2-4 [c]Gen 10:14; Deut 2:23; Amos 9:7

5 [a]Jer 48:37; Mic 1:16 [b]Judg 1:18; Jer 25:20; Amos 1:7, 8; Zeph 2:4, 7; Zech 9:5 [c]Jer 16:6; 41:5

6 [a]Judg 7:20; Jer 12:12; Ezek 21:3-5

7 [1]Lit *you* [a]Is 10:6; Ezek 14:17 [b]Mic 6:9

48:1 [a]Is 15:1; Ezek 25:9

48:1 [1]Or *dismayed* [b]Num 32:3, 38; Jer 48:22 [c]Num 32:37; Jer 48:23; Ezek 25:9
2 [1]I.e. a city of Moab [a]Num 21:25; Jer 48:34, 45; 49:3
3 [a]Is 15:5; Jer 48:5, 34
5 [1]Lit *distresses of outcry* [a]Is 15:5
6 [a]Jer 51:6
7 [a]Ps 52:7; Is 59:4; Jer 9:23 [b]Num 21:29; 1 Kin 11:33; Jer 48:13, 46
8 [a]Josh 13:9, 17, 21
9 [1]Or *salt* [2]Or *fall in ruins* [a]Ps 11:1; Is 16:2; Jer 48:28 [b]Jer 44:22
10 [a]Jer 11:3 [b]1 Kin 20:39, 40, 42; 2 Kin 13:19 [c]Jer 47:6, 7
11 [1]Lit *his* [2]Lit *his flavor has stayed in him* [a]Jer 22:21; Ezek 16:49; Zech 1:15 [b]Zeph 1:12 [c]Nah 2:2
12 [1]Lit *their*
13 [a]Is 45:16; Jer 48:39 [b]Judg 11:24 [c]1 Kin 12:29; Hos 8:5, 6
14 [a]Ps 33:16; Is 10:13-16

"Woe to [b]Nebo, for it has been destroyed;
[c]Kiriathaim has been put to shame, it has been captured;
The lofty stronghold has been put to shame
and [1]shattered.
2 "There is praise for Moab no longer;
In [a]Heshbon they have devised calamity against her:
'Come and let us cut her off from *being* a nation!'
You too, [1]Madmen, will be silenced;
The sword will follow after you.
3 "The sound of an outcry from [a]Horonaim,
'Devastation and great destruction!'
4 "Moab is broken,
Her little ones have sounded out a cry *of distress.*
5 "For by the ascent of [a]Luhith
They will ascend with continual weeping;
For at the descent of Horonaim
They have heard the [1]anguished cry of destruction.
6 "[a]Flee, save your lives,
That you may be like a juniper in the wilderness.
7 "For because of your [a]trust in your own achievements
and treasures,
Even you yourself will be captured;
And [b]Chemosh will go off into exile
Together with his priests and his princes.
8 "A destroyer will come to every city,
So that no city will escape;
The valley also will be ruined
And the [a]plateau will be destroyed,
As the LORD has said.
9 "Give [1a]wings to Moab,
For she will [2]flee away;
And her cities will become a [b]desolation,
Without inhabitants in them.
10 "[a]Cursed be the one who does the LORD's
work [b]negligently,
And cursed be the one who restrains his [c]sword
from blood.

11 "Moab has been [a]at ease since his youth;
He has also been [b]undisturbed, *like wine* on [1]its dregs,
And he has not been [c]emptied from vessel to vessel,
Nor has he gone into exile.
Therefore [2]he retains his flavor,
And his aroma has not changed.
12 "Therefore behold, the days are coming," declares the LORD,
"when I will send to him those who tip *vessels,* and they will tip
him over, and they will empty his vessels and shatter [1]his jars.
13 "And Moab will be [a]ashamed of [b]Chemosh, as the house of
Israel was ashamed of [c]Bethel, their confidence.
14 "How can you say, 'We are [a]mighty warriors,
And men valiant for battle'?

INSIGHT

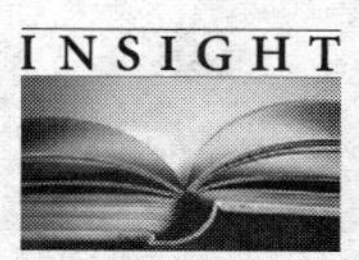

Chemosh was a Moabite god who was believed to provide the people with land. During his reforms King Josiah desecrated a temple built by Solomon for Chemosh (2 Kings 23:13).

15 "Moab has been destroyed and [1]men have gone up to
[2]his cities;
His choicest [3a]young men have also gone down to the
slaughter,"
Declares the [b]King, whose name is the LORD of hosts.
16 "The disaster of Moab will [a]soon come,
And his calamity has swiftly hastened.
17 "Mourn for him, all you who *live* around him,
Even all of you who know his name;
Say, 'How has the mighty [1a]scepter been broken,
A staff of splendor!'
18 "[a]Come down from your glory
And sit [1]on the parched ground,
O [b]daughter dwelling in [c]Dibon,
For the destroyer of Moab has come up against you,
He has ruined your strongholds.
19 "Stand by the road and keep watch,
O inhabitant of [a]Aroer;
[b]Ask him who flees and her who escapes
And say, 'What has happened?'
20 "Moab has been put to shame, for it has been [1]shattered.
Wail and cry out;
Declare by the [a]Arnon
That Moab has been destroyed.
21 "Judgment has also come upon the plain, upon Holon, [a]Jahzah
and against [b]Mephaath,
22 against Dibon, Nebo and Beth-diblathaim,
23 against Kiriathaim, Beth-gamul and [a]Beth-meon,
24 against [a]Kerioth, Bozrah and all the cities of the land of
Moab, far and near.
25 "The [a]horn of Moab has been cut off and his [b]arm broken,"
declares the LORD.
26 "[a]Make him drunk, for he has [1]become [b]arrogant toward the
LORD; so Moab will [2]wallow in his vomit, and he also will
become a laughingstock.
27 "Now was not Israel a [a]laughingstock to you? Or was he
[1b]caught among thieves? For each time you speak about him
you [c]shake *your head in scorn.*
28 "Leave the cities and dwell among the [a]crags,
O inhabitants of Moab,
And be like a [b]dove that nests
Beyond the mouth of the chasm.
29 "[a]We have heard of the pride of Moab—he *is* very proud—
Of his haughtiness, his [b]pride, his arrogance and
[1]his self-exaltation.
30 "I know his [a]fury," declares the LORD,
"But it is futile;
His idle boasts have accomplished nothing.
31 "Therefore I will [a]wail for Moab,
Even for all Moab will I cry out;
[1]I will moan for the men of [b]Kir-heres.

15 [1]Lit *one has* [2]Lit *her* [3]I.e. warriors [a]Is 40:30, 31; Jer 50:27 [b]Jer 46:18; 51:57; Mal 1:14

16 [a]Is 13:22

17 [1]Or *rod* [a]Is 9:4; 14:5

18 [1]Lit *in thirst* [a]Is 47:1 [b]Jer 46:19 [c]Num 21:30; Josh 13:9, 17; Is 15:2; Jer 48:22

19 [a]Deut 2:36; Josh 12:2 [b]1 Sam 4:13, 14, 16

20 [1]Or *dismayed* [a]Num 21:13

21 [a]Num 21:23; Is 15:4; Jer 48:34 [b]Josh 13:18

23 [a]Josh 13:17

24 [a]Jer 48:41; Amos 2:2

25 [a]Ps 75:10; Zech 1:19-21 [b]Job 22:9; Ps 10:15

26 [1]Or *magnified himself against* [2]Or *splash into* [a]Jer 25:15 [b]Ex 5:2; Jer 48:42; Dan 5:23

27 [1]Or *found* [a]Lam 2:15-17; Mic 7:8-10 [b]Jer 2:26 [c]Job 16:4; Jer 18:16

28 [a]Judg 6:2; Is 2:19; Jer 49:16; Obad 3 [b]Ps 55:6; Song 2:14

29 [1]Lit *elevation of his heart* [a]Is 16:6; Zeph 2:8 [b]Job 40:11, 12; Ps 138:6

30 [a]Is 37:28

31 [1]Another reading is *He* [a]Is 15:5; 16:7, 11 [b]2 Kin 3:25; Is 16:7, 11; Jer 48:36

32 "More than the [a]weeping for [b]Jazer
I will weep for you, O vine of Sibmah!
Your tendrils stretched across the sea,
They reached to the sea of Jazer;
Upon your summer fruits and your grape harvest
The destroyer has fallen.
33 "So [a]gladness and joy are taken away
From the fruitful field, even from the land of Moab.
And I have made the wine to [b]cease from the wine presses;
No one will tread *them* with shouting,
The shouting will not be shouts *of joy.*
34 "[a]From the outcry at Heshbon even to [b]Elealeh, even to Jahaz
they have [1]raised their voice, from [c]Zoar even to Horonaim *and*
to Eglath-shelishiyah; for even the waters of Nimrim will become
desolate.
35 "I will make an end of Moab," declares the LORD, "the one
who offers *sacrifice* on the [a]high place and the one who [1b]burns
incense to his gods.
36 "Therefore My [a]heart [1]wails for Moab like flutes; My heart
also [1]wails like flutes for the men of Kir-heres. Therefore they
have [b]lost the abundance it produced.
37 "For [a]every head is bald and every beard cut short; there are
gashes on all the hands and [b]sackcloth on the loins.
38 "On all the [a]housetops of Moab and in its streets [1]there is
lamentation everywhere; for I have broken Moab like an
undesirable [b]vessel," declares the LORD.
39 "How [1]shattered it is! *How* they have wailed! How Moab has
turned his back—he is ashamed! So Moab will become a
laughingstock and an [a]object of terror to all around him."

40 For thus says the LORD:
"Behold, one will [a]fly swiftly like an eagle
And [b]spread out his wings against Moab.
41 "Kerioth has been captured
And the strongholds have been seized,
So the [a]hearts of the mighty men of Moab in that day
Will be like the heart of a [b]woman in labor.
42 "Moab will be [a]destroyed from *being* a people
Because he has [1]become [b]arrogant toward the LORD.
43 "[a]Terror, pit and snare are *coming* upon you,
O inhabitant of Moab," declares the LORD.
44 "The one who [a]flees from the terror
Will fall into the pit,
And the one who climbs up out of the pit
Will be caught in the snare;
For I shall bring upon her, *even* upon Moab,
The year of their [b]punishment," declares the LORD.

45 "In the shadow of Heshbon
The fugitives stand without strength;
For a fire has gone forth from Heshbon
And a [a]flame from the midst of [b]Sihon,

32 [a]Is 16:8, 9 [b]Num 21:32
33 [a]Is 16:10; Jer 25:10; Joel 1:12 [b]Is 5:10; Hag 2:16
34 [1]Lit *given forth* [a]Is 15:4-6 [b]Num 32:3, 37 [c]Gen 13:10; 14:2; Is 15:5, 6
35 [1]Or *offers up in smoke* [a]Is 15:2; 16:12 [b]Jer 7:9; 11:13
36 [1]Lit *sounds* [a]Is 15:5; 16:11 [b]Is 15:7
37 [a]Is 15:2; Jer 16:6; 41:5; 47:5 [b]Gen 37:34; Is 15:3; 20:2
38 [1]Lit *all of it is lamentation* [a]Is 22:1 [b]Jer 19:10, 11; 22:28; 25:34
39 [1]Or *dismayed* [a]Ezek 26:16
40 [a]Deut 28:49; Jer 49:22; Hos 8:1; Hab 1:8 [b]Is 8:8
41 [a]Jer 49:22 [b]Is 13:8; 21:3; Jer 30:6; Mic 4:9, 10
42 [1]Or *magnified himself against* [a]Ps 83:4; Jer 48:2 [b]Is 37:23; Jer 48:26
43 [a]Is 24:17, 18; Lam 3:47
44 [a]1 Kin 19:17; Is 24:18; Amos 5:19 [b]Jer 46:21
45 [a]Num 21:28, 29 [b]Num 21:21, 26; Ps 135:11

And it has devoured the [c]forehead of Moab
And the scalps of the [1]riotous revelers.
46 “[a]Woe to you, Moab!
The people of [b]Chemosh have perished;
For your sons have been taken away captive
And your daughters into captivity.
47 “Yet I will [a]restore the [1]fortunes of Moab
In the [2]latter days,” declares the LORD.
Thus far the judgment on Moab.

Chapter 49 Theme ____________________

49 Concerning the sons of [a]Ammon. Thus says the LORD:
“Does Israel have no sons?
Or has he no heirs?
Why then has [1]Malcam taken possession of Gad
And his people settled in its cities?
2 “Therefore behold, the days are coming,” declares the LORD,
“That I will cause a [1a]trumpet blast of war to be heard
Against [b]Rabbah of the sons of Ammon;
And it will become a desolate heap,
And her [c]towns will be set on fire.
Then Israel will take [d]possession of his possessors,”
Says the LORD.
3 “Wail, O [a]Heshbon, for [b]Ai has been destroyed!
Cry out, O daughters of Rabbah,
[c]Gird yourselves with sackcloth and lament,
And rush back and forth inside the walls;
For [1]Malcam will [d]go into exile
Together with his priests and his princes.
4 “How [a]boastful you are about the valleys!
Your valley is flowing *away,*
O [b]backsliding daughter
Who trusts in her [c]treasures, *saying,*
‘[d]Who will come against me?’
5 “Behold, I am going to bring [a]terror upon you,”
Declares the Lord [1]GOD of hosts,
“From all *directions* around you;
And each of you will be [b]driven out [2]headlong,
With no one to gather the [c]fugitives together.
6 “But afterward I will [a]restore
The [1]fortunes of the sons of Ammon,”
Declares the LORD.

7 Concerning [a]Edom.
Thus says the LORD of hosts,
“Is there no longer any [b]wisdom in [c]Teman?
Has good counsel been lost to the prudent?
Has their wisdom decayed?
8 “Flee away, turn back, dwell in the depths,
O inhabitants of [a]Dedan,

INSIGHT

Malcam, also called Milcom, was the national god of Ammon. When King Solomon was old, he worshiped Malcam on the high places he built just outside Jerusalem. King Josiah desecrated these high places during his reforms (1 Kings 11:1-8, 33; 2 Kings 23:13).

45 [1]Lit *sons of tumult* [c]Num 24:17

46 [a]Num 21:29 [b]Judg 11:24; 1 Kin 11:7; Jer 48:7

47 [1]Or *captivity* [2]Lit *end of the days* [a]Jer 12:14-17; 49:6, 39

49:1 [1]In 1 Kin 11:5, 33 and Zeph 1:5, *Milcom* [a]Deut 23:3, 4; 2 Chr 20:1; Ezek 21:28-32; 25:2-10; Amos 1:13-15; Zeph 2:8-11

2 [1]Or *shout of* [a]Num 10:9; Jer 4:19 [b]Deut 3:11; 2 Sam 11:1; Ezek 21:20 [c]Josh 17:11, 16 [d]Is 14:2

3 [1]Cf v 1 [a]Jer 48:2 [b]Josh 7:2-5; 8:1-29; Ezra 2:28 [c]Is 32:11; Jer 48:37 [d]Jer 46:25; 48:7

4 [a]Jer 9:23 [b]Jer 31:22 [c]Ps 62:10; Ezek 28:4, 5; 1 Tim 6:17 [d]Jer 21:13

5 [1]Heb *YHWH,* usually rendered *LORD* [2]Lit *before him* [a]Jer 48:43f; 49:29 [b]Jer 16:16; 46:5 [c]Lam 4:15

6 [1]Or *captivity* [a]Jer 48:47; 49:39

7 [a]Gen 25:30; 32:3; Is 34:5, 6; Jer 25:21; Ezek 25:12; Amos 1:11; Obad 1-21 [b]Job 2:11; Jer 8:9 [c]Gen 36:11, 15, 34; Jer 49:20

8 [a]Is 21:13; Jer 25:23

8 [1]Or *brought* [2]Or *punished* [b]Jer 46:21; Mal 1:3, 4

For I [1]will bring the [b]disaster of Esau upon him
At the time I [2]punish him.
9 "[a]If grape gatherers came to you,
Would they not leave gleanings?
If thieves *came* by night,
They would destroy *only* [1]until they had enough.
10 "But I have [a]stripped Esau bare,
I have uncovered his hiding places
So that he will not be able to conceal himself;
His [1]offspring has been destroyed along with his [2]relatives
And his neighbors, and [b]he is no more.
11 "Leave your [1a]orphans behind, I will keep *them* alive;
And let your [b]widows trust in Me."
12 For thus says the LORD, "Behold, those [1]who were not
sentenced to drink the [a]cup will certainly drink *it,* and are you
the one who will be [b]completely acquitted? You will not be
acquitted, but you will certainly drink *it.*
13 "For I have [a]sworn by Myself," declares the LORD, "that
[b]Bozrah will become an [c]object of horror, a reproach, a ruin
and a curse; and all its cities will become perpetual ruins."
14 I have [a]heard a message from the LORD,
And an [b]envoy is sent among the nations, *saying,*
"[c]Gather yourselves together and come against her,
And rise up for battle!"
15 "For behold, I have made you small among the nations,
Despised among men.
16 "As for the terror of you,
The arrogance of your heart has deceived you,
O you who live in the clefts of [1]the [a]rock,
Who occupy the height of the hill.
Though you make your nest as [b]high as an eagle's,
I will [c]bring you down from there," declares the LORD.
17 "Edom will become an [a]object of horror; everyone who passes
by it will be horrified and will [b]hiss at all its wounds.
18 "Like the [a]overthrow of Sodom and Gomorrah with its
neighbors," says the LORD, "[b]no one will live there, nor will a
son of man reside in it.
19 "[a]Behold, one will come up like a lion from the [1b]thickets of
the Jordan against [2]a perennially watered pasture; for in an instant
I will make him run away from it, and whoever is [c]chosen I shall
appoint over it. For who is [d]like Me, and who will summon Me
into court? And who then is the shepherd [e]who can stand
against Me?"
20 Therefore hear the [a]plan of the LORD which He has planned
against Edom, and His purposes which He has purposed against
the inhabitants of Teman: surely they will drag them off, *even*
the little ones of the flock; surely He will make their [1]pasture
[b]desolate because of them.
21 The [a]earth has quaked at the noise of their downfall. There
is an outcry! The noise of it has been heard at the [1]Red Sea.

9 [1]Lit *their sufficiency* [a]Obad 5

10 [1]Lit *seed* [2]Lit *brothers* [a]Jer 13:26 [b]Is 17:14

11 [1]Or *fatherless* [a]Ps 68:5; Hos 14:3 [b]Ps 68:5; Zech 7:10

12 [1]Lit *whose judgment was not to* [a]Jer 25:15 [b]Jer 25:28, 29; 1 Pet 4:17

13 [a]Gen 22:16; Is 45:23; Jer 44:26; Amos 6:8 [b]Gen 36:33; 1 Chr 1:44; Is 34:6; 63:1; Amos 1:12 [c]Is 34:9-15; Jer 18:16

14 [a]Obad 1-4 [b]Is 18:2; 30:4 [c]Jer 50:14

16 [1]Or *Sela* [a]2 Kin 14:7; Jer 48:28 [b]Job 39:27; Is 14:13-15 [c]Amos 9:2

17 [a]Jer 18:16; 49:13; 50:13; Ezek 35:7 [b]1 Kin 9:8; Jer 51:37

18 [a]Gen 19:24, 25; Deut 29:23; Jer 50:40; Amos 4:11; Zeph 2:9 [b]Job 18:15-18; Jer 49:33

19 [1]Lit *pride* [2]Or *an enduring habitation* [a]Jer 50:44 [b]Josh 3:15; Jer 12:5 [c]Num 16:5 [d]Ex 15:11; Is 46:9 [e]Job 41:10

20 [1]Or *habitation* [a]Is 14:24, 27; Jer 50:45 [b]Mal 1:3, 4

21 [1]Lit *Sea of Reeds* [a]Jer 50:46; Ezek 26:15, 18

22 Behold, [1]He will mount up and [a]swoop like an eagle and
spread out His wings [2]against Bozrah; and the [b]hearts of the
mighty men of Edom in that day will be like the heart of a
woman in labor.

23 Concerning [a]Damascus.
"[b]Hamath and [c]Arpad are put to shame,
For they have heard bad news;
They are [d]disheartened.
There is anxiety by the sea,
It [e]cannot be calmed.
24 "Damascus has become helpless;
She has turned away to flee,
And panic has gripped her;
[a]Distress and pangs have taken hold of her
Like a woman in childbirth.
25 "How [1]the [a]city of praise has not been deserted,
The town of My joy!
26 "Therefore, her [a]young men will fall in her streets,
And all the men of war will be [1]silenced in that day,"
declares the LORD of hosts.
27 "I will [a]set fire to the wall of Damascus,
And it will devour the [1]fortified towers of [b]Ben-hadad."

28 Concerning [a]Kedar and the kingdoms of Hazor, which
Nebuchadnezzar king of Babylon defeated. Thus says the LORD,
"Arise, go up to Kedar
And devastate the [1b]men of the east.
29 "They will take away their tents and their flocks;
They will carry off for themselves
Their tent [a]curtains, all their goods and their [b]camels,
And they will call out to one another, '[c]Terror on
every side!'
30 "Run away, flee! Dwell in the depths,
O inhabitants of Hazor," declares the LORD;
"For [a]Nebuchadnezzar king of Babylon has formed a plan
against you
And devised a scheme against you.
31 "Arise, go up against a nation which is [a]at ease,
Which lives securely," declares the LORD.
"It has [b]no gates or bars;
They [c]dwell alone.
32 "Their camels will become plunder,
And their many cattle for booty,
And I will [a]scatter to all the winds those who [b]cut the
corners *of their hair;*
And I will bring their disaster from every side,"
declares the LORD.
33 "Hazor will become a [a]haunt of jackals,
A desolation forever;
No one will live there,
Nor will a son of man reside in it."

34 That which came as the word of the LORD to Jeremiah the

22 [1]Or *one* [2]Or *over* [a]Jer 4:13; 48:40; Hos 8:1 [b]Is 13:8; Jer 30:6; 48:41

23 [a]Gen 14:15; 15:2; 2 Kin 5:12; 2 Chr 16:2; Is 7:8; 17:1; Amos 1:3; Acts 9:2 [b]Num 13:21; Is 10:9; Jer 39:5; Amos 6:2 [c]2 Kin 18:34; 19:13; Is 10:9 [d]Ex 15:15; Nah 2:10 [e]Is 57:20

24 [a]Is 13:8

25 [1]Or *deserted is the city of praise* [a]Jer 33:9; 51:41

26 [1]Or *destroyed* [a]Jer 11:22; 50:30; Amos 4:10

27 [1]Or *palaces* [a]Jer 43:12; Amos 1:3-5 [b]1 Kin 15:18-20; 2 Kin 13:3

28 [1]Lit *sons* [a]Gen 25:13; Ps 120:5; Is 21:16, 17; Jer 2:10; Ezek 27:21 [b]Job 1:3; Is 11:14

29 [a]Hab 3:7 [b]1 Chr 5:21 [c]Jer 46:5

30 [a]Jer 25:9; 27:6

31 [a]Judg 18:7; Is 47:8 [b]Is 42:11 [c]Num 23:9; Deut 33:28; Mic 7:14

32 [a]Ezek 5:10; 12:14, 15 [b]Jer 9:26; 25:23

33 [a]Is 13:20-22; Jer 9:11; 10:22; 51:37; Zeph 2:9, 13-15; Mal 1:3

prophet concerning [a]Elam, [b]at the beginning of the reign of
Zedekiah king of Judah, saying:
35 "Thus says the LORD of hosts,
'Behold, I am going to [a]break the bow of Elam,
The [1]finest of their might.
36 'I will bring upon Elam the [a]four winds
From the four ends of heaven,
And will [b]scatter them to all these winds;
And there will be no nation
To which the outcasts of Elam will not go.
37 'So I will [1]shatter Elam before their enemies
And before those who seek their lives;
And I will [a]bring calamity upon them,
Even My [b]fierce anger,' declares the LORD,
'And I will [c]send out the sword after them
Until I have consumed them.
38 'Then I will set My throne in Elam
And destroy [1]out of it king and princes,'
Declares the LORD.
39 'But it will come about in the last days
That I will [a]restore the [1]fortunes of Elam,'"
Declares the LORD.

Chapter 50 Theme ____________________________________

50 The word which the LORD spoke concerning [a]Babylon,
the land of the Chaldeans, through Jeremiah the prophet:
2 "[a]Declare and proclaim among the nations.
Proclaim it and [b]lift up a standard.
Do not conceal *it but* say,
'[c]Babylon has been captured,
[d]Bel has been put to shame, [1]Marduk has been [2]shattered;
Her [e]images have been put to shame, her idols have
been shattered.'
3 "For a nation has come up against her out of the [a]north; it
will make her land [b]an object of horror, and there will be [c]no
inhabitant in it. Both man and beast have wandered off, they
have gone away!
4 "In those days and at that time," declares the LORD, "the
sons of Israel will come, *both* they and the sons of Judah [a]as
well; they will go along [b]weeping as they go, and it will be [c]the
LORD their God they will seek.
5 "They will [a]ask for the way to Zion, *turning* their faces [1]in
its direction; [2]they [3]will come that they may join themselves to
the LORD *in* an [b]everlasting covenant that will not be forgotten.
6 "My people have become [a]lost sheep;
[b]Their shepherds have led them astray.
They have made them turn aside *on* the [c]mountains;
They have gone along from mountain to hill
And have forgotten their [d]resting place.

34 [a]Gen 10:22; 14:1, 9; Is 11:11; Jer 25:25; Ezek 32:24; Dan 8:2 [b]2 Kin 24:17, 18; Jer 28:1

35 [1]Lit *first* [a]Ps 46:9; Is 22:6; Jer 51:56

36 [a]Dan 7:2; 8:8; Rev 7:1 [b]Jer 49:32; Ezek 5:10; Amos 9:9

37 [1]Or *dismay* [a]Jer 6:19 [b]Jer 30:24 [c]Jer 9:16; 48:2

38 [1]Or *from there*

39 [1]Or *captivity* [a]Jer 48:47

50:1 [a]Gen 10:10; 11:9; 2 Kin 17:24; Is 13:1; 47:1; Dan 1:1; Rev 14:8

2 [1]Heb *Merodach* [2]Or *dismayed* [a]Jer 4:16 [b]Jer 51:27 [c]Jer 51:31 [d]Is 46:1 [e]Jer 51:47

3 [a]Is 13:17; Jer 50:9; 51:11, 27 [b]Is 14:22, 23; Jer 50:13 [c]Jer 9:10, 11; Zeph 1:3

4 [a]Is 11:12, 13; Jer 3:18; 31:31; 33:7; Hos 1:11 [b]Ezra 3:12, 13; Ps 126:5; Jer 31:9 [c]Hos 3:5

5 [1]Lit *hither* [2]M.T. reads *come ye!* [3]Or *will have come* [a]Is 35:8; Jer 6:16 [b]Is 55:3; Jer 32:40; Heb 8:6-10

6 [a]Is 53:6; Ezek 34:15, 16; Matt 9:36; 10:6 [b]Jer 23:11-14 [c]Jer 13:16; Ezek 34:6 [d]Jer 33:12; 50:19

INSIGHT

Marduk and ***Bel*** were Babylonian deities. Bel was the Babylonian equivalent of Baal, acknowledged as the lord of heaven.

7 "All who came upon them have devoured them;
And their adversaries have said, '[a]We are not guilty,
Inasmuch as they have sinned against the LORD
who is the [b]habitation of righteousness,
Even the LORD, the [c]hope of their fathers.'

8 "Wander away from the [a]midst of Babylon
And [1]go forth from the land of the Chaldeans;
Be also like male goats [2]at the head of the flock.
9 "For behold, I am going to [a]arouse and bring up
against Babylon
A horde of great nations from the land of the north,
And they will draw up *their* battle lines against her;
From there she will be taken captive.
Their arrows will be like [1]an expert warrior
Who does not return empty-handed.
10 "[1a]Chaldea will become plunder;
All who plunder her will have enough," declares the LORD.

11 "Because you are glad, because you are jubilant,
O you who [a]pillage My heritage,
Because you skip about [1]like a threshing [b]heifer
And neigh like [2]stallions,
12 Your [a]mother [1]will be greatly ashamed,
She who gave you birth [1]will be humiliated.
Behold, *she will be* the least of the nations,
A [b]wilderness, a parched land and a desert.
13 "Because of the indignation of the LORD she will [a]not
be inhabited,
But she will be [b]completely desolate;
Everyone who passes by Babylon [c]will be horrified
And will hiss because of all her wounds.
14 "Draw up your battle lines against Babylon on every side,
All you who [1]bend the bow;
Shoot at her, do not be sparing with *your* arrows,
For she has [a]sinned against the LORD.
15 "Raise your battle cry against her on every side!
She has [a]given [1]herself up, her pillars have fallen,
Her [b]walls have been torn down.
For this is the [c]vengeance of the LORD:
Take vengeance on her;
[d]As she has done *to others, so* do to her.
16 "Cut off the [a]sower from Babylon
And the one who wields the sickle at the time of harvest;
From before [1]the [b]sword of the oppressor
[c]They will each turn back to his own people
And they will each flee to his own land.

17 "Israel is a [a]scattered [1]flock, the [b]lions have driven *them*
away. The first one *who* devoured him was the [c]king of Assyria,
and this last one *who* has broken his bones is [d]Nebuchadnezzar
king of Babylon.

7 [a]Jer 2:3; Zech 11:5 [b]Jer 31:23; 40:2, 3 [c]Ps 22:4; Jer 14:8; 17:13

8 [1]Another reading is *let them go forth* [2]Or *in front of* [a]Is 48:20; Jer 51:6; Rev 18:4

9 [1]So some mss and versions; M.T. reads *a warrior who makes childless* [a]Jer 51:1

10 [1]Or *the Chaldeans* [a]Jer 51:24, 35; Ezek 11:24

11 [1]Another reading is *in the grass* [2]Lit *mighty ones* [a]Jer 12:14 [b]Jer 46:20

12 [1]Or *has become* [a]Jer 15:9 [b]Jer 22:6; 51:43

13 [a]Jer 34:22 [b]Jer 51:26 [c]Jer 18:16; 49:17

14 [1]Lit *tread* (in order to string) [a]Hab 2:8, 17

15 [1]Lit *her hand* [a]1 Chr 29:24; 2 Chr 30:8; Lam 5:6 [b]Jer 50:44; 51:58 [c]Jer 46:10 [d]Ps 137:8; Rev 18:6

16 [1]Or *the oppressing sword* [a]Joel 1:11 [b]Jer 25:38; 46:16 [c]Is 13:14

17 [1]Lit *sheep* [a]Joel 3:2 [b]Jer 2:15; 4:7 [c]2 Kin 15:19; 17:6; 18:9-13 [d]2 Kin 24:1, 10-12; 25:1-7

18 [a]Is 10:12; Ezek 31:3, 11, 12; Nah 3:7, 18, 19

18 "Therefore thus says the LORD of hosts, the God of Israel:
'Behold, I am going to punish the king of Babylon and his land,
just as I [a]punished the king of Assyria.
19 'And I will [a]bring Israel back to his pasture and he will
graze on Carmel and Bashan, and his [1]desire will be satisfied in
the [b]hill country of Ephraim and Gilead.

19 [1]Lit *soul* [a]Is 65:10; Jer 31:10; 33:12; Ezek 34:13 [b]Jer 31:6

20 'In those days and at that time,' declares the LORD, 'search
will be made for the iniquity of Israel, but [a]there will be none;
and for the sins of Judah, but they will not be found; for I will
pardon those [b]whom I leave as a remnant.'

20 [a]Is 43:25; Jer 31:34; Mic 7:19 [b]Is 1:9

21 "Against the land of [1]Merathaim, go up against it,
And against the inhabitants of [2a]Pekod.
Slay and [3]utterly destroy them," declares the LORD,
"And do according to all that I have commanded you.

21 [1]Or *Double Rebellion* [2]Or *Punishment* [3]Lit *put under the ban* [a]Ezek 23:23

22 "The [a]noise of battle is in the land,
And great destruction.

22 [a]Jer 4:19-21; 51:54-56

23 "How the [a]hammer of the whole earth
Has been cut off and broken!
How Babylon has become
An object of horror among the nations!

23 [a]Jer 51:20-24

24 "I [a]set a snare for you and you were also [b]caught,
O Babylon,
While you yourself were not aware;
You have been found and also seized
Because you have engaged in [c]conflict with the LORD."

24 [a]Jer 48:43, 44 [b]Jer 51:31; Dan 5:30, 31 [c]Job 9:4; 40:2, 9

25 The LORD has opened His armory
And has brought forth the [a]weapons of His indignation,
For it is a [b]work of the Lord [1]GOD of hosts
In the land of the Chaldeans.

25 [1]Heb *YHWH,* usually rendered *LORD* [a]Is 13:5 [b]Jer 50:15; 51:12, 25, 55

26 Come to her from the [1]farthest border;
[a]Open up her barns,
Pile her up like heaps
And [2b]utterly destroy her,
Let nothing be left to her.

26 [1]Lit *end* [2]Lit *put under the ban* [a]Is 45:3; Jer 50:10 [b]Is 14:23

27 [a]Put all her young bulls to the sword;
Let them [b]go down to the slaughter!
Woe be upon them, for their [c]day has come,
The time of their punishment.

27 [a]Is 34:7 [b]Jer 48:10 [c]Ps 37:13; Jer 46:21; 48:44; Ezek 7:7

28 There is a [a]sound of fugitives and refugees from the
land of Babylon,
To declare in Zion the [b]vengeance of the LORD our God,
Vengeance for His [c]temple.

28 [a]Is 48:20 [b]Ps 149:6-9; Jer 50:15; 51:10 [c]Lam 1:10; 2:6, 7

29 "Summon [1]many against Babylon,
All those who [2]bend the bow:
Encamp against her on every side,
Let there be no escape[3].
Repay her according to her work;
[a]According to all that she has done, *so* do to her;

29 [1]Another reading is *archers* [2]Lit *tread* (in order to string) [3]Some mss add *to her* [a]Ps 137:8; Jer 50:15; 51:56; 2 Thess 1:6

For she has become [b]arrogant against the LORD,
Against the Holy One of Israel.
30 "Therefore her [a]young men will fall in her streets,
And all her men of war will be [1b]silenced in that day,"
declares the LORD.
31 "Behold, [a]I am against you, O [1]arrogant one,"
Declares the Lord [2]GOD of hosts,
"For your day has come,
The time [3]when I will punish you.
32 "The [1a]arrogant one will stumble and fall
With no one to raise him up;
And I will [b]set fire to his cities
And it will devour all his environs."

33 Thus says the LORD of hosts,
"The sons of Israel are oppressed,
And the sons of Judah as well;
And [a]all who took them captive have held them fast,
They have refused to let them go.
34 "Their [a]Redeemer is strong, [b]the LORD of hosts is His name;
He will vigorously [c]plead their case
So that He may [d]bring rest to [1]the earth,
But turmoil to the inhabitants of Babylon.
35 "A [a]sword against the Chaldeans," declares the LORD,
"And against the inhabitants of Babylon
And against her [b]officials and her [c]wise men!
36 "A sword against the [a]oracle priests, and they will
become fools!
A sword against her [b]mighty men, and they will
be [1c]shattered!
37 "A sword against [1]their [a]horses and against [1]their chariots
And against all the [2b]foreigners who are in the midst of her,
And they will become [c]women!
A sword against her treasures, and they will be plundered!
38 "A [1a]drought on her waters, and they will be dried up!
For it is a land of [b]idols,
And they are mad over fearsome idols.

39 "Therefore the [a]desert creatures will live *there* along with
the jackals;
The ostriches also will live in it,
And it will [b]never again be inhabited
Or dwelt in from generation to generation.
40 "As when God overthrew [a]Sodom
And Gomorrah with its neighbors," declares the LORD,
"No man will live there,
Nor will *any* son of man reside in it.

41 "Behold, a people is coming [a]from the north,
And a great nation and many kings
Will be aroused from the remote parts of the earth.

29 [b]Ex 10:3; Jer 49:16; Dan 4:37

30 [1]Or *made lifeless* or *destroyed* [a]Is 13:17, 18; Jer 9:21; 18:21; 49:26; 51:4 [b]Jer 51:57

31 [1]Lit *arrogance* [2]Heb *YHWH*, usually rendered *LORD* [3]Another reading is *of your punishment* [a]Jer 21:13; Nah 2:13

32 [1]Lit *arrogance* [a]Is 10:12-15 [b]Jer 21:14; 49:27

33 [a]Is 14:17; 58:6

34 [1]Or their *land* [a]Prov 23:11; Is 43:14; Jer 15:21; 31:11; Rev 18:8 [b]Is 47:4; Jer 32:18; 51:19 [c]Jer 51:36; Mic 7:9 [d]Is 14:3-7

35 [a]Jer 47:6; Hos 11:6 [b]Dan 5:1, 2 [c]Dan 5:7, 8

36 [1]Or *dismayed* [a]Is 44:25 [b]Jer 49:22 [c]Nah 3:13

37 [1]Lit *his* [2]Lit *mixed multitude* [a]Ps 20:7, 8; Jer 51:21, 22 [b]Jer 25:20; Ezek 30:5 [c]Jer 48:41; 51:30; Nah 3:13

38 [1]Another reading is *sword* [a]Is 44:27; Jer 51:32, 36; Rev 16:12 [b]Is 46:1, 6, 7

39 [a]Is 13:21; 34:14; Rev 18:2 [b]Is 13:20; Jer 25:12

40 [a]Gen 19:24, 25; Is 13:19; Jer 49:18; Luke 17:28-30; 2 Pet 2:6; Jude 7

41 [a]Is 13:2-5; Jer 6:22; 50:3, 9; 51:27, 28

42 "They [a]seize *their* bow and javelin;
They are [b]cruel and have no mercy.
Their [c]voice roars like the sea;
And they ride on [d]horses,
[e]Marshalled like a man for the battle
Against you, O daughter of Babylon.
43 "The [a]king of Babylon has heard the report about them,
And his hands hang limp;
[b]Distress has gripped him,
Agony like a woman in childbirth.
44 "[a]Behold, one will come up like a lion from the [1]thicket of
the Jordan to [2]a perennially watered pasture; for in an instant I
will make them run away from it, and whoever is [b]chosen I will
appoint over it. For who is [c]like Me, and who will summon Me
into court? And who then is the shepherd who can [d]stand before
Me?"
45 Therefore hear the [a]plan of the LORD which He has planned
against Babylon, and His purposes which He has purposed
against the land of the Chaldeans: [b]surely they will drag them
off, *even* the little ones of the flock; surely He will make their
[1]pasture desolate because of them.
46 At the [1]shout, "Babylon has been seized!" the [a]earth is
shaken, and an [b]outcry is heard among the nations.

Chapter 51 Theme ________________

51 Thus says the LORD:
"Behold, I am going to arouse against Babylon
And against the inhabitants of [1]Leb-kamai
[2]The [a]spirit of a destroyer.
2 "I will dispatch [1]foreigners to Babylon that they may
[a]winnow her
And may devastate her land;
For on every side they will be opposed to her
In the day of *her* calamity.
3 "[1]Let not [2]him who [3a]bends his bow [3]bend *it,*
[1]Nor let him rise up in his [b]scale-armor;
So do not spare her young men;
Devote all her army to destruction.
4 "They will fall down [1]slain in the land of the Chaldeans,
And [a]pierced through in their streets."

5 For [a]neither Israel nor Judah has been [1]forsaken
By his God, the LORD of hosts,
Although their land is [b]full of guilt
[2]Before the Holy One of Israel.
6 [a]Flee from the midst of Babylon,
And each of you save his life!
Do not be [1b]destroyed in her [2]punishment,
For this is the [c]LORD's time of vengeance;
He is going to [d]render recompense to her.

42 [a]Jer 6:23 [b]Is 13:17, 18; 47:6 [c]Is 5:30 [d]Jer 8:16; 47:3; Hab 1:8 [e]Jer 50:9, 14; Joel 2:5

43 [a]Jer 51:31 [b]Jer 30:6; 49:24

44 [1]Lit *pride* [2]Or *an enduring habitation* [a]Jer 49:19-21 [b]Num 16:5 [c]Is 46:9 [d]Job 41:10; Jer 30:21

45 [1]Or *habitation* [a]Ps 33:11; Is 14:24; Jer 51:10, 11 [b]Jer 49:20

46 [1]Lit *voice* [a]Jer 10:10; 49:21; Ezek 26:18; 31:16 [b]Is 5:7; 15:5; Jer 46:12; 51:54; Ezek 27:28

51:1 [1]Cryptic name for Chaldea; or *the heart of those who rise up against Me* [2]Or *a destroying wind* [a]Jer 4:11, 12; 23:19; Hos 13:15

2 [1]Some versions read *winnowers* [a]Is 41:16; Jer 15:7; Matt 3:12

3 [1]M.T. reads *Against him who* [2]I.e. the Chaldean defender [3]Lit *tread(s)* (in order to string) [a]Jer 50:14, 29 [b]Jer 46:4

4 [1]Or *wounded* [a]Is 13:15; 14:19; Jer 49:26; 50:30, 37

5 [1]Lit *widowed* [2]Lit *From* [a]Is 54:7, 8; Jer 33:24-26 [b]Hos 4:1, 2

6 [1]Or *silenced* or *made lifeless* [2]Or *penalty for iniquity* [a]Jer 50:8, 28; Rev 18:4 [b]Num 16:26 [c]Jer 50:15 [d]Jer 25:14

7 Babylon has been a golden [a]cup in the hand of the LORD,
Intoxicating all the earth.
The [b]nations have drunk of her wine;
Therefore the nations are [c]going mad.
8 Suddenly [a]Babylon has fallen and been broken;
[b]Wail over her!
[c]Bring [1]balm for her pain;
Perhaps she may be healed.
9 We applied healing to Babylon, but she was not healed;
Forsake her and [a]let us each go to his own country,
For her judgment has [b]reached to heaven
And [1]towers up to the very skies.
10 The LORD has [a]brought [1]about our vindication;
Come and let us [b]recount in Zion
The work of the LORD our God!

11 [a]Sharpen the arrows, fill the quivers!
The LORD has aroused the spirit of the kings of the Medes,
Because His purpose is against Babylon to destroy it;
For it is the [b]vengeance of the LORD, vengeance for
His temple.
12 [a]Lift up a [1]signal against the walls of Babylon;
Post a strong guard,
Station [2]sentries,
Place men in ambush!
For the LORD has both [b]purposed and performed
What He spoke concerning the inhabitants of Babylon.
13 O you who [a]dwell by many waters,
Abundant in [b]treasures,
Your end has come,
The [1]measure of your [2c]end.
14 The [a]LORD of hosts has sworn by Himself:
"Surely I will fill you with a [1]population like [b]locusts,
And they will cry out with [2]shouts of victory over you."

15 *It is* [a]He who made the earth by His power,
Who established the world by His wisdom,
And by His understanding He [b]stretched out the heavens.
16 When He utters His [a]voice, *there is* a tumult of waters in
the heavens,
And He causes the [b]clouds to ascend from the end
of the earth;
He makes lightning for the rain
And brings forth the [c]wind from His storehouses.
17 [a]All mankind is stupid, devoid of knowledge;
Every goldsmith is put to shame by his [1]idols,
For his molten images are [b]deceitful,
And there is no breath in them.
18 They are [a]worthless, a work of mockery;
In the time of their punishment they will perish.

7 [a]Jer 25:15; Hab 2:16; Rev 14:8; 17:4 [b]Rev 14:8; 18:3 [c]Jer 25:16

8 [1]Or *balsam resin* [a]Is 21:9; Jer 50:2; Rev 14:8; 18:2 [b]Is 13:6; Rev 18:9 [c]Jer 46:11

9 [1]Lit *is lifted* [a]Is 13:14; Jer 46:16; 50:16 [b]Ezra 9:6; Rev 18:5

10 [1]Lit *forth* [a]Ps 37:6; Mic 7:9 [b]Is 40:2; Jer 50:28

11 [a]Jer 46:4, 9; Joel 3:9, 10 [b]Jer 50:28

12 [1]Or *standard* [2]Or *watchmen* [a]Is 13:2; Jer 50:2; 51:27 [b]Jer 4:28; 23:20; 51:29

13 [1]Lit *cubit* [2]Lit *being cut off* [a]Rev 17:1 [b]Is 45:3 [c]Is 57:17; Hab 2:9-11

14 [1]Or *mankind* [2]I.e. like the song of grape treaders [a]Jer 49:13 [b]Jer 51:27; Nah 3:15

15 [a]Gen 1:1; Jer 10:12-16; 51:15-19 [b]Job 9:8; Ps 146:5, 6; Jer 32:17; Acts 14:15; Rom 1:20

16 [a]Job 37:2-6; Ps 18:13 [b]Ps 135:7; Jer 10:13 [c]Jon 1:4

17 [1]Or *graven images* [a]Is 44:18-20; Jer 10:14 [b]Hab 2:18, 19

18 [a]Jer 18:15

19 The [a]portion of Jacob is not like these;
For the [1]Maker of all is He,
And of the [2]tribe of His inheritance;
The [b]LORD of hosts is His name.
20 *He says,* "You are My [1a]war-club, *My* weapon of war;
And with you I [b]shatter nations,
And with you I destroy kingdoms.
21 "With you I [a]shatter the horse and his rider,
And with you I shatter the [b]chariot and its rider,
22 And with you I shatter [a]man and woman,
And with you I shatter old man and [b]youth,
And with you I shatter young man and virgin,
23 And with you I shatter the shepherd and his flock,
And with you I shatter the farmer and his team,
And with you I shatter governors and prefects.
24 "But I will repay Babylon and all the inhabitants of [a]Chaldea
for [b]all their evil that they have done in Zion before your eyes,"
declares the LORD.
25 "Behold, [a]I am against you, [b]O destroying mountain,
Who destroys the whole earth," declares the LORD,
"And I will stretch out My hand against you,
And roll you down from the crags,
And I will make you a [c]burnt out mountain.
26 "They will not take from you *even* a stone for a corner
Nor a stone for foundations,
But you will be [a]desolate forever," declares the LORD.

27 [a]Lift up a [1]signal in the land,
Blow a trumpet among the nations!
Consecrate the nations against her,
Summon against her the [b]kingdoms of [c]Ararat, Minni
and [d]Ashkenaz;
Appoint a marshal against her,
Bring up the [e]horses like bristly locusts.
28 Consecrate the nations against her,
The kings of the Medes,
[1]Their governors and all [1]their [2]prefects,
And every land of [3]their dominion.
29 So the [a]land quakes and writhes,
For the purposes of the LORD against Babylon stand,
To make the land of Babylon
[1]A [b]desolation without inhabitants.
30 The [a]mighty men of Babylon have ceased fighting,
They stay in the strongholds;
[b]Their strength is [1]exhausted,
They are becoming [b]*like* women;
Their dwelling places are set on fire,
The [c]bars of her *gates* are broken.
31 One [1a]courier runs to meet [1]another,
And one [2b]messenger to meet [2]another,

19 [1]Lit *Fashioner* [2]Or *Scepter;* cf Num 24:17 [a]Ps 73:26; Jer 10:16 [b]Jer 50:34

20 [1]Lit *shatterer* [a]Is 10:5; 41:15, 16; Jer 50:23 [b]Is 8:9; 41:15, 16; Mic 4:12, 13

21 [a]Ex 15:1 [b]Ex 15:4; Is 43:17

22 [a]2 Chr 36:17; Is 13:15, 16 [b]Is 13:18

24 [a]Jer 50:10 [b]Jer 50:15, 29

25 [a]Jer 50:31 [b]Is 13:2; Zech 4:7 [c]Rev 8:8

26 [a]Is 13:19-22; Jer 50:13; 51:29

27 [1]Or *standard* [a]Is 13:2-5; 18:3; Jer 50:2; 51:12 [b]Jer 50:3, 9 [c]Gen 8:4; 2 Kin 19:37; Is 37:38 [d]Gen 10:3 [e]Jer 50:42

28 [1]Lit *Her* [2]I.e. lieutenant governors [3]Lit *his*

29 [1]Or *An object of horror* [a]Jer 8:16; 10:10; 50:46; Amos 8:8 [b]Is 13:19, 20; 47:11; Jer 50:13; 51:26, 43

30 [1]Lit *dried up* [a]Ps 76:5; Jer 50:15, 36, 37 [b]Is 13:7, 8; Nah 3:13 [c]Is 45:1, 2; Lam 2:9; Amos 1:5; Nah 3:13

31 [1]Lit *runner* [2]Lit *announcer* [a]2 Chr 30:6 [b]2 Sam 18:19-31

To tell the king of Babylon
That his city has been captured from end *to end;*
32 The fords also have been seized,
And they have burned the marshes with fire,
And the men of war are terrified.

33 For thus says the LORD of hosts, the God of Israel:
"The daughter of Babylon is like a [a]threshing floor
At the time [1]it is stamped firm;
Yet in a little while the time of [b]harvest will come for her."

34 "Nebuchadnezzar king of Babylon has [a]devoured me
and crushed me,
He has set me down *like* an [b]empty vessel;
He has [c]swallowed me like a monster,
He has filled his stomach with my delicacies;
He has washed me away.
35 "May the [a]violence *done* to me and to my flesh be
upon Babylon,"
The [1]inhabitant of Zion will say;
And, "May my blood be upon the inhabitants
of Chaldea,"
Jerusalem will say.
36 Therefore thus says the LORD,
"Behold, I am going to [a]plead your case
And [b]exact full vengeance for you;
And [c]I will dry up her [1]sea
And make her fountain dry.
37 "[a]Babylon will become a heap *of ruins,* a haunt of jackals,
An [b]object of horror and hissing, without inhabitants.
38 "They will roar together like [a]young lions,
They will growl like lions' cubs.
39 "When they become heated up, I will serve *them* their
banquet
And [a]make them drunk, that they may become jubilant
And may [b]sleep a perpetual sleep
And not wake up," declares the LORD.
40 "I will bring them down like [1]lambs [a]to the slaughter,
Like rams together with male goats.

41 "How [1a]Sheshak has been captured,
And [b]the praise of the whole earth been seized!
How Babylon has become an object of horror among
the nations!
42 "The [1a]sea has come up over Babylon;
She has been engulfed with its tumultuous waves.
43 "Her cities have become an [a]object of horror,
A parched land and a desert,
A land in which [b]no man lives
And through which no son of man passes.

33 [1]Lit *of treading it* [a]Is 21:10; 41:15, 16; Mic 4:13 [b]Is 17:5; Hos 6:11; Joel 3:13; Rev 14:15

34 [a]Jer 50:17 [b]Is 24:1-3 [c]Job 20:15; Jer 51:44

35 [1]Lit *inhabitress* [a]Ps 137:8

36 [1]Or *broad river* [a]Ps 140:12 [b]Jer 51:6, 11; Rom 12:19 [c]Jer 50:38

37 [a]Rev 18:2 [b]Jer 25:9

38 [a]Jer 2:15

39 [a]Jer 25:27; 48:26; 51:57 [b]Ps 76:5

40 [1]Or *young rams* [a]Jer 48:15; 50:27

41 [1]Cryptic name for Babylon [a]Jer 25:26 [b]Jer 49:25

42 [1]Or *broad river* [a]Is 8:7, 8; Jer 51:55; Dan 9:26

43 [a]Jer 50:12 [b]Is 13:20; Jer 2:6

44 [a]Is 46:1; Jer 50:2 [b]Ezra 1:7, 8 [c]Is 2:2 [d]Jer 50:15; 51:58
45 [a]Is 48:20; Jer 50:8, 28; 51:6; Rev 18:4 [b]Gen 19:12-16; Acts 2:40
46 [1]Lit *in the* [2]Lit *the* [a]Is 43:5; Jer 46:27, 28 [b]2 Kin 19:7; Is 13:3-5 [c]Is 19:2
47 [a]Is 21:9; 46:1, 2; Jer 50:2; 51:52 [b]Jer 50:12, 35-37
48 [a]Is 44:23; 48:20; 49:13; Rev 18:20 [b]Jer 50:3
49 [a]Ps 137:8; Jer 50:29 [b]Rev 18:24
50 [1]Lit *come upon your heart* [a]Jer 44:28 [b]Deut 4:29-31; Ps 137:6
51 [a]Ps 44:15 [b]Ps 74:3-8; Lam 1:10
52 [a]Jer 50:38
53 [1]Lit *the height of her strength* [a]Gen 11:4; Job 20:6; Ps 139:8-10; Is 14:12-14; Jer 49:16; Amos 9:2; Obad 4 [b]Is 13:3
54 [a]Jer 48:3-5; 50:22, 46
55 [1]Or *voice* [2]Lit *is given* [a]Ps 18:4; 69:2; 124:2, 4, 5; Jer 51:42

44 "[a]I will punish Bel in Babylon,
And I will make what he has swallowed [b]come out of his mouth;
And the nations will no longer [c]stream to him.
Even the [d]wall of Babylon has fallen down!

45 "[a]Come forth from her midst, My people,
And each of you [b]save yourselves
From the fierce anger of the LORD.
46 "Now [a]so that your heart does not grow faint,
And you are not afraid at the [b]report that *will be* heard in the land—
For the report will come [1]one year,
And after that [2]another report in [2]another year,
And violence *will be* in the land
With [c]ruler against ruler—
47 Therefore behold, days are coming
When I will punish the [a]idols of Babylon;
And her whole land will be [b]put to shame
And all her slain will fall in her midst.
48 "Then [a]heaven and earth and all that is in them
Will shout for joy over Babylon,
For [b]the destroyers will come to her from the north,"
Declares the LORD.

49 [a]Indeed Babylon is to fall *for* the slain of Israel,
As also for Babylon [b]the slain of all the earth have fallen.
50 You [a]who have escaped the sword,
Depart! Do not stay!
[b]Remember the LORD from afar,
And let Jerusalem [1]come to your mind.
51 [a]We are ashamed because we have heard reproach;
Disgrace has covered our faces,
For [b]aliens have entered
The holy places of the LORD'S house.

52 "Therefore behold, the days are coming,"
declares the LORD,
"When I will punish her [a]idols,
And the mortally wounded will groan throughout her land.
53 "Though Babylon should [a]ascend to the heavens,
And though she should fortify [1]her lofty stronghold,
From [b]Me destroyers will come to her," declares the LORD.

54 The [a]sound of an outcry from Babylon,
And of great destruction from the land of the Chaldeans!
55 For the LORD is going to destroy Babylon,
And He will make *her* loud [1]noise vanish from her.
And their [a]waves will roar like many waters;
The tumult of their voices [2]sounds forth.

56 For the [a]destroyer is coming against her, against Babylon,
And her mighty men will be captured,
Their [b]bows are shattered;
For the LORD is a God of [c]recompense,
He will fully repay.
57 "I will [a]make her princes and her wise men drunk,
Her governors, her prefects and her mighty men,
That they may sleep a [b]perpetual sleep and not wake up,"
[c]Declares the King, whose name is the LORD of hosts.
58 Thus says the LORD of hosts,
"The broad [a]wall of Babylon will be completely razed
And her high [b]gates will be set on fire;
So the peoples will [c]toil for nothing,
And the nations become [d]exhausted *only* for fire."
59 The [1]message which Jeremiah the prophet commanded
Seraiah the son of [a]Neriah, the grandson of Mahseiah, when he
went with [b]Zedekiah the king of Judah to Babylon in the fourth
year of his reign. (Now Seraiah was quartermaster.)
60 So Jeremiah [a]wrote in a single [1]scroll all the calamity which
would come upon Babylon, *that is,* all these words which have
been written concerning Babylon.
61 Then Jeremiah said to Seraiah, "As soon as you come to
Babylon, then see that you read all these words aloud,
62 and say, 'You, O LORD, have [1]promised concerning this place
to [a]cut it off, so that there will be [b]nothing dwelling in it,
[2]whether man or beast, but it will be a perpetual desolation.'
63 "And as soon as you finish reading this [1]scroll, you will tie a
stone to it and [a]throw it into the middle of the Euphrates,
64 and say, 'Just so shall Babylon sink down and [a]not rise
again because of the calamity that I am going to bring upon
her; and they will become [b]exhausted.'" [c]Thus far are the
words of Jeremiah.

Chapter 52 Theme ______________________

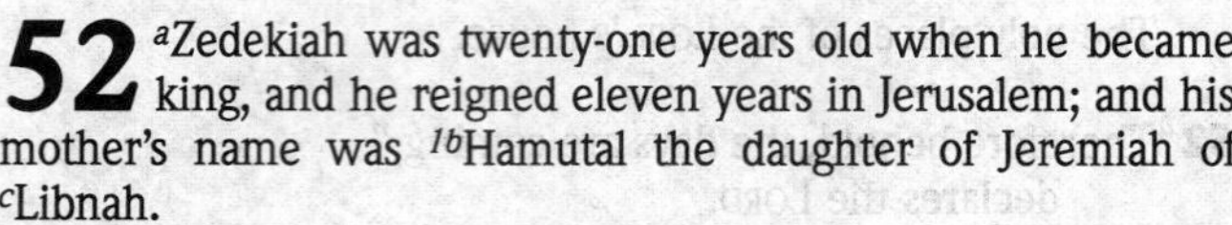

52 [a]Zedekiah was twenty-one years old when he became
king, and he reigned eleven years in Jerusalem; and his
mother's name was [1b]Hamutal the daughter of Jeremiah of
[c]Libnah.

2 He did [a]evil in the sight of the LORD like all that [b]Jehoiakim
had done.
3 For through the [a]anger of the LORD *this* came about in
Jerusalem and Judah until He cast them out from His presence.
And Zedekiah [b]rebelled against the king of Babylon.
4 [a]Now it came about in the ninth year of his reign, on the
tenth *day* of the tenth month, that Nebuchadnezzar king of
Babylon came, he and all his army, against Jerusalem, camped
against it and built a [b]siege wall all around [1]it.
5 [a]So the city was under siege until the eleventh year of King
Zedekiah.
6 On the ninth *day* of the [a]fourth month the [b]famine was so
severe in the city that there was no food for the people of the land.

56 [a]Jer 51:48, 53; Hab 2:8 [b]Ps 46:9; 76:3 [c]Deut 32:35; Ps 94:1, 2; Jer 51:6, 24

57 [a]Jer 25:27 [b]Ps 76:5, 6 [c]Jer 46:18; 48:15

58 [a]Jer 50:15 [b]Is 45:1, 2 [c]Hab 2:13 [d]Jer 9:5; 51:64; Lam 5:5

59 [1]Lit *word* [a]Jer 32:12; 36:4; 45:1 [b]Jer 28:1; 52:1

60 [1]Or *book* [a]Is 30:8; Jer 30:2, 3; 36:2, 4, 32

62 [1]Lit *spoken* [2]Lit *from man even to beast* [a]Is 13:19-22; 14:22, 23; Jer 50:3, 13, 39, 40 [b]Jer 51:43; Ezek 35:9

63 [1]Or *book* [a]Jer 19:10, 11; Rev 18:21

64 [a]Nah 1:8, 9 [b]Jer 51:58 [c]Job 31:40; Ps 72:20

52:1 [1]Another reading is *Hamital* [a]2 Kin 24:18; 2 Chr 36:11 [b]2 Kin 23:31; 24:18 [c]Josh 10:29; 2 Kin 8:22; Is 37:8

2 [a]1 Kin 14:22; 2 Kin 24:19; 2 Chr 36:12 [b]Jer 36:30, 31

3 [a]2 Kin 24:20; Is 3:1, 4, 5 [b]2 Chr 36:13; Ezek 17:12-16

4 [1]Lit *against it* [a]2 Kin 25:1; Jer 39:1; Ezek 24:1, 2; Zech 8:19 [b]Jer 32:24

5 [a]2 Kin 25:2

6 [a]Jer 39:2 [b]2 Kin 25:3; Is 3:1; Jer 38:9; Ezek 4:16; 5:16; 14:13

7 Then the city was [a]broken into, and all the [b]men of war
fled and went forth from the city at night by way of the gate
between the two walls which *was* by the king's garden, though
the Chaldeans were [1c]all around the city. And they went by
way of the Arabah.
8 But the army of the Chaldeans pursued the king and
[a]overtook Zedekiah in the [1]plains of Jericho, and all his army
was scattered from him.
9 Then they captured the king and [a]brought him up to the
king of Babylon at [b]Riblah in the land of [c]Hamath, and he
[1]passed sentence on him.
10 The king of Babylon [a]slaughtered the sons of Zedekiah
before his eyes, and he also slaughtered all the [1]princes of
Judah in Riblah.
11 Then he [a]blinded the eyes of Zedekiah; and the king of
Babylon bound him with bronze fetters and brought him to
Babylon and put him in prison until the day of his death.
12 [a]Now on the tenth *day* of the fifth month, which was the
[b]nineteenth year of King Nebuchadnezzar, king of Babylon,
[c]Nebuzaradan the captain of the bodyguard, [1]who was in the
service of the king of Babylon, came to Jerusalem.
13 He [a]burned the house of the LORD, the [b]king's house and all
the houses of Jerusalem; even every large house he burned
with fire.
14 So all the army of the Chaldeans who *were* with the captain
of the guard [a]broke down all the walls around Jerusalem.
15 Then Nebuzaradan the captain of the guard [a]carried away
into exile some of the poorest of the people, the rest of the
people who were left in the city, the [1b]deserters who had
deserted to the king of Babylon and the rest of the artisans.
16 But [a]Nebuzaradan the captain of the guard left some of the
poorest of the land to be vinedressers and [1]plowmen.
17 Now the bronze [a]pillars which belonged to the house of the
LORD and the [b]stands and the bronze [c]sea, which were in the
house of the LORD, the Chaldeans broke in pieces and carried
all their bronze to Babylon.
18 They also took away the [a]pots, the shovels, the snuffers,
the basins, the [1]pans and all the bronze vessels which were
used in *temple* service.
19 The captain of the guard also took away the [a]bowls, the
firepans, the basins, the pots, the lampstands, the [1]pans and the
drink offering bowls, what was fine gold and what was fine silver.
20 The two pillars, the one sea, and the twelve bronze bulls
that were under [1]the sea, *and* the stands, which King Solomon
had made for the house of the LORD—the bronze of all these
vessels was [a]beyond weight.
21 As for the pillars, the [a]height of each pillar *was* eighteen
[1]cubits, and [2]it *was* twelve cubits in [a]circumference and four
fingers in thickness, *and* hollow.
22 Now a [a]capital of bronze was on it; and the height of each
capital was five cubits, with network and [b]pomegranates upon

7 [1]Lit *against the city on every side* [a]2 Kin 25:4; Jer 39:2 [b]Jer 39:4-7; 51:32 [c]Ezek 33:21

8 [1]Lit *Arabah* [a]Jer 21:7; 32:4; 34:21; 37:17; 38:23

9 [1]Lit *spoke judgments with* [a]2 Kin 25:6; Jer 32:4; 39:5 [b]Num 34:11; Jer 39:5 [c]Num 13:21; Josh 13:5

10 [1]Or *commanders* [a]2 Kin 25:7; Jer 22:30; 39:6

11 [a]Jer 39:7; Ezek 12:13

12 [1]Lit *stood before the king* [a]2 Kin 25:8-21; Zech 7:5; 8:19 [b]2 Kin 24:12; 25:8; Jer 52:29 [c]Jer 39:9

13 [a]1 Kin 9:8; 2 Kin 25:9; 2 Chr 36:19; Ps 74:6-8; 79:1; Is 64:10, 11; Lam 2:7; Mic 3:12 [b]Jer 39:8

14 [a]2 Kin 25:10; Neh 1:3

15 [1]Lit *fallers who had fallen* [a]2 Kin 25:11 [b]Jer 39:9

16 [1]Or *unpaid laborers* [a]2 Kin 25:12; Jer 39:10; 40:2-6

17 [a]1 Kin 7:15-22; 2 Kin 25:13; Jer 27:19-22; 52:20-23 [b]1 Kin 7:27-37 [c]1 Kin 7:23-26

18 [1]Or *spoons* for incense [a]Ex 27:3; 1 Kin 7:40, 45; 2 Kin 25:14

19 [1]Or *spoons* for incense [a]1 Kin 7:49, 50; 2 Kin 25:15

20 [1]So Gr and Syriac; Heb omits *the sea* [a]1 Kin 7:47; 2 Kin 25:16

21 [1]I.e. One cubit equals approx 18 in. [2]Lit *a line of 12 cubits would encircle it* [a]1 Kin 7:15; 2 Kin 25:17; 2 Chr 3:15

22 [a]1 Kin 7:16; 2 Kin 25:17 [b]1 Kin 7:20, 42

the capital all around, all of bronze. And the second pillar was
like these, including pomegranates.
23 There were ninety-six [1]exposed pomegranates; all [a]the
pomegranates *numbered* a hundred on the network all around.
24 Then the captain of the guard took [a]Seraiah the chief priest
and [b]Zephaniah the second priest, with the three [1c]officers of
the temple.
25 He also took from the city one official who was overseer of
the men of war, and seven [1]of the [a]king's advisers who were
found in the city, and the scribe of the commander of the army
who mustered the people of the land, and sixty men of the
people of the land who were found in the midst of the city.
26 Nebuzaradan the captain of the guard took them and
[a]brought them to the king of Babylon at Riblah.
27 Then the king of Babylon [a]struck them down and put them
to death at Riblah in the land of Hamath. So Judah was [b]led
away into exile from its land.
28 These are the people whom [a]Nebuchadnezzar carried away
into exile: in the [1]seventh year 3,023 Jews;
29 in the eighteenth year of Nebuchadnezzar 832 persons
from Jerusalem;
30 in the twenty-third year of Nebuchadnezzar, [a]Nebuzaradan
the captain of the guard carried into exile 745 Jewish people;
there were 4,600 persons in all.
31 [a]Now it came about in the thirty-seventh year of the exile
of Jehoiachin king of Judah, in the twelfth month, on the
twenty-fifth of the month, that [1]Evil-merodach king of Babylon,
in the *first* year of his reign, [2b]showed favor to Jehoiachin king
of Judah and brought him out of prison.
32 [a]Then he spoke kindly to him and set his throne above the
thrones of the kings who *were* with him in Babylon.
33 So [1]Jehoiachin [a]changed his prison clothes, and [2b]had his
meals in [3]the king's presence regularly all the days of his life.
34 For his allowance, a [a]regular allowance was given him by
the king of Babylon, a daily portion all the days of his life until
the day of his death.

23 [1]Lit *windward* [a]1 Kin 7:20

24 [1]Lit *keepers of the door* [a]2 Kin 25:18; 1 Chr 6:14; Ezra 7:1 [b]2 Kin 25:18; Jer 21:1; 29:25, 29; 37:3 [c]1 Chr 9:19; Jer 35:4

25 [1]Lit *men of those seeing the king's face* [a]2 Kin 25:19; Esth 1:14

26 [a]2 Kin 25:20

27 [a]2 Kin 25:21; Ezek 8:11-18 [b]Is 6:11, 12; 27:10; 32:13, 14; Jer 13:19; 20:4; 25:9-11; 39:9; Ezek 33:28; Mic 4:10

28 [1]Or possibly *seventeenth* [a]2 Kin 24:2, 3, 12-16; 2 Chr 36:20; Ezra 2:1; Neh 7:6; Dan 1:1-3

30 [a]2 Kin 25:11; Jer 39:9

31 [1]Or *Awil-Marduk* ("Man of Marduk") [2]Lit *lifted up the head of* [a]2 Kin 25:27 [b]Gen 40:13, 20; Ps 3:3; 27:6

32 [a]2 Kin 25:28

33 [1]Lit *he* [2]Lit *ate* [3]Lit *his presence* [a]Gen 41:14, 42; 2 Kin 25:29 [b]2 Sam 9:7, 13; 1 Kin 2:7

34 [a]2 Sam 9:10; 2 Kin 25:30

Theme of Jeremiah:

Author:

Date:

Purpose:

Key Words:

- nations
- word(s) (when it refers to the word of the Lord)
- destroy (pluck, uproot)
- plant (build, restore)
- listen (hear)
- return (repent, turn)
- wickedness (sin, iniquity, wicked)
- heart
- forsaken (forsake)
- heal (healing, healed)
- covenant
- concerning
- north
- Babylon (Chaldeans from chapter 20 on)
- calamity (wrath)
- woe
- famine

SEGMENT DIVISIONS		CHAPTER THEMES
		1
		2
		3
		4
		5
		6
		7
		8
		9
		10
		11
		12
		13
		14
		15
		16
		17
		18
		19
		20
		21
		22
		23
		24
		25
		26

Segment Divisions

		Chapter Themes
		27
		28
		29
		30
		31
		32
		33
		34
		35
		36
		37
		38
		39
		40
		41
		42
		43
		44
		45
		46
		47
		48
		49
		50
		51
		52

LAMENTATIONS איכה EKHA

Lamentations is a book of wailings that are read annually by the Jews as a reminder of the fall of Jerusalem and destruction of the temple. They serve as a reminder of an avoidable tragedy caused by sin—and of a God who judges, but keeps His covenant forever.

These expressions of grief were written sometime between the destruction of Jerusalem and the return of the remnant after 70 years of captivity. Although Judah's plight is desperate, it is not hopeless when the people remember, "The LORD's lovingkindnesses indeed never cease, for His compassions never fail. They are new every morning; great is Your faithfulness" (3:22-23).

THINGS TO DO

1. There are five laments in this book; each begins a new chapter. Lamentations is written as poetry. While the fifth lament has 22 verses, which correspond to the number of letters in the Hebrew alphabet, it is not an acrostic like the other four laments. In those, the acrostic form in Hebrew is the first letter of the first word in each verse (three verses for chapter 3) and follows the letter sequence in the Hebrew alphabet, Aleph through Tav. As you read chapter by chapter, note how each lament begins and who or what the lament centers on.
2. Mark the key words (and their synonyms) listed on LAMENTATIONS AT A GLANCE on page 1315.
3. Note the personification of Jerusalem and Judah. Jerusalem is personified as a woman. The personification is seen in the first lines of Lamentations: "How lonely sits the city… she has become like a widow." List what happened to Jerusalem and why; this is key. Note her emotions, the anguish because of her children, the thoughts and memories she has to deal with.
4. Carefully observe and list what you learn about God, His character, His judgments, and why He acts as He does. For example, 1:5 states that God caused Judah grief because of Judah's sin. God brought about Judah's captivity because of Judah's transgressions.
5. Lamentations gives a more definitive understanding of what took place during the Babylonian siege of Jerusalem. In the margin of the text, list what you learn. For example, 1:10 says the nations entered the sanctuary, the house of God, where only Jewish priests were to go. Verse 11 reveals there was a famine—people were seeking bread and giving away precious things in order to get it. (You saw this if you studied Jeremiah.)
6. Determine the theme of each chapter. Write the theme in your Bible next to each chapter number and on LAMENTATIONS AT A GLANCE.
7. Complete LAMENTATIONS AT A GLANCE.

THINGS TO THINK ABOUT

1. What would happen if we considered our future—if we weighed the consequences of our actions—before we acted?
2. God's judgment can take many forms. The sovereign God rules. None can stay His hand or say to Him, "What have You done?" for He does according to His will in the army of heaven and among the inhabitants of the earth (Daniel 4:34-35). Do you think you can sin and go unchastened by God? Judgment must begin at the house of God. Look at 1 Corinthians 11:31-32.
3. Why do you think God deals with sin as He does? How should you respond? Read chapter 3 on your knees so your "dancing" need not be turned into "mourning."

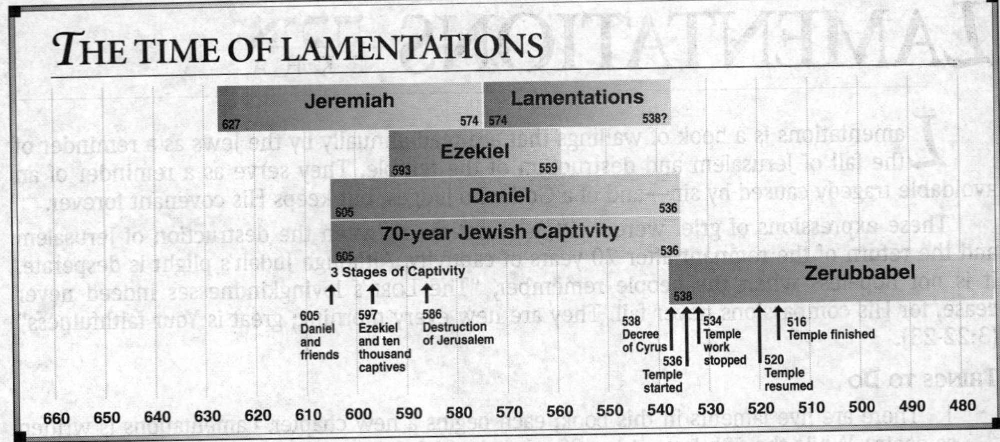

Chapter 1 Theme ______________________

1 How [a]lonely sits the city
That was [b]full of people!
She has become like a [c]widow
Who was *once* [d]great among the nations!
She who was a princess among the [1]provinces
Has become a [e]forced laborer!
2 She [a]weeps bitterly in the night
And her tears are on her cheeks;
She has none to comfort her
Among all her [b]lovers.
All her friends have [c]dealt treacherously with her;
They have become her enemies.
3 [a]Judah has gone into exile [1]under affliction
And [1]under [2]harsh servitude;
She dwells [b]among the nations,
But she has found no rest;
All [c]her pursuers have overtaken her
In the midst of [3]distress.
4 The roads [1]of Zion are in mourning
Because [a]no one comes to the appointed feasts.
All her gates are [b]desolate;
Her priests are groaning,
Her [c]virgins are afflicted,
And she herself [2]is [d]bitter.
5 Her adversaries have become [1]her masters,
Her enemies [2]prosper;
For the LORD has [a]caused her grief
Because of the multitude of her transgressions;
Her little ones have gone away
As captives before the adversary.

1:1 [1]Or *districts* [a]Is 3:26 [b]Is 22:2 [c]Is 54:4 [d]1 Kin 4:21; Ezra 4:20; Jer 31:7 [e]2 Kin 23:35; Jer 40:9

2 [a]Ps 6:6; 77:2-6; Lam 1:16 [b]Jer 2:25; 3:1; 22:20-22 [c]Job 19:13, 14; Ps 31:11; Mic 7:5

3 [1]Or *by reason of* [2]Lit *great* [3]Or *narrow places* [a]Jer 13:19 [b]Lev 26:39; Deut 28:64-67 [c]2 Kin 25:4, 5

4 [1]Or *to* [2]Or *suffers bitterly* [a]Is 24:4-6; Lam 2:6, 7 [b]Jer 9:11; 10:22 [c]Lam 2:10, 21 [d]Joel 1:8-13

5 [1]Lit *head* [2]Or *are at ease* [a]Ps 90:7, 8; Ezek 8:17, 18; 9:9, 10

6 All her [a]majesty
Has departed from the daughter of Zion;
Her princes have become like deer
That have found no pasture;
And they have [1b]fled without strength
Before the pursuer.
7 In the days of her affliction and homelessness
[a]Jerusalem remembers all her precious things
That were from the days of old,
When her people fell into the hand of the adversary
And [b]no one helped her.
The adversaries saw her,
They [c]mocked at her [1]ruin.
8 Jerusalem sinned [a]greatly,
Therefore [b]she has become an unclean thing.
All who honored her despise her
Because they have seen her nakedness;
Even [c]she herself groans and turns away.
9 Her [a]uncleanness was in her skirts;
She [1]did not consider her [b]future.
Therefore she has [2c]fallen astonishingly;
[d]She has no comforter.
"[e]See, O LORD, my affliction,
For the enemy has [f]magnified himself!"
10 The adversary has stretched out his hand
Over all her precious things,
For she has seen the [a]nations enter her sanctuary,
The ones whom You commanded
That they should [b]not enter into Your congregation.
11 All her people groan [a]seeking bread;
They have given their precious things for food
To [b]restore their [1]lives themselves.
"See, O LORD, and look,
For I am [c]despised."
12 "Is [a]it nothing to all you who pass this way?
Look and see if there is any [1]pain like my [1]pain
Which was severely dealt out to me,
Which the [b]LORD inflicted on the day of His
[c]fierce anger.
13 "From on high He sent fire into my [a]bones,
And it [1]prevailed *over them.*
He has spread a [b]net for my feet;
He has turned me back;
He has made me [c]desolate,
[2]Faint all day long.
14 "The [a]yoke of my transgressions is bound;
By His hand they are knit together.
They have [b]come upon my neck;
He has made my strength [1]fail.
The Lord [c]has given me into the hands
Of *those against whom* I am not able to stand.

6 [1]Lit *gone* [a]Jer 13:18 [b]2 Kin 25:4, 5

7 [1]Lit *cessation* [a]Ps 42:4; 77:5-9 [b]Jer 37:7; Lam 4:17 [c]Ps 79:4; Jer 48:27

8 [a]Is 59:2-13; Lam 1:5, 20 [b]Lam 1:17 [c]Lam 1:11, 21, 22

9 [1]Lit *did not remember her latter end* [2]Lit *come down* [a]Jer 2:34; Ezek 24:13 [b]Deut 32:29; Is 47:7 [c]Is 3:8; Jer 13:17, 18 [d]Eccl 4:1; Jer 16:7 [e]Ps 25:18; 119:153 [f]Ps 74:23; Zeph 2:10

10 [a]Ps 74:4-8; Is 64:10, 11; Jer 51:51 [b]Deut 23:3

11 [1]Lit *soul* [a]Jer 38:9; 52:6 [b]1 Sam 30:12 [c]Jer 15:19

12 [1]Or *sorrow* [a]Jer 18:16; 48:27 [b]Jer 30:23, 24 [c]Is 13:13; Jer 4:8

13 [1]Or *descended, overthrew* [2]Or *Sick* [a]Job 30:30; Ps 22:14; Hab 3:16 [b]Job 19:6; Ps 66:11 [c]Jer 44:6

14 [1]Lit *stumble* [a]Prov 5:22; Is 47:6 [b]Jer 28:13, 14 [c]Jer 32:3, 5; Ezek 25:4, 7

15 "The [a]Lord has rejected all my strong men
In my midst;
He has called an appointed [1]time against me
To crush my [b]young men;
The Lord has [c]trodden *as in* a wine press
The virgin daughter of Judah.
16 "For these things I [a]weep;
[1]My eyes run down with water;
Because far from me is a [b]comforter,
One who restores my soul.
My children are desolate
Because the enemy has prevailed."
17 Zion [a]stretches out her hands;
There is no one to comfort her;
The LORD has [b]commanded concerning Jacob
That the ones round about him should be
his adversaries;
[c]Jerusalem has become an unclean thing among them.
18 "The LORD is [a]righteous;
For I have [b]rebelled against His [1]command;
Hear now, all peoples,
And [c]behold my [2]pain;
[d]My virgins and my young men
Have gone into captivity.
19 "I [a]called to my lovers, *but* they deceived me;
My [b]priests and my elders perished in the city
While they sought food to [c]restore [1]their strength
themselves.
20 "See, O LORD, for I am in distress;
My [1a]spirit is greatly troubled;
My heart is overturned within me,
For I have been very [b]rebellious.
In the street the sword [2]slays;
In the house it is like death.
21 "They have heard that I [a]groan;
There is no one to comfort me;
All my enemies have heard of my [1]calamity;
They are [b]glad that You have done *it*.
Oh, that You would bring the day which You have
proclaimed,
That they may become [c]like me.
22 "Let all their wickedness come before You;
And [a]deal with them as You have dealt with me
For all my transgressions;
For my groans are many and my heart is faint."

Chapter 2 Theme ____________________

2 How the Lord has [a]covered the daughter of Zion
With a cloud in His anger!
He has [b]cast from heaven to earth

15 [1]Or *feast* [a]Is 41:2; Jer 13:24; 37:10 [b]Jer 6:11; 18:21 [c]Mal 4:3

16 [1]Lit *My eye, my eye* [a]Jer 14:17; Lam 2:11, 18; 3:48, 49 [b]Ps 69:20; Eccl 4:1; Lam 1:2

17 [a]Is 1:15; Jer 4:31 [b]2 Kin 24:2-4; Jer 12:9 [c]Lam 1:8

18 [1]Lit *mouth* [2]Or *sorrow* [a]Ps 119:75; Jer 12:1 [b]1 Sam 12:14, 15; Jer 4:17 [c]Lam 1:12 [d]Deut 28:32, 41

19 [1]Lit *their soul* [a]Job 19:13-19; Lam 1:2 [b]Jer 14:15; Lam 2:20 [c]Lam 1:11

20 [1]Lit *inward parts are in ferment* [2]Lit *bereaves* [a]Is 16:11; Lam 2:11 [b]Jer 14:20

21 [1]Lit *evil* [a]Lam 1:4, 8, 22 [b]Ps 35:15; Jer 50:11; Lam 2:15 [c]Is 14:5, 6; 47:6, 11; Jer 30:16

22 [a]Neh 4:4, 5; Ps 137:7, 8

2:1 [a]Ezek 30:18 [b]Is 14:12-15; Ezek 28:14-16

The [c]glory of Israel,
And has not remembered His [d]footstool
In the day of His anger.
2 The Lord has [a]swallowed up; He has not spared
All the habitations of Jacob.
In His wrath He has [b]thrown down
The strongholds of the daughter of Judah;
He has [c]brought *them* down to the ground;
He has [d]profaned the kingdom and its princes.
3 In fierce anger He has cut off
[1]All the [a]strength of Israel;
He has [b]drawn back His right hand
From before the enemy.
And He has [c]burned in Jacob like a flaming fire
Consuming round about.
4 He has bent His [a]bow like an enemy;
He has set His right hand like an adversary
And slain all that were [b]pleasant to the eye;
In the tent of the daughter of Zion
He has [c]poured out His wrath like fire.
5 The Lord has become like an [a]enemy.
He has [b]swallowed up Israel;
He has swallowed up all its [c]palaces,
He has destroyed its strongholds
And [d]multiplied in the daughter of Judah
Mourning and moaning.
6 And He has violently treated His [1]tabernacle like
a garden *booth;*
He has [a]destroyed His appointed [2]meeting place.
The LORD has [b]caused to be forgotten
The appointed feast and sabbath in Zion,
And He has [c]despised king and priest
In the indignation of His anger.
7 The Lord has [a]rejected His altar,
He has abandoned His sanctuary;
He [b]has delivered into the hand of the enemy
The walls of her palaces.
They have made a [c]noise in the house of the LORD
As in the day of an appointed feast.
8 The LORD [1]determined to destroy
The wall of the daughter of Zion.
He has [a]stretched out a line,
He has not restrained His hand from [2]destroying,
And He has [b]caused rampart and wall to lament;
They have languished together.
9 Her [a]gates have sunk into the ground,
He has destroyed and broken her bars.
Her king and her princes are among the nations;
The [b]law is no more.
Also, her prophets find
[c]No vision from the LORD.

1 [c]Is 64:11 [d]Ps 99:5; 132:7

2 [a]Ps 21:9; Lam 3:43 [b]Lam 2:5; Mic 5:11, 14 [c]Is 25:12; 26:5 [d]Ps 89:39, 40; Is 43:28

3 [1]Lit *Every horn* [a]Ps 75:5, 10; Jer 48:25 [b]Ps 74:11; Jer 21:4, 5 [c]Is 42:25; Jer 21:14

4 [a]Job 6:4; 16:13; Lam 3:12, 13 [b]Ezek 24:25 [c]Is 42:25; Jer 7:20

5 [a]Jer 30:14 [b]Lam 2:2 [c]Jer 52:13; Lam 2:2 [d]Jer 9:17-20

6 [1]Lit *booth* [2]Or *feast* [a]Jer 52:13 [b]Jer 17:27; Lam 1:4; Zeph 3:18 [c]Lam 4:16

7 [a]Ps 78:59-61; Is 64:11; Ezek 7:20-22 [b]Jer 33:4, 5; 52:13 [c]Ps 74:3-8

8 [1]Lit *thought* [2]Lit *swallowing up* [a]2 Kin 21:13; Is 34:11; Amos 7:7-9 [b]Is 3:26; Jer 14:2

9 [a]Neh 1:3 [b]Hos 3:4 [c]Jer 14:14; 23:16; Ezek 7:26

10 The elders of the daughter of Zion
[a]Sit on the ground, they [b]are silent.
They have thrown [c]dust on their heads;
They have girded themselves with [d]sackcloth.
The [e]virgins of Jerusalem
Have bowed their heads to the ground.
11 My [a]eyes fail because of tears,
My [1b]spirit is greatly troubled;
My [2c]heart is poured out on the earth
[d]Because of the [3]destruction of the daughter of my people,
When [e]little ones and infants faint
In the streets of the city.
12 They say to their mothers,
"[a]Where is grain and wine?"
As they faint like a wounded man
In the streets of the city,
As their [b]life is poured out
On their mothers' bosom.
13 How shall I admonish you?
To what [a]shall I compare you,
O daughter of Jerusalem?
To what shall I liken you as I comfort you,
O [b]virgin daughter of Zion?
For your [1]ruin is as vast as the sea;
Who can [c]heal you?
14 Your [a]prophets have seen for you
False and foolish *visions;*
And they have not [b]exposed your iniquity
So as to restore you from captivity,
But they have [c]seen for you false and misleading [1]oracles.
15 All who pass along the way
[a]Clap their hands *in derision* at you;
They [b]hiss and shake their heads
At the daughter of Jerusalem,
"Is this the city of which they said,
'[c]The perfection of beauty,
[d]A joy to all the earth'?"
16 All [a]your enemies
Have opened their mouths wide against you;
They hiss and [b]gnash *their* teeth.
They say, "We have [c]swallowed *her* up!
Surely this is the [d]day for which we waited;
We have reached *it,* we have seen *it.*"
17 The LORD has [a]done what He purposed;
He has accomplished His word
Which He commanded from days of old.
He has thrown down [b]without sparing,
And He has caused the enemy to [c]rejoice over you;
He has [d]exalted the [1]might of your adversaries.
18 Their [a]heart cried out to the Lord,
"O [b]wall of the daughter of Zion,

10 [a]Job 2:13; Is 3:26; 47:1 [b]Amos 8:3 [c]Job 2:12; Ezek 27:30 [d]Is 15:3; Jon 3:6-8 [e]Lam 1:4

11 [1]Lit *inward parts are in ferment* [2]Lit *liver* [3]Lit *breaking* [a]Lam 1:16; 3:48, 51 [b]Jer 4:19 [c]Job 16:13 [d]Is 22:4; Lam 4:10 [e]Jer 44:7; Lam 2:19

12 [a]Jer 5:17 [b]Job 30:16; Ps 42:4; 62:8

13 [1]Lit *breaking* [a]Lam 1:12 [b]Is 37:22 [c]Jer 8:22; 30:12-15

14 [1]Lit *burdens* [a]Jer 23:25-29; 29:8, 9 [b]Is 58:1; Ezek 23:36; Mic 3:8 [c]Jer 23:36; Ezek 22:25, 28

15 [a]Job 27:23; Ezek 25:6 [b]Ps 22:7; Is 37:22; Jer 18:16; 19:8; Zeph 2:15 [c]Ps 50:2 [d]Ps 48:2

16 [a]Job 16:10; Ps 22:13; Lam 3:46 [b]Job 16:9; Ps 35:16; 37:12 [c]Ps 56:2; 124:3; Jer 51:34 [d]Obad 12-15

17 [1]Lit *horn* [a]Jer 4:28 [b]Lam 2:1, 2; Ezek 5:11; 7:8, 9; 8:18 [c]Ps 35:24, 26; 89:42; Is 14:29 [d]Deut 28:43, 44; Lam 1:5

18 [a]Ps 119:145; Hos 7:14 [b]Lam 2:8; Hab 2:11

Let *your* [c]tears run down like a river day and night;
Give yourself no relief,
Let [1]your eyes have no rest.
19 "Arise, cry aloud in the [a]night
At the beginning of the night watches;
[b]Pour out your heart like water
Before the presence of the Lord;
Lift up your hands to Him
For the [c]life of your little ones
Who are [d]faint because of hunger
At the head of every street."
20 See, O LORD, and look!
With [a]whom have You dealt thus?
Should women [b]eat their [1]offspring,
The little ones who were [2]born healthy?
Should [c]priest and prophet be slain
In the sanctuary of the Lord?
21 On the ground in the streets
Lie [a]young and old;
My [b]virgins and my young men
Have fallen by the sword.
You have slain *them* in the day of Your anger,
You have slaughtered, [c]not sparing.
22 You called as in the day of an appointed feast
My [a]terrors on every side;
And there was [b]no one who escaped or survived
In the day of the LORD's anger.
Those [c]whom I [1]bore and reared,
My enemy annihilated them.

Chapter 3 Theme ______________________

3 I am the man who has [a]seen affliction
Because of the rod of His wrath.
2 He has driven me and made me walk
In [a]darkness and not in light.
3 Surely against me He has [a]turned His hand
Repeatedly all the day.
4 He has caused my [a]flesh and my skin to waste away,
He has [b]broken my bones.
5 He has [a]besieged and encompassed me with [b]bitterness
and hardship.
6 In [a]dark places He has made me dwell,
Like those who have long been dead.
7 He has [a]walled me in so that I cannot go out;
He has made my [1b]chain heavy.
8 Even when I cry out and call for help,
He [a]shuts out my prayer.
9 He has [a]blocked my ways with hewn stone;
He has made my paths crooked.
10 He is to me like a bear lying in wait,
Like a lion in secret places.

18 [1]Lit *the daughter of your eye* [c]Ps 119:136; Jer 9:1; Lam 1:2, 16; 3:48, 49

19 [a]Ps 42:3; Is 26:9 [b]1 Sam 1:15; Ps 42:4; 62:8 [c]Lam 2:11 [d]Is 51:20

20 [1]Lit *fruit* [2]Or *tenderly cared for* [a]Ex 32:11; Deut 9:26 [b]Jer 19:9; Lam 4:10 [c]Ps 78:64; Jer 14:15; 23:11, 12

21 [a]2 Chr 36:17; Jer 6:11 [b]Ps 78:62, 63 [c]Jer 13:14; Zech 11:6

22 [1]Lit *bore healthy* or, *tenderly cared for* [a]Ps 31:13; Is 24:17; Jer 6:25 [b]Jer 11:11 [c]Jer 16:2-4; 44:7

3:1 [a]Ps 88:7, 15, 16

2 [a]Job 30:26; Is 59:9; Jer 4:23

3 [a]Ps 38:2; Is 5:25

4 [a]Ps 31:9, 10; 38:2-8; 102:3-5 [b]Ps 51:8; Is 38:13

5 [a]Job 19:8 [b]Jer 23:15; Lam 3:19

6 [a]Ps 88:5, 6; 143:3

7 [1]Lit *bronze piece* [a]Job 3:23; 19:8 [b]Jer 40:4

8 [a]Job 30:20; Ps 22:2

9 [a]Is 63:17; Hos 2:6

11 He has turned aside my ways and [a]torn me to pieces;
He has made me desolate.
12 He [a]bent His bow
And [b]set me as a target for the arrow.
13 He made the [1]arrows of His [a]quiver
To enter into my [2]inward parts.
14 I have become a [a]laughingstock to all my people,
Their *mocking* [b]song all the day.
15 He has [a]filled me with bitterness,
He has made me drunk with wormwood.
16 He has [a]broken my teeth with [b]gravel;
He has made me cower in the [c]dust.
17 My soul has been rejected [a]from peace;
I have forgotten [1]happiness.
18 So I say, "My strength has perished,
And *so has* my [a]hope from the LORD."

19 Remember my affliction and my [1]wandering,
the [a]wormwood and bitterness.
20 Surely [a]my soul remembers
And is [b]bowed down within me.
21 This I recall to my mind,
Therefore I have [a]hope.
22 The LORD's [a]lovingkindnesses [1]indeed never cease,
[b]For His compassions never fail.
23 *They* are new [a]every morning;
Great is [b]Your faithfulness.
24 "The LORD is my [a]portion," says my soul,
"Therefore I [b]have hope in Him."
25 The LORD is good to those who [a]wait for Him,
To the [1]person who [b]seeks Him.
26 *It is* good that he [a]waits silently
For the salvation of the LORD.
27 *It is* good for a man that he should bear
The yoke in his youth.
28 Let him [a]sit alone and be silent
Since He has laid *it* on him.
29 Let him [1]put his mouth in the [a]dust,
Perhaps there is [b]hope.
30 Let him give his [a]cheek to [1]the smiter,
Let him be filled with reproach.
31 For the Lord will [a]not reject forever,
32 For if He causes grief,
Then He will have [a]compassion
According to His abundant lovingkindness.
33 For He [a]does not afflict [1]willingly
Or grieve the sons of men.
34 To crush under His feet
All the prisoners of the [1]land,
35 To [1]deprive a man of [a]justice
In the presence of the Most High,

11 [a]Job 16:12, 13; Jer 15:3; Hos 6:1
12 [a]Ps 7:12; Lam 2:4 [b]Job 6:4; 7:20; Ps 38:2
13 [1]Lit *sons* [2]Lit *kidneys* [a]Jer 5:16
14 [a]Ps 22:6, 7; 123:4; Jer 20:7 [b]Job 30:9; Lam 3:63
15 [a]Jer 9:15
16 [a]Ps 3:7; 58:6 [b]Prov 20:17 [c]Jer 6:26
17 [1]Lit *good* [a]Is 59:11; Jer 12:12
18 [a]Job 17:15; Ezek 37:11
19 [1]Or *bitterness* [a]Jer 9:15; Lam 3:5, 15
20 [a]Job 21:6 [b]Ps 42:5, 6, 11; 43:5; 44:25
21 [a]Ps 130:7
22 [1]Or *that we are not consumed* [a]Ps 78:38; Jer 3:12; 30:11 [b]Mal 3:6
23 [a]Is 33:2; Zeph 3:5 [b]Heb 10:23
24 [a]Ps 16:5; 73:26 [b]Ps 33:18
25 [1]Lit *soul* [a]Ps 27:14; Is 25:9 [b]Is 26:9
26 [a]Ps 37:7
28 [a]Jer 15:17
29 [1]Lit *give* [a]Job 16:15; 40:4 [b]Jer 31:17
30 [1]Lit *his* [a]Job 16:10; Is 50:6
31 [a]Ps 77:7; 94:14; Is 54:7-10
32 [a]Ps 78:38; 106:43-45; Hos 11:8
33 [1]Lit *from His heart* [a]Ps 119:67, 71, 75; Ezek 33:11; Heb 12:10
34 [1]Or *earth*
35 [1]Or *turn aside a man's case* [a]Ps 140:12; Prov 17:15

36 [1]Lit *make crooked* [2]Lit *see* [a]Jer 22:3; Hab 1:13
37 [1]Lit *this* [a]Ps 33:9-11
38 [1]Lit *the evil* things *and the good* [a]Job 2:10; Is 45:7; Jer 32:42
39 [1]Or *human being* [2]Or *on the basis of* [a]Jer 30:15; Mic 7:9; Heb 12:5, 6
40 [a]Ps 119:59; 139:23, 24; 2 Cor 13:5
41 [1]Lit *toward* our [a]Ps 25:1; 28:2; 141:2
42 [a]Neh 9:26; Jer 14:20; Dan 9:5 [b]2 Kin 24:4; Jer 5:7, 9
43 [a]Lam 2:21 [b]Ps 83:15; Lam 3:66 [c]Lam 2:2, 17, 21
44 [a]Ps 97:2 [b]Lam 3:8; Zech 7:13
45 [a]1 Cor 4:13
46 [a]Job 30:9, 10; Ps 22:6-8; Lam 2:16
47 [a]Is 24:17, 18; Jer 48:43, 44
48 [1]Lit *eye brings* [a]Ps 119:136; Jer 9:1, 18; Lam 1:16; 2:11, 18
49 [a]Ps 77:2; Jer 14:17
50 [a]Ps 80:14; Is 63:15; Lam 5:1
52 [a]Ps 35:7, 19 [b]1 Sam 26:20; Ps 11:1; 124:7
53 [1]Lit *my life* [2]Or *cast stones* [a]Jer 37:16; 38:6, 9 [b]Dan 6:17
54 [a]Ps 69:2; Jon 2:3-5
55 [a]Ps 130:1; Jon 2:2
56 [a]Job 34:28 [b]Ps 55:1
57 [a]Ps 145:18 [b]Is 41:10, 14
58 [a]Jer 50:34 [b]Ps 34:22
59 [a]Jer 18:19, 20 [b]Ps 26:1; 43:1

36 To [1a]defraud a man in his lawsuit—
Of these things the Lord does not [2]approve.
37 Who is [1]there who speaks and it [a]comes to pass,
Unless the Lord has commanded *it?*
38 *Is it* not from the mouth of the Most High
That [1a]both good and ill go forth?

39 Why should *any* living [1]mortal, or *any* man,
Offer [a]complaint [2]in view of his sins?
40 Let us [a]examine and probe our ways,
And let us return to the LORD.
41 We [a]lift up our heart [1]and hands
Toward God in heaven;
42 We have [a]transgressed and rebelled,
You have [b]not pardoned.
43 You have covered *Yourself* with [a]anger
And [b]pursued us;
You have slain *and* [c]have not spared.
44 You have [a]covered Yourself with a cloud
So that [b]no prayer can pass through.
45 *You have made us mere* [a]offscouring and refuse
In the midst of the peoples.
46 All our enemies have [a]opened their mouths against us.
47 [a]Panic and pitfall have befallen us,
Devastation and destruction;
48 My [1a]eyes run down with streams of water
Because of the destruction of the daughter
of my people.
49 My eyes pour down [a]unceasingly,
Without stopping,
50 Until the LORD [a]looks down
And sees from heaven.
51 My eyes bring pain to my soul
Because of all the daughters of my city.
52 My enemies [a]without cause
Hunted me down [b]like a bird;
53 They have silenced [1]me [a]in the pit
And have [2b]placed a stone on me.
54 Waters flowed [a]over my head;
I said, "I am cut off!"
55 I [a]called on Your name, O LORD,
Out of the lowest pit.
56 You have [a]heard my voice,
"[b]Do not hide Your ear from my *prayer for* relief,
From my cry for help."
57 You [a]drew near when I called on You;
You said, "[b]Do not fear!"
58 O Lord, You [a]have pleaded my soul's cause;
You have [b]redeemed my life.
59 O LORD, You have [a]seen my oppression;
[b]Judge my case.

60 You have seen all their vengeance,
All their [a]schemes against me.
61 You have heard their [a]reproach, O LORD,
All their schemes against me.
62 The [a]lips of my assailants and their whispering
Are against me all day long.
63 Look on their [a]sitting and their rising;
[b]I am their mocking song.
64 You will [a]recompense them, O LORD,
According to the work of their hands.
65 You will give them [1a]hardness of heart,
Your curse will be on them.
66 You will [a]pursue them in anger and destroy them
From under the [b]heavens of the LORD!

Chapter 4 Theme ________________________

4 How [a]dark the gold has become,
How the pure gold has changed!
The sacred stones are poured out
At the [1]corner of every street.
2 The precious sons of Zion,
Weighed against fine gold,
How they are regarded as [a]earthen jars,
The work of a potter's hands!
3 Even [a]jackals offer the breast,
They nurse their young;
But the daughter of my people has become [b]cruel
Like [c]ostriches in the wilderness.
4 The [a]tongue of the infant cleaves
To the roof of its mouth because of [b]thirst;
The little ones [c]ask for bread,
But no one breaks *it* for them.
5 Those who ate [a]delicacies
Are desolate in the streets;
Those [1]reared in purple
Embrace ash pits.
6 For the [1]iniquity of the daughter of my people
Is greater than the [2a]sin of Sodom,
Which was [b]overthrown as in a moment,
And no hands were [3]turned toward her.
7 Her [1]consecrated ones were [a]purer than snow,
They were whiter than milk;
They were more ruddy *in* [2]body than corals,
Their polishing *was like* [3b]lapis lazuli.
8 Their appearance is [a]blacker than soot,
They are not recognized in the streets;
Their [b]skin is shriveled on their bones,
It is withered, it has become like wood.
9 Better are those [1a]slain with the sword
Than those [1]slain with hunger;

60 [a]Jer 11:19
61 [a]Ps 74:18; 89:50; Lam 5:1; Zeph 2:8
62 [a]Ps 59:7, 12; 140:3; Ezek 36:3
63 [a]Ps 139:2 [b]Job 30:9; Lam 3:14
64 [a]Ps 28:4; Jer 51:6, 24, 56
65 [1]Or *insolence* [a]Ex 14:8; Deut 2:30; Is 6:10
66 [a]Lam 3:43 [b]Ps 8:3
4:1 [1]Lit *head* [a]Ezek 7:19-22
2 [a]Is 30:14; Jer 19:1, 11
3 [a]Is 13:22; 34:13 [b]Is 49:15; Ezek 5:10 [c]Job 39:14-17
4 [a]Ps 22:15 [b]Jer 14:3 [c]Lam 2:12
5 [1]Lit *established in crimson* [a]Jer 6:2; Amos 6:3-7
6 [1]Or *punishment for iniquity* [2]Or *punishment for sin* [3]Or *wrung over her* [a]Gen 19:24 [b]Gen 19:25; Jer 20:16
7 [1]Or *Nazirites* [2]Lit *bones* [3]Heb *sappir* [a]Ps 51:7 [b]Ex 24:10; Job 28:16
8 [a]Job 30:30; Lam 5:10 [b]Job 19:20; Ps 102:3-5
9 [1]Lit *pierced* [a]Jer 16:4

9 [2]Lit *flow away* [3]Lit *my fields* [b]Lev 26:39; Ezek 24:23

10 [a]Lev 26:29; Deut 28:57; 2 Kin 6:29; Jer 19:9; Lam 2:20; Ezek 5:10 [b]Deut 28:53-55

11 [a]Jer 7:20; Lam 2:17; Ezek 22:31 [b]Deut 32:22; Jer 17:27

12 [a]Deut 29:24 [b]Jer 21:13

13 [a]Jer 5:31; 6:13; Lam 2:14; Ezek 22:26-28 [b]Jer 2:30; 26:8, 9; Matt 23:31

14 [a]Deut 28:28, 29; Is 29:10; 56:10; 59:9, 10 [b]Is 1:15 [c]Jer 2:34

15 [1]Or *they* (men) *cried to them* [a]Lev 13:45, 46 [b]Jer 49:5

16 [1]Lit *lift up the faces of* [a]Is 9:14-16; Jer 52:24-27

17 [1]Lit *our help* [a]Jer 37:7; Lam 1:7 [b]Ezek 29:6, 7, 16

18 [1]Lit *full* [a]Jer 16:16 [b]Jer 5:31; Ezek 7:2-12; Amos 8:2

19 [a]Is 5:26-28; 30:16, 17; Jer 4:13; Hab 1:8

20 [a]Gen 2:7 [b]2 Sam 1:14; 19:21 [c]Jer 39:5; 52:9 [d]Dan 4:12

21 [a]Ps 137:7; Jer 25:21 [b]Obad 16

For they [2b]pine away, being stricken
For lack of the fruits of [3]the field.
10 The hands of compassionate women
[a]Boiled their own children;
They became [b]food for them
Because of the destruction of the daughter of my people.
11 The LORD has [a]accomplished His wrath,
He has poured out His fierce anger;
And He has [b]kindled a fire in Zion
Which has consumed its foundations.
12 The kings of the earth did not believe,
Nor *did* any of [a]the inhabitants of the world,
That the adversary and the enemy
Could [b]enter the gates of Jerusalem.
13 Because of the sins of her [a]prophets
And the iniquities of her priests,
Who have shed in her midst
The [b]blood of the righteous;
14 They wandered, [a]blind, in the streets;
They were defiled with [b]blood
So that no one could touch their [c]garments.
15 "Depart! [a]Unclean!" [1]they cried of themselves.
"Depart, depart, do not touch!"
So they [b]fled and wandered;
Men among the nations said,
"They shall not continue to dwell *with us.*"
16 The presence of the LORD has scattered them,
He will not continue to regard them;
They did not [1a]honor the priests,
They did not favor the elders.
17 Yet our eyes failed,
Looking for [1]help was [a]useless;
In our watching we have watched
For a [b]nation that could not save.
18 They [a]hunted our steps
So that we could not walk in our streets;
Our [b]end drew near,
Our days were [1]finished
For our end had come.
19 Our pursuers were [a]swifter
Than the eagles of the sky;
They chased us on the mountains,
They waited in ambush for us in the wilderness.
20 The [a]breath of our nostrils, the [b]LORD's anointed,
Was [c]captured in their pits,
Of whom we had said, "Under his [d]shadow
We shall live among the nations."
21 Rejoice and be glad, O daughter of [a]Edom,
Who dwells in the land of Uz;
But the [b]cup will come around to you as well,
You will become drunk and make yourself naked.

22 *The punishment* of your iniquity has been [a]completed,
O daughter of Zion;
He will exile you no longer.
But He [b]will punish your iniquity, O daughter of Edom;
He will expose your sins!

Chapter 5 Theme ___________________________

5 Remember, O LORD, what has befallen us;
Look, and see our [a]reproach!
2 Our inheritance has been turned over to [a]strangers,
Our [b]houses to aliens.
3 We have become orphans [a]without a father,
Our mothers are like widows.
4 [1]We have to pay for our drinking [a]water,
Our wood comes *to us* at a price.
5 [1]Our pursuers are at our necks;
We are worn out, there is [a]no rest for us.
6 We have [1]submitted to [a]Egypt *and* Assyria [2]to get enough bread.
7 Our [a]fathers sinned, *and* are no more;
It is we who have borne their iniquities.
8 [a]Slaves rule over us;
There is [b]no one to deliver us from their hand.
9 We get our bread [1]at the [a]risk of our lives
[2]Because of the sword in the wilderness.
10 Our skin has become as [a]hot as an oven,
Because of [1]the burning heat of famine.
11 They ravished the [a]women in Zion,
The virgins in the cities of Judah.
12 Princes were hung by their hands;
[1a]Elders were not respected.
13 Young men [1a]worked at the grinding mill,
And youths [b]stumbled under *loads* of wood.
14 Elders [1]are gone from the gate,
Young men from their [a]music.
15 The joy of our hearts has [a]ceased;
Our dancing has been turned into mourning.
16 The [a]crown has fallen from our head;
[b]Woe to us, for we have sinned!
17 Because of this our [a]heart is faint,
Because of these things our [b]eyes are dim;
18 Because of [a]Mount Zion which lies desolate,
[b]Foxes prowl in it.

19 [a]You, O LORD, [1]rule forever;
Your [b]throne is from generation to generation.
20 Why do You [a]forget us forever?
Why do You forsake us [1]so long?
21 [a]Restore us to You, O LORD, that we may be restored;
Renew [b]our days as of old,
22 Unless [a]You have utterly rejected us
And are exceedingly [b]angry with us.

22 [a]Is 40:2; Jer 33:7, 8 [b]Jer 49:10; Mal 1:3, 4

5:1 [a]Ps 44:13-16

2 [a]Is 1:7; Hos 8:7, 8 [b]Zeph 1:13

3 [a]Ex 22:24; Jer 15:8; 18:21

4 [1]Lit *We drink our water for silver* [a]Is 3:1

5 [1]Lit *We have been pursued upon* [a]Neh 9:36, 37

6 [1]Lit *given the hand to* [2]Lit *to be satisfied with* [a]Hos 9:3; 12:1

7 [a]Jer 14:20; 16:12

8 [a]Neh 5:15 [b]Ps 7:2; Zech 11:6

9 [1]Lit *with our soul* [2]Or *In the face of* [a]Jer 40:9-12

10 [1]Or *the ravages of hunger* [a]Job 30:30; Lam 4:8

11 [a]Is 13:16; Zech 14:2

12 [1]Lit *The faces of elders* [a]Is 47:6; Lam 4:16

13 [1]Lit *carry* [a]Judg 16:21 [b]Jer 7:18

14 [1]Lit *have ceased* [a]Is 24:8; Jer 7:34

15 [a]Jer 25:10; Amos 8:10

16 [a]Job 19:9; Ps 89:39; Jer 13:18 [b]Is 3:9-11

17 [a]Is 1:5 [b]Job 17:7; Lam 2:11

18 [a]Mic 3:12 [b]Neh 4:3

19 [1]Lit *sit* [a]Ps 102:12, 25-27 [b]Ps 45:6

20 [1]Lit *to length of days* [a]Ps 13:1; 44:24

21 [a]Ps 80:3; Jer 31:18 [b]Is 60:20-22

22 [a]Ps 60:1, 2; Jer 7:29 [b]Is 64:9

Theme of Lamentations:

Author:

Date:

Purpose:

Key Words:

how

Zion (Jerusalem, the city)

anger (wrath)

transgressions (sin, iniquity, wickedness)

destroy (destroyed, destruction)

affliction (afflict)

desolate

little ones (children, infants)

eyes

SEGMENT DIVISIONS		CHAPTER THEMES
		1
		2
		3
		4
		5

EZEKIEL

In 622 B.C. the book of the law was found in the house of the Lord. When it was brought to King Josiah, he wept, for he saw the awfulness of Judah's sin and knew that God's wrath burned against them. Although Josiah was determined that Judah would walk after the Lord and keep His commandments, the prophetess Huldah told him that after his death God would have to bring judgment upon Judah, for they had forsaken God (see 2 Kings 22).

God's judgment on Judah began when King Josiah tried to stop Pharaoh Neco, king of Egypt, on his way to Carchemish on the Euphrates in 609 B.C. (see 2 Chronicles 35:20-27). Neco killed Josiah on the plain of Megiddo. Then four years later, in 605 B.C., Neco was defeated at Carchemish by Nebuchadnezzar, king of Babylon (see Jeremiah 46:2).

Ezekiel was 18 years old when a handful of the nobles and princes were captured by King Nebuchadnezzar and taken from Judah to Babylon. Among them were a 15-year-old boy named Daniel, and his three friends, Hananiah, Mishael, and Azariah. Ezekiel, however, was left behind. At age 30 he would be eligible for the priesthood and would spend his life in service to God in the temple at Jerusalem. Or so it seemed.

For almost ten years things were relatively quiet in Judah. The prophets were bringing good news, prophesying peace. The people loved it and continued in their sin. Only one lonely voice disturbed their peace—the voice of Jeremiah.

Then Jehoiakim, king of Judah, rebelled against Nebuchadnezzar (2 Kings 23:36–24:4). When Jehoiakim died, Jehoiachin became king, and in 597 B.C. Nebuchadnezzar once again besieged Jerusalem. This time 10,000 people were taken captive into Babylon, and Ezekiel, who would soon have been eligible for the priesthood, was among them. Never again would he see Jerusalem or the temple where he was to serve. Both would be destroyed by Nebuchadnezzar in 586 B.C.

But Ezekiel would see another temple and another Jerusalem—one which would be called *Jehovah-shammah,* the Lord is there! For at age 30, Ezekiel had a vision.

THINGS TO DO

In order to understand the depth and magnitude of the book of Ezekiel, you need to study it again and again. However, if you do the following, you will gain a good understanding of it.

General Instructions

1. Ezekiel has many references to time. These are important and need to be marked with a clock and colored green for ease of identification. Ezekiel 1:1-2 establishes the historical setting of Ezekiel's ministry. The other references to time give you the historical timing of his visions and prophecies.

   a. Every time you mark references to time, look at the calendar on page 1320 to see what month Ezekiel is referring to. (Follow the sacred calendar highlighted in black.)

   b. Ezekiel 1:2 is a parenthesis and serves as an explanation of the timing of verse 2. Read 2 Kings 24:8–25:21 for a good overview of the historical setting. This will help you understand the timing of Ezekiel's prophecies.

      1) As you read, look for Jehoiachin's name, mark it in a distinctive way, and watch when he goes into exile. Also note who is made king when Jehoiachin goes into exile.

      2) In the margins of 2 Kings 24–25, record the dates of Jerusalem's first, second, and third sieges. (Jehoiachin was taken captive when Nebuchadnezzar besieged Jerusalem the second time.) The first siege is recorded in 2 Kings 24:1-7 and

occurred in 605 B.C. The second siege is recorded in 2 Kings 24:10-16 and occurred in 597 B.C. (Ezekiel was taken captive during the second siege.) The third and final siege is recorded in 2 Kings 25:1-21. It began in 588 B.C., and by 586 B.C. the city was captured and destroyed.

3) Read Ezekiel 1:1-3 and record what you learn about Ezekiel under "Author" on the EZEKIEL AT A GLANCE chart on page 1401.

4) Now read Numbers 4:3 and observe at what age a man began his priestly service. Then look at Ezekiel 1 and compare this with the way Ezekiel is described and the year he had his first visions from God. Verse 2 tells you what year it was in relationship to the second siege of Jerusalem, the year when Jehoiachin went into exile.

2. Now that you have the historical setting, as you read the dates of all the other visions or prophecies in Ezekiel, you can know that the dates are calculated from the time of Jehoiachin's and Ezekiel's exile in 597 B.C.

3. If you learn anything new about God, record your insight in the margin next to a △ (for God).

4. Key repeated words and phrases to mark throughout the book are listed on EZEKIEL AT A GLANCE. Write them on an index card, color code each in a distinctive way, and then use the card as a bookmark while you study Ezekiel. Double-underline in green all geographical locations.

Chapters 1–3: Ezekiel's Call

1. Read chapters 1–3 and mark the key repeated words. Also, mark *listen,* and if it is negative, put a slash through it like this: \.

2. As you go through these chapters one at a time, interrogate the text with the "5 W's and an H." Ask questions such as: What does Ezekiel see? How are they described? Where are they? Where is Ezekiel? What is he told to do? Why is he told to do it? When is Ezekiel to speak?

3. You may want to summarize your observations in your notebook. Note what Ezekiel is called to do and how he is to do it. Also note to whom he is sent and why.

4. In summary form in your notebook, list everything you observe from the text about Ezekiel, the people to whom he was sent, and the glory of the Lord.

5. Record the theme of each chapter on EZEKIEL AT A GLANCE and in your Bible.

Chapters 4–24: Prophecies about Judah and Jerusalem

1. Read through this segment one chapter at a time. On the first reading of a chapter, mark every reference to the time of a vision. Also mark the key words that are on your bookmark.

   a. Watch for and mark the phrase *know that I am the Lord*. This is a key phrase used throughout the remainder of Ezekiel, so add this to your bookmark. Every time you see this phrase, observe who is going to know and how they will know it.

   b. When you mark *Spirit*, *heart*, and *the glory of God*, you may want to list what you learn about each from that chapter.

   c. Add *covenant* to your list of key words. When it is used in a chapter, list what you learn about it in your notebook. Also watch for additional key repeated words.

2. Now read through each chapter again. Watch for every reference to the *son of man*. In your notebook, note God's instructions to Ezekiel, the son of man. Note to whom or to what he was to speak and how. Note whether it was by symbolic acts, messages, visions, parables, or signs. Also note why he was to speak in that way and the significance of his action. Note when Ezekiel's mouth is shut and opened. This is important.

3. Record the theme of each chapter as you have done previously.

Chapters 25–32: Prophecies about the Nations

1. Read through this segment one chapter at a time. On the first reading mark the key words. Watch for the phrase *know that I am the Lord*, and again observe who is going to know and how they will know it.

2. On the second reading of the chapter, identify and record in the margin the nation to whom the prophecy is given and the ruler—if he is mentioned. Also observe and note what will happen to the nation and why.

3. Make sure you note or mark *when* the word of the Lord came to Ezekiel.

4. Record the theme of each chapter as you have done previously.

Chapters 33–39: Prophecies about Israel's Restoration

1. Read each chapter and once again:

   a. Mark the references to time, noting when the visions or prophecies were given to Ezekiel. As you look at these, you may want to consult the chart "The Prophetic Points of History" on page 1094.

   b. Mark every key word. In your notebook list what you learn from marking *covenant* and then compare it with what you observed about covenant in Ezekiel 16–17.

   c. Continue noting the same observations from marking every occurrence of *know that I am the Lord*. Also list what you learn about the *Spirit*, *heart*, and *the glory of God*.

2. List God's instructions to Ezekiel ("the son of man"). Note to whom or to what he was to speak and what the message was to be. As you look at the prophecy, list what is going to happen, to whom or what it will happen, and when it will happen. Put a symbol next to any indication of timing. Also note any symbolic acts he was to perform and why.

3. List the theme of each chapter as before.

Chapters 40–48: Prophecies about the Temple

1. As you begin observing this final segment, read 40:1-5. In a distinctive way, mark when this final vision is given. Then in your notebook, record who gives it, how, where, and what Ezekiel is to do.

2. Read each chapter carefully and do the following:

   a. Mark key words as before; however, add to your list *temple (sanctuary, house)*, *holy*, *offering*, and *gate (entrance)*. Watch for the reference to the Eastern Gate.

   b. Watch for and record the reason for the vision of the temple and its measurements. Also note what you learn about *the glory of the Lord*, the *Spirit*, and their relationship to the temple or sanctuary. Compare this with what you saw in Ezekiel 8–11.

   c. Warning: This last segment of Ezekiel may seem a little boring after the first 39 chapters. Don't get bogged down in all the temple measurements. Don't miss the last verse of Ezekiel, since it names "the city." It's *Jehovah-shammah!*

   d. In your notebook, list the main points, instructions, or events of each chapter.

3. See the chart "The Tribes, the Prince's Portion, the City, the Sanctuary" on page 1399.

4. Record the theme of these chapters as you have done before. Then complete EZEKIEL AT A GLANCE. Go back to each vision Ezekiel had, note the year when it occurred, and from your calendar record the name of the month and the day. (Follow the sacred calendar highlighted in black.) Then transfer this information to the segment division portion of EZEKIEL AT A GLANCE.

Things to Think About

1. As you think about God's call on Ezekiel's life, what do you see about Ezekiel's responsibility as a watchman that you could apply to your own life? If the people wouldn't listen, was Ezekiel still to speak (Ezekiel 2–3; 33)? Remember that the things in the Old Testament were written for our example, encouragement, and perseverance (1 Corinthians 10:6,11; Romans 15:4).

2. Before Ezekiel ever shared God's message he was told to eat it, take it to heart, and listen closely to the Lord (Ezekiel 3). What lessons can you learn from his example? How would what you are doing in this inductive study Bible help you? What do you need to remember as you work your way through the Bible?

3. What have you learned about God and His ways from studying Ezekiel? God took Israel as His wife. Christians are espoused to Jesus Christ, their heavenly Bridegroom (2 Corinthians 11:2-3). Have you, like Israel, played the harlot spiritually and hurt God's heart (Ezekiel 6:9; James 4:4)? If so, what do you need to do? If not, what should you do so that you never do?

4. In Ezekiel 20:33 God tells Israel, "As I live…surely with a mighty hand and with an outstretched arm and with wrath poured out, I shall be king over you." Think about this verse in the light of the character and position of God and in the light of Philippians 2:5-11. Have you genuinely confessed Jesus Christ as your Lord, your King who has a right to rule over you?

5. What have you observed from marking the word *covenant*? What have you learned about the heart of stone and the Spirit dwelling within (Ezekiel 36)? Read 2 Corinthians 3 and see how this parallels what Ezekiel says. Do you have a heart of stone, or flesh? Where is the Spirit of God in relationship to you? Is He within? Read Ezekiel 36:26-27.

6. What have you learned about prophecy from Ezekiel that you could use in sharing God's Word with the Jews? What about the prophecies of Ezekiel 36–37 and the way they already are being fulfilled? And what do you learn about Israel's future in respect to Ezekiel 38–39? This is of great interest to Jews.

7. What have you learned about the holiness of God? What effect will it have on your life?

Chapter 1 Theme ____________

592 B.C.

1 Now it came about in the thirtieth year, on the fifth *day* of the
fourth month, while I was by the [a]river Chebar among the
exiles, the [b]heavens were opened and I saw [1c]visions of God.
2 (On the fifth of the month [1]in the [a]fifth year of King
Jehoiachin's exile,
3 the [a]word of the LORD came expressly to Ezekiel the priest,
son of Buzi, in the [b]land of the Chaldeans by the river Chebar;
and there [c]the hand of the LORD came upon him.)
4 As I looked, behold, a [a]storm wind was coming from the
north, a great cloud with fire flashing forth continually and a
bright light around it, and in its midst something like [b]glowing
metal in the midst of the fire.

1:1 [1]Some ancient mss and versions read *a vision* [a]Ezek 3:23; 10:15, 20 [b]Matt 3:16; Mark 1:10; Luke 3:21; Acts 7:56; 10:11; Rev 4:1; 19:11 [c]Ex 24:10; Num 12:6; Is 1:1; 6:1; Ezek 8:3; 11:24; 40:2; Dan 8:1, 2
2 [1]Lit *it was* [a]2 Kin 24:12-15; Ezek 8:1; 20:1
3 [a]2 Pet 1:21 [b]Ezek 12:13 [c]1 Kin 18:46; 2 Kin 3:15; Ezek 3:14, 22
4 [a]Is 21:1; Jer 23:19; Ezek 13:11, 13 [b]Ezek 1:27; 8:2

INSIGHT

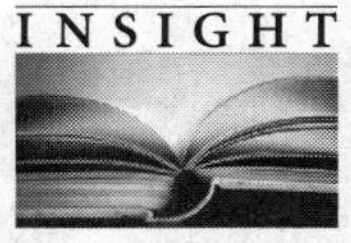

According to Numbers 4:3, men entered the priestly service at the age of thirty.

The Jewish Calendar

Babylonian names (B) for the months are still used today for the Jewish calendar. Canaanite names (C) were used prior to the Babylonian captivity in 586 B.C. Four are mentioned in the Old Testament. **Adar-Sheni** is an intercalary month used every two to three years or seven times in 19 years.

1st month	2nd month	3rd month	4th month
Nisan (B) Abib (C) March-April	Iyyar (B) Ziv (C) April-May	Sivan (B) May-June	Tammuz (B) June-July
7th month	*8th month*	*9th month*	*10th month*
5th month	**6th month**	**7th month**	**8th month**
Ab (B) July-August	Elul (B) August-September	Tishri (B) Ethanim (C) September-October	Marcheshvan (B) Bul (C) October-November
11th month	*12th month*	*1st month*	*2nd month*
9th month	**10th month**	**11th month**	**12th month**
Chislev (B) November-December	Tebeth (B) December-January	Shebat (B) January-February	Adar (B) February-March
3rd month	*4th month*	*5th month*	*6th month*

Sacred calendar appears in black • Civil calendar appears in gray

5 Within it there were figures resembling [a]four living beings.
And this was their appearance: they had human [b]form.
6 Each of them had [a]four faces and [b]four wings.
7 Their legs were straight and [1]their feet were like a calf's
hoof, and they gleamed like [a]burnished bronze.
8 Under their wings on their [a]four sides *were* human [b]hands.
As for the faces and wings of the four of them,
9 their wings touched one another; *their faces* did [a]not turn
when they moved, each [b]went straight forward.
10 As for the [a]form of their faces, *each* had the [b]face of a man;
[1]all four had the face of a lion on the right and the face of a bull
on the left, and [1]all four had the face of an eagle.
11 Such were their faces. Their wings were spread out above; each
had two touching another *being,* and [a]two covering their bodies.
12 And [a]each went straight forward; [b]wherever the spirit was
about to go, they would go, without turning as they went.
13 [1]In the midst of the living beings there was something that
looked like burning coals of [a]fire, [2]like torches darting back and
forth among the living beings. The fire was bright, and lightning
was [3]flashing from the fire.
14 And the living beings [a]ran to and fro like bolts of [b]lightning.
15 Now as I looked at the living beings, behold, there was one
[a]wheel on the earth beside the living beings, [1]for *each of* the
four of them.
16 The [a]appearance of the wheels and their workmanship *was*
like [1]sparkling [b]beryl, and all four of them had the same form,
their appearance and workmanship *being* as if [2]one wheel
were within another.
17 Whenever they [1]moved, they [1]moved in any of their four
[2]directions without [a]turning as they [1]moved.
18 As for their rims they were lofty and awesome, and the
rims of all four of them were [a]full of eyes round about.
19 [a]Whenever the living beings [1]moved, the wheels [1]moved
with them. And whenever the living beings [b]rose from the
earth, the wheels rose *also.*

5 [a]Ezek 10:15, 17, 20; Rev 4:6-8 [b]Ezek 1:26
6 [a]Ezek 1:10; 10:14, 21 [b]Ezek 1:23
7 [1]Lit *the soles of their feet* [a]Dan 10:6; Rev 1:15
8 [a]Ezek 1:17; 10:11 [b]Ezek 10:8, 21
9 [a]Ezek 1:17 [b]Ezek 1:12; 10:22
10 [1]Lit *the four of them* [a]Rev 4:7 [b]Ezek 10:14
11 [a]Is 6:2; Ezek 1:23
12 [a]Ezek 1:9 [b]Ezek 1:20
13 [1]So with some ancient versions; Heb *as the likeness of the living beings* [2]Lit *like the appearance of* [3]Lit *coming out* [a]Ps 104:4; Rev 4:5
14 [a]Zech 4:10 [b]Matt 24:27; Luke 17:24
15 [1]Lit *for his four faces* [a]Ezek 1:19-21; 10:9
16 [1]Lit *the look of beryl* [2]Lit *the wheel in the midst of the wheel* [a]Ezek 10:9-11 [b]Ezek 10:9; Dan 10:6
17 [1]Lit *went* [2]Lit *sides* [a]Ezek 1:9, 12; 10:11
18 [a]Ezek 10:12; Rev 4:6, 8
19 [1]Lit *went* [a]Ezek 10:16 [b]Ezek 10:19

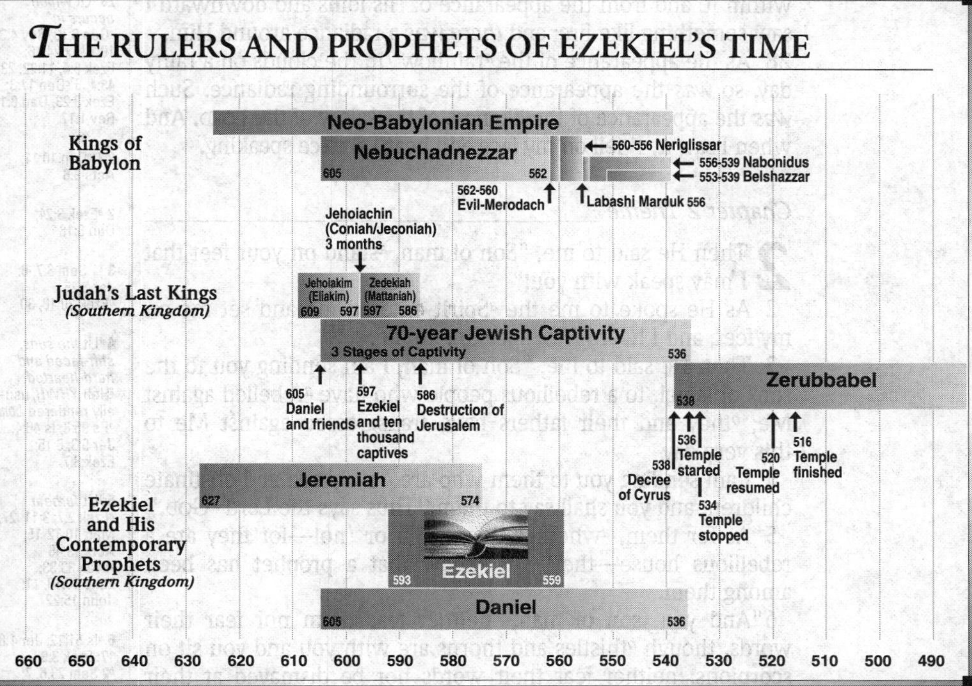

20 ᵃWherever the spirit was about to go, they would go in that
direction[1]. And the wheels rose close beside them; for the spirit
of the living [2]beings *was* in the wheels.
21 ᵃWhenever those went, these went; and whenever those
stood still, these stood still. And whenever those rose from the
earth, the wheels rose close beside them; for the spirit of the
living [1]beings *was* in the wheels.
22 Now ᵃover the heads of the living [1]beings *there was*
something like an expanse, like the awesome gleam of [2]crystal,
spread out over their heads.
23 Under the expanse their wings *were stretched out* straight,
one toward the other; each one also had ᵃtwo wings covering
its body on the one side and on the other.
24 I also heard the sound of their wings like the ᵃsound of
abundant waters as they went, like the ᵇvoice of [1]the Almighty,
a sound of tumult like the ᶜsound of an army camp; whenever
they stood still, they dropped their wings.
25 And there came a voice from above the ᵃexpanse that was
over their heads; whenever they stood still, they dropped their
wings.
26 Now ᵃabove the expanse that was over their heads there
was something ᵇresembling a throne, like [1c]lapis lazuli in
appearance; and on that which resembled a throne, high up,
was a figure with the appearance of a ᵈman.
27 Then I [1]noticed from the appearance of His loins and upward
something ᵃlike [2]glowing metal that looked like fire all around

20 [1]M.T. adds *the spirit to go* [2]M.T. reads *being* ᵃEzek 1:12
21 [1]M.T. reads *being* ᵃEzek 10:17
22 [1]So some ancient mss and versions; M.T. reads *being* [2]Or *ice* ᵃEzek 10:1
23 ᵃEzek 1:6, 11
24 [1]Heb *Shaddai* ᵃEzek 43:2; Rev 1:15; 19:6 ᵇEzek 10:5 ᶜ2 Kin 7:6; Dan 10:6
25 ᵃEzek 1:22; 10:1
26 [1]Heb *eben-sappir* ᵃEzek 1:22; 10:1 ᵇIs 6:1; Ezek 10:1; Dan 7:9 ᶜEx 24:10; Is 54:11 ᵈEzek 43:6, 7; Rev 1:13
27 [1]Lit *saw* [2]Or *electrum* ᵃEzek 1:4; 8:2

within it, and from the appearance of His loins and downward I
saw something like fire; and *there was* a radiance around Him.
28 As the appearance of the [a]rainbow [1]in the clouds on a rainy
day, so *was* the appearance of the surrounding radiance. Such
was the appearance of the likeness of the [b]glory of the LORD. And
when I saw *it,* I [c]fell on my face and heard a voice speaking.

Chapter 2 Theme ______________________________

2 Then He said to me, "Son of man, [a]stand on your feet that
I may speak with you!"
2 As He spoke to me the [a]Spirit entered me and set me on
my feet; and I heard *Him* speaking to me.
3 Then He said to me, "Son of man, I am sending you to the
sons of Israel, to a rebellious people who have [a]rebelled against
Me; [b]they and their fathers have transgressed against Me to
this very day.
4 "I am sending you to them who are [1a]stubborn and obstinate
children, and you shall say to them, 'Thus says the Lord [2]GOD.'
5 "As for them, [a]whether they listen or [1]not—for they are a
rebellious house—they will [b]know that a prophet has been
among them.
6 "And you, son of man, [a]neither fear them nor fear their
words, though [b]thistles and thorns are with you and you sit on
scorpions; neither fear their words nor be dismayed at their
presence, for they are a rebellious house.
7 "But you shall [a]speak My words to them [b]whether they
listen or [1]not, for they are rebellious.
8 "Now you, son of man, listen to what I am speaking to you;
do not be rebellious like that rebellious house. Open your mouth
and [a]eat what I am giving you."
9 Then I looked, and behold, a [a]hand was extended to me;
and lo, a [1b]scroll *was* in it.
10 When He spread it out before me, it was written on the
front and back, and written on it were lamentations, mourning
and [a]woe.

Chapter 3 Theme ______________________________

3 Then He said to me, "Son of man, eat what you find; [a]eat
this scroll, and go, speak to the house of Israel."
2 So I [a]opened my mouth, and He fed me this scroll.
3 He said to me, "Son of man, feed your stomach and [a]fill
your [1]body with this scroll which I am giving you." Then I [b]ate
it, and it was sweet as [c]honey in my mouth.
4 Then He said to me, "Son of man, [1]go to the house of
Israel and speak with My words to them.
5 "For [a]you are not being sent to a people of [1b]unintelligible
speech or difficult language, *but* to the house of Israel,
6 nor to many peoples of [1]unintelligible speech or difficult
language, whose words you cannot understand. [2]But I have
sent you to them [3]who should listen to you;

28 [1]Lit *which occurs in* [a]Gen 9:13; Rev 4:3; 10:1 [b]Ex 24:16; Ezek 8:4; 11:22, 23; 43:4, 5 [c]Gen 17:3; Ezek 3:23; Dan 8:17; Rev 1:17

2:1 [a]Dan 10:11; Acts 9:6

2 [a]Ezek 3:24; Dan 8:18

3 [a]1 Sam 8:7, 8; Jer 3:25 [b]Ezek 20:18, 30

4 [1]Lit *the sons, stiff-faced and hard-hearted* [2]Heb *YHWH,* usually rendered *LORD* [a]Ps 95:8; Is 48:4; Jer 5:3; 6:15; Ezek 3:7

5 [1]Lit *forbear* [a]Ezek 2:7; 3:11, 27; Matt 10:12-15; Acts 13:46 [b]Ezek 33:33; Luke 10:10, 11; John 15:22

6 [a]Is 51:12; Jer 1:8, 17; Ezek 3:9 [b]2 Sam 23:6, 7; Ezek 28:24; Mic 7:4

7 [1]Lit *forbear* [a]Jer 1:7, 17; Ezek 3:10, 17 [b]Ezek 2:5

8 [a]Jer 15:16; Ezek 3:3; Rev 10:9

9 [1]Lit *scroll of a book* [a]Ezek 8:3 [b]Jer 36:2; Ezek 3:1; Rev 5:1-5; 10:8-11

10 [a]Is 3:11; Rev 8:13

3:1 [a]Ezek 2:9

2 [a]Jer 25:17

3 [1]Lit *inward parts* [a]Jer 6:11; 20:9 [b]Jer 15:16 [c]Ps 19:10; 119:103; Rev 10:9, 10

4 [1]Lit *go, come*

5 [1]Lit *deepness of lip and heaviness of tongue* [a]Jon 1:2; Acts 14:11; 26:17 [b]Is 28:11; 33:19

6 [1]Lit *deepness of lip and heaviness of tongue* [2]Or *If I had sent you to them, they would listen to you* [3]Lit *they*

7 yet the house of Israel will not be willing to listen to you,
since they are [a]not willing to listen to Me. Surely the whole
house of Israel is [1]stubborn and obstinate.
8 "Behold, I have made your face as hard as their faces and
your forehead as hard as their foreheads.
9 "Like [1]emery harder than flint I have made your forehead.
Do not be afraid of them or be dismayed before them, though
they are a rebellious house."
10 Moreover, He said to me, "Son of man, take into your heart
all My [a]words which I will speak to you and listen [1]closely.
11 "[1]Go to the exiles, to the sons of your people, and speak to
them and tell them, whether they listen or [2]not, 'Thus says the
Lord [3]GOD.'"
12 Then the [a]Spirit lifted me up, and I heard a great [b]rumbling
sound behind me, "Blessed be the glory of the LORD [1]in His place."
13 And I *heard* the sound of the wings of the living beings
touching one another and the sound of the [a]wheels beside
them, even a great rumbling sound.
14 So the Spirit lifted me up and took me away; and I went
embittered in the rage of my spirit, and [a]the hand of the LORD
was strong on me.
15 Then I came to the exiles who lived beside the river Chebar
at Tel-abib, and I sat there [a]seven days where they were living,
causing consternation among them.
16 [a]At the end of seven days the word of the LORD came to me,
saying,
17 "Son of man, I have appointed you a [a]watchman to the house
of Israel; whenever you hear a word from My mouth, [b]warn
them from Me.
18 "When I say to the wicked, 'You will surely die,' and you do
not warn him or speak out to warn the wicked from his wicked
way that he may live, that wicked man shall die in his iniquity,
but his [a]blood I will require at your hand.
19 "Yet if you have [a]warned the wicked and he does not turn
from his wickedness or from his wicked way, he shall die in his
iniquity; but you have [b]delivered yourself.
20 "Again, [a]when a righteous man turns away from his
righteousness and commits iniquity, and I place an [b]obstacle
before him, he will die; since you have not warned him, he shall
die in his sin, and his righteous deeds which he has done shall
not be remembered; but his blood I will require at your hand.
21 "However, if you have [a]warned [1]the righteous man that the
righteous should not sin and he does not sin, he shall surely live
because he took warning; and you have delivered yourself."
22 The hand of the LORD was on me there, and He said to me,
"Get up, go out to the plain, and there I will [a]speak to you."
23 So I got up and went out to the plain; and behold, the
[a]glory of the LORD was standing there, like the glory which [b]I
saw by the river Chebar, and I fell on my face.
24 The [a]Spirit then entered me and made me stand on my
feet, and He spoke with me and said to me, "Go, shut yourself
up in your house.

7 [1]Lit *of a hard forehead and a stiff heart* [a]1 Sam 8:7
9 [1]Lit *corundum*
10 [1]Lit *with your ears* [a]Job 22:22; Ezek 2:8; 3:1-3
11 [1]Lit *Go, come* [2]Lit *forbear* [3]Heb *YHWH,* usually rendered LORD
12 [1]Or *from* [a]Ezek 3:14; 8:3; Acts 8:39 [b]Acts 2:2
13 [a]Ezek 1:15; 10:16, 17
14 [a]2 Kin 3:15
15 [a]Job 2:13
16 [a]Jer 42:7
17 [a]Is 52:8; 56:10; 62:6; Jer 6:17; Ezek 33:7-9 [b]2 Chr 19:10; Is 58:1; Hab 2:1
18 [a]Ezek 3:20; 33:6, 8
19 [a]2 Kin 17:13, 14; Ezek 33:3, 9 [b]Ezek 14:14, 20; Acts 18:6; 1 Tim 4:16
20 [a]Ps 125:5; Ezek 18:24; 33:18; Zeph 1:6 [b]Is 8:14; Jer 6:21; Ezek 14:3, 7-9
21 [1]Lit *him, the righteous* [a]Acts 20:31
22 [a]Acts 9:6
23 [a]Ezek 1:28; Acts 7:55 [b]Ezek 1:1
24 [a]Ezek 2:2

25 "As for you, son of man, they will [a]put ropes on you and bind you with them so that you cannot go out among them.

26 "Moreover, [a]I will make your tongue stick to [1]the roof of your mouth so that you will be mute and cannot be a man who rebukes them, for they are a rebellious house.

27 "But [a]when I speak to you, I will open your mouth and you will say to them, 'Thus says the Lord [1]GOD.' He who hears, let him hear; and he who refuses, let him refuse; [b]for they are a rebellious house.

Chapter 4 Theme ______________________

4

"Now you son of man, [a]get yourself a brick, place it before you and inscribe a city on it, Jerusalem.

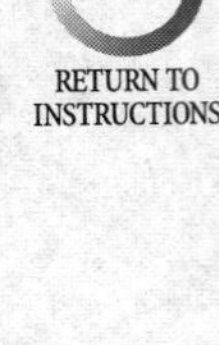

2 "Then [a]lay siege against it, build a siege wall, [1]raise up a ramp, pitch camps and place battering rams against it all around.

3 "Then get yourself an iron plate and set it up as an iron wall between you and the city, and set your face toward it so that [a]it is under siege, and besiege it. This is a [b]sign to the house of Israel.

4 "As for you, lie down on your left side and lay the iniquity of the house of Israel on it; you shall [a]bear their iniquity for the number of days that you lie on it.

5 "For I have assigned you a number of days corresponding to the years of their iniquity, three hundred and ninety days; thus [a]you shall bear the iniquity of the house of Israel.

6 "When you have completed these, you shall lie down a second time, *but* on your right side and bear the iniquity of the house of Judah; I have assigned it to you for forty days, a day for [a]each year.

7 "Then you shall set your face toward the siege of Jerusalem with your arm bared and [a]prophesy against it.

8 "Now behold, I will [a]put ropes on you so that you cannot turn from one side to the other until you have completed the days of your siege.

9 "But as for you, take wheat, barley, beans, lentils, millet and [a]spelt, put them in one vessel and make them into bread for yourself; you shall eat it according to the number of the days that you lie on your side, three hundred and ninety days.

10 "Your food which you eat *shall be* [a]twenty shekels a day by weight; you shall eat it from time to time.

11 "The water you drink shall be the sixth part of a hin by measure; you shall drink it from time to time.

12 "You shall eat it as a barley cake, having baked *it* in their sight over human [a]dung."

13 Then the LORD said, "Thus will the sons of Israel eat their bread [a]unclean among the nations where I will banish them."

14 But I said, "[a]Ah, Lord [1]GOD! Behold, I have [b]never been defiled; for from my youth until now I have never eaten what [c]died of itself or was torn by beasts, nor has any [d]unclean meat ever entered my mouth."

25 [a]Ezek 4:8

26 [1]Lit *your palate* [a]Luke 1:20, 22

27 [1]Heb *YHWH,* usually rendered LORD [a]Ezek 24:27; 33:22 [b]Ezek 12:2, 3

4:1 [a]Is 20:2; Jer 13:1; 18:2; 19:1

2 [1]Lit *cast* [a]Jer 6:6; Ezek 21:22

3 [a]Jer 39:1, 2; Ezek 5:2 [b]Is 8:18; 20:3; Ezek 12:6, 11; 24:24-27

4 [a]Lev 10:17; 16:22; Num 18:1

5 [a]Num 14:34

6 [a]Num 14:34; Dan 9:24-26; 12:11, 12; Rev 11:2, 3

7 [a]Ezek 21:2

8 [a]Ezek 3:25

9 [a]Ex 9:32; Is 28:25

10 [a]Ezek 45:12

12 [a]Is 36:12

13 [a]Dan 1:8; Hos 9:3

14 [1]Heb *YHWH,* usually rendered LORD [a]Jer 1:6; Ezek 9:8; 20:49 [b]Acts 10:14 [c]Lev 17:15; 22:8; Ezek 44:31 [d]Deut 14:3; Is 65:4; 66:17

15 Then He said to me, "See, I will give you cow's dung in
place of human dung over which you will prepare your bread."
16 Moreover, He said to me, "Son of man, behold, I am going to
[a]break the staff of bread in Jerusalem, and they will eat bread
by [b]weight and with anxiety, and drink water by [c]measure and
in horror,
17 because bread and water will be scarce; and they will be
appalled with one another and [a]waste away in their iniquity.

Chapter 5 Theme ________________________

5 "As for you, son of man, take a [a]sharp sword; take and [1]use
it *as* a barber's razor on your head and beard. Then take
[b]scales for weighing and divide [2]the hair.
2 "One third you shall burn in the fire at the center of the city,
when the [a]days of the siege are completed. Then you shall take
one third and strike *it* with the sword all around [1]the city, and
one third you shall scatter to the wind; and I will [b]unsheathe a
sword behind them.
3 "Take also a few in number from [1]them and bind them in
the edges of your *robes*.
4 "Take again some of them and throw them into the fire and
burn them in the fire; from it a fire will [1]spread to all the house
of Israel.
5 "Thus says the Lord [1]GOD, 'This is [a]Jerusalem; I have set her
at the [b]center of the nations, with lands around her.
6 'But she has rebelled against My ordinances more wickedly
than the nations and against My statutes [a]more than the lands
which surround her; for they have [b]rejected My ordinances
and have not walked [1]in My statutes.'
7 "Therefore, thus says the Lord GOD, 'Because you have [a]more
turmoil than the nations which surround you *and* have not
walked in My statutes, nor observed My ordinances, nor
observed the ordinances of the nations which surround you,'
8 therefore, thus says the Lord GOD, 'Behold, I, even I, am
[a]against you, and I will [b]execute judgments among you in the
sight of the nations.
9 'And because of all your abominations, I will do among you
what I have [a]not done, and the like of which I will never do
again.
10 'Therefore, [a]fathers will eat *their* sons among you, and sons
will eat their fathers; for I will execute judgments on you and
[b]scatter all your remnant to every wind.
11 'So as I live,' declares the Lord GOD, 'surely, because you
have [a]defiled My sanctuary with all your [b]detestable idols and
with all your abominations, therefore I will also withdraw, and
My eye will have no pity and I will not spare.
12 'One third of you will die by [a]plague or be consumed by
famine among you, one third will fall by the sword around you,
and one third I will [b]scatter to every wind, and I will [c]unsheathe
a sword behind them.

16 [a]Lev 26:26; Is 3:1; Ezek 5:16; 14:13 [b]Ezek 4:10, 11; 12:19 [c]Lam 5:4; Ezek 12:18, 19

17 [a]Lev 26:39; Ezek 24:23; 33:10

5:1 [1]Lit *make it pass over your head* [2]Lit *them* [a]Lev 21:5; Is 7:20; Ezek 44:20 [b]Dan 5:27

2 [1]Lit *it* [a]Jer 39:1, 2; Ezek 4:2-8 [b]Lev 26:33

3 [1]Lit *there*

4 [1]Lit *go out*

5 [1]Heb *YHWH,* usually rendered LORD, and so throughout the ch [a]Jer 6:6; Ezek 4:1 [b]Deut 4:6; Lam 1:1; Ezek 16:14

6 [1]Lit *in them, My statutes* [a]2 Kin 17:8-20; Ezek 16:47, 48, 51 [b]Neh 9:16, 17; Ps 78:10; Jer 11:10; Zech 7:11

7 [a]2 Kin 21:9-11; 2 Chr 33:9; Jer 2:10, 11

8 [a]Jer 21:5, 13; Ezek 15:7; 21:3; Zech 14:2 [b]Jer 24:9; Ezek 5:15; 11:9

9 [a]Dan 9:12; Amos 3:2; Matt 24:21

10 [a]Lev 26:29; Jer 19:9; Lam 4:10 [b]Ps 44:11; Ezek 5:2, 12; 6:8; 12:14; Amos 9:9; Zech 2:6; 7:14

11 [a]Jer 7:9-11; Ezek 8:5, 6, 16 [b]Jer 16:18; Ezek 7:20

12 [a]Jer 15:2; 21:9; Ezek 5:17; 6:11, 12 [b]Ezek 5:2, 10; Amos 9:9; Zech 2:6 [c]Jer 43:10, 11; 44:27; Ezek 5:2; 12:14

13 ‘Thus My anger will be spent and I will [1]satisfy My wrath on
them, and I will be [2a]appeased; then they will know that I, the
LORD, have [b]spoken in My zeal when I have spent My wrath upon
them.
14 ‘Moreover, I will make you a desolation and a [a]reproach among
the nations which surround you, in the sight of all who pass by.
15 ‘So [1]it will be a reproach, a reviling, a [a]warning and an
object of horror to the nations who surround you when I
[b]execute judgments against you in anger, wrath and raging
rebukes. I, the LORD, have spoken.
16 ‘When I send against them the [1]deadly arrows of famine
which [2]were for the destruction of those whom I will send to
destroy you, then I will also intensify the famine upon you and
break the staff of bread.
17 ‘Moreover, [a]I will send on you famine and wild beasts, and
they will bereave you of children; [b]plague and bloodshed also
will pass through you, and I will bring the sword on you. I, the
LORD, have spoken.’”

Chapter 6 Theme ______________________________

6 And the word of the LORD came to me saying,
2 “Son of man, set your face toward the [a]mountains of Israel,
and prophesy against them
3 and say, ‘Mountains of Israel, listen to the word of the Lord
[1]GOD! Thus says the Lord [1]GOD to the mountains, the hills, the
ravines and the valleys: “Behold, I Myself am going to bring a
sword on you, and [a]I will destroy your high places.
4 “So your [a]altars will become desolate and your incense altars
will be smashed; and I will make your slain fall in front of your
idols.
5 “I will also lay the dead bodies of the sons of Israel in front
of their idols; and I will scatter your [a]bones around your altars.
6 “In all your dwellings, [a]cities will become waste and the
high places will be desolate, that your altars may become waste
and [1]desolate, your [b]idols may be broken and brought to an
end, your incense altars may be cut down, and your works may
be blotted out.
7 “The slain will fall among you, and you will know that I am
the LORD.
8 “However, I will leave a [a]remnant, for you will have those
who [b]escaped the sword among the nations when you are
scattered among the countries.
9 “Then those of you who escape will [a]remember Me among
the nations to which they will be carried captive, how I have
[1b]been hurt by their adulterous hearts which turned away from
Me, and by their eyes which played the harlot after their idols;
and they will [c]loathe themselves in their own sight for the evils
which they have committed, for all their abominations.
10 “Then they will know that I am the LORD; I have not said in
vain [1]that I would inflict this disaster on them.”’

13 [1]Lit *cause to rest* [2]Lit *comforted* [a]Is 1:24 [b]Is 59:17; Ezek 36:5, 6; 38:19

14 [a]Ps 74:3-10; 79:1-4; Ezek 22:4

15 [1]Ancient versions read *you* [a]Is 26:9; Jer 22:8, 9; 1 Cor 10:11 [b]Is 66:15, 16; Ezek 5:8; 25:17

16 [1]Lit *evil* [2]Or *are for destruction, which I will send*

17 [a]Lev 26:22; Rev 6:8 [b]Ezek 38:22

6:2 [a]Ezek 36:1

3 [1]Heb *YHWH*, usually rendered *LORD* [a]Lev 26:30

4 [a]Lev 26:30; 2 Chr 14:5; Is 27:9; Ezek 6:6

5 [a]2 Kin 23:14, 16, 20; Jer 8:1, 2

6 [1]So some ancient versions; Heb *bear their guilt* [a]Lev 26:31; Is 6:11; Ezek 5:14 [b]Ezek 6:4; Mic 1:7; Zech 13:2

8 [a]Is 6:13; Jer 30:11 [b]Jer 44:14, 28; Ezek 7:16; 14:22

9 [1]Lit *been broken*, or, *broken for Myself their* [a]Deut 4:29; 30:2; Jer 51:50 [b]Ps 78:40; Is 7:13; 43:24; Hos 11:8 [c]Job 42:6; Ezek 20:43; 36:31

10 [1]Lit *to do this evil to*

11 "Thus says the Lord [1]GOD, 'Clap your hand, [a]stamp your foot
and say, "[b]Alas, because of all the evil abominations of the
house of Israel, which will fall by [c]sword, famine and plague!
12 "He who is [a]far off will die by the plague, and he who is near
will fall by the sword, and he who remains and is besieged will
die by the famine. Thus will I [b]spend My wrath on them.
13 "Then you will know that I am the LORD, when their [a]slain
are among their idols around their altars, on [b]every high hill,
on all the tops of the mountains, under every green tree and
under every leafy oak—the places where they offered soothing
aroma to all their idols.
14 "So throughout all their habitations I will [a]stretch out My
hand against them and make the land more desolate and waste
than the wilderness toward Diblah; thus they will know that I
am the LORD."'"

Chapter 7 Theme

7 Moreover, the word of the LORD came to me saying,
2 "And you, son of man, thus says the Lord [1]GOD to the land
of Israel, 'An [a]end! The end is coming on the four corners of the
land.
3 'Now the end is upon you, and I will send My anger against
you; I will judge you according to your ways and bring all your
abominations upon you.
4 'For My eye will have no pity on you, nor will I spare *you*,
but I will [a]bring your ways upon you, and your abominations
will be among you; then you will [b]know that I am the LORD!'
5 "Thus says the Lord [1]GOD, 'A [a]disaster, unique disaster,
behold it is coming!
6 'An end is coming; the end has come! It has [a]awakened
against you; behold, it has come!
7 'Your doom has come to you, O inhabitant of the land. The
[a]time has come, the [b]day is near—tumult rather than joyful
shouting on the mountains.
8 'Now I will shortly [a]pour out My wrath on you and spend
My anger against you; [b]judge you according to your ways and
bring on you all your abominations.
9 'My eye will show no pity nor will I spare. I will [1]repay you
according to your ways, while your abominations are in your
midst; then you will know that I, the LORD, do the smiting.
10 'Behold, the day! Behold, it is coming! *Your* doom has gone
forth; the [a]rod has budded, arrogance has blossomed.
11 'Violence [1]has grown into a rod of [a]wickedness. None of
them *shall remain*, none of their people, none of their [b]wealth,
nor anything eminent among them.
12 'The [a]time has come, the day has arrived. Let not the
[b]buyer rejoice nor the seller mourn; for [c]wrath is against all
their multitude.
13 'Indeed, the seller will not [1a]regain [2]what he sold as long as
[3]they *both* live; for the vision regarding all their multitude will

11 [1]Heb *YHWH,* usually rendered *LORD* [a]Ezek 25:6 [b]Ezek 9:4 [c]Ezek 5:12; 7:15
12 [a]Dan 9:7 [b]Lam 4:11, 22; Ezek 5:13
13 [a]Ezek 6:4-7 [b]1 Kin 14:23; 2 Kin 16:4; Is 57:5-7; Ezek 20:28; Hos 4:13
14 [a]Is 5:25; 9:12; Ezek 14:13; 20:33, 34
7:2 [1]Heb *YHWH,* usually rendered *LORD* [a]Ezek 7:3, 5, 6; 11:13; Amos 8:2, 10
4 [a]Ezek 11:21; 22:31; Hos 9:7 [b]Ezek 6:7, 14; 7:27
5 [1]Heb *YHWH,* usually rendered *LORD* [a]2 Kin 21:12, 13; Nah 1:9
6 [a]Zech 13:7
7 [a]Ezek 7:12; 12:23-25, 28 [b]Is 22:5
8 [a]Is 42:25; Ezek 9:8; 14:19; Nah 1:6 [b]Ezek 7:3; 33:20; 36:19
9 [1]Lit *give*
10 [a]Ps 89:32; Is 10:5
11 [1]Lit *has risen* [a]Ps 73:8; 125:3; Is 59:6-8 [b]Zeph 1:18
12 [a]Ezek 7:5-7, 10; 1 Cor 7:29-31; James 5:8, 9 [b]Prov 20:14; 1 Cor 7:30 [c]Is 5:13, 14; Ezek 6:11, 12; 7:14
13 [1]Lit *return to* [2]Lit *thing sold,* i.e. his inherited land [3]Lit *their life among the living ones* [a]Lev 25:24-28, 31

not [4]be averted, nor will any of them maintain his life by his
iniquity.
14 'They have [a]blown the trumpet and made everything ready,
but no one is going to the battle, for My wrath is against all
[1]their multitude.
15 'The [a]sword is outside and the plague and the famine are
within. He who is in the field will die by the sword; famine
and the plague will also consume those in the city.
16 'Even when their survivors [a]escape, they will be on the
mountains like [b]doves of the valleys, all of them [1c]mourning,
each over his own iniquity.
17 'All [a]hands will hang limp and all knees will [1]become *like*
water.
18 'They will [a]gird themselves with sackcloth and [b]shuddering
will overwhelm them; and shame *will be* on all faces and
[c]baldness on all their heads.
19 'They will [a]fling their silver into the streets and their gold
will become an abhorrent thing; their [b]silver and their gold will
not be able to deliver them in the day of the wrath of the LORD.
They cannot satisfy their [1]appetite nor can they fill their
stomachs, for their iniquity has become an occasion of stumbling.
20 'They transformed the beauty of His ornaments into pride,
and [a]they made the images of their abominations *and* their
detestable things with it; therefore I will make it an abhorrent
thing to them.
21 'I will give it into the hands of the [a]foreigners as plunder
and to the wicked of the earth as spoil, and they will profane it.
22 'I will also turn My [a]face from them, and they will profane
My secret place; then robbers will enter and profane it.
23 '[a]Make the chain, for the land is full of [1b]bloody crimes and
the city is [c]full of violence.
24 'Therefore, I will bring the worst of the [a]nations, and they
will possess their houses. I will also make the [b]pride of the
strong ones cease, and their [c]holy places will be profaned.
25 'When anguish comes, they will seek [a]peace, but there will
be none.
26 '[a]Disaster will come upon disaster and [b]rumor will be *added*
to rumor; then they will seek a [c]vision from a prophet, but the
[d]law will be lost from the priest and [e]counsel from the elders.
27 'The king will mourn, the prince will be [a]clothed with horror,
and the hands of the people of the land will [1]tremble. According
to their conduct I will deal with them, and by their judgments I
will judge them. And they will know that I am the LORD.'"

Chapter 8 Theme ____________________

591 B.C.

8 It came about in the sixth year, on the fifth *day* of the sixth
month, as I was sitting in my house with the elders of Judah
sitting before me, that the hand of the Lord [1]GOD fell on me there.
2 Then I looked, and behold, a likeness as the appearance of [1]a
man; from His loins and downward *there was* the [a]appearance

13 [4]Lit *return*
14 [1]Lit *her* [a]Num 10:9; Jer 4:5
15 [a]Jer 14:18; Ezek 5:12; 6:11, 12; 12:16
16 [1]Lit *moaning* [a]Ezra 9:15; Is 37:31; Ezek 6:8; 14:22 [b]Is 38:14 [c]Is 59:11; Nah 2:7
17 [1]Lit *run with water* [a]Is 13:7; Ezek 21:7; 22:14; Heb 12:12
18 [a]Is 15:3; Ezek 27:31; Amos 8:10 [b]Job 21:6; Ps 55:5 [c]Ezek 27:31
19 [1]Lit *soul* [a]Is 2:20; 30:22 [b]Prov 11:4; Zeph 1:18
20 [a]Jer 7:30
21 [a]2 Kin 24:13; Ps 74:2-8; Jer 52:13
22 [a]Jer 18:17; Ezek 39:23, 24
23 [1]Lit *judgment of blood* [a]Jer 27:2 [b]Ezek 9:9; Hos 4:2 [c]Ezek 8:17
24 [a]Ezek 21:31; 28:7 [b]Ezek 33:28 [c]2 Chr 7:20; Ezek 24:21
25 [a]Ezek 13:10, 16
26 [a]Is 47:11; Jer 4:20 [b]Ezek 21:7 [c]Jer 21:2; 37:17 [d]Ps 74:9; Ezek 22:26; Mic 3:6 [e]Jer 18:18; Ezek 11:2
27 [1]Lit *be terrified* [a]Job 8:22; Ps 35:26; 109:18, 29; Ezek 26:16
8:1 [1]Heb *YHWH*, usually rendered *LORD*
2 [1]Lit *fire* [a]Ezek 1:27

of fire, and from His loins and upward the appearance of
brightness, like the appearance [b]of [2]glowing metal.
3 He stretched out the form of a hand and caught me by a
lock of my head; and the [a]Spirit lifted me up between earth and
heaven and brought me in the visions of God to Jerusalem, to the
entrance of the [1]north gate of the inner *court,* where the seat of
the idol of jealousy, which [b]provokes to jealousy, was *located.*
4 And behold, the [a]glory of the God of Israel *was* there, like
the appearance which I saw in the plain.
5 Then He said to me, "Son of man, [a]raise your eyes now
toward the north." So I raised my eyes toward the north, and
behold, to the north of the altar gate *was* this [b]idol of jealousy
at the entrance.
6 And He said to me, "Son of man, do you see what they are
doing, the great [a]abominations which the house of Israel are
committing here, so that I would be far from My sanctuary?
But yet you will see still greater abominations."
7 Then He brought me to the entrance of the court, and
when I looked, behold, a hole in the wall.
8 He said to me, "Son of man, now [a]dig through the wall." So
I dug through the wall, and behold, an entrance.
9 And He said to me, "Go in and see the wicked abominations
that they are committing here."
10 So I entered and looked, and behold, every form of creeping
things and beasts *and* detestable things, with all the idols of the
house of Israel, were carved on the wall all around.
11 Standing in front of them were [a]seventy [b]elders of the
house of Israel, with Jaazaniah the son of Shaphan standing
among them, each man with his [c]censer in his hand and the
fragrance of the cloud of incense rising.
12 Then He said to me, "Son of man, do you see what the
elders of the house of Israel are committing in the dark, each
man in the room of his carved images? For they say, '[a]The LORD
does not see us; the LORD has [b]forsaken the land.'"
13 And He said to me, "Yet you will see still greater abominations which they are committing."
14 Then He brought me to the entrance of the [a]gate of the
LORD'S house which *was* toward the north; and behold, women
were sitting there weeping for Tammuz.
15 He said to me, "Do you see *this,* son of man? Yet you will
see still greater abominations than these."
16 Then He brought me into the inner court of the LORD'S house.
And behold, at the entrance to the temple of the LORD, between
the porch and the altar, *were* about twenty-five men with their
[a]backs to the temple of the LORD and their faces toward the east;
and [b]they were [1]prostrating themselves eastward toward the sun.
17 He said to me, "Do you see *this,* son of man? Is it too light
a thing for the house of Judah to commit the abominations
which they have committed here, that they have [a]filled the
land with violence and [b]provoked Me repeatedly? For behold,
they are putting the twig to their nose.

2 [2]Or *electrum* [b]Ezek 1:4, 27

3 [1]Lit *facing north* [a]Ezek 3:12; 11:1 [b]Ex 20:4; Deut 32:16

4 [a]Ezek 1:28; 3:22, 23

5 [a]Jer 3:2; Zech 5:5 [b]Ps 78:58; Jer 7:30; 32:34; Ezek 8:3

6 [a]2 Kin 23:4, 5; Ezek 5:11; 8:9, 17

8 [a]Is 29:15

11 [a]Num 11:16, 25; Luke 10:1 [b]Jer 19:1 [c]Num 16:17, 35

12 [a]Ps 14:1; Is 29:15; Ezek 9:9 [b]Ps 10:11

14 [a]Ezek 44:4; 46:9

16 [1]I.e. worshiping [a]2 Chr 29:6; Jer 2:27; Ezek 23:39 [b]Deut 4:19; 17:3; Job 31:26-28; Jer 44:17

17 [a]Ezek 7:11, 23; 9:9; Amos 3:10; Mic 2:2 [b]Jer 7:18, 19; Ezek 16:26

18 "Therefore, I indeed will deal in wrath. My eye will have no
pity nor will I spare; and [a]though they cry in My ears with a
loud voice, yet I will not listen to them."

Chapter 9 Theme ____________________

9 Then He cried out in my hearing with a loud [a]voice saying,
"Draw near, [1]O executioners of the city, each with his
destroying weapon in his hand."
2 Behold, six men came from the direction of the upper gate
which faces north, each with his shattering weapon in his hand;
and among them was [a]a certain man clothed in linen with a
[1]writing case at his loins. And they went in and stood beside
the bronze altar.
3 Then the [a]glory of the God of Israel went up from the cherub
on which it had been, to the threshold of the [1]temple. And He
called to the man clothed in linen at whose loins was the
writing case.
4 The LORD said to him, "Go through the midst of the city,
even through the midst of Jerusalem, and put a [a]mark on the
foreheads of the men who [b]sigh and groan over all the
abominations which are being committed in its midst."
5 But to the others He said in my hearing, "Go through the
city after him and strike; do not let your eye have pity and do
not spare.
6 "[1]Utterly [a]slay old men, young men, maidens, little children,
and women, but do not [b]touch any man on whom is the mark;
and you shall [c]start from My sanctuary." So they started with
the [2]elders who *were* before the [3]temple.
7 And He said to them, "[a]Defile the [1]temple and fill the courts
with the slain. Go out!" Thus they went out and struck down
the people in the city.
8 As they were striking *the people* and I *alone* was left, I [a]fell
on my face and cried out [1]saying, "[b]Alas, Lord [2]GOD! Are You
destroying the whole remnant of Israel [3]by pouring out Your
wrath on Jerusalem?"
9 Then He said to me, "The iniquity of the house of Israel
and Judah is very, very great, and the land is [a]filled with blood
and the city is [b]full of perversion; for [c]they say, 'The LORD has
forsaken the land, and the LORD does not see!'
10 "But as for Me, [a]My eye will have no pity nor will I spare,
but [b]I will bring their conduct upon their heads."
11 Then behold, the man clothed in linen at whose loins was
the [1]writing case [2]reported, saying, "I have done just as You
have commanded me."

Chapter 10 Theme ____________________

10 Then I looked, and behold, in the [1a]expanse that was over
the heads of the cherubim something like a [b]sapphire
stone, in appearance resembling a [c]throne, appeared above them.

18 [a]Is 1:15; Jer 11:11; Mic 3:4; Zech 7:13

9:1 [1]Lit *you who punish* [a]Is 6:8

2 [1]Or *scribal inkhorn* [a]Lev 16:4

3 [1]Lit *house* [a]Ezek 10:4; 11:22, 23

4 [a]Ex 12:7, 13; Ezek 9:6; 2 Cor 1:22; 2 Tim 2:19; Rev 7:2, 3; 9:4; 14:1 [b]Ps 119:53, 136; Jer 13:17; Ezek 6:11; 21:6

6 [1]Lit *To destruction* [2]Or *old men* [3]Lit *house* [a]2 Chr 36:17 [b]Ex 12:23; Rev 9:4 [c]Jer 25:29; Amos 3:2; Luke 12:47

7 [1]Lit *house* [a]2 Chr 36:17; Ezek 7:20-22

8 [1]Lit *and said* [2]Heb *YHWH*, usually rendered LORD [3]Lit *by Your pouring* [a]1 Chr 21:16 [b]Ezek 11:13; Amos 7:2-6

9 [a]2 Kin 21:16; Jer 2:34; Ezek 7:23; 22:2, 3 [b]Ezek 22:29; Mic 3:1-3; 7:3 [c]Job 22:13; Ps 10:11; 94:7; Is 29:15; Ezek 8:12

10 [a]Is 65:6; Ezek 8:18; 24:14 [b]Ezek 7:4; 11:21; Hos 9:7

11 [1]Or *inkhorn* [2]Lit *brought back word*

10:1 [1]Or *firmament* [a]Ezek 1:22, 26 [b]Ex 24:10 [c]Rev 4:2, 3

2 And He spoke to the man clothed in linen and said, "Enter between the [a]whirling wheels under the [1]cherubim and fill your hands with [b]coals of fire from between the cherubim and scatter *them* over the city." And he entered in my sight.

3 Now the cherubim were standing on the right side of the [1]temple when the man entered, and the cloud filled the [a]inner court.

4 Then the [a]glory of the LORD went up from the cherub to the threshold of the temple, and the [b]temple was filled with the cloud and the court was filled with the [c]brightness of the glory of the LORD.

5 Moreover, the sound of the wings of the cherubim was heard as far as the outer court, like the [a]voice of [1]God Almighty when He speaks.

6 It came about when He commanded the man clothed in linen, saying, "Take fire from between the whirling wheels, from between the cherubim," he entered and stood beside a wheel.

7 Then the cherub stretched out his hand from between the cherubim to the fire which was between the cherubim, took *some* and put *it* into the hands of the one clothed in linen, who took *it* and went out.

8 The cherubim appeared to have the form of a man's hand under their wings.

9 Then I looked, and behold, [a]four wheels beside the cherubim, one wheel beside each cherub; and the appearance of the wheels *was* like the gleam of a [1b]Tarshish stone.

10 As for their appearance, all four of them had the same likeness, as if one wheel were within another wheel.

11 When they moved, they went [a]in *any of* their four [1]directions without turning as they went; but they followed in the direction which [2]they faced, without turning as they went.

12 Their [a]whole body, their backs, their hands, their wings and the [b]wheels were full of eyes all around, the wheels belonging to all four of them.

13 The wheels were called in my hearing, the whirling wheels.

14 And [a]each one had four faces. The first face *was* the face of a cherub, the second face *was* the face of a man, the third the face of a lion, and the fourth the face of an eagle.

15 Then the cherubim rose up. They are the [a]living beings that I saw by the river Chebar.

16 Now when the cherubim moved, the wheels would go beside them; also when the cherubim lifted up their wings to rise from the ground, the wheels would not turn from beside them.

17 When [1]the cherubim [a]stood still, [1]the wheels would stand still; and when they rose up, [1]the wheels would rise with them, for the spirit of the living beings *was* in them.

18 Then the glory of the LORD departed from the threshold of the temple and stood [a]over the cherubim.

19 When [a]the cherubim departed, they lifted their wings and rose up from the earth in my sight with the wheels beside them; and they stood still at the entrance of the east gate of the

2 [1]So with Gr; Heb *cherub* [a]Ezek 1:15-21; 10:13 [b]Ps 18:10-13; Is 6:6; Ezek 1:13; Rev 8:5

3 [1]Lit *house*, and so throughout the ch [a]Ezek 8:3, 16

4 [a]Ezek 9:3; 11:22, 23 [b]Ex 40:34, 35; Is 6:1-4 [c]Ezek 1:28

5 [1]Heb *El Shaddai* [a]Job 40:9; Ezek 1:24; Rev 10:3

9 [1]Perhaps, *beryl* [a]Ezek 1:15-17 [b]Dan 10:6; Rev 21:20

11 [1]Lit *sides* [2]Lit *the head turned* [a]Ezek 1:17

12 [a]Rev 4:6, 8 [b]Ezek 1:18

14 [a]1 Kin 7:29, 36; Ezek 1:6, 10; 10:21; Rev 4:7

15 [a]Ezek 1:3, 5

17 [1]Lit *they* [a]Ezek 1:21

18 [a]Ps 18:10

19 [a]Ezek 11:22

LORD's house, and the glory of the God of Israel [1]hovered over
them.
20 These are the [a]living beings that I saw beneath the God of
Israel by [b]the river Chebar; so I knew that they *were* cherubim.
21 [a]Each one had four faces and each one four wings, and
beneath their wings *was* the form of human hands.
22 As for the likeness of their faces, they were the same faces
whose appearance I had seen by the river Chebar. Each one
went straight ahead.

Chapter 11 Theme ________________________________

11 Moreover, the [a]Spirit lifted me up and brought me to the
east gate of the LORD's house which faced eastward. And
behold, *there were* twenty-five men at the entrance of the gate,
and among them I saw Jaazaniah son of Azzur and [b]Pelatiah son
of Benaiah, leaders of the people.
2 He said to me, "Son of man, these are the men who devise
iniquity and [a]give evil advice in this city,
3 who say, '*The time* is not near to build houses. [1]This [a]*city*
is the pot and we are the flesh.'
4 "Therefore, [a]prophesy against them, son of man, prophesy!"
5 Then the Spirit of the LORD fell upon me, and He said to
me, "Say, 'Thus says the LORD, "So you think, house of Israel,
for [a]I know [1]your [b]thoughts.
6 "You have [a]multiplied your slain in this city, filling its streets
with [1]them."
7 'Therefore, thus says the Lord [1]GOD, "Your [a]slain whom you
have laid in the midst of [2]the city are the flesh and this *city* is
the pot; but [3]I will [b]bring you out of it.
8 "You have [a]feared a sword; so I will [b]bring a sword upon
you," the Lord GOD declares.
9 "And I will bring you out of the midst of [1]the city and deliver
you into the hands of [a]strangers and [b]execute judgments against
you.
10 "You will [a]fall by the sword. I will judge you to the [b]border
of Israel; so you shall know that I am the LORD.
11 "This *city* will [a]not be a pot for you, nor will you be flesh in
the midst of it, *but* I will judge you to the border of Israel.
12 "Thus you will know that I am the LORD; for you have not
walked in My statutes nor have you [a]executed My ordinances,
but have acted according to the ordinances of the [b]nations
around you."'"
13 Now it came about as I prophesied, that [a]Pelatiah son of
Benaiah died. Then I fell on my face and cried out with a loud
voice and said, "[b]Alas, Lord GOD! Will You bring the remnant of
Israel to a complete end?"
14 Then the word of the LORD came to me, saying,
15 "Son of man, your brothers, your [1]relatives, [2]your fellow
exiles and the whole house of Israel, all of them, *are those* to
whom the inhabitants of Jerusalem have said, 'Go far from the
LORD; this land has been given [a]us as a possession.'

19 [1]Lit *over them from above*
20 [a]Ezek 1:5, 22, 26; 10:15 [b]Ezek 1:1
21 [a]Ezek 1:6, 8; 10:14; 41:18, 19
11:1 [a]Ezek 3:12, 14; 8:3; 11:24; 43:5 [b]Ezek 11:13
2 [a]Ps 2:1, 2; 52:2; Is 30:1; Jer 5:5; Mic 2:1
3 [1]Or *This is* [a]Jer 1:13; Ezek 11:7, 11; 24:3, 6
4 [a]Ezek 3:4, 17
5 [1]Lit *what comes up in your spirit* [a]Jer 11:20; 17:10 [b]Ezek 38:10
6 [1]Lit *the slain* [a]Is 1:15; Ezek 7:23; 22:2-6, 9, 12, 27
7 [1]Heb *YHWH*, usually rendered *LORD*, and so throughout the ch [2]Lit *it* [3]So with Gr; Heb *he will bring you out* [a]Ezek 24:3-13; Mic 3:2, 3 [b]2 Kin 25:18-22; Jer 52:24-27; Ezek 11:9
8 [a]Prov 10:24; Is 66:4 [b]Job 3:25; Is 24:17, 18
9 [1]Lit *it* [a]Deut 28:36, 49, 50; Ps 106:41 [b]Ezek 5:8; 16:41
10 [a]Jer 52:9, 10 [b]2 Kin 14:25
11 [a]Ezek 11:3, 7; 24:3, 6
12 [a]Ezek 18:8, 9 [b]Ezek 8:10, 14, 16
13 [a]Ezek 11:1 [b]Ezek 9:8
15 [1]Lit *brothers* [2]So with Gr and some ancient versions; Heb *the men of your redemption* [a]Ezek 33:24

16 "Therefore say, 'Thus says the Lord GOD, "Though I had
removed them far away among the nations and though I had
scattered them among the countries, yet I was a [a]sanctuary for
them a little while in the countries where they had gone."'
17 "Therefore say, 'Thus says the Lord GOD, "I will [a]gather you
from the peoples and assemble you out of the countries among
which you have been scattered, and I will give you the land of
Israel."'
18 "When they come there, they will [a]remove all its [b]detestable
things and all its abominations from it.
19 "And I will [a]give them one heart, and put a new spirit within
[1]them. And I will take the [b]heart of stone out of their flesh and
give them a [c]heart of flesh,
20 that they may [a]walk in My statutes and keep My ordinances
and do them. Then they will be [b]My people, and I shall be
their God.
21 "[1]But as for those whose hearts go after their [a]detestable
things and abominations, I will [b]bring their conduct down on
their heads," declares the Lord GOD.
22 Then the cherubim [a]lifted up their wings with the wheels
beside them, and [b]the glory of the God of Israel [1]hovered over
them.
23 The [a]glory of the LORD went up from the midst of the city
and [b]stood over the mountain which is east of the city.
24 And the [a]Spirit lifted me up and brought me in a vision by
the Spirit of God to the exiles [1]in Chaldea. So the vision that I
had seen [2b]left me.
25 Then I [a]told the exiles all the things that the LORD had
shown me.

Chapter 12 Theme

12 Then the word of the LORD came to me, saying,
2 "Son of man, you live in the [a]midst of the [b]rebellious
house, who [c]have eyes to see but do not see, ears to hear but
do not hear; for they are a rebellious house.
3 "Therefore, son of man, prepare for yourself baggage for
exile and go into exile by day in their sight; even go into exile
from your place to another place in their sight. [a]Perhaps they
will [1]understand though they are a rebellious house.
4 "Bring your baggage out by day in their sight, as baggage for
exile. Then you will go out [a]at evening in their sight, as those
going into exile.
5 "Dig a hole through the wall in their sight and [1]go out
through it.
6 "Load *the baggage* on *your* shoulder in their sight *and* carry
it out in the dark. You shall [a]cover your face so that you cannot
see the land, for I have set you as a [b]sign to the house of Israel."
7 I [a]did so, as I had been commanded. By day I [b]brought out
my baggage like the baggage of an exile. Then in the evening I
dug through the wall with my hands; I went out in the dark
and carried *the baggage* on *my* shoulder in their sight.

16 [a]Ps 31:20; 90:1; 91:9; Is 8:14; Jer 29:7, 11

17 [a]Is 11:11-16; Jer 3:12, 18; 24:5; Ezek 20:41, 42; 28:25

18 [a]Ezek 37:23 [b]Ezek 5:11; 7:20

19 [1]So with Gr and many mss; Heb *you* [a]Jer 24:7; 32:39; Ezek 18:31; 36:26 [b]Zech 7:12; Rom 2:4, 5 [c]2 Cor 3:3

20 [a]Ps 105:45; Ezek 36:27 [b]Ezek 14:11

21 [1]Lit *And to the heart of their detestable things and their abomination their heart goes* [a]Jer 16:18; Ezek 11:18 [b]Ezek 9:10; 16:43

22 [1]Lit *over them from above* [a]Ezek 10:19 [b]Ezek 43:2

23 [a]Ezek 8:4 [b]Zech 14:4

24 [1]I.e. Babylonia [2]Lit *went up from* [a]Ezek 8:3; 11:1; 37:1; 2 Cor 12:2-4 [b]Acts 10:16

25 [a]Ezek 2:7; 3:4, 17, 27

12:2 [a]Is 6:5 [b]Ps 78:40; Is 1:23; Ezek 2:7, 8 [c]Is 6:9f; 43:8; Jer 5:21; Matt 13:13, 14; Mark 4:12; 8:18; Luke 8:10; John 9:39-41; 12:40; Acts 28:26f; Rom 11:8

3 [1]Or *see that they are* [a]Jer 26:3; 36:3, 7; Luke 20:13; 2 Tim 2:25

4 [a]2 Kin 25:4; Jer 39:4; Ezek 12:12

5 [1]Lit *bring it out*

6 [a]1 Sam 28:8; Ezek 12:12, 13 [b]Is 8:18; 20:3; Ezek 4:3; 12:11; 24:24

7 [a]Ezek 24:18; 37:7, 10 [b]Ezek 12:3-6

8 In the morning the word of the LORD came to me, saying,
9 "Son of man, has not the house of Israel, the [a]rebellious
house, said to you, '[b]What are you doing?'
10 "Say to them, 'Thus says the Lord [1]GOD, "This [2a]burden
concerns the prince in Jerusalem as well as all the house of
Israel who are [3]in it."'
11 "Say, 'I am [1]a [a]sign to you. As I have done, so it will be done
to them; they will [b]go into exile, into captivity.'
12 "The [a]prince who is among them will load *his baggage* on
his shoulder in the dark and go out. [1]They will dig a hole
through the wall to bring *it* out. He will cover his face so that
he can not see the land with *his* eyes.
13 "I will also spread My [a]net over him, and he will be caught
in My snare. And I will bring him to Babylon in the land of the
Chaldeans; yet he will [b]not see it, though he will die there.
14 "I will [a]scatter to every wind all who are around him, his
helpers and all his troops; and I will draw out a sword after them.
15 "So they will [a]know that I am the LORD when I scatter them
among the nations and spread them among the countries.
16 "But I will [1]spare a few of them from the [a]sword, the famine
and the pestilence that they may tell all their abominations
among the nations where they go, and [2]may [b]know that I am
the LORD."
17 Moreover, the word of the LORD came to me saying,
18 "Son of man, [a]eat your bread with trembling and drink your
water with quivering and anxiety.
19 "Then say to the people of the land, 'Thus says the Lord
GOD concerning the inhabitants of Jerusalem in the land of
Israel, "They will eat their bread with anxiety and drink their
water with horror, because [1]their land will be [2a]stripped of its
fullness on account of the violence of all who live in it.
20 "The inhabited [a]cities will be laid waste and the [b]land will
be a desolation. So you will know that I am the LORD."'"
21 Then the word of the LORD came to me, saying,
22 "Son of man, what is this [a]proverb you *people* have
concerning the land of Israel, saying, 'The [b]days are long and
every [c]vision fails'?
23 "Therefore say to them, 'Thus says the Lord GOD, "I will
make this proverb cease so that they will no longer use it as a
proverb in Israel." But tell them, "[a]The days draw near as well
as the [1]fulfillment of every vision.
24 "For there will no longer be any [1a]false vision or flattering
divination within the house of Israel.
25 "For I the LORD will speak, and whatever [a]word I speak will
be performed. It will no longer be delayed, for in [b]your days, O
[c]rebellious house, I will speak the word and perform it,"
declares the Lord GOD.'"
26 Furthermore, the word of the LORD came to me, saying,
27 "Son of man, behold, the house of Israel is saying, 'The vision
that he sees is for [a]many [1]years *from now,* and he prophesies of
times far off.'

9 [a]Ezek 2:5-8; 12:1-3 [b]Ezek 17:12; 20:49; 24:19

10 [1]Heb *YHWH,* usually rendered *LORD,* and so throughout the ch [2]Or *oracle* [3]Lit *in their midst* [a]2 Kin 9:25; Is 13:1; Ezek 12:3-8

11 [1]Lit *your sign* [a]Ezek 12:6 [b]Jer 15:2; 52:15, 28-30; Ezek 12:3

12 [1]I.e. the king's attendants [a]2 Kin 25:4; Jer 39:4; 52:7; Ezek 12:6

13 [a]Is 24:17, 18; Ezek 17:20; 19:8; Hos 7:12 [b]Jer 39:7; 52:11

14 [a]2 Kin 25:4, 5; Ezek 5:2; 17:21

15 [a]Ezek 6:7, 14; 12:16, 20

16 [1]Lit *leave over* [2]Or *they will know* [a]Ezek 7:15; 14:21 [b]Jer 22:8, 9

18 [a]Lam 5:9; Ezek 4:16

19 [1]Lit *her* [2]Lit *desolate* [a]Jer 10:22; Ezek 6:6, 7, 14; Mic 7:13; Zech 7:14

20 [a]Is 3:26; Jer 4:7; Ezek 5:14 [b]Is 7:23, 24; Jer 25:9; Ezek 36:3

22 [a]Ezek 16:44; 18:2, 3 [b]Jer 5:12; Ezek 11:3; 12:27; Amos 6:3; 2 Pet 3:4 [c]Ezek 7:26

23 [1]Lit *word* [a]Ps 37:13; Joel 2:1; Zeph 1:14

24 [1]Lit *vain* [a]Jer 14:13-16; Ezek 13:6, 23; Zech 13:2-4

25 [a]Num 14:28-34; Is 14:24; Ezek 6:10; 12:28 [b]Jer 16:9; Hab 1:5 [c]Ezek 12:2

27 [1]Lit *days* [a]Ezek 12:22; Dan 10:14

28 "Therefore say to them, 'Thus says the Lord GOD, "None of
My words will be delayed any longer. Whatever word I speak
will be performed,"'" declares the Lord GOD.

Chapter 13 Theme ______________________________

13 Then the word of the LORD came to me saying,
2 "Son of man, prophesy against the [a]prophets of Israel
who prophesy, and say to those who prophesy from their own
[1]inspiration, '[b]Listen to the word of the LORD!
3 'Thus says the Lord [1]GOD, "Woe to the [a]foolish prophets
who are following their own spirit and have [b]seen nothing.
4 "O Israel, your prophets have been like foxes among ruins.
5 "You have not [a]gone up into the [b]breaches, nor did you
build the wall around the house of Israel to stand in the battle
on the [c]day of the LORD.
6 "They see [1a]falsehood and lying divination who are saying,
'The LORD declares,' when the LORD has not sent them; [b]yet
they hope for the fulfillment of *their* word.
7 "[a]Did you not see a false vision and speak a lying divination
when you said, 'The LORD declares,' but it is not I who have
spoken?"'"
8 Therefore, thus says the Lord GOD, "Because you have
spoken [1]falsehood and seen a lie, therefore behold, [a]I am against
you," declares the Lord GOD.
9 "So My hand will be against the [a]prophets who see false
visions and utter lying divinations. They will [1]have no place in
the council of My people, [b]nor will they be written down in
the register of the house of Israel, nor will they enter the land
of Israel, [2]that you may know that I am the Lord GOD.
10 "It is definitely because they have [a]misled My people by
saying, '[b]Peace!' when there is [c]no peace. And when anyone
builds a wall, behold, they plaster it over with whitewash;
11 *so* tell those who plaster *it* over with whitewash, that it
will fall. A [a]flooding rain will come, and you, O hailstones, will
fall; and a violent wind will break out.
12 "Behold, when the wall has fallen, will you not be asked,
'Where is the plaster with which you plastered *it?*'"
13 Therefore, thus says the Lord GOD, "I will make a violent
wind break out in My wrath. There will also be in My anger a
flooding rain and [a]hailstones to consume *it* in wrath.
14 "So I will tear down the wall which you plastered over with
whitewash and bring it down to the ground, so that its
[a]foundation is laid bare; and when it falls, you will be
[b]consumed in its midst. And you will [c]know that I am the LORD.
15 "Thus I will spend My wrath on the wall and on those who
have plastered it over with whitewash; and I will say to you,
'The wall [1]is gone and its plasterers are gone,
16 *along with* the prophets of Israel who prophesy to Jerusalem,
and who [a]see visions of peace for her when there is [b]no peace,'
declares the Lord GOD.

13:2 [1]Lit *heart* [a]Is 9:15; Jer 37:19; Ezek 22:25, 28 [b]Is 1:10; Amos 7:16
3 [1]Heb *YHWH,* usually rendered *LORD,* and so throughout the ch [a]Lam 2:14; Hos 9:7; Zech 11:15 [b]Jer 23:28-32
5 [a]Ps 106:23; Jer 23:22; Ezek 22:30 [b]Is 58:12 [c]Is 13:6, 9; Ezek 7:19
6 [1]Lit *vanity* [a]Jer 29:8; Ezek 22:28 [b]Jer 28:15; 37:19
7 [a]Ezek 22:28
8 [1]Lit *vanity* [a]Ezek 5:8; 21:3; Nah 2:13
9 [1]Lit *not be in* [2]Or *and you will know* [a]Jer 20:3-6; 28:15-17 [b]Ps 69:28; 87:6; Jer 17:13; Dan 12:1
10 [a]Jer 23:32; 50:6 [b]Jer 6:14; 8:11; 14:13 [c]Ezek 7:25; 13:16
11 [a]Ezek 38:22
13 [a]Ex 9:24, 25; Ps 18:12, 13; Is 30:30; Rev 11:19; 16:21
14 [a]Mic 1:6; Hab 3:13 [b]Jer 6:15; 14:15 [c]Ezek 13:9
15 [1]Lit *is not . . . are not*
16 [a]Jer 6:14; 8:11; Ezek 13:10 [b]Is 57:21

17 "Now you, son of man, set your face against the daughters of
your people who are [a]prophesying [b]from their own [1]inspiration.
Prophesy against them
18 and say, 'Thus says the Lord GOD, "Woe to the women who
sew *magic* bands on [1]all wrists and make veils for the heads of
persons of every stature to [a]hunt down [2]lives! Will you hunt
down the [2]lives of My people, but preserve the [2]lives *of others*
for yourselves?
19 "[a]For handfuls of barley and fragments of bread, you have
profaned Me to My people to put to death [1]some who should
not die and to [b]keep [1]others alive who should not live, by your
lying to My people who listen to lies."'"
20 Therefore, thus says the Lord GOD, "Behold, I am against
your *magic* bands by which you hunt [1]lives there as [2]birds and
I will tear them from your arms; and I will let [1]them go, even
those [1]lives whom you hunt as [2]birds.
21 "I will also tear off your veils and [a]deliver My people from
your hands, and they will no longer be in your hands to be
hunted; and you will know that I am the LORD.
22 "Because you [a]disheartened the righteous with falsehood
when I did not cause him grief, but have [1b]encouraged the
wicked not to [c]turn from his wicked way *and* preserve his life,
23 therefore, you women will no longer see [1a]false visions or
practice divination, and I will [b]deliver My people out of your
hand. Thus you will [c]know that I am the LORD."

Chapter 14 Theme ______________________

14 Then some [a]elders of Israel came to me and [b]sat down
before me.
2 And the word of the LORD came to me, saying,
3 "Son of man, these men have [a]set up their idols in their
hearts and have [b]put right before their faces the stumbling
block of their iniquity. Should I be [c]consulted by them at all?
4 "Therefore speak to them and tell them, 'Thus says the Lord
[1]GOD, "Any man of the house of Israel who sets up his idols in
his heart, puts right before his face the stumbling block of his
iniquity, and *then* comes to the prophet, I the LORD will be
brought to give him an answer in [2]the matter in view of the
[a]multitude of his idols,
5 in order to lay hold of [1a]the hearts of the house of Israel
who are [2b]estranged from Me through all their idols."'
6 "Therefore say to the house of Israel, 'Thus says the Lord
GOD, "[a]Repent and turn away from your idols and turn your
faces away from all your [b]abominations.
7 "For anyone of the house of Israel or of the [a]immigrants who
stay in Israel who separates himself from Me, sets up his idols
in his heart, puts right before his face the stumbling block of
his iniquity, and *then* comes to the prophet to inquire of Me for
himself, [b]I the LORD will be brought to answer him in My own
person.

17 [1]Lit *heart* [a]Judg 4:4; 2 Kin 22:14; Luke 2:36; Acts 21:9 [b]Ezek 13:2; Rev 2:20

18 [1]Lit *all joints of the hand;* M.T. reads *of my hands* [2]Or *souls* [a]2 Pet 2:14

19 [1]Or *souls* [a]Prov 28:21; Mic 3:5 [b]Jer 23:14, 17

20 [1]Lit *souls* [2]Or *flying ones*

21 [a]Ps 91:3; 124:7

22 [1]Lit *strengthen the hands of* [a]Amos 5:12 [b]Jer 23:14; 34:16, 22 [c]Ezek 18:21, 27, 30-32; 33:14-16

23 [1]Lit *vanity* [a]Ezek 12:24; 13:6; Mic 3:6; Zech 13:3 [b]Ezek 13:21; 34:10 [c]Ezek 13:9, 21

14:1 [a]2 Kin 6:32; Ezek 8:1; 20:1 [b]Is 29:13; Ezek 33:31, 32

3 [a]Ezek 20:16 [b]Ezek 7:19; 14:4, 7; Zeph 1:3 [c]Is 1:15; Jer 11:11; Ezek 20:3, 31

4 [1]Heb *YHWH,* usually rendered *LORD,* and so throughout the ch [2]Lit *it* [a]1 Kin 21:20-24; 2 Kin 1:16; Is 66:4

5 [1]Lit *their* [2]Or *all estranged from Me through their idols* [a]Jer 17:10; Zech 7:12 [b]Is 1:4; Jer 2:11; Zech 11:8

6 [a]1 Sam 7:3; Neh 1:9; Is 2:20; 30:22; 55:6, 7; Ezek 18:30 [b]Ezek 8:6; 14:4

7 [a]Ex 12:48; 20:10 [b]Ezek 14:4

8"I will [a]set My face against that man and make him a [b]sign
and [1]a proverb, and I will cut him off from among My people.
So you will know that I am the LORD.
9"But if the prophet is [1]prevailed upon to speak a word, it is
I, the LORD, who have [1]prevailed upon that prophet, and I will
stretch out My hand against him and [a]destroy him from among
My people Israel.
10"They will bear *the punishment of* their iniquity; as the
iniquity of the inquirer is, so the iniquity of the prophet will be,
11 in order that the house of Israel may no longer [a]stray from
Me and no longer [b]defile themselves with all their transgressions.
Thus they will be [c]My people, and I shall be their God,"'
declares the Lord GOD."
12 Then the word of the LORD came to me saying,
13"Son of man, if a country sins against Me by [a]committing
unfaithfulness, and I stretch out My hand against it, [1]destroy its
[b]supply of bread, send famine against it and cut off from it both
man and beast,
14 even [a]*though* these three men, [b]Noah, [c]Daniel and [d]Job
were in its midst, by their *own* righteousness they could *only*
deliver [e]themselves," declares the Lord GOD.
15"If I were to cause [a]wild beasts to pass through the land and
they [1]depopulated it, and it became desolate so that no one
would pass through it because of the beasts,
16 *though* these three men were in its midst, as I live,"
declares the Lord GOD, "they could not deliver either *their* sons
or *their* daughters. [a]They alone would be delivered, but the
country would be desolate.
17"Or *if* I should [a]bring a sword on that country and say, 'Let
the sword pass through the country and [b]cut off man and beast
from it,'
18 even *though* these three men were in its midst, as I live,"
declares the Lord GOD, "they could not deliver either *their* sons
or *their* daughters, but they alone would be delivered.
19"Or *if* I should send a [a]plague against that country and pour
out My wrath in blood on it to cut off man and beast from it,
20 even *though* Noah, Daniel and Job were in its midst, as I
live," declares the Lord GOD, "they could not deliver either
their son or *their* daughter. They would deliver only themselves
by their righteousness."
21 For thus says the Lord GOD, "How much more when [a]I
send My four [1]severe judgments against Jerusalem: sword,
famine, wild beasts and plague to cut off man and beast from it!
22"Yet, behold, [1]survivors will be left in it who will be brought
out, *both* sons and daughters. Behold, they are going to come
forth to you and you will [a]see their conduct and actions; then
you will be [b]comforted for the calamity which I have brought
against Jerusalem for everything which I have brought upon it.
23"Then they will comfort you when you see their conduct
and actions, for you will know that I have not done [a]in vain
whatever I did [1]to it," declares the Lord GOD.

8 [1]Lit *proverbs* [a]Jer 44:11; Ezek 15:7 [b]Is 65:15; Ezek 5:15

9 [1]Or *enticed* [a]Jer 6:14, 15; 14:15

11 [a]Ezek 44:10, 15; 48:11 [b]Ezek 11:18; 37:23 [c]Ezek 11:20; 34:30; 36:28

13 [1]Lit *break the staff* [a]Ezek 15:8; 20:27 [b]Lev 26:26; Is 3:1; Ezek 4:16

14 [a]Jer 15:1 [b]Gen 6:8; 7:1; Heb 11:7 [c]Ezek 28:3; Dan 1:6; 9:21; 10:11 [d]Job 1:1, 5; 42:8, 9 [e]Ezek 16:18, 20; 18:20

15 [1]Lit *bereave of children* [a]Lev 26:22; Num 21:6; Ezek 5:17; 14:21

16 [a]Gen 19:29; Ezek 18:20

17 [a]Lev 26:25; Ezek 5:12; 21:3, 4 [b]Ezek 25:13; Zeph 1:3

19 [a]Jer 14:12; Ezek 5:12; 14:21

21 [1]Lit *evil* [a]Ezek 5:17; 33:27; Amos 4:6-10; Rev 6:8

22 [1]Lit *escaped ones* [a]Ezek 12:16; 36:20 [b]Ezek 16:54; 31:16; 32:31

23 [1]Or *in* [a]Jer 22:8, 9

Chapter 15 Theme ______________________________

15 Then the word of the LORD came to me, saying,
2 "Son of man, how is the wood of the [a]vine *better* than
any wood of a branch which is among the trees of the forest?
3 "Can wood be taken from it to make [1]anything, or can *men*
take a peg from it on which to hang any vessel?
4 "[1]If it has been put into the [a]fire for fuel, *and* the fire has
consumed both of its ends and its middle part has been
charred, is it *then* useful for [2]anything?
5 "Behold, while it is intact, it is not made into [1]anything. How
much less, when the fire has consumed it and it is charred, can
it still be made into [1]anything!
6 "Therefore, thus says the Lord [1]GOD, 'As the wood of the
vine among the trees of the forest, which I have given to the
fire for fuel, so have I given up the inhabitants of Jerusalem;
7 and I [a]set My face against them. *Though* they have [b]come
out of the fire, yet the fire will consume them. Then you will
know that I am the LORD, when I set My face against them.
8 'Thus I will make the land desolate, because they have
[a]acted unfaithfully,'" declares the Lord GOD.

Chapter 16 Theme ______________________________

16 Then the word of the LORD came to me, saying,
2 "Son of man, [a]make known to Jerusalem her abominations
3 and say, 'Thus says the Lord [1]GOD to Jerusalem, "Your
origin and your birth are from the land of the Canaanite, your
father was an Amorite and your mother a Hittite.
4 "As for your birth, [a]on the day you were born your navel cord
was not cut, nor were you washed with water for cleansing;
you were not rubbed with salt or even wrapped in cloths.
5 "No eye looked with pity on you to do any of these things
for you, to have compassion on you. Rather you were thrown
out into the [1a]open field, [2]for you were abhorred on the day
you were born.
6 "When I passed by you and saw you squirming in your
blood, I said to you *while you were* in your blood, 'Live!' Yes, I
said to you *while you were* in your blood, 'Live!'
7 "I [a]made you [1]numerous like plants of the field. Then you
grew up, became tall and reached the age for fine ornaments;
your breasts were formed and your hair had grown. Yet you
were naked and bare.
8 "Then I passed by you and saw you, and behold, [1]you were at
the time for love; so I [a]spread My skirt over you and covered your
nakedness. I also [b]swore to you and [c]entered into a covenant
with you so that you [d]became Mine," declares the Lord GOD.
9 "Then I bathed you with water, washed off your blood from
you and [a]anointed you with oil.
10 "I also clothed you with [a]embroidered cloth and put sandals
of porpoise skin on your feet; and I wrapped you with fine
linen and covered you with silk.

15:2 [a]Ps 80:8-16; Is 5:1-7; Hos 10:1

3 [1]Lit *a work*

4 [1]Or *Behold* [2]Lit *a work* [a]Is 27:11; Ezek 15:6; 19:14

5 [1]Lit *a work*

6 [1]Heb *YHWH,* usually rendered *LORD,* and so throughout the ch

7 [a]Lev 26:17; Ps 34:16; Jer 21:10; Ezek 14:8 [b]1 Kin 19:17; Is 24:18; Amos 9:1-4

8 [a]Ezek 14:13; 17:20

16:2 [a]Is 58:1; Ezek 20:4; 22:2

3 [1]Heb *YHWH,* usually rendered *LORD,* and so throughout the ch

4 [a]Hos 2:3

5 [1]Lit *surface* [2]Lit *in the loathing of your soul* [a]Deut 32:10

7 [1]Lit *a myriad* [a]Ex 1:7; Deut 1:10

8 [1]Lit *your time was* [a]Ruth 3:9; Jer 2:2 [b]Gen 22:16-18 [c]Ex 24:7, 8 [d]Ex 19:5; Ezek 20:5; Hos 2:19, 20

9 [a]Ruth 3:3

10 [a]Ex 26:36; Ezek 16:13, 18; 26:16; 27:7, 16

11 "I adorned you with ornaments, put [a]bracelets on your
hands and a [b]necklace around your neck.
12 "I also put a [a]ring in your nostril, earrings in your ears and a
[b]beautiful crown on your head.
13 "Thus you were adorned with [a]gold and silver, and your
dress was of fine linen, silk and embroidered cloth. You ate fine
flour, honey and oil; so you were exceedingly beautiful and
advanced to [b]royalty.
14 "Then your [a]fame went forth among the nations on account
of your beauty, for it was [b]perfect because of My splendor
which I bestowed on you," declares the Lord GOD.
15 "But you [a]trusted in your beauty and [b]played the harlot
because of your fame, and you poured out your harlotries on
every passer-by [1]who might be *willing.*
16 "You took some of your clothes, made for yourself high
places of various colors and played the harlot on them, [1]which
should never come about nor happen.
17 "You also took your beautiful [1a]jewels *made* of My gold and
of My silver, which I had given you, and made for yourself male
images that you might play the harlot with them.
18 "Then you took your embroidered cloth and covered them,
and offered My oil and My incense before them.
19 "Also [a]My bread which I gave you, fine flour, oil and honey
with which I fed you, [1]you would offer before them for a
soothing aroma; so it happened," declares the Lord GOD.
20 "Moreover, you took your sons and daughters whom you had
borne to [a]Me and [b]sacrificed them to [1]idols to be devoured.
Were your harlotries so small a matter?
21 "You slaughtered [a]My children and offered them up to [1]idols
by [b]causing them to pass through *the fire.*
22 "Besides all your abominations and harlotries you did not
remember the days of [a]your youth, when you were naked and
bare and squirming in your blood.
23 "Then it came about after all your wickedness ('Woe, woe to
you!' declares the Lord GOD),
24 that you built yourself a [a]shrine and made yourself a [b]high
place in every square.
25 "You built yourself a high place at the top of [a]every street
and made your beauty abominable, and you spread your legs to
every passer-by to multiply your harlotry.
26 "You also played the harlot with the Egyptians, your [1]lustful
neighbors, and multiplied your harlotry to [a]make Me angry.
27 "Behold now, I have stretched out My hand against you and
diminished your rations. And I delivered you up to the desire
of those who hate you, the [a]daughters of the Philistines, who
are ashamed of your lewd conduct.
28 "Moreover, you played the harlot with the [a]Assyrians because
you were not satisfied; you played the harlot with them and still
were not satisfied.
29 "You also multiplied your harlotry with the land of merchants,
Chaldea, yet even with this you were not satisfied."'"

11 [a]Gen 24:22, 47; Is 3:19; Ezek 23:42 [b]Gen 41:42; Prov 1:9

12 [a]Gen 24:47; Is 3:21 [b]Is 28:5; Jer 13:18; Ezek 16:14

13 [a]Ps 45:13, 14; Ezek 16:17 [b]1 Sam 10:1; 1 Kin 4:21

14 [a]1 Kin 10:1, 24 [b]Ps 50:2; Lam 2:15

15 [1]Lit *to whom it might be* [a]Ezek 16:25; 27:3 [b]Is 57:8; Jer 2:20

16 [1]Lit *things which had not happened nor will it be*

17 [1]Lit *articles of beauty* [a]Ezek 16:11, 12

19 [1]Lit *and you...offer it* [a]Hos 2:8

20 [1]Lit *them* [a]Ex 13:2, 12; Deut 29:11, 12 [b]Ps 106:37, 38; Jer 7:31; Ezek 20:31; 23:37

21 [1]Lit *them* [a]Ex 13:2 [b]2 Kin 17:17; Jer 19:5

22 [a]Jer 2:2

24 [a]Jer 11:13; Ezek 16:31, 39; 20:28, 29 [b]Ps 78:58; Is 57:7

25 [a]Prov 9:14

26 [1]Lit *great of flesh* [a]Jer 7:18, 19; Ezek 8:17

27 [a]Is 9:12; Ezek 16:57

28 [a]2 Kin 16:7, 10-18; 2 Chr 28:16, 20-23; Jer 2:18, 36; Ezek 23:12; Hos 10:6

30 "How [a]languishing is your heart," declares the Lord GOD,
"while you do all these things, the actions of a [1b]bold-faced harlot.
31 "When you built your shrine at the beginning of every street
and made your high place in every square, in [a]disdaining
money, you were not like a harlot.
32 "You adulteress wife, who takes strangers instead of her
husband!
33 "[1]Men give gifts to all harlots, but you [a]give your gifts to all
your lovers to bribe them to come to you from every direction
for your harlotries.
34 "Thus you are different from those women in your
harlotries, in that no one plays the harlot [1]as you do, because you
give money and no money is given you; thus you are different."
35 Therefore, O harlot, hear the word of the LORD.
36 Thus says the Lord GOD, "Because your lewdness was
poured out and your nakedness uncovered through your
harlotries with your lovers and with all your detestable [a]idols,
and because of the blood of your sons which you gave to [1]idols,
37 therefore, behold, I will [a]gather all your lovers with whom
you took pleasure, even all those whom you loved *and* all those
whom you [b]hated. So I will gather them against you from every
direction and [c]expose your nakedness to them that they may
see all your nakedness.
38 "Thus I will [a]judge you like women who commit adultery or
shed blood are judged; and I will bring on you the blood of
[b]wrath and jealousy.
39 "I will also give you into [1]the hands of your lovers, and they
will tear down your shrines, demolish your high places, [a]strip
you of your clothing, take away your [2]jewels, and will leave you
naked and bare.
40 "They will [1]incite a [a]crowd against you and they will stone
you and cut you to pieces with their swords.
41 "They will [a]burn your houses with fire and execute judgments
on you in the sight of many women. Then I will [b]stop you from
playing the harlot, and you will also no longer pay [1]your lovers.
42 "So I [a]will calm My fury against you and My jealousy will
depart from you, and I will be pacified and angry [b]no more.
43 "Because you have [a]not remembered the days of your youth
but [1]have [b]enraged Me by all these things, behold, I in turn
will [c]bring your conduct down on your own head," declares
the Lord GOD, "so that you will not commit this lewdness on
top of all your *other* abominations.
44 "Behold, everyone who quotes [a]proverbs will quote *this*
proverb concerning you, saying, '[1]Like mother, [1]like daughter.'
45 "You are the daughter of your mother, who loathed her
husband and children. You are also the [a]sister of your sisters,
who [b]loathed their husbands and children. Your mother was a
Hittite and your father an Amorite.
46 "Now your [a]older sister is Samaria, who lives [1]north of you
with her [2]daughters; and your younger sister, who lives [3]south
of you, is [b]Sodom with her [2]daughters.

30 [1]Lit *domineering* [a]Prov 9:13; Is 1:3; Jer 4:22 [b]Is 3:9; Jer 3:3

31 [a]Is 52:3

33 [1]Lit *They* [a]Is 57:9; Ezek 16:41; Hos 8:9, 10

34 [1]Lit *after you*

36 [1]Lit *them* [a]Jer 19:5; Ezek 20:31; 23:37

37 [a]Jer 13:22, 26; Ezek 23:9, 22; Hos 2:3, 10; Nah 3:5, 6 [b]Ezek 23:17, 28 [c]Is 47:3

38 [a]Ezek 23:45 [b]Ps 79:3, 5; Jer 18:21; Ezek 23:25; Zeph 1:17

39 [1]Lit *their hands, and they* [2]Lit *articles of beauty* [a]Ezek 23:26; Hos 2:3

40 [1]Lit *bring up an assembly* [a]Ezek 23:47; Hab 1:6-10

41 [1]Lit *a harlot's hire* [a]2 Kin 25:9; Jer 39:8; 52:13 [b]Ezek 23:48

42 [a]2 Sam 24:25; Ezek 5:13; 21:17; Zech 6:8 [b]Is 40:1, 2; 54:9, 10; Ezek 39:29

43 [1]So with ancient versions; Heb *are angry against* [a]Ps 78:42; 106:13; Ezek 16:22 [b]Is 63:10; Ezek 6:9 [c]Ezek 11:21; 22:31

44 [1]Lit *Her* [a]1 Sam 24:13; Ezek 12:22, 23; 18:2, 3

45 [a]Ezek 23:2 [b]Is 1:4; Ezek 23:37-39; Zech 11:8

46 [1]Lit *on your left* [2]I.e. environs; so through v 55 [3]Lit *from your right* [a]Jer 3:8-11; Ezek 23:4 [b]Gen 13:10-13; 18:20; Ezek 16:48, 49, 53-56, 61

47 "Yet you have not merely walked in their ways or done according to their abominations; but, as if that were [a]too little, you acted [b]more corruptly in all your conduct than they.

48 "As I live," declares the Lord GOD, "Sodom, your sister and her daughters have [a]not done as you and your daughters have done.

49 "Behold, this was the guilt of your sister Sodom: she and her daughters had [a]arrogance, [b]abundant food and [c]careless ease, but she did not [1]help the [d]poor and needy.

50 "Thus they were haughty and committed [a]abominations before Me. Therefore I [b]removed them [1]when I saw *it.*

51 "Furthermore, Samaria did not commit half of your sins, for you have multiplied your abominations more than they. Thus you have made your sisters appear [a]righteous by all your abominations which you have committed.

52 "Also bear your disgrace in that you have [1]made judgment favorable for your sisters. Because of your sins in which you acted [a]more abominably than they, they are more in the right than you. Yes, be also ashamed and bear your disgrace, in that you made your sisters appear righteous.

53 "Nevertheless, I will restore their captivity, the captivity of Sodom and her daughters, the captivity of Samaria and her daughters, and [1]along with them [2]your own captivity,

54 in order that you may bear your humiliation and feel [a]ashamed for all that you have done when you become [b]a consolation to them.

55 "Your sisters, Sodom with her daughters and Samaria with her daughters, [1]will return to their former state, and you with your daughters will *also* return to your former state.

56 "As *the name of* your sister Sodom was not heard from your lips in your day of pride,

57 before your [a]wickedness was uncovered, [1]so now you have become the [b]reproach of the daughters of [2]Edom and of all who are around her, of the daughters of the Philistines—those surrounding *you* who despise you.

58 "You have [a]borne *the penalty of* your lewdness and abominations," the LORD declares.

59 For thus says the Lord GOD, "I will also do with you as you have done, you who have [a]despised the oath by breaking the covenant.

60 "Nevertheless, I will remember My covenant with you in the days of your youth, and I will establish an [a]everlasting covenant with you.

61 "Then you will [a]remember your ways and be ashamed when you receive your sisters, *both* your older and your younger; and I will give them to you as daughters, but not because of your covenant.

62 "Thus I will [a]establish My covenant with you, and you shall [b]know that I am the LORD,

63 so that you may [a]remember and be ashamed and [b]never open your mouth anymore because of your humiliation, when I

47 [a]1 Kin 16:31 [b]2 Kin 21:9; Ezek 5:6; 16:48, 51

48 [a]Matt 10:15; 11:23, 24

49 [1]Lit *grasp the hand of* [a]Gen 19:9; Ps 138:6; Is 3:9; Ezek 28:2, 9, 17 [b]Gen 13:10; Is 22:13; Amos 6:4-6 [c]Luke 12:16-20; 16:19 [d]Ezek 18:7, 12, 16

50 [1]Many ancient mss and versions read *as you have seen* [a]Gen 13:13; 18:20; 19:5 [b]Gen 19:24, 25

51 [a]Jer 3:8-11

52 [1]Lit *mediated for* [a]Ezek 16:47, 48, 51

53 [1]Lit *in their midst* [2]Lit *the captivity of your captivity*

54 [a]Jer 2:26 [b]Ezek 14:22, 23

55 [1]Heb includes *will return . . . state* after Sodom also

57 [1]Lit *as at the time of* [2]So with many mss and one version; M.T. *Aram* [a]Ezek 16:36, 37 [b]2 Kin 16:5-7; 2 Chr 28:5, 6, 18-23; Ezek 5:14, 15; 22:4

58 [a]Ezek 23:49

59 [a]Is 24:5; Ezek 17:19

60 [a]Is 55:3; Jer 32:38-41; Ezek 37:26

61 [a]Jer 50:4, 5; Ezek 6:9

62 [a]Ezek 20:37; 34:25; 37:26 [b]Jer 24:7; Ezek 20:43, 44

63 [a]Ezek 36:31, 32; Dan 9:7, 8 [b]Ps 39:9; Rom 3:19

have [c]forgiven you for all that you have done," the Lord GOD
declares.

Chapter 17 Theme ______________________________

17 Now the word of the LORD came to me saying,
2 "Son of man, propound a riddle and speak a [a]parable to
the house of Israel,
3 [1]saying, 'Thus says the Lord [2]GOD, "A great [a]eagle with [b]great
wings, long pinions and a full plumage of many colors came to
[c]Lebanon and took away the top of the cedar.
4 "He plucked off the topmost of its young twigs and brought
it to a land of merchants; he set it in a city of traders.
5 "He also took some of the seed of the land and planted it in
[1a]fertile soil. He [2]placed *it* beside abundant waters; he set it
like a [b]willow.
6 "Then it sprouted and became a low, spreading vine with its
branches turned toward him, but its roots remained under it.
So it became a vine and yielded shoots and sent out branches.
7 "But there was [1]another great eagle with great wings and
much plumage; and behold, this vine bent its roots toward him
and sent out its branches toward him from the beds where it
was [a]planted, that he might water it.
8 "It was planted in good [1]soil beside abundant waters, that it
might yield branches and bear fruit *and* become a splendid vine."'
9 "Say, 'Thus says the Lord GOD, "Will it thrive? Will he not
pull up its roots and cut off its fruit, so that it withers—so that
all its sprouting leaves wither? And neither by great [1]strength
nor by many people can it be raised from its roots *again.*
10 "Behold, though it is planted, will it thrive? Will it not
[a]completely wither as soon as the east wind strikes it—wither
on the beds where it grew?"'"
11 Moreover, the word of the LORD came to me, saying,
12 "Say now to the [a]rebellious house, 'Do you not [b]know what
these things *mean?*' Say, 'Behold, the [c]king of Babylon came to
Jerusalem, took its king and princes and brought them to him
in Babylon.
13 'He took one of the royal [1a]family and made a covenant with
him, [2]putting him under [b]oath. He also took away the [c]mighty
of the land,
14 that the kingdom might [a]be [1]in subjection, not exalting
itself, *but* keeping his covenant that it might continue.
15 'But he [a]rebelled against him by sending his envoys to
Egypt that they might give him horses and many [1]troops. Will
he succeed? Will he who does such things [b]escape? Can he
indeed break the covenant and escape?
16 'As I live,' declares the Lord GOD, 'Surely in the [1]country of
the king who [2]put him on the throne, whose oath he [a]despised
and whose covenant he broke, [3b]in Babylon he shall die.
17 '[a]Pharaoh with *his* mighty army and great company will not
[1]help him in the war, when they cast up ramps and build siege
walls to cut off many lives.

63 [c]Ps 65:3; 78:38; 79:9

17:2 [a]Ezek 20:49; 24:3

3 [1]Lit *and you shall say* [2]Heb *YHWH,* usually rendered *LORD,* and so throughout the ch [a]Jer 48:40; Ezek 17:12; Hos 8:1 [b]Dan 4:22 [c]Jer 22:23

5 [1]Lit *a field of seed* [2]Lit *took* [a]Deut 8:7-9 [b]Is 44:4

7 [1]So with several ancient versions; M.T. *one* [a]Ezek 31:4

8 [1]Lit *field*

9 [1]Lit *arm*

10 [a]Ezek 19:14; Hos 13:15

12 [a]Ezek 2:3-5 [b]Ezek 12:9-11; 24:19 [c]2 Kin 24:11, 12, 15; Ezek 1:2; 17:3

13 [1]Lit *seed* [2]Lit *and caused him to enter into an oath* [a]2 Kin 24:17; Ezek 17:5 [b]2 Chr 36:13 [c]2 Kin 24:15, 16

14 [1]Lit *low* [a]Ezek 29:14

15 [1]Lit *people* [a]2 Kin 24:20; 2 Chr 36:13; Jer 52:3; Ezek 17:7 [b]Jer 34:3; 38:18, 23; Ezek 17:18

16 [1]Lit *place* [2]Lit *made him king* [3]Lit *with him in Babylon* [a]2 Kin 24:17, 20; Ezek 16:59; 17:13, 18, 19 [b]Jer 52:11; Ezek 12:13

17 [1]Lit *act with* [a]Is 36:6; Jer 37:5, 7; Ezek 29:6, 7

18 'Now he despised the oath by breaking the covenant, and
behold, he [1a]pledged his allegiance, yet did all these things; he
shall not escape.'"
19 Therefore, thus says the Lord GOD, "As I live, surely My
oath which he despised and My covenant which he broke, I
will [1]inflict on his head.
20 "I will spread My [a]net over him, and he will be [b]caught in
My snare. Then I will bring him to Babylon and [c]enter into
judgment with him there *regarding* the unfaithful act which he
has committed against Me.
21 "All the [1a]choice men in all his troops will fall by the sword,
and the survivors will be scattered to every wind; and you will
know that I, the LORD, have spoken."
22 Thus says the Lord GOD, "I will also take *a sprig* from the
lofty top of the cedar and set *it* out; I will pluck from the
topmost of its young twigs a tender one and I will plant *it* on a
[a]high and lofty mountain.
23 "On the high mountain of Israel I will plant it, that it may
bring forth boughs and bear fruit and become a stately [a]cedar.
And birds of every [1]kind will [2]nest under it; they will [2]nest in
the shade of its branches.
24 "All the [a]trees of the field will know that I am the LORD; I
bring down the high tree, exalt the low tree, dry up the green
tree and make the dry tree [b]flourish. I am the LORD; I have
spoken, and I will perform *it.*"

Chapter 18 Theme ____________________

18 Then the word of the LORD came to me, saying,
2 "[a]What do you mean by using this proverb concerning
the land of Israel, saying,
'[b]The fathers eat the sour grapes,
But the children's teeth [1]are set on edge'?
3 "As I live," declares the Lord [1]GOD, "you are surely not
going to use this proverb in Israel anymore.
4 "Behold, [a]all [1]souls are Mine; the [2]soul of the father as well
as the [2]soul of the son is Mine. The [3]soul who [b]sins will die.
5 "But if a man is righteous and practices justice and righteousness,
6 and does not [a]eat at the mountain *shrines* or [b]lift up his
eyes to the idols of the house of Israel, or [c]defile his neighbor's
wife or approach a woman during her menstrual period—
7 if a man does not oppress anyone, but [a]restores to the
debtor his pledge, [b]does not commit robbery, *but* [c]gives his
bread to the hungry and covers the naked with clothing,
8 if he does not lend *money* on [a]interest or take [b]increase, *if*
he keeps his hand from iniquity *and* [c]executes true justice
between man and man,
9 *if* he walks in [a]My statutes and My ordinances so as to deal
faithfully—[b]he is righteous *and* will surely [c]live," declares the
Lord GOD.

18 [1]Lit *gave his hand* [a]1 Chr 29:24

19 [1]Lit *give it*

20 [a]Ezek 12:13; 32:3 [b]Jer 39:5-7 [c]Jer 2:35; Ezek 20:35, 36

21 [1]So many ancient mss and versions; M.T. *fugitives* [a]2 Kin 25:5, 11; Ezek 5:2, 10, 12-14

22 [a]Ps 72:16; Ezek 20:40; 37:22

23 [1]Lit *wing* [2]Lit *dwell* [a]Ps 92:12

24 [a]Ps 96:12; Is 55:12 [b]Amos 9:11

18:2 [1]Lit *become dull* [a]Is 3:15 [b]Jer 31:29; Lam 5:7

3 [1]Heb *YHWH,* usually rendered *LORD,* and so throughout the ch

4 [1]Or *lives* [2]Or *life* [3]Or *person* [a]Num 16:22; 27:16; Is 42:5; 57:16 [b]Ezek 18:20; Rom 6:23

6 [a]Ezek 6:13; 18:15; 22:9 [b]Deut 4:19; Ezek 18:12, 15; 20:24; 33:25 [c]Ezek 18:15; 22:11

7 [a]Deut 24:13; Ezek 33:15; Amos 2:8 [b]Lev 19:13; Amos 3:10 [c]Deut 15:11; Ezek 18:16; Matt 25:35-40; Luke 3:11

8 [a]Ex 22:25; Deut 23:19, 20 [b]Lev 25:36 [c]Zech 7:9; 8:16

9 [a]Lev 18:5 [b]Rom 8:1 [c]Amos 5:4; Hab 2:4; Rom 1:17

10 "Then he may [1]have a violent son who sheds blood and who
does any of these things to a brother
11 (though he himself did not do any of these things), that is, he
even eats at the mountain *shrines,* and [a]defiles his neighbor's
wife,
12 oppresses the [a]poor and needy, [b]commits robbery, does not
restore a pledge, but lifts up his eyes to the idols *and* [c]commits
abomination,
13 he [a]lends *money* on interest and takes increase; will he live?
He will not live! He has committed all these abominations, he
will surely be put to death; his [b]blood will be [1]on his own head.
14 "Now behold, he [1]has a son who has observed all his father's
sins which he committed, and [a]observing does not do likewise.
15 "He does not eat at the mountain *shrines* or lift up his eyes
to the idols of the house of Israel, or defile his neighbor's wife,
16 or oppress anyone, or retain a pledge, or commit robbery,
but he [a]gives his bread to the hungry and covers the naked
with clothing,
17 he keeps his hand from [1]the poor, does not take interest or
increase, *but* executes My ordinances, and walks in My statutes;
[a]he will not die for his father's iniquity, he will surely live.
18 "As for his father, because he practiced extortion, robbed *his*
brother and did what was not good among his people, behold,
he will die for his iniquity.
19 "Yet you say, '[a]Why should the son not bear the punishment
for the father's iniquity?' When the son has practiced [b]justice
and righteousness and has observed all My statutes and done
them, he shall surely live.
20 "The person who [a]sins will die. The [b]son will not bear the
punishment for the father's iniquity, nor will the father bear
the punishment for the son's iniquity; the [c]righteousness of the
righteous will be upon himself, and the wickedness of the
wicked will be upon himself.
21 "But if the [a]wicked man turns from all his sins which he has
committed and observes all My statutes and practices justice
and righteousness, he shall surely live; he shall not die.
22 "[a]All his transgressions which he has committed will not be
remembered against him; because of his [b]righteousness which
he has practiced, he will live.
23 "[a]Do I have any pleasure in the death of the wicked,"
declares the Lord GOD, "[1]rather than that he should [b]turn from
his ways and live?
24 "But when a righteous man [a]turns away from his righteousness,
commits iniquity and does according to all the abominations
that a wicked man does, will he live? [b]All his righteous deeds
which he has done will not be remembered for his [c]treachery
which he has committed and his sin which he has committed;
for them he will die.
25 "Yet you say, '[a]The way of the Lord is not right.' Hear now,
O house of Israel! Is [b]My way not right? Is it not your ways that
are not right?

10 [1]Lit *beget*

11 [a]1 Cor 6:9

12 [a]Amos 4:1; Zech 7:10 [b]Is 59:6, 7; Jer 22:3, 17; Ezek 7:23; 18:7, 16, 18 [c]2 Kin 21:11; Ezek 8:6, 17

13 [1]Lit *on him* [a]Ex 22:25 [b]Ezek 33:4, 5

14 [1]Lit *begets* [a]2 Chr 29:6-10; 34:21

16 [a]Job 31:16, 20; Ps 41:1; Is 58:7, 10; Ezek 18:7

17 [1]So M.T.; Gr reads *iniquity* as in v 8 [a]Rom 2:7

19 [a]Ex 20:5; Jer 15:4; Ezek 18:2 [b]Ezek 18:9; 20:18-20; Zech 1:3-6

20 [a]2 Kin 14:6; 22:18-20; Ezek 18:4 [b]Deut 24:16; Jer 31:30 [c]1 Kin 8:32; Is 3:10, 11; Matt 16:27; Rom 2:6-9

21 [a]Ezek 18:27, 28; 33:12, 19

22 [a]Is 43:25; Jer 50:20; Ezek 18:24; 33:16; Mic 7:19 [b]Ps 18:20-24

23 [1]Lit *is it not* [a]Ezek 18:32; 33:11 [b]Ps 147:11; Mic 7:18

24 [a]1 Sam 15:11; 2 Chr 24:2, 17-22; Ezek 3:20; 18:26; 33:18 [b]Ezek 18:22; Gal 3:3, 4 [c]Prov 21:16; Ezek 17:20; 20:27

25 [a]Ezek 18:29; 33:17, 20; Mal 2:17; 3:13-15 [b]Gen 18:25; Jer 12:1; Zeph 3:5

27 [a]Is 1:18; 55:7

26 "When a righteous man turns away from his righteousness,
commits iniquity and dies because of it, for his iniquity which
he has committed he will die.
27 "Again, when a wicked man turns away [a]from his wickedness
which he has committed and practices justice and righteousness,
he will save his life.

30 [a]Ezek 14:6; 33:11; Hos 12:6

28 "Because he considered and turned away from all his
transgressions which he had committed, he shall surely live; he
shall not die.
29 "But the house of Israel says, 'The way of the Lord is not
right.' Are My ways not right, O house of Israel? Is it not your
ways that are not right?

31 [a]Is 1:16, 17; 55:7 [b]Ps 51:10; Ezek 11:19; 36:26

30 "Therefore I will judge you, O house of Israel, each according to his conduct," declares the Lord GOD. "[a]Repent and turn
away from all your transgressions, so that iniquity may not
become a stumbling block to you.

32 [a]Ezek 18:23; 33:11

31 "[a]Cast away from you all your transgressions which you
have committed and make yourselves a [b]new heart and a new
spirit! For why will you die, O house of Israel?
32 "For I have [a]no pleasure in the death of anyone who dies,"
declares the Lord GOD. "Therefore, repent and live."

19:1 [a]Ezek 2:10; 19:14 [b]2 Kin 23:29, 30, 34; 24:6, 12; 25:5-7

Chapter 19 Theme ____________________

19 "As for you, take up a [a]lamentation for the [b]princes of Israel
2 and say,

2 [1]Or *Why did your mother, a lioness, lie down among lions; among young lions rear her cubs?*

'[1]What was your mother?
A lioness among lions!
She lay down among young lions,
She reared her cubs.
3 'When she brought up one of her cubs,
He became a lion,
And he learned to tear *his* prey;
He devoured men.

4 [a]2 Kin 23:34; 2 Chr 36:4, 6

4 'Then nations heard about him;
He was captured in their pit,
And they [a]brought him with hooks
To the land of Egypt.

5 [1]Lit *one*

5 'When she saw, as she waited,
That her hope was lost,
She took [1]another of her cubs
And made him a young lion.

6 [a]2 Kin 24:9; 2 Chr 36:9

6 'And he [a]walked about among the lions;
He became a young lion,
He learned to tear *his* prey;
He devoured men.

7 [1]So Targum; M.T. *knew* [2]Or *widows*

7 'He [1]destroyed their [2]fortified towers
And laid waste their cities;
And the land and its fullness were appalled
Because of the sound of his roaring.

8 [a]2 Kin 24:11

8 'Then [a]nations set against him
On every side from *their* provinces,

And they spread their net over him;
He was captured in their pit.
9 '[a]They put him in a cage with hooks
And [b]brought him to the king of Babylon;
They brought him in hunting nets
So that his voice would be heard no more
On the mountains of Israel.
10 'Your mother was [a]like a vine in your [1]vineyard,
Planted by the waters;
It was fruitful and full of branches
Because of abundant waters.
11 'And it had [1a]strong branches *fit* for scepters of rulers,
And its [b]height was raised above the clouds
So that it was seen in its height with the mass of its branches.
12 'But it was [a]plucked up in fury;
It was [b]cast down to the ground;
And the [c]east wind dried up its fruit.
Its [1d]strong branch [2]was torn off
So that [3]it withered;
The fire consumed it.
13 'And now it is planted in the [a]wilderness,
In a dry and thirsty land.
14 'And [a]fire has gone out from *its* branch;
It has consumed its shoots *and* fruit,
So that there is not in it a [1]strong branch,
A scepter to rule.'"
This is a lamentation, and has become a lamentation.

Chapter 20 Theme ____________________

590 B.C.

20 Now in the seventh year, in the fifth *month*, on the
tenth of the month, [1]certain of the [a]elders of Israel
came to inquire of the LORD, and sat before me.
2 And the word of the LORD came to me saying,
3 "Son of man, speak to the elders of Israel and say to them,
'Thus says the Lord [1]GOD, "Do you come to inquire of Me? As I
live," declares the Lord GOD, "[a]I will not be inquired of by
you."'
4 "Will you judge them, will you judge them, son of man?
[a]Make them know the abominations of their fathers;
5 and say to them, 'Thus says the Lord GOD, "On the day
when I [a]chose Israel and [1]swore to the [2]descendants of the
house of Jacob and made Myself known to them in the land of
Egypt, when I [1]swore to them, saying, [b]I am the LORD your God,
6 on that day I swore to them, [a]to bring them out from the
land of Egypt into a land that I had [1]selected for them, [b]flowing
with milk and honey, which is [c]the glory of all lands.
7 "I said to them, '[a]Cast away, each of you, the detestable
things of his eyes, and [b]do not defile yourselves with the idols
of Egypt; [c]I am the LORD your God.'

9 [a]2 Chr 36:6 [b]2 Kin 24:15

10 [1]So with some ancient mss; M.T. *blood* [a]Ps 80:8-11

11 [1]Lit *rods of strength* [a]Ps 80:15 [b]Ezek 31:3

12 [1]Lit *rods of her strength* [2]So Gr; M.T. *they were* [3]So Gr; M.T. *they* [a]Jer 31:28 [b]Lam 2:1; Ezek 28:17 [c]Ezek 17:10; Hos 13:15 [d]Is 27:11; Ezek 19:11

13 [a]2 Kin 24:12-16; Ezek 19:10; 20:35; Hos 2:3

14 [1]Lit *rod of strength* [a]Ezek 15:4; 20:47, 48

20:1 [1]Lit *men* [a]Ezek 8:1, 11, 12

3 [1]Heb *YHWH,* usually rendered *LORD,* and so throughout the ch [a]Ezek 14:3

4 [a]Ezek 16:2; 22:2; Matt 23:32

5 [1]Lit *lifted up My hand,* and so throughout the ch [2]Lit *seed* [a]Ex 6:6-8 [b]Ex 6:2, 3

6 [1]Lit *spied out* [a]Jer 32:22 [b]Ex 13:5; 33:3 [c]Ps 48:2

7 [a]Ex 20:4, 5; 22:20 [b]Lev 18:3; Deut 29:16-18 [c]Ex 20:2

8 "But they [a]rebelled against Me and were not willing to listen
to Me; [1]they did not cast away the detestable things of their
eyes, nor did they forsake the [b]idols of Egypt.
Then I [2]resolved to [c]pour out My wrath on them, to
accomplish My anger against them in the midst of the land of
Egypt.
9 "But I acted [a]for the sake of My name, that it should [b]not be
profaned in the sight of the nations among whom they *lived,* in
whose sight I made Myself known to them by bringing them
out of the land of Egypt.
10 "So I took them out of the land of Egypt and brought them
into the [a]wilderness.
11 "I gave them My [a]statutes and informed them of My
ordinances, by [b]which, if a man [1]observes them, he will live.
12 "Also I gave them My sabbaths to be a [a]sign between Me
and them, that they might know that I am the LORD who
sanctifies them.
13 "But the house of Israel [a]rebelled against Me in the
wilderness. They did not walk in My statutes and they rejected
My ordinances, [b]by which, if a man [1]observes them, he will
live; and My [c]sabbaths they greatly profaned. Then I [2]resolved
to [d]pour out My wrath on them in the wilderness, to annihilate
them.
14 "But I acted for the sake of My name, that it should not be
profaned in the sight of the nations, before whose sight I had
brought them out.
15 "Also [a]I swore to them in the wilderness that I would not
bring them into the land which I had given them, flowing with
milk and honey, which is the glory of all lands,
16 because they rejected My ordinances, and as for My
statutes, they did not walk in them; they even profaned My
sabbaths, for their [a]heart continually went after their idols.
17 "Yet My eye spared them rather than destroying them, and I
did not cause their [a]annihilation in the wilderness.
18 "I said to their [1a]children in the wilderness, '[b]Do not walk in
the statutes of your fathers or keep their ordinances or defile
yourselves with their idols.
19 '[a]I am the LORD your God; [b]walk in My statutes and keep
My ordinances and [1]observe them.
20 '[a]Sanctify My sabbaths; and they shall be a sign between
Me and you, that you may know that I am the LORD your God.'
21 "But the [a]children rebelled against Me; they did not walk in
My statutes, nor were they careful to observe My ordinances,
by which, *if* a man observes them, he will live; they profaned
My sabbaths. So I [1]resolved to pour out My wrath on them, to
accomplish My anger against them in the wilderness.
22 "But I [a]withdrew My hand and acted [b]for the sake of My
name, that it should not be profaned in the sight of the nations
in whose sight I had brought them out.
23 "Also I swore to them in the wilderness that I would [a]scatter
them among the nations and disperse them among the lands,

8 [1]Lit *each one* [2]Lit *said* [a]Deut 9:7; Is 63:10 [b]Ex 32:1-9 [c]Ezek 5:13; 7:8; 20:13, 21

9 [a]Ex 32:11-14; Ezek 20:14, 22; 36:21, 22 [b]Ezek 39:7

10 [a]Ex 19:1

11 [1]Lit *does* [a]Ex 20:1-23:33 [b]Lev 18:5; Ezek 20:13

12 [a]Ex 31:13, 17; Ezek 20:20

13 [1]Lit *does* [2]Lit *said* [a]Num 14:11, 12, 22; Ezek 20:8 [b]Lev 18:5 [c]Is 56:6; Ezek 20:21 [d]Ex 32:10; Deut 9:8; Ezek 20:8, 21

15 [a]Num 14:30; Ps 95:11; 106:26

16 [a]Ezek 11:21; 14:3-7; 20:8

17 [a]Jer 4:27; 5:18; Ezek 11:13

18 [1]Lit *sons* [a]Num 14:31; Deut 4:3-6 [b]Zech 1:4

19 [1]Lit *do* [a]Ex 6:7; 20:2 [b]Deut 5:32, 33; 6:1, 2; 8:1, 2; 11:1; 12:1

20 [a]Jer 17:22

21 [1]Lit *said* [a]Num 21:5; 25:1-3

22 [a]Job 13:21; Ps 78:38; Ezek 20:17 [b]Is 48:9-11; Jer 14:7, 21; Ezek 20:9, 14

23 [a]Lev 26:33; Deut 4:27; 28:64

24 because they had not observed My ordinances, but had
rejected My statutes and had profaned My sabbaths, and [a]their
eyes were [1]on the idols of their fathers.
25 "I also gave them statutes that were [a]not good and
ordinances by which they could not live;
26 and I pronounced them [a]unclean because of their gifts, in
that they [b]caused all [1]their firstborn to pass through *the fire* so
that I might make them desolate, in order that they might
[c]know that I am the LORD."'
27 "Therefore, son of man, [a]speak to the house of Israel and say
to them, 'Thus says the Lord GOD, "Yet in this your fathers
have [b]blasphemed Me by [c]acting treacherously against Me.
28 "When I had [a]brought them into the land which I swore to
give to them, then they saw every [b]high hill and every leafy tree,
and they offered there their sacrifices and there they presented
the provocation of their offering. There also they made their
soothing aroma and there they poured out their drink offerings.
29 "Then I said to them, 'What is the high place to which you
go?' So its name is called [1]Bamah to this day."'
30 "Therefore, say to the house of Israel, 'Thus says the Lord
GOD, "Will you defile yourselves [1]after the manner of your
[a]fathers and play the harlot after their detestable things?
31 "[1]When you offer your gifts, when you [a]cause your sons to
pass through the fire, you are defiling yourselves with all your
idols to this day. And shall I be inquired of by you, O house of
Israel? As I live," declares the Lord GOD, "I will not be inquired
of by you.
32 "What [a]comes [1]into your mind will not come about, when
you say: 'We will be like the nations, like the tribes of the
lands, [b]serving wood and stone.'
33 "As I live," declares the Lord GOD, "surely with a mighty
hand and with an [a]outstretched arm and with wrath poured
out, I shall be [b]king over you.
34 "I will [a]bring you out from the peoples and gather you from
the lands where you are scattered, with a mighty hand and
with an outstretched arm and with [b]wrath poured out;
35 and I will bring you into the [a]wilderness of the peoples,
and there I will enter into judgment with you face to face.
36 "As I [a]entered into judgment with your fathers in the
[b]wilderness of the land of Egypt, so I will enter into judgment
with you," declares the Lord GOD.
37 "I will make you [a]pass under the rod, and I will bring you
into the bond of the covenant;
38 and I will [a]purge from you the rebels and those who
transgress against Me; I will bring them out of the land where
they sojourn, but they will [b]not enter the [1]land of Israel. Thus
you will know that I am the LORD.
39 "As for you, O house of Israel," thus says the Lord GOD,
"[a]Go, serve everyone his idols; [1]but later you will surely listen to
Me, and My holy name you will [b]profane no longer with your
gifts and with your idols.

24 [1]Lit *after* [a]Ezek 6:9

25 [a]Ps 81:12; Is 66:4; Rom 1:21-25, 28

26 [1]Lit *that which opens the womb* [a]Lev 18:21; 20:2-5; Is 63:17; Ezek 20:30; Rom 11:8 [b]Jer 7:31; 19:4-9 [c]Ezek 6:7; 20:12, 20

27 [a]Ezek 2:7; 3:4, 11, 27 [b]Num 15:30; Rom 2:24 [c]Ezek 18:24; 39:23, 26

28 [a]Josh 23:3, 14; Neh 9:22-26; Ps 78:55; Jer 2:7 [b]1 Kin 14:23; Ps 78:58; Is 57:5-7; Jer 3:6; Ezek 6:13

29 [1]Or *High Place*

30 [1]Lit *in the way of* [a]Judg 2:19; Jer 7:26; 16:12

31 [1]Lit *In your lifting up* [a]Ps 106:37-39; Jer 7:31; Ezek 16:20; 20:26

32 [1]Lit *upon your spirit* [a]Ezek 11:5 [b]Jer 2:25; 44:17

33 [a]Jer 21:5 [b]Jer 51:57

34 [a]Is 27:12, 13; Ezek 20:38; 34:16 [b]Jer 42:18; 44:6; Lam 2:4

35 [a]Ezek 19:13; 20:36; Hos 2:14

36 [a]Num 11:1-35; Ps 106:15; Ezek 20:13, 21; 1 Cor 10:5-10 [b]Deut 32:10

37 [a]Lev 27:32; Jer 33:13

38 [1]Lit *ground* or *soil* [a]Ezek 34:17-22; Amos 9:9, 10; Zech 13:8, 9; Mal 3:3; 4:1-3 [b]Num 14:29, 30; Ps 95:11; Ezek 13:9; 20:15, 16; Heb 4:3

39 [1]Or *and afterwards, if you will not listen to Me, but* [a]Jer 44:25, 26 [b]Is 1:13-15; Ezek 23:38, 39; 43:7

40 "For on My holy mountain, on the high mountain of Israel,"
declares the Lord GOD, "there the whole house of Israel, [a]all of
them, will serve Me in the land; there I will [b]accept them and
there I will [1]seek your contributions and the choicest of your
gifts, with all your holy things.
41 "[1]As a soothing aroma I will accept you when I [a]bring you
out from the peoples and gather you from the lands where you
are scattered; and I will prove Myself [b]holy among you in the
sight of the nations.
42 "And [a]you will know that I am the LORD, [b]when I bring you
into the land of Israel, into the [c]land which I swore to give to
your forefathers.
43 "There you will [a]remember your ways and all your deeds with
which you have defiled yourselves; and you will [b]loathe yourselves
in your own [1]sight for all the evil things that you have done.
44 "Then [a]you will know that I am the LORD when I have dealt
with you [b]for My name's sake, not according to your evil ways
or according to your corrupt deeds, O house of Israel," declares
the Lord GOD.'"
45 [1]Now the word of the LORD came to me, saying,
46 "Son of man, set your face toward [1]Teman, and speak out
against the [a]south and [b]prophesy against the [c]forest [2]land of the
Negev,
47 and say to the forest of the Negev, 'Hear the word of the
LORD: thus says the Lord GOD, "Behold, I am about to [a]kindle a
fire in you, and it will consume every [1]green tree in you, as well
as every dry tree; the blazing flame will not be quenched and
[2b]the whole surface from south to north will be burned by it.
48 "All flesh will see that I, the LORD, have kindled it; it shall
[a]not be quenched."'"
49 Then I said, "Ah Lord GOD! They are saying of me, 'Is he
not *just* speaking [a]parables?'"

Chapter 21 Theme ____________________

21 [1]And the word of the LORD came to me saying,
2 "Son of man, [a]set your face toward Jerusalem, and
[1b]speak against the sanctuaries and prophesy against the land of
Israel;
3 and say to the land of Israel, 'Thus says the LORD, "Behold,
[a]I am against you; and I will draw My sword out of its sheath
and cut off from you the [b]righteous and the wicked.
4 "Because I will cut off from you the righteous and the
wicked, therefore My sword will go forth from its sheath
against [a]all flesh from south *to* north.
5 "Thus all flesh will know that I, the LORD, have drawn My
sword out of its sheath. It will [a]not return *to its sheath* again."'
6 "As for you, son of man, groan with breaking [1]heart and
bitter grief, groan in their sight.
7 "And when they say to you, 'Why do you groan?' you shall
say, 'Because of the [a]news that is coming; and [b]every heart will

40 [1]Or *require* [a]Is 66:23; Ezek 37:22, 24 [b]Is 56:7; 60:7; Ezek 43:12, 27

41 [1]Lit *With* [a]Is 27:12, 13; Ezek 11:17; 28:25 [b]Is 5:16; Ezek 28:25; 36:23

42 [a]Ezek 36:23; 38:23 [b]Ezek 11:17; 34:13; 36:24 [c]Ezek 20:6, 15

43 [1]Lit *faces* [a]Ezek 6:9; 16:61, 63; Hos 5:15 [b]Jer 31:18; Ezek 36:31; Zech 12:10

44 [a]Ezek 24:24 [b]Ezek 36:22

45 [1]Ch 21:1 in Heb

46 [1]Or *the South* [2]Lit *of the field* [a]Jer 13:19; Ezek 21:4 [b]Ezek 21:2; Amos 7:16 [c]Is 30:6-11

47 [1]Lit *moist* [2]Or *all the faces* [a]Is 9:18, 19; Jer 21:14 [b]Is 13:8

48 [a]Jer 7:20; 17:27

49 [a]Ezek 17:2; Matt 13:13; John 16:25

21:1 [1]Ch 21:6 in Heb

2 [1]Lit *flow* [a]Ezek 20:46; 25:2; 28:21 [b]Job 29:22; Ezek 20:46

3 [a]Jer 21:13; Ezek 5:8; Nah 2:13; 3:5 [b]Is 57:1

4 [a]Jer 12:12; Ezek 7:2; 20:47

5 [a]1 Sam 3:12; Jer 23:20; Ezek 21:30; Nah 1:9

6 [1]Lit *loins*

7 [a]Ezek 7:26 [b]Is 13:7; Nah 2:10

melt, all hands will be feeble, every spirit will [1]faint and all
knees will [2]be weak as water. Behold, it comes and it will
happen,' declares the Lord [3]GOD."

8 Again the word of the LORD came to me, saying,

9 "Son of man, prophesy and say, 'Thus says the LORD.' Say,
'[a]A sword, a sword sharpened
And also polished!
10 'Sharpened to make a [a]slaughter,
Polished [1]to flash like lightning!'
Or shall we rejoice, the [2]rod of My son [b]despising every tree?
11 "It is given to be polished, that it may be handled; the sword
is sharpened and polished, to give it into the hand of the slayer.
12 "[a]Cry out and wail, son of man; for it is against My people, it
is against all the [b]officials of Israel. They are delivered over to
the sword with My people, therefore strike *your* thigh.
13 "For *there is* a testing; and what if even the [1]rod which
despises will be no more?" declares the Lord GOD.

14 "You therefore, son of man, prophesy and clap *your* hands
together; and let the sword be [a]doubled the third time, the
sword for the slain. It is the sword for the great one slain,
which surrounds them,
15 that *their* [a]hearts may melt, and many [b]fall at all their [c]gates.
I have given the glittering sword. Ah! It is made *for striking*
like lightning, it is wrapped up *in readiness* for slaughter.
16 "[1]Show yourself sharp, go to the right; set yourself; go to the
left, wherever your [2]edge is appointed.
17 "I will also clap My hands together, and I will [1a]appease My
wrath; I, the LORD, have spoken."

18 The word of the LORD came to me saying,
19 "As for you, son of man, [1a]make two ways for the sword of
the king of Babylon to come; both of them will go out of one
land. And [2]make a signpost; [3]make it at the head of the way to
the city.
20 "You shall [1]mark a way for the sword to come to [a]Rabbah of
the sons of Ammon, and to Judah into [b]fortified Jerusalem.
21 "For the king of Babylon stands at the [1]parting of the way, at
the head of the two ways, to use [a]divination; he [b]shakes the
arrows, he consults the [2c]household idols, he looks at the liver.
22 "Into his right hand came the divination, 'Jerusalem,' to [a]set
battering rams, to open the mouth [1]for slaughter, to lift up the
voice with a battle cry, to set battering rams against the gates,
to cast up ramps, to build a siege wall.
23 "And it will be to them like a false divination in their eyes;
[a]they have *sworn* solemn oaths. But he [b]brings iniquity to
remembrance, that they may be seized.

24 "Therefore, thus says the Lord GOD, 'Because you have made
your iniquity to be remembered, in that your transgressions are
uncovered, so that in all your deeds your sins appear—because
you have come to remembrance, you will be seized with the hand.
25 'And you, O slain, wicked one, the prince of Israel, whose
[a]day has come, in the time of the [1]punishment of the end,'

7 [1]Lit *be dim* [2]Lit *flow* [3]Heb *YHWH,* usually rendered LORD, and so throughout the ch

9 [a]Deut 32:41

10 [1]Lit *lightning to be to her* [2]Or *scepter* [a]Is 34:5, 6 [b]Ps 110:5, 6; Ezek 20:47

12 [a]Ezek 21:6; Joel 1:13 [b]Ezek 21:25; 22:6

13 [1]Or *scepter*

14 [a]Lev 26:21, 24; 2 Kin 24:1, 10-16; 25:1

15 [a]Josh 2:11; 2 Sam 17:10; Ps 22:14; Ezek 21:7 [b]Is 59:10; Jer 13:16; 18:15 [c]Jer 17:27; Ezek 21:19

16 [1]Or *Unite yourself* [2]Lit *face*

17 [1]Lit *cause to rest* [a]Ezek 5:13

19 [1]Or *set for yourself* [2]Lit *cut out a hand* [3]Lit *cut it* [a]Jer 1:10; Ezek 4:1-3

20 [1]Lit *set* [a]Deut 3:11; Jer 49:2; Ezek 25:5; Amos 1:14 [b]Ps 48:12, 13; 125:1, 2

21 [1]Lit *mother* [2]Heb *teraphim* [a]Num 22:7; 23:23 [b]Prov 16:33 [c]Gen 31:19, 30; Judg 17:5; 18:17, 20

22 [1]Lit *in* [a]Ezek 4:2; 26:9

23 [a]Ezek 17:16, 18 [b]Num 5:15; Ezek 21:24; 29:16

25 [1]Or *iniquity* [a]Ps 37:13; Ezek 7:2, 3, 7

26 thus says the Lord GOD, 'Remove the turban and take off
the [a]crown; this *will* [1]no longer *be* the same. [b]Exalt that which
is low and abase that which is high.
27 '[a]A ruin, a ruin, a ruin, I will make it. This also will be no
more until [b]He comes whose right it is, and I will give it *to Him.*'
28 "And you, son of man, prophesy and say, 'Thus says the Lord
GOD concerning the sons of Ammon and concerning their
[a]reproach,' and say: 'A sword, a sword is drawn, polished for the
slaughter, to cause it [1]to [b]consume, that it may be like lightning—
29 while they see for you [a]false visions, while they divine lies for
you—to place you on the necks of the wicked who are slain,
whose day has come, in the [b]time of the [1]punishment of the end.
30 '[a]Return *it* to its sheath. In the [b]place where you were
created, in the land of your origin, I will judge you.
31 'I will [a]pour out My indignation on you; I will [b]blow on you
with the fire of My wrath, and I will give you into the hand of
brutal men, [1c]skilled in destruction.
32 'You will be [1a]fuel for the fire; your blood will be in the midst
of the land. You will [b]not be remembered, for I, the LORD, have
spoken.'"

Chapter 22 Theme ____________________

22 Then the word of the LORD came to me, saying,
2 "And you, son of man, will you judge, will you judge
the bloody city? Then cause her to know all her abominations.
3 "You shall say, 'Thus says the Lord [1]GOD, "A city [a]shedding
blood in her midst, so that her time will come, and that makes
idols, contrary to her *interest,* for defilement!
4 "You have become [a]guilty by [1]the blood which you have shed,
and defiled by your idols which you have made. Thus you have
brought your [2]day near and have come to your years; therefore
I have made you a [b]reproach to the nations and a mocking to
all the lands.
5 "Those who are near and those who are far from you will
mock you, you of ill repute, full of [a]turmoil.
6 "Behold, the [a]rulers of Israel, each according to his [1]power,
have been in you for the purpose of shedding blood.
7 "They have [a]treated father and mother lightly within you.
The [b]alien they have oppressed in your midst; the [c]fatherless
and the widow they have wronged in you.
8 "You have [a]despised My holy things and [b]profaned My sabbaths.
9 "Slanderous men have been in you for the purpose of
shedding blood, and in you they have eaten at the mountain
shrines. In your midst they have [a]committed acts of lewdness.
10 "In you [1]they have [a]uncovered *their* fathers' nakedness; in you
they have humbled her who was [b]unclean in her menstrual
impurity.
11 "One has committed abomination with his [a]neighbor's wife
and another has lewdly defiled his [b]daughter-in-law. And
another in you has [c]humbled his sister, his father's daughter.

26 [1]Lit *not this* [a]Jer 13:18; Ezek 16:12 [b]Ps 75:7; Ezek 17:24

27 [a]Hag 2:21, 22 [b]Ps 2:6; 72:7, 10; Jer 23:5, 6; Ezek 34:24; 37:24

28 [1]Lit *to finish* [a]Ezek 36:15; Zeph 2:8-10 [b]Is 31:8; Jer 12:12; 46:10, 14

29 [1]Or *iniquity* [a]Jer 27:9; Ezek 13:6-9; 22:28 [b]Ezek 21:25; 35:5

30 [a]Jer 47:6, 7 [b]Ezek 25:5

31 [1]Or *artisans of* [a]Ezek 14:19; 25:7; Nah 1:6 [b]Ps 18:15; Is 30:33; Ezek 22:20, 21; Hag 1:9 [c]Jer 4:7; 6:22, 23; 51:20-23; Hab 1:6, 10

32 [1]Lit *food* [a]Ezek 20:47, 48; Mal 4:1 [b]Ezek 25:10

22:3 [1]Heb *YHWH,* usually rendered *LORD,* and so throughout the ch [a]Ezek 22:6, 27; 23:37, 45

4 [1]Lit *your* [2]Lit *days* [a]2 Kin 21:16; Ezek 24:7, 8 [b]Ps 44:13, 14; Ezek 5:14, 15; 16:57

5 [a]Is 22:2

6 [1]Lit *arm* [a]Is 1:23; Ezek 22:27

7 [a]Ex 20:12; Lev 20:9; Deut 5:16; 27:16 [b]Ex 22:21f; 23:9; Deut 24:17; Jer 7:6; Zech 7:10 [c]Ex 22:22; Ezek 22:25; Mal 3:5

8 [a]Ezek 22:26 [b]Ezek 20:13, 21, 24; 23:38, 39

9 [a]Ezek 23:29; Hos 4:2, 10, 14

10 [1]Lit *he has* [a]Lev 18:8 [b]Lev 18:19; Ezek 18:6

11 [a]Ezek 18:11; 33:26 [b]Lev 18:15 [c]2 Sam 13:11-14

12"In you they have [a]taken bribes to shed blood; you have taken
[b]interest and profits, and you have injured your neighbors for
gain by [c]oppression, and you have [d]forgotten Me," declares the
Lord GOD.
13"Behold, then, I smite My hand at your [a]dishonest gain
which you have acquired and at [1]the bloodshed which is among
you.
14"Can [a]your heart endure, or can your hands be strong in the
days that I will deal with you? [b]I, the LORD, have spoken and
will act.
15"I will [a]scatter you among the nations and I will disperse you
through the lands, and I will [b]consume your uncleanness from you.
16"You will profane yourself in the sight of the nations, and
you will [a]know that I am the LORD."'"
17 And the word of the LORD came to me, saying,
18"Son of man, the house of Israel has become [a]dross to Me;
all of them are [b]bronze and tin and iron and lead in the
[c]furnace; they are the dross of silver.
19"Therefore, thus says the Lord GOD, 'Because all of you have
become dross, therefore, behold, I am going to gather you into
the midst of Jerusalem.
20 'As they gather silver and bronze and iron and lead and tin
into the [a]furnace to blow fire on it in order to melt *it,* so I will
gather *you* in My anger and in My wrath and I will lay you
there and melt you.
21 'I will gather you and blow on you with the fire of My wrath,
and you will be melted in the midst of it.
22 'As silver is melted in the furnace, so you will be melted in
the midst of it; and you will know that I, the LORD, have
[a]poured out My wrath on you.'"
23 And the word of the LORD came to me, saying,
24"Son of man, say to her, 'You are a land that is [a]not cleansed
or rained on in the day of indignation.'
25"There is a [a]conspiracy of her prophets in her midst like a
roaring lion tearing the prey. They have [b]devoured lives; they
have taken treasure and precious things; they have made many
[c]widows in the midst of her.
26"Her [a]priests have done violence to My law and have
[b]profaned My holy things; they have made no [c]distinction
between the holy and the profane, and they have not taught the
difference between the [d]unclean and the clean; and they hide
their eyes from My sabbaths, and I am profaned among them.
27"Her princes within her are like wolves tearing the prey, by
shedding blood *and* [a]destroying lives in order to get [b]dishonest
gain.
28"Her prophets have smeared whitewash for them, seeing
[a]false visions and divining lies for them, saying, 'Thus says the
Lord GOD,' when the LORD has not spoken.
29"The people of the land have practiced [a]oppression and
committed robbery, and they have wronged the poor and
needy and have [b]oppressed the sojourner without justice.

12 [a]Ex 23:8; Deut 16:19; 27:25; Mic 7:2, 3 [b]Lev 25:36; Deut 23:19 [c]Lev 19:13 [d]Ps 106:21; Ezek 23:35

13 [1]Lit *your* [a]Is 33:15; Amos 2:6-8; Mic 2:2

14 [a]Ezek 21:7 [b]Ezek 17:24

15 [a]Deut 4:27; Neh 1:8; Ezek 20:23; Zech 7:14 [b]Ezek 23:27, 48

16 [a]Ps 83:18; Ezek 6:7

18 [a]Ps 119:119; Is 1:22; Lam 4:1 [b]Jer 6:28-30 [c]Prov 17:3; Is 48:10

20 [a]Is 1:25

22 [a]Ezek 20:8, 33; Hos 5:10

24 [a]Is 9:13; Jer 2:30; Ezek 24:13; Zeph 3:2

25 [a]Jer 11:9; Hos 6:9 [b]Jer 2:34; Ezek 13:19; 22:27 [c]Jer 15:8; Ezek 22:7

26 [a]Jer 2:8, 26; Ezek 7:26 [b]1 Sam 2:12-17, 22; Ezek 22:8 [c]Lev 10:10; Ezek 44:23 [d]Hag 2:11-14

27 [a]Ezek 22:25 [b]Ezek 22:13

28 [a]Jer 23:25-32; Ezek 13:6

29 [a]Is 5:7; Ezek 9:9; 22:7; Amos 3:10 [b]Ex 23:9

30 "I [a]searched for a man among them who would [b]build up
the wall and [c]stand in the gap before Me for the land, so that I
would not destroy it; but I found [1]no one.
31 "Thus I have poured out My [a]indignation on them; I have
consumed them with the fire of My wrath; [b]their way I have
brought upon their heads," declares the Lord GOD.

Chapter 23 Theme ______________________

23 The word of the LORD came to me again, saying,
2 "Son of man, there were [a]two women, the daughters
of one mother;
3 and they played the harlot in Egypt. They [a]played the harlot
in their youth; there their breasts were pressed and there their
virgin bosom was handled.
4 "Their names were Oholah the elder and Oholibah her sister.
And they became Mine, and they bore sons and daughters. And
as for their names, Samaria is Oholah and Jerusalem is Oholibah.
5 "Oholah played the harlot [1]while she was Mine; and she
lusted after her lovers, after the [a]Assyrians, *her* neighbors,
6 who were clothed in purple, [a]governors and officials, all of
them desirable young men, horsemen riding on horses.
7 "She bestowed her harlotries on them, all of whom *were* the
choicest [1]men of Assyria; and with all whom she lusted after,
with all their idols she [a]defiled herself.
8 "She did not forsake her harlotries [a]from *the time in* Egypt;
for in her youth [1]men had lain with her, and they handled her
virgin bosom and poured out their [2]lust on her.
9 "Therefore, I gave her into the hand of her [a]lovers, into the
hand of the [1]Assyrians, after whom she lusted.
10 "They [a]uncovered her nakedness; they took her sons and her
daughters, but they slew her with the sword. Thus she became
a [1]byword among women, and they executed judgments on her.
11 "Now her sister Oholibah saw *this,* yet she was [a]more
corrupt in her lust than she, and her harlotries were more than
the harlotries of her sister.
12 "She lusted after the [1a]Assyrians, governors and officials, the
ones near, magnificently dressed, horsemen riding on horses,
all of them desirable young men.
13 "I saw that she had defiled herself; they both took [1]the same
way.
14 "So she increased her harlotries. And she saw men [a]portrayed
on the wall, images of the [b]Chaldeans portrayed with vermilion,
15 girded with belts on their loins, with flowing turbans on their
heads, all of them looking like officers, [1]like the [2]Babylonians
in Chaldea, the land of their birth.
16 "[1]When she saw them she [a]lusted after them and sent
messengers to them in Chaldea.
17 "The [1a]Babylonians came to her to the bed of love and
defiled her with their harlotry. And when she had been defiled
by them, [2]she became disgusted with them.

30 [1]Lit *not* [a]Is 59:16; 63:5; Jer 5:1 [b]Ezek 13:5 [c]Ps 106:23; Jer 15:1

31 [a]Is 10:5; 13:5; 30:27; Ezek 22:20 [b]Ezek 7:3, 8, 9; 9:10; 16:43; Rom 2:8, 9

23:2 [a]Ezek 16:46

3 [a]Lev 17:7; Jer 3:9

5 [1]Lit *under Me* [a]2 Kin 15:19; 16:7; 17:3; Ezek 16:28; Hos 5:13; 8:9, 10

6 [a]Ezek 23:12, 13

7 [1]Lit *sons of Asshur* [a]Ezek 20:7; 22:3, 4; Hos 5:3; 6:10

8 [1]Lit *they* [2]Lit *harlotry* [a]Ex 32:4; 1 Kin 12:28; 2 Kin 10:29; 17:16; Ezek 23:3, 19

9 [1]Lit *sons of Asshur* [a]Ezek 16:37; 23:22

10 [1]Lit *name* [a]Ezek 16:37, 41

11 [a]Jer 3:8-11; Ezek 16:51

12 [1]Lit *sons of Asshur* [a]2 Kin 16:7

13 [1]Lit *one*

14 [a]Ezek 8:10 [b]Ezek 16:29

15 [1]Lit *the likeness of* [2]Lit *sons of Babel*

16 [1]Lit *At the sight of her eyes* [a]Ezek 23:20; Matt 5:28

17 [1]Lit *sons of Babel* [2]Lit *her soul* [a]2 Kin 24:17

18 "She [a]uncovered her harlotries and uncovered her nakedness;
then [1]I became [b]disgusted with her, as [1]I had become disgusted
with her [c]sister.
19 "Yet she multiplied her harlotries, remembering the days of
her youth, when she played the harlot in the land of Egypt.
20 "She [a]lusted after their paramours, whose flesh is *like* the
flesh of donkeys and whose issue is *like* the issue of horses.
21 "Thus you longed for the [a]lewdness of your youth, when
[1]the Egyptians handled your bosom because of the breasts of
your youth.
22 "Therefore, O Oholibah, thus says the Lord [1]GOD, 'Behold I
will arouse your lovers against you, from whom [2]you were
alienated, and I will bring them against you from every side:
23 the [1a]Babylonians and all the [b]Chaldeans, [c]Pekod and Shoa
and Koa, *and* all the [2d]Assyrians with them; desirable young
men, governors and officials all of them, officers and [3]men of
renown, all of them riding on horses.
24 'They will come against you with weapons, [a]chariots and
[1]wagons, and with a company of peoples. They will set
themselves against you on every side with buckler and shield
and helmet; and I will commit the [b]judgment to them, and they
will judge you according to their customs.
25 'I will set My [a]jealousy against you, that they may deal with
you in wrath. They will remove your nose and your ears; and your
[1]survivors will fall by the sword. They will take your [b]sons and
your daughters; and your [1]survivors will be consumed by the fire.
26 'They will also [a]strip you of your clothes and take away your
[b]beautiful jewels.
27 'Thus [a]I will make your lewdness and your harlotry *brought*
from the land of Egypt to cease from you, so that you will not
lift up your eyes to them or remember Egypt anymore.'
28 "For thus says the Lord GOD, 'Behold, I will give you into
the hand of those whom you [a]hate, into the hand of those from
whom [1]you were alienated.
29 'They will [a]deal with you in hatred, take all your property,
and leave you naked and bare. And the nakedness of your
harlotries will be uncovered, both your lewdness and your
harlotries.
30 'These things will be done to you because you have [a]played
the harlot with the nations, because you have defiled yourself
with their idols.
31 'You have walked in the way of your sister; therefore I will
give [a]her cup into your hand.'
32 "Thus says the Lord GOD,

'You will [a]drink your sister's cup,
Which is deep and wide.
[1]You will be [b]laughed at and held in derision;
It contains much.

33 'You will be filled with [a]drunkenness and sorrow,
The cup of horror and desolation,
The cup of your sister Samaria.

18 [1]Lit *My soul* [a]Jer 8:12; Ezek 21:24; 23:10 [b]Ps 78:59; 106:40; Jer 12:8 [c]Ezek 23:9; Amos 5:21

20 [a]Ezek 16:26; 17:15

21 [1]So two mss; M.T. *from Egypt* [a]Jer 3:9; Ezek 23:3

22 [1]Heb *YHWH,* usually rendered *LORD,* and so throughout the ch [2]Lit *your soul was alienated*

23 [1]Lit *sons of Babylon* [2]Lit *sons of Assyria* [3]Lit *the called ones* [a]2 Kin 20:14-17; Ezek 21:19; 23:14-17 [b]2 Kin 24:2; Job 1:17; Is 23:13 [c]Jer 50:21 [d]Gen 2:14; 25:18; Ezra 6:22

24 [1]Lit *wheels* [a]Jer 47:3; Ezek 26:10; Nah 2:3, 4 [b]Jer 39:5, 6; Ezek 16:38; 23:45

25 [1]Lit *remainder* [a]Ex 34:14; Ezek 5:13; 8:17, 18; Zeph 1:18 [b]Ezek 23:47; Hos 2:4

26 [a]Jer 13:22; Ezek 16:39; 23:29 [b]Is 3:18-23

27 [a]Ezek 16:41

28 [1]Lit *your soul was alienated* [a]Jer 21:7-10; 34:20; Ezek 16:37; 23:17, 22

29 [a]Deut 28:48; Ezek 23:25, 26, 45-47

30 [a]Ezek 6:9

31 [a]2 Kin 21:13; Jer 7:14, 15; Ezek 23:33

32 [1]Or *It will be for jesting and deriding because of its great size* [a]Ps 60:3; Is 51:17; Jer 25:15 [b]Ezek 5:14, 15; 16:57; 22:4, 5

33 [a]Jer 25:15, 16, 27; Hab 2:16

34 'You will [a]drink it and drain it.
Then you will gnaw its fragments
And tear your breasts;
for I have spoken,' declares the Lord GOD.
35 "Therefore, thus says the Lord GOD, 'Because you have
[a]forgotten Me and [b]cast Me behind your back, bear now the
punishment of your lewdness and your harlotries.'"
36 Moreover, the LORD said to me, "Son of man, will you [a]judge
Oholah and Oholibah? Then [b]declare to them their abominations.
37 "For they have committed adultery, and blood is on their
hands. Thus they have committed adultery with their idols and
even caused their sons, [a]whom they bore to Me, to pass
through *the fire* to [1]them as food.
38 "Again, they have done this to Me: they have [a]defiled My
sanctuary on the same day and have [b]profaned My sabbaths.
39 "For when they had slaughtered their children for their
idols, they entered My [a]sanctuary on the same day to profane
it; and lo, thus they did within My house.
40 "Furthermore, [1]they have even sent for men who come
from afar, to whom a messenger was sent; and lo, they came—
for whom you bathed, [a]painted your eyes and [b]decorated
yourselves with ornaments;
41 and you sat on a splendid [a]couch with a [b]table arranged
before it on which you had set My [c]incense and My [c]oil.
42 "The sound of a [1a]carefree multitude was with her; and
[b]drunkards were brought from the wilderness with men of the
[2]common sort. And they put [c]bracelets on [3]the hands of the
women and beautiful crowns on their heads.
43 "Then I said concerning her who was [a]worn out by adulteries,
'[1]Will they now commit adultery with her when she is *thus?*'
44 "[1]But they went in to her as they would go in to a harlot. Thus
they went in to Oholah and to Oholibah, the lewd women.
45 "But they, righteous men, will [a]judge them with the judgment
of adulteresses and with the judgment of women who shed blood,
because they are adulteresses and blood is on their hands.
46 "For thus says the Lord GOD, 'Bring up a company against
them and give them over to [a]terror and plunder.
47 'The company will [a]stone them with stones and cut them
down with their swords; they will slay their sons and their
daughters and [b]burn their houses with fire.
48 'Thus I will make lewdness cease from the land, that all
women may be admonished and not commit [1]lewdness as you
have done.
49 'Your lewdness [1]will be [a]requited upon you, and you will
bear the penalty of *worshiping* your idols; thus you will know
that I am the Lord GOD.'"

34 [a]Ps 75:8; Is 51:17
35 [a]Is 17:10; Jer 3:21; Ezek 22:12; Hos 8:14; 13:6 [b]1 Kin 14:9; Jer 2:27; 32:33
36 [a]Jer 1:10; Ezek 20:4; 22:2 [b]Is 58:1; Ezek 16:2; Mic 3:8
37 [1]I.e. idols [a]Ezek 16:20; 20:26
38 [a]2 Kin 21:4, 7; Ezek 5:11; 7:20 [b]Jer 17:27; Ezek 20:13, 24
39 [a]Jer 7:9-11
40 [1]Or *you* (women) [a]2 Kin 9:30; Jer 4:30 [b]Is 3:18-23; Ezek 16:13-16
41 [a]Esth 1:6; Is 57:7; Amos 6:4 [b]Is 65:11; Ezek 44:16 [c]Jer 44:17; Hos 2:8
42 [1]Lit *at ease* [2]Lit *multitude of mankind* [3]Lit *their hands* [a]Ezek 16:49; Amos 6:3-6 [b]Jer 51:7 [c]Gen 24:30; Ezek 16:11, 12
43 [1]Or *Now they will commit adultery with her, and she with them* [a]Ezek 23:3
44 [1]Or *And*
45 [a]Ezek 16:38
46 [a]Jer 15:4; 24:9; 29:18
47 [a]Lev 20:10; Ezek 16:40 [b]Jer 39:8
48 [1]Lit *according to your lewdness*
49 [1]Lit *they will give* [a]Is 59:18; Ezek 7:4, 9; 9:10; 23:35

Chapter 24 Theme ______________________

24

And the word of the LORD came to me in the ninth year,
in the tenth month, on the tenth of the month, saying,

588 B.C.

2 "Son of man, write the name of the day, this very day. The
king of Babylon [1]has [a]laid siege to Jerusalem this very day.
3 "Speak a [a]parable to the [b]rebellious house and say to them,
'Thus says the Lord [1]GOD,
"Put on the [c]pot, put *it* on and also pour water in it;
4 [1a]Put in it the pieces,
Every good piece, the thigh and the shoulder;
Fill *it* with choice bones.
5 "Take the [a]choicest of the flock,
And also pile [1]wood under [2]the pot.
Make it boil vigorously.
Also seethe its bones in it."

6 'Therefore, thus says the Lord GOD,
"Woe to the [a]bloody city,
To the pot in which there is rust
And whose rust has not gone out of it!
Take out of it piece after piece,
[1]Without making a choice.
7 "For her blood is in her midst;
She placed it on the bare rock;
She did not [a]pour it on the ground
To cover it with dust.
8 "That it may [a]cause wrath to come up to take vengeance,
I have put her blood on the bare rock,
That it may not be covered."
9 'Therefore, thus says the Lord GOD,
"[a]Woe to the bloody city!
I also will make the pile great.
10 "Heap on the wood, kindle the fire,
[1]Boil the flesh well
And mix in the spices,
And let the bones be burned.
11 "Then [a]set it empty on its coals
So that it may be hot
And its bronze may [1]glow
And its [b]filthiness may be melted in it,
Its rust consumed.
12 "She has [a]wearied *Me* with toil,
Yet her great rust has not gone from her;
Let her rust *be* in the fire!
13 "In your filthiness is lewdness.
Because I *would* have cleansed you,
Yet you are [a]not clean,
You will not be cleansed from your filthiness again
Until I have [1b]spent My wrath on you.
14 "I, the LORD, have spoken; it is [a]coming and I will act. I will not
relent, and I will not [b]pity and I will not be sorry; [c]according to
your ways and according to your deeds [1]I will judge you,"
declares the Lord GOD.'"
15 And the word of the LORD came to me saying,

24:2 [1]Lit *leaned on* [a]2 Kin 25:1; Jer 39:1; 52:4

3 [1]Heb *YHWH,* usually rendered *LORD,* and so throughout the ch [a]Ps 78:2; Ezek 17:2; 20:49 [b]Is 1:2; 30:1, 9; Ezek 2:3, 6, 8 [c]Jer 1:13, 14; Ezek 11:3, 7, 11; 24:6

4 [1]Lit *Gather her pieces* [a]Mic 3:2, 3

5 [1]Lit *bones* [2]Lit *it* [a]Jer 39:6; 52:10, 24-27

6 [1]Lit *No lot has fallen on it* [a]2 Kin 24:3, 4; Ezek 22:2, 3, 27; Mic 7:2; Nah 3:1

7 [a]Lev 17:13; Deut 12:16

8 [a]Is 26:21

9 [a]Ezek 24:6; Hab 2:12

10 [1]Lit *Complete*

11 [1]Lit *become hot* [a]Jer 21:10; Mal 4:1 [b]Ezek 22:15; 23:27

12 [a]Jer 9:5

13 [1]Lit *caused to rest* [a]Jer 6:28-30; Ezek 22:24 [b]Ezek 5:13; 8:18

14 [1]So with several ancient mss and versions; M.T. *they* [a]Ps 33:9; Is 55:11 [b]Jer 13:14; Ezek 9:10 [c]Is 3:11; Ezek 18:30; 36:19

16 "Son of man, behold, I am about to take from you the
[a]desire of your eyes with a [b]blow; but you shall not [c]mourn and
you shall not weep, and your [d]tears shall not come.
17 "Groan silently; make [a]no mourning for the dead. Bind on
your turban and put your shoes on your feet, and do not cover
your mustache and [b]do not eat the bread of men."
18 So I spoke to the people in the morning, and in the evening
my wife died. And in the morning I did as I was commanded.
19 The people said to me, "Will you not tell us what these
things that you are doing mean for us?"
20 Then I said to them, "The word of the LORD came to me
saying,
21 'Speak to the house of Israel, "Thus says the Lord GOD,
'Behold, I am about to profane My sanctuary, the pride of your
power, the [a]desire of your eyes and the delight of your soul;
and your [b]sons and your daughters whom you have left behind
will fall by the sword.
22 'You will do as I have done; you will not cover *your* mustache
and you will not eat the bread of men.
23 'Your turbans will be on your heads and your shoes on your
feet. You [a]will not mourn and you will not weep, but [b]you will
rot away in your iniquities and you will groan [1]to one another.
24 'Thus Ezekiel will be a [a]sign to you; according to all that he
has done you will do; when it comes, then you will know that I
am the Lord GOD.'"
25 'As for you, son of man, will *it* not be on the day when I
take from them their [a]stronghold, the joy of their [1]pride, the
desire of their eyes and [2]their heart's delight, their sons and
their daughters,
26 that on that day he who [a]escapes will come to you with
information for *your* ears?

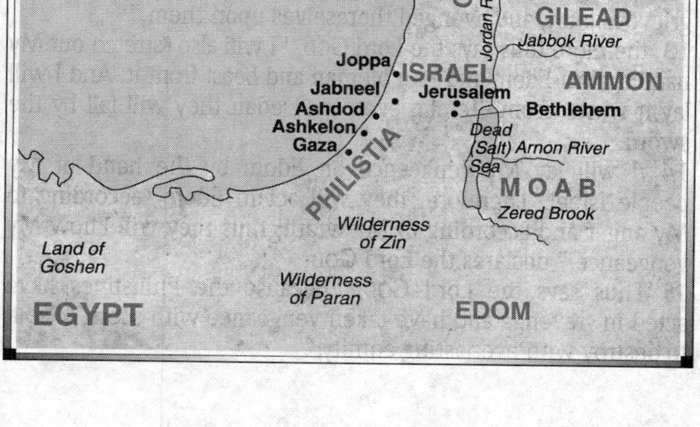

The Nations of Ezekiel's Prophecies

16 [a]Song 7:10; Ezek 24:18 [b]Job 23:2 [c]Jer 16:5; 22:10 [d]Jer 13:17

17 [a]Lev 21:10-12 [b]Jer 16:7; Hos 9:4

21 [a]Ps 27:4; 84:1; Ezek 24:16 [b]Jer 6:11; 16:3, 4; Ezek 23:25, 47

23 [1]Lit *a man to his brother* [a]Job 27:15; Ps 78:64 [b]Lev 26:39; Ezek 33:10

24 [a]Ezek 4:3; Luke 11:29, 30

25 [1]Or *beauty* [2]Lit *the lifting up of their soul* [a]Ps 48:2; 50:2; Ezek 24:21

26 [a]1 Sam 4:12; Job 1:15-19

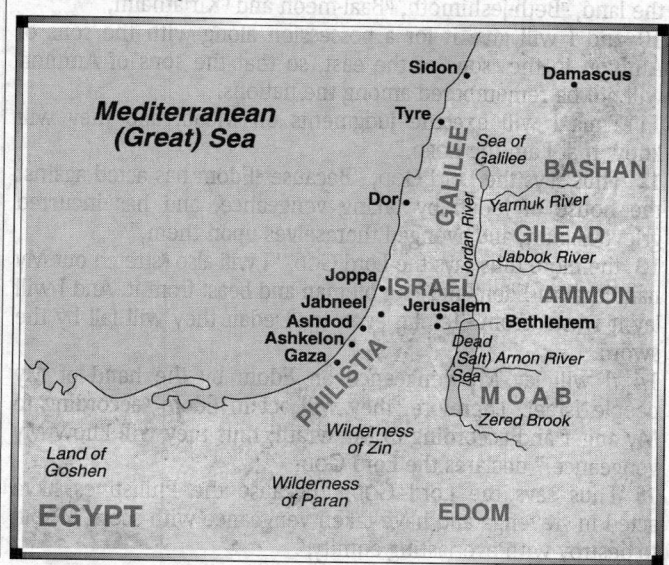

27 'On that day your [a]mouth will be opened to him who escaped,
and you will speak and be mute no longer. Thus you will be a
sign to them, and they will know that I am the LORD.'"

Chapter 25 Theme ______________________________

RETURN TO INSTRUCTIONS

25 And the word of the LORD came to me saying,
2 "Son of man, set your face toward the [a]sons of
Ammon and prophesy against them,
3 and say to the sons of Ammon, 'Hear the word of the Lord
[1]GOD! Thus says the Lord GOD, "Because you said, '[a]Aha!'
against My sanctuary when it was profaned, and against the
land of Israel when it was made desolate, and against the house
of Judah when they went into exile,
4 therefore, behold, I am going to give you to the [a]sons of the
east for a possession, and they will set their encampments
among you and make their dwellings among you; they will [b]eat
your fruit and drink your milk.
5 "I will make [a]Rabbah a pasture for camels and the sons of
Ammon a resting place for flocks. Thus you will know that I am
the LORD."
6 'For thus says the Lord GOD, "Because you have [a]clapped
your hands and stamped your feet and [b]rejoiced with all the
scorn of your soul against the land of Israel,
7 therefore, behold, I have [a]stretched out My hand against
you and I will give you for [b]spoil to the nations. And I will [c]cut
you off from the peoples and [d]make you perish from the lands;
I will destroy you. Thus you will [e]know that I am the LORD."
8 'Thus says the Lord GOD, "Because [a]Moab and Seir say,
'Behold, the house of Judah is like all the nations,'
9 therefore, behold, I am going to [1]deprive the flank of Moab
of *its* cities, of its cities which are on its [2]frontiers, the glory of
the land, [a]Beth-jeshimoth, [b]Baal-meon and [c]Kiriathaim,
10 and I will give it for a possession along with the sons of
Ammon to the [a]sons of the east, so that the sons of Ammon
will not be remembered among the nations.
11 "Thus I will execute judgments on Moab, and they will
know that I am the LORD."
12 'Thus says the Lord GOD, "Because [a]Edom has acted against
the house of Judah by taking vengeance, and has incurred
grievous guilt, and avenged themselves upon them,"
13 therefore thus says the Lord GOD, "I will also [a]stretch out My
hand against Edom and [b]cut off man and beast from it. And I will
lay it waste; from [c]Teman even to [d]Dedan they will fall by the
sword.
14 "[a]I will lay My vengeance on Edom by the hand of My
people Israel. Therefore, they will act in Edom [b]according to
My anger and according to My wrath; thus they will know My
vengeance," declares the Lord GOD.
15 'Thus says the Lord GOD, "Because the Philistines have
acted in [a]revenge and have taken vengeance with scorn of soul
to destroy with everlasting enmity,"

27 [a]Ezek 3:26; 33:22

25:2 [a]Jer 49:1-6; Amos 1:13-15; Zeph 2:9

3 [1]Heb *YHWH,* usually rendered *LORD,* and so throughout the ch [a]Ps 70:2, 3; Ezek 21:28; 25:6; 26:2; 36:2

4 [a]Judg 6:3, 33; 1 Kin 4:30 [b]Deut 28:33, 51; Is 1:7

5 [a]Deut 3:11; 2 Sam 12:26; Jer 49:2; Ezek 21:20

6 [a]Job 27:23; Nah 3:19 [b]Obad 12; Zeph 2:8, 10

7 [a]Ezek 25:13, 16; Zeph 1:4 [b]Is 33:4; Ezek 26:5 [c]Ezek 21:32 [d]Amos 1:14, 15 [e]Ezek 6:14

8 [a]Is 15:1; Jer 48:1; Amos 2:1, 2

9 [1]Lit *open* [2]Lit *end* [a]Num 33:49; Josh 12:3; 13:20 [b]Num 32:3, 38; Josh 13:17; 1 Chr 5:8; Jer 48:23 [c]Num 32:37; Josh 13:19; Jer 48:1, 23

10 [a]Ezek 25:4

12 [a]2 Chr 28:17; Ps 137:7; Jer 49:7-22

13 [a]Jer 49:8, 13 [b]Ezek 29:8; Mal 1:3, 4 [c]Gen 36:34; Jer 49:7; Amos 1:12 [d]Jer 25:23; 49:8

14 [a]Is 11:14 [b]Ezek 35:11

15 [a]Is 14:29-31; Ezek 25:6, 12; Joel 3:4

16 therefore thus says the Lord GOD, "Behold, I will [a]stretch out
My hand against the Philistines, even cut off the [b]Cherethites
and destroy the remnant of the seacoast.
17 "I will execute great vengeance on them with wrathful
rebukes; and they will [a]know that I am the LORD when I lay My
vengeance on them."'"

Chapter 26 Theme ______________________

26 Now in the eleventh year, on the first of the month,
the word of the LORD came to me saying,

586 B.C.

2 "Son of man, because [a]Tyre has said concerning Jerusalem,
'Aha, the [b]gateway of the peoples is broken; it has [1c]opened to
me. I shall be filled, *now that* she is laid waste,'
3 therefore thus says the Lord [1]GOD, 'Behold, I am against
you, O Tyre, and I will bring up [a]many nations against you, as
the [b]sea brings up its waves.
4 'They will [a]destroy the walls of Tyre and break down her
towers; and I will scrape her debris from her and make her a
bare rock.
5 'She will be a place for the spreading of nets in the midst of
the sea, for I have spoken,' declares the Lord GOD, 'and she
will become [a]spoil for the nations.
6 'Also her [a]daughters who are [1]on the mainland will be slain
by the sword, and they will know that I am the LORD.'"
7 For thus says the Lord GOD, "Behold, I will bring upon Tyre
from the north Nebuchadnezzar king of Babylon, [a]king of
kings, with horses, [b]chariots, cavalry and [1]a great army.
8 "He will slay your daughters [1]on the mainland with the
sword; and he will make [a]siege walls against you, cast up a
[b]ramp against you and raise up a large shield against you.
9 "The blow of his battering rams he will direct against your
walls, and with his [1]axes he will break down your towers.
10 "Because of the multitude of his [a]horses, the dust *raised by*
them will cover you; your walls will [b]shake at the noise of
cavalry and [1]wagons and chariots when he [c]enters your gates
as men enter a city that is breached.
11 "With the hoofs of his [a]horses he will trample all your streets.
He will slay your people with the sword; and your strong pillars
will [b]come down to the ground.
12 "Also they will make a spoil of your riches and a prey of your
[a]merchandise, [b]break down your walls and destroy your [c]pleasant
houses, and [1]throw your stones and your timbers and your
debris [d]into the water.
13 "So I will [1]silence the sound of your [a]songs, and the sound of
your [b]harps will be heard no more.
14 "I will make you a bare rock; you will be a place for the
spreading of nets. You will be [a]built no more, for I the [b]LORD
have spoken," declares the Lord GOD.
15 Thus says the Lord GOD to Tyre, "Shall not the [a]coastlands
[b]shake at the sound of your fall when the wounded groan,
when the slaughter occurs in your midst?

16 [a]Jer 25:20; 47:1-7 [b]1 Sam 30:14; Zeph 2:5
17 [a]Ps 9:16
26:2 [1]Lit *turned* [a]2 Sam 5:11; Is 23:1; Jer 25:22 [b]Is 62:10 [c]Ezek 25:8; 35:10
3 [1]Heb *YHWH,* usually rendered LORD, and so throughout the ch [a]Mic 4:11 [b]Is 5:30; Jer 50:42; 51:42
4 [a]Is 23:11; Ezek 26:9; Amos 1:10
5 [a]Ezek 25:7; 29:19
6 [1]Lit *in the field* [a]Ezek 16:46, 53; 26:8
7 [1]Lit *an assembly, even many people* [a]Ezra 7:12; Is 10:8; Jer 52:32; Dan 2:37, 47 [b]Ezek 23:24; Nah 2:3, 4
8 [1]Lit *in the field* [a]Jer 52:4; Ezek 21:22 [b]Jer 32:24
9 [1]Lit *swords*
10 [1]Lit *wheels* [a]Jer 4:13; 47:3 [b]Ezek 26:15; 27:28 [c]Jer 39:3
11 [a]Is 5:28; Hab 1:8 [b]Is 26:5; Jer 43:13
12 [1]Lit *put* [a]Is 23:8, 18; Ezek 27:3-27; Zech 9:3 [b]Jer 52:14 [c]2 Chr 32:27; Amos 5:11 [d]Ezek 27:27, 32, 34; 28:8
13 [1]Lit *cause to cease* [a]Is 23:16; 24:8, 9; Amos 6:5 [b]Is 5:12; Rev 18:22
14 [a]Deut 13:16; Job 12:14; Mal 1:4 [b]Is 14:27
15 [a]Ezek 26:18; 27:35 [b]Jer 49:21; Ezek 31:16

16 "Then all the princes of the sea will [a]go down from their
thrones, remove their robes and strip off their embroidered
garments. They will [b]clothe themselves with [1]trembling; they will
sit on the ground, [c]tremble every moment and be appalled at you.
17 "They will take up a [a]lamentation over you and say to you,
'[b]How you have perished, O inhabited one,
From the seas, O renowned city,
Which was [c]mighty on the sea,
She and her inhabitants,
Who [1]imposed [2]her terror
On all her inhabitants!
18 'Now the [a]coastlands will tremble
On the day of your fall;
Yes, the coastlands which are by the sea
Will be terrified at your [b]passing.'"
19 For thus says the Lord GOD, "When I make you a desolate
city, like the cities which are not inhabited, when I [a]bring up
the deep over you and the great waters cover you,
20 then I will bring you down with those who [a]go down to the
pit, to the people of old, and I will make you dwell in the [b]lower
parts of the earth, like the ancient waste places, with those
who go down to the pit, so that you will not [1]be inhabited; but
I will set [c]glory in the land of the living.
21 "I will [1]bring [a]terrors on you and you will be no more;
though you will be sought, [b]you will never be found again,"
declares the Lord GOD.

Chapter 27 Theme ____________________

27 Moreover, the word of the LORD came to me saying,
2 "And you, son of man, [a]take up a lamentation over Tyre;
3 and say to Tyre, [a]who dwells at the [1]entrance to the sea,
[b]merchant of the peoples to many coastlands, 'Thus says the
Lord [2]GOD,
"O Tyre, you have said, 'I am perfect in beauty.'
4 "Your borders are in the heart of the seas;
Your builders have perfected your beauty.
5 "They have [1]made all *your* planks of fir trees from [a]Senir;
They have taken a cedar from Lebanon to make a mast
for you.
6 "Of [a]oaks from [b]Bashan they have made your oars;
With ivory they have [1]inlaid your deck of boxwood from
the coastlands of [c]Cyprus.
7 "Your sail was of fine embroidered linen from Egypt
So that it became your [1]distinguishing mark;
Your [2]awning was [3a]blue and purple from the coastlands
of [b]Elishah.
8 "The inhabitants of Sidon and [a]Arvad were your rowers;
Your [b]wise men, O Tyre, were [1]aboard; they were your pilots.
9 "The elders of [a]Gebal and her wise men were with you
repairing your seams;

16 [1]Lit *tremblings* [a]Jon 3:6 [b]Job 8:22; Ps 35:26; Ezek 7:27; 1 Pet 5:5 [c]Ezek 32:10; Hos 11:10

17 [1]Lit *put* [2]Lit *their* [a]Ezek 19:1, 14; 27:2, 32; 32:2, 16 [b]Is 14:12; Jer 48:39; 50:23 [c]Ezek 27:3, 10, 11; 28:2

18 [a]Is 41:5; Ezek 26:15; 27:35 [b]Is 23:5-7, 10, 11

19 [a]Is 8:7, 8; Ezek 26:3

20 [1]Or *return* [a]Is 14:9, 10; Ezek 32:30 [b]Ps 88:6; Amos 9:2; Jon 2:2, 6 [c]Jer 33:9; Zech 2:8

21 [1]Lit *give you terrors* [a]Ezek 26:15, 16; 27:36 [b]Rev 18:21

27:2 [a]Jer 9:10, 17-20; Ezek 28:12

3 [1]Lit *entrances* [2]Heb *YHWH,* usually rendered LORD, and so throughout the ch [a]Ezek 28:2 [b]Is 23:3

5 [1]Lit *built* [a]Deut 3:9; 1 Chr 5:23; Song 4:8

6 [1]Lit *made* [a]Is 2:13; Zech 11:2 [b]Num 21:33; Is 2:13; Jer 22:20 [c]Gen 10:4; Is 23:1, 12; Jer 2:10

7 [1]Or *standard* [2]Lit *covering* [3]Or *violet* [a]Ex 25:4; Jer 10:9 [b]Gen 10:4

8 [1]Lit *in you* [a]Gen 10:18; 1 Chr 1:16; Ezek 27:11 [b]1 Kin 9:27

9 [a]Josh 13:5; 1 Kin 5:18

All the ships of the sea and their sailors were with you
In order to deal in your merchandise.
10 “[a]Persia and [a]Lud and [a]Put were in your army, your men of
war. They hung shield and helmet in you; they set forth your
splendor.
11 “The sons of Arvad and your army were on your walls, *all*
around, and the [1]Gammadim were in your towers. They hung
their shields on your walls *all* around; they perfected your beauty.
12 “Tarshish was your customer because of the abundance of
all *kinds* of wealth; with silver, iron, tin and lead they paid for
your wares.
13 “[a]Javan, [a]Tubal and [b]Meshech, they were your traders; with
the [c]lives of men and vessels of bronze they paid for your
merchandise.
14 “Those from [a]Beth-togarmah gave horses and war horses and
mules for your wares.
15 “The sons of [a]Dedan were your traders. Many coastlands were
[1]your market; [b]ivory tusks and ebony they brought as your
payment.
16 “[a]Aram was your customer because of the abundance of
your [1]goods; they paid for your wares with [b]emeralds, purple,
[c]embroidered work, fine linen, coral and rubies.
17 “Judah and the land of Israel, they were your traders; with
the wheat of [a]Minnith, [1]cakes, honey, oil and balm they paid
for your merchandise.
18 “[a]Damascus was your customer because of the abundance of
your [1]goods, because of the abundance of all *kinds* of wealth,
because of the wine of Helbon and white wool.
19 “Vedan and Javan paid for your wares [1]from Uzal; wrought
iron, cassia and [2]sweet cane were among your merchandise.
20 “[a]Dedan traded with you in saddlecloths for riding.
21 “[a]Arabia and all the princes of Kedar, they were [1]your
customers for [b]lambs, rams and goats; for these they were your
customers.
22 “The traders of [a]Sheba and Raamah, they traded with you;
they paid for your wares with the best of all *kinds* of [b]spices,
and with all *kinds* of precious stones and gold.
23 “Haran, Canneh, [a]Eden, the traders of Sheba, Asshur *and*
Chilmad traded with you.
24 “They traded with you in choice garments, in clothes of
[1]blue and embroidered work, and in carpets of many colors *and*
tightly wound cords, *which were* among your merchandise.
25 “The [a]ships of Tarshish were [1]the carriers for your merchandise.
And you were filled and were very [2]glorious
In the heart of the seas.

26 “Your rowers have brought you
Into [a]great waters;
The [b]east wind has broken you
In the heart of the seas.

10 [a]Ezek 30:5; 38:5
11 [1]Or *valorous ones*
13 [a]Gen 10:2; Is 66:19; Ezek 27:19 [b]Gen 10:2; Ezek 38:2; 39:1 [c]Joel 3:3; Rev 18:13
14 [a]Gen 10:3; Ezek 38:6
15 [1]Lit *the market of your hand* [a]Jer 25:23; Ezek 25:13; 27:20 [b]1 Kin 10:22; Rev 18:12
16 [1]Lit *works* [a]Judg 10:6; Is 7:1-8; Ezek 16:57 [b]Ezek 28:13 [c]Ezek 16:13, 18
17 [1]Heb *pannag* [a]Judg 11:33
18 [1]Lit *works* [a]Gen 14:15; Is 7:8; Jer 49:23; Ezek 47:16-18
19 [1]Or *with yarn* [2]Or *calamus*
20 [a]Gen 25:3
21 [1]Lit *customers of your hand* [a]Is 21:13 [b]Is 60:7
22 [a]Gen 10:7; Is 60:6; Ezek 38:13 [b]Gen 43:11; 1 Kin 10:2
23 [a]2 Kin 19:12; Is 37:12; Amos 1:5
24 [1]Or *violet*
25 [1]Lit *your travelers* [2]Lit *honored* [a]Is 2:16
26 [a]Ezek 26:19 [b]Ps 48:7; Jer 18:17; Acts 27:14

27 "Your wealth, your wares, your merchandise,
Your sailors and your pilots,
Your repairers of seams, your dealers in merchandise
And all your men of war who are in you,
With all your company that is in your midst,
Will fall into the heart of the seas
On the day of your overthrow.
28 "At the sound of the cry of your pilots
The pasture lands will [a]shake.
29 "All who handle the oar,
The [a]sailors *and* all the pilots of the sea
Will come down from their ships;
They will stand on the land,
30 And they will [a]make their voice heard over you
And will cry bitterly.
They will [b]cast dust on their heads,
They will [c]wallow in ashes.
31 "Also they will make themselves [a]bald for you
And [b]gird themselves with sackcloth;
And they will [c]weep for you in bitterness of soul
With bitter mourning.
32 "Moreover, in their wailing they will take up a [a]lamentation for you
And lament over you:
'Who is like Tyre,
Like her who is silent in the midst of the sea?
33 'When your wares went out from the seas,
You satisfied many peoples;
With the [a]abundance of your wealth and your merchandise
You enriched the kings of earth.
34 '[1]Now that you are [a]broken by the seas
In the depths of the waters,
Your [b]merchandise and all your company
Have fallen in the midst of you.
35 'All the [a]inhabitants of the coastlands
Are appalled at you,
And their kings are horribly afraid;
They are troubled in countenance.
36 'The merchants among the peoples [a]hiss at you;
You have become [1]terrified
And you [b]will cease to be forever."'"

Chapter 28 Theme ____________________

28 The word of the LORD came again to me, saying,
2 "Son of man, say to the [1]leader of Tyre, 'Thus says the Lord [2]GOD,
"Because your heart is lifted up
And you have said, '[a]I am a god,
I sit in the seat of [3]gods

28 [a]Ezek 26:10, 15, 18

29 [a]Rev 18:17-19

30 [a]Is 23:1-6; Ezek 26:17 [b]1 Sam 4:12; 2 Sam 1:2; Lam 2:10; Rev 18:19 [c]Jer 6:26; Jon 3:6

31 [a]Is 15:2; Ezek 29:18 [b]Is 22:12; Ezek 7:18 [c]Is 16:9; 22:4

32 [a]Ezek 26:17; 27:2; 28:12

33 [a]Ezek 27:12, 18; 28:4, 5

34 [1]Lit *The time* [a]Ezek 26:12; 27:26, 27 [b]Zech 9:3, 4

35 [a]Is 23:6; Ezek 26:16

36 [1]Lit *terrors* [a]Jer 18:16; 19:8; 49:17; 50:13; Zeph 2:15 [b]Ps 37:10, 36

28:2 [1]Or *ruler, prince* [2]Heb *YHWH,* usually rendered *LORD,* and so throughout the ch [3]Or *God* [a]Is 14:14; 47:8; Ezek 28:9; 2 Thess 2:4

In the heart of the seas';
Yet you are a [b]man and not God,
Although you make your heart like the heart of God—
3 Behold, you are wiser than [a]Daniel;
There is no secret that is a match for you.
4 "By your wisdom and understanding
You have acquired [a]riches for yourself
And have acquired gold and silver for your treasuries.
5 "By your great wisdom, by your [a]trade
You have increased your riches
And your [b]heart is lifted up because of your riches—
6 Therefore thus says the Lord GOD,
'Because you have [a]made your heart
Like the heart of God,
7 Therefore, behold, I will bring [a]strangers upon you,
The [b]most ruthless of the nations.
And they will draw their swords
Against the beauty of your wisdom
And defile your splendor.
8 'They will bring you down to the pit,
And you will die the [a]death of those who are slain
In the heart of the seas.
9 'Will you still say, "I am a god,"
In the presence of your slayer,
Though you are a man and not God,
In the hands of those who wound you?
10 'You will die the death of the [a]uncircumcised
By the hand of strangers,
For I have spoken!' declares the Lord GOD!"'"
11 Again the word of the LORD came to me saying,
12 "Son of man, [a]take up a lamentation over the king of Tyre
and say to him, 'Thus says the Lord GOD,
"You [1]had the seal of perfection,
Full of wisdom and perfect in beauty.
13 "You were in [a]Eden, the garden of God;
[b]Every precious stone was your covering:
The [c]ruby, the topaz and the diamond;
The beryl, the onyx and the jasper;
The lapis lazuli, the turquoise and the emerald;
And the gold, the workmanship of your [1][d]settings
and [2]sockets,
Was in you.
On the day that you were created
They were prepared.
14 "You were the [a]anointed cherub who [1]covers,
And I placed you *there.*
You were on the holy [b]mountain of God;
You walked in the midst of the [c]stones of fire.
15 "You were [a]blameless in your ways
From the day you were created
Until [b]unrighteousness was found in you.

2 [b]Ps 9:20; 82:6, 7; Is 31:3; Ezek 28:9
3 [a]Dan 1:20; 2:20-23, 28; 5:11, 12
4 [a]Ezek 27:33; Zech 9:2, 3
5 [a]Ezek 27:12; Hos 12:7, 8 [b]Job 31:24, 25; Ps 52:7; Ezek 28:2; Hos 13:6
6 [a]Ex 9:17; Ezek 28:2
7 [a]Ezek 26:7 [b]Ezek 30:11; 31:12; 32:12; Hab 1:6-8
8 [a]Ezek 27:26, 27, 34
10 [a]1 Sam 17:26, 36; Ezek 31:18; 32:30
12 [1]Lit *were the one sealing a pattern* [a]Ezek 19:1; 26:17; 27:2
13 [1]Or *tambourines* [2]Or *flutes* [a]Gen 2:8; Is 51:3; Ezek 31:8, 9, 16; 36:35 [b]Ezek 27:16, 22 [c]Ex 28:17-20 [d]Is 24:8; 30:32
14 [1]Or *guards* [a]Ex 25:17-20; 30:26; 40:9; Ezek 28:16 [b]Ezek 20:40; 28:16 [c]Ezek 28:13, 16; Rev 18:16
15 [a]Ezek 27:3, 4; 28:3-6, 12 [b]Ezek 28:17, 18

16 "By the [a]abundance of your trade
[1]You were internally [b]filled with violence,
And you sinned;
Therefore I have cast you as profane
From the mountain of God.
And I have destroyed you, O [2]covering cherub,
From the midst of the stones of fire.
17 "Your heart was lifted up because of your [a]beauty;
You [b]corrupted your wisdom by reason of your splendor.
I cast you to the ground;
I put you before [c]kings,
That they may see you.
18 "By the multitude of your iniquities,
In the unrighteousness of your trade
You profaned your sanctuaries.
Therefore I have brought [a]fire from the midst of you;
It has consumed you,
And I have turned you to [b]ashes on the earth
In the eyes of all who see you.
19 "All who know you among the peoples
Are appalled at you;
You have become [1a]terrified
And you will cease to be [b]forever." ' "

20 And the word of the LORD came to me saying,
21 "Son of man, [a]set your face toward [b]Sidon, prophesy against
her
22 and say, 'Thus says the Lord GOD,
"Behold, I am against you, O Sidon,
And I will [1]be glorified in your midst.
Then they will know that I am the LORD when I [a]execute judgments in her,
And I will manifest My holiness in her.
23 "For [a]I will send pestilence to her
And blood to her streets,
And the [b]wounded will [1]fall in her midst
By the sword upon her on every side;
Then they will know that I am the LORD.
24 "And there will be no more for the house of Israel a
[a]prickling brier or a painful thorn from any round about them
who scorned them; then they will know that I am the Lord
GOD."
25 'Thus says the Lord GOD, "When I [a]gather the house of
Israel from the peoples among whom they are scattered, and
will manifest My holiness in them in the sight of the nations,
then they will [b]live in their [1]land which I gave to My servant
Jacob.
26 "They will [a]live in it securely; and they will [b]build houses,
plant vineyards and live securely when I [c]execute judgments
upon all who scorn them round about them. Then they will
know that I am the LORD their God." ' "

16 [1]Lit *They filled your midst* [2]Or *guardian* [a]Ezek 27:12 [b]Ezek 8:17; Hab 2:8, 17

17 [a]Ezek 27:3, 4; 28:7 [b]Is 19:11 [c]Ezek 26:16

18 [a]Amos 1:9, 10 [b]Mal 4:3

19 [1]Lit *terrors* [a]Ezek 26:21; 27:36 [b]Jer 51:64

21 [a]Ezek 6:2; 25:2 [b]Gen 10:15, 19; Is 23:2, 4; Ezek 27:8

22 [1]Or *glorify Myself* [a]Ezek 28:26; 30:19

23 [1]Or *be judged* [a]Ezek 38:22 [b]Jer 51:52

24 [a]Num 33:55; Josh 23:13; Is 55:13; Ezek 2:6

25 [1]Lit *ground* [a]Ps 106:47; Is 11:12, 13; Jer 32:37; Ezek 20:41; 34:13, 27 [b]Jer 23:8; 27:11

26 [a]Jer 23:6; Ezek 34:25-28; 38:8 [b]Jer 32:15, 43, 44; Amos 9:13, 14 [c]Ezek 25:11; 28:22

Chapter 29 Theme ______________________

587 B.C.

29 In the [a]tenth year, in the tenth *month,* on the twelfth of
the month, the word of the LORD came to me saying,
2 "Son of man, set your face against [a]Pharaoh king of Egypt
and prophesy against him and against all [b]Egypt.
3 "Speak and say, 'Thus says the Lord [1]GOD,
"Behold, I am against you, Pharaoh king of Egypt,
The great [2a]monster that lies in the midst of his [3]rivers,
That [b]has said, 'My Nile is mine, and I myself have made *it.*'
4 "I will put [a]hooks in your jaws
And make the fish of your [1]rivers cling to your scales.
And I will bring you up out of the midst of your [1]rivers,
And all the fish of your [1]rivers will cling to your scales.
5 "I will [a]abandon you to the wilderness, you and all the fish
of your [1]rivers;
You will fall on the [2]open field; you will not be brought
together or [3b]gathered.
I have given you for [c]food to the beasts of the earth and to
the birds of the sky.
6 "Then all the inhabitants of Egypt will know that I am
the LORD,
Because they have been *only* a [a]staff *made* of reed to the
house of Israel.
7 "When they took hold of you with the hand,
You [a]broke and tore all their [1]hands;
And when they leaned on you,
You broke and made all their loins [2]quake."
8 'Therefore thus says the Lord GOD, "Behold, I will [a]bring
upon you a sword and I will cut off from you man and beast.
9 "The [a]land of Egypt will become a desolation and waste.
Then they will know that I am the LORD.
Because [1]you [b]said, 'The Nile is mine, and I have made *it,*'
10 therefore, behold, I am [a]against you and against your [1]rivers,
and I will make the land of Egypt an utter waste and desolation,
from Migdol *to* Syene and even to the border of [2]Ethiopia.
11 "A man's foot will [a]not pass through it, and the foot of a
beast will not pass through it, and it will not be inhabited for
forty years.
12 "So I will make the land of Egypt a desolation in the [a]midst of
desolated lands. And her cities, in the midst of cities that are laid
waste, will be desolate forty years; and I will [b]scatter the Egyptians
among the nations and disperse them among the lands."
13 'For thus says the Lord GOD, "At the end of forty years I will
[a]gather the Egyptians from the peoples [1]among whom they were
scattered.
14 "I will turn the fortunes of Egypt and make them return to
the land of [a]Pathros, to the land of their origin, and there they
will be a lowly kingdom.
15 "It will be the [a]lowest of the kingdoms, and it will never
again lift itself up above the nations. And I will make them so
small that they will not [b]rule over the nations.

29:1 [a]Ezek 26:1; 29:17; 30:20
2 [a]Jer 44:30 [b]Is 19:1-17; Jer 46:2-26; Ezek 30:1-32:32
3 [1]Heb *YHWH,* usually rendered *LORD,* and so throughout the ch [2]Lit *tannim* [3]Or *Nile* [a]Is 27:1; Ezek 32:2 [b]Ezek 29:9; 30:12
4 [1]Or *Nile* [a]2 Kin 19:28; Ezek 38:4
5 [1]Or *Nile* [2]Lit *faces of the field* [3]Or with several mss and Targum, *buried* [a]Ezek 32:4-6 [b]Jer 8:2; 25:33 [c]Jer 7:33; 34:20; Ezek 39:4
6 [a]2 Kin 18:21; Is 36:6
7 [1]So with some ancient versions; M.T. *shoulders* [2]Lit *stand* [a]2 Kin 18:21; Is 36:6; Ezek 17:15-17
8 [a]Jer 46:13; Ezek 14:17
9 [1]Lit *he* [a]Ezek 29:10-12; 30:7, 8, 13-19 [b]Prov 16:18; 18:12; Ezek 29:3
10 [1]Or *Nile* [2]Lit *Cush* [a]Ezek 13:8; 21:3; 26:3; 29:3
11 [a]Jer 43:11, 12; 46:19; Ezek 32:13
12 [a]Jer 25:15-19; 27:6-11; Ezek 30:7 [b]Jer 46:19; Ezek 30:23, 26
13 [1]Lit *where* [a]Is 19:22; Jer 46:26
14 [a]Is 11:11; Jer 44:1, 15; Ezek 30:14
15 [a]Ezek 17:6, 14; 30:13; Zech 10:11 [b]Ezek 31:2; 32:2; Nah 3:8-10

16 "And it will never again be the [a]confidence of the house of
Israel, [1b]bringing to mind the iniquity of their having turned
[2]to Egypt. Then they will know that I am the Lord GOD."'"
570 B.C. 17 Now in the [a]twenty-seventh year, in the first *month,* on the
first of the month, the word of the LORD came to me saying,
18 "Son of man, [a]Nebuchadnezzar king of Babylon made his
army labor [1]hard against Tyre; every head was made [b]bald and
every shoulder was rubbed bare. But he and his army had no
wages from Tyre for the labor that he had [2]performed against
it."
19 Therefore thus says the Lord GOD, "Behold, I [a]will give the
land of Egypt to Nebuchadnezzar king of Babylon. And he will
carry off her [1b]wealth and capture her spoil and seize her
plunder; and it will be wages for his army.
20 "I have given him the land of Egypt *for* his labor which he
[1a]performed, because they acted for Me," declares the Lord
GOD.
21 "On that day I will make a [a]horn sprout for the house of Israel,
and I will [1b]open your mouth in their midst. Then they will know
that I am the LORD."

Chapter 30 Theme ____________________________

30 The word of the LORD came again to me saying,
2 "Son of man, prophesy and say, 'Thus says the Lord
[1]GOD,

"[a]Wail, 'Alas for the day!'
3 "For the day is near,
Even [a]the day of the LORD is near;
It will be a day of [b]clouds,
A time *of doom* for the nations.
4 "A sword will come upon Egypt,
And anguish will be in [1]Ethiopia;
When the slain fall in Egypt,
They [a]take away her [2]wealth,
And her foundations are torn down.
5 "[1]Ethiopia, Put, Lud, all [2a]Arabia, [3]Libya and the [4]people of
the land [5]that is in league will fall with them by the sword."
6 'Thus says the LORD,
"Indeed, those who support [a]Egypt will fall
And the pride of her power will come down;
From Migdol *to* Syene
They will fall within her by the sword,"
Declares the Lord GOD.
7 "They will be desolate
In the [a]midst of the desolated lands;
And her cities will be
In the midst of the devastated cities.
8 "And they will [a]know that I am the LORD,
When I set a [b]fire in Egypt
And all her helpers are broken.

16 [1]Lit *causing to remember* [2]Lit *after them* [a]Is 20:5; 30:1-3; 31:1; 36:6; Ezek 17:15; 29:6, 7 [b]Is 64:9; Jer 14:10; Ezek 21:23; Hos 8:13

17 [a]Ezek 24:1; 26:1; 29:1; 30:20; 40:1

18 [1]Lit *a great labor* [2]Lit *labored* [a]Jer 25:9; 27:6; Ezek 26:7-12 [b]Jer 48:37; Ezek 27:31

19 [1]Or *multitude* [a]Ezek 30:10, 24, 25; 32:11 [b]Jer 43:10-13; Ezek 30:14

20 [1]Lit *labored* [a]Is 10:6, 7; 45:1-3; Jer 25:9

21 [1]Lit *give you an opening of the mouth* [a]1 Sam 2:10; Ps 92:10; 132:17 [b]Ezek 3:27; 24:27; 33:22; Amos 3:7, 8; Luke 21:15

30:2 [1]Heb *YHWH,* usually rendered *LORD,* and so throughout the ch [a]Is 13:6; 15:2; Ezek 21:12; Joel 1:5, 11, 13

3 [a]Ezek 7:19; 13:5; Joel 1:15; 2:1; Obad 15 [b]Ezek 30:18; 32:7; 34:12

4 [1]Lit *Cush* [2]Or *multitude* [a]Ezek 29:19

5 [1]Lit *Cush* [2]Or *the mixed people* [3]Or *Cub* [4]Lit *sons* [5]Lit *of the covenant* [a]Jer 25:20, 24

6 [a]Is 20:3-6

7 [a]Jer 25:18-26; Ezek 29:12

8 [a]Ps 58:11; Ezek 29:6, 9, 16 [b]Ezek 22:31; 30:14, 16; Amos 1:4, 7, 10, 12, 14

9 [1]Lit *Cush* [a]Is 18:1, 2 [b]Is 47:8; Ezek 38:11; 39:6 [c]Is 19:17; 23:5; Ezek 32:9, 10

10 [1]Or *people;* lit *crowd,* and so throughout the ch [a]Ezek 29:19

11 [a]Ezek 28:7

12 [1]Lit *her fullness* [a]Ezek 29:3, 9 [b]Is 19:4

13 [1]Or *futile ones* [2]Or *Noph* [a]Is 2:18 [b]Is 19:13; Jer 2:16; 44:1; 46:14; Ezek 30:16

14 [1]Or *No* [a]Is 11:11; Jer 44:1, 15; Ezek 29:14 [b]Ps 78:12, 43; Is 19:11, 13 [c]Jer 46:25; Ezek 30:15, 16; Nah 3:8

15 [1]Or *Pelusium* [2]Or *No*

16 [1]Or *Pelusium* [2]Or *No* [3]Or *Noph* [4]Or *adversaries*

17 [1]Or *Aven* [2]Lit *they* [a]Gen 41:45; 46:20

18 [1]So with many mss and ancient versions; M.T. *restrain* [a]Jer 43:8-13 [b]Ezek 30:3 [c]Lev 26:13; Is 10:27; Jer 27:2; 28:10, 13; 30:8; Ezek 34:27

19 [a]Ps 9:16; Ezek 5:8, 15; 25:11; 30:14

20 [a]Ezek 26:1; 29:1, 17; 31:1

21 [1]Lit *to give healing* [2]Lit *to put a bandage, to wrap it* [a]Ps 10:15; 37:17; Ezek 30:24 [b]Jer 30:13; 46:11

22 [a]Jer 46:25; Ezek 29:3 [b]2 Kin 24:7; Jer 37:7 [c]Jer 46:21

23 [a]Ezek 29:12; 30:17, 18, 26

9 "On that day [a]messengers will go forth from Me in ships to
frighten [b]secure [1]Ethiopia; and [c]anguish will be on them as on
the day of Egypt; for behold, it comes!"

10 'Thus says the Lord GOD,
"[a]I will also make the [1]hordes of Egypt cease
By the hand of Nebuchadnezzar king of Babylon.
11 "He and his people with him,
[a]The most ruthless of the nations,
Will be brought in to destroy the land;
And they will draw their swords against Egypt
And fill the land with the slain.
12 "Moreover, I will make the [a]Nile canals dry
And [b]sell the land into the hands of evil men.
And I will make the land desolate
And [1]all that is in it,
By the hand of strangers; I the LORD have spoken."

13 'Thus says the Lord GOD,
"I will also [a]destroy the idols
And make the [1]images cease from [2b]Memphis.
And there will no longer be a prince in the land of Egypt;
And I will put fear in the land of Egypt.
14 "I will make [a]Pathros desolate,
Set a fire in [b]Zoan
And execute judgments on [1c]Thebes.
15 "I will pour out My wrath on [1]Sin,
The stronghold of Egypt;
I will also cut off the hordes of [2]Thebes.
16 "I will set a fire in Egypt;
[1]Sin will writhe in anguish,
[2]Thebes will be breached
And [3]Memphis *will have* [4]distresses daily.
17 "The young men of [1a]On and of Pi-beseth
Will fall by the sword,
And [2]the women will go into captivity.
18 "In [a]Tehaphnehes the day will [1]be [b]dark
When I [c]break there the yoke bars of Egypt.
Then the pride of her power will cease in her;
A cloud will cover her,
And her daughters will go into captivity.
19 "Thus I will [a]execute judgments on Egypt,
And they will know that I am the LORD."'"

20 In the [a]eleventh year, in the first *month,* on the seventh of 586 B.C.
the month, the word of the LORD came to me saying,
21 "Son of man, I have [a]broken the arm of Pharaoh king of Egypt;
and, behold, it has not been [b]bound up [1]for healing [2]or wrapped
with a bandage, that it may be strong to hold the sword.
22 "Therefore thus says the Lord GOD, 'Behold, I am [a]against
Pharaoh king of Egypt and will break his arms, both the strong
and the [b]broken; and I will make the sword [c]fall from his hand.
23 'I will [a]scatter the Egyptians among the nations and disperse
them among the lands.

24 'For I will [a]strengthen the arms of the king of Babylon and put [b]My sword in his hand; and I will break the arms of Pharaoh, so that he will groan before him with the groanings of a wounded man.
25 'Thus I will strengthen the arms of the king of Babylon, but the arms of Pharaoh will fall. Then they will know that I am the LORD, when I put My sword into the hand of the king of Babylon and he [a]stretches it out against the land of Egypt.
26 'When I scatter the Egyptians among the nations and disperse them among the lands, then they will know that I am the LORD.'"

Chapter 31 Theme ____________________

586 B.C.

31 In the [a]eleventh year, in the third *month,* on the first of the month, the word of the LORD came to me saying,
2 "Son of man, say to Pharaoh king of Egypt and to his [a]hordes,
'Whom are you like in your greatness?
3 'Behold, Assyria *was* a [a]cedar in Lebanon
With beautiful branches and forest shade,
And [1b]very high,
And its top was among the [2]clouds.
4 'The [a]waters made it grow, the [1]deep made it high.
With its rivers it continually [2]extended all around its planting place,
And sent out its channels to all the trees of the field.
5 'Therefore [a]its height was loftier than all the trees of the field
And its boughs became many and its branches long
Because of [b]many waters [1]as it spread them out.
6 'All the [a]birds of the heavens nested in its boughs,
And under its branches all the beasts of the field gave birth,
And all great nations lived under its shade.
7 'So it was beautiful in its greatness, in the length of its branches;
For its [1]roots extended to many waters.
8 'The [a]cedars in [b]God's garden [1]could not match it;
The [2]cypresses [1]could not compare with its boughs,
And the plane trees [3]could not match its branches.
No tree in [b]God's garden [1]could compare with it in its beauty.
9 'I made it beautiful with the multitude of its branches,
And all the trees of [a]Eden, which were in the [a]garden of God, were jealous of it.
10 'Therefore thus says the Lord [1]GOD, "Because [2]it is high in stature and has set its top among the [3]clouds, and its [a]heart is haughty in its loftiness,
11 therefore I will give it into the hand of a [1a]despot of the nations; he will thoroughly deal with it. According to its wickedness I have [b]driven it away.

24 [a]Neh 6:9; Is 45:1, 5; Ezek 30:10, 25; Zech 10:12 [b]Ezek 30:11, 25; Zeph 2:12

25 [a]Josh 8:18; 1 Chr 21:16; Is 5:25

31:1 [a]Jer 52:5, 6; Ezek 30:20; 32:1

2 [a]Ezek 29:19; 30:10; Nah 3:9

3 [1]Lit *high of stature* [2]So Gr; M.T. *thick boughs* [a]Is 10:33, 34; Ezek 17:3, 4, 22; 31:16; Dan 4:10, 20-23 [b]Is 10:33; Ezek 31:5, 10

4 [1]I.e. subterranean waters [2]Lit *was going* [a]Ezek 17:5, 8; Rev 17:1, 15

5 [1]Lit *in its sending forth* [a]Dan 4:11 [b]Ps 1:3; Ezek 17:5

6 [a]Ezek 17:23; 31:13; Dan 4:12, 21; Matt 13:32

7 [1]Lit *root was*

8 [1]Lit *did* [2]Or *Phoenician junipers* [3]Lit *were not like* [a]Ps 80:10; Ezek 31:3 [b]Gen 2:8, 9; 13:10; Is 51:3; Ezek 28:13; 31:16, 18

9 [a]Gen 2:8, 9; 13:10; Is 51:3; Ezek 28:13; 31:16, 18

10 [1]Heb *YHWH,* usually rendered *LORD,* and so throughout the ch [2]Lit *you are* [3]Or *thick boughs* [a]2 Chr 32:25; Is 10:12; 14:13, 14; Ezek 28:17; Dan 5:20

11 [1]Or *mighty one* [a]Ezek 30:10, 11; 32:11, 12; Dan 5:18, 19 [b]Deut 18:12; Nah 3:18

12 “[a]Alien [b]tyrants of the nations have cut it down and left it;
on the [c]mountains and in all the valleys its branches have fallen
and its boughs have been broken in all the ravines of the land.
And all the peoples of the earth have [d]gone down from its
shade and left it.
13 “On its ruin all the [a]birds of the heavens will dwell, and all
the beasts of the field will be on its *fallen* branches
14 so that all the trees by the waters may not be exalted in
their stature, nor set their top among the [1]clouds, nor their
[2]well-watered mighty ones stand *erect* in their height. For they
have all been given over to death, to the [a]earth beneath, among
the sons of men, with those who go down to the pit.”
15 ‘Thus says the Lord GOD, “On the day when it went down to
Sheol I [a]caused lamentations; I closed the [1]deep over it and
held back its rivers. And *its* many waters were stopped up, and
I made Lebanon [2]mourn for it, and all the trees of the field
wilted away on account of it.
16 “I made the nations [a]quake at the sound of its fall when I
made it [b]go down to Sheol with those who go down to the pit;
and all the [1]well-watered trees of Eden, the choicest and best
of [c]Lebanon, were [d]comforted in the earth beneath.
17 “They also [a]went down with it to Sheol to those who were
[b]slain by the sword; and those who were its [1]strength lived
[c]under its shade among the nations.
18 “To which among the trees of Eden are you thus [1]equal in
glory and greatness? Yet you will be brought down with the
trees of Eden to the earth beneath; you will lie in the midst of
the [a]uncircumcised, with those who were slain by the sword.
[b]So is Pharaoh and all his hordes!”’ declares the Lord GOD.”

Chapter 32 Theme ________________________

32 In the [a]twelfth year, in the twelfth *month,* on the first
of the month, the word of the LORD came to me saying, 585 B.C.
2 “Son of man, take up a [a]lamentation over Pharaoh king of
Egypt and say to him,
‘You [1]compared yourself to a young [b]lion
of the nations,
Yet you are like the [c]monster in the seas;
And you [d]burst forth in your rivers
And muddied the waters with your feet
And [2]fouled their rivers.’”
3 Thus says the Lord [1]GOD,
“Now I will [a]spread My net over you
With a company of many peoples,
And they shall lift you up in My net.
4 “I will leave you on the land;
I will cast you on the [1]open field.
And I will cause all the [a]birds of the heavens
to dwell on you,
And I will satisfy the beasts of the whole earth [2]with you.

12 [a]Ezek 7:21; 28:7; 30:12; Hab 1:6 [b]Ezek 28:7; 30:11; 32:12 [c]Ezek 32:5; 35:8 [d]Ezek 31:17; Dan 4:14; Nah 3:17, 18

13 [a]Is 18:6; Ezek 29:5; 31:6; 32:4

14 [1]Or *thick boughs* [2]Lit *drinkers of water* [a]Num 16:30, 33; Ps 63:9; Ezek 26:20; 31:18; 32:24; Amos 9:2; Jon 2:2, 6; Eph 4:9

15 [1]I.e. subterranean waters [2]Lit *be darkened* [a]Ezek 32:7; Nah 2:10

16 [1]Lit *drinkers of water* [a]Ezek 26:15; 27:28; Hag 2:7 [b]Is 14:15; Ezek 32:18 [c]Is 14:8; Hab 2:17 [d]Ezek 14:22, 23; 32:31

17 [1]Lit *arm* [a]Ps 9:17 [b]Ezek 32:20f [c]Ezek 31:3, 6; Dan 4:12

18 [1]Lit *like* [a]Jer 9:25, 26; Ezek 28:10; 32:19, 21 [b]Ps 52:7; Matt 13:19

32:1 [a]Ezek 30:20; 31:1; 32:17; 33:21

2 [1]Or *were like* [2]Lit *fouled by stamping* [a]Ezek 19:1; 27:2; 28:12; 32:16 [b]Jer 4:7; Ezek 19:2-6; Nah 2:11-13 [c]Is 27:1; Ezek 29:3 [d]Jer 46:7, 8

3 [1]Heb *YHWH,* usually rendered *LORD,* and so throughout the ch [a]Ezek 12:13

4 [1]Lit *surface of the field* [2]Lit *from* [a]Is 18:6

5 "I will lay your flesh [a]on the mountains
And fill the valleys with your refuse.
6 "I will also make the land drink the discharge of your [a]blood
As far as the mountains,
And the ravines will be full of you.
7 "And when *I* [a]extinguish you,
I will [b]cover the heavens and darken their [c]stars;
I will cover the [d]sun with a cloud
And the moon will not give its light.
8 "All the shining [a]lights in the heavens
I will darken over you
And will set darkness on your land,"
Declares the Lord GOD.
9 "I will also [a]trouble the hearts of many peoples when I [b]bring
your destruction among the nations, into lands which you have
not known.
10 "I will make many peoples [a]appalled at you, and their kings
will be horribly afraid of you when I brandish My sword before
them; and [b]they will tremble every moment, every man for his
own life, on the day of your fall."
11 For [a]thus says the Lord GOD, "The sword of the king of
Babylon will come upon you.
12 "By the swords of the mighty ones I will cause your hordes
to fall; all of them are [a]tyrants of the nations,
And they will [b]devastate the pride of Egypt,
And all its hordes will be destroyed.
13 "I will also destroy all its cattle from beside many waters;
And [a]the foot of man will not muddy them anymore
And the hoofs of beasts will not muddy them.
14 "Then I will make their waters settle
And will cause their rivers to run like oil,"
Declares the Lord GOD.
15 "When I make the land of Egypt a [a]desolation,
And the land is destitute of that which filled it,
When I smite all those who live in it,
Then they shall [b]know that I am the LORD.
16 "This is a [a]lamentation and they shall [1]chant it. The daughters
of the nations shall [1]chant it. Over Egypt and over all her hordes
they shall [1]chant it," declares the Lord GOD.
585 B.C. **17** In the [a]twelfth year, on the [a]fifteenth of the month, the
word of the LORD came to me saying,
18 "Son of man, [a]wail for the hordes of Egypt and [b]bring it
down, her and the daughters of the powerful nations, to the
[c]nether world, with those who go down to the pit;
19 'Whom do you surpass in beauty?
Go down and make your bed with the [a]uncircumcised.'
20 "They shall fall in the midst of those who are slain by the
sword. [1]She is given over to the sword; they have [a]drawn her
and all her hordes away.
21 "The [a]strong among the mighty ones shall speak of him *and*
his helpers from the midst of Sheol, 'They have gone down,
they lie still, the uncircumcised, slain by the sword.'

5 [a]Ezek 31:12
6 [a]Ex 7:17; Is 34:3, 7; Ezek 35:6; Rev 14:20
7 [a]Job 18:5, 6; Prov 13:9 [b]Ex 10:21-23; Is 34:4; Ezek 30:3, 18; 34:12 [c]Is 13:10 [d]Joel 2:2, 31; 3:15; Amos 8:9; Matt 24:29; Mark 13:24f; Luke 21:25; Rev 6:12; 8:12
8 [a]Gen 1:14
9 [a]Ezek 27:29-32; 28:19; Rev 18:10-15 [b]Ex 15:14-16
10 [a]Ezek 27:35 [b]Ezek 26:16
11 [a]Jer 46:26
12 [a]Ezek 28:7 [b]Ezek 28:19
13 [a]Ezek 29:11
15 [a]Ps 107:33, 34; Ezek 29:12, 19, 20 [b]Ex 7:5; 14:4, 18; Ps 9:16; 83:17, 18; Ezek 6:7; 30:19, 26
16 [1]Or *lament* [a]2 Sam 1:17; 3:33, 34; 2 Chr 35:25; Jer 9:17; Ezek 26:17; 32:2
17 [a]Ezek 31:1; 32:1; 33:21
18 [a]Is 16:9; Ezek 21:6; 32:2, 16; Mic 1:8 [b]Jer 1:10; Ezek 43:3; Hos 6:5 [c]Ezek 31:14, 16, 18; 32:24
19 [a]Jer 9:25, 26; Ezek 31:18; 32:21, 24, 29, 30
20 [1]Or *The sword is given* [a]Ps 28:3
21 [a]Is 14:9-12; Ezek 32:27

22 "[a]Assyria is there and all her company; [1]her graves are
round about [2]her. All of them are slain, fallen by the sword,
23 whose [a]graves are set in the remotest parts of the pit and her
company is round about her grave. All of them are slain, fallen
by the sword, who [1]spread terror in the land of the living.
24 "[a]Elam is there and all her hordes around her grave; all of
them slain, fallen by the sword, who went down uncircumcised
to the [b]lower parts of the earth, who instilled their terror in the
[c]land of the living and [d]bore their disgrace with those who went
down to the pit.
25 "They have made a [a]bed for her among the slain with all her
hordes. Her graves are around it, they are all uncircumcised,
slain by the sword (although their terror was [1]instilled in the
land of the living), and they bore their disgrace with those who
go down to the pit; [2]they were put in the midst of the slain.
26 "[a]Meshech, [b]Tubal and all their hordes are there; their graves
[1]surround them. All of them were slain by the sword [c]uncir-
cumcised, though they instilled their terror in the land of the
living.
27 "[a]Nor do they lie beside the fallen [1b]heroes of the uncircumcised, who went down to Sheol with their weapons of war
and whose swords were laid under their heads; but the punishment for their [c]iniquity rested on their bones, though the
terror of *these* [1]heroes *was once* in the land of the living.
28 "But in the midst of the uncircumcised you will be broken
and lie with those slain by the sword.
29 "There also is [a]Edom, its kings and all its [1]princes, who [2]for
all their might are laid with those slain by the sword; they will lie
with the uncircumcised and with those who go down to the pit.
30 "There also are the [1]chiefs of the [a]north, all of them, and all
the [b]Sidonians, who in spite of the terror resulting from their
might, in shame went down with the slain. So they lay down
uncircumcised with those slain by the sword and bore their
disgrace with those who go down to the pit.
31 "These Pharaoh will see, and he will be [a]comforted for all
his hordes slain by the sword, *even* Pharaoh and all his army,"
declares the Lord GOD.
32 "Though I instilled a terror of him in the land of the living,
yet he will be made to lie down among *the* uncircumcised
along with those slain by the sword, *even* Pharaoh and all his
hordes," declares the Lord GOD.

Chapter 33 Theme ____________________

33 And the word of the LORD came to me, saying,
2 "Son of man, speak to the [a]sons of your people and
say to them, 'If I bring a sword upon a land, and the people of
the land take one man from among them and make him their
watchman,
3 and he sees the sword coming upon the land and [a]blows
on the trumpet and warns the people,

22 [1]Lit *his* [2]Lit *him* [a]Ezek 27:23; 31:3, 16
23 [1]Lit *gave,* and so throughout the ch [a]Is 14:15
24 [a]Gen 10:22; 14:1; Is 11:11; Jer 25:25; 49:34-39 [b]Ezek 26:20; 31:14, 18; 32:18 [c]Job 28:13; Ps 27:13; 52:5; 142:5; Is 38:11; Jer 11:19 [d]Ezek 16:52, 54; 32:25, 30
25 [1]Lit *given* [2]So with ancient versions; M.T. reads *he was* [a]Ps 139:8
26 [1]Lit *are around him* [a]Gen 10:2; Ezek 27:13; 38:2, 3; 39:1 [b]Gen 10:2; Is 66:19; Ezek 27:13; 38:2, 3; 39:1 [c]Ezek 32:19
27 [1]Or *mighty ones* [a]Is 14:18, 19 [b]Job 3:13-15; Ezek 32:21 [c]Job 20:11; Ps 109:18
29 [1]Or *leaders* [2]Or *in* [a]Is 34:5-15; Jer 49:7-22; Ezek 25:13; 35:9, 15
30 [1]Or *princes* [a]Jer 1:15; 25:26; Ezek 38:6, 15; 39:2 [b]Jer 25:22; Ezek 28:21-23
31 [a]Ezek 14:22; 31:16
33:2 [a]Ezek 3:11; 33:12, 17, 30; 37:18
3 [a]Neh 4:18-20; Is 58:1; Ezek 33:9; Hos 8:1; Joel 2:1

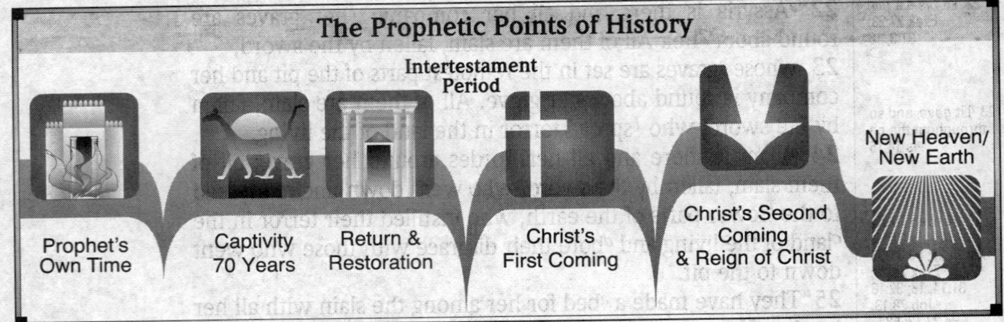

4 then he who hears the sound of the trumpet and [a]does not
take warning, and a sword comes and takes him away, his
[b]blood will be on his *own* head.
5 'He heard the sound of the trumpet but did not take warning;
his blood will be on himself. But had he taken warning, he
would have [a]delivered his life.
6 'But if the watchman sees the sword coming and does not
blow the trumpet and the people are not warned, and a sword
comes and takes a person from them, he is [a]taken away [1]in his
iniquity; but his [b]blood I will require from the watchman's hand.'
7 "Now as for you, son of man, I have [1a]appointed you a
watchman for the house of Israel; so you will hear a [2]message
from My mouth and give them [b]warning from Me.
8 "When I say to the wicked, 'O wicked man, you will [a]surely
die,' and you do not speak to warn the wicked from his way,
that wicked man shall die in his iniquity, but his blood I will
require from your hand.
9 "But if you on your part warn a wicked man to turn from his
way and he [a]does not turn from his way, he will die in his
iniquity, but you have [b]delivered your life.
10 "Now as for you, son of man, say to the house of Israel,
'Thus you have spoken, saying, "Surely our transgressions and
our sins are upon us, and we are [a]rotting away in them; [b]how
then can we [1]survive?"'
11 "Say to them, '[a]As I live!' declares the Lord [1]GOD, 'I take [b]no
pleasure in the death of the wicked, but rather that the wicked
[c]turn from his way and live. [d]Turn back, turn back from your
evil ways! Why then will you die, O house of Israel?'
12 "And you, son of man, say to [1]your fellow citizens, 'The
[a]righteousness of a righteous man will not deliver him in the
day of his transgression, and as for the wickedness of the
wicked, he will [b]not stumble because of it in the day when he
turns from his wickedness; whereas a righteous man will not
be able to live [2]by his righteousness on the day when he
commits sin.'
13 "When I say to the righteous he will surely live, and he *so*
trusts in his righteousness that he [a]commits iniquity, none of
his righteous deeds will be remembered; but in that same
iniquity of his which he has committed he will die.

4 [a]2 Chr 25:16; Jer 6:17; Zech 1:4 [b]Ezek 18:13; 33:5, 9; Acts 18:6

5 [a]Ex 9:19-21; Heb 11:7

6 [1]Or *for,* and so throughout the ch [a]Ezek 18:20, 24; 33:8, 9 [b]Ezek 3:18, 20

7 [1]Or *given* [2]Lit *word* [a]Is 62:6; Ezek 3:17-21 [b]Jer 1:17; 26:2; Ezek 2:7, 8; Acts 5:20

8 [a]Is 3:11; Ezek 18:4, 13, 18, 20; 33:14

9 [a]Acts 13:40, 41, 46 [b]Ezek 3:19, 21; Acts 20:26

10 [1]Lit *live* [a]Lev 26:39; Ezek 4:17; 24:23 [b]Is 49:14; Ezek 37:11

11 [1]Heb *YHWH,* usually rendered *LORD,* and so throughout the ch [a]Is 49:18; Ezek 5:11 [b]Ezek 18:23, 32; Hos 11:8 [c]Jer 31:20; 1 Tim 2:4; 2 Pet 3:9 [d]Is 55:6, 7; Jer 3:22; Ezek 18:30, 31; Hos 14:1; Acts 3:19

12 [1]Lit *the sons of your people* [2]Lit *by it* [a]Ezek 3:18; 18:24; 33:20 [b]2 Chr 7:14; Ezek 18:21; 33:19

13 [a]Ezek 18:26; Heb 10:38; 2 Pet 2:20, 21

14 "But when I say to the wicked, 'You will surely die,' and he
[a]turns from his sin and practices [b]justice and righteousness,
15 *if a* wicked man restores a pledge, [a]pays back what he has
taken by robbery, walks by the [b]statutes [1]which ensure life
without committing iniquity, he shall surely live; he shall not die.
16 "[a]None of his sins that he has committed will be remembered
against him. He has practiced justice and righteousness; he shall
surely live.
17 "Yet [1]your fellow citizens say, 'The way of the Lord is not
right,' when it is their own way that is not right.
18 "When the righteous turns from his righteousness and
[a]commits iniquity, then he shall die in [1]it.
19 "But when the wicked turns from his wickedness and
practices justice and righteousness, he will live by them.
20 "Yet you say, '[a]The way of the Lord is not right.' O house of
Israel, I will judge each of you according to his ways."
21 Now [a]in the [b]twelfth year of our exile, on the fifth of the
tenth month, the [1]refugees from Jerusalem came to me, saying,
"[c]The city has been [2]taken."

585 B.C.

22 Now the [a]hand of the LORD had been upon me in the
evening, before the [1]refugees came. And He [b]opened my mouth
[2]at the time *they* came to me in the morning; so my mouth was
[c]opened and I was no longer [3]speechless.
23 Then the word of the LORD came to me saying,
24 "Son of man, they who [a]live in these waste places in the land
of Israel are saying, '[b]Abraham was *only* one, yet he possessed
the land; so to [c]us who are many the land has been given as a
possession.'
25 "Therefore say to them, 'Thus says the Lord GOD, "You eat
meat with the [a]blood *in it,* lift up your eyes to your idols as you
shed blood. [b]Should you then possess the land?
26 "You [1a]rely on your sword, you commit abominations and
each of you defiles his neighbor's wife. Should you then possess
the land?"'
27 "Thus you shall say to them, 'Thus says the Lord GOD, "As I
live, surely those who are in the waste places will [a]fall by the
sword, and whoever is in the [1]open field I will give to the
beasts to be devoured, and those who are in the strongholds
and in the [b]caves will die of pestilence.
28 "I will [a]make the land a desolation and a waste, and the
[b]pride of her power will cease; and the mountains of Israel will
be desolate so that no one will pass through.
29 "Then they will know that I am the LORD, when I make the
land a desolation and a waste because of all their abominations
which they have committed."'
30 "But as for you, son of man, [1]your fellow citizens who talk
about you by the walls and in the doorways of the houses,
speak to one another, each to his brother, saying, '[a]Come now and
hear what the [2]message is which comes forth from the LORD.'
31 "They come to you as people come, and sit before you *as*
My people and hear your words, but they do not do them, for

14 [a]Is 55:7; Jer 18:7, 8; Ezek 18:27; 33:8, 19; Hos 14:1, 4 [b]Mic 6:8
15 [1]Lit *of life* [a]Ex 22:1-4; Lev 6:4, 5; Luke 19:8 [b]Ps 119:59; 143:8; Ezek 20:11
16 [a]Is 1:18; 43:25; Ezek 18:22
17 [1]Lit *the sons of your people*
18 [1]Lit *them* [a]Ezek 3:20; 18:24; 33:12, 13
20 [a]Ezek 18:25
21 [1]Or *refugee* [2]Lit *smitten* [a]Ezek 31:1; 32:1, 17 [b]Jer 39:1, 2; 40:1; 52:4-7; Ezek 24:1, 2 [c]2 Kin 25:10; Jer 39:8
22 [1]Lit *refugee* [2]Lit *until he came* [3]Or *mute* [a]Ezek 1:3; 8:1; 37:1 [b]Ezek 3:26, 27; 24:27 [c]Luke 1:64
24 [a]Jer 39:10; 40:7; Ezek 33:27 [b]Is 51:2; Luke 3:8; Acts 7:5; Rom 4:12 [c]Ezek 11:15
25 [a]Lev 17:10, 12, 14; Deut 12:16, 23; 15:23 [b]Jer 7:9, 10
26 [1]Lit *stand* [a]Mic 2:1, 2; Zeph 3:3
27 [1]Lit *surface of the field* [a]Jer 15:2, 3; 42:22; Ezek 5:12 [b]1 Sam 13:6; Is 2:19
28 [a]Ezek 5:14; 6:14; Mic 7:13 [b]Ezek 7:24; 24:21; 30:6
30 [1]Lit *the sons of your people* [2]Lit *word* [a]Is 29:13; 58:2; Ezek 14:3; 20:3, 31

they do the lustful desires *expressed* by their [a]mouth, *and* their
heart goes after their [b]gain.
32 "Behold, you are to them like a sensual song by one who
has a [a]beautiful voice and plays well on an instrument; for they
hear your words but they do not practice them.
33 "So when it [a]comes to pass—[1]as surely it will—then they
will know that a prophet has been in their midst."

Chapter 34 Theme ______________________________

34 Then the word of the LORD came to me saying,
2 "Son of man, prophesy against the [a]shepherds of
Israel. Prophesy and say to [1]those shepherds, 'Thus says the
Lord [2]GOD, "Woe, shepherds of Israel who have been [3b]feeding
themselves! Should not the shepherds [3c]feed the flock?
3 "You [a]eat the fat and clothe yourselves with the wool, you
[b]slaughter the fat *sheep* without [1]feeding the flock.
4 "Those who are sickly you have not strengthened, the
[1]diseased you have not healed, [a]the broken you have not
bound up, the scattered you have not brought back, nor have
you [b]sought for the lost; but with force and with severity you
have dominated them.
5 "They were [a]scattered for lack of a shepherd, and they
became [b]food for every beast of the field and were scattered.
6 "My flock [a]wandered through all the mountains and on
every high hill; [b]My flock was scattered over all the surface of
the earth, and there was [c]no one to search or seek *for them.*"'"
7 Therefore, you shepherds, hear the word of the LORD:
8 "As I live," declares the Lord GOD, "surely because My flock
has become a [a]prey, My flock has even become food for all the
beasts of the field for lack of a shepherd, and My shepherds did
not search for My flock, but *rather* the shepherds fed
themselves and did not feed My flock;
9 therefore, you shepherds, hear the word of the LORD:
10 'Thus says the Lord GOD, "Behold, I am [a]against the
shepherds, and I will demand My [1]sheep [2]from them and make
them [b]cease from feeding [1]sheep. So the shepherds will not
[3]feed themselves anymore, but I will [c]deliver My flock from
their mouth, so that they will not be food for them."'"
11 For thus says the Lord GOD, "Behold, I Myself will [a]search
for My sheep and seek them out.
12 "[a]As a shepherd [1]cares for his herd in the day when he is
among his scattered [2]sheep, so I will [1b]care for My [2]sheep and
will deliver them from all the places to which they were
scattered on a [c]cloudy and gloomy day.
13 "I will bring them out from the peoples and gather them
from the countries and bring them to their own land; and I will
[a]feed them on the mountains of Israel, by the [b]streams, and in
all the inhabited places of the land.
14 "I will feed them in a [a]good pasture, and their grazing ground
will be on the mountain heights of Israel. There they will lie

31 [a]Ps 78:36, 37; Is 29:13; 1 John 3:18 [b]Ezek 22:13, 27; Luke 12:15

32 [a]Mark 6:20

33 [1]Lit *behold, it is coming* [a]Jer 28:9; Ezek 33:29

34:2 [1]Lit *them, the shepherds* [2]Heb *YHWH,* usually rendered *LORD,* and so throughout the ch [3]Lit *pasturing, pasture* [a]Jer 2:8; 3:15; 10:21; 12:10 [b]Jer 23:1; Ezek 22:25; 34:8-10; Mic 3:1-3, 11 [c]Ps 78:71, 72; Is 40:11; Ezek 34:14, 15; John 10:11; 21:15-17

3 [1]Lit *pasturing* [a]Zech 11:16 [b]Ezek 22:25, 27

4 [1]Lit *sick* [a]Zech 11:16 [b]Matt 9:36; 10:6; 18:12, 13; Luke 15:4

5 [a]Num 27:17; 2 Chr 18:16; Jer 10:21; 23:2; 50:6, 7; Matt 9:36; Mark 6:34 [b]Ezek 34:8, 28

6 [a]Jer 40:11, 12; Ezek 7:16; 1 Pet 2:25 [b]John 10:16 [c]Ps 142:4

8 [a]Acts 20:29

10 [1]Or (a) *flock* [2]Lit *from their hand* [3]Lit *pasture,* and so throughout the ch [a]Jer 21:13; Ezek 5:8; 13:8; 34:2; Zech 10:3 [b]1 Sam 2:29, 30; Jer 52:24-27 [c]Ps 72:12-14; Ezek 13:23

11 [a]Ezek 11:17; 20:41

12 [1]Or *seek(s) out* [2]Or *flock* [a]Jer 31:10 [b]Is 40:11; 56:8; Jer 23:3; 31:8; Luke 19:10; John 10:16 [c]Jer 13:16; Ezek 30:3; Joel 2:2

13 [a]Ezek 34:23; 36:29, 30; Mic 7:14 [b]Is 30:25

14 [a]Ps 23:2; Jer 31:12-14, 25; John 10:9

down on good grazing ground and feed in [1b]rich pasture on the
mountains of Israel.
15 "I will [a]feed My flock and I will [1]lead them to rest," declares
the Lord GOD.
16 "I will seek the lost, bring back the scattered, bind up the
broken and strengthen the sick; but the [a]fat and the strong I
will destroy. I will [b]feed them with judgment.
17 "As for you, My flock, thus says the Lord GOD, 'Behold, I
will [a]judge between one [1]sheep and another, between the rams
and the male goats.
18 'Is it too [a]slight a thing for you that you should feed in the
good pasture, that you must tread down with your feet the rest
of your pastures? Or that you should drink of the clear waters,
that you must [1]foul the rest with your feet?
19 'As for My flock, they must eat what you tread down with
your feet and drink what you [1]foul with your feet!'"
20 Therefore, thus says the Lord GOD to them, "Behold, I,
even I, will judge between the fat sheep and the lean sheep.
21 "Because you push with side and with shoulder, and [a]thrust
at all the [1]weak with your horns until you have scattered them
[2]abroad,
22 therefore, I will [a]deliver My flock, and they will no longer
be a prey; and I will judge between one sheep and another.
23 "Then I will [a]set over them one [b]shepherd, My servant
[c]David, and he will feed them; he will feed them himself and
be their shepherd.
24 "And I, the LORD, will be their God, and My servant [a]David
will be prince among them; I the LORD have spoken.
25 "I will make a [a]covenant of peace with them and [b]eliminate
harmful beasts from the land so that they may [c]live securely in
the wilderness and sleep in the woods.
26 "I will make them and the places around My hill a [a]blessing.
And I will cause [b]showers to come down in their season; they
will be showers of [c]blessing.
27 "Also the tree of the field will yield its fruit and the earth
will yield its increase, and they will be [a]secure on their land.
Then they will know that I am the LORD, when I have [b]broken
the bars of their yoke and have delivered them from the hand
of those who enslaved them.
28 "They will no longer be a prey to the nations, and the beasts
of the earth will not devour them; but they will [a]live securely,
and no one will make *them* afraid.
29 "I will establish for them a [a]renowned planting place, and
they will [b]not again be [1]victims of famine in the land, and they
will not [c]endure the insults of the nations anymore.
30 "Then they will know that [a]I, the LORD their God, am with
them, and that they, the house of Israel, are My people,"
declares the Lord GOD.
31 "As for you, My [a]sheep, the [b]sheep of My pasture, you are
men, and I am your God," declares the Lord GOD.

14 [1]Lit *fat* [b]Ezek 28:25, 26; 36:29, 30

15 [1]Lit *cause them to lie down* [a]Ps 23:1, 2; Ezek 34:23

16 [a]Is 10:16 [b]Is 49:26

17 [1]Or *lamb* [a]Ezek 20:38; 34:20-22; Mal 4:1; Matt 25:32

18 [1]Lit *foul by trampling* [a]Num 16:9, 13; 2 Sam 7:19; Is 7:13

19 [1]Lit *foul by trampling*

21 [1]Or *sick* [2]Lit *to the outside* [a]Deut 33:17; Dan 8:4; Luke 13:14-16

22 [a]Ps 72:12-14; Jer 23:3; Ezek 34:10

23 [a]Rev 7:17 [b]Is 40:11; John 10:11 [c]Jer 30:9; Ezek 37:24

24 [a]Is 55:3; Jer 30:9; Ezek 37:24, 25; Hos 3:5

25 [a]Ezek 16:60; 20:37; 37:26 [b]Job 5:22, 23; Is 11:6-9 [c]Jer 33:16; Ezek 28:26; 34:27, 28

26 [a]Gen 12:2; Ezek 34:14 [b]Deut 11:13-15; 28:12 [c]Lev 25:21; Is 44:3

27 [a]Ezek 38:8, 11 [b]Lev 26:13; Is 52:2, 3; Jer 30:8

28 [a]Jer 30:10; Ezek 39:26

29 [1]Lit *those gathered* [a]Is 4:2; 60:21; 61:3 [b]Ezek 34:26, 27; 36:29 [c]Ezek 36:6, 15

30 [a]Ps 46:7, 11; Ezek 14:11; 36:28

31 [a]Ps 78:52; 80:1; Ezek 36:38 [b]Ps 100:3; Jer 23:1

Chapter 35 Theme ________________________________

35 Moreover, the word of the LORD came to me saying,
2 "Son of man, set your face against [a]Mount Seir, and
prophesy against it
3 and say to it, 'Thus says the Lord [1]GOD,
"Behold, I am against you, Mount Seir,
And I will [a]stretch out My hand against you
And make you a [b]desolation and a waste.
4 "I will [a]lay waste your cities
And you will become a desolation.
Then you will know that I am the LORD.
5 "Because you have had everlasting [a]enmity and have
[1]delivered the sons of Israel to the power of the sword at the time
of their calamity, at the time of the [2b]punishment of the end,
6 therefore as I live," declares the Lord GOD, "I will [1]give you
over to [a]bloodshed, and bloodshed will pursue you; since you
have not hated bloodshed, therefore bloodshed will pursue you.
7 "I will make Mount Seir a waste and a desolation and I will
cut off from it the one who passes through and returns.
8 "I will [a]fill its mountains with its slain; on your hills and in
your valleys and in all your ravines those slain by the sword
will [1]fall.
9 "I will make you an everlasting [a]desolation and your cities
will not be inhabited. Then you will know that I am the LORD.
10 "Because you have [a]said, 'These two nations and these two
lands will be mine, and we will possess [1]them,' although the
[b]LORD was there,
11 therefore as I live," declares the Lord GOD, "I will deal *with*
you [a]according to your anger and according to your envy which
you showed because of your hatred against them; so I will
[b]make Myself known among them when I judge you.
12 "Then you will know [1]that I, the LORD, have heard all your
revilings which you have spoken against the mountains of Israel
saying, 'They are laid desolate; they are [a]given to us for food.'
13 "And you have [1a]spoken arrogantly against Me and have
multiplied your words against Me; [b]I have heard *it.*"
14 'Thus says the Lord GOD, "As all the [a]earth rejoices, I will
make you a desolation.
15 "As you [a]rejoiced over the inheritance of the house of Israel
because it was desolate, [b]so I will do to you. You will be a
[c]desolation, O Mount Seir, and all Edom, all of it. Then they will
know that I am the LORD."'

35:2 [a]Gen 36:8; Ezek 25:12; 36:5

3 [1]Heb *YHWH,* usually rendered *LORD,* and so throughout the ch [a]Jer 6:12; 15:6; Ezek 25:13 [b]Jer 49:13, 17, 18; Ezek 35:7

4 [a]Ezek 6:6; 35:9; Mal 1:3, 4

5 [1]Lit *poured* [2]Or *iniquity* [a]Ps 137:7; Ezek 25:12, 15; 36:5; Amos 1:11; Obad 10 [b]Ezek 7:2; 21:25, 29

6 [1]Lit *prepare you for* [a]Is 63:2-6; Ezek 16:38; 32:6

8 [1]Lit *fall in them* [a]Is 34:5, 6; Ezek 31:12; 32:4, 5; 39:4, 5

9 [a]Jer 49:13; Ezek 25:13

10 [1]Lit *it* [a]Ps 83:4-12; Ezek 36:2, 5 [b]Ps 48:1-3; 132:13, 14; Is 12:6; Ezek 48:35; Zeph 3:15

11 [a]Ps 137:7; Ezek 25:14; Amos 1:11 [b]Ps 9:16; 73:17, 18

12 [1]Or *that I am the LORD: I have heard* [a]Jer 50:7; Ezek 36:2

13 [1]Lit *made great with your mouth* [a]Is 10:13, 14; 36:20; Jer 48:26, 42; Dan 11:36 [b]Jer 7:11; 29:23

14 [a]Is 44:23; 49:13; Jer 51:48

15 [a]Jer 50:11; Lam 4:21 [b]Obad 15 [c]Is 34:5, 6; Ezek 35:3, 4

INSIGHT

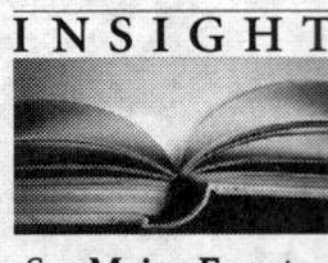

See **Major Events in Israel's History** on page 2087. Notice the section from 1948 through modern times.

Chapter 36 Theme ________________________________

36 "And you, son of man, prophesy to the mountains of
Israel and say, 'O mountains of Israel, hear the word of
the LORD.
2 'Thus says the Lord [1]GOD, "Because the enemy has spoken
against you, 'Aha!' and, 'The everlasting [2a]heights have become
our possession,'

36:2 [1]Heb *YHWH,* usually rendered *LORD,* and so throughout the ch [2]Heb *Bamoth* [a]Deut 32:13; Ps 78:69; Is 58:14; Hab 3:19

3 therefore prophesy and say, 'Thus says the Lord GOD, "[1]For
good reason they have made you [a]desolate and crushed you
from every side, that you would become a possession of the
rest of the nations and you have been taken up in the [2b]talk
and the whispering of the people."'"
4 'Therefore, O [a]mountains of Israel, hear the word of the
Lord GOD. Thus says the Lord GOD to the mountains and to the
hills, to the ravines and to the valleys, to the desolate wastes
and to the forsaken cities which have become a [b]prey and a
derision to the rest of the nations which are round about,
5 therefore thus says the Lord GOD, "Surely in the fire of My
[a]jealousy I have spoken against the [b]rest of the nations, and
against all Edom, who [1]appropriated My land for themselves as
a possession with wholehearted [c]joy *and* with scorn of soul, to
drive it out for a prey."
6 'Therefore prophesy concerning the land of Israel and say to
the mountains and to the hills, to the ravines and to the valleys,
"Thus says the Lord GOD, 'Behold, I have spoken in My jealousy
and in My wrath because you have [a]endured the insults of the
nations.'
7 "Therefore thus says the Lord GOD, 'I have [1]sworn that surely
the nations which are around you will themselves endure their
insults.
8 'But you, O mountains of Israel, you will [a]put forth your
branches and bear your fruit for My people Israel; for they will
soon come.
9 'For, behold, I am for you, and I will [a]turn to you, and you
will be [b]cultivated and sown.
10 'I will multiply men on you, [a]all the house of Israel, all of it;
and the [b]cities will be inhabited and the waste places will be
rebuilt.
11 'I will multiply on you man and beast; and they will increase
and be fruitful; and I will cause you to be inhabited as you were
[a]formerly and will [1]treat you [b]better than at the first. Thus you
will know that I am the LORD.
12 'Yes, I will cause [a]men—My people Israel—to walk on you
and possess you, so that you will become their [b]inheritance and
never again [c]bereave them of children.'
13 "Thus says the Lord GOD, 'Because they say to you, "You are a
[a]devourer of men and have bereaved your [1]nation of children,"
14 therefore you will no longer devour men and no longer
bereave your nation of children,' declares the Lord GOD.
15 "I will not let you hear [a]insults from the nations anymore,
nor will you bear [b]disgrace from the peoples any longer, nor
will you cause your nation to [c]stumble any longer," declares the
Lord GOD.'"
16 Then the word of the LORD came to me saying,
17 "Son of man, when the house of Israel was living in their
own land, they [a]defiled it by their ways and their deeds; their
way before Me was like [b]the uncleanness of a woman in her
impurity.

3 [1]Lit *Because;* or *By the cause* [2]Lit *lip of the tongue* [a]Jer 2:15 [b]Ps 44:13, 14; Jer 18:16; Ezek 35:13

4 [a]Deut 11:11; Ezek 36:1, 6, 8 [b]Ezek 34:8, 28

5 [1]Lit *gave* [a]Ezek 5:13; 36:6; 38:19 [b]Jer 25:9, 15-29; Ezek 36:3 [c]Jer 50:11; Ezek 35:15; Mic 7:8

6 [a]Ps 74:10; 123:3, 4; Ezek 34:29

7 [1]Lit *lifted up My hand*

8 [a]Is 4:2; 27:6; Ezek 17:23; 34:26-29

9 [a]Lev 26:9 [b]Ezek 28:26; 34:14; 36:34

10 [a]Is 27:6; 49:17-23; Ezek 37:21, 22 [b]Jer 31:27, 28; 33:12; Ezek 36:33

11 [1]Lit *cause good* [a]Jer 30:18; Ezek 16:55; Mic 7:14 [b]Job 42:12; Is 51:3

12 [a]Ezek 34:13, 14 [b]Ezek 47:14 [c]Jer 15:7; Ezek 22:12, 27

13 [1]Or *nations,* and so throughout the ch [a]Num 13:32

15 [a]Is 60:14; Ezek 34:29; 36:7 [b]Ps 89:50; Is 54:4; Ezek 22:4 [c]Is 63:13; Jer 13:16; 18:15

17 [a]Jer 2:7 [b]Lev 15:19

18 "Therefore I [a]poured out My wrath on them for the blood
which they had shed on the land, because they had defiled it
with their idols.
19 "Also I [a]scattered them among the nations and they were
dispersed throughout the lands. [b]According to their ways and
their deeds I judged them.
20 "When they came to the nations where they went, they
[a]profaned My holy name, because it was said of them, 'These
are the [b]people of the LORD; yet they have come out of His land.'
21 "But I had [1]concern for My [a]holy name, which the house of
Israel had profaned among the nations where they went.
22 "Therefore say to the house of Israel, 'Thus says the Lord
GOD, "It is [a]not for your sake, O house of Israel, that I am about
to act, but for My holy name, which you have profaned among
the nations where you went.
23 "I will [a]vindicate the holiness of My great name which has
been profaned among the nations, which you have profaned in
their midst. Then the [b]nations will know that I am the LORD,"
declares the Lord GOD, "when I prove Myself holy among you
in their sight.
24 "For I will [a]take you from the nations, gather you from all
the lands and bring you into your own land.
25 "Then I will [a]sprinkle clean water on you, and you will be
clean; I will cleanse you from all your [b]filthiness and from all
your [c]idols.
26 "Moreover, I will give you a [a]new heart and put a new spirit
within you; and I will remove the [b]heart of stone from your
flesh and give you a heart of flesh.
27 "I will [a]put My Spirit within you and cause you to walk in
My statutes, and you will be careful to observe My ordinances.
28 "You will live in the land that I gave to your forefathers; so
you will be [a]My people, and I will be your God.
29 "Moreover, I will save you from all your uncleanness; and I
will call for the grain and multiply it, and I [a]will not [1]bring a
famine on you.
30 "I will [a]multiply the fruit of the tree and the produce of the
field, so that you will not receive again the disgrace of famine
among the nations.
31 "Then you will [a]remember your evil ways and your deeds
that were not good, and you will loathe yourselves in your own
sight for your iniquities and your abominations.
32 "I am not doing *this* [a]for your sake," declares the Lord GOD,
"let it be known to you. Be ashamed and confounded for your
ways, O house of Israel!"
33 'Thus says the Lord GOD, "On the day that I cleanse you
from all your iniquities, I will cause the [a]cities to be inhabited,
and the [b]waste places will be rebuilt.
34 "The desolate land will be cultivated instead of being a
desolation in the sight of everyone who passes by.
35 "They will say, 'This desolate land has become like the
[a]garden of Eden; and the waste, desolate and ruined cities are
fortified *and* inhabited.'

18 [a]2 Chr 34:21, 25; Lam 2:4; 4:11; Ezek 22:20, 22

19 [a]Deut 28:64; Ezek 5:12; 22:15; Amos 9:9 [b]Ezek 24:14; 39:24; Rom 2:6

20 [a]Is 52:5; Ezek 12:16; Rom 2:24 [b]Jer 33:24

21 [1]Lit *compassion* [a]Ps 74:18; Is 48:9; Ezek 20:44

22 [a]Deut 7:7, 8; 9:5, 6; Ezek 36:32

23 [a]Is 5:16; Ezek 20:41; 38:23; 39:7, 25 [b]Ps 102:15; 126:2

24 [a]Is 43:5, 6; Ezek 34:13; 37:21

25 [a]Num 19:17-19; Ps 51:7; Titus 3:5, 6; Heb 9:13, 19; 10:22 [b]Is 4:4; Zech 13:1 [c]Is 2:18, 20; Hos 14:3, 8

26 [a]Ps 51:10; Ezek 11:19; 18:31; John 3:3, 5; 2 Cor 5:17 [b]Ezek 11:19; Zech 7:12

27 [a]Is 44:3; 59:21; Ezek 37:14; 39:29; Joel 2:28, 29

28 [a]Ezek 14:11; 37:23, 27

29 [1]Lit *put* [a]Ezek 34:27, 29; Hos 2:21-23

30 [a]Lev 26:4; Ezek 34:27

31 [a]Ezek 16:61-63; 20:43

32 [a]Deut 9:5

33 [a]Ezek 36:10; Zech 8:7, 8 [b]Is 58:12

35 [a]Is 51:3; Ezek 31:9; Joel 2:3

36 "Then the nations that are left round about you will know
that I, the LORD, have rebuilt the ruined places *and* planted that
which was desolate; I, the LORD, have spoken and [a]will do it."
37 'Thus says the Lord GOD, "This also I will let the house of
Israel ask Me to do for them: I will increase their men like a flock.
38 "Like the [a]flock [1]for sacrifices, like the flock at Jerusalem
during her appointed feasts, so will the waste cities be filled with
[b]flocks of men. Then they will know that I am the LORD."'"

Chapter 37 Theme

37 The [a]hand of the LORD was upon me, and He [b]brought
me out [1]by the Spirit of the LORD and set me down in
the middle of the [c]valley; and it was full of bones.
2 He caused me to pass among them round about, and behold,
there were very many on the surface of the valley; and lo, *they
were* very dry.
3 He said to me, "Son of man, [a]can these bones live?" And I
answered, "O Lord [1]GOD, [b]You know."
4 Again He said to me, "[a]Prophesy over these bones and say
to them, 'O dry bones, [b]hear the word of the LORD.'
5 "Thus says the Lord GOD to these bones, 'Behold, I will
cause [1a]breath to enter you that you may come to life.
6 'I will put sinews on you, make flesh grow back on you,
cover you with skin and put breath in you that you may come
alive; and you will [a]know that I am the LORD.'"
7 So I prophesied [a]as I was commanded; and as I prophesied,
there was a [1]noise, and behold, a rattling; and the bones came
together, bone to its bone.
8 And I looked, and behold, sinews were on them, and flesh
grew and skin covered them; but there was no breath in them.
9 Then He said to me, "Prophesy to the breath, prophesy,
son of man, and say to the breath, 'Thus says the Lord GOD,
"Come from the four winds, O breath, and [a]breathe on these
slain, that they [b]come to life."'"
10 So I prophesied as He commanded me, and the [a]breath
came into them, and they came to life and stood on their feet,
an [b]exceedingly great army.
11 Then He said to me, "Son of man, these bones are the
[a]whole house of Israel; behold, they say, 'Our [b]bones are dried
up and our hope has perished. We are [1]completely [c]cut off.'
12 "Therefore prophesy and say to them, 'Thus says the Lord
GOD, "Behold, I will open your graves and [a]cause you to come
up out of your graves, My people; and I will bring you into the
land of Israel.
13 "Then you will know that I am the LORD, when I have
opened your graves and caused you to come up out of your
graves, My people.
14 "I will [a]put My [1]Spirit within you and you will come to life,
and I will place you on your own land. Then you will know
that I, the LORD, have spoken and done it," declares the LORD.'"

36 [a]Ezek 17:24; 22:14; 37:14; Hos 14:4-9

38 [1]Lit *of holy things* [a]1 Kin 8:63; 2 Chr 35:7-9; John 2:14 [b]Ps 74:1; 100:3; Jer 23:1; John 10:7, 9, 16

37:1 [1]Or *in* [a]Ezek 1:3; 33:22; 40:1 [b]Ezek 8:3; 11:24; 43:5; Acts 8:39 [c]Jer 7:32-8:2

3 [1]Heb *YHWH,* usually rendered *LORD,* and so throughout the ch [a]Ezek 26:19 [b]Deut 32:39; 1 Sam 2:6

4 [a]Ezek 37:9, 12 [b]Jer 22:29; Ezek 36:1

5 [1]Or *spirit,* and so throughout the ch [a]Gen 2:7; Ps 104:29, 30; Ezek 37:9, 10, 14

6 [a]Is 49:23; Ezek 35:9; 38:23; 39:6; Joel 2:27; 3:17

7 [1]Lit *voice;* or *thunder* [a]Jer 13:5-7

9 [a]Ps 104:30 [b]Hos 13:14

10 [a]Rev 11:11 [b]Jer 30:19; 33:22

11 [1]Lit *cut off to ourselves* [a]Jer 33:24; Ezek 36:10; 39:25 [b]Ps 141:7 [c]Ps 88:5; Lam 3:54

12 [a]Deut 32:39; 1 Sam 2:6; Is 26:19; 66:14; Hos 13:14

14 [1]Or *breath* [a]Is 32:15; Ezek 11:19; 36:27; 37:6, 9; 39:29; Joel 2:28, 29; Zech 12:10

15 The word of the LORD came again to me saying,
16 "And you, son of man, take for yourself [a]one stick and write
on it, 'For [b]Judah and for the sons of Israel, his companions';
then take another stick and write on it, 'For [c]Joseph, the stick
of Ephraim and all the house of Israel, his companions.'
17 "Then [a]join them for yourself one to another into one stick,
that they may become one in your hand.
18 "When the sons of your people speak to you saying, 'Will
you not declare to us [a]what you mean by these?'
19 say to them, 'Thus says the Lord GOD, "Behold, I will take
the stick of Joseph, which is in the hand of Ephraim, and the
tribes of Israel, his companions; and I will put them with it,
with the stick of Judah, and make them one stick, and they will
be one in My hand."'
20 "The sticks on which you write will be in your hand before
their eyes.
21 "Say to them, 'Thus says the Lord GOD, "Behold, I will [a]take
the sons of Israel from among the nations where they have
gone, and I will gather them from every side and bring them
into their own land;
22 and I will make them [a]one nation in the land, on the
mountains of Israel; and [b]one king will be king for all of them;
and they will no longer be two nations and no longer be divided
into two kingdoms.
23 "They will [a]no longer defile themselves with their idols, or
with their detestable things, or with any of their transgressions;
but [b]I will deliver them from all their [1]dwelling places in which
they have sinned, and will cleanse them. And they will be My
people, and I will be their God.
24 "My servant [a]David will be king over them, and they will all
have [b]one shepherd; and they will walk in My ordinances and
keep My statutes and observe them.
25 "They will live on the land that I gave to Jacob My servant,
in which your fathers lived; and they will live on it, they, and
their sons and their sons' sons, forever; and [a]David My servant
will be their prince forever.
26 "I will make a [a]covenant of peace with them; it will be an
[b]everlasting covenant with them. And I will [1]place them and
[c]multiply them, and will set My [d]sanctuary in their midst forever.
27 "My [a]dwelling place also will be with them; and [b]I will be
their God, and they will be My people.
28 "And the nations will know that I am the LORD [a]who sanctifies
Israel, when My sanctuary is in their midst forever."'"

Chapter 38 Theme ____________________________________

See map on page 2242.

38 And the word of the LORD came to me saying,
2 "Son of man, set your face toward [a]Gog of the land of
[b]Magog, the [1]prince of [c]Rosh, [d]Meshech and [d]Tubal, and prophesy against him
3 and say, 'Thus says the Lord [1]GOD, "Behold, I am against
you, O Gog, [2]prince of Rosh, Meshech and Tubal.

16 [a]Num 17:2, 3 [b]2 Chr 10:17; 11:11-17; 15:9 [c]1 Kin 12:16-20; 2 Chr 10:19

17 [a]Is 11:13; Jer 50:4; Ezek 37:22-24; Hos 1:11; Zeph 3:9

18 [a]Ezek 12:9; 17:12; 20:49; 24:19

21 [a]Is 43:5, 6; Jer 29:14; Ezek 36:24; 39:27; Amos 9:14, 15

22 [a]Jer 3:18; 50:4, 5; Ezek 36:10 [b]Ezek 34:23, 24; 37:24

23 [1]Another reading is *backslidings* [a]Ezek 36:25 [b]Ezek 36:28, 29

24 [a]Jer 30:9; Ezek 34:24; 37:25; Hos 3:5 [b]Ps 78:71; Is 40:11; Ezek 34:23

25 [a]Is 11:1; Ezek 37:24; Zech 6:12

26 [1]Lit *give* [a]Ezek 16:62; 20:37; 34:25 [b]Ps 89:3, 4; Is 55:3; 59:21; Ezek 16:60 [c]Jer 30:19; Ezek 36:10, 11, 37 [d]Ezek 20:40; 43:7

27 [a]John 1:14; Rev 21:3 [b]Ezek 37:23; 2 Cor 6:16

28 [a]Ex 31:13; Ezek 20:12

38:2 [1]Or *chief prince of Meshech* [a]Ezek 38:3, 14, 16, 18; 39:1, 11; Rev 20:8 [b]Gen 10:2; Ezek 39:6; Rev 20:8 [c]Ezek 38:3; 39:1 [d]Ezek 27:13; 38:3; 39:1

3 [1]Heb *YHWH,* usually rendered *LORD,* and so throughout the ch [2]Or *chief prince of Meshech*

4 "I will turn you about and put hooks into your jaws, and I
will [a]bring you out, and all your army, [b]horses and horsemen,
all of them [1]splendidly attired, a great company *with* buckler
and shield, all of them wielding swords;
5 [a]Persia, [1b]Ethiopia and [c]Put with them, all of them *with*
shield and helmet;
6 [a]Gomer with all its troops; [b]Beth-togarmah *from* the remote
parts of the north with all its troops—many peoples with you.
7 "[a]Be prepared, and prepare yourself, you and all your
companies that are assembled about you, and be a guard for
them.
8 "[a]After many days you will be summoned; in the latter years
you will come into the land that is restored from the sword,
whose inhabitants have been [b]gathered from many [1]nations to
the [c]mountains of Israel which had been a continual waste; but
[2]its people were brought out from the [1]nations, and they are
[d]living securely, all of them.
9 "You will go up, you will come [a]like a storm; you will be like
a [b]cloud covering the land, you and all your troops, and many
peoples with you."
10 'Thus says the Lord GOD, "It will come about on that day,
that [1]thoughts will come into your mind and you will [a]devise
an evil plan,
11 and you will say, 'I will go up against the land of [1a]unwalled
villages. I will go against those who are [b]at rest, that live securely,
all of them living without walls and having no bars or gates,
12 to [a]capture spoil and to seize plunder, to turn your hand
against the waste places which are *now* inhabited, and against the
people who are gathered from the nations, who have acquired
cattle and goods, who live at the [1]center of the world.'
13 "[a]Sheba and [b]Dedan and the merchants of [c]Tarshish with all its
[1]villages will say to you, 'Have you come to capture spoil? Have
you assembled your company to seize plunder, to carry away silver
and gold, to take away cattle and goods, to capture great [d]spoil?'"'
14 "Therefore prophesy, son of man, and say to Gog, 'Thus says
the Lord GOD, "On that day when My people Israel are [a]living
securely, will you not know *it?*
15 "[a]You will come from your place out of the remote parts of
the north, you and many peoples with you, all of them riding
on horses, a great assembly and a mighty army;
16 and you will come up against My people Israel like a cloud
to cover the land. It shall come about in the last days that I will
bring you against My land, so that the nations may [a]know Me
when I am [b]sanctified through you before their eyes, O Gog."
17 'Thus says the Lord GOD, "Are you the one of whom I spoke
in former days through My servants the prophets of Israel, who
[a]prophesied in those days for *many* years that I would bring
you against them?
18 "It will come about on that day, when Gog comes against
the land of Israel," declares the Lord GOD, "that My fury will
mount up in My [a]anger.

4 [1]Or *clothed in full armor* [a]Is 43:17 [b]Ezek 38:15; Dan 11:40
5 [1]Lit *Cush* [a]2 Chr 36:20; Ezra 1:1; Ezek 27:10; Dan 8:20 [b]Gen 10:6-8; Ezek 30:4, 5 [c]Ezek 27:10; 30:5
6 [a]Gen 10:2, 3 [b]Gen 10:3; Ezek 27:14
7 [a]Is 8:9
8 [1]Lit *peoples* [2]Lit *it was* [a]Is 24:22 [b]Is 11:11; Ezek 36:24; 37:21; 38:12; 39:27, 28 [c]Ezek 34:13; 36:1-8 [d]Ezek 38:11, 14; 39:26
9 [a]Is 5:28; 21:1; 25:4; 28:2; Jer 4:13 [b]Ezek 30:18; 38:16; Joel 2:2
10 [1]Lit *words* [a]Ps 36:4; Mic 2:1
11 [1]Or *open country* [a]Zech 2:4 [b]Jer 49:31
12 [1]Lit *navel* [a]Is 10:6; Ezek 29:19
13 [1]Or *young lions* [a]Ezek 27:22, 23 [b]Ezek 25:13; 27:15, 20 [c]Ezek 27:12 [d]Is 10:6; 33:23; Jer 15:13
14 [a]Jer 23:6; Ezek 38:8, 11; Zech 2:5, 8
15 [a]Ezek 39:2
16 [a]Ps 83:18; Ezek 36:23; 38:23 [b]Is 5:16; 8:13; 29:23; Ezek 28:22
17 [a]Is 5:26-29; 34:1-6; 63:1-6; 66:15, 16; Joel 3:9-14
18 [a]Ps 18:8, 15

19 "In My [a]zeal and in My blazing wrath I declare *that* on that day
there will surely be a great [1b]earthquake in the land of Israel.
20 "[a]The fish of the sea, the birds of the heavens, the beasts of
the field, all the creeping things that creep on the earth, and all
the men who are on the face of the earth will shake at My
presence; the [b]mountains also will be thrown down, the steep
pathways will [1]collapse and every wall will fall to the ground.
21 "I will call for a [a]sword against [1]him on all My mountains,"
declares the Lord GOD. "[b]Every man's sword will be against his
brother.
22 "With pestilence and with blood I will enter into [a]judgment
with him; and I will rain on him and on his troops, and on the
many peoples who are with him, [1]a torrential rain, with
[b]hailstones, fire and brimstone.
23 "I will magnify Myself, sanctify Myself, and [a]make Myself
known in the sight of many nations; and they will know that I
am the LORD."'

Chapter 39 Theme ______________________________

39 "And [a]you, son of man, prophesy against Gog and say,
'Thus says the Lord [1]GOD, "Behold, I am against you, O
Gog, [2]prince of Rosh, Meshech and Tubal;
2 and I will turn you around, drive you on, take you up from
the remotest parts of the north and bring you against the
mountains of Israel.
3 "I will [a]strike your bow from your left hand and dash down
your arrows from your right hand.
4 "You will [a]fall on the mountains of Israel, you and all your
troops and the peoples who are with you; I will give you as
[b]food to every [1]kind of predatory bird and beast of the field.
5 "You will fall on the [1]open field; for it is I who have spoken,"
declares the Lord GOD.
6 "And I will send [a]fire upon Magog and those who inhabit the
[b]coastlands in safety; and they will know that I am the LORD.
7 "My [a]holy name I will make known in the midst of My people
Israel; and I will not let My holy name be [b]profaned anymore.
And the [c]nations will know that I am the LORD, the [d]Holy One
in Israel.
8 "Behold, it is coming and it shall be done," declares the
Lord GOD. "That is the day of which I have spoken.
9 "Then those who inhabit the cities of Israel will [a]go out and
make [b]fires with the weapons and burn *them,* both shields and
bucklers, bows and arrows, war clubs and spears, and for seven
years they will make fires of them.
10 "They will not take wood from the field or gather firewood
from the forests, for they will make fires with the weapons; and
they will take the spoil of those who despoiled them and seize the
[a]plunder of those who plundered them," declares the Lord GOD.
11 "On that day I will give Gog a burial ground there in Israel,
the valley of those who pass by east of the sea, and it will block

19 [1]Or *shaking* [a]Deut 32:22; Ps 18:7, 8; Ezek 5:13; 36:5, 6; Nah 1:2; Heb 12:29 [b]Joel 3:16; Hag 2:6, 7, 21

20 [1]Lit *fall* [a]Jer 4:24, 25; Hos 4:3; Nah 1:4-6 [b]Zech 14:4

21 [1]I.e. Gog [a]Ezek 14:17 [b]Judg 7:22; 1 Sam 14:20; 2 Chr 20:23; Hag 2:22

22 [1]Lit *an overflowing* [a]Is 66:16; Jer 25:31 [b]Ps 11:6; 18:12-14; Is 28:17

23 [a]Ps 9:16; Ezek 37:28; 38:16

39:1 [1]Heb *YHWH,* usually rendered *LORD,* and so throughout the ch [2]Or *chief prince of Meshech* [a]Ezek 38:2

3 [a]Ps 76:3; Jer 21:4, 5; Ezek 30:21-24; Hos 1:5

4 [1]Lit *wing* [a]Is 14:24, 25; Ezek 39:17-20 [b]Ezek 29:5; 32:4, 5; 33:27

5 [1]Lit *face of the*

6 [a]Ezek 30:8, 16; 38:19, 22; Amos 1:4, 7, 10; Nah 1:6 [b]Ps 72:10; Is 66:19; Jer 25:22

7 [a]Ezek 36:20-22; 39:25 [b]Ex 20:7; Ezek 20:9, 14, 39 [c]Ezek 38:16, 23 [d]Is 12:6; 43:3, 14; 55:5; 60:9, 14

9 [a]Is 66:24; Mal 1:5 [b]Josh 11:6; Ps 46:9

10 [a]Is 14:2; 33:1; Mic 5:8; Hab 2:8

off those who would pass by. So they will bury Gog there with
all his [1]horde, and they will call *it* the valley of [2]Hamon-gog.
12 "For seven months the house of Israel will be burying them
in order to [a]cleanse the land.
13 "Even all the people of the land will bury *them;* and it will
be [1]to their [a]renown *on* the day that I [b]glorify Myself," declares
the Lord GOD.
14 "They will set apart men who will constantly pass through
the land, [a]burying those who were passing through, even those
left on the surface of the ground, in order to cleanse it. At the
end of seven months they will make a search.
15 "As those who pass through the land pass through and
anyone sees a man's bone, then he will [1]set up a marker by it
until the buriers have buried it in the valley of [2]Hamon-gog.
16 "And even *the* name of *the* city will be Hamonah. So they
will cleanse the land."'
17 "As for you, son of man, thus says the Lord GOD, 'Speak to
every [1]kind of [a]bird and to every [a]beast of the field, "Assemble
and come, gather from every side to My sacrifice which I am
going to [b]sacrifice for you, as a great sacrifice on the mountains
of Israel, that you may eat flesh and drink blood.
18 "You will [a]eat the flesh of mighty men and drink the blood
of the princes of the earth, as *though they were* [b]rams, lambs,
goats and [c]bulls, all of them fatlings of [d]Bashan.
19 "So you will eat fat until you are glutted, and drink blood until
you are drunk, from My sacrifice which I have sacrificed for you.
20 "You will be glutted at My table with [a]horses and charioteers,
with mighty men and all the men of war," declares the Lord
GOD.
21 "And I will set My [a]glory among the nations; and all the
nations will see My judgment which I have executed and My
hand which I have laid on them.
22 "And the house of Israel will [a]know that I am the LORD their
God from that day onward.
23 "The nations will know that the house of Israel went into
exile for their [a]iniquity because they acted treacherously
against Me, and I [b]hid My face from them; so I gave them into
the hand of their adversaries, and all of them fell by the sword.
24 "[a]According to their uncleanness and according to their
transgressions I dealt with them, and I hid My face from them."'"
25 Therefore thus says the Lord GOD, "Now I will [1a]restore the
fortunes of Jacob and have mercy on the whole [b]house of
Israel; and I will be [c]jealous for My holy name.
26 "They will [1a]forget their disgrace and all their treachery which
they [2]perpetrated against Me, when they [b]live securely on their
own land with [c]no one to make *them* afraid.
27 "When I [a]bring them back from the peoples and gather them
from the lands of their enemies, then I shall be [b]sanctified
[1]through them in the sight of the many nations.
28 "Then they will know that I am the LORD their God because
I made them go into exile among the nations, and then gathered

11 [1]Lit *crowd* [2]Or *the multitude of Gog*
12 [a]Deut 21:23; Ezek 39:14, 16
13 [1]Or *a memorial for them* [a]Jer 33:9; Zeph 3:19, 20 [b]Ezek 28:22
14 [a]Jer 14:16
15 [1]Lit *build* [2]Or *the multitude of Gog*
17 [1]Lit *wing* [a]Is 56:9; Jer 12:9; Ezek 39:4; Rev 19:17, 18 [b]Is 34:6, 7; Jer 46:10; Zeph 1:7
18 [a]Ezek 29:5; Rev 19:18 [b]Jer 51:40 [c]Jer 50:27 [d]Ps 22:12; Amos 4:1
20 [a]Ps 76:5, 6; Ezek 38:4; Hag 2:22; Rev 19:18
21 [a]Ex 9:16; Is 37:20; Ezek 36:23; 38:16, 23; 39:13
22 [a]Jer 24:7
23 [a]Jer 22:8, 9; 44:22; Ezek 36:18, 19 [b]Is 1:15; 59:2; Ezek 39:29
24 [a]2 Kin 17:7; Jer 2:17, 19; 4:18; Ezek 36:19
25 [1]Or *return the captivity* [a]Is 27:12, 13; Jer 33:7; Ezek 34:13 [b]Jer 31:1; Ezek 36:10; 37:21, 22; Hos 1:11 [c]Ex 20:5; Nah 1:2
26 [1]Another reading is *bear* [2]Lit *did treacherously* [a]Ezek 16:63; 20:43; 36:31 [b]1 Kin 4:25; Ezek 34:25-28 [c]Is 17:2; Mic 4:4
27 [1]Lit *in* [a]Ezek 36:24; 37:21 [b]Ezek 36:23; 38:16, 23

them *again* to their own land; and I will leave none of them there any longer.
29 "I will not hide My face from them any longer, for I will have [a]poured out My Spirit on the house of Israel," declares the Lord GOD.

Chapter 40 Theme ____________________

572 B.C.

40 In the [a]twenty-fifth year of our exile, at the beginning of the year, on the tenth of the month, in the fourteenth year after the [b]city was [1]taken, on that same day the [c]hand of the LORD was upon me and He brought me there.
2 In the [a]visions of God He brought me into the land of Israel and set me on a very [b]high mountain, and on it [c]to the south *there was* a [d]structure like a city.
3 So He brought me there; and behold, there was a man whose appearance was like the appearance of [a]bronze, with a [b]line of flax and a [c]measuring [1]rod in his hand; and he was standing in the gateway.
4 The man said to me, "[a]Son of man, [b]see with your eyes, hear with your ears, and give attention to all that I am going to show you; for you have been brought here in order to show *it* to you. [c]Declare to the house of Israel all that you see."
5 And behold, there was a [a]wall on the outside of the [1]temple all around, and in the man's hand was a measuring rod of six cubits, *each of which was* a cubit and a [2]handbreadth. So he measured the thickness of the [3]wall, one rod; and the height, one rod.
6 Then he went to the gate which faced [a]east, went up its steps and measured the threshold of the gate, one rod [1]in width; and the other threshold *was* one rod [1]in width.
7 The [a]guardroom *was* one rod long and one rod wide; and *there were* five cubits between the guardrooms. And the threshold of the gate by the porch of the gate [1]facing inward *was* one rod.
8 Then he measured the porch of the gate [1]facing inward, one rod.
9 He measured the porch of the gate, eight cubits; and its side pillars, two cubits. And the porch of the gate was [1]faced inward.
10 The guardrooms of the gate toward the east *numbered* three on each side; the three of them had the same measurement. The side pillars also had the same measurement on each side.
11 And he measured the width of the [1]gateway, ten cubits, and the length of the gate, thirteen cubits.
12 *There was* a [1]barrier *wall* one cubit *wide* in front of the guardrooms on each side; and the guardrooms *were* six cubits *square* on each side.
13 He measured the gate from the roof of the one guardroom to the roof of the other, a width of twenty-five cubits from *one* door to *the* door opposite.

RETURN TO INSTRUCTIONS

29 [a]Is 32:15; Ezek 36:27; 37:14; Joel 2:28

40:1 [1]Lit *struck* [a]Ezek 32:1, 17; 33:21 [b]2 Kin 25:1-7; Jer 39:1-9; 52:4-11; Ezek 33:21 [c]Ezek 1:3; 3:14, 22; 37:1

2 [a]Ezek 1:1; 8:3; Dan 7:1, 7 [b]Is 2:2, 3; Ezek 17:23; 20:40; 37:22; Mic 4:1; Rev 21:10 [c]Ps 48:2; Is 14:13 [d]1 Chr 28:12, 19

3 [1]Lit *reed,* and so throughout the ch [a]Ezek 1:7; Dan 10:6; Rev 1:15 [b]Ezek 47:3; Zech 2:1, 2 [c]Rev 11:1; 21:15

4 [a]Ezek 2:1, 3, 6, 8; 44:5 [b]Ezek 2:7, 8; 44:5 [c]Is 21:10; Jer 26:2; Acts 20:27

5 [1]Lit *house* [2]I.e. 204 in. [3]Lit *building* [a]Is 26:1; Ezek 42:20

6 [1]Or *in depth* [a]Ezek 8:16; 11:1; 40:20; 43:1

7 [1]Lit *from the house* [a]Ezek 40:10-16, 21, 29, 33, 36

8 [1]Lit *from the house*

9 [1]Lit *from the house*

11 [1]Lit *entrance of the gate*

12 [1]Lit *border*

14 He made the side pillars sixty cubits *high;* the gate *extended*
round about to the side pillar of the [a]courtyard.
15 *From* the front of the entrance gate to the front of the inner
porch of the gate *was* fifty cubits.
16 *There were* [1a]shuttered windows *looking* toward the
guardrooms, and toward their side pillars within the gate all
around, and likewise for the porches. And *there were* windows
all around inside; and on *each* side pillar *were* [b]palm tree
ornaments.
17 Then he brought me into the [a]outer court, and behold,
there were [b]chambers and a pavement made for the court all
around; thirty chambers [1]faced the pavement.
18 The pavement (*that is,* the lower pavement) *was* by the
[1]side of the gates, corresponding to the length of the gates.
19 Then he measured the width from the front of the [a]lower
gate to the front of the exterior of the inner court, a [b]hundred
cubits on the east and on the north.
20 *As for* the [a]gate of the outer court which faced the north,
he measured its length and its width.
21 [1]It had three [a]guardrooms on each side; and its [b]side pillars
and its porches [2]had the same measurement as the first gate.
Its length *was* [c]fifty cubits and the width [d]twenty-five cubits.
22 Its [a]windows and its porches and its palm tree ornaments
had the same measurements as the [b]gate which faced toward
the east; and [1]it was reached by seven [c]steps, and its [2]porch
was in front of them.
23 The inner court had a gate opposite the gate on the north
as well as *the gate* on the east; and he measured a [a]hundred
cubits from gate to gate.
24 Then he led me toward the south, and behold, there was a
[a]gate toward the south; and he measured its [b]side pillars and its
porches according to [1]those same measurements.
25 [1]The gate and its porches had [a]windows all around like
[2]those other windows; the length *was* [b]fifty cubits and the
width twenty-five cubits.
26 *There were* seven [a]steps going up to it, and its porches
were in front of them; and it had [b]palm tree ornaments on its
side pillars, one on each side.
27 The inner court had a gate toward the [a]south; and he
measured from gate to gate toward the south, a [b]hundred cubits.
28 Then he brought me to the inner court by the south gate;
and he measured the south gate [a]according to those same
measurements.
29 Its [a]guardrooms also, its side pillars and its [b]porches *were*
according to those same measurements. And [1]the gate and its
porches had [b]windows all around; it *was* [c]fifty cubits long and
twenty-five cubits wide.
30 *There were* [a]porches all around, twenty-five cubits long and
five cubits wide.
31 Its porches *were* toward the outer court; and [a]palm tree
ornaments *were* on its side pillars, and its stairway *had* eight
[b]steps.

14 [a]Ex 27:9; 1 Chr 28:6; Ps 100:4; Is 62:9; Ezek 8:7; 42:1

16 [1]Or *beveled inwards* [a]1 Kin 6:4; Ezek 41:16, 26 [b]1 Kin 6:29, 32, 35; 2 Chr 3:5; Ezek 40:22, 26, 31, 34, 37; 41:18-20, 25, 26

17 [1]Lit *to* [a]Ezek 10:5; 42:1; 46:21; Rev 11:2 [b]2 Kin 23:11; 1 Chr 9:26; 23:28; 2 Chr 31:11; Ezek 40:38

18 [1]Lit *shoulder*

19 [a]Ezek 40:23, 27; 46:1, 2 [b]Ezek 40:23, 27

20 [a]Ezek 40:6

21 [1]Lit *its guardrooms were three* [2]Lit *were* [a]Ezek 40:7 [b]Ezek 40:16, 30 [c]Ezek 40:15 [d]Ezek 40:13

22 [1]Lit *they were going up into it* [2]Or *porches* [a]Ezek 40:16 [b]Ezek 40:6 [c]Ezek 40:26, 31, 34, 37, 49

23 [a]Ezek 40:19, 27

24 [1]Lit *these measurements,* and so throughout the ch [a]Ezek 40:6, 20, 35; 46:9 [b]Ezek 40:21

25 [1]Lit *It* [2]Lit *these windows* [a]Ezek 40:16, 22, 29 [b]Ezek 40:21, 33

26 [a]Ezek 40:6, 22 [b]Ezek 40:16

27 [a]Ezek 40:23, 32 [b]Ezek 40:19

28 [a]Ezek 40:32, 35

29 [1]Lit *it* [a]Ezek 40:7, 10, 21 [b]Ezek 40:16, 22, 25 [c]Ezek 40:21

30 [a]Ezek 40:16, 21

31 [a]Ezek 40:16 [b]Ezek 40:22, 26, 34, 37

32 He brought me into the [a]inner court toward the east. And
he measured the gate [b]according to those same measurements.
33 Its [a]guardrooms also, its side pillars and its porches *were*
according to those same measurements. And [1]the gate and its
porches had [b]windows all around; it *was* [c]fifty cubits long and
twenty-five cubits wide.
34 Its [a]porches *were* toward the outer court; and [a]palm tree
ornaments *were* on its side pillars, on each side, and its
stairway *had* eight [b]steps.
35 Then he brought me to the [a]north gate; and he measured *it*
according to those same measurements,
36 *with* its [a]guardrooms, its side pillars and its [b]porches. And
[1]the gate had [b]windows all around; the length *was* [c]fifty cubits
and the width twenty-five cubits.
37 Its side pillars *were* toward the outer court; and [a]palm tree
ornaments *were* on its side pillars on each side, and its
stairway had eight [b]steps.
38 A [a]chamber with its doorway was by the side pillars at the
gates; there they [b]rinse the burnt offering.
39 In the porch of the gate *were* two [a]tables on each side, on
which to slaughter the [b]burnt offering, the sin offering and the
guilt offering.
40 On the outer [1]side, [2]as one went up to the [3]gateway toward
the north, *were* two tables; and on the other [1]side of the porch
of the gate *were* two tables.
41 Four [a]tables *were* on each side [1]next to the gate; *or,* eight
tables on which they slaughter *sacrifices.*
42 For the burnt offering *there were* four [a]tables of [b]hewn
stone, a cubit and a half long, a cubit and a half wide and one
cubit high, on which they lay the instruments with which they
slaughter the [a]burnt offering and the sacrifice.
43 The double [1]hooks, one handbreadth in length, were
installed [2]in the house all around; and on the tables *was* the
flesh of the offering.
44 From the outside to the [a]inner gate were [1b]chambers for
the [c]singers in the inner court, *one of* which was at the [2]side of
the north gate, with [3]its front toward the south, and one at the
[2]side of the [4]south gate facing toward the north.
45 He said to me, "This is the [a]chamber which faces toward
the south, *intended* for the priests who [b]keep charge of the
[1]temple;
46 but the [a]chamber which faces toward the north is for the
priests who [b]keep charge of the altar. These are the [c]sons of
Zadok, who from the sons of Levi [d]come near to the LORD to
minister to Him."
47 He measured the court, a *perfect* square, a [a]hundred cubits
long and a hundred cubits wide; and the altar was in front of
the [1]temple.
48 Then he brought me to the [a]porch of the [1]temple and
measured *each* side pillar of the porch, five cubits on each side;
and the width of the gate was three cubits on each side.

32 [a]Ezek 40:28-31, 35 [b]Ezek 40:28

33 [1]Lit *it* [a]Ezek 40:29 [b]Ezek 40:16 [c]Ezek 40:21

34 [a]Ezek 40:16 [b]Ezek 40:22, 37

35 [a]Ezek 40:27, 32; 44:4; 47:2

36 [1]Lit *it* [a]Ezek 40:7, 29 [b]Ezek 40:16 [c]Ezek 40:21

37 [a]Ezek 40:16 [b]Ezek 40:34

38 [a]1 Chr 28:12; Neh 13:5, 9; Jer 35:4; 36:10; Ezek 40:17; 41:10; 42:13 [b]2 Chr 4:6

39 [a]Ezek 40:42 [b]Lev 1:3-17; Ezek 46:2

40 [1]Lit *shoulder* [2]Lit *to the one going up* [3]Lit *entrance of the gate*

41 [1]Lit *by the shoulder of* [a]Ezek 40:39, 40

42 [a]Ezek 40:39 [b]Ex 20:25

43 [1]Or *ledges* [2]Or *inside*

44 [1]Gr reads *in two chambers* [2]Lit *shoulder* [3]Lit *their* [4]Gr reads *east* [a]Ezek 40:23, 27 [b]Ezek 40:17, 38 [c]1 Chr 6:31, 32; 16:41-43; 25:1-7

45 [1]Or *house* [a]Ezek 40:17, 38 [b]1 Chr 9:23; Ps 134:1

46 [a]Ezek 40:17, 38 [b]Lev 6:12, 13; Ezek 44:15 [c]1 Kin 2:35; Ezek 43:19; 48:11 [d]Lev 10:3; Num 16:5, 40; Ezek 42:13; 45:4

47 [1]Lit *house* [a]Ezek 40:19, 23, 27

48 [1]Lit *house* [a]1 Kin 6:3; 2 Chr 3:4

49 The length of the porch *was* twenty cubits and the width
eleven cubits; and at the [a]stairway by which it was ascended
were [b]columns belonging to the side pillars, one on each side.

Chapter 41 Theme ____________________

41 Then he [a]brought me to the [1b]nave and measured the [c]side
pillars; six cubits wide on each side *was* the width of the
[2]side pillar.
2 The width of the entrance *was* ten cubits and the [1]sides of
the entrance *were* five cubits on each side. And he measured [2]the
length of the nave, [a]forty cubits, and the width, [a]twenty cubits.
3 Then he went [1a]inside and measured each [b]side pillar of
the doorway, two cubits, and the doorway, six cubits *high;* and
the width of the doorway, seven cubits.
4 He measured its length, [a]twenty cubits, and the width,
twenty cubits, before the [b]nave; and he said to me, "This is the
[c]most holy *place.*"
5 Then he measured the wall of the [1]temple, six cubits; and
the width of the [a]side chambers, four cubits, all around about
the house on every side.
6 [a]The side chambers were in three stories, [1]one above
another, and [2]thirty in each story; and [3]the side chambers
[b]extended to the wall which *stood* on [4]their inward side all
around, that they might be fastened, and not be fastened into
the wall of the temple *itself.*
7 The side chambers surrounding the temple were wider at
each successive story. Because the [a]structure surrounding the
temple went upward by stages on all sides of the temple,
therefore the width of the temple *increased* as it went higher;
and thus one went up from the lowest *story* to the highest by
way of the [1]second *story.*
8 I saw also that the house had a raised [1]platform all around;
the foundations of the side chambers were a full rod of [a]six
[2]long cubits *in height.*
9 The [1]thickness of the outer wall of the side chambers *was*
five cubits. But the [a]free space between the side chambers
belonging to the temple
10 and the *outer* [a]chambers *was* twenty cubits in width all
around the temple on every side.
11 The [1]doorways of the [2]side chambers toward the [a]free
space *consisted of* one doorway toward the north and another
doorway toward the south; and the width of the [a]free space
was five cubits all around.
12 The [a]building that *was* in front of the [b]separate area at the
side toward the west *was* seventy cubits wide; and the wall of
the building *was* five cubits [1]thick all around, and its length
was ninety cubits.
13 Then he measured the temple, a [a]hundred cubits long; the
[b]separate area with the [c]building and its walls *were* also a
[a]hundred cubits long.

49 [a]Ezek 40:31, 34, 37 [b]1 Kin 7:15-22; 2 Chr 3:17; Jer 52:17-23; Rev 3:12

41:1 [1]I.e. the main inner hall [2]Lit *tent* [a]Ezek 40:2, 3, 17 [b]Ezek 41:21, 23 [c]Ezek 40:9; 41:3

2 [1]Lit *shoulders* [2]Lit *its length,* [a]1 Kin 6:2, 17; 2 Chr 3:3

3 [1]I.e. of the inner sanctuary [a]Ezek 40:16 [b]Ezek 41:1

4 [a]1 Kin 6:20 [b]1 Kin 6:5 [c]Ex 26:33, 34; 1 Kin 6:16; 7:50; 8:6; 2 Chr 5:7; Heb 9:3-8

5 [1]Lit *house,* and so throughout the ch [a]1 Kin 6:5; Ezek 41:6-11

6 [1]Lit *chamber upon chamber* [2]Lit *thirty times* [3]Lit *they were coming* [4]Lit *the inside of the side chambers* [a]1 Kin 6:5-10 [b]1 Kin 6:6, 10

7 [1]Lit *middle* [a]1 Kin 6:8

8 [1]Lit *height* [2]Or *to the joint* [a]Ezek 40:5

9 [1]Lit *width* [a]Ezek 41:11

10 [a]Ezek 40:17

11 [1]Lit *doorway* [2]Lit *side chamber* [a]Ezek 41:9

12 [1]Lit *wide* [a]Ezek 41:13, 15; 42:1 [b]Ezek 41:14; 42:10, 13

13 [a]Ezek 40:47 [b]Ezek 41:13-15; 42:1, 10, 13 [c]Ezek 41:12

14 Also the width of the front of the temple and *that of* the
separate [1]areas along the east *side totaled* a hundred cubits.
15 He measured the length of the [a]building [1]along the front of
the [b]separate area behind it, with a [2c]gallery on each side, a
hundred cubits; *he* also *measured* the inner nave and the
porches of the court.
16 The [a]thresholds, the [1b]latticed windows and the [2c]galleries
round about their [d]three stories, opposite the threshold, were
[e]paneled with wood all around, and *from* the ground to the
windows (but the windows were covered),
17 over the entrance, and to the inner house, and on the outside,
and on all the wall all around inside and outside, by measurement.
18 It was [1]carved with [a]cherubim and [b]palm trees; and a palm
tree was between cherub and cherub, and every cherub had
two faces,
19 a [a]man's face toward the palm tree on one side and a young
[a]lion's face toward the palm tree on the other side; they were
[1]carved on all the house all around.
20 From the ground to above the entrance [a]cherubim and [a]palm
trees were [1]carved, as well as *on* the wall of the nave.
21 The [a]doorposts of the [b]nave were square; as for the front of
the sanctuary, the appearance of one doorpost was like that of
the other.
22 The [a]altar *was* of wood, three cubits high and its length
two cubits; its corners, its [1]base and its [2]sides *were* of wood.
And he said to me, "This is the [b]table that is before the LORD."
23 The [a]nave and the [b]sanctuary each had a double [c]door.
24 Each of the doors had two leaves, two [1a]swinging leaves;
two *leaves* for one door and two leaves for the other.
25 Also there were [1]carved on them, on the doors of the nave,
[a]cherubim and [a]palm trees like those [1]carved on the walls; and
there was a [2b]threshold of wood on the front of the porch outside.
26 *There were* [1a]latticed windows and [b]palm trees on one side
and on the other, on the sides of the [c]porch; thus *were* the
[d]side chambers of the house and the [2]thresholds.

Chapter 42 Theme ____________________

42 Then he [a]brought me out into the [b]outer court, the way
[c]toward the north; and he brought me to the [d]chamber
which *was* opposite the [e]separate area and opposite the [f]build-
ing toward the north.
2 Along the length, *which was* a [a]hundred cubits, *was* the
north door; the width *was* fifty cubits.
3 Opposite the [a]twenty *cubits* which belonged to the inner
court, and opposite the [b]pavement which belonged to the outer
court, *was* [1c]gallery corresponding to [1]gallery in three stories.
4 Before the [a]chambers *was* an inner walk ten cubits wide, a
way of one *hundred* cubits; and their openings *were* on the north.
5 Now the upper chambers *were* [1]smaller because the
[2a]galleries took more *space* away from them than from the
lower and middle ones in the building.

14 [1]Lit *area*
15 [1]Lit *to* [2]Or *passageway* [a]Ezek 41:12, 13; 42:1 [b]Ezek 41:14; 42:1, 10, 13 [c]Ezek 41:16; 42:3, 5
16 [1]Or *framed* [2]Or *passageways* [a]Is 6:4; Ezek 10:18; 40:6; 41:25 [b]1 Kin 6:4; Ezek 40:16, 25; 41:26 [c]Ezek 41:15 [d]Ezek 42:3 [e]1 Kin 6:15
18 [1]Lit *made* [a]1 Kin 6:29, 32, 35; 7:36; Ezek 41:20, 25 [b]2 Chr 3:5; Ezek 40:16
19 [1]Lit *made* [a]Ezek 1:10; 10:14
20 [1]Lit *made* [a]Ezek 41:18
21 [a]1 Kin 6:33; Ezek 40:9, 14, 16; 41:1 [b]Ezek 41:1
22 [1]Lit *length* [2]Lit *walls* [a]Ex 30:1-3; 1 Kin 6:20; Rev 8:3 [b]Ex 25:23, 30; Lev 24:6; Ezek 23:41; 44:16; Mal 1:7, 12
23 [a]Ezek 41:1 [b]Ezek 41:4 [c]1 Kin 6:31-35
24 [1]Or *turning* [a]1 Kin 6:34
25 [1]Lit *made* [2]Or *canopy of wood over* [a]Ezek 41:18 [b]Ezek 41:16
26 [1]Or *framed* [2]Or *canopies* [a]Ezek 41:16 [b]Ezek 40:16 [c]Ezek 40:9, 48 [d]Ezek 41:5
42:1 [a]Ezek 40:17, 28, 48; 41:1 [b]Ezek 40:17, 20 [c]Ezek 40:20 [d]Ezek 40:17; 42:4 [e]Ezek 41:12; 42:10, 13 [f]Ezek 41:12
2 [a]Ezek 41:13
3 [1]Or *passageway* [a]Ezek 41:10 [b]Ezek 40:17 [c]Ezek 41:15, 16; 42:5
4 [a]Ezek 46:19
5 [1]Lit *shorter* [2]Or *passageways* [a]Ezek 42:3

6 For they *were* in [a]three stories and had no pillars like the pillars of the courts; therefore *the upper chambers* were [1]set back from the ground upward, more than the lower and middle ones.

7 As for the [a]outer wall by the side of the chambers, toward the outer court facing the chambers, its length *was* fifty cubits.

8 For the length of the chambers which *were* in the outer court *was* fifty cubits; and behold, *the length of those* facing the temple *was* a [a]hundred cubits.

9 Below these chambers *was* the [a]entrance on the east side, as one enters them from the outer court.

10 In the [1]thickness of the [a]wall of the court toward the east, facing the [b]separate area and facing the building, *there were* [c]chambers.

11 The [a]way in front of them *was* like the appearance of the chambers which *were* on the north, according to their length so was their width, and all their exits *were* both according to their arrangements and openings.

12 Corresponding to the openings of the chambers which were toward the south was an opening at the head of the way, the way in front of the [a]wall toward the east, as one enters them.

13 Then he said to me, "The north chambers *and* the south chambers, which are opposite the [a]separate area, they are the [b]holy chambers where the priests who are [c]near to the LORD shall eat the [d]most holy things. There they shall lay the most holy things, the grain offering, the sin offering and the guilt offering; for the place is holy.

14 "When the priests enter, then they shall not go out into the outer court from the sanctuary [1]without [a]laying there their [b]garments in which they minister, for they are holy. They shall put on other garments; then they shall approach that which is for the people."

15 Now when he had finished measuring the inner house, he brought me out by the way of the [a]gate which faced toward the east and measured it all around.

16 He measured on the east side with the measuring reed five hundred reeds by the [a]measuring reed.

17 He measured on the north side five hundred reeds by the measuring reed.

18 On the south side he measured five hundred reeds with the measuring reed.

19 He turned to the west side *and* measured five hundred reeds with the measuring reed.

20 He measured it [1]on the four sides; it had a [a]wall all around, the [b]length five hundred and the [b]width five hundred, to [c]divide between the holy and the profane.

Chapter 43 Theme ______________________________

43

Then he led me to the [a]gate, the gate facing toward the east;

2 and behold, the [a]glory of the God of Israel was coming from the way of the [b]east. And His [c]voice was like the sound of many waters; and the earth [d]shone with His glory.

---

6 [1]Or *reduced* [a]Ezek 41:6

7 [a]Ezek 42:10, 12

8 [a]Ezek 41:13, 14

9 [a]Ezek 44:5; 46:19

10 [1]Lit *width* [a]Ezek 42:7 [b]Ezek 42:1, 13 [c]Ezek 40:17

11 [a]Ezek 42:4

12 [a]Ezek 42:7

13 [a]Ezek 42:1, 10 [b]Ex 29:31; Lev 7:6; 10:13, 14, 17 [c]Lev 10:3; Deut 21:5; Ezek 40:46 [d]Lev 6:25, 29; 14:13; Num 18:9, 10

14 [1]Lit *but there they shall lay* [a]Ezek 44:19 [b]Ex 29:4-9; Lev 8:7, 13; Is 61:10; Zech 3:4, 5

15 [a]Ezek 40:6; 43:1

16 [a]Ezek 40:3

20 [1]Lit *toward the four winds* [a]Is 60:18; Ezek 40:5; Zech 2:5 [b]Ezek 45:2; Rev 21:16 [c]Ezek 22:26; 44:23; 48:15

43:1 [a]Ezek 10:19; 40:6; 42:15; 43:4; 44:1; 46:1

2 [a]Is 6:3; Ezek 1:28; 3:23; 10:18, 19 [b]Ezek 11:23 [c]Ezek 1:24; Rev 1:15; 14:2 [d]Ezek 1:28; 10:4; Rev 18:1

3 And *it was* like the appearance of the vision which I saw, like the [a]vision which I saw when [1]He came to [b]destroy the city. And the visions *were* like the vision which I saw by the [c]river Chebar; and I [d]fell on my face.

4 And the glory of the LORD came into the house by the way of the gate facing toward the [a]east.

5 And the [a]Spirit lifted me up and brought me into the inner court; and behold, the [b]glory of the LORD filled the house.

6 Then I heard one speaking to me from the house, while a [a]man was standing beside me.

7 He said to me, "Son of man, *this is* the place of My [a]throne and the place of the soles of My feet, where I will [b]dwell among the sons of Israel forever. And the house of Israel will not again defile My holy name, neither they nor their kings, by their harlotry and by the [1c]corpses of their kings [2]when they die,

8 by setting their threshold by My threshold and their door post beside My door post, with *only* the wall between Me and them. And they have [a]defiled My holy name by their abominations which they have committed. So I have consumed them in My anger.

9 "Now let them [a]put away their harlotry and the [1]corpses of their kings far from Me; and I will [b]dwell among them forever.

10 "As for you, son of man, [1a]describe the [2]temple to the house of Israel, that they may be [b]ashamed of their iniquities; and let them measure the [3c]plan.

11 "If they are ashamed of all that they have done, make known to them the [1]design of the house, its structure, its [a]exits, its entrances, all its designs, all its statutes[2], and all its laws. And write *it* [b]in their sight, so that they may observe its whole [1]design and all its statutes and [c]do them.

12 "This is the [1]law of the house: its entire [2]area on the top of the [a]mountain all around *shall be* most holy. Behold, this is the [1]law of the house.

13 "And these are the measurements of the [a]altar by cubits (the [b]cubit being a cubit and a handbreadth): the [1]base *shall be* a cubit and the width a cubit, and its border on its edge round about one span; and this *shall be* the *height* of the [2]base of the altar.

14 "From the base on the ground to the lower [a]ledge *shall be* two cubits and the width one cubit; and from the smaller ledge to the larger ledge *shall be* four cubits and the width [1]one cubit.

15 "The [1]altar hearth *shall be* four cubits; and from the [1]altar hearth shall extend upwards four [a]horns.

16 "Now the [1]altar hearth *shall be* twelve *cubits* long by twelve wide, [a]square in its four sides.

17 "The ledge *shall be* fourteen *cubits* long by fourteen wide in its four sides, the border around it *shall be* half a cubit and its base *shall be* a cubit round about; and its [a]steps shall [1b]face the east."

18 And He said to me, "[a]Son of man, thus says the Lord [1]GOD, 'These are the statutes for the altar on the day it is built, to offer [b]burnt offerings on it and to [c]sprinkle blood on it.

3 [1]So with some mss and some ancient versions; M.T. *I* [a]Ezek 1:4-28 [b]Jer 1:10; Ezek 9:1, 5; 32:18 [c]Ezek 1:3; 10:20 [d]Ezek 1:28; 3:23

4 [a]Ezek 10:19; 11:23; 43:2

5 [a]Ezek 3:14; 8:3; 11:1, 24; 2 Cor 12:2-4 [b]Ezek 10:4

6 [a]Ezek 1:26; 40:3

7 [1]Or *monuments* as in Ugaritic [2]Or *in their high places* [a]Ps 47:8; Ezek 1:26 [b]Ezek 37:26, 28 [c]Lev 26:30; Ezek 6:5, 13

8 [a]Ezek 8:3, 16

9 [1]Or *monuments* as in Ugaritic [a]Ezek 18:30, 31 [b]Ezek 37:26-28; 43:7

10 [1]Lit *declare* [2]Lit *house* [3]Lit *perfection* or *pattern* [a]Ezek 40:4 [b]Ezek 16:61, 63; 43:11 [c]Ezek 28:12

11 [1]Or *form(s)* [2]M.T. repeats *and all its designs* after *statutes* [a]Ezek 44:5 [b]Ezek 12:3 [c]Ezek 11:20; 36:27

12 [1]Or *instruction for* [2]Lit *border* [a]Ezek 40:2

13 [1]Lit *lap* [2]Or *back* [a]Ex 27:1-8; 2 Chr 4:1 [b]Ezek 40:5; 41:8

14 [1]Lit *the* [a]Ezek 43:17, 20; 45:19

15 [1]Or *ariel* shall [a]Ex 27:2; Lev 9:9; 1 Kin 1:50; Ps 118:27

16 [1]Or *ariel* shall [a]Ex 27:1

17 [1]Or *be on the east side* [a]Ex 20:26 [b]Ezek 40:6

18 [1]Heb *YHWH,* usually rendered *LORD,* and so throughout the ch [a]Ezek 2:1 [b]Ex 40:29 [c]Lev 1:5, 11; Heb 9:21, 22

19 'You shall give to the Levitical priests who are from the
offspring of [a]Zadok, who draw [b]near to Me to minister to Me,'
declares the Lord GOD, 'a [c]young bull for a [d]sin offering.
20 'You shall take some of its blood and put it on its four [a]horns
and on the four corners of the [b]ledge and on the border round
about; thus you shall [c]cleanse it and make atonement for it.
21 'You shall also take the bull for the sin offering, and it *shall*
be [a]burned in the appointed place of the house, outside the
sanctuary.
22 'On the second day you shall offer a [a]male goat without
blemish for a sin offering, and they shall [b]cleanse the altar as
they cleansed *it* with the bull.
23 'When you have finished cleansing *it,* you shall present a
[a]young bull without blemish and a [b]ram without blemish from
the flock.
24 'You shall present them before the LORD, and the priests
shall throw [a]salt on them, and they shall offer them up as a
burnt offering to the LORD.
25 '[a]For seven days you shall prepare daily a goat for a sin
offering; also a young bull and a ram from the flock, without
blemish, shall be prepared.
26 'For seven days they shall make atonement for the altar and
purify it; so shall they [1]consecrate it.
27 'When they have completed the days, it shall be that on the
[a]eighth day and onward, the priests shall [1]offer your burnt
offerings on the altar, and your [b]peace offerings; and I will
[c]accept you,' declares the Lord GOD."

Chapter 44 Theme ______________________

44 Then He brought me back by the way of the [a]outer gate
of the sanctuary, which faces the east; and it was shut.
2 The LORD said to me, "This gate shall be shut; it shall not
be opened, and no one shall enter by it, for the [a]LORD God of
Israel has entered by it; therefore it shall be shut.
3 "As for the [a]prince, he shall sit in it as prince to [b]eat bread
before the LORD; he shall [c]enter by way of the [d]porch of the
gate and shall go out [1]by the same way."
4 Then He brought me by way of the [a]north gate to the front
of the house; and I looked, and behold, the [b]glory of the LORD
filled the house of the LORD, and I [c]fell on my face.
5 The LORD said to me, "Son of man, [1a]mark well, see with
your eyes and hear with your ears all that I say to you concerning
all the [b]statutes of the house of the LORD and concerning all its
laws; and [1]mark well the entrance of the house, with all exits
of the sanctuary.
6 "You shall say to the [1a]rebellious ones, to the house of Israel,
'Thus says the Lord [2]GOD, "[b]Enough of all your abominations,
O house of Israel,
7 when you brought in [a]foreigners, [b]uncircumcised in heart
and uncircumcised in flesh, to be in My sanctuary to profane it,

19 [a]1 Kin 2:35; Ezek 40:46; 44:15 [b]Num 16:5, 40 [c]Lev 4:3; Ezek 43:23; 45:18 [d]Ezek 45:19; Heb 7:27

20 [a]Lev 8:15; 9:9; Ezek 43:15 [b]Ezek 43:14, 17 [c]Lev 16:19; Ezek 43:22, 26

21 [a]Ex 29:14; Lev 4:12; Heb 13:11

22 [a]Ezek 43:25 [b]Ezek 43:20, 26

23 [a]Ex 29:1, 10; Ezek 45:18 [b]Ex 29:1

24 [a]Lev 2:13; Num 18:19; Mark 9:49, 50; Col 4:6

25 [a]Ex 29:35-37; Lev 8:33, 35

26 [1]Lit *fill its hands*

27 [1]Lit *make* [a]Lev 9:1 [b]Lev 3:1; 17:5 [c]Ezek 20:40

44:1 [a]Ezek 40:6, 17; 42:14

2 [a]Ezek 43:2-4

3 [1]Lit *by his way* [a]Ezek 34:24; 37:25 [b]Gen 31:54; Ex 24:9-11 [c]Ezek 46:2, 8-10 [d]Ezek 40:9

4 [a]Ezek 40:20, 40 [b]Is 6:3, 4; Ezek 1:28; 3:23; 43:4, 5; Hag 2:7 [c]Ezek 1:28; 43:3

5 [1]Lit *set your heart on* [a]Deut 32:46; Ezek 40:4 [b]Deut 12:32; Ezek 43:10, 11

6 [1]Lit *rebellion* [2]Heb *YHWH,* usually rendered *LORD,* and so throughout the ch [a]Ezek 2:5-7; 3:9 [b]Ezek 45:9; 1 Pet 4:3

7 [a]Ex 12:43-49 [b]Lev 26:41; Deut 10:16; Jer 4:4; 9:26

even My house, when you [c]offered My food, the fat and the
blood; for they [d]made My covenant void—*this* in addition to all
your abominations.
8 "And you have not [a]kept charge of My holy things yourselves,
but you have set *foreigners* [1]to keep charge of My sanctuary."
9 'Thus says the Lord GOD, "[a]No foreigner uncircumcised in
heart and uncircumcised in flesh, of all the foreigners who are
among the sons of Israel, shall enter My sanctuary.
10 "But the Levites who went far from Me when Israel went
astray, who [a]went astray from Me after their idols, shall [b]bear
the punishment for their iniquity.
11 "Yet they shall be [a]ministers in My sanctuary, having [b]oversight
at the gates of the house and [c]ministering in the house; they
shall [d]slaughter the burnt offering and the sacrifice for the
people, and they shall [e]stand before them to minister to them.
12 "Because they ministered to them [a]before their idols and
became a [b]stumbling block of iniquity to the house of Israel,
therefore I have [1c]sworn against them," declares the Lord GOD,
"that they shall [d]bear *the punishment for* their iniquity.
13 "And they shall [a]not come near to Me to serve as a priest to
Me, nor come near to any of My holy things, to the things that
are most holy; but they will [b]bear their shame and their
abominations which they have committed.
14 "Yet I will [1]appoint them [2]to [a]keep charge of the house, of
all its service and of all that shall be done in it.
15 "But the [a]Levitical priests, the sons of [b]Zadok, who [c]kept
charge of My sanctuary when the sons of Israel [d]went astray
from Me, shall come near to Me to minister to Me; and they
shall [e]stand before Me to offer Me the [f]fat and the blood,"
declares the Lord GOD.
16 "They shall [a]enter My sanctuary; they shall come near to My
[b]table to minister to Me and keep My charge.
17 "It shall be that when they enter at the gates of the inner
court, they shall be clothed with [a]linen garments; and wool
shall not [1]be on them while they are ministering in the gates of
the inner court and in the house.
18 "Linen [a]turbans shall be on their heads and [b]linen undergarments shall be on their loins; they shall not gird themselves
with *anything which makes them* sweat.
19 "When they go out into the outer court, into the outer court
to the people, they shall [a]put off their garments in which they
have been ministering and lay them in the holy chambers;
then they shall put on other garments so that they will [b]not
transmit holiness to the people with their garments.
20 "Also they shall [a]not shave their heads, yet they shall not [b]let
their locks [1]grow long; they shall only trim *the hair of* their heads.
21 "[a]Nor shall any of the priests drink wine when they enter
the inner court.
22 "And they shall not [1]marry a widow or a [a]divorced woman
but shall [b]take virgins from the offspring of the house of Israel,
or a widow who is the widow of a priest.

7 [c]Lev 22:25 [d]Gen 17:14
8 [1]Lit *as keepers of My charge in My* [a]Lev 22:2; Num 18:7
9 [a]Ezek 44:7; Joel 3:17; Zech 14:21
10 [a]2 Kin 23:8, 9; Ezek 22:26; 44:12 [b]Num 18:23
11 [a]Num 3:5-37; 4:1-33; 18:2-7 [b]1 Chr 26:1-19 [c]Ezek 40:45; 44:14 [d]2 Chr 29:34; 30:17 [e]Num 16:9
12 [1]Lit *lifted up My hand* [a]2 Kin 16:10-16 [b]Ezek 14:3, 4 [c]Ezek 20:15, 23 [d]Ezek 44:10
13 [a]Num 18:3 [b]Ezek 16:61, 63; 39:26
14 [1]Lit *give* [2]Lit *keepers of the charge* [a]Num 18:4; 1 Chr 23:28-32; Ezek 44:11
15 [a]Jer 33:18-22 [b]Ezek 40:46; 43:19; 48:11 [c]Num 18:7; Ezek 40:45 [d]Ezek 44:10; 48:11 [e]Zech 3:1, 7 [f]Lev 3:16, 17; 17:5, 6; Ezek 44:7
16 [a]Num 18:5, 7, 8 [b]Ezek 41:22; Mal 1:7, 12
17 [1]Lit *come upon* [a]Ex 28:42, 43; 39:27-29; Rev 19:8
18 [a]Ex 28:40; Is 3:20; Ezek 24:17, 23 [b]Ex 28:42; Lev 16:4
19 [a]Lev 6:10; 16:4, 23, 24; Ezek 42:14 [b]Lev 6:27; Ezek 46:20
20 [1]Or *hang loose* [a]Lev 21:5 [b]Num 6:5
21 [a]Lev 10:9
22 [1]Lit *take as wives for themselves* [a]Lev 21:7, 14 [b]Lev 21:13

23 "Moreover, they shall teach My people *the* [a]*difference*
between the holy and the profane, and cause them to discern
between the unclean and the clean.
24 "In a dispute [a]they shall take their stand to judge; they shall
judge it according to My ordinances. They shall also keep My
laws and My statutes in all My [b]appointed feasts and [c]sanctify
My sabbaths.
25 "[1a]They shall not go to a dead person to defile *themselves;*
however, for father, for mother, for son, for daughter, for
brother, or for a sister who has not had a husband, they may
defile themselves.
26 "After he is [a]cleansed, seven days shall [1]elapse for him.
27 "On the day that he goes into the sanctuary, into the [a]inner
court to minister in the sanctuary, he shall offer his [b]sin offering,"
declares the Lord GOD.
28 "And it shall be with regard to an inheritance for them, *that*
[a]I am their inheritance; and you shall give them no possession
in Israel—I am their possession.
29 "They shall [a]eat the grain offering, the sin offering and the
guilt offering; and every [1b]devoted thing in Israel shall be theirs.
30 "The first of all the [a]first fruits of every kind and every
[1]contribution of every kind, from all your [1]contributions, shall
be for the priests; you shall also give to the priest the [b]first of
your [2]dough to cause a [c]blessing to rest on your house.
31 "The priests shall not eat any bird or beast that has [a]died a
natural death or has been torn to pieces.

Chapter 45 Theme ____________________

45 "And when you [a]divide by lot the land for inheritance,
you shall offer [1]an [b]allotment to the LORD, a [c]holy portion of the land; the length shall be the length of 25,000 [d]*cubits,* and the width shall be [2]20,000. It shall be holy within all
its boundary round about.
2 "Out of this there shall be for the holy place a square round
about [a]five hundred by five hundred *cubits,* and fifty cubits for
its [1b]open space round about.
3 "From this [1]area you shall measure a length of 25,000 *cubits*
and a width of 10,000 *cubits;* and in it shall be the sanctuary,
the most holy place.
4 "It shall be the holy portion of the land; it shall be for the
[a]priests, the ministers of the sanctuary, who [b]come near to
minister to the LORD, and it shall be a place for their houses
and a holy place for the sanctuary.
5 "*An area* [a]25,000 *cubits* in length and 10,000 in width shall
be for the Levites, the ministers of the house, *and* for their
possession [1]cities to dwell in.
6 "You shall give the [a]city possession of *an area* 5,000 *cubits*
wide and 25,000 *cubits* long, alongside the [1]allotment of the
holy portion; it shall be for the whole house of Israel.
7 "The [a]prince shall have *land* on either side of the holy
[1]allotment and the [2]property of the city, adjacent to the holy

23 [a]Lev 10:10; Ezek 22:26; Hos 4:6; Mic 3:9-11; Zeph 3:4; Hag 2:11-13; Mal 2:6-8

24 [a]Deut 17:8, 9; 19:17; 21:5; 1 Chr 23:4; 2 Chr 19:8-10 [b]Lev 23:2, 4, 44 [c]Ezek 20:12, 20

25 [1]Lit *He* [a]Lev 21:1-4

26 [1]Lit *be counted* [a]Num 19:13-19

27 [a]Ezek 44:17 [b]Lev 5:3, 6; Num 6:9-11

28 [a]Num 18:20; Deut 10:9; 18:1, 2; Josh 13:33

29 [1]Or *dedicated* [a]Num 18:9, 14; Josh 13:14 [b]Lev 27:21, 28; Num 18:14

30 [1]Or *heave offering(s)* [2]Or *coarse meal* [a]Num 18:12, 13; 2 Chr 31:4-6, 10; Neh 10:35-37 [b]Num 15:20, 21 [c]Mal 3:10

31 [a]Lev 22:8; Deut 14:21; Ezek 4:14

45:1 [1]Or *a contribution* [2]Or with Gr *10,000* [a]Num 34:13; Josh 13:7; 14:3; Ezek 47:21; 48:29 [b]Ezek 48:8, 9 [c]Zech 14:20, 21 [d]Ezek 42:16; 45:2

2 [1]Or *pasture land* [a]Ezek 42:20 [b]Ezek 27:28

3 [1]Lit *measure*

4 [a]Ezek 48:10, 11 [b]Num 16:5; Ezek 40:45; 43:19

5 [1]So with Gr; M.T. *twenty chambers* [a]Ezek 48:13

6 [1]Or *contribution* [a]Ezek 48:15-18, 30-35

7 [1]Or *contribution* [2]Lit *possession* [a]Ezek 34:24; 37:24; 46:16-18; 48:21

[1]allotment and the [2]property of the city, on the west side
toward the west and on the east side toward the east, and in
length comparable to one of the portions, from the west border
to the east border.
8 "This shall be his land for a possession in Israel; so My princes
shall no longer [a]oppress My people, but they shall give *the rest
of* the land to the house of Israel [b]according to their tribes."
9 'Thus says the Lord [1]GOD, "[a]Enough, you princes of Israel;
put away [b]violence and destruction, and [c]practice justice and
righteousness. Stop your [d]expropriations from My people,"
declares the Lord GOD.
10 "You shall have [a]just balances, a just [b]ephah and a just [b]bath.
11 "The ephah and the bath shall be [1]the same quantity, so that
the bath will contain a tenth of a [a]homer and the ephah a tenth
of a homer; [2]their standard shall be according to the homer.
12 "The [a]shekel shall be twenty [a]gerahs; twenty shekels,
twenty-five shekels, *and* fifteen shekels shall be your [1]maneh.
13 "This is the offering that you shall offer: a sixth of an ephah
from a homer of wheat; a sixth of an ephah from a homer of
barley;
14 and the prescribed portion of oil (*namely,* the bath of oil), a
tenth of a bath from *each* kor (*which is* ten baths *or* a homer,
for ten baths are a homer);
15 and one sheep from *each* flock of two hundred from the
watering places of Israel—for a [a]grain offering, for a burnt
offering and for peace offerings, to [b]make atonement for them,"
declares the Lord GOD.
16 "[a]All the people of the land shall [1]give to this offering for the
[b]prince in Israel.
17 "It shall be the [a]prince's part *to provide* the [b]burnt offerings,
the grain offerings and the drink offerings, at the [c]feasts, on the
[d]new moons and on the sabbaths, at all the appointed feasts of
the house of Israel; he shall provide the sin offering, the grain
offering, the burnt offering and the [e]peace offerings, to make
atonement for the house of Israel."
18 'Thus says the Lord GOD, "In the [a]first *month,* on the first of
the month, you shall take a young bull [b]without blemish and
[c]cleanse the sanctuary.
19 "The priest shall take some of the blood from the sin offering
and put *it* on the door posts of the house, on the [a]four corners
of the [b]ledge of the altar and on the posts of the gate of the
inner court.
20 "Thus you shall do on the seventh *day* of the month for
everyone who goes [a]astray or is [1]naive; so you shall make
[b]atonement for the house.
21 "In the [a]first *month,* on the fourteenth day of the month,
you shall have the [b]Passover, a feast of seven days; unleavened
bread shall be eaten.
22 "On that day the prince shall provide for himself and all the
people of the land a [a]bull for a sin offering.
23 "*During* the [a]seven days of the feast he shall provide as a
[b]burnt offering to the LORD [c]seven bulls and seven rams

7 [1]Or *contribution* [2]Lit *possession*
8 [a]Is 11:3-5; Jer 23:5; Ezek 19:7; 22:27; 46:18 [b]Josh 11:23
9 [1]Heb *YHWH,* usually rendered *LORD,* and so throughout the ch [a]Ezek 44:6 [b]Jer 6:7; Ezek 7:11, 23; 8:17 [c]Jer 22:3; Zech 8:16 [d]Neh 5:1-5
10 [a]Lev 19:36; Deut 25:15; Prov 16:11; Amos 8:4-6; Mic 6:10, 11 [b]Is 5:10
11 [1]Lit *one* [2]Lit *its measure* [a]Is 5:10
12 [1]Or *mina* [a]Ex 30:13; Lev 27:25; Num 3:47
15 [a]Ezek 45:17 [b]Lev 1:4; 6:30
16 [1]Lit *be* [a]Ex 30:14, 15 [b]Is 16:1
17 [a]Ezek 46:4-12 [b]1 Kin 8:64; 1 Chr 16:2; 2 Chr 31:3 [c]Lev 23:1-44; Num 28:1-29:39 [d]Is 66:23 [e]1 Kin 8:63; Ezek 43:27
18 [a]Ex 12:2 [b]Lev 22:20; Heb 9:14 [c]Lev 16:16, 33; Ezek 43:22, 26
19 [a]Lev 16:18-20; Ezek 43:20 [b]Ezek 43:14, 17, 20
20 [1]Lit *simple* [a]Lev 4:27; Ps 19:12 [b]Lev 16:20; Ezek 45:15, 18
21 [a]Num 28:16f [b]Ex 12:1-24; Lev 23:5-8
22 [a]Lev 4:14
23 [a]Lev 23:8 [b]Num 28:16-25 [c]Num 23:1, 2; Job 42:8

without blemish on every day of the seven days, and a male
goat daily for a sin offering.
24 “He shall provide as a [a]grain offering an ephah [1]with a bull,
an ephah [1]with a ram and a hin of oil [1]with an ephah.
25 “In the [a]seventh *month,* on the fifteenth day of the month,
at the feast, he shall provide like this, seven days [1]for the sin
offering, the burnt offering, the grain offering and the oil.”

Chapter 46 Theme ______________________________

46 ‘Thus says the Lord [1]GOD, “The [a]gate of the [b]inner
court facing east shall be [c]shut the six [d]working days;
but it shall be opened on the [e]sabbath day and opened on the
day of the [f]new moon.
2 “The [a]prince shall enter by way of the porch of the gate from
outside and stand by the [b]post of the gate. Then the priests shall
provide his burnt offering and his peace offerings, and he shall
worship at the threshold of the gate and then go out; but the
gate shall not be [c]shut until the evening.
3 “The [a]people of the land shall also worship at the doorway of
that gate before the LORD on the sabbaths and on the [b]new moons.
4 “The [a]burnt offering which the prince shall offer to the LORD
on the sabbath day shall be [b]six lambs without blemish and a
ram without blemish;
5 and the [a]grain offering shall be an ephah [1]with the ram,
and the grain offering [1]with the lambs [2]as much as he is [b]able
to give, and a hin of oil [1]with an ephah.
6 “On the day of the [a]new moon *he shall offer* a young bull
without blemish, also six lambs and a ram, *which* shall be
without blemish.
7 “And he shall provide a [a]grain offering, an ephah [1]with the
bull and an ephah [1]with the ram, and [1]with the lambs as
[2]much as he is [b]able, and a hin of oil [1]with an ephah.
8 “When the [a]prince enters, he shall go in by way of the
porch of the gate and go out [1]by the same way.
9 “But when the people of the land come [a]before the LORD at
the appointed feasts, he who enters by way of the north gate to
worship shall go out by way of the south gate. And he who
enters by way of the south gate shall go out by way of the north
gate. [1]No one shall return by way of the gate by which he
entered but shall go straight out.
10 “When they go in, the prince shall go in [a]among them; and
when they go out, [1]he shall go out.
11 “At the [a]festivals and the appointed feasts the [b]grain offering
shall be an ephah [1]with a bull and an ephah [1]with a ram, and
[1]with the lambs as [2]much as one is able to give, and a hin of oil
[1]with an ephah.
12 “When the prince provides a [a]freewill offering, a burnt
offering, or peace offerings *as* a freewill offering to the LORD,
the gate facing east shall be [b]opened for him. And he shall
provide his burnt offering and his peace offerings as he does on

24 [1]Lit *for* [a]Num 28:12-15; Ezek 46:5-7
25 [1]Lit *according to* [a]Lev 23:33-43; Num 29:12-38; 2 Chr 5:3; 7:8, 10
46:1 [1]Heb *YHWH,* usually rendered *LORD,* and so throughout the ch [a]Ezek 45:19 [b]Ezek 8:16; 10:3 [c]Ezek 44:1, 2 [d]Ex 20:9 [e]Is 66:23; Ezek 45:17 [f]Ezek 45:18; 46:3, 6
2 [a]Ezek 44:3; 46:8 [b]Ezek 45:19 [c]Ezek 46:12
3 [a]Luke 1:10 [b]Ezek 46:1
4 [a]Ezek 45:17 [b]Num 28:9
5 [1]Lit *for* [2]Lit *a gift of his hand* [a]Num 28:12; Ezek 45:24; 46:7, 11 [b]Ezek 46:7
6 [a]Ezek 46:1
7 [1]Lit *for* [2]Lit *his hand can reach* [a]Ezek 46:5 [b]Lev 14:21; Deut 16:17; Ezek 46:5
8 [1]Lit *by its way* [a]Ezek 44:3; 46:2
9 [1]Lit *He shall not* [a]Ex 34:23; Ps 84:7; Mic 6:6
10 [1]So with many mss and the ancient versions; M.T. *they* [a]2 Sam 6:14, 15; 1 Chr 29:20, 22; 2 Chr 6:3; 7:4; Ps 42:4
11 [1]Lit *for* [2]Lit *a gift of his hand* [a]Ezek 45:17 [b]Ezek 46:5, 7
12 [a]Lev 23:38; 2 Chr 29:31 [b]Ezek 44:3; 46:1, 2, 8

the [c]sabbath day. Then he shall go out, and the gate shall be
shut after he goes out.
13 "And you shall provide a [a]lamb a year old without blemish
for a burnt offering to the LORD daily; [b]morning by morning you
shall provide it.
14 "Also you shall provide a grain offering with it morning by
morning, a [a]sixth of an ephah and a third of a hin of oil to
moisten the fine flour, a grain offering to the LORD continually
by a perpetual [1]ordinance.
15 "Thus they shall provide the lamb, the grain offering and the
oil, morning by morning, for a [a]continual burnt offering."
16 'Thus says the Lord GOD, "If the prince gives a [a]gift *out of*
his inheritance to any of his sons, it shall belong to his sons; it
is their possession by inheritance.
17 "But if he gives a gift from his inheritance to one of his
servants, it shall be his until the [a]year of liberty; then it shall
return to the prince. His inheritance *shall be* only his sons'; it
shall belong to them.
18 "The prince shall [a]not take from the people's inheritance,
[1b]thrusting them out of their possession; he shall give his sons
inheritance from his own possession so that My people will not
be scattered, anyone from his possession."'"
19 Then he brought me through the [a]entrance, which *was* at the
side of the gate, into the holy chambers for the priests, which
faced north; and behold, there *was* a place at the extreme rear
toward the west.
20 He said to me, "This is the place where the priests shall
boil the [a]guilt offering and the sin offering *and* where they shall
[b]bake the grain offering, in order that they may not bring *them*
out into the outer court to transmit holiness to the people."
21 Then he brought me out into the outer court and led me
across to the four corners of the court; and behold, in every
corner of the court *there was* a *small* court.
22 In the four corners of the court *there were* enclosed courts,
forty *cubits* long and thirty wide; these four in the corners
were [1]the same size.
23 *There was* a row *of masonry* round about in them, around
the four of them, and boiling places were made under the rows
round about.
24 Then he said to me, "These are the boiling [1]places where
the ministers of the house shall boil the sacrifices of the people."

Chapter 47 Theme ______________________

47 Then he brought me back to the [a]door of the house;
and behold, [b]water was flowing from under the threshold of the house toward the east, for the house faced east. And
the water was flowing down from under, from the right side of
the house, from south of the altar.
2 He brought me out by way of the north gate and led me
around [1]on the outside to the outer gate by way of *the gate* that
faces east. And behold, water was trickling from the south side.

12 [c]Ezek 45:17

13 [a]Num 28:3-5 [b]Is 50:4

14 [1]Lit *statute* [a]Num 28:5

15 [a]Ex 29:42; Num 28:6

16 [a]2 Chr 21:3

17 [a]Lev 25:10

18 [1]Lit *oppressing* [a]Ezek 45:8 [b]1 Kin 21:19; Ezek 22:27; Mic 2:1, 2

19 [a]Ezek 42:9; 44:5

20 [a]2 Chr 35:13; Ezek 44:29 [b]Lev 2:4-7

22 [1]Lit *one measure*

24 [1]Lit *houses*

47:1 [a]Ezek 41:2, 23-25 [b]Ps 46:4; Is 30:25; 55:1; Jer 2:13; Joel 3:18; Zech 13:1; 14:8; Rev 22:1, 17

2 [1]Lit *by way of*

3 When the man went out toward the east with a line in his
hand, he measured a thousand cubits, and he led me through
the water, water *reaching* the ankles.
4 Again he measured a thousand and led me through the water,
water *reaching* the knees. Again he measured a thousand and
led me through *the water,* water *reaching* the loins.
5 Again he measured a thousand; *and it was* a river that I
could not ford, for the water had risen, *enough* water to swim
in, a [a]river that could not be forded.
6 He said to me, "Son of man, have you [a]seen *this?*" Then he
brought me [1]back to the bank of the river.
7 Now when I had returned, behold, on the bank of the river
there *were* very many [a]trees on the one side and on the other.
8 Then he said to me, "These waters go out toward the eastern
region and go down into the [a]Arabah; then they go toward the
sea, being made to flow into the [b]sea, and the waters *of the sea*
become [1]fresh.
9 "It will come about that every living creature which swarms
in every place where the [1]river goes, will live. And there will
be very many fish, for these waters go there and *the others*
[2]become fresh; so [a]everything will live where the river goes.
10 "And it will come about that [a]fishermen will stand beside it;
from [b]Engedi to Eneglaim there will be a place for the [c]spreading
of nets. Their fish will be according to their kinds, like the fish
of the [d]Great Sea, [e]very many.
11 "But its swamps and marshes will not become [1]fresh; they
will be [2]left for [a]salt.
12 "[a]By the river on its bank, on one side and on the other, will
grow all *kinds of* [b]trees for food. Their [c]leaves will not wither
and their fruit will not fail. They will bear every month because
their water flows from the sanctuary, and their fruit will be for
food and their [d]leaves for healing."
13 Thus says the Lord [1]GOD, "This *shall be* the [a]boundary by
which you shall divide the land for an inheritance among the
twelve tribes of Israel; Joseph *shall have* two [b]portions.
14 "You shall divide it for an inheritance, each one [1]equally
with the other; for I [2a]swore to give it to your forefathers, and
this land shall fall to you [3]as an inheritance.
15 "This *shall be* the boundary of the land: on the [a]north side, from
the Great Sea *by* the way of Hethlon, to the entrance of [1b]Zedad;
16 [1a]Hamath, Berothah, Sibraim, which is between the border
of [b]Damascus and the border of Hamath; Hazer-hatticon, which
is by the border of Hauran.
17 "The boundary shall [1]extend from the sea *to* [a]Hazar-enan *at*
the border of Damascus, and on the north toward the north is
the border of Hamath. This is the north side.
18 "The [a]east side, from between Hauran, Damascus, [b]Gilead
and the land of Israel, *shall be* the [c]Jordan; from the *north* border
to the eastern sea you shall measure. This is the east side.
19 "The [a]south side toward the south *shall extend* from [b]Tamar
as far as the waters of [c]Meribath-kadesh, to the [d]brook *of Egypt*
and to the [e]Great Sea. This is the south side toward the south.

5 [a]Is 11:9; Hab 2:14

6 [1]Lit *and caused me to return* [a]Ezek 8:6; 40:4; 44:5

7 [a]Is 60:13, 21; 61:3; Ezek 47:12

8 [1]Lit *healed* [a]Deut 3:17; Is 35:6, 7; 41:17-19; 44:3 [b]Josh 3:16

9 [1]Lit *two rivers* [2]Lit *are healed* [a]Is 12:3; 55:1; John 4:14; 7:37, 38

10 [a]Matt 4:19; 13:47; Luke 5:10 [b]Gen 14:7; Josh 15:62; 1 Sam 23:29; 24:1; 2 Chr 20:2 [c]Ezek 26:5, 14 [d]Num 34:6; Ps 104:25; Ezek 47:15; 48:28 [e]Luke 5:5-9; John 21:6

11 [1]Lit *healed* [2]Lit *given* [a]Deut 29:23

12 [a]Ezek 47:7; Rev 22:2 [b]Gen 2:9 [c]Ps 1:3; Jer 17:8 [d]Rev 22:2

13 [1]Heb *YHWH,* usually rendered *LORD,* and so throughout the ch [a]Num 34:2-12 [b]Gen 48:5; Ezek 48:4, 5

14 [1]Lit *like his brother* [2]Lit *lifted up My hand* [3]Lit *in* [a]Deut 1:8; Ezek 20:6

15 [1]Or *Hamath* [a]Num 34:7-9 [b]Num 34:8

16 [1]Or *Zedad* [a]Num 13:21; Is 10:9; Ezek 47:17, 20; 48:1; Zech 9:2 [b]Gen 14:15; Ezek 47:17, 18; 48:1

17 [1]Lit *be* [a]Num 34:9

18 [a]Num 34:10-12 [b]Gen 37:25; Jer 50:19 [c]Gen 13:10, 11

19 [a]Num 34:3-5 [b]Ezek 48:28 [c]Deut 32:51 [d]Num 34:5; 1 Kin 8:65; Is 27:12 [e]Ezek 47:10, 15

20 "The [a]west side *shall be* the Great Sea, from the *south* border
to a point opposite [1b]Lebo-hamath. This is the west side.
21 "So you shall divide this land among yourselves according to
the tribes of Israel.
22 "You shall divide it by [a]lot for an inheritance among yourselves
and among the [b]aliens who stay in your midst, who bring forth
sons in your midst. And they shall be to you as the native-born
among the sons of Israel; they shall be allotted an [c]inheritance
with you among the tribes of Israel.
23 "And in the tribe with which the alien stays, there you shall
give *him* his inheritance," declares the Lord GOD.

Chapter 48 Theme ______________________

48 "Now [a]these are the names of the tribes: from the northern extremity, [1]beside the way of Hethlon to [2]Lebo-
hamath, *as far as* Hazar-enan *at* the border of Damascus, toward
the north [1]beside Hamath, [3]running from east to west, [b]Dan,
one *portion.*
2 "Beside the border of Dan, from the east side to the west
side, [a]Asher, one *portion.*
3 "Beside the border of Asher, from the east side to the west
side, [a]Naphtali, one *portion.*
4 "Beside the border of Naphtali, from the east side to the
west side, [a]Manasseh, one *portion.*
5 "Beside the border of Manasseh, from the east side to the
west side, [a]Ephraim, one *portion.*
6 "Beside the border of Ephraim, from the east side to the
west side, [a]Reuben, one *portion.*
7 "Beside the border of Reuben, from the east side to the west
side, [a]Judah, one *portion.*
8 "And beside the border of Judah, from the east side to the
west side, shall be the [1]allotment which you shall [2]set apart,
25,000 [3]*cubits* in width, and in length like one of the portions,
from the east side to the west side; and the [a]sanctuary shall be
in the middle of it.
9 "The allotment that you shall set apart to the LORD *shall be*
25,000 *cubits* in length and 10,000 in width.
10 "The holy allotment shall be for these, *namely* for the
[a]priests, toward the north 25,000 *cubits in length,* toward the
west 10,000 in width, toward the east 10,000 in width, and
toward the south 25,000 in length; and the sanctuary of the
LORD shall be in its midst.
11 "*It shall be* for the priests who are sanctified of the [a]sons of
Zadok, who have kept My charge, who did not go astray when
the sons of Israel went astray as the [b]Levites went astray.
12 "It shall be an allotment to them from the allotment of the
land, a most holy place, by the border of the Levites.
13 "Alongside the border of the priests the Levites *shall have*
25,000 *cubits* in length and 10,000 in width. The whole length
shall be 25,000 *cubits* and the width 10,000.

20 [1]Or *entrance of Hamath*
[a]Num 34:6
[b]Judg 3:3; 2 Chr 7:8; Ezek 48:1; Amos 6:14

22 [a]Num 26:55, 56
[b]Is 14:1; 56:6, 7
[c]Acts 11:18; 15:9; Eph 2:12-14; 3:6; Col 3:11

48:1 [1]Lit *at the hand of*
[2]Or *the entrance of Hamath*
[3]Lit *and there shall be to it an east and west side*
[a]Ex 1:1
[b]Josh 19:40-48

2 [a]Josh 19:24-31

3 [a]Josh 19:32-39

4 [a]Josh 13:29-31; 17:1-11

5 [a]Josh 16:5-9; 17:8-10, 14-18

6 [a]Josh 13:15-21

7 [a]Josh 15:1-63; 19:9

8 [1]Or *contribution,* and so throughout the ch
[2]Lit *offer*
[3]Or possibly *reeds,* and so throughout the ch
[a]Is 12:6; 33:20-22; Ezek 45:3, 4

10 [a]Ezek 44:28; 45:4

11 [a]Ezek 40:46; 44:15
[b]Ezek 44:10, 12

14 “Moreover, they [a]shall not sell or exchange any of it, or
alienate this [1]choice *portion* of land; for it is holy to the LORD.
15 “The remainder, 5,000 *cubits* in width and 25,000 [1]in
length, shall be for [a]common use for the city, for dwellings and
for [2]open spaces; and the city shall be in its midst.
16 “These *shall be* its measurements: the north side 4,500
cubits, the south side [a]4,500 *cubits,* the east side 4,500 *cubits,*
and the west side 4,500 *cubits.*
17 “The city shall have [1]open spaces: on the north 250 *cubits,* on
the south 250 *cubits,* on the east 250 *cubits,* and on the west
250 *cubits.*
18 “The remainder of the length alongside the holy allotment
shall be 10,000 *cubits* toward the east and 10,000 toward the
west; and it shall be [1]alongside the holy allotment. And its
produce shall be food for the workers of the city.
19 “The workers of the city, out of all the tribes of Israel, shall
cultivate it.
20 “The whole allotment *shall be* 25,000 by 25,000 *cubits;*
you shall [1]set apart the holy allotment, a [2]square, with the
[3]property of the city.
21 “The [a]remainder *shall be* for the prince, on the one side and
on the other of the holy allotment and of the [1]property of the
city; in front of the 25,000 *cubits* of the allotment toward the
east border and westward in front of the 25,000 toward the
west border, alongside the portions, *it shall be* for the prince.
And the holy allotment and the sanctuary of the house shall be
in the middle of it.
22 “Exclusive of the [1]property of the Levites and the [1]property
of the city, *which* are in the middle of that which belongs to
the prince, *everything* between the border of Judah and the
border of Benjamin shall be for the prince.

The Tribes, the Prince's Portion, the City, the Sanctuary

23 “As for the rest of the tribes: from the east side to the west
side, [a]Benjamin, one *portion.*
24 “Beside the border of
Benjamin, from the east side
to the west side, [a]Simeon,
one *portion.*
25 “Beside the border of
Simeon, from the east side
to the west side, [a]Issachar,
one *portion.*
26 “Beside the border of
Issachar, from the east side
to the west side, [a]Zebulun,
one *portion.*
27 “Beside the border of
Zebulun, from the east side
to the west side, [a]Gad, one
portion.
28 “And beside the border
of Gad, at the south side

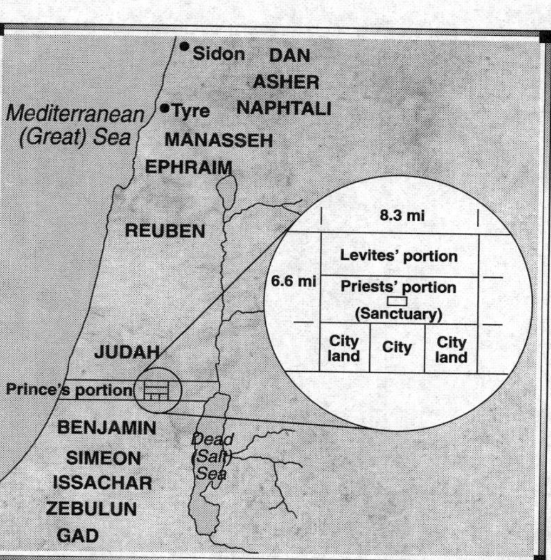

14 [1]Lit *first* or *first fruits* [a]Lev 25:32-34; 27:10, 28, 33
15 [1]Lit *in front* [2]Or *pasture land* [a]Ezek 42:20; 45:6
16 [a]Rev 21:16
17 [1]Or *pasture land*
18 [1]Or *exactly as*
20 [1]Lit *offer* [2]Lit *fourth* [3]Or *possession*
21 [1]Or *possession* [a]Ezek 34:24; 45:7; 48:22
22 [1]Or *possession*
23 [a]Josh 18:21-28
24 [a]Josh 19:1-9
25 [a]Josh 19:17-23
26 [a]Josh 19:10-16
27 [a]Josh 13:24-28

toward the south, the border shall be from [a]Tamar to the
waters of Meribath-kadesh, to the brook *of Egypt,* to the [b]Great
Sea.
29 "This is the [a]land which you shall divide by lot to the tribes of
Israel for an inheritance, and these are their *several* portions,"
declares the Lord [1]GOD.
30 "These are the exits of the city: on the [a]north side, 4,500
cubits by measurement,
31 [1]shall be the gates of the city, [2a]named for the tribes of
Israel, three gates toward the north: the gate of Reuben, one;
the gate of Judah, one; the gate of Levi, one.
32 "On the east side, 4,500 *cubits,* [1]shall be three gates: the
gate of Joseph, one; the gate of Benjamin, one; the gate of Dan,
one.
33 "On the south side, 4,500 *cubits* by measurement, [1]shall be
three gates: the gate of Simeon, one; the gate of Issachar, one;
the gate of Zebulun, one.
34 "On the west side, 4,500 *cubits, shall be* three gates: the
gate of Gad, one; the gate of Asher, one; the gate of Naphtali,
one.
35 "*The city shall be* 18,000 *cubits* round about; and the [a]name
of the city from *that* day *shall be,* '[1]The [b]LORD is there.'"

28 [a]Gen 14:7; 2 Chr 20:2; Ezek 47:19 [b]Ezek 47:10, 15, 19, 20

29 [1]Heb *YHWH,* usually rendered *LORD* [a]Ezek 47:13-20

30 [a]Ezek 48:32-34

31 [1]Lit *and* [2]Lit *according to the names of* [a]Rev 21:12, 13

32 [1]Lit *and*

33 [1]Lit *and*

35 [1]Heb *YHWH-shammah* [a]Jer 23:6; 33:16 [b]Is 12:6; 14:32; 24:23; Jer 3:17; 8:19; 14:9; Ezek 35:10; Joel 3:21; Zech 2:10; Rev 21:3; 22:3

Ezekiel at a Glance

Theme of Ezekiel:

Author:

Date:

Purpose:

Key Words:

- the word of the Lord
- prophesy
- son of man
- covenant
- vision(s)
- the glory of God (the Lord)
- Spirit (spirit)
- know that I am the Lord
- iniquity (sin, abominations)
- rebelled (rebellious)
- sword
- wrath
- mountain(s)
- heart
- harlot (harlotries, adultery)
- blood
- sanctuary (temple)
- the day of the Lord

Segment Divisions		Chapter Themes
		1
		2
		3
		4
		5
		6
		7
		8
		9
		10
		11
		12
		13
		14
		15
		16
		17
		18
		19
		20
		21
		22
		23
		24

SEGMENT DIVISIONS

		CHAPTER THEMES
		25
		26
		27
		28
		29
		30
		31
		32
		33
		34
		35
		36
		37
		38
		39
		40
		41
		42
		43
		44
		45
		46
		47
		48

DANIEL דניאל DANIYEL

Daniel's prophetic ministry began and ended in Babylon. When Nebuchadnezzar first besieged Jerusalem in 605 B.C., Daniel, who was about 15 years old, was among the captives taken to Babylon.

As Moses predicted, Israel lost her place of supremacy among the nations because she did not obey God. Instead of being the head, Israel became the tail to be wagged by the Gentiles (Deuteronomy 28). Yet, because the gifts and calling of God are irrevocable, when the fulness of the Gentiles is complete, all Israel will be saved, for the Deliverer will come out of Zion and take away Israel's sin (see Romans 11:25-30). All this becomes evident as the prophecies of Daniel unfold.

Things to Do

What the skeleton is to the body, Daniel is to prophecy. All the other prophecies in the Old and New Testaments add flesh to Daniel's bones. If you carefully and thoroughly observe Daniel and discover exactly what the text says, you will find that Daniel's prophecies become increasingly clear and more exciting with every new observation.

General Instructions

Read through Daniel one chapter at a time. Don't hurry. Simply do the following assignment on each chapter. Record all your notes in the margin of the chapter. As you read, answer the following questions and record the answers in the margin of the text:

1. When do the events of this chapter occur? Mark every reference to time with a clock ⏲, using a distinctive color so you can see it immediately.
2. What king/kingdom is ruling at the time? Record this in the margin along with a notation of the "when" of the chapter. For instance, in the margin of chapter 1 you would put the following:

   Third year of Jehoiakim, king of Judah
   Nebuchadnezzar was king of Babylon
3. Who are the main characters in the chapter?
4. What, in general, is the chapter about?
5. Record the theme or event of the chapter on the DANIEL AT A GLANCE chart on page 1433 and in your Bible. Then in the margin list the key points or happenings connected with the main event of the chapter.
6. If a vision or dream is recorded, note in the margin who had the vision or dream and what the vision or dream was about. Also, if you sketch or draw the vision or dream, you will better remember and understand it.
7. Read "From 931 B.C. Until the Birth of Christ" beginning on page 2088.

Chapters 1–6

1. Read Daniel 1 through 6 again chapter by chapter. This time do the following:
   a. Color code every reference to God. Watch for the repeated reference to God as the "Most High" and color this also. When you gain a new insight into God's character, power, ways, or sovereignty, put a △ in the margin and record what you learned. Then meditate on how you can apply each truth to your own life.
   b. In your notebook, list everything you learn about Daniel: his character, his relationship to God and to others, and how he handles and responds to various situations.

c. Mark in a distinctive way the following key repeated words: *kingdom (dominion)*, *rules (ruler)*, *dream*, *mystery (mysteries)*, and *Nebuchadnezzar* (including pronouns). Put these on an index card and use it as a bookmark. Also watch for and mark key repeated words that appear in individual chapters. If there is room, you may want to summarize in your notebook what you learn about Nebuchadnezzar.

2. Study the historical chart on page 1407. In the light of what you have observed in the text and on the chart, see if the first six chapters of Daniel come in chronological order.

Chapters 7–12

1. As you prepare to go through these final chapters of Daniel, review what you have observed in chapters 7 through 12 and what you recorded on DANIEL AT A GLANCE. Do you see any difference between the first six chapters of Daniel and the last six?

a. Are the last six chapters chronological?

b. Who had the dreams/visions in each of these major segments?

c. Record your insights to these two questions on DANIEL AT A GLANCE under "Segment Divisions." Show the chronology or lack of it on one line, and then on the other write the main theme or emphasis of these two major divisions of Daniel.

2. Read Daniel 7 through 12 again chapter by chapter. Do the following:

a. As you read each chapter mark the following key words: *vision*, *kingdom (empire, authority, power, dominion)*, *horn(s)*, *saints*, *man of high esteem*, *end (end time, appointed time, time of the end)*, *covenant*, *Michael*, *Gabriel*, and *God*. Mark every reference to the fourth beast in Daniel 9.

b. List everything you learn about Daniel from observing the text.

Understanding the Visions and Dreams in Daniel

1. When you come to a vision, observe the details of the vision carefully. Watch the references to numbers. See if the text interprets the vision. In chapter 7, list in the margin or your notebook all that you learn about the little horn.

2. After you observe chapter 7, compare it with chapter 2.

a. If you didn't do a sketch of the vision in chapter 2, stop and do it. Then do a sketch of the vision in chapter 7. What parallels do you see? Which chapter gives more details of the events encompassed in the vision? Pay attention to those details when you sketch out the vision.

b. Mark any references to time with a clock. In biblical reckoning "time, times, and half a time" is the equivalent of 3 1/2 years. Note what precedes a period of time and what brings it to an end.

3. When you observe chapter 8, list everything you learn about the ram and the goat. In a distinctive way mark every pronoun which refers to the small horn of 8:9. Then list everything you observe from the text about this horn. Ask the "5 W's and an H": Where did it come from? What does it do and where? When does it happen? How long does it last?

4. When you observe Daniel 9:24-27, follow those verses chronologically.

a. Number from 1 to 6 in the text the six things in Daniel 9:24 that will be accomplished in 70 weeks (sevens).

b. Observe who the 70 weeks pertain to. Then in your notebook draw a line and put in the sequence of events. For example:

|Seven weeks|______________________(you complete the drawing).
Decree

Note when the prophecy begins (what starts it) and what happens at each interval of time. Note what happens after the seven weeks and 62 weeks and what happens during the last week (the seventieth week) mentioned in 9:27.

c. Observe who destroys the city and the sanctuary, and their relationship to the prince who is to come in 9:26. A historical fact that might help is that Jerusalem was destroyed in A.D. 70 by Titus, a Roman general.

5. Read chapters 10–12 as one unit and then concentrate on the message and vision of chapters 11–12.

a. Mark every reference to time, including the word *then,* which shows the sequence of events.

b. Chapter 11 is not an easy chapter to understand apart from a grasp of history. It was written years before the fact, but many people are not familiar with this period of time. When you read about the kings of the south and the north, keep in mind that they are so named because of their geographical relationship to Israel, the Beautiful Land.

c. As you read through the chapter, consult the chart HISTORY OF ISRAEL'S RELATIONSHIP TO THE KINGS OF DANIEL 11 on page 1427. In 11:1-35 there are approximately 135 prophetic statements, which have all been fulfilled. The accuracy of Daniel's prophecies regarding the Gentile nations and their relationship to Israel has staggered the minds of some theologians. Many even say that because of its historical accuracy, Daniel had to be written sometime after the Maccabean period in the second century B.C. However, the book of Daniel clearly refers to Daniel as the author, and so does our Lord Jesus Christ (see Matthew 24:15).

d. If you have not done so, make a list of everything you learned about the despicable person in Daniel 11:22-35. Many scholars link this description to Antiochus IV Epiphanes. To date, no person in history has yet fulfilled the description given in 11:36-45.

e. Reading *Josephus, the Essential Writings* (Kregel, 1988) will help you understand the intertestament period, the 400 silent years from Malachi to Matthew. It also gives insight into Rome's role in Israel's history and tells more about the various kings mentioned in Daniel 11:1-35, especially Antiochus IV Epiphanes.

f. Observe the transition from 11:45 to 12:1 chronologically. Mark all references to time and the events connected with them. Observe this chapter very carefully.

6. When you study the dreams and visions in Daniel, remember that Nebuchadnezzar's dream in chapter 2 gives a broad overview and that every vision that follows begins to fill in the details. Now that you have finished observing Daniel, you might want to study the chart PROPHETIC OVERVIEW OF DANIEL on page 1432 and see how it compares with the text and your understanding of it.

7. Finally, determine how the book of Daniel can be segmented. Note these under "Segment Divisions" on DANIEL AT A GLANCE. Then complete the chart.

Things to Think About

1. Keeping in mind the meaning of Daniel's name, "God is my judge," think about how Daniel lived. Review what you observed of his life and character and determine to be a Daniel. You have His promise, "The people who know their God will display strength

and take action" (Daniel 11:32b). If you are God's child, you also have God's Spirit and His grace (John 14:17; 1 Corinthians 15:10).

2. What did Daniel know about God that would help him accept what happened to him? How does this understanding of God help you deal with the situations and circumstances of your life?

3. How does your understanding of future events help you understand and deal with what is happening in history? Have you thought about using Daniel as a tool in sharing the gospel with others? Many times prophecy will open the door when nothing else will.

Chapter 1 Theme __________________________

1 In the third year of the reign of [a]Jehoiakim king of Judah,
[b]Nebuchadnezzar king of Babylon came to Jerusalem and
besieged it.
2 The [a]Lord gave Jehoiakim king of Judah into his hand,
along with some of the [b]vessels of the house of God; and he
brought them to the land of [c]Shinar, to the house of his [1]god,
and he brought the vessels into the treasury of his [1d]god.
3 Then the king [1]ordered Ashpenaz, the chief of his [2]officials,
to bring in some of the sons of Israel, including some of the
[3]royal [a]family and of the nobles,
4 youths in whom was [a]no defect, who were good-looking,
showing [b]intelligence in every *branch of* wisdom, endowed
with understanding and discerning knowledge, and who had
ability for [1]serving in the king's [2]court; and *he ordered him* to
teach them the [3]literature and [c]language of the [d]Chaldeans.
5 The king appointed for them a daily ration from the [a]king's
choice food and from the wine which he drank, and *appointed*
that they should be [1]educated three years, at the end of which
they were to [2b]enter the king's personal service.
6 Now among them from the sons of Judah were [a]Daniel,
Hananiah, Mishael and Azariah.
7 Then the commander of the officials assigned *new* names to
them; and to Daniel he assigned *the name* [a]Belteshazzar, to
Hananiah [b]Shadrach, to Mishael [b]Meshach and to Azariah
[b]Abed-nego.
8 But Daniel [1]made up his mind that he would not [a]defile
himself with the [b]king's choice food or with the [c]wine which
he drank; so he sought *permission* from the commander of the
officials that he might not defile himself.
9 Now God granted Daniel [1a]favor and compassion in the
sight of the commander of the officials,
10 and the commander of the officials said to Daniel, "I am afraid
of my lord the king, who has appointed your food and your drink;

1:1 [a]2 Kin 24:1; 2 Chr 36:5, 6 [b]Jer 25:1; 52:12, 28-30

2 [1]Or *gods* [a]Is 42:24; Dan 2:37, 38 [b]2 Chr 36:7; Jer 27:19, 20; Dan 5:2 [c]Gen 10:10; 11:2; Is 11:11; Zech 5:11 [d]Jer 50:2; 51:44

3 [1]Or *said to* [2]Or *eunuchs,* and so throughout the ch [3]Lit *seed of the* [a]2 Kin 24:15; Is 39:7

4 [1]Lit *standing* [2]Lit *palace* [3]Or *writing* [a]2 Sam 14:25 [b]Dan 1:17 [c]Is 36:11; Jer 5:15; Dan 2:4 [d]Dan 2:2, 4, 5, 10; 3:8; 4:7; 5:7, 11, 30; 9:1

5 [1]Or *reared* [2]Lit *stand before the king* [a]Dan 1:8 [b]1 Sam 16:22; Dan 1:19

6 [a]Ezek 14:14, 20; 28:3; Matt 24:15

7 [a]Dan 2:26; 4:8; 5:12 [b]Dan 2:49; 3:12

8 [1]Lit *set upon his heart* [a]Lev 11:47; Ezek 4:13, 14; Hos 9:3, 4 [b]Ps 141:4; Dan 1:5 [c]Deut 32:38; Dan 5:4

9 [1]Lit *loving-kindness* [a]Gen 39:21; 1 Kin 8:50; Job 5:15, 16; Ps 106:46; Prov 16:7

10 [1]Lit *make my head guilty*

12 [a]Dan 1:16

13 [1]Lit *seen*

15 [1]Lit *fat of flesh* [a]Ex 23:25; Prov 10:22

16 [1]Lit *take away* [a]Dan 1:12

17 [1]Or *writing* [a]1 Kin 3:12, 28; Job 32:8; Dan 1:20; 2:21, 23; Acts 7:22 [b]Dan 2:19; 7:1; 8:1

18 [1]Lit *said* [2]Lit *to bring them in* [3]Lit *brought in*

for why should he see your faces looking more haggard than
the youths who are your own age? Then you would [1]make me
forfeit my head to the king."
11 But Daniel said to the overseer whom the commander of
the officials had appointed over Daniel, Hananiah, Mishael and
Azariah,
12 "Please test your servants for ten days, and let us be [a]given
some vegetables to eat and water to drink.
13 "Then let our appearance be [1]observed in your presence
and the appearance of the youths who are eating the king's
choice food; and deal with your servants according to what you
see."
14 So he listened to them in this matter and tested them for
ten days.
15 At the end of ten days their appearance seemed [a]better and
[1]they were fatter than all the youths who had been eating the
king's choice food.
16 So the overseer continued to [1]withhold their choice food and
the wine they were to drink, and kept [a]giving them vegetables.
17 As for these four youths, [a]God gave them knowledge and
intelligence in every *branch of* [1]literature and wisdom; Daniel
even understood all *kinds of* [b]visions and dreams.
18 Then at the end of the days which the king had [1]specified [2]for
presenting them, the commander of the officials [3]presented
them before Nebuchadnezzar.

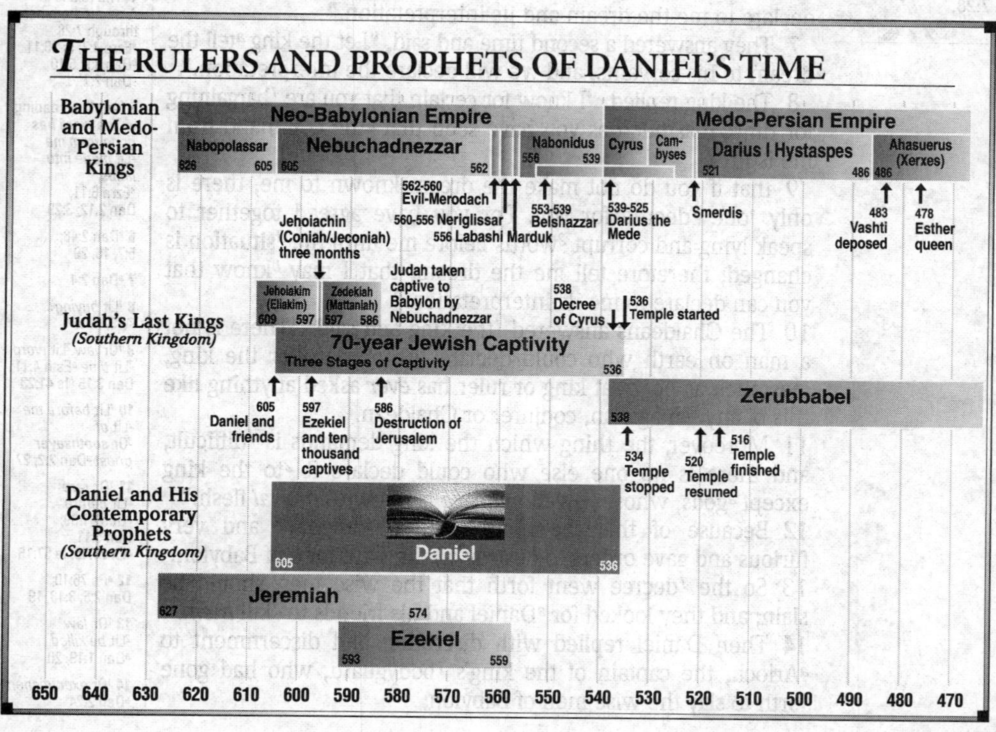

19 The king talked with them, and out of them all not one was
found like [a]Daniel, Hananiah, Mishael and Azariah; so they
[1b]entered the king's personal service.
20 As for every matter of [a]wisdom [1]and understanding about
which the king consulted them, he found them [b]ten times [c]better
than all the [2d]magicians *and* conjurers who *were* in all his realm.
21 And Daniel [1]continued until the [a]first year of Cyrus the king.

Chapter 2 Theme ________________________________

2 Now in the second year of the reign of Nebuchadnezzar,
Nebuchadnezzar [1a]had dreams; and his spirit was troubled
and his [b]sleep [2]left him.
2 Then the king [1]gave orders to call in the [2a]magicians, the
conjurers, the sorcerers and the [3]Chaldeans to tell the king his
dreams. So they came in and stood before the king.
3 The king said to them, "I [1a]had a dream and my spirit [2]is
anxious to [3]understand the dream."
4 Then the Chaldeans spoke to the king in [1a]Aramaic: "[b]O
king, live forever! [c]Tell the dream to your servants, and we will
declare the interpretation."
5 The king replied to the Chaldeans, "[1]The command from
me is firm: if you do not make known to me the dream and its
interpretation, you will be [2a]torn limb from limb and your
houses will be made a rubbish heap.
6 "But if you declare the dream and its interpretation, you will
receive from me [a]gifts and a reward and great honor; therefore
declare to me the dream and its interpretation."
7 They answered a second time and said, "Let the king [a]tell the
dream to his servants, and we will declare the interpretation."
8 The king replied, "I know for certain that you are [1]bargaining
for time, inasmuch as you have seen that [2]the command from
me is firm,
9 that if you do not make the dream known to me, there is
only [a]one [1]decree for you. For you have agreed together to
speak lying and corrupt [2]words before me until the [3]situation is
changed; therefore tell me the dream, that I may [b]know that
you can declare to me its interpretation."
10 The Chaldeans answered [1]the king and said, "There is not
a man on earth who could declare the matter [2]for the king,
inasmuch as no great king or ruler has *ever* asked anything like
this of any [3a]magician, conjurer or Chaldean.
11 "Moreover, the thing which the king demands is [1]difficult,
and there is no one else who could declare it [2]to the king
except [a]gods, whose [b]dwelling place is not with *mortal* flesh."
12 Because of this the king became [a]indignant and very
furious and gave orders to destroy all the wise men of Babylon.
13 So the [1]decree went forth that the wise men should be
slain; and they looked for [a]Daniel and his friends to [2]kill *them.*
14 Then Daniel replied with discretion and discernment to
[a]Arioch, the captain of the king's [1]bodyguard, who had gone
forth to slay the wise men of Babylon;

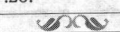

INSIGHT

Daniel was written in Aramaic and Hebrew. The Aramaic portion is from 2:4 through 7:28.

19 [1]Lit *stood before the king* [a]Dan 1:6, 7 [b]Gen 41:46; Dan 1:5

20 [1]Lit *of* [2]Or *soothsayer priests* [a]1 Kin 4:30, 31; Dan 1:17 [b]Gen 31:7; Num 14:22; Neh 4:12; Job 19:3 [c]Dan 2:27, 28, 46, 48 [d]Is 19:3; Dan 2:2; 4:18; 5:7

21 [1]Lit *was until* [a]Dan 6:28; 10:1

2:1 [1]Lit *dreamed dreams* [2]Lit *was gone upon him* [a]Gen 40:5-8; 41:1, 8; Job 33:15-17; Dan 2:3; 4:5 [b]Esth 6:1; Dan 6:18

2 [1]Lit *said to call* [2]Or *soothsayer priests* [3]Or *master astrologers,* and so throughout the ch [a]Gen 41:8; Ex 7:11; Is 47:12, 13; Dan 1:20; 2:10, 27; 4:6; 5:7

3 [1]Lit *dreamed* [2]Lit *was troubled* [3]Lit *know* [a]Gen 40:8; 41:15; Dan 4:5

4 [1]The text is in Aramaic from here through 7:28 [a]Ezra 4:7; Is 36:11 [b]Dan 3:9; 5:10 [c]Dan 2:7

5 [1]Another reading is *The word has gone from me* [2]Lit *made into limbs* [a]Ezra 6:11; Dan 2:12; 3:29

6 [a]Dan 2:48; 5:7, 16, 29

7 [a]Dan 2:4

8 [1]Lit *buying* [2]V 5, note 1

9 [1]Or *law* [2]Lit *word* [3]Lit *time* [a]Esth 4:11; Dan 3:15 [b]Is 41:23

10 [1]Lit *before the* [2]Lit *of* [3]Or *soothsayer priest* [a]Dan 2:2, 27

11 [1]Or *rare* [2]Lit *before* [a]Gen 41:39; Dan 5:11 [b]Ex 29:45; Is 57:15

12 [a]Ps 76:10; Dan 2:5; 3:13, 19

13 [1]Or *law* [2]Lit *be killed* [a]Dan 1:19, 20

14 [1]Or *executioners* [a]Dan 2:24

15 he said to Arioch, the king's commander, "For what reason is
the [1]decree from the king *so* [2]urgent?" Then Arioch informed
Daniel about the matter.
16 So Daniel went in and requested of the king that he would
[1]give him time, in order that he might declare the interpretation
to the king.
17 Then Daniel went to his house and informed his friends,
[a]Hananiah, Mishael and Azariah, about the matter,
18 so that they might [a]request compassion from the God of
heaven concerning this mystery, so that Daniel and his friends
would not be [b]destroyed with the rest of the wise men of
Babylon.
19 Then the mystery was revealed to Daniel in a night [a]vision.
Then Daniel blessed the God of heaven;
20 Daniel said,

"Let the name of God be [a]blessed forever and ever,
For [b]wisdom and power belong to Him.
21 "It is He who [a]changes the times and the epochs;
He [b]removes kings and [1]establishes kings;
He gives [c]wisdom to wise men
And knowledge to [2]men of understanding.
22 "It is He who [a]reveals the profound and hidden things;
[b]He knows what is in the darkness,
And the [c]light dwells with Him.
23 "To You, O [a]God of my fathers, I give thanks and praise,
For You have given me [b]wisdom and power;
Even now You have made known to me what we
[c]requested of You,
For You have made known to us the king's matter."

24 Therefore, Daniel went in to Arioch, whom the king had
appointed to destroy the wise men of Babylon; he went and
spoke to him as follows: "[a]Do not destroy the wise men of
Babylon! Take me [1]into the king's presence, and I will declare
the interpretation to the king."
25 Then Arioch hurriedly [a]brought Daniel [1]into the king's
presence and spoke to him as follows: "I have found a man
among the [2b]exiles from Judah who can make the interpretation
known to the king!"
26 The king said to Daniel, whose name was [a]Belteshazzar,
"Are you able to make known to me the dream which I have
seen and its interpretation?"
27 Daniel answered before the king and said, "As for the
mystery about which the king has inquired, neither [a]wise men,
conjurers, [1]magicians *nor* diviners are able to declare *it* to the king.
28 "However, there is a [a]God in heaven who reveals mysteries,
and He has made known to King Nebuchadnezzar what will
take place in the [1b]latter days. This was your dream and the
[c]visions [2]in your mind *while* on your bed.
29 "As for you, O king, *while* on your bed your thoughts
[1]turned to what would take place [2]in the future; and [a]He who
reveals mysteries has made known to you what will take place.

15 [1]Or *law* [2]Or *harsh*
16 [1]Or *appoint a time for him*
17 [a]Dan 1:6
18 [a]Esth 4:15, 16; Is 37:4; Jer 33:3; Ezek 36:37; Dan 2:23 [b]Gen 18:28; Mal 3:18
19 [a]Num 12:6; Job 33:15, 16; Dan 1:17; 7:2, 7, 13
20 [a]Ps 103:1, 2; 113:1, 2; 115:18; 145:1, 2, 21 [b]1 Chr 29:11, 12; Job 12:13, 16-22; Dan 2:21-23
21 [1]Or *sets up* [2]Lit *knowers* [a]Ps 31:15; Dan 2:9; 7:25 [b]Job 12:18; Ps 75:6, 7; Dan 4:17, 32 [c]1 Kin 3:9, 10; 4:29; James 1:5
22 [a]Job 12:22; Ps 25:14; Dan 2:19, 28 [b]Job 26:6; Ps 139:12; Is 45:7; Jer 23:24; Heb 4:13 [c]Ps 36:9; Dan 5:11, 14; James 1:17; 1 John 1:5
23 [a]Gen 31:42; Ex 3:15 [b]Dan 1:17; 2:21 [c]Ps 21:2, 4; Dan 2:18, 29, 30
24 [1]Lit *in before the king* [a]Dan 2:12, 13; Acts 27:24
25 [1]Lit *in before the king* [2]Lit *sons of the exile of* [a]Gen 41:14 [b]Dan 1:6; 5:13; 6:13
26 [a]Dan 1:7; 4:8; 5:12
27 [1]Or *soothsayer priests* [a]Dan 2:2, 10, 11; 5:7, 8
28 [1]Lit *end of the days* [2]Lit *of your head* [a]Gen 40:8; 41:16; Dan 2:22, 45 [b]Gen 49:1; Is 2:2; Dan 10:14; Mic 4:1 [c]Dan 4:5
29 [1]Lit *came up* [2]Lit *after this* [a]Dan 2:23, 47

30 "But as for me, this mystery has not been revealed to me for
any [a]wisdom [1]residing in me more than *in* any *other* living man,
but for the purpose of making the interpretation known to the
king, and that you may [2]understand the [b]thoughts of your [3]mind.
31 "You, O king, were looking and behold, there was a single
great statue; that statue, which was large and [1]of extraordinary
splendor, was standing in front of you, and its appearance was
[a]awesome.
32 "The [a]head of that statue *was made* of fine gold, its breast
and its arms of silver, its belly and its thighs of bronze,
33 its legs of iron, its feet partly of iron and partly of clay.
34 "You [1]continued looking until a [a]stone was cut out [b]without
hands, and it struck the statue on its feet of iron and clay and
[c]crushed them.
35 "Then the iron, the clay, the bronze, the silver and the gold
were crushed [1]all at the same time and became [a]like chaff from
the summer threshing floors; and the wind carried them away so
that [b]not a trace of them was found. But the stone that struck
the statue became a great [c]mountain and filled the whole earth.
36 "This *was* the dream; now we will tell [a]its interpretation
before the king.
37 "You, O king, are the [a]king of kings, to whom the God of
heaven has given the [1]kingdom, the [b]power, the strength and
the glory;
38 and wherever the sons of men dwell, *or* the [a]beasts of the
field, or the birds of the sky, He has given *them* into your hand
and has caused you to rule over them all. You are the head of gold.
39 "After you there will arise another kingdom inferior to you,
then another third kingdom of bronze, which will rule over all
the earth.
40 "Then there will be a [a]fourth kingdom as strong as iron;
inasmuch as iron crushes and shatters all things, so, like iron
that breaks in pieces, it will crush and break all these in pieces.
41 "In that you saw the feet and toes, partly of potter's clay and
partly of iron, it will be a divided kingdom; but it will have in it
the toughness of iron, inasmuch as you saw the iron mixed
with [1]common clay.
42 "*As* the toes of the feet *were* partly of iron and partly of
pottery, *so* some of the kingdom will be strong and part of it
will be brittle.
43 "And in that you saw the iron mixed with [1]common clay,
they will combine with one another [2]in the seed of men; but
they will not adhere to one another, even as iron does not
combine with pottery.
44 "In the days of those kings the [a]God of heaven will [b]set up a
[c]kingdom which will never be destroyed, and *that* kingdom
will not be [1]left for another people; it will [d]crush and put an
end to all these kingdoms, but it will itself endure forever.
45 "Inasmuch as you saw that a [a]stone was cut out of the
mountain without hands and that it crushed the iron, the
bronze, the clay, the silver and the gold, the [b]great God has

INSIGHT

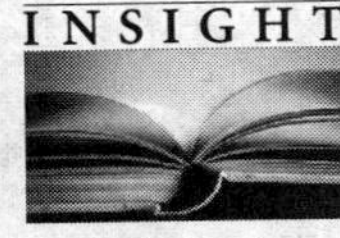

For a clear understanding of the empires represented in the statue, consult the timeline on pages NISB-45 through NISB-48, and the historical account on pages 2087 through 2098.

30 [1]Lit *which is* [2]Lit *know* [3]Lit *heart* [a]Gen 41:16; Dan 1:17 [b]Ps 139:2; Amos 4:13

31 [1]Lit *its splendor was surpassing* [a]Hab 1:7

32 [a]Dan 2:38

34 [1]Lit *were* [a]Dan 2:45 [b]Dan 8:25; Zech 4:6 [c]Ps 2:9; Is 60:12

35 [1]Lit *like one* [a]Ps 1:4; Is 17:13; 41:15, 16; Hos 13:3 [b]Ps 37:10, 36 [c]Is 2:2; Mic 4:1

36 [a]Dan 2:24

37 [1]Or *sovereignty* [a]Is 47:5; Jer 27:6, 7; Ezek 26:7 [b]Ps 62:11

38 [a]Ps 50:10, 11; Dan 4:21, 22

40 [a]Dan 7:23

41 [1]Lit *clay of mud*

43 [1]Lit *clay of mud* [2]Or *with*

44 [1]Or *passed on to* [a]Dan 2:28, 37 [b]Is 9:6, 7 [c]Ps 145:13; Ezek 37:25; Dan 4:3, 34; 6:26; 7:14, 27; Mic 4:7; Luke 1:32, 33 [d]Ps 2:9; Is 60:12; Dan 2:34, 35

45 [a]Dan 2:34 [b]Deut 10:17; 2 Sam 7:22; Ps 48:1; Jer 32:18, 19; Dan 2:29; Mal 1:11

made known to the king what [c]will take place [1]in the future; so
the dream is true and its interpretation is trustworthy."
46 Then King Nebuchadnezzar fell on his face and did [a]homage
to Daniel, and gave orders to present to him an offering and
[1b]fragrant incense.
47 The king answered Daniel and said, "Surely [a]your God is a
[b]God of gods and a Lord of kings and a [c]revealer of mysteries,
since you have been able to reveal this mystery."
48 Then the king [1a]promoted Daniel and gave him many great
gifts, and he made him ruler over the whole [b]province of
Babylon and chief [2]prefect over all the wise men of Babylon.
49 And Daniel made request of the king, and he [a]appointed
[b]Shadrach, Meshach and Abed-nego over the administration of
the province of Babylon, while Daniel *was* at the king's [1c]court.

45 [1]Lit *after this* [c]Gen 41:28, 32

46 [1]Lit *sweet odors* [a]Dan 3:5, 7; Acts 10:25; 14:13; Rev 19:10; 22:8 [b]Lev 26:31; Ezra 6:10

47 [a]Dan 3:15; 4:25 [b]Deut 10:17; Ps 136:2, 3; Dan 11:36 [c]Dan 2:22, 30; Amos 3:7

48 [1]Lit *made great* [2]Lit *of the prefects* [a]Gen 41:39-43; Dan 2:6; 5:16, 29 [b]Dan 3:1, 12, 30

49 [1]Lit *gate* [a]Dan 3:12 [b]Dan 1:7 [c]Esth 2:19, 21; Amos 5:15

Chapter 3 Theme ______________________________

3 Nebuchadnezzar the king made an [a]image of gold, the
height of which *was* sixty [1]cubits *and* its width six [1]cubits;
he set it up on the plain of Dura in the [b]province of Babylon.
2 Then Nebuchadnezzar the king sent *word* to assemble the
[a]satraps, the prefects and the governors, the counselors, the
treasurers, the judges, the magistrates and all the rulers of the
provinces to come to the dedication of the image that
Nebuchadnezzar the king had set up.
3 Then the satraps, the prefects and the governors, the
counselors, the treasurers, the judges, the magistrates and all
the rulers of the provinces were assembled for the dedication
of the image that Nebuchadnezzar the king had set up; and
they stood before the image that Nebuchadnezzar had set up.
4 Then the herald loudly proclaimed: "To you [1]the command
is given, [a]O peoples, nations and *men of every* [2]language,
5 that at the moment you [a]hear the sound of the horn, flute,
[1]lyre, [2]trigon, [3]psaltery, bagpipe and all kinds of music, you are to
fall down and worship the golden image that Nebuchadnezzar
the king has set up.

3:1 [1]I.e. One cubit equals approx 18 in. [a]1 Kin 12:28; Is 46:6; Jer 16:20; Dan 2:31; Hos 2:8; 8:4; Hab 2:19 [b]Dan 2:48; 3:30

2 [a]Dan 3:3, 27; 6:1-7

4 [1]Lit *they command* [2]Lit *tongue* [a]Dan 3:7; 4:1; 6:25

5 [1]Or *zither* [2]I.e. triangular lyre [3]Or *a type of harp* [a]Dan 3:7, 10, 15

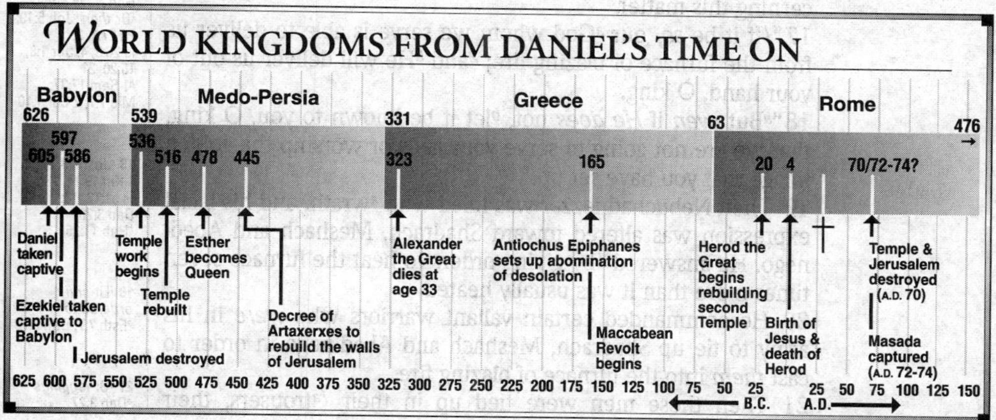

6 "But whoever does not fall down and worship shall
[1]immediately be [a]cast into the midst of a [b]furnace of blazing fire."
7 Therefore at that time, when all the peoples heard the sound
of the horn, flute, [1]lyre, trigon, psaltery, bagpipe and all kinds of
music, all the peoples, nations and *men of every* [2]language fell
down *and* worshiped the golden image that Nebuchadnezzar
the king had set up.
8 For this reason at that time certain [a]Chaldeans came
forward and [1b]brought charges against the Jews.
9 They responded and said to Nebuchadnezzar the king: "[a]O
king, live forever!
10 "You, O king, have [a]made a decree that every man who hears
the sound of the horn, flute, [1]lyre, trigon, psaltery, and bagpipe
and all kinds of music, is to [b]fall down and worship the golden
image.
11 "But whoever does not fall down and worship shall be cast
into the midst of a furnace of blazing fire.
12 "There are certain Jews whom you have [a]appointed over the
administration of the province of Babylon, *namely* Shadrach,
Meshach and Abed-nego. These men, O king, have disregarded
you; they do not serve your gods or worship the golden image
which you have set up."
13 Then Nebuchadnezzar in [a]rage and anger gave orders to
bring Shadrach, Meshach and Abed-nego; then these men
were brought before the king.
14 Nebuchadnezzar responded and said to them, "Is it true,
Shadrach, Meshach and Abed-nego, that you do not serve [a]my
gods or worship the golden image that I have set up?
15 "Now if you are ready, [a]at the moment you hear the sound
of the horn, flute, [1]lyre, trigon, psaltery and bagpipe and all kinds
of music, to fall down and worship the image that I have made,
very well. But if you do not worship, you will [2]immediately be
[b]cast into the midst of a furnace of blazing fire; and [c]what god
is there who can deliver you out of my hands?"
16 [a]Shadrach, Meshach and Abed-nego replied to the king, "O
Nebuchadnezzar, we do not need to give you an answer concerning this matter.
17 "[1]If it be *so,* our [a]God whom we serve is able to deliver us
from the furnace of blazing fire; [2]and [b]He will deliver us out of
your hand, O king.
18 "[a]But *even* if *He does* not, [b]let it be known to you, O king,
that we are not going to serve your gods or worship the golden
image that you have set up."
19 Then Nebuchadnezzar was filled with [a]wrath, and his facial
expression was altered toward Shadrach, Meshach and Abed-
nego. He answered [1]by giving orders to heat the furnace seven
times more than it was usually heated.
20 He commanded certain valiant warriors who *were* in his
army to tie up Shadrach, Meshach and Abed-nego in order to
cast *them* into the furnace of blazing fire.
21 Then these men were tied up in their [1a]trousers, their

6 [1]Or *in the same hour* [a]Dan 3:11, 15, 21; 6:7 [b]Jer 29:22; Ezek 22:18-22; Matt 13:42, 50; Rev 9:2; 14:11

7 [1]V 5, notes 1, 2, 3 [2]Lit *tongue*

8 [1]Lit *ate the pieces of* [a]Dan 2:2, 10; 4:7 [b]Ezra 4:12-16; Esth 3:8, 9; Dan 6:12, 13

9 [a]Dan 2:4; 5:10; 6:6, 21

10 [1]V 5, notes 1, 2, 3 [a]Esth 3:12-14; Dan 3:4-6; 6:12 [b]Dan 3:5, 7, 15

12 [a]Dan 2:49

13 [a]Dan 2:12; 3:19

14 [a]Is 46:1; Jer 50:2; Dan 3:1; 4:8

15 [1]V 5, notes 1, 2, 3 [2]Or *in the same hour* [a]Dan 3:5 [b]Dan 3:6 [c]Ex 5:2; Is 36:18-20; Dan 2:47

16 [a]Dan 1:7; 3:12

17 [1]Or *If our God . . . is able* [2]Or *then* [a]Job 5:19; Ps 27:1, 2; Is 26:3, 4; Jer 1:8; 15:20, 21 [b]1 Sam 17:37; Mic 7:7; 2 Cor 1:10

18 [a]Josh 24:15; 1 Kin 19:14, 18; Is 51:12, 13; Dan 3:28 [b]Heb 11:25

19 [1]Lit *and ordered to* [a]Esth 7:7; Dan 3:13

21 [1]Or *leggings* [a]Dan 3:27

[2]coats, their caps and their *other* clothes, and were cast into
the midst of the furnace of blazing fire.
22 For this reason, because the king's [1]command *was* [2a]urgent
and the furnace had been made extremely hot, the flame of the
fire slew those men who carried up Shadrach, Meshach and
Abed-nego.
23 But these three men, Shadrach, Meshach and Abed-nego,
[a]fell into the midst of the furnace of blazing fire *still* tied up.
24 Then Nebuchadnezzar the king was astounded and stood
up in haste; he said to his high officials, "Was it not three men
we cast bound into the midst of the fire?" They replied to the
king, "Certainly, O king."
25 He said, "Look! I see four men loosed *and* [a]walking *about*
in the midst of the fire [1]without harm, and the appearance of
the fourth is like a son of *the* [b]gods!"
26 Then Nebuchadnezzar came near to the door of the furnace
of blazing fire; he responded and said, "Shadrach, Meshach and
Abed-nego, come out, you servants of the [a]Most High God, and
come here!" Then Shadrach, Meshach and Abed-nego [b]came
out of the midst of the fire.
27 The [a]satraps, the prefects, the governors and the king's
high officials gathered around *and* saw in regard to these men
that the [b]fire had no [1]effect on [2]the bodies of these men nor was
the hair of their head singed, nor were their [3c]trousers
[4]damaged, nor had the smell of fire *even* come upon them.
28 Nebuchadnezzar responded and said, "Blessed be the [a]God
of Shadrach, Meshach and Abed-nego, who has [b]sent His angel
and delivered His servants who put their [c]trust in Him, [1]violating
the king's command, and yielded up their bodies so as [d]not to
serve or worship any god except their own God.
29 "Therefore I [a]make a decree that any people, nation or tongue
that speaks anything offensive against the God of [b]Shadrach,
Meshach and Abed-nego shall be torn limb from limb and their
[c]houses reduced to a rubbish heap, inasmuch as there is [d]no
other god who is able to deliver in this way."
30 Then the king [a]caused Shadrach, Meshach and Abed-nego
to prosper in the province of Babylon.

Chapter 4 Theme ____________________

4 [1]Nebuchadnezzar the king to all the peoples, nations, and
men of every [2]language that live in all the earth: "May your
[3a]peace abound!
2 "It has seemed good to me to declare the signs and wonders
which the [a]Most High God has done for me.
3 "How great are His [a]signs
And how mighty are His wonders!
His [b]kingdom is an everlasting kingdom
And His dominion is from generation to generation.
4 "[1]I, Nebuchadnezzar, was at ease in my house and [a]flourishing
in my palace.

---

21 [2]Or *cloaks*
22 [1]Lit *word* [2]Or *harsh* [a]Ex 12:33; Dan 2:15
23 [a]Is 43:2
25 [1]Lit *there is no injury in them* [a]Ps 91:3-9; Is 43:2 [b]Jer 1:8, 19; 15:21
26 [a]Dan 3:17; 4:2 [b]Deut 4:20; 1 Kin 8:51; Jer 11:4
27 [1]Lit *power over* [2]Lit *their* [3]Or *cloaks* [4]Lit *changed* [a]Dan 3:2, 3 [b]Is 43:2; Heb 11:34 [c]Dan 3:21
28 [1]Lit *and changed the king's word* [a]Dan 2:47; 3:15-17 [b]Ps 34:7, 8; Is 37:36; Dan 3:25; 6:22; Acts 5:19; 12:7 [c]Ps 22:4, 5; 40:4; 84:12; Is 12:2; 26:3, 4; 50:10; Jer 17:7 [d]Dan 3:16-18
29 [a]Dan 6:26 [b]Dan 1:7, 19; 2:17, 49; 3:12 [c]Ezra 6:11; Dan 2:5 [d]Dan 2:47; 3:15
30 [a]Dan 2:49; 3:12
4:1 [1]Ch 3:31 in Aram [2]Lit *tongue* [3]Or *welfare* or *prosperity* [a]Ezra 4:17; Dan 6:25
2 [a]Dan 3:26; 4:17, 24, 25, 32, 34
3 [a]Ps 77:19; 105:27; Is 25:1; Dan 6:27 [b]Dan 2:44; 4:34; 6:26
4 [1]Ch 4:1 in Aram [a]Ps 30:6; Is 47:7, 8

5 "I saw a [a]dream and it made me fearful; and *these* fantasies *as*
I lay on my bed and the [b]visions [1]in my mind kept alarming me.
6 "So I gave orders to [a]bring into my presence all the wise men
of Babylon, that they might make known to me the interpretation of the dream.
7 "Then the [1a]magicians, the conjurers, the [2]Chaldeans and
the diviners came in and I related the dream [3]to them, but they
could not make its [b]interpretation known to me.
8 "But finally Daniel came in before me, whose name is
[a]Belteshazzar according to the name of my god, and in whom is
[1b]a spirit of the holy gods; and I related the dream [2]to him, *saying,*
9 'O Belteshazzar, [a]chief of the magicians, since I know that
[b]a spirit of the holy gods is in you and [c]no mystery baffles you,
[d]tell *me* the visions of my dream which I have seen, along with
its interpretation.
10 'Now *these were* the [a]visions [1]in my mind *as I lay* on my
bed: I was looking, and behold, *there was* a [b]tree in the midst
of the [2]earth and its height *was* great.
11 'The tree grew large and became strong
And its height [a]reached to the sky,
And it *was* visible to the end of the whole earth.
12 'Its foliage *was* [a]beautiful and its fruit abundant,
And in it *was* food for all.
The [b]beasts of the field found [c]shade under it,
And the [d]birds of the sky dwelt in its branches,
And all [1]living creatures fed themselves from it.
13 'I was looking in the [a]visions [1]in my mind *as I lay* on my
bed, and behold, [b]an *angelic* watcher, a [c]holy one, descended
from heaven.
14 'He shouted out and spoke as follows:
"[a]Chop down the tree and cut off its branches,
Strip off its foliage and scatter its fruit;
Let the [b]beasts flee from under it
And the birds from its branches.
15 "Yet [a]leave the stump [1]with its roots in the ground,
But with a band of iron and bronze *around it*
In the new grass of the field;
And let him be drenched with the dew of heaven,
And let [2]him share with the beasts in the grass
of the earth.
16 "Let his [1]mind be changed from *that of* a man
And let a beast's [1]mind be given to him,
And let [a]seven [2]periods of time pass over him.
17 "This sentence is by the decree of the *angelic* watchers
And the decision is a command of the holy ones,
In order that the living may [a]know
That the Most High is ruler over the realm of mankind,
And [b]bestows it on whom He wishes
And sets over it the [c]lowliest of men."
18 'This is the dream *which* I, King Nebuchadnezzar, have seen.
Now you, Belteshazzar, tell *me* its interpretation, inasmuch as

5 [1]Lit *of my head* [a]Dan 2:3 [b]Dan 2:1, 28; 4:10, 13

6 [a]Gen 41:8; Dan 2:2

7 [1]Or *soothsayer priests,* and so throughout the ch [2]Or *master astrologers* [3]Lit *before* [a]Gen 41:8; Dan 2:10, 27; 5:7 [b]Is 44:25; Jer 27:9, 10; Dan 2:7

8 [1]Or possibly *the Spirit of the holy God,* and so throughout the ch [2]Lit *before* [a]Dan 1:7; 2:26; 5:12 [b]Dan 4:9, 18; 5:11, 14

9 [a]Dan 1:20; 2:48; 5:11 [b]Gen 41:38; Dan 4:8 [c]Ezek 28:3; Dan 2:47 [d]Gen 41:15; Dan 2:4, 5

10 [1]Lit *of my head* [2]Or *land,* and so throughout the ch [a]Dan 4:5 [b]Ezek 31:3, 6

11 [a]Deut 9:1; Dan 4:21, 22

12 [1]Lit *flesh* [a]Ezek 31:7 [b]Jer 27:6; Ezek 31:6 [c]Lam 4:20 [d]Ezek 17:23; Matt 13:32; Luke 13:19

13 [1]Lit *of my head* [a]Dan 7:1 [b]Dan 4:17, 23 [c]Deut 33:2; Ps 89:7; Dan 8:13

14 [a]Ezek 31:10-14; Dan 4:23; Matt 3:10; 7:19; Luke 13:7-9 [b]Ezek 31:12, 13; Dan 4:12

15 [1]Lit *of* [2]Lit *his portion be with* [a]Job 14:7-9

16 [1]Lit *heart* [2]I.e. years [a]Dan 4:23, 25, 32

17 [a]Ps 9:16; 83:18; Dan 2:21; 5:21 [b]Jer 27:5-7; Dan 4:25; 5:18, 19 [c]1 Sam 2:8; Dan 11:21

none of the [a]wise men of my kingdom is able to make known
to me the interpretation; but you are able, for a [b]spirit of the
holy gods is in you.'
19 "Then Daniel, whose name is Belteshazzar, was appalled for
a while as his [a]thoughts alarmed him. The king responded and
said, 'Belteshazzar, do not [b]let the dream or its interpretation
alarm you.' Belteshazzar replied, '[c]My lord, *if only* the dream
applied to those who hate you and its interpretation to [d]your
adversaries!
20 'The [a]tree that you saw, which became large and grew strong,
whose height reached to the sky and was visible to all the earth
21 and whose foliage *was* beautiful and its fruit abundant, and
in which *was* food for all, under which the beasts of the field
dwelt and in whose branches the birds of the sky lodged—
22 it is [a]you, O king; for you have become great and grown
strong, and your [1]majesty has become great and reached to the
sky and your [b]dominion to the end of the earth.
23 'In that the king saw an *angelic* watcher, a holy one,
descending from heaven and saying, "[a]Chop down the tree and
destroy it; yet leave the stump [1]with its roots in the ground,
but with a band of iron and bronze *around it* in the new grass
of the field, and let him be drenched with the dew of heaven,
and let [2]him share with the beasts of the field until [b]seven
[3]periods of time pass over him,"
24 this is the interpretation, O king, and this is the decree of
the Most High, which has [a]come upon my lord the king:
25 that you be [a]driven away from mankind and your dwelling
place be with the beasts of the field, and you be given grass to eat
like cattle and be drenched with the dew of heaven; and seven
[1]periods of time will pass over you, until you recognize that the
[b]Most High is ruler over the realm of mankind and [c]bestows it
on whomever He wishes.
26 'And in that it was commanded to [a]leave the stump [1]with the
roots of the tree, your kingdom will be [2]assured to you after you
recognize that *it is* [b]Heaven *that* rules.
27 'Therefore, O king, may my [a]advice be pleasing to you:
[1b]break away now from your sins by *doing* righteousness and
from your iniquities by [c]showing mercy to *the* poor, in case
there may be a [d]prolonging of your prosperity.'
28 "All *this* [a]happened to Nebuchadnezzar the king.
29 "[a]Twelve months later he was walking on the *roof of* the
royal palace of Babylon.
30 "The king [1]reflected and said, 'Is this not Babylon the [a]great,
which I myself have built as a royal [2]residence by the might of
my power and for the glory of my majesty?'
31 "While the word *was* in the king's mouth, a voice [1]came from
heaven, *saying,* 'King Nebuchadnezzar, to you it is declared:
[2]sovereignty has been removed from you,
32 and [a]you will be driven away from mankind, and your
dwelling place *will be* with the beasts of the field. You will be
given grass to eat like cattle, and [b]seven [1]periods of time will pass

18 [a]Gen 41:8, 15; Dan 4:7; 5:8, 15 [b]Dan 4:8, 9
19 [a]Jer 4:19; Dan 7:15, 28; 8:27; 10:16, 17 [b]1 Sam 3:17; Dan 4:4, 5 [c]2 Sam 18:31; Dan 4:24; 10:16 [d]2 Sam 18:32
20 [a]Dan 4:10-12
22 [1]Lit *greatness* [a]2 Sam 12:7; Dan 2:37, 38 [b]Jer 27:6, 7
23 [1]Lit *of* [2]Lit *his portion be with* [3]I.e. years [a]Dan 4:14, 15 [b]Dan 4:16
24 [a]Job 40:11, 12; Ps 107:40
25 [1]I.e. years [a]Dan 4:33; 5:21 [b]Ps 83:18; Jer 27:5; Dan 4:2, 17 [c]Dan 2:37; 4:17; 5:21
26 [1]Lit *of* [2]Lit *enduring* [a]Dan 4:15, 23 [b]Dan 2:18, 19, 28, 37, 44; 4:31
27 [1]Or *redeem now your sins* [a]Gen 41:33-37 [b]Prov 28:13; Is 55:6, 7; Ezek 18:7, 21, 22; Acts 8:22 [c]Ps 41:1-3; Is 58:6, 7, 10 [d]1 Kin 21:29; Jon 3:9
28 [a]Num 23:19; Zech 1:6
29 [a]2 Pet 3:9
30 [1]Lit *answered* [2]Lit *house* [a]Hab 2:4
31 [1]Lit *fell* [2]Or *kingdom*
32 [1]I.e. years [a]Dan 4:25 [b]Dan 4:16

over you until you recognize that the [c]Most High is ruler over
the realm of mankind and bestows it on whomever He wishes.'
33 "Immediately the word concerning Nebuchadnezzar was
fulfilled; and he was [a]driven away from mankind and began
eating grass like cattle, and his body was drenched with the
dew of heaven until his hair had grown like eagles' *feathers*
and his nails like birds' *claws.*
34 "But at the end of [1]that period, I, Nebuchadnezzar, raised my
eyes toward heaven and my [2]reason returned to me, and I blessed
the [a]Most High and praised and honored [b]Him who lives forever;
For His dominion is an [c]everlasting dominion,
And His kingdom *endures* from generation to generation.
35 "[a]All the inhabitants of the earth are accounted as nothing,
But [b]He does according to His will in the host of heaven
And *among* the inhabitants of earth;
And [c]no one can [1]ward off His hand
Or say to Him, '[d]What have You done?'
36 "At that time my [1a]reason returned to me. And my majesty
and [b]splendor were [2]restored to me for the glory of my kingdom,
and my counselors and my nobles began seeking me out; so I
was reestablished in my [3]sovereignty, and surpassing [c]greatness
was added to me.
37 "Now I, Nebuchadnezzar, praise, exalt and honor the King
of [a]heaven, for [b]all His works are [1]true and His ways [2]just, and
He is able to humble those who [c]walk in pride."

Chapter 5 Theme ________________

5 Belshazzar the king [1]held a great [a]feast for a thousand of
his nobles, and he was drinking wine in the presence of
the thousand.
2 When Belshazzar tasted the wine, he gave orders to bring
the gold and silver [a]vessels which Nebuchadnezzar his [1]father
had taken out of the temple which *was* in Jerusalem, so that
the king and his nobles, his wives and his concubines might
drink from them.
3 Then they brought the gold vessels that had been taken out
of the temple, the house of God which *was* in Jerusalem; and the
king and his nobles, his wives and his concubines drank from
them.
4 They [a]drank the wine and praised the gods of [b]gold and
silver, of bronze, iron, wood and stone.
5 Suddenly the fingers of a man's hand emerged and began
writing opposite the lampstand on the plaster of the wall of the
king's palace, and the king saw the [1]back of the hand that did
the writing.
6 Then the king's [1a]face grew pale and his thoughts alarmed
him, and his [b]hip joints went slack and his [c]knees began knocking
together.
7 The king called aloud to bring in the [a]conjurers, the
[1]Chaldeans and the diviners. The king spoke and said to the

32 [c]Dan 4:17

33 [a]Dan 4:25; 5:21

34 [1]Lit *the days* [2]Lit *knowledge* [a]Dan 4:2; 5:18, 21 [b]Ps 102:24-27; Dan 6:26; 12:7; Rev 4:10 [c]Ps 145:13; Jer 10:10; Dan 4:3; Mic 4:7; Luke 1:33

35 [1]Lit *strike against* [a]Ps 39:5; Is 40:15, 17 [b]Ps 33:11; 115:3; 135:6; Dan 6:27 [c]Job 42:2; Is 43:13 [d]Job 9:12; Is 45:9; Rom 9:20

36 [1]Lit *knowledge* [2]Lit *returning* [3]Or *kingdom* [a]2 Chr 33:12, 13; Dan 4:34 [b]Dan 2:31 [c]Prov 22:4; Dan 4:22

37 [1]Lit *truth* [2]Lit *justice* [a]Dan 4:26; 5:23 [b]Deut 32:4; Ps 33:4, 5; Is 5:16 [c]Ex 18:11; Job 40:11, 12; Dan 5:20

5:1 [1]Lit *made* [a]Esth 1:3; Is 22:12-14

2 [1]Or *forefather,* and so throughout the ch [a]2 Kin 24:13; 25:15; Ezra 1:7-11; Dan 1:2

4 [a]Is 42:8; Dan 5:23; Rev 9:20 [b]Ps 115:4; 135:15; Is 40:19, 20; Dan 3:1; Hab 2:19

5 [1]Or *palm*

6 [1]Lit *brightness changed for him* [a]Dan 5:9, 10; 7:28 [b]Ps 69:23 [c]Ezek 7:17; 21:7; Nah 2:10

7 [1]Or *master astrologers* [a]Is 44:25; 47:13; Dan 4:6, 7; 5:11, 15

wise men of Babylon, "Any man who can read this inscription
and explain its interpretation to me shall be [b]clothed with
purple and *have* a [c]necklace of gold around his neck, and have
authority as [2d]third *ruler* in the kingdom."
8 Then all the king's wise men came in, but [a]they could not
read the inscription or make known its interpretation to the king.
9 Then King Belshazzar was greatly [a]alarmed, his [1b]face grew
even paler, and his nobles were perplexed.
10 The queen entered the banquet [1]hall because of the words of
the king and his nobles; the queen spoke and said, "[a]O king, live
forever! Do not let your thoughts alarm you or your [2]face be pale.
11 "There is a [a]man in your kingdom in whom is [1]a [b]spirit of the
holy gods; and in the days of your father, illumination, insight and
wisdom like the wisdom of the gods were found in him. And King
Nebuchadnezzar, your father, your father [2c]the king, appointed
him chief of the [3]magicians, conjurers, [4]Chaldeans *and* diviners.
12 "*This was* because an [a]extraordinary spirit, knowledge and
insight, interpretation of dreams, explanation of enigmas and
solving of difficult problems were found in this Daniel, whom
the king named [b]Belteshazzar. Let Daniel now be summoned
and he will declare the interpretation."
13 Then Daniel was brought in before the king. The king spoke
and said to Daniel, "Are you that Daniel who is one of the [1a]exiles
from Judah, whom my father the king [b]brought from Judah?
14 "Now I have heard about you that [1]a spirit of the gods is in
you, and that illumination, insight and extraordinary wisdom
have been found in you.
15 "Just now the [a]wise men *and* the conjurers were brought in
before me that they might read this inscription and make its
interpretation known to me, but they [b]could not declare the
interpretation of the [1]message.
16 "But I personally have heard about you, that you are able to
give interpretations and solve difficult problems. Now if you
are able to read the inscription and make its [a]interpretation
known to me, you will be [b]clothed with purple and *wear* a
necklace of gold around your neck, and you will have authority
as the [1]third *ruler* in the kingdom."
17 Then Daniel answered and said before the king, "[1]Keep
your [a]gifts for yourself or give your rewards to someone else;
however, I will read the inscription to the king and make the
interpretation known to him.
18 "[1]O king, the [a]Most High God [b]granted [2]sovereignty,
[c]grandeur, glory and majesty to Nebuchadnezzar your father.
19 "Because of the grandeur which He bestowed on him, all
the peoples, nations and *men of every* [1]language feared and
trembled before him; [a]whomever he wished he killed and
whomever he wished he spared alive; and whomever he
wished he elevated and whomever he wished he humbled.
20 "But when his heart was [a]lifted up and his spirit became so
[1b]proud that he behaved arrogantly, he was [c]deposed from his
royal throne and *his* glory was taken away from him.

7 [2]Or *a triumvir* [b]Gen 41:42-44; Dan 5:16, 29 [c]Ezek 16:11 [d]Dan 2:48; 5:16, 29; 6:2, 3

8 [a]Gen 41:8; Dan 2:27; 4:7; 5:15

9 [1]Lit *brightness was changing upon him* [a]Job 18:11; Is 21:2-4; Jer 6:24; Dan 2:1; 5:6 [b]Is 13:6-8

10 [1]Lit *house* [2]Lit *brightness be changed* [a]Dan 3:9; 6:6

11 [1]Or possibly *the Spirit of the holy God* [2]Or *O king* [3]Or *soothsayer priests* [4]Or *master astrologers* [a]Gen 41:11-15; Dan 2:47 [b]Dan 4:8, 9, 18; 5:14 [c]Dan 2:48

12 [a]Dan 5:14; 6:3 [b]Dan 1:7; 4:8

13 [1]Lit *sons of the exile* [a]Ezra 4:1; 6:16, 19, 20; Dan 2:25; 6:13 [b]Dan 1:1, 2

14 [1]Or possibly *the Spirit of God*

15 [1]Lit *word* [a]Dan 5:7 [b]Is 47:12f; Dan 5:8

16 [1]Or *triumvir* [a]Gen 40:8 [b]Dan 5:7, 29

17 [1]Lit *Let... be for* [a]2 Kin 5:16

18 [1]Lit *You, O king* [2]Or *the kingdom* [a]Dan 4:2; 5:21 [b]Dan 2:37, 38; 4:17 [c]Jer 25:9; 27:5-7

19 [1]Lit *tongue* [a]Dan 2:12, 13; 3:6; 11:3, 16, 36

20 [1]Lit *strong* [a]Ex 9:17; Job 15:25; Is 14:13-15; Dan 4:30, 31 [b]2 Kin 17:14; 2 Chr 36:13 [c]Job 40:11, 12; Jer 13:18

21 "He was also [a]driven away from [1]mankind, and his heart
was made like *that of* beasts, and his dwelling place *was* with
the [b]wild donkeys. He was given grass to eat like cattle, and his
body was drenched with the dew of heaven until he
recognized that the [c]Most High God is ruler over the realm of
mankind and *that* He sets over it whomever He wishes.
22 "Yet you, his [1]son, Belshazzar, have [a]not humbled your
heart, [2]even though you knew all this,
23 but you have [a]exalted yourself against the [b]Lord of heaven;
and they have brought the vessels of His house before you, and
you and your nobles, your wives and your concubines have
been drinking wine from them; and you have praised the [c]gods
of silver and gold, of bronze, iron, wood and stone, which do
not see, hear or understand. But the God [d]in whose hand are
your life-breath and all your [e]ways, you have not glorified.
24 "Then the [1a]hand was sent from Him and this inscription
was written out.
25 "Now this is the inscription that was written out: '[1]MENĒ,
[1]MENĒ, [2]TEKĒL, [3]UPHARSIN.'
26 "This is the interpretation of the [1]message: 'MENĒ'—God
has numbered your kingdom and [a]put an end to it.
27 "'TEKĒL'—you have been [a]weighed on the scales and found
deficient.
28 "'PERĒS'—your kingdom has been divided and given over
to the [a]Medes and [1]Persians."
29 Then Belshazzar gave orders, and they [a]clothed Daniel with
purple and *put* a necklace of gold around his neck, and issued a
proclamation concerning him that he *now* had authority as the
[1]third *ruler* in the kingdom.
30 That same night [a]Belshazzar the Chaldean king was [b]slain.
31 [1]So [a]Darius the Mede received the kingdom at about the
age of sixty-two.

Chapter 6 Theme ______________________________

6 [1]It seemed good to Darius to appoint 120 satraps over the
kingdom, that they would be in charge of the whole kingdom,
2 and over them three commissioners (of whom [a]Daniel was
one), that these satraps might be accountable to them, and that
the king might not suffer [b]loss.
3 Then this Daniel began distinguishing himself [1]among the
commissioners and satraps because [2]he possessed an [a]extraordinary spirit, and the king planned to appoint him over the
[b]entire kingdom.
4 Then the commissioners and satraps began [a]trying to find a
ground of accusation against Daniel in regard to [1]government
affairs; but they could find [b]no ground of accusation or
evidence of corruption, inasmuch as he was faithful, and no
negligence or corruption was *to be* found in him.
5 Then these men said, "We will not find any ground of
accusation against this Daniel unless we find *it* against him
with regard to the [a]law of his God."

21 [1]Lit *the sons of man* [a]Job 30:3-7; Dan 4:32, 33 [b]Job 39:5-8 [c]Ex 9:14-16; Ps 83:17, 18; Ezek 17:24; Dan 4:17, 34, 35

22 [1]Or *descendant* [2]Lit *inasmuch as you* [a]Ex 10:3; 2 Chr 33:23; 36:12

23 [a]2 Kin 14:10; Is 2:12; 37:23; Jer 50:29; Dan 5:3, 4 [b]Dan 4:37 [c]Ps 115:4-8; Is 37:19; Hab 2:18, 19 [d]Job 12:10 [e]Job 31:4; Ps 139:3; Prov 20:24; Jer 10:23

24 [1]Lit *palm of the hand* [a]Dan 5:5

25 [1]Or *a mina* (50 shekels) from verb "to number" [2]Or *a shekel* from verb "to weigh" [3]Or *and half-shekels* (sing: *perēs*) from verb "to divide"

26 [1]Lit *word* [a]Is 13:6, 17-19; Jer 50:41-43

27 [a]Job 31:6; Ps 62:9

28 [1]Aram: *Pāras* [a]Is 13:17; 21:2; 45:1, 2; Dan 5:31; 6:8, 28; Acts 2:9

29 [1]Or *triumvir* [a]Dan 5:7, 16

30 [a]Dan 5:1, 2 [b]Is 21:4-9; 47:9; Jer 51:11, 31, 39, 57

31 [1]Ch 6:1 in Aram [a]Dan 6:1; 9:1

6:1 [1]Ch 6:2 in Aram

2 [a]Dan 2:48, 49; 5:16, 29 [b]Ezra 4:22; Esth 7:4

3 [1]Lit *above* [2]Lit *there was in him* [a]Dan 5:12, 14; 9:23 [b]Gen 41:40; Esth 10:3

4 [1]Lit *the kingdom* [a]Gen 43:18; Judg 14:4; Jer 20:10; Dan 3:8; Luke 20:20 [b]Dan 6:22; Luke 20:26; 23:14, 15; Phil 2:15; 1 Pet 2:12; 3:16

5 [a]Acts 24:13-16, 20, 21

6 Then these commissioners and satraps came [1]by agreement
to the king and spoke to him as follows: "King Darius, [a]live forever!
7 "All the [a]commissioners of the kingdom, the prefects and the
satraps, the high officials and the governors have [b]consulted
together that the king should establish a statute and enforce an
injunction that anyone who makes a petition to any god or man
besides you, O king, for thirty days, shall [c]be cast into the lions'
[1]den.
8 "Now, O king, [a]establish the injunction and sign the document so that it may not be changed, according to the [b]law of
the Medes and Persians, which [1]may not be revoked."
9 Therefore King Darius [a]signed the document, that is, the
injunction.
10 Now when Daniel knew that the document was signed, he
entered his house (now in his roof chamber he had windows
open [a]toward Jerusalem); and he continued [b]kneeling on his
knees three times a day, [c]praying and [d]giving thanks before his
God, [1]as he had been doing previously.
11 Then these men came [1a]by agreement and found Daniel
making petition and supplication before his God.
12 Then they approached and [a]spoke before the king about
the king's injunction, "Did you not sign an injunction that any
man who makes a petition to any god or man besides you, O
king, for thirty days, is to be cast into the lions' den?" The king
replied, "The statement is true, according to the [b]law of the
Medes and Persians, which [1]may not be revoked."
13 Then they answered and spoke before the king, "[a]Daniel,
who is one of the [1]exiles from Judah, pays [b]no attention to you,
O king, or to the injunction which you signed, but keeps
making his petition three times a day."
14 Then, as soon as the king heard this statement, he was
deeply [a]distressed and set *his* mind on delivering Daniel; and
even until sunset he kept exerting himself to rescue him.
15 Then these men came [1]by agreement to the king and said
to the king, "Recognize, O king, that it is a [a]law of the Medes
and Persians that no injunction or statute which the king
establishes may be changed."
16 Then the king gave orders, and Daniel was brought in and
[a]cast into the lions' den. The king spoke and said to Daniel,
"[1b]Your God whom you constantly serve will Himself deliver you."
17 A [a]stone was brought and laid over the mouth of the den;
and the king sealed it with his own signet ring and with the
signet rings of his nobles, so that nothing would be changed in
regard to Daniel.
18 Then the king went off to his palace and spent the night
[a]fasting, and no entertainment was brought before him; and his
[b]sleep fled from him.
19 Then the king arose at dawn, at the break of day, and went
in haste to the lions' den.
20 When he had come near the den to Daniel, he cried out
with a troubled voice. The king spoke and said to Daniel,

6 [1]Or *thronging* [a]Neh 2:3; Dan 2:4; 5:10; 6:21

7 [1]Or *pit,* and so throughout the ch [a]Dan 3:2, 27 [b]Ps 59:3; 62:4; 64:2-6; 83:1-3 [c]Ps 10:9; Dan 3:6; 6:16

8 [1]Lit *does not pass away* [a]Esth 3:12; 8:10; Is 10:1 [b]Esth 1:19; 8:8; Dan 6:12, 15

9 [a]Ps 118:9; 146:3

10 [1]Or *because* [a]1 Kin 8:44, 48, 49; Ps 5:7; Jon 2:4 [b]Ps 55:17; 95:6 [c]Dan 9:4-19 [d]Ps 34:1; Phil 4:6; 1 Thess 5:17, 18

11 [1]Or *thronging* [a]Ps 37:32, 33; Dan 6:6

12 [1]Lit *does not pass away* [a]Dan 3:8-12; Acts 16:19-21 [b]Esth 1:19; Dan 6:8, 15

13 [1]Lit *sons of the exile* [a]Dan 2:25; 5:13 [b]Esth 3:8; Dan 3:12; Acts 5:29

14 [a]Mark 6:26

15 [1]Or *thronging* [a]Esth 8:8; Ps 94:20, 21; Dan 6:8, 12

16 [1]Or *May your God . . . Himself deliver you* [a]2 Sam 3:39; Jer 38:5; Dan 6:7 [b]Job 5:19; Ps 37:39, 40; Is 41:10; Dan 3:17, 28; 6:20; 2 Cor 1:10

17 [a]Lam 3:53; Matt 27:66

18 [a]2 Sam 12:16, 17 [b]Esth 6:1; Ps 77:4; Dan 2:1

"Daniel, servant of the living God, has [a]your God, whom you
constantly serve, been [b]able to deliver you from the lions?"
21 Then Daniel spoke [1]to the king, "[a]O king, live forever!
22 "My God [a]sent His angel and [b]shut the lions' mouths and they
have not harmed me, inasmuch as [1]I was found innocent before
Him; and also [2]toward you, O king, I have committed no crime."
23 Then the king was very pleased and gave orders for Daniel
to be taken up out of the den. So Daniel was taken up out of
the den and [a]no injury whatever was found on him, because he
had [b]trusted in his God.
24 The king then gave orders, and they brought those men
who had [1]maliciously accused Daniel, and they [a]cast them, their
[b]children and their wives into the lions' den; and they had not
reached the bottom of the den before the lions overpowered
them and crushed all their bones.
25 Then Darius the king wrote to all the [a]peoples, nations and
men of every [1]language who were living in all the land: "[b]May
your [2]peace abound!
26 "[1]I [a]make a decree that in all the dominion of my kingdom
men are to fear and tremble before the God of Daniel;
For He is the [b]living God and [c]enduring forever,
And [d]His kingdom is one which will not be destroyed,
And His dominion *will be* [2]forever.
27 "He delivers and rescues and performs [a]signs and wonders
In heaven and on earth,
Who has *also* delivered Daniel from the [1]power of the lions."
28 So this [a]Daniel enjoyed success in the reign of Darius and
in the reign of [b]Cyrus the Persian.

Chapter 7 Theme ______________________

7 In the first year of Belshazzar king of Babylon Daniel saw a
[a]dream and visions [1]in his mind *as he lay* on his bed; then he
[b]wrote the dream down *and* related the [2]*following* summary of [3]it.
2 Daniel [1]said, "I was [a]looking in my vision by night, and
behold, the [b]four winds of heaven were stirring up the great sea.
3 "And four great [a]beasts were coming up from the sea,
different from one another.
4 "The first *was* [a]like a lion and had *the* wings of an eagle. I
kept looking until its wings were plucked, and it was lifted up
from the ground and made to stand on two feet like a man; a
human [1]mind also was given to it.
5 "And behold, another beast, a second one, resembling a
bear. And it was raised up on one side, and three ribs *were* in
its mouth between its teeth; and thus they said to it, 'Arise,
devour much meat!'
6 "After this I kept looking, and behold, another one, [a]like a
leopard, which had on its [1]back four wings of a bird; the beast
also had [b]four heads, and dominion was given to it.
7 "After this I kept looking in the night visions, and behold, a
[a]fourth beast, dreadful and terrifying and extremely strong; and
it had large iron teeth. It devoured and crushed and trampled

RETURN TO INSTRUCTIONS

20 [a]Dan 6:16, 27 [b]Gen 18:14; Num 11:23; Jer 32:17; Dan 3:17

21 [1]Lit *with* [a]Dan 2:4; 6:6

22 [1]Lit *innocence was found for me* [2]Lit *before* [a]Num 20:16; Is 63:9; Dan 3:28; Acts 12:11; Heb 1:14 [b]Ps 91:11-13; 2 Tim 4:17; Heb 11:33

23 [a]Dan 3:25, 27 [b]1 Chr 5:20; 2 Chr 20:20; Ps 118:8, 9; Is 26:3; Dan 3:17, 28

24 [1]Lit *eaten the pieces of Daniel* [a]Deut 19:18, 19; Esth 7:10 [b]Deut 24:16; 2 Kin 14:6; Esth 9:10

25 [1]Lit *tongue* [2]Or *welfare* or *prosperity* [a]Ezra 1:1, 2; Esth 3:12; 8:9; Dan 4:1 [b]Ezra 4:17; 1 Pet 1:2

26 [1]Lit *From me a decree is made* [2]Lit *to the end* [a]Ezra 6:8-12; 7:13, 21; Dan 3:29 [b]Dan 4:34; 6:20; Hos 1:10; Rom 9:26 [c]Ps 93:1, 2; Mal 3:6 [d]Dan 2:44; 4:3; 7:14, 27; Luke 1:33

27 [1]Lit *hand* [a]Dan 4:2, 3

28 [a]Dan 1:21 [b]2 Chr 36:22, 23; Dan 10:1

7:1 [1]Lit *of his head* [2]Or *beginning* [3]Lit *words* [a]Job 33:14-16; Dan 1:17; 2:1, 26-28; 4:5-9; Joel 2:28 [b]Jer 36:4, 32

2 [1]Lit *spoke and said* [a]Dan 7:7, 13 [b]Rev 7:1

3 [a]Dan 7:17; Rev 13:1; 17:8

4 [1]Lit *heart* [a]Jer 4:7

6 [1]Or *sides* [a]Rev 13:2 [b]Dan 8:22

7 [a]Dan 7:19, 20, 23

down the remainder with its feet; and it was different from all
the beasts that were before it, and it had [b]ten horns.
8 "While I was contemplating the horns, behold, [a]another horn,
a little one, came up among them, and three of the first horns
were pulled out by the roots before it; and behold, [1]this horn
possessed eyes like the eyes of a man and [b]a mouth uttering
great *boasts.*

9 "I kept looking
Until [a]thrones were set up,
And the Ancient of Days took *His* seat;
His [b]vesture *was* like white snow
And the [c]hair of His head like pure wool.
His [d]throne *was* [1]ablaze with flames,
Its [e]wheels *were* a burning fire.
10 "A river of [a]fire was flowing
And coming out from before Him;
[b]Thousands upon thousands were attending Him,
And myriads upon myriads were standing before Him;
The [c]court sat,
And [d]the books were opened.

11 "Then I kept looking because of the sound of the [1]boastful
words which the horn was speaking; I kept looking until the beast
was slain, and its body was destroyed and given to the [a]burning
[2]fire.
12 "As for the rest of the beasts, their dominion was taken
away, but an extension of life was granted to them for an
appointed period of time.

13 "I kept looking in the night visions,
And behold, with the clouds of heaven
One like a [a]Son of Man was coming,
And He came up to the Ancient of Days
And was presented before Him.
14 "And to Him was given [a]dominion,
Glory and [1b]a kingdom,
[c]That all the peoples, nations and *men of every* [2]language
Might serve Him.
[d]His dominion is an everlasting dominion
Which will not pass away;
[e]And His kingdom is one
Which will not be destroyed.

15 "As for me, Daniel, my spirit was distressed [1]within me, and
the [a]visions [2]in my mind kept [b]alarming me.
16 "I approached one of those who were [a]standing by and
began asking him the [1]exact meaning of all this. So he [b]told me
and made known to me the interpretation of these things:
17 'These great beasts, which are four *in number,* are four kings
who will arise from the earth.
18 'But the [1a]saints of the Highest One will [b]receive the kingdom
and possess the kingdom forever, [2]for all ages to come.'
19 "Then I desired to know the [1]exact meaning of the [a]fourth
beast, which was different from all [2]the others, exceedingly

7 [b]Rev 12:3; 13:1

8 [1]Lit *in this horn were eyes* [a]Dan 8:9 [b]Rev 13:5, 6

9 [1]Lit *flames of fire* [a]Rev 20:4 [b]Mark 9:3 [c]Rev 1:14 [d]Ezek 1:13, 26 [e]Ezek 10:2, 6

10 [a]Ps 18:8; 50:3; 97:3; Is 30:27, 33 [b]Deut 33:2; 1 Kin 22:19; Rev 5:11 [c]Ps 96:11-13; Dan 7:22, 26 [d]Dan 12:1; Rev 20:11-15

11 [1]Lit *great* [2]Lit *of the fire* [a]Rev 19:20; 20:10

13 [a]Matt 24:30; 26:64; Mark 13:26; 14:62; Luke 21:27; Rev 1:7, 13; 14:14

14 [1]Or *sovereignty* [2]Lit *tongue* [a]Dan 7:27; John 3:35; 1 Cor 15:27; Eph 1:20-22; Phil 2:9-11; Rev 1:6; 11:15 [b]Dan 2:37 [c]Ps 72:11; 102:22 [d]Mic 4:7; Luke 1:33 [e]Heb 12:28

15 [1]Lit *in the midst of its sheath* [2]Lit *of my head* [a]Dan 7:1 [b]Dan 4:19; 7:28

16 [1]Lit *truth concerning* [a]Zech 1:9, 19; Rev 5:5; 7:13, 14 [b]Dan 8:16, 17; 9:22

18 [1]Lit *holy ones* [2]Lit *and unto the age of the ages* [a]Dan 7:22, 25, 27 [b]Ps 149:5-9; Is 60:12-14; Dan 7:14; Rev 2:26, 27; 20:4; 22:5

19 [1]Lit *truth concerning* [2]Lit *of them* [a]Dan 7:7, 8

dreadful, with its teeth of iron and its claws of bronze, *and which*
devoured, crushed and trampled down the remainder with its feet,
20 and *the meaning* of the ten horns that *were* on its head and
the other *horn* which came up, and before which three *of them*
fell, namely, that horn which had eyes and a mouth uttering
great *boasts* and [1]which was larger in appearance than its
associates.
21 "I kept looking, and that horn was [a]waging war with the
[1]saints and overpowering them
22 until the Ancient of Days came and [a]judgment was [1]passed
in favor of the [2]saints of the Highest One, and the time arrived
when the [2]saints took possession of the kingdom.
23 "Thus he said: 'The fourth beast will be a fourth kingdom
on the earth, which will be different from all the *other* kingdoms and will devour the whole earth and tread it down and
crush it.
24 'As for the [a]ten horns, out of this kingdom ten kings will
arise; and another will arise after them, and he will be different
from the previous ones and will subdue three kings.
25 'He will [a]speak [1]out against the [b]Most High and [c]wear down
the [2]saints of the Highest One, and he will intend to make
[d]alterations in times and in law; and [3]they will be given into his
hand for a [4e]time, [4]times, and half a [4]time.
26 'But the court will sit *for judgment,* and his dominion will
be [a]taken away, [1]annihilated and destroyed [2]forever.
27 'Then the [1a]sovereignty, the dominion and the greatness of *all*
the kingdoms under the whole heaven will be given to the people
of the [2]saints of the Highest One; His kingdom *will be* an [b]ever-
lasting kingdom, and all the dominions will [c]serve and obey Him.'
28 "[1]At this point the revelation ended. As for me, Daniel, my
thoughts were [a]greatly alarming me and my [2]face grew pale,
but I [b]kept the matter [3]to myself."

INSIGHT

The maps on pages 2246, 2247 show the boundaries of the Babylonian, Persian, Greek, and Roman Empires as they relate to the nations today.

Chapter 8 Theme

The Beautiful Land

8 In the third year of the reign of Belshazzar the king a
vision appeared to me, [1]Daniel, subsequent to the one
which appeared to me [2]previously.

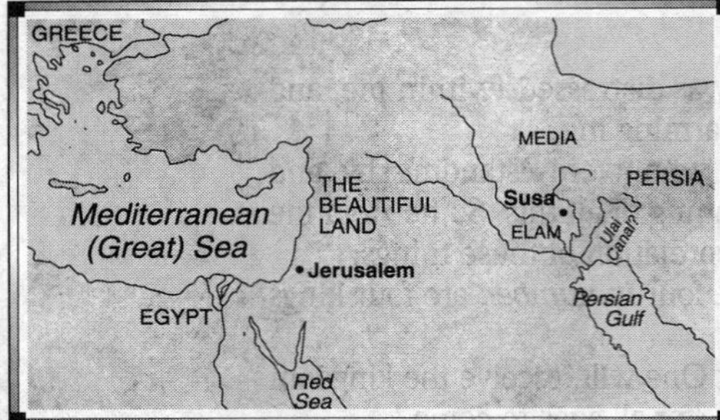

2 I [a]looked in the vision,
and while I was looking I was
in the citadel of [b]Susa, which
is in the province of [c]Elam;
and I looked in the vision and
I myself was beside the Ulai
[1]Canal.
3 Then I lifted my eyes and
looked, and behold, a [a]ram
which had two horns was
standing in front of the
[1]canal. Now the two horns *were* [2]long, but one *was* [2]longer
than the other, with the [2]longer one coming up last.

20 [1]Lit *its appearance was larger*
21 [1]Lit *holy ones* [a]Rev 11:7; 13:7
22 [1]Lit *given for* [2]Lit *holy ones* [a]Dan 7:10; 1 Cor 6:2, 3
24 [a]Dan 7:7; Rev 17:12
25 [1]Lit *words* [2]Lit *holy ones* [3]I.e. the saints [4]I.e. year(s) [a]Dan 11:36; Rev 13:6 [b]Dan 3:26; 4:2, 17, 34 [c]Rev 13:7; 18:24 [d]Dan 2:21 [e]Dan 12:7; Rev 12:14
26 [1]Lit *to annihilate and to destroy* [2]Lit *to the end* [a]Rev 17:14; 19:2
27 [1]Or *kingdom* [2]Lit *holy ones* [a]Is 54:3; Dan 7:14, 18, 22; Rev 20:4 [b]Ps 145:13; Is 9:7; Dan 2:44; 4:34; 7:14; Luke 1:33; Rev 11:15; 22:5 [c]Ps 2:6-12; 22:27; 72:11; 86:9; Is 60:12; Rev 11:1
28 [1]Lit *To here the end of the word* [2]Lit *brightness was changing upon me* [3]Lit *in my heart* [a]Dan 4:19 [b]Luke 2:19, 51
8:1 [1]Lit *I, Daniel* [2]Lit *at the beginning*
2 [1]Or *river* [a]Num 12:6; Dan 7:2, 15; 8:3 [b]Neh 1:1; Esth 1:2; 2:8 [c]Gen 10:22; 14:1; Is 11:11; Jer 25:25; Ezek 32:24
3 [1]Or *river* [2]Lit *high(er)* [a]Dan 8:20

4 I saw the ram [a]butting westward, northward, and southward,
and no *other* beasts could stand before him nor was there
anyone to rescue from his [1]power, but [b]he did as he pleased
and magnified *himself.*
5 While I was observing, behold, a male goat was coming from
the west over the surface of the whole earth without touching the
ground; and the [1]goat *had* a [a]conspicuous horn between his eyes.
6 He came up to the ram that had the two horns, which I
had seen standing in front of the [1]canal, and rushed at him in
his mighty wrath.
7 I saw him come beside the ram, and he was enraged at
him; and he struck the ram and shattered his two horns, and
the ram had no strength to withstand him. So he hurled him to
the ground and trampled on him, and there was none to rescue
the ram from his [1]power.
8 Then the male goat magnified *himself* exceedingly. But as
soon as [a]he was mighty, the [b]large horn was broken; and in its
place there came up four conspicuous *horns* toward the [c]four
winds of heaven.
9 Out of one of them came forth a rather [a]small horn which
grew exceedingly great toward the south, toward the east, and
toward the [1b]Beautiful *Land.*
10 It grew up to the host of heaven and caused some of the
host and some of the [a]stars to fall to the earth, and it [b]trampled
them down.
11 It even [a]magnified *itself* [1]to be equal with the [2]Commander
of the host; and it removed the [b]regular sacrifice from Him, and
the place of His sanctuary was thrown down.
12 And on account of transgression the host will be given over
to the horn along with the regular sacrifice; and it will [a]fling
truth to the ground and perform *its will* and prosper.
13 Then I heard a [a]holy one speaking, and another holy one said
to that particular one who was speaking, "[b]How long will the
vision *about* the regular sacrifice apply, [1]while the transgression
causes horror, so as to allow both the holy place and the host
[2]to be [c]trampled?"
14 He said to me, "For [a]2,300 evenings *and* mornings; then
the holy place will be [1]properly restored."
15 When [a]I, Daniel, had seen the vision, I sought [1]to
understand it; and behold, standing before me was one [2]who
looked like a [b]man.
16 And I heard the voice of a man between *the banks of* Ulai,
and he called out and said, "[a]Gabriel, give this *man* an
understanding of the vision."
17 So he came near to where I was standing, and when he came
I was frightened and [a]fell on my face; but he said to me, "Son of
man, understand that the vision pertains to the [b]time of the end."
18 Now while he was talking with me, I [a]sank into a deep sleep
with my face to the ground; but he [b]touched me and made me
stand [1]upright.
19 He said, "Behold, I am going to [a]let you know what will

4 [1]Lit *hand* [a]Deut 33:17; 1 Kin 22:11; Ezek 34:21 [b]Dan 11:3
5 [1]Lit *buck* [a]Dan 8:8, 21; 11:3
6 [1]Or *river*
7 [1]Lit *hand*
8 [a]2 Chr 26:16; Dan 5:20 [b]Dan 8:22 [c]Dan 7:2; Rev 7:1
9 [1]I.e. Palestine [a]Dan 8:23 [b]Ps 48:2; Dan 11:16, 41
10 [a]Is 14:13; Jer 48:26; Rev 12:4 [b]Dan 7:7; 8:7
11 [1]Lit *up to the* [2]Or *Prince* [a]2 Kin 19:22, 23; 2 Chr 32:15-17; Is 37:23; Dan 8:25; 11:36, 37 [b]Ezek 46:14; Dan 11:31; 12:11
12 [a]Is 59:14
13 [1]Or possibly *and the transgression that horrifies* [2]Lit *as a trampling* [a]Dan 4:13, 23; 1 Pet 1:12 [b]Ps 74:10; 79:5; Is 6:11; Dan 12:6, 8; Rev 6:10 [c]Is 63:18; Jer 12:10; Luke 21:24; Heb 10:29; Rev 11:2
14 [1]Lit *vindicated* [a]Dan 7:25; 12:7, 11; Rev 11:2, 3; 12:14; 13:5
15 [1]Lit *under-standing* [2]Lit *like the appearance of a man* [a]Dan 8:1 [b]Dan 7:13; 10:16, 18
16 [a]Dan 9:21; Luke 1:19, 26
17 [a]Ezek 1:28; 44:4; Dan 2:46; Rev 1:17 [b]Dan 8:19; 11:35, 40
18 [1]Lit *on my standing* [a]Dan 10:9; Luke 9:32 [b]Ezek 2:2; Dan 10:10, 16, 18
19 [a]Dan 8:15-17

occur at the final period of the indignation, for *it* pertains to the appointed time of the end.

20 "The [a]ram which you saw with the two horns represents the kings of Media and Persia.

21 "The shaggy [1]goat *represents* the [2]kingdom of Greece, and the large horn that is between his eyes is the first king.

22 "The [a]broken *horn* and the four *horns that* arose in its place *represent* four kingdoms *which* will arise from *his* nation, although not with his power.

23 "In the latter period of their [1]rule,
When the transgressors have [2]run *their course,*
A king will arise,
[3]Insolent and skilled in [4]intrigue.

24 "His power will be mighty, but not by his *own* power,
And he will [1a]destroy to an extraordinary degree
And prosper and perform *his will;*
He will [1]destroy mighty men and [2]the holy people.

25 "And through his shrewdness
He will cause deceit to succeed by his [1]influence;
And he will magnify *himself* in his heart,
And he will [2]destroy many while *they are* [3]at ease.
He will even [4a]oppose the Prince of princes,
But he will be broken [b]without [1]human agency.

26 "The vision of the evenings and mornings
Which has been told is [a]true;
But [b]keep the vision secret,
For *it* pertains to many [c]days *in the future.*"

27 Then I, Daniel, was [1a]exhausted and sick for days. Then I got up *again* and [b]carried on the king's business; but I was astounded at the vision, and there was none to [2]explain *it.*

Chapter 9 Theme

9 In the first year of [a]Darius the son of Ahasuerus, of Median descent, who was made king over the kingdom of the Chaldeans—

2 in the first year of his reign, I, Daniel, observed in the books the number of the years which was *revealed as* the word of the LORD to [a]Jeremiah the prophet for the completion of the desolations of Jerusalem, *namely,* [a]seventy years.

3 So I [1]gave my attention to the Lord God to seek *Him by* prayer and supplications, with fasting, sackcloth and ashes.

4 I prayed to the LORD my God and confessed and said, "Alas, O Lord, the [a]great and awesome God, who [b]keeps His covenant and lovingkindness for those who love Him and keep His commandments,

5 [a]we have sinned, committed iniquity, acted wickedly and [b]rebelled, even [c]turning aside from Your commandments and ordinances.

6 "Moreover, we have not [a]listened to Your servants the prophets, who spoke in Your name to our kings, our princes, our fathers and all the people of the land.

20 [a]Dan 8:3

21 [1]Lit *buck* [2]Lit *king*

22 [a]Dan 8:8

23 [1]Or *kingdom* [2]Lit *finished* [3]Lit *Strong of face* [4]Or *ambiguous speech*

24 [1]Or *corrupt* [2]Lit *people of the saints* [a]Dan 8:11-13; 11:36; 12:7

25 [1]Lit *hand* [2]Or *corrupt* [3]Or *secure* [4]Lit *stand against* [a]Dan 8:11 [b]Job 34:20; Dan 2:34, 45

26 [a]Dan 10:1 [b]Ezek 12:27; Dan 12:4, 9; Rev 22:10 [c]Dan 10:14

27 [1]Or *done in* [2]Lit *make me understand* [a]Dan 7:28; 8:17; Hab 3:16 [b]Dan 2:48

9:1 [a]Dan 5:31; 11:1

2 [a]2 Chr 36:21; Ezra 1:1; Jer 25:11, 12; 29:10; Zech 7:5

3 [1]Lit *set my face*

4 [a]Deut 7:21; Neh 9:32 [b]Deut 7:9

5 [a]1 Kin 8:48; Neh 9:33; Ps 106:6; Is 64:5-7; Jer 14:7 [b]Lam 1:18, 20 [c]Ps 119:176; Is 53:6; Dan 9:11

6 [a]2 Chr 36:16; Jer 44:4, 5

7 "[a]Righteousness belongs to You, O Lord, but to us [1b]open
shame, as it is this day—to the men of Judah, the inhabitants of
Jerusalem and all Israel, those who are nearby and those who
are far away in [c]all the countries to which You have driven them,
because of their unfaithful deeds which they have committed
against You.
8 "[1]Open shame belongs to us, O Lord, to our kings, our
princes and our fathers, because we have sinned against You.
9 "To the Lord our God *belong* [a]compassion and forgiveness,
[1]for we have [b]rebelled against Him;
10 nor have we obeyed the voice of the LORD our God, to walk
in His [1]teachings which He [a]set before us through His servants
the prophets.
11 "Indeed [a]all Israel has transgressed Your law and turned
aside, not obeying Your voice; so the [b]curse has been poured
out on us, along with the oath which is written in the law of
Moses the servant of God, for we have sinned against Him.
12 "Thus He has [a]confirmed His words which He had spoken
against us and against our [1b]rulers who ruled us, to bring on us
great calamity; for under the whole heaven there has [c]not been
done *anything* like what was done to Jerusalem.
13 "As it is written in the [a]law of Moses, all this calamity has come
on us; yet we have [b]not [1]sought the favor of the LORD our God by
[c]turning from our iniquity and [2]giving attention to Your truth.
14 "Therefore the LORD has [1a]kept the calamity in store and
brought it on us; for the LORD our God is [b]righteous with
respect to all His deeds which He has done, but we have not
obeyed His voice.
15 "And now, O Lord our God, who have [a]brought Your people
out of the land of Egypt with a mighty hand and have [b]made a
name for Yourself, as it is this day—we have sinned, we have
been wicked.
16 "O Lord, in accordance with all Your [1]righteous acts, let
now Your [a]anger and Your wrath turn away from Your city Jerusalem, Your [b]holy mountain; for because of our sins and the
iniquities of our fathers, Jerusalem and Your people *have
become* a [c]reproach to all those around us.
17 "So now, our God, listen to the prayer of Your servant and to
his supplications, and for [1]Your sake, O Lord, [a]let Your face
shine on Your [b]desolate sanctuary.
18 "O my God, [a]incline Your ear and hear! Open Your eyes and
[b]see our desolations and the city which is [c]called by Your name;
for we are not [1d]presenting our supplications before You on
account of [2]any merits of our own, but on account of Your great
compassion.
19 "O Lord, hear! O Lord, forgive! O Lord, listen and take
action! For Your own sake, O my God, [a]do not delay, because
Your city and Your people are called by Your name."
20 Now while I was [a]speaking and praying, and [b]confessing
my sin and the sin of my people Israel, and [1]presenting my
supplication before the LORD my God in behalf of the holy
mountain of my God,

7 [1]Lit *the shame of face* [a]Jer 23:6; 33:16; Dan 9:18 [b]Ps 44:15; Jer 2:26, 27; 3:25 [c]Deut 4:27

8 [1]Lit *The shame of face*

9 [1]Or *though* [a]Neh 9:17; Ps 130:4 [b]Ps 106:43; Jer 14:7; Dan 9:5, 6

10 [1]Or *laws* [a]2 Kin 17:13-15; 18:12

11 [a]Is 1:3, 4; Jer 8:5-10 [b]Deut 27:15-26

12 [1]Lit *judges who judged us* [a]Is 44:26; Jer 44:2-6; Lam 2:17; Zech 1:6 [b]Job 12:17; Ps 82:2-7; 148:11 [c]Lam 1:12; 2:13; Ezek 5:9

13 [1]Lit *softened the face of* [2]Or *having insight into* [a]Lev 26:14-45; Deut 28:15-68; Dan 9:11 [b]Job 36:13; Is 9:13; Jer 2:30; 5:3 [c]Jer 31:18

14 [1]Lit *watched over the evil* [a]Jer 31:28; 44:27 [b]Ps 51:14; Dan 9:7

15 [a]Deut 5:15 [b]Neh 9:10; Jer 32:20

16 [1]Lit *righteousnesses* [a]Jer 32:31, 32 [b]Ps 87:1-3; Dan 9:20; Joel 3:17; Zech 8:3 [c]Ezek 5:14

17 [1]Lit *the sake of the Lord* [a]Num 6:24-26; Ps 80:3, 7, 19 [b]Lam 5:18

18 [1]Lit *causing to fall* [2]Lit *our righteousnesses* [a]Is 37:17 [b]Ps 80:14 [c]Jer 7:10-12 [d]Jer 36:7

19 [a]Ps 44:23; 74:10, 11

20 [1]Lit *causing to fall* [a]Ps 145:18; Is 58:9; Dan 9:3; 10:12 [b]Is 6:5

21 while I was still speaking in prayer, then the man [a]Gabriel,
whom I had seen in the vision [1]previously, [2]came to me [3]in *my*
extreme weariness about the time of the [b]evening offering.
22 He gave *me* instruction and talked with me and said, "O
Daniel, I have now come forth to give you insight with
[a]understanding.
23 "At the [a]beginning of your supplications the [1]command was
issued, and I have come to tell *you,* for you are [2b]highly
esteemed; so give heed to the message and gain [c]understanding
of the vision.
24 "Seventy [1a]weeks have been decreed for your people and
your holy city, to [2]finish the transgression, to [3]make an end of
sin, to [b]make atonement for iniquity, to bring in [c]everlasting
righteousness, to seal up vision and [4]prophecy and to anoint
the most holy *place.*
25 "So you are to know and discern *that* from the issuing of a
[1a]decree to restore and rebuild Jerusalem until [2b]Messiah the
[c]Prince *there will be* seven weeks and sixty-two weeks; it will
be built again, with [3]plaza and moat, even in times of distress.
26 "Then after the sixty-two weeks the [1]Messiah will be [a]cut
off and have [2]nothing, and the people of the prince who is to
come will [b]destroy the city and the sanctuary. And [3]its end *will*
come with a [c]flood; even to the end [4]there will be war;
desolations are determined.
27 "And he will make a firm covenant with the many for one
week, but in the middle of the week he will put a stop to sacrifice
and grain offering; and on the wing of [1a]abominations *will come*
one who [2]makes desolate, even until a [b]complete destruction, one
that is decreed, is poured out on the one who [2]makes desolate."

Chapter 10 Theme ____________________

10 In the third year of [a]Cyrus king of Persia a [1]message was
revealed to [b]Daniel, who was named Belteshazzar; and the
[1c]message was true and *one of* great [2]conflict, but he understood the [1]message and had an [d]understanding of the vision.
2 In those days, I, Daniel, had been [a]mourning for three entire
weeks.
3 I [a]did not eat any [1]tasty food, nor did meat or wine enter
my mouth, nor did I use any ointment at all until the entire
three weeks were completed.
4 On the twenty-fourth day of the first month, while I was by
the bank of the great [a]river, that is, the [1]Tigris,
5 I lifted my eyes and looked, and behold, there was a certain
man [a]dressed in linen, whose waist was [b]girded with *a belt of*
pure [c]gold of Uphaz.
6 His body also *was* like [1]beryl, his face [2]had the appearance
of lightning, [a]his eyes were like flaming torches, his arms and
feet like the gleam of polished bronze, and the sound of his
words like the sound of a [3]tumult.
7 Now I, Daniel, [a]alone saw the vision, while the [b]men who
were with me did not see the vision; nevertheless, a great

INSIGHT

The word *weeks* in Hebrew is ***Shabuim*** and means "sevens." There is no indication whether the "sevens" refer to seven days, weeks, months, or years. Seventy sevens (or weeks) is 490. So, if the six things of Daniel 9:24 were not completed within 490 days, weeks, or months, it would be logical to assume that the *sevens* refers to sevens of years. A decree to rebuild and restore Jerusalem was issued by King Artaxerxes of Medo-Persia in 445 B.C. (see Nehemiah 1:1–2:8). This began the 490 years.

21 [1]Lit *at the beginning* [2]Lit *was reaching;* or *touching* [3]Lit *wearied with weariness* [a]Dan 8:16; Luke 1:19, 26 [b]Ex 29:39; 1 Kin 18:36; Ezra 9:4

22 [a]Dan 8:16; 10:21; Zech 1:9

23 [1]Lit *word went out* [2]Lit *desirable;* or *precious* [a]Dan 10:12 [b]Dan 10:11, 19 [c]Matt 24:15

24 [1]Or *units of seven,* and so throughout the ch [2]Or *restrain* [3]Another reading is *seal up sins* [4]Lit *prophet* [a]Lev 25:8; Num 14:34; Ezek 4:5, 6 [b]2 Chr 29:24; Is 53:10; Rom 5:10 [c]Is 51:6, 8; 56:1; Jer 23:5, 6; Rom 3:21, 22

25 [1]Lit *word* [2]Or *an anointed one* [3]Or *streets* [a]Ezra 4:24; 6:1-15; Neh 2:1-8; 3:1 [b]John 1:41; 4:25 [c]Is 9:6; Dan 8:11, 25

26 [1]Or *anointed one* [2]Or *no one* [3]Or *his* [4]Or *war will be decreed for desolations* [a]Is 53:8; Mark 9:12; Luke 24:26 [b]Matt 24:2; Mark 13:2; Luke 19:43, 44 [c]Nah 1:8

27 [1]Or *detestable things* [2]Or *causes horror* [a]Dan 11:31; Matt 24:15; Mark 13:14; Luke 21:20 [b]Is 10:23; 28:22

10:1 [1]Lit *word* [2]Or *warfare* [a]Dan 1:21; 6:28 [b]Dan 1:7 [c]Dan 8:26 [d]Dan 1:17; 2:21

2 [a]Ezra 9:4, 5; Neh 1:4

3 [1]Lit *bread of desirability* [a]Dan 6:18

4 [1]Heb *Hiddekel* [a]Ezek 1:3; Dan 8:2

5 [a]Ezek 9:2; Dan 12:6, 7 [b]Rev 1:13; 15:6 [c]Jer 10:9

6 [1]Or *yellow serpentine* [2]Lit *like* [3]Or *roaring* [a]Rev 1:14; 2:18; 19:12

7 [a]2 Kin 6:17-20 [b]Acts 9:7

History of Israel's Relationship to the Kings of Daniel 11

Alexander the Great
336-323 B.C.
The Large Horn of the Shaggy Goat of Greece (8:21)
Twenty-two years after Alexander's death, Greece was divided among four of his generals (8:22):

Lysimachus	**Cassander**	**Ptolemy I Soter**	**Seleucus I Nicator**
took Thrace and Bithynia	took Macedonia	took Egypt	took Syria

Only Ptolemy I Soter and Seleucus I Nicator relate to Israel.

Kings of the South—Egypt		**Kings of the North—Syria**
*1. Ptolemy I Soter, 323-285 B.C. (11:5)		1. Seleucus I Nicator, 312-281 B.C. (11:5)
		2. Antiochus I Soter (not referred to in Daniel)
*2. Ptolemy II Philadelphus, 285-245 B.C. (11:6)	*Marriage*	3. Antiochus II Theos, 262-246 B.C. (11:6)
*3. Ptolemy III Euergetes, 245-221 B.C. (11:7-9)	*2 Wars*	4. Seleucus II Callinicus, 246-226 B.C. (11:7-9)
		5. Seleucus III Ceraunus, 226-223 B.C. (11:10)
*4. Ptolemy IV Philopator, 221-203 B.C. (11:11, 12)	*2 Wars*	*6. Antiochus III the Great, 223-187 B.C. (11:10, 11, 13, 15-19)
*5. Ptolemy V Epiphanes, 203-181 B.C. (11:14, 15, 17)	*War/Marriage*	*7. Seleucus IV Philopator, 187-175 B.C. (11:20)
6. Ptolemy VI Philometor, 181-145 B.C. (11:25)		*8. **Antiochus IV Epiphanes**, 175-163 B.C. (11:21-35) *(younger son of Antiochus III the Great)*

** These kings ruled Israel*

[c]dread fell on them, and they ran away to hide themselves.
8 So I was [a]left alone and saw this great vision; yet [b]no strength
was left in me, for my [1]natural color turned to [2]a deathly pallor,
and I retained no strength.
9 But I heard the sound of his words; and as soon as I heard
the sound of his words, I [a]fell into a deep sleep on my face,
with my face to the ground.
10 Then behold, a hand [a]touched me and set me trembling on
my [1]hands and knees.
11 He said to me, "O [a]Daniel, man of [1]high esteem, [b]understand the words that I am about to tell you and [c]stand [2]upright,
for I have now been sent to you." And when he had spoken
this word to me, I stood up [d]trembling.
12 Then he said to me, "[a]Do not be afraid, Daniel, for from
the first day that you set your heart on understanding *this* and
on [b]humbling yourself before your God, your words were heard,
and I have come in response [c]to your words.
13 "But the prince of the kingdom of Persia was [1]withstanding
me for twenty-one days; then behold, [a]Michael, one of the chief
princes, came to help me, for I had been left there with the
kings of Persia.
14 "Now I have come to [a]give you an understanding of what
will happen to your people in the [1b]latter days, for the vision
pertains to [c]the days yet *future*."
15 When he had spoken to me according to these words, I
[1]turned my face toward the ground and became [a]speechless.

7 [c]Ezek 12:18
8 [1]Lit *splendor* [2]Lit *corruption* [a]Gen 32:24 [b]Dan 7:28; 8:27; Hab 3:16
9 [a]Gen 15:12; Job 4:13; Dan 8:18
10 [1]Lit *knees and the palms of my hands* [a]Jer 1:9; Dan 8:18
11 [1]Lit *desirability; or preciousness* [2]Lit *upon your standing* [a]Dan 10:19 [b]Dan 8:16, 17 [c]Ezek 2:1 [d]Job 4:14, 15
12 [a]Is 41:10, 14; Dan 10:19 [b]Dan 9:20-23; 10:2, 3 [c]Acts 10:30, 31
13 [1]Lit *standing opposite* [a]Dan 10:21; 12:1; Jude 9; Rev 12:7
14 [1]Lit *end of the days* [a]Dan 8:16; 9:22 [b]Deut 31:29; Dan 2:28 [c]Dan 8:26; 12:4, 9
15 [1]Lit *set* [a]Ezek 3:26; 24:27; Luke 1:20

16 And behold, [1a]one who resembled a human being was
[b]touching my lips; then I opened my mouth and spoke and said to
him who was standing before me, "O my lord, as a result of the
vision [2c]anguish has come upon me, and I have retained no strength.
17 "For [a]how can such a servant of my lord talk with such as
my lord? As for me, there remains just now [b]no strength in me,
nor has any breath been left in me."
18 Then *this* one with human appearance touched me again
and [a]strengthened me.
19 He said, "O man of [1]high esteem, [a]do not be afraid. Peace
[2]be with you; take [b]courage and be courageous!" Now as soon
as he spoke to me, I received strength and said, "May my lord
speak, for you have [c]strengthened me."
20 Then he said, "Do you [1]understand why I came to you? But
I shall now return to fight against the [2]prince of Persia; so I am
going forth, and behold, the [2a]prince of [3]Greece is about to come.
21 "However, I will tell you what is inscribed in the writing of
[a]truth. Yet there is no one who [1]stands firmly with me against
these *forces* except [b]Michael your prince.

INSIGHT

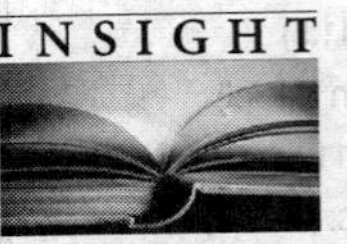

Read about the Persian, Greek, and Maccabean periods of Israel's history on pages 2089-2093 in this Bible. The next four Persian kings after Cyrus were Cambyses, Darius I, Xerxes, and Artaxerxes.

Chapter 11 Theme ____________________

11

"In the [a]first year of Darius the Mede, [1]I arose to be [2]an
encouragement and a protection for him.
2 "And now I will tell you the [a]truth. Behold, three more kings
are going to arise [1]in Persia. Then a fourth will gain far more riches
than all *of them;* as soon as he becomes strong through his riches,
[2]he will arouse the whole *empire* against the realm of [3b]Greece.
3 "And a [a]mighty king will arise, and he will rule with great
authority and [b]do as he pleases.
4 "But as soon as he has arisen, his kingdom will be broken
up and parceled out [a]toward the [b]four [1]points of the compass,
though not to his *own* descendants, nor according to his authority
which he wielded, for his sovereignty will be [c]uprooted and *given*
to others besides [2]them.
5 "Then the [a]king of the South will grow strong, [1]along with
one of his princes [2]who will gain ascendancy over him and
obtain dominion; his domain *will be* a great dominion *indeed.*
6 "After some years they will form an alliance, and the daughter
of the king of the South will come to the [a]king of the North to
carry out [1]a peaceful arrangement. But she will not retain her
[2]position of power, nor will he remain with his [3]power, but she will
be given up, along with those who brought her in and the one
who sired her as well as he who supported her in *those* times.
7 "But one of the [1]descendants of her line will arise in his place,
and he will come against *their* army and enter the [a]fortress of
the king of the North, and he will deal with them and display
great strength.
8 "Also their [a]gods with their [1]metal images *and* their precious
vessels of silver and gold he will take into captivity to Egypt,
and he on his part will [2]refrain from *attacking* the king of the
North for *some* years.

16 [1]Lit *as a likeness of sons of man* [2]Lit *my pains have* [a]Dan 8:15 [b]Is 6:7; Jer 1:9 [c]Dan 7:15, 28; 8:17, 27; 10:8, 9

17 [a]Ex 24:10, 11; Is 6:1-5 [b]Dan 10:8

18 [a]Is 35:3, 4

19 [1]Lit *desirability;* or *preciousness* [2]Lit *to you* [a]Judg 6:23; Is 43:1; Dan 10:12 [b]Josh 1:6, 7, 9; Is 35:4 [c]Ps 138:3; 2 Cor 12:9

20 [1]Lit *know* [2]I.e. Satanic angel [3]Heb *Javan* [a]Dan 8:21; 11:2

21 [1]Lit *shows himself strong* [a]Dan 12:4 [b]Dan 10:13; Rev 12:7

11:1 [1]Lit *my standing up* was [2]Lit *for a strengthener* [a]Dan 5:31; 9:1

2 [1]Lit *for* [2]Or they *all will stir up the realm of Greece* [3]Heb *Javan* [a]Dan 8:26; 10:1, 21 [b]Dan 8:21; 10:20

3 [a]Dan 8:5, 21 [b]Dan 5:19; 8:4; 11:16, 36

4 [1]Lit *winds of the heaven* [2]I.e. his descendants [a]Dan 8:8, 22 [b]Jer 49:36; Ezek 37:9; Dan 7:2; 8:8; Zech 2:6; Rev 7:1 [c]Jer 12:15, 17; 18:7

5 [1]Lit *and* [2]Lit *and he* [a]Dan 11:9, 11, 14, 25, 40

6 [1]Or *an equitable agreement* [2]Lit *strength of arm* [3]Lit *arm* [a]Dan 11:7, 13, 15, 40

7 [1]Lit *branch of her roots* [a]Dan 11:19, 38, 39

8 [1]Lit *cast images* [2]Or *stand against the king* [a]Is 37:19; 46:1, 2; Jer 43:12, 13

9 "Then [1]the latter will enter the realm of the king of the South, but will return to his *own* land.

10 "His sons will [1]mobilize and assemble a multitude of great forces; and one of them will keep on coming and [a]overflow and pass through, that he may [2]again wage war up to his *very* fortress.

11 "The [a]king of the South will be enraged and go forth and fight [1]with the king of the North. Then the latter will raise a great multitude, but *that* multitude will be given into [2]the hand of the *former.*

12 "When the multitude is carried away, his heart will be lifted up, and he will cause tens of thousands to fall; yet he will not prevail.

13 "For the king of the North will again raise a greater multitude than the former, and [1]after an [a]interval of some years he will [2]press on with a great army and much equipment.

14 "Now in those times many will rise up against the king of the South; the violent ones among your people will also lift themselves up in order to fulfill the vision, but they will [1]fall down.

15 "Then the king of the North will come, cast up a [a]siege ramp and capture a well-fortified city; and the forces of the South will not stand *their ground,* not even [1]their choicest troops, for there will be no strength to make a stand.

16 "But he who comes against him will [a]do as he pleases, and [b]no one will *be able to* withstand him; he will also stay *for a time* in the [1c]Beautiful Land, with destruction in his hand.

17 "He will [a]set his face to come with the power of his whole kingdom, [1]bringing with him [2]a proposal of peace which he will put into effect; he will also give him the daughter of women to ruin it. But she will not take a stand *for him* or be [3]on his side.

18 "Then he will turn his face to the [a]coastlands and capture many. But a commander will put a stop to his scorn against him; moreover, he will [b]repay him for his scorn.

19 "So he will turn his face toward the fortresses of his own land, but he will [a]stumble and fall and be [b]found no more.

20 "Then in his place one will arise who will [a]send an [1]oppressor through the [2]Jewel of *his* kingdom; yet within a few days he will be shattered, though not in anger nor in battle.

21 "In his place a despicable person will arise, on whom the honor of kingship has not been conferred, but he will come in a time of tranquility and [a]seize the kingdom by intrigue.

22 "The overflowing [a]forces will be flooded away before him and shattered, and also the prince of the covenant.

23 "After an alliance is made with him he will practice deception, and he will go up and gain power with a small *force of* people.

24 "[1]In a time of tranquility he will enter the [a]richest *parts* of the [2]realm, and he will accomplish what his fathers never did, nor his [3]ancestors; he will distribute plunder, booty and possessions among them, and he will devise his schemes against strongholds, but *only* for a time.

25 "He will stir up his strength and [1]courage against the [a]king of the South with a large army; so the king of the South will mobilize an extremely large and mighty army for war; but he will not stand, for schemes will be devised against him.

9 [1]Lit *he will,* and so throughout the ch

10 [1]Or *wage war* [2]Or *return and wage* [a]Is 8:8; Jer 46:7, 8; 51:42; Dan 11:26, 40

11 [1]Lit *with him, with* [2]Lit *his hand* [a]Dan 11:5

13 [1]Lit *at the end of the times, years* [2]Or *keep on coming* [a]Dan 4:16; 12:7

14 [1]Lit *stumble,* and so throughout the ch

15 [1]Lit *the people of its choice ones* [a]Jer 6:6; Ezek 4:2; 17:17

16 [1]I.e. Palestine [a]Dan 5:19; 11:3, 36 [b]Josh 1:5 [c]Dan 8:9; 11:41

17 [1]Lit *and* [2]Lit *equitable things* [3]Lit *for him;* i.e. for her father [a]2 Kin 12:17; Ezek 4:3, 7

18 [a]Gen 10:5; Is 66:19; Jer 2:10; 31:10; Zeph 2:11 [b]Hos 12:14

19 [a]Ps 27:2; Jer 46:6 [b]Job 20:8; Ps 37:36; Ezek 26:21

20 [1]Or *exactor* of tribute [2]Lit *adornment;* i.e. probably Jerusalem and its temple [a]Is 60:17

21 [a]2 Sam 15:6

22 [a]Dan 9:26; 11:10

24 [1]Lit *Into tranquility and the richest . . . he will enter* [2]Or *province* [3]Lit *fathers' fathers* [a]Num 13:20; Neh 9:25; Ezek 34:14

25 [1]Lit *heart* [a]Dan 11:5

26 "Those who eat his choice food will [1]destroy him, and his
army will [2a]overflow, but many will fall down slain.
27 "As for both kings, their hearts will be *intent* on [a]evil, and
they will [b]speak lies *to each other* at the same table; but it will
not succeed, for the [c]end is still *to come* at the appointed time.
28 "Then he will return to his land with much [1]plunder; but
his heart will be *set* against the holy covenant, and he will take
action and *then* return to his *own* land.
29 "At the appointed time he will return and come into the
South, but [1]this last time it will not turn out the way it did before.
30 "For ships of [1a]Kittim will come against him; therefore he
will be disheartened and will return and become enraged at
the holy covenant and take action; so he will come back and
show regard for those who forsake the holy covenant.
31 "Forces from him will arise, [a]desecrate the sanctuary fortress,
and do away with the regular sacrifice. And they will set up the
[b]abomination [1]of desolation.
32 "By [a]smooth *words* he will [1]turn to godlessness those who
act wickedly toward the covenant, but the people who know
their God will display [b]strength and take action.
33 "[1a]Those who have insight among the people will give
understanding to the many; yet they will [b]fall by sword and by
flame, by captivity and by plunder for *many* days.
34 "Now when they fall they will be granted a little help, and
many will [a]join with them in [b]hypocrisy.
35 "Some of [1]those who have insight will fall, in order to [a]refine,
[b]purge and make them [2c]pure until the [d]end time; because *it is*
still *to come* at the appointed time.
36 "Then the king will [a]do as he pleases, and he will exalt and
[b]magnify himself above every god and will [c]speak [1]monstrous
things against the [d]God of gods; and he will prosper until the
[e]indignation is finished, for that which is [f]decreed will be done.
37 "He will show no regard for the [1]gods of his fathers or for
the desire of women, nor will he show regard for any *other*
god; for he will magnify himself above *them* all.
38 "But [1]instead he will honor a god of fortresses, a god whom
his fathers did not know; he will honor *him* with gold, silver,
costly stones and treasures.
39 "He will take action against the strongest of fortresses with
the help of a foreign god; he will give great honor to [1]those
who acknowledge *him* and will cause them to rule over the
many, and will parcel out land for a price.
40 "At the [a]end time the [b]king of the South will collide with him,
and the [c]king of the North will [d]storm against him with chariots,
with horsemen and with many ships; and he will enter
countries, [e]overflow *them* and pass through.
41 "He will also enter the [1a]Beautiful Land, and many *countries*
will fall; but these will be rescued out of his hand: Edom,
[b]Moab and the foremost of the sons of [c]Ammon.
42 "Then he will stretch out his hand against *other* countries,
and the land of Egypt will not escape.

26 [1]Lit *break* [2]Or *be swept away, and many* [a]Dan 11:10, 40

27 [a]Ps 52:1; 64:6 [b]Ps 12:2; Jer 9:3-5; 41:1-3 [c]Dan 8:19; 11:35, 40; Hab 2:3

28 [1]Lit *possessions*

29 [1]Lit *it will not happen as the first and as the last*

30 [1]I.e. Cyprus [a]Gen 10:4; Num 24:24; Is 23:1, 12; Jer 2:10

31 [1]Lit *that makes desolate;* or *that causes horror* [a]Dan 8:11-13; 12:11 [b]Dan 9:27; Matt 24:15; Mark 13:14

32 [1]Or *pollute those* [a]Dan 11:21, 34 [b]Mic 5:7-9; Zech 9:13-16; 10:3-6

33 [1]Or *Instructors of the people* [a]Mal 2:7 [b]Matt 24:9; John 16:2; Heb 11:36-38

34 [a]Matt 7:15; Acts 20:29, 30 [b]Dan 11:21, 32; Rom 16:18

35 [1]Or *the instructors* [2]Lit *white* [a]Deut 8:16; Prov 17:3; Dan 12:10; Zech 13:9; Mal 3:2, 3 [b]John 15:2 [c]Rev 7:14 [d]Dan 11:27

36 [1]Lit *extraordinary* [a]Dan 5:19; 11:3, 16 [b]Is 14:13; Dan 5:20; 8:11, 25; 2 Thess 2:4 [c]Rev 13:5, 6 [d]Deut 10:17; Ps 136:2; Dan 2:47 [e]Is 10:25; 26:20; Dan 8:19 [f]Dan 9:27

37 [1]Or *God*

38 [1]Lit *in his place*

39 [1]Lit *the one who acknowledges*

40 [a]Dan 11:27, 35; 12:4, 9 [b]Dan 11:11, 25 [c]Dan 11:7, 13, 15 [d]Is 5:28; Jer 4:13 [e]Dan 11:10, 26

41 [1]I.e. Palestine [a]Dan 8:9; 11:16 [b]Jer 48:47 [c]Jer 49:6

43 "But he will [1]gain control over the hidden treasures of gold
and silver and over all the precious things of Egypt; and
[a]Libyans and [b]Ethiopians *will follow* at his [2]heels.
44 "But rumors from the East and from the North will disturb
him, and he will go forth with great wrath to destroy and
[1]annihilate many.
45 "He will pitch the tents of his royal pavilion between the
seas and the beautiful [a]Holy Mountain; yet he will come to his
end, and no one will help him.

Chapter 12 Theme ______________________________

12 "Now at that time [a]Michael, the great prince who stands
guard over the sons of your people, will arise. And there
will be a [b]time of distress [c]such as never occurred since there
was a nation until that time; and at that time your people,
everyone who is found written in the [d]book, will be rescued.
2 "[a]Many of those who sleep in the dust of the ground will
awake, [b]these to everlasting life, but the others to disgrace *and*
everlasting [1]contempt.
3 "[1]Those who have [a]insight will [b]shine brightly like the
brightness of the [2]expanse of heaven, and those who [c]lead the
many to righteousness, like the stars forever and ever.
4 "But as for you, Daniel, [a]conceal these words and [b]seal up
the book until the [c]end of time; [d]many will go back and forth,
and knowledge will increase."
5 Then I, Daniel, looked and behold, two others were standing,
one on this bank of the river and the other on that bank of the river.
6 And [a]one said to the man [b]dressed in linen, who was above
the waters of the river, "[c]How long *will it be* until the end of
these wonders?"
7 I heard the man dressed in linen, who was above the
waters of the river, [1]as he [a]raised his right hand and his left
toward heaven, and swore by [b]Him who lives forever that it
would be for a [2c]time, [2]times, and half *a* [2]*time;* and as soon as
[3]they finish [d]shattering the [4]power of the holy people, all these
events will be completed.
8 As for me, I heard but could not understand; so I said, "My
lord, what *will be* the [1]outcome of these *events?*"
9 He said, "Go *your way,* Daniel, for *these* words are concealed
and [a]sealed up until the end time.
10 "[a]Many will be purged, [1]purified and refined, but the [b]wicked
will act wickedly; and none of the wicked will understand, but
[2]those who [c]have insight will understand.
11 "From the time that the regular sacrifice is abolished and the
[1a]abomination of desolation is set up, *there will be* 1,290 days.
12 "How [a]blessed is he who keeps waiting and attains to the
[b]1,335 days!
13 "But as for you, go *your way* to the [1]end; then you will enter
into [a]rest and rise *again* for your [b]allotted portion at the end of
the [2]age."

43 [1]Or *rule over* [2]Lit *footsteps* [a]2 Chr 12:3; Nah 3:9 [b]2 Chr 12:3; Ezek 30:4, 5; Nah 3:9
44 [1]Lit *devote to destruction*
45 [a]Is 11:9; 27:13; 65:25; 66:20; Dan 9:16, 20
12:1 [a]Dan 10:13, 21; Rev 12:7 [b]Rev 7:14; 16:18 [c]Jer 30:7; Ezek 5:9; Dan 9:12; Matt 24:21; Mark 13:19 [d]Dan 7:10; 10:21
2 [1]Lit *abhorrence* [a]Is 26:19; Ezek 37:12-14 [b]Matt 25:46; John 5:28, 29
3 [1]Or *The instructors will* [2]Or *firmament* [a]Dan 11:33, 35; 12:10 [b]John 5:35 [c]Is 53:11; Dan 11:33
4 [a]Dan 8:26; 12:9 [b]Is 8:16; Dan 12:9; Rev 22:10 [c]Dan 8:17; 12:9, 13 [d]Is 11:9; 29:18, 19; Dan 11:33
6 [a]Dan 8:16; Zech 1:12, 13 [b]Ezek 9:2; Dan 10:5 [c]Dan 8:13; 12:8; Matt 24:3; Mark 13:4
7 [1]Lit *and* [2]I.e. year(s) [3]Lit *to finish* [4]Lit *hand* [a]Ezek 20:5; Rev 10:5, 6 [b]Dan 4:34 [c]Dan 7:25; Rev 12:14 [d]Dan 8:24; Luke 21:24
8 [1]Or *final end*
9 [a]Dan 12:4
10 [1]Lit *made white* [2]Or *the instructors will* [a]Zech 13:9 [b]Is 32:6, 7; Rev 22:11 [c]Dan 12:3; Hos 14:9; John 7:17; 8:47
11 [1]Or *horrible abomination* [a]Dan 9:27; 11:31; Matt 24:15; Mark 13:14
12 [a]Is 30:18 [b]Dan 8:14; Rev 11:2; 12:6; 13:5
13 [1]I.e. end of your life [2]Lit *days* [a]Is 57:2; Rev 14:13 [b]Ps 16:5

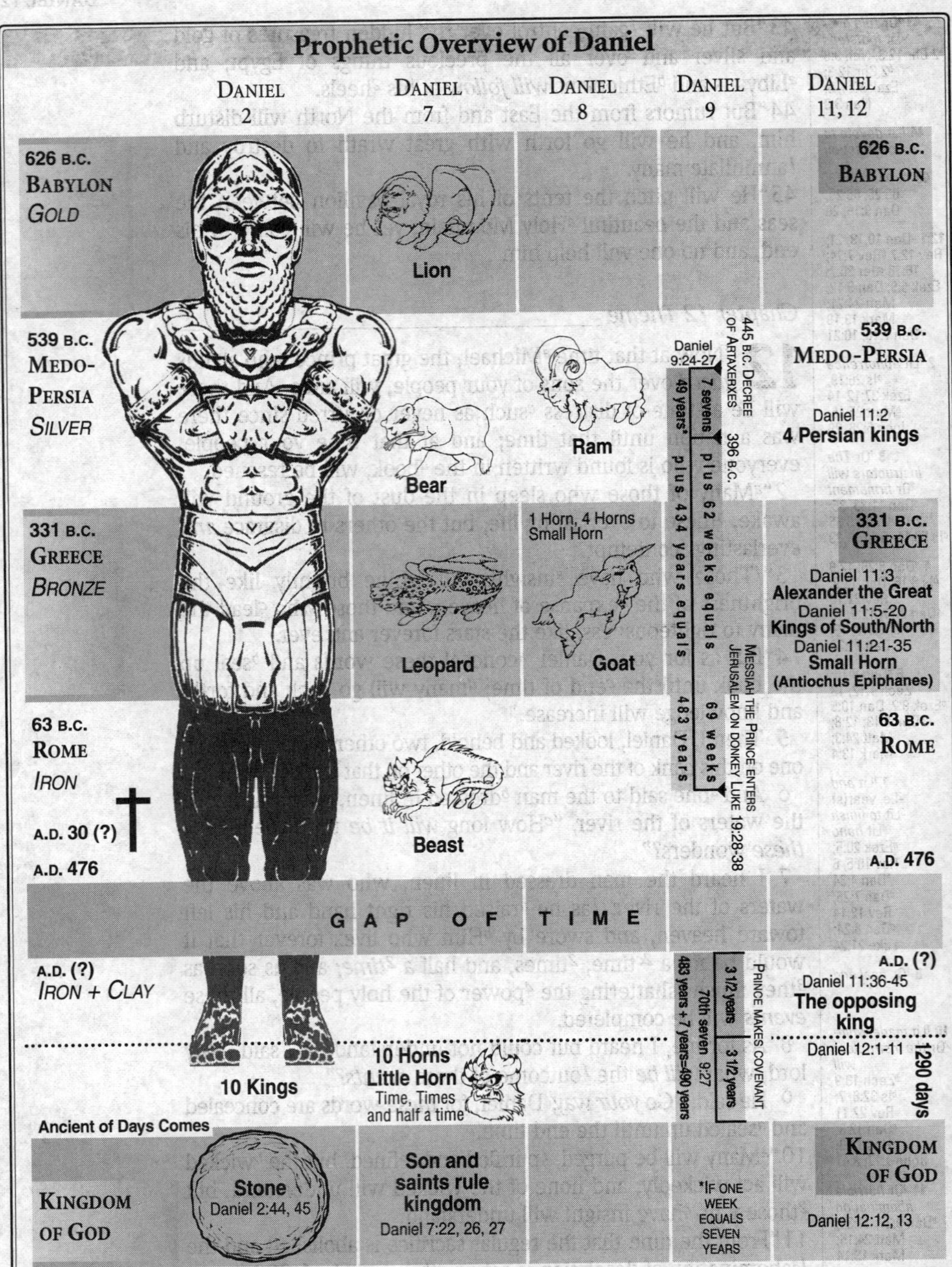
Prophetic Overview of Daniel
DANIEL 2
DANIEL 7
DANIEL 8
DANIEL 9
DANIEL 11, 12
626 B.C.
BABYLON
GOLD
Lion
626 B.C.
BABYLON
539 B.C.
MEDO-PERSIA
SILVER
Bear
Ram
Daniel 9:24-27
445 B.C. DECREE OF ARTAXERXES
7 sevens
49 years*
396 B.C.
plus 62 weeks equals
plus 434 years equals
69 weeks
483 years
MESSIAH THE PRINCE ENTERS JERUSALEM ON DONKEY LUKE 19:28-38
539 B.C.
MEDO-PERSIA
Daniel 11:2
4 Persian kings
331 B.C.
GREECE
BRONZE
Leopard
1 Horn, 4 Horns
Small Horn
Goat
331 B.C.
GREECE
Daniel 11:3
Alexander the Great
Daniel 11:5-20
Kings of South/North
Daniel 11:21-35
Small Horn
(Antiochus Epiphanes)
63 B.C.
ROME
IRON
A.D. 30 (?)
A.D. 476
Beast
63 B.C.
ROME
A.D. 476
GAP OF TIME
A.D. (?)
IRON + CLAY
PRINCE MAKES COVENANT
3 1/2 years
3 1/2 years
70th seven 9:27
483 years + 7 years=490 years
A.D. (?)
Daniel 11:36-45
The opposing king
Daniel 12:1-11
1290 days
10 Kings
10 Horns
Little Horn
Time, Times and half a time
Ancient of Days Comes
KINGDOM OF GOD
Stone
Daniel 2:44, 45
Son and saints rule kingdom
Daniel 7:22, 26, 27
*IF ONE WEEK EQUALS SEVEN YEARS
KINGDOM OF GOD
Daniel 12:12, 13

Daniel at a Glance

Theme of Daniel:

Author:

Date:

Purpose:

Key Words:

Segment Divisions

			Kings/ Kingdom	Chapter Themes
				1
				2
				3
				4
				5
				6
				7
				8
				9
				10
				11
				12

To get a better idea of the empires that play a crucial role in Daniel's prophecies, see the maps on pages 2246, 2247.

HOSEA הושע HOSHEA

God had entered into a covenant with Israel. Yet from the time of Jeroboam son of Nebat's reign through that of Jeroboam (II), son of Joash, the northern kingdom of Israel continued to play the harlot. God begged her to return to Him, but she would not listen. God's heart was grieved. If only Israel could understand; if only she could see what she was doing to the One who had betrothed her to Himself. If only she could see what her infidelity was doing to her children! Then the word of the Lord came to Hosea with a surprising message: "Go, take to yourself a wife of harlotry and have children."

Things to Do

Chapters 1–3

1. The first three chapters of Hosea provide the setting for Hosea's prophetic message to the northern kingdom of Israel. Read these three chapters as you would a story; just remember it is a true story.
2. Read through Hosea 1 again. As you read:
   a. Mark every occurrence of the word *harlotry*.
   b. In your notebook, draw a simple family tree that shows whom Hosea married and the names of their children. Under each family member write a brief description of what the person was like or what his or her name meant. If your Bible has reference notes in the margin, consult them if you have problems discerning the meanings of the children's names.
   c. Observe what this chapter teaches about the sons of Israel and the sons of Judah.
3. Now go back and read the introduction, which precedes "Things to Do." Then:
   a. Read 1 Kings 11:26-40, where God tells Jeroboam what He will do after King Solomon's death. Notice why God does what He does.
   b. Read 1 Kings 12, which tells of the fulfillment of God's word to Jeroboam. This chapter describes how the kingdom of Israel was divided into the northern kingdom, consisting of ten tribes, and the southern kingdom, consisting of two tribes. Pay attention to what Jeroboam does, since the northern kingdom no longer has access to Jerusalem and the temple, where they were to worship God three times a year.
   c. Read Hosea 1:2 again and then Hosea 3:1. Watch the word *as* in 3:1.
   d. In the margin of chapter 1 write why Hosea was told by God to marry Gomer. This will help you see why chapters 1 through 3 provide the setting for Hosea's message to the northern kingdom of Israel.
4. Keeping in mind what you have seen thus far, read Hosea 2 and do the following:
   a. Mark every occurrence of the word *harlotry* and the phrase *in that day*.
   b. Check your Bible's reference notes for 2:1 and either write in the text what *Ammi* and *Ruhamah* mean or highlight the reference note.
   c. Carefully observe what the children are to say to their mother and why.
   d. Read chapters 1 and 2 and underline every occurrence of *the Lord said* or *declares the Lord*. Then highlight or mark in a distinctive way every occurrence of *I will*. Then decide who is speaking throughout chapter 2 and who the *her* and *she* refer to.

e. Finally, read each *I will* in chapter 2. Watch the sequence of events and summarize the type of action taken in these "I wills." Also watch what happens to *her*. Record your insights in your notebook.

f. When you come to 2:23, read your Bible's reference notes on this verse and compare this with 1:6,9; 2:1.

5. In the light of all you have seen in chapters 1 and 2, read chapter 3 and do the following:

a. In a distinctive way mark the word *love.*

b. Summarize in your notebook what God tells Hosea to do and why.

c. Read 3:5 and mark *in the last days*, but before you choose how to mark it, see if you notice any parallel to *in that day* in chapter 2. If you think any of these references pertain to *the day of the Lord*, record your insights on the chart on page 2076.

6. Write the themes of each of the first three chapters on the HOSEA AT A GLANCE chart on page 1453. Then record the chapter theme in your Bible.

Chapters 4–14

1. Keeping in mind the setting of Hosea 1–3, read through Hosea 4–14 chapter by chapter. As you do:

a. Mark in a distinctive way the following key words (with their synonyms or pronouns): *harlot (harlotry), knowledge, covenant, return, woe, iniquity (guilt, wickedness, sin)*. Also mark the phrases *I will, from Me,* and *against Me (the Lord)*. Write these words on an index card and use it as a bookmark.

b. Also mark *Judah, Israel,* and *Ephraim,* each in its own distinctive way. As you do, remember that Ephraim was one of the ten tribes that comprised the northern kingdom of Israel. After Pekah took the throne in Israel, Tiglath-pileser, king of Assyria, came against him and took all of the kingdom captive in 733 B.C. except Ephraim and western Manasseh. Ten years later the remainder of the northern kingdom was completely destroyed by the Assyrians in 722 B.C. Thus Ephraim refers to what remained of Israel in those last ten years. Remember this as you read.

2. After you read a chapter and mark key words and the references to *Judah, Israel,* and *Ephraim,* compile your insights on the chart on page 1452.

3. As you read through the remainder of Hosea, remember that this is a passionate discourse because of God's relationship to Israel, the relationship of a husband to his wife (Ezekiel 16; Jeremiah 3:6-8), and of a father to his children (Hosea 11:1-3; Jeremiah 31:20). Remember also that because it is passionate, there is quite a bit of repetition, but not without purpose.

4. As you finish reading each chapter, summarize the theme of each one and record it on HOSEA AT A GLANCE and in your Bible. Also, when you finish the book, decide on its theme and record it on the chart. Then fill in the remainder of the chart.

Things to Think About

In 2 Corinthians 11:2 Paul wrote, "I am jealous for you with a godly jealousy; for I betrothed you to one husband, so that to Christ I might present you as a pure virgin."

1. Are there any similarities between your relationship to Jesus Christ and Israel's relationship to God? How are you pleasing your heavenly Bridegroom? Are you breaking God's heart in any way?

2. What do you need to do?

3. How do you think God will respond, and why?

THE RULERS AND PROPHETS OF HOSEA'S TIME

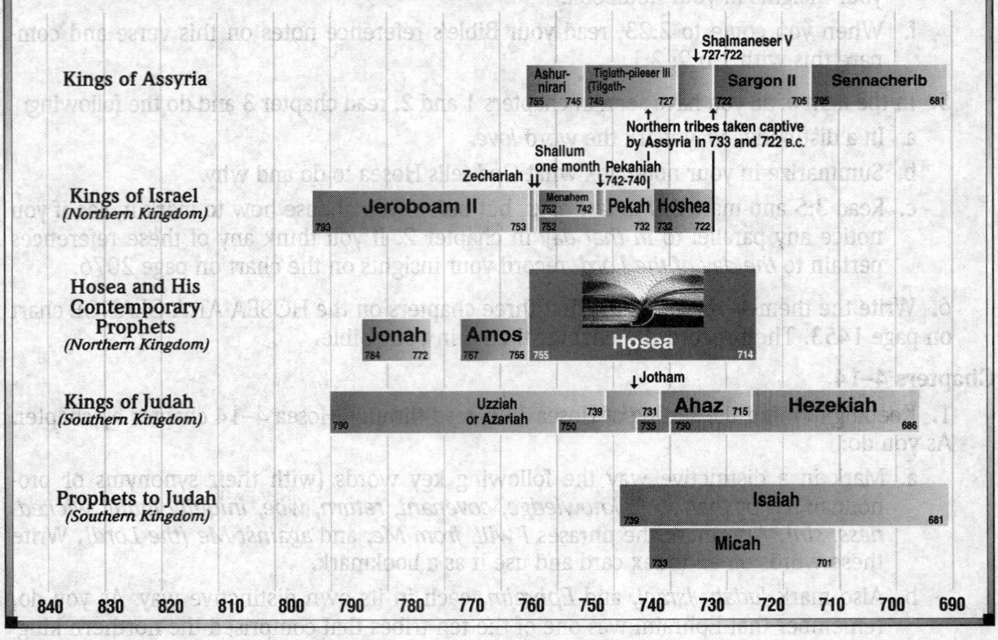

Kings of Assyria
Shalmaneser V ↓727-722
Ashur-nirari 755 745
Tiglath-pileser III (Tiglath- 745 727
Sargon II 722 705
Sennacherib 705 681
Northern tribes taken captive by Assyria in 733 and 722 B.C.

Kings of Israel (Northern Kingdom)
Jeroboam II 793 753
Zechariah ⇊
Shallum one month
Pekahiah ↓742-740
Menahem 752 742
Pekah 752 732
Hoshea 732 722

Hosea and His Contemporary Prophets (Northern Kingdom)
Jonah 784 772
Amos 767 755
Hosea 755 714

Kings of Judah (Southern Kingdom)
Uzziah or Azariah 790 739
↓Jotham 750 731
Ahaz 735 715
Hezekiah 730 686

Prophets to Judah (Southern Kingdom)
Isaiah 739 681
Micah 733 701

840 830 820 810 800 790 780 770 760 750 740 730 720 710 700 690

INSIGHT

Only one Israelite king, Jeroboam (often referred to as Jeroboam II), is mentioned in Hosea 1:1. Because Hosea mentions the names of the kings of Judah, we can know the other kings who ruled Israel during Hosea's ministry.

Chapter 1 Theme ______________________

1 The word of the LORD which came to [a]Hosea the son of Beeri,
during the days of [b]Uzziah, [c]Jotham, [d]Ahaz *and* [e]Hezekiah,
kings of Judah, and during the days of [f]Jeroboam the son of
Joash, king of Israel.
2 When the LORD first spoke through Hosea, the LORD said to
Hosea, "[a]Go, take to yourself a wife of harlotry and *have* children
of harlotry; for [b]the land commits flagrant harlotry, [1]forsaking
the LORD."
3 So he went and took Gomer the daughter of Diblaim, and
she conceived and [a]bore him a son.
4 And the LORD said to him, "Name him [a]Jezreel; for yet a little
while, and [b]I will [1]punish the house of Jehu for the bloodshed of
Jezreel, and [c]I will put an end to the kingdom of the house of
Israel.
5 "On that day I will [a]break the bow of Israel in the [b]valley of
Jezreel."
6 Then she conceived again and gave birth to a daughter.
And [1]the LORD said to him, "Name her [2]Lo-ruhamah, for I will
no longer [a]have compassion on the house of Israel, that I would
ever forgive them.
7 "But I will have [a]compassion on the house of Judah and

1:1 [a]Rom 9:25 [b]2 Chr 26:1-23; Is 1:1; Amos 1:1 [c]2 Kin 15:5, 7, 32-38; 2 Chr 27:1-9 [d]2 Kin 16:1-20; 2 Chr 28:1-27; Is 1:1; 7:1-17; Mic 1:1 [e]2 Kin 18:1-20:21; 2 Chr 29:1-32:33; Mic 1:1 [f]2 Kin 13:13; 14:23-29; Amos 1:1

2 [1]Lit *from not following after* [a]Hos 3:1 [b]Deut 31:16; Jer 3:1; Ezek 23:3-21; Hos 2:5; 5:3

3 [a]Ezek 23:4

4 [1]Lit *visit the bloodshed of Jezreel on the house of Jehu* [a]Hos 2:22 [b]2 Kin 10:11 [c]2 Kin 15:8-10

5 [a]Jer 49:35; Ezek 39:3 [b]Josh 17:16; Judg 6:33

6 [1]Lit *He* [2]I.e. she has not obtained compassion [a]Hos 2:4

7 [a]2 Kin 19:29-35; Is 30:18

[b]deliver them by the LORD their God, and will not deliver them
by [c]bow, sword, battle, horses or horsemen."
8 When she had weaned Lo-ruhamah, she conceived and gave
birth to a son.
9 And [1]the LORD said, "Name him [2]Lo-ammi, for you are not
My people and I am not [3]your God."

10 [1]Yet the number of the sons of Israel
Will be like the [a]sand of the sea,
Which cannot be measured or numbered;
And [b]in the place
Where it is said to them,
"You are [c]not My people,"
It will be said to them,
"*You are* the [d]sons of the living God."
11 And the [a]sons of Judah and the sons of Israel will be
[b]gathered together,
And they will appoint for themselves [c]one leader,
And they will go up from the land,
For great will be the day of Jezreel.

Chapter 2 Theme ______________________________

2 [1]Say to your brothers, "[2]Ammi," and to your sisters,
"[3]Ruhamah."
2 "Contend with your mother, [a]contend,
For she is [b]not my wife, and I am not her husband;
And let her put away her [c]harlotry from her face
And her adultery from between her breasts,
3 Or I will strip her [a]naked
And expose her as on the [b]day when she was born.
I will also [c]make her like a wilderness,
Make her like desert land
And slay her with [d]thirst.
4 "Also, I will have no compassion on her children,
Because they are [a]children of harlotry.
5 "For their mother has [a]played the harlot;
She who conceived them has acted shamefully.
For she said, '[a]I will go after my lovers,
Who [b]give *me* my bread and my water,
My wool and my flax, my [c]oil and my drink.'
6 "Therefore, behold, I will [a]hedge up [1]her way with [b]thorns,
And I will build [2]a wall against her so that she cannot find
her [c]paths.
7 "She will [a]pursue her lovers, but she will not overtake them;
And she will seek them, but will not find *them.*
Then she will say, '[b]I will go back to my [c]first husband,
For it was [d]better for me then than now!'

8 "For she does [a]not know that it was [b]I who gave her the grain,
the new wine and the oil,

7 [b]Jer 25:5, 6; Zech 9:9, 10 [c]Ps 44:3-7; Zech 4:6
9 [1]Lit *He* [2]I.e. not my people [3]Lit *yours*
10 [1]Ch 2:1 in Heb [a]Gen 22:17; 32:12; Jer 33:22 [b]Rom 9:26 [c]Is 65:1; Hos 1:9 [d]Is 63:16; 64:8; John 1:12; 1 Pet 2:10
11 [a]Is 11:12 [b]Jer 23:5, 6; 50:4, 5; Ezek 37:21-24 [c]Jer 30:21; Hos 3:5
2:1 [1]Ch 2:3 in Heb [2]I.e. my people [3]I.e. she has obtained compassion
2 [a]Ezek 23:45; Hos 2:5; 4:5 [b]Is 50:1 [c]Jer 3:1, 9, 13
3 [a]Jer 13:22; Ezek 16:7, 22, 39 [b]Ezek 16:4 [c]Is 32:13, 14; Hos 13:15 [d]Jer 14:3; Amos 8:11-13
4 [a]Jer 13:14
5 [a]Is 1:21; Jer 2:25; 3:1, 2; Hos 3:1 [b]Jer 44:17, 18; Hos 2:12 [c]Hos 2:8
6 [1]So with some ancient versions; Heb *your* [2]Lit *her wall so that* [a]Job 19:8; Lam 3:7, 9 [b]Hos 9:6; 10:8 [c]Jer 18:15
7 [a]Hos 5:13 [b]Luke 15:17, 18 [c]Jer 2:2; 3:1; Ezek 16:8; 23:4 [d]Jer 14:22; Hos 13:6
8 [a]Is 1:3 [b]Ezek 16:19

And lavished on her silver and gold,
Which they [1]used for Baal.
9 "Therefore, I will [a]take back My grain at [1]harvest time
And My new wine in its season.
I will also take away My wool and My flax
Given to cover her nakedness.
10 "And then I will [a]uncover her lewdness
In the sight of her lovers,
And no one will rescue her out of My hand.
11 "I will also [a]put an end to all her gaiety,
Her [b]feasts, her [c]new moons, her sabbaths
And all her festal assemblies.
12 "I will [a]destroy her vines and fig trees,
Of which she said, 'These are my wages
Which my lovers have given me.'
And I will [b]make them a forest,
And the [c]beasts of the field will devour them.
13 "I will punish her for the [a]days of the Baals
When she used to [1b]offer sacrifices to them
And [c]adorn herself with her [2]earrings and jewelry,
And follow her lovers, so that she [d]forgot Me,"
declares the LORD.

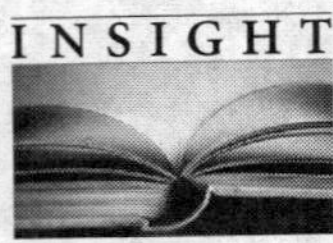

INSIGHT

Baal, which meant "lord, owner, possessor," or "husband," was the Canaanite god of fertility. ***Baal*** was part of several compound names for locations where Canaanite deities were worshiped, such as Baal-peor.

14 "Therefore, behold, I will allure her,
[a]Bring her into the wilderness
And speak [1]kindly to her.
15 "Then I will give her her [a]vineyards from there,
And [b]the valley of Achor as a door of hope.
And she will [1c]sing there as in the days of her youth,
As in the [d]day when she came up from the land of Egypt.
16 "It will come about in that day," declares the LORD,
"That you will call Me [1a]Ishi
And will no longer call Me [2]Baali.
17 "For [a]I will remove the names of the Baals from her mouth,
So that they will be [1]mentioned by their names no more.
18 "In that day I will also make a covenant for them
With the [a]beasts of the field,
The birds of the sky
And the creeping things of the ground.
And I will [1b]abolish the bow, the sword and war
from the land,
And will make them [c]lie down in safety.
19 "I will [a]betroth you to Me forever;
Yes, I will betroth you to Me in [b]righteousness
and in justice,
In lovingkindness and in compassion,
20 And I will betroth you to Me in faithfulness.
Then you will [a]know the LORD.

21 "It will come about in that day that [a]I will respond,"
declares the LORD.

8 [1]Or *made into the*

9 [1]Lit *its time* [a]Hos 8:7; 9:2

10 [a]Ezek 16:37

11 [a]Jer 7:34; 16:9 [b]Hos 3:4; Amos 5:21; 8:10 [c]Is 1:13, 14

12 [a]Jer 5:17; 8:13 [b]Is 5:5; 7:23 [c]Hos 13:8

13 [1]Or *burn incense* [2]Or *nose rings* [a]Hos 4:13; 11:2 [b]Jer 7:9 [c]Ezek 16:12, 17; 23:40 [d]Hos 4:6; 8:14; 13:6

14 [1]Lit *upon her heart* [a]Ezek 20:33-38

15 [1]Or *give answer* [a]Ezek 28:25, 26 [b]Josh 7:26 [c]Jer 2:1-3; Ezek 16:8-14 [d]Hos 11:1; 12:9, 13; 13:4

16 [1]I.e. my husband [2]I.e. my master, or my Baal [a]Is 54:5; Hos 2:7

17 [1]Or *remembered* [a]Ex 23:13; Josh 23:7; Ps 16:4

18 [1]Lit *break* [a]Job 5:23; Is 11:6-9; Ezek 34:25 [b]Is 2:4; Ezek 39:1-10 [c]Lev 26:5; Jer 23:6; Ezek 34:25

19 [a]Is 62:4, 5 [b]Is 1:27; 54:6-8

20 [a]Jer 31:33, 34; Hos 6:6; 13:4

21 [a]Is 55:10; Zech 8:12; Mal 3:10, 11

"I will respond to the heavens, and they will respond
to the earth,
22 And the [a]earth will respond to the grain, to the new wine
and to the oil,
And they will respond to [1]Jezreel.
23 "I will [a]sow her for Myself in the land.
[b]I will also have compassion on [1]her who had not obtained
compassion,
And [c]I will say to [2]those who were [d]not My people,
'You are My people!'
And [3]they will say, '*You are* my God!'"

Chapter 3 Theme ______________________

3 Then the LORD said to me, "Go again, love a [1]woman *who*
is loved by *her* [2]husband, yet an adulteress, even [a]as the
LORD loves the sons of Israel, though they turn to other gods
and love raisin [b]cakes."
2 So I [a]bought her for myself for fifteen *shekels* of silver and a
homer and a [1]half of barley.
3 Then I said to her, "You shall [a]stay with me for many days.
You shall not play the harlot, nor shall you have a [1]man; so I
will also be toward you."
4 For the sons of Israel will remain for many days [a]without
king or prince, [b]without sacrifice or *sacred* [c]pillar and without
[d]ephod or [1e]household idols.
5 Afterward the sons of Israel will [a]return and seek the LORD
their God and [b]David their king; and [c]they will come trembling
to the LORD and to His goodness in the last days.

Chapter 4 Theme ______________________

4 [a]Listen to the word of the LORD, O sons of Israel,
For the LORD has a [b]case against the inhabitants of the land,
Because there is [c]no [1]faithfulness or [2]kindness
Or [d]knowledge of God in the land.
2 *There is* [a]swearing, [b]deception, [c]murder, [d]stealing
and [e]adultery.
They employ violence, so that [f]bloodshed [1]follows bloodshed.
3 Therefore the land [a]mourns,
And everyone who lives in it languishes
Along with the beasts of the field and the birds of the sky,
And also the fish of the sea [1]disappear.

4 Yet let no one [1a]find fault, and let none offer reproof;
For your people are like those who [b]contend with the priest.
5 So you will [a]stumble by day,
And the prophet also will stumble with you by night;
And I will destroy your [b]mother.
6 [a]My people are destroyed for lack of knowledge.
Because you have [b]rejected knowledge,
I also will [c]reject you from being My priest.

22 [1]I.e. God sows [a]Jer 31:12; Joel 2:19

23 [1]Heb *Lo-ruhamah* [2]Heb *Lo-ammi* [3]Lit *he* [a]Jer 31:27 [b]Hos 1:6 [c]Rom 9:25; 1 Pet 2:10 [d]Hos 1:9

3:1 [1]I.e. Gomer [2]Lit *companion* [a]Jer 3:20 [b]2 Sam 6:19; 1 Chr 16:3; Song 2:5

2 [1]Heb *lethech* [a]Ruth 4:10

3 [1]Or *husband* [a]Deut 21:13

4 [1]Heb *teraphim* [a]Hos 10:3; 13:10, 11 [b]Dan 9:27; 11:31; 12:11; Hos 2:11 [c]Hos 10:1, 2 [d]Ex 28:4-12; 1 Sam 23:9-12 [e]Gen 31:19, 34; Judg 17:5; 18:14, 17; 1 Sam 15:23

5 [a]Jer 50:4, 5 [b]Jer 30:9; Ezek 34:24 [c]Is 2:2, 3; Jer 31:9

4:1 [1]Or *truth* [2]Or *loyalty* [a]Hos 5:1 [b]Hos 12:2; Mic 6:2 [c]Is 59:4; Jer 7:28 [d]Jer 4:22

2 [1]Lit *touches* [a]Deut 5:11; Hos 10:4 [b]Hos 7:3; 10:13; 11:12 [c]Gen 4:8; Hos 6:9 [d]Deut 5:19; Hos 7:1 [e]Deut 5:18; Hos 7:4 [f]Hos 6:8; 12:14

3 [1]Lit *are taken away* [a]Is 24:4; 33:9; Amos 5:16; Zeph 1:3

4 [1]Lit *contend* [a]Ezek 3:26; Amos 5:10, 13 [b]Deut 17:12

5 [a]Ezek 14:3, 7; Hos 5:5 [b]Jer 15:8; Hos 2:2, 5

6 [a]Is 5:13 [b]Hos 4:14; Mal 2:7, 8 [c]Zech 11:8, 9, 15-17

Since you have [d]forgotten the [e]law of your God,
I also will forget your children.

7 The more they [a]multiplied, the more they sinned
against Me;
I will [b]change their glory into shame.
8 They [a]feed on the [1]sin of My people
And [b]direct their desire toward their iniquity.
9 And it will be, like people, [a]like priest;
So I will [b]punish them for their ways
And repay them for their deeds.
10 [a]They will eat, but not have enough;
They will [b]play the harlot, but not increase,
Because they have [1c]stopped giving heed to the LORD.

11 Harlotry, [a]wine and new wine take away the
[1]understanding.
12 My people [a]consult their wooden idol, and their *diviner's*
wand informs them;
For a spirit of harlotry has led *them* astray,
And they have played the harlot, *departing*
[1]from their God.
13 They offer sacrifices on the [a]tops of the mountains
And [1b]burn incense on the hills,
[c]Under oak, poplar and terebinth,
Because their shade is pleasant.
Therefore your daughters play the harlot
And your [2]brides commit adultery.
14 I will not punish your daughters when they play the harlot
Or your [1]brides when they commit adultery,
For *the men* themselves go apart with harlots
And offer sacrifices with [a]temple prostitutes;
So the people without understanding are [2]ruined.

15 Though you, Israel, play the harlot,
Do not let Judah become guilty;
Also do not go to [a]Gilgal,
Or go up to Beth-aven
[b]And take the oath:
"As the LORD lives!"
16 Since Israel is [a]stubborn
Like a stubborn heifer,
[1]Can the LORD now [b]pasture them
Like a lamb in a large field?
17 Ephraim is joined to [a]idols;
[b]Let him alone.
18 Their liquor gone,
They play the harlot continually;
[a]Their [1]rulers dearly love shame.
19 [a]The wind wraps them in its wings,
And they will be ashamed because of their sacrifices.

INSIGHT

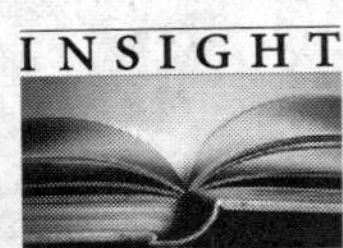

After Pekah took the throne in Israel, Tiglath-pileser, king of Assyria, came against him in 733 B.C. and took captive all of the kingdom except Ephraim and western Manasseh. Ten years later the remainder of the northern kingdom was completely destroyed by the Assyrians in 722 B.C. Thus Ephraim is a reference to what remained of Israel in those last ten years.

6 [d]Hos 2:13; 8:14; 13:6 [e]Hos 8:1, 12

7 [a]Hos 10:1; 13:6 [b]Hab 2:16

8 [1]Or *sin offering* [a]Hos 10:13 [b]Is 56:11; Mic 3:11

9 [a]Is 24:2; Jer 5:31 [b]Hos 8:13; 9:9

10 [1]Lit *forsaken giving heed; or forsaken the* LORD *to practice (v 11) harlotry* [a]Lev 26:26; Is 65:13; Mic 6:14 [b]Hos 7:4 [c]Hos 9:17

11 [1]Lit *heart* [a]Prov 20:1; Is 5:12; 28:7

12 [1]Lit *from under* [a]Is 44:19; Jer 2:27

13 [1]Or *offer sacrifices* [2]Or *daughters-in-law* [a]Jer 3:6 [b]Hos 2:13; 11:2 [c]Is 1:29; Jer 2:20

14 [1]Or *daughters-in-law* [2]Lit *thrust down* [a]Deut 23:17

15 [a]Hos 9:15; 12:11 [b]Jer 5:2; 44:26; Amos 8:14

16 [1]Or *Now the* LORD *will pasture . . . field* [a]Ps 78:8 [b]Is 5:17; 7:25

17 [a]Hos 13:2 [b]Ps 81:12; Hos 4:4

18 [1]Lit *shields* [a]Mic 3:11

19 [a]Hos 12:1; 13:15

5:1 [a]Hos 9:8
2 [1]Or *waded deep in slaughter* [a]Hos 9:15 [b]Is 29:15; Hos 4:2; 6:9
3 [a]Amos 3:2; 5:12
4 [a]Hos 4:12 [b]Hos 4:6, 14
5 [a]Hos 7:10 [b]Ezek 23:31-35
6 [a]Hos 8:13; Mic 6:6, 7 [b]Prov 1:28; Is 1:15; Jer 14:12 [c]Ezek 8:6
7 [1]Lit *strange* [2]Lit *portions* [a]Is 48:8; Jer 3:20; Hos 6:7 [b]Hos 2:4 [c]Is 1:14; Hos 2:11
8 [a]Joel 2:1 [b]Hos 9:9; 10:9 [c]Judg 5:14
9 [a]Is 28:1-4; Hos 9:11-17 [b]Is 37:3 [c]Is 46:10; Zech 1:6
10 [a]Deut 19:14; 27:17 [b]Ezek 7:8 [c]Ps 32:6; 93:3, 4
11 [1]Or with some ancient versions, *follow nothingness* [a]Deut 28:33 [b]Mic 6:16
12 [a]Ps 39:11; Is 51:8
13 [1]Or *ulcer* [2]Or *the avenging king* or *the great king* [a]Hos 7:11; 8:9; 12:1 [b]Hos 10:6 [c]Jer 30:12-15
14 [a]Ps 7:2; Hos 13:7, 8; Amos 3:4 [b]Ps 50:22 [c]Mic 5:8
15 [1]Or *bear their punishment* [a]Is 64:7-9; Jer 3:13, 14 [b]Ps 50:15; 78:34; Jer 2:27; Hos 3:5

Chapter 5 Theme ______________________________

5 Hear this, O priests!
Give heed, O house of Israel!
Listen, O house of the king!
For the judgment applies to you,
For you have been a [a]snare at Mizpah
And a net spread out on Tabor.
2 The [a]revolters have [1b]gone deep in depravity,
But I will chastise all of them.
3 I [a]know Ephraim, and Israel is not hidden from Me;
For now, O Ephraim, you have played the harlot,
Israel has defiled itself.
4 Their deeds will not allow them
To return to their God.
For a [a]spirit of harlotry is within them,
And they [b]do not know the LORD.
5 Moreover, the [a]pride of Israel testifies against him,
And Israel and Ephraim stumble in their iniquity;
[b]Judah also has stumbled with them.
6 They will [a]go with their flocks and herds
To seek the LORD, but they will [b]not find *Him;*
He has [c]withdrawn from them.
7 They have [a]dealt treacherously against the LORD,
For they have borne [1b]illegitimate children.
Now the [c]new moon will devour them with their [2]land.

8 [a]Blow the horn in [b]Gibeah,
The trumpet in Ramah.
Sound an alarm at Beth-aven:
"[c]Behind you, Benjamin!"
9 Ephraim will become a [a]desolation in the [b]day of rebuke;
Among the tribes of Israel I [c]declare what is sure.
10 The princes of Judah have become like those who [a]move a boundary;
On them I will [b]pour out My wrath [c]like water.
11 Ephraim is [a]oppressed, crushed in judgment,
[b]Because he was determined to [1]follow *man's* command.
12 Therefore I am like a [a]moth to Ephraim
And like rottenness to the house of Judah.
13 When Ephraim saw his sickness,
And Judah his [1]wound,
Then Ephraim went to [a]Assyria
And sent to [2b]King Jareb.
But he is [c]unable to heal you,
Or to cure you of your [1]wound.
14 For I *will be* [a]like a lion to Ephraim
And like a young lion to the house of Judah.
[b]I, even I, will tear to pieces and go away,
I will carry away, and there will be [c]none to deliver.
15 I will go away *and* return to My place
Until they [1a]acknowledge their guilt and seek My face;
In their affliction they will earnestly [b]seek Me.

Chapter 6 Theme ______________________________

6 "[a]Come, let us return to the LORD.
For [b]He has torn *us,* but [c]He will heal us;
He has [1]wounded *us,* but He will [d]bandage us.
2 "He will [a]revive us after two days;
He will [b]raise us up on the third day,
That we may live before Him.
3 "So let us [a]know, let us press on to know the LORD.
His [b]going forth is as certain as the dawn;
And He will come to us like the [c]rain,
Like the spring rain watering the earth."

4 What shall I do with you, O [a]Ephraim?
What shall I do with you, O Judah?
For your [1]loyalty is like a [b]morning cloud
And like the dew which goes away early.
5 Therefore I have [a]hewn *them* in pieces by the prophets;
I have slain them by the [b]words of My mouth;
And the judgments on you are *like* the light that goes forth.
6 For [a]I delight in loyalty [b]rather than sacrifice,
And in the knowledge of God rather than burnt offerings.
7 But [a]like [1]Adam they have [b]transgressed the covenant;
There they have [c]dealt treacherously against Me.
8 [a]Gilead is a city of wrongdoers,
Tracked with [b]bloody *footprints.*
9 And as [a]raiders wait for a man,
So a band of priests [b]murder on the way to Shechem;
Surely they have committed [1c]crime.
10 In the house of Israel I have seen a [a]horrible thing;
Ephraim's [b]harlotry is there, Israel has defiled itself.
11 Also, O Judah, there is a [a]harvest appointed for you,
When I [b]restore the fortunes of My people.

Chapter 7 Theme ______________________________

7 When I [a]would heal Israel,
The iniquity of Ephraim is uncovered,
And the evil deeds of Samaria,
For they deal [b]falsely;
The thief enters in,
[c]Bandits raid outside,
2 And they do not [1]consider in their hearts
That I [a]remember all their wickedness.
Now their [b]deeds are all around them;
They are before My face.
3 [a]With their wickedness they make the [b]king glad,
And the princes with their [c]lies.
4 They are [a]all adulterers,
Like an oven heated by the baker
Who ceases to stir up *the fire*
From the kneading of the dough until it is leavened.

6:1 [1]Lit *struck* [a]Jer 50:4, 5 [b]Deut 32:39; Hos 5:14 [c]Jer 30:17; Hos 14:4 [d]Is 30:26

2 [a]Ps 30:5 [b]1 Cor 15:4

3 [a]Is 2:3; Mic 4:2 [b]Ps 19:6; Mic 5:2 [c]Job 29:23; Ps 72:6; Joel 2:23

4 [1]Or *lovingkindness* [a]Hos 7:1; 11:8 [b]Ps 78:34-37; Hos 13:3

5 [a]1 Sam 15:32, 33; Jer 1:10; 5:14 [b]Jer 23:29

6 [a]Matt 9:13; 12:7 [b]Is 1:11

7 [1]Or *men* [a]Job 31:33 [b]Hos 8:1 [c]Hos 5:7

8 [a]Hos 12:11 [b]Hos 4:2

9 [1]Or *lewdness* [a]Hos 7:1 [b]Jer 7:9, 10; Hos 4:2 [c]Ezek 22:9; 23:27; Hos 2:10

10 [a]Jer 5:30, 31; 23:14 [b]Hos 5:3

11 [a]Jer 51:33; Joel 3:13 [b]Zeph 2:7

7:1 [a]Ezek 24:13; Hos 6:4; 7:13; 11:8 [b]Hos 4:2 [c]Hos 6:9

2 [1]Lit *say to their heart* [a]Ps 25:7; Jer 14:10; 17:1; Hos 8:13; 9:9; Amos 8:7 [b]Jer 2:19; 4:18; Hos 4:9

3 [a]Rom 1:32 [b]Jer 28:1-4; Hos 7:5; Mic 7:3 [c]Hos 4:2; 11:12

4 [a]Jer 9:2; 23:10

5 On the [1]day of our king, the princes [a]became sick
with the heat of wine;
He stretched out his hand with [b]scoffers,
6 For their hearts are like an [a]oven
As they approach their [1]plotting;
Their [2]anger [3]smolders all night,
In the morning it burns like a flaming fire.
7 All of them are hot like an oven,
And they consume their [a]rulers;
All their kings have fallen.
[b]None of them calls on Me.

8 Ephraim [a]mixes himself with the [1]nations;
Ephraim has become a cake not turned.
9 [a]Strangers devour his strength,
Yet he [b]does not know *it;*
Gray hairs also are sprinkled on him,
Yet he does not know *it.*
10 Though the [a]pride of Israel testifies against him,
Yet [b]they have not returned to the LORD their God,
Nor have they sought Him, for all this.
11 So [a]Ephraim has become like a silly dove,
[b]without [1]sense;
They call to [c]Egypt, they go to [d]Assyria.
12 When they go, I will [a]spread My net over them;
I will bring them down like the birds of the sky.
I will [b]chastise them in accordance with the [1]proclamation
to their assembly.
13 [a]Woe to them, for they have [b]strayed from Me!
Destruction is theirs, for they have rebelled against Me!
I [c]would redeem them, but they speak lies against Me.
14 And [a]they do not cry to Me from their heart
When they wail on their beds;
For the sake of grain and new wine they [1b]assemble
themselves,
They [c]turn away from Me.
15 Although I trained *and* strengthened their arms,
Yet they [a]devise evil against Me.
16 They turn, *but* not [1]upward,
They are like a [a]deceitful bow;
Their princes will fall by the sword
Because of the [2b]insolence of their tongue.
This *will be* their [c]derision in the land of Egypt.

Chapter 8 Theme ______________________________

8 [a]*Put* the trumpet to your [1]lips!
[b]Like an eagle *the enemy comes* [c]against the house
of the LORD,
Because they have [d]transgressed My covenant
And rebelled against My [e]law.

5 [1]I.e. a festive occasion [a]Is 28:1, 7 [b]Is 28:14

6 [1]Lit *ambush* [2]So with some ancient versions; M.T. *baker* [3]Lit *sleeps* [a]Ps 21:9

7 [a]Hos 13:10 [b]Is 64:7

8 [1]Lit *peoples* [a]Ps 106:35

9 [a]Is 1:7; Hos 8:7 [b]Hos 4:6

10 [a]Hos 5:5 [b]Is 9:13

11 [1]Lit *heart* [a]Hos 11:11 [b]Hos 4:6, 11, 14; 5:4 [c]Hos 8:13; 9:3, 6 [d]Hos 5:13; 8:9; 12:1

12 [1]Lit *report* [a]Ezek 12:13 [b]Lev 26:14-39; Deut 28:15

13 [a]Hos 9:12 [b]Jer 14:10; Ezek 34:6; Hos 9:17 [c]Jer 51:9; Hos 7:1; Matt 23:37

14 [1]Or with Gr and many ancient mss *gash themselves* [a]Job 35:9-11; Hos 8:2; Zech 7:5 [b]Judg 9:27; Amos 2:8; Mic 2:11 [c]Hos 13:16

15 [a]Nah 1:9

16 [1]Or possibly *to the Most High* [2]Lit *indignation;* or *cursing* [a]Ps 78:57 [b]Ps 12:3, 4; 17:10; 73:9; Dan 7:25; Mal 3:13, 14 [c]Ezek 23:32; Hos 9:3, 6

8:1 [1]Lit *palate* [a]Jer 4:13; Hos 5:8 [b]Hab 1:8 [c]Deut 28:49 [d]Hos 6:7 [e]Hos 4:6

2 [a]They cry out to Me,
"My God, [b]we of Israel know You!"
3 Israel has rejected the good;
The enemy will pursue him.
4 [a]They have set up kings, but not by Me;
They have appointed princes, but I did not know *it.*
With their [b]silver and gold they have made idols
for themselves,
That [1]they might be cut off.
5 [1]He has rejected your [a]calf, O Samaria, *saying,*
"My anger burns against them!"
How long will they be incapable of [b]innocence?
6 For from Israel is even this!
A [a]craftsman made it, so it is not God;
Surely the calf of Samaria will be broken to [1]pieces.
7 For [a]they sow the wind
And they reap the [b]whirlwind.
The standing grain has no [1]heads;
It yields [c]no [2]grain.
Should it yield, strangers would swallow it up.

8 Israel is [a]swallowed up;
They are now among the nations
Like a [b]vessel in which no one delights.
9 For they have gone up to [a]Assyria,
Like [b]a wild donkey all alone;
Ephraim has [c]hired [1]lovers.
10 Even though they hire *allies* among the nations,
Now I will [a]gather them up;
And they will begin [b]to [1]diminish
Because of the burden of the [c]king of princes.

11 Since Ephraim has [a]multiplied altars for sin,
They have become altars of sinning for him.
12 Though [a]I wrote for him ten thousand *precepts* of My [b]law,
They are regarded as a strange thing.
13 As for My [a]sacrificial gifts,
They [b]sacrifice the flesh and eat *it,*
But the LORD has taken no delight in them.
Now He will [c]remember their iniquity,
And [d]punish *them* for their sins;
They will return to [e]Egypt.
14 For Israel has [a]forgotten his Maker and [b]built palaces;
And Judah has multiplied fortified cities,
But I will send a [c]fire on its cities that it may consume its
palatial dwellings.

Chapter 9 Theme ____________________

9 [a]Do not rejoice, O Israel, [1]with exultation like the [2]nations!
For you have [b]played the harlot, [3]forsaking your God.
You have loved *harlots'* earnings on [4]every threshing floor.

2 [a]Ps 78:34; Hos 7:14 [b]Titus 1:16

4 [1]Lit *he* [a]2 Kin 15:13, 17, 25; Hos 13:10, 11 [b]Hos 2:8; 13:1, 2

5 [1]Or *Your calf has rejected you* [a]Hos 10:5; 13:2 [b]Ps 19:13; Jer 13:27

6 [1]Or *splinters* [a]Hos 13:2

7 [1]Lit *growth* [2]Or *meal* [a]Prov 22:8 [b]Is 66:15; Nah 1:3 [c]Hos 2:9

8 [a]2 Kin 17:6; Jer 51:34 [b]Jer 22:28; 25:34

9 [1]Lit *loves* [a]Hos 7:11 [b]Jer 2:24 [c]Ezek 16:33, 34

10 [1]Or *suffer for awhile* [a]Ezek 16:37; 22:20 [b]Jer 42:2 [c]Is 10:8

11 [a]Hos 10:1

12 [a]Deut 4:6, 8 [b]Hos 4:6

13 [a]Hos 5:6 [b]Jer 6:20; 7:21 [c]Jer 14:10; Hos 7:2; Luke 12:2; 1 Cor 4:5 [d]Hos 4:9; 9:7 [e]Hos 9:3, 6

14 [a]Deut 32:18; Hos 2:13; 4:6; 13:6 [b]Is 9:9, 10 [c]Jer 17:27

9:1 [1]Lit *to* [2]Lit *peoples* [3]Lit *away from your God* [4]Lit *all threshing floors of grain* [a]Is 22:12, 13; Hos 10:5 [b]Hos 4:12

2 Threshing floor and wine press will [a]not feed them,
And the new wine will fail [1]them.
3 They will not remain in [a]the LORD's land,
But Ephraim will return to [b]Egypt,
And in [c]Assyria they will eat [d]unclean *food.*
4 They will not pour out drink offerings of [a]wine
to the LORD,
[b]Their sacrifices will not please Him.
Their bread will [1]*be* like [2]mourners' bread;
All who eat of it will be [c]defiled,
For their bread will be for [3]themselves *alone;*
It will not enter the house of the LORD.
5 [a]What will you do on the day of the appointed festival
And on the day of the [b]feast of the LORD?
6 For behold, they will go because of destruction;
Egypt will gather them up, [a]Memphis will bury them.
Weeds will take over their treasures of silver;
[b]Thorns *will be* in their tents.

7 The days of [a]punishment have come,
The days of [b]retribution have come;
[1]Let Israel know *this!*
The prophet is a [c]fool,
The [2]inspired man is [d]demented,
Because of the grossness of your [e]iniquity,
And *because* your hostility is *so* great.
8 Ephraim *was* a watchman with my God, a prophet;
Yet the snare of a bird catcher is in all his ways,
And there is *only* hostility in the house of his God.
9 They have gone [a]deep [1]in depravity
As in the days of [b]Gibeah;
He will [c]remember their iniquity,
He will punish their sins.

10 I found Israel like [a]grapes in the wilderness;
I saw your forefathers as the [b]earliest fruit on the fig tree
in its first *season.*
But they came to [c]Baal-peor and devoted themselves
to [1d]shame,
And they became as [e]detestable as that which they loved.
11 As for Ephraim, their [a]glory will fly away like a bird—
No birth, no pregnancy and no conception!
12 Though they bring up their children,
Yet I will bereave them [1]until not a man is left.
Yes, [a]woe to them indeed when I depart from them!
13 Ephraim, as I have seen,
Is planted in a pleasant meadow like [a]Tyre;
But Ephraim will bring out his children for slaughter.
14 Give them, O LORD—what will You give?
Give them a [a]miscarrying womb and dry breasts.

2 [1]Lit *her* [a]Hos 2:9
3 [a]Lev 25:23; Jer 2:7 [b]Hos 7:16; 8:13 [c]Hos 7:11 [d]Ezek 4:13
4 [1]Lit be *to them* [2]Or *bread of misfortune* [3]Lit *their appetite* [a]Ex 29:40 [b]Jer 6:20; Hos 8:13 [c]Hag 2:13, 14
5 [a]Is 10:3; Jer 5:31 [b]Hos 2:11; Joel 1:13
6 [a]Is 19:13; Jer 2:16; 44:1; 46:14, 19; Ezek 30:13, 16 [b]Is 5:6; 7:23; Hos 10:8
7 [1]Or *Israel will know it* [2]Lit *man of the spirit* [a]Is 10:3; Jer 10:15; Mic 7:4; Luke 21:22 [b]Is 34:8; Jer 16:18; 25:14 [c]Lam 2:14; Ezek 13:3, 10 [d]Is 44:25 [e]Ezek 14:9, 10
9 [1]Lit *they have corrupted* [a]Is 31:6 [b]Judg 19:12, 16-30; Hos 10:9 [c]Hos 7:2; 8:13
10 [1]I.e. Baal [a]Mic 7:1 [b]Jer 24:2 [c]Num 25:1-5; Ps 106:28, 29 [d]Jer 11:13; Hos 4:18 [e]Ps 115:8; Ezek 20:8
11 [a]Hos 4:7; 10:5
12 [1]Lit *without a man* [a]Deut 31:17; Hos 7:13
13 [a]Ezek 26:1-21
14 [a]Hos 9:11

15 All their evil is at [a]Gilgal;
Indeed, I came to hate them there!
Because of the [b]wickedness of their deeds
I will drive them out of My house!
I will love them no more;
All their princes are [c]rebels.
16 [a]Ephraim is stricken, their root is dried up,
They will bear [b]no fruit.
Even though they bear children,
I will slay the [c]precious ones of their womb.
17 My God will cast them away
Because they have [a]not listened to Him;
And they will be [b]wanderers among the nations.

Chapter 10 Theme __________________________________

10 Israel is a [1]luxuriant [a]vine;
He produces fruit for himself.
The more his fruit,
The more altars he [b]made;
The [2]richer his land,
The better [3]he made the *sacred* [c]pillars.
2 Their heart is [1a]faithless;
Now they must bear their [b]guilt.
[2]The LORD will [c]break down their altars
And destroy their *sacred* pillars.

3 Surely now they will say, "We have [a]no king,
For we do not revere the LORD.
As for the king, what can he do for us?"
4 They speak *mere* words,
[1]With [a]worthless oaths they make covenants;
And [b]judgment sprouts like poisonous weeds in the furrows of the field.
5 The inhabitants of Samaria will fear
For the [1a]calf of [b]Beth-aven.
Indeed, its people will mourn for it,
And its [c]idolatrous priests [2]will cry out over it,
Over its [d]glory, since it has departed from it.
6 The thing itself will be carried to [a]Assyria
As tribute to [1b]King Jareb;
Ephraim will [2]be [c]seized with shame
And Israel will be ashamed of its [d]own counsel.
7 Samaria will be [a]cut off *with* her king
Like a stick on the surface of the water.
8 Also the [a]high places of Aven, the [b]sin of Israel, will be destroyed;
[c]Thorn and thistle will grow on their altars;
Then they will [d]say to the mountains,
"Cover us!" And to the hills, "Fall on us!"
9 From the days of Gibeah you have sinned, O Israel;
There they stand!

15 [a]Hos 4:15; 12:11 [b]Hos 4:9; 7:2; 12:2 [c]Is 1:23; Hos 5:2

16 [a]Hos 5:11 [b]Hos 8:7 [c]Ezek 24:21

17 [a]Hos 4:10 [b]Hos 7:13

10:1 [1]Or *degenerate* [2]Or *better* [3]Lit *they* [a]Is 5:1-7; Ezek 15:1-6 [b]Jer 2:28; Hos 8:11; 12:11 [c]1 Kin 14:23; Hos 3:4

2 [1]Lit *smooth* [2]Lit *He* [a]1 Kin 18:21; Zeph 1:5 [b]Hos 13:16 [c]Hos 10:8; Mic 5:13

3 [a]Ps 12:4; Is 5:19

4 [1]Or *Swearing falsely in making a covenant* [a]Ezek 17:13-19; Hos 4:2 [b]Deut 31:16, 17; 2 Kin 17:3, 4; Amos 5:7

5 [1]So with some ancient versions; Heb *calves* [2]Or who *used to rejoice over* [a]Hos 8:5, 6 [b]Hos 4:15; 5:8 [c]2 Kin 23:5 [d]Hos 9:11

6 [1]Or *the avenging king* or *the great king* [2]Lit *receive shame* [a]Hos 11:5 [b]Hos 5:13 [c]Hos 4:7 [d]Is 30:3; Jer 7:24

7 [a]Hos 13:11

8 [a]Hos 4:13 [b]1 Kin 12:28-30; 13:34 [c]Is 32:13; Hos 9:6; 10:2 [d]Is 2:19; Luke 23:30; Rev 6:16

10 [1]Or *bind* [a]Ezek 5:13 [b]Hos 4:9 [c]Jer 16:16

11 [a]Jer 50:11; Hos 4:16; Mic 4:13 [b]Jer 28:14

12 [1]Or *loyalty* [2]Or *teach* [a]Prov 11:18 [b]Jer 4:3 [c]Hos 12:6 [d]Hos 6:3 [e]Is 44:3; 45:8

13 [a]Job 4:8; Prov 22:8; Gal 6:7, 8 [b]Hos 4:2; 7:3; 11:12 [c]Ps 33:16

14 [a]Is 17:3 [b]Hos 13:16

11:1 [a]Hos 2:15; 12:9, 13; 13:4 [b]Ex 4:22, 23; Matt 2:15

2 [1]I.e. God's prophets [a]2 Kin 17:13-15 [b]Hos 2:13; 4:13 [c]Is 65:7; Jer 18:15

3 [1]So ancient versions; Heb *He . . . His* [a]Deut 1:31; 32:10, 11 [b]Ps 107:20; Jer 30:17

4 [a]Jer 31:2, 3 [b]Lev 26:13 [c]Ex 16:32; Ps 78:25

5 [1]Lit *He* [2]Lit *his* [a]Hos 7:16

6 [1]Lit *his* [a]Hos 13:16 [b]Lam 2:9 [c]Hos 4:16, 17

7 [1]I.e. God's prophets [2]Lit *him;* i.e. Israel [a]Jer 3:6, 7; 8:5

Will not the battle against the sons of iniquity
overtake them in Gibeah?
10 When it is My [a]desire, I will [1b]chastise them;
And [c]the peoples will be gathered against them
When they are bound for their double guilt.

11 Ephraim is a trained [a]heifer that loves to thresh,
But I will [b]come over her fair neck *with a yoke;*
I will harness Ephraim,
Judah will plow, Jacob will harrow for himself.
12 [a]Sow with a view to righteousness,
Reap in accordance with [1]kindness;
[b]Break up your fallow ground,
For it is time to [c]seek the LORD
Until He [d]comes to [2e]rain righteousness on you.
13 You have [a]plowed wickedness, you have reaped injustice,
You have eaten the fruit of [b]lies.
Because you have trusted in your way,
in your [c]numerous warriors,
14 Therefore a tumult will arise among your people,
And all your [a]fortresses will be destroyed,
As Shalman destroyed Beth-arbel on the day of battle,
When [b]mothers were dashed in pieces with *their* children.
15 Thus it will be done to you at Bethel because of
your great wickedness.
At dawn the king of Israel will be completely cut off.

Chapter 11 Theme ________________________

11 When Israel *was* a youth I loved him,
And [a]out of Egypt I [b]called My son.
2 The more [1a]they called them,
The more they went from [1]them;
They kept [b]sacrificing to the Baals
And [c]burning incense to idols.
3 Yet it is I who taught Ephraim to walk,
[1]I [a]took them in My arms;
But they did not know that I [b]healed them.
4 I [a]led them with cords of a man, with bonds of love,
And [b]I became to them as one who lifts the yoke
from their jaws;
And I bent down *and* [c]fed them.

5 [1]They will not return to the land of Egypt;
But Assyria—he will be [2]their king
Because they [a]refused to return *to Me.*
6 The [a]sword will whirl against [1]their cities,
And will demolish [1]their gate bars
And [b]consume *them* because of their [c]counsels.
7 So My people are bent on [a]turning from Me.
Though [1]they call [2]them to *the One* on high,
None at all exalts *Him.*

8 [a]How can I give you up, O Ephraim?
How can I surrender you, O Israel?
How can I [1]make you like [b]Admah?
How can I treat you like [b]Zeboiim?
My heart is turned over within Me,
[2]All My compassions are kindled.
9 I will [a]not execute My fierce anger;
I will not destroy Ephraim [b]again.
For [c]I am God and not man, the [d]Holy One in your midst,
And I will not come in [1]wrath.
10 They will [a]walk after the LORD,
He will [b]roar like a lion;
Indeed He will roar
And *His* sons will come [c]trembling from the west.
11 They will come trembling like birds from [a]Egypt
And like [b]doves from the land of [a]Assyria;
And I will [c]settle them in their houses,
declares the LORD.

12 [1]Ephraim surrounds Me with [a]lies
And the house of Israel with deceit;
Judah is also unruly against God,
Even against the Holy One who is faithful.

Chapter 12 Theme ____________________

12 [1]Ephraim feeds on [a]wind,
And pursues the [b]east wind continually;
He multiplies lies and violence.
Moreover, [2]he makes a covenant with Assyria,
And oil is carried to Egypt.
2 The LORD also has a [a]dispute with Judah,
And will punish Jacob [b]according to his ways;
He will repay him according to his deeds.
3 In the womb he [a]took his brother by the heel,
And in his maturity he [b]contended with God.
4 Yes, he wrestled with the angel and prevailed;
He wept and [a]sought His favor.
He found Him at [b]Bethel
And there He spoke with us,
5 Even the LORD, the God of hosts,
The LORD is His [1a]name.
6 Therefore, [a]return to your God,
[b]Observe [1]kindness and justice,
And [c]wait for your God continually.
7 A [1]merchant, in whose hands are false [a]balances,
He loves to oppress.
8 And Ephraim said, "Surely I have become [a]rich,
I have found wealth for myself;
In all my labors they will find in me
[b]No iniquity, which *would be* sin."

8 [1]Lit *give* [2]Lit *Together* [a]Hos 6:4; 7:1 [b]Gen 14:8; Deut 29:23

9 [1]Lit *excitement* [a]Deut 13:17 [b]Jer 26:3; 30:11 [c]Num 23:19 [d]Is 5:24; 12:6; 41:14, 16

10 [a]Hos 3:5; 6:1-3 [b]Is 31:4; Joel 3:16; Amos 1:2 [c]Is 66:2, 5

11 [a]Is 11:11 [b]Is 60:8; Hos 7:11 [c]Ezek 28:25, 26; 34:27, 28

12 [1]Ch 12:1 in Heb [a]Hos 4:2; 7:3

12:1 [1]Ch 12:2 in Heb [2]Lit *they make* [a]Jer 22:22 [b]Gen 41:6; Ezek 17:10

2 [a]Hos 4:1; Mic 6:2 [b]Hos 4:9; 7:2

3 [a]Gen 25:26 [b]Gen 32:28

4 [a]Gen 32:26 [b]Gen 28:13-19; 35:10-15

5 [1]Lit *memorial* [a]Ex 3:15

6 [1]Or *loyalty* [a]Hos 6:1-3; 10:12 [b]Mic 6:8 [c]Mic 7:7

7 [1]Or *Canaanite* [a]Prov 11:1; Amos 8:5; Mic 6:11

8 [a]Ps 62:10; Hos 13:6; Rev 3:17 [b]Hos 4:8; 14:1

9 But I *have been* the LORD your God since
the land of Egypt;
I will make you [a]live in tents again,
As in the days of the appointed festival.
10 I have also spoken to the [a]prophets,
And I [1]gave numerous visions,
And through the prophets I gave [b]parables.
11 Is there iniquity *in* Gilead?
Surely they are worthless.
In Gilgal they sacrifice bulls,
Yes, [a]their altars are like the stone heaps
Beside the furrows of the field.

12 Now [a]Jacob fled to the [1]land of Aram,
And [b]Israel worked for a wife,
And for a wife he kept *sheep.*
13 But by a [a]prophet the LORD brought Israel from Egypt,
And by a prophet he was kept.
14 [a]Ephraim has provoked to bitter anger;
So his Lord will leave his [b]bloodguilt on him
And bring back his [c]reproach to him.

Chapter 13 Theme ____________________

13 [a]When Ephraim [1]spoke, *there was* trembling.
He [b]exalted himself in Israel,
But through [c]Baal he [2]did wrong and died.
2 And now they sin more and more,
And make for themselves [a]molten images,
Idols [1b]skillfully made from their silver,
All of them the [c]work of craftsmen.
They say of them, "Let the [2]men who sacrifice
kiss the [d]calves!"
3 Therefore they will be like the [a]morning cloud
And like dew which [1]soon disappears,
Like [b]chaff which is blown away from the
threshing floor
And like [c]smoke from a [2]chimney.

4 Yet I *have been* the [a]LORD your God
Since the land of Egypt;
And you were not to know [b]any god except Me,
For there is no savior [c]besides Me.
5 I [1a]cared for you in the wilderness,
[b]In the land of drought.
6 As *they had* their pasture, they became [a]satisfied,
And being satisfied, their [b]heart became proud;
Therefore they [c]forgot Me.
7 So I will be [a]like a lion to them;
Like a [b]leopard I will [1]lie in wait by the wayside.

9 [a]Lev 23:42
10 [1]Lit *multiplied the vision* [a]2 Kin 17:13; Jer 7:25 [b]Ezek 17:2; 20:49
11 [a]Hos 8:11; 10:1, 2
12 [1]Lit *field* [a]Gen 28:5 [b]Gen 29:20
13 [a]Ex 14:19-22; Is 63:11-14
14 [a]2 Kin 17:7-18 [b]Ezek 18:10-13 [c]Dan 11:18; Mic 6:16
13:1 [1]Or *spoke with trembling* [2]Or *became guilty* [a]Job 29:21, 22 [b]Judg 8:1; 12:1 [c]Hos 2:8-17; 11:2
2 [1]Or *according to their own understanding* [2]Lit *sacrificers of* or, *(among) mankind* [a]Is 46:6; Jer 10:4; Hos 2:8 [b]Is 44:17-20 [c]Hos 8:6 [d]Hos 8:5, 6; 10:5
3 [1]Lit *goes away early* [2]Lit *window* [a]Hos 6:4 [b]Ps 1:4; Is 17:13; Dan 2:35 [c]Ps 68:2
4 [a]Hos 12:9 [b]Ex 20:3; 2 Kin 18:35 [c]Is 43:11; 45:21, 22
5 [1]Or *knew* [a]Deut 2:7; 32:10 [b]Deut 8:15
6 [a]Deut 8:12, 14; 32:13-15; Jer 5:7 [b]Hos 7:14 [c]Hos 2:13; 4:6; 8:14
7 [1]Or *watch* [a]Lam 3:10; Hos 5:14 [b]Jer 5:6

8 I will encounter them [a]like a bear robbed of her cubs,
And I will tear open [1]their chests;
There I will also [b]devour them like a lioness,
As a wild beast would tear them.

9 *It is* your destruction, O Israel,
[1]That *you are* [a]against Me, against your [b]help.
10 Where now is your [a]king
That he may save you in all your cities,
And your [b]judges of whom you [1]requested,
"Give me a king and princes"?
11 I [a]gave you a king in My anger
And [b]took him away in My wrath.

12 The iniquity of Ephraim is bound up;
His sin is [a]stored up.
13 The pains of [a]childbirth come upon him;
He is [b]not a wise son,
For [1]it is not the time that he should [c]delay at the opening
of the womb.
14 Shall I [a]ransom them from the [1]power of Sheol?
Shall I redeem them from death?
[b]O Death, where are your thorns?
O Sheol, where is your sting?
[c]Compassion will be hidden from My sight.

15 Though he [a]flourishes among the [1]reeds,
An [b]east wind will come,
The wind of the LORD coming up from the wilderness;
And his fountain will [c]become dry
And his spring will be dried up;
It will [d]plunder *his* treasury of every precious article.
16 [1]Samaria will be held [a]guilty,
For she has [b]rebelled against her God.
[c]They will fall by the [d]sword,
Their little ones will be [e]dashed in pieces,
And their pregnant [f]women will be ripped open.

Chapter 14 Theme ______________________________

14 [1a]Return, O Israel, to the LORD your God,
For you have stumbled [2]because of your [b]iniquity.
2 Take words with you and return to the LORD.
Say to Him, "[a]Take away all iniquity
And [1]receive *us* graciously,
That we may [b]present [2]the fruit of our lips.
3 "Assyria will not save us,
We will [a]not ride on horses;
Nor will we say again, '[b]Our god,'
To the [c]work of our hands;
For in [d]You the [1]orphan finds mercy."

8 [1]Lit *the enclosure of their heart* [a]2 Sam 17:8 [b]Ps 50:22

9 [1]Or *But in Me is your help* [a]Jer 2:17, 19; Mal 1:12, 13 [b]Deut 33:26, 29

10 [1]Lit *said* [a]2 Kin 17:4; Hos 8:4 [b]1 Sam 8:5, 6

11 [a]1 Sam 8:7; 10:17-24 [b]1 Sam 15:26; 1 Kin 14:7-10; Hos 10:7

12 [a]Deut 32:34, 35; Job 14:17; Rom 2:5

13 [1]Lit *it is the time that he should not tarry at the breaking forth of children* [a]Is 13:8; Mic 4:9, 10 [b]Deut 32:6; Hos 5:4 [c]Is 37:3; 66:9

14 [1]Lit *hand* [a]Ps 49:15; Ezek 37:12, 13 [b]1 Cor 15:55 [c]Jer 20:16; 31:35-37

15 [1]Or *brothers* [a]Gen 49:22; Hos 10:1 [b]Gen 41:6; Jer 4:11, 12; Ezek 17:10; 19:12 [c]Jer 51:36 [d]Jer 20:5

16 [1]Ch 14:1 in Heb [a]Hos 10:2 [b]Hos 7:14 [c]2 Kin 8:12 [d]Hos 11:6 [e]Hos 10:14 [f]2 Kin 15:16

14:1 [1]Ch 14:2 in Heb [2]Or *in* [a]Hos 6:1; 10:12; 12:6; Joel 2:13 [b]Hos 4:8; 5:5; 9:7

2 [1]Or *accept that which is good* [2]So with ancient versions; M.T. *our lips as bulls* [a]Mic 7:18, 19 [b]Ps 51:16, 17; Hos 6:6; Heb 13:15

3 [1]Or *fatherless* [a]Ps 33:17; Is 31:1 [b]Hos 8:6; 13:2 [c]Hos 4:12 [d]Ps 10:14; 68:5

4 [a]Is 57:18; Hos 6:1 [b]Zeph 3:17 [c]Is 12:1

5 [1]Lit *strike his roots* [a]Prov 19:12; Is 26:19 [b]Song 2:1; Matt 6:28 [c]Is 35:2

6 [1]Lit *go* [2]Or *splendor* [a]Jer 11:16 [b]Song 4:11

7 [1]Or *return, they will raise grain* [a]Ezek 17:23 [b]Hos 2:21, 22

8 [1]Lit *him* [a]Job 34:32; Hos 14:3 [b]Is 41:19 [c]Ezek 17:23

9 [a]Ps 107:43; Jer 9:12 [b]Ps 111:7, 8; Prov 10:29; Zeph 3:5 [c]Is 26:7 [d]Is 1:28

4 I will [a]heal their apostasy,
I will [b]love them freely,
For My anger has [c]turned away from them.
5 I will be like the [a]dew to Israel;
He will blossom like the [b]lily,
And he will [1]take root like *the cedars of* [c]Lebanon.
6 His shoots will [1]sprout,
And his [2]beauty will be like the [a]olive tree
And his fragrance like *the cedars of* [b]Lebanon.
7 Those who [a]live in his shadow
Will [1]again raise [b]grain,
And they will blossom like the vine.
His renown *will be* like the wine of Lebanon.

8 O Ephraim, what more have I to do with [a]idols?
It is I who answer and look after [1]you.
I am like a luxuriant [b]cypress;
From [c]Me comes your fruit.

9 [a]Whoever is wise, let him understand these things;
Whoever is discerning, let him know them.
For the [b]ways of the LORD are right,
And the [c]righteous will walk in them,
But [d]transgressors will stumble in them.

God's Response to Israel's Sin

Their Iniquity	The Immediate or Long-Range Consequences

Their Future or Hope

Hosea at a Glance

Theme of Hosea:

Author:

Date:

Purpose:

Key Words:

Segment Divisions		Chapter Themes
		1
		2
		3
		4
		5
		6
		7
		8
		9
		10
		11
		12
		13
		14

JOEL יואל YO'EL

Although we know nothing about Joel himself nor the exact time of his writing, what we read in this short prophetic book is significant. When Peter preached on Pentecost, he explained Pentecost in the light of a prophecy in Joel (Acts 2:14-21; Joel 2:28-32).

Joel uses a present-day plague to call God's people to repentance. As he does this, Joel, like the other prophets, warns them of the coming day of the Lord—a day that is as sure as the promises of God.

Things to Do

1. Read through Joel and mark the key words listed on the JOEL AT A GLANCE chart on page 1461.

2. To correctly interpret Joel, you must pay attention to the time when certain events occur. Joel switches from the present to the future. To pick this up, watch for and mark the words *then* and *now*. Mark any references to time with a clock. Also, observe the sequence of events.

3. As you read through Joel, note the following and record what you learn in the appropriate section on the JOEL OBSERVATIONS CHART on page 1462.

   a. What is going to happen to the people, the land, the nations, and the animals and who or what is going to do it.

   b. What the people are to do and why.

   c. How God will respond and the effect it will have on the people.

   d. When applicable, note when any of the above will happen.

4. Although we don't know when Joel prophesied, many believe it was during the days of Joash. See the chart THE RULERS AND PROPHETS OF JOEL'S TIME on page 1455.

5. Record the theme of each chapter on JOEL AT A GLANCE as well as in your Bible. Then fill in the rest of the chart. Be sure to record the theme or message of Joel.

6. *The day of the Lord* is an important day prophetically. Record your insights on the chart beginning on page 2076. As you do, note the reference (book, chapter, and verse) that you took your information from so you can find it later.

Things to Think About

1. What do you see happening in the world, in your nation? Could it be the judgment of the Lord? What could you and others learn from Joel's exhortations? What could you do?

2. Have you failed God in any way? According to what you have seen in Joel, is there a chance to return to Him? What could you do? How can you apply the message of Joel to your life? What do you think would happen if your church collectively repented and returned to the Lord in this manner? Think about it and ask God what to do.

1:1 [a]Jer 1:2; Ezek 1:3; Hos 1:1 [b]Acts 2:16

2 [a]Hos 4:1; 5:1 [b]Job 8:8; Joel 1:14 [c]Jer 30:7; Joel 2:2

3 [a]Ex 10:2; Ps 78:4

4 [a]Deut 28:38; Joel 2:25; Amos 4:9 [b]Nah 3:15, 16 [c]Is 33:4

5 [a]Joel 3:3 [b]Is 32:10

6 [1]Lit *come up against* [a]Joel 2:2, 11, 25 [b]Rev 9:8

7 [1]Or *a stump* [a]Is 5:6; Amos 4:9

8 [a]Is 22:12 [b]Joel 1:13; Amos 8:10

Chapter 1 Theme ____________________

1 The [a]word of the LORD that came to [b]Joel, the son of Pethuel:
2 [a]Hear this, O [b]elders,
And listen, all inhabitants of the land.
[c]Has *anything like* this happened in your days
Or in your fathers' days?
3 [a]Tell your sons about it,
And *let* your sons *tell* their sons,
And their sons the next generation.

4 What the [a]gnawing locust has left, the swarming locust
has eaten;
And what the [b]swarming locust has left, the creeping
locust has eaten;
And what the creeping locust has left, the [c]stripping locust
has eaten.
5 Awake, [a]drunkards, and weep;
And wail, all you wine drinkers,
On account of the sweet wine
That is [b]cut off from your mouth.
6 For a [a]nation has [1]invaded my land,
Mighty and without number;
[b]Its teeth are the teeth of a lion,
And it has the fangs of a lioness.
7 It has [a]made my vine a waste
And my fig tree [1]splinters.
It has stripped them bare and cast *them* away;
Their branches have become white.

8 [a]Wail like a virgin [b]girded with sackcloth
For the bridegroom of her youth.

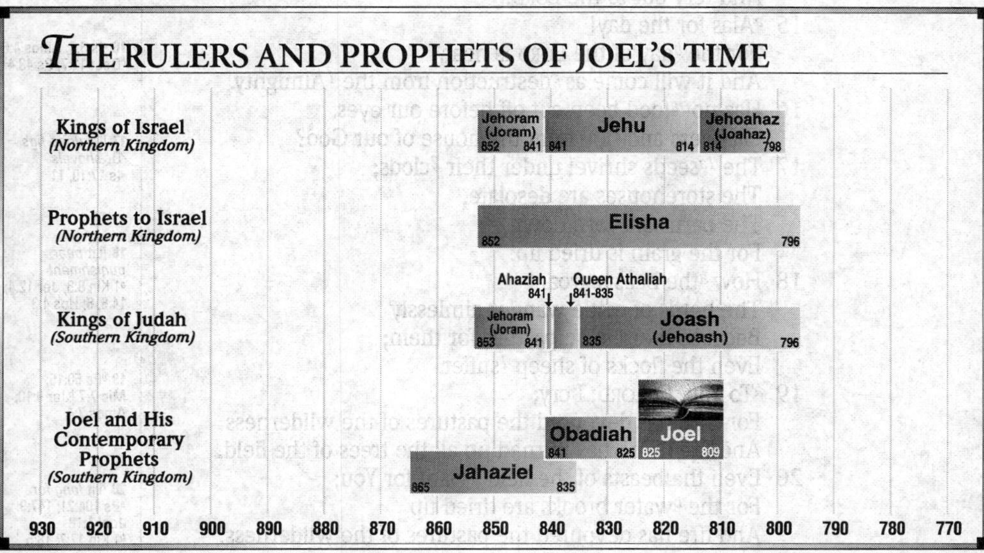

9 The [a]grain offering and the drink offering are cut off
From the house of the LORD.
The [b]priests mourn,
The ministers of the LORD.
10 The field is [a]ruined,
[b]The land mourns;
For the grain is ruined,
The new wine dries up,
Fresh oil [1]fails.
11 [1a]Be ashamed, O farmers,
Wail, O vinedressers,
For the wheat and the barley;
Because the [b]harvest of the field is destroyed.
12 The [a]vine dries up
And the fig tree [1]fails;
The [b]pomegranate, the [c]palm also, and the [2d]apple tree,
All the trees of the field dry up.
Indeed, [e]rejoicing dries up
From the sons of men.

13 [a]Gird yourselves *with sackcloth*
And lament, O priests;
[b]Wail, O ministers of the altar!
Come, [c]spend the night in sackcloth
O ministers of my God,
For the grain offering and the drink offering
Are withheld from the house of your God.
14 [a]Consecrate a fast,
Proclaim a [b]solemn assembly;
Gather the elders
And all the inhabitants of the land
To the house of the LORD your God,
And [c]cry out to the LORD.
15 [a]Alas for the day!
For the [b]day of the LORD is near,
And it will come as [c]destruction from the [1]Almighty.
16 Has not [a]food been cut off before our eyes,
Gladness and [b]joy from the house of our God?
17 The [1a]seeds shrivel under their [2]clods;
The storehouses are desolate,
The barns are torn down,
For the grain is dried up.
18 How [a]the beasts groan!
The herds of cattle wander aimlessly
Because there is no pasture for them;
Even the flocks of sheep [1]suffer.
19 [a]To You, O LORD, I cry;
For [b]fire has devoured the pastures of the wilderness
And the flame has burned up all the trees of the field.
20 Even the beasts of the field [1a]pant for You;
For the [b]water brooks are dried up
And fire has devoured the pastures of the wilderness.

9 [a]Hos 9:4; Joel 1:13; 2:14 [b]Joel 2:17

10 [1]Lit *wastes away* [a]Is 24:4, 7 [b]Jer 12:11

11 [1]Or *The farmers are ashamed, The vinedressers wail* [a]Jer 14:4; Amos 5:16 [b]Is 17:11; Jer 9:12

12 [1]Lit *wastes away* [2]Or *apricot* [a]Joel 1:10; Hab 3:17 [b]Hag 2:19 [c]Song 7:8 [d]Song 2:3 [e]Is 16:10; 24:11; Jer 48:33

13 [a]Jer 4:8; Ezek 7:18 [b]Jer 9:10 [c]1 Kin 21:27

14 [a]Joel 2:15, 16 [b]Lev 23:36 [c]Jon 3:8

15 [1]Heb *Shaddai* [a]Is 13:9; Jer 30:7; Amos 5:16 [b]Joel 2:1, 11, 31 [c]Is 13:6; Ezek 7:2-12

16 [a]Is 3:7; Amos 4:6 [b]Deut 12:7; Ps 43:4

17 [1]Or *dried figs* [2]Or *shovels* [a]Is 17:10, 11

18 [1]Lit *bear punishment* [a]1 Kin 8:5; Jer 12:4; 14:5, 6; Hos 4:3

19 [a]Ps 50:15; Mic 7:7 [b]Jer 9:10; Amos 7:4

20 [1]Lit *long for* [a]Ps 104:21; 147:9; Joel 1:18 [b]1 Kin 17:7; 18:5

2:1 [a]Jer 4:5; Joel 2:15; Zeph 1:16 [b]Joel 1:15; 2:11, 31; 3:14; Obad 15; Zeph 1:14
2 [a]Joel 2:10, 31; Amos 5:18; Zeph 1:15 [b]Joel 1:6; 2:11, 25 [c]Lam 1:12; Dan 9:12; 12:1; Joel 1:2
3 [a]Ps 97:3; Is 9:18, 19 [b]Is 51:3; Ezek 36:35 [c]Ex 10:5, 15; Ps 105:34, 35; Zech 7:14
4 [a]Rev 9:7
5 [1]Lit *Like the noise of chariots* [2]Lit *noise* [a]Rev 9:9 [b]Is 5:24; 30:30
6 [1]Or *become flushed* [a]Is 13:8; Nah 2:10 [b]Jer 30:6
7 [1]Lit *in his ways* [a]Prov 30:27
8 [1]Lit *fall* [2]Lit *weapon, probably javelin*
9 [a]Ex 10:6 [b]Jer 9:21; John 10:1
10 [a]Ps 18:7; Joel 3:16; Nah 1:5 [b]Is 13:10; 34:4; Jer 4:23; Ezek 32:7, 8; Joel 2:31; 3:15; Matt 24:29; Rev 8:12
11 [a]Ps 46:6; Is 13:4; Jer 25:30; Joel 3:16 [b]Joel 2:25 [c]Jer 50:34; Rev 18:8 [d]Jer 30:7; Joel 1:15; 2:1, 31; 3:14; Zeph 1:14, 15; Rev 6:17 [e]Ezek 22:14; Mal 3:2
12 [a]Deut 4:29; Jer 4:1, 2; Ezek 33:11; Hos 12:6

Chapter 2 Theme ______________________

2 [a]Blow a trumpet in Zion,
And sound an alarm on My holy mountain!
Let all the inhabitants of the land tremble,
For the [b]day of the LORD is coming;
Surely it is near,
2 A day of [a]darkness and gloom,
A day of clouds and thick darkness.
As the dawn is spread over the mountains,
So there is a [b]great and mighty people;
There has [c]never been *anything* like it,
Nor will there be again after it
To the years of many generations.
3 A [a]fire consumes before them
And behind them a flame burns.
The land is [b]like the garden of Eden before them
But a [c]desolate wilderness behind them,
And nothing at all escapes them.
4 Their [a]appearance is like the appearance of horses;
And like war horses, so they run.
5 [1]With a [a]noise as of chariots
They leap on the tops of the mountains,
Like the [2]crackling of a [b]flame of fire consuming
the stubble,
Like a mighty people arranged for battle.
6 Before them the people are in [a]anguish;
All [b]faces [1]turn pale.
7 They run like mighty men,
They climb the wall like soldiers;
And they each [a]march [1]in line,
Nor do they deviate from their paths.
8 They do not crowd each other,
They march everyone in his path;
When they [1]burst through the [2]defenses,
They do not break ranks.
9 They rush on the city,
They run on the wall;
They climb into the [a]houses,
They [b]enter through the windows like a thief.
10 Before them the earth [a]quakes,
The heavens tremble,
The [b]sun and the moon grow dark
And the stars lose their brightness.
11 The LORD [a]utters His voice before [b]His army;
Surely His camp is very great,
For [c]strong is he who carries out His word.
The [d]day of the LORD is indeed great and
very awesome,
And [e]who can endure it?
12 "Yet even now," declares the LORD,
"[a]Return to Me with all your heart,

And with [b]fasting, weeping and mourning;
13 And [a]rend your heart and not [b]your garments."
Now return to the LORD your God,
For He is [c]gracious and compassionate,
Slow to anger, abounding in lovingkindness
And [d]relenting of evil.
14 Who knows [a]whether He will *not* turn and relent
And leave a [b]blessing behind Him,
Even [c]a grain offering and a drink offering
For the LORD your God?
15 [a]Blow a trumpet in Zion,
[b]Consecrate a fast, proclaim a solemn assembly,
16 Gather the people, [a]sanctify the congregation,
Assemble the elders,
Gather the children and the nursing infants.
Let the [b]bridegroom come out of his room
And the bride out of her *bridal* chamber.
17 Let the priests, the LORD's ministers,
Weep [a]between the porch and the altar,
And let them say, "[b]Spare Your people, O LORD,
And do not make Your inheritance a [c]reproach,
A byword among the nations.
Why should they among the peoples say,
'[d]Where is their God?'"

18 Then the LORD [1]will be [a]zealous for His land
And [2]will have [b]pity on His people.
19 The LORD [1]will answer and say to His people,
"Behold, I am going to [a]send you grain, new wine
and oil,
And you will be satisfied *in full* with [2]them;
And I will [b]never again make you a reproach
among the nations.
20 "But I will remove the [a]northern *army* far from you,
And I will drive it into a parched and desolate land,
And its vanguard into the [b]eastern sea,
And its rear guard into the [c]western sea.
And its [d]stench will arise and its foul smell
will come up,
For it has done great things."

21 [a]Do not fear, O land, rejoice and be glad,
For the LORD has done [b]great things.
22 Do not fear, beasts of the field,
For the [a]pastures of the wilderness have turned green,
For the tree has borne its fruit,
The fig tree and the vine have yielded [1]in full.
23 So rejoice, O [a]sons of Zion,
And [b]be glad in the LORD your God;
For He has [c]given you [1]the early rain for
your vindication.

12 [b]Dan 9:3

13 [a]Ps 34:18; 51:17; Is 57:15 [b]Gen 37:34; 2 Sam 1:11; Job 1:20; Jer 41:5 [c]Ex 34:6 [d]Jer 18:8; 42:10; Amos 7:3, 6

14 [a]Jer 26:3; Jon 3:9 [b]Hag 2:19 [c]Joel 1:9, 13

15 [a]Num 10:3; 2 Kin 10:20 [b]Joel 1:14

16 [a]1 Sam 16:5; 2 Chr 29:5 [b]Ps 19:5

17 [a]2 Chr 8:12; Ezek 8:16 [b]Ex 32:11, 12; Is 37:20; Amos 7:2, 5 [c]Ps 44:13; 74:10 [d]Ps 42:10; 79:10; 115:2

18 [1]Or *was zealous* [2]Or *had pity* [a]Zech 1:14; 8:2 [b]Is 60:10; 63:9, 15

19 [1]Or *answered and said* [2]Lit *it* [a]Jer 31:12; Hos 2:21, 22; Joel 1:10; Mal 3:10 [b]Ezek 34:29; 36:15

20 [a]Jer 1:14, 15 [b]Zech 14:8 [c]Deut 11:24 [d]Is 34:3; Amos 4:10

21 [a]Is 54:4; Jer 30:10; Zeph 3:16, 17 [b]Ps 126:3; Joel 2:26

22 [1]Lit *their wealth* [a]Ps 65:12, 13

23 [1]I.e. autumn; or possibly *the teacher for righteousness* [a]Ps 149:2 [b]Is 12:2-6 [c]Deut 11:14; Is 41:16; Jer 5:24; Hab 3:18; Zech 10:7

And He has poured down for you the rain,
The [2]early and [3d]latter rain [4]as before.
24 The threshing floors will be full of grain,
And the vats will [a]overflow with the new wine and oil.
25 "Then I will make up to you for the years
That the swarming [a]locust has eaten,
The creeping locust, the stripping locust
and the gnawing locust,
My great army which I sent among you.
26 "You will have plenty to [a]eat and be satisfied
And [b]praise the name of the LORD your God,
Who has [c]dealt wondrously with you;
Then My people will [d]never be put to shame.
27 "Thus you will [a]know that I am in the midst of Israel,
And that I am the LORD your God,
And there is [b]no other;
And My people will never be [c]put to shame.

28 "[1a]It will come about after this
That I will [b]pour out My Spirit on all [2c]mankind;
And your sons and daughters will prophesy,
Your old men will dream dreams,
Your young men will see visions.
29 "Even on the [a]male and female servants
I will pour out My Spirit in those days.
30 "I will [a]display wonders in the sky and on the earth,
Blood, fire and columns of smoke.
31 "The [a]sun will be turned into darkness
And the moon into blood
Before the [b]great and awesome day of the LORD comes.
32 "And it will come about that [a]whoever calls on the name
of the LORD
Will be delivered;
For [b]on Mount Zion and in Jerusalem
There will be those who [c]escape,
As the LORD has said,
Even among the [d]survivors whom the LORD calls.

Chapter 3 Theme ____________________

3 "[1]For behold, [a]in those days and at that time,
When I [b]restore the fortunes of Judah and Jerusalem,
2 I will [a]gather all the nations
And bring them down to the [b]valley of [1]Jehoshaphat.
Then I will [c]enter into judgment with them there
On behalf of My people and My inheritance, Israel,
Whom they have [d]scattered among the nations;
And they have [e]divided up My land.
3 "They have also [a]cast lots for My people,
[1b]Traded a boy for a harlot
And sold a girl for wine that they may drink.

23 [2]I.e. autumn [3]I.e. spring [4]So with ancient versions; Heb *in the first* [d]Lev 26:4; Hos 6:3; Zech 10:1
24 [a]Lev 26:10; Amos 9:13; Mal 3:10
25 [a]Joel 1:4-7; 2:2-11
26 [a]Lev 26:5; Deut 11:15; Is 62:9 [b]Deut 12:7; Ps 67:5-7 [c]Ps 126:2, 3; Is 25:1 [d]Is 45:17
27 [a]Lev 26:11, 12; Joel 3:17, 21 [b]Is 45:5, 6 [c]Is 49:23
28 [1]Ch 3:1 in Heb [2]Lit *flesh* [a]Acts 2:17-21 [b]Is 32:15; 44:3; Ezek 39:29; Zech 12:10 [c]Is 40:5; 49:26
29 [a]1 Cor 12:13; Gal 3:28
30 [a]Matt 24:29; Mark 13:24, 25; Luke 21:11, 25, 26; Acts 2:19
31 [a]Is 13:10; 34:4; Joel 2:10; 3:15; Matt 24:29; Mark 13:24; Luke 21:25; Acts 2:20; Rev 6:12, 13 [b]Is 13:9; Zeph 1:14-16; Mal 4:1, 5
32 [a]Jer 33:3; Acts 2:21; Rom 10:13 [b]Is 46:13; Rom 11:26 [c]Is 4:2; Obad 17 [d]Is 11:11; Jer 31:7; Mic 4:7; Rom 9:27
3:1 [1]Ch 4:1 in Heb [a]Jer 30:3; Ezek 38:14 [b]Jer 16:15
2 [1]I.e. YHWH judges [a]Is 66:18; Mic 4:12; Zech 14:2 [b]Joel 3:12, 14 [c]Is 66:16; Jer 25:31; Ezek 38:22 [d]Jer 50:17; Ezek 34:6 [e]Ezek 35:10; 36:1-5
3 [1]Lit *Given* [a]Obad 11; Nah 3:10 [b]Amos 2:6

The Valley of Jehoshaphat (see Joel 3:12)

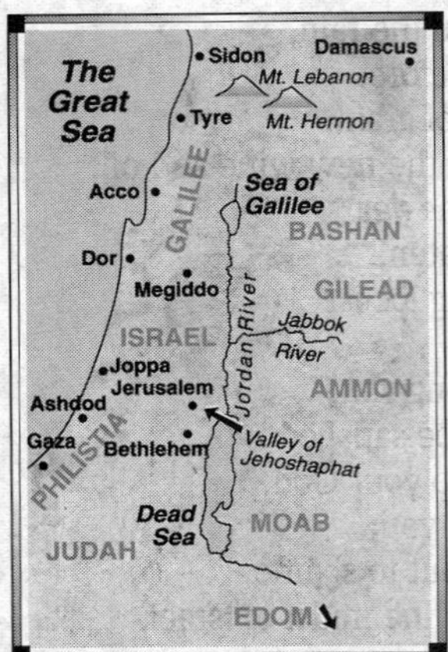

4 "Moreover, what are you to
Me, O [a]Tyre, Sidon and all the
regions of [b]Philistia? Are you
rendering Me a recompense? But
if you do recompense Me, swiftly
and speedily I will [c]return your
recompense on your head.
5 "Since you have [a]taken My
silver and My gold, brought My
precious [1]treasures to your temples,
6 and sold the [a]sons of Judah
and Jerusalem to the [1]Greeks in
order to remove them far from
their territory,
7 behold, I am going to [a]arouse
them from the place where you have sold them, and return
your recompense on your head.
8 "Also I will [a]sell your sons and your daughters into the hand
of the sons of Judah, and they will sell them to the [b]Sabeans, to
a distant nation," for the LORD has spoken.

9 [a]Proclaim this among the nations:
[b]Prepare a war; [c]rouse the mighty men!
Let all the soldiers draw near, let them come up!
10 [a]Beat your plowshares into swords
And your pruning hooks into spears;
[b]Let the weak say, "I am a mighty man."
11 [1a]Hasten and come, all you surrounding nations,
And gather yourselves there.
Bring down, O LORD, Your [b]mighty ones.
12 Let the nations be aroused
And come up to the [a]valley of [1]Jehoshaphat,
For there I will sit to [b]judge
All the surrounding nations.
13 [a]Put in the sickle, for the [b]harvest is ripe.
Come, [c]tread, for the [d]wine press is full;
The vats overflow, for their [e]wickedness is great.
14 [a]Multitudes, multitudes in the [b]valley of [1]decision!
For the [c]day of the LORD is near in the valley of [1]decision.
15 The [a]sun and moon grow dark
And the stars lose their brightness.
16 The LORD [a]roars from Zion
And [b]utters His voice from Jerusalem,
And the [c]heavens and the earth tremble.
But the LORD is a [d]refuge for His people
And a [e]stronghold to the sons of Israel.
17 Then you will [a]know that I am the LORD your God,
Dwelling in Zion, My [b]holy mountain.
So Jerusalem will be [c]holy,
And [d]strangers will pass through it no more.

18 And in that day
The [a]mountains will drip with [1]sweet wine,

INSIGHT

Sabeans are the descendants of Seba, the son of Cush or possibly of Sheba, the son of Raamah (see Genesis 10:7). Sabeans destroyed Job's flocks, herds, and servants. They were known as traveling merchants. The term *Sabeans* could have been adapted to refer to foreign or nomadic merchants.

4 [a]Is 23:1-18; Amos 1:9, 10; Zech 9:2-4; Matt 11:21, 22; Luke 10:13, 14 [b]Is 14:29-31; Jer 47:1-7; Ezek 25:15-17; Amos 1:6-8; Zech 9:5-7 [c]Is 34:8; 59:18

5 [1]Lit *goodly things* [a]2 Kin 12:18; 2 Chr 21:16, 17

6 [1]Lit *sons of Javan* [a]Ezek 27:13

7 [a]Is 43:5, 6; Jer 23:8; Zech 9:13

8 [a]Is 14:2; 60:14 [b]Job 1:15; Ps 72:10; Ezek 38:13

9 [a]Jer 51:27 [b]Jer 6:4; Ezek 38:7; Mic 3:5 [c]Is 8:9, 10; Jer 46:3, 4; Zech 14:2, 3

10 [a]Is 2:4; Mic 4:3 [b]Zech 12:8

11 [1]Or *Lend aid* [a]Ezek 38:15, 16 [b]Is 13:3

12 [1]I.e. YHWH judges [a]Joel 3:2, 14 [b]Ps 7:6; 96:13; 98:9; Is 2:4; 3:13

13 [a]Rev 14:14-19 [b]Jer 51:33; Hos 6:11 [c]Rev 14:19, 20; 19:15 [d]Is 63:3; Lam 1:15 [e]Gen 18:20

14 [1]I.e. God's verdict [a]Is 34:2-8 [b]Joel 3:2, 12 [c]Joel 1:15; 2:1, 11, 31

15 [a]Joel 2:10, 31

16 [a]Hos 11:10; Amos 1:2 [b]Joel 2:11 [c]Ezek 38:19; Joel 2:10; Hag 2:6 [d]Ps 61:3; Is 33:16; Jer 17:17 [e]Jer 16:19; Nah 1:7

17 [a]Joel 2:27 [b]Is 11:9; 56:7; Ezek 20:40 [c]Is 4:3; Obad 17 [d]Is 52:1; Nah 1:15

18 [1]Lit *freshly pressed out grape juice* [a]Amos 9:13

18 [2]Or *acacias* [b]Ex 3:8 [c]Is 30:25; 35:6 [d]Ezek 47:1-12

And the hills will [b]flow with milk,
And all the [c]brooks of Judah will flow with water;
And a [d]spring will go out from the house of the LORD
To water the valley of [2]Shittim.

19 [1]Lit *of the sons* [a]Obad 10

19 Egypt will become a waste,
And Edom will become a desolate wilderness,
Because of the [a]violence [1]done to the sons of Judah,
In whose land they have shed innocent blood.

20 [a]Ezek 37:25; Amos 9:15

20 But Judah will be [a]inhabited forever
And Jerusalem for all generations.

21 [a]Is 4:4

21 And I will [a]avenge their blood which I have not avenged,
For the LORD dwells in Zion.

JOEL AT A GLANCE

Theme of Joel:

Author:

Date:

Purpose:

Key Words:

- locust
- Zion
- day of the Lord
- return
- I will
- never again
- then
- now
- nations
- sackcloth
- Spirit
- land (God's)

SEGMENT DIVISIONS		CHAPTER THEMES
		1
		2
		3

Joel Observations Chart

What Happens to the People

What the People Are to Do

What Is the Effect on People

What Happens to the Land Before and During Judgment

What Happens to the Land After Judgment

What Happens to the Animals

What God Will Do—"I will"

What Happens to the Nations and Why

The Day of the Lord

AMOS עָמוֹס AMOS

While the cows of Bashan (the best of breeds raised in Canaan) grazed and were pampered in the northern Transjordan region, the Israelites of the northern kingdom went up to worship at Bethel, burning incense and presenting their sacrifices at the altar.

Bethel was one of two places where Jeroboam son of Nebat, the first king of Israel (the northern kingdom), had set up the golden calves (see 1 Kings 12–13). He felt he had to. When the 12 tribes divided into two kingdoms, those of the northern kingdom were cut off from Jerusalem. Jerusalem now belonged to the two tribes of the southern kingdom, Judah and Benjamin. If Jeroboam's people went to celebrate the feasts in Jerusalem at the temple as God commanded, they might defect to the southern kingdom.

So Jeroboam commissioned his own priests and instituted his own feast. The people would worship as they pleased, where they pleased. Those who did not go to Bethel could go to Gilgal, another principal place of worship. In Gilgal they could present their thank offerings with leaven, proclaim their freewill offerings, and even worship other gods.

Israel became prosperous and politically secure. It was a golden era. Surely God was pleased with Israel—or that is what they supposed until a shepherd from the small city of Tekoa, just ten miles south of Jerusalem, appeared on the scene.

Then the Word of the Lord came.

Things to Do

General Instructions

1. In order to understand the historical setting of Amos, do the following:
   a. Read Amos 1:1 and then record what you learn about Amos on the AMOS AT A GLANCE chart on page 1478 under "Author." Then under "Date" record the information that gives you a clue as to the time of these visions (see Zechariah 14:5). Under "Purpose" fill in Amos's reason for writing (see Amos 1:1).
   b. Study the historical chart on page 1465, which shows Amos's relationship to the kings of Israel and Judah. Remember, Amos is a prophet to the northern kingdom.
   c. Read 2 Chronicles 26:1-23; 2 Kings 14:23–15:7. When you come across Azariah, remember that this is another name for King Uzziah, who ruled over the southern kingdom.
2. Record the key words on AMOS AT A GLANCE on an index card and use this as a bookmark. Other key words will be added in the upcoming segments. As you mark the key words, compile a list of the information you glean by examining the key word in the light of how it might answer the "5 W's and an H."
3. Observe references to God carefully. Note the extent of His sovereignty. Draw a △ in the margin of every verse that reveals God's authority and power and what He is sovereign over.

As you read through Amos, you will find three key phrases that divide the book into three segments. Therefore, your instructions will be divided accordingly.

Chapters 1–2

1. Read Amos 1 and 2 and mark each occurrence of the phrase *Thus says the Lord, for three transgressions of* ________ *and for four*. Note whose transgressions God is going to deal with in each incident.

2. Read what follows each of the statements you have marked. Look for another key repeated phrase and mark or color it in a distinctive way.

3. Then observe why God will not revoke their punishment and what the punishment will be. Note their punishment by marking each occurrence of *I will*.

4. In 2:4,6 God deals with the southern kingdom, Judah, and with the northern kingdom, Israel. To understand why God speaks to them separately, look at Amos 1:1 and notice to whom Amos was sent as a prophet (see the chart on page 1465). Keep this in mind as you study Amos.

5. Record the theme of the first two chapters on AMOS AT A GLANCE and in your Bible.

Chapters 3–6

1. The second key repeated phrase is *hear this word*. Read Amos 3–6 and distinctively mark each occurrence of this phrase.

2. Read Amos 3–6 a second time. As you read these messages from the Lord, ask the "5 W's and an H." Ask questions such as: Who is speaking? To whom? What is being said? What is going to happen? When will it happen? Where will it take place? Why will it happen? How will it happen? (Remember, you won't always find answers to every question.)

3. Mark key repeated words or phrases. Marking every *I will* as it refers to God and asking the "5 W's and an H" will help you see what God is going to do. Watch for *yet* and *returned* in chapter 4 and *seek* in chapter 5. Mark every reference to *the day of the Lord* and record your insights on the chart beginning on page 2076.

4. In your notebook, list important insights about God, Israel, what the people are doing wrong, and what they don't like.

5. Record the chapter themes as you have done previously.

Chapters 7–9

1. The key repeated phrase that sets off the last segment of Amos is *thus the Lord God showed me*. Read these last three chapters and mark each occurrence of this phrase.

2. As you read through this final segment of Amos, watch what Amos was shown and how he responds. Also observe the response to Amos's prophecy and how Amos deals with this.

3. In chapter 8 you see one final *hear this*. Pay careful attention to what God is going to do. Compare 8:8 with 1:1.

4. Although the phrase *thus the Lord God showed me* is not used in 9:1, can you see that *I saw the Lord...and He said* could be Amos's fifth vision, which parallels those you marked in chapters 7 and 8? If so, mark it as you did the others.

5. Mark the *I will*'s of God and any other key words or phrases.

6. Record the chapter themes along with the theme of Amos.

7. Record your insights from Amos on *the day of the Lord* on the chart beginning on page 2076.

8. Finally, watch how the book of Amos closes. What is God's promise? Recall any reference to the land. Has this promise regarding the land of Israel been fulfilled? Think of Israel's history.

Things to Think About

1. Has wealth, the ease of life, the possession of things, the pursuit of happiness led to complacency in your worship? Are you worshiping God His way or your way?

2. Review the list of Israel's sins. Are you guilty of any of these? According to what you read in Amos, could Israel or the other nations sin and not reap the consequences? Can you?

3. What is the purpose of God's judgments? When God decides to judge, what can we do? What can we expect?

THE RULERS AND PROPHETS OF AMOS'S TIME

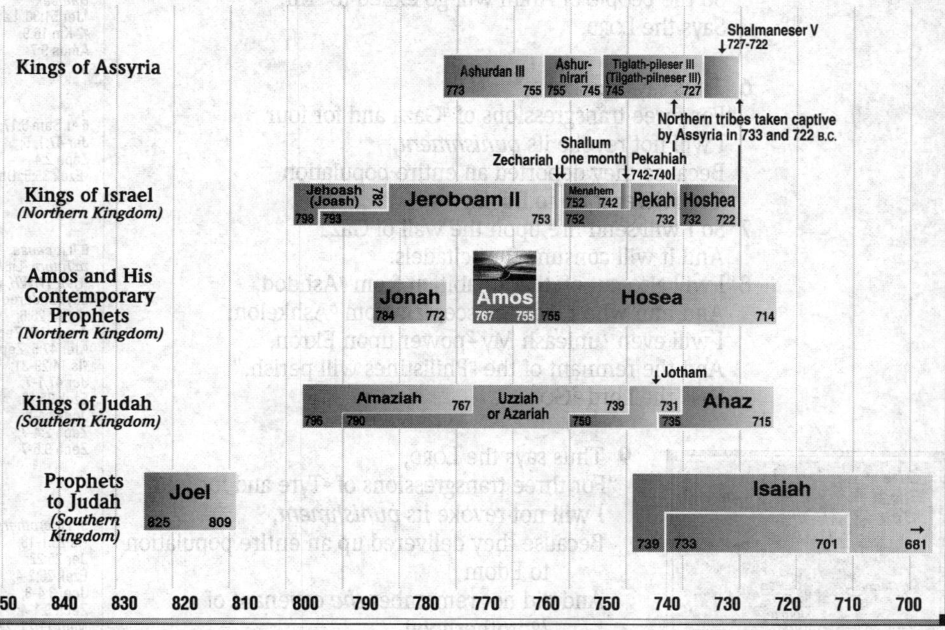

Kings of Assyria

Ashurdan III 773–755; Ashur-nirari 755–745; Tiglath-pileser III (Tilgath-pileser III) 745–727; Shalmaneser V 727-722

Northern tribes taken captive by Assyria in 733 and 722 B.C.

Kings of Israel *(Northern Kingdom)*

Jehoash (Joash) 798–782; Jeroboam II 793–753; Zechariah; Shallum one month; Menahem 752–742; Pekahiah 742-740; Pekah 752–732; Hoshea 732–722

Amos and His Contemporary Prophets *(Northern Kingdom)*

Jonah 784–772; Amos 767–755; Hosea 755–714

Kings of Judah *(Southern Kingdom)*

Amaziah 796–767; Uzziah or Azariah 790–739; Jotham 750–731; Ahaz 735–715

Prophets to Judah *(Southern Kingdom)*

Joel 825–809; Isaiah 739–681 →; 733–701

850 840 830 820 810 800 790 780 770 760 750 740 730 720 710 700

Chapter 1 Theme ____________________

1:1 [1]Lit *saw concerning* [a]Amos 7:14 [b]2 Sam 14:2; Jer 6:1 [c]2 Chr 26:1-23; Is 1:1 [d]2 Kin 14:23-29; Hos 1:1; Amos 7:10, 11 [e]Zech 14:5

2 [1]Lit *head* [a]Is 42:13; Jer 25:30; Joel 3:16 [b]Jer 12:4; Joel 1:18, 19 [c]Amos 9:3

3 [a]Amos 2:1, 4, 6 [b]Is 8:4; 17:1-3; Jer 49:23-27; Zech 9:1

1 The words of Amos, who was among the [a]sheepherders from
[b]Tekoa, which he [1]envisioned in visions concerning Israel in
the days of [c]Uzziah king of Judah, and in the days of [d]Jeroboam
son of Joash, king of Israel, two years before the [e]earthquake.
2 He said,
"The [a]LORD roars from Zion
And from Jerusalem He utters His voice;
And the shepherds' [b]pasture grounds mourn,
And the [1c]summit of Carmel dries up."

3 Thus says the LORD,
"For [a]three transgressions of [b]Damascus and for four

INSIGHT

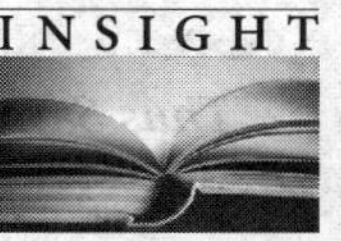

There are two Zions referred to in the Scriptures: the earthly Zion, Jerusalem, and the heavenly Zion, where God's throne is. Zion is also referred to as the city of God.

I will not [1]revoke its *punishment,*
Because they threshed Gilead with *implements*
of sharp iron.
4 "So I will send fire upon the house of Hazael
And it will consume the citadels of [a]Ben-hadad.
5 "I will also [a]break the *gate* bar of Damascus,
And cut off the inhabitant from the [1]valley of Aven,
And him who holds the scepter, from Beth-eden;
So the people of Aram will go exiled to [b]Kir,"
Says the LORD.

6 Thus says the LORD,
"For three transgressions of [a]Gaza and for four
I will not revoke its *punishment,*
Because they deported an entire population
To [b]deliver *it* up to Edom.
7 "So I will send fire upon the wall of Gaza
And it will consume her citadels.
8 "I will also cut off the inhabitant from [a]Ashdod,
And him who holds the scepter, from [b]Ashkelon;
I will even [1]unleash My [2]power upon Ekron,
And the remnant of the [c]Philistines will perish,"
Says the Lord [3]GOD.

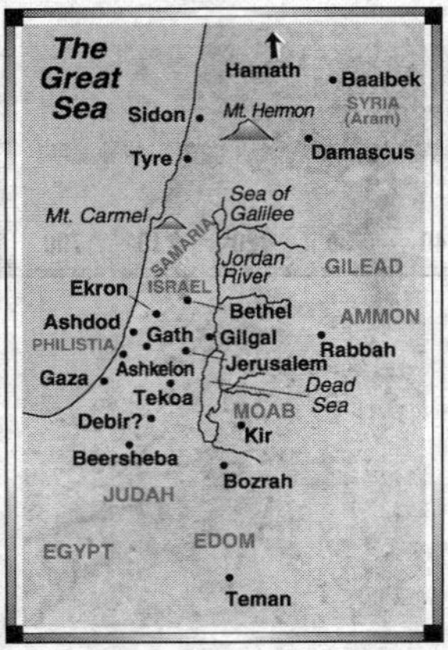

9 Thus says the LORD,
"For three transgressions of [a]Tyre and for four
I will not revoke its *punishment,*
Because they delivered up an entire population
to Edom
And did not remember *the* covenant of
[1b]brotherhood.
10 "So I will [a]send fire upon the wall of Tyre
And it will consume her citadels."

11 Thus says the LORD,
"For three transgressions of [a]Edom and for four
I will not revoke its *punishment,*
Because he [b]pursued his brother with
the sword,
While he [1]stifled his compassion;
His anger also [c]tore continually,
And he maintained his fury forever.
12 "So I will send fire upon [a]Teman
And it will consume the citadels of Bozrah."

13 Thus says the LORD,
"For three transgressions of the sons of [a]Ammon
and for four
I will not revoke its *punishment,*
Because they [b]ripped open the pregnant women of Gilead
In order to [c]enlarge their borders.

Thus Says the Lord to...

3 [1]Lit *cause it to turn back,* and so throughout the ch

4 [a]1 Kin 20:1; 2 Kin 6:24

5 [1]Possibly, *Baalbek* [a]Jer 51:30; Lam 2:9 [b]2 Kin 16:9; Amos 9:7

6 [a]1 Sam 6:17; Jer 47:1, 5; Zeph 2:4 [b]Ezek 35:5; Obad 11

8 [1]Lit *cause to return* [2]Lit *hand* [3]Heb *YHWH,* usually rendered LORD [a]2 Chr 26:6; Amos 3:9; Zech 9:6 [b]Jer 47:5; Zeph 2:4 [c]Is 14:29-31; Jer 47:1-7; Ezek 25:16; Joel 3:4-8; Zeph 2:4-7; Zech 9:5-7

9 [1]Lit *brothers* [a]Is 23:1-18; Jer 25:22; Ezek 26:2-4; Joel 3:4-8; Zech 9:1-4; Matt 11:21, 22; Luke 10:13, 14 [b]1 Kin 9:11-14

10 [a]Zech 9:4

11 [1]Lit *corrupted* [a]Is 34:5, 6; 63:1-6; Jer 49:7-22; Ezek 25:12-14; 35:1-15; Obad 1-14; Mal 1:2-5 [b]Num 20:14-21; 2 Chr 28:17; Obad 10-12 [c]Is 57:16; Mic 7:18

12 [a]Jer 49:7, 20; Obad 9

13 [a]Jer 49:1-6; Ezek 21:28-32; 25:2-7; Zeph 2:8, 9 [b]2 Kin 15:16; Hos 13:16 [c]Is 5:8; Ezek 35:10

14 "So I will kindle a fire on the wall of [a]Rabbah
And it will consume her citadels
Amid [1b]war cries on the day of battle,
And a [c]storm on the day of tempest.
15 "Their [a]king will go into exile,
He and his princes together," says the LORD.

Chapter 2 Theme ____________________

2 Thus says the LORD,
"For three transgressions of [a]Moab and for four
I will not [1]revoke its *punishment,*
Because he [b]burned the bones of the king of Edom to lime.
2 "So I will send fire upon Moab
And it will consume the citadels of [a]Kerioth;
And Moab will die amid [b]tumult,
With [1]war cries and the sound of a trumpet.
3 "I will also cut off the [1a]judge from her midst
And slay all her [b]princes with him," says the LORD.

4 Thus says the LORD,
"For three transgressions of [a]Judah and for four
I will not revoke its *punishment,*
Because they [b]rejected the law of the LORD
And have not kept His statutes;
Their [1c]lies also have led them astray,
Those after which their [d]fathers walked.
5 "So I will [a]send fire upon Judah
And it will consume the citadels of Jerusalem."

6 Thus says the LORD,
"For three transgressions of [a]Israel and for four
I will not revoke its *punishment,*
Because they [b]sell the righteous for money
And the needy for a pair of sandals.
7 "These who [1]pant after the *very* dust of the earth
on the head of the [a]helpless
Also [b]turn aside the way of the humble;
And a [c]man and his father [2]resort to the same [3]girl
In order to profane My holy name.
8 "On garments [a]taken as pledges they stretch out
beside [b]every altar,
And in the house of their God they [c]drink the wine
of those who have been fined.

9 "Yet it was I who destroyed the [a]Amorite before them,
[1]Though his [b]height *was* like the height of cedars
And he *was* strong as the oaks;
I even destroyed his [c]fruit above and his root below.
10 "It was I who [a]brought you up from the land of Egypt,
And I led you in the wilderness [b]forty years

14 [1]Or *shouts* [a]Deut 3:11; 1 Chr 20:1; Jer 49:2 [b]Ezek 21:22; Amos 2:2 [c]Is 29:6; 30:30

15 [a]Jer 49:3

2:1 [1]Lit *cause it to turn back,* and so throughout the ch [a]Is 15:1-16:14; 25:10-12; Jer 48:1-47; Ezek 25:8-11; Zeph 2:8, 9 [b]2 Kin 3:26, 27

2 [1]Or *shouts* [a]Jer 48:24, 41 [b]Jer 48:45

3 [1]Or *executive officer* [a]Ps 2:10; 141:6; Amos 5:7, 12; 6:12 [b]Job 12:21; Is 40:23

4 [1]Or *false gods* [a]2 Kin 17:19; Hos 12:2; Amos 3:2 [b]Judg 2:17-20; 2 Kin 22:11-17; Jer 6:19; 8:9 [c]Is 9:15, 16; 28:15; Jer 16:19; Hab 2:18 [d]Jer 9:14; 16:11, 12; Ezek 20:18, 24, 30

5 [a]Jer 17:27; 21:10; Hos 8:14

6 [a]2 Kin 18:11, 12 [b]Joel 3:3; Amos 5:11, 12; 8:6

7 [1]Or *trample* or, *snap at the head of the helpless on the dust* [2]Lit *go* [3]Possibly a harlot, or a temple prostitute [a]Amos 8:4; Mic 2:2, 9 [b]Amos 5:12 [c]Hos 4:14

8 [a]Ex 22:26 [b]Amos 3:14 [c]Amos 4:1; 6:6

9 [1]Lit *Whose height* [a]Num 21:23-25; Josh 10:12 [b]Num 13:32 [c]Ezek 17:9; Mal 4:1

10 [a]Ex 12:51; 20:2; Amos 3:1; 9:7 [b]Deut 2:7

[1]That you might take possession of the land
of the [c]Amorite.
11 "Then I [a]raised up some of your sons to be prophets
And some of your young men to be [b]Nazirites.
Is this not so, O sons of Israel?" declares the LORD.
12 "But you made the Nazirites drink wine,
And you commanded the prophets saying, 'You [a]shall not
prophesy!'
13 "Behold, I am [1a]weighted down beneath you
As a wagon [2]is weighted down when filled with sheaves.
14 "[1a]Flight will perish from the swift,
And the stalwart will not strengthen his power,
Nor the [b]mighty man save his [2]life.
15 "He who [a]grasps the bow will not stand *his ground,*
The swift of foot will not escape,
Nor will he who rides the [b]horse save his [1]life.
16 "Even the [1]bravest among the warriors will [a]flee naked in
that day," declares the LORD.

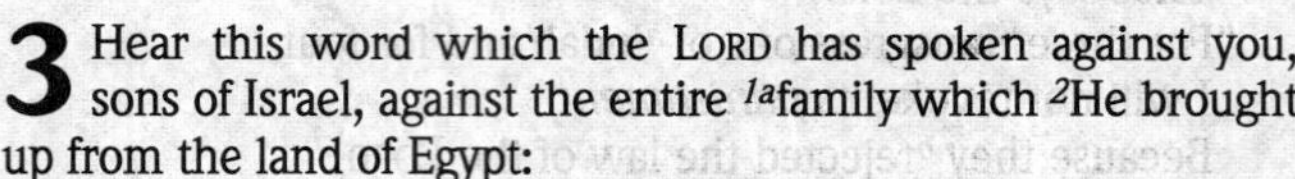
Chapter 3 Theme ______________________

3 Hear this word which the LORD has spoken against you,
sons of Israel, against the entire [1a]family which [2]He brought
up from the land of Egypt:
2 "[a]You only have I [1]chosen among all the families
of the earth;
Therefore I will [2b]punish you for all your iniquities."
3 Do two men walk together unless they have made an
[1]appointment?
4 Does a [a]lion roar in the forest when he has no prey?
Does a young lion [1]growl from his den unless he has
captured *something?*
5 Does a bird fall into a trap on the ground when there is no
[1]bait in it?
Does a trap spring up from the earth when it captures
nothing at all?
6 If a [a]trumpet is blown in a city will not the
people tremble?
If a [b]calamity occurs in a city has not the LORD done it?
7 [1]Surely the Lord [2]GOD does nothing
Unless He [a]reveals His secret counsel
To His servants the prophets.
8 A [a]lion has roared! Who will not fear?
The [b]Lord [1]GOD has spoken! [c]Who can but prophesy?
9 Proclaim on the citadels in [a]Ashdod and on the citadels in the
land of Egypt and say, "Assemble yourselves on the [b]mountains
of Samaria and see *the* great tumults within her and *the*
[c]oppressions in her midst.
10 "But they [a]do not know how to do what is right," declares the
LORD, "these who [b]hoard up [1]violence and devastation in their
citadels."

10 [1]Lit *To possess* [c]Ex 3:8
11 [a]Deut 18:18; Jer 7:25 [b]Num 6:2, 3; Judg 13:5
12 [a]Is 30:10; Jer 11:21; Amos 7:13, 16; Mic 2:6
13 [1]Or *tottering* [2]Or *totters* [a]Is 1:14
14 [1]Or *A place of refuge* [2]Lit *soul* [a]Is 30:16, 17 [b]Ps 33:16; Jer 9:23
15 [1]Lit *soul* [a]Jer 51:56; Ezek 39:3 [b]Is 31:3
16 [1]Lit *stout of heart* [a]Judg 4:17
3:1 [1]I.e. nation [2]Lit *I* [a]Jer 8:3; 13:11
2 [1]Lit *known* [2]Lit *visit* [a]Gen 18:19; Ex 19:5, 6; Deut 4:32-37; 7:6 [b]Jer 14:10; Ezek 20:36; Dan 9:12; Rom 2:9
3 [1]Or *agreement*
4 [1]Lit *give his voice* [a]Ps 104:21; Hos 5:14; 11:10
5 [1]Or *striker-bar set*
6 [a]Jer 4:5, 19, 21; 6:1; Hos 5:8; Zeph 1:16 [b]Is 14:24-27; 45:7
7 [1]Or *For* [2]Heb *YHWH* [a]Gen 6:13; 18:17; Jer 23:22; Dan 9:22; John 15:15
8 [1]Heb *YHWH,* usually rendered *LORD,* and so throughout the ch [a]Amos 1:2 [b]Jon 1:1-3; 3:1-3 [c]Jer 20:9; Acts 4:20
9 [a]1 Sam 5:1 [b]Amos 4:1; 6:1 [c]Amos 5:11; 8:6
10 [1]I.e. the booty from violence [a]Ps 14:4; Jer 4:22; Amos 5:7; 6:12 [b]Hab 2:8-10; Zeph 1:9; Zech 5:3, 4

11 Therefore, thus says the Lord GOD,
"An [a]enemy, even one surrounding the land,
Will pull down your [1]strength from you
And your [b]citadels will be looted."
12 Thus says the LORD,
"Just as the shepherd [1a]snatches from the lion's mouth
a couple of legs or a piece of an ear,
So will the sons of Israel dwelling in Samaria
be [2]snatched away—
With *the* [b]corner of a bed and *the* [3c]cover of a couch!
13 "Hear and [a]testify against the house of Jacob,"
Declares the Lord GOD, the God of hosts.
14 "For on the day that I punish Israel's transgressions,
I will also punish the altars of [a]Bethel;
The horns of the altar will be cut off
And they will fall to the ground.
15 "I will also smite the [1a]winter house together
with the [b]summer house;
The houses of [2c]ivory will also perish
And the [d]great houses will come to an end,"
Declares the LORD.

Chapter 4 Theme ______________________________

4 Hear this word, you cows of [a]Bashan who are on
the [b]mountain of Samaria,
Who [c]oppress the poor, who crush the needy,
Who say to [1]your husbands, "Bring now, that we may
[d]drink!"
2 The Lord [1]GOD has [a]sworn by His [b]holiness,
"Behold, the days are coming upon you
When [2]they will take you away with [c]meat hooks,
And the last of you with [d]fish hooks.
3 "You will [a]go out *through* breaches *in the walls,*
Each one straight before her,
And you [1]will be cast to Harmon," declares the LORD.

4 "Enter Bethel and transgress;
In Gilgal multiply transgression!
[a]Bring your sacrifices every morning,
Your tithes every three days.
5 "[1]Offer a [a]thank offering also from that which is leavened,
And proclaim [b]freewill offerings, make them known.
For so you [c]love *to do,* you sons of Israel,"
Declares the Lord GOD.

6 "But I gave you also [a]cleanness of teeth in all your cities
And lack of bread in all your places,
Yet you have [b]not returned to Me," declares the LORD.
7 "Furthermore, I [a]withheld the rain from you
While *there were* still three months until harvest.

11 [1]Or *stronghold* [a]Amos 6:14 [b]Amos 2:5

12 [1]Or *delivers* [2]Or *delivered* [3]Lit *damask* [a]1 Sam 17:34-37 [b]Ps 132:3 [c]Esth 1:6; 7:8; Amos 6:4

13 [a]Ezek 2:7

14 [a]2 Kin 23:15; Hos 10:5-8, 14, 15; Amos 4:4; 5:5, 6; 7:10, 13

15 [1]Or *autumn* [2]I.e. ivory inlay [a]Jer 36:22 [b]Judg 3:20 [c]1 Kin 22:39; Ps 45:8 [d]Amos 2:5; 6:11

4:1 [1]Lit *their lords* [a]Ps 22:12; Ezek 39:18 [b]Amos 3:9; 6:1 [c]Amos 5:11; 8:6 [d]Amos 2:8; 6:6

2 [1]Heb *YHWH,* usually rendered *LORD,* and so throughout the ch [2]Lit *he* [a]Amos 6:8; 8:7 [b]Ps 89:35 [c]Is 37:29; Ezek 38:4 [d]Jer 16:16; Ezek 29:4; Hab 1:15

3 [1]So Gr; M.T. reads *will cast* [a]Jer 52:7

4 [a]Num 28:3; Amos 5:21, 22

5 [1]Lit *Offer up in smoke* [a]Lev 7:13 [b]Lev 22:18-21 [c]Jer 7:9, 10; Hos 9:1, 10

6 [a]Is 3:1; Jer 14:18 [b]Is 9:13; Jer 5:3; Hag 2:17

7 [a]Deut 11:17; 2 Chr 7:13; Is 5:6

Then I would send rain on one city
And on [b]another city I would not send rain;
One part would be rained on,
While the part not rained on would dry up.
8 "So two or three cities would stagger to another city
to drink [a]water,
But would [b]not be satisfied;
Yet you have [c]not returned to Me," declares the LORD.
9 "I [a]smote you with scorching *wind* and mildew;
And the [b]caterpillar was devouring
Your many gardens and vineyards, fig trees
and olive trees;
Yet you have [c]not returned to Me," declares the LORD.
10 "I sent a [a]plague among you after the manner of Egypt;
I [b]slew your young men by the sword along with your
[c]captured horses,
And I made the [d]stench of your camp rise up
in your nostrils;
Yet you have [e]not returned to Me," declares the LORD.
11 "I overthrew you, as [a]God overthrew Sodom and Gomorrah,
And you were like a [b]firebrand snatched from a blaze;
Yet you have [c]not returned to Me," declares the LORD.
12 "Therefore thus I will do to you, O Israel;
Because I will do this to you,
Prepare to [a]meet your God, O Israel."
13 For behold, He who [a]forms mountains and [b]creates
the wind
And [c]declares to man what are His thoughts,
He who [d]makes dawn into darkness
And [e]treads on the high places of the earth,
[f]The LORD God of hosts is His name.

Chapter 5 Theme ____________________

5 Hear this word which I take up for you as a [a]dirge,
O house of Israel:
2 She has fallen, she will [a]not rise again—
The [b]virgin Israel.
She *lies* neglected on her land;
There is [c]none to raise her up.
3 For thus says the Lord [1]GOD,
"The city which goes forth a thousand *strong*
Will have a [a]hundred left,
And the one which goes forth a hundred *strong*
Will have [b]ten left to the house of Israel."

4 For thus says the LORD to the house of Israel,
"[a]Seek Me [b]that you may live.
5 "But do not [1]resort to [a]Bethel
And do not come to [b]Gilgal,
Nor cross over to [c]Beersheba;

7 [b]Ex 9:4, 26; 10:22, 23

8 [a]1 Kin 18:5; Jer 14:4 [b]Ezek 4:16, 17; Hag 1:6 [c]Jer 3:7

9 [a]Deut 28:22; Hag 2:17 [b]Joel 1:4, 7; Amos 7:1, 2 [c]Jer 3:10

10 [a]Ex 9:3; Lev 26:25; Deut 28:27, 60; Ps 78:50 [b]Jer 11:22; 18:21; 48:15 [c]2 Kin 13:3, 7 [d]Joel 2:20 [e]Is 9:13

11 [a]Gen 19:24, 25; Deut 29:23; Is 13:19 [b]Zech 3:2 [c]Jer 23:14

12 [a]Is 32:11; 64:2; Jer 5:22

13 [a]Job 38:4-7; Ps 65:6; Is 40:12 [b]Ps 135:7; Jer 10:13 [c]Dan 2:28, 30 [d]Jer 13:16; Joel 2:2; Amos 5:8 [e]Mic 1:3 [f]Is 47:4; Jer 10:16; Amos 5:8, 27; 9:6

5:1 [a]Jer 7:29; 9:10, 17; Ezek 19:1

2 [a]Amos 8:14 [b]Jer 14:17 [c]Is 51:18; Jer 50:32

3 [1]Heb *YHWH,* usually rendered *LORD,* and so throughout the ch [a]Is 6:13 [b]Amos 6:9

4 [a]Deut 4:29; 32:46, 47; Jer 29:13 [b]Is 55:3

5 [1]Lit *seek* [a]1 Kin 12:28, 29; Amos 3:14; 4:4; 7:10, 13 [b]1 Sam 7:16; 11:14 [c]Gen 21:31-33; Amos 8:14

For Gilgal will certainly go into captivity
And Bethel will [2]come to trouble.
6 "[a]Seek the LORD that you may live,
Or He will break forth like a [b]fire, [1]O house of Joseph,
And it will consume with none to quench *it* for Bethel,
7 *For* those who turn [a]justice into wormwood
And [1]cast righteousness down to the earth."

8 He who made the [a]Pleiades and Orion
And [b]changes deep darkness into morning,
[1]Who also [c]darkens day *into* night,
Who [d]calls for the waters of the sea
And pours them out on the surface of the earth,
The [e]LORD is His name.
9 It is He who [a]flashes forth *with* destruction upon the strong,
So that [b]destruction comes upon the fortress.

10 They hate him who [a]reproves in the [1]gate,
And they [b]abhor him who speaks *with* integrity.
11 Therefore because you [1]impose heavy rent on the poor
And exact a tribute of grain from them,
Though you have built [a]houses of well-hewn stone,
Yet you will not live in them;
You have planted pleasant vineyards, yet you will [b]not
drink their wine.
12 For I know your transgressions are many and your sins
are great,
You who [a]distress the righteous *and* accept bribes
And [1]turn aside the poor in the [2]gate.
13 Therefore at [1]such a time the prudent person [a]keeps silent,
for it is an evil time.

14 Seek good and not evil, that you may live;
And thus may the LORD God of hosts be with you,
[a]Just as you have said!
15 [a]Hate evil, love good,
And establish justice in the [1]gate!
Perhaps the LORD God of hosts
[b]May be gracious to the [c]remnant of Joseph.

16 Therefore thus says the LORD God of hosts, the Lord,
"There is [a]wailing in all the plazas,
And in all the streets they say, 'Alas! Alas!'
They also call the [b]farmer to mourning
And [1c]professional mourners to lamentation.
17 "And in all the [a]vineyards *there is* wailing,
Because I will pass through the midst of you," says the LORD.

18 Alas, you who are longing for the [a]day of the LORD,
For what purpose *will* the day of the LORD *be* to you?
It *will be* [b]darkness and not light;

5 [2]Or *become iniquity*

6 [1]Or in *the house* [a]Is 55:3, 6, 7; Amos 5:14 [b]Deut 4:24

7 [1]Lit *they have put down* [a]Amos 2:3; 5:12; 6:12

8 [1]Lit *And He darkened* [a]Job 9:9; 38:31 [b]Job 12:22; 38:12; Is 42:16 [c]Ps 104:20 [d]Ps 104:6-9; Amos 9:6 [e]Amos 4:13

9 [a]Is 29:5; Amos 2:14 [b]Mic 5:11

10 [1]I.e. the place where court was held [a]Is 29:21; Amos 5:15 [b]1 Kin 22:8; Is 59:15; Jer 17:16-18

11 [1]Another reading is *trample upon* [a]Amos 3:15; 6:11 [b]Mic 6:15

12 [1]Lit *they turn* [2]I.e. the place where court was held [a]Is 1:23; 5:23; Amos 2:6

13 [1]Lit *that time* [a]Eccl 3:7; Hos 4:4

14 [a]Mic 3:11

15 [1]I.e. the place where court was held [a]Ps 97:10; Rom 12:9 [b]Joel 2:14 [c]Mic 5:3, 7, 8

16 [1]Lit *those who know lamentation* [a]Jer 9:10, 18-20; Amos 8:3 [b]Joel 1:11 [c]2 Chr 35:25; Jer 9:17

17 [a]Is 16:10; Jer 48:33

18 [a]Is 5:19; Jer 30:7; Joel 1:15; 2:1, 11, 31 [b]Is 5:30; Joel 2:2

19 As when a man [a]flees from a lion
And a bear meets him,
[1]Or goes home, leans his hand against the wall
And a snake bites him.
20 *Will* not the day of the LORD *be* [a]darkness instead of light,
Even gloom with no brightness in it?

21 "I hate, I [a]reject your festivals,
Nor do I [1b]delight in your solemn assemblies.
22 "Even though you [a]offer up to Me burnt offerings
and your grain offerings,
I will not accept *them;*
And I will not *even* look at the [b]peace offerings
of your fatlings.
23 "Take away from Me the noise of your songs;
I will not even listen to the sound of your harps.
24 "But let [a]justice roll down like waters
And righteousness like an ever-flowing stream.
25 "[1a]Did you present Me with sacrifices and grain offerings in
the wilderness for forty years, O house of Israel?
26 "[a]You also carried along [1]Sikkuth your king and [2]Kiyyun, your
images, [3]the star of your gods which you made for yourselves.
27 "Therefore, I will make you go into exile beyond Damascus,"
says the LORD, whose name is the God of hosts.

Chapter 6 Theme ______________________________

6 [a]Woe to those who are at ease in Zion
And to those who *feel* secure in the mountain of Samaria,
The [b]distinguished men of the foremost of nations,
To whom the house of Israel comes.
2 Go over to [a]Calneh and look,
And go from there to [b]Hamath the great,
Then go down to [c]Gath of the Philistines.
Are [1]they better than these kingdoms,
Or is their territory greater than yours?
3 Do you [a]put off the day of calamity,
And would you [b]bring near the seat of violence?

4 Those who recline on beds of ivory
And sprawl on their [a]couches,
And [b]eat lambs from the flock
And calves from the midst of the stall,
5 Who improvise to the sound of the harp,
And like David have [1]composed [a]songs for themselves,
6 Who [a]drink wine from [1]sacrificial bowls
While they anoint themselves with the finest of oils,
Yet they have not [b]grieved over the ruin of Joseph.
7 Therefore, they will now [a]go into exile at the head
of the exiles,
And the [b]sprawlers' [1]banqueting will [2]pass away.

19 [1]Or *Then* [a]Job 20:24; Is 24:17, 18; Jer 15:2, 3; 48:44

20 [a]Is 13:10; Zeph 1:15

21 [1]Lit *like to smell* [a]Is 1:11-16; 66:3; Amos 4:4, 5; 8:10 [b]Lev 26:31; Jer 14:12; Hos 5:6

22 [a]Is 66:3; Mic 6:6, 7 [b]Lev 7:11-15; Amos 4:5

24 [a]Jer 22:3; Ezek 45:9; Mic 6:8

25 [1]Or *You presented Me with the sacrifices and a grain offering* [a]Deut 32:17; Josh 24:14; Neh 9:18-21; Acts 7:42, 43

26 [1]Or *Sakkuth (Saturn)* or *shrine of your Moloch* [2]Or *Kaiwan (Saturn)* or *stands of* [3]Or *your star gods* [a]Acts 7:43

6:1 [a]Is 32:9-11; Zeph 1:12; Luke 6:24 [b]Ex 19:5; Amos 3:2

2 [1]Or *you* [a]Gen 10:10; Is 10:9 [b]1 Kin 8:65; 2 Kin 18:34; Is 10:9 [c]1 Sam 5:8; 2 Chr 26:6

3 [a]Is 56:12; Amos 9:10 [b]Amos 3:10

4 [a]Amos 3:12 [b]Ezek 34:2, 3

5 [1]Or *invented musical instruments* [a]1 Chr 15:16; 23:5; Is 5:12

6 [1]Lit *sprinkling basins* [a]Amos 2:8; 4:1 [b]Ezek 9:4

7 [1]Or *cultic feasts* [2]Lit *turn aside* [a]Amos 7:11, 17 [b]1 Kin 20:16-21; Dan 5:4-6, 30

8 The Lord [1]GOD has [a]sworn by Himself, the LORD God of
hosts has declared:
"I [b]loathe the arrogance of Jacob,
And [2]detest his [c]citadels;
Therefore I will [d]deliver up *the* city and [3]all
it contains."
9 And it will be, if [a]ten men are left in one house, they will die.
10 Then one's [1]uncle, or his [2a]undertaker, will lift him up to
carry out *his* bones from the house, and he will say to the one
who is in the innermost part of the house, "Is anyone else with
you?" And that one will say, "No one." Then he will [3]answer,
"[b]Keep quiet. For [4]the name of the LORD is [c]not to be mentioned."
11 For behold, the LORD is going to [a]command that the [b]great
house be smashed to pieces and the small house to fragments.
12 Do horses run on rocks?
Or does one plow [1]them with oxen?
Yet you have turned [a]justice into poison
And the fruit of righteousness into [2]wormwood,
13 You who rejoice in [1a]Lodebar,
[2]And say, "Have we not [b]by our *own* strength taken
[3]Karnaim for ourselves?"
14 "For behold, [a]I am going to raise up a nation against you,
O house of Israel," declares the LORD God of hosts,
"And they will afflict you from the [b]entrance of Hamath
To the [b]brook of the Arabah."

Chapter 7 Theme ____

7 Thus the Lord [1]GOD showed me, and behold, He was form-
ing a [a]locust-swarm [2]when the spring crop began to sprout.
And behold, the spring crop *was* after the king's [3]mowing.
2 And it came about, [1]when it had [a]finished eating the
vegetation of the land, that I said,
"[b]Lord GOD, please pardon!
[2]How can Jacob stand,
For he is [c]small?"
3 The LORD [1a]changed His mind about this.
"It shall not be," said the LORD.
4 Thus the Lord GOD showed me, and behold, the Lord GOD
was calling to contend *with them* by [a]fire, and it consumed the
great deep and began to consume the [1]farm land.
5 Then I said,
"[a]Lord GOD, please stop!
[b]How can Jacob stand, for he is small?"
6 The LORD [1a]changed His mind about this.
"This too shall not be," said the Lord GOD.
7 Thus He showed me, and behold, the Lord was standing
[1]by a [2]vertical wall with a plumb line in His hand.
8 The LORD said to me, "[a]What do you see, Amos?" And I
said, "A plumb line." Then the Lord said,
"Behold I am about to put a [b]plumb line

8 [1]Heb *YHWH,* usually rendered *LORD* [2]Lit *hate* [3]Lit *its fullness* [a]Gen 22:16; Jer 22:5; 51:14; Amos 4:2; 8:7 [b]Lev 26:30; Deut 32:19; Ps 106:40; Amos 5:21 [c]Amos 3:10, 11 [d]Hos 11:6

9 [a]Amos 5:3

10 [1]Or *beloved one* [2]Lit *one who burns him* [3]Lit *say* [4]Lit *not to make mention of the name of* [a]1 Sam 31:12 [b]Amos 5:13; 8:3 [c]Jer 44:26; Ezek 20:39

11 [a]Is 55:11 [b]2 Kin 25:9; Amos 3:15; 5:11

12 [1]Another reading is *the sea with oxen* [2]I.e. bitterness [a]1 Kin 21:7-13; Is 59:13, 14; Hos 10:4; Amos 5:7, 11, 12

13 [1]Lit *a thing of nothing* [2]Lit *Who* [3]Lit *a pair of horns* [a]Job 8:14, 15; Ps 2:2-4; Luke 12:19, 20 [b]Ps 75:4, 5; Is 28:14, 15

14 [a]Jer 5:15 [b]Num 34:7, 8; 1 Kin 8:65; 2 Kin 14:25

7:1 [1]Heb *YHWH,* usually rendered *LORD,* and so throughout the ch [2]Lit *at the beginning of the coming up of* [3]Or *shearings* [a]Joel 1:4; Amos 4:9; Nah 3:15

2 [1]Lit *if* [2]Lit *As who* [a]Ex 10:15 [b]Jer 14:7, 20, 21; Ezek 9:8; 11:13 [c]Is 37:4; Jer 42:2

3 [1]Or *relented* [a]Deut 32:36; Jer 26:19; Hos 11:8; Amos 5:15; Jon 3:10

4 [1]Lit *portion* [a]Deut 32:22; Is 66:15, 16; Amos 2:5

5 [a]Ps 85:4; Joel 2:17 [b]Amos 7:2

6 [1]Or *relented* [a]Ps 106:45; Amos 7:3; Jon 3:10

7 [1]Or *upon* [2]Lit *wall of a plumb line*

8 [a]Jer 1:11; Amos 8:2 [b]2 Kin 21:13; Is 28:17; 34:11; Lam 2:8

RETURN TO INSTRUCTIONS

In the midst of My people Israel.
I will [1c]spare them no longer.
9 "The [a]high places of Isaac will be desolated
And the [b]sanctuaries of Israel laid waste.
Then I will [c]rise up against the house of Jeroboam
with the sword."
10 Then Amaziah, the [a]priest of Bethel, sent *word* to [b]Jeroboam
king of Israel, saying, "Amos has [c]conspired against you in the
midst of the house of Israel; the land is unable to endure all his
words.
11 "For thus Amos says, 'Jeroboam will die by the sword and
Israel will certainly go from its land into exile.'"
12 Then Amaziah said to Amos, "[a]Go, you seer, flee away to
the land of Judah and there eat bread and there do your
prophesying!
13 "But [a]no longer prophesy at Bethel, for it is a [b]sanctuary of
the king and a royal [1]residence."
14 Then Amos replied to Amaziah, "I am not a prophet, nor
am I the [a]son of a prophet; for I am a herdsman and a [1]grower
of sycamore figs.
15 "But the LORD took me from [1]following the flock and the
LORD said to me, 'Go [a]prophesy to My people Israel.'
16 "Now hear the word of the LORD: you are saying, 'You [a]shall
not prophesy against Israel [b]nor shall you [1]speak against the
house of Isaac.'
17 "Therefore, thus says the LORD, 'Your [a]wife will become a
harlot in the city, your [b]sons and your daughters will fall by the
sword, your land will be parceled up by a *measuring* line and
you yourself will die [1]upon [c]unclean soil. Moreover, Israel will
certainly go from its land into exile.'"

Chapter 8 Theme ______________________________

8 Thus the Lord [1]GOD showed me, and behold, *there was* a
basket of summer fruit.
2 He said, "What do you see, Amos?" And [a]I said, "A basket
of summer fruit." Then the LORD said to me, "The [b]end has
come for My people Israel. I will [1c]spare them no longer.
3 "[1]The [a]songs of the palace will turn to [b]wailing in that day,"
declares the Lord GOD. "Many *will be* the [c]corpses; in every
place [2]they will cast them forth [3]in silence."
4 Hear this, you who [1a]trample the needy, to do away with
the humble of the land,
5 saying,
"When will the [a]new moon [1]be over,
So that we may sell grain,
And the [b]sabbath, that we may open the wheat *market,*
To make the [2]bushel smaller and the shekel bigger,
And to [c]cheat with [3]dishonest scales,

8 [1]Lit *pass him by* [c]Jer 15:6; Ezek 7:4-9; Amos 8:2

9 [a]Gen 46:1; Hos 10:8; Mic 1:5 [b]Lev 26:31; Is 63:18; Jer 51:51; Amos 7:13 [c]2 Kin 15:8-10; Amos 7:11

10 [a]1 Kin 12:31, 32; 13:33 [b]2 Kin 14:23, 24 [c]Jer 26:8-11; 38:4

12 [a]Matt 8:34

13 [1]Lit *house* [a]Amos 2:12; Acts 4:18 [b]1 Kin 12:29, 32; Amos 7:9

14 [1]Or *nipper* [a]1 Kin 20:35; 2 Kin 2:3, 5; 4:38; 2 Chr 19:2

15 [1]Lit *behind* [a]Jer 1:7; Ezek 2:3, 4

16 [1]Lit *flow* [a]Amos 2:12; 7:13 [b]Deut 32:2; Ezek 20:46; 21:2

17 [1]Or *in an unclean land* [a]Hos 4:13, 14 [b]Jer 14:16 [c]2 Kin 17:6; Ezek 4:13; Hos 9:3

8:1 [1]Heb *YHWH,* usually rendered *LORD,* and so throughout the ch

2 [1]Lit *pass him by* [a]Jer 24:3 [b]Ezek 7:2, 3, 6 [c]Amos 7:8

3 [1]Or *They will howl the palace songs* [2]Lit *he has thrown* [3]Or *hush!* [a]Amos 5:23; 6:4, 5; 8:10 [b]Amos 5:16 [c]Amos 6:8-10

4 [1]Or *snap at* [a]Ps 14:4; Prov 30:14; Amos 2:7; 5:11, 12

5 [1]Lit *pass by* [2]Lit *ephah* [3]Lit *balances of deception* [a]Num 28:11; 2 Kin 4:23 [b]Ex 31:13-17; Neh 13:15 [c]Hos 12:7; Mic 6:11

6 So as to [a]buy the helpless for [1]money
And the needy for a pair of sandals,
And *that* we may sell the refuse of the wheat?"

7 The LORD has [a]sworn by the [b]pride of Jacob,
"Indeed, I will [c]never forget any of their deeds.
8 "Because of this will not the land [a]quake
And everyone who dwells in it [b]mourn?
Indeed, all of it will [c]rise up like the Nile,
And it will be tossed about
And subside like the Nile of Egypt.
9 "It will come about in that day," declares the Lord GOD,
"That I will make the [a]sun go down at noon
And [b]make the earth dark in [1]broad daylight.
10 "Then I will [a]turn your festivals into mourning
And all your songs into [1]lamentation;
And I will bring [b]sackcloth on everyone's loins
And baldness on every head.
And I will make it [c]like *a time of* mourning
for an only son,
And the end of it will be like a bitter day.

11 "Behold, days are coming," declares the Lord GOD,
"When I will send a famine on the land,
Not a famine for bread or a thirst for water,
But rather [a]for hearing the words of the LORD.
12 "People will stagger from sea to sea
And from the north even to the east;
They will go to and fro to [a]seek the word of the LORD,
But they will not find *it.*
13 "In that day the beautiful [a]virgins
And the young men will [b]faint from thirst.
14 "*As for* those who swear by the [1a]guilt of Samaria,
Who say, 'As your god lives, O [b]Dan,'
And, 'As the way of [c]Beersheba lives,'
They will fall and [d]not rise again."

Chapter 9 Theme ____________

9 I saw the Lord standing beside the [a]altar, and He said,
"Smite the capitals so that the [b]thresholds will shake,
And [c]break them on the heads of them all!
Then I will [d]slay the rest of them with the sword;
They will [e]not have a fugitive who will flee,
Or a refugee who will escape.
2 "Though they dig into [a]Sheol,
From there will My hand take them;
And though they [b]ascend to heaven,
From there will I bring them down.
3 "Though they hide on the summit of Carmel,
I will [a]search them out and take them from there;

6 [1]Lit *silver* [a]Amos 2:6
7 [a]Amos 4:2 [b]Deut 33:26, 29; Ps 68:34; Amos 6:8 [c]Ps 10:11; Hos 7:2; 8:13
8 [a]Ps 18:7; 60:2; Is 5:25 [b]Hos 4:3 [c]Jer 46:7, 8; Amos 9:5
9 [1]Lit *a day of light* [a]Job 5:14; Is 13:10; Jer 15:9; Mic 3:6 [b]Is 59:9, 10; Amos 4:13; 5:8
10 [1]Or *a dirge* [a]Job 20:23; Amos 5:21 [b]Is 15:2, 3; Jer 48:37; Ezek 7:18; 27:31 [c]Jer 6:26; Zech 12:10
11 [a]1 Sam 3:1; 2 Chr 15:3; Ps 74:9; Ezek 7:26; Mic 3:6
12 [a]Ezek 20:3, 31
13 [a]Lam 1:18; 2:21 [b]Is 41:17; Hos 2:3
14 [1]Or *Ashimah* [a]Hos 8:5 [b]1 Kin 12:28, 29 [c]Amos 5:5 [d]Amos 5:2
9:1 [a]Amos 3:14 [b]Zeph 2:14 [c]Ps 68:21; Hab 3:13 [d]Amos 7:17 [e]Jer 11:11
2 [a]Ps 139:8 [b]Jer 51:53; Obad 4
3 [a]Jer 16:16

And though they [b]conceal themselves from My sight
on the floor of the sea,
From there I will command the [c]serpent and it will
bite them.
4 "And though they go into [a]captivity before their enemies,
From there I will command the sword that it slay them,
And I will [b]set My eyes against them for evil and
not for good."

5 The Lord [1]GOD of hosts,
The One who [a]touches the land so that it melts,
And [b]all those who dwell in it mourn,
And all of it rises up like the Nile
And subsides like the Nile of Egypt;
6 The One who builds His [1a]upper chambers in the heavens
And has founded His vaulted dome over the earth,
He who [b]calls for the waters of the sea
And [c]pours them out on the face of the earth,
[d]The LORD is His name.

7 "Are you not as the sons of [a]Ethiopia to Me,
O sons of Israel?" declares the LORD.
"Have I not brought up Israel from the land of Egypt,
And the [b]Philistines from Caphtor and the [c]Arameans
from [d]Kir?
8 "Behold, the [a]eyes of the Lord GOD are on the sinful
kingdom,
And I will [b]destroy it from the face of the earth;
Nevertheless, I will [c]not totally destroy the house of Jacob,"
Declares the LORD.
9 "For behold, I am commanding,
And I will [a]shake the house of Israel among all nations
As *grain* is shaken in a sieve,
But not a [1]kernel will fall to the ground.
10 "All the [a]sinners of My people will die by the sword,
Those who say, '[b]The calamity will not overtake
or confront us.'

11 "In that day I will [a]raise up the fallen [1b]booth of David,
And wall up its [c]breaches;
I will also raise up its ruins
And rebuild it as in the [d]days of old;
12 [a]That they may possess the remnant of [b]Edom
And all the [1]nations who are [c]called by My name,"
Declares the LORD who does this.

13 "Behold, days are coming," declares the LORD,
"When the [a]plowman will overtake the reaper
And the treader of grapes him who sows seed;
When the [b]mountains will drip sweet [c]wine
And all the hills will be dissolved.

3 [b]Job 34:22; Ps 139:9, 10 [c]Is 27:1

4 [a]Lev 26:33 [b]Lev 17:10; Jer 21:10; 39:16; 44:11

5 [1]Heb *YHWH,* usually rendered LORD, and so throughout the ch [a]Ps 104:32; 144:5; Is 64:1; Mic 1:4 [b]Amos 8:8

6 [1]Or *stairs* [a]Ps 104:3, 13 [b]Amos 5:8 [c]Ps 104:6 [d]Amos 4:13

7 [a]2 Chr 14:9, 12; Is 20:4; 43:3 [b]Deut 2:23; Jer 47:4 [c]Amos 1:5 [d]2 Kin 16:9; Is 22:6

8 [a]Jer 44:27; Amos 9:4 [b]Amos 7:17; 9:10 [c]Jer 5:10; 30:11; 31:35, 36; Joel 2:32; Amos 3:12; Obad 17

9 [1]Or *pebble* [a]Is 30:28; Luke 22:31

10 [a]Is 33:14; Zech 13:8 [b]Amos 6:3

11 [1]Or *shelter* or *tabernacle* [a]Acts 15:16-18 [b]Is 16:5 [c]Ps 80:12 [d]Is 63:11; Jer 46:26

12 [1]Or *Gentiles* [a]Obad 19 [b]Num 24:18; Is 11:14 [c]Is 43:7

13 [a]Lev 26:5 [b]Joel 3:18 [c]Gen 49:11

14 [1]Or *fortunes*
[a]Ps 53:6; Is 60:4; Jer 30:3, 18
[b]Is 61:4; 65:21
[c]Jer 24:6; 31:28

15 [a]Is 60:21; Ezek 34:28; 37:25

14 "Also I will [a]restore the [1]captivity of My people Israel,
And they will [b]rebuild the ruined cities and live *in them;*
They will also [c]plant vineyards and drink their wine,
And make gardens and eat their fruit.
15 "I will also plant them on their land,
And [a]they will not again be rooted out from their land
Which I have given them,"
Says the LORD your God.

Amos at a Glance

Theme of Amos:

Segment Divisions

		Chapter Themes
		1
		2
		3
		4
		5
		6
		7
		8
		9

Author:

Date:

Purpose:

Key Words:

Amos

Israel

land

nations (other than Israel)

Edom

covenant

any reference to the name of the Lord

any reference to famine

OBADIAH עוֹבַדְיָה OVADYA

God said that whoever touched Israel touched the apple (pupil) of His eye. According to Obadiah 1:10-14, Edom had touched God's eye.

Scholars are divided about whether the incident referred to in these verses occurred during the reign of Jehoram (853–841 B.C.), when the Philistines and the Arabs invaded Jerusalem, or during Babylon's sieges of Jerusalem (between 605 and 586 B.C.). However, the exact date is not critical to the message of the book. What we do know is that in both instances Edom did not respond as God wanted, and thus came this report through "the Lord's servant," which is the meaning of Obadiah's name.

Things to Do

1. Read this book once without stopping in order to get an overview of Obadiah's message.

2. Read through Obadiah again, and in a distinctive way mark the key words (along with their synonyms and pronouns) listed on the OBADIAH AT A GLANCE chart on page 1482.

3. Remember that Jacob and Esau were brothers, born to Rebekah and Isaac. If you want to refresh your memory, read Genesis 27:1–28:9; 32:1–33:20; Romans 9:10-13; and Numbers 20:14-21. Genesis 36 gives the genealogy of Esau and says, "Esau is Edom." It also names Esau as the father of the Edomites.

   Although the people of Edom (descendants of Esau) and Israel (descendants of Jacob) are related (Amos 1:11-12), biblical history records many conflicts between them. Look at the map on page 1481 and notice the proximity of Edom to Israel. Edom was a constant threat to Israel, repeatedly thwarting the nation and blocking Judah's access to the Gulf of Elat (Aqaba).

4. Now read through Obadiah again, asking the "5 W's and an H." Ask questions such as: Who is speaking? To whom? Why? What is the message? What is going to happen? To whom? How? Summarize your observations in the margin of the text.

5. Look at a map and find the Negev and the other places mentioned at the end of Obadiah. These are real lands and real people, and what God says will happen to them *will* happen.

6. Since Obadiah is just one chapter, record the theme (subject) of each paragraph on OBADIAH AT A GLANCE and then fill in the rest of the chart, including the theme of Obadiah.

7. The day of the Lord is an important day prophetically. Record your insights on *the day of the Lord* on the DAY OF THE LORD chart on page 2076.

Things to Think About

1. Sometimes when tragic and unjust things happen, we wonder where God is. If He is righteous, just, and omnipotent, why doesn't He intervene? What do you learn from Obadiah that helps answer these questions? What can you learn from this for your own life?

2. How should we respond to the tragedies of others, the dark hours of our enemies? What does God think when we use their tragedy to our advantage?

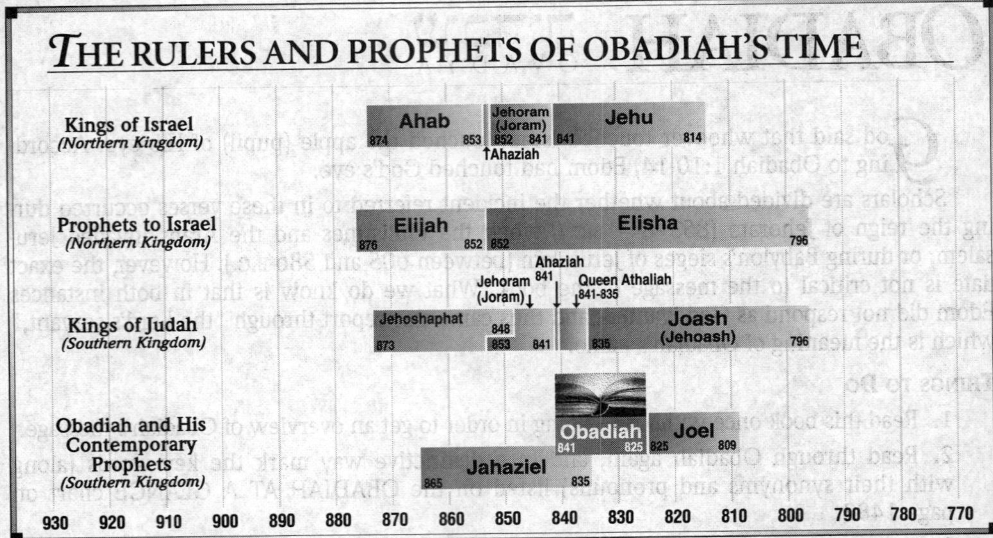

Chapter 1 Theme ____________________

1 The vision of Obadiah.
Thus says the Lord [1]GOD concerning [a]Edom—
[b]We have heard a report from the LORD,
And an [c]envoy has been sent among the nations *saying,*
"[d]Arise and let us go against her for battle"—
2 "Behold, I will make you [a]small among the nations;
You are greatly despised.
3 "The [a]arrogance of your heart has deceived you,
You who live in the clefts of [1]the [b]rock,
In the loftiness of your dwelling place,
Who say in your heart,
'[c]Who will bring me down to earth?'
4 "Though you [a]build high like the eagle,
Though you set your nest among the [b]stars,
From there I will bring you down," declares the LORD.
5 "If [a]thieves came to you,
If [1]robbers by night—
O how you will be ruined!—
Would they not steal *only* [2]until they had enough?
If grape gatherers came to you,
[b]Would they not leave *some* gleanings?
6 "O how Esau will be [a]ransacked,
And his hidden treasures searched out!
7 "All the [a]men [1]allied with you
Will send you forth to the border,
And the men at peace with you
Will deceive you and overpower you.

1:1 [1]Heb *YHWH,* usually rendered LORD
[a]Ps 137:7; Is 21:11, 12; 34:1-17; 63:1-6; Jer 49:7-22; Ezek 25:12-14; 35:15; Joel 3:19; Amos 1:11, 12; Mal 1:4
[b]Jer 49:14-16; Obad 1-4
[c]Is 18:2; 30:4
[d]Jer 6:4, 5

2 [a]Num 24:18; Is 23:9

3 [1]Or *Sela*
[a]Is 16:6; Jer 49:16
[b]2 Kin 14:7; 2 Chr 25:11f
[c]Is 14:13-15; Rev 18:7

4 [a]Job 20:6, 7; Hab 2:9
[b]Is 14:12-15

5 [1]Lit *devastators of the night*
[2]Lit *their sufficiency*
[a]Jer 49:9
[b]Deut 24:21

6 [a]Jer 49:10

7 [1]Lit *of your covenant*
[a]Jer 30:14

They who eat your [b]bread
Will set an ambush for you.
(There is [c]no understanding [2]in him.)
8 "Will I not on that day," declares the LORD,
"[a]Destroy wise men from Edom
And understanding from the mountain of Esau?
9 "Then your [a]mighty men will be dismayed, O [b]Teman,
So that everyone may be [c]cut off from the mountain
of Esau by slaughter.

10 "Because of [a]violence to your brother Jacob,
[1]You will be covered *with* shame,
[b]And you will be cut off forever.
11 "On the day that you [a]stood aloof,
On the day that strangers carried off his wealth,
And foreigners entered his gate
And [b]cast lots for Jerusalem—
[c]You too were as one of them.
12 "[a]Do not [1]gloat over your brother's day,
The day of his misfortune.
And [b]do not rejoice over the sons of Judah
In the day of their destruction;
Yes, [c]do not [2]boast
In the day of *their* distress.
13 "Do not enter the gate of My people
In the [a]day of their disaster.
Yes, you, do not [1]gloat over their calamity
In the day of their disaster.
And do not [b]loot their wealth
In the day of their disaster.
14 "Do not [a]stand at the fork of the road
To cut down their fugitives;
And do not imprison their survivors
In the day of their distress.

15 "For the [a]day of the LORD draws near on all the nations.
[b]As you have done, it will be done to you.
Your [c]dealings will return on your own head.
16 "Because just as you [a]drank on [b]My holy mountain,
All the nations [c]will drink continually.
They will drink and [1]swallow
And become as if they had never existed.
17 "But on Mount [a]Zion there will be those who escape,
And it will be holy.
And the house of Jacob will [b]possess their possessions.
18 "Then the house of Jacob will be a [a]fire
And the house of Joseph a flame;
But the house of Esau *will be* as stubble.
And they will set [1]them on fire and consume [1]them,
So that there will be [b]no survivor of the house of Esau,"
For the LORD has spoken.

7 [2]I.e. in Esau; or *of it* [b]Ps 41:9 [c]Is 19:11; Jer 49:7
8 [a]Job 5:12-14; Is 29:14
9 [a]Jer 49:22 [b]Gen 36:11; 1 Chr 1:45; Job 2:11; Jer 49:7; Ezek 25:13; Amos 1:12; Hab 3:3 [c]Is 34:5-8; 63:1-3; Obad 5
10 [1]Lit *Shame will cover you* [a]Gen 27:41; Ezek 25:12; Joel 3:19; Amos 1:11 [b]Ezek 35:9
11 [a]Ps 83:5, 6; 137:7; Amos 1:6, 9 [b]Joel 3:3; Nah 3:10 [c]Ezek 35:10
12 [1]Lit *look on* [2]Lit *make your mouth large* [a]Mic 4:11; 7:10 [b]Prov 17:5; Ezek 35:15; 36:5 [c]Ps 31:18; Ezek 35:12
13 [1]Lit *look on* [a]Ezek 35:5 [b]Ezek 35:10; 36:2, 3
14 [a]Is 16:3, 4
15 [a]Ezek 30:3; Joel 1:15; 2:1, 11, 31; Amos 5:18, 20 [b]Jer 50:29; 51:56; Hab 2:8 [c]Ezek 35:11
16 [1]Or *stagger* [a]Jer 49:12 [b]Joel 3:17 [c]Is 51:22, 23; Jer 25:15, 16
17 [a]Is 4:2, 3 [b]Is 14:1, 2; Amos 9:11-15
18 [1]I.e. the people of Esau [a]Is 5:24; 9:18, 19; Zech 12:6 [b]Jer 11:23; Amos 1:8

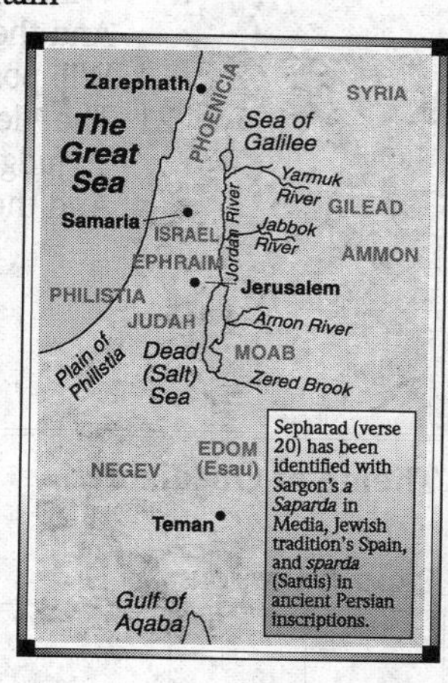

Possessions Given by the Lord

19 Then *those of* the [1]Negev will [a]possess the
mountain of Esau,
And *those of* the [2]Shephelah the [b]Philistine *plain;*
Also, [c]possess the territory of Ephraim and the territory
of Samaria,
And Benjamin *will possess* Gilead.
20 And the exiles of this host of the sons of Israel,
Who are *among* the Canaanites as far as [a]Zarephath,
And the exiles of Jerusalem who are in Sepharad
Will possess the [b]cities of the Negev.
21 The [a]deliverers will ascend Mount Zion
To judge the mountain of Esau,
And the [b]kingdom will be the LORD's.

19 [1]I.e. South country [2]I.e. the foothills [a]Is 11:14; Amos 9:12 [b]Is 11:14 [c]Jer 31:5; 32:44

20 [a]1 Kin 17:9; Luke 4:26 [b]Jer 32:44; 33:13

21 [a]Neh 9:27 [b]Ps 22:28; 47:7-9; 67:4; Zech 14:9; Rev 11:15

OBADIAH AT A GLANCE

Theme of Obadiah:

SEGMENT DIVISIONS

		PARAGRAPH THEMES
		VERSES 1-9
		VERSES 10-14
		VERSES 15-21

Author:

Date:

Purpose:

Key Words:

the day

day of the Lord

Edom (Esau)

Jacob (Judah)

the nations

Mount Zion (My holy mountain)

declares the Lord (or any phrase having to do with the Lord speaking or reporting)

JONAH יוֹנָה YONA

Just before God commissioned Amos and Hosea as prophets to the northern kingdom to warn Israel of the impending invasion by the Assyrians, He appointed the prophet Jonah to go to Nineveh, the capital of Assyria. Yet 50 years later, in 722 B.C., Assyria would take the last portion of the northern kingdom into captivity.

God knew what Assyria would do. Why, then, did He bother to send Jonah to the wicked city of Nineveh? Because of who God is. The focus of Jonah is not a man trapped in the belly of a great fish; the focus is people engraved on the heart of God.

Things to Do

1. Before you read through Jonah, look up 2 Kings 14:23-27, which mentions Jonah and his ministry during the reign of Jeroboam II son of Joash, king of Israel. At that time Shalmaneser IV was king of Assyria.

2. In a distinctive way mark the key words listed on the JONAH AT A GLANCE chart on page 1487. Double-underline in green every geographical reference. Mark all references to time with a clock 🕒.

3. Mark references to God with a triangle; you'll learn awesome things about Him.

4. Record the theme of each chapter on JONAH AT A GLANCE and in your Bible next to the chapter number. Then fill in the rest of the chart.

Things to Think About

1. What or who evokes compassion in your heart? Contrast Jonah's heart with God's heart. How does your heart compare with God's? Does it long for the same things? Why?

2. Is there something that you know God wants you to do that you haven't done? What can you learn from Jonah's life?

3. How did Jesus view the story of Jonah? Read Matthew 12:39-41; 16:4. Will you accept as truth what Jesus accepted as fact—or did Jesus compare His resurrection to a mythological tale?

Chapter 1 Theme ______________________

1:1 [a]2 Kin 14:25; Matt 12:39-41; 16:4; Luke 11:29, 30, 32

2 [a]Gen 10:11; 2 Kin 19:36; Is 37:37; Nah 1:1; Zeph 2:13 [b]Is 58:1 [c]Gen 18:20; Hos 7:2

3 [a]Is 23:1, 6, 10; Jer 10:9 [b]Gen 4:16; Ps 139:7, 9, 10 [c]Josh 19:46; 2 Chr 2:16; Ezra 3:7; Acts 9:36, 43

4 [1]Lit *be broken* [a]Ps 107:23-28; 135:6, 7

5 [1]Lit *vessels* [2]Lit *from upon them* [a]1 Kin 18:26 [b]Acts 27:18, 19, 38

1 The word of the LORD came to [a]Jonah the son of Amittai saying,
2 "Arise, go to [a]Nineveh the great city and [b]cry against it, for
their [c]wickedness has come up before Me."
3 But Jonah rose up to flee to [a]Tarshish [b]from the presence of
the LORD. So he went down to [c]Joppa, found a ship which was
going to Tarshish, paid the fare and went down into it to go
with them to Tarshish from the presence of the LORD.
4 The [a]LORD hurled a great wind on the sea and there was a
great storm on the sea so that the ship was about to [1]break up.
5 Then the sailors became afraid and every man cried to [a]his
god, and they [b]threw the [1]cargo which was in the ship into the
sea to lighten *it* [2]for them. But Jonah had gone below into the
hold of the ship, lain down and fallen sound asleep.

6 So the captain approached him and said, "How is it that
you are sleeping? Get up, [a]call on your god. Perhaps *your* [b]god
will be concerned about us so that we will not perish."
7 Each man said to his mate, "Come, let us [a]cast lots so we
may [1]learn on whose account this calamity *has struck* us." So
they cast lots and the [b]lot fell on Jonah.
8 Then they said to him,
"[a]Tell us, now! On whose
account *has* this calamity
struck us? What is your
[b]occupation? And where do
you come from? What is
your country? From what
people are you?"
9 He said to them, "I am
a [a]Hebrew, and I [b]fear the
LORD [c]God of heaven who
[d]made the sea and the dry
land."

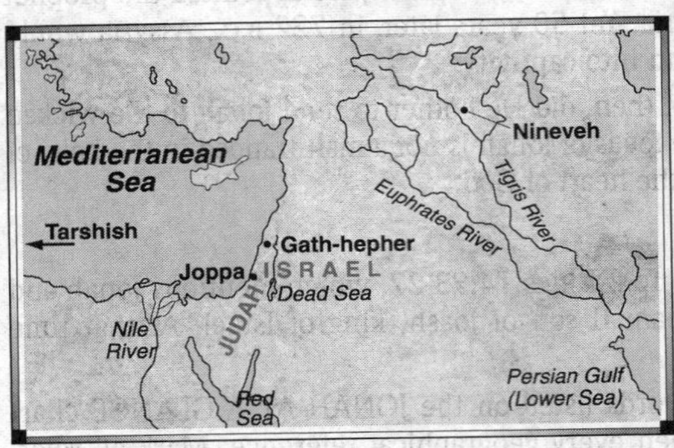

Jonah's Journey

10 Then the men became extremely frightened and they said to
him, "[1]How could you do this?" For the men knew that he was
[a]fleeing from the presence of the LORD, because he had told them.
11 So they said to him, "What should we do to you that the
sea may become calm [1]for us?"—for the sea was becoming
increasingly stormy.
12 He said to them, "Pick me up and throw me into the sea.
Then the sea will become calm [1]for you, for I know that [a]on
account of me this great storm *has come* upon you."
13 However, the men [1]rowed *desperately* to return to land but
they could not, for the sea was becoming *even* stormier against
them.
14 Then they called on the [a]LORD and said, "We earnestly
pray, O LORD, do not let us perish on account of this man's life
and do not put innocent blood on us; for [b]You, O LORD, have
done as You have pleased."
15 So they picked up Jonah, threw him into the sea, and the
sea [a]stopped its raging.
16 Then the men feared the LORD greatly, and they offered a
sacrifice to the LORD and made [a]vows.
17 [1]And the LORD appointed a great fish to swallow Jonah, and
Jonah was in the [a]stomach of the fish three days and three
nights.

Chapter 2 Theme ____________________

2 [1]Then Jonah prayed to the LORD his God [a]from the stomach of the fish,
2 and he said,
"I [a]called out of my distress to the LORD,
And He answered me.
I cried for help from the [1]depth of [b]Sheol;
You heard my voice.

6 [a]Ps 107:28 [b]2 Sam 12:22; Amos 5:15; Jon 3:9

7 [1]Lit *know* [a]Josh 7:14-18; 1 Sam 10:20, 21; 14:41, 42; Acts 1:23-26 [b]Num 32:23; Prov 16:33

8 [a]Josh 7:19; 1 Sam 14:43 [b]Gen 47:3; 1 Sam 30:13

9 [a]Gen 14:13; Ex 1:15; 2:13 [b]2 Kin 17:25, 28, 32, 33 [c]Ezra 1:2; Neh 1:4; Ps 136:26; Dan 2:18 [d]Neh 9:6; Ps 95:5; 146:6

10 [1]Lit *What is this you have done* [a]Job 27:22; Jon 1:3

11 [1]Lit *from upon us*

12 [1]Lit *from upon you* [a]2 Sam 24:17; 1 Chr 21:17

13 [1]Lit *dug their oars into the water*

14 [a]Ps 107:28; Jon 1:16 [b]Ps 115:3; 135:6; Dan 4:34, 35

15 [a]Ps 65:7; 93:3, 4; 107:29

16 [a]Ps 50:14; 66:13, 14

17 [1]Ch 2:1 in Heb [a]Matt 12:40; 16:4

2:1 [1]Ch 2:2 in Heb [a]Job 13:15; Ps 130:1, 2; Lam 3:53-56

2 [1]Lit *belly* [a]1 Sam 30:6; Ps 18:4-6; 22:24; 120:1 [b]Ps 18:5, 6; 86:13; 88:1-7

3 “For You had [a]cast me into the deep,
Into the heart of the seas,
And the current [1]engulfed me.
All Your [b]breakers and billows passed over me.
4 “So I said, ‘I have been [a]expelled from [1]Your sight.
Nevertheless I will look again [b]toward Your holy temple.’
5 “[a]Water encompassed me to the [1]point of death.
The great [b]deep [2]engulfed me,
Weeds were wrapped around my head.
6 “I [a]descended to the roots of the mountains.
The earth with its [b]bars *was* around me forever,
But You have [c]brought up my life from [1]the pit,
O LORD my God.
7 “While [1]I was [a]fainting away,
I [b]remembered the LORD,
And my [c]prayer came to You,
Into [d]Your holy temple.
8 “Those who [a]regard [1]vain idols
Forsake their faithfulness,
9 But I will [a]sacrifice to You
With the voice of thanksgiving.
That which I have vowed I will [b]pay.
[c]Salvation is from the LORD.”
10 Then the LORD commanded the [a]fish, and it vomited Jonah
up onto the dry land.

3 [1]Lit *surrounded* [a]Ps 69:1, 2, 14, 15; Lam 3:54 [b]Ps 42:7
4 [1]Lit *before Your eyes* [a]Ps 31:22; Jer 7:15 [b]1 Kin 8:38; 2 Chr 6:38; Ps 5:7
5 [1]Lit *soul* [2]Lit *surrounded* [a]Lam 3:54 [b]Ps 69:1, 2
6 [1]Or *corruption* [a]Ps 18:5; 116:3 [b]Is 38:10; Matt 16:18 [c]Job 33:28; Ps 16:10; 30:3; Is 38:17
7 [1]Lit *my soul . . . within me* [a]Ps 142:3 [b]Ps 77:10, 11; 143:5 [c]2 Chr 30:27; Ps 18:6 [d]Ps 11:4; 65:4; Jon 2:4; Mic 1:2; Hab 2:20
8 [1]Lit *empty vanities* [a]2 Kin 17:15; Ps 31:6; Jer 10:8
9 [a]Ps 50:14, 23; Jer 33:11; Hos 14:2 [b]Job 22:27; Eccl 5:4, 5 [c]Ps 3:8; Is 45:17
10 [a]Jon 1:17

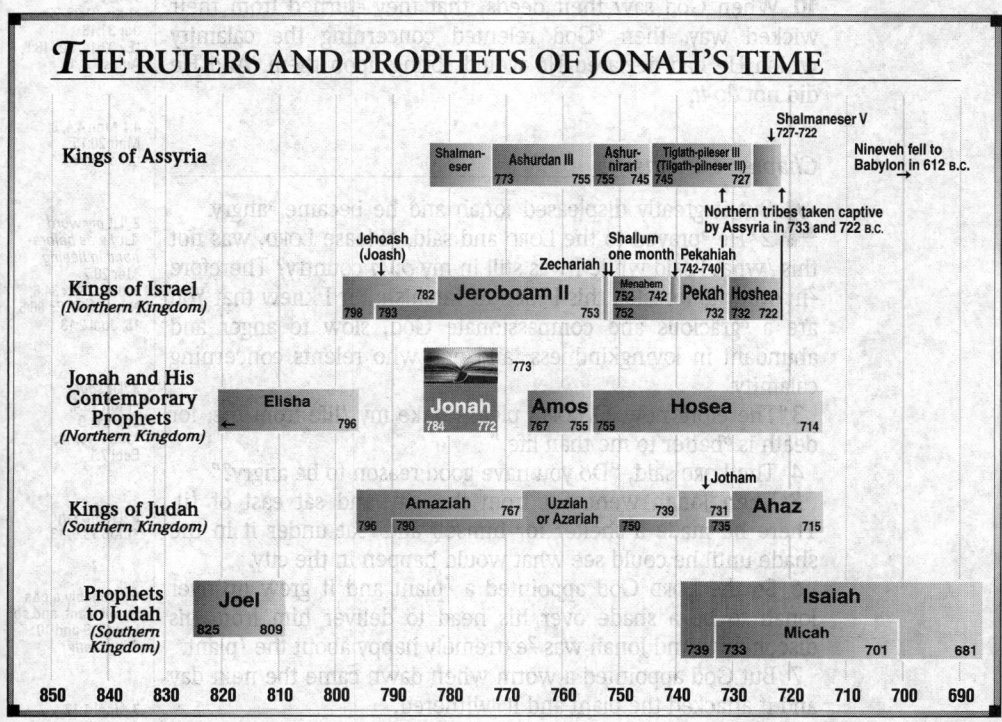

THE RULERS AND PROPHETS OF JONAH'S TIME

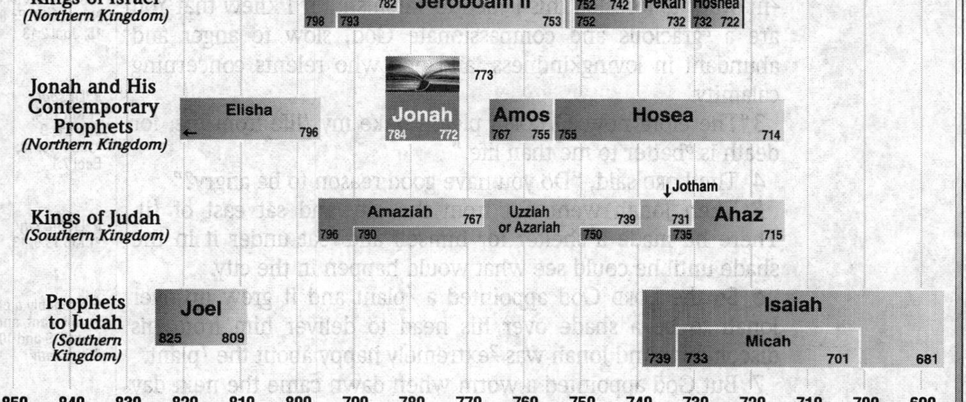

Kings of Assyria
Shalmaneser 773
Ashurdan III 773–755
Ashur-nirari 755–745
Tiglath-pileser III (Tilgath-pilneser III) 745–727
Shalmaneser V 727-722
Nineveh fell to Babylon in 612 B.C.
Northern tribes taken captive by Assyria in 733 and 722 B.C.

Kings of Israel *(Northern Kingdom)*
Jehoash (Joash) 798–782
Jeroboam II 793–753
Zechariah
Shallum one month
Menahem 752–742
Pekahiah 742-740
Pekah 752–732
Hoshea 732–722

Jonah and His Contemporary Prophets *(Northern Kingdom)*
Elisha 796
Jonah 784–772
773
Amos 767–755
Hosea 755–714

Kings of Judah *(Southern Kingdom)*
Amaziah 796–767
Uzziah or Azariah 790–739
Jotham 750–731
Ahaz 735–715

Prophets to Judah *(Southern Kingdom)*
Joel 825–809
Isaiah 739–681
Micah 733–701

850 840 830 820 810 800 790 780 770 760 750 740 730 720 710 700 690

Chapter 3 Theme ________________________________

3 Now the word of the LORD came to Jonah the second time,
saying,
2 "Arise, go to [a]Nineveh the great city and [b]proclaim to it the
proclamation which I am going to tell you."
3 So Jonah arose and went to Nineveh according to the word
of the LORD. Now Nineveh was [1]an [a]exceedingly great city, a
three days' walk.
4 Then Jonah began to go through the city one day's walk;
and he [a]cried out and said, "Yet forty days and Nineveh will be
overthrown."
5 Then the people of Nineveh believed in God; and they
called a [a]fast and put on sackcloth from the greatest to the least
of them.
6 When the word reached the king of Nineveh, he arose
from his throne, laid aside his robe from him, [a]covered *himself*
with sackcloth and sat on the [1]ashes.
7 He issued a [a]proclamation and it said, "In Nineveh by the
decree of the king and his nobles: Do not let man, beast, herd,
or flock taste a thing. Do not let them eat or drink water.
8 "But both man and beast must be covered with sackcloth;
and let [1]men [a]call on God earnestly that each may [b]turn from
his wicked way and from the violence which is in [2]his hands.
9 "[a]Who knows, God may turn and relent and withdraw His
burning anger so that we will not perish."
10 When God saw their deeds, that they [a]turned from their
wicked way, then [b]God relented concerning the calamity
which He had declared He would [1]bring upon them. And He
did not do *it*.

Chapter 4 Theme ________________________________

4 But it greatly displeased Jonah and he became [a]angry.
2 He [a]prayed to the LORD and said, "Please LORD, was not
this [1]what I said while I was still in my *own* country? Therefore
[2]in order to forestall this I [b]fled to Tarshish, for I knew that You
are a [c]gracious and compassionate God, slow to anger and
abundant in lovingkindness, and one who relents concerning
calamity.
3 "Therefore now, O LORD, please [a]take my [1]life from me, for
death is [b]better to me than life."
4 The LORD said, "Do you have good reason to be angry?"
5 Then Jonah went out from the city and sat east of [1]it.
There he made a shelter for himself and [a]sat under it in the
shade until he could see what would happen in the city.
6 So the LORD God appointed a [1]plant and it grew up over
Jonah to be a shade over his head to deliver him from his
discomfort. And Jonah was [2]extremely happy about the [1]plant.
7 But God appointed a worm when dawn came the next day
and it attacked the plant and it [a]withered.

3:2 [a]Zeph 2:13 [b]Jer 1:17; Ezek 2:7

3 [1]Lit *a great city to God* [a]Jon 1:2; 4:11

4 [a]Matt 12:41; Luke 11:32

5 [a]Dan 9:3; Joel 1:14

6 [1]Or *dust* [a]Esth 4:1-4; Jer 6:26; Ezek 27:30, 31

7 [a]2 Chr 20:3; Ezra 8:21; Jon 3:5

8 [1]Lit *them* [2]Lit *their* [a]Ps 130:1; Jon 1:6, 14 [b]Is 1:16-19; 55:6, 7; Jer 18:11

9 [a]2 Sam 12:22; Joel 2:14

10 [1]Lit *do* [a]1 Kin 21:27-29; Jer 31:18 [b]Ex 32:14; Jer 18:8; Amos 7:3, 6

4:1 [a]Jon 4:4, 9; Matt 20:15; Luke 15:28

2 [1]Lit *my word* [2]Lit *I was beforehand in fleeing* [a]Jer 20:7 [b]Jon 1:3 [c]Ex 34:6; Num 14:18; Ps 86:5, 15; Joel 2:13

3 [1]Lit *soul* [a]1 Kin 19:4; Job 6:8, 9 [b]Job 7:15, 16; Eccl 7:1

5 [1]Lit *the city* [a]1 Kin 19:9, 13

6 [1]Probably a castor oil plant, and so in vv 7, 9 and 10 [2]Lit *greatly*

7 [a]Joel 1:12

8 [a]Ezek 19:12; Hos 13:15 [b]Ps 121:6; Is 49:10 [c]Jon 4:3

10 [1]Lit *was a son of a night* [2]Lit *a son of a night*

11 [a]Jon 3:10 [b]Deut 1:39; Is 7:16 [c]Ps 36:6

8 When the sun came up God appointed a scorching [a]east
wind, and the [b]sun beat down on Jonah's head so that he
became faint and begged with *all* his soul to die, saying, "[c]Death
is better to me than life."
9 Then God said to Jonah, "Do you have good reason to be
angry about the plant?" And he said, "I have good reason to be
angry, even to death."
10 Then the LORD said, "You had compassion on the plant for
which you did not work and *which* you did not cause to grow,
which [1]came up overnight and perished [2]overnight.
11 "Should I not [a]have compassion on Nineveh, the great city
in which there are more than 120,000 persons who do not
[b]know *the difference* between their right and left hand, as well
as many [c]animals?"

Jonah at a Glance

Theme of Jonah:

Author:

Date:

Purpose:

Key Words:
- Jonah
- compassion (compassionate)
- relent(s)
- turn (turned)
- pray (any reference to prayer or calling out to God)
- perish
- Lord (God) appointed
- anger (angry)
- calamity (and synonyms)

Segment Divisions		Chapter Themes
		1
		2
		3
		4

MICAH מיכה MIKHA

Micah knew his calling and was ready to fulfill it, for Micah knew his God. What a contrast he is to the prophet Jonah! Micah, whose name means "who is like Jehovah," reminds a rebellious people that "the LORD is coming forth from *His* place."

THINGS TO DO

1. Micah 1:1 gives the historical setting of Micah. Read it carefully and answer as many of the "5 W's and an H" as you can concerning the who, when, where, why, what, and how of this book.

The reigns of Jotham, Ahaz, and Hezekiah, three kings of Judah, cover the years 750–686 B.C. Remember that Assyria conquered the northern kingdom in 722 B.C. and Babylon destroyed the southern kingdom in 586 B.C.

2. For the historical background of the kings of Judah mentioned in Micah 1:1, read 2 Kings 15:32–20:21 and 2 Chronicles 27:1–33:20.

3. Read through Micah to get an overview of the book. It divides into three messages, each of which starts with "hear" or "hear now." Mark Micah 1:2; 3:1; 6:1. Study the book accordingly.

4. Read one chapter of Micah at a time or, if you prefer, one message at a time. As you observe the text of each chapter:

a. Mark the key words listed (with their synonyms and pronouns) on the MICAH AT A GLANCE chart on page 1499. You will find it helpful to record these on an index card that you can use as a bookmark while you study Micah.

b. Mark references to time with a clock ⏲, such as *when, then, in that day, in the last days*.

c. Since Micah's prophecy concerns Samaria (representing the northern kingdom of Israel) and Jerusalem (representing the southern kingdom of Judah), next to the word *Samaria* in Micah 1:1 write "NK" for northern kingdom. Next to the word *Jerusalem* write "SK" for southern kingdom.

As you observe the text, watch which kingdom Micah is referring to. Observe what is said regarding their sins, the consequences of their sin, their future, and the remnant. If it will help, list your insights in your notebook.

d. Watch what God is going to do and to whom. Always note to whom Micah is referring.

e. List everything you learn about Micah and what he is to do.

f. Record the theme or subject of each chapter in your Bible and on MICAH AT A GLANCE. When you finish the last chapter of Micah, complete the chart.

5. Record your insights from Micah on the last days on the chart on page 2076 if you think these pertain to the day of the Lord.

THINGS TO THINK ABOUT

1. Review what you have learned about God the Father and the Son in this book. Meditate on these truths. Tell God you want to know Him more intimately and ask Him to open the eyes of your understanding. Ask Him to show you how to live in light of who He is.

2. Micah 4:12 says the nations do not know the thoughts of the Lord, nor do they understand His purpose. Yet the child of God can know these things through studying His Word. Amos said, "Surely the Lord GOD does nothing unless He reveals His secret

counsel to His servants the prophets" (3:7). God's secret counsel and His plan for the future is in the Word of God. Are you ordering your life in such a way that you take time to study His Word?

3. What have you learned about the unchanging love and compassion of God in pardoning your sins? Are you living accordingly?

4. Although you may not be able to trust in others, can you trust in God? Are you trusting Him? Can He trust you? In Micah 6:6-8 God tells you how to approach Him and what He requires. Will you live accordingly?

Chapter 1 Theme ______________________

1 The [a]word of the LORD which came *to* [b]Micah of Moresheth
in the days of [c]Jotham, [d]Ahaz *and* [e]Hezekiah, kings of Judah,
which he saw concerning Samaria and Jerusalem.

2 Hear, O peoples, all of [1]you;
[a]Listen, O earth and [2]all it contains,
And let the Lord [3]GOD be a [b]witness against you,
The Lord from His holy temple.
3 For behold, the LORD is [a]coming forth from His place.
He will come down and [b]tread on the high places
of the [1]earth.
4 [a]The mountains will melt under Him
And the valleys will be split,
Like wax before the fire,
Like water poured down a steep place.
5 All this is for the rebellion of Jacob
And for the sins of the house of Israel.
What is the [a]rebellion of Jacob?
Is it not [b]Samaria?
What is the [c]high [1]place of Judah?
Is it not Jerusalem?
6 For I will make Samaria a [a]heap of ruins [1]in the open country,
[b]Planting places for a vineyard.
I will [c]pour her stones down into the valley
And will [d]lay bare her foundations.
7 All of her [a]idols will be smashed,
All of her earnings will be burned with fire
And all of her images I will make desolate,
For she collected *them* from a [b]harlot's earnings,
And to the earnings of a harlot they will return.

8 Because of this I must lament and wail,
I must go [a]barefoot and naked;
I must make a lament like the [b]jackals
And a mourning like the ostriches.
9 For her [1a]wound is incurable,
For [b]it has come to Judah;
It has reached the [c]gate of my people,
Even to Jerusalem.

1:1 [a]2 Pet 1:21 [b]Jer 26:18 [c]2 Kin 15:5, 32-38; 2 Chr 27:1-9; Is 1:1; Hos 1:1 [d]2 Kin 16:1-20; 2 Chr 28:1-27; Is 7:1-12 [e]2 Kin 18:1-20; 2 Chr 29:1-31

2 [1]Lit *them* [2]Lit *its fullness* [3]Heb *YHWH,* usually rendered LORD [a]Jer 6:19; 22:29 [b]Is 50:7

3 [1]Or *land* [a]Is 26:21 [b]Amos 4:13

4 [a]Ps 97:5; Is 64:1, 2; Nah 1:5

5 [1]Lit *places* [a]Jer 2:19 [b]Is 7:9; Amos 8:14 [c]2 Chr 34:3, 4

6 [1]Lit *of the field* [a]2 Kin 19:25; Mic 3:12 [b]Jer 31:5; Amos 5:11 [c]Lam 4:1 [d]Ezek 13:14

7 [a]Deut 9:21; 2 Chr 34:7 [b]Deut 23:18; Is 23:17

8 [a]Is 32:11 [b]Is 13:21, 22

9 [1]Lit *wounds* [a]Is 3:26; Jer 30:12, 15 [b]2 Kin 18:13; Is 8:7, 8 [c]Mic 1:12

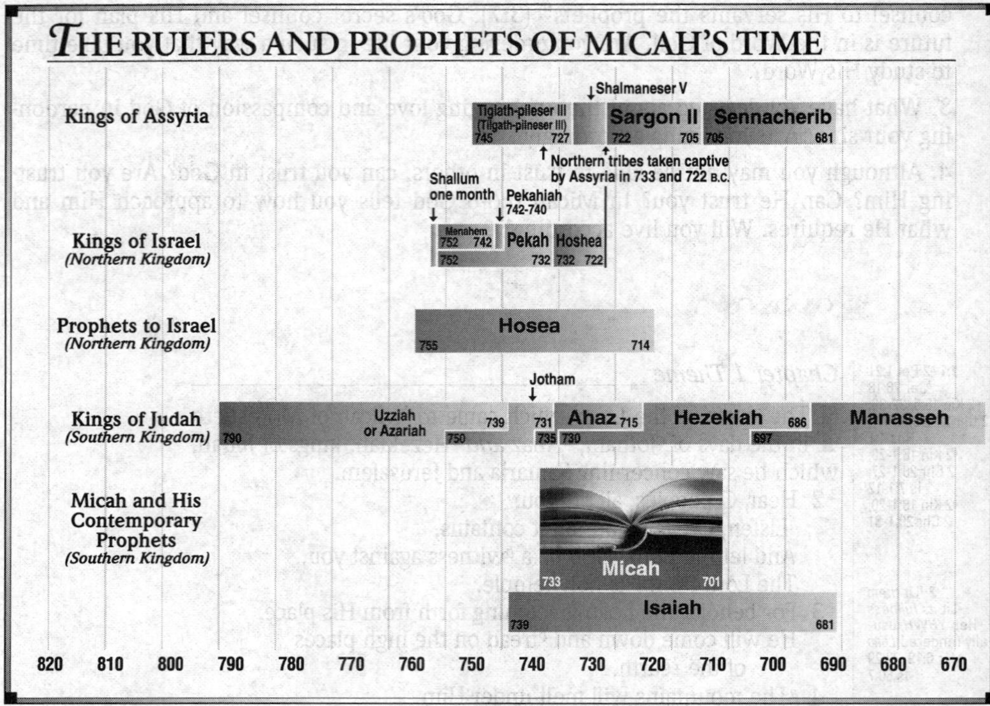

10 [a]Tell it not in Gath,
Weep not at all.
At [1]Beth-le-aphrah roll yourself in the dust.
11 [1]Go on your way, inhabitant of [2]Shaphir, in [a]shameful
nakedness.
The inhabitant of [3b]Zaanan does not [4]escape.
The lamentation of [5]Beth-ezel: "He will take from you
its [6]support."
12 For the inhabitant of [1]Maroth
Becomes weak [a]waiting for good,
Because a calamity has come down from the LORD
To the [b]gate of Jerusalem.
13 Harness the chariot to the team of horses,
O inhabitant of [a]Lachish—
She was the beginning of sin
To the daughter of Zion—
Because in you were found
The [b]rebellious acts of Israel.
14 Therefore you will give parting [a]gifts
On behalf of Moresheth-gath;
The houses of [b]Achzib *will* become a [c]deception
To the kings of Israel.
15 Moreover, I will bring on you
The one who takes possession,
O inhabitant of [1a]Mareshah.
The glory of Israel will enter [b]Adullam.

10 [1]I.e. house of dust [a]2 Sam 1:20

11 [1]I.e. Go into captivity [2]I.e. pleasantness [3]I.e. going out [4]Lit *go out* [5]I.e. house of removal [6]Lit *standing place* [a]Ezek 23:29 [b]Josh 15:37

12 [1]I.e. bitterness [a]Is 59:9-11; Jer 14:19 [b]Mic 1:9

13 [a]Josh 10:3; 2 Kin 14:19; Is 36:2 [b]Mic 1:5

14 [a]2 Kin 16:8 [b]Josh 15:44 [c]Jer 15:18

15 [1]I.e. possession [a]Josh 15:44 [b]Josh 12:15; 15:35; 2 Sam 23:13

16 Make yourself [a]bald and cut off your hair,
Because of the children of your delight;
Extend your baldness like the eagle,
For they will [b]go from you into exile.

Chapter 2 Theme ______________________

2 Woe to those who [a]scheme iniquity,
Who work out evil on their beds!
[1b]When morning comes, they do it,
For it is in the [c]power of their hands.
2 They [a]covet fields and then [b]seize *them,*
And houses, and take *them* away.
They [1c]rob a man and his house,
A man and his inheritance.
3 Therefore thus says the LORD,
"Behold, I am [a]planning against this [b]family a calamity
From which you [c]cannot remove your necks;
And you will not walk [d]haughtily,
For it will be an [e]evil time.
4 "On that day they will [a]take up against you a [1]taunt
And [2b]utter a bitter lamentation *and* say,
'We are completely [c]destroyed!
He exchanges the portion of my people;
How He removes it from me!
To the apostate He [d]apportions our fields.'
5 "Therefore you will have no one [1a]stretching
a measuring line
For you by lot in the assembly of the LORD.
6 '[a]Do not [1]speak out,' *so* they [1]speak out.
But if [2]they do [b]not [1]speak out concerning these things,
[c]Reproaches will not be turned back.
7 "Is it being said, O house of Jacob:
'Is the Spirit of the LORD [a]impatient?
Are these His doings?'
Do not My words [b]do good
To the one [c]walking uprightly?
8 "[1]Recently My people have arisen as an [a]enemy—
You [b]strip the [2]robe off the garment
From [c]unsuspecting passers-by,
From those returned from war.
9 "The women of My people you [a]evict,
Each *one* from her pleasant house.
From her children you take My [b]splendor forever.
10 "Arise and go,
For this is no place [a]of rest
Because of the [b]uncleanness that brings on destruction,
A painful destruction.
11 "If a man walking after wind and [a]falsehood
Had told lies *and said,*

16 [a]Is 22:12 [b]2 Kin 17:6; Amos 7:11, 17

2:1 [1]Lit *In the light of the morning* [a]Ps 36:4; Is 32:7; Nah 1:11 [b]Hos 7:6, 7 [c]Gen 31:29; Deut 28:32; Prov 3:27

2 [1]Lit *oppress* [a]Jer 22:17; Amos 8:4 [b]Is 5:8 [c]1 Kin 21:1-15

3 [a]Deut 28:48; Jer 18:11 [b]Jer 8:3; Amos 3:1, 2 [c]Lam 1:14; 5:5 [d]Is 2:11, 12 [e]Amos 5:13

4 [1]Or *proverb* [2]Lit *lament* [a]Hab 2:6 [b]Jer 9:10, 17-21; Mic 1:8 [c]Is 6:11; 24:3; Jer 4:13 [d]Jer 6:12; 8:10

5 [1]Lit *casting* [a]Num 34:13, 16-29; Deut 32:8; Josh 18:4, 10

6 [1]Lit *flow* [2]I.e. God's prophets [a]Is 30:10; Amos 2:12; 7:16 [b]Is 29:10; Mic 3:6 [c]Mic 6:16

7 [a]Is 50:2; 59:1 [b]Ps 119:65, 68, 116; Jer 15:16 [c]Ps 15:2; 84:11

8 [1]Lit *And yesterday* [2]Or *ornaments* [a]Jer 12:8 [b]Mic 3:2, 3; 7:2, 3 [c]Ps 120:6, 7

9 [a]Jer 10:20 [b]Ezek 39:21; Hab 2:14

10 [a]Deut 12:9 [b]Ps 106:38

11 [a]Jer 5:31

'I will [1]speak out to you concerning [b]wine and liquor,'
He would be [2]spokesman to [c]this people.

12 "I will surely [a]assemble all of you, Jacob,
I will surely gather the [b]remnant of Israel.
I will put them together like sheep in the fold;
Like a flock in the midst of its pasture
They will be noisy with men.
13 "The breaker goes up before them;
They break out, pass through the gate and go out by it.
So their king goes on before them,
And the LORD at their head."

Chapter 3 Theme ________________________

3 And I said,
"[a]Hear now, heads of Jacob
And rulers of the house of Israel.
Is it not for you to [b]know justice?
2 "You who hate good and love evil,
Who [a]tear off their skin from them
And their flesh from their bones,
3 Who [a]eat the flesh of my people,
Strip off their skin from them,
Break their bones
And [b]chop *them* up as for the pot
And as meat in a kettle."
4 Then they will [a]cry out to the LORD,
But He will not answer them.
Instead, He will [b]hide His face from them at that time
Because they have [c]practiced evil deeds.

5 Thus says the LORD concerning the prophets who [a]lead my
people astray;
When they have *something* to bite with their teeth,
They [b]cry, "Peace,"
But against him who puts nothing in their mouths
They declare holy war.
6 Therefore *it will be* [a]night for you—without vision,
And darkness for you—without divination.
The [b]sun will go down on the prophets,
And the day will become dark over them.
7 The seers will be [a]ashamed
And the [b]diviners will be embarrassed.
Indeed, they will all [c]cover *their* [1]mouths
Because there is [d]no answer from God.
8 On the other hand [a]I am filled with power—
With the Spirit of the LORD—
And with justice and courage
To [b]make known to Jacob his rebellious act,
Even to Israel his sin.

11 [1]Lit *flow* [2]Lit *one who flows* oracles [b]Is 28:7 [c]Is 30:10, 11

12 [a]Mic 4:6, 7 [b]Mic 5:7, 8; 7:18

3:1 [a]Is 1:10; Mic 3:9 [b]Ps 82:1-5; Jer 5:5

2 [a]Ps 53:4; Ezek 22:27; Mic 2:8; 7:2, 3

3 [a]Ps 14:4; 27:2; Zeph 3:3 [b]Ezek 11:3, 6, 7

4 [a]Ps 18:41; Prov 1:28; Is 1:15; Jer 11:11 [b]Deut 31:17; Is 59:2 [c]Is 3:11; Mic 7:13

5 [a]Is 3:12; 9:15, 16; Jer 14:14, 15 [b]Jer 6:14

6 [a]Is 8:20-22; 29:10-12 [b]Is 59:10

7 [1]Lit *mustache* [a]Zech 13:4 [b]Is 44:25; 47:12-14 [c]Mic 7:16 [d]1 Sam 28:6; Mic 3:4

8 [a]Is 61:1, 2; Jer 1:18 [b]Is 58:1

9 [a]Mic 1:1 [b]Ps 58:1, 2; Is 1:23

9 Now hear this, [a]heads of the house of Jacob
And rulers of the house of Israel,
Who [b]abhor justice
And twist everything that is straight,

10 [a]Jer 22:13, 17; Hab 2:12

10 Who [a]build Zion with bloodshed
And Jerusalem with violent injustice.

11 [a]Is 1:23; Mic 7:3 [b]Jer 6:13 [c]Is 48:2

11 Her leaders pronounce [a]judgment for a bribe,
Her [b]priests instruct for a price
And her prophets divine for money.
Yet they lean on the LORD saying,
"[c]Is not the LORD in our midst?
Calamity will not come upon us."

12 [1]Lit *house* [a]Jer 26:18 [b]Ps 79:1; Jer 9:11 [c]Mic 4:1

12 Therefore, on account of you
[a]Zion will be plowed as a field,
[b]Jerusalem will become a heap of ruins,
And the [c]mountain of the [1]temple *will become*
high places of a forest.

Chapter 4 Theme ______________________

4:1 [1]Lit *on* [a]Is 2:2-4; Dan 2:28; 10:14; Hos 3:5 [b]Ezek 43:12; Mic 3:12; Zech 8:3 [c]Ps 22:27; 86:9; Jer 3:17

4 And it will come about in the [a]last days
That the [b]mountain of the house of the LORD
Will be established [1]as the chief of the mountains.
It will be raised above the hills,
And the [c]peoples will stream to it.

2 [a]Zech 2:11; 14:16 [b]Is 2:3; Jer 31:6 [c]Ps 25:8, 9, 12; Is 54:13 [d]Is 42:1-4; Zech 14:8, 9

2 [a]Many nations will come and say,
"[b]Come and let us go up to the mountain of the LORD
And to the house of the God of Jacob,
That [c]He may teach us about His ways
And that we may walk in His paths."
For [d]from Zion will go forth the law,
Even the word of the LORD from Jerusalem.

3 [1]Lit *at a distance* [2]Lit *learn* [a]Is 2:4; 11:3-5 [b]Joel 3:10

3 And He will [a]judge between many peoples
And render decisions for mighty, [1]distant nations.
Then they will hammer their swords [b]into plowshares
And their spears into pruning hooks;
Nation will not lift up sword against nation,
And never again will they [2]train for war.

4 [a]1 Kin 4:25; Zech 3:10 [b]Lev 26:6; Jer 30:10 [c]Is 1:20; 40:5

4 Each of them will [a]sit under his vine
And under his fig tree,
With [b]no one to make *them* afraid,
For the [c]mouth of the LORD of hosts has spoken.

5 [a]2 Kin 17:29 [b]Zech 10:12 [c]Josh 24:15; Is 26:8, 13

5 Though all the peoples walk
Each in the [a]name of his god,
As for us, [b]we will walk
In the name of the [c]LORD our God forever and ever.

6 [a]Zeph 3:19 [b]Ps 147:2; Ezek 34:13, 16; 37:21

6 "In that day," declares the LORD,
"I will assemble the [a]lame
And [b]gather the outcasts,
Even those whom I have afflicted.

7 "I will make the lame a [a]remnant
And the outcasts a strong nation,
And the [b]LORD will reign over them in Mount Zion
From now on and forever.
8 "As for you, [1][a]tower of the flock,
[2]Hill of the daughter of Zion,
To you it will come—
Even the [b]former dominion will come,
The kingdom of the daughter of Jerusalem.

9 "Now, why do you [a]cry out loudly?
Is there no king among you,
Or has your [b]counselor perished,
That agony has gripped you like a woman in childbirth?
10 "[a]Writhe and labor to give birth,
Daughter of Zion,
Like a woman in childbirth;
For now you will [b]go out of the city,
Dwell in the field,
And go to Babylon.
[c]There you will be rescued;
[d]There the LORD will redeem you
From the hand of your enemies.
11 "And now [a]many nations have been assembled
against you
Who say, 'Let her be polluted,
And let our eyes [1]gloat over Zion.'
12 "But they do not [a]know the thoughts of the LORD,
And they do not understand His purpose;
For He has gathered them like sheaves
to the threshing floor.
13 "Arise and [a]thresh, daughter of Zion,
For your horn I will make iron
And your hoofs I will make bronze,
That you may [b]pulverize many peoples,
That you may [c]devote to the LORD their unjust gain
And their wealth to the Lord of all the earth.

Chapter 5 Theme ________________________________

5 "[1]Now muster yourselves in troops, daughter of troops;
[2]They have laid siege against us;
With a rod they will [a]smite the judge of Israel
on the cheek.
2 "[1]But as for [a]you, Bethlehem Ephrathah,
Too little to be among the clans of Judah,
From [b]you One will go forth for Me to be [c]ruler in Israel.
[2]His goings forth are [d]from long ago,
From the days of eternity."
3 Therefore He will [a]give them *up* until the time
When she [b]who is in labor has borne a child.

7 [a]Mic 5:7, 8; 7:18 [b]Is 24:23

8 [1]Heb *Migdal-eder* [2]Heb *Ophel of* [a]Ps 48:3, 12; 61:3; Mic 2:12 [b]Is 1:26; Zech 9:10

9 [a]Jer 8:19 [b]Is 3:1-3

10 [a]Mic 5:3 [b]2 Kin 20:18; Hos 2:14 [c]Is 43:14; 45:13; Mic 7:8-12 [d]Is 48:20; 52:9-12

11 [1]Lit *look on* [a]Is 5:25-30; 17:12-14

12 [a]Ps 147:19, 20

13 [a]Is 41:15 [b]Jer 51:20-23 [c]Is 60:9

5:1 [1]Ch 4:14 in Heb [2]Lit *He has* [a]1 Kin 22:24; Job 16:10; Lam 3:30

2 [1]Ch 5:1 in Heb [2]Or *His appearances are from long ago, from days of old* [a]Gen 35:19; 48:7; Ruth 4:11; Matt 2:6 [b]Is 11:1; Luke 2:4; John 7:42 [c]Jer 30:21; Zech 9:9 [d]Ps 102:25; Prov 8:22, 23

3 [a]Hos 11:8; Mic 4:10; 7:13 [b]Mic 4:9, 10

Then the [c]remainder of His brethren
Will return to the sons of Israel.
4 And He will arise and [a]shepherd *His flock*
In the strength of the LORD,
In the majesty of the name of the LORD His God.
And they will [1]remain,
Because [2]at that time He will be great
To the [b]ends of the earth.
5 This One [a]will be *our* peace.

When the [b]Assyrian invades our land,
When he tramples on our [1]citadels,
Then we will raise against him
Seven shepherds and eight leaders of men.
6 They will [a]shepherd the land of Assyria with the sword,
The land of [b]Nimrod at its entrances;
And He will [c]deliver *us* from the Assyrian
When he attacks our land
And when he tramples our territory.

7 Then the [a]remnant of Jacob
Will be among many peoples
Like [b]dew from the LORD,
Like [c]showers on vegetation
Which do not wait for man
Or delay for the sons of men.
8 The remnant of Jacob
Will be among the nations,
Among many peoples
[a]Like a lion among the beasts of the forest,
Like a young lion among flocks of sheep,
Which, if he passes through,
[b]Tramples down and [c]tears,
And there is [d]none to rescue.
9 Your hand will be [a]lifted up against your adversaries,
And all your enemies will be cut off.

10 "It will be in that day," declares the LORD,
"[a]That I will cut off your [b]horses from among you
And destroy your chariots.
11 "I will also cut off the [a]cities of your land
And tear down all your [b]fortifications.
12 "I will cut off [a]sorceries from your hand,
And you will have fortune-tellers no more.
13 "[a]I will cut off your carved images
And your *sacred* pillars from among you,
So that you will no longer bow down
To the work of your hands.
14 "I will root out your [1a]Asherim from among you
And destroy your cities.

3 [c]Is 10:20-22; Mic 5:7, 8

4 [1]Or *live* in safety [2]Lit *now* [a]Is 40:11; 49:9; Ezek 34:13-15, 23, 24; Mic 7:14 [b]Is 45:22; 52:10

5 [1]Or *palaces* [a]Is 9:6; Luke 2:14; Eph 2:14; Col 1:20 [b]Is 8:7, 8; 10:24-27

6 [a]Nah 2:11-13; Zeph 2:13 [b]Gen 10:8-11 [c]Is 14:25; 37:36, 37

7 [a]Mic 2:12; 4:7; 5:3; 7:18 [b]Deut 32:2; Ps 110:3; Hos 14:5 [c]Ps 72:6; Is 44:3

8 [a]Gen 49:9; Num 24:9 [b]Ps 44:5; Is 41:15, 16; Mic 4:13; Zech 10:5 [c]Hos 5:14 [d]Ps 50:22

9 [a]Ps 10:12; 21:8; Is 26:11

10 [a]Zech 9:10 [b]Deut 17:16; Is 2:7; Hos 14:3

11 [a]Is 1:7; 6:11 [b]Is 2:12-17; Hos 10:14; Amos 5:9

12 [a]Deut 18:10-12; Is 2:6; 8:19

13 [a]Is 2:18; 17:8; Ezek 6:9

14 [1]I.e. wooden symbols of a female deity [a]Ex 34:13; Is 17:8; 27:9

15 "And I will [a]execute vengeance in anger and wrath
On the nations which have not obeyed."

Chapter 6 Theme ______________________________

6 Hear now what the LORD is saying,
"Arise, plead your case [1]before the mountains,
And let the hills hear your voice.
2 "Listen, you mountains, to the indictment of the LORD,
And you enduring [a]foundations of the earth,
Because the [b]LORD has a case against His people;
Even with Israel He will dispute.
3 "[a]My people, [b]what have I done to you,
And [c]how have I wearied you? Answer Me.
4 "Indeed, I [a]brought you up from the land of Egypt
And [b]ransomed you from the house of slavery,
And I sent before you [c]Moses, Aaron and [d]Miriam.
5 "My people, remember now
What [a]Balak king of Moab counseled
And what Balaam son of Beor answered him,
And from [b]Shittim to [c]Gilgal,
So [1]that you might know the [d]righteous acts of the LORD."

6 [a]With what shall I come to the LORD
And bow myself before the God on high?
Shall I come to Him with [b]burnt offerings,
With yearling calves?
7 Does the LORD take delight in [a]thousands of rams,
In ten thousand rivers of oil?
Shall I present my [b]firstborn *for* my rebellious acts,
The fruit of my body for the sin of my soul?
8 He has [a]told you, O man, what is good;
And [b]what does the LORD require of you
But to [c]do justice, to [d]love [1]kindness,
And to walk [2e]humbly with your God?

9 The voice of the LORD will call to the city—
And it is sound wisdom to fear Your name:
"Hear, O tribe. Who has appointed [1]its time?
10 "Is there yet a man in the wicked house,
Along with treasures of [a]wickedness
And a [1b]short measure *that is* cursed?
11 "Can I justify wicked [a]scales
And a bag of deceptive weights?
12 "For the rich men of *the* [1]city are full of [a]violence,
Her residents speak [b]lies,
And their [c]tongue is deceitful in their mouth.
13 "So also I will make *you* [a]sick, striking you down,
[b]Desolating *you* because of your sins.
14 "You will eat, but you will [a]not be satisfied,
And your [1]vileness will be in your midst.

15 [a]Is 1:24; 65:12

6:1 [1]Lit *with*

2 [a]2 Sam 22:16; Ps 104:5 [b]Is 1:18; Hos 4:1; 12:2

3 [a]Ps 50:7 [b]Jer 2:5 [c]Is 43:22, 23

4 [a]Ex 12:51; 20:2 [b]Deut 7:8 [c]Ex 4:10-16; Ps 77:20 [d]Ex 15:20

5 [1]Lit *to know* [a]Num 22:5, 6 [b]Num 25:1; Josh 2:1; 3:1 [c]Josh 4:19; 5:9, 10 [d]1 Sam 12:7; Is 1:27

6 [a]Ps 40:6-8 [b]Ps 51:16, 17

7 [a]Ps 50:9; Is 1:1; 40:16 [b]Lev 18:21; 20:1-5; 2 Kin 16:3; Jer 7:31

8 [1]Or *loyalty* [2]Or *circumspectly* [a]Deut 30:15 [b]Deut 10:12 [c]Is 56:1; Jer 22:3 [d]Hos 6:6 [e]Is 57:15; 66:2

9 [1]Lit *it*

10 [1]Lit *shrunken ephah* [a]Jer 5:26, 27; Amos 3:10 [b]Ezek 45:9, 10; Amos 8:5

11 [a]Lev 19:36; Hos 12:7

12 [1]Lit *her* [a]Is 1:23; 5:7; Amos 6:3, 4; Mic 2:1, 2 [b]Jer 9:2-6, 8; Hos 7:13; Amos 2:4 [c]Is 3:8

13 [a]Mic 1:9 [b]Is 1:7; 6:11

14 [1]Or possibly *garbage* or *excreta* [a]Is 9:20

14 [b]Is 30:6

You will *try to* remove *for safekeeping,*
But you will [b]not preserve *anything,*
And what you do preserve I will give to the sword.
15 "You will sow but you will [a]not reap.
You will tread the olive but will not anoint
yourself with oil;
And the grapes, but you will [b]not drink wine.
16 "The statutes of [a]Omri
And all the works of the house of [b]Ahab are observed;
And in their devices you [c]walk.
Therefore I will give you up for [d]destruction
And [1]your inhabitants for [e]derision,
And you will bear the [f]reproach of My people."

15 [a]Deut 28:38-40; Jer 12:13 [b]Amos 5:11; Zeph 1:13

16 [1]Lit *her* [a]1 Kin 16:25, 26 [b]1 Kin 16:29-33 [c]Jer 7:24 [d]Jer 18:16; Mic 6:13 [e]Jer 19:8; 25:9, 18; 29:18 [f]Ps 44:13; Jer 51:51; Hos 12:14

Chapter 7 Theme ______________________

7 Woe is me! For I am
Like the fruit pickers, like the [a]grape gatherers.
There is not a cluster of grapes to eat,
Or a [b]first-ripe fig *which* [1]I crave.
2 The [1]godly person has [a]perished from the land,
And there is no upright *person* among men.
All of them lie in wait for [b]bloodshed;
Each of them hunts the other with a [c]net.
3 Concerning evil, both hands do it [a]well.
The prince asks, also the judge, for a [b]bribe,
And a great man speaks the desire of his soul;
So they weave it together.
4 The best of them is like a [a]briar,
The most upright like a [b]thorn hedge.
The day when you post your watchmen,
Your [c]punishment will come.
Then their [d]confusion will occur.
5 Do not [a]trust in a neighbor;
Do not have confidence in a friend.
From her who lies in your bosom
Guard [1]your lips.
6 For [a]son treats father contemptuously,
Daughter rises up against her mother,
Daughter-in-law against her mother-in-law;
[b]A man's enemies are the men of his own household.

7:1 [1]Lit *my soul* [a]Is 24:13 [b]Is 28:4; Hos 9:10

2 [1]Or *loyal* [a]Is 57:1 [b]Is 59:7; Mic 3:10 [c]Jer 5:26; Hos 5:1

3 [a]Prov 4:16, 17 [b]Amos 5:12; Mic 3:11

4 [a]Ezek 2:6; 28:24 [b]Nah 1:10 [c]Is 10:3; Hos 9:7 [d]Is 22:5

5 [1]Lit *openings of your mouth* [a]Jer 9:4

6 [a]Matt 10:21, 35; Luke 12:53 [b]Matt 10:36

7 But as for me, I will [a]watch expectantly for the LORD;
I will [b]wait for the God of my salvation.
My [c]God will hear me.
8 [a]Do not rejoice over me, O [b]my enemy.
Though I fall I will [c]rise;
Though I dwell in darkness, the LORD is a [d]light for me.

9 I will bear the indignation of the LORD
Because I have sinned against Him,

7 [a]Hab 2:1 [b]Ps 130:5; Is 25:9 [c]Ps 4:3

8 [a]Prov 24:17; Obad 12 [b]Mic 7:10 [c]Amos 9:11 [d]Is 9:2

Until He [a]pleads my case and executes justice for me.
He will bring me out to the [b]light,
And I will see His [1c]righteousness.
10 Then my enemy will see,
And shame will cover her who [a]said to me,
"Where is the LORD your God?"
My eyes will look on her;
[1]At that time she will [2]be [b]trampled down
Like mire of the streets.
11 *It will be* a day for [a]building your walls.
On that day will your boundary be extended.
12 It *will be* a day when [1]they will [a]come to you
From Assyria and the cities of Egypt,
From Egypt even to the [2]Euphrates,
Even from sea to sea and mountain to mountain.
13 And the earth will become [a]desolate because of her
inhabitants,
On account of the [b]fruit of their deeds.

14 [a]Shepherd Your people with Your [b]scepter,
The flock of Your [1]possession
Which dwells by itself in the woodland,
In the midst of [2]a fruitful field.
Let them feed in [c]Bashan and Gilead
[d]As in the days of old.
15 "As in the days when you came out from the land of Egypt,
I will show [1a]you miracles."
16 Nations [a]will see and be ashamed
Of all their might.
They will [b]put *their* hand on *their* mouth,
Their ears will be deaf.
17 They will [a]lick the dust like a serpent,
Like [b]reptiles of the earth.
They will come [c]trembling out of their [1]fortresses;
To the LORD our God they will come in [d]dread
And they will be afraid before You.
18 Who is a God like You, who [a]pardons iniquity
And passes over the rebellious act of the [b]remnant
of His [1]possession?
He does not [c]retain His anger forever,
Because He [d]delights in [2]unchanging love.
19 He will again have compassion on us;
[a]He will tread our iniquities under foot.
Yes, You will [b]cast all [1]their sins
Into the depths of the sea.
20 You will give [1a]truth to Jacob
And [2]unchanging love to Abraham,
Which You [b]swore to our forefathers
From the days of old.

9 [1]I.e. right dealing [a]Jer 50:34 [b]Ps 37:6; Is 42:7, 16 [c]Is 46:13; 56:1

10 [1]Lit *Now* [2]Lit *become a trampled* place [a]Joel 2:17 [b]Is 51:23; Zech 10:5

11 [a]Is 54:11; Amos 9:11

12 [1]Lit *he* [2]Lit *River* [a]Is 19:23-25; 60:4, 9

13 [a]Jer 25:11; Mic 6:13 [b]Is 3:10, 11; Mic 3:4

14 [1]Or *inheritance* [2]Or *Carmel* [a]Ps 95:7; Is 40:11; 49:10; Mic 5:4 [b]Lev 27:32; Ps 23:4 [c]Jer 50:19 [d]Amos 9:11

15 [1]Lit *him* [a]Ex 3:20; 34:10; Ps 78:12

16 [a]Is 26:11 [b]Mic 3:7

17 [1]Lit *fastnesses* [a]Ps 72:9; Is 49:23 [b]Deut 32:24 [c]Ps 18:45 [d]Is 25:3; 59:19

18 [1]Or *inheritance* [2]Or *lovingkindness* [a]Ex 34:7, 9; Is 43:25 [b]Mic 2:12; 4:7; 5:7, 8 [c]Ps 103:8, 9, 13 [d]Jer 32:41

19 [1]Several ancient versions read *our* [a]Jer 50:20 [b]Is 38:17; 43:25; Jer 31:34

20 [1]Or *faithfulness* [2]Or *lovingkindness* [a]Gen 24:27; 32:10 [b]Deut 7:8, 12

MICAH AT A GLANCE

Theme of Micah:

Author:

Date:

Purpose:

Key Words:

- Samaria
- Jerusalem
- Jacob
- Israel
- Judah
- Zion
- destroy(ed) (destruction)
- remnant
- in that day (in the last days)
- My (Your, His) people
- sin (iniquity, evil)

SEGMENT DIVISIONS		CHAPTER THEMES
		1
		2
		3
		4
		5
		6
		7

NAHUM נחום
NACHUM

One hundred years had passed since Jonah went to Nineveh to proclaim its destruction. Now another prophet, Nahum, proclaims his vision from God regarding Nineveh, the capital of Assyria. What a sharp contrast between Nahum's prophetic message and the meaning of his name—comforter!

Assyria sat smugly on her throne. Assyria had conquered Israel in 722 B.C. In 701 B.C., under Sennacherib's rule, the Assyrians had invaded Judah. Rabshakeh, Sennacherib's general, had boasted to Judah that none of the gods of the nations they had conquered had been able to deliver their people. To Hezekiah, king of Judah, he proclaimed, "Do not let your God in whom you trust deceive you saying, 'Jerusalem will not be given into the hand of the king of Assyria.' Behold, you have heard what the kings of Assyria have done to all the lands, destroying them completely. So will you be spared?" (2 Kings 19:10-11).

But God did spare Judah. Sennacherib, king of Assyria, returned to Nineveh and died there.

Yet that wasn't the end of the story. God had a message for Nineveh, the capital of Assyria, who at the time of Nahum's prophecy sat at the pinnacle of wealth and power, secure behind her impregnable walls. Or so she thought.

THINGS TO DO

1. If you have time, read Jonah to see what God said to the people of Nineveh 100 years earlier and how they responded.

2. Begin your study by reading through Nahum and marking every reference to *Nineveh* (pronouns and synonyms such as "wicked one", or "bloody city") in a distinctive color or way. Sometimes you will find it difficult to discern who the "you" refers to—Nineveh or someone else such as Jacob in 2:2. Do not mark the text until you are sure.

3. Study the historical chart on the next page to see the context of the book.

4. Read Nahum chapter by chapter and do the following:

   a. Mark each in its own distinctive way the following two phrases: "I am against you" and "I will."

   b. Nahum tells us much about God. Carefully observe the text and then in the margin summarize what you learn about God. For instance, 1:4 tells us that God rules over nature. Write that in your list in the margin under the title "God" or the symbol △.

   c. Look at every place you marked *Nineveh.* List in your notebook what you learn from marking these references.

5. Record the theme or subject of each chapter on NAHUM AT A GLANCE on page 1506 and in your Bible. Also, record the theme of the book and complete any other information requested on the chart.

THINGS TO THINK ABOUT

1. What do you learn about the justice of God and the certainty of His Word from this book? Is this the kind of God you can trust? Why?

2. Is there anything that can stop God from doing what He says or plans?

3. Can compassionate people deliver this kind of message? What if you were impressed by God to bring this kind of warning to others? Would you? What would motivate you or hinder you? By the way, remember the meaning of Nahum's name.

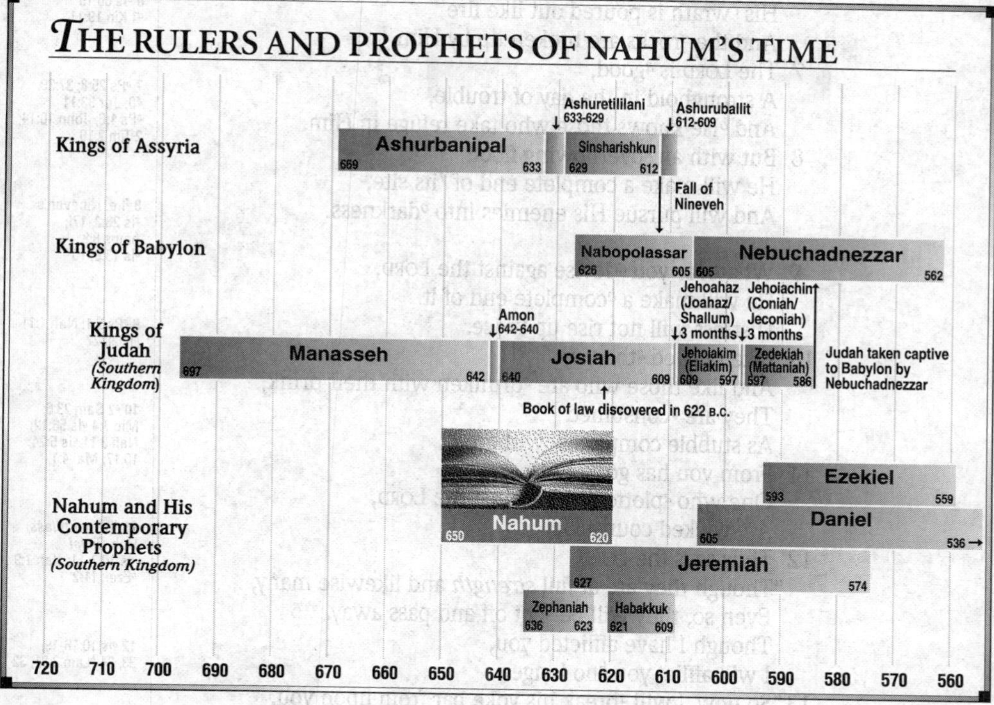

Chapter 1 Theme

1 The [1a]oracle of [b]Nineveh. The book of the vision of Nahum
the Elkoshite.

2 A [a]jealous and avenging God is the LORD;
The LORD is [b]avenging and [1]wrathful.
The LORD takes [c]vengeance on His adversaries,
And He reserves wrath for His enemies.

3 The LORD is [a]slow to anger and great in power,
And the LORD will by no means leave *the guilty*
unpunished.
In [b]whirlwind and storm is His way,
And [c]clouds are the dust beneath His feet.

4 He [a]rebukes the sea and makes it dry;
He dries up all the rivers.
[b]Bashan and Carmel wither;
The blossoms of Lebanon wither.

5 Mountains [a]quake because of Him
And the hills [b]dissolve;
Indeed the earth is [c]upheaved by His presence,
The [d]world and all the inhabitants in it.

6 [a]Who can stand before His indignation?
Who can endure the [b]burning of His anger?

1:1 [1]Or *burden* [a]Is 13:1; 19:1; Jer 23:33, 34; Hab 1:1; Zech 9:1; Mal 1:1 [b]2 Kin 19:36; Jon 1:2; Nah 2:8; Zeph 2:13

2 [1]Lit *a possessor of wrath* [a]Ex 20:5; Josh 24:19 [b]Deut 32:35, 41 [c]Ps 94:1

3 [a]Ex 34:6, 7; Neh 9:17; Ps 103:8 [b]Ex 19:16; Is 29:6 [c]Ps 104:3; Is 19:1

4 [a]Josh 3:15, 16; Ps 106:9; Is 50:2; Matt 8:26 [b]Is 33:9

5 [a]Ex 19:18; 2 Sam 22:8; Ps 18:7 [b]Mic 1:4 [c]Is 24:1, 20 [d]Ps 98:7

6 [a]Jer 10:10; Mal 3:2 [b]Is 13:13

His [c]wrath is poured out like fire
And the [d]rocks are broken up by Him.
7 The LORD is [a]good,
A stronghold in the day of trouble,
And [b]He knows those who take refuge in Him.
8 But with an [a]overflowing flood
He will make a complete end of [1]its site,
And will pursue His enemies into [b]darkness.

9 Whatever you [a]devise against the LORD,
He will make a [b]complete end of it.
Distress will not rise up twice.
10 Like tangled [a]thorns,
And like those who are [b]drunken with their drink,
They are [c]consumed
As stubble completely withered.
11 From you has gone forth
One who [a]plotted evil against the LORD,
A [1b]wicked counselor.
12 Thus says the LORD,
"Though they are at full *strength* and likewise many,
Even so, they will be [a]cut off and pass away.
Though I have afflicted you,
I will afflict you [b]no longer.
13 "So now, I will [a]break his yoke bar from upon you,
And I will tear off your shackles."

14 The LORD has issued a command concerning [1]you:
"[2]Your name will [a]no longer be perpetuated.
I will cut off [3b]idol and [4]image
From the house of your gods.
I will prepare your [c]grave,
For you are contemptible."

15 [1]Behold, [a]on the mountains the feet of him who brings
good news,
Who announces peace!
[b]Celebrate your feasts, O Judah;
Pay your vows.
For [c]never again will the [2]wicked one pass through you;
He is [d]cut off completely.

Chapter 2 Theme ______________________

2 [1]The one who [a]scatters has come up against [2]you.
Man the fortress, watch the road;
[3]Strengthen your back, [4]summon all *your* strength.
2 For the LORD will restore the [a]splendor of Jacob
[b]Like the splendor of Israel,
Even though devastators have devastated them
And [c]destroyed their vine branches.

6 [c]Is 66:15 [d]1 Kin 19:11

7 [a]Ps 25:8; 37:39, 40; Jer 33:11 [b]Ps 1:6; John 10:14; 2 Tim 2:19

8 [1]I.e. Nineveh's [a]Is 28:2, 17f; Amos 8:8 [b]Is 13:9, 10

9 [a]Ps 2:1; Nah 1:11 [b]Is 28:22

10 [a]2 Sam 23:6; Mic 7:4 [b]Is 56:12; Nah 3:11 [c]Is 5:24; 10:17; Mal 4:1

11 [1]Or *worthless;* Heb *Belial* [a]Is 10:7-11; Nah 1:9 [b]Ezek 11:2

12 [a]Is 10:16-19, 33, 34 [b]Lam 3:31, 32

13 [a]Is 9:4; 10:27; Jer 2:20

14 [1]I.e. the king of Nineveh [2]Lit *No more of your name will be sown* [3]Or *a graven image* [4]Lit *cast* metal *image* [a]Job 18:17; Ps 109:13; Is 14:22 [b]Is 46:1, 2; Mic 5:13, 14 [c]Ezek 32:22, 23

15 [1]Ch 2:1 in Heb [2]Or *worthless one;* Heb *Belial* [a]Is 40:9; 52:7; Rom 10:15 [b]Lev 23:2, 4 [c]Is 52:1; Joel 3:17 [d]Is 29:7, 8

2:1 [1]Ch 2:2 in Heb [2]Lit *your face* [3]Lit *Make strong your loins* [4]Lit *strengthen power greatly* [a]Jer 51:20-23

2 [a]Is 60:15 [b]Ezek 37:21-23 [c]Ps 80:12, 13

3 The shields of [1]his mighty men are *colored* red,
The warriors are dressed in [a]scarlet,
The chariots are *enveloped* in [2]flashing steel
[3]When he is prepared *to march,*
And the cypress [b]*spears* are brandished.
4 The [a]chariots race madly in the streets,
They rush wildly in the [1]squares,
Their appearance is like torches,
They dash to and fro like lightning flashes.
5 He remembers his [a]nobles;
They [b]stumble in their march,
They hurry to her wall,
And the [1]mantelet is set up.
6 The gates of the rivers are opened
And the palace is dissolved.
7 It is fixed:
She is stripped, she is carried away,
And her handmaids are [a]moaning like the sound
of doves,
[b]Beating on their [1]breasts.

8 Though Nineveh *was* like a pool of water throughout
her days,
Now they are fleeing;
"Stop, stop,"
But [a]no one turns back.
9 Plunder the silver!
Plunder the [a]gold!
For there is no limit to the treasure—
Wealth from every kind of desirable object.
10 She is [a]emptied! Yes, she is desolate and waste!
[b]Hearts are melting and knees knocking!
Also anguish is in [1]the whole body
And all their [c]faces are grown pale!
11 Where is the den of the lions
And the feeding place of the [a]young lions,
Where the lion, lioness and lion's cub prowled,
With nothing to disturb *them?*
12 The lion tore enough for his cubs,
[1]Killed *enough* for his lionesses,
And filled his lairs with prey
And his dens with torn flesh.
13 "Behold, [a]I am against you," declares the LORD of hosts. "I
will [b]burn up her chariots in smoke, a sword will devour your
young lions; I will [c]cut off your prey from the land, and no
longer will the voice of your messengers be heard."

Chapter 3 Theme ____________________

3 [a]Woe to the bloody city, completely full of lies *and* pillage;
Her prey never departs.

3 [1]I.e. those attacking Nineveh [2]Lit *fire of steel* [3]Lit *On the day of his preparation* [a]Ezek 23:14, 15 [b]Job 39:23

4 [1]Lit *broad places* [a]Is 66:15; Jer 4:13; Ezek 26:10; Nah 3:2, 3

5 [1]Lit *covering* used in a siege [a]Nah 3:18 [b]Jer 46:12

7 [1]Lit *hearts* [a]Is 38:14; 59:11 [b]Is 32:12

8 [a]Jer 46:5; 47:3

9 [a]Rev 18:12, 16

10 [1]Lit *all the loin* [a]Is 24:1; 34:10-13; Nah 2:2 [b]Ps 22:14; Is 13:7, 8; Ezek 21:7 [c]Joel 2:6

11 [a]Is 5:29

12 [1]Lit *Strangled*

13 [a]Jer 21:13; Ezek 5:8; Nah 3:5 [b]Josh 11:6, 9; Ps 46:9 [c]Is 49:24, 25; Nah 3:1

3:1 [a]Ezek 24:6, 9

2 The [a]noise of the whip,
The noise of the rattling of the wheel,
Galloping horses
And [1]bounding chariots!
3 Horsemen charging,
Swords flashing, [a]spears gleaming,
[b]Many slain, a mass of corpses,
And [1c]countless dead bodies—
They stumble over [2]the dead bodies!
4 *All* because of the [a]many harlotries of the harlot,
The charming one, the [b]mistress of sorceries,
Who [c]sells nations by her harlotries
And families by her sorceries.
5 "Behold, [a]I am against you," declares the LORD of hosts;
"And I will [1b]lift up your skirts over your face,
And [c]show to the nations your nakedness
And to the kingdoms your disgrace.
6 "I will [a]throw [1]filth on you
And [b]make you vile,
And set you up as a [c]spectacle.
7 "And it will come about that all who see you
Will [1]shrink from you and say,
'Nineveh is devastated!
[a]Who will grieve for her?'
Where will I seek comforters for you?"

8 Are you better than [1a]No-amon,
Which was situated by the [b]waters of the Nile,
With water surrounding her,
Whose rampart *was* [2]the sea,
Whose wall *consisted* of [2]the sea?
9 [a]Ethiopia was *her* might,
And Egypt too, without limits.
[b]Put and [c]Lubim were among [1]her helpers.
10 Yet she [a]became an exile,
She went into captivity;
Also her [b]small children were dashed to pieces
[c]At the head of every street;
They [d]cast lots for her honorable men,
And all her great men were bound with fetters.
11 You too will become [a]drunk,
You will be [b]hidden.
You too will search for a refuge from the enemy.
12 All your fortifications are [a]fig trees with [1b]ripe fruit—
When shaken, they fall into the eater's mouth.
13 Behold, your people are [a]women in your midst!
The gates of your land are [b]opened wide
to your enemies;
Fire consumes your gate bars.
14 [a]Draw for yourself water for the siege!
[b]Strengthen your fortifications!

INSIGHT

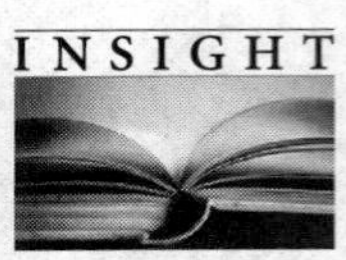

No-amon refers to ***Thebes***, the Greek name for No, the capital of Egypt. Since Nahum reminds Nineveh of the fall of No-amon (Thebes), his prophecy had to come after 661 B.C. and before Nineveh was destroyed in 612 B.C. by the Babylonians, Medes, and Scythians.

2 [1]Lit *skipping* [a]Job 39:22-25; Jer 47:3; Nah 2:3, 4

3 [1]Lit *there is no end to* [2]Lit *their* [a]Hab 3:11 [b]Is 34:3; 66:16 [c]Is 37:36; Ezek 39:4

4 [a]Is 23:17; Ezek 16:25-29; Rev 17:1, 2 [b]Is 47:9, 12, 13 [c]Rev 18:3

5 [1]Lit *uncover your* [a]Jer 50:31; Ezek 26:3; Nah 2:13 [b]Is 47:2, 3; Jer 13:26 [c]Ezek 16:37

6 [1]Lit *detestable things* [a]Job 9:31 [b]Job 30:8; Mal 2:9 [c]Is 14:16; Jer 51:37

7 [1]Lit *flee* [a]Is 51:19; Jer 15:5

8 [1]I.e. the city of Amon: Thebes [2]I.e. the Nile [a]Jer 46:25; Ezek 30:14-16 [b]Is 19:6-8

9 [1]Lit *your* [a]Is 20:5 [b]Jer 46:9; Ezek 27:10; 30:5; 38:5 [c]2 Chr 12:3; 16:8

10 [a]Is 19:4; 20:4 [b]Ps 137:9; Is 13:16; Hos 13:16 [c]Lam 2:19 [d]Joel 3:3; Obad 11

11 [a]Is 49:26; Jer 25:27; Nah 1:10 [b]Is 2:10, 19; Hos 10:8

12 [1]Lit *first fruits* [a]Rev 6:13 [b]Is 28:4

13 [a]Is 19:16; Jer 50:37; 51:30 [b]Is 45:1, 2; Nah 2:6

14 [a]2 Chr 32:3, 4 [b]Nah 2:1

15 [a]Is 66:15, 16; Nah 2:13; 3:13 [b]Joel 1:4

16 [1]I.e. strips vegetation; or *molts* [a]Is 23:8

17 [1]Or *officials* [a]Rev 9:7 [b]Jer 51:27

18 [a]Ps 76:5, 6; Is 56:10; Jer 51:57 [b]Jer 50:18 [c]Nah 2:5 [d]1 Kin 22:17; Is 13:14

19 [1]Lit *your report* [a]Jer 46:11; Mic 1:9 [b]Jer 30:12 [c]Job 27:23; Lam 2:15

Go into the clay and tread the mortar!
Take hold of the brick mold!
15 There [a]fire will consume you,
The sword will cut you down;
It will [b]consume you as the locust *does.*

Multiply yourself like the creeping locust,
Multiply yourself like the swarming locust.
16 You have increased your [a]traders more than the stars
of heaven—
The creeping locust [1]strips and flies away.
17 Your [1a]guardsmen are like the swarming locust.
Your [b]marshals are like hordes of grasshoppers
Settling in the stone walls on a cold day.
The sun rises and they flee,
And the place where they are is not known.
18 Your shepherds are [a]sleeping, O [b]king of Assyria;
Your [c]nobles are lying down.
Your people are [d]scattered on the mountains
And there is no one to regather *them.*
19 There is [a]no relief for your breakdown,
Your [b]wound is incurable.
All who hear [1]about you
Will [c]clap *their* hands over you,
For on whom has not your evil passed continually?

Nahum at a Glance

Theme of Nahum:

Segment Divisions

		Chapter Themes
		1
		2
		3

Author:

Date:

Purpose:

Key Words:

I am against you

I will

Nineveh (and all references to it)

HABAKKUK חבקוק CHAVAQQUQ

"The righteous will live by his faith." This truth, which pierced Martin Luther's heart and as a result brought about a reformation, comes from Habakkuk 2:4. Paul echoed it in Romans and Galatians, but its roots are in the Old Testament, where God affirms that salvation has always been by faith and faith alone.

And what is the setting of the verse that unshackled Luther and brought him into a vital relationship with the living God? You will discover this as you study Habakkuk, a book that ends with a crescendo of faith even in anticipation of Judah's darkest of hours.

THINGS TO DO

General Instructions

As you read Habakkuk it is critical for you to know whether God is speaking or Habakkuk. Since the book is only three chapters long, read through Habakkuk and note in the margin when God speaks or when Habakkuk speaks. Try it on your own and then look at the HABAKKUK AT A GLANCE chart on page 1514 for the segment divisions, which show who is speaking when.

Chapter 1

1. An "oracle" can be translated "a burden." What is Habakkuk's burden; what is bothering him? Mark the key repeated word *why* and you'll discover the answer.

2. Read through Habakkuk 1 and mark every reference to *Habakkuk* in one color and every reference to the *Lord* (including personal pronouns) in another color. Then observe (and list, if you want) everything you learn about the Lord as a personality and what He is going to do.

3. The Chaldeans, another name for the Babylonians, invaded the southern kingdom of Judah three times. In 605 B.C., Daniel and many nobles were taken captive. Then in 597 B.C., Ezekiel and 10,000 others were taken captive. The final siege occurred from 588 to 586 B.C., when Jerusalem and the temple were destroyed. Mark every reference to the *Chaldeans*—and observe what they will do and what will happen to them. Also, from this point onward, mark *nations.*

4. Study the historical chart on page 1509 and notice the relationship between the time of Habakkuk's writing and the Babylonian invasion.

Chapter 2

1. Mark every reference, including pronouns, to the *proud* or *haughty man.* Then in your notebook, list what he is like and with whom he is contrasted.

2. Mark each use of *woe* and observe to whom the woe is going to come, why it will come, and what will happen when it comes. If you want to, summarize this in your notebook.

3. Mark every reference to the *Lord* and record in the margin any new insights about Him.

Chapter 3

1. Habakkuk's prayer is an intensely emotional poem. A statement is made and is followed by a similar statement that heightens the meaning or repeats the truth in another way. Read the prayer again, keeping its form in mind.

2. As you read, ask the "5 W's and an H": Who is doing what? To whom or what? When will it be done? Why will it be done? What specifically is going to happen? How? Observe everything you learn about the Lord from this chapter.

3. What does this chapter say about Habakkuk and his relationship to God? Record this in your notebook. Then compare what you write with 2:4. How is Habakkuk going to live? Have his circumstances changed?

4. Fill in the appropriate sections of HABAKKUK AT A GLANCE, recording the theme of each paragraph, each chapter, and the book itself. Fill in any other information asked for on the chart. Also record the theme of each chapter in your Bible.

Things to Think About

1. What do you learn about God—His ways, His Word, His character? If He is the same yesterday, today, and forever, how would such insight into God influence your relationship to Him and to His Word? How would this affect your response to your circumstances?

2. What have you learned about the haughty or proud? God says in James 4 that He resists the proud. Can you understand why? Can you see any element of pride or haughtiness in your life that you need to deal with?

3. Review what you learned about the woes pronounced by God. Ask God to search your heart. Would these woes be applicable to you because of your lifestyle? Do you need to confess anything to God and receive His forgiveness and cleansing (see 1 John 1:9)?

4. As you look at how Habakkuk begins and ends, think about what effected the difference in Habakkuk and then apply it to your own life. Are you questioning or doubting God and His ways, and is it causing despair? What do you need to do?

Chapter 1 Theme ______________________________

1 The [1a]oracle which Habakkuk the prophet saw.
2 [a]How long, O LORD, will I call for help,
And You will not hear?
I cry out to You, "Violence!"
Yet You do [b]not save.
3 Why do You make me [a]see iniquity,
And cause *me* to look on wickedness?
Yes, [b]destruction and violence are before me;
[c]Strife exists and contention arises.
4 Therefore the [a]law is [1]ignored
And justice [2]is never upheld.
For the wicked [b]surround the righteous;
Therefore justice comes out [c]perverted.

5 "[a]Look among the nations! Observe!
Be astonished! [b]Wonder!
Because *I am* doing [c]something in your days—
You would not believe if [1]you were told.
6 "For behold, I am [a]raising up the Chaldeans,
That [1]fierce and impetuous people
Who march [2]throughout the earth
To [3b]seize dwelling places which are not theirs.

1:1 [1]Or *burden* [a]Is 13:1; Nah 1:1
2 [a]Ps 13:1, 2; 22:1, 2 [b]Jer 14:9
3 [a]Ps 55:9-11; Jer 20:18 [b]Jer 20:8 [c]Jer 15:10
4 [1]Or *ineffective;* lit *numbed* [2]Lit *never goes forth* [a]Ps 58:1, 2; 119:126; Is 59:12-14 [b]Ps 22:12; Is 1:21-23 [c]Is 5:20; Ezek 9:9
5 [1]Lit *it* [a]Acts 13:41 [b]Is 29:9 [c]Is 29:14; Ezek 12:22-28
6 [1]Lit *bitter* [2]Lit *the breadth of* [3]Lit *take possession of* [a]2 Kin 24:2; Jer 4:11-13 [b]Jer 8:10

7 “They are dreaded and [a]feared;
Their [b]justice and [1]authority [2]originate
with themselves.
8 “Their [a]horses are swifter than leopards
And [1]keener than [b]wolves in the evening.
Their [2]horsemen come galloping,
Their horsemen come from afar;
They fly like an [c]eagle swooping *down* to devour.
9 “All of them come for violence.
[1]Their horde of [a]faces *moves* forward.
They collect captives like sand.
10 “They [a]mock at kings
And rulers are a laughing matter to them.
They [b]laugh at every fortress
And [c]heap up rubble to capture it.
11 “Then they will sweep through *like* the [a]wind
and pass on.
But they will be held [b]guilty,
They whose [c]strength is their god.”

12 Are You not from [a]everlasting,
O LORD, my God, my Holy One?
We will not die.
You, O LORD, have [b]appointed them to judge;
And You, O [c]Rock, have established them to correct.

7 [1]Lit *eminence* [2]Lit *proceeds from* [a]Is 18:2, 7 [b]Jer 39:5-9

8 [1]Or *more eager to attack* [2]Or *steeds paw the ground* [a]Jer 4:13 [b]Zeph 3:3 [c]Ezek 17:3; Hos 8:1

9 [1]Or *The eagerness of their faces* [a]2 Kin 12:17; Dan 11:17

10 [a]2 Chr 36:6, 10; Is 37:13 [b]Is 10:9; 14:16 [c]Jer 32:24; Ezek 26:8

11 [a]Jer 4:11, 12 [b]Jer 2:3 [c]Dan 4:30; Hab 1:16

12 [a]Deut 33:27; Ps 90:2; Mal 3:6 [b]Is 10:5, 6; Mal 3:5 [c]Deut 32:4

THE RULERS AND PROPHETS OF HABAKKUK'S TIME

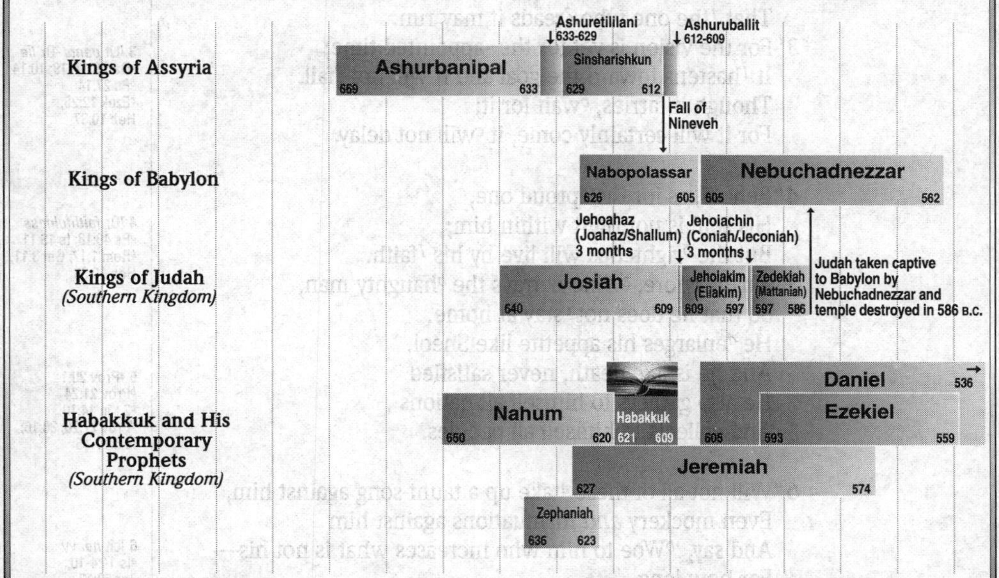

Kings of Assyria
Ashurbanipal 669–633
Ashuretililani 633-629
Sinsharishkun 629–612
Ashuruballit 612-609
Fall of Nineveh

Kings of Babylon
Nabopolassar 626–605
Nebuchadnezzar 605–562

Kings of Judah *(Southern Kingdom)*
Josiah 640–609
Jehoahaz (Joahaz/Shallum) 3 months
Jehoiakim (Eliakim) 609–597
Jehoiachin (Coniah/Jeconiah) 3 months
Zedekiah (Mattaniah) 597–586
Judah taken captive to Babylon by Nebuchadnezzar and temple destroyed in 586 B.C.

Habakkuk and His Contemporary Prophets *(Southern Kingdom)*
Nahum 650–620
Habakkuk 621–609
Daniel 605–536 →
Ezekiel 593–559
Jeremiah 627–574
Zephaniah 636–623

720 710 700 690 680 670 660 650 640 630 620 610 600 590 580 570 560

13 *Your* eyes are too [a]pure to [1]approve evil,
And You can not look on wickedness *with favor.*
Why do You [b]look with favor
On those who deal [c]treacherously?
Why are You [d]silent when the wicked [e]swallow up
Those more righteous than they?
14 *Why* have You made men like the fish of the sea,
Like creeping things without a ruler over them?
15 *The Chaldeans* [a]bring all of them up with a hook,
[b]Drag them away with their net,
And gather them together in their fishing net.
Therefore they rejoice and are glad.
16 Therefore they offer a sacrifice to their net
And [1]burn incense to their fishing net;
Because through [a]these things their [2]catch is [3]large,
And their food is [4]plentiful.
17 Will they therefore empty their [a]net
And continually [b]slay nations without sparing?

Chapter 2 Theme ______________________________

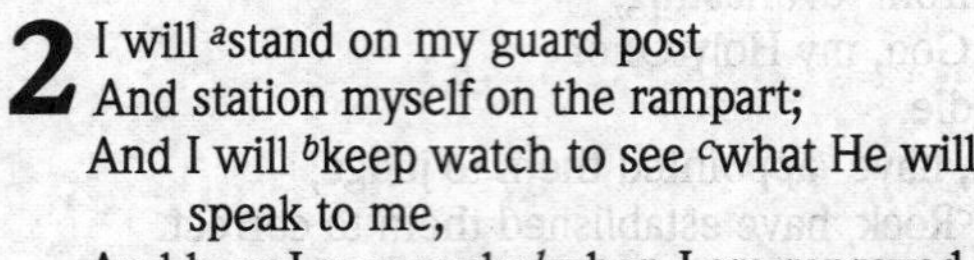

2 I will [a]stand on my guard post
And station myself on the rampart;
And I will [b]keep watch to see [c]what He will
speak to me,
And how I may reply [1]when I am reproved.
2 Then the LORD answered me and said,
"[a]Record the vision
And inscribe *it* on tablets,
That [1]the one who [2]reads it may run.
3 "For the vision is yet for the [a]appointed time;
It [1]hastens toward the goal and it will not [2]fail.
Though it tarries, [b]wait for it;
For it will certainly come, it [c]will not delay.

4 "Behold, as for the [a]proud one,
His soul is not right within him;
But the [b]righteous will live by his [1]faith.
5 "Furthermore, [a]wine betrays the [b]haughty man,
So that he does not [c]stay at home.
He [d]enlarges his appetite like Sheol,
And he is like death, never satisfied.
He also gathers to himself all nations
And collects to himself all peoples.

6 "Will not all of these [a]take up a taunt-song against him,
Even mockery *and* insinuations against him
And say, '[b]Woe to him who increases what is not his—
For how long—
And makes himself [1]rich with loans?'

RETURN TO INSTRUCTIONS

13 [1]Lit *look at* [a]Ps 11:4-6; 34:15, 16 [b]Jer 12:1, 2 [c]Is 24:16 [d]Ps 50:21 [e]Ps 35:25

15 [a]Jer 16:16; Amos 4:2 [b]Ps 10:9

16 [1]Or *sacrifice* [2]Lit *portion* [3]Lit *fat;* or *plentiful* [4]Lit *the fat portion* [a]Jer 44:17

17 [a]Is 19:8 [b]Is 14:5, 6

2:1 [1]Lit *upon my reproof* [a]Is 21:8 [b]Ps 5:3 [c]Ps 85:8

2 [1]Or *one may read it fluently* [2]Or *is to proclaim it* [a]Deut 27:8; Rom 15:4; Rev 1:19

3 [1]Lit *pants* [2]Or *lie* [a]Dan 8:17, 19; 10:14 [b]Ps 27:14 [c]Ezek 12:25; Heb 10:37

4 [1]Or *faithfulness* [a]Ps 49:18; Is 13:11 [b]Rom 1:17; Gal 3:11; Heb 10:38

5 [a]Prov 20:1 [b]Prov 21:24 [c]2 Kin 14:10 [d]Prov 27:20; 30:16; Is 5:11-15

6 [1]Lit *heavy* [a]Is 14:4-10; Jer 50:13 [b]Job 20:15-29; Hab 2:12

7 "Will not [1]your creditors [a]rise up suddenly,
And those who [2]collect from you awaken?
Indeed, you will become plunder for them.
8 "Because you have [a]looted many nations,
All the remainder of the peoples will loot you—
Because of human bloodshed and violence [1]done
to the land,
To the town and all its inhabitants.

9 "Woe to him who gets [a]evil gain for his house
To [b]put his nest on high,
To be delivered from the hand of calamity!
10 "You have devised a [a]shameful thing for your house
By cutting off many peoples;
So you are [b]sinning against yourself.
11 "Surely the [a]stone will cry out from the wall,
And the rafter will answer it from the [1]framework.

12 "Woe to him who [a]builds a city with bloodshed
And founds a town with [1]violence!
13 "Is it not indeed from the LORD of hosts
That peoples [a]toil for fire,
And nations grow weary for nothing?
14 "For the earth will be [a]filled
With the knowledge of the glory of the LORD,
As the waters cover the sea.

15 "Woe to you who make [1]your neighbors drink,
Who mix in your venom even to make *them* drunk
So as to look on their nakedness!
16 "You will be filled with disgrace rather than honor.
Now you yourself [a]drink and [1]expose your *own* nakedness.
The [b]cup in the LORD's right hand will come around
to you,
And [c]utter disgrace *will come* upon your glory.
17 "For the [a]violence [1]done to Lebanon will [2]overwhelm you,
And the devastation of *its* beasts [3]by which you
terrified them,
[b]Because of human bloodshed and [c]violence [4]done
to the land,
To the town and all its inhabitants.

18 "What [a]profit is the [1]idol when its maker has carved it,
Or [2]an image, a [b]teacher of falsehood?
For *its* maker [c]trusts in his *own* handiwork
When he fashions speechless idols.
19 "Woe to him who [a]says to a *piece of* wood, '[b]Awake!'
To a mute stone, 'Arise!'
And that is *your* teacher?
Behold, it is overlaid with [c]gold and silver,
And there is [d]no breath at all inside it.

7 [1]Lit *those who bite you* [2]Lit *violently shake you* [a]Prov 29:1
8 [1]Lit *of the land* [a]Is 33:1; Jer 27:7; Zech 2:8
9 [a]Jer 22:13; Ezek 22:27 [b]Jer 49:16
10 [a]2 Kin 9:26; Nah 1:14; Hab 2:16 [b]Jer 26:19
11 [1]Lit *wood* [a]Josh 24:27; Luke 19:40
12 [1]Or *injustice* [a]Mic 3:10; Nah 3:1
13 [a]Is 50:11; Jer 51:58
14 [a]Ps 22:27; Is 11:9; Zech 14:9
15 [1]Lit *his neighbor*
16 [1]Lit *show yourself uncircumcised;* or *stagger;* so DSS and ancient versions [a]Lam 4:21 [b]Jer 25:15, 17 [c]Nah 3:6
17 [1]Lit *of Lebanon* [2]Lit *cover* [3]Lit which *terrified them* [4]Lit *of the land* [a]Joel 3:19; Zech 11:1 [b]Ps 55:23; Hab 2:8 [c]Jer 51:35; Hab 2:8
18 [1]Or *a graven image* [2]Lit a *cast* metal *image* [a]Is 42:17; 44:9; Jer 2:27, 28 [b]Jer 10:8, 14; Zech 10:2 [c]Ps 115:4, 8
19 [a]Jer 2:27, 28; 10:3 [b]1 Kin 18:26-29 [c]Ps 135:15-18; Jer 10:4, 9, 14 [d]Ps 135:17

20 "But the [a]LORD is in His holy temple.
[1]Let all the earth [b]be silent before Him."

Chapter 3 Theme ______________________________

RETURN TO INSTRUCTIONS

3 A prayer of Habakkuk the prophet, according to [1]Shigionoth.
2 LORD, I have [a]heard [1]the report about You *and* [2]I [b]fear.
O LORD, [c]revive [d]Your work in the midst of the years,
In the midst of the years make it known;
In wrath remember [3e]mercy.

3 God comes from [a]Teman,
And the Holy One from Mount [b]Paran. Selah.
His [c]splendor covers the heavens,
And the [d]earth is full of His praise.
4 *His* [a]radiance is like the sunlight;
He has rays *flashing* from His hand,
And there is the hiding of His [b]power.
5 Before Him goes [a]pestilence,
And [b]plague comes [1]after Him.
6 He stood and surveyed the earth;
He looked and [a]startled the nations.
Yes, the perpetual mountains were shattered,
The ancient hills [1]collapsed.
His ways are [b]everlasting.
7 I saw the tents of Cushan under [a]distress,
The tent curtains of the land of [b]Midian were trembling.

8 Did the LORD rage against the [a]rivers,
Or *was* Your anger against the rivers,
Or *was* Your wrath against the [b]sea,
That You [c]rode on Your horses,
On Your [d]chariots of salvation?
9 Your [a]bow was made bare,
The rods of [1]chastisement were sworn. Selah.
You [b]cleaved the earth with rivers.
10 The mountains saw You *and* quaked;
The downpour of waters swept by.
The deep [a]uttered forth its voice,
It lifted high its hands.
11 [a]Sun *and* moon stood in their places;
They went away at the [b]light of Your arrows,
At the radiance of Your gleaming spear.
12 In indignation You [a]marched through the earth;
In anger You [1b]trampled the nations.
13 You went forth for the [a]salvation of Your people,
For the salvation of Your [b]anointed.
You struck the [c]head of the house of the evil
To lay him open from [1]thigh to neck. Selah.
14 You pierced with his [a]own [1]spears
The head of his [2]throngs.
They [b]stormed in to scatter [3]us;

20 [1]Lit *Hush before Him, all the earth* [a]Mic 1:2 [b]Zeph 1:7; Zech 2:13

3:1 [1]I.e. a highly emotional poetic form

2 [1]Or *Your report* [2]Or *I stand in awe of Your work, O LORD; In the midst of the years revive it,* [3]Or *compassion* [a]Job 42:5 [b]Ps 119:120; Jer 10:7 [c]Ps 71:20; 85:6 [d]Ps 44:1-8; Hab 1:5 [e]Num 14:19; 2 Sam 24:15-17; Is 54:8

3 [a]Jer 49:7; Amos 1:12; Obad 9 [b]Gen 21:21; Deut 33:2 [c]Ps 113:4; 148:13 [d]Ps 48:10

4 [a]Ps 18:12 [b]Job 26:14

5 [1]Lit *at His feet* [a]Ex 12:29, 30; Num 16:46-49 [b]Num 11:1-3; Ps 18:12, 13

6 [1]Lit *bowed;* or *sank down* [a]Job 21:18; Ps 35:5 [b]Hab 1:12

7 [a]Ex 15:14-16 [b]Num 31:7, 8; Judg 7:24, 25; 8:12

8 [a]Ex 7:19, 20; Josh 3:16; Is 50:2 [b]Ex 14:16, 21; Ps 114:3, 5 [c]Deut 33:26; Ps 18:10; Hab 3:15 [d]Ps 68:17

9 [1]Lit *word* [a]Ps 7:12, 13; Hab 3:11 [b]Ps 78:16; 105:41

10 [a]Ps 93:3; 98:7, 8

11 [a]Josh 10:12-14 [b]Ps 18:14

12 [1]Or *thresh* [a]Ps 68:7 [b]Is 41:15; Jer 51:33; Mic 4:13

13 [1]Lit *foundation* [a]Ex 15:2; 2 Sam 5:20; Ps 68:19, 20 [b]Ps 20:6; 28:8 [c]Ps 68:21; 110:6

14 [1]Lit *shafts* [2]Or *warriors* or *villagers* [3]Lit *me* [a]Judg 7:22 [b]Dan 11:40; Zech 9:14

14 [c]Ps 10:8; 64:2-5

15 [a]Ps 77:19; Hab 3:8 [b]Ex 15:8

16 [1]Lit *belly* [2]Or *To come upon the people who will* [a]Dan 10:8; Hab 3:2 [b]Job 30:17, 30; Jer 23:9 [c]Luke 21:19 [d]Jer 5:15

17 [1]Lit *produce* [a]Joel 1:10-12; Amos 4:9; 2 Cor 4:8, 9 [b]Mic 6:15 [c]Joel 1:18 [d]Jer 5:17

18 [a]Ex 15:1, 2; Job 13:15; Is 61:10; Rom 5:2, 3 [b]Ps 46:1-5; Phil 4:4 [c]Ps 25:5; 27:1; Is 12:2

19 [1]Heb *YHWH,* usually rendered *LORD* [a]Ps 18:32, 33; 27:1; 46:1; Is 45:24 [b]2 Sam 22:34 [c]Deut 33:29

Their exultation *was* like those
Who [c]devour the oppressed in secret.
15 You [a]trampled on the sea with Your horses,
On the [b]surge of many waters.

16 I heard and my [1]inward parts [a]trembled,
At the sound my lips quivered.
Decay enters my [b]bones,
And in my place I tremble.
Because I must [c]wait quietly for the day of distress,
[2]For the [d]people to arise *who* will invade us.
17 Though the [a]fig tree should not blossom
And there be no [1]fruit on the vines,
Though the yield of the [b]olive should fail
And the fields produce no food,
Though the [c]flock should be cut off from the fold
And there be [d]no cattle in the stalls,
18 Yet I will [a]exult in the LORD,
I will [b]rejoice in the [c]God of my salvation.
19 The Lord [1]GOD is my [a]strength,
And [b]He has made my feet like hinds' *feet,*
And makes me walk on my [c]high places.

For the choir director, on my stringed instruments.

Theme of Habakkuk:

SEGMENT DIVISIONS

	WHO IS SPEAKING	PARAGRAPH THEMES	CHAPTER THEMES
	HABAKKUK SPEAKS	1:1-4	1
	GOD SPEAKS	1:5-11	
	HABAKKUK SPEAKS	1:12-17	
	GOD SPEAKS	2:1-3	2
		2:4, 5	
		2:6-8	
		2:9-11	
		2:12-14	
		2:15-17	
		2:18-20	
	HABAKKUK PRAYS	3:1, 2	3
		3:3-7	
		3:8-15	
		3:16-19	

Author:

Date:

Purpose:

Key Words:

ZEPHANIAH צְפַנְיָה TZ^eFANYA

During the latter years of King Josiah's reign, Israel was a spiritual oasis surrounded by apostasy—the abandonment of faith.

We do not know exactly when Zephaniah's prophecy came, although it was during Josiah's reign (640–609 B.C.). However, some argument can be made from the text that Zephaniah's prophecy motivated Josiah's reforms. In 2 Chronicles 34:3 we read "in the eighth year of his (Josiah's) reign (about 632 B.C.) while he was still a youth, he began to seek the God of his father David; and in the twelfth year he began to purge Judah and Jerusalem..." In 622 B.C., the book of the Law was found in the house of God. Whenever Zephaniah's prophecy came, it came full gale, a stormy blast calling God's people to humility and righteousness in the face of the day of the Lord's anger.

Things to Do

1. Zephaniah 1:1 gives the genealogy of Zephaniah and also the historical setting of the book. Record your insights about the author on the ZEPHANIAH AT A GLANCE chart on page 1522. If you want a more thorough picture of the historical setting of Zephaniah, read 2 Kings 22:1–23:30 and 2 Chronicles 34:1–35:27.

2. Consult the historical chart on page 1516 to see the relationship of his prophecy to the Babylonian captivity and the destruction of Nineveh.

3. Read Zephaniah paragraph by paragraph, watching carefully for the references to the different peoples and places. Double-underline in green every reference to the various peoples and cities (Moab, Ammon, etc.). Note what is said about each one.

   a. Be careful to note when there is a change of subject. Watch carefully what happens in 3:1. Although Jerusalem is not mentioned by name at the beginning of chapter 3, the prophecy changes from Nineveh (the Assyrian capital) to Jerusalem.

   b. Decide on the theme or subject covered in each paragraph and record this under "Paragraph Themes" on ZEPHANIAH AT A GLANCE.

4. Now read Zephaniah chapter by chapter and mark the key words listed on ZEPHANIAH AT A GLANCE.

   a. Watch for any other key words as you read chapter by chapter and mark these.

   b. As you mark *the day*, *in* or *on that day,* and *the day of the Lord* notice what will happen in that day and how it relates, if at all, to the day of the Lord. (Remember, prophecy can have a near and a distant fulfillment. If you are not familiar with interpreting prophecy, you can read "Guidelines for Interpreting Predictive Prophecy" on page 2101.)

   c. Note what God will do, to whom, and why. Also note what effect it will have on Israel.

5. Record what you learn about *the day of the Lord* on the chart on page 2076.

6. Fill in ZEPHANIAH AT A GLANCE. Record the theme of each chapter and of the book in the designated spaces. Then record the chapter theme in your Bible.

Things to Think About

1. The day of the Lord is also mentioned in the New Testament. One such reference is in 1 Thessalonians 5:1-11. If the day of the Lord is yet future, what should you be doing to prepare for the time of its approaching?

2. What do you learn about the nation of Israel and its future? Are you using these truths in sharing the good news of Jesus Christ with God's people, the Jews?

3. Think about what you have learned about God from Zephaniah and how such knowledge should affect the way you live.

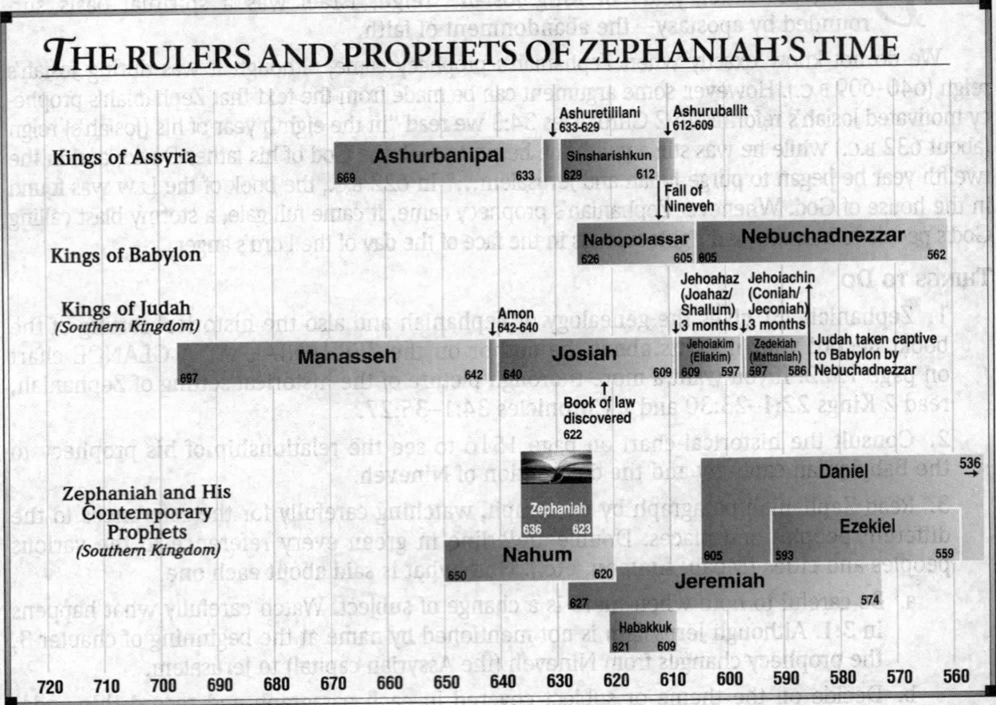

Chapter 1 Theme ____________________

1 The word of the LORD which came to Zephaniah son of
Cushi, son of Gedaliah, son of Amariah, son of Hezekiah, in
the days of [a]Josiah son of [b]Amon, king of Judah:

2 "I will completely [a]remove all *things*
From the face of the [1]earth," declares the LORD.

3 "I will remove [a]man and beast;
I will remove the [b]birds of the sky
And the fish of the sea,
And the [1c]ruins along with the wicked;
And I will cut off man from the face of the [2]earth,"
declares the LORD.

4 "So I will [a]stretch out My hand against Judah
And against all the inhabitants of Jerusalem.
And I will [b]cut off the remnant of Baal from this place,
And the names of the [c]idolatrous priests along with
the priests.

1:1 [a]2 Kin 22:1, 2; 2 Chr 34:1-33; Jer 1:2; 22:11 [b]2 Kin 21:18-26; 2 Chr 33:20-25

2 [1]Lit *ground* [a]Gen 6:7; Jer 7:20; Ezek 33:27, 28

3 [1]Or *stumbling blocks* [2]Lit *ground* [a]Is 6:11, 12 [b]Jer 4:25; 9:10 [c]Ezek 7:19; 14:3, 4, 8

4 [a]Jer 6:12; Ezek 6:14 [b]Mic 5:13 [c]2 Kin 23:5; Hos 10:5

5 [1]Or *their king;* M.T. *Malcam,* probably a variant spelling of Milcom [a]2 Kin 23:12; Jer 19:13 [b]Jer 5:2, 7; 7:9, 10 [c]1 Kin 11:5, 33; Jer 49:1

6 [a]Is 1:4; Hos 7:10 [b]Is 9:13

7 [1]Lit *Hush* [2]Heb *YHWH,* usually rendered *LORD* [a]Hab 2:20; Zech 2:13 [b]Zeph 1:14 [c]Is 34:6; Jer 46:10 [d]1 Sam 16:5; Is 13:3

8 [a]Is 24:21; Hab 1:10 [b]Is 2:6

9 [1]Or *Lord* [a]Jer 5:27; Amos 3:10

10 [1]I.e. a district of Jerusalem [a]2 Chr 33:14; Neh 3:3; 12:39 [b]2 Chr 34:22 [c]Ezek 6:13

11 [1]I.e. a district of Jerusalem [2]Or *merchant people will* [a]Zeph 2:5; Zech 14:21 [b]Job 27:16, 17; Hos 9:6

12 [1]Lit *thickening on their lees* [a]Jer 16:16, 17; Ezek 9:4-11; Amos 9:1-3 [b]Jer 48:11; Amos 6:1 [c]Ezek 8:12; 9:9

13 [a]Jer 15:13; 17:3 [b]Amos 5:11; Mic 6:15

14 [1]Lit *There* [a]Jer 30:7; Joel 2:11; Mal 4:5 [b]Ezek 7:7, 12; 30:3; Joel 1:15; 3:14; Zeph 1:7 [c]Ezek 7:16-18

15 [a]Is 22:5 [b]Joel 2:2, 31; Amos 5:18-20

16 [a]Is 27:13; Jer 4:19 [b]Is 2:12-15

5 "And those who bow down on the [a]housetops to the host of heaven,
And those who bow down *and* [b]swear to the LORD and *yet* swear by [1c]Milcom,
6 And those who have [a]turned back from following the LORD,
And those who have [b]not sought the LORD or inquired of Him."

7 [1a]Be silent before the Lord [2]GOD!
For the [b]day of the LORD is near,
For the LORD has prepared a [c]sacrifice,
He has [d]consecrated His guests.
8 "Then it will come about on the day of the LORD's sacrifice
That I will [a]punish the princes, the king's sons
And all who clothe themselves with [b]foreign garments.
9 "And I will punish on that day all who leap on the *temple* threshold,
Who fill the house of their [1]lord with [a]violence and deceit.
10 "On that day," declares the LORD,
"There will be the sound of a cry from the [a]Fish Gate,
A wail from the [1b]Second Quarter,
And a loud crash from the [c]hills.
11 "Wail, O inhabitants of the [1]Mortar,
For all the [2]people of [a]Canaan will be silenced;
All who weigh out [b]silver will be cut off.
12 "It will come about at that time
That I will [a]search Jerusalem with lamps,
And I will punish the men
Who are [1b]stagnant in spirit,
Who say in their hearts,
'The LORD will [c]not do good or evil!'
13 "Moreover, their wealth will become [a]plunder
And their houses desolate;
Yes, [b]they will build houses but not inhabit *them,*
And plant vineyards but not drink their wine."

14 Near is the [a]great [b]day of the LORD,
Near and coming very quickly;
Listen, the day of the LORD!
[1]In it the warrior [c]cries out bitterly.
15 A day of wrath is that day,
A day of [a]trouble and distress,
A day of destruction and desolation,
A day of [b]darkness and gloom,
A day of clouds and thick darkness,
16 A day of [a]trumpet and battle cry
Against the [b]fortified cities
And the high corner towers.

17 I will bring [a]distress on men
So that they will walk [b]like the blind,
Because they have sinned against the LORD;
And their [c]blood will be poured out like dust
And their [d]flesh like dung.
18 Neither their [a]silver nor their gold
Will be able to deliver them
On the day of the LORD'S wrath;
And [b]all the earth will be devoured
In the fire of His jealousy,
For He will [c]make a complete end,
Indeed a terrifying one,
Of all the inhabitants of the earth.

17 [a]Jer 10:18 [b]Deut 28:29 [c]Ezek 24:7, 8 [d]Jer 8:2; 9:22

18 [a]Ezek 7:19 [b]Zeph 3:8 [c]Gen 6:7; Ezek 7:5-7

The Nations of the Lord's Anger

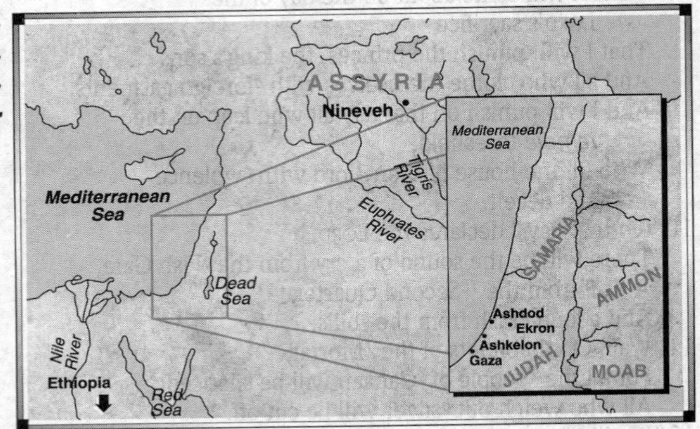

Chapter 2 Theme ______________________

2 Gather yourselves together, yes, [a]gather,
O nation [b]without [1]shame,
2 Before the decree [1]takes effect—
The day passes [a]like the chaff—
Before the [b]burning anger of the LORD comes upon you,
Before the [c]day of the LORD'S anger comes upon you.
3 [a]Seek the LORD,
All you [b]humble of the [1]earth
Who have carried out His [2]ordinances;
[c]Seek righteousness, seek humility.
Perhaps you will be [d]hidden
In the day of the LORD'S anger.

4 For [a]Gaza will be abandoned
And Ashkelon a desolation;
[a]Ashdod will be driven out at noon
And [a]Ekron will be uprooted.
5 Woe to the inhabitants of the seacoast,
The nation of the [1a]Cherethites!
The word of the LORD is [b]against you,

2:1 [1]Or *longing* [a]2 Chr 20:4; Joel 1:14 [b]Jer 3:3; 6:15

2 [1]Lit *is born* [a]Is 17:13; Hos 13:3 [b]Lam 4:11; Nah 1:6 [c]Zeph 1:18

3 [1]Or *land* [2]Or *justice* [a]Ps 105:4; Amos 5:6 [b]Ps 22:26; Is 11:4 [c]Amos 5:14, 15 [d]Ps 57:1; Is 26:20

4 [a]Amos 1:7, 8; Zech 9:5-7

5 [1]I.e. a segment of the Philistines with roots in Crete [a]Ezek 25:16 [b]Amos 3:1

INSIGHT

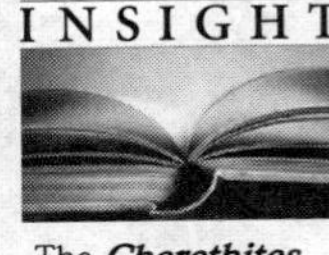

The ***Cherethites*** were probably paid soldiers of the Philistines. David used some of these soldiers as personal bodyguards. Both Ezekiel and Zephaniah pronounced judgment on them.

O [c]Canaan, land of the Philistines;
And I will [d]destroy you
So that there will be [e]no inhabitant.
6 So the seacoast will be [a]pastures,
With [1]caves for shepherds and folds for flocks.
7 And the coast will be
For the [a]remnant of the house of Judah,
They will [b]pasture on it.
In the houses of Ashkelon they will lie down at evening;
For the LORD their God will [c]care for them
And [d]restore their fortune.

8 "I have heard the [1a]taunting of Moab
And the [b]revilings of the sons of Ammon,
With which they have [2]taunted My people
And [3c]become arrogant against their territory.
9 "Therefore, as I live," declares the LORD of hosts,
The God of Israel,
"Surely [a]Moab will be like [b]Sodom
And the sons of [c]Ammon like [d]Gomorrah—
A place possessed by nettles and salt pits,
And a perpetual desolation.
The remnant of My people will [e]plunder them
And the remainder of My nation will inherit them."
10 This they will have in return for their [a]pride, because they
have [1b]taunted and [2]become arrogant against the people of the
LORD of hosts.
11 The LORD will be [a]terrifying to them, for He will [1]starve [b]all
the gods of the earth; and all the [c]coastlands of the nations will
[d]bow down to Him, everyone from his *own* place.
12 "You also, O [a]Ethiopians, will be slain by My sword."
13 And He will [a]stretch out His hand against the north
And destroy [b]Assyria,
And He will make [c]Nineveh a desolation,
Parched like the wilderness.
14 Flocks will lie down in her midst,
[1]All beasts which range in herds;
Both the [2a]pelican and the hedgehog
Will lodge in [3]the tops of her pillars;
[4]Birds will sing in the window,
Desolation *will be* on the threshold;
For He has laid bare the cedar work.
15 This is the [a]exultant city
Which [b]dwells securely,
Who says in her heart,
"[c]I am, and there is no one besides me."
How she has become a [d]desolation,
A resting place for beasts!
[e]Everyone who passes by her will hiss
And wave his hand *in contempt.*

5 [c]Zeph 1:11 [d]Is 14:29, 30 [e]Zeph 3:6
6 [1]Or *meadows* or *wells* [a]Is 5:17; 7:25
7 [a]Is 11:16 [b]Is 32:14 [c]Ex 4:31; Ps 80:14 [d]Jer 32:44; Zeph 3:20
8 [1]Lit *reproach* [2]Lit *reproached* [3]Lit *made* themselves *great* [a]Ezek 25:8 [b]Ezek 25:3 [c]Amos 1:13
9 [a]Is 15:1-9; Jer 48:1-47; Amos 2:1-3 [b]Gen 19:24 [c]Jer 49:1-6; Ezek 25:1-10 [d]Deut 29:23 [e]Is 11:14
10 [1]Lit *reproached* [2]Lit *made* themselves *great* [a]Is 16:6 [b]Zeph 2:8
11 [1]Lit *make lean* [a]Joel 2:11 [b]Zeph 1:4 [c]Is 24:15 [d]Ps 72:8-11; Zeph 3:9
12 [a]Is 18:1-7; 20:4, 5; Ezek 30:4-9
13 [a]Is 14:26; Zeph 1:4 [b]Is 10:16; Mic 5:6 [c]Nah 3:7
14 [1]Or *All* kinds of *beasts in crowds;* lit *Every* kind of *beast of a nation* [2]Or *owl* or *jackdaw* [3]Lit *her capitals* [4]Lit *A voice* [a]Is 14:23; 34:11
15 [a]Is 22:2 [b]Is 32:9, 11; 47:8 [c]Is 47:8; Ezek 28:2, 9 [d]Is 32:14 [e]Jer 18:16; 19:8

Chapter 3 Theme ______________________

3 Woe to her who is [a]rebellious and [b]defiled,
The [c]tyrannical city!
2 She [a]heeded no voice,
She [b]accepted no instruction.
She did not [c]trust in the LORD,
She did not [d]draw near to her God.
3 Her [a]princes within her are roaring lions,
Her judges are [b]wolves at evening;
They leave nothing for the morning.
4 Her prophets are [a]reckless, treacherous men;
Her [b]priests have profaned the sanctuary.
They have done violence to the law.
5 The LORD is [a]righteous [b]within her;
He will [c]do no injustice.
[d]Every morning He brings His justice to light;
He does not fail.
But the unjust [e]knows no shame.
6 "I have cut off nations;
Their corner towers are in ruins.
I have made their streets [a]desolate,
With no one passing by;
Their [b]cities are laid waste,
Without a man, [c]without an inhabitant.
7 "I said, 'Surely you will revere Me,
[a]Accept instruction.'
So her dwelling will [b]not be cut off
According to all that I have appointed concerning her.
But they were eager to [c]corrupt all their deeds.

8 "Therefore [a]wait for Me," declares the LORD,
"For the day when I rise up as a witness.
Indeed, My decision is to [b]gather nations,
To assemble kingdoms,
To pour out on them My indignation,
All My burning anger;
For [c]all the earth will be devoured
By the fire of My zeal.
9 "For then I will [1]give to the peoples [a]purified lips,
That all of them may [b]call on the name of the LORD,
To serve Him [2]shoulder to shoulder.
10 "From beyond the rivers of [a]Ethiopia
My [1]worshipers, [2]My dispersed ones,
Will [b]bring My offerings.
11 "In that day you will [a]feel no shame
Because of all your deeds
By which you have rebelled against Me;
For then I will remove from your midst
Your [b]proud, exulting ones,
And you will never again be haughty
On My [c]holy mountain.

3:1 [a]Jer 5:23 [b]Ezek 23:30 [c]Jer 6:6

2 [a]Jer 7:23-28 [b]Jer 2:30; 5:3; 2 Tim 3:16 [c]Ps 78:22; Jer 13:25 [d]Ps 73:28

3 [a]Ezek 22:27 [b]Jer 5:6; Hab 1:8

4 [a]Judg 9:4 [b]Ezek 22:26; Mal 2:7, 8

5 [a]Deut 32:4 [b]Zeph 3:15, 17 [c]Ps 92:15 [d]Job 7:18 [e]Zeph 2:1

6 [a]Jer 9:12; Zech 7:14; Matt 23:38 [b]Lev 26:31; Is 6:11 [c]Zeph 2:5

7 [a]Job 36:10; Ps 32:8; 1 Tim 1:5 [b]Jer 7:7 [c]Hos 9:9

8 [a]Ps 27:14; Is 30:18; Hab 2:3 [b]Ezek 38:14-23; Joel 3:2 [c]Zeph 1:18

9 [1]Lit *change* [2]Lit *with one shoulder* [a]Is 19:18; 57:19 [b]Ps 22:27; 86:9; Hab 2:14; Zeph 2:11

10 [1]Or *suppliants* [2]Lit *the daughter of My dispersed ones* [a]Ps 68:31; Is 18:1 [b]Is 60:6, 7

11 [a]Is 45:17; 54:4; Joel 2:26, 27 [b]Is 2:12; 5:15 [c]Is 11:9; 56:7; Ezek 20:40

12 "But I will leave among you
A [a]humble and lowly people,
And they will [b]take refuge in the name of the LORD.
13 "The [a]remnant of Israel will [b]do no wrong
And [c]tell no lies,
Nor will a deceitful tongue
Be found in their mouths;
For they will [d]feed and lie down
With no one to make them tremble."

14 Shout for joy, O daughter of Zion!
[a]Shout *in triumph,* O Israel!
Rejoice and exult with all *your* heart,
O daughter of Jerusalem!
15 The LORD has taken away [a]*His* judgments against you,
He has cleared away your enemies.
The King of Israel, the LORD, is [b]in your midst;
You will [c]fear disaster no more.
16 [a]In that day it will be said to Jerusalem:
"[b]Do not be afraid, O Zion;
[c]Do not let your hands fall limp.
17 "The LORD your God is [a]in your midst,
A [1b]victorious warrior.
He will [c]exult over you with joy,
He will [2]be quiet in His love,
He will rejoice over you with shouts of joy.
18 "I will gather those who [a]grieve about the appointed feasts—
They [1]came from you, *O Zion;*
The reproach *of exile* is a burden on [2]them.
19 "Behold, I am going to deal at that time
With all your [a]oppressors,
I will save the [b]lame
And gather the outcast,
And I will turn their [c]shame into [d]praise and renown
In all the earth.
20 "At that time I will [a]bring you in,
Even at the time when I gather you together;
Indeed, I will give you [b]renown and praise
Among all the peoples of the earth,
When I [c]restore your fortunes before your eyes,"
Says the LORD.

12 [a]Is 14:30 [b]Is 14:32; 50:10; Nah 1:7; Zech 13:8, 9

13 [a]Is 10:20-22; Mic 4:7; Zeph 2:7 [b]Ps 119:3; Jer 31:33; Zeph 3:5 [c]Zech 8:3, 16; Rev 14:5 [d]Ezek 34:13-15

14 [a]Zech 9:9

15 [a]Ps 19:9; John 5:30; Rev 18:20 [b]Ezek 37:26-28; Zeph 3:5 [c]Is 54:14

16 [a]Is 25:9 [b]Is 35:3, 4 [c]Job 4:3; Heb 12:12

17 [1]Lit *A warrior who saves* [2]Or with some ancient versions, *renew* you *in* [a]Zeph 3:5, 15 [b]Is 63:1 [c]Is 62:5

18 [1]Lit *were* [2]Lit *her* [a]Ps 42:2-4; Ezek 9:4

19 [a]Is 60:14 [b]Ezek 34:16; Mic 4:6 [c]Ezek 16:27, 57 [d]Is 60:18; 62:7; Zech 8:23

20 [a]Ezek 37:12, 21 [b]Deut 26:18, 19; Is 56:5; 66:22 [c]Jer 29:14; Joel 3:1; Zeph 2:7

Zephaniah at a Glance

Theme of Zephaniah:

Segment Divisions	Paragraph Themes	Chapter Themes
	1:1-6	1
	1:7-13	
	1:14-18	
	2:1-3	2
	2:4-7	
	2:8-11	
	2:12-15	
	3:1-7	3
	3:8-13	
	3:14-20	

Author:

Date:

Purpose:

Key Words:

- I will (the Lo will, He will)
- the day of the Lord (the day or on that day
- remnant (remainder)
- every referen to God's peop nation (daugh of Zion)
- nations (kingdoms, peoples)
- desolation
- in your midst

HAGGAI חַגַּי CHAGGAI

Discouragement reigned. Only a remnant returned to Jerusalem after the 70 years of exile—a small remnant in comparison to the number of people taken captive. Many Jews were reluctant to leave Babylon to return to Jerusalem. The land of their captors had become home. The Babylonians had allowed them to establish businesses and build houses. Their children, while born in captivity, were secure. Why should they leave?

It was a small remnant that returned to rebuild the temple, which soon became a discouraging task. Their zeal dwindled. What was begun enthusiastically was forgotten before God's house was completed. For about 16 years the temple stood unfinished and ignored.

Then about 520 B.C., the word of the Lord came to Haggai.

THINGS TO DO

1. Read through the book of Haggai once, and then read it again and mark in a distinctive color every occurrence of the word *people* (the people in general), including the appropriate pronouns. Also, mark every reference to *the house of the Lord,* also called *the temple*.
2. Having done that, did you notice a pattern to the book of Haggai? Read through the text again and mark with the symbol of a clock 🕒 every reference to specific dates as seen in 1:1,15 and 2:1,10,20. The sacred portion of the Jewish calendar on page 1525 can help you see the "when" of the message.
3. Now read Haggai again and, in a distinctive way, mark every occurrence of the phrases *the word of the Lord came by the prophet Haggai, the word of the Lord came by Haggai the prophet,* and *Haggai, the messenger of the Lord spoke by commission of the Lord*. When you finish, you will see that Haggai is a series of messages.
4. Now read Haggai, one message at a time.
   a. As you do, mark the key words listed on the HAGGAI AT A GLANCE chart on page 1527, along with their synonyms and pronouns.
   b. After you have read each message and marked key words, observe the content of each message by asking the "5 W's and an H." Ask: What is the specific message, and to whom was it given? What has happened? To whom? Why? What is going to happen? What are they to believe or do? Summarize and record what you learn about each message in the section for "Paragraph Themes" on HAGGAI AT A GLANCE.
   c. Observe what you learn from marking *Lord of hosts,* with the appropriate pronouns, *people, temple, consider,* and *shake*. It would be good to make a list of what you observe about each.
5. To get the historical setting of Haggai, read Ezra 4:24–6:22. Then study the two charts on pages 1524 and 1525. The first gives the historical setting of Haggai. Note who Darius is, and note that Darius is mentioned in Haggai. Also note when the temple work started and stopped under Ezra and when it resumed under Haggai.
6. Complete HAGGAI AT A GLANCE. Record the theme of each chapter in the appropriate places. Then record the chapter theme in your Bible next to the chapter number. Finally, write out the theme of the book and fill in any other information needed.

THINGS TO THINK ABOUT

1. Have you given too much attention and time to your personal affairs and needs but neglected the things of God that are important for the spreading of the gospel or the furtherance of His work?

2. What might God be trying to say when cataclysmic events take place? Do you take advantage of these things to turn people's attention and thoughts to God?

3. When discouraged in your service to God, do you quit, or do you courageously persevere, determined to be faithful and to leave the outcome to God?

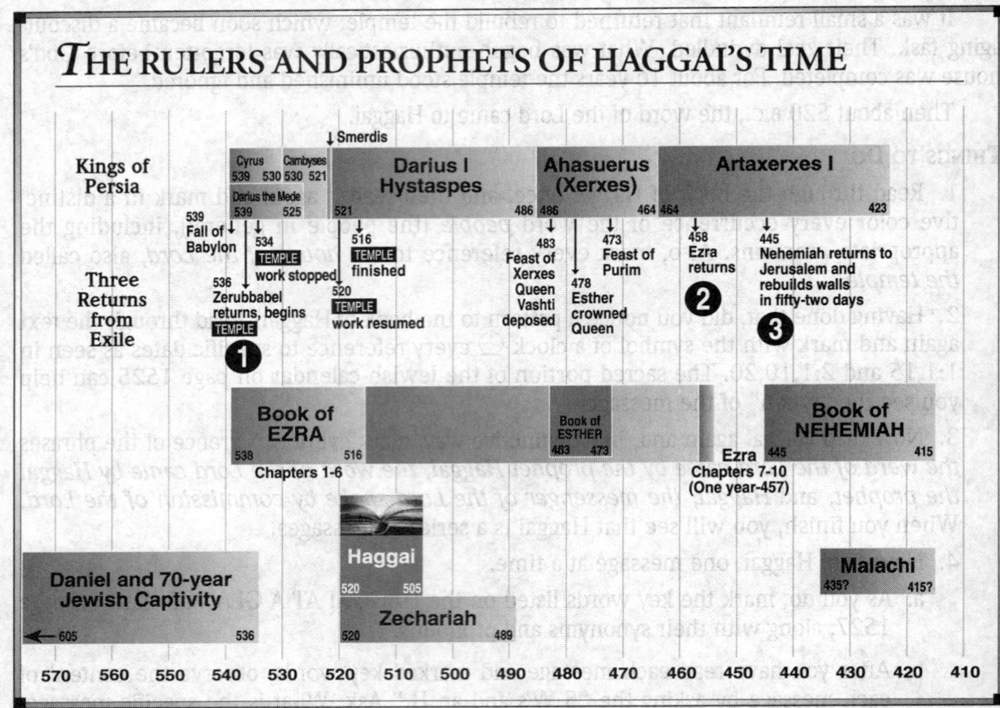

Chapter 1 Theme ______________________________

1 In the [a]second year of Darius the king, on the first day of the
sixth month, the word of the LORD came by the prophet
[b]Haggai to [c]Zerubbabel the son of Shealtiel, [d]governor of Judah,
and to [e]Joshua the son of Jehozadak, the high priest, saying,
2 "Thus says the LORD of [1]hosts, 'This people says, "The time
has not come, *even* the time for the house of the LORD to be
rebuilt."'"
3 Then the word of the LORD came by Haggai the prophet,
saying,
4 "Is it time for you yourselves to dwell in your paneled
houses while this house [a]*lies* desolate?"

1:1 [a]Ezra 4:24 [b]Ezra 5:1; 6:14; Hag 1:3, 12, 13; 2:1, 10, 20 [c]Ezra 2:2; Neh 7:7; Hag 1:12, 14; Zech 4:6; Matt 1:12, 13 [d]1 Kin 10:15; Ezra 5:3 [e]Zech 6:11

2 [1]Lit *hosts, saying*

4 [a]Jer 33:10, 12; Hag 1:9

The Jewish Calendar

Babylonian names (B) for the months are still used today for the Jewish calendar. Canaanite names (C) were used prior to the Babylonian captivity in 586 B.C. Four are mentioned in the Old Testament. **Adar-Sheni** is an intercalary month used every two to three years or seven times in 19 years.

1st month	2nd month	3rd month	4th month
Nisan (B) Abib (C) March-April	Iyyar (B) Ziv (C) April-May	Sivan (B) May-June	Tammuz (B) June-July
7th month	*8th month*	*9th month*	*10th month*
5th month	**6th month**	**7th month**	**8th month**
Ab (B) July-August	Elul (B) August-September	Tishri (B) Ethanim (C) September-October	Marcheshvan (B) Bul (C) October-November
11th month	*12th month*	*1st month*	*2nd month*
9th month	**10th month**	**11th month**	**12th month**
Chislev (B) November-December	Tebeth (B) December-January	Shebat (B) January-February	Adar (B) February-March
3rd month	*4th month*	*5th month*	*6th month*

Sacred calendar appears in black • Civil calendar appears in gray

5 Now therefore, thus says the LORD of hosts, "[1]Consider your ways!

6 "You have [a]sown much, but [1]harvest little; *you* eat, but *there is* not *enough* to be satisfied; *you* drink, but *there is* [2]not *enough* to become drunk; *you* put on clothing, but no one is warm *enough;* and he who earns, earns wages *to put* into a purse with holes."

7 Thus says the LORD of hosts, "[1]Consider your ways!

8 "Go up to the [1]mountains, bring wood and [a]rebuild the [2]temple, that I may be [b]pleased with it and be [c]glorified," says the LORD.

9 "[a]*You* look for much, but behold, *it comes* to little; when you bring *it* home, I [b]blow it *away.* Why?" declares the LORD of hosts, "Because of My house which [c]*lies* desolate, while each of you runs to his own house.

10 "Therefore, because of you the [a]sky has withheld [1]its dew and the earth has withheld its produce.

11 "I called for a [a]drought on the land, on the mountains, on the grain, on the new wine, on the oil, on what the ground produces, on [b]men, on cattle, and on [c]all the labor of [1]your hands."

12 Then [a]Zerubbabel the son of Shealtiel, and [b]Joshua the son of Jehozadak, the high priest, with all the remnant of the people, [c]obeyed the voice of the LORD their God and the words of Haggai the prophet, as the LORD their God had sent him. And the people [1d]showed reverence for the LORD.

13 Then Haggai, the [a]messenger of the LORD, spoke [1]by the commission of the LORD to the people saying, "'[b]I am with you,' declares the LORD."

14 So the LORD stirred up the spirit of [a]Zerubbabel the son of Shealtiel, [a]governor of Judah, and the spirit of Joshua the son of Jehozadak, the high priest, and the spirit of all the [b]remnant of the people; and they came and [c]worked on the house of the LORD of hosts, their God,

15 on the twenty-fourth day of the sixth month in the second year of Darius the king.

5 [1]Lit *Set your heart on*

6 [1]Lit *bring in* [2]Lit *not becoming drunk* [a]Deut 28:38-40; Hos 8:7; Hag 1:9, 10; 2:16, 17

7 [1]Lit *Set your heart on*

8 [1]Lit *mountain* [2]Lit *house* [a]1 Kin 6:1 [b]Ps 132:13, 14 [c]Hag 2:7, 9

9 [a]Prov 27:20; Eccl 1:8 [b]Is 40:7 [c]Hag 1:4

10 [1]Lit *from dew* [a]Deut 28:23, 24; 1 Kin 17:1; Joel 1:18-20

11 [1]Lit *the palms* [a]Jer 14:2-6; Mal 3:9, 11 [b]Deut 28:22 [c]Hag 2:17

12 [1]Lit *feared before* [a]Hag 1:1 [b]Hag 1:14; 2:2 [c]Is 1:19; 1 Thess 2:13 [d]Deut 31:12, 13; Ps 112:1; Is 50:10

13 [1]Or *the message* [a]Is 44:26; Ezek 3:17; Mal 2:7; 3:1 [b]Ps 46:11; Is 41:10; 43:2

14 [a]Hag 1:1; 2:2, 21 [b]Hag 1:12 [c]Ezra 5:2; Neh 4:6

Chapter 2 Theme ______________________________

2 On the twenty-first of the seventh month, the word of the LORD came by [a]Haggai the prophet saying,

2 "Speak now to [a]Zerubbabel the son of Shealtiel, [a]governor of Judah, and to [a]Joshua the son of Jehozadak, the high priest, and to the [b]remnant of the people saying,

3 'Who is [a]left among you who saw this [1]temple in its [b]former glory? And how do you see it now? Does it not [2]seem to you like nothing [3]in comparison?

4 'But now [1a]take courage, Zerubbabel,' declares the LORD, 'take courage also, Joshua son of Jehozadak, the high priest, and all you people of the land take courage,' declares the LORD, 'and work; for [b]I am with you,' declares the LORD of hosts.

5 'As for the [1a]promise which I [2]made you when you came out of Egypt, [3]My [b]Spirit is abiding in your midst; [c]do not fear!'

6 "For thus says the LORD of hosts, '[a]Once more [1]in a [b]little while, I am going to [c]shake the heavens and the earth, the sea also and the dry land.

7 'I will shake [a]all the nations; and [1]they will come with the [b]wealth of all nations, and I will [c]fill this house with glory,' says the LORD of hosts.

8 'The [a]silver is Mine and the gold is Mine,' declares the LORD of hosts.

9 'The latter [a]glory of this house will be greater than the [b]former,' says the LORD of hosts, 'and in this place I will give [c]peace,' declares the LORD of hosts."

10 On the [a]twenty-fourth of the ninth *month,* in the second year of Darius, the word of the LORD came to Haggai the prophet, saying,

11 "Thus says the LORD of hosts, '[a]Ask now the priests *for* a [1]ruling:

12 'If a man carries [a]holy meat in the [1]fold of his garment, and touches bread with [2]this fold, or cooked food, wine, oil, or any *other* food, will it become holy?'" And the priests answered, "No."

13 Then Haggai said, "[a]If one who is unclean from a [1]corpse touches any of these, will *the latter* become unclean?" And the priests answered, "It will become unclean."

14 Then Haggai said, "'[a]So is this people. And so is this nation before Me,' declares the LORD, 'and so is every work of their hands; and what they offer there is unclean.

15 'But now, do [1a]consider from this day [2]onward: before one [b]stone was placed on another in the temple of the LORD,

16 [1]from that time *when* one came to a *grain* heap of twenty *measures,* there would be only ten; and *when* one came to the wine vat to draw fifty [2]measures, there would be *only* twenty.

17 'I smote you *and* every work of your hands with [a]blasting wind, mildew and hail; [1]yet you *did* not *come back* to Me,' declares the LORD.

18 'Do [1a]consider from this day [2]onward, from the [b]twenty-fourth day of the ninth *month;* from the day when the temple of the LORD was [c]founded, [1]consider:

2:1 [a]Hag 1:1

2 [a]Hag 1:1 [b]Hag 1:12

3 [1]Lit *house* [2]Lit *in your eyes* [3]Lit *like it* [a]Ezra 3:12 [b]Hag 2:9

4 [1]Lit *be strong* [a]Deut 31:23; 1 Chr 22:13; 28:20; Zech 8:9; Eph 6:10 [b]2 Sam 5:10; Acts 7:9

5 [1]Lit *word* [2]Lit *cut with* [3]Or *while . . . was standing* [a]Ex 19:4-6; 29:45, 46; 33:12-14; 34:8-10 [b]Neh 9:20; Is 63:11, 14 [c]Is 41:10, 13; Zech 8:13

6 [1]Lit *it is a little* [a]Heb 12:26 [b]Is 10:25; 29:17 [c]Hag 2:21

7 [1]Or *the desire of all nations will come* [a]Dan 2:44; Joel 3:9, 16 [b]Is 60:4-9 [c]1 Kin 8:11; Is 60:7

8 [a]1 Chr 29:14, 16; Is 60:17

9 [a]Zech 2:5 [b]Hag 2:3 [c]Is 9:6, 7; 66:12

10 [a]Hag 2:20

11 [1]Lit *law* [a]Deut 17:8-11; Mal 2:7

12 [1]Lit *wing* [2]Lit *his wing* [a]Ex 29:37; Lev 6:27, 29; 7:6; Ezek 44:19; Matt 23:19

13 [1]Lit *soul* [a]Lev 22:4-6; Num 19:22

14 [a]Prov 15:8; Is 1:11-15

15 [1]Lit *set your heart* [2]Or *backward* [a]Hag 1:5, 7; 2:18 [b]Ezra 3:10; 4:24

16 [1]Lit *since they were* [2]Or *troughs full*

17 [1]Or *but what did we have in common?* [a]Deut 28:22; 1 Kin 8:37; Amos 4:9

18 [1]Lit *set your heart* [2]Or *backward* [a]Deut 32:29; Hag 2:15 [b]Hag 2:10 [c]Ezra 5:1, 2; Zech 8:9, 12

19 [a]Ps 128:1-6; Jer 31:12, 14; Mal 3:10
20 [a]Hag 2:10
21 [a]Ezra 5:2; Hag 1:1; Zech 4:6-10 [b]Hag 2:6; Heb 12:26, 27
22 [1]Or *Gentiles* [a]Ezek 26:16; Zeph 3:8 [b]Mic 7:16 [c]Ps 46:9; Ezek 39:20; Mic 5:10 [d]Amos 2:15 [e]Judg 7:22; 2 Chr 20:23
23 [1]Or *seal* [a]Song 8:6; Jer 22:24 [b]Is 42:1; 43:10

19 'Is the seed still in the barn? Even including the vine, the
fig tree, the pomegranate and the olive tree, it has not borne
fruit. Yet from this day on I will [a]bless *you.*'"
20 Then the word of the LORD came a second time to Haggai
on the [a]twenty-fourth *day* of the month, saying,
21 "Speak to [a]Zerubbabel governor of Judah, saying, 'I am going
to [b]shake the heavens and the earth.
22 'I will [a]overthrow the thrones of kingdoms and destroy the
[b]power of the kingdoms of the [1]nations; and I will [c]overthrow
the chariots and their riders, and the [d]horses and their riders
will go down, [e]everyone by the sword of another.'
23 'On that day,' declares the LORD of hosts, 'I will take you,
Zerubbabel, son of Shealtiel, My servant,' declares the LORD,
'and I will make you like a [1a]signet *ring,* for [b]I have chosen
you,'" declares the LORD of hosts.

HAGGAI AT A GLANCE

Theme of Haggai:

SEGMENT DIVISIONS	PARAGRAPH THEMES	CHAPTER THEMES
	1:1-11	1
	1:12-15	
	2:1-9	2
	2:10-19	
	2:20-23	

Author:

Date:

Purpose:

Key Words:

people

the house of the Lord (the temple)

Lord of hosts

consider

shake

ZECHARIAH זכריה ZEKHARYA

The earth was peaceful and quiet. All the nations were at rest...except for Israel. From Israel's perspective, it looked as if God had abandoned His people and forgotten His holy city, Jerusalem. Jerusalem's walls were torn down, Solomon's temple had been destroyed, and now a partially rebuilt temple stood on its site. Even if this temple were to be completed, it would not begin to equal Solomon's.

The majority of God's people had settled in their land of exile and were reluctant to return to Jerusalem. Only a remnant had come back, and they were a discouraged lot who soon abandoned the rebuilding of the house of God. But then the word of the Lord came—first through Haggai and then Zechariah.

Born in Babylon, Zechariah was among the remnant who returned to Jerusalem under the leadership of Zerubbabel and Joshua. Although he belonged to the priestly line, Zechariah, like Haggai his predecessor, was to be God's prophet to the discouraged remnant.

And so, about 520 to 519 B.C., the word of the Lord came to Zechariah—a needed word, an encouraging word...a word for the future, a word of hope.

THINGS TO DO

General Instructions

If you are going to have a good understanding of Zechariah, it will help to put the book into its historical context. Although this will take extra study, it will be worthwhile.

Ezra gives the historical setting of Zechariah; therefore, if you have not studied Ezra, read it before you start Zechariah. Ezra, like Zechariah, is a post-exilic book, which simply means it was written after the Jews were in exile under the Babylonians (Chaldeans). Ezra records the return of a remnant to Jerusalem under the reign and decree of Cyrus, a Persian king who ruled from 539 to 530 B.C. The Babylonians conquered Judah, and then the Medes and Persians conquered the Babylonians.

1. As you read Ezra, observe what is said regarding rebuilding the temple, since the temple plays a key role in Ezra and Zechariah. Also, watch for any reference to Zerubbabel and to Jeshua, who is called Joshua in Zechariah. Joshua is also called Jeshua in Nehemiah, another post-exilic book that focuses on the rebuilding of the walls of Jerusalem.

2. If you have not studied Haggai, study it next since Haggai and Zechariah are contemporaries.

Chapters 1–8

1. The book of Zechariah divides into two segments: chapters 1 through 8 and chapters 9 through 14. As you read the first segment, mark every occurrence of the phrase *the word of the Lord came*. There will be slight variations to the wording (e.g., *the word of the Lord of hosts came*). However, mark each occurrence the same way. Then in the margin, note the main point of the Lord's message. Also, if the text tells you when the word came, draw a clock 🕒 in the text. Consult the historical chart on page 1530 for the chronological setting of these messages.

2. As you read, also watch for the phrases *what do you see?, the Lord showed me, I saw*, and *I lifted up my eyes*. In the margin write "Vision," and then note briefly what the vision was. As you do this, you will see many correlations between *the word of the Lord* and the vision.

3. Watch for and mark in a distinctive way the following key words or phrases, along with their synonyms or pronouns: *listen (stopped their ears from hearing), return, again,*

temple (house of the Lord), nations, Judah, Jerusalem, I will dwell in your midst (I will be the glory in her midst or any reference to the Lord's coming), *remnant*, and *seventy years.* Record these key words and phrases on an index card and use it as a bookmark as you study Zechariah. You will find it helpful to color or mark these phrases in the same way you mark them in the text.

4. Zechariah contains many prophecies regarding the Messiah's first and final comings, the nation of Israel and Jerusalem, and the future of the nations. Therefore, as you read Zechariah chapter by chapter, watch for these prophecies and note them under the appropriate columns on the chart ZECHARIAH'S PROPHETIC REVELATIONS on page 1546.

5. God's name, Jehovah-sabaoth, Lord of hosts, is used repeatedly. Mark these occurrences. Then as you study Zechariah, in your notebook keep a list of all you learn about God.

6. After you study each chapter, record its theme (subject) on the ZECHARIAH AT A GLANCE chart on page 1547 under the appropriate chapter number and then in your Bible next to the chapter number.

Chapters 9–14

1. As you read through this segment, watch for the same key words and/or phrases you marked in chapters 1 through 8, but add to your list *covenant, in that day*, and any reference to the Lord as *King*.

2. Also mark the phrase *the burden of the word of the Lord*. The occurrences of this phrase divide these final chapters of Zechariah into segments.

3. After you mark the key words and phrases in this segment, list in the margin or on the chart ZECHARIAH'S PROPHETIC REVELATIONS what you learn about each. If you believe *that day* refers to the day of the Lord, also record your insights on the chart on page 2076.

4. When you read chapter 13, watch what will happen to the *two parts* and *the third.* Watch the pronouns *they* and *them*. Mark the third part as *remnant.* You may want to record in your notebook all you learn about *the third*—the remnant that survives.

5. In chapter 14 you will see a reference to the Feast of Booths. On pages 214 and 215, you will find a chart called THE FEASTS OF ISRAEL. As you look at the chart, note the significance of the Feast of Booths (or Tabernacles, as it is sometimes called).

6. Record the theme of each chapter as you did previously. When you finish, write the theme of Zechariah on ZECHARIAH AT A GLANCE. Record the main theme of the two major segment divisions and fill in the other information requested on the chart.

7. Since Haggai and Zechariah were contemporaries, it would be interesting to note how the messages given by the Lord to these two prophets correlate in time. After you have studied both books, look at the "time symbols" in both books and note when the messages came in relationship to each other. List the messages in the order of their occurrence.

Things to Think About

1. As you studied Zechariah, were you touched by the awesomeness of God's sovereignty? What does it mean to you personally to realize that God reigns supreme over the nations? That He has declared things before they have come to pass, and that as He has purposed, so it shall be? If He can handle nations, can He handle your life?

2. Do you take time to listen—really listen—to what God says in His Word? If you have not listened, God's invitation to return to Him is still there in Zechariah for you. Believe Him…and return.

3. How can you apply the truth of Zechariah 4:6-7 to your own life? Remember, the things

that were written in the Old Testament were written for our encouragement and perseverance. They are not simply historical records; they are the bread of life by which we live.

4. God said, "The Lord is coming; He will dwell in our midst." Revelation 22:12 tells us that when He comes, He will reward us according to our deeds. Are you prepared? According to 1 John 3:2-3 the coming of the Lord is a purifying hope. What do you need to do in order not to be ashamed at His coming?

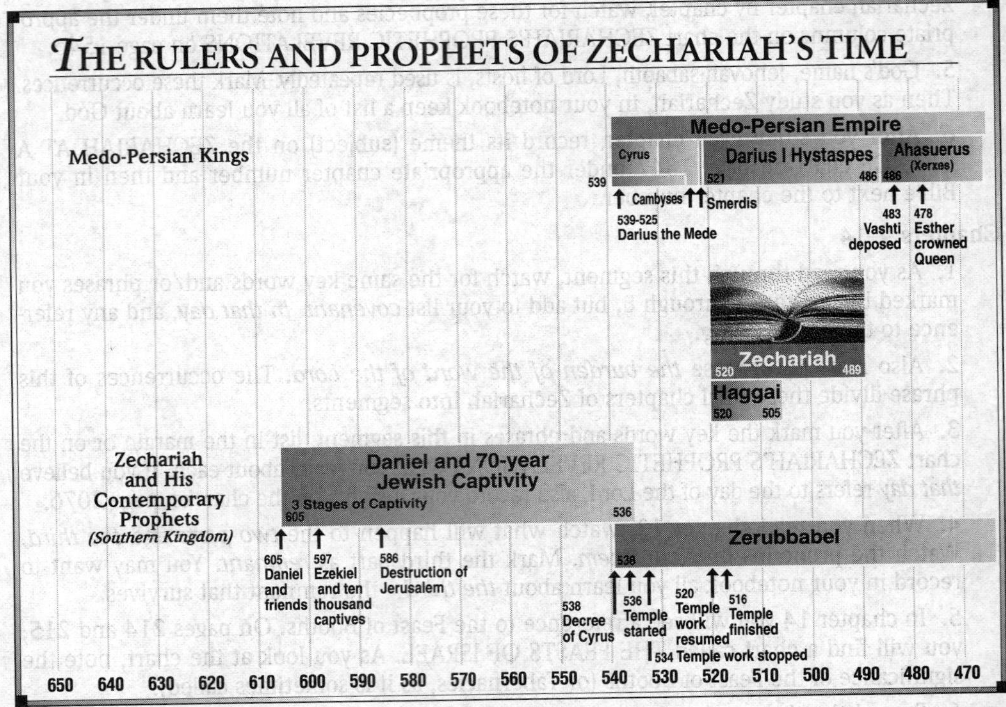

Chapter 1 Theme ______________________

1 In the eighth month of the second year of [a]Darius, the word
of the LORD came to [b]Zechariah the prophet, the son of
Berechiah, the son of [c]Iddo saying,

2 "The LORD was very [a]angry with your fathers.

3 "Therefore say to them, 'Thus says the LORD of hosts, "[a]Return
to Me," declares the LORD of hosts, "that I may return to you,"
says the LORD of hosts.

4 "Do not be [a]like your fathers, to whom the [b]former prophets
proclaimed, saying, 'Thus says the LORD of hosts, "[c]Return now
from your evil ways and from your evil deeds."' But they did
[d]not listen or give heed to Me," declares the LORD.

5 "Your [a]fathers, where are they? And the [b]prophets, do they
live forever?

1:1 [a]Ezra 4:24; 6:15; Hag 1:15; 2:10; Zech 1:7; 7:1 [b]Ezra 5:1; 6:14; Zech 7:1; Matt 23:35; Luke 11:51 [c]Neh 12:4, 16

2 [a]2 Chr 36:16; Jer 44:6; Ezek 8:18; Zech 1:15

3 [a]Is 31:6; 44:22; Mal 3:7

4 [a]Ps 78:8; 106:6, 7 [b]2 Chr 24:19; 36:15 [c]Is 1:16-19; Jer 4:1; Ezek 33:11 [d]Jer 6:17; 11:7, 8

5 [a]Lam 5:7 [b]John 8:52

The Jewish Calendar

Babylonian names (B) for the months are still used today for the Jewish calendar. Canaanite names (C) were used prior to the Babylonian captivity in 586 B.C. Four are mentioned in the Old Testament. **Adar-Sheni** is an intercalary month used every two to three years or seven times in 19 years.

1st month	2nd month	3rd month	4th month
Nisan (B) Abib (C) March-April	Iyyar (B) Ziv (C) April-May	Sivan (B) May-June	Tammuz (B) June-July
7th month	*8th month*	*9th month*	*10th month*
5th month	**6th month**	**7th month**	**8th month**
Ab (B) July-August	Elul (B) August-September	Tishri (B) Ethanim (C) September-October	Marcheshvan (B) Bul (C) October-November
11th month	*12th month*	*1st month*	*2nd month*
9th month	**10th month**	**11th month**	**12th month**
Chislev (B) November-December	Tebeth (B) December-January	Shebat (B) January-February	Adar (B) February-March
3rd month	*4th month*	*5th month*	*6th month*

Sacred calendar appears in black • Civil calendar appears in gray

6 "But did not My words and My statutes, which I commanded
My servants the prophets, [a]overtake your fathers? Then they
repented and said, '[b]As the LORD of hosts purposed to do to us
in accordance with our ways and our deeds, so He has dealt
with us.'"'"
7 On the twenty-fourth day of the eleventh month, which is
the month Shebat, in the second year of Darius, the word of
the LORD came to Zechariah the prophet, the son of Berechiah,
the son of Iddo, as follows:
8 I saw at night, and behold, a man was riding on a [a]red horse,
and he was standing among the [b]myrtle trees which were in
the ravine, with red, sorrel and [c]white horses behind him.
9 Then I said, "My [a]lord, what are these?" And the [b]angel who
was speaking with me said to me, "I will show you what these
are."
10 And the man who was standing among the myrtle trees
answered and said, "These are those whom the LORD has sent
to [1][a]patrol the earth."
11 So they answered the angel of the LORD who was [a]standing
among the myrtle trees and said, "We have [1]patrolled the earth,
and behold, [b]all the earth is [2]peaceful and quiet."
12 Then the angel of the LORD said, "O LORD of hosts, [a]how
long will You [b]have no compassion for Jerusalem and the cities
of Judah, with which You have been [c]indignant these [d]seventy
years?"
13 The LORD answered the [a]angel who was speaking with me
with [1]gracious words, [b]comforting words.
14 So the angel who was speaking with me said to me,
"[a]Proclaim, saying, 'Thus says the LORD of hosts, "I am [b]exceed-
ingly jealous for Jerusalem and Zion.
15 "But I am very [a]angry with the nations who are [b]at ease; for
while I was only a little angry, they [1][c]furthered the disaster."
16 'Therefore thus says the LORD, "I will [a]return to Jerusalem
with compassion; My [b]house will be built in it," declares the

6 [a]Jer 12:16, 17; 44:28, 29; Amos 9:10 [b]Lam 2:17

8 [a]Zech 6:2; Rev 6:4 [b]Neh 8:15; Is 41:19; 55:13; Zech 1:10, 11 [c]Zech 6:3; Rev 6:2

9 [a]Zech 1:19; 4:4, 5, 13; 6:4 [b]Zech 2:3; 5:5

10 [1]Lit *walk about through* [a]Job 1:7; Zech 1:11; 4:10; 6:5-8

11 [1]Lit *walked about through* [2]Lit *sitting* [a]Zech 1:8, 10 [b]Is 14:7

12 [a]Ps 74:10; Jer 12:4; Hab 1:2 [b]Ps 102:13; Jer 30:18 [c]Ps 102:10; Jer 15:17 [d]Jer 25:11; 29:10; Dan 9:2; Zech 7:5

13 [1]Lit *good* [a]Zech 1:9; 4:1 [b]Is 40:1, 2; 57:18

14 [a]Is 40:2, 6; Zech 1:17 [b]Zech 8:2

15 [1]Lit *helped for evil* [a]Zech 1:2 [b]Ps 123:4; Jer 48:11 [c]Amos 1:11

16 [a]Is 54:8-10; Zech 2:10, 11 [b]Ezra 6:14, 15; Zech 4:9

LORD of hosts, "and a measuring [c]line will be stretched over Jerusalem."'
17 "Again, proclaim, saying, 'Thus says the LORD of hosts, "My [a]cities will again overflow with prosperity, and the LORD will again [b]comfort Zion and again [c]choose Jerusalem."'"
18 [1]Then I lifted up my eyes and looked, and behold, *there were* four horns.
19 So I said to the angel who was speaking with me, "What are these?" And he answered me, "These are the [a]horns which have scattered Judah, Israel and Jerusalem."
20 Then the LORD showed me four [a]craftsmen.
21 I said, "What are these coming to do?" And he said, "These are the [a]horns which have scattered Judah so that no man lifts up his head; but these *craftsmen* have come to terrify them, to [b]throw down the horns of the nations who have lifted up *their* horns against the land of Judah in order to scatter it."

Chapter 2 Theme ______________________

2 [1]Then I lifted up my eyes and looked, and behold, *there was* a man with a [a]measuring line in his hand.
2 So I said, "Where are you going?" And he said to me, "To [a]measure Jerusalem, to see how wide it is and how long it is."
3 And behold, the [a]angel who was speaking with me was going out, and another angel was coming out to meet him,
4 and said to him, "Run, speak to that [a]young man, saying, '[b]Jerusalem will be inhabited [1c]without walls because of the [d]multitude of men and cattle within it.
5 'For I,' declares the LORD, 'will be a [a]wall of fire [1]around her, and I will be the [b]glory in her midst.'"
6 "[1]Ho there! [a]Flee from the land of the north," declares the LORD, "for I have [b]dispersed you as the four winds of the heavens," declares the LORD.
7 "Ho, Zion! [a]Escape, you who are living with the daughter of Babylon."
8 For thus says the LORD of hosts, "After [1a]glory He has sent Me against the nations which plunder you, for he who touches you, touches the [2b]apple of His eye.
9 "For behold, I will [a]wave My hand over them so that they will be [b]plunder for their slaves. Then you will know that the LORD of hosts has sent Me.
10 "[a]Sing for joy and be glad, O daughter of Zion; for behold I am coming and I will [b]dwell in your midst," declares the LORD.
11 "[a]Many nations will join themselves to the LORD in that day and will become My people. Then I will [b]dwell in your midst, and you will [c]know that the LORD of hosts has sent Me to you.
12 "The LORD will [1a]possess Judah as His portion in the holy land, and will again [b]choose Jerusalem.
13 "[1a]Be silent, all flesh, before the LORD; for He is [b]aroused from His holy habitation."

16 [c]Jer 31:39; Zech 2:2, 4
17 [a]Is 44:26; 61:4 [b]Is 51:3 [c]Zech 2:12
18 [1]Ch 2:1 in Heb
19 [a]1 Kin 22:11; Ps 75:4, 5; Amos 6:13 mg
20 [a]Is 44:12; 54:16
21 [a]Zech 1:19 [b]Ps 75:10
2:1 [1]Ch 2:5 in Heb [a]Jer 31:39; Ezek 40:3; 47:3; Zech 1:16
2 [a]Jer 31:39; Ezek 40:3; Rev 21:15-17
3 [a]Zech 1:9
4 [1]Lit like *unwalled villages;* or like *open country* [a]Jer 1:6; Dan 1:4; 1 Tim 4:12 [b]Zech 1:17; 8:4 [c]Ezek 38:11 [d]Is 49:20; Jer 30:19; 33:22
5 [1]Lit *to her* [a]Is 4:5; 26:1; 60:18 [b]Hag 2:9; Zech 2:10, 11
6 [1]Lit *Ho! Ho!* [a]Jer 3:18 [b]Jer 31:10; Ezek 11:16
7 [a]Is 48:20; Jer 51:6
8 [1]Or *the glory* [2]Lit *pupil* [a]Is 60:7-9 [b]Deut 32:10; Ps 17:8
9 [a]Is 19:16 [b]Is 14:2
10 [a]Is 65:18, 19; Zech 9:9 [b]Zech 2:5; 8:3
11 [a]Mic 4:2 [b]Zech 2:5, 10 [c]Zech 2:9
12 [1]Or *inherit* [a]Deut 32:9; Ps 33:12; Jer 10:16 [b]2 Chr 6:6; Ps 132:13, 14; Zech 1:17
13 [1]Lit *Hush* [a]Hab 2:20; Zeph 1:7 [b]Ps 78:65; Is 51:9

Chapter 3 Theme ______________________________

3 Then he showed me [a]Joshua the high priest standing
before the angel of the LORD, and [1b]Satan standing at his
right hand to accuse him.
2 The LORD said to Satan, "[a]The LORD rebuke you, Satan!
Indeed, the LORD who has [b]chosen Jerusalem rebuke you! Is
this not a [c]brand plucked from the fire?"
3 Now Joshua was clothed with [a]filthy garments and standing
before the angel.
4 He spoke and said to those who were standing before him,
saying, "[a]Remove the filthy garments from him." Again he said
to him, "See, I have [b]taken your iniquity away from you and
[1]will [c]clothe you with festal robes."
5 Then I said, "Let them put a clean [a]turban on his head." So
they put a clean turban on his head and clothed him with
garments, while the angel of the LORD was standing by.
6 And the angel of the LORD admonished Joshua, saying,
7 "Thus says the LORD of hosts, 'If you will [a]walk in My ways
and if you will perform My service, then you will also [b]govern
My house and also have charge of My [c]courts, and I will grant
you [1]free access among these who are standing *here*.
8 'Now listen, Joshua the high priest, you and your friends
who are sitting in front of you—indeed they are men who are a
[a]symbol, for behold, I am going to bring in My servant the
[1b]Branch.
9 'For behold, the stone that I have set before Joshua; on one
stone are [a]seven eyes. Behold, I will engrave an inscription on
it,' declares the LORD of hosts, 'and I will [b]remove the iniquity
of that land in one day.
10 'In that day,' declares the LORD of hosts, 'every one of you
will invite his neighbor to *sit* under *his* [a]vine and under *his* fig
tree.'"

Chapter 4 Theme ______________________________

4 Then [a]the angel who was speaking with me returned and
[b]roused me, as a man who is awakened from his sleep.
2 He said to me, "[a]What do you see?" And I said, "I see, and
behold, a [b]lampstand all of gold with its bowl on the top of it,
and its [c]seven lamps on it with seven spouts belonging to each
of the lamps which are on the top of it;
3 also [a]two olive trees by it, one on the right side of the bowl
and the other on its left side."
4 Then I said to the angel who was speaking with me saying,
"What are these, [a]my lord?"
5 So [a]the angel who was speaking with me answered and said
to me, "[b]Do you not know what these are?" And I said, "No,
my lord."
6 Then he [1]said to me, "This is the word of the LORD to
[a]Zerubbabel saying, '[b]Not by might nor by power, but by My
[c]Spirit,' says the LORD of hosts.

3:1 [1]Or the *Adversary* or *Accuser* [a]Ezra 5:2; Hag 1:1; Zech 6:11 [b]1 Chr 21:1; Job 1:6; Ps 109:6; Rev 12:10

2 [a]Mark 9:25; Jude 9 [b]Zech 2:12 [c]Amos 4:11; Jude 23

3 [a]Ezra 9:15; Is 4:4; 64:6

4 [1]Lit *to clothe* [a]Is 43:25; Ezek 36:25 [b]Mic 7:18, 19; Zech 3:9 [c]Is 52:1; 61:10

5 [a]Job 29:14; Is 3:23

7 [1]Lit *goings* [a]1 Kin 3:14 [b]Deut 17:9, 12 [c]Is 62:9

8 [1]Lit *Sprout* [a]Is 8:18; 20:3; Ezek 12:11 [b]Is 11:1; 53:2; Jer 23:5; 33:15; Zech 6:12

9 [a]Zech 4:10 [b]Jer 31:34; 50:20; Zech 3:4

10 [a]1 Kin 4:25; Is 36:16; Mic 4:4

4:1 [a]Zech 1:9 [b]1 Kin 19:5-7; Jer 31:26

2 [a]Jer 1:13; Zech 5:2 [b]Ex 25:31, 37; Jer 52:19 [c]Rev 4:5

3 [a]Zech 4:11; Rev 11:4

4 [a]Zech 1:9; 4:5, 13; 6:4

5 [a]Zech 1:9; 4:1 [b]Zech 4:13

6 [1]Lit *said to me, saying* [a]Ezra 5:2; Hag 2:4, 5 [b]Is 11:2-4; 30:1; Hos 1:7 [c]2 Chr 32:7, 8; Eph 6:17

7 'What are you, O great [a]mountain? Before Zerubbabel *you*
will become a plain; and he will bring forth the top stone with
[b]shouts of "Grace, grace to it!"'"
8 Also the word of the LORD came to me, saying,
9 "The hands of Zerubbabel have [a]laid the foundation of this
house, and his hands will [b]finish *it.* Then you will know that
the LORD of hosts has sent me to [1]you.
10 "For who has despised the day of [a]small things? [1]But these
[b]seven will be glad when they see the [2c]plumb line in the hand
of Zerubbabel—*these are* the [d]eyes of the LORD which [e]range to
and fro throughout the earth."
11 Then I said to him, "What are these [a]two olive trees on the
right of the lampstand and on its left?"
12 And I answered the second time and said to him, "What
are the two olive [1]branches which are beside the two golden
pipes, which empty the golden *oil* from themselves?"
13 So he answered me, saying, "[a]Do you not know what these
are?" And I said, "No, [b]my lord."
14 Then he said, "These are the two [1a]anointed ones who are
[b]standing by the [c]Lord of the whole earth."

Chapter 5 Theme ____________________________

5 Then I lifted up my eyes again and looked, and behold,
there was a flying [a]scroll.
2 And he said to me, "[a]What do you see?" And I answered, "I
see a flying scroll; its length is twenty [1]cubits and its width ten
cubits."
3 Then he said to me, "This is the [a]curse that is going forth
over the face of the whole [1]land; surely everyone who [b]steals
will be purged away according to [2]the writing on one side, and
everyone who [c]swears will be purged away according to [2]the
writing on the other side.
4 "I will [a]make it go forth," declares the LORD of hosts, "and it
will [b]enter the house of the [c]thief and the house of the one
who swears falsely by My name; and it will spend the night
within that house and [d]consume it with its timber and stones."
5 Then [a]the angel who was speaking with me went out and
said to me, "Lift up now your eyes and see what this is going
forth."
6 I said, "What is it?" And he said, "This is the [1a]ephah going
forth." Again he said, "This is their [2]appearance in all the [3]land
7 (and behold, a lead cover was lifted up); and this is a woman
sitting inside the ephah."
8 Then he said, "This is [a]Wickedness!" And he threw her
down into the middle of the ephah and cast the lead weight on
its [1]opening.
9 Then I lifted up my eyes and looked, and there two women
were coming out with the wind in their wings; and they had
wings like the wings of a [a]stork, and they lifted up the ephah
between the earth and the heavens.

7 [a]Ps 114:4, 6; Is 40:4; Jer 51:25; Nah 1:5; Zech 14:4, 5 [b]Ezra 3:10, 11; Ps 84:11

9 [1]Lit *you* (plural) [a]Ezra 3:8-10; 5:16; Hag 2:18 [b]Ezra 6:14, 15; Zech 6:12, 13

10 [1]Or *But they will rejoice when they see . . . Zerubbabel. These seven are the eyes of the LORD* [2]Lit *plummet stone* [a]Neh 4:2-4; Amos 7:2, 5; Hag 2:3 [b]Zech 3:9; Rev 8:2 [c]Amos 7:7, 8 [d]2 Chr 16:9; Prov 15:3; Jer 16:17 [e]Zech 1:10; Rev 5:6

11 [a]Zech 4:3; Rev 11:4

12 [1]Or *clusters*

13 [a]Zech 4:5 [b]Zech 4:4, 5

14 [1]Lit *sons of fresh oil* [a]Ex 29:7; 40:15; 1 Sam 16:1, 12, 13; Is 61:1-3; Dan 9:24-26 [b]Zech 3:1-7 [c]Mic 4:13

5:1 [a]Jer 36:2; Ezek 2:9; Rev 5:1

2 [1]I.e. One cubit equals approx 18 in. [a]Zech 4:2

3 [1]Or *earth* [2]Lit *it* [a]Is 24:6; 43:28; Jer 26:6 [b]Ex 20:15; Lev 19:11; Mal 3:8, 9 [c]Lev 19:12; Is 48:1; Jer 5:2; Zech 5:4

4 [a]Mal 3:5 [b]Hos 4:2, 3 [c]Jer 2:26 [d]Lev 14:34, 35; Job 18:15

5 [a]Zech 1:9

6 [1]I.e. Approx one bu [2]Lit *eye;* some ancient versions read *iniquity* [3]Or *earth* [a]Lev 19:36; Amos 8:5

8 [1]Lit *mouth* [a]Hos 12:7; Amos 8:5; Mic 6:11

9 [a]Lev 11:13, 19; Ps 104:17; Jer 8:7

10 I said to the angel who was speaking with me, "Where are
they taking the ephah?"
11 Then he said to me, "To build a [1]temple for her in the land
of [a]Shinar; and when it is prepared, she will be set there on her
own pedestal."

Chapter 6 Theme ____________________

6 Now I lifted up my eyes again and looked, and behold,
[a]four chariots were coming forth from between the two
mountains; and the mountains *were* bronze mountains.
2 With the first chariot *were* [a]red horses, with the second
chariot [b]black horses,
3 with the third chariot [a]white horses, and with the fourth
chariot strong [b]dappled horses.
4 Then I spoke and said to the angel who was speaking with
me, "[a]What are these, my lord?"
5 The angel replied to me, "These are the [a]four spirits of
heaven, going forth after standing before the Lord of all the
earth,
6 with one of which the black horses are going forth to the
[a]north country; and the white ones go forth after them, while
the dappled ones go forth to the [b]south country.
7 "When the strong ones went out, they [1]were eager to go to
[2a]patrol the earth." And He said, "Go, [2]patrol the earth." So
they [3]patrolled the earth.
8 Then He cried out to me and spoke to me saying, "See,
those who are going to the land of the north have [1a]appeased
My wrath in the land of the north."
9 The [a]word of the LORD also came to me, saying,
10 "[a]Take *an offering* from the exiles, from Heldai, Tobijah and
Jedaiah; and you go the same day and enter the house of Josiah
the son of Zephaniah, where they have arrived from Babylon.
11 "Take silver and gold, make an *ornate* [a]crown and set *it* on
the head of [b]Joshua the son of Jehozadak, the high priest.
12 "Then say to him, 'Thus says the LORD of hosts, "Behold, a
man whose name is [1a]Branch, for He will [2b]branch out from
where He is; and He will [c]build the temple of the LORD.
13 "Yes, it is He who will build the temple of the LORD, and He
who will [a]bear the honor and sit and [b]rule on His throne. Thus,
He will be a [c]priest on His throne, and the counsel of peace
will be between the two [1]offices."'
14 "Now the [a]crown will become a reminder in the temple of
the LORD to Helem, Tobijah, Jedaiah and [1]Hen the son of
Zephaniah.
15 "[a]Those who are far off will come and [1]build the temple of
the LORD." Then you will [b]know that the LORD of hosts has sent
me to you. And it will take place if you completely [c]obey the
LORD your God.

11 [1]Lit *house* [a]Gen 10:10; 11:2; 14:1; Is 11:11; Dan 1:2
6:1 [a]Dan 7:3; 8:22; Zech 1:18; 6:5
2 [a]Zech 1:8; Rev 6:4 [b]Rev 6:5
3 [a]Rev 6:2 [b]Rev 6:8
4 [a]Zech 1:9
5 [a]Jer 49:36; Ezek 37:9; Dan 7:2; 11:4; Matt 24:31; Rev 7:1
6 [a]Jer 1:14, 15; 4:6; 6:1; 25:9; 46:10; Ezek 1:4 [b]Is 43:6; Dan 11:5
7 [1]Lit *sought to go* [2]Lit *walk about through* [3]Lit *walked about through* [a]Zech 1:10
8 [1]Lit *caused My spirit to rest in* [a]Ezek 5:13; 24:13; Zech 1:15
9 [a]Zech 1:1; 7:1; 8:1
10 [a]Ezra 7:14-16; 8:26-30; Jer 28:6
11 [a]2 Sam 12:30; Ps 21:3; Song 3:11 [b]Ezra 3:2; Hag 1:1; Zech 3:1
12 [1]Lit *Sprout* [2]Lit *sprout up* [a]Is 4:2; 11:1; Jer 23:5; 33:15; Zech 3:8 [b]Is 53:2 [c]Ezra 3:8, 10; Amos 9:11; Zech 4:6-9
13 [1]Lit *of them* [a]Is 9:6; 11:10; 22:24; 49:5, 6 [b]Is 9:7 [c]Ps 110:1, 4
14 [1]I.e. Josiah [a]Zech 6:11
15 [1]Lit *build in* [a]Is 56:6-8; 60:10 [b]Zech 2:9-11; 4:9 [c]Is 58:10-14; Jer 7:23; Zech 3:7

Chapter 7 Theme ____________________

7 In the fourth year of King Darius, the word of the LORD
came to Zechariah on the fourth *day* of the ninth month,
which is [a]Chislev.
2 Now *the town of* Bethel had sent Sharezer and Regem-
melech and [1]their men to [2a]seek the favor of the LORD,
3 speaking to the [a]priests who belong to the house of the
LORD of hosts, and to the prophets, saying, "Shall I weep in the
[b]fifth month [1]and abstain, as I have done these many years?"
4 Then the word of the LORD of hosts came to me, saying,
5 "Say to all the people of the land and to the priests, 'When
you fasted and mourned in the fifth and seventh months [1]these
[a]seventy years, was it actually for [b]Me that you fasted?
6 'When you eat and drink, [1]do you not eat for yourselves and
do you not drink for yourselves?
7 'Are not *these* the words which the LORD [a]proclaimed by the
former prophets, when Jerusalem was inhabited and [1b]prosperous
along with its cities around it, and the [2c]Negev and the
[3]foothills were inhabited?'"
8 Then the word of the LORD came to Zechariah saying,
9 "Thus has the LORD of hosts said, '[a]Dispense true justice and
practice [b]kindness and compassion each to his brother;
10 and [a]do not oppress the widow or the [1]orphan, the [2]stranger
or the poor; and do [b]not devise evil in your hearts against one
another.'
11 "But they [a]refused to pay attention and [1b]turned a stubborn
shoulder and [2c]stopped their ears from hearing.
12 "They made their [a]hearts *like* [1b]flint [2]so that they could not
hear the law and the [c]words which the LORD of hosts had sent
by His Spirit through the [d]former prophets; therefore great
[e]wrath came from the LORD of hosts.
13 "And just as [a]He called and they would not listen, so [b]they
called and I would not listen," says the LORD of hosts;
14 "but I [1a]scattered them with a [b]storm wind among all the
nations whom they have not known. Thus the land is [c]desolated
behind them [2]so that [d]no one went back and forth, for they
[e]made the pleasant land desolate."

Chapter 8 Theme ____________________

8 Then the word of the LORD of hosts came, saying,
2 "Thus says the LORD of hosts, 'I am [a]exceedingly jealous
for Zion, yes, with great wrath I am jealous for her.'
3 "Thus says the LORD, 'I will return to Zion and will [a]dwell in
the midst of Jerusalem. Then Jerusalem will be called the City
of [b]Truth, and the mountain of the LORD of hosts *will be called*
the Holy Mountain.'
4 "Thus says the LORD of hosts, '[a]Old men and old women will
again sit in the [1]streets of Jerusalem, each man with his staff in
his hand because of [2]age.
5 'And the [1]streets of the city will be filled with [a]boys and
girls playing in its [1]streets.'

7:1 [a]Neh 1:1
2 [1]Lit *his* [2]Lit *soften the face of* [a]1 Kin 13:6; Jer 26:19; Zech 8:21
3 [1]Lit *abstaining;* or *dedicating myself* [a]Ezra 3:10-12 [b]Zech 8:19
5 [1]Lit *and these* [a]Zech 1:12 [b]Is 1:11, 12; 58:5
6 [1]Lit *is it not you who eat and you who drink*
7 [1]Or *at ease* [2]I.e. South country [3]Heb *Shephelah* [a]Is 1:16-20; Jer 7:5, 23; Zech 1:4 [b]Jer 22:21 [c]Jer 13:19; 32:44
9 [a]Ezek 18:8; 45:9; Zech 8:16 [b]2 Sam 9:7; Job 6:14; Mic 6:8
10 [1]Or *fatherless* [2]Or *resident alien* [a]Ex 22:22; Ps 72:4; Jer 7:6 [b]Ps 21:11; Mic 2:1; Zech 8:17
11 [1]Lit *gave* [2]Lit *made heavy* [a]Jer 5:3; 8:5; 11:10 [b]Jer 7:26; 17:23 [c]Ps 58:4; Jer 5:21
12 [1]Lit *corundum* [2]Lit *from hearing* [a]2 Chr 36:13; Ezek 2:4; 3:7-9 [b]Jer 17:1; Ezek 3:9 [c]Zech 7:7 [d]Neh 9:30 [e]2 Chr 36:16; Dan 9:11, 12
13 [a]Jer 11:10, 14; 14:12 [b]Prov 1:24-28; Is 1:15
14 [1]Lit *stormed them away upon all* [2]Lit *from passing and from returning* [a]Deut 4:27; 28:64 [b]Jer 23:19 [c]Jer 44:6 [d]Is 60:15 [e]Jer 12:10
8:2 [a]Zech 1:14
3 [a]Zech 2:10, 11 [b]Zech 8:16, 19
4 [1]Or *squares* [2]Lit *the multitude of days* [a]Is 65:20
5 [1]Or *squares* [a]Jer 30:19, 20; 31:12, 13

6 "Thus says the LORD of hosts, 'If it is [1a]too difficult in the sight of the remnant of this people in those days, will it also be [1b]too difficult in My sight?' declares the LORD of hosts.

7 "Thus says the LORD of hosts, 'Behold, I am going to save My people from the land of the [1a]east and from the land of the [2]west;

8 and I will [a]bring them *back* and they will [b]live in the midst of Jerusalem; and they shall be [c]My people, and I will be their God in [1]truth and righteousness.'

9 "Thus says the LORD of hosts, 'Let your hands be [a]strong, you who are listening in these days to these words from the mouth of the [b]prophets, *those* who *spoke* in the day that the foundation of the house of the LORD of hosts was laid, to the end that the temple might be built.

10 'For before those days there was [a]no wage for man or any wage for animal; and for him who went out or came in there was no [1b]peace because of [2]his enemies, and I [c]set all men one against another.

11 'But now I will [a]not [1]treat the remnant of this people as in the former days,' declares the LORD of hosts.

12 'For *there will be* [a]peace for the seed: the vine will yield its fruit, the land will yield its produce and the heavens will give their [b]dew; and I will cause the remnant of this people to inherit [c]all these *things.*

13 'It will come about that just as you were a [a]curse among the nations, O house of Judah and house of Israel, so I will save you that you may become a [b]blessing. Do not fear; let your [c]hands be strong.'

14 "For thus says the LORD of hosts, 'Just as I [a]purposed to do harm to you when your fathers provoked Me to wrath,' says the LORD of hosts, 'and I have not [b]relented,

15 so I have again purposed in these days to [a]do good to Jerusalem and to the house of Judah. [b]Do not fear!

16 'These are the things which you should do: speak the [a]truth to one another; [b]judge with truth and judgment for peace in your [1]gates.

17 'Also let none of you [a]devise evil in your heart against another, and do not love [1b]perjury; for all these are what I [c]hate,' declares the LORD."

18 Then the word of the LORD of hosts came to me, saying,

19 "Thus says the LORD of hosts, 'The fast of the [a]fourth, the fast of the [b]fifth, the fast of the [c]seventh and the fast of the [d]tenth *months* will become [e]joy, gladness, and [1]cheerful feasts for the house of Judah; so [f]love truth and peace.'

20 "Thus says the LORD of hosts, '*It will* yet *be* that [a]peoples will come, even the inhabitants of many cities.

21 'The inhabitants of one will go to another, saying, "Let us go at once to [a]entreat the favor of the LORD, and to seek the LORD of hosts; [1]I will also go."

22 'So [a]many peoples and mighty nations will come to seek the LORD of hosts in Jerusalem and to [b]entreat the favor of the LORD.'

6 [1]Or *wonderful* [a]Ps 118:23; 126:1-3 [b]Jer 32:17, 27

7 [1]Lit *rising* [2]Lit *setting sun* [a]Ps 107:3; Is 11:11; 27:12, 13; 43:5

8 [1]Or *faithfulness* [a]Zeph 3:20; Zech 10:10 [b]Jer 3:17; Ezek 37:25 [c]Ezek 11:20; 36:28; Zech 2:11

9 [a]1 Chr 22:13; Is 35:4; Hag 2:4 [b]Ezra 5:1; 6:14

10 [1]Or *safety* [2]Lit *the adversary* [a]Hag 2:15-19 [b]2 Chr 15:5 [c]Is 19:2; Amos 3:6; 9:4

11 [1]Lit *be to the* [a]Ps 103:9; Is 12:1; Hag 2:19

12 [a]Lev 26:3-6 [b]Gen 27:28; Deut 33:13, 28; Hos 13:3 [c]Is 61:7; Obad 17

13 [a]Jer 29:18; Dan 9:11 [b]Ps 72:17; Is 19:24, 25; Ezek 34:26; Zech 14:11 [c]Zech 8:9

14 [a]Jer 31:28 [b]Jer 4:28; Ezek 24:14

15 [a]Jer 29:11; Mic 7:18-20 [b]Zech 8:13

16 [1]I.e. the place where court was held [a]Ps 15:2; Prov 12:17-19; Zech 8:3; Eph 4:25 [b]Is 9:7; 11:4, 5; Zech 7:9

17 [1]Lit *false oath* [a]Prov 3:29; Jer 4:14; Zech 7:10 [b]Zech 5:4; Mal 3:5 [c]Prov 6:16-19; Hab 1:13

19 [1]Or *goodly* [a]2 Kin 25:3, 4; Jer 39:2 [b]Zech 7:3, 5 [c]2 Kin 25:25; Zech 7:5 [d]Jer 52:4 [e]Ps 30:11; Is 12:1 [f]Zech 8:16; Luke 1:74, 75

20 [a]Ps 117:1; Jer 16:19; Mic 4:2, 3; Zech 2:11; 14:16

21 [1]Or *let me go too* [a]Zech 7:2

22 [a]Is 2:2, 3; 25:7; 49:6, 22, 23; 60:3-12 [b]Zech 8:21

23 "Thus says the LORD of hosts, 'In those days ten men from
all the [1]nations will [2a]grasp the [3]garment of a Jew, saying, "Let
us go with you, for we have heard that God is with you."'"

23 [1]Lit *languages of the nations* [2]Lit *grasp, and they will grasp* [3]Or *corner of the garment* [a]Is 45:14, 24; 60:14

Chapter 9 Theme ______________________________

RETURN TO INSTRUCTIONS

God's Judgment Pronounced

9 The [1]burden of the word of the LORD is against the land of
Hadrach, with [a]Damascus as its resting place (for the eyes
of men, especially of all the tribes of Israel, are toward the
LORD),

9:1 [1]Or *oracle* [a]Is 17:1; Jer 49:23-27; Amos 1:3-5

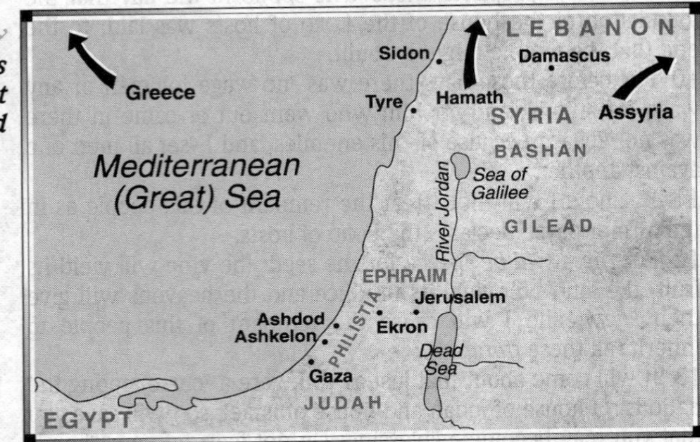

2 And [a]Hamath also, which borders on it;
[b]Tyre and [c]Sidon, [1]though [2]they are [b]very wise.
3 For Tyre built herself a [a]fortress
And [b]piled up silver like dust,
And [c]gold like the mire of the streets.
4 Behold, the Lord will [a]dispossess her
And cast her wealth into the sea;
And she will be [b]consumed with fire.
5 Ashkelon will see *it* and be afraid.
Gaza too will writhe in great pain;
Also Ekron, for her expectation has been confounded.
Moreover, the king will perish from Gaza,
And Ashkelon will not be inhabited.
6 And a [1]mongrel race will dwell in [a]Ashdod,
And I will cut off the pride of the Philistines.
7 And I will remove their blood from their mouth
And their detestable things from between their teeth.
Then they also will be a remnant for our God,
And be like a [1]clan in Judah,
And Ekron like a Jebusite.
8 But I will camp around My house [1]because of an army,
Because of [a]him who passes by and returns;
And [b]no oppressor will pass over them anymore,
For now I have seen with My eyes.

2 [1]Or *because* [2]I.e. they think they are [a]Jer 49:23 [b]Ezek 28:2-5, 12 [c]Ezek 28:21

3 [a]Josh 19:29; 2 Sam 24:7 [b]Job 27:16; Ezek 27:33; 28:4, 5 [c]1 Kin 10:21, 27

4 [a]Ezek 26:3-5 [b]Ezek 28:18

6 [1]Lit *bastard will* [a]Amos 1:8; Zeph 2:4

7 [1]Or *chief*

8 [1]Or *as a guard, so that none will go back and forth* [a]Is 52:1 [b]Is 54:14; 60:18

9 [a]Rejoice greatly, O daughter of Zion!
Shout *in triumph,* O daughter of Jerusalem!
Behold, your [b]king is coming to you;
He is [1c]just and [d]endowed with salvation,
[e]Humble, and mounted on a donkey,
Even on a [f]colt, the [2]foal of a donkey.
10 I will [a]cut off the chariot from Ephraim
And the [b]horse from Jerusalem;
And the [c]bow of war will be cut off.
And He will speak [d]peace to the nations;
And His [e]dominion will be from sea to sea,
And from the [1]River to the ends of the earth.

11 As for you also, because of the [a]blood of *My* covenant
with you,
I have set your [b]prisoners free from the [1]waterless pit.
12 Return to the [1a]stronghold, O prisoners [2]who have
the [b]hope;
This very day I am declaring that I will restore [c]double
to you.
13 For I will [a]bend Judah [1]as My bow,
I will fill the bow with Ephraim.
And I will stir up your sons, O Zion, against your sons,
O [b]Greece;
And I will make you like a [c]warrior's sword.
14 Then the LORD will appear [a]over them,
And His [b]arrow will go forth like lightning;
And the Lord [1]GOD will blow the [c]trumpet,
And will march in the [d]storm winds of the south.
15 [a]The LORD of hosts will defend them.
And they will [b]devour and trample on the [c]sling stones;
And they will drink *and* be [d]boisterous as with wine;
And they will be filled like a *sacrificial* basin,
Drenched like the [e]corners of the altar.
16 And the LORD their God will [a]save them in that day
As the flock of His people;
For *they are as* the stones of a [b]crown,
[1]Sparkling in His land.
17 For what [1a]comeliness and [b]beauty *will be* [2]theirs!
Grain will make the young men flourish, and new wine
the virgins.

Chapter 10 Theme ______________________

10 Ask [a]rain from the LORD at the time of the
spring rain—
The LORD who [b]makes the [1]storm clouds;
And He will give them [c]showers of rain, vegetation
in the field to *each* man.
2 For the [a]teraphim speak [1]iniquity,
And the [b]diviners see [2]lying visions

9 [1]Or *vindicated and victorious* [2]Lit *son of a female donkey* [a]Zeph 3:14, 15; Zech 2:10 [b]Ps 110:1; Is 9:6, 7; Jer 23:5, 6; Matt 21:5; John 12:15 [c]Zeph 3:5 [d]Is 43:3, 11 [e]Is 57:15 [f]Judg 10:4; Is 30:6

10 [1]I.e. Euphrates [a]Hos 1:7 [b]Mic 5:10 [c]Hos 2:18 [d]Is 57:19; Mic 4:2-4 [e]Ps 72:8; Is 60:12

11 [1]Lit *cistern in which there is no water* [a]Ex 24:8; Heb 10:2 [b]Is 24:22; 51:14

12 [1]Or *Stronghold* [2]Lit *of the hope* [a]Jer 16:19; Joel 3:16 [b]Jer 14:8; 17:13; Heb 6:18, 19 [c]Is 61:7

13 [1]Lit *for Me* [a]Jer 51:20 [b]Joel 3:6 [c]Ps 45:3

14 [1]Heb *YHWH,* usually rendered LORD [a]Is 31:5; Zech 2:5 [b]Ps 18:14; Hab 3:11 [c]Is 27:13 [d]Is 21:1; 66:15

15 [a]Is 37:35; Zech 12:8 [b]Zech 12:6 [c]Job 41:28 [d]Ps 78:65 [e]Ex 27:2

16 [1]Or *Displayed over* [a]Jer 31:10, 11 [b]Is 62:3

17 [1]Lit *goodness* [2]Lit *his* [a]Jer 31:12, 14 [b]Ps 27:4; Is 33:17

10:1 [1]Or *thunderbolts* [a]Joel 2:23 [b]Jer 10:13 [c]Is 30:23

2 [1]Or *futility* [2]Lit *a lie* [a]Ezek 21:21; Hos 3:4 [b]Jer 27:9

And tell [c]false dreams;
They comfort in vain.
Therefore *the people* [3]wander like [d]sheep,
They are afflicted, because there is no shepherd.
3 "My [a]anger is kindled against the shepherds,
And I will punish the [1]male goats;
For the LORD of hosts has [b]visited His flock,
the house of Judah,
And will make them like His majestic horse in battle.
4 "From [1]them will come the [a]cornerstone,
From [1]them the tent peg,
From [1]them the bow of [b]battle,
From [1]them every [2]ruler, *all* of them together.
5 "They will be as mighty men,
[a]Treading down *the enemy* in the mire of the streets
in battle;
And they will fight, for the LORD *will be* with them;
And the [b]riders on horses will be put to shame.
6 "I will [a]strengthen the house of Judah,
And I will [b]save the house of Joseph,
And I will [1c]bring them back,
Because I have had [d]compassion on them;
And they will be as though I had [e]not rejected them,
For I am the LORD their God and I will [f]answer them.
7 "Ephraim will be like a mighty man,
And their heart will be glad as if *from* wine;
Indeed, their [a]children will see *it* and be glad,
[1]Their heart will rejoice in the LORD.
8 "I will [a]whistle for them to gather them together,
For I have redeemed them;
And they will be as [b]numerous as they [1c]were before.
9 "When I [1]scatter them among the peoples,
They will [a]remember Me in far countries,
And they with their children will live and come back.
10 "I will [a]bring them back from the land of Egypt
And gather them from Assyria;
And I will bring them into the land of
[b]Gilead and Lebanon
[1]Until [c]no *room* can be found for them.
11 "And they will pass through the [a]sea *of* distress
And He will strike the waves in the sea,
So that all the depths of the [b]Nile will dry up;
And the pride of [c]Assyria will be brought down
And the scepter of [d]Egypt will depart.
12 "And I will [a]strengthen them in the LORD,
And in His name [b]they will walk," declares the LORD.

Chapter 11 Theme ____________________

11

Open your doors, O Lebanon,
That a [a]fire may feed on your [b]cedars.

2 [3]Lit *journey* [c]Jer 23:32 [d]Ezek 34:5, 8; Matt 9:36; Mark 6:34

3 [1]I.e. leaders [a]Jer 25:34-36 [b]Ezek 34:12

4 [1]Lit *him* [2]Or *oppressor* [a]Luke 20:17; Eph 2:20; 1 Pet 2:6 [b]Jer 51:20; Zech 9:10

5 [a]2 Sam 22:43 [b]Amos 2:15; Hag 2:22

6 [1]Or *make them dwell* [a]Zech 10:12 [b]Zech 8:7; 9:16 [c]Zech 8:8 [d]Is 54:8; Zech 1:16 [e]Is 54:4 [f]Zech 13:9

7 [1]Or *Let their heart rejoice* [a]Is 54:13; Ezek 37:25

8 [1]Lit *were numerous* [a]Is 5:26; 7:18, 19 [b]Jer 33:22; Rev 7:9 [c]Jer 30:20; Ezek 36:11

9 [1]Lit *sow* [a]1 Kin 8:47, 48; Ezek 6:9

10 [1]Lit *And* [a]Is 11:11 [b]Jer 50:19 [c]Is 49:19, 20

11 [a]Is 51:9, 10 [b]Is 19:5-7 [c]Zeph 2:13 [d]Ezek 30:13

12 [a]Zech 10:6 [b]Mic 4:5

11:1 [a]Jer 22:6, 7 [b]Ezek 31:3

2 Wail, O [1]cypress, for the cedar has fallen,
Because the glorious *trees* have been destroyed;
Wail, O oaks of Bashan,
For the [2]impenetrable forest has come down.
3 There is a sound of the shepherds' [a]wail,
For their glory is ruined;
There is a [b]sound of the young lions' roar,
For the [1]pride of the Jordan is ruined.
4 Thus says the LORD my God, "Pasture the flock *doomed* to
[a]slaughter.
5 "Those who buy them slay them and [1]go [a]unpunished, and
each of those who sell them says, 'Blessed be the LORD, for [b]I
have become rich!' And their [c]own shepherds have no pity on
them.
6 "For I will [a]no longer have pity on the inhabitants of the land,"
declares the LORD; "but behold, I will [b]cause the men to [1]fall,
each into another's [2]power and into the [2]power of his king;
and they will strike the land, and I will [c]not deliver *them* from
their [2]power."
7 So I [a]pastured the flock *doomed* to slaughter, [1]hence the
[b]afflicted of the flock. And I took for myself two [c]staffs: the one
I called [2d]Favor and the other I called [3e]Union; so I pastured
the flock.
8 Then I annihilated the three shepherds in [a]one month, for
my soul was impatient with them, and their soul also [1]was
weary of me.
9 Then I said, "I will not pasture you. What is to [a]die, [1]let it
die, and what is to be annihilated, [2]let it be annihilated; and
[3]let those who are left eat one another's flesh."
10 I took my staff [1a]Favor and cut it in pieces, to [2b]break my
covenant which I had made with all the peoples.
11 So it was [1]broken on that day, and [2]thus the [a]afflicted of the
flock who were watching me realized that it was the word of
the LORD.
12 I said to them, "If it is good in your sight, give *me* my [a]wages;
but if not, [1]never mind!" So they weighed out [b]thirty *shekels* of
silver as my wages.
13 Then the LORD said to me, "Throw it to the [a]potter, *that*
magnificent price at which I was valued by them." So I took
the thirty *shekels* of silver and threw them to the potter in the
house of the LORD.
14 Then I cut in pieces my second staff [1a]Union, to [b]break the
brotherhood between Judah and Israel.
15 The LORD said to me, "Take again for yourself the equipment
of a [1a]foolish shepherd.
16 "For behold, I am going to raise up a shepherd in the land
who will [a]not care for the perishing, seek the scattered, heal
the broken, or sustain the one standing, but will [b]devour the
flesh of the fat *sheep* and tear off their hoofs.
17 "[a]Woe to the worthless shepherd
Who leaves the flock!

2 [1]Or *juniper* [2]Another reading is *forest of the vintage*
3 [1]Or *jungle* [a]Jer 25:34-36 [b]Jer 2:15; 50:44
4 [a]Ps 44:22; Zech 11:7
5 [1]Lit *are not held guilty* [a]Jer 50:7 [b]Hos 12:8; 1 Tim 6:9 [c]Ezek 34:2, 3
6 [1]Lit *find* [2]Lit *hand* [a]Jer 13:14 [b]Is 9:19-21; Mic 7:2-6; Zech 14:13 [c]Ps 50:22; Mic 5:8
7 [1]Another reading is *for the sheep dealers* [2]Or *Pleasantness* [3]Or *Cords* [a]Zech 11:4 [b]Jer 39:10; Zeph 3:12 [c]Ezek 37:16 [d]Ps 27:4; 90:17; Zech 11:10 [e]Ps 133:1; Ezek 37:16-23; Zech 11:14
8 [1]Or *detested* [a]Hos 5:7
9 [1]Or *will die* [2]Or *will be annihilated* [3]Or *those . . . will eat* [a]Jer 15:2
10 [1]Or *Pleasantness* [2]Or *annul* [a]Zech 11:7 [b]Ps 89:39; Jer 14:21
11 [1]Or *annulled* [2]Another reading is *the sheep dealers who* [a]Zeph 3:12
12 [1]Lit *cease* [a]1 Kin 5:6; Mal 3:5 [b]Gen 37:28; Ex 21:32; Matt 26:15; 27:9, 10
13 [a]Matt 27:3-10; Acts 1:18, 19
14 [1]Or *Cords* [a]Zech 11:7 [b]Is 9:21; Zech 11:6
15 [1]Or *useless* [a]Is 6:10-12; Zech 11:17
16 [a]Jer 23:2 [b]Ezek 34:2-6
17 [a]Jer 23:1; Zech 10:2; 11:15

A [b]sword will be on his arm
And on his right eye!
His [c]arm will be totally withered
And his right eye will be [1]blind."

Chapter 12 Theme ______________________________

12 The [1]burden of the word of the LORD concerning Israel.
Thus declares the LORD who [a]stretches out the heavens,
[b]lays the foundation of the earth, and [c]forms the spirit of man
within him,
2 "Behold, I am going to make Jerusalem a [a]cup [1]that causes
reeling to all the peoples around; and when the siege is against
Jerusalem, it will also be against [b]Judah.
3 "It will come about in that day that I will make Jerusalem a
heavy [a]stone for all the peoples; all who lift it will be [b]severely
[1]injured. And all the [c]nations of the earth will be gathered
against it.
4 "In that day," declares the LORD, "I will strike every horse
with bewilderment and his rider with madness. But I will
[1]watch over the house of Judah, while I strike every horse of
the peoples with blindness.
5 "Then the clans of Judah will say in their hearts, '[1]A strong
support for us are the inhabitants of Jerusalem through the
LORD of hosts, their God.'
6 "In that day I will make the clans of Judah like a [a]firepot
among pieces of wood and a flaming torch among sheaves, so
they will consume on the right hand and on the left all the
surrounding peoples, while the [b]inhabitants of Jerusalem again
dwell on their own sites in Jerusalem.
7 "The LORD also will [a]save the tents of Judah first, so that the
glory of the house of [b]David and the glory of the inhabitants of
Jerusalem will not be magnified above Judah.
8 "In that day the LORD will [a]defend the inhabitants of Jerusalem,
and the one who [1b]is feeble among them in that day will be like
David, and the house of David *will be* like [c]God, like the [d]angel
of the LORD before them.
9 "And in that day I will [1a]set about to destroy all the nations
that come against Jerusalem.
10 "I will [a]pour out on the house of David and on the inhabitants
of Jerusalem, [1]the Spirit of grace and of supplication, so that
they will look on Me whom they have [b]pierced; and they will
mourn for Him, as one [c]mourns for an only son, and they will
weep bitterly over Him like the bitter weeping over a firstborn.
11 "In that day there will be great [a]mourning in Jerusalem, like
the mourning of Hadadrimmon in the [1]plain of [2]Megiddo.
12 "The land will mourn, every family by itself; the family of the
house of David by itself and their wives by themselves; the family
of the house of Nathan by itself and their wives by themselves;
13 the family of the house of Levi by itself and their wives by
themselves; the family of the Shimeites by itself and their
wives by themselves;

17 [1]Lit *completely dimmed* [b]Jer 50:35-37 [c]Ezek 30:21, 22

12:1 [1]Or *oracle* [a]Is 42:5; 44:24; Jer 51:15 [b]Job 26:7; Ps 102:25, 26; Heb 1:10-12 [c]Is 57:16; Heb 12:9

2 [1]Lit *of reeling* [a]Ps 75:8; Is 51:22, 23 [b]Zech 14:14

3 [1]Lit *scratched* [a]Dan 2:34, 35, 44, 45 [b]Matt 21:44 [c]Zech 14:2

4 [1]Lit *open My eyes*

5 [1]Lit *My strength is*

6 [a]Is 10:17, 18; Obad 18; Zech 11:1 [b]Zech 2:4; 8:3-5

7 [a]Jer 30:18 [b]Amos 9:11

8 [1]Or *stumbles* [a]Joel 3:16; Zech 9:14, 15 [b]Lev 26:8; Josh 23:10; Mic 7:8 [c]Ps 8:5; 82:6 [d]Ex 14:19; 33:2

9 [1]Lit *seek to* [a]Zech 14:2, 3

10 [1]Or *a spirit* [a]Is 44:3; Ezek 39:29; Joel 2:28, 29 [b]John 19:37; Rev 1:7 [c]Jer 6:26; Amos 8:10

11 [1]I.e. broad valley [2]Heb *Megiddon* [a]Matt 24:30; Rev 1:7

13:1 [a]Jer 2:13; 17:13 [b]Ps 51:2, 7; Is 1:16-18; John 1:29 [c]Num 19:17; Is 4:4; Ezek 36:25

14 all the families that remain, every family by itself and their
wives by themselves.

Chapter 13 Theme ____________________

13 "In that day a [a]fountain will be opened for the house of
David and for the inhabitants of Jerusalem, for [b]sin and
for [c]impurity.

2 [a]Ex 23:13; Hos 2:17 [b]Jer 23:14, 15 [c]1 Kin 22:22; Ezek 36:25, 29

2 "It will come about in that day," declares the LORD of hosts,
"that I will [a]cut off the names of the idols from the land, and
they will no longer be remembered; and I will also remove the
[b]prophets and the [c]unclean spirit from the land.

3 [a]Jer 23:34 [b]Deut 18:20; Ezek 14:9 [c]Jer 23:25 [d]Deut 13:6-11; Matt 10:37

3 "And if anyone still [a]prophesies, then his father and mother
who gave birth to him will say to him, 'You shall [b]not live, for
you have spoken [c]falsely in the name of the LORD'; and his
[d]father and mother who gave birth to him will pierce him
through when he prophesies.

4 [a]Jer 6:15; 8:9; Mic 3:7 [b]2 Kin 1:8; Is 20:2; Matt 3:4

4 "Also it will come about in that day that the prophets will each
be [a]ashamed of his vision when he prophesies, and they will not
put on a [b]hairy robe in order to deceive;

5 [1]Lit *caused another to buy me* [a]Amos 7:14

5 but he will say, 'I am [a]not a prophet; I am a tiller of the
ground, for a man [1]sold me as a slave in my youth.'

6 [1]Lit *hands* [2]Lit *those who love me* [a]2 Kin 9:24

6 "And one will say to him, 'What are these wounds [a]between
your [1]arms?' Then he will say, '*Those* with which I was wounded
in the house of [2]my friends.'

7 [1]Or *upon* [a]Jer 47:6; Ezek 21:3-5 [b]Is 40:11; Ezek 34:23, 24; 37:24; Mic 5:2, 4 [c]Ps 2:2; Jer 23:5, 6 [d]Is 53:4, 5, 10; Matt 26:31; Mark 14:27 [e]Is 1:25

7 "Awake, O [a]sword, against My [b]Shepherd,
And against the man, My [c]Associate,"
Declares the LORD of hosts.
"[d]Strike the Shepherd that the sheep may be scattered;
And I will [e]turn My hand [1]against the little ones.
8 "It will come about in all the land,"
Declares the LORD,
"That [a]two parts in it will be cut off *and* perish;
But the third will be left in it.

8 [a]Is 6:13; Ezek 5:2-4, 12

9 "And I will bring the third part through the [a]fire,
Refine them as silver is refined,
And test them as gold is tested.
They will [b]call on My name,
And I will [c]answer them;
I will say, 'They are [d]My people,'
And they will say, 'The LORD is my God.'"

9 [a]Is 48:10; Mal 3:3 [b]Ps 34:15-17; 50:15; Zech 12:10 [c]Is 58:9; 65:24; Jer 29:11-13; Zech 10:6 [d]Hos 2:23

Chapter 14 Theme ____________________

14:1 [a]Is 13:6, 9; Joel 2:1; Mal 4:1 [b]Zech 14:14

14 Behold, a [a]day is coming for the LORD when [b]the spoil
taken from you will be divided among you.

2 [a]Zech 12:2, 3 [b]Is 13:16

2 For I will [a]gather all the nations against Jerusalem to battle,
and the city will be captured, the [b]houses plundered, the
women ravished and half of the city exiled, but the rest of the
people will not be cut off from the city.

3 [1]Lit *His day of fighting* [a]Zech 9:14, 15

3 Then the LORD will go forth and [a]fight against those nations,
as [1]when He fights on a day of battle.

4 In that day His feet will [a]stand on the Mount of Olives,
which is in front of Jerusalem on the east; and the Mount of
Olives will be [b]split in its middle from east to west by a very
large valley, so that half of the mountain will move toward the
north and the other half toward the south.
5 You will flee by the valley of My mountains, for the valley
of the mountains will reach to Azel; yes, you will flee just as
you fled before the [a]earthquake in the days of Uzziah king of
Judah. [b]Then the LORD, my God, will come, *and* all the holy
ones with [1]Him!
6 In that day there will be [a]no light; the [1]luminaries will
dwindle.
7 For it will be [a]a unique day which is [b]known to the LORD,
neither day nor night, but it will come about that at [c]evening
time there will be light.
8 And in that day [a]living waters will flow out of Jerusalem,
half of them toward the eastern sea and the other half toward
the western sea; it will be in summer as well as in winter.
9 And the LORD will be [a]king over all the earth; in that day
the LORD will be *the only* [b]one, and His name *the only* one.
10 All the land will be changed into a plain from [a]Geba to
[b]Rimmon south of Jerusalem; but [1]Jerusalem will [c]rise and
[d]remain on its site from [e]Benjamin's Gate as far as the place of
the First Gate to the [f]Corner Gate, and from the [g]Tower of
Hananel to the king's wine presses.
11 [1]People will live in it, and there will [a]no longer be a curse,
for Jerusalem will [b]dwell in security.
12 Now this will be the plague with which the LORD will strike
all the peoples who have gone to war against Jerusalem; their
flesh will [a]rot while they stand on their feet, and their eyes will
rot in their sockets, and their tongue will rot in their mouth.
13 It will come about in that day that a great panic from the LORD
will [1]fall on them; and they will [a]seize one another's hand, and
the hand of one will [2]be lifted against the hand of another.
14 [a]Judah also will fight at Jerusalem; and the [b]wealth of all
the surrounding nations will be gathered, gold and silver and
garments in great abundance.
15 So also like this [a]plague will be the plague on the horse, the
mule, the camel, the donkey and all the cattle that will be in
those camps.
16 Then it will come about that any who are left of all the
nations that went against Jerusalem will [a]go up from year to
year to worship the King, the LORD of hosts, and to celebrate
the [b]Feast of Booths.
17 And it will be that whichever of the families of the earth
does not go up to Jerusalem to worship the [a]King, the LORD of
hosts, there will be [b]no rain on them.
18 If the family of Egypt does not go up or enter, then no *rain
will fall* on them; it will be the [a]plague with which the LORD
smites the nations who do not go up to celebrate the Feast of
Booths.

4 [a]Ezek 11:23 [b]Is 64:1, 2; Ezek 47:1-10; Mic 1:3, 4; Hab 3:6; Zech 4:7; 14:8

5 [1]So the versions; Heb *You* [a]Is 29:6; Amos 1:1 [b]Ps 96:13; Is 66:15, 16; Matt 16:27; 25:31

6 [1]Lit *glorious ones will congeal* [a]Is 13:10; Jer 4:23; Ezek 32:7, 8; Joel 2:30, 31; Acts 2:16, 19

7 [a]Jer 30:7; Amos 8:9 [b]Is 45:21; Acts 15:18 [c]Is 58:10; Rev 22:5

8 [a]Ezek 47:1-12; Joel 3:18; John 7:38; Rev 22:1, 2

9 [a]Is 2:2-4; 45:23; Zech 9:9; 14:16, 17 [b]Deut 6:4; Is 45:21-24

10 [1]Lit *it* [a]1 Kin 15:22 [b]Josh 15:32; Judg 20:45, 47 [c]Is 2:2; Amos 9:11 [d]Jer 30:18; Zech 12:6 [e]Jer 37:13; 38:7 [f]2 Kin 14:13 [g]Jer 31:38

11 [1]Lit *They* [a]Zech 8:13; Rev 22:3 [b]Jer 23:5, 6; Ezek 34:25-28

12 [a]Lev 26:16; Deut 28:21, 22

13 [1]Lit *be among* [2]Lit *rise up against* [a]Zech 11:6

14 [a]Zech 12:2, 5 [b]Is 23:18; Zech 14:1

15 [a]Zech 14:12

16 [a]Is 60:6-9; 66:18-21, 23 [b]Lev 23:34-44

17 [a]Zech 14:9, 16 [b]Jer 14:3-6; Amos 4:7

18 [a]Zech 14:12, 15

19 [1]Lit *sin*

19 This will be the [1]punishment of Egypt, and the [1]punishment
of all the nations who do not go up to celebrate the Feast of
Booths.

20 [a]Ex 28:36-38
[b]Ezek 46:20

20 In that day there will *be inscribed* on the bells of the
horses, "[a]HOLY TO THE LORD." And the [b]cooking pots in the
LORD's house will be like the bowls before the altar.

21 [1]Or *merchant*
[a]Neh 8:10;
Rom 14:6, 7;
1 Cor 10:31
[b]Zeph 1:11

21 Every cooking pot in Jerusalem and in Judah will be [a]holy
to the LORD of hosts; and all who sacrifice will come and take of
them and boil in them. And there will no longer be a
[1][b]Canaanite in the house of the LORD of hosts in that day.

Zechariah's Prophetic Revelations

Concerning Messiah, Judah, and Jerusalem	Concerning the Nations	Concerning Messiah, the Savior and King

Zechariah at a Glance

Theme of Zechariah:

Author:

Date:

Purpose:

Key Words:

Segment Divisions		Chapter Themes
		1
		2
		3
		4
		5
		6
		7
		8
		9
		10
		11
		12
		13
		14

MALACHI מַלְאָכִי
MAL'AKHI

Because they had not obeyed the word of the Lord, in 586 B.C. the children of Israel were taken into captivity. The nation that was once the head became the tail, just as God had spoken through His prophet Moses. And just as God had decreed through Jeremiah the prophet, the children of Israel's captivity lasted for 70 years.

In 538 B.C. Cyrus, the king of Persia, issued a decree allowing the children of Israel to return to Jerusalem and rebuild their temple. It was just as God had said when Isaiah prophesied 150 years earlier. Zerubbabel finished the temple, just as God promised. In 445 B.C. the Persian King Artaxerxes permitted Nehemiah to return to Jerusalem and rebuild its walls, just as Daniel had prophesied.

Over and over, the children of Israel saw that God stood by His word. Just as Solomon wrote in Proverbs, the hearts of kings were in God's hands, and He could turn them wherever He wanted. Why, then, did the remnant of Israel think that they could live and worship any way they wanted once they returned from their 70 years of exile and settled again in Israel? Had they grown tired of waiting for the fulfillment of the prophecies that promised that the Messiah would reign as King over all the earth? Had God abandoned them as He had Esau's descendants? Did they think He would allow the heathen nations who had come against them to go unpunished? Or were they entertaining thoughts that God really did not love them, that He would not keep His covenant promises?

Whatever it was, once again the remnant became apathetic in their relationship with God. So He spoke one more time through Malachi, whose name means "my messenger." It was sometime around 433 B.C. And then came a famine for hearing the word of the Lord (Amos 8:11).

THINGS TO DO

1. Since Malachi is a short book, read it without interruption so you can get a perspective of the book as a whole before you observe it chapter by chapter. As you read, catch the atmosphere of this book. Remember, this was written to people who had been sent into exile because of disobedience and then had returned to their land, just as God had promised.
2. Now read through Malachi one chapter at a time, doing the following:
   a. In a distinctive way or color mark the key words listed on the MALACHI AT A GLANCE chart on page 1554. Write these key words on an index card you can use as a bookmark while you study Malachi.
   b. As you mark every reference to *you say* or *said,* watch what the priests and/or the people say and how God answers.
   c. You may want to note in the margin with whom God is upset, why He is upset, and what He tells them to do or what He is going to do as a result.
   d. Observe what will happen to those who fear His name and to those who do not.
   e. Note God's call to return to Him, how they are to return, and what will happen if they do.
3. When you finish each chapter, decide what the main subject or theme of that chapter is and record it on MALACHI AT A GLANCE and in your Bible.
4. As you read the final chapter of Malachi, read Deuteronomy 28–30, which speaks of the blessings or curses upon those who obey or disobey the law given by Moses.

5. God was silent for 400 years after He spoke through His prophet Malachi. His silence was broken when an angel appeared to Zacharias with the news that he and Elizabeth would give birth to a son. Read Luke 1:5-17 and Matthew 11:2-15, and see how these passages relate to God's final promise in Malachi. Record the essence of that promise in the margin of Malachi 4, and write next to it the cross-references in Luke and Matthew.

6. Record what you learn about the *day of the Lord* on the chart on page 2076.

Things to Think About

1. What do you learn from God's word to the priests that you can apply to your own life? Read through the list you compiled on "the priests" and remember that if you belong to the Lord Jesus Christ, you are part of a kingdom of priests to God. What kind of a priest are you? In principle, do you think God expects anything less of you as a Christian? For instance, what do you offer the Lord of your time and talents, your tithe and offering? Do you give others instructions according to the Word of the Lord or according to the current philosophy of the world? What about your covenant relationship with your mate?

2. Are you tired of serving God? Or do you fear Him? If so, what is God's promise to you?

Chapter 1 Theme ______________________________

1 The [1a]oracle of the word of the LORD to [b]Israel through
[2]Malachi.
2 "I have [a]loved you," says the LORD. But you say, "How have
You loved us?" "*Was* not Esau Jacob's brother?" declares the LORD.
"Yet I [b]have loved Jacob;
3 but I have hated Esau, and I have [a]made his mountains a
desolation and *appointed* his inheritance for the jackals of the
wilderness."
4 Though Edom says, "We have been [a]beaten down, but we
will [1b]return and build up the ruins"; thus says the LORD of hosts,
"They may [c]build, but I will tear down; and *men* will call them
the [2]wicked territory, and the people [3]toward whom the LORD
is indignant [d]forever."
5 Your eyes will see this and you will say, "[a]The LORD [1]be
magnified beyond the [2]border of Israel!"
6 "'A son [a]honors *his* father, and a servant his master. Then if
I am a [b]father, where is My honor? And if I am a master, where is
My [1]respect?' says the LORD of hosts to you, O [c]priests who despise
My name. But you say, 'How have we despised Your name?'
7 "*You* are presenting [a]defiled [1b]food upon My altar. But you
say, 'How have we defiled You?' In that you say, 'The [c]table of
the LORD is to be despised.'
8 "But when you present the [a]blind for sacrifice, is it not evil?
And when you present the lame and sick, is it not evil? [1]Why
not offer it to your [b]governor? Would he be pleased with you?
Or would he receive you kindly?" says the LORD of hosts.

1:1 [1]Lit *burden* [2]Or *My messenger* [a]Is 13:1; Nah 1:1; Hab 1:1; Zech 9:1 [b]Mal 2:11
2 [a]Deut 4:37; 7:8; 23:5; Is 41:8, 9; Jer 31:3; John 15:12 [b]Rom 9:13
3 [a]Jer 49:10, 16-18; Ezek 35:3, 4, 7, 8, 15
4 [1]Or *rebuild the ruins* [2]Lit *border of wickedness* [3]Or *whom the LORD has cursed* [a]Jer 5:17 [b]Is 9:9, 10 [c]Amos 3:15; 5:11; 6:11 [d]Ezek 35:9; Obad 10
5 [1]Or *will be great* [2]Or *territory* [a]Ps 35:27; Mic 5:4
6 [1]Lit *fear* [a]Ex 20:12; Prov 30:11, 17 [b]Deut 1:31; Is 1:2; Jer 3:4; Mal 2:10 [c]Zeph 3:4; Mal 2:1-9
7 [1]Lit *bread* [a]Mal 1:8, 13 [b]Lev 3:11; 21:6, 8 [c]Mal 1:12
8 [1]Lit *Offer it, please* [a]Lev 22:22; Deut 15:21 [b]Hag 1:1

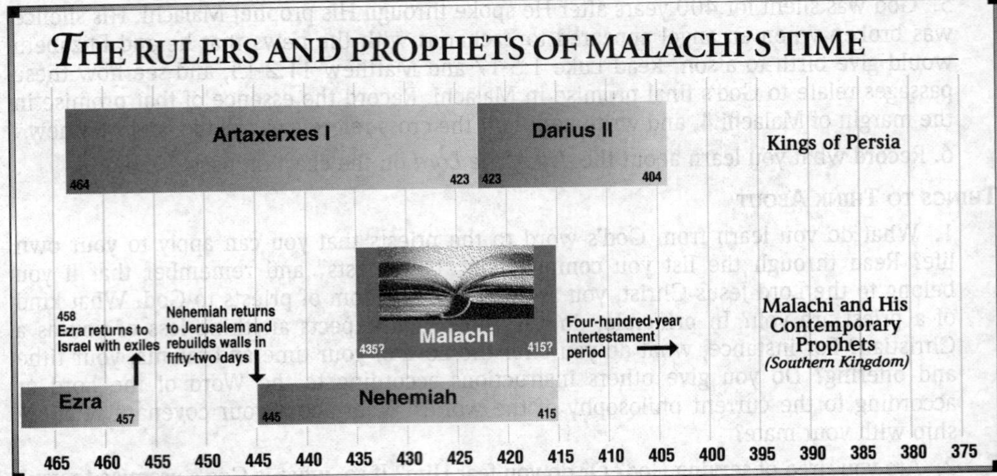

9 "But now [1]will you not [a]entreat God's favor, that He may be
gracious to us? [2]With such an offering on your part, will He
[b]receive any of you kindly?" says the LORD of hosts.
10 "Oh that there were one among you who would [a]shut the
[1]gates, that you might not uselessly kindle *fire on* My altar! I
am not pleased with you," says the LORD of hosts, "[b]nor will I
accept an offering from [2]you.
11 "For from the [a]rising of the sun even to its setting, [b]My name
will be [c]great among the nations, and in every place [d]incense is
going to be offered to My name, and a grain offering *that is*
pure; for My name *will be* [e]great among the nations," says the
LORD of hosts.
12 "But you are [a]profaning it, in that you say, 'The table of the
Lord is defiled, and as for its fruit, its food is to be despised.'
13 "You also say, '[1]My, how [a]tiresome it is!' And you disdain-
fully sniff at it," says the LORD of hosts, "and you bring what
was taken by [b]robbery and *what is* [c]lame or sick; so you bring
the offering! Should I [d]receive that from your hand?" says the
LORD.
14 "But cursed be the [a]swindler who has a male in his flock
and vows it, but sacrifices a [b]blemished animal to the Lord, for
I am a great [c]King," says the LORD of hosts, "and My name is
[1][d]feared among the [2]nations."

Chapter 2 Theme ________________________________

2 "And now this commandment is for you, O priests.
2 "If you do [a]not listen, and if you do not take it to heart to
give honor to My name," says the LORD of hosts, "then I will
send the [b]curse upon you and I will curse your blessings; and
indeed, I have [c]cursed them *already,* because you are not taking
it to heart.
3 "Behold, I am going to [a]rebuke your [1]offspring, and I will

9 [1]Lit *entreat, please* [2]Lit *This has been from your hand* [a]Jer 27:18; Joel 2:12-14 [b]Amos 5:22

10 [1]Or *doors* [2]Lit *your hand* [a]Is 1:13 [b]Jer 14:10, 12; Hos 5:6

11 [a]Is 45:6 [b]Ps 111:9 [c]Is 66:18, 19 [d]Is 60:6 [e]Is 12:4, 5; 54:5; Jer 10:6, 7

12 [a]Mal 1:7

13 [1]Lit *Behold it is weariness* [a]Is 43:22 [b]Lev 6:4; Is 61:8 [c]Mal 1:8 [d]Mal 1:10

14 [1]Or *revered* [2]Or *Gentiles* [a]Acts 5:1-4 [b]Lev 22:18-20 [c]Zech 14:9 [d]Zeph 2:11

2:2 [a]Lev 26:14, 15; Deut 28:15 [b]Deut 28:16-20 [c]Mal 3:9

3 [1]Lit *seed* [a]Lev 26:16; Deut 28:38

[b]spread [2]refuse on your faces, the [2]refuse of your [c]feasts; and
you will be taken away [3]with it.
4 "Then you will know that I have sent this commandment to
you, [1]that My [a]covenant may [2]continue with Levi," says the
LORD of hosts.
5 "My covenant with him was *one of* life and [a]peace, and I
gave them to him *as an object of* [1]reverence; so he [2b]revered
Me and stood in awe of My name.
6 "[1a]True instruction was in his mouth and unrighteousness
was not found on his lips; he walked [b]with Me in peace and
uprightness, and he [c]turned many back from iniquity.
7 "For the lips of a priest should preserve [a]knowledge, and
[1]men should [b]seek [2]instruction from his mouth; for he is the
[c]messenger of the LORD of hosts.
8 "But as for you, you have turned aside from the way; you
have caused many to [a]stumble [1]by the instruction; you have
[2b]corrupted the covenant of Levi," says the LORD of hosts.
9 "So [a]I also have made you despised and [b]abased [1]before all the
people, just as you are not keeping My ways but are showing
[c]partiality in the [2]instruction.
10 "Do we not all have [a]one father? [b]Has not one God created
us? Why do we deal [c]treacherously each against his brother so
as to profane the [d]covenant of our fathers?
11 "Judah has dealt [a]treacherously, and an abomination has been
committed in Israel and in Jerusalem; for Judah has [b]profaned
the sanctuary of the LORD [1]which He loves and has married the
daughter of a foreign god.
12 "*As* for the man who does this, may the [a]LORD cut off from
the tents of Jacob *everyone* who awakes and answers, or who
[b]presents [1]an offering to the LORD of hosts.
13 "This is [1]another thing you do: you cover the altar of the LORD
with tears, with weeping and with groaning, because He [a]no
longer regards the [2]offering or accepts *it with* favor from your
hand.
14 "Yet you say, 'For what reason?' Because the LORD has been
a witness between you and the [a]wife of your youth, against
whom you have dealt [b]treacherously, though she is your
companion and your wife by covenant.
15 "[1]But not one has [a]done *so* who has a remnant of the Spirit.
And [2]what did *that* one *do* while he was seeking a [b]godly
[3]offspring? Take heed then to your spirit, and let no one deal
[c]treacherously against the wife of your youth.
16 "For [1]I hate [2a]divorce," says the LORD, the God of Israel,
"and [3]him who covers his garment with [4b]wrong," says the
LORD of hosts. "So take heed to your spirit, that you do not deal
treacherously."
17 You have [a]wearied the LORD with your words. Yet you say,
"How have we wearied *Him?*" In that you say, "[b]Everyone who
does evil is good in the sight of the LORD, and He [c]delights in
them," or, "[d]Where is the God of [e]justice?"

3 [2]Or *vomit* [3]Lit *to* [b]Nah 3:6 [c]Ex 29:14

4 [1]Or *to be My covenant with* [2]Lit *be* [a]Num 3:11-13, 45; 18:21; Neh 13:29; Mal 3:1

5 [1]Or *fear* [2]Or *feared* [a]Num 25:12 [b]Num 25:7, 8, 13

6 [1]Or *Law of truth* [a]Ps 119:142, 151, 160 [b]Deut 33:8, 9; Ps 37:37 [c]Jer 23:22

7 [1]Lit *they* [2]Or *law* [a]Lev 10:11; Neh 8:7 [b]Num 27:21; Deut 17:8-11; Jer 18:18; Ezek 7:26 [c]Hag 1:13

8 [1]Or *in the law* [2]Or *violated* [a]Jer 18:15 [b]Num 25:12, 13; Neh 13:29; Ezek 44:10

9 [1]Lit *to* [2]Or *law* [a]Nah 3:6 [b]Ezek 7:26 [c]Deut 1:17; Mic 3:11

10 [a]Is 63:16; 64:8; Jer 31:9; 1 Cor 8:6; Eph 4:6 [b]Acts 17:24f [c]Jer 9:4, 5 [d]Ex 19:4-6; 24:3, 7, 8

11 [1]Or *in that He has loved and married* [a]Jer 3:7-9 [b]Ezra 9:1, 2

12 [1]Or *a grain offering* [a]Ezek 24:21; Hos 9:12 [b]Mal 1:10, 13

13 [1]Lit *second* [2]Or *grain offering* [a]Jer 11:14; 14:12

14 [a]Is 54:6 [b]Jer 9:2; Mal 3:5

15 [1]Or *Did He not make one, although He had the remnant* [2]Or *why one? He sought a godly offspring* [3]Lit *seed* [a]Gen 2:24; Matt 19:4, 5 [b]Ruth 4:12; 1 Sam 2:20 [c]Ex 20:14; Lev 20:10

16 [1]Lit *He hates* [2]Lit *sending away* [3]Lit *he covers* [4]Or *violence* [a]Deut 24:1; Matt 5:31; 19:6-8 [b]Ps 73:6; Is 59:6

17 [a]Is 43:22, 24 [b]Is 5:20; Zeph 1:12 [c]Job 9:24 [d]2 Pet 3:4 [e]Is 5:19; Jer 17:15

Chapter 3 Theme ______________________

3 "[a]Behold, I am going to send [b]My [1]messenger, and he will
[2c]clear the way before Me. And the Lord, whom you seek,
will suddenly come to His temple; [3]and the [1d]messenger of the
covenant, in whom you delight, behold, He is coming," says
the LORD of hosts.
2 "But who can [a]endure the day of His coming? And who can
stand when He appears? For He is like a [b]refiner's fire and like
[1]fullers' soap.
3 "He will sit as a smelter and purifier of silver, and He will
[a]purify the sons of Levi and refine them like gold and silver, so
that they may [b]present to the LORD [1]offerings in righteousness.
4 "Then the [1]offering of Judah and Jerusalem will be [a]pleasing
to the LORD as in the [b]days of old and as in former years.
5 "Then I will draw near to you for judgment; and I will be a
swift witness against the [a]sorcerers and against the [b]adulterers
and against those who [c]swear falsely, and against those who
oppress the [d]wage earner in his wages, the [e]widow and the
[1]orphan, and those who turn aside the [2f]alien and do not [3]fear
Me," says the LORD of hosts.
6 "For [1]I, the LORD, [a]do not change; therefore you, O sons of
Jacob, [2]are not consumed.
7 "From the [a]days of your fathers you have turned aside from
My statutes and have not kept *them.* [b]Return to Me, and I will
return to you," says the LORD of hosts. "But you say, 'How shall
we return?'
8 "Will a man [1]rob God? Yet you are robbing Me! But you say,
'How have we robbed You?' In [a]tithes and [2]offerings.
9 "You are [a]cursed with a curse, for you are [1]robbing Me, the
whole nation *of you!*
10 "[a]Bring the whole tithe into the storehouse, so that there
may be [1]food in My house, and test Me now in this," says the
LORD of hosts, "if I will not [b]open for you the windows of
heaven and [c]pour out for you a blessing until [2d]it overflows.
11 "Then I will rebuke the [a]devourer for you, so that it will not
[1]destroy the fruits of the ground; nor will your vine in the field
cast *its grapes,*" says the LORD of hosts.
12 "[a]All the nations will call you blessed, for you shall be a
[b]delightful land," says the LORD of hosts.
13 "Your words have been [1]arrogant against Me," says the
LORD. "Yet you say, 'What have we spoken against You?'
14 "You have said, 'It is [a]vain to serve God; and what [b]profit is
it that we have kept His charge, and that we have walked in
mourning before the LORD of hosts?
15 'So now we [a]call the arrogant blessed; not only are the
doers of wickedness built up but they also test God and
[b]escape.'"
16 Then those who [1]feared the LORD spoke to one another,
and the LORD [a]gave attention and heard *it,* and a [b]book of
remembrance was written before Him for those who [1]fear the
LORD and who esteem His name.

3:1 [1]Or *angel* [2]Or *prepare* [3]Or *even* [a]Matt 11:10, 14; Mark 1:2; Luke 1:76; 7:27 [b]Hag 1:13; John 1:6, 7 [c]Is 40:3 [d]Is 63:9

2 [1]Lit *laundrymen's* [a]Is 33:14; Ezek 22:14; Rev 6:17 [b]Zech 13:9; Matt 3:10-12; 1 Cor 3:13-15

3 [1]Or *grain offerings* [a]Is 1:25; Dan 12:10 [b]Ps 4:5; 51:19

4 [1]Or *grain offering* [a]Ps 51:17-19 [b]2 Chr 7:1-3, 12

5 [1]Or *fatherless* [2]Or *sojourner* [3]Or *revere* [a]Deut 18:10; Jer 27:9, 10 [b]Ezek 22:9-11 [c]Jer 5:2; 7:9; Zech 5:4 [d]Lev 19:13 [e]Ex 22:22-24 [f]Deut 27:19

6 [1]Or *I am the LORD; I do not* [2]Or *have not come to an end* [a]Num 23:19; James 1:17

7 [a]Jer 7:25, 26; 16:11, 12 [b]Zech 1:3

8 [1]Or *defraud* [2]Or *heave offerings* [a]Neh 13:11, 12

9 [1]Or *defrauding* [a]Mal 2:2

10 [1]Lit *prey* [2]Or *there is not* room *enough* [a]Lev 27:30; Num 18:21-24; Deut 12:6; 14:22-29; Neh 13:12 [b]Ps 78:23-29 [c]Ezek 34:26 [d]Lev 26:3-5

11 [1]Lit *ruin* [a]Joel 1:4; 2:25

12 [a]Is 61:9 [b]Is 62:4

13 [1]Lit *strong*

14 [a]Jer 2:25; 18:12 [b]Is 58:3

15 [a]Is 2:22; Mal 4:1 [b]Jer 7:10

16 [1]Or *revere(d)* [a]Ps 34:15; Jer 31:18-20 [b]Is 4:3; Dan 12:1

17 “They will be [a]Mine,” says the LORD of hosts, “on the [b]day
that I [1]prepare *My* [2c]own possession, and I will [3]spare them as
a man [3d]spares his own son who serves him.”
18 So you will again [a]distinguish between the righteous and
the wicked, between one who serves God and one who does
not serve Him.

Chapter 4 Theme ______________________________

4 “[1]For behold, the day is coming, [a]burning like a furnace;
and all the arrogant and every evildoer will be [b]chaff; and
the day that is coming will [c]set them ablaze,” says the LORD of
hosts, “so that it will leave them neither root nor branch.”
2 “But for you who [1]fear My name, the [a]sun of righteousness
will rise with [b]healing in its wings; and you will go forth and
[c]skip about like calves from the stall.
3 “You will [a]tread down the wicked, for they will be [b]ashes
under the soles of your feet [c]on the day [1]which I am preparing,”
says the LORD of hosts.
4 “[1a]Remember the law of Moses My servant, *even the* statutes
and ordinances which I commanded him in Horeb for all Israel.
5 “Behold, I am going to send you [a]Elijah the prophet before
the coming of the great and terrible day of the LORD.
6 “He will [1a]restore the hearts of the fathers to *their* children
and the hearts of the children to their fathers, so that I will not
come and [b]smite the land with a [2]curse.”

17 [1]Lit *make* [2]Or *special treasure* [3]Or *have (has) compassion on* [a]Is 43:1 [b]Is 4:2 [c]Ex 19:5; Deut 7:6; Is 43:21; 1 Pet 2:9 [d]Ps 103:13

18 [a]Gen 18:25; Amos 5:15

4:1 [1]Ch 3:19 in Heb [a]Ps 21:9; Nah 1:5, 6; Mal 3:2, 3; 2 Pet 3:7 [b]Is 5:24; Obad 18 [c]Is 9:18, 19

2 [1]Or *revere* [a]2 Sam 23:4; Is 30:26; 60:1 [b]Jer 30:17; 33:6 [c]Is 35:6

3 [1]Or *when I act* [a]Job 40:12; Is 26:6; Mic 5:8 [b]Ezek 28:18 [c]Mal 3:17

4 [1]Ch 3:22 in Heb [a]Deut 4:23; 8:11, 19

5 [a]Matt 11:14; 17:10-13; Mark 9:11-13; Luke 1:17; John 1:21

6 [1]Or *turn* [2]Or *ban of destruction* [a]Luke 1:17 [b]Is 11:4; Rev 19:15

Malachi at a Glance

Theme of Malachi:

Segment Divisions

	Chapter Themes
	1
	2
	3
	4

Author:

Date:

Purpose:

Key Words:

Lord of hosts

you say (said)

profane (profaned)

My name (or Your name)

priest(s)

offering (sacrifices)

curse

covenant

treacherously

fear (reverence)

THE NEW TESTAMENT

The Genealogy of Jesus the Christ

Adam (1 Chronicles 1, 2; Luke 3)
Seth
Enosh
Cainan
Mahalaleel
Jared
Enoch
Methuselah
Lamech
Noah
Shem
Arphaxad
Cainan
Shelah
Heber
Peleg
Reu
Serug
Nahor
Terah
Abraham (1 Chronicles 3; Matthew 1; Luke 3)
Isaac
Jacob
Judah
Perez
Hezron
Ram
Admin
Amminadab
Nahshon
Salmon—Rahab
Boaz—Ruth
Obed
Jesse

David

Nathan (Luke 3)
Mattatha
Menna
Melea
Eliakim
Jonam
Joseph
Judah
Simeon
Levi
Matthat
Jorim
Eliezer
Joshua
Er
Elmadam
Cosam
Addi
Melchi
Neri
Shealtiel
Zerubbabel
Rhesa
Joanan
Joda
Josech
Semein
Mattathias
Maath
Naggai
Hesli
Nahum
Amos
Mattathias
Joseph
Jannai
Melchi
Levi
Matthat
Eli
Mary

Solomon (1 Chronicles 3; Matthew 1)
Rehoboam
Abijah
Asa
Jehoshaphat
Joram (Jehoram)
Ahaziah
Joash
Amaziah
Uzziah (Azariah)
Jotham
Ahaz
Hezekiah
Manasseh
Amon
Josiah
Jehoiakim
Jeconiah (Jehoiachin)
Shealtiel
Zerubbabel (Matthew 1)
Abihud
Eliakim
Azor
Zadok
Achim
Eliud
Eleazar
Matthan
Jacob
Joseph

The Holy Spirit
Luke 1:35

Jesus
("Being supposedly the son of Joseph" [Luke 3:23])

Bible Cities in the Time of Jesus

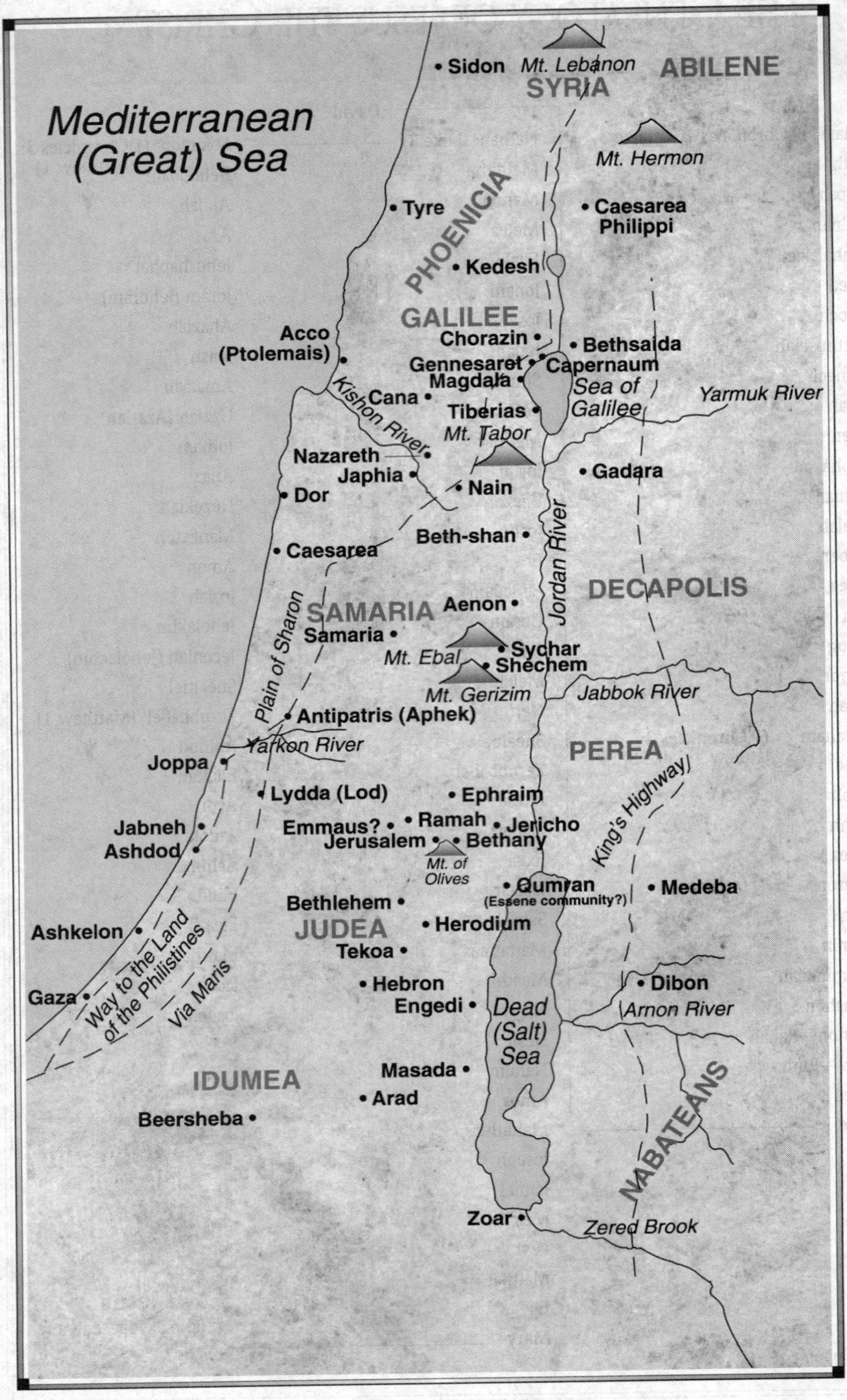

Mediterranean (Great) Sea
Sidon
Mt. Lebanon
ABILENE
SYRIA
Mt. Hermon
Tyre
PHOENICIA
Caesarea Philippi
Kedesh
GALILEE
Acco (Ptolemais)
Chorazin
Bethsaida
Gennesaret
Capernaum
Magdala
Sea of Galilee
Cana
Kishon River
Tiberias
Yarmuk River
Mt. Tabor
Nazareth
Japhia
Gadara
Nain
Dor
Beth-shan
Caesarea
Jordan River
DECAPOLIS
Plain of Sharon
Aenon
SAMARIA
Samaria
Sychar
Mt. Ebal
Shechem
Mt. Gerizim
Jabbok River
Antipatris (Aphek)
Yarkon River
PEREA
Joppa
King's Highway
Lydda (Lod)
Ephraim
Jabneh
Emmaus?
Ramah
Jericho
Ashdod
Jerusalem
Bethany
Mt. of Olives
Qumran (Essene community?)
Medeba
Bethlehem
Ashkelon
JUDEA
Herodium
Way to the Land of the Philistines
Tekoa
Via Maris
Hebron
Dibon
Gaza
Engedi
Dead (Salt) Sea
Arnon River
Masada
IDUMEA
NABATEANS
Arad
Beersheba
Zoar
Zered Brook

*M*ATTHEW

God promised Abraham that all the nations of the earth would be blessed through his seed (Genesis 12:3; 15:1-6). Where was this son of Abraham?

God promised Isaiah that a child would be born, a son would be given, and the government would rest on His shoulders. His name would be Wonderful Counselor, Mighty God, Eternal Father, Prince of Peace. There would be no end to the increase of His government or of peace. He would occupy the throne of David (Isaiah 9:6-7). Where was this son of David?

No one knew until a baby's cry went up from Bethlehem Ephrathah. Magi from the East arrived in Jerusalem saying, "Where is He who has been born King of the Jews?" The One who was to be ruler in Israel (Micah 5:2), the son of David, the son of Abraham, had been born. Matthew writes about this King of the Jews.

Things to Do

1. From the first verse, Matthew's purpose is clear: to show that Jesus was the long-awaited King, the son of David, the Messiah whose coming was prophesied throughout the Old Testament.

   There is a pattern to Matthew that repeats itself and divides the Gospel into six segments. Matthew presents certain facts concerning the person and work of Jesus, which he then follows with an account of Jesus' teaching. Each teaching account is brought to a conclusion with one of the following three phrases: "When Jesus had finished these words," "finished giving instructions," or "finished these parables."

   Therefore before you read through Matthew chapter by chapter, mark in a distinctive way each occurrence of a dividing phrase in 7:28; 11:1; 13:53; 19:1; and 26:1. Remember, these phrases conclude that particular teaching. Then the cycle begins again.

2. Now read Matthew chapter by chapter, keeping in mind these six segments. As you read:
   a. In a distinctive way mark in the text the key words listed on MATTHEW AT A GLANCE on page 1613. Mark every reference to time with a green clock 🕒. Double-underline in green all geographical locations and locate them on the map on page 1558.
      1) List on page 1758 what you learn about *king* or *kingdom.*
      2) In addition to these key words, watch for other key repeated words or phrases.
   b. Using the same color each time, underline or highlight each reference to or quotation from an Old Testament prophecy that shows Jesus as the promised King. Then in the margin, write the word "prophecy." (In the NASB, you can easily spot the Old Testament quotes because they are printed in small capital letters.)
   c. Watch for the events, works, or facts that demonstrate who Jesus Christ is.
   d. When you read Jesus' teaching on a particular subject, in your notebook make a list of the main points covered in His teaching. If it is a prophetic teaching, pay attention to time phrases or indicators, including *then* and *when*. Watch for the progression of events.
   e. Record the main theme or event of each chapter in your Bible next to the chapter number and on MATTHEW AT A GLANCE.

3. Chapters 26 through 28 give an account of the final events in the life of Jesus. Record the progression of events on the chart THE ARREST, TRIAL, AND CRUCIFIXION OF JESUS

CHRIST on page 1757 or the chart THE ACCOUNT OF JESUS' RESURRECTION on page 1760. Note the chapter and verse of each insight for future reference.

4. When you record the circumstances surrounding the resurrection of Jesus Christ, also note any postresurrection appearances that are recorded in Matthew. After you do this for all four Gospels you will have comprehensive notes on all that took place. Remember, Luke gives the consecutive order of events and therefore becomes a chronological plumb line for the other Gospel records.

5. List and consolidate everything you learn from Matthew about the kingdom of God in your notebook. Be sure to note the chapter and verse for future reference. You can transfer this information to the chart on page 1758.

6. Complete MATTHEW AT A GLANCE. Under "Segment Divisions," record the theme of each segment of Matthew. There is also a blank line for any other segment divisions you might see.

Things to Think About

1. Have you bowed your knee to Jesus as King in your life? Read Matthew 7:21-27 and think about the difference between *merely hearing* something and *hearing and living accordingly.* Which best describes you?

2. Can you explain from Scripture why Jesus is the King of the promised kingdom?

3. Do you realize that Jesus' final words to His disciples in Matthew 28:19-20 are your responsibility also? What are you doing in order to fulfill His Great Commission? As you go, are you making disciples? Are you teaching them to observe all that He has commanded?

Chapter 1 Theme ______________________

1 The [1]record of the genealogy of [2]Jesus [3]the Messiah, [a]the son
of David, [b]the son of Abraham:
2 Abraham [1]was the father of Isaac, [2]Isaac the father of Jacob,
and Jacob the father of [3]Judah and his brothers.
3 Judah was the father of Perez and Zerah by Tamar, [a]Perez was
the father of Hezron, and Hezron the father of [1]Ram.
4 Ram was the father of Amminadab, Amminadab the father of
Nahshon, and Nahshon the father of Salmon.
5 Salmon was the father of Boaz by Rahab, Boaz was the father
of Obed by Ruth, and Obed the father of Jesse.
6 Jesse was the father of David the king.
David [a]was the father of Solomon by [1]Bathsheba who had
been the wife of Uriah.
7 Solomon [a]was the father of Rehoboam, Rehoboam the
father of Abijah, and Abijah the father of [1]Asa.
8 Asa was the father of Jehoshaphat, Jehoshaphat the father
of [1]Joram, and Joram the father of Uzziah.
9 Uzziah was the father of [1]Jotham, Jotham the father of
Ahaz, and Ahaz the father of Hezekiah.
10 Hezekiah was the father of Manasseh, Manasseh the father
of [1]Amon, and Amon the [a]father of Josiah.

INSIGHT

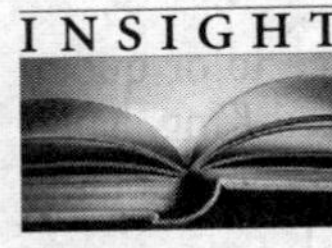

See **The Genealogy of Jesus the Christ** on page 1557.

1:1 [1]Lit *book* [2]Heb *Yeshua* (*Joshua*), meaning *The Lord saves* [3]Gr *Christos* (*Christ*), Gr for *Messiah*, which means *Anointed One* [a]2 Sam 7:12-16; Ps 89:3f; 132:11; Is 9:6f; 11:1; Matt 9:27; Luke 1:32, 69; John 7:42; Acts 13:23; Rom 1:3; Rev 22:16 [b]Matt 1:1-6: *Luke 3:32-34;* Gen 22:18; Gal 3:16
2 [1]Lit *fathered,* and throughout the genealogy [2]Lit *and . . . ,* and throughout the genealogy [3]Gr *Judas;* names of people in the Old Testament are given in their Old Testament form
3 [1]Gr *Aram* [a]Ruth 4:18-22; 1 Chr 2:1-15; Matt 1:3-6
6 [1]Lit *her of Uriah* [a]2 Sam 11:27; 12:24
7 [1]Gr *Asaph* [a]1 Chr 3:10ff
8 [1]Also Gr for *Jehoram* in 2 King 8:16; cf 1 Chron 3:11
9 [1]Gr *Joatham*
10 [1]Gr *Amos* [a]1 Chr 3:14

11 Josiah became the father of [1]Jeconiah and his brothers, at
the time of the [a]deportation to Babylon.
12 After the [a]deportation to Babylon: Jeconiah became the
father of [1]Shealtiel, and Shealtiel the father of Zerubbabel.
13 Zerubbabel was the father of [1]Abihud, Abihud the father of
Eliakim, and Eliakim the father of Azor.
14 Azor was the father of Zadok, Zadok the father of Achim,
and Achim the father of Eliud.
15 Eliud was the father of Eleazar, Eleazar the father of Matthan,
and Matthan the father of Jacob.
16 Jacob was the father of Joseph the husband of Mary, by
whom Jesus was born, [a]who is called [1]the Messiah.
17 So all the generations from Abraham to David are fourteen
generations; from David to the [a]deportation to Babylon,
fourteen generations; and from the [a]deportation to Babylon to
[1]the Messiah, fourteen generations.
18 Now the birth of Jesus [1]Christ was as follows: when His
[a]mother Mary had been [2]betrothed to Joseph, before they came
together she was [b]found to be with child by the Holy Spirit.
19 And Joseph her husband, being a righteous man and not
wanting to disgrace her, planned [1a]to send her away secretly.
20 But when he had considered this, behold, an angel of the
Lord appeared to him in a dream, saying, "[a]Joseph, son of
David, do not be afraid to take Mary as your wife; for [1]the
Child who has been [2]conceived in her is of the Holy Spirit.
21 "She will bear a Son; and [a]you shall call His name Jesus, for
[1]He [b]will save His people from their sins."
22 Now all this [1]took place to fulfill what was [a]spoken by the
Lord through the prophet:

11 [1]*Jehoiachin* in 2 Kin 24:15 [a]2 Kin 24:14f; Jer 27:20; Matt 1:17
12 [1]Gr *Salathiel* [a]2 Kin 24:14f; Jer 27:20; Matt 1:17
13 [1]Gr *Abioud*, usually spelled *Abiud*
16 [1]Gr *Christos* (*Christ*) [a]Matt 27:17, 22; Luke 2:11; John 4:25
17 [1]Gr *Christos* (*Christ*) [a]2 Kin 24:14f; Jer 27:20; Matt 1:11, 12
18 [1]I.e. The Messiah [2]The first stage of marriage in Jewish culture, usually lasting for a year before the wedding night, more legal than an engagement [a]Matt 12:46; Luke 1:27 [b]Luke 1:35
19 [1]Or *to divorce her* [a]Deut 22:20-24; 24:1-4; John 8:4, 5
20 [1]Lit *that which* [2]Lit *begotten* [a]Luke 2:4
21 [1]Lit *He Himself* [a]Luke 1:31; 2:21 [b]Luke 2:11; John 1:29; Acts 4:12; 5:31; 13:23, 38, 39; Col 1:20-23
22 [1]Lit *has happened* [a]Luke 24:44; Rom 1:2-4

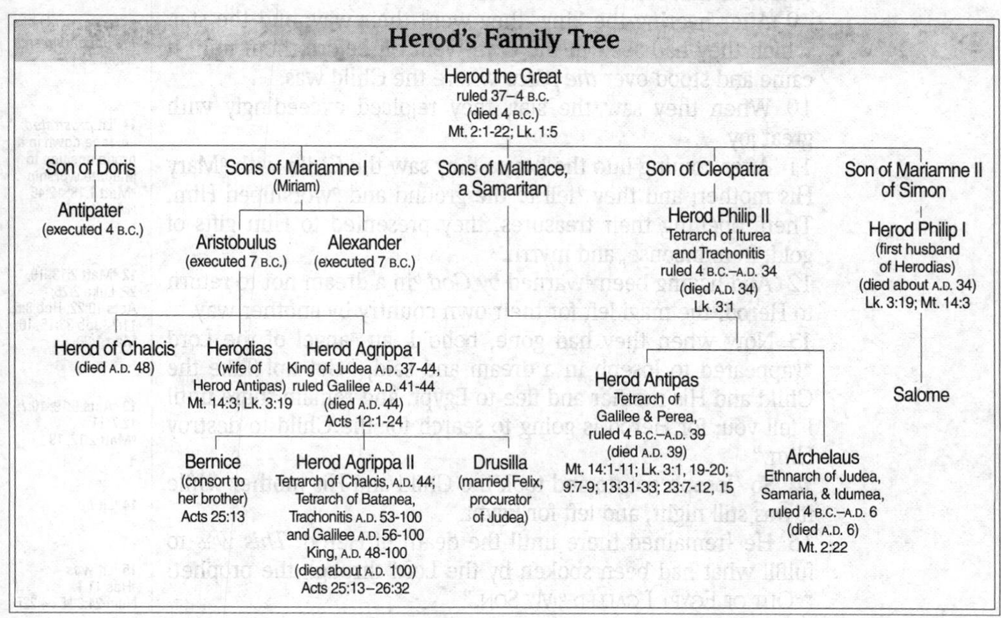

23 "[a]BEHOLD, THE VIRGIN SHALL BE WITH [b]CHILD AND SHALL BEAR A
SON, AND THEY SHALL CALL HIS NAME [1]IMMANUEL," which
translated means, "[c]GOD WITH US."
24 And Joseph [1]awoke from his sleep and did as the angel of
the Lord commanded him, and took *Mary* as his wife,
25 [1]but kept her a virgin until she [a]gave birth to a Son; and
[b]he called His name Jesus.

Chapter 2 Theme ____________________

2 Now after Jesus was [a]born in Bethlehem of Judea in the days
of [b]Herod the king, [1]magi from the east arrived in Jerusalem,
saying,
2 "Where is He who has been born [a]King of the Jews? For we
saw [b]His star in the east and have come to worship Him."
3 When Herod the king heard *this,* he was troubled, and all
Jerusalem with him.
4 Gathering together all the chief priests and scribes of the
people, he inquired of them where the [1]Messiah was to be born.
5 They said to him, "[a]In Bethlehem of Judea; for this is what
has been written [1]by the prophet:
6 '[a]AND YOU, BETHLEHEM, LAND OF JUDAH,
ARE BY NO MEANS LEAST AMONG THE LEADERS OF JUDAH;
FOR OUT OF YOU SHALL COME FORTH A RULER
WHO WILL [b]SHEPHERD MY PEOPLE ISRAEL.'"
7 Then Herod secretly called the magi and determined from
them [1]the exact time [a]the star appeared.
8 And he sent them to Bethlehem and said, "Go and search
carefully for the Child; and when you have found *Him,* report
to me, so that I too may come and worship Him."
9 After hearing the king, they went their way; and the star,
which they had seen in the east, went on before them until it
came and stood over *the place* where the Child was.
10 When they saw the star, they rejoiced exceedingly with
great joy.
11 After coming into the house they saw the Child with [a]Mary
His mother; and they [1]fell to the ground and [b]worshiped Him.
Then, opening their treasures, they presented to Him gifts of
gold, frankincense, and myrrh.
12 And having been [a]warned *by God* [b]in a dream not to return
to Herod, the magi left for their own country by another way.
13 Now when they had gone, behold, an [a]angel of the Lord
*[b]appeared to Joseph in a dream and said, "Get up! Take the
Child and His mother and flee to Egypt, and remain there until
I tell you; for Herod is going to search for the Child to destroy
Him."
14 So [1]Joseph got up and took the Child and His mother while
it was still night, and left for Egypt.
15 He [1]remained there until the death of Herod. *This was* to
fulfill what had been spoken by the Lord through the prophet:
"[a]OUT OF EGYPT I CALLED [b]MY SON."

23 [1]Or *Emmanuel* [a]Is 7:14 [b]Is 9:6, 7 [c]Is 8:10

24 [1]Lit *got up*

25 [1]Lit *and was not knowing her* [a]Luke 2:7 [b]Matt 1:21; Luke 2:21

2:1 [1]A caste of wise men specializing in astronomy, astrology, and natural science [a]Mic 5:2; Luke 2:4-7 [b]Luke 1:5

2 [a]Jer 23:5; 30:9; Zech 9:9; Matt 27:11; Luke 19:38; 23:38; John 1:49 [b]Num 24:17

4 [1]Gr *Christos (Christ)*

5 [1]Or *through* [a]John 7:42

6 [a]Mic 5:2; John 7:42 [b]John 21:16

7 [1]Lit *the time of the appearing star* [a]Num 24:17

11 [1]Lit *prostrated;* i.e. face down in a prone position to indicate worship [a]Matt 1:18; 12:46 [b]Matt 14:33

12 [a]Matt 2:13, 19, 22; Luke 2:26; Acts 10:22; Heb 8:5; 11:7 [b]Job 33:15, 16; Matt 1:20

13 [a]Acts 5:19; 10:7; 12:7-11 [b]Matt 2:12, 19

14 [1]Lit *he*

15 [1]Lit *was* [a]Hos 11:1; Num 24:8 [b]Ex 4:22f

16 Then when Herod saw that he had been tricked by [a]the
magi, he became very enraged, and sent and [b]slew all the male
children who were in Bethlehem and all its vicinity, from two
years old and under, according to the time which he had
determined from the magi.
17 Then what had been spoken through Jeremiah the prophet
was fulfilled:
18 "[a]A VOICE WAS HEARD IN RAMAH,
WEEPING AND GREAT MOURNING,
RACHEL WEEPING FOR HER CHILDREN;
AND SHE REFUSED TO BE COMFORTED,
BECAUSE THEY WERE NO MORE."
19 But when Herod died, behold, an angel of the Lord
*[a]appeared in a dream to Joseph in Egypt, and said,
20 "Get up, take the Child and His mother, and go into the land
of Israel; for those who sought the Child's life are dead."
21 So [1]Joseph got up, took the Child and His mother, and
came into the land of Israel.
22 But when he heard that Archelaus was reigning over Judea
in place of his father Herod, he was afraid to go there. Then
after being [a]warned *by God* in a dream, he left for the regions
of Galilee,
23 and came and lived in a city called [a]Nazareth. *This was* to
fulfill what was spoken through the prophets: "He shall be
called a [b]Nazarene."

Chapter 3 Theme ______________________

3 Now [a]in those days [b]John the Baptist *[1]came, [2]preaching
in the [c]wilderness of Judea, saying,
2 "[a]Repent, for [b]the kingdom of heaven [1]is at hand."
3 For this is the [a]one referred to [1]by Isaiah the prophet when
he said,
"[b]THE VOICE OF ONE [2]CRYING IN THE WILDERNESS,
'[c]MAKE READY THE WAY OF THE LORD,
MAKE HIS PATHS STRAIGHT!'"
4 Now John himself had [1a]a garment of camel's hair and a
leather belt around his waist; and his food was [b]locusts and
wild honey.
5 Then Jerusalem [a]was going out to him, and all Judea and all
[b]the district around the Jordan;
6 and they were being [a]baptized by him in the Jordan River,
as they confessed their sins.
7 But when he saw many of the [a]Pharisees and [b]Sadducees
coming for baptism, he said to them, "You [c]brood of vipers,
who warned you to flee from [d]the wrath to come?
8 "[a]Therefore bear fruit [b]in keeping with repentance;
9 and do not suppose that you can say to yourselves, '[a]We
have Abraham for our father'; for I say to you that from these
stones God is able to raise up children to Abraham.
10 "The [a]axe is already laid at the root of the trees; therefore

16 [a]Matt 2:1 [b]Is 59:7
18 [a]Jer 31:15
19 [a]Matt 1:20; 2:12, 13, 22
21 [1]Lit *he*
22 [a]Matt 2:12, 13, 19
23 [a]Luke 1:26; 2:39; John 1:45, 46 [b]Mark 1:24; John 18:5, 7; 19:19
3:1 [1]Or *arrived*, or *appeared* [2]Or *proclaiming as a herald* [a]Matt 3:1-12: *Mark 1:3-8; Luke 3:2-17;* John 1:6-8, 19-28 [b]Matt 11:11-14; 16:14 [c]Josh 15:61; Judg 1:16
2 [1]Lit *has come near* [a]Matt 4:17 [b]Dan 2:44; Matt 4:17, 23; 6:10; 10:7; Mark 1:15; Luke 10:9f; 11:20; 21:31
3 [1]Or *through* [2]Or *shouting* [a]Luke 1:17, 76 [b]Is 40:3 [c]John 1:23
4 [1]Lit *his garment* [a]2 Kin 1:8; Zech 13:4; Matt 11:8; Mark 1:6 [b]Lev 11:22
5 [a]Mark 1:5 [b]Luke 3:3
6 [a]Matt 3:11, 13-16; Mark 1:5; John 1:25, 26; 3:23; Acts 1:5; 2:38-41; 10:37
7 [a]Matt 16:1ff; 23:13, 15 [b]Matt 22:23; Acts 4:1; 5:17; 23:6ff [c]Matt 12:34; 23:33 [d]1 Thess 1:10
8 [a]Luke 3:8; Eph 5:8, 9 [b]Acts 26:20
9 [a]Luke 3:8; 16:24; John 8:33, 39, 53; Acts 13:26; Rom 4:1; 9:7, 8; Gal 3:29
10 [a]Luke 3:9

[b]every tree that does not bear good fruit is cut down and thrown
into the fire.
11 "As for me, [a]I baptize you [1]with water for repentance, but
He who is coming after me is mightier than I, and I am not fit
to remove His sandals; [b]He will baptize you [1]with the Holy
Spirit and fire.
12 "His [a]winnowing fork is in His hand, and He will thoroughly
clear His threshing floor; and He will [b]gather His wheat into the
barn, but He will burn up the [c]chaff with [d]unquenchable fire."
13 [a]Then Jesus *arrived [b]from Galilee at the Jordan *coming* to
John, to be baptized by him.
14 But John tried to prevent Him, saying, "I have need to be
baptized by You, and do You come to me?"
15 But Jesus answering said to him, "Permit *it* at this time; for
in this way it is fitting for us [a]to fulfill all righteousness." Then
he *permitted Him.
16 After being baptized, Jesus came up immediately from the
water; and behold, the heavens were opened, and [1][a]he saw the
Spirit of God descending as a dove *and* [2]lighting on Him,
17 and behold, a voice out of the heavens said, "[a]This is [1]My
beloved Son, in whom I am well-pleased."

Chapter 4 Theme ____________________

4 [a]Then Jesus was led up by the Spirit into the wilderness [b]to
be tempted by the devil.
2 And after He had [a]fasted forty days and forty nights, He
[1]then became hungry.
3 And [a]the tempter came and said to Him, "If You are the
[b]Son of God, command that these stones become bread."
4 But He answered and said, "It is written, '[a]MAN SHALL NOT
LIVE ON BREAD ALONE, BUT ON EVERY WORD THAT PROCEEDS OUT OF
THE MOUTH OF GOD.'"
5 Then the devil *took Him into [a]the holy city and had Him
stand on the pinnacle of the temple,
6 and *said to Him, "If You are the Son of God, throw
Yourself down; for it is written,

'[a]HE WILL COMMAND HIS ANGELS CONCERNING YOU';

and

'ON *their* HANDS THEY WILL BEAR YOU UP,
SO THAT YOU WILL NOT STRIKE YOUR FOOT AGAINST A STONE.'"

7 Jesus said to him, "[1]On the other hand, it is written, '[a]YOU
SHALL NOT PUT THE LORD YOUR GOD TO THE TEST.'"
8 [a]Again, the devil *took Him to a very high mountain and
*showed Him all the kingdoms of the world and their glory;
9 and he said to Him, "[a]All these things I will give You, if You
fall down and [1]worship me."
10 Then Jesus *said to him, "Go, Satan! For it is written, '[a]YOU
SHALL WORSHIP THE LORD YOUR GOD, AND [1]SERVE HIM ONLY.'"
11 Then the devil *left Him; and behold, [a]angels came and
began to minister to Him.

10 [b]Ps 92:12-14; Matt 7:19; John 15:2

11 [1]The Gr here can be translated *in, with* or *by* [a]Mark 1:4, 8; Luke 3:16; John 1:26f; Acts 1:5; 8:36, 38; 11:16 [b]John 1:33; Acts 2:3, 4; Titus 3:5

12 [a]Is 30:24; 41:16; Jer 15:7; 51:2; Luke 3:17 [b]Matt 13:30 [c]Ps 1:4 [d]Is 66:24; Jer 7:20; Matt 13:41, 42; Mark 9:43, 48

13 [a]Matt 3:13-17: *Mark 1:9-11; Luke 3:21, 22;* John 1:31-34 [b]Matt 2:22

15 [a]Ps 40:7, 8; John 4:34; 8:29

16 [1]Or *He* [2]Lit *coming upon Him* [a]Mark 1:10; Luke 3:22; John 1:32; Acts 7:56

17 [1]Or *My Son, the Beloved* [a]Ps 2:7; Is 42:1; Matt 12:18; 17:5; Mark 9:7; Luke 9:35; John 12:28

4:1 [a]Matt 4:1-11: *Mark 1:12, 13; Luke 4:1-13* [b]Heb 4:15; James 1:14

2 [1]Lit *later became;* or *afterward became* [a]Ex 34:28; 1 Kin 19:8

3 [a]1 Thess 3:5 [b]Matt 14:33; 26:63; Mark 3:11; 5:7; Luke 1:35; 4:41; John 1:34, 49; Acts 9:20

4 [a]Deut 8:3

5 [a]Neh 11:1, 18; Dan 9:24; Matt 27:53

6 [a]Ps 91:11, 12

7 [1]Lit *Again* [a]Deut 6:16

8 [a]Matt 16:26; 1 John 2:15-17

9 [1]Lit *prostrate Yourself* [a]1 Cor 10:20f

10 [1]Or *fulfill religious duty to Him* [a]Deut 6:13; 10:20

11 [a]Matt 26:53; Luke 22:43; Heb 1:14

12 Now when Jesus heard that [a]John had been taken into
custody, [b]He withdrew into Galilee;
13 and leaving Nazareth, He came and [a]settled in Capernaum,
which is by the sea, in the region of Zebulun and Naphtali.
14 *This was* to fulfill what was spoken through Isaiah the
prophet:
15 "[a]THE LAND OF ZEBULUN AND THE LAND OF NAPHTALI,
[1]BY THE WAY OF THE SEA, BEYOND THE JORDAN, GALILEE OF
THE [2]GENTILES—
16 "[a]THE PEOPLE WHO WERE SITTING IN DARKNESS SAW A GREAT LIGHT,
AND THOSE WHO WERE SITTING IN THE LAND AND SHADOW
OF DEATH,
UPON THEM A LIGHT DAWNED."

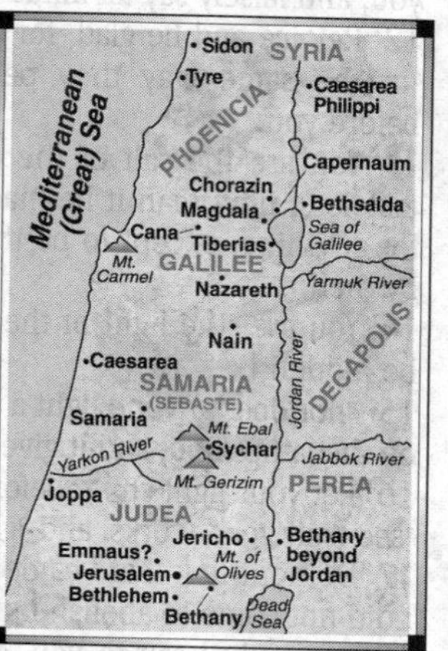

Israel in the Time of Christ

17 [a]From that time Jesus began
to [1]preach and say, "[b]Repent, for
the kingdom of heaven is at
hand."
18 [a]Now as Jesus was walking
by [b]the Sea of Galilee, He saw
two brothers, [c]Simon who was
called Peter, and Andrew his
brother, casting a net into the
sea; for they were fishermen.
19 And He *said to them,
"[1]Follow Me, and I will make
you fishers of men."
20 Immediately they left their
nets and followed Him.
21 Going on from there He saw two other brothers, [1a]James
the *son* of Zebedee, and [2]John his brother, in the boat with
Zebedee their father, mending their nets; and He called them.
22 Immediately they left the boat and their father, and
followed Him.
23 Jesus was going [a]throughout all Galilee, [b]teaching in their
synagogues and [c]proclaiming the [1]gospel of the kingdom, and
[d]healing every kind of disease and every kind of sickness
among the people.
24 The news about Him spread [a]throughout all Syria; and they
brought to Him all who were ill, those suffering with various
diseases and pains, [b]demoniacs, [1c]epileptics, [d]paralytics; and He
healed them.
25 Large crowds [a]followed Him from Galilee and [b]*the* Decapolis
and Jerusalem and Judea and *from* [c]beyond the Jordan.

Chapter 5 Theme ______________________________

5 [a]When Jesus saw the crowds, He went up on [b]the [1]moun-
tain; and after He sat down, His disciples came to Him.
2 [a]He opened His mouth and *began* to teach them, saying,
3 "[1a]Blessed are the [2]poor in spirit, for [b]theirs is the kingdom
of heaven.

12 [a]Matt 14:3; Mark 1:14; Luke 3:20; John 3:24 [b]Mark 1:14; Luke 4:14; John 1:43; 2:11
13 [a]Matt 11:23; Mark 1:21; 2:1; Luke 4:23, 31; John 2:12; 4:46f
15 [1]Or *Toward the sea* [2]Lit *nations,* usually non-Jewish [a]Is 9:1
16 [a]Is 9:2; 60:1-3; Luke 2:32
17 [1]Or *proclaim* [a]Mark 1:14, 15 [b]Matt 3:2
18 [a]Matt 4:18-22: *Mark 1:16-20;* Luke 5:2-11; John 1:40-42 [b]Matt 15:29; Mark 7:31; Luke 5:1; John 6:1 [c]Matt 10:2; 16:18; John 1:40-42
19 [1]Lit *Come here after Me*
21 [1]Or *Jacob;* James is the Eng form of Jacob [2]Gr *Joannes,* Heb *Johanan* [a]Matt 10:2; 20:20
23 [1]Or *good news* [a]Mark 1:39; Luke 4:14, 44 [b]Matt 9:35; 13:54; Mark 1:21; 6:2; 10:1; Luke 4:15; 6:6; 13:10; John 6:59; 18:20 [c]Matt 3:2; 9:35; 24:14; Mark 1:14; Luke 4:43; 8:1; 16:16; Acts 20:25; 28:31 [d]Matt 8:16; 9:35; 14:14; 15:30; 19:2; 21:14; Mark 1:34; 3:10; Luke 4:40; 7:21; Acts 10:38
24 [1]Lit *moonstruck* [a]Mark 7:26; Luke 2:2; Acts 15:23; 18:18; 20:3; 21:3; Gal 1:21 [b]Matt 8:16, 28, 33; 9:32; 12:22; 15:22; Mark 1:32; 5:15, 16, 18; Luke 8:36; John 10:21 [c]Matt 17:15 [d]Matt 8:6; 9:2, 6; Mark 2:3-5, 9; Luke 5:24
25 [a]Mark 3:7, 8; Luke 6:17 [b]Mark 5:20; 7:31 [c]Matt 4:15
5:1 [1]Or *hill* [a]Matt ch 5-7; Luke 6:20-49 [b]Mark 3:13; Luke 6:17; 9:28; John 6:3, 15
2 [a]Matt 13:35; Acts 8:35; 10:34; 18:14
3 [1]I.e. fortunate or prosperous, and so through v 11 [2]I.e. those who are not spiritually arrogant [a]Matt 5:3-12; Luke 6:20-23 [b]Matt 5:10; 19:14; 25:34; Mark 10:14; Luke 6:20; 22:29f

4 "Blessed are [a]those who mourn, for they shall be comforted.
5 "Blessed are [a]the [1]gentle, for they shall inherit the earth.
6 "Blessed are [a]those who hunger and thirst for righteousness,
for they shall be satisfied.
7 "Blessed are [a]the merciful, for they shall receive mercy.
8 "Blessed are [a]the pure in heart, for [b]they shall see God.
9 "Blessed are the peacemakers, for [a]they shall be called sons
of God.
10 "Blessed are those who have been [a]persecuted for the sake
of righteousness, for [b]theirs is the kingdom of heaven.
11 "Blessed are you when *people* [a]insult you and persecute
you, and falsely say all kinds of evil against you because of Me.
12 "Rejoice and be glad, for your reward in heaven is great; for
[a]in the same way they persecuted the prophets who were
before you.
13 "You are the salt of the earth; but [a]if the salt has become
tasteless, how [1]can it be made salty *again?* It is no longer good
for anything, except to be thrown out and trampled under foot
by men.
14 "You are [a]the light of the world. A city set on a [1]hill cannot
be hidden;
15 [a]nor does *anyone* light a lamp and put it under a [1]basket, but
on the lampstand, and it gives light to all who are in the house.
16 "Let your light shine before men in such a way that they may
[a]see your good works, and [b]glorify your Father who is in heaven.
17 "Do not think that I came to abolish the [a]Law or the Prophets;
I did not come to abolish but to fulfill.
18 "For truly I say to you, [a]until heaven and earth pass away,
not [1]the smallest letter or stroke shall pass from the Law until
all is accomplished.
19 "Whoever then annuls one of the least of these
commandments, and teaches [1]others *to do* the same, shall be
called least [a]in the kingdom of heaven; but whoever [2]keeps and
teaches *them,* he shall be called great in the kingdom of
heaven.
20 "For I say to you that unless your [a]righteousness surpasses
that of the scribes and Pharisees, you will not enter the
kingdom of heaven.
21 "[a]You have heard that [1]the ancients were told, '[b]YOU SHALL
NOT COMMIT MURDER' and 'Whoever commits murder shall be
[2]liable to [c]the court.'
22 "But I say to you that everyone who is angry with his
brother shall be [1]guilty before [a]the court; and whoever says to
his brother, '[2]You good-for-nothing,' shall be [1]guilty before
[3b]the supreme court; and whoever says, 'You fool,' shall be
[1]guilty *enough to go* into the [4c]fiery hell.
23 "Therefore if you are [a]presenting your [1]offering at the altar, and
there remember that your brother has something against you,
24 leave your [1]offering there before the altar and go; first be
[a]reconciled to your brother, and then come and present your
[1]offering.

4 [a]Is 61:2; John 16:20; Rev 7:17
5 [1]Or *humble, meek* [a]Ps 37:11
6 [a]Is 55:1, 2; John 4:14; 6:48ff; 7:37
7 [a]Prov 11:17; Matt 6:14, 15; 18:33-35
8 [a]Ps 24:4 [b]Heb 12:14; 1 John 3:2; Rev 22:4
9 [a]Matt 5:45; Luke 6:35; Rom 8:14
10 [a]1 Pet 3:14 [b]Matt 5:3; 19:14; 25:34; Mark 10:14; Luke 6:20; 22:29f
11 [a]1 Pet 4:14
12 [a]2 Chr 36:16; Matt 23:37; Acts 7:52; 1 Thess 2:15; Heb 11:33ff; James 5:10
13 [1]Lit *will* [a]Mark 9:50; Luke 14:34f
14 [1]Or *mountain* [a]Prov 4:18; John 8:12; 9:5; 12:36
15 [1]Or *peck-measure* [a]Mark 4:21; Luke 8:16; 11:33; Phil 2:15
16 [a]1 Pet 2:12 [b]Matt 9:8
17 [a]Matt 7:12
18 [1]Lit *one iota* (Heb yodh) or *one projection of a letter* (serif) [a]Matt 24:35; Luke 16:17
19 [1]Gr *anthropoi* [2]Lit *does* [a]Matt 11:11
20 [a]Luke 18:11, 12
21 [1]Lit *it was said to the ancients* [2]Or *guilty before* [a]Matt 5:27, 33, 38, 43 [b]Ex 20:13; Deut 5:17 [c]Deut 16:18; 2 Chr 19:5f
22 [1]Or *liable to* [2]Or *empty-head;* Gr *Raka (Raca)* fr Aram *reqa* [3]Lit *the Sanhedrin* [4]Lit *Gehenna of fire* [a]Deut 16:18; 2 Chr 19:5f [b]Matt 10:17; 26:59; Mark 13:9; 14:55; 15:1; Luke 22:66; John 11:47; Acts 4:15; 5:21; 6:12; 22:30; 23:1; 24:20 [c]Matt 5:29f; 10:28; 18:9; 23:15, 33; Mark 9:43ff; Luke 12:5; James 3:6
23 [1]Or *gift* [a]Matt 5:24
24 [1]Or *gift* [a]Rom 12:17, 18

25 "[a]Make friends quickly with your opponent at law while you
are with him on the way, so that your opponent may not hand
you over to the judge, and the judge to the officer, and you be
thrown into prison.
26 "Truly I say to you, [a]you will not come out of there until you
have paid up the last [1]cent.
27 "[a]You have heard that it was said, '[b]YOU SHALL NOT COMMIT
ADULTERY';
28 but I say to you that everyone who looks at a woman [a]with
lust for her has already committed adultery with her in his heart.
29 "[a]If your right eye makes you [1]stumble, tear it out and
throw it from you; for it is better for you [2]to lose one of the
parts of your body, [3]than for your whole body to be thrown into
[4b]hell.
30 "[a]If your right hand makes you [1]stumble, cut it off and
throw it from you; for it is better for you [2]to lose one of the
parts of your body, [3]than for your whole body to go into [4b]hell.
31 "It was said, '[a]WHOEVER SENDS HIS WIFE AWAY, LET HIM GIVE HER
A CERTIFICATE OF DIVORCE';
32 [a]but I say to you that everyone who [1]divorces his wife,
except for *the* reason of unchastity, makes her commit adultery;
and whoever marries a [2]divorced woman commits adultery.
33 "Again, [a]you have heard that [1]the ancients were told, '[2b]YOU
SHALL NOT [3]MAKE FALSE VOWS, BUT SHALL FULFILL YOUR [4]VOWS TO THE
LORD.'
34 "But I say to you, [a]make no oath at all, either by heaven, for
it is [b]the throne of God,
35 or by the earth, for it is the [a]footstool of His feet, or [1]by
Jerusalem, for it is [b]THE CITY OF THE GREAT KING.
36 "Nor shall you make an oath by your head, for you cannot
make one hair white or black.
37 "But let your statement be, 'Yes, yes' *or* 'No, no'; anything
beyond these is [1]of [a]evil.
38 "[a]You have heard that it was said, '[b]AN EYE FOR AN EYE, AND A
TOOTH FOR A TOOTH.'
39 "But I say to you, do not resist an evil person; but [a]whoever
slaps you on your right cheek, turn the other to him also.
40 "If anyone wants to sue you and take your [1]shirt, let him
have your [2]coat also.
41 "Whoever [1]forces you to go one mile, go with him two.
42 "[a]Give to him who asks of you, and do not turn away from
him who wants to borrow from you.
43 "[a]You have heard that it was said, '[b]YOU SHALL LOVE YOUR
NEIGHBOR [c]and hate your enemy.'
44 "But I say to you, [a]love your enemies and pray for those who
persecute you,
45 so that you may [1]be [a]sons of your Father who is in heaven;
for He causes His sun to rise on *the* evil and *the* good, and
sends rain on *the* righteous and *the* unrighteous.
46 "For [a]if you love those who love you, what reward do you
have? Do not even the tax collectors do the same?

25 [a]Prov 25:8f; Luke 12:58
26 [1]Lit *quadrans* (equaling two mites); i.e. 1/64 of a daily wage [a]Luke 12:59
27 [a]Matt 5:21, 33, 38, 43 [b]Ex 20:14; Deut 5:18
28 [a]2 Sam 11:2-5; Job 31:1; Matt 15:19; James 1:14, 15
29 [1]I.e. sin [2]Lit *that one . . . be lost* [3]Lit *not your whole body* [4]Gr *Gehenna* [a]Matt 18:9; Mark 9:47 [b]Matt 5:22
30 [1]I.e. sin [2]Lit *that one . . . be lost* [3]Lit *not your whole body* [4]Gr *Gehenna* [a]Matt 18:8; Mark 9:43 [b]Matt 5:22
31 [a]Deut 24:1, 3; Jer 3:1; Matt 19:7; Mark 10:4
32 [1]Or *sends away* [2]Or *sent away* [a]Matt 19:9; Mark 10:11f; Luke 16:18; 1 Cor 7:11f
33 [1]Lit *it was said to the ancients* [2]*you* and *your* are singular here [3]Or *break your vows* [4]Lit *oaths* [a]Matt 5:21, 27, 38, 43; 23:16ff [b]Lev 19:12; Num 30:2; Deut 23:21, 23
34 [a]James 5:12 [b]Is 66:1; Matt 23:22
35 [1]Or *toward* [a]Is 66:1; Acts 7:49 [b]Ps 48:2
37 [1]Or *from the evil one* [a]Matt 6:13; 13:19, 38; John 17:15; 2 Thess 3:3; 1 John 2:13f; 3:12; 5:18f
38 [a]Matt 5:21, 27, 33, 43 [b]Ex 21:24; Lev 24:20; Deut 19:21
39 [a]Matt 5:39-42: *Luke 6:29, 30;* 1 Cor 6:7
40 [1]Lit *tunic;* i.e. a garment worn next to the body [2]Lit *cloak;* i.e. an outer garment
41 [1]Lit *will force*
42 [a]Deut 15:7-11; Luke 6:34f; 1 Tim 6:18
43 [a]Matt 5:21, 27, 33, 38 [b]Lev 19:18 [c]Deut 23:3-6
44 [a]Luke 6:27f; 23:34; Acts 7:60; Rom 12:20
45 [1]Or *show yourselves to be* [a]Matt 5:9; Luke 6:35; Acts 14:17
46 [a]Luke 6:32

47 "If you greet only your brothers, what more are you doing
than others? Do not even the Gentiles do the same?
48 "Therefore [1a]you are to be perfect, as your heavenly Father
is perfect.

Chapter 6 Theme ______________________

6 "Beware of practicing your righteousness before men [a]to
be noticed by them; otherwise you have no reward with
your Father who is in heaven.
2 "So when you [1]give to the poor, do not sound a trumpet
before you, as the hypocrites do in the synagogues and in the
streets, so that they [a]may be honored by men. [b]Truly I say to
you, they have their reward in full.
3 "But when you [1]give to the poor, do not let your left hand
know what your right hand is doing,
4 so that your [1]giving will be in secret; and [a]your Father who
sees *what is done* in secret will reward you.
5 "When you pray, you are not to be like the hypocrites; for
they love to [a]stand and pray in the synagogues and on the
street corners [1b]so that they may be seen by men. [c]Truly I say
to you, they have their reward in full.
6 "But you, when you pray, [a]go into your inner room, close
your door and pray to your Father who is in secret, and [b]your
Father who sees *what is done* in secret will reward you.
7 "And when you are praying, do not use meaningless
repetition as the Gentiles do, for they suppose that they will be
heard for their [a]many words.
8 "So do not be like them; for [a]your Father knows what you
need before you ask Him.
9 "[a]Pray, then, in this way:
'Our Father who is in heaven,
Hallowed be Your name.
10 '[a]Your kingdom come.
[b]Your will be done,
On earth as it is in heaven.
11 '[a]Give us this day [1]our daily bread.
12 'And [a]forgive us our debts, as we also have forgiven
our debtors.
13 'And do not lead us into temptation, but [a]deliver us from
[1b]evil. [2][For Yours is the kingdom and the power and
the glory forever. Amen.']
14 "[a]For if you forgive [1]others for their transgressions, your
heavenly Father will also forgive you.
15 "But [a]if you do not forgive [1]others, then your Father will not
forgive your transgressions.
16 "[a]Whenever you fast, do not put on a gloomy face as the
hypocrites *do,* for they [1]neglect their appearance so that they will
be noticed by men when they are fasting. [b]Truly I say to you,
they have their reward in full.
17 "But you, when you fast, [a]anoint your head and wash your face

48 [1]Lit *you shall be* [a]Lev 19:2; Deut 18:13; 2 Cor 7:1; Phil 3:12-15

6:1 [a]Matt 6:5, 16; 23:5

2 [1]Or *give alms* [a]Matt 6:5, 16; 23:5 [b]Matt 6:5, 16; Luke 6:24

3 [1]Or *give alms*

4 [1]Or *alms* [a]Jer 17:10; Matt 6:6, 18; Heb 4:13

5 [1]Lit *to be apparent to men* [a]Mark 11:25; Luke 18:11, 13 [b]Matt 6:1, 16 [c]Matt 6:2, 16; Luke 6:24

6 [a]Is 26:20; Matt 26:36-39; Acts 9:40 [b]Matt 6:4, 18

7 [a]1 Kin 18:26f

8 [a]Ps 38:9; 69:17-19; Matt 6:32; Luke 12:30

9 [a]Matt 6:9-13: *Luke 11:2-4*

10 [a]Matt 3:2; 4:17 [b]Matt 26:42; Luke 22:42; Acts 21:14

11 [1]Or *our bread for tomorrow* [a]Prov 30:8; Is 33:16; Luke 11:3

12 [a]Ex 34:7; Ps 32:1; 130:4; Matt 9:2; 26:28; Eph 1:7; 1 John 1:7-9

13 [1]Or *the evil one* [2]This clause not found in early mss [a]John 17:15; 1 Cor 10:13; 2 Thess 3:3; 2 Tim 4:18; 2 Pet 2:9; 1 John 5:18 [b]Matt 5:37

14 [1]Gr *anthropoi* [a]Matt 7:2; Mark 11:25f; Eph 4:32; Col 3:13

15 [1]Gr *anthropoi* [a]Matt 18:35

16 [1]Lit *distort their faces,* i.e. discolor their faces with makeup [a]Is 58:5 [b]Matt 6:2

17 [a]Ruth 3:3; 2 Sam 12:20

18 so that your fasting will not be noticed by men, but by your
Father who is in secret; and your [a]Father who sees *what is
done* in secret will reward you.
19 "[a]Do not store up for yourselves treasures on earth, where
moth and rust destroy, and where thieves break in and steal.
20 "But store up for yourselves [a]treasures in heaven, where
neither moth nor rust destroys, and where thieves do not break
in or steal;
21 for [a]where your treasure is, there your heart will be also.
22 "[a]The eye is the lamp of the body; so then if your eye is
[1]clear, your whole body will be full of light.
23 "But if [a]your eye is [1]bad, your whole body will be full of
darkness. If then the light that is in you is darkness, how great
is the darkness!
24 "[a]No one can serve two masters; for either he will hate the
one and love the other, or he will be devoted to one and
despise the other. You cannot serve God and [1b]wealth.
25 "[a]For this reason I say to you, [1]do not be [b]worried about
your [2]life, *as to* what you will eat or what you will drink; nor
for your body, *as to* what you will put on. Is not life more than
food, and the body more than clothing?
26 "[a]Look at the birds of the [1]air, that they do not sow, nor reap
nor gather into barns, and *yet* your heavenly Father feeds them.
Are you not worth much more than they?
27 "And who of you by being [a]worried can [b]add a *single* [1]hour
to his [2]life?
28 "And why are you [a]worried about clothing? Observe how
the lilies of the field grow; they do not toil nor do they spin,
29 yet I say to you that not even [a]Solomon in all his glory
clothed himself like one of these.
30 "But if God so clothes the [a]grass of the field, which is *alive*
today and tomorrow is thrown into the furnace, *will He* not
much more *clothe* you? [b]You of little faith!
31 "Do not [a]worry then, saying, 'What will we eat?' or 'What will
we drink?' or 'What will we wear for clothing?'
32 "For the Gentiles eagerly seek all these things; for [a]your
heavenly Father knows that you need all these things.
33 "But [1]seek first [2]His kingdom and His righteousness, and [a]all
these things will be [3]added to you.
34 "So do not [a]worry about tomorrow; for tomorrow will [1]care
for itself. [2]Each day has enough trouble of its own.

Chapter 7 Theme ______________________

7 "[a]Do not judge so that you will not be judged.
2 "For in the way you judge, you will be judged; and [1a]by
your standard of measure, it will be measured to you.
3 "Why do you [a]look at the speck that is in your brother's eye,
but do not notice the log that is in your own eye?
4 "[a]Or how [1]can you say to your brother, 'Let me take the
speck out of your eye,' and behold, the log is in your own eye?

18 [a]Matt 6:4, 6
19 [a]Prov 23:4; Matt 19:21; Luke 12:21, 33; 18:22; 1 Tim 6:9, 10; Heb 13:5; James 5:2
20 [a]Matt 19:21; Luke 12:33; 1 Tim 6:19
21 [a]Luke 12:34
22 [1]Or *healthy;* or *sincere* [a]Matt 6:22, 23: *Luke 11:34, 35*
23 [1]Or *evil* [a]Matt 20:15; Mark 7:22
24 [1]Gr *mamonas,* for Aram *mamon* (mammon); i.e. wealth, etc, personified as an object of worship [a]1 Kin 18:21; Luke 16:13; Gal 1:10; James 4:4 [b]Luke 16:9, 11, 13
25 [1]Or *stop being worried* [2]Lit *soul* [a]Matt 6:25-33: *Luke 12:22-31* [b]Matt 6:27, 28, 31, 34; Luke 10:41; 12:11, 22; Phil 4:6; 1 Pet 5:7
26 [1]Lit *heaven* [a]Job 35:11; 38:41; Ps 104:27, 28; Matt 10:29ff; Luke 12:24
27 [1]Lit *cubit* (approx 18 in.) [2]Or *height* [a]Matt 6:25, 28, 31, 34; Luke 10:41; 12:11, 22; Phil 4:6; 1 Pet 5:7 [b]Ps 39:5
28 [a]Matt 6:25, 27, 31, 34; Luke 10:41; 12:11, 22; Phil 4:6; 1 Pet 5:7
29 [a]1 Kin 10:4-7; 2 Chr 9:4-6, 20-22
30 [a]James 1:10, 11; 1 Pet 1:24 [b]Matt 8:26; 14:31; 16:8
31 [a]Matt 6:25, 27, 28, 34; Luke 10:41; 12:11, 22; Phil 4:6; 1 Pet 5:7
32 [a]Matt 6:8; Phil 4:19
33 [1]Or *continually seek* [2]Or *the kingdom* [3]Or *provided* [a]Matt 19:28; Mark 10:29f; Luke 18:29f; 1 Tim 4:8
34 [1]Lit *worry about itself* [2]Lit *Sufficient for the day is its evils* [a]Matt 6:25, 27, 28, 31; Luke 10:41; 12:11, 22; Phil 4:6; 1 Pet 5:7
7:1 [a]Matt 7:1-5: *Luke 6:37f, 41f;* Rom 14:10, 13
2 [1]Lit *by what measure you measure* [a]Mark 4:24; Luke 6:38
3 [a]Rom 2:1
4 [1]Lit *will* [a]Luke 6:42

5 "You hypocrite, first take the log out of your own eye, and then
you will see clearly to take the speck out of your brother's eye.
6 "[a]Do not give what is holy to dogs, and do not throw your
pearls before swine, or they will trample them under their feet,
and turn and tear you to pieces.
7 "[1a]Ask, and [b]it will be given to you; [2]seek, and you will find;
[3]knock, and it will be opened to you.
8 "For everyone who asks receives, and he who seeks finds,
and to him who knocks it will be opened.
9 "Or what man is there among you [1]who, when his son asks
for a loaf, [2]will give him a stone?
10 "Or [1]if he asks for a fish, he will not give him a snake, will he?
11 "If you then, being evil, know how to give good gifts to your
children, [a]how much more will your Father who is in heaven
give what is good to those who ask Him!
12 "In everything, [a]therefore, [1]treat people the same way you
want [2]them to treat you, for [b]this is the Law and the Prophets.
13 "[a]Enter through the narrow gate; for the gate is wide and
the way is broad that leads to destruction, and there are many
who enter through it.
14 "For the gate is small and the way is narrow that leads to
life, and there are few who find it.
15 "Beware of the [a]false prophets, who come to you in sheep's
clothing, but inwardly are [b]ravenous wolves.
16 "You will [1a]know them by their fruits. [2]Grapes are not
gathered from thorn *bushes* nor figs from thistles, are they?
17 "So [a]every good tree bears good fruit, but the bad tree bears
bad fruit.
18 "A good tree cannot produce bad fruit, nor can a bad tree
produce good fruit.
19 "[a]Every tree that does not bear good fruit is cut down and
thrown into the fire.
20 "So then, you will [1]know them [a]by their fruits.
21 "[a]Not everyone who says to Me, 'Lord, Lord,' will enter the
kingdom of heaven, but he who does the will of My Father
who is in heaven *will enter.*
22 "[a]Many will say to Me on [b]that day, 'Lord, Lord, did we not
prophesy in Your name, and in Your name cast out demons,
and in Your name perform many [1]miracles?'
23 "And then I will declare to them, 'I never knew you; [a]DEPART
FROM ME, YOU WHO PRACTICE LAWLESSNESS.'
24 "Therefore [a]everyone who hears these words of Mine and
[1]acts on them, [2]may be compared to a wise man who built his
house on the rock.
25 "And the rain fell, and the [1]floods came, and the winds blew
and slammed against that house; and *yet* it did not fall, for it
had been founded on the rock.
26 "Everyone who hears these words of Mine and does not
[1]act on them, will be like a foolish man who built his house
on the sand.
27 "The rain fell, and the [1]floods came, and the winds blew and
slammed against that house; and it fell—and great was its fall."

6 [a]Matt 15:26

7 [1]Or *Keep asking* [2]Or *keep seeking* [3]Or *keep knocking* [a]Matt 7:7-11: *Luke 11:9-13* [b]Matt 18:19; 21:22; Mark 11:24; John 14:13; 15:7, 16; 16:23f; James 1:5f; 1 John 3:22; 5:14f

9 [1]Lit *whom his son will ask* [2]Lit *he will not give him a stone, will he?*

10 [1]Lit *also will ask*

11 [a]Ps 84:11; Is 63:7; Rom 8:32; James 1:17

12 [1]Lit *you, too, do so for them* [2]Lit *people;* Gr *anthropoi* [a]Luke 6:31 [b]Matt 22:40; Rom 13:8ff; Gal 5:14

13 [a]Luke 13:24

15 [a]Matt 24:11, 24; Mark 13:22; Luke 6:26; Acts 13:6; 2 Pet 2:1; 1 John 4:1; Rev 16:13; 19:20; 20:10 [b]Ezek 22:27; John 10:12; Acts 20:29

16 [1]Or *recognize* [2]Lit *They do not gather* [a]Matt 7:20; 12:33; Luke 6:44; James 3:12

17 [a]Matt 12:33, 35

19 [a]Matt 3:10; Luke 3:9; 13:7; John 15:2, 6

20 [1]Or *recognize* [a]Matt 7:16; 12:33; Luke 6:44; James 3:12

21 [a]Luke 6:46

22 [1]Or *works of power* [a]Matt 25:11f; Luke 13:25ff [b]Matt 10:15

23 [a]Ps 6:8; Matt 25:41; Luke 13:27

24 [1]Lit *does* [2]Lit *will* [a]Matt 7:24-27: *Luke 6:47-49;* Matt 16:18; James 1:22-25

25 [1]Lit *rivers*

26 [1]Lit *do*

27 [1]Lit *rivers*

28 [1a]When Jesus had finished these words, [b]the crowds were amazed at His teaching;

29 for He was teaching them as *one* having authority, and not as their scribes.

Chapter 8 Theme ______________________________

8 When [1]Jesus came down from the mountain, [2]large crowds followed Him.

2 And [a]a leper came to Him and [1b]bowed down before Him, and said, "Lord, if You are willing, You can make me clean."

3 Jesus stretched out His hand and touched him, saying, "I am willing; be cleansed." And immediately his [a]leprosy was cleansed.

4 And Jesus *said to him, "[a]See that you tell no one; but [b]go, [c]show yourself to the priest and present the [1]offering that Moses commanded, as a testimony to them."

5 And [a]when [1]Jesus entered Capernaum, a centurion came to Him, imploring Him,

6 and saying, "[1]Lord, my [2]servant is [3]lying [a]paralyzed at home, fearfully tormented."

7 Jesus *said to him, "I will come and heal him."

8 But the centurion said, "[1]Lord, I am not worthy for You to come under my roof, but just [2]say the word, and my [3]servant will be healed.

9 "For I also am a man under [a]authority, with soldiers under me; and I say to this one, 'Go!' and he goes, and to another, 'Come!' and he comes, and to my slave, 'Do this!' and he does *it*."

10 Now when Jesus heard *this*, He marveled and said to those who were following, "Truly I say to you, I have not found such great faith [1]with anyone in Israel.

11 "I say to you that many [a]will come from east and west, and [1]recline *at the table* with Abraham, Isaac and Jacob in the kingdom of heaven;

12 but [a]the sons of the kingdom will be cast out into [b]the outer darkness; in that place [c]there will be weeping and gnashing of teeth."

13 And Jesus said to the centurion, "Go; [1]it shall be done for you [a]as you have believed." And the [2]servant was healed that *very* [3]moment.

14 [a]When Jesus came into Peter's [1]home, He saw his mother-in-law lying sick in bed with a fever.

15 He touched her hand, and the fever left her; and she got up and [1]waited on Him.

16 When evening came, they brought to Him many [a]who were demon-possessed; and He cast out the spirits with a word, and [b]healed all who were ill.

17 *This was* to fulfill what was spoken through Isaiah the prophet: "[a]HE HIMSELF TOOK OUR INFIRMITIES AND [1]CARRIED AWAY OUR DISEASES."

18 Now when Jesus saw a crowd around Him, [a]He gave orders to depart to the other side *of the sea.*

---

28 [1]Lit *And it happened when* [a]Matt 11:1; 13:53; 19:1; 26:1 [b]Matt 13:54; 22:33; Mark 1:22; 6:2; 11:18; Luke 4:32; John 7:46

8:1 [1]Lit *He* [2]Lit *many*

2 [1]Or *worshiped* [a]Matt 8:2-4: *Mark 1:40-44; Luke 5:12-14* [b]Matt 9:18; 15:25; 18:26; 20:20; John 9:38; Acts 10:25

3 [a]Matt 11:5; Luke 4:27

4 [1]Lit *gift* [a]Matt 9:30; 12:16; 17:9; Mark 1:44; 3:12; 5:43; 7:36; 8:30; 9:9; Luke 4:41; 8:56; 9:21 [b]Mark 1:44; Luke 5:14; 17:14 [c]Lev 13:49; 14:2ff

5 [1]Lit *He* [a]Matt 8:5-13: *Luke 7:1-10*

6 [1]Or *Sir* [2]Lit *boy* [3]Lit *thrown down* [a]Matt 4:24

8 [1]Or *Sir* [2]Lit *say with a word* [3]Lit *boy*

9 [a]Mark 1:27; Luke 9:1

10 [1]One early ms reads *not even in Israel*

11 [1]Or *dine* [a]Is 49:12; 59:19; Mal 1:11; Luke 13:29

12 [a]Matt 13:38 [b]Matt 22:13; 25:30 [c]Matt 13:42, 50; 22:13; 24:51; 25:30; Luke 13:28

13 [1]Or *let it be done;* i.e. a command [2]Lit *boy* [3]Lit *hour* [a]Matt 9:22, 29

14 [1]Or *house* [a]Matt 8:14-16: *Mark 1:29-34; Luke 4:38-41*

15 [1]Or *served*

16 [a]Matt 4:24 [b]Matt 4:23; 8:33

17 [1]Or *removed* [a]Is 53:4

18 [a]Mark 4:35; Luke 8:22

19 [a]Then a scribe came and said to Him, "Teacher, I will
follow You wherever You go."
20 Jesus *said to him, "The foxes have holes and the birds of
the [1]air *have* [2]nests, but [a]the Son of Man has nowhere to lay
His head."
21 Another of the disciples said to Him, "Lord, permit me first
to go and bury my father."
22 But Jesus *said to him, "[a]Follow Me, and allow the dead to
bury their own dead."
23 [a]When He got into the boat, His disciples followed Him.
24 And behold, there arose [1]a great storm on the sea, so that
the boat was being covered with the waves; but Jesus Himself
was asleep.
25 And they came to *Him* and woke Him, saying, "[a]Save *us,*
Lord; we are perishing!"
26 He *said to them, "Why are you [1]afraid, [a]you men of little
faith?" Then He got up and rebuked the winds and the sea, and
[2]it became perfectly calm.
27 The men were amazed, and said, "What kind of a man is
this, that even the winds and the sea obey Him?"

Galilee

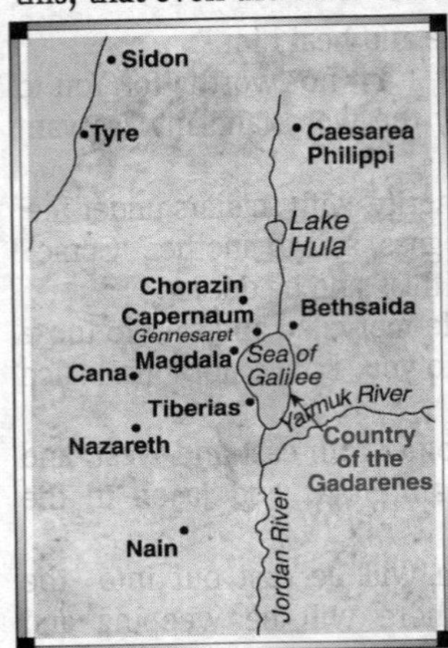

28 [a]When He came to the
other side into the country of
the Gadarenes, two men who
were [b]demon-possessed met Him
as they were coming out of the
tombs. *They were* so extremely
violent that no one could pass
by that way.
29 And they cried out, saying,
"[1a]What business do we have
with each other, Son of God?
Have You come here to torment
us before [2]the time?"
30 Now there was a herd of
many swine feeding at a distance
from them.
31 The demons *began* to entreat Him, saying, "If You *are going to*
cast us out, send us into the herd of swine."
32 And He said to them, "Go!" And they came out and went
into the swine, and the whole herd rushed down the steep
bank into the sea and perished in the waters.
33 The herdsmen ran away, and went to the city and reported
everything, [1]including what had happened to the [a]demoniacs.
34 And behold, the whole city came out to meet Jesus; and
when they saw Him, [a]they implored Him to leave their region.

Chapter 9 Theme ______________________

9 Getting into a boat, Jesus crossed over *the sea* and came to
[a]His own city.
2 [a]And they brought to Him a [b]paralytic lying on a bed. Seeing

19 [a]Matt 8:19-22: *Luke 9:57-60*

20 [1]Or *sky* [2]Or *roosting places* [a]Dan 7:13; Matt 9:6; 12:8, 32, 40; 13:41; 16:13, 27f; 17:9; 19:28; 26:64; Mark 8:38; Luke 12:8; 18:8; 21:36; John 1:51; 3:13f; 6:27; 12:34; Acts 7:56

22 [a]Matt 9:9; Mark 2:14; Luke 9:59, 60; John 1:43; 21:19

23 [a]Matt 8:23-27: *Mark 4:36-41; Luke 8:22-25*

24 [1]Lit *a shaking*

25 [a]Matt 8:2; 9:18

26 [1]Or *cowardly* [2]Lit *a great calm occurred* [a]Matt 6:30; 14:31; 16:8; 17:20

28 [a]Matt 8:28-34: *Mark 5:1-17; Luke 8:26-37* [b]Matt 4:24

29 [1]Lit *What is to us and to you* (a Heb idiom) [2]I.e. the appointed time of judgment [a]Judg 11:12; 2 Sam 16:10; 19:22; 1 Kin 17:18; 2 Kin 3:13; 2 Chr 35:21; Mark 1:24; 5:7; Luke 4:34; 8:28; John 2:4

33 [1]Lit *and the things of* [a]Matt 4:24

34 [a]Amos 7:12; Acts 16:39

9:1 [a]Matt 4:13; Mark 5:21

2 [a]Matt 9:2-8: *Mark 2:3-12; Luke 5:18-26* [b]Matt 4:24; 9:6

their faith, Jesus said to the paralytic, "[c]Take courage, [1]son; [d]your sins are forgiven."

3 And some of the scribes said [1]to themselves, "This *fellow* [a]blasphemes."

4 And Jesus [a]knowing their thoughts said, "Why are you thinking evil in your hearts?

5 "Which is easier, to say, '[a]Your sins are forgiven,' or to say, 'Get up, and walk'?

6 "But so that you may know that [a]the Son of Man has authority on earth to forgive sins"—then He *said to the [b]paralytic, "Get up, pick up your bed and go home."

7 And he got up and [1]went home.

8 But when the crowds saw *this,* they were [1]awestruck, and [a]glorified God, who had given such authority to men.

9 [a]As Jesus went on from there, He saw a man called [b]Matthew, sitting in the tax collector's booth; and He *said to him, "[c]Follow Me!" And he got up and followed Him.

10 Then it happened that as [1]Jesus was reclining *at the table* in the house, behold, many tax collectors and [2]sinners came and were dining with Jesus and His disciples.

11 When the Pharisees saw *this,* they said to His disciples, "[a]Why is your Teacher eating with the tax collectors and sinners?"

12 But when Jesus heard *this,* He said, "*It is* not [a]those who are healthy who need a physician, but those who are sick.

13 "But go and learn [1a]what this means: '[b]I DESIRE [2]COMPASSION, [3]AND NOT SACRIFICE,' for [c]I did not come to call the righteous, but sinners."

14 Then the disciples of John *came to Him, asking, "Why do we and [a]the Pharisees fast, but Your disciples do not fast?"

15 And Jesus said to them, "The [1]attendants of the bridegroom cannot mourn as long as the bridegroom is with them, can they? But the days will come when the bridegroom is taken away from them, and then they will fast.

16 "But no one puts [1]a patch of unshrunk cloth on an old garment; for [2]the patch pulls away from the garment, and a worse tear results.

17 "Nor do *people* put new wine into old wineskins; otherwise the wineskins burst, and the wine pours out and the wineskins are ruined; but they put new wine into fresh wineskins, and both are preserved."

18 [a]While He was saying these things to them, [1]a *synagogue* [2]official came and [3b]bowed down before Him, and said, "My daughter has just died; but come and lay Your hand on her, and she will live."

19 Jesus got up and *began* to follow him, and *so did* His disciples.

20 And a woman who had been suffering from a hemorrhage for twelve years, came up behind Him and touched [a]the [1]fringe of His [2]cloak;

21 for she was saying [1]to herself, "If I only [a]touch His garment, I will [2]get well."

2 [1]Lit *child* [c]Matt 9:22; 14:27; Mark 6:50; 10:49; John 16:33; Acts 23:11 [d]Mark 2:5, 9; Luke 5:20, 23; 7:48

3 [1]Lit *among* [a]Mark 3:28, 29

4 [a]Matt 12:25; Luke 6:8; 9:47

5 [a]Matt 9:2, 6; Mark 2:5, 9; Luke 5:20, 23; 7:48

6 [a]Matt 8:20; John 5:27 [b]Matt 4:24; 9:2

7 [1]Or *departed*

8 [1]Lit *afraid* [a]Matt 5:16; 15:31; Mark 2:12; Luke 2:20; 5:25, 26; 7:16; 13:13; 17:15; 23:47; John 15:8; Acts 4:21; 11:18; 21:20; 2 Cor 9:13; Gal 1:24

9 [a]Matt 9:9-17: *Mark 2:14-22; Luke 5:27-38* [b]Matt 10:3; Mark 2:14; 3:18; Luke 6:15; Acts 1:13 [c]Matt 8:22

10 [1]Lit *He* [2]I.e. irreligious Jews

11 [a]Matt 11:19; Mark 2:16; Luke 5:30; 15:2

12 [a]Mark 2:17; Luke 5:31

13 [1]Lit *what is* [2]Or *mercy* [3]I.e. more than [a]Matt 12:7 [b]Hos 6:6 [c]Mark 2:17; Luke 5:32; 1 Tim 1:15

14 [a]Luke 18:12

15 [1]Lit *sons of the wedding place*

16 [1]Lit *that which is put on* [2]Lit *that which fills up*

18 [1]Or *one* [2]Lit *ruler* [3]Or *worshiped* [a]Matt 9:18-26: *Mark 5:22-43; Luke 8:41-56* [b]Matt 8:2

20 [1]I.e. tassel fringe with a blue cord [2]Or *outer garment* [a]Num 15:38; Deut 22:12; Matt 14:36; 23:5

21 [1]Lit *in herself* [2]Lit *be saved* [a]Matt 14:36; Mark 3:10; Luke 6:19

22 But Jesus turning and seeing her said, "Daughter, [a]take
courage; [b]your faith has [1]made you well." [2]At once the woman
was [3]made well.
23 When Jesus came into the [1]official's house, and saw [a]the
flute-players and the crowd in noisy disorder,
24 He said, "Leave; for the girl [a]has not died, but is asleep."
And they *began* laughing at Him.
25 But [a]when the crowd had been sent out, He entered and
[b]took her by the hand, and the girl [1]got up.
26 [a]This news spread throughout all that land.
27 As Jesus went on from there, two blind men followed Him,
crying out, "Have mercy on us, [a]Son of David!"
28 When He entered the house, the blind men came up to
Him, and Jesus *said to them, "Do you believe that I am able to
do this?" They *said to Him, "Yes, Lord."
29 Then He touched their eyes, saying, "[1]It shall be done to
you [a]according to your faith."
30 And their eyes were opened. And Jesus [a]sternly warned
them: "See that no one knows *about this!*"
31 But they went out and [a]spread the news about Him
throughout all that land.
32 As they were going out, [a]a mute, [b]demon-possessed man
[1]was brought to Him.
33 After the demon was cast out, the mute man spoke; and
the crowds were amazed, *and were* saying, "[a]Nothing like this
has [1]ever been seen in Israel."
34 But the Pharisees were saying, "He [a]casts out the demons
by the ruler of the demons."
35 Jesus was going through all the cities and villages, [a]teaching
in their synagogues and proclaiming the gospel of the kingdom,
and healing every kind of disease and every kind of sickness.
36 [a]Seeing the [1]people, He felt compassion for them, [b]because
they were [2]distressed and [3]dispirited like sheep [4]without a
shepherd.
37 Then He *said to His disciples, "[a]The harvest is plentiful,
but the workers are few.
38 "Therefore beseech the Lord of the harvest to send out
workers into His harvest."

Chapter 10 Theme ____________________

10 Jesus [a]summoned His twelve disciples and gave them
authority over unclean spirits, to cast them out, and to
[b]heal every kind of disease and every kind of sickness.
2 [a]Now the names of the twelve apostles are these: The first,
[b]Simon, who is called Peter, and [b]Andrew his brother; and
[1c]James the son of Zebedee, and [2]John his brother;
3 [a]Philip and [1]Bartholomew; [b]Thomas and [c]Matthew the tax
collector; [2d]James the son of Alphaeus, and [e]Thaddaeus;
4 Simon the [1]Zealot, and [a]Judas Iscariot, the one who betrayed
Him.

22 [1]Lit *saved you* [2]Lit *from that hour* [3]Lit *saved* [a]Matt 9:2 [b]Matt 9:29; 15:28; Mark 5:34; 10:52; Luke 7:50; 8:48; 17:19; 18:42
23 [1]Lit *ruler's* [a]2 Chr 35:25; Jer 9:17; 16:6; Ezek 24:17
24 [a]John 11:13; Acts 20:10
25 [1]Or *was raised up* [a]Acts 9:40 [b]Mark 9:27
26 [a]Matt 4:24; 9:31; 14:1; Mark 1:28, 45; Luke 4:14, 37; 5:15; 7:17
27 [a]Matt 1:1; 12:23; 15:22; 20:30, 31; 21:9, 15; 22:42; Mark 10:47, 48; 12:35; Luke 18:38, 39; 20:41f
29 [1]Or *Let it be done;* Gr command [a]Matt 8:13; 9:22
30 [a]Matt 8:4
31 [a]Matt 4:24; 9:26; 14:1; Mark 1:28, 45; Luke 4:14, 37; 5:15; 7:17
32 [1]Lit *they brought* [a]Matt 12:22, 24 [b]Matt 4:24
33 [1]Lit *ever appeared* [a]Mark 2:12
34 [a]Matt 12:24; Mark 3:22; Luke 11:15; John 7:20f
35 [a]Matt 4:23; Mark 1:14
36 [1]Lit *crowds* [2]Or *harassed* [3]Lit *thrown down* [4]Lit *not having* [a]Matt 14:14; 15:32; Mark 6:34; 8:2 [b]Num 27:17; Ezek 34:5; Zech 10:2; Mark 6:34
37 [a]Luke 10:2
10:1 [a]Mark 3:13-15; 6:7 [b]Matt 9:35; Luke 9:1
2 [1]Or *Jacob;* James is the Eng form of Jacob [2]Gr *Joannes,* Heb *Johanan* [a]Matt 10:2-4: *Mark 3:16-19; Luke 6:14-16; Acts 1:13* [b]Matt 4:18 [c]Matt 4:21
3 [1]I.e. son of Talmai (Aram) [2]Or *Jacob* [a]John 1:43ff [b]John 11:16; 14:5; 20:24ff; 21:2 [c]Matt 9:9 [d]Mark 15:40 [e]Mark 3:18; Luke 6:16; Acts 1:13
4 [1]Or *Cananaean* [a]Matt 26:14; Luke 22:3; John 6:71; 13:2, 26

5 [a]These twelve Jesus sent out after instructing them: “Do
not [1]go [2]in *the* way of *the* Gentiles, and do not enter *any* city of
the [b]Samaritans;
6 but rather go to [a]the lost sheep of the house of Israel.
7 “And as you go, [1]preach, saying, ‘[a]The kingdom of heaven
[2]is at hand.’
8 “Heal *the* sick, raise *the* dead, cleanse *the* lepers, cast out
demons. Freely you received, freely give.
9 “[a]Do not acquire gold, or silver, or copper for your money belts,
10 or a [1]bag for *your* journey, or even two [2]coats, or sandals,
or a staff; for [a]the worker is worthy of his [3]support.
11 “And whatever city or village you enter, inquire who is
worthy in it, and stay [1]at his house until you leave *that city.*
12 “As you enter the [1]house, [a]give it your [2]greeting.
13 “If the house is worthy, [1]give it your *blessing of* peace. But if
it is not worthy, [2]take back your *blessing of* peace.
14 “Whoever does not receive you, nor heed your words, as you
go out of that house or that city, [a]shake the dust off your feet.
15 “Truly I say to you, [a]it will be more tolerable for *the* land of
[b]Sodom and Gomorrah in [c]the day of judgment than for that city.
16 “[a]Behold, I send you out as sheep in the midst of wolves; so
[1]be [b]shrewd as serpents and [c]innocent as doves.
17 “But beware of men, for they will hand you over to *the*
[a]courts and scourge you [b]in their synagogues;
18 and you will even be brought before governors and kings
for My sake, as a testimony to them and to the Gentiles.
19 “[a]But when they hand you over, [b]do not worry about how or
what you are to say; for it will be given you in that hour what
you are to say.
20 “For [a]it is not you who speak, but *it is* the Spirit of your
Father who speaks in you.
21 “[a]Brother will betray brother to death, and a father *his* child;
and [b]children will rise up against parents and [1]cause them to
be put to death.
22 “[a]You will be hated by all because of My name, but [b]it is the
one who has endured to the end who will be saved.
23 “But whenever they [a]persecute you in [1]one city, flee to [2]the
next; for truly I say to you, you will not finish *going through*
the cities of Israel [b]until the Son of Man comes.
24 “[a]A [1]disciple is not above his teacher, nor a slave above his
master.
25 “It is enough for the disciple that he become like his
teacher, and the slave like his master. [a]If they have called the
head of the house [1b]Beelzebul, how much more *will they malign*
the members of his household!
26 “Therefore do not [a]fear them, [b]for there is nothing concealed
that will not be revealed, or hidden that will not be known.
27 “[a]What I tell you in the darkness, speak in the light; and what
you hear *whispered* in *your* ear, proclaim [b]upon the housetops.

5 [1]Or *go off* [2]Or *on the road of* (Gr *hodos: way* or *road*) [a]Mark 6:7; Luke 9:2 [b]2 Kin 17:24ff; Luke 9:52; 10:33; 17:16; John 4:9, 39f; 8:48; Acts 8:25
6 [a]Matt 15:24
7 [1]Or *proclaim* [2]Lit *has come near* [a]Matt 3:2
9 [a]Matt 10:9-15: *Mark 6:8-11; Luke 9:3-5; 10:4-12;* Luke 22:35
10 [1]Or *knapsack, or beggar's bag* [2]Or *inner garments* [3]Lit *nourishment* [a]1 Cor 9:14; 1 Tim 5:18
11 [1]Lit *there until*
12 [1]Or *household* [2]I.e. the familiar Heb blessing, “Peace be to this house!” [a]1 Sam 25:6; Ps 122:7, 8
13 [1]Lit *your peace is to come upon it* [2]Lit *your peace is to return to you*
14 [a]Acts 13:51
15 [a]Matt 11:22, 24 [b]Matt 11:24; 2 Pet 2:6; Jude 7 [c]Matt 7:22; 11:22, 24; 12:36; Acts 17:31; 1 Thess 5:4; Heb 10:25; 2 Pet 2:9; 3:7; 1 John 4:17; Jude 6
16 [1]Or *show yourselves to be* [a]Luke 10:3 [b]Gen 3:1; Matt 24:25; Rom 16:19 [c]Hos 7:11
17 [a]Matt 5:22 [b]Matt 23:34; Mark 13:9; Luke 12:11; Acts 5:40; 22:19; 26:11
19 [a]Matt 10:19-22: *Mark 13:11-13; Luke 21:12-17* [b]Matt 6:25; Luke 12:11, 12
20 [a]Luke 12:12; Acts 4:8; 13:9; 2 Cor 13:3
21 [1]Lit *put them to death* [a]Matt 10:35, 36; Mark 13:12 [b]Mic 7:6
22 [a]Matt 24:9; Luke 21:17; John 15:18ff [b]Matt 24:13; Mark 13:13
23 [1]Lit *this* [2]Lit *the other* [a]Matt 23:34 [b]Matt 16:27f
24 [1]Or *student* [a]Luke 6:40; John 13:16; 15:20
25 [1]Or *Beezebul: ruler of demons* [a]Matt 9:34 [b]2 Kin 1:2; Matt 12:24, 27;

25 Mark 3:22; Luke 11:15, 18, 19
26 [a]Matt 10:26-33: *Luke 12:2-9* [b]Mark 4:22; Luke 8:17; 12:2; 1 Cor 4:5
27 [a]Luke 12:3 [b]Matt 24:17; Acts 5:20

28 "Do not fear those who kill the body but are unable to kill the soul; but rather [a]fear Him who is able to destroy both soul and body in [1b]hell.

29 "[a]Are not two sparrows sold for a [1]cent? And *yet* not one of them will fall to the ground apart from your Father.

30 "But [a]the very hairs of your head are all numbered.

31 "So do not fear; [a]you are more valuable than many sparrows.

32 "Therefore [a]everyone who [1]confesses Me before men, I will also confess [2]him before My Father who is in heaven.

33 "But [a]whoever [1]denies Me before men, I will also deny him before My Father who is in heaven.

34 "[a]Do not think that I came to [1]bring peace on the earth; I did not come to bring peace, but a sword.

35 "For I came to [a]SET A MAN AGAINST HIS FATHER, AND A DAUGHTER AGAINST HER MOTHER, AND A DAUGHTER-IN-LAW AGAINST HER MOTHER-IN-LAW;

36 and [a]A MAN'S ENEMIES WILL BE THE MEMBERS OF HIS HOUSEHOLD.

37 "[a]He who loves father or mother more than Me is not worthy of Me; and he who loves son or daughter more than Me is not worthy of Me.

38 "And [a]he who does not take his cross and follow after Me is not worthy of Me.

39 "[a]He who has found his [1]life will lose it, and he who has lost his [1]life for My sake will find it.

40 "[a]He who receives you receives Me, and [b]he who receives Me receives Him who sent Me.

41 "[a]He who receives a prophet in *the* name of a prophet shall receive a prophet's reward; and he who receives a righteous man in the name of a righteous man shall receive a righteous man's reward.

42 "And [a]whoever in the name of a disciple gives to one of these [1]little ones even a cup of cold water to drink, truly I say to you, he shall not lose his reward."

Chapter 11 Theme ______________________

11 [a]When Jesus had finished [1]giving instructions to His twelve disciples, He departed from there [b]to teach and [2]preach in their cities.

2 [a]Now when [b]John, [1]while imprisoned, heard of the works of Christ, he sent *word* by his disciples

3 and said to Him, "Are You [a]the [1]Expected One, or shall we look for someone else?"

4 Jesus answered and said to them, "Go and report to John what you hear and see:

5 [a]*the* BLIND RECEIVE SIGHT and *the* lame walk, *the* lepers are cleansed and *the* deaf hear, *the* dead are raised up, and *the* [b]POOR HAVE THE [1]GOSPEL PREACHED TO THEM.

6 "And blessed is he [1]who [a]does not [2]take offense at Me."

7 As these men were going *away,* Jesus began to speak to the

28 [1]Gr *Gehenna* [a]Heb 10:31 [b]Matt 5:22; Luke 12:5

29 [1]Gr *assarion,* the smallest copper coin [a]Luke 12:6

30 [a]1 Sam 14:45; 2 Sam 14:11; 1 Kin 1:52; Luke 21:18; Acts 27:34

31 [a]Matt 12:12

32 [1]Lit *will confess in Me* [2]Lit *in him* [a]Luke 12:8; Rev 3:5

33 [1]Lit *will deny* [a]Mark 8:38; Luke 9:26; 2 Tim 2:12

34 [1]Lit *cast* [a]Matt 10:34, 35: *Luke 12:51-53*

35 [a]Mic 7:6; Matt 10:21; Luke 12:53

36 [a]Mic 7:6; Matt 10:21

37 [a]Deut 33:9; Luke 14:26

38 [a]Matt 16:24; Mark 8:34; Luke 9:23; 14:27

39 [1]Or *soul* [a]Matt 16:25; Mark 8:35; Luke 9:24; 17:33; John 12:25

40 [a]Matt 18:5; Luke 10:16; John 13:20; Gal 4:14 [b]Mark 9:37; Luke 9:48; John 12:44

41 [a]Matt 25:44, 45

42 [1]I.e. humble [a]Matt 25:40; Mark 9:41

11:1 [1]Or *commanding* [2]Or *proclaim* [a]Matt 7:28 [b]Matt 9:35; Luke 23:5

2 [1]Lit *in prison* [a]Matt 11:2-19: *Luke 7:18-35;* Matt 4:12 [b]Matt 14:3; Mark 6:17; Luke 9:7ff

3 [1]Lit *Coming One* [a]Ps 118:26; Matt 11:10; John 6:14; 11:27; Heb 10:37

5 [1]Or *good news* [a]Is 35:5f; Matt 8:3; 12:13 [b]Is 61:1; Luke 4:18

6 [1]Lit *whoever* [2]Or *stumble over Me* [a]Matt 5:29; 13:57; 24:10; 26:31; Mark 6:3; John 6:61; 16:1

crowds about John, "What did you go out into [a]the wilderness
to see? A reed shaken by the wind?
8 "[1]But what did you go out to see? A man dressed in soft
clothing? Those who wear soft *clothing* are in kings'
[2]palaces!
9 "[1]But what did you go out to see? [a]A prophet? Yes, I tell you,
and one who is more than a prophet.
10 "This is the one about whom it [1]is written,
'[a]BEHOLD, I SEND MY MESSENGER [2]AHEAD OF YOU,
WHO WILL PREPARE YOUR WAY BEFORE YOU.'
11 "Truly I say to you, among those born of women there has
not arisen *anyone* greater than John the Baptist! Yet the one
who is [1]least in the kingdom of heaven is greater than he.
12 "[a]From the days of John the Baptist until now the kingdom
of heaven [1]suffers violence, and violent men [2]take it by force.
13 "For all the prophets and the Law prophesied until John.
14 "And if you are willing to accept *it,* John himself is [a]Elijah
who [1]was to come.
15 "[a]He who has ears to hear, [1]let him hear.
16 "But to what shall I compare this generation? It is like children
sitting in the market places, who call out to the other *children,*
17 and say, 'We played the flute for you, and you did not
dance; we sang a dirge, and you did not [1]mourn.'
18 "For John came neither [a]eating nor [b]drinking, and they say,
'[c]He has a demon!'
19 "The Son of Man came eating and drinking, and they say,
'Behold, a gluttonous man and a [1]drunkard, [a]a friend of tax
collectors and [2]sinners!' Yet wisdom is vindicated by her deeds."
20 Then He began to denounce the cities in which most of
His [1a]miracles were done, because they did not repent.
21 "[a]Woe to you, Chorazin! Woe to you, [b]Bethsaida! For if the
[1]miracles had occurred in [c]Tyre and [c]Sidon which occurred in
you, they would have repented long ago in [2d]sackcloth and ashes.
22 "Nevertheless I say to you, [a]it will be more tolerable for Tyre
and Sidon in [b]*the* day of judgment than for you.
23 "And you, [a]Capernaum, will not be exalted to heaven, will
you? You will [b]descend to [c]Hades; for if the [1]miracles had
occurred in [d]Sodom which occurred in you, it would have
remained to this day.
24 "Nevertheless I say to you that [a]it will be more tolerable for
the land of [b]Sodom in *the* day of judgment, than for you."
25 [a]At that [1]time Jesus said, "I praise You, [b]Father, Lord of
heaven and earth, that [c]You have hidden these things from *the*
wise and intelligent and have revealed them to infants.
26 "Yes, [a]Father, for this way was well-pleasing in Your sight.
27 "[a]All things have been handed over to Me by My Father;
and no one knows the Son except the Father; nor does anyone
know the Father [b]except the Son, and anyone to whom the Son
wills to reveal *Him.*
28 "[a]Come to Me, all [1]who are weary and heavy-laden, and I
will give you rest.

7 [a]Matt 3:1
8 [1]Or *Well then,* [2]Lit *houses*
9 [1]Or *Well then,* [a]Matt 14:5; 21:26; Luke 1:76; 20:6
10 [1]Lit *has been written* [2]Lit *before your face* [a]Mal 3:1; Mark 1:2
11 [1]Or *less*
12 [1]Or *is forcibly entered* [2]Or *seize it for themselves* [a]Luke 16:16
14 [1]Or *is going to come* [a]Mal 4:5; Matt 17:10-13; Mark 9:11-13; Luke 1:17; John 1:21
15 [1]Or *hear!* Or *listen!* [a]Matt 13:9, 43; Mark 4:9, 23; Luke 8:8; 14:35; Rev 2:7, 11, 17, 29; 3:6, 13, 22; 13:9
17 [1]Lit *beat the breast*
18 [a]Matt 3:4 [b]Luke 1:15 [c]Matt 9:34; John 7:20; 8:48f, 52; 10:20
19 [1]Or *winedrinker* [2]I.e. irreligious Jews [a]Matt 9:11; Luke 5:29-32; 15:2
20 [1]Or *works of power* [a]Luke 10:13-15
21 [1]Or *works of power* [2]I.e. symbols of mourning [a]Matt 11:21-23: *Luke 10:13-15* [b]Mark 6:45; 8:22; Luke 9:10; John 1:44; 12:21 [c]Matt 11:22; 15:21; Mark 3:8; 7:24, 31; Luke 4:26; 6:17; Acts 12:20; 27:3 [d]Rev 11:3
22 [a]Matt 10:15; 11:24 [b]Matt 10:15; 12:36; Rev 20:11, 12
23 [1]Or *works of power* [a]Matt 4:13 [b]Is 14:13, 15; Ezek 26:20; 31:14; 32:18, 24 [c]Matt 16:18; Luke 10:15; 16:23; Acts 2:27, 31; Rev 1:18; 6:8; 20:13f [d]Matt 10:15
24 [a]Matt 10:15; 11:22 [b]Matt 10:15
25 [1]Or *occasion* [a]Matt 11:25-27: *Luke 10:21, 22* [b]Luke 22:42; 23:34; John 11:41; 12:27, 28 [c]Ps 8:2; 1 Cor 1:26ff
26 [a]Luke 22:42; 23:34; John 11:41; 12:27, 28
27 [a]Matt 28:18; John 3:35; 13:3; 17:2 [b]John 7:29; 10:15; 17:25
28 [1]Or *who work to exhaustion* [a]Jer 31:25; John 7:37

29 "Take My yoke upon you and [a]learn from Me, for I am gentle
and humble in heart, and [b]YOU WILL FIND REST FOR YOUR SOULS.
30 "For [a]My yoke is [1]easy and My burden is light."

Chapter 12 Theme ______________________

12 [a]At that [1]time Jesus went through the grainfields on the
Sabbath, and His disciples became hungry and began to
[b]pick the heads *of grain* and eat.
2 But when the Pharisees saw *this,* they said to Him, "Look,
Your disciples do what [a]is not lawful to do on a Sabbath."
3 But He said to them, "Have you not read what David did
when he became hungry, he and his companions,
4 how he entered the house of God, and [a]they ate the
[1]consecrated bread, which was not lawful for him to eat nor for
those with him, but for the priests alone?
5 "Or have you not read in the Law, that on the Sabbath the
priests in the temple [1]break the Sabbath and are innocent?
6 "But I say to you that something [a]greater than the temple is
here.
7 "But if you had known what this [1]means, '[a]I DESIRE [2]COMPASSION,
AND NOT A SACRIFICE,' you would not have condemned the
innocent.
8 "For [a]the Son of Man is Lord of the Sabbath."
9 [a]Departing from there, He went into their synagogue.
10 And a man *was there* whose hand was withered. And they
questioned [1]Jesus, asking, "[a]Is it lawful to heal on the
Sabbath?"—so that they might accuse Him.
11 And He said to them, "[a]What man [1]is there among you who
[2]has a sheep, and if it falls into a pit on the Sabbath, will he not
take hold of it and lift it out?
12 "[a]How much more valuable then is a man than a sheep! So
then, it is lawful to do [1]good on the Sabbath."
13 Then He *said to the man, "Stretch out your hand!" [a]He
stretched it out, and it was restored to [1]normal, like the other.
14 But the Pharisees went out and [1a]conspired against Him, *as
to* how they might destroy Him.
15 But Jesus, [1]aware of *this,* withdrew from there. Many
followed Him, and [a]He healed them all,
16 and [a]warned them not to [1]tell who He was.
17 *This was* to fulfill what was spoken through Isaiah the
prophet:
18 "[a]BEHOLD, MY [1]SERVANT WHOM I [2]HAVE CHOSEN;
[b]MY BELOVED IN WHOM MY SOUL [3]IS WELL-PLEASED;
[c]I WILL PUT MY SPIRIT UPON HIM,
[a]AND HE SHALL PROCLAIM [4]JUSTICE TO THE [5]GENTILES.
19 "[a]HE WILL NOT QUARREL, NOR CRY OUT;
NOR WILL ANYONE HEAR HIS VOICE IN THE STREETS.
20 "[a]A BATTERED REED HE WILL NOT BREAK OFF,
AND A SMOLDERING WICK HE WILL NOT PUT OUT,
UNTIL HE [1]LEADS [2]JUSTICE TO VICTORY.

29 [a]John 13:15; Eph 4:20; Phil 2:5; 1 Pet 2:21; 1 John 2:6 [b]Jer 6:16

30 [1]Or *comfortable, or pleasant* [a]1 John 5:3

12:1 [1]Or *occasion* [a]Matt 12:1-8: *Mark 2:23-28; Luke 6:1-5* [b]Deut 23:25

2 [a]Matt 12:10; Luke 13:14; 14:3; John 5:10; 7:23; 9:16

4 [1]Or *showbread;* lit *loaves of presentation* [a]1 Sam 21:6

5 [1]Or *profane*

6 [a]2 Chr 6:18; Is 66:1, 2; Matt 12:41, 42

7 [1]Lit *is* [2]Or *mercy* [a]Hos 6:6; Matt 9:13

8 [a]Matt 8:20; 12:32, 40

9 [a]Matt 12:9-14: *Mark 3:1-6; Luke 6:6-11*

10 [1]Lit *Him* [a]Matt 12:2; Luke 13:14; 14:3; John 5:10; 7:23; 9:16

11 [1]Lit *will be from you* [2]Lit *will have* [a]Luke 14:5

12 [1]Lit *well* [a]Matt 10:31; Luke 14:1-6

13 [1]Lit *health* [a]Matt 8:3; Acts 28:8

14 [1]Lit *took counsel* [a]Matt 26:4; Mark 14:1; Luke 22:2; John 7:30, 44; 8:59; 10:31, 39; 11:53

15 [1]Lit *knowing* [a]Matt 4:23

16 [1]Lit *make Him known* [a]Matt 8:4; 9:30; 17:9

18 [1]Lit *Child* [2]Lit *chose* [3]Or *took pleasure* [4]Or *judgment* [5]Or *nations* [a]Is 42:1 [b]Matt 3:17; 17:5 [c]Luke 4:18; John 3:34

19 [a]Is 42:2

20 [1]Or *puts forth* [2]Or *judgment* [a]Is 42:3

21 "[a]AND IN HIS NAME THE [1]GENTILES WILL HOPE."
22 [a]Then a [b]demon-possessed man *who was* blind and mute
was brought to [1]Jesus, and He healed him, so that the mute
man spoke and saw.
23 All the crowds were amazed, and were saying, "This man
cannot be the [a]Son of David, can he?"
24 But when the Pharisees heard *this,* they said, "This man
[a]casts out demons only by [1]Beelzebul the ruler of the demons."
25 [a]And [b]knowing their thoughts Jesus said to them, "[1]Any
kingdom divided against itself is laid waste; and [1]any city or
house divided against itself will not stand.
26 "If [a]Satan casts out Satan, he [1]is divided against himself;
how then will his kingdom stand?
27 "If I [a]by [1]Beelzebul cast out demons, [b]by whom do your sons
cast *them* out? For this reason they will be your judges.
28 "But [a]if I cast out demons by the Spirit of God, then the
kingdom of God has come upon you.
29 "Or how can anyone enter the strong man's house and carry
off his property, unless he first binds the strong *man?* And then
he will plunder his house.
30 "[a]He who is not with Me is against Me; and he who does
not gather with Me scatters.
31 "[a]Therefore I say to you, any sin and blasphemy shall be
forgiven people, but blasphemy against the Spirit shall not be
forgiven.
32 "[a]Whoever [1]speaks a word against the Son of Man, it shall
be forgiven him; but whoever [1]speaks against the Holy Spirit, it
shall not be forgiven him, either in [b]this age or in the *age* to
come.
33 "Either make the tree good and its fruit good, or make the
tree bad and its fruit bad; for [a]the tree is known by its fruit.
34 "[a]You brood of vipers, how can you, being evil, speak [1]what
is good? [b]For the mouth speaks out of that which fills the heart.
35 "[a]The good man brings out of *his* good treasure [1]what is good;
and the evil man brings out of *his* evil treasure [2]what is evil.
36 "But I tell you that every [1]careless word that people [2]speak,
they shall give an accounting for it in [a]the day of judgment.
37 "For [1]by your words you will be justified, and [1]by your
words you will be condemned."
38 Then some of the scribes and Pharisees said to Him,
"Teacher, [a]we want to see a [1]sign from You."
39 But He answered and said to them, "[a]An evil and
adulterous generation craves for a [1]sign; and *yet* no [1]sign will
be given to it but the [1]sign of Jonah the prophet;
40 for just as [a]JONAH WAS THREE DAYS AND THREE NIGHTS IN THE
BELLY OF THE SEA MONSTER, so will [b]the Son of Man be [c]three days
and three nights in the heart of the earth.
41 "[a]The men of Nineveh will stand up with this generation at
the judgment, and will condemn it because [b]they repented at
the preaching of Jonah; and behold, [c]something greater than
Jonah is here.

21 [1]Or *nations* [a]Rom 15:12
22 [1]Lit *Him* [a]Matt 12:22, 24: *Luke 11:14, 15;* Matt 9:32, 34 [b]Matt 4:24; 2 Thess 2:9
23 [a]Matt 9:27
24 [1]Or *Beezebul;* i.e. ruler of demons [a]Matt 9:34
25 [1]Lit *Every* [a]Matt 12:25-29: *Mark 3:23-27; Luke 11:17-22* [b]Matt 9:4
26 [1]Lit *was* [a]Matt 4:10; 13:19
27 [1]V 24, note 1 [a]Matt 9:34 [b]Acts 19:13
28 [a]1 John 3:8
30 [a]Mark 9:40; Luke 9:50; 11:23
31 [a]Matt 12:31, 32; Mark 3:28-30; Luke 12:10
32 [1]Lit *will speak* [a]Luke 12:10 [b]Matt 13:22, 39; Mark 10:30; Luke 16:8; 18:30; 20:34, 35; Eph 1:21; 1 Tim 6:17; 2 Tim 4:10; Titus 2:12; Heb 6:5
33 [a]Matt 7:16-18; Luke 6:43, 44; John 15:4-7
34 [1]Lit *good things* [a]Matt 3:7; 23:33; Luke 3:7 [b]1 Sam 24:13; Is 32:6; Matt 12:34, 35; 15:18; Luke 6:45; Eph 4:29; James 3:2-12
35 [1]Lit *good things* [2]Lit *evil things* [a]Prov 10:20, 21; 25:11, 12; Matt 13:52; Col 4:6
36 [1]Or *useless* [2]Lit *will speak* [a]Matt 10:15
37 [1]Or *in accordance with*
38 [1]I.e. attesting miracle [a]Matt 16:1; Mark 8:11, 12; Luke 11:16; John 2:18; 6:30; 1 Cor 1:22
39 [1]I.e. attesting miracle [a]Matt 12:39-42: *Luke 11:29-32;* Matt 16:4
40 [a]Jon 1:17 [b]Matt 8:20 [c]Matt 16:21
41 [a]Jon 1:2 [b]Jon 3:5 [c]Matt 12:6, 42

42 "[a]*The* Queen of *the* South will rise up with this generation
at the judgment and will condemn it, because she came from
the ends of the earth to hear the wisdom of Solomon; and behold,
[b]something greater than Solomon is here.
43 "[a]Now when the unclean spirit goes out of a man, it passes
through waterless places seeking rest, and does not find *it*.
44 "Then it says, 'I will return to my house from which I came';
and when it comes, it finds *it* unoccupied, swept, and put in order.
45 "Then it goes and takes along with it seven other spirits
more wicked than itself, and they go in and live there; and [a]the
last state of that man becomes worse than the first. That is the
way it will also be with this evil generation."
46 [a]While He was still speaking to the crowds, behold, His [b]mother
and [c]brothers were standing outside, seeking to speak to Him.
47 Someone said to Him, "Behold, Your mother and Your
brothers are standing outside seeking to speak to You."[1]
48 But [1]Jesus answered the one who was telling Him and said,
"Who is My mother and who are My brothers?"
49 And stretching out His hand toward His disciples, He said,
"Behold My mother and My brothers!
50 "For whoever does the will of My Father who is in heaven,
he is My brother and sister and mother."

Chapter 13 Theme ____________________

13 That day Jesus went out of [a]the house and was sitting [b]by
the sea.
2 And [1]large crowds gathered to Him, so [a]He got into a boat
and sat down, and the whole crowd was standing on the beach.
3 And He spoke many things to them in [a]parables, saying,
"Behold, the sower went out to sow;
4 and as he sowed, some *seeds* fell beside the road, and the
birds came and ate them up.
5 "Others fell on the rocky places, where they did not have
much soil; and immediately they sprang up, because they had
no depth of soil.
6 "But when the sun had risen, they were scorched; and
because they had no root, they withered away.
7 "Others fell [1]among the thorns, and the thorns came up and
choked them out.
8 "And others fell on the good soil and *yielded a crop, some
a [a]hundredfold, some sixty, and some thirty.
9 "[a]He who has ears, [1]let him hear."
10 And the disciples came and said to Him, "Why do You
speak to them in parables?"
11 [1]Jesus answered them, "[a]To you it has been granted to know
the mysteries of the kingdom of heaven, but to them it has not
been granted.
12 "[a]For whoever has, to him *more* shall be given, and he will
have an abundance; but whoever does not have, even what he
has shall be taken away from him.
13 "Therefore I speak to them in parables; because while [a]seeing

INSIGHT

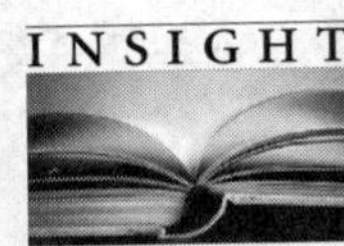

See the section on *Parables*, under **Figures of Speech**, on page 2104.

42 [a]1 Kin 10:1; 2 Chr 9:1 [b]Matt 12:6, 41

43 [a]Matt 12:43-45: *Luke 11:24-26*

45 [a]Mark 5:9; Luke 11:26; Heb 6:4-8; 2 Pet 2:20

46 [a]Matt 12:46-50: *Mark 3:31-35; Luke 8:19-21* [b]Matt 1:18; 2:11ff; 13:55; Luke 1:43; 2:33f, 48, 51; John 2:1, 5, 12; 19:25f; Acts 1:14 [c]Matt 13:55; Mark 6:3; John 2:12; 7:3, 5, 10; Acts 1:14; 1 Cor 9:5; Gal 1:19

47 [1]This verse is not found in early mss

48 [1]Lit *He*

13:1 [a]Matt 9:28; 13:36 [b]Matt 13:1-15: *Mark 4:1-12; Luke 8:4-10;* Mark 2:13

2 [1]Lit *Many* [a]Luke 5:3

3 [a]Matt 13:10ff; Mark 4:2ff

7 [1]Lit *upon*

8 [a]Gen 26:12; Matt 13:23

9 [1]Or *hear!* Or *listen!* [a]Matt 11:15; Rev 2:7, 11, 17, 29; 3:6, 13, 22

11 [1]Lit *He* [a]Matt 19:11; 20:23; John 6:65; 1 Cor 2:10; Col 1:27; 1 John 2:20, 27

12 [a]Matt 25:29; Mark 4:25; Luke 8:18; 19:26

13 [a]Deut 29:4; Is 42:19, 20; Jer 5:21; Ezek 12:2

50 and [a]will throw them into the furnace of fire; in that place
[b]there will be weeping and gnashing of teeth.
51 "Have you understood all these things?" They *said to Him,
"Yes."
52 And [1]Jesus said to them, "Therefore every scribe who has
become a disciple of the kingdom of heaven is like a head of a
household, who brings out of his treasure things new and old."
53 [a]When Jesus had finished these parables, He departed from
there.
54 [a]He came to [1]His hometown and [b]*began* teaching them in
their synagogue, so that [c]they were astonished, and said, "Where
did this man *get* this wisdom and *these* [2]miraculous powers?
55 "Is not this the carpenter's son? Is not [a]His mother called
Mary, and His [a]brothers, James and Joseph and Simon and Judas?
56 "And [a]His sisters, are they not all with us? Where then *did*
this man *get* all these things?"
57 And they took [a]offense at Him. But Jesus said to them, "[b]A
prophet is not without honor except in his [1]hometown and in
his *own* household."
58 And He did not do many [1]miracles there because of their
unbelief.

Chapter 14 Theme

14 [a]At that [1]time [b]Herod the tetrarch heard the news about
Jesus,
2 and said to his servants, "[a]This is John the Baptist; [1]he has
risen from the dead, and that is why miraculous powers are at
work in him."
3 For when [a]Herod had John arrested, he bound him and put
him [b]in prison because of [c]Herodias, the wife of his brother
Philip.
4 For John had been saying to him, "[a]It is not lawful for you
to have her."
5 Although Herod wanted to put him to death, he feared the
crowd, because they regarded [1]John as [a]a prophet.
6 But when Herod's birthday came, the daughter of
[a]Herodias danced [1]before *them* and pleased [b]Herod,
7 so *much* that he promised with an oath to give her
whatever she asked.
8 Having been prompted by her mother, she *said, "Give me
here on a platter the head of John the Baptist."
9 Although he was grieved, the king commanded *it* to be
given because of his oaths, and because of [1]his dinner guests.
10 He sent and had John beheaded in the prison.
11 And his head was brought on a platter and given to the
girl, and she brought it to her mother.
12 His disciples came and took away the body and buried [1]it;
and they went and reported to Jesus.
13 [a]Now when Jesus heard *about John,* He withdrew from there
in a boat to a secluded place by Himself; and when the [1]people
heard *of this,* they followed Him on foot from the cities.

50 [a]Matt 13:42 [b]Matt 8:12
52 [1]Lit *He*
53 [a]Matt 7:28
54 [1]Or *His own part of the country* [2]Or *miracles* [a]Matt 13:54-58: *Mark 6:1-6* [b]Matt 4:23 [c]Matt 7:28
55 [a]Matt 12:46
56 [a]Mark 6:3
57 [1]Or *own part of the country* [a]Matt 11:6 [b]Mark 6:4; Luke 4:24; John 4:44
58 [1]Or *works of power*
14:1 [1]Or *occasion* [a]Matt 14:1-12: *Mark 6:14-29;* Matt 14:1, 2: *Luke 9:7-9* [b]Mark 8:15; Luke 3:1, 19; 8:3; 13:31; 23:7f, 11f, 15; Acts 4:27; 12:1
2 [1]Or *he, himself* [a]Matt 16:14; Mark 6:14; Luke 9:7
3 [a]Matt 14:1-12: *Mark 6:14-29;* Mark 8:15; Luke 3:1, 19; 8:3; 13:31; 23:7f, 11f, 15; Acts 4:27; 12:1 [b]Matt 4:12; 11:2 [c]Matt 14:6; Mark 6:17, 19, 22; Luke 3:19f
4 [a]Lev 18:16; 20:21
5 [1]Lit *him* [a]Matt 11:9
6 [1]Lit *in the midst* [a]Matt 14:3; Mark 6:17, 19, 22; Luke 3:19 [b]Matt 14:1-12: *Mark 6:14-29;* Mark 8:15; Luke 3:1, 19; 8:3; 13:31; 23:7f, 11f, 15; Acts 4:27; 12:1
9 [1]Lit *those who reclined* at the table *with him*
12 [1]Lit *him*
13 [1]Lit *the crowds* [a]Matt 14:13-21: *Mark 6:32-44; Luke 9:10-17; John 6:1-13;* Matt 15:32-38

14 When He went [1]ashore, He [a]saw a large crowd, and felt
compassion for them and [b]healed their sick.
15 When it was evening, the disciples came to Him and said,
"This place is desolate and the hour is already [1]late; so send the
crowds away, that they may go into the villages and buy food
for themselves."
16 But Jesus said to them, "They do not need to go away; you
give them *something* to eat!"
17 They *said to Him, "We have here only [a]five loaves and
two fish."
18 And He said, "Bring them here to Me."
19 Ordering the [1]people to [2]sit down on the grass, He took
the five loaves and the two fish, and looking up toward heaven,
He [a]blessed *the food,* and breaking the loaves He gave them to
the disciples, and the disciples *gave them* to the crowds,
20 and they all ate and were satisfied. They picked up what
was left over of the broken pieces, twelve full [a]baskets.
21 There were about five thousand men who ate, besides
women and children.
22 [a]Immediately He [1]made the disciples get into the boat and
go ahead of Him to the other side, while He sent the crowds
away.
23 After He had sent the crowds away, [a]He went up on the
mountain by Himself to pray; and when it was evening, He was
there alone.
24 But the boat was already [1]a long distance from the land,
[2]battered by the waves; for the wind was [3a]contrary.
25 And in [a]the [1]fourth watch of the night He came to them,
walking on the sea.
26 When the disciples saw Him walking on the sea, they were
terrified, and said, "It is [a]a ghost!" And they cried out [1]in fear.
27 But immediately Jesus spoke to them, saying, "[a]Take courage,
it is I; [b]do not be afraid."
28 Peter said to Him, "Lord, if it is You, command me to come
to You on the water."
29 And He said, "Come!" And Peter got out of the boat, and
walked on the water and came toward Jesus.
30 But seeing the wind, he became frightened, and beginning
to sink, he cried out, "Lord, save me!"
31 Immediately Jesus stretched out His hand and took hold of
him, and *said to him, "[a]You of little faith, why did you doubt?"
32 When they got into the boat, the wind stopped.
33 And those who were in the boat worshiped Him, saying,
"You are certainly [a]God's Son!"
34 [a]When they had crossed over, they came to land at
[b]Gennesaret.
35 And when the men of that place [1]recognized Him, they
sent *word* into all that surrounding district and brought to Him
all who were sick;
36 and they implored Him that they might just touch [a]the
fringe of His cloak; and as many as [b]touched *it* were cured.

14 [1]Lit *out* [a]Matt 9:36 [b]Matt 4:23

15 [1]Lit *past*

17 [a]Matt 16:9

19 [1]Lit *crowds* [2]Lit *recline* [a]1 Sam 9:13; Matt 15:36; 26:26; Mark 6:41; 8:7; 14:22; Luke 24:30; Acts 27:35; Rom 14:6

20 [a]Matt 16:9; Mark 6:43; 8:19; Luke 9:17; John 6:13

22 [1]Lit *compelled* [a]Matt 14:22-33: *Mark 6:45-51; John 6:15-21*

23 [a]Mark 6:46; Luke 6:12; 9:28; John 6:15

24 [1]Lit *many stadia from;* a stadion was about 600 feet or about 182 meters [2]Lit *tormented* [3]Or *adverse* [a]Acts 27:4

25 [1]I.e. 3-6 a.m. [a]Matt 24:43; Mark 13:35

26 [1]Lit *from* [a]Luke 24:37

27 [a]Matt 9:2 [b]Matt 17:7; 28:5, 10; Mark 6:50; Luke 1:13, 30; 2:10; 5:10; 12:32; John 6:20; Rev 1:17

31 [a]Matt 6:30; 8:26; 16:8

33 [a]Matt 4:3

34 [a]Matt 14:34-36: *Mark 6:53-56;* John 6:24, 25 [b]Mark 6:53; Luke 5:1

35 [1]Or *knew*

36 [a]Matt 9:20 [b]Matt 9:21; Mark 3:10; 6:56; 8:22; Luke 6:19

Chapter 15 Theme ____

15 [a]Then some Pharisees and scribes *came to Jesus [b]from
Jerusalem and said,
2 "Why do Your disciples break the tradition of the elders? For
they [a]do not wash their hands when they eat bread."
3 And He answered and said to them, "Why do you
yourselves transgress the commandment of God for the sake of
your tradition?
4 "For God said, '[a]HONOR YOUR FATHER AND MOTHER,' and, '[b]HE
WHO SPEAKS EVIL OF FATHER OR MOTHER IS TO [1]BE PUT TO DEATH.'
5 "But you say, 'Whoever says to *his* father or mother,
"Whatever I have that would help you has been [1]given *to God,*"
6 he is not to honor his father or his mother[1].' And *by this*
you invalidated the word of God for the sake of your tradition.
7 "You hypocrites, rightly did Isaiah prophesy of you:
8 '[a]THIS PEOPLE HONORS ME WITH THEIR LIPS,
BUT THEIR HEART IS FAR AWAY FROM ME.
9 'BUT IN VAIN DO THEY WORSHIP ME,
TEACHING AS [a]DOCTRINES THE PRECEPTS OF MEN.'"
10 After Jesus called the crowd to Him, He said to them,
"Hear and understand.
11 "[a]*It is* not what enters into the mouth *that* defiles the man,
but what proceeds out of the mouth, this defiles the man."
12 Then the disciples *came and *said to Him, "Do You know that
the Pharisees were [1]offended when they heard this statement?"
13 But He answered and said, "[a]Every plant which My
heavenly Father did not plant shall be uprooted.
14 "Let them alone; [a]they are blind guides [1]of the blind. And [b]if
a blind man guides a blind man, both will fall into a pit."
15 Peter [1]said to Him, "[a]Explain the parable to us."
16 [1]Jesus said, "Are you still lacking in understanding also?
17 "Do you not understand that everything that goes into the
mouth passes into the stomach, and is [1]eliminated?
18 "But [a]the things that proceed out of the mouth come from
the heart, and those defile the man.
19 "[a]For out of the heart come evil thoughts, murders,
adulteries, [1]fornications, thefts, false witness, slanders.
20 "These are the things which defile the man; but to eat with
unwashed hands does not defile the man."
21 [a]Jesus went away from there, and withdrew into the
district of [b]Tyre and [b]Sidon.
22 And a Canaanite woman from that region came out and
began to cry out, saying, "Have mercy on me, Lord, [a]Son of
David; my daughter is cruelly [b]demon-possessed."
23 But He did not answer her a word. And His disciples came
and implored Him, saying, "Send her away, because she keeps
shouting [1]at us."
24 But He answered and said, "I was sent only to [a]the lost
sheep of the house of Israel."
25 But she came and [a]*began* [1]to bow down before Him,
saying, "Lord, help me!"

15:1 [a]Matt 15:1-20: *Mark 7:1-23* [b]Mark 3:22; 7:1; John 1:19; Acts 25:7
2 [a]Luke 11:38
4 [1]Lit *die the death* [a]Ex 20:12; Deut 5:16 [b]Ex 21:17; Lev 20:9
5 [1]Lit *a gift;* i.e. an offering
6 [1]I.e. by supporting them with it
8 [a]Is 29:13
9 [a]Col 2:22
11 [a]Matt 15:18; Acts 10:14, 15; 1 Tim 4:3
12 [1]Lit *caused to stumble*
13 [a]Is 60:21; 61:3; John 15:2; 1 Cor 3:9
14 [1]Later mss add *of the blind* [a]Matt 23:16, 24 [b]Luke 6:39
15 [1]Lit *answered and said* [a]Matt 13:36
16 [1]Lit *and He*
17 [1]Lit *thrown out into the latrine*
18 [a]Matt 12:34; Mark 7:20
19 [1]I.e. sexual immorality [a]Gal 5:19ff
21 [a]Matt 15:21-28: *Mark 7:24-30* [b]Matt 11:21
22 [a]Matt 9:27 [b]Matt 4:24
23 [1]Lit *behind us*
24 [a]Matt 10:6
25 [1]Or *worshiped* [a]Matt 8:2

26 And He answered and said, "It is not [1]good to take the
children's bread and throw it to the dogs."
27 But she said, "Yes, Lord; [1]but even the dogs feed on the
crumbs which fall from their masters' table."
28 Then Jesus said to her, "O woman, [a]your faith is great; it
shall be done for you as you wish." And her daughter was
healed [1]at once.
29 [a]Departing from there, Jesus went along by [b]the Sea of
Galilee, and having gone up on the mountain, He was sitting
there.
30 And [1]large crowds came to Him, bringing with them *those*
who were lame, crippled, blind, mute, and many others, and
they laid them down at His feet; and [a]He healed them.
31 So the crowd marveled as they saw the mute speaking, the
crippled [1]restored, and the lame walking, and the blind seeing;
and they [a]glorified the God of Israel.
32 [a]And Jesus called His disciples to Him, and said, "[b]I feel
compassion for the [1]people, because they [2]have remained with
Me now three days and have nothing to eat; and I do not want
to send them away hungry, for they might faint on the way."
33 The disciples *said to Him, "Where would we get so many
loaves in *this* desolate place to satisfy such a large crowd?"
34 And Jesus *said to them, "How many loaves do you have?"
And they said, "Seven, and a few small fish."
35 And He directed the [1]people to [2]sit down on the ground;
36 and He took the seven loaves and the fish; and [a]giving
thanks, He broke them and started giving them to the disciples,
and the disciples *gave them* to the people.
37 And they all ate and were satisfied, and they picked up what
was left over of the broken pieces, seven large [a]baskets full.
38 And those who ate were four thousand men, besides
women and children.
39 And sending away the crowds, Jesus got into [a]the boat and
came to the region of [b]Magadan.

Chapter 16 Theme ____________________

16 [a]The [b]Pharisees and Sadducees came up, and testing Jesus,
they [c]asked Him to show them a [1]sign from heaven.
2 But He replied to them, "[1a]When it is evening, you say, '*It*
will be fair weather, for the sky is red.'
3 "And in the morning, '*There will be* a storm today, for the
sky is red and threatening.' [a]Do you know how to discern the
[1]appearance of the sky, but cannot *discern* the signs of the
times?
4 "[a]An evil and adulterous generation seeks after a [1]sign; and
a [1]sign will not be given it, except the sign of Jonah." And He
left them and went away.
5 And the disciples came to the other side *of the sea,* but
they had forgotten to bring *any* bread.

26 [1]Or *proper*

27 [1]Lit *for*

28 [1]Lit *from that hour* [a]Matt 9:22

29 [a]Matt 15:29-31; Mark 7:31-37 [b]Matt 4:18

30 [1]Lit *many* [a]Matt 4:23

31 [1]Or *healthy* [a]Matt 9:8

32 [1]Lit *crowd* [2]Lit *are remaining* [a]Matt 15:32-39: *Mark 8:1-10;* Matt 14:13-21 [b]Matt 9:36

35 [1]Lit *crowd* [2]Lit *recline*

36 [a]Matt 14:19; 26:27; Luke 22:17, 19; John 6:11, 23; Acts 27:35; Rom 14:6

37 [a]Matt 16:10; Mark 8:8, 20; Acts 9:25

39 [a]Mark 3:9 [b]Mark 8:10

16:1 [1]Or *attesting miracle* [a]Matt 16:1-12: *Mark 8:11-21* [b]Matt 3:7; 16:6, 11, 12 [c]Matt 12:38; Luke 11:16

2 [1]Early mss do not contain the rest of v 2 and v 3 [a]Luke 12:54f

3 [1]Lit *face* [a]Luke 12:56

4 [1]Or *attesting miracle* [a]Matt 12:39; Luke 11:29

6 And Jesus said to them, "Watch out and [a]beware of the [1]leaven of the [b]Pharisees and Sadducees."

7 They began to discuss *this* among themselves, saying, "*He said that* because we did not bring *any* bread."

8 But Jesus, aware of this, said, "[a]You men of little faith, why do you discuss among yourselves that you have no bread?

9 "Do you not yet understand or remember [a]the five loaves of the five thousand, and how many baskets *full* you picked up?

10 "Or [a]the seven loaves of the four thousand, and how many large baskets *full* you picked up?

11 "How is it that you do not understand that I did not speak to you concerning bread? But [a]beware of the [1]leaven of the [b]Pharisees and Sadducees."

12 Then they understood that He did not say to beware of the leaven of bread, but of the teaching of the [a]Pharisees and Sadducees.

13 [a]Now when Jesus came into the district of [b]Caesarea Philippi, He was asking His disciples, "Who do people say that [c]the Son of Man is?"

14 And they said, "Some *say* [a]John the Baptist; and others, [1][b]Elijah; but still others, [2]Jeremiah, or one of the prophets."

15 He *said to them, "But who do you say that I am?"

16 Simon Peter answered, "You are [1][a]the Christ, [b]the Son of [c]the living God."

17 And Jesus said to him, "Blessed are you, [a]Simon [1]Barjona, because [b]flesh and blood did not reveal *this* to you, but My Father who is in heaven.

18 "I also say to you that you are [1][a]Peter, and upon this [2]rock I will build My church; and the gates of [b]Hades will not overpower it.

19 "I will give you [a]the keys of the kingdom of heaven; and [b]whatever you bind on earth [1]shall have been bound in heaven, and whatever you loose on earth [2]shall have been loosed in heaven."

20 [a]Then He [1]warned the disciples that they should tell no one that He was [2][b]the Christ.

21 [a]From that time [1]Jesus began to show His disciples that He must go to Jerusalem, and [b]suffer many things from the elders and chief priests and scribes, and be killed, and be raised up on the third day.

22 Peter took Him aside and began to rebuke Him, saying, "[1]God forbid *it,* Lord! This shall never [2]happen to You."

23 But He turned and said to Peter, "Get behind Me, [a]Satan! You are a stumbling block to Me; for you are not setting your mind on [1]God's interests, but man's."

24 Then Jesus said to His disciples, "If anyone wishes to come after Me, he must deny himself, and [a]take up his cross and follow Me.

25 "For [a]whoever wishes to save his [1]life will lose it; but whoever loses his [1]life for My sake will find it.

26 "For what will it profit a man if he gains the whole world

6 [1]Or *yeast* [a]Mark 8:15; Luke 12:1 [b]Matt 3:7
8 [a]Matt 6:30; 8:26; 14:31
9 [a]Matt 14:17-21
10 [a]Matt 15:34-38
11 [1]Or *yeast* [a]Matt 16:6; Mark 8:15; Luke 12:1 [b]Matt 3:7; 16:6, 12
12 [a]Matt 3:7; 5:20
13 [a]Matt 16:13-16: *Mark 8:27-29; Luke 9:18-20* [b]Mark 8:27 [c]Matt 8:20; 16:27, 28
14 [1]Gr *Elias* [2]Gr *Jeremias* [a]Matt 14:2 [b]Matt 17:10; Mark 6:15; Luke 9:8; John 1:21
16 [1]I.e. the Messiah [a]Matt 1:16; 16:20; John 11:27 [b]Matt 4:3 [c]Ps 42:2; Matt 26:63; Acts 14:15; Rom 9:26; 2 Cor 3:3; 6:16; 1 Thess 1:9; 1 Tim 3:15; 4:10; Heb 3:12; 9:14; 10:31; 12:22; Rev 7:2
17 [1]I.e. son of Jonah [a]John 1:42; 21:15-17 [b]1 Cor 15:50; Gal 1:16; Eph 6:12; Heb 2:14
18 [1]Gr *Petros,* a stone [2]Gr *petra,* large rock; bedrock [a]Matt 4:18 [b]Matt 11:23
19 [1]Gr *estai dedemenon,* fut. pft. pass. [2]Gr *estai lelumenon,* fut. pft. pass. [a]Is 22:22; Rev 1:18; 3:7 [b]Matt 18:18; John 20:23
20 [1]Or *strictly admonished* [2]I.e. the Messiah [a]Matt 8:4; Mark 8:30; Luke 9:21 [b]Matt 1:16; 16:16; John 11:27
21 [1]Two early mss read *Jesus Christ* [a]Matt 16:21-28: *Mark 8:31-9:1; Luke 9:22-27* [b]Matt 12:40; 17:9, 12, 22f; 20:18f; 27:63; Mark 9:12, 31; Luke 17:25; 18:32; 24:7; John 2:19
22 [1]Lit (God be) *merciful to You* [2]Lit *be*
23 [1]Lit *the things of God* [a]Matt 4:10
24 [a]Matt 10:38; Luke 14:27
25 [1]Or *soul* [a]Matt 10:39

and forfeits his soul? Or what will a man give in exchange for
his soul?
27 "For the [a]Son of Man [b]is going to come in the glory of His
Father with His angels, and [c]WILL THEN [1]REPAY EVERY MAN
ACCORDING TO HIS [2]DEEDS.
28 "Truly I say to you, there are some of those who are
standing here who will not taste death until they see the [a]Son
of Man [b]coming in His kingdom."

Chapter 17 Theme ______________________

17 [a]Six days later Jesus *took with Him [b]Peter and [1]James
and John his brother, and *led them up on a high mountain by themselves.
2 And He was transfigured before them; and His face shone
like the sun, and His garments became as white as light.
3 And behold, Moses and Elijah appeared to them, talking
with Him.
4 Peter said to Jesus, "Lord, it is good for us to be here; if You
wish, [a]I will make three [1]tabernacles here, one for You, and
one for Moses, and one for Elijah."
5 While he was still speaking, a bright cloud overshadowed
them, and behold, [a]a voice out of the cloud said, "[b]This is My
beloved Son, with whom I am well-pleased; listen to Him!"
6 When the disciples heard *this,* they fell [1]face down to the
ground and were terrified.
7 And Jesus came to *them* and touched them and said, "Get
up, and [a]do not be afraid."
8 And lifting up their eyes, they saw no one except Jesus
Himself alone.
9 [a]As they were coming down from the mountain, Jesus
commanded them, saying, "[b]Tell the vision to no one until [c]the
Son of Man has [d]risen from the dead."
10 And His disciples asked Him, "Why then do the scribes say
that [a]Elijah must come first?"
11 And He answered and said, "Elijah is coming and will
restore all things;
12 but I say to you that Elijah already came, and they did not
recognize him, but did [1]to him whatever they wished. So also
[a]the Son of Man is going to suffer [2]at their hands."
13 Then the disciples understood that He had spoken to them
about John the Baptist.
14 [a]When they came to the crowd, a man came up to Jesus,
falling on his knees before Him and saying,
15 "[1]Lord, have mercy on my son, for he is a [2a]lunatic and is
very ill; for he often falls into the fire and often into the water.
16 "I brought him to Your disciples, and they could not cure
him."
17 And Jesus answered and said, "You unbelieving and
perverted generation, how long shall I be with you? How long
shall I put up with you? Bring him here to Me."

27 [1]Or *recompense* [2]Lit *doing* [a]Matt 8:20 [b]Matt 10:23; 24:3, 27, 37, 39; 26:64; Mark 8:38; 13:26; Luke 21:27; John 21:22; Acts 1:11; 1 Cor 15:23; 1 Thess 1:10; 4:16; 2 Thess 1:7, 10; 2:1, 8; James 5:7f; 2 Pet 1:16; 3:4, 12; 1 John 2:28; Rev 1:7 [c]Ps 62:12; Prov 24:12; Rom 2:6; 14:12; 1 Cor 3:13; 2 Cor 5:10; Eph 6:8; Col 3:25; Rev 2:23; 20:12; 22:12

28 [a]Matt 8:20 [b]Matt 10:23; 24:3, 27, 37, 39; 26:64; Mark 8:38; 13:26; Luke 21:27; John 21:22; Acts 1:11; 1 Cor 15:23; 1 Thess 1:10; 4:16; 2 Thess 1:7, 10; 2:1, 8; James 5:7f; 2 Pet 1:16; 3:4, 12; 1 John 2:28; Rev 1:7

17:1 [1]Or *Jacob* [a]Matt 17:1-8: *Mark 9:2-8; Luke 9:28-36* [b]Matt 26:37; Mark 5:37; 13:3

4 [1]Or *sacred tents* [a]Mark 9:5; Luke 9:33

5 [a]Mark 1:11; Luke 3:22; 2 Pet 1:17f [b]Is 42:1; Matt 3:17; 12:18

6 [1]Lit *on their faces*

7 [a]Matt 14:27

9 [a]Matt 17:9-13: *Mark 9:9-13* [b]Matt 8:4 [c]Matt 8:20; 17:12, 22 [d]Matt 16:21

10 [a]Mal 4:5; Matt 11:14; 16:14

12 [1]Lit *in him;* or *in his case* [2]Lit *by them* [a]Matt 8:20; 17:9, 22

14 [a]Matt 17:14-19: *Mark 9:14-28;* Matt 17:14-18: *Luke 9:37-42*

15 [1]Or *Sir* [2]Or moonstruck; Gr *seleniazo* [a]Matt 4:24

18 And Jesus rebuked him, and the demon came out of him,
and the boy was cured [1]at once.
19 Then the disciples came to Jesus privately and said, "Why
could we not drive it out?"
20 And He *said to them, "Because of the littleness of your
faith; for truly I say to you, [a]if you have faith [1]the size of [b]a
mustard seed, you will say to [c]this mountain, 'Move from here to
there,' and it will move; and [d]nothing will be impossible to you.
21 ["[1a]But this kind does not go out except by prayer and
fasting."]
22 [a]And while they were gathering together in Galilee, Jesus
said to them, "The Son of Man is going to be [1]delivered into
the hands of men;
23 and [a]they will kill Him, and He will be raised on the third
day." And they were deeply grieved.
24 When they came to Capernaum, those who collected [a]the
[1]two-drachma *tax* came to Peter and said, "Does your teacher
not pay [a]the [1]two-drachma *tax?*"
25 He *said, "Yes." And when he came into the house, Jesus
spoke to him first, saying, "What do you think, Simon? From
whom do the kings of the earth collect [a]customs or [b]poll-tax,
from their sons or from strangers?"
26 When Peter said, "From strangers," Jesus said to him,
"Then the sons are [1]exempt.
27 "However, so that we do not [1a]offend them, go to the sea
and throw in a hook, and take the first fish that comes up; and
when you open its mouth, you will find [2]a shekel. Take that
and give it to them for you and Me."

Chapter 18 Theme ______________________________

18 [a]At that [1]time the disciples came to Jesus and said,
"[b]Who then is greatest in the kingdom of heaven?"
2 And He called a child to Himself and set him [1]before them,
3 and said, "Truly I say to you, unless you [1]are converted and
[a]become like children, you will not enter the kingdom of
heaven.
4 "Whoever then humbles himself as this child, he is the
greatest in the kingdom of heaven.
5 "And whoever receives one such child in My name receives
Me;
6 but [a]whoever [b]causes one of these little ones who believe
in Me to stumble, it [1]would be better for him to have a [2]heavy
millstone hung around his neck, and to be drowned in the
depth of the sea.
7 "Woe to the world because of *its* stumbling blocks! For [a]it is
inevitable that stumbling blocks come; but woe to that man
through whom the stumbling block comes!
8 "[a]If your hand or your foot causes you to stumble, cut it off
and throw it from you; it is better for you to enter life crippled

18 [1]Lit *from that hour*
20 [1]Lit *as* [a]Matt 21:21f; Mark 11:23f; Luke 17:6 [b]Matt 13:31; Luke 17:6 [c]Matt 17:9; 1 Cor 13:2 [d]Mark 9:23; John 11:40
21 [1]Early mss do not contain this v [a]Mark 9:29
22 [1]Or *betrayed* [a]Matt 17:22, 23: *Mark 9:30-32; Luke 9:44, 45*
23 [a]Matt 16:21; 17:9
24 [1]Equivalent to two denarii or two days' wages, paid as a temple tax [a]Ex 30:13; 38:26
25 [a]Rom 13:7 [b]Matt 22:17, 19
26 [1]Or *free*
27 [1]Lit *cause them to stumble* [2]Lit *standard coin,* which was a shekel [a]Matt 5:29, 30; 18:6, 8, 9; Mark 9:42, 43, 45, 47; Luke 17:2; John 6:61; 1 Cor 8:13
18:1 [1]Lit *hour* [a]Matt 18:1-5: *Mark 9:33-37; Luke 9:46-48* [b]Luke 22:24
2 [1]Lit *in their midst*
3 [1]Lit *are turned* [a]Matt 19:14; Mark 10:15; Luke 18:17; 1 Cor 14:20; 1 Pet 2:2
6 [1]Lit *is better* [2]Lit *millstone turned by a donkey* [a]Mark 9:42; Luke 17:2; 1 Cor 8:12 [b]Matt 17:27
7 [a]Luke 17:1; 1 Cor 11:19; 1 Tim 4:1
8 [a]Matt 5:30; Mark 9:43

or lame, than [1]to have two hands or two feet and be cast into
the eternal fire.
9 "[a]If your eye causes you to stumble, pluck it out and throw
it from you. It is better for you to enter life with one eye, than
[1]to have two eyes and be cast into the [2b]fiery hell.
10 "See that you do not despise one of these little ones, for I say
to you that [a]their angels in heaven continually see the face of
My Father who is in heaven.
11 ["[1a]For the Son of Man has come to save that which was
lost.]
12 "What do you think? [a]If any man has a hundred sheep, and
one of them has gone astray, does he not leave the ninety-nine on
the mountains and go and search for the one that is straying?
13 "If it turns out that he finds it, truly I say to you, he rejoices
over it more than over the ninety-nine which have not gone
astray.
14 "So it is not *the* will [1]of your Father who is in heaven that
one of these little ones perish.
15 "[a]If your brother sins[1], go and [2]show him his fault [3]in
private; if he listens to you, you have won your brother.
16 "But if he does not listen *to you,* take one or two more with
you, so that [a]BY THE MOUTH OF TWO OR THREE WITNESSES EVERY
[1]FACT MAY BE CONFIRMED.
17 "If he refuses to listen to them, [a]tell it to the church; and if
he refuses to listen even to the church, [b]let him be to you as [1]a
Gentile and [1]a tax collector.
18 "Truly I say to you, [a]whatever you [1]bind on earth [2]shall have
been bound in heaven; and whatever you [3]loose on earth [2]shall
have been loosed in heaven.
19 "Again I say to you, that if two of you agree on earth about
anything that they may ask, [a]it shall be done for them [1]by My
Father who is in heaven.
20 "For where two or three have gathered together in My
name, [a]I am there in their midst."
21 Then Peter came and said to Him, "Lord, [a]how often shall
my brother sin against me and I forgive him? Up to [b]seven
times?"
22 Jesus *said to him, "I do not say to you, up to seven times,
but up to [a]seventy times seven.
23 "For this reason [a]the kingdom of heaven [1]may be compared
to a king who wished to [b]settle accounts with his slaves.
24 "When he had begun to settle *them,* one who owed him
[1]ten thousand talents was brought to him.
25 "But since he [1a]did not have *the means* to repay, his lord
commanded him [b]to be sold, along with his wife and children
and all that he had, and repayment to be made.
26 "So the slave fell *to the ground* and [a]prostrated himself
before him, saying, 'Have patience with me and I will repay
you everything.'
27 "And the lord of that slave felt compassion and released him
and [a]forgave him the [1]debt.

8 [1]Lit *having;* Gr part.

9 [1]Lit *having;* Gr part. [2]Lit *Gehenna of fire* [a]Matt 5:29; Mark 9:47 [b]Matt 5:22

10 [a]Luke 1:19; Acts 12:15; Rev 8:2

11 [1]Early mss do not contain this v [a]Luke 19:10

12 [a]Matt 18:12-14: *Luke 15:4-7*

14 [1]Lit *before*

15 [1]Late mss add *against you* [2]Or *reprove* [3]Lit *between you and him alone* [a]Lev 19:17; Luke 17:3; Gal 6:1; 2 Thess 3:15; James 5:19

16 [1]Lit *word* [a]Deut 19:15; John 8:17; 2 Cor 13:1; 1 Tim 5:19; Heb 10:28

17 [1]Lit *the* [a]1 Cor 6:1ff [b]2 Thess 3:6, 14f

18 [1]Or *forbid* [2]Gr fut. pft. pass. [3]Or *permit* [a]Matt 16:19; John 20:23

19 [1]Lit *from* [a]Matt 7:7

20 [a]Matt 28:20

21 [a]Matt 18:15 [b]Luke 17:4

22 [a]Gen 4:24

23 [1]Lit *was compared to* [a]Matt 13:24 [b]Matt 25:19

24 [1]A talent was worth more than fifteen years' wages of a laborer

25 [1]Or *was unable to* [a]Luke 7:42 [b]Ex 21:2; Lev 25:39; 2 Kin 4:1; Neh 5:5

26 [a]Matt 8:2

27 [1]Or *loan* [a]Luke 7:42

28 [1]The denarius was a day's wages
30 [1]Lit *but*
33 [a]Matt 6:12; Eph 4:32
35 [1]Lit *your hearts* [a]Matt 6:14
19:1 [a]Matt 7:28 [b]Matt 19:1-9: *Mark 10:1-12*
2 [1]Lit *many* [a]Matt 4:23
3 [1]Lit *Him* [2]Or *send away* [a]Matt 5:31
4 [a]Gen 1:27; 5:2
5 [a]Gen 2:24; Eph 5:31 [b]1 Cor 6:16
7 [a]Deut 24:1-4; Matt 5:31
8 [1]Or *send away*
9 [1]Or *sends away* [2]Lit *fornication* [3]Some early mss read *makes her commit adultery* [4]Some early mss add *and he who marries a divorced woman commits adultery* [a]Matt 5:32

28 "But that slave went out and found one of his fellow slaves
who owed him a hundred [1]denarii; and he seized him and
began to choke *him,* saying, 'Pay back what you owe.'
29 "So his fellow slave fell *to the ground* and *began* to plead
with him, saying, 'Have patience with me and I will repay you.'
30 "But he was unwilling [1]and went and threw him in prison
until he should pay back what was owed.
31 "So when his fellow slaves saw what had happened, they
were deeply grieved and came and reported to their lord all
that had happened.
32 "Then summoning him, his lord *said to him, 'You wicked
slave, I forgave you all that debt because you pleaded with me.
33 '[a]Should you not also have had mercy on your fellow slave,
in the same way that I had mercy on you?'
34 "And his lord, moved with anger, handed him over to the
torturers until he should repay all that was owed him.
35 "[a]My heavenly Father will also do the same to you, if each of
you does not forgive his brother from [1]your heart."

Chapter 19 Theme ____________________

19 [a]When Jesus had finished these words, He departed from
Galilee and [b]came into the region of Judea beyond the
Jordan;
2 and [1]large crowds followed Him, and [a]He healed them there.
3 *Some* Pharisees came to [1]Jesus, testing Him and asking,
"[a]Is it lawful *for a man* to [2]divorce his wife for any reason at
all?"
4 And He answered and said,
"Have you not read [a]that He
who created *them* from the
beginning MADE THEM MALE AND
FEMALE,
5 and said, '[a]FOR THIS REASON A
MAN SHALL LEAVE HIS FATHER AND
MOTHER AND BE JOINED TO HIS
WIFE, AND [b]THE TWO SHALL BECOME
ONE FLESH'?
6 "So they are no longer two,
but one flesh. What therefore
God has joined together, let no
man separate."
7 They *said to Him, "[a]Why
then did Moses command to GIVE
HER A CERTIFICATE OF DIVORCE AND
SEND *her* AWAY?"
8 He *said to them, "Because of your hardness of heart Moses
permitted you to [1]divorce your wives; but from the beginning
it has not been this way.
9 "And I say to you, [a]whoever [1]divorces his wife, except for
[2]immorality, and marries another woman [3]commits adultery[4]."

Judea

10 The disciples *said to Him, "If the relationship of the man
with his wife is like this, it is better not to marry."
11 But He said to them, "[a]Not all men *can* accept this
statement, but [b]*only* those to whom it has been given.
12 "For there are eunuchs who were born that way from their
mother's womb; and there are eunuchs who were made
eunuchs by men; and there are *also* eunuchs who made
themselves eunuchs for the sake of the kingdom of heaven. He
who is able to accept *this,* let him accept *it.*"
13 [a]Then *some* children were brought to Him so that He
might lay His hands on them and pray; and the disciples
rebuked them.
14 But Jesus said, "[1][a]Let the children alone, and do not hinder
them from coming to Me; for [b]the kingdom of heaven belongs
to such as these."
15 After laying His hands on them, He departed from there.
16 [a]And someone came to Him and said, "Teacher, what good
thing shall I do that I may obtain [b]eternal life?"
17 And He said to him, "Why are you asking Me about what
is good? There is *only* One who is good; but [a]if you wish to
enter into life, keep the commandments."
18 *Then* he *said to Him, "Which ones?" And Jesus said, "[a]YOU
SHALL NOT COMMIT MURDER; YOU SHALL NOT COMMIT ADULTERY;
YOU SHALL NOT STEAL; YOU SHALL NOT BEAR FALSE WITNESS;
19 [a]HONOR YOUR FATHER AND MOTHER; and [b]YOU SHALL LOVE YOUR
NEIGHBOR AS YOURSELF."
20 The young man *said to Him, "All these things I have kept;
what am I still lacking?"
21 Jesus said to him, "If you wish to be [1]complete, go *and* [a]sell
your possessions and give to *the* poor, and you will have
[b]treasure in heaven; and come, follow Me."
22 But when the young man heard this statement, he went
away grieving; for he was one who owned much property.
23 And Jesus said to His disciples, "Truly I say to you, [a]it is
hard for a rich man to enter the kingdom of heaven.
24 "Again I say to you, [a]it is easier for a camel to go through the
eye of a needle, than for a rich man to enter the kingdom of God."
25 When the disciples heard *this,* they were very astonished
and said, "Then who can be saved?"
26 And looking at *them* Jesus said to them, "[a]With people this
is impossible, but with God all things are possible."
27 Then Peter said to Him, "Behold, we have left everything
and followed You; what then will there be for us?"
28 And Jesus said to them, "Truly I say to you, that you who
have followed Me, in the regeneration when [a]the Son of Man
will sit on [1]His glorious throne, [b]you also shall sit upon twelve
thrones, judging the twelve tribes of Israel.
29 "And [a]everyone who has left houses or brothers or sisters or
father or mother [1]or children or farms for My name's sake, will
receive [2]many times as much, and will inherit eternal life.
30 "[a]But many *who are* first will be last; and *the* last, first.

11 [a]1 Cor 7:7ff [b]Matt 13:11

13 [a]Matt 19:13-15: *Mark 10:13-16; Luke 18:15-17*

14 [1]Or *Permit the children* [a]Matt 18:3; Mark 10:15; Luke 18:17; 1 Cor 14:20; 1 Pet 2:2 [b]Matt 5:3

16 [a]Matt 19:16-29: *Mark 10:17-30; Luke 18:18-30;* Luke 10:25-28 [b]Matt 25:46

17 [a]Lev 18:5; Neh 9:29; Ezek 20:21

18 [a]Ex 20:13-16; Deut 5:17-20

19 [a]Ex 20:12; Deut 5:16 [b]Lev 19:18

21 [1]Or *perfect* [a]Luke 12:33; 16:9; Acts 2:45; 4:34f [b]Matt 6:20

23 [a]Matt 13:22; Mark 10:23f; Luke 18:24

24 [a]Mark 10:25; Luke 18:25

26 [a]Gen 18:14; Job 42:2; Jer 32:17; Zech 8:6; Mark 10:27; Luke 1:37; 18:27

28 [1]Lit *the throne of His glory* [a]Matt 25:31 [b]Luke 22:30; Rev 3:21; 4:4; 11:16; 20:4

29 [1]One early ms adds *or wife* [2]One early ms reads *a hundred times* [a]Matt 6:33; Mark 10:29f; Luke 18:29f

30 [a]Matt 20:16; Mark 10:31; Luke 13:30

Chapter 20 Theme ____________________

20 "For [a]the kingdom of heaven is like [1]a landowner who
went out early in the morning to hire laborers for his
[b]vineyard.
2 "When he had agreed with the laborers for a [1]denarius for
the day, he sent them into his vineyard.
3 "And he went out about the [1]third hour and saw others
standing idle in the market place;
4 and to those he said, 'You also go into the vineyard, and
whatever is right I will give you.' And *so* they went.
5 "Again he went out about the [1]sixth and the ninth hour, and
did [2]the same thing.
6 "And about the [1]eleventh *hour* he went out and found
others standing *around;* and he *said to them, 'Why have you
been standing here idle all day long?'
7 "They *said to him, 'Because no one hired us.' He *said to
them, 'You go into the vineyard too.'
8 "When [a]evening came, the [1]owner of the vineyard *said to
his [b]foreman, 'Call the laborers and pay them their wages,
beginning with the last *group* to the first.'
9 "When those *hired* about the eleventh hour came, each one
received a [1]denarius.
10 "When those *hired* first came, they thought that they would
receive more; [1]but each of them also received a denarius.
11 "When they received it, they grumbled at the landowner,
12 saying, 'These last men have worked *only* one hour, and
you have made them equal to us who have borne the burden
and the [a]scorching heat of the day.'
13 "But he answered and said to one of them, '[a]Friend, I am
doing you no wrong; did you not agree with me for a denarius?
14 'Take what is yours and go, but I wish to give to this last
man the same as to you.
15 'Is it not lawful for me to do what I wish with what is my
own? Or is your [a]eye [1]envious because I am [2]generous?'
16 "So [a]the last shall be first, and the first last."
17 [a]As Jesus was about to go up to Jerusalem, He took the
twelve *disciples* aside by themselves, and on the way He said
to them,
18 "Behold, we are going up to Jerusalem; and the Son of Man
[a]will be [1]delivered to the chief priests and scribes, and they
will condemn Him to death,
19 and [a]will hand Him over to the Gentiles to mock and scourge
and crucify *Him,* and on [b]the third day He will be raised up."
20 [a]Then the mother of [b]the sons of Zebedee came to [1]Jesus
with her sons, [c]bowing down and making a request of Him.
21 And He said to her, "What do you wish?" She *said to
Him, "Command that in Your kingdom these two sons of mine
[a]may sit one on Your right and one on Your left."
22 But Jesus answered, "You do not know what you are
asking. Are you able [a]to drink the cup that I am about to
drink?" They *said to Him, "We are able."

20:1 [1]Lit *a man, a landowner* [a]Matt 13:24 [b]Matt 21:28, 33
2 [1]The denarius was a day's wages
3 [1]I.e. 9 a.m.
5 [1]I.e. noon and 3 p.m. [2]Lit *similarly*
6 [1]I.e. 5 p.m.
8 [1]Or *lord* [a]Lev 19:13; Deut 24:15 [b]Luke 8:3
9 [1]The denarius was a day's wages
10 [1]Lit *each one a denarius*
12 [a]Jon 4:8; Luke 12:55; James 1:11
13 [a]Matt 22:12; 26:50
15 [1]Lit *evil* [2]Lit *good* [a]Deut 15:9; Matt 6:23; Mark 7:22
16 [a]Matt 19:30; Mark 10:31; Luke 13:30
17 [a]Matt 20:17-19: *Mark 10:32-34; Luke 18:31-33*
18 [1]Or *betrayed* [a]Matt 16:21
19 [a]Matt 27:2; Acts 2:23; 3:13; 4:27; 21:11 [b]Matt 16:21; 17:23; Luke 18:32f
20 [1]Lit *Him* [a]Matt 20:20-28: *Mark 10:35-45* [b]Matt 4:21; 10:2 [c]Matt 8:2
21 [a]Matt 19:28
22 [a]Is 51:17, 22; Jer 49:12; Matt 26:39, 42; Luke 22:42; John 18:11

23 He *said to them, "[a]My cup you shall drink; but to sit on
My right and on *My* left, this is not Mine to give, [b]but it is for
those for whom it has been [c]prepared by My Father."
24 And hearing *this,* the ten became indignant with the two
brothers.
25 [a]But Jesus called them to Himself and said, "You know that
the rulers of the Gentiles lord it over them, and *their* great men
exercise authority over them.
26 "It is not this way among you, [a]but whoever wishes to
become great among you shall be your servant,
27 and whoever wishes to be first among you shall be your
slave;
28 just as [a]the Son of Man [b]did not come to be served, but to
serve, and to give His [1]life a ransom for many."
29 [a]As they were leaving Jericho, a large crowd followed Him.
30 And two blind men sitting by the road, hearing that Jesus
was passing by, cried out, "Lord, [a]have mercy on us, [b]Son of
David!"
31 The crowd sternly told them to be quiet, but they cried out
all the more, "Lord, [a]Son of David, have mercy on us!"
32 And Jesus stopped and called them, and said, "What do you
want Me to do for you?"
33 They *said to Him, "Lord, *we want* our eyes to be opened."
34 Moved with compassion, Jesus touched their eyes; and
immediately they regained their sight and followed Him.

Chapter 21 Theme ______________________

21 [a]When they had approached Jerusalem and had come to
Bethphage, at [b]the Mount of Olives, then Jesus sent two
disciples,
2 saying to them, "Go into the village opposite you, and
immediately you will find a donkey tied *there* and a colt with
her; untie them and bring them to Me.
3 "If anyone says anything to you, you shall say, 'The Lord has
need of them,' and immediately
he will send them."
4 [a]This [1]took place to fulfill
what was spoken through the
prophet:
5 "[a]SAY TO THE DAUGHTER OF
ZION,
'BEHOLD YOUR KING IS COMING
TO YOU,
GENTLE, AND MOUNTED ON A
DONKEY,
EVEN ON A COLT, THE FOAL OF
A BEAST OF BURDEN.'"
6 The disciples went and did
just as Jesus had instructed
them,

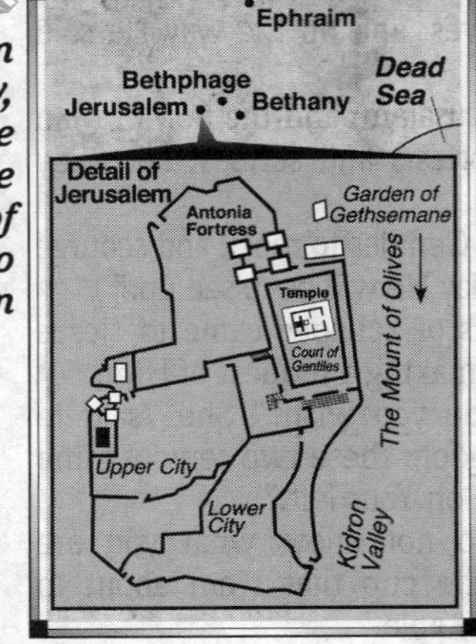

From Bethany, Bethphage across the Mount of Olives into Jerusalem

23 [a]Acts 12:2; Rev 1:9 [b]Matt 13:11 [c]Matt 25:34

25 [a]Matt 20:25-28; Luke 22:25-27

26 [a]Matt 23:11; Mark 9:35; 10:43; Luke 22:26

28 [1]Or *soul* [a]Matt 8:20 [b]Matt 26:28; John 13:13ff; 2 Cor 8:9; Phil 2:7; 1 Tim 2:6; Titus 2:14; Heb 9:28; Rev 1:5

29 [a]Matt 20:29-34: *Mark 10:46-52; Luke 18:35-43;* Matt 9:27-31

30 [a]Matt 9:27 [b]Matt 20:31

31 [a]Matt 9:27

21:1 [a]Matt 21:1-9: *Mark 11:1-10; Luke 19:29-38* [b]Matt 24:3; 26:30; Mark 11:1; 13:3; 14:26; Luke 19:29, 37; 21:37; 22:39; John 8:1; Acts 1:12

4 [1]Lit *has happened* [a]Matt 21:4-9: *Mark 11:7-10; Luke 19:35-38; John 12:12-15*

5 [a]Is 62:11; Zech 9:9

7 [1]Lit *them*

7 and brought the donkey and the colt, and laid their coats
on them; and He sat on [1]the coats.

8 [a]2 Kin 9:13

8 Most of the crowd [a]spread their coats in the road, and
others were cutting branches from the trees and spreading
them in the road.

9 [a]Matt 9:27 [b]Ps 118:26 [c]Luke 2:14

9 The crowds going ahead of Him, and those who followed,
were shouting,

"Hosanna to the [a]Son of David;
[b]BLESSED IS HE WHO COMES IN THE NAME OF THE LORD;
Hosanna [c]in the highest!"

11 [a]Matt 21:26; Mark 6:15; Luke 7:16, 39; 13:33; 24:19; John 1:21, 25; 4:19; 6:14; 7:40; 9:17; Acts 3:22f; 7:37 [b]Matt 2:23

10 When He had entered Jerusalem, all the city was stirred,
saying, "Who is this?"
11 And the crowds were saying, "This is [a]the prophet Jesus,
from [b]Nazareth in Galilee."

12 [a]Matt 21:12-16: *Mark 11:15-18; Luke 19:45-47;* Matt 21:12, 13: *John 2:13-16* [b]Ex 30:13 [c]Lev 1:14; 5:7; 12:8

12 [a]And Jesus entered the temple and drove out all those who
were buying and selling in the temple, and overturned the
tables of the [b]money changers and the seats of those who were
selling [c]doves.

13 [1]Lit *cave* [a]Is 56:7 [b]Jer 7:11

13 And He *said to them, "It is written, '[a]MY HOUSE SHALL BE
CALLED A HOUSE OF PRAYER'; but you are making it a [b]ROBBERS'
[1]DEN."

14 [a]Matt 4:23

14 And *the* blind and *the* lame came to Him in the temple,
and [a]He healed them.

15 [a]Matt 9:27

15 But when the chief priests and the scribes saw the
wonderful things that He had done, and the children who were
shouting in the temple, "Hosanna to the [a]Son of David," they
became indignant

16 [a]Ps 8:2; Matt 11:25

16 and said to Him, "Do You hear what these *children* are
saying?" And Jesus *said to them, "Yes; have you never read,
'[a]OUT OF THE MOUTH OF INFANTS AND NURSING BABIES YOU HAVE
PREPARED PRAISE FOR YOURSELF'?"

17 [a]Matt 26:6; Mark 11:1, 11, 12; 14:3; Luke 19:29; 24:50; John 11:1, 18; 12:1

17 And He left them and went out of the city to [a]Bethany, and
spent the night there.
18 [a]Now in the morning, when He was returning to the city,
He became hungry.

18 [a]Matt 21:18-22: *Mark 11:12-14, 20-24*

19 Seeing a lone [a]fig tree by the road, He came to it and found
nothing on it except leaves only; and He *said to it, "No longer
shall there ever be *any* fruit from you." And at once the fig tree
withered.

19 [a]Luke 13:6-9

20 Seeing *this,* the disciples were amazed and asked, "How
did the fig tree wither *all* at once?"

21 [a]Matt 17:20; Mark 11:23; Luke 17:6; James 1:6

21 And Jesus answered and said to them, "Truly I say to you,
[a]if you have faith and do not doubt, you will not only do what
was done to the fig tree, but even if you say to this mountain,
'Be taken up and cast into the sea,' it will happen.

22 [a]Matt 7:7

22 "And [a]all things you ask in prayer, believing, you will
receive."

23 [a]Matt 21:23-27: *Mark 11:27-33; Luke 20:1-8* [b]Matt 26:55

23 [a]When He entered the temple, the chief priests and the
elders of the people came to Him [b]while He was teaching, and
said, "By what authority are You doing these things, and who
gave You this authority?"

24 Jesus said to them, "I will also ask you one [1]thing, which if you tell Me, I will also tell you by what authority I do these things.
25 "The baptism of John was from what *source,* from heaven or from men?" And they *began* reasoning among themselves, saying, "If we say, 'From heaven,' He will say to us, 'Then why did you not believe him?'
26 "But if we say, 'From men,' we fear the [1]people; for they all regard John as [a]a prophet."
27 And answering Jesus, they said, "We do not know." He also said to them, "Neither will I tell you by what authority I do these things.
28 "But what do you think? A man had two [1]sons, and he came to the first and said, '[2]Son, go work today in the [a]vineyard.'
29 "And he answered, 'I will not'; but afterward he regretted it and went.
30 "The man came to the second and said the same thing; and he answered, 'I *will,* sir'; but he did not go.
31 "Which of the two did the will of his father?" They *said, "The first." Jesus *said to them, "Truly I say to you that [a]the tax collectors and prostitutes [1]will get into the kingdom of God before you.
32 "For John came to you in the way of righteousness and you did not believe him; but [a]the tax collectors and prostitutes did believe him; and you, seeing *this,* did not even feel remorse afterward so as to believe him.
33 "Listen to another parable. [a]There was a [1]landowner who [b]PLANTED A [c]VINEYARD AND PUT A WALL AROUND IT AND DUG A WINE PRESS IN IT, AND BUILT A TOWER, and rented it out to [2]vine-growers and [d]went on a journey.
34 "When the [1]harvest time approached, he [a]sent his slaves to the vine-growers to receive his produce.
35 "The vine-growers took his slaves and beat one, and killed another, and stoned a third.
36 "Again he [a]sent another group of slaves larger than the first; and they did the same thing to them.
37 "But afterward he sent his son to them, saying, 'They will respect my son.'
38 "But when the vine-growers saw the son, they said among themselves, 'This is the heir; come, let us kill him and seize his inheritance.'
39 "They took him, and threw him out of the vineyard and killed him.
40 "Therefore when the [1]owner of the vineyard comes, what will he do to those vine-growers?"
41 They *said to Him, "He will bring those wretches to a wretched end, and [a]will rent out the vineyard to other vine-growers who will pay him the proceeds at the *proper* seasons."
42 Jesus *said to them, "Did you never read in the Scriptures,

'[a]THE STONE WHICH THE BUILDERS REJECTED,
THIS BECAME THE CHIEF CORNER *stone;*

24 [1]Lit *word*

26 [1]Lit *crowd* [a]Matt 11:9; Mark 6:20

28 [1]Lit *children* [2]Lit *Child* [a]Matt 20:1; 21:33

31 [1]Lit *are getting into* [a]Luke 7:29, 37-50

32 [a]Luke 3:12; 7:29f

33 [1]Lit *a man, head of a household* [2]Or *tenant farmers,* also vv 34, 35, 38, 40 [a]Matt 21:33-46: *Mark 12:1-12; Luke 20:9-19* [b]Is 5:1, 2 [c]Matt 20:1; 21:28 [d]Matt 25:14

34 [1]Lit *the fruit season* [a]Matt 22:3

36 [a]Matt 22:4

40 [1]Lit *lord*

41 [a]Matt 8:11f; Acts 13:46; 18:6; 28:28

42 [a]Ps 118:22f; Acts 4:11; Rom 9:33; 1 Pet 2:7

THIS CAME ABOUT FROM THE LORD,
AND IT IS MARVELOUS IN OUR EYES'?
43 "Therefore I say to you, the kingdom of God will be taken
away from you and given to a [1]people, producing the fruit of it.
44 "And [a]he who falls on this stone will be broken to pieces;
but on whomever it falls, it will scatter him like dust."
45 When the chief priests and the Pharisees heard His
parables, they understood that He was speaking about them.
46 When they sought to seize Him, they [a]feared the [1]people,
because they considered Him to be a [b]prophet.

Chapter 22 Theme ______________________

22 Jesus spoke to them again in parables, saying,
2 "[a]The kingdom of heaven [1]may be compared to [2]a
king who [3]gave a [b]wedding feast for his son.
3 "And he [a]sent out his slaves to call those who had been
invited to the wedding feast, and they were unwilling to come.
4 "Again he [a]sent out other slaves saying, 'Tell those who
have been invited, "Behold, I have prepared my dinner; my
oxen and my fattened livestock are *all* butchered and everything
is ready; come to the wedding feast."'
5 "But they paid no attention and went their way, one to his
own [1]farm, another to his business,
6 and the rest seized his slaves and mistreated them and
killed them.
7 "But the king was enraged, and he sent his armies and
destroyed those murderers and set their city on fire.
8 "Then he *said to his slaves, 'The wedding is ready, but
those who were invited were not worthy.
9 'Go therefore to [a]the main highways, and as many as you
find *there,* invite to the wedding feast.'
10 "Those slaves went out into the streets and gathered
together all they found, both evil and good; and the wedding
hall was filled with [1]dinner guests.
11 "But when the king came in to look over the dinner guests,
he saw [a]a man there who was not dressed in wedding clothes,
12 and he *said to him, '[a]Friend, how did you come in here
without wedding clothes?' And the man was speechless.
13 "Then the king said to the servants, 'Bind him hand and
foot, and throw him into [a]the outer darkness; in that place
there will be weeping and gnashing of teeth.'
14 "For many are [1a]called, but few *are* [a]chosen."
15 [a]Then the Pharisees went and [1]plotted together how they
might trap Him [2]in what He said.
16 And they *sent their disciples to Him, along with the
[a]Herodians, saying, "Teacher, we know that You are truthful
and teach the way of God in truth, and [1]defer to no one; for
You are not partial to any.
17 "Tell us then, what do You think? Is it [1]lawful to give a [a]poll-
tax to [b]Caesar, or not?"

43 [1]Lit *nation*
44 [a]Is 8:14, 15
46 [1]Lit *crowds* [a]Matt 21:26 [b]Matt 21:11
22:2 [1]Lit *was compared to* [2]Lit *a man, a king* [3]Lit *made* [a]Matt 13:24; 22:2-14; Luke 14:16-24 [b]Luke 12:36; John 2:2
3 [a]Matt 21:34
4 [a]Matt 21:36
5 [1]Or *field*
9 [a]Ezek 21:21; Obad 14
10 [1]Lit *those reclining* at the table
11 [a]2 Kin 10:22; Zech 3:3, 4
12 [a]Matt 20:13; 26:50
13 [a]Matt 8:12; 25:30; Luke 13:28
14 [1]Or *invited* [a]Matt 24:22; 2 Pet 1:10; Rev 17:14
15 [1]Lit *took counsel* [2]Lit *in word* [a]Matt 22:15-22: *Mark 12:13-17; Luke 20:20-26*
16 [1]Lit *it is not a concern to You about anyone;* i.e. You do not seek anyone's favor [a]Mark 3:6; 8:15; 12:13
17 [1]Or *permissible* [a]Matt 17:25 [b]Luke 2:1; 3:1

18 But Jesus perceived their [1]malice, and said, "Why are you
testing Me, you hypocrites?
19 "Show Me the [a]coin *used* for the poll-tax." And they brought
Him a [1]denarius.
20 And He *said to them, "Whose likeness and inscription is this?"
21 They *said to Him, "Caesar's." Then He *said to them,
"[a]Then render to Caesar the things that are Caesar's; and to
God the things that are God's."
22 And hearing *this,* they were amazed, and [a]leaving Him,
they went away.
23 [a]On that day *some* [b]Sadducees (who say [c]there is no
resurrection) came to Jesus and questioned Him,
24 asking, "Teacher, Moses said, '[a]IF A MAN DIES HAVING NO
CHILDREN, HIS BROTHER AS NEXT OF KIN SHALL MARRY HIS WIFE, AND
RAISE UP CHILDREN FOR HIS BROTHER.'
25 "Now there were seven brothers with us; and the first married
and died, and having no children left his wife to his brother;
26 so also the second, and the third, down to the seventh.
27 "Last of all, the woman died.
28 "In the resurrection, therefore, whose wife of the seven will
she be? For they all had *married* her."
29 But Jesus answered and said to them, "You are mistaken,
[a]not [1]understanding the Scriptures nor the power of God.
30 "For in the resurrection they neither [a]marry nor are given in
marriage, but are like angels in heaven.
31 "But regarding the resurrection of the dead, have you not
read what was spoken to you by God:
32 '[a]I AM THE GOD OF ABRAHAM, AND THE GOD OF ISAAC, AND THE
GOD OF JACOB'? He is not the God of the dead but of the living."
33 When the crowds heard *this,* [a]they were astonished at His
teaching.
34 [a]But when the Pharisees heard that Jesus had silenced [b]the
Sadducees, they gathered themselves together.
35 One of them, [1][a]a lawyer, asked Him *a question,* testing Him,
36 "Teacher, which is the great commandment in the Law?"
37 And He said to him, "'[a]YOU SHALL LOVE THE LORD YOUR GOD WITH
ALL YOUR HEART, AND WITH ALL YOUR SOUL, AND WITH ALL YOUR MIND.'
38 "This is the great and [1]foremost commandment.
39 "The second is like it, '[a]YOU SHALL LOVE YOUR NEIGHBOR AS
YOURSELF.'
40 "[a]On these two commandments depend the whole Law and
the Prophets."
41 [a]Now while the Pharisees were gathered together, Jesus
asked them a question:
42 "What do you think about [1]the Christ, whose son is He?"
They *said to Him, "[a]*The son* of David."
43 He *said to them, "Then how does David [1][a]in the Spirit
call Him 'Lord,' saying,
44 '[a]THE LORD SAID TO MY LORD,
"SIT AT MY RIGHT HAND,
UNTIL I PUT YOUR ENEMIES BENEATH YOUR FEET"'?

18 [1]Or *wickedness*
19 [1]The denarius was a day's wages [a]Matt 17:25
21 [a]Mark 12:17; Luke 20:25; Rom 13:7
22 [a]Mark 12:12
23 [a]Matt 22:23-33: *Mark 12:18-27; Luke 20:27-40* [b]Matt 3:7 [c]Acts 23:8
24 [a]Deut 25:5
29 [1]Or *knowing* [a]John 20:9
30 [a]Matt 24:38; Luke 17:27
32 [a]Ex 3:6
33 [a]Matt 7:28
34 [a]Matt 22:34-40: *Mark 12:28-31;* Luke 10:25-37 [b]Matt 3:7
35 [1]I.e. an expert in the Mosaic Law [a]Luke 7:30; 10:25; 11:45, 46, 52; 14:3; Titus 3:13
37 [a]Deut 6:5
38 [1]Or *first*
39 [a]Lev 19:18; Matt 19:19; Gal 5:14
40 [a]Matt 7:12
41 [a]Matt 22:41-46: *Mark 12:35-37; Luke 20:41-44*
42 [1]I.e. the Messiah [a]Matt 9:27
43 [1]Or *by inspiration* [a]2 Sam 23:2; Rev 1:10; 4:2
44 [a]Ps 110:1; Matt 26:64; Mark 16:19; Acts 2:34f; 1 Cor 15:25; Heb 1:13; 10:13

45 "If David then calls Him 'Lord,' how is He his son?"
46 [a]No one was able to answer Him a word, nor did anyone
dare from that day on to ask Him [1]another question.

Chapter 23 Theme ____

23 [a]Then Jesus spoke to the crowds and to His disciples,
2 saying: "[a]The scribes and the Pharisees have seated
themselves in the chair of Moses;
3 therefore all that they tell you, do and observe, but do not do
according to their deeds; for they say *things* and do not do *them.*
4 "[a]They tie up heavy burdens and lay them on men's
shoulders, but they themselves are unwilling to move them with
so much as a finger.
5 "But they do all their deeds [a]to be noticed by men; for they
[b]broaden their [1]phylacteries and lengthen [c]the tassels *of their*
garments.
6 "They [a]love the place of honor at banquets and the chief
seats in the synagogues,
7 and respectful greetings in the market places, and being
called [a]Rabbi by men.
8 "But [a]do not be called [b]Rabbi; for One is your Teacher, and
you are all brothers.
9 "Do not call *anyone* on earth your father; for [a]One is your
Father, He who is in heaven.
10 "Do not be called [1]leaders; for One is your Leader, *that is,*
Christ.
11 "[a]But the greatest among you shall be your servant.
12 "[a]Whoever exalts himself shall be humbled; and whoever
humbles himself shall be exalted.
13 "[a]But woe to you, scribes and Pharisees, hypocrites, [b]because
you shut off the kingdom of heaven [1]from [2]people; for you do not
enter in yourselves, nor do you allow those who are entering to
go in.
14 ["[1]Woe to you, scribes and Pharisees, hypocrites, because
[a]you devour widows' houses, and for a pretense you make long
prayers; therefore you will receive greater condemnation.]
15 "Woe to you, scribes and Pharisees, hypocrites, because you
travel around on sea and land to make one [1a]proselyte; and
when he becomes one, you make him twice as much a son of
[2b]hell as yourselves.
16 "Woe to you, [a]blind guides, who say, '[b]Whoever swears by
the [1]temple, *that* is nothing; but whoever swears by the gold of
the [1]temple is obligated.'
17 "You fools and blind men! [a]Which is [1]more important, the
gold or the [2]temple that sanctified the gold?
18 "And, 'Whoever swears by the altar, *that* is nothing, but
whoever swears by the [1]offering on it, he is obligated.'
19 "You blind men, [a]which is [1]more important, the [2]offering,
or the altar that sanctifies the [2]offering?
20 "Therefore, [1]whoever swears by the altar, swears *both* by
[2]the altar and by everything on it.

46 [1]Lit *any longer* [a]Mark 12:34; Luke 14:6; 20:40

23:1 [a]Matt 23:1-7: *Mark 12:38, 39; Luke 20:45, 46*

2 [a]Deut 33:3f; Ezra 7:6, 25; Neh 8:4

4 [a]Luke 11:46; Acts 15:10

5 [1]I.e. small cases containing Scripture texts worn on the left arm and forehead for religious purposes [a]Matt 6:1, 5, 16 [b]Ex 13:9; Deut 6:8; 11:18 [c]Matt 9:20

6 [a]Luke 11:43; 14:7; 20:46

7 [a]Matt 23:8; 26:25, 49; Mark 9:5; 10:51; 11:21; John 1:38, 49; 3:2, 26; 4:31; 6:25; 9:2; 11:8; 20:16

8 [a]James 3:1 [b]Matt 23:7; 26:25, 49; Mark 9:5; 10:51; 11:21; 14:45; John 1:38, 49; 3:2, 26; 4:31; 6:25; 9:2; 11:8; 20:16

9 [a]Matt 6:9; 7:11

10 [1]Or *teachers*

11 [a]Matt 20:26

12 [a]Luke 14:11; 18:14

13 [1]Lit *in front of* [2]Gr *anthropoi* [a]Matt 23:15, 16, 23, 25, 27, 29 [b]Luke 11:52

14 [1]This v not found in early mss [a]Mark 12:40; Luke 20:47

15 [1]Or *convert* [2]Gr *Gehenna* [a]Acts 2:10; 6:5; 13:43 [b]Matt 5:22

16 [1]Or *sanctuary* [a]Matt 15:14; 23:24 [b]Matt 5:33-35

17 [1]Lit *greater* [2]Or *sanctuary* [a]Ex 30:29

18 [1]Or *gift*

19 [1]Lit *greater* [2]Or *gift* [a]Ex 29:37

20 [1]Lit *he who* [2]Lit *it*

21 "And [1]whoever swears by the [2]temple, swears *both* by [3]the temple and by Him who [a]dwells within it.

22 "And [1]whoever swears by heaven, [a]swears *both* by the throne of God and by Him who sits upon it.

23 "[a]Woe to you, scribes and Pharisees, hypocrites! For you tithe mint and dill and [1]cummin, and have neglected the weightier provisions of the law: justice and mercy and faithfulness; but these are the things you should have done without neglecting the others.

24 "You [a]blind guides, who strain out a gnat and swallow a camel!

25 "Woe to you, scribes and Pharisees, hypocrites! For [a]you clean the outside of the cup and of the dish, but inside they are full [1]of robbery and self-indulgence.

26 "You blind Pharisee, first [a]clean the inside of the cup and of the dish, so that the outside of it may become clean also.

27 "[a]Woe to you, scribes and Pharisees, hypocrites! For you are like whitewashed tombs which on the outside appear beautiful, but inside they are full of dead men's bones and all uncleanness.

28 "So you, too, outwardly appear righteous to men, but inwardly you are full of hypocrisy and lawlessness.

29 "[a]Woe to you, scribes and Pharisees, hypocrites! For you build the tombs of the prophets and adorn the monuments of the righteous,

30 and say, 'If we had been *living* in the days of our fathers, we would not have been partners with them in *shedding* the blood of the prophets.'

31 "So you testify against yourselves, that you [a]are [1]sons of those who murdered the prophets.

32 "Fill up, then, the measure *of the guilt* of your fathers.

33 "You serpents, [a]you brood of vipers, how [1]will you escape the [2]sentence of [3b]hell?

34 "[a]Therefore, behold, [b]I am sending you prophets and wise men and scribes; some of them you will kill and crucify, and some of them you will [c]scourge in your synagogues, and [d]persecute from city to city,

35 so that upon you may fall *the guilt of* all the righteous blood shed on earth, from the blood of righteous [a]Abel to the blood of Zechariah, the [b]son of Berechiah, whom [c]you murdered between the [1]temple and the altar.

36 "Truly I say to you, all these things will come upon [a]this generation.

37 "[a]Jerusalem, Jerusalem, who [b]kills the prophets and stones those who are sent to her! How often I wanted to gather your children together, [c]the way a hen gathers her chicks under her wings, and you were unwilling.

38 "Behold, [a]your house is being left to you desolate!

39 "For I say to you, from now on you will not see Me until you say, '[a]BLESSED IS HE WHO COMES IN THE NAME OF THE LORD!'"

21 [1]Lit *he who* [2]Or *sanctuary* [3]Lit *it* [a]1 Kin 8:13; Ps 26:8; 132:14

22 [1]Lit *he who* [a]Is 66:1; Matt 5:34

23 [1]Similar to caraway seeds [a]Matt 23:13; Luke 11:42

24 [a]Matt 23:16

25 [1]Or *as a result of* [a]Mark 7:4; Luke 11:39f

26 [a]Mark 7:4; Luke 11:39f

27 [a]Luke 11:44; Acts 23:3

29 [a]Luke 11:47f

31 [1]Or *descendants* [a]Matt 23:34, 37; Acts 7:51f

33 [1]Lit *would* [2]Or *judgment* [3]Gr *Gehenna* [a]Matt 3:7; Luke 3:7 [b]Matt 5:22

34 [a]Matt 23:34-36; Luke 11:49-51 [b]2 Chr 36:15, 16 [c]Matt 10:17 [d]Matt 10:23

35 [1]Or *sanctuary* [a]Gen 4:8ff; Heb 11:4 [b]Zech 1:1 [c]2 Chr 24:21

36 [a]Matt 10:23; 24:34

37 [a]Matt 23:37-39: *Luke 13:34, 35* [b]Matt 5:12 [c]Ruth 2:12

38 [a]1 Kin 9:7f; Jer 22:5

39 [a]Ps 118:26; Matt 21:9

Chapter 24 Theme ____________________

24 [a]Jesus [b]came out from the temple and was going away
[1]when His disciples came up to point out the temple
buildings to Him.
2 And He said to them, "Do you not see all these things?
Truly I say to you, [a]not one stone here will be left upon another,
which will not be torn down."
3 As He was sitting on [a]the Mount of Olives, the disciples
came to Him privately, saying, "Tell us, when will these things
happen, and what *will be* the sign of [b]Your coming, and of the
[1]end of the age?"
4 And Jesus answered and said to them, "[a]See to it that no
one misleads you.
5 "For [a]many will come in My name, saying, 'I am the [1]Christ,'
and will mislead many.
6 "You will be hearing of [a]wars and rumors of wars. See that
you are not frightened, for *those things* must take place, but
that is not yet the end.
7 "For [a]nation will rise against nation, and kingdom against
kingdom, and in various places there will be [b]famines and
earthquakes.
8 "[a]But all these things are *merely* the beginning of birth pangs.
9 "[a]Then they will deliver you to tribulation, and will kill you,
and [b]you will be hated by all nations because of My name.
10 "At that time many will [1a]fall away and will [2]betray one
another and hate one another.
11 "Many [a]false prophets will arise and will mislead many.
12 "Because lawlessness is increased, [1]most people's love will
grow cold.
13 "[a]But the one who endures to the end, he will be saved.
14 "This [a]gospel of the kingdom [b]shall be preached in the
whole [1c]world as a testimony to all the nations, and then the
end will come.
15 "Therefore when you see the [a]ABOMINATION OF DESOLATION
which was spoken of through Daniel the prophet, standing in
[b]the holy place ([c]let the reader understand),
16 then those who are in Judea must flee to the mountains.
17 "[1]Whoever is on [a]the housetop must not go down to get the
things out that are in his house.
18 "[1]Whoever is in the field must not turn back to get his cloak.
19 "But [a]woe to those who are pregnant and to those who are
nursing babies in those days!
20 "But pray that your flight will not be in the winter, or on a
Sabbath.
21 "For then there will be a [a]great tribulation, such as has not
occurred since the beginning of the world until now, nor ever will.
22 "Unless those days had been cut short, no [1]life would have
been saved; but for [a]the sake of the [2]elect those days will be
cut short.
23 "[a]Then if anyone says to you, 'Behold, here is the [1]Christ,'
or '[2]There *He is,*' do not believe *him.*

24:1 [1]Lit *and* [a]Matt 24:1-51: *Mark 13; Luke 21:5-36* [b]Matt 21:23
2 [a]Luke 19:44
3 [1]Or *consummation* [a]Matt 21:1 [b]Matt 16:27f; 24:27, 37, 39
4 [a]Jer 29:8
5 [1]I.e. the Messiah [a]Matt 24:11, 24; Acts 5:36f; 1 John 2:18; 4:3
6 [a]Rev 6:4
7 [a]2 Chr 15:6; Is 19:2; Rev 6:8, 12 [b]Acts 11:28; Rev 6:5, 6
8 [a]Matt 24:8-20; Luke 21:12-24
9 [a]Matt 10:17; John 16:2 [b]Matt 10:22; John 15:18ff
10 [1]Lit *be caused to stumble* [2]Or *hand over* [a]Matt 11:6
11 [a]Matt 7:15; 24:24
12 [1]Lit *the love of many*
13 [a]Matt 10:22
14 [1]Lit *inhabited earth* [a]Matt 4:23 [b]Rom 10:18; Col 1:6, 23 [c]Luke 2:1; 4:5; Acts 11:28; 17:6, 31; 19:27; Rom 10:18; Heb 1:6; 2:5; Rev 3:10; 16:14
15 [a]Dan 9:27; 11:31; 12:11 [b]Mark 13:14; Luke 21:20; John 11:48; Acts 6:13f; 21:28 [c]Mark 13:14; Rev 1:3
17 [1]Lit *He who* [a]1 Sam 9:25; 2 Sam 11:2; Matt 10:27; Luke 5:19; 12:3; 17:31; Acts 10:9
18 [1]Lit *He who*
19 [a]Luke 23:29
21 [a]Dan 12:1; Joel 2:2; Matt 24:29
22 [1]Lit *flesh* [2]Or *chosen ones* [a]Matt 22:14; 24:24, 31; Luke 18:7
23 [1]I.e. Messiah [2]Lit *here* [a]Luke 17:23f

INSIGHT

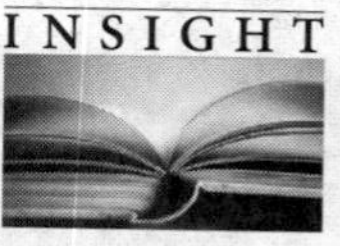

See the illustration of the temple mount on NISB-40.

24 "For false Christs and [a]false prophets will arise and will [1]show great [2b]signs and wonders, so as to mislead, if possible, even [c]the [3]elect.

25 "Behold, I have told you in advance.

26 "So if they say to you, 'Behold, He is in the wilderness,' do not go out, *or,* 'Behold, He is in the inner rooms,' do not believe *them.*

27 "[a]For just as the lightning comes from the east and flashes even to the west, so will the [b]coming of the [c]Son of Man be.

28 "[a]Wherever the corpse is, there the [1]vultures will gather.

29 "But immediately after the [a]tribulation of those days [b]THE SUN WILL BE DARKENED, AND THE MOON WILL NOT GIVE ITS LIGHT, AND [c]THE STARS WILL FALL from [1]the sky, and the powers of [1]the heavens will be shaken.

30 "And then [a]the sign of the Son of Man will appear in the sky, and then all the tribes of the earth will mourn, and they will see [b]the SON OF MAN COMING ON THE CLOUDS OF THE SKY with power and great glory.

31 "And [a]He will send forth His angels with [b]A GREAT TRUMPET and THEY WILL GATHER TOGETHER His [1c]elect from [d]the four winds, from one end of the sky to the other.

32 "Now learn the parable from the fig tree: when its branch has already become tender and puts forth its leaves, you know that summer is near;

33 so, you too, when you see all these things, [1]recognize that [2]He is near, *right* [a]at the [3]door.

34 "Truly I say to you, [a]this [1]generation will not pass away until all these things take place.

35 "[a]Heaven and earth will pass away, but My words will not pass away.

36 "But [a]of that day and hour no one knows, not even the angels of heaven, nor the Son, but the Father alone.

37 "For [1]the [a]coming of the Son of Man will be [b]just like the days of Noah.

38 "For as in those days before the flood they were eating and drinking, [a]marrying and giving in marriage, until the day that [b]Noah entered the ark,

39 and they did not [1]understand until the flood came and took them all away; so will the [a]coming of the Son of Man be.

40 "Then there will be two men in the field; one [1]will be taken and one [1]will be left.

41 "[a]Two women *will be* grinding at the [1b]mill; one [2]will be taken and one [2]will be left.

42 "Therefore [a]be on the alert, for you do not know which day your Lord is coming.

43 "But [1]be sure of this, that [a]if the head of the house had known [b]at what time of the night the thief was coming, he would have been on the alert and would not have allowed his house to be [2]broken into.

44 "For this reason [a]you also must be ready; for [b]the Son of Man is coming at an hour when you do not think *He will.*

24 [1]Lit *give* [2]Or *attesting miracles* [3]Or *chosen ones* [a]Matt 7:15; 24:11 [b]John 4:48; 2 Thess 2:9 [c]Matt 22:14; 24:22, 31; Luke 18:7

27 [a]Luke 17:24 [b]Matt 24:3, 37, 39 [c]Matt 8:20

28 [1]Or *eagles* [a]Job 39:30; Ezek 39:17; Hab 1:8; Luke 17:37

29 [1]Or *heaven* [a]Matt 24:21 [b]Is 13:10; 24:23; Ezek 32:7; Joel 2:10, 31; 3:15f; Amos 5:20; 8:9; Zeph 1:15; Matt 24:29-35; Acts 2:20; Rev 6:12-17; 8:12 [c]Is 34:4; Rev 6:13

30 [a]Matt 24:3; Rev 1:7 [b]Dan 7:13; Matt 16:27; 24:3, 37, 39

31 [1]Or *chosen ones* [a]Matt 13:41 [b]Ex 19:16; Deut 30:4; Is 27:13; Zech 9:14; 1 Cor 15:52; 1 Thess 4:16; Heb 12:19; Rev 8:2; 11:15 [c]Matt 24:22 [d]Dan 7:2; Zech 2:6; Rev 7:1

33 [1]Or *know* [2]Or *it* [3]Lit *doors* [a]James 5:9; Rev 3:20

34 [1]Or *race* [a]Matt 10:23; 16:28; 23:36

35 [a]Matt 5:18; Mark 13:31; Luke 21:33

36 [a]Mark 13:32; Acts 1:7

37 [1]Lit *just as . . . were the days* [a]Matt 16:27; 24:3, 30, 39 [b]Gen 6:5; 7:6-23; Luke 17:26f

38 [a]Matt 22:30 [b]Gen 7:7

39 [1]Lit *know* [a]Matt 16:27; 24:3, 30, 37

40 [1]Lit *is*

41 [1]I.e. handmill [2]Lit *is* [a]Luke 17:35 [b]Ex 11:5; Deut 24:6; Is 47:2

42 [a]Matt 24:43, 44; 25:10, 13; Luke 12:39f; 21:36

43 [1]Lit *know this* [2]Lit *dug through* [a]Matt 24:42, 44; 25:10, 13; Luke 12:39f; 21:36 [b]Matt 14:25; Mark 6:48; 13:35; Luke 12:38

44 [a]Matt 24:42, 43; 25:10, 13; Luke 12:39f; 21:36 [b]Matt 24:27

45 "[a]Who then is the [b]faithful and [c]sensible slave whom his
[1]master [d]put in charge of his household to give them their food
at the proper time?
46 "Blessed is that slave whom his [1]master finds so doing when
he comes.
47 "Truly I say to you that [a]he will put him in charge of all his
possessions.
48 "But if that evil slave says in his heart, 'My [1]master [2]is not
coming for a long time,'
49 and begins to beat his fellow slaves and eat and drink with
drunkards;
50 the [1]master of that slave will come on a day when he does
not expect *him* and at an hour which he does not know,
51 and will [1]cut him in pieces and [2]assign him a place with the
hypocrites; in that place there will be [a]weeping and gnashing of
teeth.

Chapter 25 Theme ____________________

25 "Then [a]the kingdom of heaven will be comparable to ten
virgins, who took their [b]lamps and went out to meet
the bridegroom.
2 "Five of them were foolish, and five were [a]prudent.
3 "For when the foolish took their lamps, they took no oil
with them,
4 but the [a]prudent took oil in flasks along with their lamps.
5 "Now while the bridegroom was delaying, they all got
drowsy and *began* to sleep.
6 "But at midnight there was a shout, 'Behold, the bridegroom!
Come out to meet *him*.'
7 "Then all those virgins rose and trimmed their lamps.
8 "The foolish said to the prudent, 'Give us some of your oil,
for our lamps are going out.'
9 "But the [a]prudent answered, 'No, there will not be enough
for us and you *too;* go instead to the dealers and buy *some* for
yourselves.'
10 "And while they were going away to make the purchase,
the bridegroom came, and those who were [a]ready went in
with him to [b]the wedding feast; and [c]the door was shut.
11 "Later the other virgins also came, saying, '[a]Lord, lord, open
up for us.'
12 "But he answered, 'Truly I say to you, I do not know you.'
13 "[a]Be on the alert then, for you do not know the day nor the
hour.
14 "[a]For *it is* just like a man [b]*about* to go on a journey, who
called his own slaves and entrusted his possessions to them.
15 "To one he gave five [1a]talents, to another, two, and to
another, one, each according to his own ability; and he [b]went
on his journey.
16 "Immediately the one who had received the five [a]talents
went and traded with them, and gained five more talents.

45 [1]Or *lord* [a]Matt 24:45-51: *Luke 12:42-46* [b]Matt 25:21, 23; Luke 16:10 [c]Matt 7:24; 10:16; 25:2ff [d]Matt 25:21, 23

46 [1]Or *lord*

47 [a]Matt 25:21, 23

48 [1]Or *lord* [2]Lit *lingers*

50 [1]Or *lord*

51 [1]Or *severely scourge him* [2]Lit *appoint his portion* [a]Matt 8:12

25:1 [a]Matt 13:24 [b]John 18:3; Acts 20:8; Rev 4:5; 8:10

2 [a]Matt 7:24; 10:16; 25:2ff

4 [a]Matt 7:24; 10:16; 25:2ff

9 [a]Matt 7:24; 10:16; 25:2ff

10 [a]Matt 24:42ff [b]Luke 12:35f [c]Matt 7:21ff; Luke 13:25

11 [a]Matt 7:21ff; Luke 13:25

13 [a]Matt 24:42ff

14 [a]Matt 25:14-30; Luke 19:12-27 [b]Matt 21:33

15 [1]A talent was worth about fifteen years' wages of a laborer [a]Matt 18:24; Luke 19:13 [b]Matt 21:33

16 [a]Matt 18:24; Luke 19:13

17 "In the same manner the one who *had received* the two
talents gained two more.
18 "But he who received the one *talent* went away, and dug *a*
hole in the ground and hid his [1]master's money.
19 "Now after a long time the master of those slaves *came and
*[a]settled accounts with them.
20 "The one who had received the five [a]talents came up and
brought five more talents, saying, 'Master, you entrusted five
talents to me. See, I have gained five more talents.'
21 "His master said to him, 'Well done, good and [a]faithful slave.
You were faithful with a few things, I will [b]put you in charge of
many things; enter into the joy of your [1]master.'
22 "Also the one who *had received* the two [a]talents came up
and said, 'Master, you entrusted two talents to me. See, I have
gained two more talents.'
23 "His master said to him, 'Well done, good and [a]faithful slave.
You were faithful with a few things, I will put you in charge of
many things; enter into the joy of your master.'
24 "And the one also who had received the one [a]talent came up
and said, 'Master, I knew you to be a hard man, reaping where
you did not sow and gathering where you scattered no *seed.*
25 'And I was afraid, and went away and hid your talent in the
ground. See, you have what is yours.'
26 "But his master answered and said to him, 'You wicked, lazy
slave, you knew that I reap where I did not sow and gather
where I scattered no *seed.*
27 'Then you ought to have put my money [1]in the bank, and on
my arrival I would have received my *money* back with interest.
28 'Therefore take away the talent from him, and give it to the
one who has the ten talents.'
29 "[a]For to everyone who has, *more* shall be given, and he will
have an abundance; but from the one who does not have, even
what he does have shall be taken away.
30 "Throw out the worthless slave into [a]the outer darkness; in
that place there will be weeping and gnashing of teeth.
31 "But when [a]the Son of Man comes in His glory, and all the
angels with Him, then [b]He will sit on His glorious throne.
32 "All the nations will be [a]gathered before Him; and He will
separate them from one another, [b]as the shepherd separates
the sheep from the goats;
33 and He will put the sheep [a]on His right, and the goats [b]on
the left.
34 "Then the King will say to those on His right, 'Come, you
who are blessed of My Father, [a]inherit the kingdom prepared
for you [b]from the foundation of the world.
35 'For [a]I was hungry, and you gave Me *something* to eat; I
was thirsty, and you gave Me *something* to drink; [b]I was a
stranger, and you invited Me in;
36 [a]naked, and you clothed Me; I was sick, and you [b]visited
Me; [c]I was in prison, and you came to Me.'
37 "Then the righteous will answer Him, 'Lord, when did we

18 [1]Or *lord's*

19 [a]Matt 18:23

20 [a]Matt 18:24; Luke 19:13

21 [1]Or *lord* [a]Matt 24:45, 47; 25:23 [b]Luke 12:44; 22:29; Rev 3:21; 21:7

22 [a]Matt 18:24; Luke 19:13

23 [a]Matt 24:45, 47; 25:21

24 [a]Matt 18:24; Luke 19:13

27 [1]Lit *to the bankers*

29 [a]Matt 13:12; Mark 4:25; Luke 8:18; John 15:2

30 [a]Matt 8:12; 22:13; Luke 13:28

31 [a]Matt 16:27f; 1 Thess 4:16; 2 Thess 1:7; Heb 9:28; Jude 14; Rev 1:7 [b]Matt 19:28

32 [a]Matt 13:49; 2 Cor 5:10 [b]Ezek 34:17, 20

33 [a]1 Kin 2:19; Ps 45:9 [b]Eccl 10:2

34 [a]Matt 5:3; 19:29; Luke 12:32; 1 Cor 6:9; 15:50; Gal 5:21; James 2:5 [b]Matt 13:35; Luke 11:50; John 17:24; Eph 1:4; Heb 4:3; 9:26; 1 Pet 1:20; Rev 13:8; 17:8

35 [a]Is 58:7; Ezek 18:7, 16; James 2:15, 16 [b]Job 31:32; Heb 13:2

36 [a]Is 58:7; Ezek 18:7, 16; James 2:15, 16 [b]James 1:27 [c]2 Tim 1:16f

see You hungry, and feed You, or thirsty, and give You *something*
to drink?
38 'And when did we see You a stranger, and invite You in, or
naked, and clothe You?
39 'When did we see You sick, or in prison, and come to You?'
40 "[a]The King will answer and say to them, 'Truly I say to you,
[b]to the extent that you did it to one of these brothers of Mine,
even the least *of them,* you did it to Me.'
41 "Then He will also say to those on His left, '[a]Depart from
Me, accursed ones, into the [b]eternal fire which has been
prepared for [c]the devil and his angels;
42 for I was hungry, and you gave Me *nothing* to eat; I was
thirsty, and you gave Me nothing to drink;
43 I was a stranger, and you did not invite Me in; naked, and
you did not clothe Me; sick, and in prison, and you did not visit
Me.'
44 "Then they themselves also will answer, 'Lord, when did we
see You hungry, or thirsty, or a stranger, or naked, or sick, or in
prison, and did not [1]take care of You?'
45 "Then He will answer them, 'Truly I say to you, to the
extent that you did not do it to one of the least of these, you
did not do it to Me.'
46 "These will go away into [a]eternal punishment, but the
righteous into [b]eternal life."

Chapter 26 Theme ____________________

26 [a]When Jesus had finished all these words, He said to
His disciples,
2 "[a]You know that after two days [b]the Passover is coming, and
the Son of Man is *to be* [c]handed over for crucifixion."
3 [a]Then the chief priests and the elders of the people were
gathered together in [b]the court of the high priest, named
[c]Caiaphas;
4 and they [a]plotted together to seize Jesus by stealth and kill
Him.
5 But they were saying, "Not during the festival, [a]otherwise a
riot might occur among the people."
6 [a]Now when Jesus was in [b]Bethany, at the home of Simon
the leper,
7 [a]a woman came to Him with an alabaster vial of very costly
perfume, and she poured it on His head as He reclined *at the
table.*
8 But the disciples were indignant when they saw *this,* and
said, "Why this waste?
9 "For this *perfume* might have been sold for a high price and
the money given to the poor."
10 But Jesus, aware of this, said to them, "Why do you bother
the woman? For she has done a good deed to Me.
11 "For you always have [a]the poor with you; but you do not
always have Me.

40 [a]Matt 25:34; Luke 19:38; Rev 17:14; 19:16 [b]Prov 19:17; Matt 10:42; Heb 6:10
41 [a]Matt 7:23 [b]Mark 9:48; Luke 16:24; Jude 7 [c]Matt 4:10; Rev 12:9
44 [1]Or *serve*
46 [a]Dan 12:2; John 5:29; Acts 24:15 [b]Matt 19:29; John 3:15f, 36; 5:24; 6:27, 40, 47, 54; 17:2f; Acts 13:46, 48; Rom 2:7; 5:21; 6:23; Gal 6:8; 1 John 5:11
26:1 [a]Matt 7:28
2 [a]Matt 26:2-5: *Mark 14:1, 2; Luke 22:1, 2* [b]John 11:55; 13:1 [c]Matt 10:4
3 [a]John 11:47 [b]Matt 26:58, 69; 27:27; Mark 14:54, 66; 15:16; Luke 22:55; John 18:15 [c]Matt 26:57; Luke 3:2; John 11:49; 18:13, 14, 24, 28; Acts 4:6
4 [a]Matt 12:14
5 [a]Matt 27:24
6 [a]Matt 26:6-13: *Mark 14:3-9;* Luke 7:37-39; John 12:1-8 [b]Matt 21:17
7 [a]Luke 7:37f
11 [a]Deut 15:11; Mark 14:7; John 12:8

RETURN TO INSTRUCTIONS

INSIGHT
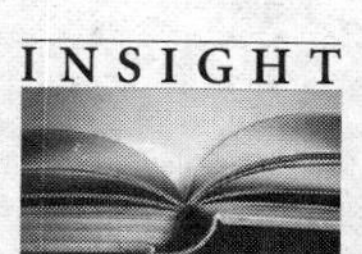
See the chart **The Feasts of Israel** located on pages 214, 215.

12 "For when she poured this perfume on My body, she did it
[a]to prepare Me for burial.
13 "Truly I say to you, [a]wherever this gospel is preached in the
whole world, what this woman has done will also be spoken of
in memory of her."
14 [a]Then one of the twelve, named [b]Judas Iscariot, went to the
chief priests
15 and said, "What are you willing to give me [1]to [2a]betray
Him to you?" And [b]they weighed out thirty [3]pieces of silver to
him.
16 From then on he *began* looking for a good opportunity to
[1]betray [2]Jesus.
17 [a]Now on the first *day* of [b]Unleavened Bread the disciples
came to Jesus and asked, "Where do You want us to prepare for
You to eat the Passover?"
18 And He said, "Go into the city to [a]a certain man, and say to
him, 'The Teacher says, "[b]My time is near; I *am to* keep the
Passover at your house with My disciples."'"
19 The disciples did as Jesus had directed them; and they
prepared the Passover.
20 [a]Now when evening came, Jesus was reclining *at the table*
with the twelve disciples.
21 As they were eating, He said, "[a]Truly I say to you that one
of you will betray Me."
22 Being deeply grieved, they [1]each one began to say to Him,
"Surely not I, Lord?"
23 And He answered, "[a]He who dipped his hand with Me in
the bowl is the one who will betray Me.
24 "The Son of Man *is to* go, [a]just as it is written of Him; but
woe to that man by whom the Son of Man is betrayed! [b]It
would have been good [1]for that man if he had not been born."
25 And [a]Judas, who was betraying Him, said, "Surely it is not
I, [b]Rabbi?" Jesus *said to him, "[c]You have said *it* yourself."
26 [a]While they were eating, Jesus took *some* bread, and
[1b]after a blessing, He broke *it* and gave *it* to the disciples, and
said, "Take, eat; this is My body."
27 And when He had taken a cup and given thanks, He gave *it*
to them, saying, "Drink from it, all of you;
28 for [a]this is My blood of the covenant, which is poured out
for [b]many for forgiveness of sins.
29 "But I say to you, I will not drink of this fruit of the vine
from now on until that day when I drink it new with you in
My Father's kingdom."
30 [a]After singing a hymn, they went out to [b]the Mount of Olives.
31 Then Jesus *said to them, "You will all [1a]fall away because
of Me this night, for it is written, '[b]I WILL STRIKE DOWN THE
SHEPHERD, AND THE SHEEP OF THE FLOCK SHALL BE [c]SCATTERED.'
32 "But after I have been raised, [a]I will go ahead of you to
Galilee."
33 But Peter said to Him, "*Even* though all may [1]fall away
because of You, I will never fall away."

12 [a]John 19:40
13 [a]Mark 14:9
14 [a]Matt 26:14-16: *Mark 14:10, 11; Luke 22:3-6* [b]Matt 10:4; 26:25, 47; 27:3; John 6:71; 12:4; 13:26; Acts 1:16
15 [1]Lit *and I will* [2]Or *deliver* [3]I.e. silver shekels [a]Matt 10:4 [b]Ex 21:32; Zech 11:12
16 [1]Or *deliver* [2]Lit *Him*
17 [a]Matt 26:17-19: *Mark 14:12-16; Luke 22:7-13* [b]Ex 12:18-20
18 [a]Mark 14:13; Luke 22:10 [b]John 7:6, 8
20 [a]Matt 26:20-24: *Mark 14:17-21*
21 [a]Luke 22:21-23; John 13:21f
22 [1]Or *one after another*
23 [a]Ps 41:9; John 13:18, 26
24 [1]Lit *for him if that man had not been born* [a]Matt 26:31, 54, 56; Mark 9:12; Luke 24:25-27, 46; Acts 17:2f; 26:22f; 1 Cor 15:3; 1 Pet 1:10f [b]Matt 18:7; Mark 14:21
25 [a]Matt 26:14 [b]Matt 23:7; 26:49 [c]Matt 26:64; 27:11; Luke 22:70
26 [1]Lit *having blessed* [a]Matt 26:26-29: *Mark 14:22-25; Luke 22:17-20; 1 Cor 11:23-25;* 1 Cor 10:16 [b]Matt 14:19
28 [a]Ex 24:8; Heb 9:20 [b]Matt 20:28
30 [a]Matt 26:30-35: *Mark 14:26-31; Luke 22:31-34* [b]Matt 21:1
31 [1]Or *stumble* [a]Matt 11:6 [b]Zech 13:7 [c]John 16:32
32 [a]Matt 28:7, 10, 16; Mark 16:7
33 [1]Or *stumble*

34 Jesus said to him, "[a]Truly I say to you that [b]this *very* night,
before a rooster crows, you will deny Me three times."
35 Peter *said to Him, "[a]Even if I have to die with You, I will
not deny You." All the disciples said the same thing too.
36 [a]Then Jesus *came with them to a place called [b]Gethsemane,
and *said to His disciples, "Sit here while I go over there and pray."
37 And He took with Him [a]Peter and the two sons of Zebedee,
and began to be grieved and distressed.
38 Then He *said to them, "[a]My soul is deeply grieved, to the
point of death; remain here and [b]keep watch with Me."
39 And He went a little beyond *them,* and fell on His face and
prayed, saying, "My Father, if it is possible, let [a]this cup pass
from Me; [b]yet not as I will, but as You will."
40 And He *came to the disciples and *found them sleeping,
and *said to Peter, "So, you *men* could not [a]keep watch with
Me for one hour?
41 "[a]Keep watching and praying that you may not enter into
temptation; [b]the spirit is willing, but the flesh is weak."
42 He went away again a second time and prayed, saying,
"My Father, if this [a]cannot pass away unless I drink it, [b]Your
will be done."
43 Again He came and found them sleeping, for their eyes
were heavy.
44 And He left them again, and went away and prayed a third
time, saying the same thing once more.
45 Then He *came to the disciples and *said to them, "[1]Are
you still sleeping and resting? Behold, [a]the hour is at hand and
the Son of Man is being betrayed into the hands of sinners.
46 "Get up, let us be going; behold, the one who betrays Me is
at hand!"
47 [a]While He was still speaking, behold, [b]Judas, one of the
twelve, came up [1]accompanied by a large crowd with swords and
clubs, *who came* from the chief priests and elders of the people.
48 Now he who was betraying Him gave them a sign, saying,
"Whomever I kiss, He is the one; seize Him."
49 Immediately Judas went to
Jesus and said, "Hail, [a]Rabbi!" and
kissed Him.
50 And Jesus said to him,
"[a]Friend, *do* what you have come
for." Then they came and laid
hands on Jesus and seized Him.
51 And behold, [a]one of those
who were with Jesus [1]reached
and drew out his [b]sword, and
struck the [a]slave of the high
priest and [2]cut off his ear.
52 Then Jesus *said to him, "Put
your sword back into its place; for
[a]all those who take up the sword
shall perish by the sword.

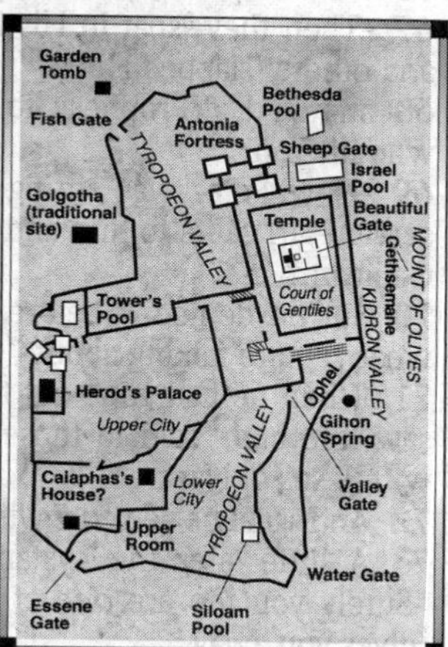

Jerusalem of the New Testament

34 [a]Matt 26:75; John 13:38 [b]Mark 14:30
35 [a]John 13:37
36 [a]Matt 26:36-46: *Mark 14:32-42; Luke 22:40-46* [b]Mark 14:32; Luke 22:39; John 18:1
37 [a]Matt 4:21; 17:1; Mark 5:37
38 [a]John 12:27 [b]Matt 26:40, 41
39 [a]Matt 20:22 [b]Matt 26:42; Mark 14:36; Luke 22:42; John 6:38
40 [a]Matt 26:38
41 [a]Matt 26:38 [b]Mark 14:38
42 [a]Matt 20:22 [b]Matt 26:39; Mark 14:36; Luke 22:42; John 6:38
45 [1]Or *Keep on sleeping therefore* [a]Mark 14:41; John 12:27; 13:1
47 [1]Lit *and with him* [a]Matt 26:47-56: *Mark 14:43-50; Luke 22:47-53; John 18:3-11* [b]Matt 26:14
49 [a]Matt 23:7; 26:25
50 [a]Matt 20:13; 22:12
51 [1]Lit *extended the hand* [2]Lit *took off* [a]Mark 14:47; Luke 22:50; John 18:10 [b]Luke 22:38
52 [a]Gen 9:6; Rev 13:10

53 "Or do you think that I cannot appeal to My Father, and He
will at once put at My disposal more than twelve [1a]legions of
[b]angels?
54 "How then will [a]the Scriptures be fulfilled, *which say* that it
must happen this way?"
55 At that time Jesus said to the crowds, "Have you come out
with swords and clubs to arrest Me as *you would* against a
robber? [a]Every day I used to sit in the temple teaching and you
did not seize Me.
56 "But all this has taken place to fulfill [a]the Scriptures of the
prophets." Then all the disciples left Him and fled.
57 [a]Those who had seized Jesus led Him away to [b]Caiaphas,
the high priest, where the scribes and the elders were gathered
together.
58 But [a]Peter was following Him at a distance as far as the
[b]courtyard of the high priest, and entered in, and sat down
with the [1c]officers to see the outcome.
59 Now the chief priests and the whole [1a]Council kept trying
to obtain false testimony against Jesus, so that they might put
Him to death.
60 They did not find *any,* even though many false witnesses
came forward. But later on [a]two came forward,
61 and said, "This man stated, '[a]I am able to destroy the
[1]temple of God and to rebuild it [2]in three days.'"
62 The high priest stood up and said to Him, "Do You not
answer? What is it that these men are testifying against You?"
63 But [a]Jesus kept silent. [b]And the high priest said to Him, "I
[1c]adjure You by [d]the living God, that You tell us whether You
are [2]the Christ, [e]the Son of God."
64 Jesus *said to him, "[a]You have said it *yourself;* nevertheless
I tell you, [1]hereafter you will see [b]THE SON OF MAN SITTING AT THE
RIGHT HAND OF POWER, and [c]COMING ON THE CLOUDS OF HEAVEN."
65 Then the high priest [a]tore his [1]robes and said, "He has
blasphemed! What further need do we have of witnesses?
Behold, you have now heard the blasphemy;
66 what do you think?" They answered, "[a]He deserves death!"
67 [a]Then they [b]spat in His face and beat Him with their fists;
and others [1]slapped Him,
68 and said, "[a]Prophesy to us, You [1]Christ; who is the one
who hit You?"
69 [a]Now Peter was sitting outside in the [b]courtyard, and a
servant-girl came to him and said, "You too were with Jesus the
Galilean."
70 But he denied *it* before them all, saying, "I do not know
what you are talking about."
71 When he had gone out to the gateway, another *servant-girl*
saw him and *said to those who were there, "This man was
with Jesus of Nazareth."
72 And again he denied *it* with an oath, "I do not know the man."
73 A little later the bystanders came up and said to Peter,
"Surely you too are *one* of them; [a]for even the way you talk
[1]gives you away."

53 [1]A legion equaled 6,000 troops [a]Mark 5:9, 15; Luke 8:30 [b]Matt 4:11

54 [a]Matt 26:24

55 [a]Mark 12:35; 14:49; Luke 4:20; 19:47; 20:1; 21:37; John 7:14, 28; 8:2, 20; 18:20

56 [a]Matt 26:24

57 [a]Matt 26:57-68: *Mark 14:53-65; John 18:12f, 19-24* [b]Matt 26:3

58 [1]Or *servants* [a]John 18:15 [b]Matt 26:3 [c]Matt 5:25; John 7:32, 45f; 19:6; Acts 5:22, 26

59 [1]Or *Sanhedrin* [a]Matt 5:22

60 [a]Deut 19:15

61 [1]Or *sanctuary* [2]Or *after* [a]Matt 27:40; Mark 14:58; 15:29; John 2:19; Acts 6:14

63 [1]Or *charge You under oath* [2]I.e. the Messiah [a]Matt 27:12, 14; John 19:9 [b]Matt 26:63-66; Luke 22:67-71 [c]Lev 5:1 [d]Matt 16:16 [e]Matt 4:3

64 [1]Or *from now on* [a]Matt 26:25 [b]Ps 110:1; Mark 14:62 [c]Dan 7:13; Matt 16:27f

65 [1]Or *outer garments* [a]Num 14:6; Mark 14:63; Acts 14:14

66 [a]Lev 24:16; John 19:7

67 [1]Or *beat Him with rods* [a]Is 50:6; Matt 26:67, 68; Luke 22:63-65; John 18:22 [b]Matt 27:30; Mark 10:34

68 [1]I.e. the Messiah [a]Mark 14:65; Luke 22:64

69 [a]Matt 26:69-75: *Mark 14:66-72; Luke 22:55-62; John 18:16-18, 25-27* [b]Matt 26:3

73 [1]Lit *makes you evident* [a]Mark 14:70; Luke 22:59; John 18:26

74 Then he began to curse and swear, "I do not know the man!"
And immediately a rooster crowed.
75 And Peter remembered the word which Jesus had said,
"[a]Before a rooster crows, you will deny Me three times." And
he went out and wept bitterly.

Chapter 27 Theme ______________________________

27 [a]Now when morning came, all the chief priests and the
elders of the people conferred together against Jesus to
put Him to death;
2 and they bound Him, and led Him away and [a]delivered
Him to [b]Pilate the governor.
3 Then when [a]Judas, who had betrayed Him, saw that He
had been condemned, he felt remorse and returned [b]the thirty
[1]pieces of silver to the chief priests and elders,
4 saying, "I have sinned by betraying innocent blood." But
they said, "What is that to us? [a]See *to that* yourself!"
5 And he threw the pieces of silver into [a]the temple sanctuary
and departed; and [b]he went away and hanged himself.
6 The chief priests took the pieces of silver and said, "It is
not lawful to put them into the temple treasury, since it is the
price of blood."
7 And they conferred together and [1]with the money bought
the Potter's Field as a burial place for strangers.
8 [a]For this reason that field has been called the Field of Blood
to this day.
9 Then that which was spoken through Jeremiah the prophet
was fulfilled: "[a]AND [1]THEY TOOK THE THIRTY PIECES OF SILVER, THE
PRICE OF THE ONE WHOSE PRICE HAD BEEN SET by the sons of Israel;
10 [a]AND [1]THEY GAVE THEM FOR THE POTTER'S FIELD, AS THE LORD
DIRECTED ME."
11 [a]Now Jesus stood before the governor, and the governor
questioned Him, saying, "Are You the [b]King of the Jews?" And
Jesus said to him, "[c]*It is as* you say."
12 And while He was being accused by the chief priests and
elders, [a]He did not answer.
13 Then Pilate *said to Him, "Do You not hear how many
things they testify against You?"
14 And [a]He did not answer him with regard to even a *single*
[1]charge, so the governor was quite amazed.
15 [a]Now at *the* feast the governor was accustomed to release
for the [1]people *any* one prisoner whom they wanted.
16 At that time they were holding a notorious prisoner, called
Barabbas.
17 So when the people gathered together, Pilate said to them,
"Whom do you want me to release for you? Barabbas, or Jesus
[a]who is called Christ?"
18 For he knew that because of envy they had handed Him over.
19 [a]While he was sitting on the judgment seat, his wife sent
him *a message,* saying, "Have nothing to do with that
[b]righteous Man; for [1]last night I suffered greatly [c]in a dream
because of Him."

75 [a]Matt 26:34
27:1 [a]Mark 15:1; Luke 22:66; John 18:28
2 [a]Matt 20:19 [b]Luke 3:1; 13:1; 23:12; Acts 3:13; 4:27; 1 Tim 6:13
3 [1]Or *silver shekels* [a]Matt 26:14 [b]Matt 26:15
4 [a]Matt 27:24
5 [a]Matt 26:61; Luke 1:9, 21 [b]Acts 1:18
7 [1]Lit *from them*
8 [a]Acts 1:19
9 [1]Or *I took;* cf Zech 11:13 [a]Zech 11:12
10 [1]Some early mss read *I gave* [a]Zech 11:13
11 [a]Matt 27:11-14: *Mark 15:2-5; Luke 23:2, 3; John 18:29-38* [b]Matt 2:2 [c]Matt 26:25
12 [a]Matt 26:63; John 19:9
14 [1]Lit *word* [a]Matt 27:12; Mark 15:5; Luke 23:9; John 19:9
15 [1]Lit *crowd* [a]Matt 27:15-26: *Mark 15:6-15; Luke 23:17-25;* John 18:39-19:16
17 [a]Matt 1:16; 27:22
19 [1]Lit *today* [a]John 19:13; Acts 12:21; 18:12, 16f; 25:6, 10, 17 [b]Matt 27:24 [c]Gen 20:6; 31:11; Num 12:6; Job 33:15; Matt 1:20; 2:12f, 19, 22

20 But the chief priests and the elders persuaded the crowds
to [a]ask for Barabbas and to put Jesus to death.
21 But the governor [1]said to them, "Which of the two do you
want me to release for you?" And they said, "Barabbas."
22 Pilate *said to them, "Then what shall I do with Jesus [a]who
is called Christ?" They all *said, "[1]Crucify Him!"
23 And he said, "Why, what evil has He done?" But they kept
shouting all the more, saying, "[1]Crucify Him!"
24 When Pilate saw that he was accomplishing nothing, but
rather that [a]a riot was starting, he took water and [b]washed his
hands in front of the crowd, saying, "I am innocent of [c]this
Man's blood; [d]see *to that* yourselves."
25 And all the people said, "[a]His blood shall be on us and on
our children!"
26 Then he released Barabbas [1]for them; but after having
Jesus [a]scourged, he handed Him over to be crucified.
27 [a]Then the soldiers of the governor took Jesus into [b]the
[1]Praetorium and gathered the whole *Roman* [2c]cohort around Him.
28 They stripped Him and [a]put a scarlet robe on Him.
29 [a]And after twisting together a crown of thorns, they put it
on His head, and a [1]reed in His right hand; and they knelt down
before Him and mocked Him, saying, "[b]Hail, King of the Jews!"
30 [a]They spat on Him, and took the reed and *began* to beat
Him on the head.
31 [a]After they had mocked Him, they took the *scarlet* robe off
Him and put His *own* garments back on Him, and led Him
away to crucify Him.
32 [a]As they were coming out, they found a man of [b]Cyrene
named Simon, [1]whom they pressed into service to bear His cross.
33 [a]And when they came to a place called [b]Golgotha, which
means Place of a Skull,
34 [a]they gave Him [b]wine to drink mixed with gall; and after
tasting *it,* He was unwilling to drink.
35 And when they had crucified Him, [a]they divided up His
garments among themselves by casting [1]lots.
36 And sitting down, they *began* to [a]keep watch over Him there.
37 And above His head they put up the charge against Him
[1]which read, "[a]THIS IS JESUS THE KING OF THE JEWS."
38 At that time two robbers *were crucified with Him, one on
the right and one on the left.
39 And those passing by were [1]hurling abuse at Him, [a]wagging
their heads
40 and saying, "[a]You who *are going to* destroy the temple and
rebuild it in three days, save Yourself! [b]If You are the Son of God,
come down from the cross."
41 In the same way the chief priests also, along with the scribes
and elders, were mocking *Him* and saying,
42 "[a]He saved others; [1]He cannot save Himself. [b]He is the King
of Israel; let Him now come down from the cross, and we will
believe in Him.
43 "[a]HE TRUSTS IN GOD; LET GOD RESCUE *Him* now, IF HE [1]DELIGHTS
IN HIM; for He said, 'I am the Son of God.'"

INSIGHT

The ***Praetorium*** was used as the temporary Roman military headquarters or as the palace in Jerusalem to house the Roman governor. It was either a building next to Herod's palace or the Antonia Fortress beside the temple mount complex. See the map on page 1607 and the illustration of the temple mount on page NISB-40.

20 [a]Acts 3:14
21 [1]Lit *answered and said to them*
22 [1]Lit *Let Him be crucified* [a]Matt 1:16
23 [1]Lit *Let Him be crucified*
24 [a]Matt 26:5 [b]Deut 21:6-8 [c]Matt 27:19 [d]Matt 27:4
25 [a]Josh 2:19; Acts 5:28
26 [1]Or *to them* [a]Mark 15:15; Luke 23:16; John 19:1
27 [1]I.e. the governor's official residence [2]Or *battalion* [a]Matt 27:27-31: *Mark 15:16-20* [b]Matt 26:3; John 18:28, 33; 19:9 [c]Acts 10:1
28 [a]Mark 15:17; John 19:2
29 [1]Or *staff;* i.e. to mimic a king's scepter [a]Mark 15:17; John 19:2 [b]Mark 15:18; John 19:3
30 [a]Matt 26:67; Mark 10:34; 14:65; 15:19
31 [a]Mark 15:20
32 [1]Lit *this one* [a]Matt 27:32: *Mark 15:21; Luke 23:26;* John 19:17 [b]Acts 2:10; 6:9; 11:20; 13:1
33 [a]Matt 27:34-44: *Mark 15:22-32; Luke 23:33-43; John 19:17-24* [b]Luke 23:33; John 19:17
34 [a]Ps 69:21 [b]Mark 15:23
35 [1]Lit *a lot* [a]Ps 22:18
36 [a]Matt 27:54
37 [1]Lit *written* [a]Mark 15:26; Luke 23:38; John 19:19
39 [1]Or *blaspheming* [a]Job 16:4; Ps 22:7; 109:25; Lam 2:15; Mark 15:29
40 [a]Matt 26:61; John 2:19 [b]Matt 27:42
42 [1]Or *can He not save Himself?* [a]Mark 15:31; Luke 23:35 [b]Matt 27:37; Luke 23:37; John 1:49; 12:13
43 [1]Or *takes pleasure in;* or *cares for him* [a]Ps 22:8

44 [a]Luke 23:39-43
45 [1]I.e. noon [2]Or *occurred* [3]I.e. 3 p.m. [a]Matt 27:45-56: *Mark 15:33-41; Luke 23:44-49*
46 [a]Ps 22:1
48 [a]Ps 69:21; Mark 15:36; Luke 23:36; John 19:29
49 [1]Lit *Permit that we see* [2]Some early mss read *And another took a spear and pierced His side, and there came out water and blood* (cf John 19:34)
50 [a]Mark 15:37; Luke 23:46; John 19:30
51 [1]Or *curtain* [a]Matt 27:51-56: *Mark 15:38-41;* Luke 23:47-49 [b]Ex 26:31ff; Mark 15:38; Luke 23:45; Heb 9:3 [c]Matt 27:54
52 [1]Or *holy ones* [a]Acts 7:60
53 [a]Matt 4:5
54 [1]Or *a son of God* or *a son of a god* [a]Mark 15:39; Luke 23:47 [b]Matt 27:36 [c]Matt 27:51 [d]Matt 4:3; 27:43
55 [1]Or *caring for Him* [a]Mark 15:40f; Luke 23:49; John 19:25 [b]Mark 15:41; Luke 8:2, 3
56 [a]Matt 28:1; Mark 15:40, 47; 16:9; Luke 8:2; John 19:25; 20:1, 18 [b]Matt 20:20
57 [a]Matt 27:57-61: *Mark 15:42-47; Luke 23:50-56; John 19:38-42*
60 [a]Matt 27:66; 28:2; Mark 16:4
61 [a]Matt 27:56; 28:1
62 [1]Lit *which is after* [a]Mark 15:42; Luke 23:54; John 19:14, 31, 42
63 [a]Matt 16:21; 17:23; 20:19; Mark 8:31; 9:31; 10:34; Luke 9:22; 18:31-33
65 [a]Matt 27:66; 28:11
66 [a]Matt 27:65; 28:11 [b]Dan 6:17 [c]Matt 27:60; 28:2; Mark 16:4

44 [a]The robbers who had been crucified with Him were also
insulting Him with the same words.
45 [a]Now from the [1]sixth hour darkness [2]fell upon all the land
until the [3]ninth hour.
46 About the ninth hour Jesus cried out with a loud voice,
saying, "[a]ELI, ELI, LAMA SABACHTHANI?" that is, "MY GOD, MY
GOD, WHY HAVE YOU FORSAKEN ME?"
47 And some of those who were standing there, when they
heard it, *began* saying, "This man is calling for Elijah."
48 [a]Immediately one of them ran, and taking a sponge, he filled
it with sour wine and put it on a reed, and gave Him a drink.
49 But the rest *of them* said, "[1]Let us see whether Elijah will
come to save Him[2]."
50 And Jesus [a]cried out again with a loud voice, and yielded
up His spirit.
51 [a]And behold, [b]the [1]veil of the temple was torn in two from
top to bottom; and [c]the earth shook and the rocks were split.
52 The tombs were opened, and many bodies of the [1]saints
who had [a]fallen asleep were raised;
53 and coming out of the tombs after His resurrection they
entered [a]the holy city and appeared to many.
54 [a]Now the centurion, and those who were with him
[b]keeping guard over Jesus, when they saw [c]the earthquake and
the things that were happening, became very frightened and
said, "Truly this was [1d]the Son of God!"
55 [a]Many women were there looking on from a distance, who
had followed Jesus from Galilee while [1b]ministering to Him.
56 Among them was [a]Mary Magdalene, and Mary the mother
of James and Joseph, and [b]the mother of the sons of Zebedee.
57 [a]When it was evening, there came a rich man from
Arimathea, named Joseph, who himself had also become a
disciple of Jesus.
58 This man went to Pilate and asked for the body of Jesus.
Then Pilate ordered it to be given *to him.*
59 And Joseph took the body and wrapped it in a clean linen cloth,
60 and laid it in his own new tomb, which he had hewn out
in the rock; and he rolled [a]a large stone against the entrance of
the tomb and went away.
61 And [a]Mary Magdalene was there, and the other Mary, sitting
opposite the grave.
62 Now on the next day, [1]the day after [a]the preparation, the
chief priests and the Pharisees gathered together with Pilate,
63 and said, "Sir, we remember that when He was still alive
that deceiver said, '[a]After three days I *am to* rise again.'
64 "Therefore, give orders for the grave to be made secure until
the third day, otherwise His disciples may come and steal Him
away and say to the people, 'He has risen from the dead,' and
the last deception will be worse than the first."
65 Pilate said to them, "You have a [a]guard; go, make it *as*
secure as you know how."
66 And they went and made the grave secure, and along with
[a]the guard they set a [b]seal on [c]the stone.

Chapter 28 Theme ______________________

28 [a]Now after the Sabbath, as it began to dawn toward the
first *day* of the week, [b]Mary Magdalene and the other
Mary came to look at the grave.
2 And behold, a severe earthquake had occurred, for [a]an
angel of the Lord descended from heaven and came and rolled
away [b]the stone and sat upon it.
3 And [a]his appearance was like lightning, and his clothing as
white as snow.
4 The guards shook for fear of him and became like dead men.
5 The angel said to the women, "[1a]Do not be afraid; for I
know that you are looking for Jesus who has been crucified.
6 "He is not here, for He has risen, [a]just as He said. Come, see
the place where He was lying.
7 "Go quickly and tell His disciples that He has risen from the
dead; and behold, He is going ahead of you [a]into Galilee, there
you will see Him; behold, I have told you."
8 And they left the tomb quickly with fear and great joy and
ran to report it to His disciples.
9 And behold, Jesus met them [1]and greeted them. And they
came up and took hold of His feet and worshiped Him.
10 Then Jesus *said to them, "[1a]Do not be afraid; go and take
word to [b]My brethren to leave [c]for Galilee, and there they will
see Me."
11 Now while they were on their way, some of [a]the guard
came into the city and reported to the chief priests all that had
happened.
12 And when they had assembled with the elders and consulted
together, they gave a large sum of money to the soldiers,
13 and said, "You are to say, 'His disciples came by night and
stole Him away while we were asleep.'
14 "And if this should come to [a]the governor's ears, we will
win him over and [1]keep you out of trouble."
15 And they took the money and did as they had been
instructed; and this story was widely [a]spread among the Jews,
and is [b]to this day.
16 But the eleven disciples proceeded [a]to Galilee, to the
mountain which Jesus had designated.
17 When they saw Him, they worshiped *Him;* but [a]some were
doubtful.
18 And Jesus came up and spoke to them, saying, "[a]All
authority has been given to Me in heaven and on earth.
19 "[1a]Go therefore and [b]make disciples of [c]all the nations,
[d]baptizing them in the name of the Father and the Son and the
Holy Spirit,
20 teaching them to observe all that I commanded you; and lo,
[a]I am with you [1]always, even to [b]the end of the age."

28:1 [a]Matt 28:1-8: *Mark 16:1-8; Luke 24:1-10;* John 20:1-8 [b]Matt 27:56, 61

2 [a]Luke 24:4; John 20:12 [b]Matt 27:66; Mark 16:4

3 [a]Dan 7:9; 10:6; Mark 9:3; John 20:12; Acts 1:10

5 [1]Or *Stop being afraid* [a]Matt 14:27; 28:10; Rev 1:17

6 [a]Matt 12:40; 16:21; 27:63

7 [a]Matt 26:32; 28:10, 16; Mark 16:7

9 [1]Lit *saying hello*

10 [1]Or *Stop being afraid* [a]Matt 14:27; 28:5 [b]John 20:17; Rom 8:29; Heb 2:11f, 17 [c]Matt 26:32; 28:7, 16

11 [a]Matt 27:65, 66

14 [1]Lit *make you free from care* [a]Matt 27:2

15 [a]Matt 9:31; Mark 1:45 [b]Matt 27:8

16 [a]Matt 26:32; 28:7, 10; Mark 15:41; 16:7

17 [a]Mark 16:11

18 [a]Dan 7:13f; Matt 11:27; 26:64; Rom 14:9; Eph 1:20-22; Phil 2:9f; Col 2:10; 1 Pet 3:22

19 [1]Or *Having gone;* Gr aorist part. [a]Mark 16:15f [b]Matt 13:52; Acts 1:8; 14:21 [c]Matt 25:32; Luke 24:47 [d]Acts 2:38; 8:16; Rom 6:3; 1 Cor 1:13, 15ff; Gal 3:27

20 [1]Lit *all the days* [a]Matt 18:20; Acts 18:10 [b]Matt 13:39

Theme of Matthew:

Author:

Date:

Purpose:

Key Words:

king (kingdom, kingdom of heaven, kingdom of God)

fulfilled

mark every reference to the devil or demons

covenant

Spirit (Holy Spirit)

believe (faith)

disciples (disciple)

sign (signs)

SEGMENT DIVISIONS

		CHAPTER THEMES
		1
		2
		3
		4
		5
		6
		7
		8
		9
		10
		11
		12
		13
		14
		15
		16
		17
		18
		19
		20
		21
		22
		23
		24
		25
		26
		27
		28

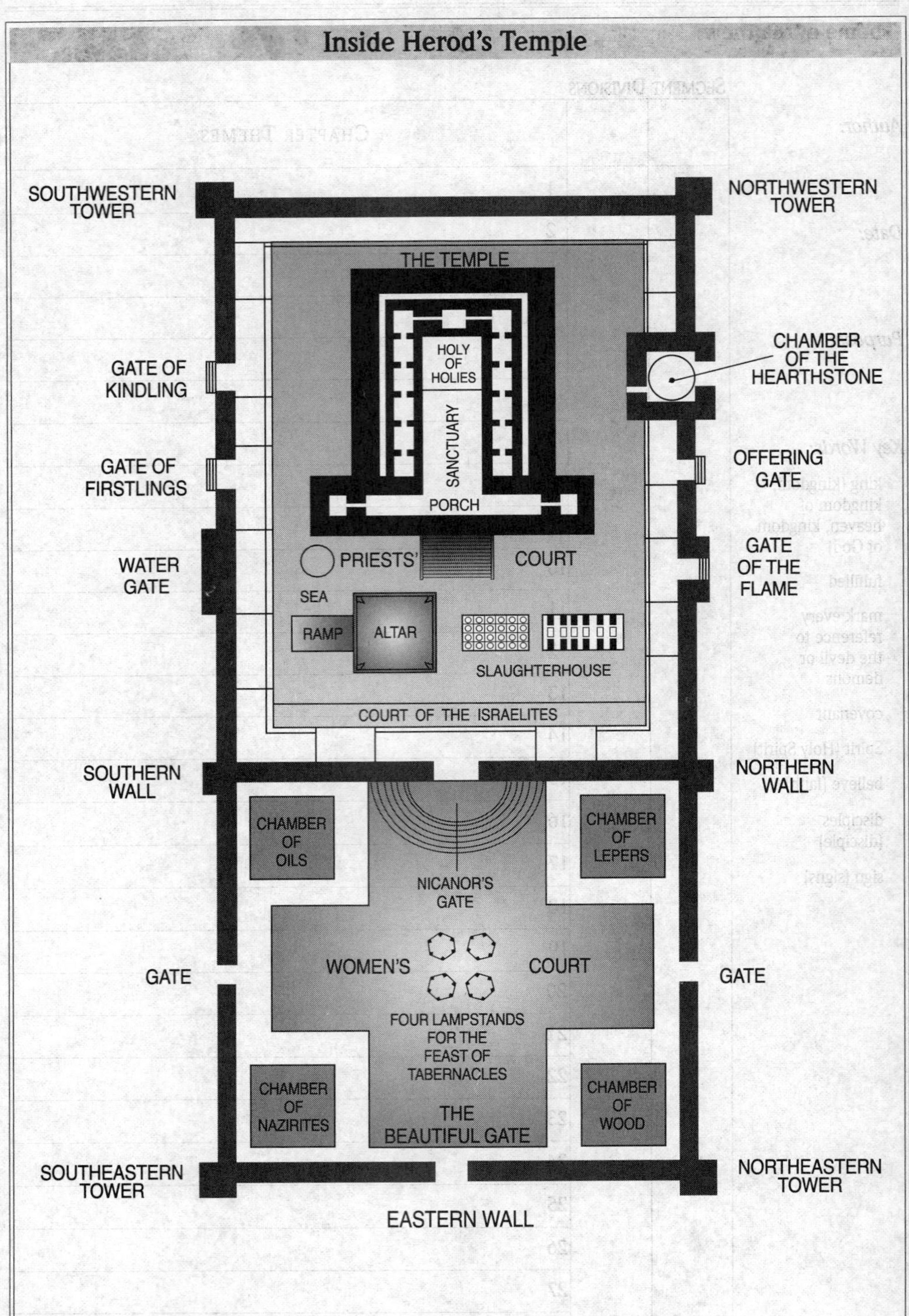
Inside Herod's Temple
SOUTHWESTERN TOWER
NORTHWESTERN TOWER
THE TEMPLE
HOLY OF HOLIES
SANCTUARY
PORCH
CHAMBER OF THE HEARTHSTONE
GATE OF KINDLING
GATE OF FIRSTLINGS
OFFERING GATE
WATER GATE
GATE OF THE FLAME
PRIESTS' COURT
SEA
RAMP
ALTAR
SLAUGHTERHOUSE
COURT OF THE ISRAELITES
SOUTHERN WALL
NORTHERN WALL
CHAMBER OF OILS
CHAMBER OF LEPERS
NICANOR'S GATE
WOMEN'S COURT
GATE
GATE
FOUR LAMPSTANDS FOR THE FEAST OF TABERNACLES
CHAMBER OF NAZIRITES
CHAMBER OF WOOD
THE BEAUTIFUL GATE
SOUTHEASTERN TOWER
NORTHEASTERN TOWER
EASTERN WALL

MARK

Jesus was clearly born to be King of the Jews, as Matthew points out. However, the gospel was not just for the Jews; it was for the whole world. Before Jesus would reign as King of kings, He would be servant of all by dying for mankind. Mark writes of the works and authority of the One who came not to be served but to serve, and to give His life a ransom for many.

THINGS TO DO

Mark is a fast-paced Gospel which emphasizes Jesus' works rather than His teachings. Although Jesus is referred to as a teacher a number of times, Mark shows Jesus' power and authority through the works He does as He goes about His Father's business.

In reading this Gospel you will notice the repeated use of the word *immediately* as Mark takes his reader from one event in the life of Jesus to another. These events and the works of Jesus show the reader Jesus' power and authority as the servant of God and man.

Chapters 1–13

Read through all of the instructions below before you begin working on chapters 1–13.

1. Although the emphasis in the Gospel of Mark is on the works of Jesus that show His divine power, Mark opens his Gospel by declaring the deity of Jesus Christ. He also gives an account of the events that took place prior to and in preparation for Jesus' ministry. Read Mark 1:1-13 and list in your notebook the following:

   a. The facts that declare the deity of Jesus Christ.

   b. The events that took place in Jesus' life prior to His public ministry.

2. Now read Mark chapter by chapter, and in a distinctive way mark in the text the key words listed on the MARK AT A GLANCE chart on page 1650.

   a. Record these key words on an index card and use it as a bookmark while you study this Gospel. Mark references to time with a green clock ⏲ so they're distinctive.

   b. Double-underline in green each geographical location, whether it is a city, a region, or a place, such as the temple or the synagogue. Noting these will help in your overall understanding of the events in Jesus' life.

3. Chapters 1–3 cover events (including healings and miracles) that demonstrate Jesus' authority.

   a. As you look at each event, observe how it demonstrates Jesus' authority, how the people respond, and what Jesus has authority over.

   b. Record your insights in your notebook by listing the event and then under that event noting how the people, religious leaders, disciples, and others responded. For example:

      Healing on Sabbath
      Pharisees counsel to destroy Him

   c. After you have recorded these demonstrations and responses, be sure to record the scope of Jesus' authority. For example, next to the illustration above, you might write, "Authority over Sabbath." Look at His works. Watch for Jesus' power over nature, demons, disease, and so on. Ask God to show you how this demonstration of Jesus' power declares His deity. Also, notice how these events portray Jesus as a Servant.

d. Throughout these chapters, Jesus faces the accusations and rejection of the Jewish religious leaders of His day. Each time the scribes, Pharisees, or Sadducees accuse Jesus, He reasons with them. Mark that conflict in the margin with a star.

4. Record in your notebook the main points of Jesus' teachings, whether the teaching comes as a result of healing, casting out demons, working a miracle, or responding to a question from either the disciples or the multitude. Also note the response of those who hear the teaching.

5. Look at every reference to the kingdom of God you marked and do the following:

a. Note when Jesus increases His emphasis on the kingdom of God.

b. Underline every prediction of Jesus' death and resurrection and note how it coincides with Jesus' emphasis on the kingdom of God.

c. Observe that in the first part of Mark, Jesus defines the kingdom of God, and then at chapter 9 the emphasis shifts to how to enter the kingdom.

d. Compile the *main* teachings from Mark about the kingdom of God on page 1758. Note the chapter and verse as you do this.

6. After you finish reading and marking each chapter, record the theme of that chapter on MARK AT A GLANCE. Also record it in your Bible.

Chapters 14–16

1. When you read Mark's account, record the progression of events during the trial, death, burial, and resurrection of Christ on the charts on pages 1757 and 1760 and in your notebook. Note the chapter and verse beside each insight.

a. When you record the circumstances surrounding the resurrection of Jesus Christ, also note any postresurrection appearances recorded in Mark. After you do this for all four Gospels you will have comprehensive notes on everything that took place at this time in our Lord's life.

b. As you do this, remember that because Luke gives the consecutive order of events, it is a plumb line for the other Gospel records.

2. Complete MARK AT A GLANCE. Fill in any segment divisions you have seen from studying the book.

Things to Think About

1. People often say that Mark shows the servant aspect of Jesus' ministry. Although the word *servant* is used only four times, Mark 10:45 says that Jesus "did not come to be served, but to serve, and to give His life a ransom for many." How like your Lord are you in that respect? Would others regard you as a servant? Or do they see you as having to be "number one"? What is it to be "number one" in God's eyes?

2. Jesus talks about discipleship in this Gospel. According to Jesus, what is required of disciples? Can you consider yourself a true disciple of Jesus Christ? Why? Think about Mark 8:34-36 and 10:28-31.

3. Can you say with Peter, "You are the Christ, the Son of the living God"? (Matthew 16:16). And will you listen to Jesus as the Father commands?

Chapter 1 Theme ______________________

1 The beginning of the gospel of Jesus Christ, [a]the Son of God.
2 [a]As it is written in Isaiah the prophet:
"[b]BEHOLD, I SEND MY MESSENGER [1]AHEAD OF YOU,
WHO WILL PREPARE YOUR WAY;
3 [a]THE VOICE OF ONE CRYING IN THE WILDERNESS,
'MAKE READY THE WAY OF THE LORD,
MAKE HIS PATHS STRAIGHT.'"
4 John the Baptist appeared in the wilderness [1a]preaching a
baptism of repentance for the [b]forgiveness of sins.
5 And all the country of Judea was going out to him, and all
the people of Jerusalem; and they were being baptized by him
in the Jordan River, confessing their sins.
6 John was clothed with camel's hair and *wore* [a]a leather belt
around his waist, and [1]his diet was locusts and wild honey.
7 And he was [1]preaching, and saying, "After me One is coming
who is mightier than I, and I am not fit to stoop down and untie
the thong of His sandals.
8 "I baptized you [1]with water; but He will baptize you [1]with
the Holy Spirit."
9 [a]In those days Jesus [b]came from Nazareth in Galilee and
was baptized by John in the Jordan.
10 Immediately coming up out of the water, He saw the heavens
[1]opening, and the Spirit like a dove descending upon Him;
11 and a voice came out of the heavens: "[a]You are My beloved
Son, in You I am well-pleased."
12 [a]Immediately the Spirit *impelled Him *to go* out into the
wilderness.
13 And He was in the wilderness forty days being tempted by
[a]Satan; and He was with the wild beasts, and the angels were
ministering to Him.
14 [a]Now after John had been [1]taken into custody, Jesus came
into Galilee, [2b]preaching the gospel of God,
15 and saying, "[a]The time is fulfilled, and the kingdom of God
[1]is at hand; [b]repent and [2]believe in the gospel."
16 [a]As He was going along by the Sea of Galilee, He saw
Simon and Andrew, the brother of Simon, casting a net in the
sea; for they were fishermen.
17 And Jesus said to them, "Follow Me, and I will make you
become fishers of men."
18 Immediately they left their nets and followed Him.
19 Going on a little farther, He saw [1]James the son of Zebedee,
and John his brother, who were also in the boat mending the
nets.
20 Immediately He called them; and they left their father
Zebedee in the boat with the hired servants, and went away [1]to
follow Him.
21 [a]They *went into Capernaum; and immediately on the
Sabbath [b]He entered the synagogue and *began* to teach.
22 [a]They were amazed at His teaching; for He was teaching
them as *one* having authority, and not as the scribes.

1:1 [a]Matt 4:3
2 [1]Lit *before your face* [a]Mark 1:2-8: *Matt 3:1-11; Luke 3:2-16* [b]Mal 3:1; Matt 11:10; Luke 7:27
3 [a]Is 40:3; Matt 3:3; Luke 3:4; John 1:23
4 [1]Or *proclaiming* [a]Acts 13:24 [b]Luke 1:77
6 [1]Lit *he was eating* [a]2 Kin 1:8
7 [1]Or *proclaiming*
8 [1]The Gr here can be translated *in, with* or *by*
9 [a]Mark 1:9-11: *Matt 3:13-17; Luke 3:21, 22* [b]Matt 2:23; Luke 2:51
10 [1]Or *being parted*
11 [a]Ps 2:7; Is 42:1; Matt 3:17; 12:18; Mark 9:7; Luke 3:22
12 [a]Mark 1:12, 13: *Matt 4:1-11; Luke 4:1-13*
13 [a]Matt 4:10
14 [1]Lit *delivered up* [2]Or *proclaiming* [a]Matt 4:12 [b]Matt 4:23
15 [1]Lit *has come near* [2]Or *put your trust in* [a]Gal 4:4; Eph 1:10; 1 Tim 2:6; Titus 1:3 [b]Matt 3:2; Acts 20:21
16 [a]Mark 1:16-20: *Matt 4:18-22;* Luke 5:2-11; John 1:40-42
19 [1]Or *Jacob*
20 [1]Lit *after Him*
21 [a]Mark 1:21-28: *Luke 4:31-37* [b]Matt 4:23; Mark 1:39; 10:1
22 [a]Matt 7:28

23 Just then there was a man in their synagogue with an unclean spirit; and he cried out,

24 saying, "[a]What [1]business do we have with each other, Jesus [2]of [b]Nazareth? Have You come to destroy us? I know who You are—[c]the Holy One of God!"

25 And Jesus rebuked him, saying, "Be quiet, and come out of him!"

26 Throwing him into convulsions, the unclean spirit cried out with a loud voice and came out of him.

27 They were all [a]amazed, so that they debated among themselves, saying, "What is this? A new teaching with authority! He commands even the unclean spirits, and they obey Him."

28 Immediately the news about Him spread everywhere into all the surrounding district of Galilee.

29 [a]And immediately after they came [b]out of the synagogue, they came into the house of Simon and Andrew, with [1]James and John.

30 Now Simon's mother-in-law was lying sick with a fever; and immediately they *spoke to [1]Jesus about her.

31 And He came to her and raised her up, taking her by the hand, and the fever left her, and she [1]waited on them.

32 [a]When evening came, [b]after the sun had set, they *began* bringing to Him all who were ill and those who were [c]demon-possessed.

33 And the whole [a]city had gathered at the door.

34 And He [a]healed many who were ill with various diseases, and cast out many demons; and He was not permitting the demons to speak, because they knew who He was.

35 [a]In the early morning, while it was still dark, Jesus got up, left *the house,* and went away to a secluded place, and [b]was praying there.

36 Simon and his companions searched for Him;

37 they found Him, and *said to Him, "Everyone is looking for You."

38 He *said to them, "Let us go somewhere else to the towns nearby, so that I may [1]preach there also; for that is what I came for."

39 [a]And He went into their synagogues throughout all Galilee, [1]preaching and casting out the demons.

40 [a]And a leper *came to Jesus, beseeching Him and [b]falling on his knees before Him, and saying, "If You are willing, You can make me clean."

41 Moved with compassion, Jesus stretched out His hand and touched him, and *said to him, "I am willing; be cleansed."

42 Immediately the leprosy left him and he was cleansed.

43 And He sternly warned him and immediately sent him away,

44 and He *said to him, "[a]See that you say nothing to anyone; but [a]go, show yourself to the priest and [b]offer for your cleansing what Moses commanded, as a testimony to them."

45 But he went out and began to [a]proclaim it freely and to [a]spread the news around, to such an extent that [1]Jesus could no longer publicly enter a city, but [2]stayed out in unpopulated areas; and [b]they were coming to Him from everywhere.

24 [1]Lit *What to us and to You* (a Heb idiom) [2]Lit *the Nazarene* [a]Matt 8:29 [b]Matt 2:23; Mark 10:47; 14:67; 16:6; Luke 4:34; 24:19; Acts 24:5 [c]Luke 1:35; 4:34; John 6:69; Acts 3:14

27 [a]Mark 10:24, 32; 16:5, 6

29 [1]*Or Jacob* [a]Mark 1:29-31: *Matt 8:14, 15; Luke 4:38, 39* [b]Mark 1:21, 23

30 [1]Lit *Him*

31 [1]Or *served*

32 [a]Mark 1:32-34: *Matt 8:16, 17; Luke 4:40, 41* [b]Matt 8:16; Luke 4:40 [c]Matt 4:24

33 [a]Mark 1:21

34 [a]Matt 4:23

35 [a]Mark 1:35-38: *Luke 4:42, 43* [b]Matt 14:23; Luke 5:16

38 [1]Or *proclaim*

39 [1]Or *proclaiming* [a]Matt 4:23; 9:35; Mark 1:23; 3:1

40 [a]Mark 1:40-44: *Matt 8:2-4; Luke 5:12-14* [b]Matt 8:2; Mark 10:17; Luke 5:12

44 [a]Matt 8:4 [b]Lev 14:1-32

45 [1]Lit *He* [2]Lit *was* [a]Matt 28:15; Luke 5:15 [b]Mark 2:2, 13; 3:7; Luke 5:17; John 6:2

Chapter 2 Theme ______________________

2 When He had come back to Capernaum several days afterward, it was heard that He was at home.

2 And [a]many were gathered together, so that there was no longer room, not even near the door; and He was speaking the word to them.

3 [a]And they *came, bringing to Him a [b]paralytic, carried by four men.

4 Being unable to [1]get to Him because of the crowd, they [a]removed the roof [2]above Him; and when they had dug an opening, they let down the pallet on which the [b]paralytic was lying.

5 And Jesus seeing their faith *said to the paralytic, "[1]Son, [a]your sins are forgiven."

6 But some of the scribes were sitting there and reasoning in their hearts,

7 "Why does this man speak that way? He is blaspheming; [a]who can forgive sins [1]but God alone?"

8 Immediately Jesus, aware [1]in His spirit that they were reasoning that way within themselves, *said to them, "Why are you reasoning about these things in your hearts?

9 "Which is easier, to say to the [a]paralytic, 'Your sins are forgiven'; or to say, 'Get up, and pick up your pallet and walk'?

10 "But so that you may know that the Son of Man has authority on earth to forgive sins"—He *said to the paralytic,

11 "I say to you, get up, pick up your pallet and go home."

12 And he got up and immediately picked up the pallet and went out in the sight of everyone, so that they were all amazed and [a]were glorifying God, saying, "[b]We have never seen anything like this."

13 And He went out again by the seashore; and [a]all the [1]people were coming to Him, and He was teaching them.

14 [a]As He passed by, He saw [1b]Levi the *son* of Alphaeus sitting in the tax booth, and He *said to him, "[c]Follow Me!" And he got up and followed Him.

15 And it *[1]happened that He was reclining *at the table* in his house, and many tax collectors and [2]sinners [3]were dining with Jesus and His disciples; for there were many of them, and they were following Him.

16 When [a]the scribes of the Pharisees saw that He was eating with the sinners and tax collectors, they said to His disciples, "[b]Why is He eating and drinking with tax collectors and [1]sinners?"

17 And hearing *this*, Jesus *said to them, "[a]*It is* not those who are healthy who need a physician, but those who are sick; I did not come to call the righteous, but sinners."

18 [a]John's disciples and the Pharisees were fasting; and they *came and *said to Him, "Why do John's disciples and the disciples of the Pharisees fast, but Your disciples do not fast?"

19 And Jesus said to them, "While the bridegroom is with them, [1]the attendants of the bridegroom cannot fast, can they? So long as they have the bridegroom with them, they cannot fast.

2:2 [a]Mark 1:45; 2:13
3 [a]Mark 2:3-12: *Matt 9:2-8; Luke 5:18-26* [b]Matt 4:24
4 [1]Lit *bring to* [2]Lit *where He was* [a]Luke 5:19 [b]Matt 4:24
5 [1]Lit *child* [a]Matt 9:2
7 [1]Lit *if not one, God* [a]Is 43:25
8 [1]Lit *by*
9 [a]Matt 4:24
12 [a]Matt 9:8 [b]Matt 9:33
13 [1]Lit *crowd* [a]Mark 1:45
14 [1]also called *Matthew* [a]Mark 2:14-17: *Matt 9:9-13; Luke 5:27-32* [b]Matt 9:9 [c]Matt 8:22
15 [1]Lit *happens* [2]I.e. irreligious Jews [3]Lit *were reclining with*
16 [1]I.e. irreligious Jews [a]Luke 5:30; Acts 23:9 [b]Matt 9:11
17 [a]Matt 9:12, 13; Luke 5:31, 32
18 [a]Mark 2:18-22: *Matt 9:14-17; Luke 5:33-38*
19 [1]Lit *sons of the bridal-chamber*

20 "But the [a]days will come when the bridegroom is taken
away from them, and then they will fast in that day.
21 "No one sews [1]a patch of unshrunk cloth on an old garment;
otherwise [2]the patch pulls away from it, the new from the old,
and a worse tear results.
22 "No one puts new wine into old wineskins; otherwise the
wine will burst the skins, and the wine is lost and the skins *as*
well; but *one puts* new wine into fresh wineskins."
23 [a]And it happened that He was passing through the grainfields
on the Sabbath, and His disciples began to make their way along
while [b]picking the heads *of grain.*
24 The Pharisees were saying to Him, "Look, [a]why are they
doing what is not lawful on the Sabbath?"
25 And He *said to them, "Have you never read what David
did when he was in need and he and his companions became
hungry;
26 how he entered the house of God in the time of [a]Abiathar
the high priest, and ate the [1]consecrated bread, which [b]is not
lawful for *anyone* to eat except the priests, and he also gave it
to those who were with him?"
27 Jesus said to them, "[a]The Sabbath [1]was made [2]for man, and
[b]not man [2]for the Sabbath.
28 "So the Son of Man is Lord even of the Sabbath."

Chapter 3 Theme ______________________

3 [a]He [b]entered again into a synagogue; and a man was there
whose hand was withered.
2 [a]They were watching Him *to see* if He would heal him on
the Sabbath, [b]so that they might accuse Him.
3 He *said to the man with the withered hand, "[1]Get up and
come forward!"
4 And He *said to them, "Is it lawful to do good or to do harm
on the Sabbath, to save a life or to kill?" But they kept silent.
5 After [a]looking around at them with anger, grieved at their
hardness of heart, He *said to the man, "Stretch out your hand."
And he stretched it out, and his hand was restored.
6 The Pharisees went out and immediately *began* [1]conspiring
with the [a]Herodians against Him, *as to* how they might destroy
Him.
7 [a]Jesus withdrew to the sea with His disciples; and [b]a great
multitude from Galilee followed; and *also* from Judea,
8 and from Jerusalem, and from [a]Idumea, and beyond the
Jordan, and the vicinity of [b]Tyre and Sidon, a great number of
people heard of all that He was doing and came to Him.
9 [a]And He told His disciples that a boat should stand ready for
Him because of the crowd, so that they would not crowd Him;
10 for He had [a]healed many, with the result that all those who
had [b]afflictions pressed around Him in order to [c]touch Him.
11 Whenever the unclean spirits saw Him, they would fall
down before Him and shout, "You are [a]the Son of God!"

20 [a]Matt 9:15; Luke 17:22

21 [1]Lit *that which is put on* [2]Lit *that which fills up*

23 [a]Mark 2:23-28: *Matt 12:1-8; Luke 6:1-5* [b]Deut 23:25

24 [a]Matt 12:2

26 [1]Or *showbread;* lit *loaves of presentation* [a]1 Sam 21:1; 2 Sam 8:17; 1 Chr 24:6 [b]Lev 24:9

27 [1]Or *came into being* [2]Lit *because for the sake of* [a]Ex 23:12; Deut 5:14 [b]Col 2:16

3:1 [a]Mark 3:1-6: *Matt 12:9-14; Luke 6:6-11* [b]Mark 1:21, 39

2 [a]Luke 6:7; 14:1; 20:20 [b]Matt 12:10; Luke 6:7; 11:54

3 [1]Lit *Arise into the midst*

5 [a]Luke 6:10

6 [1]Lit *giving counsel* [a]Matt 22:16; Mark 12:13

7 [a]Mark 3:7-12: *Matt 12:15, 16; Luke 6:17-19* [b]Matt 4:25; Luke 6:17

8 [a]Josh 15:1, 21; Ezek 35:15; 36:5 [b]Matt 11:21

9 [a]Mark 4:1; Luke 5:1-3

10 [a]Matt 4:23 [b]Mark 5:29, 34; Luke 7:21 [c]Matt 9:21; 14:36; Mark 6:56; 8:22

11 [a]Matt 4:3

12 And He [a]earnestly warned them not to [1]tell who He was.
13 And He *went up on [a]the mountain and *[b]summoned
those whom He Himself wanted, and they came to Him.
14 And He appointed twelve, so that they would be with Him
and that He *could* send them out to preach,
15 and to have authority to cast out the demons.
16 And He appointed the twelve: [a]Simon (to whom He gave
the name Peter),
17 and [1]James, the *son* of Zebedee, and John the brother of
[1]James (to them He gave the name Boanerges, which means,
"Sons of Thunder");
18 and Andrew, and Philip, and Bartholomew, and Matthew,
and Thomas, and [1]James the son of Alphaeus, and Thaddaeus,
and Simon the [2]Zealot;
19 and Judas Iscariot, who betrayed Him.
20 And He *came [1a]home, and the [b]crowd *gathered again,
[c]to such an extent that they could not even eat [2]a meal.
21 When [a]His own [1]people heard *of this,* they went out to take
custody of Him; for they were saying, "[b]He has lost His senses."
22 The scribes who came down [a]from Jerusalem were saying,
"He is possessed by [1b]Beelzebul," and "[c]He casts out the
demons by the ruler of the demons."
23 [a]And He called them to Himself and began speaking to
them in [b]parables, "How can [c]Satan cast out Satan?
24 "If a kingdom is divided
against itself, that kingdom
cannot stand.
25 "If a house is divided
against itself, that house
will not be able to stand.
26 "If [a]Satan has risen up
against himself and is
divided, he cannot stand,
but [1]he is finished!
27 "[a]But no one can enter
the strong man's house and
plunder his property unless
he first binds the strong
man, and then he will
plunder his house.
28 "[a]Truly I say to you, all
sins shall be forgiven the
sons of men, and whatever
blasphemies they utter;
29 but [a]whoever blasphemes against the Holy Spirit never has
forgiveness, but is guilty of an eternal sin"—
30 because they were saying, "He has an unclean spirit."
31 [a]Then His mother and His brothers *arrived, and standing
outside they sent *word* to Him and called Him.
32 A crowd was sitting around Him, and they *said to Him,
"Behold, Your mother and Your brothers are outside looking for
You."

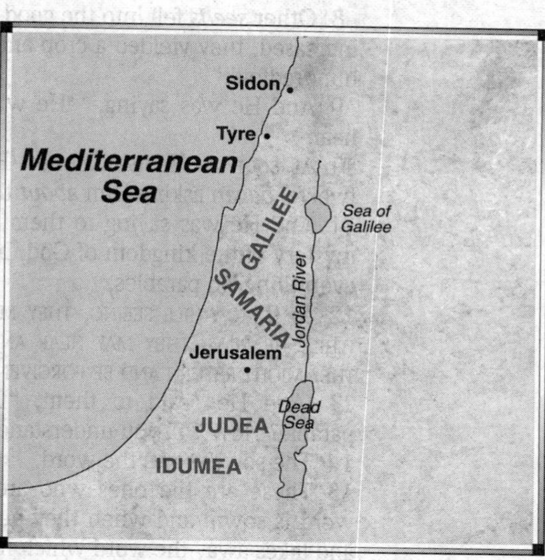

Regions from Which People Came to See Jesus (Mark 3:7-8)

12 [1]Lit *make Him known* [a]Matt 8:4
13 [a]Matt 5:1; Luke 6:12 [b]Matt 10:1; Mark 6:7; Luke 9:1
16 [a]Mark 3:16-19: *Matt 10:2-4; Luke 6:14-16;* Acts 1:13
17 [1]Or *Jacob*
18 [1]Or *Jacob* [2]Or *Cananaean*
20 [1]Lit *into a house* [2]Lit *bread* [a]Mark 2:1; 7:17; 9:28 [b]Mark 1:45; 3:7 [c]Mark 6:31
21 [1]Or *kinsmen* [a]Mark 3:31f [b]John 10:20; Acts 26:24
22 [1]Or *Beezebul;* others read *Beelzebub* [a]Matt 15:1 [b]Matt 10:25; 11:18 [c]Matt 9:34
23 [a]Mark 3:23-27: *Matt 12:25-29; Luke 11:17-22* [b]Matt 13:3ff; Mark 4:2ff [c]Matt 4:10
26 [1]Lit *he has an end* [a]Matt 4:10
27 [a]Is 49:24, 25
28 [a]Matt 12:31, 32; Mark 3:28-30; Luke 12:10
29 [a]Luke 12:10
31 [a]Mark 3:31-35: *Matt 12:46-50; Luke 8:19-21*

33 Answering them, He *said, "Who are My mother and My
brothers?"
34 Looking about at those who were sitting around Him, He
*said, "[a]Behold My mother and My brothers!
35 "For whoever [a]does the will of God, he is My brother and
sister and mother."

Chapter 4 Theme ______________________________

4 [a]He began to teach again [b]by the sea. And such a very large
crowd gathered to Him that [c]He got into a boat in the sea
and sat down; and the whole crowd was by the sea on the land.
2 And He was teaching them many things in [a]parables, and
was saying to them in His teaching,
3 "Listen *to this!* Behold, the sower went out to sow;
4 as he was sowing, some *seed* fell beside the road, and the
birds came and ate it up.
5 "Other *seed* fell on the rocky *ground* where it did not have
much soil; and immediately it sprang up because it had no
depth of soil.
6 "And after the sun had risen, it was scorched; and because
it had no root, it withered away.
7 "Other *seed* fell among the thorns, and the thorns came up
and choked it, and it yielded no crop.
8 "Other *seeds* fell into the good soil, and as they grew up and
increased, they yielded a crop and produced thirty, sixty, and a
hundredfold."
9 And He was saying, "[a]He who has ears to hear, [1]let him
hear."
10 As soon as He was alone, [1]His followers, along with the
twelve, *began* asking Him *about* the parables.
11 And He was saying to them, "To you has been given the
mystery of the kingdom of God, but [a]those who are outside get
everything [b]in parables,
12 so that [a]WHILE SEEING, THEY MAY SEE AND NOT PERCEIVE, AND
WHILE HEARING, THEY MAY HEAR AND NOT UNDERSTAND, OTHERWISE
THEY MIGHT RETURN AND BE FORGIVEN."
13 [a]And He *said to them, "Do you not understand this
parable? How will you understand all the parables?
14 "The sower sows the word.
15 "These are the ones who are beside the road where the
word is sown; and when they hear, immediately [a]Satan comes
and takes away the word which has been sown in them.
16 "In a similar way these are the ones on whom seed was
sown on the rocky *places,* who, when they hear the word,
immediately receive it with joy;
17 and they have no *firm* root in themselves, but are *only*
temporary; then, when affliction or persecution arises because
of the word, immediately they [1]fall away.
18 "And others are the ones on whom seed was sown among
the thorns; these are the ones who have heard the word,

INSIGHT

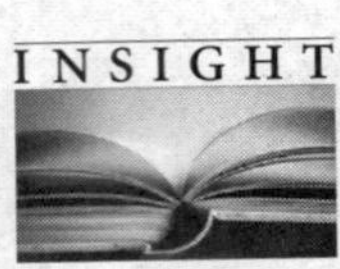

See the section on *Parables*, under **Figures of Speech**, on page 2104.

34 [a]Matt 12:49

35 [a]Eph 6:6; Heb 10:36; 1 Pet 4:2; 1 John 2:17

4:1 [a]Mark 4:1-12: *Matt 13:1-15; Luke 8:4-10* [b]Mark 2:13; 3:7 [c]Luke 5:1-3

2 [a]Matt 13:3ff; Mark 3:23; 4:2ff

9 [1]Or *hear!;* or *listen!* [a]Matt 11:15; Mark 4:23; Rev 2:7, 11, 17, 29

10 [1]Lit *those about Him*

11 [a]1 Cor 5:12f; Col 4:5; 1 Thess 4:12; 1 Tim 3:7 [b]Mark 3:23; 4:2

12 [a]Is 6:9f; 43:8; Jer 5:21; Ezek 12:2; Matt 13:14; Luke 8:10; John 12:40; Rom 11:8

13 [a]Mark 4:13-20: *Matt 13:18-23; Luke 8:11-15*

15 [a]Matt 4:10f; 1 Pet 5:8; Rev 20:2, 3, 7-10

17 [1]Lit *are caused to stumble*

19 but the worries of [a]the [1]world, and the [b]deceitfulness of
riches, and the desires for other things enter in and choke the
word, and it becomes unfruitful.
20 "And those are the ones on whom seed was sown on the
good soil; and they hear the word and accept it and [a]bear fruit,
thirty, sixty, and a hundredfold."
21 And He was saying to them, "[a]A lamp is not brought to be
put under a [1]basket, is it, or under a bed? Is it not *brought* to
be put on the lampstand?
22 "[a]For nothing is hidden, except to be revealed; nor has
anything been secret, but that it would come to light.
23 "[a]If anyone has ears to hear, let him hear."
24 And He was saying to them, "Take care what you listen to.
[1a]By your standard of measure it will be measured to you; and
more will be given you besides.
25 "[a]For whoever has, to him *more* shall be given; and whoever
does not have, even what he has shall be taken away from him."
26 And He was saying, "The kingdom of God is like a man
who casts seed upon the soil;
27 and he goes to bed at night and gets up by day, and the
seed sprouts and grows—how, he himself does not know.
28 "The soil produces crops by itself; first the blade, then the
head, then the mature grain in the head.
29 "But when the crop permits, he immediately [1a]puts in the
sickle, because the harvest has come."
30 [a]And He said, "How shall we [1b]picture the kingdom of
God, or by what parable shall we present it?
31 "*It is* like a mustard seed, which, when sown upon the soil,
though it is smaller than all the seeds that are upon the soil,
32 yet when it is sown, it grows up and becomes larger than
all the garden plants and forms large branches; so that [a]THE
BIRDS OF THE [1]AIR can NEST UNDER ITS SHADE."
33 With many such parables He was speaking the word to
them, so far as they were able to hear it;
34 and He did not speak to them [a]without a parable; but He
was [b]explaining everything privately to His own disciples.
35 [a]On that day, when evening came, He *said to them, "Let
us go over to the other side."
36 [1]Leaving the crowd, they *took Him along with them [a]in
the boat, just as He was; and other boats were with Him.
37 And there *arose a fierce gale of wind, and the waves were
breaking over the boat so much that the boat was already filling
up.
38 Jesus Himself was in the stern, asleep on the cushion; and
they *woke Him and *said to Him, "Teacher, do You not care
that we are perishing?"
39 And He got up and [a]rebuked the wind and said to the sea,
"Hush, be still." And the wind died down and [1]it became
perfectly calm.
40 And He said to them, "Why are you [1]afraid? [a]Do you still
have no faith?"

19 [1]Or *age* [a]Matt 13:22; Rom 12:2; Eph 2:2; 6:12 [b]Prov 23:4; 1 Tim 6:9, 10, 17

20 [a]John 15:2ff; Rom 7:4

21 [1]Or *peck-measure* [a]Matt 5:15; Luke 8:16; 11:33

22 [a]Matt 10:26; Luke 8:17; 12:2

23 [a]Matt 11:15; 13:9, 43; Mark 4:9; Luke 8:8; 14:35; Rev 3:6, 13, 22; 13:9

24 [1]Lit *By what measure you measure* [a]Matt 7:2; Luke 6:38

25 [a]Matt 13:12; 25:29; Luke 8:18; 19:26

29 [1]Lit *sends forth* [a]Joel 3:13

30 [1]Lit *compare* [a]Mark 4:30-32: *Matt 13:31, 32; Luke 13:18, 19* [b]Matt 13:24

32 [1]Or *sky* [a]Ezek 17:23; Ps 104:12; Ezek 31:6; Dan 4:12

34 [a]Matt 13:34; John 10:6; 16:25 [b]Luke 24:27

35 [a]Mark 4:35-41: *Matt 8:18, 23-27; Luke 8:22, 25*

36 [1]Or *Sending away* [a]Mark 3:9; 4:1; 5:2, 21

39 [1]Lit *a great calm occurred* [a]Ps 65:7; 89:9; 107:29; Matt 8:26; Luke 8:24

40 [1]Or *cowardly* [a]Matt 14:31; Luke 8:25

41 They became very much afraid and said to one another, "Who then is this, that even the wind and the sea obey Him?"

Chapter 5 Theme ______________________

5 [a]They came to the other side of the sea, into the country of the Gerasenes.

2 When He got out of [a]the boat, immediately a man from the tombs [b]with an unclean spirit met Him,

3 and he had his dwelling among the tombs. And no one was able to bind him anymore, even with a chain;

4 because he had often been bound with shackles and chains, and the chains had been torn apart by him and the shackles broken in pieces, and no one was strong enough to subdue him.

5 Constantly, night and day, he was screaming among the tombs and in the mountains, and gashing himself with stones.

6 Seeing Jesus from a distance, he ran up and bowed down before Him;

7 and shouting with a loud voice, he *said, "[1a]What business do we have with each other, Jesus, [b]Son of [c]the Most High God? I implore You by God, do not torment me!"

8 For He had been saying to him, "Come out of the man, you unclean spirit!"

9 And He was asking him, "What is your name?" And he *said to Him, "My name is [a]Legion; for we are many."

10 And he *began* to implore Him earnestly not to send them out of the country.

11 Now there was a large herd of swine feeding [1]nearby on the mountain.

12 *The demons* implored Him, saying, "Send us into the swine so that we may enter them."

13 Jesus gave them permission. And coming out, the unclean spirits entered the swine; and the herd rushed down the steep bank into the sea, about two thousand *of them;* and they were drowned in the sea.

14 Their herdsmen ran away and reported it in the city and in the country. And *the people* came to see what it was that had happened.

15 They *came to Jesus and *observed the man who had been [a]demon-possessed sitting down, [b]clothed and [c]in his right mind, the very man who had had the "[d]legion"; and they became frightened.

16 Those who had seen it described to them how it had happened to the [a]demon-possessed man, and *all* about the swine.

17 And they began to [a]implore Him to leave their region.

18 [a]As He was getting into the boat, the man who had been [b]demon-possessed was imploring Him that he might [1]accompany Him.

19 And He did not let him, but He *said to him, "[a]Go home to your people and report to them [1]what great things the Lord has done for you, and *how* He had mercy on you."

5:1 [a]Mark 5:1-17: *Matt 8:28-34; Luke 8:26-37*

2 [a]Mark 3:9; 4:1, 36; 5:21 [b]Mark 1:23

7 [1]Lit *What to me and to you* (a Heb idiom) [a]Matt 8:29 [b]Matt 4:3 [c]Luke 8:28; Acts 16:17; Heb 7:1

9 [a]Matt 26:53; Mark 5:15; Luke 8:30

11 [1]Lit *there*

15 [a]Matt 4:24; Mark 5:16, 18 [b]Luke 8:27 [c]Luke 8:35 [d]Mark 5:9

16 [a]Matt 4:24; Mark 5:15

17 [a]Matt 8:34; Acts 16:39

18 [1]Lit *be with Him* [a]Mark 5:18-20: *Luke 8:38, 39* [b]Matt 4:24; Mark 5:15, 16

19 [1]Or *everything that* [a]Luke 8:39

20 And he went away and began to [a]proclaim in [b]Decapolis
[1]what great things Jesus had done for him; and everyone was
amazed.
21 [a]When Jesus had crossed over again in [b]the boat to the other
side, a large crowd gathered around Him; and so He [1]stayed [c]by
the seashore.
22 [a]One of [b]the synagogue [1]officials named Jairus *came up,
and on seeing Him, *fell at His feet
23 and *implored Him earnestly, saying, "My little daughter is
at the point of death; *please* come and [a]lay Your hands on her,
so that she will [1]get well and live."
24 And He went off with him; and a large crowd was following
Him and pressing in on Him.
25 A woman who had had a hemorrhage for twelve years,
26 and had endured much at the hands of many physicians,
and had spent all that she had and was not helped at all, but
rather had grown worse—
27 after hearing about Jesus, she came up in the crowd behind
Him and touched His [1]cloak.
28 For she [1]thought, "If I just touch His garments, I will [2]get
well."
29 Immediately the flow of her blood was dried up; and she
felt in her body that she was healed of her [a]affliction.
30 Immediately Jesus, perceiving in Himself that [a]the power
proceeding from Him had gone forth, turned around in the
crowd and said, "Who touched My garments?"
31 And His disciples said to Him, "You see the crowd pressing
in on You, and You say, 'Who touched Me?'"
32 And He looked around to see the woman who had done this.
33 But the woman fearing and trembling, aware of what had
happened to her, came and fell down before Him and told Him
the whole truth.
34 And He said to her, "Daughter, [a]your faith has [1]made you
well; [b]go in peace and be healed of your [c]affliction."
35 While He was still speaking, they *came from the *house of*
the [a]synagogue official, saying, "Your daughter has died; why
trouble the Teacher anymore?"
36 But Jesus, overhearing what was being spoken, *said to the
[a]synagogue official, "[b]Do not be afraid *any longer,* only [1]believe."
37 And He allowed no one to accompany Him, except [a]Peter
and [1]James and John the brother of [1]James.
38 They *came to the house of the [a]synagogue official; and He
*saw a commotion, and *people* loudly weeping and wailing.
39 And entering in, He *said to them, "Why make a commotion
and weep? The child has not died, but is asleep."
40 They *began* laughing at Him. But putting them all out, He
*took along the child's father and mother and His own
companions, and *entered *the room* where the child was.
41 Taking the child by the hand, He *said to her, "Talitha kum!"
(which translated means, "Little girl, [a]I say to you, get up!").
42 Immediately the girl got up and *began* to walk, for she was

20 [1]Or *everything that* [a]Ps 66:16 [b]Matt 4:25; Mark 7:31

21 [1]Lit *was* [a]Matt 9:1; Luke 8:40 [b]Mark 4:36 [c]Mark 4:1

22 [1]Or *rulers* [a]Mark 5:22-43: *Matt 9:18-26; Luke 8:41-56* [b]Matt 9:18; Mark 5:35, 36, 38; Luke 8:49; 13:14; Acts 13:15; 18:8, 17

23 [1]Lit *be saved* [a]Mark 6:5; 7:32; 8:23; 16:18; Luke 4:40; 13:13; Acts 6:6; 9:17; 28:8

27 [1]Or *outer garment*

28 [1]Lit *was saying* [2]Lit *be saved*

29 [a]Mark 3:10; 5:34

30 [a]Luke 5:17

34 [1]Lit *saved you* [a]Matt 9:22 [b]Luke 7:50; 8:48; Acts 16:36; James 2:16 [c]Mark 3:10; 5:29

35 [a]Mark 5:22

36 [1]Or *keep on believing* [a]Mark 5:22 [b]Luke 8:50

37 [1]Or *Jacob;* James is the Eng form of Jacob [a]Matt 17:1; 26:37

38 [a]Mark 5:22

41 [a]Luke 7:14; Acts 9:40

twelve years old. And immediately they were completely
astounded.
43 And He [a]gave them strict orders that no one should know
about this, and He said that *something* should be given her to eat.

Chapter 6 Theme ________________________________

6 [a]Jesus went out from there and *came into [1b]His hometown; and His disciples *followed Him.
2 When the Sabbath came, He began [a]to teach in the synagogue;
and the [b]many listeners were astonished, saying, "Where did
this man *get* these things, and what is *this* wisdom given to
Him, and such [1]miracles as these performed by His hands?
3 "Is not this [a]the carpenter, [b]the son of Mary, and brother of
[1]James and Joses and Judas and Simon? Are not [c]His sisters
here with us?" And they took [d]offense at Him.
4 Jesus said to them, "[a]A prophet is not without honor
except in [1b]his hometown and among his *own* relatives and in
his *own* household."
5 And He could do no [1]miracle there except that He [a]laid His
hands on a few sick people and healed them.
6 And He wondered at their unbelief.
[a]**A**nd He was going around the villages teaching.
7 [a]And [b]He *summoned the twelve and began to send them
out [c]in pairs, and gave them authority over the unclean spirits;
8 [a]and He instructed them that they should take nothing for
their journey, except a mere staff—no bread, no [1]bag, no
money in their belt—
9 but [1]*to* wear sandals; and *He added,* "Do not put on two
[2]tunics."
10 And He said to them, "Wherever you enter a house, stay
there until you [1]leave town.
11 "Any place that does not receive you or listen to you, as you
go out from there, [a]shake the dust [1]off the soles of your feet for
a testimony against them."
12 [a]They went out and [1]preached that *men* should repent.
13 And they were casting out many demons and [a]were
anointing with oil many sick people and healing them.
14 [a]And King Herod heard *of it,* for His name had become
well known; and *people* were saying, "[b]John the Baptist has
risen from the dead, and that is why these miraculous powers
are at work in Him."
15 But others were saying, "He is [a]Elijah." And others were
saying, "*He is* [b]a prophet, like one of the prophets *of old.*"
16 But when Herod heard *of it,* he kept saying, "John, whom I
beheaded, has risen!"
17 For Herod himself had sent and had John arrested and
bound in prison on account of [a]Herodias, the wife of his
brother Philip, because he had married her.
18 For John had been saying to Herod, "[a]It is not lawful for
you to have your brother's wife."

43 [a]Matt 8:4

6:1 [1]Or *His own part of the country* [a]Mark 6:1-6: *Matt 13:54-58* [b]Matt 13:54, 57; Luke 4:16, 23

2 [1]Or *works of power* [a]Matt 4:23; Mark 10:1 [b]Matt 7:28

3 [1]Or *Jacob* [a]Matt 13:55 [b]Matt 12:46 [c]Matt 13:56 [d]Matt 11:6

4 [1]Or *his own part of the country* [a]Matt 13:57; John 4:44 [b]Mark 6:1

5 [1]Or *work of power* [a]Mark 5:23

6 [a]Matt 9:35; Mark 1:39; 10:1; Luke 13:22

7 [a]Mark 6:7-11: *Matt 10:1, 9-14; Luke 9:1, 3-5;* Luke 10:4-11 [b]Matt 10:1, 5; Mark 3:13; Luke 9:1 [c]Luke 10:1

8 [1]Or *knapsack* or *beggar's bag* [a]Matt 10:10

9 [1]Lit *being shod with* [2]Or *inner garments*

10 [1]Lit *go out from there*

11 [1]Lit *under your feet* [a]Matt 10:14; Acts 13:51

12 [1]Or *proclaimed as a herald* [a]Matt 11:1; Luke 9:6

13 [a]James 5:14

14 [a]Mark 6:14-29: *Matt 14:1-12;* Mark 6:14-16: *Luke 9:7-9* [b]Matt 14:2; Luke 9:19

15 [a]Matt 16:14; Mark 8:28 [b]Matt 21:11

17 [a]Matt 14:3; Luke 3:19

18 [a]Matt 14:4

19 [a]Herodias had a grudge against him and wanted to put him
to death and could not *do so;*
20 for [a]Herod was afraid of John, knowing that he was a
righteous and holy man, and he kept him safe. And when he
heard him, he was very perplexed; [1]but he [2]used to enjoy
listening to him.
21 A strategic day came when Herod on his birthday [a]gave a
banquet for his lords and [1]military commanders and the
leading men [b]of Galilee;
22 and when the daughter of [a]Herodias herself came in and
danced, she pleased Herod and [1]his dinner guests; and the king
said to the girl, "Ask me for whatever you want and I will give
it to you."
23 And he swore to her, "Whatever you ask of me, I will give
it to you; up to [a]half of my kingdom."
24 And she went out and said to her mother, "What shall I ask
for?" And she said, "The head of John the Baptist."
25 Immediately she came in a hurry to the king and asked,
saying, "I want you to give me at once the head of John the
Baptist on a platter."
26 And although the king was very sorry, *yet* because of his oaths
and because of [1]his dinner guests, he was unwilling to refuse her.
27 Immediately the king sent an executioner and commanded
him to bring *back* his head. And he went and had him beheaded
in the prison,
28 and brought his head on a platter, and gave it to the girl;
and the girl gave it to her mother.
29 When his disciples heard *about this,* they came and took
away his body and laid it in a tomb.
30 [a]The [b]apostles *gathered together with Jesus; and they
reported to Him all that they had done and taught.
31 And He *said to them, "Come away by yourselves to a
secluded place and rest a while." (For there were many *people*
coming and going, and [a]they did not even have time to eat.)
32 [a]They went away in [b]the boat to a secluded place by
themselves.
33 *The people* saw them going, and many recognized *them*
and ran there together on foot from all the cities, and got there
ahead of them.
34 When Jesus went [1]ashore, He [a]saw a large crowd, and He
felt compassion for them because [b]they were like sheep
without a shepherd; and He began to teach them many things.
35 When it was already quite late, His disciples came to Him
and said, "[1]This place is desolate and it is already quite late;
36 send them away so that they may go into the surrounding
countryside and villages and buy themselves [1]something to eat."
37 But He answered them, "You give them *something* to eat!"
[a]And they *said to Him, "Shall we go and spend two hundred
[1][b]denarii on bread and give them *something* to eat?"
38 And He *said to them, "How many loaves do you have? Go
look!" And when they found out, they *said, "Five, and two fish."

19 [a]Matt 14:3
20 [1]Lit *and* [2]Lit *was hearing him gladly* [a]Matt 21:26
21 [1]I.e. chiliarchs, in command of a thousand troops [a]Esth 1:3; 2:18 [b]Luke 3:1
22 [1]Lit *those who reclined at the table with him* [a]Matt 14:3
23 [a]Esth 5:3, 6; 7:2
26 [1]Lit *those reclining at the table*
30 [a]Luke 9:10 [b]Matt 10:2; Mark 3:14; Luke 6:13; 9:10; 17:5; 22:14; 24:10; Acts 1:2, 26
31 [a]Mark 3:20
32 [a]Mark 6:32-44: *Matt 14:13-21; Luke 9:10-17; John 6:5-13;* Mark 8:2-9 [b]Mark 3:9; 4:36; 6:45
34 [1]Lit *out* [a]Matt 9:36 [b]Num 27:17; 1 Kin 22:17; 2 Chr 18:16; Zech 10:2
35 [1]Lit *The*
36 [1]Lit *what they may eat*
37 [1]The denarius was equivalent to one day's wage [a]John 6:7 [b]Matt 18:28; Luke 7:41

39 And He commanded them all to [1]sit down by groups on
the green grass.
40 They [1]sat down in groups of hundreds and of fifties.
41 And He took the five loaves and the two fish, and looking
up toward heaven, He [a]blessed *the food* and broke the loaves
and He kept giving *them* to the disciples to set before them;
and He divided up the two fish among them all.
42 They all ate and were satisfied,
43 and they picked up twelve full [a]baskets of the broken pieces,
and also of the fish.
44 There were [a]five thousand men who ate the loaves.
45 [a]Immediately Jesus made His disciples get into [b]the boat
and go ahead of *Him* to the other side to [c]Bethsaida, while He
Himself was sending the crowd away.
46 After [a]bidding them farewell, He left [b]for the mountain to
pray.
47 When it was evening, the boat was in the middle of the
sea, and He was alone on the land.
48 Seeing them [1]straining at the oars, for the wind was against
them, at about the [2a]fourth watch of the night He *came to
them, walking on the sea; and He intended to pass by them.
49 But when they saw Him walking on the sea, they supposed
that it was a ghost, and cried out;
50 for they all saw Him and were [1]terrified. But immediately
He spoke with them and *said to them, "[a]Take courage; it is I,
[b]do not be afraid."
51 Then He got into [a]the boat with them, and the wind
stopped; and they were utterly astonished,
52 for [a]they [1]had not gained any insight from the *incident of*
the loaves, but [2]their heart [b]was hardened.
53 [a]When they had crossed over they came to land at
Gennesaret, and moored to the shore.
54 When they got out of the boat, immediately *the people*
recognized Him,
55 and ran about that whole country and began to carry here
and there on their pallets those who were sick, to [1]the place
they heard He was.
56 Wherever He entered villages, or cities, or countryside,
they were laying the sick in the market places, and imploring
Him that they might just [a]touch [b]the fringe of His cloak; and as
many as touched it were being cured.

Chapter 7 Theme ____________

7 [a]The Pharisees and some of the scribes gathered around
Him when they had come [b]from Jerusalem,
2 and had seen that some of His disciples were eating their
bread with [a]impure hands, that is, unwashed.
3 (For the Pharisees and all the Jews do not eat unless they
[1]carefully wash their hands, *thus* observing the [a]traditions of
the elders;

39 [1]Lit *recline*

40 [1]Lit *reclined*

41 [a]Matt 14:19

43 [a]Matt 14:20

44 [a]Matt 14:21

45 [a]Mark 6:45-51: *Matt 14:22-32; John 6:15-21* [b]Mark 6:32 [c]Matt 11:21; Mark 8:22

46 [a]Acts 18:18, 21; 2 Cor 2:13 [b]Matt 14:23

48 [1]Lit *harassed in rowing* [2]I.e. 3-6 a.m. [a]Matt 24:43; Mark 13:35

50 [1]Or *troubled* [a]Matt 9:2 [b]Matt 14:27

51 [a]Mark 6:32

52 [1]Lit *had not understood on the basis of* [2]Or *their mind was closed, made dull,* or *insensible* [a]Mark 8:17ff [b]Rom 11:7

53 [a]Mark 6:53-56: *Matt 14:34-36;* John 6:24, 25

55 [1]Lit *where they were hearing that He was*

56 [a]Mark 3:10 [b]Matt 9:20; Num 15:37-40

7:1 [a]Mark 7:1-23: *Matt 15:1-20* [b]Matt 15:1

2 [a]Matt 15:2; Mark 7:5; Luke 11:38; Acts 10:14, 28; 11:8; Rom 14:14; Heb 10:29; Rev 21:27

3 [1]Lit *with the fist* [a]Mark 7:5, 8, 9, 13; Gal 1:14

4 and *when they come* from the market place, they do not
eat unless they [1]cleanse themselves; and there are many other
things which they have received in order to observe, such as
the [2]washing of [a]cups and pitchers and copper pots.)
5 The Pharisees and the scribes *asked Him, "Why do Your
disciples not walk according to the [a]tradition of the elders, but
eat their bread with [b]impure hands?"
6 And He said to them, "Rightly did Isaiah prophesy of you
hypocrites, as it is written:
'[a]THIS PEOPLE HONORS ME WITH THEIR LIPS,
BUT THEIR HEART IS FAR AWAY FROM ME.
7 '[a]BUT IN VAIN DO THEY WORSHIP ME,
TEACHING AS DOCTRINES THE PRECEPTS OF MEN.'
8 "Neglecting the commandment of God, you hold to the
[a]tradition of men."
9 He was also saying to them, "You are experts at setting aside
the commandment of God in order to keep your [a]tradition.
10 "For Moses said, '[a]HONOR YOUR FATHER AND YOUR MOTHER'; and,
'[b]HE WHO SPEAKS EVIL OF FATHER OR MOTHER, IS TO [1]BE PUT TO DEATH';
11 but you say, 'If a man says to *his* father or *his* mother,
whatever I have that would help you is [a]Corban (that is to say,
[1]given *to God*),'
12 you no longer permit him to do anything for *his* father or
his mother;
13 *thus* invalidating the word of God by your [a]tradition which
you have handed down; and you do many things such as that."
14 After He called the crowd to Him again, He *began* saying to
them, "Listen to Me, all of you, and understand:
15 there is nothing outside the man which can defile him if it
goes into him; but the things which proceed out of the man are
what defile the man.
16 ["[1]If anyone has ears to hear, let him hear."]
17 When he had left the crowd *and* entered [a]the house, [b]His
disciples questioned Him about the parable.
18 And He *said to them, "Are you so lacking in understanding
also? Do you not understand that whatever goes into the man
from outside cannot defile him,
19 because it does not go into his heart, but into his stomach,
and [1]is eliminated?" (*Thus He* declared [a]all foods [b]clean.)
20 And He was saying, "[a]That which proceeds out of the man,
that is what defiles the man.
21 "For from within, out of the heart of men, proceed the evil
thoughts, [1]fornications, thefts, murders, adulteries,
22 deeds of coveting *and* wickedness, *as well as* deceit,
sensuality, [1a]envy, slander, [2]pride *and* foolishness.
23 "All these evil things proceed from within and defile the man."
24 [a]Jesus got up and went away from there to the region of
[b]Tyre[1]. And when He had entered a house, He wanted no one
to know *of it;* [2]yet He could not escape notice.
25 But after hearing of Him, a woman whose little daughter
had an unclean spirit immediately came and fell at His feet.

4 [1]Or *sprinkle* [2]Lit *baptizing* [a]Matt 23:25
5 [a]Mark 7:3, 8, 9, 13; Gal 1:14 [b]Mark 7:2
6 [a]Is 29:13
7 [a]Is 29:13
8 [a]Mark 7:3, 5, 9, 13; Gal 1:14
9 [a]Mark 7:3, 5, 8, 13; Gal 1:14
10 [1]Lit *die the death* [a]Ex 20:12; Deut 5:16 [b]Ex 21:17; Lev 20:9
11 [1]Or *a gift,* i.e. an offering [a]Lev 1:2; Matt 27:6
13 [a]Mark 7:3, 5, 8, 9; Gal 1:14
16 [1]Early mss do not contain this verse
17 [a]Mark 2:1; 3:20; 9:28 [b]Matt 15:15
19 [1]Lit *goes out into the latrine* [a]Rom 14:1-12; Col 2:16 [b]Luke 11:41; Acts 10:15; 11:9
20 [a]Matt 15:18; Mark 7:23
21 [1]I.e. acts of sexual immorality
22 [1]Lit *an evil eye* [2]Or *arrogance* [a]Matt 6:23; 20:15
24 [1]Two early mss add *and Sidon* [2]Lit *and* [a]Mark 7:24-30: *Matt 15:21-28* [b]Matt 11:21; Mark 7:31

26 Now the woman was a [1]Gentile, of the Syrophoenician race.
And she kept asking Him to cast the demon out of her daughter.
27 And He was saying to her, "Let the children be satisfied first,
for it is not [1]good to take the children's bread and throw it to
the dogs."
28 But she answered and *said to Him, "Yes, Lord, *but* even
the dogs under the table feed on the children's crumbs."
29 And He said to her, "Because of this [1]answer go; the
demon has gone out of your daughter."
30 And going back to her home, she found the child [1]lying on
the bed, the demon having left.
31 [a]Again He went out from the region of [b]Tyre, and came
through Sidon to [c]the Sea of Galilee, within the region of
[d]Decapolis.
32 They *brought to Him one who was deaf and spoke with
difficulty, and they *implored Him to [a]lay His hand on him.
33 [a]Jesus took him aside from the crowd, by himself, and put
His fingers into his ears, and after [a]spitting, He touched his
tongue *with the saliva;*
34 and looking up to heaven with a deep [a]sigh, He *said to
him, "Ephphatha!" that is, "Be opened!"
35 And his ears were opened, and the [1]impediment of his
tongue [2]was removed, and he *began* speaking plainly.
36 And [a]He gave them orders not to tell anyone; but the more
He ordered them, the more widely they [b]continued to proclaim it.
37 They were utterly astonished, saying, "He has done all things
well; He makes even the deaf to hear and the mute to speak."

Chapter 8 Theme ______________________

8 In those days, when there was again a large crowd and
they had nothing to eat, [a]Jesus called His disciples and
*said to them,
2 "[a]I feel compassion for the [1]people because they have
remained with Me now three days and have nothing to eat.
3 "If I send them away hungry to their homes, they will faint on
the way; and some of them have come from a great distance."
4 And His disciples answered Him, "Where will anyone be
able *to find enough* [1]bread here in *this* desolate place to satisfy
these people?"
5 And He was asking them, "How many loaves do you have?"
And they said, "Seven."
6 And He *directed the [1]people to [2]sit down on the ground;
and taking the seven loaves, He gave thanks and broke them,
and started giving them to His disciples to [3]serve to them, and
they served them to the [1]people.
7 They also had a few small fish; and [a]after He had blessed
them, He ordered these to be [1]served as well.
8 And they ate and were satisfied; and they picked up seven
large [a]baskets full of what was left over of the broken pieces.
9 About four thousand were *there;* and He sent them away.

26 [1]Lit *Greek*
27 [1]Or *proper*
29 [1]Lit *word*
30 [1]Lit *thrown*
31 [a]Mark 7:31-37: *Matt 15:29-31* [b]Matt 11:21; Mark 7:24 [c]Matt 4:18 [d]Matt 4:25; Mark 5:20
32 [a]Mark 5:23
33 [a]Mark 8:23
34 [a]Mark 8:12
35 [1]Or *bond* [2]Lit *was loosed*
36 [a]Matt 8:4 [b]Mark 1:45
8:1 [a]Mark 8:1-9: *Matt 15:32-39;* Mark 6:34-44
2 [1]Lit *crowd* [a]Matt 9:36; Mark 6:34
4 [1]Lit *loaves*
6 [1]Lit *crowd* [2]Lit *recline* [3]Lit *set before*
7 [1]Lit *set before them* [a]Matt 14:19
8 [a]Matt 15:37; Mark 8:20

10 And immediately He entered the boat with His disciples
and came to the district of [a]Dalmanutha.
11 [a]The Pharisees came out and began to argue with Him,
[b]seeking from Him a [1]sign from heaven, [2]to test Him.
12 [a]Sighing deeply [1]in His spirit, He *said, "Why does this
generation seek for a [2]sign? Truly I say to you, [3b]no [2]sign will
be given to this generation."
13 Leaving them, He again embarked and went away to the
other side.
14 And they had forgotten to take bread, and did not have
more than one loaf in the boat with them.
15 And He was giving orders to them, saying, "[a]Watch out!
Beware of the leaven of the Pharisees and the leaven of [b]Herod."
16 They *began* to discuss with
one another *the fact* that they
had no bread.
17 And Jesus, aware of this, *said
to them, "Why do you discuss *the
fact* that you have no bread? [a]Do
you not yet see or understand? Do
you have a [1]hardened heart?
18 "[a]HAVING EYES, DO YOU NOT SEE?
AND HAVING EARS, DO YOU NOT
HEAR? And do you not remember,
19 when I broke [a]the five loaves
for the five thousand, how many
[b]baskets full of broken pieces you
picked up?" They *said to Him,
"Twelve."
20 "When *I broke* [a]the seven for the four thousand, how many
large [b]baskets full of broken pieces did you pick up?" And they
*said to Him, "Seven."
21 And He was saying to them, "[a]Do you not yet understand?"
22 And they *came to [a]Bethsaida. And they *brought a blind
man to Jesus and *implored Him to [b]touch him.
23 Taking the blind man by the hand, He [a]brought him out of
the village; and after [a]spitting on his eyes and [b]laying His hands
on him, He asked him, "Do you see anything?"
24 And he [1]looked up and said, "I see men, for [2]I see *them*
like trees, walking around."
25 Then again He laid His hands on his eyes; and he looked
intently and was restored, and *began* to see everything clearly.
26 And He sent him to his home, saying, "Do not even enter
[a]the village."
27 [a]Jesus went out, along with His disciples, to the villages of
[b]Caesarea Philippi; and on the way He questioned His disciples,
saying to them, "Who do people say that I am?"
28 [a]They told Him, saying, "John the Baptist; and others *say*
Elijah; but others, one of the prophets."
29 And He *continued* by questioning them, "But who do you
say that I am?" [a]Peter *answered and *said to Him, "You are
[1]the Christ."

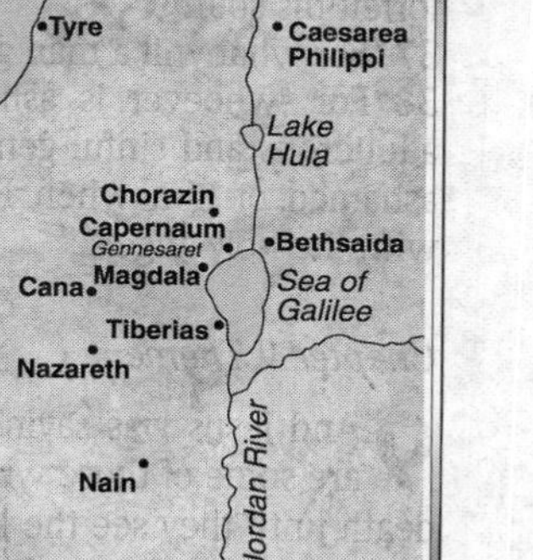

Galilee

10 [a]Matt 15:39
11 [1]Or *attesting miracle* [2]Lit *testing Him* [a]Mark 8:11-21: *Matt 16:1-12* [b]Matt 12:38
12 [1]Or *to Himself* [2]Or *attesting miracle* [3]Lit *if a sign shall be given* [a]Mark 7:34 [b]Matt 12:39
15 [a]Matt 16:6; Luke 12:1 [b]Matt 14:1; 22:16
17 [1]Or *dull, insensible* [a]Mark 6:52
18 [a]Jer 5:21; Ezek 12:2; Mark 4:12
19 [a]Mark 6:41-44 [b]Matt 14:20
20 [a]Mark 8:6-9 [b]Mark 8:8
21 [a]Mark 6:52
22 [a]Matt 11:21; Mark 6:45 [b]Mark 3:10
23 [a]Mark 7:33 [b]Mark 5:23
24 [1]Or *gained sight* [2]Or *they look to me*
26 [a]Mark 8:23
27 [a]Mark 8:27-29: *Matt 16:13-16; Luke 9:18-20* [b]Matt 16:13
28 [a]Mark 6:14; Luke 9:7, 8
29 [1]I.e. the Messiah [a]John 6:68, 69

INSIGHT

The exact location of ***Dalmanutha*** is unknown. However, it is believed to be another name for *Magdala,* or the name for a nearby region.

30 And [a]He [1]warned them to tell no one about Him.
31 [a]And He began to teach them that [b]the Son of Man must suffer
many things and be rejected by the elders and the chief priests
and the scribes, and be killed, and after three days rise again.
32 And He was stating the matter [a]plainly. And Peter took
Him aside and began to rebuke Him.
33 But turning around and seeing His disciples, He rebuked
Peter and *said, "Get behind Me, [a]Satan; for you are not setting
your mind on [1]God's interests, but man's."
34 And He summoned the crowd with His disciples, and said
to them, "If anyone wishes to come after Me, he must deny
himself, and [a]take up his cross and follow Me.
35 "For [a]whoever wishes to save his [1]life will lose it, but
whoever loses his [1]life for My sake and the gospel's will save it.
36 "For what does it profit a man to gain the whole world, and
forfeit his soul?
37 "For what will a man give in exchange for his soul?
38 "For [a]whoever is ashamed of Me and My words in this
adulterous and sinful generation, [b]the Son of Man will also be
ashamed of him when He [c]comes in the glory of His Father
with the holy angels."

Chapter 9 Theme ______________________________

9 And Jesus was saying to them, "[a]Truly I say to you, there
are some of those who are standing here who will not taste
death until they see the kingdom of God after it has come with
power."
2 [a]Six days later, Jesus *took with Him [b]Peter and [1]James and
John, and *brought them up on a high mountain by themselves.
And He was transfigured before them;
3 and [a]His garments became radiant and exceedingly white,
as no launderer on earth can whiten them.
4 Elijah appeared to them along with Moses; and they were
talking with Jesus.
5 Peter *said to Jesus, "[a]Rabbi, it is good for us to be here; [b]let
us make three [1]tabernacles, one for You, and one for Moses, and
one for Elijah."
6 For he did not know what to answer; for they became
terrified.
7 Then a cloud [1]formed, overshadowing them, and [a]a voice
[1]came out of the cloud, "[b]This is My beloved Son, [2]listen to Him!"
8 All at once they looked around and saw no one with them
anymore, except Jesus alone.
9 [a]As they were coming down from the mountain, He [b]gave
them orders not to relate to anyone what they had seen, [1]until
the Son of Man rose from the dead.
10 They [1]seized upon [2]that statement, discussing with one
another [3]what rising from the dead meant.
11 They asked Him, saying, "*Why is it* that the scribes say that
[a]Elijah must come first?"

30 [1]Or *strictly admonished* [a]Matt 8:4; 16:20; Luke 9:21

31 [a]Mark 8:31-9:1: *Matt 16:21-28; Luke 9:22-27* [b]Matt 16:21

32 [a]John 10:24; 11:14; 16:25, 29; 18:20

33 [1]Lit *the things of God* [a]Matt 4:10

34 [a]Matt 10:38; Luke 14:27

35 [1]Or *soul* [a]Matt 10:39; Luke 17:33; John 12:25

38 [a]Matt 10:33; Luke 9:26; Heb 11:16 [b]Matt 8:20 [c]Matt 16:27; Mark 13:26; Luke 9:26

9:1 [a]Matt 16:28; Mark 13:26; Luke 9:27

2 [1]Or *Jacob* [a]Mark 9:2-8: *Matt 17:1-8; Luke 9:28-36* [b]Mark 5:37

3 [a]Matt 28:3

5 [1]Or *sacred tents* [a]Matt 23:7 [b]Matt 17:4; Luke 9:33

7 [1]Or *occurred* [2]Or *give constant heed* [a]2 Pet 1:17f [b]Matt 3:17; Mark 1:11; Luke 3:22

9 [1]Lit *except when* [a]Mark 9:9-13: *Matt 17:9-13* [b]Matt 8:4; Mark 5:43; 7:36; 8:30

10 [1]Or *kept to themselves* [2]Lit *the statement* [3]Lit *what was the rising from the dead*

11 [a]Mal 4:5; Matt 11:14

12 And He said to them, "Elijah does first come and restore all
things. And *yet* how is it written of [a]the Son of Man that [b]He
will suffer many things and be treated with contempt?
13 "But I say to you that Elijah has [1]indeed come, and they did
to him whatever they wished, just as it is written of him."
14 [a]When they came *back* to the disciples, they saw a large
crowd around them, and *some* scribes arguing with them.
15 Immediately, when the entire crowd saw Him, they were
[a]amazed and *began* running up to greet Him.
16 And He asked them, "What are you discussing with them?"
17 And one of the crowd answered Him, "Teacher, I brought
You my son, possessed with a spirit which makes him mute;
18 and [1]whenever it seizes him, it [2]slams him *to the ground*
and he foams *at the mouth,* and grinds his teeth and [3]stiffens
out. I told Your disciples to cast it out, and they could not *do it.*"
19 And He *answered them and *said, "O unbelieving
generation, how long shall I be with you? How long shall I put
up with you? Bring him to Me!"
20 They brought [1]the boy to Him. When he saw Him,
immediately the spirit threw him into a convulsion, and falling
to the ground, he *began* rolling around and foaming *at the mouth.*
21 And He asked his father, "How long has this been happening
to him?" And he said, "From childhood.
22 "It has often thrown him both into the fire and into the
water to destroy him. But if You can do anything, take pity on
us and help us!"
23 And Jesus said to him, "'If You can?' [a]All things are possible
to him who believes."
24 Immediately the boy's father cried out and said, "I do
believe; help my unbelief."
25 When Jesus saw that [a]a crowd was [1]rapidly gathering, He
rebuked the unclean spirit, saying to it, "You deaf and mute spirit,
I [2]command you, come out of him and do not enter him [3]again."
26 After crying out and throwing him into terrible convulsions,
it came out; and *the boy* became so much like a corpse that
most *of them* said, "He is dead!"
27 But Jesus took him by the hand and raised him; and he got up.
28 When He came [a]into *the* house, His disciples *began*
questioning Him privately, "Why could we not drive it out?"
29 And He said to them, "This kind cannot come out by
anything but prayer."
30 [a]From there they went out and *began* to go through
Galilee, and He did not want anyone to know *about it.*
31 For He was teaching His disciples and telling them, "[a]The Son
of Man is to be [1]delivered into the hands of men, and they will kill
Him; and when He has been killed, He will rise three days later."
32 But [a]they [1]did not understand *this* statement, and they
were afraid to ask Him.
33 [a]They came to Capernaum; and when He [1]was in [b]the
house, He *began* to question them, "What were you discussing
on the way?"

12 [a]Mark 9:31 [b]Matt 16:21; 26:24
13 [1]Lit *also*
14 [a]Mark 9:14-28: *Matt 17:14-19; Luke 9:37-42*
15 [a]Mark 14:33; 16:5, 6
18 [1]Or *wherever* [2]Or *tears him* [3]Or *withers away*
20 [1]Lit *him*
23 [a]Matt 17:20; John 11:40
25 [1]Or *running together* [2]Or *I Myself command* [3]Or *from now on* [a]Mark 9:15
28 [a]Mark 2:1; 7:17
30 [a]Mark 9:30-32: *Matt 17:22, 23; Luke 9:43-45*
31 [1]Or *betrayed* [a]Matt 16:21; Mark 8:31; 9:12
32 [1]Lit *were not knowing* [a]Luke 2:50; 9:45; 18:34; John 12:16
33 [1]Lit *had come* [a]Mark 9:33-37: *Matt 18:1-5; Luke 9:46-48* [b]Mark 3:19

34 But they kept silent, for on the way [a]they had discussed
with one another which *of them was* the greatest.
35 Sitting down, He called the twelve and *said to them, "[a]If
anyone wants to be first, [1]he shall be last of all and servant of all."
36 Taking a child, He set him [1]before them, and taking him in
His arms, He said to them,
37 "[a]Whoever receives [1]one child like this in My name receives
Me; and whoever receives Me does not receive Me, but Him
who sent Me."
38 [a]John said to Him, "Teacher, we saw someone casting out
demons in Your name, and [b]we tried to prevent him because
he was not following us."
39 But Jesus said, "Do not hinder him, for there is no one
who will perform a miracle in My name, and be able soon
afterward to speak evil of Me.
40 "[a]For he who is not against us is [1]for us.
41 "For [a]whoever gives you a cup of water to drink [1]because of
your name as *followers* of Christ, truly I say to you, he will not
lose his reward.
42 "[a]Whoever causes one of these [1]little ones who believe to
stumble, it [2]would be better for him if, with a heavy millstone
hung around his neck, he [3]had been cast into the sea.
43 "[a]If your hand causes you to stumble, cut it off; it is better
for you to enter life crippled, than, having your two hands, to
go into [1b]hell, into the [c]unquenchable fire,
44 [[1]where THEIR WORM DOES NOT DIE, AND THE FIRE IS NOT
QUENCHED.]
45 "If your foot causes you to stumble, cut it off; it is better for you
to enter life lame, than, having your two feet, to be cast into [1a]hell,
46 [[1]where THEIR WORM DOES NOT DIE, AND THE FIRE IS NOT
QUENCHED.]
47 "[a]If your eye causes you to stumble, throw it out; it is better
for you to enter the kingdom of God with one eye, than, having
two eyes, to be cast into [1b]hell,
48 [a]where THEIR WORM DOES NOT DIE, AND [b]THE FIRE IS NOT
QUENCHED.
49 "For everyone will be salted with fire.
50 "Salt is good; but [a]if the salt becomes unsalty, with what will
you [1]make it salty *again?* [b]Have salt in yourselves, and [c]be at
peace with one another."

Chapter 10 Theme ______________________________

10 [a]Getting up, He *went from there to the region of Judea
and beyond the Jordan; crowds *gathered around Him
again, and, [b]according to His custom, He once more *began* to
teach them.
2 *Some* Pharisees came up to Jesus, testing Him, and *began* to
question Him whether it was lawful for a man to [1]divorce a wife.
3 And He answered and said to them, "What did Moses
command you?"

34 [a]Matt 18:4; Mark 9:50; Luke 22:24

35 [1]Or *let him be* [a]Matt 20:26; 23:11; Mark 10:43, 44; Luke 22:26

36 [1]Lit *in their midst*

37 [1]Lit *one of such children* [a]Matt 10:40; Luke 10:16; John 13:20

38 [a]Mark 9:38-40: *Luke 9:49, 50* [b]Num 11:27-29

40 [1]Or *on our side* [a]Matt 12:30; Luke 11:23

41 [1]Lit *in a name that you are Christ's* [a]Matt 10:42

42 [1]I.e. humble [2]Lit *is better for him if a millstone turned by a donkey is hung* [3]Lit *has been thrown* [a]Matt 18:6; Luke 17:2; 1 Cor 8:12

43 [1]Gr *Gehenna* [a]Matt 5:30; 18:8 [b]Matt 5:22 [c]Matt 3:12; 25:41

44 [1]Vv 44 and 46, which are identical to v 48, are not found in the early mss

45 [1]Gr *Gehenna* [a]Matt 5:22

46 [1]V 44, note 1

47 [1]Gr *Gehenna* [a]Matt 5:29; 18:9 [b]Matt 5:22

48 [a]Is 66:24 [b]Matt 3:12; 25:41

50 [1]Lit *season it* [a]Matt 5:13; Luke 14:34f [b]Col 4:6 [c]Mark 9:34; Rom 12:18; 2 Cor 13:11; 1 Thess 5:13

10:1 [a]Mark 10:1-12: *Matt 19:1-9* [b]Matt 4:23; 26:55; Mark 1:21; 2:13; 4:2; 6:2, 6, 34; 12:35; 14:49

2 [1]Or *send away*

4 They said, "[a]Moses permitted *a man* TO WRITE A CERTIFICATE
OF DIVORCE AND [1]SEND *her* AWAY."
5 But Jesus said to them, "[1a]Because of your hardness of
heart he wrote you this commandment.
6 "But [a]from the beginning of creation, *God* [b]MADE THEM MALE
AND FEMALE.
7 "[a]FOR THIS REASON A MAN SHALL LEAVE HIS FATHER AND MOTHER,[1]
8 [a]AND THE TWO SHALL BECOME ONE FLESH; so they are no longer
two, but one flesh.
9 "What therefore God has joined together, let no man separate."
10 In the house the disciples *began* questioning Him about
this again.
11 And He *said to them, "[a]Whoever [1]divorces his wife and
marries another woman commits adultery against her;
12 and [a]if she herself [1]divorces her husband and marries
another man, she is committing adultery."
13 [a]And they were bringing children to Him so that He might
touch them; but the disciples rebuked them.
14 But when Jesus saw this, He was indignant and said to
them, "Permit the children to come to Me; do not hinder
them; [a]for the kingdom of God belongs to such as these.
15 "Truly I say to you, [a]whoever does not receive the kingdom
of God like a child will not enter it *at all.*"
16 And He [a]took them in His arms and *began* blessing them,
laying His hands on them.
17 [a]As He was setting out on a journey, a man ran up to Him
and [b]knelt before Him, and asked Him, "Good Teacher, what
shall I do to [c]inherit eternal life?"
18 And Jesus said to him, "Why do you call Me good? No one
is good except God alone.
19 "You know the commandments, '[a]DO NOT MURDER, DO NOT
COMMIT ADULTERY, DO NOT STEAL, DO NOT BEAR FALSE WITNESS, Do
not defraud, HONOR YOUR FATHER AND MOTHER.'"
20 And he said to Him, "Teacher, I have kept [a]all these things
from my youth up."
21 Looking at him, Jesus felt a love for him and said to him, "One
thing you lack: go and sell all you possess and give to the poor,
and you will have [a]treasure in heaven; and come, follow Me."
22 But at these words [1]he was saddened, and he went away
grieving, for he was one who owned much property.
23 And Jesus, looking around, *said to His disciples, "[a]How hard
it will be for those who are wealthy to enter the kingdom of God!"
24 The disciples [a]were amazed at His words. But Jesus
*answered again and *said to them, "Children, how hard it is
to enter the kingdom of God!
25 "[a]It is easier for a camel to go through the eye of a needle
than for a rich man to enter the kingdom of God."
26 They were even more astonished and said to Him, "[1]Then
who can be saved?"
27 Looking at them, Jesus *said, "[a]With people it is impossible,
but not with God; for all things are possible with God."

4 [1]Or *divorce* her [a]Deut 24:1, 3; Matt 5:31
5 [1]Or *With reference to* [a]Matt 19:8
6 [a]Mark 13:19; 2 Pet 3:4 [b]Gen 1:27; 5:2
7 [1]Many late mss add *and shall cling to his wife* [a]Gen 2:24
8 [a]Gen 2:24
11 [1]Or *sends away* [a]Matt 5:32
12 [1]Or *sends away* [a]1 Cor 7:11, 13
13 [a]Mark 10:13-16: *Matt 19:13-15; Luke 18:15-17*
14 [a]Matt 5:3
15 [a]Matt 18:3; 19:14; Luke 18:17; 1 Cor 14:20; 1 Pet 2:2
16 [a]Mark 9:36
17 [a]Mark 10:17-31: *Matt 19:16-30; Luke 18:18-30* [b]Mark 1:40 [c]Matt 25:34; Luke 10:25; 18:18; Acts 20:32; Eph 1:18; 1 Pet 1:4
19 [a]Ex 20:12-16; Deut 5:16-20
20 [a]Matt 19:20
21 [a]Matt 6:20
22 [1]Or *he became gloomy*
23 [a]Matt 19:23
24 [a]Mark 1:27
25 [a]Matt 19:24
26 [1]Lit *And*
27 [a]Matt 19:26

28 [a]Peter began to say to Him, "Behold, we have left everything
and followed You."
29 Jesus said, "Truly I say to you, [a]there is no one who has left
house or brothers or sisters or mother or father or children or
farms, for My sake and for the gospel's sake,
30 [1]but that he will receive a hundred times as much now in
[2]the present age, houses and brothers and sisters and mothers
and children and farms, along with persecutions; and in [a]the
age to come, eternal life.
31 "But [a]many *who are* first will be last, and the last, first."
32 [a]They were on the road going up to Jerusalem, and Jesus
was walking on ahead of them; and they [b]were amazed, and
those who followed were fearful. And again He took the twelve
aside and began to tell them what was going to happen to Him,
33 *saying,* "Behold, we are going up to Jerusalem, and [a]the Son
of Man will be [1]delivered to the chief priests and the scribes;
and they will condemn Him to death and will [2]hand Him over
to the Gentiles.
34 "They will mock Him and [a]spit on Him, and scourge Him
and kill *Him,* and three days later He will rise again."
35 [1a]James and John, the two sons of Zebedee, *came up to
Jesus, saying, "Teacher, we want You to do for us whatever we
ask of You."
36 And He said to them, "What do you want Me to do for you?"
37 They said to Him, "[1]Grant that we [a]may sit, one on Your
right and one on *Your* left, in Your glory."
38 But Jesus said to them, "You do not know what you are
asking. Are you able [a]to drink the cup that I drink, or [b]to be
baptized with the baptism with which I am baptized?"
39 They said to Him, "We are able." And Jesus said to them,
"The cup that I drink [a]you shall drink; and you shall be
baptized with the baptism with which I am baptized.
40 "But to sit on My right or on *My* left, this is not Mine to
give; [a]but it is for those for whom it has been prepared."
41 [a]Hearing *this,* the ten began to feel indignant with [1]James
and John.
42 Calling them to Himself, Jesus *said to them, "You know
that those who are recognized as rulers of the Gentiles lord it
over them; and their great men exercise authority over them.
43 "But it is not this way among you, [a]but whoever wishes to
become great among you shall be your servant;
44 and whoever wishes to be first among you shall be slave of all.
45 "For even the Son of Man [a]did not come to be served, but to
serve, and to give His [1]life a ransom for many."
46 [a]Then they *came to Jericho. And [b]as He was leaving
Jericho with His disciples and a large crowd, a blind beggar
named Bartimaeus, the son of Timaeus, was sitting by the road.
47 When he heard that it was Jesus the [a]Nazarene, he began
to cry out and say, "Jesus, [b]Son of David, have mercy on me!"
48 Many were sternly telling him to be quiet, but he kept
crying out all the more, "[a]Son of David, have mercy on me!"

28 [a]Matt 4:20-22
29 [a]Matt 6:33; 19:29; Luke 18:29f
30 [1]Lit *if not* [2]Lit *this time* [a]Matt 12:32
31 [a]Matt 19:30; 20:16; Luke 13:30
32 [a]Mark 10:32-34: *Matt 20:17-19; Luke 18:31-33* [b]Mark 1:27
33 [1]Or *betrayed* [2]Or *betray* [a]Mark 8:31; 9:12
34 [a]Matt 16:21; 26:67; 27:30; Mark 9:31; 14:65
35 [1]Or *Jacob* [a]Mark 10:35-45: *Matt 20:20-28*
37 [1]Lit *Give to us* [a]Matt 19:28
38 [a]Matt 20:22 [b]Luke 12:50
39 [a]Acts 12:2; Rev 1:9
40 [a]Matt 13:11
41 [1]Or *Jacob* [a]Mark 10:42-45; Luke 22:25-27
43 [a]Matt 20:26; 23:11; Mark 9:35; Luke 22:26
45 [1]Or *soul* [a]Matt 20:28
46 [a]Mark 10:46-52: *Matt 20:29-34; Luke 18:35-43* [b]Luke 18:35; 19:1
47 [a]Mark 1:24 [b]Matt 9:27
48 [a]Matt 9:27

49 And Jesus stopped and said, "Call him *here.*" So they *called
the blind man, saying to him, "[a]Take courage, stand up! He is
calling for you."
50 Throwing aside his cloak, he jumped up and came to Jesus.
51 And answering him, Jesus said, "What do you want Me to
do for you?" And the blind man said to Him, "[1a]Rabboni, *I want*
to regain my sight!"
52 And Jesus said to him, "Go; [a]your faith has [1]made you
well." Immediately he regained his sight and *began* following
Him on the road.

Chapter 11 Theme ________________________________

11 [a]As they *approached Jerusalem, at Bethphage and [b]Bethany,
near [c]the Mount of Olives, He *sent two of His disciples,
2 and *said to them, "Go into the village opposite you, and
immediately as you enter it, you will find a colt tied *there,* on
which no one yet has ever sat; untie it and bring it *here.*
3 "If anyone says to you, 'Why are you doing this?' you say, 'The
Lord has need of it'; and immediately he [1]will send it back here."
4 They went away and found a colt tied at the door, outside
in the street; and they *untied it.
5 Some of the bystanders were saying to them, "What are
you doing, untying the colt?"
6 They spoke to them just as Jesus had told *them,* and they
gave them permission.
7 [a]They *brought the colt to Jesus and put their coats on it;
and He sat on it.
8 And many spread their coats in the road, and others *spread*
leafy branches which they had cut from the fields.
9 Those who went in front and those who followed were
shouting:
"Hosanna!
[a]BLESSED IS HE WHO COMES IN THE NAME OF THE LORD;
10 Blessed *is* the coming kingdom of our father David;
Hosanna [a]in the highest!"
11 [a]Jesus entered Jerusalem *and came* into the temple; and
after looking around at everything,
[b]He left for Bethany with the
twelve, since it was already late.
12 [a]On the next day, when they
had left Bethany, He became
hungry.
13 Seeing at a distance a fig
tree in leaf, He went *to see* if
perhaps He would find anything
on it; and when He came to it,
He found nothing but leaves, for
it was not the season for figs.
14 He said to it, "May no one
ever eat fruit from you again!"
And His disciples were listening.

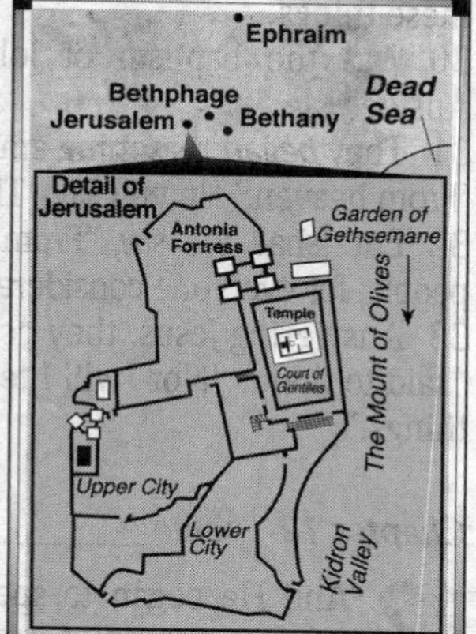

From Bethany, Bethphage across the Mount of Olives into Jerusalem

49 [a]Matt 9:2
51 [1]I.e. My Master [a]Matt 23:7; John 20:16
52 [1]Lit *saved you* [a]Matt 9:22
11:1 [a]Mark 11:1-10: *Matt 21:1-9; Luke 19:29-38* [b]Matt 21:17 [c]Matt 21:1
3 [1]Lit *sends*
7 [a]Mark 11:7-10: *Matt 21:4-9; Luke 19:35-38; John 12:12-15*
9 [a]Ps 118:26; Matt 21:9
10 [a]Matt 21:9
11 [a]Matt 21:12 [b]Matt 21:17
12 [a]Mark 11:12-14, 20-24: *Matt 21:18-22*

15 [a]Then they *came to Jerusalem. And He entered the temple
and began to drive out those who were buying and selling in
the temple, and overturned the tables of the money changers
and the seats of those who were selling [1]doves;
16 and He would not permit anyone to carry [1]merchandise
through the temple.
17 And He *began* to teach and say to them, "Is it not written,
'[a]MY HOUSE SHALL BE CALLED A HOUSE OF PRAYER FOR ALL THE NATIONS'?
[b]But you have made it a ROBBERS' [1]DEN."
18 The chief priests and the scribes heard *this,* and [a]*began*
seeking how to destroy Him; for they were afraid of Him, for
[b]the whole crowd was astonished at His teaching.
19 [a]When evening came, [1]they would go out of the city.
20 [a]As they were passing by in the morning, they saw the fig
tree withered from the roots *up.*
21 Being reminded, Peter *said to Him, "[a]Rabbi, look, the fig
tree which You cursed has withered."
22 And Jesus *answered saying to them, "[a]Have faith in God.
23 "[a]Truly I say to you, whoever says to this mountain, 'Be taken up
and cast into the sea,' and does not doubt in his heart, but believes
that what he says is going to happen, it will be *granted* him.
24 "Therefore I say to you, [a]all things for which you pray and
ask, believe that you have received them, and they will be
granted you.
25 "Whenever you [a]stand praying, [b]forgive, if you have anything
against anyone, so that your Father who is in heaven will also
forgive you your transgressions.
26 ["[1a]But if you do not forgive, neither will your Father who
is in heaven forgive your transgressions."]
27 They *came again to Jerusalem. [a]And as He was walking in
the temple, the chief priests and the scribes and the elders
*came to Him,
28 and *began* saying to Him, "By what authority are You doing
these things, or who gave You this authority to do these things?"
29 And Jesus said to them, "I will ask you one question, and
you answer Me, and *then* I will tell you by what authority I do
these things.
30 "Was the baptism of John from heaven, or from men?
Answer Me."
31 They *began* reasoning among themselves, saying, "If we say,
'From heaven,' He will say, 'Then why did you not believe him?'
32 "But [1]shall we say, 'From men'?"—they were afraid of the
people, for everyone considered John to have been a real prophet.
33 Answering Jesus, they *said, "We do not know." And Jesus
*said to them, "Nor [1]will I tell you by what authority I do these
things."

Chapter 12 Theme ____________________

12 [a]And He began to speak to them in parables: "[b]A man
[c]PLANTED A VINEYARD AND PUT A [1]WALL AROUND IT, AND DUG A

15 [1]Lit *the doves* [a]Mark 11:15-18: *Matt 21:12-16; Luke 19:45-47;* John 2:13-16

16 [1]Lit *a vessel;* i.e. a receptacle or implement of any kind

17 [1]Lit *cave* [a]Is 56:7 [b]Jer 7:11

18 [a]Matt 21:46; Mark 12:12; Luke 20:19; John 7:1 [b]Matt 7:28

19 [1]I.e. Jesus and His disciples [a]Matt 21:17; Mark 11:11; Luke 21:37

20 [a]Mark 11:12-14, 20-24: *Matt 21:19-22*

21 [a]Matt 23:7

22 [a]Matt 17:20; 21:21f

23 [a]Matt 17:20; 1 Cor 13:2

24 [a]Matt 7:7f

25 [a]Matt 6:5 [b]Matt 6:14

26 [1]Early mss do not contain this v [a]Matt 6:15; 18:35

27 [a]Mark 11:27-33: *Matt 21:23-27; Luke 20:1-8*

32 [1]Or *if we say*

33 [1]Lit *do I tell*

12:1 [1]Or *fence* [a]Mark 3:23; 4:2ff [b]Mark 12:1-12: *Matt 21:33-46; Luke 20:9-19* [c]Is 5:1, 2

VAT UNDER THE WINE PRESS AND BUILT A TOWER, and rented it out to [2]vine-growers and went on a journey.

2 "At the *harvest* time he sent a slave to the vine-growers, in order to receive *some* of the produce of the vineyard from the vine-growers.

3 "They took him, and beat him and sent him away empty-handed.

4 "Again he sent them another slave, and they wounded him in the head, and treated him shamefully.

5 "And he sent another, and that one they killed; and *so with* many others, beating some and killing others.

6 "He had one more *to send,* a beloved son; he sent him last *of all* to them, saying, 'They will respect my son.'

7 "But those vine-growers said to one another, 'This is the heir; come, let us kill him, and the inheritance will be ours!'

8 "They took him, and killed him and threw him out of the vineyard.

9 "What will the [1]owner of the vineyard do? He will come and destroy the vine-growers, and will give the vineyard to others.

10 "Have you not even read this Scripture:
'[a]THE STONE WHICH THE BUILDERS REJECTED,
THIS BECAME THE CHIEF CORNER *stone;*

11 [a]THIS CAME ABOUT FROM THE LORD,
AND IT IS MARVELOUS IN OUR EYES'?"

12 [a]And they were seeking to seize Him, and *yet* they feared the [1]people, for they understood that He spoke the parable against them. And *so* [b]they left Him and went away.

13 [a]Then they *sent some of the Pharisees and [b]Herodians to Him in order to [c]trap Him in a statement.

14 They *came and *said to Him, "Teacher, we know that You are truthful and [1]defer to no one; for You are not partial to any, but teach the way of God in truth. Is it [2]lawful to pay a poll-tax to Caesar, or not?

15 "Shall we pay or shall we not pay?" But He, knowing their hypocrisy, said to them, "Why are you testing Me? Bring Me a [1]denarius to look at."

16 They brought *one.* And He *said to them, "Whose likeness and inscription is this?" And they said to Him, "Caesar's."

17 And Jesus said to them, "[a]Render to Caesar the things that are Caesar's, and to God the things that are God's." And they [1]were amazed at Him.

18 [a]*Some* Sadducees (who say that there is no resurrection) *came to Jesus, and *began* questioning Him, saying,

19 "Teacher, Moses wrote for us that [a]IF A MAN'S BROTHER DIES and leaves behind a wife AND LEAVES NO CHILD, HIS BROTHER SHOULD [1]MARRY THE WIFE AND RAISE UP CHILDREN TO HIS BROTHER.

20 "There were seven brothers; and the first took a wife, and died leaving no children.

21 "The second one [1]married her, and died leaving behind no children; and the third likewise;

22 and *so* [1]all seven left no children. Last of all the woman died also.

12:1 [2]Or *tenant farmers,* also vv 2, 7, 9
9 [1]Lit *lord*
10 [a]Ps 118:22
11 [a]Ps 118:23
12 [1]Lit *crowd* [a]Mark 11:18 [b]Matt 22:22
13 [a]Mark 12:13-17: *Matt 22:15-22; Luke 20:20-26* [b]Matt 22:16 [c]Luke 11:54
14 [1]Lit *it is not a concern to You about anyone;* i.e. You do not seek anyone's favor [2]Or *permissible*
15 [1]The denarius was a day's wages
17 [1]Or *were greatly marveling* [a]Matt 22:21
18 [a]Mark 12:18-27: *Matt 22:23-33; Luke 20:27-38;* Acts 23:8
19 [1]Lit *take* [a]Deut 25:5
21 [1]Lit *took*
22 [1]Lit *the seven*

23 "In the resurrection, [1]when they rise again, which one's
wife will she be? For [2]all seven had married her."
24 Jesus said to them, "Is this not the reason you are
mistaken, that you do not [1]understand the Scriptures or the
power of God?
25 "For when they rise from the dead, they neither marry nor
are given in marriage, but are like angels in heaven.
26 "But [1]regarding the fact that the dead rise again, have you
not read in the book of Moses, [a]in the *passage* about *the
burning* bush, how God spoke to him, saying, '[b]I AM THE GOD
OF ABRAHAM, AND THE GOD OF ISAAC, and the God of Jacob'?
27 "[a]He is not the God [1]of the dead, but of the living; you are
greatly mistaken."
28 [a]One of the scribes came and heard them arguing, and
[b]recognizing that He had answered them well, asked Him,
"What commandment is the [1]foremost of all?"
29 Jesus answered, "The foremost is, '[a]HEAR, O ISRAEL! THE
LORD OUR GOD IS ONE LORD;
30 [a]AND YOU SHALL LOVE THE LORD YOUR GOD WITH ALL YOUR
HEART, AND WITH ALL YOUR SOUL, AND WITH ALL YOUR MIND, AND
WITH ALL YOUR STRENGTH.'
31 "The second is this, '[a]YOU SHALL LOVE YOUR NEIGHBOR AS
YOURSELF.' There is no other commandment greater than
these."
32 The scribe said to Him, "Right, Teacher; You have truly
stated that [a]HE IS ONE, AND THERE IS NO ONE ELSE BESIDES HIM;
33 [a]AND TO LOVE HIM WITH ALL THE HEART AND WITH ALL THE
UNDERSTANDING AND WITH ALL THE STRENGTH, AND TO LOVE ONE'S
NEIGHBOR AS HIMSELF, [b]is much more than all burnt offerings and
sacrifices."
34 When Jesus saw that he had answered intelligently, He said
to him, "You are not far from the kingdom of God." [a]After that,
no one would venture to ask Him any more questions.
35 [a]And Jesus *began* to say, as He [b]taught in the temple, "How
is it that the scribes say that [1]the Christ is the [c]son of David?
36 "David himself said [1]in the Holy Spirit,
'[a]THE LORD SAID TO MY LORD,
"SIT AT MY RIGHT HAND,
UNTIL I PUT YOUR ENEMIES BENEATH YOUR FEET."'
37 "David himself calls Him 'Lord'; so in what sense is He his
son?" And [a]the large crowd [1]enjoyed listening to Him.
38 [a]In His teaching He was saying: "Beware of the scribes
who like to walk around in long robes, and *like* [b]respectful
greetings in the market places,
39 and chief seats in the synagogues and places of honor at
banquets,
40 [a]who devour widows' houses, and for appearance's sake
offer long prayers; these will receive greater condemnation."
41 [a]And He sat down opposite [b]the treasury, and *began*
observing how the people were [c]putting [1]money into the
treasury; and many rich people were putting in large sums.

INSIGHT

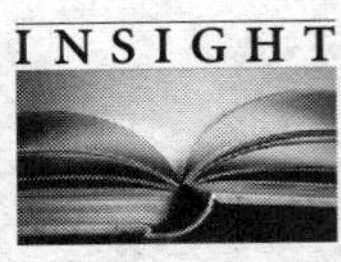

The treasury was in the women's court of the temple, where there were thirteen trumpet-shaped offering receptacles. See the illustration of the floor plan of Herod's Temple on page 1614, and see the illustration of Herod's Temple on page NISB-38.

23 [1]Early mss do not contain *when they rise again* [2]Lit *the seven*

24 [1]Or *know*

26 [1]Lit *concerning the dead, that they rise* [a]Luke 20:37; Rom 11:2 [b]Ex 3:6

27 [1]Or *of corpses* [a]Matt 22:32; Luke 20:38

28 [1]Or *first* [a]Mark 12:28-34: *Matt 22:34-40; Luke 10:25-28;* 20:39f [b]Matt 22:34; Luke 20:39

29 [a]Deut 6:4

30 [a]Deut 6:5

31 [a]Lev 19:18

32 [a]Deut 4:35

33 [a]Deut 6:5 [b]1 Sam 15:22; Hos 6:6; Mic 6:6-8; Matt 9:13; 12:7

34 [a]Matt 22:46

35 [1]I.e. the Messiah [a]Mark 12:35-37: *Matt 22:41-46; Luke 20:41-44* [b]Matt 26:55; Mark 10:1 [c]Matt 9:27

36 [1]Or *by* [a]Ps 110:1

37 [1]Lit *was gladly hearing Him* [a]John 12:9

38 [a]Mark 12:38-40: *Matt 23:1-7; Luke 20:45-47* [b]Matt 23:7; Luke 11:43

40 [a]Luke 20:47

41 [1]I.e. copper coins [a]Mark 12:41-44: *Luke 21:1-4* [b]John 8:20 [c]2 Kin 12:9

42 A poor widow came and put in two [1]small copper coins, which amount to a [2]cent.

43 Calling His disciples to Him, He said to them, "Truly I say to you, this poor widow put in more than all [1]the contributors to the treasury;

44 for they all put in out of their [1]surplus, but she, out of her poverty, put in all she owned, [2]all she had [a]to live on."

Chapter 13 Theme ____

13 [a]As He was going out of the temple, one of His disciples *said to Him, "Teacher, behold [1]what wonderful stones and [1]what wonderful buildings!"

2 And Jesus said to him, "Do you see these great buildings? [a]Not one stone will be left upon another which will not be torn down."

3 As He was sitting on [a]the Mount of Olives opposite the temple, [b]Peter and [1]James and John and Andrew were questioning Him privately,

4 "Tell us, when will these things be, and what *will be* the [1]sign when all these things are going to be fulfilled?"

5 And Jesus began to say to them, "See to it that no one misleads you.

6 "Many will come in My name, saying, '[a]I am *He!*' and will mislead many.

7 "When you hear of wars and rumors of wars, do not be frightened; *those things* must take place; but *that is* not yet the end.

8 "For nation will rise up against nation, and kingdom against kingdom; there will be earthquakes in various places; there will *also* be famines. These things are *merely* the beginning of birth pangs.

9 "But [1]be on your guard; for they will [a]deliver you to *the* [2]courts, and you will be flogged [a]in *the* synagogues, and you will stand before governors and kings for My sake, as a testimony to them.

10 "[a]The gospel must first be preached to all the nations.

11 "[a]When they [1]arrest you and hand you over, do not worry beforehand about what you are to say, but say whatever is given you in that hour; for it is not you who speak, but *it is* the Holy Spirit.

12 "Brother will betray brother to death, and a father *his* child; and children will rise up against parents and [1]have them put to death.

13 "[a]You will be hated by all because of My name, but the one who endures to the end, he will be saved.

14 "But [a]when you see the [b]ABOMINATION OF DESOLATION standing where it should not be (let the reader understand), then those who are in Judea must flee to the mountains.

15 "[a]The one who is on the housetop must not go down, or go in to get anything out of his house;

42 [1]Gr *lepta* [2]Gr *quadrans;* i.e. 1/64 of a denarius

43 [1]Lit *those who were putting in*

44 [1]Or *abundance* [2]Lit *her whole livelihood* [a]Luke 8:43; 15:12, 30; 21:4

13:1 [1]Lit *how great* [a]Mark 13:1-37: *Matt 24; Luke 21:5-36*

2 [a]Luke 19:44

3 [1]Or *Jacob* [a]Matt 21:1 [b]Matt 17:1

4 [1]Or *attesting miracle*

6 [a]John 8:24

9 [1]Lit *look to yourselves* [2]Or *Sanhedrin* or *Council* [a]Matt 10:17

10 [a]Matt 24:14

11 [1]Lit *lead* [a]Mark 13:11-13: *Matt 10:19-22; Luke 21:12-17*

12 [1]Lit *put them to death*

13 [a]Matt 10:22; John 15:21

14 [a]Matt 24:15f [b]Dan 9:27; 11:31; 12:11

15 [a]Luke 17:31

16 and the one who is in the field must not turn back to get his coat.
17 "But woe to those who are pregnant and to those who are nursing babies in those days!
18 "But pray that it may not happen in the winter.
19 "For those days will be a *time of* tribulation such as has not occurred [a]since the beginning of the creation which God created until now, and never will.
20 "Unless the Lord had shortened *those* days, no [1]life would have been saved; but for the sake of the [2]elect, whom He chose, He shortened the days.
21 "And then if anyone says to you, 'Behold, here is [1]the Christ'; or, 'Behold, *He is* there'; do not believe *him;*
22 for false Christs and [a]false prophets will arise, and will show [1b]signs and [b]wonders, in order to lead astray, if possible, the elect.
23 "But take heed; behold, I have told you everything in advance.
24 "But in those days, after that tribulation, [a]THE SUN WILL BE DARKENED AND THE MOON WILL NOT GIVE ITS LIGHT,
25 [a]AND THE STARS WILL BE FALLING from heaven, and the powers that are in [1]the heavens will be shaken.
26 "Then they will see [a]THE SON OF MAN [b]COMING IN CLOUDS with great power and glory.
27 "And then He will send forth the angels, and [a]will gather together His [1]elect from the four winds, [b]from the farthest end of the earth to the farthest end of heaven.
28 "Now learn the parable from the fig tree: when its branch has already become tender and puts forth its leaves, you know that summer is near.
29 "Even so, you too, when you see these things happening, [1]recognize that [2]He is near, *right* at the [3]door.
30 "Truly I say to you, this [1]generation will not pass away until all these things take place.
31 "Heaven and earth will pass away, but My words will not pass away.
32 "[a]But of that day or hour no one knows, not even the angels in heaven, nor the Son, but the Father *alone.*
33 "Take heed, [a]keep on the alert; for you do not know when the *appointed* time [1]will come.
34 "[a]*It is* like a man away on a journey, *who* upon leaving his house and [1]putting his slaves in charge, *assigning* to each one his task, also commanded the doorkeeper to stay on the alert.
35 "Therefore, [a]be on the alert—for you do not know when the [1]master of the house is coming, whether in the evening, at midnight, or [b]when the rooster crows, or [c]in the morning—
36 in case he should come suddenly and find you [a]asleep.
37 "What I say to you I say to all, '[a]Be on the alert!'"

Chapter 14 Theme ____________________

14 [a]Now [b]the Passover and Unleavened Bread were two days away; and the chief priests and the scribes [c]were seeking how to seize Him by stealth and kill *Him;*

19 [a]Dan 12:1; Mark 10:6

20 [1]Lit *flesh* [2]Or *chosen ones*

21 [1]I.e. the Messiah

22 [1]Or *attesting miracles* [a]Matt 7:15 [b]Matt 24:24; John 4:48

24 [a]Is 13:10; Ezek 32:7; Joel 2:10, 31; 3:15; Rev 6:12

25 [1]Or *heaven* [a]Is 34:4; Rev 6:13

26 [a]Dan 7:13; Rev 1:7 [b]Matt 16:27; Mark 8:38

27 [1]Or *chosen ones* [a]Deut 30:4 [b]Zech 2:6

29 [1]Or *know* [2]Or *it* [3]Lit *doors*

30 [1]Or *race*

32 [a]Matt 24:36; Acts 1:7

33 [1]Lit *is* [a]Eph 6:18; Col 4:2

34 [1]Lit *giving the authority to* [a]Luke 12:36-38

35 [1]Lit *lord* [a]Matt 24:42; Mark 13:37 [b]Mark 14:30 [c]Matt 14:25; Mark 6:48

36 [a]Rom 13:11

37 [a]Matt 24:42; Mark 13:35

14:1 [a]Mark 14:1, 2: *Matt 26:2-5; Luke 22:1, 2* [b]Ex 12:1-27; Mark 14:12; John 11:55; 13:1 [c]Matt 12:14

2 for they were saying, "Not during the festival, otherwise
there might be a riot of the people."
3 [a]While He was in [b]Bethany at the home of Simon the leper,
and reclining *at the table,* there came a woman with an
alabaster vial of very [c]costly perfume of pure [1]nard; *and* she
broke the vial and poured it over His head.
4 But some were indignantly *remarking* to one another,
"Why has this perfume been wasted?
5 "For this perfume might have been sold for over three
hundred [1]denarii, and *the money* given to the poor." And they
were scolding her.
6 But Jesus said, "Let her alone; why do you bother her? She
has done a good deed to Me.
7 "For you always have [a]the poor with you, and whenever you
wish you can do good to them; but you do not always have Me.
8 "She has done what she could; [a]she has anointed My body
beforehand for the burial.
9 "Truly I say to you, [a]wherever the gospel is preached in the
whole world, what this woman has done will also be spoken of
in memory of her."
10 [a]Then Judas Iscariot, [b]who was one of the twelve, went off
to the chief priests in order to [1]betray Him to them.
11 They were glad when they heard *this,* and promised to
give him money. And he *began* seeking how to betray Him at
an opportune time.
12 [a]On the first day of [b]Unleavened Bread, when [1]the Passover
lamb was being [c]sacrificed, His disciples *said to Him, "Where
do You want us to go and prepare for You to eat the Passover?"
13 And He *sent two of His disciples and *said to them, "Go
into the city, and a man will meet you carrying a pitcher of water;
follow him;
14 and wherever he enters, say to the owner of the house,
'The Teacher says, "Where is My [a]guest room in which I may
eat the Passover with My disciples?"'
15 "And he himself will show you a large upper room furnished
and ready; prepare for us there."
16 The disciples went out and came to the city, and found *it*
just as He had told them; and they prepared the Passover.
17 [a]When it was evening He *came with the twelve.
18 As they were reclining *at the table* and eating, Jesus said,
"Truly I say to you that one of you will [1]betray Me—[2]one who
is eating with Me."
19 They began to be grieved and to say to Him one by one,
"Surely not I?"
20 And He said to them, "*It is* one of the twelve, [1]one who
dips with Me in the bowl.
21 "For the Son of Man *is to* go just as it is written of Him; but
woe to that man [1]by whom the Son of Man is betrayed! *It
would have been* good [2]for that man if he had not been born."
22 [a]While they were eating, He took *some* bread, and [1]after a
[b]blessing He broke *it,* and gave *it* to them, and said, "Take *it;*
this is My body."

3 [1]An aromatic oil extracted from an East Indian plant [a]Mark 14:3-9: *Matt 26:6-13;* Luke 7:37-39; John 12:1-8 [b]Matt 21:17 [c]Matt 26:6f; John 12:3

5 [1]The denarius was equivalent to a day's wages

7 [a]Deut 15:11; Matt 26:11; John 12:8

8 [a]John 19:40

9 [a]Matt 26:13

10 [1]Or *hand Him over* [a]Mark 14:10, 11: *Matt 26:14-16; Luke 22:3-6* [b]John 6:71

12 [1]Lit *they were sacrificing* [a]Mark 14:12-16: *Matt 26:17-19; Luke 22:7-13* [b]Matt 26:17 [c]Deut 16:5; Mark 14:1; Luke 22:7; 1 Cor 5:7

14 [a]Luke 22:11

17 [a]Mark 14:17-21: *Matt 26:20-24; Luke 22:14, 21-23;* John 13:18ff

18 [1]Or *deliver Me over* [2]Or *the one*

20 [1]Or *the one*

21 [1]Or *through* [2]Lit *for him if that man had not been born*

22 [1]Lit *having blessed* [a]Mark 14:22-25: *Matt 26:26-29; Luke 22:17-20; 1 Cor 11:23-25;* Mark 10:16 [b]Matt 14:19

23 And when He had taken a cup *and* given thanks, He gave *it*
to them, and they all drank from it.
24 And He said to them, "This is My [a]blood of the [b]covenant,
which is poured out for many.
25 "Truly I say to you, I will never again drink of the fruit of the
vine until that day when I drink it new in the kingdom of God."
26 [a]After singing a hymn, they went out to [b]the Mount of Olives.
27 [a]And Jesus *said to them, "You will all [1]fall away, because it
is written, '[b]I WILL STRIKE DOWN THE SHEPHERD, AND THE SHEEP SHALL
BE SCATTERED.'
28 "But after I have been raised, [a]I will go ahead of you to Galilee."
29 But Peter said to Him, "*Even* though all may [1]fall away, yet
I will not."
30 And Jesus *said to him, "Truly I say to you, that [1a]this very
night, before [b]a rooster crows twice, you yourself will deny Me
three times."
31 But *Peter* kept saying insistently, "*Even* if I have to die with
You, I will not deny You!" And they all were saying the same
thing also.
32 [a]They *came to a place named Gethsemane; and He *said
to His disciples, "Sit here until I have prayed."
33 And He *took with Him Peter and [1]James and John, and
began to be very [a]distressed and troubled.
34 And He *said to them, "[a]My soul is deeply grieved to the
point of death; remain here and keep watch."
35 And He went a little beyond *them,* and fell to the ground
and *began* to pray that if it were possible, [a]the hour might
[1]pass Him by.
36 And He was saying, "[a]Abba! Father! All things are possible
for You; remove this cup from Me; [b]yet not what I will, but
what You will."
37 And He *came and *found them sleeping, and *said to Peter,
"Simon, are you asleep? Could you not keep watch for one hour?
38 "[a]Keep watching and praying that you may not come into
temptation; the spirit is willing, but the flesh is weak."
39 Again He went away and prayed, saying the same [1]words.
40 And again He came and found them sleeping, for their eyes
were very heavy; and they did not know what to answer Him.
41 And He *came the third time, and *said to them, "[1]Are
you still sleeping and resting? It is enough; [a]the hour has come;
behold, the Son of Man is being [2]betrayed into the hands of
sinners.
42 "Get up, let us be going; behold, the one who betrays Me is
at hand!"
43 [a]Immediately while He was still speaking, Judas, one of the
twelve, *came up [1]accompanied by a crowd with swords and clubs,
who were from the chief priests and the scribes and the elders.
44 Now he who was betraying Him had given them a signal,
saying, "Whomever I kiss, He is the one; seize Him and lead
Him away [1]under guard."
45 After coming, Judas immediately went to Him, saying,
"[a]Rabbi!" and kissed Him.

24 [a]Ex 24:8 [b]Jer 31:31-34

26 [a]Matt 26:30 [b]Matt 21:1

27 [1]Or *stumble* [a]Mark 14:27-31: *Matt 26:31-35* [b]Zech 13:7

28 [a]Matt 28:16

29 [1]Or *stumble*

30 [1]Lit *today, on this night* [a]Matt 26:34 [b]Mark 14:68, 72; John 13:38

32 [a]Mark 14:32-42: *Matt 26:36-46; Luke 22:40-46*

33 [1]Or *Jacob* [a]Mark 9:15; 16:5, 6

34 [a]Matt 26:38; John 12:27

35 [1]Lit *pass from Him* [a]Matt 26:45; Mark 14:41

36 [a]Rom 8:15; Gal 4:6 [b]Matt 26:39

38 [a]Matt 26:41

39 [1]Lit *word*

41 [1]Or *Keep on sleeping therefore* [2]Or *delivered* [a]Mark 14:35

43 [1]Lit *and with him* [a]Mark 14:43-50: *Matt 26:47-56; Luke 22:47-53; John 18:3-11*

44 [1]Lit *safely*

45 [a]Matt 23:7

46 They laid hands on Him and seized Him.
47 But one of those who stood by drew his sword, and struck
the slave of the high priest and [1]cut off his ear.
48 And Jesus said to them, "Have you come out with swords
and clubs to arrest Me, as *you would* against a robber?
49 "Every day I was with you [a]in the temple teaching, and you
did not seize Me; but *this has taken place* to fulfill the Scriptures."
50 And they all left Him and fled.
51 A young man was following Him, wearing *nothing but* a
linen sheet over *his* naked *body;* and they *seized him.
52 But he [1]pulled free of the linen sheet and escaped naked.
53 [a]They led Jesus away to the high priest; and all the chief
priests and the elders and the scribes *gathered together.
54 Peter had followed Him at a distance, [a]right into [b]the
courtyard of the high priest; and he was sitting with the [1]officers
and [c]warming himself at the [2]fire.
55 Now the chief priests and the whole [1a]Council kept trying
to obtain testimony against Jesus to put Him to death, and they
were not finding any.
56 For many were giving false testimony against Him, but
their testimony was not consistent.
57 Some stood up and *began* to give false testimony against
Him, saying,
58 "We heard Him say, '[a]I will destroy this [1]temple made with
hands, and in three days I will build another made without hands.'"
59 Not even in this respect was their testimony consistent.
60 The high priest stood up *and came* forward and questioned
Jesus, saying, "Do You not answer? [1]What is it that these men
are testifying against You?"
61 [a]But He kept silent and did not answer. [b]Again the high
priest was questioning Him, and [1]saying to Him, "Are You [2]the
Christ, the Son of the Blessed *One?*"
62 And Jesus said, "I am; and you shall see [a]THE SON OF MAN
SITTING AT THE RIGHT HAND OF POWER, and [b]COMING WITH THE CLOUDS
OF HEAVEN."
63 [a]Tearing his clothes, the high priest *said, "What further
need do we have of witnesses?
64 "You have heard the [a]blasphemy; how does it seem to you?"
And they all condemned Him to be deserving of death.
65 Some began to [a]spit at Him, and [1b]to blindfold Him, and to
beat Him with their fists, and to say to Him, "[c]Prophesy!" And
the officers [2]received Him with [3]slaps *in the face.*
66 [a]As Peter was below in [b]the courtyard, one of the servant-
girls of the high priest *came,
67 and seeing Peter [a]warming himself, she looked at him and
*said, "You also were with Jesus the [b]Nazarene."
68 But he denied *it,* saying, "I neither know nor understand
what you are talking about." And he [a]went out onto the
[1]porch.[2]
69 The servant-girl saw him, and began once more to say to
the bystanders, "This is *one* of them!"

47 [1]Lit *took off*
49 [a]Mark 12:35; Luke 19:47; 21:37
52 [1]Lit *left behind*
53 [a]Mark 14:53-65: *Matt 26:57-68; John 18:12f, 19-24*
54 [1]Or *servants* [2]Lit *light* [a]Mark 14:68 [b]Matt 26:3 [c]Mark 14:67; John 18:18
55 [1]Or *Sanhedrin* [a]Matt 5:22
58 [1]Or *sanctuary* [a]Matt 26:61; Mark 15:29; John 2:19
60 [1]Or *what do these testify?*
61 [1]Lit *says* [2]I.e. the Messiah [a]Matt 26:63 [b]Mark 14:61-63: *Matt 26:63ff; Luke 22:67-71*
62 [a]Ps 110:1; Mark 13:26 [b]Dan 7:13
63 [a]Num 14:6; Matt 26:65; Acts 14:14
64 [a]Lev 24:16
65 [1]Or *cover over His face* [2]Or *treated* [3]Or *blows with rods* [a]Matt 26:67; Mark 10:34 [b]Esth 7:8 [c]Matt 26:68; Luke 22:64
66 [a]Mark 14:66-72: *Matt 26:69-75; Luke 22:56-62; John 18:16-18, 25-27* [b]Mark 14:54
67 [a]Mark 14:54 [b]Mark 1:24
68 [1]Or *forecourt, gateway* [2]Later mss add *and a rooster crowed* [a]Mark 14:54

70 But again [a]he denied it. And after a little while the bystanders
were again saying to Peter, "Surely you are *one* of them, [b]for
you are a Galilean too."
71 But he began to [1]curse and swear, "I do not know this man
you are talking about!"
72 Immediately a rooster crowed a second time. And Peter
remembered how Jesus had made the remark to him, "Before
[a]a rooster crows twice, you will deny Me three times." [1]And he
began to weep.

Chapter 15 Theme ____________________

15 [a]Early in the morning the chief priests with the elders and
scribes and the whole [1b]Council, immediately held a
consultation; and binding Jesus, they led Him away and delivered Him to Pilate.
2 [a]Pilate questioned Him, "Are
You the King of the Jews?" And He
*answered him, "*It is as* you say."
3 The chief priests *began* to
accuse Him [1]harshly.
4 Then Pilate questioned Him
again, saying, "Do You not answer?
See how many charges they bring
against You!"
5 But Jesus [a]made no further
answer; so Pilate was amazed.
6 [a]Now at *the* feast he used to
release for them *any* one prisoner
whom they requested.
7 The man named Barabbas had
been imprisoned with the insur-
rectionists who had committed murder in the insurrection.
8 The crowd went up and began asking him *to do* as he had
been accustomed to do for them.
9 Pilate answered them, saying, "Do you want me to release
for you the King of the Jews?"
10 For he was aware that the chief priests had handed Him
over because of envy.
11 But the chief priests stirred up the crowd [a]*to ask* him to
release Barabbas for them instead.
12 Answering again, Pilate said to them, "Then what shall I
do with Him whom you call the King of the Jews?"
13 They shouted [1]back, "Crucify Him!"
14 But Pilate said to them, "Why, what evil has He done?" But
they shouted all the more, "Crucify Him!"
15 Wishing to satisfy the crowd, Pilate released Barabbas for
them, and after having Jesus [a]scourged, he handed Him over to
be crucified.
16 [a]The soldiers took Him away into [b]the [1]palace (that is, the
Praetorium), and they *called together the whole *Roman*
[2c]cohort.

Jerusalem of the New Testament

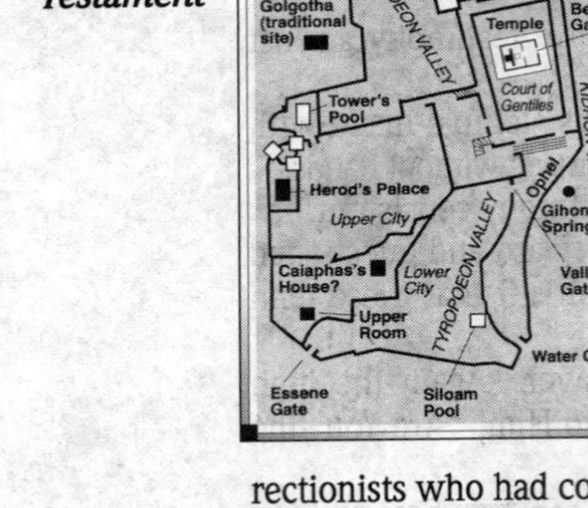

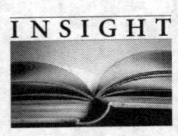

INSIGHT

The ***Praetorium*** was used as the temporary Roman military headquarters or as the palace in Jerusalem to house the Roman governor. It was either a building next to Herod's palace or the Antonia Fortress beside the temple mount complex. See the map above and the illustration of the temple mount on page NISB-40.

70 [a]Mark 14:68 [b]Matt 26:73; Luke 22:59

71 [1]Or *put himself under a curse*

72 [1]Or *Thinking of this, he began weeping* or *Rushing out, he began weeping* [a]Mark 14:30, 68

15:1 [1]Or *Sanhedrin* [a]Matt 27:1 [b]Matt 5:22

2 [a]Mark 15:2-5: *Matt 27:11-14; Luke 23:2, 3; John 18:29-38*

3 [1]Or *of many things*

5 [a]Matt 27:12

6 [a]Mark 15:6-15: *Matt 27:15-26; Luke 23:18-25; John 18:39-19:16*

11 [a]Acts 3:14

13 [1]Or *again*

15 [a]Matt 27:26

16 [1]Or *court* [2]Or *battalion* [a]Mark 15:16-20: *Matt 27:27-31* [b]Matt 26:3; 27:27 [c]Acts 10:1

17 They *dressed Him up in purple, and after twisting a
crown of thorns, they put it on Him;
18 and they began to acclaim Him, "Hail, King of the Jews!"
19 They kept beating His head with a [1]reed, and spitting on
Him, and kneeling and bowing before Him.
20 After they had mocked Him, they took the purple robe off
Him and put His *own* garments on Him. And they *led Him
out to crucify Him.
21 [a]They *pressed into service a passer-by coming from the
country, Simon of Cyrene (the father of Alexander and [b]Rufus),
to bear His cross.
22 [a]Then they *brought Him to the place [b]Golgotha, which is
translated, Place of a Skull.
23 They tried to give Him [a]wine mixed with myrrh; but He
did not take it.
24 And they *crucified Him, and *[a]divided up His garments
among themselves, casting [1]lots for them *to decide* [2]what each
man should take.
25 It was the [1a]third hour [2]when they crucified Him.
26 The inscription of the charge against Him [1]read, "[a]THE
KING OF THE JEWS."
27 They *crucified two robbers with Him, one on His right
and one on His left.
28 [[1]And the Scripture was fulfilled which says, "And He was
numbered with transgressors."]
29 Those passing by were [1]hurling abuse at Him, [a]wagging
their heads, and saying, "Ha! You who *are going to* [b]destroy the
temple and rebuild it in three days,
30 save Yourself, and come down from the cross!"
31 In the same way the chief priests also, along with the
scribes, were mocking *Him* among themselves and saying,
"[a]He saved others; [1]He cannot save Himself.
32 "Let *this* Christ, [a]the King of Israel, now come down from
the cross, so that we may see and believe!" [b]Those who were
crucified with Him were also insulting Him.
33 [a]When the [1b]sixth hour came, darkness [2]fell over the
whole land until the [3b]ninth hour.
34 At the [a]ninth hour Jesus cried out with a loud voice, "[b]ELOI,
ELOI, LAMA SABACHTHANI?" which is translated, "MY GOD, MY
GOD, WHY HAVE YOU FORSAKEN ME?"
35 When some of the bystanders heard it, they *began* saying,
"Behold, He is calling for Elijah."
36 Someone ran and filled a sponge with sour wine, put it on
a reed, and gave Him a drink, saying, "[1]Let us see whether
Elijah will come to take Him down."
37 [a]And Jesus uttered a loud cry, and breathed His last.
38 [a]And the veil of the temple was torn in two from top to
bottom.
39 [a]When the centurion, who was standing [1]right in front of
Him, saw [2]the way He breathed His last, he said, "Truly this
man was [3]the Son of God!"

19 [1]Or *staff* (made of a reed)
21 [a]Mark 15:21: *Matt 27:32; Luke 23:26* [b]Rom 16:13
22 [a]Mark 15:22-32: *Matt 27:33-44; Luke 23:33-43; John 19:17-24* [b]Luke 23:33; John 19:17
23 [a]Matt 27:34
24 [1]Lit *a lot upon* [2]Lit *who should take what* [a]Ps 22:18; John 19:24
25 [1]I.e. 9 a.m. [2]Lit *and* [a]Mark 15:33
26 [1]Lit *had been inscribed* [a]Matt 27:37
28 [1]Early mss do not contain this v
29 [1]Or *blaspheming* [a]Ps 22:7; 109:25; Matt 27:39 [b]Mark 14:58; John 2:19
31 [1]Or *can He not save Himself?* [a]Matt 27:42; Luke 23:35
32 [a]Matt 27:42; Mark 15:26 [b]Matt 27:44; Mark 15:27; Luke 23:39-43
33 [1]I.e. noon [2]Or *occurred* [3]I.e. 3 p.m. [a]Mark 15:33-41: *Matt 27:45-56; Luke 23:44-49* [b]Matt 27:45f; Mark 15:25; Luke 23:44
34 [a]Matt 27:45f; Mark 15:25; Luke 23:44 [b]Ps 22:1; Matt 27:46
36 [1]Lit *Permit that we see;* or *Hold off, let us see*
37 [a]Matt 27:50; Luke 23:46; John 19:30
38 [a]Ex 26:31-33; Matt 27:51; Luke 23:45
39 [1]Or *opposite Him* [2]Lit *that He thus* [3]Or *a son of God* or *son of a god* [a]Matt 27:54; Mark 15:45; Luke 23:47

40 [a]There were also *some* women looking on from a distance,
among whom *were* Mary Magdalene, and Mary the mother of
[1]James [b]the [2]Less and Joses, and [c]Salome.
41 When He was in Galilee, they used to follow Him and
[1a]minister to Him; and *there were* many other women who
came up with Him to Jerusalem.
42 [a]When evening had already come, because it was [b]the
preparation day, that is, the day before the Sabbath,
43 Joseph of Arimathea came, a [a]prominent member of the
Council, who himself was [b]waiting for the kingdom of God;
and he [c]gathered up courage and went in before Pilate, and
asked for the body of Jesus.
44 Pilate wondered if He was dead by this time, and summoning
the centurion, he questioned him as to whether He was already
dead.
45 And ascertaining this from [a]the centurion, he granted the
body to Joseph.
46 Joseph bought a linen cloth, took Him down, wrapped Him
in the linen cloth and laid Him in a tomb which had been hewn
out in the rock; and he rolled a stone against the entrance of
the tomb.
47 [a]Mary Magdalene and Mary the *mother* of Joses were looking
on *to see* where He was laid.

Chapter 16 Theme ______________________

16 [a]When the Sabbath was over, [b]Mary Magdalene, and
Mary the *mother* of [1]James, and Salome, [c]bought spices,
so that they might come and anoint Him.
2 Very early on the first day of the week, they *came to the
tomb when the sun had risen.
3 They were saying to one another, "Who will roll away [a]the
stone for us from the entrance of the tomb?"
4 Looking up, they *saw that the stone had been rolled away,
[1]although it was extremely large.
5 [a]Entering the tomb, they saw a young man sitting at the
right, wearing a white robe; and they [b]were amazed.
6 And he *said to them, "[a]Do not be amazed; you are looking
for Jesus the [b]Nazarene, who has been crucified. [c]He has risen;
He is not here; behold, *here is* the place where they laid Him.
7 "But go, tell His disciples and Peter, '[a]He is going ahead of
you to Galilee; there you will see Him, just as He told you.'"
8 They went out and fled from the tomb, for trembling and
astonishment had gripped them; and they said nothing to
anyone, for they were afraid.
9 [[1]Now after He had risen early on the first day of the week,
He first appeared to [a]Mary Magdalene, from whom He had cast
out seven demons.
10 [a]She went and reported to those who had been with Him,
while they were mourning and weeping.
11 When they heard that He was alive and had been seen by
her, [a]they refused to believe it.

40 [1]Or *Jacob* [2]Lit *little* (either in stature or age) [a]Mark 15:40, 41: *Matt 27:55f;* Luke 23:49; John 19:25 [b]Luke 19:3 [c]Mark 16:1

41 [1]Or *wait on* [a]Matt 27:55f

42 [a]Mark 15:42-47: *Matt 27:57-61; Luke 23:50-56; John 19:38-42* [b]Matt 27:62

43 [a]Matt 27:57; Luke 23:50, 51; Acts 13:50; 17:12 [b]Matt 27:57; Luke 2:25, 38; 23:51; John 19:38 [c]John 19:38

45 [a]Mark 15:39

47 [a]Matt 27:56; Mark 15:40; 16:1

16:1 [1]Or *Jacob* [a]Mark 16:1-8: *Matt 28:1-8; Luke 24:1-10;* John 20:1-8 [b]Mark 15:47 [c]Luke 23:56; John 19:39f

3 [a]Matt 27:60; Mark 15:46; 16:4

4 [1]Lit *for*

5 [a]John 20:11, 12 [b]Mark 9:15

6 [a]Mark 9:15 [b]Mark 1:24 [c]Matt 28:6; Luke 24:6

7 [a]Matt 26:32; Mark 14:28

9 [1]Later mss add vv 9-20 [a]Matt 27:56; John 20:14

10 [a]John 20:18

11 [a]Matt 28:17; Mark 16:13, 14; Luke 24:11, 41; John 20:25

12 After that, [a]He appeared in a different form [b]to two of them
while they were walking along on their way to the country.
13 They went away and reported it to the others, but they
[a]did not believe them either.
14 Afterward [a]He appeared [b]to the eleven themselves as they
were reclining *at the table;* and He reproached them for their
[c]unbelief and hardness of heart, because they had not believed
those who had seen Him after He had risen.
15 And He said to them, "[a]Go into all the world and preach
the gospel to all creation.
16 "[a]He who has believed and has been baptized shall be
saved; but he who has disbelieved shall be condemned.
17 "These [1]signs will accompany those who have believed: [a]in
My name they will cast out demons, they will [b]speak with new
tongues;
18 they will [a]pick up serpents, and if they drink any deadly
poison, it will not hurt them; they will [b]lay hands on the sick,
and they will recover."
19 So then, when the Lord Jesus had [a]spoken to them, He [b]was
received up into heaven and [c]sat down at the right hand of God.
20 And they went out and preached everywhere, while the
Lord worked with them, and confirmed the word by the [1]signs
that followed.]

[[2]*And they promptly reported all these instructions to Peter and his companions. And after that, Jesus Himself sent out through them from east to west the sacred and imperishable proclamation of eternal salvation.*]

20 [1]Or *attesting miracles* [2]A few late mss and versions contain this paragraph, usually after v 8; a few have it at the end of ch

12 [a]Mark 16:14; John 21:1, 14 [b]Luke 24:13-35
13 [a]Matt 28:17; Mark 16:11, 14; Luke 24:11, 41; John 20:25
14 [a]Mark 16:12; John 21:1, 14 [b]Luke 24:36; John 20:19, 26; 1 Cor 15:5 [c]Matt 28:17; Mark 16:11, 13; Luke 24:11, 41; John 20:25
15 [a]Matt 28:19; Acts 1:8
16 [a]John 3:18, 36; Acts 16:31
17 [1]Or *attesting miracles* [a]Mark 9:38; Luke 10:17; Acts 5:16; 8:7; 16:18; 19:12 [b]Acts 2:4; 10:46; 19:6; 1 Cor 12:10, 28, 30; 13:1; 14:2
18 [a]Luke 10:19; Acts 28:3-5 [b]Mark 5:23
19 [a]Acts 1:3 [b]Luke 9:51; 24:51; John 6:62; 20:17; Acts 1:2, 9-11; 1 Tim 3:16 [c]Ps 110:1; Luke 22:69; Acts 7:55f; Rom 8:34; Eph 1:20; Col 3:1; Heb 1:3; 8:1; 10:12; 12:2; 1 Pet 3:22

Mark at a Glance

Theme of Mark:

Segment Divisions

		Chapter Themes
		1
		2
		3
		4
		5
		6
		7
		8
		9
		10
		11
		12
		13
		14
		15
		16

Author:

Date:

Purpose:

Key Words:

immediately

authority (power)

kingdom of God

mark every reference to Satan or demons

covenant

Spirit

LUKE

In Matthew we see Jesus as King of the Jews. In Mark we see Him as the Servant who came to give His life a ransom for many. Then Luke, writing with the carefulness of a historian, takes us "in consecutive order" through the days of the Son of Man. In this Gospel we see the fulfillment of the things written about Him in the law of Moses, the Prophets, and the Psalms, things that no other Gospel records.

THINGS TO DO

1. Luke's purpose in writing is stated in Luke 1:1-4; record this on LUKE AT A GLANCE on page 1709.
2. As you read chapter by chapter, be sure to do the following:
   a. Mark in the text the key words listed on LUKE AT A GLANCE.
   b. Mark references to time with a green clock. The references will come in many different forms, from the mention of actual days or years to the naming of a Jewish feast, a chief priest, or a king. The chart on Herod's family tree on page 1658 will help. This part of your study will keep before you the timing and sequence of the events in Jesus' life. These are critical to Luke's purpose.
   c. It is also important to note where each event takes place. Double-underline in green every reference to places, cities, or regions. Locate these on the map on page 1661.
   d. Observe the main events and teachings covered in each chapter. (Note: Much of the material in Luke 1–3; 10–18 is unique to Luke.)
      1) As you list each event in the margin of the text, color code or mark it in a distinctive way so it can be recognized as an event. This will help you see at a glance the chronology of events in Luke. Consult the chart THE LIFE OF CHRIST on page 1710.
      2) Pay attention to the setting and the response of those who are listening or participating in what is happening. Observe where Jesus is, His relationships to people, what social events He is involved in, and what He expects from people.
   e. *Disciple(s)* is a key word. You may want to make a list of everything you learn from marking it.
   f. If Jesus tells a parable or tells of an incident such as the rich man and Lazarus dying (Luke 16), note what provokes Jesus to do so.
   g. Record the theme of each chapter in your Bible and on LUKE AT A GLANCE. Do the same for the theme of the book as you complete the chart.
3. Record the facts concerning Jesus' betrayal, arrest, trial, crucifixion, resurrection, post-resurrection appearances, and ascension on the appropriate charts on pages 1757 and 1760. Note the chapter and verse for each insight. After you do this for all four Gospels you will have comprehensive notes on what took place at this time in our Lord's life.
4. Record on pages 1758 and 1759 the information you glean from marking every reference to the *kingdom of God* in Luke.

THINGS TO THINK ABOUT

1. Have you been slow of heart to believe all that Moses and the prophets wrote about Jesus Christ? Do you see Jesus as the Son of Man, the fulfillment of prophecy, the Christ, the Son of God? Have you bowed to Him as Lord of your life? Are you a true disciple?

2. Jesus reached out to the hurting, the sinners, and the outcasts. He visited in their homes. He was available and accessible. What about you? Do you have compassion on these people? Are you wasting your life on self or are you investing in others? What did you learn from watching Christ's response to others that you can apply to your life?

3. If Jesus needed to withdraw often to a lonely place to pray, what about you? Is prayer a high priority in your life? Do you understand and incorporate the principles of prayer that Jesus taught in the Gospel of Luke?

Chapter 1 Theme ______________________

1 Inasmuch as many have undertaken to compile an account
of the things [1a]accomplished among us,
2 just as they were handed down to us by those who [a]from
the beginning [1]were [b]eyewitnesses and [2c]servants of [d]the [3]word,
3 it seemed fitting for me as well, [a]having [1]investigated
everything carefully from the beginning, to write *it* out for you
[b]in consecutive order, [c]most excellent [d]Theophilus;
4 so that you may know the exact truth about the things you
have been [1a]taught.
5 [a]In the days of Herod, king of Judea, there was a priest
named [1]Zacharias, of the [b]division of [2]Abijah; and he had a wife
[3]from the daughters of Aaron, and her name was Elizabeth.
6 They were both [a]righteous in the sight of God, walking
[b]blamelessly in all the commandments and requirements of the
Lord.
7 But they had no child, because Elizabeth was barren, and
they were both advanced in [1]years.
8 Now it happened *that* while [a]he was performing his priestly
service before God in the *appointed* order of his division,
9 according to the custom of the priestly office, he was
chosen by lot [a]to enter the temple of the Lord and burn incense.
10 And the whole multitude of the people were in prayer
[a]outside at the hour of the incense offering.
11 And [a]an angel of the Lord appeared to him, standing to the
right of the altar of incense.
12 Zacharias was troubled when he saw *the angel,* and [a]fear
[1]gripped him.
13 But the angel said to him, "[a]Do not be afraid, Zacharias, for
your petition has been heard, and your wife Elizabeth will bear
you a son, and [b]you will [1]give him the name John.
14 "You will have joy and gladness, and many will rejoice at his
birth.
15 "For he will be great in the sight of the Lord; and he will
[a]drink no wine or liquor, and he will be filled with the Holy
Spirit [1]while yet in his mother's womb.
16 "And he will [a]turn many of the sons of Israel back to the
Lord their God.

1:1 [1]Or *on which there is full conviction* [a]Rom 4:21; 14:5; Col 2:2; 4:12; 1 Thess 1:5; 2 Tim 4:17; Heb 6:11; 10:22

2 [1]Lit *became* [2]Or *ministers* [3]I.e. gospel [a]John 15:27; Acts 1:21f [b]2 Pet 1:16; 1 John 1:1 [c]Acts 26:16; 1 Cor 4:1; Heb 2:3 [d]Mark 4:14; 16:20; Acts 8:4; 14:25; 16:6; 17:11

3 [1]Or *followed* [a]1 Tim 4:6 [b]Acts 11:4; 18:23 [c]Acts 23:26; 24:3; 26:25 [d]Acts 1:1

4 [1]Or *orally instructed in* [a]Acts 18:25; Rom 2:18; 1 Cor 14:19; Gal 6:6

5 [1]I.e. Zechariah [2]Gr *Abia* [3]I.e. of priestly descent [a]Matt 2:1 [b]1 Chr 24:10

6 [a]Gen 7:1; Acts 2:25; 8:21 [b]Phil 2:15; 3:6; 1 Thess 3:13

7 [1]Lit *days*

8 [a]1 Chr 24:19; 2 Chr 8:14; 31:2

9 [a]Ex 30:7f

10 [a]Lev 16:17

11 [a]Luke 2:9; Acts 5:19

12 [1]Or *fell upon* [a]Luke 2:9

13 [1]Lit *call his name* [a]Matt 14:27; Luke 1:30 [b]Luke 1:60, 63

15 [1]Lit *from* [a]Num 6:3; Judg 13:4; Matt 11:18; Luke 7:33

16 [a]Matt 3:2, 6; Luke 3:3

17 "It is he who will [a]go *as a forerunner* before Him in the
spirit and power of [b]Elijah, [c]TO TURN THE HEARTS OF THE FATHERS
BACK TO THE CHILDREN, and the disobedient to the attitude of the
righteous, so as to [a]make ready a people prepared for the Lord."
18 Zacharias said to the angel, "How will I know this *for certain?*
For [a]I am an old man and my wife is advanced in [1]years."
19 The angel answered and said to him, "I am [a]Gabriel, who
[1b]stands in the presence of God, and I have been sent to speak
to you and to bring you this good news.
20 "And behold, you shall be silent and unable to speak until
the day when these things take place, because you did not
believe my words, which will be fulfilled in their proper time."
21 The people were waiting for Zacharias, and were wondering
at his delay in the temple.
22 But when he came out, he was unable to speak to them;
and they realized that he had seen a vision in the temple; and
he [a]kept [1]making signs to them, and remained mute.
23 When the days of his priestly service were ended, he went
back home.
24 After these days Elizabeth his wife became pregnant, and
she [1]kept herself in seclusion for five months, saying,
25 "This is the way the Lord has dealt with me in the days when
He looked *with favor* upon *me,* to [a]take away my disgrace among
men."
26 Now in the sixth month the angel [a]Gabriel was sent from
God to a city in Galilee called [b]Nazareth,
27 to [a]a virgin [1]engaged to a man whose name was Joseph, [b]of
the [2]descendants of David; and the virgin's name was [3]Mary.
28 And coming in, he said to her, "Greetings, [1]favored one!
The Lord [2]*is* with you."
29 But she [a]was very perplexed at *this* statement, and kept
pondering what kind of salutation this was.
30 The angel said to her, "[a]Do not be afraid, Mary; for you
have found favor with God.
31 "And behold, you will conceive in your womb and bear a
son, and you [a]shall name Him Jesus.
32 "He will be great and will be called the Son of [a]the Most
High; and the Lord God will give Him [b]the throne of His father
David;
33 [a]and He will reign over the house of Jacob forever, [b]and His
kingdom will have no end."
34 Mary said to the angel, "How [1]can this be, since I [2]am a
virgin?"
35 The angel answered and said to her, "[a]The Holy Spirit will
come upon you, and the power of [b]the Most High will overshadow you; and for that reason [c]the [1]holy Child shall be called
[d]the Son of God.
36 "And behold, even your relative Elizabeth has also conceived
a son in her old age; and [1]she who was called barren is now in
her sixth month.
37 "For [1a]nothing will be impossible with God."

17 [a]Luke 1:76 [b]Matt 11:14 [c]Mal 4:6

18 [1]Lit *days* [a]Gen 17:17

19 [1]Lit *stand beside* [a]Dan 8:16; 9:21; Luke 1:26 [b]Matt 18:10

22 [1]Or *beckoning to* or *nodding to* [a]Luke 1:62

24 [1]Lit *was hidden*

25 [a]Gen 30:23; Is 4:1; 25:8

26 [a]Luke 1:19 [b]Matt 2:23

27 [1]Or *betrothed;* i.e. the first stage of marriage in Jewish culture, usually lasting for a year before the wedding night. More legal than engagement [2]Lit *house* [3]Gr *Mariam;* i.e. Heb Miriam; so throughout Luke [a]Matt 1:18 [b]Matt 1:16, 20; Luke 2:4

28 [1]Or *woman richly blessed* [2]Or *be*

29 [a]Luke 1:12

30 [a]Matt 14:27; Luke 1:13

31 [a]Is 7:14; Matt 1:21, 25; Luke 2:21

32 [a]Mark 5:7; Luke 1:35, 76; 6:35; Acts 7:48 [b]2 Sam 7:12, 13, 16; Is 9:7

33 [a]Matt 1:1 [b]2 Sam 7:13, 16; Ps 89:36, 37; Dan 2:44; 7:14, 18, 27; Matt 28:18

34 [1]Lit *will* [2]Lit *know no man*

35 [1]Lit *the holy thing begotten* [a]Matt 1:18 [b]Luke 1:32 [c]Mark 1:24 [d]Matt 4:3; John 1:34, 49; 20:31

36 [1]Lit *this is the sixth month to her who*

37 [1]Lit *not any word* [a]Gen 18:14; Jer 32:17; Matt 19:26

38 And Mary said, "Behold, the [1]bondslave of the Lord; may it
be done to me according to your word." And the angel departed
from her.
39 Now [1]at this time Mary arose and went in a hurry to [a]the
hill country, to a city of Judah,
40 and entered the house of Zacharias and greeted Elizabeth.
41 When Elizabeth heard Mary's greeting, the baby leaped in
her womb; and Elizabeth was [a]filled with the Holy Spirit.
42 And she cried out with a loud voice and said, "Blessed *are*
you among women, and blessed *is* the fruit of your womb!
43 "And [1]how has it *happened* to me, that the mother of [a]my
Lord would come to me?
44 "For behold, when the sound of your greeting reached my
ears, the baby leaped in my womb for joy.
45 "And [a]blessed *is* she who [1]believed that there would be a
fulfillment of what had been spoken to her [2]by the Lord."
46 And Mary said:
"[a]My soul [1b]exalts the Lord,
47 And [a]my spirit has rejoiced in [b]God my Savior.
48 "For [a]He has had regard for the humble state of His [1]bondslave;
For behold, from this time on all generations will count
me [b]blessed.
49 "For the Mighty One has done great things for me;
And holy is His name.
50 "[a]AND HIS MERCY IS [1]UPON GENERATION AFTER GENERATION
TOWARD THOSE WHO FEAR HIM.
51 "[a]He has done [1]mighty deeds with His arm;
He has scattered *those who were* proud in the [2]thoughts
of their heart.
52 "He has brought down rulers from *their* thrones,
And has [a]exalted those who were humble.
53 "[a]HE HAS FILLED THE HUNGRY WITH GOOD THINGS;
And sent away the rich empty-handed.
54 "He has given help to Israel His servant,
[1]In remembrance of His mercy,
55 [a]As He spoke to our fathers,
[b]To Abraham and his [1]descendants forever."
56 And Mary stayed with her about three months, and *then*
returned to her home.
57 Now the time [1]had come for Elizabeth to give birth, and she
gave birth to a son.
58 Her neighbors and her relatives heard that the Lord had
[1a]displayed His great mercy toward her; and they were rejoicing
with her.
59 And it happened that on [a]the eighth day they came to
circumcise the child, and they were going to call him Zacharias,
[1]after his father.
60 But his mother answered and said, "No indeed; but [a]he shall
be called John."
61 And they said to her, "There is no one among your
relatives who is called by that name."

38 [1]I.e. female slave

39 [1]Lit *in these days* [a]Josh 20:7; 21:11; Luke 1:65

41 [a]Luke 1:67; Acts 2:4; 4:8; 9:17

43 [1]Lit *from where this to me* [a]Luke 2:11

45 [1]Or *believed, because there will be* [2]Lit *from* [a]Luke 1:20, 48

46 [1]Lit *makes great* [a]Luke 1:46-53: *1 Sam 2:1-10* [b]Ps 34:2f

47 [a]Ps 35:9; Hab 3:18 [b]1 Tim 1:1; 2:3; Titus 1:3; 2:10; 3:4; Jude 25

48 [1]I.e. female slave [a]Ps 138:6 [b]Luke 1:45

50 [1]Lit *unto generations and generations* [a]Ps 103:17

51 [1]Lit *might* [2]Lit *thought, attitude* [a]Ps 98:1; 118:15

52 [a]Job 5:11

53 [a]Ps 107:9

54 [1]Lit *So as to remember*

55 [1]Lit *seed* [a]Gen 17:19; Ps 132:11; Gal 3:16 [b]Gen 17:7

57 [1]Lit *was fulfilled*

58 [1]Lit *magnified* [a]Gen 19:19

59 [1]Lit *after the name of* [a]Gen 17:12; Lev 12:3; Luke 2:21; Phil 3:5

60 [a]Luke 1:13, 63

62 And they [a]made signs to his father, as to what he wanted
him called.
63 And he asked for a tablet and wrote as follows, "[a]His name is
John." And they were all astonished.
64 [a]And at once his mouth was opened and his tongue *loosed,*
and he *began* to speak in praise of God.
65 Fear came on all those living around them; and all these
matters were being talked about in all [a]the hill country of
Judea.
66 All who heard them kept them in mind, saying, "What then
will this child *turn out to* be?" For [a]the hand of the Lord was
certainly with him.
67 And his father Zacharias [a]was filled with the Holy Spirit,
and [b]prophesied, saying:
68 "[a]Blessed *be* the Lord God of Israel,
For He has visited us and accomplished [b]redemption for
His people,
69 And has raised up a [a]horn of salvation for us
In the house of David [b]His servant—
70 [a]As He spoke by the mouth of His holy prophets
[b]from of old—
71 [1a]Salvation [b]FROM OUR ENEMIES,
And FROM THE HAND OF ALL WHO HATE US;
72 [a]To show mercy toward our fathers,
[b]And to remember His holy covenant,
73 [a]The oath which He swore to Abraham our father,
74 To grant us that we, being rescued from the hand
of our enemies,
Might serve Him without fear,
75 [a]In holiness and righteousness before Him all our days.
76 "And you, child, will be called the [a]prophet of [b]the Most High;
For you will go on [c]BEFORE THE LORD TO [d]PREPARE HIS WAYS;
77 To give to His people *the* knowledge of salvation
[1]By [a]the forgiveness of their sins,
78 Because of the tender mercy of our God,
With which [a]the Sunrise from on high will visit us,
79 [a]TO SHINE UPON THOSE WHO SIT IN DARKNESS AND THE SHADOW
OF DEATH,
To guide our feet into the [b]way of peace."
80 [a]And the child continued to grow and to become strong in
spirit, and he lived in the deserts until the day of his public
appearance to Israel.

Chapter 2 Theme ______________________

2 Now in those days a decree went out from [a]Caesar Augustus,
that a census be taken of [b]all [1]the inhabited earth.
2 [1]This was the first census taken while [2]Quirinius was
governor of [a]Syria.
3 And everyone was on his way to register for the census,
each to his own city.

62 [a]Luke 1:22
63 [a]Luke 1:13, 60
64 [a]Luke 1:20
65 [a]Luke 1:39
66 [a]Acts 11:21
67 [a]Luke 1:41; Acts 2:4, 8; 9:17 [b]Joel 2:28
68 [a]1 Kin 1:48; Ps 41:13; 72:18; 106:48 [b]Luke 1:71; 2:38; Heb 9:12
69 [a]1 Sam 2:1, 10; Ps 18:2; 89:17; 132:17; Ezek 29:21 [b]Matt 1:1
70 [a]Rom 1:2 [b]Acts 3:21
71 [1]Or *Deliverance* [a]Luke 1:68 [b]Ps 106:10
72 [a]Mic 7:20 [b]Ps 105:8f, 42; 106:45
73 [a]Gen 22:16ff; Heb 6:13
75 [a]Eph 4:24
76 [a]Matt 11:9 [b]Luke 1:32 [c]Mal 3:1; Matt 11:10; Mark 1:2; Luke 7:27 [d]Luke 1:17
77 [1]Or *Consisting in* [a]Jer 31:34; Mark 1:4
78 [a]Mal 4:2; Eph 5:14; 2 Pet 1:19
79 [a]Is 9:2 [b]Is 59:8; Matt 4:16
80 [a]Luke 2:40
2:1 [1]I.e. the Roman empire [a]Matt 22:17; Luke 3:1 [b]Matt 24:14
2 [1]Or *This took place as a first census* [2]Gr *Kyrenios* [a]Matt 4:24

4 Joseph also went up from Galilee, from the city of
Nazareth, to Judea, to the city of David which is called
Bethlehem, because [a]he was of the house and family of David,
5 in order to register along with Mary, who was engaged to
him, and was with child.
6 While they were there, the days were completed for her to
give birth.
7 And she [a]gave birth to her firstborn son; and she wrapped
Him in cloths, and laid Him in a [1]manger, because there was
no room for them in the inn.
8 In the same region there were *some* shepherds staying out
in the fields and keeping watch over their flock by night.
9 And [a]an angel of the Lord suddenly [b]stood before them,
and the glory of the Lord shone around them; and they were
terribly frightened.
10 But the angel said to them, "[a]Do not be afraid; for behold, I
bring you good news of great joy which will be for all the
people;
11 for today in the city of David there has been born for you a
[a]Savior, who is [1b]Christ [c]the Lord.
12 "[a]This *will be* a sign for you: you will find a baby wrapped in
cloths and lying in a [1]manger."
13 And suddenly there appeared with the angel a multitude of
the heavenly host praising God and saying,
14 "[a]Glory to God in the highest,
And on earth peace among men [1b]with whom
He is pleased."
15 When the angels had gone away from them into heaven,
the shepherds *began* saying to one another, "Let us go straight
to Bethlehem then, and see this thing that has happened which
the Lord has made known to us."
16 So they came in a hurry and found their way to Mary and
Joseph, and the baby as He lay in the [1]manger.
17 When they had seen this, they made known the statement
which had been told them about this Child.
18 And all who heard it wondered at the things which were
told them by the shepherds.
19 But Mary [a]treasured all these things, pondering them in
her heart.
20 The shepherds went back, [a]glorifying and praising God for
all that they had heard and seen, just as had been told them.
21 And when [a]eight days had passed, [1]before His circumcision,
[b]His name was *then* called Jesus, the name given by the angel
before He was conceived in the womb.
22 [a]And when the days for their purification according to the
law of Moses were completed, they brought Him up to
Jerusalem to present Him to the Lord
23 (as it is written in the Law of the Lord, "[a]EVERY *firstborn*
MALE THAT OPENS THE WOMB SHALL BE CALLED HOLY TO THE LORD"),
24 and to offer a sacrifice according to what was said in the Law
of the Lord, "[a]A PAIR OF TURTLEDOVES OR TWO YOUNG PIGEONS."

4 [a]Luke 1:27

7 [1]Or *feeding trough* [a]Matt 1:25

9 [a]Luke 1:11; Acts 5:19 [b]Luke 24:4; Acts 12:7

10 [a]Matt 14:27

11 [1]I.e. Messiah [a]Matt 1:21; John 4:42; Acts 5:31 [b]Matt 1:16; 16:16, 20; John 11:27 [c]Luke 1:43; Acts 2:36; 10:36

12 [1]Or *feeding trough* [a]1 Sam 2:34; 2 Kin 19:29; 20:8f; Is 7:11, 14

14 [1]Lit *of good pleasure;* or *of good will* [a]Matt 21:9; Luke 19:38 [b]Luke 3:22; Eph 1:9; Phil 2:13

16 [1]Or *feeding trough*

19 [a]Luke 2:51

20 [a]Matt 9:8

21 [1]Lit *so as to circumcise Him* [a]Gen 17:12; Lev 12:3; Luke 1:59 [b]Matt 1:21, 25; Luke 1:31

22 [a]Lev 12:6-8

23 [a]Ex 13:2, 12; Num 3:13; 8:17

24 [a]Lev 5:11; 12:8

25 And there was a man in Jerusalem whose name was Simeon; and this man was [a]righteous and devout, [b]looking for the consolation of Israel; and the Holy Spirit was upon him.

26 And [a]it had been revealed to him by the Holy Spirit that he would not [b]see death before he had seen the Lord's [1]Christ.

27 And he came in the Spirit into the temple; and when the parents brought in the child Jesus, [1a]to carry out for Him the custom of the Law,

28 then he took Him into his arms, and blessed God, and said,

29 "Now Lord, You are releasing Your bond-servant to depart in
peace,
[a]According to Your word;

30 For my eyes have [a]seen Your salvation,

31 Which You have prepared in the presence of all peoples,

32 [a]A LIGHT [1]OF REVELATION TO THE GENTILES,
And the glory of Your people Israel."

33 And His father and [a]mother were amazed at the things which were being said about Him.

34 And Simeon blessed them and said to Mary [a]His mother, "Behold, this *Child* is appointed for [b]the fall and [1]rise of many in Israel, and for a sign to be opposed—

35 and a sword will pierce even your own soul—to the end that thoughts from many hearts may be revealed."

36 And there was a [a]prophetess, [1]Anna the daughter of Phanuel, of [b]the tribe of Asher. She was advanced in [2]years [c]and had lived with *her* husband seven years after her [3]marriage,

37 and then as a widow to the age of eighty-four. She never left the temple, serving night and day with [a]fastings and prayers.

38 At that very [1]moment she came up and *began* giving thanks to God, and continued to speak of Him to all those who were [a]looking for the redemption of Jerusalem.

39 When they had performed everything according to the Law of the Lord, they returned to Galilee, to [a]their own city of Nazareth.

40 [a]The Child continued to grow and become strong, [1]increasing in wisdom; and the grace of God was upon Him.

41 Now His parents went to Jerusalem every year at [a]the Feast of the Passover.

42 And when He became twelve, they went up *there* according to the custom of the Feast;

43 and as they were returning, after spending the [a]full number of days, the boy Jesus stayed behind in Jerusalem. But His parents were unaware of it,

44 but supposed Him to be in the caravan, and went a day's journey; and they *began* looking for Him among their relatives and acquaintances.

45 When they did not find Him, they returned to Jerusalem looking for Him.

46 Then, after three days they found Him in the temple, sitting in the midst of the teachers, both listening to them and asking them questions.

25 [a]Luke 1:6 [b]Mark 15:43; Luke 2:38; 23:51
26 [1]I.e. Messiah [a]Matt 2:12 [b]Ps 89:48; John 8:51; Heb 11:5
27 [1]Lit *to do for Him according to* [a]Luke 2:22
29 [a]Luke 2:26
30 [a]Ps 119:166, 174; Is 52:10; Luke 3:6
32 [1]Or *for* [a]Is 9:2; 42:6; 49:6, 9; 51:4; 60:1-3; Matt 4:16; Acts 13:47; 26:23
33 [a]Matt 12:46
34 [1]Or *resurrection* [a]Matt 12:46 [b]Matt 21:44; 1 Cor 1:23; 2 Cor 2:16; 1 Pet 2:8
36 [1]Or *Hannah* [2]Lit *days* [3]Lit *virginity* [a]Luke 2:38; Acts 21:9 [b]Josh 19:24 [c]1 Tim 5:9
37 [a]Luke 5:33; Acts 13:3; 14:23; 1 Tim 5:5
38 [1]Lit *hour* [a]Luke 1:68; 2:25
39 [a]Matt 2:23; Luke 1:26; 2:51; 4:16
40 [1]Lit *becoming full of* [a]Luke 1:80; 2:52
41 [a]Ex 12:11; 23:15; Deut 16:1-6
43 [a]Ex 12:15

47 And all who heard Him [a]were amazed at His understanding
and His answers.
48 When they saw Him, they were astonished; and [a]His
mother said to Him, "[1]Son, why have You treated us this way?
Behold, [b]Your father and I [2]have been anxiously looking for You."
49 And He said to them, "Why is it that you were looking for
Me? Did you not know that [a]I had to be in My Father's [1]*house?*"
50 But [a]they did not understand the statement which He [1]had
made to them.
51 And He went down with them and came to [a]Nazareth, and
He continued in subjection to them; and [b]His mother [c]treasured
all *these* [1]things in her heart.
52 And Jesus kept increasing in wisdom and [1]stature, and in
[a]favor with God and men.

47 [a]Matt 7:28; 13:54; 22:33; Mark 1:22; 6:2; 11:18; Luke 4:32; John 7:15
48 [1]Or *Child* [2]Lit *are looking* [a]Matt 12:46 [b]Luke 2:49; 3:23; 4:22
49 [1]Or *affairs;* lit *in the things of My Father* [a]John 4:34; 5:36
50 [1]Lit *had spoken* [a]Mark 9:32; Luke 9:45; 18:34
51 [1]Lit *words* [a]Luke 2:39 [b]Matt 12:46 [c]Luke 2:19
52 [1]Or *age* [a]Luke 2:40

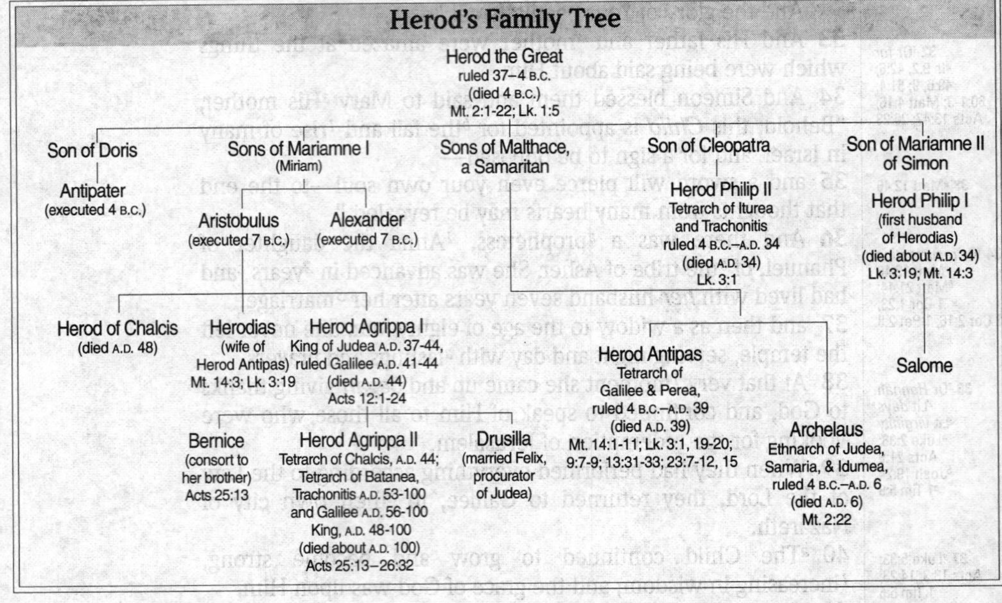

Chapter 3 Theme ____________________

3 Now in the fifteenth year of the reign of Tiberius Caesar,
when [a]Pontius Pilate was governor of Judea, and [b]Herod
was tetrarch of Galilee, and his brother Philip was tetrarch of
the region of Ituraea and Trachonitis, and Lysanias was tetrarch
of Abilene,
2 in the high priesthood of [a]Annas and [b]Caiaphas, [c]the word
of God came to John, the son of Zacharias, in the wilderness.
3 And he came into all [a]the district around the Jordan,
preaching a baptism of repentance for the forgiveness of sins;
4 as it is written in the book of the words of Isaiah the prophet,
"[a]THE VOICE OF ONE CRYING IN THE WILDERNESS,
'MAKE READY THE WAY OF THE LORD,
MAKE HIS PATHS STRAIGHT.

3:1 [a]Matt 27:2 [b]Matt 14:1
2 [a]John 18:13, 24; Acts 4:6 [b]Matt 26:3 [c]Luke 3:3-10: *Matt 3:1-10; Mark 1:3-5*
3 [a]Matt 3:5
4 [a]Is 40:3

5 [1]Or *leveled* [a]Is 40:4
6 [1]Or *mankind* [a]Is 40:5 [b]Luke 2:30
7 [a]Matt 12:34; 23:33
8 [1]Or *in* [a]Luke 5:21; 13:25, 26; 14:9 [b]John 8:33
9 [a]Matt 7:19; Luke 13:6-9
10 [a]Luke 3:12, 14; Acts 2:37, 38
11 [a]Is 58:7; 1 Tim 6:17, 18; James 2:14-20
12 [a]Luke 7:29
13 [1]Or *Exact*
14 [a]Ex 20:16; 23:1 [b]Phil 4:11
15 [1]Or *reasoning* or *debating* [2]I.e. the Messiah [a]John 1:19f
16 [1]The Gr here can be translated *in, with* or *by* [a]Luke 3:16, 17: *Matt 3:11, 12; Mark 1:7, 8*
17 [a]Is 30:24 [b]Mark 9:43, 48
19 [a]Matt 14:3; Mark 6:17 [b]Matt 14:1; Luke 3:1

5 '[a]EVERY RAVINE WILL BE FILLED,
AND EVERY MOUNTAIN AND HILL WILL BE [1]BROUGHT LOW;
THE CROOKED WILL BECOME STRAIGHT,
AND THE ROUGH ROADS SMOOTH;
6 [a]AND ALL [1]FLESH WILL [b]SEE THE SALVATION OF GOD.'"
7 So he *began* saying to
the crowds who were going
out to be baptized by him,
"[a]You brood of vipers, who
warned you to flee from the
wrath to come?
8 "Therefore bear fruits in
keeping with repentance,
and [a]do not begin to say [1]to
yourselves, '[b]We have Abraham for our father,' for I say
to you that from these
stones God is able to raise
up children to Abraham.
9 "Indeed the axe is already
laid at the root of the trees;
so [a]every tree that does not
bear good fruit is cut down
and thrown into the fire."

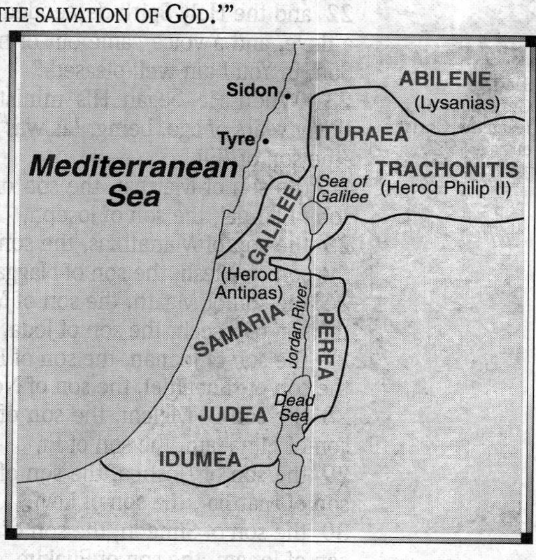

The Regions of the Tetrarchs

10 And the crowds were questioning him, saying, "[a]Then
what shall we do?"
11 And he would answer and say to them, "The man who has
two tunics is to [a]share with him who has none; and he who
has food is to do likewise."
12 And *some* [a]tax collectors also came to be baptized, and
they said to him, "Teacher, what shall we do?"
13 And he said to them, "[1]Collect no more than what you
have been ordered to."
14 *Some* soldiers were questioning him, saying, "And *what
about* us, what shall we do?" And he said to them, "Do not
take money from anyone by force, or [a]accuse *anyone* falsely,
and [b]be content with your wages."
15 Now while the people were in a state of expectation and all
were [1]wondering in their hearts about John, [a]as to whether he
was [2]the Christ,
16 [a]John answered and said to them all, "As for me, I baptize
you with water; but One is coming who is mightier than I, and
I am not fit to untie the thong of His sandals; He will baptize
you [1]with the Holy Spirit and fire.
17 "His [a]winnowing fork is in His hand to thoroughly clear His
threshing floor, and to gather the wheat into His barn; but He
will burn up the chaff with [b]unquenchable fire."
18 So with many other exhortations he preached the gospel to
the people.
19 But when [a]Herod the tetrarch was reprimanded by him
because of [a]Herodias, his brother's wife, and because of all the
wicked things which [b]Herod had done,

20 Herod also added this to them all: [a]he locked John up in
prison.
21 [a]Now when all the people were baptized, Jesus was also
baptized, and while He was [b]praying, heaven was opened,
22 and the Holy Spirit descended upon Him in bodily form like
a dove, and a voice came out of heaven, "[a]You are My beloved
Son, in You I am well-pleased."
23 [a]When He began His ministry, Jesus Himself was about
thirty years of age, being, [1]as was supposed, the son of [b]Joseph,
[2]the son of [3]Eli,
24 the son of Matthat, the son of Levi, the son of Melchi, the
son of Jannai, the son of Joseph,
25 the son of Mattathias, the son of Amos, the son of Nahum,
the son of [1]Hesli, the son of Naggai,
26 the son of Maath, the son of Mattathias, the son of Semein,
the son of Josech, the son of Joda,
27 the son of Joanan, the son of Rhesa, [a]the son of Zerubbabel,
the son of [1]Shealtiel, the son of Neri,
28 the son of Melchi, the son of Addi, the son of Cosam, the
son of Elmadam, the son of Er,
29 the son of [1]Joshua, the son of Eliezer, the son of Jorim, the
son of Matthat, the son of Levi,
30 the son of Simeon, the son of [1]Judah, the son of Joseph, the
son of Jonam, the son of Eliakim,
31 the son of Melea, the son of Menna, the son of Mattatha,
the son of Nathan, the son of David,
32 [a]the son of Jesse, the son of Obed, the son of Boaz, the son
of [1]Salmon, the son of [2]Nahshon,
33 the son of Amminadab, the son of Admin, the son of [1]Ram,
the son of Hezron, the son of Perez, the son of Judah,
34 the son of Jacob, the son of Isaac, [a]the son of Abraham, the
son of Terah, the son of Nahor,
35 the son of Serug, the son of [1]Reu, the son of Peleg, the son
of [2]Heber, the son of Shelah,
36 the son of Cainan, the son of Arphaxad, the son of Shem,
[a]the son of Noah, the son of Lamech,
37 the son of Methuselah, the son of Enoch, the son of Jared,
the son of Mahalaleel, the son of Cainan,
38 the son of Enosh, the son of Seth, the son of Adam, the son
of God.

INSIGHT

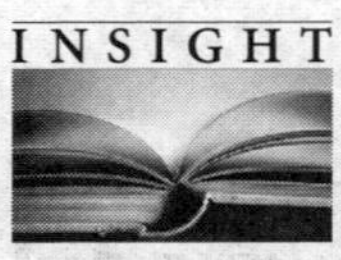

See **The Genealogy of Jesus the Christ** on page 1557.

Chapter 4 Theme

4 [a]Jesus, full of the Holy Spirit, [b]returned from the Jordan
and was led around [1]by the Spirit in the wilderness
2 for [a]forty days, being tempted by the devil. And He ate
nothing during those days, and when they had ended, He
became hungry.
3 And the devil said to Him, "If You are the Son of God, tell
this stone to become bread."
4 And Jesus answered him, "It is written, '[a]MAN SHALL NOT
LIVE ON BREAD ALONE.'"

20 [a]John 3:24

21 [a]Luke 3:21, 22: *Matt 3:13-17; Mark 1:9-11* [b]Matt 14:23; Luke 5:16; 9:18, 28f

22 [a]Ps 2:7; Is 42:1; Matt 3:17; 17:5; Mark 1:11; Luke 9:35; 2 Pet 1:17

23 [1]Lit *as it was being thought* [2]Lit *of Eli,* and so throughout the genealogy [3]Also spelled *Heli* [a]Matt 4:17; Acts 1:1 [b]Matt 1:16; Luke 3:23-27

25 [1]Also spelled *Esli*

27 [1]Gr *Salathiel;* names of people in the Old Testament are given in their Old Testament form through v 38 [a]Matt 1:12

29 [1]Gr *Jesus*

30 [1]Gr *Judas*

32 [1]Gr *Sala* [2]Gr *Naasson* [a]Luke 3:32-34: *Matt 1:1-6*

33 [1]Gr *Arni*

34 [a]Luke 3:34-36: *Gen 11:26-30; 1 Chr 1:24-27*

35 [1]Gr *Ragau* [2]Gr *Eber*

36 [a]Luke 3:36-38: *Gen 5:3-32; 1 Chr 1:1-4*

4:1 [1]Or *under the influence of;* lit *in* [a]Luke 4:1-13: *Matt 4:1-11; Mark 1:12, 13* [b]Luke 3:3

2 [a]Ex 34:28; 1 Kin 19:8

4 [a]Deut 8:3

5 [a]And he led Him up and showed Him all the kingdoms of
[1b]the world in a moment of time.
6 And the devil said to Him, "I will give You all this domain
and [1]its glory; [a]for it has been handed over to me, and I give it
to whomever I wish.
7 "Therefore if You [1]worship before me, it shall all be Yours."
8 Jesus answered him, "It is written, '[a]YOU SHALL WORSHIP THE
LORD YOUR GOD AND SERVE HIM ONLY.'"
9 [a]And he led Him to Jerusalem and had Him stand on the
pinnacle of the temple, and said to Him, "If You are the Son of
God, throw Yourself down from here;
10 for it is written,

'[a]HE WILL COMMAND HIS ANGELS CONCERNING YOU
TO GUARD YOU,'

11 and,

'[a]ON *their* HANDS THEY WILL BEAR YOU UP,
SO THAT YOU WILL NOT STRIKE YOUR FOOT AGAINST A STONE.'"

12 And Jesus answered and said to him, "It is said, '[a]YOU SHALL
NOT PUT THE LORD YOUR GOD TO THE TEST.'"
13 When the devil had finished every temptation, he left Him
until an opportune time.
14 And [a]Jesus returned to Galilee in the power of the Spirit,
and [b]news about Him spread through all the surrounding district.
15 And He *began* [a]teaching in their synagogues and was
praised by all.
16 And He came to [a]Nazareth, where He had been brought
up; and as was His custom, [b]He entered the synagogue on the
Sabbath, and [c]stood up to read.
17 And the [1]book of the prophet Isaiah was handed to Him.
And He opened the [1]book and found the place where it was
written,
18 "[a]THE SPIRIT OF THE LORD IS UPON ME,
BECAUSE HE ANOINTED ME TO PREACH THE GOSPEL TO THE POOR.
HE HAS SENT ME TO PROCLAIM RELEASE TO THE CAPTIVES,
AND RECOVERY OF SIGHT TO THE BLIND,
TO SET FREE THOSE WHO ARE OPPRESSED,
19 [a]TO PROCLAIM THE FAVORABLE
YEAR OF THE LORD."
20 And He [a]closed the [1]book,
gave it back to the attendant and
[b]sat down; and the eyes of all in
the synagogue were fixed on Him.
21 And He began to say to them,
"Today this Scripture has been
fulfilled in your [1]hearing."
22 And all were [1]speaking well
of Him, and wondering at the
[2]gracious words which [3]were
falling from His lips; and they
were saying, "[a]Is this not Joseph's
son?"

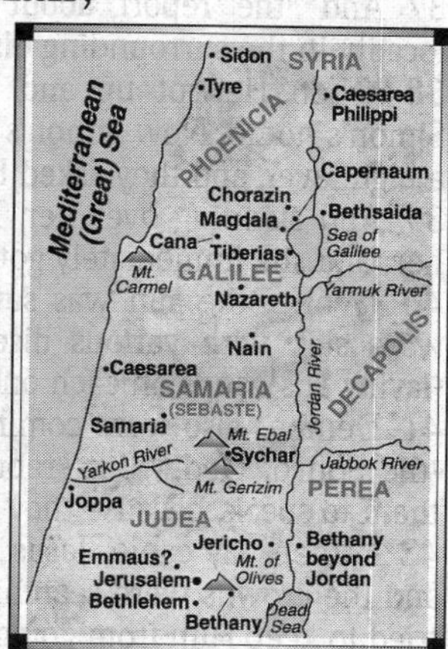

Israel in the Time of Christ

5 [1]Lit *the inhabited earth* [a]Matt 4:8-10 [b]Matt 24:14
6 [1]Lit *their* (referring to the kingdoms in v 5) [a]1 John 5:19
7 [1]Or *bow down before*
8 [a]Deut 6:13; 10:20; Matt 4:10
9 [a]Matt 4:5-7
10 [a]Ps 91:11
11 [a]Ps 91:12
12 [a]Deut 6:16
14 [a]Matt 4:12 [b]Matt 9:26; Luke 4:37
15 [a]Matt 4:23
16 [a]Luke 2:39, 51 [b]Matt 13:54; Mark 6:1f [c]Acts 13:14-16
17 [1]Or *scroll*
18 [a]Is 61:1; Matt 11:5; 12:18; John 3:34
19 [a]Is 61:2; Lev 25:10
20 [1]Or *scroll* [a]Luke 4:17 [b]Matt 26:55
21 [1]Lit *ears*
22 [1]Or *testifying* [2]Or *words of grace* [3]Lit *were proceeding out of His mouth* [a]Matt 13:55; Mark 6:3; John 6:42

23 And He said to them, "No doubt you will quote this proverb
to Me, 'Physician, heal yourself! Whatever we heard was done
[a]at Capernaum, do here in [b]your hometown as well.'"
24 And He said, "Truly I say to you, [a]no prophet is welcome in
his hometown.
25 "But I say to you in truth, there were many widows in Israel
[a]in the days of Elijah, when the sky was shut up for three years
and six months, when a great famine came over all the land;
26 and yet Elijah was sent to none of them, but [a]only to
[1]Zarephath, *in the land* of [b]Sidon, to a woman who was a
widow.
27 "And there were many lepers in Israel in the time of Elisha
the prophet; and none of them was cleansed, but [a]only Naaman
the Syrian."
28 And all *the people* in the synagogue were filled with rage
as they heard these things;
29 and they got up and [a]drove Him out of the city, and led
Him to the brow of the hill on which their city had been built,
in order to throw Him down the cliff.
30 But [a]passing through their midst, He went His way.
31 And [a]He came down to [b]Capernaum, a city of Galilee, and
He was teaching them on the Sabbath;
32 and [a]they were amazed at His teaching, for [b]His [1]message
was with authority.
33 In the synagogue there was a man [1]possessed by the spirit
of an unclean demon, and he cried out with a loud voice,
34 "Let us alone! [1a]What business do we have with each other,
Jesus [2]of [b]Nazareth? Have You come to destroy us? I know who
You are—[b]the Holy One of God!"
35 But Jesus [a]rebuked him, saying, "Be quiet and come out of
him!" And when the demon had thrown him down in the midst
of the people, he came out of him without doing him any harm.
36 And amazement came upon them all, and they *began*
talking with one another saying, "What is [1]this message? For
[a]with authority and power He commands the unclean spirits
and they come out."
37 And [a]the report about Him was spreading into every
locality in the surrounding district.
38 [a]Then He got up and *left* the synagogue, and entered
Simon's home. Now Simon's mother-in-law was [b]suffering from
a high fever, and they asked Him [1]to help her.
39 And standing over her, He [a]rebuked the fever, and it left
her; and she immediately got up and [1]waited on them.
40 [a]While [b]the sun was setting, all those who had any *who*
were sick with various diseases brought them to Him; and
[c]laying His hands on each one of them, He was [d]healing them.
41 Demons also were coming out of many, shouting, "You are
[a]the Son of God!" But [b]rebuking them, He would [c]not allow
them to speak, because they knew Him to be [1]the Christ.
42 [a]When day came, Jesus left and went to a secluded place;
and the crowds were searching for Him, and came to Him and
tried to keep Him from going away from them.

23 [a]Matt 4:13; Mark 1:21ff; 2:1ff; Luke 4:35ff; John 4:46ff [b]Mark 6:1; Luke 2:39, 51; 4:16

24 [a]Matt 13:57; Mark 6:4; John 4:44

25 [a]1 Kin 17:1; 18:1; James 5:17

26 [1]Gr *Sarepta* [a]1 Kin 17:9 [b]Matt 11:21

27 [a]2 Kin 5:1-14

29 [a]Num 15:35; Acts 7:58; Heb 13:12

30 [a]John 10:39

31 [a]Luke 4:31-37: *Mark 1:21-28* [b]Matt 4:13; Luke 4:23

32 [1]Lit *word* [a]Matt 7:28 [b]Luke 4:36; John 7:46

33 [1]Lit *having a spirit*

34 [1]Lit *What to us and to you* (a Heb idiom) [2]Lit *the Nazarene* [a]Matt 8:29 [b]Mark 1:24

35 [a]Matt 8:26; Mark 4:39; Luke 4:39, 41; 8:24

36 [1]Or *this word, that with authority . . . come out?* [a]Luke 4:32

37 [a]Luke 4:14

38 [1]Lit *about her* [a]Luke 4:38, 39: *Matt 8:14, 15; Mark 1:29-31* [b]Matt 4:24

39 [1]Or *served* [a]Luke 4:35, 41

40 [a]Luke 4:40, 41: *Matt 8:16, 17; Mark 1:32-34* [b]Mark 1:32 [c]Mark 5:23 [d]Matt 4:23

41 [1]I.e. the Messiah [a]Matt 4:3 [b]Luke 4:35 [c]Matt 8:16; Mark 1:34

42 [a]Luke 4:42, 43: *Mark 1:35-38*

43 But He said to them, "I must preach the kingdom of God to
the other cities also, [a]for I was sent for this purpose."
44 So He kept on preaching in the synagogues [a]of [1]Judea.

Chapter 5 Theme ______________________________

5 [a]Now it happened that while the crowd was pressing around
Him and listening to the word of God, He was standing by
[b]the lake of Gennesaret;
2 and He saw two boats lying at the edge of the lake; but the
fishermen had gotten out of them and were washing their nets.
3 And [a]He got into one of the boats, which was Simon's, and
asked him to put out a little way from the land. And He sat
down and *began* teaching the [1]people from the boat.
4 When He had finished speaking, He said to Simon, "Put
out into the deep water and [a]let down your nets for a catch."
5 Simon answered and said, "[a]Master, [b]we worked hard all
night and caught nothing, but [1]I will do as You say *and* let
down the nets."
6 When they had done this, [a]they enclosed a great quantity
of fish, and their nets *began* to break;
7 so they signaled to their partners in the other boat for them
to come and help them. And they came and filled both of the
boats, so that they began to sink.
8 But when Simon Peter saw *that,* he fell down at Jesus' [1]feet,
saying, "Go away from me Lord, for I am a sinful man!"
9 For amazement had seized him and all his companions
because of the catch of fish which they had taken;
10 and so also *were* [1]James and John, sons of Zebedee, who
were partners with Simon. And Jesus said to Simon, "[a]Do not
fear, from now on you will be [b]catching men."
11 When they had brought their boats to land, [a]they left
everything and followed Him.
12 [a]While He was in one of the cities, behold, *there was* a
man [1]covered with leprosy; and when he saw Jesus, he fell on
his face and implored Him, saying, "Lord, if You are willing,
You can make me clean."
13 And He stretched out His hand and touched him, saying, "I
am willing; be cleansed." And immediately the leprosy left him.
14 And He ordered him to tell no one, "But go and [a]show
yourself to the priest and make an offering for your cleansing,
just as Moses commanded, as a testimony to them."
15 But [a]the news about Him was spreading even farther, and
large crowds were gathering to hear *Him* and to be healed of
their sicknesses.
16 But Jesus Himself would *often* slip away [1]to the [2]wilderness
and [a]pray.
17 [1]One day He was teaching; and [a]there were *some* Pharisees
and [b]teachers of the law sitting *there,* who had [c]come from
every village of Galilee and Judea and *from* Jerusalem; and [d]the
power of the Lord was *present* for Him to perform healing.

43 [a]Mark 1:38
44 [1]I.e. the country of the Jews (including Galilee) [a]Matt 4:23
5:1 [a]Matt 4:18-22; Mark 1:16-20; Luke 5:1-11; John 1:40-42 [b]Num 34:11; Deut 3:17; Josh 12:3; 13:27; Matt 4:18
3 [1]Lit *crowds* [a]Matt 13:2; Mark 3:9, 10; 4:1
4 [a]John 21:6
5 [1]Lit *upon Your word* [a]Luke 8:24; 9:33, 49; 17:13 [b]John 21:3
6 [a]John 21:6
8 [1]Lit *knees*
10 [1]Or *Jacob* [a]Matt 14:27 [b]2 Tim 2:26
11 [a]Matt 4:20, 22; 19:29; Mark 1:18, 20; Luke 5:28
12 [1]Lit *full of* [a]Luke 5:12-14: *Matt 8:2-4; Mark 1:40-44*
14 [a]Lev 13:49; 14:2ff
15 [a]Matt 9:26
16 [1]Lit *in* [2]Or *deserted places* [a]Matt 14:23; Mark 1:35; Luke 6:12
17 [1]Lit *On one of the days* [a]Matt 15:1 [b]Luke 2:46 [c]Mark 1:45 [d]Mark 5:30; Luke 6:19; 8:46

18 [a]And *some* men *were* carrying on a [1]bed a man who was
paralyzed; and they were trying to bring him in and to set him
down in front of Him.
19 But not finding any *way* to bring him in because of the crowd,
they went up on [a]the roof and let him down [b]through the tiles
with his stretcher, into the middle *of the crowd,* in front of Jesus.
20 Seeing their faith, He said, "[1]Friend, [a]your sins are forgiven
you."
21 The scribes and the Pharisees [a]began to reason, saying,
"[b]Who is this *man* who speaks blasphemies? [c]Who can forgive
sins, but God alone?"
22 But Jesus, [1]aware of their reasonings, answered and said to
them, "Why are you reasoning in your hearts?
23 "Which is easier, to say, 'Your sins have been forgiven you,'
or to say, 'Get up and walk'?
24 "But, so that you may know that the Son of Man has authority
on earth to forgive sins,"—He said to the [a]paralytic—"I say to
you, get up, and pick up your stretcher and go home."
25 Immediately he got up before them, and picked up what he
had been lying on, and went home [a]glorifying God.
26 [1]They were all struck with astonishment and *began*
[a]glorifying God; and they were filled [b]with fear, saying, "We
have seen remarkable things today."
27 [a]After that He went out and noticed a tax collector named
[1b]Levi sitting in the tax booth, and He said to him, "Follow Me."
28 And he [a]left everything behind, and got up and *began* to
follow Him.
29 And [a]Levi gave a big reception for Him in his house; and
there was a great crowd of [b]tax collectors and other *people*
who were reclining *at the table* with them.
30 [a]The Pharisees and their scribes *began* grumbling at His
disciples, saying, "Why do you eat and drink with the tax
collectors and [1]sinners?"
31 And Jesus answered and said to them, "[a]*It is* not those who
are well who need a physician, but those who are sick.
32 "I have not come to call the righteous but sinners to
repentance."
33 And they said to Him, "[a]The disciples of John often fast and
offer prayers, the *disciples* of the Pharisees also do [1]the same,
but Yours eat and drink."
34 And Jesus said to them, "You cannot make the [1]attendants of
the bridegroom fast while the bridegroom is with them, can you?
35 "[a]But *the* days will come; and when the bridegroom is taken
away from them, then they will fast in those days."
36 And He was also telling them a parable: "No one tears a
piece of cloth from a new garment and puts it on an old
garment; otherwise he will both tear the new, and the piece
from the new will not match the old.
37 "And no one puts new wine into old wineskins; otherwise
the new wine will burst the skins and it will be spilled out, and
the skins will be ruined.

18 [1]Or *stretcher* [a]Luke 5:18-26: *Matt 9:2-8; Mark 2:3-12*
19 [a]Matt 24:17 [b]Mark 2:4
20 [1]Lit *Man* [a]Matt 9:2
21 [a]Luke 3:8 [b]Luke 7:49 [c]Is 43:25
22 [1]Or *perceiving*
24 [a]Matt 4:24
25 [a]Matt 9:8
26 [1]Lit *Astonishment took them all* [a]Matt 9:8 [b]Luke 1:65; 7:16
27 [1]Also called *Matthew* [a]Luke 5:27-39: *Matt 9:9-17; Mark 2:14-22* [b]Matt 9:9
28 [a]Luke 5:11
29 [a]Matt 9:9 [b]Luke 15:1
30 [1]I.e. irreligious Jews [a]Mark 2:16; Luke 15:2; Acts 23:9
31 [a]Matt 9:12, 13; Mark 2:17
33 [1]Or *likewise* [a]Matt 9:14; Mark 2:18
34 [1]Lit *sons of the bridal-chamber*
35 [a]Matt 9:15; Mark 2:20; Luke 17:22

38 “But new wine must be put into fresh wineskins.
39 “And no one, after drinking old *wine* wishes for new; for he
says, ‘The old is good *enough.*’ ”

Chapter 6 Theme ________________________________

6 [a]Now it happened that He was passing through *some* grainfields on a Sabbath; and His disciples [b]were picking the heads
of grain, rubbing them in their hands, and eating *the grain.*
2 But some of the Pharisees said, “Why do you do what [a]is
not lawful on the Sabbath?”
3 And Jesus answering them said, “Have you not even read
[a]what David did when he was hungry, he and those who were
with him,
4 how he entered the house of God, and took and ate the
[1]consecrated bread which [a]is not lawful for any to eat except
the priests alone, and gave it to his companions?”
5 And He was saying to them, “The Son of Man is Lord of
the Sabbath.”
6 [a]On another Sabbath He entered [b]the synagogue and was
teaching; and there was a man there [1]whose right hand was
withered.
7 The scribes and the Pharisees [a]were watching Him closely
to see if He healed on the Sabbath, so that they might find
reason to accuse Him.
8 But He [a]knew [1]what they were thinking, and He said to the
man with the withered hand, “Get up and [2]come forward!”
And he got up and [3]came forward.
9 And Jesus said to them, “I ask you, is it lawful to do good
or to do harm on the Sabbath, to save a life or to destroy it?”
10 After [a]looking around at them all, He said to him, “Stretch
out your hand!” And he did *so;* and his hand was restored.
11 But they themselves were filled with [1]rage, and discussed
together what they might do to Jesus.
12 It was [1]at this time that He went off to [a]the mountain to
[b]pray, and He spent the whole night in prayer to God.
13 And when day came, [a]He called His disciples to Him and
chose twelve of them, whom He also named as [b]apostles:
14 Simon, whom He also named Peter, and Andrew his
brother; and [1]James and John; and Philip and Bartholomew;
15 and [a]Matthew and Thomas; James *the son* of Alphaeus, and
Simon who was called the Zealot;
16 Judas *the son* of James, and Judas Iscariot, who became a
traitor.
17 Jesus [a]came down with them and stood on a level place;
and *there was* [b]a large crowd of His disciples, and a great
throng of people from all Judea and Jerusalem and the coastal
region of [c]Tyre and Sidon,
18 who had come to hear Him and to be healed of their
diseases; and those who were troubled with unclean spirits
were being cured.

6:1 [a]Luke 6:1-5: *Matt 12:1-8; Mark 2:23-28* [b]Deut 23:25
2 [a]Matt 12:2
3 [a]1 Sam 21:6
4 [1]Or *showbread;* lit *loaves of presentation* [a]Lev 24:9
6 [1]Lit *and his* [a]Luke 6:6-11: *Matt 12:9-14; Mark 3:1-6;* Luke 6:1 [b]Matt 4:23
7 [a]Mark 3:2
8 [1]Lit *their thoughts* [2]Lit *stand into the middle* [3]Lit *stood* [a]Matt 9:4
10 [a]Mark 3:5
11 [1]Lit *folly*
12 [1]Lit *in these days* [a]Matt 5:1 [b]Matt 14:23; Luke 5:16; 9:18, 28
13 [a]Luke 6:13-16: *Matt 10:2-4; Mark 3:16-19; Acts 1:13* [b]Mark 6:30
14 [1]Or *Jacob,* also vv 15 and 16
15 [a]Matt 9:9
17 [a]Luke 6:12 [b]Matt 4:25; Mark 3:7, 8 [c]Matt 11:21

19 And all the [1]people were trying to [a]touch Him, for [b]power
was coming from Him and healing *them* all.
20 And turning His gaze toward His disciples, He *began* to say,
"[a]Blessed *are* [1]you *who are* poor, for [b]yours is the kingdom of
God.
21 "Blessed *are* [1]you who hunger now, for you shall be
satisfied. Blessed *are* you who weep now, for you shall laugh.
22 "[a]Blessed are you when men hate you, and [b]ostracize you,
and insult you, and scorn your name as evil, for the sake of the
Son of Man.
23 "Be glad in that day and [a]leap *for joy,* for behold, your
reward is great in heaven. For [b]in the same way their fathers
used to [1]treat the prophets.
24 "But woe to [a]you who are rich, for [b]you are receiving your
comfort in full.
25 "Woe to you who [1]are well-fed now, for you shall be hungry.
Woe *to you* who laugh now, for you shall mourn and weep.
26 "Woe *to you* when all men speak well of you, for their
fathers used to [1]treat the [a]false prophets in the same way.
27 "But I say to you who hear, [a]love your enemies, do good to
those who hate you,
28 bless those who curse you, [a]pray for those who [1]mistreat you.
29 "[a]Whoever hits you on the cheek, offer him the other also;
and whoever takes away your [1]coat, do not withhold your
[2]shirt from him either.
30 "Give to everyone who asks of you, and whoever takes away
what is yours, do not demand it back.
31 "[1a]Treat others the same way you want [2]them to treat you.
32 "[a]If you love those who love you, what credit is *that* to you?
For even sinners love those who love them.
33 "If you do good to those who do good to you, what credit is
that to you? For even sinners do the same.
34 "[a]If you lend to those from whom you expect to receive,
what credit is *that* to you? Even sinners lend to sinners in
order to receive back the same *amount.*
35 "But [a]love your enemies, and do good, and lend, [1]expecting
nothing in return; and your reward will be great, and you will
be [b]sons of [c]the Most High; for He Himself is kind to ungrateful
and evil *men.*
36 "[1]Be merciful, just as your Father is merciful.
37 "[a]Do not judge, and you will not be judged; and do not
condemn, and you will not be condemned; [1b]pardon, and you
will be pardoned.
38 "Give, and it will be given to you. They will [1]pour [a]into your
lap a [b]good measure—pressed down, shaken together, *and*
running over. For by your standard of measure it will be
measured to you in return."
39 And He also spoke a parable to them: "[a]A blind man cannot
guide a blind man, can he? Will they not both fall into a pit?
40 "[a]A [1]pupil is not above his teacher; but everyone, after he
has been fully trained, will [2]be like his teacher.

19 [1]Lit *crowd* [a]Matt 9:21; 14:36; Mark 3:10 [b]Luke 5:17
20 [1]Lit *the* [a]Matt 5:3-12; Luke 6:20-23 [b]Matt 5:3
21 [1]Lit *the*
22 [a]1 Pet 4:14 [b]John 9:22; 16:2
23 [1]Lit *do to* [a]Mal 4 [b]2 Chr 36:16; Acts 7:52
24 [a]Luke 16:25; James 5:1 [b]Matt 6:2
25 [1]Lit *having been filled*
26 [1]Lit *do to* [a]Matt 7:15
27 [a]Matt 5:44; Luke 6:35
28 [1]Or *revile* [a]Matt 5:44; Luke 6:35
29 [1]I.e. outer garment [2]Or *tunic;* i.e. garment worn next to body [a]Luke 6:29, 30: *Matt 5:39-42*
31 [1]Lit *Do to* [2]Lit *people* [a]Matt 7:12
32 [a]Matt 5:46
34 [a]Matt 5:42
35 [1]Or *not despairing at all* [a]Luke 6:27 [b]Matt 5:9 [c]Luke 1:32
36 [1]Or *Become*
37 [1]Lit *release* [a]Luke 6:37-42: *Matt 7:1-5* [b]Matt 6:14; Luke 23:16; Acts 3:13
38 [1]Lit *give* [a]Mark 4:24 [b]Ps 79:12; Is 65:6, 7; Jer 32:18
39 [a]Matt 15:14
40 [1]Or *disciple* [2]Or *reach his teacher's level* [a]Matt 10:24; John 13:16; 15:20

41 "Why do you look at the speck that is in your brother's eye,
but do not notice the log that is in your own eye?
42 "Or how can you say to your brother, 'Brother, let me take
out the speck that is in your eye,' when you yourself do not see
the log that is in your own eye? You hypocrite, first take the log
out of your own eye, and then you will see clearly to take out
the speck that is in your brother's eye.
43 "[a]For there is no good tree which produces bad fruit, nor, [1]on
the other hand, a bad tree which produces good fruit.
44 "[a]For each tree is known by its own fruit. For men do not
gather figs from thorns, nor do they pick grapes from a briar
bush.
45 "[a]The good man out of the good [1]treasure of his heart brings
forth what is good; and the evil *man* out of the evil *treasure* brings
forth what is evil; [b]for his mouth speaks from [2]that which fills
his heart.
46 "[a]Why do you call Me, 'Lord, Lord,' and do not do what I say?
47 "[a]Everyone who comes to Me and hears My words and [1]acts
on them, I will show you whom he is like:
48 he is like a man building a house, who [1]dug deep and laid a
foundation on the rock; and when a flood occurred, the [2]torrent
burst against that house and could not shake it, because it had
been well built.
49 "But the one who has heard and has not acted *accordingly,*
is like a man who built a house on the ground without any
foundation; and the [1]torrent burst against it and immediately it
collapsed, and the ruin of that house was great."

Chapter 7 Theme ________________________________

7 [a]When He had completed all His discourse in the hearing
of the people, [b]He went to Capernaum.
2 And a centurion's slave, [1]who was highly regarded by him,
was sick and about to die.
3 When he heard about Jesus, [a]he sent some [1]Jewish elders
asking Him to come and [2]save the life of his slave.
4 When they came to Jesus, they earnestly implored Him,
saying, "He is worthy for You to grant this to him;
5 for he loves our nation and it was he who built us our
synagogue."
6 Now Jesus *started* on His way with them; and when He
was not far from the house, the centurion sent friends, saying
to Him, "[1]Lord, do not trouble Yourself further, for I am not
worthy for You to come under my roof;
7 for this reason I did not even consider myself worthy to
come to You, but *just* [1]say the word, and my [2]servant will be
healed.
8 "For I also am a man placed under authority, with soldiers
under me; and I say to this one, 'Go!' and he goes, and to
another, 'Come!' and he comes, and to my slave, 'Do this!' and
he does it."

43 [1]Lit *again* [a]Luke 6:43, 44: *Matt 7:16, 18, 20*

44 [a]Matt 7:16; 12:33

45 [1]Or *treasury, storehouse* [2]Lit *the abundance of* [a]Matt 12:35 [b]Matt 12:34

46 [a]Mal 1:6; Matt 7:21

47 [1]Lit *does* [a]Luke 6:47-49: *Matt 7:24-27;* James 1:22ff

48 [1]Lit *dug and went deep* [2]Lit *river*

49 [1]Lit *river*

7:1 [a]Matt 7:28 [b]Luke 7:1-10: *Matt 8:5-13*

2 [1]Lit *to whom he was honorable*

3 [1]Lit *elders of the Jews* [2]Lit *bring safely through, rescue* [a]Matt 8:5

6 [1]Or *Sir*

7 [1]Lit *say with a word* [2]Or *boy*

9 Now when Jesus heard this, He marveled at him, and
turned and said to the crowd that was following Him, "I say to
you, [a]not even in Israel have I found such great faith."
10 When those who had been sent returned to the house,
they found the slave in good health.
11 Soon afterwards He went to a city called Nain; and His
disciples were going along with Him, [1]accompanied by a large
crowd.
12 Now as He approached the gate of the city, [1]a dead man
was being carried out, the [2]only son of his mother, and she was
a widow; and a sizeable crowd from the city was with her.
13 When [a]the Lord saw her, He felt compassion for her, and
said to her, "[1]Do not weep."
14 And He came up and touched the coffin; and the bearers
came to a halt. And He said, "Young man, I say to you, arise!"
15 The [1]dead man sat up and began to speak. And *Jesus* gave
him back to his mother.
16 [a]Fear gripped them all, and they *began* [b]glorifying God,
saying, "A great [c]prophet has arisen among us!" and, "God has
[1]visited His people!"
17 [a]This report concerning Him went out all over Judea and in
all the surrounding district.
18 [a]The disciples of John reported to him about all these things.
19 Summoning [1]two of his disciples, John sent them to [a]the
Lord, saying, "Are You the [2]Expected One, or do we look for
someone else?"
20 When the men came to Him, they said, "John the Baptist
has sent us to You, to ask, 'Are You the [1]Expected One, or do
we look for someone else?'"
21 At that [1]very time He [a]cured many *people* of diseases and
[b]afflictions and evil spirits; and He gave sight to many *who
were* blind.
22 And He answered and said to them, "Go and report to John
what you have seen and heard: *the* [a]BLIND RECEIVE SIGHT, *the*
lame walk, *the* lepers are cleansed, and *the* deaf hear, *the* dead
are raised up, *the* [b]POOR HAVE THE GOSPEL PREACHED TO THEM.
23 "Blessed is he [1]who does not take offense at Me."
24 When the messengers of John had left, He began to speak
to the crowds about John, "What did you go out into the
wilderness to see? A reed shaken by the wind?
25 "[1]But what did you go out to see? A man dressed in soft
[2]clothing? Those who are splendidly clothed and live in luxury
are *found* in royal palaces!
26 "But what did you go out to see? A prophet? Yes, I say to
you, and one who is more than a prophet.
27 "This is the one about whom it is written,

'[a]BEHOLD, I SEND MY MESSENGER [1]AHEAD OF YOU,
WHO WILL PREPARE YOUR WAY BEFORE YOU.'

28 "I say to you, among those born of women there is no one
greater than John; yet he who is [1]least in the kingdom of God
is greater than he."

9 [a]Matt 8:10; Luke 7:50

11 [1]Lit *and*

12 [1]Lit *one who had died* [2]Or *only begotten*

13 [1]Or *Stop weeping* [a]Luke 7:19; 10:1; 11:1, 39; 12:42; 13:15; 17:5, 6; 18:6; 19:8; 22:61; 24:34; John 4:1; 6:23; 11:2

15 [1]Or *corpse*

16 [1]Or *cared for* [a]Luke 5:26 [b]Matt 9:8 [c]Matt 21:11; Luke 7:39

17 [a]Matt 9:26

18 [a]Luke 7:18-35: *Matt 11:2-19*

19 [1]Lit *a certain two* [2]Lit *Coming One* [a]Luke 7:13; 10:1; 11:1, 39; 12:42; 13:15; 17:5, 6; 18:6; 19:8; 22:61; 24:34; John 4:1; 6:23; 11:2

20 [1]Lit *Coming One*

21 [1]Lit *hour* [a]Matt 4:23 [b]Mark 3:10

22 [a]Is 35:5 [b]Is 61:1

23 [1]Lit *whoever*

25 [1]Or *Well then, what* [2]Or *garments*

27 [1]Lit *before Your face* [a]Mal 3:1; Matt 11:10; Mark 1:2

28 [1]Or *less*

29 When all the people and the tax collectors heard *this,* they
[1]acknowledged [a]God's justice, [b]having been baptized with [c]the
baptism of John.
30 But the Pharisees and the [1a]lawyers rejected God's purpose
for themselves, not having been baptized by [2]John.
31 "To what then shall I compare the men of this generation,
and what are they like?
32 "They are like children who sit in the market place and call
to one another, and they say, 'We played the flute for you, and
you did not dance; we sang a dirge, and you did not weep.'
33 "For John the Baptist has come [a]eating no bread and drinking
no wine, and you say, 'He has a demon!'
34 "The Son of Man has come eating and drinking, and you say,
'Behold, a gluttonous man and a [1]drunkard, a friend of tax
collectors and [2]sinners!'
35 "Yet wisdom [a]is vindicated by all her children."
36 Now one of the Pharisees was requesting Him to [1]dine with
him, and He entered the Pharisee's house and reclined *at the table.*
37 [a]And there was a woman in the city who was a [1]sinner;
and when she learned that He was reclining *at the table* in the
Pharisee's house, she brought an alabaster vial of perfume,
38 and standing behind *Him* at His feet, weeping, she began
to wet His feet with her tears, and kept wiping them with the
hair of her head, and kissing His feet and anointing them with
the perfume.
39 Now when the Pharisee who had invited Him saw this, he
said to himself, "If this man were [a]a prophet He would know
who and what sort of person this woman is who is touching
Him, that she is a [1]sinner."
40 And Jesus answered him, "Simon, I have something to say
to you." And he [1]replied, "Say it, Teacher."
41 "A moneylender had two debtors: one owed five hundred
[1a]denarii, and the other fifty.
42 "When they [a]were unable to repay, he graciously forgave
them both. So which of them will love him more?"
43 Simon answered and said, "I suppose the one whom he
forgave more." And He said to him, "You have judged correctly."
44 Turning toward the woman, He said to Simon, "Do you see
this woman? I entered your house; you [a]gave Me no water for
My feet, but she has wet My feet with her tears and wiped
them with her hair.
45 "You [a]gave Me no kiss; but she, since the time I came in,
has not ceased to kiss My feet.
46 "[a]You did not anoint My head with oil, but she anointed My
feet with perfume.
47 "For this reason I say to you, her sins, which are many, have
been forgiven, for she loved much; but he who is forgiven
little, loves little."
48 Then He said to her, "[a]Your sins have been forgiven."
49 Those who were reclining *at the table* with Him began to
say [1]to themselves, "[a]Who is this *man* who even forgives sins?"

29 [1]Or *justified God* [a]Luke 7:35 [b]Matt 21:32; Luke 3:12 [c]Acts 18:25; 19:3

30 [1]I.e. experts in the Mosaic Law [2]Lit *him* [a]Matt 22:35

33 [a]Luke 1:15

34 [1]Or *wine-drinker* [2]I.e. irreligious Jews

35 [a]Luke 7:29

36 [1]Lit *eat*

37 [1]I.e. an immoral woman [a]Matt 26:6-13; Mark 14:3-9; Luke 7:37-39; John 12:1-8

39 [1]I.e. an immoral woman [a]Luke 7:16; John 4:19

40 [1]Lit *says*

41 [1]The denarius was equivalent to a day's wages [a]Matt 18:28; Mark 6:37

42 [a]Matt 18:25

44 [a]Gen 18:4; 19:2; 43:24; Judg 19:21; 1 Tim 5:10

45 [a]2 Sam 15:5

46 [a]2 Sam 12:20; Ps 23:5; Eccl 9:8; Dan 10:3

48 [a]Matt 9:2; Mark 2:5, 9; Luke 5:20, 23

49 [1]Or *among* [a]Luke 5:21

50 And He said to the woman, "[a]Your faith has saved you; [b]go
in peace."

Chapter 8 Theme ____________________________

8 Soon afterwards, He *began* going around from one city and
village to another, [a]proclaiming and preaching the kingdom
of God. The twelve were with Him,
2 and *also* [a]some women who had been healed of evil spirits
and sicknesses: [b]Mary who was called Magdalene, from whom
seven demons had gone out,
3 and Joanna the wife of Chuza, [a]Herod's [b]steward, and
Susanna, and many others who were contributing to their support
out of their private means.
4 [a]When a large crowd was coming together, and those from
the various cities were journeying to Him, He spoke by way of
a parable:
5 "The sower went out to sow his seed; and as he sowed,
some fell beside the road, and it was trampled under foot and
the birds of the [1]air ate it up.
6 "Other *seed* fell on rocky *soil,* and as soon as it grew up, it
withered away, because it had no moisture.
7 "Other *seed* fell among the thorns; and the thorns grew up
with it and choked it out.
8 "Other *seed* fell into the good soil, and grew up, and produced
a crop a hundred times as great." As He said these things, He
would call out, "[a]He who has ears to hear, [1]let him hear."
9 [a]His disciples *began* questioning Him as to what this parable
meant.
10 And He said, "[a]To you it has been granted to know the
mysteries of the kingdom of God, but to the rest *it is* in parables,
so that [b]SEEING THEY MAY NOT SEE, AND HEARING THEY MAY NOT
UNDERSTAND.
11 "Now the parable is this: [a]the seed is the word of God.
12 "Those beside the road are those who have heard; then the
devil comes and takes away the word from their heart, so that
they will not believe and be saved.
13 "Those on the rocky *soil are* those who, when they hear,
receive the word with joy; and these have no *firm* root; [1]they
believe for a while, and in time of temptation fall away.
14 "The *seed* which fell among the thorns, these are the ones
who have heard, and as they go on their way they are choked
with worries and riches and pleasures of *this* life, and bring no
fruit to maturity.
15 "But the *seed* in the good soil, these are the ones who have
heard the word in an honest and good heart, and hold it fast,
and bear fruit with [1]perseverance.
16 "Now [a]no one after lighting a lamp covers it over with a
container, or puts it under a bed; but he puts it on a lampstand,
so that those who come in may see the light.
17 "[a]For nothing is hidden that will not become evident, nor
anything secret that will not be known and come to light.

50 [a]Matt 9:22; Luke 17:19; 18:42 [b]Mark 5:34; Luke 8:48

8:1 [a]Matt 4:23

2 [a]Matt 27:55; Mark 15:40, 41; Luke 23:49, 55 [b]Matt 27:56; Mark 16:9

3 [a]Matt 14:1 [b]Matt 20:8

4 [a]Luke 8:4-8: *Matt 13:2-9; Mark 4:1-9*

5 [1]Lit *heaven*

8 [1]Or *hear!* Or *listen!* [a]Matt 11:15; Mark 7:16; Luke 14:35; Rev 2:7, 11, 17, 29; 3:6, 13, 22; 13:9

9 [a]Luke 8:9-15: *Matt 13:10-23; Mark 4:10-20*

10 [a]Matt 13:11 [b]Is 6:9; Matt 13:14; Acts 28:26

11 [a]1 Pet 1:23

13 [1]Lit *who believe*

15 [1]Or *steadfastness*

16 [a]Matt 5:15; Mark 4:21; Luke 11:33

17 [a]Matt 10:26; Mark 4:22; Luke 12:2

18 "So take care how you listen; [a]for whoever has, to him *more*
shall be given; and whoever does not have, even what he
[1]thinks he has shall be taken away from him."
19 [a]And His mother and brothers came to Him, and they were
unable to get to Him because of the crowd.
20 And it was reported to Him, "Your mother and Your
brothers are standing outside, wishing to see You."
21 But He answered and said to them, "My mother and My
brothers are these [a]who hear the word of God and do it."
22 [a]Now on one of *those* days Jesus and His disciples got into
a boat, and He said to them, "Let us go over to the other side of
[b]the lake." So they launched out.
23 But as they were sailing along He fell asleep; and a fierce
gale of wind descended on [a]the lake, and they *began* to be
swamped and to be in danger.
24 They came to Jesus and woke Him up, saying, "[a]Master,
Master, we are perishing!" And He got up and [b]rebuked the
wind and the surging waves, and they stopped, and [1]it became
calm.
25 And He said to them, "Where is your faith?" They were
fearful and amazed, saying to one another, "Who then is this,
that He commands even the winds and the water, and they
obey Him?"
26 [a]Then they sailed to the country of the Gerasenes, which is
opposite Galilee.
27 And when He came out onto the land, He was met by a
man from the city who was possessed with demons; and who
had not put on any clothing for a long time, and was not living
in a house, but in the tombs.
28 Seeing Jesus, he cried out and fell before Him, and said in a
loud voice, "[1a]What business do we have with each other, Jesus,
Son of [b]the Most High God? I beg You, do not torment me."
29 For He had commanded the unclean spirit to come out of
the man. For it had seized him many times; and he was bound
with chains and shackles and kept under guard, and *yet* he
would break his bonds and be driven by the demon into the
desert.
30 And Jesus asked him, "What is your name?" And he said,
"[a]Legion"; for many demons had entered him.
31 They were imploring Him not to command them to go
away into [a]the abyss.
32 Now there was a herd of many swine feeding there on the
mountain; and *the demons* implored Him to permit them to
enter [1]the swine. And He gave them permission.
33 And the demons came out of the man and entered the
swine; and the herd rushed down the steep bank into [a]the lake
and was drowned.
34 When the herdsmen saw what had happened, they ran
away and reported it in the city and *out* in the country.
35 *The people* went out to see what had happened; and they
came to Jesus, and found the man from whom the demons had

18 [1]Or *seems to have* [a]Matt 13:12; 25:29; Luke 19:26
19 [a]Luke 8:19-21: *Matt 12:46-50; Mark 3:31-35*
21 [a]Luke 11:28
22 [a]Luke 8:22-25: *Matt 8:23-27; Mark 4:36-41* [b]Luke 5:1f; 8:23
23 [a]Luke 5:1f; 8:22
24 [1]Lit *a calm occurred* [a]Luke 5:5 [b]Luke 4:39
26 [a]Luke 8:26-37: *Matt 8:28-34; Mark 5:1-17*
28 [1]Lit *What to me and to you* (a Heb idiom) [a]Matt 8:29 [b]Mark 5:7
30 [a]Matt 26:53
31 [a]Rom 10:7; Rev 9:1f, 11; 11:7; 17:8; 20:1, 3
32 [1]Lit *them*
33 [a]Luke 5:1f; 8:22

gone out, sitting down [a]at the feet of Jesus, clothed and in his
right mind; and they became frightened.
36 Those who had seen it reported to them how the man who
was [a]demon-possessed had been [1]made well.
37 And all the people of the country of the Gerasenes and the
surrounding district asked Him to leave them, for they were
gripped with great fear; and He got into a boat and returned.
38 [a]But the man from whom the demons had gone out was
begging Him that he might [1]accompany Him; but He sent him
away, saying,
39 "Return to your house and describe what great things God
has done for you." So he went away, proclaiming throughout
the whole city what great things Jesus had done for him.
40 [a]And as Jesus returned, the [1]people welcomed Him, for they
had all been waiting for Him.
41 [a]And there came a man named Jairus, and he was an
[1b]official of the synagogue; and he fell at Jesus' feet, and *began*
to implore Him to come to his house;
42 for he had an [1]only daughter, about twelve years old, and she
was dying. But as He went, the crowds were pressing against
Him.
43 And a woman who had a hemorrhage for twelve years, and
could not be healed by anyone,
44 came up behind Him and touched the fringe of His [1]cloak,
and immediately her hemorrhage stopped.
45 And Jesus said, "Who is the one who touched Me?" And
while they were all denying it, Peter said, "[a]Master, the [1]people
are crowding and pressing in on You."
46 But Jesus said, "Someone did touch Me, for I was aware
that [a]power had gone out of Me."
47 When the woman saw that she had not escaped notice, she
came trembling and fell down before Him, and declared in the
presence of all the people the reason why she had touched
Him, and how she had been immediately healed.
48 And He said to her, "Daughter, [a]your faith has [1]made you
well; [b]go in peace."
49 While He was still speaking, someone *came from *the house
of* [a]the synagogue official, saying, "Your daughter has died; do
not trouble the Teacher anymore."
50 But when Jesus heard *this,* He answered him, "[a]Do not be
afraid *any longer;* only believe, and she will be [1]made well."
51 When He came to the house, He did not allow anyone to
enter with Him, except Peter and John and James, and the
girl's father and mother.
52 Now they were all weeping and [a]lamenting for her; but He
said, "Stop weeping, for she has not died, but [b]is asleep."
53 And they *began* laughing at Him, knowing that she had died.
54 He, however, took her by the hand and called, saying,
"Child, arise!"
55 And her spirit returned, and she got up immediately; and
He gave orders for *something* to be given her to eat.

35 [a]Luke 10:39

36 [1]Or *saved* [a]Matt 4:24

38 [1]Lit *be with* [a]Luke 8:38, 39: *Mark 5:18-20*

40 [1]Lit *crowd* [a]Matt 9:1; Mark 5:21

41 [1]Lit *ruler* [a]Luke 8:41-56: *Matt 9:18-26; Mark 5:22-43* [b]Mark 5:22; Luke 8:49

42 [1]Or *only begotten*

44 [1]Or *outer garment*

45 [1]Lit *crowds* [a]Luke 5:5

46 [a]Luke 5:17

48 [1]Or *saved you* [a]Matt 9:22 [b]Mark 5:34; Luke 7:50

49 [a]Luke 8:41

50 [1]Or *saved* [a]Mark 5:36

52 [a]Matt 11:17; Luke 23:27 [b]John 11:13

56 Her parents were amazed; but He [a]instructed them to tell
no one what had happened.

Chapter 9 Theme ________________________________

9 [a]And He called the twelve together, and gave them power
and authority over all the demons and to heal diseases.
2 And He sent them out to [a]proclaim the kingdom of God
and to perform healing.
3 And He said to them, "[a]Take nothing for *your* journey,
[b]neither a staff, nor a [1]bag, nor bread, nor money; and do not
even have [2]two tunics apiece.
4 "Whatever house you enter, stay there [1]until you leave that
city.
5 "And as for those who do not receive you, as you go out from
that city, [a]shake the dust off your feet as a testimony against them."
6 Departing, they *began* going [1]throughout the villages,
[a]preaching the gospel and healing everywhere.
7 [a]Now [b]Herod the tetrarch heard of all that was happening;
and he was greatly perplexed, because it was said by some that
[c]John had risen from the dead,
8 and by some that [a]Elijah had appeared, and by others that
one of the prophets of old had risen again.
9 Herod said, "I myself had John beheaded; but who is this
man about whom I hear such things?" And [a]he kept trying to
see Him.
10 [a]When the apostles returned, they gave an account to Him
of all that they had done. [b]Taking them with Him, He withdrew
by Himself to a city called [c]Bethsaida.
11 But the crowds were aware of this and followed Him; and
welcoming them, He *began* speaking to them about the
kingdom of God and curing those who had need of healing.
12 Now the day [1]was ending, and the twelve came and said to
Him, "Send the crowd away, that they may go into the
surrounding villages and countryside and find lodging and get
[2]something to eat; for here we are in a desolate place."
13 But He said to them, "You give them *something* to eat!"
And they said, "We have no more than five loaves and two
fish, unless perhaps we go and buy food for all these people."
14 (For there were about five thousand men.) And He said to
His disciples, "Have them [1]sit down *to eat* [a]in groups of about
fifty each."
15 They did so, and had them all [1]sit down.
16 Then He took the five loaves and the two fish, and looking
up to heaven, He blessed them, and broke *them,* and kept
giving *them* to the disciples to set before the [1]people.
17 And they all ate and were satisfied; and [1]the broken pieces
which they had left over were picked up, twelve [a]baskets *full.*
18 [a]And it happened that while He was [b]praying alone, the
disciples were with Him, and He questioned them, saying,
"Who do the [1]people say that I am?"

56 [a]Matt 8:4
9:1 [a]Matt 10:5; Mark 6:7
2 [a]Matt 10:7
3 [1]Or *knapsack* or *beggar's bag* [2]Or *inner garments* [a]Luke 9:3-5: *Matt 10:9-15; Mark 6:8-11;* Luke 10:4-12; 22:35 [b]Matt 10:10; Mark 6:8; Luke 22:35f
4 [1]Lit *and leave from there*
5 [a]Luke 10:11; Acts 13:51
6 [1]Or *from village to village* [a]Mark 6:12; Luke 8:1
7 [a]Luke 9:7-9: *Matt 14:1, 2;* Mark 6:14f [b]Matt 14:1; Luke 3:1; 13:31; 23:7 [c]Matt 14:2
8 [a]Matt 16:14
9 [a]Luke 23:8
10 [a]Mark 6:30 [b]Luke 9:10-17: *Matt 14:13-21; Mark 6:32-44; John 6:5-13* [c]Matt 11:21
12 [1]Lit *began to decline* [2]Lit *provisions*
14 [1]Lit *recline* [a]Mark 6:39
15 [1]Lit *recline*
16 [1]Lit *crowd*
17 [1]Lit *that which was left over to them of the broken pieces was* [a]Matt 14:20
18 [1]Lit *crowds* [a]Luke 9:18-20: *Matt 16:13-16; Mark 8:27-29* [b]Matt 14:23; Luke 6:12; 9:28

19 They answered and said, "John the Baptist, and others *say*
Elijah; but others, that one of the prophets of old has risen again."
20 And He said to them, "But who do you say that I am?" And
Peter answered and said, "[a]The [1]Christ of God."
21 But He [1a]warned them and instructed *them* not to tell this
to anyone,
22 [a]saying, "[b]The Son of Man must suffer many things and be
rejected by the elders and chief priests and scribes, and be
killed and be raised up on the third day."
23 And He was saying to *them* all, "[a]If anyone wishes to come
after Me, he must deny himself, and take up his cross daily and
follow Me.
24 "For [a]whoever wishes to save his [1]life will lose it, but whoever
loses his [1]life for My sake, he is the one who will save it.
25 "For what is a man profited if he gains the whole world, and
[a]loses or forfeits himself?
26 "[a]For whoever is ashamed of Me and My words, the Son of
Man will be ashamed of him when He comes in His glory, and
the glory of the Father and of the holy angels.
27 "But I say to you truthfully, [a]there are some of those standing
here who will not taste death until they see the kingdom of God."
28 [a]Some eight days after these sayings, He took along [b]Peter
and John and James, and [c]went up on the mountain [d]to pray.
29 And while He was [a]praying, the appearance of His face
[b]became different, and His clothing *became* white *and* [1]gleaming.
30 And behold, two men were talking with Him; and they
were Moses and Elijah,
31 who, appearing in [1]glory, were speaking of His [a]departure
which He was about to accomplish at Jerusalem.
32 Now Peter and his companions [a]had been overcome with
sleep; but when they were fully awake, they saw His glory and
the two men standing with Him.
33 And as [1]these were leaving Him, Peter said to Jesus, "[a]Master,
it is good for us to be here; [b]let us make three [2]tabernacles: one
for You, and one for Moses, and one for Elijah"—[c]not realizing
what he was saying.
34 While he was saying this, a cloud [1]formed and *began* to
overshadow them; and they were afraid as they entered the
cloud.
35 Then [a]a voice came out of the cloud, saying, "[b]This is My
Son, *My* Chosen One; listen to Him!"
36 And when the voice [1]had spoken, Jesus was found alone.
And [a]they kept silent, and reported to no one in those days any
of the things which they had seen.
37 [a]On the next day, when they came down from the
mountain, a large crowd met Him.
38 And a man from the crowd shouted, saying, "Teacher, I beg
You to look at my son, for he is my [1]only *boy,*
39 and a spirit seizes him, and he suddenly screams, and it
throws him into a convulsion with foaming *at the mouth;* and
only with difficulty does it leave him, mauling him *as it leaves.*

20 [1]I.e. Messiah [a]John 6:68f

21 [1]Or *strictly admonished* [a]Matt 8:4; 16:20; Mark 8:30

22 [a]Luke 9:22-27: *Matt 16:21-28; Mark 8:31-9:1* [b]Matt 16:21; Luke 9:44

23 [a]Matt 10:38; Luke 14:27

24 [1]Or *soul* [a]Matt 10:39; Luke 17:33; John 12:25

25 [a]Heb 10:34

26 [a]Matt 10:33; Luke 12:9

27 [a]Matt 16:28

28 [a]Luke 9:28-36: *Matt 17:1-8; Mark 9:2-8* [b]Matt 17:1 [c]Matt 5:1 [d]Luke 3:21; 5:16; 6:12; 9:18

29 [1]Lit *flashing like lightning* [a]Luke 3:21; 5:16; 6:12; 9:18 [b]Mark 16:12

31 [1]Or *splendor* [a]2 Pet 1:15

32 [a]Matt 26:43; Mark 14:40

33 [1]Lit *they* [2]Or *sacred tents* [a]Luke 5:5; 9:49 [b]Matt 17:4; Mark 9:5 [c]Mark 9:6

34 [1]Lit *occurred*

35 [a]2 Pet 1:17f [b]Is 42:1; Matt 3:17; 12:18; Mark 1:11; Luke 3:22

36 [1]Lit *occurred* [a]Matt 17:9; Mark 9:9f

37 [a]Luke 9:37-42: *Matt 17:14-18; Mark 9:14-27*

38 [1]Or *only begotten*

40 "I begged Your disciples to cast it out, and they could not."
41 And Jesus answered and said, "You unbelieving and
perverted generation, how long shall I be with you and put up
with you? Bring your son here."
42 While he was still approaching, the demon [1]slammed him *to
the ground* and threw him into a convulsion. But Jesus rebuked
the unclean spirit, and healed the boy and gave him back to his
father.
43 And they were all amazed at the [1a]greatness of God.
[b]**B**ut while everyone was marveling at all that He was doing,
He said to His disciples,
44 "Let these words sink into your ears; [a]for the Son of Man is
going to be [1]delivered into the hands of men."
45 But [a]they [1]did not understand this statement, and it was
concealed from them so that they would not perceive it; and
they were afraid to ask Him about this statement.
46 [a]An argument [1]started among them as to which of them
might be the greatest.
47 But Jesus, [a]knowing [1]what they were thinking in their heart,
took a child and stood him by His side,
48 and said to them, "[a]Whoever receives this child in My name
receives Me, and whoever receives Me receives Him who sent
Me; [b]for the one who is least among all of you, this is the one
who is great."
49 [a]John answered and said, "[b]Master, we saw someone casting
out demons in Your name; and we tried to prevent him because
he does not follow along with us."
50 But Jesus said to him, "Do not hinder *him;* [a]for he who is
not against you is [1]for you."
51 When the days were approaching for [a]His [1]ascension, He
[2]was determined [b]to go to Jerusalem;
52 and He sent messengers on ahead of Him, and they went and
entered a village of the [a]Samaritans to [1]make arrangements for
Him.
53 But they did not receive Him, [a]because [1]He was traveling
toward Jerusalem.
54 When His disciples [a]James and John saw *this,* they said,
"Lord, do You want us to [b]command fire to come down from
heaven and consume them?"
55 But He turned and rebuked them, [[1]and said, "You do not
know what kind of spirit you are of;
56 for the Son of Man did not come to destroy men's lives, but
to save them."] And they went on to another village.
57 [a]As they were going along the road, [b]someone said to Him,
"I will follow You wherever You go."
58 And Jesus said to him, "The foxes have holes and the birds
of the [1]air *have* [2]nests, but [a]the Son of Man has nowhere to lay
His head."
59 And He said to another, "[a]Follow Me." But he said, "Lord,
permit me first to go and bury my father."
60 But He said to him, "Allow the dead to bury their own

42 [1]Or *tore him*
43 [1]Or *majesty* [a]2 Pet 1:16 [b]Luke 9:43-45: *Matt 17:22f; Mark 9:30-32*
44 [1]Or *betrayed* [a]Luke 9:22
45 [1]Lit *were not knowing* [a]Mark 9:32
46 [1]Lit *entered in* [a]Luke 9:46-48: *Matt 18:1-5; Mark 9:33-37;* Luke 22:24
47 [1]Lit *the reasoning;* or *argument* [a]Matt 9:4
48 [a]Matt 10:40; Luke 10:16; John 13:20 [b]Luke 22:26
49 [a]Luke 9:49, 50: *Mark 9:38-40* [b]Luke 5:5; 9:33
50 [1]Or *on your side* [a]Matt 12:30; Luke 11:23
51 [1]Lit *taking up* [2]Lit *set His face* [a]Mark 16:19 [b]Luke 13:22; 17:11; 18:31; 19:11, 28
52 [1]Or *prepare* [a]Matt 10:5; Luke 10:33; 17:16; John 4:4
53 [1]Lit *His face was proceeding toward* [a]John 4:9
54 [a]Mark 3:17 [b]2 Kin 1:9-16
55 [1]Early mss do not contain bracketed portion
57 [a]Luke 9:51 [b]Luke 9:57-60: *Matt 8:19-22*
58 [1]Or *sky* [2]Or *roosting-places* [a]Matt 8:20
59 [a]Matt 8:22

dead; but as for you, go and [a]proclaim everywhere the kingdom
of God."
61 Another also said, "I will follow You, Lord; but [a]first permit
me to say good-bye to those at home."
62 But Jesus said to him, "[a]No one, after putting his hand to
the plow and looking back, is fit for the kingdom of God."

Chapter 10 Theme ______________________________

10 Now after this [a]the Lord appointed [1]seventy [b]others, and
sent them [c]in pairs ahead of Him to every city and place
where He Himself was going to come.
2 And He was saying to them, "[a]The harvest is plentiful, but
the laborers are few; therefore beseech the Lord of the harvest
to send out laborers into His harvest.
3 "Go; [a]behold, I send you out as lambs in the midst of wolves.
4 "[a]Carry no money belt, no [1]bag, no shoes; and greet no one
on the way.
5 "Whatever house you enter, first say, 'Peace *be* to this house.'
6 "If a [1]man of peace is there, your peace will rest on him; but
if not, it will return to you.
7 "Stay in [1]that house, eating and drinking [2]what they give you;
for [a]the laborer is worthy of his wages. Do not keep moving
from house to house.
8 "Whatever city you enter and they receive you, [a]eat what is
set before you;
9 and heal those in it who are sick, and say to them, '[a]The
kingdom of God has come near to you.'
10 "But whatever city you enter and they do not receive you,
go out into its streets and say,
11 '[a]Even the dust of your city which clings to our feet we wipe
off *in protest* against you; yet [1]be sure of this, that [b]the
kingdom of God has come near.'
12 "I say to you, [a]it will be more tolerable in that day for [b]Sodom
than for that city.
13 "[a]Woe to you, [b]Chorazin! Woe to you, [b]Bethsaida! For if the
[1]miracles had been performed in [b]Tyre and Sidon which
occurred in you, they would have repented long ago, sitting in
[2c]sackcloth and ashes.
14 "But it will be more tolerable for [a]Tyre and Sidon in the
judgment than for you.
15 "And you, [a]Capernaum, will not be exalted to heaven, will
you? You will be brought down to Hades!
16 "[a]The one who listens to you listens to Me, and [b]the one
who rejects you rejects Me; and he who rejects Me rejects the
One who sent Me."
17 The [1]seventy returned with joy, saying, "Lord, even [a]the
demons are subject to us in Your name."
18 And He said to them, "I was watching [a]Satan fall from
heaven like lightning.
19 "Behold, I have given you authority to [a]tread on serpents

60 [a]Matt 4:23

61 [a]1 Kin 19:20

62 [a]Phil 3:13

10:1 [1]Some mss read *seventy-two* [a]Luke 7:13 [b]Luke 9:1f, 52 [c]Mark 6:7

2 [a]Matt 9:37, 38; John 4:35

3 [a]Matt 10:16

4 [1]Or *knapsack* or *beggar's bag* [a]Matt 10:9-14; Mark 6:8-11; Luke 9:3-5; 10:4-12

6 [1]Lit *son of peace;* i.e. a person inclined toward peace

7 [1]Lit *the house itself* [2]Lit *the things from them* [a]Matt 10:10; 1 Cor 9:14; 1 Tim 5:18

8 [a]1 Cor 10:27

9 [a]Matt 3:2; 10:7; Luke 10:11

11 [1]Lit *know* [a]Matt 10:14; Mark 6:11; Luke 9:5; Acts 13:51 [b]Matt 3:2; 10:7; Luke 10:9

12 [a]Gen 19:24-28; Matt 10:15; 11:24 [b]Matt 10:15

13 [1]Or *works of power* [2]i.e. symbols of mourning [a]Luke 10:13-15: *Matt 11:21-23* [b]Is 23:1-18; Ezek 26:1-28:26; Joel 3:4-8; Matt 11:21 [c]Rev 11:3

14 [a]Matt 11:21

15 [a]Is 14:13-15; Matt 4:13; 11:23

16 [a]Matt 10:40; Mark 9:37; Luke 9:48; John 13:20; Gal 4:14 [b]John 12:48; 1 Thess 4:8

17 [1]Some mss read *seventy-two* [a]Mark 16:17

18 [a]Matt 4:10

19 [a]Ps 91:13; Mark 16:18

and scorpions, and over all the power of the enemy, and
nothing will injure you.
20 "Nevertheless do not rejoice in this, that the spirits are
subject to you, but rejoice that [a]your names are recorded in
heaven."
21 [a]At that very [1]time He rejoiced greatly in the Holy Spirit,
and said, "I [2]praise You, O Father, Lord of heaven and earth,
that You have hidden these things from *the* wise and intelligent
and have revealed them to infants. Yes, Father, for this way was
well-pleasing in Your sight.
22 "[a]All things have been handed over to Me by My Father,
and [b]no one knows who the Son is except the Father, and who
the Father is except the Son, and anyone to whom the Son
wills to reveal *Him.*"
23 [a]Turning to the disciples, He said privately, "Blessed *are*
the eyes which see the things you see,
24 for I say to you, that many prophets and kings wished to
see the things which you see, and did not see *them,* and to
hear the things which you hear, and did not hear *them.*"
25 [a]And a [1b]lawyer stood up and put Him to the test, saying,
"Teacher, what shall I do to inherit eternal life?"
26 And He said to him, "What is written in the Law? [1]How
does it read to you?"
27 And he answered, "[a]YOU SHALL LOVE THE LORD YOUR GOD WITH
ALL YOUR HEART, AND WITH ALL YOUR SOUL, AND WITH ALL YOUR
STRENGTH, AND WITH ALL YOUR MIND; AND YOUR NEIGHBOR AS YOURSELF."
28 And He said to him, "You have answered correctly; [a]DO
THIS AND YOU WILL LIVE."
29 But wishing [a]to justify himself, he said to Jesus, "And who
is my neighbor?"
30 Jesus replied and said, "A man was [a]going down from
Jerusalem to Jericho, and fell among robbers, and they stripped
him and [1]beat him, and went away leaving him half dead.
31 "And by chance a priest was going down on that road, and
when he saw him, he passed by on the other side.
32 "Likewise a Levite also, when he came to the place and saw
him, passed by on the other side.
33 "But a [a]Samaritan, who was on a journey, came upon him;
and when he saw him, he felt compassion,
34 and came to him and bandaged up his wounds, pouring oil
and wine on *them;* and he put him on his own beast, and
brought him to an inn and took care of him.
35 "On the next day he took out two [1]denarii and gave them to
the innkeeper and said, 'Take care of him; and whatever more
you spend, when I return I will repay you.'
36 "Which of these three do you think proved to be a neighbor
to the man who fell into the robbers' *hands?*"
37 And he said, "The one who showed mercy toward him."
Then Jesus said to him, "Go and do [1]the same."
38 Now as they were traveling along, He entered a village;
and a woman named [a]Martha welcomed Him into her home.

20 [a]Ex 32:32; Ps 69:28; Is 4:3; Ezek 13:9; Dan 12:1; Phil 4:3; Heb 12:23; Rev 3:5; 13:8; 17:8; 20:12, 15; 21:27

21 [1]Lit *hour* [2]Or *acknowledge to You* [a]Luke 10:21, 22: *Matt 11:25-27*

22 [a]John 3:35 [b]John 10:15

23 [a]Luke 10:23, 24: *Matt 13:16, 17*

25 [1]I.e. an expert in the Mosaic Law [a]Luke 10:25-28: *Matt 22:34-40; Mark 12:28-31;* Matt 19:16-19 [b]Matt 22:35

26 [1]Lit *How do you read?*

27 [a]Deut 6:5; Lev 19:18

28 [a]Lev 18:5; Ezek 20:11; Matt 19:17

29 [a]Luke 16:15

30 [1]Lit *laid blows upon* [a]Luke 18:31; 19:28

33 [a]Matt 10:5; Luke 9:52

35 [1]The denarius was equivalent to a day's wages

37 [1]Or *likewise*

38 [a]Luke 10:40f; John 11:1, 5, 19ff, 30, 39; 12:2

39 She had a sister called [a]Mary, who was [b]seated at the Lord's
feet, listening to His word.
40 But [a]Martha was distracted with [1]all her preparations; and
she came up *to Him* and said, "Lord, do You not care that my
sister has left me to do all the serving alone? Then tell her to
help me."
41 But the Lord answered and said to her, "[a]Martha, Martha,
you are [b]worried and bothered about so many things;
42 [a]but *only* one thing is necessary, for [b]Mary has chosen the
good part, which shall not be taken away from her."

Chapter 11 Theme ______________________

11 It happened that while [1]Jesus was praying in a certain place,
after He had finished, one of His disciples said to Him,
"Lord, teach us to pray just as John also taught his disciples."
2 And He said to them, "[a]When you pray, say:
'[1]Father, hallowed be Your name.
Your kingdom come.
3 'Give us [a]each day our [1]daily bread.
4 'And forgive us our sins,
For we ourselves also forgive everyone who [a]is indebted
to us.
And lead us not into temptation.'"
5 Then He said to them, "[1]Suppose one of you has a friend,
and goes to him at midnight and says to him, 'Friend, lend me
three loaves;
6 for a friend of mine has come to me from a journey, and I
have nothing to set before him';
7 and from inside he answers and says, 'Do not bother me;
the door has already been shut and my children [1]and I are in
bed; I cannot get up and give you *anything*.'
8 "I tell you, even though he will not get up and give him
anything because he is his friend, yet [a]because of his
[1]persistence he will get up and give him as much as he needs.
9 "So I say to you, [1a]ask, and it will be given to you; [2]seek,
and you will find; [3]knock, and it will be opened to you.
10 "For everyone who asks, receives; and he who seeks, finds;
and to him who knocks, it will be opened.
11 "Now [1]suppose one of you fathers is asked by his son for a
[2]fish; he will not give him a snake instead of a fish, will he?
12 "Or *if* he is asked for an egg, he will not give him a scorpion,
will he?
13 "[a]If you then, being evil, know how to give good gifts to
your children, how much more will *your* [1]heavenly Father give
the Holy Spirit to those who ask Him?"
14 [a]And He was casting out a demon, and it was mute; when
the demon had gone out, the mute man spoke; and the crowds
were amazed.
15 But some of them said, "He casts out demons [a]by [b]Beelzebul,
the ruler of the demons."

39 [a]Luke 10:42; John 11:1f, 19f, 28, 31f, 45; 12:3 [b]Luke 8:35; Acts 22:3

40 [1]Lit *much service* [a]Luke 10:38, 41; John 11:1, 5, 19ff, 30, 39; 12:2

41 [a]Luke 10:38, 40; John 11:1, 5, 19ff, 30, 39; 12:2 [b]Matt 6:25

42 [a]Ps 27:4; John 6:27 [b]Luke 10:39; John 11:1f, 19f, 28, 31f, 45; 12:3

11:1 [1]Lit *He*

2 [1]Later mss add phrases from Matt 6:9-13 to make the two passages closely similar [a]Luke 11:2-4: *Matt 6:9-13*

3 [1]Or *bread for the coming day* or *needful bread* [a]Acts 17:11

4 [a]Luke 13:4 mg

5 [1]Lit *Which one of you will have*

7 [1]Lit *with me*

8 [1]Lit *shamelessness* [a]Luke 18:1-5

9 [1]Or *keep asking* [2]Or *keep seeking* [3]Or *keep knocking* [a]Luke 11:9-13: *Matt 7:7-11*

11 [1]Lit *which of you, a son, will ask the father* [2]Two early mss insert *loaf, he will not give him a stone, will he, or for a*

13 [1]Lit *Father from heaven* [a]Matt 7:11; Luke 18:7f

14 [a]Luke 11:14, 15: *Matt 12:22, 24;* Matt 9:32-34

15 [a]Matt 9:34 [b]Matt 10:25

16 Others, [1]to test *Him,* [a]were demanding of Him a [2]sign from heaven.

17 [a]But He knew their thoughts and said to them, "[1]Any kingdom divided against itself is laid waste; and a house *divided* against [2]itself falls.

18 "If [a]Satan also is divided against himself, how will his kingdom stand? For you say that I cast out demons by [b]Beelzebul.

19 "And if I by [a]Beelzebul cast out demons, by whom do your sons cast them out? So they will be your judges.

20 "But if I cast out demons by the [a]finger of God, then [b]the kingdom of God has come upon you.

21 "When [1]a strong *man,* fully armed, guards his own house, his possessions are [2]undisturbed.

22 "But when someone stronger than he attacks him and overpowers him, he takes away from him all his armor on which he had relied and distributes his plunder.

23 "[a]He who is not with Me is against Me; and he who does not gather with Me, scatters.

24 "[a]When the unclean spirit goes out of [1]a man, it passes through waterless places seeking rest, and not finding any, it says, 'I will return to my house from which I came.'

25 "And when it comes, it finds it swept and put in order.

26 "Then it goes and takes *along* seven other spirits more evil than itself, and they go in and live there; and the last state of that man becomes worse than the first."

27 While [1]Jesus was saying these things, one of the women in the crowd raised her voice and said to Him, "[a]Blessed is the womb that bore You and the breasts at which You nursed."

28 But He said, "On the contrary, blessed are [a]those who hear the word of God and observe it."

29 As the crowds were increasing, He began to say, "[a]This generation is a wicked generation; it [b]seeks for a [1]sign, and *yet* no [1]sign will be given to it but the [1]sign of Jonah.

30 "For just as [a]Jonah became a [1]sign to the Ninevites, so will the Son of Man be to this generation.

31 "The [a]Queen of the South will rise up with the men of this generation at the judgment and condemn them, because she came from the ends of the earth to hear the wisdom of Solomon; and behold, something greater than Solomon is here.

32 "The men of Nineveh will stand up with this generation at the judgment and condemn it, because [a]they repented at the preaching of Jonah; and behold, something greater than Jonah is here.

33 "[a]No one, after lighting a lamp, puts it away in a cellar nor under a basket, but on the lampstand, so that those who enter may see the light.

34 "[a]The eye is the lamp of your body; when your eye is [1]clear, your whole body also is full of light; but when it is [2]bad, your body also is full of darkness.

35 "Then watch out that the light in you is not darkness.

16 [1]Lit *testing* [2]Or *attesting miracle* [a]Matt 12:38; 16:1; Mark 8:11

17 [1]Lit *every* [2]Lit *a house* [a]Luke 11:17-22: *Matt 12:25-29; Mark 3:23-27*

18 [a]Matt 4:10 [b]Matt 10:25

19 [a]Matt 10:25

20 [a]Ex 8:19 [b]Matt 3:2

21 [1]Lit *the* [2]Lit *in peace*

23 [a]Matt 12:30; Mark 9:40

24 [1]Lit *the* [a]Luke 11:24-26: *Matt 12:43-45*

27 [1]Lit *He* [a]Luke 23:29

28 [a]Luke 8:21

29 [1]Or *attesting miracle* [a]Luke 11:29-32: *Matt 12:39-42;* Matt 16:4; Mark 8:12 [b]Matt 12:38; Luke 11:16

30 [1]Or *attesting miracle* [a]Jon 3:4

31 [a]1 Kin 10:1-10; 2 Chr 9:1-12

32 [a]Jon 3:5

33 [a]Matt 5:15; Mark 4:21; Luke 8:16

34 [1]Or *healthy* [2]Or *evil* [a]Luke 11:34, 35: *Matt 6:22, 23*

36 "If therefore your whole body is full of light, with no dark
part in it, it will be wholly illumined, as when the lamp illumines
you with its rays."
37 Now when He had spoken, a Pharisee *asked Him to have
lunch with him; and He went in, and reclined *at the table.*
38 When the Pharisee saw it, he was surprised that He had
not first [1a]ceremonially washed before the [2]meal.
39 But [a]the Lord said to him, "Now [b]you Pharisees clean the
outside of the cup and of the platter; but [1]inside of you, you are
full of robbery and wickedness.
40 "[a]You foolish ones, did not He who made the outside make
the inside also?
41 "But [a]give that which is within as charity, and [1]then all
things are [b]clean for you.
42 "[a]But woe to you Pharisees! For you [b]pay tithe of mint and
rue and every *kind of* garden herb, and *yet* disregard justice
and the love of God; but these are the things you should have
done without neglecting the others.
43 "Woe to you Pharisees! For you [a]love the chief seats in the
synagogues and the respectful greetings in the market places.
44 "[a]Woe to you! For you are like [1]concealed tombs, and the
people who walk over *them* are unaware *of it.*"
45 One of the [1a]lawyers *said to Him in reply, "Teacher, when
You say this, You insult us too."
46 But He said, "Woe to you [a]lawyers as well! For [b]you weigh
men down with burdens hard to bear, [1]while you yourselves
will not even touch the burdens with one of your fingers.
47 "[a]Woe to you! For you build the [1]tombs of the prophets, and
it was your fathers *who* killed them.
48 "So you are witnesses and approve the deeds of your fathers;
because it was they who killed them, and you build *their tombs.*
49 "For this reason also [a]the wisdom of God said, '[b]I will send
to them prophets and apostles, and *some* of them they will kill
and *some* they will [1]persecute,
50 so that the blood of all the prophets, shed [a]since the foundation
of the world, may be [1]charged against this generation,
51 from [a]the blood of Abel to [b]the blood of Zechariah, who
was killed between the altar and the house *of God;* yes, I tell
you, it shall be [1]charged against this generation.'
52 "Woe to you [1a]lawyers! For you have taken away the key of
knowledge; [b]you yourselves did not enter, and you hindered
those who were entering."
53 When He left there, the scribes and the Pharisees began to
be very hostile and to question Him closely on many subjects,
54 [a]plotting against Him [b]to catch [1]*Him* in something He
might say.

Chapter 12 Theme ______________________________

12 Under these circumstances, after [1]so many thousands of
[2]people had gathered together that they were stepping

38 [1]Lit *baptized* [2]Or *lunch* [a]Matt 15:2; Mark 7:3f

39 [1]Lit *your inside is full* [a]Luke 7:13 [b]Matt 23:25f

40 [a]Luke 12:20; 1 Cor 15:36

41 [1]Lit *behold* [a]Luke 12:33; 16:9 [b]Mark 7:19; Titus 1:15

42 [a]Matt 23:23 [b]Lev 27:30; Luke 18:12

43 [a]Matt 23:6f; Mark 12:38f; Luke 14:7; 20:46

44 [1]Or *indistinct, unseen* [a]Matt 23:27

45 [1]I.e. experts in the Mosaic Law [a]Matt 22:35; Luke 11:46, 52

46 [1]Lit *and* [a]Matt 22:35; Luke 11:45, 52 [b]Matt 23:4

47 [1]Or *monuments to* [a]Matt 23:29ff

49 [1]Or *drive out* [a]1 Cor 1:24, 30; Col 2:3 [b]Matt 23:34-36

50 [1]Or *required of* [a]Matt 25:34

51 [1]Or *required of* [a]Gen 4:8 [b]2 Chr 24:20, 21

52 [1]I.e. experts in the Mosaic Law [a]Matt 22:35; Luke 11:45, 46 [b]Matt 23:13

54 [1]Lit *something out of His mouth* [a]Mark 3:2; Luke 20:20; Acts 23:21 [b]Mark 12:13

12:1 [1]Lit *myriads* [2]Lit *the crowd*

on one another, He began saying to His disciples first *of all,*
"[a]Beware of the leaven of the Pharisees, which is hypocrisy.
2 "[a]But there is nothing covered up that will not be revealed,
and hidden that will not be known.
3 "Accordingly, whatever you have said in the dark will be
heard in the light, and what you have [1]whispered in the inner
rooms will be proclaimed upon [a]the housetops.
4 "I say to you, [a]My friends, do not be afraid of those who kill
the body and after that have no more that they can do.
5 "But I will [1]warn you whom to fear: [a]fear the One who,
after He has killed, has authority to cast into [2b]hell; yes, I tell
you, fear Him!
6 "Are not [a]five sparrows sold for two [1]cents? *Yet* not one of
them is forgotten before God.
7 "[a]Indeed, the very hairs of your head are all numbered. Do
not fear; you are more valuable than many sparrows.
8 "And I say to you, everyone who [a]confesses Me before men,
the Son of Man will confess him also before the angels of God;
9 but [a]he who denies Me before men will be denied [b]before
the angels of God.
10 "[a]And everyone who [1]speaks a word against the Son of
Man, it will be forgiven him; but he who blasphemes against
the Holy Spirit, it will not be forgiven him.
11 "When they bring you before [a]the synagogues and the rulers
and the authorities, do not [b]worry about how or what you are
to speak in your defense, or what you are to say;
12 for [a]the Holy Spirit will teach you in that very hour what
you ought to say."
13 Someone [1]in the crowd said to Him, "Teacher, tell my
brother to divide the *family* inheritance with me."
14 But He said to him, "[a]Man, who appointed Me a judge or
arbitrator over you?"
15 Then He said to them, "[a]Beware, and be on your guard
against every form of greed; for not *even* when one has an
abundance does his life consist of his possessions."
16 And He told them a parable, saying, "The land of a rich
man was very productive.
17 "And he began reasoning to himself, saying, 'What shall I
do, since I have no place to store my crops?'
18 "Then he said, 'This is what I will do: I will tear down my
barns and build larger ones, and there I will store all my grain
and my goods.
19 'And I will say to my soul, "Soul, [a]you have many goods laid
up for many years *to come;* take your ease, eat, drink *and* be
merry."'
20 "But God said to him, '[a]You fool! This *very* night [1b]your soul is
required of you; and [c]*now* who will own what you have prepared?'
21 "So is the man who [a]stores up treasure for himself, and is
not rich toward God."
22 And He said to His disciples, "[a]For this reason I say to you,
[1]do not worry about *your* [2]life, *as to* what you will eat; nor for
your body, *as to* what you will put on.

12:1 [a]Matt 16:6, 11f; Mark 8:15
2 [a]Luke 12:2-9: *Matt 10:26-33;* Matt 10:26; Mark 4:22; Luke 8:17
3 [1]Lit *spoken in the ear* [a]Matt 10:27; 24:17
4 [a]John 15:13-15
5 [1]Or *show* [2]Gr *Gehenna* [a]Heb 10:31 [b]Matt 5:22
6 [1]Gr *assaria,* the smallest of copper coins [a]Matt 10:29
7 [a]Matt 10:30
8 [a]Matt 10:32; Luke 15:10; Rom 10:9
9 [a]Matt 10:33; Luke 9:26 [b]Luke 15:10
10 [1]Lit *will speak* [a]Matt 12:31, 32; Mark 3:28-30
11 [a]Matt 10:17 [b]Matt 6:25; 10:19; Mark 13:11; Luke 12:22; 21:14
12 [a]Matt 10:20; Luke 21:15
13 [1]Lit *out of*
14 [a]Mic 6:8; Rom 2:1, 3; 9:20
15 [a]1 Tim 6:6-10
19 [a]Eccl 11:9
20 [1]Lit *they are demanding your soul from you* [a]Jer 17:11; Luke 11:40 [b]Job 27:8 [c]Ps 39:6
21 [a]Luke 12:33
22 [1]Or *stop being worried* [2]Lit *soul* [a]Luke 12:22-31: *Matt 6:25-33*

23 "For life is more than food, and the body more than
clothing.
24 "Consider the [a]ravens, for they neither sow nor reap; they
have no storeroom nor [b]barn, and *yet* God feeds them; how
much more valuable you are than the birds!
25 "And which of you by worrying can add a *single* [1a]hour to
his [2]life's span?
26 "If then you cannot do even a very little thing, why do you
worry about other matters?
27 "Consider the lilies, how they grow: they neither toil nor
spin; but I tell you, not even [a]Solomon in all his glory clothed
himself like one of these.
28 "But if God so clothes the grass in the field, which is *alive*
today and tomorrow is thrown into the furnace, how much
more *will He clothe* you? [a]You men of little faith!
29 "And do not seek what you will eat and what you will drink,
and do not [a]keep worrying.
30 "For [1]all these things the nations of the world eagerly seek;
but your Father knows that you need these things.
31 "But seek His kingdom, and [a]these things will be added to
you.
32 "[a]Do not be afraid, [b]little flock, for [c]your Father has chosen
gladly to give you the kingdom.
33 "[a]Sell your possessions and give to charity; make yourselves
money belts which do not wear out, [b]an unfailing treasure in
heaven, where no thief comes near nor moth destroys.
34 "For [a]where your treasure is, there your heart will be also.
35 "[1a]Be dressed in [b]readiness, and *keep* your lamps lit.
36 "Be like men who are waiting for their master when he
returns from the wedding feast, so that they may immediately
open *the door* to him when he comes and knocks.
37 "Blessed are those slaves whom the master will find [a]on the
alert when he comes; truly I say to you, that [b]he will gird
himself *to serve,* and have them recline *at the table,* and will
come up and wait on them.
38 "[a]Whether he comes in the [1]second watch, or even in the
[2]third, and finds *them* so, blessed are those *slaves.*
39 "[a]But [1]be sure of this, that if the head of the house had
known at what hour the thief was coming, he would not have
allowed his house to be [2b]broken into.
40 "[a]You too, be ready; for the Son of Man is coming at an hour
that you do not [1]expect."
41 Peter said, "Lord, are You addressing this parable to us, or
[a]to everyone *else* as well?"
42 And [a]the Lord said, "[b]Who then is the faithful and sensible
[c]steward, whom his master will put in charge of his [1]servants,
to give them their rations at the proper time?
43 "Blessed is that [a]slave whom his [1]master finds so doing
when he comes.
44 "Truly I say to you that he will put him in charge of all his
possessions.

24 [a]Job 38:41 [b]Luke 12:18

25 [1]Lit *cubit* (approx 18 in.) [2]Or *height* [a]Ps 39:5

27 [a]1 Kin 10:4-7; 2 Chr 9:3-6

28 [a]Matt 6:30

29 [a]Matt 6:31

30 [1]Or *these things all the nations of the world*

31 [a]Matt 6:33

32 [a]Matt 14:27 [b]John 21:15-17 [c]Eph 1:5, 9

33 [a]Matt 19:21; Luke 11:41; 18:22 [b]Matt 6:20; Luke 12:21

34 [a]Matt 6:21

35 [1]Lit *Let your loins be girded* [a]Matt 25:1ff [b]Eph 6:14; 1 Pet 1:13

37 [a]Matt 24:42 [b]Luke 17:8; John 13:4

38 [1]I.e. 9 p.m. to midnight [2]I.e. midnight to 3 a.m. [a]Matt 24:43

39 [1]Lit *know* [2]Lit *dug through* [a]Luke 12:39, 40: *Matt 24:43, 44* [b]Matt 6:19

40 [1]Lit *think, suppose* [a]Mark 13:33; Luke 21:36

41 [a]Luke 12:47, 48

42 [1]Lit *service* [a]Luke 7:13 [b]Luke 12:42-46: *Matt 24:45-51* [c]Matt 24:45; Luke 16:1ff

43 [1]Or *lord* [a]Luke 12:42

45 [1]Lit *is delaying to come*
45 "But if that slave says in his heart, 'My master [1]will be a
long time in coming,' and begins to beat the slaves, *both* men
and women, and to eat and drink and get drunk;
47 [a]Deut 25:2; James 4:17
46 the master of that slave will come on a day when he does
not expect *him* and at an hour he does not know, and will cut
him in pieces, and assign him a place with the unbelievers.
48 [1]Lit *blows* [a]Lev 5:17; Num 15:29f [b]Matt 13:12
47 "And that slave who knew his master's will and did not get
ready or act in accord with his will, will [a]receive many lashes,
48 but the one who did not [a]know *it,* and committed deeds
worthy of [1]a flogging, will receive but few. [b]From everyone
who has been given much, much will be required; and to
49 [1]Or *came* [2]Lit *what do I wish if . . . ?*
whom they entrusted much, of him they will ask all the more.
49 "I [1]have come to cast fire upon the earth; and [2]how I wish it
were already kindled!
50 [1]Lit *be baptized with* [a]Mark 10:38
50 "But I have a [a]baptism to [1]undergo, and how distressed I am
until it is accomplished!
51 "[a]Do you suppose that I came to grant peace on earth? I tell
you, no, but rather division;
51 [a]Luke 12:51-53: *Matt 10:34-36*
52 for from now on five *members* in one household will be
divided, three against two and two against three.
53 "They will be divided, [a]father against son and son against
53 [a]Mic 7:6; Matt 10:21
father, mother against daughter and daughter against mother,
mother-in-law against daughter-in-law and daughter-in-law
against mother-in-law."
54 [a]Matt 16:2f
54 And He was also saying to the crowds, "[a]When you see a
cloud rising in the west, immediately you say, 'A shower is
coming,' and so it turns out.
55 [a]Matt 20:12
55 "And when *you see* a south wind blowing, you say, 'It will
be a [a]hot day,' and it turns out *that way.*
56 [1]Lit *how* [a]Matt 16:3
56 "You hypocrites! [a]You know how to analyze the appearance of
the earth and the sky, but [1]why do you not analyze this present
time?
57 "And [a]why do you not even on your own initiative judge
57 [a]Luke 21:30
what is right?
58 "For [a]while you are going with your opponent to appear before
58 [1]Lit *be released from him* [a]Luke 12:58, 59: *Matt 5:25, 26*
the magistrate, on *your* way *there* make an effort to [1]settle with
him, so that he may not drag you before the judge, and the judge
turn you over to the officer, and the officer throw you into prison.
59 "I say to you, you will not get out of there until you have
paid the very last [1a]cent."

59 [1]Gr *lepton;* i.e. 1/128 of a denarius [a]Mark 12:42

Chapter 13 Theme ______________________

13:1 [1]I.e. shed along with [a]Matt 27
13 Now on the same occasion there were some present
who reported to Him about the Galileans whose blood
[a]Pilate had [1]mixed with their sacrifices.
2 And Jesus said to them, "[a]Do you suppose that these
Galileans were *greater* sinners than all *other* Galileans because
2 [a]John 9:2f
they suffered this *fate?*
3 "I tell you, no, but unless you [1]repent, you will all likewise
3 [1]Or *are repentant*
perish.

4 "Or do you suppose that those eighteen on whom the tower
in [a]Siloam fell and killed them were *worse* [1b]culprits than all
the men who live in Jerusalem?
5 "I tell you, no, but unless you repent, you will all likewise
perish."
6 And He *began* telling this parable: "A man had [a]a fig tree
which had been planted in his vineyard; and he came looking
for fruit on it and did not find any.
7 "And he said to the vineyard-keeper, 'Behold, for three years
I have come looking for fruit on this fig tree [1]without finding
any. [a]Cut it down! Why does it even use up the ground?'
8 "And he answered and said to him, 'Let it alone, sir, for this
year too, until I dig around it and put in fertilizer;
9 and if it bears fruit next year, *fine;* but if not, cut it down.'"
10 And He was [a]teaching in one of the synagogues on the
Sabbath.
11 And there was a woman who for eighteen years had had [a]a
sickness caused by a spirit; and she was bent double, and could
not straighten up at all.
12 When Jesus saw her, He called her over and said to her,
"Woman, you are freed from your sickness."
13 And He [a]laid His hands on her; and immediately she was
made erect again and *began* [b]glorifying God.
14 But [a]the synagogue official, indignant because Jesus [b]had
healed on the Sabbath, *began* saying to the crowd in response,
"[c]There are six days in which work should be done; so come
during them and get healed, and not on the Sabbath day."
15 But [a]the Lord answered him and said, "You hypocrites, [b]does
not each of you on the Sabbath untie his ox or his donkey from
the stall and lead him away to water *him?*
16 "And this woman, [a]a daughter of Abraham as she is, whom
[b]Satan has bound for eighteen long years, should she not have
been released from this bond on the Sabbath day?"
17 As He said this, all His opponents were being humiliated;
and [a]the entire crowd was rejoicing over all the glorious things
being done by Him.
18 So [a]He was saying, "[b]What is the kingdom of God like, and
to what shall I compare it?
19 "It is like a mustard seed, which a man took and threw into
his own garden; and it grew and became a tree, and [a]THE BIRDS
OF THE [1]AIR NESTED IN ITS BRANCHES."
20 And again He said, "[a]To what shall I compare the kingdom
of God?
21 "[a]It is like leaven, which a woman took and hid in [b]three
[1]pecks of flour until it was all leavened."
22 And He was passing through from one city and village to
another, teaching, and [a]proceeding on His way to Jerusalem.
23 And someone said to Him, "Lord, are there *just* a few who
are being saved?" And He said to them,
24 "[a]Strive to enter through the narrow door; for many, I tell
you, will seek to enter and will not be able.

4 [1]Lit *debtors* [a]Neh 3:15; Is 8:6; John 9:7, 11 [b]Matt 6:12; Luke 11:4

6 [a]Matt 21:19

7 [1]Lit *and I do not find* [a]Matt 3:10; 7:19; Luke 3:9

10 [a]Matt 4:23

11 [a]Luke 13:16

13 [a]Mark 5:23 [b]Matt 9:8

14 [a]Mark 5:22 [b]Matt 12:2; Luke 14:3 [c]Ex 20:9; Deut 5:13

15 [a]Luke 7:13 [b]Luke 14:5

16 [a]Luke 19:9 [b]Matt 4:10; Luke 13:11

17 [a]Luke 18:43

18 [a]Luke 13:18, 19: *Matt 13:31, 32; Mark 4:30-32* [b]Matt 13:24; Luke 13:20

19 [1]Or *sky* [a]Ezek 17:23

20 [a]Matt 13:24; Luke 13:18

21 [1]Gr *sata* [a]Luke 13:20, 21: *Matt 13:33* [b]Matt 13:33

22 [a]Luke 9:51

24 [a]Matt 7:13

25 [a]Matt 25:10 [b]Matt 7:22; 25:11 [c]Matt 7:23; 25:12; Luke 13:27

25 "Once the head of the house gets up and [a]shuts the door,
and you begin to stand outside and knock on the door, saying,
'[b]Lord, open up to us!' then He will answer and say to you, '[c]I
do not know where you are from.'

26 [a]Luke 3:8

26 "Then you will [a]begin to say, 'We ate and drank in Your
presence, and You taught in our streets';

27 [a]Luke 13:25 [b]Ps 6:8; Matt 25:41

27 and He will say, 'I tell you, [a]I do not know where you are
from; [b]DEPART FROM ME, ALL YOU EVILDOERS.'

28 [a]Matt 8:12; 22:13; 25:30

28 "[a]In that place there will be weeping and gnashing of teeth
when you see Abraham and Isaac and Jacob and all the prophets
in the kingdom of God, but yourselves being thrown out.

29 [a]Matt 8:11

29 "And they [a]will come from east and west and from north
and south, and will recline *at the table* in the kingdom of God.

30 [a]Matt 19:30; 20:16; Mark 10:31

30 "And behold, [a]*some* are last who will be first and *some* are
first who will be last."

31 [a]Matt 14:1; Luke 3:1; 9:7; 23:7

31 Just at that time some Pharisees approached, saying to
Him, "Go away, leave here, for [a]Herod wants to kill You."

32 [1]Or *am perfected* [a]Heb 2:10; 5:9; 7:28

32 And He said to them, "Go and tell that fox, 'Behold, I cast
out demons and perform cures today and tomorrow, and the
third *day* I [1a]reach My goal.'

33 [a]John 11:9 [b]Matt 21:11

33 "Nevertheless [a]I must journey on today and tomorrow and
the next *day;* for it cannot be that a [b]prophet would perish
outside of Jerusalem.

34 [a]Luke 13:34, 35: *Matt 23:37-39;* Luke 19:41 [b]Matt 23:37

34 "[a]O Jerusalem, Jerusalem, *the city* that kills the prophets and
stones those sent to her! How often I wanted to gather your
children together, [b]just as a hen *gathers* her brood under her
wings, and you would not *have it!*

35 [a]Ps 118:26; Matt 21:9; Luke 19:38

35 "Behold, your house is left to you *desolate;* and I say to you,
you will not see Me until *the time* comes when you say,
'[a]BLESSED IS HE WHO COMES IN THE NAME OF THE LORD!'"

Chapter 14 Theme ______________________

14:1 [1]I.e. members of the Sanhedrin [a]Mark 3:2

14 It happened that when He went into the house of one of
the [1]leaders of the Pharisees on *the* Sabbath to eat bread,
[a]they were watching Him closely.

2 [1]Lit *behold*

2 And [1]there in front of Him was a man suffering from dropsy.

3 [1]I.e. experts in Mosaic Law [a]Matt 22:35 [b]Matt 12:2; Luke 13:14

3 And Jesus answered and spoke to the [1a]lawyers and
Pharisees, saying, "[b]Is it lawful to heal on the Sabbath, or not?"
4 But they kept silent. And He took hold of him and healed
him, and sent him away.

5 [1]Lit *Whose son of you . . . will fall* [a]Matt 12:11; Luke 13:15

5 And He said to them, "[1a]Which one of you will have a son
or an ox fall into a well, and will not immediately pull him out
on a Sabbath day?"

6 [a]Matt 22:46; Luke 20:40

6 [a]And they could make no reply to this.

7 [a]Matt 23:6

7 And He *began* speaking a parable to the invited guests
when He noticed how [a]they had been picking out the places of
honor *at the table,* saying to them,

8 [1]Lit *recline at* [a]Prov 25:6, 7

8 "When you are invited by someone to a wedding feast, [a]do
not [1]take the place of honor, for someone more distinguished
than you may have been invited by him,

9 and he who invited you both will come and say to you,
'Give *your* place to this man,' and then [a]in disgrace you [1]proceed
to occupy the last place.
10 "But when you are invited, go and recline at the last place,
so that when the one who has invited you comes, he may say
to you, 'Friend, [a]move up higher'; then you will have honor in
the sight of all who [1]are at the table with you.
11 "[a]For everyone who exalts himself will be humbled, and he
who humbles himself will be exalted."
12 And He also went on to say to the one who had invited
Him, "When you give a luncheon or a dinner, do not invite your
friends or your brothers or your relatives or rich neighbors,
otherwise they may also invite you in return and *that* will be
your repayment.
13 "But when you give a [1]reception, invite *the* poor, *the* crippled,
the lame, *the* blind,
14 and you will be blessed, since they [1]do not have *the means*
to repay you; for you will be repaid at [a]the resurrection of the
righteous."
15 When one of those who were reclining *at the table* with
Him heard this, he said to Him, "[a]Blessed is everyone who will
eat bread in the kingdom of God!"
16 But He said to him, "[a]A man was giving a big dinner, and
he invited many;
17 and at the dinner hour he sent his slave to say to those
who had been invited, 'Come; for everything is ready now.'
18 "But they all alike began to make excuses. The first one said
to him, 'I have bought a [1]piece of land and I need to go out and
look at it; [2]please consider me excused.'
19 "Another one said, 'I have bought five yoke of oxen, and I
am going to try them out; [1]please consider me excused.'
20 "Another one said, '[a]I have married a wife, and for that
reason I cannot come.'
21 "And the slave came *back* and reported this to his master.
Then the head of the household became angry and said to his
slave, 'Go out at once into the streets and lanes of the city and
bring in here the poor and crippled and blind and lame.'
22 "And the slave said, 'Master, what you commanded has
been done, and still there is room.'
23 "And the master said to the slave, 'Go out into the highways
and along the hedges, and compel *them* to come in, so that my
house may be filled.
24 'For I tell you, none of those men who were invited shall taste
of my dinner.'"
25 Now [1]large crowds were going along with Him; and He
turned and said to them,
26 "[a]If anyone comes to Me, and does not [1]hate his own father
and mother and wife and children and brothers and sisters,
yes, and even his own life, he cannot be My disciple.
27 "Whoever does not [a]carry his own cross and come after Me
cannot be My disciple.

9 [1]Lit *begin* [a]Luke 3:8

10 [1]Lit *recline* at the table [a]Prov 25:6, 7

11 [a]2 Sam 22:28; Prov 29:23; Matt 23:12; Luke 1:52; 18:14; James 4:10

13 [1]Or *banquet*

14 [1]Or *are unable to* [a]John 5:29; Acts 24:15; Rev 20:4, 5

15 [a]Rev 19:9

16 [a]Matt 22:2-14; Luke 14:16-24

18 [1]Or *field* [2]Lit *I request you*

19 [1]Lit *I request you*

20 [a]Deut 24:5; 1 Cor 7:33

25 [1]Lit *many*

26 [1]I.e. by comparison of his love for Me [a]Matt 10:37

27 [a]Matt 10:38; 16:24; Mark 8:34; Luke 9:23

28 "For which one of you, when he wants to build a tower,
does not first sit down and calculate the cost to see if he has
enough to complete it?
29 "Otherwise, when he has laid a foundation and is not able
to finish, all who observe it begin to ridicule him,
30 saying, 'This man began to build and was not able to finish.'
31 "Or what king, when he sets out to meet another king in
battle, will not first sit down and [a]consider whether he is
strong enough with ten thousand *men* to encounter the one
coming against him with twenty thousand?
32 "Or else, while the other is still far away, he sends [1]a
delegation and asks for terms of peace.
33 "So then, none of you can be My disciple who [a]does not
give up all his own possessions.
34 "Therefore, salt is good; but [a]if even salt has become tasteless,
with what will it be seasoned?
35 "It is useless either for the soil or for the manure pile; it is
thrown out. [a]He who has ears to hear, [1]let him hear."

Chapter 15 Theme

15 Now all the [a]tax collectors and the [1]sinners were coming
near Him to listen to Him.
2 Both the Pharisees and the scribes *began* to grumble,
saying, "This man receives sinners and [a]eats with them."
3 So He told them this parable, saying,
4 "[a]What man among you, if he has a hundred sheep and has
lost one of them, does not leave the ninety-nine in the [1]open
pasture and go after the one which is lost until he finds it?
5 "When he has found it, he lays it on his shoulders, rejoicing.
6 "And when he comes home, he calls together his friends
and his neighbors, saying to them, 'Rejoice with me, for I have
found my sheep which was lost!'
7 "I tell you that in the same way, there will be *more* joy in
heaven over one sinner who repents than over ninety-nine
righteous persons who need no repentance.
8 "Or what woman, if she has ten [1]silver coins and loses one
coin, does not light a lamp and sweep the house and search
carefully until she finds it?
9 "When she has found it, she calls together her friends and
neighbors, saying, 'Rejoice with me, for I have found the coin
which I had lost!'
10 "In the same way, I tell you, there is joy [a]in the presence of
the angels of God over one sinner who repents."
11 And He said, "A man had two sons.
12 "The younger of them said to his father, 'Father, give me [a]the
share of the estate that falls to me.' So he divided his [1b]wealth
between them.
13 "And not many days later, the younger son gathered
everything together and went on a journey into a distant
country, and there he squandered his estate with loose living.

31 [a]Prov 20:18
32 [1]Or *an embassy*
33 [a]Phil 3:7; Heb 11:26
34 [a]Matt 5:13; Mark 9:50
35 [1]Or *hear!* Or *listen!* [a]Matt 11:15
15:1 [1]I.e. irreligious Jews [a]Luke 5:29
2 [a]Matt 9:11
4 [1]Lit *wilderness* [a]Matt 18:12-14; Luke 15:4-7
8 [1]Gr *drachmas,* one drachma was a day's wages
10 [a]Matt 10:32; Luke 15:7
12 [1]Lit *living* [a]Deut 21:17 [b]Mark 12:44; Luke 15:30

14 "Now when he had spent everything, a severe famine
occurred in that country, and he began to be impoverished.
15 "So he went and [1]hired himself out to one of the citizens of
that country, and he sent him into his fields to feed swine.
16 "And he would have gladly filled his stomach with the [1]pods
that the swine were eating, and no one was giving *anything* to
him.
17 "But when he came to [1]his senses, he said, 'How many of
my father's hired men have more than enough bread, but I am
dying here with hunger!
18 'I will get up and go to my father, and will say to him,
"Father, I have sinned against heaven, and [1]in your sight;
19 I am no longer worthy to be called your son; make me as
one of your hired men."'
20 "So he got up and came to [1]his father. But while he was still
a long way off, his father saw him and felt compassion *for him*,
and ran and [2a]embraced him and kissed him.
21 "And the son said to him, 'Father, I have sinned against heaven
and in your sight; I am no longer worthy to be called your son.'
22 "But the father said to his slaves, 'Quickly bring out [a]the
best robe and put it on him, and [b]put a ring on his hand and
sandals on his feet;
23 and bring the fattened calf, kill it, and let us eat and celebrate;
24 for this son of mine was [a]dead and has come to life again;
he was lost and has been found.' And they began to celebrate.
25 "Now his older son was in the field, and when he came and
approached the house, he heard music and dancing.
26 "And he summoned one of the servants and *began* inquiring
what these things could be.
27 "And he said to him, 'Your brother has come, and your
father has killed the fattened calf because he has received him
back safe and sound.'
28 "But he became angry and was not willing to go in; and his
father came out and *began* pleading with him.
29 "But he answered and said to his father, 'Look! For so many
years I have been serving you and I have never [1]neglected a
command of yours; and *yet* you have never given me a young
goat, so that I might celebrate with my friends;
30 but when this son of yours came, who has devoured your
[1a]wealth with prostitutes, you killed the fattened calf for him.'
31 "And he said to him, 'Son, you [1]have always been with me,
and all that is mine is yours.
32 'But we had to celebrate and rejoice, for this brother of
yours was [a]dead and *has begun* to live, and *was* lost and has
been found.'"

Chapter 16 Theme ______________________________

16 Now He was also saying to the disciples, "There was a
rich man who had a manager, and this *manager* was
[1]reported to him as [a]squandering his possessions.

15 [1]Lit *was joined to*

16 [1]I.e. of the carob tree

17 [1]Lit *himself*

18 [1]Lit *before you*

20 [1]Lit *his own* [2]Lit *fell on his neck* [a]Gen 45:14; 46:29; Acts 20:37

22 [a]Zech 3:4; Rev 6:11 [b]Gen 41:42

24 [a]Matt 8:22; Luke 9:60; 15:32; Rom 11:15; Eph 2:1, 5; 5:14; Col 2:13; 1 Tim 5:6

29 [1]Or *disobeyed*

30 [1]Lit *living* [a]Prov 29:3; Luke 15:12

31 [1]Lit *are always with me*

32 [a]Luke 15:24

16:1 [1]Or *accused* [a]Luke 15:13

2 "And he called him and said to him, 'What is this I hear about you? Give an accounting of your management, for you can no longer be manager.'

3 "The manager said to himself, 'What shall I do, since my [1]master is taking the management away from me? I am not strong enough to dig; I am ashamed to beg.

4 'I know what I shall do, so that when I am removed from the management people will welcome me into their homes.'

5 "And he summoned each one of his [1]master's debtors, and he *began* saying to the first, 'How much do you owe my master?'

6 "And he said, 'A hundred [1]measures of oil.' And he said to him, 'Take your bill, and sit down quickly and write fifty.'

7 "Then he said to another, 'And how much do you owe?' And he said, 'A hundred [1]measures of wheat.' He *said to him, 'Take your bill, and write eighty.'

8 "And his [1]master praised the unrighteous manager because he had acted shrewdly; for the sons of [a]this age are more shrewd in relation to their own [2]kind than the [b]sons of light.

9 "And I say to you, [a]make friends for yourselves by means of the [1b]wealth of unrighteousness, so that when it fails, [c]they will receive you into the eternal dwellings.

10 "[a]He who is faithful in a very little thing is faithful also in much; and he who is unrighteous in a very little thing is unrighteous also in much.

11 "Therefore if you have not been faithful in the *use of* unrighteous [1a]wealth, who will entrust the true *riches* to you?

12 "And if you have not been faithful in *the use of* that which is another's, who will give you that which is your own?

13 "[a]No [1]servant can serve two masters; for either he will hate the one and love the other, or else he will be devoted to one and despise the other. You cannot serve God and [2b]wealth."

14 Now the Pharisees, who were [a]lovers of money, were listening to all these things and [b]were scoffing at Him.

15 And He said to them, "You are those who [a]justify yourselves [1]in the sight of men, but [b]God knows your hearts; for that which is highly esteemed among men is detestable [1]in the sight of God.

16 "[a]The Law and the Prophets *were proclaimed* until John; since that time [b]the gospel of the kingdom of God [1]has been preached, and everyone is forcing his way into it.

17 "[a]But it is easier for heaven and earth to pass away than for one [1]stroke of a letter of the Law to fail.

18 "[a]Everyone who [1]divorces his wife and marries another commits adultery, and he who marries one who is [2]divorced from a husband commits adultery.

19 "Now there was a rich man, and he habitually dressed in purple and fine linen, joyously living in splendor every day.

20 "And a poor man named Lazarus [a]was laid at his gate, covered with sores,

21 and longing to be fed with the *crumbs* which were falling from the rich man's table; besides, even the dogs were coming and licking his sores.

3 [1]Or *lord*

5 [1]Or *lord's*

6 [1]Gr *baths,* a Heb unit of measure equaling about 7 1/2 gal.

7 [1]Gr *kors,* one kor equals between 10 and 12 bu

8 [1]Or *lord* [2]Lit *generation* [a]Matt 12:32; Luke 20:34 [b]John 12:36; Eph 5:8; 1 Thess 5:5

9 [1]Gr *mamonas,* for Aram *mamon* (mammon); i.e. wealth, etc, personified as an object of worship [a]Matt 19:21; Luke 11:41; 12:33 [b]Matt 6:24; Luke 16:11, 13 [c]Luke 16:4

10 [a]Matt 25:21, 23

11 [1]Gr *mamonas,* for Aram *mamon* (mammon); i.e. wealth, etc, personified as an object of worship [a]Luke 16:9

13 [1]Or *house-servant* [2]Gr *mamonas,* for Aram *mamon* (mammon); i.e. wealth, etc, personified as an object of worship [a]Matt 6:24 [b]Luke 16:9

14 [a]2 Tim 3:2 [b]Luke 23:35

15 [1]Lit *before* [a]Luke 10:29; 18:9, 14 [b]1 Sam 16:7; Prov 21:2; Acts 1:24; Rom 8:27

16 [1]Lit *is preached* [a]Matt 11:12f [b]Matt 4:23

17 [1]I.e. projection of a letter (serif) [a]Matt 5:18

18 [1]Or *sends away* [2]Or *sent away* [a]Matt 5:32; 1 Cor 7:10, 11

20 [a]Acts 3:2

22 "Now the poor man died and was carried away by the angels
to [a]Abraham's bosom; and the rich man also died and was buried.
23 "In [a]Hades he lifted up his eyes, being in torment, and *saw
Abraham far away and Lazarus in his bosom.
24 "And he cried out and said, '[a]Father Abraham, have mercy
on me, and send Lazarus so that he may dip the tip of his finger
in water and cool off my tongue, for I am in agony in [b]this flame.'
25 "But Abraham said, 'Child, remember that [a]during your life
you received your good things, and likewise Lazarus bad things;
but now he is being comforted here, and you are in agony.
26 'And [1]besides all this, between us and you there is a great
chasm fixed, so that those who wish to come over from here to
you will not be able, and *that* none may cross over from there
to us.'
27 "And he said, 'Then I beg you, father, that you send him to
my father's house—
28 for I have five brothers—in order that he may [a]warn them,
so that they will not also come to this place of torment.'
29 "But Abraham *said, 'They have [a]Moses and the Prophets;
let them hear them.'
30 "But he said, 'No, [a]father Abraham, but if someone goes to
them from the dead, they will repent!'
31 "But he said to him, 'If they do not listen to Moses and the
Prophets, they will not be persuaded even if someone rises
from the dead.'"

Chapter 17 Theme ____________________

17 He said to His disciples, "[a]It is inevitable that [1]stumbling
blocks come, but woe to him through whom they come!
2 "[a]It [1]would be better for him if a millstone were hung
around his neck and he were thrown into the sea, than that he
would cause one of these little ones to stumble.
3 "[1]Be on your guard! [a]If your brother sins, rebuke him; and if
he repents, forgive him.
4 "And if he sins against you [a]seven times a day, and returns
to you seven times, saying, 'I repent,' [1]forgive him."
5 [a]The apostles said to [b]the Lord, "Increase our faith!"
6 And [a]the Lord said, "If you [1]had faith like [b]a mustard seed,
you would say to this [c]mulberry tree, 'Be uprooted and be
planted in the sea'; and it would [2]obey you.
7 "Which of you, having a slave plowing or tending sheep,
will say to him when he has come in from the field, 'Come
immediately and [1]sit down to eat'?
8 "But will he not say to him, '[a]Prepare something for me to
eat, and *properly* [1]clothe yourself and serve me while I eat and
drink; and [2]afterward you [3]may eat and drink'?
9 "He does not thank the slave because he did the things
which were commanded, does he?
10 "So you too, when you do all the things which are commanded
you, say, 'We are unworthy slaves; we have done *only* that
which we ought to have done.'"

22 [a]John 1:18; 13:23

23 [a]Matt 11:23

24 [a]Luke 3:8; 16:30; 19:9 [b]Matt 25:41

25 [a]Luke 6:24

26 [1]Lit *in all these things*

28 [a]Acts 2:40; 8:25; 10:42; 18:5; 20:21ff; 23:11; 28:23; Gal 5:3; Eph 4:17; 1 Thess 2:11; 4:6

29 [a]Luke 4:17; John 5:45-47; Acts 15:21

30 [a]Luke 3:8; 16:24; 19:9

17:1 [1]Or *temptations to sin* [a]Matt 18:7; 1 Cor 11:19; 1 Tim 4:1

2 [1]Lit *is* [a]Matt 18:6; Mark 9:42; 1 Cor 8:12

3 [1]Lit *Take heed to yourselves* [a]Matt 18:15

4 [1]Lit *you shall forgive* [a]Matt 18:21f

5 [a]Mark 6:30 [b]Luke 7:13

6 [1]Lit *have* [2]Lit *have obeyed* [a]Luke 7:13 [b]Matt 13:31; 17:20; Mark 4:31; Luke 13:19 [c]Luke 19:4

7 [1]Lit *recline*

8 [1]Lit *gird* [2]Lit *after these things* [3]Lit *will* [a]Luke 12:37

11 While He was [a]on the way to Jerusalem, [b]He was passing
[1]between Samaria and Galilee.
12 As He entered a village, ten leprous men who [a]stood at a
distance met Him;
13 and they raised their voices, saying, "Jesus, [a]Master, have
mercy on us!"
14 When He saw them, He said to them, "[a]Go and show yourselves to the priests." And as they were going, they were cleansed.
15 Now one of them, when he saw that he had been healed,
turned back, [a]glorifying God with a loud voice,
16 and he fell on his face at His feet, giving thanks to Him.
And he was a [a]Samaritan.
17 Then Jesus answered and said, "Were there not ten cleansed?
But the nine—where are they?
18 "[1]Was no one found who returned to [a]give glory to God,
except this foreigner?"
19 And He said to him, "Stand up and go; [a]your faith [1]has
made you well."
20 Now having been questioned by the Pharisees [a]as to when
the kingdom of God was coming, He answered them and said,
"The kingdom of God is not coming with [1b]signs to be observed;
21 nor will [a]they say, 'Look, here *it is!*' or, 'There *it is!*' For
behold, the kingdom of God is [1]in your midst."
22 And He said to the disciples, "[a]The days will come when
you will long to see one of the days of the Son of Man, and you
will not see it.
23 "[a]They will say to you, 'Look there! Look here!' Do not go
away, and do not run after *them.*
24 "[a]For just like the lightning, when it flashes out of one part
[1]of the sky, shines to the other part [1]of the sky, so will the Son
of Man be in His day.
25 "[a]But first He must suffer many things and be rejected by
this generation.
26 "[a]And just as it happened [b]in the days of Noah, so it will be
also in the days of the Son of Man:
27 they were eating, they were drinking, they were marrying,
they were being given in marriage, until the day that Noah
entered the ark, and the flood came and destroyed them all.
28 "[1]It was the same as happened in [a]the days of Lot: they
were eating, they were drinking, they were buying, they were
selling, they were planting, they were building;
29 but on the day that Lot went out from Sodom it rained fire
and [1]brimstone from heaven and destroyed them all.
30 "It will be [1]just the same on the day that the Son of Man [a]is
revealed.
31 "On that day, the one who is [a]on the housetop and whose
goods are in the house must not go down to take them out; and
likewise the one who is in the field must not turn back.
32 "[a]Remember Lot's wife.
33 "[a]Whoever seeks to keep his [1]life will lose it, and whoever
loses *his life* will preserve it.

11 [1]Lit *through the middle of;* or *along the borders of* [a]Luke 9:51 [b]Luke 9:52ff; John 4:3f
12 [a]Lev 13:45f
13 [a]Luke 5:5
14 [a]Lev 14:1-32; Matt 8:4; Luke 5:14
15 [a]Matt 9:8
16 [a]Matt 10:5
18 [1]Lit *Were there not found those who* [a]Matt 9:8
19 [1]Lit *has saved you* [a]Matt 9:22; Luke 18:42
20 [1]Lit *observation* [a]Luke 19:11; Acts 1:6 [b]Luke 14:1
21 [1]Or *within you* [a]Luke 17:23
22 [a]Matt 9:15; Mark 2:20; Luke 5:35
23 [a]Matt 24:23; Mark 13:21; Luke 21:8
24 [1]Lit *under heaven* [a]Matt 24:27
25 [a]Matt 16:21; Luke 9:22
26 [a]Luke 17:26, 27: *Matt 24:37-39* [b]Gen 6:5-8; 7
28 [1]Lit *In the same way as* [a]Gen 19
29 [1]I.e. burning sulfur
30 [1]Lit *according to the same things* [a]Matt 16:27; 1 Cor 1:7; Col 3:4; 2 Thess 1:7; 1 Pet 1:7; 4:13; 1 John 2:28
31 [a]Matt 24:17, 18; Mark 13:15f; Luke 21:21
32 [a]Gen 19:26
33 [1]Or *soul* [a]Matt 10:39

34 "I tell you, on that night there will be two in one bed; one
will be taken and the other will be left.
35 "[a]There will be two women grinding at the same place; one
will be taken and the other will be left.
36 ["[1a]Two men will be in the field; one will be taken and the
other will be left."]
37 And answering they *said to Him, "Where, Lord?" And He
said to them, "[a]Where the body *is,* there also the [1]vultures will
be gathered."

Chapter 18 Theme ________________________

18 Now He was telling them a parable to show that at all
times they [a]ought to pray and not to [b]lose heart,
2 saying, "In a certain city there was a judge who did not
fear God and did not [a]respect man.
3 "There was a widow in that city, and she kept coming to
him, saying, '[1]Give me legal protection from my opponent.'
4 "For a while he was unwilling; but afterward he said to
himself, 'Even though I do not fear God nor [a]respect man,
5 yet [a]because this widow bothers me, I will [1]give her legal
protection, otherwise by continually coming she will [2b]wear
me out.'"
6 And [a]the Lord said, "Hear what the unrighteous judge *said;
7 now, will not God [a]bring about justice for His [b]elect who
cry to Him day and night, [1]and will He [c]delay long over them?
8 "I tell you that He will bring about justice for them quickly.
However, when the Son of Man comes, [a]will He find [1]faith on
the earth?"
9 And He also told this parable to some people who [a]trusted
in themselves that they were righteous, and [b]viewed others
with contempt:
10 "Two men [a]went up into the temple to pray, one a Pharisee
and the other a tax collector.
11 "The Pharisee [a]stood and was praying this to himself: 'God,
I thank You that I am not like other people: swindlers, unjust,
adulterers, or even like this tax collector.
12 'I [a]fast twice a week; I [b]pay tithes of all that I get.'
13 "But the tax collector, [a]standing some distance away, [b]was
even unwilling to lift up his eyes to heaven, but [c]was beating
his breast, saying, 'God, be [1]merciful to me, the sinner!'
14 "I tell you, this man went to his house justified rather than
the other; [a]for everyone who exalts himself will be humbled,
but he who humbles himself will be exalted."
15 [a]And they were bringing even their babies to Him so that
He would touch them, but when the disciples saw it, they
began rebuking them.
16 But Jesus called for them, saying, "Permit the children to
come to Me, and do not hinder them, for the kingdom of God
belongs to such as these.
17 "Truly I say to you, [a]whoever does not receive the kingdom
of God like a child will not enter it *at all.*"

35 [a]Matt 24:41

36 [1]Early mss do not contain this v [a]Matt 24:40

37 [1]Or *eagles* [a]Matt 24:28

18:1 [a]Luke 11:5-10 [b]2 Cor 4:1

2 [a]Luke 18:4; 20:13; Heb 12:9

3 [1]Lit *Do me justice*

4 [a]Luke 18:2; 20:13; Heb 12:9

5 [1]Lit *do her justice* [2]Lit *hit me under the eye* [a]Luke 11:8 [b]1 Cor 9:27

6 [a]Luke 7:13

7 [1]Or *and yet He is very patient toward them* [a]Rev 6:10 [b]Matt 24:22; Rom 8:33; Col 3:12; 2 Tim 2:10; Titus 1:1 [c]2 Pet 3:9

8 [1]Lit *the faith* [a]Luke 17:26ff

9 [a]Luke 16:15 [b]Rom 14:3, 10

10 [a]1 Kin 10:5; 2 Kin 20:5, 8; Acts 3:1

11 [a]Matt 6:5; Mark 11:25; Luke 22:41

12 [a]Matt 9:14 [b]Luke 11:42

13 [1]Or *propitious* [a]Matt 6:5; Mark 11:25; Luke 22:41 [b]Ezra 9:6 [c]Luke 23:48

14 [a]Matt 23:12; Luke 14:11

15 [a]Luke 18:15-17: *Matt 19:13-15; Mark 10:13-16*

17 [a]Matt 18:3; 19:14; Mark 10:15; 1 Cor 14:20; 1 Pet 2:2

18 [a]A ruler questioned Him, saying, "Good Teacher, what shall
I do to inherit eternal life?"
19 And Jesus said to him, "Why do you call Me good? No one
is good except God alone.
20 "You know the commandments, '[a]DO NOT COMMIT ADULTERY,
DO NOT MURDER, DO NOT STEAL, DO NOT BEAR FALSE WITNESS,
HONOR YOUR FATHER AND MOTHER.'"
21 And he said, "All these things I have kept from *my* youth."
22 When Jesus heard *this,* He said to him, "One thing you still
lack; [a]sell all that you possess and distribute it to the poor, and
you shall have [b]treasure in heaven; and come, follow Me."
23 But when he had heard these things, he became very sad,
for he was extremely rich.
24 And Jesus looked at him and said, "[a]How hard it is for
those who are wealthy to enter the kingdom of God!
25 "For [a]it is easier for a camel to [1]go through the eye of a
needle than for a rich man to enter the kingdom of God."
26 They who heard it said, "Then who can be saved?"
27 But He said, "[a]The things that are impossible with people
are possible with God."
28 Peter said, "Behold, [a]we have left [1]our own *homes* and
followed You."
29 And He said to them, "Truly I say to you, [a]there is no one
who has left house or wife or brothers or parents or children,
for the sake of the kingdom of God,
30 who will not receive many times as much at this time and
in [a]the age to come, eternal life."
31 [a]Then He took the twelve aside and said to them, "Behold,
[b]we are going up to Jerusalem, and [c]all things which are written
through the prophets about the Son of Man will be accomplished.
32 "[a]For He will be [1]handed over to the Gentiles, and will be
mocked and mistreated and spit upon,
33 and after they have scourged Him, they will kill Him; and
the third day He will rise again."
34 But [a]the disciples understood none of these things, and *the
meaning of* this statement was hidden from them, and they did
not comprehend the things that were said.
35 [a]As [1][b]Jesus was approaching Jericho, a blind man was
sitting by the road begging.
36 Now hearing a crowd going by, he *began* to inquire what
this was.
37 They told him that Jesus of Nazareth was passing by.
38 And he called out, saying, "Jesus, [a]Son of David, have mercy
on me!"
39 Those who led the way were sternly telling him to be
quiet; but he kept crying out all the more, "[a]Son of David, have
mercy on me!"
40 And Jesus stopped and commanded that he be brought to
Him; and when he came near, He questioned him,
41 "What do you want Me to do for you?" And he said, "Lord, *I
want* to regain my sight!"

18 [a]Luke 18:18-30: *Matt 19:16-29; Mark 10:17-30;* Luke 10:25-28
20 [a]Ex 20:12-16; Deut 5:16-20
22 [a]Matt 19:21; Luke 12:33 [b]Matt 6:20
24 [a]Matt 19:23; Mark 10:23f
25 [1]Lit *enter* [a]Matt 19:24; Mark 10:25
27 [a]Matt 19:26
28 [1]Lit *our own things* [a]Luke 5:11
29 [a]Matt 6:33; 19:29; Mark 10:29f
30 [a]Matt 12:32
31 [a]Luke 18:31-33: *Matt 20:17-19; Mark 10:32-34* [b]Luke 9:51 [c]Ps 22; Is 53
32 [1]Or *betrayed* [a]Matt 16:21
34 [a]Mark 9:32; Luke 9:45
35 [1]Lit *He* [a]Luke 18:35-43: *Matt 20:29-34; Mark 10:46-52* [b]Matt 20:29; Mark 10:46; Luke 19:1
38 [a]Matt 9:27; Luke 18:39
39 [a]Luke 18:38

42 And Jesus said to him, "[1]Receive your sight; [a]your faith has
[2]made you well."
43 Immediately he regained his sight and *began* following
Him, [a]glorifying God; and when [b]all the people saw it, they
gave praise to God.

Chapter 19 Theme ______________________

19 He [a]entered Jericho and was passing through.
2 And there was a man called by the name of Zaccheus;
he was a chief tax collector and he was rich.
3 Zaccheus was trying to see who Jesus was, and was unable
because of the crowd, for he was small in stature.
4 So he ran on ahead and climbed up into a [1a]sycamore tree
in order to see Him, for He was about to pass through that way.
5 When Jesus came to the place, He looked up and said to him,
"Zaccheus, hurry and come down, for today I must stay at your
house."
6 And he hurried and came down and received Him [1]gladly.
7 When they saw it, they all *began* to grumble, saying, "He
has gone [1]to be the guest of a man who is a sinner."
8 Zaccheus stopped and said to [a]the Lord, "Behold, Lord, half
of my possessions I [1]will give to the poor, and if I have
[b]defrauded anyone of anything, I [1]will give back [c]four times as
much."
9 And Jesus said to him, "Today salvation has come to this
house, because he, too, is [a]a son of Abraham.
10 "For [a]the Son of Man has come to seek and to save that
which was lost."
11 While they were listening to these things, Jesus went on to
tell a parable, because [a]He was near Jerusalem, and they
supposed that [b]the kingdom of God was going to appear
immediately.
12 So He said, "[a]A nobleman went to a distant country to
receive a kingdom for himself, and *then* return.
13 "And he called ten of his slaves, and gave them ten [1]minas
and said to them, 'Do business *with this* [2]until I come *back.*'
14 "But his citizens hated him and sent [1]a delegation after him,
saying, 'We do not want this man to reign over us.'
15 "When he returned, after receiving the kingdom, he ordered
that these slaves, to whom he had given the money, be called
to him so that he might know what business they had done.
16 "The first appeared, saying, '[1]Master, your [2]mina has made
ten minas more.'
17 "And he said to him, 'Well done, good slave, because you have
been [a]faithful in a very little thing, you are to be in authority
over ten cities.'
18 "The second came, saying, 'Your [1]mina, [2]master, has made
five minas.'
19 "And he said to him also, 'And you are to be over five
cities.'

42 [1]Lit *Regain your sight* [2]Lit *saved you* [a]Matt 9:22

43 [a]Matt 9:8 [b]Luke 9:43; 13:17; 19:37

19:1 [a]Luke 18:35

4 [1]I.e. fig-mulberry [a]1 Kin 10:27; 1 Chr 27:28; 2 Chr 1:15; 9:27; Ps 78:47; Is 9:10; Luke 17:6

6 [1]Lit *rejoicing*

7 [1]Or *to find lodging*

8 [1]Lit *am giving* [a]Luke 7:13 [b]Luke 3:14 [c]Ex 22:1; Lev 6:5; Num 5:7; 2 Sam 12:6

9 [a]Luke 3:8; 13:16; Rom 4:16; Gal 3:7

10 [a]Matt 18:11

11 [a]Luke 9:51 [b]Luke 17:20

12 [a]Matt 25:14-30; Luke 19:12-27

13 [1]A mina is equal to about 100 days' wages [2]Lit *while I am coming*

14 [1]Or *an embassy*

16 [1]Lit *Lord* [2]V 13, note 1

17 [a]Luke 16:10

18 [1]V 13, note 1 [2]Lit *lord*

22 [1]Lit *Out of your own mouth*
26 [a]Matt 13:12; Mark 4:25; Luke 8:18
27 [a]Luke 19:14 [b]Matt 22:7; Luke 20:16
28 [a]Mark 10:32 [b]Luke 9:51
29 [1]Or *hill . . . Olive Grove;* Mount of Olives [a]Luke 19:29-38: *Matt 21:1-9; Mark 11:1-10* [b]Matt 21:17 [c]Luke 21:37; Acts 1:12
33 [1]Lit *lords*
35 [a]Luke 19:35-38: *Matt 21:4-9; Mark 11:7-10; John 12:12-15*
37 [1]Lit *rejoicing* [2]Or *works of power* [a]Matt 21:1; Luke 19:29 [b]Luke 18:43
38 [a]Ps 118:26 [b]Matt 2:2; 25:34 [c]Matt 21:9; Luke 2:14
39 [1]Lit *from* [a]Matt 21:15f
40 [a]Hab 2:11

20 "Another came, saying, 'Master, here is your mina, which I
kept put away in a handkerchief;
21 for I was afraid of you, because you are an exacting man;
you take up what you did not lay down and reap what you did
not sow.'
22 "He *said to him, '[1]By your own words I will judge you, you
worthless slave. Did you know that I am an exacting man, taking
up what I did not lay down and reaping what I did not sow?
23 'Then why did you not put my money in the bank, and
having come, I would have collected it with interest?'
24 "Then he said to the bystanders, 'Take the mina away from
him and give it to the one who has the ten minas.'
25 "And they said to him, 'Master, he has ten minas *already.*'
26 "[a]I tell you that to everyone who has, more shall be given,
but from the one who does not have, even what he does have
shall be taken away.
27 "But [a]these enemies of mine, who did not want me to reign
over them, bring them here and [b]slay them in my presence."
28 After He had said these things, He [a]was going on ahead,
[b]going up to Jerusalem.
29 [a]When He approached Bethphage and [b]Bethany, near the
[1]mount that is called [c]Olivet, He
sent two of the disciples,
30 saying, "Go into the village
ahead of *you;* there, as you enter,
you will find a colt tied on which
no one yet has ever sat; untie it
and bring it *here.*
31 "If anyone asks you, 'Why are
you untying it?' you shall say, 'The
Lord has need of it.'"
32 So those who were sent went
away and found it just as He had
told them.

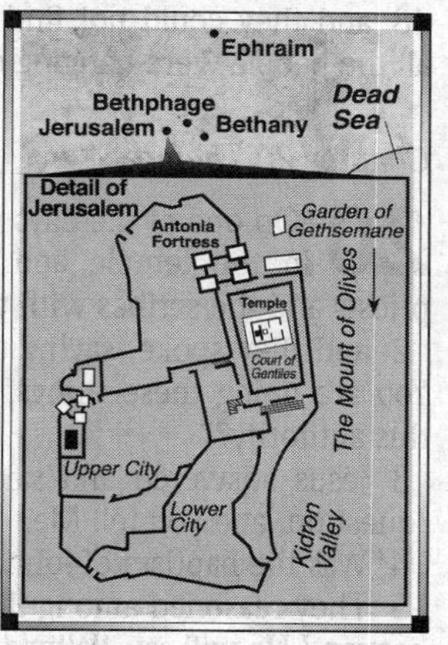

From Bethany, Bethphage across the Mount of Olives into Jerusalem

33 As they were untying the colt, its [1]owners said to them,
"Why are you untying the colt?"
34 They said, "The Lord has need of it."
35 They brought it to Jesus, [a]and they threw their coats on the
colt and put Jesus *on it.*
36 As He was going, they were spreading their coats on the road.
37 As soon as He was approaching, near the descent of [a]the
Mount of Olives, the whole crowd of the disciples began to
[b]praise God [1]joyfully with a loud voice for all the [2]miracles
which they had seen,
38 shouting:

"[a]BLESSED IS THE [b]KING WHO COMES IN THE NAME OF THE LORD;
Peace in heaven and [c]glory in the highest!"

39 [a]Some of the Pharisees [1]in the crowd said to Him, "Teacher,
rebuke Your disciples."
40 But Jesus answered, "I tell you, if these become silent, [a]the
stones will cry out!"

41 When He approached *Jerusalem,* He saw the city and [a]wept over it,

42 saying, "If you had known in this day, even you, the things which make for peace! But now they have been hidden from your eyes.

43 "For the days will come upon you [1]when your enemies will [a]throw up a [2]barricade against you, and [b]surround you and hem you in on every side,

44 and they will level you to the ground and your children within you, and [a]they will not leave in you one stone upon another, because you did not recognize [b]the time of your visitation."

45 [a]Jesus entered the temple and began to drive out those who were selling,

46 saying to them, "It is written, '[a]AND MY HOUSE SHALL BE A HOUSE OF PRAYER,' [b]but you have made it a ROBBERS' [1]DEN."

47 And [a]He was teaching daily in the temple; but the chief priests and the scribes and the leading men among the people [b]were trying to destroy Him,

48 and they could not find [1]anything that they might do, for all the people were hanging on to [2]every word He said.

Chapter 20 Theme ________________________________

20 [a]On one of the days while [b]He was teaching the people in the temple and [c]preaching the gospel, the chief priests and the scribes with the elders [d]confronted *Him,*

2 and they spoke, saying to Him, "Tell us by what authority You are doing these things, or who is the one who gave You this authority?"

3 Jesus answered and said to them, "I will also ask you a [1]question, and you tell Me:

4 "Was the baptism of John from heaven or from men?"

5 They reasoned among themselves, saying, "If we say, 'From heaven,' He will say, 'Why did you not believe him?'

6 "But if we say, 'From men,' all the people will stone us to death, for they are convinced that John was a [a]prophet."

7 So they answered that they did not know where *it came* from.

8 And Jesus said to them, "Nor [1]will I tell you by what authority I do these things."

9 [a]And He began to tell the people this parable: "A man planted a vineyard and rented it out to [1]vine-growers, and went on a journey for a long time.

10 "At the *harvest* time he sent a slave to the vine-growers, so that they would give him *some* of the produce of the vineyard; but the vine-growers beat him and sent him away empty-handed.

11 "And he proceeded to send another slave; and they beat him also and treated him shamefully and sent him away empty-handed.

41 [a]Luke 13:34, 35

43 [1]Lit *and* [2]I.e. a dirt wall or mound for siege purposes [a]Eccl 9:14; Is 29:3; 37:33; Jer 6:6; Ezek 4:2; 26:8 [b]Luke 21:20

44 [a]Matt 24:2; Mark 13:2; Luke 21:6 [b]1 Pet 2:12

45 [a]Luke 19:45, 46: *Matt 21:12, 13; Mark 11:15-17;* John 2:13-16

46 [1]Lit *cave* [a]Is 56:7; Jer 7:11; Matt 21:13; Mark 11:17 [b]Jer 7:11

47 [a]Matt 26:55; Luke 21:37 [b]Luke 20:19

48 [1]Lit *what they would do* [2]Lit *Him, listening*

20:1 [a]Luke 20:1-8: *Matt 21:23-27; Mark 11:27-33* [b]Matt 26:55 [c]Luke 8:1 [d]Acts 4:1; 6:12

3 [1]Lit *word*

6 [a]Matt 11:9; Luke 7:29, 30

8 [1]Lit *do I tell*

9 [1]Or *tenant farmers,* also vv 10, 14, 16 [a]Luke 20:9-19: *Matt 21:33-46; Mark 12:1-12*

13 [1]Lit *lord*
[a]Luke 18:2

15 [1]Lit *lord*

16 [a]Matt 21:41; Mark 12:9; Luke 19:27
[b]Rom 3:4, 6, 31; 6:2, 15; 7:7, 13; 9:14; 11:1, 11; 1 Cor 6:15; Gal 2:17; 3:21; 6:14

17 [1]Lit *He*
[a]Ps 118:22
[b]Eph 2:20; 1 Pet 2:6

18 [a]Matt 21:44

19 [a]Luke 19:47

20 [1]Lit *falsely represented themselves*
[2]Lit *take hold of His word*
[a]Luke 20:20-26: *Matt 22:15-22; Mark 12:13-17;* Mark 3:2
[b]Luke 11:54; 20:26
[c]Matt 27:2

21 [1]Lit *do not receive a face*

22 [1]Or *permissible*
[a]Matt 17:25; Luke 23:2

24 [1]The denarius was a day's wages
[2]Lit *image*

25 [a]Matt 22:21; Mark 12:17

26 [1]Lit *catch His statement*
[a]Luke 11:54

27 [a]Luke 20:27-40: *Matt 22:23-33; Mark 12:18-27*
[b]Acts 23:8

28 [1]Lit *take*
[a]Deut 25:5

31 [1]Lit *took*
[2]Lit *the seven also*
[3]Lit *left no children, and died*

33 [1]Lit *the* [2]Lit *had her as wife*

12 "And he proceeded to send a third; and this one also they
wounded and cast out.
13 "The [1]owner of the vineyard said, 'What shall I do? I will
send my beloved son; perhaps they will [a]respect him.'
14 "But when the vine-growers saw him, they reasoned with
one another, saying, 'This is the heir; let us kill him so that the
inheritance will be ours.'
15 "So they threw him out of the vineyard and killed him.
What, then, will the [1]owner of the vineyard do to them?
16 "He will come and [a]destroy these vine-growers and will give
the vineyard to others." When they heard it, they said, "[b]May
it never be!"
17 But [1]Jesus looked at them and said, "What then is this that
is written:

'[a]THE STONE WHICH THE BUILDERS REJECTED,
THIS BECAME [b]THE CHIEF CORNER *stone*'?

18 "[a]Everyone who falls on that stone will be broken to pieces;
but on whomever it falls, it will scatter him like dust."
19 The scribes and the chief priests [a]tried to lay hands on Him
that very hour, and they feared the people; for they understood
that He spoke this parable against them.
20 [a]So they watched Him, and sent spies who [1]pretended to
be righteous, in order [b]that they might [2]catch Him in some
statement, so that they *could* deliver Him to the rule and the
authority of [c]the governor.
21 They questioned Him, saying, "Teacher, we know that You
speak and teach correctly, and You [1]are not partial to any, but
teach the way of God in truth.
22 "Is it [1]lawful for us [a]to pay taxes to Caesar, or not?"
23 But He detected their trickery and said to them,
24 "Show Me a [1]denarius. Whose [2]likeness and inscription
does it have?" They said, "Caesar's."
25 And He said to them, "Then [a]render to Caesar the things
that are Caesar's, and to God the things that are God's."
26 And they were unable to [1a]catch Him in a saying in the
presence of the people; and being amazed at His answer, they
became silent.
27 [a]Now there came to Him some of the [b]Sadducees (who say
that there is no resurrection),
28 and they questioned Him, saying, "Teacher, Moses wrote for
us that [a]IF A MAN'S BROTHER DIES, having a wife, AND HE IS CHILDLESS,
HIS BROTHER SHOULD [1]MARRY THE WIFE AND RAISE UP CHILDREN TO HIS
BROTHER.
29 "Now there were seven brothers; and the first took a wife
and died childless;
30 and the second
31 and the third [1]married her; and in the same way [2]all seven
[3]died, leaving no children.
32 "Finally the woman died also.
33 "In the resurrection therefore, which one's wife will she be?
For [1]all seven [2]had married her."

34 Jesus said to them, "The sons of [a]this age marry and are
given in marriage,
35 but those who are considered worthy to attain to [a]that age
and the resurrection from the dead, neither marry nor are
given in marriage;
36 for they cannot even die anymore, because they are like
angels, and are [a]sons of God, being sons of the resurrection.
37 "But that the dead are raised, even Moses showed, in [a]the
passage about the burning bush, where he calls the Lord [b]THE
GOD OF ABRAHAM, AND THE GOD OF ISAAC, AND THE GOD OF JACOB.
38 "[a]Now He is not the God of the dead but of the living; for
[b]all live to Him."
39 Some of the scribes answered and said, "Teacher, You have
spoken well."
40 For [a]they did not have courage to question Him any longer
about anything.
41 [a]Then He said to them, "How *is it that* they say [1]the Christ
is [b]David's son?
42 "For David himself says in the book of Psalms,
'[a]THE LORD SAID TO MY LORD,
"SIT AT MY RIGHT HAND,
43 [a]UNTIL I MAKE YOUR ENEMIES A FOOTSTOOL FOR YOUR FEET."'
44 "Therefore David calls Him 'Lord,' and how is He his son?"
45 [a]And while all the people were listening, He said to the
disciples,
46 "Beware of the scribes, [a]who like to walk around in long
robes, and love respectful greetings in the market places, and
chief seats in the synagogues and places of honor at banquets,
47 who devour widows' houses, and for appearance's sake
offer long prayers. These will receive greater condemnation."

INSIGHT

The treasury was in the women's court of the temple, where there were thirteen trumpet-shaped offering receptacles. See the illustration of the floor plan of Herod's Temple on page 1614, and see the illustration of Herod's Temple on page NISB-38.

Chapter 21 Theme ______________________________

21 [a]And He looked up and saw the rich putting their gifts
into the treasury.
2 And He saw a poor widow putting [1]in [a]two [2]small copper
coins.
3 And He said, "Truly I say to you, this poor widow put in
more than all *of them;*
4 for they all out of their [1]surplus put into the [2]offering; but
she out of her poverty put in all [3]that she had [a]to live on."
5 [a]And while some were talking about the temple, that it
was adorned with beautiful stones and votive gifts, He said,
6 "*As for* these things which you are looking at, the days will
come in which [a]there will not be left one stone upon another
which will not be torn down."
7 They questioned Him, saying, "Teacher, when therefore
will these things happen? And what *will be* the [1]sign when
these things are about to take place?"
8 And He said, "See to it that you are not misled; for many
will come in My name, saying, '[a]I am *He,*' and, 'The time is
near.' [b]Do not go after them.

34 [a]Matt 12:32; Luke 16:8
35 [a]Matt 12:32; Luke 16:8
36 [a]Rom 8:16f; 1 John 3:1, 2
37 [a]Mark 12:26 [b]Ex 3:6
38 [a]Matt 22:32; Mark 12:27 [b]Rom 14:8
40 [a]Matt 22:46; Luke 14:6
41 [1]I.e. the Messiah [a]Luke 20:41-44: *Matt 22:41-46; Mark 12:35-37* [b]Matt 9:27
42 [a]Ps 110:1
43 [a]Ps 110:1
45 [a]Luke 20:45-47: *Matt 23:1-7; Mark 12:38-40*
46 [a]Luke 11:43; 14:7
21:1 [a]Luke 21:1-4: *Mark 12:41-44*
2 [1]Lit *there* [2]Gr *lepta* [a]Mark 12:42
4 [1]Or *abundance* [2]Lit *gifts* [3]Lit *the living that she had* [a]Mark 12:44
5 [a]Luke 21:5-36: *Matt 24; Mark 13*
6 [a]Luke 19:44
7 [1]Or *attesting miracle*
8 [a]John 8:24 [b]Luke 17:23

9 "When you hear of wars and disturbances, do not be terrified;
for these things must take place first, but the end *does* not
follow immediately."
10 Then He continued by saying to them, "Nation will rise
against nation and kingdom against kingdom,
11 and there will be great earthquakes, and in various places
plagues and famines; and there will be terrors and great [1]signs
from heaven.
12 "But before all these things, [a]they will lay their hands on you
and will persecute you, delivering you to the synagogues and
prisons, [1]bringing you before kings and governors for My name's
sake.
13 "[a]It will lead to [1]an opportunity for your testimony.
14 "[a]So make up your minds not to prepare beforehand to
defend yourselves;
15 for [a]I will give you [1]utterance and wisdom which none of
your opponents will be able to resist or refute.
16 "But you will be betrayed even by parents and brothers and
relatives and friends, and they will put *some* of you to death,
17 and you will be hated by all because of My name.
18 "Yet [a]not a hair of your head will perish.
19 "[a]By your endurance you will gain your [1]lives.
20 "But when you see Jerusalem [a]surrounded by armies, then
[1]recognize that her desolation is near.
21 "Then those who are in Judea must flee to the mountains,
and those who are in the midst of [1]the city must leave, and
[a]those who are in the country must not enter [1]the city;
22 because these are [a]days of vengeance, so that all things
which are written will be fulfilled.
23 "Woe to those who are pregnant and to those who are
nursing babies in those days; for [a]there will be great distress
upon the [1]land and wrath to this people;
24 and they will fall by [a]the edge of the sword, and will be led
captive into all the nations; and [b]Jerusalem will be [c]trampled under
foot by the Gentiles until [d]the times of the Gentiles are fulfilled.
25 "There will be [1]signs in sun and moon and stars, and on the
earth dismay among nations, in perplexity at the roaring of the
sea and the waves,
26 men fainting from fear and the expectation of the things
which are coming upon the [1]world; for the powers of [2]the
heavens will be shaken.
27 "[a]Then they will see [b]THE SON OF MAN COMING IN A CLOUD
with power and great glory.
28 "But when these things begin to take place, straighten up and
lift up your heads, because [a]your redemption is drawing near."
29 Then He told them a parable: "Behold the fig tree and all
the trees;
30 as soon as they put forth *leaves,* you see it and [a]know for
yourselves that summer is now near.
31 "So you also, when you see these things happening, [1]recognize
that [a]the kingdom of God is near.

11 [1]Or *attesting miracles*

12 [1]Lit *being brought* [a]Luke 21:12-17: *Matt 10:19-22; Mark 13:11-13*

13 [1]Lit *a testimony for you* [a]Phil 1:12

14 [a]Luke 12:11

15 [1]Lit *a mouth* [a]Luke 12:12

18 [a]Matt 10:30; Luke 12:7

19 [1]Lit *souls* [a]Matt 10:22; 24:13; Rom 2:7; 5:3f; Heb 10:36; James 1:3; 2 Pet 1:6

20 [1]Lit *know* [a]Luke 19:43

21 [1]Lit *her* [a]Luke 17:31

22 [a]Is 63:4; Dan 9:24-27; Hos 9:7

23 [1]Or *earth* [a]Dan 8:19; 1 Cor 7:26

24 [a]Gen 34:26; Ex 17:13; Heb 11:34 [b]Is 63:18; Dan 8:13 [c]Rev 11:2 [d]Rom 11:25

25 [1]Or *attesting miracles*

26 [1]Lit *inhabited earth* [2]Or *heaven*

27 [a]Matt 16:27; 24:30; 26:64; Mark 13:26 [b]Dan 7:13; Rev 1:7

28 [a]Luke 18:7

30 [a]Luke 12:57

31 [1]Lit *know* [a]Matt 3:2

32 "Truly I say to you, this [1]generation will not pass away until
all things take place.
33 "[a]Heaven and earth will pass away, but My words will not
pass away.
34 "[a]Be on guard, so that your hearts will not be weighted
down with dissipation and drunkenness and the worries of life,
and that day will not come on you suddenly like a trap;
35 for it will come upon all those who dwell on the face of all
the earth.
36 "But [a]keep on the alert at all times, praying that you may
have strength to escape all these things that are about to take
place, and to [b]stand before the Son of Man."
37 Now [1]during the day He was [a]teaching in the temple, but
[2b]at evening He would go out and spend the night on [3c]the
mount that is called [4]Olivet.
38 And all the people would get up [a]early in the morning *to
come* to Him in the temple to listen to Him.

Chapter 22 Theme ____________________

22 [a]Now the Feast of Unleavened Bread, which is called
the [b]Passover, was approaching.
2 The chief priests and the scribes [a]were seeking how they
might put Him to death; for they were afraid of the people.
3 [a]And [b]Satan entered into Judas who was called Iscariot,
[1]belonging to the number of the twelve.
4 And he went away and discussed with the chief priests and
[a]officers how he might betray Him to them.
5 They were glad and agreed to give him money.
6 So he consented, and *began* seeking a good opportunity to
betray Him to them [1]apart from the crowd.
7 [a]Then came the *first* day of Unleavened Bread on which
[b]the Passover *lamb* had to be sacrificed.
8 And Jesus sent [a]Peter and John, saying, "Go and prepare
the Passover for us, so that we may eat it."
9 They said to Him, "Where do You want us to prepare it?"
10 And He said to them, "When you have entered the city, a
man will meet you carrying a pitcher of water; follow him into
the house that he enters.
11 "And you shall say to the owner of the house, 'The Teacher
says to you, "Where is the guest room in which I may eat the
Passover with My disciples?"'
12 "And he will show you a large, furnished upper room; prepare
it there."
13 And they left and found *everything* just as He had told
them; and they prepared the Passover.
14 [a]When the hour had come, He reclined *at the table,* and
[b]the apostles with Him.
15 And He said to them, "I have earnestly desired to eat this
Passover with you before I suffer;
16 for I say to you, I shall never again eat it [a]until it is fulfilled
in the kingdom of God."

32 [1]Or *race*

33 [a]Matt 5:18; Luke 16:17

34 [a]Matt 24:42-44; Mark 4:19; Luke 12:40, 45; 1 Thess 5:2ff

36 [a]Mark 13:33; Luke 12:40 [b]Luke 1:19; Rev 7:9; 8:2; 11:4

37 [1]Lit *days* [2]Lit *nights* [3]Or *the hill* [4]Or *Olive Grove* [a]Matt 26:55; Luke 19:47 [b]Mark 11:19 [c]Matt 21:1

38 [a]John 8:2

22:1 [a]Luke 22:1, 2: *Matt 26:2-5; Mark 14:1, 2;* Ex 12:1-27 [b]John 11:55; 13:1

2 [a]Matt 12:14

3 [1]Lit *being of* [a]Luke 22:3-6: *Matt 26:14-16; Mark 14:10, 11* [b]Matt 4:10; John 13:2, 27

4 [a]1 Chr 9:11; Neh 11:11; Luke 22:52; Acts 4:1; 5:24, 26

6 [1]Or *without a disturbance*

7 [a]Luke 22:7-13: *Matt 26:17-19; Mark 14:12-16* [b]Mark 14:12

8 [a]Acts 3:1, 11; 4:13, 19; 8:14; Gal 2:9

14 [a]Matt 26:20; Mark 14:17 [b]Mark 6:30

16 [a]Luke 14:15; 22:18, 30; Rev 19:9

17 [a]And when He had taken a cup *and* [b]given thanks, He said,
"Take this and share it among yourselves;
18 for [a]I say to you, I will not drink of the fruit of the vine
from now on until the kingdom of God comes."
19 And when He had taken *some* bread *and* [a]given thanks, He
broke it and gave it to them, saying, "This is My body which is
given for you; do this in remembrance of Me."
20 And in the same way *He took* the cup after they had eaten,
saying, "This cup which is [a]poured out for you is the [b]new
covenant in My blood.
21 "[a]But behold, the hand of the one betraying Me is with [1]Mine
on the table.
22 "For indeed, the Son of Man is going [a]as it has been
determined; but woe to that man by whom He is betrayed!"
23 And they began to discuss among themselves which one of
them it might be who was going to do this thing.
24 And there arose also [a]a dispute among them *as to* which
one of them was regarded to be greatest.
25 [a]And He said to them, "The kings of the Gentiles lord it
over them; and those who have authority over them are called
'Benefactors.'
26 "But *it is* not this way with you, [a]but the one who is the
greatest among you must become like [b]the youngest, and the
leader like the servant.
27 "For [a]who is greater, the one who reclines *at the table* or the
one who serves? Is it not the one who reclines *at the table?* But
[b]I am among you as the one who serves.
28 "You are those who have stood by Me in My [a]trials;
29 and just as My Father has granted Me a [a]kingdom, I grant you
30 that you may [a]eat and drink at My table in My [b]kingdom,
and [c]you will sit on thrones judging the twelve tribes of Israel.
31 "Simon, Simon, behold, [a]Satan has [1]demanded *permission*
to [b]sift you like wheat;
32 but I [a]have prayed for you, that your faith may not fail; and
you, when once you have turned again, [b]strengthen your
brothers."
33 [a]But he said to Him, "Lord, with You I am ready to go both
to prison and to death!"
34 And He said, "I say to you, Peter, the rooster will not crow
today until you have denied three times that you know Me."
35 And He said to them, "[a]When I sent you out without
money belt and bag and sandals, you did not lack anything, did
you?" They said, "*No,* nothing."
36 And He said to them, "But now, [1]whoever has a money
belt is to take it along, likewise also a bag, and [1]whoever has
no sword is to sell his [2]coat and buy one.
37 "For I tell you that this which is written must be fulfilled in
Me, '[a]AND HE WAS NUMBERED WITH TRANSGRESSORS'; for [b]that
which refers to Me has *its* [1]fulfillment."
38 They said, "Lord, look, here are two [a]swords." And He said
to them, "It is enough."

17 [a]Luke 22:17-20: *Matt 26:26-29; Mark 14:22-25; 1 Cor 11:23-25;* 1 Cor 10:16 [b]Matt 14:19
18 [a]Matt 26:29; Mark 14:25
19 [a]Matt 14:19
20 [a]Matt 26:28; Mark 14:24 [b]Ex 24:8; Jer 31:31; 1 Cor 11:25; 2 Cor 3:6; Heb 8:8, 13; 9:15
21 [1]Lit *Me* [a]Luke 22:21-23: *Matt 26:21-24; Mark 14:18-21;* Ps 41:9; John 13:18, 21, 22, 26
22 [a]Acts 2:23; 4:28; 10:42; 17:31
24 [a]Mark 9:34; Luke 9:46
25 [a]Luke 22:25-27: *Matt 20:25-28; Mark 10:42-45*
26 [a]Matt 23:11; Mark 9:35; Luke 9:48 [b]1 Pet 5:5
27 [a]Luke 12:37 [b]Matt 20:28; John 13:12-15
28 [a]Heb 2:18; 4:15
29 [a]Matt 5:3; 2 Tim 2:12
30 [a]Luke 22:16 [b]Matt 5:3; 2 Tim 2:12 [c]Matt 19:28
31 [1]Or *obtained by asking* [a]Job 1:6-12; 2:1-6; Matt 4:10 [b]Amos 9:9
32 [a]John 17:9, 15 [b]John 21:15-17
33 [a]Luke 22:33, 34: *Matt 26:33-35; Mark 14:29-31; John 13:37, 38*
35 [a]Matt 10:9f; Mark 6:8; Luke 9:3ff; 10:4
36 [1]Lit *he who* [2]Or *outer garment*
37 [1]Lit *end* [a]Is 53:12 [b]John 17:4; 19:30
38 [a]Luke 22:36, 49

39 [a]And He came out and proceeded [b]as was His custom to
[c]the Mount of Olives; and the disciples also followed Him.
40 [a]When He arrived at the place, He said to them, "[b]Pray
that you may not enter into temptation."
41 And He withdrew from them about a stone's throw, and He
[a]knelt down and *began* to pray,
42 saying, "Father, if You are willing, remove this [a]cup from
Me; [b]yet not My will, but Yours be done."
43 [1]Now an [a]angel from heaven appeared to Him, strengthening
Him.
44 And [a]being in agony He was praying very fervently; and His
sweat became like drops of blood, falling down upon the ground.
45 When He rose from prayer, He came to the disciples and
found them sleeping from sorrow,
46 and said to them, "Why are you sleeping? Get up and [a]pray
that you may not enter into temptation."
47 [a]While He was still speaking, behold, a crowd *came,* and
the one called Judas, one of the twelve, was preceding them;
and he approached Jesus to kiss Him.
48 But Jesus said to him, "Judas, are you betraying the Son of
Man with a kiss?"
49 When those who were around Him saw what was going to
happen, they said, "Lord, shall we strike with the [a]sword?"
50 And one of them struck the slave of the high priest and cut
off his right ear.
51 But Jesus answered and said, "[1]Stop! No more of this." And
He touched his ear and healed him.
52 Then Jesus said to the chief priests and [a]officers of the
temple and elders who had come against Him, "Have you come
out with swords and clubs [b]as you would against a robber?
53 "While I was with you daily in the temple, you did not lay
hands on Me; but [1]this hour and the power of darkness are
yours."
54 [a]Having arrested Him, they led Him *away* and brought Him
to the house of the high priest; but [b]Peter was following at a
distance.
55 [a]After they had kindled a fire in the middle of [b]the courtyard
and had sat down together, Peter was sitting among them.
56 And a servant-girl, seeing him as he sat in the firelight and
looking intently at him, said, "This man was with Him too."
57 But he denied *it,* saying, "Woman, I do not know Him."
58 A little later, [a]another saw him and said, "You are *one* of
them too!" But Peter said, "Man, I am not!"
59 After about an hour had passed, another man *began* to
insist, saying, "Certainly this man also was with Him, [a]for he is
a Galilean too."
60 But Peter said, "Man, I do not know what you are talking
about." Immediately, while he was still speaking, a rooster crowed.
61 [a]The Lord turned and looked at Peter. And Peter remembered
the word of the Lord, how He had told him, "[b]Before a rooster
crows today, you will deny Me three times."

39 [a]Matt 26:30; Mark 14:26; John 18:1 [b]Luke 21:37 [c]Matt 21:1

40 [a]Luke 22:40-46: *Matt 26:36-46; Mark 14:32-42* [b]Matt 6:13; Luke 22:46

41 [a]Matt 26:39; Mark 14:35; Luke 18:11

42 [a]Matt 20:22 [b]Matt 26:39

43 [1]Most early mss do not contain vv 43 and 44 [a]Matt 4:11

44 [a]Heb 5:7

46 [a]Luke 22:40

47 [a]Luke 22:47-53: *Matt 26:47-56; Mark 14:43-50; John 18:3-11*

49 [a]Luke 22:38

51 [1]Or *"Let Me at least do this," and He touched*

52 [a]Luke 22:4 [b]Luke 22:37

53 [1]Lit *this is your hour and power of darkness*

54 [a]Matt 26:57; Mark 14:53 [b]Matt 26:58; Mark 14:54; John 18:15

55 [a]Luke 22:55-62: *Matt 26:69-75; Mark 14:66-72; John 18:16-18, 25-27* [b]Matt 26:3

58 [a]John 18:26

59 [a]Matt 26:73; Mark 14:70

61 [a]Luke 7:13 [b]Luke 22:34

62 And he went out and wept bitterly.
63 [a]Now the men who were holding [1]Jesus in custody were
mocking Him and beating Him,
64 and they blindfolded Him and were asking Him, saying,
"[a]Prophesy, who is the one who hit You?"
65 And they were saying many other things against Him,
[a]blaspheming.
66 [a]When it was day, [b]the [1]Council of elders of the people
assembled, both chief priests and scribes, and they led Him
away to their [c]council *chamber,* saying,
67 "[a]If You are the [1]Christ, tell us." But He said to them, "If I
tell you, you will not believe;
68 and if I ask a question, you will not answer.
69 "[a]But from now on [b]THE SON OF MAN WILL BE SEATED AT THE
RIGHT HAND of the power OF GOD."
70 And they all said, "Are You [a]the Son of God, then?" And
He said to them, "[1][b]Yes, I am."
71 Then they said, "What further need do we have of testimony?
For we have heard it ourselves from His own mouth."

Chapter 23 Theme

23 Then the whole body of them got up and [a]brought Him
before Pilate.
2 [a]And they began to accuse Him, saying, "We found this
man [b]misleading our nation and [c]forbidding to pay taxes to
Caesar, and saying that He Himself is [1]Christ, a King."
3 So Pilate asked Him, saying, "Are You the King of the
Jews?" And He answered him and said, "[a]*It is as* you say."
4 Then Pilate said to the chief priests and the crowds, "[a]I
find no guilt in this man."
5 But they kept on insisting, saying, "He stirs up the people,
teaching all over Judea, [a]starting from Galilee even as far as this
place."
6 When Pilate heard it, he asked whether the man was a
Galilean.
7 And when he learned that He belonged to Herod's
jurisdiction, he sent Him to [a]Herod, who himself also was in
Jerusalem [1]at that time.
8 Now Herod was very glad when he saw Jesus; for [a]he had
wanted to see Him for a long time, because he had been hearing
about Him and was hoping to see some [1]sign performed by Him.
9 And he questioned Him [1]at some length; but [a]He answered
him nothing.
10 And the chief priests and the scribes were standing there,
accusing Him vehemently.
11 And Herod with his soldiers, after treating Him with
contempt and mocking Him, [a]dressed Him in a gorgeous robe
and sent Him back to Pilate.
12 Now [a]Herod and Pilate became friends with one another that
very day; for before they had been enemies with each other.

63 [1]Lit *Him* [a]Matt 26:67f; Mark 14:65; John 18:22f

64 [a]Matt 26:68; Mark 14:65

65 [a]Matt 27:39

66 [1]Or *Sanhedrin* [a]Matt 27:1f; Mark 15:1; John 18:28 [b]Acts 22:5 [c]Matt 5:22

67 [1]I.e. Messiah [a]Matt 26:63-66; Mark 14:61-63; Luke 22:67-71; John 18:19-21

69 [a]Matt 26:64; Mark 14:62; 16:19 [b]Ps 110:1

70 [1]Lit *You say that I am* [a]Matt 4:3 [b]Matt 26:64; 27:11; Luke 23:3

23:1 [a]Matt 27:2; Mark 15:1; John 18:28

2 [1]I.e. Messiah [a]Luke 23:2, 3: *Matt 27:11-14; Mark 15:2-5; John 18:29-37* [b]Luke 23:14 [c]Luke 20:22; John 18:33ff; 19:12; Acts 17:7

3 [a]Luke 22:70

4 [a]Matt 27:23; Mark 15:14; Luke 23:14, 22; John 18:38; 19:4, 6

5 [a]Matt 4:12

7 [1]Lit *in these days* [a]Matt 14:1; Mark 6:14; Luke 3:1; 9:7; 13:31

8 [1]Or *attesting miracle* [a]Luke 9:9

9 [1]Lit *in many words* [a]Matt 27:12, 14; Mark 15:5; John 19:9

11 [a]Matt 27:28

12 [a]Acts 4:27

Jerusalem of the New Testament

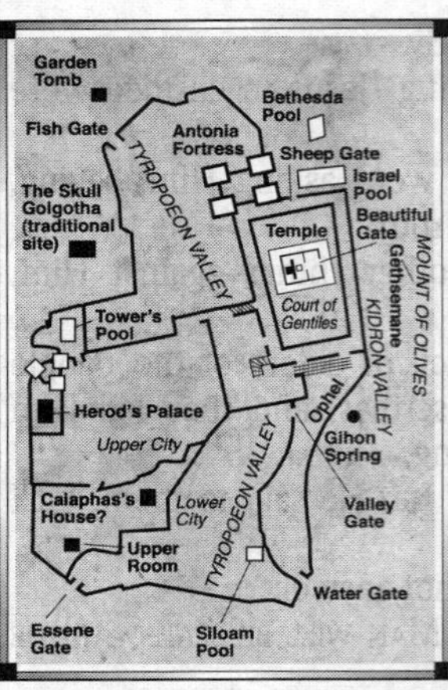

13 Pilate summoned the chief
priests and the [a]rulers and the
people,
14 and said to them, "You
brought this man to me as one
who [a]incites the people to
rebellion, and behold, having
examined Him before you, I
[b]have found no guilt in this man
regarding the charges which you
make against Him.
15 "No, nor has [a]Herod, for he
sent Him back to us; and behold,
nothing deserving death has
been done by Him.
16 "Therefore I will [a]punish Him and release Him."
17 [[1]Now he was obliged to release to them at the feast one
prisoner.]
18 But they cried out all together, saying, "[a]Away with this
man, and release for us Barabbas!"
19 (He was one who had been thrown into prison for an
insurrection made in the city, and for murder.)
20 Pilate, wanting to release Jesus, addressed them again,
21 but they kept on calling out, saying, "Crucify, crucify Him!"
22 And he said to them the third time, "Why, what evil has
this man done? I have found in Him no guilt *demanding* death;
therefore I will [a]punish Him and release Him."
23 But they were insistent, with loud voices asking that He be
crucified. And their voices *began* to prevail.
24 And Pilate pronounced sentence that their demand be
granted.
25 And he released the man they were asking for who had
been thrown into prison for insurrection and murder, but he
delivered Jesus to their will.
26 [a]When they led Him away, they seized a man, Simon of
[b]Cyrene, coming in from the country, and placed on him the
cross to carry behind Jesus.
27 And following Him was a large crowd of the people, and of
women who were [1a]mourning and lamenting Him.
28 But Jesus turning to them said, "Daughters of Jerusalem,
stop weeping for Me, but weep for yourselves and for your
children.
29 "For behold, the days are coming when they will say,
'[a]Blessed are the barren, and the wombs that never bore, and
the breasts that never nursed.'
30 "Then they will begin TO [a]SAY TO THE MOUNTAINS, 'FALL ON US,'
AND TO THE HILLS, 'COVER US.'
31 "For if they do these things [1]when the tree is green, what
will happen [2]when it is dry?"
32 [a]Two others also, who were criminals, were being led away
to be put to death with Him.

13 [a]Luke 23:35; John 7:26, 48; 12:42; Acts 3:17; 4:5, 8; 13:27

14 [a]Luke 23:2 [b]Luke 23:4

15 [a]Luke 9:9

16 [a]Matt 27:26; Mark 15:15; Luke 23:22; John 19:1; Acts 16:37

17 [1]Early mss do not contain this v

18 [a]Luke 23:18-25: *Matt 27:15-26; Mark 15:6-15;* John 18:39-19:16

22 [a]Luke 23:16

26 [a]Luke 23:26: *Matt 27:32; Mark 15:21;* John 19:17 [b]Matt 27:32

27 [1]Lit *beating the breast* [a]Luke 8:52

29 [a]Matt 24:19; Luke 11:27; 21:23

30 [a]Hos 10:8; Is 2:19, 20; Rev 6:16

31 [1]Lit *in the green tree* [2]Lit *in the dry*

32 [a]Matt 27:38; Mark 15:27; John 19:18

33 [a]When they came to the place called [1]The Skull, there they
crucified Him and the criminals, one on the right and the other
on the left.
34 [1]But Jesus was saying, "[a]Father, forgive them; for they do
not know what they are doing." [b]And they cast lots, dividing
up His garments among themselves.
35 And the people stood by, looking on. And even the [a]rulers
were sneering at Him, saying, "He saved others; [b]let Him save
Himself if this is the [1]Christ of God, His Chosen One."
36 The soldiers also mocked Him, coming up to Him, [a]offering
Him sour wine,
37 and saying, "[a]If You are the King of the Jews, save Yourself!"
38 Now there was also an inscription above Him, "[a]THIS IS
THE KING OF THE JEWS."
39 [a]One of the criminals who were hanged *there* was [1]hurling
abuse at Him, saying, "Are You not the [2]Christ? [b]Save Yourself
and us!"
40 But the other answered, and rebuking him said, "Do you
not even fear God, since you are under the same sentence of
condemnation?
41 "And we indeed *are suffering* justly, for we are receiving [1]what
we deserve for our deeds; but this man has done nothing wrong."
42 And he was saying, "Jesus, remember me when You come
[1]in Your kingdom!"
43 And He said to him, "Truly I say to you, today you shall be
with Me in [a]Paradise."
44 [a]It was now about [1b]the sixth hour, and darkness [2]fell over
the whole land until [3]the ninth hour,
45 [1]because the sun was obscured; and [a]the veil of the temple
was torn [2]in two.
46 And Jesus, [a]crying out with a loud voice, said, "Father,
[b]INTO YOUR HANDS I COMMIT MY SPIRIT." Having said this, He
breathed His last.
47 [a]Now when the centurion saw what had happened, he
began [b]praising God, saying, "Certainly this man was [1]innocent."
48 And all the crowds who came together for this spectacle,
when they observed what had happened, *began* to return,
[1a]beating their breasts.
49 [a]And all His acquaintances and [a]the women who
accompanied Him from Galilee were standing at a distance,
seeing these things.
50 [a]And a man named Joseph, who was a [b]member of the
Council, a good and righteous man
51 (he had not consented to their plan and action), *a man*
from Arimathea, a city of the Jews, who was [a]waiting for the
kingdom of God;
52 this man went to Pilate and asked for the body of Jesus.
53 And he took it down and wrapped it in a linen cloth, and laid
Him in a tomb cut into the rock, where no one had ever lain.
54 It was [a]the [1]preparation day, and the Sabbath was about to
[2]begin.

33 [1]In Lat *Calvarius;* or *Calvary* [a]Luke 23:33-43: *Matt 27:33-44; Mark 15:22-32; John 19:17-24*

34 [1]Some early mss do not contain *But Jesus was saying . . . doing* [a]Matt 11:25; Luke 22:42 [b]Ps 22:18; John 19:24

35 [1]I.e. Messiah [a]Luke 23:13 [b]Matt 27:43

36 [a]Matt 27:48

37 [a]Matt 27:43

38 [a]Matt 27:37; Mark 15:26; John 19:19

39 [1]Or *blaspheming* [2]I.e. Messiah [a]Matt 27:44; Mark 15:32; Luke 23:39-43 [b]Luke 23:35, 37

41 [1]Lit *things worthy of what we have done*

42 [1]Or *into*

43 [a]2 Cor 12:4; Rev 2:7

44 [1]I.e. noon [2]Or *occurred* [3]I.e. 3 p.m. [a]Luke 23:44-49: *Matt 27:45-56; Mark 15:33-41* [b]John 19:14

45 [1]Lit *the sun failing* [2]Lit *in the middle* [a]Ex 26:31-33; Matt 27:51

46 [a]Matt 27:50; Mark 15:37; John 19:30 [b]Ps 31:5

47 [1]Lit *righteous* [a]Matt 27:54; Mark 15:39 [b]Matt 9:8

48 [1]I.e. as a traditional sign of mourning or contrition [a]Luke 8:52; 18:13

49 [a]Matt 27:55f; Mark 15:40f; Luke 8:2; John 19:25

50 [a]Luke 23:50-56: *Matt 27:57-61; Mark 15:42-47; John 19:38-42* [b]Mark 15:43

51 [a]Mark 15:43; Luke 2:25

54 [1]I.e. preparation for the Sabbath [2]Lit *dawn* [a]Matt 27:62; Mark 15:42

55 Now [a]the women who had come with Him out of Galilee
followed, and saw the tomb and how His body was laid.
56 Then they returned and [a]prepared spices and perfumes.
And [b]on the Sabbath they rested according to the commandment.

Chapter 24 Theme ______________________

24 [a]But on the first day of the week, at early dawn, they
came to the tomb bringing the spices which they had
prepared.
2 And they found the stone rolled away from the tomb,
3 but when they entered, they did not find the body of [a]the
Lord Jesus.
4 While they were perplexed about this, behold, [a]two men
suddenly [b]stood near them in dazzling clothing;
5 and as *the women* were terrified and bowed their faces to
the ground, *the men* said to them, "Why do you seek the living
One among the dead?
6 "He is not here, but He [a]has [1]risen. Remember how He
spoke to you [b]while He was still in Galilee,
7 saying that [a]the Son of Man must be delivered into the hands
of sinful men, and be crucified, and the third day rise again."
8 And [a]they remembered His words,
9 and returned from the tomb and reported all these things
to the eleven and to all the rest.
10 Now they were [a]Mary Magdalene and Joanna and Mary the
mother of James; also the other women with them were telling
these things to [b]the apostles.
11 But these words appeared [1]to them as nonsense, and they
[a]would not believe them.
12 But Peter got up and [a]ran to the tomb; stooping and looking
in, he *saw the linen wrappings [1]only; and he went away [b]to
his home, marveling at what had happened.
13 And behold, [a]two of them were going that very day to a
village named Emmaus, which was [1]about seven miles from
Jerusalem.
14 And they were talking with each other about all these
things which had taken place.
15 While they were talking and discussing, Jesus Himself
approached and *began* traveling with them.
16 But [a]their eyes were prevented from recognizing Him.
17 And He said to them, "What are these words that you are
exchanging with one another as you are walking?" And they
stood still, looking sad.
18 One *of them,* named Cleopas, answered and said to Him,
"Are You [1]the only one visiting Jerusalem and unaware of the
things which have happened here in these days?"
19 And He said to them, "What things?" And they said to Him,
"The things about [a]Jesus the Nazarene, who was a [b]prophet
mighty in deed and word in the sight of God and all the people,

55 [a]Luke 23:49

56 [a]Mark 16:1; Luke 24:1 [b]Ex 20:10f; Deut 5:14

24:1 [a]Luke 24:1-10: *Matt 28:1-8; Mark 16:1-8;* John 20:1-8

3 [a]Luke 7:13; Acts 1:21

4 [a]John 20:12 [b]Luke 2:9; Acts 12:7

6 [1]Or *been raised* [a]Mark 16:6 [b]Matt 17:22f; Mark 9:30f; Luke 9:44; 24:44

7 [a]Matt 16:21; Luke 24:46

8 [a]John 2:22

10 [a]Matt 27:56 [b]Mark 6:30

11 [1]Lit *in their sight* [a]Mark 16:11

12 [1]Or *by themselves* [a]John 20:3-6 [b]John 20:10

13 [1]Lit *60 stadia;* one stadion was about 600 ft [a]Mark 16:12

16 [a]Luke 24:31; John 20:14; 21:4

18 [1]Or *visiting Jerusalem alone*

19 [a]Mark 1:24 [b]Matt 21:11

20 and how the chief priests and our [a]rulers delivered Him to
the sentence of death, and crucified Him.
21 "But we were hoping that it was He who was going to
[a]redeem Israel. Indeed, besides all this, it is the third day since
these things happened.
22 "But also some women among us amazed us. [a]When they
were at the tomb early in the morning,
23 and did not find His body, they came, saying that they had
also seen a vision of angels who said that He was alive.
24 "Some of those who were with us went to the tomb and
found it just exactly as the women also had said; but Him they
did not see."
25 And He said to them, "O foolish men and slow of heart to
believe in all that [a]the prophets have spoken!
26 "[a]Was it not necessary for the [1]Christ to suffer these things
and to enter into His glory?"
27 Then beginning [1]with [a]Moses and [1]with all the [b]prophets,
He explained to them the things concerning Himself in all the
Scriptures.
28 And they approached the village where they were going,
and [a]He acted as though He were going farther.
29 But they urged Him, saying, "Stay with us, for it is *getting*
toward evening, and the day [1]is now nearly over." So He went
in to stay with them.
30 When He had reclined *at the table* with them, He took the
bread and [a]blessed *it,* and breaking *it,* He *began* giving *it* to them.
31 Then their [a]eyes were opened and they recognized Him;
and He vanished from [1]their sight.
32 They said to one another, "[1]Were not our hearts burning
within us while He was speaking to us on the road, while He
[a]was [2]explaining the Scriptures to us?"
33 And they got up that very hour and returned to Jerusalem,
and [a]found gathered together the eleven and [b]those who were
with them,
34 saying, "[a]The Lord has really risen and [b]has appeared to
Simon."
35 They *began* to relate [1]their experiences on the road and
how [a]He was recognized by them in the breaking of the bread.
36 While they were telling these things, [a]He Himself stood in
their midst and *said to them, "Peace be to you."
37 But they were startled and frightened and thought that
they were seeing [a]a spirit.
38 And He said to them, "Why are you troubled, and why do
doubts arise in your [1]hearts?
39 "[a]See My hands and My feet, that it is I Myself; [b]touch Me and
see, for a spirit does not have flesh and bones as you see that I
have."
40 And when He had said this, He showed them His hands
and His feet.
41 While they still [1a]could not believe *it* because of their joy and
amazement, He said to them, "[b]Have you anything here to eat?"

20 [a]Luke 23:13
21 [a]Luke 1:68
22 [a]Luke 24:1ff
25 [a]Matt 26:24
26 [1]I.e. Messiah [a]Luke 24:7, 44ff; Heb 2:10; 1 Pet 1:11
27 [1]Lit *from* [a]Gen 3:15; 12:3; Num 21:9 [John 3:14]; Deut 18:15 [John 1:45]; John 5:46 [b]2 Sam 7:12-16; Is 7:14 [Matt 1:23]; Is 9:1f [Matt 4:15f]; Is 42:1 [Matt 12:18ff]; Is 53:4 [Matt 8:17; Luke 22:37]; Dan 7:13 [Matt 24:30]; Mic 5:2 [Matt 2:6]; Zech 9:9 [Matt 21:5]; Acts 13:27
28 [a]Mark 6:48
29 [1]Lit *has now declined*
30 [a]Matt 14:19
31 [1]Lit *them* [a]Luke 24:16
32 [1]Lit *Was not our heart* [2]Lit *opening* [a]Luke 24:45
33 [a]Mark 16:13 [b]Acts 1:14
34 [a]Luke 24:6 [b]1 Cor 15:5
35 [1]Lit *the things* [a]Luke 24:30f
36 [a]Mark 16:14
37 [a]Matt 14:26; Mark 6:49
38 [1]Lit *heart*
39 [a]John 20:20, 27 [b]John 20:27; 1 John 1:1
41 [1]Lit *were disbelieving* [a]Luke 24:11 [b]John 21:5

42 They gave Him a piece of a broiled fish;
43 and He took it and [a]ate *it* before them.
44 Now He said to them, "[a]These are My words which I
spoke to you while I was still with you, that all things which
are written about Me in the [b]Law of Moses and the Prophets
and [c]the Psalms must be fulfilled."
45 Then He [a]opened their [1]minds to understand the Scriptures,
46 and He said to them, "[a]Thus it is written, that the [1]Christ
would suffer and [b]rise again from the dead the third day,
47 and that [a]repentance [1]for forgiveness of sins would be
proclaimed [2]in His name to [b]all the nations, beginning from
Jerusalem.
48 "You are [a]witnesses of these things.
49 "And behold, [a]I am sending forth the promise of My Father
upon you; but [b]you are to stay in the city until you are clothed
with power from on high."
50 And He led them out as far as [a]Bethany, and He lifted up
His hands and blessed them.
51 While He was blessing them, He parted from them and
was carried up into heaven.
52 And they, after worshiping Him, returned to Jerusalem
with great joy,
53 and were continually in the temple [1]praising God.

43 [a]Acts 10:41

44 [a]Luke 9:22, 44f; 18:31-34; 22:37 [b]Luke 24:27 [c]Ps 2:7ff [Acts 13:33]; Ps 16:10 [Acts 2:27]; Ps 22:1-18 [Matt 27:34-46]; Ps 69:1-21 [John 19:28ff]; Ps 72; 110:1 [Matt 22:43f]; Ps 118:22f [Matt 21:42]

45 [1]Lit *mind* [a]Luke 24:32; Acts 16:14; 1 John 5:20

46 [1]I.e. Messiah [a]Luke 24:26, 44 [b]Luke 24:7

47 [1]Later mss read *and forgiveness* [2]Or *on the basis of* [a]Acts 5:31; 10:43; 13:38; 26:18 [b]Matt 28:19

48 [a]Acts 1:8, 22; 2:32; 3:15; 4:33; 5:32; 10:39, 41; 13:31; 1 Pet 5:1

49 [a]John 14:26 [b]Acts 1:4

50 [a]Matt 21:17; Acts 1:12

53 [1]Lit *blessing*

Luke at a Glance

Theme of Luke:

Author:

Date:

Purpose:

Key Words:

- kingdom (kingdom of God)
- Son of Man
- mark every reference to the devil or demons
- covenant
- pray (prayer, etc.)
- disciple(s)
- sins (sinner)
- every reference to Jesus' second coming

Segment Divisions			Chapter Themes
		1	
		2	
		3	
		4	
		5	
		6	
		7	
		8	
		9	
		10	
		11	
		12	
		13	
		14	
		15	
		16	
		17	
		18	
		19	
		20	
		21	
		22	
		23	
		24	

Life of Christ Showing Coverage by Luke (Shaded Area)

PREPARATION | PUBLIC MINISTRY | SACRIFICE

OBSCURITY (VANISHING)
POPULARITY (DECLINING)
OPPOSITION (INCREASING)

OPENING EVENTS — 4 months
EARLY MINISTRIES — 8 months
EXTENDED MINISTRIES — 4 months; 10 months
SPECIALIZED MINISTRIES — 6 months
CONCLUDING MINISTRIES — 3 months; 3 months
2 months

BIRTH
JOHN INTRODUCES JESUS John 1:19ff
JESUS CLEANSES TEMPLE John 2:13ff
JESUS RETURNS TO GALILEE Mark 1:14
JESUS ORDAINS THE TWELVE Luke 6:12ff
TO TYRE AND SIDON Matthew 15:21
TO FEAST OF TABERNACLES John 7:10
BEYOND JORDAN John 10:40
TRIUMPHAL ENTRY Matthew 21:1
DEATH
RESURRECTION
40 days
ASCENSION

EARLY JUDEAN | EARLY GALILEAN | MIDDLE GALILEAN | LATER GALILEAN | LATER JUDEAN | PEREAN

5 B.C. | FIRST YEAR | — | SECOND YEAR | — | THIRD YEAR

ANNUAL PASSOVERS: John 2:13 | John 5:1 | John 6:4 | John 11:55

Luke: Luke 1 | Luke 4:13 | Luke 4:14 | Luke 6:12 | Luke 9:17 | Luke 9:18 | Luke 9:51 | Luke 13:22 | Luke 19:28 | Luke 24

Used by permission. Jensen, Irving L. *Luke: A Self-Study Guide.* Chicago: Moody Press, 1970.

JOHN

God in the flesh! What would He be like? What would He do? How would He live in relationship to the Father once He came to earth? And how would people know He was God? Would He force people to believe in Him? What about those who refused to believe He was God? And what of those who believed, who followed Him? What would God in the flesh expect from them?

God in the flesh. The incarnation would be hard for some to believe, but their belief or unbelief would be a matter of life or death.

Three other Gospels had been written, and years had passed. One more Gospel was needed, one which would answer these questions and more, one which would illumine the shadows of doubt. So the apostle John answered God's call to write a fourth and final Gospel to explain the One who came to reveal the Father. It was about A.D. 85.

THINGS TO DO

1. Although the author of John is not identified by name, tradition holds that it was the apostle John. Read John 21:20-25 and note how the author identifies himself. You might want to put this reference or information under "Author" on the JOHN AT A GLANCE chart on page 1756.

2. To understand the purpose of John read John 20:30-31. Record this on JOHN AT A GLANCE. Keep John's purpose in mind as you study this Gospel.

Chapters 1–12

1. Carefully read this segment chapter by chapter, observing what the author includes to accomplish his purpose.
   a. Mark the following key words and their synonyms: *believe, life, sign, judge (judgment), witness, love, sin, true (truth), Spirit,* and *king (kingdom)*.
   b. Write the key words on an index card and mark them in the same way you mark them in your Bible. Use this as a bookmark.
   c. Also mark any other repeated key words that are pertinent to the message of the chapter.
2. As you read each of the first 12 chapters, ask the "5 W's and an H": Who? What? Where? When? Why? and How? Observe the events and the people.
   a. *Events:* What is happening? For example, "Nicodemus came to Jesus by night."
   b. *Geographic locations:* Where is this event taking place? For example, John was baptizing at Bethany beyond the Jordan. Double-underline in green all geographical locations.
   c. *Timing of events:* When is this event taking place? For example, "on the third day," or "before the Feast of the Passover." Mark time phrases with a green clock ◷. When Jesus attends a feast, put a clock in the margin and write the name of the feast. (Consult the chart on pages 214, 215.)
   d. *Portrayals of Jesus Christ:* How is Jesus pictured or described? For example: "the Word," "the Lamb of God," etc. You may want to note this in the margin.
   e. *Signs and Miracles:* The signs John recorded were for the purpose of leading people to believe that Jesus is the Christ, the Son of God. Look for these signs or miracles and note them with a special symbol in the margin. For example, Jesus turned water into wine. The text says this was the beginning of His signs.

f. *References that show the deity of Jesus* (references that show that Jesus is God, such as "I am"). Each time you note such a reference, write *Deity* in the margin, and under it, record the next reference to His deity. This will give you a good chain of cross-references.

g. *Witnesses:* Throughout his Gospel, John refers to those who bear witness to Jesus. Who are these witnesses and what is their witness? For example, John said, "I myself have seen, and have testified that this is the Son of God" (John 1:34).

3. Determine the main subject or theme of each chapter and then record it in your Bible next to the chapter number and on JOHN AT A GLANCE.

Chapters 13–17

1. This segment brings a change in Jesus' ministry as He draws away with the disciples in order to prepare them for what is to come. Make a new list of key words on a bookmark: ***believe, love, works, commandments, fruit, abide, ask, truth (truly), witness,*** and ***devil (Satan, ruler of this world)***. (Go back to chapter 12 and mark the references to *ruler of this world.)*

2. Mark in the text in a distinctive way all references, including pronouns, to the Holy Spirit. Then list in your notebook everything you learn about the Holy Spirit. This is especially important in chapters 14 through 16.

3. List in your notebook any specific instructions or commandments that Jesus gives the disciples.

4. Record the main theme of each chapter as you did before.

Chapters 18–21

1. The final chapters of John give an account of the events surrounding the arrest, trial, crucifixion, resurrection, and the postresurrection appearances of Jesus Christ. As you read each chapter:

   a. Mark the following key words and their synonyms: ***witness, believe, love, truth (true), life, signs,*** and ***king (kingdom)***.

   b. Record the progression of events from Jesus' arrest through His resurrection and postresurrection appearances, noting chapters and verses on the appropriate charts on pages 1757 and 1760. Remember that since Luke gives the chronological order of events, it becomes a plumb line for the other Gospel records.

2. Once again determine the theme of each chapter and record it as you have done previously.

3. Compile what John teaches about the King and the kingdom on the chart on pages 1758 and 1759. John 3 contains the only two references to the kingdom. The other references to Jesus as the King are in the first and last segments of John.

4. Complete JOHN AT A GLANCE by doing the following:

   a. Review your chapter themes of John and determine the theme of the book. Record this in the appropriate place on JOHN AT A GLANCE.

   b. You will notice a section titled "Segment Divisions" and two lines where you can record "Signs and Miracles" and "Portrayals of Jesus Christ." Review the information you have recorded in the margins. Record your observations on the appropriate segment division line. For example, in chapter 1 Jesus is referred to as "the Lamb of God." Record that fact at chapter 1 under "Portrayals of Jesus Christ." This will give you a visual picture of the structure of John.

Things to Think About

1. Do you really believe that Jesus is God and live accordingly? And what if you don't? (see John 8:24).

2. Do you know how to take another person through the Scriptures to show him that Jesus is God?

3. Do people know that you are a disciple of Jesus Christ because of your love for others and because you have continued in His Word?

4. Are you relying on the Spirit of God to comfort you, help you, bear witness through you, do the work of God through you, and guide you into all truth?

5. Do you look at other Christians and wonder why God deals differently with you than He does with them? Do you need to hear His words to Peter in John 21:22, "If I want him to remain until I come, what is that to you? You follow Me!"? Are you willing to follow Jesus wherever He leads, even if you have to do it alone? Are you telling others about Him?

Chapter 1 Theme ____________________

1 [a]In the beginning was [b]the Word, and the Word was [c]with
God, and [d]the Word was God.
2 [1]He was in the beginning with God.
3 [a]All things came into being through Him, and apart from
Him nothing came into being that has come into being.
4 [a]In Him was life, and the life was [b]the Light of men.
5 [a]The Light shines in the darkness, and the darkness did not
[1]comprehend it.
6 There [1]came a man sent from God, whose name was [a]John.
7 [1]He came [2a]as a witness, to testify about the Light, [b]so that
all might believe through him.
8 [1a]He was not the Light, but *he came* to testify about the Light.
9 There was [a]the true Light [1]which, coming into the world,
enlightens every man.
10 He was in the world, and [a]the world was made through
Him, and the world did not know Him.
11 He came to His [1]own, and those who were His own did
not receive Him.
12 But as many as received Him, to them He gave the right to
become [a]children of God, *even* [b]to those who believe in His name,
13 [a]who were [1]born, not of [2]blood nor of the will of the flesh
nor of the will of man, but of God.
14 And [a]the Word [b]became flesh, and [1c]dwelt among us, and
[d]we saw His glory, glory as of [2]the only begotten from the
Father, full of [e]grace and [f]truth.

1:1 [a]Gen 1:1; Col 1:17; 1 John 1:1 [b]John 1:14; Rev 19:13 [c]John 17:5; 1 John 1:2 [d]Phil 2:6

2 [1]Lit *This one*

3 [a]John 1:10; 1 Cor 8:6; Col 1:16; Heb 1:2

4 [a]John 5:26; 11:25; 14:6 [b]John 8:12; 9:5; 12:46

5 [1]Or *overpower* [a]John 3:19

6 [1]Or *came into being* [a]Matt 3:1

7 [1]Lit *This one* [2]Lit *for testimony* [a]John 1:15, 19, 32; 3:26; 5:33 [b]John 1:12; Acts 19:4; Gal 3:26

8 [1]Lit *That one* [a]John 1:20

9 [1]Or *which enlightens every person coming into the world* [a]1 John 2:8

10 [a]1 Cor 8:6; Col 1:16; Heb 1:2

11 [1]Or *own things, possessions, domain*

12 [a]John 11:52; Gal 3:26 [b]John 1:7; 3:18; 1 John 3:23; 5:13

13 [1]Or *begotten* [2]Lit *bloods* [a]John 3:5f; James 1:18; 1 Pet 1:23; 1 John 2:29; 3:9

14 [1]Or *tabernacled;* i.e. lived temporarily [2]Or *unique, only one of His kind* [a]Rev 19:13 [b]Rom 1:3; Gal 4:4; Phil 2:7f; 1 Tim 3:16; Heb 2:14; 1 John 1:1f; 4:2; 2 John 7 [c]Rev 21:3 [d]Luke 9:32; John 2:11; 17:22, 24; 2 Pet 1:16f; 1 John 1:1 [e]John 1:17; Rom 5:21; 6:14 [f]John 8:32; 14:6; 18:37

15 John *[a]testified about Him and cried out, saying, "This was
He of whom I said, '[b]He who comes after me [1]has a higher
rank than I, [c]for He existed before me.'"
16 For of His [a]fullness [1]we have all received, and [2]grace upon
grace.
17 For [a]the Law was given through Moses; [b]grace and [c]truth
[1]were realized through Jesus Christ.
18 [a]No one has seen God at any time; [b]the only begotten God
who is [c]in the bosom of the Father, [d]He has explained *Him.*
19 This is [a]the testimony of John, when [b]the Jews sent to him
priests and Levites [c]from Jerusalem to ask him, "Who are you?"
20 And he confessed and did not deny, but confessed, "[a]I am
not [1]the Christ."
21 They asked him, "What then? Are you [a]Elijah?" And he *said,
"I am not." "Are you [b]the Prophet?" And he answered, "No."
22 Then they said to him, "Who are you, so that we may give an
answer to those who sent us? What do you say about yourself?"
23 He said, "I am [a]A VOICE OF ONE CRYING IN THE WILDERNESS, 'MAKE
STRAIGHT THE WAY OF THE LORD,' as Isaiah the prophet said."
24 Now they had been sent from the Pharisees.
25 They asked him, and said to him, "Why then are you
baptizing, if you are not the [1]Christ, nor Elijah, nor [a]the Prophet?"
26 John answered them saying, "[a]I baptize [1]in water, *but*
among you stands One whom you do not know.
27 "*It is* [a]He who comes after me, the [b]thong of whose sandal I
am not worthy to untie."
28 These things took place in Bethany [a]beyond the Jordan,
where John was baptizing.
29 The next day he *saw Jesus coming to him and *said,
"Behold, [a]the Lamb of God who [b]takes away the sin of the
world!
30 "This is He on behalf of whom I said, '[a]After me comes a
Man who [1]has a higher rank than I, [b]for He existed before me.'
31 "I did not recognize [1]Him, but so that He might be
manifested to Israel, I came baptizing [2]in water."
32 John [a]testified saying, "[b]I have seen the Spirit descending
as a dove out of heaven, and He remained upon Him.
33 "I did not recognize [1]Him, but He who sent me to baptize
[2]in water said to me, 'He upon whom you see the Spirit
descending and remaining upon Him, [a]this is the One who
baptizes [2]in the Holy Spirit.'
34 "I myself have seen, and have testified that this is [a]the Son
of God."
35 Again [a]the next day John was standing [1]with two of his
disciples,
36 and he looked at Jesus as He walked, and *said, "Behold,
[a]the Lamb of God!"
37 The two disciples heard him speak, and they followed Jesus.

34 [a]Matt 4:3; John 1:49
35 [1]Lit *and* [a]John 1:29
36 [a]John 1:29

15 [1]Lit *has become before me* [a]John 1:7 [b]Matt 3:11; John 1:27, 30 [c]John 1:30
16 [1]Lit *we all received* [2]Lit *grace for grace* [a]Eph 1:23; 3:19; 4:13; Col 1:19; 2:9
17 [1]Lit *came to be* [a]John 7:19 [b]John 1:14; Rom 5:21; 6:14 [c]John 8:32; 14:6; 18:37
18 [a]Ex 33:20; John 6:46; Col 1:15; 1 Tim 6:16; 1 John 4:12 [b]John 3:16, 18; 1 John 4:9 [c]Luke 16:22; John 13:23 [d]John 3:11
19 [a]John 1:7 [b]John 2:18, 20; 5:10, 15f, 18; 6:41, 52; 7:1, 11, 13, 15, 35; 8:22, 48, 52, 57; 9:18, 22; 10:24, 31, 33 [c]Matt 15:1
20 [1]I.e. the Messiah [a]Luke 3:15f; John 3:28
21 [a]Matt 11:14; 16:14 [b]Deut 18:15, 18; Matt 21:11; John 1:25
23 [a]Is 40:3; Matt 3:3; Mark 1:3; Luke 3:4
25 [1]I.e. Messiah [a]Deut 18:15, 18; Matt 21:11; John 1:21
26 [1]The Gr here can be translated *in, with* or *by* [a]Matt 3:11; Mark 1:8; Luke 3:16; Acts 1:5
27 [a]Matt 3:11; John 1:30 [b]Matt 3:11; Mark 1:7; Luke 3:16
28 [a]John 3:26; 10:40
29 [a]Is 53:7; John 1:36; Acts 8:32; 1 Pet 1:19; Rev 5:6, 8, 12f; 6:1 [b]Matt 1:21; 1 John 3:5
30 [1]Lit *has become before me* [a]Matt 3:11; John 1:27 [b]John 1:15
31 [1]I.e. as the Messiah [2]The Gr here can be translated *in, with* or *by*
32 [a]John 1:7 [b]Matt 3:16; Mark 1:10; Luke 3:22
33 [1]I.e. as the Messiah [2]The Gr here can be translated *in, with* or *by* [a]Matt 3:11; Mark 1:8; Luke 3:16; Acts 1:5

38 And Jesus turned and saw them following, and *said to
them, "What do you seek?" They said to Him, "[a]Rabbi (which
translated means Teacher), where are You staying?"
39 He *said to them, "Come, and you will see." So they came
and saw where He was staying; and they stayed with Him that
day, for it was about the [1]tenth hour.
40 [a]One of the two who heard John *speak* and followed Him,
was Andrew, Simon Peter's brother.
41 He *found first his own brother Simon and *said to him,
"We have found the [a]Messiah" (which translated means [1]Christ).
42 He brought him to Jesus. Jesus looked at him and said,
"You are Simon the son of [1a]John; you shall be called [b]Cephas"
(which is translated [2c]Peter).
43 [a]The next day He purposed to go into [b]Galilee, and He
*found [c]Philip. And Jesus *said to him, "[d]Follow Me."
44 Now [a]Philip was from [b]Bethsaida, of the city of Andrew
and Peter.
45 [a]Philip *found [b]Nathanael and *said to him, "We have
found Him of whom [c]Moses in the Law and *also* [c]the Prophets
wrote—Jesus of [d]Nazareth, [e]the son of Joseph."
46 Nathanael said to him, "[a]Can any good thing come out of
Nazareth?" [b]Philip *said to him, "Come and see."
47 Jesus saw Nathanael coming to Him, and *said of him,
"Behold, an [a]Israelite indeed, in whom there is no deceit!"
48 Nathanael *said to Him, "How do You know me?" Jesus
answered and said to him, "Before [a]Philip called you, when
you were under the fig tree, I saw you."
49 Nathanael answered Him, "[a]Rabbi, You are [b]the Son of
God; You are the [c]King of Israel."
50 Jesus answered and said to him, "Because I said to you that
I saw you under the fig tree, do you believe? You will see
greater things than these."
51 And He *said to him, "Truly, truly, I say to you, you will
see [a]the heavens opened and [b]the angels of God ascending and
descending on [c]the Son of Man."

Chapter 2 Theme ____________________

2 On [a]the third day there was a wedding in [b]Cana of Galilee,
and the [c]mother of Jesus was there;
2 and both Jesus and His [a]disciples were invited to the
wedding.
3 When the wine ran out, the mother of Jesus *said to Him,
"They have no wine."
4 And Jesus *said to her, "[a]Woman, [1b]what does that have to
do with us? [c]My hour has not yet come."
5 His [a]mother *said to the servants, "Whatever He says to
you, do it."
6 Now there were six stone waterpots set there [a]for the
Jewish custom of purification, containing [1]twenty or thirty
gallons each.

38 [a]Matt 23:7f; John 1:49
39 [1]Perhaps 10 a.m. (Roman time)
40 [a]Matt 4:18-22; Mark 1:16-20; Luke 5:2-11; John 1:40-42
41 [1]Gr *Anointed One* [a]Dan 9:25; John 4:25
42 [1]Gr *Joannes* [2]I.e. Rock or Stone [a]Matt 16:17; John 21:15-17 [b]1 Cor 1:12; 3:22; 9:5; 15:5; Gal 1:18; 2:9, 11, 14 [c]Matt 16:18
43 [a]John 1:29, 35 [b]Matt 4:12; John 1:28; 2:11 [c]Matt 10:3; John 1:44-48; 6:5, 7; 12:21f; 14:8f [d]Matt 8:22
44 [a]Matt 10:3; John 1:44-48; 6:5, 7; 12:21f; 14:8f [b]Matt 11:21
45 [a]Matt 10:3; John 1:44-48; 6:5, 7; 12:21f; 14:8f [b]John 1:46-49; 21:2 [c]Luke 24:27 [d]Matt 2:23 [e]Luke 2:48; 3:23; 4:22; John 6:42
46 [a]John 7:41, 52 [b]Matt 10:3; John 1:44-48; 6:5, 7; 12:21f; 14:8f
47 [a]Rom 9:4
48 [a]Matt 10:3; John 1:44-48; 6:5, 7; 12:21f; 14:8f
49 [a]John 1:38 [b]John 1:34 [c]Matt 2:2; 27:42; Mark 15:32; John 12:13
51 [a]Ezek 1:1; Matt 3:16; Luke 3:21; Acts 7:56; 10:11; Rev 19:11 [b]Gen 28:12 [c]Matt 8:20
2:1 [a]John 1:29, 35, 43 [b]John 2:11; 4:46; 21:2 [c]Matt 12:46
2 [a]John 1:40-49; 2:12, 17, 22; 3:22; 4:2, 8, 27; 6:8, 12, 16, 22, 24, 60f, 66; 7:3; 8:31
4 [1]Lit *what to Me and to you* (a Hebrew idiom) [a]John 19:26 [b]Matt 8:29 [c]John 7:6, 8, 30; 8:20
5 [a]Matt 12:46
6 [1]Lit *two or three measures* [a]Mark 7:3f; John 3:25

7 Jesus *said to them, "Fill the waterpots with water." So
they filled them up to the brim.
8 And He *said to them, "Draw *some* out now and take it to
the [1]headwaiter." So they took it *to him.*
9 When the headwaiter tasted the water [a]which had become
wine, and did not know where it came from (but the servants
who had drawn the water knew), the headwaiter *called the
bridegroom,
10 and *said to him, "Every man serves the good wine first,
and when *the people* [a]have [1]drunk freely, *then he serves* the
poorer *wine; but* you have kept the good wine until now."
11 This beginning of *His* [1a]signs Jesus did in Cana of [b]Galilee,
and manifested His [c]glory, and His disciples believed in Him.
12 After this He went down to [a]Capernaum, He and His
[b]mother and *His* [b]brothers and His [c]disciples; and they stayed
there a few days.

Jesus Ministers from Capernaum to Jerusalem

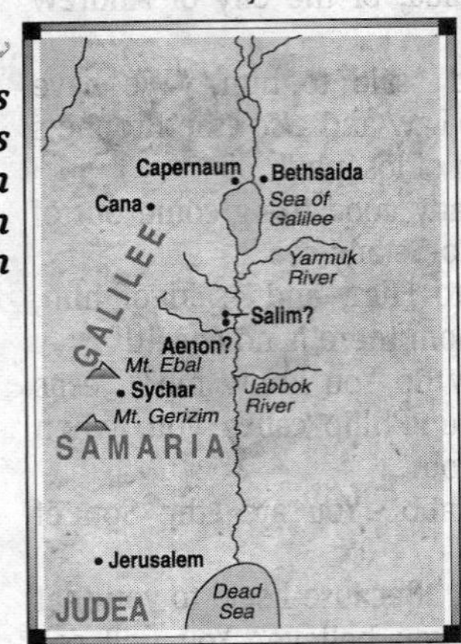

13 [a]The Passover of the Jews
was near, and Jesus [b]went up to
Jerusalem.
14 [a]And He found in the temple
those who were selling oxen and
sheep and doves, and the money
changers seated *at their tables.*
15 And He made a scourge of
cords, and drove *them* all out of
the temple, with the sheep and
the oxen; and He poured out the
coins of the money changers and
overturned their tables;
16 and to those who were selling
[a]the doves He said, "Take these
things away; stop making [b]My
Father's house a [1]place of business."
17 His [a]disciples remembered that it was written, "[b]ZEAL FOR
YOUR HOUSE WILL CONSUME ME."
18 [a]The Jews then said to Him, "[b]What sign do You show us
[1]as your authority for doing these things?"
19 Jesus answered them, "[a]Destroy this [1]temple, and in three
days I will raise it up."
20 [a]The Jews then said, "It took [b]forty-six years to build this
[1]temple, and will You raise it up in three days?"
21 But He was speaking of [a]the [1]temple of His body.
22 So when He was raised from the dead, His [a]disciples
[b]remembered that He said this; and they believed [c]the
Scripture and the word which Jesus had spoken.
23 Now when He was in Jerusalem at [a]the Passover, during
the feast, many believed in His name, [b]observing His signs
which He was doing.
24 But Jesus, on His part, was not entrusting Himself to them,
for [a]He knew all men,
25 and because He did not need anyone to testify concerning
man, [a]for He Himself knew what was in man.

8 [1]Or *steward*

9 [a]John 4:46

10 [1]Or *have become drunk* [a]Matt 24:49; Luke 12:45; Acts 2:15; 1 Cor 11:21; Eph 5:18; 1 Thess 5:7; Rev 17:2, 6

11 [1]Or *attesting miracles;* i.e. one which points to the supernatural power of God in redeeming grace [a]John 2:23; 3:2; 4:54; 6:2, 14, 26, 30; 7:31; 9:16; 10:41; 11:47; 12:18, 37; 20:30 [b]John 1:43 [c]John 1:14

12 [a]Matt 4:13 [b]Matt 12:46 [c]John 2:2

13 [a]Deut 16:1-6; John 5:1; 6:4; 11:55 [b]Luke 2:41; John 2:23

14 [a]John 2:14-16: *Matt 21:12ff; Mark 11:15, 17; Luke 19:45f;* Mal 3:1ff

16 [1]Lit *house* [a]Matt 21:12 [b]Luke 2:49

17 [a]John 2:2 [b]Ps 69:9

18 [1]Lit *that You do these* [a]John 1:19 [b]Matt 12:38

19 [1]Or *sanctuary* [a]Matt 26:61; 27:40; Mark 14:58; 15:29; Acts 6:14

20 [1]Or *sanctuary* [a]John 1:19 [b]Ezra 5:16

21 [1]Or *sanctuary* [a]1 Cor 6:19

22 [a]John 2:2 [b]Luke 24:8; John 2:17; 12:16; 14:26 [c]Ps 16:10; Luke 24:26f; John 20:9; Acts 13:33

23 [a]John 2:13 [b]John 2:11

24 [a]Acts 1:24; 15:8

25 [a]Matt 9:4; John 1:42, 47; 6:61, 64; 13:11

Chapter 3 Theme ______________________________

3 Now there was a man of the Pharisees, named [a]Nicodemus,
a [b]ruler of the Jews;
2 this man came to Jesus by night and said to Him, "[a]Rabbi,
we know that You have come from God *as* a teacher; for no
one can do these [1b]signs that You do unless [c]God is with him."
3 Jesus answered and said to him, "Truly, truly, I say to you,
unless one [a]is born [1]again he cannot see [b]the kingdom of God."
4 Nicodemus *said to Him, "How can a man be born when
he is old? He cannot enter a second time into his mother's
womb and be born, can he?"
5 Jesus answered, "Truly, truly, I say to you, unless one is born
of [a]water and the Spirit he cannot enter into [b]the kingdom of God.
6 "[a]That which is born of the flesh is flesh, and that which is
born of the Spirit is spirit.
7 "Do not be amazed that I said to you, 'You must be born
[1]again.'
8 "[a]The wind blows where it wishes and you hear the sound
of it, but do not know where it comes from and where it is
going; so is everyone who is born of the Spirit."
9 Nicodemus said to Him, "How can these things be?"
10 Jesus answered and said to him, "Are you [a]the teacher of
Israel and do not understand these things?
11 "Truly, truly, I say to you, [a]we speak of what we know and
[b]testify of what we have seen, and [b]you do not accept our
testimony.
12 "If I told you earthly things and you do not believe, how will
you believe if I tell you heavenly things?
13 "[a]No one has ascended into heaven, but [b]He who descended
from heaven: [c]the Son of Man.
14 "As [a]Moses lifted up the serpent in the wilderness, even so
must [b]the Son of Man [c]be lifted up;
15 so that whoever [1]believes will [a]in Him have eternal life.
16 "For God so [a]loved the world, that He [b]gave His [1c]only
begotten Son, that whoever [d]believes in Him shall not perish,
but have eternal life.
17 "For God [a]did not send the Son into the world [b]to judge the
world, but that the world might be saved through Him.
18 "[a]He who believes in Him is not judged; he who does not
believe has been judged already, because he has not believed in
the name of [b]the [1]only begotten Son of God.
19 "This is the judgment, that [a]the Light has come into the
world, and men loved the darkness rather than the Light, for
[b]their deeds were evil.
20 "[a]For everyone who does evil hates the Light, and does not
come to the Light for fear that his deeds will be exposed.
21 "But he who [a]practices the truth comes to the Light, so that
his deeds may be manifested as having been wrought in God."
22 After these things Jesus and His [a]disciples came into the
land of Judea, and there He was spending time with them and
[b]baptizing.

3:1 [a]John 7:50; 19:39 [b]Luke 23:13; John 7:26, 48
2 [1]Or *attesting miracles* [a]Matt 23:7; John 3:26 [b]John 2:11 [c]John 9:33; 10:38; 14:10f; Acts 2:22; 10:38
3 [1]Or *from above* [a]2 Cor 5:17; 1 Pet 1:23 [b]Matt 19:24; 21:31; Mark 9:47; 10:14f; John 3:5
5 [a]Ezek 36:25-27; Eph 5:26; Titus 3:5 [b]Matt 19:24; 21:31; Mark 9:47; 10:14f; John 3:3
6 [a]John 1:13; 1 Cor 15:50
7 [1]Or *from above*
8 [a]Ps 135:7; Eccl 11:5; Ezek 37:9
10 [a]Luke 2:46; 5:17; Acts 5:34
11 [a]John 1:18; 7:16f; 8:26, 28; 12:49; 14:24 [b]John 3:32
13 [a]Deut 30:12; Prov 30:4; Acts 2:34; Rom 10:6; Eph 4:9 [b]John 3:31; 6:38, 42 [c]Matt 8:20
14 [a]Num 21:9 [b]Matt 8:20 [c]John 8:28; 12:34
15 [1]Or *believes in Him will have eternal life* [a]John 20:31; 1 John 5:11-13
16 [1]Or *unique,* only one of His kind [a]Rom 5:8; Eph 2:4; 2 Thess 2:16; 1 John 4:10; Rev 1:5 [b]Rom 8:32; 1 John 4:9 [c]John 1:18; 3:18; 1 John 4:9 [d]John 3:36; 6:40; 11:25f
17 [a]John 3:34; 5:36, 38; 6:29, 38, 57; 7:29; 8:42; 10:36; 11:42; 17:3, 8, 18, 21, 23, 25; 20:21 [b]Luke 19:10; John 8:15; 12:47; 1 John 4:14
18 [1]Or *unique,* only one of His kind [a]Mark 16:16; John 5:24 [b]John 1:18; 1 John 4:9
19 [a]John 1:4; 8:12; 9:5; 12:46 [b]John 7:7
20 [a]John 3:20, 21; Eph 5:11, 13
21 [a]1 John 1:6
22 [a]John 2:2 [b]John 4:1, 2

23 John also was baptizing in Aenon near Salim, because there
was much water there; and *people* were coming and were
being baptized—
24 for [a]John had not yet been thrown into prison.
25 Therefore there arose a discussion on the part of John's
disciples with a Jew about [a]purification.
26 And they came to John and said to him, "[a]Rabbi, He who
was with you [b]beyond the Jordan, to whom you [c]have testified,
behold, He is baptizing and all are coming to Him."
27 John answered and said, "[a]A man can receive nothing
unless it [b]has been given him from heaven.
28 "You yourselves [1]are my witnesses that I said, '[a]I am not the
[2]Christ,' but, 'I have been sent ahead of Him.'
29 "He who has the bride is [a]the bridegroom; but the friend of
the bridegroom, who stands and hears him, rejoices greatly
because of the bridegroom's voice. So this [b]joy of mine has
been made full.
30 "He must increase, but I must decrease.
31 "[a]He who comes from above is above all, [b]he who is of the
earth is from the earth and speaks of the earth. [a]He who comes
from heaven is above all.
32 "What He has seen and heard, of that He [a]testifies; and [a]no
one receives His testimony.
33 "He who has received His testimony [a]has set his seal to *this,*
that God is true.
34 "For He whom God has [a]sent speaks the words of God; [1b]for
He gives the Spirit without measure.
35 "[a]The Father loves the Son and [b]has given all things into His
hand.
36 "He who [a]believes in the Son has eternal life; but he who
[b]does not [1]obey the Son will not see life, but the wrath of God
abides on him."

Chapter 4 Theme ____________________

4 Therefore when [a]the Lord knew that the Pharisees had
heard that Jesus was making and [b]baptizing more disciples
than John
2 (although [a]Jesus Himself was not baptizing, but His [b]disciples
were),
3 He left [a]Judea and went away [b]again into Galilee.
4 And He had to pass through [a]Samaria.
5 So He *came to a city of [a]Samaria called Sychar, near [b]the
parcel of ground that [c]Jacob gave to his son Joseph;
6 and Jacob's well was there. So Jesus, being wearied from His
journey, was sitting thus by the well. It was about [1]the sixth hour.
7 There *came a woman of Samaria to draw water. Jesus
*said to her, "Give Me a drink."
8 For His [a]disciples had gone away into [b]the city to buy food.
9 Therefore the [a]Samaritan woman *said to Him, "How is it
that You, being a Jew, ask me for a drink since I am a Samaritan
woman?" (For [b]Jews have no dealings with Samaritans.)

INSIGHT

It is difficult to pinpoint who the ***Samaritans*** are racially. However, it is believed that after the Assyrians conquered the northern kingdom, they "imported" people into Samaria. Some of the Jews married these importees. Their offspring were called Samaritans. When the Jews returned after the captivity, the Samaritans wanted a share in rebuilding the temple but were rejected because of their pagan practices. The enmity continued through the time of Jesus (see 2 Kings 17:33 and Ezra 4:2, 3).

24 [a]Matt 4:12; 14:3; Mark 6:17; Luke 3:20

25 [a]John 2:6

26 [a]Matt 23:7; John 3:2 [b]John 1:28 [c]John 1:7

27 [a]1 Cor 4:7; Heb 5:4 [b]James 1:17

28 [1]Lit *testify for me* [2]I.e. Messiah [a]John 1:20, 23

29 [a]Matt 9:15; 25:1 [b]John 15:11; 16:24; 17:13; Phil 2:2; 1 John 1:4; 2 John 12

31 [a]Matt 28:18; John 3:13; 8:23 [b]1 Cor 15:47; 1 John 4:5

32 [a]John 3:11

33 [a]John 6:27; Rom 4:11; 15:28; 1 Cor 9:2; 2 Cor 1:22; Eph 1:13; 4:30; 2 Tim 2:19; Rev 7:3-8

34 [1]Lit *because He does not give the Spirit by measure* [a]John 3:17 [b]Matt 12:18; Luke 4:18; Acts 1:2; 10:38

35 [a]Matt 28:18; John 5:20; 17:2 [b]Matt 11:27; Luke 10:22

36 [1]Or *believe* [a]John 3:16 [b]Acts 14:2; Heb 3:18

4:1 [a]Luke 7:13 [b]John 3:22, 26; 1 Cor 1:17

2 [a]John 3:22, 26; 1 Cor 1:17 [b]John 2:2

3 [a]John 3:22 [b]John 2:11f

4 [a]Luke 9:52

5 [a]Luke 9:52 [b]Gen 33:19; Josh 24:32 [c]Gen 48:22; John 4:12

6 [1]Perhaps 6 p.m. Roman time or noon Jewish time

8 [a]John 2:2 [b]John 4:5, 39

9 [a]Luke 9:52 [b]Ezra 4:3-6, 11ff; Matt 10:5; John 8:48; Acts 10:28

10 Jesus answered and said to her, "If you knew the gift of God,
and who it is who says to you, 'Give Me a drink,' you would
have asked Him, and He would have given you [a]living water."
11 She *said to Him, "[1]Sir, You have nothing to draw with and
the well is deep; where then do You get that [a]living water?
12 "You are not greater than our father Jacob, are You, who [a]gave
us the well, and drank of it himself and his sons and his cattle?"
13 Jesus answered and said to her, "Everyone who drinks of
this water will thirst again;
14 but whoever drinks of the water that I will give him [a]shall
never thirst; but the water that I will give him will become in
him a well of water springing up to [b]eternal life."
15 The woman *said to Him, "[1]Sir, [a]give me this water, so I
will not be thirsty nor come all the way here to draw."
16 He *said to her, "Go, call your husband and come here."
17 The woman answered and said, "I have no husband." Jesus
*said to her, "You have correctly said, 'I have no husband';
18 for you have had five husbands, and the one whom you
now have is not your husband; this you have said truly."
19 The woman *said to Him, "[1]Sir, I perceive that You are [a]a
prophet.
20 "[a]Our fathers worshiped in [b]this mountain, and you *people*
say that [c]in Jerusalem is the place where men ought to worship."
21 Jesus *said to her, "Woman, believe Me, [a]an hour is coming
when [b]neither in this mountain nor in Jerusalem will you
worship the Father.
22 "[a]You worship what you do not know; we worship what we
know, for [b]salvation is from the Jews.
23 "But [a]an hour is coming, and now is, when the true
worshipers will worship the Father [b]in spirit and truth; for
such people the Father seeks to be His worshipers.
24 "God is [1]spirit, and those who worship Him must worship
[a]in spirit and truth."
25 The woman *said to Him, "I know that [a]Messiah is coming
([b]He who is called Christ); when that One comes, He will
declare all things to us."
26 Jesus *said to her, "[a]I who speak to you am *He*."
27 At this point His [a]disciples came, and they were amazed
that He had been speaking with a woman, yet no one said,
"What do You seek?" or, "Why do You speak with her?"
28 So the woman left her waterpot, and went into the city and
*said to the men,
29 "Come, see a man [a]who told me all the things that I *have*
done; [b]this is not [1]the Christ, is it?"
30 They went out of the city, and were coming to Him.
31 Meanwhile the disciples were urging Him, saying, "[a]Rabbi,
eat."
32 But He said to them, "I have food to eat that you do not
know about."
33 So the [a]disciples were saying to one another, "No one
brought Him *anything* to eat, did he?"

10 [a]Jer 2:13; John 4:14; 7:37f; Rev 7:17; 21:6; 22:1, 17
11 [1]Or *Lord* [a]Jer 2:13; John 4:14; 7:37f; Rev 7:17; 21:6; 22:1, 17
12 [a]John 4:6
14 [a]John 6:35; 7:38 [b]Matt 25:46; John 6:27
15 [1]Or *Lord* [a]John 6:35
19 [1]Or *Lord* [a]Matt 21:11; Luke 7:16, 39; 24:19; John 6:14; 7:40; 9:17
20 [a]Gen 33:20; John 4:12 [b]Deut 11:29; Josh 8:33 [c]Luke 9:53
21 [a]John 4:23; 5:25, 28; 16:2, 32 [b]Mal 1:11; 1 Tim 2:8
22 [a]2 Kin 17:28-41 [b]Is 2:3; Rom 3:1f; 9:4f
23 [a]John 4:21; 5:25, 28; 16:2, 32 [b]Phil 3:3
24 [1]Or *Spirit* [a]Phil 3:3
25 [a]Dan 9:25; John 1:41 [b]Matt 1:16; 27:17, 22; Luke 2:11
26 [a]John 8:24, 28, 58; 9:37; 13:19
27 [a]John 4:8
29 [1]I.e. the Messiah [a]John 4:17f [b]Matt 12:23; John 7:26, 31
31 [a]Matt 23:7; 26:25, 49; Mark 9:5; 11:21; 14:45; John 1:38, 49; 3:2, 26; 6:25; 9:2; 11:8
33 [a]Luke 6:13-16; John 1:40-49; 2:2

34 Jesus *said to them, "My food is to [a]do the will of Him who sent Me and to [b]accomplish His work.

35 "Do you not say, 'There are yet four months, and *then* comes the harvest'? Behold, I say to you, lift up your eyes and look on the fields, that they are white [a]for harvest.

36 "Already he who reaps is receiving [a]wages and is gathering [b]fruit for [c]life eternal; so that he who sows and he who reaps may rejoice together.

37 "For in this *case* the saying is true, '[a]One sows and another reaps.'

38 "I sent you to reap that for which you have not labored; others have labored and you have entered into their labor."

39 From [a]that city many of the Samaritans believed in Him because of the word of the woman who testified, "[b]He told me all the things that I *have* done."

40 So when the Samaritans came to Jesus, they were asking Him to stay with them; and He stayed there two days.

41 Many more believed because of His word;

42 and they were saying to the woman, "It is no longer because of what you said that we believe, for we have heard for ourselves and know that this One is indeed [a]the Savior of the world."

43 After [a]the two days He went forth from there into Galilee.

44 For Jesus Himself testified that [a]a prophet has no honor in his own country.

45 So when He came to Galilee, the Galileans received Him, [a]having seen all the things that He did in Jerusalem at the feast; for they themselves also went to the feast.

46 Therefore He came again to [a]Cana of Galilee [b]where He had made the water wine. And there was a royal official whose son was sick at [c]Capernaum.

47 When he heard that Jesus had come [a]out of Judea into Galilee, he went to Him and was imploring *Him* to come down and heal his son; for he was at the point of death.

48 So Jesus said to him, "Unless you *people* see [1a]signs and [a]wonders, you *simply* will not believe."

49 The royal official *said to Him, "[1]Sir, come down before my child dies."

50 Jesus *said to him, "[a]Go; your son lives." The man believed the word that Jesus spoke to him and started off.

51 As he was now going down, *his* slaves met him, saying that his [1]son was living.

52 So he inquired of them the hour when he began to get better. Then they said to him, "Yesterday at the [1]seventh hour the fever left him."

53 So the father knew that *it was* at that hour in which Jesus said to him, "Your son lives"; and he himself believed and [a]his whole household.

54 This is again a [a]second [1]sign that Jesus performed when He had [b]come out of Judea into Galilee.

34 [a]John 5:30; 6:38 [b]John 5:36; 17:4; 19:28, 30

35 [a]Matt 9:37, 38; Luke 10:2

36 [a]Prov 11:18; 1 Cor 9:17f [b]Rom 1:13 [c]Matt 19:29; John 3:36; 4:14; 5:24; Rom 2:7; 6:23

37 [a]Job 31:8; Mic 6:15

39 [a]John 4:5, 30 [b]John 4:29

42 [a]Matt 1:21; Luke 2:11; John 1:29; Acts 5:31; 13:23; 1 Tim 4:10; 1 John 4:14

43 [a]John 4:40

44 [a]Matt 13:57; Mark 6:4; Luke 4:24

45 [a]John 2:23

46 [a]John 2:1 [b]John 2:9 [c]Luke 4:23; John 2:12

47 [a]John 4:3, 54

48 [1]Or *attesting miracles* [a]Dan 4:2f; 6:27; Matt 24:24; Mark 13:22; Acts 2:19, 22, 43; 4:30; 5:12; 6:8; 7:36; 14:3; 15:12; Rom 15:19; 1 Cor 1:22; 2 Cor 12:12; 2 Thess 2:9; Heb 2:4

49 [1]Or *Lord*

50 [a]Matt 8:13

51 [1]Or *boy*

52 [1]Perhaps 7 p.m. Roman time or 1 p.m. Jewish time

53 [a]Acts 11:14

54 [1]Or *attesting miracle* [a]John 2:11 [b]John 4:45f

Chapter 5 Theme ______________________________

5 After these things there was [a]a feast of the Jews, and Jesus
went up to Jerusalem.
2 Now there is in Jerusalem by [a]the sheep *gate* a pool, which
is called [b]in [1]Hebrew [2]Bethesda, having five porticoes.
3 In these lay a multitude of those who were sick, blind,
lame, and withered, [[1]waiting for the moving of the waters;
4 for an angel of the Lord went down at certain seasons into
the pool and stirred up the water; whoever then first, after the
stirring up of the water, stepped in was made well from
whatever disease with which he was afflicted.]
5 A man was there who had been [1]ill for thirty-eight years.
6 When Jesus saw him lying *there,* and knew that he had
already been a long time *in that condition,* He *said to him,
"Do you wish to get well?"
7 The sick man answered Him, "Sir, I have no man to put
me into the pool when [a]the water is stirred up, but while I am
coming, another steps down before me."
8 Jesus *said to him, "[a]Get up, pick up your pallet and walk."
9 Immediately the man became well, and picked up his
pallet and *began* to walk.
[a]**N**ow it was the Sabbath on that day.
10 So [a]the Jews were saying to the man who was cured, "It is
the Sabbath, and [b]it is not permissible for you to carry your
pallet."
11 But he answered them, "He who made me well was the
one who said to me, 'Pick up your pallet and walk.'"
12 They asked him, "Who is the man who said to you, 'Pick
up *your pallet* and walk'?"
13 But the man who was healed did not know who it was, for
Jesus had slipped away while there was a crowd in *that* place.
14 Afterward Jesus *found him in the temple and said to him,
"Behold, you have become well; do not [a]sin anymore, [b]so that
nothing worse happens to you."
15 The man went away, and told [a]the Jews that it was Jesus
who had made him well.
16 For this reason [a]the Jews were persecuting Jesus, because
He was doing these things on the Sabbath.
17 But He answered them, "My Father is working until now,
and I Myself am working."
18 For this reason therefore [a]the Jews [b]were seeking all the
more to kill Him, because He not only was breaking the
Sabbath, but also was calling God His own Father, [c]making
Himself equal with God.
19 Therefore Jesus answered and was saying to them, "Truly,
truly, I say to you, [a]the Son can do nothing of Himself, unless *it
is* something He sees the Father doing; for whatever [1]the
Father does, these things the Son also does in like manner.
20 "[a]For the Father loves the Son, and shows Him all things
that He Himself is doing; and *the Father* will show Him
[b]greater works than these, so that you will marvel.

5:1 [a]Deut 16:1; John 2:13

2 [1]I.e. Jewish Aramaic [2]Some early mss read *Bethsaida* or *Bethzatha* [a]Neh 3:1, 32; 12:39 [b]John 19:13, 17, 20; 20:16; Acts 21:40; Rev 9:11; 16:16

3 [1]Early mss do not contain the remainder of v 3, nor v 4

5 [1]Lit *in his sickness*

7 [a]John 5:4

8 [a]Matt 9:6; Mark 2:11; Luke 5:24

9 [a]John 9:14

10 [a]John 1:19; 5:15, 16, 18 [b]Neh 13:19; Jer 17:21f; Matt 12:2; Luke 6:2; John 7:23; 9:16

14 [a]Mark 2:5; John 8:11 [b]Ezra 9:14

15 [a]John 1:19; 5:16, 18

16 [a]John 1:19; 5:10, 15, 18

18 [a]John 1:19; 5:15, 16 [b]John 5:16; 7:1 [c]John 10:33; 19:7

19 [1]Lit *that One* [a]Matt 26:39; John 5:30; 6:38; 8:28; 12:49; 14:10

20 [a]Matt 3:17; John 3:35; 2 Pet 1:17 [b]John 14:12

21 "For just as the Father raises the dead and [a]gives them life,
even so [b]the Son also gives life to whom He wishes.
22 "For not even the Father judges anyone, but [a]He has given
all judgment to the Son,
23 so that all will honor the Son even as they honor the
Father. [a]He who does not honor the Son does not honor the
Father who sent Him.
24 "Truly, truly, I say to you, he who hears My word, and
[a]believes Him who sent Me, has eternal life, and [b]does not
come into judgment, but has [c]passed out of death into life.
25 "Truly, truly, I say to you, [a]an hour is coming and now is,
when [b]the dead will hear the voice of the Son of God, and
those who [c]hear will live.
26 "For just as the Father has life in Himself, even so He [a]gave
to the Son also to have life in Himself;
27 and He gave Him authority to [a]execute judgment, because
He is [1]*the* Son of Man.
28 "Do not marvel at this; for [a]an hour is coming, in which [b]all
who are in the tombs will hear His voice,
29 and will come forth; [a]those who did the good *deeds* to a
resurrection of life, those who committed the evil *deeds* to a
resurrection of judgment.
30 "[a]I can do nothing on My own initiative. As I hear, I judge;
and [b]My judgment is just, because I do not seek My own will,
but [c]the will of Him who sent Me.
31 "[a]If I *alone* testify about Myself, My testimony is not [1]true.
32 "There is [a]another who testifies of Me, and I know that the
testimony which He gives about Me is true.
33 "You have sent to John, and he [a]has testified to the truth.
34 "But [a]the testimony which I receive is not from man, but I
say these things so that you may be saved.
35 "He was [a]the lamp that was burning and was shining and
you [b]were willing to rejoice for [1]a while in his light.
36 "But the testimony which I have is greater than *the
testimony of* John; for [a]the works which the Father has given
Me [b]to accomplish—the very works that I do—testify about
Me, that the Father [c]has sent Me.
37 "And the Father who sent Me, [a]He has testified of Me. You
have neither heard His voice at any time nor seen His form.
38 "You do not have [a]His word abiding in you, for you do not
believe Him whom He [b]sent.
39 "[1a]You search the Scriptures because you think that in them
you have eternal life; it is [b]these that testify about Me;
40 and you are unwilling to come to Me so that you may have
life.
41 "[a]I do not receive glory from men;
42 but I know you, that you do not have the love of God in
yourselves.
43 "I have come in My Father's name, and you do not receive
Me; [a]if another comes in his own name, you will receive him.
44 "How can you believe, when you [a]receive [1]glory from one

21 [a]Rom 4:17; 8:11 [b]John 11:25

22 [a]John 5:27; 9:39; Acts 10:42; 17:31

23 [a]Luke 10:16; 1 John 2:23

24 [a]John 3:18; 12:44; 20:31; 1 John 5:13 [b]John 3:18 [c]1 John 3:14

25 [a]John 4:21, 23; 5:28 [b]Luke 15:24 [c]John 6:60; 8:43, 47; 9:27

26 [a]John 1:4; 6:57

27 [1]Or *a son of man* [a]John 9:39; Acts 10:42; 17:31

28 [a]John 4:21 [b]John 11:24; 1 Cor 15:52

29 [a]Dan 12:2; Matt 25:46; Acts 24:15

30 [a]John 5:19 [b]John 8:16 [c]John 4:34; 6:38

31 [1]I.e. admissible as legal evidence [a]John 8:14

32 [a]John 5:37

33 [a]John 1:7, 15, 19, 32; 3:26-30

34 [a]John 5:32; 1 John 5:9

35 [1]Lit *an hour* [a]2 Sam 21:17; 2 Pet 1:19 [b]Mark 1:5

36 [a]Matt 11:4; John 2:23; 10:25, 38; 14:11; 15:24 [b]John 4:34 [c]John 3:17

37 [a]Matt 3:17; Mark 1:11; Luke 3:22; 24:27; John 8:18; 1 John 5:9

38 [a]1 John 2:14 [b]John 3:17

39 [1]Or (a command) *Search the Scriptures!* [a]John 7:52; Rom 2:17ff [b]Luke 24:25, 27; Acts 13:27

41 [a]John 5:44; 7:18; 1 Thess 2:6

43 [a]Matt 24:5

44 [1]Or *honor* or *fame* [a]John 5:41

another and you do not seek [b]the [1]glory that is from [c]the *one
and* only God?
45 "Do not think that I will accuse you before the Father; the
one who accuses you is [a]Moses, in whom you have set your hope.
46 "For if you believed Moses, you would believe Me, for [a]he
wrote about Me.
47 "But [a]if you do not believe his writings, how will you
believe My words?"

Chapter 6 Theme __________________________________

6 After these things [a]Jesus went away to the other side of
[b]the Sea of Galilee (or [c]Tiberias).
2 A large crowd followed Him, because they saw the [1a]signs
which He was performing on those who were sick.
3 Then [a]Jesus went up on the mountain, and there He sat
down with His disciples.
4 Now [a]the Passover, the feast of the Jews, was near.
5 Therefore Jesus, lifting up His eyes and seeing that a large
crowd was coming to Him, *said to [a]Philip, "Where are we to
buy bread, so that these may eat?"
6 This He was saying to [a]test him, for He Himself knew what
He was intending to do.
7 [a]Philip answered Him, "[b]Two hundred [1]denarii worth of
bread is not sufficient for them, for everyone to receive a little."
8 One of His [a]disciples, [b]Andrew, Simon Peter's brother, *said
to Him,
9 "There is a lad here who has five barley loaves and two
[a]fish, but what are these for so many people?"
10 Jesus said, "Have the people [1]sit down." Now there was
[a]much grass in the place. So the men [1]sat down, in number
about [b]five thousand.
11 Jesus then took the loaves, and [a]having given thanks, He
distributed to those who were seated; likewise also of the [b]fish
as much as they wanted.
12 When they were filled, He *said to His [a]disciples, "Gather
up the leftover fragments so that nothing will be lost."
13 So they gathered them up, and filled twelve [a]baskets with
fragments from the five barley loaves which were left over by
those who had eaten.
14 Therefore when the people saw the [1]sign which He had
performed, they said, "This is truly the [a]Prophet who is to
come into the world."
15 So Jesus, perceiving that they were [1]intending to come and
take Him by force [a]to make Him king, [b]withdrew again to [c]the
mountain by Himself alone.
16 Now when evening came, His [a]disciples went down to the
sea,
17 and after getting into a boat, they *started to* cross the sea
[a]to Capernaum. It had already become dark, and Jesus had not
yet come to them.

44 [1]Or *honor* or *fame* [b]Rom 2:29 [c]John 17:3; 1 Tim 1:17
45 [a]John 9:28; Rom 2:17ff
46 [a]Luke 24:27
47 [a]Luke 16:29, 31
6:1 [a]John 6:1-13: *Matt 14:13-21; Mark 6:32-44; Luke 9:10-17* [b]Matt 4:18; Luke 5:1 [c]John 6:23; 21:1
2 [1]Or *attesting miracles* [a]John 2:11, 23; 3:2; 6:14, 30; 11:47; 12:18, 37; 20:30
3 [a]Matt 5:1; Mark 3:13; Luke 6:12; 9:28; John 6:15
4 [a]Deut 16:1; John 2:13
5 [a]John 1:43
6 [a]2 Cor 13:5; Rev 2:2
7 [1]The denarius was equivalent to a day's wages [a]John 1:43 [b]Mark 6:37
8 [a]John 2:2 [b]John 1:40
9 [a]John 6:11; 21:9, 10, 13
10 [1]Lit *recline(d)* [a]Mark 6:39 [b]Matt 14:21
11 [a]Matt 15:36; John 6:23 [b]John 6:9; 21:9, 10, 13
12 [a]John 2:2
13 [a]Matt 14:20
14 [1]Or *attesting miracle* [a]Matt 11:3; 21:11; John 1:21
15 [1]Or *about* [a]John 18:36f [b]John 6:15-21: *Matt 14:22-33; Mark 6:45-51* [c]John 6:3
16 [a]John 2:2
17 [a]Mark 6:45; John 6:24, 59

INSIGHT

See the chart **The Feasts of Israel** located on pages 214, 215.

18 The sea *began* to be stirred up because a strong wind was
blowing.
19 Then, when they had rowed about [1]three or four miles,
they *saw Jesus walking on the sea and drawing near to the
boat; and they were frightened.
20 But He *said to them, "It is I; [1a]do not be afraid."
21 So they were willing to receive Him into the boat, and
immediately the boat was at the land to which they were going.
22 The next day [a]the crowd that stood on the other side of the
sea saw that there was no other small boat there, except one,
and that Jesus [b]had not entered with His disciples into the
boat, but *that* His disciples had gone away alone.
23 There came other small boats from [a]Tiberias near to the
place where they ate the bread after the [b]Lord [c]had given thanks.
24 So when the crowd saw that Jesus was not there, nor His
disciples, they themselves got into the small boats, and [a]came
to Capernaum seeking Jesus.
25 When they found Him on the other side of the sea, they
said to Him, "[a]Rabbi, when did You get here?"
26 Jesus answered them and said, "Truly, truly, I say to you,
you [a]seek Me, not because you saw [b]signs, but because you ate
of the loaves and were filled.
27 "Do not [a]work for the food which perishes, but for the food
which endures to [b]eternal life, which [c]the Son of Man will give
to you, for on Him the Father, God, [d]has set His seal."
28 Therefore they said to Him, "What shall we do, so that we
may work the works of God?"
29 Jesus answered and said to them, "This is [a]the work of
God, that you believe in Him whom He [b]has sent."
30 So they said to Him, "[a]What then do You do for a [b]sign, so
that we may see, and believe You? What work do You perform?
31 "[a]Our fathers ate the manna in the wilderness; as it is
written, '[b]HE GAVE THEM BREAD OUT OF HEAVEN TO EAT.'"
32 Jesus then said to them, "Truly, truly, I say to you, it is not
Moses who has given you the bread out of heaven, but it is My
Father who gives you the true bread out of heaven.
33 "For the bread of God is [1]that which [a]comes down out of
heaven, and gives life to the world."
34 Then they said to Him, "Lord, always [a]give us this bread."
35 Jesus said to them, "[a]I am the bread of life; he who comes
to Me will not hunger, and he who believes in Me [b]will never
thirst.
36 "But [a]I said to you that you have seen Me, and yet do not
believe.
37 "[a]All that the Father gives Me will come to Me, and the one
who comes to Me I will certainly not cast out.
38 "For [a]I have come down from heaven, [b]not to do My own
will, but [c]the will of Him who [d]sent Me.
39 "This is the will of Him who sent Me, that of [a]all that He has
given Me I [b]lose nothing, but [c]raise it up on the last day.
40 "For this is the will of My Father, that everyone who

19 [1]Lit *25 or 30 stadia*

20 [1]Or *stop being afraid* [a]Matt 14:27

22 [a]John 6:2 [b]John 6:15ff

23 [a]John 6:1 [b]Luke 7:13 [c]John 6:11

24 [a]Matt 14:34; Mark 6:53; John 6:17, 59

25 [a]Matt 23:7

26 [a]John 6:24 [b]John 6:2, 14, 30

27 [a]Is 55:2 [b]John 3:15f; 4:14; 6:40, 47, 54; 10:28; 17:2f [c]Matt 8:20; John 6:53, 62 [d]John 3:33

29 [a]1 Thess 1:3; James 2:22; 1 John 3:23; Rev 2:26 [b]John 3:17

30 [a]Matt 12:38 [b]John 6:2, 14, 26

31 [a]Ex 16:4, 15, 21; Num 11:8; John 6:49, 58 [b]Ps 78:24; Ex 16:4, 15; Neh 9:15; Ps 105:40

33 [1]Or *He who comes* [a]John 6:41, 50

34 [a]John 4:15

35 [a]John 6:48, 51 [b]John 4:14

36 [a]John 6:26

37 [a]John 6:39; 17:2, 24

38 [a]John 3:13 [b]Matt 26:39 [c]John 4:34; 5:30 [d]John 6:29

39 [a]John 6:37; 17:2, 24 [b]John 17:12; 18:9 [c]Matt 10:15; John 6:40, 44, 54; 11:24

[a]beholds the Son and [b]believes in Him will have eternal life,
and I Myself will [c]raise him up on the last day."
41 [a]Therefore the Jews were grumbling about Him, because
He said, "I am the bread that [b]came down out of heaven."
42 They were saying, "[a]Is not this Jesus, the son of Joseph,
whose father and mother [b]we know? How does He now say, '[c]I
have come down out of heaven'?"
43 Jesus answered and said to them, "Do not grumble among
yourselves.
44 "No one can come to Me unless the Father who sent Me
[a]draws him; and I will [b]raise him up on the last day.
45 "It is written [a]in the prophets, '[b]AND THEY SHALL ALL BE [c]TAUGHT
OF GOD.' Everyone who has heard and learned from the Father,
comes to Me.
46 "[a]Not that anyone has seen the Father, except the One who
is from God; He has seen the Father.
47 "Truly, truly, I say to you, he who believes [a]has eternal life.
48 "[a]I am the bread of life.
49 "[a]Your fathers ate the manna in the wilderness, and they died.
50 "This is the bread which [a]comes down out of heaven, so
that one may eat of it and [b]not die.
51 "[a]I am the living bread that [b]came down out of heaven; if
anyone eats of this bread, [c]he will live forever; and the bread
also which I will give [d]for the life of the world is [e]My flesh."
52 [a]Then the Jews [b]*began* to argue with one another, saying,
"How can this man give us *His* flesh to eat?"
53 So Jesus said to them, "Truly, truly, I say to you, unless you
eat the flesh of [a]the Son of Man and drink His blood, you have
no life in yourselves.
54 "He who eats My flesh and drinks My blood has eternal life,
and I will [a]raise him up on the last day.
55 "For My flesh is true food, and My blood is true drink.
56 "He who eats My flesh and drinks My blood [a]abides in Me,
and I in him.
57 "As the [a]living Father [b]sent Me, and I live because of the
Father, so he who eats Me, he also will live because of Me.
58 "This is the bread which [a]came down out of heaven; not as [b]the
fathers ate and died; he who eats this bread [c]will live forever."
59 These things He said [a]in the synagogue as He taught [b]in
Capernaum.
60 Therefore many of His [a]disciples, when they heard *this*
said, "[b]This is a difficult statement; who can listen to it?"
61 But Jesus, [a]conscious that His disciples grumbled at this,
said to them, "Does this [b]cause you to stumble?
62 "*What* then if you see [a]the Son of Man [b]ascending to where
He was before?
63 "[a]It is the Spirit who gives life; the flesh profits nothing; [b]the
words that I have spoken to you are spirit and are life.
64 "But there are [a]some of you who do not believe." For Jesus
[b]knew from the beginning who they were who did not believe,
and [c]who it was that would [1]betray Him.

40 [a]John 12:45; 14:17, 19 [b]John 3:16 [c]Matt 10:15; John 6:39, 44, 54; 11:24
41 [a]John 1:19; 6:52 [b]John 6:33, 51, 58
42 [a]Luke 4:22 [b]John 7:27f [c]John 6:38, 62
44 [a]Jer 31:3; Hos 11:4; John 6:65; 12:32 [b]John 6:39
45 [a]Acts 7:42; 13:40; Heb 8:11 [b]Is 54:13; Jer 31:34 [c]Phil 3:15; 1 Thess 4:9; 1 John 2:27
46 [a]John 1:18
47 [a]John 3:36; 5:24; 6:51, 58; 11:26
48 [a]John 6:35, 51
49 [a]John 6:31, 58
50 [a]John 6:33 [b]John 3:36; 5:24; 6:47, 51, 58; 11:26
51 [a]John 6:35, 48 [b]John 6:41, 58 [c]John 3:36; 5:24; 6:47, 58; 11:26 [d]John 1:29; 3:14f; Heb 10:10; 1 John 4:10 [e]John 6:53-56
52 [a]John 1:19; 6:41 [b]John 9:16; 10:19
53 [a]Matt 8:20; John 6:27, 62
54 [a]John 6:39
56 [a]John 15:4f; 17:23; 1 John 2:24; 3:24; 4:15f
57 [a]Matt 16:16; John 5:26 [b]John 3:17; 6:29, 38
58 [a]John 6:33, 41, 51 [b]John 6:31, 49 [c]John 3:36; 5:24; 6:47, 51; 11:26
59 [a]Matt 4:23 [b]John 6:24
60 [a]John 2:2; 6:66; 7:3 [b]John 6:52
61 [a]John 6:64 [b]Matt 11:6
62 [a]Matt 8:20; John 6:27, 53 [b]Mark 16:19; John 3:13
63 [a]2 Cor 3:6 [b]John 6:68
64 [1]Or *hand Him over* [a]John 6:60, 66 [b]John 2:25 [c]Matt 10:4; John 6:71; 13:11

65 And He was saying, "For this reason I have [a]said to you,
that no one can come to Me unless [b]it has been granted him
from the Father."
66 As a result of this many of His [a]disciples [b]withdrew and
were not walking with Him anymore.
67 So Jesus said to [a]the twelve, "You do not want to go away
also, do you?"
68 [a]Simon Peter answered Him, "Lord, to whom shall we go?
You have [b]words of eternal life.
69 "We have believed and have come to know that You are [a]the
Holy One of God."
70 Jesus answered them, "[a]Did I Myself not choose you, [b]the
twelve, and *yet* one of you is [c]a devil?"
71 Now He meant Judas [a]*the son* of Simon Iscariot, for he,
[b]one of [c]the twelve, [1]was going to betray Him.

Chapter 7 Theme ______________________________

7 After these things Jesus [a]was walking in Galilee, for He
was unwilling to walk in Judea because [b]the Jews [c]were
seeking to kill Him.
2 Now the feast of the Jews, [a]the Feast of Booths, was near.
3 Therefore His [a]brothers said to Him, "Leave here and go
into Judea, so that Your [b]disciples also may see Your works
which You are doing.
4 "For no one does anything in secret [1]when he himself seeks
to be *known* publicly. If You do these things, show Yourself to
the world."
5 For not even His [a]brothers were believing in Him.
6 So Jesus *said to them, "[a]My time is not yet here, but your
time is always opportune.
7 "[a]The world cannot hate you, but it hates Me because I
testify of it, that [b]its deeds are evil.
8 "Go up to the feast yourselves; I do not go up to this feast
because [a]My time has not yet fully come."
9 Having said these things to them, He stayed in Galilee.
10 But when His [a]brothers had gone up to the feast, then He
Himself also went up, not publicly, but as if, in secret.
11 [a]So the Jews [b]were seeking Him at the feast and were
saying, "Where is He?"
12 There was much grumbling among the crowds concerning
Him; [a]some were saying, "He is a good man"; others were
saying, "No, on the contrary, He leads the people astray."
13 Yet no one was speaking openly of Him for [a]fear of the
Jews.
14 But when it was now the midst of the feast Jesus went up
into the temple, and *began to* [a]teach.
15 [a]The Jews then were astonished, saying, "How has this
man [b]become learned, having never been educated?"
16 So Jesus answered them and said, "[a]My teaching is not
Mine, but His who sent Me.

65 [a]John 6:37, 44 [b]Matt 13:11; John 3:27

66 [a]John 2:2; 7:3 [b]John 6:60, 64

67 [a]Matt 10:2; John 2:2; 6:70f; 20:24

68 [a]Matt 16:16 [b]John 6:63; 12:49f; 17:8

69 [a]Mark 1:24; 8:29; Luke 9:20

70 [a]John 15:16, 19 [b]Matt 10:2; John 2:2; 6:71; 20:24 [c]John 8:44; 13:2, 27; 17:12

71 [1]Or *was intending to* [a]John 12:4; 13:2, 26 [b]Mark 14:10 [c]Matt 10:2; John 2:2; 6:70; 20:24

7:1 [a]John 4:3; 6:1; 11:54 [b]John 1:19; 7:11, 13, 15, 35 [c]John 5:18; 7:19; 8:37, 40; 11:53

2 [a]Lev 23:34; Deut 16:13, 16; Zech 14:16-19

3 [a]Matt 12:46; Mark 3:21; John 7:5, 10 [b]John 6:60

4 [1]Lit *and*

5 [a]Matt 12:46; Mark 3:21; John 7:3, 10

6 [a]Matt 26:18; John 2:4; 7:8, 30

7 [a]John 15:18f [b]John 3:19f

8 [a]John 7:6

10 [a]Matt 12:46; Mark 3:21; John 7:3, 5

11 [a]John 7:13, 15, 35 [b]John 11:56

12 [a]John 7:40-43

13 [a]John 9:22; 12:42; 19:38; 20:19

14 [a]Matt 26:55; John 7:28

15 [a]John 1:19; 7:11, 13, 35 [b]Acts 26:24

16 [a]John 3:11

17 "[a]If anyone is willing to do His will, he will know of the
teaching, whether it is of God or *whether* I speak from Myself.
18 "He who speaks from himself [a]seeks his own glory; but He
who is seeking the glory of the One who sent Him, He is true,
and there is no unrighteousness in Him.
19 "[a]Did not Moses give you the Law, and *yet* none of you
carries out the Law? Why do you [b]seek to kill Me?"
20 The crowd answered, "[a]You have a demon! Who seeks to
kill You?"
21 Jesus answered them, "I did [a]one [1]deed, and you all marvel.
22 "For this reason [a]Moses has given you circumcision (not
because it is from Moses, but from [b]the fathers), and on *the*
Sabbath you circumcise a man.
23 "[a]If a man receives circumcision on *the* Sabbath so that the
Law of Moses will not be broken, are you angry with Me
because I made an entire man well on *the* Sabbath?
24 "Do not [a]judge according to appearance, but [1]judge with
righteous judgment."
25 So some of the people of Jerusalem were saying, "Is this
not the man whom they are seeking to kill?
26 "Look, He is speaking publicly, and they are saying nothing
to Him. [a]The rulers do not really know that this is [1]the Christ,
do they?
27 "However, [a]we know where this man is from; but whenever
the Christ may come, no one knows where He is from."
28 Then Jesus cried out in the temple, [a]teaching and saying,
"[b]You both know Me and know where I am from; and [c]I have
not come of Myself, but He who sent Me is true, whom you do
not know.
29 "[a]I know Him, because [b]I am from Him, and [c]He sent Me."
30 So they [a]were seeking to seize Him; and no man laid his
hand on Him, because His [b]hour had not yet come.
31 But [a]many of the crowd believed in Him; and they were
saying, "[b]When [1]the Christ comes, He will not perform more
[2c]signs than those which this man has, will He?"
32 The Pharisees heard the crowd muttering these things about
Him, and the chief priests and the Pharisees sent [a]officers to
[b]seize Him.
33 Therefore Jesus said, "[a]For a little while longer I am with
you, then [b]I go to Him who sent Me.
34 "[a]You will seek Me, and will not find Me; and where I am,
you cannot come."
35 [a]The Jews then said to one another, "[b]Where does this man
intend to go that we will not find Him? He is not intending to
go to [c]the Dispersion among [d]the Greeks, and teach the Greeks,
is He?
36 "What is this statement that He said, '[a]You will seek Me,
and will not find Me; and where I am, you cannot come'?"
37 Now on [a]the last day, the great *day* of the feast, Jesus stood
and cried out, saying, "[1b]If anyone is thirsty, [2]let him come to
Me and drink.

17 [a]Ps 25:9, 14; Prov 3:32; Dan 12:10; John 3:21; 8:43f
18 [a]John 5:41; 8:50, 54; 12:43
19 [a]John 1:17 [b]Mark 11:18; John 7:1
20 [a]Matt 11:18; John 8:48f, 52; 10:20
21 [1]Or *work* [a]John 5:2-9, 16; 7:23
22 [a]Lev 12:3 [b]Gen 17:10ff; 21:4; Acts 7:8
23 [a]Matt 12:2; John 5:9, 10
24 [1]Lit *judge the righteous judgment* [a]Lev 19:15; Is 11:3; Zech 7:9; John 8:15
26 [1]I.e. the Messiah [a]Luke 23:13; John 3:1
27 [a]John 6:42; 7:41f; 9:29
28 [a]John 7:14 [b]John 6:42; 7:14f; 9:29 [c]John 8:42
29 [a]Matt 11:27; John 8:55; 17:25 [b]John 6:46 [c]John 3:17
30 [a]Matt 21:46; John 7:32, 44; 10:39 [b]John 7:6; 8:20
31 [1]I.e. the Messiah [2]Or *attesting miracles* [a]John 2:23; 8:30; 10:42; 11:45; 12:11, 42 [b]John 7:26 [c]John 2:11
32 [a]Matt 26:58; John 7:45f [b]Matt 12:14
33 [a]John 12:35; 13:33; 14:19; 16:16-19 [b]John 14:12, 28; 16:5, 10, 17, 28; 20:17
34 [a]John 7:36; 8:21; 13:33
35 [a]John 7:1 [b]John 8:22 [c]Ps 147:2; Is 11:12; 56:8; Zeph 3:10; James 1:1; 1 Pet 1:1 [d]John 12:20; Acts 14:1; 17:4; 18:4; Rom 1:16
36 [a]John 7:34; 8:21; 13:33
37 [1]Vv 37-38 may also be read: *If anyone is thirsty, . . . let him come . . . , he who believes in me as . . .* [2]Or *let him keep coming to Me and let him keep drinking* [a]Lev 23:36; Num 29:35; Neh 8:18 [b]John 4:10, 14; 6:35

38 "He who believes in Me, [a]as the Scripture said, 'From [1]his
innermost being will flow rivers of [b]living water.'"
39 But this He spoke [a]of the Spirit, whom those who believed
in Him were to receive; for [b]the Spirit was not yet *given,*
because Jesus was not yet [c]glorified.
40 *Some* of the people therefore, when they heard these
words, were saying, "This certainly is [a]the Prophet."
41 Others were saying, "This is [1]the Christ." Still others were
saying, "[a]Surely [1]the Christ is not going to come from Galilee,
is He?
42 "Has not the Scripture said that the Christ comes from [a]the
descendants of David, and from Bethlehem, the village where
David was?"
43 So [a]a division occurred in the crowd because of Him.
44 [a]Some of them wanted to seize Him, but no one laid hands
on Him.
45 The [a]officers then came to the chief priests and Pharisees,
and they said to them, "Why did you not bring Him?"
46 The [a]officers answered, "[b]Never has a man spoken the way
this man speaks."
47 The Pharisees then answered them, "[a]You have not also been
led astray, have you?
48 "[a]No one of [b]the rulers or Pharisees has believed in Him,
has he?
49 "But this crowd which does not know the Law is accursed."
50 [a]Nicodemus (he who came to Him before, being one of
them) *said to them,
51 "[a]Our Law does not judge a man unless it first hears from
him and knows what he is doing, does it?"
52 They answered him, "[a]You are not also from Galilee, are
you? Search, and see that no prophet arises out of Galilee."
53 [[1]Everyone went to his home.

Chapter 8 Theme ____________________

8 But Jesus went to [a]the Mount of Olives.
2 Early in the morning He came again into the temple,
and all the people were coming to Him; and [a]He sat down and
began to teach them.
3 The scribes and the Pharisees *brought a woman caught in
adultery, and having set her in the center *of the court,*
4 they *said to Him, "Teacher, this woman has been caught
in adultery, in the very act.
5 "Now in the Law [a]Moses commanded us to stone such
women; what then do You say?"
6 They were saying this, [a]testing Him, [b]so that they might
have grounds for accusing Him. But Jesus stooped down and
with His finger wrote on the ground.
7 But when they persisted in asking Him, [a]He straightened
up, and said to them, "[b]He who is without sin among you, let
him *be the* [c]first to throw a stone at her."

38 [1]Lit *out of his belly* [a]Is 44:3; 55:1; 58:11 [b]John 4:10

39 [a]Joel 2:28; John 1:33 [b]John 20:22; Acts 1:4f; 2:4, 33; 19:2 [c]John 12:16, 23; 13:31f; 16:14; 17:1

40 [a]Matt 21:11; John 1:21

41 [1]I.e. the Messiah [a]John 1:46; 7:52

42 [a]Ps 89:4; Mic 5:2; Matt 1:1; 2:5f; Luke 2:4ff

43 [a]John 9:16; 10:19

44 [a]John 7:30

45 [a]John 7:32

46 [a]John 7:32 [b]Matt 7:28

47 [a]John 7:12

48 [a]John 12:42 [b]Luke 23:13; John 7:26

50 [a]John 3:1; 19:39

51 [a]Ex 23:1; Deut 17:6; 19:15; Prov 18:13; Acts 23:3

52 [a]John 1:46; 7:41

53 [1]Later mss add the story of the adulterous woman, numbering it as John 7:53-8:11

8:1 [a]Matt 21:1

2 [a]Matt 26:55; John 8:20

5 [a]Lev 20:10; Deut 22:22f

6 [a]Matt 16:1; 19:3; 22:18, 35; Mark 8:11; 10:2; 12:15; Luke 10:25; 11:16 [b]Mark 3:2

7 [a]John 8:10 [b]Matt 7:1; Rom 2:1 [c]Deut 17:7

8 Again He stooped down and wrote on the ground.
9 When they heard it, they *began* to go out one by one,
beginning with the older ones, and He was left alone, and the
woman, where she was, in the center *of the court.*
10 [a]Straightening up, Jesus said to her, "Woman, where are
they? Did no one condemn you?"
11 She said, "No one, [1]Lord." And Jesus said, "[a]I do not
condemn you, either. Go. From now on [b]sin no more."]
12 Then Jesus again spoke to them, saying, "[a]I am the Light of
the world; [b]he who follows Me will not walk in the darkness,
but will have the Light of life."
13 So the Pharisees said to Him, "[a]You are testifying about
Yourself; Your testimony is not [1]true."
14 Jesus answered and said to them, "[a]Even if I testify about
Myself, My testimony is [1]true, for I know [b]where I came from
and where I am going; but [c]you do not know where I come
from or where I am going.
15 "[a]You judge [1]according to the flesh; [b]I am not judging anyone.
16 "But even [a]if I do judge, My judgment is true; for I am not
alone *in it,* but I and the Father who sent Me.
17 "Even in [a]your law it has been written that the testimony of
[b]two men is [1]true.
18 "I am He who testifies about Myself, and [a]the Father who
sent Me testifies about Me."
19 So they were saying to Him, "Where is Your Father?" Jesus
answered, "You know neither Me nor My Father; [a]if you knew
Me, you would know My Father also."
20 These words He spoke in [a]the treasury, as [b]He taught in
the temple; and no one seized Him, because [c]His hour had not
yet come.
21 Then He said again to them, "I go away, and [a]you will seek
Me, and [b]will die in your sin; where I am going, you cannot
come."
22 So [a]the Jews were saying, "Surely He will not kill Himself,
will He, since He says, '[b]Where I am going, you cannot come'?"
23 And He was saying to them, "[a]You are from below, I am
from above; [b]you are of this world, [c]I am not of this world.
24 "Therefore I said to you that you [a]will die in your sins; for
unless you believe that [1b]I am *He,* [a]you will die in your sins."
25 So they were saying to Him, "Who are You?" Jesus said to
them, "[1]What have I been saying to you *from* the beginning?
26 "I have many things to speak and to judge concerning you,
but [a]He who sent Me is true; and [b]the things which I heard
from Him, these I speak to the world."
27 They did not realize that He had been speaking to them
about the Father.
28 So Jesus said, "When you [a]lift up the Son of Man, then you
will know that [1b]I am *He,* and [c]I do nothing on My own
initiative, but I speak these things as the Father taught Me.
29 "And He who sent Me is with Me; [a]He [1]has not left Me
alone, for [b]I always do the things that are pleasing to Him."

10 [a]John 8:7
11 [1]Or *Sir* [a]John 3:17 [b]John 5:14
12 [a]John 1:4; 9:5; 12:35 [b]Matt 5:14
13 [1]Or *valid* [a]John 5:31
14 [1]Or *valid* [a]John 18:37; Rev 1:5; 3:14 [b]John 8:42; 13:3; 16:28 [c]John 7:28; 9:29
15 [1]I.e. by a carnal standard [a]1 Sam 16:7; John 7:24 [b]John 3:17
16 [a]John 5:30
17 [1]I.e. valid or admissible [a]Deut 17:6; 19:15 [b]Matt 18:16
18 [a]John 5:37; 1 John 5:9
19 [a]John 7:28; 8:55; 14:7, 9; 16:3
20 [a]Mark 12:41, 43; Luke 21:1 [b]John 7:14; 8:2 [c]John 7:30
21 [a]John 7:34 [b]John 8:24
22 [a]John 1:19; 8:48, 52, 57 [b]John 7:35
23 [a]John 3:31 [b]1 John 4:5 [c]John 17:14, 16
24 [1]Most authorities associate this with Ex 3:14, *I AM WHO I AM* [a]John 8:21 [b]Matt 24:5; Mark 13:6; Luke 21:8; John 4:26; 8:28, 58; 13:19
25 [1]*Or That which I have been saying to you from the beginning*
26 [a]John 3:33; 7:28 [b]John 8:40; 12:49; 15:15
28 [1]Lit *I AM* (v 24 note) [a]John 3:14; 12:32 [b]Matt 24:5; Mark 13:6; Luke 21:8; John 4:26; 8:24, 58; 13:19 [c]John 3:11; 5:19
29 [1]Or *did not leave* [a]John 8:16; 16:32 [b]John 4:34

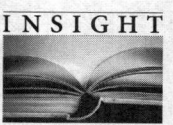

INSIGHT

The treasury was in the women's court of the temple, where there were thirteen trumpet-shaped offering receptacles. See the illustration of the floor plan of Herod's Temple on page 1614, and see the illustration of Herod's Temple on page NISB-38.

30 As He spoke these things, [a]many came to believe in Him.
31 So Jesus was saying to those Jews who had believed Him, "[a]If
you continue in My word, *then* you are truly [b]disciples of Mine;
32 and [a]you will know the truth, and [b]the truth will make you
free."
33 They answered Him, "[a]We are Abraham's descendants and
have never yet been enslaved to anyone; how is it that You say,
'You will become free'?"
34 Jesus answered them, "Truly, truly, I say to you, [a]everyone
who commits sin is the slave of sin.
35 "[a]The slave does not remain in the house forever; [b]the son
does remain forever.
36 "So if the Son [a]makes you free, you will be free indeed.
37 "I know that you are [a]Abraham's descendants; yet [b]you seek
to kill Me, because My word [1]has no place in you.
38 "I speak the things which I have seen [1]with *My* Father; therefore you also do the things which you heard from [a]*your* father."
39 They answered and said to Him, "Abraham is [a]our father."
Jesus *said to them, "[b]If you are Abraham's children, do the
deeds of Abraham.
40 "But as it is, [a]you are seeking to kill Me, a man who has
[b]told you the truth, which I heard from God; this Abraham did
not do.
41 "You are doing the deeds of [a]your father." They said to Him,
"We were not born of fornication; [b]we have one Father: God."
42 Jesus said to them, "If God were your Father, [a]you would
love Me, [b]for I proceeded forth and have come from God, for I
have [c]not even come on My own initiative, but [1d]He sent Me.
43 "Why do you not understand [1a]what I am saying? *It is*
because you cannot [b]hear My word.
44 "[a]You are of [b]*your* father the devil, and [c]you want to do the
desires of your father. [d]He was a murderer from the beginning,
and does not stand in the truth because [e]there is no truth in him.
Whenever he speaks [1]a lie, he [f]speaks from his own *nature,* for
he is a liar and the father of [2]lies.
45 "But because [a]I speak the truth, you do not believe Me.
46 "Which one of you convicts Me of sin? If [a]I speak truth, why
do you not believe Me?
47 "[a]He who is of God hears the words of God; for this reason
you do not hear *them,* because you are not of God."
48 [a]The Jews answered and said to Him, "Do we not say
rightly that You are a [b]Samaritan and [c]have a demon?"
49 Jesus answered, "I do not [a]have a demon; but I honor My
Father, and you dishonor Me.
50 "But [a]I do not seek My glory; there is One who seeks and
judges.
51 "Truly, truly, I say to you, if anyone [a]keeps My word he will
never [b]see death."
52 [a]The Jews said to Him, "Now we know that You [b]have a
demon. Abraham died, and the prophets *also;* and You say, 'If
anyone [c]keeps My word, he will never [d]taste of death.'

30 [a]John 7:31
31 [a]John 15:7; 2 John 9 [b]John 2:2
32 [a]John 1:14, 17 [b]John 8:36; Rom 8:2; 2 Cor 3:17; Gal 5:1, 13; James 2:12; 1 Pet 2:16
33 [a]Matt 3:9; Luke 3:8; John 8:37, 39
34 [a]Rom 6:16; 2 Pet 2:19
35 [a]Gen 21:10; Gal 4:30 [b]Luke 15:31
36 [a]John 8:32
37 [1]Or *makes no progress* [a]Matt 3:9; John 8:39 [b]John 7:1; 8:40
38 [1]Or *in the presence of* [a]John 8:41, 44
39 [a]Matt 3:9; John 8:37 [b]Rom 9:7; Gal 3:7
40 [a]John 7:1; 8:37 [b]John 8:26
41 [a]John 8:38, 44 [b]Deut 32:6; Is 63:16; 64:8
42 [1]Lit *that One* [a]1 John 5:1 [b]John 13:3; 16:28, 30; 17:8 [c]John 7:28 [d]John 3:17
43 [1]Or *My way of speaking* [a]John 8:33, 39, 41 [b]John 5:25
44 [1]Lit *the lie* [2]Lit *it* [a]1 John 3:8 [b]John 8:38, 41 [c]John 7:17 [d]Gen 3:4; 1 John 3:8, 15 [e]1 John 2:4 [f]Matt 12:34
45 [a]John 18:37
46 [a]John 18:37
47 [a]1 John 4:6
48 [a]John 1:19 [b]Matt 10:5; John 4:9 [c]John 7:20
49 [a]John 7:20
50 [a]John 5:41; 8:54
51 [a]John 8:55; 14:23; 15:20; 17:6 [b]Matt 16:28; Luke 2:26; John 8:52; Heb 2:9; 11:5
52 [a]John 1:19 [b]John 7:20 [c]John 8:55; 14:23; 15:20; 17:6 [d]John 8:51

53 "Surely You [a]are not greater than our father Abraham, who
died? The prophets died too; whom do You make Yourself out
to be?"
54 Jesus answered, "[a]If I glorify Myself, My glory is nothing; [b]it
is My Father who glorifies Me, of whom you say, 'He is our God';
55 and [a]you have not come to know Him, [b]but I know Him;
and if I say that I do not know Him, I will be [c]a liar like you,
[b]but I do know Him and [d]keep His word.
56 "[a]Your father Abraham [b]rejoiced [1]to see My day, and he saw
it and was glad."
57 [a]So the Jews said to Him, "You are not yet fifty years old, and
have You seen Abraham?"
58 Jesus said to them, "Truly, truly, I say to you, before Abraham
[1]was born, [a]I am."
59 Therefore they [a]picked up stones to throw at Him, but
Jesus [1b]hid Himself and went out of the temple.

Chapter 9 Theme ______________________

9 As He passed by, He saw a man blind from birth.
2 And His disciples asked Him, "[a]Rabbi, who sinned, [b]this
man or his [c]parents, that he would be born blind?"
3 Jesus answered, "*It was* neither *that* this man sinned, nor
his parents; but *it was* so [a]that the works of God might be
displayed in him.
4 "We must work the works of Him who sent Me [a]as long as
it is day; night is coming when no one can work.
5 "While I am in the world, I am [a]the Light of the world."
6 When He had said this, He [a]spat on the ground, and made
clay of the spittle, and applied the clay to his eyes,
7 and said to him, "Go, wash in [a]the pool of Siloam" (which
is translated, Sent). So he went away and [b]washed, and [c]came
back seeing.
8 Therefore the neighbors, and those who previously saw him
as a beggar, were saying, "Is not this the one who used to [a]sit
and beg?"
9 Others were saying, "This is he," *still* others were saying,
"No, but he is like him." [1]He kept saying, "I am the one."
10 So they were saying to him, "How then were your eyes
opened?"
11 He answered, "The man who is called Jesus made clay, and
anointed my eyes, and said to me, 'Go to [a]Siloam and wash'; so
I went away and washed, and I received sight."
12 They said to him, "Where is He?" He *said, "I do not know."
13 They *brought to the Pharisees the man who was formerly
blind.
14 [a]Now it was a Sabbath on the day when Jesus made the
clay and opened his eyes.
15 [a]Then the Pharisees also were asking him again how he
received his sight. And he said to them, "He applied clay to my
eyes, and I washed, and I see."

53 [a]John 4:12
54 [a]John 8:50 [b]John 7:39
55 [a]John 8:19; 15:21 [b]John 7:29 [c]John 8:44 [d]John 8:51; 15:10
56 [1]Lit *in order that he might see* [a]John 8:37, 39 [b]Matt 13:17; Heb 11:13
57 [a]John 1:19
58 [1]Lit *came into being* [a]Ex 3:14; John 1:1; 17:5, 24
59 [1]Lit *was hidden* [a]Matt 12:14; John 10:31; 11:8 [b]John 12:36
9:2 [a]Matt 23:7 [b]Luke 13:2; John 9:34; Acts 28:4 [c]Ex 20:5
3 [a]John 11:4
4 [a]John 7:33; 11:9; 12:35; Gal 6:10
5 [a]Matt 5:14; John 1:4; 8:12; 12:46
6 [a]Mark 7:33; 8:23
7 [a]Neh 3:15; Is 8:6; Luke 13:4; John 9:11 [b]2 Kin 5:13f [c]Is 29:18; 35:5; 42:7; Matt 11:5; John 11:37
8 [a]Acts 3:2, 10
9 [1]Lit *That one*
11 [a]John 9:7
14 [a]John 5:9
15 [a]John 9:10

16 Therefore some of the Pharisees were saying, "This man is
not from God, because He [a]does not keep the Sabbath." But
others were saying, "How can a man who is a sinner perform
such [1b]signs?" And [c]there was a division among them.
17 So they *said to the blind man [a]again, "What do you say
about Him, since He opened your eyes?" And he said, "He is a
[b]prophet."
18 [a]The Jews then did not believe *it* of him, that he had been
blind and had received sight, until they called the parents of
the very one who had received his sight,
19 and questioned them, saying, "Is this your son, who you
say was born blind? Then how does he now see?"
20 His parents answered them and said, "We know that this is
our son, and that he was born blind;
21 but how he now sees, we do not know; or who opened his
eyes, we do not know. Ask him; he is of age, he will speak for
himself."
22 His parents said this because they [a]were afraid of the Jews;
for the Jews [b]had already agreed that if anyone confessed Him
to be [1]Christ, [c]he was to be put out of the synagogue.
23 For this reason his parents said, "[a]He is of age; ask him."
24 So a second time they called the man who had been blind,
and said to him, "[a]Give glory to God; we know that [b]this man
is a sinner."
25 He then answered, "Whether He is a sinner, I do not
know; one thing I do know, that though I was blind, now I see."
26 So they said to him, "What did He do to you? How did He
open your eyes?"
27 He answered them, "[a]I told you already and you did not
[b]listen; why do you want to hear *it* again? You do not want to
become His disciples too, do you?"
28 They reviled him and said, "You are His disciple, but [a]we
are disciples of Moses.
29 "We know that God has spoken to Moses, but as for this
man, [a]we do not know where He is from."
30 The man answered and said to them, "Well, here is an
amazing thing, that you do not know where He is from, and *yet*
He opened my eyes.
31 "We know that [a]God does not hear sinners; but if anyone is
God-fearing and does His will, He hears him.
32 "[1]Since the beginning of time it has never been heard that
anyone opened the eyes of a person born blind.
33 "[a]If this man were not from God, He could do nothing."
34 They answered him, "[a]You were born entirely in sins, and
are you teaching us?" So they [b]put him out.
35 Jesus heard that they had [a]put him out, and finding him,
He said, "Do you believe in the [b]Son of Man?"
36 He answered, "[a]Who is He, [1]Lord, that I may believe in
Him?"
37 Jesus said to him, "You have both seen Him, and [a]He is the
one who is talking with you."

16 [1]Or *attesting miracles* [a]Matt 12:2; Luke 13:14; John 5:10; 7:23 [b]John 2:11 [c]John 6:52; 7:12, 43; 10:19

17 [a]John 9:15 [b]Deut 18:15; Matt 21:11

18 [a]John 1:19; 9:22

22 [1]I.e. the Messiah [a]John 7:13 [b]John 7:45-52 [c]Luke 6:22; John 12:42; 16:2

23 [a]John 9:21

24 [a]Josh 7:19; Ezra 10:11; Rev 11:13 [b]John 9:16

27 [a]John 9:15 [b]John 5:25

28 [a]John 5:45; Rom 2:17

29 [a]John 8:14

31 [a]Job 27:8f; 35:13; Ps 34:15f; 66:18; 145:19; Prov 15:29; 28:9; Is 1:15; James 5:16ff

32 [1]Lit *From the age it was not heard*

33 [a]John 3:2; 9:16

34 [a]John 9:2 [b]John 9:22, 35; 3 John 10

35 [a]John 9:22, 34; 3 John 10 [b]Matt 4:3

36 [1]Or *Sir* [a]Rom 10:14

37 [a]John 4:26

38 And he said, "Lord, I believe." And he [a]worshiped Him.
39 And Jesus said, "[a]For judgment I came into this world, so
that [b]those who do not see may see, and that [c]those who see
may become blind."
40 Those of the Pharisees who were with Him heard these
things and said to Him, "[a]We are not blind too, are we?"
41 Jesus said to them, "[a]If you were blind, you would have no
sin; but [1]since you say, '[b]We see,' your sin remains.

Chapter 10 Theme ____________________________

10 "Truly, truly, I say to you, he who does not enter by the
door into the fold of the sheep, but climbs up some other
way, he is [a]a thief and a robber.
2 "But he who enters by the door is [a]a shepherd of the sheep.
3 "To him the doorkeeper opens, and the sheep hear [a]his
voice, and he calls his own sheep by name and [b]leads them
out.
4 "When he puts forth all his own, he goes ahead of them,
and the sheep follow him because they know [a]his voice.
5 "A stranger they simply will not follow, but will flee from
him, because they do not know [a]the voice of strangers."
6 This [a]figure of speech Jesus spoke to them, but they did not
understand what those things were which He had been saying
to them.
7 So Jesus said to them again, "Truly, truly, I say to you, I am
[a]the door of the sheep.
8 "All who came before Me are [a]thieves and robbers, but the
sheep did not hear them.
9 "[a]I am the door; if anyone enters through Me, he will be
saved, and will go in and out and find pasture.
10 "The thief comes only to steal and kill and destroy; I came
that they [a]may have life, and [1]have *it* abundantly.
11 "[a]I am the good shepherd; the good shepherd [b]lays down
His life for the sheep.
12 "He who is a hired hand, and not a [a]shepherd, who is not
the owner of the sheep, sees the wolf coming, and leaves the
sheep and flees, and the wolf snatches them and scatters *them.*
13 "*He flees* because he is a hired hand and is not concerned
about the sheep.
14 "[a]I am the good shepherd, and [b]I know My own and My
own know Me,
15 even as [a]the Father knows Me and I know the Father; and
[b]I lay down My life for the sheep.
16 "I have [a]other sheep, which are not of this fold; I must bring
them also, and they will hear My voice; and they will become
[b]one flock *with* [c]one shepherd.
17 "For this reason the Father loves Me, because I [a]lay down
My life so that I may take it again.
18 "[a]No one has taken it away from Me, but I [b]lay it down on
My own initiative. I have authority to lay it down, and I have

38 [a]Matt 8:2
39 [a]John 3:19; 5:22, 27 [b]Luke 4:18 [c]Matt 13:13; 15:14
40 [a]Rom 2:19
41 [1]Lit *now* [a]John 15:22, 24 [b]Prov 26:12
10:1 [a]John 10:8
2 [a]John 10:11f
3 [a]John 10:4f, 16, 27 [b]John 10:9
4 [a]John 10:5, 16, 27
5 [a]John 10:4, 16, 27
6 [a]John 16:25, 29; 2 Pet 2:22
7 [a]John 10:1f, 9
8 [a]Jer 23:1f; Ezek 34:2ff; John 10:1
9 [a]John 10:1f, 9
10 [1]Or *have abundance* [a]John 5:40
11 [a]Is 40:11; Ezek 34:11-16, 23; John 10:14; Heb 13:20; 1 Pet 5:4; Rev 7:17 [b]John 10:15, 17, 18; 15:13; 1 John 3:16
12 [a]John 10:2
14 [a]John 10:11 [b]John 10:27
15 [a]Matt 11:27; Luke 10:22 [b]John 10:11, 17, 18
16 [a]Is 56:8 [b]John 11:52; 17:20f; Eph 2:13-18; 1 Pet 2:25 [c]Ezek 34:23; 37:24
17 [a]John 10:11, 15, 18
18 [a]Matt 26:53; John 2:19; 5:26 [b]John 10:11, 15, 17

authority to take it up again. [c]This commandment I received
from My Father."
19 [a]A division occurred again among the Jews because of these
words.
20 Many of them were saying, "He [a]has a demon and [b]is
insane. Why do you listen to Him?"
21 Others were saying, "These are not the sayings of one
[a]demon-possessed. [b]A demon cannot open the eyes of the
blind, can he?"
22 At that time the Feast of the Dedication took place at
Jerusalem;
23 it was winter, and Jesus was walking in the temple in the
portico of [a]Solomon.
24 [a]The Jews then gathered around Him, and were saying to
Him, "How long [1]will You keep us in suspense? If You are [2]the
Christ, tell us [b]plainly."
25 Jesus answered them, "[a]I told you, and you do not believe;
[b]the works that I do in My Father's name, these testify of Me.
26 "But you do not believe because [a]you are not of My sheep.
27 "My sheep [a]hear My voice, and [b]I know them, and they
follow Me;
28 and I give [a]eternal life to them, and they will never perish;
and [b]no one will snatch them out of My hand.
29 "[1]My Father, who has given *them* to Me, is greater than all;
and no one is able to snatch *them* out of the Father's hand.
30 "[a]I and the Father are [1]one."
31 The Jews [a]picked up stones again to stone Him.
32 Jesus answered them, "I showed you many good works
from the Father; for which of them are you stoning Me?"
33 The Jews answered Him, "For a good work we do not
stone You, but for [a]blasphemy; and because You, being a man,
[b]make Yourself out *to be* God."
34 Jesus answered them, "Has it not been written in [a]your
[b]Law, '[c]I SAID, YOU ARE GODS'?
35 "If he called them gods, to whom the word of God came
(and the Scripture cannot be broken),
36 do you say of Him, whom the Father [a]sanctified and [b]sent
into the world, 'You are blaspheming,' because I said, '[c]I am
the Son of God'?
37 "[a]If I do not do the works of My Father, do not believe Me;
38 but if I do them, though you do not believe Me, believe
[a]the works, so that you may [1]know and understand that [b]the
Father is in Me, and I in the Father."
39 Therefore [a]they were seeking again to seize Him, and [b]He
eluded their grasp.
40 And He went away [a]again beyond the Jordan to the place
where John was first baptizing, and He was staying there.
41 Many came to Him and were saying, "While John
performed no [a]sign, yet [b]everything John said about this man
was true."
42 [a]Many believed in Him there.

18 [c]John 14:31; 15:10; Phil 2:8; Heb 5:8

19 [a]John 7:43; 9:16

20 [a]John 7:20 [b]Mark 3:21

21 [a]Matt 4:24 [b]Ex 4:11; John 9:32f

23 [a]Acts 3:11; 5:12

24 [1]Lit *do You lift up our soul* [2]I.e. the Messiah [a]John 1:19; 10:31, 33 [b]Luke 22:67; John 16:25

25 [a]John 8:56, 58 [b]John 5:36; 10:38

26 [a]John 8:47

27 [a]John 10:4, 16 [b]John 10:14

28 [a]John 17:2f; 1 John 2:25; 5:11 [b]John 6:37, 39

29 [1]One early ms reads *What My Father has given Me is greater than all*

30 [1]Or *a unity;* or *one essence* [a]John 17:21ff

31 [a]John 8:59

33 [a]Lev 24:16 [b]John 5:18

34 [a]John 8:17 [b]John 12:34; 15:25; Rom 3:19; 1 Cor 14:21 [c]Ps 82:6

36 [a]Jer 1:5; John 6:69 [b]John 3:17 [c]John 5:17f; 10:30

37 [a]John 10:25; 15:24

38 [1]Lit *know and continue knowing* [a]John 10:25; 14:11 [b]John 14:10f, 20; 17:21, 23

39 [a]John 7:30 [b]Luke 4:30; John 8:59

40 [a]John 1:28

41 [a]John 2:11 [b]John 1:27, 30, 34; 3:27-30

42 [a]John 7:31

Chapter 11 Theme ____

11 Now a certain man was sick, Lazarus of [a]Bethany, the village of Mary and her sister [b]Martha.
2 It was the Mary who [a]anointed [b]the Lord with ointment,
and wiped His feet with her hair, whose brother Lazarus was
sick.
3 So the sisters sent *word* to Him, saying, "[a]Lord, behold, [b]he
whom You love is sick."
4 But when Jesus heard *this,* He said, "This sickness is not to
end in death, but for [a]the glory of God, so that the Son of God
may be glorified by it."
5 Now Jesus loved [a]Martha and her sister and Lazarus.
6 So when He heard that he was sick, He then stayed two
days *longer* in the place where He was.
7 Then after this He *said to the disciples, "[a]Let us go to
Judea again."
8 The disciples *said to Him, "[a]Rabbi, the Jews were just
now seeking [b]to stone You, and are You going there again?"
9 Jesus answered, "[a]Are there not twelve hours in the day? If
anyone walks in the day, he does not stumble, because he sees
the light of this world.
10 "But if anyone walks in the night, he stumbles, because the
light is not in him."
11 This He said, and after that He *said to them, "Our [a]friend
Lazarus [b]has fallen asleep; but I go, so that I may awaken him
out of sleep."
12 The disciples then said to Him, "Lord, if he has fallen asleep,
he will [1]recover."
13 Now [a]Jesus had spoken of his death, but they thought that
He was speaking of [1]literal sleep.
14 So Jesus then said to them plainly, "Lazarus is dead,
15 and I am glad for your sakes that I was not there, so that
you may believe; but let us go to him."
16 [a]Therefore Thomas, who is called [1b]Didymus, said to *his*
fellow disciples, "Let us also go, so that we may die with Him."
17 So when Jesus came, He found that he had already been in
the tomb [a]four days.
18 Now [a]Bethany was near Jerusalem, about [1]two miles off;
19 and many of [a]the Jews had come to [b]Martha and Mary, [c]to
console them concerning *their* brother.
20 [a]Martha therefore, when she heard that Jesus was coming,
went to meet Him, but [a]Mary [1]stayed at the house.
21 Martha then said to Jesus, "[a]Lord, [b]if You had been here,
my brother would not have died.
22 "Even now I know that [a]whatever You ask of God, God will
give You."
23 Jesus *said to her, "Your brother will rise again."
24 Martha *said to Him, "[a]I know that he will rise again in
the resurrection on the last day."
25 Jesus said to her, "[a]I am the resurrection and the life; he
who believes in Me will live even if he dies,

11:1 [a]Matt 21:17; John 11:18 [b]Luke 10:38; John 11:5, 19ff
2 [a]Luke 7:38; John 12:3 [b]Luke 7:13; John 11:3, 21, 32; 13:13f
3 [a]Luke 7:13; John 11:2, 21, 32; 13:13f [b]John 11:5, 11, 36
4 [a]John 9:3; 10:38; 11:40
5 [a]John 11:1
7 [a]John 10:40
8 [a]Matt 23:7 [b]John 8:59; 10:31
9 [a]Luke 13:33; John 9:4; 12:35
11 [a]John 11:3 [b]Matt 27:52; Mark 5:39; John 11:13; Acts 7:60
12 [1]Lit *be saved*
13 [1]Lit *the slumber of sleep* [a]Matt 9:24; Luke 8:52
16 [1]I.e. the Twin [a]Matt 10:3; Mark 3:18; Luke 6:15; John 14:5; 20:26-28; Acts 1:13 [b]John 20:24; 21:2
17 [a]John 11:39
18 [1]Lit *15 stadia* (9,090 ft) [a]John 11:1
19 [a]John 1:19; 11:8 [b]John 11:1 [c]1 Sam 31:13; 1 Chr 10:12; Job 2:11; John 11:31
20 [1]Lit *was sitting* [a]Luke 10:38-42
21 [a]John 11:2 [b]John 11:32, 37
22 [a]John 9:31; 11:41f
24 [a]Dan 12:2; John 5:28f; Acts 24:15
25 [a]John 1:4; 5:26; 6:39f; Rev 1:18

26 and everyone who lives and believes in Me [a]will never die.
Do you believe this?"
27 She *said to Him, "Yes, Lord; I have believed that You are
[1a]the Christ, the Son of God, *even* [2b]He who comes into the
world."
28 When she had said this, she [a]went away and called Mary
her sister, saying secretly, "[b]The Teacher is here and is calling
for you."
29 And when she heard it, she *got up quickly and was
coming to Him.
30 Now Jesus had not yet come into the village, but [a]was still
in the place where Martha met Him.
31 [a]Then the Jews who were with her in the house, and
[b]consoling her, when they saw that Mary got up quickly and
went out, they followed her, supposing that she was going to
the tomb to weep there.
32 Therefore, when Mary came where Jesus was, she saw
Him, and fell at His feet, saying to Him, "[a]Lord, [b]if You had
been here, my brother would not have died."
33 When Jesus therefore saw her weeping, and [a]the Jews who
came with her *also* weeping, He [b]was deeply moved in spirit
and [1c]was troubled,
34 and said, "Where have you laid him?" They *said to Him,
"Lord, come and see."
35 Jesus [a]wept.
36 So [a]the Jews were saying, "See how He [b]loved him!"
37 But some of them said, "Could not this man, who [a]opened
the eyes of the blind man, [1]have kept this man also from
dying?"
38 So Jesus, again being deeply moved within, *came to the
tomb. Now it was a [a]cave, and a stone was lying against it.
39 Jesus *said, "Remove the stone." Martha, the sister of the
deceased, *said to Him, "Lord, by this time [1]there will be a
stench, for he has been *dead* [a]four days."
40 Jesus *said to her, "[a]Did I not say to you that if you believe,
you will see the glory of God?"
41 So they removed the [a]stone. Then Jesus [b]raised His eyes,
and said, "[c]Father, I thank You that You have heard Me.
42 "I knew that You always hear Me; but [a]because of the
[1]people standing around I said it, so that they may believe that
[b]You sent Me."
43 When He had said these things, He cried out with a loud
voice, "Lazarus, come forth."
44 The man who had died came forth, [a]bound hand and foot
with wrappings, and [b]his face was wrapped around with a
cloth. Jesus *said to them, "Unbind him, and let him go."
45 [a]Therefore many of the Jews [b]who came to Mary, and [c]saw
what He had done, believed in Him.
46 But some of them went to the [a]Pharisees and told them the
things which Jesus had done.
47 Therefore [a]the chief priests and the Pharisees [b]convened a

26 [a]John 6:47, 50, 51; 8:51
27 [1]I.e. the Messiah [2]The Coming One was the Messianic title [a]Matt 16:16; Luke 2:11 [b]John 6:14
28 [a]John 11:30 [b]Matt 26:18; Mark 14:14; Luke 22:11; John 13:13
30 [a]John 11:20
31 [a]John 11:19, 33 [b]John 11:19
32 [a]John 11:2 [b]John 11:21
33 [1]Lit *troubled Himself* [a]John 11:19 [b]John 11:38 [c]John 12:27; 13:21
35 [a]Luke 19:41; John 11:33
36 [a]John 11:19 [b]John 11:3
37 [1]Lit *have caused that this man also not die* [a]John 9:7
38 [a]Matt 27:60; Mark 15:46; Luke 24:2; John 20:1
39 [1]Lit *he stinks* [a]John 11:17
40 [a]John 11:4, 23ff
41 [a]Matt 27:60; Mark 15:46; Luke 24:2; John 20:1 [b]John 17:1; Acts 7:55 [c]Matt 11:25
42 [1]Lit *crowd* [a]John 12:30; 17:21 [b]John 3:17
44 [a]John 19:40 [b]John 20:7
45 [a]John 7:31 [b]John 11:19; 12:17f [c]John 2:23
46 [a]John 7:32, 45; 11:57
47 [a]John 7:32, 45; 11:57 [b]Matt 26:3

27 "[a]Now My soul has become troubled; and what shall I say,
'[b]Father, save Me from [c]this hour'? But for this purpose I came
to this hour.
28 "[a]Father, glorify Your name." Then a [b]voice came out of
heaven: "I have both glorified it, and will glorify it again."
29 So the crowd *of people* who stood by and heard it were
saying that it had thundered; others were saying, "[a]An angel
has spoken to Him."
30 Jesus answered and said, "[a]This voice has not come for My
sake, but for your sakes.
31 "[a]Now judgment is upon this world; now [b]the ruler of this
world will be cast out.
32 "And I, if I [a]am lifted up from the earth, will [b]draw all men
to Myself."
33 But He was saying this [a]to indicate the kind of death by
which He was to die.
34 The crowd then answered Him, "We have heard out of [a]the
Law that [1b]the Christ is to remain forever; and how can You say,
'The [c]Son of Man must be [d]lifted up'? Who is this [c]Son of Man?"
35 So Jesus said to them, "[a]For a little while longer [b]the Light
is among you. [c]Walk while you have the Light, so that darkness
will not overtake you; he who [d]walks in the darkness does not
know where he goes.
36 "While you have the Light, [a]believe in the Light, so that you
may become [b]sons of Light."
These things Jesus spoke, and He went away and [1c]hid
Himself from them.
37 But though He had performed so many [1]signs before them,
yet they were not believing in Him.
38 *This was* to fulfill the word of Isaiah the prophet which he
spoke: "[a]LORD, WHO HAS BELIEVED OUR REPORT? AND TO WHOM HAS
THE ARM OF THE LORD BEEN REVEALED?"
39 For this reason they could not believe, for Isaiah said again,
40 "[a]HE HAS BLINDED THEIR EYES AND HE [b]HARDENED THEIR HEART, SO
THAT THEY WOULD NOT SEE WITH THEIR EYES AND PERCEIVE WITH THEIR
HEART, AND [1]BE CONVERTED AND I HEAL THEM."
41 These things Isaiah said because [a]he saw His glory, and [b]he
spoke of Him.
42 Nevertheless [a]many even of [b]the rulers believed in Him,
but [c]because of the Pharisees they were not confessing *Him*,
for fear that they would be [1d]put out of the synagogue;
43 [a]for they loved the [1]approval of men rather than the [1]approval
of God.
44 And Jesus cried out and said, "[a]He who believes in Me,
does not believe in Me but in Him who sent Me.
45 "[a]He who sees Me sees the One who sent Me.
46 "[a]I have come *as* Light into the world, so that everyone who
believes in Me will not remain in darkness.
47 "If anyone hears My sayings and does not keep them, I do
not judge him; for [a]I did not come to judge the world, but to
save the world.

27 [a]Matt 26:38; Mark 14:34; John 11:33 [b]Matt 11:25 [c]John 12:23
28 [a]Matt 11:25 [b]Matt 3:17; 17:5; Mark 1:11; 9:7; Luke 3:22; 9:35
29 [a]Acts 23:9
30 [a]John 11:42
31 [a]John 3:19; 9:39; 16:11 [b]John 14:30; 16:11; 2 Cor 4:4; Eph 2:2; 6:12; 1 John 4:4; 5:19
32 [a]John 3:14; 8:28; 12:34 [b]John 6:44
33 [a]John 18:32; 21:19
34 [1]I.e. the Messiah [a]John 10:34 [b]Ps 110:4; Is 9:7; Ezek 37:25; Dan 7:14 [c]Matt 8:20 [d]John 3:14; 8:28; 12:32
35 [a]John 7:33; 9:4 [b]John 12:46; 1 John 2:10 [c]Gal 6:10; Eph 5:8 [d]1 John 1:6; 2:11
36 [1]Lit *was hidden* [a]John 12:46 [b]Luke 16:8; John 8:12 [c]John 8:59
37 [1]Or *attesting signs*
38 [a]Is 53:1; Rom 10:16
40 [1]Lit *be turned;* i.e. turn about [a]Is 6:10; Matt 13:14f [b]Mark 6:52
41 [a]Is 6:1ff [b]Luke 24:27
42 [1]I.e. excommunicated [a]John 7:48; 12:11 [b]Luke 23:13 [c]John 7:13 [d]John 9:22
43 [1]Or *glory* [a]John 5:41, 44
44 [a]Matt 10:40; John 5:24
45 [a]John 14:9
46 [a]John 1:4; 3:19; 8:12; 9:5; 12:35f
47 [a]John 3:17; 8:15f

48“[a]He who rejects Me and does not receive My sayings, has
one who judges him; [b]the word I spoke is what will judge him
at [c]the last day.
49“[a]For I did not speak [1]on My own initiative, but the Father
Himself who sent Me [b]has given Me a commandment *as to*
what to say and what to speak.
50“I know that [a]His commandment is eternal life; therefore
the things I speak, I speak [b]just as the Father has told Me.”

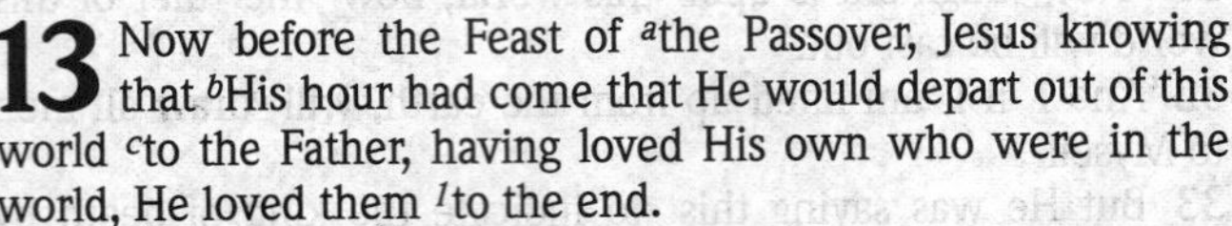
Chapter 13 Theme ______________________________

13 Now before the Feast of [a]the Passover, Jesus knowing
that [b]His hour had come that He would depart out of this
world [c]to the Father, having loved His own who were in the
world, He loved them [1]to the end.
2 During supper, [a]the devil having already put into the heart
of [b]Judas Iscariot, *the son* of Simon, to betray Him,
3 *Jesus,* [a]knowing that the Father had given all things into
His hands, and that [b]He had come forth from God and was
going back to God,
4 *got up from supper, and *laid aside His garments; and
taking a towel, He [a]girded Himself.
5 Then He *poured water into the basin, and began to [a]wash
the disciples' feet and to wipe them with the towel with which
He was girded.
6 So He *came to Simon Peter. He *said to Him, “Lord, do You
wash my feet?”
7 Jesus answered and said to him, “What I do you do not
realize now, but you will understand [a]hereafter.”
8 Peter *said to Him, “Never shall You wash my feet!” Jesus
answered him, “[a]If I do not wash you, [b]you have no part with
Me.”
9 Simon Peter *said to Him, “Lord, *then wash* not only my
feet, but also my hands and my head.”
10 Jesus *said to him, “He who has bathed needs only to
wash his feet, but is completely clean; and [a]you are clean, but
not all *of you.*”
11 For [a]He knew the one who was betraying Him; for this
reason He said, “Not all of you are clean.”
12 So when He had washed their feet, and [a]taken His garments
and reclined *at the table* again, He said to them, “Do you know
what I have done to you?
13“You call Me [a]Teacher and [b]Lord; and [1]you are right, for *so*
I am.
14“If I then, [a]the Lord and the Teacher, washed your feet, you
also ought to wash one another's feet.
15“For I gave you [a]an example that you also should do as I did
to you.
16“Truly, truly, I say to you, [a]a slave is not greater than his master,
nor *is* [b]one who is sent greater than the one who sent him.
17“If you know these things, you are [a]blessed if you do them.

48 [a]Luke 10:16 [b]Deut 18:18f; John 5:45ff; 8:47 [c]Matt 10:15; John 6:39; Acts 17:31; 1 Pet 1:5; 2 Pet 3:3, 7; Heb 10:25

49 [1]Lit *of Myself* [a]John 3:11; 7:16; 8:26, 28, 38; 14:10, 24 [b]John 14:31; 17:8

50 [a]John 6:68 [b]John 5:19; 8:28

13:1 [1]Or *to the uttermost;* or *eternally* [a]John 2:13; 11:55 [b]John 12:23 [c]John 13:3; 16:28

2 [a]John 6:70; 13:27 [b]John 6:71

3 [a]John 3:35 [b]John 8:42

4 [a]Luke 12:37; 17:8

5 [a]Gen 18:4; 19:2; 43:24; Judg 19:21; Luke 7:44; 1 Tim 5:10

7 [a]John 13:12ff

8 [a]Ps 51:2, 7; Ezek 36:25; Acts 22:16; 1 Cor 6:11; Heb 10:22 [b]Deut 12:12; 2 Sam 20:1; 1 Kin 12:16

10 [a]John 15:3; Eph 5:26

11 [a]John 6:64; 13:2

12 [a]John 13:4

13 [1]Lit *you say well* [a]John 11:28 [b]John 11:2; 1 Cor 12:3; Phil 2:11

14 [a]John 11:2; 1 Cor 12:3; Phil 2:11

15 [a]1 Pet 5:3

16 [a]Matt 10:24; Luke 6:40; John 15:20 [b]2 Cor 8:23; Phil 2:25

17 [a]Matt 7:24ff; Luke 11:28; James 1:25

18 “[a]I do not speak of all of you. I know the ones I have
[b]chosen; but *it is* [c]that the Scripture may be fulfilled, ‘[d]HE WHO
EATS MY BREAD HAS LIFTED UP HIS HEEL AGAINST ME.’
19 “From now on [a]I am telling you before *it* comes to pass, so
that when it does occur, you may believe that [b]I am *He.*
20 “Truly, truly, I say to you, [a]he who receives whomever I
send receives Me; and he who receives Me receives Him who
sent Me.”
21 When Jesus had said this, He [a]became troubled in spirit, and
testified and said, “Truly, truly, I say to you, that [b]one of you
will [1]betray Me.”
22 The disciples *began* looking at one another, [a]at a loss *to
know* of which one He was speaking.
23 There was reclining on [a]Jesus’ bosom one of His disciples,
[b]whom Jesus loved.
24 So Simon Peter *gestured to him, and *said to him, “Tell
us who it is of whom He is speaking.”
25 He, [a]leaning back thus on Jesus’ bosom, *said to Him,
“Lord, who is it?”
26 Jesus then *answered, “That is the one for whom I shall
dip the morsel and give it to him.” So when He had dipped the
morsel, He *took and *gave it to Judas, [a]*the son* of Simon Iscariot.
27 After the morsel, [a]Satan then [b]entered into him. Therefore
Jesus *said to him, “What you do, do quickly.”
28 Now no one of those reclining *at the table* knew for what
purpose He had said this to him.
29 For some were supposing, because Judas [a]had the money
box, that Jesus was saying to him, “Buy the things we have
need of [b]for the feast”; or else, that he should [c]give something
to the poor.
30 So after receiving the morsel he went out immediately; and
[a]it was night.
31 Therefore when he had gone out, Jesus *said, “Now [1]is
[a]the Son of Man [b]glorified, and [c]God [1]is glorified in Him;
32 [1]if God is glorified in Him, [a]God will also glorify Him in
Himself, and will glorify Him immediately.
33 “[a]Little children, I am with you [b]a little while longer. [c]You
will seek Me; and as I said to the Jews, now I also say to you,
‘Where I am going, you cannot come.’
34 “A [a]new commandment I give to you, [b]that you love one
another, [c]even as I have loved you, that you also love one another.
35 “[a]By this all men will know that you are My disciples, if you
have love for one another.”
36 Simon Peter *said to Him, “Lord, where are You going?”
Jesus answered, “[a]Where I go, you cannot follow Me now; but
[b]you will follow later.”
37 Peter *said to Him, “Lord, why can I not follow You right
now? [a]I will lay down my life for You.”
38 Jesus *answered, “Will you lay down your life for Me? Truly,
truly, I say to you, [a]a rooster will not crow until you deny Me
three times.

18 [a]John 13:10f [b]John 6:70; 15:16, 19 [c]John 15:25; 17:12; 18:32; 19:24, 36 [d]Ps 41:9; Matt 26:21ff; Mark 14:18f; Luke 22:21ff; John 13:21, 22, 26

19 [a]John 14:29; 16:4 [b]John 8:24

20 [a]Matt 10:40; Mark 9:37; Luke 9:48; 10:16; Gal 4:14

21 [1]Or *hand Me over* [a]John 11:33 [b]Matt 26:21f; Mark 14:18ff; Luke 22:21ff; John 13:18, 22, 26

22 [a]Matt 26:21ff; Mark 14:18ff; Luke 22:21ff; John 13:18, 21, 26

23 [a]John 1:18 [b]John 19:26; 20:2; 21:7, 20

25 [a]John 21:20

26 [a]John 6:71

27 [a]Matt 4:10 [b]Luke 22:3; John 13:2

29 [a]John 12:6 [b]John 13:1 [c]John 12:5

30 [a]Luke 22:53

31 [1]Or *was* [a]Matt 8:20 [b]John 7:39 [c]John 14:13; 17:4; 1 Pet 4:11

32 [1]Most early mss do not contain this phrase [a]John 17:1

33 [a]1 John 2:1 [b]John 7:33 [c]John 7:34

34 [a]John 15:12, 17; 1 John 2:7f; 3:11, 23; 2 John 5 [b]Lev 19:18; Matt 5:44; Gal 5:14; 1 Thess 4:9; Heb 13:1; 1 Pet 1:22; 1 John 4:7 [c]Eph 5:2; 1 John 4:10f

35 [a]1 John 3:14; 4:20

36 [a]John 13:33; 14:2; 16:5 [b]John 21:18f; 2 Pet 1:14

37 [a]John 13:37, 38: *Matt 26:33-35; Mark 14:29-31; Luke 22:33-34*

38 [a]Mark 14:30; John 18:27

Chapter 14 Theme ______________________

14 "[a]Do not let your heart be troubled; [1]believe in God,
believe also in Me.
2 "In My Father's house are many dwelling places; if it were
not so, I would have told you; for [a]I go to prepare a place for
you.
3 "If I go and prepare a place for you, [a]I will come again and
receive you to Myself, that [b]where I am, *there* you may be also.
4 "And you know the way where I am going."
5 [a]Thomas *said to Him, "Lord, we do not know where You
are going, how do we know the way?"
6 Jesus *said to him, "I am [a]the way, and [b]the truth, and [c]the
life; no one comes to the Father but through Me.
7 "[a]If you had known Me, you would have known My Father
also; from now on you [b]know Him, and have [c]seen Him."
8 [a]Philip *said to Him, "Lord, show us the Father, and it is
enough for us."
9 Jesus *said to him, "Have I been so long with you, and *yet*
you have not come to know Me, Philip? [a]He who has seen Me
has seen the Father; how *can* you say, 'Show us the Father'?
10 "Do you not believe that [a]I am in the Father, and the Father
is in Me? [b]The words that I say to you I do not speak on My
own initiative, but the Father abiding in Me does His works.
11 "Believe Me that [a]I am in the Father and the Father is in
Me; otherwise [b]believe because of the works themselves.
12 "Truly, truly, I say to you, he who believes in Me, the works
that I do, he will do also; and [a]greater *works* than these he will
do; because [b]I go to the Father.
13 "[a]Whatever you ask in My name, that will I do, so that [b]the
Father may be glorified in the Son.
14 "If you ask Me anything [a]in My name, I will do *it*.
15 "[a]If you love Me, you will keep My commandments.
16 "I will ask the Father, and He will give you another [1a]Helper,
that He may be with you forever;
17 *that is* [a]the Spirit of truth, [b]whom the world cannot receive,
because it does not see Him or know Him, *but* you know Him
because He abides with you and will be in you.
18 "I will not leave you as orphans; [a]I will come to you.
19 "[1a]After a little while [b]the world will no longer see Me, but
you *will* see Me; [c]because I live, you will live also.
20 "[a]In that day you will know that [b]I am in My Father, and you
in Me, and I in you.
21 "[a]He who has My commandments and keeps them is the
one who loves Me; and [b]he who loves Me will be loved by My
Father, and I will love him and will [c]disclose Myself to him."
22 [a]Judas (not Iscariot) *said to Him, "Lord, what then has
happened [b]that You are going to disclose Yourself to us and not
to the world?"
23 Jesus answered and said to him, "[a]If anyone loves Me, he
will [b]keep My word; and [c]My Father will love him, and We
[d]will come to him and make Our abode with him.

14:1 [1]Or *you believe in God* [a]John 14:27; 16:22, 24
2 [a]John 13:33, 36
3 [a]John 14:18, 28 [b]John 12:26
5 [a]John 11:16
6 [a]John 10:9; Rom 5:2; Eph 2:18; Heb 10:20 [b]John 1:14 [c]John 1:4; 11:25; 1 John 5:20
7 [a]John 8:19 [b]1 John 2:13 [c]John 6:46
8 [a]John 1:43
9 [a]John 1:14; 12:45; Col 1:15; Heb 1:3
10 [a]John 10:38; 14:11, 20 [b]John 5:19; 14:24
11 [a]John 10:38; 14:10, 20 [b]John 5:36
12 [a]John 4:37f; 5:20 [b]John 7:33; 14:28
13 [a]Matt 7:7 [b]John 13:31
14 [a]John 15:16; 16:23f
15 [a]John 14:21, 23; 15:10; 1 John 5:3; 2 John 6
16 [1]Gr *Paracletos,* one called along-side to help; or *Comforter, Advocate, Intercessor* [a]John 7:39; 14:26; 15:26; 16:7; Rom 8:26; 1 John 2:1
17 [a]John 15:26; 16:13; 1 John 4:6; 5:7 [b]1 Cor 2:14
18 [a]John 14:3, 28
19 [1]Lit *Yet a little and the world* [a]John 7:33 [b]John 16:16, 22 [c]John 6:57
20 [a]John 16:23, 26 [b]John 10:38; 14:11
21 [a]John 14:15, 23; 15:10; 1 John 5:3; 2 John 6 [b]John 14:23; 16:27 [c]Ex 33:18f; Prov 8:17
22 [a]Luke 6:16; Acts 1:13 [b]Acts 10:40, 41
23 [a]John 14:15, 21; 15:10; 1 John 5:3; 2 John 6 [b]John 8:51; 1 John 2:5 [c]John 14:21 [d]2 Cor 6:16; Eph 3:17; 1 John 2:24; Rev 3:20; 21:3

24 "He who does not love Me [a]does not keep My words; and
[b]the word which you hear is not Mine, but the Father's who
sent Me.
25 "These things I have spoken to you while abiding with you.
26 "But the [a]Helper, the Holy Spirit, [b]whom the Father will
send in My name, [c]He will teach you all things, and [d]bring to
your remembrance all that I said to you.
27 "[a]Peace I leave with you; My peace I give to you; not as the
world gives do I give to you. [b]Do not let your heart be troubled,
nor let it be fearful.
28 "[a]You heard that I said to you, 'I go away, and [b]I will come to
you.' If you loved Me, you would have rejoiced because [c]I go to
the Father, for [d]the Father is greater than I.
29 "Now [a]I have told you before it happens, so that when it
happens, you may believe.
30 "I will not speak much more with you, for [a]the ruler of the
world is coming, and he has nothing in Me;
31 but so that the world may know that I love the Father, [1]I do
exactly as [a]the Father commanded Me. Get up, [b]let us go from
here.

Chapter 15 Theme ____________________________________

15 "[a]I am the true vine, and My Father is the [b]vinedresser.
2 "Every branch in Me that does not bear fruit, He takes
away; and every *branch* that bears fruit, He [1]prunes it so that it
may bear more fruit.
3 "[a]You are already [1]clean because of the word which I have
spoken to you.
4 "[a]Abide in Me, and I in you. As the branch cannot bear fruit
[1]of itself unless it abides in the vine, so neither *can* you unless
you abide in Me.
5 "I am the vine, you are the branches; he who abides in Me
and I in him, he [a]bears much fruit, for apart from Me you can
do nothing.
6 "If anyone does not abide in Me, he is [a]thrown away as a
branch and dries up; and they gather them, and cast them into
the fire and they are burned.
7 "If you abide in Me, and My words abide in you, [a]ask
whatever you wish, and it will be done for you.
8 "My [a]Father is glorified by this, that you bear much fruit,
and *so* [1b]prove to be My disciples.
9 "Just as [a]the Father has loved Me, I have also loved you; abide
in My love.
10 "[a]If you keep My commandments, you will abide in My
love; just as [b]I have kept My Father's commandments and abide
in His love.
11 "[a]These things I have spoken to you so that My joy may be
in you, and *that* your [b]joy may be made full.
12 "This is [a]My commandment, that you love one another, just
as I have loved you.

24 [a]John 14:23 [b]John 7:16; 14:10
26 [a]John 14:16 [b]Luke 24:49; John 1:33; 15:26; 16:7; Acts 2:33 [c]John 16:13f; 1 John 2:20, 27 [d]John 2:22
27 [a]John 16:33; 20:19; Phil 4:7; Col 3:15 [b]John 14:1
28 [a]John 14:2-4 [b]John 14:3, 18 [c]John 14:12 [d]John 10:29; Phil 2:6
29 [a]John 13:19
30 [a]John 12:31
31 [1]Lit *and as the Father . . . so I do* [a]John 10:18; 12:49 [b]John 13:1; 18:1
15:1 [a]Ps 80:8ff; Is 5:1ff; Ezek 19:10ff; Matt 21:33ff [b]Matt 15:13; Rom 11:17; 1 Cor 3:9
2 [1]Lit *cleans;* used to describe pruning
3 [1]I.e. pruned like a branch [a]John 13:10; 17:17; Eph 5:26
4 [1]Lit *from* [a]John 6:56; 15:4-7; 1 John 2:6
5 [a]John 15:16
6 [a]John 15:2
7 [a]Matt 7:7; John 15:16
8 [1]Or *become My disciples* [a]Matt 5:16 [b]John 8:31
9 [a]John 3:35; 17:23, 24, 26
10 [a]John 14:15 [b]John 8:29
11 [a]John 17:13 [b]John 3:29
12 [a]John 13:34; 15:17; 1 John 3:23; 2 John 5

13 "[a]Greater love has no one than this, that one [b]lay down his life for his friends.

14 "You are My [a]friends if [b]you do what I command you.

15 "No longer do I call you slaves, for the slave does not know what his master is doing; but I have called you friends, for [a]all things that I have heard from My Father I have made known to you.

16 "[a]You did not choose Me but I chose you, and appointed you that you would go and [b]bear fruit, and *that* your fruit would remain, so that [c]whatever you ask of the Father in My name He may give to you.

17 "This [a]I command you, that you love one another.

18 "[a]If the world hates you, [1]you know that it has hated Me before *it hated* you.

19 "If you were of the world, the world would love its own; but because you are not of the world, but [a]I chose you out of the world, [b]because of this the world hates you.

20 "Remember the word that I said to you, '[a]A slave is not greater than his master.' If they persecuted Me, [b]they will also persecute you; if they [c]kept My word, they will keep yours also.

21 "But all these things they will do to you [a]for My name's sake, [b]because they do not know the One who sent Me.

22 "[a]If I had not come and spoken to them, they would not have [1]sin, but now they have no excuse for their sin.

23 "He who hates Me hates My Father also.

24 "[a]If I had not done among them [b]the works which no one else did, they would not have [1]sin; but now they have both seen and hated Me and My Father as well.

25 "But *they have done this* to fulfill the word that is written in their [a]Law, '[b]THEY HATED ME WITHOUT A CAUSE.'

26 "When the [1a]Helper comes, [b]whom I will send to you from the Father, *that is* [c]the Spirit of truth who proceeds from the Father, [d]He will testify about Me,

27 [1]and [a]you *will* testify also, because you have been with Me [b]from the beginning.

Chapter 16 Theme ______________________

16 "[a]These things I have spoken to you so that you may be kept from [b]stumbling.

2 "[1]They will [a]make you outcasts from the synagogue, but [b]an hour is coming for everyone [c]who kills you to think that he is offering service to God.

3 "These things they will do [a]because they have not known the Father or Me.

4 "But these things I have spoken to you, [a]so that when their hour comes, you [1]may remember that I told you of them. These things I did not say to you [b]at the beginning, because I was with you.

5 "But now [a]I am going to Him who sent Me; and none of you asks Me, '[b]Where are You going?'

13 [a]Rom 5:7f [b]John 10:11

14 [a]Luke 12:4 [b]Matt 12:50

15 [a]John 8:26; 16:12

16 [a]John 6:70; 13:18; 15:19 [b]John 15:5 [c]John 14:13; 15:7; 16:23

17 [a]John 15:12

18 [1]Or (imperative) *know that* [a]John 7:7; 1 John 3:13

19 [a]John 15:16 [b]Matt 10:22; 24:9; John 17:14

20 [a]Matt 10:24; John 13:16 [b]1 Cor 4:12; 2 Cor 4:9; 2 Tim 3:12 [c]John 8:51

21 [a]Matt 10:22; 24:9; Mark 13:13; Luke 21:12, 17; Acts 4:17; 5:41; 9:14; 26:9; 1 Pet 4:14; Rev 2:3 [b]John 8:19, 55; 16:3; 17:25; Acts 3:17; 1 John 3:1

22 [1]I.e. guilt [a]John 9:41; 15:24

24 [1]I.e. guilt [a]John 9:41; 15:21 [b]John 5:36; 10:37

25 [a]John 10:34 [b]Ps 35:19; 69:4

26 [1]Gr *Paracletos*, one called alongside to help; or *Comforter, Advocate, Intercessor* [a]John 14:16 [b]John 14:26 [c]John 14:17 [d]1 John 5:7

27 [1]Or (imperative) *and bear witness* [a]Luke 24:48; John 19:35; 21:24; 1 John 1:2; 4:14 [b]Luke 1:2

16:1 [a]John 15:18-27 [b]Matt 11:6

2 [1]Or *They will have you excommunicated* [a]John 9:22 [b]John 4:21; 16:25 [c]Is 66:5; Acts 26:9-11; Rev 6:9

3 [a]John 8:19, 55; 15:21; 17:25; Acts 3:17; 1 John 3:1

4 [1]Or *will remember them, that I told you* [a]John 13:19 [b]Luke 1:2

5 [a]John 7:33; 16:10, 17, 28 [b]John 13:36; 14:5

6 "But because I have said these things to you, [a]sorrow has
filled your heart.
7 "But I tell you the truth, it is to your advantage that I go
away; for if I do not go away, the [1a]Helper will not come to you;
but if I go, [b]I will send Him to you.
8 "And He, when He comes, will convict the world concerning
sin and righteousness and judgment;
9 concerning sin, [a]because they do not believe in Me;
10 and concerning [a]righteousness, because [b]I go to the Father
and you no longer see Me;
11 [a]and concerning judgment, because the ruler of this world
has been judged.
12 "I have many more things to say to you, but you cannot bear
them now.
13 "But when He, [a]the Spirit of truth, comes, He will [b]guide you
into all the truth; for He will not speak on His own initiative,
but whatever He hears, He will speak; and He will disclose to
you what is to come.
14 "He will [a]glorify Me, for He will take of Mine and will disclose
it to you.
15 "[a]All things that the Father has are Mine; therefore I said
that He takes of Mine and will disclose *it* to you.
16 "[a]A little while, and [b]you will no longer see Me; and again a
little while, and [c]you will see Me."
17 *Some* of His disciples then said to one another, "What is
this thing He is telling us, '[a]A little while, and you will not see
Me; and again a little while, and you will see Me'; and,
'because [b]I go to the Father'?"
18 So they were saying, "What is this that He says, 'A little
while'? We do not know what He is talking about."
19 [a]Jesus knew that they wished to question Him, and He said
to them, "Are you deliberating together about this, that I said,
'A little while, and you will not see Me, and again a little while,
and you will see Me'?
20 "Truly, truly, I say to you, that [a]you will weep and lament,
but the world will rejoice; you will grieve, but [b]your grief will
be turned into joy.
21 "[a]Whenever a woman is in labor she has [1]pain, because her
hour has come; but when she gives birth to the child, she no
longer remembers the anguish because of the joy that a [2]child
has been born into the world.
22 "Therefore [a]you too have grief now; but [b]I will see you
again, and your heart will rejoice, and no one *will* take your joy
away from you.
23 "[a]In that day [b]you will not question Me about anything.
Truly, truly, I say to you, [c]if you ask the Father for anything in
My name, He will give it to you.
24 "[a]Until now you have asked for nothing in My name; ask
and you will receive, so that your [b]joy may be made full.
25 "These things I have spoken to you in [1a]figurative language;
[b]an hour is coming when I will no longer speak to you in
[1]figurative language, but will tell you plainly of the Father.

6 [a]John 14:1; 16:22

7 [1]Gr *Paracletos,* one called alongside to help; or *Comforter, Advocate, Intercessor* [a]John 14:16 [b]John 14:26

9 [a]John 15:22, 24

10 [a]Acts 3:14; 7:52; 17:31; 1 Pet 3:18 [b]John 16:5

11 [a]John 12:31

13 [a]John 14:17 [b]John 14:26

14 [a]John 7:39

15 [a]John 17:10

16 [a]John 7:33 [b]John 14:18-24; 16:16-24 [c]John 16:22

17 [a]John 16:16 [b]John 16:5

19 [a]Mark 9:32; John 6:61

20 [a]Mark 16:10; Luke 23:27 [b]John 20:20

21 [1]Lit *grief* [2]Lit *human being* [a]Is 13:8; 21:3; 26:17; 66:7; Hos 13:13; Mic 4:9; 1 Thess 5:3

22 [a]John 16:6 [b]John 16:16

23 [a]John 14:20; 16:26 [b]John 16:19, 30 [c]John 15:16

24 [a]John 14:14 [b]John 3:29; 15:11

25 [1]Lit *proverbs;* or *figures of speech* [a]Matt 13:34; John 10:6; 16:29 [b]John 16:2

26 "[a]In that day [b]you will ask in My name, and I do not say to
you that I will request of the Father on your behalf;
27 for [a]the Father Himself loves you, because you have loved
Me and [b]have believed that [c]I came forth from the Father.
28 "[a]I came forth from the Father and have come into the
world; I am leaving the world again and [b]going to the Father."
29 His disciples *said, "Lo, now You are speaking plainly and
are not [1]using [a]a figure of speech.
30 "Now we know that You know all things, and have no need
for anyone to question You; by this we [a]believe that You [b]came
from God."
31 Jesus answered them, "Do you now believe?
32 "Behold, [a]an hour is coming, and has *already* come, for [b]you
to be scattered, each to [c]his own *home,* and to leave Me alone;
and *yet* [d]I am not alone, because the Father is with Me.
33 "These things I have spoken to you, so that [a]in Me you may
have peace. [b]In the world you have tribulation, but [c]take
courage; [d]I have overcome the world."

Chapter 17 Theme ____________________

17 Jesus spoke these things; and [a]lifting up His eyes to heaven,
He said, "Father, the hour has come; [b]glorify Your Son, that
the Son may glorify You,
2 even as [a]You gave Him authority over all flesh, that [b]to [1]all
whom You have given Him, [c]He may give eternal life.
3 "This is eternal life, that they may know You, [a]the only true
God, and Jesus Christ whom [b]You have sent.
4 "[a]I glorified You on the earth, [1b]having accomplished the
work which You have given Me to do.
5 "Now, Father, [a]glorify Me together with Yourself, with the
glory which I had [b]with You before the world was.
6 "[a]I have manifested Your name to the men whom [b]You gave
Me out of the world; they were [c]Yours and You gave them to
Me, and they have [d]kept Your word.
7 "Now they have come to know that everything You have
given Me is from You;
8 for [a]the words which You gave Me [b]I have given to them;
and they received *them* and truly understood that [c]I came forth
from You, and they believed that [d]You sent Me.
9 "[a]I ask on their behalf; [b]I do not ask on behalf of the world,
but of those whom [c]You have given Me; for [d]they are Yours;
10 and [a]all things that are Mine are Yours, and Yours are
Mine; and I have been glorified in them.
11 "I am no longer in the world; and *yet* [a]they themselves are
in the world, and [b]I come to You. [c]Holy Father, keep them in
Your name, *the name* [d]which You have given Me, that [e]they
may be one even as We *are.*
12 "While I was with them, I was keeping them in Your name
[a]which You have given Me; and I guarded them and [b]not one of
them perished but [c]the [1]son of perdition, so that the [d]Scripture
would be fulfilled.

26 [a]John 14:20; 16:23 [b]John 16:19, 30
27 [a]John 14:21, 23 [b]John 2:11; 16:30 [c]John 8:42
28 [a]John 8:42; 16:30 [b]John 13:1, 3; 16:5, 10, 17
29 [1]Lit *saying a proverb* [a]Matt 13:34; John 10:6; 16:25
30 [a]John 2:11; 16:27 [b]John 8:42; 16:28
32 [a]John 4:23; 16:2, 25 [b]Zech 13:7; Matt 26:31 [c]John 19:27 [d]John 8:29
33 [a]John 14:27 [b]John 15:18ff [c]Matt 9:2 [d]Rom 8:37; 2 Cor 2:14; 4:7ff; 6:4ff; Rev 3:21; 12:11
17:1 [a]John 11:41 [b]John 7:39; 13:31f
2 [1]Lit *everything that You have given Him, to them He may* [a]John 3:35 [b]John 10:28 [c]John 6:37, 39; 17:6, 9, 24
3 [a]John 5:44 [b]John 3:17; 17:8, 21, 23, 25
4 [1]Or *by accomplishing* [a]John 13:31 [b]Luke 22:37; John 4:34
5 [a]John 17:1 [b]John 1:1; 8:58; 17:24; Phil 2:6
6 [a]John 17:26 [b]John 6:37, 39; 17:2, 9, 24 [c]John 17:9 [d]John 8:51
8 [a]John 6:68; 12:49 [b]John 15:15; 17:14, 26 [c]John 8:42; 16:27, 30 [d]John 3:17; 17:18, 21, 23, 25
9 [a]Luke 22:32; John 14:16 [b]Luke 23:34; John 17:20f [c]John 6:37, 39; 17:2, 6, 24 [d]John 17:6
10 [a]John 16:15
11 [a]John 13:1 [b]John 7:33; 17:13 [c]John 17:25 [d]John 17:6; Phil 2:9; Rev 19:12 [e]John 17:21f; Rom 12:5; Gal 3:28
12 [1]Heb idiom for one destined to perish [a]John 17:6; Phil 2:9; Rev 19:12 [b]John 6:39; 18:9 [c]John 6:70 [d]Ps 41:9; John 13:18

13 "But now [a]I come to You; and [b]these things I speak in the
world so that they may have My [c]joy made full in themselves.
14 "I have given them Your word; and [a]the world has hated
them, because [b]they are not of the world, even as I am not of
the world.
15 "I do not ask You to take them out of the world, but to keep
them [1]from [2a]the evil *one.*
16 "[a]They are not of the world, even as I am not of the world.
17 "[a]Sanctify them in the truth; Your word is truth.
18 "As [a]You sent Me into the world, [b]I also have sent them into
the world.
19 "For their sakes I [a]sanctify Myself, that they themselves also
may be [b]sanctified [c]in truth.
20 "I do not ask on behalf of these alone, but for those also
who believe in Me through their word;
21 that they may all be one; [a]even as You, Father, *are* in Me
and I in You, that they also may be in Us, [b]so that the world
may [1]believe that [c]You sent Me.
22 "The [a]glory which You have
given Me I have given to them,
that they may be one, just as
We are one;
23 [a]I in them and You in Me,
that they may be perfected [1]in
unity, so that the world may
[2]know that [b]You sent Me, and
[c]loved them, even as You have
loved Me.
24 "Father, I desire that [a]they
also, whom You have given Me,
[b]be with Me where I am, so that
they may see My [c]glory which
You have given Me, for You
loved Me before [d]the foundation
of the world.
25 "O [a]righteous Father, [1]although [b]the world has not known
You, yet I have known You; and these have known that [c]You
sent Me;
26 and [a]I have made Your name known to them, and will
make it known, so that [b]the love with which You loved Me
may be in them, and I in them."

Jerusalem of the New Testament

Chapter 18 Theme ________________

18 When Jesus had spoken these words, [a]He went forth
with His disciples over [b]the [1]ravine of the Kidron, where
there was [c]a garden, in which He entered [2]with His disciples.
2 Now Judas also, who was [1]betraying Him, knew the place,
for Jesus had [a]often met there with His disciples.
3 [a]Judas then, having received [b]the *Roman* [1]cohort and
[c]officers from the chief priests and the Pharisees, *came there
with lanterns and [d]torches and weapons.

13 [a]John 7:33; 17:11 [b]John 15:11 [c]John 3:29

14 [a]John 15:19 [b]John 8:23; 17:16

15 [1]Or *out of* the power of [2]Or *evil* [a]Matt 5:37

16 [a]John 17:14

17 [a]John 15:3

18 [a]John 3:17; 17:3, 8, 21, 23, 25 [b]Matt 10:5; John 4:38; 20:21

19 [a]John 15:13 [b]John 15:3 [c]2 Cor 7:14; Col 1:6; 1 John 3:18

21 [1]Gr tense indicates *continually believe* [a]John 10:38; 17:11, 23 [b]John 17:8 [c]John 3:17; 17:3, 8, 18, 23, 25

22 [a]John 1:14; 17:24

23 [1]Lit *into one* [2]Gr tense indicates *continually know* [a]John 10:38; 17:11, 21 [b]John 3:17; 17:3, 8, 18, 21, 25 [c]John 16:27

24 [a]John 17:2 [b]John 12:26 [c]John 1:14; 17:22 [d]Matt 25:34; John 17:5

25 [1]Lit *even the world* [a]John 17:11; 1 John 1:9 [b]John 7:29; 15:21 [c]John 3:17; 17:3, 8, 18, 21, 23

26 [a]John 17:6 [b]John 15:9

18:1 [1]Lit *winter-torrent* [2]Lit *and* [a]Matt 26:30, 36; Mark 14:26, 32; Luke 22:39 [b]2 Sam 15:23; 1 Kin 2:37; 15:13; 2 Kin 23:4, 6, 12; 2 Chr 15:16; 29:16; 30:14; Jer 31:40 [c]Matt 26:36; Mark 14:32; John 18:26

2 [1]Or *handing Him over* [a]Luke 21:37; 22:39

3 [1]Normally 600 men; *a battalion* [a]John 18:3-11: *Matt 26:47-56; Mark 14:43-50; Luke 22:47-53* [b]John 18:12; Acts 10:1 [c]John 7:32; 18:12, 18 [d]Matt 25:1

4 So Jesus, [a]knowing all the things that were coming upon
Him, went forth and *said to them, "[b]Whom do you seek?"
5 They answered Him, "Jesus the Nazarene." He *said to
them, "I am *He.*" And Judas also, who was betraying Him, was
standing with them.
6 So when He said to them, "I am *He,*" they drew back and
fell to the ground.
7 Therefore He again asked them, "[a]Whom do you seek?"
And they said, "Jesus the Nazarene."
8 Jesus answered, "I told you that I am *He;* so if you seek
Me, let these go their way,"
9 to fulfill the word which He spoke, "[a]Of those whom You
have given Me I lost not one."
10 Simon Peter then, [a]having a sword, drew it and struck the
high priest's slave, and cut off his right ear; and the slave's
name was Malchus.
11 So Jesus said to Peter, "Put the sword into the sheath; [a]the
cup which the Father has given Me, shall I not drink it?"
12 [a]So [b]the *Roman* [1]cohort and the [2]commander and the
[b]officers of the Jews, arrested Jesus and bound Him,
13 and led Him to [a]Annas first; for he was father-in-law of
[b]Caiaphas, who was high priest that year.
14 Now Caiaphas was the one who had advised the Jews that
[a]it was expedient for one man to die on behalf of the people.
15 [a]Simon Peter was following Jesus, and *so was* another
disciple. Now that disciple was known to the high priest, and
entered with Jesus into [b]the court of the high priest,
16 [a]but Peter was standing at the door outside. So the other
disciple, who was known to the high priest, went out and spoke
to the doorkeeper, and brought Peter in.
17 [a]Then the slave-girl who kept the door *said to Peter, "[b]You
are not also *one* of this man's disciples, are you?" He *said, "I
am not."
18 Now the slaves and the [a]officers were standing *there,*
having made [b]a charcoal fire, for it was cold and they were
[c]warming themselves; and Peter was also with them, standing
and warming himself.
19 [a]The high priest then questioned Jesus about His disciples,
and about His teaching.
20 Jesus answered him, "I [a]have spoken openly to the world; I
always [b]taught in [1]synagogues and [c]in the temple, where all the
Jews come together; and I spoke nothing in secret.
21 "Why do you question Me? Question those who have heard
what I spoke to them; they know what I said."
22 When He had said this, one of the [a]officers standing nearby
[b]struck Jesus, saying, "Is that the way You answer the high
priest?"
23 [a]Jesus answered him, "If I have spoken wrongly, testify of
the wrong; but if rightly, why do you strike Me?"
24 [a]So Annas sent Him bound to [a]Caiaphas the high priest.
25 [a]Now [b]Simon Peter was standing and warming himself. So

4 [a]John 6:64; 13:1, 11 [b]John 18:7
7 [a]John 18:4
9 [a]John 17:12
10 [a]Matt 26:51; Mark 14:47
11 [a]Matt 20:22; 26:39; Mark 14:36; Luke 22:42
12 [1]Or *battalion* [2]I.e. chiliarch, in command of a thousand troops [a]John 18:12f: *Matt 26:57ff* [b]John 18:3
13 [a]Luke 3:2; John 18:24 [b]Matt 26:3; John 11:49, 51
14 [a]John 11:50
15 [a]Matt 26:58; Mark 14:54; Luke 22:54 [b]Matt 26:3; John 18:24, 28
16 [a]John 18:16-18: *Matt 26:69f; Mark 14:66-68; Luke 22:55-57*
17 [a]Acts 12:13 [b]John 18:25
18 [a]John 18:3 [b]John 21:9 [c]Mark 14:54, 67
19 [a]John 18:19-24: *Matt 26:59-68; Mark 14:55-65; Luke 22:63-71*
20 [1]Lit *a synagogue* [a]John 7:26; 8:26 [b]Matt 4:23; John 6:59 [c]Matt 26:55
22 [a]John 18:3 [b]John 19:3
23 [a]Matt 5:39; Acts 23:2-5
24 [a]John 18:13
25 [a]John 18:25-27: *Matt 26:71-75; Mark 14:69-72; Luke 22:58-62* [b]John 18:18

they said to him, "[c]You are not also *one* of His disciples, are
you?" He denied *it,* and said, "I am not."
26 One of the slaves of the high priest, being a relative of the
one [a]whose ear Peter cut off, *said, "Did I not see you in [b]the
garden with Him?"
27 Peter then denied *it* again, and immediately [a]a rooster
crowed.
28 [a]Then they *led Jesus from [b]Caiaphas into [c]the [1]Praetorium,
and it was early; and they themselves did not enter into [c]the
[1]Praetorium so that [d]they would not be defiled, but might eat
the Passover.
29 [a]Therefore Pilate went out to them and *said, "What
accusation do you bring against this Man?"
30 They answered and said to him, "If this Man were not an
evildoer, we would not have delivered Him to you."
31 So Pilate said to them, "Take Him yourselves, and judge
Him according to your law." The Jews said to him, "We are not
permitted to put anyone to death,"
32 to fulfill [a]the word of Jesus which He spoke, signifying by
what kind of death He was about to die.
33 Therefore Pilate [a]entered again into the Praetorium, and
summoned Jesus and said to Him, "[b]Are You the King of the
Jews?"
34 Jesus answered, "Are you saying this [1]on your own initiative,
or did others tell you about Me?"
35 Pilate answered, "I am not a Jew, am I? Your own nation
and the chief priests delivered You to me; what have You done?"
36 Jesus answered, "[a]My kingdom [1]is not of this world. If My
kingdom were of this world, then My servants would be
fighting so that I would not be handed over to the Jews; but as
it is, My kingdom is not [2]of this realm."
37 Therefore Pilate said to Him, "So You are a king?" Jesus
answered, "[a]You say *correctly* that I am a king. For this I have
been born, and for this I have come into the world, [b]to testify
to the truth. [c]Everyone who is of the truth hears My voice."
38 Pilate *said to Him, "What is truth?"

And when he had said this, he [a]went out again to the Jews
and *said to them, "[b]I find no guilt in Him.
39 "[a]But you have a custom that I release someone [1]for you at
the Passover; do you wish then that I release [1]for you the King
of the Jews?"
40 So they cried out again, saying, "[a]Not this Man, but
Barabbas." Now Barabbas was a robber.

Chapter 19 Theme ____________________

19 Pilate then took Jesus and [1a]scourged Him.
2 [a]And the soldiers twisted together a crown of thorns
and put it on His head, and put a purple robe on Him;
3 and they *began* to come up to Him and say, "[a]Hail, King of
the Jews!" and to [b]give Him slaps *in the face.*

25 [c]John 18:17
26 [a]John 18:10 [b]John 18:1
27 [a]John 13:38
28 [1]I.e. governor's official residence [a]Matt 27:2; Mark 15:1; Luke 23:1 [b]John 18:13 [c]Matt 27:27; John 18:33; 19:9 [d]John 11:55; Acts 11:3
29 [a]John 18:29-38: *Matt 27:11-14; Mark 15:2-5; Luke 23:2, 3*
32 [a]Matt 20:19; 26:2; Mark 10:33f; Luke 18:32f; John 3:14; 8:28; 12:32f
33 [a]John 18:28, 29; 19:9 [b]Luke 23:3; John 19:12
34 [1]Lit *from yourself*
36 [1]Or *is not derived from* [2]Lit *from here* [a]Matt 26:53; Luke 17:21; John 6:15
37 [a]Matt 27:11; Mark 15:2; Luke 22:70; 23:3 [b]John 1:14; 3:32; 8:14 [c]John 8:47; 1 John 4:6
38 [a]John 18:33; 19:4 [b]Luke 23:4; John 19:4, 6
39 [1]Or *to you* [a]John 18:39-19:16: *Matt 27:15-26; Mark 15:6-15; Luke 23:18-25*
40 [a]Acts 3:14
19:1 [1]Or *had Him scourged* [a]Matt 27:26
2 [a]Matt 27:27-30: *Mark 15:16-19*
3 [a]Matt 27:29; Mark 15:18 [b]John 18:22

INSIGHT

The ***Praetorium*** was used as the temporary Roman military headquarters or as the palace in Jerusalem to house the Roman governor. It was either a building next to Herod's palace or the Antonia Fortress beside the temple mount complex. See the map on page 1747 and the illustration of the temple mount on page NISB-40.

4 Pilate [a]came out again and *said to them, "Behold, I am
bringing Him out to you so that you may know that [b]I find no
guilt in Him."
5 Jesus then came out, [a]wearing the crown of thorns and the
purple robe. *Pilate* *said to them, "Behold, the Man!"
6 So when the chief priests and the [a]officers saw Him, they
cried out saying, "Crucify, crucify!" Pilate *said to them, "Take
Him yourselves and crucify Him, for [b]I find no guilt in Him."
7 The Jews answered him, "[a]We have a law, and by that law
He ought to die because He [b]made Himself out *to be* the Son of
God."
8 Therefore when Pilate heard this statement, he was *even*
more afraid;
9 and he [a]entered into the [1]Praetorium again and *said to
Jesus, "Where are You from?" But [b]Jesus gave him no answer.
10 So Pilate *said to Him, "You do not speak to me? Do You
not know that I have authority to release You, and I have
authority to crucify You?"
11 Jesus answered, "[a]You would have no authority [1]over Me,
unless it had been given you from above; for this reason [b]he
who delivered Me to you has *the* greater sin."
12 As a result of this Pilate [1]made efforts to release Him, but
the Jews cried out saying, "[a]If you release this Man, you are no
friend of Caesar; everyone who makes himself out *to be* a king
[2]opposes Caesar."
13 Therefore when Pilate heard these words, he brought Jesus
out, and [a]sat down on the judgment seat at a place called [1]The
Pavement, but [b]in [2]Hebrew, Gabbatha.
14 Now it was [a]the day of preparation for the Passover; it was
about the [1b]sixth hour. And he *said to the Jews, "Behold, [c]your
King!"
15 So they cried out, "[a]Away with *Him,* away with *Him,* crucify
Him!" Pilate *said to them, "Shall I crucify your King?" The chief
priests answered, "We have no king but Caesar."
16 So he then [a]handed Him over to them to be crucified.
17 [a]They took Jesus, therefore, and He went out, [1b]bearing His
own cross, to the place called [c]the Place of a Skull, which is
called [d]in [2]Hebrew, Golgotha.
18 There they crucified Him, and with Him [a]two other men,
one on either side, and Jesus in between.
19 Pilate also wrote an inscription and put it on the cross. It
was written, "[a]JESUS THE NAZARENE, [b]THE KING OF THE
JEWS."
20 Therefore many of the Jews read this inscription, for the
place where Jesus was crucified was near the city; and it was
written [a]in [1]Hebrew, Latin *and* in Greek.
21 So the chief priests of the Jews were saying to Pilate, "Do
not write, '[a]The King of the Jews'; but that He said, 'I am [a]King
of the Jews.'"
22 Pilate answered, "[a]What I have written I have written."
23 Then [a]the soldiers, when they had crucified Jesus, took His

4 [a]John 18:33, 38 [b]Luke 23:4; John 18:38; 19:6
5 [a]John 19:2
6 [a]Matt 26:58; John 18:3 [b]Luke 23:4; John 18:38; 19:4
7 [a]Lev 24:16; Matt 26:63-66 [b]John 5:18; 10:33
9 [1]I.e. governor's official residence [a]John 18:33 [b]Matt 26:63; 27:12, 14; John 18:34-37
11 [1]Lit *against* [a]Rom 13:1 [b]John 18:13f, 28ff; Acts 3:13
12 [1]Lit *was seeking to* [2]Or *speaks against* [a]Luke 23:2; John 18:33ff
13 [1]Gr *The Lithostrotos* [2]I.e. Jewish Aramaic [a]Matt 27:19 [b]John 5:2; 19:17, 20
14 [1]Perhaps 6 a.m. [a]Matt 27:62; John 19:31, 42 [b]Matt 27:45; Mark 15:25 [c]John 19:19, 21
15 [a]Luke 23:18
16 [a]Matt 27:26; Mark 15:15; Luke 23:25
17 [1]Lit *bearing the cross for Himself* [2]I.e. Jewish Aramaic [a]John 19:17-24: *Matt 27:33-44; Mark 15:22-32; Luke 23:33-43* [b]Matt 27:32; Mark 15:21; Luke 14:27; 23:26 [c]Luke 23:33 [d]John 19:13
18 [a]Luke 23:32
19 [a]Matt 27:37; Mark 15:26; Luke 23:38 [b]John 19:14, 21
20 [1]I.e. Jewish Aramaic [a]John 19:13
21 [a]John 19:14, 19
22 [a]Gen 43:14; Esth 4:16
23 [a]Matt 27:35; Mark 15:24; Luke 23:34

outer garments and made [b]four parts, a part to every soldier and
also the [1]tunic; now the tunic was seamless, woven [2]in one
piece.
24 So they said to one another, "[a]Let us not tear it, but cast
lots for it, *to decide* whose it shall be"; [b]*this was* to fulfill the
Scripture: "THEY [c]DIVIDED MY OUTER GARMENTS AMONG THEM, AND
FOR MY CLOTHING THEY CAST [1]LOTS."
25 Therefore the soldiers did these things.
[a]**B**ut standing by the cross of Jesus were [b]His mother, and His
mother's sister, Mary the *wife* of Clopas, and [c]Mary Magdalene.
26 When Jesus then saw His mother, and [a]the disciple whom
He loved standing nearby, He *said to His mother, "[b]Woman,
behold, your son!"
27 Then He *said to the disciple, "Behold, your mother!"
From that hour the disciple took her into [a]his own *household.*
28 After this, Jesus, [a]knowing that all things had already been
accomplished, [b]to fulfill the Scripture, *said, "[c]I am thirsty."
29 A jar full of sour wine was standing there; so [a]they put a
sponge full of the sour wine upon *a branch of* hyssop and
brought it up to His mouth.
30 Therefore when Jesus had received the sour wine, He said,
"[a]It is finished!" And He bowed His head and [b]gave up His spirit.
31 Then the Jews, because it was [a]the day of preparation, so
that [b]the bodies would not remain on the cross on the Sabbath
([1]for that Sabbath was a [c]high day), asked Pilate that their legs
might be broken, and *that* they might be taken away.
32 So the soldiers came, and broke the legs of the first man
and of the other who was [a]crucified with Him;
33 but coming to Jesus, when they saw that He was already
dead, they did not break His legs.
34 But one of the soldiers pierced His side with a spear, and
immediately [a]blood and water came out.
35 And he who has seen has [a]testified, and his testimony is
true; and he knows that he is telling the truth, so that you also
may believe.
36 For these things came to pass [a]to fulfill the Scripture, "[b]NOT
A BONE OF HIM SHALL BE [1]BROKEN."
37 And again another Scripture says, "[a]THEY SHALL LOOK ON
HIM WHOM THEY PIERCED."
38 [a]After these things Joseph of Arimathea, being a disciple of
Jesus, but a [b]secret *one* for [c]fear of the Jews, asked Pilate that
he might take away the body of Jesus; and Pilate granted
permission. So he came and took away His body.
39 [a]Nicodemus, who had first come to Him by night, also
came, [b]bringing a [1]mixture of [c]myrrh and aloes, about a
[d]hundred [2]pounds *weight.*
40 So they took the body of Jesus and [a]bound it in [b]linen
wrappings with the spices, as is the burial custom of the Jews.
41 Now in the place where He was crucified there was a
garden, and in the garden a [a]new tomb [b]in which no one had
yet been laid.

23 [1]Gr *khiton,* the garment worn next to the skin [2]Lit *from the upper part through the whole* [b]Acts 12:4
24 [1]Lit *a lot* [a]Ex 28:32; Matt 27:35; Mark 15:24; Luke 23:34 [b]John 19:28, 36f [c]Ps 22:18
25 [a]Matt 27:55f; Mark 15:40f; Luke 23:49 [b]Matt 12:46 [c]Luke 8:2; John 20:1, 18
26 [a]John 13:23 [b]John 2:4
27 [a]Luke 18:28; John 1:11; 16:32; Acts 21:6
28 [a]John 13:1; 17:4 [b]John 19:24, 36f [c]Ps 69:21
29 [a]John 19:29, 30: *Matt 27:48, 50; Mark 15:36f; Luke 23:36*
30 [a]John 17:4 [b]Matt 27:50; Mark 15:37; Luke 23:46
31 [1]Lit *for the day of that Sabbath was great* [a]John 19:14, 42 [b]Deut 21:23; Josh 8:29; 10:26f [c]Ex 12:16
32 [a]John 19:18
34 [a]1 John 5:6, 8
35 [a]John 15:27; 21:24
36 [1]Or *crushed* or *shattered* [a]John 19:24, 28 [b]Ex 12:46; Num 9:12; Ps 34:20
37 [a]Zech 12:10; Rev 1:7
38 [a]John 19:38-42: *Matt 27:57-61; Mark 15:42-47; Luke 23:50-56* [b]Mark 15:43 [c]John 7:13
39 [1]Two early mss read *package of* [2]Lit *100 litras* (12 oz each) [a]John 3:1 [b]Mark 16:1 [c]Ps 45:8; Prov 7:17; Song 4:14; Matt 2:11 [d]John 12:3
40 [a]Matt 26:12; Mark 14:8; John 11:44 [b]Luke 24:12; John 20:5, 7
41 [a]Matt 27:60 [b]Luke 23:53

42 Therefore because of the Jewish day of [a]preparation, since
the tomb was [b]nearby, they laid Jesus there.

Chapter 20 Theme ______________________________

20 [a]Now on the first *day* of the week [b]Mary Magdalene
*came early to the tomb, while it *was still dark, and
*saw [c]the stone *already* taken away from the tomb.
2 So she *ran and *came to Simon Peter and to the other
[a]disciple whom Jesus loved, and *said to them, "[b]They have
taken away the Lord out of the tomb, and we do not know
where they have laid Him."
3 [a]So Peter and the other disciple went forth, and they were
going to the tomb.
4 The two were running together; and the other disciple ran
ahead faster than Peter and came to the tomb first;
5 and [a]stooping and looking in, he *saw the [b]linen wrappings
lying *there;* but he did not go in.
6 And so Simon Peter also *came, following him, and entered
the tomb; and he *saw the linen wrappings lying *there,*
7 and [a]the face-cloth which had been on His head, not lying
with the [b]linen wrappings, but rolled up in a place by itself.
8 So the other disciple who [a]had first come to the tomb then
also entered, and he saw and believed.
9 For as yet [a]they did not understand the Scripture, [b]that He
must rise again from the dead.
10 So the disciples went away again [a]to their own homes.
11 [a]But Mary was standing outside the tomb weeping; and so,
as she wept, she [b]stooped and looked into the tomb;
12 and she *saw [a]two angels in white sitting, one at the head
and one at the feet, where the body of Jesus had been lying.
13 And they *said to her, "[a]Woman, why are you weeping?"
She *said to them, "Because [b]they have taken away my Lord,
and I do not know where they have laid Him."
14 When she had said this, she turned around and *[a]saw Jesus
standing *there,* and [b]did not know that it was Jesus.
15 Jesus *said to her, "[a]Woman, why are you weeping? Whom
are you seeking?" Supposing Him to be the gardener, she *said
to Him, "Sir, if you have carried Him away, tell me where you
have laid Him, and I will take Him away."
16 Jesus *said to her, "Mary!" She turned and *said to Him [a]in
[1]Hebrew, "[b]Rabboni!" (which means, Teacher).
17 Jesus *said to her, "Stop clinging to Me, for I have not yet
ascended to the Father; but go to [a]My brethren and say to them,
'I [b]ascend to My Father and your Father, and My God and your
God.'"
18 [a]Mary Magdalene *came, [b]announcing to the disciples, "I
have seen the Lord," and *that* He had said these things to her.
19 So when it was evening on that day, the first *day* of the
week, and when the doors were shut where the disciples
were, for [a]fear of the Jews, Jesus came and stood in their midst
and *said to them, "[1b]Peace *be* with you."

42 [a]John 19:14, 31 [b]John 19:20, 41

20:1 [a]John 20:1-8: *Matt 28:1-8; Mark 16:1-8; Luke 24:1-10* [b]John 19:25; 20:18 [c]Matt 27:60, 66; 28:2; Mark 15:46; 16:3f; Luke 24:2; John 11:38

2 [a]John 13:23 [b]John 20:13

3 [a]Luke 24:12; John 20:3-10

5 [a]John 20:11 [b]John 19:40

7 [a]John 11:44 [b]John 19:40

8 [a]John 20:4

9 [a]Matt 22:29; John 2:22 [b]Luke 24:26ff, 46

10 [a]Luke 24:12

11 [a]Mark 16:5 [b]John 20:5

12 [a]Matt 28:2f; Mark 16:5; Luke 24:4

13 [a]John 20:15 [b]John 20:2

14 [a]Matt 28:9; Mark 16:9 [b]John 21:4

15 [a]John 20:13

16 [1]I.e. Jewish Aramaic [a]John 5:2 [b]Matt 23:7; Mark 10:51

17 [a]Matt 28:10 [b]Mark 12:26; 16:19; John 7:33

18 [a]John 20:1 [b]Mark 16:10; Luke 24:10, 23

19 [1]Lit *Peace to you* [a]John 7:13 [b]Luke 24:36; John 14:27; 20:21, 26

20 [a]Luke 24:39, 40; John 19:34 [b]John 16:20, 22

20 And when He had said this, [a]He showed them both His
hands and His side. The disciples then [b]rejoiced when they
saw the Lord.

21 [a]Luke 24:36; John 14:27; 20:19, 26 [b]John 17:18

21 So Jesus said to them again, "[a]Peace *be* with you; [b]as the
Father has sent Me, I also send you."
22 And when He had said this, He breathed on them and
*said to them, "Receive the Holy Spirit.

23 [1]I.e. have previously been forgiven [a]Matt 16:19; 18:18

23 "[a]If you forgive the sins of any, *their sins* [1]have been
forgiven them; if you retain the *sins* of any, they have been
retained."

24 [1]I.e. the Twin [a]John 11:16 [b]John 6:67

24 But [a]Thomas, one of [b]the twelve, called [1a]Didymus, was
not with them when Jesus came.

25 [a]John 20:20 [b]Mark 16:11

25 So the other disciples were saying to him, "We have seen
the Lord!" But he said to them, "Unless I see in [a]His hands the
imprint of the nails, and put my finger into the place of the
nails, and put my hand into His side, [b]I will not believe."

26 [1]Or *A week later* [2]Or *locked* [a]Luke 24:36; John 14:27; 20:19, 21

26 [1]After eight days His disciples were again inside, and
Thomas with them. Jesus *came, the doors having been [2]shut,
and stood in their midst and said, "[a]Peace *be* with you."

27 [a]Luke 24:40; John 20:25

27 Then He *said to Thomas, "[a]Reach here with your finger,
and see My hands; and reach here your hand and put it into
My side; and do not be unbelieving, but believing."

29 [a]1 Pet 1:8

28 Thomas answered and said to Him, "My Lord and my God!"
29 Jesus *said to him, "Because you have seen Me, have you
believed? [a]Blessed *are* they who did not see, and *yet* believed."

30 [1]Or *attesting miracles* [a]John 21:25 [b]John 2:11

30 [a]Therefore many other [1b]signs Jesus also performed in the
presence of the disciples, which are not written in this book;

31 [1]I.e. the Messiah [a]John 19:35 [b]Matt 4:3 [c]John 3:15

31 but these have been written [a]so that you may believe that
Jesus is [1]the Christ, [b]the Son of God; and that [c]believing you
may have life in His name.

Chapter 21 Theme ____________________

21:1 [1]Or *made Himself visible* [a]Mark 16:12; John 21:14 [b]John 20:19, 26 [c]John 6:1

21 After these things Jesus [1a]manifested Himself [b]again to
the disciples at the [c]Sea of Tiberias, and He manifested
Himself in this way.

2 [1]I.e. the Twin [a]John 11:16 [b]John 1:45ff [c]John 2:1 [d]Matt 4:21; Mark 1:19; Luke 5:10

2 Simon Peter, and [a]Thomas called [1]Didymus, and [b]Nathanael
of [c]Cana in Galilee, and [d]the *sons* of Zebedee, and two others
of His disciples were together.

3 [a]Luke 5:5

3 Simon Peter *said to them, "I am going fishing." They
*said to him, "We will also come with you." They went out
and got into the boat; and [a]that night they caught nothing.

4 [a]Luke 24:16; John 20:14

4 But when the day was now breaking, Jesus stood on the
beach; yet the disciples did not [a]know that it was Jesus.

5 [1]Lit *something eaten with bread* [a]Luke 24:41

5 So Jesus *said to them, "Children, [a]you do not have [1]any
fish, do you?" They answered Him, "No."

6 [a]Luke 5:4ff

6 And He said to them, "[a]Cast the net on the right-hand side
of the boat and you will find *a catch*." So they cast, and then they
were not able to haul it in because of the great number of fish.

7 [a]John 13:23; 21:20

7 [a]Therefore that disciple whom Jesus loved *said to Peter,
"It is the Lord." So when Simon Peter heard that it was the

Lord, he put his outer garment on (for he was stripped *for*
work), and threw himself into the sea.
8 But the other disciples came in the little boat, for they
were not far from the land, but about [1]one hundred yards
away, dragging the net *full* of fish.
9 So when they got out on the land, they *saw a charcoal
[a]fire *already* laid and [b]fish placed on it, and bread.
10 Jesus *said to them, "Bring some of the [a]fish which you
have now caught."
11 Simon Peter went up and drew the net to land, full of large
fish, a hundred and fifty-three; and although there were so
many, the net was not torn.
12 Jesus *said to them, "Come *and* have [a]breakfast." None of
the disciples ventured to question Him, "Who are You?"
knowing that it was the Lord.
13 Jesus *came and *took [a]the bread and *gave *it* to them,
and the [b]fish likewise.
14 This is now the [a]third time that Jesus [1]was manifested to
the disciples, after He was raised from the dead.
15 So when they had [a]finished breakfast, Jesus *said to Simon
Peter, "Simon, *son* of John, do you [1b]love Me more than
these?" He *said to Him, "Yes, Lord; You know that I [2]love
You." He *said to him, "Tend [c]My lambs."
16 He *said to him again a second time, "Simon, *son* of John,
do you [1]love Me?" He *said to Him, "Yes, Lord; You know that
I [2]love You." He *said to him, "[a]Shepherd My sheep."
17 He *said to him the third time, "Simon, *son* of John, do
you [1]love Me?" Peter was grieved because He said to him [a]the
third time, "Do you [1]love Me?" And he said to Him, "Lord,
[b]You know all things; You know that I [1]love You." Jesus *said to
him, "[c]Tend My sheep.
18 "Truly, truly, I say to you, when you were younger, you used
to gird yourself and walk wherever you wished; but when you
grow old, you will stretch out your hands and someone else
will gird you, and bring you where you do not wish to *go*."
19 Now this He said, [a]signifying by [b]what kind of death he
would glorify God. And when He had spoken this, He *said to
him, "[c]Follow Me!"
20 Peter, turning around, *saw the [a]disciple whom Jesus loved
following *them;* the one who also had [b]leaned back on His
bosom at the supper and said, "Lord, who is the one who
betrays You?"
21 So Peter seeing him *said to Jesus, "Lord, and what about
this man?"
22 Jesus *said to him, "If I want him to remain [a]until I come,
what *is that* to you? You [b]follow Me!"
23 Therefore this saying went out among [a]the brethren that
that disciple would not die; yet Jesus did not say to him that he
would not die, but *only,* "If I want him to remain [b]until I come,
what *is that* to you?"

8 [1]Lit *200 cubits*

9 [a]John 18:18 [b]John 6:9, 11; 21:10, 13

10 [a]John 6:9, 11; 21:9, 13

12 [a]John 21:15

13 [a]John 21:9 [b]John 6:9, 11; 21:9, 10

14 [1]Or *made Himself visible* [a]John 20:19, 26

15 [1]Gr *agapao* [2]Gr *phileo* [a]John 21:12 [b]Matt 26:33; Mark 14:29; John 13:37 [c]Luke 12:32

16 [1]Gr *agapao* [2]Gr *phileo* [a]Matt 2:6; Acts 20:28; 1 Pet 5:2; Rev 7:17

17 [1]Gr *phileo* [a]John 13:38 [b]John 16:30 [c]John 21:15, 16

19 [a]John 12:33; 18:32 [b]2 Pet 1:14 [c]Matt 8:22; 16:24; John 21:22

20 [a]John 21:7 [b]John 13:25

22 [a]Matt 16:27f; 1 Cor 4:5; 11:26; James 5:7; Rev 2:25 [b]Matt 8:22; 16:24; John 21:19

23 [a]Acts 1:15 [b]Matt 16:27f; 1 Cor 4:5; 11:26; James 5:7; Rev 2:25

24 [a]John 15:27

24 This is the disciple who [a]is testifying to these things and
wrote these things, and we know that his testimony is true.
25 And there are also [a]many other things which Jesus did,
which if they *were written in detail, I suppose that even the
world itself *would not contain the books that *would be
written.

25 [a]John 20:30

John at a Glance

Theme of John:

Segment Divisions

	Portrayals of Jesus Christ	Signs and Miracles	Ministry	Chapter Themes
			To Israel	1
				2
				3
				4
				5
				6
				7
				8
				9
				10
				11
			To Disciples	12
				13
				14
				15
				16
				17
			To All Mankind	18
				19
				20
			To Dis-ciples	21

Author:

Date:

Purpose:

Key Words:
(including synonyms)

The Arrest, Trial, and Crucifixion of Jesus Christ

Matthew	Mark	Luke	John
		Luke gives consecutive order of events in Jesus' life (Luke 1:3)	

What the Gospels Teach about the

Matthew	Mark

Luke	John

The Account of Jesus' Resurrection

Matthew	Mark	Luke	John
		Luke gives consecutive order of events in Jesus' life (Luke 1:3)	

Postresurrection Appearances

ACTS

"I'm going away."

The 11 heard nothing else. The promise of another Helper, the Holy Spirit, fell on deaf ears. The thought that they could do the works that Jesus had done—and even greater—must have seemed preposterous to them.

Jesus had died and been buried. But three days later He arose from the dead! For more than 40 days the disciples saw, heard, and touched the Word of Life as He spoke with them of things concerning the kingdom of God. He commissioned His disciples to reach the world, and then once again He was gone, taken away before their very eyes! Before He left, He promised to send the Spirit to empower them, to teach them, and to guide them.

Then came Pentecost and the acts of the apostles. Luke wrote Theophilus all about it in the book of Acts, which was probably written about A.D. 63.

THINGS TO DO

General Instructions

1. In a distinctive way mark in the text every occurrence of the key words (along with their synonyms and pronouns) listed on the ACTS AT A GLANCE chart on page 1820. Record these key words on an index card that you can use as a bookmark while studying Acts.
2. Mark every reference to time with the symbol of a green clock 🕒. Do this throughout the book of Acts whether the time is indicated by an event (such as a feast) or by mentioning a certain period of months or years. Also, double-underline in green every geographical location.

Chapters 1–2

In the first two chapters of the book of Acts, Luke gives an account of Christ's ascension and the Holy Spirit's coming.

1. Read chapter 1, looking for Jesus' instructions and promises to the apostles.
   a. In your notebook list everything you learn from the references to the Holy Spirit.
   b. Note the main events that occur in this chapter by either marking these events within the text or listing them in the margin.
2. Acts 1:8 gives an outline for the book of Acts. Remember this as you read Acts. Observe when the gospel goes from Jerusalem and Judea to Samaria and the outermost parts of the world.
3. As you read chapter 2:
   a. Keep in mind that in the NASB any Scripture printed in small caps indicates that the Scripture is either an Old Testament quotation or an allusion to an Old Testament text. Observe how much is taken from the Old Testament.
   b. List in the margin the main events that occur. As you note them, ask the "5 W's and an H": Who? What? When? Where? Why? and How? For example, ask: Who was present on the day of Pentecost? What happened? Whom did it affect? What was their response? Why did they respond as they did? How did they hear?
   c. As you mark key words, watch the word *promise* and note its relationship to the Spirit. Compare this with Acts 1:4-5.

d. Observe the main points in Peter's sermon on the day of Pentecost. Note what he emphasized in his sermon and the result.

4. Determine the theme of each of these chapters. Then record the themes on ACTS AT A GLANCE and in your Bible.

Chapters 3–7

1. As you study, do the following:
   a. Read each chapter in the light of the "5 W's and an H." What happens in that chapter? Where and when did it happen? Who is involved? How are things done or said?
   b. Mark every reference to the Holy Spirit and then list what you learn about the Holy Spirit, His ministry, and the results. Also mark in the text the other key words listed on ACTS AT A GLANCE. Remember to use your bookmark.
   c. If a message is proclaimed in these chapters, you may want to record in your notebook the main points of that message and the effect of the message on those who hear it.
2. Determine the theme of each chapter and then record the theme as before.

Chapters 8–12

1. Read Acts 8:1-8 and then Acts 1:8. What do you see happening in Acts 8 that is a change from the first seven chapters? Note this in the margin of chapter 8.

2. Read chapters 8 through 11 carefully, as significant events occur in these chapters. As you read:
   a. List the main events in each chapter. Who does what? When? Where is it done? What is said? What is the result? Who is affected? How does it happen? Don't add to the text, but simply observe it and record in your notebook what you learn.
   b. Mark key words and list everything you learn about the Holy Spirit in your notebook. This is crucial to chapters 8, 10, and 11. Note to whom the Holy Spirit comes.
   c. Record the theme of each chapter in your Bible and on ACTS AT A GLANCE.

3. As you read and study chapter 12, keep in mind that this is a pivotal chapter. At this point the focus of the book turns from Peter's ministry to that of Paul (Saul).

Chapters 13–28

1. Included in these chapters is an account of Paul's missionary journeys: Paul's first missionary journey in 13–14; Paul's second missionary journey in 15:36–18:22; and Paul's third missionary journey in 18:23–21:17.

   For easy reference, write and color code in the margin where each journey begins.

2. As you study these chapters, mark the key repeated words. Add the word *synagogue* to your list. Also keep in mind what you learned from Acts 1:8 and watch carefully the work of the Spirit throughout these chapters. In your notebook, note your insights.
   a. Examine each chapter with the "5 W's and an H." Note in the text who accompanies Paul, where they go, and what happens. Trace each of Paul's journeys on the maps on pages 1787, 1794, and 1800.
   b. Carefully observe each time the gospel is proclaimed, whether to an individual or a group. Watch how Paul reasons with Jews and Gentiles. Also, note what their response is and how Paul handles it.

3. In several instances you will notice Paul giving his testimony. Compare each of these instances with Acts 9 and the account of Paul's conversion. This will give you a more complete picture of all that happened on that significant day.

4. Record the theme of each chapter on ACTS AT A GLANCE and in your Bible. Then determine the main subject for the book of Acts and record it. Complete the chart and record the ways you might segment the book of Acts according to its themes.

THINGS TO THINK ABOUT

1. What have you learned from Acts about the Holy Spirit and your responsibility to be a witness for the Lord Jesus Christ?

2. Based on what you saw in the sermons that were preached and the personal witnesses that were given, what would you include in your witness? Where would the emphasis be?

3. As you studied the lives of the early apostles and the commitment of the early church, how has God spoken to your heart? Stop and think about how they lived, and then think about how you are living. Do you have the Holy Spirit living inside you? Isn't He the same today, yesterday, and forever? If you are filled with the Holy Spirit and are not quenching Him, what should be happening in your life?

Chapter 1 Theme ______

1 The first account I [1]composed, [a]Theophilus, about all that
Jesus [b]began to do and teach,
2 until the day when He [a]was taken up *to heaven,* after He
[b]had [1]by the Holy Spirit given orders to [c]the apostles whom He
had [d]chosen.
3 To [1]these [a]He also presented Himself alive after His suffering,
by many convincing proofs, appearing to them over *a period of*
forty days and speaking of [b]the things concerning the kingdom
of God.
4 [1]Gathering them together, He commanded them [a]not to
leave Jerusalem, but to wait for [2b]what the Father had promised,
"Which," *He said,* "you heard of from Me;
5 for [a]John baptized with water, but you will be baptized
[1]with the Holy Spirit [2b]not many days from now."
6 So when they had come together, they were asking Him,
saying, "Lord, [a]is it at this time You are restoring the kingdom
to Israel?"
7 He said to them, "It is not for you to know times or epochs
which [a]the Father has fixed by His own authority;
8 but you will receive power [a]when the Holy Spirit has come
upon you; and you shall be [b]My witnesses both in Jerusalem,
and in all Judea and [c]Samaria, and even to [d]the remotest part of
the earth."
9 And after He had said these things, [a]He was lifted up while
they were looking on, and a cloud received Him out of their sight.

1:1 [1]Lit *made* [a]Luke 1:3 [b]Luke 3:23
2 [1]Or *through* [a]Mark 16:19; Acts 1:9, 11, 22 [b]Matt 28:19f; Mark 16:15; John 20:21f; Acts 10:42 [c]Mark 6:30 [d]John 13:18; Acts 10:41
3 [1]Lit *whom* [a]Matt 28:17; Mark 16:12, 14; Luke 24:34, 36; John 20:19, 26; 21:1, 14; 1 Cor 15:5-7 [b]Acts 8:12; 19:8; 28:23, 31
4 [1]Or *eating with;* or *lodging with* [2]Lit *the promise of the Father* [a]Luke 24:49 [b]John 14:16, 26; 15:26; Acts 2:33
5 [1]Or *in* [2]Lit *not long after these many days* [a]Matt 3:11; Mark 1:8; Luke 3:16; John 1:33; Acts 11:16 [b]Acts 2:1-4
6 [a]Matt 17:11; Mark 9:12; Luke 17:20; 19:11
7 [a]Matt 24:36; Mark 13:32
8 [a]Acts 2:1-4 [b]Luke 24:48; John 15:27 [c]Acts 8:1, 5, 14 [d]Matt 28:19; Mark 16:15; Rom 10:18; Col 1:23
9 [a]Luke 24:50, 51; Acts 1:2

10 And as they were gazing intently into [1]the sky while He was going, behold, [a]two men in white clothing stood beside them.

11 They also said, "[a]Men of Galilee, why do you stand looking into [1]the sky? This Jesus, who [b]has been taken up from you into heaven, will [c]come in just the same way as you have watched Him go into heaven."

12 Then they [a]returned to Jerusalem from the [1b]mount called [2]Olivet, which is near Jerusalem, a [3]Sabbath day's journey away.

13 When they had entered *the city,* they went up to [a]the upper room where they were staying; [b]that is, Peter and John and [1]James and Andrew, Philip and Thomas, Bartholomew and Matthew, [1]James *the son* of Alphaeus, and Simon the Zealot, and [c]Judas *the* [2]*son* of [1]James.

14 These all with one mind [a]were continually devoting themselves to prayer, along with [b]*the* women, and Mary the [c]mother of Jesus, and with His [c]brothers.

15 [1]At this time Peter stood up in the midst of [a]the brethren (a gathering of about one hundred and twenty [2]persons was there together), and said,

16 "Brethren, [a]the Scripture had to be fulfilled, which the Holy Spirit foretold by the mouth of David concerning Judas, [b]who became a guide to those who arrested Jesus.

17 "For he was [a]counted among us and received his share in [b]this ministry."

18 (Now this man [a]acquired a field with [b]the price of his wickedness, and falling headlong, he burst open in the middle and all his intestines gushed out.

19 And it became known to all who were living in Jerusalem; so that in [a]their own language that field was called Hakeldama, that is, Field of Blood.)

20 "For it is written in the book of Psalms,

'[a]LET HIS HOMESTEAD BE MADE DESOLATE,
AND LET NO ONE DWELL IN IT';

and,

'[b]LET ANOTHER MAN TAKE HIS [1]OFFICE.'

21 "Therefore it is necessary that of the men who have accompanied us all the time that [a]the Lord Jesus went in and out [1]among us—

22 [a]beginning [1]with the baptism of John until the day that He [b]was taken up from us—one of these *must* become a [c]witness with us of His resurrection."

23 So they put forward two men, Joseph called Barsabbas (who was also called Justus), and [a]Matthias.

24 And they [a]prayed and said, "You, Lord, [b]who know the hearts of all men, show which one of these two You have chosen

25 to [1]occupy [a]this ministry and [b]apostleship from which Judas turned aside to go to his own place."

26 And they [1a]drew lots for them, and the lot fell [2]to [b]Matthias; and he was [3]added to [c]the eleven apostles.

INSIGHT

There were 150 Jewish colonies in major population centers throughout the Roman Empire. Many Jews came from these centers to Jerusalem to celebrate the feasts. Jesus' followers who spoke in tongues (known dialects) were Galilean Jews, yet they spoke in the languages of the men attending the Feast of Pentecost.

10 [1]Or *heaven* [a]Luke 24:4; John 20:12
11 [1]Or *heaven* [a]Acts 2:7; 13:31 [b]Mark 16:19; Acts 1:9, 22 [c]Matt 16:27f; Acts 3:21
12 [1]Or *hill* [2]Or *Olive Grove* [3]I.e. 2K cubits, or approx 3/5 mile [a]Luke 24:52 [b]Matt 21:1
13 [1]Or *Jacob* [2]Or *brother* [a]Mark 14:15; Luke 22:12; Acts 9:37, 39; 20:8 [b]Acts 1:13: *Matt 10:2-4; Mark 3:16-19; Luke 6:14-16* [c]John 14:22
14 [a]Acts 2:42; 6:4; Rom 12:12; Eph 6:18; Col 4:2 [b]Luke 8:2f [c]Matt 12:46
15 [1]Lit *In these days* [2]Lit *names* [a]John 21:23; Acts 6:3; 9:30; 10:23; 11:1, 12, 26, 29; 12:17; 14:2; 15:1, 3, 22, 23, 32f, 40; 16:2, 40; 17:6, 10, 14; 18:18, 27; 21:7, 17; 22:5; 28:14f; Rom 1:13
16 [a]John 13:18; 17:12; Acts 1:20 [b]Matt 26:47; Mark 14:43; Luke 22:47; John 18:3
17 [a]John 6:70f [b]Acts 1:25; 20:24; 21:19
18 [a]Matt 27:3-10 [b]Matt 26:14f
19 [a]Matt 27:8; Acts 21:40
20 [1]Lit *position as overseer* [a]Ps 69:25 [b]Ps 109:8
21 [1]Lit *to us* [a]Luke 24:3
22 [1]Lit *from* [a]Matt 3:16; Mark 1:1-4, 9; Luke 3:21 [b]Mark 16:19; Acts 1:2 [c]Acts 1:8; 2:32
23 [a]Acts 1:26
24 [a]Acts 6:6; 13:3; 14:23 [b]1 Sam 16:7; Jer 17:10; Acts 15:8; Rom 8:27
25 [1]Lit *take the place of* [a]Acts 1:17 [b]Rom 1:5; 1 Cor 9:2; Gal 2:8
26 [1]Lit *gave* [2]Or *upon* [3]Lit *voted together with* [a]Lev 16:8; Josh 14:2; 1 Sam 14:41f; Neh 10:34; 11:1; Prov 16:33 [b]Acts 1:23 [c]Acts 2:14

Chapter 2 Theme ________________________________

2 When [a]the day of Pentecost [1]had come, they were all together in one place.

2 And suddenly there came from heaven a noise like a violent rushing wind, and it filled [a]the whole house where they were sitting.

3 And there appeared to them tongues as of fire [1]distributing themselves, and [2]they [3]rested on each one of them.

4 And they were all [a]filled with the Holy Spirit and began to [b]speak with other [1]tongues, as the Spirit was giving them [2]utterance.

5 Now there were Jews living in Jerusalem, [a]devout men from every nation under heaven.

6 And when [a]this sound occurred, the crowd came together, and were bewildered because each one of them was hearing them speak in his own [1]language.

7 [a]They were amazed and astonished, saying, "[1]Why, are not all these who are speaking [b]Galileans?

8 "And how is it that we each hear *them* in our own [1]language [2]to which we were born?

9 "Parthians and Medes and Elamites, and residents of Mesopotamia, Judea and [a]Cappadocia, [b]Pontus and [1c]Asia,

10 [a]Phrygia and [b]Pamphylia, Egypt and the districts of Libya around [c]Cyrene, and [1d]visitors from Rome, both Jews and [2e]proselytes,

11 Cretans and Arabs—we hear them in our *own* tongues speaking of the mighty deeds of God."

12 And [a]they all continued in amazement and great perplexity, saying to one another, "What does this mean?"

13 But others were mocking and saying, "[a]They are full of [1]sweet wine."

14 But Peter, [1]taking his stand with [a]the eleven, raised his voice and declared to them: "Men of Judea and all you who live

INSIGHT

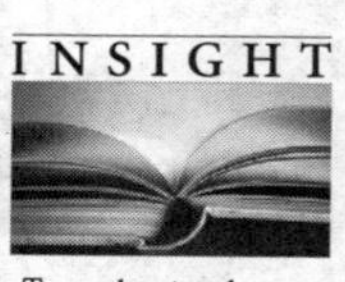

To understand the significance of Pentecost, see the chart **The Feasts of Israel** located on pages 214, 215.

Men from Every Nation at Pentecost

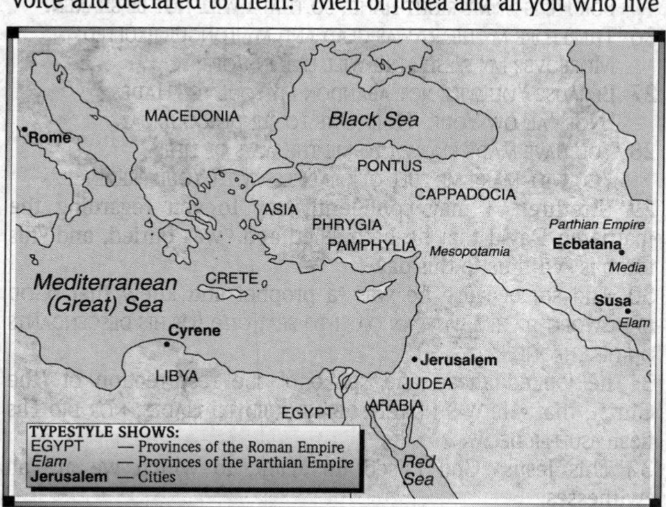

2:1 [1]Lit *was being fulfilled* [a]Lev 23:15f; Acts 20:16; 1 Cor 16:8

2 [a]Acts 4:31

3 [1]Or *being distributed* [2]Lit *it* [3]Or *sat*

4 [1]Or *languages* [2]Or *ability to speak out* [a]Matt 10:20; Acts 1:5, 8; 4:8, 31; 6:3, 5; 7:55; 8:17; 9:17; 11:15; 13:9, 52 [b]Mark 16:17; 1 Cor 12:10f; 14:21

5 [a]Luke 2:25; Acts 8:2

6 [1]Or *dialect* [a]Acts 2:2

7 [1]Lit *Behold* [a]Acts 2:12 [b]Matt 26:73; Acts 1:11

8 [1]Or *dialect* [2]Lit *in*

9 [1]I.e. west coast province of Asia Minor [a]1 Pet 1:1 [b]Acts 18:2; 1 Pet 1:1 [c]Acts 6:9; 16:6; 19:10; 20:4; 21:27; 24:18; 27:2; Rom 16:5; 1 Cor 16:19; 2 Cor 1:8; 2 Tim 1:15; Rev 1:4

10 [1]Lit *the sojourning Romans* [2]I.e. Gentile converts to Judaism [a]Acts 16:6; 18:23 [b]Acts 13:13; 14:24; 15:38; 27:5 [c]Matt 27:32 [d]Acts 17:21 [e]Matt 23:15

12 [a]Acts 2:7

13 [1]I.e. new wine [a]1 Cor 14:23

14 [1]Or *being put forward* as spokesman [a]Acts 1:26

in Jerusalem, let this be known to you and give heed to my
words.
15 "For these men are not drunk, as you suppose, [a]for it is *only*
the [1]third hour of the day;
16 but this is what was spoken of through the prophet Joel:
17 '[a]AND IT SHALL BE IN THE LAST DAYS,' God says,
'THAT I WILL POUR FORTH OF MY SPIRIT ON ALL
[1]MANKIND;
AND YOUR SONS AND YOUR DAUGHTERS SHALL PROPHESY,
AND YOUR YOUNG MEN SHALL SEE VISIONS,
AND YOUR OLD MEN SHALL DREAM DREAMS;
18 EVEN ON MY BONDSLAVES, BOTH MEN AND WOMEN,
I WILL IN THOSE DAYS POUR FORTH OF MY SPIRIT
And they shall prophesy.
19 'AND I WILL GRANT WONDERS IN THE SKY ABOVE
AND SIGNS ON THE EARTH BELOW,
BLOOD, AND FIRE, AND VAPOR OF SMOKE.
20 'THE SUN WILL BE TURNED INTO DARKNESS
AND THE MOON INTO BLOOD,
BEFORE THE GREAT AND GLORIOUS DAY OF THE LORD SHALL COME.
21 'AND IT SHALL BE THAT [a]EVERYONE WHO CALLS ON THE NAME OF
THE LORD WILL BE SAVED.'
22 "Men of Israel, listen to these words: [a]Jesus the Nazarene,
[b]a man [1]attested to you by God with [2]miracles and [c]wonders
and [3]signs which God performed through Him in your midst,
just as you yourselves know—
23 this *Man,* delivered over by the [a]predetermined plan and
foreknowledge of God, [b]you nailed to a cross by the hands of
[1]godless men and put *Him* to death.
24 "[1]But [a]God raised Him up again, putting an end to the [2]agony
of death, since it [b]was impossible for Him to be held [3]in its power.
25 "For David says of Him,
'[a]I SAW THE LORD ALWAYS IN MY PRESENCE;
FOR HE IS AT MY RIGHT HAND, SO THAT I WILL NOT BE SHAKEN.
26 'THEREFORE MY HEART WAS GLAD AND MY TONGUE EXULTED;
MOREOVER MY FLESH ALSO WILL LIVE IN HOPE;
27 BECAUSE YOU WILL NOT ABANDON MY SOUL TO [a]HADES,
[b]NOR [1]ALLOW YOUR [2]HOLY ONE TO [3]UNDERGO DECAY.
28 'YOU HAVE MADE KNOWN TO ME THE WAYS OF LIFE;
YOU WILL MAKE ME FULL OF GLADNESS WITH YOUR PRESENCE.'
29 "[1]Brethren, I may confidently say to you regarding the
[a]patriarch David that he both [b]died and [c]was buried, and [d]his
tomb is [2]with us to this day.
30 "And so, because he was [a]a prophet and knew that [b]GOD
HAD SWORN TO HIM WITH AN OATH TO SEAT *one* [1]OF HIS DESCENDANTS
ON HIS THRONE,
31 he looked ahead and spoke of the resurrection of [1]the
Christ, that [a]HE WAS NEITHER ABANDONED TO HADES, NOR DID His
flesh [2]SUFFER DECAY.
32 "This Jesus [a]God raised up again, to which we are all
[b]witnesses.

15 [1]I.e. 9 a.m. [a]1 Thess 5:7

17 [1]Lit *flesh* [a]Joel 2:28-32

21 [a]Rom 10:13

22 [1]Or *exhibited* or *accredited* [2]Or *works of power* [3]Or *attesting miracles* [a]Acts 3:6; 4:10; 10:38 [b]John 3:2 [c]John 4:48; Acts 2:19, 43

23 [1]Lit *men without the Law;* i.e. pagan [a]Luke 22:22; Acts 3:18; 4:28; 1 Pet 1:20 [b]Matt 27:35; Mark 15:24; Luke 23:33; 24:20; John 19:18; Acts 3:13

24 [1]Lit *Whom God raised up* [2]Lit *birth pains* [3]Lit *by it* [a]Matt 28:5, 6; Mark 16:6; Luke 24:5, 6; Acts 2:32; 3:15, 26; 4:10; 5:30; 10:40; 13:30, 33, 34, 37; 17:31; Rom 4:24; 6:4; 8:11; 10:9; 1 Cor 6:14; 15:15; 2 Cor 4:14; Gal 1:1; Eph 1:20; Col 2:12; 1 Thess 1:10; Heb 13:20; 1 Pet 1:21 [b]John 20:9

25 [a]Ps 16:8-11

27 [1]Lit *give* [2]Or *devout* or *pious* [3]Lit *see corruption* [a]Matt 11:23; Acts 2:31 [b]Acts 13:35

29 [1]Lit *Men brothers* [2]Lit *among* [a]Acts 7:8f; Heb 7:4 [b]Acts 13:36 [c]1 Kin 2:10 [d]Neh 3:16

30 [1]Lit *of the fruit of his loins* [a]Matt 22:43 [b]Ps 132:11; 2 Sam 7:12f; Ps 89:3f

31 [1]I.e. the Messiah [2]Lit *see corruption* [a]Matt 11:23; Acts 2:27

32 [a]Acts 2:24; 3:15, 26; 4:10; 5:30; 10:40; 13:30, 33, 34, 37; 17:31; Rom 4:24; 6:4; 8:11; 10:9; 1 Cor 6:14; 15:15; 2 Cor 4:14; Gal 1:1; Eph 1:20; Col 2:12; 1 Thess 1:10; Heb 13:20; 1 Pet 1:21 [b]Acts 1:8

33 "Therefore having been exalted [1a]to the right hand of God,
and [b]having received from the Father [c]the promise of the Holy
Spirit, He has [d]poured forth this which you both see and hear.
34 "For it was not David who ascended into [1]heaven, but he
himself says:

'[a]THE LORD SAID TO MY LORD,
"SIT AT MY RIGHT HAND,
35 UNTIL I MAKE YOUR ENEMIES A FOOTSTOOL FOR YOUR FEET."'

36 "Therefore let all the [a]house of Israel know for certain that
God has made Him both [b]Lord and [1]Christ—this Jesus [c]whom
you crucified."
37 Now when they heard *this,* they were [1]pierced to the heart,
and said to Peter and the rest of the apostles, "[2]Brethren, [3a]what
shall we do?"
38 Peter *said* to them, "[a]Repent, and each of you be [b]baptized
in the name of Jesus Christ for the forgiveness of your sins; and
you will receive the gift of the Holy Spirit.
39 "For [a]the promise is for you and your children and for all who
are [b]far off, as many as the Lord our God will call to Himself."
40 And with many other words he solemnly [a]testified and
kept on exhorting them, saying, "[1]Be saved from this [b]perverse
generation!"
41 So then, those who had received his word were baptized; and
that day there were added about three thousand [1a]souls.
42 They were [a]continually devoting themselves to the apostles'
teaching and to fellowship, to [b]the breaking of bread and [1a]to
prayer.
43 [1]Everyone kept feeling a sense of awe; and many [a]wonders
and [2]signs were taking place through the apostles.
44 And all those who had believed [1]were together and [a]had all
things in common;
45 and they [a]*began* selling their property and possessions and
were sharing them with all, as anyone might have need.
46 [a]Day by day continuing with one mind in the temple, and
[b]breaking bread [1]from house to house, they were taking their
[2]meals together with gladness and [3]sincerity of heart,
47 praising God and [a]having favor with all the people. And the
Lord [b]was adding [1]to their number day by day [c]those who were
being saved.

Chapter 3 Theme ____________________

3 Now [a]Peter and John were going up to the temple at the
[1]ninth *hour,* [b]the hour of prayer.
2 And [a]a man who had been lame from his mother's womb
was being carried along, whom they [b]used to set down every
day at the gate of the temple which is called Beautiful, [c]in order
to beg [1]alms of those who were entering the temple.
3 When he saw [a]Peter and John about to go into the temple,
he *began* asking to receive alms.
4 But Peter, along with John, [a]fixed his gaze on him and said,
"Look at us!"

33 [1]Or *by* [a]Mark 16:19; Acts 5:31 [b]Acts 1:4 [c]John 7:39; Gal 3:14 [d]Acts 2:17; 10:45
34 [1]Lit *the heavens* [a]Ps 110:1; Matt 22:44f
36 [1]I.e. Messiah [a]Ezek 36:22, 32, 37; 45:6 [b]Acts 2:23 [c]Luke 2:11
37 [1]Or *wounded in conscience* [2]Lit *Men brothers* [3]Or *what are we to do* [a]Luke 3:10, 12, 14
38 [a]Mark 1:15; Luke 24:47; Acts 3:19; 5:31; 20:21 [b]Mark 16:16; Acts 8:12, 16; 22:16
39 [a]Is 44:3; 54:13; 57:19; Joel 2:32; Rom 9:4; Eph 2:12 [b]Eph 2:13, 17
40 [1]Or *Escape* [a]Luke 16:28 [b]Deut 32:5; Matt 17:17; Phil 2:15
41 [1]I.e. persons [a]Acts 3:23; 7:14; 27:37; Rom 13:1; 1 Pet 3:20; Rev 16:3
42 [1]Lit *the prayers* [a]Acts 1:14 [b]Luke 24:30; Acts 2:46; 20:7; 1 Cor 10:16
43 [1]Lit *fear was occurring to every soul* [2]Or *attesting miracles* [a]Acts 2:22
44 [1]One early ms does not contain *were* and *and* [a]Acts 4:32, 37; 5:2
45 [a]Matt 19:21; Acts 4:34
46 [1]Or *in the various private homes* [2]Lit *food* [3]Or *simplicity* [a]Acts 5:42 [b]Luke 24:30; Acts 2:42; 20:7; 1 Cor 10:16
47 [1]Lit *together* [a]Acts 5:13 [b]Acts 2:41; 4:4; 5:14; 6:1, 7; 9:31, 35, 42; 11:21, 24; 14:1, 21; 16:5; 17:12 [c]1 Cor 1:18
3:1 [1]I.e. 3 p.m. [a]Luke 22:8; Acts 3:3, 4, 11 [b]Ps 55:17; Matt 27:45; Acts 10:30
2 [1]Or *a gift of charity* [a]Acts 14:8 [b]Luke 16:20 [c]John 9:8; Acts 3:10
3 [a]Luke 22:8; Acts 3:1, 4, 11
4 [a]Acts 10:4

RETURN TO INSTRUCTIONS

5 And he *began* to give them his attention, expecting to receive
something from them.
6 But Peter said, "I do not possess silver and gold, but what I do
have I give to you: [a]In the name of Jesus Christ the Nazarene—
walk!"
7 And seizing him by the right hand, he raised him up; and
immediately his feet and his ankles were strengthened.
8 [1a]With a leap he stood upright and *began* to walk; and he
entered the temple with them, walking and leaping and praising
God.
9 And [a]all the people saw him walking and praising God;
10 and they were taking note of him as being the one who used
to [a]sit at the Beautiful Gate of the temple to *beg* alms, and they
were filled with wonder and amazement at what had happened
to him.
11 While he was clinging to [a]Peter and John, all the people ran
together to them at the so-called [1b]portico of Solomon, full of
amazement.
12 But when Peter saw *this,* he replied to the people, "Men of
Israel, why are you amazed at this, or why do you gaze at us, as
if by our own power or piety we had made him walk?
13 "[a]The God of Abraham, Isaac and Jacob, [b]the God of our
fathers, has glorified His [1c]servant Jesus, *the one* whom [d]you
delivered and disowned in the presence of [e]Pilate, when he
had [f]decided to release Him.
14 "But you disowned [a]the Holy and Righteous One and [b]asked
for a murderer to be granted to you,
15 but put to death the [1a]Prince of life, *the one* whom [b]God
raised from the dead, *a fact* to which we are [c]witnesses.
16 "And on the basis of faith [a]in His name, *it is* [1]the name of
Jesus which has strengthened this man whom you see and
know; and the faith which *comes* through Him has given him
this perfect health in the presence of you all.
17 "And now, brethren, I know that you acted [a]in ignorance,
just as your [b]rulers did also.
18 "But the things which [a]God announced beforehand by the
mouth of all the prophets, [b]that His [1]Christ would suffer, He has
thus fulfilled.
19 "Therefore [a]repent and return, so that your sins may be
wiped away, in order that [b]times of refreshing may come from
the presence of the Lord;
20 and that He may send Jesus, the [1]Christ appointed for you,
21 [a]whom heaven must receive until *the* [1]period of [b]restoration
of all things about which [c]God spoke by the mouth of His holy
prophets from ancient time.
22 "Moses said, '[a]THE LORD GOD WILL RAISE UP FOR YOU A PROPHET
[1]LIKE ME FROM YOUR BRETHREN; TO HIM YOU SHALL GIVE HEED to
everything He says to you.
23 '[a]And it will be that every [b]soul that does not heed that
prophet [c]shall be utterly destroyed from among the people.'
24 "And likewise, [a]all the prophets who have spoken, from
Samuel and *his* successors onward, also announced these days.

6 [a]Acts 2:22; 3:16; 4:10

8 [1]Lit *leaping up* [a]Acts 14:10

9 [a]Acts 4:16, 21

10 [a]John 9:8; Acts 3:2

11 [1]Or *colonnade* [a]Luke 22:8; Acts 3:3, 4 [b]John 10:23; Acts 5:12

13 [1]Or *Son* [a]Matt 22:32 [b]Ex 3:13, 15; Acts 5:30; 7:32; 22:14 [c]Acts 3:26; 4:27, 30 [d]Matt 20:19; John 19:11; Acts 2:23 [e]Matt 27:2 [f]Luke 23:4

14 [a]Mark 1:24; Acts 4:27; 7:52; 2 Cor 5:21 [b]Matt 27:20; Mark 15:11; Luke 23:18, 25

15 [1]Or *Author* [a]Acts 5:31; Heb 2:10; 12:2 [b]Acts 2:24 [c]Luke 24:48

16 [1]Lit *His name* [a]Acts 3:6

17 [a]Luke 23:34; John 15:21; Acts 13:27; 26:9; Eph 4:18 [b]Luke 23:13

18 [1]Or *Anointed One;* i.e. Messiah [a]Acts 2:23 [b]Luke 24:27; Acts 17:3; 26:23

19 [a]Acts 2:38; 26:20 [b]2 Thess 1:7; Heb 4:1ff

20 [1]Or *Anointed One;* i.e. Messiah

21 [1]Lit *periods, times* [a]Acts 1:11 [b]Matt 17:11; Rom 8:21 [c]Luke 1:70

22 [1]Or *as* He raised up *me* [a]Deut 18:15, 18; Acts 7:37

23 [a]Deut 18:19 [b]Acts 2:41 [c]Lev 23:29

24 [a]Luke 24:27; Acts 17:3; 26:23

25 "It is you who are [a]the sons of the prophets and of the
[b]covenant which God [1]made with your fathers, saying to
Abraham, '[c]AND IN YOUR SEED ALL THE FAMILIES OF THE EARTH SHALL
BE BLESSED.'
26 "For you [a]first, God [b]raised up His [1]Servant and sent Him to
bless you by turning every one *of you* from your wicked ways."

Chapter 4 Theme ______________________

4 As they were speaking to the people, the priests and [a]the
captain of the temple *guard* and [b]the Sadducees [c]came up
to them,
2 being greatly disturbed because they were teaching the
people and proclaiming [1a]in Jesus the resurrection from the dead.
3 And they laid hands on them and [a]put them in jail until the
next day, for it was already evening.
4 But many of those who had heard the [1]message believed;
and [a]the number of the men came to be about five thousand.
5 On the next day, their [a]rulers and elders and scribes were
gathered together in Jerusalem;
6 and [a]Annas the high priest *was there,* and [b]Caiaphas and
John and Alexander, and all who were of high-priestly descent.
7 When they had placed them in the center, they *began to*
inquire, "By what power, or in what name, have you done this?"
8 Then Peter, [1a]filled with the Holy Spirit, said to them,
"[2b]Rulers and elders of the people,
9 if we are [1]on trial today for [a]a benefit done to a sick man,
[2]as to how this man has been made well,
10 let it be known to all of you and to all the people of Israel,
that [1a]by the name of Jesus Christ the Nazarene, whom you
crucified, whom [b]God raised from the dead—[1]by [2]this *name*
this man stands here before you in good health.
11 "[1a]He is the [b]STONE WHICH WAS [c]REJECTED by you, THE BUILDERS,
but WHICH BECAME THE CHIEF CORNER *stone.*
12 "And there is salvation in [a]no one else; for there is no other
name under heaven that has been given among men by which
we must be saved."
13 Now as they observed the [a]confidence of [b]Peter and John
and understood that they were uneducated and untrained men,
they were amazed, and [c]*began* to recognize them [1]as having
been with Jesus.
14 And seeing the man who had been healed standing with
them, they had nothing to say in reply.
15 But when they had ordered them to leave the [1a]Council,
they *began* to confer with one another,
16 saying, "[a]What shall we do with these men? For the fact
that a [b]noteworthy [1]miracle has taken place through them is
apparent to all who live in Jerusalem, and we cannot deny it.
17 "But so that it will not spread any further among the people,
let us warn them to speak no longer to any man [a]in this name."
18 And when they had summoned them, they [a]commanded
them not to speak or teach at all [1]in the name of Jesus.

25 [1]Lit *covenanted* [a]Acts 2:39 [b]Rom 9:4f [c]Gen 22:18
26 [1]Or *Son* [a]Matt 15:24; John 4:22; Acts 13:46; Rom 1:16; 2:9f [b]Acts 2:24
4:1 [a]Luke 22:4 [b]Matt 3:7 [c]Luke 20:1; Acts 6:12
2 [1]Or *in the case of* [a]Acts 3:15; 17:18
3 [a]Acts 5:18
4 [1]Lit *word* [a]Acts 2:41
5 [a]Luke 23:13; Acts 4:8
6 [a]Luke 3:2 [b]Matt 26:3
8 [1]Or *having* just *been filled* [2]Lit *Rulers of the people and elders* [a]Acts 2:4; 13:9 [b]Luke 23:13; Acts 4:5
9 [1]Lit *answering* [2]Or *by whom* [a]Acts 3:7f
10 [1]Or *in* [2]Or *Him* [a]Acts 2:22; 3:6 [b]Acts 2:24
11 [1]Lit *This One* [a]Matt 21:42 [b]Ps 118:22 [c]Mark 9:12
12 [a]Matt 1:21; Acts 10:43; 1 Tim 2:5
13 [1]Lit *that they had been* [a]Acts 4:31 [b]Luke 22:8; Acts 4:19 [c]John 7:15
15 [1]Or *Sanhedrin* [a]Matt 5:22
16 [1]Or *sign* [a]John 11:47 [b]Acts 3:7-10
17 [a]John 15:21
18 [1]Or *on the basis of* [a]Acts 5:28f

19 But [a]Peter and John answered and said to them, "[b]Whether it is right in the sight of God to give heed to you rather than to God, you be the judge;

20 for [a]we cannot stop speaking about what we have seen and heard."

21 When they had threatened them further, they let them go (finding no basis on which to punish them) [a]on account of the people, because they were all [b]glorifying God for what had happened;

22 for the man was more than forty years old on whom this [1]miracle of healing had been performed.

23 When they had been released, they went to their own *companions* and reported all that the chief priests and the elders had said to them.

24 And when they heard *this,* they lifted their voices to God with one accord and said, "O [1]Lord, it is You who [a]MADE THE HEAVEN AND THE EARTH AND THE SEA, AND ALL THAT IS IN THEM,

25 who [a]by the Holy Spirit, *through* the mouth of our father David Your servant, said,

'[b]WHY DID THE [1]GENTILES RAGE,
AND THE PEOPLES DEVISE FUTILE THINGS?

26 '[a]THE KINGS OF THE EARTH [1]TOOK THEIR STAND,
AND THE RULERS WERE GATHERED TOGETHER
AGAINST THE LORD AND AGAINST HIS [2b]CHRIST.'

27 "For truly in this city there were gathered together against Your holy [1a]servant Jesus, whom You anointed, both [b]Herod and [c]Pontius Pilate, along with [d]the [2]Gentiles and the peoples of Israel,

28 to do whatever Your hand and [a]Your purpose predestined to occur.

29 "And [1]now, Lord, take note of their threats, and grant that Your bond-servants may [a]speak Your word with all [b]confidence,

30 while You extend Your hand to heal, and [1a]signs and wonders take place through the name of Your holy [2b]servant Jesus."

31 And when they had prayed, the [a]place where they had gathered together was shaken, and they were all [b]filled with the Holy Spirit and *began* to [c]speak the word of God with [d]boldness.

32 And the [1]congregation of those who believed were of one heart and soul; and not one *of them* [2]claimed that anything belonging to him was his own, but [a]all things were common property to them.

33 And [a]with great power the apostles were giving [b]testimony to the resurrection of the Lord Jesus, and abundant grace was upon them all.

34 For there was not a needy person among them, for all who were owners of land or houses [a]would sell them and bring the [1]proceeds of the sales

35 and [a]lay them at the apostles' feet, and they would be [b]distributed to each as any had need.

36 Now Joseph, a Levite of [a]Cyprian birth, who was also called

19 [a]Acts 4:13 [b]Acts 5:28f

20 [a]1 Cor 9:16

21 [a]Acts 5:26 [b]Matt 9:8

22 [1]Or *sign*

24 [1]Or *Master* [a]Ex 20:11; Neh 9:6; Ps 146:6

25 [1]Or *nations* [a]Acts 1:16 [b]Ps 2:1

26 [1]Or *approached* [2]Or *Anointed One;* i.e. Messiah [a]Ps 2:2 [b]Dan 9:24f; Luke 4:18; Acts 10:38; Heb 1:9

27 [1]Or *Son* [2]Or *nations* [a]Acts 3:13; 4:30 [b]Matt 14:1; Luke 23:7-11 [c]Matt 27:2; Mark 15:1; Luke 23:1, 12; John 18:28, 29 [d]Matt 20:19

28 [a]Acts 2:23

29 [1]Or *as for the present situation* [a]Phil 1:14 [b]Acts 4:13, 31; 14:3

30 [1]Or *attesting miracles* [2]Or *Son* [a]John 4:48 [b]Acts 3:13; 4:27

31 [a]Acts 2:1 [b]Acts 2:4 [c]Phil 1:14 [d]Acts 4:13; 14:3

32 [1]Or *multitude* [2]Lit *was saying* [a]Acts 2:44

33 [a]Acts 1:8 [b]Luke 24:48

34 [1]Lit *the prices of the things being sold* [a]Matt 19:21; Acts 2:45

35 [a]Acts 4:37; 5:2 [b]Acts 2:45; 6:1

36 [a]Acts 11:19f; 13:4; 15:39; 21:3, 16; 27:4

[b]Barnabas by the apostles (which translated means Son of
[1c]Encouragement),
37 and who owned a tract of land, sold it and brought the money
and [a]laid it at the apostles' feet.

Chapter 5 Theme ________________________

5 But a man named Ananias, with his wife Sapphira, sold a
piece of property,
2 and [a]kept back *some* of the price for himself, with his wife's
[1]full knowledge, and bringing a portion of it, he [b]laid it at the
apostles' feet.
3 But Peter said, "Ananias, why has [a]Satan filled your heart to
lie [b]to the Holy Spirit and to [c]keep back *some* of the price of
the land?
4 "While it remained *unsold,* did it not remain your own?
And after it was sold, was it not [1]under your control? Why is it
that you have [2]conceived this deed in your heart? You have not
lied to men but [a]to God."
5 And as he heard these words, Ananias [a]fell down and
breathed his last; and [b]great fear came over all who heard of it.
6 The young men got up and [a]covered him up, and after
carrying him out, they buried him.
7 Now there elapsed an interval of about three hours, and
his wife came in, not knowing what had happened.
8 And Peter responded to her, "Tell me whether you sold the
land [1a]for such and such a price?" And she said, "Yes, [1]that was
the price."
9 Then Peter *said* to her, "Why is it that you have agreed
together to [a]put [b]the Spirit of the Lord to the test? Behold, the
feet of those who have buried your husband are at the door,
and they will carry you out *as well.*"
10 And immediately she [a]fell at his feet and breathed her last,
and the young men came in and found her dead, and they
carried her out and buried her beside her husband.
11 And [a]great fear came over the whole church, and over all
who heard of these things.
12 [1]At the hands of the apostles many [a]signs and wonders were
taking place among the people; and they were all with one
accord in [b]Solomon's portico.
13 But none of the rest dared to associate with them; however,
[a]the people held them in high esteem.
14 And all the more [a]believers in the Lord, multitudes of men
and women, were constantly [b]added to *their number,*
15 to such an extent that they even carried the sick out into
the streets and laid them on cots and pallets, so that when Peter
came by [a]at least his shadow might fall on any one of them.
16 Also the [1]people from the cities in the vicinity of Jerusalem
were coming together, bringing people who were sick [2]or afflicted
with unclean spirits, and they were all being healed.
17 But the high priest rose up, along with all his associates

36 [1]Or *Exhortation* or *Consolation* [b]Acts 9:27; 11:22, 30; 12:25; 13:1, 2, 7; 1 Cor 9:6; Gal 2:1, 9, 13; Col 4:10 [c]Acts 2:40; 11:23; 13:15; 1 Cor 14:3; 1 Thess 2:3

37 [a]Acts 4:35; 5:2

5:2 [1]Or *collusion* [a]Acts 5:3 [b]Acts 4:35, 37

3 [a]Matt 4:10; Luke 22:3; John 13:2, 27 [b]Acts 5:4, 9 [c]Acts 5:2

4 [1]Or *in your authority* [2]Lit *placed* [a]Acts 5:3, 9

5 [a]Ezek 11:13; Acts 5:10 [b]Acts 2:43; 5:11

6 [a]John 19:40

8 [1]Lit *for so much* [a]Acts 5:2

9 [a]Acts 15:10 [b]Acts 5:3, 4

10 [a]Ezek 11:13; Acts 5:5

11 [a]Acts 2:43; 5:5

12 [1]Lit *Through* [a]John 4:48 [b]John 10:23; Acts 3:11

13 [a]Acts 2:47; 4:21

14 [a]2 Cor 6:15 [b]Acts 2:47; 11:24

15 [a]Acts 19:12

16 [1]Lit *multitude* [2]Lit *and*

(that is [a]the sect of [b]the Sadducees), and they were filled with
jealousy.
18 They laid hands on the apostles and [a]put them in a public jail.
19 But during the night [a]an angel of the Lord opened the gates
of the prison, and taking them out he said,
20 "Go, stand and [1]speak to the people in the temple [2a]the
whole message of this Life."
21 Upon hearing *this,* they entered into the temple [a]about
daybreak and *began* to teach.
Now when [b]the high priest and his associates came, they
called [c]the [1]Council together, even all the Senate of the sons of
Israel, and sent *orders* to the prison house for them to be brought.
22 But [a]the officers who came did not find them in the prison;
and they returned and reported back,
23 saying, "We found the prison house locked quite securely
and the guards standing at the doors; but when we had opened
up, we found no one inside."
24 Now when [a]the captain of the temple *guard* and the chief
priests heard these words, they were greatly perplexed about
them as to what [1]would come of this.
25 But someone came and reported to them, "The men whom
you put in prison are standing in the temple and teaching the
people!"
26 Then [a]the captain went along with [b]the officers and
proceeded to bring them *back* without violence (for [c]they were
afraid of the people, that they might be stoned).
27 When they had brought them, they stood them [1]before
[a]the Council. The high priest questioned them,
28 saying, "We gave you [a]strict orders not to continue
teaching in this name, and [1]yet, you have filled Jerusalem with
your teaching and [b]intend to bring this man's blood upon us."
29 But Peter and the apostles answered, "[a]We must obey God
rather than men.
30 "[a]The God of our fathers [b]raised up Jesus, [1]whom you had
[c]put to death by hanging Him on a [2]cross.
31 "[a]He is the one whom God exalted [1]to His right hand as a
[2b]Prince and a [c]Savior, to grant [d]repentance to Israel, and
forgiveness of sins.
32 "And we are [a]witnesses [1]of these things; and [b]*so is* the Holy
Spirit, whom God has given to those who obey Him."
33 But when they heard this, they were [a]cut [1]to the quick and
intended to kill them.
34 But a Pharisee named [a]Gamaliel, a [b]teacher of the Law,
respected by all the people, stood up in [c]the Council and gave
orders to put the men outside for a short time.
35 And he said to them, "Men of Israel, take care what you
propose to do with these men.
36 "For some time ago Theudas rose up, [a]claiming to be
somebody, and a group of about four hundred men joined up
with him. [1]But he was killed, and all who [2]followed him were
dispersed and came to nothing.

17 [a]Acts 15:5 [b]Matt 3:7; Acts 4:1

18 [a]Acts 4:3

19 [a]Matt 1:20, 24; 2:13, 19; 28:2; Luke 1:11; 2:9; Acts 8:26; 10:3; 12:7, 23; 27:23

20 [1]Or *continue to speak* [2]Lit *all the words* [a]John 6:63, 68

21 [1]Or *Sanhedrin* [a]John 8:2 [b]Acts 4:6 [c]Matt 5:22; Acts 5:27, 34, 41

22 [a]Matt 26:58; Acts 5:26

24 [1]Lit *this would become* [a]Acts 4:1; 5:26

26 [a]Acts 5:24 [b]Acts 5:22 [c]Acts 4:21; 5:13

27 [1]Lit *in* [a]Matt 5:22; Acts 5:21, 34, 41

28 [1]Lit *behold* [a]Acts 4:18 [b]Matt 23:35; 27:25; Acts 2:23, 36; 3:14f; 7:52

29 [a]Acts 4:19

30 [1]Or *on whom you had laid violent hands* [2]Lit *wood* [a]Acts 3:13 [b]Acts 2:24 [c]Acts 10:39; 13:29; Gal 3:13; 1 Pet 2:24

31 [1]Or *by* [2]Or *Leader* [a]Acts 2:33 [b]Acts 3:15 [c]Luke 2:11 [d]Luke 24:47; Acts 2:38

32 [1]One early ms adds *in Him* [a]Luke 24:48 [b]John 15:26; Acts 15:28; Rom 8:16; Heb 2:4

33 [1]Or *in their hearts* [a]Acts 2:37; 7:54

34 [a]Acts 22:3 [b]Luke 2:46; 5:17 [c]Acts 5:21

36 [1]Lit *Who was killed* [2]Lit *were obeying* [a]Acts 8:9; Gal 2:6; 6:3

37 "After this man, Judas of Galilee rose up in the days of [a]the
census and drew away *some* people after him; he too perished,
and all those who [1]followed him were scattered.
38 "So in the present case, I say to you, stay away from these
men and let them alone, for if this plan or [1]action [a]is of men, it
will be overthrown;
39 but if it is of God, you will not be able to overthrow them;
or else you may even be found [a]fighting against God."
40 They [1]took his advice; and after calling the apostles in, they
[a]flogged them and ordered them not to [2]speak in the name of
Jesus, and *then* released them.
41 So they went on their way from the presence of the
[1a]Council, [b]rejoicing that they had been considered worthy to
suffer shame [c]for *His* name.
42 [a]And every day, in the temple and [1]from house to house,
they [2]kept right on teaching and [3b]preaching Jesus *as* the
[4]Christ.

Chapter 6 Theme ____

6 Now [1]at this time while the [a]disciples were [b]increasing *in
number,* a complaint arose on the part of the [2c]Hellenistic
Jews against the *native* [d]Hebrews, because their [e]widows were
being overlooked in [f]the daily serving *of food.*
2 So the twelve summoned the [1]congregation of the disciples
and said, "It is not desirable for us to neglect the word of God
in order to serve tables.
3 "Therefore, [a]brethren, select from among you seven men of
good reputation, [b]full of the Spirit and of wisdom, whom we may
put in charge of this task.
4 "But we will [a]devote ourselves to prayer and to the [1]ministry
of the word."
5 The statement found approval with the whole [1]congregation;
and they chose [a]Stephen, a man [b]full of faith and of the Holy
Spirit, and [c]Philip, Prochorus, Nicanor, Timon, Parmenas and
[2]Nicolas, a [3d]proselyte from [e]Antioch.
6 And these they brought before the apostles; and after [a]praying,
they [b]laid their hands on them.
7 [a]The word of God kept on spreading; and [b]the number of
the disciples continued to increase greatly in Jerusalem, and a
great many of the priests were becoming obedient to [c]the faith.
8 And Stephen, full of grace and power, was performing great
[a]wonders and [1]signs among the people.
9 But some men from what was called the Synagogue of the
Freedmen, *including* both [a]Cyrenians and [b]Alexandrians, and
some from [c]Cilicia and [1d]Asia, rose up and argued with Stephen.
10 But they were unable to cope with the wisdom and the
Spirit with which he was speaking.
11 Then they secretly induced men to say, "We have heard
him speak blasphemous words against Moses and *against* God."
12 And they stirred up the people, the elders and the scribes,

37 [1]Lit *were obeying* [a]Luke 2:2
38 [1]Or *work* [a]Mark 11:30
39 [a]Prov 21:30; Acts 11:17
40 [1]Lit *were persuaded by him* [2]Lit *be speaking* [a]Matt 10:17
41 [1]Or *Sanhedrin* [a]Acts 5:21 [b]1 Pet 4:14, 16 [c]John 15:21
42 [1]Or *in the various private homes* [2]Lit *were not ceasing to* [3]Lit *telling the good news of* [4]I.e. Messiah [a]Acts 2:46 [b]Acts 8:35; 11:20; 17:18; Gal 1:16
6:1 [1]Lit *in these days* [2]Jews who adopted the Gr language and much of Gr culture through acculturation [a]Acts 11:26 [b]Acts 2:47; 6:7 [c]Acts 9:29; 11:20 [d]2 Cor 11:22; Phil 3:5 [e]Acts 9:39, 41; 1 Tim 5:3 [f]Acts 4:35; 11:29
2 [1]Lit *multitude*
3 [a]John 21:23; Acts 1:15 [b]Acts 2:4
4 [1]Or *service* [a]Acts 1:14
5 [1]Lit *multitude* [2]Gr *Nikolaos* [3]I.e. a Gentile convert to Judaism [a]Acts 6:8ff; 11:19; 22:20 [b]Acts 6:3; 11:24 [c]Acts 8:5ff; 21:8 [d]Matt 23:15 [e]Acts 11:19
6 [a]Acts 1:24 [b]Num 8:10; 27:18; Deut 34:9; Mark 5:23; Acts 8:17ff; 9:17; 13:3; 19:6; 1 Tim 4:14; 2 Tim 1:6; Heb 6:2
7 [a]Acts 12:24; 19:20 [b]Acts 6:1 [c]Acts 13:8; 14:22; Gal 1:23; 6:10; Jude 3, 20
8 [1]Or *attesting miracles* [a]John 4:48
9 [1]I.e. west coast province of Asia Minor [a]Matt 27:32; Acts 2:10 [b]Acts 18:24 [c]Acts 15:23, 41; 21:39; 22:3; 23:34; 27:5; Gal 1:21 [d]Acts 16:6; 19:10; 21:27; 24:18

and they [a]came up to him and dragged him away and brought
him [1]before [b]the [2]Council.
13 They put forward [a]false witnesses who said, "This man
incessantly speaks against this [b]holy place and the Law;
14 for we have heard him say that [a]this Nazarene, Jesus, will
destroy this place and alter [b]the customs which Moses handed
down to us."
15 And fixing their gaze on him, all who were sitting in the
[1a]Council saw his face like the face of an angel.

Chapter 7 Theme ______________________________

7 The high priest said, "Are these things so?"
2 And he said, "Hear me, [a]brethren and fathers! [b]The God of
glory [c]appeared to our father Abraham when he was in Mesopotamia, before he lived in [1]Haran,
3 and said to him, '[a]LEAVE YOUR COUNTRY AND YOUR RELATIVES,
AND COME INTO THE LAND THAT I WILL SHOW YOU.'
4 "[a]Then he left the land of the Chaldeans and settled in
[1]Haran. [b]From there, after his father died, *God* had him move
to this country in which you are now living.
5 "But He gave him no inheritance in it, not even a foot of
ground, and *yet,* even when he had no child, [a]He promised that
HE WOULD GIVE IT TO HIM AS A POSSESSION, AND TO HIS DESCENDANTS
AFTER HIM.
6 "But [a]God spoke to this effect, that his DESCENDANTS WOULD
BE ALIENS IN A FOREIGN LAND, AND THAT THEY WOULD [1]BE ENSLAVED
AND MISTREATED FOR FOUR HUNDRED YEARS.
7 "'AND WHATEVER NATION TO WHICH THEY WILL BE IN BONDAGE I
MYSELF WILL JUDGE,' said God, 'AND [a]AFTER THAT THEY WILL COME
OUT AND [1]SERVE ME IN THIS PLACE.'
8 "And He [a]gave him [1]the covenant of circumcision; and so
[b]*Abraham* became the father of Isaac, and circumcised him on
the eighth day; and [c]Isaac *became the father of* Jacob, and
[d]Jacob *of* the twelve [e]patriarchs.
9 "The patriarchs [a]became jealous of Joseph and sold him into
Egypt. *Yet* God was with him,
10 and rescued him from all his afflictions, and [a]granted him
favor and wisdom in the sight of Pharaoh, king of Egypt, and he
made him governor over Egypt and all his household.
11 "Now [a]a famine came over all Egypt and Canaan, and great
affliction *with it,* and our fathers [1]could find no food.
12 "But [a]when Jacob heard that there was grain in Egypt, he
sent our fathers *there* the first time.
13 "On the second *visit* [a]Joseph [1]made himself known to his
brothers, and [b]Joseph's family was disclosed to Pharaoh.
14 "Then [a]Joseph sent *word* and invited Jacob his father and all
his relatives to come to him, [b]seventy-five [1c]persons *in all.*
15 "And [a]Jacob went down to Egypt and *there* he and our
fathers died.
16 "*From there* they were removed to [1a]Shechem and laid in

12 [1]Lit *into* [2]Or *Sanhedrin* [a]Luke 20:1; Acts 4:1 [b]Matt 5:22

13 [a]Matt 26:59-61; Acts 7:58 [b]Matt 24:15; Acts 21:28; 25:8

14 [a]Matt 26:61 [b]Acts 15:1; 21:21; 26:3; 28:17

15 [1]Or *Sanhedrin* [a]Matt 5:22

7:2 [1]Gr *Charran* [a]Acts 22:1 [b]Ps 29:3; 1 Cor 2:8 [c]Gen 11:31; 15:7

3 [a]Gen 12:1

4 [1]Gr *Charran* [a]Gen 11:31; 15:7 [b]Gen 12:4, 5

5 [a]Gen 12:7; 13:15; 15:18; 17:8

6 [1]Lit *enslave them and mistreat them* [a]Gen 15:13f

7 [1]Or *worship* [a]Ex 3:12

8 [1]Or *a* [a]Gen 17:10ff [b]Gen 21:2-4 [c]Gen 25:26 [d]Gen 29:31ff; 30:5ff; 35:23ff [e]Acts 2:29

9 [a]Gen 37:11, 28; 39:2, 21f; 45:4

10 [a]Gen 39:21; 41:40-46; Ps 105:21

11 [1]Lit *were not finding* [a]Gen 41:54f; 42:5

12 [a]Gen 42:2

13 [1]Or *was made known* [a]Gen 45:1-4 [b]Gen 45:16

14 [1]Lit *souls* [a]Gen 45:9, 10, 17, 18 [b]Gen 46:26f; Ex 1:5; Deut 10:22 [c]Acts 2:41

15 [a]Gen 46:1-7; 49:33; Ex 1:6

16 [1]Gr *Sychem* [a]Gen 23:16; 33:19; 50:13; Josh 24:32

the tomb which Abraham had purchased for a sum of money
from the sons of [2]Hamor in [1]Shechem.
17 "But as the [a]time of the promise was approaching which God
had assured to Abraham, [b]the people increased and multiplied
in Egypt,
18 until [a]THERE AROSE ANOTHER KING OVER EGYPT WHO KNEW
NOTHING ABOUT JOSEPH.
19 "It was he who took [a]shrewd advantage of our race and
mistreated our fathers so that they would [1b]expose their infants
and they would not survive.
20 "It was at this time that [a]Moses was born; and he was lovely
[1]in the sight of God, and he was nurtured three months in his
father's home.
21 "And after he had been set outside, [a]Pharaoh's daughter [1]took
him away and nurtured him as her own son.
22 "Moses was educated in all [a]the learning of the Egyptians,
and he was a man of power in words and deeds.
23 "But when he was approaching the age of forty, [a]it entered
his [1]mind to visit his brethren, the sons of Israel.
24 "And when he saw one *of them* being treated unjustly, he
defended him and took vengeance for the oppressed by striking
down the Egyptian.
25 "And he supposed that his brethren understood that God
was granting them [1]deliverance [2]through him, but they did not
understand.
26 "[a]On the following day he appeared to them as they were
fighting together, and he tried to reconcile them in peace, saying,
'Men, you are brethren, why do you injure one another?'
27 "But the one who was injuring his neighbor pushed him away,
saying, '[a]WHO MADE YOU A RULER AND JUDGE OVER US?
28 '[a]YOU DO NOT MEAN TO KILL ME AS YOU KILLED THE EGYPTIAN
YESTERDAY, DO YOU?'
29 "At this remark, [a]MOSES FLED AND BECAME AN ALIEN IN THE
LAND OF [1]MIDIAN, where he [b]became the father of two sons.
30 "After forty years had passed, [a]AN ANGEL APPEARED TO HIM IN
THE WILDERNESS OF MOUNT Sinai, IN THE FLAME OF A BURNING
THORN BUSH.
31 "When Moses saw it, he marveled at the sight; and as he
approached to look *more* closely, there came the voice of the
Lord:
32 '[a]I AM THE GOD OF YOUR FATHERS, THE GOD OF ABRAHAM AND ISAAC
AND JACOB.' Moses shook with fear and would not venture to look.
33 "[a]BUT THE LORD SAID TO HIM, '[b]TAKE OFF THE SANDALS FROM YOUR
FEET, FOR THE PLACE ON WHICH YOU ARE STANDING IS HOLY GROUND.
34 '[a]I HAVE CERTAINLY SEEN THE OPPRESSION OF MY PEOPLE IN EGYPT
AND HAVE HEARD THEIR GROANS, AND I HAVE COME DOWN TO RESCUE
THEM; [1b]COME NOW, AND I WILL SEND YOU TO EGYPT.'
35 "This Moses whom they [a]disowned, saying, 'WHO MADE YOU
A RULER AND A JUDGE?' is the one whom God [1]sent *to be* both a
ruler and a deliverer with the [2]help of the angel who appeared
to him in the thorn bush.

16 [1]Gr *Sychem* [2]Gr *Emmor*
17 [a]Gen 15:13 [b]Ex 1:7f
18 [a]Ex 1:8
19 [1]Or *put out to die* [a]Ex 1:10f, 16ff [b]Ex 1:22
20 [1]Lit *to God* [a]Ex 2:2; Heb 11:23
21 [1]Or *adopted him* [a]Ex 2:5f, 10
22 [a]1 Kin 4:30; Is 19:11
23 [1]Lit *heart* [a]Ex 2:11f; Heb 11:24-26
25 [1]Or *salvation* [2]Lit *through his hand*
26 [a]Ex 2:13f
27 [a]Ex 2:14; Acts 7:35
28 [a]Ex 2:14
29 [1]Gr *Madiam* [a]Ex 2:15, 22 [b]Ex 18:3, 4
30 [a]Ex 3:1f; Is 63:9
32 [a]Ex 3:6; Matt 22:32
33 [a]Ex 3:5 [b]Josh 5:15
34 [1]Lit *and now come!* [a]Ex 3:7f [b]Ex 3:10
35 [1]Lit *has sent* [2]Lit *hand* [a]Ex 2:14; Acts 7:27

36 "[a]This man led them out, performing [b]wonders and [1]signs in
the land of Egypt and in the Red Sea and in the [c]wilderness for
forty years.
37 "This is the Moses who said to the sons of Israel, '[a]GOD WILL
RAISE UP FOR YOU A PROPHET [1]LIKE ME FROM YOUR BRETHREN.'
38 "This is the one who was in [a]the [1]congregation in the
wilderness together with [b]the angel who was speaking to him on
Mount Sinai, and *who was* with our fathers; and he received
[c]living [d]oracles to pass on to you.
39 "Our fathers were unwilling to be obedient to him, but
[a]repudiated him and in their hearts turned back to Egypt,
40 [a]SAYING TO AARON, 'MAKE FOR US GODS WHO WILL GO BEFORE
US; FOR THIS MOSES WHO LED US OUT OF THE LAND OF EGYPT—WE DO
NOT KNOW WHAT HAPPENED TO HIM.'
41 "[1]At that time [a]they made a [2]calf and brought a sacrifice to
the idol, and were rejoicing in [b]the works of their hands.
42 "But God [a]turned away and delivered them up to [1]serve the
[2]host of heaven; as it is written in the book of the prophets, '[b]IT
WAS NOT TO ME THAT YOU OFFERED VICTIMS AND SACRIFICES [c]FORTY
YEARS IN THE WILDERNESS, WAS IT, O HOUSE OF ISRAEL?
43 '[a]YOU ALSO TOOK ALONG THE TABERNACLE OF MOLOCH AND THE STAR
OF THE GOD [1]ROMPHA, THE IMAGES WHICH YOU MADE TO WORSHIP. I
ALSO WILL REMOVE YOU BEYOND BABYLON.'
44 "Our fathers had [a]the tabernacle of testimony in the wilderness, just as He who spoke to Moses directed *him* to make it
[b]according to the pattern which he had seen.
45 "And having received it in their turn, our fathers [a]brought it
in with [1]Joshua upon dispossessing the [2]nations whom God
drove out before our fathers, until the time of David.
46 "[a]*David* found favor in God's sight, and [b]asked that he might
find a dwelling place for the [1]God of Jacob.
47 "But it was [a]Solomon who built a house for Him.
48 "However, [a]the Most High does not dwell in *houses* made
by *human* hands; as the prophet says:
49 '[a]HEAVEN IS MY THRONE,
AND EARTH IS THE FOOTSTOOL OF MY FEET;
WHAT KIND OF HOUSE WILL YOU BUILD FOR ME?' says the Lord,
'OR WHAT PLACE IS THERE FOR MY REPOSE?
50 '[a]WAS IT NOT MY HAND WHICH MADE ALL THESE THINGS?'
51 "You men who are [a]stiff-necked and uncircumcised in heart
and ears are always resisting the Holy Spirit; you are doing just
as your fathers did.
52 "[a]Which one of the prophets did your fathers not persecute?
They killed those who had previously announced the coming of
[b]the Righteous One, whose betrayers and murderers [c]you have
now become;
53 you who received the law as [a]ordained by angels, and *yet*
did not keep it."
54 Now when they heard this, they were [a]cut to the quick,
and they *began* gnashing their teeth at him.
55 But being [a]full of the Holy Spirit, he [b]gazed intently into

36 [1]Or *attesting miracles* [a]Ex 12:41; 33:1; Heb 8:9 [b]Ex 7:3; 14:21; John 4:48 [c]Ex 16:35; Num 14:33; Ps 95:8-10; Acts 7:42; 13:18; Heb 3:8f

37 [1]Or *as* He raised up *me* [a]Deut 18:15, 18; Acts 3:22

38 [1]Gr *ekklesia* [a]Ex 19:17 [b]Acts 7:53 [c]Deut 32:47; Heb 4:12 [d]Rom 3:2; Heb 5:12; 1 Pet 4:11

39 [a]Num 14:3f

40 [a]Ex 32:1, 23

41 [1]Lit *in those days* [2]Or *young bull* [a]Ex 32:4, 6 [b]Rev 9:20

42 [1]Or *worship* [2]I.e. heavenly bodies [a]Josh 24:20; Is 63:10; Jer 19:13; Ezek 20:39 [b]Amos 5:25 [c]Acts 7:36

43 [1]Other mss spell it: *Romphan,* or *Rempham,* or *Raiphan,* or *Rephan* [a]Amos 5:26, 27

44 [a]Ex 25:8, 9; 38:21 [b]Ex 25:40

45 [1]Gr *Jesus* [2]Or *Gentiles* [a]Deut 32:49; Josh 3:14ff; 18:1; 23:9; 24:18; Ps 44:2f

46 [1]The earliest mss read *house* instead of *God;* the Septuagint reads *God* [a]2 Sam 7:8ff; Ps 132:1-5; Acts 13:22 [b]2 Sam 7:1-16; 1 Chr 17:1-14

47 [a]1 Kin 6:1-38; 8:20; 2 Chr 3:1-17

48 [a]Luke 1:32

49 [a]Is 66:1; Matt 5:34f

50 [a]Is 66:2

51 [a]Ex 32:9; 33:3, 5; Lev 26:41; Num 27:14; Is 63:10; Jer 6:10; 9:26

52 [a]2 Chr 36:15f; Matt 5:12; 23:31, 37 [b]Acts 3:14; 22:14; 1 John 2:1 [c]Acts 3:14; 5:28

53 [a]Deut 33:2; Acts 7:38; Gal 3:19; Heb 2:2

54 [a]Acts 5:33

55 [a]Acts 2:4 [b]John 11:41

heaven and saw the glory of God, and Jesus standing [c]at the
right hand of God;
56 and he said, "Behold, I see the [a]heavens opened up and [b]the
Son of Man standing at the right hand of God."
57 But they cried out with a loud voice, and covered their ears
and rushed at him with one impulse.
58 When they had [a]driven him out of the city, they *began*
stoning *him;* and [b]the witnesses [c]laid aside their robes at the
feet of [d]a young man named Saul.
59 They went on stoning Stephen as he [a]called on *the Lord*
and said, "Lord Jesus, receive my spirit!"
60 Then [a]falling on his knees, he cried out with a loud voice,
"Lord, [b]do not hold this sin against them!" Having said this, he
[1c]fell asleep.

Chapter 8 Theme ________________________

8 [a]Saul was in hearty agreement with putting him to death.
And on that day a great persecution [1]began against [b]the
church in Jerusalem, and they were all [c]scattered throughout the
regions of Judea and [d]Samaria, except the apostles.
2 *Some* devout men buried Stephen, and made loud
lamentation over him.
3 But [a]Saul *began* ravaging the church, entering house after
house, and [b]dragging off men and women, he would put them in
prison.
4 Therefore, those [a]who had been scattered went about
[1b]preaching the word.
5 [a]Philip went down to the city of Samaria and *began*
proclaiming [1]Christ to them.
6 The crowds with one accord were giving attention to what
was said by Philip, as they heard and saw the [1]signs which he
was performing.
7 For *in the case of* many who had [a]unclean spirits, they
were coming out *of them* shouting with a loud voice; and many
who had been [b]paralyzed and lame were healed.
8 So there was [a]much rejoicing in that city.
9 Now there was a man named Simon, who formerly was
practicing [a]magic in the city and astonishing the people of
Samaria, [b]claiming to be someone great;
10 and they all, from smallest to greatest, were giving attention
to him, saying, "[a]This man is what is called the Great Power of
God."
11 And they were giving him attention because he had for a
long time astonished them with his [a]magic arts.
12 But when they believed Philip [a]preaching the good news
about the kingdom of God and the name of Jesus Christ, they
were being [b]baptized, men and women alike.
13 Even Simon himself believed; and after being baptized, he
continued on with Philip, and as he observed [a]signs and [b]great
miracles taking place, he was constantly amazed.

55 [c]Mark 16:19
56 [a]John 1:51 [b]Matt 8:20
58 [a]Lev 24:14, 16; Luke 4:29 [b]Deut 13:9f; 17:7; Acts 6:13 [c]Acts 22:20 [d]Acts 8:1; 22:20; 26:10
59 [a]Acts 9:14, 21; 22:16; Rom 10:12-14; 1 Cor 1:2; 2 Tim 2:22
60 [1]I.e. died [a]Luke 22:41 [b]Matt 5:44; Luke 23:34 [c]Dan 12:2; Matt 27:52; John 11:11f; Acts 13:36; 1 Cor 15:6, 18, 20; 1 Thess 4:13ff; 2 Pet 3:4
8:1 [1]Lit *occurred* [a]Acts 7:58; 22:20; 26:10 [b]Acts 9:31 [c]Acts 8:4; 11:19 [d]Acts 1:8; 8:5, 14; 9:31
3 [a]Acts 9:1, 13, 21; 22:4, 19; 26:10f; 1 Cor 15:9; Gal 1:13; Phil 3:6; 1 Tim 1:13 [b]James 2:6
4 [1]Or *bringing the good news of* [a]Acts 8:1 [b]Acts 8:12; 15:35
5 [1]I.e. the Messiah [a]Acts 6:5; 8:26, 30
6 [1]Or *attesting miracles*
7 [a]Mark 16:17 [b]Matt 4:24
8 [a]John 4:40-42; Acts 8:39
9 [a]Acts 8:11; 13:6 [b]Acts 5:36
10 [a]Acts 14:11; 28:6
11 [a]Acts 8:9; 13:6
12 [a]Acts 1:3; 8:4 [b]Acts 2:38
13 [a]Acts 8:6 [b]Acts 19:11

RETURN TO INSTRUCTIONS

14 Now when [a]the apostles in Jerusalem heard that Samaria
had received the word of God, they sent them [b]Peter and John,
15 who came down and prayed for them [a]that they might
receive the Holy Spirit.
16 For He had [a]not yet fallen upon any of them; they had
simply been [b]baptized [1]in the name of the Lord Jesus.
17 Then they [a]*began* laying their hands on them, and they
were [b]receiving the Holy Spirit.
18 Now when Simon saw that the Spirit was bestowed through
the laying on of the apostles' hands, he offered them money,
19 saying, "Give this authority to me as well, so that everyone
on whom I lay my hands may receive the Holy Spirit."
20 But Peter said to him, "May your silver perish with you,
because you thought you could [a]obtain the gift of God with
money!
21 "You have [a]no part or portion in this [1]matter, for your heart
is not [b]right before God.
22 "Therefore repent of this wickedness of yours, and pray the
Lord that, [a]if possible, the intention of your heart may be
forgiven you.
23 "For I see that you are in the gall of bitterness and in [a]the
[1]bondage of iniquity."
24 But Simon answered and said, "[a]Pray to the Lord for me
yourselves, so that nothing of what you have said may come
upon me."
25 So, when they had solemnly [a]testified and spoken [b]the
word of the Lord, they started back to Jerusalem, and were
[c]preaching the gospel to many villages of the [d]Samaritans.
26 But [a]an angel of the Lord spoke to [b]Philip saying, "Get up and
go south to the road that descends from Jerusalem to [c]Gaza."
([1]This is a desert *road.*)
27 So he got up and went; and [a]there was an Ethiopian
eunuch, a court official of Candace, queen of the Ethiopians,
who was in charge of all her treasure; and he [b]had come to
Jerusalem to worship,
28 and he was returning and sitting in his [1]chariot, and was
reading the prophet Isaiah.
29 Then [a]the Spirit said to Philip, "Go up and join this [1]chariot."
30 Philip ran up and heard him reading Isaiah the prophet,
and said, "Do you understand what you are reading?"
31 And he said, "Well, how could I, unless someone guides
me?" And he invited Philip to come up and sit with him.
32 Now the passage of Scripture which he was reading was this:

"[a]HE WAS LED AS A SHEEP TO SLAUGHTER;
AND AS A LAMB BEFORE ITS SHEARER IS SILENT,
SO HE DOES NOT OPEN HIS MOUTH.

33 "[a]IN HUMILIATION HIS JUDGMENT WAS TAKEN AWAY;
WHO WILL [1]RELATE HIS [2]GENERATION?
FOR HIS LIFE IS REMOVED FROM THE EARTH."

34 The eunuch answered Philip and said, "Please *tell me,* of
whom does the prophet say this? Of himself or of someone else?"

INSIGHT

See the "Insight" about the **Samaritans** on page 1718.

14 [a]Acts 8:1 [b]Luke 22:8

15 [a]Acts 2:38; 19:2

16 [1]Lit *into* [a]Matt 28:19; Acts 19:2 [b]Acts 2:38; 10:48

17 [a]Mark 5:23; Acts 6:6 [b]Acts 2:4

20 [a]2 Kin 5:16; Is 55:1; Dan 5:17; Matt 10:8; Acts 2:38

21 [1]Or *teaching;* lit *word* [a]Deut 10:9; 12:12; Eph 5:5 [b]Ps 78:37

22 [a]Is 55:7

23 [1]Lit *bond* [a]Is 58:6

24 [a]Gen 20:7; Ex 8:8; Num 21:7; James 5:16

25 [a]Luke 16:28 [b]Acts 13:12 [c]Acts 8:40 [d]Matt 10:5

26 [1]Or *This city is deserted* [a]Acts 5:19; 8:29 [b]Acts 8:5 [c]Gen 10:19

27 [a]Ps 68:31; 87:4; Is 56:3ff [b]1 Kin 8:41f; John 12:20

28 [1]Or *carriage*

29 [1]Or *carriage* [a]Acts 8:39; 10:19; 11:12; 13:2; 16:6, 7; 20:23; 21:11; 28:25; Heb 3:7

32 [a]Is 53:7

33 [1]Or *describe* [2]Or *family* or *origin* [a]Is 53:8

Sequence of Events in Paul's Life After His Conversion*

**There are differing opinions on these dates. For continuity's sake this chart will be the basis for dates pertaining to Paul's life.*

Scripture	Year A.D.	Event
Acts 9:1-25	33–34	Conversion, time in Damascus
	35–47	Some silent years, except we know that Paul:
Gal. 1:17		1. Spent time in Arabia and Damascus (3 years)
Acts 9:26; Gal. 1:18		2. Made first visit to Jerusalem
Acts 9:30–11:26; Gal. 1:21		3. Went to Tarsus, Syria-Cilicia area
Acts 11:26		4. Was with Barnabas in Antioch
Acts 11:27-30		5. With Barnabas took relief to brethren in Judea, and Paul's second visit to Jerusalem
Acts 12:23	44	Herod Agrippa I dies
Acts 12:25–13:3		6. Returned to Antioch; was sent out with Barnabas by church at Antioch
Acts 15:1-35; Gal. 2:1	47–48	**First missionary journey:** *Galatians written(?)*
	(14 years, Gal. 2:1)	Proconsul Sergius Paulus on Paphos
Acts 15:36–18:22	49	Apostolic Council at Jerusalem—Paul visits Jerusalem *(Galatians written?)*
Acts 15:36–18:22	49–51	**Second missionary journey:** *1 and 2 Thessalonians written*—1½ years in Corinth, Acts 18:11
	51–52	Gallio known to be proconsul in Corinth
Acts 18:23–21:17	52–56	**Third missionary journey:** *1 and 2 Corinthians and Romans written*—1 Corinthians from Ephesus, 2 Corinthians from Macedonia, Romans from Corinth
Acts 21:18-23		
Acts 24–26	56	Paul goes to Jerusalem and is arrested; held in Caesarea
Acts 27–28:15	57–59	Appearance before Felix and Drusilla; before Festus—appeals to Caesar; before Agrippa
Acts 28:16-31	59–60	Went from Caesarea to Rome
	60–62	First Roman imprisonment; *Ephesians, Philemon, Colossians, and Philippians written—2 years in prision*
	62	Paul's release; possible trip to Spain
	62	Paul in Macedonia: *1 Timothy written*
	62	Paul goes to Crete
	63–64	*Titus written*
	64	Paul taken to Rome and imprisoned: *2 Timothy written*
		Paul is absent from the body and present with the Lord *(Others put Paul's conversion about A.D. 35, his death at A.D. 68.)*

35 [a]Matt 5:2 [b]Luke 24:27; Acts 17:2; 18:28; 28:23 [c]Acts 5:42
36 [a]Acts 10:47
37 [1]Early mss do not contain this v
38 [1]Or *carriage*
39 [1]Lit *for he was going* [a]1 Kin 18:12; 2 Kin 2:16; Ezek 3:12, 14; 8:3; 11:1, 24; 43:5; 2 Cor 12:2
40 [1]Or *was found* [2]OT: Ashdod [a]Josh 11:22; 1 Sam 5:1 [b]Acts 8:25 [c]Acts 9:30; 10:1, 24; 11:11; 12:19; 18:22; 21:8, 16; 23:23, 33; 25:1, 4, 6, 13
9:1 [1]Later called Paul [2]Lit *threat* [a]Acts 9:1-22; 22:3-16; 26:9-18 [b]Acts 8:3; 9:13-21
2 [a]Acts 9:14, 21; 22:5; 26:10 [b]Matt 10:17 [c]Gen 14:15; 2 Cor 11:32; Gal 1:17 [d]John 14:6; Acts 18:25f; 19:9, 23; 22:4; 24:14, 22
3 [a]1 Cor 15:8

35 Then Philip [a]opened his mouth, and [b]beginning from this
Scripture he [c]preached Jesus to him.
36 As they went along the road they came to some water; and
the eunuch *said, "Look! Water! [a]What prevents me from being
baptized?"
37 [[1]And Philip said, "If you believe with all your heart, you
may." And he answered and said, "I believe that Jesus Christ is
the Son of God."]
38 And he ordered the [1]chariot to stop; and they both went
down into the water, Philip as well as the eunuch, and he
baptized him.
39 When they came up out of the water, [a]the Spirit of the Lord
snatched Philip away; and the eunuch no longer saw him, [1]but
went on his way rejoicing.
40 But Philip [1]found himself at [2a]Azotus, and as he passed
through he [b]kept preaching the gospel to all the cities until he
came to [c]Caesarea.

Chapter 9 Theme ________________________

9 [a]Now [1]Saul, still [b]breathing [2]threats and murder against
the disciples of the Lord, went to the high priest,
2 and asked for [a]letters from him to [b]the synagogues at
[c]Damascus, so that if he found any belonging to [d]the Way, both
men and women, he might bring them bound to Jerusalem.
3 As he was traveling, it happened that he was approaching
Damascus, and [a]suddenly a light from heaven flashed around him;

4 and [a]he fell to the ground and heard a voice saying to him,
"Saul, Saul, why are you persecuting Me?"
5 And he said, "Who are You, Lord?" And He *said,* "I am Jesus
whom you are persecuting,
6 but get up and enter the city, and [a]it will be told you what
you must do."
7 The men who traveled with him [a]stood speechless, [b]hearing
the [1]voice but seeing no one.
8 Saul got up from the ground, and [a]though his eyes were
open, he [1]could see nothing; and leading him by the hand,
they brought him into [b]Damascus.
9 And he was three days without sight, and neither ate nor
drank.
10 Now there was a disciple at [a]Damascus named [b]Ananias;
and the Lord said to him in [c]a vision, "Ananias." And he said,
"Here I am, Lord."
11 And the Lord *said* to him, "Get up and go to the street called
Straight, and inquire at the house of Judas for a man from
[a]Tarsus named Saul, for he is praying,
12 and he has seen [1]in a vision a man named Ananias come in
and [a]lay his hands on him, so that he might regain his sight."
13 But Ananias answered, "Lord, I have heard from many
about this man, [a]how much harm he did to [b]Your [1]saints at
Jerusalem;
14 and here he [a]has authority from the chief priests to bind all
who [b]call on Your name."
15 But the Lord said to him, "Go, for [a]he is a chosen [1]instrument
of Mine, to bear My name before [b]the Gentiles and [c]kings and
the sons of Israel;
16 for [a]I will show him how much he must suffer for My
name's sake."
17 So Ananias departed and entered the house, and after [a]laying
his hands on him said, "[b]Brother Saul, the Lord Jesus, who
appeared to you on the road by which you were coming, has
sent me so that you may regain your sight and be [c]filled with
the Holy Spirit."
18 And immediately there fell from his eyes something like
scales, and he regained his sight, and he got up and was baptized;
19 and he took food and was strengthened.
Now [a]for several days he was with [b]the disciples who were
at Damascus,
20 and immediately he *began* to proclaim Jesus [a]in the
synagogues, [1]saying, "He is [b]the Son of God."
21 All those hearing him continued to be amazed, and were
saying, "Is this not he who in Jerusalem [a]destroyed those who
[b]called on this name, and *who* had come here for the purpose
of bringing them bound before the chief priests?"
22 But Saul kept increasing in strength and confounding the Jews
who lived at Damascus by proving that this *Jesus* is the [1]Christ.
23 When [a]many days had elapsed, [b]the Jews plotted together
to do away with him,

4 [a]Acts 22:7; 26:14

6 [a]Acts 9:16

7 [1]Or *sound* [a]Acts 26:14 [b]John 12:29f; Acts 22:9

8 [1]Lit *was seeing* [a]Acts 9:18; 22:11 [b]Gen 14:15; 2 Cor 11:32; Gal 1:17

10 [a]Gen 14:15; 2 Cor 11:32; Gal 1:17 [b]Acts 22:12 [c]Acts 10:3, 17, 19; 11:5; 12:9; 16:9f; 18:9

11 [a]Acts 9:30; 11:25; 21:39; 22:3

12 [1]A few early mss do not contain *in a vision* [a]Mark 5:23; Acts 6:6; 9:17

13 [1]Or *holy ones* [a]Acts 8:3 [b]Acts 9:32, 41; 26:10; Rom 1:7; 15:25, 26, 31; 16:2, 15; 1 Cor 1:2

14 [a]Acts 9:2, 21 [b]Acts 7:59

15 [1]Or *vessel* [a]Acts 13:2; Rom 1:1; 9:23; Gal 1:15; Eph 3:7 [b]Acts 22:21; 26:17; Rom 1:5; 11:13; 15:16; Gal 1:16; 2:7ff; Eph 3:1, 8; 1 Tim 2:7; 2 Tim 4:17 [c]Acts 25:22f; 26:1, 32; 2 Tim 4:17

16 [a]Acts 20:23; 21:4, 11, 13; 2 Cor 6:4f; 11:23-27; 1 Thess 3:3

17 [a]Mark 5:23; Acts 6:6; 9:12 [b]Acts 22:13 [c]Acts 2:4

19 [a]Acts 26:20 [b]Acts 9:26, 38; 11:26

20 [1]Lit *that* [a]Acts 13:5, 14; 14:1; 16:13; 17:2, 10; 18:4, 19; 19:8 [b]Matt 4:3; Acts 9:22; 13:33

21 [a]Acts 8:3; 9:13; Gal 1:13, 23 [b]Acts 9:14

22 [1]I.e. Messiah

23 [a]Gal 1:17, 18 [b]1 Thess 2:16

24 but [a]their plot became known to Saul. [b]They were also
watching the gates day and night so that they might put him to
death;
25 but his disciples took him by night and let him down
through *an opening in* the wall, lowering him in a large basket.
26 [a]When he came to Jerusalem, he was trying to associate
with the disciples; [1]but they were all afraid of him, not
believing that he was a disciple.
27 But [a]Barnabas took hold of him and brought him to the
apostles and described to them how he had [b]seen the Lord on
the road, and that He had talked to him, and how [c]at Damascus
he had [d]spoken out boldly in the name of Jesus.
28 And he was with them, [1]moving about freely in Jerusalem,
[a]speaking out boldly in the name of the Lord.
29 And he was talking and arguing with the [1a]Hellenistic
Jews; but they were attempting to put him to death.
30 But when [a]the brethren learned *of it,* they brought him
down to [b]Caesarea and [c]sent him away to [d]Tarsus.
31 So [a]the church throughout all Judea and Galilee and Samaria
[1]enjoyed peace, being built up; and going on in the fear of the Lord
and in the comfort of the Holy Spirit, it continued to increase.
32 Now as Peter was traveling through all *those regions,* he
came down also to [a]the [1]saints who lived at [2b]Lydda.
33 There he found a man named Aeneas, who had been bed-
ridden eight years, for he was paralyzed.
34 Peter said to him, "Aeneas, Jesus Christ heals you; get up
and make your bed." Immediately he got up.
35 And all who lived at [1a]Lydda and [b]Sharon saw him, and
they [c]turned to the Lord.
36 Now in [a]Joppa there was a disciple named Tabitha (which
translated *in Greek* is called [1]Dorcas); this woman was abounding
with deeds of kindness and charity which she continually did.
37 And it happened [1]at that time that she fell sick and died;
and when they had washed her body, they laid it in an [a]upper
room.
38 Since Lydda was near [a]Joppa, [b]the disciples, having heard
that Peter was there, sent two men to him, imploring him, "Do
not delay in coming to us."
39 So Peter arose and went with them. When he arrived, they
brought him into the [a]upper room; and all the [b]widows stood
beside him, weeping and showing all the [1]tunics and garments
that Dorcas used to make while she was with them.
40 But Peter [a]sent them all out and [b]knelt down and prayed,
and turning to the body, he said, "[c]Tabitha, arise." And she
opened her eyes, and when she saw Peter, she sat up.
41 And he gave her his hand and raised her up; and calling
[a]the [1]saints and [b]widows, he presented her alive.
42 It became known all over [a]Joppa, and [b]many believed in
the Lord.
43 And Peter stayed many days in [a]Joppa with [b]a tanner *named*
Simon.

24 [a]Acts 20:3, 19; 23:12, 30; 25:3 [b]2 Cor 11:32f

26 [1]Lit *and* [a]Acts 22:17-20; 26:20

27 [a]Acts 4:36 [b]Acts 9:3-6 [c]Acts 9:20, 22 [d]Acts 4:13, 29; 9:29

28 [1]Lit *going in and going out* [a]Acts 4:13, 29; 9:29

29 [1]Jews who adopted the Gr language and much of Gr culture through accultura-tion [a]Acts 6:1

30 [a]Acts 1:15 [b]Acts 8:40 [c]Gal 1:21 [d]Acts 9:11

31 [1]Lit *was having* [a]Acts 5:11; 8:1; 16:5

32 [1]Or *holy ones* [2]OT: Lod [a]Acts 9:13 [b]1 Chr 8:12; Ezra 2:33; Neh 7:37; 11:35

35 [1]OT: Lod [a]1 Chr 8:12; Ezra 2:33; Neh 7:37; 11:35 [b]1 Chr 5:16; 27:29; Is 33:9; 35:2; 65:10 [c]Acts 2:47; 9:42; 11:21

36 [1]I.e. Gazelle [a]Josh 19:46; 2 Chr 2:16; Ezra 3:7; Jon 1:3; Acts 9:38, 42f; 10:5, 8, 23, 32; 11:5, 13

37 [1]Lit *in those days* [a]Acts 1:13; 9:39

38 [a]Josh 19:46; 2 Chr 2:16; Ezra 3:7; Jon 1:3; Acts 9:36, 42f; 10:5, 8, 23, 32; 11:5, 13 [b]Acts 11:26

39 [1]Or *inner garments* [a]Acts 1:13; 9:37 [b]Acts 6:1

40 [a]Matt 9:25 [b]Luke 22:41; Acts 7:60 [c]Mark 5:41

41 [1]Or *holy ones* [a]Acts 9:13, 32 [b]Acts 6:1

42 [a]Josh 19:46; 2 Chr 2:16; Jon 1:3; Acts 9:38, 42f; 10:5, 8, 23, 32; 11:5, 13 [b]Acts 9:35

43 [a]Josh 19:46; 2 Chr 2:16; Ezra 3:7; Jon 1:3; Acts 9:38, 42f; 10:5, 8, 23, 32; 11:13, 15 [b]Acts 10:6

Chapter 10 Theme ______________________________

10 Now *there was* a man at [a]Caesarea named Cornelius, a
centurion of what was [b]called the Italian [1]cohort,
2 a devout man and [a]one who feared God with all his household, and [b]gave many [1]alms to the *Jewish* people and prayed to
God continually.
3 About [a]the [1]ninth hour of the day he clearly saw [b]in a
vision [c]an angel of God who had *just* come in and said to him,
"Cornelius!"
4 And [a]fixing his gaze on him and being much alarmed, he
said, "What is it, Lord?" And he said to him, "Your prayers and
[1]alms [b]have ascended [c]as a memorial before God.
5 "Now dispatch *some* men to [a]Joppa and send for a man
named Simon, who is also called Peter;
6 he is staying with a tanner *named* [a]Simon, whose house is
by the sea."
7 When the angel who was speaking to him had left, he
summoned two of his [1]servants and a devout soldier of those
who were his personal attendants,
8 and after he had explained everything to them, he sent
them to [a]Joppa.
9 On the next day, as they were on their way and approaching
the city, [a]Peter went up on [b]the housetop about [c]the [1]sixth
hour to pray.
10 But he became hungry and was desiring to eat; but while
they were making preparations, he [a]fell into a trance;
11 and he *saw [a]the [1]sky opened up, and an [2]object like a great
sheet coming down, lowered by four corners to the ground,
12 and there were in it all *kinds of* four-footed animals and
[1]crawling creatures of the earth and birds of the [2]air.
13 A voice came to him, "Get up, Peter, [1]kill and eat!"
14 But Peter said, "By no means, [a]Lord, for [b]I have never
eaten anything [1]unholy and unclean."
15 Again a voice *came* to him a second time, "[a]What God has
cleansed, no *longer* consider [1]unholy."
16 This happened three times, and immediately the [1]object
was taken up into the [2]sky.
17 Now while Peter was greatly perplexed in [1]mind as to what
[a]the vision which he had seen might be, behold, [b]the men who
had been sent by Cornelius, having asked directions for Simon's
house, appeared at the gate;
18 and calling out, they were asking whether Simon, who was
also called Peter, was staying there.
19 While Peter was reflecting on [a]the vision, [b]the Spirit said to
him, "Behold, [1]three men are looking for you.
20 "But get up, go downstairs and [a]accompany them [1]without
misgivings, for I have sent them Myself."
21 Peter went down to the men and said, "Behold, I am the one
you are looking for; what is the reason for which you have come?"
22 They said, "Cornelius, a centurion, a righteous and [a]God-
fearing man well spoken of by the entire nation of the Jews,

10:1 [1]Or *battalion* [a]Acts 8:40; 10:24 [b]Matt 27:27; Mark 15:16; John 18:3, 12; Acts 21:31; 27:1

2 [1]Or *gifts of charity* [a]Acts 10:22, 35; 13:16, 26 [b]Luke 7:4f

3 [1]I.e. 3 p.m. [a]Acts 3:1 [b]Acts 9:10; 10:17, 19 [c]Acts 5:19

4 [1]Or *deeds of charity* [a]Acts 3:4 [b]Rev 8:4 [c]Matt 26:13; Phil 4:18; Heb 6:10

5 [a]Acts 9:36

6 [a]Acts 9:43

7 [1]Or *household slaves*

8 [a]Acts 9:36

9 [1]I.e. noon [a]Acts 10:9-32; 11:5-14 [b]Jer 19:13; 32:29; Zeph 1:5; Matt 24:17 [c]Ps 55:17; Acts 10:3

10 [a]Acts 11:5; 22:17

11 [1]Or *heaven* [2]Or *vessel* [a]John 1:51

12 [1]Or *reptiles* [2]Or *heaven*

13 [1]Or *sacrifice*

14 [1]Or *profane;* lit *common* [a]Matt 8:2ff; John 4:11ff; Acts 9:5; 22:8 [b]Lev 11:20-25; Deut 14:4-20; Ezek 4:14; Dan 1:8; Acts 10:28

15 [1]Lit *make common* [a]Matt 15:11; Mark 7:19; Rom 14:14; 1 Cor 10:25ff; 1 Tim 4:4f; Titus 1:15

16 [1]Or *vessel* [2]Or *heaven*

17 [1]Lit *himself* [a]Acts 10:3 [b]Acts 10:8

19 [1]One early ms reads *two* [a]Acts 10:3 [b]Acts 8:29

20 [1]Lit *doubting nothing* [a]Acts 15:7-9

22 [a]Acts 10:2

[b]was *divinely* directed by a [c]holy angel to send for you *to come*
to his house and hear [1d]a message from you."
23 So he invited them in and gave them lodging.
And on the next day he got up and went away with them,
and [a]some of [b]the brethren from [c]Joppa accompanied him.
24 On the following day he entered [a]Caesarea. Now Cornelius
was waiting for them and had called together his relatives and
close friends.
25 When Peter entered, Cornelius met him, and fell at his feet
and [1a]worshiped *him.*
26 But Peter raised him up, saying, "[a]Stand up; I too am *just* a
man."
27 As he talked with him, he entered and *found [a]many people
assembled.
28 And he said to them, "You yourselves know how [a]unlawful
it is for a man who is a Jew to associate with a foreigner or to
visit him; and *yet* [b]God has shown me that I should not call any
man [1]unholy or unclean.
29 "That is why I came without even raising any objection when
I was sent for. So I ask for what reason you have sent for me."
30 Cornelius said, "[a]Four days ago to this hour, I was praying
in my house during [b]the [1]ninth hour; and behold, [c]a man stood
before me in shining garments,
31 and he *said, 'Cornelius, your prayer has been heard and
your [1]alms have been remembered before God.
32 'Therefore send to [a]Joppa and invite Simon, who is also called
Peter, to come to you; he is staying at the house of Simon *the*
tanner by the sea.'
33 "So I sent for you immediately, and you have [1]been kind
enough to come. Now then, we are all here present before God
to hear all that you have been commanded by the Lord."
34 [a]Opening his mouth, Peter said:
"**I** most certainly understand *now* that [b]God is not one to
show partiality,
35 but [a]in every nation the man who [1b]fears Him and [2]does
what is right is welcome to Him.
36 "The word which He sent to the sons of Israel, [a]preaching
[1b]peace through Jesus Christ (He is [c]Lord of all)—
37 you yourselves know the thing which took place throughout
all Judea, starting from Galilee, after the baptism which John
proclaimed.
38 "[1]*You know of* [a]Jesus of Nazareth, how God [b]anointed Him
with the Holy Spirit and with power, [2c]and *how* He went about
doing good and healing all who were oppressed by the devil,
for [d]God was with Him.
39 "We are [a]witnesses of all the things He did both in the [1]land
of the Jews and in Jerusalem. They also [b]put Him to death by
hanging Him on a [2]cross.
40 "[a]God raised Him up on the third day and granted that He
become visible,
41 [a]not to all the people, but to [b]witnesses who were chosen

22 [1]Lit *words* [b]Matt 2:12 [c]Mark 8:38; Luke 9:26; Rev 14:10 [d]Acts 11:14

23 [a]Acts 10:45; 11:12 [b]Acts 1:15 [c]Acts 9:36

24 [a]Acts 8:40; 10:1

25 [1]Or *prostrated himself in reverence* [a]Matt 8:2

26 [a]Acts 14:15; Rev 19:10; 22:8f

27 [a]Acts 10:24

28 [1]Or *profane;* lit *common* [a]John 4:9; 18:28; Acts 11:3 [b]Acts 10:14f, 35; 15:9

30 [1]I.e. 3 to 4 p.m. [a]Acts 10:9, 22f [b]Acts 3:1; 10:3 [c]Acts 10:3-6, 30-32

31 [1]Or *deeds of charity*

32 [a]John 4:9; 18:28; Acts 11:3

33 [1]Lit *done well in coming*

34 [a]Matt 5:2 [b]Deut 10:17; 2 Chr 19:7; Rom 2:11; Gal 2:6; Eph 6:9; Col 3:25; 1 Pet 1:17

35 [1]Or *reverences* [2]Lit *works righteousness* [a]Acts 10:28 [b]Acts 10:2

36 [1]Or *the gospel of peace* [a]Acts 13:32 [b]Luke 1:79; 2:14; Rom 5:1; Eph 2:17 [c]Matt 28:18; Acts 2:36; Rom 10:12

38 [1]Or *How God anointed Jesus of Nazareth* [2]Lit *who went* [a]Acts 2:22 [b]Acts 4:26 [c]Matt 4:23 [d]John 3:2

39 [1]Or *countryside* [2]Lit *wood* [a]Luke 24:48; Acts 10:41 [b]Acts 5:30

40 [a]Acts 2:24

41 [a]John 14:19, 22; 15:27 [b]Luke 24:48; Acts 10:39

beforehand by God, *that is,* to us [c]who ate and drank with Him
after He arose from the dead.
42 "And He [a]ordered us to [1]preach to the people, and solemnly
to [b]testify that this is the One who has been [c]appointed by God
as [d]Judge of the living and the dead.
43 "Of Him [a]all the prophets bear witness that through [b]His name
everyone who believes in Him receives forgiveness of sins."
44 While Peter was still speaking these words, [a]the Holy Spirit
fell upon all those who were listening to the [1]message.
45 [a]All the [1]circumcised believers who came with Peter were
amazed, because the gift of the Holy Spirit had been [b]poured
out on the Gentiles also.
46 For they were hearing them [a]speaking with tongues and
exalting God. Then Peter answered,
47 "[a]Surely no one can refuse the water for these to be baptized
who [b]have received the Holy Spirit just as we *did,* can he?"
48 And he [a]ordered them to be baptized [b]in the name of Jesus
Christ. Then they asked him to stay on for a few days.

Chapter 11 Theme ________________________

11 Now the apostles and [a]the brethren who were throughout
Judea heard that the Gentiles also had received the word
of God.
2 And when Peter came up to Jerusalem, [1a]those who were
circumcised took issue with him,
3 saying, "[a]You [1]went to uncircumcised men and ate with them."
4 But Peter began *speaking* [1]and *proceeded* to explain to
them [a]in orderly sequence, saying,
5 "[a]I was in the city of Joppa praying; and in a trance I saw [b]a
vision, an [1]object coming down like a great sheet lowered by
four corners from [2]the sky; and it came right down to me,
6 and when I had fixed my gaze on it and was observing it [1]I
saw the four-footed animals of the earth and the wild beasts
and the [2]crawling creatures and the birds of the [3]air.
7 "I also heard a voice saying to me, 'Get up, Peter; [1]kill and eat.'
8 "But I said, 'By no means, Lord, for nothing [1]unholy or
unclean has ever entered my mouth.'
9 "But a voice from heaven answered a second time, '[a]What
God has cleansed, no longer [1]consider unholy.'
10 "This happened three times, and everything was drawn
back up into [1]the sky.
11 "And behold, at that moment three men appeared at the house
in which we were *staying,* having been sent to me from [a]Caesarea.
12 "[a]The Spirit told me to go with them [1b]without misgivings.
[c]These six brethren also went with me and we entered the
man's house.
13 "And he reported to us how he had seen the angel [1]standing
in his house, and saying, 'Send to Joppa and have Simon, who
is also called Peter, brought here;
14 and he will speak [a]words to you by which you will be
saved, you and [b]all your household.'

41 [c]Luke 24:43; Acts 1:4 mg

42 [1]Or *proclaim* [a]Acts 1:2 [b]Luke 16:28 [c]Luke 22:22 [d]John 5:22, 27; Acts 17:31; 2 Tim 4:1; 1 Pet 4:5

43 [a]Acts 3:18 [b]Luke 24:47; Acts 2:38; 4:12

44 [1]Lit *word* [a]Acts 11:15; 15:8

45 [1]Lit *believers from among the circumcision;* i.e. Jewish Christians [a]Acts 10:23 [b]Acts 2:33, 38

46 [a]Mark 16:17; Acts 2:4; 19:6

47 [a]Acts 8:36 [b]Acts 2:4; 10:44f; 11:17; 15:8

48 [a]1 Cor 1:14-17 [b]Acts 2:38; 8:16; 19:5

11:1 [a]Acts 1:15

2 [1]Lit *those of the circumcision;* i.e. Jewish Christians [a]Acts 10:45

3 [1]Or *entered the house of* [a]Matt 9:11; Acts 10:28; Gal 2:12

4 [1]Lit *and was explaining* [a]Luke 1:3

5 [1]Or *vessel* [2]Or *heaven* [a]Acts 10:9-32; 11:5-14 [b]Acts 9:10

6 [1]Lit *and I saw* [2]Or *reptiles* [3]Or *heaven*

7 [1]Or *sacrifice*

8 [1]Or *profane;* lit *common*

9 [1]Lit *make common* [a]Acts 10:15

10 [1]Or *heaven*

11 [a]Acts 8:40

12 [1]Or *without making any distinction* [a]Acts 8:29 [b]Acts 15:9; Rom 3:22 [c]Acts 10:23

13 [1]Or *after he had stood in his house and said*

14 [a]Acts 10:22 [b]John 4:53; Acts 10:2; 16:15, 31-34; 18:8; 1 Cor 1:16

15 "And as I began to speak, [a]the Holy Spirit fell upon them
just [b]as *He did* upon us at the beginning.
16 "And I remembered the word of the Lord, how He used to
say, '[a]John baptized with water, but you will be baptized [1]with
the Holy Spirit.'
17 "Therefore if [a]God gave to them the same gift as *He gave* to
us also after believing in the Lord Jesus Christ, [b]who was I that
I could [1]stand in God's way?"
18 When they heard this, they [1]quieted down and [a]glorified
God, saying, "Well then, God has granted to the Gentiles also
the [b]repentance *that leads* to life."
19 [a]So then those who were scattered because of the
[1]persecution that occurred in connection with Stephen made
their way [2]to [b]Phoenicia and [c]Cyprus and [d]Antioch, speaking
the word to no one except to Jews alone.
20 But there were some of them, men of [a]Cyprus and [b]Cyrene,
who came to [c]Antioch and *began* speaking to the [1d]Greeks also,
[2e]preaching the Lord Jesus.
21 And [a]the hand of the Lord was with them, and [b]a large
number who believed turned to the Lord.
22 The [1]news about them [2]reached the ears of the church at
Jerusalem, and they sent [a]Barnabas off [3]to [b]Antioch.
23 Then when he arrived and [1]witnessed [a]the grace of God,
he rejoiced and *began* to encourage them all with [2]resolute
heart to remain *true* to the Lord;
24 for he was a good man, and [a]full of the Holy Spirit and of
faith. And [b]considerable [1]numbers were [2]brought to the Lord.
25 And he left for [a]Tarsus to look for Saul;
26 and when he had found him, he brought him to [a]Antioch.
And for an entire year they [1]met with the church and taught
considerable [2]numbers; and [b]the disciples were first called
[c]Christians in [a]Antioch.
27 Now [1]at this time [a]some prophets came down from Jerusalem
to [b]Antioch.
28 One of them named [a]Agabus stood up and *began* to indicate
[1]by the Spirit that there would certainly be a great famine [b]all
over the [2]world. [3]And this took place in the *reign* of [c]Claudius.
29 And in the proportion that any of [a]the disciples had means,
each of them determined to send *a contribution* for the [1]relief
of [b]the brethren living in Judea.
30 [a]And this they did, sending it [1]in charge of [b]Barnabas and
Saul to the [c]elders.

Chapter 12 Theme ____

12 Now about that time [1]Herod the king laid hands on some
who belonged to the church in order to mistreat them.
2 And he [a]had James the brother of John [b]put to death with a
sword.
3 When he saw that it [a]pleased the Jews, he proceeded to arrest
Peter also. Now [1]it was during [b]the days of Unleavened Bread.

15 [a]Acts 10:44 [b]Acts 2:4
16 [1]Or *in* [a]Acts 1:5
17 [1]Lit *prevent God* [a]Acts 10:45, 47 [b]Acts 5:39
18 [1]Lit *became silent* [a]Matt 9:8 [b]2 Cor 7:10
19 [1]Lit *tribulation* [2]Lit *as far as* [a]Acts 8:1, 4 [b]Acts 15:3; 21:2 [c]Acts 4:36 [d]Acts 6:5; 11:20, 22, 27; 13:1; 14:26; 15:22f, 30, 35; 18:22; Gal 2:11
20 [1]Lit *Hellenists;* people who lived by Greek customs and culture [2]Or *bringing the good news of* [a]Acts 4:36 [b]Matt 27:32; Acts 2:10; 6:9; 13:1 [c]Acts 6:5; 11:19, 22, 27; 13:1; 14:26; 15:22f, 30, 35; 18:22; Gal 2:11 [d]John 7:35; Acts 6:1 [e]Acts 5:42
21 [a]Luke 1:66 [b]Acts 2:47
22 [1]Lit *word* [2]Lit *was heard in* [3]Lit *as far as* [a]Acts 4:36 [b]Acts 6:5; 11:19, 20, 27; 13:1; 18:22; Gal 2:11
23 [1]Lit *saw* [2]Lit *purpose of heart* [a]Acts 13:43; 14:26; 15:40; 20:24, 32
24 [1]Lit *crowd was* [2]Lit *added* [a]Acts 2:4 [b]Acts 2:47; 5:14; 11:21
25 [a]Acts 9:11
26 [1]Or *were gathered together* [2]Lit *crowd* [a]Acts 6:5; 11:20, 22, 27 [b]John 2:2; Acts 1:15 [c]Acts 26:28; 1 Pet 4:16
27 [1]Lit *in these days* [a]Luke 11:49; Acts 2:17; 13:1; 1 Cor 12:10, 28f [b]Acts 6:5; 11:20, 22, 26; 13:1; 14:26; 15:22f, 30, 35; 18:22; Gal 2:11
28 [1]Or *through* [2]Lit *inhabited earth* [3]Lit *which* [a]Acts 21:10 [b]Matt 24:14 [c]Acts 18:2
29 [1]Lit *service* [a]John 2:2; Acts 1:15; 6:1f; 9:19, 25, 26, 38; 11:26; 13:52; 14:20, 22, 28 [b]Acts 11:1
30 [1]Lit *by the hand of* [a]Acts 12:25 [b]Acts 4:36 [c]Acts 14:23; 15:2, 4, 6, 22f; 16:4; 20:17; 21:18; 1 Tim 5:17, 19; Titus 1:5; James 5:14; 1 Pet 5:1; 2 John 1; 3 John 1
12:1 [1]I.e. Herod Agrippa I
2 [a]Matt 4:21; 20:23 [b]Mark 10:39
3 [1]Lit *they were the days* [a]Acts 24:27; 25:9 [b]Ex 12:15; 23:15; Acts 20:6

4 When he had seized him, he put him in prison, delivering
him to four [1a]squads of soldiers to guard him, intending after
[b]the Passover to bring him out before the people.
5 So Peter was kept in the prison, but prayer for him was
being made fervently by the church to God.
6 On [1]the very night when Herod was about to bring him
forward, Peter was sleeping between two soldiers, [a]bound with
two chains, and guards in front of the door were watching over
the prison.
7 And behold, [a]an angel of the Lord suddenly [b]appeared and
a light shone in the cell; and he struck Peter's side and woke him
up, saying, "Get up quickly." And [c]his chains fell off his hands.
8 And the angel said to him, "Gird yourself and [1]put on your
sandals." And he did so. And he *said to him, "Wrap your cloak
around you and follow me."
9 And he went out and continued to follow, and he did not
know that what was being done by the angel was real, but
thought he was seeing [a]a vision.
10 When they had passed the first and second guard, they
came to the iron gate that leads into the city, which [a]opened for
them by itself; and they went out and went along one street,
and immediately the angel departed from him.
11 When Peter [a]came [1]to himself, he said, "Now I know for
sure that [b]the Lord has sent forth His angel and rescued me
from the hand of Herod and from all [2]that the Jewish people
were expecting."
12 And when he realized *this,* he went to the house of Mary,
the mother of [a]John who was also called Mark, where many
were gathered together and [b]were praying.
13 When he knocked at the door of the gate, [a]a servant-girl
named Rhoda came to answer.
14 When she recognized Peter's voice, [a]because of her joy she
did not open the gate, but ran in and announced that Peter was
standing in front of the gate.
15 They said to her, "You are out of your mind!" But she kept
insisting that it was so. They kept saying, "It is [a]his angel."
16 But Peter continued knocking; and when they had opened
the door, they saw him and were amazed.
17 But [a]motioning to them with his hand to be silent, he
described to them how the Lord had led him out of the prison.
And he said, "Report these things to [1b]James and [c]the brethren."
Then he left and went to another place.
18 Now when day came, there was no small disturbance
among the soldiers *as to* [1]what could have become of Peter.
19 When Herod had searched for him and had not found him,
he examined the guards and ordered that they [a]be led away *to*
execution. Then he went down from Judea to [b]Caesarea and
was spending time there.
20 Now he was very angry with the people of [a]Tyre and Sidon;
and with one accord they came to him, and having won over
Blastus the king's chamberlain, they were asking for peace,
because [b]their country was fed by the king's country.

4 [1]Lit *quaternions;* a quaternion was composed of four soldiers [a]John 19:23 [b]Ex 12:1-27; Mark 14:1; Acts 12:3

6 [1]Lit *that night* [a]Acts 21:33

7 [a]Acts 5:19 [b]Luke 2:9; 24:4 [c]Acts 16:26

8 [1]Lit *bind*

9 [a]Acts 9:10

10 [a]Acts 5:19; 16:26

11 [1]Lit *in himself* [2]Lit *the expectation of the people of the Jews* [a]Luke 15:17 [b]Dan 3:28; 6:22

12 [a]Acts 12:25; 13:5, 13; 15:37, 39; Col 4:10; 2 Tim 4:11; Philem 24; 1 Pet 5:13 [b]Acts 12:5

13 [a]John 18:16f

14 [a]Luke 24:41

15 [a]Matt 18:10

17 [1]Or *Jacob* [a]Acts 13:16; 19:33; 21:40 [b]Mark 6:3; Acts 15:13; 21:18; 1 Cor 15:7; Gal 1:19; 2:9, 12 [c]Acts 1:15

18 [1]Lit *what therefore had become*

19 [a]Acts 16:27; 27:42 [b]Acts 8:40

20 [a]Matt 11:21 [b]1 Kin 5:11; Ezra 3:7; Ezek 27:17

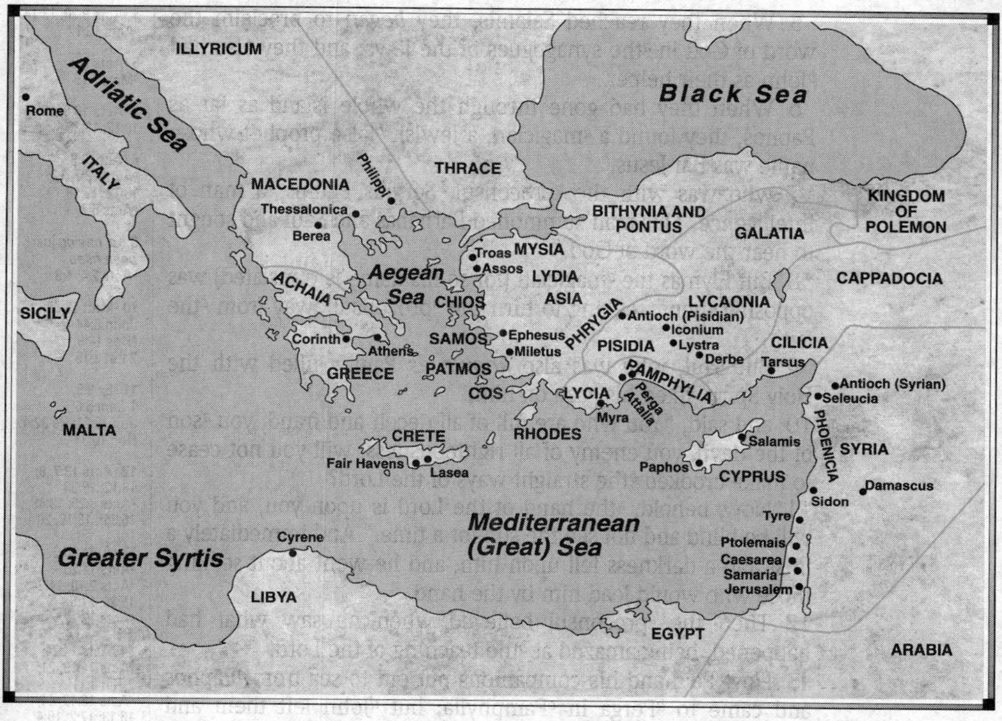

Paul's First Missionary Journey (Acts 13, 14)

21 On an appointed day Herod, having put on his royal apparel,
took his seat on the [1]rostrum and *began* delivering an address to
them.
22 The people kept crying out, "The voice of a god and not of a
man!"
23 And immediately [a]an angel of the Lord struck him because he
did not give God the glory, and he was eaten by worms and [1]died.
24 But [a]the word of the Lord continued to grow and to be
multiplied.
25 And [a]Barnabas and [a]Saul returned [1]from Jerusalem [b]when
they had fulfilled their [2]mission, taking along with *them* [c]John,
who was also called Mark.

Chapter 13 Theme ______________________

13 Now there were at [a]Antioch, in the [b]church that was *there,*
[c]prophets and [d]teachers: [e]Barnabas, and Simeon who
was called Niger, and Lucius of [f]Cyrene, and Manaen who had
been brought up with [g]Herod the tetrarch, and Saul.
2 While they were ministering to the Lord and fasting, [a]the
Holy Spirit said, "Set apart for Me [b]Barnabas and Saul for [c]the
work to which I have called them."
3 Then, when they had fasted and [a]prayed and [b]laid their
hands on them, [c]they sent them away.
4 So, being [a]sent out by the Holy Spirit, they went down to
Seleucia and from there they sailed to [b]Cyprus.

21 [1]Or *judgment seat*
23 [1]Lit *breathed his last breath* [a]2 Sam 24:16; 2 Kin 19:35; Acts 5:19
24 [a]Acts 6:7; 19:20
25 [1]Two early mss read *to Jerusalem* [2]Lit *ministry* [a]Acts 4:36; 13:1ff [b]Acts 11:30 [c]Acts 12:12
13:1 [a]Acts 11:19 [b]Acts 11:26 [c]Acts 11:27; 15:32; 19:6; 21:9; 1 Cor 11:4f; 13:2, 8f; 14:29, 32, 37 [d]Rom 12:6f; 1 Cor 12:28f; Eph 4:11; James 3:1 [e]Acts 4:36 [f]Matt 27:32; Acts 11:20 [g]Matt 14:1
2 [a]Acts 8:29; 13:4 [b]Acts 4:36 [c]Acts 9:15
3 [a]Acts 1:24 [b]Acts 6:6 [c]Acts 13:4; 14:26
4 [a]Acts 13:2f [b]Acts 4:36

5 When they reached Salamis, they *began* to proclaim the
word of God in [a]the synagogues of the Jews; and they also had
[b]John as their helper.
6 When they had gone through the whole island as far as
Paphos, they found a [a]magician, a Jewish [b]false prophet whose
name was Bar-Jesus,
7 who was with the [a]proconsul, Sergius Paulus, a man of
intelligence. This man summoned Barnabas and Saul and sought
to hear the word of God.
8 But Elymas the [a]magician (for so his name is translated) was
opposing them, seeking to turn the [b]proconsul away from [c]the
faith.
9 But Saul, who was also *known as* Paul, [1a]filled with the
Holy Spirit, fixed his gaze on him,
10 and said, "You who are full of all deceit and fraud, you [a]son
of the devil, you enemy of all righteousness, will you not cease
to make crooked [b]the straight ways of the Lord?
11 "Now, behold, [a]the hand of the Lord is upon you, and you
will be blind and not see the sun for a time." And immediately a
mist and a darkness fell upon him, and he went about seeking
those who would lead him by the hand.
12 Then the [a]proconsul believed when he saw what had
happened, being amazed at [b]the teaching of the Lord.
13 Now Paul and his companions put out to sea from [a]Paphos
and came to [b]Perga in [c]Pamphylia; but [d]John left them and
returned to Jerusalem.
14 But going on from Perga, they arrived at [a]Pisidian [b]Antioch, and
on [c]the Sabbath day they went into [d]the synagogue and sat down.
15 After [a]the reading of the Law and [b]the Prophets [c]the
synagogue officials sent to them, saying, "Brethren, if you have
any word of exhortation for the people, say it."
16 Paul stood up, and [a]motioning with his hand said,
"**M**en of Israel, and [b]you who fear God, listen:
17 "The God of this people Israel [a]chose our fathers and [1b]made
the people great during their stay in the land of Egypt, and with
an uplifted arm [c]He led them out from it.
18 "For [a]a period of about forty years [b]He put up with them in
the wilderness.
19 "[a]When He had destroyed [b]seven nations in the land of
Canaan, He [c]distributed their land as an inheritance—*all of
which took* [d]about four hundred and fifty years.
20 "After these things He [a]gave *them* judges until [b]Samuel the
prophet.
21 "Then they [a]asked for a king, and God gave them [b]Saul the
son of Kish, a man of the tribe of Benjamin, for forty years.
22 "After He had [a]removed him, He raised up David to be their
king, concerning whom He also testified and said, '[b]I HAVE
FOUND DAVID the son of Jesse, A MAN AFTER MY HEART, who will
do all My [1]will.'
23 "[a]From the descendants of this man, [b]according to promise,
God has brought to Israel [c]a Savior, Jesus,

5 [a]Acts 9:20; 13:14 [b]Acts 12:12
6 [a]Acts 8:9 [b]Matt 7:15
7 [a]Acts 13:8, 12; 18:12; 19:38
8 [a]Acts 8:9 [b]Acts 13:7, 12; 18:12; 19:38 [c]Acts 6:7
9 [1]Or *having* just *been filled* [a]Acts 2:4; 4:8
10 [a]Matt 13:38; John 8:44 [b]Hos 14:9; 2 Pet 2:15
11 [a]Ex 9:3; 1 Sam 5:6f; Job 19:21; Ps 32:4; Heb 10:31
12 [a]Acts 13:7, 8; 18:12; 19:38 [b]Acts 8:25; 13:49; 15:35f; 19:10, 20
13 [a]Acts 13:6 [b]Acts 14:25 [c]Acts 2:10; 14:24; 15:38; 27:5 [d]Acts 12:12
14 [a]Acts 14:24 [b]Acts 14:19, 21; 2 Tim 3:11 [c]Acts 13:42, 44; 16:13; 17:2; 18:4 [d]Acts 9:20; 13:5
15 [a]Acts 15:21; 2 Cor 3:14f [b]Acts 13:27 [c]Mark 5:22
16 [a]Acts 12:17 [b]Acts 10:2; 13:26
17 [1]Or *exalted* [a]Ex 6:1, 6; 13:14, 16; Deut 7:6-8; Acts 7:17ff [b]Ex 1:7 [c]Ex 12:51
18 [a]Num 14:34; Acts 7:36 [b]Deut 1:31
19 [a]Acts 7:45 [b]Deut 7:1 [c]Josh 14:1; 19:51; Ps 78:55 [d]Judg 11:26; 1 Kin 6:1
20 [a]Judg 2:16 [b]1 Sam 3:20; Acts 3:24
21 [a]1 Sam 8:5 [b]1 Sam 9:1f; 10:1, 21
22 [1]Lit *wishes* [a]1 Sam 15:23, 26, 28; 16:1, 13 [b]1 Sam 13:14; Ps 89:20; Acts 7:46
23 [a]Matt 1:1 [b]Acts 13:32f [c]Luke 2:11; John 4:42

24 after [a]John had proclaimed before [1]His coming a [b]baptism
of repentance to all the people of Israel.
25 "And while John [a]was completing his course, [b]he kept saying,
'What do you suppose that I am? I am not *He*. But behold, one
is coming after me the sandals of whose feet I am not worthy
to untie.'
26 "Brethren, sons of Abraham's family, and those among you
who fear God, to us the message of [a]this salvation has been sent.
27 "For those who live in Jerusalem, and their [a]rulers, [b]recog-
nizing neither Him nor the [1]utterances of [c]the prophets which
are [d]read every Sabbath, fulfilled *these* by condemning *Him.*
28 "And though they found no ground for *putting Him to*
death, they [a]asked Pilate that He be [1]executed.
29 "When they had [a]carried out all that was written concerning
Him, [b]they took Him down from [c]the [1]cross and [d]laid Him in a
tomb.
30 "But God [a]raised Him from the dead;
31 and for many days [a]He appeared to those who came up with
Him from Galilee to Jerusalem, the very ones who are now [b]His
witnesses to the people.
32 "And we [a]preach to you the good news of [b]the promise made
to the fathers,
33 that God has fulfilled this *promise* [1]to our children in that
He [a]raised up Jesus, as it is also written in the second Psalm,
'[b]YOU ARE MY SON; TODAY I HAVE BEGOTTEN YOU.'
34 "*As for the fact* that He [a]raised Him up from the dead, no
longer to return to decay, He has spoken in this way: '[b]I WILL
GIVE YOU THE HOLY *and* [1]SURE *blessings* OF DAVID.'
35 "Therefore He also says in another *Psalm,* '[a]YOU WILL NOT
[1]ALLOW YOUR [2]HOLY ONE TO [3]UNDERGO DECAY.'
36 "For [a]David, after he had [1]served [b]the purpose of God in his
own generation, [c]fell asleep, and was laid among his fathers
and [2]underwent decay;
37 but He whom God [a]raised did not [1]undergo decay.
38 "Therefore let it be known to you, brethren, that [a]through
[1]Him forgiveness of sins is proclaimed to you,
39 and [1]through Him [a]everyone who believes is [2]freed [3]from
all things, from which you could not be [2]freed [3]through the
Law of Moses.
40 "Therefore take heed, so that the thing spoken of [a]in the
Prophets may not come upon *you:*
41 '[a]BEHOLD, YOU SCOFFERS, AND MARVEL, AND [1]PERISH;
FOR I AM ACCOMPLISHING A WORK IN YOUR DAYS,
A WORK WHICH YOU WILL NEVER BELIEVE, THOUGH SOMEONE
SHOULD DESCRIBE IT TO YOU.'"
42 As [1]Paul and Barnabas were going out, the people kept begging
that these [2]things might be spoken to them the next [a]Sabbath.
43 Now when *the meeting of* the synagogue had broken up,
many of the Jews and of the [a]God-fearing [1b]proselytes followed
Paul and Barnabas, who, speaking to them, were urging them
to continue in [c]the grace of God.

24 [1]Lit *the face of His entering* [a]Mark 1:1-4; Acts 1:22; 19:4 [b]Luke 3:3
25 [a]Acts 20:24 [b]Matt 3:11; Mark 1:7; Luke 3:16; John 1:20, 27
26 [a]John 6:68; Acts 4:12; 5:20; 13:46; 28:28
27 [1]Lit *voices* [a]Luke 23:13 [b]Acts 3:17 [c]Luke 24:27 [d]Acts 13:15
28 [1]Lit *destroyed* [a]Matt 27:22, 23; Mark 15:13, 14; Luke 23:21-23; John 19:15; Acts 3:14
29 [1]Lit *wood* [a]Acts 26:22 [b]Luke 23:53 [c]Acts 5:30 [d]Matt 27:57-61; Mark 15:42-47; Luke 23:50-56; John 19:38-42
30 [a]Acts 2:24; 13:33, 34, 37
31 [a]Acts 1:3 [b]Luke 24:48
32 [a]Acts 5:42; 14:15 [b]Acts 13:23; 26:6; Rom 1:2; 4:13; 9:4
33 [1]Late mss read *to us their children* [a]Acts 2:24; 13:30, 34, 37 [b]Ps 2:7
34 [1]Lit *trustworthy* [a]Acts 2:24; 13:30, 33, 37 [b]Is 55:3
35 [1]Lit *give* [2]Or *Devout* or *Pious* [3]Lit *see corruption* [a]Ps 16:10; Acts 2:27
36 [1]Or *served his own generation by the purpose of God* [2]Lit *saw corruption* [a]Acts 2:29 [b]Acts 13:22; 20:27 [c]1 Kin 2:10; Acts 8:1
37 [1]Lit *see corruption* [a]Acts 2:24; 13:30, 33, 34
38 [1]Lit *this One* [a]Luke 24:47; Acts 2:38
39 [1]Lit *in* or *by* [2]Lit *justified* [3]Lit *by* [a]Acts 10:43; Rom 3:28; 10:4
40 [a]Luke 24:44; John 6:45; Acts 7:42
41 [1]Lit *disappear* [a]Hab 1:5
42 [1]Lit *they* [2]Lit *words* [a]Acts 13:14
43 [1]I.e. Gentile converts to Judaism [a]Acts 13:50; 16:14; 17:4, 17; 18:7 [b]Matt 23:15 [c]Acts 11:23

44 The next [a]Sabbath nearly the whole city assembled to hear
the word of [1]the Lord.
45 But when [a]the Jews saw the crowds, they were filled with
jealousy and *began* contradicting the things spoken by Paul,
and were [1]blaspheming.
46 Paul and Barnabas spoke out boldly and said, "It was
necessary that the word of God be spoken to you [a]first; since
you repudiate it and judge yourselves unworthy of eternal life,
behold, [b]we are turning to the Gentiles.
47 "For so the Lord has commanded us,

'[a]I HAVE PLACED YOU AS A [b]LIGHT FOR THE GENTILES,
THAT YOU MAY [1]BRING SALVATION TO THE END OF THE EARTH.'"

48 When the Gentiles heard this, they *began* rejoicing and
glorifying [a]the word of [1]the Lord; and as many as [b]had been
appointed to eternal life believed.
49 And [a]the word of the Lord was being spread through the
whole region.
50 But [a]the Jews incited the [1b]devout women [c]of prominence
and the leading men of the city, and instigated a persecution
against Paul and Barnabas, and drove them out of their [2]district.
51 But [a]they shook off the dust of their feet *in protest* against
them and went to [b]Iconium.
52 And the disciples were continually [a]filled with joy and with
the Holy Spirit.

Chapter 14 Theme ________________________________

14 In [a]Iconium [b]they entered the synagogue of the Jews
together, and spoke in such a manner [c]that a large number of people believed, both of Jews and of [d]Greeks.
2 But [a]the Jews who [1b]disbelieved stirred up the [2]minds of
the Gentiles and embittered them against [c]the brethren.
3 Therefore they spent a long time *there* [a]speaking boldly *with
reliance* upon the Lord, who was testifying to the word of His
grace, granting that [1b]signs and wonders be done by their hands.
4 [a]But the [1]people of the city were divided; and some [2]sided
with [b]the Jews, and some with [c]the apostles.
5 And when an attempt was made by both the Gentiles and
[a]the Jews with their rulers, to mistreat and to [b]stone them,
6 they became aware of it and fled to the cities of [a]Lycaonia,
[b]Lystra and [c]Derbe, and the surrounding region;
7 and there they continued to [a]preach the gospel.
8 At [a]Lystra [b]a man was sitting who had no strength in his
feet, lame from his mother's womb, who had never walked.
9 This man was listening to Paul as he spoke, who, [a]when he
had fixed his gaze on him and had seen that he had [b]faith to be
[1]made well,
10 said with a loud voice, "Stand upright on your feet." [a]And
he leaped up and *began* to walk.
11 When the crowds saw what Paul had done, they raised
their voice, saying in the [a]Lycaonian language, "[b]The gods have
become like men and have come down to us."

44 [1]One early ms reads *God* [a]Acts 13:14

45 [1]Or *slandering* him [a]Acts 13:50; 14:2, 4, 5, 19; 1 Thess 2:16

46 [a]Acts 3:26; 9:20; 13:5, 14 [b]Acts 18:6; 19:9; 22:21; 26:20; 28:28

47 [1]Lit *be for salvation* [a]Is 42:6; 49:6 [b]Luke 2:32

48 [1]Two early mss read *God* [a]Acts 13:12 [b]Rom 8:28ff; Eph 1:4f, 11

49 [a]Acts 13:12

50 [1]Or *worshiping* [2]Lit *boundaries* [a]Acts 13:45; 14:2, 4, 5, 19; 1 Thess 2:14ff [b]Acts 13:43; 16:14; 17:4, 17; 18:7 [c]Mark 15:43

51 [a]Matt 10:14; Mark 6:11; Luke 9:5; 10:11; Acts 18:6 [b]Acts 14:1, 19, 21; 16:2; 2 Tim 3:11

52 [a]Acts 2:4

14:1 [a]Acts 13:51; 14:19, 21; 16:2; 2 Tim 3:11 [b]Acts 13:5 [c]Acts 2:47 [d]John 7:35; Acts 18:4

2 [1]Or *disobeyed* [2]Lit *souls* [a]Acts 13:45, 50; 14:4, 5, 19; 1 Thess 2:14ff [b]John 3:36 [c]Acts 1:15

3 [1]Or *attesting miracles* [a]Acts 4:29f; 20:32; Heb 2:4 [b]John 4:48

4 [1]Lit *multitude* [2]Lit *were* [a]Acts 17:4f; 19:9; 28:24 [b]Acts 13:45, 50; 14:2, 5, 19; 1 Thess 2:14ff [c]Acts 14:14

5 [a]Acts 13:45, 50; 14:2, 4, 19; 1 Thess 2:14ff [b]Acts 14:19

6 [a]Acts 14:11 [b]Acts 14:8, 21; 16:1f; 2 Tim 3:11 [c]Acts 14:20; 16:1; 20:4

7 [a]Acts 14:15, 21; 16:10

8 [a]Acts 14:6, 21; 16:1f; 2 Tim 3:11 [b]Acts 3:2

9 [1]Lit *saved* [a]Acts 3:4; 10:4 [b]Matt 9:28

10 [a]Acts 3:8

11 [a]Acts 14:6 [b]Acts 8:10; 28:6

12 And they *began* calling Barnabas, [1]Zeus, and Paul, [2]Hermes,
because he was [3]the chief speaker.
13 The priest of Zeus, whose *temple* was [1]just outside the city,
brought oxen and garlands to the gates, and [a]wanted to offer
sacrifice with the crowds.
14 But when [a]the apostles Barnabas and Paul heard of it, they
[b]tore their [1]robes and rushed out into the crowd, crying out
15 and saying, "Men, why are you doing these things? We are
also [a]men of the same nature as you, and [b]preach the gospel to
you that you should turn from these [1c]vain things to a [d]living
God, [e]WHO MADE THE HEAVEN AND THE EARTH AND THE SEA AND ALL
THAT IS IN THEM.
16 "[1]In the generations gone by He [a]permitted all the [2]nations
to [b]go their own ways;
17 and yet [a]He did not leave Himself without witness, in that
He did good and [b]gave you rains from heaven and fruitful
seasons, [1]satisfying your hearts with food and gladness."
18 *Even* saying these things, with difficulty they restrained the
crowds from offering sacrifice to them.
19 But [a]Jews came from [b]Antioch and [c]Iconium, and having
won over the crowds, they [d]stoned Paul and dragged him out
of the city, supposing him to be dead.
20 But while [a]the disciples stood around him, he got up and
entered the city. The next day he went away with Barnabas to
[b]Derbe.
21 After they had [a]preached the gospel to that city and had
[b]made many disciples, they returned to [c]Lystra and to [d]Iconium
and to [e]Antioch,
22 strengthening the souls of [a]the disciples, encouraging them
to continue in [b]the faith, and *saying,* "[c]Through many tribulations
we must enter the kingdom of God."
23 When [a]they had appointed [b]elders for them in every
church, having [c]prayed with fasting, they [d]commended them to
the Lord in whom they had believed.
24 They passed through [a]Pisidia and came into [b]Pamphylia.
25 When they had spoken the word in [a]Perga, they went
down to Attalia.
26 From there they sailed to [a]Antioch, from [b]which they had
been [c]commended to the grace of God for the work that they
had [1]accomplished.
27 When they had arrived and gathered the church together,
they *began* to [a]report all things that God had done with them
and [1]how He had opened a [b]door of faith to the Gentiles.
28 And they spent [1]a long time with [a]the disciples.

Chapter 15 Theme ______________________

15 [a]Some men came down from Judea and *began* teaching
[b]the brethren, "Unless you are [c]circumcised according to
[d]the custom of Moses, you cannot be saved."

12 [1]Lat *Jupiter,* the chief pagan god [2]Lat *Mercury,* considered the messenger or spokesman for the pagan gods of Greece and Rome [3]Lit *the leader of the speaking*
13 [1]Lit *in front of* [a]Dan 2:46
14 [1]Or *outer garments* [a]Acts 14:4 [b]Num 14:6; Matt 26:65; Mark 14:63
15 [1]I.e. idols [a]Acts 10:26; James 5:17 [b]Acts 13:32; 14:7, 21 [c]Deut 32:21; 1 Sam 12:21; Jer 8:19; 14:22; 1 Cor 8:4 [d]Matt 16:16 [e]Ex 20:11; Ps 146:6; Acts 4:24; 17:24; Rev 14:7
16 [1]Lit *Who in the generations gone by permitted* [2]Or *Gentiles* [a]Acts 17:30 [b]Ps 81:12; Mic 4:5
17 [1]Lit *filling* [a]Acts 17:26f; Rom 1:19f [b]Deut 11:14; Job 5:10; Ps 65:10f; Ezek 34:26f; Joel 2:23
19 [a]Acts 13:45, 50; 14:2, 4, 5; 1 Thess 2:14ff [b]Acts 13:14; 14:21, 26 [c]Acts 13:51; 14:1, 21 [d]Acts 14:5; 2 Cor 11:25; 2 Tim 3:11
20 [a]Acts 11:26; 14:22, 28 [b]Acts 14:6
21 [a]Acts 14:7 [b]Acts 2:47 [c]Acts 14:6 [d]Acts 13:51; 14:1, 19 [e]Acts 13:14; 14:19, 26
22 [a]Acts 11:26; 14:28 [b]Acts 6:7 [c]Mark 10:30; John 15:18, 20; 16:33; Acts 9:16; 1 Thess 3:3; 2 Tim 3:12; 1 Pet 2:21; Rev 1:9
23 [a]2 Cor 8:19; Titus 1:5 [b]Acts 11:30 [c]Acts 1:24; 13:3 [d]Acts 20:32
24 [a]Acts 13:14 [b]Acts 13:13
25 [a]Acts 13:13
26 [1]Lit *fulfilled* [a]Acts 11:19 [b]Acts 13:3 [c]Acts 11:23; 15:40
27 [1]Lit *that* [a]Acts 15:3, 4, 12; 21:19 [b]1 Cor 16:9; 2 Cor 2:12; Col 4:3; Rev 3:8
28 [1]Lit *not a little* [a]Acts 11:26; 14:22
15:1 [a]Acts 15:24 [b]Acts 1:15; 15:3, 22, 32 [c]Lev 12:3; Acts 15:5; 1 Cor 7:18; Gal 2:11, 14; 5:2f [d]Acts 6:14

2 And when Paul and Barnabas had [1]great dissension and
[a]debate with them, [b]*the brethren* determined that Paul and
Barnabas and some others of them should go up to Jerusalem to
the [c]apostles and elders concerning this issue.
3 Therefore, being [a]sent on their way by the church, they
were passing through both [b]Phoenicia and Samaria, [c]describing
in detail the conversion of the Gentiles, and were bringing
great joy to all [d]the brethren.
4 When they arrived at Jerusalem, they were received by the
church and [a]the apostles and the elders, and they [b]reported all
that God had done with them.
5 But some of [a]the sect of the [b]Pharisees who had believed
stood up, saying, "It is necessary to [c]circumcise them and to
direct them to observe the Law of Moses."
6 [a]The apostles and the elders came together to [1]look into
this [2]matter.
7 After there had been much [a]debate, Peter stood up and
said to them, "Brethren, you know that [1]in the early days [b]God
made a choice among you, that by my mouth the Gentiles would
hear the word of [c]the gospel and believe.
8 "And God, [a]who knows the heart, testified to them [b]giving
them the Holy Spirit, just as He also did to us;
9 and [a]He made no distinction between us and them,
[b]cleansing their hearts by faith.
10 "Now therefore why do you [a]put God to the test by placing
upon the neck of the disciples a yoke which [b]neither our
fathers nor we have been able to bear?
11 "But we believe that we are saved through [a]the grace of the
Lord Jesus, in the same way as they also are."
12 All the people kept silent, and they were listening to
Barnabas and Paul as they were [a]relating what [b]signs and wonders
God had done through them among the Gentiles.
13 After they had stopped speaking, [1a]James answered, saying,
"Brethren, listen to me.
14 "[a]Simeon has related how God first concerned Himself
about taking from among the Gentiles a people for His name.
15 "With this the words of [a]the Prophets agree, just as it is written,
16 '[a]AFTER THESE THINGS [b]I will return,
AND I WILL REBUILD THE [1]TABERNACLE OF DAVID WHICH
HAS FALLEN,
AND I WILL REBUILD ITS RUINS,
AND I WILL RESTORE IT,
17 [a]SO THAT THE REST OF [1]MANKIND MAY SEEK THE LORD,
AND ALL THE GENTILES [2b]WHO ARE CALLED BY MY NAME,'
18 [a]SAYS THE LORD, WHO [1b]MAKES THESE THINGS KNOWN
FROM LONG AGO.
19 "Therefore it is [a]my judgment that we do not trouble those
who are turning to God from among the Gentiles,
20 but that we write to them that they abstain from [1a]things
contaminated by idols and from [b]fornication and from [c]what is
strangled and from blood.

2 [1]Lit *not a little* [a]Acts 15:7 [b]Gal 2:2 [c]Acts 11:30; 15:4, 6, 22, 23; 16:4

3 [a]Acts 20:38; 21:5; Rom 15:24; 1 Cor 16:6, 11; 2 Cor 1:16; Titus 3:13; 3 John 6 [b]Acts 11:19 [c]Acts 14:27; 15:4, 12 [d]Acts 1:15; 15:22, 32

4 [a]Acts 11:30; 15:6, 22, 23; 16:4 [b]Acts 14:27; 15:12

5 [a]Acts 5:17; 24:5, 14; 26:5; 28:22 [b]Matt 3:7; Acts 26:5 [c]1 Cor 7:18; Gal 2:11, 14; 5:2f

6 [1]Lit *see about* [2]Lit *word* [a]Acts 11:30; 15:4, 22, 23; 16:4

7 [1]Lit *from days of old* [a]Acts 15:2 [b]Acts 10:19f [c]Acts 20:24

8 [a]Acts 1:24 [b]Acts 2:4; 10:44, 47

9 [a]Acts 10:28, 34; 11:12 [b]Acts 10:43

10 [a]Acts 5:9 [b]Matt 23:4; Gal 5:1

11 [a]Rom 3:24; 5:15; 2 Cor 13:14; Eph 2:5-8

12 [a]Acts 14:27; 15:3, 4 [b]John 4:48

13 [1]Or *Jacob* [a]Acts 12:17

14 [a]Acts 15:7; 2 Pet 1:1

15 [a]Acts 13:40

16 [1]Or *tent* [a]Amos 9:11 [b]Jer 12:15

17 [1]Gr *anthropoi* [2]Lit *upon whom My name is called* [a]Amos 9:12 [b]Deut 28:10; Is 63:19; Jer 14:9; Dan 9:19; James 2:7

18 [1]Or *does these things* which were *known* [a]Amos 9:12 [b]Is 45:21

19 [a]Acts 15:28; 21:25

20 [1]Lit *the pollutions of* [a]Ex 34:15-17; Dan 1:8; Acts 15:29; 1 Cor 8:7, 13; 10:7f, 14-28; Rev 2:14, 20 [b]Lev 18:6-23 [c]Gen 9:4; Lev 3:17; 7:26; 17:10, 14; 19:26; Deut 12:16, 23; 15:23; 1 Sam 14:33

21 "For [a]Moses from ancient generations has in every city
those who preach him, since [1]he is read in the synagogues
every Sabbath."
22 Then it seemed good to [a]the apostles and the elders, with
the whole church, to choose men from among them to send to
[b]Antioch with Paul and Barnabas—Judas called Barsabbas, and
[c]Silas, leading men among [d]the brethren,
23 and they [1]sent this letter by them,

"[a]The apostles and the brethren who are elders, to [b]the
brethren in [c]Antioch and [d]Syria and [e]Cilicia who are
from the Gentiles, [f]greetings.

24 "Since we have heard that [a]some [1]of our number to whom
we gave no instruction have [b]disturbed you with *their*
words, unsettling your souls,

25 [a]it seemed good to us, having [1]become of one mind, to
select men to send to you with our beloved Barnabas and
Paul,

26 men who have [1a]risked their lives for the name of our
Lord Jesus Christ.

27 "Therefore we have sent [a]Judas and [b]Silas, who themselves will also report the same things by word *of mouth.*

28 "For [a]it seemed good to [b]the Holy Spirit and to [c]us to lay
upon you no greater burden than these essentials:

29 that you abstain from [a]things sacrificed to idols and from
[a]blood and from [a]things strangled and from [a]fornication;
[1]if you keep yourselves free from such things, you will
do well. Farewell."

30 So when they were sent away, [a]they went down to Antioch;
and having gathered the [1]congregation together, they delivered
the letter.
31 When they had read it, they rejoiced because of its [1]en-
couragement.
32 [a]Judas and [b]Silas, also being [c]prophets themselves, [1]encouraged
and strengthened [d]the brethren with a lengthy message.
33 After they had spent time *there,* they were sent away from
the brethren [a]in peace to those who had [b]sent them out.
34 [[1]But it seemed good to Silas to remain there.]
35 But [a]Paul and Barnabas stayed in Antioch, teaching and
[b]preaching with many others also, [c]the word of the Lord.
36 After some days Paul said to Barnabas, "Let us return and
visit the brethren in [a]every city in which we proclaimed [b]the
word of the Lord, *and see* how they are."
37 Barnabas wanted to take [a]John, called Mark, along with them
also.
38 But Paul kept insisting that they should not take him along
who had [a]deserted them [1]in Pamphylia and had not gone with
them to the work.
39 And there occurred such a sharp disagreement that they
separated from one another, and Barnabas took [a]Mark with him
and sailed away to [b]Cyprus.

21 [1]I.e. the books of Moses, Gen through Deut [a]Acts 13:15; 2 Cor 3:14f

22 [a]Acts 15:2 [b]Acts 11:20 [c]Acts 15:27, 32, 40; 16:19, 25, 29; 17:4, 10, 14f; 18:5; 2 Cor 1:19; 1 Thess 1:1; 2 Thess 1:1; 1 Pet 5:12 [d]Acts 15:1

23 [1]Lit *wrote by their hand* [a]Acts 15:2 [b]Acts 15:1 [c]Acts 11:20 [d]Matt 4:24; Acts 15:41; Gal 1:21 [e]Acts 6:9 [f]Acts 23:26; James 1:1; 2 John 10f

24 [1]Lit *from us* [a]Acts 15:1 [b]Gal 1:7; 5:10

25 [1]Or *met together* [a]Acts 15:28

26 [1]Lit *given over* [a]Acts 9:23ff; 14:19

27 [a]Acts 15:22, 32 [b]Acts 15:22

28 [a]Acts 15:25 [b]Acts 5:32; 15:8 [c]Acts 15:19, 25

29 [1]Lit *from which keeping yourselves free* [a]Acts 15:20

30 [1]Or *multitude* [a]Acts 15:22f

31 [1]Or *exhortation*

32 [1]Or *exhorted* [a]Acts 15:22, 27 [b]Acts 15:22 [c]Acts 13:1 [d]Acts 15:1

33 [a]Mark 5:34; Acts 16:36; 1 Cor 16:11; Heb 11:31 [b]Acts 15:22

34 [1]Early mss do not contain this v

35 [a]Acts 12:25 [b]Acts 8:4 [c]Acts 13:12

36 [a]Acts 13:4, 13, 14, 51; 14:6, 24f [b]Acts 13:12

37 [a]Acts 12:12

38 [1]Lit *from* [a]Acts 13:13

39 [a]Acts 12:12; 15:37; Col 4:10 [b]Acts 4:36

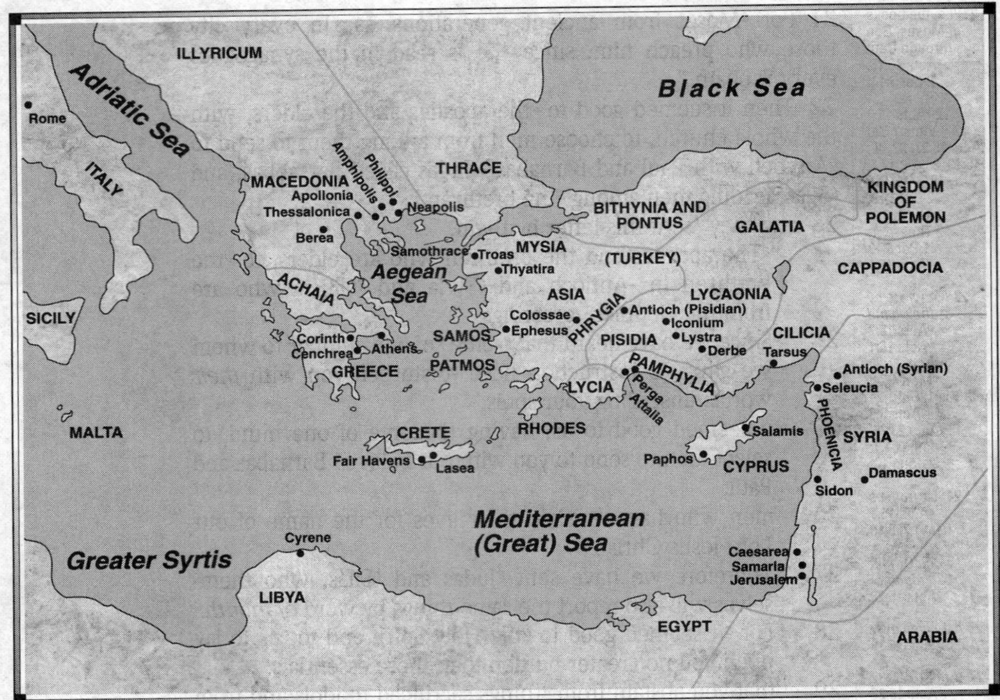

Paul's Second Missionary Journey (Acts 15:36–18:22)

40 But Paul chose [a]Silas and left, being [b]committed by the
brethren to the grace of the Lord.
41 And he was traveling through [a]Syria and [b]Cilicia,
strengthening the churches.

Chapter 16 Theme ______________________

16 Paul came also to [a]Derbe and to [a]Lystra. And a disciple
was there, named [b]Timothy, the son of a [c]Jewish woman
who was a believer, but his father was a Greek,
2 and he was well spoken of by [a]the brethren who were in
[b]Lystra and [c]Iconium.
3 Paul wanted this man to [1]go with him; and he [a]took him
and circumcised him because of the Jews who were in those
parts, for they all knew that his father was a Greek.
4 Now while they were passing through the cities, they were
delivering [a]the decrees which had been decided upon by [b]the
apostles and [c]elders who were in Jerusalem, for them to observe.
5 So [a]the churches were being strengthened [1]in the faith,
and were [b]increasing in number daily.
6 They passed through the [1a]Phrygian and [b]Galatian region,
having been forbidden by the Holy Spirit to speak the word in
[2c]Asia;
7 and after they came to [a]Mysia, they were trying to go into
[b]Bithynia, and the [c]Spirit of Jesus did not permit them;
8 and passing by [a]Mysia, they came down to [b]Troas.

40 [a]Acts 15:22 [b]Acts 11:23; 14:26

41 [a]Matt 4:24; Acts 15:23 [b]Acts 6:9

16:1 [a]Acts 14:6 [b]Acts 17:14f; 18:5; 19:22; 20:4; Rom 16:21; 1 Cor 4:17; 16:10; 2 Cor 1:1, 19; Phil 1:1; 2:19; Col 1:1; 1 Thess 1:1; 3:2, 6; 2 Thess 1:1; 1 Tim 1:2, 18; 6:20; 2 Tim 1:2; Philem 1; Heb 13:23 [c]2 Tim 1:5; 3:15

2 [a]Acts 16:40 [b]Acts 14:6 [c]Acts 13:51

3 [1]Lit *go out* [a]Gal 2:3

4 [a]Acts 15:28f [b]Acts 15:2 [c]Acts 11:30

5 [1]Or *in faith* [a]Acts 9:31 [b]Acts 2:47

6 [1]Or *Phrygia and the Galatian region* [2]I.e. west coast province of Asia Minor [a]Acts 2:10; 18:23 [b]Acts 18:23; 1 Cor 16:1; Gal 1:2; 3:1; 2 Tim 4:10; 1 Pet 1:1 [c]Acts 2:9

7 [a]Acts 16:8 [b]1 Pet 1:1 [c]Luke 24:49; Acts 8:29; Rom 8:9; Gal 4:6; Phil 1:19; 1 Pet 1:11

8 [a]Acts 16:7 [b]Acts 16:11; 20:5f; 2 Cor 2:12; 2 Tim 4:13

9 [a]A vision appeared to Paul in the night: a man of [b]Macedonia was standing and appealing to him, and saying, "Come over to Macedonia and help us."
10 When he had seen [a]the vision, immediately [b]we sought to [1]go into Macedonia, concluding that God had called us to [c]preach the gospel to them.
11 So putting out to sea from [a]Troas, we ran [b]a straight course to Samothrace, and on the day following to Neapolis;
12 and from there to [a]Philippi, which is a leading city of the district of [b]Macedonia, [c]a *Roman* colony; and we were staying in this city for some days.
13 And on [a]the Sabbath day we went outside the gate to a riverside, where we were supposing that there would be a place of prayer; and we sat down and began speaking to the women who had assembled.
14 A woman named Lydia, from the city of [a]Thyatira, a seller of purple fabrics, [b]a worshiper of God, was listening; [1]and the Lord [c]opened her heart to respond to the things spoken by Paul.
15 And when she and [a]her household had been baptized, she urged us, saying, "If you have judged me to be faithful to the Lord, come into my house and stay." And she prevailed upon us.
16 It happened that as we were going to [a]the place of prayer, a slave-girl having [b]a spirit of divination met us, who was bringing her masters much profit by fortune-telling.
17 Following after Paul and us, she kept crying out, saying, "These men are bond-servants of [a]the Most High God, who are proclaiming to you [1]the way of salvation."
18 She continued doing this for many days. But Paul was greatly annoyed, and turned and said to the spirit, "I command you [a]in the name of Jesus Christ to come out of her!" And it came out at that very [1]moment.
19 But when her masters saw that their hope of [a]profit was [1]gone, they seized [b]Paul and Silas and [c]dragged them into the market place before the authorities,
20 and when they had brought them to the chief magistrates, they said, "These men are throwing our city into confusion, being Jews,
21 and [a]are proclaiming customs which it is not lawful for us to accept or to observe, being [b]Romans."
22 The crowd rose up together against them, and the chief magistrates tore their [1]robes off them and proceeded to order [2]*them* to be [a]beaten with rods.
23 When they had struck them with many blows, they threw them into prison, commanding [a]the jailer to guard them securely;
24 [1]and he, having received such a command, threw them into the inner prison and fastened their feet in [a]the [2]stocks.
25 But about midnight [a]Paul and Silas were praying and [b]singing hymns of praise to God, and the prisoners were listening to them;
26 and suddenly [a]there came a great earthquake, so that the foundations of the prison house were shaken; and immediately [b]all the doors were opened and everyone's [c]chains were unfastened.

9 [a]Acts 9:10 [b]Acts 16:10, 12; 18:5; 19:21f, 29; 20:1, 3; 27:2; Rom 15:26

10 [1]Lit *go out* [a]Acts 9:10 [b][we] Acts 16:10-17; 20:5-15; 21:1-18; 27:1-28:16 [c]Acts 14:7

11 [a]Acts 16:8; 20:5f; 2 Cor 2:12; 2 Tim 4:13 [b]Acts 21:1

12 [a]Acts 20:6; Phil 1:1; 1 Thess 2:2 [b]Acts 16:9, 10; 18:5; 19:21f, 29; 20:1, 3; 27:2; Rom 15:26 [c]Acts 16:21

13 [a]Acts 13:14

14 [1]Lit *whose heart the Lord opened* [a]Rev 1:11; 2:18, 24 [b]Acts 13:43; 18:7 [c]Luke 24:45

15 [a]Acts 11:14

16 [a]Acts 16:13 [b]Lev 19:31; 20:6, 27; Deut 18:11; 1 Sam 28:3, 7; 2 Kin 21:6; 1 Chr 10:13; Is 8:19

17 [1]Lit *a way* [a]Mark 5:7

18 [1]Lit *hour* [a]Mark 16:17

19 [1]Lit *gone out* [a]Acts 16:16; 19:25f [b]Acts 15:22, 40; 16:25, 29 [c]Acts 8:3; 17:6f; 21:30; James 2:6

21 [a]Esth 3:8 [b]Acts 16:12

22 [1]Or *outer garments* [2]Lit *to beat with rods* [a]2 Cor 11:25; 1 Thess 2:2

23 [a]Acts 16:27, 36

24 [1]Lit *who* [2]Lit *wood* [a]Job 13:27; 33:11; Jer 20:2f; 29:26

25 [a]Acts 16:19 [b]Eph 5:19

26 [a]Acts 4:31 [b]Acts 12:10 [c]Acts 12:7

27 When [a]the jailer awoke and saw the prison doors opened, he drew his sword and was about [b]to kill himself, supposing that the prisoners had escaped.

28 But Paul cried out with a loud voice, saying, "Do not harm yourself, for we are all here!"

29 And he called for lights and rushed in, and trembling with fear he fell down before [a]Paul and Silas,

30 and after he brought them out, he said, "Sirs, [a]what must I do to be saved?"

31 They said, "[a]Believe in the Lord Jesus, and you will be saved, you and [b]your household."

32 And they spoke the word of [1]the Lord to him together with all who were in his house.

33 And he took them [a]that *very* hour of the night and washed their wounds, and immediately he was baptized, he and all his *household.*

34 And he brought them into his house and set [1]food before them, and rejoiced [2]greatly, having believed in God with [a]his whole household.

35 Now when day came, the chief magistrates sent their policemen, saying, "Release those men."

36 And [a]the jailer reported these words to Paul, *saying,* "The chief magistrates have sent to release you. Therefore come out now and go [b]in peace."

37 But Paul said to them, "They have beaten us in public without trial, [a]men who are Romans, and have thrown us into prison; and now are they sending us away secretly? No indeed! But let them come themselves and bring us out."

38 The policemen reported these words to the chief magistrates. [a]They were afraid when they heard that they were Romans,

39 and they came and appealed to them, and when they had brought them out, they kept begging them [a]to leave the city.

40 They went out of the prison and entered *the house of* [a]Lydia, and when they saw [b]the brethren, they [1]encouraged them and departed.

Chapter 17 Theme ____________________

17 Now when they had traveled through Amphipolis and Apollonia, they came to [a]Thessalonica, where there was a synagogue of the Jews.

2 And [a]according to Paul's custom, he went to them, and for three [b]Sabbaths reasoned with them from [c]the Scriptures,

3 [1]explaining and [2]giving evidence that the [3]Christ [a]had to suffer and [b]rise again from the dead, and *saying,* "[c]This Jesus whom I am proclaiming to you is the [3]Christ."

4 [a]And some of them were persuaded and joined [b]Paul and Silas, [1]along with a large number of the [c]God-fearing [d]Greeks and [2]a number of the [e]leading women.

5 But [a]the Jews, becoming jealous and taking along some wicked men from the market place, formed a mob and set the

27 [a]Acts 16:23, 36 [b]Acts 12:19

29 [a]Acts 16:19

30 [a]Acts 2:37; 22:10

31 [a]Mark 16:16 [b]Acts 11:14; 16:15

32 [1]Two early mss read *God*

33 [a]Acts 16:25

34 [1]Lit *a table* [2]Or *greatly with his whole household, having believed in God* [a]Acts 11:14; 16:15

36 [a]Acts 16:27 [b]Acts 15:33

37 [a]Acts 22:25-29

38 [a]Acts 22:29

39 [a]Matt 8:34

40 [1]Or *exhorted* [a]Acts 16:14 [b]Acts 1:15; 16:2

17:1 [a]Acts 17:11, 13; 20:4; 27:2; Phil 4:16; 1 Thess 1:1; 2 Thess 1:1; 2 Tim 4:10

2 [a]Acts 9:20; 17:10, 17 [b]Acts 13:14 [c]Acts 8:35

3 [1]Lit *opening* [2]Lit *placing before* [3]I.e. Messiah [a]Acts 3:18 [b]John 20:9 [c]Acts 9:22; 18:5, 28

4 [1]Lit *and a large* [2]Lit *not a few* [a]Acts 14:4 [b]Acts 15:22, 40; 17:10, 14f [c]Acts 13:43; 17:17 [d]John 7:35 [e]Acts 13:50

5 [a]Acts 17:13; 1 Thess 2:14ff

city in an uproar; and attacking the house of [b]Jason, they were
seeking to bring them out to the people.
6 When they did not find them, they *began* [a]dragging Jason
and some brethren before the city authorities, shouting, "These
men who have upset [1b]the world have come here also;
7 [1]and Jason [a]has welcomed them, and they all act [b]contrary
to the decrees of Caesar, saying that there is another king, Jesus."
8 They stirred up the crowd and the city authorities who
heard these things.
9 And when they had received a [1]pledge from [a]Jason and the
others, they released them.
10 [a]The brethren immediately sent [b]Paul and Silas away by night
to [c]Berea, [1]and when they arrived, they went into [d]the synagogue
of the Jews.
11 Now these were more noble-minded than those in
[a]Thessalonica, [1]for they received the word with [2]great eagerness,
examining the Scriptures daily *to see* whether these things
were so.
12 Therefore [a]many of them believed, [1]along with a number
of [b]prominent Greek [c]women and men.
13 But when the Jews of [a]Thessalonica found out that the
word of God had been proclaimed by Paul in [b]Berea also, they
came there as well, agitating and stirring up the crowds.
14 Then immediately [a]the brethren sent Paul out to go as far
as the sea; and [b]Silas and [c]Timothy remained there.
15 Now [a]those who escorted Paul brought him as far as [b]Athens;
and receiving a command for [c]Silas and Timothy to [d]come to
him as soon as possible, they left.
16 Now while Paul was waiting for them at [a]Athens, his spirit
was being provoked within him as he was observing the city
full of idols.
17 So he was reasoning [a]in the synagogue with the Jews and
[b]the God-fearing *Gentiles,* and in the market place every day
with those who happened to be present.
18 And also some of the Epicurean and Stoic philosophers
were [1]conversing with him. Some were saying, "What would
[a]this [2]idle babbler wish to say?" Others, "He seems to be a
proclaimer of strange deities,"—because he was preaching
[b]Jesus and the resurrection.
19 And they [a]took him and brought him [1]to the [2b]Areopagus,
saying, "May we know what [c]this new teaching is [3]which you
are proclaiming?
20 "For you are bringing some strange things to our ears; so we
want to know what these things mean."
21 (Now all the Athenians and the strangers [a]visiting there used
to spend their time in nothing other than telling or hearing
something new.)
22 So Paul stood in the midst of the [1]Areopagus and said, "Men
of [a]Athens, I observe that you are very [b]religious in all respects.
23 "For while I was passing through and examining the [a]objects
of your worship, I also found an altar with this inscription, 'TO

5 [b]Acts 17:6, 7, 9; Rom 16:21

6 [1]Lit *the inhabited earth* [a]Acts 16:19f [b]Matt 24:14; Acts 17:31

7 [1]Lit *whom Jason has welcomed* [a]Luke 10:38; James 2:25 [b]Luke 23:2

9 [1]Or *bond* [a]Acts 17:5

10 [1]Lit *who when . . . arrived went* [a]Acts 1:15; 17:6, 14f [b]Acts 17:4 [c]Acts 17:13; 20:4 [d]Acts 17:1f

11 [1]Lit *who received* [2]Lit *all* [a]Acts 17:1

12 [1]Lit *and not a few* [a]Acts 2:47 [b]Mark 15:43 [c]Acts 13:50

13 [a]Acts 17:1 [b]Acts 17:10; 20:4

14 [a]Acts 1:15; 17:6, 10 [b]Acts 15:22; 17:4, 10 [c]Acts 16:1

15 [a]Acts 15:3 [b]Acts 17:16, 21f; 18:1; 1 Thess 3:1 [c]Acts 17:14 [d]Acts 18:5

16 [a]Acts 17:15, 21f; 18:1; 1 Thess 3:1

17 [a]Acts 9:20; 17:2 [b]Acts 17:4

18 [1]Or *disputing* [2]I.e. one who makes his living by picking up scraps [a]1 Cor 1:20; 4:10 [b]Acts 4:2; 17:31f

19 [1]Or *before* [2]Or *Hill of Ares,* god of war [3]Lit *which is being spoken by you* [a]Acts 23:19 [b]Acts 17:22 [c]Mark 1:27

21 [a]Acts 2:10

22 [1]Or *the Council of the Areopagus* [a]Acts 17:15 [b]Acts 25:19

23 [a]2 Thess 2:4

AN UNKNOWN GOD.' Therefore what [b]you worship in
ignorance, this I proclaim to you.
24 "[a]The God who made the world and all things in it, since He
is [b]Lord of heaven and earth, does not [c]dwell in temples made
with hands;
25 nor is He served by human hands, [a]as though He needed
anything, since He Himself gives to all *people* life and breath
and all things;
26 and [a]He made from one *man* every nation of mankind to live
on all the face of the earth, having [b]determined *their* appointed
times and the boundaries of their habitation,
27 that they would seek God, if perhaps they might grope for
Him and find Him, [a]though He is not far from each one of us;
28 for [a]in Him we live and move and [1]exist, as even some of
your own poets have said, 'For we also are His children.'
29 "Being then the children of God, we [a]ought not to think that
the Divine Nature is like gold or silver or stone, an image formed
by the art and thought of man.
30 "Therefore having [a]overlooked [b]the times of ignorance, God is
[c]now declaring to men that all *people* everywhere should repent,
31 because He has fixed [a]a day in which [b]He will judge [1c]the
world in righteousness [2]through a Man whom He has [d]appointed,
having furnished proof to all men [3]by [e]raising Him from the dead."
32 Now when they heard of [a]the resurrection of the dead,
some *began* to sneer, but others said, "We shall hear you [1]again
concerning this."
33 So Paul went out of their midst.
34 But some men joined him and believed, among whom also
were Dionysius the [a]Areopagite and a woman named Damaris
and others with them.

Chapter 18 Theme ____________________

18 After these things he left [a]Athens and went to [b]Corinth.
2 And he found a Jew named [a]Aquila, a native of [b]Pontus,
having recently come from [c]Italy with his wife [a]Priscilla, because
[d]Claudius had commanded all the Jews to leave Rome. He
came to them,
3 and because he was of the same trade, he stayed with them
and [a]they were working, for by trade they were tent-makers.
4 And he was reasoning [a]in the synagogue every [b]Sabbath
and trying to persuade [c]Jews and Greeks.
5 But when [a]Silas and Timothy [b]came down from [c]Macedonia,
Paul *began* devoting himself completely to the word, solemnly
[d]testifying to the Jews that [e]Jesus was the [1]Christ.
6 But when they resisted and blasphemed, he [a]shook out his
garments and said to them, "Your [b]blood *be* on your own
heads! I am clean. From now on I will go [c]to the Gentiles."
7 Then he left there and went to the house of a man named
[1]Titius Justus, [a]a worshiper of God, whose house was next to
the synagogue.

23 [b]John 4:22
24 [a]Is 42:5; Acts 14:15 [b]Deut 10:14; Ps 115:16; Matt 11:25 [c]1 Kin 8:27; Acts 7:48
25 [a]Job 22:2; Ps 50:10-12
26 [a]Mal 2:10 [b]Deut 32:8; Job 12:23
27 [a]Deut 4:7; Jer 23:23f; Acts 14:17
28 [1]Lit *are* [a]Job 12:10; Dan 5:23
29 [a]Is 40:18ff; Rom 1:23
30 [a]Acts 14:16; Rom 3:25 [b]Acts 17:23 [c]Luke 24:47; Acts 26:20; Titus 2:11f
31 [1]Lit *the inhabited earth* [2]Lit *by* or *in* [3]Or *when He raised* [a]Matt 10:15 [b]Ps 9:8; 96:13; 98:9; John 5:22, 27; Acts 10:42 [c]Matt 24:14; Acts 17:6 [d]Luke 22:22 [e]Acts 2:24
32 [1]Lit *also again* [a]Acts 17:18, 31
34 [a]Acts 17:19, 22
18:1 [a]Acts 17:15 [b]Acts 18:8; 19:1; 1 Cor 1:2; 2 Cor 1:1, 23; 6:11; 2 Tim 4:20
2 [a]Acts 18:18, 26; Rom 16:3; 1 Cor 16:19; 2 Tim 4:19 [b]Acts 2:9 [c]Acts 27:1, 6; Heb 13:24 [d]Acts 11:28
3 [a]Acts 20:34; 1 Cor 4:12; 9:14f; 2 Cor 11:7; 12:13; 1 Thess 2:9; 4:11; 2 Thess 3:8
4 [a]Acts 9:20; 18:19 [b]Acts 13:14 [c]Acts 14:1
5 [1]I.e. Messiah [a]Acts 15:22; 16:1; 17:14 [b]Acts 17:15 [c]Acts 16:9 [d]Luke 16:28; Acts 20:21 [e]Acts 17:3; 18:28
6 [a]Neh 5:13; Acts 13:51 [b]2 Sam 1:16; 1 Kin 2:33; Ezek 18:13; 33:4, 6, 8; Matt 27:25; Acts 20:26 [c]Acts 13:46
7 [1]One early ms reads *Titus;* two other early mss omit the name [a]Acts 13:43; 16:14

8 [a]Crispus, [b]the leader of the synagogue, believed in the Lord
[c]with all his household, and many of the [d]Corinthians when
they heard were believing and being baptized.
9 And the Lord said to Paul in the night by [a]a vision, "Do not
be afraid *any longer,* but go on speaking and do not be silent;
10 for I am with you, and no man will attack you in order to
harm you, for I have many people in this city."
11 And he settled *there* a year and six months, teaching the
word of God among them.
12 But while Gallio was [a]proconsul of [b]Achaia, [c]the Jews with
one accord rose up against Paul and brought him before [d]the
judgment seat,
13 saying, "This man persuades men to worship God contrary
to [a]the law."
14 But when Paul was about to [a]open his mouth, Gallio said to
the Jews, "If it were a matter of wrong or of vicious crime, O
Jews, it would be reasonable for me to put up with you;
15 but if there are [a]questions about words and names and your
own law, look after it yourselves; I am unwilling to be a judge
of these matters."
16 And he drove them away from [a]the judgment seat.
17 And they all took hold of [a]Sosthenes, [b]the leader of the
synagogue, and *began* beating him in front of [c]the judgment
seat. But Gallio was not concerned about any of these things.
18 Paul, having remained many days longer, [a]took leave of [b]the
brethren and put out to sea for [c]Syria, and with him were
[d]Priscilla and [d]Aquila. In [e]Cenchrea [1]he [f]had his hair cut, for
he was keeping a vow.
19 They came to [a]Ephesus, and he left them there. Now he
himself entered [b]the synagogue and reasoned with the Jews.
20 When they asked him to stay for a longer time, he did not
consent,
21 but [a]taking leave of them and saying, "I will return to you
again [b]if God wills," he set sail from [c]Ephesus.
22 When he had landed at [a]Caesarea, he went up and greeted
the church, and went down to [b]Antioch.
23 And having spent some time *there,* he left and passed succes-
sively through the [a]Galatian region and Phrygia, strengthening
all the disciples.
24 Now a Jew named [a]Apollos, an [b]Alexandrian by birth, [1]an
eloquent man, came to [c]Ephesus; and he was mighty in the
Scriptures.
25 This man had been instructed in [a]the way of the Lord; and
being fervent in spirit, he was speaking and teaching accurately
the things concerning Jesus, being acquainted only with [b]the
baptism of John;
26 and [1]he began to speak out boldly in the synagogue. But
when [a]Priscilla and Aquila heard him, they took him aside and
explained to him [b]the way of God more accurately.
27 And when he wanted to go across to [a]Achaia, [b]the brethren
encouraged him and wrote to [c]the disciples to welcome him;

8 [a]1 Cor 1:14 [b]Mark 5:22 [c]Acts 11:14 [d]Acts 18:1; 19:1; 1 Cor 1:2; 2 Cor 1:1, 23; 6:11; 2 Tim 4:20

9 [a]Acts 9:10

12 [a]Acts 13:7 [b]Acts 18:27; 19:21; Rom 15:26; 1 Cor 16:15; 2 Cor 1:1; 9:2; 11:10; 1 Thess 1:7f [c]1 Thess 2:14ff [d]Matt 27:19

13 [a]John 19:7; Acts 18:15

14 [a]Matt 5:2

15 [a]Acts 23:29; 25:19

16 [a]Matt 27:19

17 [a]1 Cor 1:1 [b]Acts 18:8 [c]Matt 27:19

18 [1]Lit *having his hair cut* [a]Mark 6:46 [b]Acts 1:15; 18:27 [c]Matt 4:24 [d]Acts 18:2, 26 [e]Rom 16:1 [f]Num 6:2, 5, 9, 18; Acts 21:24

19 [a]Acts 18:21, 24; 19:1, 17, 26, 28, 34f; 20:16f; 21:29; 1 Cor 15:32; 16:8; Eph 1:1; 1 Tim 1:3; 2 Tim 1:18; 4:12; Rev 1:11; 2:1 [b]Acts 18:4

21 [a]Mark 6:46 [b]Rom 1:10; 15:32; 1 Cor 4:19; 16:7; Heb 6:3; James 4:15; 1 Pet 3:17 [c]Acts 18:19, 24; 19:1, 17, 26, 28, 34f; 20:16f; 21:29; 1 Cor 15:32; 16:8; Eph 1:1; 1 Tim 1:3; 2 Tim 1:18; 4:12; Rev 1:11; 2:1

22 [a]Acts 8:40 [b]Acts 11:19

23 [a]Acts 16:6

24 [1]Or *a learned man* [a]Acts 19:1; 1 Cor 1:12; 3:5, 6, 22; 4:6; 16:12; Titus 3:13 [b]Acts 6:9 [c]Acts 18:19

25 [a]Acts 9:2; 18:26 [b]Luke 7:29; Acts 19:3

26 [1]Lit *this man* [a]Acts 18:2, 18 [b]Acts 18:25

27 [a]Acts 18:12; 19:1 [b]Acts 18:18 [c]Acts 11:26

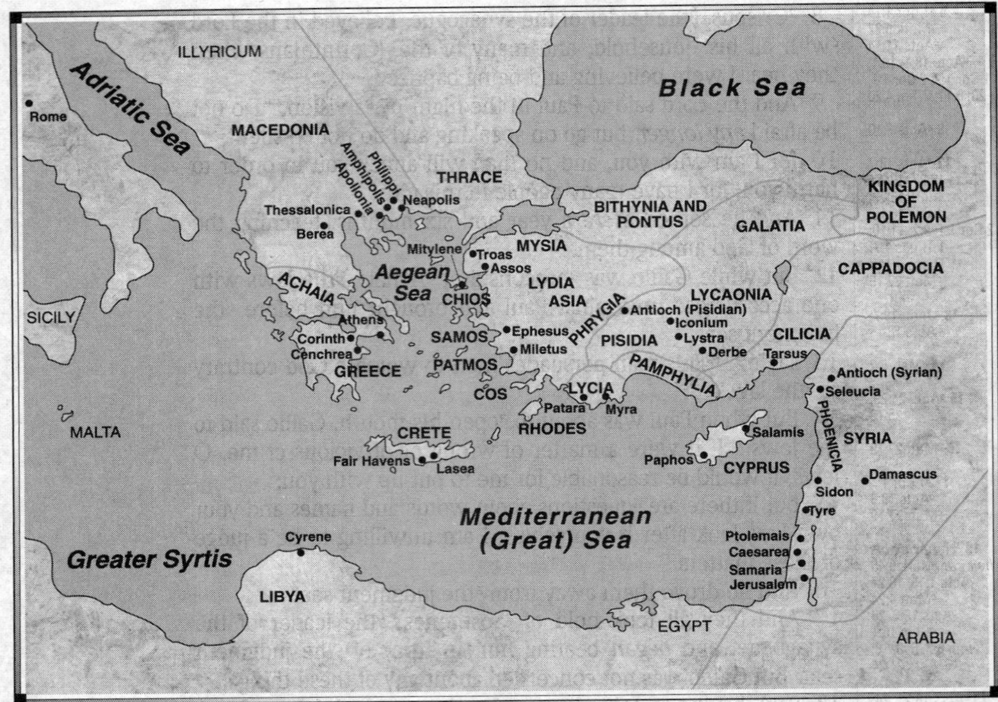

Paul's Third Missionary Journey (Acts 18:23–21:17)

and when he had arrived, he greatly [1]helped those who had
believed through grace,
28 for he powerfully refuted the Jews in public, demonstrating
[a]by the Scriptures that [b]Jesus was the [1]Christ.

Chapter 19 Theme ____

19 It happened that while [a]Apollos was at [b]Corinth, Paul
passed through the [c]upper country and came to [d]Ephesus,
and found some disciples.
2 He said to them, "[a]Did you receive the Holy Spirit when you
believed?" And they *said* to him, "No, [b]we have not even heard
whether [1]there is a Holy Spirit."
3 And he said, "Into what then were you baptized?" And they
said, "[a]Into John's baptism."
4 Paul said, "[a]John baptized with the baptism of repentance,
telling the people [b]to believe in Him who was coming after
him, that is, in Jesus."
5 When they heard this, they were [a]baptized [1]in the name of
the Lord Jesus.
6 And when Paul had [a]laid his hands upon them, the Holy
Spirit came on them, and they *began* [b]speaking with tongues
and [c]prophesying.
7 There were in all about twelve men.
8 And he entered [a]the synagogue and continued speaking
out boldly for three months, reasoning and persuading *them*
[b]about the kingdom of God.

27 [1]Or *helped greatly through grace those who had believed*

28 [1]I.e. Messiah [a]Acts 8:35 [b]Acts 18:5

19:1 [a]Acts 18:24; 1 Cor 1:12; 3:5, 6, 22; 4:6; 16:12; Titus 3:13 [b]Acts 18:1 [c]Acts 18:23 [d]Acts 18:21, 24; 19:17, 26, 28, 34f; 20:16f; 21:29; 1 Cor 15:32; 16:8; Eph 1:1; 1 Tim 1:3; 2 Tim 1:18; 4:12; Rev 1:11; 2:1

2 [1]Or *the Holy Spirit has been given* [a]Acts 8:15f; 11:16f [b]John 7:39

3 [a]Luke 7:29; Acts 18:25

4 [a]Matt 3:11; Mark 1:4, 7, 8; Luke 3:16; John 1:26, 27; Acts 13:24 [b]John 1:7

5 [1]Lit *into* [a]Acts 8:12, 16; 10:48

6 [a]Acts 6:6; 8:17 [b]Mark 16:17; Acts 2:4; 10:46 [c]Acts 13:1

8 [a]Acts 9:20; 18:26 [b]Acts 1:3

9 But when [a]some were becoming hardened and disobedient,
speaking evil of [b]the Way before the [1]people, he withdrew from
them and took away [c]the disciples, reasoning daily in the school
of Tyrannus.
10 This took place for [a]two years, so that all who lived in [1b]Asia
heard [c]the word of the Lord, both Jews and Greeks.
11 God was performing [a]extraordinary [1]miracles by the hands
of Paul,
12 [a]so that handkerchiefs or aprons were even carried from his
body to the sick, and the diseases left them and [b]the evil spirits
went out.
13 But also some of the Jewish [a]exorcists, who went from place
to place, attempted to name over those who had the evil spirits
the name of the Lord Jesus, saying, "I adjure you by Jesus whom
Paul preaches."
14 Seven sons of one Sceva, a Jewish chief priest, were doing this.
15 And the evil spirit answered and said to them, "I recognize
Jesus, and I know about Paul, but who are you?"
16 And the man, in whom was the evil spirit, leaped on them
and subdued all of them and overpowered them, so that they
fled out of that house naked and wounded.
17 This became known to all, both Jews and Greeks, who
lived in [a]Ephesus; and fear fell upon them all and the name of
the Lord Jesus was being magnified.
18 Many also of those who had believed kept coming, confessing
and disclosing their practices.
19 And many of those who practiced magic brought their books
together and *began* burning them in the sight of everyone; and
they counted up the price of them and found it [1]fifty thousand
[a]pieces of silver.
20 So [1a]the word of the Lord [b]was growing mightily and
prevailing.
21 Now after these things were finished, Paul purposed in the
[1]Spirit to [a]go to Jerusalem [b]after he had passed through
[c]Macedonia and [d]Achaia, saying, "After I have been there, [e]I
must also see Rome."
22 And having sent into [a]Macedonia two of [b]those who
ministered to him, [c]Timothy and [d]Erastus, he himself stayed in
[1e]Asia for a while.
23 About that time there occurred no small disturbance
concerning [a]the Way.
24 For a man named Demetrius, a silversmith, who made silver
shrines of [1]Artemis, [a]was bringing no little [2]business to the
craftsmen;
25 these he gathered together with the workmen of similar
trades, and said, "Men, you know that our prosperity [1]depends
upon this business.
26 "You see and hear that not only in [a]Ephesus, but in almost
all of [1b]Asia, this Paul has persuaded and turned away a
considerable number of people, saying that [2c]gods made with
hands are no gods *at all.*

9 [1]Lit *multitude* [a]Acts 14:4 [b]Acts 9:2; 19:23 [c]Acts 11:26; 19:30
10 [1]I.e. west coast province of Asia Minor [a]Acts 19:8; 20:31 [b]Acts 16:6; 19:22, 26, 27 [c]Acts 13:12; 19:20
11 [1]Or *works of power* [a]Acts 8:13
12 [a]Acts 5:15 [b]Mark 16:17
13 [a]Matt 12:27; Luke 11:19
17 [a]Acts 18:19
19 [1]Probably fifty thousand Greek drachmas; a drachma approximated a day's wage [a]Luke 15:8
20 [1]Or *according to the power of the Lord the word was growing* [a]Acts 19:10 [b]Acts 6:7; 12:24
21 [1]Or *spirit* [a]Acts 20:16, 22; 21:15; Rom 15:25; 2 Cor 1:16 [b]Acts 20:1; 1 Cor 16:5 [c]Acts 16:9; 19:22, 29; Rom 15:26; 1 Thess 1:7f [d]Acts 18:12 [e]Acts 23:11; Rom 15:24, 28
22 [1]I.e. west coast province of Asia Minor [a]Acts 16:9; 19:21, 29 [b]Acts 13:5; 19:29; 20:34; 2 Cor 8:19 [c]Acts 16:1 [d]Rom 16:23; 2 Tim 4:20 [e]Acts 19:10
23 [a]Acts 19:9
24 [1]Lat *Diana* [2]Or *profit* [a]Acts 16:16, 19f
25 [1]Lit *is from*
26 [1]V 22, note 1 [2]Lit *those* [a]Acts 18:19 [b]Acts 19:10 [c]Deut 4:28; Ps 115:4; Is 44:10-20; Jer 10:3ff; Acts 17:29; 1 Cor 8:4; 10:19; Rev 9:20

27 "Not only is there danger that this trade of ours fall into
disrepute, but also that the temple of the great goddess [1]Artemis
be regarded as worthless and that she whom all of [2a]Asia and [b]the
[3]world worship will even be dethroned from her magnificence."
28 When they heard *this* and were filled with rage, they
began crying out, saying, "Great is [1]Artemis of the [a]Ephesians!"
29 The city was filled with the confusion, and they rushed
[1]with one accord into the theater, dragging along [a]Gaius and
[b]Aristarchus, Paul's traveling [c]companions from [d]Macedonia.
30 And when Paul wanted to go into the [1]assembly, [a]the
disciples would not let him.
31 Also some of the [1]Asiarchs who were friends of his sent to
him and repeatedly urged him not to [2]venture into the theater.
32 [a]So then, some were shouting one thing and some another,
for the [1]assembly was in confusion and the majority did not
know [2]for what reason they had come together.
33 Some of the crowd [1]concluded *it was* Alexander, since the
Jews had put him forward; and having [a]motioned with his hand,
Alexander was intending to make a defense to the [2]assembly.
34 But when they recognized that he was a Jew, a *single*
outcry arose from them all as they shouted for about two hours,
"Great is [1]Artemis of the Ephesians!"
35 After quieting the crowd, the town clerk *said, "Men of
[a]Ephesus, what man is there after all who does not know that
the city of the Ephesians is guardian of the temple of the great
[1]Artemis and of the *image* which fell down from [2]heaven?
36 "So, since these are undeniable facts, you ought to keep
calm and to do nothing rash.
37 "For you have brought these men *here* who are neither
[a]robbers of temples nor blasphemers of our goddess.
38 "So then, if Demetrius and the craftsmen who are with him
have a complaint against any man, the courts are in session and
[1a]proconsuls are *available;* let them bring charges against one
another.
39 "But if you want anything beyond this, it shall be settled in
the [1]lawful [2]assembly.
40 "For indeed we are in danger of being accused of a riot in
connection with today's events, since there is no *real* cause *for
it,* and in this connection we will be unable to account for this
disorderly gathering."
41 After saying this he dismissed the [1]assembly.

Chapter 20 Theme ________________

20 After the uproar had ceased, Paul sent for [a]the disciples,
and when he had exhorted them and taken his leave of
them, he left [b]to go to [c]Macedonia.
2 When he had gone through those districts and had given
them much exhortation, he came to Greece.
3 And *there* he spent three months, and when [a]a plot was
formed against him by the Jews as he was about to set sail for
[b]Syria, he decided to return through [c]Macedonia.

27 [1]Lat *Diana* [2]V 22, note 1 [3]Lit *the inhabited earth* [a]Acts 19:10 [b]Matt 24:14

28 [1]Lat *Diana* [a]Acts 18:19

29 [1]Or *together* [a]Acts 20:4 [b]Acts 20:4; 27:2; Col 4:10; Philem 24 [c]Acts 13:5; 19:22; 20:34; 2 Cor 8:19 [d]Acts 16:9; 19:22

30 [1]Lit *people* [a]Acts 19:9

31 [1]I.e. political or religious officials of the province of Asia [2]Lit *give himself*

32 [1]Gr *ekklesia* [2]Or *on whose account* [a]Acts 21:34

33 [1]Or *advised Alexander* [2]Lit *people* [a]Acts 12:17

34 [1]Lat *Diana*

35 [1]Lat *Diana* [2]Lit *Zeus;* Lat *Jupiter* [a]Acts 18:19

37 [a]Rom 2:22

38 [1]Or *provincial governors* [a]Acts 13:7

39 [1]Or *regular* [2]Gr *ekklesia*

41 [1]Gr *ekklesia*

20:1 [a]Acts 11:26 [b]Acts 19:21 [c]Acts 16:9; 20:3

3 [a]Acts 9:23f; 20:19 [b]Matt 4:24 [c]Acts 16:9; 20:1

4 And [1]he was accompanied by Sopater of [a]Berea, *the son* of
Pyrrhus, and by [b]Aristarchus and Secundus of the [c]Thessalonians,
and [b]Gaius of [d]Derbe, and [e]Timothy, and [f]Tychicus and
[g]Trophimus of [2h]Asia.
5 But these had gone on ahead and were waiting for [a]us at
[b]Troas.
6 [a]We sailed from [b]Philippi after [c]the days of Unleavened
Bread, and came to them at [d]Troas within five days; and there
we stayed seven days.
7 On [a]the first day of the week, when [b]we were gathered
together to [c]break bread, Paul *began* talking to them, intending to
leave the next day, and he prolonged his [1]message until midnight.
8 There were many [a]lamps in the [b]upper room where we
were gathered together.
9 And there was a young man named [1]Eutychus sitting [2]on
the window sill, sinking into a deep sleep; and as Paul kept on
talking, he was overcome by sleep and fell down from the third
floor and was picked up dead.
10 But Paul went down and [a]fell upon him, and after embracing
him, he [b]said, "[1]Do not be troubled, for his life is in him."
11 When he had gone *back* up and had [a]broken the bread and
[1]eaten, he talked with them a long while until daybreak, and
then left.
12 They took away the boy alive, and were [1]greatly comforted.
13 But [a]we, going ahead to the ship, set sail for Assos, intending
from there to take Paul on board; for so he had arranged it,
intending himself to go [1]by land.
14 And when he met us at Assos, we took him on board and
came to Mitylene.
15 Sailing from there, we arrived the following day opposite
Chios; and the next day we crossed over to Samos; and the day
following we came to [a]Miletus.
16 For Paul had decided to sail past [a]Ephesus so that he would
not have to spend time in [1b]Asia; for he was hurrying [c]to be in
Jerusalem, if possible, [d]on the day of Pentecost.
17 From Miletus he sent to [a]Ephesus and called to him [b]the
elders of the church.
18 And when they had come to him, he said to them,
"**Y**ou yourselves know, [a]from the first day that I set foot in
[1]Asia, how I was with you the whole time,
19 serving the Lord with all humility and with tears and with
trials which came upon me [1]through [a]the plots of the Jews;
20 how I [a]did not shrink from declaring to you anything that
was profitable, and teaching you publicly and [1]from house to
house,
21 solemnly [a]testifying to both Jews and Greeks of [b]repentance
toward God and [c]faith in our Lord Jesus Christ.
22 "And now, behold, bound by the [1]Spirit, [a]I am on my way to
Jerusalem, not knowing what will happen to me there,
23 except that [a]the Holy Spirit solemnly [b]testifies to me in
every city, saying that [c]bonds and afflictions await me.

4 [1]Lit *there accompanied him* [2]I.e. west coast province of Asia Minor [a]Acts 17:10 [b]Acts 19:29 [c]Acts 17:1 [d]Acts 14:6 [e]Acts 16:1 [f]Eph 6:21; Col 4:7; 2 Tim 4:12; Titus 3:12 [g]Acts 21:29; 2 Tim 4:20 [h]Acts 16:6; 20:16, 18

5 [a]Acts 16:10; 20:5-15 [b]Acts 16:8

6 [a]Acts 16:10; 20:5-15 [b]Acts 16:12 [c]Acts 12:3 [d]Acts 16:8

7 [1]Lit *word, speech* [a]1 Cor 16:2; Rev 1:10 [b]Acts 16:10; 20:5-15 [c]Acts 2:42; 20:11

8 [a]Matt 25:1 [b]Acts 1:13

9 [1]*Eutychus* means *Good fortune*, i.e. 'Lucky' [2]Or *at the window*

10 [1]Or *Stop being troubled* [a]1 Kin 17:21; 2 Kin 4:34 [b]Matt 9:23f; Mark 5:39

11 [1]Lit *tasted* [a]Acts 2:42; 20:7

12 [1]Lit *not moderately*

13 [1]Or *on foot* [a]Acts 16:10; 20:5-15

15 [a]Acts 20:17; 2 Tim 4:20

16 [1]I.e. west coast province of Asia Minor [a]Acts 18:19 [b]Acts 16:6; 20:4, 18 [c]Acts 19:21; 20:6, 22; 1 Cor 16:8 [d]Acts 2:1

17 [a]Acts 18:19 [b]Acts 11:30

18 [1]V 16, note 1 [a]Acts 18:19; 19:1, 10; 20:4, 16

19 [1]Lit *by* [a]Acts 20:3

20 [1]Or *in the various private homes* [a]Acts 20:27

21 [a]Luke 16:28; Acts 18:5; 20:23, 24 [b]Acts 2:38; 11:18; 26:20 [c]Acts 24:24; 26:18; Eph 1:15; Col 2:5; Philem 5

22 [1]Or *in spirit* [a]Acts 17:16; 20:16

23 [a]Acts 8:29 [b]Luke 16:28; Acts 18:5; 20:21, 24 [c]Acts 9:16; 21:33

24 "But [a]I do not consider my life of any account as dear to
myself, so that I may [b]finish my course and [c]the ministry which
I received from the Lord Jesus, to [d]testify solemnly of the
gospel of [e]the grace of God.
25 "And now, behold, I know that all of you, among whom I
went about [a]preaching the kingdom, will no longer see my face.
26 "Therefore, I [1]testify to you this day that [a]I am [2]innocent of
the blood of all men.
27 "For I [a]did not shrink from declaring to you the whole
[b]purpose of God.
28 "Be on guard for yourselves and for all [a]the flock, among
which the Holy Spirit has made you [1]overseers, to shepherd [b]the
church of God which [c]He [2]purchased [3]with His own blood.
29 "I know that after my departure [a]savage wolves will come in
among you, not sparing [b]the flock;
30 and from among your own selves men will arise, speaking
perverse things, to draw away [a]the disciples after them.
31 "Therefore be on the alert, remembering that night and day
for a period of [a]three years I did not cease to admonish each one
[b]with tears.
32 "And now I [a]commend you to God and to [b]the word of His
grace, which is able to [c]build *you* up and to give *you* [d]the
inheritance among all those who are sanctified.
33 "[a]I have coveted no one's silver or gold or clothes.
34 "You yourselves know that [a]these hands ministered to my
own needs and to the [b]men who were with me.
35 "In everything I showed you that by working hard in this
manner you must help the weak and remember the words of
the Lord Jesus, that He Himself said, 'It is more blessed to give
than to receive.'"
36 When he had said these things, he [a]knelt down and prayed
with them all.
37 And [1]they *began* to weep aloud and [2a]embraced Paul, and
repeatedly kissed him,
38 [1]grieving especially over [a]the word which he had spoken,
that they would not see his face again. And they were
[b]accompanying him to the ship.

Chapter 21 Theme ______________________

21 When [a]we had parted from them and had set sail, we ran
[b]a straight course to Cos and the next day to Rhodes and
from there to Patara;
2 and having found a ship crossing over to [a]Phoenicia, we
went aboard and set sail.
3 When we came in sight of [a]Cyprus, leaving it on the left,
we kept sailing to [b]Syria and landed at [c]Tyre; for there the ship
was to unload its cargo.
4 After looking up [a]the disciples, we stayed there seven days;
and they kept telling Paul [1b]through the Spirit not to set foot in
Jerusalem.

24 [a]Acts 21:13 [b]Acts 13:25; 2 Tim 4:7 [c]Acts 1:17 [d]Luke 16:28; Acts 18:5; 20:21 [e]Acts 11:23; 20:32

25 [a]Matt 4:23; Acts 28:31

26 [1]Or *call you to witness* [2]Lit *pure from* [a]Acts 18:6

27 [a]Acts 20:20 [b]Acts 13:36

28 [1]Or *bishops* [2]Lit *acquired* [3]Lit *through* [a]Luke 12:32; John 21:15-17; Acts 20:29; 1 Pet 5:2f [b]Matt 16:18; Rom 16:16; 1 Cor 10:32 [c]Eph 1:7, 14; Titus 2:14; 1 Pet 1:19; 2:9; Rev 5:9

29 [a]Ezek 22:27; Matt 7:15 [b]Luke 12:32; John 21:15-17; Acts 20:28; 1 Pet 5:2f

30 [a]Acts 11:26

31 [a]Acts 19:8, 10; 24:17 [b]Acts 20:19

32 [a]Acts 14:23 [b]Acts 14:3; 20:24 [c]Acts 9:31 [d]Acts 26:18; Eph 1:14; 5:5; Col 1:12; 3:24; Heb 9:15; 1 Pet 1:4

33 [a]1 Cor 9:4-18; 2 Cor 11:7-12; 12:14-18; 1 Thess 2:5f

34 [a]Acts 18:3 [b]Acts 19:22

36 [a]Acts 9:40; 21:5; Luke 22:41

37 [1]Lit *a considerable weeping of all occurred* [2]Lit *threw themselves on Paul's neck* [a]Luke 15:20

38 [1]Lit *suffering pain* [a]Acts 20:25 [b]Acts 15:3

21:1 [a][we] Acts 16:10; 21:1-18 [b]Acts 16:11

2 [a]Acts 11:19; 21:3

3 [a]Acts 4:36; 21:16 [b]Matt 4:24 [c]Acts 12:20; 21:7

4 [1]I.e. because of impressions made by the Spirit [a]Acts 11:26; 21:16 [b]Acts 20:23; 21:11

5 When [1]our days there were ended, we left and started on
our journey, while they all, with wives and children, [a]escorted
us until *we were* out of the city. After [b]kneeling down on the
beach and praying, we said farewell to one another.
6 Then we went on board the ship, and they returned [a]home
again.
7 When we had finished the voyage from [a]Tyre, we arrived
at Ptolemais, and after greeting [b]the brethren, we stayed with
them for a day.
8 On the next day we left and came to [a]Caesarea, and
entering the house of [b]Philip the [c]evangelist, who was [b]one of
the seven, we stayed with him.
9 Now this man had four virgin daughters who were
[a]prophetesses.
10 As we were staying there for some days, a prophet named
[a]Agabus came down from Judea.
11 And coming to us, he [a]took Paul's belt and bound his own
feet and hands, and said, "This [b]is what the Holy Spirit says: 'In
this way the Jews at Jerusalem will [c]bind the man who owns
this belt and [d]deliver him into the hands of the Gentiles.'"
12 When we had heard this, we as well as the local residents
began begging him [a]not to go up to Jerusalem.
13 Then Paul answered, "What are you doing, weeping and
breaking my heart? For [a]I am ready not only to be bound, but
even to die at Jerusalem for [b]the name of the Lord Jesus."
14 And since he would not be persuaded, we fell silent,
remarking, "[a]The will of the Lord be done!"
15 After these days we got ready and [a]started on our way up to
Jerusalem.
16 *Some* of [a]the disciples from [b]Caesarea also came with us,
taking us to Mnason of [c]Cyprus, a [d]disciple of long standing
with whom we were to lodge.
17 After we arrived in Jerusalem, [a]the brethren received us
gladly.
18 And the following day Paul went in with us to [1a]James, and
all [b]the elders were present.
19 After he had greeted them, he [a]*began* to relate one by one
the things which God had done among the Gentiles through
his [b]ministry.
20 And when they heard it they *began* [a]glorifying God; and
they said to him, "You see, brother, how many [1]thousands
there are among the Jews of those who have believed, and they
are all [b]zealous for the Law;
21 and they have been told about you, that you are [a]teaching all
the Jews who are among the Gentiles to forsake Moses, telling
them [b]not to circumcise their children nor to [1]walk according
to [c]the customs.
22 "What, then, is *to be done?* They will certainly hear that
you have come.
23 "Therefore do this that we tell you. We have four men who
[1a]are under a vow;

5 [1]Lit *we had completed the days* [a]Acts 15:3 [b]Luke 22:41; Acts 9:40; 20:36
6 [a]John 19:27
7 [a]Acts 12:20; 21:3 [b]Acts 1:15; 21:17
8 [a]Acts 8:40; 21:16 [b]Acts 6:5; 8:5 [c]Eph 4:11; 2 Tim 4:5
9 [a]Luke 2:36; Acts 13:1; 1 Cor 11:5
10 [a]Acts 11:28
11 [a]1 Kin 22:11; Is 20:2; Jer 13:1-11; 19:1, 11; John 18 [b]Acts 8:29 [c]Acts 9:16; 21:33 [d]Matt 20:19
12 [a]Acts 21:15
13 [a]Acts 20:24 [b]Acts 5:41; 9:16
14 [a]Luke 22:42
15 [a]Acts 21:12
16 [a]Acts 21:4 [b]Acts 8:40 [c]Acts 4:36; 21:3 [d]Acts 15:7
17 [a]Acts 1:15; 21:7
18 [1]Or *Jacob* [a]Acts 12:17 [b]Acts 11:30
19 [a]Acts 14:27 [b]Acts 1:17
20 [1]Lit *ten thousands* [a]Matt 9:8 [b]Acts 15:1; 22:3; Rom 10:2; Gal 1:14
21 [1]I.e. observe or live by [a]Acts 21:28 [b]Acts 15:19ff; 1 Cor 7:18f [c]Acts 6:14
23 [1]Lit *have a vow on them* [a]Num 6:13-21; Acts 18:18

24 take them and [a]purify yourself along with them, and [1]pay their
expenses so that they may [b]shave their [2]heads; and all will know
that there is nothing to the things which they have been told about
you, but that you yourself also walk orderly, keeping the Law.
25 "But concerning the Gentiles who have believed, we wrote,
[a]having decided that they should abstain from [1]meat sacrificed
to idols and from blood and from what is strangled and from
fornication."
26 Then Paul [1]took the men, and the next day, [a]purifying
himself along with them, [b]went into the temple giving notice of
the completion of the days of purification, until the sacrifice
was offered for each one of them.
27 When [a]the seven days were almost over, [b]the Jews from
[1c]Asia, upon seeing him in the temple, *began* to stir up all the
crowd and laid hands on him,
28 crying out, "Men of Israel, come to our aid! [a]This is the
man who preaches to all men everywhere against our people
and the Law and this place; and besides he has even brought
Greeks into the temple and has [b]defiled this holy place."
29 For they had previously seen [a]Trophimus the [b]Ephesian in
the city with him, and they supposed that Paul had brought
him into the temple.
30 Then all the city was provoked, and [1]the people rushed
together, and taking hold of Paul they [a]dragged him out of the
temple, and immediately the doors were shut.
31 While they were seeking to kill him, a report came up to
the [1]commander of the [a]*Roman* [2]cohort that all Jerusalem was
in confusion.
32 At once he [a]took along *some* soldiers and centurions and
ran down to them; and when they saw the [1]commander and
the soldiers, they stopped beating Paul.
33 Then the [1]commander came up and took hold of him, and
ordered him to be [a]bound with [b]two chains; and he *began*
asking who he was and what he had done.
34 But among the crowd [a]some were shouting one thing *and*
some another, and when he could not find out the [1]facts because
of the uproar, he ordered him to be brought into [b]the barracks.
35 When he got to [a]the stairs, he was carried by the soldiers
because of the violence of the [1]mob;
36 for the multitude of the people kept following them, shouting,
"[a]Away with him!"
37 As Paul was about to be brought into [a]the barracks, he said
to the [1]commander, "May I say something to you?" And he *said,
"Do you know Greek?
38 "Then you are not [a]the Egyptian who some [1]time ago stirred
up a revolt and led the four thousand men of the Assassins out
[b]into the wilderness?"
39 But Paul said, "[a]I am a Jew of Tarsus in [b]Cilicia, a citizen of no
insignificant city; and I beg you, allow me to speak to the people."
40 When he had given him permission, Paul, standing on [a]the
stairs, [b]motioned to the people with his hand; and when there [1]was
a great hush, he spoke to them in the [2c]Hebrew dialect, saying,

24 [1]Lit *spend on them* [2]Lit *head* [a]John 11:55; Acts 21:26; 24:18 [b]Acts 18:18

25 [1]Lit *the thing* [a]Acts 15:19f, 29

26 [1]Or *took the men the next day, and purifying himself* [a]John 11:55; Acts 21:24; 24:18 [b]Num 6:13; Acts 24:18

27 [1]I.e. west coast province of Asia Minor [a]Num 6:9, 13-20 [b]Acts 20:19; 24:18 [c]Acts 16:6

28 [a]Acts 6:13 [b]Matt 24:15; Acts 6:13f; 24:6

29 [a]Acts 20:4 [b]Acts 18:19

30 [1]Lit *a running together of the people occurred* [a]2 Kin 11:15; Acts 16:19; 26:21

31 [1]I.e. chiliarch, in command of one thousand troops [2]Or *battalion* [a]Acts 10:1

32 [1]V 31, note 1 [a]Acts 23:27

33 [1]V 31, note 1 [a]Acts 20:23; 21:11; 22:29; 26:29; 28:20; Eph 6:20; 2 Tim 1:16; 2:9 [b]Acts 12:6

34 [1]Lit *certainty* [a]Acts 19:32 [b]Acts 21:37; 22:24; 23:10, 16, 32

35 [1]Lit *crowd* [a]Acts 21:40

36 [a]Luke 23:18; John 19:15; Acts 22:22

37 [1]V 31, note 1 [a]Acts 21:34; 22:24; 23:10, 16, 32

38 [1]Lit *days* [a]Acts 5:36 [b]Matt 24:26

39 [a]Acts 9:11; 22:3 [b]Acts 6:9

40 [1]Lit *occurred* [2]I.e. Jewish Aramaic [a]Acts 21:35 [b]Acts 12:17 [c]John 5:2; Acts 1:19; 22:2; 26:14

Chapter 22 Theme ______________________________

22 “[a]Brethren and fathers, hear my defense which I now
offer to you.”
2 And when they heard that he was addressing them in the
[1a]Hebrew dialect, they became even more quiet; and he *said,
3 “[a]I am [b]a Jew, born in [c]Tarsus of [d]Cilicia, but brought up in
this city, educated [1]under [e]Gamaliel, [2f]strictly according to the law
of our fathers, being zealous for God just as [g]you all are today.
4 “[a]I persecuted this [b]Way to the death, binding and putting
both men and women into prisons,
5 as also [a]the high priest and all [b]the Council of the elders
[1]can testify. From them I also [c]received letters to [d]the brethren,
and started off for [c]Damascus in order to bring even those who
were there to Jerusalem [2]as prisoners to be punished.
6 “[a]But it happened that as I was on my way, approaching
Damascus about noontime, a very bright light suddenly flashed
from heaven all around me,
7 and I fell to the ground and heard a voice saying to me,
‘Saul, Saul, why are you persecuting Me?’
8 “And I answered, ‘Who are You, Lord?’ And He said to me,
‘I am [a]Jesus the Nazarene, whom you are persecuting.’
9 “And those who were with me [a]saw the light, to be sure, but
[b]did not [1]understand the voice of the One who was speaking to me.
10 “And I said, ‘[a]What shall I do, Lord?’ And the Lord said to me,
‘Get up and go on into Damascus, and there you will be told of
all that has been appointed for you to do.’
11 “But since I [a]could not see because of the [1]brightness of that
light, I was led by the hand by those who were with me and
came into Damascus.
12 “A certain [a]Ananias, a man who was devout by the standard
of the Law, *and* [b]well spoken of by all the Jews who lived there,
13 came to me, and standing near said to me, ‘[a]Brother Saul,
receive your sight!’ And [1b]at that very time I looked up at him.
14 “And he said, ‘[a]The God of our fathers has [b]appointed you to
know His will and to [c]see the [d]Righteous One and to hear an
[1]utterance from His mouth.
15 ‘For you will be [a]a witness for Him to all men of [b]what you
have seen and heard.
16 ‘Now why do you delay? [a]Get up and be baptized, and
[b]wash away your sins, [c]calling on His name.’
17 “It happened when I [a]returned to Jerusalem and was praying
in the temple, that I [b]fell into a trance,
18 and I saw Him saying to me, ‘[a]Make haste, and get out of
Jerusalem quickly, because they will not accept your testimony
about Me.’
19 “And I said, ‘Lord, they themselves understand that in one
synagogue after another [a]I used to imprison and [b]beat those
who believed in You.
20 ‘And [a]when the blood of Your witness Stephen was being
shed, I also was standing by approving, and watching out for
the coats of those who were slaying him.’

22:1 [a]Acts 7:2
2 [1]I.e. Jewish Aramaic [a]Acts 21:40
3 [1]Lit *at the feet of* [2]Lit *according to the strictness of the ancestral law* [a]Acts 9:1-22; 22:3-16; 26:9-18 [b]Acts 21:39 [c]Acts 9:11 [d]Acts 6:9 [e]Acts 5:34 [f]Acts 23:6; 26:5; Phil 3:6 [g]Acts 21:20
4 [a]Acts 8:3; 22:19f; 26:9-11 [b]Acts 9:2
5 [1]Lit *testifies for me* [2]Lit *having been bound* [a]Acts 9:1 [b]Luke 22:66; Acts 5:21; 1 Tim 4:14 [c]Acts 9:2 [d]Acts 2:29; 3:17; 13:26; 23:1; 28:17, 21; Rom 9:3
6 [a]Acts 22:6-11: *Acts 9:3-8; 26:12-18*
8 [a]Acts 26:9
9 [1]Or *hear* (with comprehension) [a]Acts 26:13 [b]Acts 9:7
10 [a]Acts 16:30
11 [1]Lit *glory* [a]Acts 9:8
12 [a]Acts 9:10 [b]Acts 6:3; 10:22
13 [1]Or *instantly;* lit *at the very hour* [a]Acts 9:17 [b]Acts 9:18
14 [1]Or *message;* lit *voice* [a]Acts 3:13 [b]Acts 9:15; 26:16 [c]Acts 9:17; 26:16; 1 Cor 9:1; 15:8 [d]Acts 7:52
15 [a]Acts 23:11; 26:16 [b]Acts 22:14
16 [a]Acts 9:18 [b]Acts 2:38; 1 Cor 6:11; Eph 5:26; Heb 10:22 [c]Acts 7:59
17 [a]Acts 9:26; 26:20 [b]Acts 10:10
18 [a]Acts 9:29
19 [a]Acts 8:3; 22:4 [b]Matt 10:17; Acts 26:11
20 [a]Acts 7:58f; 8:1; 26:10

21 "And He said to me, 'Go! For I will send you far away [a]to
the Gentiles.'"
22 They listened to him up to this statement, and *then* they
raised their voices and said, "[a]Away with such a fellow from
the earth, for [b]he should not be allowed to live!"
23 And as they were crying out and [a]throwing off their cloaks
and [b]tossing dust into the air,
24 the [1]commander ordered him to be brought into [a]the
barracks, stating that he should be [b]examined by scourging so
that he might find out the reason why they were shouting
against him that way.
25 But when they stretched him out [1]with thongs, Paul said to
the centurion who was standing by, "Is it [2]lawful for you to
scourge [a]a man who is a Roman and uncondemned?"
26 When the centurion heard *this,* he went to the [1]commander
and told him, saying, "What are you about to do? For this man
is a Roman."
27 The [1]commander came and said to him, "Tell me, are you
a Roman?" And he said, "Yes."
28 The [1]commander answered, "I acquired this citizenship with
a large sum of money." And Paul said, "But I was actually born
a citizen."
29 Therefore those who were about to [a]examine him
immediately [1]let go of him; and the [2]commander also [b]was afraid
when he found out that he was a Roman, and because he had
[3c]put him in chains.
30 But on the next day, [a]wishing to know for certain why he
had been accused by the Jews, he [b]released him and ordered
the chief priests and all [c]the [1]Council to assemble, and brought
Paul down and set him before them.

Chapter 23 Theme ______________________

23 Paul, looking intently at [a]the [1]Council, said, "[b]Brethren,
[c]I have [2]lived my life with a perfectly good conscience
before God up to this day."
2 The high priest [a]Ananias commanded those standing
beside him [b]to strike him on the mouth.
3 Then Paul said to him, "God is going to strike you, [a]you
whitewashed wall! Do you [b]sit to try me according to the Law,
and in violation of the Law order me to be struck?"
4 But the bystanders said, "Do you revile God's high priest?"
5 And Paul said, "I was not aware, brethren, that he was high
priest; for it is written, '[a]YOU SHALL NOT SPEAK EVIL OF A RULER OF
YOUR PEOPLE.'"
6 But perceiving that one group were [a]Sadducees and the
other Pharisees, Paul *began* crying out in [b]the [1]Council,
"[c]Brethren, [d]I am a Pharisee, a son of Pharisees; I am on trial
for [e]the hope and resurrection of the dead!"
7 As he said this, there occurred a dissension between the
Pharisees and Sadducees, and the assembly was divided.

21 [a]Acts 9:15

22 [a]Acts 21:36; 1 Thess 2:16 [b]Acts 25:24

23 [a]Acts 7:58 [b]2 Sam 16:13

24 [1]I.e. chiliarch, in command of one thousand troops [a]Acts 21:34 [b]Acts 22:29

25 [1]Or *for the whip* [2]Interrogation by torture was a procedure used with slaves [a]Acts 16:37

26 [1]V 24, note 1

27 [1]V 24, note 1

28 [1]V 24, note 1

29 [1]Lit *withdrew from* [2]V 24, note 1 [3]Lit *bound him* [a]Acts 22:24 [b]Acts 16:38 [c]Acts 21:33

30 [1]Or *Sanhedrin* [a]Acts 23:28 [b]Acts 21:33 [c]Matt 5:22

23:1 [1]Or *Sanhedrin* [2]Or *conducted myself as a citizen* [a]Acts 22:30; 23:6, 15, 20, 28 [b]Acts 22:5 [c]Acts 24:16; 2 Cor 1:12; 2 Tim 1:3

2 [a]Acts 24:1 [b]John 18:22

3 [a]Matt 23:27 [b]Lev 19:15; Deut 25:2; John 7:51

5 [a]Ex 22:28

6 [1]Or *Sanhedrin* [a]Matt 3:7; 22:23 [b]Acts 22:30; 23:1, 15, 20, 28 [c]Acts 22:5 [d]Acts 26:5; Phil 3:5 [e]Acts 24:15, 21; 26:8

8 For [a]the Sadducees say that there is no resurrection, nor an
angel, nor a spirit, but the Pharisees acknowledge them all.
9 And there occurred a great uproar; and some of [a]the
scribes of the Pharisaic party stood up and *began* to argue
heatedly, saying, "[b]We find nothing wrong with this man;
[c]suppose a spirit or an angel has spoken to him?"
10 And as a great dissension was developing, the [1]commander
was afraid Paul would be torn to pieces by them and ordered
the troops to go down and take him away from them by force,
and bring him into [a]the barracks.
11 But on [a]the night *immediately* following, the Lord stood at
his side and said, "[b]Take courage; for [c]as you have [d]solemnly
witnessed to My cause at Jerusalem, so you must witness at
Rome also."
12 When it was day, [a]the Jews formed a [1]conspiracy and [b]bound
themselves under an oath, saying that they would neither eat
nor drink until they had killed Paul.
13 There were more than forty who formed this plot.
14 They came to the chief priests and the elders and said, "We
have [a]bound ourselves under a solemn oath to taste nothing
until we have killed Paul.
15 "Now therefore, you [1]and [a]the [2]Council notify the [3]commander
to bring him down to you, as though you were going to determine his case by a more thorough investigation; and we for our
part are ready to slay him before he comes near *the place.*"
16 But the son of Paul's sister heard of their ambush, [1]and he
came and entered [a]the barracks and told Paul.
17 Paul called one of the centurions to him and said, "Lead this
young man to the [1]commander, for he has something to report
to him."
18 So he took him and led him to the [1]commander and *said,
"Paul [a]the prisoner called me to him and asked me to lead this
young man to you since he has something to tell you."
19 The [1]commander took him by the hand and stepping aside,
began to inquire of him privately, "What is it that you have to
report to me?"
20 And he said, "[a]The Jews have agreed to ask you to bring
Paul down tomorrow to [b]the [1]Council, as though they were
going to inquire somewhat more thoroughly about him.
21 "So do not [1]listen to them, for more than forty of them are
[a]lying in wait for him who have [b]bound themselves under a
curse not to eat or drink until they slay him; and now they are
ready and waiting for the promise from you."
22 So the [1]commander let the young man go, instructing him,
"Tell no one that you have notified me of these things."
23 And he called to him two of the centurions and said, "Get
two hundred soldiers ready by [1]the third hour of the night to
proceed to [a]Caesarea, [2]with seventy horsemen and two hundred
[3]spearmen."
24 *They were* also to provide mounts to put Paul on and bring
him safely to [a]Felix the governor.

8 [a]Matt 22:23; Mark 12:18; Luke 20:27
9 [a]Mark 2:16; Luke 5:30 [b]Acts 23:29 [c]John 12:29; Acts 22:6ff
10 [1]I.e. chiliarch, in command of one thousand troops [a]Acts 21:34; 23:16, 32
11 [a]Acts 18:9 [b]Matt 9:2 [c]Acts 19:21 [d]Luke 16:28; Acts 28:23
12 [1]Or *mob* [a]Acts 9:23; 23:30; 1 Thess 2:16 [b]Acts 23:14, 21
14 [a]Acts 23:12, 21
15 [1]Lit *with* [2]Or *Sanhedrin* [3]V 10, note 1 [a]Acts 22:30; 23:1, 6, 20, 28
16 [1]Or *having been present* with them, *and he entered* [a]Acts 21:34; 23:10, 32
17 [1]V 10, note 1
18 [1]V 10, note 1 [a]Eph 3:1
19 [1]V 10, note 1
20 [1]Or *Sanhedrin* [a]Acts 23:14f [b]Acts 22:30; 23:1, 6, 15, 28
21 [1]Lit *be persuaded by them* [a]Acts 23:12, 14 [b]Luke 11:54
22 [1]V 10, note 1
23 [1]I.e. 9 p.m. [2]Lit *and* [3]Or *slingers* or *bowmen* [a]Acts 8:40; 23:33
24 [a]Acts 23:26, 33; 24:1, 3, 10; 25:14

25 And he wrote a letter having this form:
26 "Claudius Lysias, to the [a]most excellent governor Felix,
[b]greetings.
27 "When this man was arrested by the Jews and was about to
be slain by them, [a]I came up to them with the troops and
rescued him, [b]having learned that he was a Roman.
28 "And [a]wanting to ascertain the charge for which they were
accusing him, I [b]brought him down to their [1c]Council;
29 and I found him to be accused over [a]questions about
their Law, but [1]under [b]no accusation deserving death or
[2]imprisonment.
30 "When I was [a]informed that there would be [b]a plot against
the man, I sent him to you at once, also instructing [c]his
accusers to [1]bring charges against him before you."
31 So the soldiers, in accordance with their orders, took Paul
and brought him by night to Antipatris.
32 But the next day, leaving [a]the horsemen to go on with him,
they returned to [b]the barracks.
33 When these had come to [a]Caesarea and delivered the letter
to [b]the governor, they also presented Paul to him.
34 When he had read it, he asked from what [a]province he
was, and when he learned that [b]he was from Cilicia,
35 he said, "I will give you a hearing after your [a]accusers arrive
also," giving orders for him to be [b]kept in Herod's [1]Praetorium.

Chapter 24 Theme ____

24 After [a]five days the high priest [b]Ananias came down
with some elders, [1]with an [2]attorney *named* Tertullus,
and they [3]brought charges to [c]the governor against Paul.
2 After *Paul* had been summoned, Tertullus began to accuse
him, saying *to the governor,*
"Since we have through you attained much peace, and since
by your providence reforms are being carried out for this nation,
3 we acknowledge *this* in every way and everywhere, [a]most
excellent Felix, with all thankfulness.
4 "But, that I may not weary you any further, I beg you [1]to
grant us, by your kindness, a brief hearing.
5 "For we have found this man a real pest and a fellow who
stirs up dissension among all the Jews throughout [1]the world,
and a ringleader of the [a]sect of the Nazarenes.
6 "And he even tried to [a]desecrate the temple; and [1]then we
arrested him. [[2]We wanted to judge him according to our own
Law.
7 "But Lysias the commander came along, and with much
violence took him out of our hands,
8 ordering his accusers to come before you.] By examining
him yourself concerning all these matters you will be able to
ascertain the things of which we accuse him."
9 [a]The Jews also joined in the attack, asserting that these
things were so.

26 [a]Luke 1:3; Acts 24:3; 26:25 [b]Acts 15:23

27 [a]Acts 21:32f [b]Acts 22:25-29

28 [1]Or *Sanhedrin* [a]Acts 22:30 [b]Acts 23:10 [c]Acts 23:1

29 [1]Lit *having* [2]Lit *bonds* [a]Acts 18:15; 25:19 [b]Acts 23:9; 25:25; 26:31; 28:18

30 [1]Lit *speak against him* [a]Acts 23:20f [b]Acts 9:24; 23:12 [c]Acts 23:35; 24:19; 25:16

32 [a]Acts 23:23 [b]Acts 23:10

33 [a]Acts 8:40; 23:23 [b]Acts 23:24, 26; 24:1, 3, 10; 25:14

34 [a]Acts 25:1 [b]Acts 6:9; 21:39

35 [1]I.e. governor's official residence [a]Acts 23:30; 24:19; 25:16 [b]Acts 24:27

24:1 [1]Lit *and* [2]Lit *orator* [3]Or *presented their evidence* or *case* [a]Acts 24:11 [b]Acts 23:2 [c]Acts 23:24

3 [a]Acts 23:26; 26:25

4 [1]Lit *to hear . . . briefly*

5 [1]Lit *the inhabited earth* [a]Acts 15:5; 24:14

6 [1]Lit *also* [2]The early mss do not contain the remainder of v 6, v 7, nor the first part of v 8 [a]Acts 21:28

9 [a]1 Thess 2:16

also with confidence, since I am persuaded that none of these
things escape his notice; for this has not been done in a [2]corner.
27 "King Agrippa, do you believe the Prophets? I know that you
[1]do."
28 Agrippa *replied* to Paul, "[1]In a short time you [2]will persuade
me to [3]become a [a]Christian."
29 And Paul *said*, "[1]I would wish to God, that whether [2]in a
short or long time, not only you, but also all who hear me this
day, might become such as I am, except for these [a]chains."
30 [a]The king stood up and the governor and Bernice, and those
who were sitting with them,
31 and when they had gone aside, they *began* talking to one
another, saying, "[a]This man is not doing anything worthy of
death or [1]imprisonment."
32 And Agrippa said to Festus, "This man might have been [a]set
free if he had not [b]appealed to Caesar."

Chapter 27 Theme ______________________________

27 When it was decided that [a]we [b]would sail for [c]Italy, they
proceeded to deliver Paul and some other prisoners to a
centurion of the Augustan
[1d]cohort named Julius.
2 And embarking in an
Adramyttian ship, which was
about to sail to the regions
along the coast of [1a]Asia, we
put out to sea accompanied
by [b]Aristarchus, a [c]Macedonian of [d]Thessalonica.
3 The next day we put in
at [a]Sidon; and Julius [b]treated
Paul with consideration and
[c]allowed him to go to his
friends and receive care.

Paul Sails from Caesarea to Rome

4 From there we put out to sea and sailed under the shelter
of [a]Cyprus because [b]the winds were contrary.
5 When we had sailed through the sea along the coast of
[a]Cilicia and [b]Pamphylia, we landed at Myra in Lycia.
6 There the centurion found an [a]Alexandrian ship sailing for
[b]Italy, and he put us aboard it.
7 When we had sailed slowly for a good many days, and with
difficulty had arrived off Cnidus, [a]since the wind did not permit
us *to go* farther, we sailed under the shelter of [b]Crete, off Salmone;
8 and with difficulty [a]sailing past it we came to a place called
Fair Havens, near which was the city of Lasea.
9 When considerable time had passed and the voyage was
now dangerous, since even [a]the [1]fast was already over, Paul
began to admonish them,
10 and said to them, "Men, I perceive that the voyage will
certainly be with [a]damage and great loss, not only of the cargo
and the ship, but also of our lives."

26 [2]I.e. a hidden or secret place

27 [1]Lit *believe*

28 [1]Or *With a little* [2]Or *are trying to convince* [3]Lit *make* [a]Acts 11:26

29 [1]Or *I would pray to* [2]Or *with a little or with much* [a]Acts 21:33

30 [a]Acts 25:23

31 [1]Lit *bonds* [a]Acts 23:29

32 [a]Acts 28:18 [b]Acts 25:11

27:1 [1]Or *battalion* [a][we] Acts 16:10; 27:1-28 [b]Acts 25:12, 25 [c]Acts 18:2; 27:6 [d]Acts 10:1

2 [1]I.e. west coast province of Asia Minor [a]Acts 2:9 [b]Acts 19:29 [c]Acts 16:9 [d]Acts 17:1

3 [a]Matt 11:21 [b]Acts 27:43 [c]Acts 24:23

4 [a]Acts 4:36 [b]Acts 27:7

5 [a]Acts 6:9 [b]Acts 13:13

6 [a]Acts 28:11 [b]Acts 18:2; 27:1

7 [a]Acts 27:4 [b]Acts 2:11; 27:12f, 21; Titus 1:5, 12

8 [a]Acts 27:13

9 [1]I.e. Day of Atonement in September or October, which was a dangerous time of year for navigation [a]Lev 16:29-31; 23:27-29; Num 29:7

10 [a]Acts 27:21

11 But the centurion was more persuaded by the [a]pilot and
the [1]captain of the ship than by what was being said by Paul.
12 Because the harbor was not suitable for wintering, the
majority reached a decision to put out to sea from there, if
somehow they could reach Phoenix, a harbor of [a]Crete, facing
southwest and northwest, and spend the winter *there.*
13 [1]When a moderate south wind came up, supposing that
they had attained their purpose, they weighed anchor and
began [a]sailing along [b]Crete, close *inshore.*
14 But before very long there [a]rushed down from [1]the land a
violent wind, called [2]Euraquilo;
15 and when the ship was caught *in it* and could not face the
wind, we gave way *to it* and let ourselves be driven along.
16 Running under the shelter of a small island called Clauda,
we were scarcely able to get the *ship's* [1]boat under control.
17 After they had hoisted it up, they used [1]supporting cables
in undergirding the ship; and fearing that they might [a]run
aground on *the shallows* of Syrtis, they let down the [2]sea
anchor and in this way let themselves be driven along.
18 The next day as we were being violently storm-tossed, [1]they
began to [a]jettison the cargo;
19 and on the third day they threw the ship's tackle overboard
with their own hands.
20 Since neither sun nor stars appeared for many days, and no
small storm was assailing *us,* from then on all hope of our being
saved was gradually abandoned.
21 [1]When they had gone a long time without food, then Paul
stood up in their midst and said, "[a]Men, you ought to have
[2]followed my advice and not to have set sail from [b]Crete and
[3]incurred this [a]damage and loss.
22 "*Yet* now I urge you to [a]keep up your courage, for there will
be no loss of life among you, but *only* of the ship.
23 "For this very night [a]an angel of the God to whom I belong
and [b]whom I serve [c]stood before me,
24 saying, 'Do not be afraid, Paul; [a]you must stand before Caesar;
and behold, God has granted you [b]all those who are sailing
with you.'
25 "Therefore, [a]keep up your courage, men, for I believe God
that [1]it will turn out exactly as I have been told.
26 "But we must [a]run aground on a certain [b]island."
27 But when the fourteenth night came, as we were being
driven about in the Adriatic Sea, about midnight the sailors
began to surmise that [1]they were approaching some land.
28 They took soundings and found *it to be* twenty fathoms;
and a little farther on they took another sounding and found *it
to be* fifteen fathoms.
29 Fearing that we might [a]run aground somewhere on the [1]rocks,
they cast four anchors from the stern and [2]wished for daybreak.
30 But as the sailors were trying to escape from the ship and
had let down [a]the *ship's* boat into the sea, on the pretense of
intending to lay out anchors from the bow,

11 [1]Or *owner* [a]Rev 18:17

12 [a]Acts 2:11; 27:13, 21; Titus 1:5, 12

13 [1]Lit *a south wind having gently blown* [a]Acts 27:8 [b]Acts 2:11; 27:12f, 21; Titus 1:5, 12

14 [1]Lit *it* [2]I.e. a northeaster [a]Mark 4:37

16 [1]Or *skiff:* a small boat in tow or carried on board for emergency use, transportation to and from shore, etc.

17 [1]Lit *helps* [2]Or *gear* [a]Acts 27:26, 29

18 [1]Lit *they were doing a throwing out* [a]Jon 1:5; Acts 27:38

21 [1]Lit *there being much abstinence from food* [2]Lit *obeyed me* [3]Lit *gained* [a]Acts 27:10 [b]Acts 27:7

22 [a]Acts 27:25, 36

23 [a]Acts 5:19 [b]Rom 1:9 [c]Acts 18:9; 23:11; 2 Tim 4:17

24 [a]Acts 23:11 [b]Acts 27:31, 42, 44

25 [1]Lit *it will be* [a]Acts 27:22, 36

26 [a]Acts 27:17, 29 [b]Acts 28:1

27 [1]Lit *some land was approaching them*

29 [1]Lit *rough places* [2]Lit *they were praying for it to become day* [a]Acts 27:17, 26

30 [a]Acts 27:16

31 Paul said to the centurion and to the soldiers, "Unless these
men remain in the ship, you yourselves cannot be saved."
32 Then the soldiers cut away the [a]ropes of the *ship's* boat and
let it fall away.
33 Until the day was about to dawn, Paul was encouraging them
all to take some food, saying, "Today is the fourteenth day that
you have been constantly watching and going without eating,
having taken nothing.
34 "Therefore I encourage you to take some food, for this is for
your preservation, for [a]not a hair from the head of any of you
will perish."
35 Having said this, he took bread and [a]gave thanks to God in
the presence of all, and he broke it and began to eat.
36 All [a]of them [1]were encouraged and they themselves also took
food.
37 All of us in the ship were two hundred and seventy-six
[1a]persons.
38 When they had eaten enough, they *began* to lighten the
ship by [a]throwing out the wheat into the sea.
39 When day came, [a]they [1]could not recognize the land; but
they did observe a bay with a beach, and they resolved to drive
the ship onto it if they could.
40 And casting off [a]the anchors, they left them in the sea while at
the same time they were loosening the ropes of the rudders; and
hoisting the foresail to the wind, they were heading for the beach.
41 But striking a [1]reef where two seas met, they ran the vessel
aground; and the prow stuck fast and remained immovable, but
the stern *began* to be broken up by the force *of the waves.*
42 The soldiers' plan was to [a]kill the prisoners, so that none *of
them* would swim away and escape;
43 but the centurion, [a]wanting to bring Paul safely through,
kept them from their intention, and commanded that those
who could swim should [1]jump overboard first and get to land,
44 and the rest *should follow,* some on planks, and others on
various things from the ship. And so it happened that [a]they all
were brought safely to land.

Chapter 28 Theme

28 When [a]they had been brought safely through, [b]then we
found out that [c]the island was called [1]Malta.
2 [a]The [1]natives showed us extraordinary kindness; for because
of the rain that had set in and because of the cold, they kindled
a fire and [b]received us all.
3 But when Paul had gathered a bundle of sticks and laid
them on the fire, a viper came out [1]because of the heat and
fastened itself on his hand.
4 When [a]the [1]natives saw the creature hanging from his hand,
they *began* saying to one another, "[b]Undoubtedly this man is a
murderer, and though he has been saved from the sea, [2]justice
has not allowed him to live."

32 [a]John 2:15
34 [a]Matt 10:30
35 [a]Matt 14:19
36 [1]Lit *became cheerful* [a]Acts 27:22, 25
37 [1]Lit *souls* [a]Acts 2:41
38 [a]Jon 1:5; Acts 27:18
39 [1]Lit *were not recognizing* [a]Acts 28:1
40 [a]Acts 27:29
41 [1]Lit *place*
42 [a]Acts 12:19
43 [1]Lit *throw themselves* [a]Acts 27:3
44 [a]Acts 27:22, 31
28:1 [1]Or *Melita* [a][they] Acts 16:10; 27:1 [b]Acts 27:39 [c]Acts 27:26
2 [1]Lit *barbarians* [a]Acts 28:4; Rom 1:14; 1 Cor 14:11; Col 3:11 [b]Rom 14:1
3 [1]Or *from the heat*
4 [1]Lit *barbarians* [2]Or *Justice,* i.e. the personification of a goddess [a]Acts 28:2 [b]Luke 13:2, 4

5 However [a]he shook the creature off into the fire and
suffered no harm.
6 But they were expecting that he was about to swell up or
suddenly fall down dead. But after they had waited a long time
and had seen nothing unusual happen to him, they changed
their minds and [a]*began* to say that he was a god.
7 Now in the neighborhood of that place were lands belonging
to the leading man of the island, named Publius, who welcomed
us and entertained us courteously three days.
8 And it happened that the father of Publius was lying *in bed*
afflicted with *recurrent* fever and dysentery; and Paul went in
to see him and after he had [a]prayed, he [b]laid his hands on him
and healed him.
9 After this had happened, the rest of the people on the island
who had diseases were coming to him and getting cured.
10 They also honored us with many [1]marks of respect; and
when we were setting sail, they [2]supplied *us* with [3]all we needed.
11 At the end of three months we set sail on [a]an Alexandrian
ship which had wintered at the island, and which had [1]the
Twin Brothers for its figurehead.
12 After we put in at Syracuse, we stayed there for three days.
13 From there we sailed around and arrived at Rhegium, and a
day later a south wind sprang up, and on the second day we
came to Puteoli.
14 [1]There we found *some* [a]brethren, and were invited to stay
with them for seven days; and thus we came to Rome.
15 And the [a]brethren, when they heard about us, came from
there as far as the [1]Market of Appius and [2]Three Inns to meet us;
and when Paul saw them, he thanked God and took courage.
16 When we entered Rome, Paul was [a]allowed to stay by
himself, with the soldier who was guarding him.
17 After three days [1]Paul called together those who were [a]the
leading men of the Jews, and when they came together, he
began saying to them, "[b]Brethren, [c]though I had done nothing
against our people or [d]the customs of our [2]fathers, yet I was
delivered as a prisoner from Jerusalem into the hands of the
Romans.
18 "And when they had [a]examined me, they [b]were willing to
release me because there was [c]no ground [1]for putting me
to death.
19 "But when the Jews [1]objected, I was forced to [a]appeal to
Caesar, not that I had any accusation against my nation.
20 "For this reason, therefore, I [1]requested to see you and to
speak with you, for I am wearing [a]this chain for [b]the sake of
the hope of Israel."
21 They said to him, "We have neither received letters from
Judea concerning you, nor have any of [a]the brethren come
here and reported or spoken anything bad about you.
22 "But we desire to hear from you what [1]your views are; for
concerning this [a]sect, it is known to us that [b]it is spoken against
everywhere."

5 [a]Mark 16:18

6 [a]Acts 14:11

8 [a]Acts 9:40; James 5:14f [b]Matt 9:18; Mark 5:23; 6:5

10 [1]Lit *honors* [2]Or *put on board* [3]Lit *the things pertaining to the needs*

11 [1]Gr *the Dioscuri;* i.e. Castor and Pollux, twin sons of Zeus [a]Acts 27:6

14 [1]Lit *Where* [a]John 21:23; Acts 1:15; 6:3; 9:30; 28:15; Rom 1:13;

15 [1]Lat *Appii Forum,* a station about 43 miles from Rome [2]Lat *Tres Tabernae,* a station about 33 miles from Rome [a]Acts 1:15; 10:23; 11:1, 12, 29; 12:17

16 [a]Acts 24:23

17 [1]Lit *he* [2]Or *forefathers* [a]Acts 13:50; 25:2 [b]Acts 22:5 [c]Acts 25:8 [d]Acts 6:14

18 [1]Lit *of death in me* [a]Acts 22:24 [b]Acts 26:32 [c]Acts 23:29; 25:25; 26:31

19 [1]Lit *spoke against* [a]Acts 25:11, 21, 25; 26:32

20 [1]Or *invited you to see me and speak with me* [a]Acts 21:33 [b]Acts 26:6f

21 [a]Acts 3:17; 22:5; 28:14; Rom 9:3

22 [1]Lit *you think* [a]Acts 24:14 [b]1 Pet 2:12; 3:16; 4:14, 16

23 [a]Philem 22 [b]Luke 16:28; Acts 1:3; 23:11 [c]Acts 8:35

24 [a]Acts 14:4

26 [1]Lit *with a hearing* [2]Lit *and* [3]Lit *seeing you will see* [a]Is 6:9 [b]Matt 13:14f

27 [a]Is 6:10

28 [a]Ps 98:3; Luke 2:30; Acts 13:26 [b]Acts 9:15; 13:46

29 [1]Early mss do not contain this v

30 [1]Or *at his own expense*

31 [1]Or *proclaiming* [a]Matt 4:23; Acts 20:25; 28:23 [b]2 Tim 2:9

23 When they had set a day for Paul, they came to him at [a]his
lodging in large numbers; and he was explaining to them by
solemnly [b]testifying about the kingdom of God and trying to
persuade them concerning Jesus, [c]from both the Law of Moses
and from the Prophets, from morning until evening.
24 [a]Some were being persuaded by the things spoken, but
others would not believe.
25 And when they did not agree with one another, they *began*
leaving after Paul had spoken one *parting* word, "The Holy
Spirit rightly spoke through Isaiah the prophet to your fathers,
26 saying,

'[a]GO TO THIS PEOPLE AND SAY,
"[1][b]YOU WILL KEEP ON HEARING, [2]BUT WILL NOT UNDERSTAND;
AND [3]YOU WILL KEEP ON SEEING, BUT WILL NOT PERCEIVE;
27 [a]FOR THE HEART OF THIS PEOPLE HAS BECOME DULL,
AND WITH THEIR EARS THEY SCARCELY HEAR,
AND THEY HAVE CLOSED THEIR EYES;
OTHERWISE THEY MIGHT SEE WITH THEIR EYES,
AND HEAR WITH THEIR EARS,
AND UNDERSTAND WITH THEIR HEART AND RETURN,
AND I WOULD HEAL THEM."'

28 "Therefore let it be known to you that [a]this salvation of God
has been sent [b]to the Gentiles; they will also listen."
29 [[1]When he had spoken these words, the Jews departed,
having a great dispute among themselves.]
30 And he stayed two full years [1]in his own rented quarters
and was welcoming all who came to him,
31 [1][a]preaching the kingdom of God and teaching concerning
the Lord Jesus Christ [b]with all openness, unhindered.

Acts at a Glance

Theme of Acts:

Segment Divisions

			Chapter Themes
			1
			2
			3
			4
			5
			6
			7
			8
			9
			10
			11
			12
			13
			14
			15
			16
			17
			18
			19
			20
			21
			22
			23
			24
			25
			26
			27
			28

Author:

Date:

Purpose:

Key Words:

believe

baptized (baptism)

Holy Spirit

witness (witnesses)

word (word of God, scriptures)

gospel

saved

church

pray (praying, etc.)

raised from the dead (any reference to the resurrection)

His name (the name of Jesus)

any reference to persecution, suffering, affliction

repent (repentance)

ROMANS

The gospel Paul preached, justification by faith alone, was under siege. While many directly opposed this gospel, others twisted it to suit their own preferences. The Judaizers said salvation might be by grace but the believer is "kept" by the law. They insisted that circumcision was necessary for salvation. At the other extreme, the antinomians taught that you could be saved by grace and still live any way you wanted—even continue in sin.

Only a clear explanation of the gospel could refute such errors. Eager to prove the gospel's power to save and sanctify both Jew and Gentile, Paul, like a wise lawyer, calls the gospel to the witness stand and examines it from every angle. The result is the book of Romans, a theological masterpiece written around A.D. 56 or 57.

THINGS TO DO

1. Romans is the constitution of the Christian faith. If you understand Romans you will have a plumb line for correctly interpreting any teaching on the gospel. It is a book you need to observe over and over until you are so familiar with the text that its meaning is obvious.

   a. Ideally it would be helpful to read Romans in one sitting and color every reference to Paul. If that is not possible, read it a chapter at a time. Every time you see the word *gospel*, mark it in a distinctive way so you can easily spot it in the text.

   b. Paul gives his reasons for writing Romans in the first and the last two chapters. Record these reasons on the ROMANS OBSERVATIONS CHART on page 1846.

   c. Watch for and color every reference to the recipients that answers the "5 W's and an H" (who, what, when, where, why, and how). Record on the OBSERVATIONS CHART what you learn about them. Note whether Paul is writing to Gentiles, Jews, or both. Also record your insights about Paul on the same chart.

2. The book of Romans can be divided into five segments, each building on the previous one: chapters 1–3:20; 3:21–5; 6–8; 9–11; and 12–16. As you complete each segment, return to these instructions so you can see what you are to do.

3. Mark each of the following key words and their synonyms: *grace, faith, law, justified (justify, just), righteous (righteousness), wrath, judge (judgment), gospel, believe, sin, hope, Gentiles, Jesus Christ,* and *Spirit*. Mark references to time with a green clock 🕒. List these words on an index card to use as a bookmark when you study. Add the next group of key words to your card as you start a new section, marking the same way you plan to mark them in your Bible.

4. Watch for what *therefore*s are "there for" (don't miss Paul's points!).

Chapters 1–3:20

1. Read through Romans 1. As you mark the references to the gospel, list in your notebook all you learn about the gospel. Then note how Paul describes the unrighteousness of man. Mark *exchanged* and *God gave them over* and the events that follow.

2. In chapters 2–3:20, observe how Paul shows that all men—Jews and Gentiles—are under sin. Watch the references to the judgment of God.

3. Add the phrase *may it never be* to your key word list.

4. List in your notebook what you learn about sin, wrath, and the judgments of God.

5. From chapters 3 through 11 of Romans, Paul periodically asks an important question and then answers it. Mark each of Paul's questions. You might put a cloud like this ☁ around

each question throughout the book. Carefully read each question and note how Paul answers it.

6. When you finish observing each chapter, record the theme of that chapter in your Bible next to the chapter number and on the ROMANS AT A GLANCE chart on page 1847.

7. What do you see as the theme in this first segment of Romans? Write it (in pencil) on ROMANS AT A GLANCE in the first column under "Segment Divisions."

Chapters 3:21–5

Having established that "both Jews and Greeks [all people] are under sin" (3:9), Paul proceeds to show how God saves sinners.

1. As you read through these chapters, you will find words or phrases unique to each chapter. In chapter 4, mark *credited* and note what you learn from marking it. In chapter 5, mark and observe *death (die, died)* and *gift.*

2. List what you learn from marking key words like *righteousness* and *justified.*

3. Once again record your chapter themes on the ROMANS AT A GLANCE chart. Also write out the theme of this segment of Romans. You may want to do it in pencil to begin with.

Chapters 6–8

1. Follow the same procedure as you did in the previous segment. Add the following words and their synonyms: *flesh, life, reign, master, slaves,* and *freed from sin.*

2. Make a list of everything you learn from marking *law* and *Spirit.*

3. Mark Paul's questions and, in your notebook, list the main points of his answers.

4. Record the theme of each chapter and of this segment as you did before.

5. The ROMANS OBSERVATIONS CHART on page 1846 includes a place to record everything you learn from chapters 5 through 8 regarding our position in Adam (before we were saved) and our position in Christ (after we were saved). Do not read anything into the text; simply record what you learn.

Chapters 9–11

1. Follow the same pattern you used in the first segment and mark the same key words you marked in chapters 1 through 8. Also mark the following key words in this segment of Romans: *covenant (promise), foreknew,* predestined,* choice (chosen), Israel* (and its pronouns), *unbelief, saved (salvation*—go back and mark it in Romans 1:16), and *mercy.*

*These words are used in Romans 8:29-30. Go back and mark them, and in your notebook record what you learn from the text.

2. In this section it is critical that you follow Paul's reasoning by marking each question that he poses along with the main points of his answers. Do not read into the text meanings that aren't there. Simply let God speak as you listen. Meditate on Romans 11:33-36.

3. Record chapter and segment themes as before.

Chapters 12–16

1. At this point Paul makes a transition from explaining the doctrinal aspect of the gospel to describing how the gospel is to be lived out practically. As Paul turns from doctrine to duty, note the *therefore* (12:1) and how it relates to what has been written in the first 11 chapters of Romans. Think about what Paul is asking you to do. Is it reasonable? Why? What do you need to do?

2. Read Romans chapters 12 through 16 and identify the main topic or subject of each chapter. Also, mark the following: *love, authority (rulers), brethren (brother), Lord, Gentiles, minister (service, serving, servant), judge (judgment),* and *weak (weaknesses).*

3. Complete ROMANS AT A GLANCE. Fill in the chapter themes and segment divisions and then record the theme of Romans. (Do not forget to record your chapter themes in your Bible, too.)

Things to Think About

1. From your study of Romans, how is a person saved? Write this out.

2. Suppose someone accused you of not being a Christian. What proof could you give of the fact that you are a true child of God?

3. Do you know how to share the gospel with someone? Outline or write your testimony, incorporating the gospel into it.

4. How will your relationships to those in authority over you and to those who are your brothers and sisters in the faith change as you apply the truth of Romans to your life?

5. Are you ready to defend the gospel? Can you refute modern-day Judaizers and/or Antinomians?

Chapter 1 Theme ____________________

1 Paul, a bond-servant of Christ Jesus, [1a]called *as* an apostle,
[b]set apart for [c]the gospel of God,
2 which He [a]promised beforehand through His [b]prophets in
the holy Scriptures,
3 concerning His Son, who was born [a]of a [1]descendant of
David [b]according to the flesh,
4 who was declared [a]the Son of God with power [1]by the
resurrection from the dead, according to the [2]Spirit of holiness,
Jesus Christ our Lord,
5 through whom we have received grace and [a]apostleship [1]to
bring about *the* [b]obedience of faith among [c]all the Gentiles for
His name's sake,
6 among whom you also are the [a]called of Jesus Christ;
7 to all who are [a]beloved of God in Rome, called *as* [1b]saints:
[c]Grace to you and peace from God our Father and the Lord
Jesus Christ.
8 First, [a]I thank my God through Jesus Christ [1]for you all,
because [b]your faith is being proclaimed throughout the whole
world.
9 For [a]God, whom I [b]serve in my spirit in the *preaching of*
the gospel of His Son, is my witness *as to* how unceasingly [c]I
make mention of you,
10 always in my prayers making request, if perhaps now at
last by [a]the will of God I may succeed in coming to you.
11 For [a]I long to see you so that I may impart some spiritual
gift to you, that you may be [1]established;
12 that is, that I may be encouraged together with you *while*
among you, each of us by the other's faith, both yours and
mine.
13 [a]I do not want you to be unaware, [b]brethren, that often I
[c]have planned to come to you (and have been prevented so far) so

1:1 [1]Lit *a called apostle* [a]1 Cor 1:1; 9:1; 2 Cor 1:1 [b]Acts 9:15; 13:2; Gal 1:15 [c]Mark 1:14; Rom 15:16
2 [a]Titus 1:2 [b]Luke 1:70; Rom 3:21; 16:26
3 [1]Lit *seed* [a]Matt 1:1 [b]John 1:14; Rom 4:1; 9:3, 5; 1 Cor 10:18
4 [1]Or *as a result of* [2]Or *spirit* [a]Matt 4:3
5 [1]Lit *for obedience* [a]Acts 1:25; Gal 1:16 [b]Acts 6:7; Rom 16:26 [c]Acts 9:15
6 [a]Jude 1; Rev 17:14
7 [1]Or *holy ones* [a]Rom 5:5ff; 8:39 [b]Acts 9:13; Rom 8:28ff; 1 Cor 1:2, 24 [c]Num 6:25f; 1 Cor 1:3; 2 Cor 1:2; Gal 1:3; Eph 1:2; Phil 1:2; Col 1:2; 1 Thess 1:1; 2 Thess 1:2
8 [1]Or *concerning you all, that...* [a]1 Cor 1:4; Eph 1:15f; Phil 1:3f; Col 1:3f; 1 Thess 1:2; 2:13 [b]Acts 28:22; Rom 16:19
9 [a]Rom 9:1 [b]Acts 24:14; 2 Tim 1:3 [c]Eph 1:16; Phil 1:3f
10 [a]Acts 18:21; Rom 15:32
11 [1]Or *strengthened* [a]Acts 19:21; Rom 15:23
13 [a]Rom 11:25; 1 Cor 10:1; 12:1; 2 Cor 1:8; 1 Thess 4:13 [b]Acts 1:15; Rom 7:1; 1 Cor 1:10; 14:20, 26; Gal 3:15 [c]Acts 19:21; Rom 15:22f

INSIGHT

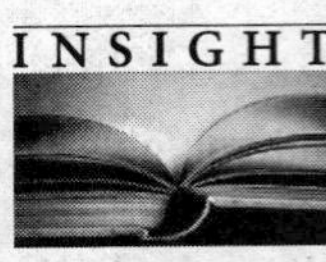

See the map on page 1800.

that I may obtain some [d]fruit among you also, even as among
the rest of the Gentiles.
14 [a]I am [1]under obligation both to Greeks and to [b]barbarians,
both to the wise and to the foolish.
15 So, for my part, I am eager to [a]preach the gospel to you also
who are in Rome.
16 For I am not [a]ashamed of the gospel, for [b]it is the power of
God for salvation to everyone who believes, to the [c]Jew first
and also to [d]the Greek.
17 For in it [a]*the* righteousness of God is revealed [1]from faith to
faith; as it is written, "[2b]BUT THE RIGHTEOUS *man* SHALL LIVE BY FAITH."
18 For [a]the wrath of God is revealed from heaven against all
ungodliness and unrighteousness of men who [b]suppress the
truth [1]in unrighteousness,
19 because [a]that which is known about God is evident [1]within
them; for God made it evident to them.
20 For [a]since the creation of the world His invisible attributes,
His eternal power and divine nature, have been clearly seen,
[b]being understood through what has been made, so that they
are without excuse.
21 For even though they knew God, they did not [1]honor Him
as God or give thanks, but they became [a]futile in their
speculations, and their foolish heart was darkened.
22 [a]Professing to be wise, they became fools,
23 and [a]exchanged the glory of the incorruptible God for an
image in the form of corruptible man and of birds and four-
footed animals and [1]crawling creatures.
24 Therefore [a]God gave them over in the lusts of their hearts to
impurity, so that their bodies would be [b]dishonored among them.
25 For they exchanged the truth of God for [1]a [a]lie, and
worshiped and served the creature rather than the Creator,
[b]who is blessed [2]forever. Amen.
26 For this reason [a]God gave them over to [b]degrading passions;
for their women exchanged the natural function for that which
is [1]unnatural,
27 and in the same way also the men abandoned the natural
function of the woman and burned in their desire toward one
another, [a]men with men committing [1]indecent acts and
receiving in [2]their own persons the due penalty of their error.
28 And just as they did not see fit [1]to acknowledge God any
longer, [a]God gave them over to a depraved mind, to do those
things which are not proper,
29 being filled with all unrighteousness, wickedness, greed,
evil; full of envy, murder, strife, deceit, malice; *they are* [a]gossips,
30 slanderers, [1a]haters of God, insolent, arrogant, boastful,
inventors of evil, [b]disobedient to parents,
31 without understanding, untrustworthy, [a]unloving, unmerciful;
32 and although they know the ordinance of God, that those
who practice such things are worthy of [a]death, they not only
do the same, but also [b]give hearty approval to those who
practice them.

13 [d]John 4:36; 15:16; Phil 1:22; Col 1:6

14 [1]Lit *debtor* [a]1 Cor 9:16 [b]Acts 28:2

15 [a]Rom 15:20

16 [a]Mark 8:38; 2 Tim 1:8, 12, 16 [b]1 Cor 1:18, 24 [c]Acts 3:26; Rom 2:9 [d]John 7:35

17 [1]Or *by* [2]Or *But he who is righteous by faith shall live* [a]Rom 3:21; 9:30; Phil 3:9 [b]Hab 2:4; Gal 3:11; Heb 10:38

18 [1]Or *by* [a]Rom 5:9; Eph 5:6; Col 3:6 [b]2 Thess 2:6f

19 [1]Or *among* [a]Acts 14:17; 17:24ff

20 [a]Mark 10:6 [b]Job 12:7-9; Ps 19:1-6; Jer 5:21f

21 [1]Lit *glorify* [a]2 Kin 17:15; Jer 2:5; Eph 4:17f

22 [a]Jer 10:14; 1 Cor 1:20

23 [1]Or *reptiles* [a]Deut 4:16-18; Ps 106:20; Jer 2:11; Acts 17:29

24 [a]Rom 1:26, 28; Eph 4:19 [b]Eph 2:3

25 [1]Lit *the lie* [2]Lit *unto the ages* [a]Is 44:20; Jer 10:14; 13:25; 16:19 [b]Rom 9:5; 2 Cor 11:31

26 [1]Lit *against nature* [a]Rom 1:24 [b]1 Thess 4:5

27 [1]Lit *the shameless deed* [2]Lit *themselves* [a]Lev 18:22; 20:13; 1 Cor 6:9

28 [1]Lit *to have God in knowledge* [a]Rom 1:24

29 [a]2 Cor 12:20

30 [1]Or *hateful to God* [a]Ps 5:5 [b]2 Tim 3:2

31 [a]2 Tim 3:3

32 [a]Rom 6:21 [b]Luke 11:48; Acts 8:1; 22:20

Chapter 2 Theme ______________________________

2 Therefore you have [a]no excuse, [1b]everyone of you who
passes judgment, for in that which [c]you judge another, you
condemn yourself; for you who judge practice the same things.
2 And we know that the judgment of God [1]rightly falls upon
those who practice such things.
3 But do you suppose this, [a]O man, [1]when you pass judgment
on those who practice such things and do the same *yourself,*
that you will escape the judgment of God?
4 Or do you think lightly of [a]the riches of His [b]kindness and
[c]tolerance and [d]patience, not knowing that the kindness of God
leads you to repentance?
5 But [1]because of your stubbornness and unrepentant heart
[a]you are storing up wrath for yourself [b]in the day of wrath and
revelation of the righteous judgment of God,
6 [a]who WILL RENDER TO EACH PERSON ACCORDING TO HIS DEEDS:
7 to those who by [a]perseverance in doing good seek for
[b]glory and honor and [c]immortality, [d]eternal life;
8 but to those who are [a]selfishly ambitious and [b]do not obey
the truth, but obey unrighteousness, wrath and indignation.
9 *There will be* [a]tribulation and distress [1]for every soul of
man who does evil, of the Jew [b]first and also of the Greek,
10 but [a]glory and honor and peace to everyone who does
good, to the Jew [b]first and also to the Greek.
11 For [a]there is no partiality with God.
12 For all who have sinned [1a]without the Law will also perish
[1]without the Law, and all who have sinned [2]under the Law will
be judged [3]by the Law;
13 for *it is* [a]not the hearers [1]of the Law *who* are [2]just before
God, but the doers [1]of the Law will be justified.
14 For when Gentiles who do not have [1]the Law do
[2a]instinctively the things of the Law, these, not having [1]the
Law, are a law to themselves,
15 in that they show [a]the work of the Law written in their
hearts, their conscience bearing witness and their thoughts
alternately accusing or else defending them,
16 on the day when, [a]according to my gospel, [b]God will judge
the secrets of men through Christ Jesus.
17 But if you bear the name "Jew" and [a]rely [1]upon the Law
and boast in God,
18 and know *His* will and [1a]approve the things that are
essential, being instructed out of the Law,
19 and are confident that you yourself are a guide to the blind,
a light to those who are in darkness,
20 a [1]corrector of the foolish, a teacher of [2]the immature, having
in the Law [a]the embodiment of knowledge and of the truth,
21 you, therefore, [a]who teach another, do you not teach
yourself? You who [1]preach that one shall not steal, do you steal?

2:1 [1]Lit *O man, everyone who* [a]Rom 1:20 [b]Luke 12:14; Rom 2:3; 9:20 [c]2 Sam 12:5-7; Matt 7:1; Luke 6:37; Rom 14:22
2 [1]Lit *is according to truth against*
3 [1]Lit *who passes judgment* [a]Luke 12:14; Rom 2:1; 9:20
4 [a]Rom 9:23; 11:33; 2 Cor 8:2; Eph 1:7, 18; 2:7; Phil 4:19; Col 1:27; 2:2; Titus 3:6 [b]Rom 11:22 [c]Rom 3:25 [d]Ex 34:6; Rom 9:22; 1 Tim 1:16; 1 Pet 3:20; 2 Pet 3:9, 15
5 [1]Or *in accordance with* [a]Deut 32:34f; Prov 1:18 [b]Ps 110:5; 2 Cor 5:10; 2 Thess 1:5; Jude 6
6 [a]Ps 62:12; Prov 24:12; Matt 16:27
7 [a]Luke 8:15; Heb 10:36 [b]Rom 2:10; Heb 2:7; 1 Pet 1:7 [c]1 Cor 15:42, 50, 53f; Eph 6:24; 2 Tim 1:10 [d]Matt 25:46
8 [a]2 Cor 12:20; Gal 5:20; Phil 1:17; 2:3; James 3:14, 16 [b]2 Thess 2:12
9 [1]Lit *upon* [a]Rom 8:35 [b]Acts 3:26; Rom 1:16; 1 Pet 4:17
10 [a]Rom 2:7; Heb 2:7; 1 Pet 1:7 [b]Rom 2:9
11 [a]Deut 10:17; Acts 10:34
12 [1]Or *without law* [2]Or *under law* [3]Or *by law* [a]Acts 2:23; 1 Cor 9:21
13 [1]Or *of law* [2]Or *righteous* [a]Matt 7:21, 24ff; John 13:17; James 1:22f, 25
14 [1]Or *law* [2]Lit *by nature* [a]Acts 10:35; Rom 1:19; 2:15
15 [a]Rom 2:14, 27
16 [a]Rom 16:25; 1 Cor 15:1; Gal 1:11; 1 Tim 1:11; 2 Tim 2:8 [b]Acts 10:42; 17:31; Rom 3:6; 14:10
17 [1]Or *upon law* [a]Mic 3:11; John 5:45; Rom 2:23; 9:4
18 [1]Or *distinguish between the things which differ* [a]Phil 1:10

20 [1]Or *instructor* [2]Lit *infants* [a]Rom 3:31; 2 Tim 1:13
21 [1]Or *proclaim* [a]Matt 23:3ff

22 You who say that one should not commit adultery, do you
commit adultery? You who abhor idols, do you [a]rob temples?
23 You who [a]boast [1]in the Law, through your breaking the
Law, do you dishonor God?
24 For "[a]THE NAME OF GOD IS BLASPHEMED AMONG THE GENTILES
[b]BECAUSE OF YOU," just as it is written.
25 For indeed circumcision is of value if you [a]practice [1]the Law;
but if you are a transgressor [2]of the Law, [b]your circumcision
has become uncircumcision.
26 [a]So if [b]the [1]uncircumcised man [c]keeps the requirements of
the Law, will not his uncircumcision be regarded as circumcision?
27 And [a]he who is physically uncircumcised, if he keeps the
Law, will he not [b]judge you who [1]though having the letter *of*
the Law and circumcision are a transgressor [2]of the Law?
28 For [a]he is not a Jew who is one outwardly, nor is
circumcision that which is outward in the flesh.
29 But [a]he is a Jew who is one inwardly; and [b]circumcision is
that which is of the heart, by the [c]Spirit, not by the letter; [d]and
his praise is not from men, but from God.

Chapter 3 Theme ______________________________

3 Then what [1]advantage has the Jew? Or what is the benefit
of circumcision?
2 Great in every respect. First of all, that [a]they were entrusted
with the [b]oracles of God.
3 What then? If [a]some [1]did not believe, their [2]unbelief will
not nullify the faithfulness of God, will it?
4 [a]May it never be! Rather, let God be found true, though
every man *be found* [b]a liar, as it is written,
"[c]THAT YOU MAY BE JUSTIFIED IN YOUR WORDS,
AND PREVAIL WHEN YOU [1]ARE JUDGED."
5 But if our unrighteousness [1a]demonstrates the righteousness of God, [b]what shall we say? The God who inflicts wrath is
not unrighteous, is He? ([c]I am speaking in human terms.)
6 [a]May it never be! For otherwise, how will [b]God judge the
world?
7 But if through my lie [a]the truth of God abounded to His
glory, [b]why am I also still being judged as a sinner?
8 And why not *say* (as we are slanderously reported and as
some claim that we say), "[a]Let us do evil that good may come"?
[1]Their condemnation is just.
9 What then? [1a]Are we better than they? Not at all; for we have
already charged that both [b]Jews and [c]Greeks are [d]all under sin;
10 as it is written,
"[a]THERE IS NONE RIGHTEOUS, NOT EVEN ONE;
11 THERE IS NONE WHO UNDERSTANDS,
THERE IS NONE WHO SEEKS FOR GOD;
12 ALL HAVE TURNED ASIDE, TOGETHER THEY HAVE BECOME USELESS;
THERE IS NONE WHO DOES GOOD,
THERE IS NOT EVEN ONE."

22 [a]Acts 19:37
23 [1]Or *in law* [a]Mic 3:11; John 5:45; Rom 2:17; 9:4
24 [a]Is 52:5; Ezek 36:20ff [b]2 Pet 2:2
25 [1]Or *law* [2]Or *of law* [a]Rom 2:13f, 27 [b]Jer 4:4; 9:25f
26 [1]Lit *uncircumcision* [a]1 Cor 7:19 [b]Rom 3:30; Eph 2:11 [c]Rom 2:25, 27; 8:4
27 [1]Lit *through the letter* [2]Or *of law* [a]Rom 3:30; Eph 2:11 [b]Matt 12:41
28 [a]John 8:39; Rom 2:17; 9:6; Gal 6:15
29 [a]Phil 3:3; Col 2:11 [b]Deut 30:6 [c]Rom 2:27; 7:6; 2 Cor 3:6 [d]John 5:44; 12:43; 1 Cor 4:5; 2 Cor 10:18
3:1 [1]Lit *is the advantage of the Jew*
2 [a]Deut 4:8; Ps 147:19; Rom 9:4 [b]Acts 7:38
3 [1]Or *were unfaithful* [2]Or *unfaithfulness* [a]Rom 10:16; Heb 4:2
4 [1]Lit *in Your judging* [a]Luke 20:16; Rom 3:6, 31 [b]Ps 116:11; Rom 3:7 [c]Ps 51:4
5 [1]Or *commends* [a]Rom 5:8; 2 Cor 6:4; 7:11 [b]Rom 4:1; 7:7; 8:31; 9:14, 30 [c]Rom 6:19; 1 Cor 9:8; 15:32; Gal 3:15
6 [a]Luke 20:16; Rom 3:4, 31 [b]Rom 2:16
7 [a]Rom 3:4 [b]Rom 9:19
8 [1]Lit *Whose* [a]Rom 6:1
9 [1]Or *Are we worse* [a]Rom 3:1 [b]Rom 2:1-29 [c]Rom 1:18-32 [d]Rom 3:19, 23; 11:32; Gal 3:22
10 [a]Ps 14:1-3; 53:1-3

13 "[a]THEIR THROAT IS AN OPEN GRAVE,
WITH THEIR TONGUES THEY KEEP DECEIVING,"
"[b]THE POISON OF ASPS IS UNDER THEIR LIPS";
14 "[a]WHOSE MOUTH IS FULL OF CURSING AND BITTERNESS";
15 "[a]THEIR FEET ARE SWIFT TO SHED BLOOD,
16 DESTRUCTION AND MISERY ARE IN THEIR PATHS,
17 AND THE PATH OF PEACE THEY HAVE NOT KNOWN."
18 "[a]THERE IS NO FEAR OF GOD BEFORE THEIR EYES."
19 Now we know that whatever the [a]Law says, it speaks to
[b]those who are [1]under the Law, so that every mouth may be
closed and [c]all the world may become accountable to God;
20 because [a]by the works [1]of the Law no flesh will be justified
in His sight; for [2b]through the Law *comes* the knowledge of
sin.
21 But now apart [1]from the Law [a]*the* righteousness of God has
been manifested, being [b]witnessed by the Law and the Prophets,
22 even *the* [a]righteousness of God through [b]faith [c]in Jesus
Christ for [d]all those [1]who believe; for [e]there is no distinction;
23 for all [1a]have sinned and fall short of the glory of God,
24 being justified as a gift [a]by His grace through [b]the redemption
which is in Christ Jesus;
25 whom God displayed publicly as [a]a [1]propitiation [2b]in His
blood through faith. *This was* to demonstrate His righteousness, [3]because in the [c]forbearance of God He [d]passed over the
sins previously committed;
26 for the demonstration, *I say,* of His righteousness at the
present time, so that He would be just and the justifier of the
one who [1]has faith in Jesus.
27 Where then is [a]boasting? It is excluded. By [b]what kind of
law? Of works? No, but by a law of faith.
28 [1]For [a]we maintain that a man is justified by faith apart from
works [2]of the Law.
29 Or [a]is God *the God* of Jews only? Is He not *the God* of
Gentiles also? Yes, of Gentiles also,
30 since indeed [a]God [b]who will justify the [1]circumcised [2]by
faith and the [3]uncircumcised through faith [c]is one.
31 Do we then nullify [1]the Law through faith? [a]May it never
be! On the contrary, we [b]establish the Law.

Chapter 4 Theme ______________________

4 What then shall we say that Abraham, [1]our forefather [a]ac-
cording to the flesh, has found?
2 For if Abraham was justified [1]by works, he has something
to boast about, but [a]not [2]before God.
3 For what does the Scripture say? "[a]ABRAHAM BELIEVED GOD,
AND IT WAS CREDITED TO HIM AS RIGHTEOUSNESS."
4 Now to the one who [a]works, his wage is not credited as a
favor, but as what is due.
5 But to the one who does not work, but [a]believes in Him
who justifies the ungodly, his faith is credited as righteousness,

13 [a]Ps 5:9 [b]Ps 140:3
14 [a]Ps 10:7
15 [a]Is 59:7f
18 [a]Ps 36:1
19 [1]Lit *in* [a]John 10:34 [b]Rom 2:12 [c]Rom 3:9
20 [1]Or *of law* [2]Or *through law* [a]Ps 143:2; Acts 13:39; Gal 2:16 [b]Rom 4:15; 5:13, 20; 7:7
21 [1]Or *from law* [a]Rom 1:17; 9:30 [b]Acts 10:43; Rom 1:2
22 [1]Or *who believe. For there is no distinction, since they all have sinned . . . and are being justified* [a]Rom 1:17; 9:30 [b]Rom 4:5 [c]Acts 3:16; Gal 2:16, 20; 3:22; Eph 3:12 [d]Rom 4:11, 16; 10:4 [e]Rom 10:12; Gal 3:28; Col 3:11
23 [1]Or *sinned* [a]Rom 3:9
24 [a]Rom 4:4f, 16; Eph 2:8 [b]1 Cor 1:30; Eph 1:7; Col 1:14; Heb 9:15
25 [1]Or *a propitiatory sacrifice* [2]Or *by* [3]Lit *because of the passing over of the sins previously committed in the forbearance of God* [a]1 John 2:2; 4:10 [b]1 Cor 5:7; Heb 9:14, 28; 1 Pet 1:19; Rev 1:5 [c]Rom 2:4 [d]Acts 14:16; 17:30
26 [1]Lit *is of the faith of Jesus*
27 [a]Rom 2:17, 23; 4:2; 1 Cor 1:29ff [b]Rom 9:31
28 [1]One early ms reads *Therefore* [2]Or *of law* [a]Acts 13:39; Rom 3:20, 21; Eph 2:9; James 2:20, 24, 26
29 [a]Acts 10:34f; Rom 9:24; 10:12; 15:9; Gal 3:28
30 [1]Lit *circumcision* [2]Lit *out of* [3]Lit *uncircumcision* [a]Rom 10:12; Gal 3:20 [b]Rom 3:22; 4:11f, 16; Gal 3:8 [c]Deut 6:4
31 [1]Or *law* [a]Luke 20:16; Rom 3:4 [b]Matt 5:17; Rom 3:4, 6; 8:4
4:1 [1]Or *our forefather, has found according to the flesh* [a]Rom 1:3
2 [1]Lit *out of* [2]Lit *toward* [a]1 Cor 1:31
3 [a]Gen 15:6; Rom 4:9, 22; Gal 3:6; James 2:23
4 [a]Rom 11:6
5 [a]John 6:29; Rom 3:22

6 just as David also speaks of the blessing on the man to
whom God credits righteousness apart from works:
7 "[a]BLESSED ARE THOSE WHOSE LAWLESS DEEDS HAVE BEEN FORGIVEN,
AND WHOSE SINS HAVE BEEN COVERED.
8 "[a]BLESSED IS THE MAN WHOSE SIN THE LORD WILL NOT [b]TAKE
INTO ACCOUNT."
9 Is this blessing then on [1a]the circumcised, or on [2]the
uncircumcised also? For [b]we say, "[c]FAITH WAS CREDITED TO
ABRAHAM AS RIGHTEOUSNESS."
10 How then was it credited? While he was [1]circumcised, or
[2]uncircumcised? Not while [1]circumcised, but while [2]uncir-
cumcised;
11 and he [a]received the sign of circumcision, [b]a seal of the
righteousness of the faith which [1]he had while uncircumcised,
so that he might be [c]the father of [d]all who believe without
being circumcised, that righteousness might be credited to
them,
12 and the father of circumcision to those who not only are of
the circumcision, but who also follow in the steps of the faith
of our father Abraham which [1]he had while uncircumcised.
13 For [a]the promise to Abraham or to his [1]descendants [b]that
he would be heir of the world was not [2]through the Law, but
through the righteousness of faith.
14 For [a]if those who are [1]of the Law are heirs, faith is made
void and the promise is nullified;
15 for [a]the Law brings about wrath, but [b]where there is no
law, there also is no violation.
16 For this reason *it is* [1]by faith, in order that *it may be* in
accordance with [a]grace, so that the promise will be guaranteed
to [b]all the [2]descendants, not only to [3]those who are of the Law,
but also to [3c]those who are of the faith of Abraham, who is [d]the
father of us all,
17 (as it is written, "[a]A FATHER OF MANY NATIONS HAVE I MADE
YOU") in the presence of Him whom he believed, *even* God,
[b]who gives life to the dead and [1c]calls into being [d]that which
does not exist.
18 In hope against hope he believed, so that he might become
[a]a father of many nations according to that which had been
spoken, "[b]SO SHALL YOUR [1]DESCENDANTS BE."
19 Without becoming weak in faith he contemplated his own
body, now [a]as good as dead since [b]he was about a hundred
years old, and [c]the deadness of Sarah's womb;
20 yet, with respect to the promise of God, he did not waver
in unbelief but grew strong in faith, [a]giving glory to God,
21 and [a]being fully assured that [b]what God had promised, He
was able also to perform.
22 Therefore [a]IT WAS ALSO CREDITED TO HIM AS RIGHTEOUSNESS.
23 Now [a]not for his sake only was it written that it was
credited to him,
24 but for our sake also, to whom it will be credited, as those
[a]who believe in Him who [b]raised Jesus our Lord from the dead,

7 [a]Ps 32:1

8 [a]Ps 32:2 [b]2 Cor 5:19

9 [1]Lit *circumcision* [2]Lit *uncircumcision* [a]Rom 3:30 [b]Rom 4:3 [c]Gen 15:6

10 [1]Lit *in circumcision* [2]Lit *in uncircumcision*

11 [1]Lit *was in uncircumcision* [a]Gen 17:10f [b]John 3:33 [c]Luke 19:9; Rom 4:16f [d]Rom 3:22; 4:16

12 [1]Lit *was in uncircumcision*

13 [1]Lit *seed* [2]Or *through law* [a]Rom 9:8; Gal 3:16, 29 [b]Gen 17:4-6; 22:17f

14 [1]Or *of law* [a]Gal 3:18

15 [a]Rom 7:7, 10-25; 1 Cor 15:56; Gal 3:10 [b]Rom 3:20

16 [1]Or *out of* [2]Lit *seed* [3]Lit *that which is* [a]Rom 3:24 [b]Rom 4:11; 9:8; 15:8 [c]Gal 3:7 [d]Luke 19:9; Rom 4:11

17 [1]Lit *calls the things which do not exist as existing* [a]Gen 17:5 [b]John 5:21 [c]Is 48:13; 51:2 [d]1 Cor 1:28

18 [1]Lit *seed* [a]Rom 4:17 [b]Gen 15:5

19 [a]Heb 11:12 [b]Gen 17:17 [c]Gen 18:11

20 [a]Matt 9:8

21 [a]Rom 14:5 [b]Gen 18:14; Heb 11:19

22 [a]Gen 15:6; Rom 4:3

23 [a]Rom 15:4; 1 Cor 9:9f; 10:11; 2 Tim 3:16f

24 [a]Rom 10:9; 1 Pet 1:21 [b]Acts 2:24

25 *He* who was [a]delivered over because of our transgressions,
and was [b]raised because of our justification.

Chapter 5 Theme ______________________________

5 [a]Therefore, having been justified by faith, [1b]we have peace
with God through our Lord Jesus Christ,
2 through whom also we have [a]obtained our introduction by
faith into this grace [b]in which we stand; and [1]we exult in hope
of the glory of God.
3 [a]And not only this, but [1]we also [b]exult in our tribulations,
knowing that tribulation brings about [c]perseverance;
4 and [a]perseverance, [b]proven character; and proven character,
hope;
5 and hope [a]does not disappoint, because the love of God has
been [b]poured out within our hearts through the Holy Spirit
who was given to us.
6 For while we were still [a]helpless, [b]at the right time [c]Christ
died for the ungodly.
7 For one will hardly die for a righteous man; [1]though
perhaps for the good man someone would dare even to die.
8 But God [a]demonstrates [b]His own love toward us, in that
while we were yet sinners, [c]Christ died for us.
9 Much more then, having now been justified [1a]by His blood,
we shall be saved [b]from the wrath *of God* through Him.
10 For if while we were [a]enemies we were reconciled to God
through the death of His Son, much more, having been
reconciled, we shall be saved [1b]by His life.
11 [a]And not only this, [1]but we also exult in God through our
Lord Jesus Christ, through whom we have now received [b]the
reconciliation.
12 Therefore, just as through [a]one man sin entered into the
world, and [b]death through sin, and [c]so death spread to all men,
because all sinned—
13 for [1]until the Law sin was in the world, but [a]sin is not
imputed when there is no law.
14 Nevertheless death reigned from Adam until Moses, even
over those who had not sinned [a]in the likeness of the offense of
Adam, who is a [1b]type of Him who was to come.
15 But [1]the free gift is not like the transgression. For if by the
transgression of [a]the one [b]the many died, much more did the
grace of God and the gift by [c]the grace of the one Man, Jesus
Christ, abound to the many.
16 The gift is not like *that which came* through the one who
sinned; for on the one hand [a]the judgment *arose* from one
transgression [1]resulting in condemnation, but on the other
hand the free gift *arose* from many transgressions [2]resulting in
justification.
17 For if by the transgression of the one, death reigned
[a]through the one, much more those who receive the abundance
of grace and of the gift of righteousness will [b]reign in life
through the One, Jesus Christ.

25 [a]Is 53:4, 5; Rom 5:6, 8; 8:32; Gal 2:20; Eph 5:2 [b]Rom 5:18; 1 Cor 15:17; 2 Cor 5:15
5:1 [1]Two early mss read *let us have* [a]Rom 3:28 [b]Rom 5:11
2 [1]Or *let us exult* [a]Eph 2:18; 3:12; Heb 10:19f; 1 Pet 3:18 [b]1 Cor 15:1
3 [1]Or *let us also exult* [a]Rom 5:11; 8:23; 9:10; 2 Cor 8:19 [b]Matt 5:12; James 1:2f [c]Luke 21:19
4 [a]Luke 21:19 [b]Phil 2:22; James 1:12
5 [a]Ps 119:116; Rom 9:33; Heb 6:18f [b]Acts 2:33; 10:45; Gal 4:6; Titus 3:6
6 [a]Rom 5:8, 10 [b]Gal 4:4 [c]Rom 4:25; 5:8; 8:32; Gal 2:20; Eph 5:2
7 [1]Lit *for*
8 [a]Rom 3:5 [b]John 3:16; 15:13; Rom 8:39 [c]Rom 4:25; 5:6; 8:32; Gal 2:20; Eph 5:2
9 [1]Or *in* [a]Rom 3:25 [b]Rom 1:18; 1 Thess 1:10
10 [1]Or *in* [a]Rom 11:28; 2 Cor 5:18f; Eph 2:3; Col 1:21f [b]Rom 8:34; Heb 7:25; 1 John 2:1
11 [1]Lit *but also exulting* [a]Rom 5:3; 8:23; 9:10; 2 Cor 8:19 [b]Rom 5:10; 11:15; 2 Cor 5:18f
12 [a]Gen 2:17; 3:6, 19; Rom 5:15-17; 1 Cor 15:21f [b]Rom 6:23; 1 Cor 15:56; James 1:15 [c]Rom 5:14, 19, 21; 1 Cor 15:22
13 [1]Or *until law* [a]Rom 4:15
14 [1]Or *foreshadowing* [a]Hos 6:7 [b]1 Cor 15:45
15 [1]Lit *not as the transgression, so also is the free gift* [a]Rom 5:12, 18, 19 [b]Rom 5:19 [c]Acts 15:11
16 [1]Lit *to condemnation* [2]Lit *to an act of righteousness* [a]1 Cor 11:32
17 [a]Gen 2:17; 3:6, 19; Rom 5:12, 15, 16; 1 Cor 15:21f [b]2 Tim 2:12; Rev 22:5

18 So then as through [a]one transgression [1]there resulted condemnation to all men, even so through one [b]act of righteousness [2]there resulted [c]justification of life to all men.

19 For as through the one man's disobedience [a]the many [b]were made sinners, even so through [c]the obedience of the One [a]the many will be made righteous.

20 [1a]The Law came in so that the transgression would increase; but where sin increased, [b]grace abounded all the more,

21 so that, as [a]sin reigned in death, even so [b]grace would reign through righteousness to eternal life through Jesus Christ our Lord.

Chapter 6 Theme ______________________

6 [a]What shall we say then? Are we to [b]continue in sin so that grace may increase?

2 [a]May it never be! How shall we who [b]died to sin still live in it?

3 Or do you not know that all of us who have been [a]baptized into [b]Christ Jesus have been baptized into His death?

4 Therefore we have been [a]buried with Him through baptism into death, so that as Christ was [b]raised from the dead through the [c]glory of the Father, so we too might walk in [d]newness of life.

5 For [a]if we have become [1]united with *Him* in the likeness of His death, certainly we shall also be [2]*in the likeness* of His resurrection,

6 knowing this, that our [a]old [1]self was [b]crucified with *Him,* in order that our [c]body of sin might be [2]done away with, so that we would no longer be slaves to sin;

7 for [a]he who has died is [1]freed from sin.

8 Now [a]if we have died with Christ, we believe that we shall also live with Him,

9 knowing that Christ, having been [a]raised from the dead, [1]is never to die again; [b]death no longer is master over Him.

10 For the death that He died, He died to sin once for all; but the life that He lives, He lives to God.

11 Even so consider yourselves to be [a]dead to sin, but alive to God in Christ Jesus.

12 Therefore do not let sin [a]reign in your mortal body so that you obey its lusts,

13 and do not go on [a]presenting [1]the members of your body to sin *as* [2]instruments of unrighteousness; but [b]present yourselves to God as those alive from the dead, and your members *as* [2]instruments of righteousness to God.

14 For [a]sin shall not [b]be master over you, for [c]you are not under law but [d]under grace.

15 What then? [a]Shall we sin because we are not under law but under grace? [b]May it never be!

16 Do you not [a]know that when you present yourselves to someone *as* [b]slaves for obedience, you are slaves of the one

18 [1]Lit *to condemnation* [2]Lit *to justification* [a]Rom 5:12, 15 [b]Rom 3:25 [c]Rom 4:25

19 [a]Rom 5:15, 18 [b]Rom 5:12; 11:32 [c]Phil 2:8

20 [1]Or *law* [a]Rom 3:20; 7:7f; Gal 3:19 [b]Rom 6:1; 1 Tim 1:14

21 [a]Rom 5:12, 14 [b]John 1:17; Rom 6:23

6:1 [a]Rom 3:5 [b]Rom 3:8; 6:15

2 [a]Luke 20:16; Rom 6:15 [b]Rom 6:11; 7:4, 6; Gal 2:19; Col 2:20; 3:3; 1 Pet 2:24

3 [a]Matt 28:19 [b]Acts 2:38; 8:16; 19:5; Gal 3:27

4 [a]Col 2:12 [b]Acts 2:24; Rom 6:9 [c]John 11:40; 2 Cor 13:4 [d]Rom 7:6; 2 Cor 5:17; Gal 6:15; Eph 4:23f; Col 3:10

5 [1]Or *united with the likeness* [2]Or *with* [a]2 Cor 4:10; Phil 3:10f; Col 2:12; 3:1

6 [1]Gr *anthropos* [2]Or *made powerless* [a]Eph 4:22; Col 3:9 [b]Gal 2:20; 5:24; 6:14 [c]Rom 7:24

7 [1]Or *acquitted* [a]1 Pet 4:1

8 [a]Rom 6:4; 2 Cor 4:10; 2 Tim 2:11

9 [1]Lit *no longer dies* [a]Acts 2:24; Rom 6:4 [b]Rev 1:18

11 [a]Rom 6:2; 7:4, 6; Gal 2:19; Col 2:20; 3:3; 1 Pet 2:24

12 [a]Rom 6:14

13 [1]Lit *your members to sin* [2]Or *weapons* [a]Rom 6:16, 19; 7:5; Col 3:5 [b]Rom 12:1; 2 Cor 5:14f; 1 Pet 2:24

14 [a]Rom 8:2, 12 [b]Rom 6:12 [c]Rom 5:18; 7:4, 6; Gal 4:21 [d]Rom 5:17, 21

15 [a]Rom 6:1 [b]Luke 20:16; Rom 6:2

16 [a]Rom 11:2; 1 Cor 3:16; 5:6; 6:2, 3, 9, 15, 16, 19; 9:13, 24 [b]John 8:34; 2 Pet 2:19

whom you obey, either of [c]sin [1]resulting in death, or of
obedience [2]resulting in righteousness?
17 But [a]thanks be to God that [1]though you were slaves of sin,
you became obedient from the heart to that [b]form of teaching
to which you were committed,
18 and having been [a]freed from sin, you became slaves of
righteousness.
19 [a]I am speaking in human terms because of the weakness of
your flesh. For just [b]as you presented your members as slaves to
impurity and to lawlessness, [1]resulting in *further* lawlessness,
so now present your members as slaves to righteousness,
[2]resulting in sanctification.
20 For [a]when you were slaves of sin, you were free in regard
to righteousness.
21 Therefore what [1a]benefit were you then [2]deriving [3]from
the things of which you are now ashamed? For the outcome of
those things is [b]death.
22 But now having been [a]freed from sin and [b]enslaved to God,
you [1]derive your [2c]benefit, [3]resulting in sanctification, and [d]the
outcome, eternal life.
23 For the wages of [a]sin is death, but the free gift of God is
[b]eternal life in Christ Jesus our Lord.

Chapter 7 Theme

7 Or do you not know, [a]brethren (for I am speaking to those
who know the law), that the law has jurisdiction over a
person as long as he lives?
2 For [a]the married woman is bound by law to her [1]husband
while he is living; but if her husband dies, she is released from
the law [2]concerning the husband.
3 So then, if while her husband is living she is joined to
another man, she shall be called an adulteress; but if her
husband dies, she is free from the law, so that she is not an
adulteress though she is joined to another man.
4 Therefore, my brethren, you also were [a]made to die [b]to the
Law [c]through the body of Christ, so that you might be joined to
another, to Him who was raised from the dead, in order that
we might bear fruit for God.
5 For while we were [a]in the flesh, the sinful passions, which
were [b]*aroused* by the Law, were at work [c]in [1]the members of
our body to bear fruit for death.
6 But now we have been [a]released from the Law, having
[b]died to that by which we were bound, so that we serve in
[c]newness of [d]the [1]Spirit and not in oldness of the letter.
7 [a]What shall we say then? Is the Law sin? [b]May it never be!
On the contrary, [c]I would not have come to know sin except
[1]through the Law; for I would not have known about [2]coveting
if the Law had not said, "[d]YOU SHALL NOT [2]COVET."
8 But sin, [a]taking opportunity [b]through the commandment,
produced in me [1]coveting of every kind; for [c]apart [2]from the
Law sin *is* dead.

16 [1]Lit *to death* [2]Lit *to righteousness* [c]Rom 6:21, 23

17 [1]Lit *you were slaves . . . but you became* [a]Rom 1:8; 2 Cor 2:14 [b]2 Tim 1:13

18 [a]John 8:32; Rom 6:22; 8:2

19 [1]Lit *to lawlessness* [2]Lit *to sanctification* [a]Rom 3:5 [b]Rom 6:13

20 [a]Matt 6:24; Rom 6:16

21 [1]Lit *fruit* [2]Lit *having* [3]Lit *in* [a]Jer 12:13; Ezek 16:63; Rom 7:5 [b]Rom 1:32; 5:12; 6:16, 23; 8:6, 13; Gal 6:8

22 [1]Lit *have* [2]Lit *fruit* [3]Lit *to sanctification* [a]John 8:32; Rom 6:18; 8:2 [b]1 Cor 7:22; 1 Pet 2:16 [c]Rom 7:4 [d]1 Pet 1:9

23 [a]Rom 1:32; 5:12; 6:16, 21; 8:6, 13; Gal 6:8 [b]Matt 25:46; Rom 5:21; 8:38, 39

7:1 [a]Rom 1:13

2 [1]Lit *living husband* [2]Lit *of* [a]1 Cor 7:39

4 [a]Rom 6:2; 7:6 [b]Rom 8:2; Gal 2:19; 5:18 [c]Col 1:22

5 [1]Lit *our members to bear* [a]Rom 8:8f; 2 Cor 10:3 [b]Rom 7:7f [c]Rom 6:13, 21, 23

6 [1]Or *spirit* [a]Rom 7:2 [b]Rom 6:2 [c]Rom 6:4 [d]Rom 2:29

7 [1]Or *through law* [2]Or *lust* [a]Rom 3:5 [b]Luke 20:16 [c]Rom 3:20; 4:15; 5:20 [d]Ex 20:17; Deut 5:21

8 [1]Or *lust* [2]Or *from law* [a]Rom 7:11 [b]Rom 3:20; 7:11 [c]1 Cor 15:56

9 I was once alive apart [1]from the Law; but when the
commandment came, sin became alive and I died;
10 and this commandment, which was [1a]to result in life,
proved [2]to result in death for me;
11 for sin, [a]taking an opportunity [b]through the commandment,
[c]deceived me and through it killed me.
12 [a]So then, the Law is holy, and the commandment is holy
and righteous and good.
13 Therefore did that which is good become *a cause of* death
for me? [a]May it never be! Rather it was sin, in order that it
might be shown to be sin by effecting my death through that
which is good, so that through the commandment sin would
become utterly sinful.
14 For we know that the Law is [a]spiritual, but I am [a]of flesh,
[b]sold [1c]into bondage to sin.
15 For what I am doing, [a]I do not understand; for I am not
practicing [b]what I *would* like to *do,* but I am doing the very
thing I hate.
16 But if I do the very thing I do not want *to do,* I agree with
[a]the Law, *confessing* that the Law is good.
17 So now, [a]no longer am I the one doing it, but sin which
dwells in me.
18 For I know that nothing good dwells in me, that is, in my
[a]flesh; for the willing is present in me, but the doing of the
good *is* not.
19 For [a]the good that I want, I do not do, but I practice the
very evil that I do not want.
20 But if I am doing the very thing I do not want, [a]I am no
longer the one doing it, but sin which dwells in me.
21 I find then [a]the [1]principle that evil is present in me, the
one who wants to do good.
22 For I joyfully concur with the law of God [1]in [a]the inner man,
23 but I see [a]a different law in [1]the members of my body,
waging war against the [b]law of my mind and making me a
prisoner [2]of [c]the law of sin which is in my members.
24 Wretched man that I am! Who will set me free from [1a]the
body of this [b]death?
25 [a]Thanks be to God through Jesus Christ our Lord! So then,
on the one hand I myself with my mind am serving the law of
God, but on the other, with my flesh [b]the law of sin.

Chapter 8 Theme ____

8 Therefore there is now no [a]condemnation for those who
are [b]in [c]Christ Jesus.
2 For [a]the law of the Spirit of life [1]in [b]Christ Jesus [c]has set
you free from the law of sin and of death.
3 For [a]what the Law could not do, [1b]weak as it was through
the flesh, God *did:* sending His own Son in [c]the likeness of
[2]sinful flesh and *as an offering* for sin, He condemned sin in
the flesh,

9 [1]Or *from law*

10 [1]Lit *to life* [2]Lit *to death* [a]Lev 18:5; Luke 10:28; Rom 10:5; Gal 3:12

11 [a]Rom 7:8 [b]Rom 3:20; 7:8 [c]Gen 3:13

12 [a]Rom 7:16; 1 Tim 1:8

13 [a]Luke 20:16

14 [1]Lit *under sin* [a]1 Cor 3:1 [b]1 Kin 21:20, 25; 2 Kin 17:17; Rom 6:6; Gal 4:3 [c]Rom 3:9

15 [a]John 15:15 [b]Rom 7:19; Gal 5:17

16 [a]Rom 7:12; 1 Tim 1:8

17 [a]Rom 7:20

18 [a]John 3:6; Rom 7:25; 8:3

19 [a]Rom 7:15

20 [a]Rom 7:17

21 [1]Lit *law* [a]Rom 7:23, 25; 8:2

22 [1]Or *concerning* [a]2 Cor 4:16; Eph 3:16; 1 Pet 3:4

23 [1]Lit *my members* [2]Lit *in* [a]Rom 6:19; Gal 5:17; James 4:1; 1 Pet 2:11 [b]Rom 7:25 [c]Rom 7:21, 25; 8:2

24 [1]Or *this body of death* [a]Rom 6:6; Col 2:11 [b]Rom 8:2

25 [a]1 Cor 15:57 [b]Rom 7:21, 23; 8:2

8:1 [a]Rom 5:16; 8:34 [b]Rom 8:9f [c]Rom 8:2, 11, 39; 16:3

2 [1]Or *has set you free in Christ Jesus* [a]1 Cor 15:45 [b]Rom 8:1, 11, 39; 16:3 [c]John 8:32, 36; Rom 6:14, 18; 7:4

3 [1]Lit *in which it was weak* [2]Lit *flesh of sin* [a]Acts 13:39; Heb 10:1ff [b]Rom 7:18f; Heb 7:18 [c]Phil 2:7; Heb 2:14, 17; 4:15

4 so that the [a]requirement of the Law might be fulfilled in us,
who [b]do not walk according to the flesh but according to the
Spirit.
5 For those who are according to the flesh set their minds on
[a]the things of the flesh, but those who are according to the
Spirit, [b]the things of the Spirit.
6 [a]For the mind set on the flesh is [b]death, but the mind set
on the Spirit is life and peace,
7 because the mind set on the flesh is [a]hostile toward God;
for it does not subject itself to the law of God, for it is not even
able *to do so,*
8 and those who are [a]in the flesh cannot please God.
9 However, you are not [a]in the flesh but in the Spirit, if
indeed the Spirit of God [b]dwells in you. But [c]if anyone does not
have the Spirit of Christ, he does not belong to Him.
10 [a]If Christ is in you, though the body is dead because of sin,
yet the spirit is [1]alive because of righteousness.
11 But if the Spirit of Him who [a]raised Jesus from the dead
dwells in you, [b]He who raised [c]Christ Jesus from the dead will
also give life to your mortal bodies [1]through His Spirit who
dwells in you.
12 So then, brethren, we are under obligation, not to the
flesh, to live according to the flesh—
13 for [a]if you are living according to the flesh, you [1]must die;
but if by the Spirit you are [b]putting to death the deeds of the
body, you will live.
14 For all who are [a]being led by the Spirit of God, these are
[b]sons of God.
15 For you [a]have not received a spirit of slavery [1]leading to
fear again, but you [b]have received [2]a spirit of adoption as sons
by which we cry out, "[c]Abba! Father!"
16 The Spirit Himself [a]testifies with our spirit that we are
[b]children of God,
17 and if children, [a]heirs also, heirs of God and fellow heirs
with Christ, [b]if indeed we suffer with *Him* so that we may also
be glorified with *Him.*
18 For I consider that the sufferings of this present time [a]are not
worthy to be compared with the [b]glory that is to be revealed to us.
19 For the [a]anxious longing of the creation waits eagerly for
[b]the revealing of the [c]sons of God.
20 For the creation [a]was subjected to [b]futility, not willingly,
but [c]because of Him who subjected it, [1]in hope
21 that [a]the creation itself also will be set free from its slavery
to corruption into the freedom of the glory of the children of
God.
22 For we know that the whole creation [a]groans and suffers
the pains of childbirth together until now.
23 [a]And not only this, but also we ourselves, having [b]the first
fruits of the Spirit, even we ourselves [c]groan within ourselves,
[d]waiting eagerly for *our* adoption as sons, [e]the redemption of
our body.

4 [a]Luke 1:6; Rom 2:26 [b]Gal 5:16, 25
5 [a]Gal 5:19-21 [b]Gal 5:22-25
6 [a]Gal 6:8 [b]Rom 6:21; 8:13
7 [a]James 4:4
8 [a]Rom 7:5
9 [a]Rom 7:5 [b]John 14:23; Rom 8:11; 1 Cor 3:16; 6:19; 2 Cor 6:16; Gal 4:6; Phil 1:19; 2 Tim 1:14; 1 John 4:13 [c]John 14:17
10 [1]Lit *life* [a]John 17:23; Gal 2:20; Eph 3:17; Col 1:27
11 [1]One early ms reads *because of* [a]Acts 2:24; Rom 6:4 [b]John 5:21 [c]Rom 8:1, 2, 39; 16:3
13 [1]Or *are going to* [a]Rom 8:6 [b]Col 3:5
14 [a]Gal 5:18 [b]Hos 1:10; Matt 5:9; John 1:12; Rom 8:16, 19; 9:8, 26; 2 Cor 6:18; Gal 3:26; 1 John 3:1; Rev 21:7
15 [1]Lit *for fear again* [2]Or *the Spirit* [a]2 Tim 1:7; Heb 2:15 [b]Rom 8:23; Gal 4:5f [c]Mark 14:36; Gal 4:6
16 [a]Acts 5:32 [b]Hos 1:10; Matt 5:9; John 1:12; Rom 8:14, 19; 9:8, 26; 2 Cor 6:18; Gal 3:26; 1 John 3:1; Rev 21:7
17 [a]Acts 20:32; Gal 3:29; 4:7; Eph 3:6; Titus 3:7; Heb 1:14; Rev 21:7 [b]2 Cor 1:5, 7; Phil 3:10; Col 1:24; 2 Tim 2:12; 1 Pet 4:13
18 [a]2 Cor 4:17; 1 Pet 4:13 [b]Col 3:4; Titus 2:13; 1 Pet 1:5; 5:1
19 [a]Phil 1:20 [b]Rom 8:18; 1 Cor 1:7f; Col 3:4; 1 Pet 1:7, 13; 1 John 3:2 [c]Hos 1:10; Matt 5:9; John 1:12; Rom 8:14, 16; 9:8, 26; 2 Cor 6:18; Gal 3:26; 1 John 3:1; Rev 21:7
20 [1]Or *in hope; because the creation* [a]Gen 3:17-19 [b]Ps 39:5f; Eccl 1:2 [c]Gen 3:17; 5:29
21 [a]Acts 3:21; 2 Pet 3:13; Rev 21:1
22 [a]Jer 12:4, 11
23 [a]Rom 5:3 [b]Rom 8:16; 2 Cor 1:22 [c]2 Cor 5:2, 4 [d]Rom 8:15, 19, 25; Gal 5:5 [e]Rom 7:24

24 For [a]in hope we have been saved, but [b]hope that is seen is
not hope; for who hopes for what he *already* sees?
25 But [a]if we hope for what we do not see, with perseverance
we wait eagerly for it.
26 In the same way the Spirit also helps our weakness; for
[a]we do not know how to pray as we should, but [b]the Spirit
Himself intercedes for *us* with groanings too deep for words;
27 and [a]He who searches the hearts knows what [b]the mind of
the Spirit is, because He [c]intercedes for the [1]saints according to
the will of God.
28 And we know that [1]God causes [a]all things to work together
for good to those who love God, to those who are [b]called
according to *His* purpose.
29 For those whom He [a]foreknew, He also [b]predestined *to*
become [c]conformed to the image of His Son, so that He would
be the [d]firstborn among many brethren;
30 and these whom He [a]predestined, He also [b]called; and
these whom He called, He also [c]justified; and these whom He
justified, He also [d]glorified.
31 [a]What then shall we say to these things? [b]If God *is* for us,
who *is* against us?
32 He who [a]did not spare His own Son, but [b]delivered Him over
for us all, how will He not also with Him freely give us all things?
33 Who will bring a charge against [a]God's elect? [b]God is the
one who justifies;
34 who is the one who [a]condemns? Christ Jesus is He who
[b]died, yes, rather who was [1c]raised, who is [d]at the right hand of
God, who also [e]intercedes for us.
35 Who will separate us from [a]the love of [1]Christ? Will
[b]tribulation, or distress, or [c]persecution, or [c]famine, or
[c]nakedness, or [c]peril, or sword?
36 Just as it is written,

"[a]For Your sake we are being put to death all day long;
We were considered as sheep to be slaughtered."

37 But in all these things we overwhelmingly [a]conquer through
[b]Him who loved us.
38 For I am convinced that neither [a]death, nor life, nor [b]angels,
nor principalities, nor [a]things present, nor things to come, nor
powers,
39 nor height, nor depth, nor any other created thing, will be
able to separate us from [a]the love of God, which is [b]in Christ
Jesus our Lord.

Chapter 9 Theme ____________________

9 [a]I am telling the truth in Christ, I am not lying, my conscience testifies with me in the Holy Spirit,
2 that I have great sorrow and unceasing grief in my heart.
3 For [a]I could [1]wish that I myself were [b]accursed, *separated*
from Christ for the sake of my brethren, my kinsmen [c]according
to the flesh,

24 [a]Rom 8:20; 1 Thess 5:8; Titus 3:7 [b]Rom 4:18; 2 Cor 5:7; Heb 11:1
25 [a]1 Thess 1:3
26 [a]Matt 20:22; 2 Cor 12:8 [b]John 14:16; Rom 8:15f; Eph 6:18
27 [1]Or *holy ones* [a]Ps 139:1f; Luke 16:15; Acts 1:24; Rev 2:23 [b]Rom 8:6 [c]Rom 8:34
28 [1]One early ms reads *all things work together for good* [a]Rom 8:32 [b]Rom 8:30; 9:24; 11:29; 1 Cor 1:9; Gal 1:6, 15; 5:8; Eph 1:11; 3:11; 2 Thess 2:14; Heb 9:15; 1 Pet 2:9; 3:9
29 [a]Rom 11:2; 1 Cor 8:3; 2 Tim 1:9; 1 Pet 1:2, 20 [b]Rom 9:23; 1 Cor 2:7; Eph 1:5, 11 [c]1 Cor 15:49; Phil 3:21 [d]Col 1:18; Heb 1:6
30 [a]Rom 9:23; 11:29; 1 Cor 2:7; Eph 1:5, 11 [b]Rom 8:28; 9:24; 1 Cor 1:9; Gal 1:6, 15; 5:8; Eph 1:11; 3:11; 2 Thess 2:14; Heb 9:15; 1 Pet 2:9; 3:9 [c]1 Cor 6:11 [d]John 17:22; Rom 8:21; 9:23
31 [a]Rom 3:5; 4:1 [b]Ps 118:6; Matt 1:23
32 [a]John 3:16; Rom 5:8 [b]Rom 4:25
33 [a]Luke 18:7 [b]Is 50:8f
34 [1]One early ms reads *raised from the dead* [a]Rom 8:1 [b]Rom 5:6f [c]Acts 2:24 [d]Mark 16:19 [e]Rom 8:27; Heb 7:25
35 [1]Two early mss read *God* [a]Rom 8:37f [b]Rom 2:9; 2 Cor 4:8 [c]1 Cor 4:11; 2 Cor 11:26f
36 [a]Ps 44:22; Acts 20:24; 1 Cor 4:9; 15:30f; 2 Cor 1:9; 4:10f; 6:9; 11:23
37 [a]John 16:33; 1 Cor 15:57 [b]Gal 2:20; Eph 5:2; Rev 1:5
38 [a]1 Cor 3:22 [b]1 Cor 15:24; Eph 1:21; 1 Pet 3:22
39 [a]Rom 5:8 [b]Rom 8:1
9:1 [a]2 Cor 11:10; Gal 1:20; 1 Tim 2:7
3 [1]Lit *pray* [a]Ex 32:32 [b]1 Cor 12:3; 16:22; Gal 1:8f [c]Rom 1:3; 11:14; Eph 6:5

RETURN TO INSTRUCTIONS

10 for with the heart a person believes, [1]resulting in righteousness, and with the mouth he confesses, [2]resulting in salvation.
11 For the Scripture says, "[a]WHOEVER BELIEVES IN HIM WILL NOT
BE [1]DISAPPOINTED."
12 For [a]there is no distinction between Jew and Greek; for the
same *Lord* is [b]Lord of [c]all, abounding in riches for all who call
on Him;
13 for "[a]WHOEVER WILL CALL ON THE NAME OF THE LORD WILL BE
SAVED."
14 How then will they call on Him in whom they have not
believed? How will they believe in Him [a]whom they have not
heard? And how will they hear without [b]a preacher?
15 How will they preach unless they are sent? Just as it is
written, "[a]HOW BEAUTIFUL ARE THE FEET OF THOSE WHO [1b]BRING
GOOD NEWS OF GOOD THINGS!"
16 However, they [a]did not all heed the [1]good news; for Isaiah
says, "[b]LORD, WHO HAS BELIEVED OUR REPORT?"
17 So faith *comes* from [a]hearing, and hearing by [b]the word [1]of
Christ.
18 But I say, surely they have never heard, have they? Indeed
they have;

"[a]THEIR VOICE HAS GONE OUT INTO ALL THE EARTH,
AND THEIR WORDS TO THE ENDS OF THE [1]WORLD."

19 But I say, surely Israel did not know, did they? First Moses
says,

"[a]I WILL [b]MAKE YOU JEALOUS BY THAT WHICH IS NOT A NATION,
BY A NATION WITHOUT UNDERSTANDING WILL I ANGER YOU."

20 And Isaiah is very bold and says,

"[a]I WAS FOUND BY THOSE WHO DID NOT SEEK ME,
I BECAME MANIFEST TO THOSE WHO DID NOT ASK FOR ME."

21 But as for Israel He says, "[a]ALL THE DAY LONG I HAVE
STRETCHED OUT MY HANDS TO A DISOBEDIENT AND OBSTINATE PEOPLE."

Chapter 11 Theme ______________________________

11 I say then, God has not [a]rejected His people, has He?
[b]May it never be! For [c]I too am an Israelite, [1]a descendant
of Abraham, of the tribe of Benjamin.
2 God [a]has not rejected His people whom He [b]foreknew. [c]Or
do you not know what the Scripture says in *the passage about*
Elijah, how he pleads with God against Israel?
3 "Lord, [a]THEY HAVE KILLED YOUR PROPHETS, THEY HAVE TORN DOWN
YOUR ALTARS, AND I ALONE AM LEFT, AND THEY ARE SEEKING MY LIFE."
4 But what [1]is the divine response to him? "[a]I HAVE KEPT for
Myself SEVEN THOUSAND MEN WHO HAVE NOT BOWED THE KNEE TO BAAL."
5 In the same way then, there has also come to be at the
present time [a]a remnant according to *God's* [1]gracious choice.
6 But [a]if it is by grace, it is no longer [1]on the basis of works,
otherwise grace is no longer grace.
7 What then? What [a]Israel is seeking, it has not obtained, but
[1]those who were chosen obtained it, and the rest were [b]hardened;

10 [1]Lit *to righteousness* [2]Lit *to salvation*
11 [1]Lit *put to shame* [a]Is 28:16; Rom 9:33
12 [a]Rom 3:22, 29 [b]Acts 10:36 [c]Rom 3:29
13 [a]Joel 2:32; Acts 2:21
14 [a]Eph 2:17; 4:21 [b]Acts 8:31; Titus 1:3
15 [1]Or *preach the gospel* [a]Is 52:7 [b]Rom 1:15; 15:20
16 [1]Or *gospel* [a]Rom 3:3 [b]Is 53:1; John 12:38
17 [1]Or *concerning Christ* [a]Gal 3:2, 5 [b]Col 3:16
18 [1]Or *inhabited earth* [a]Ps 19:4; Rom 1:8; Col 1:6, 23; 1 Thess 1:8
19 [a]Deut 32:21 [b]Rom 11:11, 14
20 [a]Is 65:1; Rom 9:30
21 [a]Is 65:2
11:1 [1]Lit *of the seed of Abraham* [a]1 Sam 12:22; Jer 31:37; 33:24-26 [b]Luke 20:16 [c]2 Cor 11:22; Phil 3:5
2 [a]Ps 94:14 [b]Rom 8:29 [c]Rom 6:16
3 [a]1 Kin 19:10, 14
4 [1]Lit *says* [a]1 Kin 19:18
5 [1]Lit *choice of grace* [a]2 Kin 19:4; Rom 9:27
6 [1]Lit *out of* [a]Rom 4:4
7 [1]Lit *the election* [a]Rom 9:31 [b]Mark 6:52; Rom 9:18; 11:25; 2 Cor 3:14

8 just as it is written,
"[a]GOD GAVE THEM A SPIRIT OF STUPOR,
EYES TO SEE NOT AND EARS TO HEAR NOT,
DOWN TO THIS VERY DAY."
9 And David says,
"[a]LET THEIR TABLE BECOME A SNARE AND A TRAP,
AND A STUMBLING BLOCK AND A RETRIBUTION TO THEM.
10 "[a]LET THEIR EYES BE DARKENED TO SEE NOT,
AND BEND THEIR BACKS FOREVER."
11 [a]I say then, they did not stumble so as to fall, did they?
[b]May it never be! But by their transgression [c]salvation *has*
come to the Gentiles, to [d]make them jealous.
12 Now if their transgression is riches for the world and their
failure is riches for the Gentiles, how much more will their
[1a]fulfillment be!
13 But I am speaking to you who are Gentiles. Inasmuch then
as [a]I am an apostle of Gentiles, I magnify my ministry,
14 if somehow I might [a]move to jealousy [b]my [1]fellow countrymen and [c]save some of them.
15 For if their rejection is the [a]reconciliation of the world,
what will *their* acceptance be but [b]life from the dead?
16 If the [a]first piece *of dough* is holy, the lump is also; and if
the root is holy, the branches are too.
17 But if some of the [a]branches were broken off, and [b]you,
being a wild olive, were grafted in among them and became
partaker with them of the [1]rich root of the olive tree,
18 do not be arrogant toward the branches; but if you are
arrogant, *remember that* [a]it is not you who supports the root,
but the root *supports* you.
19 [a]You will say then, "Branches were broken off so that I
might be grafted in."
20 Quite right, they were broken off for their unbelief, but
you [a]stand by your faith. [b]Do not be conceited, but fear;
21 for if God did not spare the natural branches, He will not
spare you, either.
22 Behold then the kindness and severity of God; to those
who fell, severity, but to you, God's [a]kindness, [b]if you continue
in His kindness; otherwise you also [c]will be cut off.
23 And they also, [a]if they do not continue in their unbelief,
will be grafted in, for God is able to graft them in again.
24 For if you were cut off from what is by nature a wild olive
tree, and were grafted contrary to nature into a cultivated olive
tree, how much more will these who are the natural *branches*
be grafted into their own olive tree?
25 For [a]I do not want you, brethren, to be uninformed of this
[b]mystery—so that you will not be [c]wise in your own
estimation—that a partial [d]hardening has happened to Israel
until the [e]fullness of the Gentiles has come in;
26 and so all Israel will be saved; just as it is written,
"[a]THE DELIVERER WILL COME FROM ZION,
HE WILL REMOVE UNGODLINESS FROM JACOB."

8 [a]Deut 29:4; Is 29:10; Matt 13:13f
9 [a]Ps 69:22
10 [a]Ps 69:23
11 [a]Rom 11:1 [b]Luke 20:16 [c]Acts 28:28 [d]Rom 11:14
12 [1]Or *fullness* [a]Rom 11:25
13 [a]Acts 9:15
14 [1]Lit *flesh* [a]Rom 11:11 [b]Gen 29:14; 2 Sam 19:12f; Rom 9:3 [c]1 Cor 1:21; 7:16; 9:22; 1 Tim 1:15; 2:4; 2 Tim 1:9; Titus 3:5
15 [a]Rom 5:11 [b]Luke 15:24, 32
16 [a]Num 15:18ff; Neh 10:37; Ezek 44:30
17 [1]Lit *root of the fatness* [a]Jer 11:16; John 15:2 [b]Eph 2:11ff
18 [a]John 4:22
19 [a]Rom 9:19
20 [a]Rom 5:2; 1 Cor 10:12; 2 Cor 1:24 [b]Rom 12:16; 1 Tim 6:17; 1 Pet 1:17
22 [a]Rom 2:4 [b]1 Cor 15:2; Heb 3:6, 14 [c]John 15:2
23 [a]2 Cor 3:16
25 [a]Rom 1:13 [b]Matt 13:11; Rom 16:25; 1 Cor 2:7-10; Eph 3:3-5, 9 [c]Rom 12:16 [d]Rom 11:7 [e]Luke 21:24; John 10:16; Rom 11:12
26 [a]Is 59:20

27 [1]Lit *the covenant from Me* [a]Is 59:21; Jer 31:33, 34; Heb 8:10 [b]Is 27:9; Heb 8:12
28 [1]Lit *According to the gospel* [2]Lit *according to the election* [a]Rom 5:10 [b]Deut 7:8; 10:15; Rom 9:5
29 [a]Rom 8:28; 1 Cor 1:26; Eph 1:18; 4:1, 4; Phil 3:14; 2 Thess 1:11; 2 Tim 1:9; Heb 3:1; 2 Pet 1:10 [b]Heb 7:21
32 [a]Rom 3:9; Gal 3:22f
33 [1]Or *and the wisdom* [a]Rom 2:4; Eph 3:8 [b]Eph 3:10; Col 2:3 [c]Job 5:9; 11:7; 15:8
34 [a]Is 40:13f; 1 Cor 2:16
35 [1]Lit *and it will be paid back* [a]Job 35:7; 41:11
36 [1]Lit *to the ages* [a]1 Cor 8:6; 11:12; Col 1:16; Heb 2:10 [b]Rom 16:27; Eph 3:21; Phil 4:20; 1 Tim 1:17; 2 Tim 4:18; 1 Pet 4:11; 5:11; 2 Pet 3:18; Jude 25; Rev 1:6; 5:13; 7:12
12:1 [1]Or *well-pleasing* [2]Or *rational* [a]1 Cor 1:10; 2 Cor 10:1-4; Eph 4:1; 1 Pet 2:11 [b]Rom 6:13, 16, 19; 1 Cor 6:20; Heb 13:15; 1 Pet 2:5
2 [1]Or *age* [2]Or *approve* [3]Or *well-pleasing* [a]1 Pet 1:14 [b]Matt 13:22; Gal 1:4; 1 John 2:15 [c]Eph 4:23; Titus 3:5 [d]Eph 5:10, 17; Col 1:9
3 [a]Rom 1:5; 15:15; 1 Cor 3:10; 15:10; Gal 2:9; Eph 3:7f [b]Rom 11:20; 12:16 [c]1 Cor 7:17; 2 Cor 10:13; Eph 4:7; 1 Pet 4:11
4 [a]1 Cor 12:12-14; Eph 4:4, 16
5 [a]1 Cor 10:17, 33 [b]1 Cor 12:20, 27; Eph 4:12, 25
6 [1]Or *in agreement with the faith* [a]Rom 12:3; 1 Cor 7:7; 12:4; 1 Pet 4:10 [b]Acts 13:1; 1 Cor 12:10
7 [1]Or *office of service* [a]Acts 6:1; 1 Cor 12:5, 28 [b]Acts 13:1; 1 Cor 12:28; 14:26

27 "[a]THIS IS [1]MY COVENANT WITH THEM,
[b]WHEN I TAKE AWAY THEIR SINS."
28 [1]From the standpoint of the gospel they are [a]enemies for
your sake, but [2]from the standpoint of *God's* choice they are
beloved for [b]the sake of the fathers;
29 for the gifts and the [a]calling of God [b]are irrevocable.
30 For just as you once were disobedient to God, but now
have been shown mercy because of their disobedience,
31 so these also now have been disobedient, that because of
the mercy shown to you they also may now be shown mercy.
32 For [a]God has shut up all in disobedience so that He may
show mercy to all.
33 Oh, the depth of [a]the riches [1]both of the [b]wisdom and
knowledge of God! [c]How unsearchable are His judgments and
unfathomable His ways!
34 For [a]WHO HAS KNOWN THE MIND OF THE LORD, OR WHO BECAME
HIS COUNSELOR?
35 Or [a]WHO HAS FIRST GIVEN TO HIM [1]THAT IT MIGHT BE PAID BACK
TO HIM AGAIN?
36 For [a]from Him and through Him and to Him are all things.
[b]To Him *be* the glory [1]forever. Amen.

Chapter 12 Theme ______________________________

12 Therefore [a]I urge you, brethren, by the mercies of God,
to [b]present your bodies a living and holy sacrifice,
[1]acceptable to God, *which is* your [2]spiritual service of worship.
2 And do not [a]be conformed to [b]this [1]world, but be
transformed by the [c]renewing of your mind, so that you may
[2d]prove what the will of God is, that which is good and
[3]acceptable and perfect.
3 For through [a]the grace given to me I say to everyone
among you [b]not to think more highly of himself than he ought
to think; but to think so as to have sound judgment, as God has
allotted to [c]each a measure of faith.
4 For [a]just as we have many members in one body and all
the members do not have the same function,
5 so we, [a]who are many, are [b]one body in Christ, and
individually members one of another.
6 Since we have gifts that [a]differ according to the grace given
to us, *each of us is to exercise them accordingly:* if [b]prophecy,
[1]according to the proportion of his faith;
7 if [1a]service, in his serving; or he who [b]teaches, in his
teaching;
8 or he who [a]exhorts, in his exhortation; he who gives, with
[1b]liberality; [c]he who [2]leads, with diligence; he who shows
mercy, with [d]cheerfulness.
9 *Let* [a]love *be* without hypocrisy. [b]Abhor what is evil; cling to
what is good.

8 [1]Or *simplicity* [2]Or *gives aid* [a]Acts 4:36; 11:23; 13:15 [b]2 Cor 8:2; 9:11, 13 [c]1 Cor 12:28; 1 Tim 5:17 [d]2 Cor 9:7
9 [a]2 Cor 6:6; 1 Tim 1:5 [b]1 Thess 5:21f

10 *Be* [a]devoted to one another in brotherly love; [1]give preference to one another [b]in honor;

11 not lagging behind in diligence, [a]fervent in spirit, [b]serving the Lord;

12 [a]rejoicing in hope, [b]persevering in tribulation, [c]devoted to prayer,

13 [a]contributing to the needs of the [1]saints, [2b]practicing hospitality.

14 [a]Bless those who persecute [1]you; bless and do not curse.

15 [a]Rejoice with those who rejoice, and weep with those who weep.

16 [a]Be of the same mind toward one another; [b]do not be haughty in mind, but [1]associate with the lowly. [c]Do not be wise in your own estimation.

17 [a]Never pay back evil for evil to anyone. [1b]Respect what is right in the sight of all men.

18 If possible, [a]so far as it depends on you, [b]be at peace with all men.

19 [a]Never take your own revenge, beloved, but [1]leave room for the wrath *of God,* for it is written, "[b]VENGEANCE IS MINE, I WILL REPAY," says the Lord.

20 "[a]BUT IF YOUR ENEMY IS HUNGRY, FEED HIM, AND IF HE IS THIRSTY, GIVE HIM A DRINK; FOR IN SO DOING YOU WILL HEAP BURNING COALS ON HIS HEAD."

21 Do not be overcome by evil, but overcome evil with good.

Chapter 13 Theme ______________________________

13 Every [1a]person is to be in [b]subjection to the governing authorities. For [c]there is no authority except [2]from God, and those which exist are established by God.

2 Therefore [1]whoever resists authority has opposed the ordinance of God; and they who have opposed will receive condemnation upon themselves.

3 For [a]rulers are not a cause of fear for [1]good behavior, but for evil. Do you want to have no fear of authority? Do what is good and you will have praise from the same;

4 for it is a minister of God to you for good. But if you do what is evil, be afraid; for it does not bear the sword for nothing; for it is a minister of God, an [a]avenger who brings wrath on the one who practices evil.

5 Therefore it is necessary to be in subjection, not only because of wrath, but also [a]for conscience' sake.

6 For because of this you also pay taxes, for *rulers* are servants of God, devoting themselves to this very thing.

7 [a]Render to all what is due them: [b]tax to whom tax *is due;* [c]custom to whom custom; fear to whom fear; honor to whom honor.

8 Owe nothing to anyone except to love one another; for [a]he who loves [1]his neighbor has fulfilled *the* law.

9 For this, "[a]YOU SHALL NOT COMMIT ADULTERY, YOU SHALL NOT MURDER, YOU SHALL NOT STEAL, YOU SHALL NOT COVET," and if

10 [1]Or *outdo one another in showing honor* [a]John 13:34; 1 Thess 4:9; Heb 13:1; 2 Pet 1:7 [b]Rom 13:7; Phil 2:3; 1 Pet 2:17

11 [a]Acts 18:25 [b]Acts 20:19

12 [a]Rom 5:2 [b]Heb 10:32, 36 [c]Acts 1:14

13 [1]Or *holy ones* [2]Lit *pursuing* [a]Rom 15:25; 1 Cor 16:15; 2 Cor 9:1; Heb 6:10 [b]Matt 25:35; 1 Tim 3:2

14 [1]Two early mss do not contain *you* [a]Matt 5:44; Luke 6:28; 1 Cor 4:12

15 [a]Job 30:25; Heb 13:3

16 [1]Or *accommodate yourself to lowly things* [a]Rom 15:5; 2 Cor 13:11; Phil 2:2; 4:2; 1 Pet 3:8 [b]Rom 11:20; 12:3 [c]Prov 3:7; Rom 11:25

17 [1]Lit *Take thought for* [a]Prov 20:22; 24:29; Rom 12:19 [b]2 Cor 8:21

18 [a]Rom 1:15 [b]Mark 9:50; Rom 14:19

19 [1]Lit *give a place* [a]Prov 20:22; 24:29; Rom 12:17 [b]Deut 32:35; Ps 94:1; 1 Thess 4:6; Heb 10:30

20 [a]2 Kin 6:22; Prov 25:21f; Matt 5:44; Luke 6:27

13:1 [1]Or *soul* [2]Lit *by* [a]Acts 2:41 [b]Titus 3:1; 1 Pet 2:13f [c]Dan 2:21; 4:17; John 19:11

2 [1]Lit *he who*

3 [1]Lit *good work* [a]1 Pet 2:14

4 [a]1 Thess 4:6

5 [a]Eccl 8; 1 Pet 2:13, 19

7 [a]Matt 22:21; Mark 12:17; Luke 20:25 [b]Luke 20:22; 23:2 [c]Matt 17:25

8 [1]Lit *the other* [a]Matt 7:12; 22:39f; John 13:34; Rom 13:10; Gal 5:14; James 2:8

9 [a]Ex 20:13ff; Deut 5:17ff

there is any other commandment, it is summed up in this
saying, "[b]YOU SHALL LOVE YOUR NEIGHBOR AS YOURSELF."
10 Love [1]does no wrong to a neighbor; therefore [a]love is the
fulfillment of *the* law.
11 *Do* this, knowing the time, that it is [a]already the hour for
you to [b]awaken from sleep; for now [1]salvation is nearer to us
than when we believed.
12 [a]The night is almost gone, and [b]the day is near. Therefore let
us lay aside [c]the deeds of darkness and put on [d]the armor of light.
13 Let us [1a]behave properly as in the day, [b]not in carousing
and drunkenness, not in sexual promiscuity and sensuality, not
in strife and jealousy.
14 But [a]put on the Lord Jesus Christ, and make no provision
for the flesh [b]in regard to *its* lusts.

Chapter 14 Theme ______

14 Now [a]accept the one who is [b]weak in faith, *but* not for
the purpose of passing judgment on his opinions.
2 [a]One person has faith that he may eat all things, but he
who is [b]weak eats vegetables *only*.
3 The one who eats is not to [a]regard with contempt the one
who does not eat, and the one who does not eat is not to
[b]judge the one who eats, for God has [c]accepted him.
4 [a]Who are you to judge the [1]servant of another? To his own
[2]master he stands or falls; and he will stand, for the Lord is able
to make him stand.
5 [a]One person [1]regards one day above another, another
regards every day *alike*. Each person must be [b]fully convinced
in his own mind.
6 He who observes the day, observes it for the Lord, and he
who eats, [1]does so for the Lord, for he [a]gives thanks to God;
and he who eats not, for the Lord he does not eat, and gives
thanks to God.
7 For not one of us [a]lives for himself, and not one dies for
himself;
8 for if we live, we live for the Lord, or if we die, we die for
the Lord; therefore [a]whether we live or die, we are the Lord's.
9 For to this end [a]Christ died and lived again, that He might
be [b]Lord both of the dead and of the living.
10 But you, why do you judge your brother? Or you again,
why do you [a]regard your brother with contempt? For [b]we will
all stand before the judgment seat of God.
11 For it is written,

"[a]AS I LIVE, SAYS THE LORD, [b]EVERY KNEE SHALL BOW TO ME,
AND EVERY TONGUE SHALL [1]GIVE PRAISE TO GOD."

12 So then [a]each one of us will give an account of himself to
God.
13 Therefore let us not [a]judge one another anymore, but
rather determine this—[b]not to put an obstacle or a stumbling
block in a brother's way.

9 [b]Lev 19:18; Matt 19:19
10 [1]Lit *works no evil* [a]Matt 7:12; 22:39f; John 13:34; Rom 13:8; Gal 5:14; James 2:8
11 [1]Or *our salvation is nearer than when* [a]1 Cor 7:29f; 10:11; James 5:8; 1 Pet 4:7; 2 Pet 3:9, 11; 1 John 2:18; Rev 1:3; 22:10 [b]Mark 13:37; 1 Cor 15:34; Eph 5:14; 1 Thess 5:6
12 [a]1 Cor 7:29f; 10:11; James 5:8; 1 Pet 4:7; 2 Pet 3:9, 11; 1 John 2:18; Rev 1:3; 22:10 [b]Heb 10:25; 1 John 2:8; Rev 1:3; 22:10 [c]Eph 5:11 [d]2 Cor 6:7; 10:4; Eph 6:11, 13; 1 Thess 5:8
13 [1]Lit *walk* [a]1 Thess 4:12 [b]Luke 21:34; Gal 5:21; Eph 5:18; 1 Pet 4:3
14 [a]Job 29:14; Gal 3:27; Eph 4:24; Col 3:10, 12 [b]Gal 5:16; 1 Pet 2:11
14:1 [a]Acts 28:2; Rom 11:15; 14:3; 15:7 [b]Rom 14:2; 15:1; 1 Cor 8:9ff; 9:22
2 [a]Rom 14:14 [b]Rom 14:1; 15:1; 1 Cor 8:9ff; 9:22
3 [a]Luke 18:9; Rom 14:10 [b]Rom 14:10, 13; Col 2:16 [c]Acts 28:2; Rom 11:15; 14:1; 15:7
4 [1]Or *house-servant* [2]Lit *lord* [a]Rom 9:20; James 4:12
5 [1]Lit *judges* [a]Gal 4:10 [b]Luke 1:1; Rom 4:21; 14:23
6 [1]Lit *eats* [a]Matt 14:19; 15:36; 1 Cor 10:30; 1 Tim 4:3f
7 [a]Rom 8:38f; 2 Cor 5:15; Gal 2:20; Phil 1:20f
8 [a]Luke 20:38; Phil 1:20; 1 Thess 5:10; Rev 14:13
9 [a]Rev 1:18; 2:8 [b]Matt 28:18; John 12:24; Phil 2:11; 1 Thess 5:10
10 [a]Luke 18:9; Rom 14:3 [b]Rom 2:16; 2 Cor 5:10
11 [1]Or *confess* [a]Is 45:23 [b]Phil 2:10f
12 [a]Matt 12:36; 16:27; 1 Pet 4:5
13 [a]Matt 7:1; Rom 14:3 [b]1 Cor 8:13

14 I know and am convinced [1]in the Lord Jesus that [a]nothing
is unclean in itself; but to him who [b]thinks anything to be
unclean, to him it is unclean.
15 For if because of food your brother is hurt, you are no
longer [a]walking according to love. [b]Do not destroy with your
food him for whom Christ died.
16 Therefore [a]do not let what is for you a good thing be [1]spoken
of as evil;
17 for the kingdom of God [a]is not eating and drinking, but
righteousness and [b]peace and [b]joy in the Holy Spirit.
18 For he who in this *way* [a]serves Christ is [b]acceptable to God
and approved by men.
19 So then [1]we [a]pursue the things which make for peace and
the [b]building up of one another.
20 [a]Do not tear down the work of God for the sake of food.
[b]All things indeed are clean, but [c]they are evil for the man who
eats [1]and gives offense.
21 [a]It is good not to eat meat or to drink wine, or *to do*
anything by which your brother stumbles.
22 The faith which you have, have [1]as your own conviction
before God. Happy is he who [a]does not condemn himself in
what he approves.
23 But [a]he who doubts is condemned if he eats, because *his*
eating is not from faith; and whatever is not from faith is sin.

Chapter 15 Theme ______________________________

15 Now we who are strong ought to bear the weaknesses of
[a]those without strength and not *just* please ourselves.
2 Each of us is to [a]please his neighbor [1]for his good, to his
[b]edification.
3 For even [a]Christ did not please Himself; but as it is written,
"[b]THE REPROACHES OF THOSE WHO REPROACHED YOU FELL ON ME."
4 For [a]whatever was written in earlier times was written for
our instruction, so that through perseverance and the
encouragement of the Scriptures we might have hope.
5 Now may the [a]God [1]who gives perseverance and encouragement grant you [b]to be of the same mind with one another
according to Christ Jesus,
6 so that with one accord you may with one [1]voice glorify
[a]the God and Father of our Lord Jesus Christ.
7 Therefore, [a]accept one another, just as Christ also accepted
[1]us to the glory of God.
8 For I say that Christ has become a servant to [a]the
circumcision on behalf of the truth of God to confirm [b]the
promises *given* to the fathers,
9 and for [a]the Gentiles to [b]glorify God for His mercy; as it is
written,

"[c]THEREFORE I WILL [1]GIVE PRAISE TO YOU AMONG THE GENTILES,
AND I WILL SING TO YOUR NAME."

10 Again he says,

"[a]REJOICE, O GENTILES, WITH HIS PEOPLE."

14 [1]Lit *through* [a]Acts 10:15; Rom 14:2, 20 [b]1 Cor 8:7

15 [a]Eph 5:2 [b]Rom 14:20; 1 Cor 8:11

16 [1]Lit *blasphemed* [a]1 Cor 10:30; Titus 2:5

17 [a]1 Cor 8:8 [b]Rom 15:13; Gal 5:22

18 [a]Rom 16:18 [b]2 Cor 8:21; Phil 4:8; 1 Pet 2:12

19 [1]Later mss read *let us pursue* [a]Ps 34:14; Rom 12:18; 1 Cor 7:15; 2 Tim 2:22; Heb 12:14 [b]Rom 15:2; 1 Cor 10:23; 14:3f, 26; 2 Cor 12:19; Eph 4:12, 29

20 [1]Lit *with offense* [a]Rom 14:15 [b]Acts 10:15; Rom 14:2, 14 [c]1 Cor 8:9-12

21 [a]1 Cor 8:13

22 [1]Lit *according to yourself* [a]1 John 3:21

23 [a]Rom 14:5

15:1 [a]Rom 14:1; Gal 6:2; 1 Thess 5:14

2 [1]Lit *for what is good to edification* [a]1 Cor 9:22; 10:24, 33; 2 Cor 13:9 [b]Rom 14:19; 1 Cor 10:23; 14:3f, 26; 2 Cor 12:19; Eph 4:12, 29

3 [a]2 Cor 8:9 [b]Ps 69:9

4 [a]Rom 4:23f; 2 Tim 3:16

5 [1]Lit *of perseverance* [a]2 Cor 1:3 [b]Rom 12:16

6 [1]Lit *mouth* [a]Rev 1:6

7 [1]One early ms reads *you* [a]Rom 14:1

8 [a]Matt 15:24; Acts 3:26 [b]Rom 4:16; 2 Cor 1:20

9 [1]Or *confess* [a]Rom 3:29; 11:30f [b]Matt 9:8 [c]2 Sam 22:50; Ps 18:49

10 [a]Deut 32:43

11 And again,
"[a]PRAISE THE LORD ALL YOU GENTILES,
AND LET ALL THE PEOPLES PRAISE HIM."
12 Again Isaiah says,
"[a]THERE SHALL COME [b]THE ROOT OF JESSE,
AND HE WHO ARISES TO RULE OVER THE GENTILES,
[c]IN HIM SHALL THE GENTILES HOPE."
13 Now may the God of hope fill you with all [a]joy and peace
in believing, so that you will abound in hope [b]by the power of
the Holy Spirit.
14 And concerning you, my brethren, I myself also am
convinced that you yourselves are full of [a]goodness, filled with
[b]all knowledge and able also to admonish one another.
15 But I have written very boldly to you on some points so as
to remind you again, because of [a]the grace that was given me
[1]from God,
16 to be [a]a minister of Christ Jesus to the Gentiles, ministering
as a priest the [b]gospel of God, so that *my* [c]offering of the
Gentiles may become acceptable, sanctified by the Holy Spirit.
17 Therefore in Christ Jesus I have found [a]reason for boasting
in [b]things pertaining to God.
18 For I will not presume to speak of anything [1]except what
[a]Christ has accomplished through me, [2]resulting in the
obedience of the Gentiles by word and deed,
19 in the power of [1a]signs and wonders, [b]in the power of the
Spirit; so that [c]from Jerusalem and round about as [d]far as
Illyricum I have [2]fully preached the gospel of Christ.
20 And thus I aspired to [a]preach the gospel, not where Christ
was *already* named, [b]so that I would not build on another
man's foundation;
21 but as it is written,
"[a]THEY WHO HAD NO NEWS OF HIM SHALL SEE,
AND THEY WHO HAVE NOT HEARD SHALL UNDERSTAND."
22 For this reason [a]I have often been prevented from coming
to you;
23 but now, with no further place for me in these regions, and
since I [a]have had for many years a longing to come to you
24 whenever I [a]go to Spain—for I hope to see you in passing,
and to be [b]helped on my way there by you, when I have first
[c]enjoyed your company [1]for a while—
25 but now, [a]I am going to Jerusalem [b]serving the [1]saints.
26 For [a]Macedonia and [b]Achaia have been pleased to make a
contribution for the poor among the [1]saints in Jerusalem.
27 Yes, they were pleased *to do so,* and they are indebted to
them. For [a]if the Gentiles have shared in their spiritual things,
they are indebted to minister to them also in material things.
28 Therefore, when I have finished this, and [a]have [1]put my
seal on this fruit of theirs, I will [b]go on by way of you to Spain.
29 I know that when [a]I come to you, I will come in the
fullness of the blessing of Christ.
30 Now I urge you, brethren, by our Lord Jesus Christ and by

11 [a]Ps 117:1
12 [a]Is 11:10 [b]Rev 5:5; 22:16 [c]Matt 12:21
13 [a]Rom 14:17 [b]Rom 15:19; 1 Cor 2:4; 1 Thess 1:5
14 [a]Eph 5:9; 2 Thess 1:11 [b]1 Cor 1:5; 8:1, 7, 10; 12:8; 13:2
15 [1]One early ms reads *by God* [a]Rom 12:3
16 [a]Acts 9:15; Rom 11:13 [b]Rom 1:1; 15:19, 20 [c]Rom 12:1; Eph 5:2; Phil 2:17
17 [a]Phil 3:3 [b]Heb 2:17; 5:1
18 [1]Lit *which Christ has not accomplished* [2]Lit *to the obedience* [a]Acts 15:12; 21:19; Rom 1:5; 2 Cor 3:5
19 [1]Or *attesting miracles* [2]Lit *fulfilled* [a]John 4:48 [b]Rom 15:13; 1 Cor 2:4; 1 Thess 1:5 [c]Acts 22:17-21 [d]Acts 20:1f
20 [a]Rom 1:15; 10:15; 15:16 [b]1 Cor 3:10; 2 Cor 10:15f
21 [a]Is 52:15
22 [a]Rom 1:13; 1 Thess 2:18
23 [a]Acts 19:21; Rom 1:10f; 15:29, 32
24 [1]Lit *in part* [a]Rom 15:28 [b]Acts 15:3 [c]Rom 1:12
25 [1]Or *holy ones* [a]Acts 19:21 [b]Acts 24:17
26 [1]V 25, note 1 [a]Acts 16:9; 1 Cor 16:5; 2 Cor 1:16; 2:13; 7:5; 8:1; 9:2, 4; 11:9; Phil 4:15; 1 Thess 1:7f; 4:10; 1 Tim 1:3 [b]Acts 18:12; 19:21
27 [a]1 Cor 9:11
28 [1]Lit *sealed to them this fruit* [a]John 3:33 [b]Rom 15:24
29 [a]Acts 19:21; Rom 1:10f; 15:23, 32

[a]the love of the Spirit, to [b]strive together with me in your
prayers to God for me,
31 that I may be [a]rescued from those who are disobedient in
Judea, and *that* my [b]service for Jerusalem may prove acceptable
to the [1c]saints;
32 so that [a]I may come to you in joy by [b]the will of God and
find *refreshing* rest in your company.
33 Now [a]the God of peace be with you all. Amen.

Chapter 16 Theme ______________________

16 I [a]commend to you our sister Phoebe, who is a [1]servant
of the church which is at [b]Cenchrea;
2 that you [a]receive her in the Lord in a manner worthy of
the [1b]saints, and that you help her in whatever matter she may
have need of you; for she herself has also been a helper of
many, [2]and of myself as well.
3 Greet [a]Prisca and Aquila, my fellow workers [b]in [c]Christ Jesus,
4 who for my life risked their own necks, to whom not only
do I give thanks, but also all the churches of the Gentiles;
5 also *greet* [a]the church that is in their house. Greet Epaenetus,
my beloved, who is the [b]first convert to Christ from [1c]Asia.
6 Greet Mary, who has worked hard for you.
7 Greet Andronicus and [1]Junias, my [a]kinsmen and my [b]fellow
prisoners, who are outstanding among the apostles, who also
[2]were [c]in Christ before me.
8 Greet Ampliatus, my beloved in the Lord.
9 Greet Urbanus, our fellow worker [a]in Christ, and Stachys
my beloved.
10 Greet Apelles, the approved [a]in Christ. Greet those who
are of the *household* of Aristobulus.
11 Greet Herodion, my [a]kinsman. Greet those of the *house-*
hold of Narcissus, who are in the Lord.
12 Greet Tryphaena and Tryphosa, workers in the Lord. Greet
Persis the beloved, who has worked hard in the Lord.
13 Greet [a]Rufus, a choice man in the Lord, also his mother
and mine.
14 Greet Asyncritus, Phlegon, Hermes, Patrobas, Hermas and
the brethren with them.
15 Greet Philologus and Julia, Nereus and his sister, and
Olympas, and all [a]the [1]saints who are with them.
16 [a]Greet one another with a holy kiss. All the churches of
Christ greet you.
17 Now I urge you, brethren, keep your eye on those who
cause dissensions and [1]hindrances [a]contrary to the teaching
which you learned, and [b]turn away from them.
18 For such men are [a]slaves, not of our Lord Christ but of
[b]their own [1]appetites; and by their [c]smooth and flattering
speech they deceive the hearts of the unsuspecting.
19 For the report of your obedience [a]has reached to all;
therefore I am rejoicing over you, but [b]I want you to be wise in
what is good and innocent in what is evil.

30 [a]Gal 5:22; Col 1:8 [b]2 Cor 1:11; Col 4:12

31 [1]V 25, note 1 [a]2 Cor 1:10; 2 Thess 3:2; 2 Tim 3:11; 4:17 [b]Rom 15:25f; 2 Cor 8:4; 9:1 [c]Acts 9:13, 15

32 [a]Rom 15:23 [b]Acts 18:21; Rom 1:10

33 [a]Rom 16:20; 2 Cor 13:11; Phil 4:9; 1 Thess 5:23; 2 Thess 3:16; Heb 13:20

16:1 [1]Or *deaconess* [a]2 Cor 3:1 [b]Acts 18:18

2 [1]Or *holy ones* [2]Lit *and of me, myself* [a]Phil 2:29 [b]Acts 9:13, 15

3 [a]Acts 18:2 [b]Rom 8:11ff; 16:7, 9, 10; 2 Cor 5:17; 12:2; Gal 1:22 [c]Rom 8:1

5 [1]I.e. west coast province of Asia Minor [a]1 Cor 16:19; Col 4:15; Philem 2 [b]1 Cor 16:15 [c]Acts 16:6

7 [1]Or *Junia* (fem) [2]Lit *have become* [a]Rom 9:3; 16:11, 21 [b]Col 4:10; Philem 23 [c]Rom 8:11ff; 16:3, 9, 10; 2 Cor 5:17; 12:2; Gal 1:22

9 [a]Rom 8:11ff; 16:3, 7, 10; 2 Cor 5:17; 12:2; Gal 1:22

10 [a]Rom 8:11ff; 16:3, 7, 9; 2 Cor 5:17; 12:2; Gal 1:22

11 [a]Rom 9:3; 16:7, 21

13 [a]Mark 15:21

15 [1]V 2, note 1 [a]Rom 16:2, 14

16 [a]1 Cor 16:20; 2 Cor 13:12; 1 Thess 5:26; 1 Pet 5:14

17 [1]Lit *occasions of stumbling* [a]1 Tim 1:3; 6:3 [b]Matt 7:15; Gal 1:8f; 2 Thess 3:6, 14; Titus 3:10; 2 John 10

18 [1]Lit *belly* [a]Rom 14:18 [b]Phil 3:19 [c]Col 2:4; 2 Pet 2:3

19 [a]Rom 1:8 [b]Jer 4:22; Matt 10:16; 1 Cor 14:20

20 [a]The God of peace will soon crush [b]Satan under your feet.
[c]The grace of our Lord Jesus be with you.
21 [a]Timothy my fellow worker greets you, and *so do* [b]Lucius
and [c]Jason and [d]Sosipater, my [e]kinsmen.
22 I, Tertius, who [a]write this letter, greet you in the Lord.
23 [a]Gaius, host to me and to the whole church, greets you.
[b]Erastus, the city treasurer greets you, and Quartus, the
brother.
24 [[1]The grace of our Lord Jesus Christ be with you all. Amen.]
25 [a]Now to Him who is able to establish you [b]according to my
gospel and the preaching of Jesus Christ, according to the
revelation of [c]the mystery which has been kept secret for [d]long
ages past,
26 but now is manifested, and by [a]the Scriptures of the prophets,
according to the commandment of the eternal God, has been
made known to all the nations, *leading* to [b]obedience of faith;
27 to the only wise God, through Jesus Christ, [a]be the glory
forever. Amen.

20 [a]Rom 15:33 [b]Matt 4:10 [c]1 Cor 16:23; 2 Cor 13:14; Gal 6:18; Phil 4:23; 1 Thess 5:28; 2 Thess 3:18; Rev 22:21

21 [a]Acts 16:1 [b][Acts 13:1] [c][Acts 17:5] [d][Acts 20:4] [e]Rom 9:3; 16:7, 11

22 [a]1 Cor 16:21; Gal 6:11; Col 4:18; 2 Thess 3:17; Philem 19

23 [a][Acts 19:29; 20:4]; 1 Cor 1:14 [b]Acts 19:22; 2 Tim 4:20

24 [1]Early mss do not contain this v

25 [a]Eph 3:20; Jude 24 [b]Rom 2:16 [c]Matt 13:35; Rom 11:25; 1 Cor 2:1, 7; 4:1; Eph 1:9; 3:3, 9; 6:19; Col 1:26f; 2:2; 4:3; 1 Tim 3:16 [d]2 Tim 1:9; Titus 1:2
26 [a]Rom 1:2 [b]Rom 1:5
27 [a]Rom 11:36

ROMANS OBSERVATIONS CHART

ABOUT PAUL

WHY HE WROTE

ABOUT THE RECIPIENTS

IN ADAM *(According to the flesh)*	IN CHRIST *(According to the Spirit)*

Romans at a Glance

Theme of Romans:

Author:

Date:

Purpose:

Key Words:

Segment Divisions

			Chapter Themes
			1
			2
			3
			4
			5
			6
			7
			8
			9
			10
			11
			12
			13
			14
			15
			16

1 CORINTHIANS

Sin abounded in the cosmopolitan city of Corinth, the chief commercial city of Greece. Corinth overlooked the narrow isthmus that connected the Greek mainland with Peloponnesus and received ships in its two harbors. The Corinthians were intrigued by Greek philosophy and captivated by the disciplined training and athletic events held at the Isthmus. At one time the city was home to at least 12 pagan temples. The people, then, desperately needed to hear the good news of Jesus Christ, the One crucified for sinners.

The worship ceremonies carried out by a thousand temple prostitutes connected with the temple of Aphrodite (the goddess of love) bred blatant immorality throughout Corinth—so much so that the Greek verb translated "to Corinthianize" meant to practice sexual immorality.

Prostitutes openly plied their wares, and meat markets thrived on sales from the sacrifices offered in the temples. The Corinthians ate well, satisfied their sexual urges without condemnation, flirted with the wisdom of men, and did all they could to keep their bodies as beautiful as those of the Greek gods. They loved to listen to great orators. For the 250,000 citizens there were almost two slaves per person. What more did Corinth need? Freedom. Freedom from sin and death. God met that need by blocking Paul at every hand on his second missionary journey until he received the Macedonian call, "Come and help us."

After establishing the Corinthian church, Paul eventually went to Ephesus, where he stayed for three years. From there he wrote his first epistle to the Corinthian believers, who so desperately needed help and correction. It was sometime between A.D. 52 and A.D. 56.

THINGS TO DO

Chapters 1–6

1. Read through these chapters and color every reference to the author in one color and every reference to the recipients in another color. Note what you observe about each from doing this.

2. Read chapters 1 through 6, one chapter at a time. As you read, keep in mind what you read in the introduction to this book. Do the following:

   a. Watch for the problems Paul deals with in his letter. You can notice these problems in one of several ways.

      1) As you read, ask the "5 W's and an H": Who? What? When? Where? Why? and How? Especially concentrate on the problems, subjects, or people mentioned. Ask questions such as: Why does Paul mention specific people by name in this chapter? Who is causing the problem? How did the Corinthians get this way? Why does Paul say what he does about himself or his ministry?

      2) Mark the following key words in the text along with *all* synonyms and pronouns: *call* (*calling,* etc.), *wisdom (wise), power, foolish, boast, spirit, arrogant, immorality, body, do you not know,* and *temple.*

      Write the key words for this segment on an index card and use it as a bookmark.

   b. As you read each of the first six chapters, note the problems Paul deals with in each chapter. In the margin make a list of these with the heading "Problems."

3. As you read, note on the OBSERVATIONS CHART on page 1871 what you learn about the Corinthians, including commands and warnings Paul gives them.

4. As you finish each chapter, summarize the theme (subject) of that chapter and record it on 1 CORINTHIANS AT A GLANCE on page 1872 and in your Bible.

5. Two things prompted Paul to write to the Corinthians, and these two things create a natural division in his epistle. Read 1 Corinthians 1:10-11, where Paul states his reason for writing. Record this reason on the 1 CORINTHIANS AT A GLANCE chart in the space under "Major Segment Divisions."

Chapters 7–16

1. The second division of 1 Corinthians is noted by a phrase that is repeated throughout the last segment of this book: *now concerning....* Read 7:1 and notice the transition. From this point on Paul deals with matters the Corinthians had questions about or issues that they needed to be instructed in.

2. Look up the following verses and underline or mark in a distinctive way the phrase *now concerning.* As you mark that phrase, mark along with it the subject matter Paul is about to deal with. The verses are 7:1; 7:25; 8:1; 12:1; 16:1. In the same way also mark in 15:1 the words *Now I make known to you, brethren, the gospel which I preached to you.* Marking these wordings will give you the topical divisions of this second segment of 1 Corinthians.

3. As you read through this last segment of 1 Corinthians, mark the following key words: *Spirit, body, love, sin (sinning), unbelieving (unbelievers), think (thinks, thinking), church (churches), idols (idolaters, idolatry), knowledge, preach, death (dead),* and *gospel.* Mark *raised* (*resurrection* in chapter 15). Make a new list of key words to use as a bookmark in this segment. (*Divisions* and *factions* are used in chapter 11. This is significant, since Paul again deals with problems while giving further instruction to the church.)

4. As you deal with each topic, ask questions such as: Why does the church have this question or problem? How are they behaving? What is their thinking? What are Paul's instructions regarding this subject? Why are they to do this? What are the consequences if they don't?

5. As Paul moves through these final matters of concern, he intermittently explains his position and ministry. Watch for these explanations and note if and how he ties them in with his subject matter.

6. Note on the OBSERVATIONS CHART what you learn from this segment about the Corinthians and the commands and warnings Paul gives them.

7. Determine and record the theme of each chapter in your Bible and on 1 CORINTHIANS AT A GLANCE.

8. Considering 7:1, give a title to the segment division for the second half of 1 Corinthians. Record your title on 1 CORINTHIANS AT A GLANCE.

9. Record the theme of 1 Corinthians and complete the 1 CORINTHIANS AT A GLANCE chart.

Things to Think About

1. Are you having any of the same problems in your own life or in your church that the Corinthians had? Do you think this letter has the answers for your problems or questions? How can you apply what you have learned?

2. According to the context of 1 Corinthians 3, what does it mean to be a carnal or fleshly Christian? Remember, context rules over all accurate interpretation.

3. Are you untaught—ignorant—concerning spiritual gifts? Do you know about one or two of them but not the others? Have you believed or even taught others in accord with

what the whole counsel of God has to say on the subject, or have you merely gone by your experience or reasoning? Do you appreciate other people's gifts even though they may be different from yours?

4. On what do you base your beliefs about marriage, divorce, and remarriage? What did you learn from 1 Corinthians 7 about these topics? Did this change your belief?

5. Is the preaching of the cross foolishness to you, or is it a demonstration of the power of God?

INSIGHT

See the map on page 1800.

Chapter 1 Theme ____________________

1 Paul, [a]called *as* an apostle of Jesus Christ [1]by [b]the will of
God, and [c]Sosthenes our [d]brother,
2 To [a]the church of God which is at [b]Corinth, to those who
have been sanctified in Christ Jesus, [1]saints [c]by calling, with all
who in every place [d]call on the name of our Lord Jesus Christ,
their *Lord* and ours:
3 [a]Grace to you and peace from God our Father and the Lord
Jesus Christ.
4 [a]I thank [1]my God always concerning you for the grace of
God which was given you in Christ Jesus,
5 that in everything you were [a]enriched in Him, in all [b]speech
and [b]all knowledge,
6 even as [a]the testimony concerning Christ was confirmed [1]in
you,
7 so that you are not lacking in any gift, [a]awaiting eagerly the
revelation of our Lord Jesus Christ,
8 [a]who will also confirm you to the end, blameless in [b]the
day of our Lord Jesus Christ.
9 [a]God is faithful, through whom you were [b]called into
[c]fellowship with His Son, Jesus Christ our Lord.
10 Now [a]I exhort you, [b]brethren, by the name of our Lord
Jesus Christ, that you all [1]agree and that there be no [2c]divisions
among you, but that you be [3]made complete in [d]the same mind
and in the same judgment.
11 For I have been informed concerning you, my brethren, by
Chloe's *people,* that there are quarrels among you.
12 Now I mean this, that [a]each one of you is saying, "I am of
Paul," and "I of [b]Apollos," and "I of [c]Cephas," and "I of Christ."
13 [1]Has Christ been divided? Paul was not crucified for you,
was he? Or were you [a]baptized [2]in the name of Paul?
14 [1]I thank God that I [a]baptized none of you except [a]Crispus
and [b]Gaius,
15 so that no one would say you were baptized [1]in my name.
16 Now I did baptize also the [a]household of Stephanas; beyond
that, I do not know whether I baptized any other.
17 [a]For Christ did not send me to baptize, but to preach the
gospel, [b]not in [1]cleverness of speech, so that the cross of Christ
would not be made void.

1:1 [1]Lit *through* [a]Rom 1:1 [b]Rom 1:10; 2 Tim 1:1 [c]Acts 18:17 [d]Acts 1:15
2 [1]Or *holy ones* [a]1 Cor 10:32 [b]Acts 18:1 [c]Rom 1:7; 8:28 [d]Acts 7:59
3 [a]Rom 1:7
4 [1]Two early mss do not contain *my* [a]Rom 1:8
5 [a]2 Cor 9:11 [b]Rom 15:14; 2 Cor 8:7
6 [1]Or *among* [a]2 Thess 1:10; 1 Tim 2:6; 2 Tim 1:8; Rev 1:2
7 [a]Luke 17:30; Rom 8:19, 23; Phil 3:20; 2 Pet 3:12
8 [a]Rom 8:19; Phil 1:6; Col 2:7; 1 Thess 3:13; 5:23 [b]Luke 17:24, 30; 1 Cor 5:5; 2 Cor 1:14; Phil 1:6, 10; 2:16; 1 Thess 5:2; 2 Thess 2:2
9 [a]Deut 7:9; Is 49:7; 1 Cor 10:13; 2 Cor 1:18; 1 Thess 5:24; 2 Thess 3:3 [b]Rom 8:28 [c]1 John 1:3
10 [1]Lit *speak the same thing* [2]Lit *schisms* [3]Or *united* [a]Rom 12:1 [b]Rom 1:13 [c]1 Cor 11:18 [d]Rom 12:16; Phil 1:27
12 [a]Matt 23:8-10; 1 Cor 3:4 [b]Acts 18:24; 1 Cor 3:22 [c]John 1:42; 1 Cor 3:22; 9:5; 15:5
13 [1]Or *Christ has been divided!* or *Christ is divided!* [2]Lit *into* [a]Matt 28:19; Acts 2:38
14 [1]Two early mss read *I give thanks that* [a]Acts 18:8 [b]Rom 16:23
15 [1]Lit *into*
16 [a]1 Cor 16:15, 17
17 [1]Lit *wisdom* [a]John 4:2; Acts 10:48 [b]1 Cor 2:1, 4, 13; 2 Cor 10:10; 11:6

18 [1]Or *perish* [2]Or *are saved* [a]1 Cor 1:21, 23, 25; 2:14; 4:10 [b]Acts 2:47; 2 Cor 2:15; 4:3; 2 Thess 2:10 [c]Rom 1:16; 1 Cor 1:24
19 [a]Is 29:14
20 [a]Job 12:17; Is 19:11f; 33:18 [b]Matt 13:22; 1 Cor 2:6, 8; 3:18, 19 [c]Rom 1:20ff [d]John 12:31; 1 Cor 1:27f; 6:2; 11:32; James 4:4
21 [1]Lit *preaching* [a]John 12:31; 1 Cor 1:27f; 6:2; 11:32; James 4:4 [b]Luke 12:32; Gal 1:15; Col 1:19 [c]1 Cor 1:18, 23, 25; 2:14; 4:10 [d]Rom 11:14; James 5:20
22 [1]Or *attesting miracles* [a]Matt 12:38
23 [1]I.e. Messiah [a]1 Cor 2:2; Gal 3:1; 5:11 [b]Luke 2:34; 1 Pet 2:8 [c]1 Cor 1:18, 21, 25; 2:14; 4:10
24 [a]Rom 8:28 [b]Rom 1:16; 1 Cor 1:18 [c]Luke 11:49; 1 Cor 1:30
25 [a]1 Cor 1:18, 21, 23; 2:14; 4:10 [b]2 Cor 13:4
26 [1]Lit *see* [2]I.e. human standards [a]Rom 11:29 [b]Matt 11:25; 1 Cor 1:20; 2:8
27 [a]James 2:5 [b]1 Cor 1:20
28 [a]1 Cor 1:20 [b]Rom 4:17 [c]Job 34:19; 1 Cor 2:6; 2 Thess 2:8; Heb 2:14
29 [1]Lit *flesh* [a]Eph 2:9
30 [1]Lit *of Him* [2]Or *both* [a]Rom 8:1; 1 Cor 4:15 [b]1 Cor 1:24 [c]Jer 23:5f; 33:16; 2 Cor 5:21; Phil 3:9 [d]1 Cor 1:2; 6:11; 1 Thess 5:23 [e]Rom 3:24; Eph 1:7, 14; Col 1:14
31 [a]Jer 9:23f; 2 Cor 10:17
2:1 [1]One early ms reads *mystery* [a]1 Cor 1:17; 2:4, 13 [b]1 Cor 2:7
2 [a]1 Cor 1:23; Gal 6:14
3 [a]1 Cor 4:10; 2 Cor 11:30; 12:5, 9f; 13:9 [b]Is 19:16; 2 Cor 7:15; Eph 6:5
4 [1]Lit *word* [a]1 Cor 1:17; 2:1, 13 [b]Rom 15:19; 1 Cor 4:20
5 [1]Lit *be* [a]2 Cor 4:7; 6:7; 12:9

18 For the word of the cross is [a]foolishness to [b]those who [1]are
perishing, but to us who [2]are being saved it is [c]the power of
God.
19 For it is written,
"[a]I WILL DESTROY THE WISDOM OF THE WISE,
AND THE CLEVERNESS OF THE CLEVER I WILL SET ASIDE."
20 [a]Where is the wise man? Where is the scribe? Where is the
debater of [b]this age? Has not God [c]made foolish the wisdom of
[d]the world?
21 For since in the wisdom of God [a]the world through its
wisdom did not *come to* know God, [b]God was well-pleased
through the [c]foolishness of the [1]message preached to [d]save
those who believe.
22 For indeed [a]Jews ask for [1]signs and Greeks search for
wisdom;
23 but we preach [1a]Christ crucified, [b]to Jews a stumbling block
and to Gentiles [c]foolishness,
24 but to those who are [a]the called, both Jews and Greeks,
Christ [b]the power of God and [c]the wisdom of God.
25 Because the [a]foolishness of God is wiser than men, and
[b]the weakness of God is stronger than men.
26 For [1]consider your [a]calling, brethren, that there were [b]not
many wise according to [2]the flesh, not many mighty, not many
noble;
27 but [a]God has chosen the foolish things of [b]the world to
shame the wise, and God has chosen the weak things of [b]the
world to shame the things which are strong,
28 and the base things of [a]the world and the despised God has
chosen, [b]the things that are not, so that He may [c]nullify the
things that are,
29 so that [a]no [1]man may boast before God.
30 But [1]by His doing you are in [a]Christ Jesus, who became to
us [b]wisdom from God, [2]and [c]righteousness and [d]sanctification,
and [e]redemption,
31 so that, just as it is written, "[a]LET HIM WHO BOASTS, BOAST IN
THE LORD."

Chapter 2 Theme ____

2 And when I came to you, brethren, I [a]did not come with
superiority of speech or of wisdom, proclaiming to you
[b]the [1]testimony of God.
2 For I determined to know nothing among you except [a]Jesus
Christ, and Him crucified.
3 I was with you in [a]weakness and in [b]fear and in much
trembling,
4 and my [1]message and my preaching were [a]not in persuasive
words of wisdom, but in demonstration of [b]the Spirit and of
power,
5 so that your faith would not [1]rest on the wisdom of men,
but on [a]the power of God.

6 Yet we do speak wisdom among those who are [a]mature; a
wisdom, however, not of [b]this age nor of the rulers of [b]this age,
who are [c]passing away;
7 but we speak God's wisdom in a [a]mystery, the hidden
wisdom which God [b]predestined before the [c]ages to our glory;
8 *the wisdom* [a]which none of the rulers of [b]this age has
understood; for if they had understood it they would not have
crucified [c]the Lord of glory;
9 but just as it is written,
"[a]THINGS WHICH EYE HAS NOT SEEN AND EAR HAS NOT HEARD,
AND *which* HAVE NOT ENTERED THE HEART OF MAN,
ALL THAT GOD HAS PREPARED FOR THOSE WHO LOVE HIM."
10 [1a]For to us God revealed *them* [b]through the Spirit; for the
Spirit searches all things, even the [c]depths of God.
11 For who among men knows the *thoughts* of a man except
the [a]spirit of the man which is in him? Even so the *thoughts* of
God no one knows except the Spirit of God.
12 Now we [a]have received, not the spirit of [b]the world, but
the Spirit who is from God, so that we may know the things
freely given to us by God,
13 which things we also speak, [a]not in words taught by
human wisdom, but in those taught by the Spirit, [1]combining
spiritual *thoughts* with spiritual *words.*
14 But [1]a [a]natural man [b]does not accept the things of the Spirit
of God, for they are [c]foolishness to him; and he cannot
understand them, because they are spiritually [2]appraised.
15 But he who is [a]spiritual appraises all things, yet he himself
is appraised by no one.
16 For [a]WHO HAS KNOWN THE MIND OF THE LORD, THAT HE WILL
INSTRUCT HIM? But [b]we have the mind of Christ.

Chapter 3 Theme

3 And I, brethren, could not speak to you as to [a]spiritual
men, but as to [b]men of flesh, as to [c]infants in Christ.
2 I gave you [a]milk to drink, not solid food; for you [b]were not
yet able *to receive it.* Indeed, even now you are not yet able,
3 for you are still fleshly. For since there is [a]jealousy and
strife among you, are you not fleshly, and are you not walking
[1b]like mere men?
4 For when [a]one says, "I am of Paul," and another, "I am of
Apollos," are you not *mere* [b]men?
5 What then is Apollos? And what is Paul? [a]Servants through
whom you believed, even [b]as the Lord gave *opportunity* to
each one.
6 [a]I planted, [b]Apollos watered, but [c]God was causing the
growth.
7 So then neither the one who plants nor the one who
waters is anything, but God who causes the growth.
8 Now he who plants and he who waters are one; but each
will [a]receive his own [1]reward according to his own labor.

6 [a]Eph 4:13; Phil 3:15; Heb 5:14; 6:1 [b]Matt 13:22; 1 Cor 1:20 [c]1 Cor 1:28
7 [a]Rom 11:25; 16:25f; 1 Cor 2:1 [b]Rom 8:29f [c]Heb 1:2; 11:3
8 [a]1 Cor 1:26; 2:6 [b]Matt 13:22; 1 Cor 1:20 [c]Acts 7:2; James 2:1
9 [a]Is 64:4; 65:17
10 [1]One early ms reads *But* [a]Matt 11:25; 13:11; 16:17; Gal 1:12; Eph 3:3, 5 [b]John 14:26 [c]Rom 11:33ff
11 [a]Prov 20:27
12 [a]Rom 8:15 [b]1 Cor 1:27
13 [1]Or *interpreting spiritual* things *for spiritual* men [a]1 Cor 1:17; 2:1, 4
14 [1]Or *an unspiritual* [2]Or *examined* [a]1 Cor 15:44, 46; James 3:15; Jude 19 mg [b]John 14:17 [c]1 Cor 1:18
15 [a]1 Cor 3:1; 14:37; Gal 6:1
16 [a]Is 40:13; Rom 11:34 [b]John 15:15
3:1 [a]1 Cor 2:15; 14:37; Gal 6:1 [b]Rom 7:14; 1 Cor 2:14 [c]1 Cor 2:6; Eph 4:14; Heb 5:13
2 [a]Heb 5:12f; 1 Pet 2:2 [b]John 16:12
3 [1]Lit *according to man* [a]Rom 13:13; 1 Cor 1:10f; 11:18 [b]1 Cor 3:4
4 [a]1 Cor 1:12 [b]1 Cor 3:3
5 [a]Rom 15:16; 2 Cor 3:3, 6; 4:1; 5:18; 6:4; Eph 3:7; Col 1:25; 1 Tim 1:12 [b]Rom 12:6; 1 Cor 3:10
6 [a]1 Cor 4:15; 9:1; 15:1; 2 Cor 10:14f [b]Acts 18:24-27; 1 Cor 1:12 [c]1 Cor 15:10
8 [1]Or *wages* [a]1 Cor 3:14; 4:5; 9:17; Gal 6:4

9 For we are God's [a]fellow workers; you are God's [1b]field,
God's [c]building.
10 According to [a]the grace of God which was given to me, like
a wise master builder [b]I laid a foundation, and [c]another is
building on it. But each man must be careful how he builds on it.
11 For no man can lay a [a]foundation other than the one which
is laid, which is Jesus Christ.
12 Now if any man builds on the foundation with gold, silver,
[1]precious stones, wood, hay, straw,
13 [a]each man's work will become evident; for [b]the day will
show it because it is *to be* revealed with fire, and the fire itself
will test [1]the quality of each man's work.
14 If any man's work which he has built on it remains, he will
[a]receive a reward.
15 If any man's work is burned up, he will suffer loss; but he
himself will be saved, yet [a]so as through fire.
16 [a]Do you not know that [b]you are a [1]temple of God and *that*
the Spirit of God dwells in you?
17 If any man destroys the [1]temple of God, God will destroy
him, for the [1]temple of God is holy, and [2]that is what you are.
18 [a]Let no man deceive himself. [b]If any man among you thinks
that he is wise in [c]this age, he must become foolish, so that he
may become wise.
19 For [a]the wisdom of this world is foolishness before God.
For it is written, "*He is* [b]THE ONE WHO CATCHES THE WISE IN THEIR
CRAFTINESS";
20 and again, "[a]THE LORD KNOWS THE REASONINGS of the wise,
THAT THEY ARE USELESS."
21 So then [a]let no one boast in men. For [b]all things belong to
you,
22 [a]whether Paul or Apollos or Cephas or the world or [b]life or
death or things present or things to come; all things belong to
you,
23 and [a]you belong to Christ; and [b]Christ belongs to God.

Chapter 4 Theme ____________________________________

4 Let a man regard us in this manner, as [a]servants of Christ
and [b]stewards of [c]the mysteries of God.
2 In this case, moreover, it is required [1]of stewards that one
be found trustworthy.
3 But to me it is a very small thing that I may be examined
by you, or by *any* human [1]court; in fact, I do not even examine
myself.
4 For I [a]am conscious of nothing against myself, yet I am not
by this [b]acquitted; but the one who examines me is the Lord.
5 Therefore [a]do not go on [1]passing judgment before [2]the time,
but wait [b]until the Lord comes who will both [c]bring to light the
things hidden in the darkness and disclose the motives of
men's hearts; and then each man's [d]praise will come to him
from God.

9 [1]Or *cultivated land* [a]Mark 16:20; 2 Cor 6:1 [b]Is 61:3; Matt 15:13 [c]1 Cor 3:16; Eph 2:20-22; Col 2:7; 1 Pet 2:5

10 [a]Rom 12:3; 1 Cor 15:10 [b]Rom 15:20; 1 Cor 3:11f [c]1 Thess 3:2

11 [a]Is 28:16; Eph 2:20; 1 Pet 2:4ff

12 [1]Or *costly*

13 [1]Lit *of what sort each man's work is* [a]1 Cor 4:5 [b]Matt 10:15; 1 Cor 1:8; 2 Thess 1:7-10; 2 Tim 1:12, 18; 4:8

14 [a]1 Cor 3:8; 4:5; 9:17; Gal 6:4

15 [a]Job 23:10; Ps 66:10, 12; Jude 23

16 [1]Or *sanctuary* [a]Rom 6:16 [b]Rom 8:9; 1 Cor 6:19; 2 Cor 6:16; Eph 2:21f

17 [1]Or *sanctuary* [2]Lit *who you are*

18 [a]Is 5:21 [b]1 Cor 8:2; Gal 6:3 [c]1 Cor 1:20

19 [a]1 Cor 1:20 [b]Job 5:13

20 [a]Ps 94:11

21 [a]1 Cor 4:6 [b]Rom 8:32

22 [a]1 Cor 1:12; 3:5, 6 [b]Rom 8:38

23 [a]1 Cor 15:23; 2 Cor 10:7; Gal 3:29 [b]1 Cor 11:3; 15:28

4:1 [a]Luke 1:2 [b]1 Cor 9:17; Titus 1:7; 1 Pet 4:10 [c]Rom 11:25; 16:25

2 [1]Lit *in*

3 [1]Lit *day*

4 [a]Acts 23:1; 2 Cor 1:12 [b]Ps 143:2; Rom 2:13

5 [1]Lit *judging anything* [2]I.e. the appointed time of judgment [a]Matt 7:1; Rom 2:1 [b]John 21:22; Rom 2:16 [c]1 Cor 3:13 [d]Rom 2:29; 1 Cor 3:8; 2 Cor 10:18

6 Now these things, brethren, I have figuratively applied to
myself and Apollos for your sakes, so that in us you may learn
not to exceed [a]what is written, so that no one of you will
[b]become [1]arrogant [c]in behalf of one against the other.
7 For who regards you as superior? [a]What do you have that
you did not receive? And if you did receive it, why do you
boast as if you had not received it?
8 You are [a]already filled, you have already become rich, you
have become kings without us; and indeed, *I* wish that you had
become kings so that we also might reign with you.
9 For, I think, God has exhibited us apostles last of all, as men
[a]condemned to death; because we [b]have become a spectacle to
the world, [1]both to angels and to men.
10 We are [a]fools for Christ's sake, but [b]you are prudent in
Christ; [c]we are weak, but you are strong; you are distinguished,
but we are without honor.
11 To this present hour we are both [a]hungry and thirsty, and
are poorly clothed, and are roughly treated, and are homeless;
12 and we toil, [a]working with our own hands; when we are
[b]reviled, we bless; when we are [c]persecuted, we endure;
13 when we are slandered, we try to [1]conciliate; we have
[a]become as the scum of the world, the dregs of all things, *even*
until now.
14 I do not write these things to [a]shame you, but to admonish
you as my beloved [b]children.
15 For if you were to have countless [a]tutors in Christ, yet *you
would* not *have* many fathers, for in [b]Christ Jesus I [c]became
your father through the [d]gospel.
16 Therefore I exhort you, be [a]imitators of me.
17 For this reason I [a]have sent to you [b]Timothy, who is my
[c]beloved and faithful child in the Lord, and he will remind you
of my ways which are in Christ, [d]just as I teach everywhere in
every church.
18 Now some have become [1a]arrogant, as though I were not
[b]coming to you.
19 But I [a]will come to you soon, [b]if the Lord wills, and I shall
find out, not the [1]words of those who are [c]arrogant but their
power.
20 For the kingdom of God does [a]not consist in [1]words but in
power.
21 What do you desire? [a]Shall I come to you with a rod, or
with love and a spirit of gentleness?

Chapter 5 Theme ______________________

5 It is actually reported that there is immorality among you,
and immorality of such a kind as does not exist even
among the Gentiles, that someone has [a]his father's wife.
2 [1]You [a]have become [2]arrogant and [1]have not [b]mourned
instead, so that the one who had done this deed would be
[c]removed from your midst.

6 [1]Lit *puffed up* [a]1 Cor 1:19, 31; 3:19f [b]1 Cor 4:18f; 8:1; 13:4 [c]1 Cor 1:12; 3:4
7 [a]John 3:27; Rom 12:3, 6; 1 Pet 4:10
8 [a]Rev 3:17f
9 [1]Or *and to angels and to men* [a]Rom 8:36; 1 Cor 15:31; 2 Cor 11:23 [b]Heb 10:33
10 [a]Acts 17:18; 26:24; 1 Cor 1:18 [b]1 Cor 1:19f; 3:18; 2 Cor 11:19 [c]1 Cor 2:3; 2 Cor 13:9
11 [a]Rom 8:35; 2 Cor 11:23-27
12 [a]Acts 18:3 [b]1 Pet 3:9 [c]John 15:20; Rom 8:35
13 [1]Or *console* [a]Lam 3:45
14 [a]1 Cor 6:5; 15:34 [b]2 Cor 6:13; 12:14; 1 Thess 2:11; 1 John 2:1; 3 John 4
15 [a]Gal 3:24f [b]1 Cor 1:30 [c]Num 11:12; 1 Cor 3:8; Gal 4:19; Philem 10 [d]1 Cor 9:12, 14, 18, 23; 15:1
16 [a]1 Cor 11:1; Phil 3:17; 4:9; 1 Thess 1:6; 2 Thess 3:9
17 [a]1 Cor 16:10 [b]Acts 16:1 [c]1 Cor 4:14; 1 Tim 1:2, 18; 2 Tim 1:2 [d]1 Cor 7:17; 14:33; 16:1; Titus 1:5
18 [1]Lit *puffed up* [a]1 Cor 4:6 [b]1 Cor 4:21
19 [1]Lit *word* [a]Acts 19:21; 20:2; 1 Cor 11:34; 16:5f; 16:7-9; 2 Cor 1:15f [b]Acts 18:21 [c]1 Cor 4:6
20 [1]Lit *word* [a]1 Cor 2:4
21 [a]2 Cor 1:23; 2:1, 3; 12:20; 13:2, 10
5:1 [a]Lev 18:8; Deut 22:30; 27:20
2 [1]Or *have you . . .?* [2]Lit *puffed up* [a]1 Cor 4:6 [b]2 Cor 7:7-10 [c]1 Cor 5:13

3 For I, on my part, though [a]absent in body but present in
spirit, have already judged him who has so committed this, as
though I were present.
4 [a]In the name of our Lord Jesus, when you are assembled,
and [1]I with you in spirit, [b]with the power of our Lord Jesus,
5 *I have decided* to [a]deliver such a one to [b]Satan for the
destruction of his flesh, so that his spirit may be saved in [c]the
day of the Lord [1]Jesus.
6 [a]Your boasting is not good. [b]Do you not know that [c]a little
leaven leavens the whole lump *of dough?*
7 Clean out the old leaven so that you may be a new lump,
just as you are *in fact* unleavened. For Christ our [a]Passover also
has been sacrificed.
8 Therefore let us celebrate the feast, [a]not with old leaven,
nor with the leaven of malice and wickedness, but with the
unleavened bread of sincerity and truth.
9 I wrote you in my letter [a]not to associate with immoral
people;
10 I *did* not at all *mean* with the immoral people of this world,
or with the covetous and swindlers, or with [a]idolaters, for then
you would have to go out of the world.
11 But [1]actually, I wrote to you not to associate [2]with any so-
called [a]brother if he is an immoral person, or covetous, or [b]an
idolater, or a reviler, or a drunkard, or a swindler—not even to
eat with such a one.
12 For what have I to do with judging [a]outsiders? [b]Do you not
judge those who are within *the church?*
13 But those who are outside, God [1]judges. [a]REMOVE THE
WICKED MAN FROM AMONG YOURSELVES.

Chapter 6 Theme ______________________________

6 Does any one of you, when he has a [1]case against his
neighbor, dare to go to law before the unrighteous and [a]not
before the [2]saints?
2 Or [a]do you not know that [b]the [1]saints will judge [c]the
world? If the world is judged by you, are you not competent *to*
[2]*constitute* the smallest law courts?
3 [a]Do you not know that we will judge angels? How much
more matters of this life?
4 So if you have law courts dealing with matters of this life, [1]do
you appoint them as judges who are of no account in the church?
5 [a]I say *this* to your shame. *Is it* so, *that* there is not among you
one wise man who will be able to decide between his [b]brethren,
6 but brother goes to law with brother, and that before
[a]unbelievers?
7 Actually, then, it is already a defeat for you, that you have
lawsuits with one another. [a]Why not rather be wronged? Why
not rather be defrauded?
8 On the contrary, you yourselves wrong and defraud. *You do*
this even to *your* [a]brethren.

3 [a]Col 2:5; 1 Thess 2:17
4 [1]Lit *my spirit, with the power* [a]2 Thess 3:6 [b]John 20:23; 2 Cor 2:10; 13:3, 10
5 [1]Two early mss do not contain *Jesus* [a]Prov 23:14; Luke 22:31; 1 Tim 1:20 [b]Matt 4:10 [c]1 Cor 1:8
6 [a]1 Cor 5:2; James 4:16 [b]Rom 6:16 [c]Hos 7:4; Matt 16:6, 12; Gal 5:9
7 [a]Mark 14:12; 1 Pet 1:19
8 [a]Ex 12:19; 13:7; Deut 16:3
9 [a]2 Cor 6:14; Eph 5:11; 2 Thess 3:6
10 [a]1 Cor 10:27
11 [1]Lit *now* [2]Lit *together if any man called a brother is* [a]Acts 1:15; 2 Thess 3:6 [b]1 Cor 10:7, 14, 20f
12 [a]Mark 4:11 [b]1 Cor 5:3-5; 6:1-4
13 [1]Or *will judge* [a]Deut 13:5; 17:7, 12; 21:21; 22:21; 1 Cor 5:2
6:1 [1]Lit *matter* [2]Or *holy ones* [a]Matt 18:17
2 [1]V 1, note 2 [2]Or *try the trivial cases?* [a]Rom 6:16 [b]Dan 7:18, 22, 27; Matt 19:28 [c]1 Cor 1:20
3 [a]Rom 6:16
4 [1]Or *appoint them . . . church*
5 [a]1 Cor 4:14; 15:34 [b]Acts 1:15; 9:13; 1 Cor 6:1
6 [a]2 Cor 6:14f; 1 Tim 5:8
7 [a]Matt 5:39f
8 [a]1 Thess 4:6

9 Or [a]do you not know that the unrighteous will not [b]inherit
the kingdom of God? [c]Do not be deceived; [d]neither fornicators,
nor idolaters, nor adulterers, nor [1]effeminate, nor homosexuals,
10 nor thieves, nor *the* covetous, nor drunkards, nor revilers,
nor swindlers, will [a]inherit the kingdom of God.
11 [a]Such were some of you; but you were [b]washed, but you
were [c]sanctified, but you were [d]justified in the name of the
Lord Jesus Christ and in the Spirit of our God.
12 [a]All things are lawful for me, but not all things are profitable. All
things are lawful for me, but I will not be mastered by anything.
13 [a]Food is for the [1]stomach and the [1]stomach is for food, but
God will [b]do away with both [2]of them. Yet the body is not for
immorality, but [c]for the Lord, and [d]the Lord is for the body.
14 Now God has not only [a]raised the Lord, but [b]will also raise
us up through His power.
15 [a]Do you not know that [b]your bodies are members of
Christ? Shall I then take away the members of Christ and make
them members of a prostitute? [c]May it never be!
16 Or [a]do you not know that the one who joins himself to a
prostitute is one body *with her?* For He says, "[b]THE TWO SHALL
BECOME ONE FLESH."
17 But the one who joins himself to the Lord is [a]one spirit
with Him.
18 [a]Flee immorality. Every *other* sin that a man commits is
outside the body, but the [1]immoral man sins against his own
body.
19 Or [a]do you not know that [b]your body is a [1]temple of the
Holy Spirit who is in you, whom you have from [2]God, and that
[c]you are not your own?
20 For [a]you have been bought with a price: therefore glorify
God in [b]your body.

Chapter 7 Theme

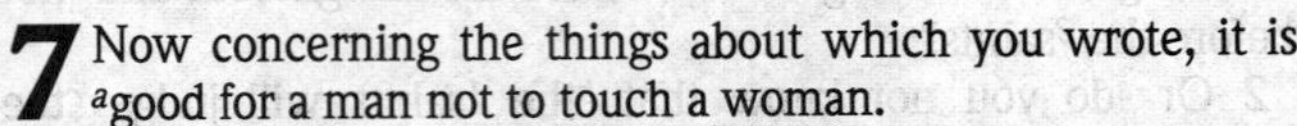

7 Now concerning the things about which you wrote, it is
[a]good for a man not to touch a woman.
2 But because of immoralities, each man is to have his own
wife, and each woman is to have her own husband.
3 The husband must [1]fulfill his duty to his wife, and likewise
also the wife to her husband.
4 The wife does not have authority over her own body, but
the husband *does;* and likewise also the husband does not have
authority over his own body, but the wife *does.*
5 [a]Stop depriving one another, except by agreement for a
time, so that you may devote yourselves to prayer, and [1]come
together again so that [b]Satan will not tempt you because of
your lack of self-control.
6 But this I say by way of concession, [a]not of command.
7 [1]Yet I wish that all men were [a]even as I myself am. However,
[b]each man has his own gift from God, one in this manner, and
another in that.

RETURN TO INSTRUCTIONS

9 [1]I.e. effeminate by perversion [a]Rom 6:16 [b]Acts 20:32; 1 Cor 15:50; Gal 5:21; Eph 5:5 [c]Luke 21:8; 1 Cor 15:33; Gal 6:7; James 1:16; 1 John 3:7 [d]Rom 13:13; 1 Cor 5:11; Gal 5:19-21; Eph 5:5; 1 Tim 1:10; Rev 21:8; 22:15

10 [a]Acts 20:32; 1 Cor 15:50; Gal 5:21; Eph 5:5

11 [a]1 Cor 12:2; Eph 2:2f; Col 3:5-7; Titus 3:3-7 [b]Acts 22:16; Eph 5:26 [c]1 Cor 1:2, 30 [d]Rom 8:30

12 [a]1 Cor 10:23

13 [1]Lit *belly* [2]Lit *it and them* [a]Matt 15:17 [b]Col 2:22 [c]1 Cor 6:15, 19 [d]Gal 5:24; Eph 5:23

14 [a]Acts 2:24 [b]John 6:39f; 1 Cor 15:23

15 [a]1 Cor 6:3 [b]Rom 12:5; 1 Cor 6:13; 12:27; Eph 5:30 [c]Luke 20:16

16 [a]1 Cor 6:3 [b]Gen 2:24; Matt 19:5; Mark 10:8; Eph 5:31

17 [a]John 17:21-23; Rom 8:9-11; 1 Cor 6:15; Gal 2:20

18 [1]Or *one who practices immorality* [a]1 Cor 6:9; 2 Cor 12:21; Eph 5:3; Col 3:5; Heb 13:4

19 [1]Or *sanctuary* [2]Or *God? And you . . . own* [a]1 Cor 6:3 [b]John 2:21; 1 Cor 3:16; 2 Cor 6:16 [c]Rom 14:7f

20 [a]Acts 20:28; 1 Cor 7:23; 1 Pet 1:18f; 2 Pet 2:1; Rev 5:9 [b]Rom 12:1; Phil 1:20

7:1 [a]1 Cor 7:8, 26

3 [1]Lit *render*

5 [1]Lit *be* [a]Ex 19:15; 1 Sam 21:5 [b]Matt 4:10

6 [a]2 Cor 8:8

7 [1]One early ms reads *For* [a]1 Cor 7:8; 9:5 [b]Matt 19:11f; Rom 12:6; 1 Cor 12:4, 11

8 But I say to the unmarried and to widows that it is [a]good
for them if they remain [b]even as I.
9 But if they do not have self-control, [a]let them marry; for it
is better to marry than to burn *with passion.*
10 But to the married I give instructions, [a]not I, but the Lord,
that the wife should not [1]leave her husband
11 (but if she does leave, she must remain unmarried, or else
be reconciled to her husband), and that the husband should
not [1]divorce his wife.
12 But to the rest [a]I say, not the Lord, that if any brother has a
wife who is an unbeliever, and she consents to live with him,
he must not [1]divorce her.
13 And a woman who has an unbelieving husband, and he
consents to live with her, she must not [1]send her husband away.
14 For the unbelieving husband is sanctified through his wife,
and the unbelieving wife is sanctified through [1]her believing
husband; for otherwise your children are unclean, but now
they are [a]holy.
15 Yet if the unbelieving one leaves, let him leave; the brother
or the sister is not under bondage in such *cases,* but God has
called [1]us [2a]to peace.
16 For how do you know, O wife, whether you will [a]save your
husband? Or how do you know, O husband, whether you will
save your wife?
17 Only, [a]as the Lord has assigned to each one, as God has
called each, in this manner let him walk. And [b]so I direct in [c]all
the churches.
18 Was any man called *when he was already* circumcised? He
is not to become uncircumcised. Has anyone been called in
uncircumcision? [a]He is not to be circumcised.
19 [a]Circumcision is nothing, and uncircumcision is nothing,
but *what matters is* [b]the keeping of the commandments of God.
20 [a]Each man must remain in that [1]condition in which he was
called.
21 Were you called while a slave? [1]Do not worry about it; but
if you are able also to become free, rather [2]do that.
22 For he who was called in the Lord while a slave, is [a]the Lord's
freedman; likewise he who was called while free, is [b]Christ's slave.
23 [a]You were bought with a price; do not become slaves of men.
24 Brethren, [a]each one is to remain with God in that *condition*
in which he was called.
25 Now concerning virgins I have [a]no command of the Lord,
but I give an opinion as one who [1b]by the mercy of the Lord is
trustworthy.
26 I think then that this is good in view of the [1]present
[a]distress, that [b]it is good for a man [2]to remain as he is.
27 Are you bound to a wife? Do not seek to be released. Are
you released from a wife? Do not seek a wife.
28 But if you marry, you have not sinned; and if a virgin marries,
she has not sinned. Yet such will have [1]trouble in this life, and
I am trying to spare you.

8 [a]1 Cor 7:1, 26 [b]1 Cor 7:7; 9:5
9 [a]1 Tim 5:14
10 [1]Lit *depart from* [a]Mal 2:16; Matt 5:32; 19:3-9; Mark 10:2-12; Luke 16:18; 1 Cor 7:6
11 [1]Or *leave his wife*
12 [1]Or *leave her* [a]1 Cor 7:6; 2 Cor 11:17
13 [1]Or *leave her husband*
14 [1]Lit *the brother* [a]Ezra 9:2; Mal 2:15
15 [1]One early ms reads *you* [2]Lit *in* [a]Rom 14:19
16 [a]Rom 11:14; 1 Pet 3:1
17 [a]Rom 12:3 [b]1 Cor 4:17 [c]1 Cor 11:16; 14:33; 2 Cor 8:18; 11:28; Gal 1:22; 1 Thess 2:14; 2 Thess 1:4
18 [a]Acts 15:1ff
19 [a]Rom 2:27, 29; Gal 3:28; 5:6; 6:15; Col 3:11 [b]Rom 2:25
20 [1]Lit *calling* [a]1 Cor 7:24
21 [1]Lit *Let it not be a care to you* [2]Lit *use*
22 [a]John 8:32, 36; Philem 16 [b]Eph 6:6; Col 3:24; 1 Pet 2:16
23 [a]1 Cor 6:20
24 [a]1 Cor 7:20
25 [1]Lit *has had mercy shown on him by the Lord to be trustworthy* [a]1 Cor 7:6 [b]2 Cor 4:1; 1 Tim 1:13, 16
26 [1]Or *impending* [2]Lit *so to be* [a]Luke 21:23; 2 Thess 2:2 [b]1 Cor 7:1, 8
28 [1]Lit *tribulation in the flesh*

29 But this I say, brethren, [a]the time has been shortened, so
that from now on those who have wives should be as though
they had none;
30 and those who weep, as though they did not weep; and
those who rejoice, as though they did not rejoice; and those
who buy, as though they did not possess;
31 and those who use the world, as though they did not [a]make
full use of it; for [b]the form of this world is passing away.
32 But I want you to be free from concern. One who is
[a]unmarried is concerned about the things of the Lord, how he
may please the Lord;
33 but one who is married is concerned about the things of
the world, how he may please his wife,
34 and *his interests* are divided. The woman who is unmarried,
and the virgin, is concerned about the things of the Lord, that
she may be holy both in body and spirit; but one who is married
is concerned about the things of the world, how she may please
her husband.
35 This I say for your own benefit; not to put a restraint upon
you, but [1]to promote what is appropriate and *to secure*
undistracted devotion to the Lord.
36 But if any man thinks that he is acting unbecomingly toward
his virgin *daughter,* if she is past her youth, and if it must be so,
let him do what he wishes, he does not sin; let [1]her marry.
37 But he who stands firm in his heart, [1]being under no constraint,
but has authority [2]over his own will, and has decided this in his
own heart, to keep his own virgin *daughter,* he will do well.
38 So then both he who gives his own virgin *daughter* in
marriage does well, and he who does not give her in marriage
will do better.
39 [a]A wife is bound as long as her husband lives; but if her
husband [1]is dead, she is free to be married to whom she wishes,
only [b]in the Lord.
40 But [a]in my opinion she is happier if she remains as she is;
and I think that I also have the Spirit of God.

Chapter 8 Theme ______________________________

8 Now concerning [a]things sacrificed to idols, we know that
we all have [b]knowledge. Knowledge [1c]makes arrogant, but
love [d]edifies.
2 [a]If anyone supposes that he knows anything, he has not yet
[b]known as he ought to know;
3 but if anyone loves God, he [a]is known by Him.
4 Therefore concerning the eating of [a]things sacrificed to
idols, we know that [1]there is [b]no such thing as an idol in the
world, and that [c]there is no God but one.
5 For even if [a]there are so-called gods whether in heaven or
on earth, as indeed there are many gods and many lords,
6 yet for us [a]there is *but* one God, [b]the Father, [c]from whom are
all things and we *exist* for Him; and [d]one Lord, Jesus Christ,
[e]by whom are all things, and we *exist* through Him.

29 [a]Rom 13:11f; 1 Cor 7:31
31 [a]1 Cor 9:18 [b]1 Cor 7:29; 1 John 2:17
32 [a]1 Tim 5:5
35 [1]Lit *for what is seemly*
36 [1]Lit *them*
37 [1]Lit *having no necessity* [2]Lit *pertaining to*
39 [1]Lit *falls asleep* [a]Rom 7:2 [b]2 Cor 6:14
40 [a]1 Cor 7:6, 25
8:1 [1]Lit *puffs up* [a]Acts 15:20; 1 Cor 8:4, 7, 10 [b]Rom 15:14; 1 Cor 8:7, 10; 10:15 [c]1 Cor 4:6 [d]Rom 14:19
2 [a]1 Cor 3:18 [b]1 Cor 13:8-12; 1 Tim 6:4
3 [a]Ps 1:6; Jer 1:5; Amos 3:2; Rom 8:29; 11:2; Gal 4:9
4 [1]Lit *nothing is an idol in the world;* i.e. an idol has no real existence [a]Acts 15:20; 1 Cor 8:1, 7, 10 [b]Acts 14:15; 1 Cor 10:19; Gal 4:8 [c]Deut 4:35, 39; 6:4; 1 Cor 8:6
5 [a]2 Thess 2:4
6 [a]Deut 4:35, 39; 6:4; Is 46:9; Jer 10:6, 7; 1 Cor 8:4 [b]Mal 2:10; Eph 4:6 [c]Rom 11:36 [d]John 13:13; 1 Cor 1:2; Eph 4:5; 1 Tim 2:5 [e]John 1:3; Col 1:16

7 However not all men [a]have this knowledge; but [b]some,
being accustomed to the idol until now, eat *food* as if it were
sacrificed to an idol; and their conscience being weak is defiled.
8 But [a]food will not [1]commend us to God; we are neither
[2]the worse if we do not eat, nor [3]the better if we do eat.
9 But [a]take care that this [1]liberty of yours does not somehow
become a stumbling block to the [b]weak.
10 For if someone sees you, who have [a]knowledge, dining in
an idol's temple, will not his conscience, if he is weak, be
strengthened to eat [b]things sacrificed to idols?
11 For through [a]your knowledge he who is weak [b]is ruined,
the brother for whose sake Christ died.
12 [a]And so, by sinning against the brethren and wounding
their conscience when it is weak, you sin [b]against Christ.
13 Therefore, [a]if food causes my brother to stumble, I will never
eat meat again, so that I will not cause my brother to stumble.

Chapter 9 Theme ____

9 Am I not [a]free? Am I not an [b]apostle? Have I not [c]seen
Jesus our Lord? Are you not [d]my work in the Lord?
2 If to others I am not an apostle, at least I am to you; for you
are the [a]seal of my [b]apostleship in the Lord.
3 My defense to those who examine me is this:
4 [1a]Do we not have a right to eat and drink?
5 [1a]Do we not have a right to take along a [2]believing wife,
even as the rest of the apostles and the [b]brothers of the Lord
and [c]Cephas?
6 Or do only [1a]Barnabas and I not have a right to refrain from
working?
7 Who at any time serves [a]as a soldier at his own expense?
Who [b]plants a vineyard and does not eat the fruit of it? Or who
tends a flock and does not [1]use the milk of the flock?
8 I am not speaking these things [a]according to [1]human
judgment, am I? Or does not the Law also say these things?
9 For it is written in the Law of Moses, "[a]YOU SHALL NOT
MUZZLE THE OX WHILE HE IS THRESHING." God is not concerned about
[b]oxen, is He?
10 Or is He speaking altogether for our sake? Yes, [a]for our sake
it was written, because [b]the plowman ought to plow in hope,
and the thresher *to thresh* in hope of sharing *the crops.*
11 [a]If we sowed spiritual things in you, is it too much if we
reap material things from you?
12 If others share the right over you, do we not more? Nevertheless, we [a]did not use this right, but we endure all things [b]so
that we will cause no hindrance to the [c]gospel of Christ.
13 [a]Do you not know that those who [b]perform sacred services
eat the *food* of the temple, *and* those who attend regularly to
the altar have their share [1]from the altar?
14 So also [a]the Lord directed those who proclaim the [b]gospel
to [c]get their living from the gospel.

7 [a]1 Cor 8:4ff [b]Rom 14:14, 22f
8 [1]Or *present* [2]Lit *lacking* [3]Lit *abounding* [a]Rom 14:17
9 [1]Lit *right* [a]Rom 14:13, 21; 1 Cor 10:28; Gal 5:13 [b]Rom 14:1; 1 Cor 8:10f
10 [a]1 Cor 8:4ff [b]Acts 15:20; 1 Cor 8:1, 4, 7
11 [a]1 Cor 8:4ff [b]Rom 14:15, 20
12 [a]Matt 18:6; Rom 14:20 [b]Matt 25:45
13 [a]Rom 14:21; 1 Cor 10:32; 2 Cor 6:3; 11:29
9:1 [a]1 Cor 9:19; 10:29 [b]Acts 14:14; Rom 1:1; 2 Cor 12:12; 1 Thess 2:6; 1 Tim 2:7; 2 Tim 1:11 [c]Acts 9:3, 17; 18:9; 22:14, 18; 23:11; 1 Cor 15:8 [d]1 Cor 3:6; 4:15
2 [a]John 3:33; 2 Cor 3:2f [b]Acts 1:25
4 [1]Lit *It is not that we have no right to eat and drink, is it?* [a]1 Cor 9:14; 1 Thess 2:6, 9; 2 Thess 3:8f
5 [1]Lit *It is not that we have no right to take along . . . Cephas, is it?* [2]Lit *sister, as wife* [a]1 Cor 7:7f [b]Matt 12:46 [c]Matt 8:14; John 1:42
6 [1]Lit *I and Barnabas* [a]Acts 4:36
7 [1]Lit *eat of* [a]2 Cor 10:4; 1 Tim 1:18; 2 Tim 2:3f [b]Deut 20:6; Prov 27:18; 1 Cor 3:6, 8
8 [1]Lit *man* [a]Rom 3:5
9 [a]Deut 25:4; 1 Tim 5:18 [b]Deut 22:1-4; Prov 12:10
10 [a]Rom 4:23f [b]2 Tim 2:6
11 [a]Rom 15:27; 1 Cor 9:14
12 [a]Acts 18:3; 20:33; 1 Cor 9:15, 18 [b]2 Cor 6:3; 11:12 [c]1 Cor 4:15; 9:14, 16, 18, 23; 2 Cor 2:12
13 [1]Lit *with* [a]Rom 6:16 [b]Lev 6:16, 26; 7:6, 31ff; Num 5:9f; 18:8-20, 31; Deut 18:1
14 [a]Matt 10:10; Luke 10:7; 1 Tim 5:18 [b]1 Cor 4:15; 9:12, 16, 18, 23; 2 Cor 2:12 [c]Luke 10:8; 1 Cor 9:4

15 But I have [a]used none of these things. And I am not writing
these things so that it will be done so in my case; for it would
be better for me to die than have any man make [b]my boast an
empty one.
16 For if I preach the gospel, I have nothing to boast of, for [a]I am
under compulsion; for woe is me if I do not preach [b]the gospel.
17 For if I do this voluntarily, I have a [a]reward; but if against
my will, I have a [b]stewardship entrusted to me.
18 What then is my [a]reward? That, when I preach the gospel,
I may offer the gospel [b]without charge, so as [c]not to make full
use of my right in the gospel.
19 For though I am [a]free from all *men,* I have made myself [b]a
slave to all, so that I may [c]win more.
20 [a]To the Jews I became as a Jew, so that I might win Jews; to
those who are under [1]the Law, as under [1]the Law though [b]not
being myself under [1]the Law, so that I might win those who
are under [1]the Law;
21 to those who are [a]without law, [b]as without law, though not
being without the law of God but [c]under the law of Christ, so
that I might win those who are without law.
22 To the [a]weak I became weak, that I might win the weak; I
have become [b]all things to all men, [c]so that I may by all means
save some.
23 I do all things for the sake of the gospel, so that I may become
a fellow partaker of it.
24 [a]Do you not know that those who run in a race all run, but
only one receives [b]the prize? [c]Run in such a way that you may win.
25 Everyone who [a]competes in the games exercises self-control
in all things. They then *do it* to receive a perishable [b]wreath,
but we an imperishable.
26 Therefore I [a]run in such a way, as not without aim; I box in
such a way, as not [b]beating the air;
27 but I [1]discipline [a]my body and make it my slave, so that, after
I have preached to others, I myself will not be disqualified.

Chapter 10 Theme ______________________

10 For [a]I do not want you to be unaware, brethren, that our
fathers were all [b]under the cloud and all [c]passed through
the sea;
2 and all were [a]baptized into Moses in the cloud and in the sea;
3 and all [a]ate the same spiritual food;
4 and all [a]drank the same spiritual drink, for they were drinking
from a spiritual rock which followed them; and the rock was
[1]Christ.
5 Nevertheless, with most of them God was not well-pleased;
for [a]they were laid low in the wilderness.
6 Now these things happened as [a]examples for us, so that we
would not crave evil things as [b]they also craved.
7 Do not be [a]idolaters, as some of them were; as it is written,
"[b]THE PEOPLE SAT DOWN TO EAT AND DRINK, AND STOOD UP TO [c]PLAY."

15 [a]Acts 18:3; 20:33; 1 Cor 9:12, 18 [b]2 Cor 11:10
16 [a]Acts 9:15; Rom 1:14 [b]1 Cor 4:15; 9:12, 14, 18, 23; 2 Cor 2:12
17 [a]John 4:36; 1 Cor 3:8; 9:18 [b]1 Cor 4:1; Gal 2:7; Eph 3:2; Phil 1:16; Col 1:25
18 [a]John 4:36; 1 Cor 3:8; 9:17 [b]Acts 18:3; 2 Cor 11:7; 12:13 [c]1 Cor 7:31; 9:12
19 [a]1 Cor 9:1 [b]2 Cor 4:5; Gal 5:13 [c]Matt 18:15; 1 Pet 3:1
20 [1]Or *law* [a]Acts 16:3; 21:23-26; Rom 11:14 [b]Gal 2:19
21 [a]Rom 2:12, 14 [b]Gal 2:3; 3:2 [c]1 Cor 7:22; Gal 6:2
22 [a]Rom 14:1; 15:1; 2 Cor 11:29 [b]1 Cor 10:33 [c]Rom 11:14
24 [a]1 Cor 9:13 [b]Phil 3:14; Col 2:18 [c]Gal 2:2; 2 Tim 4:7; Heb 12:1
25 [a]Eph 6:12; 1 Tim 6:12; 2 Tim 2:5; 4:7 [b]2 Tim 4:8; James 1:12; 1 Pet 5:4; Rev 2:10; 3:11
26 [a]Gal 2:2; 2 Tim 4:7; Heb 12:1 [b]1 Cor 14:9
27 [1]Lit *bruise* [a]Rom 8:13
10:1 [a]Rom 1:13 [b]Ex 13:21; Ps 105:39 [c]Ex 14:22, 29; Neh 9:11; Ps 66:6
2 [a]Rom 6:3; 1 Cor 1:13; Gal 3:27
3 [a]Ex 16:4, 35; Deut 8:3; Neh 9:15, 20; Ps 78:24f; John 6:31
4 [1]I.e. the Messiah [a]Ex 17:6; Num 20:11; Ps 78:15
5 [a]Num 14:29ff, 37; 26:65; Heb 3:17; Jude 5
6 [a]1 Cor 10:11 [b]Num 11:4, 34; Ps 106:14
7 [a]Ex 32:4; 1 Cor 5:11; 10:14 [b]Ex 32:6 [c]Ex 32:19

8 Nor let us act immorally, as [a]some of them [1]did, and [b]twenty-
three thousand fell in one day.
9 Nor let us try the Lord, as [a]some of them [1]did, and were
destroyed by the serpents.
10 Nor [a]grumble, as some of them [1]did, and [b]were destroyed
by the [c]destroyer.
11 Now these things happened to them as an [a]example, and
[b]they were written for our instruction, upon whom [c]the ends
of the ages have come.
12 Therefore let him who [a]thinks he stands take heed that he
does not fall.
13 No temptation has overtaken you but such as is common to
man; and [a]God is faithful, who will not allow you to be [b]tempted
beyond what you are able, but with the temptation will provide
the way of escape also, so that you will be able to endure it.
14 Therefore, my [a]beloved, flee from [b]idolatry.
15 I speak as to wise men; you judge what I say.
16 Is not the [a]cup of blessing which we bless a sharing in the
blood of Christ? Is not the [1b]bread which we break a sharing in
the body of Christ?
17 Since there is one [1]bread, we [a]who are many are one body;
for we all partake of the one [1]bread.
18 Look at [1]the nation [a]Israel; are not those who [b]eat the
sacrifices sharers in the altar?
19 What do I mean then? That a thing sacrificed to idols is
anything, or [a]that an idol is anything?
20 *No,* but *I say* that the things which the Gentiles sacrifice,
they [a]sacrifice to demons and not to God; and I do not want
you to become sharers in demons.
21 [a]You cannot drink the cup of the Lord and the cup of demons;
you cannot partake of the table of the Lord and [b]the table of
demons.
22 Or do we [a]provoke the Lord to jealousy? We are not [b]stronger
than He, are we?
23 [a]All things are lawful, but not all things are profitable. All
things are lawful, but not all things [b]edify.
24 Let no one [a]seek his own *good,* but that of his [1]neighbor.
25 [a]Eat anything that is sold in the meat market without
asking questions for conscience' sake;
26 [a]FOR THE EARTH IS THE LORD'S, AND [1]ALL IT CONTAINS.
27 If [a]one of the unbelievers invites you and you want to go,
[b]eat anything that is set before you without asking questions for
conscience' sake.
28 But [a]if anyone says to you, "This is meat sacrificed to idols,"
do not eat *it,* for the sake of the one who informed *you,* and for
conscience' sake;
29 I mean not your own conscience, but the other *man's;* for
[a]why is my freedom judged by another's conscience?
30 If I partake with thankfulness, [a]why am I slandered concerning
that for which I [b]give thanks?
31 Whether, then, you eat or drink or [a]whatever you do, do all
to the glory of God.

8 [1]Lit *acted immorally* [a]Num 25:1ff [b]Num 25:9
9 [1]Lit *made trial* [a]Num 21:5f
10 [1]Lit *grumbled* [a]Num 16:41; 17:5, 10 [b]Num 16:49 [c]Ex 12:23; 2 Sam 24:16; 1 Chr 21:15; Heb 11:28
11 [a]1 Cor 10:6 [b]Rom 4:23 [c]Rom 13:11
12 [a]Rom 11:20; 2 Pet 3:17
13 [a]1 Cor 1:9 [b]2 Pet 2:9
14 [a]Heb 6:9 [b]1 Cor 10:7, 19f; 1 John 5:21
16 [1]Lit *loaf* [a]Matt 26:27f; Mark 14:23f; Luke 22:20; 1 Cor 11:25 [b]Matt 26:26; Luke 22:19; Acts 2:42; 1 Cor 11:23f
17 [1]Lit *loaf* [a]Rom 12:5; 1 Cor 12:12f, 27; Eph 4:4, 16; Col 3:15
18 [1]Lit *Israel according to the flesh* [a]Rom 1:3 [b]Lev 7:6, 14f; Deut 12:17f
19 [a]1 Cor 8:4
20 [a]Deut 32:17; Ps 106:37; Gal 4:8; Rev 9:20
21 [a]2 Cor 6:16 [b]Is 65:11
22 [a]Deut 32:21 [b]Eccl 6:10; Is 45:9
23 [a]1 Cor 6:12 [b]Rom 14:19
24 [1]Lit *the other* [a]Rom 15:2; 1 Cor 10:33; 13:5; 2 Cor 12:14; Phil 2:21
25 [a]Acts 10:15; 1 Cor 8:7
26 [1]Lit *its fullness* [a]Ps 24:1; 50:12; 1 Tim 4:4
27 [a]1 Cor 5:10 [b]Luke 10:8
28 [a]1 Cor 8:7, 10-12
29 [a]Rom 14:16; 1 Cor 9:19
30 [a]1 Cor 9:1 [b]Rom 14:6
31 [a]Col 3:17; 1 Pet 4:11

32 [a]Give no offense either to Jews or to Greeks or to [b]the
church of God;
33 just as I also [a]please all men in all things, [b]not seeking my
own profit but the *profit* of the many, [c]so that they may be saved.

Chapter 11 Theme ____________________________

11 [a]Be imitators of me, just as I also am of Christ.
2 Now [a]I praise you because you [b]remember me in everything and [c]hold firmly to the traditions, just as I delivered them
to you.
3 But I want you to understand that [1]Christ is the [a]head of
every man, and [b]the man is the head of a woman, and God is
the [c]head of [1]Christ.
4 Every man who has *something* on his head while praying
or [a]prophesying disgraces his head.
5 But every [a]woman who has her head uncovered while
praying or prophesying disgraces her head, for she is one and
the same as the woman [1]whose head is [b]shaved.
6 For if a woman does not cover [1]her head, let her also [2]have
her hair cut off; but if it is disgraceful for a woman to [2]have her
hair cut off or [1]her head shaved, let her cover [1]her head.
7 For a man ought not to have his head covered, since he is
the [a]image and glory of God; but the woman is the glory of man.
8 For [a]man [1]does not originate from woman, but woman from
man;
9 for indeed man was not created for the woman's sake, but
[a]woman for the man's sake.
10 Therefore the woman ought to have *a symbol of* authority
on her head, because of the angels.
11 However, in the Lord, neither is woman [1]independent of
man, nor is man [1]independent of woman.
12 For as the woman [1]originates from the man, so also the man
has his birth through the woman; and [a]all things [2]originate [b]from
God.
13 [a]Judge [1]for yourselves: is it proper for a woman to pray to
God *with her head* uncovered?
14 Does not even nature itself teach you that if a man has long
hair, it is a dishonor to him,
15 but if a woman has long hair, it is a glory to her? For her
hair is given to her for a covering.
16 But if one is inclined to be contentious, [a]we have no [1]other
practice, nor have [b]the churches of God.
17 But in giving this instruction, [a]I do not praise you, because
you come together not for the better but for the worse.
18 For, in the first place, when you come together [1]as a church,
I hear that [2a]divisions exist among you; and in part I believe it.
19 For there [a]must also be factions among you, [b]so that those
who are approved may become [1]evident among you.
20 Therefore when you meet together, it is not to eat the Lord's
Supper,

32 [a]Acts 24:16; 1 Cor 8:13 [b]Acts 20:28; 1 Cor 1:2; 7:17; 11:22; 15:9; 2 Cor 1:1; Gal 1:13; Phil 3:6; 1 Tim 3:5, 15

33 [a]Rom 15:2; 1 Cor 9:22; Gal 1:10 [b]Rom 15:2; 1 Cor 13:5; 2 Cor 12:14; Phil 2:21 [c]Rom 11:14; 1 Thess 2:16

11:1 [a]1 Cor 4:16; Phil 3:17

2 [a]1 Cor 11:17, 22 [b]1 Cor 4:17; 15:2; 1 Thess 1:6; 3:6 [c]2 Thess 2:15; 3:6

3 [1]I.e. the Messiah [a]Eph 1:22; 4:15; 5:23; Col 1:18; 2:19 [b]Gen 3:16; Eph 5:23 [c]1 Cor 3:23

4 [a]Acts 13:1; 1 Thess 5:20

5 [1]Lit *who is shaved* [a]Luke 2:36; Acts 21:9; 1 Cor 14:34 [b]Deut 21:12

6 [1]Lit *herself* [2]Lit *shear herself*

7 [a]Gen 1:26; 5:1; 9:6; James 3:9

8 [1]Lit *is not from* [a]Gen 2:21-23; 1 Tim 2:13

9 [a]Gen 2:18

11 [1]Lit *without*

12 [1]Lit *is* [2]Lit *are* [a]2 Cor 5:18 [b]Rom 11:36

13 [1]Lit *in* [a]Luke 12:57

16 [1]Lit *such* [a]1 Cor 4:5; 9:1-3, 6 [b]1 Cor 7:17

17 [a]1 Cor 11:2, 22

18 [1]Lit *in church* [2]Lit *schisms* [a]1 Cor 1:10; 3:3

19 [1]Or *manifest* [a]Matt 18:7; Luke 17:1; 1 Tim 4:1; 2 Pet 2:1 [b]Deut 13:3; 1 John 2:19

21 for in your eating each one takes his own supper first; and
one is hungry and [a]another is drunk.
22 What! Do you not have houses in which to eat and drink?
Or do you despise the [a]church of God and [b]shame those who
have nothing? What shall I say to you? Shall [c]I praise you? In
this I will not praise you.
23 For [a]I received from the Lord that which I also delivered to
you, that [b]the Lord Jesus in the night in which He was betrayed
took bread;
24 and when He had given thanks, He broke it and said, "This
is My body, which is for you; do this in remembrance of Me."
25 In the same way *He took* [a]the cup also after supper, saying,
"This cup is the [b]new covenant in My blood; do this, as often
as you drink *it,* in remembrance of Me."
26 For as often as you eat this bread and drink the cup, you
proclaim the Lord's death [a]until He comes.
27 Therefore whoever eats the bread or drinks the cup of the
Lord in an unworthy manner, shall be [a]guilty of the body and
the blood of the Lord.
28 But a man must [a]examine himself, and in so doing he is to
eat of the bread and drink of the cup.
29 For he who eats and drinks, eats and drinks judgment to
himself if he does not judge the body rightly.
30 For this reason many among you are weak and sick, and a
number [1a]sleep.
31 But if we judged ourselves rightly, we would not be judged.
32 But when we are judged, we are [a]disciplined by the Lord
so that we will not be condemned along with [b]the world.
33 So then, my brethren, when you come together to eat, wait
for one another.
34 If anyone is [a]hungry, let him eat [b]at home, so that you will
not come together for judgment. The remaining matters I will
[c]arrange [d]when I come.

Chapter 12 Theme ______________

12 Now concerning [a]spiritual *gifts,* brethren, [b]I do not want
you to be unaware.
2 [a]You know that when you were pagans, *you were* [b]led
astray to the [c]mute idols, however you were led.
3 Therefore I make known to you that no one speaking [1a]by
the Spirit of God says, "Jesus is [2b]accursed"; and no one can
say, "Jesus is [c]Lord," except [1a]by the Holy Spirit.
4 Now there are [a]varieties of gifts, but the same Spirit.
5 And there are varieties of ministries, and the same Lord.
6 There are varieties of effects, but the same [a]God who works
all things in all *persons.*
7 But to each one is given the manifestation of the Spirit [a]for
the common good.
8 For to one is given the word of [a]wisdom through the Spirit,
and to another the word of [b]knowledge according to the same
Spirit;

21 [a]Jude 12
22 [a]1 Cor 10:32 [b]James 2:6 [c]1 Cor 11:2, 17
23 [a]1 Cor 15:3; Gal 1:12; Col 3:24 [b]1 Cor 11:23-25: *Matt 26:26-28; Mark 14:22-24; Luke 22:17-20;* 1 Cor 10:16
25 [a]1 Cor 10:16 [b]Ex 24:6-8; Luke 22:20; 2 Cor 3:6
26 [a]John 21:22; 1 Cor 4:5
27 [a]Heb 10:29
28 [a]Matt 26:22; 2 Cor 13:5; Gal 6:4
30 [1]I.e. are dead [a]Acts 7:60
32 [a]2 Sam 7:14; Ps 94:12; Heb 12:7-10; Rev 3:19 [b]1 Cor 1:20
34 [a]1 Cor 11:21 [b]1 Cor 11:22 [c]1 Cor 4:17; 7:17; 16:1 [d]1 Cor 4:19
12:1 [a]1 Cor 12:4; 14:1 [b]Rom 1:13
2 [a]1 Cor 6:11; Eph 2:11f; 1 Pet 4:3 [b]1 Thess 1:9 [c]Ps 115:5; Is 46:7; Jer 10:5; Hab 2:18f
3 [1]Or *in* [2]Gr *anathema* [a]Matt 22:43; 1 John 4:2f; Rev 1:10 [b]Rom 9:3 [c]John 13:13; Rom 10:9
4 [a]Rom 12:6f; 1 Cor 12:11; Eph 4:4ff, 11; Heb 2:4
6 [a]1 Cor 15:28; Eph 1:23; 4:6
7 [a]1 Cor 12:12-30; 14:26; Eph 4:12
8 [a]1 Cor 2:6; 2 Cor 1:12 [b]Rom 15:14; 1 Cor 2:11, 16; 2 Cor 2:14; 4:6; 8:7; 11:6

9 to another [a]faith [1]by the same Spirit, and to another [b]gifts
of [2]healing [1]by the one Spirit,
10 and to another the [1]effecting of [2a]miracles, and to another
[b]prophecy, and to another the [3c]distinguishing of spirits, to
another *various* [d]kinds of tongues, and to another the [e]inter-
pretation of tongues.
11 But one and the same Spirit works all these things,
[a]distributing to each one individually just as He wills.
12 For even [a]as the body is one and *yet* has many members,
and all the members of the body, though they are many, are
one body, [b]so also is Christ.
13 For [1a]by one Spirit we were all baptized into one body,
whether [b]Jews or Greeks, whether slaves or free, and we were
all made to [c]drink of one Spirit.
14 For [a]the body is not one member, but many.
15 If the foot says, "Because I am not a hand, I am not *a part* of
the body," it is not for this reason [1]any the less *a part* of the body.
16 And if the ear says, "Because I am not an eye, I am not *a*
part of the body," it is not for this reason [1]any the less *a part* of
the body.
17 If the whole body were an eye, where would the hearing be?
If the whole were hearing, where would the sense of smell be?
18 But now God has [a]placed the members, each one of them,
in the body, [b]just as He desired.
19 If they were all one member, where would the body be?
20 But now [a]there are many members, but one body.
21 And the eye cannot say to the hand, "I have no need of
you"; or again the head to the feet, "I have no need of you."
22 On the contrary, [1]it is much truer that the members of the
body which seem to be weaker are necessary;
23 and those *members* of the body which we [1]deem less
honorable, [2]on these we bestow more abundant honor, and our
less presentable members become much more presentable,
24 whereas our more presentable members have no need *of*
it. But God has *so* composed the body, giving more abundant
honor to that *member* which lacked,
25 so that there may be no [1]division in the body, but *that* the
members may have the same care for one another.
26 And if one member suffers, all the members suffer with it;
if *one* member is [1]honored, all the members rejoice with it.
27 Now you are [a]Christ's body, and [b]individually members of it.
28 And God has [1a]appointed in [b]the church, first [c]apostles,
second [d]prophets, third [e]teachers, then [2f]miracles, then [g]gifts of
healings, helps, [h]administrations, *various* [i]kinds of tongues.
29 All are not apostles, are they? All are not prophets, are they?
All are not teachers, are they? All are not *workers of* [1]miracles,
are they?
30 All do not have gifts of healings, do they? All do not speak
with tongues, do they? All do not [a]interpret, do they?
31 But [a]earnestly desire the greater gifts.
And I show you a still more excellent way.

9 [1]Or *in* [2]Lit *healings* [a]1 Cor 13:2; 2 Cor 4:13 [b]1 Cor 12:28, 30

10 [1]Lit *effects* [2]Or *works of power* [3]Lit *distinguishings* [a]1 Cor 12:28f; Gal 3:5 [b]1 Cor 11:4; 13:2, 8 [c]1 Cor 14:29; 1 John 4:1 [d]Mark 16:17; 1 Cor 12:28, 30; 13:1; 14:2ff [e]1 Cor 12:30; 14:26

11 [a]1 Cor 12:4

12 [a]Rom 12:4f; 1 Cor 10:17 [b]1 Cor 12:27

13 [1]Or *in* [a]Eph 2:18 [b]Rom 3:22; Gal 3:28; Eph 2:13-18; Col 3:11 [c]John 7:37-39

14 [a]1 Cor 12:20

15 [1]Lit *not* a part

16 [1]Lit *not* a part

18 [a]1 Cor 12:28 [b]Rom 12:6; 1 Cor 12:11

20 [a]1 Cor 12:12, 14

22 [1]Lit *to a much greater degree the members*

23 [1]Or *think to be* [2]Or *these we clothe with*

25 [1]Lit *schism*

26 [1]Lit *glorified*

27 [a]1 Cor 1:2; 12:12; Eph 1:23; 4:12; Col 1:18, 24; 2:19 [b]Rom 12:5; Eph 5:30

28 [1]Lit *set some in* [2]Or *works of power* [a]1 Cor 12:18 [b]1 Cor 10:32 [c]Eph 4:11 [d]Acts 13:1; Eph 2:20; 3:5 [e]Acts 13:1 [f]1 Cor 12:10, 29 [g]1 Cor 12:9, 30 [h]Rom 12:8 [i]1 Cor 12:10

29 [1]Or *works of power*

30 [a]1 Cor 12:10

31 [a]1 Cor 14:1, 39

Chapter 13 Theme ____

13 If I speak with the [a]tongues of men and of [b]angels, but do
not have love, I have become a noisy gong or a [c]clanging
cymbal.
2 If I have *the gift of* [a]prophecy, and know all [b]mysteries and
all [c]knowledge; and if I have [d]all faith, so as to [e]remove
mountains, but do not have love, I am nothing.
3 And if I [a]give all my possessions to feed *the poor,* and if I
[b]surrender my body [1]to be burned, but do not have love, it
profits me nothing.
4 Love [a]is patient, love is kind *and* [b]is not jealous; love does
not brag *and* is not [c]arrogant,
5 does not act unbecomingly; it [a]does not seek its own, is not
provoked, [b]does not take into account a wrong *suffered,*
6 [a]does not rejoice in unrighteousness, but [b]rejoices with the
truth;
7 [1a]bears all things, believes all things, hopes all things, endures
all things.
8 Love never fails; but if *there are gifts of* [1a]prophecy, they
will be done away; if *there are* [b]tongues, they will cease; if
there is knowledge, it will be done away.
9 For we [a]know in part and we prophesy in part;
10 but when the perfect comes, the partial will be done away.
11 When I was a child, I used to speak like a child, think like a
child, reason like a child; when I [1]became a man, I did away
with childish things.
12 For now we [a]see in a mirror [1]dimly, but then [b]face to face;
now I know in part, but then I will know fully just as I also [c]have
been fully known.
13 But now faith, hope, love, abide these three; but the [1]greatest
of these is [a]love.

Chapter 14 Theme ____

14 [a]Pursue love, yet [b]desire earnestly [c]spiritual *gifts,* but
especially that you may [d]prophesy.
2 For one who [a]speaks in a tongue does not speak to men but
to God; for no one [1]understands, but [2]in *his* spirit he speaks
[b]mysteries.
3 But one who prophesies speaks to men for [a]edification and
[b]exhortation and consolation.
4 One who [a]speaks in a tongue [b]edifies himself; but one who
[c]prophesies [b]edifies the church.
5 Now I wish that you all [a]spoke in tongues, but [b]*even* more
that you would prophesy; and greater is one who prophesies
than one who [a]speaks in tongues, unless he interprets, so that
the church may receive [c]edifying.
6 But now, brethren, if I come to you speaking in tongues,
what will I profit you unless I speak to you either by way of
[a]revelation or of [b]knowledge or of [c]prophecy or of [d]teaching?
7 Yet *even* lifeless things, either flute or harp, in producing a

13:1 [a]1 Cor 12:10 [b]2 Cor 12:4; Rev 14:2 [c]Ps 150:5
2 [a]Matt 7:22; Acts 13:1; 1 Cor 11:4; 13:8; 14:1, 39 [b]1 Cor 14:2; 15:51 [c]Rom 15:14 [d]1 Cor 12:9 [e]Matt 17:20; 21:21; Mark 11:23
3 [1]Early mss read *that I may boast* [a]Matt 6:2 [b]Dan 3:28
4 [a]Prov 10:12; 17:9; 1 Thess 5:14; 1 Pet 4:8 [b]Acts 7:9 [c]1 Cor 4:6
5 [a]1 Cor 10:24; Phil 2:21 [b]2 Cor 5:19
6 [a]2 Thess 2:12 [b]2 John 4; 3 John 3f
7 [1]Or *covers* [a]1 Cor 9:12
8 [1]Lit *prophecies* [a]1 Cor 13:2 [b]1 Cor 13:1
9 [a]1 Cor 8:2; 13:12
11 [1]Lit *have become . . . have done away with*
12 [1]Lit *in a riddle* [a]2 Cor 5:7; Phil 3:12; James 1:23 [b]Gen 32:30; Num 12:8; 1 John 3:2 [c]1 Cor 8:3
13 [1]Lit *greater* [a]Gal 5:6
14:1 [a]1 Cor 16:14 [b]1 Cor 12:31; 14:39 [c]1 Cor 12:1 [d]1 Cor 13:2
2 [1]Lit *hears* [2]Or *by the Spirit* [a]Mark 16:17; 1 Cor 12:10, 28, 30; 13:1; 14:18ff [b]1 Cor 13:2
3 [a]Rom 14:19; 1 Cor 14:5, 12, 17, 26 [b]Acts 4:36
4 [a]Mark 16:17; 1 Cor 12:10, 28, 30; 13:1; 14:18ff, 26f [b]Rom 14:19; 1 Cor 14:5, 12, 17, 26 [c]1 Cor 13:2
5 [a]Mark 16:17; 1 Cor 12:10, 28, 30; 13:1; 14:18ff, 26f [b]Num 11:29 [c]Rom 14:19; 1 Cor 14:4, 12, 17, 26
6 [a]1 Cor 14:26; Eph 1:17 [b]1 Cor 12:8 [c]1 Cor 13:2 [d]Acts 2:42; Rom 6:17; 1 Cor 14:26

sound, if they do not produce a distinction in the tones, how
will it be known what is played on the flute or on the harp?
8 For if [a]the [1]bugle produces an indistinct sound, who will
prepare himself for battle?
9 So also you, unless you utter by the tongue speech that is
clear, how will it be known what is spoken? For you will be
[a]speaking into the air.
10 There are, perhaps, a great many kinds of [1]languages in the
world, and no *kind* is without meaning.
11 If then I do not know the meaning of the language, I will
be to the one who speaks a [1a]barbarian, and the one who
speaks will be a [1]barbarian [2]to me.
12 So also you, since you are zealous of [1]spiritual *gifts,* seek to
abound for the [a]edification of the church.
13 Therefore let one who speaks in a tongue pray that he may
interpret.
14 For if I pray in a tongue, my spirit prays, but my mind is
unfruitful.
15 [a]What is *the outcome* then? I will pray with the spirit and I
will pray with the mind also; I will [b]sing with the spirit and I
will sing with the mind also.
16 Otherwise if you bless [1]in the spirit *only,* how will the one
who fills the place of the [2]ungifted say [a]the "Amen" at your
[b]giving of thanks, since he does not know what you are saying?
17 For you are giving thanks well enough, but the other
person is not [a]edified.
18 I thank God, I speak in tongues more than you all;
19 however, in the church I desire to speak five words with
my mind so that I may instruct others also, rather than ten
thousand words in a tongue.
20 [a]Brethren, [b]do not be children in your thinking; yet in evil
[c]be infants, but in your thinking be mature.
21 In [a]the Law it is written, "[b]BY MEN OF STRANGE TONGUES AND
BY THE LIPS OF STRANGERS I WILL SPEAK TO THIS PEOPLE, AND EVEN SO
THEY WILL NOT LISTEN TO ME," says the Lord.
22 So then tongues are for a sign, not to those who believe but
to unbelievers; but [a]prophecy *is for a sign,* not to unbelievers
but to those who believe.
23 Therefore if the whole church assembles together and all
speak in tongues, and [1]ungifted men or unbelievers enter, will
they not say that [a]you are mad?
24 But if all [a]prophesy, and an unbeliever or an [1]ungifted man
enters, he is [b]convicted by all, he is called to account by all;
25 [a]the secrets of his heart are disclosed; and so he will [b]fall on his
face and worship God, [c]declaring that God is certainly among you.
26 [a]What is *the outcome* then, [b]brethren? When you assemble,
[c]each one has a [d]psalm, has a [e]teaching, has a [e]revelation, has a
[f]tongue, has an [g]interpretation. Let [h]all things be done for
edification.
27 If anyone speaks in a [a]tongue, *it should be* by two or at the
most three, and *each* in turn, and one must [b]interpret;

8 [1]Lit *trumpet* [a]Num 10:9; Jer 4:19; Ezek 33:3-6; Joel 2:1

9 [a]1 Cor 9:26

10 [1]Lit *voices*

11 [1]Or *foreigner* [2]Or *in my estimation* [a]Acts 28:2

12 [1]Lit *spirits* [a]Rom 14:19; 1 Cor 14:4, 5, 17, 26

15 [a]Acts 21:22; 1 Cor 14:26 [b]Eph 5:19; Col 3:16

16 [1]Or *with the* [2]I.e. unversed in spiritual gifts [a]Deut 27:15-26; 1 Chr 16:36; Neh 5:13; 8:6; Ps 106:48; Jer 11:5; 28:6; Rev 5:14; 7:12 [b]Matt 15:36

17 [a]Rom 14:19; 1 Cor 14:4, 5, 12, 26

20 [a]Rom 1:13 [b]Eph 4:14; Heb 5:12f [c]Ps 131:2; Matt 18:3; Rom 16:19; 1 Pet 2:2

21 [a]John 10:34; 1 Cor 14:34 [b]Is 28:11f

22 [a]1 Cor 14:1

23 [1]V 16, note 2 [a]Acts 2:13

24 [1]V 16, note 2 [a]1 Cor 14:1 [b]John 16:8

25 [a]John 4:19 [b]Luke 17:16 [c]Is 45:14; Dan 2:47; Zech 8:23; Acts 4:13

26 [a]1 Cor 14:15 [b]Rom 1:13 [c]1 Cor 12:8-10 [d]Eph 5:19 [e]1 Cor 14:6 [f]1 Cor 14:2 [g]1 Cor 12:10; 14:5, 13, 27f [h]Rom 14:19

27 [a]1 Cor 14:2 [b]1 Cor 12:10; 14:5, 13, 26ff

28 but if there is no interpreter, he must keep silent in the
church; and let him speak to himself and to God.
29 Let two or three [a]prophets speak, and let the others [b]pass
judgment.
30 But if a revelation is made to another who is seated, the
first one must keep silent.
31 For you can all prophesy one by one, so that all may learn
and all may be exhorted;
32 and the spirits of prophets are subject to prophets;
33 for God is not *a God* of [a]confusion but of [1]peace, as in [b]all
the churches of the [c]saints.
34 The women are to [a]keep silent in the churches; for they
are not permitted to speak, but [b]are to subject themselves, just
as [c]the Law also says.
35 If they desire to learn anything, let them ask their own
husbands at home; for it is [1]improper for a woman to speak in
church.
36 [1]Was it from you that the word of God *first* went forth? Or
has it come to you only?
37 [a]If anyone thinks he is a prophet or [b]spiritual, let him
recognize that the things which I write to you [c]are the Lord's
commandment.
38 But if anyone does not recognize *this,* he [1]is not recognized.
39 Therefore, my brethren, [a]desire earnestly to [b]prophesy, and
do not forbid to speak in tongues.
40 But [a]all things must be done properly and in an orderly
manner.

Chapter 15 Theme ____

15 Now [a]I make known to you, brethren, the [b]gospel which
I preached to you, which also you received, [c]in which
also you stand,
2 by which also you are saved, [a]if you hold fast [1]the word
which I preached to you, [b]unless you believed in vain.
3 For [a]I delivered to you [1]as of first importance what I also
received, that Christ died [b]for our sins [c]according to the Scriptures,
4 and that He was buried, and that He was [a]raised on the
third day [b]according to the Scriptures,
5 and that [a]He appeared to [b]Cephas, then [c]to the twelve.
6 After that He appeared to more than five hundred brethren
at one time, most of whom remain until now, but some [a]have
fallen asleep;
7 then He appeared to [1][a]James, then to [b]all the apostles;
8 and last of all, as [1]to one untimely born, [a]He appeared to me
also.
9 For I am [a]the least of the apostles, [1]and not fit to be called
an apostle, because I [b]persecuted the church of God.
10 But by [a]the grace of God I am what I am, and His grace
toward me did not prove vain; but I [b]labored even more than
all of them, yet [c]not I, but the grace of God with me.

29 [a]1 Cor 13:2; 14:32, 37 [b]1 Cor 12:10
33 [1]Or *peace. As in all . . . saints, let* [a]1 Cor 14:40 [b]1 Cor 4:17; 7:17 [c]Acts 9:13
34 [a]1 Cor 11:5, 13 [b]1 Tim 2:11f; 1 Pet 3:1 [c]1 Cor 14:21
35 [1]Or *disgraceful*
36 [1]Lit *Or was*
37 [a]2 Cor 10:7 [b]1 Cor 2:15 [c]1 John 4:6
38 [1]Two early mss read *is not to be recognized*
39 [a]1 Cor 12:31 [b]1 Cor 13:2; 14:1
40 [a]1 Cor 14:33
15:1 [a]Rom 2:16; Gal 1:11 [b]Rom 2:16; 1 Cor 3:6; 4:15 [c]Rom 5:2; 11:20; 2 Cor 1:24
2 [1]Lit *to what word I* [a]Rom 11:22 [b]Gal 3:4
3 [1]Lit *among the first* [a]1 Cor 11:23 [b]John 1:29; Gal 1:4; Heb 5:1, 3; 1 Pet 2:24 [c]Is 53:5-12; Matt 26:24; Luke 24:25-27; Acts 8:32f; 17:2f; 26:22
4 [a]Matt 16:21; John 2:20ff; Acts 2:24 [b]Ps 16:8ff; Acts 2:31; 26:22f
5 [a]Luke 24:34 [b]1 Cor 1:12 [c]Mark 16:14; Luke 24:36; John 20:19
6 [a]Acts 7:60; 1 Cor 15:18, 20
7 [1]Or *Jacob* [a]Acts 12:17 [b]Luke 24:33, 36f; Acts 1:3f
8 [1]Lit *to an untimely birth* [a]Acts 9:3-8; 22:6-11; 26:12-18; 1 Cor 9:1
9 [1]Lit *who am* [a]2 Cor 12:11; Eph 3:8; 1 Tim 1:15 [b]Acts 8:3
10 [a]Rom 12:3 [b]2 Cor 11:23; Col 1:29; 1 Tim 4:10 [c]1 Cor 3:6; 2 Cor 3:5; Phil 2:13

11 Whether then *it was* I or they, so we preach and so you
believed.
12 Now if Christ is preached, that He has been raised from the
dead, how do some among you say that there [a]is no resurrection
of the dead?
13 But if there is no resurrection of the dead, not even Christ
has been raised;
14 and [a]if Christ has not been raised, then our preaching is
vain, your faith also is vain.
15 Moreover we are even found *to be* false witnesses of God,
because we testified [1]against God that He [a]raised [2]Christ, whom
He did not raise, if in fact the dead are not raised.
16 For if the dead are not raised, not even Christ has been raised;
17 and if Christ has not been raised, your faith is worthless;
[a]you are still in your sins.
18 Then those also who [a]have fallen asleep in Christ have
perished.
19 If we have hoped in Christ in this life only, we are [a]of all
men most to be pitied.
20 But now Christ [a]has been raised from the dead, the [b]first
fruits of those who [c]are asleep.
21 For since [a]by a man *came* death, by a man also *came* the
resurrection of the dead.
22 For [a]as in Adam all die, so also in [1]Christ all will be made alive.
23 But each in his own order: Christ [a]the first fruits, after that
[b]those who are Christ's at [c]His coming,
24 then *comes* the end, when He hands over [a]the kingdom to
the [b]God and Father, when He has abolished [c]all rule and all
authority and power.
25 For He must reign [a]until He has put all His enemies under
His feet.
26 The last enemy that will be [a]abolished is death.
27 For [a]HE HAS PUT ALL THINGS IN SUBJECTION UNDER HIS FEET. But
when He says, "[b]All things are put in subjection," it is evident
that He is excepted who put all things in subjection to Him.
28 When [a]all things are subjected to Him, then the Son Himself
also will be subjected to the One who subjected all things to
Him, so that [b]God may be all in all.
29 Otherwise, what will those do who are baptized for the
dead? If the dead are not raised at all, why then are they
baptized for them?
30 Why are we also [a]in danger every hour?
31 I affirm, brethren, by the boasting in you which I have in
Christ Jesus our Lord, [a]I die daily.
32 If [1]from human motives I [a]fought with wild beasts at
[b]Ephesus, what does it profit me? If the dead are not raised,
[c]LET US EAT AND DRINK, FOR TOMORROW WE DIE.
33 [a]Do not be deceived: "Bad company corrupts good morals."
34 [a]Become sober-minded [1]as you ought, and stop sinning; for
some have [b]no knowledge of God. [c]I speak *this* to your shame.
35 But [a]someone will say, "How are [b]the dead raised? And
with what kind of body do they come?"

12 [a]Acts 17:32; 23:8; 2 Tim 2:18
14 [a]1 Thess 4:14
15 [1]Or *concerning* [2]I.e. the Messiah [a]Acts 2:24
17 [a]Rom 4:25
18 [a]1 Cor 15:6; 1 Thess 4:16; Rev 14:13
19 [a]1 Cor 4:9; 2 Tim 3:12
20 [a]Acts 2:24; 1 Pet 1:3 [b]Acts 26:23; 1 Cor 15:23; Rev 1:5 [c]1 Cor 15:6; 1 Thess 4:16; Rev 14:13
21 [a]Rom 5:12
22 [1]I.e. the Messiah [a]Rom 5:14-18
23 [a]Acts 26:23; 1 Cor 15:20; Rev 1:5 [b]1 Cor 6:14; 15:52; 1 Thess 4:16 [c]1 Thess 2:19
24 [a]Dan 2:44; 7:14, 27; 2 Pet 1:11 [b]Eph 5:20 [c]Rom 8:38
25 [a]Ps 110:1; Matt 22:44
26 [a]2 Tim 1:10; Rev 20:14; 21:4
27 [a]Ps 8:6 [b]Matt 11:27; 28:18; Eph 1:22; Heb 2:8
28 [a]Phil 3:21 [b]1 Cor 3:23; 12:6
30 [a]2 Cor 11:26
31 [a]Rom 8:36
32 [1]Lit *according to man* [a]2 Cor 1:8 [b]Acts 18:19; 1 Cor 16:8 [c]Is 22:13; 56:12; Luke 12:19
33 [a]1 Cor 6:9
34 [1]Lit *righteously* [a]Rom 13:11 [b]Matt 22:29; Acts 26:8 [c]1 Cor 6:5
35 [a]Rom 9:19 [b]Ezek 37:3

36 [a]You fool! That which you [b]sow does not come to life unless it dies;

37 and that which you sow, you do not sow the body which is to be, but a bare grain, perhaps of wheat or of [1]something else.

38 But God gives it a body just as He wished, and [a]to each of the seeds a body of its own.

39 All flesh is not the same flesh, but there is one *flesh* of men, and another flesh of beasts, and another flesh of birds, and another of fish.

40 There are also heavenly bodies and earthly bodies, but the glory of the heavenly is one, and the *glory* of the earthly is another.

41 There is one glory of the sun, and another glory of the moon, and another glory of the stars; for star differs from star in glory.

42 [a]So also is the resurrection of the dead. It is sown [1b]a perishable *body,* it is raised [2c]an imperishable *body;*

43 it is sown in dishonor, it is raised in [a]glory; it is sown in weakness, it is raised in power;

44 it is sown a [a]natural body, it is raised a [b]spiritual body. If there is a natural body, there is also a spiritual *body.*

45 So also it is written, "The first [a]MAN, Adam, BECAME A LIVING SOUL." The [b]last Adam *became* a [c]life-giving spirit.

46 However, the spiritual is not first, but the natural; then the spiritual.

47 The first man is [a]from the earth, [1b]earthy; the second man is from heaven.

48 As is the earthy, so also are those who are earthy; and as is the heavenly, [a]so also are those who are heavenly.

49 Just as we have [a]borne the image of the earthy, [1]we [b]will also bear the image of the heavenly.

50 Now I say this, brethren, that [a]flesh and blood cannot [b]inherit the kingdom of God; nor does [1]the perishable inherit [2c]the imperishable.

51 Behold, I tell you a [a]mystery; we will not all sleep, but we will all be [b]changed,

52 in a moment, in the twinkling of an eye, at the last trumpet; for [a]the trumpet will sound, and [b]the dead will be raised [1]imperishable, and [c]we will be changed.

53 For this [1]perishable must put on [2a]the imperishable, and this [b]mortal must put on immortality.

54 But when this [1]perishable will have put on [2]the imperishable, and this mortal will have put on immortality, then will come about the saying that is written, "[a]DEATH IS SWALLOWED UP in victory.

55 "[a]O DEATH, WHERE IS YOUR VICTORY? O DEATH, WHERE IS YOUR STING?"

56 The sting of [a]death is sin, and [b]the power of sin is the law;

57 but [a]thanks be to God, who gives us the [b]victory through our Lord Jesus Christ.

58 [a]Therefore, my beloved brethren, be steadfast, immovable, always abounding in [b]the work of the Lord, knowing that your toil is not *in* vain in the Lord.

36 [a]Luke 11:40 [b]John 12:24
37 [1]Lit *some of the rest*
38 [a]Gen 1:11
42 [1]Lit *in corruption* [2]Lit *in incorruption* [a]Dan 12:3; Matt 13:43 [b]Rom 8:21; 1 Cor 15:50; Gal 6:8 [c]Rom 2:7
43 [a]Phil 3:21; Col 3:4
44 [a]1 Cor 2:14 [b]1 Cor 15:50
45 [a]Gen 2:7 [b]Rom 5:14 [c]John 5:21; 6:57f; Rom 8:2
47 [1]Lit *made of dust* [a]John 3:31 [b]Gen 2:7; 3:19
48 [a]Phil 3:20f
49 [1]Two early mss read *let us also* [a]Gen 5:3 [b]Rom 8:29
50 [1]Lit *corruption* [2]Lit *incorruption* [a]Matt 16:17; John 3:5f [b]1 Cor 6:9 [c]Rom 2:7
51 [a]1 Cor 13:2 [b]2 Cor 5:2, 4
52 [1]Lit *incorruptible* [a]Matt 24:31 [b]John 5:28 [c]1 Thess 4:15, 17
53 [1]Lit *corruptible* [2]Lit *incorruption* [a]Rom 2:7 [b]2 Cor 5:4
54 [1]V 53, note 1 [2]V 53, note 2 [a]Is 25:8
55 [a]Hos 13:14
56 [a]Rom 5:12 [b]Rom 3:20; 4:15; 7:8
57 [a]Rom 7:25; 2 Cor 2:14 [b]Rom 8:37; Heb 2:14f; 1 John 5:4; Rev 21:4
58 [a]2 Pet 3:14 [b]1 Cor 16:10

Chapter 16 Theme ________________________________

16 Now concerning [a]the collection for [b]the saints, as [c]I
directed the churches of [d]Galatia, so do you also.
2 On [a]the first day of every week each one of you is to [1]put
aside and save, as he may prosper, so that [b]no collections be
made when I come.
3 When I arrive, [a]whomever you may approve, I will send
them with letters to carry your gift to Jerusalem;
4 and if it is fitting for me to go also, they will go with me.
5 But I [a]will come to you after I go through [b]Macedonia, for I
[c]am going through Macedonia;
6 and perhaps I will stay with you, or even spend the winter,
so that you may [a]send me on my way wherever I may go.
7 For I do not wish to see you now [a]*just* in passing; for I
hope to remain with you for some time, [b]if the Lord permits.
8 But I will remain in [a]Ephesus until [b]Pentecost;
9 for a [a]wide door [1]for effective *service* has opened to me,
and [b]there are many adversaries.
10 Now if [a]Timothy comes, see that he is with you without
[1]cause to be afraid, for he is doing [b]the Lord's work, as I also am.
11 [a]So let no one despise him. But [b]send him on his way [c]in
peace, so that he may come to me; for I expect him with the
brethren.
12 But concerning [a]Apollos our brother, I encouraged him greatly
to come to you with the brethren; and it was not at all *his* desire
to come now, but he will come when he has opportunity.
13 [a]Be on the alert, [b]stand firm in the faith, [c]act like men, [d]be
strong.
14 Let all that you do be done [a]in love.
15 Now I urge you, brethren (you know the [a]household of
Stephanas, that [1]they were the [b]first fruits of [c]Achaia, and that
they have devoted themselves for [d]ministry to [e]the saints),
16 that [a]you also be in subjection to such men and to
everyone who helps in the work and labors.
17 I rejoice over the [1a]coming of Stephanas and Fortunatus and
Achaicus, because they have [2]supplied [b]what was lacking on
your part.
18 For they [a]have refreshed my spirit and yours. Therefore
[b]acknowledge such men.
19 The churches of [a]Asia greet you. [b]Aquila and Prisca greet
you heartily in the Lord, with [c]the church that is in their house.
20 All the brethren greet you. [a]Greet one another with a holy kiss.
21 The greeting is in [a]my own hand—[1]Paul.
22 If anyone does not love the Lord, he is to be [1a]accursed.
[2b]Maranatha.
23 [a]The grace of the Lord Jesus be with you.
24 My love be with you all in Christ Jesus. Amen.

16:1 [a]Acts 24:17; Rom 15:25f [b]Acts 9:13 [c]1 Cor 4:17 [d]Acts 16:6
2 [1]Lit *put by himself* [a]Acts 20:7 [b]2 Cor 9:4f
3 [a]2 Cor 3:1; 8:18f
5 [a]1 Cor 4:19 [b]Rom 15:26 [c]Acts 19:21
6 [a]Acts 15:3; 1 Cor 16:11
7 [a]2 Cor 1:15f [b]Acts 18:21
8 [a]Acts 18:19 [b]Acts 2:1
9 [1]Lit *and* [a]Acts 14:27 [b]Acts 19:9
10 [1]Lit *fear; for* [a]Acts 16:1; 1 Cor 4:17; 2 Cor 1:1 [b]1 Cor 15:58
11 [a]1 Tim 4:12; Titus 2:15 [b]Acts 15:3; 1 Cor 16:6 [c]Acts 15:33
12 [a]Acts 18:24; 1 Cor 1:12; 3:5f
13 [a]Matt 24:42 [b]1 Cor 15:1; Gal 5:1; Phil 1:27; 4:1; 1 Thess 3:8; 2 Thess 2:15 [c]1 Sam 4:9; 2 Sam 10:12 [d]Ps 31:24; Eph 3:16; 6:10; Col 1:11
14 [a]1 Cor 14:1
15 [1]Lit *it was* [a]1 Cor 1:16 [b]Rom 16:5 [c]Acts 18:12 [d]Rom 15:31 [e]1 Cor 16:1
16 [a]1 Thess 5:12; Heb 13:17
17 [1]Or *presence* [2]Or *made up for your absence* [a]2 Cor 7:6f [b]2 Cor 11:9; Phil 2:30
18 [a]2 Cor 7:13; Philem 7, 20 [b]Phil 2:29; 1 Thess 5:12
19 [a]Acts 16:6 [b]Acts 18:2 [c]Rom 16:5
20 [a]Rom 16:16
21 [1]Lit *Paul's* [a]Rom 16:22; Gal 6:11; Col 4:18; 2 Thess 3:17; Philem 19
22 [1]Gr *anathema* [2]I.e. O [our] Lord come! [a]Rom 9:3 [b]Phil 4:5; Rev 22:20
23 [a]Rom 16:20

1 Corinthians Observations Chart

Description of the Corinthians

Commands to the Corinthians

Warnings to the Corinthians

1 Corinthians at a Glance

Theme of 1 Corinthians:

Segment Divisions

Problems or Topics	Major Divisions	Chapter Themes
		1
		2
		3
		4
		5
		6
		7
		8
		9
		10
		11
		12
		13
		14
		15
		16

Author:

Date:

Purpose:

Key Words:

2 CORINTHIANS

Paul, the apostle to the Gentiles, was taught and appointed by Jesus Christ. Strong in faith, confident, and greatly used by God, Paul was loved by multitudes and hated by countless others. Determined that the grace of God poured out on him would not prove vain, Paul labored with more effort than anyone.

However, Paul's labor was not without cost. He endured conflicts without and fears within. Yet he persevered. What were his conflicts, his fears, his sufferings? Are they similar to yours? And how did he endure? What held him? As Paul writes his second epistle to the Corinthians from Macedonia, probably in the winter of A.D. 55, he provides answers to these questions.

Things to Do

General Instructions

1. Second Corinthians is different from Paul's other epistles. Watch the atmosphere or tone of this epistle. Paul is defending himself, which is unusual for Paul. As you read through the book, note the issues Paul addresses and what he says to the Corinthians, and you will understand what Paul is up against.

2. Study the 2 CORINTHIANS OBSERVATIONS CHART on page 1889 and see what you'll need to observe as you study 2 Corinthians chapter by chapter. Make a duplicate of this chart so you can use it as a worksheet. When you have completed it, record the information on the original chart.
   a. As you read each chapter, list everything you learn about Paul. Be sure to note the afflictions he endured: What must he do in respect to the Corinthians? What has been done to him by the Corinthians? Ask God to show you Paul's character, his heart, his joys, and his sorrows.
   b. Note what you learn about the Corinthians. Remember to ask the "5 W's and an H": What are they like? What is their relationship with Paul like? What is going on in the Corinthian church at this time? What have they said about Paul? What problems has Paul had to deal with in respect to them?
   c. What is Paul's desire or goal for the Corinthians?
   d. Titus is mentioned several times in this letter. Record what you learn about him.

3. As you read 2 Corinthians chapter by chapter, do the following:
   a. Mark in the text in a distinctive way the key words (and their synonyms and pronouns) listed on the 2 CORINTHIANS AT A GLANCE chart on page 1890. Write these on an index card that you can use as a bookmark while you study 2 Corinthians. (Hint: If you mark every reference to Satan with an appropriate symbol he will be easy to spot.)
   b. As you come to specific chapters you will notice other key words which are not listed on 2 CORINTHIANS AT A GLANCE. Mark these also.
   c. If there are several truths you learn from the use of a key word within a chapter, list in your notebook what you learn from that word. For example, list all you learn about *affliction(s)* and *sufferings*. Write the heading "Affliction/Suffering" in the margin of each chapter that has these key words. Mark the heading in a distinctive way so you can spot it easily.

4. Look for the theme (subject) of each chapter and record it in your Bible and under "Chapter Themes" on 2 CORINTHIANS AT A GLANCE.

Chapters 1–7

1. In the midst of this very personal letter, Paul gives some important insights on several subjects.
   a. Chapter 3 mentions the new covenant (which is grace) and the old covenant (which is law). These are described as ministries, and then the ministries are contrasted according to the result of each: condemnation or righteousness. Record in your notebook what you learn about each from the text.
   b. In chapter 5 Paul talks about what will happen to our earthly bodies when we die. He also discusses the judgment seat of Christ and our ministry of reconciliation. Identify how these relate to one another and what you learn about each from the text. Record any Lessons for Life ("LFL") in the margins.
   c. In chapter 7 Paul deals with two kinds of sorrow and what they produce. Don't miss this. Record your notes in your notebook.

2. What is Paul writing about in chapters 1 through 7? Is there a theme that runs through these chapters? Remember that key words reveal the themes. What key words are repeated the most in this segment?

3. How does Paul begin and end this segment?

4. Record the theme for chapters 1 through 7 on 2 CORINTHIANS AT A GLANCE under "Segment Divisions."

Chapters 8–9

1. What subject is Paul talking about in chapters 8 and 9? Note the use of the words *ministry, work,* and *service*. What ministry or work or service is he referring to?

2. Record this subject as the theme of this segment in the appropriate space on 2 CORINTHIANS AT A GLANCE.

Chapters 10–13

1. Notice when the key word *boast* first appears in the text and what happens when it appears. Note what or whom the boasting is in and what you learn.

2. In your notebook, list what you learn about Satan and spiritual warfare from these four chapters.

3. What does Paul seem to be doing in chapters 10 through 13? What opposition is there to Paul, and what is the opposition saying about him? What is his response to this opposition? Record the theme of this segment on 2 CORINTHIANS AT A GLANCE under "Segment Divisions" and complete the chart.

Things to Think About

1. What is the purpose of affliction? When you need to be comforted, do you turn to people or to God?

2. Is it always wrong to feel sorrow, to be hurt, or to have a broken heart? Is it always wrong to cause sorrow, to hurt, or to break another person's heart?

3. How do you deal with those who oppose you? How do you minister to those who are caught in the middle of a conflict and don't know who to believe?

4. Paul was human just like us; he had feelings just like we do. What can we learn from him about how we are to live and respond in spite of our feelings? When is it right to give a defense of one's self, of one's ministry?

5. Are you prepared to stand before the judgment seat of Christ?

6. What place does the ministry of giving have in your life?

7. If you were to examine yourself, would you find your Christianity genuine?

Chapter 1 Theme ______________________________

INSIGHT

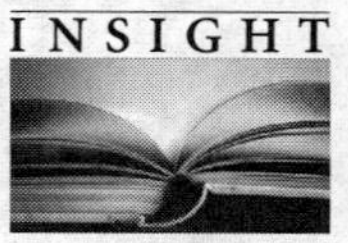

See the map on page 1800.

1 Paul, [a]an apostle of [b]Christ Jesus [c]by the will of God, and
[d]Timothy *our* brother,
To [e]the church of God which is at [f]Corinth with all the
[1]saints who are throughout [g]Achaia:
2 [a]Grace to you and peace from God our Father and the Lord
Jesus Christ.
3 [a]Blessed *be* the God and Father of our Lord Jesus Christ,
the Father of mercies and [b]God of all comfort,
4 who [a]comforts us in all our affliction so that we will be able
to comfort those who are in [1]any affliction with the comfort
with which we ourselves are comforted by God.
5 For just [a]as the sufferings of Christ are [1]ours in abundance,
so also our comfort is abundant through Christ.
6 But if we are afflicted, it is [a]for your comfort and salvation; or
if we are comforted, it is for your comfort, which is effective in
the patient enduring of the same sufferings which we also suffer;
7 and our hope for you is firmly grounded, knowing that [a]as
you are sharers of our sufferings, so also you are *sharers* of our
comfort.
8 For [a]we do not want you to be unaware, brethren, of our
[b]affliction which came *to us* in [1c]Asia, that we were burdened
excessively, beyond our strength, so that we despaired even of
life;
9 [1]indeed, we had the sentence of death within ourselves so
that we would not trust in ourselves, but in God who raises the
dead;
10 who [a]delivered us from so great a *peril of* death, and will
deliver *us,* [1]He [b]on whom we have set our hope. And He will
yet deliver us,
11 you also joining in [a]helping us through your prayers, so that
thanks may be given by [b]many persons on our behalf for the
favor bestowed on us through *the prayers of* many.
12 For our [1]proud confidence is this: the testimony of [a]our
conscience, that in holiness and [b]godly sincerity, [c]not in fleshly
wisdom but in the grace of God, we have conducted ourselves
in the world, and especially toward you.
13 For we write nothing else to you than what you read and
understand, and I hope you will understand [a]until the end;
14 just as you also partially did understand us, that we are
your reason to be proud as you also are ours, in [a]the day of our
Lord Jesus.
15 In this confidence I intended at first to [a]come to you, so
that you might [1]twice receive a [2b]blessing;
16 [1]that is, to [a]pass [2]your way into [b]Macedonia, and again
from Macedonia to come to you, and by you to be [c]helped on
my journey to Judea.
17 Therefore, I was not vacillating when I intended to do this,
was I? Or what I purpose, do I purpose [a]according to the flesh, so
that with me there will be yes, yes and no, no *at the same time?*
18 But as [a]God is faithful, [b]our word to you is not yes and no.

1:1 [1]Or *holy ones* [a]Rom 1:1; Gal 1:1; Eph 1:1; Col 1:1; 2 Tim 1:1; Titus 1:1 [b]Gal 3:26 [c]1 Cor 1:1 [d]Acts 16:1; 1 Cor 16:10; 2 Cor 1:19 [e]1 Cor 10:32 [f]Acts 18:1 [g]Acts 18:12
2 [a]Rom 1:7
3 [a]Eph 1:3; 1 Pet 1:3 [b]Rom 15:5
4 [1]Lit *every* [a]Is 51:12; 66:13; 2 Cor 7:6, 7, 13
5 [1]Lit *to us* [a]2 Cor 4:10; Phil 3:10; Col 1:24
6 [a]2 Cor 4:15; 12:15; Eph 3:1, 13; 2 Tim 2:10
7 [a]Rom 8:17
8 [1]I.e. west coast province of Asia Minor [a]Rom 1:13 [b]Acts 19:23; 1 Cor 15:32 [c]Acts 16:6
9 [1]Lit *but we ourselves*
10 [1]One early ms reads *on whom we have set our hope that He will also* [a]Rom 15:31 [b]1 Tim 4:10
11 [a]Rom 15:30; Phil 1:19; Philem 22 [b]2 Cor 4:15; 9:11f
12 [1]Lit *boasting* [a]Acts 23:1; 1 Thess 2:10; Heb 13:18 [b]2 Cor 2:17 [c]1 Cor 1:17; James 3:15
13 [a]1 Cor 1:8
14 [a]1 Cor 1:8
15 [1]Lit *have a second grace* [2]One early ms reads *joy* [a]1 Cor 4:19 [b]Rom 1:11; 15:29
16 [1]Lit *and* [2]Lit *through you into* [a]Acts 19:21; 1 Cor 16:5-7 [b]Acts 19:21; Rom 15:26 [c]Acts 15:3; 1 Cor 16:6, 11
17 [a]2 Cor 10:2f; 11:18
18 [a]1 Cor 1:9 [b]2 Cor 2:17

19 For [a]the Son of God, Christ Jesus, who was preached
among you by us—by me and [b]Silvanus and [c]Timothy—was
not yes and no, but is yes [d]in Him.
20 For [a]as many as are the promises of God, [b]in Him they are
yes; therefore also through Him is [c]our Amen to the glory of
God through us.
21 Now He who [a]establishes us with you in Christ and
[b]anointed us is God,
22 who also [a]sealed us and [b]gave *us* the Spirit in our hearts as
a [1]pledge.
23 But [a]I call God as witness [1]to my soul, that [b]to spare you I
did not come again to [c]Corinth.
24 Not that we [a]lord it over your faith, but are workers with
you for your joy; for in your faith you are [b]standing firm.

Chapter 2 Theme ______________________________

2 But I determined this [1]for my own sake, that I [a]would not
come to you in sorrow again.
2 For if I [a]cause you sorrow, who then makes me glad but the
one whom I made sorrowful?
3 This is the very thing I [a]wrote you, so that [b]when I came, I
would not have sorrow from those who ought to make me
rejoice; having [c]confidence in you all that my joy would be *the
joy* of you all.
4 For out of much affliction and anguish of heart I [a]wrote to you
with many tears; not so that you would be made sorrowful, but
that you might know the love which I have especially for you.
5 But [a]if any has caused sorrow, he has caused sorrow not to
me, but in some degree—[1]in order not to say too much—to all
of you.
6 Sufficient for such a one is [a]this punishment which *was
inflicted* by the majority,
7 so that on the contrary you should rather [a]forgive and
comfort *him,* otherwise such a one might be overwhelmed by
excessive sorrow.
8 Wherefore I urge you to reaffirm *your* love for him.
9 For to this end also [a]I wrote, so that I might [1b]put you to
the test, whether you are [c]obedient in all things.
10 But one whom you forgive anything, I *forgive* also; for
indeed what I have forgiven, if I have forgiven anything, *I did it*
for your sakes [a]in the presence of Christ,
11 so that no advantage would be taken of us by [a]Satan, for
[b]we are not ignorant of his schemes.
12 Now when I came to [a]Troas for the [b]gospel of Christ and
when a [c]door was opened for me in the Lord,
13 I [a]had no rest for my spirit, not finding [b]Titus my brother;
but [c]taking my leave of them, I went on to [d]Macedonia.
14 [a]But thanks be to God, who always [b]leads us in triumph in
Christ, and manifests through us the [c]sweet aroma of the
[d]knowledge of Him in every place.

19 [a]Matt 4:3; 16:16; 26:63 [b]Acts 15:22; 1 Thess 1:1; 2 Thess 1:1; 1 Pet 5:12 [c]Acts 18:5; 2 Cor 1:1 [d]Heb 13:8

20 [a]Rom 15:8 [b]Heb 13:8 [c]1 Cor 14:16; Rev 3:14

21 [a]1 Cor 1:8 [b]1 John 2:20, 27

22 [1]Or *down payment* [a]John 3:33 [b]Rom 8:16; 2 Cor 5:5; Eph 1:14

23 [1]Lit *upon* [a]Rom 1:9; Gal 1:20 [b]1 Cor 4:21; 2 Cor 2:1, 3 [c]2 Cor 1:1

24 [a]2 Cor 4:5; 11:20; 1 Pet 5:3 [b]Rom 11:20; 1 Cor 15:1

2:1 [1]Or *as far as I am concerned* [a]1 Cor 4:21; 2 Cor 12:21

2 [a]2 Cor 7:8

3 [a]2 Cor 2:9; 7:8, 12 [b]1 Cor 4:21; 2 Cor 12:21 [c]Gal 5:10; 2 Thess 3:4; Philem 21

4 [a]2 Cor 2:9; 7:8, 12

5 [1]Lit *so that I not be burdensome* [a]1 Cor 5:1f

6 [a]1 Cor 5:4f; 2 Cor 7:11

7 [a]Gal 6:1; Eph 4:32

9 [1]Lit *know the proof of you* [a]2 Cor 2:3f [b]2 Cor 8:2; Phil 2:22 [c]2 Cor 7:15; 10:6

10 [a]1 Cor 5:4; 2 Cor 4:6

11 [a]Matt 4:10 [b]Luke 22:31; 2 Cor 4:4; 1 Pet 5:8

12 [a]Acts 16:8 [b]Rom 1:1; 2 Cor 4:3, 4; 8:18; 9:13; 10:14; 11:4, 7; 1 Thess 3:2 [c]Acts 14:27

13 [a]2 Cor 7:5 [b]2 Cor 7:6, 13f; 8:6, 16, 23; 12:18; Gal 2:1, 3; 2 Tim 4:10; Titus 1:4 [c]Mark 6:46 [d]Rom 15:26

14 [a]Rom 1:8; 6:17; 1 Cor 15:57; 2 Cor 8:16; 9:15 [b]Col 2:15 [c]Song 1:3; Ezek 20:41; Eph 5:2; Phil 4:18 [d]1 Cor 12:8

15 For we are a [a]fragrance of Christ to God among [b]those who
are being saved and among those who are perishing;
16 [a]to the one an aroma from death to death, to the other an
aroma from life to life. And who is [b]adequate for these things?
17 For we are not like many, [1a]peddling the word of God, but
[b]as from sincerity, but as from God, we speak in Christ [c]in the
sight of God.

Chapter 3 Theme ______________________________

3 Are we beginning to [a]commend ourselves again? Or do we
need, as some, [b]letters of commendation to you or from you?
2 [a]You are our letter, written in our hearts, known and read
by all men;
3 being manifested that you are a letter of Christ, [1a]cared for
by us, written not with ink but with the Spirit of [b]the living
God, not on [c]tablets of stone but on [d]tablets of [2e]human hearts.
4 Such [a]confidence we have through Christ toward God.
5 Not that we are adequate in ourselves to consider anything
as *coming* from ourselves, but [a]our adequacy is from God,
6 who also made us adequate *as* [a]servants of a [b]new covenant,
not of [c]the letter but of the Spirit; for the letter kills, but [d]the
Spirit gives life.
7 But if the [a]ministry of death, [b]in letters engraved on stones,
came [1]with glory, [c]so that the sons of Israel could not look
intently at the face of Moses because of the glory of his face,
fading *as* it was,
8 how will the ministry of the Spirit fail to be even more with
glory?
9 For if [a]the ministry of condemnation has glory, much more
does the [b]ministry of righteousness abound in glory.
10 For indeed what had glory, in this case has no glory because
of the glory that surpasses *it.*
11 For if that which fades away *was* [1]with glory, much more
that which remains *is* in glory.
12 [a]Therefore having such a hope, [b]we use great boldness in
our speech,
13 and *are* not like Moses, [a]*who* used to put a veil over his
face so that the sons of Israel would not look intently at the end
of what was fading away.
14 But their minds were [a]hardened; for until this very day at the
[b]reading of [c]the old covenant the same veil [1]remains unlifted,
because it is removed in Christ.
15 But to this day whenever Moses is read, a veil lies over their
heart;
16 [a]but whenever a person turns to the Lord, the veil is taken
away.
17 Now the Lord is the Spirit, and where [a]the Spirit of the Lord
is, [b]*there* is liberty.
18 But we all, with unveiled face, [a]beholding as in a mirror the
[b]glory of the Lord, are being [c]transformed into the same image
from glory to glory, just as from [d]the Lord, the Spirit.

15 [a]Song 1:3; Ezek 20:41; Eph 5:2; Phil 4:18 [b]1 Cor 1:18
16 [a]Luke 2:34; John 9:39; 1 Pet 2:7f [b]2 Cor 3:5f
17 [1]Or *corrupting* [a]2 Cor 4:2; Gal 1:6-9 [b]1 Cor 5:8; 2 Cor 1:12; 1 Thess 2:4; 1 Pet 4:11 [c]2 Cor 12:19
3:1 [a]2 Cor 5:12; 10:12, 18; 12:11 [b]Acts 18:27; 1 Cor 16:3
2 [a]1 Cor 9:2
3 [1]Lit *served* [2]Lit *hearts of flesh* [a]2 Cor 3:6 [b]Matt 16:16 [c]Ex 24:12; 31:18; 32:15f; 2 Cor 3:7 [d]Prov 3:3; 7:3; Jer 17:1 [e]Jer 31:33; Ezek 11:19; 36:26
4 [a]Eph 3:12
5 [a]1 Cor 15:10
6 [a]1 Cor 3:5 [b]Jer 31:31; Luke 22:20 [c]Rom 2:29 [d]John 6:63; Rom 7:6
7 [1]Or *in glory* [a]Rom 4:15; 5:20; 7:5f; 2 Cor 3:9; Gal 3:10, 21f [b]Ex 24:12; 31:18; 32:15f; 2 Cor 3:3 [c]Ex 34:29-35; 2 Cor 3:13
9 [a]Deut 27:26; 2 Cor 3:7; Heb 12:18-21 [b]Rom 1:17; 3:21f
11 [1]Lit *through*
12 [a]2 Cor 7:4 [b]Acts 4:13, 29; 2 Cor 7:4; Eph 6:19; 1 Thess 2:2
13 [a]Ex 34:33-35; 2 Cor 3:7
14 [1]Or *remains, it not being revealed that it is done away in Christ* [a]Rom 11:7; 2 Cor 4:4 [b]Acts 13:15 [c]2 Cor 3:6
16 [a]Ex 34:34; Rom 11:23
17 [a]Is 61:1f; Gal 4:6 [b]John 8:32; Gal 5:1, 13
18 [a]1 Cor 13:12 [b]John 17:22, 24; 2 Cor 4:4, 6 [c]Rom 8:29 [d]2 Cor 3:17

Chapter 4 Theme ____________________

4 Therefore, since we have this [a]ministry, as we [b]received
mercy, we [c]do not lose heart,
2 but we have renounced the [a]things hidden because of
shame, not walking in craftiness or [b]adulterating the word of
God, but by the manifestation of truth [c]commending ourselves
to every man's conscience in the sight of God.
3 And even if our [a]gospel is [b]veiled, it is veiled [1]to [c]those
who are perishing,
4 in whose case [a]the god of [b]this [1]world has [c]blinded the minds
of the unbelieving [2]so that they might not see the [d]light of the
gospel of the [e]glory of Christ, who is the [f]image of God.
5 For we [a]do not preach ourselves but Christ Jesus as Lord,
and ourselves as your bond-servants [1]for Jesus' sake.
6 For God, who said, "[a]Light shall shine out of darkness," is
the One who has [b]shone in our hearts to give the [c]Light of the
knowledge of the glory of God in the face of Christ.
7 But we have this treasure in [a]earthen vessels, so that the
surpassing greatness of [b]the power will be of God and not from
ourselves;
8 *we are* [a]afflicted in every way, but not [b]crushed; [c]perplexed,
but not despairing;
9 [a]persecuted, but not [b]forsaken; [c]struck down, but not
destroyed;
10 [a]always carrying about in the body the dying of Jesus, so
that [b]the life of Jesus also may be manifested in our body.
11 For we who live are constantly being delivered over to
death for Jesus' sake, so that the life of Jesus also may be
manifested in our mortal flesh.
12 So death works in us, but life in you.
13 But having the same [a]spirit of faith, according to what is
written, "[b]I BELIEVED, THEREFORE I SPOKE," we also believe, therefore
we also speak,
14 knowing that He who [a]raised the Lord Jesus [b]will raise us
also with Jesus and will [c]present us with you.
15 For all things *are* [a]for your sakes, so that the grace which is
[1b]spreading to more and more people may cause the giving of
thanks to abound to the glory of God.
16 Therefore we [a]do not lose heart, but though our outer man
is decaying, yet our [b]inner man is [c]being renewed day by day.
17 For momentary, [a]light affliction is producing for us an
eternal weight of glory far beyond all comparison,
18 while we [a]look not at the things which are seen, but at the
things which are not seen; for the things which are seen are
temporal, but the things which are not seen are eternal.

Chapter 5 Theme ____________________

5 For we know that if [1]the [a]earthly [b]tent which is our house
is torn down, we have a building from God, a house [c]not
made with hands, eternal in the heavens.

4:1 [a]1 Cor 3:5 [b]1 Cor 7:25 [c]Luke 18:1; 2 Cor 4:16; Gal 6:9; Eph 3:13; 2 Thess 3:13

2 [a]Rom 6:21; 1 Cor 4:5 [b]2 Cor 2:17 [c]2 Cor 5:11f

3 [1]Lit *in* [a]2 Cor 2:12 [b]1 Cor 2:6ff; 2 Cor 3:14 [c]1 Cor 1:18; 2 Cor 2:15

4 [1]Lit *age* [2]Or *that the light . . . image of God, would not dawn* upon them [a]John 12:31 [b]Matt 13:22 [c]2 Cor 3:14 [d]Acts 26:18; 2 Cor 4:6 [e]2 Cor 3:18; 4:6 [f]John 1:18; Phil 2:6; Col 1:15; Heb 1:3

5 [1]Two early mss read *through Jesus* [a]1 Cor 4:15f; 1 Thess 2:6f

6 [a]Gen 1:3 [b]2 Pet 1:19 [c]Acts 26:18; 2 Cor 4:4

7 [a]Job 4:19; 10:9; 33:6; Lam 4:2; 2 Cor 5:1; 2 Tim 2:20 [b]Judg 7:2; 1 Cor 2:5

8 [a]2 Cor 1:8; 7:5 [b]2 Cor 6:12 [c]Gal 4:20

9 [a]John 15:20; Rom 8:35f [b]Ps 129:2; Heb 13:5 [c]Ps 37:24; Prov 24:16; Mic 7:8

10 [a]Rom 6:5; 8:36; Gal 6:17 [b]Rom 6:8

13 [a]1 Cor 12:9 [b]Ps 116:10

14 [a]Acts 2:24 [b]1 Thess 4:14 [c]Luke 21:36; Eph 5:27; Col 1:22; Jude 24

15 [1]Lit *being multiplied through the many* [a]Rom 8:28; 2 Cor 1:6 [b]1 Cor 9:19; 2 Cor 1:11

16 [a]2 Cor 4:1 [b]Rom 7:22 [c]Is 40:29, 31; Col 3:10

17 [a]Rom 8:18

18 [a]Rom 8:24; 2 Cor 5:7; Heb 11:1, 13

5:1 [1]Lit *our earthly house of the tent* [a]Job 4:19; 1 Cor 15:47; 2 Cor 4:7 [b]2 Pet 1:13f [c]Mark 14:58; Acts 7:48; Heb 9:11, 24

2 For indeed in this *house* we [a]groan, longing to be [b]clothed
with our dwelling from heaven,
3 inasmuch as we, having put it on, will not be found naked.
4 For indeed while we are in this tent, we [a]groan, being
burdened, because we do not want to be unclothed but to be
[b]clothed, so that what is [c]mortal will be swallowed up by life.
5 Now He who prepared us for this very purpose is God,
who [a]gave to us the Spirit as a [1]pledge.
6 Therefore, being always of good courage, and knowing that
[a]while we are at home in the body we are absent from the Lord—
7 for [a]we walk by faith, not by [1]sight—
8 we are of good courage, I say, and [a]prefer rather to be absent
from the body and [b]to be at home with the Lord.
9 Therefore we also have as our ambition, whether at home
or absent, to be [a]pleasing to Him.
10 For we must all appear before [a]the judgment seat of Christ,
so that each one may be recompensed for [1]his deeds in the
body, according to what he has done, whether good or bad.
11 Therefore, knowing the [a]fear of the Lord, we persuade
men, but we are made manifest to God; and I hope that we are
[b]made manifest also in your consciences.
12 We are not [a]again commending ourselves to you but *are*
giving you an [b]occasion to be proud of us, so that you will have *an*
answer for those who take pride in appearance and not in heart.
13 For if we [1]are [a]beside ourselves, it is for God; if we are of
sound mind, it is for you.
14 For the love of Christ [a]controls us, having concluded this, that
[b]one died for all, therefore all died;
15 and He died for all, so that they who live might no longer
[a]live for themselves, but for Him who died and rose again on
their behalf.
16 Therefore from now on we recognize no one [1a]according to
the flesh; even though we have known Christ [1]according to the
flesh, yet now we know *Him in this way* no longer.
17 Therefore if anyone is [a]in Christ, [1]*he is* [b]a new creature; [c]the
old things passed away; behold, new things have come.
18 Now [a]all *these* things are from God, [b]who reconciled us to
Himself through Christ and gave us the [c]ministry of reconciliation,
19 namely, that [a]God was in Christ reconciling the world to
Himself, [b]not counting their trespasses against them, and [1]He
has [2]committed to us the word of reconciliation.
20 Therefore, we are [a]ambassadors for Christ, [b]as though God
were making an appeal through us; we beg you on behalf of
Christ, be [c]reconciled to God.
21 He made Him who [a]knew no sin *to be* [b]sin on our behalf,
so that we might become the [c]righteousness of God in Him.

Chapter 6 Theme ________________________________

6 And [a]working together *with Him,* [b]we also urge you not to
receive [c]the grace of God in vain—

2 [a]Rom 8:23; 2 Cor 5:4 [b]1 Cor 15:53f; 2 Cor 5:4

4 [a]2 Cor 5:2 [b]1 Cor 15:53f; 2 Cor 5:2 [c]1 Cor 15:54

5 [1]Or *down payment* [a]Rom 8:23; 2 Cor 1:22

6 [a]Heb 11:13f

7 [1]Or *appearance* [a]1 Cor 13:12; 2 Cor 4:18

8 [a]Phil 1:23 [b]John 12:26; Phil 1:23

9 [a]Rom 14:18; Col 1:10; 1 Thess 4:1

10 [1]Lit *the things through the body* [a]Matt 16:27; Acts 10:42; Rom 2:16; 14:10, 12; Eph 6:8

11 [a]Heb 10:31; 12:29; Jude 23 [b]2 Cor 4:2

12 [a]2 Cor 3:1 [b]2 Cor 1:14; Phil 1:26

13 [1]Lit *were* [a]Mark 3:21; 2 Cor 11:1, 16ff; 12:11

14 [a]Acts 18:5 [b]Rom 5:15; 6:6f; Gal 2:20; Col 3:3

15 [a]Rom 14:7-9

16 [1]I.e. by what he is in the flesh [a]John 8:15; 2 Cor 11:18; Phil 3:4

17 [1]Or there is *a new creation* [a]Rom 16:7 [b]John 3:3; Rom 6:4; Gal 6:15 [c]Is 43:18f; 65:17; Eph 4:24; Rev 21:4f

18 [a]1 Cor 11:12 [b]Rom 5:10; Col 1:20 [c]1 Cor 3:5

19 [1]Lit *having* [2]Lit *placed in us* [a]Col 2:9 [b]Rom 4:8; 1 Cor 13:5

20 [a]Mal 2:7; Eph 6:20 [b]2 Cor 6:1 [c]Rom 5:10; Col 1:20

21 [a]Acts 3:14; Heb 4:15; 7:26; 1 Pet 2:22; 1 John 3:5 [b]Rom 3:25; 4:25; 8:3; Gal 3:13 [c]Rom 1:17; 3:21f; 1 Cor 1:30

6:1 [a]1 Cor 3:9 [b]2 Cor 5:20 [c]Acts 11:23

2 for He says,
"[a]AT THE ACCEPTABLE TIME I LISTENED TO YOU,
AND ON THE DAY OF SALVATION I HELPED YOU."
Behold, now is "THE ACCEPTABLE TIME," behold, now is "THE DAY
OF SALVATION"—
3 [a]giving no cause for offense in anything, so that the
ministry will not be discredited,
4 but in everything [a]commending ourselves as [1b]servants of
God, [c]in much endurance, in afflictions, in hardships, in distresses,
5 in [a]beatings, in imprisonments, in [b]tumults, in labors, in
sleeplessness, in [c]hunger,
6 in purity, in [a]knowledge, in [b]patience, in kindness, in the
[c]Holy Spirit, in [d]genuine love,
7 in [a]the word of truth, in [b]the power of God; by [c]the
weapons of righteousness for the right hand and the left,
8 by glory and [a]dishonor, by [b]evil report and good report;
regarded as [c]deceivers and yet [d]true;
9 as unknown [1]yet well-known, as [a]dying [1]yet behold, [b]we
live; as [2]punished [1]yet not put to death,
10 as [a]sorrowful yet always [a]rejoicing, as [b]poor yet making
many rich, as [c]having nothing [1]yet possessing [d]all things.
11 [a]Our mouth [1]has spoken freely to you, O Corinthians, our
[b]heart is opened wide.
12 You are not restrained [1]by us, but [a]you are restrained in
your own [2]affections.
13 Now in a like [a]exchange—I speak as to [b]children—open
wide *to us* also.
14 [a]Do not be [1]bound together with [b]unbelievers; for what
[c]partnership have righteousness and lawlessness, or what
fellowship has light with darkness?
15 Or what [a]harmony has Christ with [1]Belial, or [2]what has a
[b]believer in common with an [c]unbeliever?
16 Or [a]what agreement has the temple of God with idols? For
we are [b]the temple of [c]the living God; just as God said,
"[d]I WILL [e]DWELL IN THEM AND [f]WALK AMONG THEM;
AND I WILL BE THEIR GOD, AND THEY SHALL BE MY PEOPLE.
17 "[a]Therefore, [b]COME OUT FROM THEIR MIDST AND BE SEPARATE,"
says the Lord.
"AND DO NOT TOUCH WHAT IS UNCLEAN;
And I will welcome you.
18 "[a]And I will be a father to you,
And you shall be [b]sons and daughters to Me,"
Says the Lord Almighty.

Chapter 7 Theme ______________________________

7 Therefore, having these promises, [a]beloved, [b]let us cleanse
ourselves from all defilement of flesh and spirit, perfecting
holiness in the fear of God.
2 [a]Make room for us *in your hearts;* we wronged no one, we
corrupted no one, we took advantage of no one.

2 [a]Is 49:8
3 [a]1 Cor 8:9, 13; 9:12
4 [1]Or *ministers* [a]Rom 3:5 [b]1 Cor 3:5; 2 Tim 2:24f [c]Acts 9:16; 2 Cor 4:8-11; 6:4ff; 11:23-27; 12:10
5 [a]Acts 16:23 [b]Acts 19:23ff [c]1 Cor 4:11
6 [a]1 Cor 12:8; 2 Cor 11:6 [b]2 Cor 1:23; 2:10; 13:10 [c]1 Cor 2:4; 1 Thess 1:5 [d]Rom 12:9
7 [a]2 Cor 2:17; 4:2 [b]1 Cor 2:5 [c]Rom 13:12; 2 Cor 10:4; Eph 6:11ff
8 [a]1 Cor 4:10 [b]Rom 3:8; 1 Cor 4:13; 2 Cor 12:16 [c]Matt 27:63 [d]2 Cor 1:18; 4:2; 1 Thess 2:3f
9 [1]Lit *and* [2]Or *disciplined* [a]Rom 8:36 [b]2 Cor 1:8, 10; 4:11
10 [1]Lit *and* [a]John 16:22; 2 Cor 7:4; Phil 2:17; 4:4; Col 1:24; 1 Thess 1:6 [b]1 Cor 1:5; 2 Cor 8:9 [c]Acts 3:6 [d]Rom 8:32; 1 Cor 3:21
11 [1]Lit *is open to you* [a]Ezek 33:22; Eph 6:19 [b]Is 60:5; 2 Cor 7:3
12 [1]Or *in us* [2]Lit *inward parts* [a]2 Cor 7:2
13 [a]Gal 4:12 [b]1 Cor 4:14
14 [1]Lit *unequally yoked* [a]Deut 22:10; 1 Cor 5:9f [b]1 Cor 6:6 [c]Eph 5:7, 11; 1 John 1:6
15 [1]Gr *Beliar* [2]Lit *what part has a believer with an unbeliever* [a]1 Cor 10:21 [b]Acts 5:14; 1 Pet 1:21 [c]1 Cor 6:6
16 [a]1 Cor 10:21 [b]1 Cor 3:16; 6:19 [c]Matt 16:16 [d]Ex 29:45; Lev 26:12; Jer 31:1; Ezek 37:27 [e]Ex 25:8; John 14:23 [f]Rev 2:1
17 [a]Is 52:11 [b]Rev 18:4
18 [a]2 Sam 7:14; 1 Chr 17:13; Is 43:6; Hos 1:10 [b]Rom 8:14
7:1 [a]Heb 6:9 [b]1 Pet 1:15f
2 [a]2 Cor 6:12f; 12:15

3 I do not speak to condemn you, for I have said [a]before that
you are [b]in our hearts to die together and to live together.
4 Great is my [a]confidence [1]in you; great is my [b]boasting on
your behalf. I am filled with [c]comfort; I am overflowing with
[d]joy in all our affliction.
5 For even when we came into [a]Macedonia our flesh had no
rest, but we were [b]afflicted on every side: [c]conflicts without,
fears within.
6 But [a]God, who comforts the [1]depressed, [b]comforted us by
the coming of [c]Titus;
7 and not only by his coming, but also by the comfort with
which he was comforted in you, as he reported to us your longing,
your mourning, your zeal for me; so that I rejoiced even more.
8 For though I [a]caused you sorrow by my letter, I do not
regret it; though I did regret it—*for* I see that that letter caused
you sorrow, though only for a while—
9 I now rejoice, not that you were made sorrowful, but that
you were made sorrowful to *the point of* repentance; for you
were made sorrowful according to *the will of* God, so that you
might not suffer loss in anything [1]through us.
10 For the sorrow that is according to *the will of* God
produces a [a]repentance [1]without regret, *leading* to salvation,
but the sorrow of the world produces death.
11 For behold what earnestness this very thing, this [1]godly
sorrow, has produced in you: what vindication of yourselves,
what indignation, what fear, what [a]longing, what zeal, what
[b]avenging of wrong! In everything you [c]demonstrated yourselves
to be innocent in the matter.
12 So although [a]I wrote to you, *it was* not for the sake of [b]the
offender nor for the sake of the one offended, but that your
earnestness on our behalf might be made known to you in the
sight of God.
13 For this reason we have been [a]comforted.
And besides our comfort, we rejoiced even much more for
the joy of [b]Titus, because his [c]spirit has been refreshed by you all.
14 For if in anything I have [a]boasted to him about you, I was
not put to shame; but as we spoke all things to you in truth, so
also our boasting before [b]Titus proved to be *the* truth.
15 His [1]affection abounds all the more toward you, as he
remembers the [a]obedience of you all, how you received him
with [b]fear and trembling.
16 I rejoice that in everything [a]I have confidence in you.

Chapter 8 Theme ____________________

8

Now, brethren, we *wish to* make known to you the grace of
God which has been [a]given in the churches of [b]Macedonia,
2 that in a great ordeal of affliction their abundance of joy and
their deep poverty overflowed in the [a]wealth of their liberality.
3 For I testify that [a]according to their ability, and beyond
their ability, *they gave* of their own accord,

3 [a]2 Cor 6:11f [b]Phil 1:7
4 [1]Lit *toward* [a]2 Cor 3:12 [b]2 Cor 7:14; 8:24; 9:2f; 10:8; Phil 1:26; 2 Thess 1:4 [c]2 Cor 1:4 [d]2 Cor 6:10
5 [a]Rom 15:26; 2 Cor 2:13 [b]2 Cor 4:8 [c]Deut 32:25
6 [1]Or *humble* [a]2 Cor 1:3f [b]2 Cor 7:13 [c]2 Cor 2:13; 7:13f
8 [a]2 Cor 2:2
9 [1]Lit *from*
10 [1]Or leading *to a salvation without regret* [a]Acts 11:18
11 [1]Lit *sorrow according to God* [a]2 Cor 7:7 [b]2 Cor 2:6 [c]Rom 3:5
12 [a]2 Cor 2:3, 9; 7:8 [b]1 Cor 5:1f
13 [a]2 Cor 7:6 [b]2 Cor 2:13; 7:6, 14 [c]1 Cor 16:18
14 [a]2 Cor 7:4; 8:24; 9:2f; 10:8; Phil 1:26; 2 Thess 1:4 [b]2 Cor 2:13; 7:6, 13
15 [1]Lit *inward parts* [a]2 Cor 2:9 [b]1 Cor 2:3; Phil 2:12
16 [a]2 Cor 2:3
8:1 [a]2 Cor 8:5 [b]Acts 16:9
2 [a]Rom 2:4
3 [a]1 Cor 16:2; 2 Cor 8:11

RETURN TO INSTRUCTIONS

4 begging us with much urging for the [a]favor [1]of participation
in the [2b]support of the [3]saints,
5 and *this,* not as we had [1]expected, but they first [a]gave
themselves to the Lord and to us by [b]the will of God.
6 So we [a]urged [b]Titus that as he had previously [c]made a
beginning, so he would also complete in you [d]this gracious work
as well.
7 But just as you [a]abound [b]in everything, in faith and utterance
and knowledge and in all earnestness and in the [1]love we
inspired in you, *see* that you [a]abound in this gracious work also.
8 I [a]am not speaking *this* as a command, but as proving through
the earnestness of others the sincerity of your love also.
9 For you know [a]the grace of our Lord Jesus Christ, that
[b]though He was rich, yet for your sake He became poor, so that
you through His poverty might become rich.
10 I [a]give *my* opinion in this matter, for this is to your
advantage, who were the first to begin [b]a year ago not only to
do *this,* but also to desire *to do it.*
11 But now finish [1]doing it also, so that just as *there was* the
[a]readiness to desire it, so *there may be* also the completion of it
by your ability.
12 For if the readiness is present, it is acceptable [a]according to
what *a person* has, not according to what he does not have.
13 For *this* is not for the ease of others *and* for your affliction,
but by way of equality—
14 at this present time your abundance *being a supply* for
[a]their need, so that their abundance also may become *a supply*
for [a]your need, that there may be equality;
15 as it is written, "[a]HE WHO *gathered* MUCH DID NOT HAVE TOO
MUCH, AND HE WHO *gathered* LITTLE HAD NO LACK."
16 But [a]thanks be to God who [b]puts the same earnestness on
your behalf in the heart of [c]Titus.
17 For he not only accepted our [a]appeal, but being himself
very earnest, he has gone to you of his own accord.
18 We have sent along with him [a]the brother whose fame in
the things of the [b]gospel *has spread* through [c]all the churches;
19 [a]and not only *this,* but he has also been [b]appointed by the
churches to travel with us in [c]this gracious work, which is
being administered by us for the glory of the Lord Himself, and
to show our [d]readiness,
20 [1]taking precaution so that no one will discredit us in our
administration of this generous gift;
21 for we [a]have regard for what is honorable, not only in [b]the
sight of the Lord, but also in the sight of men.
22 We have sent with them our brother, whom we have often
tested and found diligent in many things, but now even more
diligent because of *his* great confidence in you.
23 As for [a]Titus, *he is* my [b]partner and fellow worker [1]among
you; as for our [c]brethren, *they are* [2d]messengers of the churches,
[e]a glory to Christ.
24 Therefore [1]openly before the churches, [2]show them the proof
of your love and of our [a]reason for boasting about you.

4 [1]Lit *and* [2]Lit *service to the saints* [3]Or *holy ones* [a]Acts 24:17; Rom 15:25f [b]Rom 15:31; 2 Cor 8:19f; 9:1, 12f

5 [1]Lit *hoped* [a]2 Cor 8:1 [b]1 Cor 1:1

6 [a]2 Cor 8:17; 12:18 [b]2 Cor 2:13; 8:16, 23 [c]2 Cor 8:10 [d]Acts 24:17; Rom 15:25f

7 [1]Lit *love from us in you;* one early ms reads *your love for us* [a]2 Cor 9:8 [b]Rom 15:14; 1 Cor 1:5; 12:8

8 [a]1 Cor 7:6

9 [a]2 Cor 13:14 [b]Matt 20:28; 2 Cor 6:10; Phil 2:6f

10 [a]1 Cor 7:25, 40 [b]1 Cor 16:2f; 2 Cor 9:2

11 [1]Lit *the doing* [a]2 Cor 8:12, 19; 9:2

12 [a]Mark 12:43f; Luke 21:3, 4; 2 Cor 9:7

14 [a]Acts 4:34; 2 Cor 9:12

15 [a]Ex 16:18

16 [a]2 Cor 2:14 [b]Rev 17:17 [c]2 Cor 2:13; 8:6, 23

17 [a]2 Cor 8:6; 12:18

18 [a]1 Cor 16:3; 2 Cor 12:18 [b]2 Cor 2:12 [c]1 Cor 4:17; 7:17

19 [a]Rom 5:3 [b]Acts 14:23; 1 Cor 16:3f [c]2 Cor 8:4, 6 [d]2 Cor 8:11, 12; 9:2

20 [1]Lit *avoiding this*

21 [a]Rom 12:17 [b]Prov 3:4; Rom 14:18

23 [1]Lit *for you* [2]Lit *apostles* [a]2 Cor 8:6 [b]Philem 17 [c]2 Cor 8:18, 22 [d]John 13:16; Phil 2:25 [e]1 Cor 11:7

24 [1]Lit *in the face of the churches* [2]Or *show the proof . . . for boasting to them about you* [a]2 Cor 7:4

Chapter 9 Theme ____________________

9 For [a]it is superfluous for me to write to you about this [b]ministry to the [1]saints;

2 for I know your readiness, of which I [a]boast about you to the [b]Macedonians, *namely,* that [c]Achaia has been prepared since [d]last year, and your zeal has stirred up most of them.

3 But I have sent the brethren, in order that our [a]boasting about you may not be made empty in this case, so that, [b]as I was saying, you may be prepared;

4 otherwise if any [a]Macedonians come with me and find you unprepared, we—not to speak of you—will be put to shame by this confidence.

5 So I thought it necessary to urge the [a]brethren that they would go on ahead to you and arrange beforehand your previously promised [1b]bountiful gift, so that the same would be ready as a [1c]bountiful gift and not [2d]affected by covetousness.

6 Now this *I say,* [a]he who sows sparingly will also reap sparingly, and he who sows [1]bountifully will also reap [1]bountifully.

7 Each one *must do* just as he has purposed in his heart, not [a]grudgingly or under compulsion, for [b]God loves a cheerful giver.

8 And [a]God is able to make all grace abound to you, so that always having all sufficiency in everything, you may have an abundance for every good deed;

9 as it is written,

"[a]HE SCATTERED ABROAD, HE GAVE TO THE POOR,
HIS RIGHTEOUSNESS [1]ENDURES FOREVER."

10 Now He who supplies [a]seed to the sower and bread for food will supply and multiply your seed for sowing and [b]increase the harvest of your righteousness;

11 you will be [a]enriched in everything for all liberality, which through us is producing [b]thanksgiving to God.

12 For the ministry of this service is not only fully supplying [a]the needs of the [1]saints, but is also overflowing [b]through many thanksgivings to God.

13 Because of the proof given by this [a]ministry, they will [b]glorify God for *your* obedience to your [c]confession of the [d]gospel of Christ and for the liberality of your [1]contribution to them and to all,

14 while they also, by prayer on your behalf, yearn for you because of the surpassing grace of God in you.

15 [a]Thanks be to God for His indescribable [b]gift!

Chapter 10 Theme ____________________

10 Now [a]I, Paul, myself [b]urge you by the [c]meekness and gentleness of Christ—I who [d]am [1]meek when face to face with you, but bold toward you when absent!

2 I ask that [a]when I am present I *need* not be bold with the confidence with which I propose to be courageous against [b]some, who regard us as if we walked [c]according to the flesh.

3 For though we walk in the flesh, we do not war [a]according to the flesh,

9:1 [1]Or *holy ones* [a]1 Thess 4:9 [b]2 Cor 8:4
2 [a]2 Cor 7:4 [b]Rom 15:26 [c]Acts 18:12 [d]2 Cor 8:10
3 [a]2 Cor 7:4 [b]1 Cor 16:2
4 [a]Rom 15:26
5 [1]Lit *blessing* [2]Lit *as covetousness* [a]2 Cor 9:3 [b]Gen 33:11; Judg 1:15; 2 Cor 9:6 [c]Phil 4:17 [d]2 Cor 12:17f
6 [1]Lit *with blessings* [a]Prov 11:24f; 22:9; Gal 6:7, 9
7 [a]Deut 15:10; 1 Chr 29:17; Rom 12:8; 2 Cor 8:12 [b]Ex 25:2
8 [a]Eph 3:20
9 [1]Lit *abides* [a]Ps 112:9
10 [a]Is 55:10 [b]Hos 10:12
11 [a]1 Cor 1:5 [b]2 Cor 1:11
12 [1]Or *holy ones* [a]2 Cor 8:14 [b]2 Cor 1:11
13 [1]Or *sharing with them* [a]Rom 15:31; 2 Cor 8:4 [b]Matt 9:8 [c]1 Tim 6:12f; Heb 3:1; 4:14; 10:23 [d]2 Cor 2:12
15 [a]2 Cor 2:14 [b]Rom 5:15f
10:1 [1]Lit *lowly* [a]Gal 5:2; Eph 3:1; Col 1:23 [b]Rom 12:1 [c]Matt 11:29; 1 Cor 4:21; Phil 4:5 [d]1 Cor 2:3f; 2 Cor 10:10
2 [a]1 Cor 4:21; 2 Cor 13:2, 10 [b]1 Cor 4:18f [c]Rom 8:4; 2 Cor 1:17
3 [a]Rom 8:4; 2 Cor 1:17

4 for the [a]weapons of our warfare are not of the flesh, but
[1]divinely powerful [b]for the destruction of fortresses.
5 *We are* destroying speculations and every [a]lofty thing raised
up against the knowledge of God, and *we are* taking every
thought captive to the [b]obedience of Christ,
6 and we are ready to punish all disobedience, whenever
[a]your obedience is complete.
7 [1a]You are looking at [2]things as they are outwardly. [b]If anyone
is confident in himself that he is Christ's, let him consider this
again within himself, that just as he is Christ's, [c]so also are we.
8 For even if [a]I boast somewhat [1]further about our [b]authority,
which the Lord gave for building you up and not for destroying
you, I will not be put to shame,
9 [1]for I do not wish to seem as if I would terrify you by my
letters.
10 For they say, "His letters are weighty and strong, but his
[1]personal presence is [a]unimpressive and [b]his speech
contemptible."
11 Let such a person consider this, that what we are in word
by letters when absent, such persons *we are* also in deed when
present.
12 For we are not bold to class or compare ourselves with
[1]some of those who [a]commend themselves; but when they
measure themselves by themselves and compare themselves
with themselves, they are without understanding.
13 But we will not boast [a]beyond *our* measure, but [1b]within
the measure of the sphere which God apportioned to us as a
measure, to reach even as far as you.
14 For we are not overextending ourselves, as if we did not
reach to you, for [a]we were the first to come even as far as you
in the [b]gospel of Christ;
15 not boasting [a]beyond *our* measure, *that is,* in [b]other men's
labors, but with the hope that as [c]your faith grows, we will be,
[1]within our sphere, [d]enlarged even more by you,
16 so as to [a]preach the gospel even to [b]the regions beyond
you, *and* not to boast [1c]in what has been accomplished in the
sphere of another.
17 But [a]HE WHO BOASTS IS TO BOAST IN THE LORD.
18 For it is not he who [a]commends himself that is approved,
but he [b]whom the Lord commends.

Chapter 11 Theme ____________________

11 I wish that you would [a]bear with me in a little [b]foolish-
ness; but [1]indeed you are bearing with me.
2 For I am jealous for you with a godly jealousy; for I
[a]betrothed you to one husband, so that to Christ I might
[b]present you *as* a pure virgin.
3 But I am afraid that, as the [a]serpent deceived Eve by his
craftiness, your minds will be led astray from the simplicity and
purity *of devotion* to Christ.

4 [1]Or *mighty before God* [a]1 Cor 9:7; 2 Cor 6:7; 1 Tim 1:18 [b]Jer 1:10; 2 Cor 10:8; 13:10

5 [a]Is 2:11f [b]2 Cor 9:13

6 [a]2 Cor 2:9

7 [1]Or *Look at . . .* or *Do you look at . . .?* [2]Lit *what is before your face* [a]John 7:24; 2 Cor 5:12 [b]1 Cor 1:12; 14:37 [c]1 Cor 9:1; 2 Cor 11:23; Gal 1:12

8 [1]Or *more abundantly* [a]2 Cor 7:4 [b]2 Cor 13:10

9 [1]Lit *so that I may not seem*

10 [1]Lit *bodily presence is weak* [a]1 Cor 2:3; 2 Cor 12:7; Gal 4:13f [b]1 Cor 1:17; 2 Cor 11:6

12 [1]Or *any* [a]2 Cor 3:1; 10:18

13 [1]Lit *according to the measure* [a]2 Cor 10:15 [b]Rom 12:3; 2 Cor 10:15f

14 [a]1 Cor 3:6 [b]2 Cor 2:12

15 [1]Lit *according to our sphere* [a]2 Cor 10:13 [b]Rom 15:20 [c]2 Thess 1:3 [d]Acts 5:13

16 [1]Lit *to the things prepared in the* [a]2 Cor 11:7 [b]Acts 19:21 [c]Rom 15:20

17 [a]Jer 9:24; 1 Cor 1:31

18 [a]2 Cor 10:12 [b]Rom 2:29; 1 Cor 4:5

11:1 [1]Or *do indeed bear with me* [a]Matt 17:17; 2 Cor 11:4, 16, 19f [b]2 Cor 5:13; 11:17, 21

2 [a]Hos 2:19f; Eph 5:26f [b]2 Cor 4:14

3 [a]Gen 3:4, 13; John 8:44; 1 Thess 3:5; 1 Tim 2:14; Rev 12:9, 15

4 For if [1]one comes and preaches [a]another Jesus whom we
have not preached, or you receive a [b]different spirit which you
have not received, or a [c]different gospel which you have not
accepted, you [d]bear *this* [e]beautifully.
5 For I consider myself [a]not in the least inferior to the [1]most
eminent apostles.
6 But even if I am [a]unskilled in speech, yet I am not *so* in
[b]knowledge; in fact, in every way we have [c]made *this* evident
to you in all things.
7 Or [a]did I commit a sin in humbling myself so that you might
be exalted, because I preached the [b]gospel of God to you [c]without
charge?
8 I robbed other churches by [a]taking wages *from them* to serve
you;
9 and when I was present with you and was in need, I was
[a]not a burden to anyone; for when [b]the brethren came from
[c]Macedonia they fully supplied my need, and in everything I kept
myself from [a]being a burden to you, [1]and will continue to do so.
10 [a]As the truth of Christ is in me, [b]this boasting of mine will
not be stopped in the regions of [c]Achaia.
11 Why? [a]Because I do not love you? [b]God knows *I do!*
12 But what I am doing I will continue to do, [a]so that I may
cut off opportunity from those who desire an opportunity to be
[1]regarded just as we are in the matter about which they are
boasting.
13 For such men are [a]false apostles, [b]deceitful workers,
disguising themselves as apostles of Christ.
14 No wonder, for even [a]Satan disguises himself as an [b]angel of
light.
15 Therefore it is not surprising if his servants also disguise
themselves as servants of righteousness, [a]whose end will be
according to their deeds.
16 [a]Again I say, let no one think me foolish; but if *you do,*
receive me even as foolish, so that I also may boast a little.
17 What I am saying, I am not saying [1a]as the Lord would, but
as [b]in foolishness, in this confidence of boasting.
18 Since [a]many boast [b]according to the flesh, I will boast also.
19 For you, [a]being *so* wise, tolerate the foolish gladly.
20 For you tolerate it if anyone [a]enslaves you, anyone [b]devours
you, anyone [c]takes advantage of you, anyone [d]exalts himself,
anyone [e]hits you in the face.
21 To *my* [a]shame I *must* say that we have been [b]weak *by
comparison.*

But in whatever respect anyone *else* [c]is bold—I [d]speak in
foolishness—I am just as bold myself.
22 Are they [a]Hebrews? [b]So am I. Are they [c]Israelites? [c]So am
I. Are they [1d]descendants of Abraham? [e]So am I.
23 Are they [a]servants of Christ?—I speak as if insane—I more
so; in [1b]far more labors, in [1c]far more imprisonments, [2d]beaten
times without number, often in [e]danger of death.
24 Five times I received from the Jews [a]thirty-nine *lashes.*

4 [1]Lit *the one who comes preaches* [a]1 Cor 3:11 [b]Rom 8:15 [c]Gal 1:6 [d]2 Cor 11:1 [e]Mark 7:9
5 [1]Or *super-apostles* [a]2 Cor 12:11; Gal 2:6
6 [a]1 Cor 1:17 [b]1 Cor 12:8; Eph 3:4 [c]2 Cor 4:2
7 [a]2 Cor 12:13 [b]Rom 1:1; 2 Cor 2:12 [c]Acts 18:3; 1 Cor 9:18
8 [a]1 Cor 4:12; 9:6; Phil 4:15, 18
9 [1]Lit *and I will keep* [a]2 Cor 12:13f, 16 [b]Acts 18:5 [c]Rom 15:26; Phil 4:15-18
10 [a]Rom 1:9; 9:1; 2 Cor 1:23; Gal 2:20 [b]1 Cor 9:15 [c]Acts 18:12
11 [a]2 Cor 12:15 [b]Rom 1:9; 2 Cor 2:17; 11:31; 12:2f
12 [1]Lit *found* [a]1 Cor 9:12
13 [a]Acts 20:30; Gal 1:7; 2:4; Phil 1:15; Titus 1:10f; 2 Pet 2:1; Rev 2:2 [b]Phil 3:2
14 [a]Matt 4:10; Eph 6:12; Col 1:13 [b]Col 1:12
15 [a]Rom 2:6; 3:8
16 [a]2 Cor 11:1
17 [1]Lit *in accordance with the Lord* [a]1 Cor 7:12, 25 [b]2 Cor 11:21
18 [a]Phil 3:3f [b]2 Cor 5:16
19 [a]1 Cor 4:10
20 [a]2 Cor 1:24; Gal 2:4; 4:3, 9; 5:1 [b]Mark 12:40 [c]2 Cor 11:3; 12:16 [d]2 Cor 10:5 [e]1 Cor 4:11
21 [a]2 Cor 6:8 [b]2 Cor 10:10 [c]2 Cor 10:2 [d]2 Cor 11:17
22 [1]Lit *seed* [a]Acts 6:1 [b]Phil 3:5 [c]Rom 9:4 [d]Gal 3:16 [e]Rom 11:1
23 [1]Lit *more abundant* [2]Lit *exceedingly in stripes* [a]1 Cor 3:5; 2 Cor 3:6; 10:7 [b]1 Cor 15:10 [c]2 Cor 6:5 [d]Acts 16:23; 2 Cor 6:5 [e]Rom 8:36
24 [a]Deut 25:3

25 Three times I was [a]beaten with rods, once I was [b]stoned, three times I was shipwrecked, a night and a day I have spent in the deep.

26 *I have been* on frequent journeys, in dangers from rivers, dangers from robbers, dangers from *my* [a]countrymen, dangers from the [b]Gentiles, dangers in the [c]city, dangers in the wilderness, dangers on the sea, dangers among [d]false brethren;

27 *I have been* in [a]labor and hardship, [1]through many sleepless nights, in [b]hunger and thirst, often [c]without food, in cold and [2d]exposure.

28 Apart from *such* [1]external things, there is the daily pressure on me *of* concern for [a]all the churches.

29 Who is [a]weak without my being weak? Who is [1]led into sin [2]without my intense concern?

30 If I have to boast, I will boast of what pertains to my [a]weakness.

31 The God and Father of the Lord Jesus, [a]He who is blessed forever, [b]knows that I am not lying.

32 In [a]Damascus the ethnarch under Aretas the king was [b]guarding the city of the Damascenes in order to seize me,

33 and I was let down in a basket [a]through a window [1]in the wall, and *so* escaped his hands.

Chapter 12 Theme ______________________

12 [a]Boasting is necessary, though it is not profitable; but I will go on to visions and [b]revelations [1]of the Lord.

2 I know a man [a]in Christ who fourteen years ago—whether in the body I do not know, or out of the body I do not know, [b]God knows—such a man was [c]caught up to the [d]third heaven.

3 And I know how such a man—whether in the body or apart from the body I do not know, [a]God knows—

4 was [a]caught up into [b]Paradise and heard inexpressible words, which a man is not permitted to speak.

5 [a]On behalf of such a man I will boast; but on my own behalf I will not boast, except in regard to *my* [b]weaknesses.

6 For if I do wish to boast I will not be [a]foolish, [b]for I will be speaking the truth; but I refrain *from this,* so that no one will credit me with more than he sees *in* me or hears from me.

7 Because of the surpassing greatness of the [a]revelations, for this reason, to keep me from exalting myself, there was given me a [b]thorn in the flesh, a [c]messenger of Satan to [1]torment me—to keep me from exalting myself!

8 Concerning this I implored the Lord [a]three times that it might leave me.

9 And He has said to me, "My grace is sufficient for you, for [a]power is perfected in weakness." Most gladly, therefore, I will rather [b]boast [1]about my weaknesses, so that the power of Christ may dwell in me.

10 Therefore [a]I am well content with weaknesses, with [1]insults, with [b]distresses, with [c]persecutions, with [b]difficulties, [d]for Christ's sake; for [e]when I am weak, then I am strong.

25 [a]Acts 16:22 [b]Acts 14:19

26 [a]Acts 9:23; 13:45, 50; 14:5; 17:5, 13; 18:12; 20:3, 19; 21:27; 23:10, 12; 25:3; 1 Thess 2:15 [b]Acts 14:5, 19; 19:23ff; 27:42 [c]Acts 21:31 [d]Gal 2:4

27 [1]Lit *often in wakefulness* [2]Lit *nakedness;* i.e. lack of clothing [a]1 Thess 2:9; 2 Thess 3:8 [b]1 Cor 4:11; Phil 4:12 [c]2 Cor 6:5 [d]1 Cor 4:11

28 [1]Or *the things unmentioned* [a]1 Cor 7:17

29 [1]Lit *made to stumble* [2]Lit *and I do not burn* [a]1 Cor 8:9, 13; 9:22

30 [a]1 Cor 2:3

31 [a]Rom 1:25 [b]2 Cor 11:11

32 [a]Acts 9:2 [b]Acts 9:24

33 [1]Lit *through* [a]Acts 9:25

12:1 [1]Or *from* [a]2 Cor 11:16, 18, 30; 12:5, 9 [b]1 Cor 14:6; 2 Cor 12:7; Gal 1:12; 2:2; Eph 3:3

2 [a]Rom 16:7 [b]2 Cor 11:11 [c]Ezek 8:3; Acts 8:39; 2 Cor 12:4; 1 Thess 4:17; Rev 12:5 [d]Deut 10:14; Ps 148:4; Eph 4:10; Heb 4:14

3 [a]2 Cor 11:11

4 [a]Ezek 8:3; Acts 8:39; 2 Cor 12:2; 1 Thess 4:17; Rev 12:5 [b]Luke 23:43

5 [a]2 Cor 12:1 [b]1 Cor 2:3; 2 Cor 12:9f

6 [a]2 Cor 5:13; 11:16f; 12:11 [b]2 Cor 7:14

7 [1]Lit *beat* [a]2 Cor 12:1 [b]Num 33:55; Ezek 28:24; Hos 2:6 [c]Job 2:6; Matt 4:10; 1 Cor 5:5

8 [a]Matt 26:44

9 [1]Lit *in* [a]1 Cor 2:5; Eph 3:16; Phil 4:13 [b]1 Cor 2:3; 2 Cor 12:5

10 [1]Or *mistreatment* [a]Rom 5:3; 8:35 [b]2 Cor 6:4 [c]2 Thess 1:4; 2 Tim 3:11 [d]2 Cor 5:15, 20 [e]2 Cor 13:4

11 I have become [a]foolish; you yourselves compelled me. Actually
I should have been commended by you, for [b]in no respect was I
inferior to the [1]most eminent apostles, even though [c]I am a nobody.
12 The [1a]signs [2]of a true apostle were performed among you
with all perseverance, by [1]signs and wonders and [3]miracles.
13 For in what respect were you treated as inferior to the rest
of the churches, except that [a]I myself did not become a burden
to you? Forgive me [b]this wrong!
14 Here [a]for this third time I am ready to come to you, and I
[b]will not be a burden to you; for I [c]do not seek what is yours,
but [d]you; for [e]children are not responsible to save up for *their*
parents, but [f]parents for *their* children.
15 I will [a]most gladly spend and be expended for your souls. If
[b]I love you more, am I to be loved less?
16 But be that as it may, I [a]did not burden you myself; nevertheless, crafty fellow that I am, I [b]took you in by deceit.
17 [a]*Certainly* I have not taken advantage of you through any of
those whom I have sent to you, have I?
18 I [a]urged [b]Titus *to go,* and I sent [c]the brother with him. Titus
did not take any advantage of you, did he? Did we not [1]conduct
ourselves [2]in the same [d]spirit *and walk* [e]in the same steps?
19 All this time [1]you have been thinking that we are defending
ourselves to you. *Actually,* [a]it is in the sight of God that we have
been speaking in Christ; and [b]all for your upbuilding, [c]beloved.
20 For I am afraid that perhaps [a]when I come I may find you
to be not what I wish and may be found by you to be not what
you wish; that perhaps *there will be* [b]strife, jealousy, [c]angry
tempers, [d]disputes, [e]slanders, [f]gossip, [g]arrogance, [h]disturbances;
21 I am afraid that when I come again my God may humiliate
me before you, and I may mourn over many of those who have
[a]sinned in the past and not repented of the [b]impurity, [1]immorality
and sensuality which they have practiced.

Chapter 13 Theme ______________________________

13 [a]This is the third time I am coming to you. [b]EVERY [1]FACT
[2]IS TO BE CONFIRMED BY THE [3]TESTIMONY OF TWO OR THREE
WITNESSES.
2 I have previously said when present the second time, and
though now absent I say in advance to those who have [a]sinned
in the past and to all the rest *as well,* that [b]if I come again I will
not [c]spare *anyone,*
3 since you are [a]seeking for proof of the [b]Christ who speaks
in me, and who is not weak toward you, but [c]mighty in you.
4 For indeed He was [a]crucified because of weakness, yet He
lives [b]because of the power of God. For we also are [c]weak [1]in
Him, yet [d]we will live with Him because of the power of God
directed toward you.
5 [a]Test yourselves *to see* if you are in the faith; [b]examine
yourselves! Or do you not recognize this about yourselves, that
Jesus Christ is in you—unless indeed you [1c]fail the test?

11 [1]Or *super-apostles* [a]2 Cor 5:13; 11:16f; 12:6 [b]1 Cor 15:10; 2 Cor 11:5 [c]1 Cor 3:7; 13:2; 15:9
12 [1]Or *attesting miracles* [2]Lit *of the apostle* [3]Or *works of power* [a]John 4:48; Rom 15:19; 1 Cor 9:1
13 [a]1 Cor 9:12, 18; 2 Cor 11:9; 12:14 [b]2 Cor 11:7
14 [a]2 Cor 1:15; 13:1, 2 [b]1 Cor 9:12, 18; 2 Cor 11:9; 12:13 [c]1 Cor 10:24, 33 [d]1 Cor 9:19 [e]1 Cor 4:14f; Gal 4:19 [f]Prov 19:14; Ezek 34:2
15 [a]Rom 9:3; 2 Cor 1:6; Phil 2:17; Col 1:24; 1 Thess 2:8; 2 Tim 2:10 [b]2 Cor 11:11
16 [a]2 Cor 11:9 [b]2 Cor 11:20
17 [a]2 Cor 9:5
18 [1]Lit *walk* [2]Or *by the same Spirit* [a]2 Cor 8:6 [b]2 Cor 2:13 [c]2 Cor 8:18 [d]1 Cor 4:21 [e]Rom 4:12
19 [1]Or *have you been thinking . . . ?* [a]Rom 9:1; 2 Cor 2:17 [b]Rom 14:19; 2 Cor 10:8; 1 Thess 5:11 [c]Heb 6:9
20 [a]1 Cor 4:21; 2 Cor 2:1-4 [b]1 Cor 1:11; 3:3 [c]Gal 5:20 [d]Rom 2:8; 1 Cor 11:19 [e]Rom 1:30; James 4:11; 1 Pet 2:1 [f]Rom 1:29 [g]1 Cor 4:6, 18; 5:2 [h]1 Cor 14:33
21 [1]I.e. sexual immorality [a]2 Cor 13:2 [b]1 Cor 6:9, 18; Gal 5:19; Col 3:5
13:1 [1]Lit *word* [2]Lit *shall be* [3]Lit *mouth* [a]2 Cor 12:14 [b]Deut 17:6; 19:15; Matt 18:16
2 [a]2 Cor 12:21 [b]1 Cor 4:21; 2 Cor 13:10 [c]2 Cor 1:23; 10:11
3 [a]2 Cor 10:1, 10 [b]Matt 10:20; 1 Cor 5:4; 7:40 [c]2 Cor 9:8; 10:4
4 [1]One early ms reads *with Him* [a]Phil 2:7f; 1 Pet 3:18 [b]Rom 1:4; 6:4; 1 Cor 6:14 [c]1 Cor 2:3; 2 Cor 13:9 [d]Rom 6:8
5 [1]Lit *are unapproved* [a]John 6:6 [b]1 Cor 11:28 [c]1 Cor 9:27

6 But I trust that you will realize that we ourselves [1]do not
fail the test.
7 Now we pray to God that you do no wrong; not that we
ourselves may appear approved, but that you may do what is
right, even though we may [1]appear unapproved.
8 For we can do nothing against the truth, but *only* for the
truth.
9 For we rejoice when we ourselves are [a]weak but you are
strong; this we also pray for, [1]that you be [b]made complete.
10 For this reason I am writing these things while absent, so
that when present [a]I *need* not use [b]severity, in accordance with
the [c]authority which the Lord gave me for building up and not
for tearing down.
11 [a]Finally, brethren, [1]rejoice, [2b]be made complete, be
comforted, [c]be like-minded, [d]live in peace; and [e]the God of
love and peace will be with you.
12 [a]Greet one another with a holy kiss.
13 [a]All the [1]saints greet you.
14 [a]The grace of the Lord Jesus Christ, and the [b]love of God,
and the [c]fellowship of the Holy Spirit, be with you all.

6 [1]Lit *are not unapproved*
7 [1]Lit *be as*
9 [1]Lit *your completion* [a]2 Cor 12:10; 13:4 [b]1 Cor 1:10; 2 Cor 13:11; Eph 4:12; 1 Thess 3:10
10 [a]2 Cor 2:3 [b]Titus 1:13 [c]1 Cor 5:4; 2 Cor 10:8
11 [1]Or *farewell* [2]Or *put yourselves in order* [a]1 Thess 4:1; 2 Thess 3:1 [b]1 Cor 1:10; 2 Cor 13:9; Eph 4:12; 1 Thess 3:10 [c]Rom 12:16 [d]Mark 9:50 [e]Rom 15:33; Eph 6:23
12 [a]Rom 16:16
13 [1]Or *holy ones* [a]Phil 4:22
14 [a]Rom 16:20; 2 Cor 8:9 [b]Rom 5:5; Jude 21 [c]Phil 2:1

2 Corinthians Observations Chart

Paul

His character	His afflictions	His conflict with the Corinthians

The Corinthians

Their strengths	Their weaknesses	Their problems with Paul

Paul's desire for the Corinthians	Insights on Titus

2 Corinthians at a Glance

Theme of 2 Corinthians:

Segment Divisions

		Chapter Themes
		1
		2
		3
		4
		5
		6
		7
		8
		9
		10
		11
		12
		13

Author:

Date:

Purpose:

Key Words:

comfort (comforted)

afflicted (affliction, suffer, sufferings)

sorrow(ful)

boast

confidence

commend(ing)

death

life

love

heart

joy (rejoice, rejoicing, rejoiced)

covenant (ministry of ____)

ministry

grace

Titus

weak (weakness)

mark references to the enemy (warfare, serpent Satan, as well as pronouns and synonyms)

GALATIANS

The gospel introduced the Jews to a new way of life—that of grace rather than law. The old covenant, with all of its regulations, was made obsolete by the new covenant (Hebrews 8:13). This transition was difficult for some Jewish believers to handle, and a group called the Judaizers sprang up. The Judaizers embraced Christianity but said that some of the old covenant rites, including circumcision, still must be observed.

As Paul, God's apostle to the Gentiles, traveled on his missionary journeys sharing the gospel of grace, many of these Judaizers followed him, teaching the necessity of keeping the law to one degree or another. They even went to Galatia. That is why Paul wrote what he did to the churches there.

We do not know when Galatians was written, but Galatians 2:1 indicates it was after Paul's trip to Jerusalem (Acts 15). However, the date it was written does not affect the message of this critical letter. The timeless truths in this epistle will liberate you to walk in that glorious freedom of a righteous life in the Spirit—truths you can glean through careful observation.

The more you read and observe the text of this book, the more you will understand Paul's words: "It is no longer I who live, but Christ lives in me; and the life which I now live in the flesh I live by faith in the Son of God, who loved me and gave Himself up for me" (Galatians 2:20).

THINGS TO DO

1. Read Acts 13 and 14 and then look at the map on page 1892 to acquaint yourself with the cities in this area. Also, review the chart on page 1893 showing the sequence of events in Paul's life after his conversion.

2. Read through Galatians and color every reference to the author in one color and every reference to the recipients in another. Then make a list of all you learn about each that answers any of the "5 W's and an H."

3. As you read, mark in the text the key words (and their synonyms and pronouns) that are listed on the GALATIANS AT A GLANCE chart on page 1902. Mark any other key words you see as you read.

   a. After you mark the key words, it's profitable to list everything you learn from the text about the key words. This will give you additional insights into Paul's message.

   b. Mark references to time with a green clock 🕒 so that they stand out distinctively. Double-underline in green all the geographical references.

   c. Jesus Christ is mentioned 38 times in Galatians. List everything you learn about Him from this book.

4. As you read through the book, note Paul's emphasis in the first two chapters and then how the focus changes in chapter 3. In chapter 3, mark *promise* and note what it is.

5. Look for the questions Paul asks the recipients of this letter. Watch for words such as *brethren, you,* and *foolish Galatians*. List them on the chart on page 1901.

   a. Think about why Paul said all he did about himself in those first two chapters. What does this have to do with what follows in the rest of his epistle?

b. Notice the progression of events in Paul's life in these chapters, cross-referencing the chart on page 1893. Trace Paul's travels on the map on page 1892.

6. Record the chapter themes on GALATIANS AT A GLANCE and in your Bible. Record the theme of the book and complete the chart, filling in the segment divisions.

THINGS TO THINK ABOUT

1. Are you living under grace or under law? Have you accepted the grace of God for your salvation but still put yourself under the law for daily living?

2. According to Galatians 5:16-21, if you live under grace, under the control of the Spirit of God, you will not be able to live a life habitually controlled by the flesh, producing the works of the flesh. Evaluate your walk according to these verses.

3. What do you boast in?

4. As you look at Paul's life, what do you learn for your own life?

Chapter 1 Theme ______________________

1 Paul, [a]an apostle ([b]not *sent* from men nor through the
agency of man, but [c]through Jesus Christ and God the
Father, who [d]raised Him from the dead),
2 and all [a]the brethren who are with me,
To [b]the churches of Galatia:
3 [a]Grace to you and peace from [1]God our Father and the
Lord Jesus Christ,
4 who [a]gave Himself for
our sins so that He might
rescue us from [b]this present
evil [1]age, according to the
will of [c]our God and Father,
5 [a]to whom *be* the glory
forevermore. Amen.
6 I am amazed that you
are so quickly deserting
[a]Him who called you [1]by
the grace of Christ, for a
[b]different gospel;
7 which is *really* not another; only there are some who are
[a]disturbing you and want to distort the gospel of Christ.
8 But even if we, or [a]an angel from heaven, should preach to
you a gospel [1]contrary to what we have preached to you, he is
to be [2b]accursed!
9 As we [a]have said before, so I say again now, [b]if any man is
preaching to you a gospel [1]contrary to what you received, he is
to be [2c]accursed!

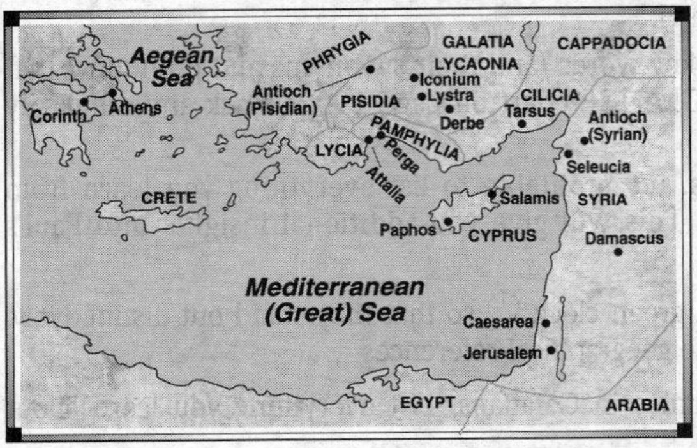

Paul's Travels as a New Believer

1:1 [a]2 Cor 1:1 [b]Gal 1:11f [c]Acts 9:15; Gal 1:15f [d]Acts 2:24

2 [a]Phil 4:21 [b]Acts 16:6; 1 Cor 16:1

3 [1]Two early mss read *God the Father, and our Lord Jesus Christ* [a]Rom 1:7

4 [1]Or *world* [a]Gal 2:20 [b]Matt 13:22; Rom 12:2; 2 Cor 4:4 [c]Phil 4:20

5 [a]Rom 11:36

6 [1]Lit *in* [a]Rom 8:28; Gal 1:15; 5:8 [b]2 Cor 11:4; Gal 1:7, 11; 2:2, 7; 5:14; 1 Tim 1:3

7 [a]Acts 15:24; Gal 5:10

8 [1]Or *other than, more than* [2]Gr *anathema* [a]2 Cor 11:14 [b]Rom 9:3

9 [1]Or *other than, more than* [2]Gr *anathema* [a]Acts 18:23 [b]Rom 16:17 [c]Rom 9:3

Sequence of Events in Paul's Life After His Conversion*

**There are differing opinions on these dates. For continuity's sake this chart will be the basis for dates pertaining to Paul's life.*

Scripture	Year A.D.	Event
Acts 9:1-25	33–34	Conversion, time in Damascus
	35–47	Some silent years, except we know that Paul:
Gal. 1:17		1. Spent time in Arabia and Damascus ⎤ *3 years*
Acts 9:26; Gal. 1:18		2. Made first visit to Jerusalem ⎦
Acts 9:30–11:26; Gal. 1:21	*14 years, Gal. 2:1*	3. Went to Tarsus, Syria-Cilicia area
Acts 11:26		4. Was with Barnabas in Antioch
Acts 11:27-30		5. With Barnabas took relief to brethren in Judea, and Paul's second visit to Jerusalem
Acts 12:23	44	Herod Agrippa I dies
Acts 12:25–13:3		6. Returned to Antioch; was sent out with Barnabas by church at Antioch
Acts 15:1-35; Gal. 2:1	47–48	**First missionary journey:** *Galatians written(?)*
		Proconsul Sergius Paulus on Paphos
Acts 15:36–18:22	49	Apostolic Council at Jerusalem—Paul visits Jerusalem *(Galatians written?)*
Acts 15:36–18:22	49–51	**Second missionary journey:** *1 and 2 Thessalonians written*—1½ years in Corinth, Acts 18:11
	51–52	Gallio known to be proconsul in Corinth
Acts 18:23–21:17	52–56	**Third missionary journey:** *1 and 2 Corinthians and Romans written*—1 Corinthians from Ephesus, 2 Corinthians from Macedonia, Romans from Corinth
Acts 21:18-23		
Acts 24–26	56	Paul goes to Jerusalem and is arrested; held in Caesarea
	57–59	Appearance before Felix and Drusilla; before Festus—appeals to Caesar; before Agrippa
Acts 27–28:15	59–60	Went from Caesarea to Rome
Acts 28:16-31	60–62	First Roman imprisonment; *Ephesians, Philemon, Colossians, and Philippians written—2 years in prision*
	62	Paul's release; possible trip to Spain
	62	Paul in Macedonia: *1 Timothy written*
	62	Paul goes to Crete
	63–64	*Titus written*
	64	Paul taken to Rome and imprisoned: *2 Timothy written*
		Paul is absent from the body and present with the Lord *(Others put Paul's conversion about A.D. 35, his death at A.D. 68.)*

10 For am I now [a]seeking the favor of men, or of God? Or am I
striving to please men? If I were still trying to please men, I
would not be a [b]bond-servant of Christ.
11 For [a]I would have you know, brethren, that the gospel
which was preached by me is [b]not according to man.
12 For [a]I neither received it from man, nor was I taught it, but
I received it through a [b]revelation of Jesus Christ.
13 For you have heard of [a]my former manner of life in Judaism,
how I [b]used to persecute [c]the church of God beyond measure
and [d]tried to destroy it;
14 and I [a]was advancing in Judaism beyond many of my
contemporaries among my [1]countrymen, being more extremely
zealous for my [b]ancestral traditions.
15 But when God, who had set me apart *even* from my
mother's womb and [a]called me through His grace, was pleased
16 to reveal His Son in me so that I might [a]preach Him among
the Gentiles, [b]I did not immediately consult with [1c]flesh and
blood,
17 [a]nor did I go up to Jerusalem to those who were apostles
before me; but I went away to Arabia, and returned once more
to [b]Damascus.
18 Then [a]three years later I went up [b]to Jerusalem to [1]become
acquainted with [c]Cephas, and stayed with him fifteen days.
19 But I did not see any other of the apostles except [1a]James,
the Lord's brother.
20 (Now in what I am writing to you, [1]I assure you [a]before God
that I am not lying.)

10 [a]1 Cor 10:33; 1 Thess 2:4 [b]Rom 1:1; Phil 1:1
11 [a]Rom 2:16; 1 Cor 15:1 [b]1 Cor 3:4; 9:8
12 [a]1 Cor 11:23; Gal 1:1 [b]1 Cor 2:10; 2 Cor 12:1; Gal 1:16; 2:2
13 [a]Acts 26:4f [b]Acts 8:3; 22:4, 5 [c]1 Cor 10:32 [d]Acts 9:21
14 [1]Lit *race* [a]Acts 22:3 [b]Jer 9:14; Matt 15:2; Mark 7:3; Col 2:8
15 [a]Is 49:1, 5; Jer 1:5; Acts 9:15; Rom 1:1; Gal 1:6
16 [1]I.e. human beings [a]Acts 9:15; Gal 2:9 [b]Acts 9:20 [c]Matt 16:17
17 [a]Acts 9:19-22 [b]Acts 9:2
18 [1]Or *visit Cephas* [a]Acts 9:22f [b]Acts 9:26 [c]John 1:42; Gal 2:9, 11, 14
19 [1]Or *Jacob* [a]Matt 12:46; Acts 12:17
20 [1]Lit *behold before God* [a]Rom 9:1; 2 Cor 1:23; 11:31

21 Then [a]I went into the regions of [b]Syria and [c]Cilicia.
22 I was *still* unknown by [1]sight to [a]the churches of Judea
which were [b]in Christ;
23 but only, they kept hearing, "He who once persecuted us is
now preaching [a]the faith which he once [b]tried to destroy."
24 And they [a]were glorifying God [1]because of me.

Chapter 2 Theme ________________________________

2 Then after an interval of fourteen years I [a]went up again to
Jerusalem with [b]Barnabas, taking [c]Titus along also.
2 [1]It was because of a [a]revelation that I went up; and I submitted
to them the [b]gospel which I preach among the Gentiles, but *I*
did so in private to those who were of reputation, for fear that I
might be [c]running, or had run, in vain.
3 But not even [a]Titus, who was with me, though he was a
Greek, was [b]compelled to be circumcised.
4 But *it was* because of the [a]false brethren secretly brought
in, who [b]had sneaked in to spy out our [c]liberty which we have
in Christ Jesus, in order to [d]bring us into bondage.
5 But we did not yield in subjection to them for even an
hour, so that [a]the truth of the gospel would remain with you.
6 But from those who [1]were of high [a]reputation (what they
were makes no difference to me; [b]God [2]shows no partiality)—
well, those who were of reputation contributed nothing to me.
7 But on the contrary, seeing that I had been [a]entrusted with
the [b]gospel [1]to the uncircumcised, just as [c]Peter *had been* [2]to
the circumcised
8 (for He who effectually worked for Peter in *his* [a]apostleship
[1]to the circumcised effectually worked for me also to the
Gentiles),
9 and recognizing [a]the grace that had been given to me,
[1b]James and [c]Cephas and John, who were [d]reputed to be [e]pillars,
gave to me and [f]Barnabas the [g]right [2]hand of fellowship, so
that we *might* [h]*go* to the Gentiles and they to the circumcised.
10 *They* only *asked* us to remember the poor—[a]the very thing
I also was eager to do.
11 But when [a]Cephas came to [b]Antioch, I opposed him to his
face, because he [1]stood condemned.
12 For prior to the coming of certain men from [1a]James, he
used to [b]eat with the Gentiles; but when they came, he *began*
to withdraw and hold himself aloof, [c]fearing [2]the party of the
circumcision.
13 The rest of the Jews joined him in hypocrisy, with the
result that even [a]Barnabas was carried away by their hypocrisy.
14 But when I saw that they [a]were not [1]straightforward about
[b]the truth of the gospel, I said to [c]Cephas in the presence of all,
"If you, being a Jew, [d]live like the Gentiles and not like the
Jews, how *is it that* you compel the Gentiles to live like Jews?[2]

14 [1]Or *progressing toward;* lit *walking straightly* [2]Some close the direct quotation here, others extend it through v 21 [a]Heb 12:13 [b]Gal 1:6; 2:5; Col 1:5 [c]Gal 1:18; 2:7, 9, 11 [d]Acts 10:28; Gal 2:12

21 [a]Acts 9:30 [b]Acts 15:23, 41 [c]Acts 6:9

22 [1]Lit *face* [a]1 Cor 7:17; 1 Thess 2:14 [b]Rom 16:7

23 [a]Acts 6:7; Gal 6:10 [b]Acts 9:21

24 [1]Lit *in me* [a]Matt 9:8

2:1 [a]Acts 15:2 [b]Acts 4:36; Gal 2:9, 13 [c]2 Cor 2:13; Gal 2:3

2 [1]Lit *according to revelation I went up* [a]Acts 15:2; Gal 1:12 [b]Gal 1:6 [c]Rom 9:16; 1 Cor 9:24ff; Gal 5:7; Phil 2:16; 2 Tim 4:7; Heb 12:1

3 [a]2 Cor 2:13; Gal 2:1 [b]Acts 16:3; 1 Cor 9:21

4 [a]Acts 15:1, 24; 2 Cor 11:13, 26; Gal 1:7 [b]2 Pet 2:1; Jude 4 [c]Gal 5:1, 13; James 1:25 [d]Rom 8:15; 2 Cor 11:20

5 [a]Gal 1:6; 2:14; Col 1:5

6 [1]Lit *seemed to be something* [2]Lit *does not receive a face* [a]2 Cor 11:5; 12:11; Gal 2:9; 6:3 [b]Acts 10:34

7 [1]Lit *of the uncircumcision* [2]Lit *of the circumcision* [a]1 Cor 9:17; 1 Thess 2:4; 1 Tim 1:11 [b]Acts 9:15; Gal 1:16 [c]Gal 1:18; 2:9, 11, 14

8 [1]Lit *of the circumcision* [a]Acts 1:25

9 [1]Or *Jacob* [2]Lit *hands* [a]Rom 12:3 [b]Acts 12:17; Gal 2:12 [c]Luke 22:8; Gal 1:18; 2:7, 11, 14 [d]2 Cor 11:5; 12:11; Gal 2:2, 6; 6:3 [e]1 Tim 3:15; Rev 3:12 [f]Acts 4:36; Gal 2:1, 13 [g]2 Kin 10:15 [h]Gal 1:16

10 [a]Acts 24:17

11 [1]Or *was to be condemned;* lit *was one who was condemned,* or, *was self-condemned* [a]Gal 1:18; 2:7, 9, 14 [b]Acts 11:19; 15:1

12 [1]Or *Jacob* [2]Or converts *from the circumcised;* lit *those from the circumcision* [a]Acts 12:17; Gal 2:9 [b]Acts 11:3 [c]Acts 11:2

13 [a]Acts 4:36; Gal 2:1, 9

15 "We *are* [a]Jews by nature and not [b]sinners from among the
Gentiles;
16 nevertheless knowing that [a]a man is not justified by the
works of [1]the Law but through faith in Christ Jesus, even we
have believed in Christ Jesus, so that we may be justified by
[b]faith in Christ and not by the works of [1]the Law; since [c]by the
works of [1]the Law no [2]flesh will be justified.
17 "But if, while seeking to be justified in Christ, we ourselves
have also been found [a]sinners, is Christ then a minister of sin?
[b]May it never be!
18 "For if I rebuild what I have *once* destroyed, I [a]prove myself
to be a transgressor.
19 "For through [1]the Law I [a]died to [1]the Law, so that I might live
to God.
20 "I have been [a]crucified with Christ; and it is no longer I
who live, but [b]Christ lives in me; and [1]the *life* which I now live
in the flesh I live by faith in [c]the Son of God, who [d]loved me
and [e]gave Himself up for me.
21 "I do not nullify the grace of God, for [a]if righteousness *comes*
through [1]the Law, then Christ died needlessly."

Chapter 3 Theme ______________________

3 [1]You foolish [a]Galatians, who has bewitched you, before
whose eyes Jesus Christ [b]was publicly portrayed *as* crucified?
2 This is the only thing I want to find out from you: did you
receive the Spirit by the works of [1]the Law, or by [2a]hearing
with faith?
3 Are you so foolish? Having begun [1]by the Spirit, are you
now [2]being perfected by the flesh?
4 Did you [1]suffer so many things in vain—[a]if indeed it was in
vain?
5 So then, does He who [a]provides you with the Spirit and
[b]works [1]miracles among you, do it by the works of [2]the Law, or
by [3c]hearing with faith?
6 [1]Even so [a]Abraham [b]BELIEVED GOD, AND IT WAS RECKONED TO
HIM AS RIGHTEOUSNESS.
7 Therefore, [1]be sure that [a]it is those who are of faith who
are [b]sons of Abraham.
8 The Scripture, foreseeing that God [1]would justify the
[2]Gentiles by faith, preached the gospel beforehand to Abraham,
saying, "[a]ALL THE NATIONS WILL BE BLESSED IN YOU."
9 So then [a]those who are of faith are blessed with [1]Abraham,
the believer.
10 For as many as are of the works of [1]the Law are under a
curse; for it is written, "[a]CURSED IS EVERYONE WHO DOES NOT ABIDE
BY ALL THINGS WRITTEN IN THE BOOK OF THE LAW, TO PERFORM THEM."
11 Now that [a]no one is justified [1]by [2]the Law before God is
evident; for, "[3b]THE RIGHTEOUS MAN SHALL LIVE BY FAITH."
12 [1]However, the Law is not [2]of faith; on the contrary, "[a]HE
WHO PRACTICES THEM SHALL LIVE [3]BY THEM."

15 [a]Phil 3:4f [b]1 Sam 15:18; Luke 24:7
16 [1]Or *law* [2]Or *mortal man* [a]Acts 13:39; Gal 3:11 [b]Rom 3:22; 9:30 [c]Ps 143:2; Rom 3:20
17 [a]Gal 2:15 [b]Luke 20:16; Gal 3:21
18 [a]Rom 3:5
19 [1]Or *law* [a]Rom 6:2; 7:4; 1 Cor 9:20
20 [1]Or *insofar as I* [a]Rom 6:6; Gal 5:24; 6:14 [b]Rom 8:10 [c]Matt 4:3 [d]Rom 8:37 [e]Gal 1:4
21 [1]Or *law* [a]Gal 3:21
3:1 [1]Lit *O* [a]Gal 1:2 [b]1 Cor 1:23; Gal 5:11
2 [1]Or *law* [2]Lit *the hearing of faith* [a]Rom 10:17
3 [1]Or *with* [2]Or *ending with*
4 [1]Or *experience* [a]1 Cor 15:2
5 [1]Or *works of power* [2]Or *law* [3]Lit *the hearing of faith* [a]2 Cor 9:10; Phil 1:19 [b]1 Cor 12:10 [c]Rom 10:17
6 [1]Lit *Just as* [a]Rom 4:3 [b]Gen 15:6
7 [1]Lit *know* [a]Rom 4:16; Gal 3:9 [b]Luke 19:9; Gal 6:16
8 [1]Lit *justifies* [2]Lit *nations* [a]Gen 12:3
9 [1]Lit *the believing Abraham* [a]Gal 3:7
10 [1]Or *law* [a]Deut 27:26
11 [1]Or *in* [2]Or *law* [3]Or *But he who is righteous by faith shall live* [a]Gal 2:16 [b]Hab 2:4; Rom 1:17; Heb 10:38
12 [1]Or *And* [2]Or *based on* [3]Or *in* [a]Lev 18:5; Rom 10:5

13 Christ [a]redeemed us from the curse of the Law, having
become a curse for us—for it is written, "[b]CURSED IS EVERYONE
WHO HANGS ON [c]A [1]TREE"—
14 in order that [a]in Christ Jesus the blessing of Abraham
might [1]come to the Gentiles, so that we [b]would receive [c]the
promise of the Spirit through faith.
15 [a]Brethren, [b]I speak [1]in terms of human relations: [c]even
though it is *only* a man's [2]covenant, yet when it has been
ratified, no one sets it aside or adds [3]conditions to it.
16 Now the promises were spoken [a]to Abraham and to his
seed. He does not say, "And to seeds," as *referring* to many, but
rather to one, "[b]And to your seed," that is, Christ.
17 What I am saying is this: the Law, which came [a]four hundred
and thirty years later, does not invalidate a covenant previously
ratified by God, so as to nullify the promise.
18 For [a]if the inheritance is [1]based on law, it is no longer
[1]based on a promise; but [b]God has granted it to Abraham by
means of a promise.
19 [a]Why the Law then? It was added [1]because of transgressions,
having been [b]ordained through angels [c]by the [2]agency of a
mediator, until [d]the seed would come to whom the promise
had been made.
20 Now [a]a mediator is not [1]for one *party only;* whereas God is
only one.
21 Is the Law then contrary to the promises of God? [a]May it
never be! For [b]if a law had been given which was able to impart
life, then righteousness [1]would indeed have been [2]based on law.
22 But the Scripture has [a]shut up [1]everyone under sin, so that
the promise by faith in Jesus Christ might be given to those
who believe.
23 But before faith came, we were kept in custody under the
law, [a]being shut up to the faith which was later to be revealed.
24 Therefore the Law has become our [a]tutor *to lead us* to
Christ, so that [b]we may be justified by faith.
25 But now that faith has come, we are no longer under a
[1a]tutor.
26 For you are all [a]sons of God through faith in [b]Christ Jesus.
27 For all of you who were [a]baptized into Christ have [b]clothed
yourselves with Christ.
28 [a]There is neither Jew nor Greek, there is neither slave nor
free man, there is [1]neither male nor female; for [b]you are all one
in [c]Christ Jesus.
29 And if [a]you [1]belong to Christ, then you are Abraham's
[2]descendants, heirs according to [b]promise.

Chapter 4 Theme ____________________

4 Now I say, as long as the heir is a [1]child, he does not differ
at all from a slave although he is [2]owner of everything,
2 but he is under guardians and [1]managers until the date set
by the father.

13 [1]Or *cross;* lit *wood* [a]Gal 4:5 [b]Deut 21:23 [c]Acts 5:30

14 [1]Or *occur* [a]Rom 4:9, 16; Gal 3:28 [b]Gal 3:2 [c]Acts 2:33; Eph 1:13

15 [1]Lit *according to man* [2]Or *will* or *testament* [3]Or *a codicil* [a]Acts 1:15; Rom 1:13; Gal 6:18 [b]Rom 3:5 [c]Heb 6:16

16 [a]Luke 1:55; Rom 4:13, 16; 9:4 [b]Acts 3:25

17 [a]Gen 15:13f; Ex 12:40; Acts 7:6

18 [1]Lit *out of, from* [a]Rom 4:14 [b]Heb 6:14

19 [1]Or *for the sake of defining* [2]Lit *hand* [a]Rom 5:20 [b]Acts 7:53 [c]Ex 20:19; Deut 5:5 [d]Gal 3:16

20 [1]Lit *of one* [a]1 Tim 2:5; Heb 8:6; 9:15; 12:24

21 [1]Or *would indeed be* [2]Lit *out of, from* [a]Luke 20:16; Gal 2:17 [b]Gal 2:21

22 [1]Lit *things* [a]Rom 11:32

23 [a]Rom 11:32

24 [a]1 Cor 4:15 [b]Gal 2:16

25 [1]Lit *child-conductor* [a]1 Cor 4:15

26 [a]Rom 8:14; Gal 4:5 [b]Rom 8:1; Gal 3:28; 4:14; 5:6, 24; Eph 1:1; Phil 1:1; Col 1:4; 1 Tim 1:12; 2 Tim 1:1; Titus 1:4

27 [a]Matt 28:19; Rom 6:3; 1 Cor 10:2 [b]Rom 13:14

28 [1]Lit *not male and female* [a]Rom 3:22; 1 Cor 12:13; Col 3:11 [b]John 17:11; Eph 2:15 [c]Rom 8:1; Gal 3:26; 4:14; 5:6, 24; Eph 1:1; Phil 1:1; Col 1:4; 1 Tim 1:12; 2 Tim 1:1; Titus 1:4

29 [1]Lit *are Christ's* [2]Lit *seed* [a]Rom 4:13; 1 Cor 3:23 [b]Rom 9:8; Gal 3:18; 4:28

4:1 [1]Or *minor* [2]Lit *lord*

2 [1]Or *stewards*

3 So also we, while we were children, were held [a]in bondage
under the [1b]elemental things of the world.
4 But when [a]the fullness of the time came, God sent forth
His Son, [b]born of a woman, born [c]under [1]the Law,
5 so that He might redeem those who were under [1]the Law,
that we might receive the adoption as [a]sons.
6 Because you are sons, [a]God has sent forth the Spirit of His
Son into our hearts, crying, "[b]Abba! Father!"
7 Therefore you are no longer a slave, but a son; and [a]if a
son, then an heir [1]through God.
8 However at that time, [a]when you did not know God, you
were [b]slaves to [c]those which by nature are no gods.
9 But now that you have come to know God, or rather to be
[a]known by God, [b]how is it that you turn back again to the weak
and worthless [1c]elemental things, to which you desire to be
enslaved all over again?
10 You [a]observe days and months and seasons and years.
11 I fear for you, that perhaps I have labored [1]over you in vain.
12 I beg of you, [a]brethren, [b]become as I *am,* for I also *have
become* as you *are.* You have done me no wrong;
13 but you know that it was because of a [1]bodily illness that I
preached the gospel to you the [2]first time;
14 and that which was a [1]trial to you in my [2]bodily condition
you did not despise or [3]loathe, but [a]you received me as an
angel of God, as [b]Christ Jesus *Himself.*
15 Where then is [1]that sense of blessing you had? For I bear
you witness that, if possible, you would have plucked out your
eyes and given them to me.
16 So have I become your enemy [a]by [1]telling you the truth?
17 They eagerly seek you, not commendably, but they wish to
shut you out so that you will seek them.
18 But it is good always to be eagerly sought in a commendable
[1]manner, and [a]not only when I am present with you.
19 [a]My children, with whom [b]I am again in labor until [c]Christ
is formed in you—
20 but I could wish to be present with you now and to change
my tone, for [a]I am perplexed about you.
21 Tell me, you who want to be under law, do you not [a]listen
to the law?
22 For it is written that Abraham had two sons, [a]one by the
bondwoman and [b]one by the free woman.
23 But [a]the son by the bondwoman [1]was born according to the
flesh, and [b]the son by the free woman through the promise.
24 [1a]This is allegorically speaking, for these *women* are two
covenants: one *proceeding* from [b]Mount Sinai bearing children
[2]who are to be [c]slaves; [3]she is Hagar.
25 Now this Hagar is Mount Sinai in Arabia and corresponds
to the present Jerusalem, for she is in slavery with her
children.
26 But [a]the Jerusalem above is free; [1]she is our mother.
27 For it is written,

3 [1]Or *rudimentary teachings* or *principles* [a]Gal 2:4; 4:8f, 24f [b]Gal 4:9; Col 2:8, 20; Heb 5:12
4 [1]Or *law* [a]Mark 1:15 [b]John 1:14; Rom 1:3; 8:3; Phil 2:7 [c]Luke 2:21f, 27
5 [1]Or *law* [a]Rom 8:14; Gal 3:26
6 [a]Acts 16:7; Rom 5:5; 8:9, 16; 2 Cor 3:17 [b]Mark 14:36; Rom 8:15
7 [1]I.e. through the gracious act of [a]Rom 8:17
8 [a]1 Cor 1:21; Eph 2:12; 1 Thess 4:5; 2 Thess 1:8 [b]Gal 4:3 [c]2 Chr 13:9; Is 37:19; Jer 2:11; 1 Cor 8:4f; 10:20
9 [1]Or *rudimentary teachings* or *principles* [a]1 Cor 8:3 [b]Col 2:20 [c]Gal 4:3
10 [a]Rom 14:5; Col 2:16
11 [1]Or *for*
12 [a]Gal 6:18 [b]2 Cor 6:11, 13
13 [1]Lit *weakness of the flesh* [2]Or *former*
14 [1]Or *temptation* [2]Lit *flesh* [3]Lit *spit out at* [a]Matt 10:40; 1 Thess 2:13 [b]Gal 3:26
15 [1]Lit *the congratulation of yourselves*
16 [1]Or *dealing truthfully with you* [a]Amos 5:10
18 [1]Or *thing* [a]Gal 4:13f
19 [a]1 John 2:1 [b]1 Cor 4:15 [c]Eph 4:13
20 [a]2 Cor 4:8
21 [a]Luke 16:29
22 [a]Gen 16:15 [b]Gen 21:2
23 [1]Lit *has been born* [a]Rom 9:7; Gal 4:29 [b]Gen 17:16ff; 18:10ff; 21:1; Gal 4:28; Heb 11:11
24 [1]Lit *Which* [2]Lit *into slavery* [3]Lit *which* [a]1 Cor 10:11 [b]Deut 33:2 [c]Gal 4:3
26 [1]Lit *which* [a]Heb 12:22; Rev 3:12; 21:2, 10

"[a]REJOICE, BARREN WOMAN WHO DOES NOT BEAR;
BREAK FORTH AND SHOUT, YOU WHO ARE NOT IN LABOR;
FOR MORE NUMEROUS ARE THE CHILDREN OF THE DESOLATE
THAN OF THE ONE WHO HAS A HUSBAND."
28 And you brethren, [a]like Isaac, are [b]children of promise.
29 But as at that time [a]he who was born according to the flesh
[b]persecuted him *who was born* according to the Spirit, [c]so it is
now also.
30 But what does the Scripture say?
"[a]CAST OUT THE BONDWOMAN AND HER SON,
FOR [b]THE SON OF THE BONDWOMAN SHALL NOT BE AN HEIR WITH
THE SON OF THE FREE WOMAN."
31 So then, brethren, we are not children of a bondwoman,
[1]but of the free woman.

Chapter 5 Theme ______________________

5 [1a]It was for freedom that Christ set us free; therefore [b]keep
standing firm and do not be subject again to a [c]yoke of
slavery.
2 Behold I, [a]Paul, say to you that if you receive [b]circumcision,
Christ will be of no benefit to you.
3 And I [a]testify again to every man who receives [b]circumcision,
that he is under obligation to [c]keep the whole Law.
4 You have been severed from Christ, you who [1]are seeking
to be justified by law; you have [a]fallen from grace.
5 For we [1]through the Spirit, [2]by faith, are [a]waiting for the
hope of righteousness.
6 For in [a]Christ Jesus [b]neither circumcision nor uncircumcision
means anything, but [c]faith working through love.
7 You were [a]running well; who hindered you from obeying
the truth?
8 This persuasion *did* not *come* from [a]Him who calls you.
9 [a]A little leaven leavens the whole lump *of dough.*
10 [a]I have confidence [1]in you in the Lord that you [b]will adopt
no other view; but the one who is [c]disturbing you will bear his
judgment, whoever he is.
11 But I, brethren, if I still preach circumcision, why am I still
[a]persecuted? Then [b]the stumbling block of the cross has been
abolished.
12 I wish that [a]those who are troubling you would even
[1b]mutilate themselves.
13 For you were called to [a]freedom, brethren; [b]only *do* not *turn*
your freedom into an opportunity for the flesh, but through
love [c]serve one another.
14 For [a]the whole Law is fulfilled in one word, in the
statement, "[b]YOU SHALL LOVE YOUR NEIGHBOR AS YOURSELF."
15 But if you [a]bite and devour one another, take care that you
are not consumed by one another.
16 But I say, [a]walk by the Spirit, and you will not carry out
[b]the desire of the flesh.

27 [a]Is 54:1
28 [a]Gal 4:23 [b]Rom 9:7ff; Gal 3:29
29 [a]Gal 4:23 [b]Gen 21:9 [c]Gal 5:11
30 [a]Gen 21:10, 12 [b]John 8:35
31 [1]V 5:1, note 1
5:1 [1]Some authorities prefer to join with 4:31 and render *but with the freedom of the free woman Christ set us free* [a]John 8:32, 36; Rom 8:15; 2 Cor 3:17; Gal 2:4; 5:13 [b]1 Cor 16:13 [c]Acts 15:10; Gal 2:4
2 [a]2 Cor 10:1 [b]Acts 15:1; Gal 5:3, 6, 11
3 [a]Luke 16:28 [b]Acts 15:1; Gal 5:2, 6, 11 [c]Rom 2:25
4 [1]Or *would be* [a]Heb 12:15; 2 Pet 3:17
5 [1]Lit *by* [2]Lit *out of* [a]Rom 8:23; 1 Cor 1:7
6 [a]Gal 3:26 [b]1 Cor 7:19; Gal 6:15 [c]Col 1:4f; 1 Thess 1:3; James 2:18, 20, 22
7 [a]Gal 2:2
8 [a]Rom 8:28; Gal 1:6
9 [a]1 Cor 5:6
10 [1]Lit *toward* [a]2 Cor 2:3 [b]Gal 5:7; Phil 3:15 [c]Gal 1:7; 5:12
11 [a]Gal 4:29; 6:12 [b]Rom 9:33; 1 Cor 1:23
12 [1]Or *cut themselves off* [a]Gal 2:4; 5:10 [b]Deut 23:1
13 [a]Gal 5:1 [b]1 Cor 8:9; 1 Pet 2:16 [c]1 Cor 9:19; Eph 5:21
14 [a]Matt 7:12; 22:40; Rom 13:8, 10; Gal 6:2 [b]Lev 19:18; Matt 19:19; John 13:34
15 [a]Gal 5:20; Phil 3:2
16 [a]Rom 8:4; 13:14; Gal 5:24f [b]Rom 13:14; Eph 2:3

17 For [a]the flesh [1]sets its desire against the Spirit, and the Spirit
against the flesh; for these are in opposition to one another, [b]so
that you may not do the things that you [2]please.
18 But if you are [a]led by the Spirit, [b]you are not under the Law.
19 Now the deeds of the flesh are evident, which are:
[1a]immorality, impurity, sensuality,
20 idolatry, [a]sorcery, enmities, [b]strife, jealousy, outbursts of anger,
[c]disputes, dissensions, [1d]factions,
21 envying, [a]drunkenness, carousing, and things like these, of
which I forewarn you, just as I have forewarned you, that those
who practice such things will not [b]inherit the kingdom of God.
22 But [a]the fruit of the Spirit is [b]love, joy, peace, patience,
kindness, goodness, faithfulness,
23 gentleness, [a]self-control; against such things [b]there is no law.
24 Now those who [1]belong to [a]Christ Jesus have [b]crucified the
flesh with its passions and [c]desires.
25 If we live by the Spirit, let us also [1]walk [a]by the Spirit.
26 Let us not become [a]boastful, challenging one another, envying
one another.

Chapter 6 Theme ____________________________

6 [a]Brethren, even if [1]anyone is caught in any trespass, you
who are [b]spiritual, [c]restore such a one [d]in a spirit of gentleness; *each one* looking to yourself, so that you too will not be
tempted.
2 [a]Bear one another's burdens, and thereby fulfill [b]the law of
Christ.
3 For [a]if anyone thinks he is something when he is nothing,
he deceives himself.
4 But each one must [a]examine his own work, and then he
will have *reason for* [b]boasting in regard to himself alone, and
not in regard to another.
5 For [a]each one will bear his own load.
6 [a]The one who is taught [b]the word is to share all good things
with the one who teaches *him.*
7 [a]Do not be deceived, [b]God is not mocked; for [c]whatever a
man sows, this he will also reap.
8 [a]For the one who sows to his own flesh will from the flesh
reap [b]corruption, but [c]the one who sows to the Spirit will from
the Spirit reap eternal life.
9 [a]Let us not lose heart in doing good, for in due time we
will reap if we [b]do not grow weary.
10 So then, [1a]while we have opportunity, let us do good to all
people, and especially to those who are of the [b]household of
[c]the faith.
11 See with what large letters I [1]am writing to you [a]with my
own hand.
12 Those who desire [a]to make a good showing in the flesh try
to [b]compel you to be circumcised, simply so that they [c]will not
be persecuted [1]for the cross of Christ.

17 [1]Lit *lusts against* [2]Lit *wish* [a]Rom 7:18, 23; 8:5ff [b]Rom 7:15ff
18 [a]Rom 8:14 [b]Rom 6:14; 7:4; 1 Tim 1:9
19 [1]I.e. sexual immorality [a]1 Cor 6:9, 18; 2 Cor 12:21
20 [1]Or *heresies* [a]Rev 21:8 [b]2 Cor 12:20 [c]Rom 2:8; James 3:14ff [d]1 Cor 11:19
21 [a]Rom 13:13 [b]1 Cor 6:9
22 [a]Matt 7:16ff; Eph 5:9 [b]Rom 5:1-5; 1 Cor 13:4; Col 3:12-15
23 [a]Acts 24:25 [b]Gal 5:18
24 [1]Lit *are of Christ Jesus* [a]Gal 3:26 [b]Rom 6:6; Gal 2:20; 6:14 [c]Gal 5:16f
25 [1]Or *follow the Spirit* [a]Gal 5:16
26 [a]Phil 2:3
6:1 [1]Gr *anthropos* [a]Gal 6:18; 1 Thess 4:1 [b]1 Cor 2:15 [c]2 Cor 2:7; 2 Thess 3:15; Heb 12:13; James 5:19f [d]1 Cor 4:21
2 [a]Rom 15:1 [b]Rom 8:2; 1 Cor 9:21; James 1:25; 2:12; 2 Pet 3:2
3 [a]Acts 5:36; 1 Cor 3:18; 2 Cor 12:11
4 [a]1 Cor 11:28 [b]Phil 1:26
5 [a]Prov 9:12; Rom 14:12; 1 Cor 3:8
6 [a]1 Cor 9:11, 14 [b]2 Tim 4:2
7 [a]1 Cor 6:9 [b]Job 13:9 [c]2 Cor 9:6
8 [a]Job 4:8; Hos 8:7; Rom 6:21 [b]1 Cor 15:42 [c]Rom 8:11; James 3:18
9 [a]1 Cor 15:58; 2 Cor 4:1 [b]Matt 10:22; Heb 12:3, 5; James 5:7f
10 [1]Or *as* [a]Prov 3:27; John 12:35 [b]Eph 2:19; Heb 3:6; 1 Pet 2:5; 4:17 [c]Acts 6:7; Gal 1:23
11 [1]Or *have written* [a]1 Cor 16:21
12 [1]Or *because of* [a]Matt 23:27f [b]Acts 15:1 [c]Gal 5:11

13 For those who [1]are circumcised do not even [a]keep [2]the
Law themselves, but they desire to have you circumcised so
that they may [b]boast in your flesh.
14 But [a]may it never be that I would boast, [b]except in the
cross of our Lord Jesus Christ, [c]through [1]which the world has
been crucified to me, and [d]I to the world.
15 For [a]neither is circumcision anything, nor uncircumcision,
but a [b]new [1]creation.
16 And those who will [1]walk by this rule, peace and mercy *be*
upon them, and upon the [a]Israel of God.
17 From now on let no one cause trouble for me, for I bear on
my body the [a]brand-marks of Jesus.
18 [a]The grace of our Lord Jesus Christ be [b]with your spirit,
[c]brethren. Amen.

13 [1]Two early mss read *have been* [2]Or *law* [a]Rom 2:25 [b]Phil 3:3

14 [1]Or *whom* [a]Luke 20:16; Gal 2:17; 3:21 [b]1 Cor 2:2 [c]Gal 2:20; Col 2:20 [d]Rom 6:2, 6; Gal 2:19f; 5:24

15 [1]Or *creature* [a]Rom 2:26, 28; 1 Cor 7:19; Gal 5:6 [b]2 Cor 5:17; Eph 2:10, 15; 4:24; Col 3:10

16 [1]Or *follow this rule* [a]Rom 9:6; Gal 3:7, 29; Phil 3:3

17 [a]Is 44:5; Ezek 9:4; 2 Cor 4:10; 11:23; Rev 13:16

18 [a]Rom 16:20 [b]2 Tim 4:22 [c]Acts 1:15; Rom 1:13; Gal 3:15; 4:12, 28, 31

GALATIANS AT A GLANCE

Theme of Galatians:

SEGMENT DIVISIONS

		CHAPTER THEMES
		1
		2
		3
		4
		5
		6

Author:

Date:

Purpose:

Key Words:

gospel

grace

law

Spirit

faith

promise

covenant

Christ (Jesus)

free (freedom)

circumcision

ƐPHESIANS

Ephesus, the fourth-largest city in the Roman Empire, was the home of the temple of the goddess called Artemis by the Greeks and Diana by the Romans. Of all the deities in Asia, none was more sought after than Artemis.

But by the time of Paul, Ephesus's position as a center of trade was lost because the harbor became unnavigable. From that point on, the worship of Artemis became the city's means of economic survival. The tourist and pilgrim trade associated with Artemis made many people in Ephesus wealthy. Silversmiths made their living selling images of this goddess and her temple. Innkeepers and restaurant owners grew rich from the large influx of worshipers who traveled great distances to see the temple of Artemis, one of the seven wonders of the world. The temple treasury even served as a bank, lending large sums of money to many, including kings. And since Artemis was the patroness of sex, prostitutes sold their bodies without condemnation in the two-story brothel on Marble Road. Although Artemis was the main attraction, all sorts of magic and sorcery were conjured up in Ephesus.

Then God sent Paul to live in Ephesus and called out for Himself a church, a light to illumine the occultic darkness of this city.

This brief glimpse into the historical and cultural setting of Ephesians should help you understand why Paul wrote what he did to the church in Ephesus. The message of this epistle is needed as much today as it was in A.D. 60 to 62, when Paul wrote it as a prisoner in Rome.

THINGS TO DO

General Instructions

1. Read Ephesians and color every reference to the author in one color, every reference to the recipients in another.

2. When you finish, read Acts 18:18-21 (Paul's first visit to Ephesus was on his second missionary journey). Then read Acts 19 for an account of Paul's second visit on his third missionary journey. This passage will help you understand why the letter to the Ephesians deals with warfare and our position in Christ more extensively than any other epistle.

Chapters 1–3

Read Ephesians 1 through 3 one chapter at a time, doing the following:

1. Mark or note each reference to God. Then make a list of everything God does.

2. Mark distinctively each reference to being *in Christ* and *in Him*. Then on the OBSERVATIONS CHART on page 1912, under the heading "Our Wealth and Position in Christ," list what believers have *in Christ.* Also, pay particular attention to the phrase *in the heavenly places,* which is key to warfare. Note the chapter and verse from which the information comes when you make your list (e.g., 1:13).

3. Mark each reference to the Holy Spirit. On the OBSERVATIONS CHART, under the heading "Our Relationship with the Holy Spirit," list what is taught about the person and work of the Holy Spirit.

4. Mark the other key words (with their synonyms and pronouns) listed on the EPHESIANS AT A GLANCE chart on page 1913. Put these on an index card and use it as a bookmark.

5. Mark distinctively each occurrence of *riches (rich)*. Then list what you learn about these riches. Remember to ask the "5 W's and an H": Who is rich and in what? How are these riches described? What is done with the riches? And so on.

6. Mark each use of *formerly*. Then on the OBSERVATIONS CHART under the heading "Our Former Lifestyle and Walk," list what Ephesians says about how believers lived before salvation.

Chapters 4–6

1. Read Ephesians 4 through 6 chapter by chapter, doing the following:
   a. Mark each occurrence of *walk*. Then on the OBSERVATIONS CHART, under the heading "Our Walk in Christ," list what is taught about the lifestyle of a believer. Also go back to 2:2,10 and mark and list what these verses teach about the believer's lifestyle. Then ask yourself: How am I to live? Why am I able to live this way?
   b. Mark the key words listed on your bookmark. Also, mark *stand firm* in chapter 6. Observe what you learn from the uses of *former(ly)* in this section of Ephesians. Note the contrast between our former lifestyle and our walk in Christ and record any new insights on page 1913.
   c. As you mark *Holy Spirit* and *in the Lord,* think about what you learn and how you are to walk in Him. Record your insights on pages 1912, 1913.

2. After you observe Ephesians 6:10-20, compare this with Ephesians 1:18-23. Note the references to *powers* and *rulers* (and their synonyms). Note what this tells you about the importance of spiritual warfare in this epistle and how believers can stand firm against the schemes of the devil.

3. On EPHESIANS AT A GLANCE:
   a. Record the theme of the book and of each chapter in the appropriate spaces. (Remember to go back and record each chapter's theme in your Bible.)
   b. As you have seen, there is a change of emphasis between chapters 3 and 4. Under "Segment Divisions" write what best summarizes the content of chapters 1–3 and then chapters 4–6.

Things to Think About

1. Stop and review all you observed and recorded about your position as a child of God. Go through chapter 1 again and note everything God has done for you. Watch for the personal pronoun *He.* Also note the phrase *according to* and the word *will*. Think about what God has done for you and why. Then thank Him and tell Him you want to live accordingly.

2. Ephesians 2:8-10 are extremely important verses. Think about what God is saying to you and ask God to show you whether you are trusting in His grace or in your works to get you to heaven. But don't stop there. Think about the relationship of good works to the life of a believer. How are you walking? Memorize these verses.

3. In your home do you live according to Ephesians 5:18–6:4?

4. Are you able to stand firm, or are you defeated by the devil's schemes? Don't forget where you are seated. Think about God's power, His strength, His armor. Do you have it on, and are you standing firm in truth, righteousness, peace, salvation, and faith? Are you able to use the Word of God as your offensive weapon?

Chapter 1 Theme ______________________________

1 Paul, [a]an apostle of [b]Christ Jesus [1c]by the will of God,
To the [2d]saints who are [3]at [e]Ephesus and [f]*who are* faithful in
[b]Christ Jesus:
2 [a]Grace to you and peace from God our Father and the Lord
Jesus Christ.
3 [a]Blessed *be* the God and Father of our Lord Jesus Christ,
who has blessed us with every spiritual blessing in [b]the heavenly
places in Christ,
4 just as [a]He chose us in Him before [b]the foundation of the
world, that we would be [c]holy and blameless before [1]Him. [d]In
love
5 [1]He [a]predestined us to [b]adoption as sons through Jesus
Christ to Himself, [c]according to the [2]kind intention of His will,
6 [a]to the praise of the glory of His grace, which He freely
bestowed on us in [b]the Beloved.
7 [a]In [1]Him we have [b]redemption [c]through His blood, the
[d]forgiveness of our trespasses, according to [e]the riches of His
grace
8 which He [1]lavished on [2]us. In all wisdom and insight
9 He [1a]made known to us the mystery of His will, [b]according
to His [2]kind intention which He [c]purposed in Him
10 with a view to an administration [1]suitable to [a]the fullness
of the times, *that is,* [b]the summing up of all things in Christ,
things [2]in the heavens and things on the earth. In Him
11 [1]also we [2a]have obtained an inheritance, having been
[b]predestined [c]according to His purpose who works all things
[d]after the counsel of His will,
12 to the end that we who were the first to hope in [1]Christ
would be [a]to the praise of His glory.
13 In [1]Him, you also, after listening to [a]the message of truth,
the gospel of your salvation—having also [2]believed, you were
[b]sealed in [1]Him with [c]the Holy Spirit of promise,
14 who is [1a]given as a pledge of [b]our inheritance, with a view to
the [c]redemption of [d]*God's own* possession, [e]to the praise of His
glory.
15 For this reason I too, [a]having heard of the faith in the Lord
Jesus which *exists* among you and [1]your love for [b]all the [2]saints,
16 [a]do not cease giving thanks for you, [b]while making mention
of you in my prayers;
17 that the [a]God of our Lord Jesus Christ, [b]the Father of glory,
may give to you a spirit of [c]wisdom and of [d]revelation in the
[1]knowledge of Him.
18 *I pray that* [a]the eyes of your heart [1]may be enlightened, so
that you will know what is the [b]hope of His [c]calling, what are
[d]the riches of the glory of [e]His inheritance in [f]the [2]saints,

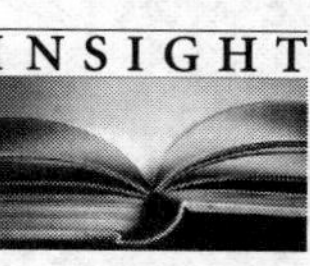

See the map on page 1800.

1:1 [1]Lit *through* [2]Or *holy ones* [3]Three early mss do not contain *at Ephesus* [a]2 Cor 1:1 [b]Rom 8:1 [c]1 Cor 1:1 [d]Acts 9:13 [e]Acts 18:19 [f]Col 1:2
2 [a]Rom 1:7
3 [a]2 Cor 1:3 [b]Eph 1:20; 2:6; 3:10; 6:12
4 [1]Or *Him, in love* [a]Eph 2:10; 2 Thess 2:13f [b]Matt 25:34 [c]Eph 5:27; Col 1:22 [d]Eph 4:2, 15, 16; 5:2
5 [1]Lit *having predestined* [2]Lit *good pleasure* [a]Acts 13:48; Rom 8:29f [b]Rom 8:14ff [c]Phil 2:13; Col 1:19
6 [a]Eph 1:12, 14 [b]Matt 3:17
7 [1]Lit *whom* [a]Col 1:14 [b]Rom 3:24; 1 Cor 1:30; Eph 1:14 [c]Acts 20:28; Rom 3:25 [d]Acts 2:38 [e]Rom 2:4; Eph 1:18; 2:7; 3:8, 16
8 [1]Lit *made abundant toward* [2]Or *us, in all wisdom and insight*
9 [1]Lit *making known* [2]Lit *good pleasure* [a]Rom 11:25; Eph 3:3 [b]1 Cor 1:21; Gal 1:15 [c]Rom 8:28; Eph 1:11
10 [1]Lit *of* [2]Lit *upon* [a]Mark 1:15 [b]Eph 3:15; Phil 2:9f; Col 1:16, 20
11 [1]Lit *in whom also* [2]Or *were made a heritage* [a]Deut 4:20; Eph 1:14; Titus 2:14 [b]Eph 1:5 [c]Rom 8:28f; Eph 3:11 [d]Rom 9:11; Heb 6:17
12 [1]I.e. the Messiah [a]Eph 1:6, 14
13 [1]Lit *whom* [2]Or *believed in Him, you were sealed* [a]Eph 4:21; Col 1:5 [b]Eph 4:30 [c]Acts 2:33
14 [1]Or *a down payment* [a]2 Cor 1:22 [b]Acts 20:32 [c]Eph 1:7 [d]Eph 1:11 [e]Eph 1:6, 12

15 [1]Three early mss do not contain *your love* [2]V 1, note 2 [a]Col 1:4; Philem 5 [b]Eph 1:1; 3:18
16 [a]Rom 1:8f; Col 1:9 [b]Rom 1:9
17 [1]Or *true knowledge* [a]John 20:17; Rom 15:6 [b]Acts 7:2; 1 Cor 2:8 [c]Col 1:9 [d]1 Cor 14:6
18 [1]Lit *being* [2]Or *holy ones* [a]Acts 26:18; 2 Cor 4:6; Heb 6:4 [b]Eph 4:4 [c]Rom 11:29 [d]Eph 1:7 [e]Eph 1:11 [f]Col 1:12

19 and what is the surpassing greatness of His power toward
us who believe. [a]*These are* in accordance with the working of
the [b]strength of His might
20 which He brought about in Christ, when He [a]raised Him
from the dead and [b]seated Him at His right hand in [c]the
heavenly *places,*
21 far above [a]all rule and authority and power and dominion,
and every [b]name that is named, not only in [c]this age but also in
the one to come.
22 And He [a]put all things in subjection under His feet, and
gave Him as [b]head over all things to the church,
23 which is His [a]body, the [b]fullness of Him who [c]fills [d]all in all.

Chapter 2 Theme ______________________

2 And you [1]were [a]dead [2]in your trespasses and sins,
2 in which you [a]formerly walked according to the [1]course
of [b]this world, according to [c]the prince of the power of the air,
of the spirit that is now working in [d]the sons of disobedience.
3 Among them we too all [a]formerly lived in [b]the lusts of our
flesh, [1]indulging the desires of the flesh and of the [2]mind, and
were [c]by nature [d]children of wrath, [e]even as the rest.
4 But God, being [a]rich in mercy, because of [b]His great love
with which He loved us,
5 even when we were [a]dead [1]in our transgressions, made us
alive together [2]with Christ ([b]by grace you have been saved),
6 and [a]raised us up with Him, and [b]seated us with Him in
[c]the heavenly *places* in [d]Christ Jesus,
7 so that in the ages to come He might show the surpassing
[a]riches of His grace in [b]kindness toward us in Christ Jesus.
8 For [a]by grace you have been saved [b]through faith; and [1]that
not of yourselves, *it is* [c]the gift of God;
9 [a]not as a result of works, so that [b]no one may boast.
10 For we are His workmanship, [a]created in [b]Christ Jesus for
[c]good works, which God [d]prepared beforehand so that we
would [e]walk in them.
11 Therefore remember that [a]formerly [b]you, the Gentiles in the
flesh, who are called "[c]Uncircumcision" by the so-called
"[c]Circumcision," *which is* performed in the flesh by human
hands—
12 *remember* that you were at that time separate from Christ,
[1a]excluded from the commonwealth of Israel, and strangers to
[b]the covenants of promise, having [c]no hope and [d]without God
in the world.
13 But now in [a]Christ Jesus you who [b]formerly were [c]far off
[1]have [c]been brought near [2d]by the blood of Christ.
14 For He Himself is [a]our peace, [b]who made both *groups into*
one and broke down the [1]barrier of the dividing wall,
15 [1]by [a]abolishing in His flesh the enmity, *which is* [b]the Law
of commandments *contained* in ordinances, so that in Himself
He might [2c]make the two into [d]one new man, *thus* establishing
[e]peace,

19 [a]Eph 3:7; Col 1:29 [b]Eph 6:10
20 [a]Acts 2:24 [b]Mark 16:19 [c]Eph 1:3
21 [a]Matt 28:18; Col 1:16 [b]Phil 2:9; Rev 19:12 [c]Matt 12:32
22 [a]Ps 8:6; 1 Cor 15:27 [b]1 Cor 11:3; Eph 4:15; Col 1:18
23 [a]1 Cor 12:27; Eph 4:12; Col 1:18, 24 [b]John 1:16; Eph 3:19 [c]Eph 4:10 [d]Col 3:11
2:1 [1]Lit *being* [2]Or *by reason of* [a]Eph 2:5; Col 2:13
2 [1]Lit *age* [a]1 Cor 6:11; Eph 2:3 [b]Eph 1:21 [c]John 12:31; Eph 6:12 [d]Eph 5:6
3 [1]Lit *doing* [2]Lit *thoughts* [a]Eph 2:2 [b]Gal 5:16f [c]Rom 2:14; Gal 2:15 [d]Rom 5:9; Col 1:21; 2 Pet 2:14 [e]Rom 5:12
4 [a]Eph 1:7 [b]John 3:16
5 [1]Or *by reason of* [2]Two early mss read *in Christ* [a]Eph 2:1 [b]Acts 15:11
6 [a]Col 2:12 [b]Eph 1:20 [c]Eph 1:3 [d]Eph 1:1; 2:10, 13
7 [a]Rom 2:4; Eph 1:7 [b]Titus 3:4
8 [1]I.e. that salvation [a]Acts 15:11; Eph 2:5 [b]1 Pet 1:5 [c]John 4:10
9 [a]Rom 3:28; 2 Tim 1:9 [b]1 Cor 1:29
10 [a]Eph 2:15; 4:24; Col 3:10 [b]Eph 1:1; 2:6, 13 [c]Titus 2:14 [d]Eph 1:4 [e]Eph 4:1
11 [a]Eph 2:2 [b]1 Cor 12:2; Eph 5:8 [c]Rom 2:28f; Col 2:11
12 [1]Or *alienated* [a]Rom 9:4; Col 1:21 [b]Gal 3:17; Heb 8:6 [c]1 Thess 4:13 [d]Gal 4:8; 1 Thess 4:5
13 [1]Lit *became;* or *were made* [2]Or *in* [a]Eph 1:1; 2:6 [b]Eph 2:2 [c]Is 57:19; Acts 2:39; Eph 2:17 [d]Rom 3:25; Col 1:20
14 [1]Lit *the dividing wall of the barrier* [a]Is 9:6; Eph 2:15; Col 3:15 [b]1 Cor 12:13; Gal 3:28; Col 3:11
15 [1]Or *the enmity, by abolishing in His flesh the Law* [2]Lit *create* [a]Eph 2:16; Col 1:21f [b]Col 2:14, 20 [c]Gal 3:28; Eph 2:10; Col 3:10, 11 [d]Gal 3:28; Col 3:10f [e]Is 9:6; Eph 2:14; Col 3:15

16 and might [a]reconcile them both in [b]one body to God
through the cross, [1]by it having [c]put to death the enmity.
17 AND [a]HE CAME AND PREACHED [b]PEACE TO YOU WHO WERE [c]FAR
AWAY, AND PEACE TO THOSE WHO WERE [c]NEAR;
18 for through Him we both have [a]our access in [b]one Spirit to
[c]the Father.
19 So then you are no longer [a]strangers and aliens, but you are
[b]fellow citizens with the [1]saints, and are of [c]God's household,
20 having been [a]built on [b]the foundation of [c]the apostles and
prophets, [d]Christ Jesus Himself being the [e]corner *stone,*
21 [a]in whom the whole building, being fitted together, is
growing into [b]a holy [1]temple in the Lord,
22 in whom you also are being [a]built together into a [b]dwelling
of God in the Spirit.

Chapter 3 Theme ________________________

3 For this reason I, Paul, [a]the prisoner of [b]Christ Jesus [c]for
the sake of you [d]Gentiles—
2 if indeed you have heard of the [a]stewardship of God's grace
which was given to me for you;
3 [a]that [b]by revelation there was [c]made known to me [d]the
mystery, [e]as I wrote before in brief.
4 [1]By referring to this, when you read you can understand
[a]my insight [2]into the [b]mystery of Christ,
5 which in other generations was not made known to the
sons of men, as it has now been revealed to His holy [a]apostles
and prophets [1]in the Spirit;
6 *to be specific,* that the Gentiles are [a]fellow heirs and [b]fellow
members of the body, and [c]fellow partakers of the promise in
[d]Christ Jesus through the gospel,
7 [a]of which I was made a [b]minister, according to the gift of
[c]God's grace which was given to me [d]according to the working
of His power.
8 To me, [a]the very least of all [1]saints, this grace was given, to
[b]preach to the Gentiles the unfathomable [c]riches of Christ,
9 and to [1]bring to light what is the administration of the [a]mystery
which for ages has been [b]hidden in God [c]who created all things;
10 so that the manifold [a]wisdom of God might now be [b]made
known through the church to the [c]rulers and the authorities in
[d]the heavenly *places.*
11 *This was* in [a]accordance with the [1]eternal purpose which
He [2]carried out in [b]Christ Jesus our Lord,
12 in whom we have boldness and [1a]confident [b]access through
faith [2]in Him.
13 Therefore I ask [1]you not [a]to lose heart at my tribulations
[b]on your behalf, [2]for they are your glory.
14 For this reason I [a]bow my knees before the Father,

16 [1]Or *in Himself* [a]2 Cor 5:18; Col 1:20, 22 [b]1 Cor 10:17; Eph 4:4 [c]Eph 2:15
17 [a]Is 57:19; Rom 10:14 [b]Acts 10:36; Eph 2:14 [c]Eph 2:13
18 [a]Rom 5:2; Eph 3:12 [b]1 Cor 12:13; Eph 4:4 [c]Col 1:12
19 [1]Or *holy ones* [a]Eph 2:12; Heb 11:13; 1 Pet 2:11 [b]Phil 3:20; Heb 12:22f [c]Gal 6:10
20 [a]1 Cor 3:9 [b]Matt 16:18; 1 Cor 3:10; Rev 21:14 [c]1 Cor 12:28; Eph 3:5 [d]1 Cor 3:11 [e]Ps 118:22; Luke 20:17
21 [1]Or *sanctuary* [a]Eph 4:15f; Col 2:19 [b]1 Cor 3:16f
22 [a]1 Cor 3:9, 16; 2 Cor 6:16 [b]Eph 3:17
3:1 [a]Acts 23:18; Eph 4:1; 2 Tim 1:8; Philem 1, 9, 23 [b]Gal 5:24 [c]2 Cor 1:6; Eph 3:13 [d]Eph 3:8
2 [a]Eph 1:10; 3:9; Col 1:25; 1 Tim 1:4
3 [a]Acts 22:17, 21; 26:16ff [b]Gal 1:12 [c]Eph 1:9; 3:4, 6, 9 [d]Rom 11:25; 16:25; Eph 3:4, 9; 6:19; Col 1:26f; 4:3 [e]Eph 1:9f; Heb 13:22; 1 Pet 5:12
4 [1]Lit *To which, when you read* [2]Lit *in* [a]2 Cor 11:6 [b]Rom 11:25; 16:25; Eph 3:3, 9; 6:19; Col 1:26f; 4:3
5 [1]Or *by* [a]1 Cor 12:28; Eph 2:20
6 [a]Gal 3:29 [b]Eph 2:16 [c]Eph 5:7 [d]Gal 5:24
7 [a]Col 1:23, 25 [b]1 Cor 3:5 [c]Acts 9:15; Rom 12:3; Eph 3:2 [d]Eph 1:19; 3:20
8 [1]Or *holy ones* [a]1 Cor 15:9 [b]Acts 9:15; Eph 3:1f [c]Rom 2:4; Eph 1:7; 3:16
9 [1]Two early mss read *make all know* [a]Rom 11:25; 16:25; Eph 3:3, 4; 6:19; Col 1:26f; 4:3 [b]Col 3:3 [c]Rev 4:11
10 [a]Rom 11:33; 1 Cor 2:7 [b]Eph 1:23; 1 Pet 1:12 [c]Eph 1:21; 6:12; Col 2:10, 15 [d]Eph 1:3

11 [1]Lit *purpose of the ages* [2]Or *formed* [a]Eph 1:11 [b]Gal 5:24; Eph 3:1
12 [1]Lit *access in confidence* [2]Lit *of Him* [a]2 Cor 3:4; Heb 4:16; 10:19, 35; 1 John 2:28; 3:21 [b]Eph 2:18
13 [1]Or *that I may not lose* [2]Lit *which are* [a]2 Cor 4:1 [b]Eph 3:1
14 [a]Phil 2:10

15 from whom [1]every family in heaven and on earth derives its
name,
16 that He would grant you, according to [a]the riches of His
glory, to be [b]strengthened with power through His Spirit in
[c]the inner man,
17 so that [a]Christ may dwell in your hearts through faith; *and*
that you, being [b]rooted and [c]grounded in love,
18 may be able to comprehend with [a]all the [1]saints what is
[b]the breadth and length and height and depth,
19 and to know [a]the love of Christ which [b]surpasses knowledge,
that you may be [c]filled up to all the [d]fullness of God.
20 [a]Now to Him who is [b]able to do far more abundantly
beyond all that we ask or think, [c]according to the power that
works within us,
21 [a]to Him *be* the glory in the church and in Christ Jesus to all
generations [1]forever and ever. Amen.

Chapter 4 Theme ______________________________

4 Therefore I, [a]the prisoner of the Lord, [b]implore you to [c]walk
in a manner worthy of the [d]calling with which you have
been [e]called,
2 with all [a]humility and gentleness, with patience, showing
tolerance for one another [b]in love,
3 being diligent to preserve the unity of the Spirit in the
[a]bond of peace.
4 *There is* [a]one body and one Spirit, just as also you were
called in one [b]hope of your calling;
5 [a]one Lord, one faith, one baptism,
6 one God and Father of all [a]who is over all and through all
and in all.
7 But [a]to each one of us [b]grace was given [c]according to the
measure of Christ's gift.
8 Therefore [1]it says,
"[a]WHEN HE ASCENDED ON HIGH,
HE [b]LED CAPTIVE A HOST OF CAPTIVES,
AND HE GAVE GIFTS TO MEN."
9 (Now this *expression,* "He [a]ascended," what [1]does it mean
except that He also [2]had descended into [b]the lower parts of the
earth?
10 He who descended is Himself also He who ascended [a]far
above all the heavens, so that He might [b]fill all things.)
11 And He [a]gave [b]some *as* apostles, and some *as* prophets,
and some *as* [c]evangelists, and some *as* pastors and [d]teachers,
12 [a]for the equipping of the [1]saints for the work of service, to
the building up of [b]the body of Christ;
13 until we all attain to [a]the unity of the faith, and of the
[1b]knowledge of the Son of God, to a [c]mature man, to the measure
of the stature [2]which belongs to the [d]fullness of Christ.
14 [1]As a result, we are [a]no longer to be children, [b]tossed here
and there by waves and carried about by every wind of doctrine,
by the trickery of men, by [c]craftiness [2]in [d]deceitful scheming;

15 [1]Or *the whole*
16 [a]Eph 1:18; 3:8 [b]1 Cor 16:13; Phil 4:13; Col 1:11 [c]Rom 7:22
17 [a]John 14:23; Rom 8:9f; 2 Cor 13:5; Eph 2:22 [b]1 Cor 3:6; Col 2:7 [c]Col 1:23
18 [1]V 8, note 1 [a]Eph 1:15 [b]Job 11:8f
19 [a]Rom 8:35, 39 [b]Phil 4:7 [c]Col 2:10 [d]Eph 1:23
20 [a]Rom 16:25 [b]2 Cor 9:8 [c]Eph 3:7
21 [1]Lit *of the age of the ages* [a]Rom 11:36
4:1 [a]Eph 3:1 [b]Rom 12:1 [c]Eph 2:10; Col 1:10; 2:6; 1 Thess 2:12 [d]Rom 11:29 [e]Rom 8:28f
2 [a]Col 3:12f [b]Eph 1:4
3 [a]Col 3:14f
4 [a]1 Cor 12:4ff; Eph 2:16, 18 [b]Eph 1:18
5 [a]1 Cor 8:6
6 [a]Rom 11:36
7 [a]1 Cor 12:7, 11 [b]Eph 3:2 [c]Rom 12:3
8 [1]Or *He* [a]Ps 68:18 [b]Col 2:15
9 [1]Lit *is it except* [2]One early ms reads *had first descended* [a]John 3:13 [b]Is 44:23
10 [a]Eph 1:20f; Heb 4:14; 7:26 [b]Eph 1:23
11 [a]Eph 4:8 [b]Acts 13:1; 1 Cor 12:28 [c]Acts 21:8 [d]Acts 13:1
12 [1]Or *holy ones* [a]2 Cor 13:9 [b]1 Cor 12:27; Eph 1:23
13 [1]Or *true knowledge* [2]Lit *of the fullness* [a]Eph 4:3, 5 [b]John 6:69; Eph 1:17; Phil 3:10 [c]1 Cor 14:20; Col 1:28; Heb 5:14 [d]John 1:16; Eph 1:23
14 [1]Lit *So that we will no longer be* [2]Lit *with regard to the scheming of deceit* [a]1 Cor 14:20 [b]James 1:6; Jude 12 [c]1 Cor 3:19; 2 Cor 4:2; 11:3 [d]Eph 6:11

15 but [1]speaking the truth [a]in love, [2]we are to [b]grow up in all *aspects* into Him who is the [c]head, *even* Christ,
16 from whom [a]the whole body, being fitted and held together [1]by what every joint supplies, according to the [2]proper working of each individual part, causes the growth of the body for the building up of itself [b]in love.
17 [a]So this I say, and affirm together with the Lord, [b]that you walk no longer just as the Gentiles also walk, in the [c]futility of their mind,
18 being [a]darkened in their understanding, [1b]excluded from the life of God because of the [c]ignorance that is in them, because of the [d]hardness of their heart;
19 and they, having [a]become callous, [b]have given themselves over to [c]sensuality [1]for the practice of every kind of impurity with greediness.
20 But you did not [a]learn [1]Christ in this way,
21 if indeed you [a]have heard Him and have [b]been taught in Him, just as truth is in Jesus,
22 that, in reference to your former manner of life, you [a]lay aside the [b]old [1]self, which is being corrupted in accordance with the [c]lusts of deceit,
23 and that you be [a]renewed in the spirit of your mind,
24 and [a]put on the [b]new [1]self, which [2c]in *the likeness of* God has been created in righteousness and holiness of the truth.
25 Therefore, [a]laying aside falsehood, [b]SPEAK TRUTH EACH ONE *of you* WITH HIS NEIGHBOR, for we are [c]members of one another.
26 [a]BE ANGRY, AND *yet* DO NOT SIN; do not let the sun go down on your anger,
27 and do not [a]give the devil [1]an opportunity.
28 He who steals must steal no longer; but rather [a]he must labor, [b]performing with his own hands what is good, [c]so that he will have *something* to share with [1]one who has need.
29 Let no [1a]unwholesome word proceed from your mouth, but only such *a word* as is good for [b]edification [2]according to the need *of the moment,* so that it will give grace to those who hear.
30 [a]Do not grieve the Holy Spirit of God, [1]by whom you were [b]sealed for the day of redemption.
31 [a]Let all bitterness and wrath and anger and clamor and slander be [b]put away from you, along with all [c]malice.
32 [a]Be kind to one another, tender-hearted, forgiving each other, [b]just as God in Christ also has forgiven [1]you.

Chapter 5 Theme ____________________________

5 [a]Therefore be imitators of God, as beloved children;
2 and [a]walk in love, just as Christ also [b]loved [1]you and [c]gave Himself up for us, an [d]offering and a sacrifice to God [2]as a [e]fragrant aroma.

15 [1]Or *holding to* or *being truthful in* [2]Or *let us grow up* [a]Eph 1:4 [b]Eph 2:21 [c]Eph 1:22
16 [1]Lit *through every joint of the supply* [2]Lit *working in measure* [a]Rom 12:4f; Col 2:19 [b]Eph 1:4
17 [a]Col 2:4 [b]Eph 2:2; 4:22 [c]Rom 1:21; Col 2:18; 1 Pet 1:18; 2 Pet 2:18
18 [1]Or *alienated* [a]Rom 1:21 [b]Eph 2:1, 12 [c]Acts 3:17; 17:30; 1 Cor 2:8; Heb 5:2; 9:7; 1 Pet 1:14 [d]Mark 3:5; Rom 11:7, 25; 2 Cor 3:14
19 [1]Or *greedy for the practice of every kind of impurity* [a]1 Tim 4:2 [b]Rom 1:24 [c]Col 3:5
20 [1]I.e. the Messiah [a]Matt 11:29
21 [a]Rom 10:14; Eph 1:13; 2:17; Col 1:5 [b]Col 2:7
22 [1]Lit *man* [a]Eph 4:25, 31; Col 3:8; Heb 12:1; James 1:21; 1 Pet 2:1 [b]Rom 6:6 [c]2 Cor 11:3; Heb 3:13
23 [a]Rom 12:2
24 [1]Lit *man* [2]Lit *according to God* [a]Rom 13:14 [b]Rom 6:4; 7:6; 12:2; 2 Cor 5:17; Col 3:10 [c]Eph 2:10
25 [a]Eph 4:22, 31; Col 3:8; Heb 12:1; James 1:21; 1 Pet 2:1 [b]Zech 8:16; Eph 4:15; Col 3:9 [c]Rom 12:5
26 [a]Ps 4:4
27 [1]Lit *a place* [a]Rom 12:19; James 4:7
28 [1]Lit *the one* [a]Acts 20:35; 1 Cor 4:12; Gal 6:10 [b]1 Thess 4:11; 2 Thess 3:8, 11f; Titus 3:8, 14 [c]Luke 3:11; 1 Thess 4:12
29 [1]Lit *rotten* [2]Lit *of the need* [a]Matt 12:34; Eph 5:4; Col 3:8 [b]Eccl 10:12; Rom 14:19; Col 4:6
30 [1]Lit *in* [a]Is 63:10; 1 Thess 5:19 [b]John 3:33; Eph 1:13
31 [a]Rom 3:14; Col 3:8, 19 [b]Eph 4:22 [c]1 Pet 2:1

32 [1]Two early mss read *us* [a]1 Cor 13:4; Col 3:12f; 1 Pet 3:8 [b]Matt 6:14f; 2 Cor 2:10
5:1 [a]Matt 5:48; Luke 6:36; Eph 4:32
2 [1]One early ms reads *us* [2]Lit *for an odor of fragrance* [a]Rom 14:15; Col 3:14 [b]John 13:34; Rom 8:37 [c]John 6:51; Rom 4:25; Gal 2:20; Eph 5:25 [d]Heb 7:27; 9:14; 10:10, 12 [e]Ex 29:18, 25; 2 Cor 2:14

3 But [a]immorality [1]or any impurity or greed must not even
be named among you, as is proper among [2]saints;
4 and *there must be no* [a]filthiness and silly talk, or coarse
jesting, which [b]are not fitting, but rather [c]giving of thanks.
5 For this you know with certainty, that [a]no [1]immoral or
impure person or covetous man, who is an idolater, has an
inheritance in the kingdom [b]of Christ and God.
6 [a]Let no one deceive you with empty words, for because of
these things [b]the wrath of God comes upon [c]the sons of
disobedience.
7 Therefore do not be [a]partakers with them;
8 for [a]you were formerly [b]darkness, but now you are Light in
the Lord; walk as [c]children of Light
9 (for [a]the fruit of the Light *consists* in all [b]goodness and
righteousness and truth),
10 [1a]trying to learn what is pleasing to the Lord.
11 [a]Do not participate in the unfruitful [b]deeds of [c]darkness,
but instead even [1d]expose them;
12 for it is disgraceful even to speak of the things which are
done by them in secret.
13 But all things become visible [a]when they are [1]exposed by
the light, for everything that becomes visible is light.
14 For this reason [1]it says,
"[a]Awake, sleeper,
And arise from [b]the dead,
And Christ [c]will shine on you."
15 Therefore [1]be careful how you [a]walk, not [b]as unwise men
but as wise,
16 [1a]making the most of your time, because [b]the days are evil.
17 So then do not be foolish, but [a]understand what the will of
the Lord is.
18 And [a]do not get drunk with wine, [1]for that is [b]dissipation,
but be [c]filled with the Spirit,
19 [a]speaking to [1]one another in [b]psalms and [c]hymns and
spiritual [d]songs, [e]singing and making melody with your heart to
the Lord;
20 [a]always giving thanks for all things in the name of our Lord
Jesus Christ to [1b]God, even the Father;
21 [1a]and be subject to one another in the [2b]fear of Christ.
22 [a]Wives, [b]*be subject* to your own husbands, [c]as to the Lord.
23 For [a]the husband is the head of the wife, as Christ also is the
[b]head of the church, He Himself [c]*being* the Savior of the body.
24 But as the church is subject to Christ, so also the wives
ought to be to their husbands in everything.
25 [a]Husbands, love your wives, just as Christ also loved the
church and [b]gave Himself up for her,
26 [a]so that He might sanctify her, having [b]cleansed her by the
[c]washing of water with [d]the word,
27 that He might [a]present to Himself the church [1]in all her
glory, having no spot or wrinkle or any such thing; but that she
would be [b]holy and blameless.

3 [1]Lit *and all* [2]Or *holy ones* [a]Col 3:5
4 [a]Matt 12:34; Eph 4:29; Col 3:8 [b]Rom 1:28 [c]Eph 5:20
5 [1]I.e. one who commits sexual immorality [a]1 Cor 6:9; Col 3:5 [b]Col 1:13
6 [a]Col 2:8 [b]Rom 1:18; Col 3:6 [c]Eph 2:2
7 [a]Eph 3:6
8 [a]Eph 2:2 [b]Acts 26:18; Col 1:12f [c]John 12:36; Rom 13:12
9 [a]Gal 5:22 [b]Rom 15:14
10 [1]Lit *proving what* [a]Rom 12:2
11 [1]Or *reprove* [a]1 Cor 5:9; 2 Cor 6:14 [b]Rom 13:12 [c]Acts 26:18; Col 1:12f [d]1 Tim 5:20
13 [1]Or *reproved* [a]John 3:20f
14 [1]Or *He* [a]Is 26:19; 51:17; 52:1; 60:1; Rom 13:11 [b]Eph 2:1 [c]Luke 1:78f
15 [1]Lit *look carefully* [a]Eph 5:2 [b]Col 4:5
16 [1]Lit *redeeming the time* [a]Col 4:5 [b]Gal 1:4; Eph 6:13
17 [a]Rom 12:2; Col 1:9; 1 Thess 4:3
18 [1]Lit *in which is* [a]Prov 20:1; 23:31f; Rom 13:13; 1 Cor 5:11; 1 Thess 5:7 [b]Titus 1:6; 1 Pet 4:4 [c]Luke 1:15
19 [1]Or *yourselves* [a]Col 3:16 [b]1 Cor 14:26 [c]Acts 16:25 [d]Rev 5:9 [e]1 Cor 14:15
20 [1]Lit *the God and Father* [a]Rom 1:8; Eph 5:4; Col 3:17 [b]1 Cor 15:24
21 [1]Lit *being subject* [2]Or *reverence* [a]Gal 5:13; Phil 2:3; 1 Pet 5:5 [b]2 Cor 5:11
22 [a]Eph 5:22-6:9: *Col 3:18-4:1* [b]1 Cor 14:34f; Titus 2:5; 1 Pet 3:1 [c]Eph 6:5
23 [a]1 Cor 11:3 [b]Eph 1:22 [c]1 Cor 6:13
25 [a]Eph 5:28, 33; Col 3:19; 1 Pet 3:7 [b]Eph 5:2
26 [a]Titus 2:14; Heb 10:10, 14, 29; 13:12 [b]2 Pet 1:9 [c]Acts 22:16; 1 Cor 6:11; Titus 3:5 [d]John 15:3; 17:17; Rom 10:8f; Eph 6:17
27 [1]Lit *glorious* [a]2 Cor 4:14; 11:2; Col 1:22 [b]Eph 1:4

28 So husbands ought also to [a]love their own wives as their
own bodies. He who loves his own wife loves himself;
29 for no one ever hated his own flesh, but nourishes and
cherishes it, just as Christ also *does* the church,
30 because we are [a]members of His [b]body.
31 [a]FOR THIS REASON A MAN SHALL LEAVE HIS FATHER AND MOTHER AND
SHALL BE JOINED TO HIS WIFE, AND THE TWO SHALL BECOME ONE FLESH.
32 This mystery is great; but I am speaking with reference to
Christ and the church.
33 Nevertheless, each individual among you also is to [a]love his
own wife even as himself, and the wife must *see to it* that she
[1b]respects her husband.

Chapter 6 Theme ____

6 [a]Children, obey your parents in the Lord, for this is right.
2 [a]HONOR YOUR FATHER AND MOTHER (which is the first commandment with a promise),
3 SO THAT IT MAY BE WELL WITH YOU, AND THAT YOU MAY LIVE LONG
ON THE EARTH.
4 [a]Fathers, do not provoke your children to anger, but [b]bring
them up in the discipline and instruction of the Lord.
5 [a]Slaves, be obedient to those who are your [1]masters
according to the flesh, with [b]fear and trembling, in the sincerity
of your heart, [c]as to Christ;
6 [a]not [1]by way of eyeservice, as [b]men-pleasers, but as [c]slaves
of Christ, [d]doing the will of God from the [2]heart.
7 With good will [1]render service, [a]as to the Lord, and not to
men,
8 [a]knowing that [b]whatever good thing each one does, this he
will receive back from the Lord, [c]whether slave or free.
9 And masters, do the same things to them, and [a]give up
threatening, knowing that [b]both their Master and yours is in
heaven, and there is [c]no partiality with Him.
10 Finally, [a]be strong in the Lord and in [b]the strength of His
might.
11 [a]Put on the full armor of God, so that you will be able to
stand firm against the [b]schemes of the devil.
12 For our [a]struggle is not against [1b]flesh and blood, but [c]against
the rulers, against the powers, against the [d]world forces of this
[e]darkness, against the [f]spiritual *forces* of wickedness in [g]the
heavenly *places.*
13 Therefore, take up [a]the full armor of God, so that you will
be able to [b]resist in [c]the evil day, and having done everything,
to stand firm.
14 Stand firm therefore, [a]HAVING GIRDED YOUR LOINS WITH TRUTH,
and HAVING [b]PUT ON THE BREASTPLATE OF RIGHTEOUSNESS,
15 and having [a]shod YOUR FEET WITH THE PREPARATION OF THE
GOSPEL OF PEACE;
16 [1]in addition to all, taking up the [a]shield of faith with which
you will be able to extinguish all the [b]flaming arrows of [c]the
evil *one.*

28 [a]Eph 5:25, 33; 1 Pet 3:7
30 [a]1 Cor 6:15; 12:27 [b]Eph 1:23
31 [a]Gen 2:24; Matt 19:5; Mark 10:7f
33 [1]Lit *fear* [a]Eph 5:25, 28; 1 Pet 3:7 [b]1 Pet 3:2, 5f
6:1 [a]Prov 6:20; 23:22; Col 3:20
2 [a]Ex 20:12; Deut 5:16
4 [a]Col 3:21 [b]Gen 18:19; Deut 6:7; 11:19; Ps 78:4; Prov 22:6; 2 Tim 3:15
5 [1]I.e. earthly masters, with fear [a]Col 3:22; 1 Tim 6:1; Titus 2:9 [b]1 Cor 2:3 [c]Eph 5:22
6 [1]Lit *according to* [2]Lit *soul* [a]Col 3:22 [b]Gal 1:10 [c]1 Cor 7:22 [d]Mark 3:35
7 [1]Lit *rendering* [a]Col 3:23
8 [a]Col 3:24 [b]Matt 16:27; 2 Cor 5:10; Col 3:24f [c]1 Cor 12:13; Col 3:11
9 [a]Lev 25:43 [b]Job 31:13ff; John 13:13; Col 4:1 [c]Deut 10:17; Acts 10:34; Col 3:25
10 [a]1 Cor 16:13; 2 Tim 2:1 [b]Eph 1:19
11 [a]Rom 13:12; Eph 6:13 [b]Eph 4:14
12 [1]Lit *blood and flesh* [a]1 Cor 9:25 [b]Matt 16:17 [c]Eph 1:21; 2:2; 3:10 [d]John 12:31 [e]Acts 26:18; Col 1:13 [f]Eph 3:10 [g]Eph 1:3
13 [a]Eph 6:11 [b]James 4:7 [c]Eph 5:16
14 [a]Is 11:5; Luke 12:35; 1 Pet 1:13 [b]Is 59:17; Rom 13:12; Eph 6:13; 1 Thess 5:8
15 [a]Is 52:7; Rom 10:15
16 [1]Lit *in all* [a]1 Thess 5:8 [b]Ps 7:13; 120:4 [c]Matt 5:37

17 And take [a]THE HELMET OF SALVATION, and the [b]sword of the
Spirit, which is [c]the word of God.
18 [1]With all [a]prayer and petition [2b]pray at all times [c]in the
Spirit, and with this in view, [3d]be on the alert with all
[e]perseverance and [f]petition for all the saints,
19 and [a]*pray* on my behalf, that utterance may be given to me
[b]in the opening of my mouth, to make known with [c]boldness
[d]the mystery of the gospel,
20 for which I am an [a]ambassador [b]in [1]chains; that [2]in
proclaiming it I may speak [c]boldly, [d]as I ought to speak.
21 [a]But that you also may know about my circumstances,
[1]how I am doing, [b]Tychicus, [c]the beloved brother and faithful
minister in the Lord, will make everything known to you.
22 [1a]I have sent him to you for this very purpose, so that you
may know [2]about us, and that he may [b]comfort your hearts.
23 [a]Peace be to the brethren, and [b]love with faith, from God
the Father and the Lord Jesus Christ.
24 Grace be with all those who love our Lord Jesus Christ
[1]with incorruptible *love.*

22 [1]Lit *Whom I have sent to you* [2]Lit *the things about us* [a]Col 4:8 [b]Col 2:2; 4:8
23 [a]Rom 15:33; Gal 6:16; 2 Thess 3:16; 1 Pet 5:14 [b]Gal 5:6; 1 Thess 5:8
24 [1]Lit *in incorruption*

17 [a]Is 59:17 [b]Is 49:2; Hos 6:5; Heb 4:12 [c]Eph 5:26; Heb 6:5

18 [1]Lit *Through* [2]Lit *praying* [3]Lit *being* [a]Phil 4:6 [b]Luke 18:1; Col 1:3; 4:2; 1 Thess 5:17 [c]Rom 8:26f [d]Mark 13:33 [e]Acts 1:14 [f]1 Tim 2:1

19 [a]Col 4:3; 1 Thess 5:25 [b]2 Cor 6:11 [c]2 Cor 3:12 [d]Eph 3:3

20 [1]Lit *a chain* [2]Two early mss read *I may speak it boldly* [a]2 Cor 5:20; Philem 9 mg [b]Acts 21:33; 28:20; Eph 3:1; Phil 1:7; Col 4:3 [c]2 Cor 3:12 [d]Col 4:4

21 [1]Lit *what* [a]Eph 6:21, 22: *Col 4:7-9* [b]Acts 20:4; 2 Tim 4:12 [c]Col 4:7

Ephesians Observations Chart

Our Wealth and Position in Christ

Ephesians Observations Chart

Our Relationship with the Holy Spirit

Our Former Lifestyle and Walk

Our Walk in Christ

Ephesians at a Glance

Theme of Ephesians:

Author:

Date:

Purpose:

Key Words:

- every reference to being in Christ (in the Lord)
- according to
- the (Holy) Spirit
- rich(es)
- in the heavenly places
- former(ly)
- grace
- power
- body (church)
- redemption
- walk
- the devil (including powers, rulers, authorities, etc.)

Segment Divisions		Chapter Themes
		1
		2
		3
		4
		5
		6

PHILIPPIANS

Blocked by the Spirit of God from going into Asia and Bithynia, Paul had a vision of a man from Macedonia asking him to come to Macedonia and help the churches there.

Confident that God had given him direction, Paul sailed with Timothy and Luke from Troas on a second missionary journey. Philippi, in Macedonia, basked in the fact that it was also a Roman colony, which ensured its citizens all the benefits of Roman citizenship.

As was his custom, when Paul reached a city, he sought out the Jews. Although there were not enough Jews living in Philippi to form a synagogue, the Jews met outside the gate by the river for prayer on the Sabbath. Little did Paul realize that he would end up in prison, for God knew there was a Roman jailer and his family who needed Jesus.

The events of that visit inaugurated the beginning of the church at Philippi, the church Paul addressed around the year A.D. 61 or 62.

THINGS TO DO

1. Familiarize yourself with the message of Philippians by marking every reference to the author in one color and to the recipients in another. Look for the verses in chapters 1 and 4 that tell where Paul is as he writes.

2. To understand the historical setting of Philippians, read Acts 15:35–17:1, which records Paul's first visit to Philippi. After his third missionary journey, Paul went to Jerusalem, where he was arrested. From there Paul was taken by a Roman guard to Caesarea, the Mediterranean seaport where the Roman consul often went to escape the heat and confines of Jerusalem. After remaining a prisoner in Caesarea for over two years, Paul, who as a Roman citizen had appealed to Caesar, was sent to Rome, where he lived under house arrest. Read Acts 28:14-31 and note how long Paul remained a prisoner at Rome. How does this compare with where Paul was when he wrote Philippians?

3. As you read Philippians chapter by chapter, do the following:
   a. Using the OBSERVATIONS CHART on pages 1921, 1922, record your insights about the author and the recipients of Philippians.
   b. In a distinctive way, mark in the text each key word (and its synonyms and pronouns) listed on the PHILIPPIANS AT A GLANCE chart on page 1923. This will help you discover the themes (main subjects) of each chapter and of the book itself. Watch for other key words that are not listed but are used within each chapter.
   c. Make a list in your notebook of everything you learn from marking your key words.
   d. List each of the instructions Paul gives to the Philippian saints on the chart PAUL'S INSTRUCTIONS TO THE PHILIPPIANS on page 1922. As you list these instructions, evaluate your life in the light of each one.

4. On PHILIPPIANS AT A GLANCE:
   a. Fill in the theme for the book and for each chapter. (Be sure you also record the chapter theme in your Bible.)
   b. Under "Segment Divisions" record what you see to be Paul's example in each chapter. Remember, in Philippians 3:17 Paul tells his readers to follow his example.
   c. In the next column under "Segment Divisions" write down what each chapter says about who or what Jesus Christ is in relation to the believer.

d. For another segment division, record a command to believers that correlates with the theme of each chapter.

Things to Think About

1. What have you learned from Philippians about your relationship to suffering as a Christian? How is it going to affect the way you respond to suffering?
2. Can you say with Paul, "For to me, to live is Christ and to die is gain"? If you can't, think about what has replaced Christ's rightful place in your life.
3. What have you learned from Jesus' example that you can apply to your own life? Do you have the attitude of Christ toward God and others? Do you regard others as more important than yourself?
4. Do you allow your circumstances to affect your peace? What is keeping you from His peace? After reading Philippians 4 do you see any way to handle life's anxieties?
5. What have you learned about your own needs and sharing with others in need?

Chapter 1 Theme ______________________________

1 [a]Paul and [b]Timothy, [c]bond-servants of [d]Christ Jesus,
To [e]all the [1f]saints in Christ Jesus who are in [g]Philippi,
[2]including the [h]overseers and [i]deacons:
2 [a]Grace to you and peace from God our Father and the Lord
Jesus Christ.
3 [a]I thank my God in all my remembrance of you,
4 always offering prayer with joy in [a]my every prayer for you all,
5 in view of your [1a]participation in the [b]gospel [c]from the first
day until now.
6 *For I am* confident of this very thing, that He who began a
good work in you will perfect it until [a]the day of Christ Jesus.
7 [1]For [a]it is only right for me to feel this way about you all,
because I [b]have you in my heart, since both in my [2c]imprison-
ment and in the [d]defense and confirmation of the [e]gospel, you
all are partakers of grace with me.
8 For [a]God is my witness, how I long for you all with the
[1]affection of [b]Christ Jesus.
9 And this I pray, that [a]your love may abound still more and
more in [b]real knowledge and all discernment,
10 so that you may [1a]approve the things that are excellent, in
order to be sincere and blameless [2]until [b]the day of Christ;
11 having been filled with the [a]fruit of righteousness which
comes through Jesus Christ, to the glory and praise of God.
12 Now I want you to know, brethren, that my circumstances
[a]have turned out for the greater progress of the [b]gospel,
13 so that my [1a]imprisonment in *the cause of* Christ has become
well known throughout the whole [2]praetorian guard and to
[b]everyone else,

1:1 [1]Or *holy ones* [2]Lit *with* [a]2 Cor 1:1 [b]Acts 16:1 [c]Rom 1:1; Gal 1:10 [d]Gal 3:26 [e]2 Cor 1:1; Col 1:2 [f]Acts 9:13 [g]Acts 16:12 [h]Acts 20:28; 1 Tim 3:1f; Titus 1:7 [i]1 Tim 3:8ff
2 [a]Rom 1:7
3 [a]Rom 1:8
4 [a]Rom 1:9
5 [1]Or *sharing in the preaching of the gospel* [a]Acts 2:42; Phil 4:15 [b]Phil 1:7; 2:22; 4:3, 15 [c]Acts 16:12-40; Phil 2:12; 4:15
6 [a]1 Cor 1:8; Phil 1:10; 2:16
7 [1]Lit *Just as it is right* [2]Lit *bonds* [a]2 Pet 1:13 [b]2 Cor 7:3 [c]Acts 21:33; Eph 6:20; Phil 1:13f, 17 [d]Phil 1:16 [e]Phil 1:5, 12, 16, 27; 2:22; 4:3, 15
8 [1]Lit *inward parts* [a]Rom 1:9 [b]Gal 3:26
9 [a]1 Thess 3:12 [b]Col 1:9
10 [1]Or *discover;* or *distinguish between the things which differ* [2]Or *for* [a]Rom 2:18 [b]1 Cor 1:8; Phil 1:6; 2:16
11 [a]James 3:18
12 [a]Luke 21:13 [b]Phil 1:5, 7, 16, 27; 2:22; 4:3, 15
13 [1]Lit *bonds* [2]Or *governor's palace* [a]Phil 1:7; 2 Tim 2:9 [b]Acts 28:30

INSIGHT

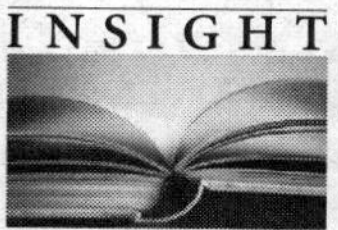

See the map on page 1800.

14 and that most of the [1]brethren, trusting in the Lord because
of my [2a]imprisonment, have [b]far more courage to speak the word
of God without fear.
15 [a]Some, to be sure, are preaching Christ even [1]from envy
and strife, but some also [1]from good will;
16 the latter *do it* out of love, knowing that I am appointed for
the defense of the [a]gospel;
17 the former proclaim Christ [a]out of selfish ambition [1]rather
than from pure motives, thinking to cause me distress in my
[2b]imprisonment.
18 What then? Only that in every way, whether in pretense or
in truth, Christ is proclaimed; and in this I rejoice.
Yes, and I will rejoice,
19 for I know that this will turn out for my [1]deliverance [a]through
your [2]prayers and the provision of [b]the Spirit of Jesus Christ,
20 according to my [a]earnest expectation and [b]hope, that I will
not be put to shame in anything, but *that* with [c]all boldness,
Christ will even now, as always, be [d]exalted in my body,
[e]whether by life or by death.
21 For to me, [a]to live is Christ and to die is gain.
22 [1]But if *I am* to live *on* in the flesh, this *will mean* [a]fruitful
labor for me; and I do not know [2]which to choose.
23 But I am hard-pressed from both *directions,* having the
[a]desire to depart and [b]be with Christ, for *that* is very much better;
24 yet to remain on in the flesh is more necessary for your sake.
25 [a]Convinced of this, I know that I will remain and continue
with you all for your progress and joy [1]in the faith,
26 so that your [a]proud confidence in me may abound in Christ
Jesus through my coming to you again.
27 Only conduct yourselves in a manner [a]worthy of the
[b]gospel of Christ, so that whether I come and see you or remain
absent, I will hear of you that you are [c]standing firm in [d]one spirit,
with one [1]mind [e]striving together for the faith of the gospel;
28 in no way alarmed by *your* opponents—which is a [a]sign of
destruction for them, but of salvation for you, and that *too,*
from God.
29 For to you [a]it has been granted for Christ's sake, not only to
believe in Him, but also to [b]suffer for His sake,
30 experiencing the same [a]conflict which [b]you saw in me, and
now hear *to be* in me.

Chapter 2 Theme ________________

2 Therefore if there is any encouragement in Christ, if there
is any consolation of love, if there is any [a]fellowship of the
Spirit, if any [1b]affection and compassion,
2 [a]make my joy complete [1]by [b]being of the same mind, main-
taining the same love, united in spirit, intent on one purpose.
3 Do nothing [1]from [2a]selfishness or [b]empty conceit, but with
humility of mind [c]regard one another as more important than
yourselves;

14 [1]Or *brethren in the Lord, trusting because of my bonds* [2]Lit *bonds* [a]Phil 1:7; 2 Tim 2:9 [b]Acts 4:31; 2 Cor 3:12; 7:4; Phil 1:20

15 [1]Lit *because of* [a]2 Cor 11:13

16 [a]Phil 1:5, 7, 12, 27; 2:22; 4:3, 15

17 [1]Lit *not sincerely* [2]Lit *bonds* [a]Rom 2:8; Phil 2:3 [b]Phil 1:7; 2 Tim 2:9

19 [1]Or *salvation* [2]Lit *supplication* [a]2 Cor 1:11 [b]Acts 16:7

20 [a]Rom 8:19 [b]Rom 5:5; 1 Pet 4:16 [c]Acts 4:31; 2 Cor 3:12; 7:4; Phil 1:14 [d]1 Cor 6:20 [e]Rom 14:8

21 [a]Gal 2:20

22 [1]Or *But if to live in the flesh, this will be fruitful labor for me, then I* [2]Lit *what I shall choose* [a]Rom 1:13

23 [a]2 Cor 5:8; 2 Tim 4:6 [b]John 12:26

25 [1]Lit *of* [a]Phil 2:24

26 [a]2 Cor 5:12; 7:4; Phil 2:16

27 [1]Lit *soul* [a]Eph 4:1 [b]Phil 1:5 [c]1 Cor 16:13; Phil 4:1 [d]Acts 4:32 [e]Jude 3

28 [a]2 Thess 1:5

29 [a]Matt 5:11, 12 [b]Acts 14:22

30 [a]Col 1:29; 2:1; 1 Thess 2:2; 1 Tim 6:12; 2 Tim 4:7; Heb 10:32; 12:1 [b]Acts 16:19-40; Phil 1:13

2:1 [1]Lit *inward parts* [a]2 Cor 13:14 [b]Col 3:12

2 [1]Lit *that you be* [a]John 3:29 [b]Rom 12:16; Phil 4:2

3 [1]Lit *according to* [2]Or *contentiousness* [a]Rom 2:8; Phil 1:17 [b]Gal 5:26 [c]Rom 12:10; Eph 5:21

4 [a]Rom 15:1f
5 [1]Or *among* [a]Matt 11:29; Rom 15:3 [b]Phil 1:1
6 [1]I.e. utilized or asserted [a]John 1:1 [b]2 Cor 4:4 [c]John 5:18; 10:33; 14:28
7 [1]I.e. laid aside His privileges [a]2 Cor 8:9 [b]Matt 20:28 [c]John 1:14; Rom 8:3; Gal 4:4; Heb 2:17
8 [1]Lit *of* [a]2 Cor 8:9 [b]Matt 26:39; John 10:18; Rom 5:19; Heb 5:8 [c]Heb 12:2
9 [a]Heb 1:9 [b]Matt 28:18; Acts 2:33; Heb 2:9 [c]Eph 1:21
10 [a]Is 45:23; Rom 14:11 [b]Eph 1:10
11 [a]John 13:13; Rom 10:9; 14:9
12 [a]Phil 1:5, 6; 4:15 [b]Heb 5:9 [c]2 Cor 7:15
13 [a]Rom 12:3; 1 Cor 12:6; 15:10; Heb 13:21 [b]Eph 1:5
14 [a]1 Cor 10:10; 1 Pet 4:9
15 [1]Or *become* [2]Or *shine* [3]Or *luminaries, stars* [a]Luke 1:6; Phil 3:6 [b]Matt 5:45; Eph 5:1 [c]Deut 32:5; Acts 2:40 [d]Matt 5:14-16
16 [1]Or *forth* [a]Phil 1:6 [b]Gal 2:2 [c]Is 49:4; Gal 4:11; 1 Thess 3:5
17 [a]2 Cor 12:15; 2 Tim 4:6 [b]Num 28:6, 7; Rom 15:16
19 [1]Or *trusting in* [a]Phil 2:23 [b]Phil 1:1
20 [a]1 Cor 16:10; 2 Tim 3:10
21 [a]1 Cor 10:24; 13:5; Phil 2:4
22 [a]Rom 5:4; Acts 16:2 [b]Acts 16:3; 1 Cor 16:10; 2 Tim 3:10 [c]1 Cor 4:17
23 [a]Phil 2:19
24 [a]Phil 1:25
25 [1]Lit *apostle* [a]Phil 4:18 [b]Rom 16:3, 9, 21; Phil 4:3; Philem 1, 24 [c]Philem 2 [d]John 13:16; 2 Cor 8:23

4 [a]do not *merely* look out for your own personal interests,
but also for the interests of others.
5 [a]Have this attitude [1]in yourselves which was also in [b]Christ
Jesus,
6 who, although He [a]existed in the [b]form of God, [c]did not
regard equality with God a thing to be [1]grasped,
7 but [1a]emptied Himself, taking the form of a [b]bond-servant,
and [c]being made in the likeness of men.
8 Being found in appearance as a man, [a]He humbled Himself
by becoming [b]obedient to the point of death, even [c]death [1]on a
cross.
9 [a]For this reason also, God [b]highly exalted Him, and bestowed
on Him [c]the name which is above every name,
10 so that at the name of Jesus [a]EVERY KNEE WILL BOW, of [b]those
who are in heaven and on earth and under the earth,
11 and that every tongue will confess that Jesus Christ is
[a]Lord, to the glory of God the Father.
12 So then, my beloved, [a]just as you have always obeyed, not
as in my presence only, but now much more in my absence,
work out your [b]salvation with [c]fear and trembling;
13 for it is [a]God who is at work in you, both to will and to
work [b]for *His* good pleasure.
14 Do all things without [a]grumbling or disputing;
15 so that you will [1]prove yourselves to be [a]blameless and
innocent, [b]children of God above reproach in the midst of a
[c]crooked and perverse generation, among whom you [2d]appear
as [3]lights in the world,
16 holding [1]fast the word of life, so that in [a]the day of Christ I
will have reason to glory because I did not [b]run in vain nor [c]toil
in vain.
17 But even if I am being [a]poured out as a drink offering upon
[b]the sacrifice and service of your faith, I rejoice and share my
joy with you all.
18 You too, *I urge you,* rejoice in the same way and share your
joy with me.
19 But I hope [1]in the Lord Jesus to [a]send [b]Timothy to you
shortly, so that I also may be encouraged when I learn of your
condition.
20 For I have no one *else* [a]of kindred spirit who will genuinely
be concerned for your welfare.
21 For they all [a]seek after their own interests, not those of
Christ Jesus.
22 But you know [a]of his proven worth, that [b]he served with me
in the furtherance of the gospel [c]like a child *serving* his father.
23 [a]Therefore I hope to send him immediately, as soon as I see
how things *go* with me;
24 and [a]I trust in the Lord that I myself also will be coming
shortly.
25 But I thought it necessary to send to you [a]Epaphroditus, my
brother and [b]fellow worker and [c]fellow soldier, who is also your
[1d]messenger and [a]minister to my need;

26 because he was longing [1]for you all and was distressed
because you had heard that he was sick.
27 For indeed he was sick to the point of death, but God had
mercy on him, and not on him only but also on me, so that I
would not have sorrow upon sorrow.
28 Therefore I have sent him all the more eagerly so that when
you see him again you may rejoice and I may be less concerned
about you.
29 [a]Receive him then in the Lord with all joy, and [b]hold men
like him in high regard;
30 because he came close to death [1a]for the work of Christ,
risking his life to [b]complete [2]what was deficient in your service
to me.

Chapter 3 Theme ______________________________

3 Finally, my brethren, [a]rejoice in the Lord. To write the same
things *again* is no trouble to me, and it is a safeguard for you.
2 Beware of the [a]dogs, beware of the [b]evil workers, beware
of the [1]false circumcision;
3 for [a]we are the *true* [1]circumcision, who [b]worship in the
Spirit of God and [c]glory in [d]Christ Jesus and put no confidence
in the flesh,
4 although [a]I myself might have confidence even in the flesh. If
anyone else has a mind to put confidence in the flesh, I far more:
5 [a]circumcised the eighth day, of the [b]nation of Israel, of the
[c]tribe of Benjamin, a [b]Hebrew of Hebrews; as to the Law, [d]a
Pharisee;
6 as to zeal, [a]a persecutor of the church; as to the [b]righteous-
ness which is in the Law, found [c]blameless.
7 But [a]whatever things were gain to me, those things I have
counted as loss for the sake of Christ.
8 More than that, I count all things to be loss [1]in view of the
surpassing value of [2a]knowing [b]Christ Jesus my Lord, [1]for
whom I have suffered the loss of all things, and count them but
rubbish so that I may gain Christ,
9 and may be found in Him, not having [a]a righteousness of
my own derived from *the* Law, but that which is through faith
in Christ, [b]the righteousness which *comes* from God on the
basis of faith,
10 that I may [a]know Him and [b]the power of His resurrection and
[1c]the fellowship of His sufferings, being [d]conformed to His death;
11 [1]in order that I may [a]attain to the resurrection from the dead.
12 Not that I have already [a]obtained *it* or have already [b]become
perfect, but I press on [1]so that I may [c]lay hold of that [2]for
which also I [d]was laid hold of by [e]Christ Jesus.
13 Brethren, I do not regard myself as having laid hold of *it*
yet; but one thing *I do:* [a]forgetting what *lies* behind and
reaching forward to what *lies* ahead,
14 I [a]press on toward the goal for the prize of the [b]upward call
of God in [c]Christ Jesus.

26 [1]One early ms reads *to see you all*

29 [a]Rom 16:2 [b]1 Cor 16:18

30 [1]Lit *because of* [2]Lit *your deficiency of service* [a]Acts 20:24 [b]1 Cor 16:17; Phil 4:10

3:1 [a]Phil 2:18; 4:4

2 [1]Lit *mutilation;* Gr *katatome* [a]Ps 22:16, 20; Gal 5:15; Rev 22:15 [b]2 Cor 11:13

3 [1]Gr *peritome* [a]Rom 2:29; 9:6; Gal 6:15 [b]Gal 5:25 [c]Rom 15:17; Gal 6:14 [d]Rom 8:39; Phil 1:1; 3:12

4 [a]2 Cor 5:16; 11:18

5 [a]Luke 1:59 [b]Rom 11:1; 2 Cor 11:22 [c]Rom 11:1 [d]Acts 22:3; 23:6; 26:5

6 [a]Acts 8:3; 22:4, 5; 26:9-11 [b]Phil 3:9 [c]Phil 2:15

7 [a]Luke 14:33

8 [1]Lit *because of* [2]Lit *the knowledge of* [a]Jer 9:23f; John 17:3; Eph 4:13; Phil 3:10; 2 Pet 1:3 [b]Rom 8:39; Phil 1:1; 3:12

9 [a]Rom 10:5; Phil 3:6 [b]Rom 9:30; 1 Cor 1:30

10 [1]Or *participation in* [a]Jer 9:23f; John 17:3; Eph 4:13; Phil 3:8; 2 Pet 1:3 [b]Rom 6:5 [c]Rom 8:17 [d]Rom 6:5; 8:36; Gal 6:17

11 [1]Lit *if somehow* [a]Acts 26:7; 1 Cor 15:23; Rev 20:5f

12 [1]Lit *if I may even* [2]Or *because also* [a]1 Cor 9:24f; 1 Tim 6:12, 19 [b]1 Cor 13:10 [c]1 Tim 6:12, 19 [d]Acts 9:5f [e]Rom 8:39; Phil 1:1; 3:3, 8

13 [a]Luke 9:62

14 [a]1 Cor 9:24; Heb 6:1 [b]Rom 8:28; 11:29; 2 Tim 1:9 [c]Phil 3:3

15 Let us therefore, as many as are [1a]perfect, have this
attitude; and if in anything you have a [b]different attitude, [c]God
will reveal that also to you;
16 however, let us keep [1a]living by that same *standard* to which
we have attained.
17 Brethren, [a]join in following my example, and observe those
who walk according to the [b]pattern you have in us.
18 For [a]many walk, of whom I often told you, and now tell
you even [b]weeping, *that they are* enemies of [c]the cross of Christ,
19 whose end is destruction, whose god is *their* [1a]appetite,
and *whose* [b]glory is in their shame, who [c]set their minds on
earthly things.
20 For [a]our [1]citizenship is in heaven, from which also we
eagerly [b]wait for a Savior, the Lord Jesus Christ;
21 who will [a]transform [1]the body of our humble state into
[b]conformity with [2]the [c]body of His glory, [d]by the exertion of
the power that He has even to [e]subject all things to Himself.

Chapter 4 Theme ______________________________

4 Therefore, my beloved brethren [1]whom I [a]long *to see,* my joy
and crown, in this way [b]stand firm in the Lord, my beloved.
2 I urge Euodia and I urge Syntyche to [1a]live in harmony in
the Lord.
3 Indeed, true companion, I ask you also to help these
women who have shared my struggle in *the cause of* the
gospel, together with Clement also and the rest of my [a]fellow
workers, whose [b]names are in the book of life.
4 [a]Rejoice in the Lord always; again I will say, rejoice!
5 Let your gentle *spirit* be known to all men. [a]The Lord is [1]near.
6 [a]Be anxious for nothing, but in everything by [b]prayer and
supplication with thanksgiving let your requests be made
known to God.
7 And [a]the peace of God, which surpasses all [1]comprehension,
will [b]guard your hearts and your [c]minds in [d]Christ Jesus.
8 Finally, brethren, [a]whatever is true, whatever is honorable,
whatever is right, whatever is pure, whatever is [1]lovely, whatever
is of good repute, if there is any excellence and if anything
worthy of praise, [2]dwell on these things.
9 The things you have learned and received and heard and
seen [a]in me, practice these things, and [b]the God of peace will
be with you.
10 But I rejoiced in the Lord greatly, that now at last [a]you have
revived your concern for me; indeed, you were concerned
before, but you lacked opportunity.
11 Not that I speak [1]from want, for I have learned to be
[2a]content in whatever circumstances I am.
12 I know how to get along with humble means, and I also
know how to live in prosperity; in any and every circumstance
I have learned the secret of being filled and going [a]hungry, both
of having abundance and [b]suffering need.

15 [1]Or *mature* [a]Matt 5:48; 1 Cor 2:6 [b]Gal 5:10 [c]John 6:45; Eph 1:17; 1 Thess 4:9
16 [1]Lit *following in line* [a]Gal 6:16
17 [a]1 Cor 4:16; 11:1; Phil 4:9 [b]1 Pet 5:3
18 [a]2 Cor 11:13 [b]Acts 20:31 [c]Gal 6:14
19 [1]Lit *belly* [a]Rom 16:18; Titus 1:12 [b]Rom 6:21; Jude 13 [c]Rom 8:5f; Col 3:2
20 [1]Lit *common-wealth* [a]Eph 2:19; Phil 1:27; Col 3:1; Heb 12:22 [b]1 Cor 1:7
21 [1]Or *our lowly body* [2]Or *His glorious body* [a]1 Cor 15:43-53 [b]Rom 8:29; Col 3:4 [c]1 Cor 15:43, 49 [d]Eph 1:19 [e]1 Cor 15:28
4:1 [1]Lit *and longed for* [a]Phil 1:8 [b]1 Cor 16:13; Phil 1:27
2 [1]Or *be of the same mind* [a]Phil 2:2
3 [a]Phil 2:25 [b]Luke 10:20
4 [a]Phil 3:1
5 [1]Or *at hand* [a]1 Cor 16:22 mg; Heb 10:37; James 5:8f
6 [a]Matt 6:25 [b]Eph 6:18; 1 Tim 2:1; 5:5
7 [1]Lit *mind* [a]Is 26:3; John 14:27; Phil 4:9; Col 3:15 [b]1 Pet 1:5 [c]2 Cor 10:5 [d]Phil 1:1; 4:19, 21
8 [1]Or *lovable and gracious* [2]Lit *ponder these things* [a]Rom 14:18; 1 Pet 2:12
9 [a]Phil 3:17 [b]Rom 15:33
10 [a]2 Cor 11:9; Phil 2:30
11 [1]Lit *according to* [2]Or *self-sufficient* [a]2 Cor 9:8; 1 Tim 6:6, 8; Heb 13:5
12 [a]1 Cor 4:11 [b]2 Cor 11:9

13 I can do all things [1]through Him who [a]strengthens me.
14 Nevertheless, you have done well to [a]share *with me* in my
affliction.
15 You yourselves also know, Philippians, that at the [1a]first
preaching of the gospel, after I left [b]Macedonia, no church
[c]shared with me in the matter of giving and receiving but you
alone;
16 for even in [a]Thessalonica you sent *a gift* more than once for
my needs.
17 [a]Not that I seek the gift itself, but I seek for the [1]profit
which increases to your account.
18 But I have received everything in full and have an abundance;
I am [1]amply supplied, having received from [a]Epaphroditus [2]what
you have sent, [3b]a fragrant aroma, an acceptable sacrifice, well-
pleasing to God.
19 And [a]my God will supply [1]all your needs according to His
[b]riches in glory in Christ Jesus.
20 Now to [a]our God and Father [b]*be* the glory [1]forever and
ever. Amen.
21 Greet every [1]saint in Christ Jesus. [a]The brethren who are
with me greet you.
22 [a]All the [1b]saints greet you, especially those of Caesar's
household.
23 [a]The grace of the Lord Jesus Christ [b]be with your spirit.

13 [1]Lit *in* [a]2 Cor 12:9; Eph 3:16; Col 1:11

14 [a]Heb 10:33; Rev 1:9

15 [1]Lit *beginning of* [a]Phil 1:5 [b]Rom 15:26 [c]2 Cor 11:9

16 [a]Acts 17:1; 1 Thess 2:9

17 [1]Lit *fruit* [a]1 Cor 9:11f; 2 Cor 9:5

18 [1]Lit *made full* [2]Lit *the things from you* [3]Lit *an odor of fragrance* [a]Phil 2:25 [b]Ex 29:18; 2 Cor 2:14; Eph 5:2

19 [1]Or *every need of yours* [a]2 Cor 9:8 [b]Rom 2:4

20 [1]Lit *to the ages of the ages* [a]Gal 1:4 [b]Rom 11:36

21 [1]Or *holy one* [a]Gal 1:2

22 [1]V 21, note 1 [a]2 Cor 13:13 [b]Acts 9:13

23 [a]Rom 16:20 [b]2 Tim 4:22

Philippians Observations Chart

Author: *Look for both pronouns and direct references*

The Recipients: *Look for* the saints, brethren, beloved, you, *or any other ways Paul addresses those to whom he is writing. (Remember to keep asking the "5 W's and an H": How does Paul describe the Philippians? What are their problems? What is his concern for them? Why is Paul writing to the Philippians?)*

(continued)

PAUL'S INSTRUCTIONS TO THE PHILIPPIANS

(continued)

Paul's Instructions to the Philippians

Philippians at a Glance

Theme of Philippians:

Author:

Date:

Purpose:

Key Words:

imprisonment

Christ Jesus

joy (rejoice)

mind (attitude)

gospel

prayer

Segment Divisions: Command to:	Segment Divisions: Jesus Is:	Segment Divisions: Paul's Example	Chapter Themes
	1:21 My Life		1
			2
3:17 Follow Paul's Example			3
		4:11 Learned to Be Content in His Circumstances	4

COLOSSIANS

Colossae was located 12 miles from Laodicea and about a hundred miles east of Ephesus in the valley of the Lycus River in the southern part of ancient Phrygia, the adopted home of Oriental mysticism. Many Jews, Phrygians, and Greeks came to Colossae because it was on a main trade route. The mixture of backgrounds made the city an interesting cultural center where all sorts of new ideas and doctrines from the East were discussed and considered.

With all these ungodly influences, it is no wonder that the Christians at Colossae were on Paul's heart during his imprisonment in Rome. He may never have seen their faces, but they belonged to his Christ and he was one with them in spirit. Physically he might be bound by chains, but he could reach them by letter. This was one way he could protect them from the wolves who were out to devour God's flock.

Paul wrote sometime around A.D. 62. His words to the faithful saints at Colossae contained a message that would be needed down through the ages. Maybe that is one of the reasons God didn't let Paul deliver this message in person.

THINGS TO DO

1. As you read Colossians, learn all you can from the text about the author to discover why he writes what he does to this particular church. This will give you the key to understanding Colossians. Following this simple procedure will help:

   a. As you read, color every reference to the author in one color and every reference to the recipients in another. Make sure you mark the synonyms and pronouns that refer either to the author or the recipients.

   b. Once you've marked the author and the recipients, study what you learn from marking the text in this way. Read through Colossians chapter by chapter, looking at each reference you marked to see if it answers any of the "5 W's and an H": Who? What? Where? Why? When? and How? Ask questions such as: Who wrote this? To whom? Where were they? What were these people like? What were their situations? What were their problems? When was this written? What seemed to be going on? Why did the author say what he did?

      Look for pronouns such as *you* and note the relationship between the author and the recipients. Ask questions like these: How did the gospel get to the Colossians? Who preached the gospel to them? What was the author's main concern for the Colossians? The answers will help you understand why this letter was written.

      Asking questions like these—answered only from what the text says—will give you insight into a book of the Bible, help you to understand the context and purpose of the book, and enable you to keep its teachings and truths in their proper context.

   c. Record insights about the author, recipients, and the author's instructions on pages 1931, 1932.

2. Now read through Colossians again, a chapter at a time. As you read:

   a. Mark the key words and phrases listed on the COLOSSIANS AT A GLANCE chart on page 1932. Mark the synonyms and pronouns for each key word and every reference to Jesus: *with Him, by Him, for Him, through Him,* and so on.

   b. In your notebook, list what you learn from marking *in Him* and other key words.

3. In chapter 2, note the warnings by looking for the phrases *see to it* and *let no one.*

a. Record these warnings along with any instructions on the OBSERVATIONS CHART.

b. With these warnings in mind, read "Understanding Gnosticism" starting on page 2100.

4. Proceed through chapters 3 and 4 in the same manner as chapters 1 and 2, adding pertinent information to your OBSERVATIONS CHART.

5. Record the theme of the book and of each chapter on the COLOSSIANS AT A GLANCE chart. Remember to record the chapter theme in your Bible. Also fill out the date the book was written, the name of the author, and his purpose for writing.

THINGS TO THINK ABOUT

1. Examine your lifestyle. What are you pursuing? Does it have eternal value? Is it drawing you closer to God or keeping you from time alone with God in prayer and in studying the Word? Are you seeking things that are above or earthly things?

2. Examine your beliefs. Are you being deluded with any modern-day philosophies or traditions that contradict the Word or aren't in the Word? Any legalistic rules that are not clearly taught in the New Testament? Any mystical teachings or prophecies that can't be supported in the Word of God or that have a tendency to add something that isn't there or that seem to be only for an elite group of people?

3. Inductive Bible study takes time. The enemy will do all he can to keep you from knowing God and His Word intimately, for truth is your major defense and offense in spiritual warfare. Are you going to make it your goal to let the Word of Christ richly dwell within you and to walk in its precepts?

4. Are you proclaiming the Lord Jesus Christ and holding firmly to all He is and all that you have in Him as He is presented in Colossians?

5. As you studied Colossians, did you see any areas in your life in which you are falling short or simply walking in disobedience to God's Word? What steps are you going to take in order to correct these?

Chapter 1 Theme ______________________

1 [a]Paul, [b]an apostle of Jesus Christ [1c]by the will of God, and
[d]Timothy [2]our brother,
2 To the [1a]saints and faithful brethren in Christ *who are* at
Colossae: [b]Grace to you and peace from God our Father.
3 [a]We give thanks to God, [b]the Father of our Lord Jesus
Christ, praying always for you,
4 [a]since we heard of your faith in Christ Jesus and the [b]love
which you have [1]for [c]all the [2]saints;
5 because of the [a]hope [b]laid up for you in [1]heaven, of which
you previously [c]heard in the word of truth, [2]the gospel
6 which has come to you, just as [1a]in all the world also it is
constantly bearing [b]fruit and [2]increasing, even as *it has been*
doing in you also since the day you [c]heard *of it* and [3]understood
the grace of God in truth;
7 just as you learned *it* from [a]Epaphras, our [b]beloved fellow
bond-servant, who is a faithful servant of Christ on our behalf,

1:1 [1]Lit *through* [2]Lit *the* [a]Phil 1:1 [b]2 Cor 1:1 [c]1 Cor 1:1 [d]2 Cor 1:1; 1 Thess 3:2
2 [1]Or *holy ones* [a]Acts 9:13 [b]Rom 1:7
3 [a]Rom 1:8 [b]Rom 15:6; 2 Cor 1:3
4 [1]Or *toward* [2]Or *holy ones* [a]Eph 1:15 [b]Gal 5:6 [c]Eph 6:18
5 [1]Lit *the heavens* [2]Or *of the gospel* [a]Acts 23:6 [b]2 Tim 4:8 [c]Eph 1:13
6 [1]Or *it is in the world* [2]Or *spreading abroad* [3]Or *came really to know* [a]Rom 10:18 [b]Rom 1:13 [c]Eph 4:21
7 [a]Col 4:12 [b]Col 4:7

Colossae

8 and he also informed
us of your [a]love in the
Spirit.
9 For this reason also,
[a]since the day we heard *of*
it, [b]we have not ceased to
pray for you and to ask
that you may be filled with
the [1c]knowledge of His
will in all spiritual [d]wisdom
and understanding,
10 so that you will [a]walk
in a manner worthy of the
Lord, [1b]to please *Him* in all respects, [c]bearing fruit in every
good work and [2]increasing in the [3]knowledge of God;
11 [a]strengthened with all power, according to [1]His glorious might,
[2]for the attaining of all steadfastness and [3]patience; [b]joyously
12 giving thanks to [a]the Father, who has qualified us [1]to share
in [b]the inheritance of the [2]saints in [c]Light.
13 [1]For He rescued us from the [2a]domain of darkness, and
transferred us to the kingdom of [3b]His beloved Son,
14 [a]in whom we have redemption, the forgiveness of sins.
15 [1]He is the [a]image of the [b]invisible God, the [c]firstborn of all
creation.
16 For [1a]by Him all things were created, [a]*both* in the heavens
and on earth, visible and invisible, whether [b]thrones or
dominions or rulers or authorities—[c]all things have been created
through Him and for Him.
17 He [1a]is before all things, and in Him all things [2]hold together.
18 He is also [a]head of [b]the body, the church; and He is [c]the
beginning, [d]the firstborn from the dead, so that He Himself will
come to have first place in everything.
19 For [1]it was [a]the *Father's* good pleasure for all [b]the [2]fullness
to dwell in Him,
20 and through Him to [a]reconcile all things to Himself, having
made [b]peace through [c]the blood of His cross; through Him, *I*
say, [d]whether things on earth or things in [1]heaven.
21 And although you were [a]formerly alienated and hostile in
mind, *engaged* in evil deeds,
22 yet He has now [a]reconciled you in His fleshly [b]body
through death, in order to [c]present you before Him [d]holy and
blameless and beyond reproach—
23 if indeed you continue in [1]the faith firmly [a]established and
steadfast, and not moved away from the [b]hope of the gospel
that you have heard, which was proclaimed [c]in all creation
under heaven, [d]and of which I, Paul, [2]was made a [3e]minister.
24 [a]Now I rejoice in my sufferings for your sake, and in my
flesh [b]I [1]do my share on behalf of [c]His body, which is the
church, in filling up what is lacking [2]in Christ's afflictions.
25 [a]Of *this church* I [1]was made a minister according to the
[b]stewardship from God bestowed on me for your benefit, so
that I might [2]fully carry out the *preaching of* the word of God,

8 [a]Rom 15:30
9 [1]Or *real knowledge* [a]Col 1:4 [b]Eph 1:16 [c]Phil 1:9 [d]Eph 1:17
10 [1]Lit *unto all pleasing* [2]Or *growing by the knowledge* [3]Or *real knowledge* [a]Eph 4:1 [b]Eph 5:10 [c]Rom 1:13
11 [1]Lit *the might of His glory* [2]Lit *unto all* [3]Or *patience with joy* [a]1 Cor 16:13 [b]Eph 4:2
12 [1]Lit *unto the portion of* [2]Or *holy ones* [a]Eph 2:18 [b]Acts 20:32 [c]Acts 26:18
13 [1]Lit *Who rescued* [2]Lit *authority* [3]Lit *the Son of His love* [a]Eph 6:12 [b]Eph 1:6
14 [a]Rom 3:24
15 [1]Lit *Who is* [a]2 Cor 4:4 [b]John 1:1 [c]Rom 8:29
16 [1]Or *in* [a]Eph 1:10 [b]Eph 1:20f; Col 2:15 [c]John 1:3; Rom 11:36; 1 Cor 8:6
17 [1]Or *has existed prior to* [2]Or *endure* [a]John 1:1; 8:58
18 [a]Eph 1:22 [b]Eph 1:23; Col 1:24; 2:19 [c]Rev 3:14 [d]Acts 26:23
19 [1]Or *all the fullness was pleased to dwell* [2]I.e. fullness of deity [a]Eph 1:5 [b]John 1:16
20 [1]Lit *the heavens* [a]2 Cor 5:18; Eph 2:16 [b]Rom 5:1; Eph 2:14 [c]Eph 2:13 [d]Col 1:16
21 [a]Rom 5:10; Eph 2:3, 12
22 [a]2 Cor 5:18; Eph 2:16 [b]Rom 7:4 [c]Eph 5:27; Col 1:28 [d]Eph 1:4
23 [1]Or *in faith* [2]Lit *became* [3]Or *servant* [a]Eph 3:17; Col 2:7 [b]Col 1:5 [c]Mark 16:15; Acts 2:5; Col 1:6 [d]Eph 3:7; Col 1:25 [e]1 Cor 3:5
24 [1]Or *representatively . . . fill up* [2]Lit *of* [a]Rom 8:17; 2 Cor 1:5; 12:15; Phil 2:17 [b]2 Tim 1:8; 2:10 [c]Col 1:18
25 [1]Lit *became* [2]Lit *make full the word of God* [a]Col 1:23 [b]Eph 3:2

26 *that is,* [a]the mystery which has been hidden from the *past*
ages and generations, but has now been manifested to His [1]saints,
27 to whom [a]God willed to make known what is [b]the riches of
the glory of this mystery among the Gentiles, which is [c]Christ
in you, the [d]hope of glory.
28 We proclaim Him, [a]admonishing every man and teaching
every man [1]with all [b]wisdom, so that we may [c]present every
man [2d]complete in Christ.
29 For this purpose also I [a]labor, [b]striving [c]according to His
[1]power, which [2]mightily works within me.

Chapter 2 Theme __________________________________

2 For I want you to know how great a [a]struggle I have on
your behalf and for those who are at [b]Laodicea, and for all
those who have not [1]personally seen my face,
2 that their [a]hearts may be encouraged, having been [b]knit
together in love, and *attaining* to all [c]the wealth [1]that comes
from the full assurance of understanding, *resulting* in a [d]true
knowledge of [e]God's mystery, *that is,* Christ *Himself,*
3 in whom are hidden all [a]the treasures of wisdom and
knowledge.
4 [a]I say this so that no one will delude you with [b]persuasive
argument.
5 For even though I am [a]absent in body, nevertheless I am
with you in spirit, rejoicing [1]to see [2]your [b]good discipline and
the [c]stability of your faith in Christ.
6 Therefore as you have received [a]Christ Jesus the Lord, *so*
[1b]walk in Him,
7 having been firmly [a]rooted *and now* being [b]built up in Him
and [c]established [1]in your faith, just as you [d]were instructed,
and overflowing [2]with gratitude.
8 [a]See to it that no one takes you captive through [b]philosophy
and empty deception, according to the tradition of men,
according to the [c]elementary principles of the world, [1]rather
than according to Christ.
9 For in Him all the [a]fullness of Deity dwells in bodily form,
10 and in Him you have been [a]made [1]complete, and [b]He is the
head [2]over all [c]rule and authority;
11 and in Him [a]you were also circumcised with a circumcision
made without hands, in the removal of [b]the body of the flesh
by the circumcision of Christ;
12 having been [a]buried with Him in baptism, in which you
were also [b]raised up with Him through faith in the working of
God, who [c]raised Him from the dead.
13 When you were [a]dead [1]in your transgressions and the
uncircumcision of your flesh, He [b]made you alive together with
Him, having forgiven us all our transgressions,
14 having canceled out [a]the certificate of debt consisting of
decrees against us, which was hostile to us; and [b]He has taken
it out of the way, having nailed it to the cross.

26 [1]Or *holy ones* [a]Rom 16:25f; Eph 3:3f; Col 2:2; 4:3
27 [a]Matt 13:11 [b]Eph 1:7, 18; 3:16 [c]Rom 8:10 [d]1 Tim 1:1
28 [1]Lit *in* [2]Or *perfect* [a]Acts 20:31; Col 3:16 [b]1 Cor 2:6f; Col 2:3 [c]Col 1:22 [d]Matt 5:48; Eph 4:13
29 [1]Lit *working* [2]Lit *in power* [a]1 Cor 15:10 [b]Col 2:1; 4:12 [c]Eph 1:19; Col 2:12
2:1 [1]Lit *in the flesh* [a]Col 1:29; 4:12 [b]Col 4:13, 15f; Rev 1:11
2 [1]Lit *of the full assurance* [a]1 Cor 14:31; Eph 6:22; Col 4:8 [b]Col 2:19 [c]Eph 1:7, 18; 3:16 [d]Matt 13:11 [e]Rom 16:25f; Eph 3:3f; Col 1:26; 4:3
3 [a]Is 11:2; Rom 11:33
4 [a]Eph 4:17 [b]Rom 16:18
5 [1]Lit *and seeing* [2]Or *your good order* [a]1 Cor 5:3 [b]1 Cor 14:40 [c]1 Pet 5:9
6 [1]Or *lead your life* [a]Gal 3:26 [b]Col 1:10
7 [1]Or *by* [2]One early ms reads *in it with* [a]Eph 3:17 [b]1 Cor 3:9; Eph 2:20 [c]1 Cor 1:8 [d]Eph 4:21
8 [1]Lit *and not* [a]1 Cor 8:9; 10:12; Gal 5:15; Heb 3:12 [b]Eph 5:6; Col 2:23; 1 Tim 6:20 [c]Gal 4:3; Col 2:20
9 [a]2 Cor 5:19; Col 1:19
10 [1]Lit *full* [2]Lit *of* [a]Eph 3:19 [b]Eph 1:21f [c]1 Cor 15:24; Eph 3:10; Col 2:15
11 [a]Rom 2:29; Eph 2:11 [b]Rom 6:6; 7:24; Gal 5:24; Col 3:5
12 [a]Rom 6:4f [b]Rom 6:5; Eph 2:6; Col 2:13; 3:1 [c]Acts 2:24
13 [1]Or *by reason of* [a]Eph 2:1 [b]Eph 2:5; Col 2:12
14 [a]Eph 2:15; Col 2:20 [b]1 Pet 2:24

15 When He had [1a]disarmed the [b]rulers and authorities, He [a]made a public display of them, having [c]triumphed over them through [2]Him.

16 Therefore no one is to [1a]act as your judge in regard to [b]food or [b]drink or in respect to a [c]festival or a [d]new moon or a [e]Sabbath [2]day—

17 things which are [a]a *mere* shadow of what is to come; but the [1]substance [2]belongs to Christ.

18 Let no one keep [1a]defrauding you of your prize by [b]delighting in [2]self-abasement and the worship of the angels, [3]taking his stand on *visions* he has seen, [4c]inflated without cause by his [d]fleshly mind,

19 and not holding fast to [a]the head, from whom [b]the entire body, being supplied and held together by the joints and [1]ligaments, grows with a growth [2]which is from God.

20 [a]If you have died with Christ [1]to the [b]elementary principles of the world, [c]why, as if you were living in the world, do you submit yourself to [d]decrees, such as,

21 "Do not handle, do not taste, do not touch!"

22 (which all *refer* [a]*to* things destined to perish [1]with use)—in accordance with the [b]commandments and teachings of men?

23 These are matters which have, to be sure, the [1]appearance of wisdom in [2a]self-made religion and self-abasement and [b]severe treatment of the body, *but are* of no value against [c]fleshly indulgence.

Chapter 3 Theme ______________________________

3 Therefore if you have been [a]raised up with Christ, keep seeking the things above, where Christ is, [b]seated at the right hand of God.

2 [1a]Set your mind on the things above, not on the things that are on earth.

3 For you have [a]died and your life is hidden with Christ in God.

4 When Christ, [a]who is our life, is revealed, [b]then you also will be revealed with Him in glory.

5 [a]Therefore [1]consider [b]the members of your earthly body as dead to [2c]immorality, impurity, passion, evil desire, and greed, which [3]amounts to idolatry.

6 For it is because of these things that [a]the wrath of God will come [1]upon the sons of disobedience,

7 and [a]in them you also once walked, when you were living [1]in them.

8 But now you also, [a]put them all aside: [b]anger, wrath, malice, slander, *and* [c]abusive speech from your mouth.

9 [1a]Do not lie to one another, since you [b]laid aside the old [2]self with its *evil* practices,

10 and have [a]put on the new self who is being [1b]renewed to a true knowledge [c]according to the image of the One who [d]created him—

10 [1]Lit *renovated* [a]Eph 4:24 [b]Rom 12:2; 2 Cor 4:16; Eph 4:23 [c]Gen 1:26; Rom 8:29 [d]Eph 2:10

15 [1]Or *divested Himself of* [2]Or *it;* i.e. the cross [a]Eph 4:8 [b]John 12:31; 1 Cor 15:24; Eph 3:10; Col 2:10 [c]2 Cor 2:14

16 [1]Lit *judge you* [2]Or *days* [a]Rom 14:3 [b]Mark 7:19; Rom 14:17; Heb 9:10 [c]Lev 23:2; Rom 14:5 [d]1 Chr 23:31; 2 Chr 31:3; Neh 10:33 [e]Mark 2:27f; Gal 4:10

17 [1]Lit *body* [2]Lit *of Christ* [a]Heb 8:5; 10:1

18 [1]Or *deciding against you* [2]Or *humility* [3]Or *going into detail about* [4]Or *conceited* [a]1 Cor 9:24; Phil 3:14 [b]Col 2:23 [c]1 Cor 4:6 [d]Rom 8:7

19 [1]Lit *bonds* [2]Lit *of God* [a]Eph 1:22 [b]Eph 1:23; 4:16

20 [1]Lit *from* [a]Rom 6:2 [b]Col 2:8 [c]Gal 4:9 [d]Col 2:14, 16

22 [1]Or *by being consumed* [a]1 Cor 6:13 [b]Is 29:13; Matt 15:9; Titus 1:14

23 [1]Lit *report;* Gr *logos* [2]Or *would-be religion* [a]Col 2:18 [b]1 Tim 4:3 [c]Rom 13:14; 1 Tim 4:8

3:1 [a]Col 2:12 [b]Ps 110:1; Mark 16:19

2 [1]Or *Be intent on* [a]Matt 16:23; Phil 3:19, 20

3 [a]Rom 6:2; 2 Cor 5:14; Col 2:20

4 [a]John 11:25; Gal 2:20 [b]1 Cor 1:7; Phil 3:21; 1 Pet 1:13; 1 John 2:28; 3:2

5 [1]Lit *put to death the members which are upon the earth* [2]Lit *fornication* [3]Lit *is* [a]Rom 8:13 [b]Col 2:11 [c]Mark 7:21f; 1 Cor 6:9f, 18; 2 Cor 12:21; Gal 5:19f; Eph 4:19; 5:3, 5

6 [1]Two early mss do not contain *upon the sons of disobedience* [a]Rom 1:18; Eph 5:6

7 [1]Or *among these* [a]Eph 2:2

8 [a]Eph 4:22 [b]Eph 4:31 [c]Eph 4:29

9 [1]Or *Stop lying* [2]Gr *anthropos* [a]Eph 4:25 [b]Eph 4:22

11 *a renewal* in which [a]there is no *distinction between* Greek
and Jew, [b]circumcised and uncircumcised, [1c]barbarian, Scythian,
[d]slave and freeman, but [e]Christ is all, and in all.
12 So, as those who have been [a]chosen of God, holy and
beloved, [b]put on a [c]heart of compassion, kindness, [d]humility,
gentleness and [1e]patience;
13 [a]bearing with one another, and [b]forgiving each other,
whoever has a complaint against anyone; [b]just as the Lord
forgave you, so also should you.
14 Beyond all these things *put on* love, which is [1a]the perfect
bond of [b]unity.
15 Let [a]the peace of Christ [1]rule in your hearts, to which
[2]indeed you were called in [b]one body; and [3]be thankful.
16 Let [a]the word of [1]Christ richly dwell within you, [2]with all
wisdom [b]teaching and admonishing [3]one another [c]with psalms
and hymns *and* spiritual songs, [d]singing [4]with thankfulness in
your hearts to God.
17 [a]Whatever you do in word or deed, *do* all in the name of
the Lord Jesus, [b]giving thanks through Him to God the Father.
18 [a]Wives, [b]be subject to your husbands, as is fitting in the Lord.
19 [a]Husbands, love your wives and do not be embittered against
them.
20 [a]Children, be obedient to your parents in all things, for this
is well-pleasing [1]to the Lord.
21 [a]Fathers, do not exasperate your children, so that they will
not lose heart.
22 [a]Slaves, in all things obey those who are your masters [1]on
earth, [b]not with [2]external service, as those who *merely* please
men, but with sincerity of heart, fearing the Lord.
23 Whatever you do, do your work [1]heartily, [a]as for the Lord
[2]rather than for men,
24 [a]knowing that from the Lord you will receive the reward
[1]of [b]the inheritance. It is the Lord Christ whom you [c]serve.
25 For [a]he who does wrong will receive the consequences of
the wrong which he has done, and [1b]that without partiality.

Chapter 4 Theme ______________________

4 Masters, grant to your slaves justice and fairness, [a]knowing
that you too have a Master in heaven.
2 [a]Devote yourselves to prayer, keeping alert in it with *an*
attitude of thanksgiving;
3 praying at the same time [a]for us as well, that God will open
up to us a [b]door for [c]the word, so that we may speak forth [d]the
mystery of Christ, for which I have also [e]been imprisoned;
4 that I may make it clear [a]in the way I ought to speak.
5 [1a]Conduct yourselves with wisdom toward [b]outsiders,
[2c]making the most of the opportunity.
6 [a]Let your speech always be [1]with grace, *as though* seasoned
with [b]salt, so that you will know how you should [c]respond to each
person.

11 [1]I.e. those who were not Greeks, either by birth or by culture [a]Rom 10:12; 1 Cor 12:13; Gal 3:28 [b]1 Cor 7:19; Gal 5:6 [c]Acts 28:2 [d]Eph 6:8 [e]Eph 1:23
12 [1]I.e. forbearance toward others [a]Luke 18:7 [b]Eph 4:24 [c]Luke 1:78; Gal 5:22f; Phil 2:1 [d]Eph 4:2; Phil 2:3 [e]1 Cor 13:4; 2 Cor 6:6
13 [a]Eph 4:2 [b]Rom 15:7; Eph 4:32
14 [1]Lit *the uniting bond of perfection* [a]Eph 4:3 [b]John 17:23; Heb 6:1
15 [1]Or *act as arbiter* [2]Lit *also* [3]Or *show yourselves thankful* [a]John 14:27 [b]Eph 2:16
16 [1]One early ms reads *the Lord* [2]Or *in* [3]Or *one another; singing with psalms...* [4]Or *by;* lit *in His grace* [a]Rom 10:17; Eph 5:26; 1 Thess 1:8 [b]Col 1:28 [c]Eph 5:19 [d]1 Cor 14:15
17 [a]1 Cor 10:31 [b]Eph 5:20; Col 3:15
18 [a]Col 3:18-4:1: *Eph 5:22-6:9* [b]Eph 5:22
19 [a]Eph 5:25; 1 Pet 3:7
20 [1]Lit *in* [a]Eph 6:1
21 [a]Eph 6:4
22 [1]Lit *according to the flesh* [2]Lit *eye-service* [a]Eph 6:5 [b]Eph 6:6
23 [1]Lit *from the soul* [2]Lit *and not* [a]Eph 6:7
24 [1]I.e. consisting of [a]Eph 6:8 [b]Acts 20:32; 1 Pet 1:4 [c]1 Cor 7:22
25 [1]Lit *there is no partiality* [a]Eph 6:8 [b]Deut 10:17; Acts 10:34; Eph 6:9
4:1 [a]Eph 6:9
2 [a]Acts 1:14; Eph 6:18
3 [a]Eph 6:19 [b]Acts 14:27 [c]2 Tim 4:2 [d]Eph 3:3, 4; 6:19 [e]Eph 6:20
4 [a]Eph 6:20
5 [1]Lit *Walk* [2]Lit *redeeming the time* [a]Eph 5:15 [b]Mark 4:11 [c]Eph 5:16
6 [1]Or *gracious* [a]Eph 4:29 [b]Mark 9:50 [c]1 Pet 3:15

7 [a]As to all my affairs, [b]Tychicus, *our* [c]beloved brother and
faithful servant and fellow bond-servant in the Lord, will bring
you information.
8 [a]*For* I have sent him to you for this very purpose, that you
may know about our circumstances and that he may
[b]encourage your hearts;
9 [1]and with him [a]Onesimus, *our* faithful and [b]beloved
brother, [c]who is one of your *number.* They will inform you
about the whole situation here.
10 [a]Aristarchus, my [b]fellow prisoner, sends you his greetings;
and *also* [c]Barnabas's cousin Mark (about whom you received
[1]instructions; [d]if he comes to you, welcome him);
11 and *also* Jesus who is called Justus; these are the only [a]fellow
workers for the kingdom of God [b]who are from the circumcision,
and they have proved to be an encouragement to me.
12 [a]Epaphras, [b]who is one of your number, a bondslave of
Jesus Christ, sends you his greetings, always [c]laboring earnestly
for you in his prayers, that you may [1]stand [2d]perfect and [3]fully
assured in all the will of God.
13 For I testify for him that he has [1]a deep concern for you
and for those who are in [a]Laodicea and Hierapolis.
14 [a]Luke, the beloved physician, sends you his greetings, and
also [b]Demas.
15 Greet the brethren who are in [a]Laodicea and also [1]Nympha
and [b]the church that is in [2]her house.
16 [a]When [1]this letter is read among you, have it also read in
the church of the Laodiceans; and you, for your part [a]read [1]my
letter *that is coming* from [b]Laodicea.
17 Say to [a]Archippus, "Take heed to the [b]ministry which you
have received in the Lord, that you may [1]fulfill it."
18 [1]I, Paul, [a]write this greeting with my own hand. [b]Remember
my [2c]imprisonment. [d]Grace be with you.

7 [a]Col 4:7-9: *Eph 6:21, 22* [b]Acts 20:4; 2 Tim 4:12 [c]Eph 6:21; Col 1:7

8 [a]Eph 6:22 [b]Col 2:2

9 [1]Lit *along with Onesimus* [a]Philem 10 [b]Col 1:7 [c]Col 4:12

10 [1]Or *orders* [a]Acts 19:29; 27:2; Philem 24 [b]Rom 16:7 [c]Acts 4:36; 12:12, 25; 15:37, 39 [d]2 Tim 4:11

11 [a]Rom 16:3 [b]Acts 11:2

12 [1]Or *stand firm* [2]Or *complete* or *mature* [3]Or *made complete* [a]Col 1:7; Philem 23 [b]Col 4:9 [c]Rom 15:30 [d]Col 1:28

13 [1]Or *much toil* or *great pain* [a]Col 2:1; 4:15f

14 [a]2 Tim 4:11; Philem 24 [b]2 Tim 4:10; Philem 24

15 [1]Or *Nymphas* (masc) [2]One early ms reads *their* [a]Col 2:1; 4:13, 16 [b]Rom 16:5

16 [1]Lit *the* [a]1 Thess 5:27; 2 Thess 3:14 [b]Col 2:1; 4:13, 15

17 [1]Or *continually fulfill* [a]Philem 2 [b]2 Tim 4:5

18 [1]Lit *The greeting by my hand of Paul* [2]Lit *bonds* [a]1 Cor 16:21 [b]Heb 13:3 [c]Phil 1:7; Col 4:3 [d]1 Tim 6:21; 2 Tim 4:22; Titus 3:15; Heb 13:25

Colossians Observations Chart

Author

Recipients

Warnings and Instructions

(continued)

Colossians Observations Chart

Colossians at a Glance

Theme of Colossians:

Segment Divisions	Chapter Themes
	1
	2
	3
	4

Author:

Date:

Purpose:

Key Words:

prayer

gospel

wisdom

knowledge

all (when it refers to completeness or totality)

faith

mystery

in Him (or before Him, through Him, etc.)

1 THESSALONIANS

Timothy joined Paul and Silas (Silvanus) while they were in Lystra on Paul's second missionary journey. Since his father was a Greek, Timothy hadn't been circumcised. Not wanting to cause any unnecessary conflicts with the Jews in those parts, Paul had Timothy circumcised. Things went smoothly on their journey until Paul had a vision of a man from Macedonia appealing to him to come and help them.

Believing this call was of God, the three went to Philippi—and the persecution began. Paul and Silas were beaten with rods and thrown into prison. Undaunted and convinced of their heavenly commission, the trio traveled on through Amphipolis and Apollonia and came to Thessalonica. There they found a Jewish synagogue, where for three Sabbaths Paul reasoned with the Thessalonians from the Scriptures. Jews and Greeks, including a number of leading women, heard and believed. The Jews who didn't like this became jealous and stirred up the city. Once again there was opposition, but this time the persecution was directed not only to the trio but also to those who had believed.

Consequently, the Thessalonian believers sent Paul, Silas, and Timothy to Berea by night where again the gospel bore fruit. When the Jews of Thessalonica heard what happened in Berea, they couldn't bear it and went there to persecute the men who were upsetting the world.

From Berea Paul went to Athens and then to Corinth. But the church at Thessalonica was on his heart. How were they doing in the midst of such adamant opposition? Paul had to find out. So about A.D. 51, while in Corinth, Paul wrote his first epistle to the church at Thessalonica.

THINGS TO DO

1. If you want to understand how the church in Thessalonica was established and the events surrounding it, read Acts 16:1–17:15.

2. Read 1 Thessalonians chapter by chapter. Mark every reference to the author(s) in one color, and every reference to the recipients in another. Include synonyms and pronouns.
   a. List what you learn about the author(s) on the chart on page 1940. Note the relationship of the author(s) to the recipients. What example do you see that's worthy of imitation?
   b. List everything you learn about the recipients. Note whom they had been serving. What happened when they heard and believed the gospel? What were they enduring, and how?
   c. Note the different problems or concerns addressed in the letter.

3. Read through the book and mark in the text the key words (along with their synonyms and pronouns) listed on the 1 THESSALONIANS AT A GLANCE chart on page 1941. When you finish, observe what you learn from marking each key word.

4. In chapters 4 and 5 are several truths about those "who have fallen asleep" and those "who are alive and remain." List what you observe about each on the OBSERVATIONS CHART at the top of page 1941. Note the progression of events in 1 Thessalonians 4:13-18. Ask the "5 W's and an H" of the text: Who is involved? What will happen? Where will they meet the Lord? When? Why are they not to sorrow? How will all this happen?

5. Record what you learn about *the day of the Lord* in chapter 5 on the chart on page 2076.

6. On 1 THESSALONIANS AT A GLANCE, record the theme of the book. Then record the theme of each chapter on the chart and in your Bible. Fill in any additional information under author, date, purpose, etc.

7. Often you will be able to note a turning point in an epistle as the author changes his emphasis. Such changes divide the book into segments. Where does the emphasis or content change in 1 Thessalonians? Note the topic in the first chapters of the book and when the subject changes. Title each segment of the book by thinking of the theme or subject discussed in the first three chapters and then in the last two chapters. Record your segment divisions on 1 THESSALONIANS AT A GLANCE.

Things to Think About

1. In this book Paul pours his life into other men who could carry on the work of the gospel. Are you spending time imparting the things God has done in your life to another person who can in turn minister to others? What can others imitate in you? Are you an example?

2. It is sometimes hard to give thanks in all things, yet that is the will of God. Go back over the last few days and think of the things that have happened in your life for which you have not given thanks. Determine in your heart to obey this command.

3. Are the circumstances in your life difficult? How are you responding? What will others say about your response? Can people imitate your walk with God?

4. Are you abstaining from sexual immorality? Are you defrauding others sexually in any way? Do you realize that if you are acting out your sexual passions in a way contrary to God's Word, God will act as the avenger against you?

5. Do you pray without ceasing (5:17) for those in your life who don't know the Lord? Do you boldly approach the Lord for answers to your problems? Do you pray consistently for others?

Chapter 1 Theme ______________________________

1 [a]Paul and [b]Silvanus and [c]Timothy,
To the [d]church of the Thessalonians in God the Father and
the Lord Jesus Christ: [e]Grace to you and peace.
2 [a]We give thanks to God always for all of you, [b]making
mention *of you* in our prayers;
3 constantly bearing in mind your [a]work of faith and labor of
[b]love and [1c]steadfastness of hope [2]in our Lord Jesus Christ in
the presence of [d]our God and Father,
4 knowing, [a]brethren beloved by God, [b]*His* choice of you;
5 for our [a]gospel did not come to you in word only, but also
[b]in power and in the Holy Spirit and with [c]full conviction; just
as you know [d]what kind of men we [1]proved to be among you
for your sake.
6 You also became [a]imitators of us and of the Lord, [b]having
received [c]the word in much tribulation with the [d]joy of the
Holy Spirit,
7 so that you became an example to all the believers in
[a]Macedonia and in [b]Achaia.

1:1 [a]2 Thess 1:1 [b]2 Cor 1:19 [c]Acts 16:1 [d]Acts 17:1 [e]Rom 1:7

2 [a]Rom 1:8; 2 Thess 1:3 [b]Rom 1:9

3 [1]Or *perseverance* [2]Lit *of* [a]John 6:29 [b]1 Cor 13:13 [c]Rom 8:25; 15:4 [d]Gal 1:4

4 [a]Rom 1:7; 2 Thess 2:13 [b]2 Pet 1:10

5 [1]Or *became* [a]1 Cor 9:14 [b]Rom 15:19 [c]Luke 1:1; Col 2:2 [d]1 Thess 2:10

6 [a]1 Cor 4:16; 11:1f [b]Acts 17:5-10 [c]2 Tim 4:2 [d]Acts 13:52; 2 Cor 6:10; Gal 5:22

7 [a]Rom 15:26 [b]Acts 18:12

8 For [a]the word of the Lord has [b]sounded forth from you, not
only in [c]Macedonia and [d]Achaia, but also [e]in every place your
faith toward God has gone forth, so that we have no need to
say anything.
9 For they themselves report about us what kind of a
[1a]reception we had [2]with you, and how you [b]turned to God
[c]from [3]idols to serve [4d]a living and true God,
10 and to [a]wait for His Son from [1]heaven, whom He [b]raised from
the dead, *that is* Jesus, who [c]rescues us from [d]the wrath to come.

Chapter 2 Theme ______________________________

2 For you yourselves know, brethren, that our [1a]coming to
you [b]was not in vain,
2 but after we had already suffered and been [a]mistreated in
[b]Philippi, as you know, we had the boldness in our God [c]to
speak to you the [d]gospel of God amid much [1e]opposition.
3 For our [a]exhortation does not *come* from [b]error or [c]impurity
or [1]by way of [d]deceit;
4 [a]but just as we have been approved by God to be [b]entrusted
with the gospel, so we speak, [c]not as pleasing men, but God
who [1d]examines our hearts.
5 For we never came [1]with flattering speech, as you know,
nor with [a]a pretext for greed—[b]God is witness—
6 nor did we [a]seek glory from men, either from you or from
others, even though as [b]apostles of Christ [1]we might have
[2]asserted our authority.
7 But we [1]proved to be [2a]gentle [3]among you, [b]as a nursing
mother [4]tenderly cares for her own children.
8 Having so fond an affection for you, we were well-pleased
to [a]impart to you not only the [b]gospel of God but also our own
[1]lives, because you had become [2]very dear to us.
9 For you recall, brethren, our [a]labor and hardship, *how*
[b]working night and day so as not to be a [c]burden to any of you,
we proclaimed to you the [d]gospel of God.
10 You are witnesses, and *so is* [a]God, [b]how devoutly and
uprightly and blamelessly we [1]behaved toward you [2]believers;
11 just as you know how we *were* [a]exhorting and encouraging
and [1b]imploring each one of you as [c]a father *would* his own
children,
12 so that you would [a]walk in a manner worthy of the God
who [b]calls you into His own kingdom and [c]glory.
13 For this reason we also constantly [a]thank God that when
you received the [b]word of God which you heard from us, you
accepted *it* [c]not *as* the word of men, but *for* what it really is,
the word of God, [d]which also performs its work in you who
believe.
14 For you, brethren, became [a]imitators of [b]the churches of
God in Christ Jesus that are [c]in Judea, for [d]you also endured
the same sufferings at the hands of your own countrymen,
[e]even as they *did* from the Jews,

8 [a]Col 3:16; 2 Thess 3:1 [b]Rom 10:18 [c]Rom 15:26 [d]Acts 18:12 [e]Rom 1:8; 16:19; 2 Cor 2:14
9 [1]Lit *entrance* [2]Lit *to* [3]Or *the idols* [4]Or *the* [a]1 Thess 2:1 [b]Acts 14:15 [c]1 Cor 12:2 [d]Matt 16:16
10 [1]Lit *the heavens* [a]Matt 16:27f; 1 Cor 1:7 [b]Acts 2:24 [c]Rom 5:9 [d]Matt 3:7; 1 Thess 2:16; 5:9
2:1 [1]Lit *entrance* [a]1 Thess 1:9 [b]2 Thess 1:10
2 [1]Or *struggle, conflict* [a]Acts 14:5; 16:19-24; Phil 1:30 [b]Acts 16:22-24 [c]Acts 17:1-9 [d]Rom 1:1 [e]Phil 1:30
3 [1]Lit *in deceit* [a]Acts 13:15 [b]2 Thess 2:11 [c]1 Thess 4:7 [d]2 Cor 4:2
4 [1]Or *approves* [a]2 Cor 2:17 [b]Gal 2:7 [c]Gal 1:10 [d]Rom 8:27
5 [1]Lit *in a word of flattery* [a]Acts 20:33; 2 Pet 2:3 [b]Rom 1:9; 1 Thess 2:10
6 [1]Lit *being able to* [2]Or *be burdensome* [a]John 5:41, 44; 2 Cor 4:5 [b]1 Cor 9:1f
7 [1]Or *became gentle* [2]Three early mss read *babes* [3]Lit *in the midst of you* [4]Or *cherishes* [a]2 Tim 2:24 [b]Gal 4:19; 1 Thess 2:11
8 [1]Or *souls* [2]Lit *beloved* [a]2 Cor 12:15; 1 John 3:16 [b]Rom 1:1
9 [a]Phil 4:16; 2 Thess 3:8 [b]Acts 18:3 [c]1 Cor 9:4f; 2 Cor 11:9 [d]Rom 1:1
10 [1]Lit *became* [2]Or *who believe* [a]1 Thess 2:5 [b]2 Cor 1:12; 1 Thess 1:5
11 [1]Or *testifying to* [a]1 Thess 5:14 [b]Luke 16:28; 1 Thess 4:6 [c]1 Cor 4:14; 1 Thess 2:7
12 [a]Eph 4:1 [b]Rom 8:28; 1 Thess 5:24; 2 Thess 2:14 [c]2 Cor 4:6; 1 Pet 5:10
13 [a]Rom 1:8; 1 Thess 1:2 [b]Rom 10:17; Heb 4:2 [c]Matt 10:20; Gal 4:14 [d]Heb 4:12
14 [a]1 Thess 1:6 [b]1 Cor 7:17; 10:32 [c]Gal 1:22 [d]Acts 17:5; 1 Thess 3:4; 2 Thess 1:4f [e]Heb 10:33f

15 [a]who both killed the Lord Jesus and [b]the prophets, and [1]drove
us out. [2]They are not pleasing to God, [2]but hostile to all men,
16 [a]hindering us from speaking to the Gentiles [b]so that they may
be saved; with the result that they always [c]fill up the measure
of their sins. But [d]wrath has come upon them [1]to the utmost.
17 But we, brethren, having been taken away from you for a
[1]short while—[a]in [2]person, not in [3]spirit—were all the more
eager with great desire [b]to see your face.
18 [1]For [a]we wanted to come to you—I, Paul, [2b]more than
once—and *yet* [c]Satan [d]hindered us.
19 For who is our hope or [a]joy or crown of exultation? Is it not
even you, in the presence of our Lord Jesus at His [1b]coming?
20 For you are [a]our glory and joy.

Chapter 3 Theme ______________________________________

3 Therefore [a]when we could endure *it* no longer, we thought
it best to be left behind at [b]Athens alone,
2 and we sent [a]Timothy, our brother and God's fellow worker
in the gospel of Christ, to strengthen and encourage you as to
your faith,
3 so that no one would be [1]disturbed by these afflictions; for
you yourselves know that [a]we have been destined for this.
4 For indeed when we were with you, we *kept* telling you in
advance that we were going to suffer affliction; [1a]and so it came
to pass, [2]as you know.
5 For this reason, [a]when I could endure *it* no longer, I also
[b]sent to [1]find out about your faith, for fear that [c]the tempter
might have tempted you, and [d]our labor would be in vain.
6 But now that [a]Timothy has come to us from you, and has
brought us good news of [b]your faith and love, and that you
always [c]think kindly of us, longing to see us just as we also long
to see you,
7 for this reason, brethren, in all our distress and affliction
we were comforted about you through your faith;
8 for now we *really* live, if you [a]stand firm in the Lord.
9 For [a]what thanks can we render to God for you in return
for all the joy with which we rejoice before our God on your
account,
10 as we [a]night and day keep praying most earnestly that we
may [b]see your face, and may [c]complete what is lacking in your
faith?
11 [a]Now may [b]our God and Father [c]Himself and Jesus our Lord
[d]direct our way to you;
12 and may the Lord cause you to increase and [a]abound in
love for one another, and for all people, just as we also *do* for
you;
13 so that He may [a]establish your hearts [b]without blame in
holiness before [c]our God and Father at the [1d]coming of our
Lord Jesus [e]with all His [2]saints.

15 [1]Or *persecuted us* [2]Lit *and* [a]Luke 24:20; Acts 2:23 [b]Matt 5:12; Acts 7:52

16 [1]Or *forever* or *altogether;* lit *to the end* [a]Acts 9:23; 13:45, 50; 14:2, 5, 19; 17:5, 13; 18:12; 21:21f, 27; 25:2, 7 [b]1 Cor 10:33 [c]Gen 15:16; Dan 8:23; Matt 23:32 [d]1 Thess 1:10

17 [1]Lit *occasion of an hour* [2]Lit *face* [3]Lit *heart* [a]1 Cor 5:3 [b]1 Thess 3:10

18 [1]Or *Because* [2]Lit *both once and twice* [a]Rom 15:22 [b]Phil 4:16 [c]Matt 4:10 [d]Rom 1:13; 15:22

19 [1]Or *presence* [a]Phil 4:1 [b]Matt 16:27; Mark 8:38; John 21:22; 1 Thess 3:13; 4:15; 5:23

20 [a]2 Cor 1:14

3:1 [a]1 Thess 3:5 [b]Acts 17:15f

2 [a]2 Cor 1:1; Col 1:1

3 [1]Or *deceived* [a]Acts 9:16; 14:22

4 [1]Lit *just as* [2]Lit *and* [a]1 Thess 2:14

5 [1]Or *to know, to ascertain* [a]Phil 2:19; 1 Thess 3:1 [b]1 Thess 3:2 [c]Matt 4:3 [d]2 Cor 6:1; Phil 2:16

6 [a]Acts 18:5 [b]1 Thess 1:3 [c]1 Cor 11:2

8 [a]1 Cor 16:13

9 [a]1 Thess 1:2

10 [a]2 Tim 1:3 [b]1 Thess 2:17 [c]2 Cor 13:9

11 [a]2 Thess 2:16 [b]Gal 1:4; 1 Thess 3:13 [c]1 Thess 4:16; 5:23; 2 Thess 2:16; 3:16; Rev 21:3 [d]2 Thess 3:5

12 [a]Phil 1:9; 1 Thess 4:1, 10; 2 Thess 1:3

13 [1]Or *presence* [2]Or *holy ones* [a]1 Cor 1:8; 1 Thess 3:2 [b]Luke 1:6 [c]Gal 1:4; 1 Thess 3:11 [d]1 Thess 2:19 [e]Matt 25:31; Mark 8:38; 1 Thess 4:17; 2 Thess 1:7

Chapter 4 Theme ________________________________

4 [a]Finally then, [b]brethren, we request and exhort you in the Lord Jesus, that as you received from us *instruction* as to how you ought to [1c]walk and [d]please God (just as you actually do [1]walk), that you [e]excel still more.

2 For you know what commandments we gave you [1]by *the authority of* the Lord Jesus.

3 For this is the will of God, your sanctification; *that is,* that you [a]abstain from [1]sexual immorality;

4 that [a]each of you know how to [1]possess his own [2b]vessel in sanctification and [c]honor,

5 not in [1a]lustful passion, like the Gentiles who [b]do not know God;

6 *and* that no man transgress and [a]defraud his brother [b]in the matter because [c]the Lord is *the* avenger in all these things, just as we also [d]told you before and solemnly warned *you.*

7 For [a]God has not called us for [b]the purpose of impurity, but [1]in sanctification.

8 So, he who rejects *this* is not rejecting man but the God who [a]gives His Holy Spirit to you.

9 Now as to the [a]love of the brethren, you [b]have no need for *anyone* to write to you, for you yourselves are [c]taught by God to love one another;

10 for indeed [a]you do practice it toward all the brethren who are in all Macedonia. But we urge you, brethren, to [b]excel still more,

11 and to make it your ambition [a]to lead a quiet life and [b]attend to your own business and [c]work with your hands, just as we commanded you,

12 so that you will [1a]behave properly toward [b]outsiders and [2c]not be in any need.

13 But [a]we do not want you to be uninformed, brethren, about those who [b]are asleep, so that you will not grieve as do [c]the rest who have [d]no hope.

14 For if we believe that Jesus died and rose again, [a]even so God will bring with Him [b]those who have fallen asleep [1]in Jesus.

15 For this we say to you [a]by the word of the Lord, that [b]we who are alive [1]and remain until [c]the coming of the Lord, will not precede [d]those who have fallen asleep.

16 For the Lord [a]Himself [b]will descend from heaven with a [1c]shout, with the voice of [d]*the* archangel and with the [e]trumpet of God, and [f]the dead in Christ will rise first.

17 Then [a]we who are alive [1]and remain will be [b]caught up together with them [c]in the clouds to meet the Lord in the air, and so we shall always [d]be with the Lord.

18 Therefore comfort one another with these words.

4:1 [1]Or *conduct yourselves* [a]2 Cor 13:11; 2 Thess 3:1 [b]Gal 6:1; 1 Thess 5:12; 2 Thess 1:3; 2:1; 3:1, 13 [c]Eph 4:1 [d]2 Cor 5:9 [e]Phil 1:9; 1 Thess 3:12; 4:10; 2 Thess 1:3
2 [1]Lit *through the Lord*
3 [1]Or *fornication* [a]1 Cor 6:18
4 [1]Or *acquire* [2]I.e. body; or wife [a]1 Cor 7:2, 9 [b]2 Cor 4:7; 1 Pet 3:7 [c]Rom 1:24
5 [1]Lit *passion of lust* [a]Rom 1:26 [b]Gal 4:8
6 [a]1 Cor 6:8 [b]2 Cor 7:11 [c]Rom 12:19; 13:4; Heb 13:4 [d]Luke 16:28; 1 Thess 2:11; Heb 2:6
7 [1]I.e. in the state or sphere of [a]1 Pet 1:15 [b]1 Thess 2:3
8 [a]Rom 5:5; 2 Cor 1:22; Gal 4:6; 1 John 3:24
9 [a]John 13:34; Rom 12:10 [b]2 Cor 9:1; 1 Thess 5:1 [c]Jer 31:33f; John 6:45; 1 John 2:27
10 [a]1 Thess 1:7 [b]1 Thess 3:12
11 [a]2 Thess 3:12 [b]1 Pet 4:15 [c]Acts 18:3; Eph 4:28; 2 Thess 3:10-12
12 [1]Lit *walk* [2]Lit *have need of nothing* [a]Rom 13:13; Col 4:5 [b]Mark 4:11 [c]Eph 4:28
13 [a]Rom 1:13 [b]Acts 7:60 [c]Eph 2:3; 1 Thess 5:6 [d]Eph 2:12
14 [1]Lit *through* [a]Rom 14:9; 2 Cor 4:14 [b]1 Cor 15:18; 1 Thess 4:13
15 [1]Lit *who* [a]1 Kin 13:17f; 20:35; 2 Cor 12:1; Gal 1:12 [b]1 Cor 15:52; 1 Thess 5:10 [c]1 Thess 2:19 [d]1 Cor 15:18; 1 Thess 4:13
16 [1]Or *cry of command* [a]1 Thess 3:11 [b]1 Thess 1:10; 2 Thess 1:7 [c]Joel 2:11 [d]Jude 9 [e]Matt 24:31 [f]1 Cor 15:23; 2 Thess 2:1; Rev 14:13
17 [1]Lit *who* [a]1 Cor 15:52; 1 Thess 5:10 [b]2 Cor 12:2 [c]Dan 7:13; Acts 1:9; Rev 11:12 [d]John 12:26

Chapter 5 Theme ________________________

5 Now as to the [a]times and the epochs, brethren, you [b]have
no need of anything to be written to you.
2 For you yourselves know full well that [a]the day of the Lord
[1]will come [b]just like a thief in the night.
3 While they are saying, "[a]Peace and safety!" then [1b]destruction
[2]will come upon them suddenly like [c]labor pains upon a woman
with child, and they will not escape.
4 But you, brethren, are not in [a]darkness, that the day would
overtake you [1b]like a thief;
5 for you are all [a]sons of light and sons of day. We are not of
night nor of [b]darkness;
6 so then let us not [a]sleep as [1b]others do, but let us be alert
and [2c]sober.
7 For those who sleep do their sleeping at night, and those
who get drunk get [a]drunk at night.
8 But since [a]we are of *the* day, let us [b]be [1]sober, having put
on the [c]breastplate of [d]faith and love, and as a [e]helmet, the
[f]hope of salvation.
9 For God has not destined us for [a]wrath, but for [b]obtaining
salvation through our Lord Jesus Christ,
10 [a]who died for us, so that whether we are awake or asleep,
we will live together with Him.
11 Therefore [1]encourage one another and [a]build up one
another, just as you also are doing.
12 But we request of you, brethren, that you [1a]appreciate
those [b]who diligently labor among you, and [c]have charge over
you in the Lord and give you [2]instruction,
13 and that you esteem them very highly in love because of
their work. [a]Live in peace with one another.
14 We urge you, brethren, admonish [a]the [1]unruly, encourage
[b]the fainthearted, help [c]the weak, be [d]patient with everyone.
15 See that [a]no one repays another with evil for evil, but always
[b]seek after that which is good for one another and for all people.
16 [a]Rejoice always;
17 [a]pray without ceasing;
18 in everything [a]give thanks; for this is God's will for you in
Christ Jesus.
19 [a]Do not quench the Spirit;
20 do not despise [a]prophetic [1]utterances.
21 But [a]examine everything *carefully;* [b]hold fast to that which
is good;
22 abstain from every [1]form of evil.
23 Now [a]may the God of peace [b]Himself sanctify you entirely;
and may your [c]spirit and soul and body be preserved complete,
[d]without blame at [e]the coming of our Lord Jesus Christ.
24 [a]Faithful is He who [b]calls you, and He also will bring it to
pass.

5:1 [a]Acts 1:7 [b]1 Thess 4:9
2 [1]Lit *is coming* [a]1 Cor 1:8 [b]Luke 21:34; 1 Thess 5:4; 2 Pet 3:10; Rev 3:3; 16:15
3 [1]Or *sudden destruction* [2]Lit *comes upon* [a]Jer 6:14; 8:11; Ezek 13:10 [b]2 Thess 1:9 [c]John 16:21
4 [1]One early ms reads *like thieves* [a]Acts 26:18; 1 John 2:8 [b]Luke 21:34; 1 Thess 5:2; 2 Pet 3:10; Rev 3:3; 16:15
5 [a]Luke 16:8 [b]Acts 26:18; 1 John 2:8
6 [1]Lit *the remaining ones* [2]Or *self-controlled* [a]Rom 13:11; 1 Thess 5:10 [b]Eph 2:3; 1 Thess 4:13 [c]1 Pet 1:13
7 [a]Acts 2:15; 2 Pet 2:13
8 [1]Or *self-controlled* [a]1 Thess 5:5 [b]1 Pet 1:13 [c]Is 59:17; Eph 6:14 [d]Eph 6:23 [e]Eph 6:17 [f]Rom 8:24
9 [a]1 Thess 1:10 [b]2 Thess 2:13f
10 [a]Rom 14:9
11 [1]Or *comfort* [a]Eph 4:29
12 [1]Lit *know* [2]Or *admonition* [a]1 Cor 16:18; 1 Tim 5:17 [b]Rom 16:6, 12; 1 Cor 15:10; 16:16 [c]Heb 13:17
13 [a]Mark 9:50
14 [1]Or *undisciplined* [a]2 Thess 3:6, 7, 11 [b]Is 35:4 [c]Rom 14:1f; 1 Cor 8:7ff; Rom 15:1 [d]1 Cor 13:4
15 [a]Matt 5:44; Rom 12:17; 1 Pet 3:9 [b]Rom 12:9; Gal 6:10; 1 Thess 5:21
16 [a]Phil 4:4
17 [a]Eph 6:18
18 [a]Eph 5:20
19 [a]Eph 4:30
20 [1]Or *gifts* [a]Acts 13:1; 1 Cor 14:31
21 [a]1 Cor 14:29; 1 John 4:1 [b]Rom 12:9; Gal 6:10; 1 Thess 5:15
22 [1]Or *appearance*

23 [a]Rom 15:33 [b]1 Thess 3:11 [c]Luke 1:46f; Heb 4:12 [d]James 1:4; 2 Pet 3:14 [e]1 Thess 2:19
24 [a]1 Cor 1:9; 2 Thess 3:3 [b]1 Thess 2:12

25 [1]Two early mss add *also* [a]Eph 6:19; 2 Thess 3:1; Heb 13:18
26 [a]Rom 16:16
27 [a]Col 4:16 [b]Acts 1:15
28 [a]Rom 16:20; 2 Thess 3:18

25 Brethren, [a]pray for us[1].
26 [a]Greet all the brethren with a holy kiss.
27 I adjure you by the Lord to [a]have this letter read to all the
[b]brethren.
28 [a]The grace of our Lord Jesus Christ be with you.

The Word Sounds Forth from Thessalonica

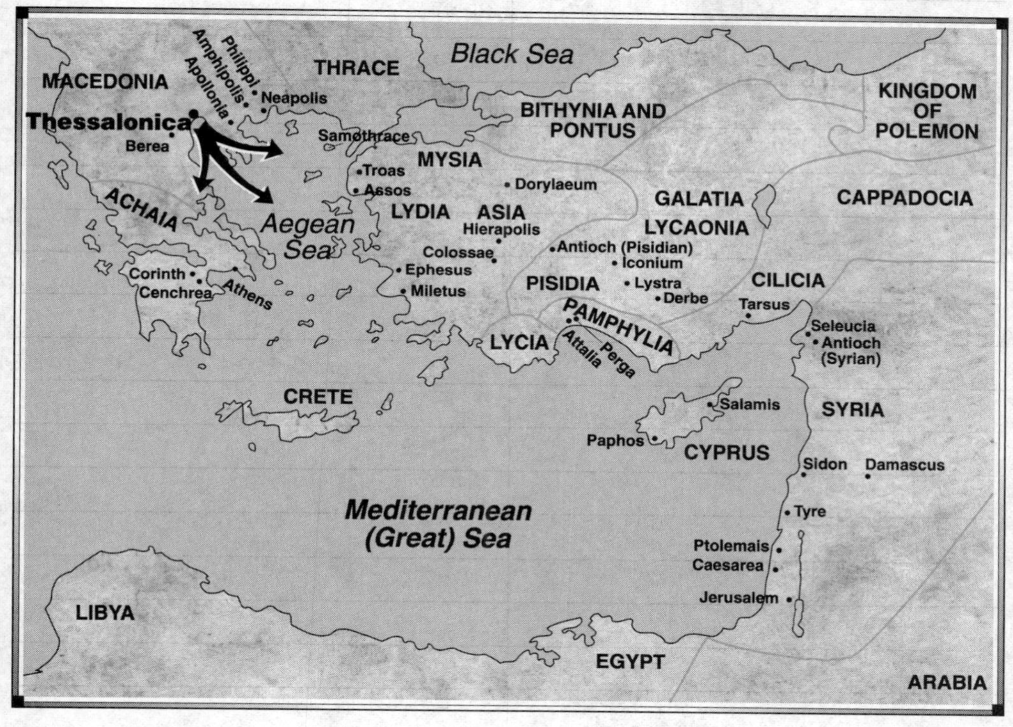

1 Thessalonians Observations Chart

Author(s)	Recipients

(continued)

1 THESSALONIANS 4:13-18		1 THESSALONIANS 5:1-11
THOSE WHO HAVE FALLEN ASLEEP	PROGRESSION OF EVENTS	THE DAY OF THE LORD
THOSE WHO ARE ALIVE AND REMAIN		

1 THESSALONIANS AT A GLANCE

Theme of 1 Thessalonians:

	SEGMENT DIVISIONS	CHAPTER THEMES
Author:		
Date:		1
Purpose:		
Key Words:		2
gospel (word)		
tribulation (suffered, affliction)		3
Spirit		
any reference to Jesus' coming		
faith		4
hope		
love		
day of the Lord		5
every reference to Satan (the tempter)		

2 THESSALONIANS

It had been four to six months since Paul wrote his first epistle to the church at Thessalonica in A.D. 51. Their persecution had not subsided, but much to Paul's joy, his labor had not been in vain; the beloved believers at Thessalonica had withstood the attacks of the tempter.

However, Paul was concerned about some things in the church. Once again, during his second missionary journey he had to take time to write—and put his distinguishing mark on this letter. The church had to know without a doubt that this letter was from him.

THINGS TO DO

1. If you haven't studied 1 Thessalonians, you should do so before you begin 2 Thessalonians. However, if you have worked through 1 Thessalonians, read it once again. Observe what Paul says about the coming of the Lord Jesus. Also give special attention to 1 Thessalonians 4:13–5:11.

2. Now read 2 Thessalonians. Mark references to the author(s) in one color and to the recipients in another. Note how 1 Thessalonians ties in with 2 Thessalonians. Look for the following information and record it on the OBSERVATIONS CHART on page 1946.

   a. What do you learn about the author and the recipients of this letter? What are the circumstances of the recipients?

   b. Paul addresses several problems that need correction. List these in the margin and on the chart. This will help you see his purpose in writing. Then note the instructions or commands related to each problem addressed. List these on your OBSERVATIONS CHART.

   c. Paul also praises the Thessalonians and encourages them about the things they are doing well. List the exhortations he includes in his letter.

   d. Be certain you record what happens to those who do not obey the gospel.

   e. From what you have observed, why do you think Paul wrote this book? Record this on 2 THESSALONIANS AT A GLANCE on page 1947 under "Purpose."

3. Read through 2 Thessalonians again, a chapter at a time, and do the following:

   a. Mark in the text the key words (including their synonyms and pronouns) listed on 2 THESSALONIANS AT A GLANCE. Also watch for any words you feel are key but aren't listed.

   b. Now go back through the key words and observe what you learned from marking these words. You may want to write your observations in your notebook.

4. On the OBSERVATIONS CHART are two more headings: "When the Day of the Lord Comes" and "When the Man of Lawlessness Is Revealed."

   a. Carefully read 2 Thessalonians 2:1-12 and list everything the chapter says must happen *before* the day of the Lord can come.

   b. Do the same for the revelation of the man of lawlessness.

   c. Record your insights on the chart THE DAY OF THE LORD on page 2076.

5. Think through each chapter and record its theme on 2 THESSALONIANS AT A GLANCE and in the appropriate place in your Bible. Also record the theme of the book, author, and date.

THINGS TO THINK ABOUT

1. How do you react to trials? Are you willing to suffer persecution? What does your response tell you and others about God? Do people see your faith? Is His love evident in your life?

2. Do you lead a disciplined life? Does your lifestyle encourage laziness in others? What are you doing for the furtherance of the kingdom? Or are you just waiting for Jesus to come back? Is this pleasing to God? Can you say, "Follow my example"?

3. When the good you do doesn't seem appreciated or even noticed, how do you feel? For whom are you doing it? Will you persevere?

4. Does what you believe about prophecy or any other doctrine come from a careful, personal study of God's Word, or does it come from what others teach you and books? Are you holding fast to what you know of the Word of God, or are you easily persuaded by "faddish" teaching?

Chapter 1 Theme ____________________

1 [a]Paul and [b]Silvanus and [c]Timothy,
To the [d]church of the Thessalonians in God our Father and the
Lord Jesus Christ:
2 [a]Grace to you and peace from God the Father and the Lord
Jesus Christ.
3 We ought always [a]to give thanks to God for you, [b]brethren,
as is *only* fitting, because your faith is greatly enlarged, and the
[c]love of each one of you toward one another grows *ever* greater;
4 therefore, we ourselves [a]speak proudly of you among [b]the
churches of God for your [1]perseverance and faith [b]in the midst
of all your persecutions and afflictions which you endure.
5 *This is* a [a]plain indication of God's righteous judgment so
that you will be [b]considered worthy of the kingdom of God, for
which indeed you are suffering.
6 [1]For after all [a]it is *only* just [2]for God to repay with affliction
those who afflict you,
7 and *to give* relief to you who are afflicted [1]and to us as well
[2a]when the Lord Jesus will be revealed [b]from heaven [c]with
[3]His mighty angels [d]in flaming fire,
8 dealing out retribution to those who [a]do not know God and
to those who [b]do not obey the gospel of our Lord Jesus.
9 These will pay the penalty of [a]eternal destruction, [b]away
from the presence of the Lord and from the glory of His power,
10 when He comes to be [a]glorified [1]in His [2]saints on that [b]day,
and to be marveled at among all who have believed—for our
[c]testimony to you was believed.
11 To this end also we [a]pray for you always, that our God will
[1b]count you worthy of your [c]calling, and fulfill every desire for
[d]goodness and the [e]work of faith with power,
12 so that the [a]name of our Lord Jesus will be glorified in you,
and you in Him, according to the grace of our God and *the*
Lord Jesus Christ.

1:1 [a]1 Thess 1:1 [b]2 Cor 1:19 [c]Acts 16:1 [d]Acts 17:1; 1 Thess 1:1
2 [a]Rom 1:7
3 [a]Rom 1:8; Eph 5:20; 1 Thess 1:2; 2 Thess 2:13 [b]1 Thess 4:1; 2 Thess 2:1 [c]1 Thess 3:12
4 [1]Or *steadfastness* [a]2 Cor 7:4; 1 Thess 2:19 [b]1 Cor 7:17; 1 Thess 2:14
5 [a]Phil 1:28 [b]Luke 20:35; 2 Thess 1:11
6 [1]Lit *If indeed* [2]Or *in the sight of* [a]Ex 23:22; Col 3:25; Heb 6:10
7 [1]Lit *along with us* [2]Lit *at the revelation of the Lord Jesus* [3]Lit *the angels of His power* [a]Luke 17:30 [b]1 Thess 4:16 [c]Jude 14 [d]Ex 3:2; 19:18; Is 66:15; Ezek 1:13; Dan 7:9; Matt 25:41; 1 Cor 3:13; Heb 10:27; 12:29; 2 Pet 3:7; Jude 7; Rev 14:10
8 [a]Gal 4:8 [b]Rom 2:8
9 [a]Phil 3:19; 1 Thess 5:3 [b]Is 2:10, 19, 21; 2 Thess 2:8
10 [1]Or *in the persons of* [2]Or *holy ones* [a]Is 49:3; John 17:10; 1 Thess 2:12 [b]Is 2:11ff; 1 Cor 3:13 [c]1 Cor 1:6; 1 Thess 2:1
11 [1]Or *make* [a]Col 1:9 [b]2 Thess 1:5 [c]Rom 11:29 [d]Rom 15:14 [e]1 Thess 1:3
12 [a]Is 24:15; 66:5; Mal 1:11; Phil 2:9ff

Chapter 2 Theme ________________________________

2 Now we request you, [a]brethren, with regard to the [1b]coming
of our Lord Jesus Christ and our [c]gathering together to Him,
2 that you not be quickly shaken from your [1]composure or be
disturbed either by a [a]spirit or a [2b]message or a [c]letter as if from
us, to the effect that [d]the day of the Lord [e]has come.
3 [a]Let no one in any way deceive you, for *it will not come*
unless the [1b]apostasy comes first, and the [c]man of lawlessness
is revealed, the [d]son of destruction,
4 who opposes and exalts himself above [1a]every so-called god
or object of worship, so that he takes his seat in the temple of
God, [b]displaying himself as being God.
5 Do you not remember that [a]while I was still with you, I
was telling you these things?
6 And you know [a]what restrains him now, so that in his time
he will be revealed.
7 For [a]the mystery of lawlessness is already at work; only [b]he
who now restrains *will do so* until he is taken out of the way.
8 Then that lawless one [a]will be revealed whom the Lord
will slay [b]with the breath of His mouth and bring to an end by
the [c]appearance of His [1]coming;
9 *that is,* the one whose [1]coming is in accord with the activity
of [a]Satan, with all power and [2b]signs and false wonders,
10 and with [1]all the deception of wickedness for [a]those who
perish, because they did not receive the love of [b]the truth so as
to be saved.
11 For this reason [a]God [1]will send upon them [2]a [b]deluding
influence so that they will believe [3]what is false,
12 in order that they all may be [1]judged who [a]did not believe
the truth, but [2b]took pleasure in wickedness.
13 [a]But we should always give thanks to God for you, [b]brethren
beloved by the Lord, because [c]God has chosen you [1]from the
beginning [d]for salvation [2e]through sanctification [3]by the Spirit
and faith in the truth.
14 It was for this He [a]called you through [b]our gospel, [1]that you
may gain the glory of our Lord Jesus Christ.
15 So then, brethren, [a]stand firm and [b]hold to the traditions
which you were taught, whether [c]by word *of mouth* or [c]by
letter [1]from us.
16 [a]Now may our Lord Jesus Christ [a]Himself and God our
Father, who has [b]loved us and given us eternal comfort and
[c]good hope by grace,
17 [a]comfort and [b]strengthen your hearts in every good work
and word.

Chapter 3 Theme ________________________________

3 [a]Finally, brethren, [b]pray for us that [c]the word of the Lord will
[1]spread rapidly and be glorified, just as *it did* also with you;
2 and that we will be [a]rescued from [1]perverse and evil men;
for not all have [2]faith.

2:1 [1]Or *presence* [a]2 Thess 1:3 [b]1 Thess 2:19 [c]Mark 13:27; 1 Thess 4:15-17
2 [1]Lit *mind* [2]Lit *word* [a]1 Cor 14:32; 1 John 4:1 [b]1 Thess 5:2; 2 Thess 2:15 [c]2 Thess 3:17 [d]1 Cor 1:8 [e]1 Cor 7:26
3 [1]Or *falling away from the faith* [a]Eph 5:6 [b]1 Tim 4:1 [c]Dan 7:25; 8:25; 11:36; 2 Thess 2:8; Rev 13:5ff [d]John 17:12
4 [1]Or *everyone who is called God* [a]1 Cor 8:5 [b]Is 14:14; Ezek 28:2
5 [a]1 Thess 3:4
6 [a]2 Thess 2:7
7 [a]Rev 17:5, 7 [b]2 Thess 2:6
8 [1]Or *presence* [a]Dan 7:25; 8:25; 11:36; 2 Thess 2:3; Rev 13:5ff [b]Is 11:4; Rev 2:16; 19:15 [c]1 Tim 6:14; 2 Tim 1:10; 4:1, 8; Titus 2:13
9 [1]Or *presence* [2]Or *attesting miracles* [a]Matt 4:10 [b]Matt 24:24; John 4:48
10 [1]Or *every deception* [a]1 Cor 1:18 [b]2 Thess 2:12, 13
11 [1]Lit *is sending* [2]Lit *an activity of error* [3]Or *the lie* [a]1 Kin 22:22; Rom 1:28 [b]1 Thess 2:3; 2 Tim 4:4
12 [1]Or *condemned* [2]Or *approved* [a]Rom 2:8 [b]Rom 1:32; 1 Cor 13:6
13 [1]One early ms reads *first fruits* [2]Lit *in* [3]Lit *of* [a]2 Thess 1:3 [b]1 Thess 1:4 [c]Eph 1:4ff [d]1 Cor 1:21; 1 Thess 2:12; 5:9; 1 Pet 1:5 [e]1 Thess 4:7; 1 Pet 1:2
14 [1]Lit *to the gaining of* [a]1 Thess 2:12 [b]1 Thess 1:5
15 [1]Lit *of* [a]1 Cor 16:13 [b]1 Cor 11:2; 2 Thess 3:6 [c]2 Thess 2:2
16 [a]1 Thess 3:11 [b]John 3:16 [c]Titus 3:7; 1 Pet 1:3
17 [a]1 Thess 3:2, 13 [b]2 Thess 3:3
3:1 [1]Lit *run* [a]1 Thess 4:1 [b]1 Thess 5:25 [c]1 Thess 1:8
2 [1]Lit *improper* [2]Or *the faith* [a]Rom 15:31

3 But [a]the Lord is faithful, [1]and He will strengthen and
protect you [2]from [b]the evil *one.*
4 We have [a]confidence in the Lord concerning you, that you
[b]are doing and will *continue to* do what we command.
5 May the Lord [a]direct your hearts into the love of God and
into the steadfastness of Christ.
6 Now we command you, brethren, [a]in the name of our Lord
Jesus Christ, that you [1b]keep away from every brother who
[2]leads an [3c]unruly life and not according to [d]the tradition which
[4]you received from us.
7 For you yourselves know how you ought to [1a]follow our
example, because we did not act in an undisciplined manner
among you,
8 nor did we [a]eat [1]anyone's bread [2]without paying for it, but
with [b]labor and hardship we *kept* [c]working night and day so
that we would not be a burden to any of you;
9 not because we do not have [a]the right *to this,* but in order
to offer ourselves [b]as a model for you, so that you would [1]follow
our example.
10 For even [a]when we were with you, we used to give you
this order: [b]if anyone is not willing to work, then he is not to
eat, either.
11 For we hear that some among you are [a]leading an undisciplined life, doing no work at all, but acting like [b]busybodies.
12 Now such persons we command and [a]exhort in the Lord
Jesus Christ to [b]work in quiet fashion and eat their own bread.
13 But as for you, [a]brethren, [b]do not grow weary of doing good.
14 If anyone does not obey our [1]instruction [2a]in this letter,
take special note of that person [3b]and do not associate with
him, so that he will be [c]put to shame.
15 *Yet* [a]do not regard him as an enemy, but [1b]admonish him as
a [c]brother.
16 Now [a]may the Lord of peace [b]Himself continually grant you
peace in every [1]circumstance. [c]The Lord be with you all!
17 [1]I, Paul, write this greeting [a]with my own hand, and this is
a distinguishing mark in every letter; this is the way I write.
18 [a]The grace of our Lord Jesus Christ be with you all.

3 [1]Lit *who will* [2]Or *from evil* [a]1 Cor 1:9; 1 Thess 5:24 [b]Matt 5:37
4 [a]2 Cor 2:3 [b]1 Thess 4:10
5 [a]1 Thess 3:11
6 [1]Or *avoid* [2]Lit *walks disorderly* [3]Or *undisciplined* [4]One early ms reads *they* [a]1 Cor 5:4 [b]Rom 16:17; 1 Cor 5:11; 2 Thess 3:14 [c]1 Thess 5:14; 2 Thess 3:7, 11 [d]1 Cor 11:2; 2 Thess 2:15
7 [1]Lit *imitate us* [a]1 Thess 1:6; 2 Thess 3:9
8 [1]Lit *from anyone* [2]Lit *freely* [a]1 Cor 9:4 [b]1 Thess 2:9 [c]Acts 18:3; Eph 4:28
9 [1]Lit *imitate us* [a]1 Cor 9:4ff [b]2 Thess 3:7
10 [a]1 Thess 3:4 [b]1 Thess 4:11
11 [a]2 Thess 3:6 [b]1 Tim 5:13; 1 Pet 4:15
12 [a]1 Thess 4:1 [b]1 Thess 4:11
13 [a]1 Thess 4:1 [b]2 Cor 4:1; Gal 6:9
14 [1]Lit *word* [2]Lit *through* [3]Lit *not to associate* [a]Col 4:16 [b]2 Thess 3:6 [c]1 Cor 4:14
15 [1]Or *keep admonishing* [a]Gal 6:1 [b]1 Thess 5:14 [c]2 Thess 3:6, 13
16 [1]Lit *way* [a]Rom 15:33 [b]1 Thess 3:11 [c]Ruth 2:4
17 [1]Lit *The greeting by my hand of Paul* [a]1 Cor 16:21
18 [a]Rom 16:20; 1 Thess 5:28

2 Thessalonians Observations Chart

Author	Recipients	Those Who Do Not Obey the Gospel

Problems/Concerns	Instructions	Exhortations

When the Day of the Lord Comes	When the Man of Lawlessness Is Revealed

2 Thessalonians at a Glance

Theme of 2 Thessalonians:

Segment Divisions	Chapter Themes
	1
	2
	3

Author:

Date:

Purpose:

Key Words:

affliction (suffering, persecutions)

coming of Jesus Christ (or synonymous references)

God

Spirit

love

faith

glory (glorified)

man of lawlessness

undisciplined (unruly)

day of the Lord (and pronouns)

truth

example (model)

1 *T*IMOTHY

Thirty years of labor for the gospel had taken its toll on Paul. His body bore the marks of a servant of Jesus Christ (Galatians 6:17). Yet the intensity of his suffering was minor compared to the intensity of his love and concern for the churches.

Undaunted by two years of house arrest in Rome, Paul pressed on toward the prize of the high calling in Christ Jesus. He intended to visit Asia, Macedonia, and possibly Spain. Spain had been on his heart before he became a prisoner of Rome.

Paul also was concerned about the church at Ephesus. Timothy, his faithful co-laborer, was pastoring that strategically important church. Possibly concerned that he might be delayed and that Timothy might need instructions to set before others as an ever-present reminder, Paul wrote to his beloved son in the faith an epistle that would become a legacy for the church, a pillar and support of the truth. It was around A.D. 62.

THINGS TO DO

1. Read 1 Timothy. Mark every reference to Paul in one color and every reference to Timothy in another. Include synonyms and pronouns. Note 1:3 and 3:14-15 to see why Paul wrote this epistle. On the 1 TIMOTHY AT A GLANCE chart on page 1957, record Paul's purpose for writing.

2. Read 1 Timothy again, one chapter at a time. On the OBSERVATIONS CHART on pages 1955, 1956:
   a. List what you learn from marking the references to Paul. Observe how he refers to himself, stating his position of authority, which qualifies him to instruct Timothy in the matters described in this letter.
   b. List what you observe from marking references to Timothy. Note where Timothy is and what his relationship is to Paul.
   c. List the commands and instructions Paul gives about specific groups of people or practices. Record what you learn about overseers (elders) and deacons. Also record what you see about general groups of believers in the church. There is a designated space for each of these groups on the OBSERVATIONS CHART.
   d. Record the specific charges Paul gives Timothy as his representative in Ephesus and as the one who is organizing and instructing the church there.

3. As you read, mark in the text the key words (with their synonyms and pronouns) listed on 1 TIMOTHY AT A GLANCE. These key words give clues about the most important and most often-mentioned instructions.

4. Unless you already recorded this on your OBSERVATIONS CHART, make a list of what you learn from the text about these key words. You'll see what is important to the health of the church.

5. What do you think the theme of 1 Timothy is? Are there problems or concerns the author must address? How does the theme relate to these concerns? Record the theme on 1 TIMOTHY AT A GLANCE and then list the theme of each chapter on the chart and in your Bible. Finally, fill in additional information under author, purpose, etc.

THINGS TO THINK ABOUT

1. Do you operate in your own church according to the principles set forth in 1 Timothy?
2. How do you esteem your local church leadership?
3. Do you pray on behalf of all men, including those in authority?

Chapter 1 Theme ______________

1 Paul, [a]an apostle of [b]Christ Jesus [c]according to the commandment of [c]God our Savior, and of [b]Christ Jesus, *who is*
our [d]hope,
2 To [a]Timothy, [a]*my* true child in *the* faith: [b]Grace, mercy *and*
peace from God the Father and [c]Christ Jesus our Lord.
3 As I urged you [1]upon my departure for [a]Macedonia, [2]remain
on at [b]Ephesus so that you
may instruct certain men not
to [c]teach strange doctrines,
4 nor to [1]pay attention to
[a]myths and endless [b]genea-
logies, which give rise to mere
[c]speculation rather than
[d]*furthering* [2]the administration of God which is by faith.
5 But the goal of our
[1a]instruction is love [b]from a
pure heart and a [c]good conscience and a sincere [d]faith.

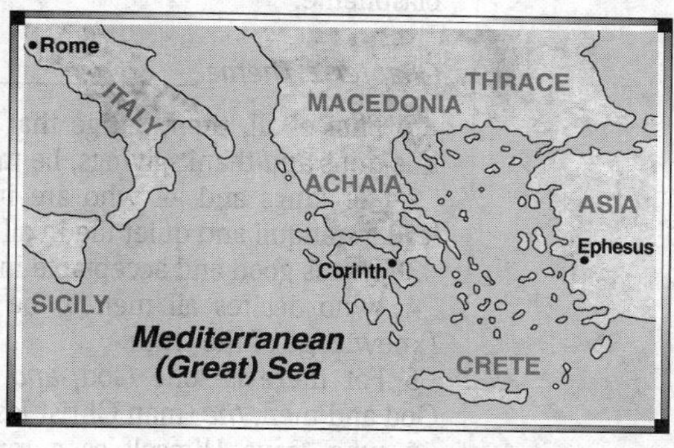

6 For some men, straying from these things, have turned
aside to [a]fruitless discussion,
7 [a]wanting to be [b]teachers of the Law, even though they do
not understand either what they are saying or the matters
about which they make confident assertions.
8 But we know that [a]the Law is good, if one uses it lawfully,
9 realizing the fact that [a]law is not made for a righteous person,
but for those who are lawless and [b]rebellious, for the [c]ungodly
and sinners, for the unholy and [d]profane, for those who kill their
fathers or mothers, for murderers
10 [1]and [2a]immoral men [1]and [b]homosexuals [1]and [c]kidnappers
[1]and [d]liars [1]and [e]perjurers, and whatever else is contrary to
[f]sound teaching,
11 according to [a]the glorious gospel of [b]the blessed God, with
which I have been [c]entrusted.
12 I thank [a]Christ Jesus our Lord, who has [b]strengthened me,
because He considered me faithful, [c]putting me into service,
13 even though I was formerly a blasphemer and a [a]persecutor
and a violent aggressor. Yet I was [b]shown mercy because [c]I
acted ignorantly in unbelief;
14 and the [a]grace of our Lord was more than abundant, with
the [b]faith and love which are *found* in Christ Jesus.
15 [a]It is a trustworthy statement, deserving full acceptance,
that [b]Christ Jesus came into the world to [c]save sinners, among
whom [d]I am foremost *of all.*
16 Yet for this reason I [a]found mercy, so that in me as the
foremost, Jesus Christ might [b]demonstrate His perfect patience
as an example for those [1]who would believe in Him for eternal
life.
17 Now to the [a]King [1]eternal, [b]immortal, [c]invisible, the [d]only
God, [e]*be* honor and glory [2]forever and ever. Amen.

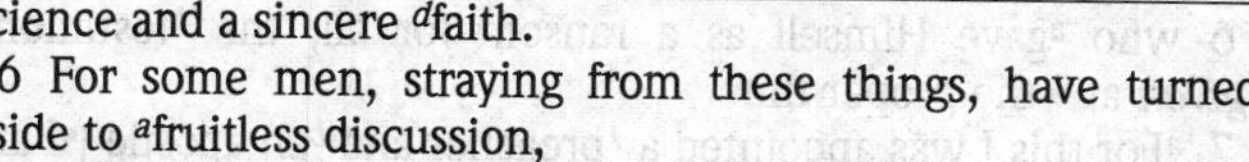

To Timothy at Ephesus

1:1 [a]2 Cor 1:1 [b]1 Tim 1:12 [c]Titus 1:3 [d]Col 1:27
2 [a]2 Tim 1:2 [b]Rom 1:7; 2 Tim 1:2; Titus 1:4 [c]1 Tim 1:12
3 [1]Lit *while going to* [2]Lit *to remain* [a]Rom 15:26 [b]Acts 18:19 [c]Rom 16:17; 2 Cor 11:4; Gal 1:6f; 1 Tim 6:3
4 [1]Or *occupy themselves with* [2]Lit *God's provision* [a]1 Tim 4:7; 2 Tim 4:4; Titus 1:14; 2 Pet 1:16 [b]Titus 3:9 [c]2 Tim 2:23 [d]Eph 3:2
5 [1]Lit *commandment* [a]1 Tim 1:18 [b]2 Tim 2:22 [c]1 Tim 1:19; 3:9; 2 Tim 1:3; 1 Pet 3:16, 21 [d]2 Tim 1:5
6 [a]Titus 1:10
7 [a]James 3:1 [b]Luke 2:46
8 [a]Rom 7:12, 16
9 [a]Gal 5:23 [b]Titus 1:6, 10 [c]1 Pet 4:18; Jude 15 [d]1 Tim 4:7; 6:20; Heb 12:16
10 [1]Lit *for* [2]Or *fornicators* [a]1 Cor 6:9 [b]Lev 18:22 [c]Ex 21:16; Rev 18:13 [d]Rev 21:8, 27; 22:15 [e]Matt 5:33 [f]1 Tim 4:6; 6:3; 2 Tim 4:3; Titus 1:9, 13; 2:1, 2
11 [a]2 Cor 4:4 [b]1 Tim 6:15 [c]Gal 2:7
12 [a]Gal 3:26 [b]Acts 9:22; Phil 4:13; 2 Tim 4:17 [c]Acts 9:15
13 [a]Acts 8:3 [b]1 Cor 7:25 [c]Acts 26:9
14 [a]Rom 5:20; 1 Cor 3:10; 2 Cor 4:15; Gal 1:13-16 [b]1 Thess 1:3; 1 Tim 2:15; 4:12; 6:11; 2 Tim 1:13; 2:22; Titus 2:2
15 [a]1 Tim 3:1; 4:9; 2 Tim 2:11; Titus 3:8 [b]Mark 2:17; Luke 15:2ff; 19:10 [c]Rom 11:14 [d]1 Cor 15:9; Eph 3:8
16 [1]Or *destined to* [a]1 Cor 7:25; 1 Tim 1:13 [b]Eph 2:7
17 [1]Lit *of the ages* [2]Lit *to the ages of the ages* [a]Rev 15:3 [b]1 Tim 6:16 [c]Col 1:15 [d]John 5:44; 1 Tim 6:15; Jude 25 [e]Rom 2:7, 10; 11:36; Heb 2:7

18 This [a]command I entrust to you, Timothy, [b]*my* [1]son, in
accordance with the [c]prophecies previously made concerning
you, that by them you [d]fight the good fight,
19 keeping [a]faith and a good conscience, which some have
rejected and suffered shipwreck in regard to [1b]their faith.
20 [1]Among these are [a]Hymenaeus and [b]Alexander, whom I
have [c]handed over to Satan, so that they will be [d]taught not to
blaspheme.

Chapter 2 Theme ____________________

2 First of all, then, I urge that [a]entreaties *and* prayers, petitions *and* thanksgivings, be made on behalf of all men,
2 [a]for kings and all who are in [1]authority, so that we may
lead a tranquil and quiet life in all godliness and [2]dignity.
3 This is good and acceptable in the sight of [a]God our Savior,
4 [a]who desires all men to be [b]saved and to [c]come to the
[1]knowledge of the truth.
5 For there is [a]one God, *and* [b]one mediator also between
God and men, *the* [c]man Christ Jesus,
6 who [a]gave Himself as a ransom for all, the [b]testimony
[1]*given* at [2c]the proper time.
7 [a]For this I was appointed a [1]preacher and [b]an apostle ([c]I am
telling the truth, I am not lying) as a teacher of [d]the Gentiles in
faith and truth.
8 Therefore [a]I want the men [b]in every place to pray, [c]lifting
up [d]holy hands, without wrath and dissension.
9 Likewise, *I want* [a]women to adorn themselves with proper
clothing, [1]modestly and discreetly, not with braided hair and
gold or pearls or costly garments,
10 but rather by means of good works, as is proper for women
making a claim to godliness.
11 [a]A woman must quietly receive instruction with entire
submissiveness.
12 [a]But I do not allow a woman to teach or exercise authority
over a man, but to remain quiet.
13 [a]For it was Adam who was first [1]created, *and* then Eve.
14 And *it was* not Adam *who* was deceived, but [a]the woman
being deceived, [1]fell into transgression.
15 But *women* will be [1]preserved through the bearing of
children if they continue in [a]faith and love and sanctity with
[2]self-restraint.

Chapter 3 Theme ____________________

3 [a]It is a trustworthy statement: if any man aspires to the [b]of-
fice of [1]overseer, it is a fine work he desires *to do.*
2 [1a]An overseer, then, must be above reproach, [b]the husband of
one wife, [c]temperate, prudent, respectable, [d]hospitable, [e]able to
teach,
3 [a]not addicted to wine [1]or pugnacious, but gentle, peaceable,
[b]free from the love of money.

18 [1]Or *child* [a]1 Tim 1:5 [b]1 Tim 1:2 [c]1 Tim 4:14 [d]2 Cor 10:4; 1 Tim 6:12; 2 Tim 2:3f; 4:7

19 [1]Lit *the* [a]1 Tim 1:5 [b]1 Tim 6:12, 21; 2 Tim 2:18

20 [1]Lit *Of* [a]2 Tim 2:17 [b]2 Tim 4:14 [c]1 Cor 5:5 [d]1 Cor 11:32; Heb 12:5ff

2:1 [a]Eph 6:18

2 [1]Or *a high position* [2]Or *seriousness* [a]Ezra 6:10; Rom 13:1

3 [a]Luke 1:47; 1 Tim 1:1; 4:10

4 [1]Or *recognition* [a]Ezek 18:23, 32; John 3:17; 1 Tim 4:10; Titus 2:11; 2 Pet 3:9 [b]Rom 11:14 [c]2 Tim 2:25; 3:7; Titus 1:1; Heb 10:26

5 [a]Rom 3:30; 10:12; 1 Cor 8:4 [b]1 Cor 8:6; Gal 3:20 [c]Matt 1:1; Rom 1:3

6 [1]Or to be given [2]Lit *its own times* [a]Matt 20:28; Gal 1:4 [b]1 Cor 1:6 [c]Mark 1:15; Gal 4:4; 1 Tim 6:15; Titus 1:3

7 [1]Or *herald* [a]Eph 3:8; 1 Tim 1:11; 2 Tim 1:11 [b]1 Cor 9:1 [c]Rom 9:1 [d]Acts 9:15

8 [a]Phil 1:12; 1 Tim 5:14; Titus 3:8 [b]John 4:21; 1 Cor 1:2; 2 Cor 2:14; 1 Thess 1:8 [c]Ps 63:4; Luke 24:50 [d]Ps 24:4; James 4:8

9 [1]Lit *with modesty* [a]1 Pet 3:3

11 [a]1 Cor 14:34; Titus 2:5

12 [a]1 Cor 14:34; Titus 2:5

13 [1]Or *formed* [a]Gen 2:7, 22; 3:16; 1 Cor 11:8ff

14 [1]Lit *has come* [a]Gen 3:6, 13; 2 Cor 11:3

15 [1]Lit *saved* [2]Or *discretion* [a]1 Tim 1:14

3:1 [1]Or *bishop* [a]1 Tim 1:15 [b]Acts 20:28; Phil 1:1

2 [1]Lit *The* [a]1 Tim 3:2-4; Titus 1:6-8 [b]Luke 2:36f; 1 Tim 5:9; Titus 1:6 [c]1 Tim 3:8, 11; Titus 2:2 [d]Rom 12:13; Titus 1:8; Heb 13:2; 1 Pet 4:9 [e]2 Tim 2:24

3 [1]Lit *not* [a]Titus 1:7 [b]1 Tim 3:8; 6:10; Titus 1:7; Heb 13:5

4 *He must be* one who [a]manages his own household well,
keeping his children under control with all dignity
5 (but if a man does not know how to manage his own
household, how will he take care of [a]the church of God?),
6 *and* not a new convert, so that he will not become [a]conceited
and fall into the [b]condemnation [1]incurred by the devil.
7 And he must [a]have a good reputation with [b]those outside
the church, so that he will not fall into reproach and [c]the snare
of the devil.
8 [a]Deacons likewise *must be* men of dignity, not [1]double-
tongued, [2b]or addicted to much wine [2c]or fond of sordid gain,
9 [a]*but* holding to the mystery of the faith with a clear
conscience.
10 [a]These men must also first be tested; then let them serve
as deacons if they are beyond reproach.
11 [1]Women *must* likewise *be* dignified, [a]not malicious gossips,
but [b]temperate, faithful in all things.
12 [a]Deacons must be [b]husbands of *only* one wife, *and* [1c]good
managers of *their* children and their own households.
13 For those who have served well as deacons [a]obtain for
themselves a [1]high standing and great confidence in the faith
that is in Christ Jesus.
14 I am writing these things to you, hoping to come to you
before long;
15 but [1]in case I am delayed, *I write* so that you will know how
[2]one ought to conduct himself in [a]the household of God, which
is the [b]church of [c]the living God, the [d]pillar and support of the
truth.
16 By common confession, great is [a]the mystery of godliness:
He who was [b]revealed in the flesh,
Was [1c]vindicated [2]in the Spirit,
[d]Seen by angels,
[e]Proclaimed among the nations,
[f]Believed on in the world,
[g]Taken up in glory.

Chapter 4 Theme __________________________

4 But [a]the Spirit explicitly says that [b]in later times some will
[1]fall away from the faith, paying attention to [c]deceitful spirits and [d]doctrines of demons,
2 by means of the hypocrisy of liars [a]seared in their own
conscience as with a branding iron,
3 *men* who [a]forbid marriage *and advocate* [b]abstaining from
foods which [c]God has created to be [d]gratefully shared in by
those who believe and know the truth.
4 For [a]everything created by God is good, and nothing is to
be rejected if it is [b]received with gratitude;
5 for it is sanctified by means of [a]the word of God and prayer.
6 In pointing out these things to [a]the brethren, you will be a
good [b]servant of Christ Jesus, *constantly* nourished on the

4 [a]1 Tim 3:12
5 [a]1 Cor 10:32; 1 Tim 3:15
6 [1]Lit *of the devil* [a]1 Tim 6:4; 2 Tim 3:4 [b]1 Tim 3:7
7 [a]2 Cor 8:21 [b]Mark 4:11 [c]1 Tim 6:9; 2 Tim 2:26
8 [1]Or *given to double-talk* [2]Lit *not* [a]Phil 1:1; 1 Tim 3:12 [b]1 Tim 5:23; Titus 2:3 [c]1 Tim 3:3; Titus 1:7; 1 Pet 5:2
9 [a]1 Tim 1:5, 19
10 [a]1 Tim 5:22
11 [1]I.e. either deacons' wives or deaconesses [a]2 Tim 3:3; Titus 2:3 [b]1 Tim 3:2
12 [1]Lit *managing well* [a]Phil 1:1; 1 Tim 3:8 [b]1 Tim 3:2 [c]1 Tim 3:4
13 [1]Lit *good* [a]Matt 25:21
15 [1]Lit *if I delay* [2]Or *you ought to conduct yourself* [a]1 Cor 3:16; 2 Cor 6:16; Eph 2:21f; 1 Pet 2:5; 4:17 [b]1 Tim 3:5 [c]Matt 16:16; 1 Tim 4:10 [d]Gal 2:9; 2 Tim 2:19
16 [1]Or *justified* [2]Or *by* [a]Rom 16:25 [b]John 1:14; 1 Pet 1:20; 1 John 3:5, 8 [c]Rom 3:4 [d]Luke 2:13; 24:4; 1 Pet 1:12 [e]Rom 16:26; 2 Cor 1:19; Col 1:23 [f]2 Thess 1:10 [g]Mark 16:19; Acts 1:9
4:1 [1]I.e. apostacize [a]John 16:13; Acts 20:23; 21:11; 1 Cor 2:10f [b]2 Thess 2:3ff; 2 Tim 3:1; 2 Pet 3:3; Jude 18 [c]1 John 4:6 [d]James 3:15
2 [a]Eph 4:19
3 [a]Heb 13:4 [b]Col 2:16, 23 [c]Gen 1:29; 9:3 [d]Rom 14:6; 1 Cor 10:30f; 1 Tim 4:4
4 [a]1 Cor 10:26 [b]Rom 14:6; 1 Cor 10:30f; 1 Tim 4:3
5 [a]Gen 1:25, 31; Heb 11:3
6 [a]Acts 1:15 [b]2 Cor 11:23

words of the faith and of the [1c]sound doctrine which you [d]have
been following.
7 But [1]have nothing to do with [a]worldly [b]fables fit only for old
women. On the other hand, discipline yourself for the purpose
of [c]godliness;
8 for [a]bodily discipline is only of little profit, but [b]godliness is
profitable for all things, since it [c]holds promise for the [d]present
life and *also* for the *life* to come.
9 [a]It is a trustworthy statement deserving full acceptance.
10 For it is for this we labor and strive, because we have fixed
[a]our hope on [b]the living God, who is [c]the Savior of all men,
especially of believers.
11 [1a]Prescribe and teach these things.
12 [a]Let no one look down on your youthfulness, but *rather* in
speech, conduct, [b]love, faith *and* purity, show yourself [c]an
example [1]of those who believe.
13 [a]Until I come, give attention to the *public* [b]reading *of
Scripture,* to exhortation and teaching.
14 Do not neglect the spiritual gift within you, which was
bestowed on you through [a]prophetic utterance with [b]the laying
on of hands by the [1c]presbytery.
15 Take pains with these things; be *absorbed* in them, so that
your progress will be evident to all.
16 [a]Pay close attention to yourself and to your teaching;
persevere in these things, for as you do this you will [1b]ensure
salvation both for yourself and for those who hear you.

Chapter 5 Theme ________________________________

5 [a]Do not sharply rebuke an [b]older man, but *rather* appeal to
him as a father, *to* [c]the younger men as brothers,
2 the older women as mothers, *and* the younger women as
sisters, in all purity.
3 Honor widows who are [a]widows indeed;
4 but if any widow has children or grandchildren, [a]they must
first learn to practice piety in regard to their own family and to
[1]make some return to their parents; for this is [b]acceptable in
the sight of God.
5 Now she who is a [a]widow indeed and who has been left
alone, [b]has fixed her hope on God and continues in [c]entreaties
and prayers night and day.
6 But she who [a]gives herself to wanton pleasure is [b]dead
even while she lives.
7 [1a]Prescribe these things as well, so that they may be above
reproach.
8 But if anyone does not provide for his own, and especially
for those of his household, he has [a]denied the faith and is
worse than an unbeliever.
9 A widow is to be [a]put on the list only if she is not less than
sixty years old, *having been* [b]the wife of one man,
10 having a reputation for [a]good works; *and* if she has brought
up children, if she has [b]shown hospitality to strangers, if she

6 [1]Lit *good* [c]1 Tim 1:10 [d]Luke 1:3; Phil 2:20, 22; 2 Tim 3:10

7 [1]Or *reject* [a]1 Tim 1:9 [b]1 Tim 1:4 [c]1 Tim 4:8; 6:3, 5f; 2 Tim 3:5

8 [a]Col 2:23 [b]1 Tim 4:7; 6:3, 5f; 2 Tim 3:5 [c]Ps 37:9, 11; Prov 19:23; 22:4; Matt 6:33 [d]Matt 6:33; 12:32; Mark 10:30

9 [a]1 Tim 1:15

10 [a]2 Cor 1:10; 1 Tim 6:17 [b]1 Tim 3:15 [c]John 4:42; 1 Tim 2:4

11 [1]Or *Keep commanding and teaching* [a]1 Tim 5:7; 6:2

12 [1]Or *to* [a]1 Cor 16:11; Titus 2:15 [b]Titus 2:7; 1 Pet 5:3 [c]1 Tim 1:14

13 [a]1 Tim 3:14 [b]2 Tim 3:15ff

14 [1]Or *board of elders* [a]1 Tim 1:18 [b]Acts 6:6; 1 Tim 5:22; 2 Tim 1:6 [c]Acts 11:30

16 [1]Lit *save both yourself and those* [a]Acts 20:28 [b]1 Cor 1:21

5:1 [a]Lev 19:32 [b]Titus 2:2 [c]Titus 2:6

3 [a]Acts 6:1; 9:39, 41; 1 Tim 5:5, 16

4 [1]Lit *give back recompenses* [a]Eph 6:2 [b]1 Tim 2:3

5 [a]Acts 6:1; 9:39, 41; 1 Tim 5:3, 16 [b]1 Cor 7:34; 1 Pet 3:5 [c]Luke 2:37; 1 Tim 2:1; 2 Tim 1:3

6 [a]James 5:5 [b]Luke 15:24; 2 Tim 3:6; Rev 3:1

7 [1]Or *Keep commanding* [a]1 Tim 4:11

8 [a]2 Tim 2:12; Titus 1:16; 2 Pet 2:1; Jude 4

9 [a]1 Tim 5:16 [b]1 Tim 3:2

10 [a]Acts 9:36; 1 Tim 6:18; Titus 2:7; 3:8; 1 Pet 2:12 [b]1 Tim 3:2

[c]has washed the [1]saints' feet, if she has [d]assisted those in
distress, *and* if she has devoted herself to every good work.
11 But refuse *to put* younger widows *on the list,* for when
they feel [a]sensual desires in disregard of Christ, they want to
get married,
12 *thus* incurring condemnation, because they have set aside
their previous [1]pledge.
13 At the same time they also learn *to be* idle, as they go around
from house to house; and not merely idle, but also [a]gossips and
[b]busybodies, talking about [c]things not proper *to mention.*
14 Therefore, I want younger *widows* to get [a]married, bear
children, [b]keep house, *and* [c]give the enemy no occasion for
reproach;
15 for some [a]have already turned aside to follow [b]Satan.
16 If any woman who is a believer [a]has *dependent* widows,
she must [b]assist them and the church must not be burdened,
so that it may assist those who are [c]widows indeed.
17 [a]The elders who [b]rule well are to be considered worthy of
double honor, especially those who [c]work hard [1]at preaching
and teaching.
18 For the Scripture says, "[a]YOU SHALL NOT MUZZLE THE OX WHILE
HE IS THRESHING," and "[b]The laborer is worthy of his wages."
19 Do not receive an accusation against an [a]elder except on
the basis of [b]two or three witnesses.
20 Those who continue in sin, [a]rebuke in the presence of all,
[b]so that the rest also will be fearful *of sinning.*
21 [a]I solemnly charge you in the presence of God and of
Christ Jesus and of *His* chosen angels, to maintain these
principles without bias, doing nothing in a *spirit of* partiality.
22 [a]Do not lay hands upon anyone *too* hastily and [1]thereby
share [b]*responsibility for* the sins of others; keep yourself [2]free
from sin.
23 No longer drink water *exclusively,* but [a]use a little wine for
the sake of your stomach and your frequent ailments.
24 The sins of some men are quite evident, going before them
to judgment; for others, their *sins* [a]follow after.
25 Likewise also, deeds that are good are quite evident, and
[a]those which are otherwise cannot be concealed.

Chapter 6 Theme ________________________

6 [a]All who are under the yoke as slaves are to regard their
own masters as worthy of all honor so [b]that the name of
God and *our* doctrine will not be [1]spoken against.
2 Those who have believers as their masters must not be
disrespectful to them because they are [a]brethren, but must serve
them all the more, because those who [1]partake of the benefit
are believers and beloved. [b]Teach and [2]preach these *principles.*
3 If anyone [a]advocates a different doctrine and does not
[1]agree with [b]sound words, those of our Lord Jesus Christ, and
with the doctrine [c]conforming to godliness,

10 [1]Or *holy ones* [c]Luke 7:44; John 13:14 [d]1 Tim 5:16
11 [a]Rev 18:7
12 [1]Lit *faith*
13 [a]3 John 10 [b]2 Thess 3:11 [c]Titus 1:11
14 [a]1 Cor 7:9; 1 Tim 4:3 [b]Titus 2:5 [c]1 Tim 6:1
15 [a]1 Tim 1:20 [b]Matt 4:10
16 [a]1 Tim 5:4 [b]1 Tim 5:10 [c]1 Tim 5:3
17 [1]Lit *in word* [a]Acts 11:30; 1 Tim 4:14; 5:19 [b]Rom 12:8 [c]1 Thess 5:12
18 [a]Deut 25:4; 1 Cor 9:9 [b]Lev 19:13; Deut 24:15; Matt 10:10; Luke 10:7; 1 Cor 9:14
19 [a]Acts 11:30; 1 Tim 4:14; 5:17 [b]Deut 17:6; 19:15; Matt 18:16
20 [a]Gal 2:14; Eph 5:11; 2 Tim 4:2 [b]2 Cor 7:11
21 [a]Luke 9:26; 1 Tim 6:13; 2 Tim 2:14; 4:1
22 [1]Lit *do not share* [2]Lit *pure* [a]1 Tim 3:10; 4:14 [b]Eph 5:11; 1 Tim 3:2-7
23 [a]1 Tim 3:8
24 [a]Rev 14:13
25 [a]Prov 10:9
6:1 [1]Or *blasphemed* [a]Eph 6:5; Titus 2:9; 1 Pet 2:18 [b]Titus 2:5
2 [1]Or *devote themselves to kindness* [2]Lit *exhort, urge* [a]Acts 1:15; Gal 3:28; Philem 16 [b]1 Tim 4:11
3 [1]Lit *come to;* or *come with* [a]1 Tim 1:3 [b]1 Tim 1:10 [c]Titus 1:1

4 he is [a]conceited *and* understands nothing; but he [1]has a morbid interest in [b]controversial questions and [c]disputes about words, out of which arise envy, strife, abusive language, evil suspicions,

5 and constant friction between [a]men of depraved mind and deprived of the truth, who [b]suppose that [1]godliness is a means of gain.

6 [a]But godliness *actually* is a means of [b]great gain when accompanied by [c]contentment.

7 For [a]we have brought nothing into the world, so we cannot take anything out of it either.

8 If we [a]have food and covering, with these we shall be content.

9 [a]But those who want to get rich fall into temptation and [b]a snare and many foolish and harmful desires which plunge men into ruin and destruction.

10 For [a]the love of money is a root of all [1]sorts of evil, and some by longing for it have [b]wandered away from the faith and pierced themselves with many griefs.

11 But [a]flee from these things, you [b]man of God, and pursue righteousness, godliness, [c]faith, [d]love, [1]perseverance *and* gentleness.

12 [a]Fight the good fight of [b]faith; [c]take hold of the eternal life [d]to which you were called, and you made the good [e]confession in the presence of [f]many witnesses.

13 [a]I charge you in the presence of God, who [1]gives life to all things, and of [b]Christ Jesus, who testified the [c]good confession [d]before Pontius Pilate,

14 that you keep the commandment without stain or reproach until the [a]appearing of our Lord Jesus Christ,

15 which He will [1]bring about at [a]the proper time—He who is [b]the blessed and [c]only Sovereign, [d]the King of [2]kings and [e]Lord of [3]lords,

16 [a]who alone possesses immortality and [b]dwells in unapproachable light, [c]whom no man has seen or can see. [a]To Him *be* honor and eternal dominion! Amen.

17 Instruct those who are rich in [a]this present world [b]not to be conceited or to [c]fix their hope on the uncertainty of riches, but on God, [d]who richly supplies us with all things to enjoy.

18 *Instruct them* to do good, to be rich in [a]good [1]works, [b]to be generous and ready to share,

19 [a]storing up for themselves the treasure of a good foundation for the future, so that they may [b]take hold of that which is life indeed.

20 O [a]Timothy, guard [b]what has been entrusted to you, avoiding [c]worldly *and* empty chatter *and* the opposing arguments of what is falsely called "knowledge"—

21 which some have professed and thus [a]gone astray [1]from [b]the faith.

[c]Grace be with you.

4 [1]Lit *is sick about* [a]1 Tim 3:6 [b]1 Tim 1:4 [c]Acts 18:15; 2 Tim 2:14
5 [1]Or *religion* [a]2 Tim 3:8; Titus 1:15 [b]Titus 1:11; 2 Pet 2:3
6 [a]Luke 12:15-21; 1 Tim 6:6-10 [b]1 Tim 4:8 [c]Phil 4:11; Heb 13:5
7 [a]Job 1:21; Eccl 5:15
8 [a]Prov 30:8
9 [a]Prov 15:27; 23:4; 28:20; Luke 12:21; 1 Tim 6:17 [b]1 Tim 3:7
10 [1]Lit *the evils* [a]Col 3:5; 1 Tim 3:3; 6:9 [b]James 5:19
11 [1]Or *steadfastness* [a]2 Tim 2:22 [b]2 Tim 3:17 [c]1 Tim 1:14 [d]2 Tim 3:10
12 [a]1 Cor 9:25f; Phil 1:30; 1 Tim 1:18 [b]1 Tim 1:19 [c]Phil 3:12; 1 Tim 6:19 [d]Col 3:15 [e]2 Cor 9:13; 1 Tim 6:13 [f]1 Tim 4:14; 2 Tim 2:2
13 [1]Or *preserves alive* [a]1 Tim 5:21 [b]Gal 3:26; 1 Tim 1:12, 15; 2:5 [c]2 Cor 9:13; 1 Tim 6:12 [d]Matt 27:2; John 18:37
14 [a]2 Thess 2:8
15 [1]Lit *show* [2]Lit *those who reign as kings* [3]Lit *those who rule as lords* [a]1 Tim 2:6 [b]1 Tim 1:11 [c]1 Tim 1:17 [d]Deut 10:17; Rev 17:14; 19:16 [e]Ps 136:3
16 [a]1 Tim 1:17 [b]Ps 104:2; James 1:17; 1 John 1:5 [c]John 1:18
17 [a]Matt 12:32; 2 Tim 4:10; Titus 2:12 [b]Ps 62:10; Luke 12:20; Rom 11:20; 1 Tim 6:9 [c]1 Tim 4:10 [d]Acts 14:17
18 [1]Or *deeds* [a]1 Tim 5:10 [b]Rom 12:8; Eph 4:28
19 [a]Matt 6:20 [b]1 Tim 6:12
20 [a]1 Tim 1:2 [b]2 Tim 1:12, 14 [c]1 Tim 1:9; 2 Tim 2:16
21 [1]Lit *concerning* [a]2 Tim 2:18 [b]1 Tim 1:19 [c]Col 4:18

1 Timothy Observations Chart

Paul	Timothy

Overseers (Elders)	Deacons	Men
	Slaves	Rich (or Those Who Want to Be)

(continued)

1 Timothy Observations Chart

Women	Charges and Instructions to Timothy
Widows	
Prayer	

1 Timothy at a Glance

Theme of 1 Timothy:

Author:	Segment Divisions	Chapter Themes
Date:		1
Purpose:		
Key Words:		2
teach		
faith		3
doctrine		
godliness		4
money (rich, riches)		
any reference to the devil		5
all references to prayer		
		6

2 *T*IMOTHY

Paul now found himself in a new set of circumstances. It was about A.D. 64 (some say A.D. 67), and Timothy was heavy on his heart. Paul had to write one last letter to his disciple, reminding Timothy of crucial matters concerning the ministry and urging him to make every effort to come quickly—before winter—because...

THINGS TO DO

1. Read 2 Timothy. Mark every reference to Paul in one color and Timothy in another. In chapters 1, 2, and 4, Paul refers to his circumstances: where he is and what is about to take place in his life. To help set the context of this letter, record on the OBSERVATIONS CHART on page 1963 anything you learn about Paul that would answer the "5 W's and an H": who, what, when, where, why, and how.

2. Read 2 Timothy again. Observe everything you marked regarding Timothy and record your insights on the OBSERVATIONS CHART.

3. As you read 2 Timothy you probably noticed the many commands and/or instructions Paul gave Timothy. These are easy to see because the verb usually comes first in the sentence and the "you" is implied. An example of this is seen in 1:13: "Retain the standard of sound words."

   a. List the instructions and/or commands Paul gives Timothy throughout the letter on the OBSERVATIONS CHART. (Note the chapter and verse in which you find each.)

   b. As you look for these instructions and/or commands, mark in the text the key words (and their synonyms and pronouns) listed on the 2 TIMOTHY AT A GLANCE chart on page 1964. When you mark references to the gospel, don't miss synonyms such as *sound words, word, Scripture, sacred writings,* etc.

4. Think back over the list of instructions and commands Paul gives Timothy and keep in mind the emphasis Paul places on the gospel. What do you think Paul's main message is to Timothy in this epistle? Record this as the theme of the book on 2 TIMOTHY AT A GLANCE.

5. Look at the book one chapter at a time and summarize the main teaching or theme of each chapter on 2 TIMOTHY AT A GLANCE and in your Bible. (Note: The theme of each chapter should relate to the general theme of the book.)

6. On 2 TIMOTHY AT A GLANCE you will see space to trace two themes, "Paul's Example" and "God's Provision," that run throughout the book. Doing this will give you additional insight into the practicality of 2 Timothy for your own life. Examine each chapter in the light of these two themes and record your insights on the appropriate spaces on the chart.

THINGS TO THINK ABOUT

1. What is your responsibility toward the gospel? To what lengths will you go in order to carry out this responsibility?

2. What are you doing to make sure you handle the Word of God accurately? Do you simply repeat what you have been taught or are you carefully studying the Word systematically?

3. Are you willing to suffer for the sake of those who would come to know the Lord Jesus Christ and receive salvation?

4. What kind of men and women do you need to beware of in these last days?

5. How are you living? Are you a coward or have you fought the good fight of faith?
6. Are you ready to die? How will you feel when you see Jesus Christ face-to-face?

Chapter 1 Theme ________________________

1 Paul, [a]an apostle of [b]Christ Jesus [1c]by the will of God, according to the promise of [d]life in Christ Jesus,
2 To [a]Timothy, my beloved [1b]son: [c]Grace, mercy *and* peace
from God the Father and Christ Jesus our Lord.
3 [a]I thank God, whom I [b]serve with a [c]clear conscience [1]the
way my forefathers did, [d]as I constantly remember you in my
[2]prayers night and day,
4 [a]longing to see you, [b]even as I recall your tears, so that I
may be filled with joy.
5 [1]For I am mindful of the [a]sincere faith within you, which
first dwelt in your grandmother Lois and [b]your mother Eunice,
and I am sure that *it is* in you as well.
6 For this reason I remind you to kindle afresh [a]the gift of
God which is in you through [a]the laying on of my hands.
7 For God has not given us a [a]spirit of [1]timidity, but of power
and love and [2]discipline.
8 Therefore [a]do not be ashamed of the [b]testimony of our Lord
or of me [c]His prisoner, but join with *me* in [d]suffering for the
[e]gospel according to the power of God,
9 who has [a]saved us and [b]called us with a holy [c]calling, [d]not
according to our works, but according to His own [b]purpose and
grace which was granted us in [e]Christ Jesus from [f]all eternity,
10 but [a]now has been revealed by the [b]appearing of our Savior
[c]Christ Jesus, who [d]abolished death and brought life and
immortality to light through the gospel,
11 [a]for which I was appointed a preacher and an apostle and a
teacher.
12 For this reason I also suffer these things, but [a]I am not
ashamed; for I know [b]whom I have believed and I am convinced
that He is able to [c]guard what I have entrusted to Him [1]until
[d]that day.
13 [1a]Retain the [b]standard of [c]sound words [d]which you have
heard from me, in the [e]faith and love which are in [f]Christ Jesus.
14 Guard, through the Holy Spirit who [a]dwells in us, the
[1b]treasure which has been entrusted to *you*.
15 You are aware of the fact that all who are in [1a]Asia [b]turned
away from me, among whom are Phygelus and Hermogenes.
16 The Lord grant mercy to [a]the house of Onesiphorus, for he
often refreshed me and [b]was not ashamed of my [1c]chains;
17 but when he was in Rome, he eagerly searched for me and
found me—
18 the Lord grant to him to find mercy from the Lord on [a]that
day—and you know very well what services he rendered at
[b]Ephesus.

1:1 [1]Lit *through* [a]2 Cor 1:1 [b]Gal 3:26 [c]1 Cor 1:1 [d]1 Tim 6:19
2 [1]Or *child* [a]Acts 16:1; 1 Tim 1:2 [b]1 Tim 1:2; 2 Tim 2:1; Titus 1:4 [c]Rom 1:7
3 [1]Lit *from my forefathers* [2]Or *petitions* [a]Rom 1:8 [b]Acts 24:14 [c]Acts 23:1; 24:16; 1 Tim 1:5 [d]Rom 1:9
4 [a]2 Tim 4:9, 21 [b]Acts 20:37
5 [1]Lit *Receiving remembrance of* [a]1 Tim 1:5 [b]Acts 16:1; 2 Tim 3:15
6 [a]1 Tim 4:14
7 [1]Or *cowardice* [2]Or *sound judgment* [a]John 14:27; Rom 8:15
8 [a]Mark 8:38; Rom 1:16; 2 Tim 1:12, 16 [b]1 Cor 1:6 [c]Eph 3:1; 2 Tim 1:16 [d]2 Tim 2:3, 9; 4:5 [e]2 Tim 1:10; 2:8
9 [a]Rom 11:14 [b]Rom 8:28ff [c]Rom 11:29 [d]Eph 2:9 [e]2 Tim 1:1 [f]Rom 16:25; Eph 1:4; Titus 1:2
10 [a]Rom 16:26 [b]2 Thess 2:8; 2 Tim 4:1, 8; Titus 2:11 [c]2 Tim 1:1 [d]1 Cor 15:26; Heb 2:14f
11 [a]1 Tim 2:7
12 [1]Or *for* [a]2 Tim 1:8, 16 [b]Titus 3:8 [c]1 Tim 6:20; 2 Tim 1:14 [d]1 Cor 1:8; 3:13; 2 Tim 1:18; 4:8
13 [1]Or *Hold the example* [a]2 Tim 3:14; Titus 1:9 [b]Rom 2:20; 6:17 [c]1 Tim 1:10 [d]2 Tim 2:2 [e]1 Tim 1:14 [f]2 Tim 1:1
14 [1]Lit *good deposit* [a]Rom 8:9 [b]1 Tim 6:20; 2 Tim 1:12
15 [1]I.e. the province of Asia [a]Acts 2:9 [b]2 Tim 4:10, 11, 16
16 [1]Lit *chain* [a]2 Tim 4:19 [b]2 Tim 1:8 [c]Eph 6:20
18 [a]1 Cor 1:8; 3:13; 2 Tim 1:12; 4:8 [b]Acts 18:19; 1 Tim 1:3

Chapter 2 Theme ______________________________

2 You therefore, my [1a]son, [b]be strong in the grace that is in
[c]Christ Jesus.
2 The things [a]which you have heard from me in the presence
of [b]many witnesses, [c]entrust these to [d]faithful men who will be
[e]able to teach others also.
3 [a]Suffer hardship with *me,* as a good [b]soldier of [c]Christ Jesus.
4 No soldier in active service [a]entangles himself in the affairs
of everyday life, so that he may please the one who enlisted
him as a soldier.
5 Also if anyone [a]competes as an athlete, he [1]does not win
the prize unless he competes according to the rules.
6 [a]The hard-working farmer ought to be the first to receive
his share of the crops.
7 Consider what I say, for the Lord will give you understanding
in everything.
8 Remember Jesus Christ, [a]risen from the dead, [b]descendant
of David, [c]according to my gospel,
9 [1]for which I [a]suffer hardship even to [b]imprisonment as a
[c]criminal; but [d]the word of God [e]is not imprisoned.
10 For this reason [a]I endure all things for [b]the sake of those
who are chosen, [c]so that they also may obtain the [d]salvation
which is in [e]Christ Jesus *and* with *it* [f]eternal glory.
11 [a]It is a trustworthy statement:
For [b]if we died with Him, we will also live with Him;
12 If we endure, [a]we will also reign with Him;
If we [1b]deny Him, He also will deny us;
13 If we are faithless, [a]He remains faithful, for [b]He cannot
deny Himself.
14 Remind *them* of these things, and solemnly [a]charge *them* in
the presence of God not to [b]wrangle about words, which is
useless *and leads* to the ruin of the hearers.
15 Be diligent to [a]present yourself approved to God as a
workman who does not need to be ashamed, accurately handling
[b]the word of truth.
16 But [a]avoid [b]worldly *and* empty chatter, for [1]it will lead to
further ungodliness,
17 and their [1]talk will spread like [2]gangrene. Among them are
[a]Hymenaeus and Philetus,
18 *men* who have gone astray from the truth saying that [a]the
resurrection has already taken place, and they upset [b]the faith
of some.
19 Nevertheless, the [a]firm foundation of God stands, having this
[b]seal, "[c]The Lord knows those who are His," and, "[d]Everyone
who names the name of the Lord is to abstain from wickedness."
20 Now in a large house there are not only gold and silver
vessels, but also vessels of wood and of earthenware, and [a]some
to honor and some to dishonor.
21 Therefore, if anyone cleanses himself from [a]these *things,* he
will be a vessel for honor, sanctified, useful to the Master,
[b]prepared for every good work.

2:1 [1]Or *child* [a]2 Tim 1:2 [b]Eph 6:10 [c]2 Tim 1:1
2 [a]2 Tim 1:13 [b]1 Tim 6:12 [c]1 Tim 1:18 [d]1 Tim 1:12 [e]2 Cor 2:14ff; 3:5
3 [a]2 Tim 1:8 [b]1 Cor 9:7; 1 Tim 1:18 [c]2 Tim 1:1
4 [a]2 Pet 2:20
5 [1]Lit *is not crowned* [a]1 Cor 9:25
6 [a]1 Cor 9:10
8 [a]Acts 2:24 [b]Matt 1:1 [c]Rom 2:16
9 [1]Lit *in which* [a]2 Tim 1:8; 2:3 [b]Phil 1:7 [c]Luke 23:32 [d]1 Thess 1:8 [e]Acts 28:31; 2 Tim 4:17
10 [a]Col 1:24 [b]Luke 18:7; Titus 1:1 [c]2 Cor 1:6; 1 Thess 5:9 [d]1 Cor 1:21 [e]2 Tim 1:1; 2:1, 3 [f]2 Cor 4:17; 1 Pet 5:10
11 [a]1 Tim 1:15 [b]Rom 6:8; 1 Thess 5:10
12 [1]Lit *will deny* [a]Matt 19:28; Luke 22:29; Rom 5:17; 8:17 [b]Matt 10:33; Luke 12:9; 1 Tim 5:8
13 [a]Rom 3:3; 1 Cor 1:9 [b]Num 23:19; Titus 1:2
14 [a]1 Tim 5:21; 2 Tim 4:1 [b]1 Tim 6:4; 2 Tim 2:23; Titus 3:9
15 [a]Rom 6:13; James 1:12 [b]Eph 1:13; James 1:18
16 [1]Lit *they will make further progress in ungodliness* [a]Titus 3:9 [b]1 Tim 1:9; 6:20
17 [1]Lit *word* [2]Or *cancer* [a]1 Tim 1:20
18 [a]1 Cor 15:12 [b]1 Tim 1:19; Titus 1:11
19 [a]Is 28:16f; 1 Tim 3:15 [b]John 3:33 [c]John 10:14; 1 Cor 8:3 [d]Luke 13:27; 1 Cor 1:2
20 [a]Rom 9:21
21 [a]1 Tim 6:11; 2 Tim 2:16-18 [b]2 Cor 9:8; Eph 2:10; 2 Tim 3:17

22 Now [a]flee from youthful lusts and pursue righteousness,
[b]faith, love *and* peace, with those who [c]call on the Lord [d]from a
pure heart.
23 But refuse foolish and ignorant [a]speculations, knowing that
they [b]produce [1]quarrels.
24 [a]The Lord's bond-servant must not be quarrelsome, but be
kind to all, [b]able to teach, patient when wronged,
25 [a]with gentleness correcting those who are in opposition, [b]if
perhaps God may grant them repentance leading to [c]the
knowledge of the truth,
26 and they may come to their senses *and escape* from [a]the snare
of the devil, having been [b]held captive [1]by him to do his will.

Chapter 3 Theme ____

3 But realize this, that [a]in the last days difficult times will come.
2 For men will be [a]lovers of self, [b]lovers of money, [c]boastful,
[c]arrogant, [d]revilers, [c]disobedient to parents, [e]ungrateful, [f]unholy,
3 [a]unloving, irreconcilable, [b]malicious gossips, without self-
control, brutal, [1c]haters of good,
4 [a]treacherous, [b]reckless, [c]conceited, [d]lovers of pleasure rather
than lovers of God,
5 holding to a form of [1a]godliness, although they have [b]denied
its power; [c]Avoid such men as these.
6 For among them are those who [1a]enter into households and
captivate [2b]weak women weighed down with sins, led on by
[c]various impulses,
7 always learning and never able to [a]come to the [1]knowledge
of the truth.
8 Just as [a]Jannes and Jambres [b]opposed Moses, so these *men*
also oppose the truth, [c]men of depraved mind, rejected in regard
to the faith.
9 But they will not make further progress; for their [a]folly will
be obvious to all, just [b]as [1]Jannes's and Jambres's folly was also.
10 Now you [a]followed my teaching, conduct, purpose, faith,
patience, [b]love, [1]perseverance,
11 [a]persecutions, *and* [b]sufferings, such as happened to me at
[c]Antioch, at [d]Iconium *and* at [e]Lystra; what [f]persecutions I
endured, and out of them all [g]the Lord rescued me!
12 Indeed, all who desire to live godly in Christ Jesus [a]will be
persecuted.
13 But evil men and impostors [a]will proceed *from bad* to
worse, [b]deceiving and being deceived.
14 You, however, [a]continue in the things you have learned and
become convinced of, knowing from whom you have learned
them,
15 and that [a]from childhood you have known [b]the sacred
writings which are able to [c]give you the wisdom that leads to
[d]salvation through faith which is in [e]Christ Jesus.
16 [a]All Scripture is [1]inspired by God and profitable for teaching,
for reproof, for correction, for [2]training in righteousness;

22 [a]1 Tim 6:11 [b]1 Tim 1:14 [c]Acts 7:59 [d]1 Tim 1:5
23 [1]Lit *fightings* [a]1 Tim 6:4; 2 Tim 2:14; Titus 3:9 [b]Titus 3:9; James 4:1
24 [a]1 Tim 3:3; Titus 1:7 [b]1 Tim 3:2
25 [a]Gal 6:1; Titus 3:2; 1 Pet 3:15 [b]Acts 8:22 [c]1 Tim 2:4
26 [1]Or *by him, to do His will* [a]1 Tim 3:7 [b]Luke 5:10
3:1 [a]1 Tim 4:1
2 [a]Phil 2:21 [b]Luke 16:14; 1 Tim 3:3; 6:10 [c]Rom 1:30 [d]2 Pet 2:10-12 [e]Luke 6:35 [f]1 Tim 1:9
3 [1]Lit *not loving good* [a]Rom 1:31 [b]1 Tim 3:11 [c]Titus 1:8
4 [a]Acts 7:52 [b]Acts 19:36 [c]1 Tim 3:6 [d]Phil 3:19
5 [1]Or *religion* [a]1 Tim 4:7 [b]1 Tim 5:8 [c]Matt 7:15; 2 Thess 3:6
6 [1]Or *creep into* [2]Or *idle* [a]Jude 4 [b]1 Tim 5:6; Titus 3:3 [c]Titus 3:3
7 [1]Or *recognition* [a]2 Tim 2:25
8 [a]Ex 7:11 [b]Acts 13:8 [c]1 Tim 6:5
9 [1]Lit *that of those* [a]Luke 6:11 [b]Ex 7:11, 12; 8:18; 9:11
10 [1]Or *steadfastness* [a]Phil 2:20, 22; 1 Tim 4:6 [b]1 Tim 6:11
11 [a]2 Cor 12:10 [b]2 Cor 1:5, 7 [c]Acts 13:14, 45, 50 [d]Acts 14:1-7, 19 [e]Acts 14:8-20 [f]2 Cor 11:23-27 [g]Rom 15:31
12 [a]John 15:20; Acts 14:22; 2 Cor 4:9f
13 [a]2 Tim 2:16 [b]Titus 3:3
14 [a]2 Tim 1:13; Titus 1:9
15 [a]2 Tim 1:5 [b]John 5:47; Rom 2:27 [c]Ps 119:98f [d]1 Cor 1:21 [e]2 Tim 1:1
16 [1]Lit *God-breathed* [2]Lit *training which is in* [a]Rom 4:23f; 15:4; 2 Pet 1:20f

17 so that [a]the man of God may be adequate, [b]equipped for
every good work.

Chapter 4 Theme ______________________

4 [a]I solemnly charge *you* in the presence of God and of
Christ Jesus, who is to [b]judge the living and the dead, and
by His [c]appearing and His kingdom:
2 preach [a]the word; be ready in season *and* out of season;
[b]reprove, rebuke, exhort, with [1]great [c]patience and instruction.
3 For [a]the time will come when they will not endure [b]sound
doctrine; but *wanting* to have their ears tickled, they will
accumulate for themselves teachers in accordance to their own
desires,
4 and [a]will turn away their ears from the truth and [b]will turn
aside to myths.
5 But you, [a]be sober in all things, [b]endure hardship, do the
work of an [c]evangelist, fulfill your [d]ministry.
6 For I am already being [a]poured out as a drink offering, and
the time of [b]my departure has come.
7 [a]I have fought the good fight, I have finished [b]the course, I
have kept [c]the faith;
8 in the future there [a]is laid up for me [b]the crown of righteousness, which the Lord, the righteous Judge, will award to me on
[c]that day; and not only to me, but also to [d]all who have loved
His [e]appearing.
9 [a]Make every effort to come to me soon;
10 for [a]Demas, having loved [b]this present [1]world, has deserted
me and gone to [c]Thessalonica; Crescens *has gone* to [2d]Galatia,
[e]Titus to Dalmatia.
11 [a]Only [b]Luke is with me. Pick up [c]Mark and bring him with
you, [d]for he is useful to me for service.
12 But [a]Tychicus I have sent to [b]Ephesus.
13 When you come bring the cloak which I left at [a]Troas with
Carpus, and the books, especially the parchments.
14 [a]Alexander the coppersmith did me much harm; [b]the Lord
will repay him according to his deeds.
15 Be on guard against him yourself, for he vigorously opposed
our [1]teaching.
16 At my first defense no one supported me, but all deserted
me; [a]may it not be counted against them.
17 But the Lord stood with me and [a]strengthened me, so that
through me [b]the proclamation might [1]be [c]fully accomplished,
and that all [d]the Gentiles might hear; and I was [e]rescued out of
[f]the lion's mouth.
18 The Lord will rescue me from every evil deed, and will
[1a]bring me safely to His [b]heavenly kingdom; [c]to [2]Him *be* the
glory forever and ever. Amen.
19 Greet Prisca and [a]Aquila, and [b]the household of Onesiphorus.
20 [a]Erastus remained at [b]Corinth, but [c]Trophimus I left sick at
[d]Miletus.

17 [a]1 Tim 6:11 [b]2 Tim 2:21; Heb 13:21
4:1 [a]1 Tim 5:21; 2 Tim 2:14 [b]Acts 10:42 [c]2 Thess 2:8; 2 Tim 1:10; 4:8
2 [1]Lit *all* [a]Gal 6:6; Col 4:3; 1 Thess 1:6 [b]1 Tim 5:20; Titus 1:13; 2:15 [c]2 Tim 3:10
3 [a]2 Tim 3:1 [b]1 Tim 1:10; 2 Tim 1:13
4 [a]2 Thess 2:11; Titus 1:14 [b]1 Tim 1:4
5 [a]1 Pet 1:13 [b]2 Tim 1:8 [c]Acts 21:8 [d]Eph 4:12; Col 4:17
6 [a]Phil 2:17 [b]Phil 1:23; 2 Pet 1:14
7 [a]1 Cor 9:25f; Phil 1:30; 1 Tim 1:18; 6:12 [b]Acts 20:24; 1 Cor 9:24 [c]2 Tim 3:10
8 [a]Col 1:5; 1 Pet 1:4 [b]1 Cor 9:25; 2 Tim 2:5; James 1:12 [c]2 Tim 1:12 [d]Phil 3:11 [e]2 Tim 4:1
9 [a]2 Tim 1:4; 4:21; Titus 3:12
10 [1]Or *age* [2]One early ms reads *Gaul* [a]Col 4:14 [b]1 Tim 6:17 [c]Acts 17:1 [d]Acts 16:6 [e]2 Cor 2:13; 8:23; Gal 2:3; Titus 1:4
11 [a]2 Tim 1:15 [b]Col 4:14; Philem 24 [c]Acts 12:12, 25; 15:37-39; Col 4:10 [d]2 Tim 2:21
12 [a]Acts 20:4; Eph 6:21, 22; Col 4:7f [b]Acts 18:19
13 [a]Acts 16:8
14 [a]Acts 19:33; 1 Tim 1:20 [b]Ps 62:12; Rom 2:6; 12:19
15 [1]Lit *words*
16 [a]Acts 7:60; 1 Cor 13:5
17 [1]Or *be fulfilled* [a]1 Tim 1:12; 2 Tim 2:1 [b]Titus 1:3 [c]2 Tim 4:5 [d]Acts 9:15; Phil 1:12ff [e]Rom 15:31; 2 Tim 3:11 [f]1 Sam 17:37; Ps 22:21
18 [1]Or *save me for* [2]Lit *Whom* [a]1 Cor 1:21 [b]1 Cor 15:50; 2 Tim 4:1; Heb 11:16; 12:22 [c]Rom 11:36; 2 Pet 3:18
19 [a]Acts 18:2 [b]2 Tim 1:16
20 [a]Acts 19:22; Rom 16:23 [b]Acts 18:1 [c]Acts 20:4; 21:29 [d]Acts 20:15

21 [a]2 Tim 4:9 [b]Titus 3:12
22 [a]Gal 6:18; Phil 4:23; Philem 25 [b]Col 4:18

21 [a]Make every effort to come before [b]winter. Eubulus greets
you, also Pudens and Linus and Claudia and all the brethren.
22 [a]The Lord be with your spirit. [b]Grace be with you.

2 Timothy Observations Chart

Paul	Timothy

2 Timothy Observations Chart

Paul's Instructions to Timothy	

2 Timothy at a Glance

Theme of 2 Timothy:

Segment Divisions

God's Provision	Paul's Example	Chapter Themes
		1
		2
Delivered Paul Out of Persecutions	Endured Persecutions	3
		4

Author:

Date:

Purpose:

Key Words:

gospel (see instructions on page 1958)

suffer (hardships, persecutions)

endure(d)

faith

ashamed

TITUS

When Paul sailed past Crete on his way to Rome, he was not the master of his own ship. He was Rome's prisoner. How wise the centurion guard would have been had he followed Paul's urging to put ashore in Crete! Despite the winds, they sailed on under much duress. As Paul had predicted, the ship was lost in Malta, the island 58 miles south of Sicily.

Paul's ship sank to the bottom of the sea; Crete had sunk to the depths of sin. Broken to pieces morally by the incessant pounding of a godless lifestyle, Crete needed the good news of the gospel. Unlike the sunken ship, however, Crete was not beyond redemption.

Whether Crete was on Paul's heart before his two years' house arrest in Rome, we don't know. We only know that once Paul was free from Rome's chains he apparently went with Titus to Crete and left him there.

As Paul wrote Titus, it was about A.D. 62. He didn't know he would return to Rome for one final imprisonment.

Things to Do

1. Read through Titus without stopping so that you understand the general content and thrust of the letter. Mark every reference to Paul in one color and Titus in another, including synonyms and pronouns. Record what you learn about each under the designated headings on the OBSERVATIONS CHART on page 1969.
2. Read Titus again, one chapter at a time. As you read each chapter:
   a. Note the groups of people mentioned in each chapter. List what you learn about each on the OBSERVATIONS CHART.
   b. Mark in the text the key words listed on the TITUS AT A GLANCE chart on page 1970. Be sure also to mark the synonyms and pronouns.
3. The commands, warnings, and instructions Paul includes in his letter to Titus help define Paul's purpose for writing. Read Titus again chapter by chapter and note each command, warning, or instruction Paul gives Titus. Either mark these with a distinguishing symbol or list them on the OBSERVATIONS CHART on page 1970 under "Instructions to Titus."
4. Listing Paul's commands, warnings, and instructions to Titus probably has helped you see the dominant subject of Titus. Look for the verses in chapters 2 and 3 regarding what Titus is to teach. They summarize the thrust of Paul's letter. These verses will help you determine the theme of the epistle. Record it on TITUS AT A GLANCE.
   a. Now summarize the theme or main message of each paragraph and then of each chapter and record these on TITUS AT A GLANCE. Also, record the chapter theme in your Bible.
   b. Fill in author, date, and purpose on the same chart.

Things to Think About

1. The world, by its lifestyle, denies God. What about you? Do you deny ungodliness and worldly desires, or do you indulge the desires of your flesh? What do your deeds say about your beliefs?
2. It is difficult always to be considerate to everyone, isn't it? When did you last fail in this area? Have you determined afresh to be gentle and uncontentious even in the most

difficult situation with the most difficult person? Your actions often will speak louder than your words ever can.

3. Your salvation was not based on performance but on the mercy and grace of God. What has your heavenly Father saved you from? Think on His goodness that brought you from death into life and brought you out of the kingdom of darkness into the kingdom of His glorious light. Have you thanked Him lately for His mercy and grace? Why not do it now? Pray for those close to you who have yet to experience the saving grace of God.

Chapter 1 Theme ____________________

1 Paul, [a]a bond-servant of God and an [b]apostle of Jesus Christ,
[1]for the faith of those [c]chosen of God and [d]the knowledge of
the truth which is [e]according to godliness,
2 in [a]the hope of eternal life, which God, [b]who cannot lie,
[c]promised [1d]long ages ago,
3 but [a]at the proper time manifested, *even* His word, in [b]the
proclamation [c]with which I was entrusted [d]according to the
commandment of [e]God our Savior,
4 To [a]Titus, [b]my true child [1]in a [c]common faith: [d]Grace and
peace from God the Father and [e]Christ Jesus our Savior.
5 For this reason I left you in [a]Crete, that you would set in order
what remains and [b]appoint [c]elders in every city as I directed you,
6 *namely,* [a]if any man is
above reproach, the [b]hus-
band of one wife, having
children who believe, not
accused of [c]dissipation or
[d]rebellion.
7 For the [1a]overseer must
be above reproach as [b]God's
steward, not [c]self-willed,
not quick-tempered, not
[d]addicted to wine, not
pugnacious, [e]not fond of
sordid gain,

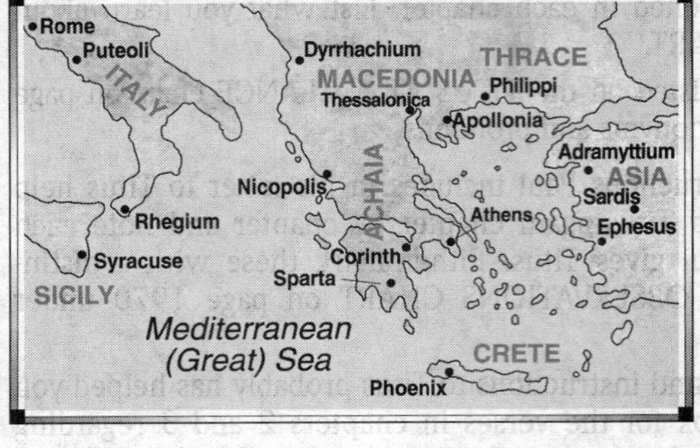

To Titus at Crete

8 but [a]hospitable, [b]loving what is good, sensible, just, devout,
self-controlled,
9 [a]holding fast the faithful word which is in accordance with
the teaching, so that he will be able both to exhort in [b]sound
doctrine and to refute those who contradict.
10 [a]For there are many [b]rebellious men, [c]empty talkers and
deceivers, especially [d]those of the circumcision,
11 who must be silenced because they are upsetting [a]whole
families, teaching [b]things they should not *teach* [c]for the sake of
sordid gain.
12 One of themselves, a prophet of their own, said, "[a]Cretans
are always liars, evil beasts, lazy gluttons."
13 This testimony is true. For this reason [a]reprove them
[b]severely so that they may be [c]sound in the faith,

1:1 [1]Or *according to* [a]Rom 1:1; James 1:1; Rev 1:1 [b]2 Cor 1:1 [c]Luke 18:7 [d]1 Tim 2:4 [e]1 Tim 6:3

2 [1]Lit *before times eternal* [a]2 Tim 1:1; Titus 3:7 [b]2 Tim 2:13; Heb 6:18 [c]Rom 1:2 [d]2 Tim 1:9

3 [a]1 Tim 2:6 [b]Rom 16:25; 2 Tim 4:17 [c]1 Tim 1:11 [d]1 Tim 1:1 [e]Luke 1:47; 1 Tim 1:1; Titus 2:10; 3:4

4 [1]Lit *according to* [a]2 Cor 2:13; 8:23; Gal 2:3; 2 Tim 4:10 [b]2 Tim 1:2 [c]2 Pet 1:1 [d]Rom 1:7 [e]1 Tim 1:12; 2 Tim 1:1

5 [a]Acts 27:7; Titus 1:12 [b]Acts 14:23 [c]Acts 11:30

6 [a]1 Tim 3:2-4; Titus 1:6-8 [b]1 Tim 3:2 [c]Eph 5:18 [d]Titus 1:10

7 [1]Or *bishop* [a]1 Tim 3:2 [b]1 Cor 4:1 [c]2 Pet 2:10 [d]1 Tim 3:3 [e]1 Tim 3:3, 8

8 [a]1 Tim 3:2 [b]2 Tim 3:3

9 [a]2 Thess 2:15; 1 Tim 1:19; 2 Tim 1:13 [b]1 Tim 1:10; Titus 2:1

10 [a]2 Cor 11:13 [b]Titus 1:6 [c]1 Tim 1:6 [d]Acts 11:2

11 [a]1 Tim 5:4; 2 Tim 3:6 [b]1 Tim 5:13 [c]1 Tim 6:5

12 [a]Acts 2:11; 27:7

13 [a]1 Tim 5:20; 2 Tim 4:2; Titus 2:15 [b]2 Cor 13:10 [c]Titus 2:2

14 not paying attention to Jewish [a]myths and [b]commandments
of men who [c]turn away from the truth.
15 [a]To the pure, all things are pure; but [b]to those who are
defiled and unbelieving, nothing is pure, but both their [c]mind
and their conscience are defiled.
16 [a]They profess to know God, but by *their* deeds they [b]deny
Him, being [c]detestable and [d]disobedient and [e]worthless [f]for
any good deed.

Chapter 2 Theme ______________________________

2 But as for you, speak the things which are fitting for
[a]sound doctrine.
2 [a]Older men are to be [b]temperate, dignified, sensible, [c]sound
[d]in faith, in love, in [1]perseverance.
3 Older women likewise are to be reverent in their behavior,
[a]not malicious gossips nor [b]enslaved to much wine, teaching
what is good,
4 so that they may [1]encourage the young women to love their
husbands, to love their children,
5 *to be* sensible, pure, [a]workers at home, kind, being [b]subject
to their own husbands, [c]so that the word of God will not be
dishonored.
6 Likewise urge [a]the young men to be [1]sensible;
7 in all things show yourself to be [a]an example of good
deeds, *with* [1]purity in doctrine, dignified,
8 sound *in* speech which is beyond reproach, so [a]that the
opponent will be put to shame, having nothing bad to say
about us.
9 *Urge* [a]bondslaves to be subject to their own masters in
everything, to be well-pleasing, not [1]argumentative,
10 not pilfering, but showing all good faith so that they will
adorn the doctrine of [a]God our Savior in every respect.
11 For the grace of God has [a]appeared, [1b]bringing salvation to
all men,
12 [1]instructing us to deny ungodliness and [a]worldly desires
and [b]to live sensibly, righteously and godly [c]in the present age,
13 looking for the blessed hope and the [a]appearing of the glory
of [1b]our great God and Savior, Christ Jesus,
14 who [a]gave Himself for us [b]to redeem us from every lawless
deed, and to [c]purify for Himself a [d]people for His own possession,
[e]zealous for good deeds.
15 These things speak and [a]exhort and [a]reprove with all
[1]authority. [b]Let no one disregard you.

Chapter 3 Theme ______________________________

3 [a]Remind them [b]to be subject to rulers, to authorities, to be
obedient, to be [c]ready for every good deed,
2 to malign no one, [a]to be peaceable, [a]gentle, [b]showing every
consideration for all men.

14 [a]1 Tim 1:4 [b]Col 2:22 [c]2 Tim 4:4

15 [a]Luke 11:41; Rom 14:20 [b]Rom 14:14, 23 [c]1 Tim 6:5

16 [a]1 John 2:4 [b]1 Tim 5:8 [c]Rev 21:8 [d]Titus 3:3 [e]2 Tim 3:8 [f]2 Tim 3:17; Titus 3:1

2:1 [a]Titus 1:9

2 [1]Or *steadfastness* [a]Philem 9 [b]1 Tim 3:2 [c]Titus 1:13 [d]1 Tim 1:2, 14

3 [a]1 Tim 3:11 [b]1 Tim 3:8

4 [1]Or *train*

5 [a]1 Tim 5:14 [b]Eph 5:22 [c]1 Tim 6:1

6 [1]Or *sensible in all things; show* [a]1 Tim 5:1

7 [1]Or *soundness;* lit *uncorruptness* [a]1 Tim 4:12

8 [a]2 Thess 3:14; 1 Pet 2:12

9 [1]Lit *contradicting* [a]Eph 6:5; 1 Tim 6:1

10 [a]Titus 1:3

11 [1]Or *to all men, bringing* [a]2 Tim 1:10; Titus 3:4 [b]1 Tim 2:4

12 [1]Or *disciplining* [a]1 Tim 6:9; Titus 3:3 [b]2 Tim 3:12 [c]1 Tim 6:17

13 [1]Or *the great God and our Savior* [a]2 Thess 2:8 [b]1 Tim 1:1; 2 Tim 1:2; Titus 1:4; 2 Pet 1:1

14 [a]1 Tim 2:6 [b]Ps 130:8; 1 Pet 1:18f [c]Ezek 37:23; Heb 1:3; 9:14; 1 John 1:7 [d]Ex 19:5; Deut 4:20; 7:6; 14:2; Eph 1:11; 1 Pet 2:9 [e]Eph 2:10; Titus 3:8; 1 Pet 3:13

15 [1]Lit *command* [a]1 Tim 4:13; 5:20; 2 Tim 4:2 [b]1 Tim 4:12

3:1 [a]2 Tim 2:14 [b]Rom 13:1 [c]2 Tim 2:21

2 [a]1 Tim 3:3; 1 Pet 2:18 [b]2 Tim 2:25

3 [a]For we also once were foolish ourselves, [b]disobedient,
[c]deceived, [d]enslaved to [e]various lusts and pleasures, spending
our life in [f]malice and [f]envy, hateful, hating one another.
4 But when the [a]kindness of [b]God our Savior and *His* love for
mankind [c]appeared,
5 [a]He saved us, [b]not on the basis of deeds which we have done
in righteousness, but [c]according to His mercy, by the [d]washing
of regeneration and [e]renewing by the Holy Spirit,
6 [a]whom He poured out upon us [b]richly through Jesus Christ
our Savior,
7 so that being justified by His grace we would be made [a]heirs
[1]according to *the* hope of eternal life.
8 [a]This is a trustworthy statement; and concerning these
things I [b]want you to speak confidently, so that those who have
[c]believed God will be careful to [d]engage in good deeds. These
things are good and profitable for men.
9 But [a]avoid [b]foolish controversies and [c]genealogies and strife
and [d]disputes about the Law, for they are [e]unprofitable and
worthless.
10 [a]Reject a [b]factious man [c]after a first and second warning,
11 knowing that such a man is [a]perverted and is sinning, being
self-condemned.
12 When I send Artemas or [a]Tychicus to you, [b]make every effort
to come to me at Nicopolis, for I have decided to [c]spend the
winter there.
13 Diligently help Zenas the [a]lawyer and [b]Apollos on their way
so that nothing is lacking for them.
14 [a]Our people must also learn to [b]engage in good [1]deeds to
meet [c]pressing needs, so that they will not be [d]unfruitful.
15 [a]All who are with me greet you. Greet those who love us
[b]in *the* faith.
[c]**G**race be with you all.

3 [a]Rom 11:30; Col 3:7 [b]Titus 1:16 [c]2 Tim 3:13 [d]Rom 6:6, 12 [e]2 Tim 3:6; Titus 2:12 [f]Rom 1:29

4 [a]Rom 2:4; Eph 2:7; 1 Pet 2:3 [b]Titus 2:10 [c]Titus 2:11

5 [a]Rom 11:14; 2 Tim 1:9 [b]Eph 2:9 [c]Eph 2:4; 1 Pet 1:3 [d]John 3:5; Eph 5:26; 1 Pet 3:21 [e]Rom 12:2

6 [a]Rom 5:5 [b]Rom 2:4; 1 Tim 6:17

7 [1]Or *of eternal life according to hope* [a]Matt 25:34; Mark 10:17; Rom 8:17, 24; Titus 1:2

8 [a]1 Tim 1:15 [b]1 Tim 2:8 [c]2 Tim 1:12 [d]Titus 2:7, 14; 3:14

9 [a]2 Tim 2:16 [b]1 Tim 1:4; 2 Tim 2:23 [c]1 Tim 1:4 [d]James 4:1 [e]2 Tim 2:14

10 [a]2 John 10 [b]Rom 16:17 [c]Matt 18:15f

11 [a]Titus 1:14

12 [a]Acts 20:4; Eph 6:21f; Col 4:7f; 2 Tim 4:12 [b]2 Tim 4:9 [c]2 Tim 4:21

13 [a]Matt 22:35 [b]Acts 18:24; 1 Cor 16:12

14 [1]Or *occupations* [a]Titus 2:8 [b]Titus 3:8 [c]Rom 12:13; Phil 4:16 [d]Matt 7:19; Phil 1:11; Col 1:10

15 [a]Acts 20:34 [b]1 Tim 1:2 [c]Col 4:18

Titus Observations Chart

Paul	Titus

Elders (Overseers)

Rebellious Men

Older Women

Young Women

Older Men

Believers in General

Bondslaves

Young Men

(continued)

Titus Observations Chart

Instructions to Titus

Titus at a Glance

Theme of Titus:

Segment Divisions	Paragraph Themes	Chapter Themes
	1:1-3	1
	1:4	
	1:5-9	
	1:10-16	
	2:1, 2	2
	2:3-5	
	2:6-8	
	2:9, 10	
	2:11-14	
	2:15	
	3:1-11	3
	3:12-14	
	3:15	

Author:

Date:

Purpose:

Key Words:

God

Jesus Christ

doctrine

word (the truth)

grace

deeds

sound

speak (speech)

sensible

PHILEMON

Slavery was a fact of life in Paul's day—a fact Paul couldn't change. But Paul could show slaves and masters how they were to behave toward one another as those redeemed by Jesus, the One who had become a bondservant on their behalf. In his epistles Paul shared these principles.

Now, however, something else had come up. Paul had to appeal to Philemon, a believer from Colossae, about a very personal matter: One of Philemon's slaves had run away, and according to Roman law he could be put to death by his master. So at about the same time Paul wrote Colossians, he wrote to Philemon from his rented quarters, where as a prisoner of Rome he also could be put to death. It was about A.D. 61 or 62.

THINGS TO DO

1. Read through Philemon and mark every reference (including pronouns and synonyms) to the author (Paul) in one color and every reference to the recipients in another.
   a. When you finish reading and marking, go back and note everything you learn about Paul on the OBSERVATIONS CHART on page 1973. Watch for Paul's reason for writing and how he goes about achieving his purpose. Record his reasons on the PHILEMON AT A GLANCE chart also on page 1973.
   b. Also note everything you learn about the recipients of Paul's letter and record this information in the appropriate section of the OBSERVATIONS CHART.
   c. Record on the OBSERVATIONS CHART everything you learn about Onesimus.
2. Carefully read the book again, marking in the text each of the key words (with their synonyms and pronouns) listed on the PHILEMON AT A GLANCE chart. Then observe what you learn from marking these words.
3. Record the theme of Philemon on PHILEMON AT A GLANCE and also in your Bible. Because Philemon is only one chapter, it is divided into paragraphs on the chart. Read the book paragraph by paragraph and record on the chart the theme of each paragraph. Then fill in the rest of the chart.

THINGS TO THINK ABOUT

1. How much do you care about others? Enough to come to another's aid, to assume the role of an advocate?
2. What can you learn from Paul's example in the way he appealed to Philemon?
3. Is there someone you need to forgive and offer restoration?
4. Can someone appeal to you to do the right thing on the basis of your character, or does he have to force your hand through rules, regulations, or some sort of a "bribe"?

Chapter 1 Theme ____________________

1 [a]Paul, [b]a prisoner of [c]Christ Jesus, and [d]Timothy [1]our brother,
To Philemon our beloved *brother* and [e]fellow worker,
2 and to Apphia [1a]our sister, and to [b]Archippus our [c]fellow
soldier, and to [d]the church in your house:

1:1 [1]Lit *the* [a]Phil 1:1 [b]Eph 3:1 [c]Gal 3:26 [d]2 Cor 1:1; Col 1:1 [e]Phil 2:25; Philem 24

2 [1]Lit *the* [a]Rom 16:1 [b]Col 4:17 [c]Phil 2:25; 2 Tim 2:3 [d]Rom 16:5

3 [a]Grace to you and peace from God our Father and the Lord
Jesus Christ.
4 [a]I thank my God always, making mention of you in my
prayers,
5 because I [a]hear of your love and of the faith which you
have toward the Lord Jesus and toward all the [1]saints;
6 *and I pray* that the fellowship of your faith may become
effective [1]through the [a]knowledge of every good thing which is
in you [2]for Christ's sake.
7 For I have come to have much [a]joy and comfort in your love,
because the [1]hearts of the [2]saints have been [b]refreshed through
you, brother.
8 Therefore, [a]though I have [1]enough confidence in Christ to
order you *to do* what is [b]proper,
9 yet for love's sake I rather [a]appeal *to you*—since I am such a
person as Paul, [1]the [b]aged, and now also [c]a prisoner of [d]Christ
Jesus—
10 I [a]appeal to you for my [b]child [1c]Onesimus, whom I have
begotten in my [2]imprisonment,
11 who formerly was useless to you, but now is useful both to
you and to me.
12 I have sent him back to you in person, that is, *sending* my
very heart,
13 whom I wished to keep with me, so that on your behalf he
might minister to me in my [1a]imprisonment for the gospel;
14 but without your consent I did not want to do anything, so
that your goodness would [a]not be, in effect, by compulsion but
of your own free will.
15 For perhaps [a]he was for this reason separated *from you* for
a while, that you would have him back forever,
16 [a]no longer as a slave, but more than a slave, [b]a beloved
brother, especially to me, but how much more to you, both [c]in
the flesh and in the Lord.
17 If then you regard me a [a]partner, accept him as *you would* me.
18 But if he has wronged you in any way or owes you anything,
charge that to my account;
19 [a]I, Paul, am writing this with my own hand, I will repay it
([b]not to [1]mention to you that you owe to me even your own
self as well).
20 Yes, brother, let me benefit from you in the Lord; [a]refresh
my heart in Christ.
21 [a]Having confidence in your obedience, I write to you, since
I know that you will do even more than what I say.
22 At the same time also prepare me a [a]lodging, for [b]I hope
that through [c]your prayers [d]I will be given to you.
23 [a]Epaphras, my [b]fellow prisoner in Christ Jesus, greets you,
24 *as do* [a]Mark, [b]Aristarchus, [c]Demas, [c]Luke, my [d]fellow
workers.
25 [a]The grace of the Lord Jesus Christ be [b]with your spirit.[1]

3 [a]Rom 1:7
4 [a]Rom 1:8f
5 [1]Or *holy ones* [a]Eph 1:15; Col 1:4; 1 Thess 3:6
6 [1]Or *in* [2]Lit *toward Christ* [a]Phil 1:9; Col 1:9; 3:10
7 [1]Lit *inward parts* [2]Or *holy ones* [a]2 Cor 7:4, 13 [b]1 Cor 16:18; Philem 20
8 [1]Lit *much* [a]2 Cor 3:12; 1 Thess 2:6 [b]Eph 5:4
9 [1]Or *an ambassador* [a]Rom 12:1 [b]Titus 2:2 [c]Philem 1 [d]Gal 3:26; 1 Tim 1:12; Philem 23
10 [1]I.e. useful [2]Lit *bonds* [a]Rom 12:1 [b]1 Cor 4:14f [c]Col 4:9
13 [1]Lit *bonds* [a]Phil 1:7; Philem 10
14 [a]2 Cor 9:7; 1 Pet 5:2
15 [a]Gen 45:5, 8
16 [a]1 Cor 7:22 [b]Matt 23:8; 1 Tim 6:2 [c]Eph 6:5; Col 3:22
17 [a]2 Cor 8:23
19 [1]Lit *say* [a]1 Cor 16:21; 2 Cor 10:1; Gal 5:2 [b]2 Cor 9:4
20 [a]Philem 7
21 [a]2 Cor 2:3
22 [a]Acts 28:23 [b]Phil 1:25; 2:24 [c]2 Cor 1:11 [d]Acts 27:24; Heb 13:19
23 [a]Col 1:7; 4:12 [b]Rom 16:7; Philem 1
24 [a]Acts 12:12, 25; 15:37-39; Col 4:10 [b]Acts 19:29; 27:2; Col 4:10 [c]Col 4:14; 2 Tim 4:10f [d]Philem 1
25 [1]One early ms adds *Amen* [a]Gal 6:18 [b]2 Tim 4:22

Philemon Observations Chart

The Author	The Recipients	Onesimus

Philemon at a Glance

Theme of Philemon:

	Segment Divisions	
Author:		Paragraph Themes
Date:		Verses 1-3
Purpose:		Verses 4-7
Key Words:		Verses 8-16
love		
appeal		Verses 17-20
slave		Verses 21, 22
		Verses 23-25

HEBREWS

Persecution increased as the gospel spread. The persecution was especially intense for Jewish believers because they had turned their back on the world and its ways, and they had abandoned the ordinances of the law, which Jews had embraced since the time of Moses. This left them in a no-man's-land. Jews as well as Gentiles who did not believe in Jesus Christ could not understand them, nor would many tolerate their newfound faith without challenge or attack.

Imagine yourself in a similar situation. What if you were wrong about Jesus Christ? What if He were not really the Messiah? And what about the new covenant? What if it didn't replace the old covenant? What if you really did need a continuing blood sacrifice for your sins? *What if...?*

So that we could be secure in our faith, God moved an unknown author to write the book we call Hebrews. No other book in the New Testament gives us what Hebrews gives us—the assurance that we have a High Priest who is touched with the feeling of our weaknesses, One who ever lives to make intercession for us, the Mediator of a new and better covenant.

Hebrews was probably written before A.D. 70 because the book makes reference to the temple as if it were still standing and the priests were still making religious sacrifices.

THINGS TO DO

1. Before you begin your study of Hebrews, read Hebrews 13:22 to discover the author's purpose for writing. Record this on the HEBREWS AT A GLANCE chart on page 1995.

2. In order to grasp the awesome truths of this book and properly interpret its difficult passages, you need to understand to whom the book is written. As you read Hebrews chapter by chapter:

   a. Mark every reference to the recipients in a specific color. Obviously the words *you, beloved,* and *brethren* refer to the recipients. However, when the author addresses the recipients he often includes himself, using the pronouns *we* and *us.* When this happens, mark these as you would other references to the recipients.

   b. Also, mark every reference to the author(s) in another distinctive color.

   c. When you finish, list everything you learn about the author and about the recipients in the appropriate columns on the OBSERVATIONS CHART on page 1993.

   d. As you saw in 13:22, Hebrews is a letter of exhortation. Watch for these exhortations. They are often introduced with the phrase *let us*. Therefore, mark every *let us* in a distinctive way. List the exhortations on the OBSERVATIONS CHART.

   e. Throughout the book you will come across occasional warnings. In Hebrews 2:1, in the first of the warnings, the author includes himself and writes, "We must pay much closer attention to what we have heard, so that we do not drift away from it."

      1) Mark each warning in a distinctive way and record that warning in the appropriate column on the OBSERVATIONS CHART on page 1994.

      2) When you note each warning, record the consequences of not heeding it. As you note the consequence, remember to whom the book is addressed. Let the text simply speak for itself. Don't read it through your theological glasses; rather, let the text say what it says.

3. As you study each chapter, do the following:

   a. Write the key words (including their synonyms and pronouns) listed on the HEBREWS

AT A GLANCE chart on page 1995 on an index card. Mark each word (and its synonyms and pronouns) in a distinctive way in the text exactly as you marked it on the card. Beginning at chapter 7, mark every occurrence of the word *covenant*. You will also discover other key words (not on your list) that occur frequently in a chapter or segment of Hebrews. Mark these in a distinctive way.

b. As you finish reading a chapter, review what you learned from marking key words. Then determine the theme or subject of that chapter. Record it in your Bible and on HEBREWS AT A GLANCE.

4. To truly appreciate and understand the book of Hebrews, you need to do the following:

a. Look back through your work and note all the times you marked *Jesus* and the pronouns referring to Him. Also look for the phrase *better*. Then, using the OBSERVATIONS CHART, list what you learn from Hebrews about our Lord.

b. There is much in Hebrews about the priesthood and about Jesus as our High Priest. Make a chart entitled THE PRIESTHOOD AND JESUS and list your information in three columns: "Insights into Priests and the Priesthood," "Insights into Jesus, Our Great High Priest," and "How This Applies to Me." Record your insights on this chart.

c. Review what you learn from marking the word *covenant* and note what the text says on a chart you might want to title A COMPARISON OF THE TWO COVENANTS: LAW AND GRACE AS TAUGHT IN HEBREWS.

5. Complete HEBREWS AT A GLANCE by doing the following:

a. Look at each of your chapter themes in order to determine the theme of Hebrews and record it on the chart.

b. Fill in the section titled "Segment Divisions."

1) Segment divisions indicate a change in the thrust or topic of the book. One change in emphasis occurs at Hebrews 10:19, where the author stops dealing with the doctrinal aspects of the truth he is sharing and begins to address the practical aspects. Record this segment division on the chart in the appropriate space.

2) Look again at the chapter themes. Are there any other divisions? If so, record them. This will help you find where a specific truth is covered in Hebrews.

Things to Think About

1. Meditate on the truths you learned about Jesus. Do you see Him as "better than..."? How supreme is He in your life?

2. As you press on to Christian maturity, are you noticing a new sense of confidence in your God? Is your faith being strengthened? Are you drawing near to God? Do you think Jesus understands what you're going through? Can He really help? Have you asked Him?

3. Are you laying aside every encumbrance that is slowing you down, and every sin, and running with endurance the race set before you? If not, what is holding you back?

4. How do you deal with persecution? How do the warnings and exhortations of Hebrews apply to your life?

5. Are you continually offering up the sacrifice of praise? What are some things you can thank God for today even though they do not necessarily seem good now? Remember, it's a *sacrifice* of praise.

Chapter 1 Theme ________________________

1 God, after He [a]spoke long ago to the fathers in [b]the prophets
in many portions and [c]in many ways,
2 [1a]in these last days [b]has spoken to us [2]in [c]His Son, whom He
appointed [d]heir of all things, [e]through whom also He made the
[3f]world.
3 [1]And He is the radiance of His glory and the exact
[a]representation of His nature, and [2b]upholds all things by the
word of His power. When He had made [c]purification of sins,
He [d]sat down at the right hand of the [e]Majesty on high,
4 having become as much better than the angels, as He has
inherited a more excellent [a]name than they.
5 For to which of the angels did He ever say,

"[a]YOU ARE MY SON,
TODAY I HAVE BEGOTTEN YOU"?

And again,

"[b]I WILL BE A FATHER TO HIM
AND HE SHALL BE A SON TO ME"?

6 And [1]when He again [a]brings the firstborn into [2b]the world,
He says,

"[c]AND LET ALL THE ANGELS OF GOD WORSHIP HIM."

7 And of the angels He says,

"[a]WHO MAKES HIS ANGELS WINDS,
AND HIS MINISTERS A FLAME OF FIRE."

8 But of the Son *He says,*

"[a]YOUR THRONE, O GOD, IS FOREVER AND EVER,
AND THE RIGHTEOUS SCEPTER IS THE SCEPTER OF [1]HIS KINGDOM.
9 "[a]YOU HAVE LOVED RIGHTEOUSNESS AND HATED LAWLESSNESS;
[b]THEREFORE GOD, YOUR GOD, HAS [c]ANOINTED YOU
WITH THE OIL OF GLADNESS ABOVE YOUR COMPANIONS."

10 And,

"[a]YOU, LORD, IN THE BEGINNING LAID THE FOUNDATION
OF THE EARTH,
AND THE HEAVENS ARE THE WORKS OF YOUR HANDS;
11 [a]THEY WILL PERISH, BUT YOU REMAIN;
[b]AND THEY ALL WILL BECOME OLD LIKE A GARMENT,
12 [a]AND LIKE A MANTLE YOU WILL ROLL THEM UP;
LIKE A GARMENT THEY WILL ALSO BE CHANGED.
BUT YOU ARE [b]THE SAME,
AND YOUR YEARS WILL NOT COME TO AN END."

13 But to which of the angels has He ever said,

"[a]SIT AT MY RIGHT HAND,
[b]UNTIL I MAKE YOUR ENEMIES
A FOOTSTOOL FOR YOUR FEET"?

14 Are they not all [a]ministering spirits, sent out to render
service for the sake of those who will [b]inherit [c]salvation?

Chapter 2 Theme ________________________

2 For this reason we must pay much closer attention to [1]what
we have heard, so that [a]we do not drift away *from it.*

1:1 [a]John 9:29; 16:13; Heb 2:2f; 3:5; 4:8; 5:5; 11:18; 12:25 [b]Acts 2:30; 3:21 [c]Num 12:6, 8; Joel 2:28

2 [1]Or *at the end of these days* [2]Lit *in Son;* or in the person of a Son [3]Lit *ages* [a]Matt 13:39; 1 Pet 1:20 [b]John 9:29 [c]John 5:26, 27; Heb 3:6; 5:8; 7:28 [d]Ps 2:8; Matt 28:18; Mark 12:7; Rom 8:17; Heb 2:8 [e]John 1:3; 1 Cor 8:6; Col 1:16 [f]1 Cor 2:7; Heb 11:3

3 [1]Lit *Who being* [2]Lit *upholding* [a]2 Cor 4:4 [b]Col 1:17 [c]Titus 2:14; Heb 9:14 [d]Mark 16:19; Heb 8:1; 10:12; 12:2 [e]2 Pet 1:17

4 [a]Eph 1:21

5 [a]Ps 2:7; Acts 13:33; Heb 5:5 [b]2 Sam 7:14

6 [1]Or *again when He brings* [2]Lit *the inhabited earth* [a]Heb 10:5 [b]Matt 24:14 [c]Ps 97:7

7 [a]Ps 104:4

8 [1]Late mss read *Your* [a]Ps 45:6

9 [a]Ps 45:7 [b]John 10:17; Phil 2:9; Heb 2:9 [c]Is 61:1, 3

10 [a]Ps 102:25

11 [a]Ps 102:26 [b]Is 51:6; Heb 8:13

12 [a]Ps 102:26, 27 [b]Heb 13:8

13 [a]Ps 110:1; Matt 22:44; Heb 1:3 [b]Josh 10:24; Heb 10:13

14 [a]Ps 103:20f; Dan 7:10 [b]Matt 25:34; Mark 10:17; Titus 3:7; Heb 6:12 [c]Rom 11:14; 1 Cor 1:21; Heb 2:3; 5:9; 9:28

2:1 [1]Lit *the things that have been heard* [a]Prov 3:21

2 For if the word [a]spoken through [b]angels proved [1]unalterable,
and [c]every transgression and disobedience received a just
[2d]penalty,
3 [a]how will we escape if we neglect so great a [b]salvation? [1]After
it was at the first [c]spoken through the Lord, it was [d]confirmed to
us by those who heard,
4 God also testifying with them, both by [a]signs and wonders
and by [b]various [1]miracles and by [2c]gifts of the Holy Spirit
[d]according to His own will.
5 For He did not subject to angels [1a]the world to come,
concerning which we are speaking.
6 But one has testified [a]somewhere, saying,
"[b]WHAT IS MAN, THAT YOU REMEMBER HIM?
OR THE SON OF MAN, THAT YOU ARE CONCERNED ABOUT HIM?
7 "[a]YOU HAVE MADE HIM [1]FOR A LITTLE WHILE LOWER
THAN THE ANGELS;
YOU HAVE CROWNED HIM WITH GLORY AND HONOR,
[2]AND HAVE APPOINTED HIM OVER THE WORKS OF YOUR HANDS;
8 [a]YOU HAVE PUT ALL THINGS IN SUBJECTION UNDER HIS FEET."
For in subjecting all things to him, He left nothing that is not
subject to him. But now [b]we do not yet see all things subjected
to him.
9 But we do see Him who was [a]made [1]for a little while lower
than the angels, *namely,* Jesus, [b]because of the suffering of death
[c]crowned with glory and honor, so that [d]by the grace of God He
might [e]taste death [f]for everyone.
10 For [a]it was fitting for Him, [b]for whom are all things, and
through whom are all things, in bringing many sons to glory, to
[c]perfect the [1d]author of their salvation through sufferings.
11 For both He who [a]sanctifies and those who [b]are [1]sanctified
are all [c]from one *Father;* for which reason He is not ashamed to
call them [d]brethren,
12 saying,
"[a]I WILL PROCLAIM YOUR NAME TO MY BRETHREN,
IN THE MIDST OF THE CONGREGATION I WILL SING YOUR PRAISE."
13 And again,
"[a]I WILL PUT MY TRUST IN HIM."
And again,
"[b]BEHOLD, I AND THE CHILDREN WHOM GOD HAS GIVEN ME."
14 Therefore, since the children share in [1a]flesh and blood,
[b]He Himself likewise also partook of the same, that [c]through
death He might render powerless [d]him who had the power of
death, that is, the devil,
15 and might free those who through [a]fear of death were subject
to slavery all their lives.
16 For assuredly He does not [1]give help to angels, but He gives
help to the [2]descendant of Abraham.
17 Therefore, He [1]had [a]to be made like His brethren in all
things, so that He might [b]become a merciful and faithful [c]high
priest in [d]things pertaining to God, to [e]make propitiation for the
sins of the people.

2 [1]Or *steadfast* [2]Or *recompense* [a]Heb 1:1 [b]Acts 7:53 [c]Heb 10:28 [d]Heb 10:35; 11:26

3 [1]Lit *Which was* [a]Heb 10:29; 12:25 [b]Rom 11:14; 1 Cor 1:21; Heb 1:14; 5:9; 9:28 [c]Heb 1:1 [d]Mark 16:20; Luke 1:2; 1 John 1:1

4 [1]Or *works of power* [2]Lit *distributions* [a]John 4:48 [b]Mark 6:14 [c]1 Cor 12:4, 11; Eph 4:7 [d]Eph 1:5

5 [1]Lit *the inhabited earth* [a]Matt 24:14; Heb 6:5

6 [a]Heb 4:4 [b]Ps 8:4

7 [1]Or *... him a little lower than ...* [2]Two early mss do not contain *And ... hands* [a]Ps 8:5, 6

8 [a]Ps 8:6; 1 Cor 15:27 [b]1 Cor 15:25

9 [1]Or *a little lower* [a]Heb 2:7 [b]Acts 2:33; 3:13; 1 Pet 1:21 [c]Phil 2:9; Heb 1:9 [d]John 3:16 [e]Matt 16:28; John 8:52 [f]Heb 7:25

10 [1]Or *leader* [a]Luke 24:26 [b]Rom 11:36 [c]Heb 5:9; 7:28 [d]Acts 3:15; 5:31

11 [1]Or *being sanctified* [a]Heb 13:12 [b]Heb 10:10 [c]Acts 17:28 [d]Matt 25:40; Mark 3:34f; John 20:17

12 [a]Ps 22:22

13 [a]Is 8:17 [b]Is 8:18

14 [1]Lit *blood and flesh* [a]Matt 16:17 [b]John 1:14 [c]1 Cor 15:54-57; 2 Tim 1:10 [d]John 12:31; 1 John 3:8

15 [a]Rom 8:15

16 [1]Lit *take hold of angels, but He takes hold of* [2]Lit *seed*

17 [1]Lit *was obligated to be* [a]Phil 2:7; Heb 2:14 [b]Heb 4:15f; 5:2 [c]Heb 3:1; 4:14f; 5:5, 10; 6:20; 7:26, 28; 8:1, 3; 9:11; 10:21 [d]Rom 15:17; Heb 5:1 [e]Dan 9:24; 1 John 2:2; 4:10

18 For since He Himself was [a]tempted in that which He has
suffered, He is able to come to the aid of those who are
tempted.

Chapter 3 Theme ____________________

3 Therefore, [a]holy brethren, partakers of a [b]heavenly calling,
consider Jesus, [c]the Apostle and [d]High Priest of our [e]con-
fession;
2 [1]He was faithful to Him who appointed Him, as [a]Moses
also was in all His house.
3 [a]For He has been counted worthy of more glory than Moses,
by just so much as the builder of the house has more honor than
the house.
4 For every house is built by someone, but the builder of all
things is God.
5 Now [a]Moses was faithful in all His house as [b]a servant, [c]for
a testimony of those things [d]which were to be spoken later;
6 but Christ *was faithful* as [a]a Son over His house—[b]whose
house we are, [c]if we hold fast our [d]confidence and the boast of
our [e]hope firm until the end.
7 Therefore, just as [a]the Holy Spirit says,
"[b]TODAY IF YOU HEAR HIS VOICE,
8 [a]DO NOT HARDEN YOUR HEARTS AS [1]WHEN THEY PROVOKED ME,
AS IN THE DAY OF TRIAL IN THE WILDERNESS,
9 [a]WHERE YOUR FATHERS TRIED *ME* BY TESTING *ME*,
AND SAW MY WORKS FOR [b]FORTY YEARS.
10 "[a]THEREFORE I WAS ANGRY WITH THIS GENERATION,
AND SAID, 'THEY ALWAYS GO ASTRAY IN THEIR HEART,
AND THEY DID NOT KNOW MY WAYS';
11 [a]AS I SWORE IN MY WRATH,
'THEY SHALL NOT ENTER MY REST.'"
12 [a]Take care, brethren, that there not be in any one of you an
evil, unbelieving heart [1]that falls away from [b]the living God.
13 But [a]encourage one another day after day, as long as it is
still called "Today," so that none of you will be hardened by the
[b]deceitfulness of sin.
14 For we have become partakers of Christ, [a]if we hold fast
the beginning of our [b]assurance firm until the end,
15 while it is said,
"[a]TODAY IF YOU HEAR HIS VOICE,
DO NOT HARDEN YOUR HEARTS, AS [1]WHEN THEY PROVOKED ME."
16 For who [a]provoked *Him* when they had heard? Indeed,
[b]did not all those who came out of Egypt *led* by Moses?
17 And with whom was He angry for forty years? Was it not
with those who sinned, [a]whose bodies fell in the wilderness?
18 And to whom did He swear [a]that they would not enter His
rest, but to those who were [b]disobedient?
19 *So* we see that they were not able to enter because of
[a]unbelief.

18 [a]Heb 4:15

3:1 [a]Acts 1:15; Heb 2:11; 3:12; 10:19; 13:22 [b]Phil 3:14 [c]John 17:3 [d]Heb 2:17; 4:14f; 5:5, 10; 6:20; 7:26, 28; 8:1, 3; 9:11; 10:21 [e]2 Cor 9:13; Heb 4:14; 10:23

2 [1]Lit *Being faithful* [a]Ex 40:16; Num 12:7; Heb 3:5

3 [a]2 Cor 3:7-11

5 [a]Ex 40:16; Num 12:7; Heb 3:2 [b]Ex 14:31; Num 12:7 [c]Deut 18:18f [d]Heb 1:1

6 [a]Heb 1:2 [b]1 Cor 3:16; 1 Tim 3:15 [c]Rom 11:22; Heb 3:14; 4:14 [d]Eph 3:12; Heb 4:16; 10:19, 35 [e]Heb 6:11; 7:19; 10:23; 11:1; 1 Pet 1:3

7 [a]Acts 28:25; Heb 9:8; 10:15 [b]Ps 95:7; Heb 3:15; 4:7

8 [1]Lit *in the provocation* [a]Ps 95:8

9 [a]Ps 95:9-11 [b]Acts 7:36

10 [a]Ps 95:10

11 [a]Ps 95:11; Heb 4:3, 5

12 [1]Lit *in falling* [a]Col 2:8; Heb 12:25 [b]Matt 16:16; Heb 9:14; 10:31; 12:22

13 [a]Heb 10:24f [b]Eph 4:22

14 [a]Heb 3:6 [b]Heb 11:1

15 [1]Lit *in the rebellion* [a]Ps 95:7f; Heb 3:7; 4:7

16 [a]Jer 32:29; 44:3, 8 [b]Num 14:2, 11, 30; Deut 1:35, 36, 38

17 [a]Num 14:29; 1 Cor 10:5

18 [a]Num 14:23; Deut 1:34f; Heb 4:2 [b]Rom 11:30-32; Heb 4:6, 11

19 [a]John 3:18, 36; Rom 11:23; Heb 3:12

Chapter 4 Theme ______________________________

4

4 Therefore, let us fear if, while a promise remains of entering
His rest, any one of you may seem to have [a]come short of it.
2 For indeed we have had good news preached to us, just as
they also; but [a]the word [1]they heard did not profit them, because
[2]it was not united by faith in those who heard.
3 For we who have believed enter that rest, just as He has
said,

"[a]AS I SWORE IN MY WRATH,
THEY SHALL NOT ENTER MY REST,"

although His works were finished [b]from the foundation of the
world.
4 For He has said [a]somewhere concerning the seventh *day:*
"[b]AND GOD [c]RESTED ON THE SEVENTH DAY FROM ALL HIS WORKS";
5 and again in this *passage,* "[a]THEY SHALL NOT ENTER MY REST."
6 Therefore, since it remains for some to enter it, and those
who formerly had good news preached to them failed to enter
because of [a]disobedience,
7 He again fixes a certain day, "Today," saying [1]through David
after so long a time just [a]as has been said before,

"[b]TODAY IF YOU HEAR HIS VOICE,
DO NOT HARDEN YOUR HEARTS."

8 For [a]if [1]Joshua had given them rest, He would not have
spoken of another day after that.
9 So there remains a Sabbath rest for the people of God.
10 For the one who has entered His rest has himself also
[a]rested from his works, as [b]God did from His.
11 Therefore let us be diligent to enter that rest, so that no one
will fall, through *following* the same [a]example of [b]disobedience.
12 For [a]the word of God is [b]living and [c]active and sharper than
any two-edged [d]sword, and piercing as far as the division of
[e]soul and [e]spirit, of both joints and marrow, and [f]able to judge
the thoughts and intentions of the heart.
13 And [a]there is no creature hidden from His sight, but all
things are [b]open and laid bare to the eyes of Him with whom
we have to do.
14 Therefore, since we have a great [a]high priest who has [b]passed
through the heavens, Jesus [c]the Son of God, let us hold fast our
[d]confession.
15 For we do not have [a]a high priest who cannot sympathize
with our weaknesses, but One who has been [b]tempted in all
things as *we are, yet* [c]without sin.
16 Therefore let us [a]draw near with [b]confidence to the throne
of grace, so that we may receive mercy and find grace to help in
time of need.

Chapter 5 Theme ______________________________

5

5 For every high priest [a]taken from among men is appointed
on behalf of men in [b]things pertaining to God, in order to
[c]offer both gifts and sacrifices [d]for sins;

4:1 [a]2 Cor 6:1; Gal 5:4; Heb 12:15
2 [1]Lit *of hearing* [2]Two early mss read *they were . . . faith with those who heard* [a]Rom 10:17; Gal 3:2; 1 Thess 2:13
3 [a]Ps 95:11; Heb 3:11 [b]Matt 25:34
4 [a]Heb 2:6 [b]Gen 2:2 [c]Ex 20:11; 31:17
5 [a]Ps 95:11; Heb 3:11
6 [a]Heb 3:18; 4:11
7 [1]Or *in* [a]Heb 3:7f [b]Ps 95:7f
8 [1]Gr *Jesus* [a]Josh 22:4
10 [a]Rev 14:13 [b]Gen 2:2; Heb 4:4
11 [a]2 Pet 2:6 [b]Heb 3:18; 4:6
12 [a]Jer 23:29; Eph 5:26; Heb 6:5; 1 Pet 1:23 [b]Acts 7:38 [c]1 Thess 2:13 [d]Eph 6:17 [e]1 Thess 5:23 [f]John 12:48; 1 Cor 14:24f
13 [a]2 Chr 16:9; Ps 33:13-15 [b]Job 26:6
14 [a]Heb 2:17 [b]Eph 4:10; Heb 6:20; 8:1; 9:24 [c]Matt 4:3; Heb 1:2; 6:6; 7:3; 10:29 [d]Heb 3:1
15 [a]Heb 2:17 [b]Heb 2:18 [c]2 Cor 5:21; Heb 7:26
16 [a]Heb 7:19 [b]Heb 3:6
5:1 [a]Ex 28:1 [b]Heb 2:17 [c]Heb 7:27; 8:3f; 9:9; 10:11 [d]1 Cor 15:3; Heb 7:27; 10:12

2 [1a]he can deal gently with the [b]ignorant and [c]misguided, since
he himself also is [2d]beset with weakness;
3 and because of it he is obligated to offer *sacrifices* [a]for sins,
[b]as for the people, so also for himself.
4 And [a]no one takes the honor to himself, but *receives it*
when he is called by God, even [b]as Aaron was.
5 So also Christ [a]did not glorify Himself so as to become a
[b]high priest, but He who [c]said to Him,

"[d]YOU ARE MY SON,
TODAY I HAVE BEGOTTEN YOU";

6 just as He says also in another *passage,*

"[a]YOU ARE A PRIEST FOREVER
ACCORDING TO [b]THE ORDER OF MELCHIZEDEK."

7 [1]In the days of His flesh, [2a]He offered up both prayers and
supplications with [b]loud crying and tears to the One [c]able to
save Him [3]from death, and He [4]was heard because of His [d]piety.
8 Although He was [a]a Son, He learned [b]obedience from the
things which He suffered.
9 And having been made [a]perfect, He became to all those who
obey Him the source of eternal salvation,
10 being designated by God as [a]a high priest according to [b]the
order of Melchizedek.
11 Concerning [1]him we have much to say, and *it is* hard to
explain, since you have become dull of hearing.
12 For though [1]by this time you ought to be teachers, you have
need again for someone to teach you [a]the [2b]elementary principles
of the [c]oracles of God, and you have come to need [d]milk and not
solid food.
13 For everyone who partakes *only* of milk is not accustomed
to the word of righteousness, for he is an [a]infant.
14 But solid food is for [a]the mature, who because of practice
have their senses [b]trained to [c]discern good and evil.

Chapter 6 Theme ____________________

6 Therefore [a]leaving [b]the [1]elementary teaching about the
[2]Christ, let us press on to [3c]maturity, not laying again a foundation of repentance from [d]dead works and of faith toward God,
2 of [a]instruction about washings and [b]laying on of hands, and
the [c]resurrection of the dead and [c]eternal judgment.
3 And this we will do, [a]if God permits.
4 For in the case of those who have once been [a]enlightened
and have tasted of [b]the heavenly gift and have been made [c]par-
takers of the Holy Spirit,
5 and [a]have tasted the good [b]word of God and the powers of
[c]the age to come,
6 and *then* have fallen away, it is [a]impossible to renew them
again to repentance, [1b]since they again crucify to themselves
the Son of God and put Him to open shame.
7 For ground that drinks the rain which often [1]falls on it and
brings forth vegetation useful to those [a]for whose sake it is also
tilled, receives a blessing from God;

2 [1]Lit *being able to* [2]Or *subject to weakness* [a]Heb 2:18; 4:15 [b]Eph 4:18; Heb 9:7 mg [c]James 5:19; 1 Pet 2:25 [d]Heb 7:28

3 [a]1 Cor 15:3; Heb 7:27; 10:12 [b]Lev 9:7; 16:6; Heb 7:27; 9:7

4 [a]Num 16:40; 18:7; 2 Chr 26:18 [b]Ex 28:1; 1 Chr 23:13

5 [a]John 8:54 [b]Heb 2:17; 5:10 [c]Heb 1:1, 5 [d]Ps 2:7

6 [a]Ps 110:4; Heb 7:17 [b]Heb 5:10; 6:20; 7:11, 17

7 [1]I.e. during Christ's earthly life [2]Lit *who having offered up* [3]Or *out of* [4]Lit *having been heard* [a]Matt 26:39, 42, 44; Mark 14:36, 39; Luke 22:41, 44 [b]Matt 27:46, 50; Mark 15:34, 37; Luke 23:46 [c]Mark 14:36 [d]Heb 11:7; 12:28

8 [a]Heb 1:2 [b]Phil 2:8

9 [a]Heb 2:10

10 [a]Heb 2:17; 5:5 [b]Heb 5:6

11 [1]Lit *whom* or *which*

12 [1]Lit *because of the time* [2]Lit *elements of the beginning* [a]Gal 4:3 [b]Heb 6:1 [c]Acts 7:38 [d]1 Cor 3:2; 1 Pet 2:2

13 [a]1 Cor 3:1; 14:20; 1 Pet 2:2

14 [a]1 Cor 2:6; Eph 4:13; Heb 6:1 [b]1 Tim 4:7 [c]Rom 14:1ff

6:1 [1]Lit *word of the beginning* [2]I.e. Messiah [3]Or *perfection* [a]Phil 3:13f [b]Heb 5:12 [c]Heb 5:14 [d]Heb 9:14

2 [a]John 3:25; Acts 19:3f [b]Acts 6:6 [c]Acts 17:31f

3 [a]Acts 18:21

4 [a]2 Cor 4:4, 6; Heb 10:32 [b]John 4:10; Eph 2:8 [c]Gal 3:2; Heb 2:4

5 [a]1 Pet 2:3 [b]Eph 6:17 [c]Heb 2:5

6 [1]Or *while* [a]Matt 19:26; Heb 10:26f; 2 Pet 2:21; 1 John 5:16 [b]Heb 10:29

7 [1]Lit *comes* [a]2 Tim 2:6

8 but if it yields thorns and thistles, it is worthless and [a]close
[1]to being cursed, and [2]it ends up being burned.
9 But, [a]beloved, we are convinced of better things concerning
you, and things that [1]accompany salvation, though we are
speaking in this way.
10 For [a]God is not unjust so as to forget [b]your work and the love
which you have shown toward His name, in having [c]ministered
and in still ministering to the [1]saints.
11 And we desire that each one of you show the same diligence
[1]so as to realize the [a]full assurance of [b]hope until the end,
12 so that you will not be sluggish, but [a]imitators of those who
through [b]faith and patience [c]inherit the promises.
13 For [a]when God made the promise to Abraham, since He
could swear by no one greater, He [b]swore by Himself,
14 saying, "[a]I WILL SURELY BLESS YOU AND I WILL SURELY MULTIPLY
YOU."
15 And so, [a]having patiently waited, he obtained the promise.
16 [a]For men swear by [1]one greater *than themselves,* and with
them [b]an oath *given* as confirmation is an end of every dispute.
17 [1]In the same way God, desiring even more to show to [a]the
heirs of the promise [b]the unchangeableness of His purpose,
[2]interposed with an oath,
18 so that by two unchangeable things in which [a]it is impossible
for God to lie, we who have [1]taken refuge would have strong
encouragement to take hold of [b]the hope set before us.
19 [1]This [a]hope we have as an anchor of the soul, a *hope* both
sure and steadfast and one which [b]enters [2]within the veil,
20 [a]where Jesus has entered as a forerunner for us, having
become a [b]high priest forever according to the order of
Melchizedek.

Chapter 7 Theme

7 For this [a]Melchizedek, king of Salem, priest of the [b]Most
High God, who met Abraham as he was returning from
the slaughter of the kings and blessed him,
2 to whom also Abraham apportioned a tenth part of all *the
spoils,* was first of all, by the translation *of his name,* king of righteousness, and then also king of Salem, which is king of peace.
3 Without father, without mother, [a]without genealogy, having
neither beginning of days nor end of life, but made like [b]the
Son of God, he remains a priest perpetually.
4 Now observe how great this man was to whom Abraham,
the [a]patriarch, [b]gave a tenth of the choicest spoils.
5 And those indeed of [a]the sons of Levi who receive the priest's
office have commandment [1]in the Law to collect [2]a tenth from
the people, that is, from their brethren, although these [3]are
descended from Abraham.
6 But the one [a]whose genealogy is not traced from them
[b]collected [1]a tenth from Abraham and [2b]blessed the one who [c]had
the promises.
7 But without any dispute the lesser is blessed by the greater.

8 [1]Lit *near to a curse* [2]Lit *whose end is for burning* [a]Gen 3:17f; Deut 29:22ff

9 [1]Or *belong to* [a]1 Cor 10:14; 2 Cor 7:1; 12:19; 1 Pet 2:11; 2 Pet 3:1; 1 John 2:7; Jude 3

10 [1]Or *holy ones* [a]Prov 19:17; Matt 10:42; 25:40; Acts 10:4 [b]1 Thess 1:3 [c]Rom 15:25; Heb 10:32-34

11 [1]Lit *to the full* [a]Heb 10:22 [b]Heb 3:6

12 [a]Heb 13:7 [b]2 Thess 1:4; James 1:3; Rev 13:10 [c]Heb 1:14

13 [a]Gal 3:15, 18 [b]Gen 22:16; Luke 1:73

14 [a]Gen 22:17

15 [a]Gen 12:4; 21:5

16 [1]Or *Him who is greater* [a]Gal 3:15 [b]Ex 22:11

17 [1]Lit *In which* [2]Or *guaranteed* [a]Heb 11:9 [b]Ps 110:4; Prov 19:21; Heb 6:18

18 [1]Lit *in which* [a]Num 23:19; Titus 1:2 [b]Heb 3:6; 7:19

19 [1]Lit *Which* hope *we have* [2]Or *inside* [a]Ps 39:7; 62:5; Acts 23:6; Rom 4:18; 5:4, 5; 1 Cor 13:13; Col 1:27; 1 Pet 1:3 [b]Lev 16:2, 15; Heb 9:3, 7

20 [a]John 14:2; Heb 4:14 [b]Ps 110:4; Heb 2:17; 5:6

7:1 [a]Gen 14:18-20; Heb 7:6 [b]Mark 5:7

3 [a]Heb 7:6 [b]Matt 4:3; Heb 7:1, 28

4 [a]Acts 2:29; 7:8f [b]Gen 14:20

5 [1]Lit *according to* [2]Or *tithes* [3]Lit *have come out of the loins of* [a]Num 18:21, 26; 2 Chr 31:4f

6 [1]Or *tithes* [2]Lit *has blessed* [a]Heb 7:3 [b]Heb 7:1f [c]Rom 4:13

8 In this case mortal men receive tithes, but in that case one
receives them, [a]of whom it is witnessed that he lives on.
9 And, so to speak, through Abraham even Levi, who received
tithes, paid tithes,
10 for he was still in the loins of his father when Melchizedek
met him.
11 [a]Now if perfection was through the Levitical priesthood (for on the basis of it [b]the people received the Law), what further need *was there* for another priest to arise [c]according to the order of Melchizedek, and not be designated according to the order of Aaron?
12 For when the priesthood is changed, of necessity there takes place a change of law also.
13 For [a]the one concerning whom [b]these things are spoken belongs to another tribe, from which no one has officiated at the altar.
14 For it is evident that our Lord [1]was [a]descended from Judah, a tribe with reference to which Moses spoke nothing concerning priests.
15 And this is clearer still, if another priest arises according to the likeness of Melchizedek,
16 who has become *such* not on the basis of a law of [1a]physical requirement, but according to the power of [b]an indestructible life.
17 For it is attested *of Him,*

"[a]YOU ARE A PRIEST FOREVER
ACCORDING TO THE ORDER OF MELCHIZEDEK."

18 For, on the one hand, there is a setting aside of a former commandment [a]because of its weakness and uselessness
19 (for [a]the Law made nothing perfect), and on the other hand there is a bringing in of a better [b]hope, through which we [c]draw near to God.
20 And inasmuch as *it was* not without an oath
21 (for they indeed became priests without an oath, but He with an oath through the One who said to Him,

"[a]THE LORD HAS SWORN
AND [b]WILL NOT CHANGE HIS MIND,
'YOU ARE A PRIEST [c]FOREVER'");

22 so much the more also Jesus has become the [a]guarantee of [b]a better covenant.
23 [1]The *former* priests, on the one hand, existed in greater numbers because they were prevented by death from continuing,
24 but Jesus, on the other hand, because He continues [a]forever, holds His priesthood permanently.
25 Therefore He is able also to [a]save [1]forever those who [b]draw near to God through Him, since He always lives to [c]make intercession for them.
26 For it was fitting for us to have such a [a]high priest, [b]holy, [c]innocent, undefiled, separated from sinners and [d]exalted above the heavens;
27 who does not need daily, like those high priests, to [a]offer up sacrifices, [b]first for His own sins and then for the *sins* of the

8 [a]Heb 5:6; 6:20

11 [a]Heb 7:18f; 8:7 [b]Heb 9:6; 10:1 [c]Heb 5:6; 7:17

13 [a]Heb 7:14 [b]Heb 7:11

14 [1]Lit *has arisen from* [a]Num 24:17; Is 11:1; Mic 5:2; Matt 2:6; Rev 5:5

16 [1]Lit *fleshly commandment;* i.e. to be a descendant of Levi [a]Heb 9:10 [b]Heb 9:14

17 [a]Ps 110:4; Heb 5:6; 6:20; 7:21

18 [a]Rom 8:3; Gal 3:21; Heb 7:11

19 [a]Acts 13:39; Rom 3:20; 7:7f; Gal 2:16; 3:21; Heb 9:9; 10:1 [b]Heb 3:6 [c]Lam 3:57; Heb 4:16; 7:25; 10:1, 22; James 4:8

21 [a]Ps 110:4; Heb 5:6; 7:17 [b]Num 23:19; 1 Sam 15:29; Rom 11:29 [c]Heb 7:23f, 28

22 [a]Ps 119:122; Is 38:14 [b]Heb 8:6

23 [1]Lit *The greater number have become priests . . .*

24 [a]Is 9:7; John 12:34; Rom 9:5; Heb 7:23f, 28

25 [1]Or *completely* [a]1 Cor 1:21 [b]Heb 7:19 [c]Rom 8:34; Heb 9:24

26 [a]Heb 2:17 [b]2 Cor 5:21; Heb 4:15 [c]1 Pet 2:22 [d]Heb 4:14

27 [a]Heb 5:1 [b]Lev 9:7; Heb 5:3

people, because this He did [c]once for all when He [d]offered up
Himself.
28 For the Law appoints men as high priests [a]who are weak,
but the word of the oath, which came after the Law, *appoints*
[b]a Son, [c]made perfect forever.

Chapter 8 Theme ______________________________

8 Now the main point in what has been said *is this:* we have
such a [a]high priest, who has taken His seat at [b]the right hand
of the throne of the [b]Majesty in the heavens,
2 a [a]minister [1]in the sanctuary and [1]in the [b]true [2]tabernacle,
which the Lord [c]pitched, not man.
3 For every [a]high priest is appointed [b]to offer both gifts and
sacrifices; so it is necessary that this *high priest* also have
something to offer.
4 Now if He were on earth, He would not be a priest at all,
since there are those who [a]offer the gifts according to the Law;
5 who serve [a]a copy and [b]shadow of the heavenly things, just as
Moses [1]was [c]warned *by God* when he was about to erect the
[2]tabernacle; for, "[d]SEE," He says, "THAT YOU MAKE all things
ACCORDING TO THE PATTERN WHICH WAS SHOWN YOU ON THE MOUNTAIN."
6 But now He has obtained a more excellent ministry, by as
much as He is also the [a]mediator of [b]a better covenant, which
has been enacted on better promises.
7 For [a]if that first *covenant* had been faultless, there would
have been no occasion sought for a second.
8 For finding fault with them, He says,
"[a]BEHOLD, DAYS ARE COMING, SAYS THE LORD,
[1]WHEN I WILL EFFECT [b]A NEW COVENANT
WITH THE HOUSE OF ISRAEL AND WITH THE HOUSE OF JUDAH;
9 [a]NOT LIKE THE COVENANT WHICH I MADE WITH THEIR FATHERS
ON THE DAY WHEN I TOOK THEM BY THE HAND
TO LEAD THEM OUT OF THE LAND OF EGYPT;
FOR THEY DID NOT CONTINUE IN MY COVENANT,
AND I DID NOT CARE FOR THEM, SAYS THE LORD.
10 "[a]FOR THIS IS THE COVENANT THAT I WILL MAKE WITH THE HOUSE
OF ISRAEL
AFTER THOSE DAYS, SAYS THE LORD:
[1]I WILL PUT MY LAWS INTO THEIR MINDS,
AND I WILL WRITE THEM [b]ON THEIR HEARTS.
AND I WILL BE THEIR GOD,
AND THEY SHALL BE MY PEOPLE.
11 "[a]AND THEY SHALL NOT TEACH EVERYONE HIS FELLOW CITIZEN,
AND EVERYONE HIS BROTHER, SAYING, 'KNOW THE LORD,'
FOR [b]ALL WILL KNOW ME,
FROM [1]THE LEAST TO THE GREATEST OF THEM.
12 "[a]FOR I WILL BE MERCIFUL TO THEIR INIQUITIES,
[b]AND I WILL REMEMBER THEIR SINS NO MORE."
13 [1]When He said, "[a]A new *covenant,*" He has made the first
obsolete. [b]But whatever is becoming obsolete and growing old
is [2]ready to disappear.

27 [c]Heb 9:12, 28; 10:10 [d]Eph 5:2; Heb 9:14, 28; 10:10, 12

28 [a]Heb 5:2 [b]Heb 1:2 [c]Heb 2:10

8:1 [a]Col 3:1; Heb 2:17; 3:1 [b]Ps 110:1; Heb 1:3

2 [1]Or *of* [2]Or *sacred tent* [a]Heb 10:11 [b]Heb 9:11, 24 [c]Ex 33:7

3 [a]Heb 2:17 [b]Rom 4:25; 5:6, 8; Gal 2:20; Eph 5:2; Heb 5:1; 8:4

4 [a]Heb 5:1; 7:27; 8:3; 9:9; 10:11

5 [1]Lit *has been* [2]Or *sacred tent* [a]Heb 9:23 [b]Col 2:17; Heb 10:1 [c]Matt 2:12; Heb 11:7; 12:25 [d]Ex 25:40

6 [a]1 Tim 2:5 [b]Luke 22:20; Heb 7:22; 8:8; 9:15; 12:24

7 [a]Heb 7:11

8 [1]Lit *And* [a]Jer 31:31 [b]Luke 22:20; 2 Cor 3:6; Heb 7:22; 8:6, 13; 9:15; 12:24

9 [a]Ex 19:5; 24:6-8; Deut 5:2, 3; Jer 31:32

10 [1]Lit *Putting my laws into . . .* [a]Jer 31:33; Rom 11:27; Heb 10:16 [b]2 Cor 3:3

11 [1]Lit *small to great of them* [a]Jer 31:34 [b]Is 54:13; John 6:45; 1 John 2:27

12 [a]Is 43:25; Jer 31:34; 50:20; Mic 7:18, 19 [b]Heb 10:17

13 [1]Or *In His saying* [2]Or *near* [a]Luke 22:20; 2 Cor 3:6; Heb 7:22; 8:6, 8; 9:15; 12:24 [b]2 Cor 5:17; Heb 1:11

Inside the Tabernacle

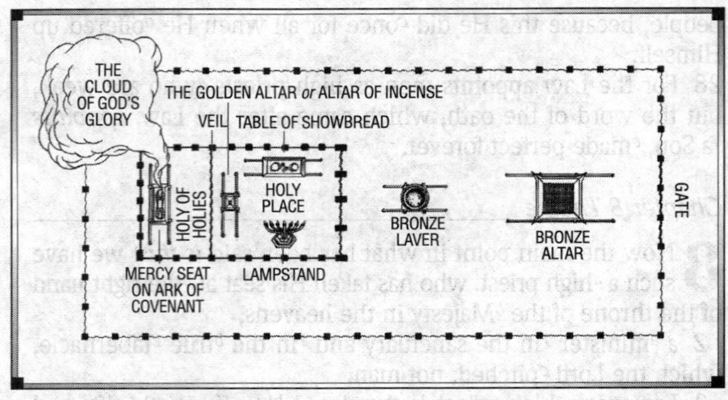

Chapter 9 Theme ______________________________

9 Now even the first *covenant* had [a]regulations of divine
worship and [b]the earthly sanctuary.
2 For there was [a]a [1]tabernacle prepared, the [2]outer one, in
which *were* [b]the lampstand and [c]the table and [d]the [3]sacred
bread; this is called the holy place.
3 Behind [a]the second veil there was a [1]tabernacle which is
called the [b]Holy of Holies,
4 having a golden [1a]altar of incense and [b]the ark of the
covenant covered on all sides with gold, in which was [c]a golden
jar holding the manna, and [d]Aaron's rod which budded, and [e]the
tables of the covenant;
5 and above it *were* the [a]cherubim of glory [b]overshadowing the
mercy seat; but of these things we cannot now speak in detail.
6 Now when these things have been so prepared, the priests
[a]are continually entering the [1]outer [2]tabernacle performing the
divine worship,
7 but into [a]the second, only [b]the high priest *enters* [c]once a
year, [d]not without *taking* blood, which he [e]offers for himself and
for the [1f]sins of the people committed in ignorance.
8 [a]The Holy Spirit *is* signifying this, [b]that the way into the holy
place has not yet been disclosed while the [1]outer tabernacle is still
standing,
9 which *is* a symbol for the present time. Accordingly [a]both
gifts and sacrifices are offered which [b]cannot make the worshiper
perfect in conscience,
10 since they *relate* only to [a]food and [b]drink and various
[c]washings, [d]regulations for the [1]body imposed until [e]a time of
reformation.
11 But when Christ appeared *as* a [a]high priest of the [b]good
things [1]to come, *He entered* through [c]the greater and more
perfect [2]tabernacle, [d]not made with hands, that is to say, [e]not of
this creation;
12 and not through [a]the blood of goats and calves, but [b]through
His own blood, He [c]entered the holy place [d]once for all, [1]having
obtained [e]eternal redemption.
13 For if [a]the blood of goats and bulls and [b]the ashes of a

9:1 [a]Heb 9:10 [b]Ex 25:8; Heb 8:2; 9:11, 24

2 [1]Or *sacred tent* [2]Lit *first* [3]Lit *loaves of presentation* [a]Ex 25:8, 9; 26:1-30 [b]Ex 25:31-39 [c]Ex 25:23-29 [d]Ex 25:30; Lev 24:5ff; Matt 12:4

3 [1]Or *sacred tent* [a]Ex 26:31-33; 40:3 [b]Ex 26:33

4 [1]Or *censer* [a]Ex 30:1-5; 37:25f [b]Ex 25:10ff; 37:1ff [c]Ex 16:32f [d]Num 17:10 [e]Ex 25:16; 31:18; 32:15; Deut 9:9, 11, 15; 10:3-5

5 [a]Ex 25:18ff [b]Ex 25:17, 20; Lev 16:2; 1 Kin 8:7

6 [1]Lit *first* [2]Or *sacred tent* [a]Num 18:2-6; 28:3

7 [1]Lit *ignorance of the people* [a]Heb 9:3 [b]Lev 16:12ff [c]Ex 30:10; Lev 16:34; Heb 10:3 [d]Lev 16:11, 14 [e]Heb 5:3 [f]Num 15:25; Heb 5:2

8 [1]Lit *first* [a]Heb 3:7 [b]John 14:6; Heb 10:20

9 [a]Heb 5:1 [b]Heb 7:19

10 [1]Lit *flesh* [a]Lev 11:2ff; Col 2:16 [b]Num 6:3 [c]Lev 11:25; Num 19:13; Mark 7:4 [d]Heb 7:16 [e]Heb 7:12

11 [1]Two early mss read *that have come* [2]Or *sacred tent* [a]Heb 2:17 [b]Heb 10:1 [c]Heb 8:2; 9:24 [d]Mark 14:58; 2 Cor 5:1 [e]2 Cor 4:18; Heb 12:27; 13:14

12 [1]Or *obtaining* [a]Lev 4:3; 16:6, 15; Heb 9:19 [b]Heb 9:14; 13:12 [c]Heb 9:24 [d]Heb 7:27 [e]Heb 5:9; 9:15

13 [a]Lev 16:15; Heb 9:19; 10:4 [b]Num 19:9, 17f

heifer sprinkling those who have been defiled sanctify for the [1]cleansing of the flesh,

14 how much more will [a]the blood of Christ, who through [1b]the eternal Spirit [c]offered Himself without blemish to God, [d]cleanse [2]your conscience from [e]dead works to serve [f]the living God?

15 For this reason [a]He is the [b]mediator of a [c]new covenant, so that, since a death has taken place for the redemption of the transgressions that were *committed* under the first covenant, those who have been [d]called may [e]receive the promise of [f]the eternal inheritance.

16 For where a [1]covenant is, there must of necessity [2]be the death of the one who made it.

17 For a [1]covenant is valid *only* when [2]men are dead, [3]for it is never in force while the one who made it lives.

18 Therefore even the first *covenant* was not inaugurated without blood.

19 For when every commandment had been [a]spoken by Moses to all the people according to the Law, [b]he took the [c]blood of the calves and the goats, with [d]water and scarlet wool and hyssop, and sprinkled both [e]the book itself and all the people,

20 saying, "[a]THIS IS THE BLOOD OF THE COVENANT WHICH GOD COMMANDED YOU."

21 And in the same way he [a]sprinkled both the [1]tabernacle and all the vessels of the ministry with the blood.

22 And according to the [1]Law, *one may* [a]almost *say,* all things are cleansed with blood, and [b]without shedding of blood there is no forgiveness.

23 Therefore it was necessary for the [a]copies of the things in the heavens to be cleansed with these, but [a]the heavenly things themselves with better sacrifices than these.

24 For Christ [a]did not enter a holy place made with hands, a *mere* copy of [b]the true one, but into [c]heaven itself, now [d]to appear in the presence of God for us;

25 nor was it that He would offer Himself often, as [a]the high priest enters [b]the holy place [a]year by year with blood that is not his own.

26 Otherwise, He would have needed to suffer often since [a]the foundation of the world; but now [b]once at [c]the consummation of the ages He has been [d]manifested to put away sin [1e]by the sacrifice of Himself.

27 And inasmuch as [a]it is [1]appointed for men to die once and after this [b]*comes* judgment,

28 so Christ also, having been [a]offered once to [b]bear the sins of many, will appear [c]a second time for [d]salvation [e]without *reference to* sin, to those who [f]eagerly await Him.

Chapter 10 Theme

10 For the Law, since it has *only* [a]a shadow of [b]the good things to come *and* not the very [1]form of things, [2]can [c]never, by the same sacrifices which they offer continually year by year, [d]make perfect those who draw near.

13 [1]Lit *purity*

14 [1]Or His *eternal spirit* [2]One early ms reads *our* [a]Heb 9:12; 13:12 [b]1 Cor 15:45; 1 Pet 3:18 [c]Eph 5:2; Heb 7:27; 10:10, 12 [d]Acts 15:9; Titus 2:14; Heb 1:3; 10:2, 22 [e]Heb 6:1 [f]Matt 16:16; Heb 3:12

15 [a]Rom 3:24 [b]1 Tim 2:5; Heb 8:6; 12:24 [c]Heb 8:8 [d]Matt 22:3ff; Rom 8:28f; Heb 3:1 [e]Heb 6:15; 10:36; 11:39 [f]Acts 20:32

16 [1]Or *testament* [2]Lit *be brought*

17 [1]Or *testament* [2]Lit *over the dead* [3]Two early mss read *for is it then . . . lives?*

19 [a]Heb 1:1 [b]Ex 24:6ff [c]Heb 9:12 [d]Lev 14:4, 7; Num 19:6, 18 [e]Ex 24:7

20 [a]Ex 24:8; Matt 26:28

21 [1]Or *sacred tent* [a]Ex 24:6; 40:9; Lev 8:15, 19; 16:14-16

22 [1]Or *Law, almost all things* [a]Lev 5:11f [b]Lev 17:11

23 [a]Heb 8:5

24 [a]Heb 4:14; 9:12 [b]Heb 8:2 [c]Heb 9:12 [d]Matt 18:10; Heb 7:25

25 [a]Heb 9:7 [b]Heb 9:2; 10:19

26 [1]Or *by His sacrifice* [a]Matt 25:34; Heb 4:3 [b]Heb 7:27; 9:12 [c]Matt 13:39; Heb 1:2 [d]1 John 3:5, 8 [e]Heb 9:12, 14

27 [1]Lit *laid up* [a]Gen 3:19 [b]2 Cor 5:10; 1 John 4:17

28 [a]Heb 7:27 [b]Is 53:12; 1 Pet 2:24 [c]Acts 1:11 [d]Heb 5:9 [e]Heb 4:15 [f]1 Cor 1:7; Titus 2:13

10:1 [1]Lit *image* [2]Two early mss read *they can* [a]Heb 8:5 [b]Heb 9:11 [c]Rom 8:3; Heb 9:9; 10:4, 11 [d]Heb 7:19

2 Otherwise, would they not have ceased to be offered,
because the worshipers, having once been cleansed, would no
longer have had [a]consciousness of sins?
3 But [a]in [1]those *sacrifices* there is a reminder of sins year by
year.
4 For it is [a]impossible for the [b]blood of bulls and goats to take
away sins.
5 Therefore, [a]when He comes into the world, He says,

"[b]SACRIFICE AND OFFERING YOU HAVE NOT DESIRED,
BUT [c]A BODY YOU HAVE PREPARED FOR ME;
6 [a]IN WHOLE BURNT OFFERINGS AND *sacrifices* FOR SIN YOU HAVE
TAKEN NO PLEASURE.
7 "[a]THEN I SAID, 'BEHOLD, I HAVE COME
(IN [b]THE SCROLL OF THE BOOK IT IS WRITTEN OF ME)
TO DO YOUR WILL, O GOD.'"

8 After saying above, "[a]SACRIFICES AND OFFERINGS AND [b]WHOLE
BURNT OFFERINGS AND *sacrifices* [c]FOR SIN YOU HAVE NOT DESIRED, NOR
HAVE YOU TAKEN PLEASURE *in them*" (which are offered according
to the Law),
9 then He [1]said, "[a]BEHOLD, I HAVE COME TO DO YOUR WILL." He
takes away the first in order to establish the second.
10 By [1]this will we have been [a]sanctified through [b]the offering
of [c]the body of Jesus Christ [d]once for all.
11 Every priest stands daily ministering and [a]offering time
after time the same sacrifices, which [b]can never take away sins;
12 but He, having offered one sacrifice [a]for [1]sins [b]for all time,
[c]SAT DOWN AT THE RIGHT HAND OF GOD,
13 waiting from that time onward [a]UNTIL HIS ENEMIES BE MADE A
FOOTSTOOL FOR HIS FEET.
14 For by one offering He has [a]perfected [b]for all time those
who are [1]sanctified.
15 And [a]the Holy Spirit also testifies to us; for after saying,

16 "[a]THIS IS THE COVENANT THAT I WILL MAKE WITH THEM
AFTER THOSE DAYS, SAYS THE LORD:
I WILL PUT MY LAWS UPON THEIR HEART,
AND ON THEIR MIND I WILL WRITE THEM,"

He then says,

17 "[a]AND THEIR SINS AND THEIR LAWLESS DEEDS
I WILL REMEMBER NO MORE."

18 Now where there is forgiveness of these things, there is no
longer *any* offering for sin.
19 Therefore, brethren, since we [a]have confidence to [b]enter
the holy place by the blood of Jesus,
20 by [a]a new and living way which He inaugurated for us
through [b]the veil, that is, His flesh,
21 and since *we have* [a]a great priest [b]over the house of God,
22 let us [a]draw near with a [1]sincere heart in [b]full assurance of
faith, having our hearts [c]sprinkled *clean* from an evil conscience
and our bodies [d]washed with pure water.
23 Let us hold fast the [a]confession of our [b]hope without
wavering, for [c]He who promised is faithful;

2 [a]1 Pet 2:19

3 [1]Lit *them there is* [a]Heb 9:7

4 [a]Heb 10:1, 11 [b]Heb 9:12f

5 [a]Heb 1:6 [b]Ps 40:6 [c]Heb 2:14; 5:7; 1 Pet 2:24

6 [a]Ps 40:6

7 [a]Ps 40:7, 8 [b]Ezra 6:2; Jer 36:2; Ezek 2:9; 3:1f

8 [a]Ps 40:6; Heb 10:5f [b]Mark 12:33 [c]Rom 8:3

9 [1]Lit *has said* [a]Ps 40:7, 8; Heb 10:7

10 [1]Lit *which* [a]John 17:19; Eph 5:26; Heb 2:11; 10:14, 29; 13:12 [b]John 6:51; Eph 5:2; Heb 7:27; 9:14, 28; 10:12 [c]Heb 2:14; 5:7; 1 Pet 2:24 [d]Heb 7:27

11 [a]Heb 5:1 [b]Mic 6:6-8; Heb 10:1, 4

12 [1]Or *sins, forever sat down* [a]Heb 5:1 [b]Heb 10:14 [c]Ps 110:1; Heb 1:3

13 [a]Ps 110:1; Heb 1:13

14 [1]Or *being sanctified* [a]Heb 10:1 [b]Heb 10:12

15 [a]Heb 3:7

16 [a]Jer 31:33; Heb 8:10

17 [a]Jer 31:34; Heb 8:12

19 [a]Heb 3:6; 10:35 [b]Heb 9:25

20 [a]Heb 9:8 [b]Heb 6:19; 9:3

21 [a]Heb 2:17 [b]1 Tim 3:15; Heb 3:6

22 [1]Lit *true* [a]Heb 7:19; 10:1 [b]Heb 6:11 [c]Ezek 36:25; Heb 9:19; 12:24; 1 Pet 1:2 [d]Acts 22:16; 1 Cor 6:11; Eph 5:26; Titus 3:5; 1 Pet 3:21

23 [a]Heb 3:1 [b]Heb 3:6 [c]1 Cor 1:9; 10:13; Heb 11:11

24 and let us consider how [a]to stimulate one another to love
and [b]good deeds,
25 not forsaking our own [a]assembling together, as is the habit
of some, but [b]encouraging *one another;* and all the more as you
see [c]the day drawing near.
26 For if we go on [a]sinning willfully after receiving [b]the
knowledge of the truth, there no longer remains a sacrifice for sins,
27 but a terrifying expectation of [a]judgment and [b]THE FURY OF A
FIRE WHICH WILL CONSUME THE ADVERSARIES.
28 [a]Anyone who has set aside the Law of Moses dies without
mercy on *the testimony of* two or three witnesses.
29 [a]How much severer punishment do you think he will
deserve [b]who has trampled under foot the Son of God, and has
regarded as unclean [c]the blood of the covenant [d]by which he
was sanctified, and has [e]insulted the Spirit of grace?
30 For we know Him who said, "[a]VENGEANCE IS MINE, I WILL
REPAY." And again, "[b]THE LORD WILL JUDGE HIS PEOPLE."
31 It is a [a]terrifying thing to fall into the hands of the [b]living God.
32 But remember [a]the former days, [1]when, after being
[b]enlightened, you endured a great [c]conflict of sufferings,
33 partly by being [a]made a public spectacle through reproaches
and tribulations, and partly by becoming [b]sharers with those
who were so treated.
34 For you [a]showed sympathy to the prisoners and accepted
[b]joyfully the seizure of your property, knowing that you have
for yourselves [c]a better possession and a lasting one.
35 Therefore, do not throw away your [a]confidence, which has
a great [b]reward.
36 For you have need of [a]endurance, so that when you have
[b]done the will of God, you may [c]receive [1]what was promised.
37 [a]FOR YET IN A VERY LITTLE WHILE,
[b]HE WHO IS COMING WILL COME, AND WILL NOT DELAY.
38 [a]BUT MY RIGHTEOUS ONE SHALL LIVE BY FAITH;
AND IF HE SHRINKS BACK, MY SOUL HAS NO PLEASURE IN HIM.
39 But [1]we are not of those who shrink back to destruction,
but of those who have faith to the [2]preserving of the soul.

Chapter 11 Theme ____________________

11 Now faith is the [1a]assurance of *things* [2b]hoped for, the [3]con-
viction of [c]things not seen.
2 For by it the [a]men of old [1b]gained approval.
3 By faith we understand that the [1a]worlds were prepared
[b]by the word of God, so that what is seen [c]was not made out of
things which are visible.
4 By faith [a]Abel offered to God a better sacrifice than Cain,
through which he [b]obtained the testimony that he was righteous,
God testifying [1]about his [c]gifts, and through [2]faith, though [d]he is
dead, he still speaks.
5 By faith [a]Enoch was taken up so that he would not [b]see
death; AND HE WAS NOT FOUND BECAUSE GOD TOOK HIM UP; for he

24 [a]Heb 13:1 [b]Titus 3:8
25 [a]Acts 2:42 [b]Heb 3:13 [c]1 Cor 3:13
26 [a]Num 15:30; Heb 6:4-8; 2 Pet 2:20f [b]1 Tim 2:4
27 [a]John 5:29; Heb 9:27 [b]Is 26:11; 2 Thess 1:7
28 [a]Deut 17:2-6; 19:15; Matt 18:16; Heb 2:2
29 [a]Heb 2:3 [b]Heb 6:6 [c]Ex 24:8; Matt 26:28; Heb 13:20 [d]Eph 5:26; Heb 9:13f; Rev 1:5 [e]1 Cor 6:11; Eph 4:30; Heb 6:4
30 [a]Deut 32:35; Rom 12:19 [b]Deut 32:36
31 [a]2 Cor 5:11 [b]Matt 16:16; Heb 3:12
32 [1]Lit *in which* [a]Heb 5:12 [b]Heb 6:4 [c]Phil 1:30
33 [a]1 Cor 4:9; Heb 12:4 [b]Phil 4:14; 1 Thess 2:14
34 [a]Heb 13:3 [b]Matt 5:12 [c]Heb 9:15; 11:16; 13:14; 1 Pet 1:4f
35 [a]Heb 10:19 [b]Heb 2:2
36 [1]Lit *the promise* [a]Luke 21:19; Heb 12:1 [b]Mark 3:35 [c]Heb 9:15
37 [a]Hab 2:3; Heb 10:25; Rev 22:20 [b]Matt 11:3
38 [a]Hab 2:4; Rom 1:17; Gal 3:11
39 [1]Lit *we are not of shrinking back . . . but of faith* [2]Or *possessing*
11:1 [1]Or *substance* [2]Or *expected* [3]Or *evidence* [a]Heb 3:14 [b]Heb 3:6 [c]Rom 8:24; 2 Cor 4:18; 5:7; Heb 11:7, 27
2 [1]Lit *obtained a good testimony* [a]Heb 1:1 [b]Heb 11:4, 39
3 [1]Lit *ages* [a]John 1:3; Heb 1:2 [b]Gen ch 1; Ps 33:6, 9; Heb 6:5; 2 Pet 3:5 [c]Rom 4:17
4 [1]I.e. by receiving his gifts [2]Lit *it* [a]Gen 4:4; Matt 23:35; 1 John 3:12 [b]Heb 11:2 [c]Heb 5:1 [d]Gen 4:8-10; Heb 12:24
5 [a]Gen 5:21-24 [b]Luke 2:26; John 8:51; Heb 2:9

obtained the witness that before his being taken up he was
pleasing to God.
6 And without faith it is impossible to please *Him,* for he
who [a]comes to God must believe that He is and *that* He is a
rewarder of those who seek Him.
7 By faith [a]Noah, being [b]warned *by God* about [c]things not yet
seen, [1d]in reverence [e]prepared an ark for the salvation of his
household, by which he condemned the world, and became an
heir of [f]the righteousness which is according to faith.
8 By faith [a]Abraham, when he was called, obeyed [1]by going
out to a place which he was to [b]receive for an inheritance; and
he went out, not knowing where he was going.
9 By faith he lived as an alien in [a]the land of promise, as in a
foreign *land,* [b]dwelling in tents with Isaac and Jacob, [c]fellow
heirs of the same promise;
10 for he was looking for [a]the city which has [b]foundations,
[c]whose architect and builder is God.
11 By faith even [a]Sarah herself received [1]ability to conceive,
even beyond the proper time of life, since she considered Him
[b]faithful who had promised.
12 Therefore there was born even of one man, and [a]him as good
as dead [1]at that, *as many descendants* [b]AS THE STARS OF HEAVEN IN
NUMBER, AND INNUMERABLE AS THE SAND WHICH IS BY THE SEASHORE.
13 [a]All these died in faith, [b]without receiving the promises, but
[c]having seen them and having welcomed them from a distance,
and [d]having confessed that they were strangers and exiles on
the earth.
14 For those who say such things make it clear that they are
seeking a country of their own.
15 And indeed if they had been [1]thinking of that *country* from
which they went out, [a]they would have had opportunity to
return.
16 But as it is, they desire a better *country,* that is, a [a]heavenly
one. Therefore [b]God is not [1]ashamed to be [c]called their God;
for [d]He has prepared a city for them.
17 By faith [a]Abraham, when he was tested, offered up Isaac,
and he who had [b]received the promises was offering up his only
begotten *son;*
18 *it was he* to whom it was said, "[a]IN ISAAC YOUR [1]DESCENDANTS
SHALL BE CALLED."
19 [1]He considered that [a]God is able to raise *people* even from
the dead, from which he also received him back [2]as a [b]type.
20 By faith [a]Isaac blessed Jacob and Esau, even regarding things
to come.
21 By faith [a]Jacob, as he was dying, blessed each of the sons of
Joseph, and [b]worshiped, *leaning* on the top of his staff.
22 By faith [a]Joseph, when he was dying, made mention of the
exodus of the sons of Israel, and gave orders concerning his bones.
23 By faith [a]Moses, when he was born, was hidden for three
months by his parents, because they saw he was a beautiful
child; and they were not afraid of the [b]king's edict.

6 [a]Heb 7:19

7 [1]Lit *having become reverent* [a]Gen 6:13-22 [b]Heb 8:5 [c]Heb 11:1 [d]Heb 5:7 [e]1 Pet 3:20 [f]Gen 6:9; Ezek 14:14, 20; Rom 4:13; 9:30

8 [1]Lit *to go out* [a]Gen 12:1-4; Acts 7:2-4 [b]Gen 12:7

9 [a]Acts 7:5 [b]Gen 12:8; 13:3, 18; 18:1, 9 [c]Heb 6:17

10 [a]Heb 12:22; 13:14 [b]Rev 21:14ff [c]Heb 11:16

11 [1]Lit *power for the laying down of seed* [a]Gen 17:19; 18:11-14; 21:2 [b]Heb 10:23

12 [1]Lit *in these things* [a]Rom 4:19 [b]Gen 15:5; 22:17; 32:12

13 [a]Matt 13:17 [b]Heb 11:39 [c]John 8:56; Heb 11:27 [d]Gen 23:4; 47:9; 1 Chr 29:15; Ps 39:12; Eph 2:19; 1 Pet 1:1; 2:11

15 [1]Or *remembering* [a]Gen 24:6-8

16 [1]Lit *ashamed of them, to be* [a]2 Tim 4:18 [b]Mark 8:38; Heb 2:11 [c]Gen 26:24; 28:13; Ex 3:6, 15; 4:5 [d]Heb 11:10; Rev 21:2

17 [a]Gen 22:1-10; James 2:21 [b]Heb 11:13

18 [1]Lit *seed* [a]Gen 21:12; Rom 9:7

19 [1]Lit *Considering* [2]Or *figuratively speaking;* lit *in a parable* [a]Rom 4:21 [b]Heb 9:9

20 [a]Gen 27:27-29, 39f

21 [a]Gen 48:1, 5, 16, 20 [b]Gen 47:31; 1 Kin 1:47

22 [a]Gen 50:24f; Ex 13:19

23 [a]Ex 2:2 [b]Ex 1:16, 22

24 By faith Moses, [a]when he had grown up, refused to be
called the son of Pharaoh's daughter,
25 choosing rather to [a]endure ill-treatment with the people of
God than to enjoy the passing pleasures of sin,
26 [a]considering the reproach of [1]Christ greater riches than the
treasures of Egypt; for he was looking to the [b]reward.
27 By faith he [a]left Egypt, not [b]fearing the wrath of the king; for
he endured, as [c]seeing Him who is unseen.
28 By faith he [1a]kept the Passover and the sprinkling of the blood,
so that [b]he who destroyed the firstborn would not touch them.
29 By faith they [a]passed through the Red Sea as though *they
were passing* through dry land; and the Egyptians, when they
attempted it, were [1]drowned.
30 By faith [a]the walls of Jericho fell down [b]after they had been
encircled for seven days.
31 By faith [a]Rahab the harlot did not perish along with those
who were disobedient, after she had welcomed the spies [1]in
peace.
32 And what more shall I say? For time will fail me if I tell of
[a]Gideon, [b]Barak, [c]Samson, [d]Jephthah, of [e]David and [f]Samuel and
the prophets,
33 who by faith [a]conquered kingdoms, [b]performed *acts of*
righteousness, [c]obtained promises, [d]shut the mouths of lions,
34 [a]quenched the power of fire, [b]escaped the edge of the sword,
from weakness were made strong, [c]became mighty in war, [c]put
foreign armies to flight.
35 [a]Women received *back* their dead by resurrection; and others
were tortured, not accepting their [1]release, so that they might
obtain a better resurrection;
36 and others [1]experienced mockings and scourgings, yes, also
[a]chains and imprisonment.
37 They were [a]stoned, they were [b]sawn in two, [1]they were
tempted, they were [c]put to death with the sword; they went
about [d]in sheepskins, in goatskins, being destitute, afflicted, [e]ill-
treated
38 (*men* of whom the world was not worthy), [a]wandering in
deserts and mountains and caves and holes [1]in the ground.
39 And all these, having [1a]gained approval through their faith,
[b]did not receive [2]what was promised,
40 because God had [1]provided [a]something better for us, so
that [b]apart from us they would not be made perfect.

Chapter 12 Theme ______________________

12 Therefore, since we have so great a cloud of witnesses
surrounding us, let us also [a]lay aside every encumbrance
and the sin which so easily entangles us, and let us [b]run with
[c]endurance the race that is set before us,
2 [1]fixing our eyes on Jesus, the [2a]author and perfecter of faith,
who for the joy set before Him [b]endured the cross, [c]despising the
shame, and has [d]sat down at the right hand of the throne of God.

24 [a]Ex 2:10, 11ff
25 [a]Heb 11:37
26 [1]I.e. the Messiah [a]Luke 14:33; Phil 3:7f [b]Heb 2:2
27 [a]Ex 2:15; 12:50f; 13:17f [b]Ex 2:14; 10:28f [c]Col 1:15; Heb 11:1, 13
28 [1]Lit *has kept* [a]Ex 12:21ff [b]Ex 12:23, 29f; 1 Cor 10:10
29 [1]Lit *swallowed up* [a]Ex 14:22-29
30 [a]Josh 6:20 [b]Josh 6:15f
31 [1]Lit *with* [a]Josh 2:9ff; 6:23; James 2:25
32 [a]Judg ch 6-8 [b]Judg ch 4, 5 [c]Judg ch 13-16 [d]Judg ch 11, 12 [e]1 Sam 16:1, 13 [f]1 Sam 1:20
33 [a]Judg ch 4, 7, 11, 14; 2 Sam 5:17-20; 8:1f; 10:12 [b]1 Sam 12:4; 2 Sam 8:15 [c]2 Sam 7:11f [d]Judg 14:6; 1 Sam 17:34ff; Dan 6:22
34 [a]Dan 3:23ff [b]Ex 18:4; 1 Sam 18:11; 19:10; 1 Kin ch 19; 2 Kin ch 6; Ps 144:10 [c]Judg 7:21; 15:8, 15f; 1 Sam 17:51f; 2 Sam 8:1-6; 10:15ff
35 [1]Lit *redemption* [a]1 Kin 17:23; 2 Kin 4:36f
36 [1]Lit *received the trial of* [a]Gen 39:20; 1 Kin 22:27; 2 Chr 18:26; Jer 20:2; 37:15
37 [1]One early ms does not contain *they were tempted* [a]1 Kin 21:13; 2 Chr 24:21 [b]2 Sam 12:31; 1 Chr 20:3 [c]1 Kin 19:10; Jer 26:23 [d]1 Kin 19:13, 19; 2 Kin 2:8, 13f; Zech 13:4 [e]Heb 11:25; 13:3
38 [1]Lit *of* [a]1 Kin 18:4, 13; 19:9
39 [1]Lit *obtained a testimony* [2]Lit *the promise* [a]Heb 11:2 [b]Heb 10:36; 11:13
40 [1]Or *foreseen* [a]Heb 11:16 [b]Rev 6:11
12:1 [a]Rom 13:12; Eph 4:22 [b]1 Cor 9:24; Gal 2:2 [c]Heb 10:36
2 [1]Lit *looking to* [2]Or *leader* [a]Heb 2:10 [b]Phil 2:8f; Heb 2:9 [c]1 Cor 1:18, 23; Heb 13:13 [d]Heb 1:3

3 For [a]consider Him who has endured such hostility by
sinners against Himself, so that you will not grow weary [1b]and
lose heart.
4 [a]You have not yet resisted [1b]to the point of shedding blood
in your striving against sin;
5 and you have forgotten the exhortation which is addressed
to you as sons,

"[a]MY SON, DO NOT REGARD LIGHTLY THE DISCIPLINE OF THE LORD,
NOR [b]FAINT WHEN YOU ARE REPROVED BY HIM;
6 [a]FOR THOSE [b]WHOM THE LORD LOVES HE DISCIPLINES,
AND HE SCOURGES EVERY SON WHOM HE RECEIVES."

7 It is for discipline that you endure; [a]God deals with you as
with sons; for what son is there whom *his* father does not
discipline?
8 But if you are without discipline, [a]of which all have become
partakers, then you are illegitimate children and not sons.
9 Furthermore, we had [1]earthly fathers to discipline us, and we
[a]respected them; shall we not much rather be subject to [b]the
Father of [2]spirits, and [c]live?
10 For they disciplined us for a short time as seemed best to
them, but He *disciplines us* for *our* good, [a]so that we may share
His holiness.
11 All discipline [a]for the moment seems not to be joyful, but
sorrowful; yet to those who have been trained by it, afterwards
it yields the [b]peaceful fruit of righteousness.
12 Therefore, [1a]strengthen the hands that are weak and the
knees that are feeble,
13 and [a]make straight paths for your feet, so that *the limb* which
is lame may not be put out of joint, but rather [b]be healed.
14 [a]Pursue peace with all men, and the [b]sanctification without
which no one will [c]see the Lord.
15 See to it that no one [a]comes short of the grace of God; that
no [b]root of bitterness springing up causes trouble, and by it
many be [c]defiled;
16 that *there be* no [a]immoral or [b]godless person like Esau,
[c]who sold his own birthright for a *single* meal.
17 For you know that even afterwards, [a]when he desired to
inherit the blessing, he was rejected, for he found no place for
repentance, though he sought for it with tears.
18 [a]For you have not come to [b]*a mountain* that can be touched
and to a blazing fire, and to darkness and gloom and whirlwind,
19 and to the [a]blast of a trumpet and the [b]sound of words which
sound was such that those who heard [c]begged that no further
word be spoken to them.
20 For they could not bear the command, "[a]IF EVEN A BEAST
TOUCHES THE MOUNTAIN, IT WILL BE STONED."
21 And so terrible was the sight, *that* Moses said, "[a]I AM FULL
OF FEAR and trembling."
22 But [a]you have come to Mount Zion and to [b]the city of [c]the
living God, [d]the heavenly Jerusalem, and to [e]myriads of [1]angels,
23 to the general assembly and [a]church of the firstborn who

3 [1]Lit *fainting in your souls* [a]Rev 2:3 [b]Gal 6:9; Heb 12:5

4 [1]Lit *as far as blood* [a]Heb 10:32ff; 13:13 [b]Phil 2:8

5 [a]Job 5:17; Prov 3:11 [b]Heb 12:3

6 [a]Prov 3:12 [b]Ps 119:75; Rev 3:19

7 [a]Deut 8:5; 2 Sam 7:14; Prov 13:24; 19:18; 23:13f

8 [a]1 Pet 5:9

9 [1]Lit *fathers of our flesh* [2]Or *our spirits* [a]Luke 18:2 [b]Num 16:22; 27:16; Rev 22:6 [c]Is 38:16

10 [a]2 Pet 1:4

11 [a]1 Pet 1:6 [b]Is 32:17; 2 Tim 4:8; James 3:17f

12 [1]Lit *make straight* [a]Is 35:3

13 [a]Prov 4:26; Gal 2:14 [b]Gal 6:1; James 5:16

14 [a]Rom 14:19 [b]Rom 6:22; Heb 12:10 [c]Matt 5:8; Heb 9:28

15 [a]2 Cor 6:1; Gal 5:4; Heb 4:1 [b]Deut 29:18 [c]Titus 1:15

16 [a]Heb 13:4 [b]1 Tim 1:9 [c]Gen 25:33f

17 [a]Gen 27:30-40

18 [a]2 Cor 3:7-13; Heb 12:18ff [b]Ex 19:12, 16ff; 20:18; Deut 4:11; 5:22

19 [a]Ex 19:16, 19; 20:18; Matt 24:31 [b]Ex 19:19; Deut 4:12 [c]Ex 20:19; Deut 5:25; 18:16

20 [a]Ex 19:12f

21 [a]Deut 9:19

22 [1]Or *angels in festive gathering, and to the church* [a]Rev 14:1 [b]Eph 2:19; Phil 3:20; Heb 11:10; Rev 21:2 [c]Heb 3:12 [d]Gal 4:26; Heb 11:16 [e]Rev 5:11

23 [a]Ex 4:22; Heb 2:12

[b]are enrolled in heaven, and to God, [c]the Judge of all, and to
the [d]spirits of *the* righteous made perfect,
24 and to Jesus, the [a]mediator of a new covenant, and to the
[b]sprinkled blood, which speaks better than [c]*the blood* of Abel.
25 [a]See to it that you do not refuse Him who is [b]speaking. For
[c]if those did not escape when they [d]refused him who [e]warned
them on earth, [1]much less *will* we *escape* who turn away from
Him who [e]*warns* from heaven.
26 And [a]His voice shook the earth then, but now He has
promised, saying, "[b]YET ONCE MORE I WILL SHAKE NOT ONLY THE
EARTH, BUT ALSO THE HEAVEN."
27 This *expression,* "Yet once more," denotes [a]the removing
of those things which can be shaken, as of created things, so
that those things which cannot be shaken may remain.
28 Therefore, since we receive a [a]kingdom which cannot be
shaken, let us [1]show gratitude, by which we may [b]offer to God
an acceptable service with reverence and awe;
29 for [a]our God is a consuming fire.

Chapter 13 Theme ______________________

13 Let [a]love of the brethren continue.
2 Do not neglect to [a]show hospitality to strangers, for by
this some have [b]entertained angels without knowing it.
3 [a]Remember [b]the prisoners, as though in prison with them,
and those who are ill-treated, since you yourselves also are in
the body.
4 [a]Marriage *is to be held* in honor among all, and the *marriage*
bed *is to be* undefiled; [b]for fornicators and adulterers God will
judge.
5 *Make sure that* your character is [a]free from the love of
money, [b]being content with what you have; for He Himself has
said, "[c]I WILL NEVER DESERT YOU, NOR WILL I EVER FORSAKE YOU,"
6 so that we confidently say,
"[a]THE LORD IS MY HELPER, I WILL NOT BE AFRAID.
WHAT WILL MAN DO TO ME?"
7 Remember [a]those who led you, who spoke [b]the word of God
to you; and considering the [1]result of their conduct, [c]imitate
their faith.
8 [a]Jesus Christ *is* the same yesterday and today and forever.
9 [a]Do not be carried away by varied and strange teachings;
for it is good for the heart to [b]be strengthened by grace, not by
[c]foods, [d]through which those who [1]were so occupied were not
benefited.
10 We have an altar [a]from which those [b]who serve the [1]taber-
nacle have no right to eat.
11 For [a]the bodies of those animals whose blood is brought
into the holy place by the high priest *as an offering* for sin, are
burned outside the camp.
12 Therefore Jesus also, [a]that He might sanctify the people
[b]through His own blood, suffered [c]outside the gate.

23 [b]Luke 10:20 [c]Gen 18:25; Ps 50:6; 94:2 [d]Heb 11:40; Rev 6:9, 11
24 [a]1 Tim 2:5; Heb 8:6; 9:15 [b]Heb 9:19; 10:22; 1 Pet 1:2 [c]Gen 4:10; Heb 11:4
25 [1]Lit *much rather we* will not *escape . . .* [a]Heb 3:12 [b]Heb 1:1 [c]Heb 2:2f; 10:28f [d]Heb 12:19 [e]Ex 20:22; Heb 8:5; 11:7
26 [a]Ex 19:18; Judg 5:4f [b]Hag 2:6
27 [a]Is 34:4; 54:10; 65:17; Rom 8:19, 21; 1 Cor 7:31; Heb 1:10ff
28 [1]Lit *have* [a]Dan 2:44 [b]Heb 13:15, 21
29 [a]Deut 4:24; 9:3; Is 33:14; 2 Thess 1:7; Heb 10:27, 31
13:1 [a]Rom 12:10; 1 Thess 4:9; 1 Pet 1:22
2 [a]Matt 25:35; Rom 12:13; 1 Pet 4:9 [b]Gen 18:1ff; 19:1f
3 [a]Col 4:18 [b]Matt 25:36; Heb 10:34
4 [a]1 Cor 7:38; 1 Tim 4:3 [b]1 Cor 6:9; Gal 5:19, 21; 1 Thess 4:6
5 [a]Eph 5:3; Col 3:5; 1 Tim 3:3 [b]Phil 4:11 [c]Deut 31:6, 8; Josh 1:5
6 [a]Ps 118:6
7 [1]Or *end of their life* [a]Heb 13:17, 24 [b]Luke 5:1 [c]Heb 6:12
8 [a]2 Cor 1:19; Heb 1:12
9 [1]Lit *walked* [a]Eph 4:14; 5:6; Jude 12 [b]2 Cor 1:21; Col 2:7 [c]Col 2:16 [d]Heb 9:10
10 [1]Or *sacred tent* [a]1 Cor 10:18 [b]Heb 8:5
11 [a]Ex 29:14; Lev 4:12, 21; 9:11; 16:27; Num 19:3, 7
12 [a]Eph 5:26; Heb 2:11 [b]Heb 9:12 [c]John 19:17

13 So, let us go out to Him outside the camp, [a]bearing His
reproach.
14 For here [a]we do not have a lasting city, but we are seeking
[b]*the city* which is to come.
15 [a]Through Him then, let us continually offer up a [b]sacrifice
of praise to God, that is, [c]the fruit of lips that [1]give thanks to
His name.
16 And do not neglect doing good and [a]sharing, for [b]with such
sacrifices God is pleased.
17 [a]Obey your leaders and submit *to them,* for [b]they keep
watch over your souls as those who will give an account. [1]Let
them do this with joy and not [2]with grief, for this would be
unprofitable for you.
18 [a]Pray for us, for we are sure that we have a [b]good
conscience, desiring to conduct ourselves honorably in all things.
19 And I urge *you* all the more to do this, [a]so that I may be
restored to you the sooner.
20 Now [a]the God of peace, who [b]brought up from the dead
the [c]great Shepherd of the sheep [1]through [d]the blood of the
[e]eternal covenant, *even* Jesus our Lord,
21 [a]equip you in every good thing to do His will, [b]working in
us that [c]which is pleasing in His sight, through Jesus Christ, [d]to
whom *be* the glory forever and ever. Amen.
22 But [a]I urge you, [b]brethren, [1]bear with [2]this [b]word of
exhortation, for [c]I have written to you briefly.
23 [1]Take notice that [a]our brother Timothy has been released,
with whom, if he comes soon, I will see you.
24 Greet [a]all of your leaders and all the [1b]saints. Those from
[c]Italy greet you.
25 [a]Grace be with you all.

13 [a]Luke 9:23; Heb 11:26; 12:2

14 [a]Heb 10:34; 12:27 [b]Eph 2:19; Heb 2:5; 11:10, 16; 12:22

15 [1]Lit *confess* [a]1 Pet 2:5 [b]Lev 7:12 [c]Is 57:19; Hos 14:2

16 [a]Rom 12:13 [b]Phil 4:18

17 [1]Lit *in order that they may do this* [2]Lit *groaning* [a]1 Cor 16:16; Heb 13:7, 24 [b]Is 62:6; Ezek 3:17; Acts 20:28

18 [a]1 Thess 5:25 [b]Acts 24:16; 1 Tim 1:5

19 [a]Philem 22

20 [1]Lit *in* [a]Rom 15:33 [b]Acts 2:24; Rom 10:7 [c]Is 63:11; John 10:11; 1 Pet 2:25 [d]Zech 9:11; Heb 10:29 [e]Is 55:3; Jer 32:40; Ezek 37:26

21 [a]1 Pet 5:10 [b]Phil 2:13 [c]Heb 12:28; 1 John 3:22 [d]Rom 11:36

22 [1]Or *listen to* [2]Lit *the* [a]Acts 13:15; Heb 3:13; 10:25; 12:5; 13:19 [b]Heb 3:1 [c]1 Pet 5:12

23 [1]Lit *Know* [a]Acts 16:1; Col 1:1

24 [1]Or *holy ones* [a]1 Cor 16:16; Heb 13:7, 17 [b]Acts 9:13 [c]Acts 18:2

25 [a]Col 4:18

Hebrews Observations Chart

Author	Exhortations
Recipients	

(continued)

HEBREWS OBSERVATIONS CHART

WARNINGS	CONSEQUENCE OF NOT LISTENING/OBEYING

THE SUPREMACY OF JESUS

Hebrews at a Glance

Theme of Hebrews:

SEGMENT DIVISIONS

Author:

unknown

Date:

Purpose:

Key Words:

Jesus (Son)

God

angels

sin (sinners)

priest (priests, priesthood)

therefore

faith (faithful)

greater

better (better than)

let us

perfect

mark the reference to the devil

covenant

		CHAPTER THEMES
		1
		2
		3
		4
		5
		6
		7
		8
		9
		10
		11
		12
		13

JAMES

What a turnaround from the day James told his half brother what to do if He wanted to be known publicly! Full of unbelief and convinced that Jesus was nothing more than his eldest brother, James told Jesus to take His disciples and go up to the Feast of Booths and do His works there. Jesus might have found more disciples there, but James was not to be numbered as one of them—at least, not until Jesus rose from the dead (see 1 Corinthians 15:7).

Convinced from that point on that Jesus was the Christ, James would lay claim not to his physical relationship to Jesus but to his spiritual relationship as a bondservant of the Lord Jesus Christ. He became a pillar of the church, a leader of the council of Jerusalem, and a friend of Peter and Paul. But most of all he was a friend of Jesus, a covenant friend for whom he would be martyred around A.D. 62.

Sometime before A.D. 50 or in the early 50s, James would write his one epistle to be included in the pages of Holy Scripture, an epistle that would show what the gospel is like when it is lived out in shoe leather.

THINGS TO DO

1. Read James in one sitting to familiarize yourself with the book as a whole.

2. Mark every reference to the recipients. James structures his writing distinctively. Once you see the pattern he uses, you will better understand the flow of the book.

   a. First, James introduces a subject by making a statement or giving an introduction. For example, in James 1:2 he says to consider it all joy when you encounter various trials.

   b. He then usually follows with more instructions concerning that particular subject, *or* he gives an illustration pertaining to the subject, *or* he gives an explanation of it.

3. As you read back through James, mark in the text the key words (and their synonyms and pronouns) listed on the JAMES AT A GLANCE chart on page 2005. Key words help you see the subjects of the book; keep in mind that some key words only appear in a portion of a book.

   a. Watch for these, including *say (says)* and *works* in chapter 2, *tongue* in chapter 3, and so on. Mark these in their own distinctive way. Also, mark any reference to the devil and his demons.

   b. When you finish, you'll find it profitable to list everything you learn from marking a key word.

4. Read James chapter by chapter:

   a. List the subjects introduced by the author on the JAMES SUBJECT BY SUBJECT chart on pages 2003–2005. Be sure to include the chapter and verse from which you took the information.

   b. Next, if the author gives instructions or illustrations regarding a particular subject, record that information in the appropriate column.

5. After you list the subjects in each chapter, determine the theme of each chapter and record these themes on JAMES AT A GLANCE and in your Bible.

6. Finally, look for the theme of James. Determine if one subject is predominant or if there is a common denominator among the subjects. The more dominant or common subject

will be the theme of James and points to the author's reason for writing. Record the theme of James on JAMES AT A GLANCE and complete the chart.

THINGS TO THINK ABOUT

1. How are you handling the trials in your life?
2. Are you a doer of the Word or a hearer only?
3. Do you show partiality in dealing with people? Are you a respecter of persons?
4. Is your faith seen by your works? If not, what should that tell you?
5. Are you a friend of the world? What do you need to do?

Chapter 1 Theme ____________________

1 [1a]James, a [b]bond-servant of God and [c]of the Lord Jesus Christ,
To [d]the twelve tribes who are [2e]dispersed abroad: [f]Greetings.
2 [a]Consider it all joy, my brethren, when you encounter
[b]various [1]trials,
3 knowing that [a]the testing of your [b]faith produces [1c]endurance.
4 And let [1a]endurance have *its* perfect [2]result, so that you may
be [3b]perfect and complete, lacking in nothing.
5 But if any of you [a]lacks wisdom, let him ask of God, who
gives to all generously and [1]without reproach, and [b]it will be
given to him.
6 But he must [a]ask in faith [b]without any doubting, for the one
who doubts is like the surf of the sea, [c]driven and tossed by the
wind.
7 For that man ought not to expect that he will receive
anything from the Lord,
8 *being* a [1a]double-minded man, [b]unstable in all his ways.
9 [a]But the [1]brother of humble circumstances is to glory in his
high position;
10 and the rich man *is to glory* in his humiliation, because [a]like
[1]flowering grass he will pass away.
11 For the sun rises with [1a]a scorching wind and [b]withers the
grass; and its flower falls off and the beauty of its appearance is
destroyed; so too the rich man in the midst of his pursuits will
fade away.
12 [a]Blessed is a man who perseveres under trial; for once he
has [1]been approved, he will receive [b]the crown of life which
the Lord [c]has promised to those who [d]love Him.
13 Let no one say when he is tempted, "[a]I am being tempted
[1]by God"; for God cannot be tempted [2]by evil, and He Himself
does not tempt anyone.
14 But each one is tempted when he is carried away and
enticed by his own lust.
15 Then [a]when lust has conceived, it gives birth to sin; and
when [b]sin [1]is accomplished, it brings forth death.

1:1 [1]Or *Jacob* [2]Lit *in the Dispersion* [a]Acts 12:17 [b]Titus 1:1 [c]Rom 1:1 [d]Luke 22:30 [e]John 7:35 [f]Acts 15:23

2 [1]Or *temptations* [a]Matt 5:12; James 1:12; 5:11 [b]1 Pet 1:6

3 [1]Or *steadfastness* [a]1 Pet 1:7 [b]Heb 6:12 [c]Luke 21:19

4 [1]V 3, note 1 [2]Lit *work* [3]Or *mature* [a]Luke 21:19 [b]Matt 5:48; Col 4:12

5 [1]Lit *does not reproach* [a]1 Kin 3:9ff; James 3:17 [b]Matt 7:7

6 [a]Matt 21:21 [b]Mark 11:23; Acts 10:20 [c]Matt 14:28-31; Eph 4:14

8 [1]Or *doubting, hesitating* [a]James 4:8 [b]2 Pet 2:14

9 [1]I.e. church member [a]Luke 14:11

10 [1]Lit *the flower of the grass* [a]1 Cor 7:31; 1 Pet 1:24

11 [1]Lit *the* [a]Matt 20:12 [b]Ps 102:4, 11; Is 40:7f

12 [1]Or *passed the test* [a]Luke 6:22; James 5:11; 1 Pet 3:14; 4:14 [b]1 Cor 9:25 [c]Ex 20:6; James 2:5 [d]1 Cor 2:9; 8:3

13 [1]Lit *from* [2]Lit *of evil things* [a]Gen 22:1

15 [1]Lit *is brought to completion* [a]Job 15:35; Ps 7:14; Is 59:4 [b]Rom 5:12; 6:23

16 [a]Do not be [1]deceived, [b]my beloved brethren.
17 Every good thing given and every perfect gift is [a]from
above, coming down from [b]the Father of lights, [c]with whom
there is no variation or [1]shifting shadow.
18 In the exercise of [a]His will He [b]brought us forth by [c]the word
of truth, so that we would be [1]a kind of [d]first fruits [2]among His
creatures.
19 [1]*This* [a]you know, [b]my beloved brethren. But everyone must
be quick to hear, [c]slow to speak *and* [d]slow to anger;
20 for [a]the anger of man does not achieve the righteousness of
God.
21 Therefore, [a]putting aside all filthiness and *all* [1]that remains of
wickedness, in [2]humility receive [b]the word implanted, which
is able to save your souls.
22 [a]But prove yourselves doers of the word, and not merely
hearers who delude themselves.
23 For if anyone is a hearer of the word and not a doer, he is
like a man who looks at his [1]natural face [a]in a mirror;
24 for *once* he has looked at himself and gone away, [1]he has
immediately forgotten what kind of person he was.
25 But one who looks intently at the perfect law, [a]the *law* of
liberty, and abides by it, not having become a forgetful hearer
but [1]an effectual doer, this man will be [b]blessed in [2]what he does.
26 If anyone thinks himself to be religious, and yet does not
[1a]bridle his tongue but deceives his *own* heart, this man's religion
is worthless.
27 Pure and undefiled religion [a]in the sight of *our* God and
Father is this: to [b]visit [c]orphans and widows in their distress,
and to keep oneself unstained [1]by [d]the world.

Chapter 2 Theme ____________________

2 [a]My brethren, [b]do not hold your faith in our [c]glorious Lord
Jesus Christ with *an attitude of* [d]personal favoritism.
2 For if a man comes into your [1]assembly with a gold ring
and dressed in [2a]fine clothes, and there also comes in a poor
man in [b]dirty clothes,
3 and you [1]pay special attention to the one who is wearing
the [a]fine clothes, and say, "You sit here in a good place," and
you say to the poor man, "You stand over there, or sit down by
my footstool,"
4 have you not made distinctions among yourselves, and
become judges [a]with evil [1]motives?
5 Listen, [a]my beloved brethren: did not [b]God choose the poor
[1]of this world *to be* [c]rich in faith and [d]heirs of the kingdom
which He [e]promised to those who love Him?
6 But you have dishonored the poor man. Is it not the rich
who oppress you and [1]personally [a]drag you into [2]court?

5 [1]Lit *to the* [a]James 1:16 [b]Job 34:19; 1 Cor 1:27f [c]Luke 12:21; Rev 2:9 [d]Matt 5:3; 25:34 [e]James 1:12
6 [1]Lit *they themselves* [2]Lit *courts* [a]Acts 8:3; 16:19

16 [1]Or *misled* [a]1 Cor 6:9 [b]Acts 1:15; James 1:2, 19; 2:1, 5, 14; 3:1, 10; 4:11; 5:12, 19

17 [1]Lit *shadow of turning* [a]John 3:3; James 3:15, 17 [b]Ps 136:7; 1 John 1:5 [c]Mal 3:6

18 [1]Or *a certain first fruits* [2]Lit *of* [a]John 1:13 [b]James 1:15; 1 Pet 1:3, 23 [c]2 Cor 6:7; Eph 1:13; 2 Tim 2:15 [d]Jer 2:3; Rev 14:4

19 [1]Or *Know* this [a]1 John 2:21 [b]Acts 1:15; James 1:2, 16; 2:1, 5, 14; 3:1, 10; 4:11; 5:12, 19 [c]Prov 10:19; 17:27 [d]Prov 16:32; Eccl 7:9

20 [a]Matt 5:22; Eph 4:26

21 [1]Lit *abundance of malice* [2]Or *gentleness* [a]Eph 4:22; 1 Pet 2:1 [b]Eph 1:13; 1 Pet 1:22f

22 [a]Matt 7:24-27; Luke 6:46-49; Rom 2:13; James 1:22-25; 2:14-20

23 [1]Lit *the face of his birth;* or *nature* [a]1 Cor 13:12

24 [1]Lit *and he*

25 [1]Lit *a doer of a work* [2]Lit *his doing* [a]John 8:32; Rom 8:2; Gal 2:4; 6:2; James 2:12; 1 Pet 2:16 [b]John 13:17

26 [1]Or *control* [a]Ps 39:1; 141:3; James 3:2-12

27 [1]Lit *from* [a]Rom 2:13; Gal 3:11 [b]Matt 25:36 [c]Deut 14:29; Job 31:16, 17, 21; Ps 146:9; Is 1:17, 23 [d]Matt 12:32; Eph 2:2; Titus 2:12; James 4:4; 2 Pet 1:4; 2:20; 1 John 2:15-17

2:1 [a]James 1:16 [b]Heb 12:2 [c]Acts 7:2; 1 Cor 2:8 [d]Acts 10:34; James 2:9

2 [1]Or *synagogue* [2]Or *bright* [a]Luke 23:11; James 2:3 [b]Zech 3:3f

3 [1]Lit *look at* [a]Luke 23:11

4 [1]Lit *reasonings* [a]Luke 18:6; John 7:24

7 [1]Lit *which has been called upon you* [a]Acts 11:26; 1 Pet 4:16
8 [1]Or *law of our King* [a]Matt 7:12 [b]Lev 19:18
9 [1]Or *Law* [a]Acts 10:34; James 2:1
10 [1]Or *Law* [a]James 3:2; 2 Pet 1:10; Jude 24 [b]Matt 5:19; Gal 5:3
11 [1]Or *Law* [a]Ex 20:14; Deut 5:18 [b]Ex 20:13; Deut 5:17
12 [a]James 1:25
13 [1]Lit *boasts against* [a]Prov 21:13; Matt 5:7; 18:32-35; Luke 6:37f
14 [1]Lit *the* [a]James 1:22ff [b]James 1:16
15 [a]Matt 25:35f; Luke 3:11
16 [1]Or *warm yourselves and fill yourselves* [a]1 John 3:17f
17 [1]Or *dead by its own standards* [a]Gal 5:6; James 2:20, 26
18 [1]Lit *will* [a]Rom 9:19 [b]Rom 3:28; 4:6; Heb 11:33 [c]James 3:13 [d]Matt 7:16f; Gal 5:6
19 [1]One early ms reads *there is one God* [a]Deut 6:4; Mark 12:29 [b]James 2:8 [c]Matt 8:29; Mark 1:24; 5:7; Luke 4:34; Acts 19:15
20 [a]Rom 9:20; 1 Cor 15:36 [b]Gal 5:6; James 2:17, 26
21 [a]Gen 22:9, 10, 12, 16-18
22 [1]Or *by the deeds* [2]Or *completed* [a]John 6:29; Heb 11:17 [b]1 Thess 1:3
23 [a]Gen 15:6; Rom 4:3 [b]2 Chr 20:7; Is 41:8
25 [a]Heb 11:31 [b]Josh 2:4, 6, 15
26 [a]Gal 5:6; James 2:17, 20
3:1 [1]Or *greater condemnation* [a]Matt 23:8; Rom 2:20f; 1 Tim 1:7 [b]James 1:16; 3:10
2 [1]Lit *word* [a]James 2:10 [b]Matt 12:34-37; James 3:2-12 [c]James 1:4 [d]James 1:26

7 [a]Do they not blaspheme the fair name [1]by which you have
been called?
8 If, however, you [a]are fulfilling the [1]royal law according to
the Scripture, "[b]YOU SHALL LOVE YOUR NEIGHBOR AS YOURSELF," you
are doing well.
9 But if you [a]show partiality, you are committing sin *and* are
convicted by the [1]law as transgressors.
10 For whoever keeps the whole [1]law and yet [a]stumbles in
one *point,* he has become [b]guilty of all.
11 For He who said, "[a]DO NOT COMMIT ADULTERY," also said, "[b]DO
NOT COMMIT MURDER." Now if you do not commit adultery, but do
commit murder, you have become a transgressor of the [1]law.
12 So speak and so act as those who are to be judged by [a]*the*
law of liberty.
13 For [a]judgment *will be* merciless to one who has shown no
mercy; mercy [1]triumphs over judgment.
14 [a]What use is it, [b]my brethren, if someone says he has faith
but he has no works? Can [1]that faith save him?
15 [a]If a brother or sister is without clothing and in need of daily
food,
16 and one of you says to them, "[a]Go in peace, [1]be warmed
and be filled," and yet you do not give them what is necessary
for *their* body, what use is that?
17 Even so [a]faith, if it has no works, is [1]dead, *being* by itself.
18 [a]But someone [1]may *well* say, "You have faith and I have
works; show me your [b]faith without the works, and I will
[c]show you my faith [d]by my works."
19 You believe that [1a]God is one. [b]You do well; [c]the demons
also believe, and shudder.
20 But are you willing to recognize, [a]you foolish fellow, that
[b]faith without works is useless?
21 [a]Was not Abraham our father justified by works when he
offered up Isaac his son on the altar?
22 You see that [a]faith was working with his works, and [1]as a
result of the [b]works, faith was [2]perfected;
23 and the Scripture was fulfilled which says, "[a]AND ABRAHAM
BELIEVED GOD, AND IT WAS RECKONED TO HIM AS RIGHTEOUSNESS," and
he was called [b]the friend of God.
24 You see that a man is justified by works and not by faith alone.
25 In the same way, was not [a]Rahab the harlot also justified by
works [b]when she received the messengers and sent them out
by another way?
26 For just as the body without *the* spirit is dead, so also [a]faith
without works is dead.

Chapter 3 Theme ______________________________

3 [a]Let not many *of you* become teachers, [b]my brethren, knowing that as such we will incur a [1]stricter judgment.
2 For we all [a]stumble in many *ways.* [b]If anyone does not
stumble in [1]what he says, he is a [c]perfect man, able to [d]bridle
the whole body as well.

3 Now [a]if we put the bits into the horses' mouths so that
they will obey us, we direct their entire body as well.
4 Look at the ships also, though they are so great and are
driven by strong winds, are still directed by a very small rudder
wherever the inclination of the pilot desires.
5 So also the tongue is a small part of the body, and *yet* it
[a]boasts of great things.

[b]See how great a forest is set aflame by such a small fire!

6 And [a]the tongue is a fire, the *very* world of iniquity; the tongue
is set among our members as that which [b]defiles the entire body,
and sets on fire the course of *our* [1]life, and is set on fire by [2c]hell.
7 For every [1]species of beasts and birds, of reptiles and
creatures of the sea, is tamed and has been tamed by the human
[1]race.
8 But no one can tame the tongue; *it is* a restless evil *and* full
of [a]deadly poison.
9 With it we bless [a]*our* Lord and Father, and with it we curse
men, [b]who have been made in the likeness of God;
10 from the same mouth come *both* blessing and cursing. My
brethren, these things ought not to be this way.
11 Does a fountain send out from the same opening *both*
[1]fresh and bitter *water?*
12 [a]Can a fig tree, my brethren, produce olives, or a vine
produce figs? Nor *can* salt water produce [1]fresh.
13 Who among you is wise and understanding? [a]Let him show
by his [b]good behavior his deeds in the gentleness of wisdom.
14 But if you have bitter [a]jealousy and [1]selfish ambition in
your heart, do not be arrogant and *so* lie against [b]the truth.
15 This wisdom is not that which comes down [a]from above,
but is [b]earthly, [1c]natural, [d]demonic.
16 For where [a]jealousy and [1]selfish ambition exist, [2]there is
disorder and every evil thing.
17 But the wisdom [a]from above is first [b]pure, then [c]peaceable,
[d]gentle, [1]reasonable, [e]full of mercy and good fruits, [f]unwavering,
without [g]hypocrisy.
18 And the [1a]seed whose fruit is righteousness is sown in
peace [2]by those who make peace.

Chapter 4 Theme ____

4 [1]What is the source of quarrels and [a]conflicts among you?
[2]Is not the source your pleasures that wage [b]war in your
members?
2 You lust and do not have; *so* you [a]commit murder. You are
envious and cannot obtain; *so* you fight and quarrel. You do not
have because you do not ask.
3 You ask and [a]do not receive, because you ask [1]with wrong
motives, so that you may spend *it* [2]on your pleasures.
4 You [a]adulteresses, do you not know that friendship with [b]the
world is [c]hostility toward God? [d]Therefore whoever wishes to
be a friend of the world makes himself an enemy of God.

3 [a]Ps 32:9

5 [a]Ps 12:3f; 73:8f [b]Prov 26:20f

6 [1]Or *existence, origin* [2]Gr *Gehenna* [a]Ps 120:2, 3; Prov 16:27 [b]Matt 12:36f; 15:11, 18f [c]Matt 5:22

7 [1]Lit *nature*

8 [a]Ps 140:3; Eccl 10:11; Rom 3:13

9 [a]James 1:27 [b]Gen 1:26; 1 Cor 11:7

11 [1]Lit *sweet*

12 [1]V 11, note 1 [a]Matt 7:16

13 [a]James 2:18 [b]1 Pet 2:12

14 [1]Or *strife* [a]Rom 2:8; 2 Cor 12:20; James 3:16 [b]1 Tim 2:4; James 1:18; 5:19

15 [1]Or *unspiritual* [a]James 1:17 [b]1 Cor 2:6; 3:19 [c]2 Cor 1:12; Jude 19 [d]2 Thess 2:9f; 1 Tim 4:1; Rev 2:24

16 [1]V 14, note 1 [2]I.e. in that place [a]Rom 2:8; 2 Cor 12:20; James 3:14

17 [1]Or *willing to yield* [a]James 1:17 [b]2 Cor 7:11; James 4:8 [c]Matt 5:9; Heb 12:11 [d]Titus 3:2 [e]Luke 6:36; James 2:13 [f]James 2:4 [g]Rom 12:9; 2 Cor 6:6

18 [1]Lit *fruit of righteousness* [2]Or *for* [a]Prov 11:18; Is 32:17; Hos 10:12; Amos 6:12; Gal 6:8; Phil 1:11

4:1 [1]Lit *From where wars and from where fightings* [2]Lit *Are they not from here,* from your [a]Titus 3:9 [b]Rom 7:23

2 [a]James 5:6; 1 John 3:15

3 [1]Lit *wickedly* [2]Lit *in* [a]1 John 3:22; 5:14

4 [a]Jer 2:2; Ezek 16:32 [b]James 1:27 [c]Rom 8:7; 1 John 2:15 [d]Matt 6:24; John 15:19

5 Or do you think that the Scripture [a]speaks to no purpose:
"[1]He [2]jealously desires [b]the Spirit which He has made to dwell
in us"?
6 But [a]He gives a greater grace. Therefore *it* says, "[b]GOD IS
OPPOSED TO THE PROUD, BUT GIVES GRACE TO THE HUMBLE."
7 [a]Submit therefore to God. [b]Resist the devil and he will flee
from you.
8 [a]Draw near to God and He will draw near to you. [b]Cleanse
your hands, you sinners; and [c]purify your hearts, you [d]double-
minded.
9 [a]Be miserable and mourn and weep; let your laughter be
turned into mourning and your joy to gloom.
10 [a]Humble yourselves in the presence of the Lord, and He
will exalt you.
11 [a]Do not speak against one another, [b]brethren. He who
speaks against a brother or [c]judges his brother, speaks against
[d]the law and judges the law; but if you judge the law, you are
not [e]a doer of the law but a judge *of it.*
12 There is *only* one [a]Lawgiver and Judge, the One who is [b]able
to save and to destroy; but [c]who are you who judge your neighbor?
13 [a]Come now, you who say, "[b]Today or tomorrow we will go
to such and such a city, and spend a year there and engage in
business and make a profit."
14 [1]Yet you do not know [2]what your life will be like tomorrow.
[a]You are *just* a vapor that appears for a little while and then
vanishes away.
15 [1]Instead, *you ought* to say, "[a]If the Lord wills, we will live
and also do this or that."
16 But as it is, you boast in your [1]arrogance; [a]all such boasting
is evil.
17 Therefore, [a]to one who knows *the* [1]right thing to do and
does not do it, to him it is sin.

Chapter 5 Theme ______________________________

5 [a]Come now, [b]you rich, [c]weep and howl for your miseries
which are coming upon you.
2 [a]Your riches have rotted and your garments have become
moth-eaten.
3 Your gold and your silver have rusted; and their rust will be
a witness against you and will consume your flesh like fire. It is
[a]in the last days that you have stored up your treasure!
4 Behold, [a]the pay of the laborers who mowed your fields,
and which has been withheld by you, cries out *against you;*
and [b]the outcry of those who did the harvesting has reached
the ears of [c]the Lord of [1]Sabaoth.
5 You have [a]lived luxuriously on the earth and led a life of
wanton pleasure; you have [1]fattened your hearts in [b]a day of
slaughter.
6 You have condemned and [1a]put to death [b]the righteous
man; he does not resist you.

5 [1]Or *The spirit which He has made to dwell in us lusts with envy* [2]Lit *desires to jealousy* [a]Num 23:19 [b]1 Cor 6:19; 2 Cor 6:16
6 [a]Is 54:7f; Matt 13:12 [b]Ps 138:6; Prov 3:34; Matt 23:12; 1 Pet 5:5
7 [a]1 Pet 5:6 [b]Eph 4:27; 6:11f; 1 Pet 5:8f
8 [a]2 Chr 15:2; Zech 1:3; Mal 3:7; Heb 7:19 [b]Job 17:9; Is 1:16; 1 Tim 2:8 [c]Jer 4:14; James 3:17; 1 Pet 1:22; 1 John 3:3 [d]James 1:8
9 [a]Neh 8:9; Prov 14:13; Luke 6:25
10 [a]Job 5:11; Ezek 21:26; Luke 1:52; James 4:6
11 [a]2 Cor 12:20; James 5:9; 1 Pet 2:1 [b]James 1:16; 5:7, 9, 10 [c]Matt 7:1; Rom 14:4 [d]James 2:8 [e]James 1:22
12 [a]Is 33:22; James 5:9 [b]Matt 10:28 [c]Rom 14:4
13 [a]James 5:1 [b]Prov 27:1; Luke 12:18-20
14 [1]Lit *Who do not* [2]Or *what* will happen *tomorrow. What kind of life is yours?* [a]Job 7:7; Ps 39:5; 102:3; 144:4
15 [1]Lit *Instead of your saying* [a]Acts 18:21
16 [1]Or *pretensions* [a]1 Cor 5:6
17 [1]Or *good* [a]Luke 12:47; John 9:41; 2 Pet 2:21
5:1 [a]James 4:13 [b]Luke 6:24; 1 Tim 6:9 [c]Is 13:6; 15:3; Ezek 30:2
2 [a]Job 13:28; Is 50:9; Matt 6:19f
3 [a]James 5:7, 8
4 [1]I.e. Hosts [a]Lev 19:13; Job 24:10f; Jer 22:13; Mal 3:5 [b]Ex 2:23; Deut 24:15; Job 31:38f [c]Rom 9:29; Is 5:9
5 [1]Lit *nourished* [a]Ezek 16:49; Luke 16:19; 1 Tim 5:6; 2 Pet 2:13 [b]Jer 12:3; 25:34
6 [1]Or *murdered* [a]James 4:2 [b]Heb 10:38; 1 Pet 4:18

7 Therefore be patient, [a]brethren, [b]until the coming of the
Lord. [c]The farmer waits for the precious produce of the soil,
being patient about it, until [1]it gets [d]the early and late rains.
8 [a]You too be patient; [b]strengthen your hearts, for [c]the coming
of the Lord is [d]near.
9 [a]Do not [1]complain, [b]brethren, against one another, so that
you yourselves may not be judged; behold, [c]the Judge is standing
[2][d]right at the [3]door.
10 As an example, [a]brethren, of suffering and patience, take [b]the
prophets who spoke in the name of the Lord.
11 We count those [a]blessed who endured. You have heard of
[b]the [1]endurance of Job and have seen [c]the [2]outcome of the
Lord's dealings, that [d]the Lord is full of compassion and *is*
merciful.
12 But above all, [a]my brethren, [b]do not swear, either by heaven
or by earth or with any other oath; but [1]your yes is to be yes,
and your no, no, so that you may not fall under judgment.
13 Is anyone among you [a]suffering? [b]*Then* he must pray. Is
anyone cheerful? He is to [c]sing praises.
14 Is anyone among you sick? *Then* he must call for [a]the elders
of the church and they are to pray over him, [1][b]anointing him
with oil in the name of the Lord;
15 and the [a]prayer [1]offered in faith will [2][b]restore the one who is
sick, and the Lord will [c]raise him up, and if he has committed
sins, [3]they will be forgiven him.
16 Therefore, [a]confess your sins to one another, and pray for
one another so that you may be [b]healed. [c]The effective [1]prayer
of a righteous man can accomplish much.
17 Elijah was [a]a man with a nature like ours, and [b]he prayed
[1]earnestly that it would not rain, and it did not rain on the
earth for [c]three years and six months.
18 Then he [a]prayed again, and [b]the [1]sky [2]poured rain and the
earth produced its fruit.
19 My brethren, [a]if any among you strays from [b]the truth and
one turns him back,
20 let him know that [1]he who turns a sinner from the error of
his way will [a]save his soul from death and will [b]cover a multitude
of sins.

18 [1]Lit *heaven* [2]Lit *gave* [a]1 Kin 18:42 [b]1 Kin 18:45
19 [a]Matt 18:15; Gal 6:1 [b]James 3:14
20 [1]Lit *he who has turned* [a]Rom 11:14; 1 Cor 1:21; James 1:21 [b]Prov 10:12; 1 Pet 4:8

7 [1]Or *he* [a]James 4:11; 5:9, 10 [b]John 21:22; 1 Thess 2:19 [c]Gal 6:9 [d]Deut 11:14; Jer 5:24; Joel 2:23

8 [a]Luke 21:19 [b]1 Thess 3:13 [c]John 21:22; 1 Thess 2:19 [d]Rom 13:11, 12; 1 Pet 4:7

9 [1]Lit *groan* [2]Lit *before* [3]Lit *doors* [a]James 4:11 [b]James 5:7, 10 [c]1 Cor 4:5; James 4:12; 1 Pet 4:5 [d]Matt 24:33; Mark 13:29

10 [a]James 4:11; 5:7, 9 [b]Matt 5:12

11 [1]Or *steadfastness* [2]Lit *end of the Lord* [a]Matt 5:10; 1 Pet 3:14 [b]Job 1:21f; 2:10 [c]Job 42:10, 12 [d]Ex 34:6; Ps 103:8

12 [1]Lit *yours is to be yes, yes, and no, no* [a]James 1:16 [b]Matt 5:34-37

13 [a]James 5:10 [b]Ps 50:15 [c]1 Cor 14:15; Col 3:16

14 [1]Lit *having anointed* [a]Acts 11:30 [b]Mark 6:13; 16:18

15 [1]Lit *of* [2]Or *save* [3]Lit *it* [a]James 1:6 [b]1 Cor 1:21; James 5:20 [c]John 6:39; 2 Cor 4:14

16 [1]Lit *supplication* [a]Matt 3:6; Mark 1:5; Acts 19:18 [b]Heb 12:13; 1 Pet 2:24 [c]Gen 18:23-32; John 9:31

17 [1]Lit *with prayer* [a]Acts 14:15 [b]1 Kin 17:1; 18:1 [c]Luke 4:25

James Subject by Subject

Subject	Instruction	Illustration/Explanation

(continued)

Subject	Instruction	Illustration/Explanation

(continued)

James Subject by Subject

Subject	Instruction	Illustration/Explanation

James at a Glance

Theme of James:

Author:

Date:

Purpose:

Key Words:

brethren

faith

perfect (perfected)

sin

rich (riches)

judge(s) (judged, judgment)

law

Segment Divisions	Chapter Themes
	1
	2
	3
	4
	5

1 PETER

The hour had come for the Shepherd to be smitten and for the sheep to be scattered. Jesus chose to spend His final hours with His eleven, preparing them for the tribulation that would come. Yet, after Jesus' resurrection and ascension, the tribulation seemed to be relatively mild. The disgruntled Pharisees wanted to shut up the men who were turning Jerusalem upside down with their teaching and miracles, but nothing seemed life threatening.

Then the first stone was thrown, and Stephen, the first martyr, was brought to the ground. Saul watched him die. In hearty agreement with Stephen's death, Saul went to the high priest to gain permission to round up those who were spreading this gospel. However, Saul's purge was short-lived, for Jesus saved him on the road to Damascus and changed his name to Paul. Yet the persecution of Christians continued. Herod, the Jewish king, became the adversary of believers. Jews who confessed Jesus as the Messiah were scattered to other Roman provinces.

However, it wasn't until the Roman emperor Nero that the persecution of Christians reached beyond the confines of Judah. Rumor had it that Nero had burned Rome so he could rebuild it as he wanted. Needing a scapegoat to divert attention from himself, Nero blamed the fire on the Christians and began the systematic persecution of God's children.

Jesus had prepared Peter for the world's tribulation; now Peter would prepare others. His first epistle was written on the eve of Nero's persecution, about A.D. 63 or 64. Nero died in A.D. 68, but not before Rome put Peter to death.

THINGS TO DO

1. Read through 1 Peter and do the following:
   a. In the initial verses of the book, Peter describes himself and states to whom he is writing. In the last verses of the book, he tells why he wrote this epistle. Mark every reference to the author in a distinctive color and every reference to the recipients in another color. Record your insights about the author and his purpose in writing on the 1 PETER AT A GLANCE chart on page 2014.
   b. Pay close attention to the recipients of 1 Peter. What is their condition? What is going on in their midst? Record what you learn on the OBSERVATIONS CHART on page 2013.

2. Look for and mark in a distinctive way the key words (and their synonyms and pronouns) listed on 1 PETER AT A GLANCE. Also remember to mark key words that you are marking throughout your Bible, including references to the devil. On a separate sheet of paper, list the truths you learn from every mention of key words. This is imperative if you want to understand 1 Peter. (Because God and Jesus Christ are each mentioned so much, you may want to mark only the instances in which you learn something new or important to remember.)

3. Peter gives the reader many commands and instructions. You notice these by the construction of the sentence. The verb usually comes first and the "you" is implied. An example is seen in 1:13: "Prepare your minds for action."
   a. In a distinctive way, mark Peter's instructions or commands. Then list these under "General Instructions" on the OBSERVATIONS CHART on page 2014.
   b. First Peter was written not only for the recipients but also for you. Think about how Peter's instructions and commands apply to your own life.

4. Peter also instructs specific groups of people such as servants, wives, husbands, etc. List his instructions to each group under the headings on the OBSERVATIONS CHART.

5. From what you have read, why are the believers to do these things? Or what future event is the motivation for living life in accordance with Peter's exhortations?

6. Finally, summarize the theme of each chapter and record it on 1 PETER AT A GLANCE and in your Bible.

THINGS TO THINK ABOUT

1. What have you learned about the way you are to live? How are you to respond to others, even when they are not living properly or treating you properly? What is Jesus' example in 1 Peter 2:21-25? Will you follow it?

2. As you think about what those believers were suffering, should you be surprised if you undergo the same? What will suffering accomplish in your life?

3. Even if you don't have a Nero in your life, is your adversary the devil still prowling about like a lion, seeking whom he may devour? What are you to do, according to 1 Peter?

4. When Jesus returns, will you be found standing firm in the true grace that has been provided you? What must you do or change in order to be prepared to see Him face-to-face?

Chapter 1 Theme ____________________

1 [a]Peter, an apostle of Jesus Christ,
To those who reside as [b]aliens, [c]scattered throughout [d]Pontus,
[e]Galatia, [d]Cappadocia, [d]Asia, and [f]Bithynia, [g]who are chosen
2 according to the [a]foreknowledge of God the Father, [b]by the
sanctifying work of the Spirit, [1]to [c]obey Jesus Christ and be
[d]sprinkled with His blood: [e]May grace and peace [2]be yours in
the fullest measure.
3 [a]Blessed be the God and Father of our Lord Jesus Christ,
who [b]according to His great mercy [c]has caused us to be born
again to [d]a living hope through the [e]resurrection of Jesus Christ
from the dead,
4 to *obtain* an [a]inheritance *which is* imperishable and undefiled
and [b]will not fade away, [c]reserved in heaven for you,
5 who are [a]protected by the power of God [b]through faith for
[c]a salvation ready [d]to be revealed in the last time.
6 [a]In this you greatly rejoice, even though now [b]for a little
while, [c]if necessary, you have been distressed by [d]various [1]trials,
7 so that the [1a]proof of your faith, *being* more precious than
gold which [2]is perishable, [b]even though tested by fire, [c]may be
found to result in praise and glory and honor at [d]the revelation
of Jesus Christ;
8 and [a]though you have not seen Him, you [b]love Him, and
though you do not see Him now, but believe in Him, you greatly
rejoice with joy inexpressible and [1]full of glory,
9 obtaining as [a]the outcome of your faith the salvation of
[1]your souls.
10 [a]As to this salvation, the prophets who [b]prophesied of the
[c]grace that *would come* to you made careful searches and
inquiries,
11 [1]seeking to know what person or time [a]the Spirit of Christ

1:1 [a]2 Pet 1:1 [b]1 Pet 2:11 [c]James 1:1 [d]Acts 2:9 [e]Acts 16:6 [f]Acts 16:7 [g]Matt 24:22; Luke 18:7
2 [1]Lit *unto obedience and sprinkling* [2]Lit *be multiplied for you* [a]Rom 8:29; 1 Pet 1:20 [b]2 Thess 2:13 [c]1 Pet 1:14, 22 [d]Heb 10:22; 12:24 [e]2 Pet 1:2
3 [a]2 Cor 1:3 [b]Gal 6:16; Titus 3:5 [c]James 1:18; 1 Pet 1:23 [d]1 Pet 1:13, 21; 3:5, 15; 1 John 3:3 [e]1 Cor 15:20; 1 Pet 3:21
4 [a]Acts 20:32; Rom 8:17; Col 3:24 [b]1 Pet 5:4 [c]2 Tim 4:8
5 [a]John 10:28; Phil 4:7 [b]Eph 2:8 [c]1 Cor 1:21; 2 Thess 2:13 [d]1 Pet 4:13; 5:1
6 [1]Or *temptations* [a]Rom 5:2 [b]1 Pet 5:10 [c]1 Pet 3:17 [d]James 1:2; 1 Pet 4:12
7 [1]Or *genuineness* [2]Lit *perishes* [a]James 1:3 [b]1 Cor 3:13 [c]Rom 2:7 [d]Luke 17:30; 1 Pet 1:13; 4:13
8 [1]Lit *glorified* [a]John 20:29 [b]Eph 3:19
9 [1]One early ms does not contain *your* [a]Rom 6:22
10 [a]Matt 13:17; Luke 10:24 [b]Matt 26:24 [c]1 Pet 1:13
11 [1]Or *inquiring* [a]2 Pet 1:21

INSIGHT

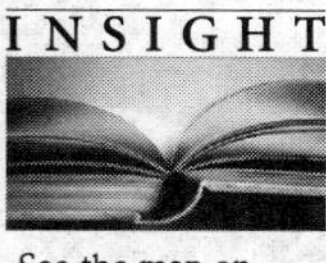

See the map on page 1800.

within them was indicating as He [b]predicted the sufferings of
Christ and the glories [2]to follow.
12 It was revealed to them that they were not serving themselves, but you, in these things which now have been announced
to you through those who [a]preached the gospel to you by [b]the
Holy Spirit sent from heaven—things into which [c]angels long
to [1]look.
13 Therefore, [1a]prepare your minds for action, [2b]keep sober *in*
spirit, fix your [c]hope completely on the [d]grace [3]to be brought to
you at [e]the revelation of Jesus Christ.
14 As [1a]obedient children, do not [2b]be conformed to the former
lusts *which were yours* in your [c]ignorance,
15 but [1a]like the Holy One who called you, [2b]be holy yourselves
also [c]in all *your* behavior;
16 because it is written, "[a]YOU SHALL BE HOLY, FOR I AM HOLY."
17 If you [a]address as Father the One who [b]impartially [c]judges
according to each one's work, conduct yourselves [d]in fear during
the time of your [e]stay *on earth;*
18 knowing that you were not [1a]redeemed with perishable
things like silver or gold from your [b]futile way of life inherited
from your forefathers,
19 but with precious [a]blood, as of a [b]lamb unblemished and
spotless, *the blood* of Christ.
20 For He was [a]foreknown before [b]the foundation of the world,
but has [c]appeared [1]in these last times [d]for the sake of you
21 who through Him are [a]believers in God, who raised Him
from the dead and [b]gave Him glory, so that your faith and [c]hope
are in God.
22 Since you have [a]in obedience to the truth [b]purified your
souls for a [1c]sincere love of the brethren, fervently love one
another from [2]the heart,
23 for you have been [a]born again [b]not of seed which is
perishable but imperishable, *that is,* through the living and
enduring [c]word of God.
24 For,

"[a]ALL FLESH IS LIKE GRASS,
AND ALL ITS GLORY LIKE THE FLOWER OF GRASS.
THE GRASS WITHERS,
AND THE FLOWER FALLS OFF,
25 [a]BUT THE WORD OF THE LORD ENDURES FOREVER."
And this is [b]the word which was [1]preached to you.

Chapter 2 Theme ______________________

2 Therefore, [a]putting aside all [1]malice and all deceit and
[2]hypocrisy and [2]envy and all [2b]slander,
2 [a]like newborn babies, long for the [1b]pure [2]milk of the
word, so that by it you may [c]grow [3]in respect to salvation,
3 if you have [a]tasted [1b]the kindness of the Lord.

2 [1]Or *unadulterated* [2]Or *spiritual* (Gr *logikos*) *milk* [3]Or *up to salvation* [a]Matt 18:3; 19:14; Mark 10:15; Luke 18:17; 1 Cor 14:20 [b]1 Cor 3:2 [c]Eph 4:15f
3 [1]Lit *that the Lord is kind* [a]Heb 6:5 [b]Ps 34:8; Titus 3:4

11 [2]Lit *after these* [b]Matt 26:24
12 [1]Or *gain a clear glimpse* [a]1 Pet 1:25; 4:6 [b]Acts 2:2-4 [c]1 Tim 3:16
13 [1]Lit *gird the loins of your mind* [2]Lit *be sober* [3]Or *which is announced* [a]Eph 6:14 [b]1 Thess 5:6, 8; 2 Tim 4:5; 1 Pet 4:7; 5:8 [c]1 Pet 1:3 [d]1 Pet 1:10 [e]1 Pet 1:7
14 [1]Lit *children of obedience* [2]Or *conform yourselves* [a]1 Pet 1:2 [b]Rom 12:2; 1 Pet 4:2f [c]Eph 4:18
15 [1]Lit *according to* [2]Or *become* [a]1 Thess 4:7; 1 John 3:3 [b]2 Cor 7:1 [c]James 3:13
16 [a]Lev 11:44f; 19:2; 20:7
17 [a]Ps 89:26; Jer 3:19; Matt 6:9 [b]Acts 10:34 [c]Matt 16:27 [d]2 Cor 7:1; Heb 12:28; 1 Pet 3:15 [e]1 Pet 2:11
18 [1]Or *ransomed* [a]Is 52:3; 1 Cor 6:20; Titus 2:14; Heb 9:12 [b]Eph 4:17
19 [a]Acts 20:28; 1 Pet 1:2 [b]John 1:29
20 [1]Lit *at the end of the times* [a]Acts 2:23; Eph 1:4; 1 Pet 1:2; Rev 13:8 [b]Matt 25:34 [c]Heb 9:26 [d]Heb 2:14
21 [a]Rom 4:24; 10:9 [b]John 17:5, 24; 1 Tim 3:16; Heb 2:9 [c]1 Pet 1:3
22 [1]Lit *unhypocritical* [2]Two early mss read *a clean heart* [a]1 Pet 1:2 [b]James 4:8 [c]John 13:34; Rom 12:10; Heb 13:1; 1 Pet 2:17; 3:8
23 [a]John 3:3; 1 Pet 1:3 [b]John 1:13 [c]Heb 4:12
24 [a]Is 40:6ff; James 1:10f
25 [1]Lit *preached as good news to you* [a]Is 40:8 [b]Heb 6:5
2:1 [1]Or *wickedness* [2]plural nouns [a]Eph 4:22, 25, 31; James 1:21 [b]James 4:11

4 And coming to Him as to a living stone which has been
[a]rejected by men, but is [1]choice and precious in the sight of God,
5 [a]you also, as living stones, [1]are being built up as a [b]spiritual
house for a holy [c]priesthood, to [d]offer up spiritual sacrifices
acceptable to God through Jesus Christ.
6 For *this* is contained in [1]Scripture:

"[a]BEHOLD, I LAY IN ZION A CHOICE STONE,
A [b]PRECIOUS CORNER *stone*,
AND HE WHO BELIEVES IN [2]HIM WILL NOT BE [3]DISAPPOINTED."

7 [a]This precious value, then, is for you who believe; but for
those who disbelieve,

"[b]THE STONE WHICH THE BUILDERS [c]REJECTED,
THIS BECAME THE VERY CORNER *stone*,"

8 and,

"[a]A STONE OF STUMBLING AND A ROCK OF OFFENSE";

[b]for they stumble because they are disobedient to the word,
[c]and to this *doom* they were also appointed.
9 But you are [a]A CHOSEN RACE, A royal [b]PRIESTHOOD, A [c]HOLY
NATION, [d]A PEOPLE FOR *God's* OWN POSSESSION, so that you may
proclaim the excellencies of Him who has called you [e]out of
darkness into His marvelous light;
10 [a]for you once were NOT A PEOPLE, but now you are THE
PEOPLE OF GOD; you had NOT RECEIVED MERCY, but now you have
RECEIVED MERCY.
11 [a]Beloved, [b]I urge you as [c]aliens and strangers to abstain
from [d]fleshly lusts which wage [e]war against the soul.
12 [a]Keep your behavior excellent among the Gentiles, so that
in the thing in which they [b]slander you as evildoers, they may
[1]because of your good deeds, as they observe *them*, [c]glorify
God [d]in the day of [2]visitation.
13 [a]Submit yourselves for the Lord's sake to every human
institution, whether to a king as the one in authority,
14 or to governors as sent [1]by him [a]for the punishment of evildoers and the [b]praise of those who do right.
15 For [1a]such is the will of God that by doing right you may
[b]silence the ignorance of foolish men.
16 *Act* as [a]free men, and [1]do not use your freedom as a covering
for evil, but *use it* as [b]bondslaves of God.
17 [a]Honor all people, [b]love the brotherhood, [c]fear God, [d]honor
the [1]king.
18 [a]Servants, be submissive to your masters with all respect, not
only to those who are good and [b]gentle, but also to those who
are [1]unreasonable.
19 For this *finds* [1]favor, if for the sake of [a]conscience toward God
a person bears up under sorrows when suffering unjustly.
20 For what credit is there if, when you sin and are harshly
treated, you endure it with patience? But if [a]when you do what
is right and suffer *for it* you patiently endure it, this *finds* [1]favor
with God.
21 For [a]you have been called for this purpose, [b]since Christ
also suffered for you, leaving you [c]an example for you to follow
in His steps,

4 [1]Lit *chosen;* or *elect* [a]1 Pet 2:7
5 [1]Or *allow yourselves to be built up;* or *build yourselves up* [a]1 Cor 3:9 [b]Gal 6:10; 1 Tim 3:15 [c]Is 61:6; 66:21; 1 Pet 2:9; Rev 1:6 [d]Rom 15:16; Heb 13:15
6 [1]Or *a scripture* [2]Or *it* [3]Or *put to shame* [a]Is 28:16; Rom 9:32, 33; 10:11; 1 Pet 2:8 [b]Eph 2:20
7 [a]2 Cor 2:16; 1 Pet 2:7, 8 [b]Ps 118:22; Matt 21:42; Luke 2:34 [c]1 Pet 2:4
8 [a]Is 8:14 [b]1 Cor 1:23; Gal 5:11 [c]Rom 9:22
9 [a]Is 43:20f; Deut 10:15 [b]Is 61:6; 66:21; 1 Pet 2:5; Rev 1:6 [c]Ex 19:6; Deut 7:6 [d]Ex 19:5; Deut 4:20; 14:2; Titus 2:14 [e]Is 9:2; 42:16; Acts 26:18; 2 Cor 4:6
10 [a]Hos 1:10; 2:23; Rom 9:25; 10:19
11 [a]Heb 6:9; 1 Pet 4:12 [b]Rom 12:1 [c]Lev 25:23; Ps 39:12; Eph 2:19; Heb 11:13; 1 Pet 1:17 [d]Rom 13:14; Gal 5:16, 24 [e]James 4:1
12 [1]Or *as a result of* [2]I.e. Christ's coming again in judgment [a]2 Cor 8:21; Phil 2:15; Titus 2:8; 1 Pet 2:15; 3:16 [b]Acts 28:22 [c]Matt 5:16; 9:8; John 13:31; 1 Pet 4:11, 16 [d]Is 10:3; Luke 19:44
13 [a]Rom 13:1
14 [1]Lit *through* [a]Rom 13:4 [b]Rom 13:3
15 [1]Lit *so* [a]1 Pet 3:17 [b]1 Pet 2:12
16 [1]Lit *not having* [a]John 8:32; James 1:25 [b]Rom 6:22; 1 Cor 7:22
17 [1]Or *emperor* [a]Rom 12:10; 13:7 [b]1 Pet 1:22 [c]Prov 24:21 [d]Matt 22:21; 1 Pet 2:13
18 [1]Or *perverse* [a]Eph 6:5 [b]James 3:17
19 [1]Or *grace* [a]Rom 13:5; 1 Pet 3:14, 16f
20 [1]V 19, note 1 [a]1 Pet 3:17
21 [a]Acts 14:22; 1 Pet 3:9 [b]1 Pet 3:18; 4:1, 13 [c]Matt 11:29; 16:24

22 WHO [a]COMMITTED NO SIN, NOR WAS ANY DECEIT FOUND IN HIS
MOUTH;
23 [1]and while being [a]reviled, He did not revile in return; while
suffering, He uttered no threats, but kept entrusting *Himself* to
Him who judges righteously;
24 and He Himself [1a]bore our sins in His body on the [2b]cross,
so that we [c]might die to [3]sin and live to righteousness; for [d]by
His [4]wounds you were [e]healed.
25 For you were [a]continually straying like sheep, but now you
have returned to the [b]Shepherd and [1]Guardian of your souls.

Chapter 3 Theme ______________________

3 [a]In the same way, you wives, [b]be submissive to your own
husbands so that even if any *of them* are disobedient to the
word, they may be [c]won without a word by the behavior of
their wives,
2 as they observe your chaste and [1]respectful behavior.
3 [a]Your adornment must not be *merely* external—braiding
the hair, and wearing gold jewelry, or putting on dresses;
4 but *let it be* [a]the hidden person of the heart, with the
imperishable quality of a gentle and quiet spirit, which is
precious in the sight of God.
5 For in this way in former times the holy women also, [a]who
hoped in God, used to adorn themselves, being submissive to
their own husbands;
6 just as Sarah obeyed Abraham, [a]calling him lord, and you
have become her children if you do what is right [1b]without
being frightened by any fear.
7 [a]You husbands in the same way, live with *your wives* in an
understanding way, as with [1b]someone weaker, since she is a
woman; and show her honor as a fellow heir of the grace of
life, so that your prayers will not be hindered.
8 [1]To sum up, [a]all of you be harmonious, sympathetic,
[b]brotherly, [c]kindhearted, and [d]humble in spirit;
9 [a]not returning evil for evil or [b]insult for insult, but [1]giving a
[c]blessing instead; for [d]you were called for the very purpose that
you might [e]inherit a blessing.
10 For,
"[a]THE ONE WHO DESIRES LIFE, TO LOVE AND SEE GOOD DAYS,
MUST KEEP HIS TONGUE FROM EVIL AND HIS LIPS
FROM SPEAKING DECEIT.
11 "[a]HE MUST TURN AWAY FROM EVIL AND DO GOOD;
HE MUST SEEK PEACE AND PURSUE IT.
12 "[a]FOR THE EYES OF THE LORD ARE TOWARD THE RIGHTEOUS,
AND HIS EARS ATTEND TO THEIR PRAYER,
BUT THE FACE OF THE LORD IS AGAINST THOSE WHO DO EVIL."
13 [a]Who is [1]there to harm you if you prove zealous for what is
good?
14 But even if you should [a]suffer for the sake of righteousness,
[b]you [1]are blessed. [c]AND DO NOT FEAR THEIR [2]INTIMIDATION, AND DO
NOT BE TROUBLED,

22 [a]Is 53:9; 2 Cor 5:21

23 [1]Lit *who* [a]Is 53:7; Heb 12:3; 1 Pet 3:9

24 [1]Or *carried... up to the cross* [2]Lit *wood* [3]Lit *sins* [4]Lit *wound;* or *welt* [a]Is 53:4, 11; 1 Cor 15:3; Heb 9:28 [b]Acts 5:30 [c]Rom 6:2, 13 [d]Is 53:5 [e]Heb 12:13; James 5:16

25 [1]Or *Bishop, Overseer* [a]Is 53:6 [b]John 10:11; 1 Pet 5:4

3:1 [a]1 Pet 3:7 [b]Eph 5:22; Col 3:18 [c]1 Cor 9:19

2 [1]Lit *with respect*

3 [a]Is 3:18ff; 1 Tim 2:9

4 [a]Rom 7:22

5 [a]1 Tim 5:5; 1 Pet 1:3

6 [1]Lit *and are not* [a]Gen 18:12 [b]1 Pet 3:14

7 [1]Lit *a weaker vessel* [a]Eph 5:25; Col 3:19 [b]1 Thess 4:4

8 [1]Or *Finally* [a]Rom 12:16 [b]1 Pet 1:22 [c]Eph 4:32 [d]Eph 4:2; Phil 2:3; 1 Pet 5:5

9 [1]Lit *blessing instead* [a]Rom 12:17; 1 Thess 5:15 [b]1 Cor 4:12; 1 Pet 2:23 [c]Luke 6:28; Rom 12:14; 1 Cor 4:12 [d]1 Pet 2:21 [e]Gal 3:14; Heb 6:14; 12:17

10 [a]Ps 34:12, 13

11 [a]Ps 34:14

12 [a]Ps 34:15, 16

13 [1]Lit *the one who will harm you* [a]Prov 16:7

14 [1]Or *would be* [2]Lit *fear* [a]Matt 5:10; 1 Pet 2:19ff; 4:15f [b]James 5:11 [c]Is 8:12f; 1 Pet 3:6

15 but [1]sanctify [a]Christ as Lord in your hearts, always *being*
ready [b]to make a [2]defense to everyone who asks you to give an
account for the [a]hope that is in you, yet [c]with gentleness and
[3d]reverence;
16 [1]and keep a [a]good conscience so that in the thing in which
[b]you are slandered, those who revile your good behavior in
Christ will be put to shame.
17 For [a]it is better, [b]if [1]God should will it so, that you suffer for
doing what is right rather than for doing what is wrong.
18 For [a]Christ also died for sins [b]once for all, *the* just for *the*
unjust, so that He might [c]bring us to God, having been put to
death [d]in the flesh, but made alive [e]in the [1]spirit;
19 in [1]which also He went and made proclamation to the spirits
now in prison,
20 who once were disobedient, when the [a]patience of God [b]kept
waiting in the days of Noah, during the construction of [c]the ark,
in which a few, that is, [d]eight [e]persons, were brought safely
through *the* [1]water.
21 [a]Corresponding to that, baptism now saves you—[b]not the
removal of dirt from the flesh, but an appeal to God [1]for a
[c]good conscience—through [d]the resurrection of Jesus Christ,
22 [a]who is at the right hand of God, [b]having gone into heaven,
[c]after angels and authorities and powers had been subjected to
Him.

Chapter 4 Theme ______________________

4 Therefore, since [a]Christ has [1]suffered in the flesh, [b]arm
yourselves also with the same purpose, because [c]he who
has [1]suffered in the flesh has ceased from sin,
2 [a]so as to live [b]the rest of the time in the flesh no longer for
the lusts of men, but for the [c]will of God.
3 For [a]the time already past is sufficient *for you* to have
carried out the desire of the Gentiles, [1b]having pursued a course
of sensuality, lusts, drunkenness, carousing, drinking parties
and [2]abominable idolatries.
4 In *all* this, they are surprised that you do not run with *them*
into the same excesses of [a]dissipation, and they [b]malign *you;*
5 but they will give account to Him who is ready to judge
[a]the living and the dead.
6 For [a]the gospel has for this purpose been [1]preached even to
those who are dead, that though they are judged in the flesh as
men, they may live in the spirit according to *the will of* God.
7 [a]The end of all things [1]is near; therefore, [b]be of sound
judgment and sober *spirit* for the purpose of [2]prayer.
8 Above all, [a]keep fervent in your love for one another, because
[b]love covers a multitude of sins.
9 [a]Be hospitable to one another without [b]complaint.
10 [a]As each one has received a *special* gift, employ it in serving
one another as good [b]stewards of the manifold grace of God.
11 [a]Whoever speaks, *is to do so* [1]as one who is speaking the
[b]utterances of God; whoever serves *is to do so* as one who is

15 [1]I.e. set apart [2]Or *argument;* or *explanation* [3]Or *fear* [a]1 Pet 1:3 [b]Col 4:6 [c]2 Tim 2:25 [d]1 Pet 1:17

16 [1]Lit *having a good* [a]1 Tim 1:5; Heb 13:18; 1 Pet 3:21 [b]1 Pet 2:12, 15

17 [1]Lit *the will of God* [a]1 Pet 2:20; 4:15f [b]Acts 18:21; 1 Pet 1:6; 2:15; 4:19

18 [1]Or *Spirit* [a]1 Pet 2:21 [b]Heb 9:26, 28; 10:10 [c]Rom 5:2; Eph 3:12 [d]Col 1:22; 1 Pet 4:1 [e]1 Pet 4:6

19 [1]Or *whom*

20 [1]I.e. the great flood [a]Rom 2:4 [b]Gen 6:3, 5, 13f [c]Heb 11:7 [d]Gen 8:18; 2 Pet 2:5 [e]Acts 2:41; 1 Pet 1:9, 22; 2:25; 4:19

21 [1]Or *from* [a]Acts 16:33; Titus 3:5 [b]Heb 9:14; 10:22 [c]1 Tim 1:5; Heb 13:18; 1 Pet 3:16 [d]1 Pet 1:3

22 [a]Mark 16:19 [b]Heb 4:14; 6:20 [c]Rom 8:38f; Heb 1:6

4:1 [1]I.e. suffered death [a]1 Pet 2:21 [b]Eph 6:13 [c]Rom 6:7

2 [a]Rom 6:2; Col 3:3 [b]1 Pet 1:14 [c]Mark 3:35

3 [1]Lit *having gone in* [2]Lit *lawless* [a]1 Cor 12:2 [b]Rom 13:13; Eph 2:2; 4:17ff

4 [a]Eph 5:18 [b]1 Pet 3:16

5 [a]Acts 10:42; Rom 14:9; 2 Tim 4:1

6 [1]I.e. preached in their lifetimes [a]1 Pet 3:18

7 [1]Lit *has come near* [2]Lit *prayers* [a]Rom 13:11; Heb 9:26; James 5:8; 1 John 2:18 [b]1 Pet 1:13

8 [a]1 Pet 1:22 [b]Prov 10:12; 1 Cor 13:4ff; James 5:20

9 [a]1 Tim 3:2; Heb 13:2 [b]Phil 2:14

10 [a]Rom 12:6f [b]1 Cor 4:1

11 [1]Lit *as utterances* [a]1 Thess 2:4; Titus 2:1, 15; Heb 13:7 [b]Acts 7:38

serving [2c]by the strength which God supplies; so that [d]in all
things God may be glorified through Jesus Christ, [e]to whom
belongs the glory and dominion forever and ever. Amen.
12 [a]Beloved, do not be surprised at the [b]fiery ordeal among
you, which comes upon you for your testing, as though some
strange thing were happening to you;
13 but to the degree that you [a]share the sufferings of Christ,
keep on rejoicing, so that also at the [b]revelation of His glory
[c]you may rejoice with exultation.
14 If you are reviled [1a]for the name of Christ, [b]you are blessed,
[c]because the Spirit of glory and of God rests on you.
15 Make sure that [a]none of you suffers as a murderer, or thief,
or evildoer, or a [1b]troublesome meddler;
16 but if *anyone suffers* as a [a]Christian, he is not to be ashamed,
but is to [b]glorify God in this name.
17 For *it is* time for judgment [a]to begin [1]with [b]the household
of God; and if *it* [c]*begins* with us first, what *will be* the outcome
for those [d]who do not obey the [e]gospel of God?
18 [a]AND IF IT IS WITH DIFFICULTY THAT THE RIGHTEOUS IS SAVED, [1]WHAT
WILL BECOME OF THE [b]GODLESS MAN AND THE SINNER?
19 Therefore, those also who suffer according to [a]the will of
God shall entrust their souls to a faithful Creator in doing what
is right.

Chapter 5 Theme ______________________________

5 [a]Therefore, I exhort the elders among you, as *your* [b]fellow
elder and [c]witness of the sufferings of Christ, and a [d]par-
taker also of the glory that is to be revealed,
2 shepherd [a]the flock of God among you, exercising oversight
[b]not under compulsion, but voluntarily, according to *the will of*
God; and [c]not for sordid gain, but with eagerness;
3 nor yet as [a]lording it over [1]those allotted to your charge,
but [2]proving to be [b]examples to the flock.
4 And when the Chief [a]Shepherd appears, you will receive
the [b]unfading [1c]crown of glory.
5 [a]You younger men, likewise, [b]be subject to *your* elders; and
all of you, clothe yourselves with [c]humility toward one another,
for [d]GOD IS OPPOSED TO THE PROUD, BUT GIVES GRACE TO THE HUMBLE.
6 Therefore [a]humble yourselves under the mighty hand of
God, that He may exalt you at the proper time,
7 casting all your [a]anxiety on Him, because He cares for you.
8 [a]Be of sober *spirit,* [b]be on the alert. Your adversary, [c]the devil,
prowls around like a roaring [d]lion, seeking someone to devour.
9 [1a]But resist him, [b]firm in *your* faith, knowing that [c]the
same experiences of suffering are being accomplished by your
[2]brethren who are in the world.
10 After you have suffered [a]for a little while, the [b]God of all
grace, who [c]called you to His [d]eternal glory in Christ, will
Himself [e]perfect, [f]confirm, strengthen *and* establish you.
11 [a]To Him *be* dominion forever and ever. Amen.

11 [2]Lit *from* [c]Eph 1:19; 6:10 [d]1 Cor 10:31; 1 Pet 2:12 [e]Rom 11:36; 1 Pet 5:11; Rev 1:6; 5:13
12 [a]1 Pet 2:11 [b]1 Pet 1:6f
13 [a]Rom 8:17; 2 Cor 1:5; 4:10; Phil 3:10 [b]2 Tim 2:12 [c]1 Pet 1:7; 5:1
14 [1]Lit *in* [a]John 15:21; Heb 11:26; 1 Pet 4:16 [b]Matt 5:11; Luke 6:22; Acts 5:41 [c]2 Cor 4:10f, 16
15 [1]Lit *one who oversees others' affairs* [a]1 Pet 2:19f; 3:17 [b]1 Thess 4:11; 2 Thess 3:11; 1 Tim 5:13
16 [a]Acts 5:41; 28:22; James 2:7 [b]1 Pet 4:11
17 [1]Lit *from* [a]Jer 25:29; Ezek 9:6; Amos 3:2 [b]1 Tim 3:15; Heb 3:6; 1 Pet 2:5 [c]Rom 2:9 [d]2 Thess 1:8 [e]Rom 1:1
18 [1]Lit *where will appear* [a]Prov 11:31; Luke 23:31 [b]1 Tim 1:9
19 [a]1 Pet 3:17
5:1 [a]Acts 11:30 [b]2 John 1; 3 John 1 [c]Luke 24:48; Heb 12:1 [d]1 Pet 1:5, 7; 4:13; Rev 1:9
2 [a]John 21:16; Acts 20:28 [b]Philem 14 [c]1 Tim 3:8
3 [1]Lit *the allotments* [2]Or *becoming* [a]Ezek 34:4; Matt 20:25f [b]John 13:15; Phil 3:17; 1 Thess 1:7; 2 Thess 3:9; 1 Tim 4:12; Titus 2:7
4 [1]Lit *wreath* [a]1 Pet 2:25 [b]1 Pet 1:4 [c]1 Cor 9:25
5 [a]Luke 22:26; 1 Tim 5:1 [b]Eph 5:21 [c]1 Pet 3:8 [d]Prov 3:34; James 4:6
6 [a]Matt 23:12; Luke 14:11; 18:14; James 4:10
7 [a]Ps 55:22; Matt 6:25
8 [a]1 Pet 1:13 [b]Matt 24:42 [c]James 4:7 [d]2 Tim 4:17
9 [1]Lit *whom resist* [2]Lit *brotherhood* [a]James 4:7 [b]Col 2:5 [c]Acts 14:22
10 [a]1 Pet 1:6 [b]1 Pet 4:10 [c]1 Cor 1:9; 1 Thess 2:12 [d]2 Cor 4:17; 2 Tim 2:10 [e]1 Cor 1:10; Heb 13:21 [f]Rom 16:25; 2 Thess 2:17; 3:3
11 [a]Rom 11:36; 1 Pet 4:11

12 [1]Lit *(as I consider)* [a]2 Cor 1:19 [b]Heb 13:22 [c]Acts 11:23; 1 Pet 1:13; 4:10 [d]1 Cor 15:1
13 [a]Acts 12:12, 25; 15:37, 39; Col 4:10; Philem 24
14 [a]Rom 16:16 [b]Eph 6:23

12 Through [a]Silvanus, our faithful brother [1](for so I regard
him), [b]I have written to you briefly, exhorting and testifying
that this is [c]the true grace of God. [d]Stand firm in it!
13 She who is in Babylon, chosen together with you, sends
you greetings, and *so does* my son, [a]Mark.
14 [a]Greet one another with a kiss of love.
[b]**P**eace be to you all who are in Christ.

1 Peter Observations Chart

Author	Recipients

General Instructions

(continued)

1 Peter Observations Chart

Instructions to

Wives

Husbands

Elders

Younger men

Servants

1 Peter at a Glance

Theme of 1 Peter:

Segment Divisions

	Chapter Themes
	1
	2
	3
	4
	5

Author:

Date:

Purpose:

Key Words:

suffering, trials (and all synonyms)

grace

glory

salvation

any reference to Jesus' future revelation

love

Holy Spirit

called

chosen

holy

2 PETER

A fisherman by trade, Peter had been captured and transformed by the Great Shepherd. Is it any wonder that even in Peter's darkest hour, the welfare of God's sheep was uppermost in his mind?

Ever since the day he stood with Jesus by a fire, the morning air full of the aroma of roasting fish, Peter had known the way he would die. But Peter would be faithful. His concern about his death and the way he would die would not override his concern for the sheep Jesus had commissioned him to feed and shepherd. And so, sometime around A.D. 63 or 64, Peter writes "to those who have received a faith of the same kind as ours."

In A.D. 64, according to tradition, Peter was crucified upside down for the Lord he once denied knowing. How Peter had grown in the grace and knowledge of his God!

THINGS TO DO

1. Read 2 Peter, marking every reference to the author in a distinctive color and every reference to the recipients in another color. Then on the OBSERVATIONS CHART on page 2020 note everything you learn about each. Observe what the author says about himself. When in his life is he writing? Who are the recipients? How are they described? Why is he writing?

2. In a distinctive way, mark in the text the key words (and their synonyms and pronouns) listed on the 2 PETER AT A GLANCE chart on page 2021. Then list on a piece of paper the truths you learn by marking these key words. Be thorough because the lists will help you see the flow of the book.

3. Read through 2 Peter again and look for specific instructions that Peter gives the readers concerning their behavior and belief. Record these on the OBSERVATIONS CHART under "Instructions." Also look for and note any people or groups of people of which Peter warns them to beware.

4. In this book, Peter states why he's writing. Look for and underline the phrase, *"I am writing to you."* Also underline other verses that indicate his purpose in writing. Record his purpose for writing on 2 PETER AT A GLANCE.

5. Summarize the message of each paragraph and record its theme on 2 PETER AT A GLANCE. Then determine the chapter themes and the book theme and record these in the appropriate places on the chart and in your Bible.

6. Mark every reference to God (and Lord, if it refers to the Father). Then list what you learn about God from this short but much-needed epistle.

7. There is a reference to *the day of the Lord* in 2 Peter. Record your insights on the chart on page 2076.

THINGS TO THINK ABOUT

1. What would it take to live your life so that you may be found spotless and blameless at Christ's coming? Are you willing?

2. Is there a danger today that false teachers will arise among the brethren, as in Peter's day? What do you need to know to be able to detect them? What is your protection?

3. How can you keep from falling from your own steadfastness? Practically, what do you need to do in order to grow in the grace and knowledge of Jesus Christ?

Chapter 1 Theme ________________________________

1 [1]Simon Peter, a [a]bond-servant and [b]apostle of Jesus Christ,
To those who have received [c]a faith of the same [2]kind as ours,
[3]by [d]the righteousness of [e]our God and Savior, Jesus Christ:
2 [a]Grace and peace be multiplied to you in [b]the knowledge of
God and of Jesus our Lord;
3 seeing that His [a]divine power has granted to us everything
pertaining to life and godliness, through the true [b]knowledge of
Him who [c]called us [1]by His own glory and [2]excellence.
4 [1]For by these He has granted to us His precious and
magnificent [a]promises, so that by them you may become
[b]partakers of *the* divine nature, having [c]escaped the [d]corruption
that is in [e]the world by lust.
5 Now for this very reason also, applying all diligence, in your
faith [a]supply [b]moral [1]excellence, and in *your* moral excellence,
[c]knowledge,
6 and in *your* knowledge, [a]self-control, and in *your* self-control,
[b]perseverance, and in *your* perseverance, [c]godliness,
7 and in *your* godliness, [a]brotherly kindness, and in *your*
brotherly kindness, love.
8 For if these *qualities* are yours and are increasing, they render
you neither useless nor [a]unfruitful in the true [b]knowledge of
our Lord Jesus Christ.
9 For he who lacks these *qualities* is [a]blind *or* short-sighted,
having forgotten *his* [b]purification from his former sins.
10 Therefore, brethren, be all the more diligent to make certain
about His [a]calling and [b]choosing you; for as long as you practice
these things, you will never [c]stumble;
11 for in this way the entrance into [a]the eternal kingdom of our
[b]Lord and Savior Jesus Christ will be [c]abundantly [d]supplied to
you.
12 Therefore, [a]I will always be ready to remind you of these
things, even though you *already* know *them,* and have been
established in [b]the truth which is present with *you.*
13 I consider it [a]right, as long as I am in [b]this *earthly* dwelling,
to [c]stir you up by way of reminder,
14 knowing that [a]the laying aside of my *earthly* dwelling is
imminent, [b]as also our Lord Jesus Christ has made clear to me.
15 And I will also be diligent that at any time after my [a]departure
you will be able to call these things to mind.
16 For we did not follow cleverly devised [a]tales when we made
known to you the [b]power and coming of our Lord Jesus Christ,
but we were [c]eyewitnesses of His majesty.
17 For when He received honor and glory from God the Father,
such an [1a]utterance as this was [2]made to Him by the [b]Majestic
Glory, "This is My beloved Son with whom I am well-pleased"—
18 and we ourselves heard this [1]utterance made from heaven
when we were with Him on the [a]holy mountain.
19 [1]*So* we have [a]the prophetic word *made* more [b]sure, to which
you do well to pay attention as to [c]a lamp shining in a dark place,
until the [d]day dawns and the [e]morning star arises [f]in your hearts.

1:1 [1]Two early mss read *Simeon* [2]Or *value* [3]Or *in* [a]Rom 1:1; Phil 1:1; James 1:1; Jude 1 [b]1 Pet 1:1 [c]Rom 1:12; 2 Cor 4:13; Titus 1:4 [d]Rom 3:21-26 [e]Titus 2:13
2 [a]Rom 1:7; 1 Pet 1:2 [b]John 17:3; Phil 3:8; 2 Pet 1:3, 8; 2:20; 3:18
3 [1]Or *to* [2]Or *virtue* [a]1 Pet 1:5 [b]John 17:3; Phil 3:8; 2 Pet 1:2, 8; 2:20; 3:18 [c]1 Thess 2:12; 2 Thess 2:14; 1 Pet 5:10
4 [1]Lit *Through which* (things) [a]2 Pet 3:9, 13 [b]Eph 4:13, 24; Heb 12:10; 1 John 3:2 [c]2 Pet 2:18, 20 [d]2 Pet 2:19 [e]James 1:27
5 [1]Or *virtue* [a]2 Pet 1:11 [b]2 Pet 1:3 [c]Col 2:3; 2 Pet 1:2
6 [a]Acts 24:25 [b]Luke 21:19 [c]2 Pet 1:3
7 [a]Rom 12:10; 1 Pet 1:22
8 [a]Col 1:10 [b]John 17:3; Phil 3:8; 2 Pet 1:2, 3; 2:20; 3:18
9 [a]1 John 2:11 [b]Eph 5:26; Titus 2:14
10 [a]Matt 22:14; Rom 11:29; 2 Pet 1:3 [b]1 Thess 1:4 [c]James 2:10; 2 Pet 3:17; Jude 24
11 [a]2 Tim 4:18 [b]2 Pet 2:20; 3:18 [c]Rom 2:4; 1 Tim 6:17 [d]2 Pet 1:5
12 [a]Phil 3:1; 1 John 2:21; Jude 5 [b]Col 1:5f; 2 John 2
13 [a]Phil 1:7 [b]2 Cor 5:1, 4; 2 Pet 1:14 [c]2 Pet 3:1
14 [a]2 Cor 5:1; 2 Tim 4:6 [b]John 13:36; 21:19
15 [a]Luke 9:31
16 [a]1 Tim 1:4; 2 Pet 2:3 [b]Mark 13:26; 14:62; 1 Thess 2:19 [c]Matt 17:1ff; Mark 9:2ff; Luke 9:28ff
17 [1]Lit *voice* [2]Lit *brought* [a]Matt 17:5; Mark 9:7; Luke 9:35 [b]Heb 1:3
18 [1]Lit *voice brought* [a]Ex 3:5; Josh 5:15
19 [1]Or *We have the even more sure prophetic word* [a]1 Pet 1:10f [b]Heb 2:2 [c]Ps 119:105 [d]Luke 1:78 [e]Rev 22:16 [f]2 Cor 4:6

20 But [a]know this first of all, that [b]no prophecy of Scripture is
a matter of one's own interpretation,
21 for [a]no prophecy was ever made by an act of human will,
but men [b]moved by the Holy Spirit spoke from God.

Chapter 2 Theme ______________________________

2 But [a]false prophets also arose among the people, just as there
will also be [b]false teachers [c]among you, who will [d]secretly
introduce [e]destructive heresies, even [f]denying the [g]Master who
[h]bought them, bringing swift destruction upon themselves.
2 Many will follow their [a]sensuality, and because of them [b]the
way of the truth will be [c]maligned;
3 and in *their* [a]greed they will [b]exploit you with [c]false words;
[d]their judgment from long ago is not idle, and their destruction
is not asleep.
4 For [a]if God did not spare angels when they sinned, but cast
them into hell and [b]committed them to pits of darkness, reserved
for judgment;
5 and did not spare [a]the ancient world, but preserved [b]Noah, a
[1]preacher of righteousness, with seven others, when He brought
a [c]flood upon the world of the ungodly;
6 and *if* He [a]condemned the cities of Sodom and Gomorrah
to destruction by reducing *them* to ashes, having made them
an [b]example to those who would [c]live ungodly *lives* thereafter;
7 and *if* He [a]rescued righteous Lot, oppressed by the [b]sensual
conduct of [c]unprincipled men
8 (for by what he saw and heard *that* [a]righteous man, while
living among them, felt *his* righteous soul tormented day after
day by *their* lawless deeds),
9 [a]*then* the Lord knows how to rescue the godly from
[1]temptation, and to keep the unrighteous under punishment for
the [b]day of judgment,
10 and especially those who [1a]indulge the flesh in *its* corrupt
desires and [b]despise authority.

Daring, [c]self-willed, they do not tremble when they [b]revile
angelic [2]majesties,
11 [a]whereas angels who are greater in might and power do
not bring a reviling judgment against them before the Lord.
12 But [a]these, like unreasoning animals, [b]born as creatures of
instinct to be captured and killed, reviling where they have no
knowledge, will in [1]the destruction of those creatures also be
destroyed,
13 suffering wrong as [a]the wages of doing wrong. They count it
a pleasure to [b]revel in the [c]daytime. They are stains and blemishes,
[b]reveling in their [1]deceptions, as they [d]carouse with you,
14 having eyes full of adultery that never cease from sin,
[a]enticing [b]unstable souls, having a heart trained in [c]greed,
[d]accursed children;
15 forsaking [a]the right way, they have gone astray, having
followed [b]the way of Balaam, the *son* of Beor, who loved [c]the
wages of unrighteousness;

20 [a]2 Pet 3:3 [b]Rom 12:6
21 [a]Jer 23:26; 2 Tim 3:16 [b]2 Sam 23:2; Luke 1:70; Acts 1:16; 3:18; 1 Pet 1:11
2:1 [a]Deut 13:1ff; Jer 6:13 [b]2 Cor 11:13 [c]Matt 7:15; 1 Tim 4:1 [d]Gal 2:4; Jude 4 [e]1 Cor 11:19; Gal 5:20 [f]Jude 4 [g]Rev 6:10 [h]1 Cor 6:20
2 [a]Gen 19:5ff; 2 Pet 2:7, 18; Jude 4 [b]Acts 16:17; 22:4; 24:14 [c]Rom 2:24
3 [a]1 Tim 6:5; 2 Pet 2:14; Jude 16 [b]2 Cor 2:17; 1 Thess 2:5 [c]Rom 16:18; 2 Pet 1:16 [d]Deut 32:35
4 [a]Jude 6 [b]Rev 20:1f
5 [1]Or *herald* [a]Ezek 26:20; 2 Pet 3:6 [b]Gen 6:8, 9; 1 Pet 3:20 [c]2 Pet 3:6
6 [a]Gen 19:24; Jude 7 [b]Is 1:9; Matt 10:15; 11:23; Rom 9:29; Jude 7 [c]Jude 15
7 [a]Gen 19:16, 29 [b]Gen 19:5ff; 2 Pet 2:2, 18; Jude 4 [c]2 Pet 3:17
8 [a]Heb 11:4
9 [1]Lit *trial;* or *temptation* [a]1 Cor 10:13; Rev 3:10 [b]Matt 10:15; Jude 6
10 [1]Lit *go after* [2]Lit *glories* [a]2 Pet 3:3; Jude 16, 18 [b]Ex 22:28; Jude 8 [c]Titus 1:7
11 [a]Jude 9
12 [1]Lit *their destruction also* [a]Jude 10 [b]Jer 12:3; Col 2:22
13 [1]One early ms reads *love feasts* [a]2 Pet 2:15 [b]Rom 13:13 [c]1 Thess 5:7 [d]1 Cor 11:21; Jude 12
14 [a]2 Pet 2:18 [b]James 1:8; 2 Pet 3:16 [c]2 Pet 2:3 [d]Eph 2:3
15 [a]Acts 13:10 [b]Num 22:5, 7; Deut 23:4; Neh 13:2; Jude 11; Rev 2:14 [c]2 Pet 2:13

16 but he received a rebuke for his own transgression, [a]*for* a
mute donkey, speaking with a voice of a man, restrained the
madness of the prophet.
17 These are [a]springs without water and mists driven by a storm,
[b]for whom the [1]black darkness has been reserved.
18 For speaking out [a]arrogant *words* of [b]vanity they [c]entice by
fleshly desires, by [d]sensuality, those who barely [e]escape from
the ones who live in error,
19 promising them freedom while they themselves are slaves
of corruption; for [a]by what a man is overcome, by this he is
enslaved.
20 For if, after they have [a]escaped the defilements of the world
by [b]the knowledge of the [c]Lord and Savior Jesus Christ, they
are again [d]entangled in them and are overcome, [e]the last state
has become worse for them than the first.
21 [a]For it would be better for them not to have known the
way of righteousness, than having known it, to turn away from
[b]the holy commandment [c]handed on to them.
22 [1]It has happened to them according to the true proverb,
"[a]A DOG RETURNS TO ITS OWN VOMIT," and, "A sow, after washing,
returns to wallowing in the mire."

Chapter 3 Theme ______________________________

3 This is now, [a]beloved, the second letter I am writing to you
in which I am [b]stirring up your sincere mind by way of
reminder,
2 that you should [a]remember the words spoken beforehand
by [b]the holy prophets and [c]the commandment of the Lord and
Savior *spoken* by your apostles.
3 [a]Know this first of all, that [b]in the last days [c]mockers will
come with *their* mocking, [d]following after their own lusts,
4 and saying, "[a]Where is the promise of His [b]coming? For *ever*
since the fathers [c]fell asleep, all continues just as it was [d]from
the beginning of creation."
5 For [1]when they maintain this, it escapes their notice that [a]by
the word of God *the* heavens existed long ago and *the* earth
was [b]formed out of water and by water,
6 through which [a]the world at that time was [b]destroyed,
being flooded with water.
7 But by His word [a]the present heavens and earth are being
reserved for [b]fire, kept for [c]the day of judgment and destruction
of ungodly men.
8 But do not let this one *fact* escape your notice, [a]beloved,
that with the Lord one day is like a thousand years, and [b]a
thousand years like one day.
9 [a]The Lord is not slow about His promise, as some count
slowness, but [b]is patient toward you, [c]not wishing for any to
perish but for all to come to repentance.
10 But [a]the day of the Lord [b]will come like a thief, in which
[c]the heavens [d]will pass away with a roar and the [e]elements will

16 [a]Num 22:21, 23, 28, 30ff

17 [1]Lit *blackness of darkness* [a]Jude 12 [b]Jude 13

18 [a]Jude 16 [b]Eph 4:17 [c]2 Pet 2:14 [d]2 Pet 2:2 [e]2 Pet 1:4; 2:20

19 [a]John 8:34; Rom 6:16

20 [a]2 Pet 2:18 [b]2 Pet 1:2 [c]2 Pet 1:11; 3:18 [d]2 Tim 2:4 [e]Matt 12:45; Luke 11:26

21 [a]Ezek 18:24; Heb 6:4ff; 10:26f; James 4:17 [b]Gal 6:2; 1 Tim 6:14; 2 Pet 3:2 [c]Jude 3

22 [1]Lit *The thing of the true proverb has happened to them* [a]Prov 26:11

3:1 [a]1 Pet 2:11; 2 Pet 3:8, 14, 17 [b]2 Pet 1:13

2 [a]Jude 17 [b]Luke 1:70; Acts 3:21; Eph 3:5 [c]Gal 6:2; 1 Tim 6:14; 2 Pet 2:21

3 [a]2 Pet 1:20 [b]1 Tim 4:1; Heb 1:2 [c]Jude 18 [d]2 Pet 2:10

4 [a]Is 5:19; Jer 17:15; Ezek 11:3; 12:22, 27; Mal 2:17; Matt 24:48 [b]1 Thess 2:19; 2 Pet 3:12 [c]Acts 7:60 [d]Mark 10:6

5 [1]Or *they are willfully ignorant of this fact, that* [a]Gen 1:6, 9; Heb 11:3 [b]Ps 24:2; 136:6

6 [a]2 Pet 2:5 [b]Gen 7:11, 12, 21f

7 [a]2 Pet 3:10, 12 [b]Is 66:15; Dan 7:9f; 2 Thess 1:7; Heb 12:29 [c]Matt 10:15; 1 Cor 3:13; Jude 7

8 [a]2 Pet 3:1 [b]Ps 90:4

9 [a]Hab 2:3; Rom 13:11; Heb 10:37 [b]Rom 2:4; Rev 2:21 [c]1 Tim 2:4; Rev 2:21

10 [a]1 Cor 1:8 [b]Matt 24:43; Luke 12:39; 1 Thess 5:2; Rev 3:3; 16:15 [c]Is 34:4; 2 Pet 3:7, 12 [d]Matt 24:35; Rev 21:1 [e]Is 24:19; Mic 1:4

10 [1]Lit *the works in it* [2]Two early mss read *discovered*
[f]2 Pet 3:7

12 [a]1 Cor 1:7
[b]2 Pet 3:7, 10
[c]Is 24:19; 34:4; Mic 1:4

13 [a]Is 65:17; 66:22
[b]Rom 8:21; Rev 21:1
[c]Is 60:21; 65:25; Rev 21:27

14 [a]1 Cor 15:58; 2 Pet 1:10 [b]2 Pet 3:1
[c]1 Pet 1:7
[d]Phil 2:15; 1 Thess 5:23; 1 Tim 6:14; James 1:27

15 [a]2 Pet 3:9
[b]Acts 9:17; 15:25; 2 Pet 3:2
[c]1 Cor 3:10; Eph 3:3

16 [a]2 Pet 3:14
[b]Heb 5:11
[c]2 Pet 2:14
[d]2 Pet 3:2

17 [a]2 Pet 3:1
[b]1 Cor 10:12
[c]2 Pet 2:18
[d]2 Pet 2:7 [e]Rev 2:5

18 [a]2 Pet 1:2
[b]2 Pet 1:11; 2:20
[c]Rom 11:36; 2 Tim 4:18; Rev 1:6

be destroyed with intense heat, and [f]the earth and [1]its works
will be [2]burned up.
11 Since all these things are to be destroyed in this way, what
sort of people ought you to be in holy conduct and godliness,
12 [a]looking for and hastening the coming of the day of God,
because of which [b]the heavens will be destroyed by burning,
and the [c]elements will melt with intense heat!
13 But according to His [a]promise we are looking for [b]new
heavens and a new earth, [c]in which righteousness dwells.
14 [a]Therefore, [b]beloved, since you look for these things, be
diligent to be [c]found by Him in peace, [d]spotless and blameless,
15 and regard the [a]patience of our Lord *as* salvation; just as
also [b]our beloved brother Paul, [c]according to the wisdom given
him, wrote to you,
16 as also in all *his* letters, speaking in them of [a]these things, [b]in
which are some things hard to understand, which the untaught
and [c]unstable distort, as *they do* also [d]the rest of the Scriptures,
to their own destruction.
17 You therefore, [a]beloved, knowing this beforehand, [b]be on
your guard so that you are not carried away by [c]the error of
[d]unprincipled men and [e]fall from your own steadfastness,
18 but grow in the grace and [a]knowledge of our [b]Lord and
Savior Jesus Christ. [c]To Him *be* the glory, both now and to the
day of eternity. Amen.

2 Peter Observations Chart

Peter	Instructions
Recipients	
	Warnings

2 Peter at a Glance

Theme of 2 Peter:

Author:

Date:

Purpose:

Key Words:

- prophecy (prophet, prophetic)
- knowledge (know, knowing, known)
- remind (reminder)
- true (truth)
- diligent (diligence)
- false teachers
- mockers
- destroyed
- promise

Segment Divisions	Paragraph Themes	Chapter Themes
	1:1-11	1
	1:12-15	
	1:16-18	
	1:19-21	
	2:1-3	2
	2:4-10	
	2:11-16	
	2:17-22	
	3:1-7	3
	3:8-10	
	3:11-13	
	3:14-18	

1 JOHN

As a boy, John thought of Jesus as just a cousin, one of the sons of Aunt Mary, his mother Salome's sister. Little did John realize that someday he would be chosen by God to be one of Jesus' twelve apostles.

John had been known as a "son of thunder" (Mark 3:17), but a transformation had taken place. Now he was called "the disciple whom Jesus loved."

Even though John's name is not mentioned in this epistle, there is much evidence that he is the author. John had been with Jesus. He had seen Him, heard Him, touched Him, and been filled with His love. This is evident as you hear John's fatherly heart for those who belong to Jesus. He loves the fathers, the young men, the little children. Yet as he writes about the antichrists and deceivers, you can hear the rumble of thunder in the background.

We don't know when John wrote this first epistle. It may have been between A.D. 85 and 95 in Ephesus before exile to the Isle of Patmos. Love—and thunder—compelled him to write. He had to protect his children from deception. He had to warn them about the brewing storm of gnosticism—a teaching that could keep them from having fellowship with him and thus with the Father and His Son (1 John 1:3).

THINGS TO DO

1. Begin your study by reading through 1 John and marking every reference to the author in one color and every reference to the recipients in another.

2. If you want to handle a passage of Scripture accurately you must always interpret it in the light of its context. Context simply means that which goes "with" *(con)* the "text." Context rules when it comes to interpretation. Identifying the author's purpose for writing will help you discern the context of a passage. What the author says, he says in the light of his purpose for writing.

   In this letter the author tells us his purpose in seven different verses: 1:4; 2:1,12-14,21, and 26. Then in 1 John 5:13 he concludes by summarizing his purpose for writing. Read these verses and record his reasons for writing on the chart I AM WRITING TO YOU on page 2029. Record on the 1 JOHN AT A GLANCE chart on page 2030 the author's purpose for writing.

3. One of the major heresies the church would face was gnosticism. Gnosticism wasn't in full bloom in John's time, but the seeds had been sown. Understanding gnosticism will help you better understand why John concentrated on the truths contained in his writing. Therefore, before you go any further, read the article "Understanding Gnosticism" starting on page 2100.

4. Now read 1 John chapter by chapter:

   a. Mark each of the key words (and their synonyms and pronouns) listed on 1 JOHN AT A GLANCE. When you finish, go to the chart 1 JOHN KEY WORDS and record the number of times each key word is used in each chapter. Then determine the number of times each word is used in 1 John. Doing this will help you see the main themes of 1 John.

   b. John uses contrasts in order to make his point: light/darkness, children of God/children of the devil, etc. Watch for these contrasts; observe what you learn from them.

5. Remember, 1 John was written "so that you may know." When you finish reading

all five chapters, trace throughout 1 John the repeated use of the word *know* and record what you learn from the text on the chart WHAT I CAN KNOW and HOW I CAN KNOW IT on page 2029. Watch the matters John deals with in respect to wrong behavior or wrong belief.

6. You may want to keep a running list of everything you learn about God, Jesus Christ, and the Spirit from this book.

7. Record the theme of each chapter on 1 JOHN AT A GLANCE and in your Bible next to the chapter number. Fill in any remaining information called for on the chart.

THINGS TO THINK ABOUT

1. Based on the criteria given in this book, how can you know whether or not you have eternal life?

2. What have you learned about sin from 1 John? Do you practice sin or righteousness?

3. Do you love the things of the world? Are you caught up in the pride of life, in boasting, or in desiring whatever your eyes see?

4. According to 1 John 3, what are you to do when your heart condemns you?

5. Does your belief about Jesus Christ match what 1 John teaches about Him?

Chapter 1 Theme ____________________________

1 What was [a]from the beginning, what we have [b]heard, what
we have [c]seen with our eyes, what we [d]have looked at and
[e]touched with our hands, concerning the [f]Word of Life—
2 and [a]the life was manifested, and we have [b]seen and
[c]testify and proclaim to you [d]the eternal life, which was [e]with
the Father and was [a]manifested to us—
3 what we have [a]seen and [b]heard we proclaim to you also, so
that you too may have fellowship with us; and indeed our
[c]fellowship is with the Father, and with His Son Jesus Christ.
4 [a]These things we write, so that our [b]joy may be made
complete.
5 [a]This is the message we have heard from Him and announce
to you, that [b]God is Light, and in Him there is no darkness at all.
6 [a]If we say that we have fellowship with Him and *yet* walk in
the darkness, we [b]lie and [c]do not practice the truth;
7 but if we [a]walk in the Light as [b]He Himself is in the Light, we
have fellowship with one another, and [c]the blood of Jesus His
Son cleanses us from all sin.
8 [a]If we say that we have no sin, we are deceiving ourselves
and the [b]truth is not in us.
9 [a]If we confess our sins, He is faithful and righteous to forgive
us our sins and [b]to cleanse us from all unrighteousness.
10 [a]If we say that we have not sinned, we [b]make Him a liar and
[c]His word is not in us.

1:1 [a]John 1:1f; 1 John 2:13, 14 [b]Acts 4:20; 1 John 1:3 [c]John 19:35; 2 Pet 1:16; 1 John 1:2 [d]John 1:14; 1 John 4:14 [e]Luke 24:39; John 20:27 [f]John 1:1, 4

2 [a]John 1:4; 1 John 3:5, 8; 5:20 [b]John 19:35; 1 John 1:1 [c]John 15:27; 1 John 4:14 [d]John 10:28; 17:3; 1 John 2:25; 5:11, 13, 20 [e]John 1:1

3 [a]John 19:35; 2 Pet 1:16; 1 John 1:1 [b]Acts 4:20; 1 John 1:1 [c]John 17:3, 21; 1 Cor 1:9

4 [a]1 John 2:1 [b]John 3:29

5 [a]John 1:19; 1 John 3:11 [b]1 Tim 6:16; James 1:17

6 [a]John 8:12; 1 John 2:11 [b]John 8:55; 1 John 2:4; 4:20 [c]John 3:21

7 [a]Is 2:5 [b]1 Tim 6:16 [c]Titus 2:14

8 [a]Job 15:14; Prov 20:9; Rom 3:10ff; James 3:2 [b]John 8:44; 1 John 2:4

9 [a]Ps 32:5; Prov 28:13 [b]Titus 2:14
10 [a]Job 15:14 [b]John 3:33; 1 John 5:10 [c]1 John 2:14

Chapter 2 Theme ________________________________

2 [a]My little children, I am [b]writing these things to you so
that you may not sin. And if anyone sins, [c]we have an
[1d]Advocate with the Father, Jesus Christ the righteous;
2 and He Himself is [a]the [1]propitiation for our sins; and not
for ours only, but also [b]for *those of* the whole world.
3 [a]By this we know that we have come to [b]know Him, if we
[c]keep His commandments.
4 The one who says, "[a]I have come to [b]know Him," and does
not keep His commandments, is a [c]liar, and [d]the truth is not in
him;
5 but whoever [a]keeps His word, in him the [b]love of God has
truly been perfected. [c]By this we know that we are in Him:
6 the one who says he [a]abides in Him [b]ought himself to walk
in the same manner as He walked.
7 [a]Beloved, I am [b]not writing a new commandment to you, but
an old commandment which you have had [c]from the beginning;
the old commandment is the word which you have heard.
8 [1]On the other hand, I am writing [a]a new commandment to
you, which is true in Him and in you, because [b]the darkness is
passing away and [c]the true Light is already shining.
9 The one who says he is in the Light and *yet* [a]hates his
[b]brother is in the darkness until now.
10 [a]The one who loves his brother abides in the Light and
there is no cause for stumbling in him.
11 But the one who [a]hates his brother is in the darkness and
[b]walks in the darkness, and does not know where he is going
because the darkness has [c]blinded his eyes.
12 I am writing to you, [a]little children, because [b]your sins have
been forgiven you for His name's sake.
13 I am writing to you, fathers, because you know Him [a]who has
been from the beginning. I am writing to you, young men,
because [b]you have overcome [c]the evil one. I have written to
you, children, because [d]you know the Father.
14 I have written to you, fathers, because you know Him [a]who
has been from the beginning. I have written to you, young men,
because you are [b]strong, and the [c]word of God abides in you,
and [d]you have overcome the evil one.
15 Do not love [a]the world nor the things in the world. [b]If
anyone loves the world, the love of the Father is not in him.
16 For all that is in the world, [a]the lust of the flesh and [b]the
lust of the eyes and [c]the boastful pride of life, is not from the
Father, but is from the world.
17 [a]The world is passing away, and *also* its lusts; but the one
who [b]does the will of God lives forever.
18 Children, [a]it is the last hour; and just as you heard that
[b]antichrist is coming, [c]even now many antichrists have appeared;
from this we know that it is the last hour.
19 [a]They went out from us, but they were not *really* of us; for if
they had been of us, they would have remained with us; but *they
went out,* [b]so that [1]it would be shown that they all are not of us.

2:1 [1]Gr *Paracletos,* one called alongside to help; or *Intercessor* [a]John 13:33; Gal 4:19; 1 John 2:12, 28; 3:7, 18; 4:4; 5:21 [b]1 John 1:4 [c]Rom 8:34; 1 Tim 2:5; Heb 7:25; 9:24 [d]John 14:16
2 [1]Or *satisfaction* [a]Rom 3:25; Heb 2:17; 1 John 4:10 [b]John 4:42; 11:51f; 1 John 4:14
3 [a]1 John 2:5; 3:24; 4:13; 5:2 [b]1 John 2:4; 3:6; 4:7f [c]John 14:15; 15:10; 1 John 3:22, 24; 5:3; Rev 12:17; 14:12
4 [a]Titus 1:10 [b]1 John 3:6; 4:7f [c]1 John 1:6 [d]1 John 1:8
5 [a]John 14:23 [b]1 John 4:12 [c]1 John 2:3; 3:24; 4:13; 5:2
6 [a]John 15:4 [b]John 13:15; 15:10; 1 Pet 2:21
7 [a]Heb 6:9; 1 John 3:2, 21; 4:1, 7, 11 [b]John 13:34; 1 John 3:11, 23; 4:21; 2 John 5 [c]1 John 2:24; 3:11; 2 John 5, 6
8 [1]Lit *Again* [a]John 13:34 [b]Rom 13:12; Eph 5:8; 1 Thess 5:4f [c]John 1:9
9 [a]1 John 2:11; 3:15; 4:20 [b]Acts 1:15; 1 John 3:10, 16; 4:20f
10 [a]John 11:9; 1 John 2:10, 11
11 [a]1 John 2:9; 3:15; 4:20 [b]John 12:35; 1 John 1:6 [c]2 Cor 4:4; 2 Pet 1:9
12 [a]1 John 2:1 [b]Acts 13:38; 1 Cor 6:11
13 [a]1 John 1:1 [b]John 16:33; 1 John 2:14; 4:4; 5:4f; Rev 2:7 [c]Matt 5:37; 1 John 2:14; 3:12; 5:18f [d]John 14:7; 1 John 2:3
14 [a]1 John 1:1 [b]Eph 6:10 [c]John 5:38; 8:37; 1 John 1:10 [d]1 John 2:13
15 [a]Rom 12:2; James 1:27 [b]James 4:4
16 [a]Rom 13:14; Eph 2:3; 1 Pet 2:11 [b]Prov 27:20 [c]James 4:16
17 [a]1 Cor 7:31 [b]Mark 3:35
18 [a]Rom 13:11; 1 Tim 4:1; 1 Pet 4:7 [b]Matt 24:5, 24; 1 John 2:22; 4:3; 2 John 7 [c]Mark 13:22; 1 John 4:1, 3
19 [1]Lit *they would be revealed* [a]Acts 20:30 [b]1 Cor 11:19

20 [1]But you have an [a]anointing from [b]the Holy One, and [c]you
all know.
21 I have not written to you because you do not know the truth,
but [a]because you do know it, and [1]because no lie is [b]of the truth.
22 Who is the liar but [a]the one who denies that Jesus is the
[1]Christ? This is [b]the antichrist, the one who denies the Father
and the Son.
23 [a]Whoever denies the Son does not have the Father; the one
who confesses the Son has the Father also.
24 As for you, let that abide in you which you heard [a]from the
beginning. If what you heard from the beginning abides in you,
you also [b]will abide in the Son and in the Father.
25 [a]This is the promise which He Himself [1]made to us: eternal
life.
26 These things I have written to you concerning those who
are trying to [a]deceive you.
27 As for you, the [a]anointing which you received from Him
abides in you, and you have no need for anyone to teach you; but
as His anointing [b]teaches you about all things, and is [c]true and is
not a lie, and just as it has taught you, [1]you abide in Him.
28 Now, [a]little children, abide in Him, so that when He
[b]appears, we may have [c]confidence and [d]not [1]shrink away from
Him in shame [2]at His [e]coming.
29 If you know that [a]He is righteous, you know that everyone
also who practices righteousness [b]is [1]born of Him.

Chapter 3 Theme ______________________

3 See [1a]how great a love the Father has bestowed on us, that
we would be called [b]children of God; and *such* we are. For
this reason the world does not know us, because [c]it did not
know Him.
2 [a]Beloved, now we are [b]children of God, and [c]it has not
appeared as yet what we will be. We know that when He
[d]appears, we will be [e]like Him, because we will [f]see Him just
as He is.
3 And everyone who has this [a]hope *fixed* on Him [b]purifies
himself, just as He is pure.
4 Everyone who practices sin also practices lawlessness; and
[a]sin is lawlessness.
5 You know that He [a]appeared in order to [b]take away sins;
and [c]in Him there is no sin.
6 No one who abides in Him [a]sins; no one who sins has seen
Him or [1b]knows Him.
7 [a]Little children, make sure no one [b]deceives you; [c]the one
who practices righteousness is righteous, just as He is righteous;
8 the one who practices sin is [a]of the devil; for the devil [1]has
sinned from the beginning. [b]The Son of God [c]appeared for this
purpose, [d]to destroy the works of the devil.

20 [1]Lit *And* [a]2 Cor 1:21; 1 John 2:27 [b]Mark 1:24; Acts 10:38 [c]Prov 28:5; Matt 13:11; John 14:26; 1 Cor 2:15f; 1 John 2:27
21 [1]Or know *that* [a]James 1:19; 2 Pet 1:12; Jude 5 [b]John 8:44; 18:37; 1 John 3:19
22 [1]I.e. Messiah [a]1 John 4:3; 2 John 7 [b]Matt 24:5, 24; 1 John 2:18; 4:3; 2 John 7
23 [a]John 8:19; 16:3; 17:3; 1 John 4:15; 5:1; 2 John 9
24 [a]1 John 2:7 [b]John 14:23; 1 John 1:3; 2 John 9
25 [1]Lit *promised us* [a]John 3:15; 6:40; 1 John 1:2
26 [a]1 John 3:7; 2 John 7
27 [1]Or *abide in Him;* Gr command [a]John 14:16; 1 John 2:20 [b]John 14:26; 1 Cor 2:12; 1 Thess 4:9 [c]John 14:17
28 [1]Lit *be put to shame from Him* [2]Or *in His presence* [a]1 John 2:1 [b]Luke 17:30; Col 3:4; 1 John 3:2 [c]Eph 3:12; 1 John 3:21; 4:17; 5:14 [d]Mark 8:38 [e]1 Thess 2:19
29 [1]Or *begotten* [a]John 7:18; 1 John 3:7 [b]John 1:13; 3:3; 1 John 3:9; 4:7; 5:1, 4, 18; 3 John 11
3:1 [1]Lit *what kind of love* [a]John 3:16; 1 John 4:10 [b]John 1:12; 11:52; Rom 8:16; 1 John 3:2, 10 [c]John 15:18, 21; 16:3
2 [a]1 John 2:7 [b]John 1:12; 11:52; Rom 8:16; 1 John 3:1, 10 [c]Rom 8:19, 23f [d]Luke 17:30; Col 3:4; 1 John 2:28 [e]Rom 8:29; 2 Pet 1:4 [f]John 17:24; 2 Cor 3:18
3 [a]Rom 15:12; 1 Pet 1:3 [b]John 17:19; 2 Cor 7:1
4 [a]Rom 4:15; 1 John 5:17
5 [a]1 John 1:2; 3:8 [b]John 1:29; 1 Pet 1:18-20; 1 John 2:2 [c]2 Cor 5:21; 1 John 2:29

6 [1]Or *has known* [a]1 John 3:9 [b]1 John 2:3; 3 John 11
7 [a]1 John 2:1 [b]1 John 2:26 [c]1 John 2:29
8 [1]Lit *sins* [a]Matt 13:38; John 8:44; 1 John 3:10 [b]Matt 4:3 [c]1 John 3:5 [d]John 12:31; 16:11

9 No one who is [1a]born of God [b]practices sin, because His seed
abides in him; and he cannot sin, because he is [1]born of God.
10 By this the [a]children of God and the [b]children of the devil
are obvious: [1]anyone who does not practice righteousness is
not of God, nor the one who [c]does not love his [d]brother.
11 [a]For this is the message [b]which you have heard from the
beginning, [c]that we should love one another;
12 not as [a]Cain, *who* was of [b]the evil one and slew his brother.
And for what reason did he slay him? Because [c]his deeds were
evil, and his brother's were righteous.
13 Do not be surprised, brethren, if [a]the world hates you.
14 We know that we have [a]passed out of death into life,
[b]because we love the brethren. He who does not love abides in
death.
15 Everyone who [a]hates his brother is a murderer; and you
know that [b]no murderer has eternal life abiding in him.
16 We know love by this, that [a]He laid down His life for us;
and [b]we ought to lay down our lives for the [c]brethren.
17 But [a]whoever has the world's goods, and sees his brother
in need and [b]closes his [1]heart [2]against him, [c]how does the love
of God abide in him?
18 [a]Little children, let us not love with word or with tongue,
but in deed and [b]truth.
19 We will know by this that we are [a]of the truth, and will
[1]assure our heart before Him
20 [1]in whatever our heart condemns us; for God is greater
than our heart and knows all things.
21 [a]Beloved, if our heart does not condemn us, we have
[b]confidence [1]before God;
22 and [a]whatever we ask we receive from Him, because we
[b]keep His commandments and do [c]the things that are pleasing
in His sight.
23 This is His commandment, that we [1a]believe in [b]the name
of His Son Jesus Christ, and love one another, just as [c]He
[2]commanded us.
24 The one who [a]keeps His commandments [b]abides in Him,
and He in him. [c]We know by this that [d]He abides in us, by the
Spirit whom He has given us.

Chapter 4 Theme ____________________

4 [a]Beloved, do not believe every [b]spirit, but test the spirits to
see whether they are from God, because [c]many false
prophets have gone out into the world.
2 By this you know the Spirit of God: [a]every spirit that
[b]confesses that [c]Jesus Christ has come in the flesh is from God;
3 and every spirit that [a]does not confess Jesus is not from God;
this is the *spirit* of the [b]antichrist, of which you have heard that
it is coming, and [c]now it is already in the world.

9 [1]Or *begotten* [a]John 1:13; 3:3; 1 John 2:29; 4:7; 5:1, 4, 18; 3 John 11 [b]1 Pet 1:23; 1 John 3:6; 5:18
10 [1]Lit *everyone* [a]John 1:12; 11:52; Rom 8:16; 1 John 3:1, 2 [b]Matt 13:38; John 8:44; 1 John 3:8 [c]Rom 13:8ff; Col 3:14; 1 Tim 1:5; 1 John 4:8 [d]1 John 2:9
11 [a]1 John 1:5 [b]1 John 2:7 [c]John 13:4f; 15:12; 1 John 4:7, 11f, 21; 2 John 5
12 [a]Gen 4:8 [b]Matt 5:37; 1 John 2:13f [c]Ps 38:20; Prov 29:10; John 8:40, 41
13 [a]John 15:18; 17:14
14 [a]John 5:24 [b]John 13:35; 1 John 2:10
15 [a]Matt 5:21f; John 8:44 [b]Gal 5:20f; Rev 21:8
16 [a]John 10:11; 15:13 [b]Phil 2:17; 1 Thess 2:8 [c]1 John 2:9
17 [1]Lit *inward parts* [2]Lit *from* [a]James 2:15f [b]Deut 15:7 [c]1 John 4:20
18 [a]1 John 2:1; 3:7 [b]2 John 1; 3 John 1
19 [1]Lit *persuade* [a]1 John 2:21
20 [1]Or *that if our heart condemns us, that God . . .*
21 [1]Lit *toward* [a]1 John 3:2 [b]1 John 2:28; 5:14
22 [a]Job 22:26f; Matt 7:7; 21:22; John 9:31 [b]1 John 2:3 [c]John 8:29; Heb 13:21
23 [1]Or *believe the name* [2]Lit *gave us a commandment* [a]John 6:29 [b]John 1:12; 2:23; 3:18 [c]John 13:34; 15:12; 1 John 2:8
24 [a]1 John 2:3 [b]John 6:56; 10:38; 1 John 2:6, 24; 4:15 [c]John 14:17; Rom 8:9, 14, 16; 1 Thess 4:8; 1 John 4:13 [d]1 John 2:5
4:1 [a]3 John 11 [b]Jer 29:8; 1 Cor 12:10; 1 Thess 5:20f; 2 Thess 2:2 [c]Jer 14:14; 2 Pet 2:1; 1 John 2:18

2 [a]1 Cor 12:3 [b]1 John 2:23 [c]John 1:14; 1 John 1:2
3 [a]1 John 2:22; 2 John 7 [b]1 John 2:18, 22 [c]2 Thess 2:3-7; 1 John 2:18

4 You are from God, [a]little children, and [b]have overcome them; because [c]greater is He who is in you than [d]he who is in the world.

5 [a]They are from the world; therefore they speak *as* from the world, and the world listens to them.

6 [a]We are from God; [b]he who knows God listens to us; [c]he who is not from God does not listen to us. By this we know [d]the spirit of truth and [e]the spirit of error.

7 [a]Beloved, let us [b]love one another, for love is from God; and [c]everyone who loves is [1d]born of God and [e]knows God.

8 The one who does not love does not know God, for [a]God is love.

9 By this the love of God was manifested [1a]in us, that [b]God has sent His [2]only begotten Son into the world so that we might live through Him.

10 In this is love, [a]not that we loved God, but that [b]He loved us and sent His Son *to be* [c]the propitiation for our sins.

11 [a]Beloved, if God so loved us, [b]we also ought to love one another.

12 [a]No one has seen God at any time; if we love one another, God abides in us, and His [b]love is perfected in us.

13 [a]By this we know that we abide in Him and He in us, because He has given us of His Spirit.

14 We have seen and [a]testify that the Father has [b]sent the Son *to be* the Savior of the world.

15 [a]Whoever confesses that [b]Jesus is the Son of God, God [c]abides in him, and he in God.

16 [a]We have come to know and have believed the love which God has [1b]for us. [c]God is love, and the one who [d]abides in love abides in God, and God abides in him.

17 By this, [a]love is perfected with us, so that we may have [b]confidence in [c]the day of judgment; because [d]as He is, so also are we in this world.

18 There is no fear in love; but [a]perfect love casts out fear, because fear [1]involves punishment, and the one who fears is not [b]perfected in love.

19 [a]We love, because He first loved us.

20 [a]If someone says, "I love God," and [b]hates his brother, he is a [c]liar; for [d]the one who does not love his brother whom he has seen, [e]cannot love God whom he has not seen.

21 And [a]this commandment we have from Him, that the one who loves God [b]should love his brother also.

Chapter 5 Theme ______________________________

5 [a]Whoever believes that Jesus is the [1]Christ is [2b]born of God, and whoever loves the [3]Father [c]loves the *child* [2]born of Him.

2 [a]By this we know that [b]we love the children of God, when we love God and [1]observe His commandments.

3 For [a]this is the love of God, that we [b]keep His commandments; and [c]His commandments are not burdensome.

4 [a]1 John 2:1 [b]1 John 2:13 [c]Rom 8:31; 1 John 3:20 [d]John 12:31
5 [a]John 15:19; 17:14, 16
6 [a]John 8:23; 1 John 4:4 [b]John 8:47; 10:3ff; 18:37 [c]1 Cor 14:37 [d]John 14:17 [e]1 Tim 4:1
7 [1]Or *begotten* [a]1 John 2:7 [b]1 John 3:11 [c]1 John 5:1 [d]1 John 2:29 [e]1 Cor 8:3; 1 John 2:3
8 [a]1 John 4:7, 16
9 [1]Or *in our case* [2]Or *unique,* only one of His kind [a]John 9:3; 1 John 4:16 [b]John 3:16f; 1 John 4:10; 5:11
10 [a]Rom 5:8, 10; 1 John 4:19 [b]John 3:16f; 1 John 4:9; 5:11 [c]1 John 2:2
11 [a]1 John 2:7 [b]1 John 4:7
12 [a]John 1:18; 1 Tim 6:16; 1 John 4:20 [b]1 John 2:5; 4:17f
13 [a]Rom 8:9; 1 John 3:24
14 [a]John 15:27; 1 John 1:2 [b]John 3:17; 4:42; 1 John 2:2
15 [a]1 John 2:23 [b]Rom 10:9; 1 John 3:23; 4:2; 5:1, 5 [c]1 John 2:24; 3:24
16 [1]Lit *in* [a]John 6:69 [b]John 9:3; 1 John 4:9 [c]1 John 4:7, 8 [d]1 John 4:12f
17 [a]1 John 2:5; 4:12 [b]1 John 2:28 [c]Matt 10:15 [d]John 17:22; 1 John 2:6; 3:1, 7, 16
18 [1]Lit *has* [a]Rom 8:15 [b]1 John 4:12
19 [a]1 John 4:10
20 [a]1 John 1:6, 8, 10; 2:4 [b]1 John 2:9, 11 [c]1 John 1:6 [d]1 John 3:17 [e]1 Pet 1:8; 1 John 4:12
21 [a]Lev 19:18; Matt 5:43f; 22:37ff; John 13:34 [b]1 John 3:11
5:1 [1]I.e. Messiah [2]Or *begotten* [3]Lit *one who begets* [a]1 John 2:22f; 4:2, 15 [b]John 1:3; 3:3; 1 John 2:29; 5:4, 18 [c]John 8:42
2 [1]Lit *do* [a]1 John 2:5 [b]1 John 3:14
3 [a]John 14:15; 2 John 6 [b]1 John 2:3 [c]Matt 11:30; 23:4

4 For whatever is [1a]born of God [b]overcomes the world; and
this is the victory that has overcome the world—our faith.
5 Who is the one who overcomes the world, but he who
[a]believes that Jesus is the Son of God?
6 This is the One who came [a]by water and blood, Jesus
Christ; not [1]with the water only, but [1]with the water and [1]with
the blood. It is [b]the Spirit who testifies, because the Spirit is
the truth.
7 For there are [a]three that testify:
8 [1]the Spirit and the water and the blood; and the three are
[2]in agreement.
9 [a]If we receive the testimony of men, the testimony of God
is greater; for the testimony of God is this, that [b]He has
testified concerning His Son.
10 The one who believes in the Son of God [a]has the testimony
in himself; the one who does not believe God has [b]made Him a
liar, because he has not believed in the testimony that God has
given concerning His Son.
11 And the testimony is this, that God has given us [a]eternal
life, and [b]this life is in His Son.
12 [a]He who has the Son has the life; he who does not have
the Son of God does not have the life.
13 [a]These things I have written to you who [b]believe in the
name of the Son of God, so that you may know that you have
[c]eternal life.
14 This is [a]the confidence which we have [1]before Him, that,
[b]if we ask anything according to His will, He hears us.
15 And if we know that He hears us *in* whatever we ask, [a]we
know that we have the requests which we have asked from
Him.
16 If anyone sees his brother [1]committing a sin not *leading* to
death, [a]he shall ask and [2]*God* will for him give life to those
who commit sin not *leading* to death. [b]There is a sin *leading* to
death; [c]I do not say that he should make request for this.
17 [a]All unrighteousness is sin, and [b]there is a sin not *leading*
to death.
18 [a]We know that [b]no one who is [1]born of God sins; but He
who was [1]born of God [c]keeps him, and [d]the evil one does not
[e]touch him.
19 [a]We know that [b]we are of God, and that [c]the whole world
lies in *the power of* the evil one.
20 And [a]we know that [b]the Son of God has come, and has
[c]given us understanding so that we may know [d]Him who is
true; and we [e]are in Him who is true, in His Son Jesus Christ.
[f]This is the true God and [g]eternal life.
21 [a]Little children, guard yourselves from [b]idols.

4 [1]Or *begotten* [a]John 1:13; 3:3; 1 John 2:29; 5:1, 18 [b]1 John 2:13; 4:4
5 [a]1 John 4:15; 5:1
6 [1]Lit *in* [a]John 19:34 [b]Matt 3:16f; John 15:26; 16:13-15
7 [a]Matt 18:16
8 [1]A few late mss add . . . *in heaven, the Father, the Word, and the Holy Spirit, and these three are one. And there are three that testify on earth, the Spirit* [2]Lit *for the one thing*
9 [a]John 5:34, 37; 8:18 [b]Matt 3:17; John 5:32, 37
10 [a]Rom 8:16; Gal 4-6; Rev 12:17 [b]John 3:18, 33; 1 John 1:10
11 [a]John 3:36; 1 John 1:2; 2:25; 4:9; 5:13, 20 [b]John 1:4
12 [a]John 3:15f, 36
13 [a]John 20:31 [b]1 John 3:23 [c]1 John 1:2; 2:25; 4:9; 5:11, 20
14 [1]Lit *toward* [a]1 John 2:28; 3:21f [b]Matt 7:7; John 14:13; 1 John 3:22
15 [a]1 John 5:18-20
16 [1]Lit *sinning* [2]Or *God will give him life,* that is, *to those who . . .* [a]James 5:15 [b]Num 15:30; Heb 6:4-6; 10:26 [c]Jer 7:16; 14:11
17 [a]1 John 3:4 [b]1 John 2:1f; 5:16
18 [1]Or *begotten* [a]1 John 5:15, 19, 20 [b]1 John 3:9 [c]James 1:27; Jude 21 [d]1 John 2:13 [e]John 14:30
19 [a]1 John 5:15, 18, 20 [b]1 John 4:6 [c]John 12:31; 17:15; Gal 1:4
20 [a]1 John 5:15, 18, 19 [b]John 8:42; 1 John 5:5 [c]Luke 24:45 [d]John 17:3; Rev 3:7 [e]John 1:18; 14:9; 1 John 2:23; Rev 3:7 [f]1 John 1:2 [g]1 John 5:11
21 [a]1 John 2:1 [b]1 Cor 10:7, 14; 1 Thess 1:9

1 John Observations Chart

I Am Writing to You

1:4	
2:1	
2:12	
2:13	
2:14	
2:21	
2:26	
5:13	

1 John Key Words

Chapter	Fellowship	Abide	Sin	Know	Love	Born of God	Write	Light	Truth
1									
2									
3									
4									
5									
Total									

What I Can Know	How I Can Know It

(continued)

1 John Observations Chart

What I Can Know	How I Can Know It

1 John at a Glance

Theme of 1 John:

Segment Divisions	Chapter Themes
	1
	2
	3
	4
	5

Author:

Date:

Purpose:

Key Words:

fellowship
abide
sin
know
love
born of God
light
truth (true)
write (writing)
world
mark every reference to the devil (or evil one

2 JOHN

A caring father can't ignore something that threatens his children. So around A.D. 90 the paternal apostle John sat down to write yet another epistle. It is short, to the point, and needful—even today.

Things to Do

1. Read through 2 John as you would a letter you had just received. Mark every reference to the author in one color and the recipients in another. Then read it again and:

   a. Mark the key words listed on the 2 JOHN AT A GLANCE chart on page 2032.

   b. List all you learn about the recipients of this letter in your notebook. Note John's feelings toward them, his instructions (or commands), his warnings, and the reason for his warnings.

2. Record the theme of 2 John in the appropriate space on 2 JOHN AT A GLANCE. Then record the theme of each paragraph and fill in any other pertinent information.

Things to Think About

1. What does this book say about someone who does not abide in the teaching of Christ? Do you know someone who could fit that description? What should you do?

2. You probably noted that verse 4 says "some" of the children are walking in truth (see also John 17:17). Are you careful to walk in all the truth you know? Do you realize that before God, you are responsible to live out the truth that has been entrusted to you?

3. According to this little epistle, what does it mean to walk in love? Are you doing this?

Chapter 1 Theme ______________________

1 [a]The elder to the [b]chosen [c]lady and her children, whom I [d]love
in truth; and not only I, but also all who [e]know the truth,
2 for [a]the sake of the truth which abides [b]in us and will be
[c]with us forever:
3 [a]Grace, mercy *and* peace will be with us, from God the Father
and from Jesus Christ, the Son of the Father, in truth and love.
4 [a]I was very glad to find *some* of your children walking in
truth, just as we have received commandment *to do* from the
Father.
5 Now I ask you, lady, [a]not as though *I were* writing to you a
new commandment, but the one which we have had [a]from the
beginning, that we [b]love one another.
6 And [a]this is love, that we walk according to His commandments. This is the commandment, [b]just as you have heard [c]from
the beginning, that you should walk in it.
7 For [a]many deceivers have [b]gone out into the world, those
who [c]do not acknowledge Jesus Christ *as* coming in the flesh.
This is [a]the deceiver and the [d]antichrist.
8 [a]Watch yourselves, [b]that you do not lose what we have
accomplished, but that you may receive a full reward.

1:1 [a]Acts 11:30; 1 Pet 5:1; 3 John 1 [b]Rom 16:13; 1 Pet 5:13; 2 John 13 [c]2 John 5 [d]1 John 3:18; 2 John 3; 3 John 1 [e]John 8:32; 1 Tim 2:4
2 [a]2 Pet 1:12 [b]1 John 1:8 [c]John 14:16
3 [a]Rom 1:7; 1 Tim 1:2
4 [a]3 John 3f
5 [a]1 John 2:7 [b]John 13:34, 35; 15:12, 17; 1 John 3:11; 4:7, 11
6 [a]1 John 2:5; 5:3 [b]1 John 2:24 [c]1 John 2:7
7 [a]1 John 2:26 [b]1 John 2:19; 4:1 [c]1 John 4:2f [d]1 John 2:18
8 [a]Mark 13:9 [b]1 Cor 3:8; Heb 10:35

9 [1]Anyone who [2]goes too far and [a]does not abide in the
teaching of Christ, does not have God; the one who abides in
the teaching, he has both the Father and the Son.
10 If anyone comes to you and does not bring this teaching,
[a]do not receive him into *your* house, and do not give him a
greeting;
11 for the one who gives him a greeting [a]participates in his
evil deeds.
12 [a]Though I have many things to write to you, I do not want
to *do so* with paper and ink; but I hope to come to you and
speak face to face, so that [1]your [b]joy may be made full.
13 The children of your [a]chosen sister greet you.

9 [1]Lit *Everyone* [2]Lit *goes on ahead* [a]John 7:16; 8:31; 1 John 2:23

10 [a]1 Kin 13:16f; Rom 16:17; 2 Thess 3:6, 14; Titus 3:10

11 [a]Eph 5:11; 1 Tim 5:22; Jude 23

12 [1]One early ms reads *our* [a]3 John 13, 14 [b]John 3:29; 1 John 1:4

13 [a]2 John 1

2 John at a Glance

Theme of 2 John:

Segment Divisions	Paragraph Themes
	Verses 1-3
	Verses 4-6
	Verses 7-11
	Verse 12
	Verse 13

Author:

Date:

Purpose:

Key Words:

truth

love

commandment(s)

teaching

walk

abide(s)

deceiver(s)

3 JOHN

Love cares about the individual. Love encourages. Love rebukes. Love walks in truth. And so, in love, John wrote a third epistle before he was exiled to Patmos, where he penned the book of Revelation. It was around A.D. 90.

Things to Do

1. Read this short letter through once. Mark every reference to the author in one color and every reference to the recipients in another. When you finish, list on a paper what you learn about each.
2. Read the book again, marking each of the key words listed on the 3 JOHN AT A GLANCE chart on page 2034.
3. Other names are mentioned. Note who they are and what is said about each person. See what you learn as you observe the contrast between these people.
4. Make a list of (or mark distinctively) the instructions and warnings John gives in this epistle.
5. Complete 3 JOHN AT A GLANCE.

Things to Think About

1. What is your testimony before others? Are you known for your love of others or for your love of yourself? Do you share what you have with others? Do you listen to others? Do you have to be first?
2. According to what John says in this epistle, what does the way you live have to do with your relationship to God?
3. Are you quick to love, to exhort, and to stand for truth? What do you need to do?

Chapter 1 Theme ____________

1 [a]The elder to the beloved [b]Gaius, whom I [c]love in truth.
2 Beloved, I pray that in all respects you may prosper and be
in good health, just as your soul prospers.
3 For I [a]was very glad when [b]brethren came and testified to
your truth, *that is,* how you [a]are walking in truth.
4 I have no greater joy than [1]this, to hear of [a]my children
[b]walking in the truth.
5 Beloved, you are acting faithfully in whatever you accomplish
for the [a]brethren, and [1]especially *when they are* [b]strangers;
6 and they have testified to your love before the church. You
will do well to [a]send them on their way in a manner [b]worthy of
God.
7 For they went out for the sake of [a]the Name, [b]accepting
nothing from the Gentiles.
8 Therefore we ought to [1]support such men, so that we may
[2]be fellow workers [3]with the truth.

1:1 [a]2 John 1 [b]Acts 19:29; 20:4; Rom 16:23; 1 Cor 1:14 [c]1 John 3:18; 2 John 1
3 [a]2 John 4 [b]Acts 1:15; Gal 6:10; 3 John 5, 10
4 [1]Lit *these things, that I hear* [a]1 Cor 4:14f; 2 Cor 6:13; Gal 4:19; 1 Thess 2:11; 1 Tim 1:2; 2 Tim 1:2; Philem 10; 1 John 2:1 [b]2 John 4
5 [1]Lit *this* [a]Acts 1:15; Gal 6:10; 3 John 3, 10 [b]Rom 12:13; Heb 13:2
6 [a]Acts 15:3; Titus 3:13 [b]Col 1:10; 1 Thess 2:12
7 [a]John 15:21; Acts 5:41; Phil 2:9 [b]Acts 20:33, 35

8 [1]Or *receive such men as guests* [2]Or *prove ourselves to be* [3]Or *for*

9 I wrote something to the church; but Diotrephes, who
loves to [a]be first among them, does not accept [1]what we say.
10 For this reason, [a]if I come, I will call attention to his deeds
which he does, unjustly accusing us with wicked words; and
not satisfied with this, he himself does not [b]receive the
[c]brethren, either, and he forbids those who desire *to do so* and
[d]puts *them* out of the church.
11 Beloved, [a]do not imitate what is evil, but what is good.
[b]The one who does good is of God; [c]the one who does evil has
not seen God.
12 Demetrius [a]has received a *good* testimony from everyone,
and from the truth itself; and we add our testimony, and [b]you
know that our testimony is true.
13 [a]I had many things to write to you, but I am not willing to
write *them* to you with pen and ink;
14 but I hope to see you shortly, and we will speak face to
face.
15 [a]Peace *be* to you. The friends greet you. Greet the friends
[b]by name.

9 [1]Lit *us* [a]2 John 9
10 [a]2 John 12 [b]2 John 10; 3 John 5 [c]Acts 1:15; Gal 6:10; 3 John 3, 5 [d]John 9:34
11 [a]Ps 34:14; 37:27 [b]1 John 2:29; 3:10 [c]1 John 3:6
12 [a]Acts 6:3; 1 Tim 3:7 [b]John 19:35; 21:24
13 [a]2 John 12
15 [a]John 20:19, 21, 26; Eph 6:23; 1 Pet 5:14 [b]John 10:3

3 John at a Glance

Theme of 3 John:

Segment Divisions	Paragraph Themes
	Verse 1
	Verses 2-4
	Verses 5-8
	Verses 9, 10
	Verses 11, 12
	Verses 13-15

Author:

Date:

Purpose:

Key Words:

truth

testimony

good

evil

JUDE

Jude had to speak up. He wasn't an apostle and he wasn't a pillar in the church, like his brother James. Although he was the half brother of the Lord Jesus Christ, Jude did not claim any relationship to Jesus Christ other than that of being His bond-servant.

Initially Jude didn't believe in Jesus (John 7:5), but finally he understood who Jesus was—the Son of God. Jude had grown up in the presence of the One who came to save His people from their sins (Matthew 1:21). No wonder Jude had to write what he did!

THINGS TO DO

1. Though only one chapter in length, Jude is a pertinent book. Read it to familiarize yourself with the content.

2. Read through Jude again. This time mark every reference to the author in one color and every reference to the recipients (including all synonyms and pronouns) in another color. When you finish, list everything you learn about the author and about the recipients in the appropriate columns on the JUDE OBSERVATIONS CHART on page 2038.

3. Now review the list of what you observed about the author and the recipients to discern the author's purpose in writing this epistle. Record this purpose on the JUDE AT A GLANCE chart on page 2039.

4. When you read through Jude, you will notice a third category of people mentioned in verse 4: the "certain persons [who] have crept in unnoticed."

   a. Read through Jude a third time and mark in a distinctive color or way every reference to these people. Watch for and mark the pronouns and various synonyms used to describe these people.

   b. Record on the OBSERVATIONS CHART all you learn about these ungodly people. When you do, it will become obvious why Jude was moved to write what he did.

5. There is a pattern in this letter. First, Jude refers to "these [ungodly] men," and then he uses Old Testament examples or illustrations to make a point. Read through Jude again and watch for this pattern. You may want to underline every Old Testament incident or reference that Jude uses. As you study, watch what the Old Testament people do and note how God deals with them. Be sure not to miss any contrasts and comparisons Jude is making between these Old Testament people and "these [ungodly] men."

6. Now read through Jude again and mark in the same way every reference to *condemnation* and *judgment,* whether it pertains to the ungodly persons or to those mentioned in the Old Testament examples. Various synonyms are used to refer to their condemnation, so watch for and mark them carefully—all in the same way.

7. Jude contains specific instructions for the recipients of his letter, whom he calls *beloved.* In the margin of the text, note the occurrence of each instruction either by writing *Instruction* in the margin or noting it with a symbol. You might want to record these instructions on the OBSERVATIONS CHART on page 2039, along with what God promises or undertakes to do on the recipients' behalf.

8. Determine a theme for Jude and write it down on JUDE AT A GLANCE.

9. Finally, look at Jude paragraph by paragraph, determine what you believe to be the theme for each paragraph, and then record it in the designated place on JUDE AT A GLANCE. Fill in any other information requested.

10. If you want to study Jude further, look up the cross-references in the margin of your Bible to the Old Testament characters and illustrations and see what you learn from each. This will deepen your insight into these ungodly men.

Things to Think About

1. Think about the promises to the "beloved in God." Spend time in prayer, praising God for what He will do on your behalf. Then think of the responsibilities that are yours and talk with God about how you are to fulfill these.

2. Review the characteristics of the ungodly. Do you know of anyone who fits this description? How does knowing this help you? What are you to do in respect to these people? Are you willing?

Chapter 1 Theme ____________________

1 [1a]Jude, a [b]bond-servant of Jesus Christ, and brother of [2]James,
To [c]those who are the called, beloved in God the Father,
and [d]kept for Jesus Christ:
2 [a]May mercy and peace and love [b]be multiplied to you.
3 [a]Beloved, while I was making every effort to write you about
our [b]common salvation, I felt the necessity to write to you
appealing that you [c]contend earnestly for [d]the faith which was
once for all [e]handed down to [f]the [1]saints.
4 For certain persons have [a]crept in unnoticed, those who were
long beforehand [1b]marked out for this condemnation, ungodly
persons who turn [c]the grace of our God into [d]licentiousness and
[e]deny our only Master and Lord, Jesus Christ.
5 Now I desire to [a]remind you, though [b]you know all things
once for all, that [1]the Lord, [c]after saving a people out of the land
of Egypt, [2]subsequently destroyed those who did not believe.
6 And [a]angels who did not keep their own domain, but
abandoned their proper abode, He has [b]kept in eternal bonds
under darkness for the judgment of the great day,
7 just as [a]Sodom and Gomorrah and the [b]cities around them,
since they in the same way as these indulged in gross immorality
and [c]went after [1]strange flesh, are exhibited as an [2d]example in
undergoing the [e]punishment of eternal fire.
8 Yet in the same way these men, also by dreaming, [a]defile
the flesh, and reject authority, and revile [1]angelic majesties.
9 But [a]Michael [b]the archangel, when he disputed with the
devil and argued about [c]the body of Moses, did not dare
pronounce against him a railing judgment, but said, "[d]The Lord
rebuke you!"
10 But [a]these men revile the things which they do not
understand; and [b]the things which they know by instinct, [a]like
unreasoning animals, by these things they are [1]destroyed.

1:1 [1]Gr *Judas* [2]Or *Jacob* [a]Matt 13:55; Mark 6:3; [Luke 6:16; John 14:22; Acts 1:13] [b]Rom 1:1 [c]Rom 1:6f [d]John 17:11f; 1 Pet 1:5; Jude 21

2 [a]Gal 6:16; 1 Tim 1:2 [b]1 Pet 1:2; 2 Pet 1:2

3 [1]Or *holy ones* [a]Heb 6:9; Jude 1, 17, 20 [b]Titus 1:4 [c]1 Tim 6:12 [d]Acts 6:7; Jude 20 [e]2 Pet 2:21 [f]Acts 9:13

4 [1]Or *written about . . . long ago* [a]Gal 2:4; 2 Tim 3:6 [b]1 Pet 2:8 [c]Acts 11:23 [d]2 Pet 2:7 [e]2 Tim 2:12; Titus 1:16; 2 Pet 2:1; 1 John 2:22

5 [1]Two early mss read *Jesus* [2]Lit *the second time* [a]2 Pet 1:12f; 3:1f [b]1 John 2:20 [c]Ex 12:51; 1 Cor 10:5-10; Heb 3:16f

6 [a]2 Pet 2:4 [b]2 Pet 2:9

7 [1]Lit *different* or *other flesh* [2]Or *example of eternal fire, in undergoing punishment* [a]Gen 19:24f; 2 Pet 2:6 [b]Deut 29:23; Hos 11:8 [c]2 Pet 2:2 [d]2 Pet 2:6 [e]Matt 25:41; 2 Thess 1:8f; 2 Pet 3:7

8 [1]Lit *glories* [a]2 Pet 2:10

9 [a]Dan 10:13, 21; 12:1; Rev 12:7 [b]1 Thess 4:16; 2 Pet 2:11 [c]Deut 34:6 [d]Zech 3:2
10 [1]Lit *corrupted* [a]2 Pet 2:12 [b]Phil 3:19

11 Woe to them! For they have gone [a]the way of Cain, and for
pay [1]they have rushed headlong into [b]the error of Balaam, and
[c]perished in the rebellion of Korah.
12 These are the men who are [1]hidden reefs [a]in your love feasts
when they feast with you [b]without fear, caring for themselves;
[c]clouds without water, [d]carried along by winds; autumn trees
without fruit, [2]doubly dead, [e]uprooted;
13 [a]wild waves of the sea, casting up [b]their own [1]shame like
foam; wandering stars, [c]for whom the [2]black darkness has been
reserved forever.
14 *It was* also about these men *that* [a]Enoch, *in* the seventh
generation from Adam, prophesied, saying, "[b]Behold, the Lord
came with [1]many thousands of His holy ones,
15 [a]to execute judgment upon all, and to convict all the ungodly
of all their ungodly deeds which they have done in an ungodly
way, and of all the harsh things which [b]ungodly sinners have
spoken against Him."
16 These are [a]grumblers, finding fault, [b]following after their
own lusts; [1]they speak [c]arrogantly, flattering people [d]for the
sake of *gaining an* advantage.
17 But you, [a]beloved, [b]ought to remember the words that were
spoken beforehand by [c]the apostles of our Lord Jesus Christ,
18 that they were saying to you, "[a]In the last time there will
be mockers, [b]following after their own ungodly lusts."
19 These are the ones who cause divisions, [1a]worldly-minded,
[2]devoid of the Spirit.
20 But you, [a]beloved, [b]building yourselves up on your most
holy [a]faith, [c]praying in the Holy Spirit,
21 keep yourselves in the love of God, [a]waiting anxiously for
the mercy of our Lord Jesus Christ to eternal life.
22 And have mercy on some, who are doubting;
23 save others, [a]snatching them out of the fire; and on some
have mercy with fear, [b]hating even the garment polluted by the
flesh.
24 [a]Now to Him who is able to keep you from stumbling, and
to [b]make you stand in the presence of His glory blameless with
[c]great joy,
25 to the [a]only [b]God our Savior, through Jesus Christ our Lord,
[c]*be* glory, majesty, dominion and authority, [d]before all time and
now and [1]forever. Amen.

11 [1]Lit *they have poured themselves out* [a]Gen 4:3-8; Heb 11:4; 1 John 3:12 [b]Num 31:16; 2 Pet 2:15; Rev 2:14 [c]Num 16:1-3, 31-35

12 [1]Or *stains* [2]Lit *twice* [a]1 Cor 11:20ff; 2 Pet 2:13 and mg [b]Ezek 34:2, 8, 10 [c]Prov 25:14; 2 Pet 2:17 [d]Eph 4:14 [e]Matt 15:13

13 [1]Or *shameless deeds* [2]Lit *blackness of darkness;* or *netherworld gloom* [a]Is 57:20 [b]Phil 3:19 [c]2 Pet 2:17; Jude 6

14 [1]Lit *His holy ten thousands* [a]Gen 5:18, 21ff [b]Deut 33:2; Dan 7:10; Matt 16:27; Heb 12:22

15 [a]2 Pet 2:6ff [b]1 Tim 1:9

16 [1]Lit *their mouth speaks* [a]Num 16:11, 41; 1 Cor 10:10 [b]2 Pet 2:10; Jude 18 [c]2 Pet 2:18 [d]2 Pet 2:3

17 [a]Jude 3 [b]2 Pet 3:2 [c]Heb 2:3

18 [a]Acts 20:29; 1 Tim 4:1; 2 Tim 3:1f; 4:3; 2 Pet 3:3 [b]Jude 4, 16

19 [1]Or *merely natural* [2]Lit *not having* [a]1 Cor 2:14f; James 3:15

20 [a]Jude 3 [b]Col 2:7; 1 Thess 5:11 [c]Eph 6:18

21 [a]Titus 2:13; Heb 9:28; 2 Pet 3:12

23 [a]Amos 4:11; Zech 3:2; 1 Cor 3:15 [b]Zech 3:3f; Rev 3:4

24 [a]Rom 16:25 [b]2 Cor 4:14 [c]1 Pet 4:13

25 [1]Lit *to all the ages* [a]John 5:44; 1 Tim 1:17 [b]Luke 1:47 [c]Rom 11:36 [d]Heb 13:8

Jude Observations Chart

The Author	The Recipients
The Ungodly	

(continued)

Jude Observations Chart

Jude's Instructions to the Beloved	God's Promises to the Beloved

Jude at a Glance

Theme of Jude:

Author:

Date:

Purpose:

Key Words:

Segment Divisions	Paragraph Themes
	Verses 1, 2
	Verses 3, 4
	Verses 5-7
	Verses 8-13
	Verses 14-16
	Verses 17-23
	Verses 24, 25

REVELATION

John, one of the sons of Zebedee, identifies himself throughout his Gospel not by his name but as "the one whom Jesus loved." John walked in faith, taking Jesus at His word, and consequently was secure in His love.

Therefore, when John was banished to the barren Isle of Patmos (and, according to tradition, submerged in a cauldron of hot oil), he remained steadfast in Jesus' love. He was faithful to his calling even in the midst of Nero's persecutions of Christians in A.D. 54 through 68 and then Domitian's in A.D. 81 through 96.

While John was exiled on Patmos, God unveiled to him the coming of the Lord Jesus Christ and what soon would come to pass—a revelation unparalleled, the last to be given. It was about A.D. 95. With John's revelation the New Testament canon of Scripture would be complete. The church could be secure. Every prophecy would be fulfilled, just as God had said.

THINGS TO DO

Chapters 1–3

1. To familiarize yourself with the first two segments of the book of Revelation, carefully read 1:1–4:1 in one sitting. (*Revelation* is a translation of the Greek word *apokalupsis,* which means "an unveiling.")

2. Mark the following key words (along with their synonyms and pronouns) in chapter 1, and then list in your notebook everything you learn from the text about these words: *Jesus Christ, God (the Father), Spirit (seven Spirits),* and *write*. Transfer this information to the chart on page 2071.

3. Revelation 1:19 gives an outline of the book of Revelation.

   a. List the three things John was to write:

      1) ______________________________

      2) ______________________________

      3) ______________________________

   b. Now look at Revelation 4:1 and note how it relates to 1:19. Revelation 4 begins the third segment of Revelation. Chapter 1 describes what John saw, and chapters 2 and 3 are "the things which are." What is the third segment that begins in 4:1?

   c. Using the terminology found in Revelation 1:19, record these three segments in the space for segment divisions on the REVELATION AT A GLANCE chart on page 2073. (The lines to divide the book into these sections are already drawn.)

4. Read Revelation 1–3 and do the following:

   a. Watch for key repeated phrases or words listed on REVELATION AT A GLANCE. Mark these in the text in a distinctive way so you can spot them immediately. Watch for a pattern in Jesus' messages as He addresses each church.

   b. Now concentrate on Jesus' messages to the churches, one church at a time. Record what you learn about each church on the chart JESUS' MESSAGES TO THE CHURCHES beginning on page 2068. When you see what is said regarding those who overcome, note how John describes overcomers in 1 John 5:4-5. Add what you learn to the chart.

5. Record the main theme of each chapter in the text next to the chapter number and on REVELATION AT A GLANCE.

Chapters 4–22

1. In the last 19 chapters of Revelation Jesus shows John "the things which will take place after these things." Read Revelation 4–22 one chapter at a time and do the following:

   a. As you read, ask the "5 W's and an H": Who? What? Why? When? Where? and How? For example, if it is an event, ask: What is happening? Who is involved? When will this happen and where? Why is this happening? How will it happen? If it is a person or a personage: Who is this? What is this person like? What does he do? When? Where? Why? What are the consequences? How will he accomplish it? These are very critical questions. If these are answered carefully after thoroughly observing the text and apart from preconceived ideas, you will learn much. Make a list of what you learn. Record your insights in your notebook.

   b. Mark key repeated words (along with their synonyms and pronouns—*he, she, it, we, they, us,* and *you*) in a distinctive way. Some key words are listed on REVELATION AT A GLANCE. Since it is a long list, write these on an index card, color code the words as you intend to mark them in the text, and use the card as a bookmark. When you finish marking these, record in your notebook what you learn from each one (unless you have been told to record that information on a chart).

   c. As you go through Revelation, let the text speak for itself. Remember, truth is revealed gradually, so don't become impatient. Simply observe what is being said without adding your own interpretation. Stay in an attitude of prayer, ask God to open the eyes of your understanding, and put away any preconceived ideas you might have.

2. Mark in a distinctive way all references to time. Observe what happens during that time. In biblical reckoning 42 months, 1260 days, and time, times and half a time all refer to a period of 3 1/2 years. Note all that happens within the framework of 3 1/2 years.

Give careful attention to *when* something begins and ends: for example, the great day of God's wrath, when the mystery of God is finished, when God begins to reign. Observe carefully the three woes and the events surrounding them. Noting the timing of these will help you understand Revelation better.

3. As you observe what happens during each of the seals, trumpets, and bowls, record your insights on the chart on page 2072, THE SEVEN SEALS, TRUMPETS, AND BOWLS. Then consider whether the seals, trumpets, and bowls happen at the same time or follow one another.

4. Babylon intermittently plays an important role from Genesis to Revelation. As you mark every reference to Babylon, carefully note whether it is referring to "the woman" or to the city. Then discern whether they are one and the same or two separate but somehow related entities. In chapters 17 and 18, where Babylon is preeminent, list what you learn from marking each reference to Babylon on the chart on pages 2074, 2075.

5. As you study Revelation, you may want to check notes you made on the chart THE DAY OF THE LORD on page 2076 to look for parallels between what you observed in other books and what you see in Daniel and in Revelation.

6. There is much to learn about God's nature in this book that you will want to remember and meditate on. Record what you learn on the chart on page 2071.

7. When you finish going through Revelation, record the chapter themes in the text and on REVELATION AT A GLANCE, along with other pertinent information called for on the chart.

8. Finally, see how various chapters of the book group according to events, places, or persons. Use your chapter themes as a guide to see when these groupings occur. Record these groupings under "Segment Divisions" on REVELATION AT A GLANCE, placing them at the chapter numbers in which they occur.

Things to Think About

Chapters 1–3

1. As you look at the Lord's message to each church, do you think the message could be for the church today? Look back through Jesus' messages to the churches in chapters 2 and 3 and note what the Spirit is saying to him who has "an ear." To whom is the Spirit speaking? What does He want you to hear? To do?

2. Think about what you have learned about Jesus Christ from these three chapters and then spend some time worshiping Him for who and what He is.

3. According to 1 John 5:4-5, and Revelation 2–3, are you an overcomer? How does it show? Is there anything you need to do that you are not presently doing so that when Jesus appears you won't be ashamed?

Chapters 4–22

1. Revelation gives insight into God's judgment upon the wicked because of what they worship. It also gives a glimpse of the way the righteous worship. How would you compare your worship with the worship described in Revelation? You might want to go back and look at the scenes where God is worshiped and use them as a pattern for worship.

2. Now that you have a better understanding of the wrath to come upon the unbeliever, what priority needs to be placed on sharing the gospel? Is witnessing a priority in your personal life?

3. Has your life been changed by Jesus Christ? Do you no longer live in habitual sin? If not, you need to be saved. Will you acknowledge the Lord Jesus Christ as God, receive His forgiveness for your sins, and let Him take full control of your life? If so, record the date in the margin. Surely you have seen that He is worthy—and trustworthy.

4. Revelation 22:12 tells us Jesus is coming, and His reward is with Him to give to everyone according to what he has done. Are you living in the light of that day?

Chapter 1 Theme ________________________

1 The Revelation of Jesus Christ, which [a]God gave Him to [b]show
to His bond-servants, [c]the things which must soon take place;
and He sent and [1]communicated *it* [d]by His angel to His bond-
servant [e]John,
2 who testified to [a]the word of God and to [b]the testimony of
Jesus Christ, *even* to all that he saw.
3 [a]Blessed is he who reads and those who hear the words of
the prophecy, and [1]heed the things which are written in it; [b]for
the time is near.
4 [a]John to [b]the seven churches that are in [c]Asia: [d]Grace to
you and peace, from [e]Him who is and who was and who [1]is to
come, and from [f]the seven Spirits who are before His throne,

1:1 [1]Or *signified* [a]John 17:8; Rev 5:7 [b]Rev 22:6 [c]Dan 2:28f; Rev 1:19 [d]Rev 17:1; 19:9f; 21:9; 22:16 [e]Rev 1:4, 9; 22:8

2 [a]Rev 1:9; 6:9; 12:17; 20:4 [b]1 Cor 1:6; Rev 12:17

3 [1]Or *keep* [a]Luke 11:28; Rev 22:7 [b]Rom 13:11; Rev 3:11; 22:7, 10, 12

4 [1]Or *is coming* [a]Rev 1:1, 9; 22:8 [b]Rev 1:11, 20 [c]Acts 2:9 [d]Rom 1:7 [e]Rev 1:8, 17; 4:8; 16:5 [f]Is 11:2; Rev 3:1; 4:5; 5:6; 8:2

5 and from Jesus Christ, [a]the faithful witness, the [b]firstborn of the dead, and the [c]ruler of the kings of the earth. To Him who [d]loves us and released us from our sins [1]by His blood—

6 and He has made us *to be* a [a]kingdom, [a]priests to [1b]His God and Father—[c]to Him *be* the glory and the dominion forever and ever. Amen.

7 [a]BEHOLD, HE IS COMING WITH THE CLOUDS, and [b]every eye will see Him, even those who pierced Him; and all the tribes of the earth will [c]mourn over Him. So it is to be. Amen.

8 "I am [a]the Alpha and the Omega," says the [b]Lord God, "[c]who is and who was and who [1]is to come, the Almighty."

9 [a]I, John, your [b]brother and [c]fellow partaker in the tribulation and [d]kingdom and [1e]perseverance *which are* in Jesus, was on the island called Patmos [f]because of the word of God and the testimony of Jesus.

10 I was [1a]in the Spirit on [b]the Lord's day, and I heard behind me a loud voice [c]like *the sound* of a trumpet,

11 saying, "[a]Write in a [1]book what you see, and send *it* to the [b]seven churches: to [c]Ephesus and to [d]Smyrna and to [e]Pergamum and to [f]Thyatira and to [g]Sardis and to [h]Philadelphia and to [i]Laodicea."

12 Then I turned to see the voice that was speaking with me. And having turned I saw [a]seven golden lampstands;

13 and [a]in the middle of the lampstands *I saw* one [b]like [1]a son of man, [c]clothed in a robe reaching to the feet, and [d]girded across His chest with a golden sash.

14 His head and His [a]hair were white like white wool, like snow; and [b]His eyes were like a flame of fire.

15 His [a]feet *were* like burnished bronze, when it has been made to glow in a furnace, and His [b]voice *was* like the sound of many waters.

16 In His right hand He held [a]seven stars, and out of His mouth came a [b]sharp two-edged sword; and His [c]face was like [d]the sun [1]shining in its strength.

17 When I saw Him, I [a]fell at His feet like a dead man. And He [b]placed His right hand on me, saying, "[c]Do not be afraid; [d]I am the first and the last,

18 and the [a]living One; and I [1b]was dead, and behold, I am alive forevermore, and I have [c]the keys of death and of Hades.

19 "Therefore [a]write [b]the things which you have seen, and the things which are, and the things which will take place [c]after these things.

20 "As for the [a]mystery of the [b]seven stars which you saw in My right hand, and the [c]seven golden lampstands: the [b]seven stars are the angels of [d]the seven churches, and the seven [e]lampstands are the seven churches.

The Seven Churches of Asia

5 [1]Or *in* [a]Rev 3:14; 19:11 [b]1 Cor 15:20; Col 1:18 [c]Rev 17:14; 19:16 [d]Rom 8:37
6 [1]Or *God and His Father* [a]Rev 5:10; 20:6 [b]Rom 15:6 [c]Rom 11:36
7 [a]Dan 7:13; 1 Thess 4:17 [b]Zech 12:10-14; John 19:37 [c]Luke 23:28
8 [1]Or *is coming* [a]Is 41:4; Rev 21:6; 22:13 [b]Rev 4:8; 11:17 [c]Rev 1:4
9 [1]Or *steadfastness* [a]Rev 1:1 [b]Acts 1:15 [c]Matt 20:23; Acts 14:22; 2 Cor 1:7; Phil 4:14 [d]2 Tim 2:12; Rev 1:6 [e]2 Thess 3:5; Rev 3:10 [f]Rev 1:2
10 [1]Or *in spirit* [a]Matt 22:43; Rev 4:2; 17:3; 21:10 [b]Acts 20:7 [c]Rev 4:1
11 [1]Or *scroll* [a]Rev 1:2, 19 [b]Rev 1:4, 20 [c]Rev 2:1 [d]Rev 2:8 [e]Rev 2:12 [f]Acts 16:14; Rev 2:18, 24 [g]Rev 3:1, 4 [h]Rev 3:7 [i]Col 2:1; Rev 3:14
12 [a]Ex 25:37; 37:23; Zech 4:2; Rev 1:20; 2:1
13 [1]Or *the Son of Man* [a]Rev 2:1 [b]Ezek 1:26; Dan 7:13; 10:16; Rev 14:14 [c]Dan 10:5 [d]Rev 15:6
14 [a]Dan 7:9 [b]Dan 7:9; 10:6; Rev 2:18; 19:12
15 [a]Ezek 1:7; Dan 10:6; Rev 2:18 [b]Ezek 1:24; 43:2; Rev 14:2; 19:6
16 [1]Lit *shines* [a]Rev 1:20; 2:1; 3:1 [b]Is 49:2; Heb 4:12; Rev 2:12, 16; 19:15 [c]Matt 17:2; Rev 10:1 [d]Judg 5:31
17 [a]Dan 8:17; 10:9, 10, 15 [b]Dan 8:18; 10:10, 12 [c]Matt 14:27; 17:7 [d]Is 41:4; 44:6; 48:12; Rev 2:8; 22:13
18 [1]Lit *became* [a]Luke 24:5; Rev 4:9f [b]Rom 6:9; Rev 2:8; 10:6; 15:7 [c]Job 38:17; Matt 11:23; 16:19; Rev 9:1; 20:1
19 [a]Rev 1:11 [b]Rev 1:12-16 [c]Rev 4:1
20 [a]Rom 11:25 [b]Rev 1:16; 2:1; 3:1 [c]Ex 25:37; 37:23; Zech 4:2; Rev 1:12; 2:1 [d]Rev 1:4, 11 [e]Matt 5:14f

Chapter 2 Theme ______________________________

2 "To the angel of the church in [a]Ephesus write:
The One who holds [b]the seven stars in His right hand, the
One who walks [1c]among the seven golden lampstands, says this:
2 '[a]I know your deeds and your toil and [1]perseverance, and
that you cannot tolerate evil men, and you [b]put to the test
those who call themselves [c]apostles, and they are not, and you
found them *to be* false;
3 and you have [1]perseverance and have endured [a]for My
name's sake, and have not grown weary.
4 'But I have *this* against you, that you have [a]left your first love.
5 'Therefore remember from where you have fallen, and [a]repent
and [b]do the [1]deeds you did at first; or else I am coming to you and
will remove your [c]lampstand out of its place—unless you repent.
6 'Yet this you do have, that you hate the deeds of the
[a]Nicolaitans, which I also hate.
7 '[a]He who has an ear, let him hear what the Spirit says to the
churches. [b]To him who overcomes, I will grant to eat of [c]the
tree of life which is in the [d]Paradise of God.'
8 "And to the angel of the church in [a]Smyrna write:
[b]The first and the last, who [1c]was dead, and has come to life,
says this:
9 'I know your [a]tribulation and your [b]poverty (but you are
[b]rich), and the blasphemy by those who [c]say they are Jews and
are not, but are a synagogue of [d]Satan.
10 'Do not fear what you are about to suffer. Behold, the devil
is about to cast some of you into prison, so that you will be
[a]tested, and you will have tribulation [b]for ten days. [1]Be [c]faithful
until death, and I will give you [d]the crown of life.
11 '[a]He who has an ear, let him hear what the Spirit says to the
churches. [b]He who overcomes will not be hurt by the [c]second
death.'
12 "And to the angel of the church in [a]Pergamum write:
The One who has [b]the sharp two-edged sword says this:
13 'I know where you dwell, where [a]Satan's throne is; and you
hold fast My name, and did not deny [b]My faith even in the
days of Antipas, My [c]witness, My [d]faithful one, who was killed
among you, [e]where Satan dwells.
14 'But [a]I have a few things against you, because you have there
some who hold the [b]teaching of Balaam, who kept teaching
Balak to put a stumbling block before the sons of Israel, [c]to eat
things sacrificed to idols and to commit *acts of* immorality.
15 'So you also have some who in the same way hold the
teaching of the [a]Nicolaitans.
16 'Therefore [a]repent; or else [b]I am coming to you quickly, and
I will make war against them with [c]the sword of My mouth.
17 '[a]He who has an ear, let him hear what the Spirit says to the
churches. [a]To him who overcomes, to him I will give *some* of
the hidden [b]manna, and I will give him a white stone, and a
[c]new name written on the stone [d]which no one knows but he
who receives it.'

2:1 [1]Lit *in the middle of* [a]Rev 1:11 [b]Rev 1:16 [c]Rev 1:12f

2 [1]Or *steadfastness* [a]Rev 2:19; 3:1, 8, 15 [b]John 6:6; 1 John 4:1 [c]2 Cor 11:13

3 [1]V 2, note 1 [a]John 15:21

4 [a]Jer 2:2; Matt 24:12

5 [1]Lit *first deeds* [a]Rev 2:16, 22; 3:3, 19 [b]Heb 10:32; Rev 2:2 [c]Matt 5:14ff; Phil 2:15; Rev 1:20

6 [a]Rev 2:15

7 [a]Matt 11:15; Rev 2:11, 17; 3:6, 13, 22; 13:9 [b]Rev 2:11, 17, 26; 3:5, 12, 21; 21:7 [c]Gen 2:9; 3:22; Prov 3:18; 11:30; 13:12; 15:4; Rev 22:2, 14 [d]Ezek 28:13; 31:8f; Luke 23:43

8 [1]Lit *became* [a]Rev 1:11 [b]Is 44:6; 48:12; Rev 1:17; 22:13 [c]Rev 1:18

9 [a]Rev 1:9 [b]2 Cor 6:10; 8:9; James 2:5 [c]Rev 3:9 [d]Matt 4:10; Rev 2:13, 24

10 [1]Or *Prove yourself faithful* [a]Rev 3:10; 13:14ff [b]Dan 1:12, 14 [c]Rev 2:13; 12:11; 17:14 [d]1 Cor 9:25; Rev 3:11

11 [a]Matt 11:15; Rev 2:7, 17, 29; 3:6, 13, 22; 13:9 [b]Rev 2:7, 17, 26; 3:5, 12, 21; 21:7 [c]Rev 20:6, 14; 21:8

12 [a]Rev 1:11 [b]Rev 1:16; 2:16

13 [a]Matt 4:10; Rev 2:24 [b]1 Tim 5:8; Rev 14:12 [c]Acts 22:20; Rev 1:5; 11:3; 17:6 [d]Rev 2:10; 12:11; 17:14 [e]Rev 2:9

14 [a]Rev 2:20 [b]Num 31:16; 2 Pet 2:15 [c]Num 25:1f; Acts 15:29; 1 Cor 10:20; Rev 2:20

15 [a]Rev 2:6

16 [a]Rev 2:5 [b]Rev 22:7, 20 [c]2 Thess 2:8; Rev 1:16

17 [a]Rev 2:7 [b]Ex 16:33; John 6:49f [c]Is 56:5; 62:2; 65:15 [d]Rev 14:3; 19:12

18 "And to the angel of the church in [a]Thyatira write:
[b]The Son of God, [c]who has [1]eyes like a flame of fire, and
His feet are like burnished bronze, says this:
19 '[a]I know your deeds, and your love and faith and service and
[1]perseverance, and that your [2]deeds of late are greater than [3]at
first.
20 'But [a]I have *this* against you, that you tolerate the woman
[b]Jezebel, who calls herself a prophetess, and she teaches and
leads My bond-servants astray so that they [c]commit *acts of*
immorality and eat things sacrificed to idols.
21 '[a]I gave her time to repent, and she [b]does not want to
repent of her immorality.
22 'Behold, I will throw her [1]on a bed *of sickness,* and those who
[a]commit adultery with her into great tribulation, unless they
repent of [2]her deeds.
23 'And I will kill her children with [1]pestilence, and all the
churches will know that I am He who [a]searches the [2]minds and
hearts; and [b]I will give to each one of you according to your
deeds.
24 'But I say to you, the rest who are in [a]Thyatira, who do not
hold this teaching, who have not known the [b]deep things of
Satan, as they call them—I [c]place no other burden on you.
25 'Nevertheless [a]what you have, hold fast [b]until I come.
26 '[a]He who overcomes, and he who keeps My deeds [b]until
the end, [c]TO HIM I WILL GIVE AUTHORITY OVER THE [1]NATIONS;
27 AND HE SHALL [1a]RULE THEM WITH A ROD OF IRON, [b]AS THE VESSELS
OF THE POTTER ARE BROKEN TO PIECES, as I also have received
authority from My Father;
28 and I will give him [a]the morning star.
29 '[a]He who has an ear, let him hear what the Spirit says to the
churches.'

Chapter 3 Theme ______________________

3 "To the angel of the church in [a]Sardis write:
He who has [b]the seven Spirits of God and [c]the seven stars,
says this: '[d]I know your deeds, that you have a name that you
are alive, [1]but you are [e]dead.
2 'Wake up, and strengthen the things that remain, which
were about to die; for I have not found your deeds completed
in the sight of My God.
3 'So [a]remember [1]what you have received and heard; and keep
it, and [a]repent. Therefore if you do not wake up, [a]I will come [b]like
a thief, and you will not know at [c]what hour I will come to you.
4 'But you have a few [1a]people in [b]Sardis who have not [c]soiled
their garments; and they will walk with Me [d]in white, for they
are worthy.
5 '[a]He who overcomes will thus be clothed in [b]white garments;
and I will not [c]erase his name from the book of life, and [d]I will
confess his name before My Father and before His angels.
6 '[a]He who has an ear, let him hear what the Spirit says to the
churches.'

18 [1]Lit *His eyes* [a]Rev 1:11; 2:24 [b]Matt 4:3 [c]Rev 1:14f

19 [1]Or *steadfastness* [2]Lit *last deeds* [3]Lit *the first* [a]Rev 2:2

20 [a]Rev 2:14 [b]1 Kin 16:31; 21:25; 2 Kin 9:7, 22, 30 [c]Acts 15:29; 1 Cor 10:20; Rev 2:14

21 [a]Rom 2:4; 2 Pet 3:9 [b]Rom 2:5; Rev 9:20f; 16:9, 11

22 [1]Lit *into* [2]One early ms reads *their* [a]Rev 17:2; 18:9

23 [1]Lit *death* [2]Lit *kidneys,* i.e. inner man [a]Ps 7:9; 26:2; 139:1; Jer 11:20; 17:10; Matt 16:27; Luke 16:15; Acts 1:24; Rom 8:27 [b]Ps 62:12

24 [a]Rev 2:18 [b]1 Cor 2:10 [c]Acts 15:28

25 [a]Rev 3:11 [b]John 21:22

26 [1]Or *Gentiles* [a]Rev 2:7 [b]Matt 10:22; Heb 3:6 [c]Ps 2:8; Rev 3:21; 20:4

27 [1]Lit *shepherd* [a]Ps 2:9; Rev 12:5; 19:15 [b]Is 30:14; Jer 19:11

28 [a]1 John 3:2; Rev 22:16

29 [a]Rev 2:7

3:1 [1]Lit *and* [a]Rev 1:11 [b]Rev 1:4 [c]Rev 1:16 [d]Rev 2:2; 3:8, 15 [e]1 Tim 5:6

3 [1]Lit *how* [a]Rev 2:5 [b]1 Thess 5:2; 2 Pet 3:10; Rev 16:15 [c]Matt 24:43; Luke 12:39f

4 [1]Lit *names* [a]Rev 11:13 [b]Rev 1:11 [c]Jude 23 [d]Eccl 9:8; Rev 3:5, 18; 4:4; 6:11; 7:9, 13f; 19:8, 14

5 [a]Rev 2:7 [b]Rev 3:4 [c]Ex 32:32f; Ps 69:28; Luke 10:20; Rev 13:8; 17:8; 20:12, 15; 21:27 [d]Matt 10:32; Luke 12:8

6 [a]Rev 2:7

7 "And to the angel of the church in [a]Philadelphia write:
[b]**H**e who is holy, [c]who is true, who has [d]the key of David,
who opens and no one will shut, and who shuts and no one
opens, says this:
8 '[a]I know your [1]deeds. Behold, I have put before you [b]an
open door which no one can shut, because you have a little
power, and have kept My word, and [c]have not denied My
name.
9 'Behold, I [1]will cause *those* of [a]the synagogue of Satan, who
say that they are Jews and are not, but lie—I will make them
[b]come and bow down [2]at your feet, and *make them* know that
[c]I have loved you.
10 'Because you have [a]kept the word of [b]My [1]perseverance, [c]I
also will keep you from the hour of [2d]testing, that *hour* which
is about to come upon the whole [3e]world, to [4]test [f]those who
dwell on the earth.
11 '[a]I am coming quickly; [b]hold fast what you have, so that no
one will take your [c]crown.
12 '[a]He who overcomes, I will make him a [b]pillar in the temple
of My God, and he will not go out from it anymore; and I will
write on him the [c]name of My God, and [d]the name of the city
of My God, [e]the new Jerusalem, which comes down out of
heaven from My God, and My [f]new name.
13 '[a]He who has an ear, let him hear what the Spirit says to the
churches.'
14 "To the angel of the church in [a]Laodicea write:
[b]**T**he Amen, [c]the faithful and true Witness, [d]the [1]Beginning
of the creation of God, says this:
15 '[a]I know your deeds, that you are neither cold nor hot; [b]I
wish that you were cold or hot.
16 'So because you are lukewarm, and neither hot nor cold, I
will [1]spit you out of My mouth.
17 'Because you say, "[a]I am rich, and have become wealthy,
and have need of nothing," and you do not know that you are
wretched and miserable and poor and blind and naked,
18 I advise you to [a]buy from Me [b]gold refined by fire so that
you may become rich, and [c]white garments so that you may
clothe yourself, and *that* [d]the shame of your nakedness will
not be revealed; and eye salve to anoint your eyes so that you
may see.
19 '[a]Those whom I love, I reprove and discipline; therefore be
zealous and [b]repent.
20 'Behold, I stand [a]at the door and [b]knock; if anyone hears My
voice and opens the door, [c]I will come in to him and will dine
with him, and he with Me.
21 '[a]He who overcomes, I will grant to him [b]to sit down with
Me on My throne, as [c]I also overcame and sat down with My
Father on His throne.
22 '[a]He who has an ear, let him hear what the Spirit says to the
churches.'"

7 [a]Rev 1:11 [b]Rev 6:10 [c]1 John 5:20; Rev 3:14; 19:11 [d]Job 12:14; Is 22:22; Matt 16:19; Rev 1:18

8 [1]Or *deeds (behold . . . shut), that you have* [a]Rev 3:1 [b]Acts 14:27 [c]Rev 2:13

9 [1]Lit *give* [2]Lit *before* [a]Rev 2:9 [b]Is 45:14; 49:23; 60:14 [c]Is 43:4; John 17:23

10 [1]Or *steadfastness* [2]Or *temptation* [3]Lit *inhabited earth* [4]Or *tempt* [a]John 17:6; Rev 3:8 [b]Rev 1:9 [c]2 Tim 2:12; 2 Pet 2:9 [d]Rev 2:10 [e]Matt 24:14; Rev 16:14 [f]Rev 6:10; 8:13; 11:10; 13:8, 14; 17:8

11 [a]Rev 1:3; 22:7, 12, 20 [b]Rev 2:25 [c]Rev 2:10

12 [a]Rev 3:5 [b]1 Kin 7:21; Jer 1:18; Gal 2:9 [c]Rev 14:1; 22:4 [d]Ezek 48:35; Rev 21:2 [e]Gal 4:26; Heb 13:14; Rev 21:2, 10 [f]Is 62:2; Rev 2:17

13 [a]Rev 3:6

14 [1]I.e. Origin or Source [a]Rev 1:11 [b]2 Cor 1:20 [c]Rev 1:5; 3:7 [d]Gen 49:3; Deut 21:17; Prov 8:22; John 1:3; Col 1:18; Rev 21:6; 22:13

15 [a]Rev 3:1 [b]Rom 12:11

16 [1]Lit *vomit*

17 [a]Hos 12:8; Zech 11:5; Matt 5:3; 1 Cor 4:8

18 [a]Is 55:1; Matt 13:44 [b]1 Pet 1:7 [c]Rev 3:4 [d]Rev 16:15

19 [a]Prov 3:12; 1 Cor 11:32; Heb 12:6 [b]Rev 2:5

20 [a]Matt 24:33; James 5:9 [b]Luke 12:36; John 10:3 [c]John 14:23

21 [a]Rev 2:7 [b]Matt 19:28; 2 Tim 2:12; Rev 2:26; 20:4 [c]John 16:33; Rev 5:5; 6:2; 17:14

22 [a]Rev 2:7

Chapter 4 Theme ____________________________________

4 After [a]these things I looked, and behold, [b]a door *standing*
open in heaven, and the first voice which I had heard, [c]like
the sound of a trumpet speaking with me, said, "[d]Come up here,
and I will [e]show you what must take place after these things."
2 Immediately I was [1a]in the Spirit; and behold, [b]a throne
was standing in heaven, and [c]One sitting on the throne.
3 And He who was sitting *was* like a [a]jasper stone and a
[b]sardius in appearance; and *there was* a [1c]rainbow around the
throne, like an [d]emerald in appearance.
4 [a]Around the throne *were* [b]twenty-four thrones; and upon
the thrones *I saw* [c]twenty-four elders [d]sitting, clothed in [e]white
garments, and [f]golden crowns on their heads.
5 Out from the throne come [a]flashes of lightning and sounds
and peals of thunder. And *there were* [b]seven lamps of fire
burning before the throne, which are [c]the seven Spirits of God;
6 and before the throne *there was something* like a [a]sea of
glass, like crystal; and in the [1]center and [b]around the throne,
[c]four living creatures [d]full of eyes in front and behind.
7 [a]The first creature *was* like a lion, and the second creature
like a calf, and the third creature had a face like that of a man,
and the fourth creature *was* like a flying eagle.
8 And the [a]four living creatures, each one of them having
[b]six wings, are [c]full of eyes around and within; and [d]day and
night [1]they do not cease to say,

> "[e]HOLY, HOLY, HOLY *is* THE [f]LORD GOD, THE ALMIGHTY, [g]WHO
> WAS AND WHO IS AND WHO [2]IS TO COME."

9 And when the living creatures give glory and honor and
thanks to Him who [a]sits on the throne, to [b]Him who lives
forever and ever,
10 the [a]twenty-four elders will [b]fall down before Him who
[c]sits on the throne, and will worship [d]Him who lives forever
and ever, and will cast their [e]crowns before the throne, saying,
11 "[a]Worthy are You, our Lord and our God, to receive glory
and honor and power; for You [b]created all things, and
because of Your will they [1]existed, and were created."

Chapter 5 Theme ____________________________________

5 I saw [1]in the right hand of Him who [a]sat on the throne a
[2b]book written inside and on the back, [c]sealed up with
seven seals.
2 And I saw a [a]strong angel proclaiming with a loud voice,
"Who is worthy to open the [1]book and to break its seals?"
3 And no one [a]in heaven or on the earth or under the earth
was able to open the [1]book or to look into it.
4 Then I *began* to weep greatly because no one was found
worthy to open the [1]book or to look into it;
5 and one of the elders *said to me, "Stop weeping; behold,
the [a]Lion that is [b]from the tribe of Judah, the [c]Root of David,
has overcome so as to open the [1]book and its seven seals."

4:1 [a]Rev 1:12ff, 19 [b]Ezek 1:1; Rev 19:11 [c]Rev 1:10 [d]Rev 11:12 [e]Rev 1:19; 22:6

2 [1]Or *in spirit* [a]Rev 1:10 [b]1 Kin 22:19; Is 6:1; Ezek 1:26; Dan 7:9; Rev 4:9f [c]Rev 4:9

3 [1]Or *halo* [a]Rev 21:11 [b]Rev 21:20 [c]Ezek 1:28; Rev 10:1 [d]Rev 21:19

4 [a]Rev 4:6; 5:11; 7:11 [b]Rev 11:16 [c]Rev 4:10; 5:6, 8, 14; 19:4 [d]Matt 19:28; Rev 20:4 [e]Rev 3:18 [f]Rev 4:10

5 [a]Ex 19:16; Rev 8:5; 11:19; 16:18 [b]Ex 25:37; Zech 4:2 [c]Rev 1:4

6 [1]Lit *middle of the throne and around* [a]Ezek 1:22; Rev 15:2; 21:18, 21 [b]Rev 4:4 [c]Ezek 1:5; Rev 4:8f; 5:6; 6:1, 6; 7:11; 14:3; 15:7; 19:4 [d]Ezek 1:18; 10:12

7 [a]Ezek 1:10; 10:14

8 [1]Lit *they have no rest, saying,* [2]Or *is coming* [a]Ezek 1:5; Rev 4:6, 9; 5:6; 6:1, 6; 7:11; 14:3; 15:7; 19:4 [b]Is 6:2 [c]Ezek 1:18; 10:12 [d]Rev 14:11 [e]Is 6:3 [f]Rev 1:8 [g]Rev 1:4

9 [a]Ps 47:8; Is 6:1; Rev 4:2 [b]Deut 32:40; Dan 4:34; 12:7; Rev 10:6; 15:7

10 [a]Rev 4:4 [b]Rev 5:8, 14; 7:11; 11:16; 19:4 [c]Ps 47:8; Is 6:1; Rev 4:2 [d]Deut 32:40; Dan 4:34; 12:7 [e]Rev 4:4; 10:6; 15:7

11 [1]Lit *were* [a]Rev 1:6; 5:12 [b]Acts 14:15; Rev 10:6; 14:7

5:1 [1]Lit *upon* [2]Or *scroll* [a]Rev 4:9; 5:7, 13 [b]Ezek 2:9, 10 [c]Is 29:11; Dan 12:4

2 [1]Or *scroll* [a]Rev 10:1; 18:21

3 [1]Or *scroll* [a]Phil 2:10; Rev 5:13

4 [1]Or *scroll*

5 [1]Or *scroll* [a]Gen 49:9 [b]Heb 7:14 [c]Is 11:1, 10; Rom 15:12; Rev 22:16

6 And I saw [1]between the throne (with the four living
creatures) and [a]the elders a [b]Lamb standing, as if [c]slain, having
seven [d]horns and [e]seven eyes, which are [f]the seven Spirits of
God, sent out into all the earth.
7 And He came and took [a]the book out of the right hand of
Him who [a]sat on the throne.
8 When He had taken the [1]book, the [a]four living creatures
and the [b]twenty-four elders [c]fell down before the [d]Lamb, each
one holding a [e]harp and [f]golden bowls full of incense, which
are the [g]prayers of the [2]saints.
9 And they *sang a [a]new song, saying,
"[b]Worthy are You to take the [1]book and to break its seals;
for You were [c]slain, and [d]purchased for God with Your
blood *men* from [e]every tribe and tongue and people and
nation.
10 "You have made them *to be* a [a]kingdom and [a]priests to
our God; and they will [b]reign upon the earth."
11 Then I looked, and I heard the voice of many angels [a]around
the throne and the [b]living creatures and the [c]elders; and the
number of them was [d]myriads of myriads, and thousands of
thousands,
12 saying with a loud voice,
"[a]Worthy is the [b]Lamb that was [b]slain to receive power
and riches and wisdom and might and honor and glory
and blessing."
13 And [a]every created thing which is in heaven and on the
earth and under the earth and on the sea, and all things in
them, I heard saying,
"To Him who [b]sits on the throne, and to the [c]Lamb, [d]*be*
blessing and honor and glory and dominion forever and
ever."
14 And the [a]four living creatures kept saying, "[b]Amen." And
the [c]elders [d]fell down and worshiped.

Chapter 6 Theme ____________________

6 Then I saw when the [a]Lamb broke one of the [b]seven seals,
and I heard one of the [c]four living creatures saying as with
a [d]voice of thunder, "Come[1]."
2 I looked, and behold, a [a]white horse, and he who sat on it
had a bow; and [b]a crown was given to him, and he went out
[c]conquering and to conquer.
3 When He broke the second seal, I heard the [a]second living
creature saying, "Come[1]."
4 And another, [a]a red horse, went out; and to him who sat
on it, it was granted to [b]take peace from the earth, and that
men would slay one another; and a great sword was given to
him.
5 When He broke the third seal, I heard the [a]third living
creature saying, "Come[1]." I looked, and behold, a [b]black horse;
and he who sat on it had a [c]pair of scales in his hand.

6 [1]Lit *in the middle of the throne and of the four living creatures, and in the middle of the elders* [a]Rev 4:4; 5:8, 14 [b]John 1:29; Rev 5:8, 12f; 13:8 [c]Rev 5:9, 12; 13:8 [d]Dan 8:3f [e]Zech 3:9; 4:10 [f]Rev 1:4

7 [a]Rev 5:1

8 [1]Or *scroll* [2]Or *holy ones* [a]Rev 4:6; 5:6, 11, 14 [b]Rev 4:4; 5:14 [c]Rev 4:10 [d]John 1:29; Rev 5:6, 12f; 13:8 [e]Rev 14:2; 15:2 [f]Rev 15:7 [g]Ps 141:2; Rev 8:3f

9 [1]Or *scroll* [a]Ps 33:3; 40:3; 98:1; 149:1; Is 42:10; Rev 14:3; 15:3 [b]Rev 4:11 [c]Rev 5:6, 12; 13:8 [d]1 Cor 6:20; Rev 14:3f [e]Dan 3:4; 5:19; Rev 7:9; 10:11; 11:9; 13:7; 14:6; 17:15

10 [a]Rev 1:6 [b]Rev 3:21; 20:4

11 [a]Rev 4:4 [b]Rev 4:6; 5:6, 8, 14 [c]Rev 4:4; 5:6, 14 [d]Dan 7:10; Heb 12:22; Jude 14; Rev 9:16

12 [a]Rev 1:6; 4:11; 5:9 [b]John 1:29; Rev 5:6, 13; 13:8

13 [a]Phil 2:10; Rev 5:3 [b]Rev 5:1 [c]John 1:29; Rev 5:6, 12f; 13:8 [d]Rom 11:36; Rev 1:6

14 [a]Rev 4:6; 5:6, 8, 11 [b]1 Cor 14:16; Rev 7:12; 19:4 [c]Rev 4:4; 5:6, 8 [d]Rev 4:10

6:1 [1]One early ms reads *and see* [a]John 1:29; Rev 5:6, 12f; 13:8 [b]Rev 5:1 [c]Rev 4:6; 5:6, 8, 11, 14 [d]Rev 14:2; 19:6

2 [a]Zech 1:8; 6:3f; Rev 19:11 [b]Zech 6:11; Rev 9:7; 14:14; 19:12 [c]Rev 3:21

3 [1]One early ms reads *and see* [a]Rev 4:7

4 [a]Zech 1:8; 6:2 [b]Matt 10:34

5 [1]One early ms reads *and see* [a]Rev 4:7 [b]Zech 6:2, 6 [c]Ezek 4:16

6 And I heard *something* like a voice in the center of the [a]four
living creatures saying, "A [1]quart of wheat for a [2]denarius, and
three [1]quarts of barley for a [2]denarius; and [b]do not damage the
oil and the wine."
7 When the Lamb broke the fourth seal, I heard the voice of
the [a]fourth living creature saying, "Come[1]."
8 I looked, and behold, an [1a]ashen horse; and he who sat on
it had the name [b]Death; and [b]Hades was following with him.
Authority was given to them over a fourth of the earth, [c]to kill
with sword and with famine and with [2]pestilence and by the
wild beasts of the earth.
9 When the Lamb broke the fifth seal, I saw [a]underneath the
[b]altar the [c]souls of those who had been slain [d]because of the
word of God, and because of the [e]testimony which they had
maintained;
10 and they cried out with a loud voice, saying, "[a]How long, O
[1b]Lord, [c]holy and true, [2]will You refrain from [d]judging and
avenging our blood on [e]those who dwell on the earth?"
11 And [a]there was given to each of them a white robe; and they
were told that they should [b]rest for a little while longer, [c]until *the
number of* their fellow servants and their brethren who were to
be killed even as they had been, would be [d]completed also.
12 I looked when He broke the sixth seal, and there was a
great [a]earthquake; and the [b]sun became black as [c]sackcloth
made of hair, and the whole moon became like blood;
13 and [a]the stars of the sky fell to the earth, [b]as a fig tree casts
its unripe figs when shaken by a great wind.
14 [a]The sky was split apart like a scroll when it is rolled up,
and [b]every mountain and island were moved out of their places.
15 Then [a]the kings of the earth and the great men and the
[1]commanders and the rich and the strong and every slave and
free man hid themselves in the caves and among the rocks of
the mountains;
16 and they *[a]said to the mountains and to the rocks, "Fall on
us and hide us from the [1]presence of Him [b]who sits on the
throne, and from the [c]wrath of the Lamb;
17 for [a]the great day of their wrath has come, and [b]who is able
to stand?"

Chapter 7 Theme ______________________

7 After this I saw [a]four angels standing at the [b]four corners of
the earth, holding back [c]the four winds of the earth, [d]so that
no wind would blow on the earth or on the sea or on any tree.
2 And I saw another angel ascending [a]from the rising of the
sun, having the [b]seal of [c]the living God; and he cried out with a
loud voice to the [d]four angels to whom it was granted to harm
the earth and the sea,
3 saying, "[a]Do not harm the earth or the sea or the trees
until we have [b]sealed the bond-servants of our God on their
[c]foreheads."

6 [1]Gr *choenix;* i.e. a dry measure almost equal to a qt [2]The denarius was equivalent to a day's wages [a]Rev 4:6f [b]Rev 7:3; 9:4
7 [1]One early ms reads *and see* [a]Rev 4:7
8 [1]Or *sickly pale* [2]Or *death* [a]Zech 6:3 [b]Prov 5:5; Hos 13:14; Matt 11:23; Rev 1:18; 20:13f [c]Jer 14:12; 15:2f; 24:10; 29:17f; Ezek 5:12, 17; 14:21; 29:5
9 [a]Ex 29:12; Lev 4:7; John 16:2 [b]Rev 14:18; 16:7 [c]Rev 20:4 [d]Rev 1:2, 9 [e]Rev 12:17
10 [1]Or *Master* [2]Lit *do You not judge and avenge* [a]Zech 1:12 [b]Luke 2:29; 2 Pet 2:1 [c]Rev 3:7 [d]Deut 32:43; Ps 79:10; Luke 18:7; Rev 19:2 [e]Rev 3:10
11 [a]Rev 3:4, 5; 7:9 [b]2 Thess 1:7; Heb 4:10; Rev 14:13 [c]Heb 11:40 [d]Acts 20:24; 2 Tim 4:7
12 [a]Matt 24:7; Rev 8:5; 11:13; 16:18 [b]Is 13:10; Joel 2:10, 31; 3:15; Matt 24:29; Mark 13:24 [c]Is 50:3; Matt 11:21
13 [a]Matt 24:29; Mark 13:25; Rev 8:10; 9:1 [b]Is 34:4
14 [a]Is 34:4; 2 Pet 3:10; Rev 20:11; 21:1 [b]Is 54:10; Jer 4:24; Ezek 38:20; Nah 1:5; Rev 16:20
15 [1]I.e. chiliarchs, in command of one thousand troops [a]Is 2:10f, 19, 21; 24:21; Rev 19:18
16 [1]Lit *face* [a]Hos 10:8; Luke 23:30; Rev 9:6 [b]Rev 4:9; 5:1 [c]Mark 3:5
17 [a]Is 63:4; Jer 30:7; Joel 1:15; 2:1f, 11, 31; Zeph 1:14f; Rev 16:14 [b]Ps 76:7; Nah 1:6; Mal 3:2; Luke 21:36
7:1 [a]Rev 9:14 [b]Is 11:12; Ezek 7:2; Rev 20:8 [c]Jer 49:36; Dan 7:2; Zech 6:5; Matt 24:31 [d]Rev 7:3; 8:7; 9:4
2 [a]Is 41:2 [b]Rev 7:3; 9:4 [c]Matt 16:16 [d]Rev 9:14
3 [a]Rev 6:6 [b]John 3:33; Rev 7:3-8 [c]Ezek 9:4, 6; Rev 13:16; 14:1, 9; 20:4; 22:4

4 And I heard the [a]number of those who were sealed, [b]one
hundred and forty-four thousand sealed from every tribe of the
sons of Israel:
5 from the tribe of Judah, twelve thousand *were* sealed,
from the tribe of Reuben twelve thousand, from the
tribe of Gad twelve thousand,
6 from the tribe of Asher twelve thousand, from the tribe of
Naphtali twelve thousand, from the tribe of Manasseh
twelve thousand,
7 from the tribe of Simeon twelve thousand, from the tribe
of Levi twelve thousand, from the tribe of Issachar
twelve thousand,
8 from the tribe of Zebulun twelve thousand, from the
tribe of Joseph twelve thousand, from the tribe of Benjamin, twelve thousand *were* sealed.
9 After these things I looked, and behold, a great multitude
which no one could count, from [a]every nation and *all* tribes and
peoples and tongues, standing [b]before the throne and [c]before
the Lamb, clothed in [d]white robes, and [e]palm branches *were* in
their hands;
10 and they cry out with a loud voice, saying,
"[a]Salvation to our God [b]who sits on the throne, and to the
Lamb."
11 And all the angels were standing [a]around the throne and
around [a]the elders and the [b]four living creatures; and they [c]fell
on their faces before the throne and worshiped God,
12 saying,
"[a]**A**men, [b]blessing and glory and wisdom and thanksgiving
and honor and power and might, *be* to our God forever and
ever. [a]Amen."
13 Then one of the elders [a]answered, saying to me, "These
who are clothed in the [b]white robes, who are they, and where
have they come from?"
14 I [1]said to him, "My lord, you know." And he said to me,
"These are the ones who come out of the [a]great tribulation,
and they have [b]washed their robes and made them [c]white in
the [d]blood of the Lamb.
15 "For this reason, they are [a]before the throne of God; and
they [b]serve Him day and night in His [1c]temple; and [d]He who
sits on the throne will spread His [e]tabernacle over them.
16 "[a]They will hunger no longer, nor thirst anymore; nor will
the sun [1]beat down on them, nor any heat;
17 for the Lamb in the center of the throne will be their
[a]shepherd, and will guide them to springs of the [1b]water of life;
and [c]God will wipe every tear from their eyes."

Chapter 8 Theme ____________________

8 When the Lamb broke the [a]seventh seal, there was silence
in heaven for about half an hour.
2 And I saw [a]the seven angels who stand before God, and
seven [b]trumpets were given to them.

4 [a]Rev 9:16 [b]Rev 14:1, 3

9 [a]Rev 5:9 [b]Rev 7:15 [c]Rev 22:3 [d]Rev 6:11; 7:14 [e]Lev 23:40

10 [a]Ps 3:8; Rev 12:10; 19:1 [b]Rev 22:3

11 [a]Rev 4:4 [b]Rev 4:6 [c]Rev 4:10

12 [a]Rev 5:14 [b]Rev 5:12

13 [a]Acts 3:12 [b]Rev 7:9

14 [1]Lit *have said* [a]Dan 12:1; Matt 24:21; Mark 13:19 [b]Zech 3:3-5; Rev 22:14 [c]Rev 6:11; 7:9 [d]Heb 9:14; 1 John 1:7

15 [1]Or *sanctuary* [a]Rev 7:9 [b]Rev 4:8f; 22:3 [c]Rev 11:19; 21:22 [d]Rev 4:9 [e]Lev 26:11; Ezek 37:27; John 1:14; Rev 21:3

16 [1]Lit *fall* [a]Ps 121:5f; Is 49:10

17 [1]Lit *waters* [a]Ps 23:1f; Matt 2:6; John 10:11 [b]John 4:14; Rev 21:6; 22:1 [c]Is 25:8; Matt 5:4; Rev 21:4

8:1 [a]Rev 5:1; 6:1, 3, 5, 7, 9, 12

2 [a]Rev 1:4; 8:6-13; 9:1, 13; 11:15 [b]1 Cor 15:52; 1 Thess 4:16

3 [a]Another angel came and stood at the [b]altar, holding a [c]golden censer; and much [d]incense was given to him, so that he might [1]add it to the [d]prayers of all the [2]saints on the [e]golden altar which was before the throne.

4 And [a]the smoke of the incense, [1]with the prayers of the [2]saints, went up before God out of the angel's hand.

5 Then the angel [1]took the censer and [a]filled it with the fire of the altar, and [b]threw it to the earth; and there followed [c]peals of thunder and sounds and flashes of lightning and an [d]earthquake.

6 [a]And the seven angels who had the seven trumpets prepared themselves to sound them.

7 The first sounded, and there came [a]hail and fire, mixed with blood, and they were thrown to the earth; and [b]a third of the earth was burned up, and [b]a third of the [c]trees were burned up, and all the green [c]grass was burned up.

8 The second angel sounded, and *something* like a great [a]mountain burning with fire was thrown into the sea; and [b]a third of the [c]sea became blood,

9 and [a]a third of the creatures which were in the sea [1]and had life, died; and a third of the [b]ships were destroyed.

10 The third angel sounded, and a great star [a]fell from heaven, burning like a torch, and it fell on a [b]third of the rivers and on the [c]springs of waters.

11 The name of the star is called Wormwood; and a [a]third of the waters became [b]wormwood, and many men died from the waters, because they were made bitter.

12 The fourth angel sounded, and a [a]third of the [b]sun and a third of the [b]moon and a [a]third of the [b]stars were struck, so that a [a]third of them would be darkened and the day would not shine for a [a]third of it, and the night in the same way.

13 Then I looked, and I heard [1]an eagle flying in [a]midheaven, saying with a loud voice, "[b]Woe, woe, woe to [c]those who dwell on the earth, because of the remaining blasts of the trumpet of the [d]three angels who are about to sound!"

Chapter 9 Theme ______________________________

9 Then the [a]fifth angel sounded, and I saw a [b]star from heaven which had fallen to the earth; and the [c]key of the [1][d]bottomless pit was given to him.

2 He opened the [1]bottomless pit, and [a]smoke went up out of the pit, like the smoke of a great furnace; and [b]the sun and the air were darkened by the smoke of the pit.

3 Then out of the smoke came [a]locusts [1]upon the earth, and power was given them, as the [b]scorpions of the earth have power.

4 They were told not to [a]hurt the [b]grass of the earth, nor any green thing, nor any tree, but only the men who do not have the [c]seal of God on their foreheads.

5 And [1]they were not permitted to kill [2]anyone, but to torment for [a]five months; and their torment was like the torment of a [b]scorpion when it [3]stings a man.

3 [1]Lit *give* [2]Or *holy ones* [a]Rev 7:2 [b]Amos 9:1; Rev 6:9 [c]Heb 9:4 [d]Ex 30:1; Rev 5:8 [e]Ex 30:3; Num 4:11; Rev 8:5; 9:13

4 [1]Or *for* [2]V 3, note 2 [a]Ps 141:2

5 [1]Lit *has taken* [a]Lev 16:12 [b]Ezek 10:2 [c]Ex 19:16; Rev 4:5; 11:19; 16:18 [d]Rev 6:12

6 [a]Rev 8:2

7 [a]Ex 9:23ff; Is 28:2; Ezek 38:22; Joel 2:30 [b]Zech 13:8, 9; Rev 8:7-12; 9:15, 18; 12:4 [c]Rev 9:4

8 [a]Jer 51:25 [b]Zech 13:8, 9; Rev 8:7-12; 9:15, 18; 12:4 [c]Ex 7:17ff; Rev 11:6; 16:3

9 [1]Lit *the ones having* [a]Zech 13:8, 9; Rev 8:7-12; 9:15, 18; 12:4 [b]Is 2:16

10 [a]Is 14:12; Rev 6:13; 9:1 [b]Zech 13:8, 9; Rev 8:7-12; 9:15, 18; 12:4 [c]Rev 14:7; 16:4

11 [a]Zech 13:8, 9; Rev 8:7-12; 9:15, 18; 12:4 [b]Jer 9:15; 23:15

12 [a]Zech 13:8, 9; Rev 8:7-12; 9:15, 18; 12:4 [b]Ex 10:21ff; Is 13:10; Ezek 32:7; Joel 2:10, 31; 3:15; Rev 6:12f

13 [1]Lit *one eagle* [a]Rev 14:6; 19:17 [b]Rev 9:12; 11:14; 12:12 [c]Rev 3:10 [d]Rev 8:2

9:1 [1]Lit *shaft of the abyss* [a]Rev 8:2 [b]Rev 8:10 [c]Rev 1:18 [d]Luke 8:31; Rev 9:2, 11

2 [1]V 1, note 1 [a]Gen 19:28; Ex 19:18 [b]Joel 2:2, 10

3 [1]Lit *into* [a]Ex 10:12-15; Rev 9:7 [b]2 Chr 10:11, 14; Ezek 2:6; Rev 9:5, 10

4 [a]Rev 6:6 [b]Rev 8:7 [c]Ezek 9:4; Rev 7:2, 3

5 [1]Lit *it was given to them* [2]Lit *them* [3]Lit *strikes* [a]Rev 9:10 [b]2 Chr 10:11, 14; Ezek 2:6; Rev 9:3, 10

6 And in those days [a]men will seek death and will not find it; they will long to die, and death flees from them.

7 The [1a]appearance of the locusts was like horses prepared for battle; and on their heads appeared to be crowns like gold, and their faces were like the faces of men.

8 They had hair like the hair of women, and their [a]teeth were like *the teeth* of lions.

9 They had breastplates like breastplates of iron; and the [a]sound of their wings was like the sound of chariots, of many horses rushing to battle.

10 They have tails like [a]scorpions, and stings; and in their [b]tails is their power to hurt men for [c]five months.

11 They have as king over them, the angel of the [a]abyss; his name in [b]Hebrew is [1c]Abaddon, and in the Greek he has the name [2]Apollyon.

12 [a]The first woe is past; behold, two woes are still coming after these things.

13 Then the sixth angel sounded, and I heard [1]a voice from the [2]four [a]horns of the [b]golden altar which is before God,

14 one saying to the sixth angel who had the trumpet, "Release the [a]four angels who are bound at the [b]great river Euphrates."

15 And the four angels, who had been prepared for the hour and day and month and year, were [a]released, so that they would kill a [b]third of [1]mankind.

16 The number of the armies of the horsemen was [a]two hundred million; [b]I heard the number of them.

17 And [1]this is how I saw [a]in the vision the horses and those who sat on them: *the riders* had breastplates *the color* of fire and of hyacinth and of [2b]brimstone; and the heads of the horses are like the heads of lions; and [c]out of their mouths proceed fire and smoke and [2b]brimstone.

18 A [a]third of [1]mankind was killed by these three plagues, by the [b]fire and the smoke and the [2]brimstone which proceeded out of their mouths.

19 For the power of the horses is in their mouths and in their tails; for their tails are like serpents and have heads, and with them they do harm.

20 The rest of [1]mankind, who were not killed by these plagues, [a]did not repent of [b]the works of their hands, so as not to [c]worship demons, and [d]the idols of gold and of silver and of brass and of stone and of wood, which can neither see nor hear nor walk;

21 and they [a]did not repent of their murders nor of their [b]sorceries nor of their [c]immorality nor of their thefts.

Chapter 10 Theme ______________________________

10 I saw another [a]strong angel [b]coming down out of heaven, clothed with a cloud; and the [c]rainbow was upon his head, and [d]his face was like the sun, and his [e]feet like pillars of fire;

2 and he had in his hand a [a]little book which was open. He placed [b]his right foot on the sea and his left on the land;

6 [a]Job 3:21; 7:15; Jer 8:3; Rev 6:16

7 [1]Lit *likenesses* [a]Joel 2:4

8 [a]Joel 1:6

9 [a]Jer 47:3; Joel 2:5

10 [a]2 Chr 10:11, 14; Ezek 2:6; Rev 9:3, 5 [b]Rev 9:19 [c]Rev 9:5

11 [1]I.e. destruction [2]I.e. destroyer [a]Luke 8:31; Rev 9:1, 2 [b]John 5:2; Rev 16:16 [c]Job 26:6; 28:22; 31:12; Ps 88:11 mg; Prov 15:11

12 [a]Rev 8:13; 11:14

13 [1]Lit *one voice* [2]Two early mss do not contain *four* [a]Ex 30:2f, 10 [b]Rev 8:3

14 [a]Rev 7:1 [b]Gen 15:18; Deut 1:7; Josh 1:4; Rev 16:12

15 [1]Gr *anthropoi* [a]Rev 20:7 [b]Rev 8:7; 9:18

16 [a]Rev 5:11 [b]Rev 7:4

17 [1]Lit *thus I saw* [2]I.e. burning sulphur [a]Dan 8:2; 9:21 [b]Rev 9:18; 14:10; 19:20; 20:10; 21:8 [c]Rev 11:5

18 [1]Gr *anthropoi* [2]I.e. burning sulphur [a]Rev 8:7; 9:15 [b]Rev 9:17

20 [1]Gr *anthropoi* [a]Rev 2:21 [b]Deut 4:28; Jer 1:16; Mic 5:13; Acts 7:41 [c]1 Cor 10:20 [d]Ps 115:4-7; 135:15-17; Dan 5:23

21 [a]Rev 9:20 [b]Is 47:9, 12; Rev 18:23 [c]Rev 17:2, 4, 5

10:1 [a]Rev 5:2 [b]Rev 18:1; 20:1 [c]Rev 4:3 [d]Matt 17:2; Rev 1:16 [e]Rev 1:15

2 [a]Rev 5:1; 10:8-10 [b]Rev 10:5, 8

3 and he cried out with a loud voice, [a]as when a lion roars;
and when he had cried out, the [b]seven peals of thunder [1]uttered
their voices.
4 When the seven peals of thunder had spoken, [a]I was about
to write; and I [b]heard a voice from heaven saying, "[c]Seal up the
things which the seven peals of thunder have spoken and do
not write them."
5 Then the angel whom I saw standing on the sea and on the
land [a]lifted up his right hand to heaven,
6 [a]and swore by [b]Him who lives forever and ever, [c]WHO CREATED
HEAVEN AND THE THINGS IN IT, AND THE EARTH AND THE THINGS IN IT,
AND THE SEA AND THE THINGS IN IT, that [d]there will be delay no
longer,
7 but in the days of the voice of the [a]seventh angel, when he
is about to sound, then [b]the mystery of God is finished, as He
[1]preached to His servants the prophets.
8 Then [a]the voice which I heard from heaven, *I heard* again
speaking with me, and saying, "Go, take [b]the [1]book which is
open in the hand of the angel who [b]stands on the sea and on
the land."
9 So I went to the angel, telling him to give me the little book.
And he *said to me, "[a]Take it and eat it; it will make your
stomach bitter, but in your mouth it will be sweet as honey."
10 I took the little book out of the angel's hand and ate it, and
in my mouth it was sweet as honey; and when I had eaten it,
my stomach was made bitter.
11 And [a]they *said to me, "You must [b]prophesy again concerning
[c]many peoples and nations and tongues and [d]kings."

Chapter 11 Theme ________________________

11 Then there was given me a [1a]measuring rod like a staff;
[2]and [b]someone said, "Get up and measure the [3]temple of
God and the altar, and those who worship in it.
2 "[1]Leave out the [a]court which is outside the [2]temple and do
not measure it, for [b]it has been given to the nations; and they
will [b]tread under foot [c]the holy city for [d]forty-two months.
3 "And I will grant *authority* to my two [a]witnesses, and they
will prophesy for [b]twelve hundred and sixty days, clothed in
[c]sackcloth."
4 These are the [a]two olive trees and the two lampstands that
stand before the Lord of the earth.
5 And if anyone wants to harm them, [a]fire flows out of their
mouth and devours their enemies; so if anyone wants to harm
them, [b]he must be killed in this way.
6 These have the power to [a]shut up the sky, so that rain will
not fall during [b]the days of their prophesying; and they have
power over the waters to [c]turn them into blood, and [d]to strike
the earth with every plague, as often as they desire.
7 When they have finished their testimony, [a]the beast that
comes up out of the [b]abyss will [c]make war with them, and
overcome them and kill them.

3 [1]Or *spoke* [a]Is 31:4; Hos 11:10 [b]Ps 29:3-9; Rev 4:5
4 [a]Rev 1:11, 19 [b]Rev 10:8 [c]Dan 8:26; 12:4, 9; Rev 22:10
5 [a]Deut 32:40; Dan 12:7
6 [a]Gen 14:22; Ex 6:8; Num 14:30; Ezek 20:5 [b]Rev 4:9 [c]Ex 20:11; Rev 4:11 [d]Rev 6:11; 12:12; 16:17; 21:6
7 [1]Lit *preached the gospel* [a]Rev 11:15 [b]Amos 3:7; Rom 16:25
8 [1]Or *scroll* [a]Rev 10:4 [b]Rev 10:2
9 [a]Jer 15:16; Ezek 2:8; 3:1-3
11 [a]Rev 11:1 [b]Ezek 37:4, 9 [c]Rev 5:9 [d]Rev 17:10, 12
11:1 [1]Lit *reed* [2]Lit *saying* [3]Or *sanctuary* [a]Ezek 40:3-42:20; Zech 2:1; Rev 21:15f [b]Rev 10:11
2 [1]Lit *throw out* [2]Or *sanctuary* [a]Ezek 40:17, 20 [b]Luke 21:24 [c]Is 52:1; Matt 4:5; 27:53; Rev 21:2, 10; 22:19 [d]Dan 7:25; 12:7; Rev 12:6; 13:5
3 [a]Rev 1:5; 2:13 [b]Dan 7:25; 12:7; Rev 12:6; 13:5 [c]Gen 37:34; 2 Sam 3:31; 1 Kin 21:27; 2 Kin 19:1f; Neh 9:1; Esth 4:1; Ps 69:11; Joel 1:13; Jon 3:5f, 8
4 [a]Ps 52:8; Jer 11:16; Zech 4:3, 11, 14
5 [a]2 Kin 1:10-12; Jer 5:14; Rev 9:17f [b]Num 16:29, 35
6 [a]1 Kin 17:1; Luke 4:25 [b]Rev 11:3 [c]Ex 7:17ff; Rev 8:8 [d]1 Sam 4:8
7 [a]Rev 13:1ff; 17:8 [b]Rev 9:1 [c]Dan 7:21; Rev 13:7

8 And their dead bodies *will lie* in the street of the [a]great city
which [1]mystically is called [b]Sodom and [c]Egypt, where also their
Lord was crucified.
9 Those from [a]the peoples and tribes and tongues and nations
will look at their dead [1]bodies for three and a half days, and
[2b]will not permit their dead bodies to be laid in a tomb.
10 And [a]those who dwell on the earth *will* rejoice over them
and celebrate; and they will [b]send gifts to one another, because
these two prophets tormented [a]those who dwell on the earth.
11 But after the three and a half days, [a]the breath of life from
God came into them, and they stood on their feet; and great
fear fell upon those who were watching them.
12 And they heard a loud voice from heaven saying to them,
"[a]Come up here." Then they [b]went up into heaven in the cloud,
and their enemies watched them.
13 And in that hour there was a great [a]earthquake, and a
tenth of the city fell; [1]seven thousand people were killed in the
earthquake, and the rest were terrified and [b]gave glory to the
[c]God of heaven.
14 The second [a]woe is past; behold, the third woe is coming
quickly.
15 Then the [a]seventh angel sounded; and there were [b]loud
voices in heaven, saying,

"[c]The kingdom of the world has become *the kingdom* of our
Lord and of [d]His [1]Christ; and [e]He will reign forever and ever."

16 And the twenty-four elders, who [a]sit on their thrones before
God, [b]fell on their faces and worshiped God,
17 saying,

"We give You thanks, [a]O Lord God, the Almighty, who are
and who were, because You have taken Your great power and
have begun to [b]reign.
18 "And [a]the nations were enraged, and [b]Your wrath came, and
[c]the time *came* for the dead to be judged, and *the time* to
[1]reward Your [d]bond-servants the prophets and the [2]saints and
those who fear Your name, [e]the small and the great, and to
destroy those who destroy the earth."

19 And [a]the [1]temple of God which is in heaven was opened;
and [b]the ark of His covenant appeared in His [1]temple, and there
were flashes of [c]lightning and sounds and peals of thunder and
an earthquake and a [d]great [2]hailstorm.

Chapter 12 Theme ____________________

12

A great [a]sign appeared [b]in heaven: [c]a woman [d]clothed
with the sun, and the moon under her feet, and on her
head a crown of twelve stars;
2 and she was with child; and she *[a]cried out, being in labor
and in pain to give birth.
3 Then [a]another sign appeared in heaven: and behold, a
great red [b]dragon having [c]seven heads and [d]ten horns, and on
his heads *were* [e]seven diadems.

8 [1]Lit *spiritually* [a]Rev 14:8; 16:19; 17:18; 18:2, 10, 16, 18, 19, 21 [b]Is 1:9, 10; 3:9; Jer 23:14; Ezek 16:46, 49 [c]Ezek 23:3, 8, 19, 27

9 [1]Lit *body* [2]Lit *do not permit* [a]Rev 5:9; 10:11 [b]1 Kin 13:22; Ps 79:2f

10 [a]Rev 3:10 [b]Neh 8:10, 12; Esth 9:19, 22

11 [a]Ezek 37:5, 9, 10, 14

12 [a]Rev 4:1 [b]2 Kin 2:11; Acts 1:9

13 [1]Lit *names of people, seven thousand* [a]Rev 6:12; 8:5; 11:19; 16:18 [b]John 9:24; Rev 14:7; 16:9; 19:7 [c]Rev 16:11

14 [a]Rev 8:13; 9:12

15 [1]I.e. Messiah [a]Rev 8:2; 10:7 [b]Rev 16:17; 19:1 [c]Rev 12:10 [d]Ps 2:2; Acts 4:26 [e]Ex 15:18; Dan 2:44; 7:14, 27; Luke 1:33

16 [a]Matt 19:28; Rev 4:4 [b]Rev 4:10

17 [a]Rev 1:8 [b]Rev 19:6

18 [1]Lit *give the reward to* [2]Or *holy ones* [a]Ps 2:1 [b]Ps 2:5; 110:5 [c]Dan 7:10; Rev 20:12 [d]Rev 10:7; 16:6 [e]Ps 115:13; Rev 13:16; 19:5

19 [1]Or *sanctuary* [2]Lit *hail* [a]Rev 4:1; 15:5 [b]Heb 9:4 [c]Rev 4:5; 8:5; 16:18 [d]Rev 16:21

12:1 [a]Matt 24:30; Rev 12:3 [b]Rev 11:19 [c]Gal 4:26 [d]Ps 104:2; Song 6:10

2 [a]Is 26:17; 66:6-9; Mic 4:9f

3 [a]Rev 12:1; 15:1 [b]Is 27:1; Rev 12:4, 7, 9, 13, 16f; 13:2, 4, 11; 16:13; 20:2 [c]Rev 13:1; 17:3, 7, 9ff [d]Dan 7:7, 20, 24; Rev 13:1; 17:12, 16 [e]Rev 13:1; 19:12

4 And his tail *swept away a [a]third of the stars of heaven and
[b]threw them to the earth. And the [c]dragon stood before the
woman who was about to give birth, so that when she gave
birth [d]he might devour her child.
5 And [a]she gave birth to a son, a male *child,* who is to [1b]rule
all the [2]nations with a rod of iron; and her child was [c]caught up
to God and to His throne.
6 Then the woman fled into the wilderness where she *had a
place prepared by God, so that there [1]she would be nourished
for [a]one thousand two hundred and sixty days.
7 And there was war in heaven, [a]Michael and his angels waging
war with the [b]dragon. The dragon and [c]his angels waged war,
8 and they were not strong enough, and there was no longer
a place found for them in heaven.
9 And the great [a]dragon was thrown down, the [b]serpent of old
who is called the devil and [c]Satan, who [d]deceives the whole
[1]world; he was [e]thrown down to the earth, and his angels were
thrown down with him.
10 Then I heard [a]a loud voice in heaven, saying,
"**N**ow the [b]salvation, and the power, and the [a]kingdom of our
God and the authority of His Christ have come, for the [c]accuser
of our brethren has been thrown down, he who accuses them
before our God day and night.
11 "And they [a]overcame him because of [b]the blood of the Lamb
and because of [c]the word of their testimony, and they [d]did not
love their life even [1]when faced with death.
12 "For this reason, [a]rejoice, O heavens and [b]you who [1]dwell in
them. [c]Woe to the earth and the sea, because [d]the devil has
come down to you, having great wrath, knowing that he has
only [e]a short time."
13 And when the [a]dragon saw that he was thrown down to the
earth, he persecuted [b]the woman who gave birth to the male
child.
14 But the [a]two wings of the great eagle were given to the
woman, so that she could fly [b]into the wilderness to her place,
where she *was nourished for [c]a time and times and half a time,
from the [1]presence of the serpent.
15 And the [a]serpent [1]poured water like a river out of his mouth
after the woman, so that he might cause her to be swept away
with the flood.
16 [1]But the earth helped the woman, and the earth opened its
mouth and drank up the river which the dragon [2]poured out of
his mouth.
17 So the dragon was enraged with the woman, and went off
to [a]make war with the rest of her [1b]children, who [c]keep the
commandments of God and [d]hold to the testimony of Jesus.

Chapter 13 Theme

13 And the dragon stood on the sand of the [1]seashore.
Then I saw a [a]beast coming up out of the sea, having [b]ten

4 [a]Rev 8:7, 12 [b]Dan 8:10 [c]Is 27:1; Rev 12:3, 7, 9, 13, 16f; 13:2, 4, 11; 16:13; 20:2 [d]Matt 2:16

5 [1]Or *shepherd* [2]Or *Gentiles* [a]Is 66:7 [b]Ps 2:9; Rev 2:27 [c]2 Cor 12:2ff

6 [1]Lit *they would nourish her for* [a]Rev 11:3; 13:5

7 [a]Dan 10:13, 21; 12:1; Jude 9 [b]Rev 12:3 [c]Matt 25:41

9 [1]Lit *inhabited earth* [a]Rev 12:3 [b]Gen 3:1; 2 Cor 11:3; Rev 12:15; 20:2 [c]Matt 4:10; 25:41 [d]Rev 13:14; 20:3, 8, 10 [e]Luke 10:18; John 12:31

10 [a]Rev 11:15 [b]Rev 7:10 [c]Job 1:11; 2:5; Zech 3:1; Luke 22:31; 1 Pet 5:8

11 [1]Lit *to death* [a]John 16:33; 1 John 2:13; Rev 15:2 [b]Rev 7:14 [c]Rev 6:9 [d]Luke 14:26; Rev 2:10

12 [1]Or *tabernacle* [a]Ps 96:11; Is 44:23; Rev 18:20 [b]Rev 13:6 [c]Rev 8:13 [d]Rev 12:9 [e]Rev 10:6

13 [a]Rev 12:3 [b]Rev 12:5

14 [1]Lit *face* [a]Ex 19:4; Deut 32:11; Is 40:31 [b]Rev 12:6 [c]Dan 7:25; 12:7

15 [1]Lit *threw* [a]Gen 3:1; 2 Cor 11:3; Rev 12:9; 20:2

16 [1]Lit *And* [2]Lit *threw*

17 [1]Lit *seed* [a]Rev 11:7; 13:7 [b]Gen 3:15 [c]1 John 2:3; Rev 14:12 [d]Rev 1:2; 6:9; 14:12; 19:10

13:1 [1]Lit *sea* [a]Dan 7:3; Rev 11:7; 13:14, 15; 15:2; 16:13; 17:8 [b]Rev 12:3

horns and [b]seven heads, and on his horns *were* [c]ten diadems,
and on his heads *were* [d]blasphemous names.
2 And the beast which I saw was [a]like a leopard, and his feet
were like *those* of [b]a bear, and his mouth like the mouth of [c]a
lion. And the [d]dragon gave him his power and his [e]throne and
great authority.
3 *I saw* one of his heads as if it had been [1]slain, and his [a]fatal
wound was healed. And the whole earth [b]was amazed *and*
followed after the beast;
4 they worshiped the [a]dragon because he [a]gave his authority
to the beast; and they worshiped the beast, saying, "[b]Who is
like the beast, and who is able to wage war with him?"
5 There was given to him a mouth [a]speaking [1]arrogant words
and blasphemies, and authority to act for [b]forty-two months
was given to him.
6 And he opened his mouth in blasphemies against God, to
blaspheme His name and His tabernacle, *that is,* [a]those who
[1]dwell in heaven.
7 It was also given to him to [a]make war with the [1]saints and
to overcome them, and authority over [b]every tribe and people
and tongue and nation was given to him.
8 All who [a]dwell on the earth will worship him, *everyone*
[b]whose name has not been [1]written [c]from the foundation of
the world in the [d]book of life of [e]the Lamb who has been slain.
9 [a]If anyone has an ear, let him hear.
10 [a]If anyone [1]*is destined* for captivity, to captivity he goes; [b]if
anyone kills with the sword, with the sword he must be killed.
Here is [c]the [2]perseverance and the faith of the [3]saints.
11 Then [a]I saw another beast coming up out of the earth; and
he had [b]two horns like a lamb and he spoke as a [c]dragon.
12 He [a]exercises all the authority of the first beast [1b]in his
presence. And he makes [c]the earth and those who dwell in it
to [d]worship the first beast, whose [e]fatal wound was healed.
13 He [a]performs great signs, so that he even makes [b]fire come
down out of heaven to the earth in the presence of men.
14 And he [a]deceives [b]those who dwell on the earth because of
[c]the signs which it was given him to perform [1d]in the presence
of the beast, telling those who dwell on the earth to make an
image to the beast who *had the [e]wound of the sword and has
come to life.
15 And it was given to him to give breath to the image of the
beast, so that the image of the beast would even [1]speak and cause
[a]as many as do not [b]worship the image of the beast to be killed.
16 And he causes all, [a]the small and the great, and the rich
and the poor, and the free men and the slaves, [1]to be given a
[b]mark on their right hand or on their forehead,
17 and *he provides* that no one will be able to buy or to sell,
except the one who has the [a]mark, *either* [b]the name of the
beast or [c]the number of his name.
18 [a]Here is wisdom. Let him who has understanding calculate
the number of the beast, for the number is that [b]of a man; and
his number is [1]six hundred and sixty-six.

1 [b]Rev 12:3 [c]Rev 12:3; 17:12 [d]Dan 7:8; 11:36; Rev 17:3
2 [a]Dan 7:6; Hos 13:7f [b]Dan 7:5 [c]Dan 7:4 [d]Rev 12:3; 13:4, 12 [e]Rev 2:13; 16:10
3 [1]Lit *slaughtered to death* [a]Rev 13:12, 14 [b]Rev 17:8
4 [a]Rev 12:3; 13:2, 12 [b]Ex 15:11; Is 46:5; Rev 18:18
5 [1]Lit *great things* [a]Dan 7:8, 11, 20, 25; 11:36; 2 Thess 2:3f [b]Rev 11:2
6 [1]Or *tabernacle* [a]Rev 7:15; 12:12
7 [1]Or *holy ones* [a]Dan 7:21; Rev 11:7 [b]Rev 5:9
8 [1]Or *written in the book . . . slain from the foundation of the world* [a]Rev 3:10; 13:12, 14 [b]Rev 3:5 [c]Matt 25:34; Rev 17:8 [d]Ps 69:28 [e]Rev 5:6
9 [a]Rev 2:7
10 [1]Or leads *into captivity* [2]Or *steadfastness* [3]Or *holy ones* [a]Is 33:1; Jer 15:2; 43:11 [b]Gen 9:6; Matt 26:52; Rev 11:18 [c]Heb 6:12; Rev 14:12
11 [a]Rev 13:1; 16:13 [b]Dan 8:3 [c]Rev 13:4
12 [1]Or *by his authority* [a]Rev 13:4 [b]Rev 13:14; 19:20 [c]Rev 13:8 [d]Rev 13:15; 14:9, 11; 16:2; 19:20; 20:4 [e]Rev 13:3
13 [a]Matt 24:24; Rev 16:14; 19:20 [b]1 Kin 18:38; Luke 9:54; Rev 11:5; 20:9
14 [1]Or *by the authority of* [a]Rev 12:9 [b]Rev 13:8 [c]2 Thess 2:9f [d]Rev 13:12; 19:20 [e]Rev 13:3
15 [1]One early ms reads *speak, and he will cause* [a]Dan 3:3ff [b]Rev 13:12; 14:9, 11; 16:2; 19:20; 20:4
16 [1]Lit *causes all, . . . that they give them a mark* [a]Rev 11:18; 19:5, 18 [b]Gal 6:17; Rev 7:3; 14:9; 20:4
17 [a]Gal 6:17; Rev 7:3; 14:9; 20:4 [b]Rev 14:11 [c]Rev 15:2
18 [1]One early ms reads 616 [a]Rev 17:9 [b]Rev 21:17

Chapter 14 Theme ______________________

14 Then I looked, and behold, [a]the Lamb *was* standing on [b]Mount Zion, and with Him [c]one hundred and forty-four thousand, having [d]His name and the [d]name of His Father written [e]on their foreheads.

2 And I heard a voice from heaven, like [a]the sound of many waters and like the [b]sound of loud thunder, and the voice which I heard *was* like *the sound* of [c]harpists playing on their harps.

3 And they *[1]sang [a]a new song before the throne and before the [b]four living creatures and the [c]elders; and [d]no one could learn the song except the [e]one hundred and forty-four thousand who had been [a]purchased from the earth.

4 [a]These are the ones who have not been defiled with women, for they [1]have kept themselves chaste. These *are* the ones who [b]follow the Lamb wherever He goes. These have been [c]purchased from among men [d]as first fruits to God and to the Lamb.

5 And [a]no lie was found in their mouth; they are [b]blameless.

6 And I saw another angel flying in [a]midheaven, having [b]an eternal gospel to preach to [c]those who [1]live on the earth, and to [d]every nation and tribe and tongue and people;

7 and he said with a loud voice, "[a]Fear God, and [b]give Him glory, because the hour of His judgment has come; worship Him who [c]made the heaven and the earth and sea and [d]springs of waters."

8 And another angel, a second one, followed, saying, "[1a]Fallen, fallen is [b]Babylon the great, she who has [c]made all the nations drink of the [d]wine of the [2]passion of her immorality."

9 Then another angel, a third one, followed them, saying with a loud voice, "If anyone [a]worships the beast and his [b]image, and receives a [c]mark on his forehead or on his hand,

10 he also will drink of the [a]wine of the wrath of God, which is mixed [1]in full strength [b]in the cup of His anger; and he will be tormented with [c]fire and [2]brimstone in the presence of the [d]holy angels and in the presence of the Lamb.

11 "And the [a]smoke of their torment goes up forever and ever; [b]they have no rest day and night, those who [c]worship the beast and his [c]image, and [1]whoever receives the [d]mark of his name."

12 Here is [a]the [1]perseverance of the [2]saints who [b]keep the commandments of God and [3c]their faith in Jesus.

13 And I heard a voice from heaven, saying, "Write, '[a]Blessed are the dead who [b]die in the Lord from now on!'" "Yes," [c]says the Spirit, "so that they may [d]rest from their labors, for their [e]deeds follow with them."

14 Then I looked, and behold, a [a]white cloud, and sitting on the cloud *was* one [b]like [1]a son of man, having a golden [c]crown on His head and a sharp sickle in His hand.

15 And another angel [a]came out of the [1]temple, crying out with a loud voice to Him who sat on the cloud, "[2b]Put in your sickle and reap, for the hour to reap has come, because the [c]harvest of the earth [3]is ripe."

14:1 [a]Rev 5:6 [b]Ps 2:6; Heb 12:22 [c]Rev 7:4; 14:3 [d]Rev 3:12 [e]Ezek 9:4; Rev 7:3
2 [a]Rev 1:15 [b]Rev 6:1 [c]Rev 5:8
3 [1]Two early mss read *sing* something *like a new song* [a]Rev 5:9 [b]Rev 4:6 [c]Rev 4:4 [d]Rev 2:17 [e]Rev 7:4; 14:1
4 [1]Lit *are chaste men* [a]Matt 19:12; 2 Cor 11:2; Eph 5:27; Rev 3:4 [b]Rev 3:4; 7:17; 17:14 [c]Rev 5:9 [d]Heb 12:23; James 1:18
5 [a]Ps 32:2; Zeph 3:13; Mal 2:6; John 1:47; 1 Pet 2:22 [b]Heb 9:14; 1 Pet 1:19; Jude 24
6 [1]Lit *sit* [a]Rev 8:13 [b]1 Pet 1:25; Rev 10:7 [c]Rev 3:10 [d]Rev 5:9
7 [a]Rev 15:4 [b]Rev 11:13 [c]Rev 4:11 [d]Rev 8:10
8 [1]Lit *Babylon . . . fell, fell, she who* [2]Or *wrath* [a]Is 21:9; Jer 51:8; Rev 18:2 [b]Dan 4:30; Rev 16:19; 17:5; 18:10 [c]Jer 51:7 [d]Rev 17:2, 4; 18:3
9 [a]Rev 13:12; 14:11 [b]Rev 13:14f; 14:11 [c]Rev 13:16
10 [1]Lit *unmixed;* in ancient times wine was usually diluted with water [2]I.e. burning sulphur [a]Is 51:17; Jer 25:15f, 27; Rev 16:19; 19:15 [b]Ps 75:8; Rev 18:6 [c]Gen 19:24; Ezek 38:22; 2 Thess 1:7; Rev 19:20; 20:10, 14f; 21:8 [d]Mark 8:38
11 [1]Lit *if anyone* [a]Is 34:8-10; Rev 18:9, 18; 19:3 [b]Rev 4:8 [c]Rev 13:12; 14:9 [d]Rev 13:17
12 [1]Or *steadfastness* [2]Or *holy ones* [3]Lit *the faith of* [a]Rev 13:10 [b]Rev 12:17 [c]Rev 2:13
13 [a]Rev 20:6 [b]1 Cor 15:18; 1 Thess 4:16 [c]Rev 2:7; 22:17 [d]Heb 4:9ff; Rev 6:11 [e]1 Tim 5:25
14 [1]Or *the Son of Man* [a]Matt 17:5 [b]Dan 7:13; Rev 1:13 [c]Ps 21:3; Rev 6:2
15 [1]Or *sanctuary* [2]Lit *Send forth* [3]Lit *has become dry* [a]Rev 11:19; 14:17; 15:6; 16:17 [b]Joel 3:13; Mark 4:29; Rev 14:18 [c]Jer 51:33; Matt 13:39-41

16 Then He who sat on the cloud [1]swung His sickle over the
earth, and the earth was reaped.
17 And another angel [a]came out of the [1]temple which is in
heaven, and he also had a sharp sickle.
18 Then another angel, [a]the one who has power over fire,
came out from [b]the altar; and he called with a loud voice to him
who had the sharp sickle, saying, "[1c]Put in your sharp sickle and
gather the clusters [2]from the vine of the earth, [d]because her
grapes are ripe."
19 So the angel [1]swung his sickle to the earth and gathered *the
clusters from* the vine of the earth, and threw them into [a]the
great wine press of the wrath of God.
20 And [a]the wine press was trodden [b]outside the city, and [c]blood
came out from the wine press, up to the horses' bridles, [1]for a
distance of [2]two hundred miles.

Chapter 15 Theme ______________________

15

15 Then I saw [a]another sign in heaven, great and marvelous,
[b]seven angels who had [c]seven plagues, *which are* [d]the
last, because in them the wrath of God is finished.
2 And I saw something like a [a]sea of glass mixed with fire,
and those who had [b]been victorious [1]over the [c]beast and [d]his
image and the [e]number of his name, standing on the [a]sea of
glass, holding [f]harps of God.
3 And they *sang the [a]song of Moses, [b]the bond-servant of
God, and the [c]song of the Lamb, saying,

"[d]Great and marvelous are Your works,
[e]O Lord God, the Almighty;
Righteous and true are Your ways,
[f]King of the [1]nations!

4 "[a]Who will not fear, O Lord, and glorify Your name?
For You alone are holy;
For [b]ALL THE NATIONS WILL COME AND WORSHIP BEFORE YOU,
FOR YOUR [1c]RIGHTEOUS ACTS HAVE BEEN REVEALED."

5 After these things I looked, and [a]the [1]temple of the
[b]tabernacle of testimony in heaven was opened,
6 and the [a]seven angels who had the seven plagues [b]came out
of the [1]temple, clothed in [2]linen, clean *and* bright, and [c]girded
around their chests with golden sashes.
7 Then one of the [a]four living creatures gave to the [b]seven
angels seven [c]golden bowls full of the [d]wrath of God, who
[e]lives forever and ever.
8 And the [1]temple was filled with [a]smoke from the glory of God
and from His power; and no one was able to enter the [1]temple
until the seven plagues of the seven angels were finished.

Chapter 16 Theme ______________________

16

16 Then I heard a loud voice from [a]the [1]temple, saying to
the [b]seven angels, "Go and [c]pour out [2]on the earth the
seven bowls of the wrath of God."

16 [1]Lit *cast*

17 [1]Or *sanctuary* [a]Rev 11:19; 14:15; 15:6; 16:17

18 [1]Lit *Send forth* [2]Lit *of* [a]Rev 16:8 [b]Rev 6:9; 8:3 [c]Joel 3:13; Mark 4:29; Rev 14:15 [d]Joel 3:13

19 [1]Lit *cast* [a]Is 63:2f; Rev 19:15

20 [1]Lit *from* [2]Lit *sixteen hundred stadia;* a stadion was approx 600 ft [a]Is 63:3; Lam 1:15; Rev 19:15 [b]Heb 13:12; Rev 11:8 [c]Gen 49:11; Deut 32:14

15:1 [a]Rev 12:1, 3 [b]Rev 15:6-8; 16:1; 17:1; 21:9 [c]Lev 26:21 [d]Rev 9:20

2 [1]Lit *from* [a]Rev 4:6 [b]Rev 12:11 [c]Rev 13:1 [d]Rev 13:14f [e]Rev 13:17 [f]Rev 5:8

3 [1]Two early mss read *ages* [a]Ex 15:1ff [b]Josh 22:5; Heb 3:5 [c]Rev 5:9f, 12f [d]Deut 32:3f; Ps 111:2; 139:14 [e]Hos 14:9; Rev 1:8 [f]1 Tim 1:17

4 [1]Or *judgments* [a]Jer 10:7; Rev 14:7 [b]Ps 86:9; Is 66:23 [c]Rev 19:8

5 [1]Or *sanctuary* [a]Rev 11:19 [b]Ex 38:21; Num 1:50; Heb 8:5; Rev 13:6

6 [1]Or *sanctuary* [2]One early ms reads *stone* [a]Rev 15:1 [b]Rev 14:15 [c]Rev 1:13

7 [a]Rev 4:6 [b]Rev 15:1 [c]Rev 5:8 [d]Rev 14:10; 15:1 [e]Rev 4:9

8 [1]Or *sanctuary* [a]Ex 19:18; 40:34f; Lev 16:2; 1 Kin 8:10f; 2 Chr 5:13f; Is 6:4

16:1 [1]Or *sanctuary* [2]Lit *into* [a]Rev 11:19 [b]Rev 15:1 [c]Ps 79:6; Jer 10:25; Ezek 22:31; Zeph 3:8; Rev 16:2ff

2 So the first *angel* went and poured out his bowl [1a]on the earth;
and it became a loathsome and malignant [b]sore on the [2]people
[c]who had the mark of the beast and who worshiped his image.
3 The second *angel* poured out his bowl [a]into the sea, and it
became blood like *that* of a dead man; and every living [1]thing
in the sea died.
4 Then the third *angel* poured out his bowl into the [a]rivers
and the springs of waters; and they [b]became blood.
5 And I heard the angel of the waters saying, "[a]Righteous are
You, [b]who are and who were, O [c]Holy One, because You [d]judged
these things;
6 for they poured out [a]the blood of saints and prophets, and
You have given them [b]blood to drink. They [1]deserve it."
7 And I heard [a]the altar saying, "Yes, O [b]Lord God, the
Almighty, [c]true and righteous are Your judgments."
8 The fourth *angel* poured out his bowl upon [a]the sun, [b]and
it was given to it to scorch men with fire.
9 Men were scorched with [1]fierce heat; and they [a]blasphemed
the name of God who has the power over these plagues, and
they [b]did not repent so as to [c]give Him glory.
10 Then the fifth *angel* poured out his bowl on the [a]throne of
the beast, and his kingdom became [b]darkened; and they gnawed
their tongues because of pain,
11 and they [a]blasphemed the [b]God of heaven because of their
pains and their [c]sores; and they [d]did not repent of their deeds.
12 The sixth *angel* poured out his bowl on the [a]great river, the
Euphrates; and [b]its water was dried up, so that [c]the way would
be prepared for the kings [d]from the [1]east.
13 And I saw *coming* out of the mouth of the [a]dragon and out
of the mouth of the [b]beast and out of the mouth of the [c]false
prophet, three [d]unclean spirits like [e]frogs;
14 for they are [a]spirits of demons, [b]performing signs, which go
out to the kings of the [c]whole [1]world, to [d]gather them together
for the war of the [e]great day of God, the Almighty.
15 ("Behold, [a]I am coming like a thief. [b]Blessed is the one
who stays awake and keeps his clothes, [c]so that he will not
walk about naked and men will not see his shame.")
16 And they [a]gathered them together to the place which [b]in
Hebrew is called [1c]Har-Magedon.
17 Then the seventh *angel* poured out his bowl upon [a]the air,
and a [b]loud voice came out of the [1c]temple from the throne,
saying, "[d]It is done."
18 And there were flashes of [a]lightning and sounds and peals
of thunder; and there was [b]a great earthquake, [c]such as there
had not been since man came to be upon the earth, so great an
earthquake *was it, and* so mighty.
19 [a]The great city was split into three parts, and the cities of
the [1]nations fell. [b]Babylon the great was [c]remembered before
God, to give her [d]the cup of the wine of [2]His fierce wrath.
20 And [a]every island fled away, and the mountains were not
found.

2 [1]Lit *into* [2]Gr *anthropoi* [a]Rev 8:7 [b]Ex 9:9-11; Deut 28:35; Rev 16:11 [c]Rev 13:15-17; 14:9
3 [1]Lit *soul* [a]Ex 7:17-21; Rev 8:8f; 11:6
4 [a]Rev 8:10 [b]Ex 7:17-20; Ps 78:44; Rev 11:6
5 [a]John 17:25 [b]Rev 11:17 [c]Rev 15:4 [d]Rev 6:10
6 [1]Lit *are worthy* [a]Rev 17:6; 18:24 [b]Is 49:26; Luke 11:49-51
7 [a]Rev 6:9; 14:18 [b]Rev 1:8 [c]Rev 15:3; 19:2
8 [a]Rev 6:12 [b]Rev 14:18
9 [1]Lit *great* [a]Rev 16:11, 21 [b]Rev 2:21 [c]Rev 11:13
10 [a]Rev 13:2 [b]Ex 10:21f; Is 8:22; Rev 8:12; 9:2
11 [a]Rev 16:9, 21 [b]Rev 11:13 [c]Rev 16:2 [d]Rev 2:21
12 [1]Lit *rising of the sun* [a]Rev 9:14 [b]Is 11:15f; 44:27; Jer 51:36 [c]Is 41:2, 25; 46:11 [d]Rev 7:2
13 [a]Rev 12:3 [b]Rev 13:1 [c]Rev 13:11, 14; 19:20; 20:10 [d]Rev 18:2 [e]Ex 8:6
14 [1]Lit *inhabited earth* [a]1 Tim 4:1 [b]Rev 13:13 [c]Rev 3:10 [d]1 Kin 22:21-23; Rev 17:14; 19:19; 20:8 [e]Rev 6:17
15 [a]Matt 24:43f; Luke 12:39f; Rev 3:3, 11 [b]Luke 12:37 [c]Rev 3:18
16 [1]Two early mss read *Armageddon* [a]Rev 19:19 [b]Rev 9:11 [c]Judg 5:19; 2 Kin 23:29f; 2 Chr 35:22; Zech 12:11
17 [1]Or *sanctuary* [a]Eph 2:2 [b]Rev 11:15 [c]Rev 14:15 [d]Rev 10:6; 21:6
18 [a]Rev 4:5 [b]Rev 6:12 [c]Dan 12:1; Matt 24:21
19 [1]Or *Gentiles* [2]Lit *wrath of His anger* [a]Rev 11:8; 17:18; 18:10, 18f, 21 [b]Rev 14:8 [c]Rev 18:5 [d]Rev 14:10
20 [a]Rev 6:14; 20:11

21 And [a]huge [1]hailstones, about [2]one hundred pounds each,
*came down from heaven upon men; and men [b]blasphemed
God because of the [c]plague of the hail, because its plague *was
extremely [3]severe.

Chapter 17 Theme ____________________

17 [a]Then one of the [b]seven angels who had the [c]seven
bowls came and spoke with me, saying, "Come here, I
will show you [d]the judgment of the [e]great harlot who [f]sits on
many waters,
2 with whom [a]the kings of the earth committed *acts of*
immorality, and [b]those who dwell on the earth were [c]made
drunk with the wine of her immorality."
3 And [a]he carried me away [1b]in the Spirit [c]into a wilderness;
and I saw a woman sitting on a [d]scarlet beast, full of [e]blasphe-
mous names, having [f]seven heads and ten horns.
4 The woman [a]was clothed in purple and scarlet, and [1]adorned
with gold and precious [2]stones and pearls, having in her hand
[b]a gold cup full of abominations and of the unclean things of
her immorality,
5 and on her forehead a name *was* written, a [a]mystery,
"[b]BABYLON THE GREAT, THE MOTHER OF HARLOTS AND
OF [c]THE ABOMINATIONS OF THE EARTH."
6 And I saw the woman drunk with [a]the blood of the [1]saints,
and with the blood of the witnesses of Jesus. When I saw her, I
wondered [2]greatly.
7 And the angel said to me, "Why [1]do you wonder? I will tell
you the [a]mystery of the woman and of the beast that carries
her, which has the [b]seven heads and the ten horns.
8 "[a]The beast that you saw [b]was, and is not, and is about to
[c]come up out of the [d]abyss and [1e]go to destruction. And [f]those
who dwell on the earth, [g]whose name has not been written in
the book of life [h]from the foundation of the world, will [i]wonder
when they see the beast, that he was and is not and will come.
9 "[a]Here is the mind which has wisdom. The [b]seven heads
are seven mountains on which the woman sits,
10 and they are seven [a]kings; five have fallen, one is, the other
has not yet come; and when he comes, he must remain a little
while.
11 "The beast which [a]was and is not, is himself also an eighth
and is *one* of the seven, and he [b]goes to destruction.
12 "The [a]ten horns which you saw are ten kings who have not
yet received a kingdom, but they receive authority as kings
with the beast [b]for one hour.
13 "These have [a]one [1]purpose, and they give their power and
authority to the beast.
14 "These will wage [a]war against the Lamb, and the Lamb will
[b]overcome them, because He is [c]Lord of lords and [c]King of
kings, and [d]those who are with Him *are the* [e]called and chosen
and faithful."

21 [1]Lit *hail* [2]Lit *the weight of a talent* [3]Lit *great* [a]Rev 8:7; 11:19 [b]Rev 16:9, 11 [c]Ex 9:18-25

17:1 [a]Rev 1:1; 21:9 [b]Rev 15:1 [c]Rev 15:7 [d]Rev 16:19 [e]Is 1:21; Jer 2:20; Nah 3:4; Rev 17:5, 15f; 19:2 [f]Jer 51:13; Rev 17:15

2 [a]Rev 2:22; 18:3, 9 [b]Rev 3:10; 17:8 [c]Rev 14:8

3 [1]Or *in spirit* [a]Rev 21:10 [b]Rev 1:10 [c]Rev 12:6, 14; 21:10 [d]Matt 27:28; Rev 18:12, 16 [e]Rev 13:1 [f]Rev 12:3; 17:7, 9, 12, 16

4 [1]Lit *gilded* [2]Lit *stone* [a]Ezek 28:13; Rev 18:12, 16 [b]Jer 51:7; Rev 18:6

5 [a]2 Thess 2:7; Rev 1:20; 17:7 [b]Rev 14:8; 16:19 [c]Rev 17:2

6 [1]Or *holy ones* [2]Lit *with great wonder* [a]Rev 16:6

7 [1]Lit *have you wondered* [a]2 Thess 2:7; Rev 1:20; 17:5 [b]Rev 17:3

8 [1]One early ms reads *is going* [a]Dan 7:7 [b]Rev 13:3, 12, 14; 17:11 [c]Rev 11:7; 13:1 [d]Rev 9:1; 13:1 [e]Rev 13:10; 17:11 [f]Rev 3:10 [g]Ps 69:28; Rev 3:5 [h]Matt 25:34; Rev 13:8 [i]Rev 13:3

9 [a]Rev 13:18 [b]Rev 17:3

10 [a]Rev 10:11

11 [a]Rev 13:3, 12, 14; 17:8 [b]Rev 13:10; 17:8

12 [a]Dan 7:24; Rev 12:3; 13:1; 17:16 [b]Rev 18:10, 17, 19

13 [1]Or *mind* [a]Rev 17:17

14 [a]Rev 16:14 [b]Rev 3:21 [c]1 Tim 6:15; Rev 19:16 [d]Rev 2:10f [e]Matt 22:14

15 And he *said to me, "The [a]waters which you saw where the
harlot sits, are [b]peoples and multitudes and nations and tongues.
16 "And the [a]ten horns which you saw, and the beast, these
will hate the harlot and will make her [b]desolate and [c]naked,
and will [d]eat her flesh and will [e]burn her up with fire.
17 "For [a]God has put it in their hearts to execute His [1]purpose
[2]by [b]having a common purpose, and by giving their kingdom to
the beast, until the [c]words of God will be fulfilled.
18 "The woman whom you saw is [a]the great city, which [1]reigns
over the kings of the earth."

Chapter 18 Theme ________________________

18 After these things I saw another [a]angel [b]coming down
from heaven, having great authority, and the earth was
[c]illumined with his glory.
2 And he cried out with a mighty voice, saying, "[1a]Fallen,
fallen is Babylon the great! She [b]has become a dwelling place of
demons and a [2]prison of every [c]unclean spirit, and a [2]prison of
every unclean and hateful bird.
3 "For all the nations [1]have drunk of the [a]wine of the [2]passion
of her immorality, and [b]the kings of the earth have committed
acts of immorality with her, and the [c]merchants of the earth
have become rich by the [3]wealth of her [4d]sensuality."
4 I heard another voice from heaven, saying, "[a]Come out of
her, my people, so that you will not participate in her sins and
receive of her plagues;
5 for her sins have [1a]piled up as high as heaven, and God has
[b]remembered her iniquities.
6 "[a]Pay her back even as she has paid, and [1]give back *to her*
double according to her deeds; in the [b]cup which she has
mixed, mix twice as much for her.
7 "[a]To the degree that she glorified herself and [b]lived
[1]sensuously, to the same degree give her torment and mourning;
for she says in her heart, '[c]I SIT *as* A QUEEN AND I AM NOT A
WIDOW, and will never see mourning.'
8 "For this reason [a]in one day her plagues will come,
[1]pestilence and mourning and famine, and she will be [b]burned
up with fire; for the Lord God who judges her [c]is strong.
9 "And [a]the kings of the earth, who committed *acts of*
immorality and [b]lived [1]sensuously with her, will [c]weep and
lament over her when they [d]see the smoke of her burning,
10 [a]standing at a distance because of the fear of her torment,
saying, '[b]Woe, woe, [c]the great city, Babylon, the strong city! For
in [d]one hour your judgment has come.'
11 "And the [a]merchants of the earth [b]weep and mourn over
her, because no one buys their cargoes any more—
12 cargoes of [a]gold and silver and precious [1]stones and pearls
and fine linen and purple and silk and scarlet, and every *kind
of* citron wood and every article of ivory and every article *made*
from very costly wood and [2]bronze and iron and marble,

15 [a]Is 8:7; Jer 47:2; Rev 17:1 [b]Rev 5:9
16 [a]Rev 17:12 [b]Rev 18:17, 19 [c]Ezek 16:37, 39 [d]Rev 19:18 [e]Rev 18:8
17 [1]Or *mind* [2]Lit *even to do one mind and to give* [a]2 Cor 8:16 [b]Rev 17:13 [c]Rev 10:7
18 [1]Lit *has a kingdom* [a]Rev 11:8; 16:19
18:1 [a]Rev 17:1, 7 [b]Rev 10:1 [c]Ezek 43:2
2 [1]Lit *Babylon . . . fell, fell* [2]Or *haunt* [a]Is 21:9; Jer 51:8; Rev 14:8 [b]Is 13:21f; 34:11, 13-15; Jer 50:39; 51:37; Zeph 2:14f [c]Rev 16:13
3 [1]Two early ancient mss read *have fallen by* [2]Lit *wrath* [3]Lit *power* [4]Or *luxury* [a]Jer 51:7; Rev 14:8 [b]Rev 17:2; 18:9 [c]Ezek 27:9-25; Rev 18:11, 15, 19, 23 [d]1 Tim 5:11; Rev 18:7, 9
4 [a]Is 52:11; Jer 50:8; 51:6, 9, 45; 2 Cor 6:17
5 [1]Lit *joined together* [a]Jer 51:9 [b]Rev 16:19
6 [1]Lit *double* to her [a]Ps 137:8; Jer 50:15, 29 [b]Rev 17:4
7 [1]Or *luxuriously* [a]Ezek 28:2-8 [b]1 Tim 5:11; Rev 18:3, 9 [c]Is 47:7f; Zeph 2:15
8 [1]Lit *death* [a]Is 47:9; Jer 50:31f; Rev 18:10 [b]Rev 17:16 [c]Jer 50:34; Rev 11:17f
9 [1]Or *luxuriously* [a]Rev 17:2; 18:3 [b]1 Tim 5:11; Rev 18:3, 7 [c]Ezek 26:16f; 27:35 [d]Rev 14:11; 18:18; 19:3
10 [a]Rev 18:15, 17 [b]Rev 18:16, 19 [c]Rev 11:8; 16:19; 18:16, 18, 19, 21 [d]Rev 17:12; 18:8, 17, 19
11 [a]Ezek 27:9-25; Rev 18:3, 15, 19, 23 [b]Ezek 27:27-34
12 [1]Lit *stone* [2]Or *brass* [a]Ezek 27:12-22; Rev 17:4

13 and cinnamon and [1]spice and incense and perfume and
frankincense and wine and olive oil and fine flour and wheat
and cattle and sheep, and *cargoes* of horses and chariots and
[2]slaves and [3a]human lives.
14 "The fruit [1]you long for has gone from you, and all things
that were luxurious and splendid have passed away from you
and *men* will no longer find them.
15 "The [a]merchants of [b]these things, who became rich from
her, will [c]stand at a distance because of the fear of her torment,
weeping and mourning,
16 saying, '[a]Woe, woe, [b]the great city, she who [c]was clothed
in fine linen and purple and scarlet, and [1]adorned with gold
and precious [2]stones and pearls;
17 for in [a]one hour such great wealth has been laid [b]waste!'
And [c]every shipmaster and every [1]passenger and sailor, and as
many as make their living by the sea, [a]stood at a distance,
18 and were [a]crying out as they [b]saw the smoke of her
burning, saying, '[c]What *city* is like [d]the great city?'
19 "And they threw [a]dust on their heads and were crying out,
weeping and mourning, saying, '[b]Woe, woe, the great city, in
which all who had ships at sea [c]became rich by her [1]wealth,
for in [b]one hour she has been laid [d]waste!'
20 "[a]Rejoice over her, O heaven, and you [1]saints and [b]apostles
and prophets, because [c]God has [2]pronounced judgment for you
against her."
21 Then [1]a [a]strong angel [b]took up a stone like a great millstone
and threw it into the sea, saying, "So will Babylon, [c]the great
city, be thrown down with violence, and [d]will not be found any
longer.
22 "And [a]the sound of harpists and musicians and flute-players
and trumpeters will not be heard in you any longer; and no
craftsman of any craft will be found in you any longer; and the
[b]sound of a mill will not be heard in you any longer;
23 and the light of a lamp will not shine in you any longer;
and the [a]voice of the bridegroom and bride will not be heard in
you any longer; for your [b]merchants were the great men of the
earth, because all the nations were deceived [c]by your sorcery.
24 "And in her was found the [a]blood of prophets and of [1]saints
and of [b]all who have been slain on the earth."

Chapter 19 Theme ____

19 After these things I heard something like a [a]loud voice of
a great multitude in heaven, saying,
"[b]**H**allelujah! [c]Salvation and [d]glory and power belong to our
God;
2 [a]BECAUSE HIS [b]JUDGMENTS ARE [c]TRUE AND RIGHTEOUS; for He
has judged the [d]great harlot who was corrupting the earth with
her immorality, and HE HAS [e]AVENGED THE BLOOD OF HIS BOND-
SERVANTS [1]ON HER."
3 And a second time they said, "[a]Hallelujah! [b]HER SMOKE RISES
UP FOREVER AND EVER."

13 [1]Gr *amomon* [2]Lit *bodies* [3]Lit *souls of people* (Gr *anthropoi*) [a]1 Chr 5:21; Ezek 27:13; 1 Tim 1:10

14 [1]Lit *of your soul's desire*

15 [a]Rev 18:3 [b]Rev 18:12, 13 [c]Rev 18:10

16 [1]Lit *gilded* [2]Lit *stone and pearl* [a]Rev 18:10, 19 [b]Rev 18:10, 18, 19, 21 [c]Rev 17:4

17 [1]Lit *one who sails to a place* [a]Rev 18:10 [b]Rev 17:16; 18:19 [c]Ezek 27:28f

18 [a]Ezek 27:30 [b]Rev 18:9 [c]Ezek 27:32; Rev 13:4 [d]Rev 18:10

19 [1]Lit *costliness* [a]Josh 7:6; Job 2:12; Lam 2:10 [b]Rev 18:10 [c]Rev 18:3, 15 [d]Rev 17:16; 18:17

20 [1]Or *holy ones* [2]Lit *judged your judgment of her* [a]Jer 51:48; Rev 12:12 [b]Luke 11:49f [c]Rev 6:10; 18:6ff; 19:2

21 [1]Lit *one* [a]Rev 5:2; 10:1 [b]Jer 51:63f [c]Rev 18:10 [d]Ezek 26:21

22 [a]Is 24:8; Ezek 26:13; Matt 9:23 [b]Eccl 12:4; Jer 25:10

23 [a]Jer 7:34; 16:9 [b]Is 23:8; Rev 6:15; 18:3 [c]Nah 3:4; Rev 9:21

24 [1]Or *holy ones* [a]Rev 16:6; 17:6 [b]Matt 23:35

19:1 [a]Jer 51:48; Rev 11:15; 19:6 [b]Ps 104:35; Rev 19:3, 4, 6 [c]Rev 7:10 [d]Rev 4:11

2 [1]Lit *from her hand* [a]Ps 19:9 [b]Rev 6:10 [c]Rev 16:7 [d]Rev 17:1 [e]Deut 32:43; 2 Kin 9:7; Rev 16:6; 18:20

3 [a]Ps 104:35; Rev 19:1, 4, 6 [b]Is 34:10; Rev 14:11

4 And the [a]twenty-four elders and the [b]four living creatures
[c]fell down and worshiped God who sits on the throne saying,
"[d]Amen. [e]Hallelujah!"
5 And a voice came from the throne, saying,
"[a]**G**ive praise to our God, all you His bond-servants, [b]you
who fear Him, the small and the great."
6 Then I heard *something* like [a]the voice of a great multitude
and like [b]the sound of many waters and like the [c]sound of
mighty peals of thunder, saying,
"[a]**H**allelujah! For the [d]Lord our God, the Almighty, reigns.
7 "Let us rejoice and be glad and [a]give the glory to Him, for
[b]the marriage of the Lamb has come and His [1c]bride has made
herself ready."
8 It was given to her to clothe herself in [a]fine linen, bright
and clean; for the fine linen is the [b]righteous acts of the [1]saints.
9 Then [a]he *said to me, "[b]Write, '[c]Blessed are those who are
invited to the marriage supper of the Lamb.'" And he *said to
me, "[d]These are true words of God."
10 Then [a]I fell at his feet to worship him. [b]But he *said to me,
"Do not do that; I am a [c]fellow servant of yours and your
brethren who [d]hold the testimony of Jesus; worship God. For
the testimony of Jesus is the spirit of prophecy."
11 And I saw [a]heaven opened, and behold, a [b]white horse, and
He who sat on it *is* called [c]Faithful and True, and in [d]righteous-
ness He judges and wages war.
12 His [a]eyes *are* a flame of fire, and on His head *are* many
[b]diadems; and He has a [c]name written *on Him* which no one
knows except Himself.
13 *He is* clothed with a [a]robe dipped in blood, and His name
is called [b]The Word of God.
14 And the armies which are in heaven, clothed in [a]fine linen,
[b]white *and* clean, were following Him on white horses.
15 [a]From His mouth comes a sharp sword, so that [b]with it He
may strike down the nations, and He will [1c]rule them with a
rod of iron; and [d]He treads the [2]wine press of the fierce wrath
of God, the Almighty.
16 And on His robe and on His thigh He has [a]a name written,
"[b]KING OF KINGS, AND LORD OF LORDS."
17 Then I saw [1]an angel standing in the sun, and he cried out
with a loud voice, saying to [a]all the birds which fly in [b]mid-
heaven, "[c]Come, assemble for the great supper of God,
18 so that you may [a]eat the flesh of kings and the flesh of
[1]commanders and the flesh of mighty men and the flesh of
horses and of those who sit on them and the flesh of all men,
[b]both free men and slaves, and [c]small and great."
19 And I saw [a]the beast and [b]the kings of the earth and their
armies assembled to make war against Him who [c]sat on the
horse and against His army.
20 And the beast was seized, and with him the [a]false prophet
who [b]performed the signs [1c]in his presence, by which he
[d]deceived those who had received the [e]mark of the beast and

4 [a]Rev 4:4, 10 [b]Rev 4:6 [c]Rev 4:10 [d]Ps 106:48; Rev 5:14 [e]Ps 104:35; Rev 19:3, 6
5 [a]Ps 22:23; 115:13; 134:1; 135:1 [b]Rev 11:18
6 [a]Jer 51:48; Rev 11:15; 19:1 [b]Ezek 1:24; Rev 1:15 [c]Rev 6:1 [d]Ps 93:1; 97:1; 99:1; Rev 1:8
7 [1]Lit *wife* [a]Rev 11:13 [b]Matt 22:2; 25:10; Luke 12:36; John 3:29; Eph 5:23, 32; Rev 19:9 [c]Matt 1:20; Rev 21:2, 9
8 [1]Or *holy ones* [a]Rev 15:6; 19:14 [b]Rev 15:4
9 [a]Rev 17:1; 19:10 [b]Rev 1:19 [c]Matt 22:2f; Luke 14:15 [d]Rev 17:17; 21:5; 22:6
10 [a]Rev 22:8 [b]Acts 10:26; Rev 22:9 [c]Rev 1:1f [d]Rev 12:17
11 [a]Ezek 1:1; John 1:51; Rev 4:1 [b]Rev 6:2; 19:19, 21 [c]Rev 3:14 [d]Ps 96:13; Is 11:4
12 [a]Dan 10:6; Rev 1:14 [b]Rev 6:2; 12:3 [c]Rev 2:17; 19:16
13 [a]Is 63:3 [b]John 1:1
14 [a]Rev 19:8 [b]Rev 3:4; 19:8
15 [1]Or *shepherd* [2]Lit *wine press of the wine of the wrath of God's anger* [a]Rev 1:16; 19:21 [b]Is 11:4; 2 Thess 2:8 [c]Ps 2:9; Rev 2:27 [d]Is 63:3; Joel 3:13; Rev 14:19, 20
16 [a]Rev 2:17; 19:12 [b]Rev 17:14
17 [1]Lit *one* [a]Rev 19:21 [b]Rev 8:13 [c]1 Sam 17:44; Jer 12:9; Ezek 39:17
18 [1]I.e. chiliarchs, in command of one thousand troops [a]Ezek 39:18-20 [b]Rev 6:15 [c]Rev 11:18; 13:16; 19:5
19 [a]Rev 11:7; 13:1 [b]Rev 16:14, 16 [c]Rev 19:11, 21
20 [1]Or *by his authority* [a]Rev 16:13 [b]Rev 13:13 [c]Rev 13:12 [d]Rev 13:14 [e]Rev 13:16f

those who [f]worshiped his image; these two were thrown alive
into the [g]lake of [h]fire which burns with [2]brimstone.
21 And the rest were killed with the sword which [a]came from
the mouth of Him who [b]sat on the horse, and [c]all the birds
were filled with their flesh.

Chapter 20 Theme ______________________________

20 Then I saw [a]an angel coming down from heaven, holding the [b]key of the abyss and a great chain [1]in his hand.
2 And he laid hold of the [a]dragon, the serpent of old, who is
the devil and Satan, and [b]bound him for a thousand years;
3 and he threw him into the [a]abyss, and shut *it* and [b]sealed *it*
over him, so that he would [c]not deceive the nations any longer,
until the thousand years were completed; after these things he
must be released for a short time.
4 Then I saw [a]thrones, and [b]they sat on them, and [c]judgment
was given to them. And I *saw* [d]the souls of those who had been
beheaded because of [1]their [e]testimony of Jesus and because of
the word of God, and those who had not [f]worshiped the beast
or his image, and had not received the [g]mark on their forehead
and on their hand; and they [h]came to life and [i]reigned with
Christ for a thousand years.
5 The rest of the dead did not come to life until the thousand
years were completed. [a]This is the first resurrection.
6 [a]Blessed and holy is the one who has a part in the first
resurrection; over these the [b]second death has no power, but
they will be [c]priests of God and of Christ and will [d]reign with
Him for a thousand years.
7 When the thousand years are completed, Satan will be
[a]released from his prison,
8 and will come out to [a]deceive the nations which are in the
[b]four corners of the earth, [c]Gog and Magog, to [d]gather them
together for the war; the number of them is like the [e]sand of
the [1]seashore.
9 And they [a]came up on the [1]broad plain of the earth and
surrounded the [b]camp of the [2]saints and the [c]beloved city, and
[d]fire came down from heaven and devoured them.
10 And [a]the devil who [a]deceived them was thrown into the
[b]lake of fire and [1]brimstone, where the [c]beast and the [c]false
prophet are also; and they will be [d]tormented day and night
forever and ever.
11 Then I saw a great white [a]throne and Him who sat upon it,
from whose [1]presence [b]earth and heaven fled away, and [c]no
place was found for them.
12 And I saw the dead, the [a]great and the small, standing
before the throne, and [1b]books were opened; and another [2]book
was opened, which is [c]*the book* of life; and the dead [a]were
judged from the things which were written in the [1]books,
[d]according to their deeds.
13 And the sea gave up the dead which were in it, and [a]death

20 [2]I.e. burning sulphur [f]Rev 13:12, 15 [g]Rev 20:10, 14f; 21:8 [h]Is 30:33; Dan 7:11; Rev 14:10

21 [a]Rev 19:15 [b]Rev 19:11, 19 [c]Rev 19:17

20:1 [1]Lit *upon* [a]Rev 10:1 [b]Rev 1:18; 9:1

2 [a]Gen 3:1; Rev 12:9 [b]Is 24:22; 2 Pet 2:4; Jude 6

3 [a]Rev 20:1 [b]Dan 6:17; Matt 27:66 [c]Rev 12:9; 20:8, 10

4 [1]Lit *the* [a]Dan 7:9 [b]Matt 19:28; Rev 3:21 [c]Dan 7:22; 1 Cor 6:2 [d]Rev 6:9 [e]Rev 1:9 [f]Rev 13:12, 15 [g]Rev 13:16f [h]John 14:19 [i]Rev 3:21; 5:10; 20:6; 22:5

5 [a]Luke 14:14; Phil 3:11; 1 Thess 4:16

6 [a]Rev 14:13 [b]Rev 2:11; 20:14 [c]Rev 1:6 [d]Rev 3:21; 5:10; 20:4; 22:5

7 [a]Rev 20:2f

8 [1]Lit *sea* [a]Rev 12:9; 20:3, 10 [b]Ezek 7:2; Rev 7:1 [c]Ezek 38:2; 39:1, 6 [d]Rev 16:14 [e]Heb 11:12

9 [1]Lit *breadth of the earth* [2]Or *holy ones* [a]Ezek 38:9, 16 [b]Deut 23:14 [c]Ps 87:2 [d]Ezek 38:22; 39:6; Rev 13:13

10 [1]I.e. burning sulphur [a]Rev 20:2f [b]Rev 19:20; 20:14, 15 [c]Rev 16:13 [d]Rev 14:10f

11 [1]Lit *face* [a]Rev 4:2 [b]Rev 6:14; 21:1 [c]Dan 2:35; Rev 12:8

12 [1]Or *scrolls* [2]Or *scroll* [a]Rev 11:18 [b]Dan 7:10 [c]Rev 3:5; 20:15 [d]Matt 16:27; Rev 2:23; 20:13

13 [a]1 Cor 15:26; Rev 1:18; 6:8; 21:4

and Hades [b]gave up the dead which were in them; and they
were judged, every one *of them* [c]according to their deeds.
14 Then [a]death and Hades were thrown into [b]the lake of fire.
This is the [c]second death, the lake of fire.
15 And if [1]anyone's name was not found written in [a]the book
of life, he was thrown into the lake of fire.

Chapter 21 Theme ______________________

21 Then I saw [a]a new heaven and a new earth; for [b]the first
heaven and the first earth passed away, and there is no
longer *any* sea.
2 And I saw [a]the holy city, [b]new Jerusalem, [c]coming down
out of heaven from God, [d]made ready as a bride adorned for
her husband.
3 And I heard a loud voice from the throne, saying, "Behold,
[a]the tabernacle of God is among men, and He will [1b]dwell
among them, and they shall be His people, and God Himself
will be among them,[2]
4 and He will [a]wipe away every tear from their eyes; and [b]there
will no longer be *any* death; [c]there will no longer be *any*
mourning, or crying, or pain; [d]the first things have passed away."
5 And [a]He who sits on the throne said, "Behold, I am [b]making
all things new." And He *said, "Write, for [c]these words are
faithful and true."
6 Then He said to me, "[1a]It is done. I am the [b]Alpha and the
Omega, the beginning and the end. [c]I will give to the one who
thirsts from the spring of the [d]water of life without cost.
7 "[a]He who overcomes will inherit these things, and [b]I will be
his God and he will be My son.
8 "[a]But for the cowardly and [1]unbelieving and abominable and
murderers and immoral persons and sorcerers and idolaters
and all liars, their part *will be* in [b]the lake that burns with fire
and [2]brimstone, which is the [c]second death."
9 [a]Then one of the seven angels who had the [b]seven bowls
[1]full of the [c]seven last plagues came and spoke with me, saying,
"[a]Come here, I will show you the [d]bride, the wife of the Lamb."
10 And [a]he carried me away [1b]in the Spirit to a great and high
mountain, and showed me [c]the holy city, Jerusalem, coming
down out of heaven from God,
11 having [a]the glory of God. Her [1]brilliance was like a very
costly stone, as a [b]stone of [c]crystal-clear jasper.
12 [1]It had a great and high wall, [1a]with twelve [b]gates, and at
the gates twelve angels; and names *were* written on them,
which are *the names* of the twelve tribes of the sons of Israel.
13 *There were* three gates on the east and three gates on the
north and three gates on the south and three gates on the west.
14 And the wall of the city had [a]twelve foundation stones, and on
them *were* the twelve names of the [b]twelve apostles of the Lamb.
15 The one who spoke with me had a [1]gold measuring [a]rod to
measure the city, and its [b]gates and its wall.

13 [b]Is 26:19 [c]Matt 16:27; Rev 2:23; 20:12

14 [a]1 Cor 15:26; Rev 1:18; 6:8; 21:4 [b]Rev 19:20; 20:10, 15 [c]Rev 20:6

15 [1]Lit *anyone was* [a]Rev 3:5; 20:12

21:1 [a]Is 65:17; 66:22; 2 Pet 3:13 [b]2 Pet 3:10; Rev 20:11

2 [a]Is 52:1; Rev 11:2; 21:10; 22:19 [b]Rev 3:12; 21:10 [c]Heb 11:10, 16; Rev 21:10 [d]Is 61:10; Rev 19:7; 21:9; 22:17

3 [1]Or *tabernacle* [2]One early ms reads, and be *their God* [a]Lev 26:11f; Ezek 37:27; 48:35; Heb 8:2; Rev 7:15 [b]John 14:23; 2 Cor 6:16

4 [a]Is 25:8; Rev 7:17 [b]1 Cor 15:26; Rev 20:14 [c]Is 35:10; 51:11; 65:19 [d]2 Cor 5:17; Heb 12:27

5 [a]Rev 4:9; 20:11 [b]2 Cor 5:17; Heb 12:27 [c]Rev 19:9; 22:6

6 [1]Lit *They are* [a]Rev 10:6; 16:17 [b]Rev 1:8; 22:13 [c]Is 55:1; John 4:10; Rev 7:17; 22:17 [d]Rev 7:17

7 [a]Rev 2:7 [b]2 Sam 7:14; Ps 89:26f; 2 Cor 6:16, 18; Rev 21:3

8 [1]Or *untrustworthy* [2]I.e. burning sulphur [a]1 Cor 6:9; Gal 5:19-21; Rev 9:21; 21:27; 22:15 [b]Rev 19:20 [c]Rev 2:11

9 [1]Lit *who were full* [a]Rev 17:1 [b]Rev 15:7 [c]Rev 15:1 [d]Rev 19:7; 21:2

10 [1]Or *in spirit* [a]Ezek 40:2; Rev 17:3 [b]Rev 1:10 [c]Rev 21:2

11 [1]Lit *luminary* [a]Is 60:1f; Ezek 43:2; Rev 15:8; 21:23; 22:5 [b]Rev 4:3; 21:18, 19 [c]Rev 4:6

12 [1]Lit *having* [a]Ezek 48:31-34 [b]Rev 21:15, 21, 25; 22:14

14 [a]Heb 11:10 [b]Acts 1:26

15 [1]Lit *measure, a gold reed* [a]Ezek 40:3; Rev 11:1 [b]Rev 21:12, 21, 25

16 The city is laid out as a square, and its length is as great as
the width; and he measured the city with the [1]rod, [2]fifteen
hundred miles; its length and width and height are equal.
17 And he measured its wall, [1]seventy-two yards, *according to*
[a]human [2]measurements, which are *also* [b]angelic *measurements.*
18 The material of the wall was [a]jasper; and the city was [b]pure
gold, like [1]clear [c]glass.
19 [a]The foundation stones of the city wall were adorned with
every kind of precious stone. The first foundation stone was
[b]jasper; the second, sapphire; the third, chalcedony; the fourth,
[c]emerald;
20 the fifth, sardonyx; the sixth, [a]sardius; the seventh, chrysolite;
the eighth, beryl; the ninth, topaz; the tenth, chrysoprase; the
eleventh, jacinth; the twelfth, amethyst.
21 And the twelve [a]gates were twelve [b]pearls; each one of the
gates was a single pearl. And the street of the city was [c]pure
gold, like transparent [d]glass.
22 I saw [a]no [1]temple in it, for the [b]Lord God the Almighty and
the [c]Lamb are its [1]temple.
23 And the city [a]has no need of the sun or of the moon to shine
on it, for [b]the glory of God has illumined it, and its lamp *is* the
[c]Lamb.
24 [a]The nations will walk by its light, and the [b]kings of the
earth [1]will bring their glory into it.
25 In the daytime (for [a]there will be no night there) [b]its gates
[c]will never be closed;
26 and [a]they will bring the glory and the honor of the nations
into it;
27 and [a]nothing unclean, and no one who practices abomination
and lying, shall ever come into it, but only those [1]whose names
are [b]written in the Lamb's book of life.

Chapter 22 Theme ________________________

22 Then [a]he showed me a [b]river of the [c]water of life, [1]clear
[d]as crystal, coming from the throne of God and of [2]the
Lamb,
2 in the middle of [a]its street. [b]On either side of the river was
[c]the tree of life, bearing twelve [1]*kinds of* fruit, yielding its fruit
every month; and the leaves of the tree were for the healing of
the nations.
3 [a]There will no longer be any curse; and [b]the throne of God
and of the Lamb will be in it, and His bond-servants will [c]serve
Him;
4 they will [a]see His face, and His [b]name *will be* on their
[c]foreheads.
5 And [a]there will no longer be *any* night; and they [1]will not
have need [b]of the light of a lamp nor the light of the sun,
because the Lord God will illumine them; and they will [c]reign
forever and ever.
6 And [a]he said to me, "[b]These words are faithful and true";
and the Lord, the [c]God of the spirits of the prophets, [d]sent His

16 [1]Lit *reed* [2]Lit *twelve thousand stadia;* a stadion was approx 600 ft

17 [1]Lit *one hundred forty-four cubits* [2]Lit *measure* [a]Deut 3:11; Rev 13:18 [b]Rev 21:9

18 [1]Lit *pure* [a]Rev 21:11 [b]Rev 21:21 [c]Rev 4:6

19 [a]Ex 28:17-20; Is 54:11f; Ezek 28:13 [b]Rev 21:11 [c]Rev 4:3

20 [a]Rev 4:3

21 [a]Rev 21:12, 15, 25 [b]Rev 17:4 [c]Rev 21:18 [d]Rev 4:6

22 [1]Or *sanctuary* [a]Matt 24:2; John 4:21 [b]Rev 1:8 [c]Rev 5:6; 7:17; 14:4

23 [a]Is 24:23; 60:19, 20; Rev 21:25; 22:5 [b]Rev 21:11 [c]Rev 5:6; 7:17; 14:4

24 [1]Lit *bring* [a]Is 60:3, 5 [b]Ps 72:10f; Is 49:23; 60:16; Rev 21:26

25 [a]Zech 14:7; Rev 21:23; 22:5 [b]Rev 21:12, 15 [c]Is 60:11

26 [a]Ps 72:10f; Is 49:23; 60:16

27 [1]Lit *who have been* [a]Is 52:1; Ezek 44:9; Zech 14:21; Rev 22:14f [b]Rev 3:5

22:1 [1]Lit *bright* [2]Or *the Lamb. In the middle of its street, and on either side of the river, was* [a]Rev 1:1; 21:9; 22:6 [b]Ps 46:4; Ezek 47:1 [c]Zech 14:8; Rev 7:17; 22:17 [d]Rev 4:6

2 [1]Or crops of *fruit* [a]Rev 21:21 [b]Ezek 47:12 [c]Gen 2:9; Rev 2:7; 22:14, 19

3 [a]Zech 14:11 [b]Rev 21:3 [c]Rev 7:15

4 [a]Ps 17:15; 42:2; Matt 5:8 [b]Rev 14:1 [c]Rev 7:3

5 [1]Lit *do not have* [a]Zech 14:7; Rev 21:25 [b]Is 60:19; Rev 21:23 [c]Dan 7:18, 27; Matt 19:28; Rom 5:17; Rev 20:4

6 [a]Rev 1:1; 21:9 [b]Rev 19:9; 21:5 [c]1 Cor 14:32; Heb 12:9 [d]Rev 1:1; 22:16

angel to show to His bond-servants the things which must soon
take place.
7 "And behold, [a]I am coming quickly. [b]Blessed is he who
[1]heeds [c]the words of the prophecy of this book."
8 [a]I, John, am the one who heard and saw these things. And
when I heard and saw, [b]I fell down to worship at the feet of the
angel who showed me these things.
9 But [a]he *said to me, "Do not do that. I am a [b]fellow servant
of yours and of your brethren the prophets and of those who
[1]heed the words of [c]this book. Worship God."
10 And he *said to me, "[a]Do not seal up [b]the words of the
prophecy of this book, [c]for the time is near.
11 "[a]Let the one who does wrong, still do wrong; and the one
who is filthy, still be filthy; and let the one who is righteous,
still practice righteousness; and the one who is holy, still keep
himself holy."
12 "Behold, [a]I am coming quickly, and My [b]reward *is* with Me,
[c]to render to every man [1]according to what he has done.
13 "I am the [a]Alpha and the Omega, [b]the first and the last, [c]the
beginning and the end."
14 Blessed are those who [a]wash their robes, so that they may
have the right to [b]the tree of life, and may [c]enter by the [d]gates
into the city.
15 [a]Outside are the [b]dogs and the sorcerers and the immoral
persons and the murderers and the idolaters, and everyone
who loves and practices lying.
16 "[a]I, Jesus, have sent [b]My angel to testify to you these things
[1c]for the churches. I am [d]the root and the [e]descendant of
David, the bright [f]morning star."
17 The [a]Spirit and the [b]bride say, "Come." And let the one
who hears say, "Come." And [c]let the one who is thirsty come;
let the one who wishes take the [d]water of life without cost.
18 I testify to everyone who hears [a]the words of the prophecy
of this book: if anyone [b]adds to them, God will add to him [c]the
plagues which are written in [d]this book;
19 and if anyone [a]takes away from the [b]words of the book of
this prophecy, God will take away his part from [c]the tree of life
and [1]from the holy city, [d]which are written in this book.
20 He who [a]testifies to these things says, "Yes, [b]I am coming
quickly." Amen. [c]Come, Lord Jesus.
21 [a]The grace of the Lord Jesus be with [1]all. Amen.

7 [1]Lit *keeps* [a]Rev 1:3; 3:3, 11; 16:15; 22:12, 20 [b]Rev 1:3; 16:15 [c]Rev 1:11; 22:9, 10, 18f
8 [a]Rev 1:1 [b]Rev 19:10
9 [1]Lit *keep* [a]Rev 19:10 [b]Rev 1:1 [c]Rev 1:11; 22:10, 18f
10 [a]Dan 8:26; Rev 10:4 [b]Rev 1:11; 22:9, 18f [c]Rev 1:3
11 [a]Ezek 3:27; Dan 12:10
12 [1]Lit *as his work is* [a]Rev 22:7 [b]Is 40:10; 62:11 [c]Ps 28:4; Jer 17:10; Matt 16:27; Rev 2:23
13 [a]Rev 1:8 [b]Is 44:6; 48:12; Rev 1:17; 2:8 [c]Rev 21:6
14 [a]Rev 7:14 [b]Gen 2:9; 3:22; Rev 22:2 [c]Rev 21:27 [d]Rev 21:12
15 [a]Matt 8:12; 1 Cor 6:9f; Gal 5:19ff; Rev 21:8 [b]Deut 23:18; Matt 7:6; Phil 3:2
16 [1]Or *concerning* [a]Rev 1:1 [b]Rev 1:1; 22:6 [c]Rev 1:4, 11; 3:22 [d]Rev 5:5 [e]Matt 1:1 [f]Matt 2:2; Rev 2:28
17 [a]Rev 2:7; 14:13 [b]Rev 21:2, 9 [c]Is 55:1; Rev 21:6 [d]Rev 7:17; 22:1
18 [a]Rev 22:7 [b]Deut 4:2; 12:32; Prov 30:6 [c]Rev 15:6-16:21 [d]Rev 22:7

19 [1]Lit *out of* [a]Deut 4:2; 12:32; Prov 30:6 [b]Rev 22:7 [c]Rev 22:2 [d]Rev 21:10-22:5
20 [a]Rev 1:2 [b]Rev 22:7 [c]1 Cor 16:22
21 [1]One early ms reads *the saints* [a]Rom 16:20

Jesus' Messages to the Churches

	Description of Jesus	Commendation to the Church	Reproof Given to the Church	Warnings and Instructions to the Church	Promise to the Overcomers
Ephesus					
Smyrna					

(continued)

Jesus' Messages to the Churches

	Description of Jesus	Commendation to the Church	Reproof Given to the Church	Warnings and Instructions to the Church	Promise to the Overcomers
Pergamum					
Thyatira					

(continued)

Jesus' Messages to the Churches

	Description of Jesus	Commendation to the Church	Reproof Given to the Church	Warnings and Instructions to the Church	Promise to the Overcomers
Sardis					
Philadelphia					
Laodicea					

What Revelation Teaches About

God	Jesus	The Holy Spirit

The Seven Seals, Trumpets, and Bowls

	Seals	Trumpets	Bowls
1st			
2nd			
3rd			
4th			
5th			
6th			
7th			

Theme of Revelation:

Author:

Date:

Purpose:

Key Words:

- God
- Jesus (Christ)
- in the Spirit
- church(es)
- throne
- mystery
- repent
- overcome(s)
- mark every reference to Satan (demons, devil, dragon)
- after these things
- and I saw (looked)
- angel(s)
- seal(s)
- nations
- trumpet(s)
- bowl(s), plague(s)
- woe
- wrath
- beast
- Babylon
- earthquake, voices, thunder, lightning

SEGMENT DIVISIONS					CHAPTER THEMES
				1	
				2	
				3	
				4	
				5	
				6	
				7	
				8	
				9	
				10	
				11	
				12	
				13	
				14	
				15	
				16	
				17	
				18	
				19	
				20	
				21	
				22	

What the Bible Teaches about Babylon

Its First Description in Scripture

Location of Babylon

The City

The Babylonian Empire *(see page 2246)*

Worship Connected with Babylon

Warnings Given about Babylon

What the Bible Teaches about Babylon

Prophecies Regarding Babylon	Destruction of Babylon
	History of Babylon's Destruction
	The City
	The Babylonian Empire
	Details Concerning Babylon's Final Destruction
	The City
	The Babylonian System

REFERENCE	HOW IT IS DESCRIBED

 (For further notetaking, this two-page chart is duplicated on pages 2078, 2079.)

What Happens in Nature	Signs of Beginning or End

(continued)

Reference	How It Is Described

What Happens in Nature	Signs of Beginning or End

STUDY HELPS

UNDERSTANDING THE VALUE OF GOD'S WORD

WHAT IS THE BIBLE?

The Bible is comprised of 66 separate writings or books. It was written over a period of approximately 1400 to 1800 years by more than 40 authors from various walks of life. While many of the authors are identified, some remain unknown.

The Bible is divided into the Old Testament, comprised of 39 books, and the New Testament, comprised of 27 books. The Old Testament, the Bible of the nation of Israel, was divided into three segments: the Law or Torah, the Prophets or Nebi'im, and the Writings or Kethubim. While the Old Testament was originally written in two Semitic languages, Hebrew and Aramaic, the vast majority of it is in Hebrew.

With the growth of the Greek Empire came the spread of the Greek language, and the Old Testament was translated into Koine (common) Greek around 250-100 B.C. This translation is referred to as the Septuagint or the LXX. It contains the same books as the Hebrew Old Testament, but the order and breakdown of the books was changed to the form now used in the Old Testament.

By the time of the Lord Jesus Christ, Koine Greek had become the popular language used throughout most of the Mediterranean world. Therefore, the New Testament was written in Koine Greek. However, a few Aramaic phrases are found in the New Testament because Aramaic was the vernacular of the people of Israel. Jesus and His disciples spoke Aramaic as well as Koine Greek. Much of the Old Testament was translated into Aramaic, and these works are referred to as the Targums.

HOW WAS THE BIBLE WRITTEN AND TRANSLATED?

The Bible itself tells us how it was written: "All Scripture is inspired by God" (2 Timothy 3:16). Men "moved by the Holy Spirit spoke from God" (2 Peter 1:21). The Greek word for inspired, *theopneustos*, means "God-breathed." The Holy Spirit carried men along, moving and guiding them as they wrote in their own words what God wanted them to say. Thus we have *verbal* inspiration, because the words of the original text were inspired by God. And because all Scripture was given by inspiration we have *plenary* inspiration, which means total or complete inspiration. Every part of the Bible is inspired. The Bible does not merely contain the words of God, but it actually is the Word of God. Thus the original writings, often called *autographs*, are inerrant—without error. This concept is called the verbal, plenary inspiration of the autographs.

Autographs

In early history, writing was done on stone, clay tablets, leather (animal skins), and papyrus scrolls. The New Testament autographs were probably written on papyrus. Papyrus, made from the inner bark of a reed plant, was formed into a paper-like material which was glued together and rolled into a scroll. Normally the writing was done on only one side of the scroll, so that as it was read it was unrolled with one hand and rolled up with the other. The scrolls were kept in a cylindrical box called a *capsa*.

According to the Jewish Talmud, the Scriptures were to be copied only on the skins of what God deemed as clean animals, such as sheep, calves, and goats. Parchment (dried animal skin) was costly but more durable and permanent than papyrus.

The Accuracy of the Copies

Eventually the scrolls were replaced by the *codex*. The codex (plural *codices*) was made from folded sheets, *quires*, which were stitched together like a book. Copies of the Old Testament were transcribed by hand under the strictest measures. The men who copied the manuscripts were called *scribes*. If one error was found the entire copy was destroyed. Thus the accuracy of the Old Testament is phenomenal. This accuracy has been confirmed by the large number of copies, by the Septuagint, and by the Dead Sea Scrolls.

More than 5000 ancient Greek copies of all or portions of the New Testament have been found. Although there are minor variances in the copied manuscripts, none affect doctrinal issues.

The Canon

The same omnipotent Sovereign who inspired men to write the Word of God led other men to recognize that these were the books which would comprise the *canon* of Scripture. The canon is the group of books which are recognized to be inspired by God. This group comprises the Old and New Testaments. The Old Testament canon of 39 books was fairly widely accepted in the days of Jesus Christ. Jesus Himself, who is one with the Father, always affirmed and never contradicted the Old Testament. Revelation, the last of the New Testament books to be written, was completed before the end of the first century A.D. By A.D. 367 Bishop Athanasius compiled the first known list of the current 27 books of the New Testament.

Translations

The Hebrew/Aramaic and Greek copies of the 66 books of the Bible are the basis of the translations made in the various languages of the world. A translator will study the original words of these copies, determine what those words mean, and then select the best way to faithfully transmit the meaning of the original words in their context into the language of their translation. This is called a *primary translation*.

A *secondary translation* occurs when a translation is made from a primary translation of another language, say English, into a third language. Thus a secondary translation is not made from a copy of the original language but from a second language translated from the original language (the primary translation).

HOW DO WE KNOW THE BIBLE IS WHAT IT CLAIMS TO BE—THE WORD OF GOD?

Believing the Bible is ultimately a matter of informed faith. You either believe what the Word of God says about itself or you don't. You either believe the testimony of Jesus Christ regarding the Word of God or you don't.

There are several areas of objective evidence that test and support the veracity of the verbal, plenary inspiration of the autographs.

First, there is *bibliographic evidence* for the Bible's authenticity. No other ancient writings have as much manuscript evidence as does the Bible. Aside from 643 copies of Homer's works, which were written about 850 B.C., the other classical works written between 450 B.C. and 10 B.C. have anywhere from 3 to 20 copies each, but the New Testament has over 5000. And not only is there more than an ample *quantity* of copies of the Bible, but the *quality* of the biblical manuscripts surpasses that of other manuscripts as well.

The passage of time is also a factor. The Dead Sea Scrolls, which date from 200 B.C. to A.D. 68, greatly reduce the time span between the writing of the Old Testament books to our earliest existing copies of the Old Testament. The time span between the autographs of the New Testament and its existing copies is between 100 and 200 years, a very low figure.

Second, there is *internal evidence* for the authenticity of the Bible. The Bible not only claims to be the Word of God, but it also states that not the smallest letter or stroke will pass away from the law (the Old Testament) until all is accomplished (Matthew 5:17, 18). Many of the writers claimed to be eyewitnesses who wrote what they saw, heard, or experienced. Although there were so many different authors who wrote over such a long time span, there are no contradictions in what they wrote. Also, what was written in the Old Testament, sealed and canonized, is often seen fulfilled in the New Testament. Thus there is the internal evidence of fulfilled prophecy.

Overview of the Bible

PRE-EXILIC

(Before the Babylonian Exile of Judah)

TORAH

(the Law, Moses, the Pentateuch)

Genesis
Exodus
Leviticus
Numbers
Deuteronomy

HISTORY

Joshua
Judges
Ruth
1 and 2 Samuel
1 and 2 Kings
1 and 2 Chronicles

PROPHECY

(in parentheses is the kingdom to which prophesied)

Jeremiah (Southern)
Obadiah (Southern)
Joel (Southern)
Jonah (Northern)
Amos (Northern)
Hosea (Northern)
Isaiah (Southern)
Micah (Southern)
Nahum (Southern)
Zephaniah (Southern)
Habakkuk (Southern)

POETRY AND WISDOM

Job
Psalms
Proverbs
Ecclesiastes
Song of Solomon

EXILIC

(During the Babylonian Exile of Judah)

PROPHECY

Daniel
Ezekiel
Jeremiah
Lamentations

POST-EXILIC

(After the Babylonian Exile of Judah)

HISTORY

1 and 2 Chronicles (written after the exile but covering events before)
Ezra
Nehemiah
Esther

PROPHECY

Haggai
Zechariah
Malachi

NEW TESTAMENT

GOSPELS

Matthew
Mark
Luke
John

HISTORY

Acts

PAUL'S EPISTLES

Romans
1 Corinthians
2 Corinthians
Galatians
Ephesians
Philippians
Colossians
1 and 2 Thessalonians
1 and 2 Timothy
Titus
Philemon

GENERAL EPISTLES

Hebrews
James
1 and 2 Peter
1, 2, and 3 John
Jude

PROPHECY

Revelation

Finally, there is an abundance of *external evidence* that supports the Bible's inerrancy. When the Bible speaks on matters of history or science, it speaks accurately. There were times when it was supposed that science or history contradicted the Bible; however, later it was discovered that all the facts had not yet been uncovered.

More recent archaeological evidence has affirmed the historicity of the Bible in a multitude of ways as it speaks regarding rulers, nations, languages, battles, customs, geographic locations, tragedies, and other events. Extrabiblical writings also affirm what the New Testament teaches about the historicity of Jesus Christ and other New Testament characters.

Have you accepted the Bible as the inerrant Word of God, profitable for teaching, reproof, correction, and training in righteousness, that you may be adequate, equipped for every good work? (2 Timothy 3:16). As you study the Bible, you will discover that it is a supernatural book... the very words of life.

Major Events in Israel's History

The Word of God takes on new life when a person understands the major events in Israel's history between the years of Abraham and the birth of Christ. Old and New Testament prophecies regarding Israel and her relationship to various world powers are seen in a new dimension.

Once you are acquainted with the religious, cultural, and political setting of Bible times, you will better understand God's plan for mankind and you will have a greater appreciation of the times in which our Lord lived and gave birth to His church.

FROM ADAM TO ABRAHAM

(The Beginning to About 2000 B.C.)

In the beginning there was no sin. Adam and Eve lived in unbroken fellowship with their Creator until they believed a lie and chose to disobey the explicit command of God. From that time on all mankind would be born in sin and bear its consequence: death.

Yet a merciful and loving God did not leave mankind in despair; He promised a Redeemer, born of a woman's seed. With the passing of time man's iniquity increased until every intent of his heart was only evil. God was grieved in His heart and "sorry that He had made man." And with that He determined to "blot out man…from the face of the land." But Noah found favor in the eyes of the Lord, for he was a righteous man, blameless in his time.

When the flood came, only those in the ark were preserved: Noah and his family, eight people in all. However, the basic sin nature of those who survived had not changed, and it wasn't long before they too were in rebellion against God. And God knew that because they were one society and had the same language, nothing which they purposed to do would be impossible for them.

So once again God intervened, though this time He didn't destroy man from the face of the earth, for He had put a rainbow in the heavens and had made a covenant which He would not break. God intervened by confusing mankind's language and scattering them over the face of the whole earth.

Then around 2000 B.C. God called a man to leave Ur of the Chaldees and go to a land which He would show him. That man's name was Abram. From Abram God would not only make a great nation, but through him He would bless all the families of the earth. Thus God made a covenant with Abram and his descendants forever, and with that covenant He changed Abram's name to Abraham, "Father of a Multitude." With that covenant also came the promise of the land of Canaan as the eternal possession of Abraham's descendants.

The Seed that God promised Adam and Eve, the One who would redeem mankind, would come not only through the seed of the woman, but also through the loins of Abraham and his descendants, Isaac and Jacob. To Isaac would be born Jacob, and to Jacob 12 sons. As God confirmed His covenant with Jacob, He changed Jacob's name to Israel, the one who fathered the heads of the 12 tribes of Israel. A covenant nation had been brought into existence by God. In the fullness of time the Redeemer, the messenger of the covenant, would come from the tribe of Judah.

But all was not well among Jacob's sons, for they were jealous of Joseph, Jacob's favorite, his firstborn by Rachel. As they plotted to take Joseph's life, Reuben and Judah intervened, and Joseph was sold into slavery and taken to Egypt. While Joseph's brothers meant this for evil, God meant it for good. Joseph went from being a slave in Potiphar's house to being a vice-regent in Pharaoh's palace via a prison. In His sovereignty God used Joseph's position in

Egypt to deliver Israel's family from famine in Canaan. They lived in Egypt for 430 years, 400 of those years as slaves. Then around 1525 B.C. a son by the name of Moses was born to two of these Hebrew slaves.

FROM THE EXODUS UNDER MOSES TO THE MONARCHY UNDER SAUL

(1445 B.C. to 1051 B.C.)

About 80 years after the birth of Moses, the sons of Israel cried out to the God of Abraham, Isaac, and Jacob because of their great affliction. God heard their cry and appeared to Moses in a burning bush. The great I AM would deliver them from the house of bondage, from the land of Egypt, and take them to the land He promised to Abraham. Moses would serve as God's spokesman, as their human deliverer, and as the one to whom God would give the pattern for the tabernacle. In the tabernacle God would give the Israelites not only the means of worshiping Him, but a picture of the Redeemer who was yet to come.

After the Israelites wandered in the wilderness for 40 years because of their unbelief, Joshua took them across the Jordan River into the promised land. The people served the Lord all the days of Joshua and the elders, and then there arose a generation who did not know the Lord, and the children of Israel served the gods of the people of Canaan and did evil in the sight of the Lord. So the Lord delivered them into the hands of their enemies. But when the people cried out to the Lord in their distress, God raised up judges from among the people. And God was with each judge all the days of his life. But when the judge died, the cycle of sin and slavery repeated itself. There was no visible king in Israel and everyone did what was right in his own eyes. Israel was to be a theocracy, with God as King, but the people did not obey their God.

Finally, in the days of Samuel, the prophet and judge, the people insisted on having a king over them like the other nations. Although this request grieved Samuel, God gave them what they wanted, for they had rejected Him.

FROM UNITED KINGDOM TO DIVIDED KINGDOM

(1051 B.C. to 931 B.C.)

Saul, Israel's first king, gave God sacrifice rather than obedience, and so God raised up a man after His own heart. David, the son of Jesse from the tribe of Judah, was anointed by God to become king.

David reigned from 1011 to 971 B.C. During that time his passion was to build a permanent dwelling for God in Jerusalem, the city of David. God saw the intent of David's heart, but because David had been a man of war, the building of the temple would be the task of David's son and successor, Solomon, born to Bathsheba.

On the day when the ark of the covenant was brought into the temple and the temple was dedicated to the Lord, Solomon fell on his face before God and reminded Him of His covenant promises. Fire came from heaven and devoured the burnt offerings, and the glory of the Lord filled the temple.

But Solomon disobeyed God. He married foreign wives and set up their idols on high places in Jerusalem. When Solomon was old, his wives turned his heart away after other gods and his heart was not wholly devoted to serving God, as the heart of his father, David, had been.

After Solomon died, God tore the kingdom of Israel in two.

FROM 931 B.C. UNTIL THE BIRTH OF CHRIST

In 931 B.C. the tribes of Judah and Benjamin formed the southern kingdom of Judah, with Jerusalem as their capital. The remaining ten tribes formed the northern kingdom of Israel and eventually made Samaria their capital. The northern kingdom immediately began to worship idols, so by 722 B.C. God allowed the Assyrians to take them captive.

Although the southern kingdom was warned by the prophets of God that they too would go into captivity if they did not repent of their disobedience and idolatry, Judah did not listen. In 605 B.C., just before Nebuchadnezzar became king of Babylon, he attacked Jerusalem and took the king and some of his nobles captive to Babylon. Among them was Daniel (Daniel 1:1, 2). In 597 B.C. Nebuchadnezzar again attacked Judah, this time taking about 10,000 captives to Babylon, Ezekiel among them. Then in 586 B.C. Babylon, now the predominant world power, conquered Judah and destroyed not only the city of Jerusalem but the magnificent temple built by Solomon during his reign over Israel.

Separated from Jerusalem and their temple, the exiles established **synagogues** as a means of preserving their faith. The synagogues became centers of learning and worship where the Jews recited the **Shema** (Deuteronomy 6:4), read from the law and the prophets, prayed, and delivered messages.

Men trained in writing who recorded events and decisions were called **scribes.** They assumed the responsibility of copying, preserving, and even teaching the Word of God in the synagogues. By New Testament times the scribes were considered experts in interpreting and teaching the law and were referred to as lawyers.

Having experienced firsthand the cursings of disobedience as promised in the book of Deuteronomy, the exiled Jews seemed to gain a new respect and appreciation for the Word of God. They saw that God meant what He said and would not alter it even for His covenant people.

It was sometime after the kingdom divided and Judah went into captivity that the exiles became known as **men of Judah** or **Jews.**

The Persian Period
(539 to 331 B.C.)

When the Medes and the Persians conquered Babylon in 539 B.C., they became the predominant world power in Babylon's stead. Daniel 5 records this invasion.

More than 100 years before Cyrus (the king of Persia) was born, Isaiah prophesied that God would raise up Cyrus to perform His desire (Isaiah 44:28). Second Chronicles 36:22, 23 records the fulfillment of God's plan: Cyrus issued a decree allowing the exiles of Judah to return to Jerusalem and rebuild their temple. Just as Jeremiah had prophesied (Jeremiah 29:10; Daniel 9:2), exactly 70 years from the time of Babylon's first attack on Jerusalem, the Israelites returned to their land.

The group which returned is referred to in Scripture as the **remnant.** ***Diaspora***, the Greek word for scattering, became the term used to describe the Jews who remained in exile among the nations.

The book of Ezra records the return of the remnant and the building of the **second temple** during the time of Haggai and Zechariah. The book of Nehemiah records the rebuilding of the walls of Jerusalem. Nehemiah and Ezra were contemporaries. Ezra is referred to as a **scribe.**

The book of Malachi records the last Old Testament prophecy given by God. After this prophecy God did not inspire canonical Scripture again for 400 years.

This 400 years of silence which followed the book of Malachi is called the **intertestament period**. Although God was silent in that He did not speak through His prophets during this time, the events of these 400 years testify to the fulfillment of much that was written by Daniel the prophet.

These years could be divided into three periods: the Greek, the Maccabean, and the beginning of the Roman period.

The Greek Period
(331 to 165 B.C.)

The Greek period encompasses three different rulerships over Jerusalem.

Under Alexander the Great (331 to 323 B.C.)

As the Persian Empire grew and threatened the security of the city-states of Greece, Philip of Macedonia sought to consolidate Greece in an effort to resist attack from Persia.

In 336 B.C. Philip was murdered, and his son, Alexander, who was about 20 years old, became king. Within two years Alexander set out to conquer Persia, whose empire now extended westward as far as Asia Minor (modern-day Turkey).

Over the next two years Alexander conquered the territory from Asia Minor to Pakistan and to Egypt, which included the land of the Jews. Although the account is not universally accepted by other historians,

Josephus, a Jewish historian who lived about A.D. 37-100, wrote that as Alexander marched into Jerusalem he was met by Jaddua and other Jewish priests dressed in their priestly garments and by the people of Jerusalem wearing white robes.

In a dream Jaddua had been told to put wreaths on the city walls in order to greet Alexander. Alexander also had a dream which coincided with this event. When Alexander was escorted into Jerusalem and shown the prophecy in Daniel 8 which described the destruction of the Medo-Persian Empire by a large horn on a goat (which represented Greece), Alexander felt the prophecy pertained to him and offered the Jews whatever they wanted. Alexander treated the Jews well and did not harm Jerusalem or their rebuilt temple.

When Alexander built the city of Alexandria in Egypt, he encouraged many Jews to settle there in order to help populate the city. Whenever Alexander conquered an area he established Greek cities and colonies, bringing in his Greek culture, ideas, and language. His goal was to consolidate his empire through a common way of life and thinking which became known as **Hellenization**. **Koine Greek** became the common language in the countries ruled by Greece and continued to be the primary language of civilization through the time of Christ. The New Testament was written in Koine Greek.

Alexander and his war-weary army returned from the Indus River Valley to Babylon in 323 B.C. History tells us he sat down and wept because there were no more territories to conquer. He died in Babylon that year at the age of 33.

Because Alexander died without an appointed heir, his kingdom fell into chaos. After 22 years of struggle among his generals, it was divided among four of them: Lysimachus, Cassander, Ptolemy I Soter, and Seleucus I Nicator. (See chart below.)

Under the Ptolemies of Egypt (323 to 204 B.C.)

Ptolemy I Soter, who took Egypt, was given Jerusalem and Judea. The Jews fared well; they were allowed to govern themselves and practice their religion without interference. Under his leadership Jews were permitted to go to Egypt. Some Jews were invited to go to Alexandria and become scholars. The Ptolemies moved Egypt's capital from Memphis to Alexandria and made it the center of learning and commerce. There the Jews were encouraged to use the Greek library, at that time the most extensive and best in the world. As a result many were caught up in philosophy and logic and drank deeply from the cup of Hellenism.

It is believed that Ptolemy II Philadelphus commissioned the translation of the Pentateuch into the Koine Greek. The Greek translation of the entire Old Testament, eventually completed about 100 B.C., was referred to as the **Septuagint** (meaning 70), or abbreviated as the **LXX**. Many of the New Testament writers quoted from the Septuagint.

Other writings produced during this intertestament period are the **Apocrypha**, the **Pseudepigrapha**, and the **Qumran Scrolls** (also called the **Dead Sea Scrolls**). The **Apocrypha** are composed of a variety of writings, including apocalyptic, wisdom, and historical literature. It is from the apocryphal book of First Maccabees that historians gained insight into the period from the Maccabean revolt through the time of John Hyrcanus. The

The Division of Alexander the Great's Empire

Lysimachus	**Cassander**	**Ptolemy I Soter**	**Seleucus I Nicator**
took	took	took	took
Thrace and Bithynia	Macedonia	Egypt	Syria

Ptolemy I Soter and Seleucus I Nicator began a succession of competing dynasties for which the land of Israel became a pawn.

(see page 1427 for the chart showing these dynasties)

Apocrypha were included in the Septuagint, although they were not part of the Hebrew Scriptures.

The **Pseudepigrapha** are a collection of writings even more extensive than the Apocrypha, but scholars cannot entirely agree on which writings comprise this group. These writings are attributed to noted people such as Adam, Abraham, Enoch, Ezra, and Baruch—but scholars agree that these claims are not authentic.

The **Qumran** or **Dead Sea Scrolls** were manuscripts apparently written or copied between 200 B.C. and A.D. 70 by a Jewish religious sect called **Essenes**. The particular community of Essenes who lived close to the Dead Sea seem to have practiced celibacy and a strictly disciplined communal lifestyle, separating themselves from others. The Dead Sea Scrolls describe the lives and beliefs of this group which lived in the last two centuries before Christ; they also include the oldest known manuscripts of the Old Testament. The scrolls are so named because they were hidden and preserved in some caves near an archaeological excavation called Khirbet Qumran on the western side of the Dead Sea.

Under the Seleucid Kings of Syria (204 to 165 B.C.)

Those ruling Syria, referred to as the kings of the north in Daniel 11, wanted the beautiful land of Israel. When Antiochus III the Great conquered Ptolemy V Epiphanes of Egypt, Jerusalem and Judea were brought under Syrian dominance.

After gaining dominance over the Jews, Antiochus was defeated by the Romans and ended up having to pay Rome a large sum of money for a period of years. To make sure he complied, Rome held his son, Antiochus IV, hostage in Rome.

Antiochus III the Great was succeeded by his son Seleucus IV Philopator, who ruled from 187-175 B.C. In 175 B.C. Antiochus IV Epiphanes (the son who had been held hostage in Rome) usurped the throne by killing his brother. He ruled until 163 B.C. He was called *Epiphanes*, which means "manifest" or "splendid."

Until this period in Israel's history, the priesthood had been a matter of birthright and the office was held for life. However, during his reign Antiochus IV Epiphanes sold the priesthood to Jason, the brother of the high priest. Jason also paid Antiochus a high price in order to build a Greek gymnasium near the temple. During this time many Jews were lured into a Hellenistic way of life. All this brought a great conflict among the orthodox Jews and the "Hellenistic" Jews. During this period the land of Israel was referred to by different regions: Judea, Samaria, Galilee, Perea, and Trachonitis.

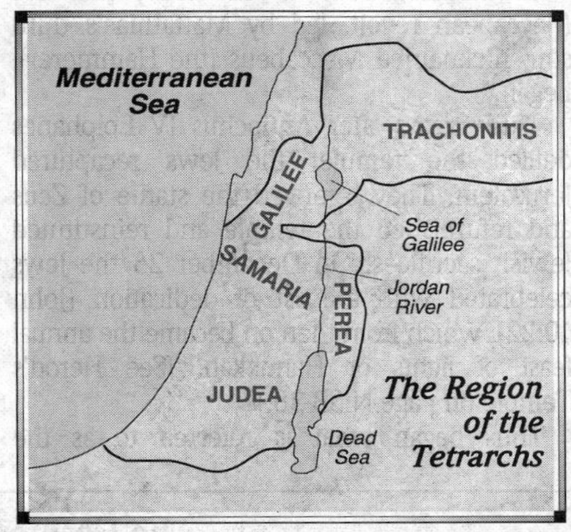

The Region of the Tetrarchs

The conflict was heightened when Antiochus IV Epiphanes sought to take the throne of Egypt but was rebuffed by Rome. Because of that and because of what he surmised as a revolt in the priesthood, Antiochus unleashed his anger on those Jews who wouldn't curry his favor or fully adopt Hellenism. He was determined to destroy Judaism. Circumcision was forbidden; those who disobeyed were put to death. Copies of the law were desecrated with heathen symbols or burned, while anyone found with a copy of the law was to be put to death. The Jews were also forbidden to celebrate the Sabbath. Then Antiochus sacrificed a pig on the altar in the temple and erected a statue of Zeus, an abomination of desolation, in the holy place (Daniel 11:31).

Finally, Antiochus sent his officers throughout the land to compel Jews to make sacrifices to Zeus.

The Maccabean Period
(165 to 63 B.C.)

When Antiochus IV Epiphanes's officer arrived in the village of Modein (which lies halfway between Jerusalem and Joppa) and commanded the aged priest Mattathias to make a sacrifice to Zeus, the officer didn't know it was the last official duty he would perform in his life. As Mattathias refused, a younger Jew stepped forward to take his place. When he did, a furious Mattathias plunged his knife not only into the Jewish volunteer but also into the Syrian officer. Mattathias fled with his five sons to the hills, and the Maccabean revolt, led by Mattathias's third son, nicknamed Maccabeus (the Hammerer), began.

Three years after Antiochus IV Epiphanes defiled the temple, the Jews recaptured Jerusalem. They removed the statue of Zeus and refurbished the temple and reinstituted Jewish sacrifices. On December 25 the Jews celebrated with a feast of dedication (John 10:22), which from then on became the annual feast of lights or Hanukkah. (See Herod's Temple on page NISB-38.)

Thus began what is referred to as the **Hasmonean Dynasty** as the descendants of Mattathias ruled Israel until Rome conquered Jerusalem in 63 B.C.

When Simon, the last surviving son of Mattathias, was murdered, Simon's son, John Hyrcanus, named himself priest and king. He ruled from 134-104 B.C. He destroyed the Samaritan temple on Mount Gerizim, and from that time on the Jews had no dealings with the Samaritans. After that Hyrcanus moved southeast and conquered the land of the Idumeans, who came from the ancient kingdom of Edom. The peoples of this land were given the choice of emigrating or converting to Judaism. This was the land of Herod the Great, who would someday become Rome's appointed king of the Jews.

During the reign of John Hyrcanus, the **Pharisees**, a religious sect of the Jews, arose from the Hasidim. The **Hasidim**, a militant religious community dedicated to the obedience of the law and the worship of God, began around 168 B.C. and was active during the Maccabean revolt. The word *Pharisee* means "separated one" and was probably used to describe these men because they separated themselves from the strong influence of

The Hasmonean Dynasty

Mattathias
Died 166/165 B.C.

John
Died 159 B.C.

Judas Maccabeus
Died 160 B.C.
(*called Maccabeus–the Hammerer*)
First leader of revolt

Simon
Led revolt
141-135 B.C.

Eleazar
Died 163 B.C.

Jonathan
Led revolt
160-141 B.C.

Judas
Died 134 B.C.

John Hyrcanus I
High priest and king, 134-104 B.C.

Mattathias
Died 134 B.C.

Judas Aristobulus I
Ruled 104-103 B.C.
married Salome Alexandra
murdered 103 B.C.

Alexander Jannaeus
High priest and king, 103-76 B.C.
married Salome Alexandra (Aristobulus's widow)
Salome ruled 76-67 B.C.

Antigonus

Hyrcanus II
High priest and governor, 63-40 B.C.,
died 30 B.C.

Aristobulus II
King 67-63 B.C.
died 49 B.C.
his granddaughter Miriam (Mariamne)
married Herod the Great

Hellenism. During New Testament times the majority of the scribes were Pharisees.

Doctrinally the Pharisees viewed the entire Old Testament as authoritative; however, they also accepted the oral tradition as equally authoritative. To the Pharisee, to study the law was true worship. They believed in life after death, the resurrection, and the existence of angels and demons. Although the Pharisees taught that the way to God was through keeping the law, they were more liberal in their interpretation of the law than were the Sadducees. The Pharisees represented the largest religious sect, but their numbers declined when they fell into John Hyrcanus's disfavor.

The **Sadducees**, a smaller religious sect comprised mostly of the upper classes, were often of the priestly line and were usually more wealthy than the Pharisees. For the most part the Pharisees were of the middle-class merchants and tradesmen. The Sadducees accepted only the **Torah** (the first five books of the Old Testament) as authoritative. While they were rigid in the observance of the law and held to its literal interpretation, they denied divine providence, the resurrection, life after death, the existence of angels and demons, and any reward or punishment after death. They opposed the oral law as obligatory or binding and were materialistic.

The Sadducees controlled the temple and its services. However, because the Sadducees leaned toward Hellenism, they were unpopular with the majority of the Jewish populace.

Aristobulus I, who succeeded his father, John Hyrcanus, married Salome Alexandra. However, when Aristobulus died, Salome married his brother Alexander Jannaeus, who became high priest and king in 103 B.C. This marriage created many enemies for Alexander Jannaeus because the high priest was to marry only a virgin.

When he died in 76 B.C., his wife, Salome Alexandra, took the throne, but as a woman she could not hold the office of high priest, so her oldest son, Hyrcanus II, assumed that position.

Civil war broke out when Salome died, because her younger son, Aristobulus II, who was supported by the Sadducees, sought to take the throne from Hyrcanus II. He was willing to give up that position, but Antipater (an Idumean and the father of Herod the Great) befriended Hyrcanus and persuaded him to seek outside help in order to regain his position as the rightful heir. Hyrcanus's forces came against Aristobulus and defeated him. He had to flee and made the temple in Jerusalem his fortress, but he was besieged by Hyrcanus's forces.

Early in this period the Hasmoneans had made a treaty with Rome in order to keep Syria, their northern neighbors, in check. Now the Roman army under Scaurus was in Syria because Seleucid rule had collapsed. Scaurus heard about the civil war in Judea and went there. Both Aristobulus and Hyrcanus sought his help. Scaurus sided with Aristobulus and had the siege lifted from Jerusalem, but the fighting continued. An appeal was made to the Roman general Pompey, who said he would settle the dispute and urged them to keep peace until he arrived. However, Aristobulus went back to Jerusalem to prepare resistance, which caused Rome's support to turn to Hyrcanus. Pompey arrived and took Aristobulus and his family captive, besieging the city for three months.

The Period of Roman Rule

(63 B.C. to A.D. 70)

In 63 B.C. Pompey conquered Jerusalem and with some of his soldiers walked into the holy of holies. Although they didn't touch any of the furnishings, they alienated the Jews, who never forgave Pompey. About 12,000 Jews died during this Roman siege of Jerusalem, a supposed attempt to settle a civil war.

Rome broke up the Hasmonean dynasty and their territory. Judea was now reduced to smaller borders and its independence lost. It was now a territory of Rome. Hyrcanus II could be the rightful priest but not king. He was now under the governor of Syria, a Roman province. Scaurus was appointed governor. Aristobulus and many Jews were taken to Rome. Not much later Gabinius, a Roman governor of Syria, took control. He entrusted the temple to Hyrcanus and changed the government of Judea.

The Jewish state was divided into five districts governed by a council that remained under the jurisdiction of the governor of Syria; Hyrcanus, the high priest, was made ruler over Jerusalem. Antipater was his chief magistrate.

The high priest presided over the **Sanhedrin**, a 71-member council comprised of both Sadducees and Pharisees, which governed the Jews under the authority of Rome. Although the Sanhedrin seemed to have autonomy in the matters of the civil and criminal government of the Jews, apparently the Sanhedrin was not allowed to put people to death without the permission of the Roman procurator. The Sanhedrin is often referred to as "the council" in the Gospels and Acts.

In 55 B.C. three men—Pompey, Crassus (the governor of Syria), and Julius Caesar—controlled Rome. Crassus, considering himself another Alexander the Great, set out to conquer the world. However, just before this he stole the treasures from the temple in Jerusalem. Crassus and his army were later destroyed by the Parthians.

Parthia, southeast of the Caspian Sea and part of the Persian Empire, had been conquered by Alexander the Great. But Rome would not conquer them until A.D. 114.

After Crassus's death, Julius Caesar took Italy and then set out to destroy Pompey. Pompey fled to Egypt, where he was assassinated. During this time Antipater supported Caesar, so out of gratitude Caesar gave him the official title of Procurator of Judea.

Antipater made his son Phasael governor of Judea and his son Herod governor of Galilee. Hyrcanus II remained high priest, although Antipater and his two sons robbed him of his authority.

In 44 B.C. Caesar was murdered by Brutus and Cassius. Civil war broke out in Rome. Cassius took control of the east. Because of the instability of Rome, Hyrcanus's rivals made a bid for power.

Antipater was murdered in 43 B.C. Antigonus, Aristobulus's son (who was supported by the Parthians), invaded the country.

At that time Herod came to the aid of Hyrcanus, who out of gratitude gave Herod a beautiful woman named Miriam. They were not married until five years later.

After that Brutus and Cassius were defeated by Mark Antony and Caesar's nephew Octavian (who would later become Caesar Augustus). Mark Antony became ruler of the east. In 40 B.C., when the Parthians invaded the region, Herod fled to Rome.

That year, at the urging of Antony and Octavian, Herod was made king of the Jews. It took him three years to rid the area of the Parthians and establish his rule in Judea. Just before laying siege to Jerusalem, Herod married Miriam (also called Mariamne), hoping that his marriage into the Hasmonean family would make him more acceptable to the Jews.

In 20 B.C. Herod began rebuilding the temple. The one built by Zerubbabel after the Babylonian exile was so pitifully small in comparison to the first temple that Herod was determined to make it larger and more magnificent than Solomon's. Although the temple itself was completed in a year-and-a-half, the construction and decoration of its outer courts continued for years, so in A.D. 26 the Jews would say, "It took forty-six years to build this temple" (John 2:20).

Herod, whose people (the Idumeans) had been forced to convert to Judaism under John Hyrcanus, was only a Jew in practice when he lived in Judea. Although Rome gave Herod the title "King of the Jews," he was never accepted by those he ruled over.

Then "in the days of Herod the king, magi from the east arrived in Jerusalem, saying, 'Where is He who has been born King of the Jews?'" (Matthew 2:1, 2).

The true King had come…the Ruler who would shepherd God's people Israel (Matthew 2:6).

Herod died in 4 B.C. But those living in Judea and Galilee saw a great light and heard with their own ears the voice of God, the King of kings.

The 400 years of silence had been broken.

Why Jesus' Birth Is Shown as 4 B.C.

The designation of years as A.D. or B.C. did not begin until the sixth century, and was not widely adopted until the eighth century. This designation was created by a highly regarded scholar named Dionysius Exiguus, who was skilled in mathematics, astronomy, and theology. Dionysius was born in Scythia, and went to Rome in 496. In the year 523, the papal chancellor Bonifatius (under Pope John I) asked Dionysius to compile a table of the dates of Easter. An existing table that covered the nineteen-year period denoted 228-247 counted the years from the beginning of the reign of the Roman emperor Diocletian, which was the custom of the time. Rather than honor Diocletian, the persecutor of Christians, Dionysius fixed the birth of Christ relative to Diocletian's reign in such a manner that it fell on 25 December (or 25 March) in the 753rd year since the founding of Rome. Thus he designated these same 19 years as *Anno Domini Nostri Jesu Christi* 532-550. Thus, Dionysius's *Anno Domini* 532 is equivalent to *Anno Diocletian* 248. Under Dionysius's scheme of dating, the year starting one week after the birth of Christ was year 1 of the era "of the Lord," or *Anno Domini* 1. According to Dionysius's calculations, A.D. 1 would have been the year of our Lord's birth. There is no "zero" year, so the preceding year is 1 B.C. (before Christ).

Research since Dionysius's time, however, indicates Christ must have been born earlier than A.D. 1. We know from the book of Matthew that Jesus was born under the reign of Herod the Great. History confirms that Herod the Great died in the year we now call 4 B.C., which means Jesus could not have been born any later than that. There is no universally accepted year of Christ's birth, but 4 B.C. is a frequently used figure, and it's the date used in all the timelines in *The New Inductive Study Bible.*

FROM CHRIST TO MODERN TIMES

Many Jewish leaders were religious, but they did not know God. When Jesus came to explain the Father, they rejected Him. They rejected God's precious cornerstone. Consequently, once again they would be banished from their land.

Jesus warned, "When you see Jerusalem surrounded by armies, then recognize that her desolation is near....for there will be great distress upon the land and wrath to this people; and they will fall by the edge of the sword, and will be led captive into all the nations; and Jerusalem will be trampled under foot by the Gentiles until the times of the Gentiles are fulfilled" (Luke 21:20, 23, 24). God had spoken. Had the people listened, they wouldn't have been caught unawares—but they refused to hear.

The Destruction of Jerusalem (A.D. 70)

The conflict between the Jews and their Roman ruler intensified. Tacitus, the Roman historian, said the Jews put up with things until the procuratorship of Gessius Florus. When the Jews rose up against Florus's army, war became inevitable. Nero commanded T. Flavius Vespasian to subdue the Jews. Vespasian reduced the Galilee and secured Judea, except for Jerusalem, Masada, and two other fortresses.

During this time, Nero committed suicide and civil war broke out in Rome. Galba, Otho, and Vitellius succeeded one another as emperor. Then the eastern legions of Rome proclaimed Vespasian emperor, and Vitellius was murdered. Vespasian put his son Titus in charge of the war and sailed for Rome. In A.D. 70 Titus besieged Jerusalem. Over one million Jews died in five months. On August 6, the ninth of Ab, Roman forces invaded the temple and, just as Jesus prophesied, not one stone was left upon the other. Jerusalem was burned. Titus went to Rome to celebrate his victory with his father.

Although some of the Jews fled to Masada, the Jewish state no longer existed. Sometime between A.D. 72-74 Masada fell to the Roman governor Flavius Silva.

Hadrian and Aelia Capitolina

In A.D. 132 the Emperor Hadrian banned circumcision and the observance of the Sabbath. He also made plans to build a temple to Zeus. These actions spurred Simon bar Kochba to lead another revolt. After Hadrian crushed the Bar Kochba revolt, Hadrian rebuilt Jerusalem in A.D. 136, named it Aelia Capitolina, and forbade the Jews entrance to the city on pain of death. That edict was enforced for about 500 years.

The Byzantine Period
(A.D. 324 to 638)

In A.D. 324 Constantine became sole emperor of Rome. In A.D. 330 the capital was moved from Rome to Byzantium, which was renamed Constantinople (present-day Istanbul, Turkey) in his honor. According to some traditions, Constantine became a Christian after seeing a vision of a cross and hearing the words, "By this sign thou shalt conquer." What is fact is that he proclaimed Christianity as the official religion of the Roman Empire.

Constantine's mother, the empress Helena, began restoring the city of David (Jerusalem), locating Christian sites and building shrines over the places associated with Christianity. Helena and the city's bishop, Macarius, built the Church of the Holy Sepulchre on the site where they believed Jesus had been buried. Byzantine churches could be seen across the land. By the fifth century the Roman Empire divided and the eastern half became the Byzantine Empire, with its capital in Constantinople. Rome became the capital of the western Roman Empire.

In the fifth century the Jews were permitted to pray on the temple mount on Tisha B'Av, the anniversary of the destruction of the temple. By the middle of this century Jerusalem was recognized as a patriarchal territory equal in status to Constantinople, Alexandria, Rome, and Antioch.

In A.D. 614 the Persians conquered the land, massacred the people, and destroyed the churches. In A.D. 629 the Byzantine emperor Heraclius reconquered Jerusalem.

The Early Muslim Period
(A.D. 638 to 1099)

Nine years later the Muslims were ruling. During this time Christians and Jews were permitted to worship freely. Jews returned to Jerusalem. The Umayyad dynasty reigned from 660-750. The prophet Mohammed's journey from Mecca to Jerusalem on his winged horse Al-buraq was linked to the temple mount, thus making it a holy site for the Muslims. In the seventh century, Caliph Abd al-Malik commissioned the building of the mosque, the Dome of the Rock, on the temple mount. Thus Jerusalem became the third-holiest city for Islam. The Arabs built only one new city, Ramle, which Suleiman made his capital in the eighth century.

The Crusader Period
(A.D. 1099 to 1244)

In 1099, at Pope Urban II's appeal, the Crusaders crossed Europe to liberate the Christian holy places from the Muslims. The city was theirs after a five-week siege. Jerusalem became the capital of the Crusader kingdom. European Christian noblemen and bourgeoisie came to settle in Jerusalem. Mosques were turned into churches, and new churches and monasteries were built. For the next 88 years, Jews and Muslims were not permitted to live in Jerusalem, but only visit it.

The Ayyubid Interlude
(A.D. 1187 to 1192)

In 1187 Saladin, the founder of the Ayyubid dynasty, took Jerusalem, destroyed the cross on top of the Dome of the Rock, and turned churches into mosques. The Jews were now allowed to return to Jerusalem. They came from North Africa, France, and England to settle alongside the Jews of Jerusalem.

Then in 1192 Richard the Lion Hearted and Phillipe Auguste of France restored the Crusader kingdom which had been conquered by Saladin. Jerusalem was divided. The temple mount and its mosques remained in Muslim hands while the other parts of the city came under Christian rule. In 1244 the Crusaders lost the city.

The Mamluk Period
(A.D. 1260 to 1517)

In 1260 Jerusalem was conquered by the Mamluks, military regiments from central Asia who were the new rulers of Egypt. The Mamluks established **madrasas** (institutes of religious instruction) and hostels for Muslim scholars and pilgrims.

The Ottoman Period
(A.D. 1517 to 1917)

The Ottoman Empire, comprised of Constantinople, Asia Minor, parts of Europe and the Balkans, Egypt, and Syria, added Israel and Judea in 1517. Jerusalem was taken from the Mamluks by Ottoman Turks. Sultan Suleiman the Magnificent had the walls which still surround Jerusalem built at this time. After his death the Jewish community became more firmly entrenched as they built the Jewish quarter along the Zion Gate. Jewish scholastic centers were established in Jerusalem and Safed. The Christians split into various eastern communities.

In 1832 the Pasha of Egypt, Mohammed Ali, denuded the Holy Land of trees as he set out to build his ships. However, his approval of Christian missions and schools, foreign consulates, and archaeological expeditions opened up Jerusalem to Western influence. In the late 1800s a political movement called Zionism sprang up in Europe. Its goal was to create a homeland for Jewish people. Jews fleeing eastern Europe and Russia and arriving in Abraham's land were quick to adopt Theodor Herzl's vision for a free state for Jews. In 1897, the first Zionist Congress was held.

The British Mandate
(A.D. 1917 to 1948)

Four hundred years of Ottoman rule came to an end on December 9, 1917. Two days later British Field Marshal Allenby entered the Citadel and Jerusalem was pronounced the capital of the country. The Balfour Declaration promised the establishment of a national home for the Jews. In 1920 and 1929 Jews and Arabs had violent clashes. The Arabs rebelled in 1936-1939, and open war erupted as Arabs and Jews fought for control over Jerusalem.

From 1939 to 1945 six million Jews were systematically murdered under the direction of Adolf Hitler. After World War II, world opinion strongly favored the establishment of a Jewish homeland. By November 1947 the tension between Jews and Arabs was so great the United Nations decided to intervene, end the Mandate, and make Jerusalem an international city. The United Nations voted 33 to 13 to partition the country west of the Jordan River into two parts—one for Arabs, one for Jews. The Jews agreed, but the Arabs rejected the plan.

The State of Israel
(May 14, 1948)

On May 14, 1948, when the British withdrew, the Jews proclaimed the independent State of Israel. The next day Israel was attacked by Iraq, Lebanon, Syria, Jordan, and Egypt. By December Israel won its independence. Jordanian soldiers, however, remained in the West Bank (biblical Judea and Samaria). Egypt held the Gaza Strip. When a cease-fire was declared in January 1949, the city was divided. Jordan held all the shrines encompassed by Suleiman's walls; the old city of Jerusalem was out-of-bounds for the Jews.

Israel prepared for the influx of more than 800,000 immigrants from 102 countries during the next seven years. Living conditions were austere, but the Jews were home! By 1957 the malarial swamps of the Hula Valley were drained and the waters of the Sea of Galilee flowed south through pipelines, bringing life to the arid Negev.

The Sinai Campaign
(1956)

In 1956 Israel executed a swift victory over Egypt in the Sinai Campaign. On the guarantee of freedom of navigation in the Straits of Tiran and the Gulf of Elath, Israel withdrew her troops from the Sinai. Then later, once again, Egyptian troops moved to Israel's borders.

The Six-Day War
(1967)

The Six-Day War broke out on June 5, 1967. During that war Israel gained control of Judea, Samaria, the Golan Heights, Gaza, and the Sinai peninsula, and reunited Jerusalem under Jewish sovereignty for the first time since the Bar Kochba revolt, more than 1800 years earlier. The Jews could finally weep at the holy wall of Jerusalem, the western wall of the sacred temple mount.

The Yom Kippur War
(1973)

In 1973, on Yom Kippur, the highest of holy days, Israel was attacked on the Golan Heights by Syria and across the Suez Canal and into Sinai by Egypt. After three weeks the Israeli defense forces finally drove the attackers back. Disengagement agreements were signed between Israel and Egypt and between Israel and Syria.

The Peace Treaty Between Israel and Egypt
(1979)

In March of 1979 Israel and Egypt signed a historic peace treaty returning the Sinai to Egypt.

On June 6, 1982, Israel launched Operation Peace for Galilee in order to remove from Lebanese territory the Palestine Liberation Organization's threat to its northern settlements.

The Middle East Gulf War
(1991)

In January 1991, when war broke out between Iraq and a coalition of nations headed by the United States of America, Iraq responded with missile attacks on Israel—although Israel was not part of the conflict and remained out of the conflict at the United States's urging. The Middle East Gulf Crisis came to an end approximately six weeks later.

The Peace Treaty Between Israel and the PLO
(1993)

In September 1993, Israel and the Palestine Liberation Organization (PLO) signed an agreement in which Israel was to give administrative control of the Gaza Strip and portions of the West Bank to the PLO by May 4, 1999, in exchange for peace. An armed Palestinian police force was to replace the Israeli Defense Forces to ensure continued security in the regions, Israel was to release some prisoners, and the PLO was to arrest terrorists who acted against Israel. Since the signing of this agreement (known as the Oslo Accord because it was negotiated in Oslo, Norway), the scheduled withdrawal of Israeli forces has proceeded more slowly than planned, and terrorism against Israeli citizens has not ended.

The words of Leviticus 25:23 seem poignant in our day: "The land, moreover, shall not be sold permanently, for the land is Mine; for you are but aliens and sojourners with Me."

The words of Zechariah the prophet remain unfulfilled, but because of all that is transpiring, they are read with new insight and great anticipation:

> *Behold, a day is coming for the LORD when the spoil taken from you will be divided among you. For I will gather all the nations against Jerusalem to battle, and the city will be captured, the houses plundered, the women ravished, and half of the city exiled, but the rest of the people will not be cut off from the city. Then the LORD will go forth and fight against those nations, as when He fights on a day of battle.*
>
> *In that day His feet will stand on the Mount of Olives, which is in front of Jerusalem on the east; and the Mount of Olives will be split in its middle from east to west by a very large valley, so that half of the mountain will move toward the north and the other half toward the south....*
>
> *Then the LORD, my God, will come, and all the holy ones with Him!...*
>
> *And the LORD will be king over all the earth; in that day the LORD will be the only one, and His name the only one* (Zechariah 14:1-4, 5, 9).
>
> *Amen. Come, Lord Jesus* (Revelation 22:20).

Historical and Grammatical Helps

The information in this section will provide you with additional tools for your inductive study of God's Word.

Take some time to familiarize yourself with the basic content of each part of this section so you will know what is at your fingertips when you need it.

THE ARK OF THE COVENANT

The one piece of furniture that is the most holy to the Jews is the ark of the covenant. The following information will help you understand why it is so important to them and why Orthodox Jews are still looking for it.

The ark, a box about 4 feet long by 2 1/2 feet wide by 2 1/2 feet high, was constructed of acacia wood and overlaid with gold inside and out. Because it symbolized God's presence, no one was allowed to touch it. Four gold rings were attached to the feet of the ark. Poles, made of acacia wood and overlaid with gold, were slipped through these rings so that the ark could be carried from place to place (Exodus 25:10-22). Only the Kohathites (a division of the Levites) were allowed to move the ark.

When the ark was in the tabernacle the cloud of God's presence hovered over the mercy seat (Leviticus 16:2; 1 Samuel 4:4). The mercy seat, made of pure gold with a gold cherub attached at each end, covered the ark of the covenant. On the day of atonement the high priest sprinkled the blood of sacrifice on the mercy seat as a covering for the sins of the people. (The Hebrew word for mercy is *kapporeth*, a covering.)

Inside the ark was the testimony, the stone tablets bearing the ten commandments (Exodus 40:20; Deuteronomy 10:2). For a period of time the ark also contained Aaron's rod which budded (Numbers 17:10) and a gold jar of manna (Hebrews 9:4).

The tabernacle, where the ark resided in the most holy place, and the furniture were made according to the pattern of God's throne in heaven. God gave Moses this pattern when He instructed him to build the tabernacle (Hebrews 8:1-5).

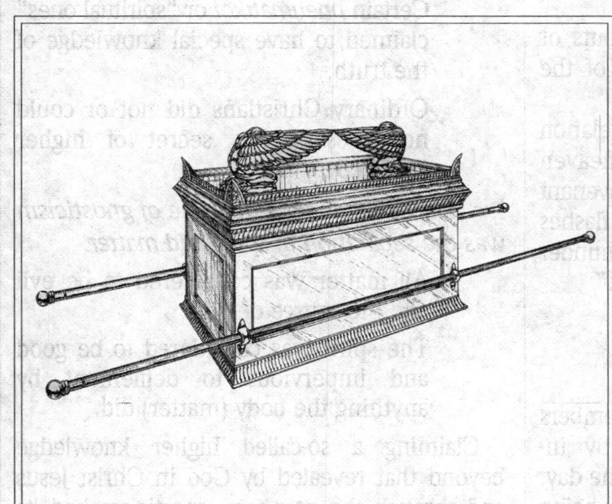

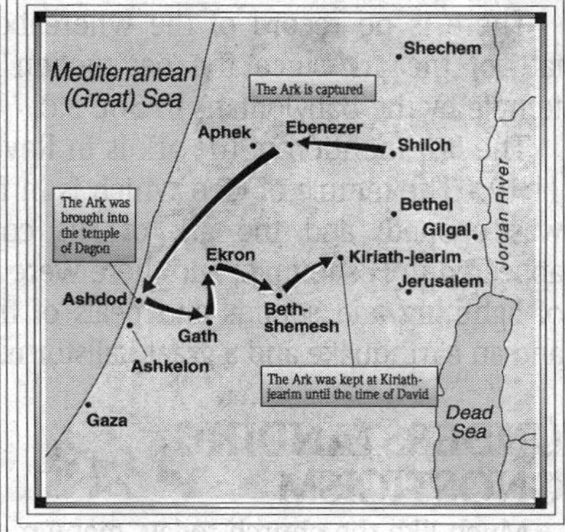

The Wanderings of the Ark

The ark journeyed before the children of Israel as they moved from Sinai to Canaan. It went before them as they crossed the Jordan River and conquered Jericho. It rested at Gilgal, Shechem, Bethel, and Shiloh. Then the Philistines at Ebenezer captured it and kept it for seven months. They took it to Aphek, Ashdod, Gath, and Ekron. From Ekron they sent it back and it ended up in Beth-shemesh. It was at Beth-shemesh that some people were killed because they looked into the ark. From there the ark was taken to Kiriath-jearim (Gibeath) and the house of Abinadab.

When David became king he wanted to move the ark to Jerusalem. The Israelites broke God's command by moving it on a cart rather than carrying it by the poles. When the ark started to fall off the cart, a man named Uzzah touched the ark and was killed by God. This incident occurred on the threshing floor of Nacon (also referred to as Chidon) (2 Samuel 6:6, 7; 1 Chronicles 13:9). The ark remained in the house of Obed-edom the Gittite, a Philistine from Gath, for three months until David had the Kohathites move it to Jerusalem. There the ark was placed in the midst of a tent (2 Chronicles 1:4).

When Solomon became king and built the temple, the ark was moved from the tent in Jerusalem to the temple, which was built on the threshing floor of Ornan (1 Chronicles 21:18; 2 Chronicles 3:1). There the ark was placed in the most holy place (1 Kings 8:6; 2 Chronicles 5:2-14).

There is no record of the whereabouts or fate of the ark since the destruction of the temple by the Babylonians in 586 B.C.

The last mention of the ark is in Revelation 11:19: "The temple of God which is in heaven was opened; and the ark of His covenant appeared in His temple, and there were flashes of lightning and sounds and peals of thunder and an earthquake and a great hailstorm."

UNDERSTANDING GNOSTICISM

Much like the church today, many members of the early church were significantly influenced by a prevailing philosophy of the day. While some of the New Testament was being written, the church in Asia was being threatened by gnosticism, a philosophy which became the major opponent of the gospel in the early apostolic church.

A familiarity with the teachings of gnosticism will give you a greater understanding of and appreciation for some of the warnings and teachings given in the epistles.

Many members of the early church were seeking enlightenment, and were easily deceived by Gnostic teachers and led astray from the simplicity and purity of devotion to Christ. Some had apparently left the church to form their own community, teaching a different gospel from what the apostles had preached. This movement away from the church caused those who remained to question what was true, and thus confusion crept in.

The term *gnosticism* comes from the Greek word *gnosis*, meaning "knowledge." Gnosticism is a philosophy which centers on a search for higher knowledge. The Gnostics taught that this knowledge was not intellectual knowledge but a knowledge which the ordinary Christian was incapable of attaining. Once a believer came into possession of this extraordinary knowledge, according to Gnostic thought, he had "salvation."

Although Gnostic philosophy took many strange and divergent turns, two axioms were basic to its teaching:

❧ *The first major Gnostic doctrine was the supremacy of knowledge.*

> Certain *pneumatikoi* or "spiritual ones" claimed to have special knowledge of the truth.
>
> Ordinary Christians did not or could not possess this secret of higher knowledge.

❧ *The second major doctrine of gnosticism was the separation of spirit and matter.*

> All matter was considered to be evil and the source of evil.
>
> The spirit was considered to be good and impervious to defilement by anything the body (matter) did.

Claiming a so-called higher knowledge beyond that revealed by God in Christ Jesus and through the prophets, gnosticism had its origins in the philosophies of the Greeks and the Romans, in the creeds of Plato and Philo, and in the religions of the East, especially those of Persia and India. As long as Christianity kept its Judaic roots, it was free from these heresies. However, when Christianity spread to Gentile territory, an attempt was made on the part of Eastern philosophical religion to form an alliance with it.

Many Gnostics allegorized the Old Testament and did not interpret its teachings literally. They strayed from the veracity of the Word, which would have exposed their erroneous teaching regarding creation, sin, and the restoration of all things. They failed to see how a supreme God, pure in spirit and essentially good, could create a universe of matter which they considered evil.

When the Gnostics embraced Christianity, they split into factions on the subject of Christ's deity. Two of the major factions taught as follows:

❧ The Docetic Gnostics denied the humanity of Jesus. The word *docetic* comes from the Greek word *dokeō*, "to seem." According to the Docetists, it was impossible for God, who was spirit and good, to become flesh, which was matter and evil, in the person of Jesus Christ. They believed that Jesus was a phantom; He didn't possess a real flesh-and-blood body. He only seemed to have a body.

❧ The Cerinthian Gnostics (followers of Cerinthus) separated the man Jesus from the *aeon*, the power of Christ. They believed that when the dove came on Jesus at His baptism, the power of Christ came and rested on the man Jesus. This power then departed before His death on the cross. So it was simply the "man" Jesus who died, not Jesus Christ, God in the flesh.

These Gnostic heresies denied that God became man and walked this earth in the person of Jesus Christ to bring redemption and salvation to mankind. Having eliminated Jesus Christ as the only way to God, the Gnostics believed they could make their own way to God through their inquiry and knowledge. Faith and one's deeds were viewed as having no significance in salvation or the life of a believer.

Understanding the basis of gnosticism and the forms of thought that it took in the early days of the Christian church will enable you to better understand the doctrinal heresy which some of the New Testament writers addressed.

GUIDELINES FOR INTERPRETING PREDICTIVE PROPHECY

From Genesis to Revelation the Bible is filled with prophecy. If you want to handle the prophecies in the Word of God accurately, the following guidelines will give you some important parameters.

The Greek word for prophecy, *propheteia*, comes from two Greek words, *pro*, meaning "forth," and *phēmi*, meaning "to speak." It means to speak forth the mind and counsel of God. According to this definition, all Scripture is in a sense prophecy.

Predictive prophecy points to a future fulfillment and is of divine origin. In *Understanding and Applying the Bible: Revised and Expanded,* Dr. Robertson McQuilkin says: "There are two purposes for predictive prophecy. The chief purpose is to affect the conduct of those who hear the prophecy. Another purpose is met only when the prophecy is fulfilled. That purpose is to build faith, to establish confidence in the God who miraculously foretold events (John 13:19; 14:29; 16:4)" (p. 281).

Some scholars divide predictive prophecy into two categories: forthtelling and foretelling. Forthtelling prophecies contain a message about the present or immediate time. (Often this is a call to godly living in the light of prophecy yet to be fulfilled.) Foretelling prophecies contain a message about what God will do in the future.

When a prophet spoke for God, the prophecy could refer to the following:

- a present or near fulfillment
- a future fulfillment
- a twofold fulfillment: a near fulfillment and then a later, future fulfillment

As you read the prophecies of the Bible, keep in mind the following guidelines and discern whether the prophecy refers to:

- the prophet's own time and/or a future time

- the captivity and/or restoration of Israel or Judah
- the first coming of Christ and any events connected with it
- the second coming of Christ
- the last days or end times

❧ *As you study prophecy, it is important to remember that the prophets did not always indicate intervals of time between events, nor did they always write their prophecies in chronological order.* For example, an Old Testament prophecy could include the first and second comings of Christ without any indication of the time span between the two comings. One such prophecy is found in Isaiah 65:17-25. In this prophecy, Isaiah first talks about the new heavens and the new earth (in which we know there is no death), and then in verses 18-25 he refers to a time when a youth dies at age 100 and the wolf and lamb lie down together. Chronologically, verse 17 will be fulfilled *after* verses 18-25 become a reality.

❧ *Always approach a prophecy as literal (in its usual, ordinary meaning) unless one of the following occurs:*

- The grammatical context shows that it is figurative language by the use of similes, metaphors, parables, allegories, symbols, or types.
- A literal interpretation violates common sense, is contrary to what the author is saying, or is contrary to what the rest of Scripture teaches.

❧ *When a prophetic passage cannot be taken literally, look for what the author is trying to convey through his figurative or symbolic language.* To discern what the author is saying, look for answers in the following places:

- within the context of the book in which the passage appears
- in any other writings of that author
- in any other prophetic writings to which the author had access (for example, other prophetic books or passages in the Word of God)

❧ *Remember that often when a prophet refers to future events, he does not use the future tense.*

❧ *When you interpret Scripture, consider the historical context of that writing, remembering that God was delivering His prophecy to a particular people at a particular time.* Granted, it might have been a prophecy with a future fulfillment, but it would still be delivered in a way that was comprehensible to those receiving that prophecy—even though they might not understand the details, the symbolism, or the full implications of the prophecy.

Make a careful historical and cultural analysis of the text. Determine the identity of all historical events, proper names, and geographical locations before you attempt to interpret the text.

❧ *Remember that the meaning of a specific prophecy could not always be understood by*

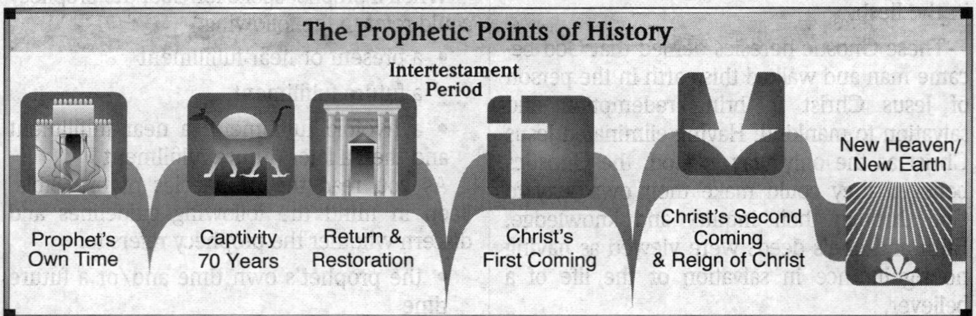

the prophet or by the people who heard the message. For example, Daniel could not understand what he had written, since it was to remain sealed until the end time (Daniel 12:8, 9).

However, many prophecies will come to light through the following:

a fulfillment as recorded in history

a fulfillment as recorded in the New Testament

an explanation given by an Old Testament or a New Testament writing (for example, Acts 4:24-28)

❧ *Remember that many New Testament prophecies include Old Testament quotations and allusions.* Scholars estimate that at least 350 Old Testament quotations or allusions appear in the book of Revelation alone. Revelation is replete with the language of Isaiah, Jeremiah, Ezekiel, Daniel, and the minor prophets. It is obvious that the author of Revelation was steeped in the Old Testament, for he talks in Old Testament phraseology. So to correctly interpret New Testament prophecy, check Old Testament cross-references.

❧ *When you study prophecy, watch for phrases which indicate periods of time.* For example, look for *in the last days, day of the Lord, day of wrath,* and *end of the age.* When you come across phrases such as these, carefully observe the things which occur during that particular time period. Then ask the following questions:

- Have these events ever occurred in history?
- Do these events coincide with any other particular period of time?
- Do these events parallel any events mentioned in another place in the Word of God?

FIGURES OF SPEECH

Although the Bible is to be interpreted literally, it is important to remember that, as with other writings, it contains figures of speech which must be interpreted for what they are and in the light of their intended purpose. As you seek to handle the Word of God accurately, you will find it helpful to understand the definitions of the different types of figures of speech.

A *figure of speech* is a word, a phrase, or an expression used in an imaginative rather than a literal sense.

Discerning the use of figures of speech is important in biblical interpretation. For example, there has been much controversy in the church over Jesus' statement regarding the bread at the Last Supper: "When He had taken some bread and given thanks, He broke it and gave it to them, saying, 'This is My body which is given for you'" (Luke 22:19). Some believe that the bread actually becomes His body (the doctrine of transubstantiation); others believe that Jesus was simply using a metaphor and that the bread is representative of His body.

Three principles for dealing with figurative language are:

- Identify the fact that the author is using figurative language.
- Identify the type of figurative language in use: simile, metaphor, hyperbole, and so on.
- Follow the guidelines for interpreting what the author meant by his use of that particular figure of speech.

You will be aided in your study of Scripture if you are able to identify when the author is using a figure of speech. The following are brief definitions of the types of figurative language used in the Bible.

❧ A *metaphor* is an implied comparison between two things which are different. In a metaphor the words of comparison—*like, as, as...so is,* and *such as*—are *not* used. An example is John 6:48, where Jesus says, "I am the bread of life."

❧ A *simile* is an expressed comparison of two different things or ideas that uses the words *like, as, as...so is,* and/or *such as.* An example is Revelation 1:14b, "His eyes were like a flame of fire."

❧ *Hyperbole* is a deliberate exaggeration for effect or emphasis. Hyperboles are found in all languages, and they are frequently used among Semitic peoples. For example, "My soul is crushed with longing" (Psalm 119:20).

❧ *Metonymy* is used when the name of one object or concept is used for that of another to which it is related. This is a figure of association. An example of a metonymy is found in the statement, "All the country of Judea was going out to him" (Mark 1:5). The metonymy is *country,* which refers to the people rather than the region itself. Note also the hyperbole: *all* the country.

❧ *Synecdoche* is another figure of association where the whole can refer to the part or the part to the whole. This is often found in the use of the term *the law*, which can refer to the Pentateuch (the first five books of the Old Testament), the ten commandments, or the whole Old Testament.

A synecdoche can also be a singular for a plural or a plural for a singular. An example is in Jeremiah 25:29. God says He is going to summon "a sword against all the inhabitants of the earth." The singular sword represents many swords.

❧ In *personification* an object is given characteristics or attributes that belong to people—for example, when the trees clap their hands and the mountains sing for joy (Isaiah 55:12).

❧ *Irony* is a statement which says the opposite of what is meant. Irony is used for emphasis or effect. When it is not easy to discern if a statement is ironic, then examine it first as a true statement. As such, does it make sense in its context? Second, examine it as figurative irony. If this makes sense and fits with the context, then accept it as irony. Otherwise, treat it as a truth.

Here are two examples of irony:

1. In 1 Kings 22:1-23, a true prophet tells the king what he wants to hear, but it is a lie. It's obvious he is using irony because the king tells him to stop prophesying falsely and to tell the truth.

2. In 1 Corinthians 4:8 Paul says to the Corinthians, "You are already filled, you have already become rich, you have become kings without us; and indeed, I wish that you had become kings so that we also might reign with you." When you read this, it is obvious the Corinthians are not kings, nor does Paul desire to reign with them.

Parables

A parable is a story which, although not usually factual, remains true to life and teaches a moral lesson or truth. Every detail of a parable will reinforce the main theme, but you shouldn't always attempt to ascribe a specific spiritual meaning and application to each point.

Jesus frequently used parables in His teaching for two reasons: to reveal truth to believers and to hide truth from those who had rejected it and/or hardened their hearts against it.

To correctly interpret a parable:

• *Determine the occasion of the parable.* Since parables clarify or emphasize a truth, discover why the parable was told. What prompted it?

• *Look for the intended meaning of the parable.* The meaning will sometimes be stated. If not, it can usually be determined by the application of the parable to the hearer.

• *Don't impose any meaning beyond what is clearly stated or applied to the hearers by the speaker of the parable.*

• *Identify the central or focal idea of the parable.* Every parable has one central theme or emphasis. No detail of the story is to be given any meaning that is independent of the main teaching of the parable.

Since a parable has one central point of emphasis, identify relevant details. To attach meaning that is not in the context of the occasion or relevant to its central emphasis is to go away from the meaning of the parable. A detail is relevant only if it reinforces the central theme of the parable.

How many sermons have you heard on the parable of the prodigal son? Many teachers violate the occasion and meaning of this parable, attaching all sorts of meanings to the details of this story. Jesus told this parable because He wanted the Pharisees to see what their hearts were like as they grumbled, "This man receives sinners and eats with them"

(Luke 15:2). In order to make His point Jesus told three consecutive parables about three things which were lost: a sheep, a coin, and a son. In each of the parables Jesus uses the following words: *lost*, *found*, *sin*, and *joy (rejoice)*. When He gets to the story of the prodigal son, He shows them the kindness of the father's heart versus the hardness of the elder brother's, and in doing so, shows the Pharisees that their hearts are like the elder brother's, not the father's.

• *Interpret parables in the context of the culture of Bible times rather than the culture of today.* For example, in the parable of the wise and foolish virgins, the central emphasis of the parable is, "Be on the alert then, for you do not know the day nor the hour" (Matthew 25:13). Understanding Eastern wedding traditions would give insight into the parable and explain why some were ready and others were not.

• *Do not establish doctrine when parables are the primary or only source for that teaching.* Parables should amplify or affirm doctrine, not establish it.

Allegory

An *allegory* is a description of one thing using the image of another—a story with an underlying meaning different from the surface facts of the story itself. Some refer to an allegory as an extended metaphor, which is an implied comparison between two different things. An allegory is a realistic or nonrealistic story created to teach one or more truths which may or may not be related.

The chart below comparing parables and allegories will help you distinguish one from the other.

When interpreting an allegory, follow these guidelines:

• List the features of the allegory.

• Note any interpretation given within the text of the allegory.

• Study the allegory's features according to sound principles of biblical exegesis. Do not contradict the clear teaching of the Word of God by interpreting an unexplained detail in an allegory in a way contrary to other truths.

• Do not try to identify all the features of an allegory.

Types

A type is a prophetic symbol designated by God.

The word *type* comes from the Greek word *tupos*. A *tupos* was a mark formed by a blow or an impression, creating a figure or an image on the object that was struck. Therefore, a type prefigures something or someone to come. That which it prefigures is called an *antitype*.

Parable	Allegory
1. Has one central point	1. Can have more than one central point
2. Teaches one truth	2. Can teach a number of truths
3. Every relevant detail reinforces the central theme or point of emphasis	3. The details of an allegory may be many and varied, relating to more than one theme
4. Can have irrelevant details; all features of the parable do not have to be identified	4. Can have irrelevant details; all the features of an allegory do not have to be identified
5. Usually the story is separate from its interpretation and application	5. Intertwines the story and the meaning
6. Interpretation usually follows the parable	6. Interpretation is found within the allegory

A type prefigures only one antitype, although it may parallel many points in the antitype. An illustration of this is the tabernacle, a type of man's redemption. According to Hebrews 10:20, the veil that separated the holy place from the holy of holies prefigured the flesh of Jesus Christ.

When determining types, although it may not be formally stated, there should be some evidence of divine affirmation of the corresponding type and antitype. For example, in Romans 5:14 we read, "Nevertheless death reigned from Adam until Moses, even over those who had not sinned in the likeness of the offense of Adam, who is a type of Him who was to come." The word translated *type* is the Greek word *tupos*. Adam was a type or figure of Christ, who was to come. In 1 Corinthians 15:45, Christ is referred to as "the last Adam." If the Word does not designate something as a type, then the Bible expositor should simply show the parallels without calling it a type.

Symbols

A symbol is a picture or an object that stands for or represents another thing. For example, the seven candlesticks mentioned in Revelation 1:20 represent the seven churches described in Revelation 2 and 3.

When noting symbols it is important to remember the following:

• *The item used as a symbol can symbolize different things.* For example, water is used to symbolize the Word of God (Ephesians 5:26) and the Holy Spirit (John 7:37-39).

• *Although a symbol can represent many things, when it does symbolize something in a given passage, a single parallel is intended.* For instance, in John 7:37-39 water symbolizes the Holy Spirit, not the Word.

• *Interpret symbols in the light of a biblical setting and culture rather than the culture of the current interpreter.*

• *Symbols are timeless and can symbolize something past, present, or future.*

LAWS OF COMPOSITION

A literary composition is an arrangement of thoughts which conveys meaning to a reader. An understanding of the laws of composition will help you discern what the author is saying.

The following laws of composition can help you in your study of the Word of God.

1. **Comparison**—to compare in order to show similarities. A comparison is the association of like things.

2. **Contrast**—to compare in order to show differences. A contrast is the association of opposites.

3. **Repetition**—to use the same word or phrase a number of times.

4. **Progression**—to extend a specific theme throughout a portion of Scripture. Many times the author will amplify what he is saying as he progresses in his writing or adds to what he has said.

5. **Climax**—a high point built by a progression from the lesser to the greater. A climax is simply an extension of the law of progression until it reaches a peak of intensity.

6. **Pivotal point**—a changing or a turning so that the elements on each side of the point differ in some way. In the Gospel of John the pivotal point comes in 11:54, when Jesus turns from ministering mainly to the public to ministering to His disciples. (Read John 11:54.) In Genesis the pivotal point of the book comes in chapter 12, where Moses turns from recording major events to tell us of major characters.

7. **Radiation**—the central or single point from or to which other truths point. An illustration of this is 1 Corinthians 15, where the truths of that chapter all radiate to resurrection.

8. **Interchange**—to alternate, in sequence, at least two main thoughts, subjects, or characteristics. This is most apparent in the Gospel of Luke. Luke opens with the announcement of the birth of John the Baptist, then moves to the announcement of Jesus' birth. He then returns to John the Baptist's birth, then to the birth of Christ. This is alternation or interchange.

9. **General to particular (or vice versa)**—to move from the extensive or general to the specific or particular. This is beautifully seen in Genesis 1 and 2. Genesis 1 gives the general overview of creation, including the creation of man, male and female, on the sixth

day. Genesis 2 moves from the general to the particular, giving more details of the creation of woman.

10. **Cause and effect (or vice versa)**—to move from the source to the consequence of it. An example of this is found in John 11. Verse 4 states that the cause of the death of Lazarus, the beloved friend of Christ, was to glorify the Son. The effect is seen in verse 45, where the people believed on Christ after seeing His power in raising Lazarus. The effect is also seen in John 12:17, 18, where once again the Son is glorified.

11. **Explanation or analysis**—the presentation of an idea or event followed by its explanation. This is expertly done by our Lord in John 6, where He multiplies the loaves and the fishes and then brings forth His discourse stating that He is the bread who gives us life.

12. **Interrogation**—the presentation of a question, usually followed by its answer. Paul masterfully uses this technique in writing Romans. Paul anticipates his readers' questions or objections, states them usually in the form of a question, and then proceeds to answer the very questions he has raised. Romans 6 beautifully demonstrates this technique.

13. **Preparation or introduction**—the presentation of background information to prepare the reader for that which follows. The purpose of the Gospel of John is to prepare the reader to believe that Jesus is the Christ, the Son of God. In John 1:1-18 the writer thoroughly introduces his subject and prepares his readers for what is to come.

14. **Summarization**—to restate the main points, to sum up, or to briefly restate particular truths. Moses does this in chapters 1 to 4 of the book of Deuteronomy as he rehearses before the children of Israel those things that took place following the exodus from Egypt. Acts 7 provides a masterful summarization by Stephen of Israel's history.

TENSE, VOICE, AND MOOD OF GREEK VERBS

There are many excellent study tools which can help you examine the text more deeply through Greek word studies. If you would like to pursue Greek word studies further, a highly recommended book is *The Complete Word Study New Testament*, by Spiros Zodhiates.

The following explanation of the tense, voice, and mood of Greek verbs will help those who do not know Greek but want a better understanding of the implications of the kind of action indicated by the verbs.

Because verbs express action, they are often the most significant element in the expression of thought. Therefore, understanding the Greek verb is a key to correct interpretation and application of Scripture. (Context is the most important key to correct interpretation and application, since the Greek words get their meaning from the context.) Three major features of Greek verbs are tense, voice, and mood.

Part of the beauty of the Greek language is that the construction of the verb clearly shows who does the action, whether the statement is a command or the passage is speaking of reality or possibility.

By thinking through a simple, concise explanation of tense, voice, and mood, new vistas of insight will be opened to you. Keep in mind that the following is a simplified and nonexhaustive summarization of a complex subject. The purpose of this information is to give you an overview of terms that are frequently used in the more technical commentaries.

Tense

(Shows the Kind of Action)

Greek verb tenses differ from English verb tenses in that the kind of action portrayed is the most significant element, and time is a relatively minor consideration.

~ Action as continuous

Present tense—continuous action. It is primarily progressive or linear; it shows action that is continuing.

Examples:

Jeff *is studying* the Bible.

John 15:4b—"As the branch *cannot bear* fruit of itself unless it *abides* in the vine, so neither can you unless you *abide* in Me."

John 15:6—"If anyone *does not abide* in Me."

Imperfect tense—continuous action, usually in the past.

Examples:

Jeff *was studying* the Bible.

John 15:19a—"If you were of the world, the world *would love* its own." (Literally, "would have been loving" its own.)

Action as completed

Perfect tense—punctiliar action in the past with the results continuing into the present. Punctiliar action is action that happens at a specific point in time.

Examples:

Jeff is being transformed by *having studied* the Bible.

John 15:3—"You are already clean because of the word which I *have spoken* to you."

John 15:10b—"Just as I *have kept* My Father's commandments and abide in His love."

Pluperfect tense—punctiliar action in the past with the results continuing in the past.

Examples:

Jeff was transformed because he *had studied* the Bible.

John 9:22—"For the Jews *had* already *agreed*."

Action as occurring

Aorist tense—punctiliar action. The aorist tense states an action as completed without regard to its duration; that is, it denotes the fact of an action without any reference to the length of that action. Compared to the present tense, the aorist tense expresses the action like a snapshot while the present tense action is like a moving picture, continuing on.

Examples:

Jeff *studied* the Bible.

John 15:4a—"*Abide* in Me, and I in you."

Future tense—indefinite action to occur in the future. Indicates continuing or punctiliar action in the future.

Examples:

Jeff *will be studying* his Bible.

John 15:7—"It *will be done* for you."

John 15:8—"*So* prove to *be* My disciples."

Voice

(Shows How the Subject Is Related to the Action)

Active voice—indicates that the subject produces the action.

Examples:

Jeff *hit* the ball.

John 15:2b—"And every branch that bears fruit, He *prunes* it."

Passive voice—indicates that the subject is acted upon.

Examples:

Jeff *was hit* by the ball.

John 15:6—"And they *are burned*."

Middle voice—indicates that the subject initiates the action and also participates in the results of the action. (This voice is unique to Greek construction.)

Examples:

Jeff *hit* himself with the ball.

John 15:26—"That is the Spirit of truth who *proceeds* from the Father, He will testify about Me."

One note of interest when looking up a verb in a Greek study tool: The middle and passive voices will have identical forms, but the context will show you if the subject is receiving the action (passive voice) or if the subject initiated the action and participated in it (middle voice).

Also, some verbs are *deponent verbs*. This means that their form in a Greek study tool may be listed as a passive or middle voice verb but their function or action is active. Usually your Greek study helps will list these as deponent verbs.

Mood

(Shows How the Action Is Related to Reality from the Speaker's Point of View)

Indicative mood—the declarative mood or mood of certainty. It is a statement of fact which assumes reality from the speaker's point of view. This mood simply states a thing as being a fact.

Examples:

Bible study *has changed* Jeff's life.

John 15:6—"He *is thrown* away as a branch and *dries* up; and they *gather* them, and *cast* them into the fire and they *are burned*."

Imperative mood—usually a command or entreaty. It is the mood of volition or will. The imperative mood in the Greek makes a demand on the will of the reader to obey the command; it is used to indicate prohibition and authority.

Examples:

Jeff, *study* your homework.

John 15:4—"*Abide* in Me."

John 15:7—"*Ask* whatever you wish."

John 15:9—"*Abide* in My love."

John 15:20—"*Remember* the word that I said to you."

One aspect which will help your study of God's Word is the understanding of the combination of the present tense and the imperative mood that is stating a negative command (a prohibition). The *present imperative prohibition* demands cessation of some act already in progress.

Example:

John 20:17—"Jesus said to her, '*Stop clinging* to Me.' " In other words, Mary was already clinging to Jesus, and Jesus was telling her to stop clinging and to go on refusing to cling to Him.

Subjunctive mood—the mood of probability. It implies some doubt regarding the reality of the action from the speaker's point of view. It expresses an uncertainty or an action which may or should happen. This is the mood used for conditional clauses, strong suggestions, or "polite" commands.

Examples:

Jeff *may have done* his homework. Jeff, if you do not do your homework, you cannot participate in the class discussion.

John 15:2—"That it *may bear* more fruit."

John 15:4b—"As the branch cannot bear fruit of itself unless it *abides* in the vine, so neither can you unless you *abide* in Me."

John 15:6—"If anyone *does not abide* in Me."

John 15:7—"If you *abide* in Me, and My words *abide* in you."

Something else which may help you in your study of God's Word is an understanding of the combination of the aorist tense and the subjunctive mood that is stating a negative command (a prohibition). The *aorist subjunctive prohibition* is a warning or an exhortation against doing a thing not yet begun.

Example:

John 13:8a—"Peter said to Him, '*Never shall* You *wash* my feet!' " In other words, Peter was telling Jesus that He was not to wash his feet and Jesus was not even to start washing his feet.

Optative mood—the mood of possibility. This mood presents no definite anticipation of realization but merely presents the action as conceivable from the speaker's point of view (used less frequently than the other moods).

Examples:

I *wish* my neighbor, Jeff, would take the Precept Bible Studies.

2 Thessalonians 3:5—"May the Lord *direct* your hearts."

Tense, Mood, and Voice of Greek Verbs

Tense

The emphasis is on the *kind* of action, not the time of action.

Tense	Kind of Action	Example
Present	Continuous action	Jeff is studying the Bible.
Imperfect	Continuous action in the past	Jeff was studying the Bible.
Perfect	Punctiliar action in the past with the results continuing into the present	Jeff is being transformed by having studied the Bible.
Pluperfect	Punctiliar action in the past with the results continuing in the past	Jeff was transformed because he had studied the Bible.
Aorist	Punctiliar action (The time can be past, present, or future but is generally past.)	Jeff studied the Bible.
Future	Generally continuous action in the future, but on occasion it can be punctiliar.	Jeff will be studying his Bible.

Tense, Mood, and Voice of Greek Verbs

Mood

The mood expresses the relationship of the action to reality from the speaker's point of view.

Mood	Relation to Reality	Usage or Meaning	Example
Indicative	Mood of certainty (reality)	Used to declare a statement of fact as something which is true. Expresses that which is actual, factual, or real from the speaker's point of view.	Bible study has changed Jeff's life.
Imperative	Mood of volition or will (potential reality)	Usually used to express a command or entreaty. Denotes intention, authority, permission, or prohibition.	Jeff, study your homework.
Subjunctive	Mood of probability (probable reality)	Used to express an action which may or should happen but which is not necessarily true at the present, from the speaker's point of view. Expresses conditional or uncertain actions.	Jeff may have done his homework.
Optative	Mood of possibility (possible reality)	Merely presents an action as conceivable from the speaker's point of view, with no definite anticipation of realization.	I wish my neighbor, Jeff, would take the Precept Bible Studies.

TENSE, MOOD, AND VOICE OF GREEK VERBS

VOICE

The voice expresses the relationship of the subject to the action.

Voice	How the Subject Is Related to the Action	Example
Active	Indicates that the subject produces the action	Jeff hit the ball.
Passive	Indicates that the subject is acted upon	Jeff was hit by the ball.
Middle	Indicates that the subject initiates the action and participates in the results of the action	Jeff hit himself with the ball.

*R*EAD *T*HROUGH THE *B*IBLE IN *O*NE *Y*EAR

Weekly Reading Plan

Week	Reading
1	Genesis 1–24
2	Genesis 25–43
3	Genesis 44–Exodus 14
4	Exodus 15–34
5	Exodus 35–Leviticus 14
6	Leviticus 15–Numbers 4
7	Numbers 5–22
8	Numbers 23–Deuteronomy 4
9	Deuteronomy 5–27
10	Deuteronomy 28–Joshua 12
11	Joshua 13–Judges 8
12	Judges 9–21; Ruth; 1 Samuel 1–4
13	1 Samuel 5–24
14	1 Samuel 25–2 Samuel 15
15	2 Samuel 16–1 Kings 7
16	1 Kings 8–22
17	2 Kings 1–18
18	2 Kings 19–1 Chronicles 12
19	1 Chronicles 13–2 Chronicles 8
20	2 Chronicles 9–32
21	2 Chronicles 33–36; Ezra; Nehemiah 1–8
22	Nehemiah 9–13; Esther; Job 1–10
23	Job 11–42
24	Psalms 1–38
25	Psalms 39–76
26	Psalms 77–109

Week	Reading
27	Psalms 110–150; Proverbs 1–4
28	Proverbs 5–31
29	Ecclesiastes; Song of Solomon; Isaiah 1–9
30	Isaiah 10–35
31	Isaiah 36–57
32	Isaiah 58–66; Jeremiah 1–10
33	Jeremiah 11–30
34	Jeremiah 31–49
35	Jeremiah 50–52; Lamentations; Ezekiel 1–12
36	Ezekiel 13–31
37	Ezekiel 32–48; Daniel 1–2
38	Daniel 3–12; Hosea
39	Joel; Amos; Obadiah; Jonah; Micah; Nahum
40	Habakkuk; Zephaniah; Haggai; Zechariah; Malachi
41	Matthew
42	Mark
43	Luke
44	John 1–14
45	John 15–21
46	Acts 1–12
47	Acts 13–28
48	Romans; 1 Corinthians
49	2 Corinthians; Galatians; Ephesians
50	Philippians; Colossians; 1 and 2 Thessalonians; 1 and 2 Timothy; Titus; Philemon
51	Hebrews; James; 1 and 2 Peter; 1 and 2 John
52	3 John; Jude; Revelation

Each week's reading has roughly the same number of verses. One suggestion for using this plan is to try to accomplish the week's goal, and not necessarily follow a precise day-by-day schedule. Use a bookmark to keep your place, and if you miss a day, on the next day just pick up where you left off, and press on toward your goal. In a year, you'll have read the Bible from Genesis to Revelation!

THREE-YEAR BIBLE STUDY PLAN

A Plan to Help You Study the Bible

Now that you have the *New Inductive Study Bible*, where should you start? What plan could you use to study through the entire Bible? Many reading plans are available, but there are few plans for systematic study.

One approach is to start with Genesis and work your way through Revelation. Or, you could start with Matthew and work your way through the New Testament first, and then the Old Testament. There are many Old Testament references in the New Testament that will make more sense if you study the Old Testament before the New Testament, but the option is yours. Whichever place you start, the following plan can help you make sense of how the books fit together and determine the pace at which you progress through the Bible.

Old Testament Study

Studying history usually makes the most sense if you work chronologically. In the Bible, the historical books teach not only history but also ongoing revelation of God to man. They progressively reveal God's plan for the redemption of mankind, from creation and the fall up to the appearing of Messiah, the Lord Jesus Christ.

The prophetic books fit into a specific chronology with the historical books. As the Old Testament reveals the history of God's people Israel, we see various prophets bringing messages from God to the kings of Israel and Judah, to the exiles, and to those who return from exile. Integrating the messages of the prophets with the messages of the historical books can help you to grasp the whole of God's message. Or, you can study the prophets after you study the historical books, so you don't interrupt the flow of your historical study. The wisdom literature can be studied separately because it is timeless and somewhat independent of the time period in which it was written, but there is still a link to the overall progressive revelation of God in time and history.

In general, we recommend studying a book of the Bible as a unit. The *New Inductive Study Bible* gives a set of directions at the beginning of each of the 66 books. Genesis through 2 Kings are in chronological order; however, 1 and 2 Chronicles and the prophets overlap these books. First Chronicles 1–9 detail the genealogies from Adam through the returning exiles from Babylon. Then starting with 1 Chronicles 10, the history of the line of David in the united kingdom then southern kingdom, Judah, is given, and the story parallels 1 Samuel 31 through 2 Kings 25. So as you study Chronicles, you can go back and compare your reading with what you learned in previous books.

New Testament Study

In general, the study of the New Testament can also proceed chronologically, but only to a point. The gospels are first, Acts gives us the development of the church, and Paul's letters overlap Acts. When reading the letters, the strict chronological order is critical only when it's obvious that one letter clearly follows the other, such as 1 and 2 Corinthians, 1 and 2 Thessalonians, 1 and 2 Timothy, and 1 and 2 Peter. The main point of these letters is the theology that is taught, not the sequence. And, of course, Revelation comes last. So the New Testament can be studied straight through.

If you have chosen to study the New Testament before the Old Testament, we would recommend that when you get to the book of Revelation, you study Daniel first, then 1 and 2 Thessalonians. You'll find many references to the Day of the Lord in Old Testament prophecy, so familiarity with the Old Testament will help.

THE OLD TESTAMENT BOOKS IN CHRONOLOGICAL RELATIONSHIP

HISTORY		WISDOM AND PROPHETS
Genesis		Job (probably between the flood and Abraham)
Exodus		
Leviticus		
Numbers		
Deuteronomy		
Joshua		
Judges		
Ruth		
1 Samuel	1 Samuel 31 = 1 Chronicles 10	
2 Samuel	2 Samuel 5–10 = 1 Chronicles 11–19 2 Samuel 21–24 = 1 Chronicles 20–29	Psalms (mostly David)
1 Kings	1 Kings 1–11 = 2 Chronicles 1–9 1 Kings 12–22 = 2 Chronicles 10–20	Proverbs (mostly Solomon), Song of Solomon, Ecclesiastes
2 Kings	2 Kings = 2 Chronicles 21–36	Obadiah = 2 Kings 9–12; 2 Chronicles 22–24 Joel = 2 Kings 12; 2 Chronicles 24 Jonah = 2 Kings 14 Amos = 2 Kings 13–15; 2 Chronicles 26 Hosea = 2 Kings 14–20; 2 Chronicles 26–32 Isaiah = 2 Kings 15–20; 2 Chronicles 26–32 Micah = 2 Kings 15–20; 2 Chronicles 27–32 Nahum = 2 Kings 21–23; 2 Chronicles 33–35 Zephaniah = 2 Kings 22; 2 Chronicles 34 Jeremiah = 2 Kings 22–25; 2 Chron. 34–36 Habakkuk = 2 Kings 22–23; 2 Chron. 34–35 Daniel = 2 Kings 24–25; 2 Chronicles 36 Ezekiel = 2 Kings 24–25; 2 Chronicles 36
1 Chronicles		
2 Chronicles		
		Lamentations
Ezra		Haggai Zechariah
Esther		
Nehemiah		Malachi

Three-Year Bible Study Plan

A Plan to Help You Study Through the Bible

Studying the Bible thoroughly can take time. An adaptation of the plan to read through the Bible in one year is to *triple* the time—that is, using three weeks to study what you would have read in one week:

Weeks	Reading
1-3	Genesis 1–24
4-6	Genesis 25–43
7-9	Genesis 44—Exodus 14
10-12	Exodus 15–34
13-15	Exodus 35—Leviticus 14
16-18	Leviticus 15—Numbers 4
19-21	Numbers 5–22
22-24	Numbers 23—Deuteronomy 4
25-27	Deuteronomy 5–27
28-30	Deuteronomy 28—Joshua 12
31-33	Joshua 13—Judges 8
34-36	Judges 9–21; Ruth; 1 Samuel 1–4
37-39	1 Samuel 5–24
40-42	1 Samuel 25—2 Samuel 15
43-45	2 Samuel 16—1 Kings 7
46-48	1 Kings 8–22
49-52	2 Kings 1–18
1-3	2 Kings 19—1 Chronicles 12
4-6	1 Chronicles 13—2 Chronicles 8
7-9	2 Chronicles 9–32
10-12	2 Chronicles 33–36; Job
13-15	Psalms 1–38
16-18	Psalms 39–76
19-21	Psalms 77–109
22-24	Psalms 110–150
25-27	Proverbs
28-30	Ecclesiastes; Song of Solomon; Obadiah; Joel; Jonah
31-33	Amos; Hosea; Isaiah 1–7
34-36	Isaiah 8–31
37-39	Isaiah 32–53
40-42	Isaiah 54–66; Micah; Nahum; Zephaniah
43-45	Jeremiah 1–18
46-48	Jeremiah 19–37
49-50	Jeremiah 38–52
51-52	Habakkuk; Daniel

Weeks	Reading
1-3	Ezekiel 1–23
4-6	Ezekiel 24–42
7-9	Ezekiel 43–48; Lamentations; Ezra
10-12	Haggai; Zechariah; Esther
13-15	Nehemiah; Malachi
16-18	Matthew
19-21	Mark
22-24	Luke
25-27	John 1–10
28-30	John 11–21
31-33	Acts 1–13
34-36	Acts 14–28
37-39	Romans
40-42	1 and 2 Corinthians; Galatians
43-45	Ephesians, Philippians; Colossians; 1 and 2 Thessalonians; 1 and 2 Timothy; Titus
46-48	Philemon; Hebrews; James; 1 and 2 Peter
49-52	1, 2, and 3 John; Jude; Revelation

A HARMONY OF THE GOSPELS

A Chronological Listing of Scriptures About the Life of Jesus

	MATTHEW	MARK	LUKE	JOHN
From Birth to Twelve Years of Age				
Introduction			1:1-4	1:1-14
Jesus' legal lineage through Joseph	1:1-17			
Jesus' natural lineage through Mary			3:23-38	
John the Baptist's birth announced			1:5-25	
Jesus' birth announced to Mary			1:26-38	
Mary's visit to Elizabeth			1:39-45	
Mary's song of joy and praise			1:46-56	
John the Baptist's birth			1:57-66	
Zechariah's prophetic song			1:67-79	
John the Baptist's early years			1:80	
Jesus' birth announced to Joseph	1:18-25			
Jesus is born in Bethlehem			2:1-7	
Angelic visit to the shepherds			2:8-20	
Circumcision of Jesus			2:21	
Jesus presented in Temple			2:22-38	
Visit of the Magi	2:1-12			
Flight into Egypt	2:13-18			
Return to Nazareth	2:19-23		2:39	
Early growth of Jesus			2:40	
Jesus at age 12 in Jerusalem for Passover			2:41-51	
Jesus' adolescence and early manhood			2:52	
John the Baptist's Ministry				
Beginning of ministry		1:1	3:1,2	
A description and his message	3:1-6	1:2-6	3:3-6	
Warnings and teachings	3:7-10		3:7-14	
His proclamation of Christ	3:11,12	1:7,8	3:15-18	
The Beginning of Jesus' Ministry				
Jesus baptized by John	3:13-17	1:9-11	3:21-23	
Jesus tempted by Satan in wilderness	4:1-11	1:12,13	4:1-13	
John's witness of Jesus as Son of God				1:15-34
Jesus' first followers				1:35-51
Jesus' first miracle—water to wine				2:1-11
Jesus visits Capernaum				2:12
First cleansing of Temple (at Passover)				2:13-25
Nicodemus' visit with Jesus				3:1-21
Jesus must increase, John must decrease				3:22-36
John imprisoned; Jesus to Galilee	4:12	1:14	3:19-20; 4:14	4:1-4
Samaritan woman at well				4:5-42
Jesus' Ministry in Galilee				
Arrival in Galilee; proclaims gospel	4:17	1:14,15	4:14,15	4:43-45

	Matthew	Mark	Luke	John
Child at Capernaum healed				4:46-54
Ministry in Nazareth; Jesus rejected			4:16-30	
Jesus goes to Capernaum	4:13-16		4:31	
Calling of Simon, Andrew, James, John	4:18-22	1:16-20	5:1-11	
Teaches in synagogue, heals demoniac		1:21-28	4:31-37	
Peter's mother-in-law, others healed	8:14-17	1:29-34	4:38-41	
Tour of towns throughout Galilee	4:23-25	1:35-39	4:42-44	
Healing of leper	8:1-4	1:40-45	5:12-16	
Healing of paralytic (hole in roof)	9:1-8	2:1-12	5:17-26	
Call of Matthew, banquet	9:9-13	2:13-17	5:27-32	
Answers objections with illustrations	9:14-17	2:18-22	5:33-39	
Lame man healed in Jerusalem on Sabbath				5:1-9
Attempts to kill Jesus				5:10-18
Jesus teaches He is equal with the Father				5:19-47
Disciples pick grain on the Sabbath	12:1-8	2:23-28	6:1-5	
Healing of man's hand on the Sabbath	12:9-14	3:1-6	6:6-11	
Withdraws to Sea of Galilee, heals many	12:15-21	3:7-12		
Selection of the 12 Disciples and Sermon on the Mount				
Lists of the 12 disciples		3:13-19	6:12-16	
Setting of the sermon	5:1,2		6:17-19	
The blessings	5:3-12		6:20-26	
Salt and light of the world	5:13-16			
The law and righteousness	5:17-20			
Interpreting the law—six contrasts	5:21-48		6:27-36	
Hypocrisy, giving, praying, fasting	6:1-18			
Avarice, judgment, handling the sacred	6:19—7:6		6:37-42	
Application of sermon	7:7-27		6:43-49	
Reaction to sermon	7:28,29			
Increasing Fame and Rejection				
Healing of the centurion's servant	8:5-13		7:1-10	
Widow's son raised from the dead			7:11-17	
John the Baptist's inquiry	11:2-19		7:18-35	
Woes upon Chorazin, Bethsaida, Capernaum	11:20-27			
Invitation to the heavy-laden	11:28-30			
Woman anoints Jesus' feet			7:36-50	
Tour with the 12 and other followers			8:1-3	
Blasphemous accusations against Jesus	12:22-37	3:20-30		
Request for a sign, Jesus' answer	12:38-45			
Natural kinship, spiritual kinship	12:46-50	3:31-35	8:19-21	
The Parables of the Kingdom				
The setting of the parables	13:1-2	4:1,2	8:4	
The parable of the sower and soils	13:3-23	4:3-25	8:5-18	
The parable of sprouting seeds		4:26-29		
The parable of the tares	13:24-30			
The parable of the mustard seed	13:31,32	4:30-32		
The parable of the leavened loaf	13:33-35	4:33,34		

	MATTHEW	MARK	LUKE	JOHN
The parable of the tares explained	13:36-43			
The parable of the treasure in the field	13:44			
The parable of the pearl of great price	13:45,46			
The parable of the fishnet	13:47-50			
The parable of the householder	13:51,52			
Growing Opposition to Jesus' Ministry				
Jesus crosses lake, calms storm	8:18-27	4:35-41	8:22-25	
Gadarene demoniacs, herd of swine	8:28-34	5:1-20	8:26-39	
Jairus' daughter, woman touches Jesus' garment	9:18-26	5:21-43	8:40-56	
More healings, another accusation	9:27-34			
Visit to Nazareth, people respond in unbelief	13:54-58	6:1-6		
End of Galilean Ministry				
Workers needed for the harvest	9:35-38	6:6		
Twelve disciples commissioned	10:1-42	6:7-11	9:1-5	
Disciples sent out	11:1	6:12,13	9:6	
Herod misidentifies Jesus as John the Baptist	14:1-12	6:14-29	9:7-9	
Return of the disciples	6:30	9:10		
Christ's Ministry Extends Beyond Galilee				
Withdrawal across Sea of Galilee	14:13,14	6:31-34	9:10,11	6:1-3
Feeding of 5,000 people	14:15-21	6:35-44	9:12-17	6:4-13
People attempt to make Jesus king	14:22,23	6:45,46		6:14,15
Jesus walks on water	14:24-33	6:47-52		6:16-21
Healings in Gennesaret	14:34-36	6:53-56		
The true bread of life				6:22-59
Some followers defect				6:60-71
Disagreement over ceremonial impurity	15:1-20	7:1-23		
Ministry in Tyre and Sidon	15:21-28	7:24-30		
Healings in Decapolis	15:29-31	7:31-37		
Jesus feeds 4,000 in Decapolis	15:32-38	8:1-9		
Jesus crosses lake to Dalmanutha	15:39	8:10		
Test from Pharisees and Sadducees	16:1-4	8:11,12		
Warning about Pharisees, Sadducees, Herodians	16:5-12	8:13-21		
Heals blind man at Bethsaida		8:22-26		
Jesus' Identity as Messiah Affirmed				
Peter confesses Jesus as the Christ	16:13-20	8:27-30	9:18-21	
Prediction of crucifixion and resurrection	16:21-26	8:31-37	9:22-25	
Coming of Son of Man, judgment	16:27,28	8:38—9:1	9:26,27	
Transfiguration of Jesus	17:1-13	9:2-13	9:28-36	
Healing of demoniac disciples couldn't heal	17:14-20 [21]	9:14-29	9:37-43	
Another prediction of death and resurrection	17:22,23	9:30-32	9:43-45	
Temple tax payment from a fish	17:24-27			
Disciples' dispute over greatness	18:1-5	9:33-37	9:46-48	
Warnings from Jesus	18:6-14	9:38-50	9:49,50	
Forgiveness toward a sinning believer	18:15-35			
Half-brothers ridicule Jesus				7:1-9

	MATTHEW	MARK	LUKE	JOHN
Departure for Jerusalem through Samaria			9:51-56	7:10
Requirements for following Jesus	8:19-22		9:57-62	
Later Judean Ministry of Christ				
People's reactions to teachings and miracles				7:11-31
Pharisees attempt to arrest Jesus				7:32-53
Jesus forgives woman caught in adultery				8:1-11
Conflict between Jesus and Pharisees				8:12-59
The 70 workers sent out			10:1-16	
The 70 workers return			10:17-24	
Parable of the Good Samaritan			10:25-37	
Jesus visits Mary and Martha			10:38-42	
Teaches disciples how to pray			11:1-13	
Blasphemous accusation against Jesus			11:14-36	
Warning about hypocrisy			12:1-12	
Warning against greed			12:13-15	
Parable of the rich fool			12:16-20	
Spiritual riches above earthly wealth			12:21-34	
Warning to be prepared			12:35-48	
Warning about future division			12:49-53	
Warning about signs of the present			12:54-59	
Repent, or perish			13:1-9	
Healing of a woman on the Sabbath			13:10-21	
Healing of a man born blind				9:1-41
Christ as the Good Shepherd and Door				10:1-18
Jews divided about Jesus				10:19-21
Attempt to stone, arrest Jesus				10:22-39
Ministry in and Around Perea				
Leaves Jerusalem, goes to Perea				10:40-42
Question about entering the kingdom			13:22-30	
Jesus' coming death			13:31-35	
Healing of man with dropsy			14:1-24	
Cost of following Jesus			14:25-35	
Parables: lost sheep, lost coin, prodigal			15:1-32	
Parable about the steward, riches			16:1-18	
The rich man and Lazarus			16:19-31	
Lessons to disciples			17:1-10	
Lazarus is sick, dies				11:1-16
Jesus raises Lazarus from the dead				11:17-45
Sanhedrin decides Jesus must die				11:46-53
Jesus withdraws to Ephraim				11:54
Healing of ten lepers			17:11-19	
Foretelling of Son of Man's coming			17:20-37	
Parable of the widow			18:1-8	
Parable of the Pharisee and publican			18:9-14	
Pharisees ask Jesus about divorce	19:1-12	10:1-12		
Little children, Jesus, the kingdom	19:13-15	10:13-16	18:15-17	

	Matthew	Mark	Luke	John
The rich young ruler	19:16-30	10:17-31	18:18-30	
Parable of landowner and laborers	20:1-16			
Prediction of death and resurrection	20:17-19	10:32-34	18:31-34	
Warning against pride: James, John	20:20-28	10:35-45		
Healing of two blind men	20:29-34	10:46-52	18:35-43	
Zacchaeus meets Jesus, is saved			19:1-10	
Parable about delay of kingdom			19:11-27	
Jesus' Last Week				
Arrival at Bethany				11:55–12:1
Mary anoints Jesus	26:6-13	14:3-9		12:2-11
Triumphal entry into Jerusalem	21:1-11, 14-17	11:1-11	19:28-44	12:12-19
Cursing of barren fig tree	21:18,19	11:12-14		
Second cleansing of temple	21:12,13	11:15-18	19:45-48	
Greeks request to see Jesus				12:20-36
Unbelievers depart from Jesus				12:36-50
Withered fig tree, lesson on faith	21:19-22	11:19-25[26]		
Christ's authority challenged	21:23-27	11:27-33	20:1-8	
Parables of two sons and the vineyard	21:28-46	12:1-12	20:9-19	
Parable of the marriage feast	22:1-14			
Question about paying taxes to Caesar	22:15-22	12:13-17	20:20-26	
Sadducees ask about the resurrection	22:23-33	12:18-27	20:27-40	
Scribe asks about greatest commandment	22:34-40	12:28-34		
Christ as David's Son and Lord	22:41-46	12:35-37	20:41-44	
Seven woes against scribes and Pharisees	23:1-36	12:38-40	20:45-47	
Jesus laments over Jerusalem	23:37-39			
The widow's two coins		12:41-44	21:1-4	
The Olivet Discourse: Jesus teaches about the temple and His return	24–25	13	21:5-36	
The Betrayal, Arrest, and Crucifixion of Jesus				
Plot by Sanhedrin to arrest and kill Jesus	26:1-5	14:1,2	21:37–22:2	
Judas agrees to betray Jesus	26:14-16	14:10,11	22:3-6	
Preparation for Passover meal	26:17-19	14:12-16	22:7-13	
Passover meal begins	26:20	14:17	22:14-16	
Jesus washes the disciples' feet				13:1-20
Jesus identifies His betrayer	26:21-25	14:18-21	22:21-23	13:21-30
Disciples argue over greatness			22:24-30	
Jesus predicts Peter's denial			22:31-38	13:31-38
The Lord's Supper established	26:26-29	14:22-25	22:17-20	
Jesus answers disciples' questions				14:1-31
The Vine and the branches				15:1-17
Expecting opposition from the world				15:18–16:4
The Holy Spirit's ministry explained				16:5-15
Jesus prophesies about His resurrection				16:16-22
Jesus promises answered prayer and peace				16:23-33
Jesus' high-priestly prayer				17

	MATTHEW	MARK	LUKE	JOHN
Jesus again predicts Peter's denial	26:30-35	14:26-31	22:39,40	18:1
Jesus' prayers in the Garden of Gethsemane	26:36-46	14:32-42	22:40-46	
Jesus betrayed and arrested, disciples flee	26:47-56	14:43-52	22:47-53	18:2-12
First Jewish trial, before Annas				18:13-24
Second Jewish trial, before Sanhedrin	26:57-68	14:53-65	22:54	
Peter denies Jesus	26:69-75	14:66-72	22:55-65	18:25-27
Third Jewish trial, before Sanhedrin	27:1	15:1	22:66-71	
Judas commits suicide	27:3-10			
First Roman trial, before Pilate	27:2,11-14	15:1-5	23:1-5	18:28-38
Second Roman trial, before Herod Antipas			23:6-12	
Third Roman trial, before Pilate	27:15-26	15:6-15	23:13-25	18:39–19:16
Jesus mocked by Roman soldiers	27:27-30	15:16-19		
Jesus goes to Golgotha	27:31-34	15:20-23	23:26-33	19:17
The crucifixion	27:35-50	15:24-37	23:33-46	19:18-37
Eyewitnesses of Jesus' death	27:51-56	15:38-41	23:45,47-49	
Jesus' body requested	27:57,58	15:42-45	23:50-52	19:38
Jesus' body buried in the tomb	27:59-61	15:46	23:53,54	19:39-42
Soldiers placed to guard the tomb	27:62-66	15:47	23:55,56	
The Resurrection and Ascension of Christ				
The resurrection on the first day of the week	28:2-4			
The tomb found empty by the women	28:1,5-8	16:1-8	24:1-10	20:1
Peter and John go to the empty tomb			24:9-11[12]	20:2-10
Jesus appears to Mary Magdalene		[16:9-11]		20:11-18
Jesus appears to the other women	28:9,10			
The soldiers' report given to Jewish priests	28:11-15			
Jesus and two disciples on road to Emmaus		[16:12,13]	24:13-32	
Two disciples give report to the others			24:33-35	
Appearance to ten disciples, Thomas absent		[16:14]	24:36-49	20:19-23
Appearance to 11 disciples, with Thomas				20:24-31
Appearance to disciples who are fishing				21:1-24
Appearance to 11 disciples in Galilee	28:16-20	[16:15-18]		
Appearance to 500 people—1 Corinthians 15:6				
Appearance to James—1 Corinthians 15:7				
Appearance to all the apostles—1 Corinthians 15:7				
Christ blesses disciples and departs (Acts 1:9-12)		[16:19,20]	24:50-53	
Conclusion				21:25

*H*ISTORICAL *C*HARTS

(in alphabetical order)

OLD TESTAMENT

Description	Book	Page
Birth Order of Jacob's Sons	Genesis	59
Camp Arrangement of Israel's Tribes	Numbers	221
David's Family Tree	2 Samuel	511
David's Family Tree Related to 1 Kings	1 Kings	549
Feasts of Israel	Leviticus	214
From the Promise of the Land to the Occupation	Joshua	355
Genealogy of Boaz	Ruth	444
Historical Chart of the Kings and Prophets of Israel and Judah	2 Kings	651
Historical Parallel of Samuel, Kings, and Chronicles	1 Chronicles	659
History of Israel	Introduction	NISB-42
History of Israel's Relationship to the Kings of Daniel 11	Daniel	1427
Israel's Division and Captivity	1 & 2 Kings	576, 649
Jewish Calendar	Leviticus, 1 Kings	201, 560
	Esther, Ezekiel	809, 1320
	Haggai, Zechariah	1525, 1531
Overlapping of the Patriarchs' Lives	Genesis	10
Period of the Judges	Judges	397
Prophetic Overview of Daniel	Daniel	1432
Prophetic Points of History	Isaiah, Ezekiel	1094, 1372
Rulers and Prophets of Amos's Time	Amos	1465
Rulers and Prophets of Daniel's Time	Daniel	1407
Rulers and Prophets of Ezekiel's Time	Ezekiel	1321
Rulers and Prophets of Habakkuk's Time	Habakkuk	1509
Rulers and Prophets of Haggai's Time	Haggai	1524
Rulers and Prophets of Hosea's Time	Hosea	1436
Rulers and Prophets of Isaiah's Time	Isaiah	1095
Rulers and Prophets of Jeremiah's Time	Jeremiah	1199
Rulers and Prophets of Joel's Time	Joel	1455
Rulers and Prophets of Jonah's Time	Jonah	1485
Rulers and Prophets of Malachi's Time	Malachi	1550
Rulers and Prophets of Micah's Time	Micah	1490
Rulers and Prophets of Nahum's Time	Nahum	1501
Rulers and Prophets of Obadiah's Time	Obadiah	1482
Rulers and Prophets of Zechariah's Time	Zechariah	1530
Rulers and Prophets of Zephaniah's Time	Zephaniah	1516
Saul's Family Tree	1 Samuel	470
Some of the Gods of Egypt	Exodus	101
Some of the Pagan Gods Worshiped by the Israelites	2 Kings	628
Three Forty-Year Periods of Moses' Life	Exodus	91
Time of Lamentations	Lamentations	1304
Times of Ezra, Nehemiah, and Esther	Ezra, Nehemiah, Esther	764, 781 808
United Kingdom Under Saul, David, and Solomon	1 Samuel	448
World Kingdoms from Daniel's Time On	Daniel	1411

NEW TESTAMENT

Description	Book	Page
Division of Alexander the Great's Empire	Bible Study Helps	2090
Genealogy of Jesus the Christ	Matthew	1557
Hasmonean Dynasty	Bible Study Helps	2092
Herod's Family Tree	Matthew, Luke	1561, 1658
Inside Herod's Temple	Matthew	1614
Life of Christ Showing Coverage by Luke	Luke	1710
Overview of the Bible	Bible Study Helps	2085
Prophetic Points of History	Bible Study Helps	2102
Sequence of Events in Paul's Life After His Conversion	Acts, Galatians	1779, 1893

*T*OPICAL *S*TUDY *C*HARTS

(in alphabetical order)

OLD TESTAMENT

Description	Book	Page
God's Response to Israel's Sin	Hosea	1452
Insights from Numbers	Numbers	287
Judges of Israel	Judges	437
Kings of Israel and Judah	2 Kings	654
Lessons from the Life of Moses	Deuteronomy	351
Lessons from the Life of Nehemiah	Nehemiah	805
Offerings and Their Purposes	Leviticus	212
Zechariah's Prophetic Revelations	Zechariah	1546

NEW TESTAMENT

Description	Book	Page
1 John Key Words	1 John	2029
Account of Jesus' Resurrection	John	1760
Arrest, Trial, and Crucifixion of Jesus Christ	John	1757
Day of the Lord, the Day of Wrath, the Day of God	Revelation	2078
I Am Writing to You	1 John	2029
James Subject by Subject	James	2003
Jesus' Messages to the Churches	Revelation	2068
Paul's Concern for the Churches at Galatia	Galatians	1901
Paul's Instructions to the Philippians	Philippians	1922
Seven Seals, Trumpets, and Bowls	Revelation	2072
What I Can Know/How I Can Know It	1 John	2029
What Revelation Teaches About God, Jesus, the Holy Spirit	Revelation	2071
What the Bible Teaches About Babylon	Revelation	2076
What the Gospels Teach About the Kingdom of God/the Kingdom of Heaven	John	1758

*M*APS

(in alphabetical order)

All maps are approximate to scale.

OLD TESTAMENT

Description	Book	Page
Assyrian Captivity of Israel	2 Kings	631
Battle at Michmash	1 Samuel	468
Beautiful Land	Daniel	1422
Border of Canaan	Numbers	282
Borders of David's Empire	1 Chronicles	690
Cedar from Lebanon	2 Chronicles	710
Cities and Geography of 2 Kings	2 Kings	605
Cities of Refuge	Numbers	284
David's Journeys: 1 Samuel 21, 22	1 Samuel	485
David's Journeys: 1 Samuel 23	1 Samuel	486
David's Journeys: 1 Samuel 24	1 Samuel	488
David's Journeys: 1 Samuel 25–27:2	1 Samuel	489
David's Journeys: 1 Samuel 27	1 Samuel	494
Death of Saul and His Sons	1 Samuel	499
Divided Kingdom: 931–586 B.C.	1 Kings,	577
	2 Chronicles	722
Elijah's Ministry	1 Kings	591
Elisha's Ministry	2 Kings	604
Exiles of Judah to Babylon	2 Kings	647
Exodus from Egypt to Canaan	Exodus	94
	Numbers	240
From Susa to Jerusalem	Nehemiah	782
Garden of Eden	Genesis	5
Gates in Nehemiah's Time	Nehemiah	784
God's Judgment Pronounced	Zechariah	1538
Israel in the Days of Samuel, Saul, and David	1 Samuel	501
Israelite Cities and Settlements in the Time of the Judges	Judges	398
Jerusalem in the Time of the Judean Monarchy	2 Kings	626
Jonah's Journey	Jonah	1484
Joshua: Occupying the Promised Land	Joshua	356
Joshua's 3-Pronged Invasion	Joshua	366
Journeys of Abraham	Genesis	20
Land Settled by the Twelve Tribes	1 Chronicles	666
Lands of Israel's Journey from Mt. Hor to Moab	Numbers	260
Lands of Israel's Journeys After the Exodus	Deuteronomy	292
Nations of Ezekiel's Prophecies	Ezekiel	1357
Nations of Jeremiah's Prophecy	Jeremiah	1279
Nations of the Lord's Anger	Zephaniah	1518
Nations That Received the Oracles	Isaiah	1112
Philistines' Attack on the Israelites	1 Samuel	466
Possessions Given by the Lord	Obadiah	1481
Ruth's Journey from Moab to Bethlehem	Ruth	440
Saul's Ascent to Kingship	1 Samuel	463
Solomon's Kingdom	1 Kings	557
Thus Says the Lord to…	Amos	1466
Tribes, the Prince's Portion, the City, the Sanctuary	Ezekiel	1399
Valley of Jehoshaphat	Joel	1460
Wanderings of the Ark	1 Samuel	455
	1 Chronicles	683
Ziklag and the Spoils	1 Samuel	497

NEW TESTAMENT

Description	Book	Page
Bible Cities in the Time of Jesus	Matthew	1558
Colossae	Colossians	1926
From Bethany, Bethphage Across the Mount of Olives into Jerusalem	Matthew	1594
	Mark	1637
	Luke, John	1695, 1738
Galilee	Matthew	1572
	Mark	1631
Israel in the Time of Christ	Matthew	1565
	Luke	1661
Jerusalem of the New Testament	Matthew	1607
	Mark	1646
	Luke, John	1704, 1747
Jesus Ministers from Capernaum to Jerusalem	John	1716
Judea	Matthew	1591
Men from Every Nation at Pentecost	Acts	1765
Paul Sails from Caesarea to Rome	Acts	1815
Paul's First Missionary Journey	Acts	1787
Paul's Second Missionary Journey	Acts	1794
Paul's Third Missionary Journey	Acts	1800
Paul's Travels as a New Believer	Galatians	1892
Region of the Roman Tetrarchs	Bible Study Helps	2091
Region of the Tetrarchs	Luke	1659
Regions from Which People Came to See Jesus	Mark	1621
Seven Churches of Asia	Revelation	2043
To Timothy at Ephesus	1 Timothy	1949
To Titus at Crete	Titus	1966
Word Sounds Forth from Thessalonica	1 Thessalonians	1939

ILLUSTRATIONS

(in alphabetical order)

OLD TESTAMENT

Description	Book	Page
Altar of Incense	Exodus	139, 153
Ark of the Covenant	Exodus, 2 Chronicles	130, 152, 713
Breastplate	Exodus	135
Bronze Altar	Exodus, 2 Chronicles	133, 153, 712
Bronze Laver	Exodus	140, 153
Bronze Stand with Bronze Basin	1 Kings, 2 Chronicles	564, 712
Close-up of Holy of Holies	1 Kings, 2 Chronicles	562, 711
Curtains	Exodus	132, 150
Ephod	Exodus	135, 155
Herod's Temple at the Time of Jesus	Introduction	NISB-38
High Priest's Garments	Exodus	136, 155
Inside the Tabernacle	Exodus, Leviticus	157, 189
Lampstand	Exodus, Leviticus, Numbers, 1 Kings, 2 Chronicles	131, 152, 203 235, 565 712
Robe of the Ephod	Exodus, 1 Chronicles	136, 156, 685
Sea on Oxen	1 Kings, 2 Chronicles	564, 712
Solomon's Temple	Introduction, 1 Kings	NISB-36, 561
Solomon's Temple: Place of Sacrifice	2 Chronicles	717
Tabernacle	Introduction	NISB-34
Table	2 Chronicles	712
Table of Showbread	Exodus	130, 152
Temple Furnishings	1 Kings	561
Temple Mount at the Time of Jesus	Introduction	NISB-40
Turban with Plate of Gold	Exodus	136, 156
Veil	Exodus	133, 151

NEW TESTAMENT

Description	Book	Page
Inside Herod's Temple	Matthew	1614
Inside the Tabernacle	Hebrews	1984

COLOR MAPS

(in alphabetical order)

Description	Page
Ancient and Modern Sites of the Exodus	2243
Development of Modern Israel	2248
Ezekiel's Vision of the Promised Land	2244
Israel's Territories: Ancient and Modern	2245
Modern Boundaries of Bible Lands	2241
Relationship of Ancient Empires to Modern Nations	2246
Settlement of the Descendants of Shem, Ham, and Japheth	2242

Historical Charts

(in Bible book order)

Old Testament

Book	Description	Page
Introduction	The History of Israel	NISB-42
Genesis	The Overlapping of the Patriarchs' Lives	10
	The Birth Order of Jacob's Sons	59
Exodus	The Three Forty-Year Periods of Moses' Life	91
	Some of the Gods of Egypt	101
Leviticus	The Jewish Calendar	201
	The Feasts of Israel	214
Numbers	Camp Arrangement of Israel's Tribes	221
Joshua	From the Promise of the Land to the Occupation	355
Judges	The Period of the Judges	397
Ruth	The Genealogy of Boaz	444
1 Samuel	The United Kingdom Under Saul, David, and Solomon	448
	Saul's Family Tree	470
2 Samuel	David's Family Tree	511
1 Kings	David's Family Tree Related to 1 Kings	549
	The Jewish Calendar	560
	Israel's Division and Captivity	576
2 Kings	Some of the Pagan Gods Worshiped by the Israelites	628
	Israel's Division and Captivity	649
	The Historical Chart of the Kings and Prophets of Israel and Judah	651
1 Chronicles	Historical Parallel of Samuel, Kings, and Chronicles	659
Ezra	The Times of Ezra, Nehemiah, and Esther	764
Nehemiah	The Times of Ezra, Nehemiah, and Esther	781
Esther	The Times of Ezra, Nehemiah, and Esther	808
	The Jewish Calendar	809
Isaiah	The Prophetic Points of History	1094
	The Rulers and Prophets of Isaiah's Time	1095
Jeremiah	The Rulers and Prophets of Jeremiah's Time	1199
Lamentations	The Time of Lamentations	1304
Ezekiel	The Jewish Calendar	1320
	The Rulers and Prophets of Ezekiel's Time	1321
	The Prophetic Points of History	1372
Daniel	The Rulers and Prophets of Daniel's Time	1407
	World Kingdoms from Daniel's Time On	1411
	History of Israel's Relationship to the Kings of Daniel 11	1427
	Prophetic Overview of Daniel	1432
Hosea	The Rulers and Prophets of Hosea's Time	1436
Joel	The Rulers and Prophets of Joel's Time	1455
Amos	The Rulers and Prophets of Amos's Time	1465
Obadiah	The Rulers and Prophets of Obadiah's Time	1480
Jonah	The Rulers and Prophets of Jonah's Time	1485
Micah	The Rulers and Prophets of Micah's Time	1490
Nahum	The Rulers and Prophets of Nahum's Time	1501
Habakkuk	The Rulers and Prophets of Habakkuk's Time	1509
Zephaniah	The Rulers and Prophets of Zephaniah's Time	1516
Haggai	The Rulers and Prophets of Haggai's Time	1524
	The Jewish Calendar	1525
Zechariah	The Rulers and Prophets of Zechariah's Time	1530
	The Jewish Calendar	1531
Malachi	The Rulers and Prophets of Malachi's Time	1550

New Testament

Book	Description	Page
Matthew	The Genealogy of Jesus the Christ	1557
	Herod's Family Tree	1561
	Inside Herod's Temple	1614
Luke	Herod's Family Tree	1658
	Life of Christ Showing Coverage by Luke	1710
Acts	Sequence of Events in Paul's Life after His Conversion	1779
Galatians	Sequence of Events in Paul's Life after His Conversion	1893
Bible Study Helps	Overview of the Bible	2085
	Division of Alexander the Great's Empire	2090
	The Hasmonean Dynasty	2092
	The Prophetic Points of History	2102

Topical Study Charts

(in Bible book order)

Old Testament

Book	Description	Page
Leviticus	The Offerings and Their Purposes	212
Numbers	Insights from Numbers	287
Deuteronomy	Lessons from the Life of Moses	351
Judges	The Judges of Israel	437
2 Kings	The Kings of Israel and Judah	654
Nehemiah	Lessons from the Life of Nehemiah	805
Hosea	God's Response to Israel's Sin	1452
Zechariah	Zechariah's Prophetic Revelations	1546

New Testament

Book	Description	Page
John	The Arrest, Trial, and Crucifixion of Jesus Christ	1757
	What the Gospels Teach about the Kingdom of God/the Kingdom of Heaven	1758
	The Account of Jesus' Resurrection	1760
Galatians	Paul's Concern for the Churches at Galatia	1901
Philippians	Paul's Instructions to the Philippians	1922
James	James Subject by Subject	2003
1 John	I Am Writing to You	2029
	1 John Key Words	2029
	What I Can Know/How I Can Know It	2029
Revelation	Jesus' Messages to the Churches	2068
	What Revelation Teaches about God, Jesus, the Holy Spirit	2071
	The Seven Seals, Trumpets, and Bowls	2072
	What the Bible Teaches about Babylon	2074
	The Day of the Lord, the Day of Wrath, the Day of God	2078

MAPS

(in Bible book order)

All maps are approximate to scale.

OLD TESTAMENT

Book	Description	Page
Genesis	The Garden of Eden	5
	Journeys of Abraham	20
Exodus	The Exodus from Egypt to Canaan	94
Numbers	The Exodus from Egypt to Canaan	240
	The Lands of Israel's Journey from Mt. Hor to Moab	260
	Border of Canaan	282
	Cities of Refuge	284
Deuteronomy	The Lands of Israel's Journeys after the Exodus	292
Joshua	Joshua: Occupying the Promised Land	356
	Joshua's 3-Pronged Invasion	366
Judges	Israelite Cities and Settlements in the Time of the Judges	398
Ruth	Ruth's Journey from Moab to Bethlehem	440
1 Samuel	The Wanderings of the Ark	455
	Saul's Ascent to Kingship	463
	The Philistines' Attack on the Israelites	466
	The Battle at Michmash	468
	David's Journeys: 1 Samuel 21–22	485
	David's Journeys: 1 Samuel 23	486
	David's Journeys: 1 Samuel 24	488
	David's Journeys: 1 Samuel 25–27:2	489
	David's Journeys: 1 Samuel 27	494
	Ziklag and the Spoils	497
	The Death of Saul and His Sons	499
	Israel in the Days of Samuel, Saul, and David	501
1 Kings	Solomon's Kingdom	557
	The Divided Kingdom: 931–586 B.C.	577
	Elijah's Ministry	591
2 Kings	Elisha's Ministry	604
	The Cities and Geography of 2 Kings	605
	Jerusalem in the Time of the Judean Monarchy	626
	The Assyrian Captivity of Israel	631
	Exiles of Judah to Babylon	647
1 Chronicles	The Land Settled by the Twelve Tribes	666
	The Wanderings of the Ark	683
	The Borders of David's Empire	690
2 Chronicles	Cedar from Lebanon	710
	The Divided Kingdom: 931–586 B.C.	722
Nehemiah	From Susa to Jerusalem	782
	The Gates in Nehemiah's Time	784
Isaiah	The Nations That Received the Oracles	1112
Jeremiah	The Nations of Jeremiah's Prophecy	1279
Ezekiel	The Nations of Ezekiel's Prophecies	1357
Ezekiel	The Tribes, the Prince's Portion, the City, the Sanctuary	1399
Daniel	The Beautiful Land	1422
Joel	The Valley of Jehoshaphat	1460
Amos	Thus Says the Lord to . . .	1466
Obadiah	Possessions Given by the Lord	1481
Jonah	Jonah's Journey	1484
Zephaniah	The Nations of the Lord's Anger	1518
Zechariah	God's Judgment Pronounced	1538

NEW TESTAMENT

Book	Description	Page
Matthew	Bible Cities in the Time of Jesus	1558
	Israel in the Time of Christ	1565
	Galilee	1572
	Judea	1591
	From Bethany, Bethphage Across the Mount of Olives into Jerusalem	1594
	Jerusalem of the New Testament	1607
Mark	Regions from Which People Came to See Jesus	1621
	Galilee	1631
	From Bethany, Bethphage Across the Mount of Olives into Jerusalem	1637
	Jerusalem of the New Testament	1646
Luke	The Region of the Tetrarchs	1659
	Israel in the Time of Christ	1661
	From Bethany, Bethphage Across the Mount of Olives into Jerusalem	1695
	Jerusalem of the New Testament	1704
John	Jesus Ministers from Capernaum to Jerusalem	1716
	From Bethany, Bethphage Across the Mount of Olives into Jerusalem	1738
	Jerusalem of the New Testament	1747
Acts	Men from Every Nation at Pentecost	1765
	Paul's First Missionary Journey	1787
	Paul's Second Missionary Journey	1794
	Paul's Third Missionary Journey	1800
	Paul Sails from Caesarea to Rome	1815
Galatians	Paul's Travels as a New Believer	1892
Colossians	Colossae	1926
1 Thessalonians	The Word Sounds Forth from Thessalonica	1939
1 Timothy	To Timothy at Ephesus	1949
Titus	To Titus at Crete	1966
Revelation	The Seven Churches of Asia	2043
Bible Study Helps	The Region of the Tetrarchs	2091

Illustrations

(in Bible book order)

Old Testament

Book	Description	Page
Introduction	The Tabernacle	NISB-34
	Solomon's Temple	NISB-36
	Herod's Temple at the Time of Jesus	NISB-38
	The Temple Mount at the Time of Jesus	NISB-40
Exodus	Ark of the Covenant	130
	Table of Showbread	130
	Lampstand	131
	Curtains	132
	Veil	133
	Bronze Altar	133
	Ephod	135
	Breastplate	135
	High Priest's Garments	136
	Robe of the Ephod	136
	Turban with Plate of Gold	136
	Altar of Incense	139
	Bronze Laver	140
	Curtains	150
	Veil	151
	Ark of the Covenant	152
	Table of Showbread	152
	Lampstand	152
	Altar of Incense	153
	Bronze Altar	153
	Bronze Laver	153
	Ephod	155
	High Priest's Garments	155
	Robe of the Ephod	156
	Turban with Plate of Gold	156
	Inside the Tabernacle	157
Leviticus	Inside the Tabernacle	189
	Lampstand	203
Numbers	Lampstand	235
1 Kings	Solomon's Temple	561
	Temple Furnishings	561
	Close-up of Holy of Holies	562
	Sea on Oxen	564
	Bronze Stand with Bronze Basin	564
	Lampstand	565
1 Chronicles	Robe of the Ephod	685
2 Chronicles	Close-up of Holy of Holies	711
	Bronze Altar	712
	Sea on Oxen	712
	Bronze Stand with Bronze Basin	712
	Lampstand	712
	Table	712
	Ark of the Covenant	713
	Solomon's Temple: Place of Sacrifice	717

New Testament

Book	Description	Page
Matthew	Inside Herod's Temple	1614
Hebrews	Inside the Tabernacle	1984

Color Maps

(in Bible book order)

Description	Page
Modern Boundaries of Bible Lands	2241
The Settlement of the Descendants of Shem, Ham, and Japheth	2242
The Ancient and Modern Sites of the Exodus	2243
Ezekiel's Vision of the Promised Land	2244
Israel's Territories: Ancient and Modern	2245
The Relationship of Ancient Empires to Modern Nations	2246
Development of Modern Israel	2248

THE NEW AMERICAN STANDARD CONCORDANCE
TO THE OLD AND NEW TESTAMENTS

A collection of the principal **common words** with their most widely used examples in text and lesser usages in reference. Related words, or synonyms follow the **key word**. The **key word** is abbreviated in the text to its first letter, e.g., "abide" is **"a."** Variants add suffixes or prefixes, e.g., "abiding" appears as **"a-ing."**

~A

AARON
brother of Moses Ex 4:14
spokesman for Moses Ex 4:28;7:1-2
as priest Ex 28:1;29:44
rod of Num 17:8; Heb 9:4
critical of Moses Num 12:1
death Deut 10:6

ABADDON
1 *region of dead* Job 26:6; Prov 15:11
2 *angel of bottomless pit* Rev 9:11

ABANDON *leave*
LORD has **a-ed** us Judg 6:13
not **a** His people 1 Sam 12:22
a the remnant 2 Kin 21:14
not **a** my soul to Ps 16:10
not **a** His people Ps 94:14
a-ed My inheritance Jer 12:7
a my soul to Hades Acts 2:27

ABASE *humble*
man will be **a-d** Is 2:11
lofty will be **a-d** Is 10:33
a the haughtiness Is 13:11
a-d before all Mal 2:9

ABATED *decreased*
water was **a** Gen 8:8
his vigor **a** Deut 34:7

ABBA *father*
A! Father Mark 14:36
we cry out, **A!** Rom 8:15

ABED-NEGO
Hebrew name Azariah Dan 1:6,7
friend of Daniel
faithful to God Dan 3:16,17
cast into furnace Dan 3:20

ABEL
son of Adam Gen 4:2
shepherd Gen 4:2
favored by God Gen 4:4
slain by Cain Gen 4:8
called righteous Matt 23:35

ABHOR *despise, detest*
associates **a** me Job 19:19
greatly **a-red** Israel Ps 78:59
nations will **a** him Prov 24:24
To the One **a-red** Is 49:7
A what is evil Rom 12:9

ABIB
early name of first month of Hebrew calendar Ex 34:18
month of Passover and Unleavened Bread Deut 16:1

ABIDE *remain, stay*
LORD **a-s** forever Ps 9:7
a in Your tent Ps 15:1
a in the shadow Ps 91:1
wrath of God **a-s** John 3:36
If you **a** in Me John 15:7
a in My love John 15:9
now faith...**a** 1 Cor 13:13
love of God **a** 1 John 3:17
God **a-s** in us 1 John 4:12

ABIGAIL
1 *wife of Nabal* 1 Sam 25:3
kind to David 1 Sam 25:18ff
wife of David 1 Sam 25:42
2 *daughter of Nahash* 2 Sam 17:25

ABIHU
son of Aaron Ex 6:23
priest Ex 28:1
disobeyed God Lev 10:1
judged by God Lev 10:2

ABIJAH
1 *son of Samuel* 1 Sam 8:2
2 *son of Jeroboam* 1 Kin 14:1
3 *son of Becher* 1 Chr 7:8
4 *line of Eleazar* 1 Chr 24:10
5 *king of Judah* 2 Chr 12:16
6 *Hezekiah's mother* 2 Chr 29:1
7 *priest* Neh 10:7;12:4

ABILITY *power, strength*
According to their **a** Ezra 2:69
a for serving Dan 1:4
a to conceive Heb 11:11

ABIMELECH
1 *king of Gerar* Gen 20:1-18
2 *king of Gerar* Gen 26:1ff
3 *king of Shechem* Judg 9:1ff
4 *priest* 1 Chr 18:16
5 *Psalm title* Ps 34

ABIRAM
opposed Moses Num 16:1ff
judged by God Num 16:25ff

ABISHAI
brother of Joab 1 Sam 26:6
warrior of David 1 Chr 18:12
aided Abner's assassination 2 Sam 3:30

ABLE *qualified*
a to judge 1 Kin 3:9
from these stones God...**a** Matt 3:9
I am **a** to do Matt 9:28
Him who is **a** Matt 10:28
a to separate us Rom 8:39
what you are **a** 1 Cor 10:13
a to comprehend Eph 3:18
be **a** to teach 2 Tim 2:2
a to save Him Heb 5:7
One who is **a** James 4:12
a to open Rev 5:3

ABNER
Saul's commander 1 Sam 17:55
loyal to David 2 Sam 3:12ff
killed by Joab 2 Sam 3:27
mourned by David 2 Sam 3:32

ABODE *habitation*
a of righteousness Jer 31:23
Our **a** with him John 14:23
their proper **a** Jude 6

ABOLISH
not come to **a** Matt 5:17
a-ing in His flesh Eph 2:15
who **a-ed** death 2 Tim 1:10

ABOMINABLE *detestable*
committed **a** deeds Ps 14:1
your beauty **a** Ezek 16:25
a idolatries 1 Pet 4:3
unbelieving and **a** Rev 21:8

ABOMINATION
hated thing
a to the Egyptians Ex 8:26
a into your house Deut 7:26
seen their **a-s** Deut 29:17
a to the LORD Prov 3:32
all their **a-s** Ezek 33:29
a of desolation Matt 24:15
a-s of the earth Rev 17:5

ABOUND *excel, plentiful*
faithful man will **a** Prov 28:20
May your peace **a** Dan 4:1
a in hope Rom 15:13
a-ing in the work 1 Cor 15:58
affection **a-s** 2 Cor 7:15
all grace **a** 2 Cor 9:8

ABOVE *over*
exalted **a** the heavens Ps 57:5
disciple is not **a** Matt 10:24
I am from **a** John 8:23

a every name Phil 2:9
exalts himself **a** 2 Thess 2:4
gift is from **a** James 1:17

ABRAHAM
covenant Gen 17:1-8
promise of Isaac Gen 17:19
asked the Lord Gen 18:22ff
offers Isaac Gen 22:9,10
death Gen 25:8
righteousness of Rom 4:3-9

ABRAHAM'S BOSOM
rabbinic terminology for Paradise Luke 16:22

ABRAM
called of God Gen 12:1-3
rescued Lot Gen 14:14-16
covenant with God Gen 15:18
name changed Gen 17:5

ABSALOM
son of David 2 Sam 13:1
his revolt 2 Sam 15:1,2
popular 2 Sam 15:6
slain by Joab 2 Sam 18:15

ABSENT *being away*
we are **a** one from Gen 31:49
a in body 1 Cor 5:3
a from the Lord 2 Cor 5:6
a from the body 2 Cor 5:8

ABSTAIN *refrain from*
a from wine Num 6:3
a-ing from foods 1 Tim 4:3
a from wickedness 2 Tim 2:19
a from fleshly lusts 1 Pet 2:11

ABUNDANCE *plenty, surplus*
seven years of **a** Gen 41:34
a of all things Deut 28:47
a of Your house Ps 36:8
a of peace Ps 72:7
a of counselors Prov 24:6
he who loves **a** Eccl 5:10
delight yourself in **a** Is 55:2
one has an **a** Luke 12:15
the **a** of grace Rom 5:17

ABUNDANT
enough, plenteous
come...find **a** water 2 Chr 32:4
a righteousness Job 37:23
a in lovingkindness Ps 86:5
comfort is **a** 2 Cor 1:5

ABUNDANTLY
they may breed **a** Gen 8:17

Populate the earth **a** Gen 9:7
will prosper you **a** Deut 30:9
drip upon man **a** Job 36:28

ABUSE (n) *insulting speech*
hurling **a** at Him Matt 27:39
was hurling **a** Luke 23:39

ABUSE (v) *hurt, molest*
a-d her all night Judg 19:25
uncircumcised...**a** me 1 Chr 10:4

ABUSIVE *filthy, vulgar*
a speech from your Col 3:8
strife, **a** language 1 Tim 6:4

ABYSS *deep, depth*
go away into the **a** Luke 8:31
descend into the **a** Rom 10:7
angel of the **a** Rev 9:11
key of the **a** Rev 20:1

ACCEPT *receive*
a the work of Deut 33:11
a good from God Job 2:10
the LORD **a-ed** Job Job 42:9
a-ed no chastening Jer 2:30
hear the word and **a** Mark 4:20
God has **a-ed** him Rom 14:3
a one another Rom 15:7

ACCEPTABLE *pleasing*
my heart Be **a** Ps 19:14
sacrifice, **a** to God Rom 12:1
a to the saints Rom 15:31
now is the **a** time 2 Cor 6:2
to God an **a** service Heb 12:28
sacrifices **a** to God 1 Pet 2:5

ACCESS *approach, entry*
grant you free **a** Zech 3:7
our **a** in one Spirit Eph 2:18

ACCOMPANY
attach to, follow
who **a** my lord 1 Sam 25:27
a-ied the king 2 Sam 19:40
a-ied by trumpets 2 Chr 5:13
allowed no one to **a** Mark 5:37
that **a** salvation Heb 6:9

ACCOMPLISH
perform, realize
a-ed deliverance 1 Sam 11:13
shall **a** my desire 1 Kin 5:9
God...**a-es** *all things* Ps 57:2
has **a-ed** His wrath Lam 4:11
a-ed redemption Luke 1:68
a His work John 4:34
I am **a-ing** a work Acts 13:41
when sin is **a-ed** James 1:15
man can **a** much James 5:16

ACCORD *agreement, union*
one **a** to fight Josh 9:2
voices...with one **a** Acts 4:24
one **a** in Solomon's Acts 5:12
crowds with one **a** Acts 8:6
one **a** they came Acts 12:20

ACCORDING
a to your word Gen 30:34
Moses did; **a** to all Ex 40:16
a to our sins Ps 103:10
a to his deeds Matt 16:27
a to the revelation Rom 16:25
heirs **a** to promise Gal 3:29
a to His riches Phil 4:19

ACCOUNT (n) *reckoning*
the **a** of the heavens Gen 2:4
On whose **a** *has* this Jon 1:8
settled **a-s** with Matt 25:19
who will give an **a** Heb 13:17

ACCOUNT (v) *reckon*
do not **a** *this* sin Num 12:11
I am **a-ed** wicked Job 9:29
You have taken **a** of Ps 56:8
are **a-ed** as nothing Dan 4:35

ACCURATELY *correctly*
teaching **a**...things Acts 18:25
a handling...word 2 Tim 2:15

ACCURSED *damned*
camp of Israel **a** Josh 6:18
be *thought* **a** Is 65:20
Depart...**a** ones Matt 25:41
he is to be **a** Gal 1:8
in greed, **a** children 2 Pet 2:14

ACCUSATION
charge of wrong
wrote an **a** against Ezra 4:6
find a ground of **a** Dan 6:4
What **a** do you John 18:29
a against my nation Acts 28:19
Do not receive an **a** 1 Tim 5:19

ACCUSE *testify against*
a-d his brother Deut 19:18
a-s you in judgment Is 54:17
He was being **a-d** Matt 27:12
a-ing...vehemently Luke 23:10
a you before the John 5:45
alternately **a-ing** Rom 2:15
not **a-d** of dissipation Titus 1:6
unjustly **a-ing** us 3 John 10

ACCUSER *complainant*
they act as my **a-s** Ps 109:4
instructing his **a-s** Acts 23:30
when the **a-s** stood Acts 25:18
a of our brethren Rev 12:10

ACHAIA
province of Greece
Acts 18:12; Rom 15:26; 1 Cor 16:15

ACHAN
stole from Jericho Josh 7:1
executed by people Josh 7:25

ACKNOWLEDGE *confess*
I **a-d** my sin Ps 32:5
all your ways **a** Him Prov 3:6
Pharisees **a** them all Acts 23:8
see fit to **a** God Rom 1:28

ACQUAINTANCE *friend*
a-s are...estranged Job 19:13
dread to my **a-s** Ps 31:11
removed my **a-s** far Ps 88:8
relatives and **a-s** Luke 2:44
And all His **a-s** Luke 23:49

ACQUAINTED
become familiar
a with all my ways Ps 139:3
a with grief Is 53:3

ACQUIRE *get, purchase*
a property in it Gen 34:10
have **a-d** Ruth Ruth 4:10
a wise counsel Prov 1:5
You have **a-d** riches Ezek 28:4
Do not **a** gold Matt 10:9

ACQUIT *declare innocent*
not **a** me of my guilt Job 10:14
A me of hidden *faults* Ps 19:12
You will not be **a-ted** Jer 49:12

ACT (n) *deed, work*
a detestable **a** Lev 20:13
mighty **a-s** as Yours Deut 3:24
every abominable **a** Deut 12:31
the **a-s** of Solomon 1 Kin 11:41
over the rebellious **a** Mic 7:18

ACT (v) *behave*
they refuse to **a** Prov 21:7
I **a-ed** ignorantly 1 Tim 1:13
So speak and so **a** James 2:12
are **a-ing** faithfully 3 John 5

ACTION *behavior, work*
a-s are weighed 1 Sam 2:3
a-s of a...harlot Ezek 16:30
plan or **a** is Acts 5:38
prepare your minds for **a** 1 Pet 1:13

ADAM
1 *first man* Gen 2:20
fall of man Gen 3:6,7
type of Christ Rom 5:14
compared to Jesus 1 Cor 15:22
2 *site in Jordan Valley* Josh 3:16

ADAR
twelfth month of Hebrew calendar Ezra 6:15
Purim observed Esth 3:7; 9:19ff

ADD
a to your yoke 1 Kin 12:11
a-ing to the wrath Neh 13:18
not **a** to His words Prov 30:6
if anyone **a-s** to them Rev 22:18

ADJURE *charge solemnly*
many times...I **a** 1 Kin 22:16
I **a** you, O daughters Song 3:5
I **a** you by Jesus Acts 19:13

ADMINISTRATION
a of the province Dan 3:12
healings, helps, **a-s** 1 Cor 12:28
in our **a** of this 2 Cor 8:20
a of the mystery Eph 3:9

ADMONISH *warn*
prophets...had **a-ed** Neh 9:26
How shall I **a** you Lam 2:13
not cease to **a** each Acts 20:31
able also to **a** one Rom 15:14
a-ing one another Col 3:16
a the unruly 1 Thess 5:14
a him as a brother 2 Thess 3:15

ADONIJAH
1 *son of David* 2 Sam 3:4
aspired to throne 1 Kin 1:5ff
pardoned 1 Kin 1:52ff
executed 1 Kin 2:25
2 *Levite* 2 Chr 17:8
3 *of the restoration* Neh 10:16

ADOPTION *acceptance*
spirit of **a** as sons Rom 8:15
to whom belongs...**a** Rom 9:4
receive the **a** as sons Gal 4:5
predestined us to **a** Eph 1:5

ADORN *array, clothe*
A yourself with Job 40:10
as a bride **a-s** herself Is 61:10
a-ed with beautiful Luke 21:5
women to **a** 1 Tim 2:9
a the doctrine of God Titus 2:10
a-ed with gold Rev 17:4
as a bride **a-ed** Rev 21:2

ADULTERER
a and the adulteress Lev 20:10
eye of the **a** waits Job 24:15
associate with **a-s** Ps 50:18
a-s, nor effeminate 1 Cor 6:9
a-s God will judge Heb 13:4

ADULTERESS
a shall surely be Lev 20:10
a who flatters with Prov 2:16
mouth of an **a** Prov 22:14
You **a** wife, who Ezek 16:32
they are **a-es** Ezek 23:45
shall be called an **a** Rom 7:3

ADULTERY
shall not commit **a** Ex 20:14
man who commits **a** Lev 20:10
a-ies of faithless Jer 3:8
worn out by **a-ies** Ezek 23:43
committed **a** with her Matt 5:28
woman commits **a** Matt 5:32
Do not commit **a** Luke 18:20
eyes full of **a** 2 Pet 2:14

ADVANCE *ahead, beyond*
old, **a-d** in age Gen 24:1
a-d *in years* 1 Sam 17:12
have told you in **a** Matt 24:25
both **a-d** in years Luke 1:7
a-ing in Judaism Gal 1:14

ADVANTAGE *benefit, profit*
lead surely to **a** Prov 21:5
What **a** does man Eccl 1:3
Wisdom has the **a** Eccl 10:10
a that I go away John 16:7

what **a** has the Jew Rom 3:1
no **a** would be taken of us 2 Cor 2:11
sake of *gaining an* **a** Jude 16

ADVERSARY *foe, opponent*
an **a** to your **a-ies** Ex 23:22
an **a** to Solomon 1 Kin 11:14
And my **a-ies** will rejoice Ps 13:4
a-ies and my enemies Ps 27:2
redeemed...from the **a** Ps 78:42
crush his **a-ies** Ps 89:23
there are many **a-ies** 1 Cor 16:9
consume the **a-ies** Heb 10:27
Your **a,** the devil 1 Pet 5:8

ADVERSITY *distress, misfortune*
death and **a** Deut 30:15
not accept **a** Job 2:10
relief from...a Ps 94:13
falls into **a** Prov 13:17
A pursues sinners Prov 13:21

ADVICE *counsel*
forsook the **a** 1 Kin 12:13
a of the young 2 Chr 10:14
a of the cunning Job 5:13
they took his **a** Acts 5:40
have followed my **a** Acts 27:21

ADVISER *counselor*
with his **a** Ahuzzath Gen 26:26
Pharaoh's wisest **a-s** Is 19:11

ADVOCATE *defender, witness*
my **a** is on high Job 16:19
A with the Father 1 John 2:1

AFFECTION *devotion, love*
set His **a** to love Deut 10:15
in your own **a-s** 2 Cor 6:12
a of Christ Jesus Phil 1:8
fond an **a** for you 1 Thess 2:8

AFFLICT (v) *oppress, trouble*
a them with hard labor Ex 1:11
not **a** any widow Ex 22:22
Egyptians...**a-ed** us Deut 26:6
bind him to **a** him Judg 16:5
the wicked **a** them 2 Sam 7:10
They **a-ed** his feet Ps 105:18
He was **a-ed** Is 63:9
will **a** you no longer Nah 1:12
were sick or **a-ed** Acts 5:16
are **a-ed** in every 2 Cor 4:8
those who **a** you 2 Thess 1:6
a-ed, ill-treated Heb 11:37

AFFLICTED (n) *troubled*
save an **a** people 2 Sam 22:28
to catch the **a** Ps 10:9
justice to the **a** Ps 82:3
LORD supports the **a** Ps 147:6
days of the **a** Prov 15:15
O **a** one Is 54:11
good news to the **a** Is 61:1

AFFLICTION *oppression*
my **a** and the toil Gen 31:42
the land of my **a** Gen 41:52
the bread of **a** Deut 16:3
LORD saw the **a** 2 Kin 14:26
You saw the **a** Neh 9:9
afflicted in their **a** Job 36:15
Look upon my **a** Ps 25:18
a severe **a** Eccl 6:2
a or persecution Mark 4:17
healed of her **a** Mark 5:29
a-s await me Acts 20:23
out of much **a** 2 Cor 2:4
great ordeal of **a** 2 Cor 8:2
to suffer **a** 1 Thess 3:4

AFRAID *dreading, fearful*
a because...naked Gen 3:10
a to look at God Ex 3:6
a and fainthearted Deut 20:8
Whoever is **a** Judg 7:3
a of the terror Ps 91:5
not **a** of the snow Prov 31:21
a to swear Eccl 9:2
a of man who dies Is 51:12
a to take Mary Matt 1:20
were **a** of Him Mark 11:18
Do not be **a,** Mary Luke 1:30
a of those who kill Luke 12:4
a of the people Luke 22:2
a that, as the serpent 2 Cor 11:3
Do not be **a** Rev 1:17

AGABUS
prophet Acts 11:28;21:10

AGE *period, year*
David reached old **a** 1 Chr 23:1
a should speak Job 32:7
either in this **a** Matt 12:32
the end of the **a** Matt 13:40
sons of this **a** are Luke 16:8
in the **a-s** to come Eph 2:7
hidden...*past* **a-s** Col 1:26
in the present **a** Titus 2:12

AGED *old*
Wisdom is...**a** men Job 12:12
a are among us Job 15:10
refined, **a** wine Is 25:6
Paul, the **a** Philem 9

AGONY *anguish*
a has seized me 2 Sam 1:9
A like...childbirth Jer 50:43
in **a** in this flame Luke 16:24
in **a** He was praying Luke 22:44
the **a** of death Acts 2:24

AGREE *consent*
if two of you **a** Matt 18:19
did you not **a** Matt 20:13
Jews had already **a-d** John 9:22
have **a-d** together Acts 5:9
words...Prophets **a** Acts 15:15
a with sound words 1 Tim 6:3

AGREEMENT *accord*
an **a** in writing Neh 9:38
Saul was in hearty **a** Acts 8:1

a has the temple 2 Cor 6:16
three are in **a** 1 John 5:8

AGRIPPA
1 *Herod Agrippa I*
see **HEROD**
2 *Herod Agrippa II*
see **HEROD**

AHAB
1 *king of Israel* 1 Kin 16:28
son of Omri 1 Kin 16:29
married Jezebel 1 Kin 16:31
idolater 1 Kin 16:33
2 *false prophet* Jer 29:21,22

AHASUERUS
1 *Persian king, Xerxes I* Ezra 4:6; Book of Esther
2 *father of Darius the Mede* Dan 9:1

AHAZ
1 *son of Jotham* 2 Kin 15:38
king of Judah 2 Kin 16:2
2 *line of Jonathan* 1 Chr 8:35

AHIJAH / AHIAH
1 *prophet of Shiloh* 1 Kin 14:2
2 *of Issachar* 1 Kin 15:27
3 *son of Jerahmeel* 1 Chr 2:25
4 *the Pelonite* 1 Chr 11:36
5 *under Nehemiah* Neh 10:26

AHIMELECH
1 *high priest* 1 Sam 22:16
gave bread and sword to David 1 Sam 21:1-9
2 *Hittite* 1 Sam 26:6,7

AHITHOPHEL
counselor of David 2 Sam 15:12; 1 Chr 27:33

AI
place near Bethel Gen 12:8
defeat of Israelites Josh 7:5
captured Josh 8:23, 29

AIJALON
1 *city of refuge* Josh 10:12
Levitical city Josh 21:24
2 *valley* Josh 19:42
3 *Zebulunite town* Judg 12:12

AIR *breeze, sky*
no **a** can come Job 41:16
They pant for **a** Jer 14:6
birds of the **a** Matt 6:26
not beating the **a** 1 Cor 9:26
speaking into the **a** 1 Cor 14:9
power of the **a** Eph 2:2
the Lord in the **a** 1 Thess 4:17

ALABASTER *whitish stone*
stones and **a** 1 Chr 29:2
pillars of **a** Song 5:15
brought an **a** vial Luke 7:37

ALARM (n) *danger, warning*
when you blow an **a** Num 10:5
The **a** of war Jer 4:19
shout of **a** at noon Jer 20:16
a on My...mountain Joel 2:1

ALARM (v) *frighten, warn*
he is not **a-ed** Job 40:23
interpretation **a** you Dan 4:19
thoughts **a-ed** him Dan 5:6
being much **a-ed** Acts 10:4
in no way **a-ed** by Phil 1:28

ALERT (n) *watch*
be on the **a** Matt 24:42
be **a** and sober 1 Thess 5:6

ALERT (v) *be watchful*
keeping **a** in it Col 4:2
let us be **a** 1 Thess 5:6

ALEXANDER
1 *son of Simon of Cyrene* Mark 15:21
2 *of priestly family* Acts 4:6
3 *Ephesian Jew* Acts 19:33
4 *apostate teacher* 1 Tim 1:20
5 *enemy of Paul* 2 Tim 4:14

ALEXANDRIAN
1 *of Alexandria* Acts 6:9
2 *ship* Acts 27:6;28:11
3 *Apollos* Acts 18:24

ALIEN *foreigner, stranger*
love for the **a** Deut 10:19
give it to the **a** Deut 14:21
Our houses to **a-s** Lam 5:2
a-s in a foreign land Acts 7:6
no longer...**a-s** Eph 2:19
he lived as an **a** Heb 11:9
I urge you as **a-s** 1 Pet 2:11

ALIENATE *estrange*
Or I shall be **a-d** Jer 6:8
a this choice *portion* Ezek 48:14
were formerly **a-d** Col 1:21

ALIVE
Is your father still **a** Gen 43:7
down **a** to Sheol Num 16:33
go down **a** to Sheol Ps 55:15
may keep **a** a heifer Is 7:21
when He was...**a** Matt 27:63
heard...He was **a** Mark 16:11
presented Himself **a** Acts 1:3
yet the spirit is **a** Rom 8:10
all will be made **a** 1 Cor 15:22
made us **a** together Eph 2:5
a in the spirit 1 Pet 3:18
I am **a** forevermore Rev 1:18

ALLEGIANCE *loyalty*
pledged **a** to King 1 Chr 29:24
he pledged his **a** Ezek 17:18

ALLIANCE *agreement*
formed a marriage **a** 1 Kin 3:1
after an **a** is made Dan 11:23

ALLIED *joined*
a...by marriage 2 Chr 18:1
throne of...**a** Ps 94:20

ALLOT *apportion, divide*
only **a** it to Israel Josh 13:6
a Him a portion Is 53:12
a-ted to each...faith Rom 12:3

ALLOTMENT *portion*
an **a** from Pharaoh Gen 47:22
as a perpetual **a** Num 18:19
Jacob is the **a** Deut 32:9
set apart the...**a** Ezek 48:20

ALLOW *permit*
not **a** the destroyer Ex 12:23
whether his body **a-s** Lev 15:3
a Your Holy One Ps 16:10
Nor **a** Your Holy One Acts 2:27
not be **a-ed** to live Acts 22:22
a you to be tempted 1 Cor 10:13
not **a** a woman 1 Tim 2:12

ALMIGHTY *all-powerful*
I am God **A** Gen 17:1
vision of the **A** Num 24:4
A has afflicted me Ruth 1:21
limits of the **A** Job 11:7
A was yet with me Job 29:5
destruction from...**A** Joel 1:15
Lord God, the **A** Rev 4:8
the **A**, reigns Rev 19:6

ALMOND
a and plane trees Gen 30:37
shaped like **a** *blossoms* Ex 37:19
and it bore ripe **a-s** Num 17:8

ALMS *charity*
a to the *Jewish* Acts 10:2
bring **a** to my nation Acts 24:17

ALONE
So He let him **a** Ex 4:26
Leave me **a**, for my Job 7:16
not live on bread **a** Matt 4:4
He was praying **a** Luke 9:18
I am not **a** *in it* John 8:16
receiving but you **a** Phil 4:15
and not by faith **a** James 2:24

ALOUD *joyful, piercing*
crying **a** as she 2 Sam 13:19
read **a** from the book Neh 13:1
I will cry **a** Ps 77:1
Sing **a** with gladness Jer 31:7
The king called **a** Dan 5:7
began to weep **a** Acts 20:37

ALPHA
first letter of Gr. alphabet Rev 1:8
title of Jesus Christ Rev 21:6
expresses eternalness of God Rev 22:13

ALTAR *place of sacrifice*
offerings on the **a** Gen 8:20
Moses built an **a** Ex 17:15
fire on the **a** Lev 6:9
Gideon built an **a** Judg 6:24
erect an **a** to 2 Sam 24:18
go to the **a** of God Ps 43:4
a-s may become waste Ezek 6:6
offering at the **a** Matt 5:23
a that sanctifies Matt 23:19
golden **a** of incense Heb 9:4
we have an **a** Heb 13:10
horns of the golden **a** Rev 9:13

ALWAYS *ever, forever*
fear the LORD...**a** Deut 14:23
He will not **a** strive Ps 103:9
fear of the LORD **a** Prov 23:17
a loses his temper Prov 29:11
will I **a** be angry Is 57:16
I am with you **a** Matt 28:20
you **a** have...poor Mark 14:7
Rejoice in the Lord **a** Phil 4:4
a be with...Lord 1 Thess 4:17
I will **a** be ready 2 Pet 1:12

AMALEKITES
descendants of Esau Gen 36:12
tribe in Negev and Sinai Ex 17:8,9; Num 14:25; 1 Sam 15:7; 1 Chr 4:43

AMASA
1 *son of Abigail* 1 Chr 2:17
Absalom's commander 2 Sam 17:25
pardoned 2 Sam 19:13
2 *an Ephraimite* 2 Chr 28:12

AMAZED
astonished, astounded
are **a** at His rebuke Job 26:11
a at His teaching Mark 1:22
heard Him were **a** Luke 2:47
Do not be **a** that I said John 3:7
were **a** and astonished Acts 2:7
whole earth was **a** Rev 13:3

AMAZEMENT *astonishment*
a came upon them Luke 4:36
with wonder and **a** Acts 3:10

AMAZIAH
1 *king of Judah* 2 Kin 12:21
son of Joash 2 Kin 14:1
2 *a Simeonite* 1 Chr 4:34
3 *son of Hilkiah* 1 Chr 6:45
4 *a priest of Bethel* Amos 7:10

AMBASSADOR *envoy*
a-s of peace weep Is 33:7
a-s for Christ 2 Cor 5:20
an **a** in chains Eph 6:20

AMBITION *design, intention*
out of selfish **a** Phil 1:17
a to lead a quiet 1 Thess 4:11
jealousy...selfish **a** James 3:14

AMBUSH (n)
cover, hiding place
a for the city Josh 8:2
rise from *your* **a** Josh 8:7
Israel set men in **a** Judg 20:29
a...behind them 2 Chr 13:13
Place men in **a** Jer 51:12

AMBUSH (v) *lie in wait*
going to **a** the city Josh 8:4
a the innocent Prov 1:11
a their own lives Prov 1:18

AMEN *so be it*
people shall say, **A** Deut 27:16
the LORD forever! **A** Ps 89:52
glory forever...**A** Phil 4:20
the **A**, the faithful Rev 3:14
A. Come, Lord Jesus Rev 22:20

AMMONITES
tribes E of Jordan Gen 19:38
defeated Israel Judg 3:13
hired Arameans 2 Sam 10:6
fought against Judah 2 Kin 24:2

AMNON
1 *eldest son of David* 2 Sam 3:2
raped his sister 2 Sam 13:2ff
ordered killed 2 Sam 13:28
2 *line of Judah* 1 Chr 4:20

AMON
1 *Ahab's governor* 1 Kin 22:26
2 *king of Judah* 2 Kin 21:18-26
3 *of the Nethinims* Neh 7:59
4 *Egyptian deity* Jer 46:25

AMORITES
tribe on both sides of Jordan Gen 15:16; Ex 34:11; Deut 1:27; Judg 11:23; Amos 2:9

AMOS
prophet to Israel Book of Amos

AMOUNT *measure*
daily **a** of bricks Ex 5:19
a of your valuation Lev 27:23
large **a** of bronze 1 Chr 18:8

AMRAM
1 *father of Moses* Ex 6:18-20; 1 Chr 23:13
2 *son of Bani* Ezra 10:34

ANAK / ANAKIM
pre-Israelite tribe of Palestine Num 13:22-33
giants Deut 2:10; Josh 14:15

ANANIAS
1 *deceived Jerusalem church* Acts 5:1-5
2 *Damascus Christian* Acts 9:10,17
3 *high priest* Acts 23:2

ANCESTORS *forefathers*
blessings of my **a** Gen 49:26
the **a** have set Deut 19:14
iniquities of their **a** Jer 11:10

ANCHOR
they weighed **a** Acts 27:13
they cast four **a-s** Acts 27:29
an **a** of the soul Heb 6:19

ANCIENT *aged, old*
of the **a** mountains Deut 33:15
the records are **a** 1 Chr 4:22
keep to the **a** path Job 22:15
O **a** doors Ps 24:9
A of Days Dan 7:9
the **a-s** were told Matt 5:21
from **a** generations Acts 15:21
not spare the **a** world 2 Pet 2:5

ANDREW
fisherman Matt 4:18
brother of Peter Matt 4:18
receives Jesus John 1:40-42
apostle Luke 6:14

ANGEL *divine messenger*
send His **a** before Gen 24:7
a-s...were ascending Gen 28:12
an **a** to Jerusalem 1 Chr 21:15
bread of **a-s** Ps 78:25
Praise Him, all His **a-s** Ps 148:2
a of His presence Is 63:9
a who was speaking Zech 4:4
command His **a-s** Matt 4:6
a Gabriel was sent Luke 1:26
they are like **a-s** Luke 20:36
two **a-s** in white John 20:12
like the face of an **a** Acts 6:15
as an **a** of light 2 Cor 11:14
worship of the **a-s** Col 2:18
entertained **a-s** Heb 13:2
God did not spare **a-s** 2 Pet 2:4
a of the church Rev 2:1

ANGEL OF THE LORD
a called to Abraham Gen 22:15
a took his stand Num 22:22
I have seen the **a** Judg 6:22
a said to Elijah 2 Kin 1:3
a destroying 1 Chr 21:12
a encamps around those Ps 34:7
a admonished Joshua Zech 3:6
a commanded him Matt 1:24
a appeared to Joseph Matt 2:13
a...opened the gates Acts 5:19

ANGER *indignation, wrath*
My **a** will be kindled Ex 22:24
Moses' **a** burned Ex 32:19
from His burning **a** Deut 13:17
a with their idols 1 Kin 16:13
not turn back His **a** Job 9:13
not rebuke me in Your **a** Ps 6:1
a is but for a moment Ps 30:5
He who is slow to **a** Prov 14:29
a man *given* to **a** Prov 22:24
a of the LORD Is 5:25
sun go down...**a** Eph 4:26
put...aside: **a** Col 3:8
slow to **a** James 1:19

ANGRY *enraged, indignant*
Why are you **a** Gen 4:6
king became very **a** Esth 1:12
that He not become **a** Ps 2:12
a man stirs up strife Prov 29:22
a beyond measure Is 64:9
and **a** no more Ezek 16:42
a with his brother Matt 5:22
Be **a**...do not sin Eph 4:26
a with this generation Heb 3:10

ANGUISH *distress, pain*
writhed in great **a** Esth 4:4
My heart is in **a** Ps 55:4
land of distress and **a** Is 30:6
A has seized us Jer 6:24
and **a** of heart 2 Cor 2:4

ANIMAL *beast, creature*
from man to **a-s** Gen 6:7
lies with an **a** Ex 22:19
the fat of the **a** Lev 7:25
wild **a-s** of the field Jer 27:6
a blemished **a** Mal 1:14
four-footed **a-s** Acts 10:12
like unreasoning **a-s** 2 Pet 2:12

ANNA
prophetess Luke 2:36

ANNAS
high priest Luke 3:2; John 18:13ff

ANNIHILATE *destroy*
to **a** all the Jews Esth 3:13
My enemy **a-d** them Lam 2:22
to destroy and **a** Dan 11:44
let it be **a-d** Zech 11:9

ANNOUNCE *proclaim*
Who **a-s** peace Is 52:7
I will **a** My words Jer 18:2
a-ing to...disciples John 20:18
a-d...the Righteous Acts 7:52

ANNUL *dismiss, make void*
he shall **a** her vow Num 30:8
husband has **a-led** Num 30:12
not **a** Your covenant Jer 14:21
a-s one of the least Matt 5:19

ANOINT (v) *sprinkle oil upon*
a them and ordain Ex 28:41
a Aaron and his sons Ex 30:30
LORD **a-ed** you king 1 Sam 15:17
a-ed my head with oil Ps 23:5
a the most holy *place* Dan 9:24
has **a-ed** My body Mark 14:8
did not **a** My head Luke 7:46
and **a-ed** my eyes John 9:11
a-ed...feet of Jesus John 12:3
a-ed Him...Holy Spirit Acts 10:38
a-ing him with oil James 5:14

ANOINTED (adj) *consecrated*
if the **a** priest sins Lev 4:3
not touch My **a** 1 Chr 16:22
a cherub who Ezek 28:14
the two **a** ones Zech 4:14

ANOINTED (n)
consecrated one
walk before My **a** 1 Sam 2:35
he is the LORD's **a** 1 Sam 24:10
against His **A** Ps 2:2

ANOINTING (adj) *consecration*
spices for the **a** oil Ex 25:6
shall be a holy **a** oil Ex 30:31
for the LORD's **a** oil Lev 10:7

ANOINTING (n) *consecration*
a will qualify them Ex 40:15
a from the Holy 1 John 2:20
His **a** teaches you 1 John 2:27

ANSWER (n) *response*
consider what **a** I 1 Chr 21:12
the king sent an **a** Ezra 4:17
Who gives a right **a** Prov 24:26
amazed at...His **a-s** Luke 2:47

ANSWER (v) *respond*
anyone who will **a** you Job 5:1
The LORD **a-ed** me Ps 118:5
Jesus **a-ing** said Matt 3:15
who **a-s** back to God Rom 9:20

ANT *insect*
to the **a**, O sluggard Prov 6:6
a-s are not a strong Prov 30:25

ANTELOPE *animal*
Like an **a** in a net Is 51:20

ANTICHRIST *foe of Christ*
a-s have appeared 1 John 2:18
This is the **a** 1 John 2:22
the *spirit* of the **a** 1 John 4:3
deceiver and the **a** 2 John 7

ANTIOCH
1 *city in Syria* Acts 6:5;11:19,26
2 *city in Galatia* Acts 13:14; 14:19

ANTIPAS
1 *Pergamum martyr* Rev 2:13
2 *Herod Antipas see* **HEROD**

ANXIETY *sorrow*
a because of my sin Ps 38:18
There is **a** by the sea Jer 49:23
casting all your **a** 1 Pet 5:7

ANXIOUS *concern, worry*
and will become **a** for us 1 Sam 9:5
not be **a** in...drought Jer 17:8
my spirit is **a** to Dan 2:3
Be **a** for nothing Phil 4:6

APART *separate*
So they set **a** Kedesh Josh 20:7
tear their fetters **a** Ps 2:3

a from your Father Matt 10:29
a from Him nothing John 1:3
a from Me you can John 15:5
faith **a** from works Rom 3:28

APOLLOS
Alexandrian Jew Acts 18:24
taught at Ephesus Acts 18:24
taught at Corinth 1 Cor 3:4,6

APOSTASY *faithlessness*
a-ies are numerous Jer 5:6
Turned away in...**a** Jer 8:5
I will heal their **a** Hos 14:4
unless the **a** comes 2 Thess 2:3

APOSTLE *sent with authority*
the twelve **a-s** Matt 10:2
named as **a-s** Luke 6:13
called *as* an **a** Rom 1:1
an **a** of Gentiles Rom 11:13
not fit to be called an **a** 1 Cor 15:9
men are false **a-s** 2 Cor 11:13
He gave some *as* **a-s** Eph 4:11
Jesus, the **A** and Heb 3:1
a-s of the Lamb Rev 21:14

APOSTLESHIP
office of apostle
received grace and **a** Rom 1:5
seal of my **a** 1 Cor 9:2
Peter in *his* **a** to Gal 2:8

APPAREL *clothing, garment*
of gold on your **a** 2 Sam 1:24
majestic in His **a** Is 63:1
put on his royal **a** Acts 12:21

APPEAL *ask, entreat*
standing and **a-ing** Acts 16:9
I **a** to Caesar Acts 25:11
Paul **a-ed** to be held Acts 25:21
a-ed to...Emperor Acts 25:25
a to *him* as a father 1 Tim 5:1
love's sake I...**a** Philem 9

APPEAR *become visible*
LORD **a-ed** to Abram Gen 12:7
glory of the LORD **a-ed** Ex 16:10
a-ed on the wings 2 Sam 22:11
and **a-ed** to many Matt 27:53
first **a-ed** to Mary Mark 16:9
who, **a-ing** in glory Luke 9:31
a-ed to them tongues Acts 2:3
we must all **a** before 2 Cor 5:10
a-ing of the glory Titus 2:13
will **a** a second time Heb 9:28
Chief Shepherd **a-s** 1 Pet 5:4
not **a-ed** as yet 1 John 3:2

APPEARANCE
countenance
handsome in...**a** Gen 39:6
the **a** of the angel Judg 13:6
at the outward **a** 1 Sam 16:7
a is blacker than soot Lam 4:8
lapis lazuli in **a** Ezek 1:26

they neglect their **a** Matt 6:16
judge according to **a** John 7:24
a of His coming 2 Thess 2:8
a of the locusts Rev 9:7

APPEASE *moderate, mollify*
I will **a** him Gen 32:20
wise man will **a** it Prov 16:14
have **a-d** My wrath Zech 6:8

APPETITE *desire, hunger*
our **a** is gone Num 11:6
a of the young lions Job 38:39
man of *great* **a** Prov 23:2
a is not satisfied Eccl 6:7
enlarges his **a** like Hab 2:5
whose god is *their* **a** Phil 3:19

APPLE *fruit*
as the **a** of the eye Ps 17:8
Like **a-s** of gold Prov 25:11
Refresh me with **a-s** Song 2:5
touches the **a** of His Zech 2:8

APPOINT
assign, commission
shall **a** *as a penalty* Ex 21:23
I will **a** over you Lev 26:16
who **a-ed** Moses 1 Sam 12:6
to **a** their relatives 1 Chr 15:16
a magistrates and Ezra 7:25
there is a harvest **a-ed** Hos 6:11
a-ed elders for them Acts 14:23
a-ed a preacher and 1 Tim 2:7
For the Law **a-s** men Heb 7:28

APPORTION *distribute*
a the inheritance Num 34:29
a this land Josh 13:7
He **a-s** our fields Mic 2:4

APPROPRIATE *suitable*
blessing **a** to him Gen 49:28
eat at the **a** time Eccl 10:17
a to repentance Acts 26:20

APPROVAL *consent*
loved the **a** of men John 12:43
give hearty **a** to Rom 1:32
men of old gained **a** Heb 11:2

APPROVE *accept, attest*
the Lord does not **a** Lam 3:36
too pure to **a** evil Hab 1:13
standing by **a-ing** Acts 22:20
and **a-d** by men Rom 14:18
present yourself **a-d** 2 Tim 2:15

AQUILA
a native of Pontus Acts 18:2
Corinthian Christian Acts 18:18
co-worker with Paul Rom 16:3

ARAB
1 *town in Judah* Josh 15:52
2 *ethnic identity* 1 Kin 10:15; Neh 2:19; Is 13:20

ARABAH
1 *desert steppe* Is 35:1,6; Jer 52:7
2 *Jordan rift valley* Deut 1:1; Josh 3:17
3 *Dead Sea* Josh 3:16; 2 Kin 14:25

ARABIA
land SE of Israel / Judah Is 21:13; Ezek 30:5; Gal 1:17;4:25

ARAM
1 *son of Shem* Gen 10:22,23
2 *line of Asher* 1 Chr 7:34
3 *ancestor of Jesus, shortened to Ram* Ruth 4:19; Matt 1:3; Luke 3:33
4 *Syria and N Mesopotamia* Num 23:7; 1 Kin 11:25; 2 Kin 13:19; Is 7:8

ARAMAIC
Semitic language 2 Kin 18:26; Ezra 4:7; Is 36:11; Dan 2:4

ARAMEANS
tribes of Aram 2 Sam 8:5; 1 Kin 20:20; 2 Kin 24:2

ARARAT
kingdom and mountain range in Armenia Gen 8:4; 2 Kin 19:37; Jer 51:27

ARAUNAH
Jebusite owner of threshing floor on Mt. Moriah 2 Sam 24:16,18
David purchases threshing floor for altar and later temple 2 Sam 24:23,24
see also **ORNAN**

ARCHANGEL
voice of *the* **a** 1 Thess 4:16
But Michael the **a** Jude 9

ARCHELAUS *see* **HEROD**

ARCHER *bowman*
the **a-s** hit him 1 Sam 31:3
a-s shot King Josiah 2 Chr 35:23
a-s equipped with bows Ps 78:9
an **a** who wounds Prov 26:10

ARCHIPPUS
Colossian Christian Col 4:17
co-worker with Paul Philem 2

AREOPAGUS
hill and council in Athens Acts 17:19,22

ARGUE *dispute, question*
I will **a** my ways Job 13:15
hastily to **a** *your case* Prov 25:8
Pharisees...**a** with Mark 8:11
scribes **a-ing** with Mark 9:14
a-ing with the...*Jews* Acts 9:29

ARGUMENT *disagreement*
Please hear my **a** Job 13:6
mouth are no **a-s** Ps 38:14
a started among them Luke 9:46

ARIEL
1 *a Moabite* 2 Sam 23:20; 1 Chr 11:22
2 *applied to Jerusalem* Is 29:1ff
3 *sent by Ezra* Ezra 8:16

ARISE *rise, stand*
A, walk about the Gen 13:17
Abraham **arose** early Gen 19:27
will **a** and play Deut 31:16
you have **a-n** early 1 Sam 29:10
arose and tore his robe Job 1:20
when God **a-s** Job 31:14
A, O LORD; save me Ps 3:7
Though war **a** Ps 27:3
A, my darling Song 2:13
a-n *anyone* greater Matt 11:11
false prophets will **a** Matt 24:11
arose from the dead Acts 10:41
a from the dead Eph 5:14

ARISTARCHUS
Thessalonian Christian Acts 20:4; 27:2
co-worker with Paul Col 4:10; Philem 24

ARK *chest, vessel*
a of gopher wood Gen 6:14
into the **a** to Noah Gen 7:9
a of acacia wood Ex 37:1
a of the covenant Josh 4:7
Noah entered the **a** Matt 24:38
a of His covenant Rev 11:19

ARM (n) *part of body*
the everlasting **a-s** Deut 33:27
a without strength Job 26:2
a-s of the wicked Ps 37:17
His holy **a** have gained Ps 98:1
a seal on your **a** Song 8:6
be carried in the **a-s** Is 60:4
took...in His **a-s** Mark 10:16
with an uplifted **a** Acts 13:17

ARM (v) *mobilize*
A men from among Num 31:3
a-ed for battle Num 32:29
a-ed with iron 2 Sam 23:7
a yourselves also 1 Pet 4:1

ARMAGEDDON
see **HAR-MAGEDON**

ARMED (adj) *mobilized*
the **a** men went Josh 6:13
their **a** camps 1 Sam 28:1
So the **a** men left 2 Chr 28:14
like an **a** man Prov 6:11

ARMOR *protective device*
a joint of the **a** 1 Kin 22:34
strip off his outer **a** Job 41:13
all his **a** on which Luke 11:22
put on...**a** of light Rom 13:12
full **a** of God Eph 6:11

ARMY *host, war*
not go out with the **a** Deut 24:5
like the **a** of God 1 Chr 12:22
a ready for battle 2 Chr 26:11
officers of the **a** Neh 2:9
forth with our **a-ies** Ps 60:10
exceedingly great **a** Ezek 37:10
a-ies...in heaven Rev 19:14
and against His **a** Rev 19:19

ARNON
river and border Num 21:13
valley in Moab Deut 2:24

AROMA *odor*
the soothing **a** Gen 8:21
his **a** has not changed Jer 48:11
through us...sweet **a** 2 Cor 2:14
a from life to life 2 Cor 2:16
as a fragrant **a** Eph 5:2

AROUSE *raise, stir*
A Yourself to help me Ps 59:4
a-s for you the spirits Is 14:9
a-d one from the north Is 41:25
He will **a** *His* zeal Is 42:13
LORD has **a-d** the spirit Jer 51:11

ARRANGE *set in order*
a what belongs on it Ex 40:4
shall **a** the pieces Lev 1:8
he **a-d** the wood 1 Kin 18:33
for so he had **a-d** it Acts 20:13

ARRAY (n)
arrangement, order
went up in martial **a** Ex 13:18
in battle **a** Josh 4:12
Worship...in holy **a** 1 Chr 16:29
holy **a,** from the womb Ps 110:3

ARRAY (v) *adorn, clothe*
Israel **a-ed** for battle Judg 20:20
let them **a** the man Esth 6:9
A yourselves before Job 33:5

ARREST *restrain*
he **a-ed** Jeremiah Jer 37:13
Herod had John **a-ed** Matt 14:3
and clubs to **a** Me Matt 26:55
proceeded to **a** Peter Acts 12:3

ARROGANCE *pride*
your **a** has come 2 Kin 19:28
Pride and **a** and Prov 8:13
a of the proud Is 13:11
a, pride, and fury Is 16:6
a of your heart Jer 49:16
you boast in your **a** James 4:16

ARROGANT *proud*
a men have risen up Ps 86:14
But a fool is **a** Prov 14:16
a toward the LORD Jer 48:26
Knowledge makes **a** 1 Cor 8:1
boastful, **a,** revilers 2 Tim 3:2
speaking...**a** *words* 2 Pet 2:18

ARROW *dart, missile*
shot an **a** past him 1 Sam 20:36
a-s of the Almighty Job 6:4
a cannot make him Job 41:28
make ready their **a** Ps 11:2
broke the flaming **a-s** Ps 76:3
sword and a sharp **a** Prov 25:18
tongue is a deadly **a** Jer 9:8
target for the **a** Lam 3:12
deadly **a-s** of famine Ezek 5:16
a-s of the evil *one* Eph 6:16

ART *craft*
with their secret **a-s** Ex 7:22
the perfumers' **a** 2 Chr 16:14

ARTAXERXES
Persian king Ezra 4:7,8;7:1,12; Neh 2:1;5:14

ARTEMIS
Greek goddess Acts 19:24ff

ARTICLE *object, vessel*
a-s of silver Gen 24:53
any wooden **a** Lev 11:32
of every precious **a** Hos 13:15
every **a** of ivory Rev 18:12

ASA
1 *king of Judah* 1 Kin 15:8-24; 2 Chr 14:8-15
2 *a Levite* 1 Chr 9:16

ASCEND *go up*
a into the hill Ps 24:3
If I **a** to heaven Ps 139:8
Who has **a-ed** into Prov 30:4
breath of man **a-s** Eccl 3:21
has **a-ed** into heaven John 3:13
Son of Man **a-ing** John 6:62
a-ed to the Father John 20:17
who **a-ed** far above Eph 4:10

ASCENT *hill, rise*
by the **a** of Heres Judg 8:13
a of the...Olives 2 Sam 15:30
Song of **A-s** Ps 120-134

ASCRIBE *attribute*
have **a-d** to David 1 Sam 18:8
A to the LORD 1 Chr 16:28
a righteousness to Job 36:3

ASH
but dust and **a-es** Gen 18:27
from the **a** heap 1 Sam 2:8
a-es on her head 2 Sam 13:19

a-es were poured 1 Kin 13:5
proverbs of **a-es** Job 13:12
repent in dust and **a-es** Job 42:6
garland instead of **a-es** Is 61:3
roll in **a-es** Jer 6:26
sackcloth and **a-es** Luke 10:13
a-es of a heifer Heb 9:13

ASHAMED *embarrassed*
naked and were not **a** Gen 2:25
Let me never be **a** Ps 71:1
a of Me...My words Mark 8:38
a...when He comes Luke 9:26
not **a** of the gospel Rom 1:16
a of the testimony 2 Tim 1:8
God is not **a** Heb 11:16
he is not to be **a** 1 Pet 4:16

ASHDOD
Philistine city Josh 15:47; 1 Sam 5:1,6; Amos 1:8

ASHER
1 *eighth son of Jacob* Gen 35:26;49:20
2 *tribe of Israel* Num 1:41;13:13; Rev 7:6
3 *town in hill country* Josh 17:7

ASHERAH
Canaanite goddess and symbol Deut 16:21; Judg 6:25
Asherim (pl) 1 Kin 14:15; Mic 5:14
Asheroth (pl) Judg 3:7; 2 Chr 19:3

ASHKELON
Philistine city Judg 1:18; 2 Sam 1:20; Jer 47:5; Zeph 2:4

ASHTORETH
1 *Near Eastern goddess* 1 Kin 11:5,33; 2 Kin 23:13
Ashtaroth (pl) Judg 2:13; 1 Sam 7:4;31:10
2 *town of Bashan in E Manasseh* Deut 1:4; Josh 13:12

ASIA
Roman province of Asia Minor Acts 6:9; Rom 16:5; Rev 1:4

ASK *appeal, beg, inquire*
whatever you **a** Ruth 3:11
Two things I **a-ed** Prov 30:7
A a sign for yourself Is 7:11
a for the ancient paths Jer 6:16
A rain from the LORD Zech 10:1
Give to him who **a-s** Matt 5:42
A, and it will be Matt 7:7
a...believing Matt 21:22
pray and **a**, believe Mark 11:24
Jews **a** for signs 1 Cor 1:22
let him **a** of God James 1:5

ASLEEP *death, rest*
sound **a**...exhausted Judg 4:21
they fall **a** Ps 90:5
not died, but is **a** Matt 9:24
in the stern, **a** Mark 4:38
Lazarus...fallen **a** John 11:11
said this, he fell **a** Acts 7:60
fallen **a** in Jesus 1 Thess 4:14

ASSAIL *attack*
will you **a** a man Ps 62:3
Whoever **a-s** you Is 54:15
storm was **a-ing** *us* Acts 27:20

ASSEMBLE *gather*
a all the congregation Lev 8:3
A the people to Me Deut 4:10
David **a-d** all Israel 1 Chr 13:5
peoples may be **a-d** Is 43:9
A...on the mountains Amos 3:9
I will...**a** all of you Mic 2:12
whole city **a-d** to Acts 13:44
a-d to make war Rev 19:19

ASSEMBLY *congregation*
holy **a** on the seventh Ex 12:16
the people of the **a** Lev 16:33
a before the rock Num 20:10
Or calls an **a** Job 11:10
a of the righteous Ps 1:5
hate the **a** of evildoers Ps 26:5
proclaim a solemn **a** Joel 2:15
I delight in...**a-ies** Amos 5:21
the **a** was divided Acts 23:7
general **a** and church Heb 12:23
comes into your **a** James 2:2

ASSOCIATE (n) *colleague*
All my **a-s** abhor me Job 19:19
high priest and...**a-s** Acts 5:21

ASSOCIATE (v) *identify with*
shall they **a** with 1 Kin 11:2
a with adulterers Ps 50:18
not **a** with a man Prov 22:24
dared to **a** with them Acts 5:13
but **a** with the lowly Rom 12:16
not **a** with him 2 Thess 3:14

ASSURANCE *confirmation*
no one has **a** of life Job 24:22
a of understanding Col 2:2
full **a** of hope Heb 6:11
full **a** of faith Heb 10:22
a of *things* hoped for Heb 11:1

ASSURE *confirm*
kingdom will be **a-d** Dan 4:26
I **a** you before God Gal 1:20
will **a** our heart 1 John 3:19

ASSYRIA
kingdom name from Asshur Gen 10:22; 1 Chr 1:17
empire in upper Mesopotamia 2 Kin 19:17; Is 19:24; Jer 2:36

ASTONISHED *amazed*
will be **a** and hiss 1 Kin 9:8
a at His teaching Matt 22:33
listeners were **a** Mark 6:2
were utterly **a** Mark 7:37
they were all **a** Luke 1:63

ASTOUNDED *astonished*
prophets will be **a** Jer 4:9
a at the vision Dan 8:27
were completely **a** Mark 5:42

ASTRAY *erring, wandering*
a like a lost sheep Ps 119:176
leading *them* **a** Is 9:16
like sheep have gone **a** Is 53:6
led My people **a** Jer 23:32
lead **a**...the elect Mark 13:22
a from the faith 1 Tim 6:21
go **a** in their heart Heb 3:10
My bond-servants **a** Rev 2:20

ATHALIAH
1 *wicked daughter of Ahab* 2 Kin 11:1; 2 Chr 21:6
wife of Jehoram 2 Chr 22:2
2 *a Benjamite* 1 Chr 8:26
3 *returned exile* Ezra 8:7

ATHENS
leading Greek city Acts 17:15ff

ATONEMENT *expiation*
by which **a** was made Ex 29:33
shall make **a** for him Lev 4:35
a before the LORD Lev 14:31
how can I make **a** 2 Sam 21:3
make **a** for iniquity Dan 9:24

ATONEMENT, DAY OF
see **DAY OF ATONEMENT**

ATTACK (n) *assault*
at the first **a** 2 Sam 17:9
king ready for the **a** Job 15:24
joined in the **a** Acts 24:9

ATTACK (v) *assault, fall upon*
that he will come and **a** Gen 32:11
adversary who **a-s** Num 10:9
and **a-ed** the camp Judg 8:11
a the Philistines 1 Sam 23:2
it **a-ed** the plant Jon 4:7
no man will **a** you Acts 18:10

ATTAIN *acquire*
I cannot **a** to it Ps 139:6
woman **a-s** honor Prov 11:16
worthy to **a** to that Luke 20:35
a-ed righteousness Rom 9:30
a to the resurrection Phil 3:11

ATTEND *pay attention to*
a to your priesthood Num 18:7
thousands were **a-ing** Dan 7:10
who **a** regularly 1 Cor 9:13
a to...business 1 Thess 4:11
ears **a** to their prayer 1 Pet 3:12

ATTENDANT *helper, servant*
the **a** of Moses Num 11:28
king's **a-s,** who served Esth 2:2
a-s of...bridegroom Mark 2:19

ATTENTION *heed, regard*
no **a** to false words Ex 5:9
gives **a** to the word Prov 16:20
pays **a** to falsehood Prov 29:12
they do not pay **a** Is 5:12
pay **a** to myths 1 Tim 1:4
a to the...reading 1 Tim 4:13

ATTIRE *covering, dress*
in his military **a** 2 Sam 20:8
cupbearers...**a** 2 Chr 9:4
Him in holy **a** 2 Chr 20:21

ATTITUDE *frame of mind*
see your father's **a** Gen 31:5
a of the righteous Luke 1:17
Have this **a** in Phil 2:5
have a different **a** Phil 3:15

AUGUSTUS
name of Caesar Octavianus Luke 2:1
see **CAESAR**

AUTHOR *source*
a of their salvation Heb 2:10
a...perfecter of faith Heb 12:2

AUTHORITY *power, right*
submit...to her **a** Gen 16:9
put...your **a** on him Num 27:20
Who gave Him **a** Job 34:13
a over...day of death Eccl 8:8
entrust him with your **a** Is 22:21
as *one* having **a** Matt 7:29
a on earth to forgive Matt 9:6
a over unclean spirits Matt 10:1
All **a**...given to Me Matt 28:18
Son of Man has **a** Luke 5:24
no **a** except from God Rom 13:1
majesty, dominion...**a** Jude 25
give **a** over...nations Rev 2:26

AVENGE *revenge*
He will **a** the blood Deut 32:43
the LORD **a** me 1 Sam 24:12
Shall I not **a** Myself Jer 5:9
I will **a** their blood Joel 3:21
a-ing our blood Rev 6:10

AVENGER *revenger*
The blood **a** himself Num 35:19
otherwise the **a** of blood Deut 19:6
a of their *evil* deeds Ps 99:8
God, an **a** who brings Rom 13:4
Lord is *the* **a** 1 Thess 4:6

AVOID *refuse*
A it, do not pass by Prov 4:15

a-ing...empty chatter 1 Tim 6:20

AWAIT *wait*
afflictions **a** me Acts 20:23
a-ing...the revelation 1 Cor 1:7
who eagerly **a** Him Heb 9:28

AWAKE *be attentive, watch*
awoke from his sleep Gen 28:16
A, a, Deborah Judg 5:12
Your likeness when I **a** Ps 17:15
dream when one **a-s** Ps 73:20
arouse or **a-n** *my* love Song 2:7
He **a-ns** My ear Is 50:4
A, a, put on strength Is 51:9
A, drunkards...weep Joel 1:5
that I may **a-n** him John 11:11
hour for you to **a-n** Rom 13:11

AWARE *know, understand*
the lad was not **a** 1 Sam 20:39
Will you not be **a** Is 43:19
But Jesus, **a** of *this* Matt 12:15
I was **a** that power Luke 8:46

AWE *fear, reverence*
stand in **a** of Him Ps 33:8
in **a** of Your words Ps 119:161
in **a** of My name Mal 2:5
feeling a sense of **a** Acts 2:43

AWESOME *fearful*
How **a** is this place Gen 28:17
angel of God, very **a** Judg 13:6
great and **a** God Neh 1:5
God is **a** majesty Job 37:22
As **a** as an army Song 6:4
a day of the LORD Joel 2:31

AXE *cutting tool*
his **a,** and his hoe 1 Sam 13:20
hammer nor **a** 1 Kin 6:7
a head fell into 2 Kin 6:5
a is already laid Luke 3:9

AZARIAH
1 *ancestor of Samuel* 1 Chr 6:36
2 *official of Solomon* 1 Kin 4:2
3 *son of Nathan* 1 Kin 4:5
4 *prophet* 2 Chr 15:1-8
5 *two sons of king Jehoshaphat* 2 Chr 21:2
6 *king of Judah, also* **Uzziah** 2 Kin 15:1; 2 Chr 26:1
7 *high priest* 1 Chr 6:10
8 *family of Merari* 2 Chr 29:12
9 *son of Hilkiah* 1 Chr 6:13,14
10 *original name of Abed-nego* Dan 1:7
the name of twelve other individuals in the OT

~B

BAAL
1 *Canaanite god(s)* Num 22:41; Judg 6:25; 1 Kin 18:40
2 *line of Reuben* 1 Chr 5:5
3 *personal name* 1 Chr 8:30
4 *place name* 1 Chr 4:33

BAAL-HANAN
1 *king of Edom* Gen 36:38
2 *servant of David* 1 Chr 27:28

BAAL-HAZOR
mountain in central Palestine 2 Sam 13:23

BAAL-HERMON
part of Mt. Hermon Judg 3:3; 1 Chr 5:23

BAAL-ZEBUB
god of Ekron 2 Kin 1:2,16
see also **BEELZEBUL**

BAASHA
king of Israel 1 Kin 15:16,32

BABEL *a city founded by Nimrod* Gen 10:10;11:9
later called Babylon

BABES *infants*
From the mouth of...**b** Ps 8:2
abundance to their **b** Ps 17:14

BABY *infant*
woe...who are nursing **b-ies** Matt 24:19
b leaped...her womb Luke 1:41
b wrapped in cloths Luke 2:12
b as He lay Luke 2:16
like newborn **b-ies** 1 Pet 2:2

BABYLON *city*
1 *on the Euphrates* 2 Kin 17:24; Jer 20:4; Ezek 29:18; Dan 4:29
2 *symbolic of godlessness* Rev 14:8;17:5

BACK *part of body*
you shall see My **b** Ex 33:23
turned his **b** to leave 1 Sam 10:9
law behind their **b-s** Neh 9:26
my sins behind Your **b** Is 38:17

BAD *evil, wrong*
b report of the land Num 13:32
basket had very **b** figs Jer 24:2
if your eye is **b** Matt 6:23
b tree bears **b** fruit Matt 7:17
B company corrupts 1 Cor 15:33

BAG *sack*
fill their **b-s** Gen 42:25
in the shepherd's **b** 1 Sam 17:40
silver in two **b-s** 2 Kin 5:23
carrying *his* **b** of seed Ps 126:6
b of...weights Mic 6:11
b for *your* journey Matt 10:10
Carry no money belt, no **b** Luke 10:4

BAGGAGE *bags, supplies*
stayed with the **b** 1 Sam 25:13
prepare...yourself **b** Ezek 12:3

BAKE *cook*
b-d unleavened bread Gen 19:3
b-d food for Pharaoh Gen 40:17
they **b-d** the dough Ex 12:39
B what you will **b** Ex 16:23
grain offering **b-d** Lev 2:4
b twelve cakes Lev 24:5
taste of cakes **b-d** Num 11:8
fire to **b** bread Is 44:15

BAKER *cook*
b for the king Gen 40:1
cooks and **b-s** 1 Sam 8:13
from the **b-s'** street Jer 37:21
oven heated by the **b** Hos 7:4

BALAAM
diviner Num 22:5-31;23:5; Josh 13:22; Rev 2:14

BALAK
king of Moab Num 22:4; Mic 6:5

BALANCE *scale*
shall have just **b-s** Lev 19:36
b-s...with my calamity Job 6:2
False **b** is an Prov 11:1
mountains in a **b** Is 40:12

BALD *hairless*
If...head becomes **b** Lev 13:41
every head is **b** Jer 48:37
head was made **b** Ezek 29:18

BALDHEAD *hairless*
mocked him...you **b** 2 Kin 2:23

BALM *aromatic ointment*
b and myrrh Gen 37:25
a present, a little **b** Gen 43:11
no **b** in Gilead Jer 8:22
Gilead and obtain **b** Jer 46:11
Bring **b** for her pain Jer 51:8
honey, oil and **b** Ezek 27:17

BALSAM *aromatic gum*
tops of the **b** trees 2 Sam 5:24
like a bed of **b** Song 5:13

BAN *set apart to God*
city...under the **b** Josh 6:17
destroy...under the **b** Josh 7:12
who violated the **b** 1 Chr 2:7
consign Jacob to the **b** Is 43:28

BAND *bond* or *group*
b-s *shall be* of silver Ex 27:10
skillfully woven **b** Ex 28:8
saw a marauding **b** 2 Kin 13:21
b of destroying angels Ps 78:49
b-s of the yoke Is 58:6

BANISH *exile*
b-ed one will not 2 Sam 14:14
assemble the **b-ed** Is 11:12
gaiety...is **b-ed** Is 24:11
where I will **b** them Ezek 4:13

BANK *slope*
b of the Nile Gen 41:3
reeds by the **b** Ex 2:3
b of the river Ezek 47:7
herd rushed down...**b** Luke 8:33

BANNER *flag, standard*
set up our **b-s** Ps 20:5
b to those who fear Ps 60:4
b over me is love Song 2:4
as an army with **b-s** Song 6:4

BANQUET *dinner, feast*
b lasting seven days Esth 1:5
brought me to *his* **b** Song 2:4
lavish **b** for all Is 25:6
place of honor at **b-s** Matt 23:6
Herod...gave a **b** Mark 6:21

BAPTISM *symbolic washing*
Sadducees coming...**b** Matt 3:7
b of repentance Mark 1:4
b with which I am Mark 10:38
with the **b** of John Luke 7:29
a **b** to undergo Luke 12:50
through **b** into death Rom 6:4
one faith, one **b** Eph 4:5
buried with Him in **b** Col 2:12

BAPTIZE *symbolic washing*
b...Holy Spirit Matt 3:11
tax collectors...**b-d** Luke 3:12
Jesus was also **b-d** Luke 3:21
sent me to **b** in water John 1:33
b-ing more disciples John 4:1
b-d with the Holy Acts 1:5
each of you be **b-d** Acts 2:38
he got up and was **b-d** Acts 9:18
household...been **b-d** Acts 16:15
John **b-d** with the Acts 19:4
b-d into Christ Jesus Rom 6:3
b-d into Moses 1 Cor 10:2
b-d into one body 1 Cor 12:13
b-d for the dead 1 Cor 15:29

BAR *metal* or *block*
b-s of your yoke Lev 26:13
a **b** of gold Josh 7:21
like **b-s** of iron Job 40:18
earth with its **b-s** Jon 2:6

BARABBAS
robber Matt 27:16; Luke 23:18
released by Pilate Matt 27:26

BARAK
Deborah's commander Judg 4:6

BARBARIAN *non-Hellenic*
obligation...to **b-s** Rom 1:14
who speaks a **b** 1 Cor 14:11
b, Scythian, slave Col 3:11

BARE (adj) *barren, uncovered*
to cover *their* **b** flesh Ex 28:42
he went to a **b** hill Num 23:3
strips the forests **b** Ps 29:9
were naked and **b** Ezek 16:7

BARE (v) *expose, uncover*
foundations...laid **b** Ps 18:15
b-d His holy arm Is 52:10
foundation is laid **b** Ezek 13:14
open and laid **b** Heb 4:13

BAREFOOT *without sandals*
priests walk **b** Job 12:19
gone naked and **b** Is 20:3

BAR-JESUS
magician Acts 13:6
see also **ELYMAS**

BARLEY *grain*
land of wheat and **b** Deut 8:8
beginning...**b** harvest Ruth 1:22
stinkweed instead...**b** Job 31:40
has five **b** loaves John 6:9

BARN *farm building*
b-s are torn down Joel 1:17
seed still in the **b** Hag 2:19
wheat into the **b** Matt 3:12
nor gather into **b-s** Matt 6:26
tear down my **b-s** Luke 12:18

BARNABAS
Cyprian by birth Acts 4:36
introduced Paul Acts 9:27
co-worker with Paul Acts 13:2,7
separated from Paul Acts 15:39

BARREN *childless, sterile*
Sarai was **b** Gen 11:30
but Rachel was **b** Gen 29:31
wrongs the **b** woman Job 24:21
Shout...O **b** one Is 54:1
Blessed are the **b** Luke 23:29

BARSABBAS
1 *Apostolic candidate, also called Joseph and Justus* Acts 1:23
2 *colleague of Paul, also called Judas* Acts 15:22

BARTHOLOMEW
apostle Matt 10:3; Luke 6:14; Acts 1:13

BARTIMAEUS
healed by Jesus Mark 10:46

BARUCH
1 *scribe* Jer 36:26;43:6
2 *priest* Neh 3:20
3 *a Judean* Neh 11:5

BASE *dishonorable*
no **b** thought Deut 15:9
b things of...world 1 Cor 1:28

BASEMATH
1 *Esau's wife* Gen 26:34
2 *daughter of Solomon* 1 Kin 4:15

BASHAN
land E of Jordan Num 21:33; Josh 13:11; Is 2:13

BASIN *bowl, vessel*
blood...in the **b** Ex 12:22
b-s...of pure gold 1 Chr 28:17
a *sacrificial* **b** Zech 9:15
water into the **b** John 13:5

BASKET *container*
got him a wicker **b** Ex 2:3
b among the reeds Ex 2:5
b of summer fruit Amos 8:1
lamp...under a **b** Matt 5:15
not...put under a **b** Mark 4:21
seven large **b-s** full Mark 8:8
twelve **b-s** *full* Luke 9:17
let down in a **b** 2 Cor 11:33

BATH *measure of capacity*
two thousand **b-s** 1 Kin 7:26
100 **b-s** of oil Ezra 7:22
only one **b** *of wine* Is 5:10
a tenth of a **b** from Ezek 45:14

BATHE *wash*
wash his clothes and **b** Lev 15:5
b his body in water Num 19:7
saw a woman **b-ing** 2 Sam 11:2
B-d in milk Song 5:12

BATHSHEBA
wife of Uriah 2 Sam 11:3
taken by David 2 Sam 11:4
wife of David 2 Sam 11:27
mother of Solomon 2 Sam 12:24

BATTLE (n) *conflict, war*
b is the LORD's 1 Sam 17:47
b is...God's 2 Chr 20:15
scents the **b** from afar Job 39:25
with strength for **b** Ps 18:39
noise of **b** is in Jer 50:22
another king in **b** Luke 14:31
horses prepared for **b** Rev 9:7

BATTLE (v) *fight*
b against the sons Judg 20:14
drew near to **b** 1 Sam 7:10
about to go to **b** 1 Chr 12:19
nations...to **b** Zech 14:2

BEACH *coast*
crowd...on the **b** Matt 13:2
Jesus stood on the **b** John 21:4
down on the **b** Acts 21:5

BEAM *log*
like a weaver's **b** 2 Sam 21:19
one was felling a **b** 2 Kin 6:5
b-s, the thresholds 2 Chr 3:7
b-s of His...chambers Ps 104:3

BEAR (n) *animal*
b came and took 1 Sam 17:34
b robbed of...cubs Prov 17:12
the **b** will graze Is 11:7
resembling a **b** Dan 7:5

BEAR (v) *sustain*
too great to **b** Gen 4:13
bore you on eagles' Ex 19:4
not **b** false witness Ex 20:16
Lord...**b-s** our burden Ps 68:19
b their iniquities Is 53:11
b the penalty Ezek 23:49
she will **b** a Son Matt 1:21
it **b-s** much fruit John 12:24
b-ing His own cross John 19:17
b fruit for God Rom 7:4
b the image of 1 Cor 15:49
B...another's burdens Gal 6:2
b the sins of many Heb 9:28
bore our sins 1 Pet 2:24

BEARD *whiskers*
infection...on the **b** Lev 13:29
seized *him* by...**b** 1 Sam 17:35
shaved...their **b-s** 2 Sam 10:4
until your **b-s** grow 1 Chr 19:5

BEARER *carrier*
the **b-s** of the ark 2 Sam 6:13
strength of...**b-s** Neh 4:10
b of good news Is 40:9

BEAST *animal, creature*
God formed every **b** Gen 2:19
Noah and all the **b-s** Gen 8:1
eliminate harmful **b-s** Lev 26:6
b-s of the field Lev 26:22
But now ask the **b-s** Job 12:7
b of the forest Ps 50:10
b also had four heads Dan 7:6
they worshiped the **b** Rev 13:4
mark of the **b** Rev 16:2

BEAT *hit, strike*
b-ing a Hebrew Ex 2:11
b out what she Ruth 2:17
b-ing tambourines Ps 68:25
B your plowshares Joel 3:10
b Him with their Matt 26:67
b-ing His head with Mark 15:19
b-ing his breast Luke 18:13
b-en us in public Acts 16:37
stopped **b-ing** Paul Acts 21:32
b-en with rods 2 Cor 11:25

BEAUTIFUL *lovely, pleasing*
daughters...were **b** Gen 6:2
Rachel was **b** Gen 29:17
foliage of **b** trees Lev 23:40
Most **b** among women Song 1:8
Branch...will be **b** Is 4:2
Your **b** sheep Jer 13:20
enter the **B** Land Dan 11:41
How **b** are the feet Rom 10:15

BEAUTIFUL GATE
see **GATES OF JERUSALEM**

BEAUTY
Your **b**...is slain 2 Sam 1:19
behold the **b** of the LORD Ps 27:4
Zion...perfection of **b** Ps 50:2
b is vain Prov 31:30
see the King in His **b** Is 33:17

BED *pallet*
My **b** will comfort me Job 7:13
make my **b** swim Ps 6:6
remember...on my **b** Ps 63:6
in **b** with a fever Matt 8:14
pick up your **b** Matt 9:6
lamp...under a **b** Mark 4:21

BEDROOM *sleeping area*
and into your **b** Ex 8:3
you speak in your **b** 2 Kin 6:12
his nurse in the **b** 2 Chr 22:11

BEELZEBUL
NT prince of the demons Matt 12:27; Luke 11:15
see also **BAAL-ZEBUB**

BEERSHEBA
well / town in Negev Gen 21:31; Judg 20:1
home of Abraham Gen 22:19
home of Isaac Gen 26:23

BEFOREHAND *prior*
do not worry **b** Mark 13:11
anointed My body **b** Mark 14:8
God announced **b** Acts 3:18
prepared **b** for glory Rom 9:23

BEG *appeal, ask*
children wander...**b** Ps 109:10
b-s during...harvest Prov 20:4
b You to look at Luke 9:38
I am ashamed to **b** Luke 16:3
who used to sit and **b** John 9:8
b-ging them to leave Acts 16:39

BEGET *bring into being, sire*
Rock who **begot** Deut 32:18
whom you will **b** 2 Kin 20:18
begotten the...dew Job 38:28
I have **begotten** You Ps 2:7
have **begotten** You Acts 13:33

BEGINNING *origin, starting*
In the **b** God created Gen 1:1
from **b** to end 1 Sam 3:12
b was insignificant Job 8:7
fear of the LORD...**b** Ps 111:10
The **b** of the gospel Mark 1:1
In the **b** was the Word John 1:1
This **b** of *His* signs John 2:11
He is the **b** Col 1:18
the **b** and the end Rev 21:6

BEGOTTEN (adj) *born one*
b from the Father John 1:14
the only **b** God John 1:18
gave His only **b** Son John 3:16
only **b** Son of God John 3:18
offering...only **b** Heb 11:17
sent His only **b** Son 1 John 4:9

BEHALF *sake of*
atonement on his **b** Lev 5:6

the Father on your **b** John 16:26
I ask on their **b** John 17:9
one man to die on **b** John 18:14
be sin on our **b** 2 Cor 5:21

BEHAVE *act*
David **b-d** himself 1 Sam 18:30
b-ing as a madman 1 Sam 21:14
b properly as in Rom 13:13
blamelessly we **b-d** 1 Thess 2:10

BEHAVIOR *conduct*
instruction in wise **b** Prov 1:3
reverent in their **b** Titus 2:3
holy...in all *your* **b** 1 Pet 1:15
the **b** of their wives 1 Pet 3:1

BEHEADED *cut off*
killed him and **b** him 2 Sam 4:7
John **b** in the prison Matt 14:10
John, whom I **b** Mark 6:16
b because of their Rev 20:4

BEHEMOTH
hippopotamus Job 40:15

BEHOLD *look, see*
upright will **b** His face Ps 11:7
b the works of the LORD Ps 46:8
b-ing as in a mirror 2 Cor 3:18
B, I stand at the door Rev 3:20

BEING *existence, life*
man became a living **b** Gen 2:7
a...**b** coming up 1 Sam 28:13
wisdom in the...**b** Job 38:36
truth in the...**b** Ps 51:6
four living **b-s** Ezek 1:5
resembled a...**b** Dan 10:16

BEL
Babylonian god, related to Baal Jer 50:2;51:44

BELA
1 *king of Edom* Gen 36:32
2 *son of Bejamin* Gen 46:21; 1 Chr 8:1
3 *a Reubenite* 1 Chr 5:8
4 *city of the plain near the Dead Sea* Gen 14:2,8
see also **ZOAR**

BELIEVE *have faith, trust*
he **b-d** in the LORD Gen 15:6
did not **b** in God Ps 78:22
naive **b-s** everything Prov 14:15
you **b** that I am able Matt 9:28
ask in prayer, **b-ing** Matt 21:22
repent and **b** Mark 1:15
they **b-d**...Scripture John 2:22
whoever **b-s** in Him John 3:16
will you **b** My words John 5:47
who **b-s** has eternal John 6:47
men will **b** in Him John 11:48
b in the Light John 12:36
not see, and *yet* **b-d** John 20:29
b-d were of one heart Acts 4:32
B in the Lord Jesus Acts 16:31
Abraham **b-d** God Rom 4:3
How will they **b** Rom 10:14
love...**b-s** all 1 Cor 13:7
whom I have **b-d** 2 Tim 1:12
comes to God must **b** Heb 11:6
demons also **b** James 2:19
do not **b** every spirit 1 John 4:1

BELIEVERS *faithful ones*
all the circumcised **b** Acts 10:45
example to all the **b** 1 Thess 1:7
toward you **b** 1 Thess 2:10

BELL
a **b**...a pomegranate Ex 39:26
b-s of the horses Zech 14:20

BELLY *stomach*
On your **b**...you go Gen 3:14
crawls on its **b** Lev 11:42
b of the sea monster Matt 12:40

BELOVED *dearly loved*
b of the LORD dwell Deut 33:12
gives to His **b** *even* Ps 127:2
b is like a gazelle Song 2:9
This is My **b** Son Matt 3:17
your upbuilding, **b** 2 Cor 12:19
stand firm...my **b** Phil 4:1
faithful and **b** brother Col 4:9
Luke, the **b** physician Col 4:14
slave, a **b** brother Philem 16
This is My **b** Son 2 Pet 1:17
the called, **b** in God Jude 1

BELSHAZZAR
ruler of Babylon Dan 5:1;7:1

BELT *waistband*
the **b** of the strong Job 12:21
leather **b** around his Matt 3:4
no money in their **b** Mark 6:8
Paul's **b** and bound Acts 21:11

BELTESHAZZAR
Daniel's Babylonian name Dan 1:7;2:26;5:12;10:1

BENAIAH
1 *son of Jehoiada* 2 Sam 8:18
captain of David 2 Sam 23:23
2 *Levitical singer* 1 Chr 15:18,20
3 *a priest* 1 Chr 15:24;16:5
the name of nine other individuals in the OT

BENEFIT *blessing, profit*
no return for the **b** 2 Chr 32:25
forget none of His **b-s** Ps 103:2
His **b-s** toward me Ps 116:12
the **b** of circumcision Rom 3:1

BEN-HADAD
1 *Ben-hadad I* 1 Kin 15:18-21
2 *Ben-hadad II* 1 Kin 20,22
3 *Ben-hadad III* 2 Kin 8:7-15;13:22

BEN-HINNOM, VALLEY OF
see **HINNOM VALLEY**

BENJAMIN
1 *son of Jacob* Gen 35:18
2 *tribe* Num 2:22
3 *of clan of Jediael* 1 Chr 7:10
4 *of the restoration* Neh 3:23

BENJAMIN GATE
see **GATES OF JERUSALEM**

BEREA
city in Macedonia visited by Paul Acts 17:10,13

BEREAVE *deprive, make sad*
be **b-d** of you both Gen 27:45
b...of your children Lev 26:22
I will **b** *them* Jer 15:7
longer **b** your nation Ezek 36:14

BERNICE
daughter of Herod Agrippa I Acts 25:13,23

BERODACH-BALADAN
king of Babylon 2 Kin 20:12
see also **MERODACH-BALADAN**

BESEECH *ask earnestly*
LORD, I **b** You Ps 116:4
do save, we **b** You Ps 118:25
leper came...**b-ing** Mark 1:40
b the Lord of the Luke 10:2

BESIEGE *assail, surround*
When you **b** a city Deut 20:19
enemies **b** them 2 Chr 6:28
was **b-ing** Jerusalem Jer 32:2
b-d...with bitterness Lam 3:5

BESTOWED *granted*
b...royal majesty 1 Chr 29:25
that the Spirit was **b** Acts 8:18
which He freely **b** Eph 1:6
b on Him the name Phil 2:9
love the Father has **b** 1 John 3:1

BETHANY
1 *E of Jerusalem* Matt 21:17
home of Mary, Martha and Lazarus John 11:1,18
2 *where John baptized* John 1:28

BETHEL
town in Benjamin Gen 12:8
N of Jerusalem Josh 8:17

BETHESDA
pool in Jerusalem John 5:2

BETH-HORON
1 *famous battle site pass NW of Jerusalem* Josh 10:10,11
2 *two towns at both ends of mountain pass* Josh 16:3,5

BETHLEHEM
1 *town S of Jerusalem* Gen 35:19
home of Ruth and Boaz Ruth 4:11
birthplace of Jesus Matt 2:1
2 *Zebulunite village* Josh 19:15

BETH-PEOR
Moabite city Deut 4:46;34:6

BETHPHAGE
village on the Mount of Olives Matt 21:1; Mark 11:1

BETHSAIDA
village on Sea of Galilee Mark 8:22; Luke 9:10
home of Philip, Andrew and Peter John 1:44

BETH-SHAN/BETH-SHEAN
city at junction of Jezreel and Jordan valleys Josh 17:11; 1 Kin 4:12; 1 Chr 7:29

BETH-SHEMESH
1 *city of Judah* Josh 15:10
2 *Issachar border city* Josh 19:22
3 *city of Naphtali* Josh 19:38

BETRAY *break faith, disloyal*
do not **b** the fugitive Is 16:3
wine **b-s** the haughty Hab 2:5
b Him to you Matt 26:15
how to **b** Him Mark 14:11
one...will **b** Me Mark 14:18
Judas, are you **b-ing** Luke 22:48

BETROTH *promise to wed*
You shall **b** a wife Deut 28:30
I will **b** you to Me Hos 2:19
Mary had been **b-ed** Matt 1:18
I **b-ed** you to one 2 Cor 11:2

BEWARE *be careful, watch*
B of practicing Matt 6:1
B of the scribes Mark 12:38
B of the leaven Luke 12:1
b...false circumcision Phil 3:2

BEYOND *over and above*
it was **b** measure Gen 41:49
remove...**b** Babylon Acts 7:43
tempted **b** what 1 Cor 10:13
b their ability 2 Cor 8:3
b all that we ask Eph 3:20
and **b** reproach Col 1:22

BEZALEL
1 *architect of tabernacle* Ex 31:1ff
2 *Israelite* Ezra 10:30

BEZER
1 *son of Zophah* 1 Chr 7:37
2 *city of refuge* Josh 20:8

BIG *large*
on the **b** toes Ex 29:20
Pharaoh...a **b** noise Jer 46:17
gave a **b** reception Luke 5:29

BILDAD
one of Job's friends
Job 2:11;18:1;42:9

BILHAH
1 *Rachel's servant* Gen 29:29
Jacob's concubine
Gen 30:3,4
2 *Simeonite town* 1 Chr 4:29

BIND *fasten, secure*
bound his son Isaac Gen 22:9
were **b-ing** sheaves Gen 37:7
b them as a sign Deut 6:8
b-s up their wounds Ps 147:3
B up the testimony Is 8:16
b up the brokenhearted
Is 61:1
b on earth Matt 16:19
and **bound** Him John 18:12
bound...a thousand Rev 20:2

BIRD *fowl*
let **b-s** fly above Gen 1:20
eat any clean **b** Deut 14:20
b-s of the heavens Ps 8:8
Flee *as* a **b** to Ps 11:1
snare of a **b** catcher Hos 9:8
b-s...*have* nests Luke 9:58

BIRTH *act of being born*
A time to give **b** Eccl 3:2
You gave me **b** Jer 2:27
b of Jesus Christ Matt 1:18
rejoice at his **b** Luke 1:14
gave **b** to a son Luke 1:57
a man blind from **b** John 9:1
in pain to give **b** Rev 12:2

BIRTHDAY *day of birth*
was Pharaoh's **b** Gen 40:20
Herod's **b** came Matt 14:6
his **b**...banquet Mark 6:21

BIRTHRIGHT *first-born rights*
First sell me your **b** Gen 25:31
He took away my **b** Gen 27:36
sold his own **b** Heb 12:16

BITE
serpent **bit** any man
Num 21:9
it **b-s** like a serpent Prov 23:32
if you **b**...one another Gal 5:15

BITHYNIA
territory on the Bosporus in Asia Minor Acts 16:7;
1 Pet 1:1

BITTER *painful, unpleasant*
b with hard labor Ex 1:14
waters of Marah...**b** Ex 15:23
b speech *as* their arrow
Ps 64:3
substitute **b** for sweet Is 5:20
Strong drink is **b** Is 24:9
fresh and **b** *water* James 3:11

BITTERNESS *unpleasantness*
in the **b** of my soul Job 10:1
because of the **b** Is 38:15
full of cursing and **b** Rom 3:14
all **b**...be put away Eph 4:31
no root of **b** Heb 12:15

BLACK *dark*
sky grew **b** with 1 Kin 18:45
darkness and **b** gloom Job 3:5
I am **b** but lovely Song 1:5
behold, a **b** horse Rev 6:5
sun became **b** Rev 6:12

BLAME *fault, responsibility*
let me bear the **b** Gen 43:9
bear the **b**...forever Gen 44:32

BLAMELESS *faultless*
show Yourself **b** 2 Sam 22:26
just *and* **b** *man* is a Job 12:4
His way is **b** Ps 18:30
b will inherit good Prov 28:10
a **b** conscience Acts 24:16
holy and **b** before Him
Eph 1:4
in the Law, found **b** Phil 3:6
spotless and **b** 2 Pet 3:14
b with great joy Jude 24

BLASPHEME *curse*
enemies...to **b** 2 Sam 12:14
name is continually **b-d**
Is 52:5
This *fellow* **b-s** Matt 9:3
b-s...Holy Spirit Mark 3:29
force them to **b** Acts 26:11
name of God is **b-d** Rom 2:24
taught not to **b** 1 Tim 1:20
b-d the God of Rev 16:11

BLASPHEMY
cursing, profanity
b against the Spirit Matt 12:31
b-ies they utter Mark 3:28
You...heard the **b** Mark 14:64
man...speaks **b-ies** Luke 5:21
stone You...for **b** John 10:33
words and **b-ies** Rev 13:5

BLAST *burst*
the **b** of Your nostrils Ex 15:8
b with the ram's horn Josh 6:5
a trumpet **b** of war Jer 49:2

BLAZING *burning*
LORD...a **b** fire Ex 3:2
furnace of **b** fire Dan 3:6
and to a **b** fire Heb 12:18

BLEMISH *imperfection, spot*
there is no **b** in you Song 4:7
six lambs without **b** Ezek 46:4
Himself without **b** Heb 9:14
stains and **b-es** 2 Pet 2:13

BLESS (v)
bestow favor or praise
God **b-ed** the...day Gen 2:3
I will greatly **b** you Gen 22:17
LORD **b-ed** the sabbath
Ex 20:11
and **b** Your inheritance
Ps 28:9
LORD will **b** His people
Ps 29:11
B the LORD Ps 103:2
generous will be **b-ed**
Prov 22:9
who **b-es** his friend
Prov 27:14
rise up and **b** her Prov 31:28
b-ed of My Father Matt 25:34
He **b-ed** *the food* Mark 6:41
b...who curse you Luke 6:28
while He was **b-ing**
Luke 24:51
you are **b-ed** if you John 13:17
B...who persecute Rom 12:14
we **b** *our* Lord James 3:9

BLESSED (adj) *favored, happy*
b be God Most High
Gen 14:20
B are you, O Israel Deut 33:29
B be the name of Job 1:21
How **b** is the man Ps 127:5
b...who finds wisdom
Prov 3:13
nations will call you **b**
Mal 3:12
B are the poor in Matt 5:3
B are the gentle Matt 5:5
B *is* the...kingdom
Mark 11:10
B *are* you among women
Luke 1:42
more **b** to give Acts 20:35
looking for...**b** hope Titus 2:13

BLESSING (n) *God's favor*
you shall be a **b** Gen 12:2
taken away your **b** Gen 27:35
a **b** and a curse Deut 11:26
curse into a **b** Neh 13:2
b of the LORD be upon
Ps 129:8
showers of **b** Ezek 34:26
pour out for you a **b** Mal 3:10
fullness of the **b** Rom 15:29
cup of **b** which we
1 Cor 10:16
inherit a **b** 1 Pet 3:9
honor and glory and **b**
Rev 5:12

BLIND (adj) *sightless*
misleads a **b** *person*
Deut 27:18
To open **b** eyes Is 42:7
b...guides a **b** man Matt 15:14
b beggar *named* Mark 10:46
b man was sitting Luke 18:35
I was **b**, now I see John 9:25

BLIND (n) *without sight*
block before the **b** Lev 19:14
I was eyes to the **b** Job 29:15
the **b** receive sight Matt 11:5
a guide to the **b** Rom 2:19

BLIND (v) *make sightless*
b-s the clear-sighted Ex 23:8
bribe to **b** my eyes 1 Sam 12:3
has **b-ed** the minds 2 Cor 4:4
darkness has **b-ed** 1 John 2:11

BLINDNESS *sightlessness*
madness and with **b**
Deut 28:28
struck them with **b** 2 Kin 6:18
every horse...with **b**
Zech 12:4

BLOOD
Whoever sheds man's **b**
Gen 9:6
bridegroom of **b** Ex 4:25
b shall be a sign Ex 12:13
not eat...any **b** Lev 3:17
land is filled with **b** Ezek 9:9
b did not reveal Matt 16:17
covenant in My **b** Luke 22:20
sweat...drops of **b** Luke 22:44
drinks My **b** abides John 6:56
Field of **B** Acts 1:19
the moon into **b** Acts 2:20
justified by His **b** Rom 5:9
sharing in the **b** 1 Cor 10:16
redemption...His **b** Eph 1:7
cleansed with **b** Heb 9:22
b, as of a lamb 1 Pet 1:19
the sea became **b** Rev 8:8
b of the saints Rev 17:6

BLOODGUILTINESS
no **b** on his account Ex 22:2
b is upon them Lev 20:11
b shall be forgiven Deut 21:8
Deliver me from **b** Ps 51:14

BLOODSHED *killing, murder*
abhors the man of **b** Ps 5:6
Men of **b** hate Prov 29:10
the **b** of Jerusalem Is 4:4
give you over to **b** Ezek 35:6
b follows **b** Hos 4:2

BLOSSOM *bloom*
the almond tree **b-s** Eccl 12:5
Israel will **b** and sprout
Is 27:6
arrogance has **b-ed** Ezek 7:10
fig tree should not **b**
Hab 3:17

BLOT *erase*
I will **b** out man Gen 6:7
b me...from Your book
Ex 32:32
b out their name Deut 9:14
sin be **b-ted** out Neh 4:5
b out all my iniquities Ps 51:9
works...be **b-ted** out Ezek 6:6

BLUE *color*
tent of **b** and purple Ex 26:36
ephod all of **b** Ex 28:31
royal robes of **b** Esth 8:15

BOANERGES
name of James and John
Mark 3:17

BOAST (n) *bragging*
soul will make its **b** Ps 34:2
the **b** of our hope Heb 3:6

BOAST (v) *brag, glory*
B no more so 1 Sam 2:3
who **b-s** of his gifts Prov 25:14

not **b** about tomorrow Prov 27:1
let not a rich man **b** Jer 9:23
b in God Rom 2:17
who **b** in the Law Rom 2:23
b...my weaknesses 2 Cor 12:9
it **b-s** of great things James 3:5

BOASTFUL *proud*
b shall not stand Ps 5:5
insolent, arrogant, **b** Rom 1:30
b pride of life 1 John 2:16

BOASTING *bragging*
Where is your **b** Judg 9:38
Where then is **b** Rom 3:27
our **b** about you 2 Cor 9:3
all such **b** is evil James 4:16

BOAT *watercraft*
slip by like reed **b-s** Job 9:26
left the **b** and their Matt 4:22
Peter got out of...**b** Matt 14:29
filled both of the **b-s** Luke 5:7
disciples into the **b** John 6:22

BOAZ
1 *husband of Ruth* Ruth 4:13
grandfather of David Ruth 4:17ff
2 *temple pillar* 2 Chr 3:17

BODY *corpse, flesh*
b cleaves to the earth Ps 44:25
lamp of the **b** Matt 6:22
perfume on My **b** Matt 26:12
this is My **b** Mark 14:22
did not find His **b** Luke 24:23
b of sin...done away Rom 6:6
redemption of our **b** Rom 8:23
present your **b-ies** Rom 12:1
b-ies are members 1 Cor 6:15
b is a temple 1 Cor 6:19
you are Christ's **b** 1 Cor 12:27
b to be burned 1 Cor 13:3
absent from the **b** 2 Cor 5:8
one **b** and one Spirit Eph 4:4
building up of the **b** Eph 4:12
wives as...own **b-ies** Eph 5:28
transform the **b** Phil 3:21
b be preserved 1 Thess 5:23
bore...sins in His **b** 1 Pet 2:24

BODYGUARD *guard, protector*
captain of the **b** put Gen 40:4
you my **b** for life 1 Sam 28:2

BOIL (n) *sore, swelling*
When...has a **b** Lev 13:18
b-s of Egypt Deut 28:27
smote Job with sore **b-s** Job 2:7

BOIL (v) *cook, heat*
not **b** a young goat in its Ex 34:26
we **b-ed** my son 2 Kin 6:29
fire causes water to **b** Is 64:2
b the guilt offering Ezek 46:20

BOISTEROUS *clamorous, loud*
woman of folly is **b** Prov 9:13
of noise, You **b** town Is 22:2
will drink *and* be **b** Zech 9:15

BOLD *brave, fearless*
wicked man...**b** face Prov 21:29
righteous are **b** as Prov 28:1
I *need* not be **b** 2 Cor 10:2

BOLDNESS *confidence*
word of God with **b** Acts 4:31
b and...access Eph 3:12
with **b** the mystery Eph 6:19

BOND *band, restraint*
neither **b** nor free 2 Kin 14:26
b of the covenant Ezek 20:37
with **b-s** of love Hos 11:4
he would break his **b-s** Luke 8:29
in the **b** of peace Eph 4:3
eternal **b-s** under Jude 6

BONDAGE *servitude, slavery*
Israel sighed...**b** Ex 2:23
the **b** of iniquity Acts 8:23
sold into **b** to sin Rom 7:14

BOND-SERVANT *servant, slave*
b-s of...Most High Acts 16:17
Paul, a **b** of Christ Rom 1:1
ourselves as your **b-s** 2 Cor 4:5
b...be quarrelsome 2 Tim 2:24
b of God...apostle Titus 1:1
His **b-s**...serve Him Rev 22:3

BONDSLAVE *servant, slave*
state of His **b** Luke 1:48
a **b** of Jesus Christ Col 4:12
Urge **b-s** to be subject Titus 2:9
use it as **b-s** of God 1 Pet 2:16

BONE
now **b** of my **b-s** Gen 2:23
the **b-s** of Joseph Josh 24:32
my **b-s** are dismayed Ps 6:2
rottenness in his **b-s** Prov 12:4
tongue breaks the **b** Prov 25:15
can these **b-s** live Ezek 37:3
dead men's **b-s** Matt 23:27
Not a **b**...be broken John 19:36

BOOK *scroll*
in a **b** as a memorial Ex 17:14
blot me...from Your **b** Ex 32:32
found the **b** of the 2 Kin 22:8
seal up the **b** Dan 12:4
not contain the **b-s** John 21:25
names are in the **b** Phil 4:3
worthy to open the **b** Rev 5:2
Lamb's **b** of life Rev 21:27

BOOK OF LIFE
God's book with names of righteous Ps 69:28; Phil 4:3; Rev 13:8;17:8;20:15

BOOTH *shelters*
b-s for his livestock Gen 33:17
live in **b-s** for seven Lev 23:42
in **b-s** during the feast Neh 8:14
sitting in the tax **b** Luke 5:27

BOOTHS, FEAST OF
see **FEASTS**

BOOTY *loot, plunder*
b that remained Num 31:32
Swift is the **b** Is 8:1
divide the **b** with Is 53:12
have his *own* life as **b** Jer 38:2

BORDER *boundary*
enlarge your **b-s** Ex 34:24
b of...city of refuge Num 35:26
the Jordan as *a* **b** Deut 3:17
God extends your **b** Deut 12:20
peace in your **b-s** Ps 147:14

BORN *brought into life*
man is **b** for trouble Job 5:7
mountains were **b** Ps 90:2
child will be **b** to us Is 9:6
land be **b** in one day Is 66:8
b King of the Jews Matt 2:2
those **b** of women Luke 7:28
b not of blood John 1:13
unless one is **b** again John 3:3
b of the Spirit John 3:6
to one untimely **b** 1 Cor 15:8
b...to a living hope 1 Pet 1:3
loves is **b** of God 1 John 4:7

BORROW *use temporarily*
if a man **b-s** *anything* Ex 22:14
you shall not **b** Deut 28:12
b-s and does not pay Ps 37:21
wants to **b** from you Matt 5:42

BOSOM *breast*
iniquity in my **b** Job 31:33
take fire in his **b** Prov 6:27
to Abraham's **b** Luke 16:22
the **b** of the Father John 1:18
reclining on Jesus' **b** John 13:23

BOTHER *pester*
conscience **b-ed** 1 Sam 24:5
you **b** the woman Matt 26:10
worried and **b-ed** Luke 10:41
this widow **b-s** me Luke 18:5

BOTTOMLESS *without bottom*
key of the **b** pit Rev 9:1
he opened the **b** pit Rev 9:2

BOUGH *branch*
Joseph is a fruitful **b** Gen 49:22
b-s of leafy trees Lev 23:40
cedars...with its **b-s** Ps 80:10
nested in its **b-s** Ezek 31:6

BOUND (adj) *fastened, tied*
Foolishness is **b** up Prov 22:15
cast **b** into the...fire Dan 3:24
A wife is **b** as long 1 Cor 7:39

BOUND (n) *boundary, limit*
utmost **b** of...hills Gen 49:26
set **b-s** for the people Ex 19:12
b-s...the mountain Ex 19:23

BOUNDARY *border, limit*
b-ies of the peoples Deut 32:8
b of light and Job 26:10
the **b-ies** of the earth Ps 74:17
set for the sea its **b** Prov 8:29
the **b** of the widow Prov 15:25

BOUNTY *generous gift*
to his royal **b** 1 Kin 10:13
crowned...with Your **b** Ps 65:11
over the **b** of the LORD Jer 31:12

BOW (n) *rainbow*
set My **b** in the cloud Gen 9:13

BOW (n) *shooting device*
his **b** remained firm Gen 49:24
a **b** of bronze 2 Sam 22:35
not trust in my **b** Ps 44:6
b-s are shattered Jer 51:56

BOW (v) *bend, worship*
nations **b** down to Gen 27:29
Israel **b-ed** *in* Gen 47:31
to Him you shall **b** 2 Kin 17:36
My soul is **b-ed** down Ps 57:6
B Your heavens, O LORD Ps 144:5
nations will **b** down Zeph 2:11
He **b-ed** His head John 19:30
every knee shall **b** Rom 14:11

BOWELS *entrails, innards*
a disease of your **b** 2 Chr 21:15
smote him in his **b** 2 Chr 21:18

BOWL *dish, jug*
golden **b** is crushed Eccl 12:6
from sacrificial **b-s** Amos 6:6
dips with Me in...**b** Mark 14:20
b-s full of the wrath Rev 15:7

BOX *container*
b with the golden 1 Sam 6:11
sashes, perfume **b-es** Is 3:20
Judas had the...**b** John 13:29

BOX *type of tree*
b tree and the cypress Is 41:19

BOY *child, lad*
she left the **b** Gen 21:15
let the **b-s** live Ex 1:17
b will lead them Is 11:6
Traded a **b** for a harlot Joel 3:3
b was cured at once Matt 17:18

BRACELETS *armlets*
two **b** for her wrists Gen 24:22
armlets and **b** Num 31:50
earrings, **b**, veils Is 3:19

BRAMBLE *briar*
trees said to the **b** Judg 9:14
fire...from the **b** Judg 9:15

BRANCH *bough*
David a righteous **B** Jer 23:5

b-es *fit* for scepters Ezek 19:11
beautiful **b-es** and Ezek 31:3
birds...in its **b-es** Luke 13:19
b-es of the palm John 12:13
b...not bear fruit John 15:2
you are the **b-es** John 15:5
is holy, the **b-es** Rom 11:16

BREACH *break*
For every **b** of trust Ex 22:9
LORD had made a **b** Judg 21:15
closed up the **b** 1 Kin 11:27
that no **b** remained Neh 6:1
Heal its **b-es** Ps 60:2

BREAD *food*
eat unleavened **b** Ex 12:20
rain **b** from heaven Ex 16:4
He will bless your **b** Ex 23:25
b of the Presence Ex 25:30
not live by **b** alone Deut 8:3
ravens brought...**b** 1 Kin 17:6
b of heaven Ps 105:40
satisfy...with **b** Ps 132:15
b *eaten* in secret Prov 9:17
eat the **b** of idleness Prov 31:27
Cast your **b**...waters Eccl 11:1
not live on **b** alone Matt 4:4
Give us...daily **b** Matt 6:11
gives you the true **b** John 6:32
I am the **b** of life John 6:35

BREAK *divide, shatter*
b down your pride Lev 26:19
never **b** My covenant Judg 2:1
broke the pitchers Judg 7:20
soft tongue **b-s** the Prov 25:15
reed He will not **b** Is 42:3
I **broke** your yoke Jer 2:20
B...fallow ground Hos 10:12
disciples **b** the Matt 15:2
waves were **b-ing** Mark 4:37
she **broke** the vial Mark 14:3
their nets *began* to **b** Luke 5:6
b his bonds Luke 8:29
b-ing the Sabbath John 5:18
did not **b** His legs John 19:33
your **b-ing** the Law Rom 2:23

BREAST *bosom*
orphan from the **b** Job 24:9
upon my mother's **b-s** Ps 22:9
b-s are like...fawns Song 7:3
b-s...never nursed Luke 23:29

BREASTPIECE *breast covering*
a **b** and an ephod Ex 28:4
make a **b** of judgment Ex 28:15
they bound the **b** Ex 39:21

BREASTPLATE *breast armor*
righteousness like a **b** Is 59:17
b of faith and love 1 Thess 5:8
like **b-s** of iron Rev 9:9

BREATH *air, spirit, wind*
the **b** of life Gen 2:7
days are *but* a **b** Job 7:16
man is a mere **b** Ps 39:11
b came into them Ezek 37:10
give **b** to the image Rev 13:15

BREATHE *inhale and exhale*
Abraham **b-d** his last Gen 25:8
such as **b** out violence Ps 27:12
garden **b**...*fragrance* Song 4:16
b on these slain Ezek 37:9
He **b-d** His last Mark 15:39
He **b-d** on them John 20:22

BRETHREN *brothers*
beating...his **b** Ex 2:11
b from all the nations Is 66:20
His **b** Will return Mic 5:3
b, why do you injure Acts 7:26
sinning against...**b** 1 Cor 8:12
dangers...false **b** 2 Cor 11:26
Peace be to the **b** Eph 6:23
faithful **b** in Christ Col 1:2
the love of the **b** 1 Thess 4:9
b...not grow weary 2 Thess 3:13
my **b,** do not swear James 5:12
our lives for the **b** 1 John 3:16
accuser of our **b** Rev 12:10

BRIAR *thistle, thorn*
b-s and thorns will come Is 5:6
land will be **b-s** Is 7:24
grapes from a **b** bush Luke 6:44

BRIBE *illegal gift*
b blinds...clear-sighted Ex 23:8
nor take a **b** Deut 10:17
who hates **b-s** will Prov 15:27
b corrupts the heart Eccl 7:7
Everyone loves a **b** Is 1:23

BRICK *clay block*
they used **b** for stone Gen 11:3
straw to make **b** as Ex 5:7
deliver...quota of **b-s** Ex 5:18
burning incense on **b-s** Is 65:3

BRIDE *newlywed*
as a **b** adorns herself Is 61:10
the voice of the **b** Jer 7:34
b out of her *bridal* Joel 2:16
He who has the **b** John 3:29
b...of the Lamb Rev 21:9

BRIDEGROOM *newlywed*
a **b** of blood to me Ex 4:25
As a **b** decks himself Is 61:10
voice of the **b** Jer 7:34
attendants of the **b** Matt 9:15
out to meet the **b** Matt 25:1

BRIDLE (n) *head harness*
My **b** in your lips 2 Kin 19:28
a **b** for the donkey Prov 26:3
up to the horses' **b-s** Rev 14:20

BRIDLE (v) *control*
not **b** his tongue James 1:26
man, able to **b** James 3:2

BRIGHT *shining*
b in the skies Job 37:21
night is as **b** as Ps 139:12
B eyes gladden Prov 15:30
b cloud...them Matt 17:5
b light...flashed Acts 22:6
the **b** morning star Rev 22:16

BRIMSTONE *sulfur*
b and fire from Gen 19:24
b and burning wind Ps 11:6
rained fire and **b** Luke 17:29
tormented with...**b** Rev 14:10
lake of fire and **b** Rev 20:10

BRING *carry, lead*
will **b** forth children Gen 3:16
Cain **brought**...offering Gen 4:3
b two of every *kind* Gen 6:19
B the ark of God 1 Sam 14:18
Kings will **b** gifts Ps 68:29
B water for the thirsty Is 21:14
B the whole tithe Mal 3:10
brought...a paralytic Matt 9:2
not...to **b** peace Matt 10:34
I **b** you good news Luke 2:10
Law **b-s** about wrath Rom 4:15
b-ing salvation Titus 2:11

BROAD *wide*
into a **b** place 2 Sam 22:20
land was **b** and 1 Chr 4:40
the sea, great and **b** Ps 104:25
dark in **b** daylight Amos 8:9
way is **b** that leads to Matt 7:13

BROKEN *crushed, separated*
My spirit is **b** Job 17:1
A **b** and a contrite heart Ps 51:17
they have **b** Your law Ps 119:126
deeps were **b** up Prov 3:20
silver cord is **b** Eccl 12:6
bind up the **b** Ezek 34:16
Scripture...be **b** John 10:35
Not a bone...**b** John 19:36
Branches were **b** off Rom 11:19

BROKENHEARTED *grieving*
LORD is near to the **b** Ps 34:18
He heals the **b** Ps 147:3
sent me to bind...**b** Is 61:1

BRONZE *metal*
implements of **b** Gen 4:22
made a **b** serpent Num 21:9
bend a bow of **b** 2 Sam 22:35
as walls of **b** Jer 1:18
third kingdom of **b** Dan 2:39
costly wood and **b** Rev 18:12

BROOD *group, offspring*
b of sinful men Num 32:14
You **b** of vipers Matt 3:7
hen *gathers* her **b** Luke 13:34

BROOK *stream, wadi*
stones from the **b** 1 Sam 17:40
by the **b** Cherith 1 Kin 17:5
deer pants for...**b-s** Ps 42:1
wisdom...bubbling **b** Prov 18:4

BROTHER *male relative*
Am I my **b-'s** Gen 4:9
b-s were jealous Gen 37:11
b-s may redeem Lev 25:48
b-s to dwell together Ps 133:1
b is born for Prov 17:17
closer than a **b** Prov 18:24
b-s of a poor man Prov 19:7
reconciled to your **b** Matt 5:24
B will betray **b** Matt 10:21
behold, His...**b-s** Matt 12:46
not forgive his **b** Matt 18:35
My **b** and sister Mark 3:35
b of yours was dead Luke 15:32
left...wife or **b-s** Luke 18:29
not even His **b-s** John 7:5
b will rise again John 11:23
b goes to law with **b** 1 Cor 6:6
my **b** to stumble 1 Cor 8:13
yet hates his **b** 1 John 2:9

BROTHERHOOD
the covenant of **b** Amos 1:9
love the **b,** fear God 1 Pet 2:17

BRUISE (n) *wound*
for wound, **b** for **b** Ex 21:25
Only **b-s,** welts and raw Is 1:6
the **b** He has inflicted Is 30:26

BRUISE (v) *batter, crush*
b him on the heel Gen 3:15
b-s me with a tempest Job 9:17

BRUTAL *fierce, vicious*
hand of **b** men Ezek 21:31
b, haters of good 2 Tim 3:3

BUD *blossom, a sprout*
flax was in **b** Ex 9:31
put forth **b-s** Num 17:8
the **b** blossoms Is 18:5

BUILD *construct, form*
Noah **built** an altar Gen 8:20
let us **b**...a city Gen 11:4
b for Me a house 1 Chr 17:12
b-ing...house of God 2 Chr 3:3
built high places 2 Chr 33:19
has **built** up Zion Ps 102:16
Unless the LORD **b-s** Ps 127:1
a time to **b** up Eccl 3:3
built his house on Matt 7:24
I will **b** My church Matt 16:18
able to **b** *you* up Acts 20:32
being **built** together Eph 2:22
stones...being **built** 1 Pet 2:5

BUILDER *fashioner, maker*
Solomon's **b-s** 1 Kin 5:18
b-s had laid the Ezra 3:10
the **b-s** rejected Matt 21:42
like a wise master **b** 1 Cor 3:10
architect and **b** is Heb 11:10

BUILDING *structure*
reconstructing this **b** Ezra 5:4
b that *was* in front Ezek 41:12
what wonderful **b-s** Mark 13:1
you are...God's **b** 1 Cor 3:9
have a **b** from God 2 Cor 5:1
whole **b,** being fitted Eph 2:21

BULB *part of plant*
a **b** and a flower Ex 25:33
b-s and their branches Ex 25:36

BULL *animal*
b of the sin offering Lev 4:20
b without blemish Ezek 45:18
blood of **b-s** and Heb 10:4

BULRUSH *marsh plant*
b in a single day Is 9:14
b-es by the Nile Is 19:7
palm branch or **b** Is 19:15

BUNDLE *package*
b...*was* in his sack Gen 42:35
the **b** of the living 1 Sam 25:29
in **b-s** to burn Matt 13:30

BURDEN (n) *load, weight*
b-s of the Egyptians Ex 6:6
the **b** of the people Num 11:17
I am a **b** to myself Job 7:20
who daily bears our **b** Ps 68:19
My **b** is light Matt 11:30
b-s hard to bear Luke 11:46
Bear one another's **b-s** Gal 6:2

BURDEN (v) *weigh down*
b-ed Me with your sins Is 43:24
were **b-ed** excessively 2 Cor 1:8
not **b** you myself 2 Cor 12:16
the church must not be **b-ed** 1 Tim 5:16

BURIAL *interment*
give me a **b** site Gen 23:4
even have a *proper* **b** Eccl 6:3
to prepare Me for **b** Matt 26:12
b custom of the Jews John 19:40

BURN (v) *consume, kindle*
Jacob's anger **b-ed** Gen 30:2
bush was **b-ing** Ex 3:2
Your anger **b** against Ex 32:11
Moses' anger **b-ed** Ex 32:19
did not **b** any cities Josh 11:13
jealousy **b** like fire Ps 79:5
to **b** their sons Jer 7:31
not to **b** the scroll Jer 36:25
will **b** up the chaff Luke 3:17
b-ed in their desire Rom 1:27
my body to be **b-ed** 1 Cor 13:3
works will be **b-ed** 2 Pet 3:10
lake of fire...**b-s** Rev 19:20

BURNING (adj)
Your **b** anger Ex 15:7
shall bewail the **b** Lev 10:6
b lips and a wicked Prov 26:23
b heat of famine Lam 5:10
b anger of the LORD Zeph 2:2

BURNISHED *polished*
gleamed like **b** bronze Ezek 1:7
feet...like **b** bronze Rev 1:15

BURNT OFFERINGS
see **OFFERINGS**

BURST *break*
great deep **b** open Gen 7:11
wine will **b** the skins Luke 5:37
he **b** open Acts 1:18

BURY *place in earth*
b-ied at...old age Gen 15:15
that I may **b** my dead Gen 23:4
b-ied the bones of Josh 24:32
go and **b** my father Matt 8:21
dead to **b** their own Matt 8:22
devout...**b-ied** Stephen Acts 8:2
that He was **b-ied** 1 Cor 15:4
b-ied...in baptism Col 2:12

BUSH *shrub*
boy under...the **b-es** Gen 21:15
the **b** was burning Ex 3:2
who dwelt in the **b** Deut 33:16
like a **b** in the desert Jer 17:6

BUSINESS *occupation, work*
until I...told my **b** Gen 24:33
carry on the *king's* **b** Esth 3:9
another to his **b** Matt 22:5
a place of **b** John 2:16
attend to your...**b** 1 Thess 4:11
engage in **b** James 4:13

BUSYBODIES *meddlers*
no work...like **b** 2 Thess 3:11
gossips and **b** 1 Tim 5:13

BUTTER
steps...bathed in **b** Job 29:6
smoother than **b** Ps 55:21
milk produces **b** Prov 30:33

BUYER *purchaser*
Bad, bad, says the **b** Prov 20:14
the **b** like the seller Is 24:2
Let not the **b** rejoice Ezek 7:12

BYSTANDERS *unlookers*
b...said to Peter Matt 26:73
the **b** heard it Mark 15:35

BYWORD *contemptible*
b among all peoples 1 Kin 9:7
a proverb and a **b** 2 Chr 7:20
He has made me a **b** Job 17:6
b among the nations Ps 44:14

~C

CAESAR
1 *Roman emperor* Matt 22:17,21; Mark 12:14; John 19:12
2 *Augustus* Luke 2:1
3 *Tiberius* Luke 3:1; John 19:12
4 *Claudius* Acts 11:28;17:7;18:2
5 *Nero* Acts 25:12;26:32; Phil 4:22

CAESAREA
Roman coastal city Acts 8:40;10:1;21:16;25:4

CAESAREA PHILIPPI
city at base of Mt. Hermon Matt 16:13; Mark 8:27

CAIAPHAS
high priest Matt 26:57; Luke 3:2; John 11:49ff; Acts 4:6

CAIN
son of Adam Gen 4:1
tiller of the ground Gen 4:2
killed his brother Gen 4:8
marked by sign Gen 4:15

CAKE *type of bread*
and make bread **c-s** Gen 18:6
took one unleavened **c** Lev 8:26
make me a...**c** 1 Kin 17:13

CALAMITY *adversity, trouble*
day of my **c** 2 Sam 22:19
sorry over the **c** 1 Chr 21:15
palate discern **c-ies** Job 6:30
c from God is Job 31:23
stumble in *time of* **c** Prov 24:16
beginning to work **c** Jer 25:29
relents concerning **c** Jon 4:2

CALCULATE *count*
shall **c** from the year Lev 25:50
c the cost Luke 14:28
c the...beast Rev 13:18

CALEB
1 *aide to Moses* Num 13:30
son of Jephunneh Num 32:12
received Hebron Josh 14:13
2 *son of Hezron* 1 Chr 2:18

CALF *animal*
tender and choice **c** Gen 18:7
into a molten **c** Ex 32:4
c and the young lion Is 11:6
skip about like **c-ves** Mal 4:2
bring the fattened **c** Luke 15:23
blood of...**c-ves** Heb 9:12

CALL *address, summon, name*
God **c-ed** the light day Gen 1:5
c upon the name Gen 4:26
c-s up the dead Deut 18:11
LORD was **c-ing**...boy 1 Sam 3:8
c-ed fine gold my trust Job 31:24
c upon the LORD Ps 18:3
those who **c** evil good Is 5:20
c His name Immanuel Is 7:14
You shall **c** Me Jer 3:19
who is **c-ed** the Messiah Matt 1:16
to **c** the righteous Matt 9:13
c-s his own sheep John 10:3
c Me Teacher and John 13:13
God has not **c-ed** 1 Thess 4:7
c-s...a prophetess Rev 2:20

CALLING *summoning*
the **c** of assemblies Is 1:13
the **c** of God Rom 11:29
For consider your **c** 1 Cor 1:26
with a holy **c** 2 Tim 1:9
His **c** and choosing 2 Pet 1:10

CALM *still*
be **c**, have no fear Is 7:4
sea may become **c** Jon 1:11
it became perfectly **c** Matt 8:26
you ought to keep **c** Acts 19:36

CAMEL *animal*
dismounted...the **c** Gen 24:64
his wives upon **c-s** Gen 31:17
a garment of **c-'s** hair Matt 3:4
c...eye of a needle Matt 19:24
clothed with **c-'s** hair Mark 1:6

CAMP (n) *lodging area*
This is God's **c** Gen 32:2
people out of the **c** Ex 19:17
outside the **c** seven Num 31:19
pitch **c-s**, and place Ezek 4:2
the **c** of the saints Rev 20:9

CAMP (v) *settle*
you shall **c** in front Ex 14:2
they shall also **c** Num 1:50
Israel **c-ed** at Gilgal Josh 5:10
I will **c** against you Is 29:3
c around My house Zech 9:8

CANA
Galilean town John 2:1,11;4:46

CANAAN
1 *son of Ham* Gen 9:18,25
2 *Syro-Palestine* Gen 13:12;42:5; Ex 16:35; Ps 105:11
3 *language (Hebrew)* Is 19:18
see also **HEBREW**
see also **JUDEAN**

CANAL *water way*
c-s will emit a stench Is 19:6
rivers *and* wide **c-s** Is 33:21
the Nile **c-s** dry Ezek 30:12
in front of the **c** Dan 8:3

CAPERNAUM
city on Sea of Galilee Matt 4:13; Luke 4:23; John 6:24,59

CAPHTOR
Crete Deut 2:23; Jer 47:4; Amos 9:7
see also **CRETE**

CAPITAL *top part of column*
height of the other **c** 1 Kin 7:16
c on the top of each 2 Chr 3:15
c-s...were on top 2 Chr 4:12

CAPPADOCIA *province in Asia Minor* Acts 2:9; 1 Pet 1:1

CAPTAIN *leader*
c of the bodyguard Gen 39:1
the **c-s** of hundreds Num 31:14
c of the host of Josh 5:14
the **c** of the ship Acts 27:11

CAPTIVE *prisoner*
firstborn of the **c** Ex 12:29
slain and the **c-s** Deut 32:42
restores his **c** people Ps 14:7
have led **c** *Your* **c-s** Ps 68:18
release to the **c-s** Luke 4:18
every thought **c** 2 Cor 10:5
having been held **c** 2 Tim 2:26

CAPTIVITY *imprisonment*
restore you from **c** Deut 30:3
land of their **c** 2 Chr 6:37
had come from the **c** Ezra 8:35
had survived the **c** Neh 1:2
destined for **c** Rev 13:10

CAPTURE *seize, take*
they **c-d** and looted Gen 34:29
c-d all his cities Deut 2:34
Can anyone **c** him Job 40:24
c...with her eyelids Prov 6:25
it **c-s** nothing at all Amos 3:5

CARAVAN *expedition*
a **c** of Ishmaelites Gen 37:25
The **c-s** of Tema Job 6:19
O **c-s** of Dedanites Is 21:13

CARCASS *corpse*
down upon the **c-es** Gen 15:11
one who touches...**c** Lev 11:39
c-es will be food Deut 28:26
c of the lion Judg 14:8
c-es of their...idols Jer 16:18

CARE (n) *concern*
into the **c** of...sons Gen 30:35
put him in my **c** Gen 42:37
friends and receive **c** Acts 27:3
c for one another 1 Cor 12:25

CARE (v) *have concern for*
He **c-d** for him Deut 32:10
No one **c-s** for...soul Ps 142:4
c for My sheep Ezek 34:12
and took **c** of him Luke 10:34
take **c** of the church 1 Tim 3:5
he **c-s** for you 1 Pet 5:7

CAREFUL *watchful, on guard*
I not be **c** to speak Num 23:12
c to observe all Deut 6:25
you shall be **c** to do Deut 8:1
be **c** not to drink Judg 13:4
be **c** how you walk Eph 5:15

CARELESS *thoughtless*
a fool is...**c** Prov 14:16
food, and **c** ease Ezek 16:49
that every **c** word Matt 12:36

CARGO *merchandise*
and they threw the **c** Jon 1:5
to unload its **c** Acts 21:3
no one buys...**c-es** Rev 18:11

CARMEL
1 *range of hills* 1 Kin 18:42; 2 Kin 4:25; Jer 46:18
2 *town in Judah* 1 Sam 15:12;25:5,40

CARPENTER *craftsman*
c-s and stonemasons 2 Sam 5:11
to the masons and **c-s** Ezra 3:7
this the **c-'s** son Matt 13:55
c, the son of Mary Mark 6:3

CARRY *bear*
LORD...**c-ied** you Deut 1:31
c an ephod before 1 Sam 2:28
Spirit...will **c** you 1 Kin 18:12
c *them* in His bosom Is 40:11
our sorrows He **c-ied** Is 53:4
c-ied away...diseases Matt 8:17
C no money belt, no bag Luke 10:4
the cross to **c** Luke 23:26
c out the desire of Gal 5:16

CART *wagon*
So Moses took the **c-s** Num 7:6
the cows to the **c** 1 Sam 6:7
sin as if with **c** ropes Is 5:18
his **c** and his horses Is 28:28

CARVE (v) *cut, fashion*
he **c-d** all the walls 1 Kin 6:29
who **c** a resting place Is 22:16
c-d with cherubim Ezek 41:18
its maker has **c-d** it Hab 2:18

CARVED (adj) *cut, etched*
with **c** engravings 1 Kin 6:29
c image of the idol 2 Chr 33:7
abdomen is **c** ivory Song 5:14

CAST *throw*
one who **c-s** a spell Deut 18:11
Joshua **c** lots for Josh 18:10
c Your law behind Neh 9:26
c *lots* for the orphans Job 6:27
c My words behind Ps 50:17
Do not **c** me away Ps 51:11
c you out of My sight Jer 7:15
will **c** out demons Mark 16:17
c fire upon...earth Luke 12:49
clothing they **c** lots John 19:24
c-ing all your anxiety 1 Pet 5:7
but **c** them into hell 2 Pet 2:4
c their crowns before Rev 4:10

CATCH *seize, trap*
shall **c** his wife Judg 21:21
to **c** the afflicted Ps 10:9
C the foxes for us Song 2:15
caught in My snare Ezek 12:13
will be **c-ing** men Luke 5:10
unable to **c** Him Luke 20:26
caught in adultery John 8:3
who **c-es** the wise 1 Cor 3:19
if anyone is **caught** Gal 6:1
child was **caught** up Rev 12:5

CATTLE *domestic animals*
c and creeping things Gen 1:24
the firstborn of **c** Ex 12:29
defect from the **c** Lev 22:19
c on a thousand hills Ps 50:10
no **c** in the stalls Hab 3:17

CAUSE (n) *purpose, reason*
the **c** of the just Ex 23:8
to death without a **c** 1 Sam 19:5
place my **c** before God Job 5:8
hate me without a **c** Ps 69:4
wounds without **c** Prov 23:29
hated...without a **c** John 15:25

CAUSE (v) *make*
I **c** My name to be Ex 20:24
c Israel to inherit Deut 1:38
has **c-d** His name Ezra 6:12
c His face to shine Ps 67:1
speech **c** you to sin Eccl 5:6
who **c** dissensions Rom 16:17
was **c-ing** the growth 1 Cor 3:6

CAVE *shelter*
buried him in the **c** Gen 25:9
escaped to the **c** 1 Sam 22:1
by fifties in a **c** 1 Kin 18:4
mountains and **c-s** Heb 11:38
hid...in the **c-s** Rev 6:15

CEASE *stop*
you shall **c** *from labor* Ex 23:12
poor will never **c** Deut 15:11
He makes wars to **c** Ps 46:9
C...consideration Prov 23:4
make this proverb **c** Ezek 12:23
c-d to kiss My feet Luke 7:45
tongues, they will **c** 1 Cor 13:8
pray without **c-ing** 1 Thess 5:17

CEDAR *tree, wood*
with the **c** wood Lev 14:6
c-s beside the waters Num 24:6
all the **c-s** of Lebanon Is 2:13
the height of **c-s** Amos 2:9

CELEBRATE *rejoice*
may **c** a feast to Me Ex 5:1
you shall **c** it in Lev 23:41
C the Passover 2 Kin 23:21
all Israel were **c-ing** 1 Chr 13:8
to **c** *the feast* 2 Chr 30:23
David...**c-ing** 1 Chr 15:29
c with my friends Luke 15:29

CENSER *incense container*
c-s for yourselves Num 16:6
his **c** in his hand Ezek 8:11
holding a golden **c** Rev 8:3
angel took the **c** Rev 8:5

CENSUS *population roll*
c of...congregation Num 1:2
number of the **c** 1 Chr 21:5
c which...David 2 Chr 2:17
the first **c** taken Luke 2:2
in the days of the **c** Acts 5:37

CENT *money*
paid up the last **c** Matt 5:26
sparrows...for a **c** Matt 10:29
amount to a **c** Mark 12:42

CENTURION *captain*
Jesus said to the **c** Matt 8:13
summoning the **c** Mark 15:44
soldiers and **c-s** Acts 21:32
gave orders to the **c** Acts 24:23

CEPHAS
apostle Peter John 1:42; 1 Cor 1:12;15:5; Gal 2:11

CERTAINTY *sureness*
know with **c** that Josh 23:13
c of the words Prov 22:21
you know with **c** Eph 5:5

CERTIFICATE *permit, record*
a **c** of divorce Deut 24:1
a **c** of divorce Matt 5:31
c of debt Col 2:14

CHAFF *husk*
consumes them as **c** Ex 15:7
c which the wind drives Ps 1:4
make the hills like **c** Is 41:15
c from the summer Dan 2:35
burn up the **c** Matt 3:12

CHAIN *band*
bound...bronze **c-s** Judg 16:21
he drew **c-s** of gold 1 Kin 6:21
whose hands are **c-s** Eccl 7:26
was bound with **c-s** Luke 8:29
c-s fell off his hands Acts 12:7
great **c** in his hand Rev 20:1

CHALDEA
S Babylonia Jer 50:10;51:24; Ezek 23:15

CHALDEANS
inhabitants of Chaldea Gen 11:28; 2 Kin 24:2; Job 1:17; Jer 24:5; Dan 5:11; Hab 1:6

CHAMBER *room*
entered his **c** Gen 43:30
in his cool roof **c** Judg 3:20
c-s of the storehouse Neh 10:38
bridegroom...his **c** Ps 19:5
to the **c-s** of death Prov 7:27
out of her *bridal* **c** Joel 2:16
c-s in the heavens Amos 9:6

CHAMPION *fighter*
c, the Philistine 1 Sam 17:23
a Savior and a **C** Is 19:20
like a dread **c** Jer 20:11

CHANGE (n) *alteration*
gave **c-s** of garments Gen 45:22
had a **c** of heart Ex 14:5
two **c-s** of clothes 2 Kin 5:23
Until my **c** comes Job 14:14
a **c** of law Heb 7:12

CHANGE (v) *alter, transform*
and **c-d** my wages Gen 31:7
He **c-s** a wilderness Ps 107:35
c-d their glory Jer 2:11
Ethiopian **c** his skin Jer 13:23
He who **c-s** the times Dan 2:21
LORD **c-d** His mind Amos 7:6
I, the LORD, do not **c** Mal 3:6
will all be **c-d** 1 Cor 15:51

CHANNEL *furrow*
Who has cleft a **c** Job 38:25
c-s of water appeared Ps 18:15
heart is *like* **c-s** Prov 21:1
sent out its **c-s** Ezek 31:4

CHANT *sing*
David **c-ed**...this 2 Sam 1:17
Jeremiah **c-ed** a 2 Chr 35:25
daughters...shall **c** Ezek 32:16

CHARACTER
and proven **c,** hope Rom 5:4
Make sure...your **c** is free Heb 13:5

CHARGE (n) *responsibility*
under Joseph's **c** Gen 39:23
keep the **c** of the LORD Lev 8:35
c of his household Matt 24:45
allotted to your **c** 1 Pet 5:3

CHARGE (n) *accusation*
far from a false **c** Ex 23:7
bring **c-s** against Acts 19:38
c against God's elect Rom 8:33

CHARGE (n) *cost*
gospel without **c** 1 Cor 9:18

CHARGE (v) *command*
Abimelech **c-d** all Gen 26:11
I **c-d** your judges Deut 1:16
Moses **c-d** us with a Deut 33:4
I solemnly **c** you 1 Tim 5:21

CHARGE (v) *exact a price*
not **c** him interest Ex 22:25
c that to my account Philem 18

CHARIOT *wagon*
Joseph prepared...**c** Gen 46:29
appeared a **c** of fire 2 Kin 2:11
Some *boast* in **c-s** Ps 20:7
c-s of God are myriads Ps 68:17
Your **c-s** of salvation Hab 3:8
I will cut off the **c** Zech 9:10
and sitting in his **c** Acts 8:28

CHARIOTEERS *warriors*
David killed 700 **c** 2 Sam 10:18
7,000 **c** and 40,000 1 Chr 19:18
with horses and **c** Ezek 39:20

CHARITY *alms*
give that...as **c** Luke 11:41
and give to **c** Luke 12:33
deeds of...**c** Acts 9:36

CHARM *beauty*
A bribe is a **c** Prov 17:8
C is deceitful Prov 31:30
with *all* your **c-s** Song 7:6

CHASE *drive, pursue*
Egyptians **c-d** after Ex 14:9
will **c** your enemies Lev 26:7
one **c** a thousand Deut 32:30
c-ing...Philistines 1 Sam 17:53
be **c-d** like chaff Is 17:13

CHASTE *pure*
c...behavior 1 Pet 3:2
kept themselves **c** Rev 14:4

CHASTEN *discipline*
Man is also **c-ed** Job 33:19
Nor **c** me in Your wrath Ps 6:1
c-ed every morning Ps 73:14
who **c-s** the nations Ps 94:10

CHASTISE *punish*
You have **c-d** me Jer 31:18
I will **c** all of them Hos 5:2

CHATTER *babbling*
worldly...empty **c** 1 Tim 6:20
avoid...empty **c** 2 Tim 2:16

CHEAT *deceive*
your father has **c-ed** Gen 31:7
c with...scales Amos 8:5

CHEBAR
river in Babylonia Ezek 3:15;10:15

CHEDORLAOMER
king of Elam Gen 14:9,17

CHEEK *part of face*
slapped me on the **c** Job 16:10
Your **c-s** are lovely Song 1:10
tears are on her **c-s** Lam 1:2
hits you on the **c** Luke 6:29

CHEERFUL
countenance and be **c** Job 9:27
joyful heart...a **c** Prov 15:13
c heart...feast Prov 15:15
God loves a **c** giver 2 Cor 9:7
Is anyone **c** James 5:13

CHEMOSH
god of Moab Judg 11:24; 1 Kin 11:7; Jer 48:13

CHERETHITES
1 *tribe on Philistine plain* 1 Sam 30:14; Ezek 25:16; Zeph 2:5
2 *David's bodyguards* 2 Sam 8:18;15:18; 1 Kin 1:38; 1 Chr 18:17

CHERISH *love*
or the wife you **c** Deut 13:6
the wife he **c-es** Deut 28:54
men **c** themselves Acts 24:15
c-es it, just as Christ Eph 5:29

CHERUB *celestial being*
He rode on a **c** 2 Sam 22:11
one **c**...ten cubits 1 Kin 6:26
c stretched out his Ezek 10:7

CHERUBIM *plural of cherub*
He stationed the **c** Gen 3:24
c had *their* wings Ex 37:9
enthroned *above*...**c** 2 Sam 6:2
c appeared to have Ezek 10:8

CHEST *box*
the priest took a **c** 2 Kin 12:9
money in the **c** 2 Kin 12:10
levies...into the **c** 2 Chr 24:10

CHEW *eat*
which **c** the cud Lev 11:4
before it was **c-ed** Num 11:33

CHIEF *head, prominent*
c-s of the sons of Gen 36:15
the **c-s** of Edom Gen 36:43
of the thirty **c** men 2 Sam 23:13
c of the magicians Dan 4:9
C Shepherd appears 1 Pet 5:4

CHILD
c grew...weaned Gen 21:8
Train up a **c** in Prov 22:6
discipline from the **c** Prov 23:13
c will be born to us Is 9:6
with **c** by the Holy Matt 1:18
take the **C** and His Matt 2:13
He called a **c** to Matt 18:2
saying, **C,** arise Luke 8:54
a woman with **c** 1 Thess 5:3

CHILDBIRTH
multiply...pain in **c** Gen 3:16
as of a woman in **c** Ps 48:6
pains of **c** come Hos 13:13
suffers the pains of **c** Rom 8:22

CHILDLESS
I am **c,** and the heir Gen 15:2
They will die **c** Lev 20:20
c among women 1 Sam 15:33
and died **c** Luke 20:29

CHILDREN
pain...bring forth **c** Gen 3:16
Are these all the **c** 1 Sam 16:11
compassion on *his* **c** Ps 103:13
c are a gift Ps 127:3
c rise up and bless Prov 31:28
c were dashed to Nah 3:10
slew all the male **c** Matt 2:16
stones...to raise up **c** Matt 3:9
c...against parents Matt 10:21
and become like **c** Matt 18:3
bringing **c** to Him Mark 10:13
Being...the **c** of God Acts 17:29
if **c,** heirs Rom 8:17

C, obey your parents Eph 6:1
My little **c** 1 John 2:1
kill her **c** with Rev 2:23

CHINNERETH / CHINNEROTH
1 *lake* Num 34:11; Josh 12:3
also **Sea of Galilee**
also **Lake of Gennesaret**
also **Sea of Tiberias**
2 *city of Naphtali* Deut 3:17; Josh 19:35
3 *plain near Galilee* Josh 11:2; 1 Kin 15:20

CHISLEV
ninth month of Hebrew calendar Neh 1:1; Zech 7:1

CHOICE *option* or *best*
Saul, a **c**...*man* 1 Sam 9:2
c men of Israel 2 Sam 10:9
And eat its **c** fruits Song 4:16
God made a **c** among Acts 15:7
God's gracious **c** Rom 11:5
His **c** of you 1 Thess 1:4

CHOIR *chorus*
c proceeded to the Neh 12:38
two **c-s** took their Neh 12:40

CHOKE *stifle*
wealth **c** the word Matt 13:22
began to **c** *him* Matt 18:28
thorns...**c-d** it Mark 4:7
c-d with worries Luke 8:14

CHOOSE *select, take*
C men for us Ex 17:9
whom the LORD **c-s** Num 16:7
C wise...discerning Deut 1:13
He **c-s** our inheritance Ps 47:4
refuse evil and **c** good Is 7:15
not God **c** the poor James 2:5

CHOP *cut*
who **c-s** your wood Deut 29:11
c-ped down...altars 2 Chr 34:7
C down the tree Dan 4:14

CHOSE *selected*
Lot **c** for himself Gen 13:11
God has **c-n** you Deut 7:6
I **c** David to be 1 Kin 8:16
when I **c** Israel Ezek 20:5
c twelve of them Luke 6:13
has **c-n** the weak 1 Cor 1:27
He **c** us in Him Eph 1:4

CHOSEN *elected, selected*
Moses His **c** one Ps 106:23
My **c** *one in whom* Is 42:1
Israel My **c** *one* Is 45:4
c ones shall inherit Is 65:9
My Son, *My* **C** One Luke 9:35
c of God, holy and Col 3:12
of *His* **c** angels 1 Tim 5:21
you are a **c** race 1 Pet 2:9

CHRIST *Messiah*
birth of Jesus **C** was Matt 1:18

C would suffer and Luke 24:46
both Lord and **C** Acts 2:36
fellow heirs with **C** Rom 8:17
are one body in **C** Rom 12:5
preach **C** crucified 1 Cor 1:23
judgment seat of **C** 2 Cor 5:10
ambassadors for **C** 2 Cor 5:20
faith in **C** Jesus Gal 2:16
as sons through Jesus **C** Eph 1:5
to live is **C** Phil 1:21
C, who is our life Col 3:4
dead in **C** will 1 Thess 4:16
coming of...**C** 2 Thess 2:1
C...high priest Heb 9:11
Advocate...Jesus **C** 1 John 2:1
with **C** for a thousand Rev 20:4

CHRISTIAN *follower of Christ*
first called **C-s** in Acts 11:26
me to become a **C** Acts 26:28
suffers as a **C** 1 Pet 4:16

CHRONICLES *book of register*
1 *of kings of Israel* 1 Kin 14:19;15:31; 2 Kin 14:28;15:26
2 *of kings of Judah* 1 Kin 14:29;15:23; 2 Kin 15:36;24:5
3 *of kings of Media / Persia* Esth 10:2

CHURCH *a called out assembly*
I will build my **c** Matt 16:18
tell it to the **c** Matt 18:17
shepherd the **c** Acts 20:28
c-es of the Gentiles Rom 16:4
together as a **c** 1 Cor 11:18
woman...speak in **c** 1 Cor 14:35
to the **c-es** of Judea Gal 1:22
Christ...head of the **c** Eph 5:23
persecutor of the **c** Phil 3:6
c of the living God 1 Tim 3:15
Spirit says to the **c-es** Rev 2:11

CILICIA
region in SE Asia Minor Acts 15:41;21:39;27:5

CINNAMON *spice*
and of fragrant **c** Ex 30:23
myrrh, aloes and **c** Prov 7:17
and **c** and spice Rev 18:13

CIRCLE *area*
sleeping inside...**c** 1 Sam 26:7
He has inscribed a **c** Job 26:10
did not sit in the **c** Jer 15:17

CIRCUIT *course*
on **c** to Bethel 1 Sam 7:16
its **c** to the other end Ps 19:6

CIRCULATE *spread*
proclamation was **c-d** Ex 36:6
LORD's people **c-ing** 1 Sam 2:24
to **c** a proclamation 2 Chr 30:5

CIRCUMCISE
be pure or *cut off*
every male...be **c-d** Gen 17:10
Abraham **c-d** his son Gen 21:4
So **c** your heart Deut 10:16
God will **c**...heart Deut 30:6
C yourselves...LORD Jer 4:4
came to **c** the child Luke 1:59
c-d the eighth day Phil 3:5

CIRCUMCISION *act of purity*
because of the **c** Ex 4:26
c is...of the heart Rom 2:29
if you receive **c** Gal 5:2
if I still preach **c** Gal 5:11
we are the *true* **c** Phil 3:3
c made without hands Col 2:11
those of the **c** Titus 1:10

CIRCUMSTANCE *condition*
spoken in right **c-s** Prov 25:11
may know...my **c-s** Eph 6:21
peace in every **c** 2 Thess 3:16
of humble **c-s** James 1:9

CISTERN *reservoir*
a **c** collecting water Lev 11:36
water from your...**c** Prov 5:15
wheel at the **c** is Eccl 12:6
prophet from the **c** Jer 38:10

CITADEL *fortress*
c of the king's 1 Kin 16:18
c of Susa Esth 2:3
in the **c** of Susa Dan 8:2
c-s of Jerusalem Amos 2:5
Proclaim on the **c-s** Amos 3:9
tramples on our **c-s** Mic 5:5

CITIES OF REFUGE
1 *Kedesh in Naphtali* Josh 20:7
2 *Shechem in Ephraim* Josh 20:7
3 *Hebron (Kiriath-arba)* Josh 20:7
4 *Bezer in Reuben* Josh 20:8
5 *Ramoth-gilead in Gad* Josh 20:8
6 *Golan in Manasseh* Josh 20:8

CITIZEN *resident*
your fellow **c-s** Ezek 33:12
fellow **c-s** who talk Ezek 33:30
c-s hated him Luke 19:14
c of no insignificant Acts 21:39
fellow **c-s** with the Eph 2:19

CITY
build...a **c** Gen 11:4
burned...their **c-ies** Num 31:10
die in my own **c** 2 Sam 19:37
glad the **c** of God Ps 46:4
LORD guards the **c** Ps 127:1
the **C** of Destruction Is 19:18
the **C** of Truth Zech 8:3
a **c** called Nazareth Matt 2:23
into the holy **c** Matt 4:5
the **c** was stirred Matt 21:10

c, shake the dust off Luke 9:5
He has prepared a **c** Heb 11:16
I saw the holy **c** Rev 21:2

CLAIM *demand*
Let darkness...**c** it Job 3:5
Do not **c** honor in Prov 25:6
c-ing to be someone Acts 8:9

CLAN *family, tribe*
c of the household Judg 9:1
and by your **c-s** 1 Sam 10:19
among...**c-s** of Judah Mic 5:2
I will make the **c-s** Zech 12:6

CLAP *applaud*
c-ped their hands 2 Kin 11:12
c-s his hands among Job 34:37
rivers **c** their hands Ps 98:8
trees...will **c** Is 55:12

CLAUDIA
Roman Christian 2 Tim 4:21

CLAUDIUS
Roman Emperor Acts 11:28;18:2
see **CAESAR**

CLAUDIUS LYSIAS
Roman tribune Acts 23:26

CLAY
dwell in houses of **c** Job 4:19
Father, We are the **c** Is 64:8
c in the potter's hand Jer 18:6
the **c** to his eyes John 9:6

CLEAN *cleansed, washed*
animals that are not **c** Gen 7:2
eat in a **c** place Lev 10:14
pronounce him **c** Lev 13:28
Create in me a **c** heart Ps 51:10
make yourselves **c** Is 1:16
You can make me **c** Matt 8:2
things are **c** for you Luke 11:41
c because of the word John 15:3

CLEANSE *purify, wash*
To **c** the house then Lev 14:49
c the house of the 2 Chr 29:15
I have **c-d** my heart Prov 20:9
I am willing; be **c-d** Matt 8:3
the lepers are **c-d** Matt 11:5
not eat unless they **c** Mark 7:4
let us **c** ourselves 2 Cor 7:1
C...you sinners James 4:8
blood...**c-s** us 1 John 1:7

CLEAR *make free* or *plain*
c-s away many nations Deut 7:1
C the way for the LORD Is 40:3
c His threshing floor Matt 3:12
Christ has made **c** 2 Pet 1:14
river...**c** as crystal Rev 22:1

CLEFT *crevice*
in the **c** of the rock Judg 15:8

the **c-s** of the cliffs Is 2:21
who live in the **c-s** Obad 3

CLEOPAS
disciple of Christ Luke 24:18

CLEVER *smart*
c in their own sight Is 5:21
cleverness of the **c** 1 Cor 1:19

CLIFF *crag*
nest is set in the **c** Num 24:21
On the **c** he dwells Job 39:28
c-s are a refuge Ps 104:18

CLIMB *ascend*
I will **c** the palm tree Song 7:8
the one who **c-s** Jer 48:44
c-ed...a sycamore Luke 19:4
c-s up...other way John 10:1

CLING *cleave*
and **c** to Him Deut 13:4
c to the LORD Josh 23:8
My soul **c-s** to You Ps 63:8
c to Your testimonies Ps 119:31
Stop **c-ing** to Me John 20:17
c to what is good Rom 12:9

CLOAK *coat, mantle*
Give me the **c** Ruth 3:15
neither bread nor **c** Is 3:7
fringe of His **c** Matt 9:20
Wrap your **c** around Acts 12:8

CLOSE *shut, stop*
and the LORD **c-d** Gen 7:16
floodgates...were **c-d** Gen 8:2
earth **c-d** over them Num 16:33
c your door...pray Matt 6:6
have **c-d** their eyes Acts 28:27
every mouth...**c-d** Rom 3:19
c-s his heart 1 John 3:17

CLOTH *fabric*
spread over *it* a **c** Num 4:6
is wrapped in a **c** 1 Sam 21:9
with embroidered **c** Ezek 16:10
in the linen **c** Mark 15:46

CLOTHE *array, dress*
C me with skin Job 10:11
meadows are **c-d** with Ps 65:13
O Zion; **C** yourself Is 52:1
God so **c-s** the grass Matt 6:30
naked...you **c-d** Me Matt 25:36
are splendidly **c-d** Luke 7:25
c-d with power Luke 24:49
c...with humility 1 Pet 5:5
c-d in the white robes Rev 7:13

CLOTHES *garments*
c of her captivity Deut 21:13
your **c** have not worn Deut 29:5
and worn-out **c** on Josh 9:5
and changed his **c** 2 Sam 12:20
without wedding **c** Matt 22:12
Tearing his **c** Mark 14:63

CLOTHING *clothes, raiment*
- reduce...her **c** Ex 21:10
- **c** did not wear out Deut 8:4
- purple are their **c** Jer 10:9
- and the body more than **c** Matt 6:25
- in sheep's **c** Matt 7:15
- **c** as white as snow Matt 28:3
- His **c** *became* white Luke 9:29
- men...in dazzling **c** Luke 24:4
- sister is without **c** James 2:15

CLOUD *mist*
- set My bow in the **c** Gen 9:13
- in a pillar of **c** Ex 13:21
- **c** where God *was* Ex 20:21
- **c** covered...mountain Ex 24:15
- **c** for a covering Ps 105:39
- voice came out...**c** Mark 9:7
- Son...coming in **c-s** Mark 13:26
- in a **c** with power Luke 21:27
- and a **c** received Him Acts 1:9

CLUB *weapon*
- went...with a **c** 2 Sam 23:21
- **C-s** are...as stubble Job 41:29
- *Like* a **c** and a Prov 25:18
- with swords and **c-s** Matt 26:47

CLUSTER *collection*
- **c-s** produced ripe Gen 40:10
- **c-s** of raisins 1 Sam 25:18
- breasts are...**c-s** Song 7:7
- gather the **c-s** Rev 14:18

COAL *charcoal*
- breath kindles **c-s** Job 41:21
- man walk on hot **c-s** Prov 6:28
- burning **c** in his hand Is 6:6
- heap burning **c-s** Rom 12:20

COAST
- **c** of the Great Sea Josh 9:1
- along the **c** of Asia Acts 27:2

COASTLAND
- inhabitants of this **c** Is 20:6
- to the **c-s** of Kittim Jer 2:10
- **c-s** shake at the Ezek 26:15
- **c-s** of the nations Zeph 2:11

COAT *cloak*
- opening...**c** of mail Ex 28:32
- with his **c** torn 2 Sam 15:32
- have your **c** also Matt 5:40
- or even two **c-s** Matt 10:10
- spread their **c-s** Mark 11:8

COBRA *snake*
- deadly poison of **c-s** Deut 32:33
- To the venom of **c-s** Job 20:14
- tread upon the...**c** Ps 91:13

COFFIN *bier*
- in a **c** in Egypt Gen 50:26
- and touched the **c** Luke 7:14

COHORT *military unit*
- the whole *Roman* **c** Matt 27:27
- called the Italian **c** Acts 10:1
- of the Augustan **c** Acts 27:1

COIN *money*
- Show Me the **c** Matt 22:19
- woman...loses one **c** Luke 15:8
- He poured out...**c-s** John 2:15

COLD *cool*
- covering against the **c** Job 24:7
- Like the **c** of snow Prov 25:13
- cup of **c** water Matt 10:42
- love will grow **c** Matt 24:12
- neither **c** nor hot Rev 3:15

COLLAPSE *fall*
- grass **c-s** into the flame Is 5:24
- pathways will **c** Ezek 38:20
- ancient hills **c-d** Hab 3:6

COLLEAGUES *co-workers*
- the rest of his **c** Ezra 4:7
- and your **c** Ezra 6:6

COLLECT *exact, take*
- **c-ed** his strength Gen 48:2
- cistern **c-ing** water Lev 11:36
- **c** captives like sand Hab 1:9
- **C** no more than Luke 3:13
- **c-ed** a tenth from Heb 7:6

COLLECTION *acquisition*
- let your **c** *of idols* Is 57:13
- no **c-s** be made 1 Cor 16:2

COLOSSAE
- *city in Asia Minor* Col 1:2

COLT *foal*
- camels and their **c-s** Gen 32:15
- Even on a **c** Zech 9:9
- and a **c** with her Matt 21:2
- on a donkey's **c** John 12:15

COLUMN *pillar, text*
- in a **c** of smoke Judg 20:40
- and marble **c-s** Esth 1:6
- read three...**c-s** Jer 36:23

COME
- **C**, let us build Gen 11:4
- **C**, let us worship Ps 95:6
- All **came** from...dust Eccl 3:20
- your king is **c-ing** Zech 9:9
- Your kingdom **c** Matt 6:10
- **C** to Me, all who Matt 11:28
- children to **c** to Me Mark 10:14
- not **c**...temptation Mark 14:38
- Son of Man **c-ing** Luke 21:27
- Father...hour has **c** John 17:1
- His judgment has **c** Rev 14:7
- I am **c-ing** quickly Rev 22:20

COMFORT (n) *consolation*
- mourning without **c** Job 30:28
- **c** in my affliction Ps 119:50
- he will give you **c** Prov 29:17
- **c** of the Holy Spirit Acts 9:31
- and God of all **c** 2 Cor 1:3
- your **c** and salvation 2 Cor 1:6

COMFORT (v) *console, cheer*
- relatives came to **c** 1 Chr 7:22
- Your rod...they **c** me Ps 23:4
- I, am He who **c-s** you Is 51:12
- To **c** all who mourn Is 61:2
- he is being **c-ed** Luke 16:25
- **c** one another 1 Thess 4:18

COMFORTER *consoler*
- Sorry **c-s** are you all Job 16:2
- **c-s,** but I found none Ps 69:20
- She has no **c** Lam 1:9
- Where will I seek **c-s** Nah 3:7

COMING (n) *arrival*
- Joseph's **c** at noon Gen 43:25
- the day of His **c** Mal 3:2
- *be* the sign of Your **c** Matt 24:3
- **c** of the Son of Man Matt 24:37
- Christ's at His **c** 1 Cor 15:23
- **c** of the Lord is James 5:8
- the promise of His **c** 2 Pet 3:4

COMMAND (n) *order*
- the **c** of the LORD Lev 24:12
- disobeyed the **c** 1 Kin 13:21
- to the king's **c** 2 Chr 35:10
- no **c** of the Lord 1 Cor 7:25
- could not bear the **c** Heb 12:20

COMMAND (v) *declare, order*
- I **c-ed** you not to eat Gen 3:11
- may **c** his children Gen 18:19
- speak all that I **c** you Ex 7:2
- bring all that I **c** Deut 12:11
- the angel...**c-ed** Matt 1:24
- **c** that these stones Matt 4:3
- **c-s** even the winds Luke 8:25
- **c-ing** the jailer Acts 16:23

COMMANDER
- *captain, general*
- the **c-s** of Israel Judg 5:9
- **c** of Saul's army 2 Sam 2:8
- his chariot **c-s** 1 Kin 9:22
- and Joab was the **c** 1 Chr 27:34
- **c** for the peoples Is 55:4
- the **C** of the host Dan 8:11
- and the flesh of **c-s** Rev 19:18

COMMANDMENT *instruction*
- and keep My **c-s** Ex 20:6
- the Ten **C-s** Ex 34:28
- and keep His **c-s** Josh 22:5
- **c** of the LORD is pure Ps 19:8
- the **c** of your father Prov 6:20
- which is the great **c** Matt 22:36
- A new **c** I give John 13:34
- will keep My **c-s** John 14:15
- I have kept...**c-s** John 15:10
- not writing a new **c** 1 John 2:7
- keep the **c-s** of God Rev 14:12

COMMEND *praise, present*
- So I **c-ed** pleasure Eccl 8:15
- I **c** you to God Acts 20:32
- food will not **c** us 1 Cor 8:8
- to **c** ourselves again 2 Cor 3:1

COMMISSION *appoint*
- **c** him in their sight Num 27:19
- He **c-ed** Joshua Deut 31:23
- king has **c-ed** me 1 Sam 21:2
- **c** it against the people Is 10:6

COMMISSIONERS *supervisors*
- and over them three **c** Dan 6:2
- Then the **c** and satraps Dan 6:4

COMMIT *entrust, practice*
- **c-ted** to Joseph's Gen 39:22
- shall not **c** adultery Ex 20:14
- have **c-ted** incest Lev 20:12
- I **c** my spirit Ps 31:5
- **C** your way to the LORD Ps 37:5
- weary...**c-ting** iniquity Jer 9:5
- Do not **c** adultery Luke 18:20
- I **c** My spirit Luke 23:46
- everyone who **c-s** sin John 8:34
- who **c-ted** no sin 1 Pet 2:22

COMMON *ordinary, shared*
- anyone of...**c** people Lev 4:27
- place of the **c** people Jer 26:23
- iron...with **c** clay Dan 2:41
- had all things in **c** Acts 2:44
- about our **c** salvation Jude 3

COMMONWEALTH *nation*
- from the **c** of Israel Eph 2:12

COMMOTION *disturbance*
- the noise of this **c** 1 Sam 4:14
- great **c** out of the Jer 10:22
- Why make a **c** and Mark 5:39

COMPANION *comrade, friend*
- are you striking your **c** Ex 2:13
- brought thirty **c-s** Judg 14:11
- And a **c** of ostriches Job 30:29
- **c** of fools will suffer Prov 13:20
- your **c** and your wife Mal 2:14
- Paul and his **c-s** Acts 13:13

COMPANY *assembly, group*
- into three **c-ies** Judg 9:43
- **c** of the godless Job 15:34
- **c** will stone them Ezek 23:47
- Bad **c** corrupts 1 Cor 15:33

COMPARE *contrast, like*
- none to **c** with You Ps 40:5
- to what shall I **c** Matt 11:16
- **c** the kingdom of Luke 13:20
- be **c-d** with the glory Rom 8:18

COMPASS
- outlines it with a **c** Is 44:13
- four points of the **c** Dan 11:4

COMPASSION *concern, love*
- God...grant you **c** Gen 43:14
- whom I will show **c** Ex 33:19
- in Your great **c** Neh 9:19
- have **c** on the poor Ps 72:13
- have **c** on Zion Ps 102:13
- His **c-s** never fail Lam 3:22
- He felt **c** for them Matt 9:36
- his father...felt **c** Luke 15:20
- put on a heart of **c** Col 3:12
- Lord is full of **c** James 5:11

COMPASSIONATE *loving*
your God is a **c** God Deut 4:31
c, Slow to anger Neh 9:17
He is gracious and **c** Joel 2:13
a gracious and **c** God Jon 4:2

COMPEL *force, press*
Egyptians **c-led** the Ex 1:13
c *them* to come in Luke 14:23
c...to be circumcised Gal 6:12

COMPETE *strive*
can you **c** with horses Jer 12:5
everyone who **c-s** 1 Cor 9:25
c-s as an athlete 2 Tim 2:5

COMPLAIN *murmur*
c-ed to Abimelech Gen 21:25
c in the bitterness Job 7:11
I will **c** and murmur Ps 55:17
Do not **c**, brethren James 5:9

COMPLAINT *grumbling*
c-s of...Israel Num 14:27
couch will ease my **c** Job 7:13
today my **c** is rebellion Job 23:2
hospitable...without **c** 1 Pet 4:9

COMPLETE (adj) *full, total*
a sabbath of **c** rest Ex 35:2
be seven **c** sabbaths Lev 23:15
not...a **c** destruction Jer 5:10
you have been made **c** Col 2:10
be perfect and **c** James 1:4
joy may be made **c** 1 John 1:4

COMPLETE (v) *finish, fulfill*
God **c-d** His work Gen 2:2
C the week of this Gen 29:27
C your work quota Ex 5:13
your days are **c** 2 Sam 7:12
house...was **c-d** 2 Chr 8:16
thousand years are **c-d** Rev 20:7

COMPOSE *write*
c words against you Job 16:4
have **c-d** songs for Amos 6:5
The first account I **c-d** Acts 1:1

COMPOSE *make calm*
c-d and quieted my Ps 131:2
I **c-d** *my soul* Is 38:13

COMPREHEND *understand*
which we cannot **c** Job 37:5
speech...no one **c-s** Is 33:19
and they did not **c** Luke 18:34
darkness did not **c** John 1:5

COMPULSION *coercion*
under **c**...let them go Ex 6:1
in effect, by **c** Philem 14
not under **c**, but 1 Pet 5:2

CONCEAL *cover, hide*
man **c-s** knowledge Prov 12:23
They do not *even* **c** *it* Is 3:9
Do not **c** *it but* Jer 50:2
was **c-ed** from them Luke 9:45

CONCEIT *pride*
selfishness or empty **c** Phil 2:3
he is **c-ed** 1 Tim 6:4
c-ed, lovers of 2 Tim 3:4

CONCEIVE *become pregnant*
Sarah **c-d** and bore a Gen 21:2
c-d all this people Num 11:12
sin my mother **c-d** me Ps 51:5
she **c-d** and gave birth Is 8:3
when lust has **c-d** James 1:15

CONCERN *have care*
master does not **c** Gen 39:8
the LORD was **c-ed** Ex 4:31
You are **c-ed** about Job 7:17
c-ed about the poor John 12:6
is married is **c-ed** 1 Cor 7:33
not **c-ed** about oxen 1 Cor 9:9

CONCUBINE *secondary wife*
Ephraim...took a **c** Judg 19:1
Now Saul had a **c** 2 Sam 3:7
king left ten **c-s** 2 Sam 15:16
three hundred **c-s** 1 Kin 11:3
in charge of the **c-s** Esth 2:14

CONDEMN *discredit, judge*
c-ing the wicked 1 Kin 8:32
my mouth will **c** me Job 9:20
he who **c-s** Me Is 50:9
will **c** Him to death Mark 10:33
do not **c**, and you Luke 6:37
you **c** yourself Rom 2:1
he stood **c-ed** Gal 2:11
our heart **c-s** us 1 John 3:20

CONDEMNATION *judgment*
receive greater **c** Mark 12:40
same sentence of **c** Luke 23:40
Their **c** is just Rom 3:8
no **c**...in Christ Rom 8:1
c upon themselves Rom 13:2
c...by the devil 1 Tim 3:6

CONDITION *state, stipulation*
with you on this **c** 1 Sam 11:2
c-s were good in 2 Chr 12:12
c in which...called 1 Cor 7:20
or adds **c-s** to it Gal 3:15

CONDUCT (n) *behavior*
queen's **c**...known Esth 1:17
turn...*from his* **c** Job 33:17
who are upright in **c** Ps 37:14
sensual **c** of...men 2 Pet 2:7
holy **c** and godliness 2 Pet 3:11

CONDUCT (v) *behave*
c-s himself arrogantly Job 15:25
c...same spirit 2 Cor 12:18
C...with wisdom Col 4:5
c yourselves in fear 1 Pet 1:17

CONDUIT *channel*
c of the upper pool 2 Kin 18:17
at the end of the **c** Is 7:3

CONFESS *acknowledge*
that he shall **c** Lev 5:5
c-ing the sins of Neh 1:6
c my transgressions Ps 32:5
c-es Me before men Matt 10:32
c-ing their sins Mark 1:5
c with your mouth Rom 10:9
If we **c** our sins 1 John 1:9
I will **c** his name Rev 3:5

CONFESSION *admission*
praying and making **c** Ezra 10:1
your **c** of the gospel 2 Cor 9:13
testified the good **c** 1 Tim 6:13
the **c** of our hope Heb 10:23

CONFIDENCE *boldness, trust*
What is this **c** 2 Kin 18:19
they lost their **c** Neh 6:16
LORD will be your **c** Prov 3:26
proud **c** is this 2 Cor 1:12
c in me may abound Phil 1:26
no **c** in the flesh Phil 3:3

CONFINE *imprison, limit*
who were **c-d** in jail Gen 40:5
he does not **c** it Ex 21:29
be **c-d** in prison Is 24:22
c-d in the court Jer 33:1

CONFINEMENT *imprisonment*
c in his master's Gen 40:7
he put me in **c** Gen 41:10

CONFIRM *establish, strengthen*
LORD **c** His word 1 Sam 1:23
c-ed Your inheritance Ps 68:9
c the work of our Ps 90:17
C-ing the word of His Is 44:26
c-ed...by the signs Mark 16:20
who will also **c** you 1 Cor 1:8

CONFIRMATION *verification*
and **c** of the gospel Phil 1:7
an oath *given* as **c** Heb 6:16

CONFLICT *contention*
one of great **c** Dan 10:1
in **c** with the LORD Jer 50:24
experiencing...**c** Phil 1:30
source of...**c-s** James 4:1

CONFORMED *being like*
c...image of His Son Rom 8:29
not be **c** to...world Rom 12:2
being **c** to His death Phil 3:10

CONFOUND *confuse*
LORD **c-ed** them Josh 10:10
c their strategy Is 19:3
c-ing the Jews Acts 9:22

CONFRONT *challenge, face*
snares of death **c-ed** 2 Sam 22:6
Days of affliction **c** Job 30:27
Arise, O LORD, **c** him Ps 17:13
the elders **c-ed** *Him* Luke 20:1

CONFUSE *perplex*
c their language Gen 11:7
Send...and **c** them Ps 144:6
They are **c-d** by wine Is 28:7

CONFUSION *disorder*
into great **c** Deut 7:23
Jerusalem was in **c** Acts 21:31
not *a God* of **c** 1 Cor 14:33

CONGREGATION *assembly*
all the **c** of Israel Ex 12:3
c shall stone him Num 15:35
strife of the **c** Num 27:14
Bless God in the **c-s** Ps 68:26
c of the godly ones Ps 149:1
the **c** of the disciples Acts 6:2
In the midst of the **c** Heb 2:12

CONJURER *magician*
magician, **c** or Dan 2:10
wise men *and* the **c-s** Dan 5:15

CONQUER *be victorious*
c-ed all the country Gen 14:7
but could not **c** it Is 7:1
c through Him Rom 8:37
out **c-ing**, and to **c** Rev 6:2

CONSCIENCE
moral obligation
David's **c** bothered 1 Sam 24:5
always a blameless **c** Acts 24:16
also for **c**' sake Rom 13:5
their **c** being weak is 1 Cor 8:7
faith with a clear **c** 1 Tim 3:9
seared in their own **c** 1 Tim 4:2
keep a good **c** 1 Pet 3:16

CONSECRATE (v) *sanctify*
sons of Israel **c** Ex 28:38
garments shall be **c-d** Ex 29:21
c it and all its Ex 40:9
C yourselves Lev 11:44
c the fiftieth year Lev 25:10
c-s his house as holy Lev 27:14
he shall **c** his head Num 6:11
C yourselves Josh 3:5
have **c-d** this house 1 Kin 9:3

CONSECRATED (adj)
sanctified
touch any **c** thing Lev 12:4
c people...LORD Deut 26:19
there is **c** bread 1 Sam 21:4
c ones were purer Lam 4:7
ate the **c** bread Matt 12:4

CONSENT *agree*
Do not listen or **c** 1 Kin 20:8
entice you, Do not **c** Prov 1:10
If you **c** and obey Is 1:19
c-s to live with him 1 Cor 7:12

CONSIDER *observe, think*
were **c-ed** unclean Neh 7:64
C my groaning Ps 5:1
he who **c-s** the helpless Ps 41:1
We are **c-ed** as sheep Ps 44:22

day of adversity **c** Eccl 7:14
c the work of His hands Is 5:12
C the ravens, for Luke 12:24
c your calling 1 Cor 1:26
He **c-ed** me faithful 1 Tim 1:12
c how to stimulate Heb 10:24
c-ed...God is able Heb 11:19

CONSIST *composed of*
reverence for Me **c-s** Is 29:13
life **c** of his Luke 12:15
does not **c** in words 1 Cor 4:20
c-ing of decrees Col 2:14

CONSOLATION *comfort*
c-s of God too small Job 15:11
Your **c-s** delight my Ps 94:19
is any **c** of love Phil 2:1

CONSOLE *soothe*
Esau is **c-ing** himself Gen 27:42
servants to **c** him 2 Sam 10:2
c-d...comforted Job 42:11
c them concerning John 11:19

CONSPIRACY *plot, scheme*
the **c** was strong 2 Sam 15:12
found **c** in Hoshea 2 Kin 17:4
from the **c-ies** of man Ps 31:20

CONSPIRE *plot against*
have **c-d** against me 1 Sam 22:8
c-d against my 2 Kin 10:9
c together against Ps 83:3
Amos...**c-d** against Amos 7:10

CONSTELLATION *stars*
a **c** in its season Job 38:32
c-s Will not flash Is 13:10

CONSTRUCT *build*
c a sanctuary for Me Ex 25:8
c siegeworks Deut 20:20

CONSTRUCTION *structure*
c of the sanctuary Ex 36:3
it has been under **c** Ezra 5:16
the **c** of the ark 1 Pet 3:20

CONSULT *confer*
c-ed with the elders 1 Kin 12:6
C the mediums Is 8:19
Without **c-ing** Me Is 30:2
people **c** their wooden Hos 4:12
not...**c** with flesh Gal 1:16

CONSUME *destroy, devour*
c-d...purchase price Gen 31:15
the bush was not **c-d** Ex 3:2
c-d the burnt offering Lev 9:24
great fire will **c** us Deut 5:25
c the cedars Judg 9:15
You **c** as a moth Ps 39:11
c-d by Your anger Ps 90:7
c-s his own flesh Eccl 4:5
fire **c-ing** the stubble Joel 2:5
Zeal...will **c** John 2:17
c your flesh like fire James 5:3

CONSUMING (adj) *destroying*
glory...like a **c** fire Ex 24:17
the flame of a **c** fire Is 29:6
our God is a **c** fire Heb 12:29

CONTAIN *hold*
cannot **c** You 1 Kin 8:27
c the burnt offering 2 Chr 7:7
c-ing twenty...gallons John 2:6
not **c** the books John 21:25
is **c-ed** in Scripture 1 Pet 2:6

CONTEMPT *scorn*
He pours **c** on nobles Job 12:21
With pride and **c** Ps 31:18
treating Him with **c** Luke 23:11
your brother with **c** Rom 14:10

CONTEND *strive*
c with him in battle Deut 2:24
c-ed...vigorously Judg 8:1
c with the Almighty Job 40:2
not **c**...without cause Prov 3:30
Who will **c** with me Is 50:8
I will not **c** forever Is 57:16
he **c-ed** with God Hos 12:3
c...for the faith Jude 3

CONTENT *satisfied*
c with your wages Luke 3:14
c with weaknesses 2 Cor 12:10
have learned to be **c** Phil 4:11
c with what you have Heb 13:5

CONTENTION *strife*
object of **c** to our Ps 80:6
the **c-s** of a wife Prov 19:13
Strife exists and **c** Hab 1:3

CONTENTIOUS *quarrelsome*
a **c**...woman Prov 21:19
with a **c** woman Prov 25:24
inclined to be **c** 1 Cor 11:16

CONTINUE *persevere, persist*
My covenant may **c** Mal 2:4
c in My word John 8:31
c in the grace of Acts 13:43
Are we to **c** in sin Rom 6:1
you **c** in the faith Col 1:23
love of the brethren **c** Heb 13:1

CONTRARY *against*
c to the command Num 24:13
for the wind was **c** Matt 14:24
grafted **c** to nature Rom 11:24
c to the teaching Rom 16:17
a gospel **c** to what Gal 1:8
c to sound teaching 1 Tim 1:10

CONTRIBUTE *give*
Josiah **c-d** to the 2 Chr 35:7
c yearly one third Neh 10:32
c-ing to their support Luke 8:3
c-ing to...the saints Rom 12:13

CONTRIBUTION *gift, offering*
to raise a **c** for Me Ex 25:2
as a **c** to the LORD Lev 7:14
c-s, the first fruits Neh 12:44
a **c** for the poor Rom 15:26
liberality of your **c** 2 Cor 9:13

CONTRITE *sorrowful*
broken and a **c** heart Ps 51:17
humble and **c** of spirit Is 66:2

CONTROL (n) *order, rule*
people were out of **c** Ex 32:25
was it not under...**c** Acts 5:4
children under **c** 1 Tim 3:4

CONTROL (v) *rule, subdue*
he **c-led** himself and Gen 43:31
Joseph could not **c** Gen 45:1
Haman **c-led** himself Esth 5:10

CONTROVERSY *dispute*
wise man has a **c** Prov 29:9
LORD has a **c** with the Jer 25:31
avoid foolish **c-ies** Titus 3:9

CONVERSE *discuss*
Stoic...were **c-ing** Acts 17:18
and **c** with him Acts 24:26

CONVERSION *change*
c of the Gentiles Acts 15:3

CONVERTED *changed*
sinners will be **c** Ps 51:13
unless you are **c** Matt 18:3
perceive...and be **c** John 12:40

CONVICT *condemn, judge*
one of you **c-s** Me John 8:46
c...concerning sin John 16:8
he is **c-ed** by all 1 Cor 14:24
to **c** all the ungodly Jude 15

CONVINCED *persuaded*
c that John was a Luke 20:6
c that neither death Rom 8:38
c in the Lord Jesus Rom 14:14
c of better things Heb 6:9

CONVOCATION *conclave*
sabbath...a holy **c** Lev 23:3
shall have a holy **c** Num 29:7

CONVULSION *paroxysm*
threw him into a **c** Mark 9:20
a **c** with foaming Luke 9:39

COOK *prepare food*
Jacob had **c-ed** stew Gen 25:29
you shall **c** and eat Deut 16:7

COOL *cold*
in the **c** of the day Gen 3:8
in his **c** roof chamber Judg 3:20
who has a **c** spirit Prov 17:27

COPPER *metal*
you can dig **c** Deut 8:9
not acquire...**c** Matt 10:9
widow...**c** coins Luke 21:2

COPY *facsimile*
c of this law on a Deut 17:18
c of...law of Moses Josh 8:32
c of the edict Esth 8:13
mere **c** of the true Heb 9:24

CORBAN *offering*
C (that is...) Mark 7:11

CORD *band, rope*
c-s of Sheol 2 Sam 22:6
c-s of affliction Job 36:8
c-s of death Ps 18:4
silver **c** is broken Eccl 12:6
the **c-s** of falsehood Is 5:18
a scourge of **c-s** John 2:15

CORINTH
city in Greece Acts 18:1
NT church site 1 Cor 1:1,2

CORNELIUS
centurion, believer Acts 10:1ff

CORNER *angle, intersection*
the chief **c** *stone* Ps 118:22
lurks by every **c** Prov 7:12
on the street **c-s** Matt 6:5
the chief **c** *stone* Mark 12:10
four **c-s** of the earth Rev 7:1

CORNER GATE
see **GATES OF JERUSALEM**

CORNERSTONE *support stone*
who laid its **c** Job 38:6
the **c** of her tribes Is 19:13
costly **c** *for the* Is 28:16
From them...the **c** Zech 10:4

CORPSE *dead body*
made unclean by a **c** Lev 22:4
Their **c-s** will rise Is 26:19
a mass of **c-s** Nah 3:3
boy...like a **c** Mark 9:26

CORRECT *reprove*
c him with the rod 2 Sam 7:14
He who **c-s** a scoffer Prov 9:7
C your son, and he Prov 29:17
C me, O LORD Jer 10:24
gentleness **c-ing** 2 Tim 2:25

CORRECTION *improvement*
Whether for **c**, or Job 37:13
refused to take **c** Jer 5:3
for reproof, for **c** 2 Tim 3:16

CORRUPT (adj) *evil, rotten*
the earth was **c** Gen 6:11
detestable and **c** Job 15:16
They are **c** Ps 14:1
all of them, are **c** Jer 6:28

CORRUPT (v) *make evil*
a bribe **c-s** the heart Eccl 7:7
c-ed your wisdom Ezek 28:17
have **c-ed** the covenant Mal 2:8
Bad company **c-s** 1 Cor 15:33
harlot who was **c-ing** Rev 19:2

CORRUPTION *decay, evil*
their **c** is in them Lev 22:25
no negligence or **c** Dan 6:4
from the flesh reap **c** Gal 6:8
c that is in the world 2 Pet 1:4
slaves of **c** 2 Pet 2:19

COSMETICS *beautifying aids*
provided her with...**c** Esth 2:9
the **c** for women Esth 2:12

COST *expense, price*
c of their lives Num 16:38
let the **c** be paid Ezra 6:4
calculate the **c** Luke 14:28
water...without **c** Rev 21:6

COSTLY *expensive*
redemption...is **c** Ps 49:8
gold, silver, **c** stones Dan 11:38
vial of...**c** perfume Mark 14:3
pearls or **c** garments 1 Tim 2:9

COUCH *bed, pallet*
he went up to my **c** Gen 49:4
falling on the **c** Esth 7:8
dissolve my **c** with my Ps 6:6
sprawl on their **c-es** Amos 6:4

COUNCIL *assembly*
not enter into their **c** Gen 49:6
the **c** of the holy ones Ps 89:7
the **c** of My people Ezek 13:9
to their **c** *chamber* Luke 22:66
conferred with his **c** Acts 25:12

COUNCIL
Sanhedrin Matt 26:59
Jewish governing body Mark 15:1,43; Luke 23:50

COUNSEL (n) *advice, opinion*
I will give you **c** Ex 18:19
Take **c** and speak up Judg 19:30
To Him belong **c** Job 12:13
not walk in the **c** Ps 1:1
Listen to **c** and Prov 19:20
the **c** of His will Eph 1:11

COUNSEL (v) *advise*
he has **c-ed** rebellion Deut 13:5
I **c** that all Israel 2 Sam 17:11
How do you **c** *me* 1 Kin 12:6
c you with My eye Ps 32:8

COUNSELOR *adviser*
the king and his **c-s** Ezra 7:15
c-s walk barefoot Job 12:17
abundance of **c-s** Prov 11:14
Wonderful **C,** Mighty Is 9:6
who became His **c** Rom 11:34

COUNT *consider, number*
c the stars, if you Gen 15:5
could not be **c-ed** 1 Kin 8:5
If I should **c** them Ps 139:18
my prayer be **c-ed** Ps 141:2
was **c-ed** among us Acts 1:17
I **c** all...loss Phil 3:8
as some **c** slowness 2 Pet 3:9

COUNTENANCE *appearance*
why has your **c** fallen Gen 4:6
LORD lift up His **c** Num 6:26
light of Your **c** Ps 4:6
an angry **c** Prov 25:23

COUNTRY *land, region*
Go forth from your **c** Gen 12:1
up into the hill **c** Deut 1:24
go out into the **c** Song 7:11
them from the **c-ies** Ezek 34:13
they are seeking a **c** Heb 11:14

COUNTRYMAN
not hate...fellow **c** Lev 19:17
among your **c-men** Deut 17:15
a man and his **c** Deut 25:11
my fellow **c-men** and Rom 11:14

COURAGE *heart, valor*
he lost **c** 2 Sam 4:1
and do not lose **c** 2 Chr 15:7
let your heart take **c** Ps 27:14
with justice and **c** Mic 3:8
Take **c**, son Matt 9:2
Take **c**, it is I Matt 14:27
c; I have overcome John 16:33
we are of good **c** 2 Cor 5:8

COURAGEOUS *brave*
Be strong and **c** Deut 31:6
be strong and very **c** Josh 1:7
I propose to be **c** 2 Cor 10:2

COURIER *messenger*
c-s went throughout 2 Chr 30:6
Letters...by **c-s** Esth 3:13
One **c** runs to meet Jer 51:31

COURSE *area, extent, way*
strong man to run his **c** Ps 19:5
on its circular **c-s** Eccl 1:6
I have finished the **c** 2 Tim 4:7
the **c** of *our* life James 3:6

COURT *area, hall, tribunal*
c of the tabernacle Ex 27:9
c of the harem Esth 2:11
a day in Your **c-s** Ps 84:10
c of the LORD's house Jer 26:2
c of the guardhouse Jer 39:15
if you have law **c-s** 1 Cor 6:4
drag you into **c** James 2:6

COURTYARD *compound*
a well in his **c** 2 Sam 17:18
c of the high priest Matt 26:58
Peter...in the **c** Mark 14:66

COVENANT *agreement*
establish My **c** Gen 6:18
for a sign of a **c** Gen 9:13
for an everlasting **c** Gen 17:13
ark of the **c** Num 10:33
My **c** of peace Num 25:12
book of the **c** 2 Kin 23:2
Remember His **c** 1 Chr 16:15
who keep His **c** Ps 103:18
I will make a new **c** Jer 31:31
forsake the holy **c** Dan 11:30
a **c** with Assyria Hos 12:1
the blood of *My* **c** Zech 9:11
cup...is the new **c** Luke 22:20
c which God made Acts 3:25
this is My **c** with Rom 11:27
servants of a new **c** 2 Cor 3:6
strangers to the **c-s** Eph 2:12
guarantee...better **c** Heb 7:22
blood of the...**c** Heb 13:20
ark of His **c** Rev 11:19

COVER (n)
c of porpoise skin Num 4:14
the **c** of a couch Amos 3:12

COVER (v) *hide, protest*
and **c** up his blood Gen 37:26
basket and **c-ed** it Ex 2:3
Whose sin is **c-ed** Ps 32:1
He will **c** you with Ps 91:4
love **c-s** all Prov 10:12
not **c** My face Is 50:6
c-ed...with sackcloth Jon 3:6
to the hills, **C** us Luke 23:30
c a multitude of sins James 5:20
love **c-s** a multitude 1 Pet 4:8

COVERING *canopy*
made...loin **c-s** Gen 3:7
spread a cloud for a **c** Ps 105:39
she makes **c-s** for Prov 31:22
sackcloth their **c** Is 50:3
given to her for a **c** 1 Cor 11:15
freedom as a **c** 1 Pet 2:16

COVET *crave, desire*
not **c** your neighbor's Ex 20:17
You shall not **c** Deut 5:21
I **c-ed** them and took Josh 7:21
They **c** fields and then Mic 2:2
c-ed no one's silver Acts 20:33

COVETOUS *desirous*
the **c** and swindlers 1 Cor 5:10
c, nor drunkards 1 Cor 6:10

COW *animal*
came up seven **c-s** Gen 41:2
c calves and does not Job 21:10
c and the bear will Is 11:7
you **c-s** of Bashan Amos 4:1

CRAFTINESS *shrewdness*
the wise in their **c** 1 Cor 3:19
not walking in **c** 2 Cor 4:2
by **c** in deceitful Eph 4:14

CRAFTSMAN *artisan*
the hands of the **c** Deut 27:15
all the **c-men** and 2 Kin 24:14
idol, a **c** casts it Is 40:19
business to...**c-men** Acts 19:24
c of any craft will Rev 18:22

CRAG *protrusion, rock*
sharp **c** on the one 1 Sam 14:4
Upon the rocky **c** Job 39:28
clefts of the **c-s** Is 57:5

CRAVE *covet, desire*
day long he is **c-ing** Prov 21:26
fig *which* I **c** Mic 7:1
generation **c-s** for Matt 12:39
would not **c** evil 1 Cor 10:6

CRAWLING *creeping*
venom of **c** things Deut 32:24
beasts and the **c** Acts 11:6
and **c** creatures Rom 1:23

CREATE *form, make*
c-d the heavens Gen 1:1
c-d man in His Gen 1:27
C in me a clean Ps 51:10
C-ing the praise of Is 57:19
c new heavens Is 65:17
one God **c-d** us Mal 2:10
c-d...for good works Eph 2:10
c-d in righteousness Eph 4:24
You **c-d** all Rev 4:11

CREATION
beginning of **c** Mark 10:6
preach...to all **c** Mark 16:15
whole **c** groans Rom 8:22
beginning of **c** 2 Pet 3:4

CREATOR *Maker*
Remember...your **C** Eccl 12:1
The **C** of Israel Is 43:15
rather than the **C** Rom 1:25
to a faithful **C** 1 Pet 4:19

CREATURE *created being*
every living **c** that Gen 1:21
winged **c** will make Eccl 10:20
and crawling **c-s** Rom 1:23
in Christ...new **c** 2 Cor 5:17
as **c-s** of instinct 2 Pet 2:12

CREDITOR *lender*
not to act as a **c** to Ex 22:25
every **c** shall release Deut 15:2
Let the **c** seize all Ps 109:11
My **c-s** did I sell you Is 50:1

CREEP *crawl*
everything that **c-s** Gen 1:25
that **c** on the earth Ezek 38:20

CREEPING *crawling*
cattle and **c** things Gen 1:24
c things and fish 1 Kin 4:33
c locust has eaten Joel 1:4
c locust strips and Nah 3:16

CRETANS
inhabitants of Crete Acts 2:11; Titus 1:12

CRETE
Mediterranean island Acts 27:7,21; Titus 1:5
see also **CAPHTOR**

CRIME *vice*
be a lustful **c** Job 31:11
committed no **c** Dan 6:22
full of bloody **c-s** Ezek 7:23
not of such **c-s** Acts 25:18

CRIMINAL *lawbreaker*
crucified...the **c-s** Luke 23:33
imprisonment as a **c** 2 Tim 2:9

CRIMSON *deep red*
purple, **c** and violet 2 Chr 2:7
like **c**...be like wool Is 1:18

CRIPPLED *lame*
a son **c** in his feet 2 Sam 4:4
enter life **c** or lame Matt 18:8
bring...**c** and blind Luke 14:21

CRISPUS
Corinthian Christian
Acts 18:8; 1 Cor 1:14

CROOKED *evil, twisted*
and **c** generation Deut 32:5
to their **c** ways Ps 125:5
What is **c** cannot be Eccl 1:15
make **c** the straight Acts 13:10
c and perverse Phil 2:15

CROP *yield of produce*
old things from the **c**
Lev 25:22
c-s to the grasshopper
Ps 78:46
c began to sprout Amos 7:1
share of the **c-s** 2 Tim 2:6

CROSS (n) *execution device*
take his **c** and Matt 10:38
down from the **c** Matt 27:40
to bear His **c** Mark 15:21
take up his **c** daily Luke 9:23
standing by the **c** John 19:25
hanging Him on a **c** Acts 5:30
c of Christ would 1 Cor 1:17
word of the **c** is 1 Cor 1:18
boast, except in the **c** Gal 6:14
even death on a **c** Phil 2:8
enemies of the **c** Phil 3:18
blood of His **c** Col 1:20
endured the **c** Heb 12:2

CROSS (v) *pass over*
you **c** the Jordan Deut 12:10
c-ed opposite Jericho
Josh 3:16
kept **c-ing** the ford
2 Sam 19:18
Jesus had **c-ed** over Mark 5:21
c-ing over to Acts 21:2

CROUCH *bow, stoop*
sin is **c-ing** at the Gen 4:7
Beneath Him **c** the Job 9:13
Nothing...but to **c** Is 10:4

CROWD *multitude*
send the **c-s** away Matt 14:15
because of the **c** Mark 2:4
He summoned the **c**
Mark 8:34
c of tax collectors Luke 5:29
Him...a large **c** Luke 23:27
they stirred up the **c** Acts 17:8

CROWN (n)
royal emblem or *top*
on the **c** of the head Gen 49:26
the **c** of their king
2 Sam 12:30
he set the royal **c** Esth 2:17
wife is the **c** of Prov 12:4
gray head is a **c** Prov 16:31
c of the drunkards Is 28:3
a **c** of thorns Matt 27:29
receive the **c** of life James 1:12
c-s before the throne Rev 4:10
golden **c** on His head
Rev 14:14

CROWN (v) *to place crown on*
c him with glory Ps 8:5
Who **c-s** you with Ps 103:4
head **c-s** you like Song 7:5
c-ed him with glory Heb 2:7

CRUCIFY *to execute on a cross*
scourge and **c** *Him* Matt 20:19
C Him Matt 27:22
Jesus...been **c-ied** Matt 28:5
c your King John 19:15
Paul was not **c-ied** 1 Cor 1:13
preach Christ **c-ied** 1 Cor 1:23
not have **c-ied** the 1 Cor 2:8
c-ied with Christ Gal 2:20
world...**c-ied** to me Gal 6:14
their Lord was **c-ied** Rev 11:8

CRUEL *fierce, harsh*
their...**c** bondage Ex 6:9
c man does...harm Prov 11:17
compassion...is **c** Prov 12:10
c and have no mercy Jer 6:23
people has become **c** Lam 4:3

CRUMBS *morsels*
dogs feed on the **c** Matt 15:27
on the children's **c** Mark 7:28

CRUSH *demolish, destroy*
a foot may **c** them Job 39:15
saves...**c-ed** in spirit Ps 34:18
lying tongue...**c-es** Prov 26:28
by **c-ing** My people Is 3:15
c-ed for our iniquities Is 53:5
LORD was pleased To **c**
Is 53:10
who **c** the needy Amos 4:1
c Satan under...feet Rom 16:20

CRY (n) *scream, sob*
great and bitter **c** Gen 27:34
the **c** of triumph Ex 32:18
c has come to Me 1 Sam 9:16
Hear my **c**, O God Ps 61:1
the **c** of Jerusalem Jer 14:2
Jesus uttered a...**c** Mark 15:37

CRY (v)
do not **c** for help Job 36:13
c aloud in the night Lam 2:19
His elect, who **c** Luke 18:7
stones will **c** out Luke 19:40
Jesus stood and **c-ied**
John 7:37

CRYSTAL *glass*
awesome gleam of **c** Ezek 1:22
sea of glass, like **c** Rev 4:6
water...clear as **c** Rev 22:1

CUB *whelp, young*
robbed of her **c-s** 2 Sam 17:8
She reared her **c-s** Ezek 19:2
lioness, and lion's **c** Nah 2:11

CUBIT *linear measure*
ark three hundred **c-s**
Gen 6:15
length was nine **c-s** Deut 3:11
gallows fifty **c-s** high Esth 5:14
the altar by **c-s** Ezek 43:13

CUD *previously swallowed food*
chews the **c** Lev 11:3
not chew **c**, it is Lev 11:7
chews the **c** Deut 14:6

CULT *religious ritual*
be a **c** prostitute Deut 23:17
male **c** prostitutes 1 Kin 14:24
male **c** prostitutes 2 Kin 23:7

CULTIVATE *till*
no man to **c** the Gen 2:5
Eden to **c** it Gen 2:15
and **c** vineyards Deut 28:39
servants shall **c** 2 Sam 9:10
and **c** faithfulness Ps 37:3

CUMMIN *plant for seasoning*
driven over **c** Is 28:27
mint and dill and **c** Matt 23:23

CUNNING *crafty*
he is very **c** 1 Sam 23:22
advice of the **c** Job 5:13
harlot and **c** of heart Prov 7:10

CUP *container*
into Pharaoh's **c** Gen 40:11
My **c** overflows Ps 23:5
the **c** of salvation Ps 116:13
a **c** of consolation Jer 16:7
c of cold water Matt 10:42
let this **c** pass Matt 26:39
washing of **c-s** and Mark 7:4
gives you a **c** of Mark 9:41
c...new covenant Luke 22:20
c of blessing 1 Cor 10:16
eat...drink the **c** 1 Cor 11:26
c full of abominations Rev 17:4

CUPBEARER *royal official*
c spoke to Pharaoh Gen 41:9
his **c-s**, and his 1 Kin 10:5
c-s and their attire 2 Chr 9:4
c to the king Neh 1:11

CURDS *butter, cheese*
he took **c** and milk Gen 18:8
she brought him **c** Judg 5:25
with honey and **c** Job 20:17

CURE *heal*
c him of his leprosy 2 Kin 5:3
c you of your wound Hos 5:13
they could not **c** him
Matt 17:16
that...time He **c-d** Luke 7:21

CURSE (n) *condemning oath*
upon myself a **c** Gen 27:12
c on Mount Ebal Deut 11:29
c to My chosen ones Is 65:15
they will become a **c** Jer 44:12
will no longer be a **c**
Zech 14:11
become a **c** for us Gal 3:13

CURSE (v) *verbally condemn*
who **c-s** you I will **c** Gen 12:3
You shall not **c** God Ex 22:28
not **c** a deaf man Lev 19:14
c-d the...anointed
2 Sam 19:21
c-d the day of his *birth* Job 3:1
began to **c** and Mark 14:71
bless and do not **c** Rom 12:14
with it we **c** men James 3:9

CURSED (adj) *under a curse*
C is the ground Gen 3:17
C be Canaan Gen 9:25
C is the man who Deut 27:15
C...who trusts Jer 17:5
C...who hangs Gal 3:13

CURTAIN *covering, drape*
on the edge of the **c** Ex 26:4
heaven like a *tent* **c** Ps 104:2
c-s of your dwellings Is 54:2
c-s of the land of Hab 3:7

CUSH
1 *area of W Asia* Gen 2:13
2 *patriarch* Gen 10:6,8
3 *region S of Egypt*
2 Kin 19:9; Is 20:3
4 *a Benjamite* Ps 7:title

CUSTODY *prison, protection*
they put him in **c** Num 15:34
into the **c** of Hegai Esth 2:3
John...taken into **c** Matt 4:12
holding Jesus in **c** Luke 22:63

CUSTOM *manner* or *tax*
it became a **c** in Judg 11:39
not pay tribute, **c** Ezra 4:13
c, He entered the Luke 4:16
burial **c** of the Jews
John 19:40
c-s...not lawful Acts 16:21
c-s of our fathers Acts 28:17
whom tax *is due;* **c** Rom 13:7

CUT *destroy, divide*
did not **c** the birds Gen 15:10
c off from the earth Ex 9:15
c down their Asherim
Ex 34:13
LORD **c** off...lips Ps 12:3
tongue will be **c** Prov 10:31
C off your hair and Jer 7:29
were **c-ting** branches
Matt 21:8
and **c** off his ear Matt 26:51
were **c** to the quick Acts 7:54
you...will be **c** off Rom 11:22

CYMBAL *musical instrument*
castanets and **c-s** 2 Sam 6:5
loud-sounding **c-s** 1 Chr 15:16
with loud **c-s** Ps 150:5
or a clanging **c** 1 Cor 13:1

CYPRESS *tree*
cedar and **c** timber 1 Kin 5:10
c and algum timber 2 Chr 2:8
Our rafters, **c-es** Song 1:17
Wail, O **c**, for the Zech 11:2

CYPRUS
Mediterranean island Is 23:1;
Acts 11:19;15:39;21:16
see also **KITTIM**

CYRENE
- *NW African port* Mark 15:21; Luke 23:26; Acts 2:10;11:20

CYRUS
- *king of Persia* 2 Chr 36:22; Is 45:1
- *decreed to rebuild Temple* Ezra 1:1;5:13

D

DAGON
- *god of Philistines* Judg 16:23; 1 Sam 5:4; 1 Chr 10:10

DAMAGE (n) *destruction*
- any **d** may be found 2 Kin 12:5
- the **d-s** of the house 2 Kin 12:6
- **d** and great loss Acts 27:10
- incurred this **d** and Acts 27:21

DAMAGE (v) *destroy, hurt*
- it will **d** the revenue Ezra 4:13
- and **d-ing** to kings Ezra 4:15
- enemy has **d-d** Ps 74:3
- So that no one...**d** it Is 27:3

DAMASCUS
- *city of Aram (Syria)* Gen 14:15; 2 Kin 5:12; Acts 9:3,27;26:20

DAN
- 1 *son of Jacob* Gen 30:6;49:16
- 2 *tribal area* Josh 19:40; Judg 18:2
- 3 *city in N Palestine* Josh 19:47

DANCE (n)
- *rhythmic movement*
- timbrels...with **d-ing** Ex 15:20
- they sing in the **d-s** 1 Sam 29:5
- will rejoice in the **d** Jer 31:13
- music and **d-ing** Luke 15:25

DANCE (v) *move rhythmically*
- from those who **d-d** Judg 21:23
- David was **d-ing** 2 Sam 6:14
- and a time to **d** Eccl 3:4
- Herodias **d-d** before Matt 14:6

DANGER *peril*
- not only is there **d** Acts 19:27
- often in **d** of death 2 Cor 11:23
- **d-s** from...Gentiles 2 Cor 11:26

DANIEL
- 1 *son of David and Abigail* 1 Chr 3:1
- 2 *priest* Ezra 8:2
- 3 *prophet* Ezek 14:14; Dan 1:6
- *see also* **BELTESHAZZAR**

DARE *presume, risk*
- who **d-s** rouse him up Gen 49:9
- who would **d** to risk Jer 30:21
- **d** from that day Matt 22:46
- did not **d** pronounce Jude 9

DARIUS
- 1 *Darius the Mede* Dan 5:31
- 2 *Darius I* Ezra 4:5; Hag 1:1
- 3 *Darius II* Neh 12:22

DARK *dim, shadow*
- not in **d** sayings Num 12:8
- **d** places of the land Ps 74:20
- live in a **d** land Is 9:2
- it was still **d** John 20:1
- shining in a **d** place 2 Pet 1:19

DARKEN *obscure*
- the land was **d-ed** Ex 10:15
- this that **d-s** counsel Job 38:2
- the stars are **d-ed** Eccl 12:2
- sun will be **d-ed** Mark 13:24
- their eyes be **d-ed** Rom 11:10

DARKNESS *gloom, shadow*
- blind...gropes in **d** Deut 28:29
- are silenced in **d** 1 Sam 2:9
- illumines my **d** 2 Sam 22:29
- that stalks in **d** Ps 91:6
- those who dwelt in **d** Ps 107:10
- as light excels **d** Eccl 2:13
- people who walk in **d** Is 9:2
- light will rise in **d** Is 58:10
- into the outer **d** Matt 22:13
- those who sit in **d** Luke 1:79
- men loved the **d** John 3:19
- turn from **d** to light Acts 26:18
- has light with **d** 2 Cor 6:14
- unfruitful deeds of **d** Eph 5:11
- in Him there is no **d** 1 John 1:5
- brother is in the **d** 1 John 2:9

DARLING *love*
- you are, my **d** Song 1:15
- Arise, my **d** Song 2:13
- my **d**, My dove Song 5:2

DATHAN
- *rebelled against Moses* Num 16:12; Ps 106:17

DAUGHTER
- **d-s** were born to them Gen 6:1
- if a man sells his **d** Ex 21:7
- inheritance to his **d** Num 27:8
- Kings' **d-s** are among Ps 45:9
- **d-s** of song Eccl 12:4
- destruction of the **d** Is 22:4
- the **d** of my people Jer 9:1
- **D** rises up against Mic 7:6
- mother against **d** Luke 12:53

DAUGHTER-IN-LAW
- said to his **d** Tamar Gen 38:11
- nakedness of your **d** Lev 18:15
- said to Ruth her **d** Ruth 2:22
- **D** against her Mic 7:6

DAVID
- *anointed* 1 Sam 16:13
- *killed Goliath* 1 Sam 17:50
- *fled from Saul* 1 Sam 19:18
- *spared Saul* 1 Sam 26:9
- *king of Judah and Israel* 2 Sam 2:4;5:3
- *covenant with God* 2 Sam 7:8
- *death* 1 Kin 2:10

DAWN (n) *daylight*
- at the approach of **d** Judg 19:25
- caused the **d** to know Job 38:12
- rise before **d** and Ps 119:147
- wings of the **d** Ps 139:9
- As the **d** is spread Joel 2:2

DAWN (v) *become light*
- the day began to **d** Judg 19:26
- when morning **d-s** Ps 46:5
- a Light **d-ed** Matt 4:16
- **d** toward the first Matt 28:1
- until the day **d-s** 2 Pet 1:19

DAY *light*
- God called the light **d** Gen 1:5
- come on a festive **d** 1 Sam 25:8
- **d**...LORD has made Ps 118:24
- what a **d** may bring Prov 27:1
- **d-s** of your youth Eccl 12:1
- a **d** of reckoning Is 2:12
- **d** of the LORD is near Is 13:6
- has despised the **d** Zech 4:10
- the **d** of His coming Mal 3:2
- Give us this **d** Matt 6:11
- raise...the last **d** John 6:39
- judge...the last **d** John 12:48
- the **d** of salvation 2 Cor 6:2
- perfect it until the **d** Phil 1:6
- **d** of the Lord 1 Thess 5:2
- **d** is like a thousand 2 Pet 3:8
- tormented **d**...night Rev 20:10

DAY OF ATONEMENT
- month is the **d** Lev 23:27
- for it is a **d** Lev 23:28

DAZZLING *blinding, bright*
- My beloved is **d** Song 5:10
- Like **d** heat Is 18:4
- near...in **d** clothing Luke 24:4

DEACONS *officer, server*
- overseers and **d** Phil 1:1
- **D** likewise *must be* 1 Tim 3:8
- let them serve as **d** 1 Tim 3:10
- **D** must be husbands 1 Tim 3:12
- served well as **d** 1 Tim 3:13

DEAD *without life*
- you are a **d** man Gen 20:3
- near to a **d** person Num 6:6
- dealt with the **d** Ruth 1:8
- forgotten as a **d** man Ps 31:12
- **d** do not praise Ps 115:17
- better than a **d** lion Eccl 9:4
- Your **d** will live Is 26:19
- not weep for the **d** Jer 22:10
- rising from the **d** Mark 9:10
- **d** will hear the John 5:25
- resurrection of the **d** Acts 23:6
- **d** in your trespasses Eph 2:1
- firstborn from the **d** Col 1:18
- living and the **d** 2 Tim 4:1
- repentance...**d** works Heb 6:1
- to those who are **d** 1 Pet 4:6
- I was **d**...I am alive Rev 1:18
- Hades gave up the **d** Rev 20:13

DEAF *without hearing*
- makes *him* mute or **d** Ex 4:11
- not curse a **d** man Lev 19:14
- Like a **d** cobra Ps 58:4
- the **d** will hear Is 29:18
- and *the* **d** hear Matt 11:5
- the **d** to hear Mark 7:37
- **d** and mute spirit Mark 9:25

DEAL *allot, barter, treat*
- let us **d** wisely Ex 1:10
- have you **d-t** with us Ex 14:11
- nor **d** falsely Lev 19:11
- **d-t** with mediums 2 Kin 21:6
- who **d** treacherously Ps 25:3
- has **d-t** bountifully Ps 116:7
- who **d** faithfully Prov 12:22
- Everyone **d-s** falsely Jer 6:13
- when I have **d-t** Ezek 20:44
- has **d-t** with me Luke 1:25

DEALINGS *actions, relations*
- no **d** with anyone Judg 18:7
- no **d** with Samaritans John 4:9
- of the Lord's **d** James 5:11

DEAR *beloved*
- Is Ephraim My **d** son Jer 31:20
- my life...as **d** to Acts 20:24
- had become very **d** 1 Thess 2:8

DEATH *cessation of life*
- **d** of the upright Num 23:10
- **d** encompassed me 2 Sam 22:5
- **d** for his own sin 2 Chr 25:4
- **D** rather than my pains Job 7:15
- no mention of You in **d** Ps 6:5
- cords of **d** encompassed Ps 18:4
- the shadow of **d** Ps 23:4
- escapes from **d** Ps 68:20
- doomed to **d** Ps 102:20
- **d** of His godly ones Ps 116:15
- who hate me love **d** Prov 8:36
- love is as strong as **d** Song 8:6
- He will swallow up **d** Is 25:8
- **D** cannot praise You Is 38:18
- no pleasure in the **d** Ezek 18:32
- **d** is better to me Jon 4:3
- is to be put to **d** Matt 15:4
- will not taste **d** Matt 16:28
- to the point of **d** Mark 14:34
- passed out of **d** John 5:24
- he will never see **d** John 8:51
- sickness is not to end in **d** John 11:4
- the agony of **d** Acts 2:24
- **d** by hanging Him Acts 10:39
- **d** reigned from Adam Rom 5:14
- wages of sin is **d** Rom 6:23
- the law of sin and of **d** Rom 8:2
- proclaim...Lord's **d** 1 Cor 11:26
- **d**, where...victory 1 Cor 15:55
- even **d** on a cross Phil 2:8
- He might taste **d** Heb 2:9

it brings forth **d** James 1:15
passed out of **d** 1 John 3:14
Be faithful until **d** Rev 2:10
had the name **D** Rev 6:8
second **d**...no power Rev 20:6

DEBATE *dispute*
d-d...themselves Mark 1:27
dissension and **d** Acts 15:2
had been much **d** Acts 15:7

DEBORAH
1 *nurse of Rebekah* Gen 35:8
2 *prophetess, judge* Judg 4:4ff

DEBT *obligation*
and pay your **d** 2 Kin 4:7
exaction of every **d** Neh 10:31
guarantors for **d-s** Prov 22:26
forgive us our **d-s** Matt 6:12

DEBTOR *borrower*
restores to the **d** Ezek 18:7
forgiven our **d-s** Matt 6:12
had two **d-s** Luke 7:41
his master's **d-s** Luke 16:5

DECAY *corruption*
own eyes see his **d** Job 21:20
Holy One to...**d** Acts 2:27
did not undergo **d** Acts 13:37

DECEASED *dead*
wife of the **d** shall Deut 25:5
the widow of the **d** Ruth 4:5
the name of the **d** Ruth 4:10
the sister of the **d** John 11:39

DECEIT
deception, falsehood, guile
full of curses and **d** Ps 10:7
in whose spirit...no **d** Ps 32:2
your tongue frames **d** Ps 50:19
D is in the heart Prov 12:20
he lays up **d** Prov 26:24
Offspring of **d** Is 57:4
houses are full of **d** Jer 5:27
house of Israel...**d** Hos 11:12
d, sensuality, envy Mark 7:22
in whom...is no **d** John 1:47
full of envy...**d** Rom 1:29
the lusts of **d** Eph 4:22
all malice and all **d** 1 Pet 2:1
nor was any **d** found 1 Pet 2:22
lips from speaking **d** 1 Pet 3:10

DECEITFUL *false*
From a **d** tongue Ps 120:2
the wicked are **d** Prov 12:5
d are the kisses of Prov 27:6
Charm is **d** and Prov 31:30
The heart is more **d** Jer 17:9
false apostles, **d** 2 Cor 11:13

DECEIVE *cheat, mislead*
have you **d-d** me Gen 29:25
Jacob **d-d** Laban Gen 31:20
d-s his companion Lev 6:2
both stolen and **d-d** Josh 7:11
Do not **d** me 2 Kin 4:28
who **d-s** his neighbor Prov 26:19
Do not **d** yourselves Jer 37:9
your heart has **d-d** you Obad 3
they keep **d-ing** Rom 3:13
Let no one **d** you Eph 5:6
d-ing and being **d-d** 2 Tim 3:13

DECEIVER *liar*
as a **d** in his sight Gen 27:12
as **d-s** and yet true 2 Cor 6:8
d and the antichrist 2 John 7

DECEPTION *falsehood*
their mind prepares **d** Job 15:35
the hills are a **d** Jer 3:23
last **d** will be worse Matt 27:64
philosophy and empty **d** Col 2:8
reveling in their **d-s** 2 Pet 2:13

DECEPTIVE *misleading*
wicked...**d** wages Prov 11:18
Do not trust in **d** words Jer 7:4
d *stream* With water Jer 15:18

DECISION
judgment, resolution
d is from the LORD Prov 16:33
in the valley of **d** Joel 3:14
My **d** is to gather Zeph 3:8
majority reached a **d** Acts 27:12

DECLARE *explain, proclaim*
Moses **d-d** to...sons Lev 23:44
d to Him the number Job 31:37
d Your faithfulness Ps 30:9
mouth...**d** Your praise Ps 51:15
d Your lovingkindness Ps 92:2
Who has **d-d** *this* Is 41:26
d-s the LORD Amos 4:11
He will **d** all things John 4:25
d-d the Son of God Rom 1:4

DECLINE *decrease*
for the shadow to **d** 2 Kin 20:10
our days have **d-d** Ps 90:9
for the day **d-s** Jer 6:4

DECREASE *abate, subside*
the water **d-d** steadily Gen 8:5
not let their cattle **d** Ps 107:38
increase...I must **d** John 3:30

DECREE (n) *judgment, order*
issued a **d** to rebuild Ezra 5:13
and **d** of the king Esth 2:8
devises mischief by **d** Ps 94:20
only one **d** for you Dan 2:9
delivering the **d-s** Acts 16:4
to the **d-s** of Caesar Acts 17:7

DECREE (v) *decide, determine*
been **d-d** against her Esth 2:1
will also **d** a thing Job 22:28
And rulers **d** justice Prov 8:15
Seventy weeks...**d-d** Dan 9:24

DEDICATE *consecrate, devote*
D yourselves today Ex 32:29
I wholly **d** the silver Judg 17:3
d-d by...David 1 Kin 7:51
David...**d-d** these 1 Chr 18:11
d-d part...the spoil 1 Chr 26:27
d-ing it to Him 2 Chr 2:4

DEDICATION *consecration*
the **d** of the altar 2 Chr 7:9
celebrated the **d** of Ezra 6:16
d of the wall Neh 12:27
d of the image Dan 3:2
assembled for the **d** Dan 3:3

DEDICATION, FEAST OF
see **FEASTS**

DEED *action* or *document*
What is this **d** Gen 44:15
for our evil **d-s** Ezra 9:13
blot out...loyal **d-s** Neh 13:14
abominable **d-s** Ps 14:1
I...sealed the **d** Jer 32:10
prophet mighty in **d** Luke 24:19
their **d-s** were evil John 3:19
d-s of the flesh are Gal 5:19
for every good **d** Titus 3:1
I know your **d-s** Rev 2:2

DEEP (adj) *far ranging*
d sleep falls on men Job 4:13
Your judgments are...**d** Ps 36:6
casts into a **d** sleep Prov 19:15
into **d** darkness Jer 13:16
the well is **d** John 4:11

DEEP (n) *abyss, depth*
fountains of the...**d** Gen 7:11
the **d** lying beneath Deut 33:13
surface of the **d** is Job 38:30
D calls to **d** Ps 42:7
The **d-s** also trembled Ps 77:16
His wonders in the **d** Ps 107:24
the springs of the **d** Prov 8:28

DEER *animal*
besides **d**, gazelles 1 Kin 4:23
d pants for the water Ps 42:1
lame will leap like a **d** Is 35:6

DEFEAT *conquer, overthrow*
d-ed...and pursued Gen 14:15
able to **d** them Num 22:6
sons of Israel **d-ed** Josh 12:7
d the Arameans 2 Kin 13:17
d-ed the Philistines 1 Chr 18:1
d-ed the entire army Jer 37:10

DEFECT (n) *blemish, spot*
No one who has a **d** Lev 21:18
one ram without **d** Num 6:14
if it has any **d** Deut 15:21
no **d** in him 2 Sam 14:25
in whom was no **d** Dan 1:4

DEFECT (v) *rebel, disobey*
d to his master 1 Chr 12:19
many **d-ed** to him 2 Chr 15:9
you have deeply **d-ed** Is 31:6

DEFEND *protect*
LORD of hosts will **d** Zech 9:15
d-ed him and took Acts 7:24
or else **d-ing** them Rom 2:15
are **d-ing** ourselves 2 Cor 12:19

DEFENSE *protection*
d-s are **d-s** of clay Job 13:12
the **d** of my life Ps 27:1
You have been a **d** Is 25:4
the **d**...of the gospel Phil 1:7

DEFILE *pollute, profane*
astray...**d-s** herself Num 5:29
d-d the high places 2 Kin 23:8
d-d the priesthood Neh 13:29
d-d Your holy temple Ps 79:1
your hands are **d-d** Is 59:3
those **d** the man Matt 15:18
is what **d-s** the man Mark 7:20
conscience...is **d-d** 1 Cor 8:7
d-s the entire body James 3:6

DEFILEMENT *filth*
her *interest*, for **d** Ezek 22:3
from all **d** of flesh 2 Cor 7:1

DEFRAUD *deprive, wrong*
whom have I **d-ed** 1 Sam 12:3
To **d** a man Lam 3:36
Do not **d** Mark 10:19
no one keep **d-ing** Col 2:18

DEITY *God, gods*
of strange **d-ies** Acts 17:18
fullness of **D** dwells Col 2:9

DELAY *hinder, linger, stall*
Do not **d** me Gen 24:56
Moses **d-ed** to come Ex 32:1
shall not **d** to pay Deut 23:21
bridegroom...**d-ing** Matt 25:5
Do not **d** in coming Acts 9:38
now why do you **d** Acts 22:16
in case I am **d-ed** 1 Tim 3:15

DELICACIES *fancy foods*
eat of their **d** Ps 141:4
Do not desire his **d** Prov 23:3
Those who ate **d** Lam 4:5

DELIGHT (n) *pleasure*
I have no **d** in you 2 Sam 15:26
Will he take **d** Job 27:10
his **d** is in the law Ps 1:2
commandments...**d** Ps 119:143
my **d** in the sons of Prov 8:31
a just weight is His **d** Prov 11:1
the **d** of kings Prov 16:13
I took great **d** Song 2:3
call the sabbath a **d** Is 58:13
My **d** is in her Is 62:4

DELIGHT (v) *desire*
LORD **d-ed** over you Deut 28:63
d in...offerings 1 Sam 15:22
d to revere Your name Neh 1:11

d in the Almighty Job 22:26
D yourself in the LORD Ps 37:4
not **d** in sacrifice Ps 51:16
Who **d** in doing evil Prov 2:14
d in my ways Prov 23:26
takes no **d** in fools Eccl 5:4
I **d** in loyalty Hos 6:6
d-s...unchanging love Mic 7:18
d-ing...self-abasement Col 2:18

DELIGHTFUL *pleasant*
d is a timely word Prov 15:23
to find **d** words Eccl 12:10
and how **d** you are Song 7:6
Is he a **d** child Jer 31:20

DELILAH
Philistine woman Judg 16:4
enticed Samson Judg 16:6-20

DELIVER *give, rescue, save*
come down to **d** them Ex 3:8
d the manslayer Num 35:25
My...power has **d-ed** Judg 7:2
can this one **d** 1 Sam 10:27
He will **d** you Job 5:19
d-ed my soul from Ps 56:13
none who can **d** Is 43:13
mind on **d-ing** Daniel Dan 6:14
d us from evil Matt 6:13
d-ed over to death 2 Cor 4:11

DELIVERANCE *salvation*
by a great **d** Gen 45:7
given this great **d** Judg 15:18
with songs of **d** Ps 32:7
a God of **d-s** Ps 68:20
d through...prayers Phil 1:19

DELIVERER *savior*
the LORD raised up a **d** Judg 3:9
gave them **d-s** Neh 9:27
my fortress and my **d** Ps 18:2
d-s...ascend Mount Obad 21
D...come from Zion Rom 11:26

DELUDE *lead astray*
they have **d-d** you Is 47:10
no one will **d** you Col 2:4
who **d** themselves James 1:22

DEMAND *order, require*
husband may **d** of him Ex 21:22
but I **d** one thing 2 Sam 3:13
captors **d-ed** of us Ps 137:3
do not **d** it back Luke 6:30
d-ing of Him a sign Luke 11:16

DEMETRIUS
1 *Ephesian smith* Acts 19:24,38
2 *a Christian* 3 John 12

DEMOLISH *destroy*
d all...high places Num 33:52
he **d-ed** its stones 2 Kin 23:15
to **d** its strongholds Is 23:11

DEMON *devil*
sacrificed to **d-s** Deut 32:17
daughters to the **d-s** Ps 106:37
after the **d** was cast Matt 9:33
sacrifice to **d-s** 1 Cor 10:20
d-s also believe James 2:19
not to worship **d-s** Rev 9:20

DEMONIACS *possessed ones*
d, epileptics Matt 4:24
what had happened to the **d** Matt 8:33

DEMON-POSSESSED
many who were **d** Matt 8:16
a mute, **d** man Matt 9:32
to the **d** man Mark 5:16
sayings of one **d** John 10:21

DEMONSTRATE *show*
God **d-s** His own love Rom 5:8
to **d** His wrath Rom 9:22
d-d yourselves to be 2 Cor 7:11
d His...patience 1 Tim 1:16

DEMONSTRATION *a showing*
for the **d,** *I say* Rom 3:26
in **d** of the Spirit 1 Cor 2:4

DEN *abode*
remains in its **d** Job 37:8
From the **d-s** of lions Song 4:8
the viper's **d** Is 11:8
cast into the lions' **d** Dan 6:7
it a robbers' **d** Mark 11:17

DENARIUS
Roman silver coin Matt 20:2,9
a day's wage Luke 20:24
Denarii (pl) John 6:7;12:5

DENOUNCE *accuse, slander*
And come, **d** Israel Num 23:7
the LORD has not **d-d** Num 23:8
let us **d** him Jer 20:10
He...to **d** the cities Matt 11:20

DENY *conceal, refuse*
Sarah **d-ied** *it* Gen 18:15
so that you do not **d** your God Josh 24:27
not **d-ied** the words Job 6:10
and **d-ing** the LORD Is 59:13
whoever **d-ies** Me Matt 10:33
has **d-ied** the faith 1 Tim 5:8
deeds they **d** *Him* Titus 1:16
us to **d** ungodliness Titus 2:12
d-ies the Son 1 John 2:23

DEPART *leave*
scepter shall not **d** Gen 49:10
sword...never **d** 2 Sam 12:10
to **d** from evil is Job 28:28
His spirit **d-s** Ps 146:4
his foolishness will not **d** Prov 27:22
turned aside and **d-ed** Jer 5:23
I never knew you; **d** Matt 7:23
d from Me, all you Luke 13:27
d and be with Christ Phil 1:23

DEPARTURE *death* or *leaving*
after their **d** from Ex 16:1
speaking of His **d** Luke 9:31
time of my **d** has 2 Tim 4:6
any time after my **d** 2 Pet 1:15

DEPEND *rely, rest*
d-ed on the weapons Is 22:8
you did not **d** on Him Is 22:11
d the whole Law Matt 22:40

DEPORTATION *exile*
after the **d** to Matt 1:12
to the **d** to Babylon Matt 1:17

DEPORTED *exiled*
d...to Babylon Ezra 5:12
d...entire population Amos 1:6

DEPOSE *release*
d you from your office Is 22:19
d-d from his royal Dan 5:20

DEPOSIT (n) *security*
in regard to a **d** Lev 6:2
d which was entrusted Lev 6:4

DEPOSIT (v) *place, put*
d them in the tent Num 17:4
d *it* in your town Deut 14:28
d...in the temple Ezra 5:15
had **d-ed** the scroll Jer 36:20

DEPRAVED *degenerate*
over to a **d** mind Rom 1:28
men of **d** mind 2 Tim 3:8

DEPRIVE *take away*
d the needy of justice Is 10:2
d-d of...my years Is 38:10
d-ing one another 1 Cor 7:5
d-d of the truth 1 Tim 6:5

DEPTH *abyss, deep*
d-s boil like a pot Job 41:31
hand are the **d-s** Ps 95:4
went down to the **d-s** Ps 107:26
sins Into the **d-s** Mic 7:19
drowned in the **d** Matt 18:6
it had no **d** of soil Mark 4:5
nor height, nor **d** Rom 8:39
the **d** of the riches Rom 11:33
even the **d-s** of God 1 Cor 2:10

DEPUTY *proconsul*
he was the only **d** 1 Kin 4:19
Solomon's...**d-ies** 1 Kin 5:16
a **d** was king 1 Kin 22:47

DERISION *laughingstock*
d among...enemies Ex 32:25
d to those around us Ps 44:13
reproach and **d** all Jer 20:8
d to the rest of the Ezek 36:4

DESCEND *go down*
angels of God...**d-ing** Gen 28:12
His glory will not **d** Ps 49:17
breath of...**d-s** Eccl 3:21
will **d** to Hades Matt 11:23
Spirit **d-ing**...dove John 1:32
d into the abyss Rom 10:7
who **d-ed**...ascended Eph 4:10

DESCENDANT *seed, offering*
your **d-s** I will give Gen 12:7
will raise up your **d** 2 Sam 7:12
His **d-s** shall endure Ps 89:36
So shall your **d-s** be Rom 4:18
you are Abraham's **d-s** Gal 3:29
to the **d** of Abraham Heb 2:16
and the **d** of David Rev 22:16

DESCENT *hill* or *heritage*
of Median **d** Dan 9:1
the **d** of the Mount Luke 19:37
were of high-priestly **d** Acts 4:6

DESCRIBE *explain*
you shall **d** the land Josh 18:6
man, **d** the temple Ezek 43:10
who had seen it **d-d** Mark 5:16

DESECRATE *defile*
d the sanctuary Dan 11:31
tried to **d** the temple Acts 24:6

DESERT (n) *wilderness*
d plains of Jericho Josh 5:10
grieved Him in the **d** Ps 78:40
better to live in a **d** Prov 21:19
in the **d** a highway Is 40:3
Rivers in the **d** Is 43:19
like a bush in the **d** Jer 17:6
he lived in the **d-s** Luke 1:80

DESERT (v) *abandon, forsake*
d-ed to the king 2 Kin 25:11
who had **d-ed** them Acts 15:38
so quickly **d-ing** Him Gal 1:6
but all **d-ed** me 2 Tim 4:16
I will never **d** you Heb 13:5

DESERTERS *changers of loyalty*
d who had deserted 2 Kin 25:11
d who had gone over Jer 39:9

DESERVE *earn, merit*
with him as he **d-d** Judg 9:16
done this **d-s** to die 2 Sam 12:5
He **d-s** death Matt 26:66
receiving what we **d** Luke 23:41

DESIGN *creation, plan*
d-s for work in gold Ex 31:4
makers of **d-s** Ex 35:35
execute any **d** which 2 Chr 2:14
All their deadly **d-s** Jer 18:23

DESIGNATE *appoint*
if he **d-s** her for Ex 21:9
one whom I **d** to 1 Sam 16:3
were **d-d** by name 1 Chr 16:41
being **d-d** by God Heb 5:10

DESIRABLE *attractive*
the tree was **d** Gen 3:6
d in your eyes 1 Kin 20:6
more **d** than gold Ps 19:10
What is **d** in a man Prov 19:22
every kind of **d** object Nah 2:9

DESIRE (n) *appetite, craving*
d...for your husband Gen 3:16
poor from *their* **d** Job 31:16
the **d-s** of your heart Ps 37:4
d of the wicked will Ps 112:10
d of the righteous Prov 10:24
d of your eyes Ezek 24:16
great man speaks the **d** Mic 7:3
d and my prayer Rom 10:1
d-s of the flesh Eph 2:3
d to depart and be Phil 1:23
evil **d,** and greed Col 3:5

DESIRE (v) *crave, wish*
your heart **d-s** Deut 14:26
as much as you **d** 1 Sam 2:16
I **d** to argue with God Job 13:3
You **d** truth Ps 51:6
not **d** his delicacies Prov 23:3
all that my eyes **d-d** Eccl 2:10
righteous men **d-d** Matt 13:17
d the greater gifts 1 Cor 12:31
d...a good showing Gal 6:12
d a better *country* Heb 11:16

DESOLATE *lonely, waste*
your sanctuaries **d** Lev 26:31
sons of the **d** one Is 54:1
high places will be **d** Ezek 6:6
d wilderness behind Joel 2:3
loaves in *this* **d** place Matt 15:33
homestead be made **d** Acts 1:20
children of the **d** Gal 4:27

DESOLATION *ruin, waste*
a **d** and a curse 2 Kin 22:19
a heap forever, a **d** Josh 8:28
D is left in the city Is 24:12
d-s of many generations Is 61:4
an everlasting **d** Ezek 35:9
the abomination of **d** Dan 11:31
day of...**d** Zeph 1:15
her **d** is near Luke 21:20

DESPAIR (n) *grief*
words of one in **d** Job 6:26
my soul is in **d** Ps 42:6
Why are you in **d** Ps 43:5

DESPAIR (v) *grieve*
Saul then will **d** 1 Sam 27:1
I...**d-ed** of all Eccl 2:20
we **d-ed** even of life 2 Cor 1:8
but not **d-ing** 2 Cor 4:8

DESPISE *reject, scorn*
d-d his birthright Gen 25:34
those who **d** Me 1 Sam 2:30
d-d...in her heart 2 Sam 6:16
not **d** the discipline Job 5:17
hate and **d** falsehood Ps 119:163
Fools **d** wisdom and Prov 1:7
wisdom...is **d-d** Eccl 9:16
has **d-d** the day of Zech 4:10
have we **d-d** Your name Mal 1:6
not **d** one of these Matt 18:10
be devoted to one and **d** Luke 16:13
do you **d**...church 1 Cor 11:22

DESPOIL *injure, lay waste*
d-ed all the cities 2 Chr 14:14
the wicked who **d** me Ps 17:9
plundered and **d-ed** Is 42:22

DESTINE *appoint*
is **d-d** for the sword Job 15:22
d you for the sword Is 65:12
things **d-d** to perish Col 2:22
not **d-d** us for wrath 1 Thess 5:9

DESTITUTE *deprived, in need*
prayer of the **d** Ps 102:17
the land is **d** Ezek 32:15
being **d,** afflicted Heb 11:37

DESTROY *abolish, ruin, waste*
to **d** all flesh Gen 6:17
so that I do not **d** you 1 Sam 15:6
would You **d** me Job 10:8
seek my life to **d** it Ps 40:14
the wicked, He will **d** Ps 145:20
that which **d-s** kings Prov 31:3
one sinner **d-s** much Eccl 9:18
stronghold is **d-ed** Is 23:14
shepherds...are **d-ing** Jer 23:1
He will **d** mighty men Dan 8:24
moth and rust **d** Matt 6:19
who is able to **d** Matt 10:28
You come to **d** us Mark 1:24
seeking...to **d** Him Mark 11:18
d the temple and Mark 15:29
flood...**d-ed** them Luke 17:27
D this temple, and John 2:19
not for **d-ing** you 2 Cor 10:8
to save and to **d** James 4:12
heavens will be **d-ed** 2 Pet 3:12
d the works of the 1 John 3:8

DESTROYER *devastator*
d of our country Judg 16:24
of the **d-s** prosper Job 12:6
d comes upon him Job 15:21
d-s and devastators Is 49:17
I will set apart **d-s** Jer 22:7

DESTRUCTION *calamity, ruin*
the **d** of my kindred Esth 8:6
God apportion **d** Job 21:17
Your tongue devises **d** Ps 52:2
Pride *goes* before **d** Prov 16:18
foolish son is **d** to Prov 19:13
called the City of **D** Is 19:18
d of the daughter of Lam 2:11
broad that leads to **d** Matt 7:13
whose end is **d** Phil 3:19
d will come 1 Thess 5:3
penalty of eternal **d** 2 Thess 1:9
bringing swift **d** upon 2 Pet 2:1

DETERMINE *decide*
to **d** whether he laid Ex 22:8
his days are **d-d** Job 14:5
d-d *their* appointed Acts 17:26
but rather **d** this Rom 14:13
d-d to know nothing 1 Cor 2:2

DETEST *despise, loathe*
carcasses you shall **d** Lev 11:11
not **d** an Egyptian Deut 23:7
d his citadels Amos 6:8

DETESTABLE *abominable*
not eat any **d** thing Deut 14:3
who is **d** and corrupt Job 15:16
swine's flesh, **d** Is 66:17
their **d** idols Jer 16:18
remove all its **d** Ezek 11:18
d...sight of God Luke 16:15

DEVASTATE *destroy, lay waste*
d-d the nations 2 Kin 19:17
Until cities are **d-d** Is 6:11
the LORD...**d-s** it Is 24:1
my tents are **d-d** Jer 4:20
d...pride of Egypt Ezek 32:12

DEVASTATION *destruction*
d of the afflicted Ps 12:5
Nor **d** or destruction Is 60:18
raise up the former **d-s** Is 61:4
d in their citadels Amos 3:10

DEVICE *plan, scheme*
By their own **d-s** Ps 5:10
not promote his *evil* **d** Ps 140:8
a man of evil **d-s** Prov 14:17
in their **d-s** you walk Mic 6:16

DEVIL *demon, Satan*
tempted by the **d** Matt 4:1
one of you is a **d** John 6:70
you son of the **d** Acts 13:10
firm against...the **d** Eph 6:11
render powerless...**d** Heb 2:14
serpent...the **d** Rev 12:9
d...into the lake Rev 20:10

DEVISE *design, scheme, plot*
d-d against the Jews Esth 9:25
d-ing a vain thing Ps 2:1
d-s mischief by decree Ps 94:20
continually **d-s** evil Prov 6:14
man who **d-s** evil Prov 12:2
He **d-s** wicked schemes Is 32:7
do not **d** evil in Zech 7:10
d futile things Acts 4:25

DEVOTE *commit, dedicate*
shall **d** to the LORD Ex 13:12
d...to the law 2 Chr 31:4
d-d to one and despise Matt 6:24
d-ing...to prayer Acts 1:14
d-d to one another Rom 12:10
D yourselves to prayer Col 4:2

DEVOTED *set apart (to God)*
d to destruction Lev 27:28
Every **d** thing in Num 18:14
d to destruction 1 Sam 15:21
d thing in Israel Ezek 44:29

DEVOTION *consecration*
his deeds of **d** 2 Chr 32:32
excessive **d** *to books* Eccl 12:12
the **d** of your youth Jer 2:2

DEVOUR *consume, swallow*
wild beast **d-ed** him Gen 37:20
the sword **d** forever 2 Sam 2:26
is **d-ed** by disease Job 18:13
fire from...**d-ed** Ps 18:8
love all words that **d** Ps 52:4
To **d** the afflicted Prov 30:14
has **d-ed** your prophets Jer 2:30
caterpillar was **d-ing** Amos 4:9
d widows' houses Mark 12:40
bite...**d** one another Gal 5:15

DEVOUT *God-fearing*
d men are taken away Is 57:1
was righteous and **d** Luke 2:25
d men, from every Acts 2:5
the **d** women Acts 13:50

DEW *drops of moisture*
God give...the **d** Gen 27:28
d fell on the camp Num 11:9
d on the fleece only Judg 6:37
on him as the **d** 2 Sam 17:12
neither **d** nor rain 1 Kin 17:1
the **d** of Hermon Ps 133:3
skies drip with **d** Prov 3:20
Like a cloud of **d** Is 18:4
drenched with the **d** Dan 4:15
sky has withheld its **d** Hag 1:10

DIALECT *language*
in the Hebrew **d** Acts 21:40
the Hebrew **d** Acts 22:2

DIAMOND *jewel*
a sapphire and a **d** Ex 28:18
With a **d** point Jer 17:1

DICTATION *spoken words*
at the **d** of Jeremiah Jer 36:4
written at the **d** of Jer 36:27
book at Jeremiah's **d** Jer 45:1

DIE *decease, expire*
you will surely **d** Gen 2:17
not eat...which **d-s** Deut 14:21
Where you **d,** I will **d** Ruth 1:17
Curse God and **d** Job 2:9
even wise men **d** Ps 49:10
fools **d** for lack of Prov 10:21
and the fool alike **d** Eccl 2:16
soul who sins will **d** Ezek 18:4
to **d** with You Matt 26:35
child has not **d-d** Mark 5:39
live even if he **d-s** John 11:25
grain of wheat...**d-s** John 12:24
she fell sick and **d-d** Acts 9:37
d-d for the ungodly Rom 5:6
we who **d-d** to sin Rom 6:2

for whom Christ **d-d** Rom 14:15
I **d** daily 1 Cor 15:31
I **d-d** to the Law Gal 2:19
to **d** is gain Phil 1:21
Jesus **d-d** and rose 1 Thess 4:14
to **d** once and after Heb 9:27
these **d-d** in faith Heb 11:13
who **d** in the Lord Rev 14:13

DIFFICULT *hard*
too **d** for the LORD Gen 18:14
test Solomon with **d** 2 Chr 9:1
anything too **d** for Me Jer 32:27
speech or **d** language Ezek 3:5
solving of **d** problems Dan 5:12
last days **d** times 2 Tim 3:1

DIG *excavate, till*
opens a pit, or **d-s** Ex 21:33
you can **d** copper Deut 8:9
they **d** into houses Job 24:16
He has **dug** a pit Ps 7:15
dug through the wall Ezek 8:8
dug a wine press Matt 21:33
until I **d** around it Luke 13:8

DIGNITY *majesty*
Preeminent in **d** Gen 49:3
What honor or **d** has Esth 6:3
all godliness and **d** 1 Tim 2:2
must be men of **d** 1 Tim 3:8

DILIGENCE *effort*
carried out with all **d** Ezra 6:12
Watch...with all **d** Prov 4:23
lagging behind in **d** Rom 12:11
show the same **d** Heb 6:11

DILIGENT *persistent*
hand of the **d** makes Prov 10:4
plans of the **d** *lead* Prov 21:5
d to present 2 Tim 2:15
d to enter that rest Heb 4:11
I will also be **d** 2 Pet 1:15

DIM *cloudy, dark*
eye was not **d** Deut 34:7
eyesight...to grow **d** 1 Sam 3:2
d because of grief Job 17:7
windows grow **d** Eccl 12:3

DIMINISH *dwindle, reduce*
you shall **d** its price Lev 25:16
d their inheritance Num 26:54
are **d-ed** and bowed Ps 107:39

DINAH
daughter of Jacob Gen 34:1,3
raped by Shechem Gen 34:2,5

DINE *eat*
men are to **d** with Gen 43:16
to **d** with a ruler Prov 23:1
came and were **d-ing** Matt 9:10

DINNER *meal*
I have prepared...**d** Matt 22:4

because of...**d** guests Mark 6:26
was giving a big **d** Luke 14:16

DIP *plunge*
d-ped the tunic in Gen 37:31
priest shall **d** his Lev 4:6
d your piece of bread Ruth 2:14
d-ped...seven times 2 Kin 5:14
d-ped...with Me Matt 26:23
who **d-s** with Me Mark 14:20
robe **d-ped** in blood Rev 19:13

DIRECT *arrange, guide, order*
LORD **d-s** his steps Prov 16:9
d your heart in the Prov 23:19
has **d-ed** the Spirit Is 40:13
walks to **d** his steps Jer 10:23
I **d-ed** the churches 1 Cor 16:1
d their entire body James 3:3

DIRECTION *path* or *order*
which turned every **d** Gen 3:24
It changes **d** Job 37:12
d of the daughter Jer 4:11
of their four **d-s** Ezek 1:17

DIRGE *lament*
for you as a **d** Amos 5:1
we sang a **d** Luke 7:32

DISAPPEAR *vanish*
For the faithful **d** Ps 12:1
When the grass **d-s** Prov 27:25
old is ready to **d** Heb 8:13

DISAPPOINT *frustrate*
and were not **d-ed** Ps 22:5
hope does not **d** Rom 5:5

DISASTER *calamity*
d was close to them Judg 20:34
d on this people Jer 6:19
because of all its **d-s** Jer 19:8
In the day of their **d** Obad 13

DISBELIEVE *doubt*
Jews who **d-d** stirred Acts 14:2
for those who **d** 1 Pet 2:7

DISCERN *understand, recognize*
would **d**...future Deut 32:29
king to **d** good 2 Sam 14:17
not **d** its appearance Job 4:16
d-ed...the youths Prov 7:7
d the...sky Matt 16:3

DISCERNMENT *judgment*
blessed be your **d** 1 Sam 25:33
asked for yourself **d** 1 Kin 3:11
not a people of **d** Is 27:11
knowledge and all **d** Phil 1:9

DISCHARGE *emission*
a **d** from his body Lev 15:2
leper or who has a **d** Lev 22:4
everyone having a **d** Num 5:2
d, or who is a leper 2 Sam 3:29
the **d** of your blood Ezek 32:6

DISCIPLE *student, learner*
to listen as a **d** Is 50:4
His twelve **d-s** Matt 10:1
d is not above his Matt 10:24
d-s rebuked them Matt 19:13
d-s left Him...fled Matt 26:56
make **d-s** of all Matt 28:19
Your **d-s** do not fast Mark 2:18
Passover...My **d-s** Mark 14:14
gaze toward His **d-s** Luke 6:20
he cannot be My **d** Luke 14:26
d-s believed in Him John 2:11
His **d-s** withdrew John 6:66
wash the **d-s'** feet John 13:5
d whom He loved John 19:26
d-s were first called Acts 11:26

DISCIPLINE (n) *chastisement*
the **d** of the LORD Deut 11:2
d of the Almighty Job 5:17
The rod of **d** Prov 22:15
to see your good **d** Col 2:5
d...of little profit 1 Tim 4:8

DISCIPLINE (v) *chastise*
as a man **d-s** his son Deut 8:5
d-d you with whips 1 Kin 12:11
D your son while Prov 19:18
I **d** my body 1 Cor 9:27
d-d by the Lord 1 Cor 11:32
father does not **d** Heb 12:7

DISCLOSE *reveal*
without **d-ing** it to 1 Sam 20:2
Esther had **d-d** what Esth 8:1
will **d** Myself to him John 14:21
d the motives of 1 Cor 4:5
secrets...are **d-d** 1 Cor 14:25

DISCOURAGE *dishearten*
d-ing the sons of Num 32:7
people of the land **d-d** Ezra 4:4
d-d with the work Neh 6:9

DISCOVER *find, uncover*
strength was not **d-ed** Judg 16:9
d the depths of God Job 11:7
man will not **d** Eccl 7:14
shamed...he is **d-ed** Jer 2:26

DISCRETION *understanding*
LORD give you **d** 1 Chr 22:12
sound wisdom and **d** Prov 3:21
woman who lacks **d** Prov 11:22
Daniel replied with **d** Dan 2:14

DISCUSS *converse, reason*
d matters of justice Jer 12:1
d...among themselves Matt 16:7
What were you **d-ing** Mark 9:33
d-ed together what Luke 6:11

DISEASE *sickness*
none of the **d-s** on you Ex 15:26
harmful **d-s** of Egypt Deut 7:15
d-d in his feet 2 Chr 16:12
d-d...not healed Ezek 34:4
heals all your **d-s** Ps 103:3
various **d-s** and pains Matt 4:24
power...to heal **d-s** Luke 9:1

DISGRACE *reproach, shame*
a **d** to us Gen 34:14
nakedness, it is a **d** Lev 20:17
sin is a **d** to Prov 14:34
not **d** the throne Jer 14:21
and bear your **d** Ezek 16:52

DISGRACEFUL *shameful*
d thing in Israel Gen 34:7
shameful and **d** son Prov 19:26
d for a woman to 1 Cor 11:6

DISGUISE *pretend*
d-d his sanity 1 Sam 21:13
Arise now, and **d** 1 Kin 14:2
king of Israel **d-d** 1 Kin 22:30
he **d-s** his face Job 24:15
d-ing...as apostles 2 Cor 11:13

DISH *bowl, plate*
prepare a savory **d** Gen 27:7
was one silver **d** Num 7:43
as one wipes a **d** 2 Kin 21:13
30 gold **d-es** Ezra 1:9

DISHEARTENED *discouraged*
not be **d** or crushed Is 42:4
you **d** the righteous Ezek 13:22

DISHONEST *untruthful*
those who hate **d** gain Ex 18:21
order to get **d** gain Ezek 22:27
cheat with **d** scales Amos 8:5

DISHONOR (n) *disgrace, shame*
to see the king's **d** Ezra 4:14
Fill their faces with **d** Ps 83:16
man conceals **d** Prov 12:16

DISHONOR (v) *disgrace, shame*
who **d-s** his father Deut 27:16
be ashamed and **d-ed** Ps 35:4
and you **d** Me John 8:49
bodies would be **d-ed** Rom 1:24
do you **d** God Rom 2:23

DISMAY *be troubled, fear*
d-ed at his presence Gen 45:3
not tremble or be **d-ed** Josh 1:9
d-ed and...afraid 1 Sam 17:11
or I will **d** you Jer 1:17
are **d-ed** and caught Jer 8:9
mighty men...be **d-ed** Obad 9

DISMISS *release, send away*
d-ed the people Josh 24:28
Solomon **d-ed** 1 Kin 2:27
priest did not **d** *any* 2 Chr 23:8

he **d-ed** the assembly Acts 19:41

DISOBEDIENCE *rebellion*
the one man's **d** Rom 5:19
in the sons of **d** Eph 2:2
d received a just Heb 2:2
same example of **d** Heb 4:11

DISOBEDIENT *rebellious*
d and rebelled Neh 9:26
hardened and **d** Acts 19:9
d to parents Rom 1:30
d...obstinate people Rom 10:21

DISPERSE *spread*
d them in Jacob Gen 49:7
d-d...the peoples Esth 3:8
d them among the Ezek 20:23
who are **d-d** abroad James 1:1

DISPLAY *declare, show*
to **d** her beauty Esth 1:11
d-ed Your splendor Ps 8:1
d their sin like Is 3:9
works of God...**d-ed** John 9:3

DISPLEASE *annoy, trouble*
if it is **d-ing** to you Num 22:34
d-ing in the sight 1 Sam 8:6
may not **d** the lords 1 Sam 29:7
d-ing in His sight Is 59:15
it greatly **d-d** Jonah Jon 4:1

DISPOSSESS *remove*
d-ed the Amorites Num 21:32
Esau **d-ed** them Deut 2:12
He will assuredly **d** Josh 3:10
d-ing the nations Acts 7:45

DISPUTE (n) *controversy*
When they have a **d** Ex 18:16
bring the **d-s** to God Ex 18:19
d in your courts Deut 17:8
a great **d** among Acts 28:29

DISPUTE (v) *contend, debate*
wished to **d** with Him Job 9:3
with Israel he will **d** Mic 6:2
without...**d-ing** Phil 2:14
He **d-d** with the devil Jude 9

DISSENSION *division*
great **d** and debate Acts 15:2
d between the Acts 23:7
those who cause **d-s** Rom 16:17
without wrath and **d** 1 Tim 2:8

DISSIPATION *intemperance*
weighted...with **d** Luke 21:34
wine, for that is **d** Eph 5:18
not accused of **d** Titus 1:6

DISSOLVE *melt*
d me in a storm Job 30:22
I **d** my couch with Ps 6:6
d-d in tears Is 15:3
And the hills **d** Nah 1:5

DISTANCE *far away*
sister stood at a **d** Ex 2:4
some **d** from the Judg 18:22
following...at a **d** Matt 26:58

welcomed...from a **d** Heb 11:13

DISTINCTION *difference*
the LORD makes a **d** Ex 11:7
d between the holy Lev 10:10
have made no **d** Ezek 22:26
He made no **d** Acts 15:9
for there is no **d** Rom 3:22
d-s among yourselves James 2:4

DISTINGUISH (v) *discern*
I **d** between good 2 Sam 19:35
not **d** the sound Ezra 3:13
d...the righteous Mal 3:18
d-ing of spirits 1 Cor 12:10

DISTINGUISHING (adj)
became your **d** mark Ezek 27:7
this is a **d** mark 2 Thess 3:17

DISTORT *pervert*
who **d-s** the justice Deut 27:19
my garment is **d-ed** Job 30:18
they **d** my words Ps 56:5
d the gospel of Christ Gal 1:7

DISTRESS *adversity, trouble*
day of my **d** Gen 35:3
When you are in **d** Deut 4:30
deliver me...**d** 1 Sam 26:24
I am in great **d** 2 Sam 24:14
cry to You in our **d** 2 Chr 20:9
refuge in the day of **d** Jer 16:19
I am in **d** Lam 1:20
d upon the land Luke 21:23
d for every soul Rom 2:9
assisted those in **d** 1 Tim 5:10
widows in their **d** James 1:27

DISTRIBUTE *apportion*
d-d by lot in Shiloh Josh 19:51
to **d** to their kinsmen Neh 13:13
d it to the poor Luke 18:22
d-ing to each one 1 Cor 12:11

DISTRICT *area, province*
the **d** of Jerusalem Neh 3:12
d around the Jordan Matt 3:5
d of Galilee Mark 1:28
the **d-s** of Libya Acts 2:10

DISTURB *annoy, bother*
Why...**d-ed** me 1 Sam 28:15
no one **d** his bones 2 Kin 23:18
d them and destroy Esth 9:24
being greatly **d-ed** Acts 4:2
one who is **d-ing** you Gal 5:10

DISTURBANCE *turmoil*
to cause a **d** in it Neh 4:8
hear of wars and **d-s** Luke 21:9
d among the soldiers Acts 12:18
arrogance, **d-s** 2 Cor 12:20

DIVIDE *apportion, separate*
that **d-s** the hoof Deut 14:6
D the living child 1 Kin 3:25
d my garments among Ps 22:18
He will **d** the booty Is 53:12
d-d up His garments Matt 27:35
d-d his wealth Luke 15:12

DIVINATION *witchcraft*
nor practice **d** or Lev 19:26
witchcraft, used **d** 2 Chr 33:6
false vision, **d** Jer 14:14
falsehood and lying **d** Ezek 13:6
a spirit of **d** met us Acts 16:16

DIVINE (adj)
pertaining to deity
in whom...**d** spirit Gen 41:38
I see a **d** being 1 Sam 28:13
D Nature...gold Acts 17:29
power and **d** nature Rom 1:20
is the **d** response Rom 11:4

DIVINE (v) *practice divination*
d-d that the LORD Gen 30:27
they **d** lies for you Ezek 21:29
d-ing lies for them Ezek 22:28
prophets **d** for money Mic 3:11

DIVINER *seer*
called for the...**d-s** 1 Sam 6:2
The **d** and the elder Is 3:2
your **d-s** deceive you Jer 29:8
d-s will be embarrassed Mic 3:7
d-s see lying visions Zech 10:2

DIVISION *dissension, segment*
d between My people Ex 8:23
divided...into **d-s** 1 Chr 23:6
d...in the crowd John 7:43
no **d-s** among you 1 Cor 1:10
d of soul and spirit Heb 4:12

DIVORCE (n) *separation*
a certificate of **d** Deut 24:1
given her a writ of **d** Jer 3:8
For I hate **d** Mal 2:16

DIVORCE (v) *separate*
he cannot **d** her Deut 22:19
husband **d-s** his wife Jer 3:1
man to **d** his wife Matt 19:3
Whoever **d-s** his Mark 10:11

DIVORCED (adj) *separated*
woman **d** from her Lev 21:7
or of a **d** woman Num 30:9
marries a **d** woman Matt 5:32
marries...who is **d** Luke 16:18

DOCTRINE *teaching*
Teaching as **d-s** the Matt 15:9
every wind of **d** Eph 4:14
to teach strange **d-s** 1 Tim 1:3
to exhort in sound **d** Titus 1:9

DOCUMENT *manuscript*
the **d** which you sent Ezra 4:18

And on the sealed **d** Neh 9:38
Darius signed the **d** Dan 6:9

DOER *workman*
recompenses the...**d** Ps 31:23
d-s of the Law will Rom 2:13
d-s of the word James 1:22
not a **d** of the law James 4:11

DOG *animal, scavenger*
Am I a **d** 1 Sam 17:43
d-s have surrounded Ps 22:16
they howl like a **d** Ps 59:6
live **d** is better than Eccl 9:4
Beware of the **d-s** Phil 3:2
d-s and the sorcerers Rev 22:15

DOMAIN *estate*
give You all this **d** Luke 4:6
the **d** of darkness Col 1:13
keep their own **d** Jude 6

DOMINION *authority, rule*
Yours is the **d** 1 Chr 29:11
places of His **d** Ps 103:22
d will be from sea Zech 9:10
and power and **d** Eph 1:21
thrones or **d-s** or Col 1:16
glory and the **d** forever Rev 1:6

DONKEY *ass*
a wild **d** of a man Gen 16:12
Balaam...to the **d** Num 22:29
the foal of a **d** Zech 9:9
you will find a **d** Matt 21:2
and mounted on a **d** Matt 21:5
a mute **d**, speaking 2 Pet 2:16

DOOR *entrance, opening*
crouching at the **d** Gen 4:7
set the **d** of the ark Gen 6:16
Uriah slept at the **d** 2 Sam 11:9
over the **d** of my lips Ps 141:3
d turns on its Prov 26:14
each had a double **d** Ezek 41:23
close your **d**...pray Matt 6:6
I am the **d** John 10:9
right at the **d** James 5:9
before you an open **d** Rev 3:8
I stand at the **d** Rev 3:20

DOORKEEPER *guard*
d-s have gathered 2 Kin 22:4
the Levites, the **d-s** 2 Chr 34:9
eunuchs who were **d-s** Esth 6:2
commanded the **d** Mark 13:34
To him the **d** opens John 10:3

DOORPOST
put it on the two **d-s** Ex 12:7
write them on the **d-s** Deut 6:9
on the seat by the **d** 1 Sam 1:9
Waiting at my **d-s** Prov 8:34

DOORWAY *entrance, opening*
the **d** of the tent Judg 4:20
d-s and doorposts 1 Kin 7:5
at my neighbor's **d** Job 31:9
chamber with its **d** Ezek 40:38

DORCAS
Tabitha, a Joppa Christian Acts 9:36-43

DOUBT (n) *unbelief*
life shall hang in **d** Deut 28:66
why do **d-s** arise Luke 24:38

DOUBT (v) *disbelieve*
why did you **d** Matt 14:31
not **d** in his heart Mark 11:23
d-s is condemned Rom 14:23
who **d-s** is like the James 1:6

DOUGH *flour mixture*
people took their **d** Ex 12:34
the first of your **d** Num 15:20
took **d**, kneaded *it* 2 Sam 13:8
knead **d** to make cakes Jer 7:18

DOVE *bird*
he sent out a **d** Gen 8:8
had wings like a **d** Ps 55:6
eyes are *like* **d-s** Song 1:15
descending as a **d** Matt 3:16
descending as a **d** John 1:32
selling the **d-s** John 2:16

DOWNFALL *collapse*
became the **d** of 2 Chr 28:23
noise of their **d** Jer 49:21

DOWNPOUR *rain*
the **d** and the rain Job 37:6
d of waters swept Hab 3:10

DOWRY *bequest*
must pay a **d** for her Ex 22:16
to the **d** for virgins Ex 22:17
d to his daughter 1 Kin 9:16

DRACHMA
Greek silver coin Neh 7:70-72; Matt 17:24

DRAG *draw, pull*
grasshopper **d-s** Eccl 12:5
D them off like sheep Jer 12:3
the dogs to **d** off Jer 15:3
Paul and **d-ged** Acts 14:19
d you into court James 2:6

DRAGON *monster, serpent*
d who *lives* in the sea Is 27:1
Who pierced the **d** Is 51:9
d stood before the Rev 12:4
he laid hold of the **d** Rev 20:2

DRAIN *empty*
blood is to be **d-ed** Lev 1:15
he **d-ed** the dew Judg 6:38
must **d** *and* drink down Ps 75:8
drink it and **d** it Ezek 23:34

DRAW *haul, pull*
out to **d** water Gen 24:13
drew him out of the Ex 2:10
but are **d-n** away Deut 30:17
He **d-s** up the drops Job 36:27
d near to my soul Ps 69:18
They are **d-ing** back Jer 46:5
redemption is **d-ing** Luke 21:28
d all men to Myself John 12:32
D near to God James 4:8

DRAWERS *servants*
wood and **d** of water Josh 9:21

DREAD (n) *fear*
in **d**...of Israel Ex 1:12
in **d** night and day Deut 28:66
d of the Jews Esth 8:17
they are in great **d** Ps 14:5
d comes like a storm Prov 1:27

DREAD (v) *fear*
what I **d** befalls me Job 3:25
Whom shall I **d** Ps 27:1
whose two kings you **d** Is 7:16
are **d-ed** and feared Hab 1:7

DREAM (n) *vision*
had a **d**, and behold Gen 28:12
man was relating a **d** Judg 7:13
flies away like a **d** Job 20:8
like a **d**, a vision Is 29:7
visions and **d-s** Dan 1:17
to Joseph in a **d** Matt 2:13

DREAM (v) *see a vision*
asleep and **d-ed** Gen 41:5
like those who **d** Ps 126:1
when a hungry man **d-s** Is 29:8
Your old men will **d** Joel 2:28

DREAMER *visionary*
Here comes this **d** Gen 37:19
If a prophet or a **d** Deut 13:1
your diviners, your **d-s** Jer 27:9

DRENCH *soak, wet*
d you with my tears Is 16:9
head is **d-ed** with dew Song 5:2
d-ed with the dew Dan 4:33

DRESS (n) *clothing*
have taken off my **d** Song 5:3
d was of fine linen Ezek 16:13
or putting on **d-es** 1 Pet 3:3

DRESS (v) *array, clothe*
d-ed in his military 2 Sam 20:8
D-ed as a harlot Prov 7:10
you **d** in scarlet Jer 4:30
d-ed Him...purple Mark 15:17

DRINK (n) *refreshment*
gave the lad a **d** Gen 21:19
or wine, or strong **d** Deut 14:26
to desire strong **d** Prov 31:4
gave Me *something* to **d** Matt 25:35
My blood is true **d** John 6:55
thirsty, give him a **d** Rom 12:20

DRINK (v)
he **drank** of the wine Gen 9:21
Do not **d** wine Lev 10:9
d from the brook 1 Kin 17:6
they all **drank** from Mark 14:23
after **d-ing** old *wine* Luke 5:39
who eats and **d-s** 1 Cor 11:29
ground that **d-s** the Heb 6:7

DRIP *drop*
clouds...They **d** Job 36:28
lips...**d** honey Song 4:11
d-ped with myrrh Song 5:5
D down, O heavens Is 45:8

DRIVE *chase, defeat*
You have **d-n** me Gen 4:14
and **drove** them away Ex 2:17
angel...**d-ing** *them* on Ps 35:5
d hard all your workers Is 58:3
drove Him out of...city Luke 4:29
drove *them* all out John 2:15
to **d** the ship Acts 27:39

DROP (n) *drip*
the **d-s** of water Job 36:27
a **d** from a bucket Is 40:15
like **d-s** of blood Luke 22:44

DROP (v) *fall*
olives will **d** off Deut 28:40
his bonds **d-ped** Judg 15:14
d off his unripe grape Job 15:33
d-ped their wings Ezek 1:24

DROSS *metallic waste*
of the earth *like* **d** Ps 119:119
Take away the **d** Prov 25:4
silver has become **d** Is 1:22
Israel has become **d** Ezek 22:18

DROUGHT *dryness*
Like heat in **d** Is 25:5
in regard to the **d** Jer 14:1
I called for a **d** Hag 1:11

DROWNED *suffocated*
d in the Red Sea Ex 15:4
to be **d** in the depth Matt 18:6
were **d** in the sea Mark 5:13

DRUNK *intoxicated*
arrows **d** with blood Deut 32:42
d, but not with wine Is 29:9
made...**d** in My wrath Is 63:6
not get **d** with wine Eph 5:18
I saw the woman **d** Rev 17:6

DRUNKARD *intoxicated person*
a glutton and a **d** Deut 21:20
song of the **d-s** Ps 69:12
Awake, **d-s**, and weep Joel 1:5
a reviler, or a **d** 1 Cor 5:11

DRUNKEN *intoxicated*
stagger like a **d** man Job 12:25
become like a **d** man Jer 23:9

DRUNKENNESS *intoxicated*
and not for **d** Eccl 10:17
weighted down...**d** Luke 21:34
in carousing and **d** Rom 13:13
envying, **d**, carousing Gal 5:21

DRY (adj) *parched, scorched*
let the **d** land appear Gen 1:9
In a **d** and weary land Ps 63:1
Better is a **d** morsel Prov 17:1
O **d** bones, hear Ezek 37:4

DRY (v) *scorch, wither*
My strength is **dried** Ps 22:15
dried up...streams Ps 74:15
I **d** up the sea Is 50:2
new wine **dries** up Joel 1:10
dries up...rivers Nah 1:4

DUE (adj) *proper, right*
In **d** time their foot Deut 32:35
food in **d** season Ps 104:27
d penalty of their Rom 1:27

DUE (n) *what is owed*
as *their* **d** forever Lev 7:34
be the priests' **d** Deut 18:3
Indeed it is Your **d** Jer 10:7

DULL *heavy, stupid*
eyes are **d** from wine Gen 49:12
Their ears **d** Is 6:10
people...become **d** Matt 13:15
become **d** of hearing Heb 5:11

DUNG *waste*
sweeps away **d** 1 Kin 14:10
dove's **d** for five 2 Kin 6:25
give you cow's **d** Ezek 4:15
their flesh like **d** Zeph 1:17

DUNGEON *prison*
put me into the **d** Gen 40:15
captive...in the **d** Ex 12:29
prisoners from the **d** Is 42:7
Jeremiah...into the **d** Jer 37:16

DUST *dirt, earth*
God formed man of **d** Gen 2:7
And **d** you will eat Gen 3:14
the poor from the **d** 1 Sam 2:8
repent in **d** and ashes Job 42:6
d before the wind Ps 18:42
Will the **d** praise You Ps 30:9
You who lie in the **d** Is 26:19
shake the **d** off Matt 10:14
the **d** of your city Luke 10:11
d on their heads Rev 18:19

DUTY *responsibility*
perform your **d** Gen 38:8
charged with any **d** Deut 24:5
the **d** of a husband's Deut 25:7
his **d** to his wife 1 Cor 7:3

DWELL *abide, live*
father of those who **d** Gen 4:20
Behold, I am **d-ing** 1 Chr 17:1
No evil **d-s** with You Ps 5:4
d on Your holy hill Ps 15:1
I will **d** in the house Ps 23:6
d among the wise Prov 15:31
have **d-t** in Jerusalem Jer 35:11
flesh, and **d-t** among John 1:14
His Spirit who **d-s** in you Rom 8:11
of God **d-s** in you 1 Cor 3:16
Christ may **d** in your Eph 3:17
d on these things Phil 4:8

DWELLING *habitation*
earth shall be your **d** Gen 27:39
name there for His **d** Deut 12:5
place for Your **d** 1 Kin 8:13
into the eternal **d-s** Luke 16:9
might find a **d** place Acts 7:46

DYED *colored*
rams' skins **d** red Ex 25:5
A spoil of **d** work Judg 5:30

E

EAGLE *bird*
bore you on **e-s'** wings Ex 19:4
the **e** swoops down Deut 28:49
swifter than **e-s** 2 Sam 1:23
with wings like **e-s** Is 40:31
the face of an **e** Ezek 1:10
was like a flying **e** Rev 4:7

EAR *hearing*
heard with our **e-s** 2 Sam 7:22
the **e** test words Job 12:11
And His **e-s** are *open* Ps 34:15
and incline your **e** Ps 45:10
He whose **e** listens Prov 15:31
e of the wise seeks Prov 18:15
e has not been open Is 48:8
let your **e** receive Jer 9:20
He who has **e-s** to Matt 11:15
and cut off his **e** Matt 26:51
fingers into his **e-s** Mark 7:33
if the **e** says 1 Cor 12:16
their **e-s** tickled 2 Tim 4:3
He who has an **e** Rev 2:7

EARLY *beforetime, soon*
they arose **e** and Gen 26:31
Let us rise **e** Song 7:12
dew which goes away **e** Hos 6:4
e on the first day Mark 16:2
at the tomb **e** Luke 24:22
the **e** and late rains James 5:7

EARNINGS *gain, wages*
her **e** she plants Prov 31:16
the **e** of a harlot Mic 1:7

EARRING *ornament*
brought...**e-s** Ex 35:22
e-s and necklaces Num 31:50
Like an **e** of gold Prov 25:12
her **e-s** and jewelry Hos 2:13

EARTH *land, world*
God created the...**e** Gen 1:1
Judge of all the **e** Gen 18:25
the **e** is the LORD's Ex 9:29
way of all the **e** Josh 23:14
His stand on the **e** Job 19:25
foundation of the **e** Job 38:4
saints...in the **e** Ps 16:3
the shields of the **e** Ps 47:9
gave birth to the **e** Ps 90:2
He established the **e** Ps 104:5
wisdom founded...**e** Prov 3:19
the **e** remains forever Eccl 1:4
made the **e** tremble Is 14:16
the circle of the **e** Is 40:22
the ends of the **e** Is 45:22
the **e** is My footstool Is 66:1
e shone with His Ezek 43:2
make the **e** dark Amos 8:9
e will be devoured Zeph 3:8
shall inherit the **e** Matt 5:5
you bind on **e** Matt 16:19
on **e** peace among Luke 2:14
glorified...on the **e** John 17:4
man is from the **e** 1 Cor 15:47
heavens and a new **e** 2 Pet 3:13
e and heaven fled Rev 20:11

EARTHENWARE *pottery*
bird in an **e** vessel Lev 14:5
holy water in an **e** Num 5:17
shatter them like **e** Ps 2:9
buy a potter's **e** jar Jer 19:1
vessels of...**e** 2 Tim 2:20

EARTHQUAKE *temblor*
LORD *was* not...**e** 1 Kin 19:11
punished with...**e** Is 29:6
be famines and **e-s** Matt 24:7
will be great **e-s** Luke 21:11
there was a great **e** Rev 6:12
killed in the **e** Rev 11:13

EARTHY *mortal*
man is...**e** 1 Cor 15:47
those who are **e** 1 Cor 15:48

EASE *free from difficulty, pain*
He who is at **e** Job 12:5
at **e** and satisfied Job 21:23
women who are at **e** Is 32:9
Woe to those...at **e** Amos 6:1
nations who are at **e** Zech 1:15

EAST *direction of compass*
spread out...to the **e** Gen 28:14
directed an **e** wind Ex 10:13
sons of the **e** were Judg 7:12
men of the **e** Job 1:3
With the **e** wind You Ps 48:7
offspring from the **e** Is 43:5
faces toward the **e** Ezek 8:16
Jerusalem on the **e** Zech 14:4
saw His star in the **e** Matt 2:2
lightning...the **e** Matt 24:27
kings from the **e** Rev 16:12

EAST GATE
see **GATES OF JERUSALEM**

EASY *without difficulty*
knowledge is **e** to one Prov 14:6
My yoke is **e** and Matt 11:30

EAT *consume, dine, feast*
shall not **e** from it Gen 3:17
they **ate** every plant Ex 10:15
not **e**...blood Lev 19:26
that we may **e** him 2 Kin 6:28
e and be satisfied Ps 22:26
not **e** the bread of Prov 31:27
will **e** curds and honey Is 7:15
words...I **ate** them Jer 15:16
e this scroll Ezek 3:1
e-ing grass like cattle Dan 4:33
what you will **e** Matt 6:25
e with unwashed Matt 15:20
Take, **e;** this is My Matt 26:26
sinners and **e-s** with Luke 15:2
e...at My table Luke 22:30
He took it and **ate** Luke 24:43
e the flesh of...Son John 6:53
Peter, kill and **e** Acts 10:13
kingdom...not **e-ing** Rom 14:17
ate...spiritual food 1 Cor 10:3
e-s...judgment 1 Cor 11:29

EBAL
1 *son of Shobal* Gen 36:23
2 *son of Joktan* 1 Chr 1:22
also **Obal** Gen 10:28
3 *mountain near Shechem* Deut 11:29

EBENEZER
a memorial stone 1 Sam 7:12

EBER
1 *line of Shem* Gen 10:21-24
progenitor of Jocktanide Arabs Gen 10:25-30
progenitor of Hebrews Gen 11:16ff
2 *a Gadite* 1 Chr 5:13
3 *son of Elpaal* 1 Chr 8:12
4 *son of Shashak* 1 Chr 8:22
5 *priest* Neh 12:20
see also **HEBER**

EDEN
1 *garden of God* Gen 2:15; Is 51:3
2 *city area* 2 Kin 19:12; Ezek 27:23
3 *son of Joah* 2 Chr 29:12

EDICT *decree*
the king's **e-s** Ezra 8:36
a royal **e** be issued Esth 1:19
king's command and **e** Esth 9:1
afraid of the king's **e** Heb 11:23

EDIFICATION *building up*
his good, to his **e** Rom 15:2
speaks to men for **e** 1 Cor 14:3
all things...for **e** 1 Cor 14:26

EDIFY *build up*
but love **e-ies** 1 Cor 8:1
not all things **e** 1 Cor 10:23
person is not **e-ied** 1 Cor 14:17

EDOM
1 *name of Esau* Gen 25:30
2 *Edomites* Num 20:18,20
3 *region or country* Gen 32:3; Judg 11:17
see also **SEIR**

EDUCATED *taught*
be **e** three years Dan 1:5
Moses was **e** in all Acts 7:22
e under Gamaliel Acts 22:3

EFFEMINATE *womanlike*
e, nor homosexuals 1 Cor 6:9

EGG
in the white of an **e** Job 6:6
gathers abandoned **e-s** Is 10:14
hatch adders' **e-s** and Is 59:5
is asked for an **e** Luke 11:12

EGLON
1 *town in Judah* Josh 10:34-37;15:39
2 *Moabite king* Judg 3:12-30

EGYPT
country in NE Africa Gen 12:10;37:25
source of food Gen 42:1,2
on the Nile Ex 4:19;7:5
conflict with Moses Ex 7:8ff
scene of Passover Ex 12:1-36

EHUD
1 *left-handed Benjamite judge of Israel* Judg 3:15,21
2 *son of Bilhan* 1 Chr 7:10
3 *progenitor of clan* 1 Chr 8:6

EKRON
Philistine city Josh 13:3; 1 Sam 5:10; Jer 25:20

ELAH
1 *Edomite* Gen 36:41
2 *valley SW of Jerusalem* 1 Sam 17:2
3 *father of Shimei* 1 Kin 4:18
4 *king of Israel* 1 Kin 16:8-10
5 *father of Hoshea* 2 Kin 15:30
6 *son of Caleb* 1 Chr 4:15
7 *son of Uzzi* 1 Chr 9:8

ELAM
1 *son of Shem* Gen 10:22
2 *son of Shashak* 1 Chr 8:24
3 *Korahite Levite* 1 Chr 26:3
4 *head of restoration family* Ezra 2:7; Neh 7:12
5 *head of restoration family* Ezra 2:31; Neh 7:34
6 *chief of people* Neh 10:14
7 *priest* Neh 12:42
8 *region E of Babylonia* Is 21:2; Dan 8:2

ELATH / ELOTH *city*
at Gulf of Aqabah 2 Kin 14:22
near Ezion-geber

EL-BETHEL
altar Gen 35:7

ELDER *aged, older*
words of her **e** son Gen 27:42
the **e-s** of Israel Ex 17:6
sits among the **e-s** Prov 31:23
Assemble the **e-s** Joel 2:16
tradition of the **e-s** Matt 15:2
chief priests and **e-s** Matt 27:12
scribes...**e-s** came Mark 11:27
Council of **e-s** of Luke 22:66
e-s of the church Acts 20:17
I saw twenty-four **e-s** Rev 4:4

ELEAZAR
1 *son of Aaron* Ex 6:23
high priest Num 20:25-28

2 *son of Abinadab* 1 Sam 7:1
3 *son of Dodo* 2 Sam 23:9
4 *a Levite* 1 Chr 23:22
5 *son of Phinehas* Ezra 8:33
6 *son of Parosh* Ezra 10:18-25
7 *priest* Neh 12:27
8 *ancestor of Jesus* Matt 1:15

ELECT *chosen*
sake of the **e** Matt 24:22
to lead astray...the **e** Mark 13:22
justice for His **e** Luke 18:7
against God's **e** Rom 8:33

ELEMENTARY *basic*
e principles of the Col 2:8
e principles of the Heb 5:12
e teaching about the Heb 6:1

ELEMENTS *physical matter*
e will be destroyed 2 Pet 3:10
the **e** will melt with 2 Pet 3:12

ELI
high priest 1 Sam 1:9; 2:12;3:6;4:18

ELIAKIM
1 *son of Hilkiah* 2 Kin 18:18;19:2
2 *son of Josiah* 2 Kin 23:34
3 *priest* Neh 12:41
4 *ancestor of Jesus* Matt 1:13
5 *ancestor of Jesus* Luke 3:30,31

ELIEZER
1 *Abraham's servant* Gen 15:2
2 *son of Moses* 1 Chr 23:15
3 *son of Becher* 1 Chr 7:8
4 *priest* 1 Chr 15:24
5 *son of Zichri* 1 Chr 27:16
6 *a prophet* 2 Chr 20:37
7 *served under Ezra* Ezra 8:16
8 *son of Jeshua* Ezra 10:18
9 *Levite* Ezra 10:10,23
10 *son Harim* Ezra 10:10,31
11 *ancestor of Jesus* Luke 3:29

ELIHU
1 *son of Tohu* 1 Sam 1:1
2 *Manassite captain* 1 Chr 12:20
3 *temple gatekeeper* 1 Chr 26:1
4 *officer of Judah* 1 Chr 27:18
5 *one of Job's friends* Job 32:17

ELIJAH
1 *prophet* 1 Kin 17:1
aided by widow 1 Kin 17:8ff
revived child 1 Kin 17:23
defeats prophets 1 Kin 18:20ff
flees Jezebel 1 Kin 19:4-8
chooses Elisha 1 Kin 19:19-21
taken up 2 Kin 2:1-11
2 *Benjamite* 1 Chr 8:27
3 *son of Harim* Ezra 10:21
4 *son of Elam* Ezra 10:26

ELIMINATE *remove*
e harmful beasts Lev 26:6
I am going to **e** Jer 16:9
stomach, and is **e-d** Mark 7:19

ELIPHAZ
1 *son of Esau* Gen 36:4
2 *one of Job's friends* Job 2:11;4:1;42:7,9

ELISHA
prophet 2 Kin 6:12
called 1 Kin 19:19-21
Elijah's successor 2 Kin 2:1ff
miracle of oil 2 Kin 4:1-7
revived child 2 Kin 4:8-37
death 2 Kin 13:20

ELIZABETH
mother of John the Baptist Luke 1:7,13,41,57

ELOQUENT *persuasive*
I have never been **e** Ex 4:10
Apollos...an **e** man Acts 18:24

ELUL
sixth month of Hebrew calendar Neh 6:15

ELYMAS
magician Acts 13:8
see also **BAR-JESUS**

EMBALM *preserve*
to **e** his father Gen 50:2
he was **e-ed** and Gen 50:26

EMBARRASSED *ashamed*
e to lift up my face Ezra 9:6
e at the gardens Is 1:29
diviners will be **e** Mic 3:7

EMBITTERED *resentful*
the people were **e** 1 Sam 30:6
e them against the Acts 14:2

EMBRACE *clasp, hug*
Esau ran...and **e-d** Gen 33:4
e...a foreigner Prov 5:20
A time to **e** Eccl 3:5
ran and **e-d** him Luke 15:20

EMBROIDERED *woven*
spoil of dyed work **e** Judg 5:30
be led...in **e** work Ps 45:14
silk, and **e** cloth Ezek 16:13
purple, **e** work Ezek 27:16

EMERALD *precious stone*
ruby, topaz and **e** Ex 28:17
throne, like an **e** Rev 4:3

EMINENT *renowned*
nor anything **e** Ezek 7:11
the most **e** apostles 2 Cor 11:5
inferior to...**e** 2 Cor 12:11

EMISSION *issuance*
man has a seminal **e** Lev 15:16
nocturnal **e** Deut 23:10

EMMAUS
village by Jerusalem Luke 24:13

EMPOWERED *authorized*
e him to eat from Eccl 5:19
God has not **e** him Eccl 6:2

EMPTY (adj) *containing nothing*
Now the pit was **e** Gen 37:24
did not return **e** 2 Sam 1:22
sent widows away **e** Job 22:9
deceive you with **e** Eph 5:6
avoid...**e** chatter 2 Tim 2:16

EMPTY (v) *remove contents*
e-ing their sacks Gen 42:35
they **e** the house Lev 14:36
I **e-ied** them out as Ps 18:42
therefore **e** their net Hab 1:17
e the golden *oil* Zech 4:12
but **e-ied** Himself Phil 2:7

ENCAMP *abide, lodge*
the tabernacle **e-s** Num 1:51
and **e-ed** together Josh 11:5
a host **e** against me Ps 27:3
angel of the LORD **e-s** Ps 34:7

ENCIRCLE *go around*
entirely **e-ing** the sea 2 Chr 4:3
he **e-d** the Ophel 2 Chr 33:14
cords...have **e-d** me Ps 119:61
Who **e** yourselves with Is 50:11

ENCOMPASS *surround*
waves of death **e** 2 Sam 22:5
e-ing the walls of 1 Kin 6:5
e-ed...with bitterness Lam 3:5
Water **e-ed** me to the Jon 2:5

ENCOURAGE *strengthen*
charge Joshua and **e** Deut 3:28
e-d him in God 1 Sam 23:16
e them in the work Ezra 6:22
Paul was **e-ing** them Acts 27:33
e one another 1 Thess 5:11
e the young women Titus 2:4

ENCOURAGEMENT *support*
I arose to be an **e** Dan 11:1
God who gives...**e** Rom 15:5
is any **e** in Christ Phil 2:1
we...would have strong **e** Heb 6:18

END (n) *extremity, goal, result*
e of all flesh has Gen 6:13
one **e** of the heavens Deut 4:32
from beginning to **e** 1 Sam 3:12
what is my **e** Job 6:11
very **e-s** of the earth Ps 2:8
wicked come to an **e** Ps 7:9
e is the way of death Prov 14:12
no **e** to all his labor Eccl 4:8
summer is **e-ed** Jer 8:20
The **e** is coming Ezek 7:2
who endures to...**e** Matt 24:13
to the **e** of the age Matt 28:20
kingdom...no **e** Luke 1:33
He loved...to the **e** John 13:1
Christ...**e** of the law Rom 10:4
beginning and the **e** Rev 21:6

END (v) *complete, stop*
border **e-ed** at the sea Josh 15:4

words of Job are **e-ed** Job 31:40
days there were **e-ed** Acts 21:5
it **e-s** up being burned Heb 6:8

ENDLESS *limitless*
writing...is **e** Eccl 12:12
and **e** genealogies 1 Tim 1:4

ENDOW *provide a gift*
God has **e-ed** me Gen 30:20
e-ed with discretion 2 Chr 2:12
to **e** those who love Prov 8:21
e-ed with salvation Zech 9:9

ENDURANCE *patience*
in much **e**, in 2 Cor 6:4
you have need of **e** Heb 10:36
let us run with **e** Heb 12:1
of the **e** of Job James 5:11

ENDURE *persevere*
will be able to **e** Ex 18:23
that I should **e** Job 6:11
while the sun **e-s** Ps 72:5
May his name **e** Ps 72:17
and your name will **e** Is 66:22
Can your heart **e** Ezek 22:14
the one who has **e-d** Matt 10:22
who **e-s** to the end Mark 13:13
e-s all things 1 Cor 13:7
discipline that you **e** Heb 12:7
blessed who **e-d** James 5:11
word...LORD **e-s** 1 Pet 1:25

ENEMY *foe*
delivered your **e-ies** Gen 14:20
Your **e-ies** perish Judg 5:31
a man finds his **e** 1 Sam 24:19
consider me Your **e** Job 13:24
make the **e**...cease Ps 8:2
presence of my **e-ies** Ps 23:5
e has persecuted my Ps 143:3
If your **e** is hungry Prov 25:21
kisses of an **e** Prov 27:6
love your **e-ies**, and Matt 5:44
e-ies with each other Luke 23:12
e of all righteousness Acts 13:10
e is hungry, feed Rom 12:20
e...be abolished 1 Cor 15:26
an **e** of God James 4:4

ENGAGE *be involved, betroth*
virgin who is not **e-d** Ex 22:16
the girl who is **e-d** Deut 22:25
e-d in their work 1 Chr 9:33
e-d to...Joseph Luke 1:27
to **e** in good deeds Titus 3:8

ENGEDI
spring and town near Dead Sea 1 Sam 23:29;24:1; Song 1:14

ENGRAVE *inscribe*
shall **e** the two stones Ex 28:11

e-d on the tablets Ex 32:16
e an inscription Zech 3:9
letters **e-d** on stones 2 Cor 3:7

ENGRAVINGS *carvings*
like the **e** of a seal Ex 28:36
the **e** of a signet Ex 39:30
carved **e** of cherubim 1 Kin 6:29

ENGULF *overwhelm, swallow*
water...to **e** them Deut 11:4
sea **e-ed** their enemies Ps 78:53
She has been **e-ed** Jer 51:42
great deep **e-ed** me Jon 2:5

ENLARGE *extend, increase*
May God **e** Japheth Gen 9:27
You will **e** my heart Ps 119:32
Sheol has **e-d** its Is 5:14
He **e-s** his appetite Hab 2:5

ENLIGHTEN *illumine*
e-ing the eyes Ps 19:8
eyes...may be **e-ed** Eph 1:18
who have...been **e-ed** Heb 6:4

ENMITY *hostility*
e Between you and Gen 3:15
had everlasting **e** Ezek 35:5
sorcery, **e-ies**, strife Gal 5:20
abolishing...the **e** Eph 2:15

ENOCH
1 *son of Cain* Gen 4:17
2 *city* Gen 4:17
3 *Methuselah's father* Gen 5:22
walked with God Gen 5:24

ENRAGE *anger*
e-d and curse their Is 8:21
jealousy **e-s** a man Prov 6:34
he became very **e-d** Matt 2:16
dragon was **e-d** with Rev 12:17

ENRICH *make wealthy*
king will **e** the 1 Sam 17:25
You greatly **e** Ps 65:9
You **e-ed** the kings Ezek 27:33

ENROLLED *recorded*
were **e** by genealogy 1 Chr 7:9
people to be **e** by Neh 7:5
e in heaven Heb 12:23

ENSLAVE *subjugate*
you have been **e-d** Is 14:3
e-d and mistreated Acts 7:6
anyone **e-s** you 2 Cor 11:20
e-d to various lusts Titus 3:3

ENSNARE *catch*
An evil man is **e-d** Prov 12:13
e him who adjudicates Is 29:21

ENTANGLE *ensnare*
camel **e-ing** her ways Jer 2:23
No soldier...**e-s** 2 Tim 2:4
sin which...**e-s** us Heb 12:1

ENTER *go in*
you shall **e** the ark Gen 6:18
He **e-s** into judgment Job 22:4
E His gates with Ps 100:4
E the rock and hide Is 2:10
He **e-s** into peace Is 57:2
Spirit **e-ed** me and Ezek 2:2
not **e** the kingdom Matt 5:20
E through the narrow gate Matt 7:13
to **e** life crippled Matt 18:8
afraid as they **e-ed** Luke 9:34
e into the kingdom John 3:5
not **e** by the door John 10:1
shall not **e** My rest Heb 3:11

ENTHRONED *exalt, make king*
e *above* the cherubim 2 Sam 6:2
LORD who is **e** *above* 1 Chr 13:6
e upon the praises of Ps 22:3
who sits **e** from of old Ps 55:19
Who is **e** on high Ps 113:5

ENTICE *deceive, seduce*
E your husband Judg 14:15
Who will **e** Ahab 2 Chr 18:19
if sinners **e** you Prov 1:10
e-d by his own lust James 1:14
e-ing unstable souls 2 Pet 2:14

ENTRAILS *inner organs*
fat that covers the **e** Ex 29:13
e and the lobe Lev 8:16
also washed the **e** Lev 9:14

ENTRANCE *doorway*
cloud...at the **e** Ex 33:10
mark well the **e** of Ezek 44:5
stone against the **e** Matt 27:60
e into the eternal 2 Pet 1:11

ENTREAT *appeal, ask*
E the LORD that he Ex 8:8
Moses **e-ed** the LORD Ex 32:11
Please **e** the LORD 1 Kin 13:6
gain if we **e** Him Job 21:15
demons *began* to **e** Matt 8:31

ENTRUST *assign, commit*
security **e-ed** *to him* Lev 6:2
He **e-ed** the vineyard Song 8:11
to whom they **e-ed** Luke 12:48
not **e-ing** Himself to John 2:24

ENVIOUS *covetous*
e of the arrogant Ps 73:3
not be **e** of evil men Prov 24:1
is your eye **e** Matt 20:15
You are **e** James 4:2

ENVIRONS *outskirts, suburbs*
the **e** of Jerusalem Jer 32:44
devour all his **e** Jer 50:32

ENVOY *agent, messenger*
e-s of the rulers 2 Chr 32:31
faithful **e** *brings* Prov 13:17
sent your **e-s** a great Is 57:9
his **e-s** to Egypt Ezek 17:15

ENVY (n) *jealousy*
full of **e,** murder Rom 1:29
preaching...from **e** Phil 1:15
out of which arise **e** 1 Tim 6:4
life in malice and **e** Titus 3:3
e and all slander 1 Pet 2:1

ENVY (v) *be discontent, jealous*
Philistines **e-ied** him Gen 26:14
e a man of violence Prov 3:31
not let your heart **e** Prov 23:17
e-ing one another Gal 5:26

EPAPHRAS
Colossian Christian Col 1:7;4:12
colleague of Paul Philem 23

EPAPHRODITUS
Philippian Christian Phil 2:25
colleague of Paul Phil 4:18

EPHAH
1 *bushel, measure of capacity* Lev 5:11; Num 5:15
2 *son of Midian* Gen 25:4; 1 Chr 1:33
3 *Caleb's concubine* 1 Chr 2:46
4 *son of Jahdai* 1 Chr 2:47

EPHESUS
city of Asia Minor Acts 18:19; 1 Cor 16:8; Rev 1:11;2:1

EPHOD
1 *priestly garment* Ex 28:6; 1 Sam 23:9; 2 Sam 6:14
2 *father of Hanniel* Num 34:23

EPHRAIM
1 *son of Joseph* Gen 41:52;48:17
2 *tribe* Josh 16:5; Judg 7:24
3 *northern kingdom* Is 7:2-17; Hos 4:17;9:3-17
4 *city* 2 Sam 13:23; John 11:54

EPHRAIM GATE
see **GATES OF JERUSALEM**

EPHRATH(AH)
1 *Bethlehem* Gen 35:19;48:7; Ruth 4:11; Mic 5:2
2 *wife of Caleb* 1 Chr 2:19,50
3 *territory* Ps 132:6

EPHRON
1 *a Hittite* Gen 23:8;50:13
2 *mountain ridge* Josh 15:9
3 *city* 2 Chr 13:19

EPICUREAN
a Greek philosophy Acts 17:18

EPOCHS *ages, seasons*
the times and the **e** Dan 2:21
to know times or **e** Acts 1:7

EQUAL *same*
shall eat **e** portions Deut 18:8
a man my **e** Ps 55:13
That I would be *his* **e** Is 40:25
have made them **e** Matt 20:12
Himself **e** with God John 5:18

EQUIP *furnish, provide*
e-ped for war Josh 4:13
e-ped for...work 2 Tim 3:17
e you in every good Heb 13:21

EQUIPMENT *implements*
the **e** for the service Ex 39:40
e for his chariots 1 Sam 8:12
e of a foolish Zech 11:15

EQUITY *equality, fairness*
eyes look with **e** Ps 17:2
have established **e** Ps 99:4
justice and **e** Prov 1:3
e *and* every good Prov 2:9

ERASTUS
Corinthian Christian Acts 19:22; Rom 16:23; 2 Tim 4:20

ERROR *mistake, sin*
can discern *his* **e-s** Ps 19:12
like an **e** which goes Eccl 10:5
e against the LORD Is 32:6
e of unprincipled 2 Pet 3:17
the spirit of **e** 1 John 4:6
rushed...into the **e** Jude 11

ESARHADDON
Assyrian king 2 Kin 19:37; Ezra 4:2; Is 37:38

ESAU
son of Isaac Gen 25:25
twin of Jacob Gen 25:26
skillful hunter Gen 25:27
sold birthright Gen 25:34
despised Jacob Gen 27:41
reconciled with Jacob Gen 33:4

ESCAPE (n) *deliverance, refuge*
there will be no **e** Job 11:20
is no **e** for me Ps 142:4
Let there be no **e** Jer 50:29
provide...**e** 1 Cor 10:13

ESCAPE (v) *elude*
slave who has **e-d** Deut 23:15
let no one **e** *or* 2 Kin 9:15
Our soul has **e-d** Ps 124:7
tells lies will not **e** Prov 19:5
how shall we **e** Is 20:6
nothing at all **e-s** Joel 2:3
had not **e-d** notice Luke 8:47
how will we **e** if Heb 2:3
it **e-s** their notice 2 Pet 3:5

ESTABLISH *confirm, found*
I will **e** My covenant Gen 17:19
how God **e-es** them Job 37:15
e-es the mountains Ps 65:6
my ways may be **e-ed** Ps 119:5
e-ed in lovingkindness Is 16:5
to **e** the heavens Is 51:16
we **e** the Law Rom 3:31
may **e** your hearts 1 Thess 3:13
e-ed in the truth 2 Pet 1:12

ESTATE *domain* or *standard*
restore your...**e** Job 8:6
us in our low **e** Ps 136:23
squandered his **e** Luke 15:13

ESTEEM (n) *honor*
man of high **e** Dan 10:11
held them in high **e** Acts 5:13

ESTEEM (v) *have high regard*
I **e** right all *Your* Ps 119:128
e-ed Him stricken Is 53:4
e-ed among men Luke 16:15
e them...in love 1 Thess 5:13

ESTHER
Hebrew name Hadassah
cousin of Mordecai Esth 2:7
Persian queen Esth 2:16-18

ESTRANGED *separated*
completely **e** from me Job 19:13
e from my brothers Ps 69:8

ETERNAL *everlasting*
e God is a dwelling Deut 33:27
E Father, Prince of Is 9:6
An **e** decree Jer 5:22
cast into the **e** fire Matt 18:8
guilty of an **e** sin Mark 3:29
to inherit **e** life Luke 10:25
He may give **e** life John 17:2
gift of God is **e** life Rom 6:23
e weight of glory 2 Cor 4:17
with the **e** purpose Eph 3:11
Now to the King **e** 1 Tim 1:17
source of **e** salvation Heb 5:9
through the **e** Spirit Heb 9:14
kept in **e** bonds Jude 6
an **e** gospel to preach Rev 14:6

ETERNITY *perpetuity*
set **e** in their heart Eccl 3:11
from **e** I am He Is 43:13
Jesus from all **e** 2 Tim 1:9
to the day of **e** 2 Pet 3:18

ETHIOPIA
NE African country Esth 1:1; Ps 68:31; Nah 3:9; Zeph 3:10

EUNICE
mother of Timothy 2 Tim 1:5

EUNUCH *chamberlain official*
seven **e-s** who served Esth 1:10
Nor let the **e** say Is 56:3
children, and *the* **e-s** Jer 41:16
made **e-s** by men Matt 19:12
an Ethiopian **e** Acts 8:27

EUPHRATES
river of Mesopotamia
Gen 2:14; Jer 13:5;46:10; Rev 9:14;16:12

EVANGELIST *proclaimer*
house of Philip the **e** Acts 21:8
and some *as* **e-s** Eph 4:11
do the work of an **e** 2 Tim 4:5

EVE
first woman Gen 2:22
wife of Adam Gen 2:23
deceived by serpent Gen 3:1-7
named by Adam Gen 3:20

EVENING *dusk, darkness*
cloud...from **e** Num 9:21
eats food before **e** 1 Sam 14:24
as the **e** offering Ps 141:2
not be idle in the **e** Eccl 11:6
When **e** came Matt 8:16

EVENT *happening*
the **e-s** of the war 2 Sam 11:18
e became sin to the 1 Kin 13:34
recorded these **e-s** Esth 9:20
time for every **e** Eccl 3:1

EVERLASTING *eternal*
e covenant between Gen 9:16
the LORD, the **E** God Gen 21:33
are the **e** arms Deut 33:27
e to **e**, You are God Ps 90:2
lovingkindness is **e** Ps 106:1
From **e** I was Prov 8:23
The **E** God, the LORD Is 40:28
e name which will Is 56:5
LORD for an **e** light Is 60:20
loved you with an **e** Jer 31:3

EVIDENCE *facts, testimony*
the **e** of witnesses Num 35:30
on the **e** of two Deut 19:15
not able to give **e** Ezra 2:59
and giving **e** Acts 17:3

EVIDENT *obvious, plain*
the tares became **e** Matt 13:26
for God made it **e** Rom 1:19
work will become **e** 1 Cor 3:13
Law before God is **e** Gal 3:11
it is **e** that our Lord Heb 7:14

EVIL *bad, wicked, wrong*
man's heart is **e** Gen 8:21
keep...from every **e** Deut 23:9
discern good and **e** 2 Sam 14:17
rebellious and **e** city Ezra 4:12
I fear no **e** Ps 23:4
repay me **e** for good Ps 35:12
turn away from **e** Prov 3:7
run rapidly to **e** Prov 6:18
returns **e** for good Prov 17:13
taken away from **e** Is 57:1
committed two **e-s** Jer 2:13
deliver us from **e** Matt 6:13
what **e** has He Matt 27:23
If you then, being **e** Luke 11:13
who does **e** hates the John 3:20
Never...**e** for **e** Rom 12:17
love of money is...**e** 1 Tim 6:10
tongue...restless **e** James 3:8

EVILDOER *wicked one*
LORD repay the **e** 2 Sam 3:39
e-s will be cut off Ps 37:9
e listens to wicked Prov 17:4
Offspring of **e-s** Is 1:4
is godless and an **e** Is 9:17
depart...you **e-s** Luke 13:27
punishment of **e-s** 1 Pet 2:14

EVIL-MERODACH
king of Babylon 2 Kin 25:27; Jer 52:31

EWE *female sheep*
seven **e** lambs Gen 21:28
e lamb without Lev 14:10
poor man's **e** lamb 2 Sam 12:4
e-s with suckling Ps 78:71
like a flock of **e-s** Song 6:6

EXACT (adj) *certain, correct*
e amount of money Esth 4:7
e meaning of all this Dan 7:16
know the **e** truth Luke 1:4
a more **e** knowledge Acts 24:22

EXACT (v) *collect*
let him **e** a fifth Gen 41:34
he shall not **e** it Deut 15:2
He **e-ed** the silver 2 Kin 23:35
You are **e-ing** usury Neh 5:7
e a tribute of grain Amos 5:11

EXALT *extol, honor, lift*
He is highly **e-ed** Ex 15:1
e-ed be God 2 Sam 22:47
He is **e-ed** in power Job 37:23
let us **e** His name Ps 34:3
e-ed far above all gods Ps 97:9
city is **e-ed** Prov 11:11
my God; I will **e** You Is 25:1
E that which is low Ezek 21:26
humbles...be **e-ed** Matt 23:12
e-ed to...right hand Acts 2:33
be **e-ed** in my body Phil 1:20
He will **e** you James 4:10

EXAMINE *investigate, search*
That You **e** him every Job 7:18
E me, O LORD, and try Ps 26:2
e my heart's *attitude* Jer 12:3
e-ing the Scriptures Acts 17:11
e-d by scourging Acts 22:24
a man must **e** himself 1 Cor 11:28

EXAMPLE *model, pattern*
the **e** of his father 2 Chr 17:3
I gave you an **e** John 13:15
e of those who 1 Tim 4:12
e of disobedience Heb 4:11
be **e-s** to the flock 1 Pet 5:3
made them an **e** 2 Pet 2:6

EXCEL *be superior*
e in...wickedness Jer 5:28
wisdom **e-s** folly Eccl 2:13
you **e**...more 1 Thess 4:1

EXCELLENCE *perfection*
greatness of Your **e** Ex 15:7
are a woman of **e** Ruth 3:11
if there is any **e** Phil 4:8
proclaim the **e-ies** of 1 Pet 2:9

EXCELLENT *outstanding*
e wife is the crown Prov 12:4
E speech is not Prov 17:7
He has done **e** things Is 12:5
e governor Felix Acts 23:26
a still more **e** way 1 Cor 12:31
a more **e** name Heb 1:4

EXCESS *too much*
he...had no **e** Ex 16:18
are in **e** among them Num 3:48
same **e-es** of dissipation 1 Pet 4:4

EXCHANGE *trade, transfer*
shall **e** *it* for money Deut 14:25
they **e-d** their glory Ps 106:20
shall not sell or **e** Ezek 48:14
e-d the truth of God Rom 1:25

EXCLUDE *refuse to admit*
e-d from...assembly Ezra 10:8
e-d all foreigners Neh 13:3
e you for My name's Is 66:5
e-d from the life of Eph 4:18

EXCUSE *justification*
began to make **e-s** Luke 14:18
no **e** for their sin John 15:22
they are without **e** Rom 1:20

EXECUTE *carry out*
e-d the justice of Deut 33:21
He has **e-d** judgment Ps 9:16
e vengeance on the Ps 149:7
Lord will **e** His word Rom 9:28
e judgment upon all Jude 15

EXERCISE *perform*
man has **e-d** authority Eccl 8:9
e-s lovingkindness Jer 9:24
e authority over Matt 20:25
e-s self-control in all 1 Cor 9:25

EXHAUSTED *used up, wearied*
sound asleep and **e** Judg 4:21
too **e** to follow 1 Sam 30:21
of flour was not **e** 1 Kin 17:16
Their strength is **e** Jer 51:30

EXHORT *admonish, urge*
and kept on **e-ing** Acts 2:40
e, with...patience 2 Tim 4:2
e in sound doctrine Titus 1:9
e and reprove Titus 2:15
e-ing and testifying 1 Pet 5:12

EXHORTATION *urging*
with many other **e-s** Luke 3:18
given them much **e** Acts 20:2
who exhorts, in his **e** Rom 12:8
this word of **e** Heb 13:22

EXILE *banishment* or *capture*
Israel away into **e** 2 Kin 17:6
people of the **e** were Ezra 4:1
captivity of the **e-s** Neh 7:6
into **e** from Jerusalem Esth 2:6

e will soon be set free Is 51:14
Israel went into e Ezek 39:23

EXIST *be, live, occur*
they had never **e-ed** Obad 16
Strife **e-s** and Hab 1:3
live and move and **e** Acts 17:28
authority...which **e** Rom 13:1

EXODUS *departure*
e of...Israel Heb 11:22

EXPANSE *firmament, vastness*
e of the heavens Gen 1:20
e of the waters Job 37:10
in His mighty **e** Ps 150:1
from above the **e** Ezek 1:25

EXPECT *await*
never **e-ed** to see Gen 48:11
e-ed good, then evil Job 30:26
which we did not **e** Is 64:3
lend, **e-ing** nothing Luke 6:35

EXPECTATION *anticipation*
your **e** is false Job 41:9
e of the wicked Prov 10:28
to my earnest **e** Phil 1:20
e of judgment Heb 10:27

EXPECTED *awaited*
Are You the **E** One Matt 11:3
Are You the **E** One Luke 7:20

EXPERIENCE *undergo*
all who had not **e-d** Judg 3:1
Your people **e** hardship Ps 60:3
e-s Your judgments Is 26:9
e-d mockings and Heb 11:36

EXPERT *very skillful*
an **e** in warfare 2 Sam 17:8
be like an **e** warrior Jer 50:9
an **e** in all customs Acts 26:3

EXPLAIN *make clear*
no one who could **e** Gen 41:24
he did not **e** to her 2 Chr 9:2
e its interpretation Dan 5:7
E the parable to us Matt 15:15
e-ing the Scriptures Luke 24:32
e-ed to him the way Acts 18:26

EXPOSE *disclose, reveal*
shame...be **e-d** Is 47:3
He will **e** your sins Lam 4:22
deeds will be **e-d** John 3:20
would **e** their infants Acts 7:19
are **e-d** by the light Eph 5:13

EXTEND *enlarge, stretch out*
God **e-s**...border Deut 12:20
e-ed lovingkindness Ezra 7:28
e-s her hand to the Prov 31:20
I **e** peace to her Is 66:12
boundary shall **e** Ezek 47:17

EXTENT *amount* or *degree*
the **e** of my days Ps 39:4
e that you did it to Matt 25:40
such an **e** that Jesus Mark 1:45

EXTERMINATE *destroy*
planned to **e** us 2 Sam 21:5
He will **e** its sinners Is 13:9

EXTERNAL *outward*
not with **e** service Col 3:22
adornment must not be...**e** 1 Pet 3:3

EXTINGUISH *put out*
they will **e** my coal 2 Sam 14:7
not **e** the lamp of 2 Sam 21:17
my days are **e-ed** Job 17:1
when *I* **e** you Ezek 32:7
e all the flaming Eph 6:16

EXTOL *praise*
God, and I will **e** Him Ex 15:2
I will **e** You, O LORD Ps 30:1
I will **e** You, my God Ps 145:1
We will **e** your love Song 1:4

EXTORTION *stealing*
practicing...**e** Jer 22:17
practiced **e**, robbed Ezek 18:18

EXTRAORDINARY *exceptional*
will bring **e** plagues Deut 28:59
His **e** work Is 28:21
insight, and **e** wisdom Dan 5:14
e miracles by Acts 19:11
showed us **e** kindness Acts 28:2

EXULT *rejoice*
heart **e-s** in the LORD 1 Sam 2:1
Let the field **e** 1 Chr 16:32
e-ed when evil befell Job 31:29
let them **e** before God Ps 68:3
I will **e** in the LORD Hab 3:18
e in our tribulations Rom 5:3

EXULTATION *jubilation*
e like the nations Hos 9:1
joy or crown of **e** 1 Thess 2:19
may rejoice with **e** 1 Pet 4:13

EYE *sight*
e-s are dull from Gen 49:12
e for **e**, tooth for Ex 21:24
be as **e-s** for us Num 10:31
his **e** was not dim Deut 34:7
right in his own **e-s** Judg 17:6
open his **e-s** that he 2 Kin 6:17
e-s of the LORD 2 Chr 16:9
was **e-s** to the blind Job 29:15
e-s...look to You Ps 145:15
Haughty **e-s**, a lying Prov 6:17
e...mocks a father Prov 30:17
e is not satisfied Eccl 1:8
To open blind **e-s** Is 42:7
e-s will bitterly weep Jer 13:17
have **e-s** to see but Ezek 12:2
I lifted my **e-s** and Dan 8:3
Your **e-s**...too pure Hab 1:13
e for an **e**, and a Matt 5:38
e...you to stumble Matt 18:9
e is the lamp Luke 11:34
the clay to his **e-s** John 9:6
which **e** has not seen 1 Cor 2:9
e-s of your heart may Eph 1:18
e-s full of adultery 2 Pet 2:14
the lust of the **e-s** 1 John 2:16
God, who has **e-s** like Rev 2:18
His **e-s** *are* a flame Rev 19:12

EYEWITNESSES *observers*
e...of the word Luke 1:2
e of His majesty 2 Pet 1:16

EZEKIEL
Hebrew prophet Ezek 1:1
called by God Ezek 1:1,3
spoke to Israel Ezek 14:1ff
taken captive Ezek 33:21
spoke to false prophets Ezek 34:2ff
spoke to nations Ezek 35:2ff
restored temple Ezek 40:1ff

EZION-GEBER
on gulf of Aqabah 1 Kin 9:26;22:48
near Elath / Eloth Deut 2:8; 2 Chr 8:17

EZRA
priest Ezra 7:1-5
scribe Ezra 7:6
sent by king Ezra 7:14,21
brought exiles Ezra 8:1-14
Nehemiah's colleague Neh 8:2-6

F

FACE *countenance*
sweat of your **f** You Gen 3:19
Abram fell on his **f** Gen 17:3
speak to Moses **f** to **f** Ex 33:11
skin of his **f** shone Ex 34:30
make His **f** shine Num 6:25
hide Your **f** from me Ps 13:1
Who seek Your **f** Ps 24:6
His **f** to shine upon us Ps 67:1
f of Your anointed Ps 84:9
makes a cheerful **f** Prov 15:13
set My **f** against you Jer 44:11
had the **f** of an eagle Ezek 1:10
Each...had four **f-s** Ezek 10:21
fast...wash your **f** Matt 6:17
they spat in His **f** Matt 26:67
like the **f** of an angel Acts 6:15
natural **f** in a mirror James 1:23
His **f** was like the sun Rev 1:16

FACT *truth*
f may be confirmed Matt 18:16
are undeniable **f-s** Acts 19:36
f is to be confirmed 2 Cor 13:1

FACTIONS *divisions*
be **f** among you 1 Cor 11:19
dissensions, **f** Gal 5:20

FADE *wither*
it **f-s**, and withers Ps 90:6
people...**f** away Is 24:4
rich man...will **f** James 1:11
will not **f** away 1 Pet 1:4

FAIL *be spent* or *fall short*
He will not **f** you Deut 4:31
none of his words **f** 1 Sam 3:19
no man's heart **f** 1 Sam 17:32
not one word...**f-ed** 1 Kin 8:56
my strength **f-s** me Ps 38:10
the olive should **f** Hab 3:17
faith may not **f** Luke 22:32
Love never **f-s** 1 Cor 13:8

FAINT *languish, swoon*
has made my heart **f** Job 23:16
soul **f-ed** within Ps 107:5
grow **f** before Me Is 57:16
I was **f-ing** away Jon 2:7
men **f-ing** from fear Luke 21:26
f when...reproved Heb 12:5

FAINTHEARTED *weak*
Do not be **f** Deut 20:3
encourage the **f** 1 Thess 5:14

FAIR HAVENS
harbor in Crete Acts 27:8

FAITH *believe, trust*
because you broke **f** Deut 32:51
Will you have **f** Job 39:12
Who keeps **f** forever Ps 146:6
will live by his **f** Hab 2:4
Seeing their **f**, Jesus Matt 9:2
f the size of a mustard seed Matt 17:20
Your **f** has saved you Luke 7:50
Increase our **f** Luke 17:5
your **f** may not fail Luke 22:32
man full of **f** Acts 6:5
of **f** to the Gentiles Acts 14:27
sanctified by **f** in Me Acts 26:18
justified by **f** Rom 5:1
f...from hearing Rom 10:17
if I have all **f** 1 Cor 13:2
your **f** also is vain 1 Cor 15:14
we walk by **f** 2 Cor 5:7
live by **f** in the Son Gal 2:20
saved through **f** Eph 2:8
one Lord, one **f** Eph 4:5
joy in the **f** Phil 1:25
stability of your **f** Col 2:5
breastplate of **f** 1 Thess 5:8
for not all have **f** 2 Thess 3:2
fall away from the **f** 1 Tim 4:1
conduct, love, **f** 1 Tim 4:12
they upset the **f** 2 Tim 2:18
sound in the **f** Titus 1:13
showing all good **f** Titus 2:10
full assurance of **f** Heb 10:22
By **f** Enoch was taken Heb 11:5
perfecter of **f** Heb 12:2
ask in **f** James 1:6
prayer offered in **f** James 5:15

power of God...**f** 1 Pet 1:5
the **f** of the saints Rev 13:10

FAITHFUL *loyal, trustworthy*
the **f** God, who keeps Deut 7:9
raise...a **f** priest 1 Sam 2:35
heart **f** before You Neh 9:8
LORD preserves the **f** Ps 31:23
commandments...**f** Ps 119:86
the LORD who is **f** Is 49:7
Well done...**f** Matt 25:23
God is **f** 1 Cor 1:9
F is He who calls 1 Thess 5:24
He considered me **f** 1 Tim 1:12
entrust...to **f** men 2 Tim 2:2
souls to a **f** Creator 1 Pet 4:19
He is **f**...to forgive 1 John 1:9
Be **f** until death Rev 2:10
called **F** and True Rev 19:11

FAITHFULNESS *loyalty*
kindness and **f** Gen 47:29
A God of **f** Deut 32:4
make known Your **f** Ps 89:1
f to all generations Ps 100:5
and mercy and **f** Matt 23:23
nullify the **f** of God Rom 3:3
kindness, goodness, **f** Gal 5:22

FAITHLESS *unbelieving*
what **f** Israel did Jer 3:6
O **f** daughter Jer 31:22
Their heart is **f** Hos 10:2
If we are **f** 2 Tim 2:13

FALL *descend* or *fail*
deep sleep to **f** upon Gen 2:21
devices let them **f** Ps 5:10
I am ready to **f** Ps 38:17
dread...had **f-en** Ps 105:38
wicked will **f** Prov 11:5
a righteous man **f-s** Prov 24:16
whether a tree **f-s** Eccl 11:3
Assyrian will **f** Is 31:8
Babylon has **f-en** Jer 51:8
f down and worship Dan 3:5
will **f** into a pit Matt 15:14
f-ing on his knees Mark 1:40
all may **f**...I will Mark 14:29
appointed for the **f** Luke 2:34
watching Satan **f** Luke 10:18
house *divided*...**f-s** Luke 11:17
f-ing headlong Acts 1:18
sinned and **f** short Rom 3:23
have **f-en** asleep 1 Cor 15:6
f-en from grace Gal 5:4
rich **f** into temptation 1 Tim 6:9
rocks, **F** on us Rev 6:16

FALLOW *unproductive*
rest and lie **f** Ex 23:11
f ground of the poor Prov 13:23

FALSE *deceitful, dishonest*
not bear a **f** report Ex 23:1
I hate every **f** way Ps 119:104
But a **f** witness Prov 12:17
f witness will not go Prov 19:5
f scale is not good Prov 20:23
F and foolish *visions* Lam 2:14
And tell **f** dreams Zech 10:2
not bear **f** witness Matt 19:18
f Christs and **f** Matt 24:24
men are **f** apostles 2 Cor 11:13
the **f** circumcision Phil 3:2
and the **f** prophet Rev 20:10

FALSEHOOD *deception*
lifted up his soul to **f** Ps 24:4
delight in **f** Ps 62:4
I hate and despise **f** Ps 119:163
Bread obtained by **f** Prov 20:17
trusted in **f** Jer 13:25
prophesying **f** in My Jer 14:14
laying aside **f** Eph 4:25

FAME *greatness*
heard of Your **f** Num 14:15
Joshua, and his **f** Josh 6:27
the **f** of Solomon 1 Kin 10:1
heard My **f** Is 66:19
f in *the things of* 2 Cor 8:18

FAMILY *household, relatives*
f-ies from the ark Gen 8:19
all the **f-ies** of Gen 12:3
f may redeem him Lev 25:49
f-ies of the Levites Num 3:20
my **f** is the least Judg 6:15
f-ies like a flock Ps 107:41
God of all the **f-ies** Jer 31:1
f-ies of the earth Amos 3:2
every **f** in heaven Eph 3:15
upsetting whole **f-ies** Titus 1:11

FAMINE *shortage of food*
a **f** in the land Gen 12:10
seven years of **f** Gen 41:27
If there is **f** 2 Chr 6:28
In **f** He will redeem Job 5:20
keep them alive in **f** Ps 33:19
f and pestilence Jer 14:12
f and wild beasts Ezek 5:17
f-s and earthquakes Matt 24:7
plagues and **f-s** Luke 21:11
Now a **f** came Acts 7:11
mourning and **f** Rev 18:8

FAMISHED *hungry, parched*
for I am **f** Gen 25:30
strength is **f** Job 18:12
honorable men are **f** Is 5:13

FAMOUS *well-known*
f in Bethlehem Ruth 4:11
men of valor, **f** men 1 Chr 5:24

FAR *distant*
f from a false charge Ex 23:7
come from a **f** country Josh 9:6
Be not **f** from me Ps 22:11
f above all gods Ps 97:9
As **f** as the east Ps 103:12
LORD is **f** from the Prov 15:29
a God **f** off Jer 23:23
heart is **f** away from Matt 15:8
f from the kingdom Mark 12:34
glory **f** beyond all 2 Cor 4:17
f above all rule Eph 1:21

FARM *agricultural land*
consume the **f** land Amos 7:4
one to his own **f** Matt 22:5
or **f-s**, for My sake Mark 10:29

FARMER *husbandman*
Does the **f** plow Is 28:24
will be your **f-s** Is 61:5
f-s...put to shame Jer 14:4
the **f** to mourning Amos 5:16

FASHION *create, form*
f-ed into a woman Gen 2:22
f us in the womb Job 31:15
He who **f-s** the hearts Ps 33:15
f a graven image Is 44:9
I am **f-ing** calamity Jer 18:11

FAST (n) *food abstinence*
Proclaim a **f** 1 Kin 21:9
you call this a **f** Is 58:5
Consecrate a **f** Joel 1:14
f was already over Acts 27:9

FAST (v) *abstain from food*
and David **f-ed** 2 Sam 12:16
maidens also will **f** Esth 4:16
you **f** for contention Is 58:4
had **f-ed** forty days Matt 4:2
whenever you **f** Matt 6:16
disciples do not **f** Mark 2:18
I **f** twice a week Luke 18:12
had **f-ed** and prayed Acts 13:3

FASTING *food abstinence*
times of **f** Esth 9:31
weak from **f** Ps 109:24
noticed...when they are **f** Matt 6:16
by prayer and **f** Matt 17:21
Pharisees were **f** Mark 2:18

FAT *animal fat* or *obese*
f of the land Gen 45:18
shall not eat any **f** Lev 7:23
Go, eat of the **f** Neh 8:10
their body is **f** Ps 73:4
Good news puts **f** Prov 15:30

FATE *destiny*
appalled at his **f** Job 18:20
one **f** befalls them Eccl 2:14
f for the righteous Eccl 9:2
one **f** for all men Eccl 9:3

FATHER *God* or *parent*
leave his **f**...mother Gen 2:24
f of a multitude Gen 17:4
Honor your **f** Ex 20:12
who strikes his **f** Ex 21:15
iniquity of the **f-s** Deut 5:9
Is not He your **F** Deut 32:6
your **f-'s** instruction Prov 1:8
son makes a **f** glad Prov 10:1
Eternal **F**, Prince of Is 9:6
all have one **f** Mal 2:10
F who sees...in secret Matt 6:4
Our **F** who is in Matt 6:9
does the will of My **F** Matt 7:21
in My **F-'s** kingdom Matt 26:29
in the glory of His **F** Mark 8:38
be in my **F-'s** *house* Luke 2:49
F, hallowed be Your Luke 11:2
F, forgive them Luke 23:34
begotten from the **F** John 1:14
my **F-'s** house a John 2:16
F...testifies John 8:18
the **f** of lies John 8:44
I and the **F** are one John 10:30
In my **F-'s** house are John 14:2
F is the vinedresser John 15:1
ask the **F** for John 16:23
I ascend to My **F** John 20:17
one God and **F** of all Eph 4:6

FATHER-IN-LAW
she sent to her **f** Gen 38:25
returned to Jethro his **f** Ex 4:18
his **f**, the girl's Judg 19:4
f of Caiaphas John 18:13

FATHERLESS *orphan*
father of the **f** Ps 68:5
He supports the **f** Ps 146:9
fields of the **f** Prov 23:10
f and the widow Ezek 22:7

FATLING *young lamb* or *kid*
sacrificed...a **f** 2 Sam 6:13
f-s...in abundance 1 Kin 1:19
f-s of Bashan Ezek 39:18

FATNESS *abundance*
f of the earth Gen 27:28
Shall I leave my **f** Judg 9:9
satisfied as with...**f** Ps 63:5
eye bulges from **f** Ps 73:7

FAULT *error, offense*
found no **f** in him 1 Sam 29:3
let no one find **f** Hos 4:4
does He still find **f** Rom 9:19
grumblers, finding **f** Jude 16

FAVOR *kind regard*
Noah found **f** Gen 6:8
I will grant...**f** Ex 3:21
show no **f** to them Deut 7:2
Why have I found **f** Ruth 2:10
surround him with **f** Ps 5:12
showed **f** to Your land Ps 85:1
obtains **f**...LORD Prov 8:35
f is like a cloud Prov 16:15
found **f** with God Luke 1:30
in **f** with God and Luke 2:52
seeking the **f** of men Gal 1:10

FEAR (n) *awe, dread, reverence*
no **f** of God in Gen 20:11
f of the LORD is clean Ps 19:9
f...is the beginning Ps 111:10
afraid of sudden **f** Prov 3:25
f...prolongs life Prov 10:27
f of man brings a Prov 29:25
they cried out in **f** Matt 14:26
guards shook for **f** Matt 28:4
men fainting from **f** Luke 21:26
for **f** of the Jews John 7:13
no **f** of God before Rom 3:18
in weakness and in **f** 1 Cor 2:3
knowing the **f** of the 2 Cor 5:11

with **f** and trembling Eph 6:5
through **f** of death Heb 2:15
love casts out **f** 1 John 4:18

FEAR (v) *be afraid, revere*
the midwives **f-ed** God Ex 1:21
Moses said...Do not **f** Ex 14:13
may learn to **f** Me Deut 4:10
not **f** other gods 2 Kin 17:37
I **f** no evil Ps 23:4
Whom shall I **f** Ps 27:1
not **f** evil tidings Ps 112:7
who **f-s** the LORD Prov 31:30
Rather, **f** God Eccl 5:7
Take courage, **f** not Is 35:4
Do not **f**, for I am Is 41:10
will **f** and tremble Jer 33:9
do not **f** them Matt 10:26
f-ed the crowd Matt 14:5
who did not **f** God Luke 18:2
slavery leading to **f** Rom 8:15
I **f** for you Gal 4:11
let us **f** if Heb 4:1

FEARFUL *terrifying*
it is a **f** thing Ex 34:10
were **f** and amazed Luke 8:25
will be **f** *of sinning* 1 Tim 5:20

FEAST *celebration*
a **f** to the LORD Ex 12:14
godless jesters at a **f** Ps 35:16
hate...appointed **f-s** Is 1:14
and cheerful **f-s** Zech 8:19
refuse of your **f-s** Mal 2:3
a wedding **f** Matt 22:2
seeking Him at the **f** John 7:11
celebrate the **f** 1 Cor 5:8
f with you without Jude 12

FEASTS
1 **Feast of Booths** Lev 23:24; Deut 16:16; 2 Chr 8:13
also **Feast of Ingathering**
2 **Feast of Dedication** John 10:22
3 **Feast of Harvest** Ex 23:16
also **Feast of Weeks**
also **Feast of Pentecost**
4 **Feast of Ingathering** Ex 23:16
also **Feast of Booths**
5 **Feast of Passover** Ex 34:25; Luke 2:41
6 **Feast of Unleavened Bread** Ex 23:15; Luke 22:1
7 **Feast of Weeks** Ex 34:22; Deut 16:10,16
also **Feast of Harvest**
also **Feast of Pentecost**
8 **Feast of Pentecost** Acts 2:1; 20:16; 1 Cor 16:8
also **Feast of Harvest**
also **Feast of Weeks**

FEEBLE *weak*
when the flock was **f** Gen 30:42
What are these **f** Jews Neh 4:2
strengthen the **f** Is 35:3
knees that are **f** Heb 12:12

FEED *eat, supply*
fed you with manna Deut 8:3
f him sparingly 1 Kin 22:27
F me with the food Prov 30:8
He **f-s** on ashes Is 44:20
f you on knowledge Jer 3:15
He **fed** me this scroll Ezek 3:2
I will **f** My flock Ezek 34:15
dogs **f** on the Matt 15:27
hungry, and **f** You Matt 25:37
fed...the *crumbs* Luke 16:21
enemy is hungry, **f** Rom 12:20

FEEL *sense, touch*
I may **f** you, my son Gen 27:21
Isaac...**felt** him and Gen 27:22
Let me **f** the pillars Judg 16:26
He **felt** compassion Matt 9:36
she **felt**...was healed Mark 5:29
Jesus **felt** a love for Mark 10:21
f-ing a sense of awe Acts 2:43
f sensual desires 1 Tim 5:11

FELIX
Roman procurator
Acts 23:26;24:25;25:14

FELL *collapse, come upon*
wall **f** down flat Josh 6:20
fire of the LORD **f** 1 Kin 18:38
the lot **f** on Jonah Jon 1:7
seeds **f** beside the Matt 13:4
He **f** asleep Luke 8:23
he **f** to the ground Acts 9:4
Holy Spirit **f** upon Acts 10:44
star **f** from heaven Rev 8:10

FELLOW *companion*
oil of joy above Your **f-s** Ps 45:7
your **f** exiles Ezek 11:15
beat his **f** slaves Matt 24:49
f heirs with Christ Rom 8:17
f citizens with the Eph 2:19
Gentiles are **f** heirs Eph 3:6
brother and **f** worker Phil 2:25
f worker in the 1 Thess 3:2
I am a **f** servant of Rev 22:9

FELLOWSHIP *companionship*
had sweet **f** together Ps 55:14
f...Holy Spirit 2 Cor 13:14
right hand of **f** Gal 2:9
f of His sufferings Phil 3:10
f is with the Father 1 John 1:3
f with one another 1 John 1:7

FEMALE *girl, woman*
and **f** He created Gen 1:27
a **f** slave Ex 21:7
f from the flock Lev 5:6
likeness of male or **f** Deut 4:16
neither male nor **f** Gal 3:28

FERTILE *productive*
a **f** land Neh 9:25
the **f** valley Is 28:4
in **f** soil Ezek 17:5

FERVENT *ardent*
being **f** in spirit Acts 18:25
f in spirit, serving Rom 12:11
keep **f** in your love 1 Pet 4:8

FESTIVAL *celebration*
celebrate a great **f** Neh 8:12
I reject your **f-s** Amos 5:21
turn your **f-s** into Amos 8:10
during the **f**, otherwise Matt 26:5

FESTUS, PORCIUS
Roman procurator of Judea
Acts 24:27;25:14,23;26:25

FETTERS *chains*
your feet put in **f** 2 Sam 3:34
they are bound in **f** Job 36:8
tear their **f** apart Ps 2:3
with **f** of iron Ps 149:8

FEVER *inflammation*
bones burn with **f** Job 30:30
in bed with a **f** Matt 8:14
from a high **f** Luke 4:38
He rebuked the **f** Luke 4:39
the **f** left him John 4:52

FIELD *productive land*
hail struck...the **f** Ex 9:25
let me go to the **f** Ruth 2:2
glean in another **f** Ruth 2:8
f of the sluggard Prov 24:30
Zion...plowed *as* a **f** Jer 26:18
the lilies of the **f** Matt 6:28
the **f** is the world Matt 13:38
shepherds...in the **f-s** Luke 2:8
Two men...in the **f** Luke 17:36
f-s...white for John 4:35
F of Blood Acts 1:19

FIERCE *violent*
anger, for it is **f** Gen 49:7
Wrath is **f** Prov 27:4
see a **f** people Is 33:19
a **f** gale of wind Mark 4:37
scorched with **f** heat Rev 16:9
f wrath of God Rev 19:15

FIERCENESS *intensity*
f of His anger Josh 7:26
the **f** of battle Is 42:25

FIERY *burning*
LORD sent **f** serpents Num 21:6
with **f** heat Deut 28:22
His arrows **f** shafts Ps 7:13
f ordeal among you 1 Pet 4:12

FIG *fruit*
they sewed **f** leaves Gen 3:7
But the **f** tree said Judg 9:11
a piece of **f** cake 1 Sam 30:12
nor **f-s** from thistles Matt 7:16
the **f** tree withered Matt 21:19
f-s from thorns Luke 6:44
under the **f** tree John 1:48
Can a **f** tree James 3:12

FIGHT *struggle*
Hebrews were **f-ing** Ex 2:13
LORD will **f** for you Ex 14:14
fought for Israel Josh 10:14
stars **fought** from Judg 5:20
and **f** our battles 1 Sam 8:20
f for your brothers Neh 4:14
f-ing against God Acts 5:39
fought the good **f** 2 Tim 4:7
so you **f** and quarrel James 4:2

FIGURATIVE *metaphorical*
in **f** language John 16:25

FIGURE *shape, type*
f-s resembling four Ezek 1:5
f...of a man Ezek 1:26
using a **f** of speech John 16:29

FILIGREE *ornamental work*
f *settings* of gold Ex 28:13
cords on the two **f** Ex 28:25

FILL (n) *satisfaction*
eat your **f** Lev 25:19
They drink their **f** Ps 36:8
drink our **f** of love Prov 7:18
its **f** of their blood Jer 46:10

FILL (v) *make full*
and **f** the earth Gen 1:28
f-ed with violence Gen 6:11
Can you **f** his skin Job 41:7
was **f-ing** with smoke Is 6:4
I am **f-ed** with power Mic 3:8
hall was **f-ed** Matt 22:10
God of hope **f** you Rom 15:13

FILTHINESS *disgustingly foul*
not washed...his **f** Prov 30:12
your **f** is lewdness Ezek 24:13
no **f** and silly talk Eph 5:4
putting aside all **f** James 1:21

FILTHY *offensive*
are full of **f** vomit Is 28:8
like a **f** garment Is 64:6
clothed...**f** garments Zech 3:3
Let...the one who is **f** Rev 22:11

FIND *discover, uncover*
not **found** a helper Gen 2:20
But Noah **found** favor Gen 6:8
sin will **f** you out Num 32:23
that you may **f** rest Ruth 1:9
he who **f-s** me **f-s** life Prov 8:35
who **f-s** a wife **f-s** Prov 18:22
f gladness and joy Is 35:10
few who **f** it Matt 7:14
has **found** his life Matt 10:39
f rest for your souls Matt 11:29
f-ing one pearl Matt 13:46
f a colt tied Mark 11:2
found...sleeping Mark 14:40
seek, and you will **f** Luke 11:9
found the Messiah John 1:41
was **found** worthy Rev 5:4

FINGER *part of hand*
the **f** of God Ex 8:19
dip his **f** in the blood Lev 4:6
six **f-s** on each 2 Sam 21:20
twenty-four **f-s** and 1 Chr 20:6
tip of his **f** in water Luke 16:24
with His **f** wrote John 8:6
Reach here with your **f** John 20:27

FINISH *complete*
Moses **f-ed** the work Ex 40:33
Solomon **f-ed** the 2 Chr 7:11
It is **f-ed** John 19:30
I may **f** my course Acts 20:24
f doing it also 2 Cor 8:11
wrath of God is **f-ed** Rev 15:1

FINS *part of fish*
that have **f** and scales Lev 11:9
anything that has **f** Deut 14:9

FIR *tree, wood*
instruments...of **f** 2 Sam 6:5
He plants a **f** Is 44:14

FIRE *burning or flame*
the **f** and the knife Gen 22:6
bush...burning with **f** Ex 3:2
pillar of **f** by night Ex 13:21
offered strange **f** Num 3:4
f of the LORD fell 1 Kin 18:38
a chariot of **f** 2 Kin 2:11
jealousy burn like **f** Ps 79:5
Israel will become a **f** Is 10:17
Is not My word like **f** Jer 23:29
the Holy Spirit and **f** Matt 3:11
with unquenchable **f** Matt 3:12
tongues as of **f** Acts 2:3
lake that burns with **f** Rev 21:8

FIREBRAND *burning wood*
who throws **F-s** Prov 26:18
you were like a **f** Amos 4:11

FIREPAN *used in worship*
a **f** full of coals Lev 16:12
the **f-s** of pure gold 2 Chr 4:22

FIRM *establish, steadfast*
his bow remained **f** Gen 49:24
stood **f** on dry ground Josh 3:17
making my footsteps **f** Ps 40:2
He made **f** the skies Prov 8:28
stand **f** in the faith 1 Cor 16:13
f foundation of God 2 Tim 2:19
hope **f** until the end Heb 3:6

FIRST *number*
f fruits of your labors Ex 23:16
f of all your produce Prov 3:9
seek **f** His kingdom Matt 6:33
f take the log out Matt 7:5
f will be last Matt 19:30
f called Christians Acts 11:26
to the Jew **f** Rom 2:10
f fruits of the Spirit Rom 8:23
He **f** loved us 1 John 4:19
I am the **f** and the Rev 1:17
left your **f** love Rev 2:4
f things have passed Rev 21:4

FIRSTBORN *oldest*
Sidon, his **f** Gen 10:15
the **f** bore a son Gen 19:37
I am Esau your **f** Gen 27:19
LORD killed every **f** Ex 13:15
birth to her **f** son Luke 2:7
church of the **f** Heb 12:23
f of the dead Rev 1:5

FIRST GATE
see **GATES OF JERUSALEM**

FISH
rule over the **f** Gen 1:26
Their **f** stink Is 50:2
a great **f** to swallow Jon 1:17
loaves and two **f** Matt 14:17
snake instead of a **f** Luke 11:11
net *full* of **f** John 21:8

FISH GATE
see **GATES OF JERUSALEM**

FISHERMEN *fishers*
f will lament Is 19:8
for they were **f** Matt 4:18
the **f** had gotten out Luke 5:2

FISHERS *fishermen*
make you **f** of men Matt 4:19
become **f** of men Mark 1:17

FIT *be suitable, worthy*
f to remove His Matt 3:11
f for the kingdom Luke 9:62
not **f** to be...apostle 1 Cor 15:9
body, being **f-ted** Eph 4:16
f-ting in the Lord Col 3:18

FIX *make firm, secure*
I will **f** your boundary Ex 23:31
f-ed her hope on God 1 Tim 5:5
f-ing...eyes on Jesus Heb 12:2
f your hope 1 Pet 1:13

FIXED *established*
the **f** festivals 1 Chr 23:31
f order of the moon Jer 31:35
is a great chasm **f** Luke 16:26

FLAME *fire*
ascended in the **f** Judg 13:20
f...the wicked Ps 106:18
f of the LORD Song 8:6
his Holy One a **f** Is 10:17
crackling of a **f** Joel 2:5
f of a burning thorn Acts 7:30
eyes *are* a **f** of fire Rev 19:12

FLAMING *burning*
the **f** sword Gen 3:24
f fire by night Is 4:5
eyes were like **f** Dan 10:6
angels in **f** fire 2 Thess 1:7

FLASH *reflect, sparkle*
why do your eyes **f** Job 15:12
lightning was **f-ing** Ezek 1:13
Polished to **f** like Ezek 21:10
He who **f-es** forth Amos 5:9
light suddenly **f-ed** Acts 22:6

FLASK *utensil*
take this **f** of oil 2 Kin 9:1
took oil in **f-s** Matt 25:4

FLATTER
Nor **f** *any* man Job 32:21
f with their tongue Ps 5:9
adulteress who **f-s** Prov 2:16
who **f-s** his neighbor Prov 29:5

FLAX *plant*
the **f** was in bud Ex 9:31
looks for wool and **f** Prov 31:13
made from combed **f** Is 19:9

FLEE *escape, run away*
arise, **f** to Haran Gen 27:43
F *as* a bird Ps 11:1
f from Your presence Ps 139:7
rulers have **fled** Is 22:3
f to Egypt Matt 2:13
left Him and **fled** Matt 26:56
fled from the tomb Mark 16:8
f from idolatry 1 Cor 10:14
f from youthful lusts 2 Tim 2:22
and heaven **fled** Rev 20:11

FLEECE *wool*
put a **f** of wool Judg 6:37
dry only on the **f** Judg 6:39
warmed with the **f** Job 31:20

FLEET *group of ships*
Solomon...built a **f** 1 Kin 9:26
sent...with the **f** 1 Kin 9:27

FLESH *body, meat*
f of my **f** Gen 2:23
shall become one **f** Gen 2:24
from my **f** I shall see Job 19:26
heart and my **f** sing Ps 84:2
All **f** is grass Is 40:6
the **f** is weak Matt 26:41
spirit...not have **f** Luke 24:39
the Word became **f** John 1:14
born of the **f** is **f** John 3:6
who eats My **f** John 6:56
children of the **f** Rom 9:8
thorn in the **f** 2 Cor 12:7
desires of the **f** Eph 2:3
polluted by the **f** Jude 23
filled with their **f** Rev 19:21

FLESHLY *carnal*
not in **f** wisdom 2 Cor 1:12
His **f** body Col 1:22
abstain from **f** lusts 1 Pet 2:11

FLIES *insects*
sent...swarms of **f** Ps 78:45
swarm of **f** *And* gnats Ps 105:31
Dead **f** make a Eccl 10:1

FLIGHT *departure*
F will perish from Amos 2:14
f will not be in Matt 24:20
foreign armies to **f** Heb 11:34

FLINT *stone*
Zipporah took a **f** Ex 4:25
f into a fountain Ps 114:8
hoofs...seem like **f** Is 5:28
emery harder than **f** Ezek 3:9
hearts *like* **f** Zech 7:12

FLOCK *goats, sheep*
a keeper of **f-s** Gen 4:2
water their father's **f** Ex 2:16
Your people like a **f** Ps 77:20
He will tend His **f** Is 40:11
scattered My **f** Jer 23:2
over their **f** by night Luke 2:8
will become one **f** John 10:16
f of God among you 1 Pet 5:2

FLOOD *overflowing of water*
I am bringing the **f** Gen 6:17
f came upon the earth Gen 7:17
end...with a **f** Dan 9:26
the **f-s** came Matt 7:25
f...destroyed Luke 17:27

FLOOR *ground, level*
threshing **f** of Atad Gen 50:11
go down to the...**f** Ruth 3:3
the **f**...with gold 1 Kin 6:30
f-s...full of grain Joel 2:24
His threshing **f** Matt 3:12
fell...from the third **f** Acts 20:9

FLOUR *ground grain*
measures of fine **f** Gen 18:6
only a handful of **f** 1 Kin 17:12
f...not exhausted 1 Kin 17:16

FLOURISH *blossom, thrive*
may the righteous **f** Ps 72:7
who did iniquity **f-ed** Ps 92:7
your bones will **f** Is 66:14
make the dry tree **f** Ezek 17:24

FLOW *pour forth*
river **f-ed** out of Eden Gen 2:10
f-ing with milk and Ex 3:8
eyelids **f** with water Jer 9:18
hills will **f** with milk Joel 3:18
f of her blood Mark 5:29
f...living water John 7:38

FLOWER *blossom*
As a **f** of the field Ps 103:15
f-s have *already* Song 2:12
to the fading **f** Is 28:1
glory like the **f** 1 Pet 1:24

FLUTE *musical instrument*
tambourine, **f**, and 1 Sam 10:5
playing on **f-s** 1 Kin 1:40
the **f** or on the harp 1 Cor 14:7
musicians...**f-players** Rev 18:22

FLY *soar*
let birds **f** above Gen 1:20
a raven, and it **flew** Gen 8:7
As sparks **f** upward Job 5:7
f-ies away like a dream Job 20:8
glory will **f** away Hos 9:11
heard an eagle **f-ing** Rev 8:13
the birds which **f** Rev 19:17

FOAL *colt*
ties *his* **f** to the vine Gen 49:11
f of a wild donkey Job 11:12
f of a beast of burden Matt 21:5

FODDER *animal food*
give his donkey f Gen 42:27
eat salted f Is 30:24

FOE *enemy*
before your f-s 1 Chr 21:12
A f and an enemy Esth 7:6
iniquity of my f-s Ps 49:5
the evil to my f-s Ps 54:5
avenge...His f-s Jer 46:10

FOLD *animal pen*
goats out of your f-s Ps 50:9
the peaceful f-s Jer 25:37
cut off from the f Hab 3:17
not of this f John 10:16

FOLLOW *imitate, pursue*
not f other gods Deut 6:14
turn back from f-ing Ruth 1:16
f the LORD your God 1 Sam 12:14
who f...wickedness Ps 119:150
bloodshed f-s Hos 4:2
He said to them, F Matt 4:19
left...and f-ed Matt 4:20
his cross, and f Me Matt 16:24
crowd was f-ing Mark 5:24
and they f Me John 10:27
Peter...f-ing Jesus John 18:15
f-ing after...lusts Jude 16
ones who f the Lamb Rev 14:4

FOLLOWERS *disciples*
His f...*began* asking Mark 4:10

FOLLY *foolishness*
this act of f Judg 19:23
of fools spouts f Prov 15:2
F is joy to him Prov 15:21
devising of f is sin Prov 24:9

FOOD *bread, meat*
shall be f for you Gen 1:29
tree was good for f Gen 3:6
in giving them f Ruth 1:6
tears have been my f Ps 42:3
it is deceptive f Prov 23:3
his f was locusts Matt 3:4
life more than f Matt 6:25
f is to do the will John 4:34
My flesh is true f John 6:55
milk...not solid f 1 Cor 3:2

FOOL *unwise person*
The f has said in his Ps 14:1
F-s despise wisdom Prov 1:7
too exalted for a f Prov 24:7
f multiplies words Eccl 10:14
The prophet is a f Hos 9:7
says, You f Matt 5:22
f-s and blind men Matt 23:17
wise, they became f-s Rom 1:22
f-s for Christ's sake 1 Cor 4:10

FOOLISH *silly, unwise*
O f and unwise Deut 32:6
a f son is a grief Prov 10:1
False and f *visions* Lam 2:14
Woe to the f Ezek 13:3
f took their lamps Matt 25:3
O f men and slow Luke 24:25
he must become f 1 Cor 3:18
You f Galatians Gal 3:1
do not be f Eph 5:17

FOOLISHNESS *folly*
The naive inherit f Prov 14:18
folly of fools is f Prov 14:24
mouth is speaking f Is 9:17
f of God is wiser 1 Cor 1:25
is f before God 1 Cor 3:19

FOOT *part of body*
she lay at his feet Ruth 3:14
six toes on each f 2 Sam 21:20
pierced...my feet Ps 22:16
the f of pride Ps 36:11
lamp to my feet Ps 119:105
their feet run to evil Prov 1:16
signals with his feet Prov 6:13
beautiful...your feet Song 7:1
feet of the afflicted Is 26:6
feet...polished bronze Dan 10:6
dust off your feet Matt 10:14
Bind...hand and f Matt 22:13
f causes you to Mark 9:45
kissing His feet Luke 7:38
anointed the feet John 12:3
the disciples' feet John 13:5
beautiful...the feet Rom 10:15
Satan under...feet Rom 16:20
worship at the feet Rev 22:8

FOOTSTEPS *path*
make His f into a way Ps 85:13
f of Your anointed Ps 89:51
my f in Your word Ps 119:133

FOOTSTOOL *foot support*
the f of our God 1 Chr 28:2
worship at His f Ps 99:5
Your enemies a f Ps 110:1
the earth is My f Is 66:1
sit down by my f James 2:3

FORBEARANCE *restraint*
By f...be persuaded Prov 25:15
in the f of God Rom 3:25

FORBID *prohibit*
if her father should f Num 30:5
f-ding to pay taxes Luke 23:2
do not f to speak 1 Cor 14:39
men who f marriage 1 Tim 4:3
he f-s those who 3 John 10

FORCE (n) *power, strength*
with a heavy f Num 20:20
captains of the f-s 2 Kin 25:23
use f against you Neh 13:21
commanders of the f-s Jer 43:5
with f and with Ezek 34:4

FORCE (v) *compel*
are f-d into bondage Neh 5:5
man f-d to labor Job 7:1
f-s you to go one mile Matt 5:41
not take...by f Luke 3:14
f them to blaspheme Acts 26:11
f-d to appeal to Acts 28:19

FORCED LABOR *work as tax*
Canaanites to f Josh 17:13
was over the f 2 Sam 20:24
will be put to f Prov 12:24

FORCED LABORERS
Solomon levied f 1 Kin 5:13
Solomon raised as f 2 Chr 8:8
men will become f Is 31:8

FORD *shallow place*
the f of the Jabbok Gen 32:22
the f-s of the Jordan Judg 12:5
f-s...been seized Jer 51:32

FOREFATHER *ancestor*
iniquity of their f-s Lev 26:40
Your first f sinned Is 43:27
I swore to your f-s Jer 11:5
Abraham, our f Rom 4:1
the way my f-s did 2 Tim 1:3

FOREHEAD *brow*
on his bald f Lev 13:42
stone...into his f 1 Sam 17:49
put a mark on the f-s Ezek 9:4
seal of God on their f-s Rev 9:4
on her f a name Rev 17:5

FOREIGN *alien, strange*
Put away the f gods Gen 35:2
sojourner in a f land Ex 2:22
sell her to a f people Ex 21:8
drank f waters 2 Kin 19:24
married f women Ezra 10:2
f armies to flight Heb 11:34

FOREIGNER *alien, stranger*
no f is to eat of it Ex 12:43
sell it to a f Deut 14:21
charge...a f Deut 23:20
since I am a f Ruth 2:10
a f in their sight Job 19:15
f-s entered his gate Obad 11

FOREKNEW *know beforehand*
whom He f, He also Rom 8:29
people whom he f Rom 11:2
He was foreknown 1 Pet 1:20

FOREKNOWLEDGE
plan and f of God Acts 2:23
f of God the Father 1 Pet 1:2

FOREMOST *first*
f commandment Matt 22:38
among whom I am f 1 Tim 1:15

FORERUNNER *goes before*
Jesus...as a f for Heb 6:20

FORESKIN
the flesh of your f Gen 17:11
cut off her son's f Ex 4:25
a hundred f-s 1 Sam 18:25
the f-s of your heart Jer 4:4

FOREST *woods*
f devoured more 2 Sam 18:8
the f of Lebanon 1 Kin 7:2
f will sing for joy 1 Chr 16:33
every beast of the f Ps 50:10
the glory of his f Is 10:18
beasts in the f, Come Is 56:9
a f is set aflame James 3:5

FORETOLD *predicted*
the Holy Spirit f Acts 1:16
just as Isaiah f Rom 9:29

FOREVER *always, eternal*
eat, and live f Gen 3:22
not strive with man f Gen 6:3
throne shall be...f 1 Chr 17:14
the LORD abides f Ps 9:7
LORD sits as King f Ps 29:10
glorify Your name f Ps 86:12
riches are not f Prov 27:24
One Who lives f Is 57:15
Christ is to remain f John 12:34
He...with you f John 14:16
He is able...to save f Heb 7:25
Son, made perfect f Heb 7:28
they will reign f Rev 22:5

FORFEIT *lose*
possessions...f-ed Ezra 10:8
f-s his own life Prov 20:2
f my head to the king Dan 1:10
and f-s his soul Matt 16:26

FORGET *forsake, neglect*
God has made me f Gen 41:51
that you do not f the LORD Deut 6:12
f-got the God who Deut 32:18
God f-s...iniquity Job 11:6
nations who f God Ps 9:17
needy...be f-gotten Ps 9:18
Do not f the afflicted Ps 10:12
They f-got His deeds Ps 78:11
do not f my teaching Prov 3:1
you will f the shame Is 54:4
My people f My name Jer 23:27
f-ting what *lies* behind Phil 3:13
f your work and Heb 6:10

FORGIVE *pardon*
f the transgression Gen 50:17
f their sin Ex 32:32
f our sins Ps 79:9
not f their iniquity Jer 18:23
f us our debts Matt 6:12
authority...to f sins Matt 9:6
f-gave him the debt Matt 18:27
can f sins but God Mark 2:7
he who is f-n little Luke 7:47
Father, f them Luke 23:34
whom you f 2 Cor 2:10
f-ing each other Eph 4:32
f-n us all our Col 2:13
righteous to f us 1 John 1:9

FORGIVENESS *pardon*
a God of f Neh 9:17
there is f with You Ps 130:4
poured out...for f Matt 26:28
repentance for f Luke 24:47
receives f of sins Acts 10:43
f of our trespasses Eph 1:7
the f of sins Col 1:14
there is no f Heb 9:22

FORK *instrument*
a three-pronged **f** 1 Sam 2:13
His winnowing **f** Matt 3:12

FORM (n) *appearance, shape*
beautiful of **f** and Gen 29:17
the **f** of the LORD Num 12:8
image in the **f** Deut 4:23
like the **f** of a man Is 44:13
in a different **f** Mark 16:12
bodily **f** like a dove Luke 3:22
f of corruptible man Rom 1:23
existed in the **f** of God Phil 2:6

FORM (v) *fashion, shape*
f-ed man of dust Gen 2:7
f-ed the dry land Ps 95:5
f-ed my inward parts Ps 139:13
One **f-ing** light Is 45:7
who **f-s** mountains Amos 4:13
f-s the spirit of man Zech 12:1
plot was **f-ed** against Acts 20:3
Christ is **f-ed** in you Gal 4:19

FORMATION *rank*
in **f** against 1 Chr 19:17
battle **f** in the 2 Chr 14:10

FORMLESS *without form*
earth was **f** and void Gen 1:2
behold, *it was* **f** Jer 4:23

FORNICATION
f-s, thefts, false Matt 15:19
were not born of **f** John 8:41
strangled and from **f** Acts 15:29

FORNICATORS
neither **f,** nor 1 Cor 6:9
f...God will judge Heb 13:4

FORSAKE
Then he **f-sook** God Deut 32:15
not fail you or **f** you Josh 1:5
f-sook the law of the 2 Chr 12:1
f Him, He will **f** you 2 Chr 15:2
God has not **f-n** us Ezra 9:9
why have You **f-n** me Ps 22:1
not **f** your mother's Prov 1:8
wicked **f** his way Is 55:7
Your sons have **f-n** Me Jer 5:7
f the idols of Egypt Ezek 20:8
have You **f-n** Me Matt 27:46
persecuted...not **f-n** 2 Cor 4:9
f-ing...assembling Heb 10:25
nor will I ever **f** you Heb 13:5

FORTIFICATIONS *stronghold*
the unassailable **f** Is 25:12
your **f** are fig trees Nah 3:12

FORTIFIED *walled*
live in the **f** cities Num 32:17
f with high walls Deut 3:5
strike every **f** city 2 Kin 3:19
f cities into Is 37:26

FORTRESS *stronghold*
God is my strong **f** 2 Sam 22:33
my rock and my **f** Ps 18:2
My refuge and my **f** Ps 91:2
wealth is his **f** Prov 10:15
f-es will be destroyed Hos 10:14

FORTUNE *one's lot*
and the **f-s** of Israel Jer 33:7
f-s of My people Hos 6:11
restore their **f** Zeph 2:7

FORTY *number*
f days and **f** nights Gen 7:4
flood...for **f** days Gen 7:17
ate the manna **f** years Ex 16:35
with the LORD **f** days Ex 34:28
fasted **f** days and **f** Matt 4:2
f days being tempted Mark 1:13

FOUL *putrid, rotten*
Nile will become **f** Ex 7:18
My wounds grow **f** Ps 38:5
f with your feet Ezek 34:19

FOUNDATION *establishment*
f-s of heaven were 2 Sam 22:8
I laid the **f** of the Job 38:4
the **f** of His throne Ps 97:2
the earth upon its **f-s** Ps 104:5
an everlasting **f** Prov 10:25
cornerstone *for* the **f** Is 28:16
a **f** on the rock Luke 6:48
the firm **f** of God 2 Tim 2:19
laid the **f** Heb 1:10
a **f** of repentance Heb 6:1

FOUNDATION GATE
see **GATES OF JERUSALEM**

FOUNDED *established*
the day it was **f** Ex 9:18
f it upon the seas Ps 24:2
by wisdom **f** the earth Prov 3:19
f His vaulted dome Amos 9:6
f on the rock Matt 7:25

FOUNTAIN *spring, well*
f-s of the great deep Gen 7:11
is the **f** of life Ps 36:9
The **f** of wisdom Prov 18:4
f of living waters Jer 2:13

FOUNTAIN GATE
see **GATES OF JERUSALEM**

FOWL *bird*
and fattened **f** 1 Kin 4:23
things and winged **f** Ps 148:10

FOX *small animal*
three hundred **f-es** Judg 15:4
f-es that are ruining Song 2:15
like **f-es** among ruins Ezek 13:4
The **f-es** have holes Matt 8:20
Go and tell that **f** Luke 13:32

FRAGMENTS *pieces*
forth His ice as **f** Ps 147:17
Gather up the...**f** John 6:12
twelve baskets with **f** John 6:13

FRAGRANCE *pleasant aroma*
oils have a pleasing **f** Song 1:3
given forth *their* **f** Song 2:13
f like *the cedars* Hos 14:6
we are a **f** of Christ 2 Cor 2:15

FRAME *structure*
f-s of the tabernacle Num 3:36
with *artistic* **f-s** 1 Kin 6:4
He...knows our **f** Ps 103:14
My **f** was not hidden Ps 139:15

FRANKINCENSE *spice*
spices with pure **f** Ex 30:34
f and the spices 1 Chr 9:29
trees of **f** Song 4:14
gold, **f,** and myrrh Matt 2:11

FREE *at liberty*
she is not to go **f** Ex 21:7
be **f** from the oath Josh 2:20
let the oppressed go **f** Is 58:6
will make you **f** John 8:32
who has died is **f-d** Rom 6:7
the **f** gift of God Rom 6:23
f from the law Rom 8:2
Christ set us **f** Gal 5:1
whether slave or **f** Eph 6:8

FREEDOM *liberty*
proclaim...**f** to Is 61:1
f of the glory Rom 8:21
you were called to **f** Gal 5:13
do not use your **f** as 1 Pet 2:16

FREEWILL OFFERINGS
see **OFFERINGS**

FRESH *new, recently prepared*
found a **f** jawbone Judg 15:15
anointed with **f** oil Ps 92:10
f water from your Prov 5:15
new wine into **f** Mark 2:22
f and bitter *water* James 3:11

FRIEND *companion, comrade*
man speaks to his **f** Ex 33:11
f-s are my scoffers Job 16:20
loved ones and my **f-s** Ps 38:11
my familiar **f** Ps 55:13
A **f** loves at all Prov 17:17
Wealth adds...**f-s** Prov 19:4
who blesses his **f** Prov 27:14
confidence in a **f** Mic 7:5
f of tax collectors Matt 11:19
F, your sins are Luke 5:20
f of the bridegroom John 3:29
his life for his **f-s** John 15:13
You are My **f-s,** if John 15:14

FRIENDSHIP
the **f** of God Job 29:4
f with the world James 4:4

FRIGHTEN *terrify*
to **f** *them* away Deut 28:26
You **f** me Job 7:14
I was **f-ed** and fell Dan 8:17
wars, do not be **f-ed** Mark 13:7

FRINGE *edge*
the **f-s** of His ways Job 26:14
touched the **f** of His Matt 9:20

FROGS
smite...with **f** Ex 8:2
f which destroyed Ps 78:45
land swarmed with **f** Ps 105:30
unclean spirits like **f** Rev 16:13

FRONTALS *prayer bands*
they shall be as **f** Deut 6:8
f on your forehead Deut 11:18
see also **PHYLACTERIES**

FROST *freezing*
and the **f** by night Gen 31:40
fine as the **f** Ex 16:14
sycamore trees with **f** Ps 78:47

FRUIT *growth, produce*
f trees...bearing **f** Gen 1:11
she took from its **f** Gen 3:6
the **f** of the womb Gen 30:2
offering of first **f-s** Lev 2:12
its **f** in its season Ps 1:3
yield **f** in old age Ps 92:14
eat its choice **f-s** Song 4:16
eaten the **f** of lies Hos 10:13
know...by their **f-s** Matt 7:16
bad tree bears bad **f** Matt 7:17
f for life eternal John 4:36
the **f** of the Spirit Gal 5:22
f in every good work Col 1:10

FRUITFUL *productive*
be **f** and multiply Gen 9:7
were **f** and increased Ex 1:7
gather a **f** harvest Ps 107:37
into the **f** land Jer 2:7
f labor for me Phil 1:22

FRUSTRATE *counteract*
to **f** their counsel Ezra 4:5
He **f-s** the plotting Job 5:12
plans are **f-d** Prov 15:22

FUEL *that which burns*
people are like **f** Is 9:19
You will be **f** Ezek 21:32

FUGITIVE *one who flees*
do not betray the **f** Is 16:3
Meet the **f** with bread Is 21:14
gather the **f-s** Jer 49:5

FULFILL *complete*
to **f** the word 2 Chr 36:21
May the LORD **f** all Ps 20:5
f-ing His word Ps 148:8
to **f** the vision Dan 11:14
the prophet was **f-ed** Matt 2:17
to abolish, but to **f** Matt 5:17
The time is **f-ed** Mark 1:15
f-ed in the kingdom Luke 22:16
Scripture...be **f-ed** John 13:18
husband must **f** his duty 1 Cor 7:3
f the law of Christ Gal 6:2
f your ministry 2 Tim 4:5

FULFILLMENT *completion*
the **f** of every vision Ezek 12:23
f of what had been Luke 1:45
f of *the* law Rom 13:10

FULL *complete, whole*
I went out **f** Ruth 1:21
The earth is **f** of Ps 33:5
until the **f** day Prov 4:18
twelve **f** baskets Matt 14:20
f of dead...bones Matt 23:27
f of the Holy Spirit Luke 4:1
also is **f** of light Luke 11:34
f of grace and truth John 1:14
f of the Spirit Acts 6:3
f armor of God Eph 6:11
f of compassion James 5:11

FULLER *one who bleaches cloth*
of the **f-'s** field 2 Kin 18:17
like **f-s'** soap Mal 3:2

FULLNESS *completeness*
Your presence is **f** of Ps 16:11
His **f** we...received John 1:16
the **f** of the Gentiles Rom 11:25
f of the time came Gal 4:4
all the **f** of God Eph 3:19
f to dwell in Him Col 1:19
the **f** of Deity dwells Col 2:9

FURIOUS *angry*
Pharaoh was **f** Gen 41:10
became **f** and very Neh 4:1
king became...**f** Dan 2:12

FURNACE *oven*
As silver tried in a **f** Ps 12:6
the **f** of affliction Is 48:10
into the midst of a **f** Dan 3:6
throw them into the **f** Matt 13:42
to glow in a **f** Rev 1:15

FURNISH *supply*
f-ed with silver bands Ex 38:17
shall **f** him liberally Deut 15:14
f-ing every kind Ps 144:13
upper room **f-ed** Mark 14:15

FURROWS *trench*
its **f** weep together Job 31:38
water its **f** Ps 65:10
weeds in the **f** Hos 10:4

FURY *anger*
brother's **f** subsides Gen 27:44
terrify them in His **f** Ps 2:5
plucked up in **f** Ezek 19:12
the **f** of a fire Heb 10:27

FUTILE *useless, vain*
go after **f** things 1 Sam 12:21
devise **f** things Acts 4:25
f in...speculations Rom 1:21

FUTURE *that which is ahead*
discern their **f** Deut 32:29
no **f** for the evil Prov 24:20
is hope for your **f** Jer 31:17
foundation for the **f** 1 Tim 6:19

~*G*

GABRIEL
angel of high rank
Dan 8:16;9:21; Luke 1:19,26

GAD
1 *son of Jacob* Gen 30:11;35:26
2 *tribe of* Num 1:25;2:14
3 *valley* 2 Sam 24:5
4 *seer, prophet* 2 Sam 24:11,18

GAIETY *cheerfulness*
g...is banished Is 24:11
an end to all her **g** Hos 2:11

GAIN (n) *profit, increase*
hate dishonest **g** Ex 18:21
Ill-gotten **g-s** do not Prov 10:2
who rejects unjust **g** Is 33:15
greedy for **g** Jer 6:13
to die is **g** Phil 1:21
fond of sordid **g** 1 Tim 3:8

GAIN (v) *acquire*
they might **g** insight Neh 8:13
have **g-ed** the victory Ps 98:1
he will **g** knowledge Prov 19:25
will **g** ascendancy Dan 11:5
g-s the whole world Matt 16:26
that I may **g** Christ Phil 3:8
may **g** the glory 2 Thess 2:14

GAIUS
1 *Macedonian* Acts 19:29
2 *companion of Paul* Acts 20:4
3 *Corinthian believer* 1 Cor 1:14
4 *addressee of 3 John* 3 John 1

GALATIA
Roman province in Asia Minor
1 Cor 16:1; 2 Tim 4:10

GALE *storm*
dust before a **g** Is 17:13
a fierce **g** of wind Mark 4:37

GALILEE
1 *district in N Palestine*
Josh 21:32; 1 Kin 9:11; Matt 2:22; Acts 10:37
2 *Sea of* Matt 4:18; Mark 7:31
also **Sea of Chinnereth**
also **Lake of Gennesaret**
also **Sea of Tiberias**

GALL *bitter herb, bitterness*
gave me **g** for my food Ps 69:21
drink...with **g** Matt 27:34
the **g** of bitterness Acts 8:23

GALLIO
governor of Achaia
Acts 18:12,17

GALLOWS *for hanging*
Have a **g**...made Esth 5:14
hanged...on the **g** Esth 7:10
his sons...on the **g** Esth 9:25

GAMALIEL
1 *head of tribe* Num 2:20;7:54
2 *Pharisee* Acts 5:34;22:3

GARDEN *planted area*
God walking in the **g** Gen 3:8
from the **g** of Eden Gen 3:23
Make my **g** breathe Song 4:16
plant **g-s**, and eat Jer 29:5
tabernacle like a **g** Lam 2:6
in the **g** with Him John 18:26
the **g** a new tomb John 19:41

GARLAND *ornament*
a **g** instead of ashes Is 61:3
brought...**g-s** to the Acts 14:13

GARMENT *clothing, dress*
God made **g-s** of skin Gen 3:21
caught him by his **g** Gen 39:12
in **g-s** of fine linen Gen 41:42
holy **g-s** for Aaron Ex 28:2
divide my **g-s** among Ps 22:18
on **g-s** of vengeance Is 59:17
g-s of glowing colors Is 63:1
g of camel's hair Matt 3:4
I just touch His **g-s** Mark 5:28
dividing up His **g-s** Luke 23:34
put his outer **g** on John 21:7
become old like a **g** Heb 1:11
clothed in white **g-s** Rev 3:5

GARRISON *defense*
g of the Philistines 1 Sam 13:4
the **g**...trembled 1 Sam 14:15
set **g-s** in the land 2 Chr 17:2

GATE *entry way*
is the **g** of heaven Gen 28:17
oppressed in the **g** Job 5:4
g-s with thanksgiving Ps 100:4
enter the **g-s** of Sheol Is 38:10
justice in the **g** Amos 5:15
Enter...narrow **g** Matt 7:13
g-s of Hades will Matt 16:18
did not open the **g** Acts 12:14

GATEKEEPERS *guards*
g for the camp 1 Chr 9:18
divisions of the **g** 1 Chr 26:12
The sons of the **g** Ezra 2:42
g, and the singers Neh 10:39

GATES OF JERUSALEM
alternate names in italics
1 **Beautiful Gate** Acts 3:10
East Gate
2 **Benjamin Gate** Jer 20:2; Zech 14:10
Gate of the Guard
Inspection Gate
Sheep Gate
3 **Corner Gate** 2 Kin 14:13; 2 Chr 26:9
4 **East Gate** Neh 3:29; Ezek 10:19;44:1
Beautiful Gate
5 **Ephraim Gate** 2 Kin 14:13; Neh 8:16
Middle Gate
Old Gate
6 **First Gate** Zech 14:10
7 **Fish Gate** 2 Chr 33:14; Neh 3:3
8 **Foundation Gate** 2 Chr 23:5
Gate of Sur
9 **Fountain Gate** Neh 2:14;12:37
gate between two walls
2 Kin 25:4; Jer 39:4
10 **Guard, Gate of the** Neh 12:39
Benjamin Gate
Inspection Gate
Sheep Gate
11 **Horse Gate** 2 Chr 23:15; Neh 3:28
12 **Inspection Gate** Neh 3:31
Benjamin Gate
Gate of the Guard
Sheep Gate
13 **Middle Gate** Jer 39:3
Ephraim Gate
Old Gate
14 **Old Gate** Neh 3:6;12:39
Ephraim Gate
Middle Gate
15 **Refuse Gate** Neh 2:13;12:31
16 **Sheep Gate** Neh 3:1
Benjamin Gate
Gate of the Guard
Inspection Gate
17 **Sur, Gate of** 2 Kin 11:6
Foundation Gate
18 **Valley Gate** 2 Chr 26:9; Neh 3:13
19 **Water Gate** Neh 3:26;8:1,3,16

GATEWAY *entrance*
the **g** of the court Ex 40:8
the **g** of the peoples Ezek 26:2

GATH
Philistine city Josh 11:22; 1 Sam 17:23; 1 Chr 20:8

GATHER *assemble, collect*
g-ed to his people Gen 25:8
g stubble for straw Ex 5:12
He **g-s** the waters Ps 33:7
G My godly ones Ps 50:5
g all nations and Is 66:18
hen **g-s** her chicks Matt 23:37
elders...were **g-ed** Matt 26:3
g...His elect Mark 13:27
G up the leftover John 6:12

GAZA
Philistine city Gen 10:19; Judg 16:1; Jer 47:5

GAZE (n) *view, glance*
Turn Your **g** away from Ps 39:13
let your **g** be fixed Prov 4:25
turning His **g** toward His Luke 6:20

GAZE (v) *look, stare*
man...**g-ing** at her Gen 24:21
and **g** after Moses Ex 33:8
eye **g-s** on their Job 17:2
LORD **g-d** upon the Ps 102:19
g-ing...into the sky Acts 1:10

GAZELLE *animal*
swift as the **g-s** 1 Chr 12:8
a **g** Or a young stag Song 2:17
like a hunted **g** Is 13:14

GEDERAH
1 *town of Judah* Josh 15:36
2 *town of Benjamin* 1 Chr 12:4

GEHAZI
servant of Elisha 2 Kin 4:12;5:20;8:4

GENEALOGY *family record*
found the book of...g Neh 7:5
g of Jesus the Messiah Matt 1:1
and endless **g-ies** 1 Tim 1:4
whose g is not traced Heb 7:6

GENERATION *age, period*
this evil **g** Deut 1:35
the righteous **g** Ps 14:5
faithfulness to all **g-s** Ps 100:5
salvation to all **g-s** Is 51:8
this **g** seek for a sign Mark 8:12
g-s...not made known Eph 3:5
and perverse **g** Phil 2:15

GENEROUS *bountiful*
g will be blessed Prov 22:9
because I am **g** Matt 20:15
g...ready to share 1 Tim 6:18

GENNESARET
1 *lake* Luke 5:1
also **Sea of Chinnereth**
also **Sea of Galilee**
also **Sea of Tiberias**
2 *land or district* Matt 14:34; Mark 6:53

GENTILES *foreigners, non-Jews*
Galilee of the **G** Matt 4:15
hand Him over to the **G** Matt 20:19
revelation to the **G** Luke 2:32
Why did the **G** rage Acts 4:25
salvation...to the **G** Rom 11:11
preach...among the **G** Gal 1:16

GENTLE *compassionate, mild*
g answer turns away Prov 15:1
I was like a **g** lamb Jer 11:19
Blessed are the **g** Matt 5:5
G, and mounted on Matt 21:5
a **g** and quiet spirit 1 Pet 3:4

GENTLENESS *kindness*
and a spirit of **g** 1 Cor 4:21
and **g** of Christ 2 Cor 10:1
g, self-control Gal 5:23
humility and **g,** with Eph 4:2

GERAR
Philistine city Gen 20:2;26:6

GERIZIM
mountain near Shechem Deut 11:29; Josh 8:33

GERSHOM
1 *son of Moses* Ex 2:22;18:3
2 *son of Levi* 1 Chr 6:16,43
3 *line of Phinehas* Ezra 8:2

GERSHON
son of Levi Gen 46:11; Ex 6:16

GETHSEMANE
garden on Mount of Olives Matt 26:36; Mark 14:32

GEZER
Canaanite city of Ephraim Josh 10:33; 1 Kin 9:17

GHOST *spirit*
resort to idols and **g-s** Is 19:3
and said, It is a **g** Matt 14:26
it was a **g** Mark 6:49

GIANT
were born to the **g** 2 Sam 21:22
from the **g-s** 1 Chr 20:6

GIBEAH
1 *village in Judah* Josh 15:57
2 *in Ephraim* Josh 24:33
3 *town of Benjamin* 1 Sam 10:26;13:2; 2 Sam 23:29

GIBEON
town in Benjamin Josh 9:3,17; 1 Kin 3:5; 1 Chr 8:29

GIDEON
son of Joash Judg 6:11,36
judge Judg 8:4-21

GIFT *present*
the sacred **g-s** Num 18:32
children are a **g** Ps 127:3
to Him **g-s** Matt 2:11
g of the Holy Spirit Acts 2:38
impart...spiritual **g** Rom 1:11
g of God is eternal Rom 6:23
desire...greater **g-s** 1 Cor 12:31
perfect **g** is from James 1:17

GIHON
1 *river of Eden* Gen 2:13
2 *Jerusalem spring* 2 Chr 32:30

GILBOA
mountain 2 Sam 1:6
where Saul died 2 Sam 21:12

GILEAD
1 *son of Machir* Num 36:1
2 *descendant of Gad* 1 Chr 5:14
3 *father of Jephthah* Judg 11:1
4 *land E of Jordan* Num 32:29
5 *mountain* Judg 7:3
6 *city* Hos 6:8

GILGAL
1 *in Arabah* Deut 11:30
2 *encampment in Jordan Valley* Josh 5:9; 1 Sam 7:16
near Jericho Josh 5:8,10
3 *in N Judah* Josh 15:7
4 *in Galilee* Josh 12:23
5 *village near Bethel* 2 Kin 2:1

GIRD *bind*
g him with the...band Ex 29:5
g up your loins like Job 38:3
g-ed me with gladness Ps 30:11
g-s herself with Prov 31:17
g-ed...with truth Eph 6:14
g-ed across His chest Rev 1:13

GIRDLE *belt, waistband*
man with a leather **g** 2 Kin 1:8
binds...with a **g** Job 12:18

GIRGASHITE(S)
Canaanite tribe Gen 10:16; Deut 7:1; Josh 24:11; Neh 9:8

GIRL *maiden*
the **g** and consult Gen 24:57
sold a **g** for wine Joel 3:3
boys and **g-s** playing Zech 8:5
the **g** has not died Matt 9:24

GIVE *bestow, yield*
g light on the earth Gen 1:17
g-n you every plant Gen 1:29
gave me from...tree Gen 3:12
in the land...God **g-s** Ex 20:12
I will **g** you rest Ex 33:14
g him to the LORD 1 Sam 1:11
G ear to my prayer Ps 17:1
gave me vinegar Ps 69:21
G me neither poverty Prov 30:8
a son will be **g-n** Is 9:6
gave birth to a Son Matt 1:25
G us this day Matt 6:11
g-ing thanks, He Matt 15:36
g you the keys Matt 16:19
authority...been **g-n** Matt 28:18
what will a man **g** Mark 8:37
body which is **g-n** Luke 22:19
gave His only...Son John 3:16
not as the world **g-s** John 14:27
gave up His spirit John 19:30
what I do have I **g** Acts 3:6
g-n among men Acts 4:12
more blessed to **g** Acts 20:35
was **g-n** me a thorn 2 Cor 12:7
always **g-ing** thanks Eph 5:20
who **gave** Himself 1 Tim 2:6
Every good thing **g-n** James 1:17
g-s a greater grace James 4:6
g-n us eternal life 1 John 5:11
to be **g-n** a mark Rev 13:16

GLAD *pleased*
g in his heart Ex 4:14
joy and a **g** heart Deut 28:47
righteous see...are **g** Job 22:19
Be **g** in the LORD Ps 32:11
g when they said Ps 122:1
son makes a father **g** Prov 10:1
Rejoice, and be **g** Matt 5:12
Be **g** in that day Luke 6:23

GLADNESS *joy*
celebrate...with **g** Neh 12:27
g...for the Jews Esth 8:17
Serve the LORD with **g** Ps 100:2
g and sincerity of Acts 2:46
With the oil of **g** Heb 1:9

GLASS *crystal*
or **g** cannot equal Job 28:17
sea of **g,** like crystal Rev 4:6

GLEAM *brilliance*
awesome **g** of crystal Ezek 1:22
g of a Tarshish stone Ezek 10:9
g of polished bronze Dan 10:6

GLEAN *gather, pick*
Nor shall you **g** Lev 19:10
Do not go to **g** Ruth 2:8
she **g-ed** in the field Ruth 2:17
g the vineyard Job 24:6
g-ing ears of grain Is 17:5

GLOOM *darkness*
cloud and thick **g** Deut 4:11
The land of utter **g** Job 10:22
darkness and **g** and Heb 12:18
and your joy to **g** James 4:9

GLORIFY *honor, worship*
g Your name forever Ps 86:12
Let the LORD be **g-ied** Is 66:5
g your Father Matt 5:16
shepherds...**g-ing** Luke 2:20
Jesus...not yet **g-ied** John 7:39
Father, **g** Your name John 12:28
God is **g-ied** in Him John 13:31
were all **g-ing** God Acts 4:21
Gentiles to **g** God Rom 15:9
g God in your body 1 Cor 6:20
did not **g** Himself Heb 5:5

GLORIOUS *exalted, great*
g name be blessed Neh 9:5
G things are spoken Ps 87:3
resting place will be **g** Is 11:10
the law great and **g** Is 42:21
g gospel of...God 1 Tim 1:11

GLORY (n) *honor, splendor*
show me Your **g** Ex 33:18
while My **g** is passing Ex 33:22
Tell of His **g** 1 Chr 16:24
King of **g** may come Ps 24:7
exchanged their **g** Ps 106:20
earth is full of His **g** Is 6:3
their **g** into shame Hos 4:7
Solomon in all his **g** Matt 6:29
g of the Lord shone Luke 2:9
G...in the highest Luke 2:14
He comes in His **g** Luke 9:26
do not seek My **g** John 8:50
short of the **g** of God Rom 3:23
all to the **g** of God 1 Cor 10:31
eternal weight of **g** 2 Cor 4:17
body of His **g** Phil 3:21
crowned Him with **g** Heb 2:7
unfading crown of **g** 1 Pet 5:4

GLORY (v) *exalt*
And **g** in Your praise 1 Chr 16:35
G in His holy name Ps 105:3
in Him they will **g** Jer 4:2
I...have reason to **g** Phil 2:16

GLUTTON *excessive eater*
g...come to poverty Prov 23:21
a companion of **g-s** Prov 28:7
evil beasts, lazy **g-s** Titus 1:12

GNASH *grind*
They **g-ed** at me Ps 35:16
He will **g** his teeth Ps 112:10
They hiss and **g** Lam 2:16
g-ing their teeth Acts 7:54

GNAT *insect*
dust...became **g-s** Ex 8:17
swarm of flies...**g-s** Ps 105:31
strain out a **g** and Matt 23:24

GO *move, proceed*
Let My people **g** Ex 7:16
God who **g-es** before Deut 1:30
where you **g**, I will **g** Ruth 1:16
the way he should **g** Prov 22:6
g one mile, **g**...two Matt 5:41
G into all...world Mark 16:15
I **g** to prepare a John 14:2
night is almost **gone** Rom 13:12

GOADS *inducements*
wise men are like **g** Eccl 12:11
kick against the **g** Acts 26:14

GOAL *end, object*
press on toward the **g** Phil 3:14
g...is love 1 Tim 1:5

GOAT *animal*
a young **g** from the flock Gen 38:17
curtains of **g-s'** *hair* Ex 26:7
not boil a young **g**...milk Ex 34:26
g for a sin offering Num 15:27
prepare a young **g** for you Judg 13:15
quilt of **g-s'** *hair* 1 Sam 19:13
g *had* a...horn Dan 8:5
shaggy **g** *represents* Dan 8:21
sheep from the **g-s** Matt 25:32
never given me a young **g** Luke 15:29
blood of **g-s**...bulls Heb 9:13

GOD *Deity, Eternal One*
In the beginning **G** Gen 1:1
G formed man of dust Gen 2:7
G sent him out Gen 3:23
G gave to Abraham Gen 28:4
tablets were **G-'s** work Ex 32:16
G is my...fortress 2 Sam 22:33
G of my salvation Ps 18:46
In **G**...put my trust Ps 56:4
Search me, O **G** Ps 139:23
word of **G** is tested Prov 30:5
servant of the living **G** Dan 6:20
I am **G** and not man Hos 11:9
Will a man rob **G** Mal 3:8
G descending...dove Matt 3:16
they shall see **G** Matt 5:8
What...**G** has joined Matt 19:6
kingdom of **G** is at Mark 1:15
My **G**, why have Mark 15:34
You the Son of **G** Luke 22:70
the Word was **G** John 1:1
No one has seen **G** John 1:18
the Lamb of **G** John 1:29
G so loved the world John 3:16
G is spirit John 4:24
voice of...Son of **G** John 5:25
obey **G** rather than Acts 5:29
judgment of **G** Rom 2:2
bear fruit for **G** Rom 7:4
we are children of **G** Rom 8:16
are a temple of **G** 1 Cor 3:16
full armor of **G** Eph 6:11
one **G**...one mediator 1 Tim 2:5
is inspired by **G** 2 Tim 3:16
word of **G** is...sharper Heb 4:12
impossible...**G** to lie Heb 6:18
G is love 1 John 4:8
great supper of **G** Rev 19:17

GOD *false deity, idols*
no other **g-s** before Me Ex 20:3
New **g-s** were chosen Judg 5:8
cast their **g-s** into Is 37:19
bowed...to other **g-s** Jer 22:9
no other **g** who is Dan 3:29
The voice of a **g** Acts 12:22
g-s...become like Acts 14:11
the **g** of this world 2 Cor 4:4

GOD, SON OF
see **SON OF GOD**

GODDESS *female deity*
Ashtoreth the **g** of 1 Kin 11:5
great **g** Artemis Acts 19:27
blasphemers of...**g** Acts 19:37

GODLESS *pagan, without God*
hope of the **g** will Job 8:13
joy of...**g** momentary Job 20:5
g man destroys his Prov 11:9
hands of **g** men Acts 2:23
become of the **g** 1 Pet 4:18

GODLINESS *holiness*
in all **g** and dignity 1 Tim 2:2
the mystery of **g** 1 Tim 3:16
g is profitable 1 Tim 4:8
to a form of **g** 2 Tim 3:5
g, brotherly kindness 2 Pet 1:7

GODLY *holy*
keeps...His **g** ones 1 Sam 2:9
g man ceases to be Ps 12:1
not forsake His **g** ones Ps 37:28
and **g** sincerity 2 Cor 1:12
to live **g** in Christ 2 Tim 3:12
rescue the **g** from 2 Pet 2:9

GOG
1 *a Reubenite* 1 Chr 5:4
2 *prince of Meshech and Tubal* Ezek 38:2
3 *symbol of godless nations* Rev 20:8
see also **MAGOG**

GOLAN
city of refuge Josh 21:27
a Levitical city 1 Chr 6:71

GOLD *precious metal*
g of that land is good Gen 2:12
mercy seat of pure **g** Ex 25:17
Almighty...be your **g** Job 22:25
more desirable than **g** Ps 19:10
refine them like **g** Mal 3:3
to Him gifts of **g** Matt 2:11
Do not acquire **g** Matt 10:9
Divine Nature...**g** Acts 17:29
coveted no...**g** Acts 20:33
city was pure **g** Rev 21:18

GOLDSMITH *gold craftsman*
g-s and...merchants Neh 3:32
g, and he makes it Is 46:6

GOLGOTHA
site of Crucifixion Matt 27:33; Mark 15:22; John 19:17

GOLIATH
Philistine giant 1 Sam 17:4,23;21:9; 1 Chr 20:5

GOMER
1 *son of Japheth* Gen 10:2
2 *group of people* Ezek 38:6
3 *wife of Hosea* Hos 1:3

GOMORRAH
city of Jordan plain Gen 10:19;14:10;19:24
probably S of Dead Sea Is 13:19; 2 Pet 2:6

GOOD *complete, right*
God saw that it was **g** Gen 1:18
knowledge of **g** and Gen 2:9
Proclaim **g** tidings 1 Chr 16:23
Do not withhold **g** Prov 3:27
joyful heart is **g** Prov 17:22
planted in **g** soil Ezek 17:8
feed in...**g** pasture Ezek 34:18
Seek **g** and not evil Amos 5:14
how to give **g** gifts Matt 7:11
Well done, **g** and Matt 25:23
sown on the **g** soil Mark 4:20
Salt is **g** Mark 9:50
No one is **g** except Luke 18:19
I am the **g** shepherd John 10:11
men of **g** reputation Acts 6:3
perseverance in...**g** Rom 2:7
nothing **g**...in me Rom 7:18
work together for **g** Rom 8:28
who bring **g** news Rom 10:15
overcome evil...**g** Rom 12:21
is of **g** repute Phil 4:8
g hope by grace 2 Thess 2:16
Fight the **g** fight 1 Tim 6:12
tasted the **g** word Heb 6:5

GOODNESS *excellence, value*
My **g** pass before you Ex 33:19
Surely **g**...will follow Ps 23:6
How great is Your **g** Ps 31:19
kindness, **g** Gal 5:22
every desire for **g** 2 Thess 1:11

GOODS *possessions, supplies*
the **g** for yourself Gen 14:21
have acquired...**g** Ezek 38:12

GORE *stab*
if an ox **g-s** a man Ex 21:28
g the Arameans 1 Kin 22:11

GOSHEN
1 *district of Egypt in Nile Delta* Gen 45:10;47:6,27
2 *S Judah region* Josh 10:41
3 *town in Judah* Josh 15:51

GOSPEL *good news*
proclaiming the **g** of Matt 4:23
preach the **g** to all Mark 16:15
not ashamed of the **g** Rom 1:16
if our **g** is veiled 2 Cor 4:3
or a different **g** 2 Cor 11:4
distort the **g** of Christ Gal 1:7
g of your salvation Eph 1:13
g of peace Eph 6:15
defense of the **g** Phil 1:16
the hope of the **g** Col 1:23
eternal **g** to preach Rev 14:6

GOSSIP *babbler*
associate with a **g** Prov 20:19
malice; *they are* **g-s** Rom 1:29
g-s and busybodies 1 Tim 5:13

GOVERN *rule*
light to **g** the day Gen 1:16
light to **g** the night Gen 1:16
when the judges **g-ed** Ruth 1:1

GOVERNMENT *authority, rule*
g...on His shoulders Is 9:6
be no end to...*His* **g** Is 9:7

GOVERNOR *ruler*
not offer it to your **g** Mal 1:8
brought before **g-s** Matt 10:18
g was quite amazed Matt 27:14
Pilate was **g** of Judea Luke 3:1
g over Egypt Acts 7:10

GRACE *benevolence, favor*
G is poured upon Your Ps 45:2
g to the afflicted Prov 3:34
g of God was upon Luke 2:40
full of **g** and truth John 1:14
g abounded...more Rom 5:20
g of our Lord Jesus Rom 16:20
My **g** is sufficient 2 Cor 12:9
by **g** you have been Eph 2:8
justified by His **g** Titus 3:7
to the throne of **g** Heb 4:16
g to the humble James 4:6

GRACIOUS *kind*
God be **g** to you Gen 43:29
g to whom I will be Ex 33:19
a **g** and...God Neh 9:31
Be **g** to me, O LORD Ps 6:2
and **g**, Slow to anger Ps 86:15
g to a poor man Prov 19:17
be **g** to...remnant Amos 5:15

GRAFT *insert, join*
I might be **g-ed** in Rom 11:19
God is able to **g** Rom 11:23
g-ed into their own Rom 11:24

GRAIN
Joseph stored up **g** Gen 41:49
glean among the...**g** Ruth 2:2
g...for your enemies Is 62:8
then the mature **g** Mark 4:28
g of wheat falls John 12:24

GRAIN OFFERING
see **OFFERINGS**

GRANDCHILDREN
G are the crown of Prov 17:6
widow has...or **g** 1 Tim 5:4

GRANDDAUGHTER
g-s, and all his Gen 46:7
g of Omri king of 2 Kin 8:26

GRANDSON
g might fear the LORD Deut 6:2
sons and thirty **g-s** Judg 12:14
master's **g** shall eat 2 Sam 9:10

GRANT *give, provide*
g this people favor Ex 3:21
have **g-ed** me life Job 10:12
g us Your salvation Ps 85:7
G that we may sit Mark 10:37
Father has **g-ed** Me Luke 22:29
g repentance to Acts 5:31
g-ing...deliverance Acts 7:25

GRAPE *fruit*
nor eat...dried **g-s** Num 6:3
of **g-s** you drank Deut 32:14
when the **g** harvest is Is 24:13
G-s are not gathered Matt 7:16
g-s from a briar Luke 6:44

GRASP *hold, seize*
hands **g** the spindle Prov 31:19
He who **g-s** the bow Amos 2:15
a thing to be **g-ed** Phil 2:6

GRASS *vegetation*
g *springs* out 2 Sam 23:4
his days are like **g** Ps 103:15
dry **g** collapses into Is 5:24
g withers, the flower Is 40:7
was given **g** to eat Dan 5:21
if God so clothes...**g** Matt 6:30
All flesh is like **g** 1 Pet 1:24
not to hurt the **g** Rev 9:4

GRASSHOPPER *insect*
the **g** in its kinds Lev 11:22
we became like **g-s** Num 13:33
inhabitants are like **g-s** Is 40:22

GRATITUDE *thankfulness*
overflowing with **g** Col 2:7
is received with **g** 1 Tim 4:4
let us show **g** Heb 12:28

GRAVE *sepulchre, tomb*
pillar of Rachel's **g** Gen 35:20
throat is an open **g** Ps 5:9
I will open your **g-s** Ezek 37:12
I will prepare your **g** Nah 1:14
made the **g** secure Matt 27:66

GRAVEN *sculptured*
make...a **g** image Deut 4:23
ashamed who serve **g** Ps 97:7
praise to **g** images Is 42:8

GRAY *color*
g hair...in sorrow Gen 42:38
with the man of **g** Deut 32:25
Both the **g-haired** Job 15:10
when *I am* old and **g** Ps 71:18
g head is a crown Prov 16:31

GRAZE *feed*
cattle...**g-ing** in 1 Chr 27:29
wolf...shall **g** Is 65:25
he will **g** on Carmel Jer 50:19

GREAT *big, excellent, grand*
made...two **g** lights Gen 1:16
make you a **g** nation Gen 12:2
lovingkindness is **g** Ps 57:10
your iniquity is **g** Jer 30:15
g day of the LORD Zeph 1:14
rejoiced...with **g** joy Matt 2:10
woman...faith is **g** Matt 15:28
good news of **g** joy Luke 2:10
reward is **g** in Luke 6:23
because of His **g** love Eph 2:4
so **g** a salvation Heb 2:3
we have a **g**...priest Heb 4:14
so **g** a cloud of Heb 12:1
g supper of God Rev 19:17
a **g** white throne Rev 20:11

GREATEST *most important*
who is the **g** among Luke 22:26
g of these is love 1 Cor 13:13
least to the **g** Heb 8:11

GREATNESS *magnitude*
Yours...is the **g** 1 Chr 29:11
g...lovingkindness Neh 13:22
g of Your compassion Ps 51:1
the **g** of His strength Is 63:1
amazed at the **g** of Luke 9:43
surpassing **g** of His Eph 1:19

GREECE
country in SE Europe
Dan 8:21;10:20;11:2; Zech 9:13; Acts 20:2

GREED *excessive desire*
caught by *their*...**g** Prov 11:6
every form of **g** Luke 12:15
wickedness, **g**, evil Rom 1:29
a pretext for **g** 1 Thess 2:5
a heart trained in **g** 2 Pet 2:14

GREEDY *craving*
had **g** desires Num 11:4
g man curses Ps 10:3
Everyone is **g** for Jer 6:13

GREEKS
people of Greece Joel 3:6; Acts 16:1,3; Rom 1:16; 1 Cor 12:13

GREEN *fertile, fruitful*
every **g** plant for Gen 1:30
lie down in **g** pastures Ps 23:2
dry up the **g** tree Ezek 17:24
nor any **g** thing Rev 9:4

GREET *hail, welcome*
g no one on the way Luke 10:4
G one another with 1 Pet 5:14

GRIEF *heartache, sorrow*
weeps because of **g** Ps 119:28
foolish son is a **g** Prov 17:25
acquainted with **g** Is 53:3
our **g-s** He Himself Is 53:4
g...turned into joy John 16:20
joy and not with **g** Heb 13:17

GRIEVE *distress, sorrow*
was **g-d** in His heart Gen 6:6
Do not be **g-d** Neh 8:10
g-d Him in the desert Ps 78:40
g-d His Holy Spirit Is 63:10
g-d at their hardness Mark 3:5
Peter was **g-d** John 21:17
not **g** the Holy Spirit Eph 4:30

GRIND *crush, press*
my wife **g** for another Job 31:10
g-ing...the poor Is 3:15
millstones and **g** meal Is 47:2
women...*be* **g-ing** Matt 24:41
and **g-s** his teeth Mark 9:18

GROAN *cry, moan*
From the city men **g** Job 24:12
man rules, people **g** Prov 29:2
wounded will **g** Jer 51:52
whole creation **g-s** Rom 8:22

GROANING *crying*
God heard their **g** Ex 2:24
O LORD, Consider my **g** Ps 5:1
g of the prisoner Ps 79:11
g-s of a wounded Ezek 30:24
g-s too deep for Rom 8:26

GROPE *move about blindly*
you will **g** at noon Deut 28:29
They **g** in darkness Job 12:25
g...like blind men Is 59:10
g for Him and find Acts 17:27

GROUND *earth, land, soil*
man of dust from...**g** Gen 2:7
Cursed is the **g** Gen 3:17
crossed on dry **g** Josh 3:17
a spirit from the **g** Is 29:4
talent in the **g** Matt 25:25
finger wrote on the **g** John 8:6
standing is holy **g** Acts 7:33
g that drinks the rain Heb 6:7

GROUNDED *established*
hope...is firmly **g** 2 Cor 1:7
rooted and **g** in love Eph 3:17

GROW *develop, increase*
Moses had **g-n** up Ex 2:11
You are **g-n** fat Deut 32:15
my spirit **g-s** faint Ps 77:3
youths **g** weary Is 40:30
sun and moon **g** dark Joel 3:15
lilies of the field **g** Matt 6:28
love will **g** cold Matt 24:12
Child continued to **g** Luke 2:40
grew strong in faith Rom 4:20
as your faith **g-s** 2 Cor 10:15
not **g** weary of 2 Thess 3:13
g in the grace 2 Pet 3:18

GROWTH *increase*
new **g** is seen Prov 27:25
God who causes the **g** 1 Cor 3:7

GRUDGE *hostile feeling*
Esau bore a **g** Gen 27:41
nor bear any **g** Lev 19:18
Herodias had a **g** Mark 6:19

GRUMBLE *complain*
they **g-d** against Moses Ex 17:3
the congregation **g** Num 14:36
g-d in their tents Ps 106:25
scribes *began* to **g** Luke 15:2
g among yourselves John 6:43

GRUMBLING *complaint*
for He hears your **g-s** Ex 16:7
g-s against Me Num 17:10
Do all...without **g** Phil 2:14

GUARD (n) *keeper*
set a **g** over me Job 7:12
be a **g** for them Ezek 38:7
g-s shook for fear Matt 28:4
Him away under **g** Mark 14:44

GUARD (v) *keep watch*
g the way to the tree Gen 3:24
g-ed the threshold 2 Kin 12:9
G-ing...justice Prov 2:8
Discretion will **g** you Prov 2:11
soldier...was **g-ing** Acts 28:16
will **g** your hearts Phil 4:7
g...from idols 1 John 5:21

GUARDHOUSE *prison*
the court of the **g** Jer 37:21
the court of the **g** Jer 38:28

GUARDIAN *overseer*
g-s of *the children* 2 Kin 10:1
under **g-s** and Gal 4:2
G of your souls 1 Pet 2:25

GUEST *visitor*
Herod and his...**g-s** Mark 6:22
Where...My **g** room Mark 14:14
to the invited **g-s** Luke 14:7
g of a...sinner Luke 19:7

GUIDANCE *counsel*
no **g**, the people fall Prov 11:14
make war by wise **g** Prov 20:18

GUIDE (n) *advisor, director*
The righteous is a **g** Prov 12:26
Woe to...blind **g-s** Matt 23:16
You blind **g-s,** who Matt 23:24
are a **g** to the blind Rom 2:19

GUIDE (v) *direct, lead*
LORD alone **g-d** him Deut 32:12
He **g-s** me in the paths Ps 23:3
g us until death Ps 48:14
my mind was **g-ing** *me* Eccl 2:3
blind...**g-s** a blind Matt 15:14
g you into...truth John 16:13
unless someone **g-s** Acts 8:31

GUILT *offence*
be free from **g** Num 5:31
according to his **g** Deut 25:2
charge me with a **g** 2 Sam 3:8
our **g** has grown Ezra 9:6
land is full of **g** Jer 51:5
must bear their **g** Hos 10:2
I find no **g** in Him John 18:38

GUILT OFFERING
see **OFFERINGS**

GUILTY *charged* or *condemned*
he sins and becomes **g** Lev 6:4
murderer...**g** of Num 35:31
as one who is **g** 2 Sam 14:13
g by the blood Ezek 22:4
g of an eternal sin Mark 3:29
has become **g** of all James 2:10

GUSHED *burst, flowed*
so that waters **g** out Ps 78:20
the rock...water **g** Is 48:21
all his intestines **g** out Acts 1:18

~H

HABAKKUK
prophet Hab 1:1;3:1

HABITATION *abode, dwelling*
from Your holy **h** Deut 26:15
a rock of **h** Ps 71:3
h-s of violence Ps 74:20
live in a peaceful **h** Is 32:18
holy and glorious **h** Is 63:15
laid waste his **h** Jer 10:25
a **h** of shepherds Jer 33:12

HABOR
river in Mesopotamia
2 Kin 17:6;18:11; 1 Chr 5:26

HADAD
1 *son of Ishmael* Gen 25:15; 1 Chr 1:30
2 *king of Edom, son of Bedad* Gen 36:35,36; 1 Chr 1:46,47
3 *king of Edom* Gen 36:39; 1 Chr 1:50,51
4 *Edomite prince* 1 Kin 11:14ff

HADASSAH
Esther's Hebrew name Esth 2:7

HADES *hell, place of dead*
will descend to **H** Matt 11:23
in **H** he lifted up Luke 16:23
abandoned to **H** Acts 2:31
see also **HELL** *and* **SHEOL**

HAGAR
Sarah's handmaiden Gen 16:1
Abraham's slave wife Gen 16:3
mother of Ishmael Gen 16:15

HAGGAI
prophet Ezra 5:1; Hag 1:1

HAGGITH
David's wife 2 Sam 3:4
mother of Adonijah 1 Kin 1:11

HAIL (n) *pieces of ice*
rained **h** on the land Ex 9:23
storehouses of the **h** Job 38:22
gave them **h** for rain Ps 105:32
plague of the **h** Rev 16:21

HAIL (v) *greeting*
H, Rabbi Matt 26:49
H, King of...Jews Matt 27:29

HAILSTONES *pieces of ice*
who died from the **h** Josh 10:11
H and coals of fire Ps 18:13
you, O **h,** will fall Ezek 13:11
h...one hundred Rev 16:21

HAIR
gray **h**...to Sheol Gen 42:38
locks of his **h** and Judg 16:14
h...bristled Job 4:15
h...like pure wool Dan 7:9
garment of camel's **h** Matt 3:4
make one **h** white Matt 5:36
h-s...all numbered Matt 10:30
His feet with her **h** John 11:2
not with braided **h** 1 Tim 2:9

HALL *corridor*
h of pillars 1 Kin 7:6
h of judgment 1 Kin 7:7
wedding **h** was Matt 22:10

HALLELUJAH *praise Yahweh*
H! Salvation and Rev 19:1
H! Her smoke rises Rev 19:3
Amen. **H** Rev 19:4
H! For the Lord our Rev 19:6

HALLOWED *consecrated, holy*
H be Your name Matt 6:9

HAM
1 *son of Noah* Gen 5:32;9:18
2 *city* Gen 14:5
3 *poetic name for Egypt* Ps 105:27;106:22

HAMAN
Persian prime minister
son of Hammedatha Esth 3:1

HAMATH
city in Aram 2 Kin 23:33;25:21

HAMMER *mallet, tool*
and seized a **h** Judg 4:21
neither **h** nor axe 1 Kin 6:7
smash with...**h-s** Ps 74:6
like a **h** which Jer 23:29

HAMON-GOG
valley where army of Gog is defeated Ezek 39:11,15

HANANIAH
1 *son of Zerubbabel* 1 Chr 3:19
2 *son of Shishak* 1 Chr 8:24
3 *musician* 1 Chr 25:4,23
4 *in Uzziah's army* 2 Chr 26:11
5 *repaired wall* Neh 3:30
6 *overseer of palace* Neh 7:2
7 *false prophet* Jer 28:15
8 *Shadrach* Dan 1:6,7
name of six other individuals

HAND *part of body*
cover you with My **h** Ex 33:22
for tooth, **h** for **h** Deut 19:21
sling was in his **h** 1 Sam 17:40
They pierced my **h-s** Ps 22:16
buries his **h** Prov 19:24
the hollow of His **h** Is 40:12
clay in the potter's **h** Jer 18:6
not let your left **h** Matt 6:3
laying His **h-s** on Mark 10:16
the right **h** of God Mark 16:19
into the **h-s** of men Luke 9:44
into Your **h-s** I Luke 23:46
reach here your **h** John 20:27
not made with **h-s** 2 Cor 5:1
lifting up holy **h-s** 1 Tim 2:8
h-s of...God Heb 10:31

HANDMAID *servant, slave*
save the son of Your **h** Ps 86:16
the son of Your **h** Ps 116:16
her **h-s** are moaning Nah 2:7

HANDSOME *attractive*
a choice and **h** *man* 1 Sam 9:2
ruddy, with a **h** 1 Sam 17:42

HANG *attach, suspend*
h you on a tree Gen 40:19
h up the veil Ex 40:8
h-ed is accursed of Deut 21:23
h-ing in an oak 2 Sam 18:10
they **h-ed** Haman Esth 7:10
he...**h-ed** himself Matt 27:5
millstone were **hung** Luke 17:2
h-ing Him on a cross Acts 5:30
who **h-s** on a tree Gal 3:13

HANNAH
mother of Samuel 1 Sam 2:21

HAPPINESS *joy*
give **h** to his wife Deut 24:5
eat your bread in **h** Eccl 9:7
I have forgotten **h** Lam 3:17

HAPPY *blessed, joyful*
Leah said, **H** am I Gen 30:13
h...man whom God Job 5:17
h...who keeps the Prov 29:18

HARAN
1 *brother of Abraham* Gen 11:27
father of Lot Gen 11:31
2 *Gershonite Levite* 1 Chr 23:9
3 *Mesopotamian city* Gen 11:32;27:43

HARD *difficult, firm*
bitter with **h** labor Ex 1:14
case that is too **h** Deut 1:17
made our yoke **h** 2 Chr 10:4
Water becomes **h** Job 38:30
h for a rich man Matt 19:23
h it is to enter Mark 10:24
worked **h** all night Luke 5:5

HARDEN *make hard, callous*
h Pharaoh's heart Ex 7:3
dust **h-s** into a mass Job 38:38
who **h-s** *his* neck Prov 29:1
h-s whom He Rom 9:18
minds were **h-ed** 2 Cor 3:14
Do not **h** your hearts Heb 3:15

HARDNESS *callousness*
give them **h** of heart Lam 3:65
Because of your **h** Matt 19:8
grieved at their **h** Mark 3:5
unbelief and **h** of Mark 16:14

HARDSHIP *difficulty*
H after **h** is with me Job 10:17
people experience **h** Ps 60:3
afflictions, in **h-s** 2 Cor 6:4
our labor and **h** 1 Thess 2:9
Suffer **h** with *me* 2 Tim 2:3

HAREM *royal wives' quarters*
best place in the **h** Esth 2:9
the court of the **h** Esth 2:11
from the **h** to the Esth 2:13
to the second **h** Esth 2:14

HARLOT *prostitute*
thought she *was* a **h** Gen 38:15
the hire of a **h** Deut 23:18
h whose name was Josh 2:1
Dressed as a **h** Prov 7:10
city has become a **h** Is 1:21
also played the **h** Ezek 16:26
Traded a boy for a **h** Joel 3:3
Mother of **H-s** Rev 17:5

HARLOTRY *prostitution*
with child by **h** Gen 38:24
profaned by **h** Lev 21:7
uncovered her **h-ies** Ezek 23:18
children of **h** Hos 1:2
spirit of **h** Hos 5:4

HARM (n) *evil, hurt*
pillar to me, for **h** Gen 31:52
h to this people Ex 5:22
keep *me* from **h** 1 Chr 4:10
Do not devise **h** Prov 3:29
great **h** to yourselves Jer 44:7
the fire without **h** Dan 3:25
did me much **h** 2 Tim 4:14

HARM (v) *damage, hurt*
David seeks to **h** 1 Sam 24:9
planning to **h** me Neh 6:2

have not **h-ed** me Dan 6:22
in order to **h** you Acts 18:10
is there to **h** you 1 Pet 3:13

HAR-MAGEDON
hill of Megiddo Rev 16:16
see also **MEGIDDO**

HARMONY *agreement*
what **h** has Christ 2 Cor 6:15
live in **h** in the Phil 4:2

HARP *musical instrument*
my **h** is turned to Job 30:31
praises...with a **h** Ps 33:2
Awake, **h** and lyre Ps 57:8
gaiety of the **h** ceases Is 24:8
each one holding a **h** Rev 5:8
holding **h-s** of God Rev 15:2

HARSH *difficult, hard*
man was **h** and evil 1 Sam 25:3
h word stirs up anger Prov 15:1
A **h** vision Is 21:2
under **h** servitude Lam 1:3

HARVEST *reap and gather*
Seedtime and **h** Gen 8:22
fruits of the wheat **h** Ex 34:22
you reap your **h** Deut 24:19
he who sleeps in **h** Prov 10:5
snow...time of **h** Prov 25:13
like rain in **h** Prov 26:1
the gladness of **h** Is 9:3
time of **h** will come Jer 51:33
Lord of the **h** Matt 9:38
h is the end of the Matt 13:39
fields...white for **h** John 4:35
h of the earth is Rev 14:15

HARVEST, FEAST OF
see **FEASTS**

HASHUM
1 *family of exiles* Ezra 2:19
2 *was with Ezra* Neh 8:4

HASTEN *accelerate*
h-ed after deceit Job 31:5
H to me, O God Ps 70:5
they **h** to shed blood Prov 1:16
bird **h-s** to the snare Prov 7:23
eye **h-s** after wealth Prov 28:22
h-ing...day of God 2 Pet 3:12

HATE *despise, loathe*
you **h** discipline Ps 50:17
who **h** the LORD Ps 81:15
I **h** every false way Ps 119:104
fools **h** knowledge Prov 1:22
withholds his rod **h-s** Prov 13:24
a time to **h** Eccl 3:8
H evil, love good Amos 5:15
For I **h** divorce Mal 2:16
good to those who **h** Luke 6:27
you will be **h-d** Luke 21:17
he who **h-s** his life John 12:25
the very thing I **h** Rom 7:15
Esau I **h-d** Rom 9:13
h-ing one another Titus 3:3
yet **h-s** his brother 1 John 2:9

HATERS *those who hate*
slanderers, **h** of God Rom 1:30
brutal, **h** of good 2 Tim 3:3

HATRED *hate, ill will*
h for my love Ps 109:5
H stirs up strife Prov 10:12
who conceals **h** *has* Prov 10:18

HAUGHTY *proud*
nor my eyes **h** Ps 131:1
H eyes, a lying Prov 6:17
h spirit before Prov 16:18
Proud, **H**, Scoffer Prov 21:24
wine betrays the **h** Hab 2:5
do not be **h** in mind Rom 12:16

HAVEN *harbor, shelter*
be a **h** for ships Gen 49:13
to their desired **h** Ps 107:30

HAVILAH
1 *second son of Cush* Gen 10:7
2 *son of Joktan* Gen 10:29; 1 Chr 1:23
3 *region encompassed by one of Eden's rivers* Gen 2:11
4 *area in W Arabia* Gen 25:18

HAWK *bird*
sea gull, and the **h** Deut 14:15
h-s will be gathered Is 34:15

HAZAEL
anointed by Elijah 1 Kin 19:15
killed Ben Hadad 2 Kin 8:15
Aramaic king 2 Kin 8:15;9:14
defeated Israel 2 Kin 10:32

HAZOR
1 *Canaanite city in N Palestine* Josh 11:11
2 *town of the Negev* Josh 15:23
3 *Benjamite city* Neh 11:33
4 *desert kingdom* Jer 49:33

HEAD *chief* or *part of body*
bruise you on the **h** Gen 3:15
anointed my **h** with oil Ps 23:5
h a garland of grace Prov 4:9
gray **h** is a crown Prov 16:31
coals on his **h** Prov 25:22
h was made bald Ezek 29:18
had four **h-s** Dan 7:6
an oath by your **h** Matt 5:36
nowhere to lay His **h** Matt 8:20
h of John the Baptist Matt 14:8
not a hair of your **h** Luke 21:18
crown...on His **h** John 19:2
God is the **h** of 1 Cor 11:3
husband is the **h** Eph 5:23

HEADLONG *headfirst*
He rushes **h** at Him Job 15:26
falling **h**, he burst Acts 1:18
h into the error Jude 11

HEAL *make well, restore*
will **h** their land 2 Chr 7:14
h-s the brokenhearted Ps 147:3
a time to **h** Eccl 3:3
H me, O LORD Jer 17:14
will **h** their apostasy Hos 14:4
h-ed all who were Matt 8:16
H *the* sick, raise Matt 10:8
h him on...Sabbath Mark 3:2
Physician, **h** yourself Luke 4:23
you may be **h-ed** James 5:16
fatal wound was **h-ed** Rev 13:3

HEALING *health, wholeness*
be **h** to your body Prov 3:8
h to the bones Prov 16:24
sorrow is beyond **h** Jer 8:18
There is no **h** for Jer 46:11
their leaves for **h** Ezek 47:12
h every kind of Matt 4:23
gifts of **h** 1 Cor 12:9
h of the nations Rev 22:2

HEALTH *soundness, wholeness*
no **h** in my bones Ps 38:3
restore you to **h** Jer 30:17
and be in good **h** 3 John 2

HEAP (n) *mound, pile*
stones and made a **h** Gen 31:46
waters stood...like a **h** Ex 15:8
made a refuse **h** Ezra 6:11
needy from the ash **h** Ps 113:7
Jerusalem a **h** of ruins Jer 9:11
altars are...**h-s** Hos 12:11

HEAP (v) *pile up, place*
h misfortunes on Deut 32:23
will **h** burning coals Prov 25:22
H on the wood Ezek 24:10
h up rubble to Hab 1:10

HEAR *listen*
h-d the sound of Gen 3:10
God **h-d** their groaning Ex 2:24
H, O Israel Deut 6:4
h the wisdom of 1 Kin 4:34
h in heaven 1 Kin 8:30
Will God **h** his cry Job 27:9
who **h** prayer Ps 65:2
h Your lovingkindness Ps 143:8
poor **h-s** no rebuke Prov 13:8
deaf will **h** words Is 29:18
bones, **h** the word Ezek 37:4
ears to **h**, let him **h** Matt 11:15
h of wars and Mark 13:7
he who **h-s** My word John 5:24
does not **h** sinners John 9:31
sheep **h** My voice John 10:27
we **h-d** of your faith Col 1:4
anyone **h-s** My voice Rev 3:20

HEARING *listening*
in the LORD's **h** 1 Sam 8:21
in the **h** of a fool Prov 23:9
fulfilled in your **h** Luke 4:21
I will give you a **h** Acts 23:35
become dull of **h** Heb 5:11

HEART
mind or *seat of emotions*
intent of man's **h** is Gen 8:21
I will harden his **h** Ex 4:21
great searchings of **h** Judg 5:16
LORD looks at the **h** 1 Sam 16:7
fool has said in his **h** Ps 14:1
meditation of my **h** Ps 19:14
My **h** is like wax Ps 22:14
in me a clean **h** Ps 51:10
and a contrite **h** Ps 51:17
Your word...in my **h** Ps 119:11
Deceit is in the **h** Prov 12:20
A joyful **h** is good Prov 17:22
to a troubled **h** Prov 25:20
bribe corrupts the **h** Eccl 7:7
a new **h** and a new Ezek 18:31
uncircumcised in **h** Ezek 44:7
are the pure in **h** Matt 5:8
adultery...in his **h** Matt 5:28
and humble in **h** Matt 11:29
h is far...from Me Matt 15:8
pondering...in her **h** Luke 2:19
pierced to the **h** Acts 2:37
cleansing their **h-s** Acts 15:9
who searches the **h-s** Rom 8:27
tablets of human **h-s** 2 Cor 3:3
not lose **h** in doing Gal 6:9
melody with your **h** Eph 5:19
intentions of the **h** Heb 4:12
deceives his *own* **h** James 1:26

HEAT *hotness, warmth*
the **h** of the day Gen 18:1
and **h** consume Job 24:19
hidden from its **h** Ps 19:6
a shade from the **h** Is 25:4
burning **h** of famine Lam 5:10
scorching **h** of the Matt 20:12
with intense **h** 2 Pet 3:10
scorched with fierce **h** Rev 16:9

HEAVE OFFERING
see **OFFERINGS**

HEAVEN *place of God* or *sky*
God created the **h-s** Gen 1:1
rain bread from **h** Ex 16:4
shut up the **h-s** Deut 11:17
thunder in the **h-s** 1 Sam 2:10
fire came...from **h** 2 Kin 1:14
make windows in **h** 2 Kin 7:2
walks...vault of **h** Job 22:14
I consider Your **h-s** Ps 8:3
h and earth praise Ps 69:34
fixed patterns of **h** Jer 33:25
lights in the **h-s** Ezek 32:8
open...windows of **h** Mal 3:10
kingdom of **h** is at Matt 3:2
voice out of the **h-s** Matt 3:17

reward in **h** is great Matt 5:12
Father who is in **h** Matt 6:9
shall have been loosed in **h** Matt 16:19
great signs from **h** Luke 21:11
Him go into **h** Acts 1:11
no...name under **h** Acts 4:12
up to the third **h** 2 Cor 12:2
citizenship is in **h** Phil 3:20
there was war in **h** Rev 12:7
new **h** and a new Rev 21:1

HEAVENLY *related to God*
h Father is perfect Matt 5:48
h Father knows that Matt 6:32
h host praising God Luke 2:13
I tell you **h** things John 3:12
Him in the **h** *places* Eph 2:6
partakers of a **h** Heb 3:1
shadow of the **h** Heb 8:5

HEAVY
burdensome, hard to lift
Moses' hands were **h** Ex 17:12
servitude was **h** on Neh 5:18
h drinkers of wine Prov 23:20
A stone is **h** Prov 27:3
Jerusalem a **h** stone Zech 12:3
eyes were very **h** Mark 14:40

HEBER
1 *son of Beriah* Gen 46:17
2 *husband of Jael* Judg 4:17
3 *son of Mered* 1 Chr 4:18
4 *son of Elpaal* 1 Chr 8:17
see also **EBER**

HEBREW(S)
1 *people* Gen 14:13; Ex 1:15;9:13; Jon 1:9
2 *language* John 19:17; Acts 22:2;26:14
see also **JUDEAN**
see also **CANAAN**

HEBRON
1 *site of Sarah's death* Gen 23:2
visited by spies Num 13:22
destroyed Josh 10:37
city of refuge Josh 20:7
residence of David 2 Sam 2:1
2 *son of Kohath* Ex 6:18
3 *son of Mareshah* 1 Chr 2:42

HEDGE *border* or *protection*
You not made a **h** Job 1:10
as a **h** of thorns Prov 15:19
along the **h-s,** and Luke 14:23

HEEL *back of foot*
bruise him on the **h** Gen 3:15
on to Esau's **h** Gen 25:26
his **h** against Me John 13:18

HEIFER *young cow*
unblemished red **h** Num 19:2
plowed with my **h** Judg 14:18
Egypt is a pretty **h** Jer 46:20
Like a stubborn **h** Hos 4:16

HEIGHT *elevation, heaven, sky*
in the **h** of heaven Job 22:12
from His holy **h** Ps 102:19
Praise Him in the **h-s** Ps 148:1
As the heavens for **h** Prov 25:3
ascend above the **h-s** Is 14:14
nor **h,** nor depth Rom 8:39

HEIR *person who inherits*
in my house is my **h** Gen 15:3
has he no **h-s** Jer 49:1
h-s also, **h-s** of God Rom 8:17
an **h** through God Gal 4:7
h-s of the kingdom James 2:5

HELIOPOLIS
ancient Egyptian city Jer 43:13
see also **ON**

HELL *place of dead*
go into the fiery **h** Matt 5:22
soul and body in **h** Matt 10:28
to be cast into **h** Mark 9:47
set on fire by **h** James 3:6
cast them into **h** 2 Pet 2:4
see also **HADES** ***AND*** **SHEOL**

HELLENISTIC JEWS
Greek speaking Jews Acts 6:1;9:29

HELMET *headpiece*
bronze **h** on his 1 Sam 17:5
h of salvation Is 59:17
take the **h** of Eph 6:17

HELP (n) *assistance, relief*
h is not within me Job 6:13
He is our **h** and our Ps 33:20
present **h** in trouble Ps 46:1
I cried for **h** Jon 2:2
gifts of...**h-s** 1 Cor 12:28

HELP (v) *aid, assist*
h-ing the Hebrew Ex 1:16
the LORD **h-ed** David 2 Sam 8:6
whence shall my **h** Ps 121:1
I will **h** you Is 41:13
Lord, **h** me Matt 15:25
h my unbelief Mark 9:24
must **h** the weak Acts 20:35
Spirit also **h-s** our Rom 8:26
earth **h-ed** the Rev 12:16

HELPER *one who assists*
h of the orphan Ps 10:14
be my **h** Ps 30:10
Behold, God is my **h** Ps 54:4
give you another **H** John 14:16
H, the Holy Spirit John 14:26

HELPLESS *weak*
the **h** has hope Job 5:16
who considers the **h** Ps 41:1
while we were still **h** Rom 5:6

HEMAN
1 *sage of Solomon* 1 Kin 4:31
2 *line of Samuel* 1 Chr 15:19

HEMORRHAGE *bleeding*
suffering from a **h** Matt 9:20
a **h** for twelve years Mark 5:25
her **h** stopped Luke 8:44

HEN *fowl*
h gathers her Matt 23:37
as a **h** *gathers* her Luke 13:34

HEPHZIBAH
Manasseh's mother 2 Kin 21:1
Hezekiah's wife 2 Kin 21:3

HERB *dried plant*
bread and bitter **h-s** Ex 12:8
fade like the green **h** Ps 37:2
h-s of...mountains Prov 27:25
sweet-scented **h-s** Song 5:13

HERD *cattle, flock*
firstborn of your **h** Deut 12:6
h, or flock taste a Jon 3:7
h of many swine Matt 8:30

HERDSMEN *keepers of flocks*
h of Abram's livestock Gen 13:7
between my **h** and Gen 13:8
the **h** ran away Matt 8:33

HERITAGE *what is inherited*
the **h** decreed to him Job 20:29
my **h** is beautiful Ps 16:6
their land as a **h** Ps 136:21
inherit the desolate **h-s** Is 49:8
you who pillage My **h** Jer 50:11

HERMES
1 *Greek god* Acts 14:12
2 *Roman Christian* Rom 16:14

HERMOGENES
Asian Christian who failed to support Paul 2 Tim 1:15

HERMON
mountain region in N Palestine Josh 11:17; Ps 42:6;133:3
N boundary of Promised Land Deut 3:8

HEROD
1 **Herod the Great**
king of Judea, Samaria, Ituraea and Traconitis Matt 2:1
ruled during Jesus' birth Matt 2:1ff
2 **Herod Archelaus**
son of Herod the Great Matt 2:22
governor of Ituraea and Traconitis
3 **Herod Antipas**
son of Herod the Great Matt 14:1
tetrarch of Galilee and Perea Luke 3:1
ruled during Jesus' ministry Luke 13:31;23:7,8,11
executed John the Baptist Matt 14:10; Mark 6:27
4 **Herod Philip I**
son of Herod the Great Mark 6:17
5 **Herod Philip II**
son of Herod the Great Luke 3:1
tetrarch of Ituraea and Traconitis
6 **Herod Agrippa I**
grandson of Herod the Great Acts 12:1
king of Judea and Samaria
persecuted the early church Acts 12:2-23
7 **Herod Agrippa II**
son of Agrippa I Acts 25:13
tetrarch of Tiberias, Abila and Traconitis
heard Paul's testimony Acts 25:23ff;26:1ff

HERODIANS
influential Jews favoring Herod Matt 22:16; Mark 3:6

HERODIAS
wife of Herod Antipas Matt 14:3; Mark 6:17
requested head of John the Baptist Matt 14:8; Mark 6:24

HETH
1 *son of Canaan* Gen 10:15
2 *Hebrew eponym for Hittites* Gen 23:10

HEW *chop, cut*
h down their Asherim Deut 7:5
H-n cisterns, vineyards Neh 9:25
h-n out in the rock Mark 15:46

HEZEKIAH
king of Judah 2 Kin 18:1
reformer 2 Kin 18:4
warrior 2 Kin 18:7,8
builder 2 Kin 20:20

HIDDEN (adj) *concealed*
Acquit me of **h** *faults* Ps 19:12
h wealth of secret Is 45:3
h snares for my feet Jer 18:22
profound and **h** Dan 2:22
some of the **h** manna Rev 2:17

HIDE *conceal, cover*
man and his wife **hid** Gen 3:8
I **h** from Abraham Gen 18:17
Moses **hid** his face Ex 3:6
h me in Sheol Job 14:13
h-ing my iniquity Job 31:33
H me in the shadow Ps 17:8
Do not **h** Your face Ps 27:9
wrongs are not **h-den** Ps 69:5
sees evil *and* **h-s** Prov 27:12
hid your talent Matt 25:25
nothing is **h-den** Mark 4:22
Jesus **hid** Himself John 8:59
h us from...Him Rev 6:16

HIDING PLACE
Clouds are a **h** Job 22:14
He lurks in a **h** Ps 10:9
You are my **h** Ps 32:7
uncovered his **h-s** Jer 49:10

HIERAPOLIS
city in Asia Minor Col 4:13

HIGH *elevated* or *heavenly*
it is still **h** day Gen 29:7
the **h** places of Baal Num 22:41
h above all nations Deut 26:19

h as the heavens Job 11:8
my advocate is on **h** Job 16:19
set him *securely* on **h** Ps 91:14
or **h** as heaven Is 7:11
to a very **h** mountain Matt 4:8
the **h** priest Matt 26:57
Son of the Most **H** Mark 5:7
from a **h** fever Luke 4:38
He ascended on **h** Eph 4:8

HIGH PLACE
worship place of God or idols
Num 22:41; 1 Sam 9:12-14

HIGH PRIEST
first in hierarchy Ex 27:21
under Aaron Ex 28:1,2
enters Holy of Holies
Ex 28:29,30; Heb 9:7
head of Sanhedrin
Matt 26:57; Acts 5:21
Jesus as High Priest
Heb 3:1;5:5-9

HIGHWAY *road*
along the king's **h** Num 20:17
h from Egypt to Is 19:23
the **H** of Holiness Is 35:8
a **h** for our God Is 40:3
Go out into the **h-s**
Luke 14:23

HILKIAH
1 *father of Eliakim*
2 Kin 18:18
2 *high priest* 2 Kin 22:4-14
3 *Merarite Levite* 1 Chr 6:45
4 *son of Hosah* 1 Chr 26:11
5 *was with Ezra* Neh 8:4
6 *returned from exile*
Neh 12:7

HILL *mountain*
the everlasting **h-s** Gen 49:26
the **h** of God 1 Sam 10:5
dwell on Your holy **h** Ps 15:1
to Your holy **h** Ps 43:3
cattle...thousand **h-s** Ps 50:10
h-s, Fall on us Hos 10:8
city set on a **h** Matt 5:14
h...brought low Luke 3:5
the brow of the **h** Luke 4:29
h-s, Cover us Luke 23:30

HINDER *delay, impede, restrain*
h meditation before Job 15:4
do not **h** them Matt 19:14
do not **h** them Luke 18:16
h-ed you from obeying Gal 5:7
prayers...not be **h-ed** 1 Pet 3:7

HINNOM
1 *valley SW of Jerusalem*
Josh 15:8; Neh 11:30
2 *person for whom valley named* 2 Kin 23:10; Jer 7:31

HIP *part of body*
the sinew of the **h** Gen 32:32
curves of your **h-s** are Song 7:1
h joints went slack Dan 5:6

HIRAM / HURAM
1 *king of Tyre* 1 Kin 5:1ff;
2 Chr 2:3,11
2 *skilled craftsman* 1 Kin 7:14;
2 Chr 4:11

HIRE (n) *wages*
it came for its **h** Ex 22:15
the **h** of a harlot Deut 23:18

HIRE (v) *engage for labor*
h...for bread 1 Sam 2:5
and **h-d** the Arameans
2 Sam 10:6
to **h**...chariots 1 Chr 19:6
he who **h-s** a fool Prov 26:10
to **h** laborers for Matt 20:1

HIRED (adj) *employed*
as a **h** man, as if Lev 25:40
oppress a **h** servant
Deut 24:14
as one of your **h** Luke 15:19
h hand...not a shepherd
John 10:12
because he is a **h** hand
John 10:13

HISS *to show dislike*
h him from his place Job 27:23
object of...**h-ing** Jer 18:16
They **h** and shake Lam 2:15
h *And* wave his hand
Zeph 2:15

HITTITES
1 *people in Palestine in patriarchal age*
Gen 15:20;49:29
2 *inhabitants of Aram during Israelite monarchy*
2 Kin 7:6; 2 Chr 8:7

HIVITES
people dispossessed by the Israelites Ex 23:28;
Josh 3:10; 2 Sam 24:7

HOGLAH
daughter of Zelophehad
Num 26:33;27:1; Josh 17:3

HOLD *grasp, retain*
Moses **held** his hand Ex 17:11
h fast to Him Deut 11:22
h fast...evil purpose Ps 64:5
heart **h** fast my words Prov 4:4
Take **h** of instruction Prov 4:13
h fast My covenant Is 56:4
h to the tradition Mark 7:8
h fast the word 1 Cor 15:2
h-ing to the mystery 1 Tim 3:9
h of the eternal 1 Tim 6:12
He **held** seven stars Rev 1:16

HOLE *opening*
the **h** of the cobra Is 11:8
a **h** in the wall Ezek 8:7
a purse with **h-s** Hag 1:6
foxes have **h-s** Matt 8:20

HOLIDAY *period of leisure*
a feast and a **h** Esth 8:17
a **h** for rejoicing Esth 9:19
mourning into a **h** Esth 9:22

HOLINESS *sacredness*
majestic in **h** Ex 15:11
H befits Your house Ps 93:5
the Highway of **H** Is 35:8
without blame in **h**
1 Thess 3:13
we may share His **h**
Heb 12:10

HOLLOW *empty space*
the **h** of a sling 1 Sam 25:29
in the **h** of His hand Is 40:12

HOLY *sacred, sanctified*
standing is **h** ground Ex 3:5
sabbath...keep it **h** Ex 20:8
you are a **h** people Deut 7:6
ten thousand **h** ones
Deut 33:2
h like the LORD 1 Sam 2:2
Worship...**h** array
1 Chr 16:29
His **h** dwelling 2 Chr 30:27
Jerusalem, the **h** city
Neh 11:1
Zion, My **h** mountain Ps 2:6
to His **h** land Ps 78:54
bless His **h** name Ps 145:21
H, H, H, is the LORD Is 6:3
the **H** One of Israel Is 30:15
what is **h** to dogs Matt 7:6
righteous and **h** man
Mark 6:20
the **H** One of God Luke 4:34
in the **h** Scriptures Rom 1:2
and **h** sacrifice Rom 12:1
with a **h** kiss Rom 16:16
h both in body 1 Cor 7:34
lifting up **h** hands 1 Tim 2:8
with a **h** calling 2 Tim 1:9
I saw the **h** city Rev 21:2

HOLY OF HOLIES
most holy place in the Tabernacle / Temple
Ex 26:33,34; 2 Chr 3:8

HOLY SPIRIT
Third Person of the Godhead
Matt 28:19; 2 Cor 13:14
Helper John 14:16,26
Giver of gifts
Rom 12:6-8; 1 Cor 12:8-11
fruit of the Spirit Gal 5:22

HOMAGE *act of reverence*
my people shall do **h**
Gen 41:40
did **h** to the LORD 1 Chr 29:20
and paid **h** to Haman Esth 3:2
did **h** to Daniel Dan 2:46

HOME *place of dwelling*
free at **h** one year Deut 24:5
God makes a **h** Ps 68:6
husband is not at **h** Prov 7:19
to his eternal **h** Eccl 12:5
Go **h** to your people
Mark 5:19
let him eat at **h** 1 Cor 11:34
at **h** in the body 2 Cor 5:6
at **h** with the Lord 2 Cor 5:8

HOMER *measure of capacity*
a **h** of barley Lev 27:16
a **h** of seed Is 5:10
from a **h** of wheat Ezek 45:13

HOMESTEAD *family dwelling*
h forlorn and forsaken Is 27:10
h be made desolate Acts 1:20

HOMOSEXUALS
effeminate, nor **h** 1 Cor 6:9
immoral men and **h**
1 Tim 1:10

HONEST *respectable, truthful*
we are **h** men Gen 42:11
painful are **h** words Job 6:25
an **h** and good heart Luke 8:15

HONEY *sweetness*
with milk and **h** Ex 3:8
swarm of bees and **h** Judg 14:8
is sweeter than **h** Judg 14:18
sweet as **h** in my Ezek 3:3
locusts and wild **h** Matt 3:4

HONEYCOMB *honey storage*
drippings of the **h** Ps 19:10
Pleasant words...a **h**
Prov 16:24

HONOR (n) *glory, great respect*
both riches and **h** 1 Kin 3:13
stripped my **h** from Job 19:9
wise will inherit **h** Prov 3:35
is not without **h** Matt 13:57
glory and **h** and Rom 2:10
Marriage...*be held* in **h**
Heb 13:4
blessing and **h** and Rev 5:13

HONOR (v) *show respect*
H your father Ex 20:12
h the aged Lev 19:32
who **h** Me I will **h** 1 Sam 2:30
am **h-ed** in the sight Is 49:5
A son **h-s** *his* father Mal 1:6
may be **h-ed** by men Matt 6:2
h-s Me with...lips Matt 15:8
does not **h** the Son John 5:23
fear God, **h** the king
1 Pet 2:17

HONORABLE *respectable*
the elder and **h** man Is 9:15
one vessel for **h** use Rom 9:21
whatever is **h** Phil 4:8

HOOF *part of animal foot*
which divide the **h** Lev 11:4
with horns and **h-s** Ps 69:31
h-s of beasts will Ezek 32:13
tear off their **h-s** Zech 11:16

HOOK *fastener*
into pruning **h-s** Is 2:4
My **h** in your nose Is 37:29
h-s into your jaws Ezek 38:4

HOPE (n) *expectation*
Where now is my **h**
Job 17:15
h of the afflicted Ps 9:18
My **h** is in You Ps 39:7
You are my **h** Ps 71:5
while there is **h** Prov 19:18
the **h** of Israel Jer 17:13
our **h** has perished
Ezek 37:11
on trial for the **h** Acts 23:6

h does not disappoint Rom 5:5
rejoicing in **h** Rom 12:12
may the God of **h** Rom 15:13
ought to plow in **h** 1 Cor 9:10
now faith, **h**, love, abide 1 Cor 13:13
h of righteousness Gal 5:5
the **h** of His calling Eph 1:18
the **h** of the gospel Col 1:23
the **h** of glory Col 1:27
the **h** of salvation 1 Thess 5:8
h of eternal life Titus 3:7
to a living **h** 1 Pet 1:3
h that is in you 1 Pet 3:15

HOPE (v)
expect with confidence
I will **h** in Him Job 13:15
For I **h** in You Ps 38:15
We **h** for justice Is 59:11
are **h-ing** for light Jer 13:16
Gentiles will **h** Matt 12:21
h-s all things 1 Cor 13:7
first to **h** in Christ Eph 1:12
I **h** in the Lord Jesus Phil 2:19
of *things* **h-d** for Heb 11:1
I **h** to come to you 2 John 12

HOPHNI
son of Eli 1 Sam 1:3;4:11

HOPHRA *see* **PHARAOH**

HOR
mountain Num 20:22,23
place of Aaron's death Num 20:28; Deut 32:50

HORDE *throng*
against Babylon A **h** Jer 50:9
h-s of grasshoppers Nah 3:17

HOREB
another name for Mount Sinai Ex 3:1; Deut 4:10; Ps 106:19

HORITES
inhabitants of Mount Seir in Edom Gen 14:6;36:29

HORN
caught...by his **h-s** Gen 22:13
h-s of the altar Ex 29:12
you shall sound a **h** Lev 25:9
with the ram's **h** Josh 6:5
h of my salvation 2 Sam 22:3
the **h**, flute, lyre Dan 3:5
it had ten **h-s** Dan 7:7

HORROR *terror*
h overwhelms me Is 21:4
object of **h** Jer 49:13
clothed with **h** Ezek 7:27
cup of **h** Ezek 23:33

HORSE *animal*
bites the **h-'s** heels Gen 49:17
h-s and chariots of 2 Kin 6:17
A **h** is a false hope Ps 33:17
whip is for the **h** Prov 26:3
slaves *riding* on **h-s** Eccl 10:7
behold, a black **h** Rev 6:5

HORSE GATE
see **GATES OF JERUSALEM**

HORSEMEN *cavalry, horse rider*
Pharaoh, his **h** and Ex 14:9
chariots and **h** 1 Kin 10:26
h riding on Ezek 23:12
H charging, Swords Nah 3:3
armies of the **h** Rev 9:16

HOSANNA
acclamation of praise
H to the Son of Matt 21:9
H in the highest Mark 11:10
H! Blessed is He John 12:13

HOSEA
prophet Hos 1:1,2

HOSHEA
1 *name of Joshua* Num 13:8,16
2 *king of Israel* 2 Kin 15:30;17:6
3 *Ephraim's officer* 1 Chr 27:20
4 *signer of covenant* Neh 10:23

HOSPITABLE *friendly*
h, able to teach 1 Tim 3:2
h, loving what is Titus 1:8
h to one another 1 Pet 4:9

HOSPITALITY *open to guests*
practicing **h** Rom 12:13
show **h** to strangers Heb 13:2

HOST *army, multitude*
all the **h** of heaven Deut 4:19
captain...LORD's **h** Josh 5:15
LORD of **h-s**, He is Ps 24:10
of the heavenly **h** Luke 2:13

HOSTILE *antagonistic*
h to...Jesus Acts 26:9
set on the flesh is **h** Rom 8:7
h to all men 1 Thess 2:15

HOT *very warm, violent*
when the sun grew **h** Ex 16:21
and **h** displeasure Deut 9:19
My heart was **h** within Ps 39:3
man walk on **h** coals Prov 6:28
neither cold nor **h** Rev 3:15

HOUR *time*
add a *single* **h** to Matt 6:27
watch...for one **h** Matt 26:40
the **h** is at hand Matt 26:45
ninth **h** Jesus cried Mark 15:34
save Me from this **h** John 12:27
the **h** has come John 17:1
the **h** of testing Rev 3:10

HOUSE *home* or *temple*
born in my **h** is my Gen 15:3
passed over the **h-s** Ex 12:27
the **h** of slavery Ex 20:2
consecrates his **h** Lev 27:14
as for me and my **h** Josh 24:15
Set your **h** in order 2 Kin 20:1
h of God forsaken Neh 13:11
h like the spider's Job 27:18
Holiness befits Your **h** Ps 93:5
LORD builds the **h** Ps 127:1
Wisdom...built her **h** Prov 9:1
in My **h** of prayer Is 56:7
O **h** of Israel Jer 18:6
his **h** on the rock Matt 7:24
My **h**...a **h** of Matt 21:13
devour widows' **h-s** Mark 12:40
guards his own **h** Luke 11:21
left **h** or wife or Luke 18:29
In My Father's **h** John 14:2
h not made...hands 2 Cor 5:1
h for a holy 1 Pet 2:5

HOUSE OF GOD / LORD
see **TEMPLE**

HOUSE OF THE LORD
see **TABERNACLE**

HOUSEHOLD *family, home*
herds and a great **h** Gen 26:14
stole the **h** idols Gen 31:19
each one with his **h** Ex 1:1
to the ways of her **h** Prov 31:27
like a head of a **h** Matt 13:52
are of God's **h** Eph 2:19
manages his own **h** 1 Tim 3:4
in the **h** of God 1 Tim 3:15

HOUSETOP *roof*
As grass on the **h-s** 2 Kin 19:26
lonely bird on a **h** Ps 102:7
upon the **h-s** Matt 10:27
Peter went...the **h** Acts 10:9

HULDAH
a Hebrew prophetess 2 Kin 22:14; 2 Chr 34:22

HUMAN *mankind, person*
the life of any **h** Lev 24:17
guilt of **h** blood Prov 28:17
they had **h** form Ezek 1:5
tablets of **h** hearts 2 Cor 3:3

HUMBLE (adj) *gentle, modest*
Moses was very **h** Num 12:3
h will inherit Ps 37:11
with the **h** is wisdom Prov 11:2
H, and mounted on Zech 9:9
gentle and **h** in Matt 11:29
along with **h** means Phil 4:12
grace to the **h** James 4:6

HUMBLE (v) *modest*
refuse to **h** yourself Ex 10:3
He might **h** you Deut 8:2
h...and pray 2 Chr 7:14
h-s...as this child Matt 18:4
H yourselves 1 Pet 5:6

HUMILIATE *embarrass*
h-d who seek my hurt Ps 71:24
do not feel **h-d** Is 54:4
His opponents...**h-d** Luke 13:17

HUMILIATION *embarrassment*
h has overwhelmed me Ps 44:15
go away together in **h** Is 45:16
let our **h** cover us Jer 3:25
In **h** His judgment Acts 8:33

HUMILITY *self-abasement*
before honor...**h** Prov 15:33
with **h** of mind Phil 2:3
clothe...with **h** 1 Pet 5:5

HUNDRED *number* or *many*
Adam had lived one **h** Gen 5:3
h of you will chase Lev 26:8
captains of **h-s** Num 31:14
h pieces of money Josh 24:32
went out by **h-s** 2 Sam 18:4
in groups of **h-s** Mark 6:40

HUNGER (n) *craving, starvation*
in **h**, in thirst Deut 28:48
lions...suffer **h** Ps 34:10
man will suffer **h** Prov 19:15
h is not satisfied Is 29:8
faint because of **h** Lam 2:19
sleeplessness, in **h** 2 Cor 6:5

HUNGER (v) *crave, need food*
the righteous to **h** Prov 10:3
are those who **h** Matt 5:6
to Me will not **h** John 6:35
They will **h** no longer Rev 7:16

HUNGRY *empty, needing food*
let you be **h** Deut 8:3
people are **h** and 2 Sam 17:29
h soul He has filled Ps 107:9
If your enemy is **h** Prov 25:21
when a **h** man dreams Is 29:8
He then became **h** Matt 4:2
disciples became **h** Matt 12:1
For I was **h** Matt 25:35
if your enemy is **h** Rom 12:20

HUNT *pursue, seek*
to **h** for game Gen 27:5
h-s a partridge 1 Sam 26:20
evil **h** the violent Ps 140:11
H-ed me down like Lam 3:52

HUNTER *seeker of game*
Nimrod a mighty **h** Gen 10:9
became a skillful **h** Gen 25:27

HUR
1 *helped Moses and Aaron* Ex 17:12;24:14
2 *Bezalel's grandfather* Ex 31:2
3 *king of Midian* Num 31:8
4 *father of Rephaiah* Neh 3:9

HURAM
a Benjamite 1 Chr 8:5
see also **HIRAM / HURAM**

HURT (n)
damage, harm, wound
Who delight in my **h** Ps 70:2
hoarded...to his **h** Eccl 5:13
your brother is **h** Rom 14:15

HURT (v) *cause pain, wound*
not allow him to **h** Gen 31:7
may be **h** by them Eccl 10:9

will not **h** or destroy Is 11:9
their power to **h** men Rev 9:10

HUSBAND *family head, spouse*
desire...your **h** Gen 3:16
honor to their **h-s** Esth 1:20
crown of her **h** Prov 12:4
is loved by *her* **h** Hos 3:1
divorces her **h** and Mark 10:12
have had five **h-s** John 4:18
if her **h** dies Rom 7:2
have her own **h** 1 Cor 7:2
unbelieving **h** is 1 Cor 7:14
h is the head of Eph 5:23
H-s, love your wives Eph 5:25
h-s of...one wife 1 Tim 3:12
adorned for her **h** Rev 21:2

HUSHAI
servant of David 2 Sam 15:32;16:17

HYMENAEUS
heretical teacher at Ephesus 1 Tim 1:20; 2 Tim 2:17

HYMN *song of praise*
h-s of thanksgiving Neh 12:46
after singing a **h** Matt 26:30
singing **h-s** of praise Acts 16:25
psalms and **h-s** and Eph 5:19

HYPOCRISY *pretense*
full of **h** and Matt 23:28
love be without **h** Rom 12:9
without **h** James 3:17

HYPOCRITE *a pretender*
as the **h-s** do Matt 6:2
and Pharisees, **h-s** Matt 23:13
You **h**, first take Luke 6:42

HYSSOP *fragrant plant*
bunch of **h** and dip it Ex 12:22
scarlet string and **h** Lev 14:4
Purify me with **h** Ps 51:7
upon *a branch of* **h** John 19:29

I

I AM
related to name of God in Hebrew
I WHO I Ex 3:14
I has sent me Ex 3:14
I the LORD Ex 6:2
I the LORD your God Lev 19:3
I the first Is 44:6
I the Son of God Matt 27:43
Jesus said, I Mark 14:62
believe that I *He* John 8:24
will know that I *He* John 8:28
before Abraham...I John 8:58
believe that I *He* John 13:19
I the Alpha and Rev 1:8
I the first and Rev 1:17

ICE *frost*
turbid because of **i** Job 6:16
womb has come...**i** Job 38:29
casts forth His **i** Ps 147:17

ICHABOD
1 *son of Phinehas* 1 Sam 4:19,20
grandson of Eli 1 Sam 14:3
2 *name commemorates departed glory from Israel* 1 Sam 4:21,22

ICONIUM
city of Asia Minor Acts 14:1,19;16:2; 2 Tim 3:11

IDLE *unemployed, uninvolved*
i man will suffer Prov 19:15
been standing here **i** Matt 20:6
this **i** babbler Acts 17:18

IDOL *false deity, image*
not make...an **i** Ex 20:4
Do not turn to **i-s** Lev 19:4
who makes an **i** or Deut 27:15
the gods...are **i-s** Ps 96:5
who blesses an **i** Is 66:3
abstain from...**i-s** Acts 15:20
guard...from **i-s** 1 John 5:21

IDOLATER *idol worshiper*
covetous, or an **i** 1 Cor 5:11
Do not be **i-s** 1 Cor 10:7
sorcerers and **i-s** Rev 21:8

IDOLATRY *idol worship*
flee from **i** 1 Cor 10:14
i, sorcery, enmities Gal 5:20
and abominable **i-ies** 1 Pet 4:3

IGNORANCE
lack of knowledge
you worship in **i** Acts 17:23
i that is in them Eph 4:18
silence the **i** of 1 Pet 2:15

IGNORANT *without knowledge*
I was senseless and **i** Ps 73:22
not **i** of his schemes 2 Cor 2:11
and **i** speculations 2 Tim 2:23

ILL *unhealthy, sick*
woman who is **i** Lev 15:33
became mortally **i** Is 38:1
lunatic and is...**i** Matt 17:15
healed many...**i** Mark 1:34

ILLEGITIMATE *bastard*
No one of **i** birth Deut 23:2
borne **i** children Hos 5:7
you are **i** children Heb 12:8

ILLNESS *infirmity, sickness*
sick with the **i** 2 Kin 13:14
after his **i** and Is 38:9
because of a bodily **i** Gal 4:13

ILLUMINE *light up*
God **i-s** my darkness Ps 18:28
fire to **i** by night Ps 105:39
glory of God has **i-d** Rev 21:23
God will **i** them Rev 22:5

IMAGE *copy, likeness*
make man in Our **i** Gen 1:26
i of God He made Gen 9:6
burn their graven **i-s** Deut 7:5
worshiped a molten **i** Ps 106:19
made an **i** of gold Dan 3:1
i and glory of God 1 Cor 11:7
i of the invisible Col 1:15
the **i** of the beast Rev 13:15

IMITATORS *followers*
be **i** of me 1 Cor 4:16
be **i** of God Eph 5:1
i of the churches 1 Thess 2:14

IMMANUEL
1 *son born to a virgin* Is 7:14
a sign to King Ahaz Is 8:8
2 *title of Jesus* Matt 1:23

IMMORAL *lewd, unchaste*
with **i** people 1 Cor 5:9
the **i** man sins 1 Cor 6:18
i men...liars 1 Tim 1:10
i or godless person Heb 12:16
and **i** persons Rev 21:8

IMMORALITY *immoral acts*
no **i** in your midst Lev 20:14
except for **i** Matt 19:9
Flee **i** 1 Cor 6:18
abstain from...**i** 1 Thess 4:3
the wine of her **i** Rev 17:2

IMMORTALITY *everlasting life*
must put on **i** 1 Cor 15:53
alone possesses **i** 1 Tim 6:16
life and **i** to light 2 Tim 1:10

IMPATIENT *restless*
the people became **i** Num 21:4
should I not be **i** Job 21:4
my soul was **i** with Zech 11:8

IMPERISHABLE *indestructible*
wreath, but we an **i** 1 Cor 9:25
will be raised **i** 1 Cor 15:52
inheritance...*is* **i** 1 Pet 1:4

IMPLEMENTS *tools, utensils*
forger of all **i** of Gen 4:22
the **i** of the oxen 1 Kin 19:21

IMPLORE *ask, beseech, entreat*
I **i** you, give glory Josh 7:19
i-d him to avert Esth 8:3
i the compassion of Job 8:5
centurion...**i-ing** Him Matt 8:5
I **i** You by God Mark 5:7
They were **i-ing** Him Luke 8:31
I **i-d** the Lord 2 Cor 12:8
i you to walk in a Eph 4:1

IMPORTED *brought in*
chariot was **i** from 1 Kin 10:29
horses were **i** 2 Chr 1:16

IMPOSE *force upon*
i-d hard labor on us Deut 26:6
whatever you **i** on 2 Kin 18:14
you **i** heavy rent Amos 5:11
i-d until a time of Heb 9:10

IMPOSSIBLE *cannot be done*
nothing...will be **i** Gen 11:6
With people this is **i** Matt 19:26
i for God to lie Heb 6:18
without faith it is **i** Heb 11:6

IMPRISON *jail, restrict*
i-ed him at Riblah 2 Kin 23:33
i his princes at will Ps 105:22
not **i** their survivors Obad 14
I used to **i** and beat Acts 22:19

IMPRISONMENT *confinement*
in **i-s**, in tumults 2 Cor 6:5
Remember my **i** Col 4:18
even to **i** as a 2 Tim 2:9

IMPURE *unclean*
her **i** discharge Lev 15:25
eating...with **i** hands Mark 7:2
no immoral or **i** person Eph 5:5

IMPURITY *uncleanness*
menstrual **i** for seven Lev 15:19
i-ies of the sons of Lev 16:19
the **i** of the nations Ezra 6:21
as slaves to **i** Rom 6:19
of **i** with greediness Eph 4:19

INCENSE *fragrant substance*
burn fragrant **i** on Ex 30:7
i as an offering Lev 2:16
gold pans, full of **i** Num 7:86
My altar, to burn **i** 1 Sam 2:28
i on the high places 2 Kin 14:4
i before the LORD 1 Chr 23:13
golden altar of **i** Heb 9:4
the smoke of the **i** Rev 8:4

INCEST *illicit sexual relations*
they...committed **i** Lev 20:12

INCITE *stir up*
i-d David against 2 Sam 24:1
Jezebel...**i-d** him 1 Kin 21:25
I will **i** Egyptians Is 19:2
who **i-s** the people Luke 23:14
Jews **i-d** the devout Acts 13:50

INCLINE *bend, lean*
i your hearts to Josh 24:23
I my heart to Your Ps 119:36
i-s toward wickedness Is 32:6
I Your ear, O LORD Is 37:17
have not **i-d** your ear Jer 35:15

INCOME *wages*
i of the wicked Prov 10:16
i with injustice Prov 16:8
abundance *with its* **i** Eccl 5:10

INCORRUPTIBLE *not impure*
glory of the **i** God Rom 1:23
Christ with **i** *love* Eph 6:24

INCREASE (n) *multiplication*
the **i** of your herd Deut 7:13
the **i** of your house 1 Sam 2:33
the LORD give you **i** Ps 115:14
i of *His* government Is 9:7

INCREASE (v) *multiply*
If riches **i**, do not Ps 62:10
the righteous **i** Prov 28:28
i-ing in wisdom Luke 2:52
i-ing in...knowledge Col 1:10
Lord cause...to **i** 1 Thess 3:12

INCURABLE *fatal, without cure*
with an **i** sickness 2 Chr 21:18
sickliness and **i** pain Is 17:11
Your wound is **i** Jer 30:12

INDIA
lower Indus valley in S Asia
Esth 1:1;8:9

INDIGNANT *be angry*
i toward His enemies Is 66:14
the ten became **i** Matt 20:24
Jesus...was **i** Mark 10:14
i because Jesus had Luke 13:14

INDIGNATION *anger*
God who has **i** Ps 7:11
Pour out Your **i** Ps 69:24
lips are filled with **i** Is 30:27
filled me with **i** Jer 15:17
stand before His **i** Nah 1:6

INFANT *child*
carries a nursing **i** Num 11:12
an **i** *who lives* Is 65:20
tongue of the **i** Lam 4:4
the mouth of **i-s** Matt 21:16
as to **i-s** in Christ 1 Cor 3:1

INFECTION *disease*
an **i** of leprosy Lev 13:2
with the scaly **i** Lev 13:31
against an **i** of Deut 24:8

INFERIOR *lower in status*
I am not **i** to you Job 12:3
i against the honorable Is 3:5
i to...apostles 2 Cor 12:11

INFINITE *unlimited*
His understanding is **i** Ps 147:5

INFLICT *strike, impose*
frogs...He had **i-ed** Ex 8:12
i all these curses Deut 30:7
i-s pain, and gives Job 5:18

INGATHERING, FEAST OF
see **FEASTS**

INHABIT *dwell*
no one would **i** Job 15:28
She shall be **i-ed** Is 44:26
build houses and **i** Is 65:21
those **i-ing** the desert Jer 9:26
who **i** the coastlands Ezek 39:6
but not **i** *them* Zeph 1:13

INHABITANT *resident*
i-s of the cities Gen 19:25
cities...without **i** Is 6:11
ruins Without **i** Jer 4:7
i-s of the seacoast Zeph 2:5
i-s of Jerusalem Zech 12:10

INHERIT *receive a legacy*
shall **i** *it* forever Ex 32:13
humble will **i** the land Ps 37:11
wise will **i** honor Prov 3:35
The naive **i** foolishness Prov 14:18
gentle...**i** the earth Matt 5:5
do to **i** eternal life Luke 10:25
not **i** the kingdom 1 Cor 6:9
might **i** a blessing 1 Pet 3:9
who overcomes will **i** Rev 21:7

INHERITANCE *bequest, legacy*
Levites for an **i** Num 18:24
the LORD is his **i** Deut 10:9
the nations as Your **i** Ps 2:8
will He forsake His **i** Ps 94:14
man leaves an **i** Prov 13:22
I...abandoned My **i** Jer 12:7
Your **i** a reproach Joel 2:17
A man and his **i** Mic 2:2
the **i** will be ours Mark 12:7
we...obtained an **i** Eph 1:11
the **i** of the saints Col 1:12
i...imperishable 1 Pet 1:4

INIQUITY *injustice, wickedness*
bear...their **i-ies** Lev 16:22
the **i** of the fathers Deut 5:9
those who plow **i** Job 4:8
O LORD, Pardon my **i** Ps 25:11
my **i** I did not hide Ps 32:5
blot out all my **i-ies** Ps 51:9
sows **i** will reap Prov 22:8
weighed down with **i** Is 1:4
the workers of **i** Is 31:2
die for his own **i** Jer 31:30
Repent...so that **i** Ezek 18:30
the bondage of **i** Acts 8:23
the *very* world of **i** James 3:6
remembered her **i-ies** Rev 18:5

INJUNCTION *decree*
establish the **i** Dan 6:8
that no **i** or statute Dan 6:15

INJURE *harm, wrong*
who seek to **i** me Ps 38:12
i-d your neighbors Ezek 22:12
nothing will **i** you Luke 10:19
do you **i** one another Acts 7:26

INJURY *wound*
there is no *further* **i** Ex 21:22
because of my **i** Jer 10:19
no **i**...was found Dan 6:23

INJUSTICE *inequity, unfairness*
do no **i** in judgment Lev 19:15
A God...without **i** Deut 32:4
there **i** on my tongue Job 6:30
They devise **i-s** Ps 64:6
is no **i** with God Rom 9:14

INK *writing liquid*
I wrote them with **i** Jer 36:18
with pen and **i** 3 John 13

INN *lodge for travelers*
no room...in the **i** Luke 2:7
brought him to...**i** Luke 10:34

INNKEEPER *traveler's host*
gave them to the **i** Luke 10:35

INNOCENCE *blamelessness*
wash my hands in **i** Ps 26:6
be incapable of **i** Hos 8:5

INNOCENT *blameless*
do not kill the **i** Ex 23:7
the blood of the **i** Deut 19:13
i before the LORD 2 Sam 3:28
the **i** mock them Job 22:19
that shed **i** blood Prov 6:17
and **i** as doves Matt 10:16
betraying **i** blood Matt 27:4
i of this Man's Matt 27:24
holy, **i**, undefiled Heb 7:26

INQUIRE *ask, seek*
to **i** of the LORD Gen 25:22
I of God, please Judg 18:5
David **i-d** of...LORD 1 Sam 23:2
you come to **i** of Me Ezek 20:3
i-d...where the Messiah Matt 2:4
i-d of them the hour John 4:52

INSANE *mad*
a demon and is **i** John 10:20
I speak as if **i** 2 Cor 11:23

INSCRIBE *carve, write*
were **i-d** in a book Job 19:23
i it on a scroll Is 30:8
and **i** a city on it Ezek 4:1
i *it* on tablets Hab 2:2

INSCRIPTION *writing*
could not read the **i** Dan 5:8
I will engrave an **i** Zech 3:9
Pilate...wrote an **i** John 19:19
i, To An Unknown Acts 17:23

INSECTS
all other winged **i** Lev 11:23

INSIGHT *discernment*
a counselor with **i** 1 Chr 26:14
according to his **i** Prov 12:8
i with understanding Dan 9:22
not gained any **i** Mark 6:52
In all wisdom and **i** Eph 1:8

INSIGNIFICANT *unimportant*
was **i** in Your eyes 2 Sam 7:19
your beginning was **i** Job 8:7
citizen of no **i** city Acts 21:39

INSOLENT *arrogant*
acts with **i** pride Prov 21:24
haters of God, **i** Rom 1:30

INSPECTION GATE
see **GATES OF JERUSALEM**

INSPIRED *stimulated*
the love we **i** in you 2 Cor 8:7
All Scripture is **i** 2 Tim 3:16

INSTINCT *natural tendency*
as creatures of **i** 2 Pet 2:12
they know by **i** Jude 10

INSTRUCT *teach*
Your good Spirit to **i** Neh 9:20
I will **i** you Ps 32:8
the wise is **i-ed** Prov 21:11
i-ed out of the Law Rom 2:18
just as you were **i-ed** Col 2:7
may **i** certain men 1 Tim 1:3

INSTRUCTION *teaching*
will walk in My **i** Ex 16:4
Heed **i** and be wise Prov 8:33
Get wisdom and **i** Prov 23:23
i-s to His twelve Matt 11:1
written for our **i** Rom 15:4
i of the Lord Eph 6:4
goal of our **i** is love 1 Tim 1:5
i about washings Heb 6:2

INSTRUMENT *object, vessel*
cut...with sharp **i-s** 1 Chr 20:3
and **i-s** of music 2 Chr 5:13
with stringed **i-s** Ps 150:4
he is a chosen **i** Acts 9:15
i-s of unrighteousness Rom 6:13

INSULT (n) *affront, indignity*
i-s of the nations Ezek 34:29
evil, or **i** for **i** 1 Pet 3:9

INSULT (v) *treat with scorn*
and do not **i** her Ruth 2:15
to **i** the LORD 2 Chr 32:17
times you have **i-ed** Job 19:3
i-ing...with the same words Matt 27:44
and **i** you Luke 6:22
i-ed the Spirit of Heb 10:29

INTEGRITY *honesty*
In the **i** of my heart Gen 20:5
dealt in truth and **i** Judg 9:19
holds fast his **i** Job 2:3
He who walks with **i** Ps 15:2
have walked in my **i** Ps 26:1
The **i** of the upright Prov 11:3

INTELLIGENCE *mental ability*
He deprives of **i** Job 12:24
gave them...**i** Dan 1:17
Paulus, a man of **i** Acts 13:7

INTELLIGENT *bright, smart*
was **i** and beautiful 1 Sam 25:3
mind of the **i** seeks Prov 15:14
from *the* wise and **i** Matt 11:25

INTEND *purpose*
Are you **i-ing** to kill Ex 2:14
I **i** to build a house 1 Kin 5:5
i to make My people Jer 23:27
i-ing to betray Him John 12:4
i-ing...to take Paul Acts 20:13

INTENTION *aim, goal*
the **i-s** of the heart 1 Chr 29:18
i of your heart Acts 8:22
kind **i** of His will Eph 1:5

INTERCEDE *plead, mediate*
i-d for the people Num 21:7
who can **i** for him 1 Sam 2:25
And **i-d** for the Is 53:12
do not **i** with Me Jer 7:16
Spirit Himself **i-s** Rom 8:26

INTERCOURSE *copulation*
not have **i** with Lev 18:20
not have **i**...animal Lev 18:23
husband has had **i** Num 5:20

INTEREST *concern or usury*
not charge him **i** Ex 22:25
not take usurious **i** Lev 25:36
i to a foreigner Deut 23:20
his money at **i** Ps 15:5
mind on God's **i-s** Matt 16:23

money...with **i** Matt 25:27
he has a morbid **i** 1 Tim 6:4

INTERMARRY
I with us Gen 34:9
shall not **i** with Deut 7:3
i with the peoples Ezra 9:14

INTERPRET *explain, translate*
no one who could **i** Gen 41:8
one who **i-s** omens Deut 18:10
He **i** the message Is 28:9
unless he **i-s** 1 Cor 14:5
pray that he may **i** 1 Cor 14:13

INTERPRETATION *explain*
i-s belong to God Gen 40:8
the dream and its **i** Judg 7:15
make its **i** known Dan 5:16
the **i** of tongues 1 Cor 12:10
of one's own **i** 2 Pet 1:20

INTIMATE *close*
my **i** friends have Job 19:14
i with the upright Prov 3:32
separates **i** friends Prov 16:28

INVADE *attack*
king of Assyria **i-d** 2 Kin 17:5
nation has **i-d** my land Joel 1:6
Assyrian **i-s** our land Mic 5:5

INVALIDATE *nullify*
i-d the word of God Matt 15:6
i-ing the word of Mark 7:13
does not **i** a covenant Gal 3:17

INVESTIGATE *examine*
the judges shall **i** Deut 19:18
the plot was **i-d** Esth 2:23
i, and to seek wisdom Eccl 7:25
having **i-d** everything Luke 1:3

INVISIBLE *unseen*
His **i** attributes Rom 1:20
image of the **i** God Col 1:15
visible and **i** Col 1:16
eternal, immortal, **i** 1 Tim 1:17

INVITE *request*
i-d us to impoverish Judg 14:15
you shall **i** Jesse 1 Sam 16:3
i-d all the king's 2 Sam 13:23
I am **i-d** by her Esth 5:12
did not **i** Me in Matt 25:43
i *the* poor Luke 14:13

IRON *metal*
was an **i** bedstead Deut 3:11
whose stones are **i** Deut 8:9
had **i** chariots Judg 1:19
made the **i** float 2 Kin 6:6
break them...rod of **i** Ps 2:9
from the **i** furnace Jer 11:4
as strong as **i** Dan 2:40
rule...rod of **i** Rev 19:15

ISAAC
birth, son of Abraham Gen 21:3
offered for sacrifice Gen 22:2
took Rebekah as wife Gen 24
father of twins Gen 25:26
blessed Jacob Gen 27:1-40

ISAIAH
prophet of Judah Is 1:1
son of Amoz 2 Kin 19:2
called Is 6:8ff
under four kings Is 1:1

ISCARIOT
geographical identity of Judas Mark 3:19; John 12:4; 13:26

ISH-BOSHETH
son of Saul 2 Sam 2:8;3:8;4:8

ISHMAEL
1 *son of Abraham* Gen 16:11;17:18;25:17
2 *son of Nethaniah* 2 Kin 25:23
3 *line of Jonathan* 1 Chr 8:38;9:44
4 *Zebadiah's father* 2 Chr 19:11
5 *son of Jehohanan* 2 Chr 23:1
6 *son of Pashhur* Ezra 10:22

ISLAND *surrounded by water*
the many **i-s** be glad Ps 97:1
He lifts up the **i-s** Is 40:15
i was called Malta Acts 28:1
every **i** fled away Rev 16:20

ISOLATE *set apart*
priest shall **i** *him* Lev 13:4
i him for seven days Lev 13:21
fortified city is **i-d** Is 27:10

ISRAEL
1 *Jacob* Gen 32:28-32;35:10;37:3
2 *line of Jacob* Gen 34:7
tribal nation Ex 1:7;4:22; Num 10:29
3 *united kingdom* 1 Sam 15:35; 1 Kin 4:1
4 *northern kingdom* 1 Kin 14:19;15:9; 2 Kin 10:29
5 *under Roman rule* Luke 2:32; John 1:49; Rom 9:6

ISSACHAR
1 *son of Jacob* Gen 30:18;49:14
2 *tribe* Num 1:29; Josh 21:28; Rev 7:7
3 *Levite* 1 Chr 26:5

ISSUE (n) *outflow, out go*
first **i** of the womb Num 3:12
offspring and **i** Is 22:24
like the **i** of horses Ezek 23:20
concerning this **i** Acts 15:2

ISSUE (v) *go forth, put forth*
Moses **i-d** a command Ex 36:6
shall **i** from you 2 Kin 20:18
decree was **i-d** at Esth 3:15
i-d a proclamation Dan 5:29

ITALY
S European country Acts 18:2;27:1,6; Heb 13:24

ITURAEA
region N of Palestine Luke 3:1
tetrarchy of Herod Philip II

IVORY *elephant tusk*
a great throne of **i** 1 Kin 10:18
silver, **i** and apes 2 Chr 9:21
Out of **i** palaces Ps 45:8
every article of **i** Rev 18:12

J

JABAL
son of Lamech Gen 4:20
father of herders

JABBOK
tributary of Jordan Gen 32:22; Num 21:24; Josh 12:2; Judg 11:13,22

JABESH-GILEAD
town of Gilead Judg 21:8ff
E of Jordan River 1 Sam 11:1,9; 2 Sam 2:4,5

JACINTH *precious stone*
a **j,** an agate Ex 28:19
the eleventh, **j** Rev 21:20

JACKALS *wild dogs*
j in their...palaces Is 13:22
ruins, A haunt of **j** Jer 9:11
a lament like the **j** Mic 1:8

JACOB
1 *son of Isaac* Gen 25:26
brother of Esau Gen 25:27
obtained birthright Gen 25:33
fled to Aram Gen 28:5,6
marriage Gen 29:1ff
wrestled angel Gen 32:24ff
name changed Gen 35:9,10
went down to Egypt Gen 46:4ff
death and burial Gen 49:28ff
2 *father of Joseph* Matt 1:15,16

JAEL
wife of Heber Judg 4:17
slayer of Sisera Judg 4:21
described as blessed Judg 5:24

JAIL *place of confinement*
put him into the **j** Gen 39:20
in **j** in the house Jer 37:15
put them in...**j** Acts 5:18

JAILER *warden*
sight of the chief **j** Gen 39:21
chief **j** did not Gen 39:23
the **j** to guard them Acts 16:23

JAIR
1 *judge of Israel* Judg 10:3
2 *son of Segub* 1 Chr 2:22
3 *father of Elhanan* 1 Chr 20:5
4 *Mordecai's father* Esth 2:5

JAIRUS
ruler of synagogue Mark 5:22; Luke 8:41

JAMES
1 *son of Zebedee* Matt 4:21
brother of John Matt 10:2
called as apostle Matt 10:2ff
martyred Acts 12:2
2 *son of Alphaeus* Matt 10:3
called as apostle Matt 10:3ff
3 *brother of Jesus* Matt 13:55; Mark 6:3
church leader Acts 12:17;15:13
4 *Judas's father* Luke 6:16

JAPHETH
son of Noah Gen 7:13;9:23,27

JAPHIA
1 *king of Lachish* Josh 10:3
2 *son of David* 2 Sam 5:15
3 *town of Zebulun* Josh 19:12

JAR *container, jug*
and a **j** of honey 1 Kin 14:3
Bring me a new **j** 2 Kin 2:20
potter's earthenware **j** Jer 19:1
j full of sour wine John 19:29

JASHAR
book quoted in Bible Josh 10:13; 2 Sam 1:18

JASON
Christian of Thessalonica Acts 17:5-9; Rom 16:21

JASPER *precious stone*
fourth row...a **j** Ex 28:20
the onyx, and the **j** Ezek 28:13
was like a **j** stone Rev 4:3
of crystal-clear **j** Rev 21:11

JAVAN
Hebrew word for Greeks or Greece Gen 10:2,4; 1 Chr 1:5,7; Is 66:19; Ezek 27:13,19

JAVELIN *spear*
Stretch out the **j** Josh 8:18
j *slung* between his 1 Sam 17:6
flashing spear and **j** Job 39:23
seize *their*...**j** Jer 50:42

JAW *part of face*
j-s of the wicked Job 29:17
cleaves to my **j-s** Ps 22:15
j teeth *like* knives Prov 30:14
hooks into your **j-s** Ezek 38:4

JAWBONE
j of a donkey Judg 15:15
threw the **j** from Judg 15:17

JEALOUS *envious, zealous*
brothers were **j** of Gen 37:11
your God, am a **j** God Ex 20:5
whose name is **J,** is Ex 34:14
j with My jealousy Num 25:11
He is a **j** God Josh 24:19
j and avenging God Nah 1:2
j for Jerusalem Zech 1:14
Jews, becoming **j** Acts 17:5
I will make you **j** Rom 10:19
love is kind...not **j** 1 Cor 13:4

JEBUS
Jerusalem Judg 19:10,11; 1 Chr 11:4,5

JEBUSITES
clan or tribe Gen 10:16
inhabitants of Jebus Ex 3:8,17; Josh 15:63; 2 Sam 24:16,18; Ezra 9:1; Zech 9:7

JECONIAH
variant of Jehoiachin's name 1 Chr 3:16,17; Esth 2:6

JEHAZIEL
1 *Benjamite warrior* 1 Chr 12:4
2 *priest* 1 Chr 16:6
3 *son of Hebron* 1 Chr 23:19
4 *son of Zechariah* 2 Chr 20:14

JEHOAHAZ
1 *son of Jehu* 2 Kin 10:35
king of Israel 2 Kin 13:1ff
2 *son of Josiah* 2 Kin 23:30-34
king of Judah 2 Kin 23:30
see also **SHALLUM** 1 Chr 3:15
3 *son of Jehoram* 2 Chr 21:17
also **Ahaziah** 2 Chr 22:1ff

JEHOASH
1 *king of Judah* 2 Kin 11:21
son of Ahaziah 2 Kin 12:1-18
2 *king of Israel* 2 Kin 13:10
son of Jehoahaz 2 Kin 13:25;14:13

JEHOIACHIN
son of Jehoiakim 2 Kin 24:6
king of Judah 2 Kin 24:8-15; 2 Chr 36:8,9; Jer 52:31,33

JEHOIADA
1 *father of Benaiah* 2 Sam 8:18
priest 1 Chr 27:5
2 *son of Benaiah* 1 Chr 27:34
3 *high priest* 2 Kin 11:4,9
4 *priest* Jer 29:26

JEHOIAKIM
son of King Josiah 2 Kin 23:34; 2 Chr 36:4
king of Judah 2 Kin 23:36; 2 Chr 36:5; Jer 22:18; Dan 1:2
father of Jehoiachin 2 Kin 24:6

JEHORAM
1 *son of Ahab* 2 Kin 3:1
king of Israel 2 Kin 3:6
2 *priest* 2 Chr 17:8
3 *Jehoshaphat's son* 2 Kin 8:16
king of Judah 2 Kin 8:25,29
see also **JORAM**

JEHOSHAPHAT
1 *son of Ahilud* 2 Sam 8:16
2 *son of Paruah* 1 Kin 4:17
3 *son of Asa* 1 Kin 15:24
king of Judah 1 Kin 22:2-51; 2 Chr 17:1-12
4 *father of Jehu* 2 Kin 9:2,14
5 *wadi E of Jerusalem* Joel 3:2,12

JEHU
1 *prophet, son of Hanani* 1 Kin 16:1,7,12; 2 Chr 19:2
2 *king of Israel* 1 Kin 19:16; 2 Kin 9:14,30; 2 Chr 22:7
3 *man of Judah* 1 Chr 2:38
4 *Simeonite* 1 Chr 4:35
5 *Benjamite* 1 Chr 12:3

JEMIMAH
daughter of Job Job 42:14

JEPHTHAH
a Gileadite Judg 11:1
judge of Israel Judg 11:2-40

JEREMIAH
1 *lived in Libnah* 2 Kin 23:31
2 *man of Manasseh* 1 Chr 5:24
3 *three individuals who joined David* 1 Chr 12:4,10,13
4 *prophet* Jer 1:1
called Jer 1:2-10
put in stocks Jer 20:2,3
life threatened Jer 26
put in prison Jer 32:2;37:13ff
taken to Egypt Jer 43:1-6
5 *son of Habazziniah* Jer 35:3
6 *priest* Neh 10:2
7 *priest from Babylon* Neh 12:1

JERICHO
city in Jordan Valley Josh 3:16
N of Dead Sea Josh 6:1; 1 Kin 16:34; Luke 18:35

JEROBOAM
1 *Solomon's warrior* 1 Kin 11:28
first king of N Kingdom 1 Kin 12:26,27; 2 Chr 10:13
made golden calves 1 Kin 12:28
2 *son of Joash* 2 Kin 14:27
king of Israel 2 Kin 14:28,29

JERUBBAAL
name of Gideon Judg 6:32
judge of Israel Judg 7:1

JERUSALEM
city called Salem Gen 14:18
city called Jebus Judg 1:21;19:10
David's capital 2 Sam 5:5,6
capital of united kingdom 1 Kin 2:36;11:42
site of temple 1 Kin 6:2;8:6,12
destroyed by Babylonians Jer 52:12-14
rebuilt by remnant Neh 2:11-20;12:27
city of Roman period Matt 2:1,3;21:1,10; Luke 13:34; Acts 11:2,22
new Jerusalem Rev 3:12;21:2,10

JESHUA
1 *line of Aaron* 1 Chr 24:11
2 *under Kore* 2 Chr 31:15
3 *high priest* Ezra 3:2; Neh 7:7
4 *of Pahath-moab* Ezra 2:6; Neh 7:11
5 *part of remnant* Ezra 2:40; Neh 7:43
6 *aided Ezra* Neh 8:7
7 *village in Judah* Neh 11:26
see also **JOSHUA**

JESHURUN
poetic name for Israel Deut 32:15;33:5,26; Is 44:2

JESSE
father of David 1 Sam 16:1,8; 2 Sam 20:1; 1 Kin 12:16; 1 Chr 2:12,13

JEST *joke, mock*
appeared...be **j-ing** Gen 19:14
Against whom do you **j** Is 57:4

JESUS
1 *name of the Lord* Matt 1:21; Luke 1:31
birth in Bethlehem Matt 1:18-25; Luke 2:1-7
youth in Nazareth Matt 2:19ff
baptized Matt 3:13ff; Mark 1:9ff; Luke 3:21; John 1:31ff
tempted Matt 4:1-11; Mark 1:12; Luke 4:1ff
called disciples Matt 4:18ff; Mark 1:16ff; Luke 5:1ff
transfigured Matt 17:1ff; Mark 9:2ff; Luke 9:28ff
triumphal entry to Jerusalem Matt 21:1ff; Mark 11:1ff; Luke 19:29ff
crucified Matt 27:31ff; Mark 15:20ff; Luke 23:26ff; John 19:16ff
resurrected Christ Matt 28:1ff; Mark 16:1ff; Luke 24:13ff; John 20:11ff
ascended to the Father Mark 16:19; Luke 24:50ff; Acts 1:9ff
2 *Jewish Christian called Justus* Col 4:11

JETHRO
priest of Midian Ex 3:1
Moses' father-in-law Ex 4:18;18:1-12

JEW(S)
originally an inhabitant of Judah, a Judean 2 Kin 16:6
Judean shortened to Jew during exile 2 Kin 25:25
synonym for Hebrew Ezra 4:12,23; Neh 4:1,2; Esth 4:3,7; Jer 34:9
later term for all Israelites in the land and in Diaspora Matt 27:11; Mark 7:3; Luke 23:51; John 4:9; Acts 22:3; Rom 3:1; Gal 3:28; Rev 2:9

JEWEL *precious stone*
precious than **j-s** Prov 3:15
better than **j-s** Prov 8:11
adorns...her **j-s** Is 61:10
the **J** of *his* kingdom Dan 11:20

JEWISH
pertaining to Jews Neh 5:1; Esth 6:13; John 2:6; Acts 13:6

JEZEBEL
1 *wife of Ahab* 1 Kin 21:5ff; 2 Kin 9:7ff
2 *woman at Thyatira* Rev 2:20

JEZREEL
1 *valley and plain* Josh 17:16; Judg 6:33; Hos 1:5
2 *fortified town* Josh 19:18; 1 Kin 18:45; 2 Kin 8:29;9:30
3 *descendant of Etam* 1 Chr 4:3
4 *son of Hosea* Hos 1:4

JOAB
1 *son of Zeruiah* 2 Sam 8:16
David's nephew 2 Sam 17:25
David's commander 2 Sam 20:23; 1 Chr 11:6
2 *son of Seraiah* 1 Chr 4:14
3 *father of those returning from captivity* Ezra 2:6;8:9; Neh 7:11

JOANNA
wife of Chuza Luke 8:3
ministered to Jesus Luke 24:10

JOASH
1 *father of Gideon* Judg 6:11,31
2 *son of Ahab* 1 Kin 22:26; 2 Chr 18:25
3 *son of Ahaziah* 2 Kin 11:2
king of Judah 2 Chr 24:1-4
4 *son of Jehoahaz* 2 Kin 13:9
king of Israel 2 Kin 13:25
5 *line of Shelah* 1 Chr 4:22
6 *son of Becher* 1 Chr 7:8
7 *a Benjamite* 1 Chr 12:3
8 *official of David* 1 Chr 27:28

JOB
pious man from Uz Job 1:1
experienced tragedy Job 2:7,8
showed great endurance Job 2:9,10; James 5:11

JOB *occupation*
workmen...**j** to **j** 2 Chr 34:13

JOCHEBED
mother of Moses Ex 6:20; Num 26:59

JOEL
1 *son of Samuel* 1 Sam 8:2
2 *line of Simeon* 1 Chr 4:35
3 *line of Reuben* 1 Chr 5:4
4 *chief of Gadites* 1 Chr 5:12
5 *ancestor of Samuel* 1 Chr 6:36
6 *son of Izrahiah* 1 Chr 7:3
7 *brother of Nathan* 1 Chr 11:38

8 *Gershonite Levite* 1 Chr 15:7;26:22
9 *son of Pedaiah* 1 Chr 27:20
10 *Kohathite Levite* 2 Chr 29:12
11 *son of Nebo* Ezra 10:43
12 *son of Zichri* Neh 11:9
13 *prophet* Joel 1:1; Acts 2:16

JOHN
1 *father of Peter* John 1:42
2 *the Baptist* Matt 3:1
baptizing Matt 3:13
beheaded Mark 6:25
birth foretold Luke 1:13
son of Zacharias Luke 1:57ff
praised by Jesus Luke 7:28
preached John 1:15
3 *the apostle* Matt 10:2
called by Jesus Matt 4:21
Sons of Thunder Mark 3:17
inner circle Matt 17:1
request refused Mark 10:35ff
assigned the care of Mary John 19:26,27
with Peter Acts 3:1,3
4 *Jewish leader* Acts 4:6
5 *Mark, evangelist* Acts 12:12,25

JOIN *bring together, couple*
j-ed to his wife Gen 2:24
do not **j** your hand Ex 23:1
j field to field Is 5:8
j...in hypocrisy Dan 11:34
God...**j-ed** together Matt 19:6
j-ed him...believed Acts 17:34
shall be **j-ed** to his wife Eph 5:31
j...*me* in suffering 2 Tim 1:8

JOINT *juncture*
bones are out of **j** Ps 22:14
together by the **j-s** Col 2:19
both **j-s** and marrow Heb 4:12

JOKTAN
person and tribe descended from Shem Gen 10:25,26,29; 1 Chr 1:19,20,23

JONAH
prophet of Israel Jon 1:1
son of Amittai 2 Kin 14:25
disobedient Jon 1:3
preached to Nineveh Jon 3:4

JONATHAN
1 *son of Gershom* Judg 18:30
2 *son of King Saul* 1 Sam 13:16;14:49
friend of David 1 Sam 18:1
3 *son of Abiathar* 2 Sam 15:36
4 *son of Shimei* 2 Sam 21:21
5 *son of Jada* 1 Chr 2:32
6 *son of Shagee* 1 Chr 11:34
7 *official of David* 1 Chr 27:25
8 *David's uncle* 1 Chr 27:32

JOPPA
seaport W of Jerusalem 2 Chr 2:16; Ezra 3:7; Jon 1:3; Acts 9:36

JORAM
1 *son of Toi* 2 Sam 8:10
2 *son of Ahab* 2 Kin 8:16
king of Israel 2 Kin 8:25
3 *line of Eliezer* 1 Chr 26:25
4 *son of Jehoshaphat* Matt 1:8
king of Judah
see also **JEHORAM**

JORDAN
1 *river in Palestine* Gen 32:10; Josh 3:17; Judg 8:4; 2 Kin 5:10; Matt 3:6
2 *valley* Gen 13:10,11

JOSEPH
1 *son of Jacob* Gen 30:23,24
sold by brothers Gen 37:28
put in prison Gen 40:3
prime minister Gen 41:41
revealed himself Gen 45:4
death Gen 50:26
2 *father of spy* Num 13:7ff
3 *son of Asaph* 1 Chr 25:9
4 *son of Bani* Ezra 10:42
5 *son of Shebaniah* Neh 12:14
6 *husband of Mary* Matt 1:18;2:13; Luke 2:16; John 6:42
7 *brother of Jesus* Matt 13:55
see also **JOSES**
8 *brother of James the Less* Matt 27:56
see also **JOSES**
9 *of Arimathea* Matt 27:57ff
in Sanhedrin (Council) Mark 15:43
disciple of Jesus John 19:38
provided tomb Matt 27:57
10 *ancestor of Jesus* Luke 3:24
11 *ancestor of Jesus* Luke 3:30
12 *surname Barsabbas* Acts 1:23
13 *Barnabas* Acts 4:36

JOSES
1 *brother of James the Less* Mark 15:40
see also **JOSEPH**
2 *brother of Jesus* Mark 6:3
see also **JOSEPH**

JOSHUA
1 *Moses' successor* Deut 31:23
attended Moses Num 11:28
chosen by God Num 27:18
encouraged by God Josh 1:1-9
charged Israel Josh 23:1ff
death Josh 24:29
2 *of Beth-shemesh* 1 Sam 6:14
3 *governor* 2 Kin 23:8
4 *high priest* Hag 1:1,12; Zech 3:1ff
see also **JESHUA**

JOSIAH
1 *son of Amon* 2 Kin 21:24
king of Judah 2 Kin 21:26
removed false worship 2 Kin 23:19,24; 2 Chr 34:33
responded to the Law 2 Chr 34:15-28
2 *son of Zephaniah* Zech 6:10

JOTHAM
1 *son of Gideon* Judg 9:5ff
2 *king of Judah* 2 Kin 15:5
son of Uzziah 2 Chr 27:2
3 *line of Caleb* 1 Chr 2:47

JOURNEY *traveling, trip*
Let us take our **j** Gen 33:12
day's **j** on the other Num 11:31
seek...a safe **j** Ezra 8:21
a bag for *your* **j** Matt 10:10
nothing for *your* **j** Luke 9:3
Sabbath day's **j** away Acts 1:12
on frequent **j-s** 2 Cor 11:26

JOURNEYED *traveled*
about as they **j** east Gen 11:2
Jacob **j** to Succoth Gen 33:17
the sons of Israel **j** Num 22:1
j from the river Ezra 8:31

JOY *delight, happiness*
raise sounds of **j** 1 Chr 15:16
shouted aloud for **j** Ezra 3:12
see His face with **j** Job 33:26
Restore to me the **j** Ps 51:12
j at Your name Ps 89:12
godly ones sing for **j** Ps 132:9
Everlasting **j** will be Is 61:7
their mourning into **j** Jer 31:13
with great **j** Matt 2:10
enter into the **j** Matt 25:21
j in heaven over one Luke 15:7
j in the Holy Spirit Rom 14:17
love, **j**, peace Gal 5:22
make my **j** complete Phil 2:2

JOYFUL *feeling gladness*
be altogether **j** Deut 16:15
j with gladness Ps 21:6
shall reap with **j** Ps 126:5
j heart is good Prov 17:22

JOYFULLY *full of joy, happy*
go **j** with the king Esth 5:14
Shout **j** to God, all Ps 66:1
They shout **j** together Is 52:8
to praise God **j** Luke 19:37

JUBAL
inventor of lyre and pipe Gen 4:21

JUBILANT *elated*
no...**j** shouting Is 16:10
Is this your **j** *city* Is 23:7
because you are **j** Jer 50:11
they may become **j** Jer 51:39

JUBILEE, YEAR OF
return of ancestral possessions every fiftieth year
year of liberty Lev 25:8ff

JUDAH
1 *son of Jacob* Gen 29:35; 37:26;44:14;49:8,10
2 *tribe* Num 1:27; Judg 1:8; 2 Sam 2:4; 1 Kin 12:20
3 *border city* Josh 19:34
4 *S kingdom* 1 Kin 14:21; 1 Chr 9:1; Ps 60:7; Jer 20:4
5 *relative of Kadmiel* Ezra 2:40
6 *urged by Ezra to put away foreign wife* Ezra 10:23
7 *Benjamite* Neh 11:9
8 *Levite who returned from captivity* Neh 12:8
9 *participant in wall dedication* Neh 12:34
10 *musician* Neh 12:36

JUDAISM *Jewish way of life*
manner of life in **J** Gal 1:13
advancing in **J** Gal 1:14

JUDAS
1 *Iscariot* Matt 10:4
used by Satan Luke 22:3
son of Simon John 6:71
treasurer John 13:29
betrayed Jesus John 18:2
2 *Jesus' brother* Matt 13:55; Mark 6:3
3 *apostle* Luke 6:16; Acts 1:13
4 *Judas of Galilee* Acts 5:37
5 *of Damascus* Acts 9:11
6 *Barsabbas* Acts 15:22,27

JUDE
brother of Jesus Matt 13:55; Mark 6:3
brother of James Jude 1

JUDEA
Roman province in Palestine based on earlier Judah Matt 2:1; Mark 1:5; Luke 2:4; John 11:7

JUDEAN
language (Hebrew) 2 Kin 18:26,28; Is 36:11,13
see also **CANAAN**
see also **HEBREW**

JUDGE (n) *leader*
J of all the earth Gen 18:25
prince or a **j** over us Ex 2:14
LORD was with the **j** Judg 2:18
For God Himself is **j** Ps 50:6
unrighteous **j** said Luke 18:6
one Lawgiver and **J** James 4:12

JUDGE (v) *pass judgment*
LORD **j** between you Gen 16:5
Moses sat to **j** the Ex 18:13
LORD will **j**...earth 1 Sam 2:10
coming to **j** the earth Ps 98:9
He will **j** the poor Is 11:4
Do not **j**...will not be **j-d** Matt 7:1
Son...world to **j** John 3:17
Law...not **j** a man John 7:51
not come to **j** the John 12:47
able to **j**...thoughts Heb 4:12
adulterers God will **j** Heb 13:4

JUDGMENT *condemnation*
I will execute **j-s** Ex 12:12

partiality in **j** Deut 1:17
let **j** be executed Ezra 7:26
will not stand in the **j** Ps 1:5
in the day of **j** Matt 10:15
j, that the light John 3:19
resurrection of **j** John 5:29
My **j** is just John 5:30
after this *comes* **j** Heb 9:27
incur a stricter **j** James 3:1
not fall under **j** James 5:12
kept for the day of **j** 2 Pet 3:7
j of the great day Jude 6
to execute **j** upon all Jude 15
His **j-s** are true Rev 19:2

JUMP *leap*
legs with which to **j** Lev 11:21
if a fox should **j** Neh 4:3
j-ed up, and came Mark 10:50

JUNIPER *tree*
slept under a **j** tree 1 Kin 19:5
The **j,** the box tree Is 60:13
like a **j** in the Jer 48:6

JUST *fair, right*
shall have **j** balances Lev 19:36
a man be **j** with God Job 25:4
Hear a **j** cause, O LORD Ps 17:1
He is **j** and endowed Zech 9:9
My judgment is **j** John 5:30
the **j** for *the* unjust 1 Pet 3:18

JUSTICE *fairness, righteousness*
shall not distort **j** Deut 16:19
Does God pervert **j** Job 8:3
j to the afflicted Job 36:6
Righteousness and **j** Ps 89:14
do not understand **j** Prov 28:5
j is turned back Is 59:14
let **j** roll down Amos 5:24
j and mercy and Matt 23:23
acknowledged...**j** Luke 7:29
grant to your slaves **j** Col 4:1

JUSTIFICATION *vindication*
because of our **j** Rom 4:25
j of life to all men Rom 5:18

JUSTIFY *declare guiltless*
how...**j** ourselves Gen 44:16
they **j** the righteous Deut 25:1
he **j-ied** himself Job 32:2
wishing to **j** himself Luke 10:29
these...He also **j-ied** Rom 8:30
God...**j-ies** Rom 8:33
seeking to be **j-ied** Gal 2:17

JUSTUS
1 *Joseph, apostolic candidate* Acts 1:23
also called **Barsabbas**
2 *Titus, Corinthian disciple* Acts 18:7
3 *Jewish Christian* Col 4:11

JUTTAH
Levitical city in Judah Josh 15:55;21:16

K

KADESH / KADESH-BARNEA
desert oasis in Negev Gen 14:7
Israelite encampment Num 13:26;33:37

KEDAR
1 *son of Ishmael* Gen 25:13
2 *tribal descendants* Is 42:11

KEDEMAH
1 *son of Ishmael* Gen 25:15
2 *tribal descendants* 1 Chr 1:31

KEDESH
1 *city in S Judah* Josh 15:23
2 *city of Issachar* 1 Chr 6:72
3 *city of Naphtali* Josh 12:22
4 *city of refuge, in Galilee* Josh 20:7

KEEP *hold, guide, preserve*
k the way of the LORD Gen 18:19
love Me and **k** My Ex 20:6
shall **k** your sabbath Lev 23:32
LORD bless you, and **k** Num 6:24
to **k** the Passover Matt 26:18
if anyone **k-s** My John 8:51
he will **k** My word John 14:23
k-ing faith and a 1 Tim 1:19
k yourself free from 1 Tim 5:22
k his tongue...evil 1 Pet 3:10

KEEPER *guard, protector*
Am I my brother's **k** Gen 4:9
been **k-s** of livestock Gen 46:32
The LORD is your **k** Ps 121:5
I, the LORD, am its **k** Is 27:3

KEILAH
1 *town of Judah* Josh 15:44; 1 Sam 23:1ff; Neh 3:17,18
2 *line of Caleb* 1 Chr 4:19

KENAZ
1 *Esau's grandson* Gen 36:10,11
2 *father of Othniel* Josh 15:17
3 *line of Caleb* 1 Chr 4:15

KENITE(S)
Canaanite tribe Gen 15:19; Num 24:21
tribe of metal-workers Judg 4:11; 1 Sam 15:6

KENIZZITE
Canaanite tribe in S Palestine and Edom Gen 15:19; Num 32:12; Josh 14:14

KEREN-HAPPUCH
daughter of Job Job 42:14

KERIOTH
1 *town of Judah* Josh 15:25
2 *town in Moab* Jer 48:41; Amos 2:2

KETURAH
second wife of Abraham Gen 25:1,4; 1 Chr 1:32,33

KEY *unlocking tool*
k-s of the kingdom Matt 16:19
the **k** of knowledge Luke 11:52
k-s of death and of Rev 1:18
k of the bottomless pit Rev 9:1

KEZIAH
daughter of Job Job 42:14

KIDNEYS *innards*
two **k** and the fat Ex 29:13
remove with the **k** Lev 3:15
He splits my **k** open Job 16:13

KIDRON
brook and valley between Jerusalem and Mount of Olives 2 Sam 15:23; 2 Kin 23:6; 2 Chr 29:16; John 18:1

KILL *take life*
for Cain **k-ed** him Gen 4:25
k-ed every firstborn Ex 13:15
who **k-s** a man shall Lev 24:21
LORD **k-s** and makes 1 Sam 2:6
Am I God, to **k** 2 Kin 5:7
jealousy **k-s** the simple Job 5:2
he **k-s** the innocent Ps 10:8
A time to **k** Eccl 3:3
unable to **k** the Matt 10:28
k-ed, and be raised Luke 9:22
do you seek to **k** Me John 7:19
Get up, Peter, **k** and Acts 10:13
the letter **k-s,** but 2 Cor 3:6
who **k** their father 1 Tim 1:9
k a third of mankind Rev 9:15

KIND (adj) *good, tender*
be **k** to this people 2 Chr 10:7
He Himself is **k** Luke 6:35
love is **k** 1 Cor 13:4
be **k** to one another Eph 4:32

KIND (n) *group, variety*
fruit after their **k** Gen 1:11
plant all **k-s** of trees Lev 19:23
all **k-s** of evil Matt 5:11
k-s of tongues 1 Cor 12:28
every **k** of impurity Eph 4:19

KINDLE *cause to burn*
anger...was **k-d** Num 11:10
His breath **k-s** coals Job 41:21
man to **k** strife Prov 26:21
all you who **k** a fire Is 50:11
k-d a fire in Zion Lam 4:11

KINDNESS *tenderness*
teaching of **k** is on Prov 31:26
to love **k,** And to Mic 6:8
with deeds of **k** Acts 9:36
k and...of God Rom 11:22
joy, peace, patience, **k** Gal 5:22
compassion, **k** Col 3:12
tasted the **k** of the 1 Pet 2:3
godliness, brotherly **k** 2 Pet 1:7

KINDRED *relative*
her people or her **k** Esth 2:10
destruction of my **k** Esth 8:6
no one...of **k** spirit Phil 2:20

KING *monarch, regent*
the **k-'s** highway Num 20:17
no **k** in Israel Judg 17:6
appoint a **k** for us 1 Sam 8:5
anointed David **k** 2 Sam 5:3
my **K** and my God Ps 5:2
The LORD is **K** forever Ps 10:16
Who is the **k** of glory Ps 24:8
will shatter **k-s** Ps 110:5
By me **k-s** reign Prov 8:15
He will...before **k-s** Prov 22:29
The Creator...your **K** Is 43:15
O **K** of the nations Jer 10:7
born **K** of the Jews Matt 2:2
Are You the **K** of Matt 27:11
your **K** is coming John 12:15
no **k** but Caesar John 19:15
K of **k-s** and Lord 1 Tim 6:15
God, honor the **k** 1 Pet 2:17

KINGDOM *domain, monarchy*
his **k** was Babel Gen 10:10
to Me a **k** of priests Ex 19:6
tear the **k** from 1 Kin 11:11
will establish his **k** 1 Chr 28:7
the **k** is the LORD's Ps 22:28
Sing to God, O **k-s** Ps 68:32
an everlasting **k** Ps 145:13
k against **k** Is 19:2
k of heaven is at Matt 3:2
showed Him...**k-s** Matt 4:8
Your **k** come Matt 6:10
sons of the **k** Matt 13:38
keys of the **k** Matt 16:19
in My Father's **k** Matt 26:29
enter the **k** of God Mark 10:24
to give you the **k** Luke 12:32
cannot see the **k** of John 3:3
preaching the **k** Acts 28:31
k of His beloved Son Col 1:13
to His heavenly **k** 2 Tim 4:18
faith conquered **k-s** Heb 11:33
heirs of the **k** James 2:5

KINSMAN *relative*
of my master's **k** Gen 24:48
he took his **k-men** Gen 31:23
a man has no **k** Lev 25:26
Naomi had a **k** of her Ruth 2:1
k-men stand afar off Ps 38:11
Herodion, my **k** Rom 16:11

KIRIATHAIM
1 *Reubenite city* Num 32:37; Josh 13:19
2 *Levitical city* 1 Chr 6:76

KIRIATH-ARBA
old name of Hebron Gen 23:2; Josh 14:15;15:13,54; Judg 1:10
city of refuge Josh 20:7

KIRIATH-JEARIM
Gibeonite town Josh 9:17; Judg 18:12; Jer 26:20

location of ark of covenant
1 Sam 6:21;7:1,2; 2 Chr 1:4

KISH
1 *father of Saul*
1 Sam 9:3;10:21
2 *son of Jeiel* 1 Chr 8:30
3 *son of Mahli* 1 Chr 23:21
4 *son of Abdi* 2 Chr 29:12
5 *a Benjamite* Esth 2:5

KISHON
battle scene Judg 4:7
river Judg 4:13;5:21
priests of Baal slain on its bank 1 Kin 18:40

KISS (n) *expression of affection*
threw a **k** from my Job 31:27
the **k-es** of his mouth Song 1:2
You gave Me no **k** Luke 7:45
betraying...with a **k**
Luke 22:48
with a holy **k** Rom 16:16
with a **k** of love 1 Pet 5:14

KISS (v) *expression of affection*
come close and **k** Gen 27:26
let me **k** my father
1 Kin 19:20
I would **k** you Song 8:1
Whomever I **k** Mark 14:44
not...to **k** My feet Luke 7:45

KITTIM
1 *grandson of Japheth*
Gen 10:4; 1 Chr 1:7
2 *island of Cyprus*
Num 24:24; Jer 2:10;
Dan 11:30

KNEAD *work dough, clay*
took flour, **k-ed** it
1 Sam 28:24
the women **k** dough Jer 7:18

KNEE *part of body*
strengthened feeble **k-s**
Job 4:4
k-s began knocking Dan 5:6
every **k** shall bow Rom 14:11
every **k** will bow Phil 2:10

KNEEL *bend, rest on knee*
made the camels **k** Gen 24:11
people **k-ed** to drink Judg 7:6
k before the LORD Ps 95:6
knelt...before Him Matt 27:29
man ran...**knelt** Mark 10:17
He **knelt** down Luke 22:41

KNIFE *cutting instrument*
k to slay his son Gen 22:10
jaw teeth *like* **k-ves**
Prov 30:14
with a scribe's **k** Jer 36:23

KNIT *joined together*
Jonathan was **k** to 1 Sam 18:1
k me together with Job 10:11
his thighs are **k** Job 40:17
His hand they are **k** Lam 1:14
k together in love Col 2:2

KNOCK *smite, strike*
his knees began **k-ing** Dan 5:6
k, and it will be Matt 7:7
stand outside and **k**
Luke 13:25
he **k-ed** at the door
Acts 12:13
at the door and **k** Rev 3:20

KNOW *experience, understand*
like one of Us, **k-ing**
Gen 3:22
make **k-n** the statutes
Ex 18:16
k that my Redeemer
Job 19:25
Make me **k** Your ways Ps 25:4
He **k-s** the secrets Ps 44:21
k that I am God Ps 46:10
made **k-n** His salvation
Ps 98:2
Try me and **k** my Ps 139:23
You **k** me Jer 12:3
left hand **k** what Matt 6:3
k...by their fruits Matt 7:20
I never **knew** you Matt 7:23
God **k-s** your hearts
Luke 16:15
you will **k** the truth John 8:32
I **k** My own John 10:14
k-ing that His hour John 13:1
k that I love You John 21:15
and **k** all mysteries 1 Cor 13:2
who **knew** no sin 2 Cor 5:21
k the love of Christ Eph 3:19
value of **k-ing** Christ Phil 3:8
k...I have believed 2 Tim 1:12
k...eternal life 1 John 5:13
I **k** your deeds Rev 2:2

KNOWLEDGE *information*
tree of the **k** of good Gen 2:9
LORD is a God of **k** 1 Sam 2:3
anyone teach God **k**
Job 21:22
k is too wonderful Ps 139:6
the beginning of **k** Prov 1:7
fools hate **k** Prov 1:22
Wise...store up **k** Prov 10:14
k increases power Prov 24:5
would He teach **k** Is 28:9
in accordance with **k**
Rom 10:2
K makes arrogant 1 Cor 8:1
k, it will be done 1 Cor 13:8
have no **k** of God 1 Cor 15:34
love...surpasses **k** Eph 3:19
treasures of...**k** Col 2:3
grow in...grace and **k**
2 Pet 3:18

KOHATH
son of Levi Gen 46:11;
Num 3:17; Josh 21:5

KOHATHITES
line of Kohath
Num 3:30;4:34; Josh 21:4

KOR *measure of capacity*
k-s of fine flour 1 Kin 4:22
20,000 **k-s** of barley
2 Chr 2:10
100 **k-s** of wheat Ezra 7:22
a bath from *each* **k** Ezek 45:14

KORAH
1 *son of Esau* Gen 36:5
2 *opposed Moses*
Num 16:8,16
3 *son of Hebron* 1 Chr 2:43
4 *a Kohathite* 1 Chr 6:37

L

LABAN
1 *Abraham's kinsman*
Gen 24:29
Rachel's father
Gen 29:10,16
2 *place in the desert* Deut 1:1

LABOR (n) *work, childbirth*
fruits of your **l-s** Ex 23:16
their **l** to the locust Ps 78:46
bread of painful **l-s** Ps 127:2
return for their **l** Eccl 4:9
in **l** and hardship 2 Cor 11:27
fruitful **l** for me Phil 1:22
faith and **l** of love 1 Thess 1:3
cried out, being in **l** Rev 12:2

LABOR (v) *toil, work*
Six days you shall **l** Ex 20:9
l in vain who build Ps 127:1
for whom am I **l-ing** Eccl 4:8
l-ed over you in vain Gal 4:11

LABORER *workman*
l-s for his vineyard Matt 20:1
Call the **l-s** and pay Matt 20:8
l-s into His harvest Luke 10:2
l is worthy of his Luke 10:7

LACHISH
city in Judah Josh 10:3;
2 Kin 14:19; 2 Chr 32:9

LACK (n) *deficiency, need*
where there is no **l** Judg 18:10
for **l** of instruction Prov 5:23
for **l** of a shepherd Ezek 34:5
l of self-control 1 Cor 7:5

LACK (v) *be deficient, need*
will not **l** anything Deut 8:9
l-ing in counsel Deut 32:28
man **l-ing** sense Prov 7:7
am I still **l-ing** Matt 19:20
One thing you **l** Mark 10:21
not **l-ing** in any gift 1 Cor 1:7
if any...**l-s** wisdom James 1:5

LAD *boy*
God heard the **l** Gen 21:17
the **l** is not *with us* Gen 44:31
the **l** was dead 2 Kin 4:32
a **l** here who has five John 6:9

LADDER *steps*
l...set on the earth
Gen 28:12

LADY *woman*
Your noble **l-ies** Ps 45:9
elder to the chosen **l** 2 John 1

LAISH
1 *a Benjamite* 1 Sam 25:44;
2 Sam 3:15
2 *place in N Palestine later called Dan* Judg 18:27,29

LAKE *pool, water*
standing by the **l** Luke 5:1
wind...on the **l** Luke 8:23
into the **l** and was Luke 8:33
into the **l** of fire Rev 20:10

LAMB *young sheep*
l for the burnt Gen 22:7
shall redeem with a **l** Ex 34:20
l without defect Lev 14:10
will dwell with the **l** Is 11:6
l...led to slaughter Is 53:7
wolf and the **l** will Is 65:25
send you out as **l-s** Luke 10:3
Behold, the **L** of God
John 1:29
Tend My **l-s** John 21:15
l before its shearer Acts 8:32
Worthy is the **L** Rev 5:12
blood of the **L** Rev 12:11

LAME *crippled, disabled*
was **l** in both feet 2 Sam 9:13
feet to the **l** Job 29:15
Then the **l** will leap Is 35:6
the **l** walk Matt 11:5
l from his mother's Acts 14:8

LAMECH
1 *in linage of Cain*
Gen 4:17,18
2 *father of Noah* Gen 5:28,29

LAMENT (n) *dirge, wail*
this **l** over Saul 2 Sam 1:17
chanted a **l** 2 Chr 35:25
I must make a **l** Mic 1:8

LAMENT (v) *mourn, wail*
house of Israel **l-ed** 1 Sam 7:2
her gates will **l** Is 3:26
fishermen will **l** Is 19:8
And **l** over you Ezek 27:32
weep and **l** over her Rev 18:9

LAMENTATION *weeping*
great...sorrowful **l** Gen 50:10
in Ramah, **L** *and* Jer 31:15
your songs into **l** Amos 8:10
made loud **l** over him Acts 8:2

LAMP *light*
You are my **l** 2 Sam 22:29
l-s of pure gold 2 Chr 4:20
his **l** goes out Job 18:6
Your word is a **l** Ps 119:105
commandment is a **l** Prov 6:23
l of the body Matt 6:22
l-s are going out Matt 25:8
l-s in the upper room
Acts 20:8
l shining in a dark 2 Pet 1:19
seven **l-s** of fire Rev 4:5

LAMPSTAND *candlestick*
l of pure gold Ex 25:31
and a chair and a **l** 2 Kin 4:10
puts it on a **l** Luke 8:16
will remove your **l** Rev 2:5

LAND *country, earth*
let the dry **l** appear Gen 1:9
famine in the **l** Gen 12:10
I have given this **l** Gen 15:18
out of the **l** of Egypt Ex 6:13

l flowing with milk Deut 6:3
in to possess the l Josh 1:11
l of their captivity 2 Chr 6:38
will heal their l 2 Chr 7:14
the l of the living Job 28:13
will inherit the l Ps 37:11
In a dry and weary l Ps 63:1
l be born in one day Is 66:8
again to this l Jer 24:6
l is filled with blood Ezek 9:9
smite the l with a Mal 4:6
darkness...all the l Matt 27:45
owned a tract of l Acts 4:37

LANDOWNER *landlord*
slaves of the l Matt 13:27
kingdom...like a l Matt 20:1
l who planted a Matt 21:33

LANGUAGE *speech, word*
according to his l Gen 10:5
earth used the same l Gen 11:1
speech or difficult l Ezek 3:5
in figurative l John 16:25
speak in his own l Acts 2:6
many kinds of **l-s** 1 Cor 14:10

LANGUISH *faint*
l-ed because of the Gen 47:13
My soul **l-es** for Ps 119:81
never l again Jer 31:12
refresh...who **l-es** Jer 31:25

LAODICEA
city in Asia Minor Col 2:1
location of early church
Col 4:15; Rev 1:11; 3:14

LAODICEANS
people of Laodicea Col 4:16

LAPIS LAZULI *precious stone*
polishing *was* like l Lam 4:7
like l in appearance Ezek 1:26
the jasper; The l Ezek 28:13

LARGE *big, great, huge*
tears in l measure Ps 80:5
a l upper room Mark 14:15
a l crowd Luke 7:11
what l letters Gal 6:11

LAST *final, utmost*
breathed his l Gen 25:8
In the l days Is 2:2
first will be l Matt 19:30
The l Adam 1 Cor 15:45
at the l trumpet 1 Cor 15:52
in these l days Heb 1:2
it is the l hour 1 John 2:18
the first and the l Rev 1:17

LATIN
language of the Roman Empire
one of three languages written on Jesus' cross John 19:20

LATTICE *trellis*
fell through the l 2 Kin 1:2
looked out...my l Prov 7:6
peering through...l Song 2:9

LAUGH *be amused, mock*
Why did Sarah l Gen 18:13
will l at violence Job 5:22
l at your calamity Prov 1:26
weep, and a time to l Eccl 3:4
began **l-ing** at Him Matt 9:24

LAUGHINGSTOCK *derision*
l among the peoples Ps 44:14
was not Israel a l Jer 48:27
I have become a l Lam 3:14

LAUGHTER *amusement*
God has made l for Gen 21:6
Even in l the heart Prov 14:13
Sorrow is better than l Eccl 7:3

LAVER *wash basin*
make a l of bronze Ex 30:18
set the l between Ex 40:7
anoint the l Ex 40:11

LAW *scripture, statute*
tablets with the l Ex 24:12
Moses wrote this l Deut 31:9
found the...l 2 Kin 22:8
walk in My l 2 Chr 6:16
l...is perfect Ps 19:7
I delight in Your l Ps 119:70
abolish the **L** or the Matt 5:17
Our **L**...not judge John 7:51
by that l He ought John 19:7
by a l of faith Rom 3:27
L brings...wrath Rom 4:15
not under l Rom 6:14
Is the **L** sin Rom 7:7
the **L** is holy Rom 7:12
L...become our tutor Gal 3:24
thereby fulfill the l Gal 6:2
L...nothing perfect Heb 7:19

LAWFUL *legal, right*
not l for him to eat Matt 12:4
Is it l to heal Matt 12:10
l...man to divorce Mark 10:2
All things are l 1 Cor 6:12

LAWGIVER *lawmaker*
The LORD is our l Is 33:22
one **L** and Judge James 4:12

LAWLESS *illegal, without law*
l one will be 2 Thess 2:8
are l and rebellious 1 Tim 1:9
from every l deed Titus 2:14

LAWYER *interpreter of law*
a **l**, asked Him *a* Matt 22:35
One of the **l-s** said Luke 11:45
Woe to you **l-s** Luke 11:52

LAY *place, put*
laid him on the altar Gen 22:9
l My hand on Egypt Ex 7:4
laid its cornerstone Job 38:6
l my glory in the dust Ps 7:5
he **l-s** up deceit Prov 26:24
laid Him in a tomb Mark 15:46
l-s down His life John 10:11
I l down My life John 10:15
have you **laid** Him John 11:34
I **L** in Zion a stone Rom 9:33
l-ing aside falsehood Eph 4:25

LAYMAN *non-ecclesiastic*
l shall not eat *them* Ex 29:33
married to a l Lev 22:12
l who comes near Num 3:10

LAZARUS
1 *beggar* Luke 16:20-25
2 *brother of Mary and Martha* John 11:1,2,5,11,43

LAZY *idle, slothful*
Because they are l Ex 5:8
You are **l**, *very* l Ex 5:17
You wicked, l slave Matt 25:26
beasts, l gluttons Titus 1:12

LEAD (n) *metal*
They sank like l Ex 15:10
an iron stylus and l Job 19:24
l is consumed by Jer 6:29
l in the furnace Ezek 22:18

LEAD (v) *direct, guide*
God **led** the people Ex 13:18
cloud by day to l Ex 13:21
l-s me beside quiet Ps 23:2
L me in Your truth Ps 25:5
led captive *Your* Ps 68:18
little boy will l Is 11:6
lamb that is **led** to Is 53:7
not l us into Matt 6:13
l astray...the elect Mark 13:22
led Him...crucify Mark 15:20
and **l-s** them out John 10:3
led by the Spirit Rom 8:14
led captive a host Eph 4:8
that **l-s** to salvation 2 Tim 3:15

LEADER *director, guide*
Let us appoint a l Num 14:4
one l of every tribe Num 34:18
l over My people 1 Kin 14:7
the l like the servant Luke 22:26
Obey your **l-s** Heb 13:17

LEADING (adj) *chief, noted*
gathered l men Ezra 7:28
number...l women Acts 17:4
l men of the Jews Acts 28:17

LEAF *foliage*
sewed fig **l-ves** Gen 3:7
sound of a driven l Lev 26:36
its l does not wither Ps 1:3
puts forth its **l-ves** Matt 24:32

LEAH
wife of Jacob Gen 29:23,30
mother of Reuben, Simeon, Levi and Judah Gen 29:32-35

LEAN (adj) *thin*
seven l...ugly cows Gen 41:27
my flesh has grown l Ps 109:24
and the l sheep Ezek 34:20

LEAN (v) *incline, rest*
may l against them Judg 16:26
l...own understanding Prov 3:5
l on the God of Israel Is 48:2

LEAP *jump, spring*
l-ing and dancing 2 Sam 6:16
I can l over a wall Ps 18:29
baby **l-ed** in her Luke 1:41
and l *for joy* Luke 6:23
l-ed up and *began* Acts 14:10

LEARN *get knowledge*
l to fear the LORD Deut 31:13
I may l Your statutes Ps 119:71
have I **l-ed** wisdom Prov 30:3
will they l war Is 2:4
l from Me Matt 11:29
l-ed to be content Phil 4:11
He **l-ed** obedience Heb 5:8

LEARNING (n) *knowledge*
increase *his* l Prov 9:9
l of the Egyptians Acts 7:22
great l is driving Acts 26:24

LEAST *insignificant*
l of my master's 2 Kin 18:24
greatest to the l 2 Chr 34:30
l in the kingdom Matt 5:19
the one who is l...is Matt 11:11
l of the apostles 1 Cor 15:9
very l of all saints Eph 3:8

LEATHER *animal skin*
man with a l girdle 2 Kin 1:8
a l belt around his Matt 3:4
and *wore* a l belt Mark 1:6

LEAVE *abandon, depart, forsake*
shall l his father Gen 2:24
arise, l this land Gen 31:13
not l me defenseless Ps 141:8
kindness and truth l Prov 3:3
l the ninety-nine Matt 18:12
Peace I l with you John 14:27
I am **l-ing**...world John 16:28
L your country Acts 7:3

LEAVEN *yeast*
no l found in your Ex 12:19
not be baked with l Lev 6:17
seven days no l shall Deut 16:4
heaven is like l Matt 13:33
little l leavens the 1 Cor 5:6

LEAVENED *raised by yeast*
whoever eats what is l Ex 12:19
with cakes of l bread Lev 7:13
not eat l bread Deut 16:3
until it was all l Matt 13:33

LEBANON
mountain range N of Israel
Josh 9:1; Judg 3:3; 1 Kin 5:6
showing God's greatness Ps 29:6
symbol of prosperity Ps 92:12

LEG *part of body*
l-s are pillars of Song 5:15
Uncover the l Is 47:2
not break His **l-s** John 19:33

LEGAL *lawful*
has a l matter Ex 24:14
Give me l protection Luke 18:3

LEGION *division, group*
twelve **l-s** of angels Matt 26:53

My name is **L** Mark 5:9
man who had...**l** Mark 5:15
L; for many demons Luke 8:30

LEMUEL
royal author of section of Proverbs Prov 31:1,4

LEND *loan*
l-ing them money Neh 5:10
l-s...on interest Ezek 18:13
l, expecting nothing Luke 6:35
l me three loaves Luke 11:5

LENDER *loaner*
becomes the **l-'s** slave Prov 22:7
l like the borrower Is 24:2

LENGTH
the **l** of the ark Gen 6:15
l of days and years Prov 3:2
breadth and **l** and Eph 3:18
l and width...equal Rev 21:16

LEOPARD *animal*
l will lie down with Is 11:6
Or the **l** his spots Jer 13:23
Like a **l** I will lie Hos 13:7
beast...was like a **l** Rev 13:2

LEPER *one having leprosy*
As for the **l** Lev 13:45
King Uzziah...a **l** 2 Chr 26:21
a **l** came to Him Matt 8:2
cleanse *the* **l-s** Matt 10:8
home of Simon the **l** Mark 14:3

LEPROSY *infectious disease*
of **l** on the skin Lev 13:2
mark of **l** on a Lev 14:34
an infection of **l** Deut 24:8
cure him of his **l** 2 Kin 5:3
his **l** was cleansed Matt 8:3

LEPROUS *having leprosy*
hand was **l** like snow Ex 4:6
is a **l** malignancy Lev 13:51
ten **l**...met Him Luke 17:12

LET *allow, permit*
L there be light Gen 1:3
L My people go Ex 5:1
L the children alone Matt 19:14
l this cup pass from Matt 26:39
Do not **l** your heart be John 14:1

LETTER *epistle* or *symbol*
a **l** sent to Solomon 2 Chr 2:11
smallest **l** or stroke Matt 5:18
You are our **l** 2 Cor 3:2
l caused you sorrow 2 Cor 7:8
large **l-s** I am writing Gal 6:11

LEVEL *flat, plain*
lead me in a **l** path Ps 27:11
path of the righteous **l** Is 26:7
stood on a **l** place Luke 6:17

LEVI
1 *son of Jacob* Gen 34:25
2 *tribe* Num 1:49; Rev 7:7
3 *two ancestors of Jesus* Luke 3:24,29
4 *apostle* Mark 2:14; Luke 5:27,29

LEVIATHAN
symbolic monster of the deep Job 3:8; Ps 104:26; Is 27:1

LEVITES
descendants of Levi Ex 6:19,25
charged with the care of the sanctuary Num 1:50; 3:41

LEVY (n) *payment, tax*
the LORD's **l** Num 31:38
l *fixed by* Moses 2 Chr 24:6

LEVY (v) *impose a tax*
l a tax for the LORD Num 31:28
l-ied forced laborers 1 Kin 9:21

LEWDNESS *lascivious, lust*
land...full of **l** Lev 19:29
not commit this **l** Ezek 16:43
I will uncover her **l** Hos 2:10

LIAR *one telling lies*
who...prove me a **l** Job 24:25
a poor man than a **l** Prov 19:22
I will be a **l** like John 8:55
hypocrisy of **l-s** 1 Tim 4:2
we make Him a **l** 1 John 1:10

LIBATION *see* **OFFERINGS**

LIBERTY *freedom*
I will walk at **l** Ps 119:45
proclaim **l** to captives Is 61:1
spy out our **l** Gal 2:4
the *law* of **l** James 1:25

LIBNAH
1 *place in wilderness* Num 33:21
2 *Canaanite city* Josh 10:29; 2 Kin 23:31
a Levitical city 1 Chr 6:57

LIBYA
country in N Africa Ezek 30:5; Acts 2:10

LICK *lap up*
dogs will **l** up your 1 Kin 21:19
his enemies **l** the dust Ps 72:9
dogs were...**l-ing** Luke 16:21

LIE (n) *false statement*
speak **l-s** go astray Ps 58:3
tells **l-s** will perish Prov 19:9
prophesy a **l** to you Jer 27:10
the father of **l-s** John 8:44
truth of God for a **l** Rom 1:25
no **l** is of the truth 1 John 2:21

LIE (v) *make false statement*
nor **l** to one another Lev 19:11
l-d to Him with their Ps 78:36
l-d about the LORD Jer 5:12
l to the Holy Spirit Acts 5:3
not **l** to one another Col 3:9
impossible...God to **l** Heb 6:18

LIE (v) *recline*
when you **l** down Deut 11:19
she **lay** at his feet Ruth 3:14
Saul **lay** sleeping 1 Sam 26:7
makes me **l** down Ps 23:2
lying in a manger Luke 2:12

LIFE *living* or *salvation*
the breath of **l** Gen 2:7
l for **l** Ex 21:23
l...is in the blood Lev 17:11
Our **l** for yours Josh 2:14
my **l** is *but* breath Job 7:7
Who redeems your **l** Ps 103:4
the springs of **l** Prov 4:23
way of **l** and...death Jer 21:8
to everlasting **l** Dan 12:2
take my **l** from me Jon 4:3
worried about your **l** Matt 6:25
loses his **l** for My Matt 16:25
His **l** a ransom for Matt 20:28
to inherit eternal **l** Mark 10:17
l is more than food Luke 12:23
but have eternal **l** John 3:16
out of death into **l** John 5:24
I am the bread of **l** John 6:35
lays down his **l** John 10:11
resurrection and...**l** John 11:25
truth, and the **l** John 14:6
lay down his **l** for John 15:13
walk in newness of **l** Rom 6:4
the Spirit gives **l** 2 Cor 3:6
Christ, who is our **l** Col 3:4
an undisciplined **l** 2 Thess 3:11
receive...crown of **l** James 1:12
lay down our **l-ves** 1 John 3:16
book of **l** of the lamb Rev 13:8

LIFEBLOOD
I will require your **l** Gen 9:5
poured out their **l** Is 63:6
l of the innocent Jer 2:34

LIFETIME *length of life*
Throughout his **l** 2 Chr 34:33
His favor is for a **l** Ps 30:5
my **l** of futility Eccl 7:15
as the **l** of a tree Is 65:22

LIFT *exalt, raise*
l up your eyes and Gen 13:14
l up your staff and Ex 14:16
l up your voice Job 38:34
One who **l-s** my head Ps 3:3
I Will **l** up my eyes Ps 121:1
will not **l** up sword Is 2:4
Spirit **l-ed** me up Ezek 3:14
Son of Man be **l-ed** John 3:14
He was **l-ed** up Acts 1:9
l-ing up holy hands 1 Tim 2:8

LIGHT *brightness, lamp*
Let there be **l** Gen 1:3
Israel had **l** in Ex 10:23
l of the wicked Job 18:5
LORD is my **l** Ps 27:1
And a **l** to my path Ps 119:105
like the **l** of dawn Prov 4:18
walk in the **l** of the Is 2:5
your **l** has come Is 60:1
stars for **l** by night Jer 31:35
the **l** of the world Matt 5:14
body will be full of **l** Matt 6:22
L of revelation to Luke 2:32
There was the true **l** John 1:9
I am the **L** John 8:12
while you have...**L** John 12:35
l of the gospel 2 Cor 4:4
walk as children of **L** Eph 5:8
Father of **l-s** James 1:17
if we walk in the **L** 1 John 1:7

LIGHTNING
flash of light in sky
thunder and **l** flashes Ex 19:16
He spreads His **l** Job 36:30
makes **l** for the rain Jer 10:13
l...from the east Matt 24:27
appearance...like **l** Matt 28:3

LIKENESS *similarity*
according to Our **l** Gen 1:26
an idol, or any **l** Ex 20:4
the **l** of sinful flesh Rom 8:3
made in the **l** of men Phil 2:7

LILY *flower*
The **l** of the valleys Song 2:1
blossom like the **l** Hos 14:5
l-ies of the field Matt 6:28

LIMIT *end, extent*
there is no **l** 1 Chr 22:16
no **l** to windy words Job 16:3
set a **l** for the rain Job 28:26
no **l** to the treasure Nah 2:9

LINE *boundary* or *cord*
draw your *border* **l** Num 34:7
ran from...battle **l** 1 Sam 4:12
a **l** into the Nile Is 19:8
plumb **l** in the hand Zech 4:10

LINEN *type of cloth*
makes **l** garments Prov 31:24
buy...a **l** waistband Jer 13:1
pulled free of the **l** sheet Mark 14:52
wrapped Him...**l** Mark 15:46
saw the **l** wrappings John 20:5
clothed in fine **l** Rev 19:14

LINTEL *horizontal crosspiece*
blood on the **l** Ex 12:23
l *and* five-sided 1 Kin 6:31

LION *wild animal*
Judah is a **l-'s** whelp Gen 49:9
a **l** or a bear 1 Sam 17:34
hunt me like a **l** Job 10:16
tear my soul like a **l** Ps 7:2
are bold as a **l** Prov 28:1
cast into the **l-s'** Dan 6:16
like a roaring **l** 1 Pet 5:8

LIPS *part of mouth*
My **l** will praise Ps 63:3

With her flattering l Prov 7:21
Your l, *my* bride Song 4:11
a man of unclean l Is 6:5
honors Me with...l Matt 15:8

LIQUOR *alcoholic drink*
concerning wine and l Mic 2:11
drink no wine or l Luke 1:15

LISTEN *hear, heed*
Pharaoh does not l Ex 7:4
l to His voice Deut 4:30
l...commandments Deut 11:27
scoffer does not l Prov 13:1
L to your father Prov 23:22
draw near to l Eccl 5:1
L to Me, O Jacob Is 48:12
L...another parable Matt 21:33
care what you l to Mark 4:24
l-ing to the word Luke 5:1
My Son...l to Him Luke 9:35

LITERATURE *writings*
teach them the l Dan 1:4
every *branch of* l Dan 1:17

LITTLE *small quantity*
a l lower than God Ps 8:5
a l boy will lead Is 11:6
You of l faith Matt 6:30
forgiven l, loves l Luke 7:47
a l leaven leavens 1 Cor 5:6
l children, abide 1 John 2:28

LIVE (v) *reside* or *be alive*
eat, and l forever Gen 3:22
does not l by bread Deut 8:3
my Redeemer **l-s** Job 19:25
Let my soul l Ps 119:175
Listen, that you may l Is 55:3
can these bones l Ezek 37:3
righteous will l by Hab 2:4
l-d in...Nazareth Matt 2:23
not l on bread alone Matt 4:4
l even if he dies John 11:25
because I l John 14:19
shall l by faith Rom 1:17
Christ died and **l-d** Rom 14:9
no longer I who l Gal 2:20
to l is Christ Phil 1:21
worship Him who **l-s** Rev 4:10

LIVER *internal organ*
the lobe of the l Ex 29:13
l of the sin offering Lev 9:10
pierces through his l Prov 7:23
he looks at the l Ezek 21:21

LIVESTOCK *domestic animals*
was very rich in l Gen 13:2
their l to Joseph Gen 47:17
l of Egypt died Ex 9:6
large number of l Num 32:1

LIVING (adj) *alive*
man became a l being Gen 2:7
voice of the l god Deut 5:26
Divide the l child 1 Kin 3:25
Son of the l God Matt 16:16
given you l water John 4:10
I am the l bread John 6:51
l and holy sacrifice Rom 12:1
became a l soul 1 Cor 15:45
temple of the l God 2 Cor 6:16
word of God is l Heb 4:12

LIVING (n) *what is alive*
mother of all *the* l Gen 3:20
land of the l Job 28:13
that the l may know Dan 4:17
God...of the l Matt 22:32
judge the l and the 1 Pet 4:5

LOAD *burden*
in all their **l-s** Num 4:27
I alone bear the l Deut 1:12

LOAF *portion of bread*
gave him a l of bread Jer 37:21
asks for a l Matt 7:9
five **l-ves** and two Matt 14:17

LO-AMMI
second son of Hosea Hos 1:9

LOAN *something lent*
your neighbor a l Deut 24:10
rich with **l-s** Hab 2:6

LOATHE *despise, detest*
I **l-d** *that* generation Ps 95:10
sated man **l-s** honey Prov 27:7
I l the arrogance of Amos 6:8

LOATHSOME *detestable*
l to the Egyptians Gen 46:34
like l food to me Job 6:7
l and malignant sore Rev 16:2

LOCK (n) *tuft of hair*
seven **l-s** of my hair Judg 16:13
flowing **l-s** of...head Song 7:5
a l of my head Ezek 8:3

LOCK (v) *secure, shut*
l the door behind 2 Sam 13:17
l-ed quite securely Acts 5:23
l up...the saints Acts 26:10

LOCUST *grasshopper*
wind brought the **l-s** Ex 10:13
you may eat: the l Lev 11:22
come in like **l-s** Judg 6:5
leap like the l Job 39:20
l-s have no king Prov 30:27
like the swarming l Nah 3:17
food was **l-s** and wild Matt 3:4

LOD / LYDDA
town of Benjamin SE of coastal Jaffa 1 Chr 8:12; Neh 11:35; Acts 9:32-38

LODGE *dwell, spend the night*
where you l, I will l Ruth 1:16
drank and **l-d** there Judg 19:4
In his neck **l-s** Job 41:22
l in the wilderness Ps 55:7

LODGING (adj) *dwelling*
fodder at the l place Gen 42:27
about at the l place Ex 4:24
A wayfarers' l place Jer 9:2

LOFTINESS *elevated, haughty*
l of man will be Is 2:11
l of your dwelling Obad 3

LOFTY *grand, high*
built You a l house 1 Kin 8:13
high and l mountain Is 57:7

LOG *beam, wood*
he who splits **l-s** Eccl 10:9
l out of your own eye Matt 7:5

LOINS *lower back*
with your l girded Ex 12:11
Gird up your l 2 Kin 4:29
l are full of anguish Is 21:3
having girded your l Eph 6:14

LOIS
grandmother of Timothy 2 Tim 1:5

LONELY *alone, isolated*
I am l and afflicted Ps 25:16
makes a home for the l Ps 68:6
How l sits the city Lam 1:1

LONG (adj) *extended*
there was a l war 2 Sam 3:1
L life is in her Prov 3:16
you make l prayers Matt 23:14
if a man has l hair 1 Cor 11:14

LONG (v) *desire, want*
Who l for death Job 3:21
my soul **l-s** for You Is 26:9
l-ing to be fed Luke 16:21
I l to see you Rom 1:11
angels l to look 1 Pet 1:12
l for the pure milk 1 Pet 2:2

LOOK *see, stare*
Do not l behind you Gen 19:17
afraid to l at God Ex 3:6
LORD **l-s** at...heart 1 Sam 16:7
L upon my affliction Ps 25:18
The sea **l-ed** and fled Ps 114:3
not l on the wine Prov 23:31
l eagerly for Him Is 8:17
l to the Holy One Is 17:7
l on Me...pierced Zech 12:10
L at the birds of Matt 6:26
l-ing up...heaven Matt 14:19
plow and **l-ing** back Luke 9:62
l on the fields John 4:35
l on Him...pierced John 19:37
l-ing for the blessed Titus 2:13
l-ing for...heavens 2 Pet 3:13

LOOSE *release*
l the cords of Orion Job 38:31
have **l-d** my bonds Ps 116:16
l on earth shall have been Matt 16:19
you l on earth Matt 18:18

LORD *personal name of God*
Old Testament
Different Hebrew words are translated as Lord
LORD *(Yahweh)* Gen 4:1; Ex 3:2,15; Ps 23:1; Is 40:31; Ezek 11:23
Lord GOD *(Adonai Yahweh)* Gen 15:2; 2 Sam 7:18,19; Is 1:24; Ezek 28:6; Hab 3:19
LORD God *(Yahweh Elohim)* Gen 2:4; Ps 59:5; 68:18; Jer 15:16; Jon 1:9
Lord *(Adonai)* Gen 18:27; Ex 4:10; Josh 3:11; Ps 68:19; Mic 4:13
LORD GOD *(Yah Yahweh)* Is 12:2
New Testament
Different Greek words are translated as Lord
Lord *(Kyrios, refers to either the Father or the Son)* Matt 1:20; John 11:2; Acts 5:19; 2 Cor 5:6; 1 Thess 4:16
Lord *(Despotes, refers to the Father)* Luke 2:29; Acts 4:24; Rev 6:10
Lord God *(Kyrios Theos, refers to either the Father or the Son)* Luke 1:32; Rev 1:8;11:17;16:7;18:8
Lord Jesus *(Kyrios Iesous)* Mark 16:19; Luke 24:3; Acts 4:33; 7:59
Lord Jesus Christ *(Kyrios Iesous Christos)* Acts 15:26; Rom 1:7;5:1; 1 Cor 1:10; Eph 1:2,3; 1 Thess 5:9; James 2:1

LORD *human master, ruler*
Hear us, my l Gen 23:6
not my l be angry Gen 31:35
Moses, my l Num 11:28
l-s of...Philistines Judg 16:27
counsel of my l Ezra 10:3
l-s of the nations Is 16:8
his l commanded Matt 18:25
write to my l Acts 25:26

LO-RUHAMAH
daughter of Hosea Hos 1:6,8

LOSE *mislay, suffer loss*
do not l courage 2 Chr 15:7
lost their confidence Neh 6:16
stars l their Joel 2:10
his life will l it Matt 10:39
that which was **lost** Matt 18:11
not l his reward Mark 9:41
whoever **l-s** his life Luke 9:24

LOSS *damage, what is lost*
might not suffer l Dan 6:2
damage and great l Acts 27:10
might not suffer l 2 Cor 7:9
all things to be l Phil 3:8

LOST (adj) *missing, ruined*
like a l sheep Ps 119:176
have become l sheep Jer 50:6
l sheep...of Israel Matt 10:6
the wine is l Mark 2:22

LOST (n) *without God*
I will seek the l Ezek 34:16
sent only to the l Matt 15:24

LOT
nephew of Abraham Gen 12:5;19:15,36

LOT *portion* or *decision process*
one **l** for the LORD Lev 16:8
clothing they cast **l-s** Ps 22:18
your **l** with us Prov 1:14
let us cast **l-s** Jon 1:7
tear it, but cast **l-s** John 19:24
l fell to Matthias Acts 1:26

LOUD *great, noisy*
very **l** trumpet sound Ex 19:16
with a **l** shout Ezra 3:13
Jesus cried...**l** voice Matt 27:50
heard...a **l** voice Rev 1:10

LOVE (n) *compassion, devotion*
l covers all Prov 10:12
in unchanging **l** Mic 7:18
l will grow cold Matt 24:12
abide in My **l** John 15:10
Greater **l** has no one John 15:13
demonstrates His...**l** Rom 5:8
separate us from...**l** Rom 8:39
l edifies 1 Cor 8:1
l is kind 1 Cor 13:4
Pursue **l** 1 Cor 14:1
l of Christ controls 2 Cor 5:14
through **l** serve one Gal 5:13
fruit...is **l** Gal 5:22
speaking...truth in **l** Eph 4:15
l of money is a root 1 Tim 6:10
for **l** is from God 1 John 4:7
God is **l** 1 John 4:16
l casts out fear 1 John 4:18
have left your first **l** Rev 2:4

LOVE (v)
who **l** Me and keep My Ex 20:6
l your neighbor as Lev 19:18
l the LORD your God Deut 6:5
the LORD **l-d** Israel 1 Kin 10:9
I **l** Your testimonies Ps 119:119
LORD **l-s** He reproves Prov 3:12
friend **l-s** at all Prov 17:17
Do not **l** sleep Prov 20:13
A time to **l** Eccl 3:8
Hate evil, **l** good Amos 5:15
do not **l** perjury Zech 8:17
l your enemies Matt 5:44
l to stand and pray Matt 6:5
God so **l-d** the world John 3:16
you **l** one another John 13:34
l-s a cheerful giver 2 Cor 9:7
Husbands, **l**...wives Eph 5:25
Do not **l** the world 1 John 2:15
whom I **l**, I reprove Rev 3:19

LOVERS *one who desires, loves*
l have been crushed Jer 22:20
I called to my **l** Lam 1:19
the hands of your **l** Ezek 16:39

I will go after my **l** Hos 2:5
l of pleasure...**l** of 2 Tim 3:4

LOVINGKINDNESS
compassion
His **l** is upon Israel Ezra 3:11
abundant in **l** and Ps 86:15
sing of the **l** of the Ps 89:1
By **l** and truth Prov 16:6
with everlasting **l** Is 54:8

LOWLAND *low hills*
country and in the **l** Deut 1:7
the Negev and the **l** Josh 10:40
sycamores in the **l** 2 Chr 1:15
the cities of the **l** Jer 32:44
see also **SHEPHELAH**

LOWLY *humble, little*
He sets on high...**l** Job 5:11
He regards the **l** Ps 138:6
associate with the **l** Rom 12:16

LOYALTY *faithfulness*
Is this your **l** 2 Sam 16:17
proclaims his own **l** Prov 20:6
I delight in **l** Hos 6:6

LUKE
associate of Paul
2 Tim 4:11; Philem 24
author of Luke and Acts
Luke 1:1; Acts 1:1
physician Col 4:14

LUKEWARM *tepid*
because you are **l** Rev 3:16

LUST *sexual desire*
looks at...woman with **l** Matt 5:28
from youthful **l-s** 2 Tim 2:22
You **l** and do not James 4:2
l of the eyes 1 John 2:16

LUXURIANT *lush, productive*
beneath...**l** tree 1 Kin 14:23
Israel is a **l** vine Hos 10:1

LUXURY *extravagance*
L is not fitting for Prov 19:10
clothed and live in **l** Luke 7:25

LUZ
1 *ancient name of Bethel*
Gen 28:19;48:3
2 *town in Aram* Judg 1:26

LYCAONIA
Roman province in Asia Minor
Acts 14:6

LYDDA *see* **LOD**

LYDIA
1 *seller of purple dyes and goods* Acts 16:14,40
2 *region on the W coast of Asia Minor* Jer 46:9

LYING (adj) *false*
with a **l** tongue Ps 109:2
hatred *has* **l** lips Prov 10:18
l pen of the scribes Jer 8:8
and **l** divination Ezek 13:6

LYRE *stringed instrument*
play the **l** and pipe Gen 4:21
prophesy with **l-s** 1 Chr 25:1
Awake, harp and **l** Ps 57:8

LYSTRA
a Lycaonian town
Acts 14:6;16:1,2

M

MACEDONIA
Roman province Acts 16:9,12
N Greece Phil 4:15; 1 Tim 1:3
visited by Paul Acts 16:10;
2 Cor 2:13

MACHIR
1 *grandson of Joseph* Josh 17:1
2 *son of Ammiel* 2 Sam 9:4,5

MACHPELAH
cave near Hebron Gen 23:17,19
Sarah's burial place Gen 23:19
Abraham buried there Gen 25:9
burial place of Jacob, Isaac, Rebekah, and Leah
Gen 49:29ff;50:13

MAD *insane*
makes a wise man **m** Eccl 7:7
nations are going **m** Jer 51:7

MADMAN *insane person*
behaving as a **m** 1 Sam 21:14
m who prophesies Jer 29:26

MADNESS *lunacy*
laughter, It is **m** Eccl 2:2
consider...**m** and folly Eccl 2:12

MAGADAN
village on the Sea of Galilee
Matt 15:39

MAGDALENE
Mary Matt 27:56,61
from village of Magdala
Mark 15:40,47; John 20:1,18

MAGI
wise men from Persia who visited Jesus, Mary, and Joseph Matt 2:1,7,16

MAGIC *sorcery*
practicing **m** Acts 8:9
who practiced **m** Acts 19:19

MAGICIAN *sorcerer, wizard*
called for...**m-s** Gen 41:8
the **m-s** of Egypt Ex 7:11
of any **m**, conjurer or Dan 2:10
found a **m** Acts 13:6

MAGISTRATE
appear before the **m** Luke 12:58
to the chief **m-s** Acts 16:20

MAGNIFY *extol, praise*
name...be **m-ied** 2 Sam 7:26
You **m** him Job 7:17
O **m** the LORD with me Ps 34:3

have **m-ied** Your word Ps 138:2
Jesus was...**m-ied** Acts 19:17
I **m** my ministry Rom 11:13

MAGOG
1 *son of Japheth* 1 Chr 1:5
2 *region in Asia Minor or further N ruled by Gog*
Ezek 38:2;39:6
see also **GOG**

MAHANAIM
city in Trans-Jordan Josh 13:26,30
city of refuge Josh 21:38
Levitical city 1 Chr 6:80

MAHER-SHALAL-HASH-BAZ
symbolic name of one of Isaiah's sons Is 8:3

MAHLAH
1 *daughter of Zelophehad*
Num 26:33;27:1; Josh 17:3
2 *a Manassite* 1 Chr 7:18

MAHLON
husband of Ruth Ruth 1:5;4:10

MAID
Hagar, Sarai's **m** Gen 16:8
gave my **m** to my Gen 30:18
I am Ruth your **m** Ruth 3:9
way of a man...a **m** Prov 30:19

MAIDENS *young woman*
at the Nile...her **m** Ex 2:5
m...tambourines Ps 68:25

MAIDSERVANT *female slave*
do...to your **m** Deut 15:17
give Your **m** a son 1 Sam 1:11
let your **m** speak 2 Sam 14:12
while your **m** slept 1 Kin 3:20

MAJESTIC *dignified, grand*
Who is like You, **m** Ex 15:11
with His **m** voice Job 37:4
How **m** is Your name Ps 8:1
They are the **m** ones Ps 16:3
m is His work Ps 111:3
by the **M** Glory 2 Pet 1:17

MAJESTY *grandeur*
Around God is...**m** Job 37:22
He is clothed with **m** Ps 93:1
The **m** of our God Is 35:2
right hand of the **M** Heb 1:3
revile angelic **m-ies** Jude 8

MAKE *cause, create, do*
Let Us **m** man in Gen 1:26
not **m** for...an idol Ex 20:4
M me know Your ways Ps 25:4
M ready the way of Matt 3:3
m you fishers of men Matt 4:19

MAKER *creator*
Where is God my **M** Job 35:10
kneel before...our **M** Ps 95:6
M of heaven and Ps 115:15
I, the LORD, am the **m** Is 44:24

MAKKEDAH
Canaanite city in Judah Josh 10:21; 15:41

MALACHI
prophet Mal 1:1

MALCHUS
servant whose ear was cut off by Peter John 18:10

MALE
m and female He Gen 1:27
lamb...unblemished **m** Ex 12:5
likeness of **m** or Deut 4:16
slew...**m** children Matt 2:16
made...**m** and female Matt 19:4
neither **m** nor female Gal 3:28

MALICE *evil, mischief*
perceived their **m** Matt 22:18
leaven of **m** and 1 Cor 5:8
wrath, **m**, slander Col 3:8
putting aside all **m** 1 Pet 2:1

MALICIOUS *harmful, spiteful*
to be a **m** witness Ex 23:1
m gossips, without 2 Tim 3:3

MALTA
island S of Sicily where Paul was shipwrecked Acts 28:1

MAMRE
1 *Abraham's dwelling place near Hebron* Gen 13:18
2 *Amorite chieftain* Gen 14:24

MAN *male*
make **m** in Our image Gen 1:26
God formed **m** of dust Gen 2:7
Elisha the **m** of God 2 Kin 5:8
m is born for trouble Job 5:7
blessed is the **m** Ps 1:1
m is a mere breath Ps 39:11
righteous **m** hates Prov 13:5
Will a **m** rob God Mal 3:8
light...before **men** Matt 5:16
fishers of **men** Mark 1:17
Sabbath...for **m** Mark 2:27
rich **m** to enter Mark 10:25
what is a **m** profited Luke 9:25
a **m**, sent from God John 1:6
How can a **m** be born John 3:4
a **m** of Macedonia Acts 16:9
through one **m** sin Rom 5:12
as is common to **m** 1 Cor 10:13
when I became a **m** 1 Cor 13:11
m...leave his father Eph 5:31

MAN, SON OF
see **SON OF MAN**

MANASSEH
1 *son of Joseph* Gen 41:51;46:20
2 *tribe and area* Num 13:11; Josh 17:1
3 *king of Judah* 2 Kin 21:1,11
4 *Pahath-moab's son* Ezra 10:30
5 *son of Hashum* Ezra 10:33

MANDRAKES *love fruit*
found **m** in the field Gen 30:14
m...fragrance Song 7:13

MANGER *feeding trough*
spend...at your **m** Job 39:9
the **m** is clean Prov 14:4
laid Him in a **m** Luke 2:7

MANIFEST *reveal*
I have **m-ed** Your name John 17:6
became **m** to those Rom 10:20
made **m** to God 2 Cor 5:11
m-ed to His saints Col 1:26

MANIFOLD *many and varied*
the **m** wisdom of God Eph 3:10
stewards...**m** grace 1 Pet 4:10

MANKIND *the human race*
God...dwell with **m** 2 Chr 6:18
All **m** is stupid Jer 51:17
His love for **m** Titus 3:4
kill a third of **m** Rev 9:15

MANNA *food of the desert*
Israel named it **m** Ex 16:31
m was like coriander Num 11:7
m ceased on the day Josh 5:12
He rained down **m** Ps 78:24
Our fathers ate the **m** John 6:31

MANNER *way*
Your **m** with those Ps 119:132
spoke in such a **m** Acts 14:1
m worthy of...saints Rom 16:2
walk in a **m** worthy Eph 4:1

MANOAH
father of Samson Judg 13:2ff

MANSLAYER
for the **m** to flee to Num 35:6
m might flee there Deut 4:42
the **m** who kills any Josh 20:3

MANTLE *cloak, garment*
threw his **m** on him 1 Kin 19:19
the **m** of Elijah 2 Kin 2:13
like a **m** You will roll Heb 1:12

MARAH
spring of bitter water Ex 15:23

MARCH *pace, walk*
m around...seven times Josh 6:4
m everyone in his path Joel 2:8

MARDUK
chief Babylonian god Jer 50:2

MARESHAH
1 *father of Hebron* 1 Chr 2:42
2 *son of Laadah* 1 Chr 4:21
3 *town in Judah* 2 Chr 11:5-8

MARK *sign, spot*
make any tattoo **m-s** Lev 19:28
m on the foreheads Ezek 9:4
m on his forehead Rev 14:9
m of the beast Rev 19:20

MARK, JOHN
author of Gospel of Mark
accompanied Paul and Barnabas Acts 13:5;15:37
cousin of Barnabas Col 4:10

MARKET
selling or *trading place*
was the **m** of nations Is 23:3
coastlands were...**m** Ezek 27:15
idle in the **m** place Matt 20:3
sold in the meat **m** 1 Cor 10:25

MARRIAGE *wedlock*
a **m** alliance with 1 Kin 3:1
nor are given in **m** Matt 22:30
M *is to be held* in honor Heb 13:4
m supper of the Lamb Rev 19:9

MARRY *join in wedlock*
m-ied foreign wives Ezra 10:10
m-ies a divorced Matt 5:32
better not to **m** Matt 19:10
neither **m** nor are Mark 12:25
m-ied woman is bound Rom 7:2
better to **m** than to 1 Cor 7:9

MARTHA
sister of Lazarus and Mary John 11:1,5

MARVEL *be amazed, wonder*
Jesus heard...**m-ed** Matt 8:10
the crowd **m-ed** Matt 15:31
m-ed at the sight Acts 7:31

MARVELOUS *extraordinary*
and see this **m** sight Ex 3:3
It is **m** in our eyes Ps 118:23
into His **m** light 1 Pet 2:9
m are Your works Rev 15:3

MARY
1 *mother of Jesus* Matt 1:16
2 *Mary Magdalene* Matt 27:56; Mark 15:40
3 *mother of James and Joseph* Matt 27:56; Mark 16:1
4 *sister of Martha and Lazarus* John 11:1
5 *mother of Mark* Acts 12:12
6 *wife of Clopas* John 19:25
7 *Roman believer* Rom 16:6

MASTER *lord, ruler*
God of...**m** Abraham Gen 24:12
m shall pierce his ear Ex 21:6
can serve two **m-s** Matt 6:24
death no longer is **m** Rom 6:9
sin shall not be **m** Rom 6:14
obedient to...your **m-s** Eph 6:5
a **M** in heaven Col 4:1

MATTHEW
tax-gatherer Matt 9:9;10:3
apostle Matt 10:3; Luke 6:15; Acts 1:13

MATTHIAS
replaced Judas Acts 1:23,26

MATURE *full grown* or *stable*
then the **m** grain Mark 4:28
those who are **m** 1 Cor 2:6
your thinking be **m** 1 Cor 14:20
food is for the **m** Heb 5:14

MATURITY *ripeness, adulthood*
bring no fruit to **m** Luke 8:14
let us press on to **m** Heb 6:1

MEAL *prepared food*
a **m** for enjoyment Eccl 10:19
not even eat a **m** Mark 3:20
washed before...**m** Luke 11:38
m-s together with Acts 2:46
for a *single* **m** Heb 12:16

MEAL OFFERING
see **OFFERINGS**

MEANINGLESS *senseless*
with **m** arguments Is 29:21
not use **m** repetition Matt 6:7

MEASURE (n) *amount*
a full and just **m** Deut 25:15
good **m**—pressed Luke 6:38
to each a **m** of faith Rom 12:3
m of Christ's gift Eph 4:7

MEASURE (v) *determine extent*
he stopped **m-ing** *it* Gen 41:49
m their former work Is 65:7
He **m-d** the gate Ezek 40:13
will be **m-d** to you Mark 4:24
rod to **m** the city Rev 21:15

MEASURING *standard*
justice the **m** line Is 28:17
was given me a **m** rod Rev 11:1

MEAT *flesh, food*
Who will give us **m** Num 11:4
LORD...you **m** Num 11:18
you may eat **m** Deut 12:20
rained **m** upon them Ps 78:27
from **m** sacrificed Acts 21:25
good not to eat **m** Rom 14:21
I will never eat **m** 1 Cor 8:13
m sacrificed...idols 1 Cor 10:28

MEDE(S)
ancient Indo-Europeans of NW Iran Dan 5:31;11:1

MEDEBA
Moabite town E of Dead Sea Josh 13:9; 1 Chr 19:7

MEDIA
country of the Medes Ezra 6:2; Esth 1:18; Is 21:2

MEDIATOR *intermediary*
by the agency of a **m** Gal 3:19

one **m**...between God 1 Tim 2:5
Jesus...**m** of a new Heb 12:24

MEDITATE *ponder*
Isaac went out to **m** Gen 24:63
His law he **m-s** day Ps 1:2
M in your heart Ps 4:4
I **m** on You in the Ps 63:6

MEDITATION *deep reflection*
m...Be acceptable Ps 19:14
m be pleasing to Him Ps 104:34
my **m** all the day Ps 119:97

MEDIUM *summons spirits*
not turn to **m-s** or Lev 19:31
m...be put to death Lev 20:27
a **m**, or a spiritist Deut 18:11
woman who is a **m** 1 Sam 28:7
will resort to...**m-s** Is 19:3

MEEKNESS *gentleness*
cause of truth and **m** Ps 45:4
m and...of Christ 2 Cor 10:1

MEET *encounter*
Esau ran to **m** him Gen 33:4
people out...to **m** God Ex 19:17
God...will **m** me Ps 59:10
Prepare to **m**...God Amos 4:12
to **m** the bridegroom Matt 25:1
m-s his accusers Acts 25:16
m...in the air 1 Thess 4:17

MEETING *assembly*
house of **m** for all Job 30:23
midst of Your **m** place Ps 74:4

MEETING, TENT OF
see **TABERNACLE**

MEGIDDO
strategic city between Manasseh and Issachar Josh 12:21; 2 Kin 9:27
plain in Jezreel Valley 2 Chr 35:22; Zech 12:11
see also **HAR-MAGEDON**

MELCHIZEDEK
1 *king of Salem* Gen 14:18,19
priest Ps 110:4
2 *type of undying priesthood* Heb 5:6,10;6:20;7:1ff

MELODY *tune*
lyre...the sound of **m** Ps 98:5
singing...making **m** Eph 5:19

MELT *dissolve*
people **m** with fear Josh 14:8
His voice...earth **m-ed** Ps 46:6
mountains **m-ed** like Ps 97:5
As silver is **m-ed** Ezek 22:22

MEMBER *part of the whole*
m-s of...household Matt 10:25
m-s one of another Rom 12:5
if one **m** suffers 1 Cor 12:26
m-s of His body Eph 5:30

MEMORIAL *commemoration*
this is My **m-name** Ex 3:15
in a book as a **m** Ex 17:14
stones...become a **m** Josh 4:7
ascended as a **m** Acts 10:4

MEMORY *remembrance*
M of him perishes Job 18:17
cut off their **m** Ps 109:15
m of the righteous Prov 10:7
spoken of in **m** of Mark 14:9

MEMPHIS
city in Egypt Is 19:13; Jer 46:19; Ezek 30:13

MENAHEM
king of Israel 2 Kin 15:14,17

MENSTRUAL
m impurity for seven Lev 15:19
a woman during...**m** Ezek 18:6

MENSTRUATION
in the days of her **m** Lev 12:2
like her bed at **m** Lev 15:26

MEPHIBOSHETH
1 *son of Jonathan* 2 Sam 4:4
also **Merib-baal** 1 Chr 8:34
2 *son of Saul* 2 Sam 21:8

MERAB
Saul's daughter 1 Sam 18:17,19

MERARI
son of Levi Gen 46:11
head of a Levitical family Ex 6:19; 2 Chr 34:12

MERCHANT *buyer / seller*
m-s procured *them* 1 Kin 10:28
m of the peoples Ezek 27:3
A **m**, in whose hands Hos 12:7
m seeking...pearls Matt 13:45
m-s of the earth Rev 18:3

MERCIFUL *compassionate*
God **m** and gracious Ps 86:15
The LORD is...and **m** Ps 145:8
The **m** man...good Prov 11:17
Blessed are the **m** Matt 5:7
as your Father is **m** Luke 6:36
m to me, the sinner Luke 18:13

MERCY *compassion*
Great are Your **m-ies** Ps 119:156
in His **m** He redeemed Is 63:9
m to *the* poor Dan 4:27
the orphan finds **m** Hos 14:3
they shall receive **m** Matt 5:7
tender **m** of our God Luke 1:78
m on whom I have **m** Rom 9:15
by the **m-ies** of God Rom 12:1
God, being rich in **m** Eph 2:4

MERCY SEAT *covering over ark*
a **m** of pure gold Ex 25:17
put the **m** on the ark Ex 26:34
in front of the **m** Ex 30:6
sprinkle it on the **m** Lev 16:15
overshadowing the **m** Heb 9:5

MERIBAH
1 *fountain of Rephidim* Ex 17:7
2 *fountain of Kadesh-Barnea* Num 27:14

MERODACH-BALADAN
king of Babylon Is 39:1
see also **BERODACH-BALADAN**

MERRY *joyful, lively*
wine makes life **m** Eccl 10:19
eat, drink *and* be **m** Luke 12:19

MESHA
1 *territorial boundary in Arabia* Gen 10:30
2 *Moabite king* 2 Kin 3:4
3 *man of Judah* 1 Chr 2:42
4 *a Benjamite* 1 Chr 8:9

MESHACH
one of three Jews thrown into furnace Dan 3:19ff
see also **MISHAEL** Dan 1:7

MESHECH
1 *son of Japheth* Gen 10:2
2 *descendants and nation* Is 66:19; Ezek 27:13

MESOPOTAMIA
land of Tigris and Euphrates Rivers Deut 23:4; Judg 3:8; 1 Chr 19:6; Acts 7:2

MESSAGE *communication*
m from God for you Judg 3:20
m...with authority Luke 4:32
m and my preaching 1 Cor 2:4
the **m** of truth Eph 1:13
m we have heard 1 John 1:5

MESSENGER *one sent*
My **m** whom I send Is 42:19
m of the LORD of hosts Mal 2:7
I send My **m** ahead Matt 11:10
m-s of the churches 2 Cor 8:23
m of Satan 2 Cor 12:7

MESSIAH
anointed one Dan 9:25,26; John 1:41;4:25
Greek: Christ

METAL
like glowing **m** Ezek 1:4
their **m** images Dan 11:8

METHUSELAH
son of Enoch Gen 5:21
grandfather of Noah Gen 5:25ff

MICAH
1 *an Ephraimite* Judg 17:1
2 *line of Reuben* 1 Chr 5:5
3 *father of Abdon* 2 Chr 34:20
4 *prophet* Jer 26:18; Mic 1:1
name of several other people

MICAIAH
1 *prophet* 1 Kin 22:8-26
2 *father of Achbor* 2 Kin 22:12
3 *wife of Rehoboam* 2 Chr 13:2
4 *under Jehoshaphat* 2 Chr 17:7
5 *line of Asaph* Neh 12:35
6 *under Nehemiah* Neh 12:41
7 *son of Gemariah* Jer 36:11

MICHAEL
1 *an archangel* Dan 10:21;12:1; Jude 9; Rev 12:7
2 *Jehoshaphat's son* 2 Chr 21:2
prince of Judah
3 *army captain* 1 Chr 12:20
4 *line of Gershom* 1 Chr 6:40
name of seven other people

MICHAL
daughter of Saul 1 Sam 18:20
David's wife 1 Sam 19:11

MIDDLE *midst*
the **m** of the garden Gen 3:3
sun stopped in the **m** Josh 10:13
m of the lampstands Rev 1:13

MIDDLE GATE
see **GATES OF JERUSALEM**

MIDHEAVEN
directly overhead
eagle flying in **m** Rev 8:13
angel flying in **m** Rev 14:6
birds which fly in **m** Rev 19:17

MIDIAN
1 *a son of Abraham* Gen 25:1,2
2 *land SE of Canaan in desert* Ex 2:15; Num 31:8; Judg 8:28

MIDIANITES
people of Midian Gen 37:36; Num 31:2; Judg 7:7

MIDST *middle, within*
God is in the **m** Ps 46:5
in the **m** of the fire Dan 3:25
Holy One in your **m** Hos 11:9
I am...in their **m** Matt 18:20

MIDWIFE *aids childbirth*
m...tied a scarlet Gen 38:28
before the **m** can get Ex 1:19

MIGDOL
1 *Israelite camp near Red Sea* Ex 14:2; Num 33:7
2 *town in Egypt* Jer 44:1

MIGHT *strength*
my firstborn; My **m** Gen 49:3
and with all your **m** Deut 6:5
With Him are...**m** Job 12:13
Not by **m** nor by Zech 4:6
strength of His **m** Eph 1:19

MIGHTY *powerful*
a **m** hunter before Gen 10:9
m...awesome God Deut 10:17
m men of valor 1 Chr 12:8
The LORD **m** in battle Ps 24:8
a **m** king will rule Is 19:4
m in the Scriptures Acts 18:24
the **m** hand of God 1 Pet 5:6

MILCAH
1 *daughter of Haran* Gen 11:29
2 *daughter of Zelophehad* Num 26:33;27:1; Josh 17:3

MILCOM
god of Ammonites
1 Kin 11:5,33; 2 Kin 23:13; Zeph 1:5
see also **MOLECH**

MILE *distance, measurement*
one **m**, go with him Matt 5:41
m-s from Jerusalem Luke 24:13

MILETUS
town in Asia Minor
Acts 20:15,17; 2 Tim 4:20

MILK
land flowing with **m** Ex 3:8
pour me out like **m** Job 10:10
m produces butter Prov 30:33
m to drink, not 1 Cor 3:2
pure **m** of the word 1 Pet 2:2

MILL *grinding stones*
sound of the...**m** Eccl 12:4
at the grinding **m** Lam 5:13
women...at the **m** Matt 24:41

MILLO
1 *fort near Shechem Beth-millo* Judg 9:6,20
2 *fortress in Jerusalem*
2 Sam 5:9; 1 Kin 9:15,24; 1 Chr 11:8; 2 Chr 32:5

MILLSTONE *grinding stone*
upper **m** in pledge Deut 24:6
woman threw...**m** Judg 9:53
m hung around Matt 18:6
stone like a great **m** Rev 18:21

MINA
measure of gold or silver coin
1 Kin 10:17; Ezra 2:69; Neh 7:71; Luke 19:13ff

MIND *memory, thought*
God tries the...**m-s** Ps 7:9
Recall it to **m** Is 46:8
I test the **m** Jer 17:10
Let his **m** be changed Dan 4:16
He opened...**m-s** Luke 24:45
with one **m** in the Acts 2:46
to a depraved **m** Rom 1:28
m set on the flesh Rom 8:7
the **m** of Christ 1 Cor 2:16
m-s were hardened 2 Cor 3:14
with humility of **m** Phil 2:3

MINDFUL *aware*
Lord be **m** of me Ps 40:17
He is **m** that we are Ps 103:14
LORD has been **m** Ps 115:12
m of the...faith 2 Tim 1:5

MINISTER (n) *one who serves*
m-s before the ark 1 Chr 16:4
spoken of *as* **m-s** Is 61:6
a **m** and a witness Acts 26:16
a **m** of Christ Jesus Rom 15:16
is Christ then a **m** Gal 2:17
I was made a **m** Eph 3:7
faithful **m** in the Eph 6:21
His **m-s** a flame of Heb 1:7
a **m** in the sanctuary Heb 8:2

MINISTER (v) *give help, serve*
to **m** as priest to Me Ex 28:1
the boy **m-ed** to 1 Sam 2:11
not stand to **m** 1 Kin 8:11
to the LORD, To **m** Is 56:6
angels were **m-ing** Mark 1:13
follow Him and **m** Mark 15:41

MINISTRY *service*
He began His **m** Luke 3:23
to the **m** of the word Acts 6:4
m of the Spirit 2 Cor 3:8
m of reconciliation 2 Cor 5:18
fulfill your **m** 2 Tim 4:5
a more excellent **m** Heb 8:6

MIRACLE *supernatural event*
Work a **m** Ex 7:9
I will perform **m-s** Ex 34:10
m-s had occurred Matt 11:21
He could do no **m** Mark 6:5
perform a **m** in My Mark 9:39
this **m** of healing Acts 4:22
works **m-s** among you Gal 3:5
wonders and...**m-s** Heb 2:4

MIRE *mud*
cast me into the **m** Job 30:19
Deliver me from the **m** Ps 69:14
wallowing in the **m** 2 Pet 2:22

MIRIAM
1 *sister of Moses and Aaron*
Ex 15:20; Num 12:4,10;20:1
2 *line of Ezrah* 1 Chr 4:17

MIRROR *image reflector*
see in a **m** dimly 1 Cor 13:12
natural face in a **m** James 1:23

MISCARRIAGE *aborted fetus*
m-s of a woman Ps 58:8

MISERABLE *bad, unhappy*
loathe this **m** food Num 21:5
m and chronic Deut 28:59
Be **m** and mourn James 4:9
m and poor and blind Rev 3:17

MISERY *sorrow, suffering*
conscious of my **m** Job 10:15
Destruction and **m** Rom 3:16

MISFORTUNE *adversity*
M will not come Jer 5:12
m which He has Jer 26:13
The day of his **m** Obad 12

MISHAEL
1 *of family of Kohath* Ex 6:22; Lev 10:4
2 *associate of Ezra* Neh 8:4
3 *Daniel's friend* Dan 1:6,7,11,19;2:17
see also **MESHACH**

MISLEAD *lead astray*
m-s a blind *person* Deut 27:18
m-led My people Ezek 13:10
that no one **m-s** you Mark 13:5
m-ing our nation Luke 23:2

MISTREAT *treat badly, wrong*
not **m**...the stranger Jer 22:3
slaves...**m-ed** them Matt 22:6
pray for...who **m** Luke 6:28
mocked and **m-ed** Luke 18:32
m and to stone them Acts 14:5

MISTRESS *woman in charge*
her **m** was despised Gen 16:4
m of the house 1 Kin 17:17
the maid like her **m** Is 24:2
the **m** of sorceries Nah 3:4

MIZPAH / MIZPEH
1 *heap of stones* Gen 31:49
2 *near Mt. Hermon* Josh 11:3
3 *village in Judah* Josh 15:38
4 *Benjamite town* Josh 18:26
5 *town in Gilead* Judg 10:17
6 *Moabite town* 1 Sam 22:3

MIZRAIM
1 *son of Ham* Gen 10:6
father of nations Gen 10:13
2 *Heb. for Egypt* 1 Chr 1:8,11

MOAB
1 *son of Lot* Gen 19:37
2 *country E of the Dead Sea*
Ex 15:15; Josh 24:9; Ruth 1:2; 2 Kin 3:7; Ps 60:8; Jer 48:1

MOCK *ridicule, scorn*
lads...**m-ed** him 2 Kin 2:23
Fools **m** at sin Prov 14:9
who **m-s** the poor Prov 17:5
soldiers also **m-ed** Luke 23:36
God is not **m-ed** Gal 6:7

MOCKERY *object of ridicule*
a **m** of the Egyptians Ex 10:2
made a **m** of me Num 22:29
a **m** of justice Prov 19:28
m *and* insinuations Hab 2:6

MOLECH
god of the Ammonites
Lev 18:21; 1 Kin 11:7; Jer 32:35
see also **MILCOM**

MOLTEN *cast metal*
made it into a **m** calf Ex 32:4
make...no **m** gods Ex 34:17
destroy...**m** images Num 33:52
capitals of **m** bronze 1 Kin 7:16
his **m** images are Jer 10:14

MONEY *currency*
take double *the* **m** Gen 43:12
not sell her for **m** Deut 21:14
time to receive **m** 2 Kin 5:26
loves **m** will not be Eccl 5:10
no **m** in their belt Mark 6:8
m in the bank Luke 19:23
love of **m** is a root 1 Tim 6:10

MONEYCHANGERS
the tables of the **m** Matt 21:12
coins of the **m** John 2:15

MONSTER *enormous animal*
created...sea **m-s** Gen 1:21
sea, or the sea **m** Job 7:12
sea **m-s** in the waters Ps 74:13
belly of the sea **m** Matt 12:40

MOON
m and...were bowing Gen 37:9
the **m** stopped Josh 10:13
m and stars to rule Ps 136:9
beautiful as...**m** Song 6:10
the **m** into blood Joel 2:31
m will not...light Matt 24:29
signs in...and **m** Luke 21:25

MORALS *principles*
Bad...good **m** 1 Cor 15:33

MORDECAI
1 *returned from exile with Zerubbabel* Ezra 2:2
2 *Esther's cousin* Esth 2:7;3:2;9:20;10:3

MORIAH
land / mountain where Abraham offered Isaac Gen 22:2
threshing floor of Araunah (Ornan) 2 Sam 24:18
site of Temple 2 Chr 3:1

MORNING *dawn*
was **m**, a fifth day Gen 1:23
Rise early in the **m** Ex 8:20
the **m** stars sang Job 38:7
m or evening sowing Eccl 11:6
the bright **m** star Rev 22:16

MORSEL *piece of bread*
have eaten my **m** Job 31:17
Better is a dry **m** Prov 17:1
After the **m**, Satan John 13:27

MORTAL *what eventually dies*
not trust...In **m** man Ps 146:3
life to your **m** bodies Rom 8:11
m...immortality 1 Cor 15:53
in our **m** flesh 2 Cor 4:11

MOSES
birth Ex 2:1-3

in Pharaoh's care Ex 2:5-10
killed an Egyptian Ex 2:11,12
exiled Ex 2:15
called by God Ex 3:1-22
opposed Pharaoh Ex 5:11
crossed Red Sea Ex 14
Ten Commandments Ex 20:1-18
saw Canaan Deut 3:23ff;34:1ff
death Deut 31:14;34:5

MOTH *insect*
crushed before the **m** Job 4:19
The **m** will eat them Is 50:9
like a **m** to Ephraim Hos 5:12
m and rust destroy Matt 6:19

MOTHER
leave...and his **m** Gen 2:24
m of all *the* living Gen 3:20
Honor...and your **m** Ex 20:12
a grief to his **m** Prov 10:1
Contend with your **m** Hos 2:2
When His **m** Mary Matt 1:18
Take...and His **m** Matt 2:13
Who is My **m** Matt 12:48
Honor your...**m** Matt 19:19
Behold, your **m** John 19:27

MOTHER-IN-LAW
who lies with his **m** Deut 27:23
Orpah kissed her **m** Ruth 1:14
m lying sick in bed Matt 8:14

MOTIVES *attitudes, intentions*
LORD weighs the **m** Prov 16:2
disclose the **m** of 1 Cor 4:5
than from pure **m** Phil 1:17
judges with evil **m** James 2:4
ask with wrong **m** James 4:3

MOUNT (n) *hill, mountain*
In the **m** of the LORD Gen 22:14
Moses on **M** Sinai Num 3:1
Israel at **M** Carmel 1 Kin 18:19
M Zion which He Ps 78:68
M of Olives...split Zech 14:4

MOUNT (v) *climb up*
to **m** his chariot 2 Chr 10:18
m up *with* wings Is 40:31
My fury will **m** up Ezek 38:18
m-ed on a donkey Zech 9:9
m-ed on a donkey Matt 21:5

MOUNT OF OLIVES
see **OLIVES, MOUNT OF**

MOUNT ZION *see* **ZION**

MOUNTAIN
sacrifice on the **m** Gen 31:54
from His holy **m** Ps 3:4
lift up...to the **m-s** Ps 121:1
lovely on the **m-s** Is 52:7
eat at the **m** shrines Ezek 18:6
m-s will melt Mic 1:4
the **m** will move Zech 14:4
m-s, Fall on us Luke 23:30
withdrew...to the **m** John 6:15
faith...remove **m-s** 1 Cor 13:2

MOURN *grieve, lament*
m her father and Deut 21:13
David **m-ed**...son 2 Sam 13:37
A time to **m** Eccl 3:4
earth **m-s** *and* withers Is 24:4
comfort all who **m** Is 61:2
Blessed...who **m** Matt 5:4
shall **m** and weep Luke 6:25
Be miserable and **m** James 4:9

MOUSE *rodent*
the mole, and the **m** Lev 11:29
five golden **mice** 1 Sam 6:4
mice that ravage 1 Sam 6:5

MOUTH
has made man's **m** Ex 4:11
m condemns you Job 15:6
From the **m** of infants Ps 8:2
Let the words of my **m** Ps 19:14
fool's **m** is his ruin Prov 18:7
your **m** is lovely Song 4:3
out of the **m** of God Matt 4:4
confess with your **m** Rom 10:9

MOVE *change position, stir*
Spirit of God...**m-ing** Gen 1:2
pillar of cloud **m-d** Ex 14:19
I will not be **m-d** Ps 10:6
all the hills **m-d** Jer 4:24
m-d with compassion Mark 1:41
He was deeply **m-d** John 11:33
in Him we live...**m** Acts 17:28
m-d by the...Spirit 2 Pet 1:21

MULE *animal*
mounted his **m** 2 Sam 13:29
Absalom...on *his* **m** 2 Sam 18:9
ride on the king's **m** 1 Kin 1:44
war horses and **m-s** Ezek 27:14

MULTIPLY *increase*
Be fruitful and **m** Gen 1:22
the fool **m-ies** words Eccl 10:14
He **m-ies** lies and Hos 12:1
and peace be **m-ied** 2 Pet 1:2

MULTITUDE *crowd, number*
father of a **m** of Gen 17:4
cover a **m** of sins James 5:20
love covers a **m** of 1 Pet 4:8

MURDER *premeditated killing*
You shall not **m** Ex 20:13
Whoever commits **m** Matt 5:21
m-ed the prophets Matt 23:31
full of envy, **m** Rom 1:29

MURDERER *killer*
m shall be put to Num 35:30
m from...beginning John 8:44
this man is a **m** Acts 28:4
no **m** has eternal 1 John 3:15

MUSIC *harmony, melody*
instruments of **m** 1 Chr 15:16
m to the LORD 2 Chr 7:6
m upon the lyre Ps 92:3
heard **m** and Luke 15:25

MUSICIAN *skilled in music*
m, a mighty man 1 Sam 16:18
the **m-s** after *them* Ps 68:25
harpists and **m-s** Rev 18:22

MUSTARD *type of plant*
kingdom...like a **m** Matt 13:31
faith the size of a **m** seed Matt 17:20
It is like a **m** seed Luke 13:19

MUTE *silent*
who makes *him* **m** Ex 4:11
I was **m** and silent Ps 39:2
a **m**...man Matt 9:32
and the **m** to speak Mark 7:37
astray to the **m** idols 1 Cor 12:2

MUZZLE *gag*
shall not **m** the ox Deut 25:4
guard...as with a **m** Ps 39:1

MYRIADS *countless*
chariots...are **m** Ps 68:17
m of angels Heb 12:22
number...was **m** Rev 5:11

MYRRH *spice*
aromatic gum...**m** Gen 43:11
Dripping with...**m** Song 5:13
frankincense and **m** Matt 2:11
mixture of **m** and John 19:39

MYRTLE *type of plant*
the **m,** and the olive Is 41:19
among the **m** trees Zech 1:11

MYSTERY *hidden truth, secret*
no **m** baffles you Dan 4:9
God's wisdom in a **m** 1 Cor 2:7
know all **m-ies** 1 Cor 13:2
into the **m** of Christ Eph 3:4
the **m** of the gospel Eph 6:19
the **m** of the faith 1 Tim 3:9

MYTHS *fables*
to pay attention to **m** 1 Tim 1:4
will turn aside to **m** 2 Tim 4:4
attention to Jewish **m** Titus 1:14

N

NAAMAH
1 *daughter of Lamech* Gen 4:22
2 *wife of Solomon* 1 Kin 14:21
3 *town in Judah* Josh 15:41

NAAMAN
1 *son, grandson, and great grandson of Benjamin* Gen 46:21; Num 26:40; 1 Chr 8:7
2 *Ben-hadad's commander* 2 Kin 5:1ff

NABAL
husband of Abigail 1 Sam 25:3ff
refused to help David

NABOTH
owner of a vineyard taken by Ahab 1 Kin 21:1-19

NADAB
1 *son of Aaron* Ex 6:23
2 *king of Israel* 1 Kin 14:20
3 *son of Shammai* 1 Chr 2:28
4 *son of Jehiel* 1 Chr 8:29,30

NAHOR
1 *Abram's grandfather* Gen 11:24ff
2 *brother of Abram* Gen 11:27;22:23
3 *city in N Mesopotamia* Gen 24:10

NAHUM
1 *prophet* Nah 1:1
2 *ancestor of Christ* Luke 3:25

NAILED (v) *attached*
you **n** to a cross Acts 2:23
n it to the cross Col 2:14

NAILS (n) *finger ends* or *pins*
and trim her **n** Deut 21:12
fasten it with **n** Jer 10:4
imprint of the **n** John 20:25

NAIVE *simple, not suspicious*
prudence to the **n** Prov 1:4
n believes everything Prov 14:15
the **n** becomes wise Prov 21:11
goes astray or is **n** Ezek 45:20

NAKED *unclothed*
n and...not ashamed Gen 2:25
n I shall return there Job 1:21
n...you clothed Me Matt 25:36

NAKEDNESS *unclothed*
the **n** of his father Gen 9:22
n of...father's sister Lev 18:12
Your **n**...be uncovered Is 47:3
shame of your **n** Rev 3:18

NAME *designation, title*
man gave **n-s** to all Gen 2:20
takes His **n** in vain Ex 20:7
blot out his **n** Deut 29:20
How majestic is Your **n** Ps 8:1
sing praises to Your **n** Ps 18:49
good **n**...desired Prov 22:1
LORD, that is My **n** Is 42:8
Hallowed be Your **n** Matt 6:9
n-s of the twelve Matt 10:2
such child in My **n** Matt 18:5
n-s are recorded Luke 10:20
will come in My **n** Luke 21:8
baptized in the **n** Acts 2:38
of faith in His **n** Acts 3:16
other **n** under heaven Acts 4:12
n-s are in the book Phil 4:3

NAOMI
woman of Bethlehem Ruth 1:1
Ruth's mother-in-law Ruth 1:4,6

NAPHTALI
1 *son of Jacob* Gen 30:8
2 *tribe / district* Num 13:14; 1 Chr 2:2; Rev 7:6

NARD *fragrant ointment*
henna with **n** plants Song 4:13
perfume of pure **n** John 12:3

NARROW *limited*
stood in a **n** path Num 22:24
Enter through the **n** gate Matt 7:13
the way is **n** Matt 7:14

NATHAN
1 *a son of David* 2 Sam 5:14; Luke 3:31
2 *prophet* 2 Sam 7:2;12:1ff
3 *son of Attai* 1 Chr 2:36
4 *helped Ezra* Ezra 8:16,17
name of several other individuals

NATHANAEL
disciple of Jesus John 1:49

NATION *government, people*
make you a great **n** Gen 12:2
priests and a holy **n** Ex 19:6
scatter...the **n-s** Lev 26:33
the **n-s** in an uproar Ps 2:1
n-s...fear the name Ps 102:15
N will not lift up sword Is 2:4
sprinkle many **n-s** Is 52:15
glory among the **n-s** Is 66:19
n...rise against **n** Matt 24:7
n not perish John 11:50
men, from every **n** Acts 2:5
tongue...people and **n** Rev 5:9

NATIVE *indigenous*
or a **n** of the land Ex 12:19
Or see his **n** land Jer 22:10
the **n-s** showed us Acts 28:2
n-s saw the creature Acts 28:4

NATURAL *normal*
died a **n** death Ezek 44:31
n man...not accept 1 Cor 2:14
is sown a **n** body 1 Cor 15:44

NATURE *essence*
of the same **n** as you Acts 14:15
n itself teach you 1 Cor 11:14
We *are* Jews by **n** Gal 2:15
of *the* divine **n** 2 Pet 1:4

NAZARENE
1 *of Nazareth* John 18:7
2 *follower of Jesus* Acts 24:5

NAZARETH
town of Galilee Matt 2:23
home of Joseph, Mary, and Jesus Luke 4:16; John 1:45

NAZIRITE
1 *one consecrated to God* Num 6:2,19,20
2 *religious vow* Judg 13:5,7; Amos 2:11,12

NEBO
1 *Moabite town* Num 32:38
2 *mountain where Moses viewed promised land* Deut 32:49; 34:1
3 *Babylonian god* Is 46:1
4 *town W of Jordan* Ezra 2:29; Neh 7:33
5 *Jew whose sons married foreign wives* Ezra 10:43

NEBUCHADNEZZAR
king of Babylon 2 Kin 24:1,10
captured Judah 1 Chr 6:15; Ezra 2:1

NEBUZARADAN
Babylonian commander responsible for destruction of Jerusalem and the Temple 2 Kin 25:8ff; Jer 39:9,10

NECK *part of body*
you shall break its **n** Ex 13:13
yoke on your **n** Deut 28:48
stiffened their **n-s** Jer 17:23
risked their own **n-s** Rom 16:4

NECKLACE *neck ornament*
n around his neck Gen 41:42
earrings and **n-s** Num 31:50
pride is their **n** Ps 73:6

NECO *see* **PHARAOH**

NEED *necessity, obligation*
sufficient for his **n** Deut 15:8
ministered to...**n-s** Acts 20:34
n-s of the saints 2 Cor 9:12
supply all your **n-s** Phil 4:19

NEEDLE
the eye of a **n** Matt 19:24
n than for a rich Mark 10:25

NEEDY *destitute, poor*
to your **n** and poor Deut 15:11
a father to the **n** Job 29:16
n will not always be Ps 9:18
the LORD hears the **n** Ps 69:33
n will lie down in Is 14:30

NEGEV
S desert region Gen 12:9; Judg 1:9; Jer 32:44; Zech 7:7

NEGLECT *disregard, ignore*
You **n-ed** the Rock Deut 32:18
who **n-s** discipline Prov 15:32
n so great a salvation Heb 2:3
n to show hospitality Heb 13:2
do not **n** doing good Heb 13:16

NEHEMIAH
1 *Jewish exile* Ezra 2:2; Neh 7:7
2 *son of Azbuk* Neh 3:16
3 *son of Hacaliah* Neh 1:1
rebuilt walls Neh 3:1ff
governor of Jerusalem Neh 8:9

NEIGHBOR *one living nearby*
not covet...**n's** wife Ex 20:17
shall love your **n** Lev 19:18
make your **n-s** drink Hab 2:15
love your **n** and Matt 5:43
And who is my **n** Luke 10:29
love your **n** as Gal 5:14

NEPHEW
and Lot his **n** Gen 12:5
Lot, Abram's **n** Gen 14:12

NEPHILIM
people of great stature Gen 6:4; Num 13:33

NEST
n is set in the cliff Num 24:21
n among the stars Obad 4
birds...*have* **n-s** Matt 8:20

NET *snare*
a **n** for my steps Ps 57:6
an antelope in a **n** Is 51:20
casting a **n** into Matt 4:18
left their **n-s** and Mark 1:18
n *full* of fish John 21:8

NETHINIM
temple servants Ezra 7:24

NEW *fresh, recent*
nothing **n** under the Eccl 1:9
Will gain **n** strength Is 40:31
a **n** spirit within Ezek 11:19
n wine into old Mark 2:22
A **n** commandment John 13:34
he is a **n** creature 2 Cor 5:17
a **n** and living way Heb 10:20
making all things **n** Rev 21:5

NEWBORN *just born*
like **n** babies, long 1 Pet 2:2

NEWNESS *freshness*
walk in **n** of life Rom 6:4
in **n** of the Spirit Rom 7:6

NEWS *report, tidings*
a day of good **n** 2 Kin 7:9
Good **n** puts fat on Prov 15:30
the **n** about Jesus Matt 14:1
n about Him spread Mark 1:28
n of great joy Luke 2:10
bring good **n** of good Rom 10:15
n of your faith 1 Thess 3:6

NICODEMUS
Pharisee John 3:1,4,9
in Sanhedrin John 7:50; 19:39

NICOLAITANS
sect in Ephesian and Pergamum church Rev 2:6,15

NICOLAS
deacon, servant Acts 6:1-6
proselyte from Antioch Acts 6:5

NIGHT *darkness*
darkness He called **n** Gen 1:5
pillar of fire by **n** Ex 13:21
meditate...day and **n** Josh 1:8
make **n** into day Job 17:12
The terror by **n** Ps 91:5
At **n** my soul longs Is 26:9
over their flock by **n** Luke 2:8
a thief in the **n** 1 Thess 5:2
tormented day and **n** Rev 20:10

NILE
river of Egypt Gen 41:1; Ex 1:22;7:20; Is 23:10

NIMROD
son of Cush Gen 10:8
a mighty hunter Gen 10:9
ruler of Shinar Gen 10:10

NINEVEH
capital of Assyria 2 Kin 19:36
visited by Jonah Jon 1:1ff

NISAN
first month of the Hebrew calendar Neh 2:1; Esth 3:7

NOAH
1 *son of Lamech* Gen 5:28,29
father of Shem, Ham, Japheth Gen 5:32
built an ark Gen 6:14-22
saved from Flood Gen 6:9;7:15;8:1;8:13
promised by God Gen 9:9-17
2 *daughter of Zelophehad* Num 26:33;27:1;36:11

NO-AMON
Egyptian city of Thebes Nah 3:8

NOBLE *lofty* or *renowned one*
king's most **n** princes Esth 6:9
speak **n** things Prov 8:6
all the **n-s** of Judah Jer 39:6

NOBLEMAN *of high rank*
the house of the **n** Job 21:28
A **n** went to Luke 19:12

NOISE *loud sound*
You who were full of **n** Is 22:2
Egypt *is but* a big **n** Jer 46:17
from heaven a **n** Acts 2:2

NOMADS *desert wanderers*
n of the desert bow Ps 72:9

NONSENSE *foolishness*
a fool speaks **n** Is 32:6
appeared...as **n** Luke 24:11

NORTH *direction of compass*
stretches out the **n** Job 26:7
Zion *in* the far **n** Ps 48:2
king of the **N** will Dan 11:13
three gates on the **n** Rev 21:13

NOSE *part of face*
the ring on her **n** Gen 24:47
n-s...cannot smell Ps 115:6
My hook in your **n** Is 37:29

NOSTRILS *nose*
breathed into his **n** Gen 2:7
breath of His **n** 2 Sam 22:16
breath of God...my **n** Job 27:3

NOTICE *attention, seen*
take **n** of me Ruth 2:10
not **n** the log Matt 7:3
deeds to be **n-d** by Matt 23:5

NOURISH *feed, sustain*
n-es and cherishes it Eph 5:29
constantly **n-ed** on 1 Tim 4:6
she would be **n-ed** Rev 12:6

NULLIFY *annul, make void*
LORD **n-ies** the counsel Ps 33:10
unbelief will not **n** Rom 3:3
the promise is **n-ied** Rom 4:14
n the grace of God Gal 2:21

NUMBER (n) *group, total*
their **n** according to Num 29:21
the **n** of the stars Ps 147:4
increasing in **n** daily Acts 16:5
his **n** is six hundred Rev 13:18

NUMBER (v) *count, enumerate*
n...by their armies Num 1:3
You **n** my steps Job 14:16
hairs...all **n-ed** Matt 10:30

NUN
father of Joshua Ex 33:11; Num 14:6; Josh 1:1

NURSE (n) *attendant*
Deborah, Rebekah's **n** Gen 35:8
and call a **n** for you Ex 2:7
n carries a nursing Num 11:12
n in the bedroom 2 Kin 11:2

NURSE (v) *suckle an infant*
Sarah...**n** children Gen 21:7
the child and **n-d** him Ex 2:9
morning to **n** my son 1 Kin 3:21
who are **n-ing** babies in Mark 13:17
breasts...never **n-d** Luke 23:29

~O

OAK *type of tree*
by the **o-s** of Mamre Gen 13:18
the diviners' **o** Judg 9:37
o-s of righteousness Is 61:3
strong as the **o-s** Amos 2:9

OAR *pole used in rowing*
no boat with **o-s** will Is 33:21
All who handle...**o** Ezek 27:29
straining at the **o-s** Mark 6:48

OATH *declaration, vow*
confirm the **o** which Deut 9:5
free from the **o** Josh 2:20
make no **o** at all Matt 5:34
priests without an **o** Heb 7:21

OBADIAH
1 *in Ahab's court* 1 Kin 18:3ff
2 *Gadite warrior* 1 Chr 12:8,9
3 *sent to teach* 2 Chr 17:7
4 *Levite, of Merari* 2 Chr 34:12
5 *son of Jehiel* Ezra 8:9
6 *signer of covenant* Neh 10:1,5
7 *prophet* Obad 1
name of five other Old Testament people

OBED
1 *son of Ruth / Boaz* Ruth 4:17
ancestor of Jesus Matt 1:5; Luke 3:32
2 *son of Ephlal* 1 Chr 2:37
3 *warrior* 1 Chr 11:26,47
4 *temple gatekeeper* 1 Chr 26:1,7
5 *father of Azariah* 2 Chr 23:1

OBED-EDOM
1 *a Gittite* 2 Sam 6:10-12
2 *temple musician* 1 Chr 15:21
3 *in charge of Temple vessels* 2 Chr 25:24

OBEDIENCE *submission*
the **o** of the peoples Gen 49:10
pretend **o** to me 2 Sam 22:45
the **o** of the One Rom 5:19
leading to **o** of faith Rom 16:26
in **o** to the truth 1 Pet 1:22

OBEDIENT *willing to obey*
we will be **o** Ex 24:7
o from the heart Rom 6:17
o to the...death Phil 2:8
Children, be **o** to Col 3:20

OBEY *follow commands, orders*
have **o-ed** My voice Gen 22:18
o My voice and keep Ex 19:5
o the LORD your God Deut 27:10
to **o** is better than 1 Sam 15:22
O-ing...His word Ps 103:20
and the sea **o** Him Matt 8:27
o God rather than Acts 5:29
o your parents Eph 6:1
O your leaders Heb 13:17
to **o** Jesus Christ 1 Pet 1:2

OBJECT *implement* or *goal*
struck...an iron **o** Num 35:16
an **o** of loathing to Ps 88:8
o like a great sheet Acts 10:11
god or **o** of worship 2 Thess 2:4

OBLIGATION *duty*
o toward the LORD Num 32:22
for his daily **o-s** 2 Chr 31:16
under **o,** not to the Rom 8:12
o to keep the...Law Gal 5:3

OBSERVE *keep* or *notice*
surely **o** My sabbaths Ex 31:13
o all My statutes Lev 19:37
you may **o** discretion Prov 5:2
the ant...**O** her ways Prov 6:6
O how the lilies Matt 6:28
o-ing the traditions Mark 7:3
the word...**o** it Luke 11:28
o days and months Gal 4:10

OBSTACLE *hindrance*
Remove *every* **o** out of Is 57:14
an **o** or a stumbling Rom 14:13

OBSTINATE *stubborn*
you are an **o** people Ex 33:3
made his heart **o** Deut 2:30
Israel is...**o** Ezek 3:7
disobedient and **o** Rom 10:21

OBTAIN *get possession of*
o children through Gen 16:2
finds a wife...**o-s** Prov 18:22
may **o** eternal life Matt 19:16
o the gift of God Acts 8:20
o-ed an inheritance Eph 1:11
for **o-ing** salvation 1 Thess 5:9

OCCUR *happen, take place*
this sign will **o** Ex 8:23
will **o** at the final Dan 8:19
otherwise a riot might **o** Matt 26:5
predestined to **o** Acts 4:28

ODED
1 *father of Azariah* 2 Chr 15:1,8
2 *prophet* 2 Chr 28:9

ODIOUS *offensive*
o in Pharaoh's sight Ex 5:21
o to the Philistines 1 Sam 13:4

OFFEND *insult* or *violate*
I will not **o** *anymore* Job 34:31
A brother **o-ed** *is* Prov 18:19
Pharisees were **o-ed** Matt 15:12

OFFENSE *anger* or *transgression*
of my *own* **o-s** Gen 41:9
they took **o** at Him Matt 13:57
of the **o** of Adam Rom 5:14
and a rock of **o** 1 Pet 2:8

OFFER (v) *give, present*
o him...as a burnt Gen 22:2
O to God a sacrifice Ps 50:14
my mouth **o-s** praises Ps 63:5
o both gifts and Heb 5:1
o-ed Himself Heb 9:14
prayer **o-ed** in faith James 5:15
o...spiritual sacrifices 1 Pet 2:5

OFFERING (n) *contribution*
freewill **o** to the LORD Ex 35:29
o of first fruits Lev 2:12
your worthless **o-s** Is 1:13
presenting your **o** Matt 5:23
any **o** for sin Heb 10:18

OFFERINGS
1 **Burnt Offering** Gen 22:13; Lev 1:17
2 **Drink Offering** Phil 2:17; 2 Tim 4:6
also **Libation**
3 **Freewill Offering** Ex 35:29; Lev 7:16
4 **Grain Offering** Lev 9:4; Josh 22:29
also **Meal Offering**
5 **Guilt Offering** Lev 5:6; Num 6:12
6 **Heave Offering** Ex 29:27,28
7 **Libation Offering** Num 6:15,17;28:9,10
also **Drink Offering**
8 **Meal Offering** 2 Kin 16:15; Ps 40:6
also **Grain Offering**
9 **Ordination Offering** Lev 8:28,31
10 **Peace Offering** Lev 4:31; Num 6:14
11 **Sin Offering** Ex 29:14; Ezek 46:20
12 **Thank Offering** 2 Chr 33:16; Jer 33:11
13 **Votive Offering** Deut 12:26;23:18
14 **Wave Offering** Lev 14:12; Num 18:18

OFFICE *function* or *position*
wield the staff of **o** Judg 5:14
priests in their **o-s** 2 Chr 35:2
to the **o** of overseer 1 Tim 3:1

OFFICIAL *one in authority*
o-s in the palace 2 Kin 20:18
o of the synagogue Luke 8:41

OFFSPRING *descendants*
o in place of Abel Gen 4:25
bring forth **o** from Is 65:9

OG
Amorite king Num 21:33; Deut 3:4; Josh 12:4

OHOLAH
symbolic for Samaria Ezek 23:4

OHOLIBAH
symbolic for Jerusalem Ezek 23:4

OHOLIBAMAH
1 *wife of Esau* Gen 36:2-25
2 *descendant of Esau* Gen 36:41

OIL
o for lighting Ex 25:6
anointed my head...**o** Ps 23:5
the **o** of joy Ps 45:7
words...softer than **o** Ps 55:21
prudent took **o** in Matt 25:4
not anoint...with **o** Luke 7:46

OINTMENT *salve*
a jar of **o** Job 41:31
anointed...with **o** John 11:2

OLD *aged, obsolete*
buried at a...**o** age Gen 15:15
too **o** to have a Ruth 1:12
honor of **o** men Prov 20:29
o men will dream Joel 2:28
wine into **o** wineskins Matt 9:17

be born when he is **o** John 3:4
o self was crucified Rom 6:6
o things passed away 2 Cor 5:17
men of **o** gained Heb 11:2
serpent of **o**...devil Rev 12:9

OLD GATE
see **GATES OF JERUSALEM**

OLIVE *tree* or *fruit*
freshly picked **o** leaf Gen 8:11
land of **o** oil and Deut 8:8
cherubim of **o** wood 1 Kin 6:23
children like **o** plants Ps 128:3

OLIVES, MOUNT OF
mountain E of Jerusalem
2 Sam 15:30; Zech 14:4; Matt 24:3; Mark 11:1
place where Jesus prayed
Matt 26:30; Luke 22:39-41

OMEGA
last letter of Gr. alphabet Rev 1:8
title of Jesus Christ Rev 21:6
expresses eternalness of God Rev 22:13

OMEN *foretells a future event*
who interprets **o-s** Deut 18:10
took this as an **o** 1 Kin 20:33

OMER *dry measure*
take an **o** apiece Ex 16:16
o is a tenth of an Ex 16:36

OMRI
1 *king of Israel* 1 Kin 16:22ff
2 *a Benjamite* 1 Chr 7:8
3 *line of Perez* 1 Chr 9:4
4 *son of Michael* 1 Chr 27:18

ON
1 *Egyptian city* Gen 41:45,50;46:20
see also **HELIOPOLIS**
2 *son of Peleth* Num 16:1

ONE *single unit*
shall become **o** flesh Gen 2:24
God, the LORD is **o** Deut 6:4
Holy **O** of Israel Ps 71:22
His chosen **o-s** Ps 105:6
Are You the...**O** Matt 11:3
joy...over **o** sinner Luke 15:7
I...Father are **o** John 10:30
they may all be **o** John 17:21
o body in Christ Rom 12:5
o died for all 2 Cor 5:14
o Lord, **o** faith Eph 4:5
o God...**o** mediator 1 Tim 2:5
husband of **o** wife 1 Tim 3:2

ONESIMUS
Christian slave of Philemon
Col 4:9; Philem 10

ONESIPHORUS
Ephesian Christian
2 Tim 1:16;4:19

ONYX *precious stone*
bdellium and the **o** Gen 2:12
o, and the jasper Ezek 28:13

OPEN (adj) *not shut, exposed*
throat is an **o** grave Ps 5:9
Better is **o** rebuke Prov 27:5
before you an **o** door Rev 3:8

OPEN (v) *expose, free, unfasten*
eyes will be **o-ed** Gen 3:5
Ezra **o-ed** the book Neh 8:5
He **o-s** their ear Job 36:10
O Lord, **o** my lips Ps 51:15
O my eyes, that I Ps 119:18
To **o** blind eyes Is 42:7
o...windows of heaven Mal 3:10
knock...will be **o-ed** Matt 7:7
o-ed a door of faith Acts 14:27
and **o-s** the door Rev 3:20
worthy to **o** the book Rev 5:2

OPHEL
citadel on S slope of Temple Mount in Jerusalem
2 Chr 27:3;33:14; Neh 3:27
home of temple servants (Nethinim) Neh 3:26;11:21

OPHIR
1 *son of Joktan* Gen 10:29
2 *gold producing region of SW Arabia* 1 Kin 10:11; Job 22:24

OPPONENT *adversary*
friends...with your **o** Matt 5:25
protection from my **o** Luke 18:3

OPPORTUNITY *occasion*
o to betray Jesus Matt 26:16
o for your testimony Luke 21:13
an **o** for the flesh Gal 5:13
not give...devil an **o** Eph 4:27

OPPOSE *contend, resist*
o the Prince of Dan 8:25
o-d the ordinance of Rom 13:2
men also **o** the truth 2 Tim 3:8
God is **o-d** to the James 4:6

OPPOSITION *hostility*
you...know My **o** Num 14:34
these are in **o** Gal 5:17
gospel...much **o** 1 Thess 2:2

OPPRESS (v) *trouble, tyrannize*
enslaved and **o-ed** Gen 15:13
Egyptians are **o-ing** Ex 3:9
not **o** your neighbor Lev 19:13
woman **o-ed** in 1 Sam 1:15
do not **o** the widow Zech 7:10
healing all...**o-ed** Acts 10:38
the rich who **o** you James 2:6

OPPRESSED (n) *afflicted*
stronghold for the **o** Ps 9:9
justice for the **o** Ps 146:7
let the **o** go free Is 58:6
devour...**o** in secret Hab 3:14
vengeance for the **o** Acts 7:24

OPPRESSION *affliction*
Do not trust in **o** Ps 62:10
o makes a...man mad Eccl 7:7
and water of **o** Is 30:20
o of My people Acts 7:34

OPPRESSOR *one who afflicts*
And crush the **o** Ps 72:4
a great **o** lacks Prov 28:16
punish all their **o-s** Jer 30:20

ORACLE *revelation*
The **o** of Balaam Num 24:3
o concerning Babylon Is 13:1
the **o** of the LORD Jer 23:33
and misleading **o-s** Lam 2:14
entrusted with the **o-s** Rom 3:2

ORDAIN *invest, set apart*
anoint...and **o** them Ex 28:41
o Aaron and his sons Ex 29:9
o-ed His covenant Ps 111:9
law as **o-ed** by angels Acts 7:53

ORDEAL *difficulty, trial*
great **o** of affliction 2 Cor 8:2
at the fiery **o** 1 Pet 4:12

ORDER (n) *arrangement*
Set your house in **o** 2 Kin 20:1
fixed **o** of the moon Jer 31:35
the **o** of Melchizedek Heb 5:6

ORDER (v) *command* or *request*
I will **o** *my prayer* Ps 5:3
o-ed him to tell no Luke 5:14
confidence...to **o** you Philem 8

ORDINANCE *statute*
o of the Passover Ex 12:43
they rejected My **o-s** Lev 26:43
o-s of the heavens Job 38:33
opposed the **o** of God Rom 13:2

ORDINATION
Aaron's ram of **o** Ex 29:26
and the **o** offering Lev 7:37
period of your **o** Lev 8:33

ORDINATION OFFERING
see **OFFERINGS**

ORIGIN *beginning, source*
of Jewish **o** Esth 6:13
o is from antiquity Is 23:7
Your **o** and your Ezek 16:3

ORIGINATE *bring into being*
not **o** from woman 1 Cor 11:8
all things **o**...God 1 Cor 11:12

ORION
constellation of stars
Job 9:9;38:31; Amos 5:8

ORNAMENT *decoration*
put off your **o-s** Ex 33:5
o of fine gold Prov 25:12
beauty of His **o-s** Ezek 7:20

ORNAN
Jebusite owner of threshing floor on Mount Moriah
1 Chr 21:15,18
sells threshing floor to David for altar and temple
1 Chr 21:25,28
see also **ARAUNAH**

ORPAH
daughter-in-law of Naomi
Ruth 1:4,14

ORPHAN *fatherless child*
not afflict any...**o** Ex 22:22
justice for the **o** Deut 10:18
helper of the **o** Ps 10:14
may plunder the **o-s** Is 10:2
Leave...**o-s** behind Jer 49:11
visit **o-s** and widows James 1:27

OSTRICH *bird*
the **o** and the owl Lev 11:16
a companion of **o-es** Job 30:29
cruel Like **o-es** Lam 4:3
mourning like the **o-es** Mic 1:8

OTHNIEL
son of Kenaz Josh 15:17
brother or nephew of Caleb
Judg 1:13;3:11

OUTBURST *sudden release*
great **o** of anger Deut 29:24
o of anger I hid My Is 54:8
jealousy, **o-s** of anger Gal 5:20

OUTCAST *rejected*
the **o-s** of Israel Ps 147:2
Hide the **o-s** Is 16:3
called you an **o** Jer 30:17
o-s from...synagogue John 16:2

OUTCRY *strong cry* or *protest*
no **o** in our streets Ps 144:14
o is heard among the Jer 50:46
a *single* **o** arose Acts 19:34

OUTSIDER *stranger*
o may not come near Num 18:4
toward **o-s** 1 Thess 4:12

OUTSTRETCHED *extended*
redeem...with an **o** arm Ex 6:6
war...with an **o** hand Jer 21:5

OUTWARD *external*
at the **o** appearance 1 Sam 16:7
is **o** in the flesh Rom 2:28

OVEN *baking, cooking vessel*
appeared a...**o** Gen 15:17
make them as a fiery **o** Ps 21:9

OVERCOME *conquer, master*
a man **o** with wine Jer 23:9
I have **o** the world John 16:33
but **o** evil with good Rom 12:21
have **o** the evil one 1 John 2:13
who **o-s** will inherit Rev 21:7

OVERFLOW *flood, inundate*
My cup **o-s** Ps 23:5
waters will **o** the Is 28:17

I am **o-ing** with joy 2 Cor 7:4
o-ing with gratitude Col 2:7

OVERLAID *decorate, spread*
o...with gold 1 Kin 6:28
vessel **o** with silver Prov 26:23
o with gold...silver Hab 2:19

OVERLOOK *ignore* or *view*
o a transgression Prov 19:11
widows were...**o-ed** Acts 6:1

OVERPOWER *subdue*
deceive you and **o** you Obad 7
Hades will not **o** Matt 16:18
attacks him and **o-s** Luke 11:22

OVERSEER *director, leader*
o in the house of Jer 29:26
the **o-s** and deacons Phil 1:1
the office of **o** 1 Tim 3:1
o...above reproach Titus 1:7

OVERSHADOW *engulf, obscure*
Most High...**o** you Luke 1:35
o-ing the mercy seat Heb 9:5

OVERSIGHT *supervision*
o of the house of 2 Kin 12:11
having **o** at...gates Ezek 44:11
exercising **o** not 1 Pet 5:2

OVERWHELM *crush, overcome*
humiliation has **o-ed** Ps 44:15
darkness will **o** me Ps 139:11
my spirit was **o-ed** Ps 142:3
o-ed by...sorrow 2 Cor 2:7

OWE *be indebted*
Pay...what you **o** Matt 18:28
O nothing to anyone Rom 13:8
that you **o** to me Philem 19

OWL *bird*
the **o**, the sea gull Deut 14:15
o of the waste places Ps 102:6
houses...full of **o-s** Is 13:21

OWN (adj) *belonging to*
man in His **o** image Gen 1:27
led...His **o** people Ps 78:52
calls his **o** sheep John 10:3
in his **o** language Acts 2:6

OWN (n) *belonging to*
He came to His **o** John 1:11
provide for his **o** 1 Tim 5:8

OWNER *possessor*
restitution to its **o** Ex 22:12
when the **o**...comes Matt 21:40
who were **o-s** of land Acts 4:34

OX *bull used as draft animal*
oxen and donkeys Gen 12:16
servant or his **o** Ex 20:17
horns of the wild **oxen** Ps 22:21
An **o** knows its owner Is 1:3
not muzzle the **o** 1 Tim 5:18

P

PACE *step, stride*
the **p** of the cattle Gen 33:14
not slow down the **p** 2 Kin 4:24

PACT *agreement*
Sheol we...made a **p** Is 28:15
p with Sheol will Is 28:18

PADDAN-ARAM
NW Mesopotamia Gen 25:20
home of Laban Gen 28:5
birthplace of most of Jacob's sons Gen 35:22-26

PAHATH-MOAB
1 *head of Jewish clan* Ezra 2:6
2 *Jewish clan* Neh 3:11

PAIN *discomfort, hurt*
multiply Your **p** Gen 3:16
p-s came upon her 1 Sam 4:19
rejoice in unsparing **p** Job 6:10
rest from your **p** Is 14:3
Your **p** is incurable Jer 30:15
bring **p** to my soul Lam 3:51
no longer be...**p** Rev 21:4

PAINFUL *hurting*
p are honest words Job 6:25
the bread of **p** labors Ps 127:2

PALACE *royal residence*
build...royal **p** 2 Chr 2:12
to the king's **p** Esth 2:8
Out of ivory **p-s** Ps 45:8
A **p** of strangers Is 25:2
luxury...royal **p-s** Luke 7:25

PALLET *bed, mat*
they let down the **p** Mark 2:4
pick up your **p** and Mark 2:9

PALM *type of tree*
the city of **p** trees Deut 34:3
flourish like the **p** Ps 92:12
branches of the **p** John 12:13

PALTI
1 *son of Raphu* Num 13:9
spy for Israel Num 13:2
2 *Michal's husband* 1 Sam 25:44

PAMPHYLIA
Roman province in Asia Minor Acts 2:10;13:13;14:24

PANIC *fear*
P seized them there Ps 48:6
P and pitfall have Lam 3:47
great **p**...will fall Zech 14:13

PANT *breathe rapidly*
deer **p-s** for the water Ps 42:1
my soul **p-s** for You Ps 42:1
I will both gasp and **p** Is 42:14
beasts...**p** for You Joel 1:20

PAPHOS
city on Cyprus Acts 13:6,13

PAPYRUS *reed plant*
p...without a marsh Job 8:11
Even in **p** vessels Is 18:2

PARABLE *story for illustration*
speak a **p** to Ezek 17:2
p of the sower Matt 13:18
heard His **p-s** Matt 21:45
p from the fig tree Mark 13:28
spoke by way of a **p** Luke 8:4

PARADISE
abode of the righteous dead Luke 23:43; 2 Cor 12:4; Rev 2:7
see also **ABRAHAM'S BOSOM**

PARALYTIC
said to the **p**, Get up Matt 9:6
p, carried by four Mark 2:3

PARAN
wilderness area in Sinai Gen 21:21; Num 13:3
place of Israelite wanderings and encampments Num 12:16
mountain in Sinai Deut 33:2

PARDON *forgive, release*
he will not **p** your Ex 23:21
May the...LORD **p** 2 Chr 30:18
O LORD, **P** my iniquity Ps 25:11
He will abundantly **p** Is 55:7
p, and you will be Luke 6:37

PARENTS *father and mother*
rise up against **p** Matt 10:21
left house or...**p** Luke 18:29
evil, disobedient to **p** Rom 1:30
Children, obey your **p** Eph 6:1
disobedient to **p** 2 Tim 3:2

PART *portion*
God...have no **p** in 2 Chr 19:7
formed my inward **p-s** Ps 139:13
have no **p** with Me John 13:8
no **p** or portion in Acts 8:21
prophesy in **p** 1 Cor 13:9
now I know in **p** 1 Cor 13:12
tongue is a small **p** James 3:5

PARTAKERS *participators*
do not be **p** with Eph 5:7
become **p** of Christ Heb 3:14
p of the Holy Spirit Heb 6:4
p of *the* divine nature 2 Pet 1:4

PARTIAL *favoring*
not be **p** to the poor Lev 19:15
you shall not be **p** Deut 16:19
now be **p** to no one Job 32:21
You are not **p** Matt 22:16

PARTIALITY *favoritism*
show **p** in judgment Deut 1:17
p is not good Prov 28:21
God shows no **p** Gal 2:6

PARTICIPATE *take part*
not **p**...deeds of Eph 5:11
p-s in his evil deeds 2 John 11
will not **p** in her sins Rev 18:4

PARTNER *comrade*
is a **p** with a thief Prov 29:24
been **p-s** with them Matt 23:30
regard me a **p** Philem 17

PASS *proceed*
LORD will **p** over the Ex 12:23
My glory is **p-ing** by Ex 33:22
heaven and earth **p** Matt 5:18
words will not **p** Matt 24:35
this cup **p** from Me Matt 26:39
p-ed out of death John 5:24
old things **p-ed** away 2 Cor 5:17
first earth **p-ed** away Rev 21:1

PASSION *desire, lust*
p is rottenness to Prov 14:30
over to degrading **p-s** Rom 1:26
flesh with its **p-s** Gal 5:24
dead to...**p** Col 3:5
not in lustful **p** 1 Thess 4:5

PASSOVER
Israel's firstborn protected from the plague of death prior to the exodus from Egypt Ex 12:1-30
Feast commemorating Israelite exodus and protection from death Ex 12:42,43; Lev 23:5; Num 9:2,12,14; Matt 26:2,18; John 19:14; Acts 12:4
see also **FEASTS**

PASTORS *shepherds of people*
and some *as* **p** Eph 4:11

PASTURE (n) *grazing field*
lie down in green **p-s** Ps 23:2
sheep of Your **p** Ps 79:13

PASTURE (v) *feed, graze*
Moses...**p-ing** the flock Ex 3:1
They will **p** on it Zeph 2:7
So I **p-d** the flock Zech 11:7

PATCH *mending cloth*
p of unshrunk cloth Matt 9:16
p pulls away from it Mark 2:21

PATH *way*
snake in the **p** Gen 49:17
the **p** of life Ps 16:11
a light to my **p** Ps 119:105
p of the upright is Prov 15:19
Make His **p-s** straight Matt 3:3

PATHROS
upper Egypt Is 11:11; Jer 44:1,15; Ezek 29:14;30:14

PATIENCE *endurance*
try the **p** of men Is 7:13
in **p**, in kindness 2 Cor 6:6
love, joy, peace, **p** Gal 5:22
exhort, with great **p** 2 Tim 4:2
endure it with **p** 1 Pet 2:20

PATIENT *bearing, enduring*
Love is **p**, love is 1 Cor 13:4
p when wronged 2 Tim 2:24
Lord...is **p** toward 2 Pet 3:9

PATMOS
Aegean island, site of John's exile Rev 1:9

PATRIARCH *father of clan*
regarding the **p** David Acts 2:29
the twelve **p-s** Acts 7:8
Abraham, the **p**, gave Heb 7:4

PATTERN *model, plan*
fixed **p-s** of heaven Jer 33:25
walk according to...**p** Phil 3:17

PAUL
heritage Acts 21:39;22:3; Phil 3:5
persecuted believers Acts 7:58; 8:1,3;9:1,2; 1 Cor 15:9
conversion and call Acts 9:1-19
name changed Acts 13:9
Jerusalem council Acts 15:2-6
missionary journeys Acts 13:1ff;15:36ff;18:23ff
apostolic defense Acts 11:5ff; Gal 1:13ff
arrest and imprisonment Acts 21:33;22:24-28:31
defense Acts 22:1ff;24:10ff; 25:10,11;26:2ff
final journey to Rome Acts 27,28
see also **SAUL**

PAULUS, SERGIUS
proconsul of Cyprus Acts 13:7

PAVEMENT *paved road*
on a **p** of stone 2 Kin 16:17
mosaic **p** of porphyry Esth 1:6
place called The **P** John 19:13

PAY *give what is due*
thief...**p** double Ex 22:7
p You my vows Ps 66:13
P back what you Matt 18:28
Never **p** back evil Rom 12:17
p the penalty 2 Thess 1:9

PEACE *calmness, tranquility*
grant **p** in the land Lev 26:6
made **p** with David 1 Chr 19:19
Seek **p**, and pursue Ps 34:14
for the **p** of Jerusalem Ps 122:6
all her paths are **p** Prov 3:17
a time for **p** Eccl 3:8
Prince of **P** Is 9:6
p...like a river Is 66:12
have withdrawn My **p** Jer 16:5
not come to bring **p** Matt 10:34
on earth **p** among Luke 2:14
P I leave with you John 14:27
we have **p** with God Rom 5:1
love, joy, **p** Gal 5:22
He Himself is our **p** Eph 2:14
gospel of **p** Eph 6:15
p of God...surpasses Phil 4:7
p through the blood Col 1:20
take **p** from the earth Rev 6:4

PEACEABLE
gentle, **p**, free from 1 Tim 3:3
be **p**, gentle Titus 3:2

PEACEMAKERS
Blessed are the **p** Matt 5:9

PEACE OFFERING
see **OFFERINGS**

PEARL *precious gem*
wisdom is above...**p-s** Job 28:18
p-s before swine Matt 7:6
one **p** of great value Matt 13:46

PEKAH
king of Israel 2 Kin 15:25ff

PEKAHIAH
king of Israel 2 Kin 15:22,23

PELEG
son of Eber Gen 10:25
descendant of Shem Gen 11:18

PENALTY *punishment*
you will bear the **p** Ezek 23:49
pay the **p** of eternal 2 Thess 1:9
received a just **p** Heb 2:2

PENIEL
where Jacob wrestled with God Gen 32:30
see also **PENUEL**

PENTECOST
Jewish feast held 50 days after Passover Acts 20:16; 1 Cor 16:8
coming of the Holy Spirit Acts 2:1
see also **FEASTS**

PENUEL
1 *tower destroyed* Judg 8:17
rebuilt 1 Kin 12:25
see also **PENIEL**
2 *father of Gedor* 1 Chr 4:4
3 *son of Shashak* 1 Chr 8:25

PEOPLE *group, nation*
they are one **p** Gen 11:6
Let My **p** go Ex 5:1
You are an obstinate **p** Ex 33:5
blessed above all **p-s** Deut 7:14
Forgive Your **p** Israel Deut 21:8
LORD loves His **p** 2 Chr 2:11
p who are called by 2 Chr 7:14
restores His captive **p** Ps 14:7
We are His **p** Ps 100:3
LORD will judge His **p** Ps 135:14
p are unrestrained Prov 29:18
p whom I formed Is 43:21
do **p** say that I am Mark 8:27
they feared the **p** Luke 20:19
die for the **p** John 11:50
not rejected His **p** Rom 11:2
every tribe and **p** Rev 13:7

PEOR
1 *mountain in Moab* Num 23:28
2 *Moabite deity* Num 25:3

PERCEIVE *be aware, discern*
p-d all the wisdom 1 Kin 10:4
listening, but do not **p** Is 6:9
p-ing in Himself Mark 5:30
p with their heart John 12:40

PERDITION *damnation*
the son of **p** John 17:12

PEREZ
son of Judah Gen 38:29

PERFECT (adj) *flawless*
His work is **p** Deut 32:4
law of the LORD is **p** Ps 19:7
heavenly Father is **p** Matt 5:48
p bond of unity Col 3:14
be **p** and complete James 1:4
p love casts out 1 John 4:18

PERFECTED *completed*
is **p** in weakness 2 Cor 12:9
love is **p** with us 1 John 4:17

PERFORM *carry out*
I will **p** miracles Ex 34:10
p My judgments Lev 18:4
p-s righteous deeds Ps 103:6
p a miracle in My Mark 9:39
John **p-ed** no sign John 10:41
p-ing great wonders Acts 6:8

PERFUME *fragrant oil*
and **p** make the heart Prov 27:9
instead of sweet **p** Is 3:24
p on My body Matt 26:12
anointed...with **p** Luke 7:46
prepared...**p-s** Luke 23:56

PERGA
city in Asia Minor Acts 13:13

PERGAMUM
city in Asia Minor Rev 1:11
early church Rev 2:12

PERISH *be destroyed*
we **p**, we are dying Num 17:12
weapons...**p-ed** 2 Sam 1:27
if I **p**, I **p** Esth 4:16
hope...will **p** Job 8:13
the wicked will **p** Ps 1:6
rod of his fury will **p** Prov 22:8
our hope has **p-ed** Ezek 37:11
little ones **p** Matt 18:14
p by the sword Matt 26:52
p, but have eternal John 3:16
for any to **p** 2 Pet 3:9

PERIZZITES
early Canaanite tribe Gen 34:30; Ex 23:23; Deut 7:1

PERMANENT *lasting*
it is a **p** ordinance Lev 6:18
p right of redemption Lev 25:32
use them as **p** slaves Lev 25:46
p home for the ark 1 Chr 28:2

PERMISSION *consent*
p they had from Cyrus Ezra 3:7

Jesus gave them **p** Mark 5:13
he had given him **p** Acts 21:40

PERMIT *allow*
not **p-ting**...demons Mark 1:34
p the children Mark 10:14
Spirit...did not **p** Acts 16:7
if the Lord **p-s** 1 Cor 16:7

PERPETUAL *lasting*
p incense before the Ex 30:8
as a **p** covenant Ex 31:16
for a **p** priesthood Ex 40:15
may sleep a **p** sleep Jer 51:39

PERSECUTE *afflict, oppress*
Why do you **p** me Job 19:22
has **p-d** my soul Ps 143:3
pray for those who **p** Matt 5:44
p you in one city Matt 10:23
why are you **p-ing** Me Acts 9:4
used to **p** the church Gal 1:13

PERSECUTION *oppression*
p arises because of Mark 4:17
p began against the Acts 8:1
a **p** against Paul Acts 13:50
distress, or **p**, or Rom 8:35

PERSEVERANCE *persistence*
by **p** in doing good Rom 2:7
tribulation brings...**p** Rom 5:3
for your **p** and faith 2 Thess 1:4
p of the saints Rev 14:12

PERSIA
ancient Near Eastern empire 2 Chr 36:20; Ezra 1:1; Esth 1:3; Ezek 27:10; Dan 8:20

PERSON *human being*
If a **p** sins Lev 4:2
hungry **p** unsatisfied Is 32:6
p...be in subjection Rom 13:1
hidden **p** of the heart 1 Pet 3:4

PERSUADE *convince, prevail on*
a ruler may be **p-d** Prov 25:15
trying to **p** Jews and Acts 18:4
p-s men to worship Acts 18:13
you will **p** me Acts 26:28

PERSUASIVE *convincing*
p words of wisdom 1 Cor 2:4
delude you with **p** Col 2:4

PERVERSE *corrupt*
a **p** and crooked Deut 32:5
A **p** heart shall depart Ps 101:4
mind will utter **p** Prov 23:33
and **p** generation Phil 2:15

PERVERT *distort, misdirect*
not **p** the justice Ex 23:6
Does God **p** justice Job 8:3
have **p-ed** their way Jer 3:21

PESTILENCE *epidemic, plague*
LORD sent a **p** 2 Sam 24:15

sword, famine, and **p** Jer 27:13
p and mourning and Rev 18:8

PETER
heritage and occupation
Matt 1:17; 4:18; John 1:42,44
called by Jesus
Mark 3:16; Luke 5:1ff
names: Cephas, Simon
Matt 4:18; Mark 3:16; John 1:42; Acts 15:14
walked on water Matt 14:28ff
confessed Jesus as Messiah
Matt 16:16; Luke 9:20
on mount of Transfiguration
Matt 17:1ff; Mark 9:2ff
denied Jesus Matt 26:70; Mark 14:70; Luke 22:58
at Pentecost Acts 2
apostle of Christ Gal 2:8; 1 Pet 1:1; 2 Pet 1:1

PETITION *request, supplication*
God...grant your **p** 1 Sam 1:17
p to any god or man Dan 6:7
p-s...be made 1 Tim 2:1

PHARAOH *title of Egyptian kings*
1 **Pharaoh,** *time of Abraham* Gen 12:15ff
2 **Pharaoh,** *time of Joseph* Gen 37:36;39:1-50:26
3 **Pharaoh,** *during oppression* Ex 1:8-2:23
4 **Pharaoh,** *during the Exodus* Ex 5:1-12:41
5 **Pharaoh,** *father of Bithiah* 1 Chr 4:17
6 **Pharaoh,** *time of David* 1 Kin 11:14ff
7 **Pharaoh,** *whose daughter married Solomon* 1 Kin 3:1;7:8;9:16
8 **Shishak,** *time of Rehoboam* 1 Kin 14:25,26
9 **So,** *time of Hoshea* 2 Kin 17:4
10 **Tirhakah,** *time of Hezekiah* 2 Kin 19:9; Is 37:9
11 **Neco,** *slew Josiah* 2 Kin 23:29,33,34
12 **Hophra,** *subject of prophecy* Jer 44:30

PHARISEES
Jewish religious party
Matt 3:7;23:13; Mark 2:18;7:3; Luke 11:42;16:14; John 3:1;11:47

PHARPAR
river of Damascus 2 Kin 5:12

PHILADELPHIA
city in Asia Minor Rev 1:11
early church Rev 3:7

PHILEMON
owner of Onesimus Philem 1
friend of Paul

PHILIP
1 *Herod Philip I, son of Herod the Great* Mark 6:17
see also **HEROD**
2 *Herod Philip II, son of Herod the Great* Luke 3:1
see also **HEROD**
3 *Philip the apostle* Matt 10:3; Mark 3:18; Luke 6:14; John 1:43ff; Acts 1:13
4 *Philip the evangelist*
Acts 6:5;8:5,29;21:8

PHILIPPI
Macedonian city
Acts 16:12;20:6

PHILIPPIANS
people of Philippi Phil 4:15

PHILISTIA
coastal area of SW Palestine
Ex 15:14; Ps 60:8;83:7; Joel 3:4

PHILISTINES
people of Philistia Gen 10:14; Josh 13:2; Judg 13:1; 1 Sam 4:2

PHINEHAS
1 *grandson of Aaron*
Num 25:7;31:6; Judg 20:28
2 *son of Eli* 1 Sam 1:3;4:4,11
3 *father of a priest* Ezra 8:33

PHOEBE
Cenchrea (Corinth) deaconess commended by Paul
Rom 16:1

PHOENICIA
coastal land N of land of Israel
Acts 11:19;21:2
visited by Paul Acts 15:3

PHRYGIA
Asia Minor province Acts 2:10
visited by Paul Acts 16:6;18:23

PHYGELUS
Asian Christian, deserted Paul
2 Tim 1:15

PHYLACTERIES *prayer bands*
as **p** on your forehead
Ex 13:16
they broaden their **p**
Matt 23:5
see also **FRONTALS**

PHYSICIAN
all worthless **p-s** Job 13:4
healthy who need a **p**
Matt 9:12
P, heal yourself Luke 4:23
Luke, the beloved **p** Col 4:14

PIECE *part, portion*
dip your **p** of bread Ruth 2:14
thirty **p-s** of silver Matt 27:3
gave Him a **p**...fish Luke 24:42
woven in one **p** John 19:23

PIERCE *penetrate*
master shall **p** his ear Ex 21:6
They **p-d** my hands Ps 22:16
He was **p-d** through Is 53:5
whom they have **p-d**
Zech 12:10
sword will **p**...soul Luke 2:35
p-d His side John 19:34
p-d to the heart Acts 2:37

PIETY *reverence*
learn to practice **p** 1 Tim 5:4
because of His **p** Heb 5:7

PILATE, PONTIUS
Roman governor of Judea
Matt 27:2; Luke 3:1
presided at Jesus' trial
Matt 27:11ff; Mark 15:2ff; Luke 23:1ff; John 18:28-38
warned by his wife Matt 27:19
orders Jesus' crucifixion
Matt 27:24ff; Mark 15:15; Luke 23:24,25; John 19:15,16

PILLAR *column* or *memorial*
became a **p** of salt Gen 19:26
p of fire by night Ex 13:21
set up...a **p** 2 Sam 18:18
hewn...her seven **p-s** Prov 9:1
feet like **p-s** of fire Rev 10:1

PILOT *steersman*
sailors, and your **p-s**
Ezek 27:27
the **p** and...captain Acts 27:11
inclination of the **p** James 3:4

PINION *wing*
p and plumage of Job 39:13
cover you with His **p-s** Ps 91:4

PINNACLE *highest point*
had Him...on the **p** Matt 4:5
p of the temple Luke 4:9

PISGAH
mountain height in Moab
Num 21:20; Josh 13:20

PISHON
river of Eden Gen 2:11

PISIDIA / PISIDIAN
district of Asia Minor
Acts 13:14;14:24

PIT *deep hole, dungeon*
full of tar **p-s** Gen 14:10
Joseph...not in the **p**
Gen 37:29
redeems...from the **p** Ps 103:4
harlot is a deep **p** Prov 23:27
silenced me in the **p** Lam 3:53
to **p-s** of darkness 2 Pet 2:4
the bottomless **p** Rev 9:1

PITCH (n) *tar*
inside and out with **p**
Gen 6:14
covered it over...**p** Ex 2:3

PITCH (v) *set up*
p-ed his tent in the
Gen 31:25
he will **p** the tents Dan 11:45
tabernacle...Lord **p-ed** Heb 8:2

PITCHER *container*
torches inside the **p-s**
Judg 7:16
Fill four **p-s** 1 Kin 18:33
carrying a **p** of Mark 14:13

PITHOM
Egyptian storage city built by Hebrew slaves Ex 1:11

PITY (n) *sympathy*
shall not show **p** Deut 19:21
I will not show **p** Jer 13:14
No eye looked with **p**
Ezek 16:5

PITY (v) *have compassion*
she had **p** on him Ex 2:6
eye shall not **p** them
Deut 7:16
P me, **p** me, O you Job 19:21
take **p** on us Mark 9:22
most to be **p-ied** 1 Cor 15:19

PLACE *area, space*
waters...into one **p** Gen 1:9
he enters the holy **p** Ex 28:29
God is a dwelling **p**
Deut 33:27
a **p** for My people 1 Chr 17:9
earth out of its **p** Job 9:6
You are my hiding **p** Ps 32:7
love the **p** of honor Matt 23:6
a **p** called Golgotha
Matt 27:33
I go to prepare a **p** John 14:2

PLAGUE *contagious disease*
no **p** will befall you Ex 12:13
Remove Your **p** from Ps 39:10
p of the hail Rev 16:21
the seven last **p-s** Rev 21:9

PLAIN *flat area*
p in...Shinar Gen 11:2
desert **p-s** of Jericho Josh 4:13
the **p** of Megiddo 2 Chr 35:22
broad **p** of the earth Rev 20:9

PLAN *design, scheme*
tabernacle...its **p** Ex 26:30
P-s *formed* long ago Is 25:1
follow our own **p-s** Jer 18:12
p and foreknowledge
Acts 2:23

PLANT (n) *growth from soil*
every **p** yielding seed
Gen 1:29
eat the **p-s** of the Gen 3:18
hail...struck every **p** Ex 9:25
God appointed a **p** Jon 4:6

PLANT (v) *put into soil*
God **p-ed** a garden Gen 2:8
p...trees for food Lev 19:23
shall **p** a vineyard Deut 28:30
A time to **p** Eccl 3:2
her earnings she **p-s**
Prov 31:16
p-ed a vineyard Mark 12:1
I **p-ed**, Apollos 1 Cor 3:6

PLATTER *shallow dish*
on a **p** the head of Matt 14:8
his head on a **p** Mark 6:28

PLAY *take part*
who **p** the lyre Gen 4:21
man who can **p** 1 Sam 16:17
p-ed the fool 1 Sam 26:21

P skillfully with a Ps 33:3
nursing child will **p** Is 11:8
not **p** the harlot Hos 3:3
We **p-ed** the flute Matt 11:17

PLEAD *appeal, beseech*
p-ed with the LORD Deut 3:23
man...**p** with God Job 16:21
LORD...**p** their case Prov 22:23
P for the widow Is 1:17
Elijah...**p-s** with God Rom 11:2

PLEASANT *pleasing*
despised the **p** land Ps 106:24
P words are a Prov 16:24
sleep...is **p** Eccl 5:12
Speak to us **p** words Is 30:10

PLEASE *satisfy*
it **p** You to bless 2 Sam 7:29
You are **p-d** with me Ps 41:11
sacrifices...not **p** Him Hos 9:4
how he may **p** his 1 Cor 7:33
p all men in all 1 Cor 10:33
striving to **p** men Gal 1:10
to walk and **p** God 1 Thess 4:1
impossible to **p** Heb 11:6

PLEASING *agreeable, gratifying*
tree that is **p** Gen 2:9
meditation be **p** Ps 104:34
not as **p** men but 1 Thess 2:4
p in His sight 1 John 3:22

PLEASURE *gratification*
old, shall I have **p** Gen 18:12
p in His people Ps 149:4
He who loves **p** *will* Prov 21:17
work for *His* good **p** Phil 2:13
lovers of **p** rather 2 Tim 3:4
passing **p-s** of sin Heb 11:25

PLEDGE *promise*
cloak as a **p** Ex 22:26
those who give **p-s** Prov 22:26
the Spirit as a **p** 2 Cor 5:5
p of our inheritance Eph 1:14

PLEIADES
constellation of stars
Job 9:9;38:31; Amos 5:8

PLENTIFUL *abundant*
shed abroad a **p** rain Ps 68:9
harvest is **p** Matt 9:37

PLOT *plan, scheme*
wicked **p-s** against Ps 37:12
you have **p-ted** *evil* Prov 30:32
Jews **p-ted** together Acts 9:23

PLOW *dig the soil*
not **p** with an ox Deut 22:10
those who **p** iniquity Job 4:8
sluggard does not **p** Prov 20:4
his hand to the **p** Luke 9:62
ought to **p** in hope 1 Cor 9:10

PLOWSHARES *blade of plow*
their swords into **p** Is 2:4
your **p** into swords Joel 3:10

PLUMB LINE *vertical line*
the **p** of emptiness Is 34:11
p In the midst of My Amos 7:8

when they see the **p** Zech 4:10

PLUNDER (n) *booty, loot*
took no **p** in silver Judg 5:19
You will become **p** Hab 2:7
wealth will become **p** Zeph 1:13

PLUNDER (v) *rob*
will **p** the Egyptians Ex 3:22
stouthearted were **p-ed** Ps 76:5
he will **p** his house Matt 12:29

POINT *particular time*
grieved, to the **p** of Matt 26:38
obedient to the **p** of Phil 2:8
to the **p** of shedding Heb 12:4

POISON *lethal substance*
P...under their lips Ps 140:3
given us **p-ed** water Jer 8:14
turned justice into **p** Amos 6:12

POLL-TAX *income and head tax*
collect customs or **p** Matt 17:25
give a **p** to Caesar Matt 22:17

POLLUTE *contaminate*
blood **p-s** the land Num 35:33
earth is also **p-d** Is 24:5

POMEGRANATE *fruit*
golden bell and a **p** Ex 28:34
p-s of blue and purple Ex 39:24
juice of my **p-s** Song 8:2
the fig tree, the **p** Hag 2:19

PONDER *think deeply*
not **p** the path of life Prov 5:6
Or **p** things...past Is 43:18

PONTUS
region in N Asia Minor
Acts 2:9; 1 Pet 1:1
homeland of Aquila Acts 18:2

POOL *pond*
of the upper **p** 2 Kin 18:17
rock into a **p** Ps 114:8
land will become a **p** Is 35:7
in the **p** of Siloam John 9:7

POOR *impoverished, needy*
p will never cease Deut 15:11
raises the **p** from the 1 Sam 2:8
or you will become **p** Prov 20:13
not rob the **p** Prov 22:22
are the **p** in spirit Matt 5:3
a **p** widow came Mark 12:42
you always have the **p** Mark 14:7
sake He became **p** 2 Cor 8:9
not God choose the **p** James 2:5

POPULATE *increase number*
P the earth abundantly Gen 9:7

whole earth was **p-d** Gen 9:19

POPULATION *people*
with all *his* great **p** Is 16:14
deported an entire **p** Amos 1:6

PORPOISE SKIN
covering of **p-s** above Ex 26:14
put sandals of **p** on Ezek 16:10

PORTICO *porch*
in the **p** of Solomon John 10:23
one accord in...**p** Acts 5:12

PORTION *part, share*
gather a day's **p** Ex 16:4
LORD's **p** is...people Deut 32:9
double **p** of...spirit 2 Kin 2:9
The LORD is my **p** Ps 119:57
joy over their **p** Is 61:7

POSSESS *control, take*
give...this land to **p** Gen 15:7
are to **p** their land Lev 20:24
go in and **p** the land Deut 1:8
p-es all the nations Ps 82:8
p-ed by Beelzebul Mark 3:22
sell all you **p** Mark 10:21
p-ed with demons Luke 8:27
do not **p** silver and Acts 3:6

POSSESSION *ownership*
for an everlasting **p** Gen 17:8
you shall be My own **p** Ex 19:5
people for His own **p** Deut 4:20
full of Your **p-s** Ps 104:24
charge of all his **p-s** Matt 24:47
selling their...**p-s** Acts 2:45

POSSIBLE *can be done*
all things are **p** Matt 19:26
p with God Luke 18:27

POSTERITY *descendants*
P will serve Him Ps 22:30
p of the wicked Ps 37:38

POT *container, vessel*
death in the **p** 2 Kin 4:40
refining **p** is for Prov 17:3
I see a boiling **p** Jer 1:13

POTIPHAR
Egyptian official who purchased Joseph Gen 39:1

POTIPHERA
Joseph's father-in-law
Gen 41:45,50;46:20

POTSHERD *piece of pottery*
p to scrape himself Job 2:8
is dried up like a **p** Ps 22:15

POTTER *one who molds clay*
clay say to the **p** Is 45:9
and You our **p** Is 64:8
as it pleased the **p** Jer 18:4
Throw it to the **p** Zech 11:13

POTTER'S FIELD
burial place bought with Judas' money Matt 27:3ff
also called **Field of Blood**

POUR *cause to flow*
p me out like milk Job 10:10
I **p** out my soul Ps 42:4
P out your heart Ps 62:8
I will **p** out My Spirit Is 44:3
P out Your wrath Jer 10:25
p out...a blessing Mal 3:10
p-ed it on His Matt 26:7
p forth of My Spirit Acts 2:17

POVERTY *destitution, want*
glutton...come to **p** Prov 23:21
neither **p** nor riches Prov 30:8
through His **p** might 2 Cor 8:9

POWER *authority, strength*
to show you My **p** Ex 9:16
from the **p** of Sheol Ps 49:15
the **p** of His works Ps 111:6
p of the tongue Prov 18:21
the **p** of the sword Jer 18:21
Not by might nor...**p** Zech 4:6
Yours is...the **p** Matt 6:13
the right hand of **p** Mark 14:62
clothed with **p** from Luke 24:49
you will receive **p** Acts 1:8
gospel...**p** of God Rom 1:16
the **p** of our Lord 1 Cor 5:4
p of sin is the law 1 Cor 15:56
p of Christ...dwell 2 Cor 12:9
prince of the **p** of Eph 2:2
p of His resurrection Phil 3:10
timidity, but of **p** 2 Tim 1:7
by the word of His **p** Heb 1:3
quenched the **p** of Heb 11:34
p-s...been subjected 1 Pet 3:22

POWERLESS *without strength*
p before this great 2 Chr 20:12
He might render **p** Heb 2:14

PRACTICE (n) *custom, habit*
evil of their **p-s** Ps 28:4
disclosing their **p-s** Acts 19:18
laid aside...*evil* **p-s** Col 3:9

PRACTICE (v) *engage in*
keep...statutes and **p** Lev 20:8
He who **p-s** deceit Ps 101:7
Who **p** righteousness Ps 106:3
p-ing hospitality Rom 12:13
learn to **p** piety 1 Tim 5:4
the one who **p-s** sin 1 John 3:8

PRAETORIAN / PRAETORIUM
guard or palace
1 *Imperial palace guards in Rome* Phil 1:13
2 *Pontius Pilate's palace in Jerusalem* Matt 27:27; Mark 15:16; John 18:28,33
3 *Herod's palace at Caesarea* Acts 23:35

PRAISE (n) *acclamation, honor*
offering of **p** Lev 19:24
sing **p-s** to Him 1 Chr 16:9
songs of **p**...hymns Neh 12:46
From You...my **p** Ps 22:25
sound His **p** abroad Ps 66:8
makes Jerusalem a **p** Is 62:7

his **p** is not from men Rom 2:29
anything worthy of **p** Phil 4:8
a sacrifice of **p** Heb 13:15
Give **p** to our God Rev 19:5

PRAISE (v) *extol, glorify*
I will **p** Him Ex 15:2
greatly to be **p-d** 1 Chr 16:25
Will the dust **p** You Ps 30:9
My lips will **p** You Ps 63:3
heavens will **p** Your Ps 89:5
P Him, sun and moon Ps 148:3
P Him with trumpet Ps 150:3
Death cannot **p** You Is 38:18
I **p** You, Father Matt 11:25
heavenly host **p-ing** Luke 2:13
disciples began to **p** Luke 19:37
leaping and **p-ing** God Acts 3:8

PRAY *ask, worship*
Abraham **p-ed** to Gen 20:17
For this boy I **p-ed** 1 Sam 1:27
found *courage* to **p** 1 Chr 17:25
For to You I **p** Ps 5:2
P for...Jerusalem Ps 122:6
p to a god who cannot Is 45:20
We earnestly **p** Jon 1:14
p for...persecute Matt 5:44
by Himself to **p** Matt 14:23
p and ask, believe Mark 11:24
until I have **p-ed** Mark 14:32
Lord, teach us to **p** Luke 11:1
they ought to **p** Luke 18:1
I have **p-ed** for you Luke 22:32
p-ed with fasting Acts 14:23
if I **p** in a tongue 1 Cor 14:14
p without ceasing 1 Thess 5:17
p for one another James 5:16
p-ing in the...Spirit Jude 20

PRAYER
I have heard your **p** 2 Chr 7:12
And my **p** is pure Job 16:17
LORD receives my **p** Ps 6:9
Give ear to my **p** Ps 55:1
p of the righteous Prov 15:29
joyful in My house of **p** Is 56:7
ask in **p**, believing Matt 21:22
you make long **p-s** Matt 23:14
whole night in **p** Luke 6:12
My house...of **p** Luke 19:46
devoting...to **p** Acts 1:14
offering **p** with joy Phil 1:4
but in everything by **p** Phil 4:6
p-s...not be hindered 1 Pet 3:7
p-s of the saints Rev 5:8

PREACH *exhort, proclaim*
Jesus began to **p** Matt 4:17
as you go, **p** Matt 10:7
teach and **p** in their Matt 11:1
p-ing...repentance Mark 1:4
p the gospel to all Mark 16:15
p the kingdom of Luke 4:43
he **p-ed** Jesus to him Acts 8:35
p...the good news Acts 13:32
How will they **p** Rom 10:15
we **p** Christ crucified 1 Cor 1:23
He...**p-ed** peace Eph 2:17
p the word 2 Tim 4:2

PREACHER *one who proclaims*
hear without a **p** Rom 10:14
appointed a **p** and an 1 Tim 2:7
Noah, a **p** of 2 Pet 2:5

PRECEPTS *commandments*
All His **p** are sure Ps 111:7
meditate on Your **p** Ps 119:15
as doctrines the **p** of Matt 15:9

PRECIOUS *beloved* or *costly*
P in the sight of Ps 116:15
like the **p** oil upon the Ps 133:2
more **p** than jewels Prov 3:15
p things...no profit Is 44:9
more **p** than gold 1 Pet 1:7
with **p** blood 1 Pet 1:19

PREDESTINED *foreordained*
purpose **p** to occur Acts 4:28
foreknew, He also **p** Rom 8:29
God **p** before the ages 1 Cor 2:7
p us to adoption Eph 1:5
p according to His Eph 1:11

PREDETERMINED
p plan...of God Acts 2:23

PREEMINENT *foremost*
P in dignity Gen 49:3

PREFECTS *Persian officials*
shatter governors...**p** Jer 51:23
the satraps, the **p** Dan 3:3

PREGNANT *with child*
womb of...**p** woman Eccl 11:5
And her womb ever **p** Jer 20:17
ripped open...**p** Amos 1:13
Elizabeth...became **p** Luke 1:24

PREPARATION *readiness*
distracted with...**p-s** Luke 10:40
Jewish day of **p** John 19:42
making **p-s**, he fell Acts 10:10
p of the gospel of Eph 6:15

PREPARE *make ready*
p a savory dish Gen 27:4
mind **p-s** deception Job 15:35
p a table before me Ps 23:5
P to meet your God Amos 4:12
will **p** Your way Matt 11:10
kingdom **p-d** for Matt 25:34
to **p** Me for burial Matt 26:12
p-d spices and Luke 23:56
I go to **p** a place John 14:2
worlds were **p-d** by Heb 11:3
p your minds for 1 Pet 1:13

PRESENCE *appearance*
My **p** shall go *with* Ex 33:14
in the **p** of my enemies Ps 23:5
the light of Your **p** Ps 44:3
tremble at Your **p** Is 64:2
the **p** of His glory Jude 24
the **p** of the Lamb Rev 14:10

PRESENT (n) *gift*
a **p** for his brother Gen 32:13
sent a **p** to the king 2 Kin 16:8
and a **p** to Hezekiah Is 39:1

PRESENT (v) *give, offer*
p you with a crown of Prov 4:9
you **p** the blind for Mal 1:8
p Him to the Lord Luke 2:22
p yourselves to God Rom 6:13
p your bodies a Rom 12:1
p you before Him holy Col 1:22

PRESERVE *protect*
no son to **p** my 2 Sam 18:18
P me, O God Ps 16:1
P my soul Ps 86:2
LORD **p-s** the simple Ps 116:6
p-d ones of Israel Is 49:6
p the unity of the Eph 4:3
be **p-d** complete 1 Thess 5:23

PRESS *compel, force*
measure, **p-ed** down Luke 6:38
I **p** on toward...goal Phil 3:14

PRETEND *deceive, feign*
p to be a mourner 2 Sam 14:2
p to be another 1 Kin 14:5
p-s to be poor Prov 13:7
spies who **p-ed** to Luke 20:20

PREVAIL *exist* or *triumph*
water **p-ed**...increased Gen 7:18
not by might...man **p** 1 Sam 2:9
Iniquities **p** against me Ps 65:3
overcome me and **p-ed** Jer 20:7

PREY *what is hunted*
birds of **p** came Gen 15:11
lion tearing the **p** Ezek 22:25
no longer be a **p** to Ezek 34:28

PRICE *cost, value*
shall increase its **p** Lev 25:16
their redemption **p** Num 18:16
p of the pardoning of Is 27:9
it is the **p** of blood Matt 27:6
p of his wickedness Acts 1:18
kept back *some*...**p** Acts 5:2
bought with a **p** 1 Cor 7:23

PRIDE *exaggerated self-esteem*
P *goes* before Prov 16:18
you an everlasting **p** Is 60:15
p of Israel testifies Hos 5:5
envy, slander, **p** Mark 7:22
boastful **p** of life 1 John 2:16

PRIEST *intermediary*
a **p** of God Most Gen 14:18
a kingdom of **p-s** Ex 19:6
Aaron's sons, the **p-s** Lev 1:5
if the anointed **p** sins Lev 4:3
p...make atonement Lev 4:31
without a teaching **p** 2 Chr 15:3
You are a **p** forever Ps 110:4
all the chief **p-s** Matt 2:4
show yourself to the **p** Matt 8:4
faithful high **p** Heb 2:17
have a great high **p** Heb 4:14
You are a **p** forever Heb 5:6

PRIESTHOOD *office of priest*
for a perpetual **p** Ex 40:15
have defiled the **p** Neh 13:29
His **p** permanently Heb 7:24
royal **p**, a holy nation 1 Pet 2:9

PRIME *fully mature period*
die in the **p** of life 1 Sam 2:33
p of life...fleeting Eccl 11:10

PRINCE *ruler*
Who made you a **p** Ex 2:14
p-s of the tribes 1 Chr 29:6
contempt upon **p-s** Ps 107:40
Do not trust in **p-s** Ps 146:3
Father, **P** of Peace Is 9:6
p-s will rule justly Is 32:1
to death the **P** of life Acts 3:15
p of...the air Eph 2:2

PRISCA / PRISCILLA
wife of Aquila Rom 16:3
co-worker with Paul
Acts 18:2,18,26; 1 Cor 16:19

PRISON *jail*
Put this man in **p** 1 Kin 22:27
my soul out of **p** Ps 142:7
beheaded in the **p** Matt 14:10
I was in **p**, and Matt 25:36
opened...the **p** Acts 5:19
spirits *now* in **p** 1 Pet 3:19

PRISONER *one who is confined*
sets the **p-s** free Ps 146:7
a notorious **p** Matt 27:16
p of the law of sin Rom 7:23
Paul, a **p** of Christ Philem 1

PRIVATE *not public*
show him his fault in **p** Matt 18:15
but *I did so* in **p** Gal 2:2

PRIZE *reward*
one receives the **p** 1 Cor 9:24
p of the upward call Phil 3:14

PROCEED *go forth*
p from evil to evil Jer 9:3
p-s out of the mouth Matt 4:4
p-s from...Father John 15:26

PROCLAIM *announce, declare*
p...name of the LORD Ex 33:19
P good tidings 1 Chr 16:23
appointed...to **p** Neh 6:7

p liberty to captives Is 61:1
p justice to the Matt 12:18
he *began* to **p** Jesus Acts 9:20
first to **p** light Acts 26:23
faith is being **p-ed** Rom 1:8
p...eternal life 1 John 1:2

PROCLAMATION *declaration*
a **p** was circulated Ex 36:6
made **p** to the spirits 1 Pet 3:19

PROCONSUL *Roman governor*
the **p**, Sergius Paulus Acts 13:7
p-s are *available* Acts 19:38

PRODUCE (n) *yield of the soil*
land will yield its **p** Lev 25:19
tithe all the **p** Deut 14:22
earth has yielded its **p** Ps 67:6
precious **p** of...soil James 5:7

PRODUCE (v) *bring forth*
milk **p-s** butter Prov 30:33
cannot **p** bad fruit Matt 7:18
they **p** quarrels 2 Tim 2:23
faith **p-s** endurance James 1:3

PROFANE *defile, desecrate*
p My holy name Lev 20:3
is **p-d** by harlotry Lev 21:7
and **p-d** My sabbaths Ezek 22:8
p-d your sanctuaries Ezek 28:18
to **p** the covenant Mal 2:10

PROFESS *confess, declare*
P-ing to be wise Rom 1:22
They **p** to know God Titus 1:16

PROFIT (n) *benefit, gain*
labor there is **p** Prov 14:23
no **p** for the charmer Eccl 10:11
not seeking my...**p** 1 Cor 10:33
business...make a **p** James 4:13

PROFIT (v) *reap an advantage*
p...my destruction Job 30:13
what does it **p** a Mark 8:36
the flesh **p-s** nothing John 6:63
it **p-s** me nothing 1 Cor 13:3

PROFITABLE *useful*
not all things are **p** 1 Cor 6:12
godliness is **p** 1 Tim 4:8
p for teaching 2 Tim 3:16

PROMINENT *well-known*
a **p** member of the Mark 15:43
of **p** Greek women Acts 17:12
p men of the city Acts 25:23

PROMISE (n) *agreement, pledge*
p of the Holy Spirit Acts 2:33
the **p** made by God Acts 26:6
the **p** is nullified Rom 4:14
children of the **p** Rom 9:8
commandment...a **p** Eph 6:2
heirs of the **p** Heb 6:17
precious...**p-s** 2 Pet 1:4
the **p** of His coming 2 Pet 3:4

PROMISED *made an agreement*
land which He had **p** Deut 9:28
p to keep Your words Ps 119:57
p long ages ago Titus 1:2
He who **p** is faithful Heb 10:23

PRONOUNCE *declare officially*
shall **p** him clean Lev 13:23
I will **p** My judgments Jer 1:16
Pilate **p-d** sentence Luke 23:24
God...**p-d** judgment Rev 18:20

PROOF *evidence*
furnished **p** to all Acts 17:31
p of your love 2 Cor 8:24
p of the Christ 2 Cor 13:3

PROPER *suitable*
fulfilled...**p** time Luke 1:20
is it **p** for a woman 1 Cor 11:13
as is **p** among saints Eph 5:3

PROPERTY *goods* or *land*
acquire **p** in it Gen 34:10
p...too great Gen 36:7
buys a slave as *his* **p** Lev 22:11
who owned much **p** Matt 19:22
selling their **p** and Acts 2:45
things...common **p** Acts 4:32

PROPHECY *proclamation*
seal up vision and **p** Dan 9:24
p...fulfilled Matt 13:14
have *the gift of* **p** 1 Cor 13:2
no **p**...of human will 2 Pet 1:21
the spirit of **p** Rev 19:10

PROPHESY *predict, proclaim*
to **p** with lyres 1 Chr 25:1
he never **p-ies** good 2 Chr 18:7
p-ing...false vision Jer 14:14
P over these bones Ezek 37:4
sons and...will **p** Joel 2:28
did we...**p** in Your Matt 7:22
P to us...Christ Matt 26:68
speaking...**p-ing** Acts 19:6
who **p-ies** edifies 1 Cor 14:4

PROPHET *spokesman for God*
Aaron shall be your **p** Ex 7:1
a **p** or a dreamer Deut 13:1
I will raise up a **p** Deut 18:18
p in your place 1 Kin 19:16
summon all...**p-s** 2 Kin 10:19
vision of...the **p** 2 Chr 32:32
Woe...foolish **p-s** Ezek 13:3
written by the **p** Matt 2:5
persecuted the **p-s** Matt 5:12
Beware...false **p-s** Matt 7:15
He...receives a **p** Matt 10:41
the **p** Jesus Matt 21:11
false **p-s**...arise Mark 13:22
p of the Most High Luke 1:76
great **p** has arisen Luke 7:16
Are you the **P** John 1:21
reading Isaiah the **p** Acts 8:30
a Jewish false **p** Acts 13:6
All are not **p-s** 1 Cor 12:29
and some *as* **p-s** Eph 4:11
beast and...false **p** Rev 20:10

PROPHETESS *speaker for God*
Miriam the **p** Ex 15:20
Deborah, a **p** Judg 4:4
there was a **p**, Anna Luke 2:36
calls herself a **p** Rev 2:20

PROPHETIC *predictive*
not...**p** utterances 1 Thess 5:20
p word...sure 2 Pet 1:19

PROPITIATION *atonement*
a **p** in His blood Rom 3:25
p for the sins Heb 2:17
He himself is the **p** 1 John 2:2
p for our sins 1 John 4:10

PROSELYTE *convert*
both Jews and **p-s** Acts 2:10
a **p** from Antioch Acts 6:5
God-fearing **p-s** Acts 13:43

PROSPER *flourish, succeed*
I will surely **p** you Gen 32:12
David was **p-ing** 1 Sam 18:14
they built and **p-ed** 2 Chr 14:7
His ways **p** at all Ps 10:5
they **p** who love you Ps 122:6

PROSPERITY *success, wealth*
my **p** has passed away Job 30:15
soul will abide in **p** Ps 25:13
saw the **p** of the wicked Ps 73:3
know how to live in **p** Phil 4:12

PROSPEROUS *successful*
exceedingly **p** Gen 30:43
make your way **p** Josh 1:8
generous man...be **p** Prov 11:25

PROSTITUTE *harlot*
Where...temple **p** Gen 38:21
male cult **p-s** in the 1 Kin 14:24
an adulterer and a **p** Is 57:3
to a **p** is one body 1 Cor 6:16

PROSTRATE *fall down flat*
p-d himself before 2 Sam 18:28
man dies and lies **p** Job 14:10
fell...**p-d** Matt 18:26

PROTECT *guard, shield*
The LORD will **p** him Ps 41:2
LORD **p-s** the strangers Ps 146:9
LORD...**p** Jerusalem Is 31:5
He will...**p** you 2 Thess 3:3
p-ed by the power of 1 Pet 1:5

PROTECTION *safe-keeping*
p has been removed Num 14:9
For wisdom is **p** Eccl 7:12
p from the storm Is 4:6
let him rely on My **p** Is 27:5

PROUD *exaggerated self-esteem*
heart will become **p** Deut 8:14
recompense to the **p** Ps 94:2
eyes and a **p** heart Prov 21:4
daughters of Zion are **p** Is 3:16
opposed to the **p** James 4:6

PROVE *establish, test*
you will be **p-d** a liar Prov 30:6
will **p** Myself holy Ezek 20:41
p to be My disciples John 15:8
p...the will of God Rom 12:2
p yourselves doers James 1:22

PROVERB *adage, short saying*
become...a **p** Deut 28:37
spoke 3,000 **p-s** 1 Kin 4:32
Israel...become a **p** 1 Kin 9:7
To understand a **p** Prov 1:6
quote this **p** to Me Luke 4:23
to the true **p** 2 Pet 2:22

PROVIDE *furnish, supply*
p for Himself...lamb Gen 22:8
p for...redemption Lev 25:24
p-d bread from heaven Neh 9:15
Who **p-s** rain for the Ps 147:8
p...way of escape 1 Cor 10:13
not **p** for his own 1 Tim 5:8
God had **p-d** Heb 11:40

PROVINCE *district* or *territory*
rulers of the **p-s** 1 Kin 20:17
holiday for the **p-s** Esth 2:18
whole **p** of Babylon Dan 2:48
arrived in the **p** Acts 25:1

PROVISION *supply, requirement*
bread of their **p** was Josh 9:5
bless her **p** Ps 132:15
p-s of the law Matt 23:23
no **p** for the flesh Rom 13:14

PROVOKE *evoke, excite*
images to **p** Me 1 Kin 14:9
who **p** God are secure Job 12:6
love...is not **p-d** 1 Cor 13:4,5
not **p** your children Eph 6:4

PROWL *roam in search*
beasts...**p** about Ps 104:20
devil, **p-s** around like 1 Pet 5:8

PRUDENT *careful, wise*
a **p** man conceals Prov 12:16
p wife is from the Prov 19:14
the **p** took oil in Matt 25:4
you are **p** in Christ 1 Cor 4:10

PRUNING *cutting*
spears into **p** hooks Is 2:4

PSALMS *sacred songs*
shout...with **p** Ps 95:2
P must be fulfilled Luke 24:44
speaking...in **p** Eph 5:19

PUBLIC *open*
of his **p** appearance Luke 1:80
beaten us in **p** Acts 16:37
refuted...Jews in **p** Acts 18:28
made a **p** display Col 2:15
made a **p** spectacle Heb 10:33

PUL
Tiglath-pileser III, king of Assyria 2 Kin 15:19; 1 Chr 5:26

PUNISH *chastise, penalize*
p them for their sin Ex 32:34
and are **p-ed** for it Prov 22:3
p the world for its Is 13:11
will **p** your iniquity Lam 4:22
p Him and release Luke 23:16
I **p-ed** them often Acts 26:11
p all disobedience 2 Cor 10:6

PUNISHMENT *penalty*
My **p** is too great Gen 4:13
p of the sword Job 19:29
fear involves **p** 1 John 4:18
the **p** of eternal fire Jude 7

PUPIL *part of eye* or *student*
as the **p** of His eye Deut 32:10
p is not above his Luke 6:40

PURCHASE *buy*
p-d with His...blood Acts 20:28
p-d for God with Your Rev 5:9

PURE *genuine, undefiled*
mercy seat of **p** gold Ex 25:17
be **p** before his Maker Job 4:17
My teaching is **p** Job 11:4
commandment...is **p** Ps 19:8
pleasant words are **p** Prov 15:26
As **p** as the sun Song 6:10
hair...like **p** wool Dan 7:9
Blessed are the **p** in Matt 5:8
whatever is **p** Phil 4:8
love from a **p** heart 1 Tim 1:5
p milk of the word 1 Pet 2:2
the city was **p** gold Rev 21:18

PURGE *remove*
p...evil from among Deut 13:5
Many will be **p-d** Dan 12:10

PURIFICATION *cleansing*
Jewish custom of **p** John 2:6
He...made **p** of sins Heb 1:3

PURIFY *make clean*
p-ied these waters 2 Kin 2:21
P me with hyssop Ps 51:7
p...a people Titus 2:14
p your hearts James 4:8
p-ied your souls 1 Pet 1:22

PURIM
Jewish festival Esth 9:26ff

PURITY *not corrupted*
who loves **p** of heart Prov 22:11
love, faith *and* **p** 1 Tim 4:12
with **p** in doctrine Titus 2:7

PURPLE *color*
a veil of blue and **p** Ex 26:31
Those reared in **p** Lam 4:5
clothed Daniel with **p** Dan 5:29
dressed Him...**p** Mark 15:17
a seller of **p** fabrics Acts 16:14
clothed in **p** and Rev 17:4

PURPOSE *intention, reason*
p of shedding blood Ezek 22:9
rejected God's **p** Luke 7:30
for this **p** I have Acts 26:16
according to *His* **p** Rom 8:28

PURSUE *chase, follow*
p the manslayer Deut 19:6
They **p** my honor Job 30:15
the enemy **p** my soul Ps 7:5
Seek peace, and **p** it Ps 34:14
Adversity **p-s** Prov 13:21
p-s righteousness Prov 21:21
may **p** strong drink Is 5:11
p righteousness 2 Tim 2:22
P peace with...men Heb 12:14

PUT *place*
p enmity Between Gen 3:15
He **p** a new song Ps 40:3
p a purple robe on Him John 19:2
p on the Lord Jesus Rom 13:14
p on the new self Eph 4:24
P on the full armor Eph 6:11

PUT
1 *son of Ham* Gen 10:6; 1 Chr 1:8
2 *African country* Jer 46:9; Ezek 27:10;30:5; Nah 3:9

Q

QUAIL *type of bird*
q-s came up and Ex 16:13
q from the sea Num 11:31

QUAKE *shake, tremble*
The mountains **q-d** Judg 5:5
made the land **q** Ps 60:2
The earth **q-d** Ps 68:8
q at Your presence Is 64:1

QUALITY *character*
test the **q** of each 1 Cor 3:13
imperishable **q** of a 1 Pet 3:4

QUANTITY *amount*
large **q-ies** of cedar 1 Chr 22:4
a great **q** of fish Luke 5:6

QUARANTINE *isolate*
shall **q** the article Lev 13:50
q the house for Lev 14:38

QUARREL (n) *altercation*
if men have a **q** Ex 21:18
So abandon the **q** Prov 17:14
are **q-s** among you 1 Cor 1:11
the source of **q-s** James 4:1

QUARREL (v) *contend, fight*
did not **q** over it Gen 26:22
Why do you **q** with me Ex 17:2
any fool will **q** Prov 20:3
those who **q** with you Is 41:12

QUART *measure*
A **q** of wheat for a Rev 6:6

QUEEN *female sovereign*
when the **q** of Sheba 1 Kin 10:1
king saw Esther the **q** Esth 5:2
The **q** of kingdoms Is 47:5
The **Q** *of the* South Matt 12:42
Candace, **q** of the Acts 8:27

QUENCH *extinguish*
donkeys **q** their thirst Ps 104:11
waters cannot **q** love Song 8:7
not **q** the Spirit 1 Thess 5:19
q-ed...power of fire Heb 11:34

QUESTION (n) *inquiry, problem*
Was it not just a **q** 1 Sam 17:29
answered all her **q-s** 2 Chr 9:2
Jesus asked...a **q** Matt 22:41
in controversial **q-s** 1 Tim 6:4

QUESTION (v) *ask*
q-ed the priests 2 Chr 31:9
Jeremiah and **q-ed** Jer 38:27
He *began* to **q** them Mark 9:33
to **q** Him closely on Luke 11:53
Q those who have John 18:21

QUICK (adj) *rapid*
is **q**-tempered exalts Prov 14:29
q to hear, slow to James 1:19

QUICK (n) *deepest feelings*
cut to the **q** and Acts 5:33
were cut to the **q** Acts 7:54

QUIET (adj) *calm, still*
he knew no **q** within Job 20:20
me beside **q** waters Ps 23:2
lead a...**q** life 1 Tim 2:2
gentle and **q** spirit 1 Pet 3:4

QUIET (v) *become calm, still*
God, do not remain **q** Ps 83:1
and **q-ed** my soul Ps 131:2
will be **q** in His love Zeph 3:17
Be **q**, and come out Mark 1:25

QUIRINIUS
Roman governor at time of Judean census Luke 2:2

QUIVER *case for holding arrows*
your **q** and your bow Gen 27:3
man whose **q** is full Ps 127:5
hidden Me in His **q** Is 49:2
q is like an open grave Jer 5:16
fill the **q-s** Jer 51:11

QUOTA *portion assigned*
complete your work **q** Ex 5:13
deliver the **q** of bricks Ex 5:18

QUOTE *repeat a passage*
who **q-s** proverbs Ezek 16:44
will **q** this proverb Luke 4:23

R

RAAMSES / RAMESES
where Joseph settled Gen 47:11
Egyptian storage city built by Hebrew slaves Ex 1:11
origin of exodus Ex 12:37; Num 33:3,5

RABBI / RABBONI
respectful form of address
Matt 23:7;26:25; Mark 10:51
master, teacher
John 1:49;6:25;11:8;20:16

RAB-MAG
title of Babylonian official Jer 39:3,13

RAB-SARIS
title of Assyrian official 2 Kin 18:17; Jer 39:3,13

RABSHAKEH
title of Assyrian official 2 Kin 18:17ff; Is 36:2,4,11

RACE (n) *nation, people*
r has intermingled Ezra 9:2
mongrel **r** will dwell Zech 9:6
advantage of our **r** Acts 7:19
you are a chosen **r** 1 Pet 2:9

RACE (n) *competition of speed*
r is not to...swift Eccl 9:11
in a **r** all run, but 1 Cor 9:24
r...set before us Heb 12:1

RACHEL
Jacob's wife Gen 29:18,28
mother of Joseph and Benjamin Gen 30:25;35:24;46:19

RADIANCE *brightness*
a **r** around Him Ezek 1:27
His **r** is like Hab 3:4
r of His glory Heb 1:3

RADIANT *shining brightly*
looked to Him...were **r** Ps 34:5
you will see and be **r** Is 60:5
His garments...**r** Mark 9:3

RAFTS *boats*
r *to go* by sea 1 Kin 5:9
bring it to you on **r** 2 Chr 2:16

RAGE (n) *violent anger*
Haman was filled...**r** Esth 3:5
with **r** as they heard Luke 4:28

RAGE (v) *be very angry*
r-s against the LORD Prov 19:3
foolish man...**r-s** Prov 29:9
Why...Gentiles **r** Acts 4:25

RAHAB
1 *harlot in Jericho* Josh 2:1
assisted spies Josh 2:4-7
family spared Josh 2:13,14;6:22,23
ancestor of Jesus Matt 1:5
example of faith Heb 11:31; James 2:25
2 *symbolic for sea monster* Job 9:13;26:12; Ps 89:10
3 *symbolic for Egypt* Ps 87:4; Is 30:7

RAID (n) *robbery*
a **r** on the land 1 Sam 23:27
a **r** on the camels Job 1:17

RAID (v) *make a sudden attack*
r *at* their heels Gen 49:19
Bandits **r** outside Hos 7:1

RAIN (n)
God had not sent **r** Gen 2:5
r fell upon the earth Gen 7:12
I shall give you **r-s** Lev 26:4
LORD sent...**r** 1 Sam 12:18
no **r** in the land 1 Kin 17:7
the mountain **r-s** Job 24:8
shed...a plentiful **r** Ps 68:9
r is over *and* gone Song 2:11
anger a flooding **r** Ezek 13:13
r on *the* righteous Matt 5:45
ground...drinks the **r** Heb 6:7

RAIN (v) *fall down, pour*
r bread from heaven Ex 16:4
the LORD **r-ed** hail Ex 9:23
it **r-ed** fire and Luke 17:29
not **r**...for three James 5:17

RAINBOW *colored arc in sky*
appearance of the **r** Ezek 1:28
a **r** around the throne Rev 4:3
r was upon his head Rev 10:1

RAISE *elevate, lift*
will **r** up a prophet Deut 18:18
LORD **r-d** up judges Judg 2:16
r-s the poor from 1 Sam 2:8
eyelids are **r-d** *in* Prov 30:13
r up shepherds over Jer 23:4
He will **r** us up Hos 6:2
Heal...**r** *the* dead Matt 10:8
He will be **r-d** up Matt 20:19
three days I will **r** John 2:19
Jesus God **r-d** up Acts 2:32
r-d a spiritual 1 Cor 15:44
r-d us up with Him Eph 2:6
God is able to **r** *people* Heb 11:19

RAISIN *dried grapes*
clusters of **r-s** 2 Sam 16:1
Sustain me with **r** Song 2:5
and love **r** cakes Hos 3:1

RAM *male sheep*
Abraham...took the **r** Gen 22:13
a **r** without defect Lev 5:15
the **r** of atonement Num 5:8
r which had two horns Dan 8:3

RAMAH
1 *city of Naphtali* Josh 19:36
2 *town of Asher* Josh 19:29
3 *town of Benjamin* Josh 18:25; Judg 4:5; 19:13
4 *town in the Negev* Josh 19:8
5 *town in Gilead* 2 Kin 8:28,29; 2 Chr 22:5,6

RAMOTH
1 *city in Gilead* Deut 4:43; Josh 20:8
see **RAMOTH-GILEAD**
2 *city in the Negev* 1 Sam 30:27
also **Ramah of the Negev**
3 *Gershonite city* 1 Chr 6:73

RAMOTH-GILEAD
Gadite city E of the Jordan Deut 4:43
city of refuge Josh 20:8
Ahab killed 1 Kin 22:29-37

RAMPART *bulwark, siege*
and **r-s** for security Is 26:1
Whose **r** *was* the sea Nah 3:8
station myself on the **r** Hab 2:1

RANK *position*
men of **r** are a lie Ps 62:9
He...has a higher **r** John 1:15
a Man...higher **r** John 1:30

RANSOM (n) *payment*
give a **r** for himself Ex 30:12
not take **r** for Num 35:31
wicked is a **r** for Prov 21:18
His life a **r** for Matt 20:28
gave Himself as a **r** 1 Tim 2:6

RANSOM (v) *redeem*
You have **r-ed** me Ps 31:5
R me because of my Ps 69:18
LORD has **r-ed** Jacob Jer 31:11
Shall I **r** them from Hos 13:14

RAVAGE *devastate*
famine will **r** the Gen 41:30
mice that **r** the land 1 Sam 6:5
r-ing the church Acts 8:3

RAVEN *type of bird*
he sent out a **r** Gen 8:7
young **r-s** which cry Ps 147:9
Consider the **r-s** Luke 12:24

RAVENOUS *wildly hungry*
Benjamin is a **r** wolf Gen 49:27
inwardly are **r** wolves Matt 7:15

RAVINE *gorge*
settle on the steep **r-s** Is 7:19
smooth *stones* of the **r** Is 57:6
Every **r** will be filled Luke 3:5

RAVISH *seize and take*
you may **r** them Judg 19:24
And their wives **r-ed** Is 13:16
r-ed...women in Zion Lam 5:11

RAZOR *instrument for shaving*
no **r** shall pass over Num 6:5
no **r** shall come upon Judg 13:5
A **r** has never come Judg 16:17
Like a sharp **r** Ps 52:2

READ
you shall **r** this Deut 31:11
r from the scroll Jer 36:6
who **r-s** it may run Hab 2:2
r-ing...Isaiah Acts 8:28
prophets...are **read** Acts 13:27
Moses is **read** 2 Cor 3:15
Blessed is he who **r-s** Rev 1:3

READY *equipped, prepared*
and **r** to forgive Ps 86:5
Let Your hand be **r** Ps 119:173
Make **r** the way Matt 3:3
you also must be **r** Matt 24:44
be **r** in season 2 Tim 4:2
r to make a defense 1 Pet 3:15

REALIZE *achieve* or *understand*
Desire **r-d** is sweet Prov 13:19
r-d through Jesus John 1:17
to **r**...assurance Heb 6:11

REALM *area, kingdom*
ruler over the **r** of Dan 4:17
kingdom is not...**r** John 18:36

REAP *cut, gather*
when you **r**...harvest Lev 19:9
iniquity will **r** vanity Prov 22:8
they **r** the whirlwind Hos 8:7
nor **r** Matt 6:26
neither sow nor **r** Luke 12:24
sows...another **r-s** John 4:37
r eternal life Gal 6:8
your sickle and **r** Rev 14:15

REAPER *harvester*
after the **r-s** Ruth 2:3
will overtake the **r** Amos 9:13
the **r-s** are angels Matt 13:39

REASON (n) *explanation*
r a man shall leave Matt 19:5
this **r** the Father John 10:17
this **r** I found mercy 1 Tim 1:16
For this **r**, rejoice Rev 12:12

REASON (v) *analyze, argue*
upright would **r** with Job 23:7
let us **r** together Is 1:18
Pharisees began to **r** Luke 5:21
r-ing in...synagogue Acts 17:17
like a child, **r** like a 1 Cor 13:11

REBEKAH
wife of Isaac Gen 24:67;26:8
mother of Esau and Jacob Gen 25:21ff

REBEL (n) *rebellious one*
Your rulers are **r-s** Is 1:23
called a **r** from birth Is 48:8
their princes are **r-s** Hos 9:15

REBEL (v) *revolt*
not **r** against the Num 14:9
r-led against...words Ps 107:11
r-led against Me Ezek 20:21

REBELLION *insurrection*
he has counseled **r** Deut 13:5
I know your **r** Deut 31:27
r is as the sin of 1 Sam 15:23
my **r** and my sin Job 13:23
children of **r** Is 57:4

REBELLIOUS *defiant*
r against the LORD Deut 9:7
r generation Ps 78:8
A **r** man seeks only Prov 17:11
stubborn and **r** heart Jer 5:23
there are many **r** Titus 1:10

REBUILD *restore*
r the house of the Ezra 1:3
let us **r** the wall Neh 2:17
r the ancient ruins Is 58:12
r it in three days Matt 26:61
r the tabernacle Acts 15:16

REBUKE (n) *reprimand*
amazed at His **r** Job 26:11
At Your **r** they fled Ps 104:7
the poor hears no **r** Prov 13:8

REBUKE (v) *scold*
r me not in Your wrath Ps 38:1
r the arrogant Ps 119:21
LORD **r** you, Satan Zech 3:2
r-d the winds Matt 8:26
Jesus **r-d** him Matt 17:18
He **r-d** the fever Luke 4:39
Do not sharply **r** 1 Tim 5:1
reprove, **r**, exhort 2 Tim 4:2

RECEIVE *encounter, take*
The LORD **r-s** my prayer Ps 6:9
r me to glory Ps 73:24
man **r-s** a bribe Prov 17:23
Freely you **r-d** Matt 10:8
who **r-s** you **r-s** Me Matt 10:40
the blind **r** sight Matt 11:5
ask...you will **r** Matt 21:22
r-d up into heaven Mark 16:19
This man **r-s** sinners Luke 15:2
as many as **r-d** Him John 1:12
r you to Myself John 14:3
R the Holy Spirit John 20:22
you will **r** power Acts 1:8
to give than to **r** Acts 20:35
one **r-s** the prize 1 Cor 9:24
r the crown of life James 1:12
whatever...ask we **r** 1 John 3:22
r-d the mark of Rev 19:20

RECHABITES
line of Jonadab Jer 35:6
strict life style Jer 35:1-18

RECKONED *accounted for*
r it to him as Gen 15:6
r among the nations Num 23:9
r...as righteousness James 2:23

RECLINE *lean, lie down*
r on beds of ivory Amos 6:4
r *at the table* in Luke 13:29
r-ing on Jesus' John 13:23

RECOGNIZE *be aware, know*
he did not **r** him Gen 27:23
Saul **r-d** David's 1 Sam 26:17
r that He is near Matt 24:33
I did not **r** Him John 1:31

RECOMPENSE (n) *reward*
the **r** of the wicked Ps 91:8

r to the proud Ps 94:2
r of God will come Is 35:4

RECOMPENSE (v) *compensate*
LORD has **r-d** me 2 Sam 22:25
He will **r** the evil Ps 54:5
But if you do **r** Me Joel 3:4

RECONCILE *bring together*
r-d to your brother Matt 5:24
be **r-d** to God 2 Cor 5:20
r them both in one Eph 2:16
r all...to Himself Col 1:20

RECONCILIATION
now received the **r** Rom 5:11
the **r** of the world Rom 11:15
the ministry of **r** 2 Cor 5:18
the word of **r** 2 Cor 5:19

RECORD (n) *document, register*
the **r-s** are ancient 1 Chr 4:22
r-s of the kings 2 Chr 33:18
discover in...**r** books Ezra 4:15
I found the...**r** Neh 7:5

RECORD (v) *register, write*
r-ed their starting Num 33:2
R the vision Hab 2:2
are **r-ed** in heaven Luke 10:20

RECOVER *reclaim, become well*
did you not **r** them Judg 11:26
Will I **r** from this 2 Kin 8:8
and they will **r** Mark 16:18

RED *color*
first came forth **r** Gen 25:25
water...**r** as blood 2 Kin 3:22
they are **r** like crimson Is 1:18
the sky is **r** Matt 16:2
a great **r** dragon Rev 12:3

RED SEA
Hebrew: Sea of Reeds Ex 10:19
body of water between Egypt and Sinai Ex 13:18; Ps 106:9; Jer 49:21

REDEEM *buy back*
I will also **r** you Ex 6:6
family may **r** him Lev 25:49
wish to **r** the field Lev 27:19
I will **r** *it* Ruth 4:4
God will **r** my soul Ps 49:15
He will **r** Israel Ps 130:8
Christ **r-ed** us Gal 3:13
He might **r** those Gal 4:5

REDEEMER *one who buys back*
left you without a **r** Ruth 4:14
know that my **R** lives Job 19:25
my rock and my **R** Ps 19:14
your **R** is the Holy Is 41:14
our Father, Our **R** Is 63:16
Their **R** is strong Jer 50:34

REDEMPTION *deliverance*
r of the land Lev 25:24
have my right of **r** Ruth 4:6
r of his soul is Ps 49:8
r is drawing near Luke 21:28
r...in Christ Jesus Rom 3:24
r of our body Rom 8:23

r through His blood Eph 1:7
in whom we have **r** Col 1:14
obtained eternal **r** Heb 9:12

REED *tall marsh grass*
set *it* among the **r-s** Ex 2:3
bruised **r** He will Is 42:3
the **r**...to beat Him Matt 27:30
and put it on a **r** Matt 27:48

REEL *stagger, sway*
earth **r-s** to and fro Is 24:20
r with strong drink Is 28:7

REFINE *purify*
r-d seven times Ps 12:6
in order to **r** Dan 11:35
R them as silver Zech 13:9
r them like gold Mal 3:3
gold **r-d** by fire Rev 3:18

REFRAIN *abstain*
not **r** from spitting Job 30:10
to **r** from working 1 Cor 9:6
r from judging Rev 6:10

REFRESH *renew, replenish*
you may **r** yourselves Gen 18:5
R me with apples Song 2:5
times of **r-ing** may Acts 3:19
r my heart in Christ Philem 20

REFUGE *protection, shelter*
in whom I take **r** 2 Sam 22:3
God is our **r** Ps 46:1
r in the LORD Ps 118:8
the **r** of lies Is 28:17
r in...distress Jer 16:19
who have taken **r** Heb 6:18

REFUGE, CITIES OF
see **CITIES OF REFUGE**

REFUSE (n) *waste*
be made a **r** heap Ezra 6:11
corpses lay like **r** Is 5:25
its waters toss up **r** Is 57:20
sell...**r** of the wheat Amos 8:6

REFUSE (v) *decline*
r you his grave Gen 23:6
r to let My people go Ex 10:4
his hands **r** to work Prov 21:25
they **r** to know Me Jer 9:6
r-d to be comforted Matt 2:18
can **r** the water Acts 10:47
not **r** Him who is Heb 12:25

REFUSE GATE
see **GATES OF JERUSALEM**

REFUTE *prove wrong*
R me if you can Job 33:5
he...**r-d** the Jews Acts 18:28
to **r** those who Titus 1:9

REGAIN *recover*
r-ed their sight Matt 20:34
want to **r** my sight Mark 10:51
he might **r** his sight Acts 9:12

REGARD (n) *respect*
LORD had **r** for Abel Gen 4:4

r to the prayer 1 Kin 8:28
have **r** for his Maker Is 17:7
r for the humble Luke 1:48

REGARD (v) *esteem, respect*
If I **r** wickedness Ps 66:18
Yet He **r-s** the lowly Ps 138:6
who **r-s** reproof Prov 15:5
highly **r-ed** by him Luke 7:2
r one another Phil 2:3
did not **r** equality Phil 2:6

REGENERATION *renewal*
r when the Son Matt 19:28
the washing of **r** Titus 3:5

REGION *area*
r of the Jordan Josh 22:10
the **r-s** of Galilee Matt 2:22
to the **r** of Judea Mark 10:1
same **r**...shepherds Luke 2:8

REGISTER *enroll, record*
r...people of Israel 2 Sam 24:4
to **r** for the census Luke 2:3

REHOBOAM
son of Solomon 1 Kin 11:43
king of Judah 1 Kin 12:16ff; 2 Chr 11:1ff

REIGN *rule*
LORD shall **r** forever Ex 15:18
Shall Saul **r** over 1 Sam 11:12
David **r-ed** over all 2 Sam 8:15
The LORD **r-s** Ps 93:1
By me kings **r** Prov 8:15
will **r** righteously Is 32:1
death **r-ed**...Adam Rom 5:14
He must **r** until 1 Cor 15:25
also **r** with Him 2 Tim 2:12
He will **r** forever Rev 11:15
will **r** with Him Rev 20:6

REJECT *decline, refuse*
have **r-ed** the LORD Num 11:20
will **r** you forever 1 Chr 28:9
not **r** the discipline Prov 3:11
A fool **r-s** his Prov 15:5
have **r-ed** this word Is 30:12
He who **r-s** unjust gain Is 33:15
r-ed My ordinances Ezek 20:13
have **r-ed** knowledge Hos 4:6
they **r-ed** the law Amos 2:4
the builders **r-ed** Matt 21:42
who **r-s** you **r-s** Me Luke 10:16
He who **r-s** Me John 12:48

REJOICE *be glad*
r before the LORD Lev 23:40
R, O nations Deut 32:43
I **r** in Your salvation 1 Sam 2:1
let the earth **r** 1 Chr 16:31
my soul shall **r** Ps 35:9
king will **r** in God Ps 63:11
Let us **r** and be glad Ps 118:24
I **r** at Your word Ps 119:162
R, young man Eccl 11:9
God will **r** over you Is 62:5
r-d exceedingly Matt 2:10

r at his birth Luke 1:14
crowd was **r-ing** Luke 13:17
you would have **r-d** John 14:28
r-ing in hope Rom 12:12
yet always **r-ing** 2 Cor 6:10
R in the Lord Phil 4:4
I **r** in my sufferings Col 1:24
r, O heavens Rev 12:12

REJOICING (n) *delight*
a holiday for **r** Esth 9:19
hills gird...with **r** Ps 65:12
Jerusalem *for* **r** Is 65:18

RELATIONS *sexual intercourse*
r with his wife Eve Gen 4:1
had no **r** with a man Judg 11:39
we may have **r** with Judg 19:22
had **r** with Hannah 1 Sam 1:19

RELATIVE *kinsman*
and to my **r-s** Gen 24:4
The man is our **r** Ruth 2:20
My **r-s** have failed Job 19:14
among his *own* **r-s** Mark 6:4
your **r** Elizabeth has Luke 1:36

RELEASE (n) *liberation*
a **r** through the land Lev 25:10
r for you the King Mark 15:9
r to the captives Luke 4:18

RELEASE (v) *set free*
he **r-d** Barabbas Matt 27:26
wanting to **r** Jesus Luke 23:20
efforts to **r** Him John 19:12
you **r-d** from a wife 1 Cor 7:27
r-d us from our sins Rev 1:5
R the four angels Rev 9:14

RELENT *yield*
I am tired of **r-ing** Jer 15:6
r...the calamity Jer 18:8
whether He will...**r** Joel 2:14
God may turn and **r** Jon 3:9

RELIEF *lessening of burden*
r and deliverance Esth 4:14
my *prayer for* **r** Lam 3:56
r of the brethren Acts 11:29

RELIGION *system of belief*
about their own **r** Acts 25:19
sect of our **r** Acts 26:5
pure and undefiled **r** James 1:27

RELIGIOUS *devout, pious*
r in all respects Acts 17:22
thinks...to be **r** James 1:26

RELY *depend, trust*
r-ied on the LORD 2 Chr 16:8
who...**r** on horses Is 31:1
r on his God Is 50:10
You **r** on your sword Ezek 33:26
r upon the Law Rom 2:17

REMAIN *abide, be left*
While the earth **r-s** Gen 8:22
R...in his place Ex 16:29

ark...not **r** with us 1 Sam 5:7
r-s yet...youngest 1 Sam 16:11
flee to Egypt, and **r** Matt 2:13
dove...**r-ed** upon John 1:32
not **r** in darkness John 12:46
not **r** on the cross John 19:31
she must **r** unmarried 1 Cor 7:11
gospel would **r** Gal 2:5
He **r-s** faithful 2 Tim 2:13

REMEMBER *recall, recollect*
God **r-ed** Noah Gen 8:1
I will **r** My covenant Gen 9:15
R the sabbath day Ex 20:8
not **r** the sins of my Ps 25:7
R also your Creator Eccl 12:1
O LORD, **R** me Jer 15:15
sin I will **r** no more Jer 31:34
Peter **r-ed** the word Matt 26:75
R Lot's wife Luke 17:32
r the words of Acts 20:35
to **r** the poor Gal 2:10

REMEMBRANCE *memory*
Your **r**, O LORD Ps 135:13
Put Me in **r** Is 43:26
a book of **r** was Mal 3:16
do this in **r** of Me Luke 22:19
in **r** of Me 1 Cor 11:25

REMNANT *remaining part*
preserve for you a **r** Gen 45:7
prayer for the **r** 2 Kin 19:4
an escaped **r** Ezra 9:8
A **r** will return Is 10:21
the **r** of Israel Jer 6:9
a **r** of the Spirit Mal 2:15
r that will be saved Rom 9:27

REMOVE *take away* or *off*
r your sandals Ex 3:5
r-d all the idols 1 Kin 15:12
He **r-d** the high 2 Kin 18:4
r the heart of stone Ezek 36:26
not fit to **r** His Matt 3:11
r this cup from Me Luke 22:42
R the stone John 11:39
as to **r** mountains 1 Cor 13:2

REND *tear*
r the heavens Is 64:1
r their garments Jer 36:24
r your heart and not Joel 2:13

RENDER *inflict, repay*
I will **r** vengeance Deut 32:41
R recompense to the Ps 94:2
r to Caesar the Matt 22:21
R to all what is due Rom 13:7

RENEW *make new, revive*
r a steadfast spirit Ps 51:10
r-ed like the eagle Ps 103:5
R our days as of old Lam 5:21
inner man...**r-ed** 2 Cor 4:16

RENOWN *fame*
men of **r** Gen 6:4
a people, for **r** Jer 13:11
shame into...and **r** Zeph 3:19

REPAIR *restore*
r the house of 1 Chr 26:27
r-ing...foundations Ezra 4:12
r of the walls Neh 4:7

REPAY *pay back*
you thus **r** the LORD Deut 32:6
so God has **repaid** Judg 1:7
LORD **r** the evildoer 2 Sam 3:39
repaid me evil for Ps 109:5
r their iniquity Jer 16:18
He will fully **r** Jer 51:56
is Mine, I will **r** Rom 12:19
no one **r-s**...evil 1 Thess 5:15

REPENT *change mind*
that He should **r** Num 23:19
r in dust and ashes Job 42:6
have refused to **r** Jer 5:3
R, for the kingdom Matt 3:2
r-ed long ago in Matt 11:21
r and believe Mark 1:15
one sinner who **r-s** Luke 15:7
R...be baptized Acts 2:38
all...should **r** Acts 17:30
r and turn to God Acts 26:20

REPENTANCE *penitence*
with water for **r** Matt 3:11
baptism of **r** Mark 1:4
r for forgiveness Luke 24:47
appropriate to **r** Acts 26:20
r without regret 2 Cor 7:10
r from dead works Heb 6:1
to come to **r** 2 Pet 3:9

REPHAIM
1 *pre-Israelite people of Palestine* Gen 14:5;15:20
people of large stature
2 *valley near Jerusalem* Josh 15:8; 2 Sam 23:13

REPHIDIM
Israelite campsite in Sinai Ex 17:1,8; Num 33:14,15

REPORT *account, statement*
not bear a false **r** Ex 23:1
r concerning Him Luke 7:17
has believed our **r** John 12:38

REPRESENTATION *likeness*
exact **r** of His nature Heb 1:3

REPRESENTATIVE *substitute*
people's **r** before God Ex 18:19
the king's **r** Neh 11:24

REPROACH (n) *dishonor*
taken away my **r** Gen 30:23
a **r** on all Israel 1 Sam 11:2
I have become a **r** Ps 31:11
with dishonor...**r** Prov 18:3
not fear the **r** of Is 51:7
the **r** of Christ Heb 11:26

REPROACH (v) *accuse, rebuke*
to **r** the living God 2 Kin 19:4
My heart does not **r** Job 27:6
foolish man **r-es** You Ps 74:22
enemies have **r-ed** me Ps 102:8
He **r-ed** them for Mark 16:14

REPROOF *correction, rebuke*
spurned all my **r** Prov 1:30
regards **r** is sensible Prov 15:5
who hates **r** will Prov 15:10
and **r** give wisdom Prov 29:15
for teaching, for **r** 2 Tim 3:16

REPROVE *correct, rebuke*
r your neighbor Lev 19:17
LORD loves He **r-s** Prov 3:12
Do not **r** a scoffer Prov 9:8
R the ruthless Is 1:17
r, rebuke, exhort 2 Tim 4:2
whom I love, I **r** Rev 3:19

REPTILE *snake*
and the sand **r** Lev 11:30
r-s of the earth Mic 7:17
r-s and creatures James 3:7

REPUTATION *character*
seven men of good **r** Acts 6:3
a **r** for good works 1 Tim 5:10

REQUEST *desire, petition*
my people as my **r** Esth 7:3
the **r** of his lips Ps 21:2
He gave them their **r** Ps 106:15
r-s be made known to Phil 4:6

REQUIRE *demand, insist*
r your lifeblood Gen 9:5
God **r** from you Deut 10:12
as each day **r-d** Ezra 3:4
your soul is **r-d** Luke 12:20
r-d of stewards 1 Cor 4:2

REQUIREMENT *necessity*
r-s of the Lord Luke 1:6
r of the Law Rom 8:4
law of physical **r** Heb 7:16

RESCUE *deliver, redeem*
O LORD, **r** my soul Ps 6:4
R the weak and needy Ps 82:4
He delivers and **r-s** Dan 6:27
The Lord will **r** me 2 Tim 4:18
r the godly from 2 Pet 2:9

RESERVE *retain, store up*
r-d a blessing for Gen 27:36
darkness...in **r** Job 20:26
lips may **r** knowledge Prov 5:2
r-s wrath for Nah 1:2
r-d in heaven 1 Pet 1:4
r-d for fire 2 Pet 3:7

RESIDE *dwell, live*
stranger who **r-s** Lev 19:34
a son of man **r** in it Jer 49:18
those who **r** as aliens 1 Pet 1:1

RESIST *oppose, withstand*
not **r** an evil person Matt 5:39
none...able to **r** Luke 21:15
r-ing the Holy Spirit Acts 7:51
whoever **r-s** authority Rom 13:2
R the devil James 4:7

RESPECT (n) *regard*
no **r** for the old Deut 28:50
where is My **r** Mal 1:6
please *Him* in all **r-s** Col 1:10
to your masters...**r** 1 Pet 2:18

RESPECT (v) *esteem*
They will **r** my son Matt 21:37
not fear God nor **r** Luke 18:4
R what is right Rom 12:17
wife...**r-s** her husband Eph 5:33

RESPOND *answer, reply*
He will **r** to them Is 19:22
r to the heavens Hos 2:21
how you should **r** Col 4:6
Peter **r-ed** to her Acts 5:8

REST (n) *remainder*
r turned and fled Judg 20:45
the **r** of the exiles Ezra 6:16
the **r** of your days Prov 19:20
I will slay the **r** Amos 9:1
to the **r**...parables Luke 8:10

REST (n) *tranquility*
r from our work Gen 5:29
sabbath of solemn **r** Lev 16:31
God gives you **r** Josh 1:13
the weary are at **r** Job 3:17
Return to your **r** Ps 116:7
whole earth is at **r** Is 14:7
there is no **r** Lam 5:5
I will give you **r** Matt 11:28
no **r** for my spirit 2 Cor 2:13
not enter My **r** Heb 3:11
no **r** day and night Rev 14:11

REST (v) *settled, refresh*
the ark **r-ed** upon Gen 8:4
glory...LORD **r-ed** Ex 24:16
Spirit **r-ed** upon Num 11:25
R in the LORD Ps 37:7
Wisdom **r-s** in Prov 14:33
government will **r** on Is 9:6
iniquity **r-ed** on Ezek 32:27
r-ed on the seventh Heb 4:4
r from their labors Rev 14:13

RESTING PLACE
dove found no **r** Gen 8:9
This is My **r** forever Ps 132:14
Do not destroy his **r** Prov 24:15
r will be glorious Is 11:10

RESTITUTION *reparation*
owner...make **r** Ex 21:34
make **r** in full Num 5:7
r for the lamb 2 Sam 12:6

RESTORE *reestablish, replace*
son he had **r-d** to 2 Kin 8:1
they **r-d** Jerusalem Neh 3:8
r His righteousness Job 33:26
He **r-s** my soul Ps 23:3
R to me the joy Ps 51:12
O God, **r** us Ps 80:3
the LORD **r-s** Zion Is 52:8
R us to You Lam 5:21
his hand was **r-d** Mark 3:5
r-ing the kingdom Acts 1:6

RESTRAIN *hold back*
the rain...was **r-ed** Gen 8:2
who can **r** Him Job 11:10
He **r-ed** His anger Ps 78:38
who **r-s** his lips Prov 10:19
Will You **r** Yourself Is 64:12

R your voice from Jer 31:16
r-ed the crowds Acts 14:18

RESULT (n) *consequence, effect*
a **r** of the anguish Is 53:11
not as a **r** of works Eph 2:9
have *its* perfect **r** James 1:4
as a **r** of the works James 2:22

RESULT (v) *follow, happen*
r-ed In reproach Jer 20:8
sin **r-ing** in death Rom 6:16
proved to **r** in death Rom 7:10
r-ing in salvation Rom 10:10

RESURRECTION
who say...no **r** Matt 22:23
r of the righteous Luke 14:14
being sons of the **r** Luke 20:36
r of judgment John 5:29
the **r** and the life John 11:25
r of the dead Acts 24:21
if there is no **r** 1 Cor 15:13
power of His **r** Phil 3:10
hope through the **r** 1 Pet 1:3
This is the first **r** Rev 20:5

RETRIBUTION *punishment*
days of **r** have come Hos 9:7
stumbling block...**r** Rom 11:9
dealing out **r** to 2 Thess 1:8

RETURN *go back* or *repay*
to dust you shall **r** Gen 3:19
r-ed me evil for 1 Sam 25:21
clouds **r** after the Eccl 12:2
a remnant...will **r** Is 10:22
ransomed...will **r** Is 51:11
r-ed to Galilee Luke 4:14
repent and **r** Acts 3:19
not **r-ing** evil for 1 Pet 3:9

REUBEN
1 *son of Jacob / Leah* Gen 29:32
2 *tribe* Ex 6:14; Num 1:21

REVEAL *expose, make known*
God had **r-ed** Himself Gen 35:7
He **r-s** mysteries Job 12:22
will **r** his iniquity Job 20:27
do not **r** the secret Prov 25:9
glory...will be **r-ed** Is 40:5
r this mystery Dan 2:47
r-ed them to infants Matt 11:25
blood did not **r** *this* Matt 16:17
Son of Man is **r-ed** Luke 17:30
glory...to be **r-ed** Rom 8:18
r-ed with fire 1 Cor 3:13
to **r** His Son in me Gal 1:16
lawlessness is **r-ed** 2 Thess 2:3
r-ed in the flesh 1 Tim 3:16

REVELATION *divine disclosure*
a **r** to Your servant 2 Sam 7:27
the **r** ended Dan 7:28
r to the Gentiles Luke 2:32
r of...judgment Rom 2:5
the **r** of the mystery Rom 16:25
awaiting...the **r** 1 Cor 1:7
through a **r** of Jesus Gal 1:12
by **r**...made known Eph 3:3
The **R** of Jesus Rev 1:1

REVENGE *vengeance*
take our **r** on him Jer 20:10
Never take...**r** Rom 12:19

REVERE *adore, venerate*
r My sanctuary Lev 19:30
nations will **r** You Is 25:3

REVERENCE *respect, awe*
you do away with **r** Job 15:4
Worship...with **r** Ps 2:11
bow in **r** for You Ps 5:7
in **r** prepared an ark Heb 11:7
service with **r** and Heb 12:28

REVILE *use abusive language*
Do you **r** God's high Acts 23:4
are **r-d,** we bless 1 Cor 4:12
r-d for the name of 1 Pet 4:14
r angelic majesties Jude 8

REVIVE *bring back to life*
they **r** the stones Neh 4:2
let your heart **r** Ps 69:32
r us again Ps 85:6
r me in Your ways Ps 119:37
r-d your concern Phil 4:10

REVOLT *rebellion*
incited **r** within it Ezra 4:15
Speaking...and **r** Is 59:13
stirred up a **r** Acts 21:38

REWARD *prize*
emptiness...his **r** Job 15:31
r for the righteous Ps 58:11
The **r** of humility Prov 22:4
chases after **r-s** Is 1:23
His **r** is with Him Is 62:11
your **r** in heaven Matt 5:12
not lose his **r** Matt 10:42
looking to the **r** Heb 11:26
receive a full **r** 2 John 8

RHODA
Christian servant girl Acts 12:13

RHODES
Mediterranean isle Acts 21:1

RIB *bone*
took one of his **r-s** Gen 2:21
r-s *were* in its mouth Dan 7:5

RICH (adj) *wealthy*
Abram was very **r** Gen 13:2
LORD makes poor...**r** 1 Sam 2:7
not a **r** man boast Jer 9:23
woe to you who are **r** Luke 6:24
a **r** man Luke 16:1
being **r** in mercy Eph 2:4
r in good works 1 Tim 6:18

RICH (n) *wealthy*
r shall not pay more Ex 30:15
the **r** above the poor Job 34:19
r among the people Ps 45:12
The **r** and the poor Prov 22:2

RICHES *wealth*
R do not profit Prov 11:4
who trusts in his **r** Prov 11:28
neither poverty nor **r** Prov 30:8
choked with...**r** Luke 8:14
abounding in **r** Rom 10:12
r of His grace Eph 1:7
r of Christ Eph 3:8
His **r** in glory Phil 4:19
uncertainty of **r** 1 Tim 6:17
Your **r** have rotted James 5:2

RIDDLE *puzzle*
propound a **r** Judg 14:12
my **r** on the harp Ps 49:4
wise and their **r-s** Prov 1:6
propound a **r** Ezek 17:2

RIGHT (adj) *correct* or *direction*
r in the sight of Deut 12:25
r in his own eyes Judg 17:6
precepts...are **r** Ps 19:8
r eye makes you Matt 5:29
what your **r** hand is Matt 6:3
Sit at My **r** hand Matt 22:44
the **r** hand of God Mark 16:19
at the **r** time Christ Rom 5:6
r hand of fellowship Gal 2:9
whatever is **r** Phil 4:8
forsaking the **r** way 2 Pet 2:15

RIGHT (n) *due, prerogative*
her conjugal **r-s** Ex 21:10
r of redemption Lev 25:32
r of the firstborn Deut 21:17
the **r-s** of the poor Prov 29:7
r-s of the afflicted Prov 31:9
my **r** in the gospel 1 Cor 9:18

RIGHTEOUS (adj) *virtuous*
Noah was a **r** man Gen 6:9
LORD is the **r** one Ex 9:27
You are more **r** 1 Sam 24:17
God is a **r** judge Ps 7:11
A **r** man hates Prov 13:5
for David a **r** Branch Jer 23:5
LORD our God is **r** Dan 9:14
ninety-nine **r** Luke 15:7
coming of the **R** One Acts 7:52
r *man* shall live by Rom 1:17
none **r**, not even one Rom 3:10
many will be made **r** Rom 5:19
prayer of a **r** man James 5:16

RIGHTEOUS (n) *moral one*
assembly of the **r** Ps 1:5
LORD tests the **r** Ps 11:5
LORD loves the **r** Ps 146:8
the paths of the **r** Prov 2:20
the **r** will flourish Prov 11:28
joy for the **r** Prov 21:15
way of the **r** is Is 26:7
they sell the **r** for Amos 2:6
sends rain on *the* **r** Matt 5:45
r into eternal life Matt 25:46

RIGHTEOUSNESS
reckoned it...as **r** Gen 15:6
will repay...his **r** 1 Sam 26:23
I put on **r** Job 29:14
in the paths of **r** Ps 23:3
judge the world in **r** Ps 96:13
declare His **r** Ps 97:6
His **r** endures forever Ps 111:3
R exalts a nation Prov 14:34
clouds pour down **r** Is 45:8
wrapped me with...**r** Is 61:10
The LORD our **r** Jer 23:6
to rain **r** on you Hos 10:12
to fulfill all **r** Matt 3:15
and thirst for **r** Matt 5:6
kingdom and His **r** Matt 6:33
you enemy of all **r** Acts 13:10
through one act of **r** Rom 5:18
breastplate of **r** Eph 6:14
pursue **r,** faith 2 Tim 2:22
the crown of **r** 2 Tim 4:8
peaceful fruit of **r** Heb 12:11
not achieve the **r** James 1:20
suffer for...**r** 1 Pet 3:14

RIMMON
1 *a Benjamite* 2 Sam 4:2
2 *Aramean deity* 2 Kin 5:18
3 *town in Simeon* Josh 19:1,7
4 *city of Zebulun* Josh 19:13
5 *rock of* Judg 20:45;21:13

RING *jewelry, ornament*
make four gold **r-s** Ex 25:26
took his signet **r** Esth 3:10
As a **r** of gold Prov 11:22
finger **r-s,** nose **r-s** Is 3:21

RIOT *tumult, uprising*
otherwise a **r** might occur Matt 26:5
a **r** was starting Matt 27:24
accused of a **r** Acts 19:40

RIPE *fully developed*
old man of **r** age Gen 35:29
produced **r** grapes Gen 40:10
the harvest is **r** Joel 3:13
harvest...is **r** Rev 14:15

RISE *go up, issue forth*
mist used to **r** from Gen 2:6
Cain **rose** up against Gen 4:8
scepter shall **r** Num 24:17
witnesses **r** up Ps 35:11
children **r** up Prov 31:28
nation will **r** Matt 24:7
r-n, just as He said Matt 28:6
children will **r** up Mark 13:12
Lord has really **r-n** Luke 24:34

RIVER
r flowed out of Eden Gen 2:10
the **r** Euphrates Josh 1:4
r of Your delights Ps 36:8
He changes **r-s** into Ps 107:33
the **r-s** of Babylon Ps 137:1
A place of **r-s** and Is 33:21
r-s in the desert Is 43:20
peace...like a **r** Is 66:12
tears...like a **r** Lam 2:18
baptized...Jordan **R** Mark 1:5
r-s of living water John 7:38
r of the water of life Rev 22:1

RIZPAH
concubine of Saul 2 Sam 3:7

ROAD *path, way*
a lion in the **r** Prov 26:13
the rough **r-s** smooth Luke 3:5

coats on the **r** Luke 19:36
the Lord on the **r** Acts 9:27

ROAR (n) *loud deep sound*
the sound of the **r** 1 Kin 18:41
young lions' **r** Zech 11:3
pass away with a **r** 2 Pet 3:10

ROAR (v) *utter a deep sound*
a voice **r-s** Job 37:4
Let the sea **r** Ps 96:11
LORD will **r** from Jer 25:30
a lion **r** in the Amos 3:4

ROAST *cook*
grain **r-ed** in the fire Lev 2:14
r-ed the...*animals* 2 Chr 35:13
lazy man...**r** Prov 12:27

ROB *steal*
bear **r-bed** of her Prov 17:12
Do not **r** the poor Prov 22:22
Will a man **r** God Mal 3:8
do you **r** temples Rom 2:22
I **r-bed**...churches 2 Cor 11:8

ROBBER *thief*
she lurks as a **r** Prov 23:28
become a den of **r-s** Jer 7:11
crucified two **r-s** Mark 15:27
fell among **r-s** Luke 10:30
a thief and a **r** John 10:1
r-s of temples Acts 19:37

ROBBERY *theft*
not vainly hope in **r** Ps 62:10
I hate **r** in the Is 61:8
they are full of **r** Matt 23:25
you are full of **r** Luke 11:39

ROBE *cloak, garment*
cut off...Saul's **r** 1 Sam 24:4
justice was like a **r** Job 29:14
r of righteousness Is 61:10
put a scarlet **r** on Matt 27:28
walk...in long **r-s** Mark 12:38
wearing a white **r** Mark 16:5
bring...the best **r** Luke 15:22
washed their **r-s** Rev 7:14
a **r** dipped in blood Rev 19:13

ROCK *stone*
the cleft of the **r** Ex 33:22
struck the **r** twice Num 20:11
R of his salvation Deut 32:15
LORD is my **r** 2 Sam 22:2
engraved in the **r** Job 19:24
my **r** and my fortress Ps 18:2
r and my Redeemer Ps 19:14
set my feet upon a **r** Ps 40:2
a **r** to stumble over Is 8:14
an everlasting **R** Is 26:4
his house on the **r** Matt 7:24
upon this **r** I will Matt 16:18
the **r-s** were split Matt 27:51
hewn out in the **r** Mark 15:46
a **r** of offense Rom 9:33

ROD *staff, stick*
fresh **r-s** of poplar Gen 30:37
r of Aaron Num 17:8
break them with a **r** Ps 2:9
Your **r** and Your staff Ps 23:4
who withholds his **r** Prov 13:24
The **r** of discipline Prov 22:15
r of My anger Is 10:5
rule them with a **r** Rev 19:15

ROLL *move*
sky will be **r-ed** up Is 34:4
let justice **r** down Amos 5:24
r-ed away the stone Matt 28:2
Who will **r** away the Mark 16:3

ROMANS
citizens of Roman Empire
John 11:48; Acts 16:21,37

ROME
Italian city Acts 2:10
Roman Empire capital Acts 18:2
Paul held there Acts 28:14,16

ROOF
brought...to the **r** Josh 2:6
r...woman bathing 2 Sam 11:2
removed the **r** above Mark 2:4
r and let him down Luke 5:19

ROOM *chamber*
the ark with **r-s** Gen 6:14
go into your inner **r** Matt 6:6
a large upper **r** Mark 14:15
no **r** for them in Luke 2:7
r for the wrath Rom 12:19

ROOSTER *bird*
The strutting **r** Prov 30:31
before a **r** crows Matt 26:34
r will not crow John 13:38

ROOT (n) *source*
the **r** of Jesse Is 11:10
no **r**, it withered Mark 4:6
if the **r** is holy Rom 11:16
of money is a **r** 1 Tim 6:10
no **r** of bitterness Heb 12:15
the **R** of David Rev 5:5

ROOT (v) *establish* or *tear out*
r out your Asherim Mic 5:14
r-ed and grounded in Eph 3:17

ROPE *cord*
them down by a **r** Josh 2:15
bound...two new **r-s** Judg 15:13
he snapped the **r-s** Judg 16:12
Instead of a belt, a **r** Is 3:24

ROSE (n) *flower*
I am the **r** of Sharon Song 2:1

ROSH
1 *son of Benjamin* Gen 46:21
2 *place of God* Ezek 38:2,3;39:1

ROT *decay*
their flesh will **r** Zech 14:12
riches have **r-ted** James 5:2

ROTTENNESS *decay*
passion is **r** to Prov 14:30
r to the house of Hos 5:12

ROUGH *jagged, uneven*
r ground become a Is 40:4
the **r** places smooth Is 45:2

ROYAL *kingly*
captured the **r** city 2 Sam 12:26
his **r** bounty 1 Kin 10:13
all the **r** offspring 2 Kin 11:1
put on her **r** robes Esth 5:1
And a **r** diadem Is 62:3
roof of the **r** palace Dan 4:29
a **r** official John 4:46
fulfilling the **r** law James 2:8
a **r** priesthood 1 Pet 2:9

RUDDY *reddish in complexion*
he was **r** 1 Sam 16:12
a youth, and **r** 1 Sam 17:42
beloved is...and **r** Song 5:10

RUHAMAH
symbolic for Israel Hos 2:1

RUIN (n) *destruction*
shall be a **r** forever Deut 13:16
become a heap of **r-s** 1 Kin 9:8
the perpetual **r-s** Ps 74:3
Jerusalem in **r-s** Ps 79:1
r of the poor is Prov 10:15
fool's mouth is his **r** Prov 18:7
rebuild its **r-s** Acts 15:16

RUIN (v) *destroy*
to **r** him without Job 2:3
the grain is **r-ed** Joel 1:10
skins will be **r-ed** Luke 5:37

RULE (n) *authority, government*
to establish his **r** 1 Chr 18:3
against the **r** of 2 Chr 21:8
will walk by this **r** Gal 6:16
above all **r** and Eph 1:21
according to the **r-s** 2 Tim 2:5

RULE (v) *govern*
r over the fish Gen 1:26
Gideon, **R** over us Judg 8:22
godless men...not **r** Job 34:30
r-s over the nations Ps 22:28
The sun to **r** by day Ps 136:8
By me princes **r** Prov 8:16
women **r** over them Is 3:12
r over the Gentiles Rom 15:12
peace of Christ **r** Col 3:15
r them with a rod Rev 2:27

RULER *king, monarch*
Joseph was the **r** Gen 42:6
nor curse a **r** Ex 22:28
no chief...or **r** Prov 6:7
your **r-s** have fled Is 22:3
Most High is **r** Dan 4:32
come forth a **R** Matt 2:6
r of the demons Matt 9:34
r-s of the Gentiles Mark 10:42
the **r** of this world John 12:31
Who made you a **r** Acts 7:27
be subject to **r-s** Titus 3:1

RUMOR *gossip, hearsay*
r will be *added* to **r** Ezek 7:26
wars and **r-s** of wars Matt 24:6

RUN *move rapidly*
to **r** his course Ps 19:5
their feet **r** to evil Prov 1:16
streams **r-ning** with Is 30:25
r and not get tired Is 40:31
rivers to **r** like oil Ezek 32:14
Peter got up and **ran** Luke 24:12
disciple **ran** ahead John 20:4
who **r** in a race 1 Cor 9:24

RUSH *move quickly*
and **r** upon the city Judg 9:33
r-es headlong at Him Job 15:26
herd **r-ed** down the Matt 8:32
horses **r-ing** to battle Rev 9:9

RUSHES *marshy plant*
Can the **r** grow Job 8:11
reeds and **r** will rot Is 19:6

RUST *corrosion*
in which there is **r** Ezek 24:6
moth and **r** destroy Matt 6:19
r will be a witness James 5:3

RUTH
Moabitess Ruth 1:4
Naomi's daughter-in-law Ruth 1:14ff
married Boaz Ruth 4:13
in Messianic line Matt 1:5

RUTHLESS *cruel*
r men attain riches Prov 11:16
Reprove the **r** Is 1:17
song of the **r** is Is 25:5
most **r** of the Ezek 28:7

S

SABAOTH
Lord of Sabaoth is same as Lord of Hosts Rom 9:29; James 5:4
see also **HOST**

SABBATH *day of rest*
Remember the **s** day Ex 20:8
LORD blessed the **s** day Ex 20:11
keep My **s-s** and Lev 26:2
Observe the **s** day Deut 5:12
new moon nor **s** 2 Kin 4:23
call the **s** a delight Is 58:13
My **s-s** to be a sign Ezek 20:12
is Lord of the **S** Matt 12:8
S was made for man Mark 2:27
to do good...on the **S** Mark 3:4
the cross on the **S** John 19:31
a **S** day's journey Acts 1:12
are read every **S** Acts 13:27
S rest for the people Heb 4:9

SABBATICAL YEAR
seventh year of rest Lev 25:5

SABEANS
people of Sheba in SW Arabia
Job 1:15; Is 45:14; Joel 3:8

SACKCLOTH *coarse cloth*
put **s** on his loins Gen 37:34
gird on **s** and lament 2 Sam 3:31
put on **s** and ashes Esth 4:1
sewed **s** over my skin Job 16:15

with fasting, **s**, and Dan 9:3
sun became black as **s** Rev 6:12

SACRED *consecrated, holy*
took all the **s** things 2 Kin 12:18
perform **s** services 1 Cor 9:13
known...**s** writings 2 Tim 3:15
table and the **s** bread Heb 9:2

SACRIFICE (n) *offering of a life*
Jacob offered a **s** Gen 31:54
a Passover **s** to Ex 12:27
s-s of righteousness Ps 4:5
The **s** of the wicked Prov 15:8
loyalty rather than **s** Hos 6:6
compassion...not **s** Matt 9:13
a **s** to the idol Acts 7:41
a living and holy **s** Rom 12:1
an acceptable **s** Phil 4:18
by the **s** of Himself Heb 9:26
s-s God is pleased Heb 13:16
offer up spiritual **s-s** 1 Pet 2:5

SACRIFICE (v) *offer a life*
we may **s** to the Lord Ex 5:3
s on it your burnt Ex 20:24
when you **s** a sacrifice Lev 22:29
they **s-d** to the LORD Judg 2:5
even **s-d** their sons Ps 106:37
s-ing to the Baals Hos 11:2
lamb had to be **s-d** Luke 22:7
they **s** to demons 1 Cor 10:20

SAD *sorrowful, unhappy*
people heard...**s** word Ex 33:4
Why is your face **s** Neh 2:2
heart is **s**, the Prov 15:13

SADDUCEES
Jewish religious party
Matt 3:7;16:11,12; Mark 12:18; Acts 5:17;23:6-8

SAFE *free from danger*
houses are **s** from fear Job 21:9
runs into it and is **s** Prov 18:10
back **s** and sound Luke 15:27

SAIL (n) *canvas for wind*
Nor spread out the **s** Is 33:23
s was...embroidered Ezek 27:7

SAIL (v) *proceed by boat*
they **s-ed** to Cyprus Acts 13:4
to **s** past Ephesus Acts 20:16
set **s** from Crete Acts 27:21

SAILOR *mariner, seaman*
s-s...knew the sea 1 Kin 9:27
s-s and your pilots Ezek 27:27
every passenger and **s** Rev 18:17

SAINTS *ones faithful to God*
s...in the earth Ps 16:3
the **s** of the Highest Dan 7:22
s...fallen asleep Matt 27:52
lock up...**s** in prisons Acts 26:10

intercedes for the **s** Rom 8:27
s will judge the 1 Cor 6:2
citizens with the **s** Eph 2:19
perseverance of the **s** Rev 14:12

SALAMIS
city on Cyprus Acts 13:5

SALEM
Jerusalem Gen 14:18; Ps 76:2; Heb 7:1,2

SALOME
1 *wife of Zebedee* Mark 15:40
mother of James and John at open tomb Mark 16:1
2 *daughter of Herodias* Matt 14:6ff; Mark 6:22-26

SALT *preservative*
became a pillar of **s** Gen 19:26
and sowed it with **s** Judg 9:45
be eaten without **s** Job 6:6
the **s** of the earth Matt 5:13
seasoned with **s** Col 4:6
can **s** water produce James 3:12

SALT SEA
the Dead Sea Gen 14:3; Num 34:3; Deut 3:17; Josh 15:2

SALT, VALLEY OF
S of Dead Sea 2 Sam 8:13; 2 Chr 25:11

SALVATION *deliverance*
For Your **s** I wait Gen 49:18
He has become my **s** Ex 15:2
scorned...his **s** Deut 32:15
S belongs to the LORD Ps 3:8
my light and my **s** Ps 27:1
lift up the cup of **s** Ps 116:13
My **s** will be forever Is 51:6
helmet of **s** on His Is 59:17
S is from the LORD Jon 2:9
eyes have seen Your **s** Luke 2:30
s in no one else Acts 4:12
power of God for **s** Rom 1:16
now is the day of **s** 2 Cor 6:2
take the helmet of **s** Eph 6:17
work out your **s** with Phil 2:12
s through our Lord 1 Thess 5:9
that leads to **s** 2 Tim 3:15
who will inherit **s** Heb 1:14
neglect so great a **s** Heb 2:3
S to our God who Rev 7:10

SAMARIA
1 *capital of N kingdom* 1 Kin 16:24; 2 Chr 18:9
2 *another name for N kingdom* 1 Kin 13:32; 2 Kin 17:24; Hos 8:5; Amos 3:9; Obad 19
3 *region of central hill country* John 4:4-7; Acts 8:1ff

SAMOTHRACE
N Aegean island Acts 16:11

SAMSON
a Hebrew judge Judg 13:24
weak in character Judg 14:1ff
slave of passion Judg 16:1ff
great strength Judg 16:5,12

SAMUEL
son of Elkanah and Hannah 1 Sam 1:20
dedicated to God 1 Sam 1:21ff
called by God 1 Sam 3:1-18
judge 1 Sam 7:15-17
opposed monarchy 1 Sam 8:6
anointed Saul 1 Sam 10:1
anointed David 1 Sam 16:12
death 1 Sam 25:1

SANBALLAT
man of Beth-horon Neh 2:10
against Nehemiah Neh 6:1ff

SANCTIFICATION *holiness*
resulting in **s** Rom 6:22
righteousness and **s** 1 Cor 1:30
will of God, your **s** 1 Thess 4:3
s by the Spirit 2 Thess 2:13
s without which no Heb 12:14

SANCTIFY *set apart to God*
S to Me every Ex 13:2
the LORD who **s-ies** Lev 22:32
They will **s** My name Is 29:23
will **s** the Holy One Is 29:23
S My sabbaths Ezek 20:20
S them in the truth John 17:17
s-ied by the...Spirit Rom 15:16
husband is **s-ied** 1 Cor 7:14
s Christ as Lord 1 Pet 3:15

SANCTUARY *place of worship*
construct a **s** for Me Ex 25:8
revere My **s** Lev 19:30
utensils of the **s** 1 Chr 9:29
into the **s** of God Ps 73:17
Praise God in His **s** Ps 150:1
beautify...My **s** Is 60:13
a minister in the **s** Heb 8:2

SAND
descendants as the **s** Gen 32:12
treasures of the **s** Deut 33:19
built...on the **s** Matt 7:26
innumerable as the **s** Heb 11:12

SANDAL *footwear*
s has not worn out Deut 29:5
fit to remove His **s-s** Matt 3:11
two coats, or **s-s** Matt 10:10

SANHEDRIN *see* **COUNCIL**

SAPPHIRA
wife of Ananias Acts 5:1-10
struck dead for lying

SAPPHIRE *precious stone*
a **s** and a diamond Ex 28:18
Inlaid with **s-s** Song 5:14
foundations...in **s-s** Is 54:11

SARAH / SARAI
wife of Abraham Gen 11:29
barren Gen 11:30
beautiful Gen 12:11
gave birth to Isaac Gen 21:2,3
death Gen 23:2

SARDIS
city in Asia Minor Rev 1:11;3:1,4

SARGON
son of Tiglath-pileser III Is 20:1
king of Assyria

SATAN
Titles:
Abaddon Rev 9:11
accuser Ps 109:6; Rev 12:10
adversary 1 Pet 5:8
Apollyon Rev 9:11
Beelzebul Matt 10:25; Mark 3:22
Belial 2 Cor 6:15
deceiver of the world Rev 12:9
devil Matt 4:1,5;25:41; John 6:70;13:2; Eph 4:27;6:11; 1 Tim 3:6,7; Heb 2:14; 1 Pet 5:8; Rev 2:10;20:2,10
dragon Rev 12:9
enemy Matt 13:28,39
evil one Matt 13:19,38; John 17:15; Eph 6:16; 1 John 2:13,14;5:18,19
father of lies John 8:44
god of this world 2 Cor 4:4
liar John 8:44
murderer John 8:44
prince of the power of the air Eph 2:2
ruler of the demons Matt 9:34; Mark 3:22
ruler of this world John 12:31;14:30;16:11
serpent of old Rev 12:9

SATISFY *be content*
eat and not be **s-ied** Lev 26:26
s-ied their desire Ps 78:30
steals To **s** himself Prov 6:30
Nor will he be **s-ied** Prov 6:35
hunger is not **s-ied** Is 29:8
to **s** the crowd Mark 15:15

SATRAPS *Persian officials*
to the king's **s** Ezra 8:36
the **s**, the governors Esth 8:9
commissioners and **s** Dan 6:4

SAUL
1 *son of Kish* 1 Sam 9:1,2
anointed 1 Sam 10:1ff
first king 1 Sam 11:15
rejected as king 1 Sam 15:11ff
jealous of David 1 Sam 18:6ff
death 1 Sam 31:4ff
2 *apostle Paul, see* **PAUL**

SAVE *deliver, rescue*
s-d by the LORD Deut 33:29
S with Your right hand Ps 60:5
He will **s** you Prov 20:22
Turn to Me, and be **s-d** Is 45:22

s you from afar Jer 30:10
he will **s** his life Ezek 18:27
will **s** His people Matt 1:21
wishes to **s** his life Matt 16:25
Son...has come to **s** Matt 18:11
faith has **s-d** you Luke 7:50
world might be **s-d** John 3:17
Father, **s** Me from John 12:27
by which we...be **s-d** Acts 4:12
be **s-d** by His life Rom 5:10
will **s** your husband 1 Cor 7:16
Jesus came...to **s** 1 Tim 1:15
One who is able to **s** James 4:12
the righteous is **s-d** 1 Pet 4:18

SAVIOR *one who saves*
My **s**, You 2 Sam 22:3
forgot God their **S** Ps 106:21
send them a **S** and a Is 19:20
no **s** besides Me Is 43:11
righteous God and a **S** Is 45:21
S, who is Christ Luke 2:11
the **S** of the world John 4:42
as a Prince and a **S** Acts 5:31
S of all men 1 Tim 4:10
appearing of our **S** 2 Tim 1:10
our great God and **S** Titus 2:13
kingdom of our...**S** 2 Pet 1:11

SAVORY *appetizing*
prepare a **s** dish for Gen 27:4
mother made **s** food Gen 27:14

SAWS *cutting tools*
set *them* under **s** 2 Sam 12:31
cut *them* with **s** 1 Chr 20:3

SAY *pronounce, speak*
God blessed...**s-ing** Gen 1:22
not **s** in your heart Deut 9:4
to the wicked God **s-s** Ps 50:16
Do not **s** to your Prov 3:28
s-s the Preacher Eccl 1:2
He will **s**, Here I am Is 58:9
Many will **s** to Me Matt 7:22
If we **s**...no sin 1 John 1:8

SAYINGS *statements*
utter dark **s** of old Ps 78:2
s of understanding Prov 1:2
s of the wise Prov 24:23
anyone hears my **s** John 12:47

SCALE *for measuring weight*
with accurate **s-s** Job 31:6
false **s** is not good Prov 20:23
been weighed on the **s-s** Dan 5:27
with dishonest **s-s** Amos 8:5
justify wicked **s-s** Mic 6:11
a pair of **s-s** in his Rev 6:5

SCAPEGOAT *for removal of sin*
lot for the **s** fell Lev 16:10
released the goat...**s** Lev 16:26

SCARLET *bright red*
tied a **s** *thread* Gen 38:28
s thread...window Josh 2:18
lips are like a **s** Song 4:3
sins are as **s** Is 1:18
put a **s** robe on Him Matt 27:28

SCATTER *spread, sprinkle*
s among the nations Lev 26:33
Brimstone is **s-ed** on Job 18:15
storm will **s** them Is 41:16
s-ing the sheep of Jer 23:1
s him like dust Matt 21:44
sheep...shall be **s-ed** Matt 26:31

SCEPTER *symbol of authority*
s shall not depart Gen 49:10
s...rise from Israel Num 24:17
A **s** of uprightness Ps 45:6
The **s** of rulers Is 14:5
s of His kingdom Heb 1:8

SCHEME *plan, plot*
s...he had devised Esth 9:25
s brings him down Job 18:7
carries out wicked **s-s** Ps 37:7
ignorant of his **s-s** 2 Cor 2:11
the **s-s** of the devil Eph 6:11

SCOFF *mock, sneer*
s-ed...His prophets 2 Chr 36:16
The Lord **s-s** at them Ps 2:4
s at all the nations Ps 59:8
were **s-ing** at Him Luke 16:14

SCOFFER *mocker*
My friends are my **s-s** Job 16:20
sit in the seat of **s-s** Ps 1:1
He who corrects a **s** Prov 9:7
Behold, you **s-s** Acts 13:41

SCORCHING *burning*
words are like **s** fire Prov 16:27
s heat or sun strike Is 49:10
appointed a **s** east wind Jon 4:8
s heat of the day Matt 20:12

SCORN *treat with contempt*
s-ed...his salvation Deut 32:15
and **s-s** a mother Prov 30:17

SCORPION *poisonous spider*
serpents and **s-s** Deut 8:15
discipline...with **s-s** 1 Kin 12:11
tread on...**s-s** Luke 10:19
not give him a **s** Luke 11:12
s-s...have power Rev 9:3

SCOURGE (n) *whip*
the **s** of the tongue Job 5:21
arouse a **s** against Is 10:26
He made a **s** of cords John 2:15

SCOURGE (v) *flog, whip*
s and crucify *Him* Matt 20:19
having Jesus **s-d** Matt 27:26
lawful for you to **s** Acts 22:25
He **s-s** every son Heb 12:6

SCRAPE *rub, scratch*
plaster that they **s** Lev 14:41
s-d the honey into Judg 14:9
potsherd to **s** himself Job 2:8

SCREEN *conceal, separate*
s the ark with the veil Ex 40:3
s-ed off the ark Ex 40:21

SCRIBE *copier, writer*
and Sheva was **s** 2 Sam 20:25
then the king's **s** 2 Chr 24:11
Ezra the **s** stood Neh 8:4
lying pen of the **s-s** Jer 8:8
chief priests and **s-s** Matt 2:4
and not as the **s-s** Mark 1:22
Where is the **s** 1 Cor 1:20

SCRIPTURE
understanding...**S-s** Matt 22:29
fulfill...**S-s** Mark 14:49
S has been fulfilled Luke 4:21
You search the **S-s** John 5:39
S cannot be broken John 10:35
mighty in the **S-s** Acts 18:24
what does the **S** say Rom 4:3
S is inspired by God 2 Tim 3:16

SCROLL *parchment*
these curses on a **s** Num 5:23
Take a **s** and write Jer 36:2
eat this **s**, and go Ezek 3:1
like a **s**...rolled Rev 6:14

SEA *body of salt water*
waters He called **s-s** Gen 1:10
s, or the **s** monster Job 7:12
founded it upon the **s-s** Ps 24:2
to the **s** in ships Ps 107:23
the waters cover the **s** Is 11:9
rebukes the **s** and Nah 1:4
walking on the **s** Matt 14:26
s *began* to be stirred John 6:18
dangers on the **s** 2 Cor 11:26
s of glass, like crystal Rev 4:6

SEA OF GALILEE
see **GALILEE, SEA OF**

SEACOAST *seashore*
remnant of the **s** Ezek 25:16
inhabitants of the **s** Zeph 2:5
s will be pastures Zeph 2:6

SEAL (n) *mark, stamp*
Your **s** and your cord Gen 38:18
the engravings of a **s** Ex 28:21
the **s** of perfection Ezek 28:12
testimony has set his **s** John 3:33
s of God on their Rev 9:4

SEAL (v) *mark, secure*
s-ed...his seal 1 Kin 21:8
s *it*...king's signet Esth 8:8
a spring **s-ed** up Song 4:12
to **s** up vision Dan 9:24
s up the book until Dan 12:4

SEARCH *examine, inquire*
LORD **s-es** all hearts 1 Chr 28:9
S me, O God, and Ps 139:23
LORD, **s** the heart Jer 17:10
s for the Child Matt 2:13
companions **s-ed** for Mark 1:36
You **s** the Scriptures John 5:39

SEASHORE *sea coast*
sand that is on the **s** Josh 11:4
the **s** in abundance 1 Kin 4:20
the dragon stood on...**s** Rev 13:1

SEASON *time of the year*
rains in their **s** Lev 26:4
grain in its **s** Job 5:26
its fruit in its **s** Ps 1:3
in **s** *and* out of **s** 2 Tim 4:2

SEAT (n) *chair, stool*
mercy **s** of pure gold Ex 25:17
sit in the **s** of scoffers Ps 1:1
sit in the **s** of gods Ezek 28:2
s-s in the synagogues Matt 23:6
before...judgment **s** Rom 14:10

SEAT (v) *sit*
s-ed at the Lord's feet Luke 10:39
coming, **s-ed**...colt John 12:15
s-ed at the right hand Col 3:1

SECRET *what is hidden*
sets *it* up in **s** Deut 27:15
the **s-s** of wisdom Job 11:6
the **s-s** of the heart Ps 44:21
bread *eaten* in **s** Prov 9:17
A gift in **s** subdues Prov 21:14
have not spoken in **s** Is 45:19
giving will be in **s** Matt 6:4
Father who sees...in **s** Matt 6:4
God will judge the **s-s** Rom 2:16

SECT *faction, party*
s of the Sadducees Acts 5:17
s of the Pharisees Acts 15:5
s of the Nazarenes Acts 24:5

SECURE *safe, stable*
overthrows the **s** Job 12:19
be **s** on their land Ezek 34:27
s in the mountain Amos 6:1
made the grave **s** Matt 27:66

SECURITY *certainty, safety*
Israel dwells in **s** Deut 33:28
in it living in **s** Judg 18:7
provides them with **s** Job 24:23
will lie down in **s** Is 14:30
will dwell in **s** Zech 14:11

SEDUCE *entice, persuade*
if a man **s-s** a virgin Ex 22:16
s you from...LORD Deut 13:10
s-d them to do evil 2 Kin 21:9
lips she **s-s** him Prov 7:21

SEE *look, perceive*
I have **s-n** God face Gen 32:30
No eye will **s** me Job 24:15
s the works of God Ps 66:5
the blind will **s** Is 29:18

s the glory of the LORD Is 35:2
to s but do not s Ezek 12:2
s your good works Matt 5:16
and the blind **s-ing** Matt 15:31
s the Son of Man Matt 16:28
s-ing their faith Mark 2:5
s-n Your salvation Luke 2:30
we **saw** His glory John 1:14
No one has **s-n** God John 1:18
s the Son of Man John 6:62
you will s Me John 16:16
may s My glory John 17:24
s in a mirror dimly 1 Cor 13:12
of things not **s-n** Heb 11:1
No one has **s-n** 1 John 4:12

SEED *descendant* or *plant*
sow your s uselessly Lev 26:16
establish your s Ps 89:4
O s of Abraham Ps 105:6
s to the sower Is 55:10
like a mustard s Matt 13:31
went out to sow his s Luke 8:5
s is the word of God Luke 8:11
s which is perishable 1 Pet 1:23
His s abides in him 1 John 3:9

SEEK *pursue, search for*
s the LORD your God Deut 4:29
pray, and s My face 2 Chr 7:14
S peace, and pursue it Ps 34:14
s me will find me Prov 8:17
man **s-s** only evil Prov 17:11
s wisdom and an Eccl 7:25
I will s the lost Ezek 34:16
time to s the LORD Hos 10:12
S good and not evil Amos 5:14
s first His kingdom Matt 6:33
s, and you will find Matt 7:7
s for a sign Mark 8:12
he who **s-s**, finds Luke 11:10
I do not s My glory John 8:50
s-ing the favor of men Gal 1:10
s-ing the things above Col 3:1

SEER *prophet*
prophets...every s 2 Kin 17:13
Who say to the **s-s** Is 30:10
Go, you s, flee away Amos 7:12
s-s will be ashamed Mic 3:7

SEIR
1 *land of Edom* Gen 32:3;36:8,9; Num 24:18; Ezek 25:8
2 *mountain range within Edom* Gen 14:6; Deut 1:2;2:4
3 *on boundary of Judah* Josh 11:17;15:10

SEIZE *grasp, take*
mother shall s him Deut 21:19
Babylon has been **s-d** Jer 50:46

and s her plunder Ezek 29:19
fields and then s *them* Mic 2:2
seeking to s Him John 7:30

SELA
rock city in Edom Judg 1:36; Is 16:1;42:11
also **Joktheel** 2 Kin 14:7
later known as Petra

SELAH
musical or liturgical sign Ps 3:2,4,8;20:3;60:4;81:7; Hab 3:3,9,13

SELEUCIA
port in N Syria Acts 13:4

SELF-CONTROL
s and the judgment Acts 24:25
your lack of s 1 Cor 7:5
gentleness, s Gal 5:23
without s, brutal 2 Tim 3:3
in *your* knowledge, s 2 Pet 1:6

SELFISH *self-centered*
the bread of a s man Prov 23:6
s ambition in your James 3:14

SELL *barter, trade*
s me your birthright Gen 25:31
s me food for money Deut 2:28
s the oil and pay 2 Kin 4:7
sold a girl for wine Joel 3:3
sold all that he had Matt 13:46
s-ing their property Acts 2:45
sold into bondage Rom 7:14

SELLER *merchant, trader*
the buyer like the s Is 24:2
a s of purple Acts 16:14

SENATE
Sanhedrin Acts 5:21
see also **COUNCIL**

SEND *convey, dispatch*
s rain on the earth Gen 7:4
he **sent** out a raven Gen 8:7
Whom shall I s Is 6:8
Lord God has **sent** Me Is 48:16
s-s rain on *the* Matt 5:45
He has **sent** Me Luke 4:18
s-ing His own Son Rom 8:3
not s her husband 1 Cor 7:13
s him...in peace 1 Cor 16:11
God **sent** forth His Son Gal 4:4

SENNACHERIB
king of Assyria 2 Kin 18:13;19:16,20; 2 Chr 32:1-22; Is 36:1;37:17

SENSUALITY
deceit, s, envy Mark 7:22
promiscuity and s Rom 13:13
themselves over to s Eph 4:19
the wealth of her s Rev 18:3

SENTENCE *judgment*
s is by the decree Dan 4:17

escape the s of hell Matt 23:33
Pilate pronounced s Luke 23:24
to the s of death Luke 24:20

SEPARATE *divide, set apart*
God **s-d** the light Gen 1:4
They s with the lip Ps 22:7
s-s intimate friends Prov 16:28
let no man s Matt 19:6
Who will s us from Rom 8:35

SEPARATION *division, isolation*
of his s to the LORD Num 6:6
his s he is holy Num 6:8
his s was defiled Num 6:12
have made a s Is 59:2

SEPHARAD
place in Assyria for Jerusalem exiles Obad 20

SEPHARVAIM
place in Aram; people relocated to Samaria 2 Kin 17:31; 18:34; Is 36:19;37:13

SERAPHIM
celestial beings Is 6:2,6

SERGIUS PAULUS
see **PAULUS, SERGIUS**

SERPENT *snake*
s was more crafty Gen 3:1
they turned into **s-s** Ex 7:12
viper and flying s Is 30:6
be shrewd as **s-s** Matt 10:16
will pick up **s-s** Mark 16:18
Moses lifted up the s John 3:14

SERVANT *helper, slave*
s of **s-s** He shall be Gen 9:25
Your s is listening 1 Sam 3:9
to shine upon Your s Ps 31:16
s-s of a new covenant 2 Cor 3:6
they **s-s** of Christ 2 Cor 11:23
s of Christ Jesus 1 Tim 4:6

SERVE *help, work for*
shall s the LORD Ex 23:25
s Him with...heart Josh 22:5
s-d as priests 1 Chr 24:2
you will s strangers Jer 5:19
God whom we s is Dan 3:17
s God and wealth Matt 6:24
If anyone **s-s** Me John 12:26
s-ing the Lord Rom 12:11
through love s one Gal 5:13

SERVICE *ministry, work*
s of righteous Is 32:17
spiritual s of worship Rom 12:1
for the work of s Eph 4:12
s with reverence Heb 12:28

SETH
son of Adam Gen 4:25,26;5:3-8; 1 Chr 1:1
line of Jesus Luke 3:38

SETTLED *arranged* or *inhabited*
Lot s in the cities Gen 13:12
cloud s over the Num 9:18
assault shall be s Deut 21:5
word is s in heaven Ps 119:89
mountains were s Prov 8:25
s in the lawful Acts 19:39

SEVEN *number*
Jacob served s years Gen 29:20
For s women...one man Is 4:1
will be s weeks Dan 9:25
s other spirits more Matt 12:45
forgive...s times Matt 18:21
John to the s churches Rev 1:4
s golden lampstands Rev 1:12

SEVERE *difficult, hard*
famine was s Gen 12:10
a very s pestilence Ex 9:3
s and lasting plagues Deut 28:59
s judgments against Ezek 14:21
a s earthquake had Matt 28:2

SEW *fasten, join*
s-ed fig leaves together Gen 3:7
s-ed sackcloth over Job 16:15
a time to s together Eccl 3:7
women who s *magic* Ezek 13:18

SEXUAL
not in s promiscuity Rom 13:13
from s immorality 1 Thess 4:3

SHACKLES *fetters*
will tear off your s Nah 1:13
s broken in pieces Mark 5:4
with chains and s Luke 8:29

SHADE *protection*
cover him with s Job 40:22
The LORD is your s Ps 121:5
lived under its s Ezek 31:6
over Jonah to be a s Jon 4:6
nest under its s Mark 4:32

SHADOW *image of shade*
days...like a s 1 Chr 29:15
the s of Your wings Ps 17:8
in the s...Almighty Ps 91:1
the **s-s** flee away Song 2:17
his s might fall on Acts 5:15
s of the heavenly Heb 8:5

SHADRACH
Hebrew: Hananiah Dan 1:7
friend of Daniel Dan 2:49;3:12-30

SHAKE *quiver, tremble*
made all my bones s Job 4:14
s my head at you Job 16:4
peace will not be **s-n** Is 54:10
s the dust off Matt 10:14
A reed **s-n** by the Matt 11:7
heavens will be **s-n** Luke 21:26

he **shook** the creature Acts 28:5
voice **shook** the earth Heb 12:26

SHALLUM
1 *king of Israel* 2 Kin 15:8-15
2 *Huldah's husband* 2 Kin 22:14
3 *son of Josiah* 1 Chr 3:15
king of Judah 2 Kin 23:31-33
called **JEHOAHAZ** 2 Kin 23:30
4 *gatekeeper* 1 Chr 9:17
5 *son of Zadok* 1 Chr 6:12
6 *time of Nehemiah* Neh 3:12
name of nine other men

SHALMANESER
king of Assyria 2 Kin 17:3;18:9

SHAME *disgrace, dishonor*
wicked be put to **s** Ps 31:17
my reproach and my **s** Ps 69:19
s to his mother Prov 29:15
wise men are put to **s** Jer 8:9
unjust knows no **s** Zeph 3:5
worthy to suffer **s** Acts 5:41
glory is in their **s** Phil 3:19
put Him to open **s** Heb 6:6

SHAMGAR
judge of Israel Judg 3:31;5:6

SHARE (n) *portion*
them take their **s** Gen 14:24
s from My offerings Lev 6:17
give me the **s** Luke 15:12
I do my **s** Col 1:24

SHARE (v) *partake, participate*
stranger does not **s** Prov 14:10
s in the inheritance Prov 17:2
s it...yourselves Luke 22:17
s all good things Gal 6:6
may **s** His holiness Heb 12:10
s the sufferings of 1 Pet 4:13

SHARON
coastal plain in central Israel Is 33:9; 65:10

SHARP *cutting*
their tongue a **s** sword Ps 57:4
S...two-edged sword Prov 5:4
Put in your **s** sickle Rev 14:18

SHATTER *break, burst*
s-ed every tree of the Ex 9:25
the mighty are **s-ed** 1 Sam 2:4
s them like earthenware Ps 2:9
s the doors of bronze Is 45:2
iron crushes and **s-s** Dan 2:40

SHAUL
1 *king of Edom* Gen 36:37,38
2 *son of Simeon* Gen 46:10
3 *Kohathite Levite* 1 Chr 6:24

SHAVE *cut* or *scrape*
he shall **s** his head Lev 14:9
s off the seven Judg 16:19
s-d off half of 2 Sam 10:4
will **s** with a razor Is 7:20

SHEAF *bundle of grain stalks*
s-ves in the field Gen 37:7
s of the first fruits Lev 23:10
among the **s-ves** Ruth 2:15

SHEARER *wool cutter*
silent before its **s-s** Is 53:7
lamb before its **s** Acts 8:32

SHEAR-JASHUB
son of Isaiah Is 7:3
name symbolizes prophecy

SHEBA
1 *son of Raamah* Gen 10:7
2 *son of Joktan* Gen 10:28
3 *grandson of Abraham* Gen 25:3
4 *Simeonite town* Josh 19:2
5 *a Benjamite* 2 Sam 20:1-7
6 *a Gadite* 1 Chr 5:13
7 *kingdom* Job 6:19; Ps 72:10,15; Jer 6:20
8 *Queen of* 2 Chr 9:1ff

SHEBAT
eleventh month of Hebrew calendar Zech 1:7

SHECHEM
1 *city in Ephraim hill country* Gen 12:6;33:18; 1 Chr 7:28
city of refuge Josh 20:7
2 *son of Hamor* Gen 34:2
3 *line of Manasseh* Num 26:31
4 *son of Shemida* 1 Chr 7:19

SHED *pour out*
Whoever **s-s** man's Gen 9:6
s streams of water Ps 119:136
hasten to **s** blood Prov 1:16
will not **s** its light Is 13:10
bribes to **s** blood Ezek 22:12
swift to **s** blood Rom 3:15
s-ding of blood Heb 9:22

SHEEP *animal*
Rachel came with...**s** Gen 29:9
not be like **s** Num 27:17
the fleece of my **s** Job 31:20
s of His pasture Ps 100:3
All of us like **s** Is 53:6
a **s** that is silent Is 53:7
will care for My **s** Ezek 34:12
lost **s** of...Israel Matt 10:6
s from the goats Matt 25:32
my **s** which was lost Luke 15:6
His life for the **s** John 10:11
s hear My voice John 10:27
Tend My **s** John 21:17
Shepherd of the **s** Heb 13:20

SHEEP GATE
see **GATES OF JERUSALEM**

SHEEPFOLDS *enclosure*
s for the flocks 2 Chr 32:28
lie down among the **s** Ps 68:13
took him from the **s** Ps 78:70

SHEEPSKINS *coverings*
they went about in **s** Heb 11:37

SHEET
hammered out gold **s-s** Ex 39:3
s over *his* naked Mark 14:51
object like a great **s** Acts 10:11

SHELTER *cover, refuge*
under the **s** of my Gen 19:8
in the **s** of Your wings Ps 61:4
a **s** to *give* shade Is 4:6
a **s** from the storm Is 32:2
made a **s** for himself Jon 4:5

SHEM
son of Noah Gen 5:32;6:10;9:27;11:11

SHEOL
place of the dead Gen 37:35; Job 7:9; Ps 49:15; Prov 15:11; Is 38:10; Ezek 32:27; Hab 2:5
see also **HADES** *and* **HELL**

SHEPHELAH
low hill country 1 Chr 27:28; Obad 19
see also **LOWLAND**

SHEPHERD (n)
sheep...have no **s** Num 27:17
The LORD is my **s** Ps 23:1
Like a **s** He Is 40:11
s-s after My own heart Jer 3:15
for lack of a **s** Ezek 34:5
raise up a **s** Zech 11:16
sheep without a **s** Matt 9:36
strike down the **s** Matt 26:31
s-s...in the fields Luke 2:8
I am the good **s** John 10:11
the great **S** Heb 13:20
the Chief **S** 1 Pet 5:4

SHEPHERD (v)
s My people 2 Sam 5:2
s My people Matt 2:6
S My sheep John 21:16
to **s** the church Acts 20:28
s the flock of God 1 Pet 5:2

SHESHBAZZAR
governor of Judah under Cyrus Ezra 5:14,16

SHIBBOLETH
test word for identification Judg 12:6

SHIELD *protection*
Abram, I am a **s** Gen 15:1
He is a **s** to all 2 Sam 22:31
My **s** is with God Ps 7:10
faithfulness is a **s** Ps 91:4
the **s** of faith Eph 6:16

SHILOH
1 *Messianic title* Gen 49:10
2 *town N of Bethel* Josh 18:1
site of tabernacle Judg 18:31

SHINAR
Babylonian plain Gen 10:10; Gen 11:2; Josh 7:21; Dan 1:2

SHINE *be radiant, glow*
his face **shone** Ex 34:29
His face **s** on you Num 6:25
Your face to **s** *upon us* Ps 80:3
light **s** before men Matt 5:16
s-s in the darkness John 1:5
lamp **s-ing** in a dark 2 Pet 1:19
Light is...**s-ing** 1 John 2:8

SHIP *boat*
a haven for **s-s** Gen 49:13
to the sea in **s-s** Ps 107:23
like merchant **s-s** Prov 31:14
escape from the **s** Acts 27:30

SHISHAK *see* **PHARAOH**

SHOOT *new growth*
s will spring from Is 11:1
like a tender **s** Is 53:2
His **s-s** will sprout Hos 14:6

SHORT *lacking*
Is My hand so **s** Is 50:2
days will be cut **s** Matt 24:22
s of the grace Heb 12:15

SHOULDER *part of body*
He bowed his **s** Gen 49:15
turned a stubborn **s** Neh 9:29
relieved his **s** Ps 81:6
government...on His **s-s** Is 9:6

SHOUT *cry out loudly*
s with a great **s** Josh 6:5
the people **s-ed** with Ezra 3:11
s for joy Ps 35:27
S joyfully to God Ps 66:1

SHOW *manifest, reveal*
land...I will **s** you Gen 12:1
s me Your glory Ex 33:18
s you the secrets Job 11:6
s Your lovingkindness Ps 17:7
s him his fault in private Matt 18:15
S us the Father John 14:9
God **s-s** no partiality Gal 2:6
s hospitality Heb 13:2
if you **s** partiality James 2:9

SHOWBREAD
tables of **s** 1 Chr 28:16
s is *set*...table 2 Chr 13:11

SHOWER *abundant flow*
roar of a *heavy* **s** 1 Kin 18:41
Like **s-s** that water Ps 72:6
be **s-s** of blessing Ezek 34:26
A **s** is coming Luke 12:54

SHREWD *cunning*
frustrates...the **s** Job 5:12
be **s** as serpents Matt 10:16

SHRINE *object of worship*
built yourself a **s** Ezek 16:24
tear down your **s-s** Ezek 16:39
who made silver **s-s** Acts 19:24

SHULAMMITE
title of young woman Song 6:13

SHUNAMMITE *from Shunem*
1 *David's nurse* 1 Kin 1:3,15;2:17,21,22

2 *hostess of Elisha* 2 Kin 4:12ff

SHUR *wilderness in NW Sinai*
Gen 16:7;20:1; Ex 15:22; 1 Sam 15:7

SHUT *close*
wilderness has s them Ex 14:3
s the lions' mouths Dan 6:22
power to s up the sky Rev 11:6

SIBBOLETH *test word for identification*
Judg 12:6

SICK *unwell*
strengthen the s Ezek 34:16
lying s with a fever Mark 1:30
Lazarus was s John 11:2
anyone among you s James 5:14

SICKLE *cutting tool*
who wields the s Jer 50:16
sharp s in His hand Rev 14:14
Put in your s Rev 14:15

SICKNESS *illness*
remove from you...s Deut 7:15
every kind of s Matt 4:23
authority over...s Matt 10:1
s is not to end in death John 11:4

SIDON
1 *son of Canaan* Gen 10:15; 1 Chr 1:13
2 *Phoenician port* Gen 10:19; Is 23:4; Ezek 28:22

SIEGE *encirclement*
throw up a s ramp 2 Kin 19:32
city came under s 2 Kin 24:10
their s towers Is 23:13
s against Jerusalem Jer 6:6
build a s wall Ezek 4:2

SIGHT *perception, vision*
pleasing to the s Gen 2:9
acceptable in Your s Ps 19:14
precious in My s Is 43:4
blind receive s Matt 11:5
three days without s Acts 9:9
by faith, not by s 2 Cor 5:7

SIGN *indication* or *wonder*
a s for Cain Gen 4:15
s of the covenant Gen 9:12
this shall be the s Ex 3:12
blood shall be a s Ex 12:13
His s-s in Egypt Ps 78:43
Ask a s for yourself Is 7:11
an everlasting s Is 55:13
a s from You Matt 12:38
s of Your coming Matt 24:3
show s-s and Mark 13:22
s-s in sun and moon Luke 21:25
beginning of *His* s-s John 2:11
s of circumcision Rom 4:11
Jews ask for s-s 1 Cor 1:22
tongues are for a s 1 Cor 14:22
s-s...false wonders 2 Thess 2:9

SIGNET *seal*
examine...whose s Gen 38:25
engravings of a s Ex 39:14
s rings of his nobles Dan 6:17

SILAS *co-worker with Paul*
Acts 15:22,32,40; 16:19,25;17:4,10,14
also **Silvanus**

SILENCE *quietness*
My soul *waits* in s Ps 62:1
war will be s-d Jer 50:30
s the ignorance 1 Pet 2:15
s in heaven Rev 8:1

SILENT *quiet*
LORD, do not keep s Ps 35:22
A time to be s Eccl 3:7
But Jesus kept s Matt 26:63
women...keep s 1 Cor 14:34

SILOAM
1 *tower in Jerusalem* Luke 13:4
2 *water pool in Jerusalem* John 9:7,11

SILVANUS *see* **SILAS**

SILVER *precious metal*
rich in...s Gen 13:2
took no plunder in s Judg 5:19
as s is refined Ps 66:10
in settings of s Prov 25:11
s has become dross Is 1:22
The s is Mine Hag 2:8
not acquire...s Matt 10:9
thirty pieces of s Matt 26:15

SIMEON
1 *son of Jacob* Gen 29:33
2 *tribe* Num 1:23; Rev 7:7
3 *devout Jew* Luke 2:25
4 *ancestor of Jesus* Luke 3:30
5 *Christian prophet* Acts 13:1
6 *Simon Peter* Acts 15:14

SIMON
1 *apostle* Matt 4:18; Mark 1:16
see also **PETER**
2 *the Zealot* Matt 10:4; Mark 3:18; Luke 6:15
3 *brother of Jesus* Matt 13:55; Mark 6:3
4 *leper* Matt 26:6; Mark 14:3
5 *a Pharisee* Luke 7:40,43
6 *of Cyrene* Matt 27:32
carried Jesus' cross Mark 15:21; Luke 23:26
7 *father of Judas* John 6:71;13:2
8 *Magus* Acts 8:9,13,18
sorcerer
9 *the tanner* Acts 9:43;10:6,32

SIMPLE *innocent* or *humble*
making wise the s Ps 19:7
LORD preserves the s Ps 116:6

SIN (n) *transgression*
please forgive my s Ex 10:17
atonement for your s Ex 32:30
purification from s Num 19:9
s will find you out Num 32:23
s of divination 1 Sam 15:23
the s-s of my youth Ps 25:7
s my mother conceived Ps 51:5
Fools mock at s Prov 14:9
bore the s of many Is 53:12
s-s of her prophets Lam 4:13
an eternal s Mark 3:29
forgive us our s-s Luke 11:4
takes away the s John 1:29
wash away your s-s Acts 22:16
wages of s is death Rom 6:23
died for our s-s 1 Cor 15:3
Him who knew no s 2 Cor 5:21
pleasures of s Heb 11:25
confess your s-s James 5:16
a multitude of s-s James 5:20
confess our s-s 1 John 1:9
s is lawlessness 1 John 3:4

SIN (v) *transgress*
When a leader s-s Lev 4:22
s against the LORD 1 Sam 14:34
Job did not s Job 1:22
s against You Ps 119:11
Father, I have s-ned Luke 15:18
s no more John 8:11
all have s-ned Rom 3:23
that you may not s 1 John 2:1

SIN
1 *wilderness in Sinai* Ex 16:1; Num 33:11,12
2 *Egyptian city* Ezek 30:15,16

SIN OFFERING
see **OFFERINGS**

SINAI
1 *mountain* Ex 19:11; Lev 26:46; Num 28:6
where Law received Ex 31:18;34:29
see also **HOREB**
2 *desert wilderness* Ex 16:1; 19:1; Num 1:19;9:5

SINCERE *without deceit*
be s and blameless Phil 1:10
mindful of the s faith 2 Tim 1:5
s love...brethren 1 Pet 1:22

SINEW *strength* or *tendon*
with bones and s-s Job 10:11
neck is an iron s Is 48:4
will put s-s on you Ezek 37:6

SINFUL *wicked*
a brood of s men Num 32:14
s generation Mark 8:38
I am a s man Luke 5:8
likeness of s flesh Rom 8:3

SING
s to the LORD Ex 15:1
s-ing and dancing 1 Sam 18:6
I will s praises 2 Sam 22:50
morning stars **sang** Job 38:7
S to Him a new song Ps 33:3
the righteous s-s Prov 29:6
birds will s Zeph 2:14
after s-ing a hymn Mark 14:26
s-ing...thankfulness Col 3:16
sang a new song Rev 5:9

SINGERS
these are the s 1 Chr 9:33
male and female s Eccl 2:8

SINK *descend, fall*
do not let me s Ps 69:14
so shall Babylon s Jer 51:64

SINNER *wrongdoer*
He instructs s-s Ps 25:8
if s-s entice you Prov 1:10
Adversity...s-s Prov 13:21
one s destroys much Eccl 9:18
a friend of...s-s Matt 11:19
one s who repents Luke 15:7
merciful to me...s Luke 18:13
God...not hear s-s John 9:31
while we were yet s-s Rom 5:8
came...to save s-s 1 Tim 1:15

SISERA
1 *Canaanite warrior* Judg 4:2ff
2 *class of Nethinim* Ezra 2:53; Neh 7:55

SISTER
She is my s Gen 12:19
We have a little s Song 8:8
a s called Mary Luke 10:39
commend...our s Rom 16:1
younger women...s-s 1 Tim 5:2

SIT *recline, rest*
Moses **sat** to judge Ex 18:13
Nor s in the seat Ps 1:1
S at My right hand Ps 110:1
lonely s-s the city Lam 1:1
s down on the grass Matt 14:19
who s in darkness Luke 1:79
dead man **sat** up Luke 7:15
where the harlot s-s Rev 17:15

SIVAN
third month of Hebrew calendar Esth 8:9

SKILL *proficiency*
filled them with s Ex 35:35
the heavens with s Ps 136:5
work of s-ed men Jer 10:9
s-ed in destruction Ezek 21:31

SKILLFUL *accomplished*
became a s hunter Gen 25:27
s player on...harp 1 Sam 16:16
praises with a s psalm Ps 47:7

SKIN *covering*
garments of s Gen 3:21
s of his face shone Ex 34:29
Clothe me with s Job 10:11
My s turns black Job 30:30
will burst the s-s Mark 2:22

SKIP *hop, leap*
children **s** about Job 21:11
Lebanon **s** like a calf Ps 29:6
go forth and **s** Mal 4:2

SKULL *bony framework of head*
head, crushing his **s** Judg 9:53
the **s** and the feet 2 Kin 9:35
Place of a **S** Matt 27:33

SKY *heavens*
sun stopped in...**s** Josh 10:13
the **s** grew black 1 Kin 18:45
witness in the **s** Ps 89:37
s will be rolled up Is 34:4
for the **s** is red Matt 16:2
will appear in the **s** Matt 24:30
s was shut up Luke 4:25
gazing...into the **s** Acts 1:10
s was split apart Rev 6:14

SLANDER (n) *defamation*
spreads **s** is a fool Prov 10:18
s-s, gossip 2 Cor 12:20
and **s** be put away Eph 4:31

SLANDER (v) *defame*
He does not **s** Ps 15:3
Whoever secretly **s-s** Ps 101:5
Do not **s** a slave Prov 30:10

SLANDERER *defamer*
s separates...friends Prov 16:28
s-s, haters of God Rom 1:30

SLAUGHTER (n) *brutal killing*
great **s** at Gibeon Josh 10:10
lamb led to the **s** Jer 11:19
as a sheep to **s** Acts 8:32
in a day of **s** James 5:5

SLAUGHTER (v) *kill*
shall **s** the bull Ex 29:11
shall **s** the lamb Lev 14:25
Who **s** the children Is 57:5
s-ed My children Ezek 16:21

SLAVE *bondservant*
The Hebrew **s** Gen 39:17
s at forced labor Gen 49:15
sold *in* a **s** sale Lev 25:42
Is Israel a **s** Jer 2:14
S-s rule over us Lam 5:8
s above his master Matt 10:24
good and faithful **s** Matt 25:21
shall be **s** of all Mark 10:44
is the **s** of sin John 8:34
neither **s** nor free Gal 3:28
as **s-s** of Christ Eph 6:6

SLAVERY *servitude*
from the house of **s** Ex 13:3
ransomed you from...**s** Mic 6:4
received a spirit of **s** Rom 8:15
to a yoke of **s** Gal 5:1

SLAY *destroy, kill*
knife to **s** his son Gen 22:10
s-s the foolish Job 5:2
Though He **s** me Job 13:15
Evil...**s** the wicked Ps 34:21
s her with thirst Hos 2:3
Lamb that was **slain** Rev 5:12

SLEEP (n) *rest*
caused a deep **s** Gen 2:21
Do not love **s** Prov 20:13
a spirit of deep **s** Is 29:10
s fled from him Dan 6:18
overcome by **s** Acts 20:9

SLEEP (v) *slumber*
why do You **s** Ps 44:23
neither slumber nor **s** Ps 121:4
who **s-s** in harvest Prov 10:5
found them **s-ing** Matt 26:43
we will not all **s** 1 Cor 15:51

SLOW *not quick*
I am **s** of speech Ex 4:10
gracious, **S** to anger Ps 103:8
to hear, **s** to speak James 1:19
Lord is not **s** 2 Pet 3:9

SLUGGARD *lazy one*
to the ant, O **s** Prov 6:6
the **s** craves Prov 13:4
the **s** buries his hand Prov 26:15

SLUMBER *sleep*
s in their beds Job 33:15
He...will not **s** Ps 121:3
None **s-s** or sleeps Is 5:27
Dreamers...love to **s** Is 56:10

SMALL *little*
both **s** and great 2 Kin 25:26
s among the nations Jer 49:15
day of **s** things Zech 4:10
For the gate is **s** Matt 7:14
a few **s** fish Mark 8:7
he was **s** in stature Luke 19:3
tongue is a **s** part James 3:5

SMILE *grin*
I **s-d** on them Job 29:24
that I may **s** *again* Ps 39:13
she **s-s** at the future Prov 31:25

SMITE *hit, strike*
s...with frogs Ex 8:2
smote Job with sore Job 2:7
sun will not **s** you Ps 121:6
righteous **s** me Ps 141:5

SMITH *worker of metal*
a vessel for the **s** Prov 25:4
created the **s** who Is 54:16
s-s from Jerusalem Jer 24:1

SMOKE *mist, vapor*
s...ascended Gen 19:28
Sinai *was* all in **s** Ex 19:18
like **s** they vanish Ps 37:20
temple was filling with **s** Is 6:4
s rises up forever Rev 19:3

SMOOTH *no roughness*
I am a **s** man Gen 27:11
five **s** stones 1 Sam 17:40
Make **s**...a highway Is 40:3
the rough roads **s** Luke 3:5
s...flattering speech Rom 16:18

SMYRNA
city in Asia Minor Rev 1:11;2:8

SNAKE *serpent*
horned **s** in the path Gen 49:17
a **s** bites him Amos 5:19
s instead of a fish Luke 11:11

SNARE *trap*
gods will be a **s** Judg 2:3
s-s of death 2 Sam 22:6
laid a **s** for me Ps 119:110
his lips are the **s** Prov 18:7
caught in My **s** Ezek 12:13
table become a **s** Rom 11:9
s of the devil 1 Tim 3:7

SNOW *ice flakes*
storehouses of the **s** Job 38:22
be whiter than **s** Ps 51:7
He gives **s** like wool Ps 147:16
Like **s** in summer Prov 26:1
as white as **s** Matt 28:3

SOBER *serious, temperate*
words of **s** truth Acts 26:25
be alert and **s** 1 Thess 5:6
Be of **s** *spirit* 1 Pet 5:8

SODOM
city S of Dead Sea Gen 10:19
home of Lot Gen 19:1,4
destroyed by God Gen 19:24

SODOMITE
one guilty of unnatural sexual practices 1 Kin 22:46

SOFT *kind*
speak to you **s** words Job 41:3
s tongue breaks the Prov 25:15

SOIL *earth, ground*
first fruits of your **s** Ex 23:19
he loved the **s** 2 Chr 26:10
fell into the good **s** Mark 4:8
produce of the **s** James 5:7

SOJOURN *visit temporarily*
S in this land Gen 26:3
stranger **s-s** with you Ex 12:48
s...land of Moab Ruth 1:1

SOJOURNER
s in a foreign land Ex 2:22
are **s-s** before You 1 Chr 29:15
oppressed the **s** Ezek 22:29

SOLDIER *military man*
s-s took Him away Mark 15:16
s-s also mocked Luke 23:36
s-s pierced His side John 19:34
a devout **s** Acts 10:7
good **s** of Christ 2 Tim 2:3

SOLEMN *deeply earnest, serious*
sabbath of **s** rest Lev 16:31
have a **s** assembly Num 29:35
sworn **s** oaths Ezek 21:23
bound...a **s** oath Acts 23:14

SOLOMON
1 *son of David* 2 Sam 12:24
king of Israel 1 Kin 1:43
ruled wisely 1 Kin 4:29,34
built the Temple 1 Kin 6:2;9:1
international fame 1 Kin 10:1
ruled foolishly 1 Kin 11:6
death 1 Kin 11:43
2 *Song of Solomon also* **Song of Songs**

SON *male descendant*
the **s-s** of Noah Gen 9:18
Take...your only **s** Gen 22:2
O Absalom, my **s** 2 Sam 18:33
to be a **s** to Me 1 Chr 28:6
s-s of God shouted Job 38:7
You are My **S** Ps 2:7
wise **s** makes a Prov 10:1
Discipline your **s** Prov 19:18
bear a **s**...Immanuel Is 7:14
Egypt I called My **s** Hos 11:1
she gave birth to a **S** Matt 1:25
This is My beloved **S** Matt 3:17
the carpenter's **s** Matt 13:55
I am the **S** of God Matt 27:43
S of Man...suffer Mark 8:31
her firstborn **s** Luke 2:7
If You are the **S** Luke 4:3
man had two **s-s** Luke 15:11
only begotten **S** John 3:16
S also gives life John 5:21
become **s-s** of Light John 12:36
sending His own **S** Rom 8:3
image of His **S** Rom 8:29
not spare His own **S** Rom 8:32
fellowship with His **S** 1 Cor 1:9
if a **s**, then an heir Gal 4:7
shall be a **S** to Me Heb 1:5
abide in the **S** 1 John 2:24
He who has the **S** 1 John 5:12

SON-IN-LAW
the **s** of the Timnite Judg 15:6
be the king's **s** 1 Sam 18:18
s of Sanballat Neh 13:28

SON OF GOD
Messianic title indicating deity of Jesus Christ
Matt 4:3;8:29;16:16; Mark 1:20;3:11;14:61; Luke 1:35; John 3:13;11:27; Acts 8:37

SON OF MAN
Messianic title of Jesus Christ
Matt 8:20;9:6; Mark 2:10;10:33; Luke 12:10;18:31; John 6:27;13:31

SONG *melody, music*
LORD is my...**s** Ex 15:2
ministered with **s** 1 Chr 6:32
gives **s-s** in the night Job 35:10
s-s of deliverance Ps 32:7
Sing to Him a new **s** Ps 33:3
A **s** of my beloved Is 5:1

Praise the LORD in **s** Is 12:5
not drink wine with **s** Is 24:9
hymns...spiritual **s-s** Eph 5:19

SORCERER *witch*
interprets...or a **s** Deut 18:10
witness against the **s-s** Mal 3:5
immoral persons...**s-s** Rev 21:8

SORCERY *witchcraft*
practiced **s** 2 Chr 33:6
idolatry, **s**, enmities Gal 5:20
deceived by your **s** Rev 18:23

SORDID *filthy*
fond of **s** gain 1 Tim 3:8
the sake of **s** gain Titus 1:11
not for **s** gain 1 Pet 5:2

SOREK
valley SW of Jerusalem
Judg 16:4

SORROW *grief, sadness*
down to Sheol in **s** Gen 42:38
life is spent with **s** Ps 31:10
man of **s-s** Is 53:3
s is beyond healing Jer 8:18
if I cause you **s** 2 Cor 2:2

SOSTHENES
1 *synagogue leader* Acts 18:17
2 *Corinthian believer* 1 Cor 1:27

SOUL *life, spirit*
her **s** was departing Gen 35:18
humble your **s-s** Lev 16:29
poured out my **s** 1 Sam 1:15
not abandon my **s** Ps 16:10
He restores my **s** Ps 23:3
my **s** pants for You Ps 42:1
Bless...LORD, O my **s** Ps 103:1
who is wise wins **s-s** Prov 11:30
s who sins will die Ezek 18:4
unable to kill the **s** Matt 10:28
exchange for his **s** Matt 16:26
My **s** is...grieved Matt 26:38
and forfeit his **s** Mark 8:36
My **s** exalts the Lord Luke 1:46
your **s** is required Luke 12:20
one heart and **s** Acts 4:32
an anchor of the **s** Heb 6:19
able to save your **s-s** James 1:21
save his **s** from James 5:20
war against the **s** 1 Pet 2:11

SOUND (adj) *accurate, stable*
s wisdom...two sides Job 11:6
I give you **s** teaching Prov 4:2
the **s** doctrine 1 Tim 4:6

SOUND (n) *noise*
s of You in...garden Gen 3:10
s of war in the camp Ex 32:17
s of a great army 2 Kin 7:6
s of many waters Ezek 43:2

SOUND (v) *express*
s His praise abroad Ps 66:8
s an alarm Joel 2:1
trumpet will **s** 1 Cor 15:52

SOUR *distasteful, tart*
eaten **s** grapes Jer 31:29
offering...**s** wine Luke 23:36

SOURCE *origin*
the **s** of sapphires Job 28:6
s of eternal salvation Heb 5:9
s of quarrels James 4:1

SOVEREIGNTY *authority*
His **s** rules over all Ps 103:19
s from Damascus Is 17:3
s will be uprooted Dan 11:4

SOW *plant, spread*
you may **s** the land Gen 47:23
s your seed uselessly Lev 26:16
who **s** in tears Ps 126:5
who **s-s** iniquity will Prov 22:8
they **s** the wind Hos 8:7
birds...do not **s** Matt 6:26
s good seed Matt 13:27
s-ed spiritual things 1 Cor 9:11
whatever a man **s-s** Gal 6:7

SOWER *planter*
seed to the **s** Is 55:10
s went out to sow Matt 13:3
s sows the word Mark 4:14

SPAIN
S European land
Rom 15:24,28

SPARE *save* or *be lenient*
did not **s** their soul Ps 78:50
No man **s-s** his brother Is 9:19
not **s** His own Son Rom 8:32
I will not **s** *anyone* 2 Cor 13:2
God did not **s** angels 2 Pet 2:4

SPEAK *proclaim, tell*
God **spoke** to Noah Gen 8:15
God **s-s** with man Deut 5:24
S of all His wonders 1 Chr 16:9
He who **s-s** falsehood Ps 101:7
and a time to **s** Eccl 3:7
the mute to **s** Mark 7:37
s of what we know John 3:11
Never has a man **spoken** John 7:46
s with other tongues Acts 2:4
we **s** God's wisdom 1 Cor 2:7
If I **s** with...tongues 1 Cor 13:1

SPEAR *weapon*
leaning on his **s** 2 Sam 1:6
s-s into pruning hooks Is 2:4
pruning hooks into **s-s** Joel 3:10
pierced...with a **s** John 19:34

SPECK *particle*
regarded as a **s** of Is 40:15
s out of your eye Matt 7:4

SPEECH *message, word*
I am slow of **s** Ex 4:10
His **s** was smoother Ps 55:21
in cleverness of **s** 1 Cor 1:17
I am unskilled in **s** 2 Cor 11:6

SPELL *incantation*
one who casts a **s** Deut 18:11
skillful caster of **s-s** Ps 58:5
power of your **s-s** Is 47:9

SPICE
s and the oil Ex 35:28
mix in the **s-s** Ezek 24:10
prepared **s-s** and Luke 23:56
wrappings with...**s-s** John 19:40

SPIES (n) *clandestine persons*
we are not **s** Gen 42:31
two men as **s** Josh 2:1
David sent out **s** 1 Sam 26:4
welcomed the **s** Heb 11:31

SPIN *make thread*
nor do they **s** Matt 6:28
neither toil nor **s** Luke 12:27

SPIRIT
S rested upon them Num 11:26
God sent an evil **s** Judg 9:23
My **s** is broken Job 17:1
renew a steadfast **s** Ps 51:10
my **s** grows faint Ps 77:3
a haughty **s** before Prov 16:18
the **S** lifted me up Ezek 3:14
his **s** was troubled Dan 2:1
four **s-s** of heaven Zech 6:5
are the poor in **s** Matt 5:3
authority over...**s-s** Matt 10:1
put My **S** upon Him Matt 12:18
blasphemy...the **S** Matt 12:31
yielded up *His* **s** Matt 27:50
S like a dove Mark 1:10
s...not have flesh Luke 24:39
born of...the **S** John 3:5
worship in **s** and John 4:24
gave up His **s** John 19:30
pour forth of My **S** Acts 2:17
Jesus, receive my **s** Acts 7:59
power of the **S** Rom 15:19
taught by the **s** 1 Cor 2:13
pray with the **s** 1 Cor 14:15
walk by the **S** Gal 5:16
fruit of the **S** is love Gal 5:22
one body and one **S** Eph 4:4
be filled with the **S** Eph 5:18
sword of the **S** Eph 6:17
not quench the **S** 1 Thess 5:19
division of soul and **s** Heb 4:12
the **s-s** *now* in prison 1 Pet 3:19
S who testifies 1 John 5:6
see also **HOLY SPIRIT**

SPIRIT OF GOD
the **S** was moving Gen 1:2
S came upon him 1 Sam 10:10
a vision by the **S** Ezek 11:24
S descending as a Matt 3:16
being led by the **S** Rom 8:14
S dwells in you 1 Cor 3:16
worship in the **S** Phil 3:3
see also **HOLY SPIRIT**

SPIRIT OF THE LORD
S came upon him Judg 3:10
S departed from 1 Sam 16:14
S gave them rest Is 63:14
filled with...the **S** Mic 3:8
S is upon Me Luke 4:18
see also **HOLY SPIRIT**

SPIRITIST *medium*
not turn to...**s-s** Lev 19:31
s...be put to death Lev 20:27
removed...the **s-s** 2 Kin 23:24

SPIRITUAL *of the spirit*
the Law is **s** Rom 7:14
s service of worship Rom 12:1
raised a **s** body 1 Cor 15:44
with every **s** blessing Eph 1:3
hymns and **s** songs Eph 5:19
offer up **s** sacrifices 1 Pet 2:5

SPIT
began to **s** at Him Mark 14:65
and **s** upon Luke 18:32
He **spat** on...ground John 9:6
I will **s** you out Rev 3:16

SPLENDOR *magnificence*
the moon going in **s** Job 31:26
displayed Your **s** Ps 8:1
Your **s** and Your majesty Ps 45:3
clothed with **s** Ps 104:1
s covers the heavens Hab 3:3

SPLIT *divide*
He **s** the rock Is 48:21
valleys will be **s** Mic 1:4
Mount...will be **s** Zech 14:4
sky was **s** apart Rev 6:14

SPOIL *booty, pillage*
he divides the **s** Gen 49:27
the **s** of the cities Deut 2:35
divide the **s** with Prov 16:19
widows may be their **s** Is 10:2
for **s** to the nations Ezek 25:7

SPONGE *absorbent matter*
taking a **s**, he filled Matt 27:48
a **s** with sour wine Mark 15:36

SPOT *speck*
Or the leopard his **s-s** Jer 13:23
no **s** or wrinkle Eph 5:27

SPOTLESS *no defects*
unblemished and **s** 1 Pet 1:19
s and blameless 2 Pet 3:14

SPREAD *stretch out*
He **s** His wings Deut 32:11
I **s** My skirt over Ezek 16:8
death **s** to all men Rom 5:12

SPRING (adj) *period, season*
has been no **s** rain Jer 3:3
Like the **s** rain Hos 6:3
s crop began to sprout Amos 7:1

SPRING (n) *water source*
went down to the **s** Gen 24:16

twelve **s-s** of water Ex 15:27
stop all **s-s** of water 2 Kin 3:19
s-s of the deep...fixed Prov 8:28
the **s-s** of salvation Is 12:3
s of the water of life Rev 21:6

SPRING (v) *jump, leap*
S up, O well Num 21:17
Truth **s-s** from the Ps 85:11
s-ing up to eternal John 4:14

SPRINKLE *scatter*
take its blood and **s** Ex 29:16
s some of the blood Lev 4:6
s *it* seven times Lev 4:17
s some of the oil Lev 14:16

SPY (v) *investigate*
Moses sent...to **s** Num 13:17
to **s** out Jericho Josh 6:25
spied out Bethel Judg 1:23
s out our liberty Gal 2:4

SQUARE *area* or *shape*
altar shall be **s** Ex 27:1
voice in the **s** Prov 1:20
city is...a **s** Rev 21:16

STAFF *rod*
s of God in his hand Ex 4:20
Your **s**, they comfort Ps 23:4
or sandals, or a **s** Matt 10:10
a mere **s**; no bread Mark 6:8

STAIN *blemish*
s of your iniquity Jer 2:22
without **s**...reproach 1 Tim 6:14

STAND *maintain position*
s before the LORD Deut 10:8
O sun, **s** still Josh 10:12
s before kings Prov 22:29
word of our God **s-s** Is 40:8
will **s** on the Mount Zech 14:4
love to **s** and pray Matt 6:5
s-ing by the cross John 19:25
why do you **s** looking Acts 1:11
s by your faith Rom 11:20
s before...judgment Rom 14:10
s firm in the faith 1 Cor 16:13
foundation...**s-s** 2 Tim 2:19
I **s** at the door Rev 3:20

STANDARD *banner* or *rule*
set up their own **s-s** Ps 74:4
set up My **s** Is 49:22
s of the Law Acts 22:12
s of sound words 2 Tim 1:13

STAR *heavenly body*
He made the **s-s** Gen 1:16
s shall come forth Num 24:17
morning **s-s** sang Job 38:7
s of the morning Is 14:12
s-s for light by night Jer 31:35
His **s** in the east Matt 2:2
morning **s** arises 2 Pet 1:19
wandering **s-s** Jude 13
s fell from heaven Rev 8:10
the bright morning **s** Rev 22:16

STATE *position*
s of expectation Luke 3:15
of our humble **s** Phil 3:21
s has become worse 2 Pet 2:20

STATEMENT *assertion*
let your **s** be Matt 5:37
trap Him in a **s** Mark 12:13
catch Him in...**s** Luke 20:20
This is a difficult **s** John 6:60

STATURE *height*
was growing in **s** 1 Sam 2:26
in wisdom and **s** Luke 2:52
he was small in **s** Luke 19:3
measure of the **s** Eph 4:13

STATUTE *law, rule*
My **s-s** and My laws Gen 26:5
a perpetual **s** Ex 29:9
keep My **s-s** Lev 18:5
Teach me Your **s-s** Ps 119:26
not walked in My **s-s** Ezek 5:7

STEADFAST *established, firm*
be **s** and not fear Job 11:15
renew a **s** spirit Ps 51:10
My heart is **s** Ps 57:7
s in righteousness Prov 11:19
be **s**, immovable 1 Cor 15:58

STEAL *rob, take*
You shall not **s** Ex 20:15
be in want and **s** Prov 30:9
thieves break in...**s** Matt 6:19
Do not **s** Mark 10:19

STEPHANAS
Corinthian Christian 1 Cor 1:16;16:15,17

STEPHEN
deacon Acts 6:5,8
martyred Acts 7:59;8:2

STEPS *distance* or *movements*
number my **s** Job 14:16
s...bathed in butter Job 29:6
His **s** do not slip Ps 37:31
s take hold of Sheol Prov 5:5
in the **s** of the faith Rom 4:12
follow in His **s** 1 Pet 2:21

STEWARD *supervisor*
and sensible **s** Luke 12:42
s-s of the mysteries 1 Cor 4:1
above reproach...**s** Titus 1:7

STEWARDSHIP *responsibility*
a **s** entrusted to me 1 Cor 9:17
s of God's grace Eph 3:2

STIFFEN *make rigid*
s your neck no longer Deut 10:16
do not **s** your neck 2 Chr 30:8
have **s-ed** their necks Jer 19:15

STILL *motionless* or *quiet*
O sun, stand **s** Josh 10:12
the storm to be **s** Ps 107:29
Why are we sitting **s** Jer 8:14
sea, Hush, be **s** Mark 4:39

STIMULATE *excite*
how to **s** my body Eccl 2:3
s one another to Heb 10:24

STING *pain*
where is your **s** 1 Cor 15:55
s of death is sin 1 Cor 15:56

STIR *agitate*
S up Yourself Ps 35:23
word **s-s** up anger Prov 15:1
man **s-s** up strife Prov 29:22
s-red up the water John 5:4

STOCKS *confinement*
put my feet in the **s** Job 13:27
Jeremiah from the **s** Jer 20:3
their feet in the **s** Acts 16:24

STOMACH *part of body*
s will be satisfied Prov 18:20
s of the fish Jon 1:17
Food is for the **s** 1 Cor 6:13
s was made bitter Rev 10:10

STONE (n) *rock*
they used brick for **s** Gen 11:3
two **s** tablets Ex 34:1
do these **s-s** mean Josh 4:6
five smooth **s-s** 1 Sam 17:40
there was no **s** seen 1 Kin 6:18
Water wears...**s-s** Job 14:19
foot against a **s** Ps 91:12
in Zion a **s** Is 28:16
take the heart of **s** Ezek 11:19
serving wood and **s** Ezek 20:32
foot against a **s** Matt 4:6
will give him a **s** Matt 7:9
rolled away the **s** Matt 28:2
s-s will cry out Luke 19:40
six **s** waterpots John 2:6
first to throw a **s** John 8:7
Remove the **s** John 11:39
s-s, wood, hay 1 Cor 3:12
as to a living **s** 1 Pet 2:4
A **s** of stumbling 1 Pet 2:8

STONE (v) *throw stones*
people will **s** us Luke 20:6
seeking to **s** You John 11:8
went on **s-ing** Stephen Acts 7:59
they **s-d** Paul Acts 14:19

STOP *cease*
the sun **s-ped** Josh 10:13
And the oil **s-ped** 2 Kin 4:6
put a **s** to sacrifice Dan 9:27
s weeping for Me Luke 23:28
s sinning 1 Cor 15:34

STORE *accumulate*
s up the grain Gen 41:35
His sin is **s-d** up Hos 13:12
s up...treasures Matt 6:20
place to **s** my crops Luke 12:17
s-d up your treasure James 5:3

STOREHOUSE *storage place*
s-s of the snow Job 38:22
wind from His **s-s** Jer 10:13
tithe into the **s** Mal 3:10

STORK *bird*
the **s**, the heron Lev 11:19
the **s** in the sky Jer 8:7
wings of a **s** Zech 5:9

STORM *tempest, whirlwind*
A refuge from the **s** Is 25:4
will come like a **s** Ezek 38:9
a great **s** on the sea Jon 1:4
mists driven by a **s** 2 Pet 2:17

STRAIGHT *direct*
Make Your way **s** Ps 5:8
make your paths **s** Prov 3:6
Make His paths **s** Matt 3:3
Make **s** the way John 1:23

STRANGE *foreign*
offered **s** fire Lev 10:1
no **s** god among you Ps 81:9
to teach **s** doctrines 1 Tim 1:3
went after **s** flesh Jude 7

STRANGER *alien, sojourner*
s-s in a land Gen 15:13
a **s** and a sojourner Gen 23:4
shall not wrong a **s** Ex 22:21
a **s** in the earth Ps 119:19
LORD protects the **s-s** Ps 146:9
violence to the **s** Jer 22:3
I was a **s** Matt 25:35
hospitality to **s-s** Heb 13:2

STRAW *stalk of grain*
s to make brick Ex 5:7
s for the horses 1 Kin 4:28
as **s** before the wind Job 21:18
wood, hay, **s** 1 Cor 3:12

STRAY *wander*
not **s** into her paths Prov 7:25
no longer **s** from Me Ezek 14:11
s-s from the truth James 5:19
s-ing like sheep 1 Pet 2:25

STREAM *current, flow*
planted by **s-s** of water Ps 1:3
The **s** of God Ps 65:9
like a rushing **s** Is 59:19

STREET *road, way*
Wisdom shouts in...**s** Prov 1:20
race madly in the **s-s** Nah 2:4
on the **s** corners Matt 6:5
s of the city...gold Rev 21:21

STRENGTH *force, power*
no longer yield its **s** Gen 4:12
The LORD is my **s** Ex 15:2
was no **s** in him 1 Sam 28:20
My **s** is dried up Ps 22:15
The LORD is my **s** Ps 28:7
s in time of trouble Ps 37:39
God is our refuge...**s** Ps 46:1
s of my salvation Ps 140:7
your **s** to women Prov 31:3
s to the weary Is 40:29
Strangers devour his **s** Hos 7:9
with all your **s** Mark 12:30
s which God supplies 1 Pet 4:11
sun shining in its **s** Rev 1:16

STRENGTHEN *make strong*
please **s** me Judg 16:28
David **s-ed** himself 1 Sam 30:6
s-ed weak hands Job 4:3
s the feeble Is 35:3
s the sick Ezek 34:16
s your brothers Luke 22:32
s-ed in the faith Acts 16:5
Him who **s-s** me Phil 4:13
s-ed with all power Col 1:11
s your hearts 2 Thess 2:17
who has **s-ed** me 1 Tim 1:12

STRETCH *extend*
I will **s** out My hand Ex 3:20
He **s-es** out the north Job 26:7
S-ing out heaven Ps 104:2
I **s-ed** out the heavens Is 45:12

STRIFE *discord, quarrel*
s between...herdsmen Gen 13:7
the **s** of tongues Ps 31:20
Hatred stirs up **s** Prov 10:12
fool's lips bring **s** Prov 18:6
puts an end to **s** Prov 18:18
of envy, murder, **s** Rom 1:29
and **s** among you 1 Cor 3:3
enmities, **s**, jealousy Gal 5:20

STRIKE *hit*
I will **s** the water Ex 7:17
you shall **s** the rock Ex 17:6
He who **s-s** a man Ex 21:12
s the timbrel Ps 81:2
you do not **s** your foot Ps 91:12
S a scoffer Prov 19:25
He will **s** the earth Is 11:4
let us **s** at him Jer 18:18
S the Shepherd Zech 13:7
s...the shepherd Matt 26:31
struck Jesus John 18:22
struck them with many blows Acts 16:23
s the earth Rev 11:6

STRIVE *contend, struggle*
not **s** with man forever Gen 6:3
He will not always **s** Ps 103:9
and **s-ing** after wind Eccl 1:14
s together with me Rom 15:30
s-ing to please men Gal 1:10
we labor and **s** 1 Tim 4:10
s-ing against sin Heb 12:4

STRONG *powerful, steadfast*
a very **s** west wind Ex 10:19
not drink...**s** drink Lev 10:9
Be **s** and courageous Deut 31:6
Israel became **s** Judg 1:28
God is...**s** fortress 2 Sam 22:33
The LORD **s** and mighty Ps 24:8
s drink a brawler Prov 20:1
their Redeemer is **s** Prov 23:11
ants are not a **s** people Prov 30:25
love is as **s** as death Song 8:6
Their Redeemer is **s** Jer 50:34
grew **s** in faith Rom 4:20
act like men, be **s** 1 Cor 16:13
be **s** in the Lord Eph 6:10
weakness...made **s** Heb 11:34
I saw a **s** angel Rev 5:2

STRONGHOLD *fortress, refuge*
David lived in the **s** 2 Sam 5:9
s and my refuge 2 Sam 22:3
s for the oppressed Ps 9:9
For God is my **s** Ps 59:9
my salvation, My **s** Ps 62:2
a **s** to the upright Prov 10:29

STRUGGLE (n) *conflict*
the days of my **s** Job 14:14
our **s** is not against Eph 6:12
have shared my **s** Phil 4:3

STRUGGLE (v) *contend*
children **s-d** together Gen 25:22
men **s**...each other Ex 21:22

STUBBLE *short stumps*
gather **s** for straw Ex 5:12
fire consumes **s** Is 5:24
give birth to **s** Is 33:11
house of Esau...**s** Obad 18

STUBBORN *obstinate*
Pharaoh's heart is **s** Ex 7:14
you are a **s** people Deut 9:6
s...generation Ps 78:8
house of Israel is **s** Ezek 3:7

STUBBORNNESS *intractable*
I know your...**s** Deut 31:27
s of their heart Ps 81:12
s...unrepentant heart Rom 2:5

STUMBLE *fall, trip*
your foot will not **s** Prov 3:23
a rock to **s** over Is 8:14
arrogant one will **s** Jer 50:32
eye makes you **s** Matt 5:29
a stone of **s-ing** Rom 9:33
all **s** in many *ways* James 3:2

STUMBLING BLOCK *obstacle*
s before the blind Lev 19:14
s of iniquity Ezek 44:12
You are a **s** to Me Matt 16:23
to Jews a **s** 1 Cor 1:23
s of the cross Gal 5:11

STUMP *part of plant*
s dies in the dry soil Job 14:8
The holy seed is its **s** Is 6:13
the **s** with the roots Dan 4:26

STUPID *foolish, senseless*
s and the senseless Ps 49:10
I am more **s** than Prov 30:2
they are altogether **s** Jer 10:8

STYLUS *marking / writing device*
an iron **s** and lead Job 19:24
with an iron **s** Jer 17:1

SUBDUE *conquer, overcome*
fill the earth, and **s** Gen 1:28
the land was **s-d** Josh 18:1
us completely **s** them Ps 74:8
s nations before him Is 45:1

SUBJECT (adj) *under authority*
s to forced labor Judg 1:30
demons are **s** to us Luke 10:17
church is **s** to Christ Eph 5:24
s to...husbands Titus 2:5
be **s** to the Father Heb 12:9

SUBJECT (v)
s him to a slave's Lev 25:39
creation was **s-ed** Rom 8:20
s themselves 1 Cor 14:34
all things are **s-ed** 1 Cor 15:28

SUBJECTION *under authority*
kingdom...in **s** Ezek 17:14
He continued in **s** Luke 2:51
s to the governing Rom 13:1
all things in **s** 1 Cor 15:27

SUBMISSIVE *yielding*
Servants, be **s** 1 Pet 2:18
s to...husbands 1 Pet 3:5

SUBMIT *yield to*
Foreigners **s** to me Ps 18:44
s yourself to decrees Col 2:20
S therefore to God James 4:7

SUBSTITUTE
s shall become holy Lev 27:10
s darkness for light Is 5:20
s bitter for sweet Is 5:20

SUCCESS *accomplishment*
grant me **s** today Gen 24:12
hands cannot attain **s** Job 5:12
Daniel enjoyed **s** Dan 6:28

SUCCESSFUL *having achieved*
make your journey **s** Gen 24:40
make Your servant **s** Neh 1:11
make his ways **s** Is 48:15

SUCCOTH
1 *Israelite camping place* Ex 12:37;13:20
2 *Gadite town in Jordan Valley* Josh 13:27; Ps 60:6

SUDDENLY *abruptly*
in case he should come **s** Mark 13:36
s...from heaven Acts 2:2

SUFFER *experience pain*
s the fate of all Num 16:29
Son of Man must **s** Mark 8:31
s and rise again Luke 24:46
worthy to **s** shame Acts 5:41
we **s** with *Him* Rom 8:17
creation...**s-s** Rom 8:22
if one member **s-s** 1 Cor 12:26
s-ing for the gospel 2 Tim 1:8
Christ also **s-ed** 1 Pet 2:21

SUFFERINGS *distress*
s of this present Rom 8:18
sharers of our **s** 2 Cor 1:7
fellowship of His **s** Phil 3:10
rejoice in my **s** Col 1:24
share the **s** of Christ 1 Pet 4:13

SUFFICIENT *enough*
s for its redemption Lev 25:26
bread is not **s** John 6:7
My grace is **s** 2 Cor 12:9

SUMMER *season*
fever heat of **s** Ps 32:4
You have made **s** Ps 74:17
Like snow in **s** Prov 26:1
know that **s** is near Matt 24:32

SUMMIT *peak, top*
Like the **s** of Lebanon Jer 22:6
hide on the **s** Amos 9:3

SUMMON *call, gather*
s-ed all Israel Deut 5:1
s all the prophets 2 Kin 10:19
He **s-s** the heavens Ps 50:4
He **s-ed** the twelve Mark 6:7

SUN *heavenly body*
when the **s** grew hot Ex 16:21
the **s** stood still Josh 10:13
chariots of the **s** 2 Kin 23:11
God is a **s** Ps 84:11
s will not smite Ps 121:6
s to rule by day Ps 136:8
new under the **s** Eccl 1:9
s go down at noon Amos 8:9
shine forth as the **s** Matt 13:43
signs in **s** Luke 21:25
not let the **s** go down Eph 4:26
clothed with the **s** Rev 12:1

SUNRISE *appearance of sun*
toward the **s** Num 3:38
Jordan toward the **s** Josh 1:15

SUNSET
Passover...at **s** Deut 16:6
dawn and the **s** shout Ps 65:8

SUNSHINE
Through **s** after rain 2 Sam 23:4
dazzling heat in the **s** Is 18:4

SUPPER *meal*
made Him a **s** John 12:2
eat the Lord's **S** 1 Cor 11:20
marriage **s** of the Rev 19:9
the great **s** of God Rev 19:17

SUPPLICATION *petition*
Make **s** to the LORD Ex 9:28
s of Your people 1 Kin 8:52
LORD has heard my **s** Ps 6:9
poor man utters **s-s** Prov 18:23
seek *Him by*...**s-s** Dan 9:3
by prayer and **s** Phil 4:6

SUPPLY *provide*
He who **s-ies** seed 2 Cor 9:10
my God will **s** Phil 4:19
s moral excellence 2 Pet 1:5

SUPPORT (n) *strength*
the LORD was my **s** 2 Sam 22:19
gave him strong **s** 1 Chr 11:10
Both supply and **s** Is 3:1
worthy of his **s** Matt 10:10

SUPPORT (v) *uphold*
Hur **s-ed** his hands Ex 17:12
will He **s**...evildoers Job 8:20
He **s-s** the fatherless Ps 146:9
ought to **s** such men 3 John 8

SUR
see **GATES OF JERUSALEM**

SURE *secure, true*
testimony...is **s** Ps 19:7
His precepts are **s** Ps 111:7
His water will be **s** Is 33:16

SURFACE *exterior*
s of the deep Gen 1:2
ark floated on the **s** Gen 7:18
water was on the **s** Gen 8:9

SURPASS *excel*
you **s** in beauty Ezek 32:19
s-ing riches of His Eph 2:7
which **s-es** knowledge Eph 3:19

SURRENDER *yield*
s me into his hand 1 Sam 23:11
How can I **s** you Hos 11:8

SURROUND *encircle*
s him with favor Ps 5:12
Sheol **s-ed** me Ps 18:5
s me with songs Ps 32:7
witnesses **s-ing** us Heb 12:1

SURVIVE *outlive*
your household will **s** Jer 38:17
how...can we **s** Ezek 33:10

SURVIVORS *continued to live*
inheritance for...**s** Judg 21:17
out of...Zion **s** 2 Kin 19:31
left us a few **s** Is 1:9
imprison their **s** Obad 14

SUSA
a Persian capital city Neh 1:1; Esth 1:2,5;3:15;9:15

SUSTAIN *provide for*
land could not **s** Gen 13:6
LORD **s-s** the righteous Ps 37:17
He will **s** you Ps 55:22
S...with raisin cakes Song 2:5

SWALLOW (n) *bird*
the **s** a nest Ps 84:3
like a **s** in *its* Prov 26:2

SWALLOW (v) *take in*
earth may **s** us up Num 16:34
He will **s** up death Is 25:8
great fish to **s** Jonah Jon 1:17
s-ed up in victory 1 Cor 15:54

SWARM *collect, gather*
Nile will **s** with frogs Ex 8:3
which **s** on the earth Lev 11:29
land **s-ed** with frogs Ps 105:30

SWEAR *take oath, vow*
s by the LORD Gen 24:3
oath which I **swore** Gen 26:3
person **s-s** thoughtlessly Lev 5:4
not **s** falsely Lev 19:12
sworn by My holiness Ps 89:35
s by My name Jer 12:16
whoever **s-s** by heaven Matt 23:22
began to...**s** Matt 26:74
brethren do not **s** James 5:12

SWEAT *perspiration*
By the **s** of your face Gen 3:19
s...like drops of Luke 22:44

SWEET *fresh, pleasant*
waters became **s** Ex 15:25
s psalmist of Israel 2 Sam 23:1
who had **s** fellowship Ps 55:14
s are Your words Ps 119:103
your sleep will be **s** Prov 3:24
Stolen water is **s** Prov 9:17
it was **s** as honey Ezek 3:3

SWIFT *fast, rapid*
horses and **s** steeds 1 Kin 4:28
s as the gazelles 1 Chr 12:8
race is not to the **s** Eccl 9:11
riding on a **s** cloud Is 19:1
s to shed blood Rom 3:15

SWINDLER *cheater*
cursed be the **s** Mal 1:14
a drunkard, or a **s** 1 Cor 5:11
revilers, nor **s-s** 1 Cor 6:10

SWINE *pig*
gold in a **s-'s** snout Prov 11:22
Who eat **s-'s** flesh Is 65:4
your pearls before **s** Matt 7:6
Send us into the **s** Mark 5:12

SWORD *weapon with blade*
flaming **s**...turned Gen 3:24
by your **s** you shall Gen 27:40
the **s** will bereave Deut 32:25
A **s** for the LORD Judg 7:20
s devour forever 2 Sam 2:26
fell on his **s** 1 Chr 10:5
tongue a sharp **s** Ps 57:4
as a two-edged **s** Prov 5:4
teeth are *like* **s-s** Prov 30:14
s against nation Is 2:4
the power of the **s** Jer 18:21
abolish...the **s** Hos 2:18
s-s into plowshares Mic 4:3
perish by the **s** Matt 26:52
s of the Spirit Eph 6:17
than any two-edged **s** Heb 4:12
s of My mouth Rev 2:16

SYCAMORE *tree*
olive and **s** trees 1 Chr 27:28
plentiful as **s-s** 2 Chr 1:15
grower of **s** figs Amos 7:14

SYCHAR
town in Samaria John 4:5
also **Shechem**

SYMPATHY *mutual feeling*
I looked for **s** Ps 69:20
s to the prisoners Heb 10:34

SYNAGOGUE *assembly*
pray in the **s-s** Matt 6:5
He went into their **s** Matt 12:9
flogged in *the* **s-s** Mark 13:9
chief seats in...**s-s** Luke 20:46
outcasts from the **s** John 16:2
taught in **s-s** John 18:20
reasoning in the **s** Acts 17:17
but are a **s** of Satan Rev 2:9

SYRIA
NE of Israel Matt 4:24; Acts 15:23,41;20:3
see also **ARAM**

T

TAANACH
Canaanite royal city Josh 12:21;21:25; Judg 5:19

TABERNACLE *assembly and area for sacrificial worship*
dwelling place of God among the Israelites Ex 25:8
construction directed by God Ex 25:9
contained Ark of the Covenant Ex 25:10
other descriptive names of the tabernacle:
house of the LORD Ex 23:19;34:26; Deut 23:18
tabernacle of the house of God 1 Chr 6:48
tabernacle of the tent of meeting Ex 39:40;40:6,29
tabernacle of the testimony Ex 38:21; Num 1:50,53
tent of meeting Ex 29:32; 30:26;38:30;38:43;40:2,6,7

TABITHA *see* **DORCAS**

TABLE *furniture*
gold **t** before the LORD Lev 24:6
You prepare a **t** Ps 23:5
crumbs...masters' **t** Matt 15:27
t-s...moneychangers Matt 21:12
dogs under the **t** Mark 7:28
drink at My **t** Luke 22:30
in order to serve **t-s** Acts 6:2
t of the Lord 1 Cor 10:21

TABLET *writing surface*
give you the stone **t-s** Ex 24:12
t-s of the testimony Ex 31:18
the **t** of their heart Jer 17:1
t-s of human hearts 2 Cor 3:3

TABOR
1 *mountain* Judg 4:6,12
2 *city in Zebulun* 1 Chr 6:77
3 *oak in Benjamin* 1 Sam 10:3

TAHPANHES
Egyptian city Jer 2:16
place where Jeremiah escaped Jer 43:7-9;44:1

TAHPENES
queen of Egypt 1 Kin 11:19,20

TAIL
grasp *it* by its **t** Ex 4:4
the foxes **t** to **t** Judg 15:4
cuts off head and **t** Is 9:14
t-s like scorpions Rev 9:10

TAKE *get, grasp*
t...the tree of life Gen 3:22
T My yoke upon Matt 11:29
T, eat; this is My Matt 26:26
t-s away the sin John 1:29
day that He was **t-n** Acts 1:22
to **t** hold of...hope Heb 6:18

TALENT
measure of weight Ex 38:27; 2 Sam 12:30; 1 Chr 20:2
measure of money 1 Kin 20:39; Matt 18:24;25:15,25

TALK (n) *conversation, speech*
argue with useless **t** Job 15:3
no...silly **t** Eph 5:4
their **t** will spread 2 Tim 2:17

TALK (v) *converse, speak*
God **t-ed** with him Gen 17:3
lips **t** of trouble Prov 24:2
who **t** about you Ezek 33:30
they were **t-ing** Luke 24:15
Paul kept on **t-ing** Acts 20:9

TALL *high*
cut...its **t** cedars 2 Kin 19:23
a nation **t** and smooth Is 18:2
grew up, became **t** Ezek 16:7

TAMAR
1 *Judah's daughter-in-law* Gen 38:6ff
2 *daughter of David* 2 Sam 13:1
3 *daughter of Absalom* 2 Sam 14:27
4 *town near the Dead Sea* 1 Kin 9:18; Ezek 47:19;48:28

TAMARISK *tree*
a **t** tree at Beersheba Gen 21:33
under the **t** tree 1 Sam 22:6

TAMBOURINE
accompanied by...**t** Is 5:12
gaiety of **t-s** ceases Is 24:8

TAMMUZ
Mesopotamian god Ezek 8:14

TARES *weeds*
t among the wheat Matt 13:25
gather up the **t** Matt 13:30
parable of the **t** Matt 13:36

TARSHISH
1 *lineage of Japheth* Gen 10:4
2 *ships of* 1 Kin 10:22;22:48; 2 Chr 9:21; Ps 48:7
3 *line of Benjamin* 1 Chr 7:6-10
4 *Persian official* Esth 1:14
5 *city* Is 66:19; Jon 1:3

TARSUS
birthplace of Paul Acts 21:39
capital of Cilicia Acts 22:3

TASKMASTERS *overseers*
appointed **t** over them Ex 1:11
Pharaoh commanded...**t** Ex 5:6

TASTE *test flavor*
As the palate **t-s** Job 34:3
O **t** and see Ps 34:8
will not **t** death Matt 16:28
t death for everyone Heb 2:9
t-d...heavenly gift Heb 6:4

TASTELESS *without taste*
Can something **t** be Job 6:6
salt has become **t** Matt 5:13

TAUNT *object of ridicule*
a **t** among all Deut 28:37
I have become their **t** Job 30:9

TAX *charge, tribute*
a **t** for the LORD Num 31:28
money for the king's **t** Neh 5:4
sitting in the **t** collector's booth Matt 9:9
pay **t-es** to Caesar Luke 20:22
t to whom **t** *is due* Rom 13:7

TAX COLLECTOR *tax gatherer*
t-s do the same Matt 5:46
many **t-s** and sinners Matt 9:10
Matthew the **t** Matt 10:3
a friend of **t-s** Matt 11:19
he was a chief **t** Luke 19:2

TEACH *instruct*
t you what...to say Ex 4:12
t them the good way 1 Kin 8:36
Can anyone **t** God Job 21:22
T me Your paths Ps 25:4
T me to do Your will Ps 143:10
would He **t** knowledge Is 28:9
He...*began* to **t** them Matt 5:2
t-ing...in parables Mark 4:2
Lord, **t** us to pray Luke 11:1
Spirit will **t** you Luke 12:12
He will **t** you all John 14:26
t strange doctrines 1 Tim 1:3
allow a woman to **t** 1 Tim 2:12
she **t-es** and leads Rev 2:20

TEACHER *instructor*
will behold your **T** Is 30:20
T, I will follow You Matt 8:19
not above his **t** Matt 10:24
why trouble the **T** Mark 5:35
the **t** of Israel John 3:10
call Me **T** and Lord John 13:13
t of the immature Rom 2:20
as pastors and **t-s** Eph 4:11
t of the Gentiles 1 Tim 2:7
false **t-s** among you 2 Pet 2:1

TEACHING (n) *instruction*
t drop as the rain Deut 32:2
your mother's **t** Prov 1:8
amazed at His **t** Matt 7:28
My **t** is not Mine John 7:16
contrary to sound **t** 1 Tim 1:10

TEAR *crying*
have seen your **t-s** 2 Kin 20:5
my **t-s** in Your bottle Ps 56:8
sow in **t-s** shall reap Ps 126:5
drench you with my **t-s** Is 16:9
eyes a fountain of **t-s** Jer 9:1
His feet with her **t-s** Luke 7:38
God...wipe every **t** Rev 7:17

TEBETH
name of the tenth month in Hebrew calendar Esth 2:16

TEL-ABIB
place in Babylonia Ezek 3:15
Jewish exiles located there

TELL *relate, speak*
not **t** the riddle Judg 14:14
T of His glory 1 Chr 16:24
t of Your righteousness Ps 71:15
t-s lies will perish Prov 19:9
t you great and mighty Jer 33:3
See that you **t** no one Matt 8:4
t you about Me John 18:34
t you the mystery Rev 17:7

TEMA
1 *son of Ishmael* Gen 25:15
2 *town in Arabia* Job 6:19; Is 21:14

TEMPER *anger*
always loses his **t** Prov 29:11
the ruler's **t** rises Eccl 10:4

TEMPEST *storm*
bruises me with a **t** Job 9:17
stormy wind *and* **t** Ps 55:8
t of destruction Is 28:2
on the day of **t** Amos 1:14

TEMPLE *structure for worship*
doorpost of the **t** 1 Sam 1:9
t is not for man 1 Chr 29:1
LORD is in His holy **t** Ps 11:4
meditate in His **t** Ps 27:4
t of the LORD Jer 7:4
pinnacle of the **t** Matt 4:5
will destroy this **t** Mark 14:58
veil of the **t** Luke 23:45
Destroy this **t**, and John 2:19
you are a **t** of God 1 Cor 3:16
t of the Holy Spirit 1 Cor 6:19
his seat in the **t** 2 Thess 2:4
the Lamb, are its **t** Rev 21:22

TEMPT *test, try*
And **t-ed** God in the Ps 106:14
being **t-ed** by Satan Mark 1:13
so that Satan will not **t** you 1 Cor 7:5
t-ed beyond what 1 Cor 10:13
Himself does not **t** James 1:13

TEMPTATION *testing, trial*
not lead us into **t** Matt 6:13
not enter into **t** Matt 26:41
time of **t** fall away Luke 8:13
t has overtaken you 1 Cor 10:13
the godly from **t** 2 Pet 2:9

TEN *number*
T Commandments Deut 10:4
it had **t** horns Dan 7:7
has the **t** talents Matt 25:28

TEND *take care of*
t his father's flock 1 Sam 17:15
He will **t** His flock Is 40:11
T My lambs John 21:15
T My sheep John 21:17

TENDER *gentle, young*
t and choice calf Gen 18:7
your heart was **t** 2 Kin 22:19
like a **t** shoot Is 53:2
t mercy of our God Luke 1:78

TENT *mobile shelter*
Abram moved his **t** Gen 13:18
man, living in **t-s** Gen 25:27
your **t-s**, O Israel 1 Kin 12:16
t-s of the destroyers Job 12:6
dwell in Your **t** forever Ps 61:4
grumbled in their **t-s** Ps 106:25
Like a shepherd's **t** Is 38:12

TENT OF MEETING
perhaps the same as the Tabernacle or at certain periods a separate meeting place Ex 33:7; Lev 1:1; Num 7:5; Josh 18:1
see also **TABERNACLE**

TENT OF TESTIMONY
see **TABERNACLE**

TERAH
father of Abraham Gen 11:24; Num 33:27; Luke 3:34

TERAPHIM
household gods, idols 2 Kin 23:24; Zech 10:2

TERRIBLE *dreadful*
and **t** wilderness Deut 8:15
t day of the LORD Mal 4:5
into **t** convulsions Mark 9:26

TERRIFY *frighten*
t-ied by the sword 1 Chr 21:30
t me by visions Job 7:14
t them with Your storm Ps 83:15
Him and were **t-ied** Mark 6:50
t you by my letters 2 Cor 10:9

TERRITORY *country, land*
smite your whole **t** Ex 8:2
God enlarges your **t** Deut 19:8
t of...inheritance Josh 19:10
possess the **t** Obad 19

TERROR *intense fear*
Sounds of **t** are in Job 15:21
t-s of thick darkness Job 24:17
t-s of Sheol came Ps 116:3
meditate on **t** Is 33:18
t-s and great signs Luke 21:11

TERTIUS
Paul's scribe Rom 16:22

TEST (n) *trial*
put God to the **t** Ps 78:18
put Him to the **t** Luke 10:25
you fail the **t** 2 Cor 13:5

TEST (v) *try*
God **t-ed** Abraham Gen 22:1
Why do you **t** the LORD Ex 17:2
she came to **t** him 1 Kin 10:1
T my mind and my Ps 26:2
word of God is **t-ed** Prov 30:5
Spirit...to the **t** Acts 5:9
fire itself will **t** 1 Cor 3:13
t the spirits to see 1 John 4:1

TESTIFY *give witness*
nor shall you **t** Ex 23:2
them **t** against him 1 Kin 21:10
I will **t** against you Ps 50:7
our sins **t** against us Is 59:12
John **t-ied** John 1:15
John **t-ied** John 1:32
Jesus Himself **t-ied** John 4:44
If I *alone* **t** John 5:31
t about Me John 15:26
you *will* **t** John 15:27
Spirit...**t-ies** Rom 8:16
three that **t** 1 John 5:7

TESTIMONY *witness*
into the ark the **t** Ex 25:16
two tablets of the **t** Ex 31:18
t of the LORD is sure Ps 19:7
t-ies are righteous Ps 119:144
Bind up the **t** Is 8:16
t to all the nations Matt 24:14
t against Jesus Matt 26:59
My **t** is true John 8:14
t of two men is true John 8:17
t concerning Christ 1 Cor 1:6
ashamed of the **t** 2 Tim 1:8
This **t** is true Titus 1:13
t of God is greater 1 John 5:9

TETRARCH
governor of a region Matt 14:1; Luke 3:1,19; Acts 13:1

THADDAEUS
apostle Matt 10:3; Mark 3:18

THANK (v) *express gratitude*
my song I shall **t** Him Ps 28:7
God, I **t** You Luke 18:11
I **t** my God always 1 Cor 1:4

THANKS (n) *gratitude*
give **t** to the LORD 1 Chr 16:7
It is good to give **t** Ps 92:1
giving **t**, He broke Matt 15:36
a cup and given **t** Matt 26:27
But **t** be to God Rom 6:17
not cease giving **t** Eph 1:16
always to give **t** 2 Thess 1:3

THANKSGIVING *gratitude*
the sacrifice of **t** Lev 7:12
with the voice of **t** Ps 26:7
His presence with **t** Ps 95:2
supplication with **t** Phil 4:6
t and honor and Rev 7:12

THEBES
Egyptian city Jer 46:25; Ezek 30:14-16

THEFT *robbery*
be sold for his **t** Ex 22:3
t-s, murders Mark 7:21

THEOPHILUS
addressee of Luke's gospel and Acts Luke 1:3; Acts 1:1

THESSALONICA
Macedonian city Acts 27:2; Phil 4:16
visited by Paul Acts 17:1,11,13

THICKET *underbrush*
ram caught in the **t** Gen 22:13
the **t** of the Jordan Jer 50:44

THIEF *robber*
that **t** shall die Deut 24:7
partner with a **t** Prov 29:24
companions of **t-ves** Is 1:23
enter...like a **t** Joel 2:9
t comes...to steal John 10:10
a **t** in the night 1 Thess 5:2

THIGH *part of leg*
hand under my **t** Gen 24:2
socket of Jacob's **t** Gen 32:25
Your sword on *Your* **t** Ps 45:3
on His **t**...a name Rev 19:16

THIN *lean*
t ears scorched Gen 41:27
t yellowish hair Lev 13:30
streams...will **t** out Is 19:6

THINK *ponder, reflect*
as he **t-s**...so he is Prov 23:7
not **t**...to abolish Matt 5:17
not to **t** more highly Rom 12:3
t like a child 1 Cor 13:11
t-s he is something Gal 6:3
beyond all that we...**t** Eph 3:20

THIRD *number*
morning, a **t** day Gen 1:13
raised...the **t** day Matt 16:21
raised on the **t** day 1 Cor 15:4
to the **t** heaven 2 Cor 12:2

THIRST (n) *craving, dryness*
for my **t**...vinegar Ps 69:21
donkeys quench...**t** Ps 104:11
not hunger or **t** Is 49:10
in Me will never **t** John 6:35
no longer...nor **t** Rev 7:16

THIRST (v) *have a craving*
My soul **t-s** for God Ps 42:2
Every one who **t-s**, come Is 55:1
t for righteousness Matt 5:6

THIRSTY *lacking water*
satisfied the **t** soul Ps 107:9
In a dry and **t** land Ezek 19:13
I was **t**, and you Matt 25:35
If anyone is **t** John 7:37
one who is **t** come Rev 22:17

THOMAS
apostle Matt 10:3; Mark 3:18; Luke 6:15
doubted Jesus' resurrection John 20:24-28

THORN *sharp point*
Both **t-s** and thistles Gen 3:18
as **t-s** in your sides Num 33:55
as a hedge of **t-s** Prov 15:19
lily among the **t-s** Song 2:2
have reaped **t-s** Jer 12:13
fell among the **t-s** Matt 13:7
a crown of **t-s** Matt 27:29
a burning **t** bush Acts 7:30
t in the flesh 2 Cor 12:7

THOUGHT *concept, idea*
t-s of his heart Gen 6:5
knows the **t-s** of man Ps 94:11
My **t-s** are not your **t-s** Is 55:8
Jesus knowing...**t-s** Matt 9:4
heart come evil **t-s** Matt 15:19
every **t** captive 2 Cor 10:5

THREAD *string*
cord of scarlet **t** Josh 2:18
lips...a scarlet **t** Song 4:3

THREE *number*
Job's **t** friends Job 2:11
or **t** have gathered Matt 18:20
deny Me **t** times Matt 26:34
t days I will raise John 2:19

THRESH *beat out*
ox while he is **t-ing** Deut 25:4
like the dust at **t-ing** 2 Kin 13:7
will **t** the mountains Is 41:15
Arise and **t** Mic 4:13

THRESHING FLOOR
winnows...at the **t** Ruth 3:2
David bought...**t** 2 Sam 24:24
clear His **t** Matt 3:12

THROAT *part of neck*
t is an open grave Ps 5:9
my **t** is parched Ps 69:3
has enlarged its **t** Is 5:14
t is an open grave Rom 3:13

THRONE *seat of sovereign*
sitting on His **t** 1 Kin 22:19
LORD's **t** is in heaven Ps 11:4
Your **t** is established Ps 93:2
it is the **t** of God Matt 5:34
sit upon twelve **t-s** Matt 19:28
Your **t**...is forever Heb 1:8
to the **t** of grace Heb 4:16
a great white **t** Rev 20:11

THRUST *cast, push*
He will **t** them out Josh 23:5
t away like thorns 2 Sam 23:6
Nor to **t** aside Prov 18:5
LORD has **t**...down Jer 46:15

THUMMIM
kept in high priest's breastplate for determining will of God Ex 28:30; Lev 8:8; Deut 33:8; Ezra 2:63; Neh 7:65

THUNDER (n)
LORD sent **t** Ex 9:23
But His mighty **t** Job 26:14
the hiding place of **t** Ps 81:7
be punished with **t** Is 29:6
sound of loud **t** Rev 14:2

THUNDER (v)
t in the heavens 1 Sam 2:10
you **t** with a voice Job 40:9
LORD also **t-ed** Ps 18:13

THYATIRA
city in Asia minor
home of Lydia Acts 16:14
early church Rev 1:11;2:18,24

TIBERIAS
city on W shore of Sea of Galilee John 6:23
Sea of Tiberias John 6:1;21:1
also **Sea of Chinnereth**
also **Sea of Galilee**
also **Lake of Gennesaret**

TIBERIUS
Roman emperor Luke 3:1
see also **CAESAR**

TIDINGS *information, news*
t of His salvation 1 Chr 16:23
not fear evil **t** Ps 112:7

TIGLATH-PILESER
Assyrian king 2 Kin 15:29;16:7,10
see also **PUL**
see also **TILGATH-PILNESER**

TIGRIS
Mesopotamian river Gen 2:14; Dan 10:4

TILGATH-PILNESER
Assyrian king 1 Chr 5:6,26; 2 Chr 28:20
see also **PUL**
see also **TIGLATH-PILESER**

TILLER *cultivator*
Cain was a **t** Gen 4:2
a **t** of the ground Zech 13:5

TIMBER *wood*
cedar and cypress **t** 1 Kin 9:11
whatever **t** you need 2 Chr 2:16
t of Lebanon Song 3:9

TIMBREL *musical instrument*
with songs, with **t** Gen 31:27
strike the **t** Ps 81:2
Praise Him with **t** Ps 150:4

TIME *day, period, season*
in **t-s** of trouble Ps 9:9
t-s are in Your hand Ps 31:15
for a **t**, **t-s**, and half Dan 12:7
t to seek the LORD Hos 10:12
signs of the **t-s** Matt 16:3
My **t** is near Matt 26:18
deny Me three **t-s** Luke 22:61
My **t** is not yet John 7:6
not...you to know **t-s** Acts 1:7
is the acceptable **t** 2 Cor 6:2
grace...in **t** of need Heb 4:16
for the **t** is near Rev 1:3

TIMOTHY
companion of Paul Acts 17:15;18:5; Phil 1:1; Col 1:1; Heb 13:23

TIRED *weary*
I am **t** of living Gen 27:46
run and not get **t** Is 40:31

TIRZAH
1 daughter of Zelophehad Num 26:33;27:1;36:11
2 royal Canaanite city 1 Kin 14:17; 2 Kin 15:14

TISHBITE
town identity of Elijah 1 Kin 17:1;21:17; 2 Kin 1:3,8

TITHE (n) *tenth*
all the **t** of the land Lev 27:30
a **t** of the **t** Num 18:26
the **t** of your grain Deut 12:17
t into the storehouse Mal 3:10
t-s of all that I get Luke 18:12
mortal men receive **t-s** Heb 7:8

TITHE (v) *pay a tithe*
shall surely **t** all Deut 14:22
you **t** mint and dill Matt 23:23

TITUS
co-worker with Paul 2 Cor 2:13;8:23; Gal 2:1

TODAY *present time*
t you...be with Me Luke 23:43
same yesterday and **t** Heb 13:8

TOGARMAH
grandson of Japheth Gen 10:1-3; 1 Chr 1:6

TOIL (n) *labor, work*
the **t** of our hands Gen 5:29
t is not *in* vain 1 Cor 15:58

TOIL (v) *work hard*
I have **t-ed** in vain Is 49:4
they do not **t** nor Matt 6:28

TOMB *grave, sepulchre*
from womb to **t** Job 10:19
you have hewn a **t** Is 22:16
like whitewashed **t-s** Matt 23:27
laid Him in a **t** Mark 15:46
Lazarus out of the **t** John 12:17
outside the **t** John 20:11

TOMORROW *future time*
not boast about **t** Prov 27:1
for **t** we may die Is 22:13
not worry about **t** Matt 6:34

TONGUE *speech, talk*
speech and slow of **t** Ex 4:10
flatter with their **t** Ps 5:9
their **t** a sharp sword Ps 57:4
a lying **t** Prov 6:17
t of the wise Prov 12:18
soft **t** breaks...bone Prov 25:15
His **t** is like...fire Is 30:27
t is a deadly arrow Jer 9:8
impediment of his **t** Mark 7:35
and his **t** *loosed* Luke 1:64
no one...tame the **t** James 3:8

TONGUE *language*
speak with new **t-s** Mark 16:17
speak with other **t-s** Acts 2:4
t-s of men...angels 1 Cor 13:1
if I pray in a **t** 1 Cor 14:14
every tribe and **t** Rev 5:9

TOOL *work instrument*
among your **t-s** Deut 23:13

nor any iron **t** 1 Kin 6:7
iron into a cutting **t** Is 44:12

TOOTH
teeth white from Gen 49:12
eye for eye, **t** for **t** Ex 21:24
and a **t** for a **t** Matt 5:38

TOPAZ *precious stone*
ruby, **t**, and emerald Ex 39:10
t of Ethiopia Job 28:19
the ninth, **t** Rev 21:20

TOPHETH
site of Baal worship in Hinnom Valley 2 Kin 23:10; Jer 7:31,32;19:6,12,14

TORMENT (n) *pain, torture*
this place of **t** Luke 16:28
their **t** was like Rev 9:5
the fear of her **t** Rev 18:15

TORMENT (v) *annoy, harass*
long will you **t** me Job 19:2
t us before the time Matt 8:29
do not **t** me Luke 8:28
Satan to **t** me 2 Cor 12:7

TORRENT *flood*
The ancient **t** Judg 5:21
t-s of destruction 2 Sam 22:5
t-s of ungodliness Ps 18:4
like an overflowing **t** Is 30:28

TOUCH *feel, handle*
not eat...or **t** it Gen 3:3
an angel **t-ing** him 1 Kin 19:5
evil will not **t** you Job 5:19
not **t** My anointed Ps 105:15
T nothing unclean Is 52:11
t the fringe of His Matt 14:36
not to **t** a woman 1 Cor 7:1

TOWER *fortress structure*
t whose top *will reach* Gen 11:4
Count her **t-s** Ps 48:12
name...strong **t** Prov 18:10
and built a **t** Matt 21:33

TOWN *city, village*
many unwalled **t-s** Deut 3:5
founds a **t** with Hab 2:12
except in his home **t** Matt 13:57

TRADE (n) *business, occupation*
abundance of your **t** Ezek 28:16
of the same **t** Acts 18:3

TRADE (v) *buy or sell*
may **t** in the land Gen 42:34
t-d with them Matt 25:16

TRADERS *merchants*
Midianite **t** passed Gen 37:28
king's **t** procured 2 Chr 1:16
in a city of **t** Ezek 17:4
increased your **t** Nah 3:16

TRADITION *custom*
sake of your **t** Matt 15:3
hold to the **t** of men Mark 7:8
hold...to the **t-s** 1 Cor 11:2
my ancestral **t-s** Gal 1:14

TRAIN *guide, instruct*
T up a child Prov 22:6
will they **t** for war Mic 4:3
t-ed to discern good Heb 5:14
heart **t-ed** in greed 2 Pet 2:14

TRAMPLE *crush, hurt*
t-s down the waves Job 9:8
let him **t** my life Ps 7:5
t-d the nations Hab 3:12
Jerusalem...**t-d** Luke 21:24

TRANCE *daze, dream*
he fell into a **t** Acts 10:10
in a **t** I saw a vision Acts 11:5
fell into a **t** Acts 22:17

TRANSFIGURED *changed*
He was **t** before them Matt 17:2

TRANSFORM *change*
t-ed by the renewing Rom 12:2
t-ed into the same 2 Cor 3:18
who will **t** the body Phil 3:21

TRANSGRESS *break, overstep*
you **t** the covenant Josh 23:16
rulers also **t-ed** Jer 2:8
they **t-ed** laws Is 24:5

TRANSGRESSION *trespass, sin*
forgives iniquity, **t** Ex 34:7
I am pure, without **t** Job 33:9
I know my **t-s** Ps 51:3
removed our **t-s** from Ps 103:12
love covers all **t-s** Prov 10:12
pierced...for our **t-s** Is 53:5
not forgive your **t-s** Matt 6:15
dead in our **t-s** Eph 2:5

TRANSGRESSOR *sinner*
teach **t-s** Your ways Ps 51:13
numbered with the **t-s** Is 53:12
a **t** of the law James 2:11

TRANSLATED
t and read before me Ezra 4:18
Immanuel...**t** means Matt 1:23
Golgotha, which is **t** Mark 15:22
Messiah...**t** means John 1:41

TRAP (n) *snare*
a snare and a **t** Josh 23:13
hidden a **t** for me Ps 142:3
table become...a **t** Rom 11:9

TRAP (v) *catch*
they might **t** Him Matt 22:15
in order to **t** Him Mark 12:13

TRAVAIL *intense pain*
t-ed nor given birth Is 23:4

TRAVEL *journey*
t by day and by night Ex 13:21
who **t** on the road Judg 5:10
Jesus...*began* **t-ing** Luke 24:15

TREACHEROUS *traitorous*
I behold the **t** Ps 119:158
t will be uprooted Prov 2:22

way of the **t** is hard Prov 13:15

TREAD *walk on*
They **t** wine presses Job 24:11
as the potter **t-s** clay Is 41:25
t on serpents Luke 10:19
t-s the wine press Rev 19:15

TREASURE (n) *valuable thing*
t-s of the sand Deut 33:19
the LORD is his **t** Is 33:6
opening their **t-s** Matt 2:11
for where your **t** is Matt 6:21
have **t** in heaven Matt 19:21
t in earthen vessels 2 Cor 4:7
stored up your **t** James 5:3

TREASURE (v) *value greatly*
I have **t-d** the words Job 23:12
Your word I have **t-d** Ps 119:11
t my commandments Prov 7:1

TREASURY *place of valuables*
t of the LORD Josh 6:19
paid from the royal **t** Ezra 6:4
fill their **t-ies** Prov 8:21
into the temple **t** Matt 27:6

TREATY *agreement, contract*
Let there be a **t** 1 Kin 15:19
go, break your **t** 2 Chr 16:3

TREE *woody plant*
fruit **t-s**...bearing Gen 1:11
t of life Gen 2:9
gave me from the **t** Gen 3:12
hang him on a **t** Deut 21:22
said to the olive **t** Judg 9:8
t *firmly* planted Ps 1:3
she is a **t** of life Prov 3:18
Beneath the apple **t** Song 8:5
like a **t** planted by Jer 17:8
under his fig **t** Mic 4:4
good **t** bears good Matt 7:17
the fig **t** withered Matt 21:19
a sycamore **t** Luke 19:4
autumn **t-s** without Jude 12
eat of the **t** of life Rev 2:7

TREMBLE *shake*
T before Him 1 Chr 16:30
pillars of heaven **t** Job 26:11
T, and do not sin Ps 4:4
make the heavens **t** Is 13:13
His soul **t-s** Is 15:4
my inward parts **t-d** Hab 3:16

TREMBLING (n) *fear, reverence*
rejoice with **t** Ps 2:11
eat...with **t** Ezek 12:18
with fear and **t** Phil 2:12

TRESPASS *fault, sin*
Saul died for his **t** 1 Chr 10:13
caught in any **t** Gal 6:1
dead in your **t-es** Eph 2:1

TRIAL *testing*
if we are on **t** today Acts 4:9
which was a **t** to you Gal 4:14
perseveres under **t** James 1:12

TRIBE *common ancestry*
twelve **t-s** of Israel Gen 49:28

a man of each **t** Num 1:4
t-s of the LORD Ps 122:4
judging...twelve **t-s** Luke 22:30
men from every **t** Rev 5:9

TRIBULATION *affliction*
will be a great **t** Matt 24:21
world you have **t** John 16:33
exult in our **t-s** Rom 5:3
my **t-s** on your behalf Eph 3:13
out of the great **t** Rev 7:14

TRIBUNAL *court*
before Caesar's **t** Acts 25:10

TRIBUTE *tax*
sons of Israel sent **t** Judg 3:15
impose...**t** or toll Ezra 7:24
exact a **t** of grain Amos 5:11

TRIGON *musical instrument*
sound of...lyre, **t** Dan 3:5

TRIUMPH *victory*
the righteous **t** Prov 28:12
t in Christ 2 Cor 2:14
mercy **t-s** over James 2:13

TROAS
city in Asia Minor Acts 16:8,11
visited by Paul Acts 20:5; 2 Cor 2:12

TROPHIMUS
companion of Paul Acts 20:4; 2 Tim 4:20
Ephesian Christian Acts 21:29

TROUBLE (n) *affliction*
forget all my **t** Gen 41:51
man is born for **t** Job 5:7
Look upon...my **t** Ps 25:18
very present help in **t** Ps 46:1
remember his **t** no Prov 31:7
t is heavy upon him Eccl 8:6
day has enough **t** Matt 6:34

TROUBLE (v) *bother, disturb*
t you in the land Num 33:55
t-s his own house Prov 11:29
also **t** the hearts Ezek 32:9
Herod...was **t-d** Matt 2:3
why **t** the Teacher Mark 5:35
your heart be **t-d** John 14:1

TROUBLED (adj) *disturbed*
songs to a **t** heart Prov 25:20
soul has become **t** John 12:27

TRUE *actual, real, reliable*
gets a **t** reward Prov 11:18
There was the **t** light John 1:9
gives you...**t** bread John 6:32
let God be found **t** Rom 3:4
signs of a **t** apostle 2 Cor 12:12
This testimony is **t** Titus 1:13
t grace of God 1 Pet 5:12
faithful and **t** Witness Rev 3:14

TRUMPET *wind instrument*
t-s of rams' horns Josh 6:6

t-s...empty pitchers Judg 7:16
Praise Him with **t** Ps 150:3
do not sound a **t** Matt 6:2
at the last **t** 1 Cor 15:52
voice like...a **t** Rev 1:10

TRUST (n) *confidence, hope*
whose **t** a spider's web Job 8:14
In God...put my **t** Ps 56:11
put My **t** in Him Heb 2:13

TRUST (v) *commit to*
t in the LORD Ps 4:5
Than to **t** in man Ps 118:8
t-s in his riches Prov 11:28
not **t** in a neighbor Mic 7:5
not **t** in ourselves 2 Cor 1:9

TRUSTWORTHY *reliable*
t witness will not lie Prov 14:5
who can find a **t** Prov 20:6
It is a **t** statement 1 Tim 3:1

TRUTH *genuineness, honesty*
walk before Me in **t** 1 Kin 2:4
speaks **t** in his heart Ps 15:2
Your word is **t** Ps 119:160
Buy **t**, and do not Prov 23:23
judge with **t** Zech 8:16
full of grace and **t** John 1:14
worship in...**t** John 4:24
t will make you free John 8:32
the way, and the **t** John 14:6
exchanged the **t** of Rom 1:25
t of the gospel Gal 2:5
speaking the **t** in love Eph 4:15
the word of **t** 2 Tim 2:15
the **t** is not in us 1 John 1:8

TUBAL
1 *son of Japheth* Gen 10:2
2 *land ruled by Gog* Ezek 38:3;39:1

TUBAL-CAIN
son of Zillah Gen 4:22
inventor of cutting tools

TUMULT *disturbance*
t of the peoples Ps 65:7
A sound of **t** Is 13:4
t of waters Jer 51:16

TUNIC *cloak, garment*
a varicolored **t** Gen 37:3
the holy linen **t** Lev 16:4

TURBAN *headdress*
a **t** of fine linen Ex 28:39
justice was like...a **t** Job 29:14
Remove the **t** Ezek 21:26

TURMOIL *tumult*
treasure and **t** with Prov 15:16
rest from your...**t** Is 14:3
ill repute, full of **t** Ezek 22:5

TURN *change* or *move*
not **t** to mediums Lev 19:31
leave you *or* **t** back Ruth 1:16
T from your evil 2 Kin 17:13
forget, nor **t** away Prov 4:5
T to Me, and be saved Is 45:22
t-ed to his own way Is 53:6
t their mourning into Jer 31:13
t...shame into praise Zeph 3:19
t from darkness to Acts 26:18
he who **t-s** a sinner James 5:20
t away from evil 1 Pet 3:11

TURTLEDOVE *bird*
t for a sin offering Lev 12:6
the voice of the **t** Song 2:12

TUTOR *teacher*
t-s in Christ 1 Cor 4:15
Law...become our **t** Gal 3:24

TWELVE *number*
t tribes of Israel Gen 49:28
summoned His **t** Matt 10:1
t legions of angels Matt 26:53
when He became **t** Luke 2:42
a crown of **t** stars Rev 12:1

TWILIGHT *darkness, dusk*
lamb...offer at **t** Ex 29:39
waits for the **t** Job 24:15
midday as in the **t** Is 59:10

TWINKLING *flicker*
in the **t** of an eye 1 Cor 15:52

TWINS *pair, two*
t in her womb Gen 25:24
T of a gazelle Song 4:5

TWO-EDGED *with two edges*
than any **t** sword Heb 4:12
His mouth...**t** sword Rev 1:16

TYRE
Phoenician seaport
Josh 19:29; Ezek 27:3; Matt 15:21; Acts 21:3

~U

UGLY *unsightly*
u and gaunt cows Gen 41:4
seven lean...**u** cows Gen 41:27

UNBELIEF *lack of faith*
wondered at their **u** Mark 6:6
help my **u** Mark 9:24
continue in their **u** Rom 11:23

UNBELIEVER *non-believer*
a place with the **u-s** Luke 12:46
wife who is an **u** 1 Cor 7:12
ungifted men or **u-s** 1 Cor 14:23
bound...with **u-s** 2 Cor 6:14
worse than an **u** 1 Tim 5:8

UNBELIEVING *doubting*
O **u** generation Mark 9:19
u husband is 1 Cor 7:14
blinded the...**u** 2 Cor 4:4
evil, **u** heart Heb 3:12

UNBLEMISHED *without defect*
shall be an **u** male Ex 12:5
u and spotless 1 Pet 1:19

UNCEASING *continuous*
u complaint in his Job 33:19
sorrow and **u** grief Rom 9:2

UNCHANGEABLENESS
the **u** of His purpose Heb 6:17

UNCIRCUMCISED
But an **u** male Gen 17:14
u heart...humbled Lev 26:41
the nations are **u** Jer 9:26
who is physically **u** Rom 2:27
the gospel to the **u** Gal 2:7

UNCIRCUMCISION
has become **u** Rom 2:25
who are called **U** Eph 2:11
the **u** of your flesh Col 2:13

UNCLEAN *not clean* or *not holy*
touches any **u** thing Lev 5:2
u in their practices Ps 106:39
man of **u** lips Is 6:5
authority over **u** Matt 10:1
u spirits entered Mark 5:13
eaten anything...**u** Acts 10:14
nothing is **u** in itself Rom 14:14

UNCOVER *expose*
to **u** her nakedness Lev 18:7
u his feet and Ruth 3:4
head **u-ed** while 1 Cor 11:5

UNDEFILED *uncorrupted*
holy, innocent, **u** Heb 7:26
marriage bed...*be* **u** Heb 13:4
pure and **u** religion James 1:27
imperishable and **u** 1 Pet 1:4

UNDERGARMENTS
u next to his flesh Lev 6:10
linen **u** shall be on Ezek 44:18

UNDERGO *experience*
Holy One to **u** decay Ps 16:10
should not **u** decay Ps 49:9
did not **u** decay Acts 13:37

UNDERSTAND *comprehend*
u-s every intent 1 Chr 28:9
To **u** a proverb Prov 1:6
O fools, **u** wisdom Prov 8:5
do not **u** justice Prov 28:5
Who can **u** it Jer 17:9
u that the vision Dan 8:17
Hear, and **u** Matt 15:10
to **u** the Scriptures Luke 24:45
Why do you not **u** John 8:43
none who **u-s** Rom 3:11
things hard to **u** 2 Pet 3:16

UNDERSTANDING
a wise and **u** people Deut 4:6
servant an **u** heart 1 Kin 3:9
Holy One is **u** Prov 9:10

UNDISCIPLINED
in an **u** manner 2 Thess 3:7
leading an **u** life 2 Thess 3:11

UNDISTURBED *peaceful*
land was **u** for forty Judg 8:28
an **u** habitation Is 33:20

UNFADING *lasting*
u crown of glory 1 Pet 5:4

UNFAITHFUL
u to her husband Num 5:27
very **u** to the LORD 2 Chr 28:19
u to our God Ezra 10:2

UNFAITHFULNESS *faithless*
u...they committed Lev 26:40
to Babylon for their **u** 1 Chr 9:1
the **u** of the exiles Ezra 9:4

UNFATHOMABLE
How...**u** His ways Rom 11:33
u riches of Christ Eph 3:8

UNFRUITFUL *not productive*
the land is **u** 2 Kin 2:19
my mind is **u** 1 Cor 14:14
u deeds of darkness Eph 5:11

UNGODLINESS *sinfulness*
torrents of **u** terrified Ps 18:4
remove **u**...Jacob Rom 11:26
lead to further **u** 2 Tim 2:16

UNGODLY *sinful, wicked*
who justifies the **u** Rom 4:5
Christ died for the **u** Rom 5:6
destruction of **u** men 2 Pet 3:7
their own **u** lusts Jude 18

UNHOLY *not holy*
no *longer* consider **u** Acts 10:15
for the **u** and profane 1 Tim 1:9

UNINTENTIONALLY
If a person sins **u** Lev 4:2
who kills a person **u** Num 35:15

UNITED *joined, union*
u as one man Judg 20:11
become **u** with *Him* Rom 6:5
love, **u** in spirit Phil 2:2
not **u** by faith Heb 4:2

UNITY *united, union*
dwell together in **u** Ps 133:1
perfected in **u** John 17:23
all attain to the **u** Eph 4:13
perfect bond of **u** Col 3:14

UNJUST *unfair*
u man is abominable Prov 29:27
For God is not **u** Heb 6:10
the just for *the* **u** 1 Pet 3:18

UNKNOWN *not known*
To An **U** God Acts 17:23
as **u** yet well-known 2 Cor 6:9

UNLEAVENED *non-fermented*
and baked **u** bread Gen 19:3
you shall eat **u** bread Ex 12:15
first day of **U** Bread Matt 26:17
you are *in fact* **u** 1 Cor 5:7

UNLEAVENED BREAD, FEAST OF *see* **FEASTS**

UNLOVED *not loved*
that Leah was **u** Gen 29:31
loved and the **u** Deut 21:15
Under an **u** woman Prov 30:23

UNMARRIED *single*
I say to the **u** 1 Cor 7:8
she must remain **u** 1 Cor 7:11

UNPRINCIPLED *unscrupulous*
conduct of **u** men 2 Pet 2:7
error of **u** men 2 Pet 3:17

UNPROFITABLE *without value*
u and worthless Titus 3:9
grief...**u** for you Heb 13:17

UNPUNISHED *not punished*
not leave him **u** Ex 20:7
shall go **u** Ex 21:19
not let him go **u** 1 Kin 2:9

UNQUENCHABLE
burn...with **u** fire Matt 3:12
into the **u** fire Mark 9:43

UNRESTRAINED *uncontrolled*
the people are **u** Prov 29:18
with **u** persecution Is 14:6

UNRIGHTEOUS *evil, wicked*
u man his thoughts Is 55:7
rain on...*the* **u** Matt 5:45
u in a...little thing Luke 16:10
God...is not **u** Rom 3:5
u will not inherit 1 Cor 6:9
u under punishment 2 Pet 2:9

UNRIGHTEOUSNESS *evil*
have no part in **u** 2 Chr 19:7
no **u** in Him Ps 92:15
not rejoice in **u** 1 Cor 13:6
cleanse us from all **u** 1 John 1:9
All **u** is sin 1 John 5:17

UNRULY *disorderly*
admonish the **u** 1 Thess 5:14
who leads an **u** life 2 Thess 3:6

UNSEARCHABLE *inscrutable*
His greatness is **u** Ps 145:3
u are His judgments Rom 11:33

UNSKILLED *lack of training*
I am **u** in speech Ex 6:12
u in speech, yet I 2 Cor 11:6

UNSTABLE *unreliable*
Her ways are **u** Prov 5:6
u in all his ways James 1:8
enticing **u** souls 2 Pet 2:14

UNWILLING *reluctant*
u to move the ark 2 Sam 6:10
they were **u** to come Matt 22:3
He was **u** to drink Matt 27:34
u to be obedient Acts 7:39

UNWISE *foolish*
foolish and **u** people Deut 32:6
walk, not as **u** men Eph 5:15

UNWORTHY *not deserving*
u of...lovingkindness Gen 32:10
We are **u** slaves Luke 17:10
u of eternal life Acts 13:46

UPRIGHT *honest, just*
the death of the **u** Num 23:10
blameless and **u** man Job 1:8
u will behold His face Ps 11:7
led you in **u** paths Prov 4:11
God made men **u** Eccl 7:29
no **u**...among men Mic 7:2
Stand **u** on your feet Acts 14:10

UPROAR *loud noise*
Why...such an **u** 1 Kin 1:41
nations in an **u** Ps 2:1
there occurred a great **u** Acts 23:9

UPROOT *tear out*
He will **u** Israel 1 Kin 14:15
He has **u-ed** my hope Job 19:10
u-ed and be planted Luke 17:6

UR
1 *city in S Mesopotamia* Gen 11:31; 15:7
original home of Abraham Gen 11:28; Neh 9:7
2 *father of Eliphal* 1 Chr 11:35

URBANUS
Roman Christian Rom 16:9

URGE *entreat*
Do not **u** me to leave Ruth 1:16
hunger **u-s** him *on* Prov 16:26
Therefore I **u** you Rom 12:1

URIAH
1 *husband of Bathsheba* 2 Sam 11:3;12:9
2 *priest under Ezra* Neh 8:4
3 *priest under Ahaz* Is 8:2
also **Urijah** 2 Kin 16:10ff
4 *time of Jeremiah* Jer 26:20

URIM
kept in high priest's breastplate for determining the will of God Ex 28:30; Lev 8:8; Num 27:21

USE *utilization*
be of **u** to God Job 22:2
for common **u** Ezek 48:15
for honorable **u** Rom 9:21
not make full **u** of 1 Cor 7:31

USEFUL *beneficial*
man be **u** to himself Job 22:2
u to me for service 2 Tim 4:11

USELESS *worthless*
they have become **u** Rom 3:12
without works is **u** James 2:20

USURY *interest*
leave off this **u** Neh 5:10
by interest and **u** Prov 28:8

UTENSILS *vessels*
table also and its **u** Ex 31:8
u of the sanctuary 1 Chr 9:29

UTTER *express*
righteous **u-s** wisdom Ps 37:30
Let my lips **u** praise Ps 119:171
He **u-s** His voice Jer 10:13
u words of...truth Acts 26:25

UTTERANCE *expression*
was giving them **u** Acts 2:4
in faith and **u** 2 Cor 8:7
u may be given Eph 6:19
through prophetic **u** 1 Tim 4:14

UZ
1 *grandson of Shem* Gen 10:23
2 *son of Nahor* Gen 22:21
3 *son of Dishan* Gen 36:28
4 *home of Job* Job 1:1
land of Uz Jer 25:20; Lam 4:21

V

VAIN *empty* or *profane*
name of...God in **v** Ex 20:7
devising a **v** thing Ps 2:1
labor in **v** who build Ps 127:1
our preaching is **v** 1 Cor 15:14

VALIANT *brave, strong*
these...**v** warriors Judg 20:46
be a **v** man for me 1 Sam 18:17
even all the **v** men 1 Chr 28:1
He drags off the **v** Job 24:22

VALLEY *ravine*
v of the Jordan Gen 13:10
the **v** of Aijalon Josh 10:12
v of the shadow of Ps 23:4
The lily of the **v-s** Song 2:1
v of the dead bodies Jer 31:40
v...full of bones Ezek 37:1
the **v** of decision Joel 3:14

VALLEY GATE
see **GATES OF JERUSALEM**

VALOR *bravery*
mighty man of **v** 1 Sam 16:18
mighty men of **v** 1 Chr 12:8

VALUE *worth*
one pearl of great **v** Matt 13:46
v of knowing Christ Phil 3:8

VANISH *disappear*
When a cloud **v-es** Job 7:9
sky will **v** like smoke Is 51:6
v-ed from...sight Luke 24:31

VANITY *futility, pride*
will reap **v** Prov 22:8
V of **v-ies!** All is **v** Eccl 1:2
arrogant *words* of **v** 2 Pet 2:18

VAPOR *smoke*
causes the **v-s** to Ps 135:7
Is a fleeting **v** Prov 21:6
You are *just* a **v** James 4:14

VARICOLORED *multicolored*
made him a **v** tunic Gen 37:3

VARIOUS *different*
v diseases and pains Matt 4:24
led on by **v** impulses 2 Tim 3:6
encounter **v** trials James 1:2
distressed by **v** trials 1 Pet 1:6

VASHTI
deposed queen of Ahasuerus Esth 1:19; 2:4

VEGETABLE *plant*
like a **v** garden Deut 11:10
Better...dish of **v-s** Prov 15:17
weak eats **v-s** *only* Rom 14:2

VEGETATION *plant life*
earth brought forth **v** Gen 1:12
ate up all **v** Ps 105:35
wither all their **v** Is 42:15

VEIL *cover, curtain*
a **v** over his face Ex 34:33
v of the sanctuary Lev 4:6
Remove your **v** Is 47:2
v of the temple Matt 27:51
enters within the **v** Heb 6:19

VENGEANCE *revenge*
not take **v** Lev 19:18
V is Mine Deut 32:35
God...executes **v** 2 Sam 22:48
LORD takes **v** on His Nah 1:2
V is Mine, I will Heb 10:30

VESSEL *utensil*
Go, borrow **v-s** 2 Kin 4:3
I am like a broken **v** Ps 31:12
v-s of wrath Rom 9:22
treasure in...**v-s** 2 Cor 4:7
be a **v** for honor 2 Tim 2:21
v-s of the potter Rev 2:27

VESTURE *apparel*
v *was* like...snow Dan 7:9

VIAL *small container*
alabaster **v** of Matt 26:7
she broke the **v** Mark 14:3

VICTORIOUS *triumphant*
A **v** warrior Zeph 3:17
v over the beast Rev 15:2

VICTORY *triumph*
LORD brought...**v** 2 Sam 23:10
had given **v** to Aram 2 Kin 5:1
the glory and the **v** 1 Chr 29:11
gained the **v** for Him Ps 98:1
v belongs to...LORD Prov 21:31
He leads justice to **v** Matt 12:20
swallowed up in **v** 1 Cor 15:54
v that has overcome 1 John 5:4

VIGOR *vitality*
nor his **v** abated Deut 34:7
grave in full **v** Job 5:26
his youthful **v** Job 20:11

VILLAGE *small town*
land of unwalled **v-s** Ezek 38:11
Go into the **v** Matt 21:2
entered a **v** Luke 10:38

VINDICATE *justify*
will **v** His people Deut 32:36
V the weak Ps 82:3
wisdom is **v-d** by Matt 11:19

VINE *stem of plant*
trees said to the **v** Judg 9:12
every man...his **v** 1 Kin 4:25
like a fruitful **v** Ps 128:3
the **v-s** in blossom Song 2:13
mother was like a **v** Ezek 19:10
Israel is a luxuriant **v** Hos 10:1
The **v** dries up Joel 1:12
fruit of the **v** Matt 26:29
I am the true **v** John 15:1

VINEDRESSER *gardener*
v-s and plowmen 2 Kin 25:12
My Father is the **v** John 15:1

VINEGAR *sour liquid*
he shall drink no **v** Num 6:3
bread in the **v** Ruth 2:14
gave me **v** to drink Ps 69:21
Like **v** to the teeth Prov 10:26

VINE-GROWERS
rented it out to **v** Matt 21:33
and destroy the **v** Mark 12:9

VINEYARD *grapevines*
Noah...planted a **v** Gen 9:20
Nor...glean your **v** Lev 19:10
Hewn cisterns, **v-s** Neh 9:25
shelter in a **v** Is 1:8
ruined My **v** Jer 12:10
laborers for his **v** Matt 20:1
Who plants a **v** 1 Cor 9:7

VIOLATE *assault* or *break*
shall not **v** his word Num 30:2
do not **v** me 2 Sam 13:12
who **v-d** the ban 1 Chr 2:7
If they **v** My statutes Ps 89:31

VIOLENCE *destructive action*
earth was filled with **v** Gen 6:11
implements of **v** Gen 49:5
such as breathe out **v** Ps 27:12
drink the wine of **v** Prov 4:17
He had done no **v** Is 53:9
not mistreat *or* do **v** Jer 22:3

VIOLENT *destructive*
a wicked, **v** man Ps 37:35
a **v**, rushing wind Acts 2:2

VIPER *snake*
v-'s tongue slays him Job 20:16
hand on the **v-'s** den Is 11:8
v and flying serpent Is 30:6
You brood of **v-s** Matt 3:7

VIRGIN *unmarried maiden*
very beautiful, a **v** Gen 24:16
if a man seduces a **v** Ex 22:16
could I gaze at a **v** Job 31:1
the **v** will rejoice Jer 31:13
v shall be with child Matt 1:23
kept her a **v** Matt 1:25
comparable to ten **v-s** Matt 25:1
v-'s name was Mary Luke 1:27
if a **v** marries 1 Cor 7:28

VISIBLE *manifest, seen*
He become **v** Acts 10:40
becomes **v** is light Eph 5:13
things which are **v** Heb 11:3

VISION *dream, foresight*
to Abram in a **v** Gen 15:1
v-s were infrequent 1 Sam 3:1
Where there is no **v** Prov 29:18
prophets find No **v** Lam 2:9
I saw **v-s** of God Ezek 1:1
in a night **v** Dan 2:19
young men...see **v-s** Joel 2:28
Tell the **v** to no one Matt 17:9
young men...see **v-s** Acts 2:17

VISIT *come* or *go to see*
v-ing the iniquity of Ex 20:5
You **v** the earth Ps 65:9
you did not **v** Me Matt 25:43
For He has **v-ed** us Luke 1:68
v orphans...widows James 1:27

VOICE *sound, speech*
have obeyed My **v** Gen 22:18
listen to His **v** Deut 4:30
v of singing men 2 Sam 19:35
You will hear my **v** Ps 5:3
the **v** of my teachers Prov 5:13
v of the turtledove Song 2:12
Give ear...hear my **v** Is 28:23
A **v** is calling Is 40:3
v came from heaven Dan 4:31
v...heard in Ramah Matt 2:18
v...out of the cloud Mark 9:7
v of one crying in Luke 3:4
v of the Son of God John 5:25
v has gone out Rom 10:18
v of *the* archangel 1 Thess 4:16
His **v** shook...earth Heb 12:26
if anyone hears My **v** Rev 3:20
with a **v** of thunder Rev 6:1

VOID *empty, invalid*
was formless and **v** Gen 1:2
make **v** the counsel Jer 19:7
faith is made **v** Rom 4:14
cross...be made **v** 1 Cor 1:17

VOMIT *throw up*
will **v** them up Job 20:15
returns to its **v** Prov 26:11
staggers in his **v** Is 19:14
and it **v-ed** Jonah Jon 2:10
returns to its own **v** 2 Pet 2:22

VOTIVE *dedicated*
his offering is a **v** Lev 7:16
choice **v** offerings Deut 12:11

VOW *solemn promise*
Jacob made a **v** Gen 28:20
v of a Nazirite Num 6:2
I shall pay my **v-s** Ps 22:25
not make false **v-s** Matt 5:33
he was keeping a **v** Acts 18:18

VOYAGE *journey*
v was now dangerous Acts 27:9

VULTURE *bird*
not eat...the **v** Deut 14:12
the **v-s** will gather Matt 24:28
the **v-s** will be gathered Luke 17:37

W

WAFER *thin cake of bread*
w-s with honey Ex 16:31
one unleavened **w** Num 6:19

WAGE *salary*
God has given...**w-s** Gen 30:18
w-s of the righteous Prov 10:16
w is not credited Rom 4:4
the **w-s** of sin Rom 6:23
worthy of his **w-s** 1 Tim 5:18

WAIL *lament, mourn*
w with a broken spirit Is 65:14
w, son of man Ezek 21:12
I must lament and **w** Mic 1:8
W, O inhabitants of Zeph 1:11
weeping and **w-ing** Mark 5:38

WAIT *expect*
For You I **w** Ps 25:5
I **w** for Your word Ps 119:81
who **w** for the LORD Is 40:31
creation **w-s** eagerly Rom 8:19
w-ing for the hope Gal 5:5

WALK *follow, go along*
w-ing in the garden Gen 3:8
W before Me Gen 17:1
w in My instruction Ex 16:4
w in My statutes Lev 26:3
w-ed forty years Josh 5:6
w before Me in truth 1 Kin 2:4
W about Zion Ps 48:12
I will **w** at liberty Ps 119:45
fool **w-s** in darkness Eccl 2:14
w in the light Is 2:5
w and not...weary Is 40:31
w-ed with Me in peace Mal 2:6
Get up, and **w** Matt 9:5
w-ed on the water Matt 14:29
w in newness of life Rom 6:4
we **w** by faith 2 Cor 5:7
w by the Spirit Gal 5:16
w in love Eph 5:2
w as children of Light Eph 5:8
if we **w** in the Light 1 John 1:7
w by its light Rev 21:24

WALL *structure*
living on the **w** Josh 2:15
So we built the **w** Neh 4:6
I can leap over a **w** Ps 18:29
w-s of Jerusalem Jer 39:8
built a siege **w** Jer 52:4
you whitewashed **w** Acts 23:3
w-s of Jericho fell Heb 11:30
a great and high **w** Rev 21:12

WANDER *roam*
w in the wilderness Num 32:13
I would **w** far away Ps 55:7
w...Your statutes Ps 119:118
people **w** like sheep Zech 10:2
w-ed...the faith 1 Tim 6:10
w-ing stars, for whom Jude 13

WANDERER *roamer*
a **w** on the earth Gen 4:12
an exile and a **w** Is 49:21
w-s among...nations Hos 9:17

WAR *battle, conflict*
when they see **w** Ex 13:17
sound of **w** in...camp Ex 32:17
land...rest from **w** Josh 11:23
He makes **w-s** to cease Ps 46:9
the weapons of **w** Ps 76:3
A time for **w** Eccl 3:8
will they learn **w** Is 2:4
w-s...rumors of **w-s** Matt 24:6
w against the law Rom 7:23
w in your members James 4:1
w against the soul 1 Pet 2:11
judges and wages **w** Rev 19:11

WARS OF THE LORD, BOOK OF
ancient Hebrew literature Num 21:14

WARM *heat*
could not keep **w** 1 Kin 1:1
the child became **w** 2 Kin 4:34
can one be **w** *alone* Eccl 4:11
no one is **w** *enough* Hag 1:6

WARN *give notice*
w the people Ex 19:21
not...**w** the wicked Ezek 33:8
w-ed...in a dream Matt 2:12
w you whom to fear Luke 12:5
Moses was **w-ed** Heb 8:5

WARRIOR *soldier*
The LORD is a **w** Ex 15:3
O valiant **w** Judg 6:12
w from his youth 1 Sam 17:33
w-s will flee naked Amos 2:16

WASH *bathe, clean*
w your feet, and rest Gen 18:4
w in the Jordan 2 Kin 5:10
w...in innocence Ps 26:6
W...from my iniquity Ps 51:2
w-ed off your blood Ezek 16:9
do not **w** their hands Matt 15:2
ceremonially **w-ed** Luke 11:38
w in the pool of John 9:7
w the disciples' feet John 13:5
w away your sins Acts 22:16
w-ed...saints' feet 1 Tim 5:10
w-ed with pure Heb 10:22
who **w** their robes Rev 22:14

WASTE (n) *wilderness*
land was laid **w** Ex 8:24
land into a salt **w** Ps 107:34
lay **w** the mountains Is 42:15
laid **w** like a desert Jer 9:12
altars may become **w** Ezek 6:6
Egypt...become a **w** Joel 3:19

WASTE (v) *destroy, use up*
he **w-d** his seed Gen 38:9
w away the eyes Lev 26:16
sick man **w-s** away Is 10:18
perfume been **w-d** Mark 14:4

WASTE PLACE *barren*
w-s of the wealthy Is 5:17
Seek Me in a **w** Is 45:19
like the ancient **w-s** Ezek 26:20
w-s will be rebuilt Ezek 36:10

WATCH (n) *guard*
at the morning **w** Ex 14:24
in the night **w-es** Ps 63:6
His eyes keep **w** Ps 66:7
keep **w** with Me Matt 26:38
w over their flock Luke 2:8
w over your souls Heb 13:17

WATCH (v) *observe*
LORD **w** between you Gen 31:49
w all my paths Job 13:27
W over your heart Prov 4:23
who **w-es** the wind Eccl 11:4
w...for the LORD Mic 7:7

WATCHMAN *one who guards*
w keeps awake in vain Ps 127:1
w-men for...morning Ps 130:6
W, how far gone is Is 21:11
I set **w-men** over you Jer 6:17
Ephraim *was* a **w** Hos 9:8

WATER (n) *flood, liquid*
moving over...the **w-s** Gen 1:2
flood of **w** came Gen 7:6
w-s *were like* a wall Ex 14:22
w of bitterness Num 5:18
the clouds dripped **w** Judg 5:4
W wears away stones Job 14:19
poured out like **w** Ps 22:14
beside quiet **w-s** Ps 23:2
Stolen **w** is sweet Prov 9:17
bread on the...**w-s** Eccl 11:1
come to the **w-s** Is 55:1
fountain of living **w-s** Jer 2:13
eyes run...with **w** Lam 1:16
knees...*like* **w** Ezek 7:17
baptize you with **w** Matt 3:11
a cup of cold **w** Matt 10:42
walked on the **w** Matt 14:29
no **w** for My feet Luke 7:44
one is born of **w** John 3:5
given you living **w** John 4:10
John baptized with **w** Acts 1:5
of **w** with the word Eph 5:26
formed out of **w** 2 Pet 3:5
by **w** and blood 1 John 5:6
sound of many **w-s** Rev 19:6

WATER (v) *make moist*
to **w** the garden Gen 2:10
I will **w** your camels Gen 24:46
w their father's flock Ex 2:16
that **w** the earth Ps 72:6
Apollos **w-ed** 1 Cor 3:6

WAVES *billows*
w of death 2 Sam 22:5
tramples down the **w** Job 9:8
Your **w** have rolled Ps 42:7
w were breaking Mark 4:37
wild **w** of the sea Jude 13

WAX *paraffin*
My heart is like **w** Ps 22:14
Like **w** before the fire Mic 1:4

WAY *manner* or *path*
guard the **w** Gen 3:24
all His **w-s** are just Deut 32:4
blameless...His **w** 2 Sam 22:33
from your evil **w-s** 2 Kin 17:13
joy of His **w** Job 8:19
w of the righteous Ps 1:6
Commit your **w** to Ps 37:5
your **w-s** acknowledge Prov 3:6
is the **w** of death Prov 14:12
Clear the **w** Is 40:3
w of the wicked Jer 12:1
Make ready the **w** Matt 3:3
Pray...in this **w** Matt 6:9
w is broad that leads Matt 7:13
teach...**w** of God Mark 12:14
into the **w** of peace Luke 1:79
I am the **w** John 14:6
belonging to the **W** Acts 9:2
the **w** of salvation Acts 16:17
unfathomable...**w-s** Rom 11:33
the **w** of escape 1 Cor 10:13
new and living **w** Heb 10:20
the **w** of the truth 2 Pet 2:2

WEAK *feeble*
I will become **w** Judg 16:17
Rescue the **w** Ps 82:4
but the flesh is **w** Matt 26:41
must help the **w** Acts 20:35
who is **w** in faith Rom 14:1
God...chosen the **w** 1 Cor 1:27

WEAKNESS *fault*
Spirit...helps our **w** Rom 8:26
bear the **w-es** Rom 15:1
w of God is stronger 1 Cor 1:25
it is sown in **w** 1 Cor 15:43
perfected in **w** 2 Cor 12:9

WEALTH *riches*
power to make **w** Deut 8:18
a man of great **w** Ruth 2:1
who trust in their **w** Ps 49:6
Honor...from your **w** Prov 3:9
W adds many friends Prov 19:4
A **w** of salvation Is 33:6
the **w** of all nations Hag 2:7
serve God and **w** Matt 6:24
deceitfulness of **w** Matt 13:22
w of their liberality 2 Cor 8:2
rich by her **w** Rev 18:19

WEAPON *armament*
girded on his **w-s** Deut 1:41
flee from the iron **w** Job 20:24
turn back the **w-s** Jer 21:4
w-s of righteousness 2 Cor 6:7

WEARY *tired*
the people were **w** 1 Sam 14:28
the **w** are at rest Job 3:17
w with my crying Ps 69:3
water to a **w** soul Prov 25:25
and not become **w** Is 40:31
sustain the **w** one Is 50:4
all who are **w** Matt 11:28
w of doing good 2 Thess 3:13

WEAVE *interlace*
You **wove** me Ps 139:13
w the spider's web Is 59:5

WEB *woven work*
loom and the **w** Judg 16:14
trust a spider's **w** Job 8:14

WEDDING *marriage*
had no **w** songs Ps 78:63
day of his **w** Song 3:11
come to the **w** feast Matt 22:4
a **w** in Cana John 2:1

WEEK *period of time*
Complete the **w** of Gen 29:27
Seventy **w-s** Dan 9:24
first *day* of the **w** Matt 28:1
I fast twice a **w** Luke 18:12

WEEKS, FEAST OF *see* **FEASTS**

WEEP *cry, sorrow*
sought *a place* to **w** Gen 43:30
do not mourn or **w** Neh 8:9
My eye **w-s** to God Job 16:20
widows could not **w** Ps 78:64
Let me **w** bitterly Is 22:4
w day and night Jer 9:1
Rachel **w-ing** for her Matt 2:18
w-ing and gnashing Matt 13:42
he...**wept** bitterly Matt 26:75
saw the city...**wept** Luke 19:41
w for yourselves Luke 23:28
Jesus **wept** John 11:35
why are you **w-ing** John 20:13
w with...who **w** Rom 12:15

WEIGH *measure out*
actions are **w-ed** 1 Sam 2:3
LORD **w-s** the motives Prov 16:2

WEIGHT *heaviness*
a full and just **w** Deut 25:15
w to the wind Job 28:25
bag of deceptive **w-s** Mic 6:11
eternal **w** of glory 2 Cor 4:17

WELCOME *gladly receive*
no prophet is **w** Luke 4:24
people **w-d** Him Luke 8:40
who fears Him...**w** Acts 10:35
she...**w-d** the spies Heb 11:31

WELL *water shaft*
sat down by a **w** Ex 2:15
w of Bethlehem 1 Chr 11:17
Like...a polluted **w** Prov 25:26
A **w** of fresh water Song 4:15
Jacob's **w** was there John 4:6

WELL-PLEASED *satisfied*
in whom I am **w** Matt 3:17
in You I am **w** Luke 3:22
God was not **w** 1 Cor 10:5

WEST *direction*
very strong **w** wind Ex 10:19
east is from the **w** Ps 103:12
gather you from the **w** Is 43:5

WHEAT *grain*
days of **w** harvest Gen 30:14
first fruits of the **w** Ex 34:22
plant **w** in rows Is 28:25
gather His **w** into Matt 3:12
to sift you like **w** Luke 22:31
unless a grain of **w** John 12:24

WHEEL *circular disk*
the **w**...is crushed Eccl 12:6
w-s like a whirlwind Is 5:28
one **w** were within Ezek 1:16
rattling of the **w** Nah 3:2

WHIRLWIND
take...Elijah by a **w** 2 Kin 2:1
comes like a **w** Prov 1:27
chariots like the **w** Jer 4:13
they reap the **w** Hos 8:7

WHISPER *talk quietly*
who hate me **w** Ps 41:7
w a prayer Is 26:16
your speech will **w** Is 29:4

WHISTLE *shrill sound*
And will **w** for it Is 5:26
LORD will **w** for the fly Is 7:18
I will **w** for them Zech 10:8

WHITE *color*
teeth **w** from milk Gen 49:12
w of an egg Job 6:6
be as **w** as snow Is 1:18
make one hair **w** Matt 5:36
clothing *became* **w** Luke 9:29
fields...**w** for harvest John 4:35
clothed in **w** robes Rev 7:9

WHITEWASHED *wall covering*
like **w** tombs Matt 23:27
you **w** wall Acts 23:3

WHOLE *entire*
water the **w** surface Gen 2:6

w earth...populated Gen 9:19
leavens the **w** lump 1 Cor 5:6
keeps the **w** law James 2:10

WICK *candle thread*
extinguished like a **w** Is 43:17
a smoldering **w** Matt 12:20

WICKED *evil, ungodly*
condemn the **w** Deut 25:1
w ones are silenced 1 Sam 2:9
counsel of the **w** Ps 1:1
the **w** spurned God Ps 10:13
The **w** strut about Ps 12:8
devises **w** plans Prov 6:18
When a **w** man dies Prov 11:7
no peace for the **w** Is 48:22
turn from his **w** way Jon 3:8
taking...some **w** men Acts 17:5
righteous and the **w** Acts 24:15

WICKEDNESS *evil*
w of man was great Gen 6:5
If I regard **w** Ps 66:18
eat the bread of **w** Prov 4:17
inclines toward **w** Is 32:6
w of My people Jer 7:12
You have plowed **w** Hos 10:13
repent of this **w** Acts 8:22
spiritual *forces* of **w** Eph 6:12

WIDOW *husband dead*
Remain a **w** Gen 38:11
not afflict any **w** Ex 22:22
sent **w-s** away empty Job 22:9
judge for the **w-s** Ps 68:5
Plead for the **w** Is 1:17
devour **w-s'** houses Matt 23:14
w put in more Mark 12:43
Honor **w-s** 1 Tim 5:3
visit orphans...**w-s** James 1:27

WIFE *married woman*
joined to his **w** Gen 2:24
man and his **w** hid Gen 3:8
shall not covet...**w** Ex 20:17
w of your youth Prov 5:18
An excellent **w** Prov 31:10
who divorces his **w** Matt 5:32
Remember Lot's **w** Luke 17:32
have his own **w** 1 Cor 7:2
head of the **w** Eph 5:23
husband of one **w** 1 Tim 3:2
w-ves, be submissive 1 Pet 3:1
w of the Lamb Rev 21:9

WILD *untamed*
w donkey of a man Gen 16:12
horns of the **w** ox Num 23:22
locusts and **w** honey Mark 1:6
being a **w** olive Rom 11:17

WILDERNESS *barren area*
water in the **w** Gen 16:7
journey into the **w** Ex 5:3
to die in the **w** Ex 14:11
forty years in the **w** Deut 29:5
pastures of the **w** Ps 65:12
roadway in the **w** Is 43:19
Have I been a **w** Jer 2:31
preaching in the **w** Matt 3:1
into the **w**...tempted Matt 4:1
crying in the **w** Mark 1:3
manna in the **w** John 6:31

WILL *attitude, purpose*
delight to do Your **w** Ps 40:8
Your **w** be done Matt 6:10
the **w** of My Father Matt 7:21
not My **w**, but Luke 22:42
nor of the **w** of man John 1:13
who resists His **w** Rom 9:19
what the **w** of God Rom 12:2
knowledge of His **w** Col 1:9
come to do Your **w** Heb 10:9
an act of human **w** 2 Pet 1:21

WIN *succeed*
wise **w-s** souls Prov 11:30
we will **w** him over Matt 28:14
that I might **w** Jews 1 Cor 9:20
won without a word 1 Pet 3:1

WIND
caused a **w** to pass Gen 8:1
scorched by...**w** Gen 41:27
will inherit **w** Prov 11:29
prophets are *as* **w** Jer 5:13
they sow the **w** Hos 8:7
reed shaken by...**w** Matt 11:7
w and the sea obey Mark 4:41
He...rebuked the **w** Luke 8:24
violent, rushing **w** Acts 2:2
every **w** of doctrine Eph 4:14
driven by strong **w-s** James 3:4

WINDOW *opening*
enter through the **w-s** Joel 2:9
open...**w-s** of heaven Mal 3:10
sitting on the **w** sill Acts 20:9
basket through a **w** 2 Cor 11:33

WINE *strong drink*
eyes...dull from **w** Gen 49:12
Do not drink **w** Lev 10:9
overflow with new **w** Prov 3:10
W is a mocker Prov 20:1
love is better than **w** Song 1:2
new **w** into old Matt 9:17
gave Him **w** to Matt 27:34
made the water **w** John 4:46
full of sweet **w** Acts 2:13
not get drunk with **w** Eph 5:18
not addicted to **w** 1 Tim 3:3

WINESKINS *animal skin bag*
These **w**...were new Josh 9:13
Like new **w** Job 32:19
wine into fresh **w** Matt 9:17

WINGS
bore you on eagles' **w** Ex 19:4
He spread His **w** Deut 32:11
under whose **w** Ruth 2:12
under His **w**...refuge Ps 91:4
with **w** like eagles Is 40:31
healing in its **w** Mal 4:2
chicks under her **w** Matt 23:37

WINK *blink*
w maliciously Ps 35:19
w-s with his eyes Prov 6:13

WINNOW *scatter*
king **w-s** the wicked Prov 20:26
You will **w** them Is 41:16
His **w-ing** fork Matt 3:12

WINTER *season*
And summer and **w** Gen 8:22
the **w** is past Song 2:11
even spend the **w** 1 Cor 16:6

WIPE *pass over, rub*
God will **w** tears Is 25:8
w-d His feet John 11:2
sins...**w-d** away Acts 3:19
w away every tear Rev 21:4

WISDOM *discernment*
the spirit of **w** Ex 28:3
w has two sides Job 11:6
the beginning of **w** Ps 111:10
Fools despise **w** Prov 1:7
w to fear Your name Mic 6:9
w given to Him Mark 6:2
kept increasing in **w** Luke 2:52
made foolish the **w** 1 Cor 1:20
any of you lacks **w** James 1:5

WISE *judicious, prudent*
not find a **w** man Job 17:10
making **w** the simple Ps 19:7
w in your own eyes Prov 3:7
the words of the **w** Prov 22:17
He is not a **w** son Hos 13:13
Who...you is **w** James 3:13

WITCHCRAFT *magic, sorcery*
who practices **w** Deut 18:10
practiced **w** and 2 Kin 21:6

WITHER *dry up*
its leaf does not **w** Ps 1:3
w...like the grass Ps 37:2
earth mourns *and* **w-s** Is 24:4
the leaf will **w** Jer 8:13
whose hand was **w-ed** Mark 3:1
the fig tree **w-ed** Mark 11:20

WITNESS (n) *testimony*
This heap is a **w** Gen 31:48
is **w** between us Judg 11:10
my **w** is in heaven Job 16:19
a **w** to the Lord Is 19:20
He came as a **w** John 1:7
you shall be My **w-es** Acts 1:8
For God is my **w** Phil 1:8
Christ, the faithful **w** Rev 1:5

WITNESS (v) *testify*
not bear false **w** Ex 20:16
w against you today Deut 4:26

WOLF *animal*
w will dwell with Is 11:6
the midst of **w-ves** Matt 10:16
w snatches them John 10:12

WOMAN *female, lady*
She shall be called **W** Gen 2:23
w...not wear man's Deut 22:5
a **w** of excellence Ruth 3:11
Man...born of **w** Job 14:1
gracious **w** attains Prov 11:16
a contentious **w** Prov 25:24
like a **w** in labor Is 42:14
looks at a **w** with lust Matt 5:28
w-en...grinding Matt 24:41
Blessed...among **w-en** Luke 1:42
W, behold, your son John 19:26
not to touch a **w** 1 Cor 7:1
w is the glory of 1 Cor 11:7
w to speak in 1 Cor 14:35
His Son, born of a **w** Gal 4:4
w clothed with...sun Rev 12:1

WOMB
nations...in your **w** Gen 25:23
Lord...closed her **w** 1 Sam 1:5
from **w** to tomb Job 10:19
formed you from the **w** Is 44:2
baby leaped in...**w** Luke 1:41

WONDER *marvel, sign*
consider the **w-s** of Job 37:14
tell of all Your **w-s** Ps 9:1
His **w-s** in the deep Ps 107:24
w-s in the sky Joel 2:30
were filled with **w** Acts 3:10

WONDERFUL *marvelous*
His **w** deeds 1 Chr 16:12
name will be called **W** Is 9:6

WOOD *cut tree*
ark of gopher **w** Gen 6:14
other gods, **w** and Deut 28:36
children gather **w** Jer 7:18
stones, **w**, hay 1 Cor 3:12

WOOL *cloth* or *hair*
of **w** and linen Deut 22:11
put a fleece of **w** on Judg 6:37
They will be like **w** Is 1:18
hair...like pure **w** Dan 7:9
white like white **w** Rev 1:14

WORD *message, speech*
to the **w** of Moses Lev 10:7
declare to you the **w** Deut 5:5
Joshua wrote...**w-s** Josh 24:26
proclaim the **w** of 1 Sam 9:27
Your **w**...confirmed 2 Chr 6:17
no limit to windy **w-s** Job 16:3
w-s of my mouth Ps 19:14
Your **w** is a lamp Ps 119:105
harsh **w** stirs up Prov 15:1
w of God is tested Prov 30:5
despised the **w** Is 5:24
w-s of a sealed book Is 29:11
speak My **w** in truth Jer 23:28
conceal these **w-s** Dan 12:4

every **w** that proceeds Matt 4:4
these **w-s** of Mine Matt 7:24
sower sows the **w** Mark 4:14
the **W** was God John 1:1
the **W** became flesh John 1:14
w-s of eternal life John 6:68
continue in My **w** John 8:31
glorifying the **w** Acts 13:48
too deep for **w-s** Rom 8:26
hearing by the **w** Rom 10:17
the **w** of the cross 1 Cor 1:18
fulfilled in one **w** Gal 5:14
no unwholesome **w** Eph 4:29
sanctified by...**w** 1 Tim 4:5
the **w** of truth 2 Tim 2:15
the faithful **w** Titus 1:9
w of God is living Heb 4:12
doers of the **w** James 1:22
pure milk of the **w** 1 Pet 2:2
the **W** of Life 1 John 1:1
The **W** of God Rev 19:13

WORK (n) *act, deed, labor*
God completed His **w** Gen 2:2
You shall **w** six days Ex 34:21
His **w** is perfect Deut 32:4
the **w** of His hands Ps 19:1
see the **w-s** of God Ps 66:5
Commit your **w-s** to Prov 16:3
let Him hasten His **w** Is 5:19
His **w** on Mount Zion Is 10:12
see your good **w-s** Matt 5:16
the **w-s** of Christ Matt 11:2
the **w** of the Law Rom 2:15
faith apart from **w-s** Rom 3:28
not...a result of **w-s** Eph 2:9
for the **w** of service Eph 4:12
began a good **w** Phil 1:6
fruit in...good **w** Col 1:10
rich in good **w-s** 1 Tim 6:18
faith without **w-s** James 2:20

WORK (v) *perform, produce*
has **w-ed** with God 1 Sam 14:45
those who **w** iniquity Ps 28:3
Who...**w-s** wonders Ps 72:18
not **w** for the food John 6:27
w together for good Rom 8:28
So death **w-s** in us 2 Cor 4:12
w out your salvation Phil 2:12
anyone is not willing to **w** 2 Thess 3:10

WORKER *laborer*
O **w** of deceit Ps 52:2
w-s of iniquity Prov 10:29
w is worthy of his Matt 10:10
God's fellow **w-s** 1 Cor 3:9
beware...evil **w-s** Phil 3:2
pure, **w-s** at home Titus 2:5

WORKMAN *craftsman*
a skillful **w** Ex 38:23
approved...as a **w** 2 Tim 2:15

WORKMANSHIP *craftsmanship*
we are His **w** Eph 2:10

WORLD *earth, humanity*
foundations of...**w** 2 Sam 22:16
He will judge the **w** Ps 9:8
first dust of the **w** Prov 8:26
the light of the **w** Matt 5:14
the field is the **w** Matt 13:38
Go into all the **w** Mark 16:15
gains the whole **w** Luke 9:25
God so loved the **w** John 3:16
Savior of the **w** John 4:42
w cannot hate you John 7:7
the Light of the **w** John 8:12
overcome the **w** John 16:33
have upset the **w** Acts 17:6
sin entered...the **w** Rom 5:12
reconciling the **w** 2 Cor 5:19
unstained by the **w** James 1:27
flood upon the **w** 2 Pet 2:5
Do not love the **w** 1 John 2:15

WORLDLY *earthly*
w fables fit only 1 Tim 4:7
avoid **w**...chatter 2 Tim 2:16

WORM *creeping animal*
But I am a **w** Ps 22:6
w-s are your covering Is 14:11
God appointed a **w** Jon 4:7
their **w** does not die Mark 9:48
he was eaten by **w-s** Acts 12:23

WORMWOOD
1 *a bitter plant* Deut 29:18
2 *used figuratively* Prov 5:4; Amos 6:12; Rev 8:11

WORRY *anxious*
not be **w-ied** about your life Matt 6:25
not **w** about tomorrow Matt 6:34
do not **w** beforehand Mark 13:11
w-ing can add a *single* Luke 12:25

WORSHIP *bow, revere*
not **w** any other god Ex 34:14
you shall **w** Him Deut 6:13
W the LORD Ps 2:11
earth will **w** You Ps 66:4
in vain do they **w** Matt 15:9
w in spirit and truth John 4:24
w in the Spirit Phil 3:3
w Him who lives Rev 4:10
who **w** the beast Rev 14:11

WORTHLESS *useless*
all **w** physicians Job 13:4
w man digs up evil Prov 16:27
your **w** offerings Is 1:13
your faith is **w** 1 Cor 15:17
w for any good Titus 1:16
man's religion is **w** James 1:26

WORTHY *having merit*
sin **w** of death Deut 21:22
w of his support Matt 10:10
is not **w** of Me Matt 10:37
is **w** of his wages Luke 10:7
manner **w** of the Rom 16:2

w of the gospel Phil 1:27
world was not **w** Heb 11:38
W is the Lamb Rev 5:12

WOUND *injury*
My **w** is incurable Job 34:6
binds up their **w-s** Ps 147:3
Your **w** is incurable Jer 30:12
bandaged...his **w-s** Luke 10:34
by His **w-s** you were 1 Pet 2:24
fatal **w** was healed Rev 13:3

WRAPPINGS *cloth coverings*
bound...with **w** John 11:44
linen **w** lying *there* John 20:5

WRATH *anger, indignation*
and in great **w** Deut 29:28
Nor chasten...in Your **w** Ps 6:1
Pour out Your **w** Ps 79:6
turns away **w** Prov 15:1
Or else My **w** will go forth Jer 4:4
spent My **w** upon Ezek 5:13
from the **w** to come Matt 3:7
w of God abides on John 3:36
God who inflicts **w** Rom 3:5
children of **w** Eph 2:3
w of God will come Col 3:6
the **w** of the Lamb Rev 6:16

WRETCHED *miserable*
in to this **w** place Num 20:5
W man that I am Rom 7:24

WRITE *enscribe*
Moses, **W** this in a Ex 17:14
W them on the tablet Prov 3:3
he **wrote** the dream Dan 7:1
w a certificate Mark 10:4
with His finger **wrote** John 8:6
w...King of the Jews John 19:21
W in a book Rev 1:11

WRITINGS *literary work*
not believe his **w** John 5:47
known the sacred **w** 2 Tim 3:15

WRITTEN *enscribed*
w by...God Ex 31:18
w in the law 2 Chr 23:18
remembrance was **w** Mal 3:16
w by the prophet Matt 2:5
about whom it is **w** Matt 11:10
Law **w** in...hearts Rom 2:15
name has not been **w** Rev 13:8
w in the Lamb's Rev 21:27

WRONG *do evil, harm*
not **w** a stranger Ex 22:21
not **w** one another Lev 25:14
I...have done **w** 2 Sam 24:17
Love does no **w** Rom 13:10

WROUGHT *accomplished*
He **w** wonders Ps 78:12
been **w** in God John 3:21

Y

YAHWEH
see **YHWH** *and* **LORD**

YEAR *period, time*
atonement...every **y** Lev 16:34
fiftieth **y**...jubilee Lev 25:11
the **y** of remission Deut 15:9
crowned the **y** with Ps 65:11
length of...**y-s** Prov 3:2
favorable **y** of the LORD Is 61:2
thirty **y-s** of age Luke 3:23
y of the LORD Luke 4:19
priest *enters,* once a **y** Heb 9:7
sacrifices...**y** by **y** Heb 10:1
y-s like one day 2 Pet 3:8
reign...thousand **y-s** Rev 20:6

YEARLING *one year old*
a **y** ewe lamb Lev 14:10
With **y** calves Mic 6:6

YEARNS *deeply moved*
my flesh **y** for You Ps 63:1
My heart **y** for him Jer 31:20

YESTERDAY *past*
we are *only* of **y** Job 8:9
thousand years...**y** Ps 90:4
same **y** and today Heb 13:8

YHWH
Hebrew tetragrammaton for name of God, probably pronounced Yahweh
Derived from Hebrew verb meaning "to be"
Translated usually as LORD
see also **LORD**
see also introductory material to NASB

YIELD *produce*
no longer **y** its Gen 4:12
land...**y** its produce Lev 25:19
Which **y-s** its fruit Ps 1:3
y-ed up *His* spirit Matt 27:50
not **y** in subjection Gal 2:5
y-s the peaceful Heb 12:11

YOKE *wooden bar*
break his **y** from Gen 27:40
iron **y** on...neck Deut 28:48
made our **y** hard 1 Kin 12:4
the **y** of their burden Is 9:4
Take My **y** upon Matt 11:29
to a **y** of slavery Gal 5:1

YOUNG *early age, youth*
he sent **y** men Ex 24:5
or two **y** pigeons Lev 15:29
glory of **y** men is Prov 20:29
y men stumble Is 40:30
like a **y** lion Hos 5:14
finding a **y** donkey John 12:14
y men...visions Acts 2:17
urge the **y** men Titus 2:6

YOUTH *young*
evil from his **y** Gen 8:21
fresher than in **y** Job 33:25
the sins of my **y** Ps 25:7
confidence from my **y** Ps 71:5
your **y** is renewed Ps 103:5
the wife of your **y** Prov 5:18
y-s grow weary Is 40:30
the reproach of my **y** Jer 31:19
life from my **y** up Acts 26:4

Z

ZACCHEUS
tax collector who followed Jesus Luke 19:2,5,8

ZACHARIAS
father of John the Baptist Luke 1:5,12,18;3:2

ZAREPHATH
scene of miracle by Elijah 1 Kin 17:9,10
Phoenician town Obad 20; Luke 4:26

ZEAL *fervor, passion*
kill them in his **z** 2 Sam 21:2
my **z** for the LORD 2 Kin 10:16
z has consumed me Ps 119:139
Your **z** for the people Is 26:11
have a **z** for God Rom 10:2
your **z** for me 2 Cor 7:7

ZEALOT
member of radical Jewish nationalist party Matt 10:4; Mark 3:18; Luke 6:15; Acts 1:13

ZEALOUS *fervent*
z for the LORD 1 Kin 19:10
all **z** for the Law Acts 21:20
z of...*gifts* 1 Cor 14:12
z for good deeds Titus 2:14
be **z** and repent Rev 3:19

ZEBEDEE
father of James and John Matt 4:21;27:56; Mark 1:19;10:35; Luke 5:10; John 21:2

ZEBULUN
1 *son of Jacob* Gen 30:20
2 *tribe* Num 34:25; Josh 21:34
3 *territory of the tribe, located in N Palestine* Josh 19:27; Judg 12:12; Is 9:1; Ezek 48:27

ZECHARIAH
1 *son of Jeiel* 1 Chr 9:35-37
2 *priest with ark* 1 Chr 15:24
3 *son of Isshiah* 1 Chr 24:25
4 *father of Iddo* 1 Chr 27:21
5 *son of Benaiah* 2 Chr 20:14
6 *son of Jehoshaphat* 2 Chr 21:2
7 *son of Jehoida* 2 Chr 24:20
8 *prophet* 2 Chr 26:5
9 *priest under Ezra* Neh 12:41
10 *minor prophet* Zech 1:1

ZELOPHEHAD
Manassite, son of Hepher Num 26:33
daughters became his heirs Num 27:1;36:2

ZEPHANIAH
1 *priest* 2 Kin 25:18
2 *Kohathite Levite* 1 Chr 6:36
3 *minor prophet* Zeph 1:1
4 *father of Josiah* Zech 6:10

ZERUBBABEL
line of David 1 Chr 3:1-19
helped rebuild temple Ezra 3:8

ZERUIAH
mother of Joab, Abishai, and Asahel 2 Sam 2:18
David's half-sister 1 Chr 2:16

ZIKLAG
town in S Judah Josh 15:31; 1 Sam 27:6; 1 Chr 12:1

ZILPAH
concubine of Jacob Gen 29:24;30:10;46:18

ZIN
wilderness in Negev Num 13:21; Deut 32:51; Josh 15:1,3

ZION
1 *hill / City of David which is Jerusalem* 2 Sam 5:7; 1 Chr 11:5
2 *after Temple built, name extended to top of hill, Mount Zion* Is 8:18;18:7; Mic 4:7
3 *applied to all of Jerusalem as city spreads* 2 Kin 19:21; Ps 69:35; Is 1:8
4 *used in the corporate sense for the people and land* Ps 97:8;149:2; Is 3:16;8:14;59:20; Joel 2:23; Zech 9:9; Rom 9:33; 1 Pet 2:3
5 *used eschatologically for heavenly Jerusalem* Is 60:14; Heb 12:22; Rev 14:1

ZIPPORAH
wife of Moses Ex 2:21;4:25

ZIV
name of the second month in Hebrew calendar 1 Kin 6:1,37

ZOAN
Egyptian delta city Num 13:22; Ps 78:12; Is 19:11; Ezek 30:14

ZOAR
city of the plain near the Dead Sea Gen 13:10;14:2;19:23,30; Deut 34:3; Jer 48:34
see also **BELA**

ZOPHAR
one of Job's friends Job 2:11;11:1;20:1;42:9

ZUZIM
pre-Israelite tribe in Palestine Gen 14:5

Study Notes

Study Notes

Study Notes

Study Notes

Study Notes

Study Notes

Study Notes

Study Notes

Study Notes

Study Notes

Study Notes

Study Notes

Modern Boundaries of Bible Lands

North America
South America
Europe
Middle East
Asia
Africa
Australia

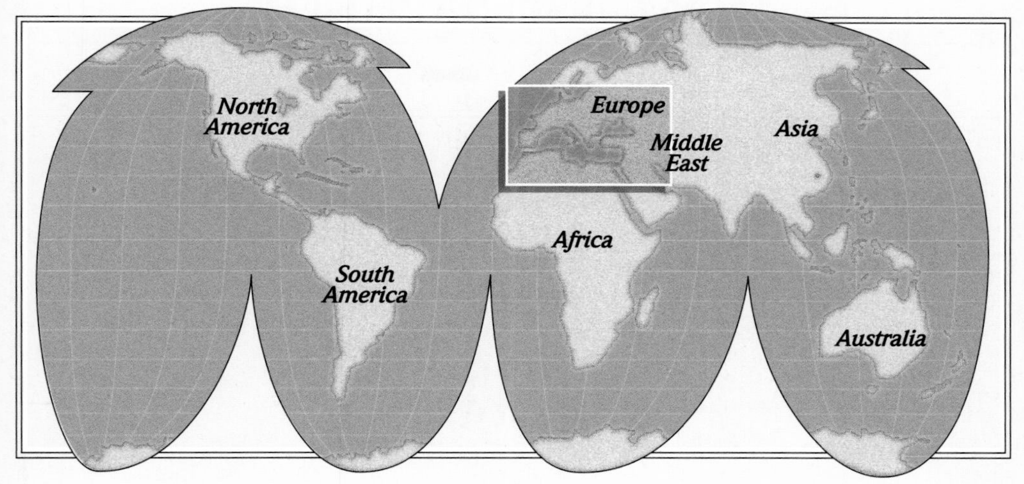

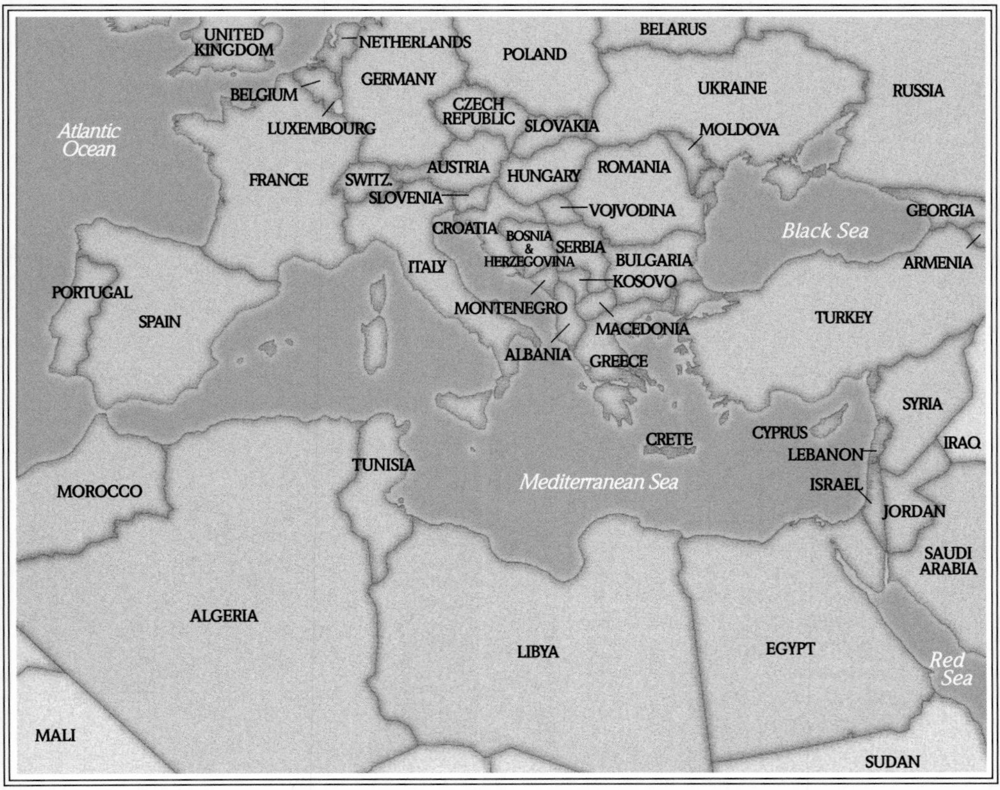

UNITED KINGDOM
NETHERLANDS
BELARUS
POLAND
GERMANY
BELGIUM
UKRAINE
RUSSIA
CZECH REPUBLIC
LUXEMBOURG
SLOVAKIA
MOLDOVA
Atlantic Ocean
AUSTRIA
FRANCE
SWITZ.
HUNGARY
ROMANIA
SLOVENIA
VOJVODINA
GEORGIA
CROATIA
BOSNIA & HERZEGOVINA
SERBIA
Black Sea
ITALY
BULGARIA
ARMENIA
PORTUGAL
KOSOVO
SPAIN
MONTENEGRO
TURKEY
MACEDONIA
ALBANIA
GREECE
SYRIA
CRETE
CYPRUS
IRAQ
LEBANON
TUNISIA
Mediterranean Sea
ISRAEL
MOROCCO
JORDAN
SAUDI ARABIA
ALGERIA
LIBYA
EGYPT
Red Sea
MALI
SUDAN

THE SETTLEMENT OF THE DESCENDANTS OF SHEM, HAM, AND JAPHETH

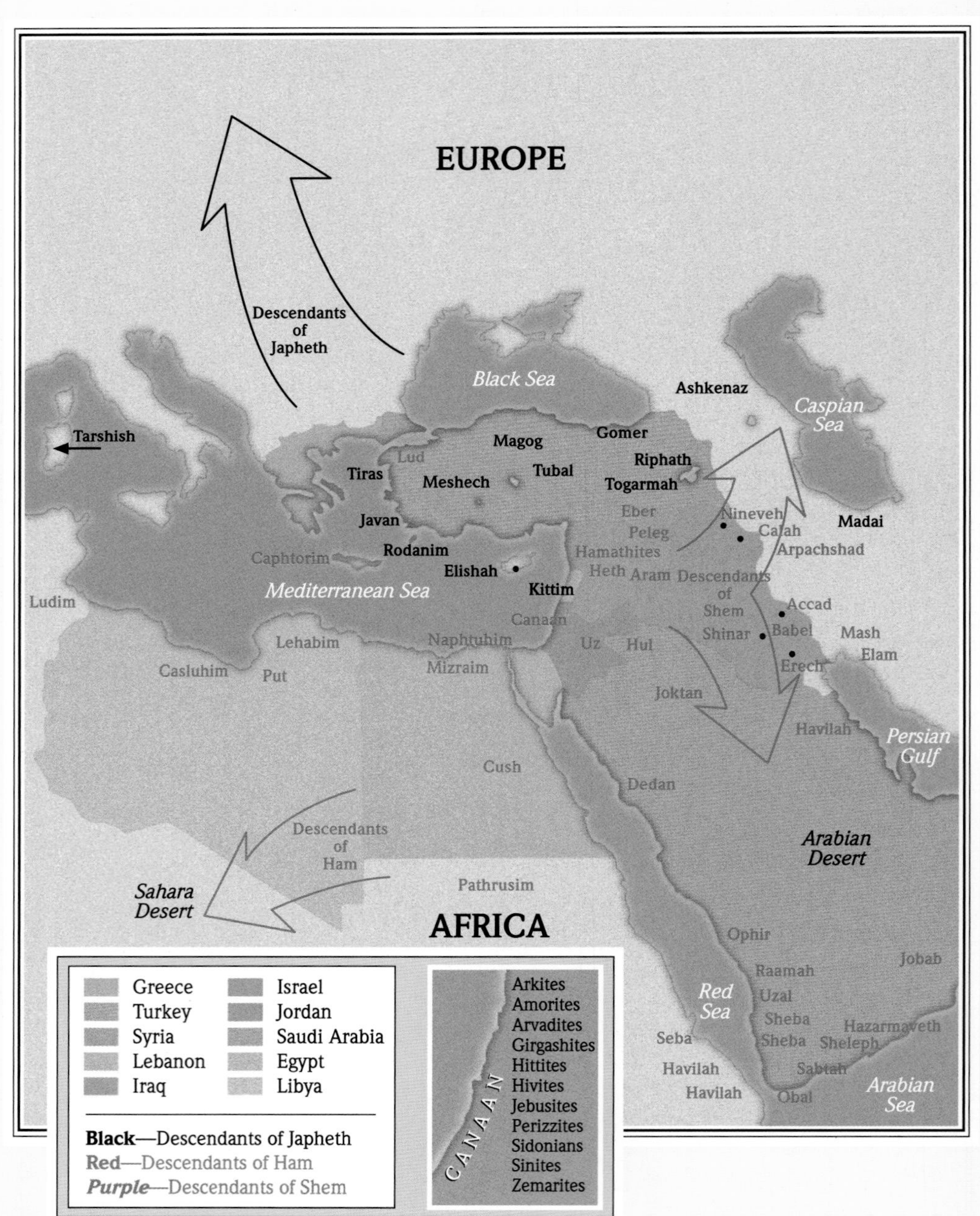
EUROPE
Descendants of Japheth
Black Sea
Ashkenaz
Caspian Sea
Tarshish
Magog
Gomer
Lud
Tiras
Meshech
Tubal
Riphath
Togarmah
Eber
Peleg
Nineveh
Calah
Madai
Javan
Arpachshad
Hamathites
Rodanim
Caphtorim
Elishah
Heth
Aram
Descendants of Shem
Kittim
Mediterranean Sea
Ludim
Accad
Canaan
Babel
Shinar
Mash
Lehabim
Naphtuhim
Uz
Hul
Elam
Erech
Casluhim
Put
Mizraim
Joktan
Havilah
Persian Gulf
Cush
Dedan
Descendants of Ham
Arabian Desert
Sahara Desert
Pathrusim
AFRICA
Ophir
Jobab
Raamah
Red Sea
Uzal
Sheba
Hazarmaveth
Seba
Sheba
Sheleph
Havilah
Sabtah
Havilah
Obal
Arabian Sea
Greece
Turkey
Syria
Lebanon
Iraq
Israel
Jordan
Saudi Arabia
Egypt
Libya
Black—Descendants of Japheth
Red—Descendants of Ham
Purple—Descendants of Shem
CANAAN
Arkites
Amorites
Arvadites
Girgashites
Hittites
Hivites
Jebusites
Perizzites
Sidonians
Sinites
Zemarites

The Ancient and Modern Sites of the Exodus

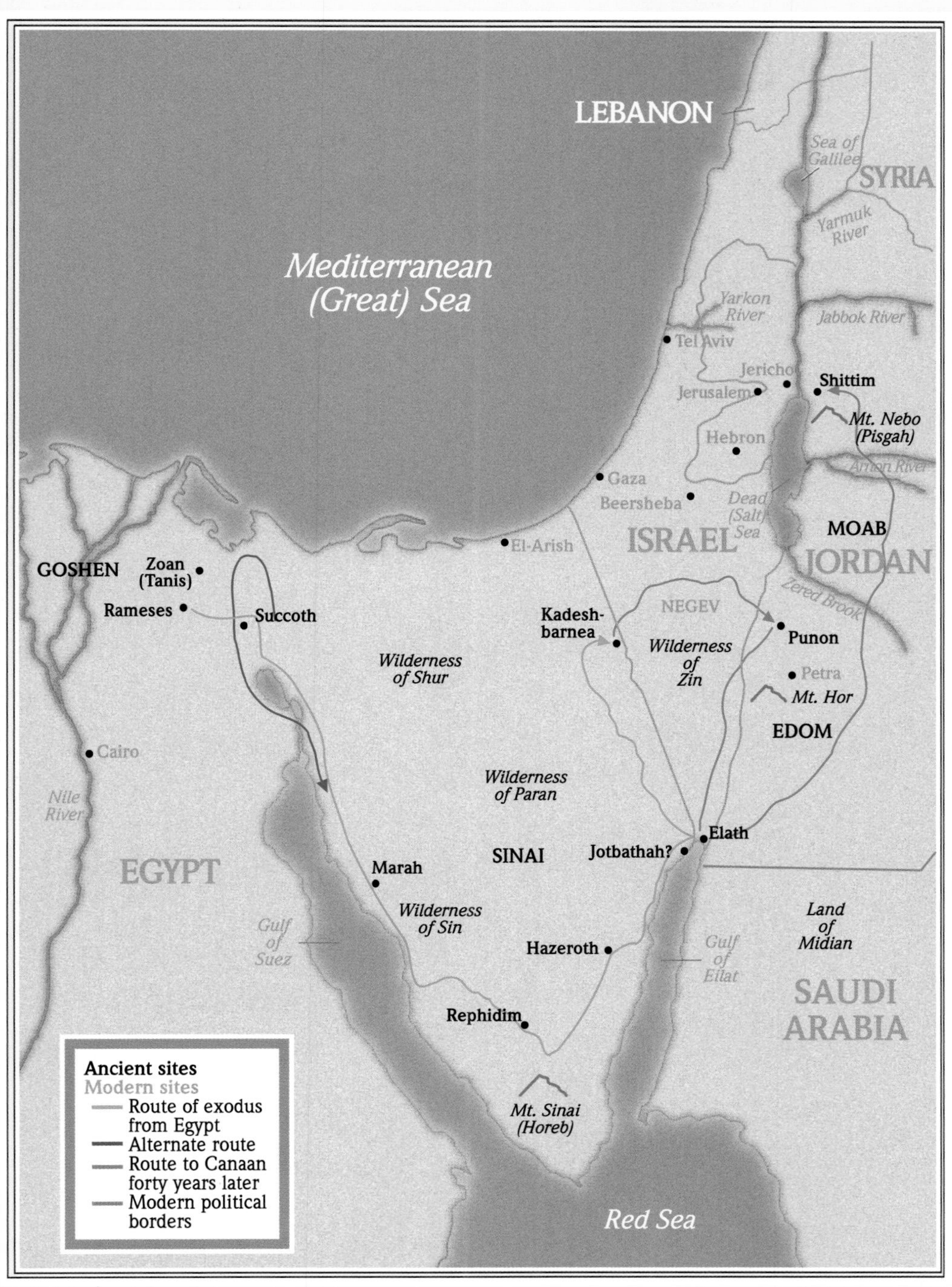

LEBANON
Sea of Galilee
SYRIA
Yarmuk River
Mediterranean (Great) Sea
Yarkon River
Jabbok River
Tel Aviv
Jericho
Shittim
Jerusalem
Mt. Nebo (Pisgah)
Hebron
Arnon River
Gaza
Beersheba
Dead (Salt) Sea
MOAB
El-Arish
ISRAEL
JORDAN
GOSHEN
Zoan (Tanis)
Rameses
Succoth
Zered Brook
NEGEV
Kadesh-barnea
Punon
Wilderness of Shur
Wilderness of Zin
Petra
Mt. Hor
EDOM
Cairo
Nile River
Wilderness of Paran
Elath
SINAI
Jotbathah?
EGYPT
Marah
Land of Midian
Wilderness of Sin
Gulf of Suez
Hazeroth
Gulf of Eilat
SAUDI ARABIA
Rephidim
Ancient sites
Modern sites
Route of exodus from Egypt
Alternate route
Route to Canaan forty years later
Modern political borders
Mt. Sinai (Horeb)
Red Sea

Ezekiel's Vision of the Promised Land

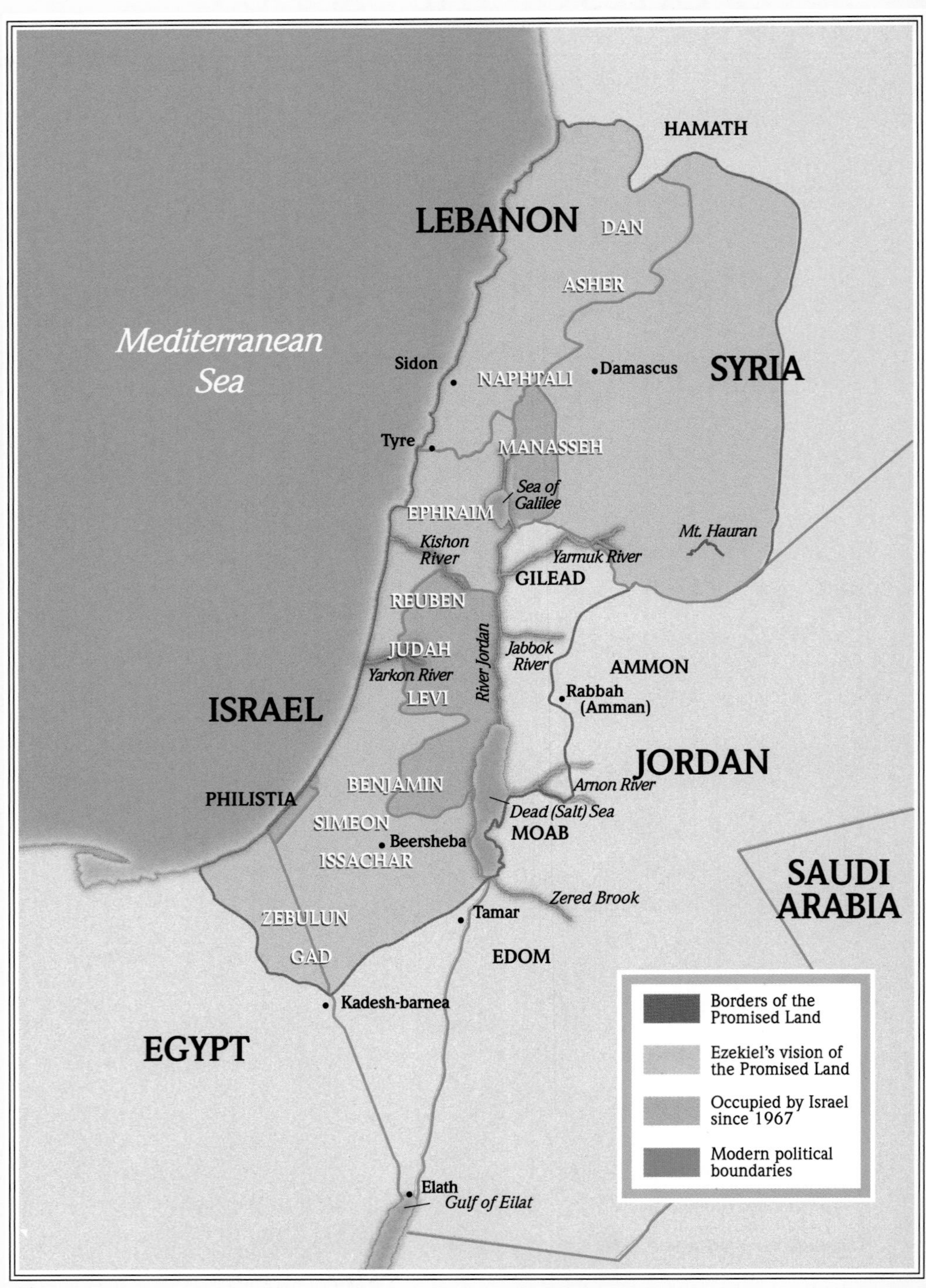

HAMATH
LEBANON
DAN
ASHER
Mediterranean Sea
Sidon
NAPHTALI
Damascus
SYRIA
Tyre
MANASSEH
Sea of Galilee
EPHRAIM
Mt. Hauran
Kishon River
Yarmuk River
GILEAD
REUBEN
JUDAH
Jabbok River
AMMON
Yarkon River
River Jordan
LEVI
Rabbah (Amman)
ISRAEL
JORDAN
BENJAMIN
Arnon River
PHILISTIA
Dead (Salt) Sea
SIMEON
MOAB
Beersheba
ISSACHAR
SAUDI ARABIA
Zered Brook
Tamar
ZEBULUN
GAD
EDOM
Kadesh-barnea
EGYPT
Elath
Gulf of Eilat
Borders of the Promised Land
Ezekiel's vision of the Promised Land
Occupied by Israel since 1967
Modern political boundaries

ISRAEL'S TERRITORIES: ANCIENT AND MODERN

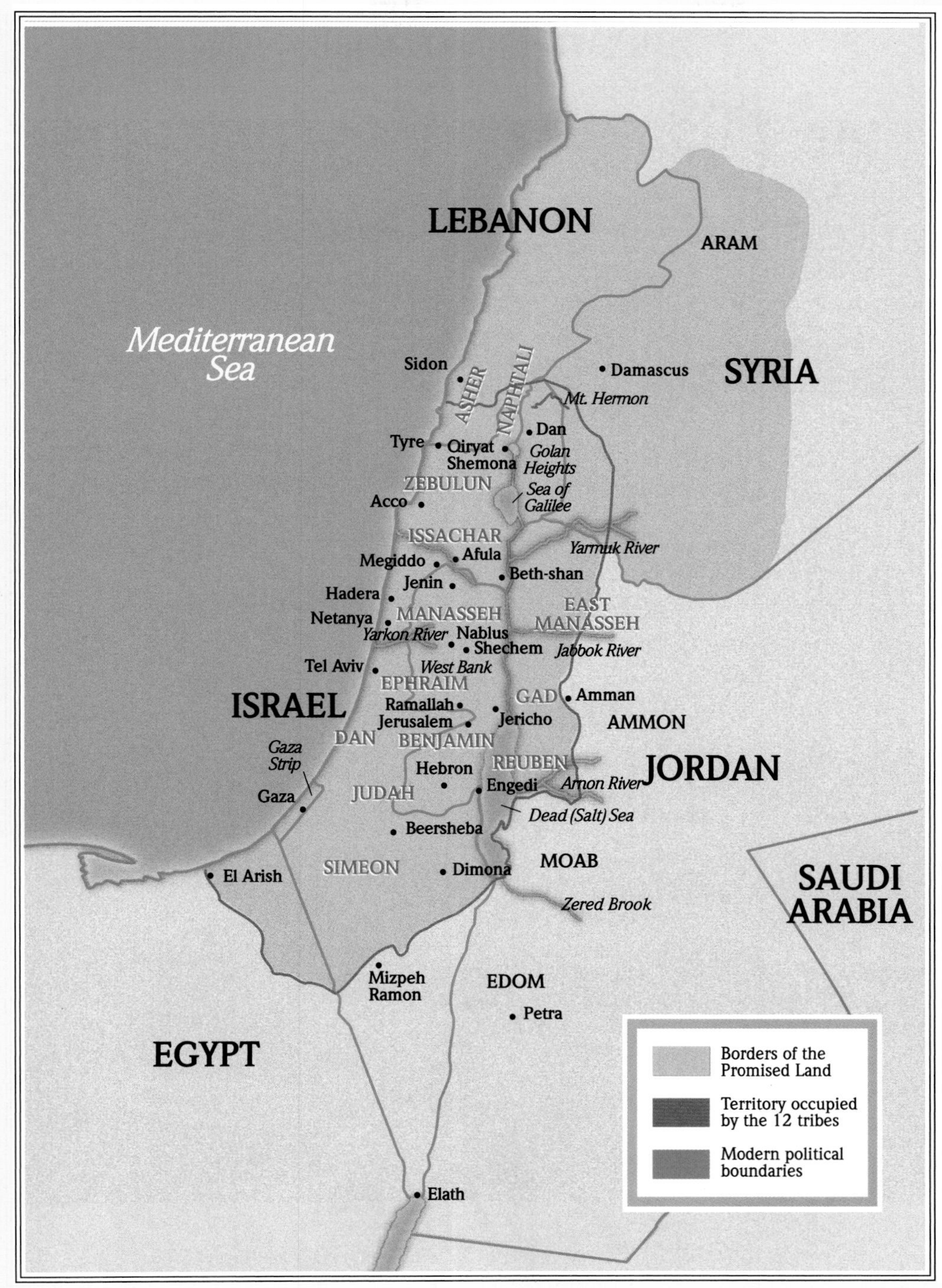

LEBANON
ARAM
Mediterranean Sea
Sidon
ASHER
NAPHTALI
Damascus
SYRIA
Mt. Hermon
Dan
Tyre
Qiryat Shemona
Golan Heights
ZEBULUN
Sea of Galilee
Acco
ISSACHAR
Afula
Yarmuk River
Megiddo
Beth-shan
Jenin
Hadera
EAST MANASSEH
Netanya
MANASSEH
Yarkon River
Nablus
Shechem
Jabbok River
Tel Aviv
West Bank
EPHRAIM
GAD
Amman
ISRAEL
Ramallah
Jericho
Jerusalem
AMMON
DAN
BENJAMIN
Gaza Strip
REUBEN
JORDAN
Hebron
Gaza
JUDAH
Engedi
Arnon River
Dead (Salt) Sea
Beersheba
SIMEON
Dimona
MOAB
El Arish
SAUDI ARABIA
Zered Brook
Mizpeh Ramon
EDOM
Petra
EGYPT
Borders of the Promised Land
Territory occupied by the 12 tribes
Modern political boundaries
Elath

BABYLONIAN EMPIRE

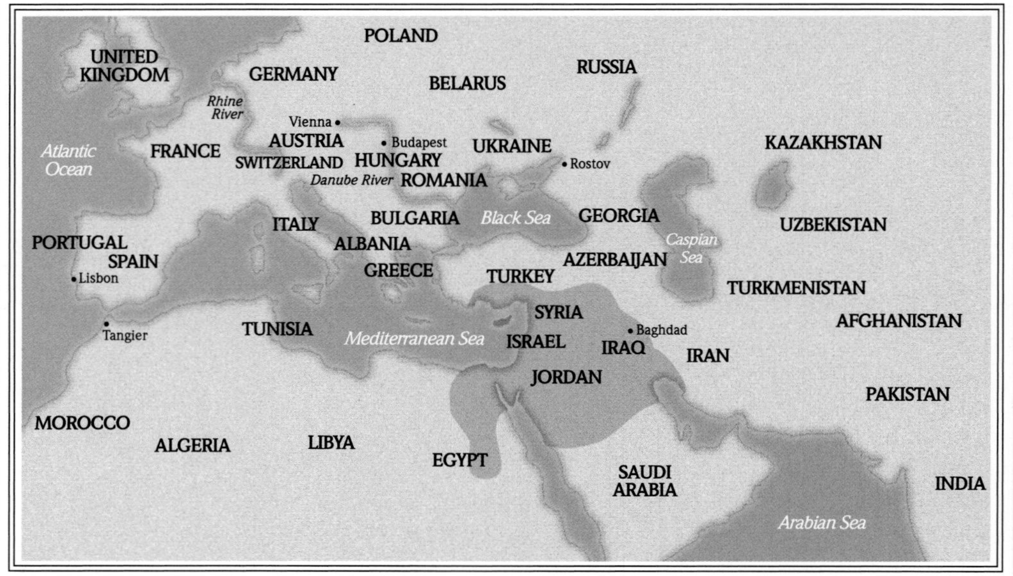

PERSIAN EMPIRE

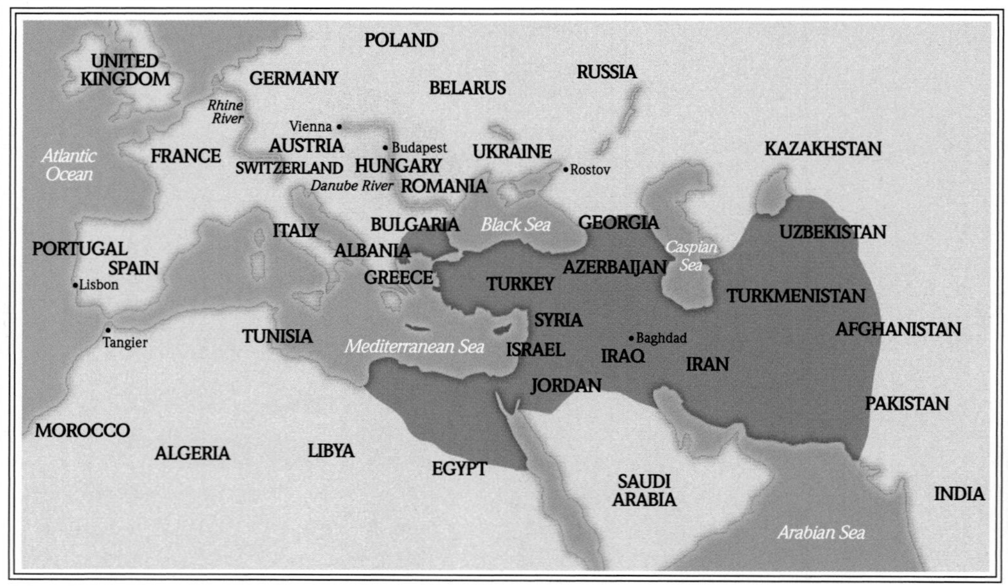

GREEK EMPIRE

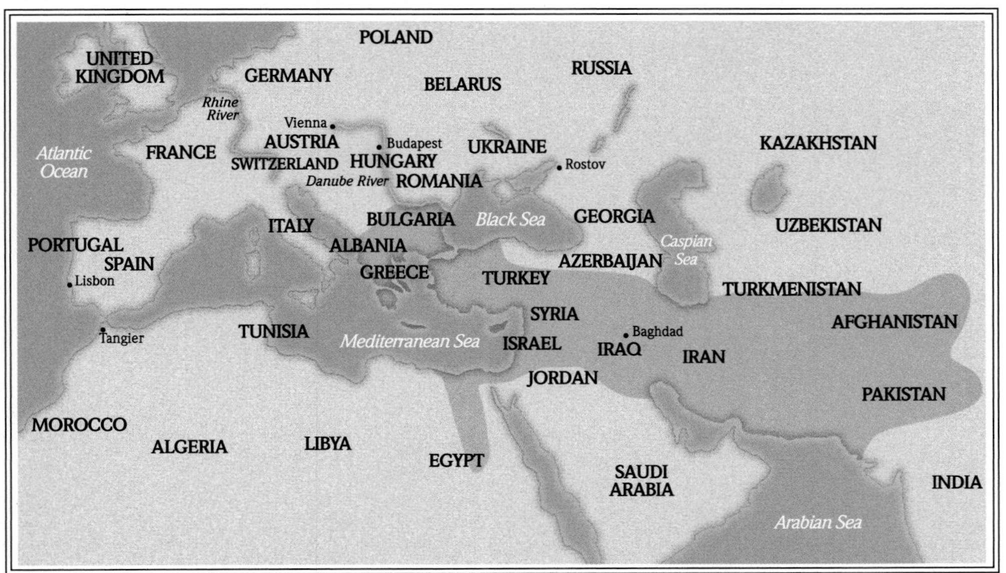

ROMAN EMPIRE

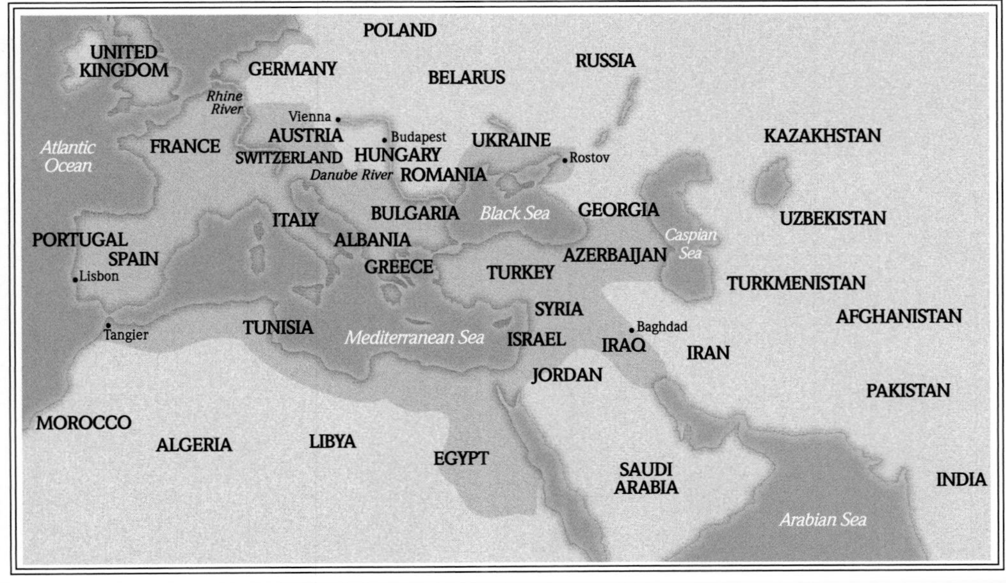

DEVELOPMENT OF MODERN ISRAEL

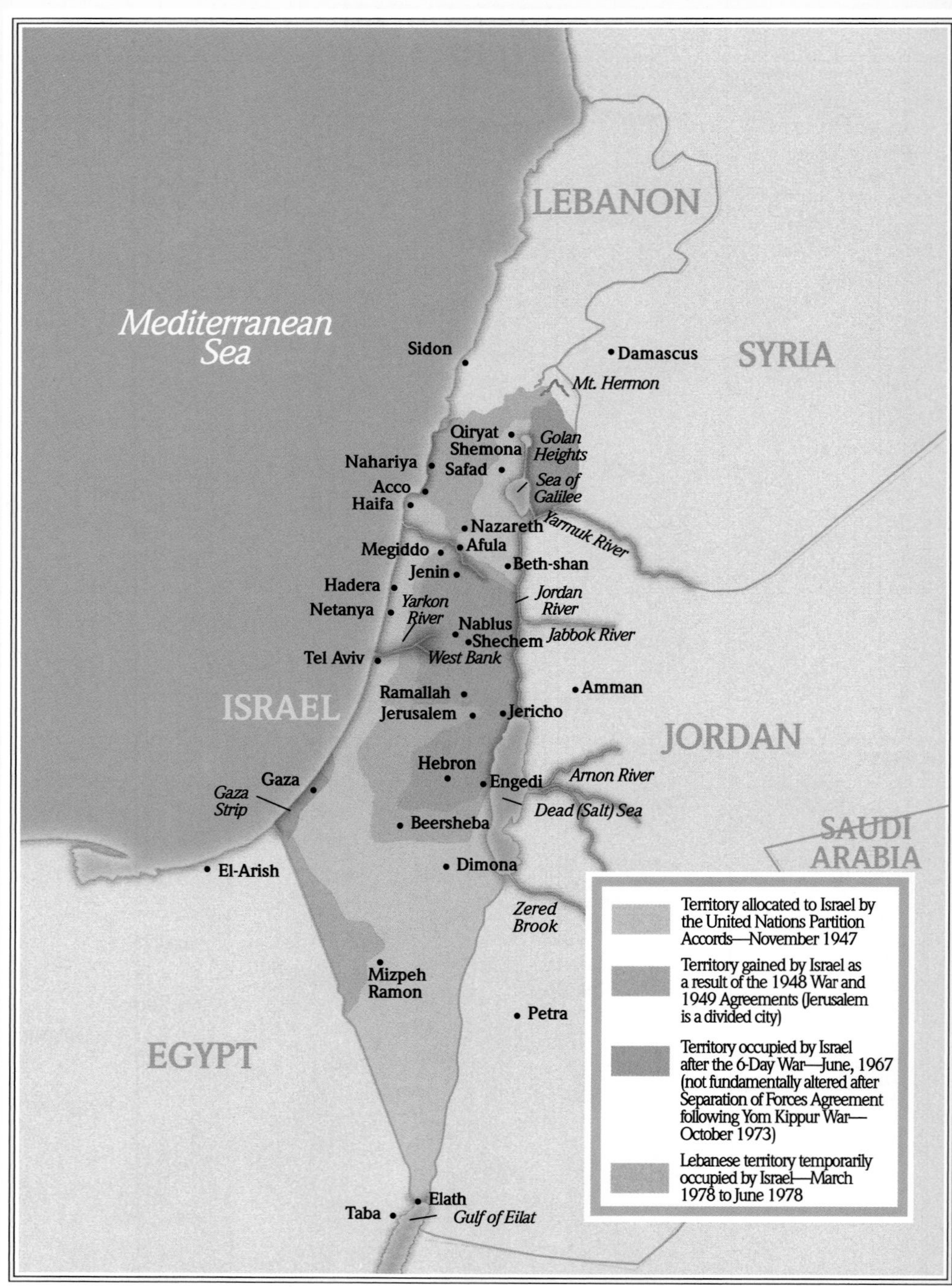
LEBANON
SYRIA
Mediterranean Sea
Sidon
Damascus
Mt. Hermon
Qiryat Shemona
Golan Heights
Nahariya
Safad
Acco
Haifa
Sea of Galilee
Nazareth
Yarmuk River
Megiddo
Afula
Jenin
Beth-shan
Hadera
Netanya
Yarkon River
Jordan River
Nablus
Shechem
Jabbok River
Tel Aviv
West Bank
Amman
ISRAEL
Ramallah
Jerusalem
Jericho
JORDAN
Hebron
Gaza
Engedi
Arnon River
Gaza Strip
Dead (Salt) Sea
Beersheba
SAUDI ARABIA
Dimona
El-Arish
Zered Brook
Mizpeh Ramon
Petra
EGYPT
Elath
Taba
Gulf of Eilat
Territory allocated to Israel by the United Nations Partition Accords—November 1947
Territory gained by Israel as a result of the 1948 War and 1949 Agreements (Jerusalem is a divided city)
Territory occupied by Israel after the 6-Day War—June, 1967 (not fundamentally altered after Separation of Forces Agreement following Yom Kippur War—October 1973)
Lebanese territory temporarily occupied by Israel—March 1978 to June 1978